AFRICA South of the Sahara 1998

AFRICA South of the Sahara 1998

TWENTY-SEVENTH EDITION

EUROPA PUBLICATIONS LIMITED

First published 1971

Twenty-Seventh Edition 1998

18 Bedford Square, London, WC1B 3JN, England

Australia and New Zealand
James Bennett (Collaroy) Pty Ltd, 4 Collaroy Street,
Collaroy, NSW 2097, Australia

Japan
Maruzen Co Ltd, POB 5050, Tokyo International 100-31

ISBN 1-85743-036-0
ISSN 0065-3896

Library of Congress Catalog Card Number 78-112271

Printed in England by
MPG Rochester Limited
Rochester, Kent

Bound by
MPG Books Limited
Bodmin, Cornwall

(Members of the Martins Printing Group)

FOREWORD

This twenty-seventh edition of AFRICA SOUTH OF THE SAHARA covers a period of significant and potentially far-reaching events in the sub-Saharan region, which have included the overthrow of one of the continent's most durable and exploitative dictatorships. Following the military defeat of the Mobutu regime in former Zaire, considerable international attention has focused on prospects for positive political and economic change in its successor state, the Democratic Republic of the Congo, together with the implications for the large numbers of refugees still displaced by the continuing civil and ethnic unrest in the central African region. This volume also chronicles and examines the continuing political uncertainties overshadowing the affairs of Angola, Nigeria, Liberia, Sudan and Somalia, as part of its coverage of developments in each of the 52 states that comprise sub-Saharan Africa.

In addition to contributions by specialist authors, commentators and researchers, all statistical and directory material in the new edition has been extensively updated, revised and expanded, and a calendar of the key political events of 1996–97 provides a convenient rapid reference guide to the year's main developments. Extensive coverage of international organizations and research bodies active in Africa is included, together with detailed background information on the continent's major agricultural and mineral commodities.

In expressing gratitude to all the contributors for their articles and advice and to the numerous governments and organizations which have returned questionnaires and provided statistical and other information, the Editor wishes to extend particular thanks to Professor Reuben Musiker, the distinguished bibliographer of Africa, for his work in updating and revising the country chapter bibliographies in this edition.

September 1997

ACKNOWLEDGEMENTS

The editors gratefully acknowledge the interest and co-operation of all the contributors to this volume, and of many national statistical and information offices in Africa and embassies and high commissions in London, Brussels, Paris and Africa, whose valued assistance in updating the material contained in AFRICA SOUTH OF THE SAHARA is greatly appreciated.

We acknowledge particular indebtedness for permission to reproduce material from the following publications: the United Nations' *Demographic Yearbook, Statistical Yearbook* and *Industrial Statistics Yearbook;* the Food and Agriculture Organization of the United Nations' *Production Yearbook, Yearbook of Fishery Statistics* and *Yearbook of Forest Products;* and *The Military Balance 1996–97,* published by the International Institute for Strategic Studies, 23 Tavistock Street, London, WC2E 7NQ, England. We acknowledge *La Zone Franc et l'Afrique* (Ediafric, Paris) and the *La Zone Franc* as the sources of some of our information on budgets in francophone Africa.

The articles on St Helena, Ascension, Tristan da Cunha and Seychelles make use of material from *A Year Book of the Commonwealth,* with the kind permission of the Controller of Her Majesty's Stationery Office.

EXPLANATORY NOTE ON THE DIRECTORY SECTION

The Directory section of each chapter is arranged under the following headings, where they apply:

THE CONSTITUTION

THE GOVERNMENT
- HEAD OF STATE
- CABINET/COUNCIL OF MINISTERS/
- POLITICAL BUREAU OF PARTY
- MINISTRY ADDRESSES

LEGISLATURE

POLITICAL ORGANIZATIONS

DIPLOMATIC REPRESENTATION

JUDICIAL SYSTEM

RELIGION

THE PRESS

PUBLISHERS

RADIO AND TELEVISION

FINANCE
- CENTRAL BANK
- STATE BANKS
- COMMERCIAL BANKS
- DEVELOPMENT BANKS
- MERCHANT BANKS
- SAVINGS BANKS
- INVESTMENT BANKS
- FOREIGN BANKS
- FINANCIAL INSTITUTIONS
- STOCK EXCHANGE
- INSURANCE

TRADE AND INDUSTRY
- PUBLIC CORPORATIONS
- DEVELOPMENT CORPORATIONS
- CHAMBERS OF COMMERCE AND INDUSTRY
- COMMERCIAL AND INDUSTRIAL ORGANIZATIONS
- EMPLOYERS' ORGANIZATIONS
- MAJOR INDUSTRIAL COMPANIES
- TRADE UNIONS
- CO-OPERATIVES

TRANSPORT
- RAILWAYS
- ROADS
- INLAND WATERWAYS
- SHIPPING
- CIVIL AVIATION

TOURISM

DEFENCE

EDUCATION

CONTENTS

CONTENTS

CONTENTS

CONTENTS

THE CONTRIBUTORS

J. A. Allan. Professor of Geography, School of Oriental and African Studies, University of London.

L. Berry. Former Professor of Geography, University of Dar es Salaam.

E. A. Boateng. Environmental consultant and educationalist.

Sir Mervyn Brown. Former British Ambassador in Madagascar. Member, Académie Malgache.

Richard Brown. Former Dean, School of African and Asian Studies, University of Sussex at Brighton.

Marisé Castro. Researcher, Amnesty International, International Secretariat, London.

Christopher Clapham. Professor of Politics and International Relations, University of Lancaster.

John I. Clarke. Professor of Geography, University of Durham.

João Gomes Cravinho. Lecturer in International Relations, University of Coímbra.

Pierre Englebert. Political Economy and Public Policy Program, University of Southern California.

Patrick Gilkes. Writer on Africa and the Third World for the BBC External Services.

Pierre Gourou. Professor of Geography, Université Libre de Bruxelles and Collège de France, Paris.

R. J. Harrison Church. Emeritus Professor of Geography, London School of Economics.

David Hilling. Senior Lecturer in Geography, Royal Holloway and Bedford New College, University of London.

Edith Hodgkinson. Writer specializing in the economies of developing countries.

Diana Hubbard. Writer specializing in the financial and economic affairs of francophone African countries.

A. MacGregor Hutcheson. Lecturer in Geography, Aberdeen College of Education.

George Kay. Head of the Department of Geography and Recreation Studies, Staffordshire University.

B. W. Langlands. Late Professor of Geography, Makerere University College, Kampala.

Bernard Lanne. Specialist on Chad and Editor-in-Chief of *La Documentation française,* Paris.

G. C. Last. Former Adviser, Ethiopian Ministry of Education and Fine Arts.

Richard Levin. Senior Lecturer, Department of Sociology, University of the Witwatersrand, Johannesburg.

I. M. Lewis. Professor of Anthropology, London School of Economics and Political Science.

John Lonsdale. Lecturer and Director of Studies in History, Trinity College, University of Cambridge.

Akin L. Mabogunje. Former Professor of Geography, University of Ibadan.

T. C. McCaskie. Lecturer in the Social History of West Africa in the Twentieth Century, Centre of West African Studies, University of Birmingham.

Andrew Manley. Writer specializing in the political and economic affairs of African countries.

Graham Matthews. Consultant in African economic and political issues.

François Misser. Writer specializing in the business and economic affairs of developing countries.

Peter K. Mitchell. Honorary Senior Research Fellow, Centre of West African Studies, University of Birmingham.

W. T. W. Morgan. Senior Lecturer, Department of Geography, University of Durham.

Gregory Mthembu-Salter. Writer specializing in the political and economic affairs of African countries.

Reuben Musiker. Professor Emeritus of Librarianship and Bibliography, University of the Witwatersrand, Johannesburg.

Thomas Ofcansky. Writer specializing in African political and economic issues.

J. D. Omer-Cooper. Former Professor of History, University of Otago.

René Pélissier. Author specializing in contemporary Spanish-speaking and Portuguese-speaking Africa.

James Pickett. Former Director, David Livingstone Institute of Overseas Development Studies, University of Strathclyde, and Economic Adviser to the Ethiopian Ministry of Planning and Economic Development.

Luisa Handem Piette. Writer specializing in African political and development issues.

Alan Rake. Managing Editor of *African Business* and *New African* magazines, London.

Filip Reyntjens. Professor of Law and Politics, Universities of Antwerp and Leuven.

Andrew D. Roberts. Professor of the History of Africa, School of Oriental and African Studies, University of London.

Christopher Saunders. Associate Professor and Head of the Department of History, University of Cape Town.

Gerhard Seibert. Social scientist specializing in African countries.

Miles Smith-Morris. Writer specializing in developing countries.

Donald L. Sparks. Associate Professor of Economics, The Citadel, Charleston, South Carolina, and Senior Fulbright Professor, University of Swaziland.

Theo Thomas. Consultant in African economic issues.

Virginia Thompson. Writer specializing in francophone Africa.

THE CONTRIBUTORS

Gill Tudor. Regional Director—Africa, Economist Intelligence Unit, London.

Linda Van Buren. Writer specializing in the business and economic affairs of African countries.

Jacques Vanderlinden. Former Professor of Law, Université Libre de Bruxelles.

Gavin Williams. Fellow and Tutor in Politics and Sociology, St Peter's College, University of Oxford.

Geoffrey J. Williams. Former Professor of Geography, University of Zambia.

John A. Wiseman. Senior Lecturer in Politics, University of Newcastle.

ABBREVIATIONS

Acad.	Academician; Academy
ACP	African, Caribbean and Pacific (States)
ADB	African Development Bank
ADF	African Development Fund
Adm.	Admiral
Admin.	Administration; Administrative; Administrator
AG	Aktiengesellschaft (limited company)
a.i.	ad interim
AIDS	Acquired Immunodeficiency Syndrome
AM	Amplitude Modulation
Apdo	Apartado (Post Box)
approx.	approximately
Apt	Apartment
Ass.	Assembly
Asscn	Association
Assoc.	Associate
Asst	Assistant
Aug.	August
auth.	authorized
Avda	Avenida (Avenue)
Ave	Avenue
Bd	Board
b/d	barrels per day
Bldg(s)	Building(s)
Blvd	Boulevard
BP	Boîte Postale (Post Box)
Br	Brother
br.(s)	branch(es)
Brig.	Brigadier
C	Centigrade; Cedi(s) (Ghana currency)
c.	circa
cap.	capital
Capt.	Captain
Cdre	Commodore
Cen.	Central
CEO	Chief Executive Officer
cf.	confer (compare)
CFA	Communauté financière africaine; Coopération financière en Afrique centrale
Ch.	Chapter
Chair.	Chairman/woman
Cie	Compagnie
c.i.f.	cost, insurance and freight
C-in-C	Commander-in-Chief
circ.	circulation
cm	centimetre(s)
cnr	corner
c/o	care of
Co	Company; County
Col	Colonel
COMESA	Common Market for Eastern and Southern Africa
Comm.	Commission
Commdr	Commander
Commdt	Commandant
Commr	Commissioner
Conf.	Conference
Confed.	Confederation
Corpn	Corporation
CP	Caixa Postal, Case Postale (Post Box)
Cpl	Corporal
Cttee	Committee
cu	cubic
cwt	hundredweight
d	died
Dec.	December
Del.	Delegate
Dep.	Deputy
dep.	deposits
Dept	Department
Devt	Development
Dir	Director
Div.	Division(al)
Dr	Doctor
Dra	Doctora
dwt	dead weight tons
E	East; Eastern; Emalangeni (Swaziland currency)
EAC	East African Community
EC	European Community
ECA	Economic Commission for Africa (UN)
ECOWAS	Economic Community of West African States
ECU	European Currency Unit(s)
Ed.(s)	Editor(s)
EDF	European Development Fund
edn	edition
EEZ	Exclusive Economic Zone
e.g.	exempli gratia (for example)
Eng.	Engineer; Engineering
EPZ	Export Processing Zone
est.	established; estimate; estimated
etc.	etcetera
EU	European Union
excl.	excluding
Exec.	Executive
exhbn(s)	exhibition(s)
f.	founded
FAO	Food and Agriculture Organization
f.a.s.	free alongside
Feb.	February
Fed.	Federation; Federal
FG	Guinea Franc
FIDES	Fonds d'investissement et de développement économique et social
Flt	Flight
FMG	Malagasy Franc
fmr(ly)	former(ly)
f.o.b.	free on board
Fr	Father
Fr.	Franc(s)
Fri.	Friday
ft	foot (feet)
g	gram(s)
GATT	General Agreement on Tariffs and Trade
GDP	Gross Domestic Product
Gen.	General
GNP	Gross National Product
Gov.	Governor
Govt	Government
GPO	General Post Office
grt	gross registered ton(s)
GWh	gigawatt hour(s)
ha	hectare(s)
HE	His Eminence; His/Her Excellency
HIV	Human Immunodeficiency Virus
hl	hectolitre(s)
HM	His/Her Majesty
HQ	Headquarters
HRH	His/Her Royal Highness
ibid.	ibidem (from the same source)
IBRD	International Bank for Reconstruction and Development (World Bank)
ID	Islamic Dinar(s)
IDA	International Development Association
i.e.	id est (that is to say)
ILO	International Labour Organisation/Office
IMF	International Monetary Fund
in	inch (inches)
Inc	Incorporated
incl.	include, including
Ind.	Independent
Ing.	Engineer
Insp.	Inspector
Inst.	Institute
Int.	International
Is	Islands
ISIC	International Standard Industrial Classification
Jan.	January
Jr	Junior
Jt	Joint

ABBREVIATIONS

K Kwacha (Malawi and Zambia currencies)
kg kilogramme(s)
km kilometre(s)
kW kilowatt(s)
kWh kilowatt hour(s)

lb pound(s)
Lda Limitada (limited company)
Le. Leone (Sierra Leone currency)
Legis. Legislative
LNG Liquefied natural gas
LPG Liquefied petroleum gas
Lt Lieutenant
Ltd Limited

M Maloti (Lesotho currency)
m metre(s)
m. million
Maj. Major
Man. Manager; Managing
Me Maître
mem. member
Mfg Manufacturing
mfr(s) manufacturer(s)
mg milligram(s)
Mgr Monseigneur, Monsignor
Mil. Military
Mlle Mademoiselle
mm millimetre(s)
Mme Madame
Mon. Monday
MP Member of Parliament
MSS manuscripts
Mt Mount
MW megawatt(s); medium wave
MWh megawatt hour(s)

N North; Northern
₦ Naira (Nigerian currency)
NA National Association (banking)
n.a. not available
Nat. National
NCO Non-Commissioned Officer
n.e.s. not elsewhere specified
No. number
Nov. November
nr near
nrt net registered ton(s)

OAU Organization of African Unity
OCAM Organisation commune africaine et mauricienne
Oct. October
OECD Organisation for Economic Co-operation and Development
OIC Organization of the Islamic Conference
OMVS Organisation pour la mise en valeur du fleuve Sénégal
OPEC Organization of the Petroleum Exporting Countries
opp. opposite
Org.(s) Organization(s)
oz ounce(s)

P Pula (Botswana currency)
p. page
p.a. per annum
Parl. Parliament(ary)
Perm. Permanent
PLC Public Limited Company
PMB Private Mail Bag
PO Post Office
POB Post Office Box
Pres. President
Prin. Principal
Prof. Professor
Propr Proprietor
Prov. Province; Provincial
Pte Private
Pty Proprietary
Pvt Private

p.u. paid up
publ.(s) published; publication(s)
Publr Publisher

q.v. quod vide (to which refer)

R Rand (South African currency)
Rd Road
regd registered
Rep. Representative
Repub. Republic
reorg. reorganized
res reserves
retd retired
Rev. Reverend
Rm Room
RMS Royal Mail Steamer
RN Royal Navy
Rs Rupee(s) (Mauritius currency)
Rt Right

S South; Southern
SA Société Anonyme, Sociedad Anónima (limited company); South Africa
SADC Southern African Development Community
SARL Sociedade Anônima de Responsabilidade Limitada (limited company)
Sat. Saturday
SDR Special Drawing Right(s)
Sec. Secretary
Secr. Secretariat
Sept. September
Sgt Sergeant
SITC Standard International Trade Classification
Soc. Society
Sq. Square
sq square (in measurements)
SR Seychelles Rupee(s)
Sr Senior
St Street; Saint, San, Santo
Sta Santa
Ste Sainte
Stn Station
Sun. Sunday
Supt Superintendent

tech. technical, technology
TEU 20-ft equivalent unit
trans. translator, translated
Treas. Treasurer
TV Television

UA Unit(s) of Account
UDEAC Union douanière et économique de l'Afrique centrale
UEE Unidade Económica Estatal
UK United Kingdom
ul. ulitsa (street)
UM Ouguiya(s) (Mauritania currency)
UN United Nations
UNCTAD United Nations Conference on Trade and Development
UNDP United Nations Development Programme
UNESCO United Nations Educational, Scientific and Cultural Organization
UNHCR United Nations High Commissioner for Refugees
UNIDO United Nations Industrial Development Organization
Univ. University
US(A) United States (of America)
USSR Union of Soviet Socialist Republics

viz. videlicet (namely)
Vol.(s) Volume(s)

W West; Western
WHO World Health Organization
WTO World Trade Organization

yr(s) year(s)

POLITICAL EVENTS IN AFRICA SOUTH OF THE SAHARA, 1996–97

1996

OCTOBER

1 Government of Nigeria announced intention to increase the number of federal states from 36 to 42.

6 Partial elections to senate in Republic of Congo.

11 and 18 Legislative elections in Mauritania.

12 Government of Gabon reshuffled.

20 New constitution of Comoros approved by referendum. Government of Mauritania resigned.
Local elections held in Gabon.

27 Government of Mali announced discovery of alleged coup plot.

NOVEMBER

1 Town of Bukavu captured by insurgent Alliance des forces démocratiques pour la libération du Congo-Zaïre (AFDL) in Zaire.

2 Town of Goma, in Zaire, falls to AFDL.

3 First round of presidential elections in Madagascar.

4 Death of Jean-Bédel Bokassa, former president of the Central African Republic.

8 Attack by alleged mercenaries on army barracks in The Gambia.

13 National assembly of Angola adopted constitutional revision extending its mandate for a further period of between two and four years.
Government reshuffle in Swaziland.

15 Renewed rioting in the Central African Republic.

18 Presidential and legislative elections in Zambia. Frederick Chiluba re-elected president.

19 Raul Vagner da Conceicão Bragança Neto appointed prime minister of São Tomé and Príncipe.

22 Cabinet reoganization in Sierra Leone.

23 Legislative elections in Niger. Majority of seats won by Union nationale des indépendants pour le renouveau démocratique.

24 Regional, municipal and rural elections in Senegal.

29 New coalition government took office in São Tomé and Príncipe.

30 Peace agreement signed in Sierra Leone between the government and the insurgent Revolutionary United Front.

DECEMBER

1 and 8 Legislative elections in Comoros.

2 New government appointed in Zambia.

5–6 19th Franco-African summit meeting held in Ouagadougu, Burkina Faso. Efforts initiated to resolve the crisis in the Central African Republic.

7 Presidential and legislative elections held in Ghana.

12 Military Conseil de salut national formally dissolved in Niger.

15 and 29 Legislative elections in Gabon.

21 New government of Niger appointed.

26 Cabinet reshuffle in Zaire.

27 Ahmed Abdou appointed prime minister of a new government in Comoros.

29 Adm. (retd) Didier Ratsiraka elected president of Madagascar in second round of voting.

1997

JANUARY

2 Elections for a new national assembly in The Gambia.

3 Inauguration of national salvation council in Somalia.

5 First round of legislative elections in Chad.

6 Government reshuffle in Mauritania.

15 Cabinet changes in Kenya.

16 New constitution of The Gambia entered into force.

24 Resignation of government of Gabon.

25 Accord resolving army mutiny signed in the Central African Republic.

26 First round of elections to the senate in Gabon.

27 Constitutional amendments approved by Burkina Faso legislature.

27–28 Appointment of new government of Gabon.

30 Michel Gbezera-Bria appointed prime minister of the Central African Republic.

FEBRUARY

3 Commencement of indefinite strike action in Swaziland.

4 New constitution of South Africa entered into force.

5 Tanzania government reorganized.

6–16 Police mutiny in Lesotho suppressed by army.

9 Second round of elections to the senate of Gabon.

14 Government of Guinea reorganized.

15 Government of Mauritania reshuffled.

18 New 'government of action' formed in the Central African Republic, with opposition representation.

21 Pascal Rakotomavo appointed prime minister of Madagascar.

23 Second round of legislative elections in Chad.

27 New government of Madagascar appointed.

MARCH

5 Strike action suspended in Swaziland.

7 New cabinet appointed in The Gambia.

15 Local government elections in Nigeria.

16 and 23 Partial elections to general council in Mayotte.

18 Government of Comoros reshuffled. Governor of the island of Nzwani (Anjouan) replaced following riots.

24 Resignation of Léon Kengo Wa Dondo as prime minister of Zaire.

APRIL

2 Etienne Tshisekedi appointed prime minister of Zaire.

3 New cabinet appointed in Zaire.

9 Gen. Likulia Bolongo appointed prime minister of Zaire. Town of Lubumbashi captured by AFDL.

10 Gen. Sani Abacha of Nigeria assumed powers to remove elected mayors and dissolve municipal councils.

11 New government of national unity and reconciliation took office in Angola.

13 First round of legislative elections in Mali.

18 Constitutional amendments adopted by legislature in Gabon.

21 Government of Sudan signed peace agreement with six insurgent groups in Southern Sudan, excluding the Sudan People's Liberation Army.

25 Constitutional court annulled the results of the first round of legislative elections in Mali.

MAY

5 Withdrawal of opposition groups from the government of the Central African Republic.

10 Archbishop Laurent Monsengwo Pasinya elected speaker of transitional legislature in Zaire.

11 Cabinet changes in Mauritania.
Presidential election in Mali.
Legislative elections in Burkina Faso.

16 Government of Chad resigned. Nassour Ouado appointed prime minister.

17 Legislative elections in Cameroon.
Troops of the AFDL entered Kinshasa. Laurent-Désiré Kabila, leader of the AFDL, declared himself president of the Democratic Republic of the Congo, as Zaire is henceforth known.

20 New government appointed in Chad.

23 Initial appointments made to cabinet of the Democratic Republic of the Congo.
Constitution of Eritrea adopted.

25 Military coup in Sierra Leone. Ahmed Tejan Kabbah deposed as president by an armed forces revolutionary council under the chairmanship of Maj. Johnny Paul Koroma.
First round of elections to French national assembly held in Réunion and Mayotte.

27 Manuel Saturnino da Costa dismissed as prime minister of Guinea-Bissau.

29 Laurent-Désiré Kabila inaugurated as president of the Democratic Republic of the Congo.

JUNE

1 Second round of elections to French national assembly held in Réunion and Mayotte.

3 Nigerian forces bombarded Freetown, Sierra Leone, in an attempt to compel military coup leaders to relinquish power.

5 Carlos Correia appointed prime minister of Guinea-Bissau.

6 New cabinet appointed in Guinea-Bissau.

7 Dr Ntsu Mokhehle, prime minister of Lesotho, resigned from governing party, the Basotho Congress Party, and formed the Lesotho Congress for Democracy, to which he transferred executive power.

9 Cabinet changes in Mauritania.

11 New government of Burkina Faso appointed.

12 Further cabinet appointments in the Democratic Republic of the Congo.

14 Government of Niger reshuffled.

17 Maj. Johnny Paul Koroma declared head of state in Sierra Leone.

19 New appointments to military high command in Niger.

20 Mauritius government coalition dissolved.

JULY

1 UN Angola Verification mission III replaced by the UN Observer Mission in Angola (MONUA).

Government of Nigeria announced a revised timetable for return to civilian government.

2 Cease-fire agreement in the Central African Republic following renewal of sporadic fighting.

New government formed in Mauritius.

9 General election in St Helena.

11 Sierra Leone suspended from meetings of the Commonwealth.

14 New cabinet appointed in Sierra Leone.

Armed confrontations between security forces and secessionists on Nzwani (Anjouan) in Comoros.

19 Presidential and legislative elections in Liberia. Charles Taylor elected president, while his National Patriotic-Party obtained a majority of seats in the legislature.

Cabinet reshuffle in Malawi.

23 Government changes in Zimbabwe.

AUGUST

2 Charles Taylor inaugurated as president of Liberia. A cabinet was subsequently formed.

3 Nzwani (Anjouan) declared its independence from Comoros.

New elections to national assembly in Mali.

5 Election of Abdallah Ibrahim as 'president' of Nzwani (Anjouan), at the head of a 13-member 'politico-administrative co-ordination'.

11 The island of Mwali (Mohéli) declared its independence from Comoros.

18 Opposition Partido del Progreso de Guinea Ecuatorial banned by government of Equatorial Guinea.

26 Frederik Willem de Klerk resigned as leader of the South African National Party.

LATE INFORMATION

ANGOLA (p. 168)
Government Change
(September 1997)

Minister of Public Works and Urbanization: (vacant).

THE COMOROS (p. 323)
Government Changes
(September 1996)

On 9 September, following an unsuccessful military attempt to suppress a separatist insurrection on the island of Nzwani (Anjouan), President Mohamed Taki Abdulkarim dismissed the government. On 12 September the president established a state transition committee to replace the former government.

REPUBLIC OF CONGO (p. 366)
Government Changes
(September 1997)

A new government was formed on 13 September 1997. Members included:

Prime Minister: Bernard Kolelas.

Minister of State for Decentralization and Regional Development: Jean-Pierre Thystère-Tchicaya.

Minister of State for Urban Planning and Public Works: Lambert Ngalibali.

Minister of State for Interior Affairs and Security: Col Philippe Bikinkita.

Minister of State for Transport and Civil Aviation: Victor Tamba-Tamba.

Minister of National Defence: Pascal Tsaty Mabiala.

Minister of the Economy, Planning and Finance: N'Guila Moungounga Nkombo.

Minister of Foreign Affairs: Destin-Arsène Tsatsy M'Boungou.

Minister of Co-operation: Grégoire Lefouoba.

Many other members of the previous government retained their posts.

MAURITANIA (p. 690)
Government Changes
(September 1997)

Minister of Justice: Sidi Mohamed Ould Mohamed Fall.

Minister of Rural Development and the Environment: Rabet Sidi Mahmoud Ould Cheikh Ahmed.

MAURITIUS (p. 705)
Government Change
(July 1997)

Minister of Economic Development and Regional Co-operation: Rundheersing Bheenick.

PART ONE
Background to the Continent

AFRICA IN RETROSPECT AND PROSPECT

GAVIN WILLIAMS

NATIONALISM AND DEVELOPMENT

The period from the Second World War to the present in Africa has been dominated by three related themes: political nationalism, communal competition and economic development. African nationalists sought state power as a means of transferring control of political office and economic resources from foreigners to Africans. The state would take responsibility for bringing 'development' to Africa. Nationalists appealed to international organizations to help bring an end to colonial rule and racist regimes, and looked to international agencies and the governments of industrial societies to fund development projects. The African state was central to achieving the goals of nationalism and development. It was the object of the struggle for power. It became the key instrument in the continuing battle to maintain power. Armed campaigns to take control of the state have contributed to the withdrawal of colonial governments and the overthrow of repressive regimes. In some cases, this has opened the way to a peaceful settlement; in others it has left a legacy of political violence and even of civil war and a collapse of state authority and social order.

Nations must be 'imagined' if they are to be formed (Anderson). The 'imagining' of African nations and ethnicities has generally taken place within and along the boundaries laid down during the scramble for Africa. Prior to colonial rule, people's identities were defined primarily by their allegiance to a ruler or leader or by their status within a political community. Pre-colonial politics had interests in incorporating settlers and slaves to strengthen their productive and military capacities. Under colonial and post-colonial regimes, political communities were defined and defined themselves according to administrative, religious and linguistic demarcations. Elites, old and new, competed to gain access to resources for themselves and their communities and to exclude others from 'their' territories.

In contemporary African usage, 'tribe' or 'ethnicity' usually refers to people speaking a common language. In some cases, these have historical links to a pre-colonial polity, such as the Zulu or Bagandan kingdoms. More commonly, such groups do not share a single pre-colonial identity. Their dialects were subsumed into a standardized written form of language only in the 20th century. Politicians seeking popular support for their claims appealed to their home communities and promised to bring to their regions, language or religious groups the benefits of development.

In February 1990 President de Klerk released Nelson Mandela and lifted the ban on the African National Congress of South Africa (ANC), the first African nationalist movement in sub-Saharan Africa. This opened the way to negotiate to end the white monopoly of political power. The independence of Eritrea from Ethiopia in 1993 and the election of Nelson Mandela as president of South Africa in April 1994 marked the culmination of the African struggle for national independence, leaving only the status of Western Sahara still unresolved. However, throughout Africa, it remained clear that the hopes invested in national independence and economic development had not been realized.

The independence of Eritrea from Ethiopia in 1993 and the election of Nelson Mandela as president of South Africa in April 1994 marked the completion of the African struggle for national independence, with only the status of Western Sahara remaining unresolved. However, throughout the rest of Africa, it was clear by 1990 that the hopes invested in national independence and economic development had not been realized. Most African states were bankrupt. Their economic policies were subject to the direction of the International Monetary Fund (IMF) and the World Bank, although the consequent strategies which governments adopted did not always meet these organizations' requirements. African rulers, whether drawn from civilian politicians or military officers, had lost moral credibility as a result of arbitrary and corrupt government, the exclusion of significant class, regional and ethnic groups from access to political decisions, and increasing economic and personal insecurity. Many governments lacked the capacity to carry through economic reforms; only a few proved able to initiate and sustain a measure of economic recovery.

One-party states and military governments, covering a wide spectrum of ideological outlooks, were confronted with popular demands for free elections and multi-party governments. In some countries these demands were met by the defeat of the ruling party in elections. In others, the ruling party was able to maintain itself in power by winning elections. Elections also legitimized the transfer of power to victorious liberation movements. In several instances, ruling cliques, and the armed groups associated with them, or in Angola an armed opposition, refused to concede power. In a number of places, governments have been unable to maintain their own authority and political order. Civil wars, exacerbated by external interventions, have left many people dead, in exile, or exposed to famine.

As at the end of the colonial period, democratic elections have provided a mechanism for deciding who is to inherit, or to retain, power. They have not always been able to proceed, nor have their results always been acceptable to those excluded from office. Political uncertainty has all too often encouraged people to resort to political violence.

The end of superpower rivalries led to peace negotiations, and sometimes agreements. The divisive and destructive results of foreign military interventions, and of the flow of arms to African clients, continued. Armed interventions, whether under US leadership and UN authority in Somalia or undertaken by combined West African armies, as in Liberia, have failed to suppress contending militias; UN troops could not prevent ethnic massacres in Rwanda. As the post-war international structure has disintegrated the USA and its allies have retreated from their vision of a 'new world order'.

NATIONALISTS, POLITICIANS AND SOLDIERS

'Seek ye first the political kingdom' advised Kwame Nkrumah. During and after the Second World War, African nationalists were able to gain widespread support from a broad coalition of groups for their demands for equal rights for all and an end to colonial and white settler rule. Workers went on strike for a living wage to match war-time and post-war price increases. Rural people variously evaded and resisted the forced cultivation of cotton, compulsory labour and the imposition of improved agricultural methods, and demanded access to more land. Traders and consumers resented the scarcity of imported goods and the monopolistic practices of foreign firms. The 'middle classes', themselves a product of mission and colonial education and the expansion of the colonial economy, sought access to political office, state and private employment, and commercial opportunities from which Europeans, and sometimes Asians, had excluded them.

African nationalists combined petitions with direct action to persuade colonial powers and settler regimes to negotiate a transfer of power. Colonial politicians were elected to the French parliament until France conferred independence on its African colonies. In some countries, suppression of strikes and political movements led nationalists to engage in armed struggle and guerrilla warfare against colonial and settler regimes. Popular demonstrations, election campaigns and armed resistance were different means by which nationalists sought to establish themselves as the *interlocuteurs valables* with whom colonial and settler governments would have to negotiate a new political settlement.

Nationalist governments, Afrikaner as well as African, looked to the state to give them control over the allocation of resources and to promote 'development'. Hence the attraction to the commercial, as well as the bureaucratic, middle classes of 'socialism' in its 'African', 'Marxist-Leninist' and other variants, and the tendency to extend state activity and intervention in the economy. Afrikaner nationalists established the precedent of mobilizing support from an ethnic group to further the political, commercial and financial ambitions of a bourgeois élite, and to utilize public resources to extend opportunities to their wider constituency. Their successors may succeed in empowering a new black élite. It is more difficult to provide resources to the African majority than it was to secure benefits for a white minority.

At independence, ruling parties acquired control of state office and the distribution of patronage. They took over an administrative apparatus which was originally designed to collect taxes, to extend colonial authority from the centre to localities through appointed intermediaries with, or without, claims to 'traditional' authority, and to provide a limited range of transport, education, health and agricultural services. These had been extended after the Second World War to implement conservationist policies and development projects. In assuming state power, revolutionary liberation movements, like constitutional nationalists, were the successors to their colonial predecessors, confronting many of the same problems and constrained by many of the same limitations. The 'new' states were ill-equipped, in their fiscal resources, administrative capacities and forms of organization, to undertake successfully the ambitious programmes they envisaged.

The new rulers sought to monopolize power and office. Their opponents usually had to choose between joining the ruling alliance or risking suppression. On the African continent, political parties have been able to contend consistently in national elections by universal adult suffrage only in Botswana, Namibia, and, more questionably, Zimbabwe; in none of these countries has the ruling party been defeated in elections. In Mauritius, the ruling coalition was defeated and replaced by the opposition in the postponed 1976 elections; since then office has been shared by changing coalitions of disparate parties.

In a number of countries—e.g. Sudan, the Democratic Republic of the Congo (then Congo-Kinshasa and subsequently Zaire), Dahomey (now Benin), Nigeria and Uganda—rival parties proved unable to settle regional conflicts and resolve their own rivalries within an agreed constitutional framework. Party competition gave way to military governments. African governments were confronted by wars of secession in Southern Sudan, in Eastern Nigeria ('Biafra'), and in Katanga (now Shaba, in the Democratic Republic of the Congo). Civil wars have also been fought to liberate countries from repressive regimes. In Uganda (in 1971) and more recently in Liberia, Sierra Leone and Rwanda, they have intensified violent conflicts and led to massacres of civilians. In Uganda (in 1979) Rwanda, Ethiopia and, in 1997, in former Zaire, the victors have generally succeeded in re-establishing political order.

The military government installed by the 1958 coup in The Sudan was itself brought to an end in 1964 by demonstrations followed by a general strike. A transitional government held elections which produced a series of coalition governments which failed to reconcile the rival claims of Islamic sects in the North or to resolve the relations of the South to the Sudanese state. Nationalist officers seized power in 1969, repressed parties of the left and right and adopted its version of *shari'a* law in 1983, exacerbating tensions with the South. Demonstrations and a general strike in 1985 brought down President Nimeri. An elected coalition government failed to resolve the *shari'a* issue and the war in the South and was replaced in 1989 by a repressive military government which turned to the National Islamic Front for political support. The South has in turn been riven by internecine military conflicts.

In Rwanda and Burundi, the prospect of independence gave rise to communal parties and political violence. In Burundi a section of the Tutsi minority retained their dominant position through their control of the army. A Hutu electoral victory in 1965 led to the suppression of the Hutu political élite and gendarmerie by the army. An abortive coup led to further massacres and exile of Hutus in 1972 and again in 1988, in response to Hutu attacks on Tutsis. Successive military regimes failed to resolve the problems of the exclusion of the Hutu majority from the army and public life. In Rwanda, by contrast, a party representing the Hutu majority came to power at independence in 1963; many Tutsi fled into exile. The conflicts in Burundi provoked further attacks on Tutsi in 1972, and the military seized power in 1973.

Governments in the Sahelian countries came into conflict with nomadic peoples, as French military administrators had done before them. In Chad this led to a series of civil wars, which involved French and Libyan troops and an unsuccessful Nigerian attempt to mediate. In Eritrea and Western Sahara, nationalist movements claimed independence for territories colonized by Italy and Spain and subsequently annexed by Ethiopia and Morocco respectively. More recently, with the collapse of the Somalian state, claims to independence have been asserted in 'Somaliland', the area formerly under British colonial rule.

In most African countries, ruling parties formed one-party states. They claimed legitimacy from their leadership of the national struggle and the needs to overcome ethnic and regional divisions and to unite the people in pursuit of 'development' or 'socialism'. During the 1960s, a series of one-party regimes in, for example, Congo-Brazzaville (now the Congo Republic), the Central African Republic, Upper Volta (Burkina Faso), Ghana and Mali were replaced by military governments, in some cases after general strikes and popular risings, and usually to popular acclaim. It appeared that the one-party state was a transitional form of government between colonial and military rule. Others followed suit between 1970–86, in Uganda, Rwanda, Niger, Chad, Mauritania, Equatorial Guinea, Guinea-Bissau, Liberia, Guinea and Lesotho.

The fate of governments and outcome of elections often depended on the alignment of the military, or even on the intervention of foreign troops. In Sierra Leone, the military intervened to prevent the opposition All-People's Congress (APC) winning the 1967 elections. A counter-coup in 1968 installed Siaka Stevens of the APC in power. He called on Guinean troops to suppress a coup in 1971 and established a one-party state in 1978. In 1985 he transferred the presidency to the head of the army, Maj.-Gen. Joseph Momoh. In Lesotho, Chief Jonathan retained power and, with South African support, suppressed the opposition following his defeat in the 1970 elections. He was removed by the military, again with South African support, in 1986. Senegalese troops suppressed a coup against the Gambian government in 1981, but did not intervene on a second occasion, in 1994. British troops suppressed mutinies in Kenya, Tanzania and Uganda in 1964. French troops based in Gabon restored President Mba to power after a coup in 1964, and have since rescued other governments from military take-overs, as in the Central African Republic in 1996, or have declined to intervene. Acting in concert with Morocco, French troops protected President Mobutu in Zaire in 1977 and 1978 and, with Belgian troops, suppressed riots there in 1991 and 1993. Since 1975, the armies and militias contending for control of government in Chad have depended upon the actions, or inaction, of French troops or on Libyan support.

Military rulers typically claim to act in the name of the whole nation against the corruption and sectionalism of politicians. They deny any political ambitions of their own, and generally promise to restore constitutional government. However, armies usually act in the interests of all or a part of the armed forces. Military interventions inherently tend to create further political instability. Coups divide armies along lines of rank and generation. Military governments inherit the problems which their civilian predecessors failed to solve; they are divided by the political and ethnic conflicts of the rest of society. They seek support by favouring specific regional or religious interests. Army officers are as susceptible as politicians to the temptations of office and even more likely to resort to authoritarian measures to deal with opposition. Coups set precedents for further coups, whether against military regimes or their civilian successors. Between 1965–79, military governments in Dahomey (thrice), Ghana (twice), and Nigeria (once) held elections and returned power to civilian politicians. Their various successors stayed in office for between one and four years before a new group of soldiers removed them.

By contrast, one-party governments survived the initial wave of military coups and provided in several countries a stable form of government for nearly three decades after independence. They included places with high rates of economic growth, such as Kenya, Malawi, Cameroon and Côte d'Ivoire, and also

Tanzania and Zambia with records of stagnation and decline. These governments were usually led by a founder of the nationalist party, in several cases of a venerable age. They successfully combined centralized, bureaucratic direction of policy and administration with a regional distribution of patronage.

Government policies were decided and implemented by ministers and civil servants, under presidential authority. In both Kenya and Tanzania, policies were administered by powerful regional or provincial commissioners, recreating the administrative forms of colonial rule. In Tanzania, Lesotho and Zimbabwe, district and village development councils provided a means for the extension of central state authority in the name of 'decentralization'.

In Kenya and Côte d'Ivoire, each group obtained some access to political offices and state resources, but larger shares were reserved to the areas from which the president came. In Côte d'Ivoire, Kenya and Zambia, several candidates were allowed to contest each parliamentary seat. These elections turned on local rivalries and the ability of candidates to secure resources for their constituents. Presidential nominations were not contested.

Governments sought to curb the capacities of trade unions for independent action and, in some cases such as Tanzania and Guinea, incorporated trade unions into the ruling parties. In several countries, including Ghana, Zambia and Nigeria, governments strengthened the funding and organization of central trade union organizations with the aim of controlling industrial unrest. These reforms increased the capacity of unions to bargain with employers, including the state. Co-opted trade union leaders lost credibility among their members. When trade unions proved unable, or unwilling, to prevent strikes, governments promoted divisions among them, undermined their funding and arrested their leaders. Strategies of incorporation and of exclusion and suppression have both proved to be of limited effectiveness in controlling workers and unions in Africa.

Independent unions emerged in South Africa from the strikes of 1973. The government proposed reforms which were designed to incorporate black workers and their unions into the existing industrial relations structures. Unions took selective advantage of the reforms to secure recognition from employers. The Congress of South African Trade Unions (COSATU) formed an alliance with the ANC and the South African Communist Party, and in 1995 secured a new Labour Relations Act which extends workers' rights within a framework of arbitration and state regulation.

Radical officers with a populist platform replaced governments, civil or military, in Congo-Brazzaville, Somalia, Dahomey, Ghana, Upper Volta and, after a series of civil wars, Uganda. In Ghana and Burkina Faso, the new regimes briefly created popular committees, together with a number of small revolutionary organizations. The ruling élites, however, soon moved to distance themselves from radical groups and to consolidate their domination of the political arena. In some cases, socialism was no more than official rhetoric. In others, it gave way to pragmatic choices. In Somalia, President Siad Barre realigned his international allegiances when the Soviet government supported the Ethiopians against his attempt to incorporate the Ogaden into Somalia by armed invasion. Confronted by extreme economic crises, the governments of Rawlings in Ghana and Museveni in Uganda proved to be apt pupils of World Bank structural adjustment policies. They were more impervious to demands for democratic elections, blaming parties and politicians for their countries' crises and conflicts.

The 1974 coup in Lisbon allowed armed liberation movements to take power in Portugal's colonies and to convert themselves into 'Marxist-Leninist' parties committed to 'socialist construction'. Emperor Haile Selassie of Ethiopia was deposed in the same year and replaced by a radical junta, the Dergue, which repressed its rivals in a savage conflict, and established a centralized form of military socialism under the slogan of 'Ethiopia First'. The governments of Mozambique and Angola were confronted by opposition movements armed and supported by the Rhodesian and South African governments and other Western sources. Cuban troops and Soviet arms were instrumental in enabling the Movimento Popular de Libertação de Angola (MPLA) to retain power and repel a South African invasion; they enabled the Dergue to defeat a Somali attack on Ethiopia in 1977–78 and to sustain their war in Eritrea and within Ethiopia itself. The USA viewed the increased Cuban and Soviet involvement in Africa with disquiet, and armed and financed regimes and political movements opposed to those aligned with the Eastern bloc.

Guerrilla war and international pressures forced the illegal white regime in Southern Rhodesia into negotiations which culminated in the emergence of independent Zimbabwe in 1980. In South Africa, the Botha government sought to devise a strategy to reform apartheid while retaining the substance of white control of power and excluding the ANC and its allies from the political process. To this end, it created three racially-based parliamentary chambers, and took measures to relegate the African population to 'Bantustans' and to urban councils. Repressive reforms and rising fiscal burdens on the African townships provoked popular resistance. The South African regime effected the assassinations of opponents both inside and outside its borders, bombed and invaded its neighbours, and escalated its war of occupation in Namibia and repression at home. Agreement between the USA and the Soviet Union secured the withdrawal of Cuban and South African forces from Angola, and opened the way to new elections in that country, although failing to bring an end to its civil war. However, the agreement did clear the way to independence for Namibia. In South Africa itself, President de Klerk recognized that reform had to be negotiated with the ANC.

A CONTINENT IN CRISIS?

Since the severe droughts in the Sahel and the Horn of Africa in the early 1970s, Africa has been presented as a continent in crisis, ravaged by famine, war, corrupt and repressive governments, and by an AIDS pandemic; phenomena which have indeed been all too common. These dramatic and selective images of parts of the continent have stood in for Africa as a whole. 'Disaster tourism' (de Waal) portrays Africans as victims, unable to cope with the problems which beset them and thus in need of emergency aid and famine relief. 'Development discourse' (Ferguson) describes African countries as backward, subsistence economies, in need of 'modernization and monetization' and therefore provided with 'development aid'.

World Bank analyses identify two main sources for these problems. One is the combination of excessive government intervention in the economy and inadequate administrative capacities (overlooking the World Bank's own part in encouraging and funding such activities.) The second is the rapid and sustained growth in population over the last three decades, which is held responsible for desertification and environmental degradation, and for inadequate food supplies and rising food imports. The solution is to reduce the birth rate and promote the adoption of yield-enhancing agricultural technologies. Neither argument nor evidence seems to be necessary to support the self-evident association of more people, less land, lower productivity and less food for everyone.

African countries are characterized by great differences in climate, soils and vegetation. The extensive arid and semi-arid regions which cover large parts of Africa, although containing a far smaller proportion of the continent's total population, have been subject to considerable climatic variations, over successive years and for much longer periods. Broadly, rainfall was generally much higher in the years between 1930–60 than in the preceding, and the subsequent, decades. The 1970s, 1980s, and early 1990s have brought droughts of varying degrees of severity to different parts of the continent.

There is little reason to attribute these trends to African farming and livestock practices. Changes in the west African climate have been linked to surface temperatures in the Atlantic, and severe droughts in southern Africa appear to be associated with the Pacific current, 'El Niño'. Models of changes in the earth's climate, e.g. of global warming, are still speculative; they cannot specify the impact of the interactions of the elements which affect the different regions of the world.

Confronted by droughts, African pastoralists and farmers have adopted a variety of responses: changing their farming practices and grazing patterns; selling livestock and other assets, in some cases land, and exploring alternative sources of food and income; seeking assistance from kin, friends and patrons; migrating to other rural areas and to towns. De Waal observes that the people of Darfur, western Sudan, when confronted by famine, were not primarily concerned to ward off starvation, but instead 'to preserve the basis of an acceptable future way of life, which involves not only material well-being but social cohesion.'

African farmers have combined numerous strategies in response to changing economic opportunities, competing demands on male and female labour, and ecological risks: adoption of high-value crops, such as tea, coffee or cocoa; substitution of less for more labour-intensive crops, such as cassava for yams; adopting more intensive forms of land use; multicropping crops with complementary ecological and labour requirements. Attempts by colonial and national governments and international agencies to improve African farming methods have had a few successes and many failures. The most effective interventions have enabled farmers to earn higher incomes by producing crops, such as tea, sugar or tobacco, for processing on terms laid down by corporate investors.

The distribution of people in relation to land resources varies considerably within, and between African countries. Appropriation of land for settler agriculture confined Africans to 'native reserves', intensifying demands on land for cultivation, grazing and residence and leading to severe erosion of soils. Demands on land for commercial ranches, large farms and irrigation schemes, have excluded pastoralists from access to seasonal grazing resources; competition for land has sometimes brought farmers into conflict with pastoralists on whom they previously relied for animal manures. In several countries, large farms have used machinery in environmentally destructive ways to clear land to grow food crops for urban markets. Smallholders tend to make more intensive use of land and to be able to sustain larger populations than large farms. In semi-arid regions, conservationary methods of cultivation tend to be labour-intensive. Migration relaxes the pressures on land use in some areas, and allows others to be opened up for cultivation.

Colonial officials in Kenya took advantage of the state of emergency in the 1950s to implement an ambitious programme of consolidation and registration of land holdings, which was designed to encourage investment in and conservation of the land, and to reduce land disputes. Land titling is a slow and expensive process. It weakens or even obliterates the claims of tenants, of women and of pastoralists to land and changes the rules by which people dispute land rights. Conferring title to land may allow possessors to protect their claims, but may also provide some with a means of extending their own claims at the expense of others, and may not confer greater security than holding land under forms of communal tenure.

After independence, the Kenyan government bought out settler farmers with loans provided by Britain and planned the redistribution of land, firstly to African farmers who would continue to farm on a large scale, secondly to selected 'yeomen' farmers, and thirdly to peasant farmers. The government was obliged to extend provision for settlement of small farmers in the face of overwhelming demand. However, the reforms of the 1960s did not conclusively resolve the land issue; in recent years, the dominance of the Rift Valley by Kikuyu farmers has been challenged by Kalenjin claimants favoured by the current regime. In Zimbabwe, land was redistributed under conditions intended to impose upon settlers the land use patterns and cultivation rules that had been resisted during the colonial period. Further land acquired for redistribution in the 1990s was initially allocated to government ministers. In South Africa, laws have been passed to restore the rights of communities dispossessed of their land and to protect the rights of labour tenants and resident farm workers. African men with appropriate economic resources and political connections were more likely to acquire land than the rural poor favoured by policy-makers. State initiatives have been taken to extend the areas allocated to Africans under the former regime. Corporate initiatives have provided opportunities for black farmers to grow sugar, wattle and fruit, while enabling industry to extend its access to land and water resources.

Political changes have reopened issues of land policy in several countries where land had been nationalized or subject to administrative direction (Ethiopia, Tanzania) or dominated by large estates (Malawi). Governments and development agencies prefer to reserve to themselves the state control of land use and of the allocation of private rights of tenure. Land reform, tenure, and land use policies all turn on the issue of who is to allocate which rights to whom.

Several millions of people in Africa have already been infected with HIV. This virus is markedly more prevalent in some parts of African countries and among specific groups, including political élites, than others. The impact of HIV and AIDS in Africa was initially greatest around the road and lake transport routes of central Africa. HIV infection and AIDS mortality increased with a doubling time of one to two years. In Africa HIV prevalence is generally greater among women than men because of the higher probability of male-to-female transmission than of female-to-male. Families and communities in Uganda have responded to the spread of AIDS by adapting existing strategies of coping with disease and mortality within the limited resources available to them. In Uganda, there is evidence of a decline in AIDS deaths, which probably reflects both the dynamics of the disease and responses to health programmes. Botswana is now believed to have the highest overall prevalance of AIDS of any country in Africa, while South Africa has the fastest growing rate of contagion. This is probably the result of the country's well developed transport facilities, which facilitate the rapid and frequent movement of people.

Christianity and Islam were established in Africa soon after their foundations, and by the end of the colonial period, most Africans adhered to one of these religions. Religious beliefs and practices have long provided a means of establishing a *modus vivendi* within wider society, and of dealing with the problems of an uncertain world. Mahdist and millennial movements offered collective deliverance from oppression. Post-colonial regimes have been confronted by the stubborn resistance of believers who reject the claims of state authorities, and occasionally by sects inspired by prophetic leaders. Many people have turned to evangelical religious movements, Christian and Islamic, to seek solutions to their private problems within a new moral and social order. Religious revivalism has thus offered alternative routes to salvation, and has also added to communal conflicts.

Rural, as well as urban people in Africa have been vulnerable to the impact of changes in climate, endemic and epidemic diseases, and changing economic conditions. They have proved their capacity to find ways of responding to familiar and unfamiliar challenges, to the extent that their resources and the constraints imposed by government actions, wars, and national and international economic changes have allowed them to do so.

FROM DEVELOPMENT TO STRUCTURAL ADJUSTMENT

In 1895 the British colonial secretary Joseph Chamberlain proclaimed the 'dual mandate', to 'develop' the 'estates' of the tropics to the mutual benefit of the native populations and the imperial power. In 1945, the post-war Labour government took up the challenge. Peasant producers of cocoa, coffee and vegetable oils were taxed through state monopoly marketing boards to contribute surplus funds to the costs of reconstructing the British economy. Across southern, central, and east Africa, agricultural officers imposed methods of cultivation, which did little to protect the soil and much to promote rural nationalism. The colonial powers extended the transport networks on which export agriculture and mining depended. France organized produce marketing and invested in irrigated agriculture on the River Niger. Félix Houphouët-Boigny, the leading Ivorian politician and planter, successfully moved the abolition of forced labour by the French parliament in 1946. Neither Belgium nor Portugal similarly restrained their capacity to command (and export) labour.

Whereas colonial development had focused on agriculture, independent governments identified development with industrial growth and the expansion of formal education. They sought to finance it from the foreign exchange and tax revenues derived from agricultural and mineral exports, supplemented by transfers of foreign 'aid' and investments. Most governments encouraged foreign and local investment in industry through protective tariffs, tax rebates, and high exchange rates. These measures facilitated the maintenance of market domination by cartels of protected firms. Several governments sought to take control of strategic industries and partially or wholly nationalized mines, as in Zambia, petroleum production, as in Nigeria, and banks, as in Tanzania, and invested in industry themselves. Governments used their powers over licenses and contracts, and in Ghana and Nigeria, introduced legislation to raise the holdings of local investors in foreign firms and in commercial activities. This enabled governments to decide who would have access to the opportunities to acquire shares and contracts.

Secondary industry expanded rapidly in South Africa under the stimuli of the 1933 increase in the price of gold and subsequently by the Second World War. After 1948 the National Party supported Afrikaner commercial and industrial interests; the mining industry allowed Afrikaner interests to take control of a major mining finance company. The share of capital owned by South African firms and the concentration of ownership continued to rise, although net foreign investment continued until the 1980s. Since 1994 African businessmen, like their Afrikaner predecessors, have been accommodated among the major financial and investment institutions, which have thus been able to circumvent any threats of anti-trust legislation.

Even in South Africa, where manufacturing exceeds production by mining and agriculture combined, industry continues to import far more in the way of machinery and other inputs than it exports. Economic expansion generated by industrial growth thus places renewed strain on the balance of payments. Investment was sustained by foreign borrowing in the 1970s. Falling gold and other export revenues, rising interest rates and capital exports precipitated a debt crisis in 1985, forcing the government to devalue the rand, declare a moratorium on debt repayments and reintroduce the 'financial rand'.

The South African example demonstrates the contradictions of import-substituting industrialization confronted by countries throughout the continent. Ironically, import-substitution replaced the import of finished with intermediate goods and with raw materials. The growth of industry therefore depended upon the sustained expansion of earnings from agriculture and mining or, temporarily, on foreign borrowing. Foreign firms invested in consumer goods industries to maintain or secure their access to African markets in which, in most African countries, the demand for goods depends ultimately on earnings from agriculture.

Several countries were able to expand their agricultural exports rapidly after independence, thus increasing their import capacity and expanding demand for industrial production. Availability of forest land for cocoa cultivation and cheap migrant labour allowed Côte d'Ivoire to repeat the expansion of cocoa production which Ghana and Nigeria had seen earlier in the century, and to supplant them as the world's leading cocoa producer. In Kenya, smallholders gained access to land and were free to grow coffee and tea which had largely been reserved to settler farmers before independence. In Zimbabwe communal area farmers with access to sufficient land sharply increased their share of maize and cotton output in the 1980s. In each of these countries, large farms and plantations continue to produce a substantial share of total output and to benefit disproportionately from government subsidies. By the 1980s, the expansion of export markets for most Ivorian and Kenyan crops had reached their limits, and prices were falling. They could no longer sustain their levels of imports of industrial inputs and consumer goods, even less service the debts they had contracted in their earlier periods of prosperity.

Peasant production stagnated or even declined in countries, notably Ghana and Uganda, as well as Nigeria, which had developed a prosperous smallholder economy in the colonial period. The marketing boards provided a boon to politicians, who used them to finance development spending, political campaigns and private business activities. Political competition turned on the ability to dispose of government revenues and intensified the struggle to monopolize political offices. Governments sought to maintain their revenues from marketing boards in a falling market and to limit inflation by maintaining the official exchange rates of their currencies at unrealistic levels, and by controlling access to foreign exchange and imported goods. These policies penalized export producers and encouraged demand for imports. The eventual outcome was a collapse of export earnings, scarcity of imports, and pervasive resort to smuggling and corruption.

Some countries, such as Mali, Tanzania and Zambia, attempted to bring the marketing of food and essential consumer goods under state control in order to control retail prices. This disrupted trade between rural areas, created local trading monopolies for those protected by state officials, encouraged the smuggling of food to neighbouring countries, discouraged local food production, increased the budget deficits, and left governments to depend on imports to meet their obligations to feed the cities.

After the sharp rise in the world price of petroleum in 1973, the leading mineral and agricultural exporters were able to borrow from banks, at high and variable interest rates, while others resorted to food aid and loans from governments and international agencies. Food aid and food imports increased rapidly in 1974, and again in the 1980s mainly to countries disrupted by war and severe drought.

In Nigeria, federal and state governments responded to rising revenues from petroleum and by increasing their expenditure to levels substantially exceeding income, thereby incurring levels of debt that could not be repaid, particularly after petroleum prices began to fall in the 1980s. Agricultural exports declined sharply, to zero in the case of groundnuts and palm oil, of which Nigeria had been the world's largest producer in 1965.

Manufacturing output increased rapidly in the first decade after independence in most African countries, albeit from a low base. Subsequently, declining access to the means to import machinery and materials led to a fall in the use of manufacturing capacity, rising unit costs and lay-offs of workers. Similarly, education and health spending increased significantly after independence. Child mortality continued to diminish and life expectancy and literacy to rise. However, these gains were undermined by declining import capacity and falling government revenues, and in some countries have even been reversed.

Foreign firms responded to political uncertainties and the problems of converting profits into 'hard' currencies by shifting away from direct investment in mining, plantations and industries into the provision of goods and managerial and financial services, paid for directly and in 'hard' currencies, often funded by development agencies or guaranteed by their own governments. The World Bank increased its lending to Africa in the 1970s, particularly for agricultural development projects. These loans funded interventionist policies, paid for fertilizer imports and contributed to the debts of African governments without making any significant impact on crop production.

In the 1980s interest rates on international loans increased, debts fell due, and export earnings decreased. In the 1990s payments for servicing debts rose, on average, to one-fifth of export earnings, representing only about one-half of the amount required to prevent a continuing rise in the totals outstanding. The World Bank and the IMF arranged rescheduling of debts and made structural adjustment loans. These loans, and the continued creditworthiness of most African governments, were conditional on the adoption of a standardized range of policies, encompassing reductions in government spending and subsidies, the liberalization of foreign trade policies and domestic marketing, the privatization of state corporations and, most crucially, currency devaluation.

These policies defined the terms on which governments would be excused from the repayment of their debts. Fiscal policies and development strategies in most African countries came to depend upon the approval of the World Bank and the IMF. They have taken over Joseph Chamberlain's mandate to develop the undeveloped economies in Africa, and other continents, in the interests of the 'less developed countries' and the global economy.

THE CONTRADICTIONS OF STRUCTURAL ADJUSTMENT

In Africa, as in Eastern Europe, strategies of economic reform preceded the movement towards political democracy. The critical element in most structural adjustment programmes (SAP) was radical devaluation of the currency. This was resisted by most governments, both because it would sharply raise the cost of imported goods, and because it would deprive them of the capacity to allocate foreign exchange and imported goods.

Devaluation is designed to encourage agricultural production by raising the price of exports and of imported food. If government spending and the money supply are not stringently controlled, the demand to exchange the national currency for foreign exchange will either lead to further devaluations, or to a renewed discrepancy between the exchange rates in official and parallel markets. Consequently, rising prices cannot be offset by raising wages and government spending. Unless other items of government spending, such as defence expenditure, are reduced, budgetary allocations for health and education spending will suffer.

The burden of SAP therefore falls most heavily on those with wage and salary incomes, who cannot pass the effects of rising prices on to others, and on students and other recipients of public services. Those who were enriched by access to state resources under a previous regime are financially well placed to take advantage of economic liberalization. Government revenues can recover if the flow of trade can be diverted from 'illegal' channels to official internal and export markets. Successful currency and trade liberalization in several countries has facilitated legal trade across African borders. In conditions of increasing unemployment and rising inflation, trade unions have generally been ineffective in protecting their members' living standards and found it hard to protect jobs, but they have asserted their independence from governments and contributed in different ways to the struggle for more democratic forms of government.

It has not been easy for the international agencies to enforce all the conditions they have sought to lay down in their negotiations with governments. Governments may meet some conditions but not others or only go half way to meeting set targets. Loan payments and assistance with rescheduling debts are used as instruments in a continuing process of negotiations between international financial institutions and governments, and within governments themselves over the adoption and implementation of economic reforms.

The effects of SAP on economic activities and distribution of incomes depend upon the mechanisms adopted to implement them. Initially, fixed exchange rates were replaced with foreign exchange auctions open to banks. The result, in Ghana and Nigeria for example, was a proliferation of banks. Foreign exchange acquired through the auction could be resold on illegal or parallel markets. In 1992 Nigeria floated the naira; rising government spending caused the exchange rate to fall further until the Abacha government fixed the rate in January 1994, at less than one-twentieth of its official exchange rate in 1986. The government was thus impelled to abandon the fixed exchange rate in 1995 and allow the naira to fall even more substantially, in relation to the US dollar. Governments seeking re-election in Ghana and Kenya in 1992 expanded the money supply, with the result that their exchange rates fell while prices rose.

The South African government drew back from the redistributive aims of the ANC's Reconstruction and Development Programme in favour of reducing the fiscal deficit inherited from the previous government and by liberalizing agricultural markets and foreign trade. The abolition of the 'financial rand' in 1995 was followed in 1997 by the relaxation of exchange controls. The country's economic revival, however, placed new strains on the balance of payments, and the exchange rate of the rand weakened against the US dollar.

The francophone African countries using the CFA franc benefited from a stable and convertible currency, which was also attractive to traders in neighbouring countries with unstable and unconvertible national currencies. The rate of exchange of the CFA franc against the French franc, however, having remained fixed since 1948, ultimately operated to discourage exports and encourage imports until it was belatedly devalued by 50% in 1994. The impact of the consequent rise in prices provoked strikes in Benin, Burkina Faso, Chad, Gabon and Niger. However, the effects of the devaluation encouraged a revival of agricultural exports, particularly in Côte d'Ivoire.

In Ghana and Uganda, rising levels of official prices for export crops attracted this trade into official channels and into rather than out of the country. Consequently, the share of government revenues in national income rose dramatically. In Ghana and Tanzania marketing boards raised the local prices of exports by less than the extent of currency devaluations, thus reducing their revenue deficits at the expense of the farmers. Uganda eventually abandoned marketing boards, but introduced a tax on windfall profits when coffee prices increased. Following the abolition of marketing boards in Nigeria, traders purchased cocoa at prices exceeding world market levels as a convenient technique for circumventing exchange control regulations. Declines in the value of the naira widened the difference between Nigerian petrol prices and those in adjoining countries; however, unpopular increases in the domestic price of petrol merely resulted in extensive smuggling, massive hoarding in anticipation of further price rises, and severe fuel shortages. Liberalization has closed some avenues of corrupt enrichment, it has been accompanied by new techniques of appropriating public resources for private use.

A number of African governments have abolished restrictions on foreign investment and transferred state enterprises to the private sector. Venture capitalists in the mining sector, and also in the development of tourism, have obtained lucrative concessions. Few African countries, however, have to date attracted significant foreign investment in industry.

SAP have encouraged official agricultural exports and allowed a modest improvement in the use of industrial capacity. Further expansion has been constrained by high interest rates, the suppression of consumer demand and the high cost of imported materials. Economic recovery drew in more imported goods than could be offset by rising exports. SAP have been accompanied by falling export prices, and rising financial outflows to service debts. A sustained net inflow of foreign exchange is needed if SAP are to generate sustained economic expansion without high inflation and further devaluations.

Some governments have negotiated substantial reductions in bilateral debt and, as in the case of Uganda, have bought back some commercial debts at a discount. The World Bank has refunded its (IBRD) debts from most African countries on concessionary IDA terms. The IMF has extended repayment of its short-term loans under its extended structural adjustment facility. However, despite these concessions, African governments continue to face debt-servicing obligations, and the external indebtedness of African countries in relation to their national income and export earnings is in aggregate far higher than those of any other region, albeit that it represents only a small proportion of total debt internationally. While this should facilitate funding from Western governments, banks and international agencies, it also diminishes the importance of doing so.

ELECTIONS, DEMOCRACY AND POWER

In the late 1980s, authoritarian governments, whether civilian or military, firmly capitalist or of 'socialist orientation' were clearly unable to resolve the economic crisis and political conflicts which confronted them. The contraction of resources at their disposal led those in power to appropriate ever larger shares. This narrowed their capacity to co-opt élites and maintain a measure of public acceptance. They lacked the credibility to persuade workers and others to accept the stringent requirements of SAP. In some cases, broadly-based opposition coalitions, such as the Movement for Multi-party Democracy in Zambia and the Forum for the Restoration of Democracy (FORD) in Kenya, emerged, variously drawing support from dissatisfied regional élites, excluded politicians or army officers, businessmen seeking equitable access to state resources, trade unions, professionals and students. In most countries, however, efforts by the politically aspirant to form effective coalitions were unsuccessful, leaving the ruling parties still in control of state institutions and patronage. Some governments sought to preserve their power by managing political reforms; others resisted changes. Radical parties and governments underwent sudden ideological conversions from 'Marxism-Leninism' to 'free enterprise' and 'indigenous capitalism'.

Some form of democratic elections have been held or scheduled in almost all African countries. In several countries, opposition parties have disputed the re-election of incumbent rulers and challenged the government's legitimacy. Newly elected presidents have often lacked majority support in legislatures and presidents and prime ministers have challenged each other's prerogatives. The weaknesses of constitutional political arrangements create scope for renewed military intervention.

President Senghor of Senegal opened the way to political change in 1974, when he licensed two opposition parties. This restriction was removed in 1981, when opposition parties multiplied. The ruling party, however, retained control of political patronage, the electoral machinery and the security services, thus tolerating opposition while maintaining power. In Nigeria, the Second Republic sought to regulate competition for the spoils of office by replacing the Westminster model with a regulated variant on the US presidential system. The National Party of Nigeria (NPN) divided its opponents and exploited its control of the electoral rules and procedures to determine the outcome of the 1983 elections, thereby discrediting the political system and opening the way to further periods of military rule.

The Babangida regime, which took power in 1985, adopted an SAP and decreed that only two political parties would be permitted to contend for office. Babangida, however, repeatedly changed the rules governing the recognition of parties and eligibility to stand for office. The result was a presidential contest in 1993 between two parties enriched by public and private funds. In the event, the military regime annulled the results of the election: Chief Abiola, who was widely regarded as having won, was insufficiently compliant to the wishes of the military. Gen. Abacha replaced both Babangida and his caretaker successor, Chief Shonekan, and later in the year dissolved the national assembly. The regime repressed demonstrations and strikes in 1993 and 1994, imprisoned Abiola in 1994 for 'treasonably' declaring himself president and secretly tried and imprisoned serving and former military officers for involvement in an alleged coup plot in 1995. The subsequent execution of nine Ogoni activists provoked widespread international condemnation, and led to Nigeria's suspension from the Commonwealth, with a contingent warning of expulsion if democracy was not restored within a period of two years. The European Union and the USA have reaffirmed their embargoes on military exports to Nigeria. Within Nigeria, the political class has remained dependent on the military to open their path to office, and have proved unable to offer a united challenge to military usurpation.

In early 1991 opposition parties triumphed in multi-party elections in the island states of Cape Verde and São Tomé and Príncipe. In Benin a series of strikes led to the calling of a national conference, which elected its own prime minister, Nicéphore Soglo, and cleared the way to legislative and presidential elections in 1991. Soglo became president and the 12 parties obtained representation in the legislature. The pattern of national conferences, representing a multiplicity of aspiring parties and other interests, was repeated in Chad, The Congo, Gabon, Madagascar, Niger, Togo and Zaire, as well as in South Africa. The dispersal of political support among a number of parties, with no stable majority party or coalition, also proved to be common to many of the new legislatures.

President Houphouët-Boigny responded to protests in Côte d'Ivoire in 1990 by calling a multi-party election, in which his party's victory demonstrated to other one-party states that power could be retained in the electoral process. In Gabon the ruling party maintained control of the national assembly in similar fashion in legislative elections in 1990, and in presidential elections three years later. In Ghana, Flt-Lt Jerry Rawlings used the state machinery in the 1992 presidential elections to defeat opposition parties whose support was limited to particular regions. In Togo, President Eyadéma, with military support, initially refused to accept the national conference's nominee as prime minister. He retained the presidency when opposition candidates withdrew from the 1993 presidential election, and has subsequently retained power through the skilled manipulation of opposition groups.

It was the Benin example, however, that persuaded a number of other single-party regimes to accept multi-party elections, while resisting the idea of a national conference. A divided opposition could not prevent Blaise Compaoré being re-elected president of Burkina Faso in 1992. Biya in Cameroon won a disputed three-way election in 1992; however, the outcome divided the opposition and highlighted the unresolved problem of relations between the anglophone and francophone areas of the country. In 1993 President Conté of Guinea obtained 52% of the vote against a divided opposition. In Guinea-Bissau, President Vieira narrowly won the second round of the presidential elections in the same year. The ruling party in Mauritania won presidential elections in 1992; most of the country's opposition parties did not take part in the subsequent legislative elections. Multi-party elections afforded little opportunity for opposition parties to challenge the repressive regime in Equatorial Guinea in 1993. Elections in Djibouti in 1993 excluded supporters of an armed opposition. In the same year President René of Seychelles obtained a clear electoral endorsement. Victorious incumbents were able to ensure their success in subsequent local parliamentary and presidential elections, which were often boycotted by their opponents.

Military interventions opened the way to the election of civilian governments in Mali (in 1992) and in Niger, where a nine-party alliance united to elect President Ousmane in 1993 against the military candidate of the previous ruling party. The transitional government in Chad was unable to prevent armed conflicts between its own forces and rival militias, and continuing internal dislocation led to the postponement of elections until 1996. Military rulers were defeated in elections in The Congo in 1992 and the Central African Republic in 1993. Madagascar, after a period of labour unrest, held presidential and legislative elections in 1992 and 1993. In Lesotho, the opposition Basotho Congress Party, which triumphed in elections held in 1993, had subsequently to face conflicts within the army and was able to retain power only after intervention by the presidents of Botswana, Zimbabwe and South Africa.

A number of newly elected presidents found that they could not presume on the support of legislators. The Madagascar national assembly impeached President Zafy in 1996, following persistent friction between the executive and legislative branches of government. President Lissouba of The Congo, lacking a parliamentary majority, dissolved the legislature in 1994 following disagreements with the majority party. In Niger, President Ousmane similarly dissolved the national assembly in 1994 but was unwilling to accept the prime minister imposed by the new majority; Col Maïnassara seized power in January 1966 and successfully arranged his election to the presidency in July. An army *coup d'etat* displaced the elected government of The Gambia in 1994; Lt Jammeh secured his election to the presidency in the following year. In Benin, opposition parties gained a majority in the 1995 legislative elections and Soglo was defeated in the 1996 presidential election by Kerekou, the country's former military dictator.

In Burundi, the Buyoya government set up a constitutional commission on 'national democratization'. In the 1993 elections, Buyoya was defeated by Ndadaye, who became Burundi's first Hutu head of state but was assassinated less than three months later by Tutsi paratroops, provoking extensive political violence and tensions between the Hutu-dominated government and the Tutsi-dominated army. In Rwanda, a peace agreement between the Hutu government and the insurgent Front patriotique rwandais (FPR) ended in 1994 when the shooting down of a plane carrying the presidents of Rwanda and Burundi was followed by genocidal massacres of political opponents and Tutsi generally by Hutu militia, ended only after the military victory of the FPR. Numerous Hutu fled to Tanzania and to Zaire, where Hutu militia continued to hold sway in refugee camps. Events in Rwanda exacerbated fears in Burundi where both armed militia and the national army were involved in ethnic massacres. The military refused to accept an African peace-keeping force and restored Buyoya to power.

In Zaire Mobutu and his supporters in the army resisted the claims of the national conference to appoint Etienne Tshisekedi prime minister, and installed their own candidate, subsequently ignoring agreements to share power with the opposition and subsequently exploiting rivalries among opposition politicians as a means of postponing elections. Mobutu's manipulation of ethnic interests to divide the opposition led to the forcible expulsion from Shaba and North Kivu of people originating from other provinces. Zairean army attacks on Tutsis in 1996 provoked an uprising, with Rwandan support, which met little resistance as it swept across the country. Laurent Kabila of the insurgent Parti de la révolution populaire took power from Mobutu in 1997 and subsequently suppressed protests against the exclusion of Tshisekedi and other opposition representatives from his new government of the Democratic Republic of the Congo.

In Zambia, President Kaunda reluctantly conceded demands for an end to one-party rule and was defeated in the 1991 elections by a trade union leader, Frederick Chiluba, with broad national support. The new government was beset by the regional rivalries, corruption and authoritarianism of its predecessor, and excluded Kaunda from contesting the 1996 presidential election. In Malawi, the electorate voted for democracy in a referendum held in 1993; President Banda was defeated in the ensuing election in 1994. The Tanzanian government held multi-party elections in 1995, securing a decisive majority on the mainland, but retaining control in Zanzibar by a questionably narrow result. In Kenya, foreign creditors insisted that President Moi agree to multi-party elections when it became clear that authoritarian rule could no longer ensure political stability. He responded by unleashing violent communal attacks, thus proving that multi-party politics would lead to tribal conflict. Meanwhile, FORD began to divide into rival regional and political factions, each asserting its claim to the presidency, thereby allowing Moi to win the presidential and parliamentary elections at the end of 1992. Subsequent attempts to form a cohesive opposition coalition have proved unsuccessful. Uganda held legislative elections in 1994 and a presidential election in 1996 without the benefit of political parties. The Swazi monarchy has continued to discourage opposition and to hold legislative elections without parties.

In Zimbabwe, the Zimbabwe African National Union–Patriotic Front (ZANU–PF) won the 1980 and 1985 elections overwhelmingly in the Shona areas, but coercion and patronage were not sufficient to defeat the Zimbabwe African People's Union (ZAPU) electorally in Matabeleland. Mugabe incorporated ZAPU into the ruling party in 1988 and proposed to set up a one-party state. In 1990, however, this proposal was jettisoned in the face of foreign disapproval and opposition from within ZANU–PF, which successfully eclipsed a disparate opposition alliance in elections held in that year. In Namibia, the South West Africa People's Organisation of Namibia (SWAPO) consolidated its victory in the 1989 independence elections, and again in the 1992 regional polls and national elections in 1994; two opposition parties retained control of regional strongholds.

In a number of countries, civil war has offered politicians the means to seek power, appropriate diamonds, timber and other natural resources, and to claim their place in peace negotiations. The overthrow of the Doe regime in Liberia in 1990, and of the Barre government in Somalia in 1991, led to violent conflicts between rival militias and the dispatch of external forces to restore order. Nigerian-led forces installed an interim government in Liberia. Rival factions agreed to replace it with a transitional council in 1993 and quarrelled over cabinet posts without giving up their arms. The conflict in Liberia spilled over into Sierra Leone. A coup in 1992 disrupted plans for democratic elections and did not bring armed rebellion to an end. Sierra Leoneans registered a clear vote for peace and against military rule when they turned out for the 1996 elections, only for the armed forces to seize power again in 1997.

The US marines opened routes for delivering food aid in parts of Somalia in 1992, but failed to remove the leaders of clan militias. US and subsequent UN peace-keeping operations were eventually terminated in 1995, leaving the country still in the grip of clan conflicts. In Angola, the anti-government União Nacional para a Independência Total de Angola (UNITA) refused to accept electoral defeat by the ruling MPLA and resorted again to war; successive peace agreements opened prospects of a coalition government. Peace negotiations between the government of Mozambique and the insurgent Resistência Nacional Moçambicana (Renamo) led to an election in 1994 in which the ruling Frente de Libertação de Moçambique (Frelimo) retained office. In both countries, the principal matter for negotiation was the division of national offices and provincial governorships.

Successful liberation movements assumed power in Ethiopia and Eritrea in 1991. Each sought to find ways of representing all ethnic groups, but were reluctant to concede the claims of such groups outside their own coalitions. In Ethiopia, however, the leading opposition groups refused to participate in legislative elections held in 1995. Many Amhara opposed the recognition of Eritrean independence and feared that their concerns would be eclipsed by rival ethnic interests dominating the government.

In South Africa, successive rounds of political negotiations eventually produced a constitution, despite the threats and use of force by those who feared exclusion from power to obstruct changes which did not accommodate their demands. The ANC predictably won the 1994 election, securing overwhelming support from African voters in most provinces. The majority of white, Indian and urban Coloured voters preferred the National Party, which won the election in the Western Cape. The Inkatha Freedom Party entered the lists at a late stage in the campaign, and accepted an agreement to allow its claim to an electoral majority in KwaZulu/Natal. Each of the three parties was included in the ANC-led government, from which the National Party withdrew in 1996. Political competition has been most evident within the political parties, who are constitutionally entitled to remove dissident members from parliament.

Elite and popular opposition to exclusion from opportunities and economic deprivation has been articulated through demands for multi-party democracy. The opening-up of political competition has brought a plethora of parties into the arena, usually lacking distinctive policies, and seeking only a chance to vie for power. National conferences and multi-party elections have provided a means for transferring power to elected rulers; they have also been used to maintain regimes in power or to broker power-sharing agreements. In a few countries they have allowed the contest for power to be decided peacefully. In many cases, opposition parties have, with more or less justification, denounced the re-election of incumbent rulers as fraudulent. None the less, the forms of multi-party democracy have opened channels of press freedom and wider political organization and debate. In other instances, however, conferences and elections have engendered confrontations between military rulers and democratic challengers, and to ethnic violence and even the renewal of civil war. Peace agreements have been negotiated and subsequently broken as signatories continue to pursue their political aims by violent means. For many young men, the use of weapons has become a means of livelihood and a way of life. Political leaders have been able to incite violence when particular groups fear that their own security and access to local resources are threatened by changes in national politics. New, and old, ruling parties have had to live with other parties but have not necessarily accepted the legitimacy of opposition. Across Africa, people are weary of soldiers and disillusioned by politicians. Politics continues to turn on the capture and uses of state power which does not provide a sufficient foundation for democratic societies.

BIBLIOGRAPHY

Akwetey, E. *Trade Unions and Democratization*. Stockholm Studies in Politics. University of Stockholm, 1994.

Allen, C., 'Understanding African Politics', in *Review of African Political Economy,* No. 65, 1995.

Allen, C., and Williams, G. (Eds). *Sociology of Developing Societies: Sub-Saharan Africa.* London, Macmillan, 1982.

Anderson, B. *Imagined Communities.* London, Verso, 1991.

Crush, J. (Ed.). *The Power of Development*. London, Routledge, 1995.

De Waal, A. *Famine that Kills: Darfur, Sudan 1984–1985.* Oxford, Clarendon Press, 1989.

Ferguson, J. *The Anti-politics Machine*. Cambridge University Press, 1990.

First, R. *The Barrel of a Gun.* London, Allen Lane, 1970.

Heyer, J., Roberts, P., and Williams, G. (Eds). *Rural Development in Tropical Africa.* London, Macmillan, 1981.

Mortimore, M. *Adapting to Drought: Farmers, Famines and Desertification in West Africa.* Cambridge University Press, 1989.

Raikes, P. *Modernising Hunger.* London, James Currey, 1988.

Richards, P. *Indigenous Agricultural Revolution.* London, Hutchinson, 1985.

ECONOMIC TRENDS IN AFRICA SOUTH OF THE SAHARA, 1997

DONALD L. SPARKS

The economies of sub-Saharan Africa are, for the most part, small and fragile, and the region is rapidly being left behind in the global economy. The region is poor: excluding South Africa, its combined gross domestic product (GDP) is approximately US $286,000m., less than that of the Netherlands. Sub-Saharan Africa accounts for less than 1% of world trade, and for only 4% of global GDP (Nigeria and South Africa jointly account for 40% of the regional total). Africa's annual GDP per caput was estimated at less than $500 in 1996, and annual income per head ranged from Mozambique's $80 to Seychelles' $6,280.

Sub-Saharan Africa has great diversities, yet the 51 states of the region share many common characteristics. They range significantly in terms of population, size and economic scale. Nigeria, the largest, had a population of 88.5m. at the 1991 census (althouth current World Bank estimates are 105m.), while 10 other countries of the region each contain less than 1m. people. Seychelles, the smallest, has a population of less than 75,000. The region's total population is about 572m. Climate and topography vary greatly and include Mediterranean, tropical and semi-tropical, desert, rain forest, savannah, mountains and plains. Some countries are more intensively urbanized than others. Zambia's urban population, for example, represents almost 50% of the country's total, while in Burundi it is only 6%. Educational levels also vary greatly; for example, 54% of all students of secondary school age are enrolled in schools in Mauritius, followed by 52% in Zimbabwe, while for Rwanda the proportion is only 2%. Mauritius has a literacy rate of about 83%, while Burkina Faso's is less than 20%. Life expectancy also varies, from 44 years in Guinea-Bissau, to an average for the region of 52 years. Some sub-Saharan countries, like South Africa, Zaire and Zimbabwe, are relatively well-endowed with natural resources, while others, such as Niger and Somalia, have few such assets. Sub-Saharan Africa contains the world's largest reserves of a number of strategic minerals, including gold, platinum, cobalt and chromium.

Given this diversity, it is accordingly difficult to draw general conclusions about the continent's economic performance as a whole during any given year. Nevertheless, some broad comparisons can be made. The region's overall economic growth rate during the past two decades has been dismal. The table below sets out some of the principal economic areas in which the region has experienced decline.

Table 1. Comparative Economic Indicators (1980–90)

	1980	1990	Percentage change
Per caput output (US dollars)	582	335	−42.5
Per caput consumption (US dollars)	465	279	−40.0
Investment (percentage of GDP)	20.2	14.2	−29.7
Export of goods (million US dollars)	48,700	31,900	−34.5
Per caput food production (US dollars)	107	94	−12.2
Poverty (percentage below poverty line)	n.a.	62	—

Source: World Bank, *World Debt Tables, 1996.*

While sub-Saharan Africa has recorded a 3.4% average annual growth rate in GDP since 1961, this is just slightly above the rate of population growth. During 1965–75 GDP per caput grew by 2.6% per year, but then stagnated. Taking inflation and population growth into account, the region's real GDP per caput actually fell by 42.5% from 1980 to 1990. The region's GDP advanced by 2.2% in real terms in 1994 and by 3.2% in 1995, according to the World Bank. The World Bank estimates that the region's GDP will increase by 3.3%–4.1% annually between 1995–2005. However, given a population increase projected at 3.2% annually, this will result in a growth rate per caput of less than 1.0%. It must be noted, however, that economic growth in sub-Saharan Africa in 1994–96 was the highest achieved in almost a decade, due primarily to policy reforms implemented by a number of governments, as well as to enhance prices for commodities and improved weather conditions. Some countries performed particularly well in 1996. Uganda's GDP rose by more than 7%, while both Zambia and Zimbabwe achieved growth rates exceeding 5%. Sustained growth has been forecast for 1996.

By virtually any economic or social indicator, sub-Saharan Africa performs less well than any other developing region. Of the 47 countries classified by the World Bank as 'least developed', 32 were in sub-Saharan Africa. In many ways sub-Saharan Africa has found itself retreating economically while other developing areas of the world are advancing strongly. For example, at independence in 1957, Ghana was more prosperous than the Republic of Korea, and in 1965 Indonesia's economic output was about the same as Nigeria's. By 1993 Indonesia's output was three times greater than that of Nigeria, while the Republic of Korea's economy was six times larger than Ghana's. Equally important, the economies of East Asia grew by 9.3% in 1994, as against the 2.2% growth recorded by sub-Sahara Africa.

Of the world's four major developing areas (sub-Saharan Africa, East Asia, South Asia and Latin America), Africa South of the Sahara has the lowest GDP per caput growth rate (which was negative during most of the 1980s), the lowest life expectancy (52 years), the lowest primary school enrolment rate (just over one-half of total eligible school-age children), the lowest literacy rate (about 50%), the smallest number of children immunized against childhood diseases (just under one-half), the lowest daily caloric intake, and the highest percentage of people living just under the international poverty line (by the year 2000, it is estimated, about 43% will be subsisting on incomes of less than $350 per year). The region also has the developing world's highest population growth rate (3.2%) and the highest rate of infant mortality (92 children out of every 1,000 die before reaching the age of five years). Of the 7.0m. infant deaths annually world-wide, 5.0m. occur in sub-Saharan Africa.

Despite the limited improvements achieved during the early and mid-1990s, almost every sub-Saharan economy declined in virtually every measurable way during the past three decades. By 1994, per caput GDP was about 15% below its level a decade earlier, and per caput income down by over one-fifth. In some of the continent's least developed countries (LDC), such as Chad and Niger, the fall has been perhaps 30% or more. The poorer countries of Africa were even poorer in 1996 than they were at their independence in the 1960s.

Africa has lost the ability to feed itself: in 1974 it imported 3.9m. metric tons of cereals, but by 1993 it had to import 18.2m. tons, almost five times the 1974 level. Food imports cost the region US $6,900m. in 1993. Food aid increased during the period 1974–89, from 0.9m. tons to 4.8m. tons of cereals. At present, about one-quarter of African population does not obtain the necessary average daily intake of calories required to sustain a healthy life. Many countries, such as Liberia, parts of Sudan and Rwanda, faced critical food shortages in 1997.

The factors underlying Africa's parlous economic condition can be broadly categorized either as 'external' or 'internal'. The major external factors include adverse movements in the terms of trade and declines in foreign aid and foreign investment. The internal factors include poor soils, widely fluctuating and harsh climates, poor human and physical infrastructure, rapid urbanization and population growth, environmental degradation, ineffective government and inappropriate public policies. Unfortunately, African governments have but limited control over many of these factors, particularly the external ones.

EXTERNAL CAUSES OF ECONOMIC DECLINE

The pillars of Africa's external relationship with the Western industrialized countries are trade, aid and investment, and the declines of all three have added to the continent's poor economic performance during the past 20 years.

Trade and Regional Co-operation

One of the most serious of these external factors is Africa's worsening terms of trade, with declining traditional exports, both in price and quantities, and increasing imports, also in both price and volume. More than one-half of sub-Saharan Africa's exports generally go to the Western industrialized countries, from which the region traditionally purchases about 80% of its imports. African countries typically produce one or two major agricultural or mineral commodities for export to the industrialized countries in the West. Primary products account for approximately 80% of the region's export revenues, about the same level as during the 1960s. Poor export performances, combined with the range of problems dealt with below, have resulted in larger deficits in most African countries' current balance-of-payments accounts. The average current account deficit rose from about 4% of GDP in the 1970s to almost 8% of GDP in the 1980s. Africa's petroleum-exporting countries were severely affected by the decline in international prices for crude petroleum and by diminished world-wide demand.

Price levels for the region's primary exports have been uneven. Prices for many agricultural commodities (including cocoa, palm oil, tea and tobacco) have risen since 1986, but prices for many others (coffee, sisal and sugar) have remained steady or fallen. Except for some petroleum producers, the 'terms of trade' for most African states worsened between 1970–81. They stabilized somewhat in the late 1980s, and by 1988 stood at about 60% of the 1970–73 level. The purchasing power of the region's exports has fallen by 22% since 1987, due primarily to the decline in world petroleum prices. Using the base year 1987 =100, the region's overall terms of trade declined to 88 by 1992. Burundi experienced the sharpest fall, of 72%, during this period. The steep decline in sub-Saharan Africa's export revenues was as much attributable to falls in volume as to relative prices. Between 1970–85 Africa's share of the world market for primary (non-petroleum) exports fell from 7% to 4% of the total. Maintenance of Africa's 7% market share would have added US$10,000m. to its overall export income. Sub-Saharan Africa's share of total world exports declined to 2.2% by 1994. Economic advance in other areas of the world suggests that increased trade and general integration into the global economy leads to swifter growth. For example, the countries that have integrated most quickly in the past decade experienced growth about three percentage points in advance of that achieved by the slowest integrating countries. The poorest group of countries are the least able to withstand the side effects of a worsening terms of trade. According to the Global Coalition for Africa, revenues from Uganda's coffee exports fell by about 50% between 1985–90, despite a rise in volume terms. Between 1970–84, the region's world market share of coffee, cotton and cocoa fell by 13%, 29% and 33% respectively. In 1996 there was a modest upturn in some commodity prices, notably coffee and cotton. These increases account in part for the improved GDP performance of the region as a whole during that year.

The import policies of the Western industrialized countries have played a major, and often negative, role in Africa's export performance. The industrialized market economies are Africa's major trading partners. However, despite a somewhat privileged access to the European Union (EU) market the African share of the African, Caribbean and Pacific (ACP) countries' participation in the EU market has declined relative to that of other developing countries. Notwithstanding the benefits of the Lomé Convention, protectionism and restrictive agricultural practices, particularly in the EU and, (to a lesser extent) the USA, have resulted in an over-supply of some agricultural commodities, and thus inhibited world-wide demand and weakened world prices. Tariff and non-tariff barriers to trade by the Western industrialized countries have discouraged value-added or semi-processed agricultural imports from African states. Moreover, as incomes increase in the industrialized countries, consumer demand for agricultural products does not advance in proportion to this rise. Additionally, industry is increasingly turning to substitutes, such as fibre optics for copper wires in telecommunications, and to beet sugar for cane sugar. Tariffs, which are already high by world comparisons, have yet to show measurable reduction in the sub-Saharan region.

According to figures published by the General Agreement on Tariffs and Trade (GATT), trade among African states is low; in 1990, regional trade accounted for only about 6% (US$4,400m.) of Africa's export volume. Equally significant was that virtually no growth was recorded during the period 1984–90. Most African states produce similar products for export, generally primary agricultural or mineral commodities, and, as most of the value added is carried out in Western industrialized countries, there is little African demand for these products. African states themselves often discourage trade by their strongly inward-orientated, import-substitution development strategies, including over-valued exchange rates and protectionist trade policies. Their transport infrastructure is geared for export to Western Europe, Japan and North America, rather than to nearby countries. In southern Africa, for example, only 4% of the export trade of the 12-member Southern African Development Community (SADC) is transacted between SADC members.

The region could exploit its comparative advantage in commodity exports only if the industrial countries will agree to support international buffer stock agreements and implement other arrangements for co-operation. African states have tried various methods of improving their trade performance, and of developing overall regional economic co-operation. There have been several attempts to form free trade areas or customs unions. Several have failed and have been abandoned, such as the colonially-imposed Central African Federation, of Zambia, Zimbabwe and Malawi, and the East African Community, comprising Kenya, Tanzania and Uganda.

One of the longest standing, and most successful, regional organizations, is the Southern African Customs Union (SACU), founded in 1969 and comprising Botswana, Lesotho, Namibia, South Africa and Swaziland. SACU permits free trade among its members and provides a common external tariff. Customs revenue is generally collected by South Africa and allocated to individual members according to a formula based on members' share of total trade. Two somewhat more recent groupings, commanding good prospects of success, are the SADC and the Economic Community of West African States (ECOWAS). ECOWAS has as its eventual goal the removal of barriers to trade, employment and movement between its 16 member states, as well as the rationalization of currency and financial payments among its members (see Part Two—Regional Organizations). This membership is drawn from francophone and lusophone as well as anglophone states, with as much economic diversity as Nigeria and Cape Verde. Owing to the political and economic disparity of its members, it is likely to be many years before any of the above objectives are fully met. The SADC (see Part Two—Regional Organizations) was established initially as the Southern African Development Co-ordination Conference (SADCC) to provide a counter, during the era of apartheid, to South Africa's economic hegemony over the region. The SADCC did not initially seek an economic association or customs union, but rather to function as sub-regional planning centre to rationalize development planning. Its reconstitution in 1992 as the SADC placed binding obligations on member countries with the aim of promoting economic integration towards a fully developed common market.

Another important grouping, the Franc Zone, was established in 1948 and now comprises, together with France, 13 former French colonies, Equatorial Guinea, a former Spanish colony and Guinea-Bisau, a former Portuguese possession (see Part Two—Regional Organizations). It operated with general success by providing a solid base of support for the members' financial and economic policies before encountering difficulties in the late 1980s. Each of the Zone's members are small states, none with a population exceeding 12m., and most are poor. A few, such as Cameroon, Congo and Gabon, are heavily reliant on petroleum export revenues. The French government guarantees the convertibility of the CFA franc, and this system automatically finances members' budgetary deficits, which aggregated at US$15m. in 1986 but had increased to $928m. by 1990.

During the early 1990s the French franc appreciated and thus made the CFA countries' exports relatively less competitive on world markets (as the value of the CFA franc also increased, its exports became more expensive). In addition, the Zone's terms of trade declined by about 45% due primarily to a fall in world commodity prices (coffee, cocoa and petroleum in particular). In 1993 per caput real income fell by 4.5% and exports declined by 3.9% in volume. In consequence of these factors, the Zone's attractiveness to potential foreign investment diminished and the outflow of capital from the CFA bloc increased. According to a study by the World Bank, the appreciation of the CFA franc against other currencies between 1986–91, with its adverse impact on trade competitiveness, had reduced the CFA countries' output by 0.2% per annum, while GDP in comparable countries outside the Franc Zone had achieved average growth of 4.5% annually during that period.

After prolonged pressure from the IMF and France to remedy the situation, in January 1994 the CFA central banks devalued the CFA franc by 50%, to French francs 1.00 = CFA francs 100 from the rate of French francs 1.00 = CFA francs 50, which had operated since 1948. (The Comoros franc, which is also aligned with the CFA franc and French franc exchange rate, was devalued by 33.3%.) The decision forestalled individual member countries from unilaterally devaluing, and also set the stage for potentially closer links, eventually leading to a common market in the region. Following the exchange rate realignment, each country introduced individual changes in fiscal, wages and structural adjustments. It was hoped that the realignment would lead to increases in agricultural output and exports, and also suppress inflation, as member governments are restricted in the growth of their respective money supplies. It should be noted, however, that in the short term the economic interests of the urban sector have been adversely affected by the devaluation, as prices for imported goods and services have increased. Indeed, in February 1994 thousands of disgruntled Senegalese massed in the streets of their capital, Dakar, when the prices of imported rice, sugar and cooking oil doubled following the devaluation. Additionally, demand for firewood rose sharply in many CFA countries as a result of rapid rises in the cost of petroleum products. This factor contributed to the already serious deforestation in many Sahelian countries. In early 1994 the IMF announced it would assist 11 of the 14 eligible member countries under its Enhanced Structural Adjustment Facility (ESAF) by providing financing on concessionary terms. Debt-relief assistance was also forthcoming from France. Almost two years after the devaluation, the IMF reported the Zone's overall economic growth as being 1.5% in 1994, with estimates of a higher rate in 1995. Côte d'Ivoire evidenced positive economic growth in 1994 for the first time in eight years.

In 1994 the six members of the francophone Customs and Economic Union of Central Africa (UDEAC) advanced their move towards fuller sub-regional integration by establishing the Economic and Monetary Community of Central Africa (CEMAC). A common external tariff was implemented, while tariffs between member states continue to be lowered and non-tariff barriers have been virtually eliminated. Another noteworthy development in regional co-operation was the initial participation of 13 southern and east African and Indian Ocean states in the Cross Border Initiative (CBI), supported by the World Bank, the African Development Bank and the EU. This initiative is aimed at liberalizing the member countries' foreign exchange systems, deregulating cross-border investments and facilitating the movement of goods, services and people among the participating countries. The CBI is voluntary, and is still in its formative stages. In 1996 Kenya, Uganda and Tanzania established the Permanent Tripartite Commission for East African Co-operation, with the aim of eliminating tariffs and co-ordinating members' infrastructure and the development of energy resources. In early 1997 the OAU inaugurated the African Economic Community, with the eventual goal of uniting the region's existing economic organizations into a single institution similar to the EU.

Foreign Debt, Aid and Investment

Three of the most obvious manifestations of external difficulties are foreign debt, declining levels of international aid and the difficulty of attracting outside investment. In 1960 the region's external debt amounted to less than US$3,000m., and the average debt-service ratio was only 2% of exports. During the 1970s and 1980s indebtedness advanced rapidly, from $84,049m. in 1980 to $223,298m. in 1995, with the debt-service ratio reaching almost 20%. By 1996 the debt-service ratio had risen to 30%. Total external debt as a percentage of exports rose from 91% in 1980 to 270% in 1995. Debt relative to total GDP has also increased, from 30.6% of GDP in 1980 to 74.1% in 1995. Of the 36 most severely indebted low-income countries listed by the World Bank in 1996, 28 were in sub-Saharan Africa.

Foreign official creditors wrote off about US$10,000m. of loans during 1989–91. These creditor nations generally converted loans to grants. The World Bank has estimated that if all the proposed debt forgiveness plans were implemented, the total debt would be reduced by perhaps $6,000m., or 8% of the total. Indeed, Africa spends four times more on debt-servicing than on the provision of health services. Without debt relief, some countries are now paying more than their exports bring in. Indeed, by the mid-1980s and continuing through the early 1990s, as much in debt-service payments was leaving Africa as foreign aid was entering. Even under the most optimistic assumptions for economic growth, seven highly indebted countries—Burundi, Guinea-Bissau, Mozambique, São Tomé and Príncipe, Sudan, the Democratic Republic of the Congo and Zambia—face an increasing scale of payments in future years to the multilateral development banks. Nevertheless, according to a recent assessment of the World Bank, African debtors and their creditors have made, 'surprisingly rapid progress' in dealing with the debt issue.

African states owe 65% of their total external debt to foreign governments, of which about US $46,000m. is owed to the 'Paris Club' of creditor countries. In 1995 the 'Paris Club' announced new terms for debt relief to Africa's poorest countries, which were defined as those with debt-to-export ratios exceeding 350%, or per caput incomes of below $500. Chad, Guinea, Guinea-Bissau, Togo and Uganda came within the ambit of these so-called 'Naples terms'. This programme allows a maximum 66.3% reduction of debt service owed to 'Paris Club' creditors. Uganda was able to reduce its indebtedness by 26% under the 'Naples terms', although its debt-service ratio was 1,227% in 1994. This programme follows a number of earlier 'Paris Club' arrangements, most notably the 'Toronto terms', which offered cancellation of up to one-third of export debt service, and a more generous 50% reduction under the 'enhanced Toronto' regime. In 1996 the World Bank and IMF launched the Heavily Indebted Poor Country (HIPC) Debt Initiative. Of the 41 countries initially defined as HIPC, 33 are in sub-Saharan Africa. Although all of the aspects of the $5,000–$7,000m. plan are yet to be finalized, it represents a major step for debt relief in the region. The HIPC initiative will be the first time the region has been accorded a scheme involving all its creditors—multilateral bodies, governments and commercial banks—in a case-by-case collaboration to share the costs of debt relief. The initiative is available only to those countries with World Bank and IMF-endorsed track records of good economic management and reform. The 'Paris Club' has agreed to reduce debt stock by as much as 80%, although commercial banks have yet to finally agree on their contributions. The World Bank will participate by way of a trust fund administered by the IDA, and the IMF will participate via its ESAF, with an initial contribution of $800m. An HIPC can be considered for 'Paris Club' relief only after three years of meeting targets, followed by a further three years of satisfactory economic performance in order to qualify for multilateral debt relief. Developing countries, however, generally view the six-year period as too long and the eligibility criteria too restrictive. The first beneficiary of the HIPC Initiative is Uganda, which is to obtain a reduction of $338m. in external debt relief in 1998. At early 1997 Burkina Faso and Mali were the only other countries eligible to participate in the initiative.

Africa's ability to service its debts has been impaired by severe falls in foreign exchange earnings. Additionally, after nearly two decades of annual increases in net foreign financial flows (including concessionary economic assistance), during the mid-1980s these flows had levelled off and actually begun to decline. These general decreases in financial intakes from all sources are the result of fewer and smaller private-sector foreign direct investments and commercial bank lending, as well as from decreased levels of 'aid' (in real terms) from traditional Western and multilateral donors. Official development assistance (ODA) continues to decline, even from traditionally generous donors. For example, Sweden reduced its ODA by 10% in 1992. Members of the OECD provided only 0.3% of their GDP in the form of ODA in 1991, as compared with 0.5% in 1982. ODA declined from US $16,700m. in 1990 (using 1994 prices) to $15,000m. in 1994. Official concessionary lending totalled $4,700m. in 1987, but declined to $4,600m. in 1993. On average, donor countries provided 0.3% of their gross national product (GNP) in 1993, well below the UN target of 0.7%. The USA provided $9,700m. in 1993 and was the second highest donor, after Japan. However, as a percentage of GNP, the US assistance level was the lowest of the OECD countries in 1994. It should be noted, however, that in 1997 the US government launched a major initiative, the US-Africa Economic Forum. Eligibility to participate in the Forum's $500m. infrastructure fund was to be extended to African countries carrying out economic reform.

International banks have been hesitant about increasing their loan commitments in Africa. Of the total US $22,500m. flow of net resources to sub-Saharan countries in 1980, about $13,000m. came as aid from official sources, with about $9,500m. provided privately, mainly by banks. By 1989 the total net flow had declined to about $21,000m., of which only $3,000m. was attributable to private sources. In 1993 only $1,300m. was disbursed in long-term loans. In 1995 about 80% of foreign direct investment to developing countries went to only 12 states, with the People's Republic of China absorbing almost one-half of the inflows. At only US$2,000m., sub-Saharan Africa was the recipient of about 1% of world-wide direct net foreign investment. Of that total, about half went to Nigeria. The level of foreign investment has been decreasing during the past decade. Africa's share of developing countries' inward investment declined from 7.5% of the total in the early 1980s to about 5.5% by the early 1990s. In 1993 sub-Saharan Africa attracted only $8 per caput in foreign capital inflows, as against almost $200 per caput in Latin America. Foreign investment has diminished for a number of reasons. The sub-Saharan region has yet to broaden its investment base beyond energy and mining, which remain the prime attractions. And, while foreign investors are attracted by the region's vast raw materials and low-wage economies, they are fearful of internal political volatility and the uncertainty of obtaining the enforcement of contracts. These considerations, combined with the deteriorating human and physical infrastructure, have virtually extinguished investor confidence.

INTERNAL CAUSES OF ECONOMIC DECLINE

Africa faces a number of 'internal' economic problems which, in the view of many analysts, outweigh the 'external' factors discussed above. Indeed, the World Bank's 1989 study on sub-Saharan Africa's quest for sustainable growth suggested that 'underlying the litany of Africa's problems is a crisis of governance'.

Governance, Social Factors and Natural Environment

Internationally, social and political stability are generally associated with higher economic growth rates. More than half of sub-Saharan Africa's countries have been caught up in civil wars, uprisings, mass migrations and famine. Ethnic conflicts and civil wars continued in 1997 in Sudan, Liberia, Somalia and both the Congo Republic and the Democratic Republic of the Congo. According to the World Bank, between 1965–85 the more unstable countries' average annual GDP per caput growth was 0.5%, while the region's 11 most politically stable countries achieved an average rate of 1.4%. In addition, many stable governments have been openly hostile toward the business community, be it foreign or domestic. For example, Ghana had at one time made it illegal to carry out 'any act with intent to sabotage the economy.' This law was interpreted with great flexibility, and some local entrepreneurs were actually executed for merely making profits. After independence, most African countries expanded the size of their civil service more rapidly than their economic growth justified. This expansion was designed to provide employment, and to the extent this reduced growth in the private sector, civil servants received lower and lower real wages. Governments became bloated and corrupt. For many, the need for better governance became critical.

Until relatively recently, most African governments did not view rapid population growth or environmental degradation as matters for concern. Indeed, until very recently most areas of the region practiced what is known as 'slash and burn' agriculture, a mode of production which can only be successful where land is abundant. The region's population has doubled since the 1960s, and at its current rate of growth it is forecast to double again in 22 years. During the past decade a succession of countries, realizing that their resources cannot service such population growth, have begun to recognize the necessity for environmental protection. Some countries of Africa have the highest rates of population growth in the world: for example, Kenya's and Côte d'Ivoire's 3.8% annual rate of natural increase is the developing world's highest. The region's projected annual growth rate of 3.2% for the years 1980–2000 compares with 2.9% for the period 1973–84. Sub-Saharan Africa's population has been forecast to reach 750m. by the year 2000. Some demographers predict that the region's population will reach 1,000m. in 20 years' time.

By 1997 about three-quarters of all African countries had family planning programmes, and some have set targets for population growth. Fertility appears to be declining in the small number of states that have established family planning services. Stemming rapid population growth in Africa is difficult because of social as well as economic factors. Most Africans live in rural areas on farms, and require large numbers of helpers. The cheapest way of obtaining such assistance is for a farmer to have more children. Because the infant mortality rate is so high (owing to poor health and nutrition), rural couples tend to want, and have, more babies. Additionally, African countries do not have organized old-age support schemes, and children are often viewed as potential providers of support for the elderly. Modern contraceptive methods, according to a recent study by the World Bank, are used by only 6% of couples in sub-Saharan Africa, as against 30% in India and 70% in China.

Rapid urbanization has also caused stresses in many African economies. Africa is still very largely rural and agricultural—some 75% of all Africans live outside cities and towns. Nevertheless, during the past generation, urbanization has increased at an alarming pace, and it has been forecast that by the year 2025 at least one-half of the population will live in cities. More than 42% of all urban-dwelling sub-Saharan Africans now reside in cities of more than 500,000 population, compared with only 8% in 1960. In fact, there were only two cities in the region with populations exceeding 500,000 in 1960. If recent trends should continue, Africa will have 60 cities with populations of more than 1m. by the year 2000, as against 19 such cities at present. Unemployment and under-employment are rampant in every major city of Africa. The population growth has put additional pressure on good agricultural and grazing lands, and on fuelwood. About 80% of the region's energy needs are supplied by fuelwood gathered by rural dwellers. In addition, population pressures add to deforestation, soil degredation and declines in agricultural output.

The informal sector has become increasingly important in the region. About 60% of the labour force, amounting to 40m. people, represent perhaps 20% of the region's total GDP. This sector has been growing at an annual rate of about 6% since the 1980s, according to the ILO. Perhaps most importantly, the 'hidden economy' absorbs 75% of new entrants into the labour market.

African states face significant problems in the provision of health services and education. Although both have improved since the mid-1960s, their levels remain the lowest in the world. Governments in Africa south of the Sahara expend less than 1% of their GDP on health care, and care is unevenly distributed throughout many countries, with most of the care centred in urban areas. According to UNICEF, several countries, including Angola, Ethiopia and Mozambique, spent more over many years on their military requirements than on health and education. With declining export receipts and general budget austerity, many African countries have been compelled to decrease their budgetary provisions for health. This has resulted in, for example, diminished levels of immunization. Less than one-half of Africa's population has access to clean, piped water, and some 80% of illness in Africa's least-developed countries (LDC) can be associated with inadequate water supplies or poor sanitation. Infant and child death rates are among the world's highest: in 17 countries of the region, infant mortality rates exceed 100 per 1,000, and in 13 states are more than 120 per 1,000.

The World Health Organization (WHO) has estimated that there are currently about 13m. adults in sub-Saharan Africa who have been infected with HIV (the virus widely believed to be the causative factor in AIDS). This figure represents about 65% of all known HIV infection world-wide. Of the 7,500m. new infections which occur daily world-wide, one-half are in sub-Saharan Africa. AIDS in Africa generally affects younger adults (20–45 year old age group) in their most economically productive years, and in Africa the educated, urban élite have been hardest hit. In fact, infection rates in urban areas are about double those of rural areas. AIDS is now the leading cause of adult death in Africa, where it is estimated that about 3.5m. women are currently infected. In Uganda about 10% of the population is thought to be infected by HIV, and the Zambian ministry of health has estimated that nearly 20% of women of child-bearing age in Zambia are HIV-infected. By the year 2000 there will probably be over 10m. orphans in Africa, and this will result in major strains on the individual governments' ability to provide housing, health care and education. Given the size of the pandemic in several central and eastern African states, it is reasonable to expect that AIDS will curtail GDP growth in several countries during the next decade. Additionally, the incidence of tuberculosis, currently the world's major infectious cause of adult deaths, has risen sharply in the recent past, claiming more than 3m. deaths world-wide in 1993. This increase has been linked to the growing AIDS incidence, as about 50% of tuberculosis patients are HIV-infected.

After initial improvements following independence, education is also declining in many sub-Saharan African countries. There has been a direct link between education and growth. Between 1960–80, the African countries which had higher percentages of children enrolled in primary school also had higher economic growth rates. A further key factor is that of increased education for women, which is clearly associated with lower fertility rates. A recent study by the World Bank found that the three countries with declining fertility—Botswana, Kenya and Zimbabwe—have the highest levels of female schooling and the lowest rates of child mortality. The study also indicated that in the Sahel, where female schooling rates are lowest, both fertility rates and child mortality have remained high. With an average of 6.3 births per female, sub-Saharan Africa has the highest fertility rate in the world.

Shortly after independence, most countries of the sub-Saharan region initiated programmes aiming to establish universal primary education. By 1980 some countries had achieved this goal. Nevertheless, according to UNESCO, enrolment ratios for primary education declined during 1980–83 in 12 African countries. For sub-Saharan Africa, an estimated 88% of primary school-aged children were enrolled in primary schools in the mid-1990s, up from 37% in 1965, but still poor in comparison with all developing countries (91%) or Western industrial countries (almost 100%). Here again, many governments have found education to be a service for which budgetary allocations may be cut back during times of fiscal crisis. African governments' emphasis on higher education at the expense of primary education has also been a negative factor for economic development. For example, average expenditures on secondary-school students per caput is some 40 times that of expeditures on primary school students as compared with a ratio of 1:16 in the Western industrialized countries. Additionally, because courses and textbooks were generally 'imported' directly from the former European colonial powers, much of the education has been inappropriate to the rural settings where most of the students live and will eventually work.

Africa's environment has been under intense pressure, especially during the past 20 years. With the increases in population discussed earlier, over-cultivation and over-grazing have turned vast areas into virtual wastelands. The United Nations Environment Programme (UNEP) has estimated that an area twice the size of India is under threat of desertification. The region annually loses about 2.7m. ha of woodland. In 1983 the FAO estimated that Africa's 700m. ha of undisturbed forest were being cleared at the rate of 3.7m. ha per year. Civil wars have also contributed to environmental degredation. In the late 1980s and early 1990s civil wars have had devastating effects on the environment in such countries as Chad, Sudan, Somalia, Mozambique and Angola. In addition, the region's 5m. displaced persons have fled not only repressive political conditions, but degraded environments unable to support them economically.

Many government leaders in the past suggested that the achievement of economic growth was inconsistent with environmental protection, and that African development could only advance at the expense of its environment. It has only been in the past few years that the two goals have been recognized as not mutually exclusive. Indeed, it is now generally accepted that sustained economic growth will be impossible without adequate environmental protection. Specifically, many nations, such as Kenya, Tanzania and South Africa will increasingly depend on tourism based on wildlife and undisturbed natural habitats. According to the World Tourism Organization, Africa attracts annually only 3.3% of the world's tourists, and absorbs less than 2% of tourism-generated revenue world-wide. In the late 1980s Lesotho, Madagascar and Mauritius became the first three African countries to develop national environmental action plans (NEAP). These NEAP are intended to create a framework for the better integration of environmental concerns into a country's economic development. By 1996 40 African states had begun the NEAP process, with support from a number of UN and bilateral donors. Loss of bio-diversity is also a serious problem as many of Africa's plant and animal numbers have been lost for ever. The long-term success of agriculture, the region's most important economic sector, ultimately will depend on the wise use of the environment.

Physical Infrastructure and the Structure of the Economies

For most countries in the region, physical infrastructure has generally deteriorated since the achievement of independence in the early and mid-1960s. Such essential services as roads, railways, ports and communications have been neglected, particularly in rural areas. Millions of US dollars worth of investment in transportation will be required if Africa is to take advantage of any improvement in agricultural output performances. Additional resources will also be needed if Africa's industrial sectors are to grow. African industry has expanded during the past generation, from about 25% of the continent's GDP in 1965 to over 30% by 1987. However, this contribution to GDP is lower than the LDC average. Manufacturing has not increased, because of low capacity utilization, limited trained manpower at all levels, small-scale domestic markets, inappropriate technology and poor plant design. Further, manufactured exports accounted for less of the total merchandise exports for Africa in 1987 than they did 25 years previously.

The structure of sub-Saharan Africa's economies has not changed dramatically since the time of independence. In 1965, agriculture accounted for 39% of GDP, and industry 19%. By 1995 agriculture had declined to less than 30%, with industry at 34%. African goals of rapid industrialization, however, did not materialize. Manufacturing advanced rapidly in the early 1960s, but then slowed to about the same average growth rate as GDP. While petroleum production expanded more swiftly, only a few states—Angola, Cameroon, Congo, Gabon and Nigeria—benefited. By the early 1990s manufacturing represented only 11% of the region's economic productivity (against 9% in 1965).

Few sub-Saharan countries have experienced rates of inflation on the scale witnessed in some parts of Latin America. During the 1980s, the rate of inflation was generally lower in countries belonging to the Franc Zone. None the less the sub-Saharan region experienced overall rates of inflation of 37.2% in 1993 of 60.7% in 1994 (following the devaluation of the CFA franc), and of 43.4% in 1995.

Many African countries' currencies appreciated in exchange rate terms during the mid-1970s. While inflation raised domestic prices, local currencies were not devalued to compensate. Thus, currencies became overvalued, meaning that their purchasing power was stronger for goods from abroad than at home, leading to increased demand for imports. Further, their exports became increasingly uncompetitive in price. As their currencies became overvalued, and foreign 'hard' currencies were in short supply, many African governments had to limit or ration foreign exchange. This in turn led to 'parallel' or 'black' markets for foreign currencies. Foreign exchange overvaluation was thus a result of inflation, which in turn was generated at least in part by escalations of government budget deficits. In addition, export and import tariff revenue provides a significant portion of African government revenues, as there is little personal or corporate taxation. As trade declines, so does government revenue, thus exacerbating budget deficits.

Agriculture and Famine

Unquestionably the leading factor behind the drastic declines in African economies has been the general neglect of agriculture. Agriculture accounts for about one-third of GDP for the continent as a whole, two-thirds of employment and 40% of export value. For virtually all African economies, the major agricultural exports consist of one or perhaps two or three primary products (cash crops such as coffee, tea, sugar, sisal, etc.) whose prices fluctuate widely from year to year on the world market. For 44 sub-Saharan African countries, their three leading agricultural exports comprise some 82% of their agricultural exports.

As suggested by the World Bank, 'if agriculture is in trouble, Africa is in trouble.' And agriculture has been in trouble for the past 25 years. The percentage of Africans lacking sufficient food has increaed from 38% to 43%: some 41 states in the region are suffering from food deficits, with undernutrition ranging from a low of 13% in Swaziland to a high of 72% in Somalia. During the same period, food production increased by only 2% annually, matched by a population growth rate of over 3%. In 1996 the FAO convened a World Food Summit, where agricultural problems were discussed at the highest international levels. As Africa is the only region where the proportion of people suffering from malnutrition is rising, the summit focused special attention on the problems of the region. The World Bank disclosed that its funding for agriculture and rural development had been reduced from US $6,000m. in 1986 to $2,600m. in 1996, and undertook to ensure that agriculture received priority attention in its agenda in Africa. On average, agricultural growth was slower during the period 1970–90 (when it rose by 1.4% annually, about one-half the rate of population growth) than in the 1960s, when it advanced at an annual rate of 2.7%.

About 180m. Africans currently suffer from chronic food insecurity, either because there is not enough food locally, or because they cannot afford enough food. Between 1980–90 the region's annual imports of cereals increased from 8.5m. tons to 18.2m. tons. Regional production of cereals did rise in 1994, however, by 9%, with the agricultural sector achieving growth of 2.0% in that year. Many Africans suffer from transitory food insecurity due to fluctuations in prices and production levels resulting from natural climatic difficulties and civil wars. A smaller number, although several million, suffer from, or are at immediate risk of famine.

As discussed above, many governments have pursued economic policies that were designed to keep urban wages and living conditions high and farm prices low by maintaining the value of currencies at high, unrealistic rates of exchange. This is understandable and obvious: political power in Africa rests in the city, not in the village or countryside. This was sometimes a matter of deliberate policy, at other times it was more a result of planned rural neglect, and on many occasions such strategies had the support of the international development community. In addition, producers were often bound by prices fixed by their governments, and at times these 'producer' prices failed to cover input costs. This resulted in farmers reducing their production for sale and reverting to subsistence agriculture.

Parastatal Organizations

Central to the understanding of direct state involvement in many African economies is the role of parastatal organizations. These organizations' influence and involvement in many African countries have been of particular concern in overall economic policy debates. After independence, most newly-formed African governments had three fundamental choices for the management and development of their economies, and for the encouragement of industrialization in the broadest sense. They could (i) nationalize existing entities; (ii) seek to attract private investment from abroad by offering favourable investment incentives (tax 'holidays', for example); or (iii) invest heavily in public enterprises. Most governments adopted combinations of all three, but virtually every national administration south of the Sahara opted for heavy parastatal involvement. At independence, the majority of new states had few other options open to them. By and large there was little African involvement in the modern sector, and almost none in the industrial sectors.

Most of the early parastatal organizations operated in natural monopoly areas: large infrastructural projects (highways, railways and dams) and social service facilities (schools, hospitals and clinics). Government soon moved into areas that had previously been dominated by the private sector (or, at least, traditionally dominated by the colonial sector in most 'mixed' economies). In the early 1990s public enterprises accounted for as much as 70% of GDP in Malawi and 58% in Tanzania. The share of parastatal bodies in employment was as high as 60% of the labour force in Mozambique in the late 1980s, and accounted for more than one-third of employment in many other countries. In the 1980s Ghana, Mozambique, Nigeria and Tanzania each operated more than 300 parastatal bodies. This expanded use of parastatal operations ideally complemented a range of domestic economic development philosophies, such as 'scientific socialism', 'humanism', 'ujamaa' or whichever term the particular African government applied to its own mode of economic planning. During this period, many governments had justifiable concerns that the private sector could not, or would not, help to improve living conditions for the poorest citizens. Most analysts have generally considered parastatal organizations to have failed, at least in terms of economic efficiency criteria. State-owned enterprises accounted for perhaps 13% of the region's GDP in 1993 (compared with almost 15% in the late 1970s), but represented a substantially higher percentage of economic output than in any of the world's other developing regions.

PRESSURES FOR ECONOMIC POLICY REFORM

African governments have been coming under increasing pressure from a variety of sources to 'liberalize' their public economic policies. During the 1970s and early 1980s, the most direct pressure came from the IMF. It insisted on 'conditionality' for its support; that is, the IMF required specific policy changes, sometimes termed 'structural adjustments', usually in the area of exchange rates (i.e. devaluation), and reductions in government spending before a new loan agreement could be signed. By 1997 35 African countries had launched structural adjustment programmes (SAP) or had borrowed from the IMF to support reform policies. Additional pressures have come from the World Bank and USAID. Specifically, the 1981 World Bank study proposed four major and basic policy changes which it felt were critical: namely, (i) the correction of overvalued exchange rates; (ii) the improvement of price incentives for exports and agriculture; (iii) the protection of industry in a more uniform and less direct way; and (iv) the reduction of direct governmental controls. Other pressures have originated and grown internally, as more people have become increasingly dissatisfied with their declining standard of living and the poor economic performance in their own countries. During the early 1990s several countries, most notably Madagascar, Mauritius, Malawi, Kenya, Tanzania, Uganda and Zimbabwe, removed restrictions on external capital transactions. This effectively closed the gap between the official exchange rate and the 'parallel', or 'black market', rate. South Africa abolished its two-tier exchange rate system in 1995, and Angola, Zambia, Ethiopia and Sierra Leone have also unified their foreign exchange systems, making foreign trade and investment less cumbersome.

Recognizing their poor past performance, African governments are currently scaling down their involvement in parastatal organizations. The growth of parastatal companies expanded more slowly in the 1980s and early 1990s than in the 1970s. Although the number of parastatal bodies remained fairly constant during the years 1980–86, at about 3,000, more than a dozen countries have reduced the number of public enterprises. In 1987 alone, according to the World Bank, nearly

100 parastatal organizations were scheduled for transfer to the private sector. Numerous African countries are now in the course either of reforming the institutional structures of parastatal bodies, or providing them with greater operating autonomy. In other cases, they are being disbanded entirely. None the less, by the mid-1990s, less than one-fifth of sub-Saharan Africa's state enterprises had been sold, of which very few were those operating in such key sectors as electricity generation, telecommunications, transport and mining. In 1991 Ghana sold 21 state agencies, but the country's state privatization agency reported that 11 were bought back by 1992. The bulk of the privatization—perhaps amounting to as much as two-thirds—has been limited to only five states: Ghana, Guinea, Mozambique, Nigeria and Senegal. Nevertheless, about 67% of structural adjustment programmes in the early 1990s involved public enterprise reform. In 1995 the ILO conducted a study on privatization of state enterprises. It found that privatization had short-term negative impacts on employment, but that over the longer term the effects appeared to have been beneficial.

In addition to the scaling back of parastatal enterprises, many governments are actively seeking the participation of the private sector, both domestic and foreign. The region has experienced a dramatic growth in stock exchanges, and in 1996 new bourses had opened, or were soon to open, in Zambia, Malawi, Uganda, Seychelles, Sudan, Swaziland and Tanzania. With the continuing sales of nationalized industries, these stock markets should gain in importance. The region has excellent potential for investment funds from domestic sources; by 1997, it was estimated, the outflow of capital to other areas of the world amounted to about US $148,000m., approximately up to 90% of the combined GDP of the countries of sub-Saharan Africa.

CURRENT OUTLOOK

Economic reforms have in general led to improved economic performance although certain sectors in most countries have experienced sharp declines. In 1994 the World Bank studied 29 countries in sub-Saharan Africa which had undertaken adjustment strategies in the 1980s. The study concluded that no African country has firmly established, in the broadest sense, a sound macro-economic policy. However, the report found that the six countries—Ghana, Tanzania, The Gambia, Burkina Faso, Nigeria and Zimbabwe—which have made the most improvement in macro-economic policies between 1981–91, also performed best in economic terms. It should be noted, however, that several of these countries were initially at such low levels of growth as to distort their actual rates of improvement. While these six countries implemented substantially improved policies, nine others achieved modest improvements, while 11 countries evidenced actual deterioration. For the six most successful states, their median rate of GDP per caput growth between 1987–91 was 0.4%, and although low, it did represent a turnaround from the 1% annual declines during the early and mid-1980s. In contrast, the other 21 countries saw median GDP per caput growth fall by 2.1%. The six best-performing countries achieved a median increase in export growth of 8%, while those 11 with ineffective policy reforms sustained an export decline of 0.7%. The best-performing countries saw their industrial growth accelerate by 6%, compared with 1.7% for the least successful 11 countries. Agricultural output advanced more quickly (by 2%) in the countries which had substantially reduced their taxation of export crops, while agricultural production declined by 1.6% in countries which taxed their farmers more. The countries which devalued their currencies increased their GDP per caput growth by an average of 2.3%, while those countries with appreciating foreign exchange rates experienced growth rate declines averaging 1.7%. The case studies were reinforced in a subsequent World Bank report.

Most observers believe there is little doubt that the region's numerous SAP have played an important part in arresting the region's sharp economic decline of the 1980s. During 1988–90 20 countries were engaged in the World Bank-led Special Programme of Assistance (SPA), which generally comprised SAP. Economic growth in these countries increased from an annual rate of 1% at the start of the 1980s to about 4% by 1992. Most importantly, this growth exceeded population growth rate, while growth in those countries not engaged in the SPA programmes was approximately one-half that of those pursuing SPA, as well as below population growth rates.

In countries as diverse as Uganda, Namibia, Ghana, and Eritrea, leaders are developing their own modes of reform. Such reform, however, must include better public management and good governance. If African governments implement their plans for economic liberalism, encompassing generally higher agricultural producer prices, revised and realistic foreign exchange rates, together with other publicly unpopular policy measures, they will require increased outside support. By the early 1990s, economic assistance to the region was being increasingly made dependent upon economic reform, and the major donor countries of the OECD had reallocated most of their economic assistance to countries implementing reform programmes. Additionally, the major multilateral donors were also reallocating their resources on this basis.

The OAU and the UN have launched a number of major initiatives supporting Africa's economic development. The African Priority Programme for Economic Recovery (AAPER) was adopted by the OAU in 1985, followed by the UN Program of Action for African Economic Recovery and Development 1986–1990 (UN–PAAERD) and the African Alternative Framework to Structural Adjustment Programs for Socio-economic Recovery and Transformation (AAF–SAP) which was proposed by the Economic Commission for Africa in 1989. This latter programme was designed to counter the effects of IMF and World Bank SAP. In 1991 the UN launched its New Agenda for the Development of Africa in the 1990s (UN–NADAF). A mid-term review of this programme was initiated by the UN in 1997.

In 1996, however, the UN launched its most ambitious programme: the US $25,000m. Special Initiative on Africa (SIA), financed principally by the World Bank. The SIA will support five major sectors: (i) water: $3,000m. will be dedicated to assure sustainable water supplies for households and farms; (ii) food security: approximately $20m. will be earmarked for soil quality improvement, desertification control and assisting the role of women; (iii) governance: $1,000m. will be devoted to capacity building to help with conflict resolution; (iv) basic human needs, including education ($14,000m. and primary health care ($6,500m.) and (v) resource mobilization: including debt relief and improved trade access. In 1997 UNCTAD established a trust fund to assist the world's 48 poorest countries (of which 34 were in sub-Saharan Africa) towards fuller integration into the world economy. About $5,000m. is being provided primarily to assist recipients to strengthen their export capabilities.

It is ironic that many of the development policies that the international donor community is now criticizing are those that they had formerly supported, especially during the 1960s, when import substitution was actively promoted. The region now employs perhaps 100,000 expatriate economic advisers at an annual cost to donors and African governments of about US$4,000m. In addition, most of these economies are small and fragile, and need some form of government protection. Large parastatal organizations continue to wield considerable power, and liberalization ultimately means competition.

Developments in South Africa will have profound and generally positive economic impacts on southern Africa and the entire region. In 1994 South Africa made a peaceful transition to majority rule. There is no doubt that South African-inspired or supported wars and destabilizations during the 1980s exposed the southern African sub-region to direct economic costs and indirectly to less easily quantifiable costs of lost economic opportunities. The region will reap a significant 'peace dividend' in the form of reduced military expenditures, more reliable transportation and transportation alternatives, increased trade and commerce, domestic and international investor confidence, increased government revenues, increased employment and general economic growth. Such a dividend should augment sub-regional GDP by as much as 1%–1.5% annually above the World Bank-projected growth of perhaps 2.5%–3.0%. The entire region might also rightly expect to benefit from South Africa's advanced training, research and technology. For example, South Africa has more university-level agricultural and technical facilities than the other SADC countries combined. The sharing of research and institution of training schemes between South Africa and its neighbours will be inhibited, however, by South Africa's own shortages in certain skills. Secondly, as expectations in

South Africa rise, it will need all of its skills to facilitate domestic economic growth.

South Africa's return to the full economic community of nations will no doubt bring significant benefits to its neighbours. Paradoxically, those with the weakest ties will probably be helped most, and those with the closest ties today will probably gain least. The potential gainers include Mozambique and Angola, and probably Malawi and Tanzania. South Africa and Angola have, for example, been meeting since 1990 to negotiate terms for South Africa to purchase and refine Angolan petroleum. There will probably be very little change for Namibia, Botswana, Lesotho or Swaziland. Their ties are so strong and extensive that it will take years to lessen them, even if there is sufficient economic rationale to do so. Except in the area of trade diversion—being able to buy from the most competitive producer in cost terms (and possibly by import-substitution) there will be little gain for these states. Zimbabwe will also probably gain little, and may indeed prove less competitive than South Africa. Moreover, it should be stressed that South Africa under majority rule will have few incentives to be unduly generous towards its smaller neighbours, and will no doubt pursue economic policies designed to enhance its own prosperity. In a wider context, however, there can be little doubt that recent political developments in South Africa will exercise generally positive effects on neighbouring countries. In 1997 South Africa will be involved in a number of important regional and international economic negotiations, including the Southern African Customs Area agreement, the formulation of new trading relationships with the EU, and the negotiations of a protocol creating a free trade area in the SADC by 2004.

As peace and stability come to other parts of the region, economic growth should follow. However, a recent World Bank report suggests that the 'peace dividend' does not necessarily immediately follow the resolution of civil war. The fact that such conflicts often do not end decisively means that armies are slow to demobilize, and military spending is not quickly reduced. Indeed, military spending actually increased by 40% in Uganda in its early years of peace after the overthrow of Gen. Idi Amin. Moreover, the conclusion of a civil war does not necessarily translate to increased security. Demobilization often results in former military personnel resorting to banditry to survive, as witnessed in Angola, Chad and Mozambique. Economic output in these countries, according to the UN, may have fallen to only one-half of the levels that would have been achieved in conditions of internal political harmony.

Africa is a resilient continent. It has withstood drastic changes during the past three centuries and especially during the past three decades. It has moved from colonial domination to independence in less than two generations. Recent history elsewhere, particularly in Asia, suggests that the unacceptable economic deterioration of the past 30 years can be reversed. As sub-Saharan Africa moves towards the year 2000 its governments have begun to realize that while many economic problems were inherited, responsibility must be taken for problems that are soluble. Rather than being hostile to foreign entrepreneurs, most African governments are now actively seeking foreign business involvement. About 35 countries have initiated SAP since the mid-1980s, and 27 have held presidential elections since 1990. By 1997 most African governments were presenting the appearance of reform, and acknowledging the parallel between political pluralism and economic development. The combination of liberalized economic policies, together with more political openness could signal the beginning of sub-Saharan Africa's transformation towards economic recovery and sustained long-term development. Dramatic, positive political and economic changes in South Africa and in other nations, which would have seemed impossible less than a decade ago, are now accepted.

As joint report issued by the World Resources Institute and the International Institute for Environment and Development succinctly states 'Sub-Saharan Africa poses the greatest challenge to world development efforts to the end of the century and beyond. Recurrent famine there is only the symptom of much deeper ills.' Africa's path ahead is difficult and uncertain. Vital questions are posed by the extent to which the region is truly committed to genuine reform, and thus whether it can finally break the cycle of poverty in which it has been trapped for the past two decades. In addition, will sub-Saharan Africa continue to be marginalized, or can it find ways to better integrate into the global economy? Will the industrial nations open their markets to competition from the region? Can the very recent, positive signs of economic growth be sustained? The last three years in this century could prove to be sub-Saharan Africa's most critical.

EUROPEAN COLONIAL RULE IN AFRICA

RICHARD BROWN

The colonial era in Africa began with the continent's hectic partition by the European powers in the final quarter of the 19th century. It ended in circumstances of equal haste less than a century later, leaving the present states of Africa as its political legacy. However, Europe had been in direct contact with sub-Saharan Africa from the mid-15th century, following the Portuguese maritime explorations. Commercial contacts gradually became dominated by the massive and destructive trade in slaves carried on by the Portuguese, Dutch, French, British and others. In all, some 14m. Africans are estimated to have been transported to the Caribbean and the Americas or to have lost their lives as a result of the trade. Colonizing efforts were few before the 19th century, but Portugal maintained a token presence in the areas that much later were extended to become Angola and Mozambique, while the Dutch initiated European settlement from Cape Town in 1652. Elsewhere the prolonged trade contacts generated only scattered European footholds along the African coasts.

Britain was the leading trafficker in slaves in the 18th century, but after 1807, when British subjects were prohibited from further participation in the slave trade, a new era began. The subsequent campaign against the slave trade of other nations; the search for new trade products such as palm oil; the onset of geographical exploration; the outburst of Christian missionary zeal; improved communications (the telegraph and steam ships); growing knowledge of tropical medicine; and Europe's new industrial might all combined to make Africa increasingly vulnerable to European colonial encroachment. The discovery of diamonds in southern Africa in 1867 and the opening of the Suez canal two years later further focused attention on the continent. Even before the main scramble for colonies began in the 1870s, Britain and France had been steadily increasing their commercial and political involvement in Africa.

Britain developed a settlement at Freetown (Sierra Leone) as a base for freed slaves from 1808, and subsequently engaged in a series of conflicts with inland Ashanti from its outposts on the Gold Coast (Ghana), while steadily increasing its influence in the Niger delta region, in Zanzibar, and in southern Africa. In mid-century Gen. Louis Faidherbe began France's expansion into the West African interior along the River Senegal from its long-held trading settlements at the river's mouth. Simultaneously, the interests of both countries grew in Madagascar, but it was France that later annexed the island (1896). During this period of colonial expansion, France extended its penetration of West Africa from existing bases in the interior as well as from enclaves on the coast. It created, too, a second colonial fiefdom in Equatorial Africa, with its administrative base in Libreville, on the Gabon coast. The result of this strategy was the emergence of two large federations of colonies: the AOF (Afrique occidentale française, 1895) eventually included Senegal, Upper Volta (Burkina Faso), Soudan (Mali), Dahomey (Benin), Guinea, Niger, Mauritania, and Côte d'Ivoire; the AEF (Afrique equatoriale française, 1908) comprised Gabon, Middle Congo (Congo Republic), Oubangui Chari (Central African Republic), and Chad. Meanwhile, in West Africa, Britain extended its foothold on the Gambian coast into a protectorate, enlarged its territorial holdings in Sierra Leone, created the Gold Coast Colony (1874, later conquering Ashanti and adding territory to the north as the scramble proceeded), and sanctioned the advance of the Royal Niger Co into the heavily populated region that subsequently, as Nigeria, became Britain's most important African colony.

The quest for colonies gained momentum as other European powers entered the field. The first of these was Belgium, whose ambitious monarch, Leopold II, created the International Association for the Exploration and Civilization of Central Africa (1876) as the means of establishing and administering a vast personal empire in the Congo basin, which was ironically named the Congo Free State. The king's infamous regime of exploitation led to international outrage and eventually, in 1908, to the transfer of the territory to the Belgian state. Another late participant in the drive to colonize Africa was Germany, which had newly emerged as a major industrial power. In 1884 its chancellor, Bismarck, declared German protectorates over Togoland, Kamerun and South West Africa (Namibia). Bismarck then moved swiftly to organize the Berlin West Africa Conference (1884–85) which created a generally agreed framework for colonial expansion so as to avert any major conflict among the European powers. Shortly afterwards Bismarck added German East Africa (Tanganyika, the mainland of modern Tanzania) to Germany's colonial possessions. (After the German defeat in the First World War, the administration of these territories passed to the victors as League of Nations mandates. South Africa obtained Namibia, Tanganyika was awarded to Britain, and Ruanda-Urundi to Belgium, while Kamerun and Togoland were each partitioned between Britain and France.)

Although Britain, as the leading European economic power, would have preferred to adhere to its traditionally gradual method of empire-building, it nevertheless emerged from the scramble as the dominant colonial power, both in terms of territory and population. Apart from its West African possessions, Britain acquired substantial holdings in eastern and southern Africa. The largest of these was the Sudan, a consequence of Britain's involvement in Egypt and the importance attached to the Suez canal. Egypt had been employing British soldier-administrators in its efforts to gain control of the Sudan, but in 1881 a Muslim cleric proclaimed himself the mahdi (supreme spiritual leader) and declared a *jihad* (holy war). In 1885, the mahdi's forces captured Khartoum, killing Gen. Gordon and causing outrage in Britain. Eventually the mahdist state was destoyed by a huge Anglo-Egyptian army led by Gen. Kitchener in 1898, just in time to forestall a parallel French expedition at Fashoda. The Sudan officially became an Anglo-Egyptian condominium, but was in effect administered as a British colony which became highly valued for its cotton production. Fertile Uganda, supposedly a key to control of the Nile valley, had been made a protectorate in 1894, and neighbouring Kenya was added by Britain the following year in order to secure access to the sea. The offshore island of Zanzibar, long a focus of British interest and commercially important as an exporter of cloves, was formally declared a protectorate in 1890. Further to the south, missionaries played an important part in the British acquisition of the land-locked Nyasaland protectorate (Malawi) in 1891.

In the extreme south, Britain had obtained the Cape Colony by treaty at the end of the Napoleonic Wars (1814), and soon found itself in conflict both with its white settlers of mainly Dutch origin (Afrikaners, or Boers), as well as with the area's many indigenous kingdoms and chieftaincies. In 1843 the British coastal colony of Natal was founded, principally as a means of containing the Afrikaners in the interior, where they established the Orange Free State and Transvaal republics. Fatefully, these developments coincided with the discovery of immense reserves of diamonds (1867) and gold (1886). The ensuing upheavals and an insatiable demand for 'cheap native labour', brought about the final conquest of the African peoples (most notably in the Zulu War, 1879). Acting on Britain's behalf, the mining magnate Cecil Rhodes organized from the Cape the further northward conquest and occupation of Southern Rhodesia (Zimbabwe) and Northern Rhodesia (Zambia), beginning in 1890: earlier Rhodes had been instrumental in Britain's acquisition of Bechuanaland (Botswana) as a protectorate, to safeguard the land route from the Cape into the interior, which had been threatened by German activity in South West Africa. Britain also obtained Basutoland (Lesotho) and the Swaziland protectorate. However, British claims to paramountcy throughout southern Africa were challenged by the two Afrikaner republics in the Boer War (1899–1902). Britain overcame the republics only with great difficulty, and then left the Afrikaners, who formed the main element of the privileged white minority, in political control of a newly-fashioned Union of South Africa which was then granted virtual independence (1910). Known as the high commission territories, Botswana, Lesotho and Swaziland, however, remained under British rule. Subsequent South Africa's ambitions to incorporate them were thwarted, and they eventually proceeded to independence in the 1960s.

Despite its economic weakness relative to the other European powers, Portugal obtained a major share of the colonial division of southern Africa. British diplomatic support helped Portugal to secure the vast colonies of Angola (including Portuguese Congo, later known as Cabinda) and Mozambique: in West Africa Portugal had long been in control of mainland (Portuguese) Guinea (now Guinea-Bissau), the Cape Verde archipelago and the islands of São Tomé and Príncipe. Spain, meanwhile, acquired the islands of Fernando Póo (Bioko) and Annobón (Pagalu), together with the mainland enclave of Río Muni, which now form the republic of Equatorial Guinea.

Some African polities themselves participated in the scramble: the kingdoms of Buganda and Ethiopia both seized opportunities to expand. Indeed, Ethiopia successfully defended itself against Italian aggression by winning a famous victory at the battle of Adowa (1896). Italy had to content itself with Eritrea and the major part of Somalia, until Mussolini's armies overran Ethiopia in 1935 (Italian occupation was ended by an Anglo-Ethiopian military expedition in 1941). Eritrea, however, was not to emerge as an independent state until 1993. Liberia, an American-inspired republic founded in 1847 and politically dominated by descendants of former slaves, remained nominally independent throughout the colonial era, but in practice became an economic dependency of US rubber-growing interests.

COLONIAL RULE

There was much resistance to the European intrusion by many of the Islamized as well as the indigenous cultures of West Africa. There were also major rebellions against the Germans in South West Africa and Tanganyika, and against the British in Southern Rhodesia; however, divisions within and between African ethnic groups, superior European weaponry and the widespread use of African troops enabled the colonial powers generally to secure control of their territorial acquisitions without great difficulty (although military operations continued in some areas until the 1920s). Boundaries were, in the main, effectively settled by 1900 or soon afterwards. Most colonies enclosed a varied assortment of societies, but many African groupings found themselves divided by the new frontiers (the Somali, for example, were split among British, French, Italian and Ethiopian administrations). Although in the long run colonialism did much to undermine previous patterns of life, its administrative policies and the development of written languages (mainly by missionaries) fostered ethnic identity, helping to replace pre-colonial cultural and political fluidity by modern tribalism. African reactions to colonialism also contributed to the growing sense of ethnic self-awareness. At the same time, members of the Western-educated indigenous élites were also exploring alternative identities based on the colonial territory (nationalism) or, indeed, on the broader concept of Pan-Africanism.

As military control gave way to civil administration, economic issues came to the fore. In the early decades of colonial rule a considerable amount of railway construction was carried out, and there was a marked development of the export-orientated economy. Colonial taxation was an important stimulus to peasant production and to wage-labour, but in the early period all colonies conscripted labour by force. In the more primitive and undeveloped colonies, (as in the Portuguese territories) coercion persisted into the 1960s. In much of West Africa and parts of East Africa, export production remained mainly in indigenous hands. Elsewhere concessionary companies (as in the Congo and AEF) or white settlers (as in South Africa and Southern Rhodesia) were the major agricultural producers. White settlers, whose interests were almost invariably given priority, were also a significant force in Kenya, and in many other colonies such as Northern Rhodesia, the Belgian Congo, Angola, Mozambique, Kamerun and Côte d'Ivoire. Mining was a dominant force in a number of areas. In South Africa, it provided the main impetus to the development of a strong industrial base by the late 1930s. Southern Rhodesia followed a similar pattern, although on a smaller scale. The important copper mines of the Katanga (Shaba) region of the Belgian Congo (Democratic Republic of the Congo) were later (in the 1920s) joined by those of Northern Rhodesia. Tin in Nigeria, gold in the Gold Coast, and, later, diamonds and uranium in Namibia augmented the primary agricultural exports of these territories. Overall, the growth of a money economy did most to change African life as different areas developed new production, supplied labour, stagnated, or developed the towns which were essential to the conduct of trade and, in the late colonial period, to the growth of manufacturing in some areas additional to that already established in South Africa.

Where settlers monopolized land and resources, colonialism tended to bear harshly on traditional African life. Elsewhere, however, the direct European impact was more muted. The very small number of European colonial officials in non-settler colonies necessitated reliance on African intermediaries to sustain rule. Such administrations had to limit their interventions in African life and rely on traditional and created chiefs to carry out day-to-day administration (although often in arbitrary and non-traditional ways); but military power was never far away in the event of any breakdown in control. By the 1920s air power could be used to transport troops quickly to suppress uprisings. The British, in particular, favoured the policy of 'indirect rule', bolstering traditional authorities as subordinate allies, but often with new powers and resources unavailable to their predecessors. Britain's colonial doctrine emphasized the separateness of its colonies from the imperial power and theoretically envisaged eventual political independence. Some degree of freedom of expression was allowed (many African newspapers flourished in British West Africa), and a limited political outlet for a circumscribed few was eventually provided through the establishment of legislative councils. In contrast, the French doctrine of assimilation theoretically envisaged Africans as citizens of a greater France, but little was done to make this a reality until after the Second World War. These contrasting British and French principles were not without influence on policy, for example in the educational sphere, and they also helped to shape the later patterns of decolonization and post-colonial relationships. Whatever the theory, all colonial regimes were deeply influenced by the racist outlook which had taken hold of the European mind in the 19th century and in practice treated their colonial subjects as inferior beings.

Racial discrimination was deeply resented by the Western-educated élites. In coastal West Africa and in South Africa the existence of these élites actually pre-dated the scramble, and soon lawyers, clergy, teachers and merchants founded moderate protest associations, such as the Aborigines' Protection Society (1897) in the Gold Coast and the Native National Congress (1912), later the African National Congress, in South Africa. By the 1920s clerks and traders in Tanganyika were able to form an African Association on a territory-wide basis. In other social strata, religious associations were often the chief vehicles for African assertion. These could be traditional, Christian, Islamic or syncretic in inspiration, and often aroused mass enthusiasm to the concern of the colonial authorities. Occasionally there were violent clashes. In 1915, the Rev. John Chilembwe led an armed uprising protesting at the recruitment of Africans for service in the First World War and at conditions for tenants on European-owned estates in Nyasaland. Worker protest appeared early in towns, and on the railways and mines. Rural protest was often about taxation (as in the 1929 riots by women in Eastern Nigeria) or commodity prices (as in the Gold Coast cocoa boycotts of the 1930s). Yet, whatever the level of discontent, prior to the Second World War the colonial grip remained unshaken.

Any complacency about the underlying state of colonial Africa had, however, already been shattered by the world economic depression beginning in 1929–30. The effects of the collapse of prices were so severe that the major European powers, Britain, France, and Belgium, began to perceive the need to provide development funds and to improve social welfare and education in their colonies if Africa's ability to export tropical products and to import finished goods was to be sustained. These ideas, however, only began to make themselves strongly felt after the Second World War, when they were to add to the ferment of change then gathering force throughout the continent.

DECOLONIZATION

Events inside and outside Africa interacted to produce the surge towards independence after 1945. The Second World War itself provided the immediate context. The war greatly weakened the colonial powers, and brought to the fore the USA, which opposed European colonial control of Africa. African troops were enrolled to fight in Asia and the Mediterranean, returning with a deep resentment at post-war conditions and the continuing colonial subordination. The victory over fascism and the enunciation of the Atlantic Charter also encouraged thoughts of liberation within the continent. Economic change intensified as both the war and its aftermath stimulated demand, and there was a surge of African migration to the towns. Economic and social grievances multiplied, especially in relation to the inadequacy of urban facilities and lack of educational opportunities. Among peasant farmers, prices, marketing arrangements and new levels of bureaucratic interference aroused intense resentment. Because of labour migration, links between town and country were close, and provided opportunities to newly militant nationalist parties in the more developed colonies such as the Gold Coast and Côte d'Ivoire to put pressure on the colonial authorities. For the democratic European powers, the increasing African discontent raised both the moral and material costs of maintaining colonial rule. In any case, with the exception of Portugal, political control was no longer regarded as essential to the safeguarding of economic interests, particularly as capitalism was becoming increasingly internationalized and the concept of possessing colonies was beginning to appear outmoded.

In French Africa, the Second World War helped directly to set in train events which were ultimately to lead to independence. Following the German defeat of France in 1940, the AEF repudiated the Vichy government and declared its support for the 'Free French' under Gen. de Gaulle. The Brazzaville Conference convened by de Gaulle in 1944 spoke in general terms of a new deal for Africans, while the new French constitution adopted in 1946 provided for direct African elections to the French national assembly. Political parties established themselves throughout francophone Africa, although their demands were for fuller rights of citizenship within the French state rather than for independence. Attempts by the French government to thwart African political progress altogether were unsuccessful. The 1956 *loi cadre* (enabling law) introduced universal suffrage, but to the dismay of many nationalist politicians the franchise was applied individually to the separate states of the two federations, so that the structures of the AOF and AEF were allowed to wither away. In 1958, de Gaulle, still attempting to salvage something of the greater France concept, organized a referendum in which only Guinea voted for full independence. By 1960, however, the remaining AOF and AEF territories had insisted upon receiving *de jure* independence, even if, despite outward appearances, they remained tied economically and militarily to France.

The events which ended the French empire in sub-Saharan Africa were hastened by concurrent developments in neighbouring British colonies, especially the Gold Coast. With no settler communities to placate, decolonization in British West Africa proceeded relatively smoothly, although much more rapidly than had been contemplated. Popular grievances gave a new edge to the political demands of the now sizeable educated middle classes, and Britain's cautious post-war moves towards granting internal self-government were soon perceived as inadequate even by the British themselves. When police fired on an ex-serviceman's peaceful demonstration in Accra (Gold Coast) in 1948, the resulting unrest, strikes and rural agitation led to major policy changes. Sensing the new mood, the militant nationalist, Kwame Nkrumah, formed the Convention People's Party (CPP) in 1949 with the slogan 'self-government now'. Its populist appeal enabled it in 1951 to overcome the more moderate United Gold Coast Convention party (of which Nkrumah had earlier been general secretary) in an election based on a new and more democratic constitution. Although in jail for sedition, Nkrumah was released and invited to become head of an independent government. This dramatic development, followed by the grant of independence in 1957 as Ghana (whose boundaries also took in the former mandated territory of British Togoland), had repercussions throughout black Africa. (In fact, the Sudan had achieved independence in the previous year, when the Anglo-Egyptian condominium was brought to an end, but this had attracted little outside attention). Nkrumah sought, with some success, to intensify African revolutionary sentiment still further by organizing an African Peoples' Conference in Accra in 1958. Nigeria's progress towards independence, meanwhile, was complicated by its enormous size and colonially imposed regional structure. Rival regional and ethnic nationalisms competed, and no one party could achieve the degree of overall dominance enjoyed by the CPP in the Gold Coast. None the less a federal Nigeria became independent in 1960, followed by Sierra Leone (1961) and The Gambia (1965).

Belgium initially remained aloof from the movement towards decolonization. It appeared to believe that its relatively advanced provision for social welfare and the rapid post-war economic growth in the Belgian Congo would enable it to avoid making political concessions and to maintain the authoritarian style of government which had characterized its administration of the territory since it took over from the Belgian king. The Belgian Congo, however, could not be insulated—any more than any other part of Africa—from the anti-colonial influences at work throughout the continent. From 1955 onwards nationalist feeling spread rapidly, despite the difficulties in building effective national parties in such a huge country. Urban riots in 1959 led to a precipitate reversal in Belgian policy: at the Brussels Round Table Conference in January 1960 it was abruptly decided that independence was to follow in only six months. Not surprisingly, the disintegration of political unity and order in the country speedily followed the termination of Belgian administration. Belgian rule in the mandated territory of Ruanda-Urundi ended in 1962, and was followed by its division into the separate countries of Rwanda and Burundi.

Meanwhile, in eastern and southern Africa, Britain was also encountering difficulties in implementing decolonization. In Uganda, where its authority rested to a large extent on an alliance with the kingdom of Buganda, British policies had tended to stratify existing ethnic divisions. The deeply ingrained internal problems which preceded independence in 1962 continued to beset Uganda for the next 25 years. In contrast, however, the nationalist movement led by Julius Nyerere in Tanganyika was exceptionally united, and there was little friction prior to independence in 1961. Three years later Tanganyika united with Zanzibar (independence, 1963) as Tanzania. In Kenya, as in other colonies with significant settler minorities, the process of decolonization was troubled. In the post-war period, the settlers of Kenya sought political domination and worked to suppress emergent African nationalism. African frustrations, particularly about access to land among the Kikuyu, and growing unrest among the urban poor, led in 1952 to the declaration of a state of emergency and the violent revolt the British knew as 'Mau Mau'. This was fiercely suppressed, but only with the help of troops from Britain, a factor which helped finally to destroy the settlers' political credibility. Kenya eventually achieved independence in 1963 under the leadership of the veteran nationalist, Jomo Kenyatta. Vilified by the settlers in the 1950s as a personification of evil, Kenyatta as head of government in fact strove to protect the economic role of the settler population and to maintain good relations with Britain.

Settler interests were more obstructive further to the south. The whites of Southern Rhodesia had obtained internal self-government as early as 1923, but in 1953 the colony was allowed by Britain to become the dominant partner in a federation with Northern Rhodesia and Nyasaland. Conflict followed with African nationalists in the two northern territories, and the federation eventually collapsed in 1963 when Britain had to concede that its policy of decolonization could only effectively apply to the two northern territories whose governments it still controlled. In 1964, Nyasaland became independent as Malawi and Northern Rhodesia as Zambia. When Britain then refused white-minority rule independence to Southern Rhodesia, its settler dominated government, led by Ian Smith, unilaterally declared independence (1965). This was resisted by Britain and condemned by the United Nations, but an ineffectual campaign of economic sanctions was defeated by support for the Smith regime by neighbouring South Africa and Portugal. African nationalists eventually succeeded in organizing the guerrilla war which in the 1970s paved the way for a negotiated settlement. With Robert Mugabe as its leader, the country became independent as Zimbabwe (1980), a development which owed much to the collapse of Portuguese rule in Africa after 1974.

During the lengthy dictatorship of Dr Salazar, Portugal regarded its African colonial possessions as inalienable, and in 1951 they were declared to be overseas provinces. However, intense political repression failed to prevent the emergence of armed resistance movements in Angola (1961), Guinea-Bissau (1963) and Mozambique (1964). Most successfully in Guinea-Bissau under the leadership of Amílcar Cabral, these guerrilla movements succeeded in mobilizing rural support. Eventually, in 1974, following the military overthrow of the Portuguese regime, progress towards internal democratization was accompanied by a determination to implement an accelerated policy of decolonization. In Angola, where the divided nationalist movement provided opportunities for external intervention on opposite sides by South African and Cuban forces, independence proved difficult to consolidate. Mozambique also suffered greatly from South Africa's policy of destabilizing its newly-independent neighbours.

During this period South Africa was itself conducting a colonial war in Namibia, which it continued to occupy in defiance of the United Nations after it had terminated the mandate in 1966. The war against the South West African People's Organisation of Namibia continued until a negotiated settlement finally led to independence in 1990, effectively concluding the colonial era in Africa.

DATES OF INDEPENDENCE OF AFRICAN COUNTRIES

IN CHRONOLOGICAL ORDER OF INDEPENDENCE—POST-WAR

Libya	24 Dec.	1951
Sudan	1 Jan.	1956
Morocco	2 March	1956
Tunisia	20 March	1956
Ghana	6 March	1957
Guinea	2 Oct.	1958
Cameroon	1 Jan.	1960
Togo	27 April	1960
Mali	20 June	1960
Senegal	20 June	1960
Madagascar	26 June	1960
The Democratic Republic of the Congo (as the Congo)	30 June	1960
Somalia	1 July	1960
Benin (as Dahomey)	1 Aug.	1960
Niger	3 Aug.	1960
Burkina Faso (as Upper Volta)	5 Aug.	1960
Côte d'Ivoire	7 Aug.	1960
Chad	11 Aug.	1960
The Central African Republic	13 Aug.	1960
Republic of Congo (Congo–Brazzaville)	15 Aug.	1960
Gabon	17 Aug.	1960
Nigeria	1 Oct.	1960
Mauritania	28 Nov.	1960
Sierra Leone	27 April	1961
Tanzania (as Tanganyika)	9 Dec.	1961
Rwanda	1 July	1962
Burundi	1 July	1962
Algeria	3 July	1962
Uganda	9 Oct.	1962
Zanzibar (now part of Tanzania)	10 Dec.	1963
Kenya	12 Dec.	1963
Malawi	6 July	1964
Zambia	24 Oct.	1964
The Gambia	18 Feb.	1965
Botswana	30 Sept.	1966
Lesotho	4 Oct.	1966
Mauritius	12 March	1968
Swaziland	6 Sept.	1968
Equatorial Guinea	12 Oct.	1968
Guinea-Bissau	10 Sept.	1974
Mozambique	25 June	1975
Cape Verde	5 July	1975
The Comoros	*6 July	1975
São Tomé and Príncipe	12 July	1975
Angola	11 Nov.	1975
Seychelles	29 June	1976
Djibouti	27 June	1977
Zimbabwe	18 April	1980
Namibia	21 March	1990
Eritrea	24 May	1993

* Date of unilateral declaration of independence, recognized by France (in respect of three of the four islands) in December 1975.

Outline Political Map of Contemporary Africa

CALENDARS, TIME RECKONING, AND WEIGHTS AND MEASURES

The Islamic Calendar

The Islamic era dates from 16 July 622, which was the beginning of the Arab year in which the *Hijra* ('flight' or migration) of the prophet Muhammad (the founder of Islam), from Mecca to Medina (in modern Saudi Arabia), took place. The Islamic or *Hijri* Calendar is lunar, each year having 354 or 355 days, the extra day being intercalated 11 times every 30 years. Accordingly, the beginning of the *Hijri* year occurs earlier in the Gregorian Calendar by a few days each year. Dates are reckoned in terms of the *anno Hegirae* (AH) or year of the Hegira (*Hijra*). The Islamic year AH 1418 began on 9 May 1997.

The year is divided into the following months:

1. Muharram	30 days	7. Rajab	30 days
2. Safar	29 ,,	8. Shaaban	29 ,,
3. Rabia I	30 ,,	9. Ramadan	30 ,,
4. Rabia II	29 ,,	10. Shawwal	29 ,,
5. Jumada I	30 ,,	11. Dhu'l-Qa'da	30 ,,
6. Jumada II	29 ,,	12. Dhu'l-Hijja	29 or 30 days

The *Hijri* Calendar is used for religious purposes throughout the Islamic world.

PRINCIPAL ISLAMIC FESTIVALS

New Year: 1st Muharram. The first 10 days of the year are regarded as holy, especially the 10th.

Ashoura: 10th Muharram. Celebrates the first meeting of Adam and Eve after leaving Paradise, also the ending of the Flood and the death of Hussain, grandson of the prophet Muhammad. The feast is celebrated with fairs and processions.

Mouloud (Birth of Muhammad): 12th Rabia I.

Leilat al-Meiraj (Ascension of Muhammad): 27th Rajab.

Ramadan (Month of Fasting).

Id al-Fitr or **Id al-Saghir** or **Küçük Bayram** (The Small Feast): Three days beginning 1st Shawwal. This celebration follows the constraint of the Ramadan fast.

Id al-Adha or **Id al-Kabir** or **Büyük Bayram** (The Great Feast, Feast of the Sacrifice): Four days beginning on 10th Dhu'l-Hijja. The principal Islamic festival, commemorating Abraham's sacrifice and coinciding with the pilgrimage to Mecca. Celebrated by the sacrifice of a sheep, by feasting and by donations to the poor.

Islamic Year	1417	1418	1419
New Year	19 May 1996	9 May 1997	28 April 1998
Ashoura	28 May 1996	18 May 1997	7 May 1998
Mouloud	28 July 1996	18 July 1997	7 July 1998
Leilat al-Meiraj	8 Dec. 1996	28 Nov. 1997	17 Nov. 1998
Ramadan begins	10 Jan. 1997	31 Dec. 1997	20 Dec. 1998
Id al-Fitr	9 Feb. 1997	30 Jan. 1998	19 Jan 1999
Id al-Adha	18 April 1997	8 April 1998	28 March 1999

Note: Local determinations may vary by one day from those given here.

The Ethiopian Calendar

The Ethiopian Calendar is solar, and is the traditional calendar of the Ethiopian Church. New Year (1st Maskarem) usually occurs on 11 September Gregorian. The Ethiopian year 1989 began on 11 September 1996.

The year is divided into 13 months, of which 12 have 30 days each. The 13th and last month (Paguemen) has five or six days, the extra day occurring in leap years. The months are as follows:

1. Maskarem
2. Tikimit
3. Hidar
4. Tahsas
5. Tir
6. Yekatit
7. Megabit
8. Maiza
9. Ginbat
10. Sene
11. Hamle
12. Nahasse
13. Paguemen

The Ethiopian Calendar is used for most purposes, religious and secular, in Ethiopia.

Standard Time

One hour behind GMT	Greenwich Mean Time (GMT)	One hour ahead of GMT	Two hours ahead of GMT	Three hours ahead of GMT	Four hours ahead of GMT
Cape Verde	Ascension Burkina Faso Côte d'Ivoire The Gambia Ghana Guinea Guinea-Bissau Liberia Mali Mauritania Morocco St Helena São Tomé and Príncipe Senegal Sierra Leone Togo Tristan da Cunha	Algeria Angola Benin Cameroon Central African Republic Chad Congo, Democratic Republic Congo, Republic Equatorial Guinea Gabon Libya Niger Nigeria Tunisia	Botswana Burundi Egypt* Lesotho Malawi Mozambique Namibia Rwanda South Africa Sudan Swaziland Zambia Zimbabwe	Comoros Djibouti Eritrea Ethiopia Kenya Madagascar Mayotte Somalia Tanzania Uganda	Mauritius Réunion Seychelles

* Egypt observes summer time, the only country in Africa to do so.

Weights and Measures

Principal weights and units of measurement in common use as alternatives to the imperial and metric systems

WEIGHT

Unit	Country	Metric equivalent	Imperial equivalent
Frazila	Tanzania (Zanzibar)	15.87 kg	35 lb
Kantar	Sudan	44.928 kg	99.05 lb
Metir or Netir	Ethiopia	453.59 grams	1 lb
Pound (Dutch)	South Africa	494 grams	1.09 lb
Wakiah	Tanzania (Zanzibar)	280 grams	9.88 oz

LENGTH

Unit	Country	Metric equivalent	Imperial equivalent
Busa	Sudan	2.54 cm	1 in
Cubito	Somalia	55.88 cm	22 in
Foot (Cape)	South Africa	31.5 cm	12.4 in
Foot (French)	Mauritius	32.5 cm	12.8 in
Kadam or Qadam	Sudan	30.48 cm	12 in
Pouce	Mauritius	2.54 cm	1 in
Senzer	Ethiopia	23.114 cm	9.1 in

CAPACITY

Unit	Country	Metric equivalent	Imperial equivalent
Ardabb or Ardeb	Sudan	198.024 litres	45.36 gallons
Bali	South Africa	46 litres	10.119 gallons
Cabaho	Ethiopia	5.91 litres	1.3 gallons
Corde	Mauritius	3.584 cu m	128 cu ft
Gantang	South Africa	9.2 litres	2.024 gallons
Kadah	Sudan	2.063 litres	3.63 pints
Keila	Sudan	16.502 litres	3.63 gallons
Kuma	Ethiopia	5 litres	1.1 gallons
Messe	Ethiopia	1.477 litres	2.6 pints
Mud or Muid	South Africa	109.1 litres	24 gallons
Ratel	Sudan	0.568 litre	1 pint

AREA

Unit	Country	Metric equivalent	Imperial equivalent
Are	Mauritius	0.01 ha	0.0247 acre
Darat or Dural	Somalia.	8,000 sq m	1.98 acres
Feddan	Sudan	4,201 sq m	1.038 acres
Gasha	Ethiopia	40 ha	99 acres
Morgen	South Africa	0.857 ha	2.117 acres

Metric to Imperial Conversions

Metric units	Imperial units	To convert Metric into Imperial units, multiply by:	To convert Imperial into Metric units, multiply by:
Weight			
Gram	Ounce (Avoirdupois)	0.035274	28.3495
Kilogram (kg)	Pound (lb)	2.204623	0.453952
Metric ton	Short ton (2,000 lb)	1.102311	0.907185
	Long ton (2,240 lb)	0.984207	1.016047
	(The short ton is in general use in the USA, while the long ton is normally used in the United Kingdom and in some other countries in the Commonwealth.)		
Length			
Centimetre (cm)	Inch (in)	0.3937008	2.54
Metre (m)	Yard (=3 feet)	1.09361	0.9144
Kilometre (km)	Mile	0.62137	1.609344
Volume			
Cubic metre (cu m)	Cubic foot	35.315	0.028317
	Cubic yard	1.30795	0.764555
Capacity			
Litre	Gallon (=8 pints)	0.219969	4.54609
	Gallon (US)	0.264172	3.78541
Area			
Square metre (sq m)	Square yard	1.19599	0.836127
Hectare (ha)	Acre	2.47105	0.404686
Square kilometre (sq km)	Square mile	0.386102	2.589988

MAJOR COMMODITIES OF AFRICA

Note: For each of the commodities in this section, there are generally two statistical tables: one relating to recent levels of production, and one indicating recent trends in prices. Each production table shows estimates of output for the world and for Africa (including northern Africa, a region not covered by this volume). In addition, the table lists the main African producing countries and, for comparison, the leading producers from outside the continent. In most cases, the table referring to prices provides indexes of export prices, calculated in US dollars. The index for each commodity is based on specific price quotations for representative grades of that commodity in countries that are major traders (excluding countries of eastern Europe and the former USSR).

Aluminium and Bauxite

Aluminium is the most abundant metallic element in the earth's crust, comprising about 8% of the total. However, it is much less widely used than steel, despite having about the same strength and only half the weight. Aluminium has important applications as a metal because of its lightness, ease of fabrication and other desirable properties. Other products of alumina (aluminium oxide) are also important industrial minerals for use as refractories, abrasives, glass manufacture, other ceramic products, catalysts and absorbers. Alumina hydrates are also used for the production of aluminium chemicals, fire retardant in carpet backing, industrial fillers in plastics and related products.

The major markets for aluminium are in building and construction, transportation, consumer durables, electrical machinery and equipment, and the packaging industry, which in the mid-1990s accounted for about 22% of all aluminium use. Although the production of aluminium is energy-intensive, its light weight results in a net saving, particularly in the transportation industry. About one-quarter of aluminium output is consumed in the manufacture of transport equipment, particularly road motor vehicles and components, where the metal is increasingly being used as a substitute for steel. In the early 1990s steel substitution accounted for about 16% of world aluminium consumption, and it has been forecast that aluminium demand by the motor vehicle industry alone could more than double, to exceed 5.7m. tons in 2010, from around 2.4m. tons in 1990. Aluminium is of great value to the aerospace industry for its weight-saving characteristics and its low cost relative to alternative materials. Aluminium-lithium alloys command considerable potential for use in this sector, although the traditional dominance of aluminium in the aerospace sector was under challenge in the 1990s from 'composites' such as carbon-epoxy, a fusion of carbon fibres and hardened resins, whose lightness and durability can exceed that of many aluminium alloys.

The world aluminium industry is dominated by seven Western producers —Alcan (Canada), Alcoa, Alumax, Reynolds, Kaiser (all USA), Pechiney (France) and Alusuisse (Switzerland). However, their level of dominance has been lessened in recent years by a major geographical shift in the location of alumina and aluminium production to areas where cheap power is available, such as Australia, Brazil, Norway, Canada and Venezuela. The Gulf states of Bahrain, Dubai and Qatar, and also Saudi Arabia, with the advantage of low energy costs, have entered the world aluminium market and are expected to become substantial producers during the 1990s, if plans for the expansion of existing capacity and the construction of new smelters are implemented. By contrast, the seven major 'integrated' producers have so far been able to retain their dominance in the markets for semi-finished and finished aluminium products.

Bauxite is the principal aluminium ore, but nepheline syenite, kaolin, shale, anorthosite and alunite are all potential alternative sources of alumina, although not currently economic to process. The developing countries, with 70% of known bauxite reserves, supply 45% of the ore required. The industry is structured in three stages: bauxite mining, alumina refining and smelting. While the high degree of 'vertical integration' (i.e. the control of successive stages of production) in the industry means that the movement of a significant proportion of trade in bauxite and alumina is in the form of intra-company transfers, and the increasing tendency to site alumina refineries on or near to bauxite deposits has resulted in a shrinking bauxite trade, there is a growing free market in alumina, serving the needs of the increasing number of independent (i.e. non-integrated) smelters.

The alumina is separated from the ore by the Bayer process. After mining, bauxite is fed to process directly if mine-run material is adequate (as in Jamaica) or is crushed and beneficiated. Where the 'as-mined' ore presents handling problems, or weight reduction is desirable, it may be dried prior to shipment.

At the alumina plant the ore is slurried with spent-liquor directly, if the soft Caribbean type is used, or, in the case of other types, it is ball-milled to reduce it to a size which will facilitate the extraction of the alumina. The bauxite slurry is then digested with caustic soda to extract the alumina from the ore while leaving the impurities as an insoluble residue. The digest conditions depend on the aluminium minerals in the ore and the impurities. The liquor, with the dissolved alumina, is then separated from the insoluble impurities by combinations of sedimentation, decantation and filtration and the residue washed to minimize the soda losses. The clarified liquor is concentrated and the alumina precipitated by seeding with hydrate. The precipitated alumina is then filtered, washed and calcined to produce alumina. The ratio of bauxite to alumina is approximately 1.95:1.

The smelting of the aluminium is generally by electrolysis in molten cryolite. Because of the high consumption of electricity by this process, alumina is usually smelted in areas where low-cost electricity is available. However, most of the electricity now used in primary smelting in the Western world is generated by hydroelectricity—a renewable energy source.

The recycling of aluminium is economically (as well as environmentally) desirable, as the process uses only 5% of the electricity required to produce a similar quantity of primary aluminium. Aluminium that has been recycled from scrap currently accounts for about 40% of the total aluminium supply in the USA, and for about 30% of Western European consumption. With the added impetus of environmental concerns, considerable growth world-wide in the recycling of used beverage cans (UBC) has been forecast for the 1990s. In the mid-1990s, according to aluminium industry estimates, the recycling rate of UBC amounted to at least 55% world-wide.

Excluding the Democratic People's Republic of Korea and the successor republics of the USSR, total world output of primary aluminium in 1994 was estimated at 15.8m. metric tons, of which African producers accounted for about 544,000 tons. The USA usually accounts for about one-third of total aluminium consumption (excluding communist and former communist countries). However, its role as a producer has declined. The USA accounted for almost 21% of world output of aluminium in 1994. US smelters have ceased to produce a surplus of ingots, and the country increasingly produces as much as it requires for fabrication and purchases the remainder from lower-cost producers elsewhere.

Guinea possesses more than one-quarter of the world's known bauxite reserves, and is the world's largest exporter of bauxite, ranking second only to Australia in terms of ore production. Some Guinean bauxite ore, which is of very high grade, is domestically processed into alumina, and some Guinean alumina is exported to Cameroon for refining. Cameroon has extensive bauxite deposits, estimated at some 1,200m. metric tons, but these have yet to be exploited. In 1996 Malawi began to seek international participation in the development of the country's 28m. metric tons of bauxite reserves at Mulanje. Ghana's bauxite reserves are estimated at 780m. tons. Although the country lacks an alumina refinery, it has Africa's second largest aluminium smelter, located at Tema and owned by the US-based Kaiser and Reynolds interests, which processes imported alumina. Sierra Leone has estimated bauxite reserves of 100m. metric tons. Exploitation of the Mkanji deposits, in the Southern province, began in 1964, but ceased in early 1995 as the result of guerrilla insurgency. Efforts to dispose of the operations, which were carried out by a subsidiary of Alusuisse, were proceeding in 1997. In 1992 the South African aluminium producer Alusaf announced that it was proceeding with plans to construct the largest smelter ever to be built in the Western world, with an annual capacity of 466,000 tons. This smelter, located at Richards Bay, entered production in June 1995 and was expected to reach full-capacity output in 1997. The achievement of this output was expected to increase total African aluminium output to more than 1m. tons annually. Proposals were pending in early 1997 to construct aluminium smelters in Mozambique, Cameroon, Nigeria and Egypt. In Nigeria, the Ikot Abasi aluminium smelter, with a projected capacity of 180,000 tons per year, entered production in early 1997.

Although world demand for aluminium advanced by an average of 3% annually from the late 1980s until 1994 (see below), industrial recession began, in 1990, to create conditions of over-supply. Despite the implementation of capacity reductions at an annual rate of 10% by the major Western producers, stock levels began to accumulate. The supply problem was exacerbated by a rapid rise, beginning in 1991, of exports by the USSR and its successor states, which had begun to accumulate substantial stocks of aluminium as a consequence of the collapse of the Soviet arms industry. The requirements of these countries for foreign exchange to restructure their economies led to a rapid acceleration in low-cost exports of high-grade aluminium to Western markets. These sales caused considerable dislocation of the market and involved the major Western producers in heavy financial losses. Producing members of the European Community (EC, now the European Union—EU) were particularly severely affected, and in August 1993 the EC imposed quota arrangements, under which aluminium imports from the former USSR were to be cut by 50% for an initial three-month period while efforts were made to negotiate an agreement that would reduce the flow of low-price imports and achieve a reduction in aluminium stocks (by then estimated to total 4.5m. tons world-wide).

Production of Bauxite (crude ore, '000 metric tons)

	1994	1995
World total	94,051*	97,020*
Africa	12,259*	12,918*
Leading African producers		
Ghana	426	513
Guinea†	11,124	12,394
Sierra Leone	700	—
Leading non-African producers		
Australia	42,159	42,655
Brazil	9,669	8,673
China, People's Repub.	7,400	8,800
Guyana†	2,093	2,093
India	4,809	5,163
Jamaica	11,571	10,858
Russia	3,633	3,632
Suriname	3,766	3,596
Venezuela	30,558	32,470

* Estimated production.

† Dried equivalent of crude ore.

Source: World Bureau of Metal Statistics.

These negotiations, which involved the EC, the USA, Canada, Norway, Australia and Russia (but in which the minor producers, Brazil, the Gulf states, Venezuela and Ukraine were not invited to take part), began in October 1993. Initially, the negotiations made little progress, and in November the market price of high-grade aluminium ingots fell to an 11-year 'low'. The resumption of negotiations in December again failed to achieve a voluntary reduction in output by the producers, largely as a result of Russia's reluctance to curtail its production. Following further meetings in January 1994, however, a Memorandum of Understanding (MOU) was finalized, under which Russia was to 'restructure' its aluminium industry and reduce its output by 500,000 tons annually. By March the major Western aluminium producers had agreed to reduce annual production by about 1.2m. tons over a maximum period of two years. Additionally, Russia was to receive US $2,000m. in loan guarantees. The MOU provided for participants to monitor world aluminium supplies and prices on a regular basis. In March the EU quota was terminated. By July the world price had recovered by about 50% on the November 1993 level.

Export Price Index for Aluminium (base: 1980 = 100)

	Average	Highest month(s)	Lowest month(s)
1985	72		
1990	93		
1994	86	110 (Nov.)	68 (Jan.)
1995	104	120 (Jan.)	95 (Nov.)
1996	87	93 (March)	78 (Oct.)

The successful operation of the MOU, combined with a strong recovery in world aluminium demand, led to the progressive reduction of stock levels and to a concurrent recovery in market prices during 1994 and 1995. Consumption in the Western industrialized countries and Japan rose by an estimated 10.3% to 17.3m. tons, representing the highest rate of annual growth since 1983. This recovery was attributed mainly to a revival in demand from the motor vehicle sector in EU countries and the USA, and to an intensified programme of public works construction in Japan. Demand for aluminium was estimated to have risen by about 13% in China, and by 7% in the less industrialized countries of the South and East Asia region. Demand in the industrialized countries advanced by 11% in 1994, and by 2.2% in 1995.

Levels of world aluminium stocks were progressively reduced during 1994, and by late 1995 it was expected that the continuing fall in stock levels could enable Western smelters to resume full capacity operation during 1996. In May 1996 stock levels were reported to have fallen to their lowest level since March

1993, and exports of aluminium from Russia, totalling 2m. tons annually, were viewed as essential to the maintenance of Western supplies. Meanwhile, progress continued to be made in arrangements under the MOU for the modernization of Russian smelters and their eventual integration into the world aluminium industry. Growth in international demand for aluminium was estimated at approximately 0.2% in 1995 and 1996, although it was forecast in early 1997 that aluminium consumption by industrialized countries would advance by 4.6% in that year. It was expected, however, that current demand would be satisfied by increased primary aluminium production, combined with sustained reductions in world levels of primary aluminium stocks.

In November 1993 the price of high-grade aluminium (minimum purity 99.7%) on the London Metal Exchange (LME) was quoted at US $ 1,023.5 (£691) per metric ton, its lowest level for about eight years. In July 1994 the London price of aluminium advanced to $ 1,529.5 (£981) per ton, although later in the month it eased to $1,414 (£924). The recovery occurred despite a steady accumulation in LME stocks of aluminium, which rose to a series of record levels over the period, increasing from 1.9m. tons at mid-1993 to 2.7m. tons in June 1994. Subsequently these holdings were considerably reduced, and the aluminium price steadily increased. In late November 1994, when LME stocks of aluminium had declined to less than 1.9m. tons, the metal was traded at $1,987.5 (£1,269) per ton.

In January 1995 there was another surge in aluminium prices, with the LME quotation rising to US $2,149.5 (£1,346) per ton, its highest level since 1990. The price of aluminium was reduced to $1,715.5 (£1,085) per ton in May 1995, but recovered to $1,945 (£1,219) in July. It retreated to $1,609.5 (£1,021) per ton in October. Throughout this period, stocks of the metal were steadily reduced. The LME's holdings on 1 May were below 1m. tons for the first time since January 1992. In October 1995 these stocks stood at 523,175 tons, their lowest level since August 1991 and only 19.7% of the June 1994 peak. Thereafter, stock levels moved generally higher, reaching 970,275 tons in October 1996. During that month the London price of aluminium fell to $1,287 (£823) per ton, its lowest level for more than two years, before recovering to more than $1,400. Although LME stocks of aluminium remained close to 1m. tons, the metal's price continued to rise and exceeded $1,500 per ton in November and December.

During the early weeks of 1997 the price of aluminium advanced further, and in March the London quotation reached US $1,665.5 (£1,030) per ton. This was the highest aluminium price recorded in the first half of the year, despite a steady decline in LME stocks of the metal, which stood at 651,675 tons in July.

Almost all the producers of primary aluminium outside communist or former communist countries are members of the International Primary Aluminium Institute (IPAI), based in London. The IPAI's membership comprises some 40 companies which collectively represent substantially all of the Western countries' production of primary aluminium. In 1993 the International Aluminium Committee was formed to represent most of the aluminium smelters in the former USSR.

Cassava (Manioc, Tapioca, Yuca) (*Manihot esculenta*)

Cassava is a perennial woody shrub, up to 5 m in height, which is cultivated mainly for its enlarged starch-rich roots, although the young shoots and leaves of the plant are also edible. The plant can be harvested at any time from seven months to three years after planting. A native of South and Central America, cassava is now one of the most important food plants in all parts of the tropics (except at the highest altitudes), having a wide range of adaptation for rainfall (500–8,000 mm per year). Cassava is also well adapted to low-fertility soils, and grows where other crops will not. It is produced mainly on marginal agricultural land, with virtually no input of fertilizers, fungicides or insecticides.

The varieties of the plant fall into two broad groups, bitter and sweet cassava, formerly classed as two separate species, *M. utilissima* and *M. dulcis* or *aipi*. The roots of the sweet variety are usually boiled and then eaten. The roots of the bitter variety are either soaked, pounded and fermented to make a paste (such as 'fufu' in west Africa), or given an additional roasting to produce 'gari'. They can also be made into flour and starch, or dried and pelletized as animal feed.

The cassava plant contains two toxic substances, linamarin and lotaustralin, in its edible roots and leaves, which release the poison cyanide, or hydrocyanic acid, when plant tissues are damaged. Sweet varieties of cassava produce as little as 20 mg of acid per kg of fresh roots, whereas bitter varieties may produce more than 1,000 mg per kg. Although traditional methods of food preparation are effective in reducing cyanogenic content to harmless levels, if roots of bitter varieties are under-processed and the diet lacks protein and iodine (as occurs during famines and wars), cyanide poisoning can cause fatalities. Despite the disadvantages of the two toxins, some farmers prefer to cultivate the bitter varieties, possibly because the cyanide helps to protect the plant from potential pests, and possibly because the texture of certain food products made from bitter varieties is preferred to that of sweet cassavas.

Cassava, which was introduced to Africa from South America in the 16th century, is the most productive source of carbohydrates and produces more calories per unit of land than any cereal crop. Although the nutrient content of the roots consists almost entirely of starch, the leaves are high in vitamins, minerals and protein and, processed as meal or eaten as a fresh vegetable ('saka saka'), provide a useful source of nutrition in many parts of Africa, especially in Zaire, the Congo basin, Sierra Leone, Malawi, Mozambique, Tanzania and Uganda. A plot of cassava may be left unattended in the ground for two years after maturity without deterioration of the roots, and the plant is resistant to prolonged drought, so the crop is valued as a famine reserve. The roots are highly perishable after harvest and, if not consumed immediately, must be processed (flour, starch, pellets, etc.).

While the area under cassava has expanded considerably in recent years, there is increasing concern that the rapid expansion of cassava root planting may threaten the fertility of the soil and subsequently other crops. Under cropping systems where no fertilizer is used, cassava is the last crop in the succession because of its particular adaptability to infertile soils and its high nutrient use-efficiency in yield terms (although there is now evidence to suggest that cassava yields increase with the use of fertilizer). With the exception of potassium, cassava produces more dry matter with fewer nutrients than most other food crops. Soil fertility is not threatened by cassava itself, but rather by the cultivation systems which employ it without fertilizer use.

Production of Cassava ('000 metric tons)

	1994	1995
World total	162,844*	163,755*
Africa	82,092*	82,973*
Leading African producers		
Angola	1,600*	1,700*
Benin	1,146	1,343
Burundi	527†	501†
Cameroon	1,600*	1,300*
Central African Repub.	518	402
Congo, Dem. Repub.	18,051	17,500*
Congo, Repub.	630*	630*
Côte d'Ivoire	1,564	1,564*
Ghana	6,025	6,899
Guinea	512	512*
Kenya	830*	840*
Madagascar	2,413†	2,420
Mozambique	3,294	4,178†
Nigeria	31,005	31,404
Tanzania	7,209	5,969
Uganda	2,080	2,625
Zambia	600*	600*
Leading non-African producers		
Brazil	24,452	25,377
India	5,784	6,000*
Indonesia	15,729	15,438
Thailand	19,091	18,164

* FAO estimate. † Unofficial figure.

As a staple source of carbohydrates in the tropics, cassava is an essential part of the diet of about 300m. people. It is cultivated on almost 9m. ha in Africa and provides more than one-half of the caloric requirements of about 200m. people in the continent. Although the area in Africa planted to cassava amounts to considerably more than one-half of the world total, Africa's output accounts for less than 49% of world production. Most of the African crop is produced by subsistence farmers and traded domestically; only a small amount enters world trade.

Since the early 1970s African cassava production has been seriously undermined by mealybug infestation. Indigenous to South America, the mealybug (*Phenacoccus manihoti*) encountered few natural enemies in Africa, and by 1990 had infected all African cassava-growing areas, with the exceptions of Uganda and Madagascar. In 1981 the parasitic wasp *Epidinocarsis lopezi* was introduced into Nigeria from Paraguay to attack the mealybug, and by 1990 *E. lopezi* was successfully established in 25 African countries. The green spider mite, also a threat to cassava cultivation, is also being successfully combated by the introduction of a natural enemy, the phytoseiid mite, which by 1997 had established a presence over 400,000 sq km in west Africa. Funding was being sought to extend the range of these operations into other cassava-producing regions of Africa. African cassava is also vulnerable to African cassava leaf mosaic disease, which, like the green spider mite, deprives the plant of chlorophyll and results in low yields. A new variety of cassava, reported to be resistant to this disease, was introduced in Uganda in 1996.

In recent years there has been interest in the utilization of cassava as an industrial raw material as well as a food crop. Cassava has the potential to become a basic energy source for ethyl alcohol (ethanol), a substitute for petroleum. 'Alcogas' (a blend of cassava alcohol and petrol) can be mixed with petrol to provide motor fuel, while the high-protein residue from its production can be used for animal feed. The possibility of utilizing cassava leaves and stems (which represent about 50% of the plant and are normally discarded) as cattle-feed concentrates has also been receiving scientific attention.

Export Price Index for Cassava (base: 1980 = 100)

	Average	Highest month(s)	Lowest month(s)
1985	52		
1990	78		
1994	86	n.a.	n.a.
1995	85	n.a.	n.a.
1996	81	82 (May, July, Aug.)	79 (Dec.)

During 1993 the average monthly import price of hard cassava pellets at the port of Rotterdam, in the Netherlands, declined from US $160 per metric ton in January to $120 per ton in November. The annual average was $137 per ton, compared with $183 in 1992.

Chromium

Chromite is the name applied both to the mineral and to the ore containing that mineral. Chromite is the only ore from which chromium is obtained, and the terms chromite ore, chromium ore and chrome ore are used interchangeably. Chromite is used by the metallurgical, chemical and refractory industries. About 87% of total demand for chromite is from the metallurgical industry, 10% from the chemical industry and 3% from the refractory industry. For the metallurgical industry, chromite ore is smelted in an electric furnace and then marketed in the form of ferrochromium. Within the metallurgical industry the major use of chromium is as an essential alloying element in stainless steel, which is valued for its toughness and resistance to most forms of corrosion. Chromium chemicals are used for wood preservation, dyeing, and tanning. Chrome plating is popular. Chromite is used as a refractory mineral.

World reserves of chromite ore are estimated to total about 1,400m. metric tons. Approximately 70% of known reserves are in South Africa, and 10% each in Zimbabwe and Kazakstan. South Africa and Kazakhstan each produce about one-third of world chromite ore supplies. South Africa, accounting for 20%–30% of the market, is the world's largest ferrochrome producer. Zimbabwe accounts for about 6% of world ferrochromium requirements. South African charge-grade, high-carbon ferrochromium (which has a chromium content of 52%–55%)

Production of Chromium Ore ('000 metric tons, gross weight)

	1994	1995
World total	9,500*	12,500*
Africa	4,201*	5,862*
African producers		
Madagascar	75	103
South Africa	3,599	5,104
Sudan	10*	10*
Zimbabwe	517	645
Leading non-African producers		
Albania	223	250*
Brazil	200*	200*
Finland	573	600*
India	1,061	1,025
Iran	140	396
Kazakhstan	2,020	2,800*
Philippines	64	78
Russia	143	150*
Turkey	790	1,050

* Estimate.

Source: British Geological Survey, *World Mineral Statistics*.

has been replacing the more expensive high- and low-carbon ferrochromium (which have a chromium content of 60%–70%) since the development, during the years 1965–75, of the Argon Oxygen Decarbonizing Process, which permits the widespread use of less costly charge-grade, high-carbon ferrochromium.

Strong demand for ferrochromium in the late 1980s, together with conditions of under-supply, generated an expansion of capacity both in South Africa and Zimbabwe. Even so, the potentially damaging effects of international boycotts and trade bans, and of civil disturbances, on South Africa's ferrochrome industry led, in the 1980s, to the development of new production capacity, generally close to ore deposits, in Brazil, Finland, Greece, India, Sweden and Turkey. However, the implementation of political change in South Africa after 1993 acted to consolidate its pre-eminence in international ferrochromium markets. In 1995 the People's Republic of China, a major importer of ferrochromium, acquired an interest in the Dilokong mine in northern South Africa, which has an estimated output capacity of 400,000 metric tons per year. Plans were outlined in the following year for the construction of a charge chrome smelter, with an annual capacity of 100,000 tons. It was expected that the extracted chromium would be exported principally to Japan and China.

Pressure on ferrochromium supplies arose from strong demand for stainless steel in the USA, Japan and Western Europe, and in 1989 and early 1990 plans for new ferrochromium plants and expansions of existing capacity were in progress. During 1989 a downward trend in US production of stainless steel permitted the rebuilding of depleted ferrochromium stocks, while an increase in supplies (resulting from the expansions in productive capacity) led to a decline in ferrochromium prices. Ferrochromium production capacity increased by an estimated 300,000 tons (equivalent to 7% of world capacity) in 1989, and by a further 300,000 tons in 1990. Despite strong demand for ferrochromium from stainless steel producers, excess production capacity led to a decline in prices, which had reached record levels in 1988. World ferrochromium production capacity was reduced in 1990 and 1991 by delays in the inauguration of new furnaces and the temporary closure of some furnace plants.

During 1992 major producers of ferrochromium continued to operate at levels substantially below full capacity. European markets for chromium and ferrochromium had been destabilized by a sharp rise in imports of the metals from Kazakhstan. This influx and the sharp decline in demand for stainless steel by the successor states of the USSR, particularly Russia, left substantial quantities of ferrochromium available to world markets. The market imbalance persisted in 1993–95, while major Western producers of ferrochromium continued to operate at levels substantially below full capacity.

Clove (*Eugenia caryophyllus*)

This tropical tree, native to Indonesia, is a small evergreen, up to 14 m high, and cloves are its dried, unopened flower-buds.

Export Price Index for Chrome Ore (base: 1980 = 100)

	Average	Highest month(s)	Lowest month(s)
1985	93		
1990	144		
1994	99	*	*
1995	131	208 (Oct.-Dec.)	99 (Jan.-Aug.)
1996	208	†	†

* The monthly index remained constant at 99 from January to December 1994.

† The monthly index remained constant at 208 from January to December 1996.

These buds are picked by hand and dried in the sun to be used as spices. The trees are planted from seed, come into bearing after eight or nine years and normally live for about 60 years. Cloves are a cyclical crop, however, and trees produce at their peak only once in every four years. Clove oil, produced by distillation of cloves, flower stalks and leaves, is used in perfumes and toiletries. The chief constituent of clove oil is eugenol, which is used as a dental anaesthetic and in toothpaste.

Cloves were an important commodity in 17th century European commerce, when supplies were closely controlled by Dutch traders in the Netherlands East Indies (now Indonesia). Clove trees were smuggled to Mauritius by French entrepreneurs in the 1700s, and a century later cloves were transplanted by Arab traders from Mauritius to the island of Zanzibar (now an autonomous part of Tanzania), where they became the principal cash crop. Formerly the world's largest exporter of cloves, Zanzibar now ranks only fourth. Clove is a notoriously volatile crop and harvests tend to proceed in a three-year cycle of good, medium and poor years. The level of marketed production has also been affected by low producer prices, smuggling and tree disease. World clove supplies have been in surplus since the early 1980s, and accumulations of clove stocks, together with depressed levels of producers' prices, have been a persistent problem for Zanzibar, which has relied on these exports for up to 90% of its foreign exchange earnings, principally from markets in Singapore, the Netherlands, India and Thailand. By the early 1990s, many growers in Zanzibar had switched to the cultivation of alternative crops, such as vanilla, cardamom and peppermint. Clove output in Zanzibar declined from 4,927 metric tons in 1994 to only 1,575 tons in 1995, although this commodity continued to provide the island's principal source of foreign exchange.

Since the early 1980s the volume and value of shipments from Madagascar have been subject to wide fluctuations, and cloves have been replaced by vanilla as the island's second most profitable export. With Zanzibar, Madagascar formerly produced most of the cloves entering world trade. However, Indonesia, which requires 30,000–35,000 tons of cloves per year to satisfy its kretek (clove) cigarette industry, became self-sufficient in clove production in the 1980s and now accounts for about 60% of world output.

Since the early 1980s the world market for cloves has been heavily oversupplied, and prices have fallen steadily, from a record US $9,600 per ton in 1980 to an all-time low of $600 per ton in 1994. In 1991 the Indonesian government, which holds substantial stocks of cloves, established a state monopoly in an attempt to stabilize the clove trade. In April 1996 the Indonesian marketing agency held stocks totalling 280,000 tons, while in 1995 international demand for cloves was approximately 80,000 tons.

Cobalt

Cobalt is usually mined as a by-product of another metal; in the case of African cobalt, this is principally copper, although cobalt is also produced from nickel-copper-cobalt ores in Botswana and Zimbabwe and from platinum ores in South Africa. It is rarely mined as the primary product of an ore, and is found in very weak concentration, generally 0.1%–0.5%. The ore must be crushed and ground after mining and subjected to a flotation process to obtain the concentrate. During the mid-1990s a new method of extraction, known as pressure acid leaching, was expected to increase substantially the rate of recovery of cobalt as a by-product when laterite nickel ore is treated. It was forecast that this technique, if widely applied, could eventually double existing annual cobalt output.

Production of Cobalt Ore (cobalt content, metric tons)

	1992	1993*
World total	27,131*	22,224
Africa	13,709*	8,776
African producers		
Botswana	208	200
Morocco	461	397
South Africa	350*	350
Zaire	5,700	2,459
Zambia†	6,910	5,300
Zimbabwe	80*	70
Non-African producers		
Australia	1,600*	1,700
Canada	5,102	5,738
Cuba	1,500*	1,500
New Caledonia	800*	800
Russia	4,000*	3,300

* Estimated production.

† Twelve months beginning 1 April of year stated.

Source: US Bureau of Mines.

About 35% of cobalt production is used in the metallic form as superalloys (in turbine engines), hardfacing and stellite. Approximately 34% is applied to chemical uses in such industries as glass manufacture, paints and inks and, increasingly, as catalysts in the processing of oil and petroleum feed stocks and synthetic materials. A further 10% is used in the manufacture of ceramics, 11% in magnetic alloys and 10% in the fabrication of hard metals. Sales agencies in the USA, Europe and the Far East market the major part of African production, which comprises about 39.5% of world cobalt output. In 1996 the major importer of cobalt was Japan.

The Democratic Republic of the Congo (DRC, formerly Zaire), possesses an estimated 65% of the world's identified cobalt reserves. These reserves also have the highest grade of the metal, with up to six tons of cobalt produced with every 100 tons of copper. Following the overthrow of the government of Zaire in May 1997, the mining, marketing and export of cobalt from the DRC have continued to be conducted by a state monopoly, La Générale des carrières et des mines (GÉCAMINES). Since 1990, however, the country's cobalt output has been adversely affected by economic dislocation, caused by internal unrest, and by thefts of cobalt, allegedly by members of the former Zairean army, which were estimated to account for 5%–25% of the total annual output. Production has also been lost as a result of the collapse of the Kamoto mine in the same year. Projects by GÉCAMINES to open up new deposits in the Shaba region were proceeding in 1996. In 1992 former Zaire was overtaken by Zambia as the world's leading cobalt producer, and in 1993 Zambian output was exceeded by that of Canada. Prospects for the restoration of internal order following the establishment of the DRC have given rise to hopes that the country can retrieve the levels of cobalt output of the early 1980s, when annual exports were in the range of 14,000–16,000 tons. In 1996 the country's export volume was estimated at only 5,000 tons, accounting for about 20% of world supplies.

Since the early 1980s Zambia has promoted the expansion of its cobalt production in an attempt to offset declines in the country's copper output. In the early 1990s three mining companies in South Africa were producing cobalt metal as a by-product of platinum production. In 1992 the Ugandan government signed an agreement with European interests for a project to extract cobalt, at an estimated rate of 1,000 tons per year for a period of 12 years, from waste dumps at the Kilembe copper mine. Financing arrangements for the construction of an extraction plant were finalized in 1996, and cobalt extraction operations were expected to begin in 1998. It was announced in 1996 that significant deposits of copper and cobalt had been identified on the northern boundary of the copper belt. Following the identification of nickel-cobalt deposits in Tanzania in the early 1990s, the exploitation of cobalt reserves, estimated at 49,000 tons, was expected to begin in 1997.

Traditional cobalt-mining may be challenged during the next 20 years by the wide-scale retrieval of manganese nodules from the world's seabeds. It is estimated that the cobalt content of each nodule is about 0.25%, although nodules recovered from the Pacific Ocean in 1983 had a cobalt content of 2.5%. Ferromanganese crusts, containing extractable cobalt, have been identified at relatively shallow depths within the USA's exclusive economic zones, which extend 370 km (200 nautical miles) into US coastal waters.

On the free market, the price of high-grade cobalt (minimum purity 99.8%) stood at more than US $14 per lb in early June 1993, but declined to $11.175 in November. Following reports of unrest in Zaire, the price of cobalt rose sharply in January 1994, reaching $22.75 per lb. The cobalt price eased to $21.00 per lb in February, but the upward trend later resumed, with the price reaching $27.00 in April. It retreated to $22.20 per lb in August. The price of cobalt increased to $28.125 per lb in October, but fell to $25.50 in December.

Another strong advance in cobalt prices occurred in early 1995, with the quotation for high-grade metal reaching US $30.40 per lb in February. The price was reduced to $27.05 per lb in April, recovered to $29.30 in May, but declined to $27.05 again in July. It advanced to $32.875 per lb in January 1996, but fell to $20.625 in August. Another recovery ensued, and in September the cobalt price reached $23.40 per lb, the highest quotation recorded during the second half of the year.

In March 1997 the free-market price of high-grade cobalt declined to US $19 per lb, its lowest level since January 1994. However, in May 1997, in response to the internal conflict in Zaire (now the DRC), the metal's price rose to $25.325 per lb. In June, following the establishment of the DRC, the price of cobalt eased to $22.50 per lb.

The Cobalt Development Institute, founded in 1982, comprises almost 40 members, including consumers, processors, merchants and the eight leading producers, including the DRC and Zambia.

Cocoa (*Theobroma cacao*)

This tree, up to 14 m tall, originated in the tropical forests of Central and South America. The first known cocoa plantations were in southern Mexico around AD 600. Cocoa first came to Europe in the 16th century. The Spanish and Portuguese introduced cocoa into Africa—on the islands of Fernando Póo (now Bioko), in Equatorial Guinea, and São Tomé and Príncipe—at the beginning of the 19th century. At the end of the century the tree was established on the African mainland, first in Ghana and then in other west African countries.

Cocoa is now widely grown in the tropics, usually at altitudes less than 300 m above sea-level, where it needs a fairly high rainfall and good soil. The cocoa tree has a much shallower tap root than, for example, the coffee bush, making cocoa more vulnerable to dry weather. Cocoa trees can take up to four years from planting before producing sufficient fruit for harvesting. They may live to 80 years or more, although the fully productive period is usually about 20 years. The tree is highly vulnerable to pests and diseases, and it is also very sensitive to climatic changes. Its fruit is a large pod, about 15–25 cm in length, which at maturity is yellow in some varieties and red in others. The ripe pods are cut from the tree, where they grow directly out of the trunk and branches. When opened, cocoa pods disclose a mass of seeds (beans) surrounded by white mucilage. After harvesting, the beans and mucilage are scooped out and fermented. Fermentation lasts several days, allowing the flavour to develop. The mature fermented beans, dull red in colour, are then dried, ready to be bagged as raw cocoa which may be further processed or exported.

Cultivated cocoa trees may be broadly divided into three groups. All west African cocoas belong to the Amazonian Forastero group, which now provides more than 80% of world cocoa production. It includes the Amelonado variety, suitable for chocolate manufacturing, grown in Ghana, Côte d'Ivoire and Nigeria. Criollo cocoa is not widely grown and is used only for luxury confectionery. The third group is Trinitario, which accounts for about 15% of world output and grows mainly in Central America and the northern regions of South America.

Cocoa processing takes place mainly in importing countries, although processing capacity was established in west Africa during the 1960s and processed products now account for a significant part of the value of its cocoa exports. The processes include shelling, roasting and grinding the beans. Almost half of each bean after shelling consists of a fat called cocoa butter. In the manufacture of cocoa powder for use as a beverage, this fat is largely removed. Cocoa is a mildly stimulating drink, because of its caffeine content, and, unlike coffee and tea, is highly nutritional.

The most important use of cocoa is in the manufacture of chocolate, of which it is the main ingredient. About 90% of all cocoa produced is used in chocolate-making, for which extra cocoa butter is added, as well as other substances such as sugar—and milk in the case of milk chocolate. Proposals that were announced in December 1993 by the consumer countries of the European Union, permitting chocolate-manufacturers in member states to add as much as 5% vegetable fats to cocoa solids and cocoa fats in the manufacture of chocolate products, have been perceived by producers as potentially damaging to the world cocoa trade. In 1995 it was estimated that the implementation of this plan could reduce world demand for cocoa beans by about 150,000 metric tons annually.

After coffee and sugar, cocoa is the most important agricultural export commodity in international trade. Recorded world exports (including re-exports) of cocoa beans totalled 1,843,820 metric tons in the 12 months ending 30 September 1995. In 1995/96 export volume was estimated to have advanced to 2,291,290 tons, of which African countries provided 1,652,570 tons. The world's leading exporters of cocoa beans in 1995/96 were Côte d'Ivoire (1,037,989 tons), Ghana (330,646 tons), Indonesia (234,174 tons), Nigeria (146,754 tons), Cameroon (105,011 tons), Ecuador (59,032 tons), the Dominican Republic (49,895 tons) and Malaysia (46,628 tons).

The principal importers of cocoa are developed countries with market economies, which account for about 80% of cocoa imports from developing countries. Recorded world imports of cocoa beans in 1995/96 were 2,321,240 tons. The principal importing countries in that year were the Netherlands (with 515,811 tons, representing 22.2% of the total), the USA (445,260 tons) and Germany (299,124 tons).

Production of Cocoa Beans
('000 metric tons, year ending 30 September)

	1994/95	1995/96*
World total	2,346	2,918
Africa	1,436	1,921
Leading African producers		
Cameroon	108	130
Congo, Dem. Repub.	4	3
Côte d'Ivoire	850	1,200
Equatorial Guinea	3	5
Ghana	310	404
Guinea	3	5
Madagascar	3	3
Nigeria	143	155
São Tomé and Príncipe	2	3
Sierra Leone	3	3
Togo	4	5
Leading non-African producers		
Brazil	225	231
Colombia	50	50
Dominican Repub.	56	55
Ecuador	80	100
Indonesia	240	300
Malaysia	120	115
Mexico	43	41
Papua New Guinea	29	36

* Estimates.

Source: International Cocoa Organization.

Côte d'Ivoire, the region's dominant producer, is also the world's principal coca grower, accounting for more than 41% of output and 45% of international coca exports in 1995/96. Since the mid-1960s, when it accounted for more than one-third of world production, Ghana's share of the world market has fallen to less than 15%, owing to the neglect of the industry and to the official policy of maintaining prices payable to producers at uneconomic levels. The decline has been exacerbated by the smuggling of cocoa to neighbouring countries, where higher prices are obtainable. The spread of plant diseases, particularly black pod and swollen shoot, have also inhibited recovery, and it was estimated by the Ghana Cocoa Board (COCOBOD) in 1995 that at least 20m. infected cocoa trees awaited removal. In recent years, however, Ghana has sought to revive cocoa production through programmes of replanting, insect spraying, storage and transport improvement. In 1992 cocoa was overtaken by gold as Ghana's main export commodity. From July 1993 COCOBOD was deprived of its monopoly, and three trading companies were licensed to purchase cocoa direct from farmers. However, COCOBOD retained exclusive control over Ghanaian cocoa exports. Among the smaller African producers, cocoa exports are a significant component of the economies of Cameroon, Equatorial Guinea, São Tomé and Príncipe and Togo. Guinea, Madagascar and the Democratic Republic of the Congo are also prominent among the region's smaller-scale producers. Although cocoa remains Nigeria's main export crop, its significance to the economy has been eclipsed by petroleum.

World prices for cocoa are highly sensitive to changes in supply and demand, making its market position volatile. Negotiations to secure international agreement on stabilizing the cocoa industry began in 1956. Full-scale cocoa conferences, under United Nations auspices, were held in 1963, 1966 and 1967, but all proved abortive. A major difficulty was the failure to agree on a fixed minimum price. In 1972 the fourth UN Cocoa Conference took place in Geneva and resulted in the first International Cocoa Agreement (ICCA), adopted by 52 countries, although the USA, the world's principal cocoa importer, did not sign. The ICCA took formal effect in October 1973. It operated for three quota years and provided for an export quota system for producing countries, a fixed price range for cocoa beans and a buffer stock to support the agreed prices. In accordance with the ICCA, the International Cocoa Organization (ICCO), based in London, was established in 1973. In March 1997 its members comprised 17 exporting countries, accounting for about three-quarters of world production and exports, excluding re-exports, of cocoa beans, and 22 importing countries, accounting for about 55% of world imports of cocoa beans. The USA, a leading importer of cocoa, is not a member. Nor is Indonesia, whose production and exports of cocoa has expanded rapidly in recent years. The governing body of the ICCO is the International Cocoa Council (ICC), established to supervise implementation of the ICCA.

A second ICCA operated during 1979–81. It was followed by an extended agreement, which was in force in 1981–87. A fourth ICCA took effect in 1987. (For detailed information on these agreements, see *Africa South of the Sahara 1991*.) During the period of these ICCA, the effective operation of cocoa price stabilization mechanisms was frequently impeded by a number of factors, principally by crop and stock surpluses, which continued to overshadow the cocoa market in the early 1990s. In addition, the achievement of ICCA objectives was affected by the divergent views of producers and consumers, led by Côte d'Ivoire, on one side, and by the USA, on the other, as to appropriate minimum price levels. Disagreements also developed over the allocation of members' export quotas and the conduct of price support measures by means of the buffer stock (which ceased to operate during 1983–88), and subsequently over the disposal of unspent buffer stock funds. The effectiveness of financial operations under the fourth ICCA was severely curtailed by the accumulation of arrears of individual members' levy payments, notably by Côte d'Ivoire and Brazil. The fourth ICCA was extended for a two-year period from October 1990, although the suspension of the economic clauses relating to cocoa price support operations rendered the agreement ineffective in terms of exerting any influence over cocoa market prices.

Preliminary discussions on a fifth ICCA, again held under UN auspices, ended without agreement in May 1992, when consumer members, while agreeing to extend the fourth ICCA for a further year (until October 1993), refused to accept producers' proposals for the creation of an export quota system as a means of stabilizing prices, on the grounds that such arrangements would not impose sufficient limits on total production to restore equilibrium between demand and supply. Additionally, no agreement was reached on the disposition of cocoa buffer stocks, then totalling 240,000 tons. At a further meeting of the ICCO, held in July, delegates again failed to reach an accord on these issues. Negotiations were renewed in November, and again in February–March 1993, when it was decided to abandon efforts to formulate arrangements under which prices would be stabilized by means of a stock-withholding scheme. At a further negotiating conference in July, however, terms were finally agreed for a new ICCA, to take effect from October, subject to its ratification by at least five exporting countries (accounting for at least 80% of total world exports) and by importing countries (representing at least 60% of total imports). Unlike previous commodity agreements sponsored by the UN, the fifth ICCA aimed to achieve stable prices by regulating supplies and promoting consumption, rather than through the operation of buffer stocks and export quotas.

The fifth ICCA, operating until September 1998, entered into effect in February 1994. Under the new agreement, buffer stocks totalling 233,000 tons that had accrued from the previous ICCA were to be released on the market at the rate of 51,000 tons annually over a maximum period of 4½ years, beginning in the 1993/94 crop season. At a meeting of the ICCO, held in October 1994, it was agreed that following the completion of the stocks reduction programme the extent of stocks held should be limited to the equivalent of three months' consumption. ICCO members also assented to a voluntary reduction in output of 75,000 tons annually, beginning in 1993/94 and terminating in 1998/99. Further measures to achieve a closer balance of production and consumption, under which the level of cocoa stocks would be maintained at 34% of world grindings during the 1996/97 crop year, were introduced by the ICCO in September 1996.

Export Price Index for Cocoa (base: 1980 = 100)

	Average	Highest month(s)	Lowest month(s)
1985	86		
1990	49		
1994	53	59 (Aug.)	47 (Feb., April)
1995	55	58 (March)	51 (Dec.)
1996	54	57 (June)	50 (March)

As the above table indicates, international prices for cocoa have generally been very low in recent years. In 1992 the average of the ICCO's daily prices (based on selected quotations from the London and New York markets) was US $1,099.5 per metric ton (49.9 US cents per lb), its lowest level since 1972. The annual average was slightly higher in 1993, at $1,117 per ton, and rose to $1,396 in 1994, to $1,433 in 1995 and to $1,456 in 1996. In 1993 the monthly average ranged from $975 per ton in March to $1,355 in December, but in 1994 it varied from $1,229 (February) to $1,552 (July). Prices were steadier in 1995, with the monthly average ranging from $1,364 per ton (in July) to $1,510 (February). The range widened again in 1996, varying from $1,339 per ton (in March) to $1,538 (June).

On the London Commodity Exchange (LCE) the price of cocoa for short-term delivery increased from £637 ($983) per ton in May 1993 to £1,003.5 in November, but it later retreated. In April 1994 the London cocoa quotation for May delivery fell to £825.5 per ton, but in July, following forecasts that the global production deficit would rise, the price reached £1,093.5 ($1,694). In September the LCE price of cocoa declined to £937.5 ($1,449) per ton, and at the end of November the quotation for December delivery was £907.5. During December, however, the cocoa price advanced to £1,045 ($1,630) per ton.

In late February 1995 the London cocoa quotation for March delivery stood at £1,056.5 per ton, but in March the price was reduced to £938 (US $1,498). The generally downward trend continued, and in late July the LCE cocoa price was £827.5 ($1,321) per ton. Prices under short-term contracts remained below £1,000 per ton until the end of the year, with the December 'spot' quotation (for immediate delivery) declining to £847.5 ($1,319) per ton.

During the first quarter of 1996 London cocoa prices continued to be depressed, but in April the short-term quotation rose to more than £1,000 per ton. In May the LCE 'spot' price reached £1,104.5 (US $1,672) per ton. Cocoa prices had increased in spite of the ICCO's forecast that supply would exceed demand in 1995/96, following four consecutive years of deficits. In July 1996, however, the 'spot' quotation in London declined from £1,049 ($1,630) per ton to £924 ($1,438) at the end of the month. The value of cocoa transactions was generally below £1,000 per ton for the remainder of the year, and in December the 'spot' price was reduced to £848.5 ($1,419).

In January and February 1997 short-term quotations for cocoa were at similarly low levels, but in March the 'spot' price on the London market rose from £894.5 (US $1,449) per ton to £1,012.5 ($1,621) in less than two weeks. London cocoa prices eased somewhat in subsequent weeks, but moved higher again in June, despite the relative strength of the British currency. On 1 July the 'spot' price stood at £1,143 ($1,895) per ton, its highest level, in terms of sterling, for more than nine years. Within three weeks, however, the price declined to about £970 (less than $1,630) per ton.

The Cocoa Producers' Alliance (COPAL), with headquarters in Lagos, Nigeria, whose 13 members include all the major producers except Indonesia, was formed in 1962 with the aim of preventing excessive price fluctuations by regulating the supply of cocoa. Members of COPAL account for about 82% of world cocoa production, with its seven African members providing about 53%. COPAL has acted in concert with successive ICCA.

The principal centres for cocoa-trading in the industrialized countries are the London Cocoa Terminal Market, in the United Kingdom, and the New York Coffee, Sugar and Cocoa Exchange, in the USA.

Coffee (*Coffea*)

This is an evergreen shrub or small tree, generally 5 m–10 m in height, indigenous to Asia and tropical Africa. Wild trees grow to 10 m but the cultivated shrubs are pruned to much lower heights. The dried seeds (beans) are roasted, ground and brewed in hot water to provide the most popular of the world's non-alcoholic beverages. Coffee is drunk in every country in the world and its consumers comprise an estimated one-third of the world's population. Although it has little nutrient value, coffee acts as a mild stimulant, owing to the presence of caffeine, an alkaloid also present in tea and cocoa.

There are about 40 species of *Coffea*, most of which grow wild in the eastern hemisphere. The species of economic importance are *C. arabica* (native to Ethiopia), which accounts for about 70%–75% of world production, and *C. canephora* (the source of robusta coffee), which accounts for all but 1% of the remainder. Arabica coffee is more aromatic but robusta, as the name implies, is a stronger plant. Coffee grows in the tropical belt, between 20°N and 20°S, and from sea-level to as much as 2,000 m above. The optimum growing conditions are found at 1,250–1,500 m above sea-level, with an average temperature of around 17°C and an average annual rainfall of 1,000–1,750 mm. Trees begin bearing fruit three to five years after planting, depending upon the variety, and give their maximum yield (up to 5 kg of fruit per year) from the sixth to the 15th year. Few shrubs remain profitable beyond 30 years.

Arabica coffee trees are grown mostly in the American tropics and supply the largest quantity and the best quality of coffee beans. In Africa and Asia arabica coffee is vulnerable in lowland areas to a serious leaf disease and consequently cultivation has been concentrated on highland areas. Some highland arabicas, such as those grown in Kenya, have a high reputation for quality.

The robusta coffee tree, grown mainly in east and west Africa, has larger leaves than arabica but the beans are generally smaller and of lower quality and price. However, robusta coffee has a higher yield than arabica as the trees are more resistant to disease. Robusta is also more suitable for the production of soluble ('instant') coffee. About 75% of African coffee is of the robusta variety. Soluble coffee accounts for more than one-fifth of world coffee consumption.

Each coffee berry, green at first but red when ripe, usually contains two beans (white in arabica, light brown in robusta) which are the commercial product of the plant. To produce the best quality arabica beans—known in the trade as 'mild' coffee—the berries are opened by a pulping machine and the beans fermented briefly in water before being dried and hulled into green coffee. Much of the crop is exported in green form. Robusta beans are generally prepared by dry-hulling. Roasting and grinding are usually undertaken in the importing countries, for economic reasons and because roasted beans rapidly lose their freshness when exposed to air.

Apart from beans, coffee produces a few minor by-products. When the coffee beans have been removed from the fruit, what remains is a wet mass of pulp and, at a later stage, the dry material of the 'hull' or fibrous sleeve that protects the beans. Coffee pulp is used as cattle feed, the fermented pulp makes a good fertilizer and coffee bean oil is an ingredient in soaps, paints and polishes.

Production of Green Coffee Beans ('000 metric tons)

	1994	1995
World total	5,604*	5,411*
Africa	1,061*	1,149*
Leading African producers		
Burundi	41	26†
Cameroon	60†	57†
Congo, Dem. Repub.	77†	76†
Côte d'Ivoire	148	194
Ethiopia	207†	228†
Guinea	30	30*
Kenya	80	93†
Madagascar	79	79†
Rwanda	2†	22†
Sierra Leone	28	25
Tanzania	34	40
Togo	26*	16
Uganda	198	220†
Leading non-African producers		
Brazil‡	1,306	926
Colombia	678†	778†
Costa Rica	150†	156†
Ecuador	187	148
El Salvador	141	135
Guatemala	212	214
Honduras	126	126
India	208†	162†
Indonesia	346	360†
Mexico	325	325
Philippines	122	124
Viet Nam	166	185

* FAO estimate.
† Unofficial figure.
‡ Data that were officially reported in terms of dry cherries have been converted into clean coffee at 50%.

More than one-half of the world's coffee is produced on smallholdings of less than 5 ha. In most producing countries, and especially in Africa, coffee is almost entirely an export crop, with little domestic consumption. Green coffee accounts for some 96% of all the coffee that is exported, with soluble and roasted coffee comprising the balance. Tariffs on green/raw coffee are usually low or non-existent. The USA is the largest single importer, although its volume of coffee purchases was overtaken in 1975 by the combined imports of the (then) nine countries of the European Community (EC, now the European Union—EU).

After petroleum, coffee is the major raw material in world trade, and the single most valuable agricultural export of the tropics. Arabica coffee accounts for about two-thirds of world production. Latin America (with 59% of world output in 1995) is the leading coffee-growing region. Africa, which formerly ranked second, was overtaken in 1993 by Asian producers. In 1994, however, African countries accounted for 18.4% of world production compared with 18% by the Asian region, and in 1995 African producers accounted for 21.2%, compared with 18.5% for Asian countries.

In every year during 1970–90, except in 1974 and 1984, Côte d'Ivoire was Africa's leading coffee producer, although since 1980 cocoa has overtaken coffee as its most important export crop. In the early 1990s more than three-quarters of the coffee trees in Côte d'Ivoire had passed their most productive age. A programme of extensive replanting was proceeding in the mid-1990s: the total area under coffee cultivation is projected to increase by 270,000 ha to 1.3m. ha by the year 2000.

The African countries which are most dependent on coffee as a source of foreign exchange are Burundi and Uganda. Coffee sales generally account for 70%–85% of Burundi's total export revenue, and in 1995 the proportion was 81%. In Uganda coffee provided 99.2% of exports in 1981, and 91% in 1990; in 1995 its contribution was 94%. Ethiopia is a significant regional producer, exceeding Côte d'Ivoire in output in each of the years

1991–95, but, with high domestic consumption and widespread smuggling, official exports accounted for only about one-quarter of total production in the early 1990s. None the less, coffee accounted for 61.6% of Ethiopia's total export earnings in 1991, and for almost 66% of foreign exchange receipts in 1994/95. The coffee sector in Rwanda, which contributed more than 60% of export revenue in 1991, has been severely affected by internal unrest, and in 1994 the bulk of that year's coffee crop was lost. Among other African countries where coffee is a major export are Cameroon, the Central African Republic, Kenya, Madagascar, Tanzania and Zaire. Angola was formerly the world's leading exporter of robusta coffee, but production during the period 1975–95 was severely disrupted by civil conflict. In 1995, however, the resumption of production in three provinces produced a crop of 2,300 tons, while plans were proceeding for the transfer to private-sector ownership of the country's major plantations during 1996. However, the full rehabilitation of Angola's coffee industry, following the political and military settlement pending in 1997, is expected to span many years. Plans have been announced for the initial rehabilitation of 50,000 ha of coffee estates over a five-year period to 2002, with the aim of achieving an annual coffee output of 60,000 tons. During 1997, the government was proceeding with the transfer of the state-controlled marketing monopoly to the private sector, and for the sale of all state-owned coffee-producing companies.

Effective international attempts to stabilize coffee prices began in 1959, when a number of producing countries made a short-term agreement to fix export quotas. After three such agreements, a five-year International Coffee Agreement (ICA), covering both producers and consumers, and introducing a quota system, was signed in 1962. This led to the establishment in 1963 of the International Coffee Organization (ICO), with its headquarters in London. In April 1996 the ICO comprised 53 members (36 exporting countries, accounting for over 90% of world supplies, and 17 importing countries, accounting, until the withdrawal of the USA in 1993, for over 80% of world imports). Subsequent ICA were negotiated in 1976, 1983 and 1994 (see below), but the system of export quotas to stabilize prices was eventually abandoned in July 1989 (for detailed information on the 1976 and 1983 agreements, see *Africa South of the Sahara 1991*.) During each successive ICA, contention arose over the allocation of members' export quotas, the operation of price support mechanisms, and, most importantly, illicit sales by some members of surplus stocks to non-members of the ICO (notably to the USSR and to countries in Eastern Europe and the Middle East). These 'leaks' of low-price coffee, often at less than one-half of the official ICA rate, also found their way to consumer members of the ICO through free ports, depressing the general market price and making it more difficult for exporters to fulfil their quotas. In the late 1980s such sales were estimated to approximate as much as one-quarter of total production by ICO members.

The issue of coffee export quotas became further complicated in the 1980s, as consumer tastes in the main importing market, the USA, and, to a lesser extent, in the EC moved away from the robustas exported by Brazil and the main African producers and in favour of the milder arabica coffees grown in Central America. Disagreements over a new system of quota allocations, taking account of coffee by variety, had the effect of undermining efforts in 1989 to preserve the economic provisions of the ICA, pending the negotiation of a new agreement. The ensuing deadlock between consumers and producers, as well as among the producers themselves, led in July to the collapse of the quota system and the suspension of the economic provisions of the ICA. The administrative clauses of the agreement, however, continued to operate and were subsequently extended until October 1993, pending an eventual settlement of the quota issue and the entering into force of a successor ICA.

With the abandonment of the ICA quotas, coffee prices fell sharply in world markets, and were further depressed by a substantial accumulation of coffee stocks held by consumers. The response by some Latin American producers was to seek to revive prices by imposing temporary suspensions of exports; this strategy, however, merely increased losses of coffee revenue. By early 1992 there had been general agreement among the ICO exporting members that the export quota mechanism should be revived; however, disagreements persisted over the allocation of quotas. In June the ICO met in London to seek agreement on transitional measures to revive the coffee market, ahead of fuller negotiations to formulate a new ICA (to take effect from 1 October). No substantive progress was made, although a 20-nation working group was formed to study means of reintroducing export controls in the next ICA. It was also proposed that the new agreement should implement coffee-export controls to all destinations, including countries that are not signatories to an ICA. It was hoped that both consuming and producing countries would agree on a successor ICA containing provisions for a target stabilization price for coffee, an equitable distribution of export quotas among the producers, and mechanisms to be used for its adjustment. Subsequent negotiations, in December 1992 and January–February 1993, ended in deadlock, although both producers and consumers agreed that any new ICA should be based on a universal quota system. In April, following further meetings of the ICO in London, it was announced that efforts to achieve a new Agreement had collapsed. In the following month Brazil and Colombia, the two largest coffee producers, were joined by some Central American producers in a scheme to limit their coffee production and exports in the 1993/94 crop year. Although world consumption of coffee exceeded the level of shipments, prices were severely depressed by surpluses of coffee stocks totalling 62m. bags (each of 60 kg), with an additional 21m. bags held in reserve by consumer companies. Prices, in real terms, stood at historic 'lows'.

In July 1993 the Latin American producers announced the formation of an Association of Coffee Producing Countries (ACPC), with headquarters in Brasília, to implement an export-withholding scheme. In the following month the Inter-African Coffee Organization (IACO, see below), whose membership includes Côte d'Ivoire, Kenya and Uganda, agreed to join the Latin American producers in a new plan to withhold 20% of output whenever market prices fell below an agreed limit. With the participation of Asian producers, a 28-member ACPC was formally established in August. (Angola was admitted to membership of the IACO and the ACPC in 1996.) Its member countries represent about two-thirds of African production and approximately 86% of coffee output world-wide.

The ACPC withholding scheme came into operation in October 1993 and gradually generated improved prices; by April 1994 market quotations for all grades and origins of coffee had achieved their highest levels since 1989. In June and July 1994 coffee prices escalated sharply, following reports that as much as 50% of the 1995/96 Brazilian crop had been damaged by frosts. In July 1994 both Brazil and Colombia announced a temporary suspension of coffee exports. The onset of drought following the Brazilian frosts further affected prospects for its 1994/95 harvest, and ensured the maintenance of a firm tone in world coffee prices during the remainder of 1994. African producers, it was forecast, would receive US $3,000m. from their 1994/95 coffee sales, compared with $900m. in 1993/94.

The intervention of speculative activity in the coffee futures market during early 1995 led to a series of price falls, despite expectations that coffee consumption in 1995/96, at a forecast 93.4m. bags, would exceed production by about 1m. bags. In an attempt to restore prices, the ACPC announced in March 1995 that it was introducing supply controls and a stock retention scheme with effect from June. In June the Brazilian authorities, holding coffee stocks of about 14.7m. bags, introduced new arrangements under which these stocks would be released for export only when the 20-day moving average of the ICO arabica coffee indicator rose about US $1.90 per lb. Prices, however, continued to decline, and in July Brazil joined Colombia, Costa Rica, El Salvador and Honduras in imposing a reduction of 16% in coffee exports for a one-year period. Later in the same month the ACPC collectively agreed to limit coffee shipments to 60.4m. bags from July 1995 to June 1996. This withholding measure would lead to a decrease of about 6m. bags in international coffee exports during this period. In May 1996 the ACPC announced that the witholding scheme was to be extended to June 1997, during which period exports would be restricted to 53.55m. bags, of which African producers were to share a quota of 12.8m. bags. Tanzania, however, withdrew from the scheme in July. In May 1997 the withholding plan was extended by the

ACPC for a further 12 months. Total exports for that period were to be limited to 52.75m. bags.

In June 1993 the members of the ICO agreed to a further extension of the ICA, to September 1994. However, the influence of the ICO, from which the USA withdrew in October 1993, was increasingly perceived as having been eclipsed by the ACPC. In 1994 the ICO agreed provisions for a new ICA, again with primarily consultative and administrative functions, to operate for a five-year period, until September 1999. The ICO has, however, continued to favour an eventual resumption of quota arrangements, which it views as the most effective means of preventing sharp fluctuations in market prices.

In February 1995 five African Producers (Burundi, Kenya, Rwanda, Tanzania and Uganda) agreed to participate in coffee price guarantee contract arrangements sponsored by the Eastern and Southern Africa Trade and Development Bank under the auspices of the Common Market for Eastern and Southern Africa (COMESA). This plan seeks to promote producer price guarantees in place of stock retention schemes. The contract guarantee arrangements would indemnify producers against prices falling below an agreed contract price, and would operate in relation to any specific trading month on coffee future markets.

Export Price Index for Coffee (base: 1980 = 100)

	Average	Highest month(s)	Lowest month(s)
1985	81		
1990	46		
1994	81	121 (Sept.)	42 (Jan.)
1995	83	97 (March)	60 (Dec.)
1996	65	72 (Feb.)	58 (Dec.)

International prices for coffee beans in the early 1990s were generally at very low levels, even in nominal terms (i.e. without taking inflation into account). On the London Commodity Exchange (LCE) the price of raw robusta coffee for short-term delivery fell in May 1992 to US $652.5 (£365) per metric ton, its lowest level, in terms of dollars, for more than 22 years. By December the London coffee price had recovered to $1,057.5 per ton (for delivery in January 1993). The LCE quotation eased to $837 (£542) per ton in January 1993, and remained within this range until August, when a sharp increase began. The coffee price advanced in September to $1,371 (£885) per ton, its highest level for the year. Thereafter, the coffee market moved within narrow limits until March 1994, when the London quotation per ton rose from $1,198.5 (£801.5) to $1,352 (£906). In April a further surge in prices began, and in May coffee was traded in London at more than $2,000 per ton for the first time since 1989. In late June 1994 there were reports from Brazil that frost had damaged the potential coffee harvest for future seasons, and the LCE quotation exceeded $3,000 per ton. In July, after further reports of frost damage to Brazilian coffee plantations, the London price reached $3,975 (£2,538) per ton. Market conditions then eased, but in September, as a drought persisted in Brazil, the LCE price of coffee increasd to $4,262.5 (£2,708) per ton, its highest level since January 1986. International coffee prices subsequently declined sharply, and in December 1994, following forecasts of a rise in production and a fall in consumption, the London quotation for January 1995 delivery stood at $2,481.5 per ton.

The coffee market later revived, and in March 1995 the LCE price reached US $3,340 (£2,112) per ton. However, in early July coffee traded in London at $2,400 (£1,501) per ton, although later in the month, after producing countries had announced plans to limit exports, the price rose to $2,932.5 (£1,837). During September the LCE 'spot' quotation (for immediate delivery) was reduced from $2,749 (£1,770) per ton to $2,227.5 (£1,441), but in November it advanced from $2,370 (£1,501) to $2,739.5 (£1,786). Coffee for short-term delivery was traded in December at less than $2,000 per ton, while longer-term quotations were considerably lower.

In early January 1996 the 'spot' price of coffee in London stood at US $1,798 (£1,159) per ton, but later in the month it reached $2,050 (£1,360). The corresponding quotation rose to $2,146.5 (£1,401) per ton in March, but declined to $1,844.5 (£1,220) in May. The 'spot' contract in July opened at $1,730.5 (£1,112) per ton, but within four weeks the price fell to $1,487 (£956), with the easing of concern about a threat of frost damage to Brazilian coffee plantations. In early September the comparable price of coffee was $1,668 (£1,070) per ton, but by the end of the month it had declined to $1,555 (£994). Coffee prices continued to fall in subsequent weeks. In November the 'spot' quotation rose to $1,571 (£934) per ton, but slumped to $1,375.5 (£819) within a week. The generally downward trend continued in December, and by the end of the year the London price of coffee (for delivery in January 1997) had been reduced to $1,259 per ton.

In early January 1997 the 'spot' price for robusta coffee stood at only US $1,237 (£734) per ton, but later in the month it reached £1,597.5 (£981). The advance in the coffee market continued in February, but in March the price per ton was reduced from $1,780 (£1,109) to $1,547.5 (£960) within two weeks. In May coffee prices rose spectacularly, in response to concerns about the scarcity of supplies and fears of frost in Brazil. The London 'spot' quotation increased from $1,595 (£986) per ton to $2,502.5 (£1,526) by the end of the month. Meanwhile, on the New York market the price of arabica coffee for short-term delivery exceeded $3 per lb for the first time since 1977. However, the rally was short-lived, and in July 1997 the London price for robusta coffee declined to less than $1,530 (about £910) per ton.

The IACO was formed in 1960, with its headquarters at Abidjan in Côte d'Ivoire. In 1995 the IACO represented 25 producer countries, all of which were also members of the ICO. The aim of the IACO is to study common problems and to encourage the harmonization of production. The ACPC, representing 28 African, Asian and Latin American producer countries, has its headquarters in London.

Copper

The ores containing copper are mainly copper sulphide or copper oxide. They are mined both underground and by open-cast or surface mining. After break-up of the ore body by explosives, the lumps of ore are crushed, ground and mixed with reagents and water in the case of sulphide ores, and then subjected to a flotation process by which copper-rich minerals are extracted. The resulting concentrate, which contains about 30% copper, is then dried, smelted and cast into anode copper, which is further refined to about 99.98% purity by electrolysis (chemical decomposition by electrical action). The cathodes are then cast into convenient shapes for working or are sold as such. Oxide ores, less important than sulphides, are treated in ways rather similar to the solvent extraction process described below.

Two alternative processes of copper extraction, both now in operation in Zambia, have been developed in recent years. The first of these techniques, and as yet of minor importance in the industry, is known as 'Torco' (treatment of refractory copper ores) and is used for extracting copper from silicate ores which were previously not treatable.

The second, and relatively low-cost, technique is the solvent extraction process. This is suited to the treatment of very low-grade oxidized ores and is currently being used on both new ores and waste dumps that have accumulated over previous years from conventional copper working. The copper in the ore or waste material is dissolved in acid and the copper-bearing leach solution is then mixed with a special organic-containing chemical reagent which selectively extracts the copper. After allowing the two layers to separate, the layer containing the copper is separated from the acid leach solution. The copper is extracted from the concentrated leach solution by means of electrolysis to produce refined cathodes.

Copper is ductile, resists corrosion and is an excellent conductor of heat and electricity. Its industrial uses are mainly in the electrical industry (about 60% of copper is made into wire for use in power cables, telecommunications, domestic and industrial wiring) and the building, engineering and chemical industries. Bronzes and brasses are typical copper alloys used for both industrial and decorative purposes. There are, however, substitutes for copper in almost all of its industrial uses, and in recent years aluminium has presented a challenge in the electrical and transport industries.

The current world reserve base of copper has been estimated by the US Bureau of Mines at 590m. metric tons. Reserves located within the Democratic Republic of the Congo (DRC) and Zambia jointly account for about 11% of the total.

Copper production is the mainstay of Zambia's economy, and copper sales normally account for about 85% of Zambia's export earnings. Mining operations are conducted by the Zambia Consolidated Copper Mines (ZCCM), and production is marketed exclusively by the state-owned Metal Marketing Corpn (MEMACO). Before being overtaken by Canada in 1983, Zambia ranked second only to Chile among the world's copper exporters. Zambian copper exports are virtually all in refined but unwrought form. About 43% of its sales are to European Union (EU) countries. Production of refined copper in Zambia entered a gradual decline in the mid-1980s; dwindling ore grades, high extraction costs, transport problems, shortages of foreign exchange, equipment and skilled labour, lack of maintenance and labour unrest combined to make the copper industry seem an unstable basis for the Zambian economy. However, following the country's change of government in 1991, a number of remedial measures, including the restructuring of ZCCM (whose transfer to private-sector ownership was scheduled to be completed by late 1998), have been carried out. A wide-ranging programme of exploration and modernization is also proceeding. In 1996 the Zambian Government declared its aim to achieve an output of 1m. tons of copper annually by the year 2000. The proposed development of the Konkola deep copper mine is a central factor in plans for the expansion of output.

The copper industry in the DRC has become increasingly vulnerable to competition from other producers, such as Chile, which have been establishing new open-cast, low-cost mines. Increasing emphasis has been placed on efforts to increase refined production capacity, and in the late 1980s about one-half of the country's copper exports were in the form of refined copper leach cathodes and blister copper. The export proportion of copper concentrates was expected to fall substantially during the 1990s. About 70% of copper exports by the DRC are to EU countries. The mining and marketing of copper in the DRC is the responsibility of the state-owned minerals enterprise, La Générale des Carrières et des Mines (GÉCAMINES), which in 1990 completed a large-scale five-year investment plan to improve copper-mining equipment and related infrastructure. However, as a result of continuing internal unrest, the copper output, which had been more than 500,000 tons per year in the mid-1980s, had declined to less than 50,000 tons in 1993 and was estimated at only 38,000 tons in 1996, respresenting less than 8% of the country's production capacity. The uncertainty of supplies from this source has been an important factor in maintaining a generally firm tone in world copper prices since 1993.

Production of Copper Ore (copper content, '000 metric tons)

	1994	1995
World total	9,418*	10,111*
Africa	673*	639*
Leading African producers		
Congo, Dem. Repub.	30	30
Namibia	29	26
South Africa	184	198
Zambia	384	342
Leading non-African producers		
Australia	416	379
Canada	617	726
Chile	2,220	2,488
China, People's Repub.	396	445
Indonesia	334	462
Mexico	306	360
Peru	405	479
Poland	377	384
Russia	448	480
USA	1,796	1,852

* Estimate.

Source: World Bureau of Metal Statistics.

South Africa is the continent's other main producer, although in the 1980s copper output began to be affected by declining grades of ore, leading to mine closures and a reduction in the level of operations to about 75% of capacity. Although as yet a minor producer, Namibia derived more than 10% of its total export revenue from copper in the late 1980s. Mining operations there are conducted by a South African-owned company, the Tsumeb Corpn Ltd (TCL), which controls four mines. While the pending closure of the mine at Tsumeb itself in the mid-1990s created a need for replacement ore for the TCL copper smelter complex, a number of new copper-mining projects were in prospect. Prominent among them was an Australian-promoted venture at Haib, with a production potential of more than 80,000 tons of cathode copper annually. Operations at this site are planned to begin in 1998. Haib, with a forecast mine life of 25 years, would form the largest single mining project ever undertaken in Namibia. In Botswana copper and nickel are mined at Selebi-Phikwe, and high-grade copper ore deposits have also been identified in the Ghanzi area. The Sanyati copper mine in Zimbabwe, with estimated ore reserves of 5.5m. tons, entered production in late 1995. Targeted output was 5,000 tons annually during the mine's expected life of eight to 10 years. The exploitation of low-grade deposits at Akjoujt, in Mauritania, ceased in 1978, but a subsequent investment programme, initiated by Arab interests, led in 1992 to the reopening of the processing plant for the recovery of gold from the accumulated tailings of copper ores. Uganda possesses a copper ore reserve base estimated to be in the range of 4m.–5m. tons, although the mines, at Kilembe, have remained closed since 1980.

The major copper-importing countries are the countries of the EU, Japan and the USA. At the close of the 1980s, demand for copper was not being satisfied in full by current production levels, which were being affected by industrial and political unrest in some of the non-African producing countries, notably Chile, with the consequence that levels of copper stocks were declining. Production surpluses, reflecting lower levels of industrial activity in the main importing countries, occurred in the early 1990s, but were followed by supply deficits, exacerbated by low levels of copper stocks. World consumption of copper was forecast to increase by 4%–5% in 1997, approximately the expected rise in mine output.

There is no international agreement between producers and consumers governing the stabilization of supplies and prices. Although most of the world's supply of primary and secondary copper is traded directly between producers and consumers, prices quoted on the London Metal Exchange and the New York Commodity Exchange provide the principal price-setting mechanism for world copper trading.

Export Price Index for Copper (base: 1980 = 100)

	Average	Highest month(s)	Lowest month(s)
1985	64		
1990	123		
1994	106	137 (Dec.)	82 (Jan.)
1995	135	141 (July)	127 (May)
1996	105	122 (May)	88 (Sept.)

On the London Metal Exchange (LME) the price of Grade 'A' copper (minimum purity 99.95%) per metric ton declined from £1,563.5 (US $2,219) in February 1993 to £1,108.5 (US $1,746) in May. From 1 July 1993 the LME replaced sterling by US dollars as the basis for pricing its copper contract. In September the London copper quotation increased to $2,011.5 (£1,304) per ton, but in October, with LME stocks of copper at a 15-year 'high', the price slumped to $1,596 (£1,079), its lowest level, in terms of US currency, for about six years. The copper price subsequently revived, with the LME quotation exceeding $1,800 per ton by the end of the year. The market remained buoyant in January 1994, although, during that month, copper stocks in LME warehouses reached 617,800 tons, their highest level since February 1978. However, stocks were quickly reduced, and the London copper price moved above $2,000 per ton in May 1994. It continued to rise, reaching $2,533.5 (£1,635) per ton in July. Concurrently, LME stocks of the metal declined to less than 340,000 tons. These holdings rose to more than 370,000 tons in September, and copper prices subsided. However, in December, with LME stocks of copper below 300,000 tons, the London price of the metal exceeded $3,000 per ton (a level not recorded for more than five years).

In January 1995 the London copper price reached US $3,055.5 (£1,939) per ton, but in May it fell to $2,721.5 (£1,728), although

LME stocks were then less than 200,000 tons. However, in July, with copper stocks reduced to about 141,000 tons, the LME price advanced to $3,216 (£2,009) per ton, its highest level, in terms of US currency, since early 1989.

The LME's holdings of copper rose to 356,800 tons in February 1996, when the price of the metal eased to US $2,492.5 (£1,609) per ton. After increasing again, the copper price fell in April to $2,479.5 (£1,624) per ton, although in early May it recovered to $2,847.5 (£1,872). In late May and June the copper market was gravely perturbed by reports that the world's largest copper-trading company, Sumitomo Corporation of Japan, had transferred, and later dismissed, its principal trader, following revelations that he had incurred estimated losses of $1,800m. in unauthorized dealings (allegedly to maintain copper prices at artificially high levels) on international markets over a 10-year period. This news led to widespread selling of copper: in late June the LME price was reduced to $1,837.5 (£1,192) per ton, although it quickly moved above $2,000 again. In July, after LME stocks had declined to 224,100 tons, the copper price reached $2,102.5 (£1,352) per ton. Stocks of copper in the LME's warehouses rose to 275,775 tons in early September, but the metal's price remained at about $2,100 per ton. After easing somewhat, the London price of copper advanced in November to $2,547.5 (£1,522) per ton, following a decline in LME stocks of the metal to 90,050 tons, their lowest level since July 1990. The copper price at the end of 1996 was $2,217 (£1,304) per ton. Meanwhile, the extent of the losses incurred in the Sumitomo scandal was revised to $2,600m.

In January 1997 the London quotation for high-grade copper reached US $2,575.5 (£1,594) per ton. The advance occurred in spite of a steady increase in LME stocks of copper, which rose to 222,500 tons in February. In June, with copper stocks reduced to 121,550 tons, the price of the metal reached $2,709.5 (£1,644) per ton.

The Intergovernmental Council of Copper Exporting Countries (CIPEC), comprising Zaire, Zambia, Chile and Peru (controlling about 70% of world copper exports but less than 50% of world output), operated as a policy co-ordinating body during 1967–92. In June 1992 the International Copper Study Group (ICSG), initially comprising 18 producing and importing countries, was formed to compile and publish statistical information. In 1995 its membership comprised 21 countries, accounting for about 80% of world trade in copper. The ICSG does not participate in trade or exercise any form of intervention in the market.

Cotton *(Gossypium)*

This is the name given to the hairs which grow on the epidermis of the seed of the plant genus *Gossypium*. The initial development of the cotton fibres takes place within a closed pod, called a boll, which, after a period of growth lasting about 50 days (depending upon climatic conditions), opens to reveal the familiar white tufts of cotton hair. After the seed cotton has been picked, the cotton fibre, or lint, has to be separated from the seeds by means of a mechanical process, known as ginning. Depending upon the variety and growing conditions, it takes about 3 metric tons of seed cotton to produce one ton of raw cotton fibre. After ginning, a fuzz of very short cotton hairs remains on the seed. These are called linters and may be removed and used in the manufacture of paper, cellulose-based chemicals, explosives, etc.

About one-half of the cotton produced in the world is used in the manufacture of clothing, about one-third is used for household textiles, and the remainder for numerous industrial products (tarpaulins, rubber reinforcement, abrasive backings, filters, high-quality papers, etc.).

The official cotton 'season' (for trade purposes) runs from 1 August to 31 July of the following year. Quantities are measured in both metric tons and bales; for statistical purposes, one bale of cotton is 226.8 kg (500 lb) gross or 217.7 kg (480 lb) net.

The price of a particular type of cotton depends upon its availability relative to demand and upon characteristics related to yarn quality and suitability for processing. These include fibre length, fineness, cleanliness, strength and colour. The most important of these is length. Generally speaking, the length of the fibre determines the quality of the yarn produced from it, with the longer fibres being preferred for the finer, stronger and more expensive yarns. Five lengths are recognized: short staple (less than 21 mm); medium staple (21–25 mm); medium-long staple (26–28 mm); long staple (28–33 mm); and extra-long staple (over 34 mm).

Production of Cotton Lint ('000 metric tons, excluding linters)

	1994	1995
World total	18,643*	19,902*
Africa	1,278*	1,445*
Leading African producers		
Benin	103	150*
Burkina Faso	67	67*
Cameroon	48*	48*
Chad	45†	61
Côte d'Ivoire	116	93
Egypt	250*	310†
Mali	110†	110*
Nigeria	105*	115*
Sudan	87†	131†
Tanzania	48	45
Togo	40†	40*
Zimbabwe	60†	37
Leading non-African producers		
Brazil	501	515*
China, People's Repub.	4,341	4,768
India	2,346	2,380†
Pakistan	1,479	1,835
Turkey	606	755†
USA	4,281	3,897
Uzbekistan	1,215	1,306*

* FAO estimate.
† Unofficial figure.

Cotton is the world's leading textile fibre. However, over the period 1960–75, as the use of synthetics grew, cotton's share in the world's total consumption of fibre declined from 68% to about 50%, despite an overall increase in cotton consumption of about 2% each year. Cotton's share later stabilized, and since the mid-1970s it has remained close to 50% of the world market. In certain areas, notably the major consumer markets of Western Europe and Japan, cotton has significantly improved its competitive position in recent years.

The area devoted to cotton cultivation totalled 31m. – 36m. ha between the 1950s and the early 1990s, accounting for about 4% of world cropped area. During the mid-1980s, however, world cotton consumption failed to keep pace with the growth in production, and the resultant surpluses led to a fall in prices, which had serious consequences for the many African countries that rely on cotton sales for a major portion of their export earnings. In the mid-1990s, despite improvements in world price levels, cotton cultivation came under pressure from food crop requirements, and the harvested areas under cotton declined world-wide from more than 35m. ha in 1995/96 to 33m. ha in 1996/97.

The leading exporters of cotton are the USA, successor states of the former USSR (of which Uzbekistan is the major cotton-producing area) and Pakistan, while the major cotton-importing countries are Russia, Japan, Indonesia, the Republic of Korea, Thailand, Italy, Taiwan, Brazil, Turkey and Germany. China, although one of the largest producing countries, is also a net importer of cotton.

Cotton is a major source of income and employment for many developing countries, both as a primary product and, increasingly, through sales of yarn, fabrics and finished goods. Cotton is the principal commercial crop, in terms of foreign exchange earnings, in Benin, Burkina Faso, Chad, Egypt, Mali, Sudan and Togo, and is second in importance in the Central African Republic, Mozambique, Senegal and Tanzania. Other African countries in which cotton is a significant source of foreign exchange, compared with other agricultural commodities, include Angola, Cameroon, Côte d'Ivoire, The Gambia, Madagascar, Malawi, Swaziland, Zambia and Zimbabwe. The cultivation of cotton is also of some economic importance in Kenya, Nigeria and Uganda.

For many years Sudan was the largest cotton producer in Africa south of the Sahara. The industry has, however, been in decline since the 1980s, not only on account of the surplus of cotton supplies on the world market, but also as a result of domestic difficulties resulting from climatic factors, an inflexible, government-dictated marketing policy and crop infestation by white-fly. Although cotton production, classification and marketing were reorganized in the late 1980s, and in 1990 special foreign exchange incentives were offered to producers, levels of output had yet to recover by the mid-1990s. The area under cotton cultivation in Sudan declined from 324,000 ha in the late 1980s to 119,000 ha in the 1992/93 crop season. In 1993/94 overseas sales of cotton represented about 20% of the total value of Sudan's exports.

Although co-operation in cotton affairs has a long history, there have been no international agreements governing the cotton trade. Proposals in recent years to link producers and consumers in price stabilization arrangements have been opposed by the USA (the world's largest cotton exporter), and by Japan and the European Union (EU). The International Cotton Advisory Committee (ICAC), an intergovernmental body, established in 1939, with its headquarters in Washington, DC, publishes statistical and economic information and provides a forum for consultation and discussion among its 39 members.

Export Price Index for Cotton Lint (base: 1980 = 100)

	Average	Highest month(s)	Lowest month(s)
1985	75		
1990	93		
1994	82	93 (Dec.)	73 (Jan.)
1995	103	120 (June)	88 (July)
1996	90	96 (April)	83 (Nov.)

The average import price of Memphis cotton lint from the USA at the port of Liverpool, in the United Kingdom, declined from US$1,792 per metric ton in 1991 to $1,378 per ton in 1992 and to $1,373 per ton in 1993. The monthly average slumped from $2,189 per ton in May 1991 to $1,318 in March 1992. It recovered to $1,572 per ton in July 1992, but retreated to $1,281 in October. The average price of US cotton rose to $1,464 per ton in March and April 1993, but was reduced to $1,257 in September and October. International prices for cotton lint are subject to considerable fluctuation on world markets, and reflect, among other factors, levels of surplus stocks. In February 1995, following a decline in stocks and forecasts of a rise in imports, prices on the 'futures' market at the New York Cotton Exchange exceeded $1 per lb for the first time since the US Civil War of the 1860s.

Diamonds

The primary source of diamonds is a rock known as kimberlite, occurring in volcanic pipes which may vary in area from a few to more than 100 ha and volcanic fissures which are considerably smaller. Among the indicator minerals for kimberlite are chrome diopside, pyrope garnet, ilmenite and zircon. Few kimberlites contain diamonds and, in ore which does, the ratio of diamond to waste is about one part per 20m. There are four methods of diamond mining, of which open-cast mining is the commonest; diamonds are recovered also by underground, alluvial and offshore mining. The diamond is separated from its ore by careful crushing and gravity concentration which maximizes the diamond's high specific gravity in a process called dense media separation. Stones are of two categories: gem qualities (used for jewellery), which are superior in terms of colour or quality; and industrial quality, about one-half of the total by weight, which are used for high-precision machining or crushed into an abrasive powder called boart.

The size of diamonds and other precious stones is measured in carats. One metric carat is equal to 0.2 gram, so one ounce avoirdupois equals 141.75 carats.

Africa is the major producing region for natural diamonds, although Australia joined the ranks of the major producers in 1983, and the Argyle diamond mine, in Western Australia, is the world's largest producing mine and main source of industrial diamonds. Output is predominantly of industrial-grade diamonds, with some lower-quality gem diamonds and a few pink diamonds. In 1996 Australian diamond output represented almost 37% of world production by volume.

Diamonds are Botswana's principal source of export earnings, normally accounting for about 80% of export receipts and 30%–35% of government revenues. Diamond production began in 1971, initially at the Orapa mine, which covers an area of 113 ha and is the world's second largest, after the Mwadui field in Tanzania (see below). In 1977 extraction began from a nearby mine at Letlhakane, and in 1982 a major new mine at Jwaneng entered production. All current diamond mining operations are conducted by the Debswana Diamond Co (Pty), which is owned equally by the Botswana government and De Beers.

About 90% of output in the Democratic Republic of the Congo (DRC), which is mainly derived from alluvial diamond-mining operations in Eastern Kasai, is industrial diamonds, of which the DRC (then known as Zaire) was the world's principal producer until it was overtaken by Australia in 1986. Since 1993 the DRC's combined output of industrial and gem diamonds has exceeded that of Botswana; the bulk of its production, however, is smuggled out of the country.

About 98% of Namibian diamonds are of gem quality, although recovery costs are high. In 1990 diamond mining commenced at Auchas, and a second mine, at Elizabeth Bay, began in 1991. Operations at the Oranjemund open-cast mine are not expected to remain economic after the year 2000, and the exploitation of an 'offshore' diamond field, extending 300 m from the coast, is proceeding. In 1996 'offshore' recoveries of gem-quality stones accounted for 34% of Namibia's diamond output. Until 1993, when the government of Namibia granted marine exploration concessions to a new privately-financed venture, the Namibian Minerals Corpn (NAMCO), Consolidated Diamond Mining (CDM), a subsidiary of the De Beers group, held exclusive rights to diamond exploration and mining in Namibia. Concession rights held by NAMCO cover three offshore areas totalling almost 2,000 sq km, containing an estimated 80m. carats of gem quality diamonds. Commercial recoveries began in late 1995. In 1994 the Namibia government and De Beers announced the formation of the Namdeb Diamond Corpn, to which the diamonds operations of CDM were transferred. Namdeb is owned 50% by De Beers and 50% by the government.

Production of Uncut Diamonds
(gem and industrial stones, million metric carats)

	1995	1996
Leading African producers		
Angola	1.9	3.8
Botswana	16.8	17.7
Central African Repub.	0.6	0.6
Congo, Dem. Repub.	20.0	21.9
Ghana	0.8	0.7
Guinea	0.5	0.5
Namibia	1.3	1.4
Sierra Leone	0.3	0.2
South Africa	9.1	10.2
Zimbabwe	0.2	0.5
Producers in other areas		
Australia	40.8	42.0
Russia	12.5	12.5
South America	2.0	1.7
Other	0.5	0.7
World total	107.9	114.5

Source: Central Selling Organisation.

Angola's diamond production, which exceeded 2m. carats in 1973, subsequently fell sharply, as a result of the civil war. Annual production recovered in the late 1980s to about 1m.–1.2m. carats, about 90% of which were of gem quality. However, official exports of Angolan diamonds declined from 1.2m. carats in 1990 to 955,000 carats in 1991. Official diamond production in Angola has subsequently revived, however, advancing from 1m. carats in 1993 to 1.9m. carats in 1995. Output advanced sharply in 1996, to 3.8m. carats. In anticipation of the future resolution of internal political strife, diamond exploration activity was gaining pace in the mid-1990s, with particular interest focused on the Catoca kimberlite, 30 km west of Saurimo, in north-eastern Angola. Covering an area of more than 660 ha, its potential reserves have been estimated at up to 200m. carats, which would establish it as one of the world's largest deposits of diamonds. Angola is known to possess substantial diamondiferous deposits, occurring in both kimberlite and alluvial formations, and in 1997 the exploration and assessment of a number of sites was proceeding, with South African,

Canadian, Brazilian and Russian technical and financial participation. In 1990 the Empresa Nacional de Diamantes de Angola (ENDIAMA, the state-controlled diamond enterprise) resumed its marketing association with the De Beers group (see below), from which it had withdrawn in 1985. Under the new arrangements (covering a five-year period from 1991), ENDIAMA was to market the entire production from Cuango, accounting for about 80% of Angola's diamond output, through the London-based Central Selling Organisation (see below). As part of the agreement, De Beers has assisted ENDIAMA with prospecting and mining operations. However, illicit prospecting and trading have continued, and it was estimated by ENDIAMA that diamonds worth \$300m.–\$500m. were smuggled out of the country in 1994.

The Mwadui diamond pipe in Tanzania is the world's largest, covering an area of 146 ha. Tanzania's diamond output was 838,000 carats in 1971, but production later declined, owing to deterioration in diamond grades, technical engineering problems and difficulties in maintaining the mines. By the late 1980s, exports from Mwadui had effectively ceased. New prospecting agreements were signed in 1993 by the Tanzania government and the De Beers operating subsidiary managing the Mwadui mine, and also with Canadian interests, which obtained mining leases and exploration licences covering almost 9,000 sq km. Following extensive rehabilitation, operations at Mwadui recommenced in August 1995. Small-scale exports were resumed in December.

South African diamond production, which is conducted at five mine locations, has been in decline since 1987. A sixth mine, Venetia (discovered in 1980 and opened in 1992), has become the country's largest producing diamond mine, accounting for about 41% of South African output in 1996. Small-scale marine mining is conducted off the west coast.

In Sierra Leone the diamond industry is faced by the dual problems of internal instability and widespread illicit digging and smuggling. Legal exports of diamonds have declined steadily since 1970, and in 1988 were estimated at only 32,000 carats, compared with 2m. carats in 1970. The exploitation of diamond reserves in the Koindu region was suspended following the seizure of the mines by guerrilla troops in May 1997. The realization of Sierra Leone's potential for expanding this resource must await the eventual restoration of a more stable political environment. Similar problems have overtaken the diamond sector in neighbouring Liberia, whose exports averaged about 200,000 carats per year in the mid-1980s (although much of this total was attributable to stones smuggled from adjoining countries and attracted to Liberia by its currency link with the US dollar). Since late 1989, civil war has effectively halted the country's diamond trade. In the Central African Republic diamonds are found in alluvial deposits, mainly in the west of the country. Here, too, there is widespread evasion of export duties, with as much as 60% of total diamond production being smuggled out of the country. In Côte d'Ivoire small-scale mining is carried out by private companies. Figures for the country's diamond production range from 20,000 carats per year (legal exports) to 250,000 carats annually (including illicit production). The diamond sector in Ghana, which has been in decline since the 1960s, was estimated in 1993 still to contain reserves of alluvial diamond deposits sufficient for 15 years' exploitation. Among the smaller-scale African producers of diamonds are Lesotho and Swaziland. In 1994 Zimbabwe began to emerge as a potentially significant regional producer. Exploration applications covering about one-third of the country's land area were lodged in 1994, and in 1996 De Beers uncovered a 17-ha diamondiferous pipe in the south of the country. The country's first operating mine, River Ranch, near Beitbridge, was opened in 1991 and completed the final stage of its expansion plans in late 1995. The mine produces mainly small diamonds. Output has been forecast to reach 300,000–400,000 carats annually.

In December 1994 an Australian-Canadian joint venture, BHP Minerals, announced that it was to open North America's first commercial diamond mine, at Lac de Gras, close to the Arctic Circle in the Northwest Territories of Canada. Production at the mine's 39 diamond-bearing pipes was scheduled to begin in October 1998. Potential output, by conventional open-pit mining, has been forecast at 4.5m. carats annually. A second North American mine, at Kelsey Lake in the Rocky Mountains of the USA, began operations in late 1995. Output of the mine's principally gem diamonds was expected to reach 150,000 carats annually when full production is reached.

In 1930 the major diamond producers formed The Diamond Corpn to act as the single channel through which most of the world's rough diamond production would be sold. To stabilize the market, the corporation puts surplus output into reserve, to be sold at a time when conditions are favourable. The corporation is now one of a group of companies, centred in London, known as the Central Selling Organisation (CSO). The CSO contracts to sell on behalf of producers and handles about 75% of world production. Almost all Africa's diamonds, although not those of Ghana and Guinea, are marketed through the CSO, which has about 160 direct clients. The CSO markets the rough diamond production of De Beers Consolidated Mines Ltd. A reorganization of De Beers' interests, undertaken in 1990, placed the CSO, together with the group's diamond stocks and other non-South African based interests, under the control of a new Swiss-domiciled corporation, De Beers Centenary AG.

In 1990 De Beers Centenary entered into an arrangement with Glavalmazzoloto (the diamond monopoly operated by the former USSR), under which 95% of rough gem diamonds destined for export were to be purchased and marketed by the CSO, affording Russia a quota of 26% of all CSO sales on the world market. This agreement, which was to operate until December 1995, was continued by the successor Russian diamond corporation, Rosalmazzoloto, and subsequently by Almazy Rossii-Sakha (ARS). In 1992 De Beers negotiated an agreement with the Russian Autonomous Republic of Sakha (Yakutia), which occupies a large part of Siberia and accounts for approximately 98% of Russian diamond output, to market the proportion of its diamond production not procured by the central diamond authority. In January 1993 the functions of this authority were transferred to an independent body, Diamonds of Russia-Sakha. It was announced in March that plans were being prepared for the creation of an exchange in Moscow for the internal marketing of rough diamonds. In December the Russian government denied allegations by De Beers that it was selling uncut diamonds on the Antwerp market (see below) in violation of the marketing agreement. In April 1994 representatives of the Russian government and diamond industry initiated negotiations with the CSO to secure modifications to the 1990 agreement which would permit Russia to market a larger proportion of its diamond production direct to independent buyers. (It was estimated that Russian sales in contravention of the agreement had amounted to US\$500m.–\$700m. in 1994.) These negotiations continued inconclusively during 1995. The agreement, which expired in December, was extended until March 1996, when a new framework was eventually formulated for the sale of Russian diamonds. Under the revised arrangements, which were to operate for a three-year period, ARS obtained the right to market approximately 14% of its exports to buyers outside the CSO. The agreement aimed to achieve a substantial reduction in the volume of diamonds circumventing the CSO marketing network, while assisting Russia in its proposed establishment of a domestic diamond-cutting industry.

In August 1995, however, it was reported that further meetings were to take place between ARS and the CSO to discuss continuing increases in sales of Russian diamonds to purchasers outside the CSO. Meanwhile, the Argyle mine in Australia (see above), whose sales accounted for about 6% of the CSO's annual intake, announced in June that it was to terminate its marketing agreement with the CSO with effect from 1 July. For the remainder of 1996 the CSO continued to purchase Russian diamonds under the terms of the agreement that had expired in December 1995, while pursuing negotiations with ARS. However, the slow progress in finalizing new arrangements, together with the continuing 'leakage' of Russian diamonds on the open market, prompted De Beers to inform the Russian government that it would cease purchasing diamonds under the existing arrangements with effect from the end of December 1996. Attempts to formulate new marketing arrangements were resumed in February 1997, and it was reported in April that agreement in principle had been reached.

Rough diamonds, of which there are currently more than 5,000 categories, are sold by the CSO in mixed packages 10 times each year at regular sales, known as 'sights', in London,

Johannesburg and Lucerne, Switzerland. Gems account for about 20% of total sales by weight, but, it is estimated, over 90% by value. After being sold by the CSO, gem diamonds are sent to be cut and polished in preparation for jewellery manufacture. The leading cutting centres are in Antwerp, Bombay, New York and Tel Aviv, which in 1993 opened an exchange for 'raw', or uncut, diamonds, with the intention of lessening the dependence of Israeli cutters on allocations from the CSO and purchases from the small, independent diamond exchange in Antwerp. The principal markets for diamond jewellery are the USA and Japan (which account for about 60% of world consumption).

The CSO provides a guaranteed market to producers and has successfully followed a policy of stockpiling diamonds during times of recession in order to stabilize prices (which are never reduced). At the end of 1996 the value of the stockpile stood at US$4,703m., an increase of about $30m. in 12 months.

Diamond prices (quoted in US dollars) were increased by 15.5% in March 1989, by 5.5% in March 1990 and by 1.5% in February 1993 (mainly in respect of stones of 0.75 carat and above). In July 1995 prices for low-grade rough diamonds were reduced by 10%–15%, while prices for large stones were raised by 2%–8%. In November prices for stones weighing 2.0 carats and above were raised by 5%, and in July 1996 prices of rough gem diamonds weighing in excess of 1.0 carat were increased by an average 7%. As there are so many varieties of diamond, the CSO price changes represent averages only. There are wide discrepancies in price, depending on such factors as rarity, colour and quality. The sales turnover of US $3,417m. recorded in 1992 by the CSO represented a six-year 'low'. Sales volume advanced strongly, however, in 1993, to $4,366m., an increase of 27.8%. This recovery was, in part, attributable to reductions in producers' quotas during 1993. Sales turnover declined marginally, to about $4,250m., in 1994, owing in part to an increase of stocks in diamond-cutting centres, and despite Russian sales outside the CSO network. A rise of 6.6% in 1995 sales turnover, to $4,531m., reflected a strong level of demand for quality gem stones, particularly in the USA and Japan. Sales turnover in 1996 advanced by almost 7%, to a record $4,834m., despite the termination of marketing arrangements with the Argyle diamond mine and the impact of direct sales by Russia.

Synthetic diamonds for industrial use have been produced since the mid-1950s by a number of companies, including De Beers, using a method which simulates the intense heat present in the geological formation of diamonds. These stones, which are always very small, account for the major proportion of all abrasive diamonds, and are used for a wide variety of industrial applications.

Gold

Gold minerals are commonly found in quartz and may occur in alluvial deposits, or in rich thin underground veins. In South Africa gold occurs in sheets of low-grade ore (reefs) which may be at great depths below ground level. Gold is associated with silver, which is its commonest by-product. Uranium oxide is another valuable by-product, particularly in the case of South Africa. Depending upon its associations, gold is separated by cyaniding, or concentrated and smelted.

Gold, silver and platinum are customarily measured in troy weight. A troy pound (now obsolete) contains 12 ounces, each of 480 grains. One troy oz is equal to 31.1 grams (1 kg = 32.15 troy oz), compared with the avoirdupois oz of 28.3 grams.

In modern times the principal function of gold has been as bullion in reserve for bank notes issued. Since the early 1970s, however, the USA has actively sought to 'demonetize' gold and so make it simply another commodity. This objective was later adopted by the IMF, which has attempted to end the position that gold occupied for many years in the international monetary system (see below).

Gold was discovered near Johannesburg, South Africa, in 1884, and its exploitation formed the basis of the country's subsequent economic prosperity. For many years, South Africa has been the world's leading gold producer, accounting in 1996 for 25.2% of world gold output outside the former Eastern bloc and for almost 80% of that mined in Africa. Since the mid-1980s, however, the South African gold industry has been adversely affected by the rising costs of extracting generally declining grades of ore from ageing and increasingly marginal (low-return) mines. Additionally, the level of world gold prices has not been sufficiently high to stimulate the active exploration and development of new mines. The share of gold in South Africa's export revenue has accordingly declined in recent years, and in 1989, for the first time, the commercial profitability of South African gold production was exceeded by profits from mining activities other than gold. In 1996 South Africa's gold production was less than 500 tons for the first time since 1956.

The relative decline of South Africa's position in world gold markets has been accompanied by the prospect of substantial increases in output as new capacity comes into production in Australia, Brazil, Canada, Indonesia, Papua New Guinea and the USA. Following the dissolution of the USSR, the successor republics, notably Russia (which accounted for about two-thirds of Soviet output) and Uzbekistan (which contains what is reputedly the world's largest open-cast gold-mine), were expected to assume a significant role in international gold trading during the 1990s. Despite adverse short-term factors, (which have included shortages of mining equipment, transport difficulties and sharp rises in the cost of electric power), proposals outlined by the Russian government in 1993 to abolish the state monopoly on gold purchases, and other measures to liberalize the market and attract foreign investment, were likely to have a significant future impact on international markets. Foreign participation in the development of gold deposits in Uzbekistan, Kazakhstan and Kyrgyzstan was proceeding in the mid-1990s. The People's Republic of China, with about 600 operating gold-mines and a further 200 dredge units, is increasing its output of gold.

Ghana, formerly a significant African producer of gold, has, since 1990, been reversing a long period of decline. Output doubled during 1990–92, and increased each year during 1993–95 as a result of the continuing rehabilitation of the country's gold industry. The dominant producer in Ghana is Ashanti Goldfields, which operates one of the world's largest gold-mines (with more than 20m. oz of proven reserves). The company was reopened to private-sector investment in 1994. Its output accounted for more than two-thirds of the country's total gold output in 1996. Exports of gold accounted for about 40% of Ghana's foreign revenue in 1995. Ashanti Goldfields has developed a major new mine at Bibani, which was expected to commence production in 1998. Other gold-mining enterprises in the country, notably the Tarkwa mine operated by Goldfields Ghana, are expected to generate further expansion in this sector in the late 1990s.

Gold was overtaken in 1980 by tobacco as Zimbabwe's major source of foreign exchange; other minor African producers include Ethiopia, Eritrea, Burkina Faso, Guinea, Sudan, Tanzania, Uganda, Zaire, Côte d'Ivoire and Namibia. Gold production in Mali was expected to increase substantially after 1997, when the exploitation of a deposit under development at Sadiola, with a potential capacity of 11 tons per year, was due to begin.

The supply of gold to Western countries, after allowing for central bank transactions and not including scrap, totalled 2,745 tons in 1993. An increase in sales, to 176 tons, by the former Eastern bloc countries (which form a significant component of international gold trading) was more than offset by a sharp fall in net official sales, to 448 tons. Mine production in that year rose by only 32 tons, to 1,904 tons. In 1994 the supply of gold declined to 2,488 tons; net official sales fell to only 80 tons, while former Eastern bloc sales declined to 109 tons. Mine output in that year was virtually static, at 1,898 tons, and in 1995 again fell only slightly, to 1,891 tons. Total Western world supply in 1995 was 2,772 tons, including Eastern bloc sales of 102 tons and net official sales of 232 tons. In 1996, in which year sales by the former Eastern bloc ceased to be separately quantified, the world supply of gold totalled 2,846 tons. Net official sales rose to 239 tons.

Total world demand for gold, including the former USSR and China, totalled 3,560 tons in 1993 and 3,357 tons in 1994. In 1995 total world demand advanced to 3,629 tons, declining to 3,490 tons in 1996. Requirements for jewellery fabrication, which accounted for 71.7% (2,551 tons) in 1993, increased to 2,610 tons (77.7%) in 1994, to 2,767 tons (76.2%) in 1995 and 2,807 tons (80.4%) in 1996. The remainder of industrial demand was absorbed mainly by medals, dentistry and the electronics industry. Of total gold fabrication in 1996 (3,290 tons), the principal consuming countries were India (13.8%), Italy (13.7%), the USA (7.5%), China (6%) and Japan (5.7%).

Production of Gold Ore (metric tons, gold content)

	1995	1996
World total*	2,269.2	2,345.5
Africa*	654.2	623.0
Leading African producers		
Congo, Dem. Repub.	10.0	8.2
Ghana	52.7	50.7
Guinea	6.5	7.0
Mali	7.8	6.1
South Africa	522.4	494.6
Tanzania	5.3	5.5
Zimbabwe	26.1	26.7
Leading non-African producers		
Australia	253.5	288.8
Brazil	67.4	64.2
Canada	150.3	163.9
Chile	48.5	56.4
China, People's Repub.*	132.6	144.6
Indonesia	74.1	92.1
Papua New Guinea	54.9	53.0
Peru	57.4	64.8
Philippines	29.4	31.1
Russia	142.1	130.0
USA	319.0	329.3
Uzbekistan*	63.6	71.0

* Estimates.

Source: Gold Fields Mineral Services Ltd.

The fabrication of official coins is another important use of gold bullion, although the demand for these coins has declined since the mid-1980s. South African 'krugerrand' coins, containing exactly 1 troy oz of pure (24-carat) gold, were first issued in 1970 and held about 70% of the world market for gold bullion coins until 1985, when international sales virtually ceased, owing to the prohibition of krugerrand imports (during 1986–90) by Japan, the European Community and the USA. A number of other countries, notably Australia, Canada, Austria, Japan and the USA, entered the gold coin market and subsequently benefited from the krugerrand embargo. However, the popularity of these bullion coins in general has been declining in recent years. Following exceptional interest in 1995 in an Austrian gold coin issue, together with the minting of a US Olympic commemorative coin, underpinning a demand increase of 27.7%, the official coin sector in 1996 relapsed to its lowest level of fabrication since 1973.

As a portable real asset which is easily convertible into cash, gold is widely esteemed as a store of value. Another distinguishing feature of gold is that new production in any one year is very small in relation to existing stocks. Much of the world's gold is in private bullion stocks, held for investment purposes, or is hoarded as a 'hedge' against inflation. Private investment stocks of gold throughout the world are estimated at 15,000–20,000 tons, the bulk of it held in France and India.

During the 19th century gold was increasingly adopted as a monetary standard, with prices set by governments. In 1919 the Bank of England allowed some South African gold to be traded in London 'at the best price obtainable'. The market was suspended in 1925–31, when sterling returned to a limited form of the gold standard, and again between 1939–54. In 1934 the official price of gold was fixed at US $35 per troy oz, and, by international agreement, all transactions in gold had to take place within narrow margins around that price. In 1960 the official gold price came under pressure from market demand. As a result, an international gold 'pool' was established in 1961 at the initiative of the USA. This 'pool' was originally a consortium of leading central banks with the object of restraining the London price of gold in case of excessive demand. It later widened into an arrangement by which eight central banks agreed that all purchases and sales of gold should be handled by the Bank of England. However, growing private demand for gold continued to exert pressure on the official price and the gold 'pool' was ended in 1968, in favour of a two-tier price system. Central banks continued to operate the official price of $35 per troy ounce, but private markets were permitted to deal freely in gold. However, the free market price did not rise significantly above the official price.

In August 1971 the US government announced that it would cease dealing freely in gold to maintain exchange rates for the dollar within previously agreed margins. This 'floating' of the dollar against other major currencies continued until December, when it was agreed to raise the official gold price to $38 per oz. Gold prices on the free market rose to $70 per oz in August 1972. In February 1973 the US dollar was devalued by a further 10%, the official gold price rising to $42.22 per oz. Thereafter the free market price rose even higher, reaching $127 per oz in June 1973. In November it was announced that the two-tier system would be terminated, and from 1974 governments were permitted to value their official gold stocks at market prices.

In 1969 the IMF introduced a new unit for international monetary dealings, the special drawing right (SDR), with a value of US $1.00, and the first allocation of SDRs was made on 1 January 1971. The SDR was linked to gold at an exchange rate of SDR 35 per troy oz. When the US dollar was devalued in December 1971 the SDR retained its gold value and a new parity with the US dollar was established. A further adjustment was made following the second dollar devaluation, in February 1973, and in July 1974 the direct link between the SDR and the US dollar was ended and the SDR was valued in terms of a weighted 'basket' of national currencies. At the same time the official gold price of SDR 35 per troy oz was retained as the IMF's basis for valuing official reserves. The SDR's average value in 1995 was $1.5170. At 30 June 1997 the exchange rate was SDR 1 = $1.3881.

In 1976 the membership of the IMF agreed on proposals for far-reaching changes in the international monetary system. These reforms, which were implemented on a gradual basis during 1977–81, included a reduction in the role of gold in the international system and the abolition of the official price of gold. (For detailed information on these arrangements, see *Africa South of the Sahara 1991*). A principal objective of the IMF plan was achieved in April 1978, when central banks were able to buy and sell gold at market prices. The physical quantity of reserve gold held by the IMF and member countries' central banks as national reserves has subsequently fallen. The USA still maintains the largest national stock of gold, although the volume of its reserves has been substantially reduced in recent years. At the end of 1949 US gold reserves were 701.8m. oz, but since the beginning of the 1980s the level has been in the range of 261.7m.–264.6m. oz. At the end of 1996 the total gold reserves held by members of the IMF, excluding countries not reporting, amounted to 906.1m. oz, of which the USA had 261.7m. oz (28.9%).

In June 1996 the 'Group of Seven' major industrial countries considered proposals by the United Kingdom and the USA whereby the IMF would release for sale between US $5,000m.–$6,000m. of its $40,000m. gold reserves to finance debt relief for the world's poorest countries, principally in Africa. The plan, which was opposed by Germany, on the grounds that it could prompt demands for similar gold sales by its central bank, remained the subject of discussion within the IMF during 1997. During 1996 substantial sales of gold bullion, jointly exceeding 500 tons, were carried out by the central banks of Belgium and the Netherlands, and the Swiss National Bank announced its intention to allocate part of its gold reserves to fund a new humanitarian foundation. In July 1997 the Reserve Bank of Australia announced that it had disposed of more than two-thirds of its bullion holdings (reducing its reserves from 247 to 80 tons) over the previous six months.

The unit of dealing in international gold markets is the 'good delivery' gold bar, weighing about 400 oz (12.5 kg). The principal centres for gold trading are London, Hong Kong and Zürich, Switzerland. The dominant markets for gold 'futures' (buying and selling for future delivery) are the Commodity Exchange in New York (COMEX) and the Tokyo Commodity Exchange (TOCOM).

A small group of dealers meet twice on each working day (morning and afternoon) to 'fix' the price of gold in the London Bullion Market, and the table above is based on the second of these daily 'fixes'. During any trading day, however, prices may fluctuate above or below these levels. In each of the five years 1988–92 the London price of gold bullion was lower at the year's end than at the beginning. The annual average for 1992 was US $344.0 per troy oz: the lowest, in real terms, since 1977. In

Gold Prices on the London Bullion Market
(afternoon 'fixes', US $ per troy oz)

	Average	Highest	Lowest
1980	612.7		
1985	317.3		
1990	383.6		
1994	384.2	396.3 (28 Sept.)	369.7 (22 April)
1995	384.1	395.6 (19 April)	372.4 (9 Jan.)
1996	387.9	414.8 (5 Feb.)	367.4 (3 Dec.)

March 1993 the price fell to $326.1 (equivalent to £227.6 sterling) per oz, its lowest level, in terms of US currency, since January 1986. However, from April 1993 there was a strong recovery in the bullion market, owing partly to speculative activity, and in late July and early August the London price exceeded $400 per oz. The gold price declined to $344 (£222) per oz in September, but ended the year at $390.75 (£264.1). The advance continued in January 1994, with the London price of gold reaching $396.5 (£266.8) per oz. In late February and early March the price eased to around $375 per oz, but in late March it moved above $390. Another decline ensued, with the gold price falling in April to less than $370 per oz, although in June the metal was traded at more than $390 again. In August the London quotation was reduced to $377 (£245) per oz. In early September the price per oz stood at $391.5 (then £253), and later in the month it moved higher in dollar terms, to $396 (£251). The quotation per oz fell in early November to $383.7, which, owing to the relative strength of the British currency, was equivalent to only £234. In terms of US currency, the price retreated further, standing at $376 (then £240.5) per oz in December.

In January 1995 the London gold price declined to US $373.0 (£240) per oz, but in April it advanced to $396.7 (£245). In dollar terms, the price remained within this range for the remainder of 1995, ending the year at $387 (£249) per oz. For 1995 as a whole, the margin between the highest and lowest bullion price was only about 6% of the annual average: the lowest level of price volatility in the gold market since 1968.

In January 1996, however, the gold market experienced a surge in prices, with the London quotation exceeding US $400 per oz. In February the price reached $416 (£274) per oz, its highest level, in terms of US currency, since February 1990. However, the rally was not sustained, and in early July 1996 the London gold price stood at $381 (£244) per oz. After a slight recovery, another decline in the price of bullion began in late September. The London quotation in early December was reduced to $367 (£222) per oz.

There was further downward movement in the gold market during the early weeks of 1997, and in January the London price was below US $350 per oz for the first time since September 1993. The price of gold fell to $339 (£206) per ounce in February 1997, recovered to $363 (£224) in March and remained within this range until June. In early July the market was further weakened by the Australian central bank's disclosure of gold sales from its reserves (see above). A few days later the London bullion price declined to $318 (£189) per oz, its lowest level for 12 years.

Groundnut (Peanut, Monkey Nut, Earth Nut) *(Arachis hypogaea)*

This is not a true nut, although the underground pod, which contains the kernels, forms a more or less dry shell at maturity. The plant is a low-growing annual herb introduced from South America, and resembles the indigenous African Bambarra groundnut, which it now outnumbers.

Each groundnut pod contains between two and four kernels, enclosed in a reddish skin. The kernels are highly nutritious because of their high content both of protein (about 30%) and oil (40%–50%). In tropical countries the crop is grown partly for domestic consumption and partly for export. Whole nuts of selected large dessert types, with the skin removed, are eaten raw or roasted. Peanut butter is made by removing the skin and germ and grinding the roasted nuts. The most important commercial use of groundnuts is the extraction of oil. Groundnut oil is used as a cooking and salad oil, as an ingredient in margarine, and, in the case of lower-quality oil, in soap manufacture. The oil is faced with strong competition from soybean, cottonseed and sunflower oils—all produced in the USA. In the early 1990s groundnut oil was the fifth most important of soft edible oils in terms of production. During the late 1980s its position in terms of exports was ninth, accounting for only 1.5% of total world exports of food oils.

Production of Groundnuts (in shell; '000 metric tons)

	1994	1995
World total	28,752*	27,973*
Africa	5,857*	5,879*
Leading African producers		
Benin	78	103
Burkina Faso	203	203*
Cameroon	100†	100†
Central African Repub.	84	86
Chad	207	55
Congo, Dem. Repub.	547	581
Côte d'Ivoire	138	147*
Egypt	117	131
Ethiopia	54*	54*
The Gambia	81	84
Ghana	176	176*
Guinea	128	170
Mali	215	215*
Mozambique	74	102†
Niger	57†	57*
Nigeria	1,453	1,502
Senegal	678	791
South Africa	142	107
Sudan	714	630*
Tanzania	72*	72*
Uganda	142	143
Zimbabwe	66	52
Leading non-African producers		
Argentina	299	339
China, People's Repub.	9,682	10,235
India	8,255	7,100
Indonesia	903†	900†
Myanmar	431	501
USA	1,927	1,570
Viet Nam	294	316

* FAO estimate. † Unofficial figure.

An oilcake, used in animal feeding, is manufactured from the groundnut residue left after oil extraction. However, trade in this groundnut meal is limited by health laws in some countries, as groundnuts can be contaminated by a mould which generates toxic and carcinogenic metabolites, the most common and most dangerous of which is aflatoxin B_1. The European Community (now the European Union) has banned imports of oilcake and meal for use as animal feed which contain more than 0.03 mg of aflatoxin per kg. The meal can be treated with ammonia, which both eliminates the aflatoxin and enriches the cake. Groundnut shells, which are usually incinerated or simply discarded as waste, are suitable for conversion into a low-cost organic fertilizer, and such production has been undertaken since the early 1970s. Although three times as much groundnut-based fertilizer per ha is required, the chemical alternatives are 20 times as expensive.

About 80% of the world's groundnut output comes from developing countries. Groundnuts are the most important of Africa's oil seeds and form the chief export crop of The Gambia and Senegal, which in the late 1980s was the world's leading groundnut exporter. Except when affected by drought, South Africa and Sudan are also important exporters. Niger and Mali, formerly significant exporters, have ceased to feature in the international groundnut trade, largely as a consequence of the Sahel drought. However, measures to revive the groundnut sector in Mali were proceeding in 1996. Groundnut harvests in southern Africa, notably in Mozambique, South Africa and Zimbabwe, were also affected by drought during the second half of the 1980s. In 1994, however, proposals were announced in Zimbabwe for a substantial expansion of groundnut cultivation.

African groundnut exports have been declining since the late 1970s, and most African countries grow the nut as a subsistence, particularly storage, crop. Senegal's groundnut production suffered from persistent drought, and also from marketing problems, in the early 1980s; however, subsequent output was substantially aided by government incentives to producers. These measures included the establishment of a groundnut price guarantee fund, which also had the unwelcome effect of attracting smuggled groundnut supplies from the neighbouring state of The Gambia. Since 1995, however, the minimum price guaranteed by the Senegal government has remained below prices obtainable on the 'black market': of a total estimated harvest of 800,000 tons in 1995/96, only about 264,000 tons were sold to the state groundnut authority.

In recent years, as the tables below make clear, prices for groundnut oil have fluctuated much more than those for groundnuts. The average import price of groundnut oil at the port of Rotterdam, in the Netherlands, declined from US $893 per metric ton in 1991 to $609 per ton in 1992, but recovered to $738 in 1993. On a monthly basis, the average price of groundnut oil per ton was reduced from $1,031 in February 1991 to $561 in September 1992, although it rose to $920 in December 1993.

Export Price Index for Groundnuts (base: 1980 = 100)

	Average	Highest month(s)	Lowest month(s)
1985	70		
1990	102		
1994	97	99 (Jan.–March)	96 (May–Dec.)
1995	92	96 (Jan.)	89 (June)
1996	84	90 (May)	78 (Nov., Dec.)

Export Price Index for Groundnut Oil (base: 1980 = 100)

	Average	Highest month(s)	Lowest month(s)
1985	107		
1990	113		
1994	120	125 (Dec.)	117 (Jan.)
1995	116	124 (Jan.)	113 (June)
1996	105	113 (Jan.)	102 (Nov., Dec.)

The African Groundnut Council, founded in 1964 with headquarters in Lagos, advises its member producing countries (The Gambia, Mali, Niger, Nigeria, Senegal, Sudan) on marketing policies and, for this purpose, has a sales promotion office in Geneva, Switzerland. Western Europe, particularly France, is the largest market for African groundnuts. The market for edible groundnuts is particularly sensitive to the level of production in the USA, which provides about one-half of world import requirements.

Iron Ore

The chief economic iron-ore minerals are magnetite and haematite. Most iron ore is processed after mining to improve its chemical and physical characteristics and is often agglomerated by pelletizing or sintering. The transformation of the ore into pig-iron is achieved through reduction by coke in blast furnaces; the proportion of ore to pig-iron yielded is usually about 1.5 or 1.6:1. Pig-iron is used to make cast iron and wrought iron products, but most of it is converted into steel by removing most of the carbon content. In the mid-1990s processing technology was being developed in the use of high-grade ore to produce direct reduced iron (DRI), which, unlike the iron used for traditional blast furnace operations, requires no melting or refining. Particular grades of steel (e.g. stainless) are made by the addition of ferro-alloys such as chromium, nickel and manganese.

Iron is, after aluminium, the second most abundant metallic element in the earth's crust, and its ore volume production is far greater than that of any other metal. Some ores contain 70% iron, while a grade of only 25% is commercially exploitable in certain areas. As the basic feedstock for the production of steel, iron ore is a major raw material in the world economy and in international trade. Because mining the ore usually involves substantial long-term investment, about 60% of trade is conducted under long-term contracts, and the mine investments are financed with some financial participation from consumers.

Iron ore is widely distributed throughout Africa, with several countries having substantial reserves of high-grade deposits (60%–68% iron). One of the world's largest unexploited iron ore deposits (an estimated 850m. metric tons, with a metal content of 64.5%) has been located in north-east Gabon, and there are future prospects for the exploitation of ore reserves in Côte d'Ivoire and Senegal. Identified reserves in Guinea include some 350m. tons of iron ore (66.7% iron) at Mt Nimba, near the border with Liberia. The two governments have developed a joint scheme to exploit the deposits for transhipment through Liberia. Ore shipments by rail through Liberia were intended to commence in 1990, but this intention has been thwarted by the civil conflict which has caused widespread dislocation of the Liberian economy. The project, which was still pending in 1997, envisaged an annual mine output of 12m. tons. It was hoped that this joint project would compensate for the expected exhaustion of Liberia's own iron reserves in the late 1990s. Liberia's largest iron ore producer, the Liberian-American-Swedish Minerals Co (LAMCO), which is jointly-controlled by government and private interests, expects to be able to sustain mine production at Yekepa, in Buchanan County, until 2006. LAMCO's mining activities have been severely disrupted since 1990 by civil disorder.

Production of Iron Ore (iron content, '000 metric tons)

	1992	1993*
World total	512,269*	517,058
Africa	28,302*	28,291
Leading African producers		
Algeria	1,250*	1,225
Egypt	1,260	1,450
Liberia	1,000	n.a.
Mauritania	5,330*	5,890
South Africa	18,350	19,100
Leading non-African producers		
Australia	72,650*	74,767
Brazil	100,000*	100,000
Canada	21,506	20,000
China, People's Repub.	67,900	74,622
India	33,800	38,200
Russia	45,000	40,000
Ukraine	40,000*	39,500
USA†	35,251	35,116
Venezuela	11,807	11,010

* Estimated production.

† Including the metal content of by-product ore.

Source: US Bureau of Mines.

The continent's leading producer of iron ore is South Africa. The industry is dominated by the Iron and Steel Corpn of South Africa (ISCOR), which operates 10 ore mines and four steel mills. Formerly state-owned, ISCOR was transferred to private-sector control in 1989. South African iron ore exports, particularly to Japan, have been an important source of foreign revenue since the late 1980s, despite declining world demand for steel.

Among the African producers, the country most dependent on the mineral as a source of foreign exchange is Mauritania, which has large deposits of high-grade ore (65%) in the Kédia region, near Zouérate. The Guelbs region, about 40 km to the north of Kédia, contains reserves of workable ores, estimated at 5,000m.–6,000m. tons. Although the metal content of Guelbs' ore, at 37%, is lower than at Kédia, enrichment processes are expected to produce an iron content of 67%, making it the richest in Mauritania. The first phase of the project, an enrichment plant, was opened in 1984, with a projected production target of 15m. tons per year by the mid-1990s, when the Kédia deposits are expected to be depleted. The second phase, involving a new mine at Oum Arwagen and another ore-enrichment plant, is scheduled to begin in the mid-1990s, with initial output forecast at 6m. tons per year. Preparations have also been proceeding for the exploitation of deposits at M'Haoudat, which are estimated to contain recoverable reserves of 100m. tons, and which, at a proposed production rate of 5.6m. tons annually, were expected to prove more economic, albeit more short-lived, than the Guelbs deposits.

The exploitation of iron ore deposits, estimated at 200m. tons, has been proceeding since 1986 in Nigeria. In 1980 Zambia discovered a deposit estimated at 20m. tons of ore (50% iron) in the west of the country, which it plans to exploit. Tanzania has sought external financing for the exploitation of ore reserves at Liganga as part of a proposed coal and steel complex, but implementation of the scheme has been delayed by cost considerations. At Falémé in eastern Senegal there exist deposits of

330m. tons of high-grade ore (60% iron) and an estimated 115m. tons of lower-grade ore. However, the depressed world iron and steel market has impeded their exploitation.

Iron ore mining in Angola has been beset by civil conflict, and ceased entirely in 1975–84. At present, output is stockpiled and the resumption of export trade in the ore depends on the eventual rehabilitation of the 520-km rail link between the mines at Cassinga and the coast. The Marampa mine in Sierra Leone has been inactive since the mid-1980s, although plans exist for the eventual resumption of operations to extract its ore deposits, which have an iron content of 69%.

Since the early 1970s world trade in iron ore has regularly exceeded 200m. metric tons (iron content) per year. In the mid-1990s the dominant exporting countries were Australia and Brazil, jointly accounting for almost 60% of iron exports world-wide. Canada, India and the successor republics of the USSR are also important exporters of iron ore. The principal importers are Japan and the countries of the European Union (EU, formerly the European Community—EC), while in the mid-1990s the People's Republic of China was becoming an increasingly significant importer. World iron ore reference prices are decided annually at a series of meetings between producers and purchasers (the steel industry accounts for about 95% of all iron ore consumption). The USA and the republics of the former USSR, although major steel-producing countries, rely on domestic ore production and take little part in the price negotiations. It is generally accepted that, because of its diversity in form and quality, iron ore is ill-suited to price stabilization through an international buffer stock arrangement, although the UN Conference on Trade and Development (UNCTAD) has, for some years, been considering proposals to improve market information by compiling statistics on iron ore production and trade, and to establish a more permanent forum for the discussion of the industry's problems. Efforts by 36 steel-exporting countries, led by the EC and the USA, to negotiate a Multilateral Steel Arrangement (MSA), aimed at the eventual elimination of trade barriers and subsidies, were suspended in 1992.

Export Price Index for Iron Ore (base: 1980 = 100)

	Average	Highest month(s)	Lowest month(s)
1985	84		
1990	124		
1994	120	128 (Oct.)	109 (Feb.)
1995	140	144 (April, July)	131 (Jan.)
1996	141	144 (Jan., Feb.)	137 (Dec.)

The index of export prices for iron ore declined to 128 in February 1997. The two leading exporters of the mineral in 1990–94 were Brazil and Australia. Exports of iron ore and concentrates (excluding agglomerates) by these two countries were valued at about US $19.5 per metric ton in 1992, but the average price declined to $17.0 per ton in 1993 and to $15.5 per ton in 1994.

The Association of Iron Ore Exporting Countries (known by its French initials as APEF) was established in 1975 to promote close co-operation among members, to safeguard their interests as iron ore exporters, to ensure the orderly growth of international trade in iron ore and to secure 'fair and remunerative' returns from its exploitation, processing and marketing. In 1995 the APEF, which also collects and disseminates information on iron ore from its secretariat in Geneva, Switzerland, had nine members, including Algeria, Liberia, Mauritania and Sierra Leone.

Maize (Indian Corn, Mealies) (*Zea mays*)

Maize is one of the world's three principal cereal crops, with wheat and rice. Originally from America, maize has been dispersed to many parts of the world. The principal varieties are dent maize (which has large, soft, flat grains) and flint maize (which has round, hard grains). Dent maize is the predominant type world-wide but flint maize is widely grown in southern Africa. Maize may be white or yellow (there is little nutritional difference), but the former is preferred for human consumption in Africa. Maize is an annual crop, planted from seed, and matures within three to five months. It requires a warm climate and ample water supplies during the growing season.

Production of Maize ('000 metric tons)

	1995	1996*
World total	511,970	574,230
Africa	39,450	36,030
Leading African producers		
Angola	240	400
Benin	600	500
Cameroon	650	660
Congo, Dem. Repub.	1,100	1,100
Côte d'Ivoire	590	560
Egypt	5,350	5,440
Ethiopia	2,200	2,800
Ghana	1,030	1,040
Kenya	2,610	2,200
Malawi	1,660	1,800
Morocco	50	240
Mozambique	940	1,000
Nigeria	3,200	2,600
Somalia	150	160
South Africa	10,100	7,660
Tanzania	2,550	2,400
Uganda	940	940
Zambia	1,410	900
Zimbabwe	2,300	1,500
Leading non-African producers		
Argentina	10,500	14,300
Brazil	32,000	34,000
China, People's Repub.	112,000	118,000
France	12,390	14,220
India†	10,270	10,000
Italy	8,450	9,600
Mexico	17,780	18,100
Romania	9,920	9,600
USA	187,310	236,000

* Provisional.

† Source: FAO.

Source: International Grains Council.

Maize is an important foodstuff in regions such as sub-Saharan Africa and the tropical zones of Latin America, where the climate precludes the extensive cultivation of other cereals. It is, however, inferior in nutritive value to wheat, being especially deficient in lysine, and tends to be replaced by wheat in diets, when the opportunity arises. In many African countries, the grain is ground into a meal, mixed with water, and boiled to produce a gruel or porridge. In other areas it is made into (unleavened) corn bread or breakfast cereals. Maize is also the source of an oil, which is used in cooking.

The high starch content of maize makes it highly suitable for animal feed, which is its main use in North America, Europe, Russia and other areas of the former USSR, and Japan. Feed use is also becoming important in some developing countries, particularly in the Far East and Latin America, but also, recently, in North Africa. Maize has a variety of industrial uses, including the preparation of ethyl alcohol (ethanol), which may be added to petrol to produce a blended motor fuel. Maize is also a source of dextrose and fructose, which can be used as artificial sweeteners, many times as sweet as sugar. The amounts of maize used for these purposes depend, critically, on its price to the users relative to that of petroleum, sugar and other potential raw materials. Maize cobs, previously discarded as a waste product, may be used as feedstock to produce various chemicals (e.g. acetic acid and formic acid).

In recent years world production of maize has generally exceeded 500m. tons annually. The USA usually accounts for one-half of the total, and the People's Republic of China (PRC), with output of around 100m. tons per year, is the next biggest producer. Apart from Egypt, most maize in Africa is grown south of the Sahara. Production there is estimated to average about 27m. tons annually, although it can exceed 30m. tons in good years and fall below 20m. tons after droughts. Maize is not grown under irrigation in most of sub-Saharan Africa, as scarce water supplies are reserved instead for higher-value export crops. Yields are therefore low. In most countries commercial farming is hindered by the lack of foreign exchange to buy essential equipment, as well as transport difficulties which make marketing expensive and uncertain. In much of Africa maize is a subsistence crop.

The region's main producer is South Africa, where, however, output is periodically affected by drought. South Africa's potential was demonstrated by the record 1993 crop (marketed in 1994), of almost 13m. tons. Drought reduced production to less than 5m. tons in 1994, although output recovered substantially in 1995, to 10m. tons. The termination of the minimum price guarantee system, following the pending deregulation of maize marketing in South Africa in 1997, may result in reduced plantings of maize in future years. In most years, the crop is equally divided between white corn (preferred for human consumption) and yellow corn, mostly used for animal feed. Zimbabwe, too, is vulnerable to drought, but good crops in the late 1980s led to acute storage problems, and official prices paid to producers of maize were reduced, in an attempt to limit the surpluses. Although marketing was liberalized in 1994, the government retains control over foreign trade. An exportable surplus was produced in 1995. However, the incidence of flooding in early 1997 diminished prospects of another favourable crop. Kenya encountered maize shortages following a drought in 1993, but, following two successive favourable harvests, the country was a significant exporter in 1996. The progressive elimination of fertilizer subsidies by the Nigerian government has prevented improved seed varieties, introduced there, from achieving their full potential. Annual production is estimated to average 3m. tons, although considerable quantities are lost as a result of inadequate storage facilities.

One of the most notable differences between maize production in developed and developing countries is in yields. In the USA, the continual development of new hybrids and the availability of adequate fertilizer and water supplies have resulted in a substantial increase in yields, interrupted only by the occasional years of drought. In good years yields exceed 8 tons per ha; a record of 8.7 tons per ha was achieved in 1994. South Africa, Kenya and Zimbabwe usually achieve yields of at least 2 tons per ha, but in much of west and central Africa yields of 1 ton per ha are normal. Although hybrid forms of maize suited to African conditions are being developed, their adoption is hindered in many countries by low producer prices, inefficient marketing arrangements, and, above all, the inability of producers to obtain regular supplies of fertilizers at economic prices.

World trade in maize reached a record 73m. tons in 1989/90 (July–June), but subsequently declined, largely because of a fall in purchases by the former USSR. Trade amounted to only 54m. tons in 1993/94. Increasing requirements for feeds by a number of countries, notably Mexico, the PRC (formerly a substantial exporter) and the Republic of Korea, raised the volume of trade to 70m. tons in 1995/96. The estimate for 1996/97 is 63m. tons.

The pre-eminent world exporter is the USA, which typically accounts for about three-quarters of the total. Its sales exceeded 58m. tons in 1995/96, when the strong world market, combined with heavy domestic demand, reduced stocks to an exceptionally low level at the close of the marketing season. Argentina, the world's second largest exporter, averages about 5m. tons annually, although, following an excellent crop, its exports reached 7m. tons in 1996/97. South Africa was a considerable maize exporter in the 1970s, and was of particular importance to neighbouring food-deficit countries as a source of white maize. In drought years, large quantities of imports may be needed to augment domestic supplies, particularly for food. In 1992 South Africa imported 4m. tons of maize, and 600,000 tons were required to supplement the disappointing 1994 crop. In better years, South Africa usually exports about 2m. tons, mainly to destinations in south and east Africa, Japan, and other countries in the Far East.

The world's principal maize importer is Japan. Its purchases averaged more than 16m. tons annually in the early 1990s, but have subsequently declined, as the Japanese market has progressively opened to imports of meat. The Republic of Korea and Taiwan, with rapidly increasing livestock production, have become substantial importers of maize in recent years; their maize imports totalled approximately 9m. tons and 6m. tons respectively in 1995/96. Imports by other Pacific basin countries have also begun to increase. In the 1980s, the USSR was a major market, but the livestock industries in the successor republics of the USSR declined sharply during the 1990s, greatly reducing feed needs. From a total of 18m. tons in 1989/90, these imports declined to 4m. tons in 1993/94 and have subsequently been less than 1m. tons annually.

Maize imports by sub-Saharan Africa vary from around 1m. tons annually in years of good crops to far higher amounts after droughts. In 1992/93, for example, these imports exceeded 8m. tons, most of which entered through South African ports, either for that country's own use or for onward transport overland to neighbouring countries.

Massive levels of carry-over stocks of maize were accumulated in the USA during the mid-1980s, reaching a high point of 124m. tons at end-August 1987. Government support programmes were successful in discouraging surplus production, but several poor harvests also contributed to the liquidation of these stocks, which were reduced to only 11m. tons at the close of the 1995/96 marketing year, at a level insufficient to maintain adequate supplies for domestic demand. Despite the harvest in 1996/97 of the second highest maize crop ever recorded, the combined forces of domestic use and export demand permitted stocks to increase to only 24m. tons.

Export Price Index for Maize (base: 1980 = 100)

	Average	Highest month(s)	Lowest month(s)
1985	57		
1990	92		
1994	75	79 (July, Aug.)	68 (Feb., March)
1995	80	101 (July)	59 (Oct., Nov.)
1996	79	86 (Jan.)	72 (Oct.)

Maize export prices, which had been especially depressed in 1993 and 1994 when import demand was low, reacted strongly to the changed market outlook. The price of US No. 2 Yellow Corn (f.o.b. Gulf Ports) was as low at US $93 per metric ton in June 1993, but reached $150 per ton by the end of 1995. As markets registered the restricted supply situation likely to prevail at the end of the season, prices advanced further, reaching $170 per ton in early March 1996, $190 in mid-April and, briefly, $214 at the end of that month, before subsiding to $190 in June. An improvement in supplies, following the favourable harvests in the USA and Argentina, caused export prices to ease to $120–$130 per ton in the first half of 1997.

Manganese

This metal is obtained from various ores containing such minerals as hausmannite, manganite and pyrolusite. The ore is usually washed or hand-sorted and then smelted to make ferromanganese (80% manganese), in which form it is chiefly used to alloy into steel, manganese steel being particularly hard and tough. Almost 95% of manganese produced is thus used in the manufacture of steel, which, on average, consumes about 6 kg of manganese per metric ton of steel. Electrolytic manganese is used to make stainless steel and in the aluminium industry. Minor uses of manganese as oxides are in dry-cell batteries, paints and varnishes, and in ceramics and glass making.

World reserves of manganese in 1993 were estimated by the US Bureau of Mines at 650m. metric tons of manganese content, of which 370m. tons are in South Africa and 150m. tons in the republics of the former USSR, principally Ukraine. These two areas account for more than 80% of the world's identified resources. Africa's second major producer, Gabon, has estimated reserves of 45m. tons.

Until overtaken by Gabon in 1990, South Africa was, during the late 1980s, the world's leading exporter of manganese ore, exporting almost three-fifths of its mine output. Where possible, South Africa's policy has been to maximize export revenues by shipping as much as possible in processed ferro-alloy form. Export volumes of ferromanganese have generally followed steel production trends, and reached a record of almost 390,000 tons in 1988. South African exports of silicomanganese more than doubled during the 1980s, reaching a record 250,000 tons in 1987. The expansion by Gabon of its manganese exports was stimulated by the opening, in 1988, of a new mineral port at Owendo. Shipments of ore by rail through the Congo to the port of Pointe-Noire, however, were suspended following a dispute in 1991.

Production of Manganese Ore
(manganese content, '000 metric tons)

	1992	1993*
World total	7,012	7,234
Africa	1,924	1,888
African producers		
Gabon†	718	674
Ghana†	106	115
Morocco†	23	23
South Africa†	1,077	1,076
Leading non-African producers		
Australia	570	865
Brazil†	647	722
China, People's Repub.†	1,060	1,080
India†	530	660
Ukraine†	1,700*	1,500

* Preliminary.
† Gross weight reported; metal content estimated.
Source: US Bureau of Mines.

Ghana, the other principal African producer, benefited in the late 1980s from government measures to revive manganese operations, assisted by loan finance from the World Bank. In 1991 a mine project was initiated that would make Burkina Faso a minor regional producer. These reserves, located at Tambao, 400 km north-west of Ouagadougou, and estimated at 19m. tons, contain an average ore content of 50% manganese. Production began in May 1993 and was targeted to reach 140,000 tons annually by 1995. In 1994 manganese production was resumed in Namibia after a lapse of almost 30 years. The Ofjosondu mine, 160 km north-east of Windhoek, was reactivated for production of medium-grade ore having a relatively low phosphorus content. Its initial annual output was projected at about 100,000 tons. Zaire, once a significant source of manganese exports, has mined only on a sporadic basis since 1980. The exploitation of manganese deposits in Angola has been interrupted by two decades of civil war. Reserves estimated at 19m. tons, with a manganese ore content of 50%, have been located in Burkina Faso. A joint venture between the government and Canadian interests to develop these resources was formed in 1995.

Extensive accumulations of manganese in marine environments have been identified. The characteristic occurrences are as nodules on deep ocean floors and as crusts on seamounts at shallower depths. Both forms are oxidic and are often termed 'ferromanganese' because they generally contain iron and manganese. The main commercial interest in both types of deposit derives from the copper, nickel and cobalt contents also present, which represent large resources of these metals. Attention was focused initially on nodules, of which the Pacific Ocean encompasses the areas with the densest coverage and highest concentration of potentially economic metals. However, the exploitation of nodules has, to date, been impeded by legal, technical and economic factors.

Export Price Index for Manganese Ore (base: 1980 = 100)

	Average	Highest month(s)	Lowest month(s)
1985	85		
1990	243		
1994	130	135 (Jan.–June)	125 (July–Dec.)
1995	125	*	*
1996	126	131 (Nov., Dec.)	125 (Jan.–Oct.)

* The monthly index remained constant at 125 throughout 1995.

The index of export prices for manganese ore remained at 131 in January and February 1997. The leading importers of manganese ores and concentrates in 1992 and 1993 were Japan, France and Norway. In the case of Norway, the average import cost of these minerals (including manganiferous iron ores) declined from US $143 per metric ton in 1991 to $132 per ton in 1992, to $105 per ton in 1993 and to $102 per ton in 1994.

Most of the Western countries' manganese ore output is sold by means of annual contracts between producers and their customers, the manufacturers of steel and ferro-alloys.

Millet and Sorghum

Millet and sorghum are often grouped together in economic analyses of world cereals, not because they are a particularly closely related species—in fact they are quite dissimilar—but because in many developing countries they are both little-traded subsistence crops. Figures for the production of the individual grains should be treated only as broad estimates in most cases. Data cover only crops harvested for grain.

Data on millet relate mainly to the following: cat-tail millet (*Pennisetum glaucum* or *typhoides*), also known as bulrush millet, pearl millet or, in India and Pakistan, as 'bajra'; finger millet (*Eleusine coracana*), known in India as 'ragi'; common or bread millet (*Panicum miliaceum*), also called 'proso'; foxtail millet (*Setaria italica*), or Italian millet; and barnyard millet (*Echinochloa crusgalli*), also often called Japanese millet.

Sorghum statistics refer mainly to the several varieties of *Sorghum vulgare,* known by various names, such as great millet, Guinea corn, kafir or kafircorn (*caffrorum*), milo (in the USA and Argentina), feterita, durra, jowar, sorgo or maicillo. Other species included in the table are Sudan grass (*S. sudanense*) and Columbus grass or sorgo negro (*S. almum*). The use of grain sorghum hybrids has resulted in a considerable increase in yields in recent years.

Millet and sorghum are cultivated particularly in semi-arid areas where there is too little rainfall to sustain maize and the temperature is too high for wheat. These two cereals constitute the staple diet of people over large areas of Africa, India, the People's Republic of China (PRC) and parts of the former USSR. They are usually consumed as porridge or unleavened bread. Both grains have good nutritive value, but are less palatable than wheat, and tend to be replaced by the latter when circumstances permit. In many African countries sorghum is used to make beer. Sorghum is also produced and used in certain countries in the western hemisphere (particularly Argentina, Mexico and the USA), where it is used mainly as an animal

Production of Millet and Sorghum ('000 metric tons)
M = Millet; S = Sorghum.

	1995	1996*
World total: M	25,070	27,000
World total: S	55,370	65,740
Africa: M	9,930	10,600
Africa: S	16,360	16,920
Leading African producers		
Burkina Faso: M	730	810
Burkina Faso: S	1,270	1,250
Chad: M	270	240
Chad: S	440	360
Egypt: S	780	760
Ethiopia: M	250	360
Ethiopia: S	1,600	1,780
Mali: M	710	770
Mali: S	710	570
Niger: M	1,770	1,830
Niger: S	270	430
Nigeria: M	3,200	3,600
Nigeria: S	5,000	4,500
Senegal: M	670	660
South Africa: S	150	340
Sudan: M	390	420
Sudan: S	2,450	3,300
Tanzania: M	310	300
Tanzania: S	610	650
Uganda: M	640	650
Uganda: S	410	400
Zimbabwe: M	80	20
Zimbabwe: S	120	30
Leading non-African producers		
Argentina: S	2,100	2,500
Australia: S	1,560	990
China, People's Repub.: M	4,350	4,300
China, People's Repub.: S	4,760	4,700
India: M	8,970	10,400
India: S	9,550	10,400
Mexico: S	5,570	6,200
USA: S	11,690	20,400

* Provisional.
Source: International Grains Council.

feed, although the high tannin content of some varieties lowers their feeding value.

World production of both sorghum and millet has been in decline for many years, as farmers have preferred to cultivate more profitable and higher-yielding crops. Because sorghum is more drought-resistant than most cereals, it tends to be grown in marginal areas, or to be substituted at short notice for maize in dry years. World production of sorghum averages about 60m. tons annually, of which Africa accounts for about one-quarter. The region's major producers are Sudan, Nigeria, Ethiopia and Burkina Faso. World millet production averages 25m. tons annually, of which about 10m. tons are grown in Africa. Mali, Niger and Nigeria are the most important producers, but most countries south of the Sahara grow at least some millet.

Millet and sorghum are grown largely for human consumption, but are gradually being replaced by wheat and rice, as those cereals become more widely available. Only low-grade sorghum is used for animal feed in Africa, but some is used for starch when maize is in short supply. Apart from food and animal feed requirements, sorghum is used in a number of countries in Asia and Africa for the production of beers and other alcoholic liquors.

World trade in sorghum ranges between 6m.–10m. tons per year, but has in recent years been at the lower end of this range, reflecting the small volume of exportable supplies. The principal exporters are the USA (which usually accounts for two-thirds of the total and holds the greater part of world sorghum stocks), Argentina and Australia. The PRC, South Africa, Sudan and Thailand are occasional exporters. Japan is the main importer, accounting for over one-third of the world market. Mexico buys sorghum in large quantities when its price is competitive with maize. Its occasional large purchases tend to make the world market for sorghum unpredictable. Little sorghum is imported by sub-Saharan Africa. Export prices for sorghum normally closely follow those of maize, although sorghum is generally slightly cheaper. The price of US No. 2 Yellow Sorghum, f.o.b. Gulf Ports, was below US $100 per ton in the second half of 1994 but rose steadily in 1995, reaching $160 per ton at the end of the year. The very restricted supply prospects for grains in general in 1996 were reflected in a firmer price trend: by May 1996 US sorghum was quoted at over $200 per ton. In common with other grains, export prices for sorghum declined in the second half of 1996, before stabilizing in early 1997. At the end of April 1997, US sorghum was quoted at $120 per ton, about $4 per ton below the price of maize.

Very little millet enters international trade, and no reliable export price series can be established.

Oil Palm (*Elaeis guineensis*)

This tree is native to west Africa and grows wild in tropical forests along the coast of that region. The entire fruit is of use commercially; palm oil is made from its pulp, and palm kernel oil from the seed. Palm oil is a versatile product and, because of its very low acid content (4%–5%), it is almost all used in food. It is used in margarine and other edible fats; as a 'shortener' for pastry and biscuits; as an ingredient in ice cream and chocolate; and in the manufacture of soaps and detergents. Palm kernel oil, which is similar to coconut oil, is also used for making soaps and fats. The sap from the stems of the tree produces palm wine, an intoxicating beverage.

Palm oil can be produced virtually through the year once the palms have reached oil-bearing age, which takes about five years. The palms continue to bear oil for 30 years or more and the yield far exceeds that of any other oil plant, with 1 ha of oil palms producing as much oil as 6 ha of groundnuts or 10–12 ha of soybeans. However, it is an intensive crop, needing considerable investment and skilled labour.

During the 1980s palm oil accounted for more than 15% of world production of vegetable oils (second only to soybean oil), owing mainly to a substantial expansion in Malaysian production. In 1989 palm oil accounted for 14.5% of world vegetable oil output, compared with 22% for soybean oil and about 11% each for sunflower and rapeseed oils. Assisted, however, by high levels of demand from Pakistan and the People's Republic of China, palm oil substantially increased its share of world vegetable oil markets in the early 1990s. In 1995 palm oil exports were expected to account for about 38% of the international trade in edible oils, with soybean oil accounting for less than 18%.

The increase in output of palm oil has posed a particular challenge to the soybean industry in the USA, which has, since the mid-1970s, been reducing its imports of palm oil. In 1988, in response to health reports that both palm and coconut oils tended to raise levels of cholesterol (a substance believed to promote arteriosclerosis in the body), several leading US food processors announced that they were to discontinue their use. These reports, however, have been vigorously challenged by palm oil producers.

Production of Palm Kernels ('000 metric tons)

	1994	1995
World total	4,444*	4,786*
Africa	747*	765*
Leading African producers		
Cameroon	55†	56†
Congo, Dem. Repub.	72*	72*
Côte d'Ivoire	32	31
Ghana	34*	34*
Guinea	53	53*
Nigeria	380†	400†
Sierra Leone	32	29
Leading non-African producers		
Brazil‡	185*	185*
Colombia	60	76†
Indonesia§	945†	1,075†
Malaysia	2,204	2,396
Papua New Guinea	66	60
Thailand	57*	57*

* FAO estimate. † Unofficial figure.
‡ Figures relate to babassu kernels.
§ Production on estates only.

Production of Palm Oil ('000 metric tons)

	1994	1995
World total	14,690*	15,805*
Africa	1,769*	1,795*
Leading African producers		
Angola	52*	52*
Cameroon	125†	130†
Congo, Dem. Repub.	181*	181*
Côte d'Ivoire	259	249
Ghana	100*	100*
Guinea	50	50*
Nigeria	837	871
Sierra Leone	50	45
Leading non-African producers		
Colombia	329	350*
Indonesia‡	4,094	4,500
Malaysia	7,221	7,811
Papua New Guinea	225*	240*
Thailand	300†	370†

* FAO estimate. † Unofficial figure.
‡ Production on estates only.

In Africa a large proportion of oil palms still grow in wild groves and the bulk of oil production is for local consumption. In export terms, Africa has, since 1980, accounted for less than 3% of world trade in palm oil, and in 1995 African exports comprised only 2% of the world market. Nigeria was the world's leading producer of palm oil until overtaken by Malaysia in 1971. The loss of Nigeria's market dominance was, in part, a result of civil war and the authorities' neglect to replace old, unproductive trees. Since the early 1980s, however, measures have been taken to revive palm oil output and to enhance the efficiency and capacity of associated mills and refineries. Foreign investment has been encouraged, as has the transfer of inefficiently managed state-owned plantations to private-sector ownership. A ban by the Nigerian government on palm oil imports, in force since 1986, was partially relaxed in 1990, however, as domestic output (of which an estimated 70% came from smallholder producers) was able to satisfy only two-thirds of a forecast annual demand of 900,000 tons.

In Benin, where the oil palm has traditionally been a staple crop of the national economy, oil palm plantations and natural palm groves cover more than 450,000 ha. Côte d'Ivoire is now

Africa's principal palm oil exporter and the fourth largest in the world, behind Malaysia (by far the largest, accounting for about 80% of all palm oil trade), Indonesia and Singapore. However, more than one-half of Côte d'Ivoire's palms were planted in 1965–70 and have passed their peak of productivity. Management and financial difficulties, as well as declining world prices for palm oil, have resulted in a scaling-down of the replanting programme, and plans to increase processing capacity have been postponed. The palm oil sector in Cameroon has similarly experienced delays in the implementation of replanting. Other African producers, notably Liberia and Ghana, also lack sufficient refinery capacity to service their palm oil output. Plans were proceeding in the early 1990s, however, for the construction by Malaysian producers of a palm oil refinery in Tanzania to process Malaysian crude palm oil. The plant, located in Dar es Salaam, would initially produce 30,000 tons of edible oils annually.

Export Price Index for Palm Oil (base: 1980 = 100)

	Average	Highest month(s)	Lowest month(s)
1985	86		
1990	49		
1994	90	123 (Dec.)	66 (Feb.)
1995	107	117 (March)	101 (Dec.)
1996	91	96 (April, Dec.)	81 (July)

Internationally, palm oil is faced with sustained competition from the other major edible lauric oils—soybean, rapeseed and sunflower oils—and these markets are subject to a complex and changing interaction of production, stocks and trade. In the longer term, prospects for palm oil exporters (particularly the higher-cost producers in sub-Saharan Africa) do not appear favourable. Technological advances in oil palm cultivation, particularly in the introduction of laboratory-produced higher-yielding varieties (HYV), may also militate against the smaller-scale producer, as, for economic and technical reasons, many HYV can be produced only on large estates, exposing smallholder cultivators to increasingly intense price pressure.

During September 1996 the import price of Malaysian palm oil in the Netherlands (c.i.f. Rotterdam) declined from US $572.5 per metric ton to $502.5 per ton. The price advanced to $585 per ton in February 1997, but fell to $500 in July.

Petroleum

Crude oils, from which petroleum fuel is derived, consist essentially of a wide range of hydrocarbon molecules which are separated by distillation in the refining process. Refined oil is treated in different ways to make the different varieties of fuel. More than four-fifths of total world oil supplies are used as fuel for the production of energy in the form of power or heating.

Petroleum, together with its associated mineral fuel, natural gas, is extracted both from onshore and offshore wells in many areas of the world. From storage tanks at the oilfield wellhead, crude petroleum is conveyed, frequently by pumping for long distances through large pipelines, to coastal depots where it is either treated in a refinery or delivered into bulk storage tanks for subsequent shipment for refining overseas. In addition to pipeline transportation of crude petroleum and refined products, natural (petroleum) gas is, in some areas, also transported through networks of pipelines. Crude petroleum varies considerably in colour and viscosity, and these variations are a determinant both of price and of end-use after refining.

In the refining process, crude petroleum is heated until vaporized. The vapours are then separately condensed, according to their molecular properties, passed through airless steel tubes and pumped into the lower section of a high cylindrical tower, as a hot mixture of vapours and liquid. The heavy unvaporized liquid flows out at the base of the tower as a 'residue' from which is obtained heavy fuel and bitumen. The vapours passing upwards then undergo a series of condensation processes that produce 'distillates', which form the basis of the various petroleum products.

The most important of these products is fuel oil, composed of heavy distillates and residues, which is used to produce heating and power for industrial purposes. Products in the kerosene group have a wide number of applications, ranging from heating fuels to the powering of aviation gas turbine engines. Gasoline (petrol) products fuel internal combustion engines (used mainly in road motor vehicles), and naphtha, a gasoline distillate, is a commercial solvent that can also be processed as a feedstock. Propane and butane, the main liquefied petroleum gases, have a wide range of industrial applications and are also used for domestic heating and cooking.

Petroleum is the leading raw material in international trade. The world's 'published proven' reserves of petroleum and natural gas liquids at 31 December 1995 were estimated to total 138,863m. metric tons, equivalent to about 1,013,700m. barrels (1 metric ton is equivalent to approximately 7.3 barrels, each of 42 US gallons or 34.97 imperial gallons, i.e. 159 litres). Of this, about 10,021m. tons (7.2%) were in Africa.

Nigeria's first petroleum discovery was made in the Niger delta region in 1956, and exports began in 1958. Production and exports increased steadily until output was disrupted by the outbreak of civil war in 1967. After the end of hostilities, in 1970, Nigeria's petroleum production greatly increased and it became the country's major industry. Since Libya restricted output in 1973, Nigeria has been Africa's leading petroleum-producing country. Being of low sulphur content and high quality, its petroleum is much in demand on the European market. Nigeria's proven reserves were estimated to be 2,853m. tons at 31 December 1995. A five-year investment programme, initiated in 1991, aimed to increase petroleum output capacity from 1.95m.–2m. barrels per day (b/d) to 2.5m. b/d by 1995. A member of the Organization of the Petroleum Exporting Countries (OPEC, see below), Nigeria accounted for 7.7% of total OPEC production of 1,309m. tons in 1996. The state petroleum enterprise, the Nigerian National Petroleum Corpn (NNPC), operates refinery facilities at Kaduna, Warri, Port Harcourt and Alesa Eleme. In 1995 their total annual capacity was 21.6m. metric tons, although Nigeria occasionally has recourse to imports of refined petroleum products in order to satisfy its domestic requirements. Petroleum sales dominate Nigeria's earnings of foreign exchange, providing about 90% of the total and accounting for approximately 80% of federal government revenue. However, considerable revenue is lost to the Nigerian government through illegal exports of oil to neighbouring countries, in the form of petrol, kerosene, diesel oil and fuel oil.

Angola's first petroleum discovery was made in 1955 near Luanda. However, the Cabinda province has a major offshore deposit, in production since 1968, which now forms the basis of Angola's oil industry. Production from Cabinda was briefly disrupted by the country's civil war, but has proceeded uninterruptedly since 1977, and output has increased steadily since 1982. In the mid-1990s Angola relied on exports of crude petroleum for about 80% of government revenue. In 1995 Angola's proven oil reserves were assessed at 741m. tons; however, with a number of oilfields currently under development and continuing discoveries of new deep-water petroleum fields, prospects exist for a considerable expansion in the petroleum sector, given an eventual settlement of the civil conflict. Most of Angola's oil output is exported in crude form, although there are plans to expand the capacity of Angola's sole refinery, at Luanda, from 1.6m. to 2m. tons annually and for the construction of a second refinery.

The Congo Republic, with proven recoverable reserves estimated at 206m. tons in 1995, entered onshore petroleum production in 1957. Subsequent expansion, however, has been in operations off shore, where significant new deposits, discovered in 1992, were expected to add 2m. tons annually to the country's petroleum output from 1996. A petroleum refinery at Pointe-Noire, with an annual capacity of 1m. tons in 1995, also processes some Angolan production. In neighbouring Gabon, whose recoverable reserves were estimated at 183.6m. tons in 1995, the exploitation of petroleum deposits began in 1956, and, as in the Congo, was increased as offshore fields came into production. In 1994 sales of petroleum and petroleum products provided more than 79% of export revenue. A member of OPEC until its withdrawal from the organization in December 1996, Gabon's output accounted for only 1.4% of OPEC's total output in 1995. In 1995 Gabon's annual refinery capacity was 861,000 metric tons.

In the early 1990s Cameroon was virtually self-sufficient in oil and petroleum products. New exploration and development projects, however, were not being actively pursued, and it has

Production of Crude Petroleum
(estimates, '000 metric tons, including natural gas liquids)

	1995	1996*
World total	3,091,789	3,164,652
Africa	319,085	334,310
Leading African producers		
Algeria	38,200	40,800
Angola	31,050	35,275
Cameroon	5,105	4,500
Congo, Repub.	8,750	10,140
Egypt	46,100	46,150
Gabon	18,200	18,500
Libya	69,500	70,125
Nigeria	94,500	100,675
Tunisia	4,385	4,325
Leading non-African producers		
Canada	90,300	90,900
China, People's Repub.†	150,350	156,365
Indonesia	74,910	75,785
Iran	180,600	183,765
Kuwait‡	100,350	102,983
Mexico	136,105	142,690
Norway	139,100	154,285
Russia	306,800	300,995
Saudi Arabia‡	403,700	404,158
United Arab Emirates	110,240	110,840
United Kingdom	128,250	131,650
USA	327,980	323,875
Venezuela	130,450	147,765

* Preliminary. † Including oil from shale and coal.
‡ Including share of production in the Neutral Zone (also known as the Partitioned Zone), divided equally between Kuwait and Saudi Arabia.
Source: The Institute of Petroleum.

been forecast that the country's proven reserves (estimated at 55m. tons in 1995) could be exhausted by the end of the decade. Cameroon's annual refinery capacity was 2.1m. tons in 1995. The Democratic Republic of the Congo (DRC) entered offshore petroleum production in 1975, operating from oilfields near the Atlantic coast and at the mouth of the River Congo. These deposits were sharply depleted during the 1980s (estimates of its proven reserves fell from 13.2m. tons in 1989 to 7.6m. tons in 1990). The level of these reserves was substantially replenished during 1991, however, raising estimates to 25.6m. tons for each of the subsequent four years. Although the DRC has a refinery capacity of 847,000 tons per year, its exceptionally heavy-grade petroleum cannot be processed locally and the DRC therefore cannot consume its own output. In June 1992 the assets of US and European oil companies were nationalised.

Côte d'Ivoire, with estimated proven reserves of 13.7m. tons in 1995, and Benin, whose proven reserves were estimated at 4m. tons in that year, are among the other smaller sub-Saharan offshore producers, which were joined in 1991 by Equatorial Guinea. The offshore Zafiro oilfield, north-west of Bioko, commenced production in October 1996, with output forecast to reach 40,000 b/d. Deposits of an estimated 52m.–58m. tons of petroleum have been identified off the coast of Senegal, but the development of these reserves (which are overwhelmingly of heavy oil) is not economically feasible at present. Chad, with identified petroleum reserves of 40m.–50m. tons, has revived plans for their exploitation, which had been interrupted by prolonged internal unrest. In late 1996 an international consortium was finalizing plans for the development of a petroleum field in Southern Chad, output from which was to be carried by a proposed pipeline, through Cameroon, to the Atlantic coast. Commercial deposits of petroleum in Southern Sudan remain unexploited, pending the resolution of internal unrest.

Among other sub-Saharan African countries where petroleum reserves are known or believed to exist, but which do not yet produce, are Guinea, Mozambique, Swaziland, Eritrea, Madagascar, South Africa and Tanzania. Exploration has also taken place in Ethiopia, Namibia, Kenya and Zimbabwe.

OPEC was formed in 1960 to maintain prices in the producing countries. Nigeria joined OPEC in 1971; however, Gabon, which became a full member in 1975, terminated its membership with effect from January 1997 (see above). The other African members are Algeria and Libya.

The four African members of OPEC formed the African Petroleum Producers' Association (APPA) in 1987. Angola, Benin, Cameroon, the DRC, the Republic of Congo, Côte d'Ivoire, Egypt and Equatorial Guinea subsequently joined the association, in which Tunisia has observer status. Apart from promoting co-operation among regional producers, the APPA, which is based in Brazzaville, in the Congo Republic, co-operates with OPEC in stabilizing oil prices.

Export Price Index for Crude Petroleum (base: 1980 = 100)

	Average	Highest month(s)	Lowest month(s)
1985	91		
1990	68		
1994	44	49 (July)	38 (March)
1995	47	51 (April, May)	44 (July, Oct.)
1996	56	65 (Oct.)	49 (Jan., Feb.)

The two leading western European producers and exporters of crude petroleum are Norway and the United Kingdom. The two countries' exports of crude petroleum earned an average of US $126 per metric ton in 1993, but only $118 per ton in 1994. In 1992 Norway's petroleum exports had an average value of $144 per ton, and those of the United Kingdom $145 per ton. The comparable averages in the previous year were, respectively, $151 and $150 per ton. Prices per barrel averaged about $20 in 1992, declined to only about $14 in late 1993, but recovered to more than $18 in mid-1994. Thereafter, international petroleum prices remained relatively stable until the early months of 1995. The price per barrel reached about $20 again in April and May 1995, but eased to $17 later in the year. In April 1996 the price of the standard grade of North Sea petroleum for short-term delivery rose to more than $23 per barrel. The surge in prices followed reports that stocks of petroleum in Western industrialized countries were at their lowest levels for 19 years. However, the advance was not sustained, and in May the price declined to less than $18 per barrel. In October another rally in the oil market took the price of North Sea petroleum to more than $25 per barrel, its highest level for more than five years. The price per barrel was generally in the range of $22–$24 for the remainder of the year.

Petroleum prices moved generally downward in the first half of 1997, and the short-term quotation for the standard North Sea grade fell to less than US $17 per barrel in June.

Platinum

This is one of a group of six related metals, also including palladium, rhodium, ruthenium, iridium and osmium. In nature, platinum is usually associated with the sulphides of iron, copper and nickel. Depending on the relative concentration of the platinum-group metals (PGM) and copper and nickel in the deposit, platinum is either the major product or a by-product of base metal production. PGM are highly resistant to corrosion, and do not oxidize in air. They are also extremely malleable and have a high melting point, giving them a wide range of industrial uses.

Although widely employed in the petroleum refining and petrochemical sectors, the principal industrial use for platinum is in catalytic converters in motor vehicles (which reduce pollution from exhaust emissions), usually accounting for about one-third of total platinum consumption by Europe (including Eastern Europe), Japan, North America and other Western countries (an estimated 31.4%, or 1,470,000 troy ounces, in 1996). The USA, Canada, Japan, Australia, Taiwan, the Republic of Korea, the European Community (EC, now the European Union—EU) and certain Latin American countries have implemented legislation to neutralize vehicle exhaust gases, and this necessitates the fitting of catalytic converters, using platinum, rhodium and palladium, to vehicles. In 1989 the EC Council of (Environment) Ministers decided to oblige vehicle manufacturers within the Community to fit three-way catalytic converters as compulsory features in passenger cars with an engine capacity of less than 1,400 cc, effective for all new models from mid-1992 and for all new cars from January 1993. It was predicted that the new measures would reduce emissions of exhaust gases by 60%–70%. The EC Commission subsequently extended similar anti-pollution requirements to larger cars, and to heavy trucks, with effect from 1995. The resultant increase in demand for automotive emission control catalysts (autocatalysts) is expected to generate a rising trend in the consumption of platinum, rhodium and palladium during the 1990s. In 1996 the EU published recommendations for stricter limits on emissions, which, if implemented, would take effect from 2000. The increasing use of palladium-rich catalysts by US and European motor vehicle manufacturers was reflected in a decline in autocatalyst demand for platinum of 30,000 oz in 1996, to 1,820,000 oz. Also of considerable potential significance to platinum demand has been the development of fuel cells incorporating platinum catalysts which produce pollution-free electricity from a controlled chemical reaction between oxygen and hydrogen. The only by-products of this reaction are carbon dioxide and water, so that the fuel cell avoids environmental damage, in contrast to the disposal of radioactive waste products from nuclear plants and the production of sulphur and nitrogen oxides at coal- and oil-fired power stations. The use of these cells in power generation, assuming that their operating costs would approximate those of conventional electricity-generating plant, could substantially increase world demand for platinum and palladium.

Alloyed platinum is very heavy and hard. Platinum's white colour makes it popular for jewellery, which accounts for the other principal source of consumption (39.5%, or 1,850,000 oz, in 1996). Japan is the world's main consumer of platinum, and its jewellery industry absorbed a record 1,480,000 oz in 1996. Industrial and other miscellaneous applications accounted for the balance of platinum consumption; these uses include platinum for minting coins and small bars purchased as an investment, petroleum refining, production of nitric acid, glass manufacture, electrical applications and dentistry. A recovery in industrial consumption, particularly in the motor vehicle industry and in jewellery fabrication, raised international demand for platinum (excluding Western sales to the People's Republic of China of 130,000 oz in 1995 and 200,000 oz in 1996) from 4,710,000 oz in 1995 to 4,680,000 oz in 1996. Supplies entering the market in 1996 declined to 4,900,000 oz from 4,990,000 oz in 1995. This decrease in supplies, the first experienced by the platinum market since 1992, reflected the impact of a labour dispute in South Africa, and a fall in shipments from Russia, from 1,280,000 oz in 1995 to 1,220,000 oz in 1996. Supplies from South Africa, which, except for 1992 and 1994, had risen in each year since 1982, declined in 1996 by 40,000 oz to 3,330,000 oz.

The US Bureau of Mines has estimated world reserves of PGM to be approximately 1,800m. oz, of which almost 90% are located in South Africa. Production is dominated by South Africa, which normally accounts for more than three-quarters of supplies to the international market. Its output comprised 68% of world supplies in 1996. An agreement that was signed in 1991 by the USSR and the South African Chamber of Mines, under which the USSR was to receive technical assistance for the development of its platinum industry, has subsequently been enlarged and extended with the Russian government. Russian PGM are produced mainly as by-products of coal and nickel mining (see below) in the far north of Siberia. Following the break-up of the former USSR in 1991, these operations were adversely affected by deterioration in plant and equipment, as the result of a lack of funds for essential maintenance. Production began to stabilize, however, in 1994, although it was estimated that in 1995 and 1996 about 1,000,000 oz of marketed shipments were supplied from Russian government platinum stocks. No supplies of PGM were exported by Russia during the first six months of 1997. In late 1995 ownership of the country's principal producer of PGM, Noril'sk Nickel, was transferred to a bank, in preparation for full privatization. The enterprise has, however, since encountered severe financial problems and was undergoing further restructuring in 1997. Canada is the third largest producer, its platinum being a by-product of its nickel production. Minor producers include the USA, Australia, Finland and Colombia. Zimbabwe, the only other African platinum producer, is developing several new mine projects, the first of which is expected to reach full production in late 1998. Elsewhere in Africa, there are known or probable deposits of platinum in Ethiopia, Kenya and Sierra Leone.

Whereas PGM are produced in Canada and Russia as by-products of copper and/or nickel production, PGM in South Africa are produced as the primary products, with nickel and copper as by-products. Another fundamental difference between the platinum deposits in South Africa and those in Russia and Canada is the ratio of platinum to palladium. In South Africa the percentage of platinum contained in PGM has, to date, exceeded that of palladium, although the ratio is expected to favour palladium in new mines being brought into production in the early 1990s (see below). In Russia, Canada and the USA there is a higher proportion of palladium than platinum.

South African production capacity was substantially increased in 1993, following the completion of a number of expansion projects which had been under development since the mid-1980s. However, the level of world platinum prices, together with rises in production costs, led to the subsequent postponement or cancellation of several expansion projects and to the closure of unprofitable operations. Similar considerations have also affected producers in North America. Proposals, announced in 1995, for the merger of the South African interests of Lonrho Platinum Division and Impala Platinum, which jointly control about 30% of world output, were vetoed in May 1996 by the EU, on the grounds that the scheme would create a duopoly in the platinum market.

Prices for Platinum

(London Platinum and Palladium Market, morning and afternoon 'fixes', US$ per troy oz)

	Average	Highest	Lowest
1990	471.7		
1994	405.3	427.5 (July)	378.5 (Jan.)
1995	424.2	461.3 (April)	398.3 (Dec.)
1996	397.3	433.0 (Feb.)	367.0 (Dec.)

For more than 17 months from mid-1994 the London price of platinum remained above US $400 per troy oz. In April 1995 the price rose to $461 (equivalent to £285 sterling) per oz, following reports that a US group had developed a new catalyst system for motor vehicles that was claimed to reduce pollution in the atmosphere. The rally in the platinum market was short-lived, however, and in December the metal's price fell to $398 (£256.5) per oz.

There was a revival of interest in precious metals during the early weeks of 1996, with the London price of platinum reaching US $433 (£285) per oz in February. As before, the advance was not sustained, and in June the platinum price was reduced to $389 (£251.5) per oz. The London quotation rose to $404.5 (£260) per oz in August, but declined to $367 (£219) in December.

During January 1997 the platinum market remained depressed, and in early February the London price fell to US $349.5 (£217) per oz, its lowest level, in terms of US currency, since March 1993. However, in late February 1997 the platinum price increased to $393.5 (£242) per oz, in response to fears of an interruption to previously plentiful supplies of Russian PGM, owing to a threatened strike at Noril'sk and to Russia's failure to settle the terms of its annual agreement to supply platinum and palladium to Japan. In May, amid continuing delays in the release of Russian platinum exports, the metal's price rose above $400 per oz. In early June the London quotation surged to $497 (£305) per oz: the highest dollar price of platinum since 1990 (the palladium price, meanwhile, rose to $240 per oz, its highest level since 1980). In July 1997, following reports that Russian sales had resumed, the platinum price eased to $396 (£235) per oz.

Rice (*Oryza*)

Rice is an annual grass belonging to the same family as (and having many similar characteristics to) small grains such as wheat, oats, rye and barley. It is principally the semi-aquatic nature of rice that distinguishes it from other grain species, and this is an important factor in determining its place of origin. In Africa and Asia, unmilled rice is referred to as 'paddy', although 'rough' rice is the common appellation in the West. After removal of the outer husk, it is called 'brown' rice. After the grain is milled to varying degrees to remove the bran layers, it is called 'milled' rice. Since rice loses 30%–40% of its weight in the milling process, most rice is traded in the milled form to save shipping expenses.

Production of Paddy Rice ('000 metric tons)

	1994	1995
World total	536,906*	553,584*
Africa	14,169*	14,148*
Leading African producers		
Congo, Dem. Repub.	414	425
Côte d'Ivoire	988	1,045
Egypt	4,583	4,789†
Guinea	532	532
Madagascar	2,360	2,596†
Mali	469	458*
Nigeria	2,427	2,548
Sierra Leone	405	284
Tanzania	614	723
Leading non-African producers		
Bangladesh	25,248	26,513†
China, People's Repub.	175,933	185,226
India	121,559	121,562†
Indonesia	46,641	49,860
Thailand	21,111	21,130
Viet Nam	23,528	24,964

* FAO estimate. † Unofficial figure.

There are two cultivated species of rice, *Oryza sativa* and *O. glaberrima*. *O. sativa*, which originated in tropical Asia, is widely grown in tropical and semi-tropical areas, while the cultivation of *O. glaberrima* is limited to the high rainfall zone of west Africa. In Africa rice is grown mainly as a subsistence crop. Methods of cultivation differ from region to region and yields tend to be low by world standards. Rice is a staple food in several African countries, including Madagascar, Tanzania and some west coast countries.

World rice production is dominated by the Asian region (which produces more than 90% of the world's total), and expanded rapidly in the 1980s. African rice production accounts for less than 3% of total world output. As the bulk of rice production is consumed mainly in the producing countries, international trade accounts for less than 5% of world output. The market is subject to great volatility and fluctuating prices. Less than 1% of the African rice crop enters international trade and more than 90% of African rice exports come from Egypt. Africa, especially in recent years, has been a substantial net importer of rice, although the volume growth in imports has been held in check by the impact of higher world rice prices on the depleted foreign exchange reserves of many African importing countries. The major African importers include Côte d'Ivoire, Nigeria, Guinea, Sierra Leone, Senegal and Madagascar, which ranks as the world's largest rice consumer per caput. However, following the completion in 1995 of the rehabilitation of its main rice-growing areas, Madagascar was expected to become self-sufficient in rice in 1996.

Africa, and especially west African countries (where rice is a staple food of 40% of the population), imports large quantities of rice from Thailand and the USA, the two major world exporters. The volume of rice imports by west African states rose by more than 5% annually during 1980-92, with consumption exceeding 9.5m. tons in the latter year.

Because rice is a relatively new crop to the region, suitable high-yielding varieties (HYV) have yet to be propagated. The development of HYV is among the activities of the 17-member West Africa Rice Development Association (WARDA), formed by the producing countries in 1970. Based in Bouaké, Côte d'Ivoire, WARDA maintains regional research stations in Côte d'Ivoire, Nigeria, Senegal and Sierra Leone, from which it conducts scientific research on crop improvement and provides technical assistance, with the aim of advancing the region towards eventual self-sufficiency in rice production.

The world's leading exporter of rice in recent years has been Thailand. The average value of Thailand's exports of milled or semi-milled rice declined from US $277 per metric ton in 1992 to $261 per ton in 1993, but rose to $321 per ton in 1994.

Export Price Index for Rice (base: 1980 = 100)

	Average	Highest month(s)	Lowest month(s)
1985	66		
1990	74		
1994	90	111 (Jan.)	71 (Oct.)
1995	84	98 (Oct.)	73 (March)
1996	93	97 (July)	88 (Dec.)

Sisal *(Agave sisalana)*

Sisal, which is not indigenous to Africa, was introduced to Tanganyika (now mainland Tanzania) from Mexico at the end of the 19th century. The leaf tissue of this plant yields hard, flexible fibres which are suitable for making rope and twine, cord matting, padding and upholstery. Sisal accounts for two-thirds of world production of hard fibres, and about three-quarters of sisal consumption is for agricultural twine. World output of sisal and other hard fibres has generally declined in recent years, owing to competition from nylons and petroleum-based synthetics (in particular, polypropylene harvest twine, which is stronger than sisal and less labour-intensive to produce), although the intensity of the competition and the success of hard fibres depend on fluctuations in the price of petroleum.

Production of Sisal ('000 metric tons)

	1994	1995
World total	294*	287*
Africa	85*	90*
Leading African producers		
Kenya	34	34*
Madagascar	17	18*
Tanzania	26	30*
Leading non-African producers		
Brazil	131	118
Mexico	36*	37*

* FAO estimate. † Unofficial figure.

In 1970 Tanzania, whose sisal is generally regarded as being of the best quality, was overtaken as the world's leading producer by Brazil. The nationalization of more than one-half of Tanzania's sisal estates in 1976, together with low prices, inefficient management and lack of equipment and spare parts, contributed to the decline of the Tanzanian crop. During the 1980s, however, the government sought to revive the industry by returning some state-owned estates to private or co-operative ownership. In 1992 the government announced that it was to return all its estates to the private sector. However, despite the introduction of a replanting programme aimed at doubling production by the mid-1990s, prospects have been overshadowed by the longer-term outlook for sisal (according to FAO projections, world demand has been falling at a rate of 7% per year). Efforts are being made, however, to create new uses in such products as specialized papers and surgical bandages. With the decline of the Tanzanian sisal sector, Kenya has emerged as Brazil's main rival, although it exports only fibre, as it has no processing industry.

Although sisal producers operate a quota system, in an attempt to improve the pricing structure of the crop, the average price of sisal was in general decline between the early 1980s and the early 1990s, as relatively stable prices for petroleum allowed polypropylene to regain its competitiveness.

Export Price Index for Sisal (base: 1980 = 100)

	Average	Highest month(s)	Lowest month(s)
1985	74		
1990	89		
1994	85	86 (Jan.–July)	83 (Oct.–Dec.)
1995	91	102 (Dec.)	85 (Jan.)
1996	116	119 (July–Nov.)	106 (Jan.)

Two main grades of sisal are exported to Europe from eastern Africa. The average import price of the less expensive grade at European ports declined from US $639 per metric ton in 1991 to $479 per ton in 1992. On a monthly basis, the lowest average price per ton in 1992 was $438 in October (compared with more than $700 in the early months of 1991). The monthly average recovered to $628 per ton in June 1993.

Sugar

Sugar is a sweet crystalline substance, which may be derived from the juices of various plants. Chemically, the basis of sugar is sucrose, one of a group of soluble carbohydrates which are important dietary sources of energy. It can be obtained from trees, including the maple and certain palms, but virtually all manufactured sugar comes from two plants, sugar beet (*Beta vulgaris*) and sugar cane, a giant perennial grass of the genus *Saccharum*.

Sugar cane, found in tropical areas, grows to a height of up to 5 m. The plant is native to Polynesia, but its distribution is now widespread. It is not necessary to plant cane every season as, if the root of the plant is left in the ground, it will grow again in the following year. This practice, known as 'ratooning', may be continued for as long as three years, when yields begin to decline. Cane is ready for cutting 12–24 months after planting, depending on local conditions. Much of the world's sugar cane is still cut by hand, but rising costs are hastening the change-over to mechanical harvesting. The cane is cut as close as possible to the ground, and the top leaves, which may be used as cattle fodder, are removed.

After cutting, the cane is loaded by hand or by machine into trucks or trailers and towed directly to a factory for processing. Sugar cane deteriorates quickly after it has been cut and should be processed as quickly as possible. At the factory the cane passes first through shredding knives or crushing rollers, which break up the hard rind and expose the inner fibre, and then to squeezing rollers, where the crushed cane is subjected to high pressure and sprayed with water. The resulting juice is heated and lime is added for clarification and the removal of impurities. The clean juice is then concentrated in evaporators. This thickened juice is next boiled in steam-heated vacuum pans until a mixture or 'massecuite' of sugar crystals and 'mother syrup' is produced. The massecuite is then spun in centrifugal machines to separate the sugar crystals (raw cane sugar) from the residual syrup (cane molasses).

The production of beet sugar follows the same process, except that the juice is extracted by osmotic diffusion. Its manufacture produces white sugar crystals which do not require further refining. In most producing countries, it is consumed domestically, although the European Union (EU), which accounts for about 15% of total world sugar production, is a net exporter of white refined sugar. Beet sugar accounts for more than one-third of world production. Production data for sugar cane and sugar beet cover generally all crops harvested, except crops grown explicitly for feed. The third table covers the production of raw sugar by the centrifugal process. In the early 1990s global output of non-centrifugal sugar (i.e. produced from sugar cane which has not undergone centrifugation) was about 12m.-13m. tons per year.

Most of the raw cane sugar produced in the world is sent to refineries outside the country of origin, unless the sugar is for local consumption. Cuba, Thailand, Brazil and India are among the few cane-producers that export part of their output as refined sugar. The refining process furtherpurifies the sugar crystals and eventually results in finished products of various grades, such as granulated, icing or castor sugar. The ratio of refined to raw sugar is usually about 0.9:1.

As well as providing sugar, quantities of cane are grown in some countries for seed, feed, fresh consumption, the manufacture of alcohol and other uses. Molasses may be used as cattle feed or fermented to produce alcoholic beverages for human consumption, such as rum, a distilled spirit manufactured in Caribbean countries. Sugar cane juice may be used to produce ethyl alcohol (ethanol). This chemical can be mixed with petroleum derivatives to produce fuel for motor vehicles. The steep rise in the price of petroleum after 1973 made the large-scale conversion of sugar cane into alcohol economically attractive (particularly to developing nations), especially as sugar, unlike petroleum, is a renewable source of energy. Several countries developed alcohol production by this means in order to reduce petroleum imports and to support cane growers. The blended fuel used in cars is known as 'gasohol', 'alcogas' or 'green petrol'. The pioneer in this field was Brazil, which established the largest 'gasohol' production programme in the world. By the late 1980s ethanol accounted for about one-half of the fuel consumption of Brazilian motorists. In Africa, 'gasohol' plants have been planned or established in Kenya, Malawi, South Africa, Tanzania and Zambia.

After the milling of sugar, the cane has dry fibrous remnants known as bagasse, which is usually burned as fuel in sugar mills but can be pulped and used for making fibreboard, particle board and most grades of paper. As the costs of imported wood pulp have risen, cane-growing regions have turned increasingly to the manufacture of paper from bagasse. A paper mill based on this process has been established in South Africa. In view of rising energy costs, some countries (such as Mauritius) are encouraging the use of bagasse as fuel for electricity production to save on foreign exchange from imports of oil. Another by-product, cachaza (which had formerly been discarded), is now being exploited as an animal feed.

In recent years sugar has encountered increased competition from other sweeteners, including maize-based products, such as isoglucose (a form of high-fructose corn syrup or HFCS), and chemical additives, such as saccharine, aspartame and xylitol. Consumption of HFCS in the USA was equivalent to about 42% of the country's sugar consumption in the late 1980s, while in Japan and the Republic of Korea HFCS accounted for 19% and 25%, respectively, of domestic sweetener use. Aspartame (APM) was the most widely used high-intensity artificial sweetener in the late 1980s, although its market dominance was expected to be challenged during the 1990s by sucralose, which is about 600

Production of Sugar Cane ('000 metric tons)

	1994	1995
World total	1,082,722*	1,160,006*
Africa	70,721*	73,107*
Leading African producers		
Egypt	13,822	13,827
Kenya	3,780*	4,300*
Madagascar	1,980	1,980*
Malawi	2,000*	2,200*
Mauritius	5,000	5,200*
Réunion	1,656	1,817
South Africa‡	15,683	16,782
Sudan	5,000*	4,800*
Swaziland	3,786	3,798
Tanzania	1,530*	1,410*
Zimbabwe	3,420	3,943†
Leading non-African producers		
Brazil	292,070	301,998
China, People's Repub.	60,927	65,417
Cuba	39,000*	36,000*
India	227,060	259,490
Mexico	40,539	42,562
Pakistan	44,427	47,168
Thailand	37,823	60,858

* FAO estimate. † Unofficial figure.

‡ Cane crushed for sugar.

Production of Sugar Beets ('000 metric tons)

	1994	1995
World total	255,144*	270,595*
Africa	4,318*	3,905*
Leading African producer		
Morocco	3,144	2,717
Leading non-African producers		
France	29,036	30,359
Germany	24,211	26,077
Russia	13,946	19,072
Ukraine	28,138	29,650
USA	28,897	25,425

* FAO estimate.

times as sweet as sugar (compared with 200–300 times for other intense sweeteners) and is more resistant to chemical deterioration than aspartame. In the late 1980s research was being conducted in the USA to formulate means of synthesizing thaumatin, a substance derived from the fruit of a west African plant, *Thaumatoccus daniellii*, which is several thousand times as sweet as sugar. If, as is widely predicted, thaumatin can be commercially produced by the year 2000, it could obtain a substantial share of the markets for both sugar and artificial sweeteners.

South Africa is the principal producer and exporter of sugar in sub-Saharan Africa. In the mid-1990s South Africa ranked as the world's seventh largest sugar exporter. In recent years, however, South Africa has been encountering increased competition from neighbouring countries, whose production costs are only about one-third of those of South Africa, in particular Swaziland and Zimbabwe. It has been forecast that by the end of the 1990s one-third of domestic demand in South Africa will be supplied by these sources. Swaziland is continental Africa's second largest sugar exporter. The majority of the country's sales of sugar are to countries of the EU, under the terms of quota agreements.

Sugar is the staple product in the economies of Mauritius and Réunion, although output is vulnerable to climatic conditions, as both islands are subject to cyclones. In Mauritius, where an estimated 90% (84,400 ha) of cultivated land is devoted to sugar production, sugar sales accounted for more than 88% of the island's export revenue in 1996 (excluding exports from the Export Processing Zone). In Réunion almost one-half of the island's 63,050 ha of cultivable land is planted with sugar cane, and sales of sugar provided 63% of export income in 1995.

The Mozambique sugar industry, formerly the country's primary source of foreign exchange, is experiencing the effects of many years of disruption and neglect. Plans to rehabilitate production at the country's six sugar complexes were pending in 1995, when only two of these locations were operational. Substantial foreign investment will be needed to revitalize the industry after more than 20 years of internal guerrilla conflict. Sugar is Malawi's third most important export commodity (after tobacco and tea), providing 7.4% of export earnings (excluding re-exports) in 1994. The development of the sugar sector in Tanzania was undergoing expansion in the mid-1990s, with the aim of reducing reliance on imports from Malawi and Zambia. Madagascar was expected to achieve self-sufficiency in sugar in 1996.

In Sudan one of the world's largest single sugar projects was inaugurated in 1981 at Kenana, south of Khartoum. The Kenana Sugar Co (in which the Sudan government has a 50% share), comprising an estate and processing facilities, has been instrumental in the elimination of sugar import costs, which were, until the mid-1980s, Sudan's single largest import item after petroleum. Sugar cane grows wild throughout Nigeria, although the country's sugar industry remains largely undeveloped. However, six sugar complexes are planned, and it is hoped that self-sufficiency in sugar will be achieved by the year 2000.

The first International Sugar Agreement (ISA) was negotiated in 1958, and its economic provisions operated until 1961. A second ISA did not come into operation until 1969. It included quota arrangements and associated provisions for regulating the price of sugar traded on the open market, and established the International Sugar Organization (ISO) to administer the agreement. However, the USA and the six original members of the EC did not participate in the ISA, and, following its expiry in 1974, it was replaced by a purely administrative interim agreement, which remained operational until the finalization of a third ISA, which took effect in 1978. The new agreement's implementation was supervised by an International Sugar Council (ISC), which was empowered to establish price ranges for sugar-trading and to operate a system of quotas and special sugar stocks. Owing to the reluctance of the USA and European Community (now EU) countries (which were not a party to the agreement) to accept export controls, the ISO ultimately lost most of its power to regulate the market, and since 1984 the activities of the organization have been restricted to recording statistics and providing a forum for discussion between producers and consumers. Subsequent ISA, without effective regulatory powers, have been in operation since 1985. (For detailed information on the successive agreements, see *Africa South of the Sahara 1991*.)

Production of Centrifugal Sugar (raw value, '000 metric tons)

	1994	1995
World total	110,915*	119,704*
Africa	7,222*	7,450*
Leading African producers		
Egypt	1,099	1,132
Ethiopia	132†	139†
Kenya	330	418†
Malawi	203	222
Mauritius	525	540
Morocco	479	477†
Réunion	177	195
South Africa	1,668	1,667
Sudan	510†	549†
Swaziland	488	482
Zambia	158†	151†
Zimbabwe	507†	512†
Leading non-African producers		
Australia	5,010†	4,901†
Brazil	12,618†	13,595†
China (incl. Taiwan)	6,822†	7,236†
Cuba	4,024†	3,400†
France	4,988	4,595
Germany	3,672	3,805
India	11,660	16,345
Mexico	3,549	4,274
Thailand	4,009†	5,571†
Ukraine	3,342	3,839
USA	7,297	6,723

* FAO estimate. † Unofficial figure.

Special arrangements for exports of African sugar exist in the successive Lomé Conventions, in operation since 1975, between the EU and a group of African, Caribbean and Pacific (ACP) countries, whereby a special Protocol on sugar, forming part of each Convention, requires the EU to import specified quantities of raw sugar annually from ACP countries.

In tandem with world output of cane and beet sugars, stock levels are an important factor in determining the prices at which sugar is traded internationally. These stocks, which were at relatively low levels in the late 1980s, increased significantly in the early 1990s, owing partly to the disruptive effects of the Gulf War on demand in the Middle East (normally a major sugar-consuming area), and also as a result of substantially increased production in Mexico and the Far East. Additionally, the output of beet sugar was expected to continue rising, as a result of substantial producers' subsidies within the EU, which, together with Australia, has been increasing the areas under sugar cane and beet. World sugar stocks were reduced in the 1993/94 trading year (September–August). However, record crops in Brazil, India and Thailand led to an increased level of sugar stocks in 1994/95. World sugar stocks continued to rise in 1995/96, and in August 1996 were forecast to advance further in 1996/97 and 1997/98. In 1993/94 world-wide consumption of raw sugar totalled 113.3m. tons, resulting in a supply deficit of 2.9m. tons. In 1994/95 higher levels of output and of consumption, at 114.5m. tons, produced a supply surplus of 1.6m. tons. The supply surplus in 1995/96, when consumption totalled 118.3m. tons, rose to 3.4m. tons, while forecasts for 1996/97, published in August 1996, projected world consumption totalling 120.6m. tons, generating a surplus in supplies of 4.2m. tons.

Most of the world's sugar output is traded at fixed prices under long-term agreements. On the free market, however, sugar prices often fluctuate with extreme volatility.

Export Price Index for Sugar (base: 1980 = 100)

	Average	Highest month(s)	Lowest month(s)
1985	15		
1990	45		
1994	43	52 (Dec.)	37 (Jan.)
1995	48	53 (Jan.)	42 (Sept.)
1996	43	46 (Feb., March, July)	38 (Nov., Dec.)

In February 1992 the import price of raw cane sugar on the London market was only US $193.0 (equivalent to £107.9

sterling) per metric ton, its lowest level, in terms of US currency, since November 1987. The London price of sugar advanced to $324.9 (£211.9) per ton in May 1993, following predictions of a world sugar deficit in 1992/93. Concurrently, sugar prices in New York were at their highest levels for three years. The London sugar price declined to $237.2 (£157.9) per ton in August 1993, but increased to $370.6 (£237.4) in December 1994.

The rise in sugar prices continued in January 1995, when the London quotation for raw sugar reached US $378.1 (£243.2) per ton, its highest level, in dollar terms, since early 1990. Meanwhile, the London price of white sugar was $426.5 (£274.4) per ton, the highest quotation for four-and-a-half years. The surge in the sugar market was partly a response to forecasts of a supply deficit in the 1994/95 season. Prices later eased, and in April 1995 raw sugar traded in London at $326.0 (£202.1) per ton. The price recovered to $373.1 (£235.6) per ton in June, but retreated to $281.5 (£179.4) in September. At the end of the year it stood at $311.5 (£200.6) per ton.

During the early months of 1996 the London price of raw sugar reached about US $330 per ton. In May the price was reduced to $262.9 (£173.3) per ton, but in July it rose to $321.4 (£206.3), despite continued forecasts of a significant sugar surplus in 1995/96. The sugar price fell to $256.3 (£156.4) per ton in early December and ended the year at $271.7.

In January 1997 the price of raw sugar declined to only US $250.8 (£154.0) per ton, but in April it reached $283.8 (£174.5).

The Group of Latin American and Caribbean Sugar Exporting Countries (GEPLACEA), with a membership of 22 Latin American and Caribbean countries, together with the Philippines, and representing about 66% of world cane production and 45% of sugar exports, complements the activities of the ISO (comprising 46 countries, including EU members, in 1996) as a forum for co-operation and research. At the end of 1992 the USA withdrew from the ISO, following a disagreement over the formulation of members' financial contributions. The USA had previously provided about 9% of the ISO's annual budget.

Tea (*Camellia sinensis*)

Tea is a beverage made by infusing in boiling water the dried young leaves and unopened leaf-buds of the tea plant, an evergreen shrub or small tree. Black and green tea are the most common finished products. The former accounts for the bulk of the world's supply and is associated with machine manufacture and, generally, the plantation system, which guarantees an adequate supply of leaf to the factory. The latter, produced mainly in China and Japan, is grown mostly on smallholdings, and much of it is consumed locally. There are two main varieties of tea, the China and the Assam, although hybrids may be obtained, such as Darjeeling. Wherever possible, data on production and trade relate to made tea, i.e. dry, manufactured tea. Where figures have been reported in terms of green (unmanufactured) leaf, appropriate allowances have been made to convert the reported amounts to the approximate equivalent weight of made tea.

Total recorded tea exports by producing countries achieved successive records in each of the years 1983–90. World exports (excluding transactions between former Soviet republics) declined in 1991 and 1992, but recovered to an estimated 1,152,000 tons in 1993. In 1994, however, export volume fell to an estimated 1,033,000 tons, before recovering to an estimated 1,080,000 tons in 1995 and an estimated 1,103,000 tons in 1996. India (the world's largest consumer) and Sri Lanka have traditionally been the two leading tea exporters, with approximately equal sales, but the quantity which they jointly supply has remained fairly stable (350,000 – 425,000 tons per year in 1977–96), so their share of the world tea trade has been declining. During the 1960s these two countries together exported more than two-thirds of all the tea sold by producing countries, but in 1996 the proportion was 34.8%. From the mid-1980s, India and Sri Lanka vied for position as the leading tea exporter. In 1989, however, the People's Republic of China (whose sales include a large proportion of green tea) was the second largest exporter, ahead of Sri Lanka. From 1990 until 1995, when it was displaced by Kenya (see below), Sri Lanka ranked as the main exporting country, and since 1992 China's tea exports have exceeded those of India. Exports of tea by

Production of Made Tea ('000 metric tons)

	1995	1996
World total	2,517.5*	2,610.6*
Africa	365.2*	384.0*
Leading African producers		
Kenya	244.5	257.2
Malawi	34.5	37.2
Rwanda	4.5*	9.0*
South Africa	10.9	9.1
Tanzania	23.7	19.8
Uganda	12.7	17.4
Zimbabwe	15.7	16.8
Leading non-African producers		
China, People's Repub.[1]	588.4	593.4
India[2]	753.9*	780.0*
Indonesia[3]	145.4	144.0*
Japan[4]	84.8	88.7
Sri Lanka	246.4	258.4
Turkey	104.7	114.5

* Provisional.

[1] Mainly green tea (413,784 tons in 1995; 422,252 tons in 1996).

[2] Including a small quantity of green tea (8,172 tons in 1995; about 8,000 tons in 1996).

[3] Including green tea (about 30,000 tons in 1995; about 30,000 tons in 1996).

[4] All green tea.

Source: International Tea Committee, *Supplement to Annual Bulletin of Statistics 1996*.

African producers accounted for about one-quarter of world trade during the early 1990s, achieving successive record shipments of 330,041 tons in 1995 and 340,395 tons in 1996, when African sales accounted for 30.8% of the world tea trade.

One of the fastest-growing exporters is Kenya, which ranked fourth in the world during 1975–92. In 1993 Kenya became the world's third largest tea supplier, and in 1994 its exports exceeded those of China, establishing it as the world's second largest exporter of tea. Kenya became the principal world exporter of tea in 1995 and again in 1996, when it accounted for 22.1% of the international tea trade and for almost 72% of African tea exports. The continuing expansion of Kenya's tea exports has followed the conservation of tea supplies by India to satisfy rising domestic consumption. Kenya has replaced India as the United Kingdom's principal supplier, providing about 40% of British tea imports. Kenya's tea sales provided 24.2% of its total export receipts in 1993, making tea the country's most valuable export crop. In 1989 a total of 84,400 ha in Kenya were planted with tea, of which almost 57,000 ha represented smallholder operations.

Malawi is Africa's second largest producer and exporter of tea. Its exports in 1996 were estimated at 34,000 tons, accounting for almost 10% of all African exports. Prior to the Amin regime and the nationalization of tea plantations in 1972, neighbouring Uganda was second only to Kenya among African producers. Uganda's tea exports were negligible by the early 1980s, but, following agreements between tea companies and the subsequent Ugandan governments, exports were resumed. There has been a sustained recovery since the early 1990s; in 1994 Uganda's exports of tea were 10,971 tons, the highest annual total since 1977. Exports in 1995 totalled 10,682 tons, and in 1996 Uganda's overseas sales of tea rose to 14,982 tons. However, Uganda's role in east African tea production continues to be eclipsed by Tanzania, whose level of exports during the 1980s ranged between 10,000–15,000 tons annually. These sales, however, advanced to 19,387 tons in 1993, declined to 18,570 tons in 1994 and rose again to a record 20,511 tons in 1995, retreating to 18,443 tons in 1996. Zimbabwe was Africa's fifth largest exporter of tea in 1996, exporting 10,413 tons in that year (compared with a record 12,768 tons in 1989, when it ranked third among African tea-exporters). Tea has traditionally been a significant component of exports from Burundi and Rwanda: these sales were estimated at 7,000 tons and 3,500 tons, respectively, in 1996. Rwanda's tea industry has been severely disrupted by recent civil unrest.

For many years the United Kingdom was the largest single importer of tea. However, the country's annual consumption of tea per person, which amounted to 4.55 kg in 1958, has declined in recent years, averaging 2.56 kg in 1990–92, 2.62 kg in 1991–93, 2.60 kg in 1992–94 and 2.53 kg in 1993–95. A similar trend was observed in other developed countries, while consumption and imports have expanded significantly in the developing countries (notably Middle East countries) and, particularly, in the USSR, which in 1990 accounted for 21.8% of world imports, having overtaken the United Kingdom in 1989 as the world's principal tea importer. This trend was interrupted in 1991, however, by a fall in Middle Eastern (particularly Iraqi) imports, as a result of the Gulf War. Internal economic factors during 1992 caused a sharp decline in tea imports by the successor republics of the USSR; in that year these purchases (excluding inter-republican trade) fell to an estimated 76,100 tons, from 166,000 tons in 1991. As a result, the United Kingdom regained its position as the leading tea importer in 1992. In 1993, the former Soviet republics (whose own tea production had fallen sharply) again displaced the United Kingdom as the major importer. In 1994 the United Kingdom was the principal importing country. In 1995, however, imports by the former USSR, at 162,349 tons, exceeded those of the United Kingdom. These republics were again the major tea importers in 1996, accounting for an estimated 172,000 tons, representing 15.4% of world tea trade. In that year the United Kingdom imported 148,452 tons (13.3%), followed by Pakistan, with 110,703 tons (9.9%).

Export Price Index for Tea (base: 1980 = 100)

	Average	Highest month(s)	Lowest month(s)
1985	112		
1990	127		
1994	206	224 (Jan.)	189 (Dec.)
1995	181	204 (Dec.)	162 (July)
1996	198	207 (Dec.)	183 (July)

Much of the tea traded internationally is sold by auction, first in the exporting country and then again in the importing country. At the weekly London auctions five categories of tea are offered for sale: 'low medium' (based on a medium Malawi tea), 'medium' (based on a medium Assam and Kenyan tea), 'good medium' (representing an above-average East African tea), 'good' (referring to teas of above-average standard) and (since April 1994) 'best available'. The average price of all grades of tea sold at London auctions increased from £1,047 sterling per metric ton in 1991 to £1,133 per ton in 1992 and to £1,238 per ton in 1993, but fell to £1,192 per ton in 1994 and to £1,036 per ton in 1995. The annual average price in 1995 was the lowest since 1988. During 1992 the monthly average ranged from £916 per ton in February to £1,494 in December. It advanced to £1,564 per ton in January 1993, declined to £1,100 in June and recovered to £1,256 in November. The average was £1,102 per ton in January 1994, but rose to £1,284 in June and September. Quotations then moved generally lower, and in July 1995 the average London tea price was only £907.5 per ton, its lowest monthly level since August 1988. The monthly average increased to £1,170.5 per ton in December 1995, but fell to £1,031 in July 1996. Based on country of origin, the highest-priced tea at London auctions during 1989–94 was that from Rwanda, which realized an average of £1,613 per ton in the latter year. The quantity of tea sold at these auctions declined from 43,658 tons in 1990 to 24,282 tons in 1995.

In 1992 the price of 'medium' tea at London auctions increased from £860 per ton in February to £1,600 in December. The quotation rose to £1,650 per ton in January 1993, but fell to £1,000 in June. Medium tea was traded at £1,250 per ton in October, but the price eased to £1,020 in November and ended the year at £1,140. The London price of this grade was reduced to £1,030 per ton in January 1994, but reached £1,250 in late February and again in June and July. By the end of the year it had declined to £1,060 per ton.

The international market for tea remained depressed during the first half of 1995. At the London auctions the price of medium tea fell to £890 per ton in March, although it recovered to £950 in May. A further slump ensued, and in September the price of this grade was reduced to only £780 per ton, its lowest level, even in nominal terms (i.e. without taking inflation into account), since 1976. Medium tea rose to £1,150 per ton in November and December 1995.

In January 1996 the London price of medium tea again reached £1,150 per ton, but by late February it had eased to £1,000. The price recovered to £1,120 per ton in late March, and was again at this level in April and May. Tea prices subsequently moved lower, and in July the quotation for medium tea stood at £930 per ton. The London price of this grade rose to £1,160 per ton in December.

The price of medium tea declined to £1,030 per ton in January 1997. Following reports that drought had reduced the crop in Kenya (which specialises in medium tea), the London quotation for this grade increased in May to £1,500 per ton, its highest level since February 1993. Prices later eased, and at the end of June 1997 medium tea traded at £1,200 per ton.

An International Tea Agreement (ITA), signed in 1933 by the governments of India, Ceylon (now Sri Lanka) and the Netherlands East Indies (now Indonesia), established the International Tea Committee (ITC), based in London, as an administrative body. Although ITA operations ceased after 1955, the ITC has continued to function as a statistical and information centre. In 1994 there were seven producer/exporter members (the tea boards or associations of Kenya, Malawi, Zimbabwe, India, Indonesia, Bangladesh and Sri Lanka), four consumer members and four associate members.

In 1969 the FAO Consultative Committee on Tea was formed and an exporters' group, meeting under this committee's auspices, set export quotas in an attempt to stabilize tea prices. These quotas have applied since 1970 but are generally regarded as too liberal to have any significant effect on prices. The perishability of tea makes the effective operation of a buffer stock very difficult, while African countries are opposed to quota arrangements and are committed to the maximum expansion of tea cultivation. India, while not favouring the revival of a formal ITA to regulate supplies and prices, has advocated greater co-operation between producers to regulate the market. The International Tea Promotion Association (ITPA), founded in 1979 and based in Nairobi, Kenya, comprises eight countries (excluding, however, India and Sri Lanka), accounting for about 35% of the world's exports of black tea. In April 1995 representatives of the tea industries of Bangladesh, China, India, Indonesia, Iran, Sri Lanka and Malawi announced their intention of forming an association of tea producers. It was hoped that Kenya would subsequently join.

Tin

The world's main tin deposits occur in the equatorial zones of Asia and Africa, in central South America and in Australia. Cassiterite is the only economically important tin-bearing mineral, and it is generally associated with tungsten, silver and tantalum minerals. There is a clear association of cassiterite with igneous rocks of granitic composition, and 'primary' cassiterite deposits occur as disseminations, or in veins and fissures in or around granites. If the primary deposits are eroded, as by rivers, cassiterite may be concentrated and deposited in 'secondary' sedimentary deposits. These secondary deposits form the bulk of the world's tin reserves. The ore is treated, generally by gravity method or flotation, to produce concentrates prior to smelting.

Tin owes its special place in industry to its unique combination of properties: low melting point, the ability to form alloys with most other metals, resistance to corrosion, non-toxicity and good appearance. Its main uses are in tinplate (about 40% of world tin consumption), in alloys (tin-lead solder, bronze, brass, pewter, bearing and type metal), and in chemical compounds (in paints, plastics, medicines, coatings and as fungicides and insecticides).

The output of tin concentrates from Nigeria, formerly Africa's main producer, has been in decline since the late 1960s, and Zaire's production has also fallen. Depressed conditions in the world tin market led, in 1990–91, to the suspension of open-cast tin mining in Namibia, formerly a significant regional producer. Following several years of increasing losses, tin production in Zimbabwe ceased in 1994. In 1992 and 1993, according to the US Bureau of Mines, Africa accounted for only 1.6% of world output of tin concentrates.

Over the period 1956–85, much of the world's tin production and trade was covered by successive international agreements, administered by the International Tin Council (ITC), based in London. The main object of each successive International Tin

Production of Tin Concentrates (tin content, metric tons)

	1992	1993*
World total (excl. USA)	178,365	178,207
Africa	3,419	2,796
Leading African producers		
Burundi	110*	50
Nigeria	186*	186
Rwanda	500*	400
South Africa	582	600
Zaire	1,020	700
Zimbabwe	950*	800
Leading non-African producers		
Australia†	6,400	8,042
Bolivia	16,516	18,634
Brazil	27,500	25,900
China, People's Repub.	43,000*	46,000
Indonesia	29,400	29,000
Malaysia	14,339	10,384
Peru	10,195	13,700
Portugal	3,000	5,300
Russia	6,000*	5,000
Thailand	11,484	7,000

* Estimated production.
† Excluding the tin content of copper-tin and tin-tungsten concentrates.
Source: US Bureau of Mines.

Agreement (ITA), of which there were six, was to stabilize prices within an agreed range by using a buffer stock to regulate the supply of tin. (For detailed information on the last of these agreements, see *Africa South of the Sahara 1991*.) The buffer stock was financed by producing countries, with voluntary contributions by some consuming countries. 'Floor' and 'ceiling' prices were fixed, and market operations conducted by a buffer stock manager who intervened, as necessary, to maintain prices within these agreed limits. For added protection, the ITA provided for the imposition of export controls if the 'floor' price was being threatened. The ITA was effectively terminated in October 1985, when the ITC's buffer stock manager informed the London Metal Exchange (LME) that he no longer had the funds with which to support the tin market. The factors underlying the collapse of the ITA included its limited membership (Bolivia and the USA, leading producing and consuming countries, were not signatories) and the accumulation of tin stocks which resulted from the widespread circumvention of producers' quota limits. The LME responded by suspending trading in tin, leaving the ITC owing more than £500m. to some 36 banks, tin smelters and metals traders. The crisis was eventually resolved in March 1990, when a financial settlement of £182.5m. was agreed between the ITC and its creditors. The ITC was itself dissolved in July.

These events lent new significance to the activities of the Association of Tin Producing Countries (ATPC), founded in 1983 by Malaysia, Indonesia and Thailand and later joined by Bolivia, Nigeria, Australia and Zaire (now the Democratic Republic of the Congo). Prior to the withdrawal of Australia and Thailand in 1996 (see below), members of the ATPC, which is based in Kuala Lumpur, Malaysia, accounted for about 45% of world production. The ATPC, which was intended to operate as a complement to the ITC and not in competition with it, introduced export quotas for tin for the year from 1 March 1987. Brazil and the People's Republic of China agreed to co-operate with the ATPC in implementing these supply restrictions, which have been renegotiated to cover succeeding years, with the aim of raising prices and reducing the level of surplus stocks. The ATPC membership has also taken stringent measures to control smuggling. Brazil and China (jointly accounting for almost 40% of world tin production) both initially held observer status at the ATPC (China became a full member in 1994, but Brazil, although it was expected to accede to full membership in 1995, decided to remain as an observer—together with Peru and Viet Nam). China and Brazil agreed to participate in the export quota arrangements, for which the ATPC has no formal powers of enforcement.

The ATPC members' combined export quota was fixed at 95,849 tons for 1991, and was reduced to 87,091 tons for 1992. However, the substantial level of world tin stocks (which stood at 38,200 tons at the end of 1992), combined with depressed demand, led to mine closures and reductions in output, with the result that members' exports in 1991 were below quota entitlements. The continuing depletion of stock levels led to a forecast by the ATPC, in May 1992, that export quotas would be removed in 1994 if these disposals continued at their current rate. The ATPC had previously set a target level for stocks of 20,000 tons, representing about six weeks of world tin consumption. Projections that world demand for tin would remain at about 160,000 tons annually, together with continued optimism about the rate of stock disposals, led the ATPC to increase its members' 1993 export quota to 89,700 tons. The persistence, however, of high levels of annual tin exports by China (estimated to have totalled 30,000 tons in 1993 and 1994, compared with its ATPC quota of 20,000 tons), together with sales of surplus defence stocks of tin by the US government, necessitated a reduction of the quota to 78,000 tons for 1994. In late 1993 prices had fallen to a 20-year 'low' and world tin stocks were estimated at 38,000-40,000 tons, owing partly to the non-observance of quota limits by Brazil and China, as well as to increased production by non-ATPC members. World tin stocks resumed their rise in early 1994, reaching 48,000 tons in June. However, the effects of reduced output, from both ATPC and non-ATPC producing countries, helped to reduce stock levels to 41,000 tons at the end of December. The continued implementation of output restrictions by ATPC members during 1995 resulted in an estimated supply shortfall in that year of 22,500 tons. In May 1996, when world tin stocks were estimated to have been reduced to 20,000 tons, the ATPC suspended its quota arrangements and announced that it was to consider their formal abolition at a meeting to be held in September. Shortly before the meeting was convened, however, Australia and Thailand announced their withdrawal from the ATPC, on the grounds that the organizations's activities had ceased to be effective in maintaining price levels favourable to tin-producers. Although China and Indonesia indicated that they would continue to support the ATPC, together with Bolivia, Malaysia and Nigeria (Zaire had ceased to be an active producer of tin), it was expected that its future activities would be limited to providing a forum for tin-producers and consumers.

Export Price Index for Tin (base: 1980 = 100)

	Average	Highest month(s)	Lowest month(s)
1985	68		
1990	42		
1994	33	37 (Nov.)	29 (Jan.)
1995	37	42 (Aug.)	32 (March)
1996	37	39 (April)	35 (Dec.)

The success, after 1985, of the ATPC in restoring orderly conditions in tin trading (partly by the voluntary quotas and partly by working towards the reduction of tin stockpiles) unofficially established it as the effective successor to the ITC as the international co-ordinating body for tin interests. The International Tin Study Group (ITSG), comprising 36 producing and consuming countries, was established by the ATPC in 1989 to assume the informational functions of the ITC. In 1991 the secretariat of the United Nations Conference on Trade and Development (UNCTAD) assumed responsibility for the publication of statistical information on the international tin market.

Although transactions in tin contracts were resumed on the LME in 1989, the Kuala Lumpur Commodity Exchange (KLCE), in Malaysia, has now become the main centre for international trading in the metal. In September 1993 the price of tin (ex-works) on the KLCE stood at only 10.78 Malaysian ringgits (RM) per kg, equivalent to £2,756 (or US $4,233) per ton. Measured in terms of US currency, international prices for tin were at their lowest level for 20 years, without taking inflation into account. In October the Malaysian tin price recovered to RM 12.71 per kg (£3,376 or $4,990 per ton), but in November it declined to RM 11.60 per kg (£3,056 or $4,545 per ton). At the end of the year, following a sharp fall in the ringgit's value, tin traded on the KLCE at RM 12.39 per kg (£3,120 or $4,608 per ton).

The rise in tin prices continued in the early weeks of 1994, and in February the Malaysian quotation reached RM 15.15 per kg

(£3,684 or US $5,449 per ton). In early March the metal's price eased to RM 14.00 per kg (£3,449 or $5,146 per ton), but later in the month it rose to RM 15.01 per kg (£3,715 or $5,515 per ton). The KLCE price was reduced in August to RM 12.99 per kg (£3,285 or $5,092 per ton), but in early November it stood at RM 16.06 per kg (then £3,896 or $6,265 per ton). At the end of the year the price was RM 15.20 per kg (£3,805 or $5,953 per ton).

The Malaysian tin price advanced strongly in January 1995, reaching RM 16.38 per kg (£4,018 or US $6,407 per ton). However, the rise was short-lived, and in early March the price declined to RM 13.33 per kg (about £3,300 or $5,200 per ton). The tin market later revived again, and in August the KLCE price of the metal reached RM 17.60 per kg (£4,569 or $7,060 per ton). International tin prices were then at their highest level for nearly six years. The recovery in the market was attributed partly to a continuing decline in tin stocks, resulting from a reduction in exports from China and in disposals from the USA's strategic reserves of the metal. However, the KLCE quotation was reduced to RM 15.36 per kg (£3,851 or $6,090 per ton) in October. At the end of the year it stood at RM 16.23 per kg (£4,117 or $6,392 per ton).

In the early months of 1996 there was a generally downward movement in international tin prices, and in March the Malaysian quotation fell to RM 15.28 per kg (£3,947 or US $6,015 per ton). In April the KLCE price of tin recovered to RM 16.24 per kg (£4,294 or $6,496 per ton). A further decline ensued, and in mid-December tin was traded at RM 14.31 per kg (£3,388 or $5,668 per ton). The Malaysian tin price ended the year at RM 14.85 per kg.

During the first six months of 1997 the price of tin on the KLCE declined by nearly 8%. The tin market moved further downward in July, with the Malaysian price falling to RM 13.52 per kg (£3,185 or US $5,398 per ton).

The International Tin Research Institute (ITRI), founded in 1932 and based in London, England, promotes scientific research and technical development in the production and use of tin. In recent years the ITRI has particularly sought to promote new end-uses for tin, especially in competition with aluminium.

Tobacco (*Nicotiana tabacum*)

Tobacco originated in South America and was used in rituals and ceremonials or as a medicine; it was smoked and chewed for centuries before its introduction into Europe. The generic name *Nicotiana* denotes the presence of the alkaloid nicotine in its leaves. The most important species in commercial tobacco cultivation is *N. tabacum.* Another species, *N. rustica,* is widely grown, but on a smaller scale, to yield cured leaf for snuff or simple cigarettes and cigars.

Production of Tobacco Leaves (farm sales weight, '000 metric tons)

	1994	1995
World total	6,559*	6,422*
Africa	411*	473*
Leading African producers		
Côte d'Ivoire	10*	10*
Kenya	10*	10*
Malawi	99†	132*
Nigeria	10*	10*
South Africa	21	22
Tanzania	18	27†
Zimbabwe	182	198
Leading non-African producers		
Brazil	519	453
China, People's Repub.	2,238	2,314
Greece	154	133†
India	563	587
Indonesia	140	146†
Italy	126	118
Turkey	187	210†
USA	718	603

* FAO estimate.

Commercially grown tobacco (from *N. tabacum*) can be divided into four major types—flue-cured, air-cured (including burley, cigar, light and dark), fire-cured and sun-cured (including oriental)—depending on the procedures used to dry or 'cure' the leaves. Each system imparts specific chemical and smoking characteristics to the cured leaf, although these may also be affected by other factors, such as the type of soil on which the crop is grown, the type and quantity of fertilizer applied to the crop, the cultivar used, the spacing of the crop in the field and the number of leaves left at topping (the removal of the terminal growing point). Each type is used, separately or in combination, in specific products (e.g. flue-cured in Virginia cigarettes). All types are grown in Africa.

As in other major producing areas, local research organizations in Africa have developed new cultivars with specific desirable chemical characteristics, disease-resistance properties and improved yields. The principal tobacco research centres are in Zimbabwe, Malawi and South Africa.

In Zimbabwe, Malawi, South Africa and, to a lesser extent, in Zambia and Tanzania, tobacco is grown mainly as a direct-labour crop on large farms, some capable of producing as much as 250 metric tons of cured leaf per year. In other parts of Africa, however, tobacco is a smallholders' crop, with each farmer cultivating, on average, 1 or 2 ha of tobacco as well as essential food crops and, usually, other cash crops. Emphasis has been placed on improving yields by the selection of cultivars, by the increased use of fertilizers, by the reduction of crop loss (through the use of crop chemicals) and by reducing hand-labour requirements through the mechanization of land-preparation and the use of crop chemicals. Where small farmers are responsible for producing the crop, harvesting remains a manual operation, as the area under tobacco and their limited financial means preclude the adoption of mechanical harvesting devices.

The principal type of tobacco that African farmers cultivate is flue-cured, and production within Africa is dominated by Malawi and Zimbabwe. The tobacco sector normally accounts for about 47% of Zimbabwe's total agricultural earnings and has in recent years provided about 22% of foreign revenue. Zimbabwean tobacco is highly regarded for its quality and flavour, and its marketability has been assisted by its relatively low tar content. Nevertheless, depressed conditions in international tobacco markets in the early 1990s were encouraging some Zimbabwean growers to switch to cotton cultivation. Following a sharp revival in international tobacco prices in 1996, however, tobacco output in Zimbabwe was forecast to rise by 17% in 1997. In 1995 tobacco sales accounted for an estimated 22% of the country's export revenues.

In the mid-1990s Malawi obtained up to 70% of its export revenue from the sale of its tobacco, principally the flue-cured, fire-cured and burley varieties. Malawi is the only significant African producer of burley tobacco, which accounts for about 15% of world exports. Production is limited to commercial estates, but since the early 1990s the government has permitted its cultivation by smallholders, in order to promote a more equitable distribution of agricultural incomes. Demand for burley tobacco has been stimulated by increased manufacturers' emphasis on low-tar cigarettes. The production of burley tobacco in Zimbabwe is being expanded.

Export Price Index for Tobacco (base: 1980 = 100)

	Average	Highest month(s)	Lowest month(s)
1985	129		
1990	125		
1994	131	141 (Feb.)	118 (Aug.)
1995	132	145 (Feb.)	129 (March–July)
1996	131	133 (Sept.–Dec.)	130 (Jan.–Aug.)

Tanzania contributes a small but significant quantity of flue-cured tobacco to the world market. South African production is increasing and quality is improving. Tobacco production in Nigeria is fairly static, and its flue-cured crop is entirely reserved for local consumption. Kenya has greatly increased its output of flue-cured leaf since commencing tobacco exports in 1984, and tobacco cultivation has recently been increasing in importance in Uganda, as part of a government programme to offset declining earnings from coffee. There are small but increasingly important exports of flue-cured tobacco from Sierra Leone and Zimbabwe. In the case of the sun- and air-cured types of tobacco, Nigeria, Malawi and South Africa account for the African crop. Modest quantities of oriental tobacco are cultivated in Malawi and South Africa.

The USA is the world's principal tobacco-exporting country. The average value of US exports of unmanufactured tobacco was US $6,302 per metric ton in 1992, $6,240 per ton in 1993 and $6,580 per ton in 1994. The country's total earnings from such exports were $1,317m. in 1994.

The International Tobacco Growers' Association (ITGA), with headquarters in the United Kingdom, was formed in 1984 by growers' groups in Argentina, Brazil, Canada, Malawi, the USA and Zimbabwe. The ITGA now includes 17 countries, accounting for more than 80% of the world's internationally traded tobacco. The ITGA provides a forum for the exchange of information among tobacco producers, and publishes data on tobacco production.

Uranium

Uranium occurs in a variety of ores, often in association with other minerals such as gold, phosphate and copper, and may be mined by open-cast, underground or *in situ* leach methods, depending on the circumstances. The concentration of uranium that is needed to form an economic mineral deposit varies widely, depending upon its geological setting and physical location. Average ore grades at operating uranium mines vary from 0.03% U to as high as 10% U, but are most frequently less than 1% U. South Africa, which accounts for about 15% of the world's uranium reserves, produces uranium concentrates as a by-product of gold mining and copper mining, and possesses uranium conversion and enrichment facilities. Both copper mining and the exploitation of phosphates by wet (phosphoric acid-yielding) processes offer a more widespread potential for by-product uranium production.

Uranium is principally used as a fuel in nuclear reactors for the production of electricity. In 1996 435 nuclear power plants generated approximately 17% of the world's electricity. Enriched uranium is used as fuel in most nuclear power stations and in the manufacture of nuclear weapons. In the latter, however, the abandonment of East–West confrontation and the prospect of significant nuclear disarmament is likely to reverse the process, with the release of substantial quantities of uranium. In 1995 a report by the OECD's Nuclear Energy Agency and the International Atomic Energy Agency estimated that probable economic reserves of uranium (excluding those in the former Eastern bloc countries and the People's Republic of China) totalled 2.2m. tons.

Because of uranium's strategic military value, there was intense prospecting activity in the 1940s and 1950s, but the market was later depressed as government purchase programmes ceased. Uranium demand fell in the late 1960s and early 1970s, until industrialized countries responded to the 1973–74 petroleum crisis by intensifying their civil nuclear power programmes. Anticipated strong demand for rapidly expanding nuclear power further improved the uranium market until the early 1980s, when lower than expected growth in electricity consumption forced nuclear power programmes to be restricted, leaving both producers and consumers with high levels of accumulated stocks requiring liquidation. A number of mining operations were also scaled down or closed. The market was further depressed in the late 1980s, in the aftermath of the accident in 1986 at the Chernobyl nuclear plant in Ukraine (then part of the USSR). At the end of 1996 there were 30 new reactors under construction. Significant growth in nuclear power programmes was notable in the Far East, especially in the People's Republic of China, Japan, the Republic of Korea and Taiwan. Other countries, such as Indonesia, Iran, Malaysia, Thailand, Turkey and Viet Nam, do not at present have nuclear power but have announced development plans. Following nine consecutive years of reduced output, uranium production achieved modest advances in both 1995 and 1996. The total of 35,324 tons in 1996, however, represented only about 55% of annual nuclear reactor requirements, necessitating recourse to inventories to meet a significant portion of world demand. During the late 1990s uranium production has widely been forecast to increase, as capacity utilization improves and plans proceed for the exploitation of new mines in Canada, Australia and the USA. Although uranium from dismantled nuclear weapons could satisfy some of the forecast increase in demand, there is uncertainty as to the timing and likely quantities of uranium that might come from this source. Nuclear electricity generating capacity has been forecast to grow at an annual compound rate of about 2% during the period 1995–2000. Annual world demand will, according to projections by the Uranium Institute, rise to 66,000 tons by the year 2000, from 60,100 tons in 1995.

Production of Uranium (uranium content of ores, metric tons)

	1995	1996*
World total	32,916	35,324
Africa	7,031	7,777
African producers		
Gabon	630	565
Namibia	2,007	2,452
Niger	2,970	3,320
South Africa	1,424	1,440
Leading non-African producers		
Australia	3,712	4,974
Canada	10,515	11,788
France	980	930
Kazakhstan	1,630	1,320
Russia	2,250	2,000
USA	2,324	2,420
Uzbekistan	1,800	1,500

*Estimates.

Source: Uranium Institute.

Canada has, in recent years, become the leading producer of uranium, accounting for about 30% of world production, and is expected to retain its position into the 21st century. South Africa has Africa's largest identified uranium resources (currently estimated at 241,000 metric tons), followed by Niger (with ore reserves of about 166,000 tons), Namibia (97,000 tons) and Gabon (15,000 tons). Uranium production has been an important component of the South African mining industry since uranium extraction began in 1951, with production reaching a record 6,146 tons in 1980. Production has subsequently declined sharply, and South Africa has been supplanted by Niger as the continent's main producer. In 1996 Niger ranked as the world's third largest producer, and fourth largest exporter, of uranium. Deliveries of ore from the world's largest open-pit uranium mine, at Rössing in Namibia, began in 1976. Output exceeded its planned level in 1980, but subsequently declined, owing to a reduction in demand and increased competition from low-cost producers. The removal of sanctions against Namibian uranium, following that country's independence from South Africa in 1990, coincided with a decline in world demand, which led to the restructuring of operations and a reduction in the workforce during 1991. However, output has subsequently been rising to satisfy higher sales commitments.

Uranium ore reserves were first identified in Gabon in 1956 and their exploitation began in 1958. During 1956–81 exploration efforts led to the discovery of several deposits: at Mounana (1956), Mikouloungou (1965), Boyindzi (1967), Oklo (1968), Okélobondo (1974) and Bagombé (1980). The deposits at Bagombé and Mikouloungou have yet to be exploited. Known reserves are sufficient for 50 years' output at current production rates. Uranium exploitation and development is handled by a consortium which is controlled mainly by French interests, but with a 25% participation by the government of Gabon. Since 1958 a total of 24,000 tons of uranium has been produced and delivered to customers. Output has recovered following a decline in production in the period 1989–92.

Uranium exploration in Niger started in the 1950s, around the Aïr mountains near Agadez, with production commencing at the Arlit mine in 1971. Niger also has a uranium mine at Akouta, where production commenced in 1978, and there are several other sites awaiting development. France purchases most of Niger's uranium production, with the remainder taken by German, Japanese and Spanish customers. Like Namibia, Niger was compelled in the early 1990s to restructure and streamline its uranium operations.

Uranium has also been found in Algeria, Botswana, the Central African Republic, Chad, Egypt, Guinea, Madagascar, Mali, Mauritania, Morocco, Nigeria, Somalia, Tanzania, Togo, Zaire and Zambia. However, in view of conditions in the world uranium market in the mid-1990s, it was uncertain if any of these deposits would be exploited in the immediate future.

The European market price for uranium oxide reached US $8.75 per lb in October 1992, but was reduced to $8.00 per lb in November and to $7.90 in December. Market conditions remained depressed in 1993, with the price moving steadily downward to $7.00 per lb in July. It fell to $6.90 per lb in August and was maintained at that level for the remainder of the year. The price of uranium oxide was adjusted to $7.00 per lb in January 1994, and to $7.10 in July. The latter remained in effect until October, when the price was reduced to $7.00 per lb again. It was increased to $7.15 per lb in December.

From the beginning of 1995 the price of uranium oxide continued to rise. In a series of upward movements, the price per lb was set at US $7.20 in January, $7.25 in February, $7.35 in April, $7.65 in June, $7.90 in July, $8.40 in August, $9.00 in September, $9.50 in October, $9.80 in November and $10.00 in December.

The price of uranium oxide was maintained at US $10.00 per lb for three months, but in March 1996 it was increased to $13.00. Further rises followed, with the price per lb set at $13.50 in April, $13.75 and then $14.50 in May, $15.00 in June and $15.50 in August. The surge in prices was attributed to steady demand and to the depletion of uranium stocks. The price of $15.50 per lb was maintained until the end of September, after which the uranium market went into a steep decline. At the end of the year the price of uranium oxide stood at $14.00 per lb.

During the first half of 1997 there was a steady series of reductions in the price of uranium oxide. The price per lb declined to US $13 in February, to $12 in April and to $10 at the end of June. Another decrease took the price to $9.70 per lb in July.

The Uranium Institute—the International Industrial Association for Energy from Nuclear Fuel—comprises mining companies, electricity utilities and nuclear fuel processors and traders from 20 countries in Europe, North America, Asia, Africa and Australia. Founded in 1975 to promote the use of uranium for peaceful purposes, the Institute organizes meetings, conducts research, and disseminates information on uranium production and the nuclear fuel industry.

Wheat (*Triticum*)

The most common species of wheat (*T. vulgare*) includes hard, semi-hard and soft varieties which have different milling characteristics but which, in general, are suitable for bread-making. Another species, *T. durum,* is grown mainly in semi-arid areas, including north Africa and the Mediterranean. This wheat is very hard and is suitable for the manufacture of semolina. In north Africa, in addition to being used for making local bread, semolina is the basic ingredient of pasta and couscous. A third species, spelt (*T. spelta*), is also included in production figures for wheat. It is grown in very small quantities in parts of Europe and is used as animal feed.

Although a most adaptable crop, wheat does not thrive in hot and humid climates. Africa's wheat production is mainly concentrated in a narrow strip along the Mediterranean coast from Morocco to Tunisia, in the Nile valley, and in parts of South Africa. Zimbabwe, Kenya, Ethiopia and Sudan also grow limited quantities, but very little is grown in west Africa. In contrast with some developing countries of Asia, the potential of improved wheat varieties has yet to be realized in much of Africa, especially south of the Sahara. One reason is the undeveloped state of the transport systems in many countries, which hinders both the distribution of production inputs (e.g. seeds and fertilizers) and the marketing of farmers' surplus produce. Until recently, many governments have also been unwilling to pay sufficiently attractive producer prices to encourage farmers to grow wheat for marketing.

Wheat production in sub-Saharan Africa averages about 4m. tons annually. South Africa accounts for about two-thirds of the total, although its output, being rain-fed, is highly variable. Large crops in the 1980s caused financial loss to the Wheat Board, as the surpluses had to be exported against subsidized competition on world markets. The policy of self-sufficiency in wheat production was modified, and marginal land taken out of production. In accordance with the country's policy of progressive deregulation, the South African Wheat Board was to be disbanded in late 1997. In the absence of tariffs or other forms of protection for domestic producers, it is expected that wheat output will continue to decline. In some other wheat-producing countries (e.g. Tanzania and Zimbabwe) the crop is grown mainly on large commercial farms, and, with the benefit of irrigation, usually yields well. Efforts to produce wheat in tropical countries, such as Nigeria and Zaire, have not as yet been successful.

Production of Wheat ('000 metric tons)

	1995	1996*
World total	539,680	580,070
Africa	13,840	21,850
Leading African producers		
Algeria	1,600	2,400
Egypt	5,700	5,740
Ethiopia	1,420	1,570
Kenya	320	350
Libya	170	170
Morocco	1,090	5,920
South Africa	1,950	2,700
Sudan	530	530
Tunisia	530	1,990
Zimbabwe	280	220
Leading non-African producers		
Australia	16,980	23,500
Canada	25,020	30,500
China, People's Repub.	102,200	108,000
France	30,860	35,860
Germany	17,800	18,350
India	65,770	62,600
Pakistan	17,000	16,910
Russia	30,100	34,900
Turkey	15,500	16,200
Ukraine	16,260	13,400
USA	59,500	62,100

* Provisional.

Source: International Grains Council.

In the long term, world wheat production has been increasing at an average rate of more than 3% per year, but there are wide year-to-year fluctuations, owing to variations in weather conditions in the main producing areas, especially the occurrence of drought. Heavy accumulations of stocks in the exporting countries during the late 1980s led their governments to adopt policies (such as export subsidies and set-asides) which aligned output more closely to demand. The low effective level of world prices discouraged wheat producers in other countries, with the consequent stagnation of total output. This situation changed abruptly in 1996, when wheat became in short supply. The resultant increase in prices acted as a stimulant to output in many producing areas, and world wheat production rose to a record 580m. tons. On average, about 70% of total consumption is directly used as human food, and about 20% for animal feed. Prior to 1990, the former Soviet Union consumed substantial quantities of wheat for feed. However, the subsequent change in economic conditions (in particular, the removal of many subsidies on output and consumption) resulted in a sharp decline in livestock and poultry numbers. The consequent fall in demand for wheat as feed offset the continuing growth in food requirements in developing countries. It was not until 1996/97, when feed requirements by the former USSR stabilized, that world consumption exceeded the previous record (set in 1990/91).

Of approximately 430m. tons of wheat used for food, Far East Asia accounts for more than one-half, and the region's consumption continues to increase. Food use in North Africa amounts to about 25m. tons annually, compared with 10m. tons per year in sub-Saharan Africa, where wheat consumption is confined mainly to urban areas.

There is more international trade in wheat than in any other cereal. The principal exporters are the USA (which accounts for about one-third of the total), the EU, Canada, Australia and Argentina. Developed countries were formerly the main markets, but the role of developing countries as importers has been steadily increasing, now accounting for about 80% of world trade. Africa's imports have recently averaged about 20m. tons per year. The major African markets are in the north (Algeria, Egypt and Morocco). Sub-Saharan Africa accounts for around 5m. tons annually, but for larger quantities in drought years, especially when white maize is not available on world markets. Imports by the region in 1995/96 were estimated at about 6m. tons.

Since 1949 nearly all world trade in wheat has been conducted under the auspices of successive international agreements, administered by the International Wheat Council (IWC) in London. The early agreements involved regulatory price controls and supply and purchase obligations, but such provisions became inoperable in more competitive market conditions, and were abandoned in 1972. The IWC subsequently concentrated on providing detailed market assessments to its members and encouraging them to confer on matters of mutual concern. A new Grains Trade Convention, which entered into force in July 1995, allows for improvements in the provision of information on all grains to members of the International Grains Council (IGC, the successor to the IWC), and enhances opportunities for consultations. In mid-1997 the IGC had a membership of 32 countries (inclusive of the EU), among them most of the major grain-exporting and importing nations. African members include Algeria, Côte d'Ivoire, Egypt, Mauritius, Morocco, South Africa and Tunisia.

Since 1967 a series of Food Aid Conventions, linked to the successive Wheat and Grains Trade Conventions, have ensured continuity of supplies of food aid in the form of cereals to needy countries. Donor members of the Convention pledge to supply minimum annual quantities of food aid to developing countries in the form of wheat and other grains suitable for human consumption. The obligations are basically quantitative, ensuring that the volume of aid is not reduced in times of very short supplies and rising grain prices. In recent seasons, upwards of 10m. tons of food aid has been provided annually under the Convention, of which 2m.–3m. tons (not all in the form of wheat) was directed to sub-Saharan Africa. The Food Aid Committee, which administers the Convention, is a focal point of international co-operation in food aid matters. A new Food Aid Convention, incorporating similar principles, entered into force on 1 July 1995. Reflecting the budgetary pressures on many governments, commitments by several donors are lower than those under the 1986 Convention, although the overall objective remains unchanged.

A lengthy period of low international wheat prices, and heavily subsidized competition among the major exporting countries, came to an end in 1995, after carry-over stocks had fallen to their lowest levels for 20 years. Markets became anxious about uncertain prospects for 1996 harvests in some of the major wheat-growing countries, especially the USA. However, by mid-1996 it was clear that crops in Canada, Western Europe and exporting countries of the southern hemisphere would be substantial, and prices fell back. With the persistence of low levels of stocks, markets remained volatile during the first half of 1997.

Export Price Index for Wheat (base: 1980 = 100)

	Average	Highest month(s)	Lowest month(s)
1985	81		
1990	82		
1994	83	89 (Jan.)	75 (July)
1995	94	110 (Dec.)	80 (March)
1996	108	136 (May)	90 (Dec.)

The export price (f.o.b. Gulf ports) of US No. 2 Hard Winter, one of the most widely-traded wheat varieties, stood at around US $140 per metric ton in mid-1994. At that time, countries benefiting from export subsidies (e.g. much of North Africa) could expect to buy wheat for at least $40 per ton less. Prices strengthened through 1995, reaching $200 per ton late in the year: by then, export subsidies were no longer available. A renewed rise in April 1996 took prices well above the previous (mid-1970s) record, reaching almost $300 per ton by the end of the month. Improved levels of supplies, augmented by substantialwheat harvests in the southern hemisphere, led to depressed price levels in the second half of 1996. However, at about $180 per ton (without subsidies available), import prices were at approximately twice the levels prevailing at the beginning of the 1990s. These higher prices caused difficulties for some of the importing developing countries, particularly in sub-Saharan Africa. In general, however, they did not substantially curtail import demand.

ACKNOWLEDGEMENTS

We gratefully acknowledge the assistance of the following organizations in the preparation of this section:

African Groundnut Council
Association of Iron Ore Exporting Countries
British-American Tobacco Co
Bureau of Mines, US Department of the Interior
Central Selling Organisation
Centro Internacional de Agricultura Tropical
Cobalt Information Centre
Copper Development Association
Cotton Research Corporation
De Beers
Food and Agricultural Organization of the UN
Gill & Duffus Group PLC
Gold Fields Mineral Services Ltd
Institute of Petroleum
Intergovernmental Council of Copper Exporting Countries
International Cocoa Organization
International Coffee Organization
International Copper Study Group
International Cotton Advisory Committee
International Grains Council
International Institute for Cotton
International Iron and Steel Institute
International Monetary Fund
International Primary Aluminium Institute
International Rice Research Institute
International Sugar Organization
International Tea Committee
Johnson Matthey PLC
Malaysian Oil Palm Growers' Council
United Nations Conference on Trade and Development
US Department of Energy
Uranium Institute
World Bureau of Metal Statistics

Sources for Agricultural Production Tables (unless otherwise indicated): FAO, *Production Yearbook 1995* (Rome 1996); FAO, *Quarterly Bulletin of Statistics,* issues to November 1996.

Source for Export Price Indexes: UN, *Monthly Bulletin of Statistics*, issues to May 1997.

RESEARCH INSTITUTES

ASSOCIATIONS AND INSTITUTIONS STUDYING AFRICA

See also Regional Organizations in Part II

ARGENTINA

Facultad de Filosophia y Letras, Seccion Interdisciplinaria de Estudios de Asia y Africa: 25 de Mayo 221, 4° piso, 1002 Buenos Aires; tel. (1) 334-7612; fax (1) 343-2733; f. 1982; multidisciplinary seminars and lectures; Dir Prof. María Elena Vela; publ. *Temas de Africa y Asia* (2 a year).

Nigeria House: Florida 142, 1337 Buenos Aires; tel. (1) 326-5543; f. 1963; library specializing in Nigerian material and general information on Africa; Dir Emilia María Sannazzari.

AUSTRALIA

African Studies Association of Australia and the Pacific: c/o ACFOA, Private Bag Daekin, Canberra, ACT 2600; tel. (6) 2851816; fax (6) 2851720.

Australian Institute of International Affairs: 32 Thesiger Court, Deakin, ACT 2600; tel. (6) 2822133; fax (6) 2852334; f. 1933; 1,800 mems; brs in all States; Pres. R. H. Searby; publs include *Australian Journal of International Affairs* (3 a year).

Indian Ocean Centre: Curtin University of Technology, GPO Box U1987, Perth 6845; tel. (8) 9221 7033; fax (8) 9221 7020; Dir Assoc. Prof. Kenneth McPherson; publ. *Indian Ocean Review* (quarterly).

AUSTRIA

Afro-Asiatisches Institut in Wien (Afro-Asian Institute in Vienna): 1090 Vienna, Türkenstrasse 3; tel. and fax (1) 3105145; f. 1959; cultural and other exchanges between Austria and African and Asian countries; economic and social research; lectures, seminars; Pres. Ing. Heinz Hödl; Gen. Sec. DI Christian Guggenberger.

Österreichische Forschungsstiftung für Entwicklungshilfe (Austrian Foundation for Development Research): 1090 Vienna, Berggasse 7; tel. (1) 3174010; fax (1) 3174015; f. 1967; documentation and information on development aid and developing countries, particularly in relation to Austria; library of 22,000 vols and 250 periodicals; publs include *Ausgewählte neue Literatur zur Entwicklungspolitik* (2 a year), *Österreichische Entwicklungspolitik* (annually).

Österreichische Gesellschaft fur Aussenpolitik und Internationale Beziehungen (Austrian Society for Foreign Policy and International Relations): 1010 Vienna, Hofburg/Schweizerhof; tel. and fax (1) 5354627; f. 1958; lectures, discussions; 360 mems; Pres. Dr Wolfgang Schallenberg; publ. *Österreichisches Jahrbuch für Internationale Politik* (annually).

Österreichisches Institut für Entwicklungshilfe und Technische Zusammenarbeit mit den Entwicklungsländern (Austrian Institute for Development Aid and Technical Co-operation with the Developing Countries): 1010 Vienna, Wipplingerstrasse 35; tel. (1) 426504; f. 1963; projects for management training; Pres Dr Hans Ingler, Erich Hofstetter.

BELGIUM

Académie Royale des sciences d'outre-mer/Koninklijke Academie voor Overzeese Wetenschappen: rue Defacqz 1, Boîte 3, 1000 Brussels; tel. (2) 538-02-11; fax (2) 539-23-53; f. 1928; the promotion of scientific knowledge of overseas areas, especially those with special development problems; 118 mems, 69 assoc. mems, 93 corresp. mems; Perm. Sec. Prof. Y. Verhasselt.

Centre international des langues, littératures et traditions d'Afrique au service de développement (CILTADE): ave des Clos 30, 1348 Louvain-la-Neuve; tel. (32) 45-06-65; fax (32) 47-25-79; Dir Dr Clementine Madiya Faik-Nzuti.

Bibliothèque africaine: 19 rue des Petites Carmes, 1000 Brussels; tel. (2) 501-35-14; fax (2) 501-36-69; f. 1885; library of 500,000 vols; large collections in the fields of African history, ethnography, economics, politics; Dir Mme Ch. Bils-Lambert.

College voor de Ontwikkelingslanden–Institute of Development Policy and Management: University of Antwerp–RUCA, Middelheimlaan 1, 2020 Antwerp; tel. (3) 218-06-60; fax (3) 218-06-66; f. 1920; conducts postgraduate study courses; library and documentation centre; Pres. Prof. Dr D. van den Bulcke; publs research reports and papers (irregular).

Fondation pour favoriser les recherches scientifiques en Afrique: 1 rue Defacqz, BP 5, 1050 Brussels; tel. (2) 269-39-05; f. 1969 to conduct scientific research in Africa with special reference to environmental management and conservation; Dir Dr A. G. Robyns; publs *Exploration des Parcs nationaux, Etudes du Continent africain.*

Institut africain/Afrika Instituut: Centre d'étude et de documentation africaines/Afrika Studie– en Dokumentatiecentrum, 65 rue Belliard, 1040 Brussels; tel. (2) 230-75-62; fax (2) 230-76-05; e-mail institutafricain@infoboard.be; f. 1970; research and documentation on African social and economic problems, with special reference to Burundi, Rwanda and the Democratic Repub. of the Congo; Dir G. de Villers; publ. *Cahiers Africains–Afrika Studies* (6 a year).

Institut d'études du développement: Université catholique de Louvain, Dépt des sciences de la population et du développement, 3 place Montesquieu, 1348 Louvain-La-Neuve; tel. (32) 47-39-35; fax (32) 47-28-05; f. 1961; Pres. J. P. H. Peemans.

Institut royal des relations internationales: 65 rue de Belliard, 4e étage, 1040 Brussels; tel. (2) 230-22-30; fax (2) 230-52-30; f. 1947; research in international relations, economics, law and politics; archives and library of 15,000 vols and 600 periodicals; Dir-Gen. Tony Hollants-Van Loocke; Exec. Dir Mme M. T. Bockstaele; publs *Studia Diplomatica* (bi-monthly), *Internationale Spectator* (monthly).

Koninklijk Museum voor Midden-Afrika/Musée royal de l'Afrique centrale: Leuvensesteenweg 13, 3080 Tervuren; tel. (2) 769-52-11; fax (2) 767-02-42; f. 1897; collections of prehistory, ethnography, nature arts and crafts; geology, mineralogy, palaeontology; zoology (entomology, ornithology, mammals, reptiles, etc.); history; economics; library of 90,000 vols and 4,500 periodicals; Dir D. Thys van den Audenaerde; publs include *Annales du Musée royal de l'Afrique centrale.*

Société belge d'etudes géographiques (Belgian Society for Geographical Studies): de Croylaan 42, 3001 Heverlee (Leuven); tel. (16) 32-24-45; fax (16) 32-29-80; f. 1931; centralizes and co-ordinates geographical research in Belgium; 395 mems; Pres. Y. Verhasselt; Sec. H. Van der Haegen; publ. *Bulletin* (2 a year).

Union royale belge pour les pays d'outre-mer: 22 rue de Stassart, 1050 Brussels; tel. (2) 511-16-93; f. 1912; fed. of 29 asscns; Chair. Pierre Andres; Gen. Sec. Oscar Libotte.

BRAZIL

Centro de Estudos Africanos (African Studies Centre): University of São Paulo, CP 8105, 05508-900 São Paulo SP; tel. and fax (11) 2109416; telex 80902; f. 1969; co-ordinating unit for all depts with African interests; specialist studies in sociology, international relations and literature concerning Africa; library; Dir Prof. Fernando A. A. Mourão; publ. *África* (annually).

Centro de Estudos Afro-Asiáticos—CEAA (Afro-Asian Studies Centre): Conjunto Universitário Candido Mendes, Rua da Assembléia 10, Conjunto 501, 20011 Rio de Janeiro RJ; tel. (21) 2213536; f. 1973; instruction and seminars; library; Dir Candido Mendes; publ. *Estudos Afro-Asiáticos.*

Centro de Estudos Afro-Orientais—CEAO (Afro-Oriental Studies Centre): Federal University of Bahia, Rua Augusto Viana s/n, Canela, 41170-290 Salvador-Bahia; tel. (71) 2452821;

f. 1959; African and Afro-Oriental Studies; library; Dir Prof. Luis César do Nascimento; publ. *Afro-Ásia* (irregular).

Centro de Estudos e Pesquisas de Cultura Yorubana (Yoruba Culture Study and Research Centre): CP 40099, CEP 20272, Rio de Janeiro RJ; tel. (21) 2930649; instruction in Yoruba language and religion; Dir Prof. Fernandes Portugal; publs include occasional papers.

Núcleo de Estudos Afro-Asiáticos (Afro-Asian Studies Unit): State University of Londrina, CP 6001, CEP 86051-970 Londrina PR; tel. (43) 371-4599; fax (43) 371-4679; f. 1985; seminars and lectures; Dir Prof. Eduardo Judas Barros; publ. *África Asia* (annually).

Núcleo Ibérico, Latino-Americano e Luso-Africano—NILALA (Iberian, Latin American and Luso-African Unit): University of Ijuí, Rua São Francisco 501, 98700 Ijuí RGS; f. 1984; lectures; Dir Prof. María Luiza de Carvalho Armando; publ. *Cadernos Luso-Africanos* (irregular).

BULGARIA

Institute for International Relations: '7 Noemvri' 1, 1040 Sofia; tel. (2) 84141; fax (2) 880448; f. 1976; attached to the Presidium of the Bulgarian Acad. of Sciences; Dir Prof. N. Carevski; publs *Afrikano-Aziatski Problemi, Meždunarodni Otnošenija.*

CANADA

Canadian Association of African Studies (CAAS): Serge Genest, c/o CAUT, Dept of Anthropology, Université Laval, Québec, PQ G1K 7P4; tel. (418) 656-2274; f. 1971; publs *Canadian Journal of African Studies* (English and French), *CAAS Newsletter* (English and French).

Canadian Council for International Co-operation: 1 Nicholas St, Suite 300, Ottawa, ON K1N 7B7; tel. (613) 241-7007; fax (613) 241-5302; f. 1968; fed. of 115 voluntary orgs promoting global development; Pres. Cameron Charlebois; Exec. Dir Betty Plewes; publs include *Newsletter* (6 a year).

Centre for African Studies: Dalhousie University, Halifax, NS B3H 4J5; tel. (902) 494-3814; telex 019-21863; fax (902) 494-2105; f. 1975; Dir Dr Jane L. Parpart; publs include *Dalhousie African Studies* series, *Dalhousie African Working Papers* series, *Briefing Papers on the African Crisis.*

Centre for Developing-Area Studies: McGill University, 3715 rue Peel, Montréal, PQ H3A 1X1; tel. (514) 398-3507; fax (514) 398-8432; Dir Dr R. Boyd; publs include *LABOUR, Capital and Society* (English and French—2 a year), discussion papers.

International Development Research Centre: POB 8500, Ottawa, ON K1G 3H9; tel. (613) 236-6163; telex 053-3753; fax (613) 238-7230; f. 1970 by the govt to support research projects designed to meet the basic needs of developing countries and to address problems associated with poverty; regional offices in Kenya, Senegal, Egypt, Singapore, Uruguay, India and South Africa; Pres. Dr Maureen O'Neill; publs include *IDRC Reports* (French, Spanish and English—weekly).

CHILE

Instituto Chileno-Zaireno de Cultura (Chilean-Zairean Cultural Institute): Casilla 144, Correo 10, Las Condes, Santiago; tel. (2) 2201464; f. 1981; affiliated inst. of the Univ. of Chile; holds seminars and exhbns and promotes cultural and academic exchanges with Zaire; Dir Ing. Gonzalo Beltrán.

PEOPLE'S REPUBLIC OF CHINA

Centre for International Studies: 22 Xianmen Dajie, POB 7411, Beijing; f. 1982; conducts research on international relations and problems; organizes academic exchanges; Gen. Dir Prof. Huan Xing.

Institute of African Studies: Siangtang University, Siangtan; tel. 24812; f. 1978.

West Asian and African Studies Institute: Chinese Academy of Social Sciences, 5 Jianguomen Nei Da Jie 5 Hao, Beijing; f. 1980; Dir. Ge Jie.

CZECH REPUBLIC

Ústav mezinárodních vztahů (Institute of International Relations): 118 50 Prague 1, Nerudova 3; tel. (2) 57320957; fax (2) 57321079; f. 1957; Dir Prof. Otto Pick; publs include *Mezinárodní politika/International Politics* (monthly), *Mezinárodní vztahy/ International Relations* (quarterly), *Perspectives—Review of Central European Affairs* (in English—2 a year).

DENMARK

Center for Udviklingsforskning (Centre for Development Research): Gammel Kongevej 5, 1610 Copenhagen V; tel. 33251200; fax 33258110; e-mail cdr@cdr.dk; f. 1969 to promote and undertake research in the economic, social and political problems of developing countries; library of 40,000 vols; Dir Dr Poul Engberg-Pedersen; publs include *Den ny Verden* (quarterly), *CDR Library Papers* (irregular), *CDR Research Reports* (in English, irregular), *CDR Working Papers* (in English—irregular).

Udenrigspolitiske Selskab (Foreign Policy Society): Amaliegade 40A, 1256 Copenhagen K; tel. 33148886; f. 1946; studies, debates, courses and conferences on international affairs; Dir Klaus Carsten Pedersen; publs *Udenrigs, Udenrigspolitiske Skrifter.*

EGYPT

African Association: 5 Ahmet Hishmat St, 11561 Zamalik, Cairo; tel. (2) 3407658; Sec.-Gen. Mohamed Fouad el-Bedewy.

Society for Coptic Archaeology: 222 Sharia Ramses, Cairo; tel. (2) 4824252; f. 1934; 360 mems; library of c. 14,700 vols; Pres. Wassif Boutros Ghali; Sec.-Gen. Dr A. Khater; publs include *Bulletin* (annually), monographs.

FRANCE

Académie des sciences d'outre-mer: 15 rue Lapérouse, 75116 Paris; tel. 1-47-20-87-93; fax 1-47-20-89-72; f. 1922; 255 mems, of which 275 mems are attached to sections on geography, politics and administration, law, economics and sociology, science and medicine, education; library of 50,000 vols and 2,500 periodicals; Perm. Sec. Gilbert Mangin; publs include *Mondes et Cultures* (quarterly).

Centre d'étude d'Afrique noire: BP 101, 33405 Talence Cedex; tel. 5-56-84-42-82; fax 5-56-84-43-24; e-mail info@cean.u-bordeaux.fr.

Centre d'études politiques et juridiques du tiers monde: Université de Paris I, 12 place du Panthéon, 75231 Paris Cedex 05; tel. 1-46-34-97-56; fax 1-46-34-97-56; f. 1965; Dir Prof. Jean-Pierre Quéneudec.

Centre d'études et de recherches sur le développement international (CERDI): Université de Clermont-Ferrand, 65 blvd François Mitterrand, 63000 Clermont-Ferrand; tel. 4-73-43-12-00; fax 4-73-43-12-28; e-mail cerdi@u-clermont1.fr; f. 1976; Dir Prof. Patrick Guillaumont.

Centre de recherches africaines: 9 rue Malher, 75181 Paris Cedex 04; tel. 1-44-78-33-40; fax 1-44-78-33-33; an inst. of the Universities of Paris I; Dir Jean Boulègue.

Centre des hautes études sur l'Afrique et l'Asie modernes: 13 rue du Four, 75006 Paris; tel. 1-44-41-38-80; fax 1-40-51-03-58; f. 1936; an affiliated inst. of Fondation nationale des sciences politiques; Dir J. P. Doumenge; publs *Notes africaines, asiatiques et caraïbes* (irregular).

Institut français de recherche scientifique pour le développement en coopération (ORSTOM): 213 rue La Fayette, 75480 Paris Cedex 10; tel. 1-48-03-77-77; telex 214627; fax 1-48-03-08-29; f. 1943, reorg. 1982; self-financing; centres, missions and rep. offices in Burkina Faso, Cameroon, the Central African Republic, Chad, the Congo Repub., Côte d'Ivoire, Gabon, Guinea, Madagascar, Mali, Niger, Senegal and Seychelles; Dir-Gen. Jean Nemo; publs include *ORSTOM News* (Quarterly).

Institut français des relations internationales: 4 rue de la Procession, 75740 Paris Cedex 15; tel. 1-40-61-60-00; fax 1-40-61-60-60; f. 1979; 900 mems; library of 30,000 vols; Chair. Maurice Faure; Dir Thierry de Montbrial; publs include *Politique étrangère* (quarterly), *Lettre d'Information* (bi-monthly), *Ramses* (annually).

Musée de l'Homme: Palais de Chaillot, 17 place du Trocadéro, 75116 Paris; tel. 1-44-05-72-72; f. 1878; library of 250,000 vols (c. 30,000 on Africa) and 5,000 periodicals; ethnography, physical anthropology, prehistory; also a research and education centre; Dirs Profs BERNARD DUPAIGNE (Ethnology), SERGE TORNAY (Black Africa), ANDRÉ LANGANEY (Anthropology), HENRY DE LUMLEY (Prehistory).

Société des africanistes (CSSF): Musée de l'Homme, Palais de Chaillot, 17 place du Trocadéro, 75116 Paris; tel. 1-47-27-72-55; f. 1931; 350 mems; Pres. MARC PIAULT; publ. *Journal des Africanistes.*

Société française d'histoire d'outre-mer: 15 rue Catulienne, 93200 Saint-Denis; tel. 1-48-13-09-89 (Wed. afternoons); fax 1-48-13-09-91; f. 1913; 500 mems; Pres. MARC MICHEL; Sec.-Gen. DANIEL LEFEVRE; publ. *Revue française d'histoire d'outre-mer* (quarterly).

GERMANY

Arbeitsstelle Politik Afrikas (African Politics Research Unit): Garystrasse 45, 14195 Berlin; f. 1967; inst. of the Free Univ. of Berlin; conducts research and documentation and offers undergraduate and graduate courses on the modern history and politics of all regions of Africa; Dir (vacant).

Deutsche Gesellschaft für Auswärtige Politik eV (German Society for Foreign Affairs): 53113 Bonn, Adenauerallee 131; tel. (228) 26750; fax (228) 2675173; f. 1955; promotes research on problems of international politics; library of 50,000 vols; 1,600 mems; Pres. Dr WERNER LAMBY; Exec. Vice-Pres. Dr DIETER VON WUERZEN; Dir Research Inst. Prof. Dr KARL KAISER; publs *Internationale Politik* (monthly), *Die Internationale Politik* (annually).

IFO–Institut für Wirtschaftsforschung (IFO–Institute for Economic Research): 81679 Munich, Postfach 860460, Poschingerstrasse 5; tel. (89) 92240; fax (89) 9224-1462; f. 1949; library of 80,000 vols; Pres. Dr KARL HEINRICH OPPENLÄNDER; publs include *Afrika-Studien, IFO-Studien zur Entwicklungsforschung, Forschungsberichte der Abteilung Entwicklungsländer.*

Informationsstelle Südliches Afrika eV (Information Centre on Southern Africa): 53227 Bonn, Königswintererstrasse 116; tel. (228) 464369; fax (228) 468177; f. 1971; research, documentation, and information on southern Africa; publs include *Afrika Süd* (6 a year).

Institut für Afrika-Kunde (Institute of African Affairs): 20354 Hamburg, Neuer Jungfernstieg 21; tel. (40) 3562523; fax (40) 3562511; f. 1963; research, documentation, information; library of 45,000 vols and 450 periodicals; Dir Dr ROLF HOFMEIER; publs include *Hamburg African Studies, Hamburger Beiträge zur Afrika-Kunde, Arbeiten aus dem Institut für Afrika-Kunde, Afrika Spectrum, Aktueller Informationsdienst Afrika, Focus Afrika.*

Institut für Afrikanistik: Leipzig University, 04109 Leipzig, Augustusplatz 9; tel. (341) 9737030; fax (341) 9737048; Dir Prof. Dr EKKEHARD WOLFF.

HUNGARY

Magyar Tudományos Akadémia Világgazdasági Kutató Intézete (Institute for World Economics of the Hungarian Academy of Sciences): 1124 Budapest, Kálló esperes u. 15; tel. (1) 319-9383; fax (1) 319-9385; f. 1965; library of 99,000 vols; Dir Prof. ANDRÁS INOTAI; publs include *Trends in World Economy* (irregular, in English), working papers (irregular, in English).

INDIA

Centre for Development Studies: Prasanth Nagar Rd, Ulloor, Thiruvananthapuram 695 011; tel. (471) 448881; telex 425227; fax (471) 447137; f. 1971; instruction and research in disciplines relevant to economic development; library of 103,600 vols; Dir Dr CHANDAN MUKHERJEE.

Centre for West Asian and African Studies: School of International Studies, Jawaharlal Nehru University, New Delhi 110 067; tel. (11) 6107676, Ext. 304; telex 73167; fax (11) 6865886; Chair. Dr GULSHAN DIETL.

Centre for African Studies: University of Mumbai, Vidyanagari Kalina Campus, Santacruz East, Mumbai 400 098; tel. (22) 6113091; fax (22) 6125711; Dir Dr V. S. SHETH.

Department of African Studies: University of Delhi, Delhi 110 007; tel. (11) 7257725, Ext. 338; fax (11) 7257336; f. 1955; Head of Dept Prof. HARJINDER SINGH; publs include *Indian Journal of African Studies.*

Indian Centre for Africa: Indian Council for Cultural Relations, Azad Bhavan, Indraprastha Estate, New Delhi 110 002; tel. (11) 3319226; telex 3161860; fax (11) 3712639; f. 1987; publ. *Africa Quarterly.*

Indian Council of World Affairs: Sapru House, Barakhamba Rd, New Delhi 110 001; tel. (11) 3317246; f. 1943; independent institution for the study of Indian and international questions; library of 123,000 vols, 624 periodicals, 2.3m. press clippings and 12,580 microfilms and microfiches; 1,500 mems; Pres. HARCHARAN SINGH JOSH; publs include *Foreign Affairs Reports* (monthly), *India Quarterly.*

Indian Society for Afro-Asian Studies: 297 Saraswati Kunj, Indraprastha Ext., New Delhi 110 092; tel. (11) 2248246; fax (11) 2425698; e-mail issas@giasdl01.vsnl.net.in; f. 1980; conducts research and holds seminars and confs; Pres. LALIT BHASIN; publs inc. *Indian Review of African Affairs* (6 a year).

ISRAEL

Harry S. Truman Research Institute for the Advancement of Peace: The Hebrew University of Jerusalem, Mt Scopus, Jerusalem 91905; tel. (2) 5882300; fax (2) 5828076; e-mail mstruman@pluto.mscc.huji.ac.il; f. 1966; conducts a broad range of research relating to non-Western and developing countries; Chair. Prof. MOSHE MA'OZ; Exec. Dir Dr EDY KAUFMAN.

Institute of Asian and African Studies: The Hebrew University of Jerusalem, Mt Scopus, Jerusalem 91905; tel. (2) 5883516; fax (2) 5322545; provides degree and postgraduate courses, covering history, social sciences and languages; Chair. Prof. ARYEH LEVIN.

International Institute—Histadrut: Bet Berl 44905, Kfar Saba; tel. (9) 987382; f. 1958 to train leadership for trade unions, co-operatives, community orgs, women's and youth groups, etc. in developing countries; library of 35,000 vols; Chair. HAIM RAMON; Dir and Prin. Dr YEHUDAH PAZ.

Moshe Dayan Center for Middle Eastern and African Studies, Shiloah Institute: Ramat-Aviv, Tel-Aviv 69978; tel. (3) 6409100; fax (3) 6415802; e-mail dayancen@ccsg.tau.ac.il; f. 1959; Dir Dr MARTIN KRAMER; publs include *Current Contents of Periodicals on the Middle East* (6 a year), *Middle East Contemporary Survey* (annually).

ITALY

The Bologna Center, Paul H. Nitze School of Advanced International Studies, The Johns Hopkins University: Via Belmeloro 11, 40126 Bologna; tel. (51) 232185; fax (51) 228505; f. 1955; graduate studies in international affairs; Dir ROBERT H. EVANS; publs include occasional papers series.

Istituto Italiano per l'Africa e l'Oriente: Via Ulisse Aldrovandi 16, 00197 Rome; tel. (6) 3221258; telex 620386; fax (6) 3225348; f. 1906; Pres. Prof. GHERARDO GNOLI; Sec.-Gen. GIANCARLO GARGARUTI; publ. *Africa* (quarterly).

Istituto per gli Studi di Politica Internazionale: Palazzo Clerici, Via Clerici 5, 20121 Milan; tel. (2) 878266; fax (2) 8692055; f. 1933 for the promotion of the study of international relations; conducts research, documentation and training; Pres. Ambassador MARCELLO GUIDI; Man. Dir Dr ENZO MARIA CALABRESE; publs include *Relazioni Internazionali* (6 a year), *Papers* (20 a year).

JAPAN

Ajia Keizai Kenkyusho (Institute of Developing Economies): 42 Ichigaya-Hommura-cho, Shinjuku-ku, Tokyo 162; tel. (3) 3353-4231; telex 32473; fax (3) 3226-8475; f. 1960; Unit of Ministry of International Trade and Industry; library of 252,000 vols; 256 mems; Chair. YOHEI MIMURA; Pres. KATSUHISA YAMADA; publs include *Ajia Keizai* (Japanese, monthly), *The Developing Economies* (English, quarterly).

Institute for the Study of Languages and Cultures of Asia and Africa: Tokyo University of Foreign Studies, 4-51-21 Nishigahara, Kita-ku, Tokyo 114; tel. (3) 3917-6111; fax (3) 3910-0613; f. 1964; library of 100,000 vols; Dir Prof. KOJI

KAMIOKA; publs *Newsletter* (3 a year), *Journal of Asian and African Studies* (2 a year).

Nihon Afurika Gakkai (Japan Asscn for African Studies): c/o Dogura and Co Ltd, 1–8 Nishihanaikecho, Koyama, Kita-ku, Kyoto 603; tel. (75) 451-4844; fax (75) 441-0436; promotes multidisciplinary African studies; Pres. H. ODA; publs *Afurika Kenkyu / Journal of African Studies* (2 a year), *Kaiho* (annually).

Nihon Kokusai Mondai Kenkyusho (Japan Inst. of International Affairs): 11F Kasumigaseki Bldg, 3-8-1 Kasumigaseki, Chiyoda-ku, Tokyo 100; tel. (3) 3503-7261; telex 2223469; fax (3) 3503-7292; f. 1959; Chair. YOSHIZANE IWASA; Pres. NOBUO MATSUNAGA; publs include *Kokusai Mondai* (International Affairs, monthly), *Japan Review of International Affairs* (Quarterly), *Roshia Kenkyu* (2 a year).

REPUBLIC OF KOREA

Institute of African Studies: Hankuk University of Foreign Studies, 270 Ly Moondong, Seoul 130-080; tel. (2) 961-4161; fax (2) 960-7898; Dir Dr WON-TAK PARK.

MEXICO

Asociación Latinoamericana de Estudios Afro-Asiáticos (Latin American Asscn for Afro-Asian Studies): El Colegio de México, Camino al Ajusco 20, Pedregal Sta Teresa, CP 10740, Mexico DF; tel. (5) 645-4954; telex 1777585; fax (5) 645-0464; f. 1976; promotes African and Asian studies in Latin America; 400 mems; Sec.-Gen. Prof. JORGE SILVA CASTILLO; publ. proceedings.

Centro de Estudios de Africa y Asia–CEAA (Centre for Asian and African Studies): El Colegio de México, Camino al Ajusco 20, Tlalpan, 01000, Mexico DF; tel. (5) 645-4954; telex 1777585; fax (5) 645-0464; f. 1964; postgraduate studies and research; library; Dir Prof. FLORA BOTTON; publs include *Estudios de Asia y Africa* (quarterly).

THE NETHERLANDS

Afrika-Studiecentrum: POB 9555, 2300 RB, Leiden; tel. (71) 5273372; fax (71) 5273344; e-mail winden@rulfsw.leidenuniv.nl.; f. 1947 to promote study of Africa, especially in the social sciences; encourages the co-operation of institutions engaged in the study of Africa; Chair. Prof. P. H. KOOIJMANS; Dir Dr G. HESSELING; publs include *African Studies Abstracts* (quarterly).

Institute of Social Studies: POB 29776, 2502 LT, The Hague; tel. (70) 4260460; telex 31491; fax (70) 4260799; e-mail studentoffice@iss.nl; f. 1952; post-graduate instruction, research and consultancy in development studies; Rector Prof. H. OPSCHOOR; publs *Development and Change* (quarterly), working papers, monograph series.

Netherlands-African Business Council: 181 Bezuidenhoutseweg, POB 10, 2501 CA, The Hague; tel. (70) 3441544; telex 32306; fax (70) 3853531; f. 1946; an information bureau, contact address and documentation centre for businessmen in African countries and in the Netherlands; Chair. Jonkheer F. J. C. MOLLERUS; Exec. Sec. R. V. D. HALL.

NORWAY

Norsk Utenrikspolitisk Institutt (Norwegian Institute of International Affairs): Grønlandsleiret 25, POB 8159 Dep, 0033 Oslo; tel. 22177050; fax 22177015; f. 1959; information and research in international relations; Pres. ÅGE DANIELSEN; Dir SVERRE LODGAARD; publs include *Internasjonal Politikk* (quarterly), *Forum for Development Studies* (2 a year), *NUPI Notat* and *NUPI Rapport* (research reports).

PAKISTAN

Pakistan Institute of International Affairs: Aiwan-e-Sadar Rd, POB 1447, Karachi 74200; tel. (21) 5682891; fax (21) 5686069; f. 1947 to study international affairs and to promote the study of international politics, economics and law; over 600 mems; library of c. 28,000 vols; Chair. FATEHYAB ALI KHAN; publs include *Pakistan Horizon* (quarterly).

POLAND

Departament Studiów i Planowania–MSZ (Dept of Studies and Planning–PISM, Ministry of Foreign Affairs): 00-950 Warsaw, Warecka 1A; tel. (22) 8263021; fax (22) 8263026; f. 1947; library of 125,000 vols; Dir Dr HENRYK SZLAJFER; publs include *Sprawy Międzynarodowe* (quarterly, in Polish and English), *Zbiór Dokumentów* (quarterly, in Polish, French, English and German), occasional papers (in English).

Instytut Krajow Rozwijajcych Sie (Institute of Developing Countries): 02-089 Warsaw, Zwirki i Wigury 93; tel. (22) 223051; undergraduate and postgraduate studies; interdisciplinary research on developing countries; Dir Prof. BOGDAR WINID; publs include *Africana Bulletin* (irregular, in French and English), *Afryka, Azja, Ameryka Łacińska* (irregular, with summaries in French and English).

Institute of Oriental Studies, Department of African Languages and Cultures, University of Warsaw: 00-927 Warsaw, Krakowskie Przedmieście 26/28; tel. (22) 200381, Ext. 517; telex 825439; fax (22) 267520; f. 1950; postgraduate studies and research in linguistics, literature, history, sociology and ethnology; Head of Dept Prof. Dr STANISŁAW PIŁASZEWICS: publ. *Studies of the Department of African Languages and Cultures.*

PORTUGAL

Amílcar Cabral Information and Documentation Centre: Rua Pinheiro Chagas, 77-2 E, 1000 Lisbon; tel. (1) 3528718; fax (1) 3534009.

Centro de Estudos Africanos (African Studies Centre): University of Coimbra, Instituto de Antropologia, Rua Arco da Traição, 3049 Coimbra; tel. (39) 29051; fax (39) 23491; f. 1982; seminars and lectures; Dir Prof. M. L. RODRIGUES DE AREIA; publ. *Publicações do Centro de Estudos Africanos.*

Centro de Estudos Sobre África e do Desenvolvimento (Centre of African and Development Studies): Instituto Superior de Economía e Gestão, Rua Miguel Lupi 20, 1200 Lisbon; tel. (1) 3925983; fax (1) 3966407; f. 1982; e-mail cesa@iseg.ult.pt; conducts research and holds seminars; publs occasional papers.

Instituto de Estudos Africanos (Institute of African Studies): Faculty of Letters, University of Lisbon, Cidade Universitária, 1669 Lisbon; literary studies and documentation centre; Dirs Prof. MANUEL FERREIRA, Prof. MANUEL VIEGAS GUERREIRO.

Instituto de Investigação Científica Tropical (Institute for Tropical Scientific Research): Ministério da Ciência e da Tecnologia, Rua da Junqueira 86-1°, 1300 Lisbon; f. 1883; tel. (1) 3622621; fax (1) 3631460; comprises 23 specialized research and development centres and a documentation centre, dealing mainly with lusophone African countries; Pres. J. A. CRUZ E SILVA; publs include monographs, serials and maps.

RUSSIA

Institute for African Studies: attached to the Dept of World Economy and International Relations, Russian Academy of Sciences, ul. Spiridonovka Tolstogo 30/I, 103001 Moscow; tel. (095) 2902752; telex 411099; fax (095) 2020786; Chair. A. M. VASSILIEV.

Moscow State University Institute of Asian and African Studies: Mokhovaja 11, 103009 Moscow; tel. (095) 2033647; fax (095) 2036476.

Scientific Council on Problems of Africa: Section of Social Sciences of Academy of Sciences, ul. Alexeya Tolstogo 30/I, 103001 Moscow; tel. (095) 2902752; Chair. AN. A. GROMYKO.

SAUDI ARABIA

King Faisal Centre for Research and Islamic Studies: POB 5149, Riyadh 11543; tel. (1) 4652255; telex 205470; f. 1983; advances research and studies into Islamic civilization; provides grants for research and organizes symposia, lectures and conferences on Islamic matters; library of over 30,000 vols and periodicals; Dir-Gen. Dr ZEID AL-HUSAIN; publ. *Newsletter.*

SOUTH AFRICA

Africa Institute of South Africa: BestMed Bldg, cnr Hamilton and Belvedere Sts, Arcadia, POB 630, Pretoria 0001; tel. (12) 328-6970; fax (12) 323-8153; f. 1960; undertakes research and collects and disseminates information on all aspects of continental Africa and its offshore islands; Dir Dr DENIS VENTER; publs include *Africa Insight* (quarterly).

Institute for Advanced Social Research: University of the Witwatersrand, 1 Jan Smuts Ave, Private Bag 3, Wits 2050, Johannesburg; tel. (11) 716-2414; telex 427125; fax (11) 716-8030; f. 1973; Dir Prof. CHARLES VAN ONSELEN.

Institute for the Study of Man in Africa (ISMA): Room 2B17, University of the Witwatersrand Medical School, York Rd, Parktown, Johannesburg 2193; tel. (11) 647-2203; fax (11) 643-4318; f. 1960 to perpetuate the work of the late Prof. Raymond A. Dart on the study of man in Africa, past and present; serves as a centre of anthropological and related field work; publs include the Raymond Dart series and occasional papers.

South African Institute of Race Relations: POB 31044, Braamfontein 2017; tel. (11) 403-3600; fax (11) 403-3671; f. 1929; research, education, publishing; library; 4,313 mems, 600 affiliated bodies; Pres. HERMANN GILIOMEE; Dir J. KANE-BERMAN; publs include *Fast Facts* (monthly), *Frontiers of Freedom* (quarterly), *South Africa Survey* (annually).

University of Cape Town Centre for African Studies: Rondebosch 7700; tel. (21) 650-2308; telex 57222085; fax (21) 689-7560; f. 1976; funded by the Harry Oppenheimer Inst. for African Studies; promotes study and research and collects source material; offers multi-disciplinary courses at undergraduate and postgraduate levels; Dir Prof. MAHMOOD MAMDANI; publs include *Social Dynamics* (bi-annually).

SPAIN

Centre d'Estudis Africans: Travessera de Gracia 100, Pral. 1, 08012 Barcelona; tel. and fax (3) 4153192; f. 1988; instruction and research; Pres. Dr ALFRED BOSCH.

Centro de Información y Documentación Africanas–CIDAF: Gaztambide 31, 28015 Madrid; tel. (1) 5441818; fax (1) 5441818; e-mail cidaf@planalfa.es; f. 1979; seminars and lectures; specialized library of 15,000 vols and periodicals; Dir Fr JOSÉ MARÍA SARASOLA CELAYA; Chief Librarian F. D. SEGURA GOMEZ; publs include *Noticias de Africa* (monthly), *Cuadernos CIDAF*.

Colegio Mayor Universitario Nuestra Señora de Africa: Avda Ramiro de Maeztu s/n, Ciudad Universitaria, 28040 Madrid; tel. (1) 5540104; fax (1) 5540401; f. 1964; attached inst. of the Complutense Univ. of Madrid and the Spanish Ministry of Foreign Affairs; linguistic studies and cultural activities; Dir OLEGARIO NEGRÍN.

Dirección de Programas de Cooperación con Iberoamérica, Asia y Africa: Vice-Rectorado de Relaciones Internacionales, Universidad de Alcalá de Henares, Plaza de Dan Diego, s/n, 28801 Alcalá de Henares (Madrid); tel. (1) 8854087; fax (1) 8854130; f. 1989; promotes and co-ordinates co-operation with African universities; organizes seminars, lectures and courses; Vice-Rector Dr LUIS BELTRÁN.

Mundo Negro: Arturo Soria 101; 28043 Madrid; tel. (1) 4152412; fax (1) 5192550; f. 1960; holds lectures; library and museum; Dir Fr ANTONIO VILLARINO RODRÍGUEZ; publ. *Mundo Negro* (monthly).

SWEDEN

Institutet för Internationell Ekonomi (Institute for International Economic Studies): Universitetsvägen 10A, 106 91 Stockholm; tel. (8) 155886; fax (8) 165886; f. 1962; attached to Stockholm University; Dir Prof. ASSAR LINDBECK.

Nordiska Afrikainstitutet (The Nordic Africa Institute): POB 1703, 751 47 Uppsala; tel. (18) 562200; fax (18) 695629; e-mail nai@nai.uu.se; f. 1962; documentation and research centre for contemporary African affairs, publication work, lectures and seminars; library of 40,000 vols and 1,000 periodicals; Dir LENNART WOHLGEMUTH; publs include *Current African Issues*, *News from Nordiska Afrikainstitutet*, seminar proceedings, research reports, discussion papers, annual report.

Utrikespolitiska Institutet (Swedish Institute of International Affairs): Lilla Nygatan 23, POB 1253, 111 82 Stockholm; tel. (8) 234060; fax (8) 201049; f. 1938; promotes studies of international affairs; library of c. 20,000 vols and 400 periodicals; Pres. Ambassador LEIF LEIFLAND; Dir Dr RUTGER LINDAHL; publs include *Världspolitikens Dagsfrågor, Världens Fakta, Internationella Studier, Länder i fickformat, Yearbook*, conference papers, research reports (in English).

SWITZERLAND

Institut universitaire d'études du développement: 24 rue Rothschild, 1211 Geneva 21; tel. (22) 9065940; fax (22) 9065923; f. 1961; a centre of higher education and research into development problems of Africa, Latin America and Asia; conducts courses, seminars and practical work; Dir JEAN-LUC MAURER; publs include *Nouveaux, Cahiers de l'IUED, Annuaire Suisse-Tiers Monde, Itinéraires.*

Institut universitaire de hautes études internationales: 132 rue de Lausanne, BP 36, 1211 Geneva 21; tel. (22) 7311730; fax (22) 7384306; f. 1927; a research and teaching institution studying international judicial, historical, political and economic questions; Dir Prof. ALEXANDER SWOBODA.

UNITED KINGDOM

African Studies Association of the United Kingdom: School of African and Oriental Studies, Thornhaugh St, Russell Sq., London, WC1H 0XG; tel. (171) 323-6253; f. 1963 to advance academic studies relating to Africa by providing facilities for the interchange of information and ideas; holds inter-disciplinary confs and symposia; 350 mems; Hon. Pres. Prof. J. D. Y. PEEL; Hon. Sec. Dr N. NELSON.

African Studies Unit: University of Leeds, Leeds, West Yorkshire, LS2 9JT; tel. (113) 2335069; a liaison unit for all depts with African interests.

Catholic Institute for International Relations (CIIR): Unit 3, Canonbury Yard, 190A New North Rd, London, N1 7BJ; tel. (171) 354-0883; fax (171) 359-0017; f. 1940; information and analysis of socio-economic, political, church and human rights issues in the developing countries; Gen. Sec. IAN LINDEN; publs include specialized studies on southern Africa and EU development policy.

Centre for Southern African Studies, York: University of York, Heslington, York, North Yorkshire, YO1 5DD; tel. (1904) 430000; telex 57933; fax (1904) 433433; Dir LANDEG WHITE.

Centre for the Study of African Economies: Institute of Economics and Statistics, University of Oxford, St Cross Bldg, Manor Rd, Oxford, OX1 3UL; tel. (1865) 271084; fax (1865) 281447; Dir Prof. P. COLLIER; publ. *Journal of African Economies* (3 a year).

Centre of African Studies: Free School Lane, Cambridge, CB2 3RQ; tel. and fax (1223) 334396; e-mail african-studies@lists.cam.ac.uk; attached inst. of the Univ. of Cambridge; Dir Dr KEITH HART.

Centre of African Studies: University of Edinburgh, Adam Ferguson Bldg, George Sq., Edinburgh, EH8 9LL, Scotland; tel. (131) 650-3878; telex 727442; fax (131) 650-6535; e-mail africanstudies@ed.ac.uk; f. 1962; postgraduate studies; Dir Prof. KENNETH KING; publs include occasional paper series and annual conference proceedings.

Centre of West African Studies: The University of Birmingham, Edgbaston, Birmingham, B15 2TT; tel. (121) 4145128; Dir ARNOLD HUGHES.

Development and Project Planning Centre: University of Bradford, Bradford, West Yorkshire, BD7 1DP; tel. (1274) 383955; fax (1274) 385280; f. 1969 to carry out postgraduate teaching, professional training, research and consultancy in project planning and management and macroeconomic policy and planning; an attached inst. of the Univ. of Bradford; Head of Centre JOHN CUSWORTH; publs include monographs and discussion papers.

Institute of Commonwealth Studies: 28 Russell Sq., London, WC1B 5DS; tel. (171) 580-5876; fax (171) 255-2160; f. 1949; conducts postgraduate research in literature, social sciences and recent history relating to the Commonwealth; library of 150,000 vols; Dir Prof. PAT CAPLAN.

Institute of Development Studies at the University of Sussex: Brighton, East Sussex, BN1 9RE; tel. (1273) 606261; fax (1273) 621202; e-mail ids@sussex.ac.uk; f. 1966; Dir K. BEZANSON.

International African Institute (IAI): School of Oriental and African Studies, Thornhaugh St, London, WC1H 0XG; tel. (171) 323-6035; fax (171) 323-6118; f. 1926 to promote the study of African peoples, their languages, cultures and social life in their traditional and modern settings; holds seminars and conducts projects; Chair. Prof. GEORGE C. BOND; Dir Prof. PAUL SPENCER; publs include *Africa* (quarterly), *Africa Bibliography* (annually), monograph and reprint series.

International Institute for Environment and Development (IIED): 3 Endsleigh St, London, WC1H 0DD; tel. (171) 388-2117; fax (171) 388-2826; f. 1971; to promote the sound management and sustainable use of natural resources; conducts research into drylands, forestry and land use, human settlements, sustainable agriculture, environmental economics, climate change and institutional co-operation; publications unit from offices in London and Buenos Aires; Exec. Dir RICHARD SANDBROOK.

Overseas Development Institute (ODI): Portland House, Stag Place, London, SW1E 5DP; tel. (171) 393-1600; fax (171) 393-1699; e-mail odi@org.uk; f. 1960 as a research centre and forum for the discussion of development issues and problems; publishes its research findings in books and working papers; Chair. Lord CAIRNS; Dir JOHN HOWELL; publs include *Development Policy Review* (quarterly), *Disasters* (quarterly).

Royal African Society: School of Oriental and African Studies, Thornhaugh St, Russell Sq., London, WC1H 0XG; tel. (171) 323-6253; f. 1901; 800 mems; Pres. Sir MICHAEL CAINE; Sec. Mrs M. L. ALLAN; publ. *African Affairs* (quarterly).

Royal Institute of International Affairs: Chatham House, 10 St James's Sq., London, SW1Y 4LE; tel. (171) 957-5700; fax (171) 957-5710; f. 1920 to study international issues; c. 3,500 mems; Chair. Lord WRIGHT; Dir Sir TIMOTHY GARDEN; Dir of Studies GEORGE JOFFÉ; publs include *International Affairs* (quarterly), *The World Today* (monthly), *Chatham House Papers, Annual Report,* special papers, discussion papers, briefing papers.

School of African and Asian Studies: University of Sussex, Falmer, Brighton, East Sussex, BN1 9QN; tel. (1273) 606755; fax (1273) 623572; Dean Dr D. A. ROBINSON.

School of Oriental and African Studies: Thornhaugh St, Russell Sq., London, WC1H 0XG; tel. (171) 637-2388; telex 262433; fax (171) 436-3844; f. 1916; a school of the Univ. of London; Dir Sir TIM LANKESTER; Sec. F. DABELL; 220 teachers, incl. 44 professors; 3,220 students; publs *The Bulletin, Calendar, Annual Report, Journal of African Law.*

School of Oriental and African Studies Library: Thornhaugh St, Russell Sq., London, WC1H 0XG; tel. (171) 637-2388; fax (171) 636-2834; f. 1916; 850,000 vols and pamphlets; 4,500 current periodicals, 50,000 maps, 6,300 microforms, 2,800 MSS and private papers collections, extensive missionary archives, all covering Asian and African languages, literatures, philosophy, religions, history, law, cultural anthropology, art and archaeology, social sciences, geography and music; Librarian MARY AUCKLAND.

UNITED STATES OF AMERICA

Africa Fund: 17 John St, 12th Floor, New York, NY 10038-4010; tel. (212) 962-1210; fax (212) 964-8570; f. 1966; conducts research and issues publs on Africa; encourages public interest in African issues; creates links between US constituencies and their African counterparts, especially among locally elected officials, trade unions and religious leaders; Pres. Bd of Trustees TILDEN J. LE MELLE; Exec. Sec. JENNIFER DAVIS.

Africa News Service: POB 3851, Durham, NC 27702; tel. (919) 286-0747; fax (919) 286-2614; f. 1973; researches and supplies broadcast and print media with information on African politics, economics and culture, international issues and US policy affecting Africa; library of 5,000 vols and newspaper archives; Pres. REED KRAMER; Exec. Editor TAMI HULTMAN.

African-American Institute: 380 Lexington Ave, New York, NY 10168; tel. (212) 949-5666; telex 666565; fax (212) 682-6174; f. 1953; organizes training programmes and offers devt assistance; maintains reps in 21 African countries; also sponsors confs and seminars; Pres. MORA MCLEAN; Exec. Vice-Pres. STEVE MCDONALD.

African-American Labor Center: 1925 K St, NW, Suite 300, Washington, DC 20006; tel. (202) 778-4600; fax (202) 778-4601; publ. *AALC Reporter.*

African and Afro-American Studies Center: University of Texas, Jester Center A232A, Austin, TX 78705; tel. (512) 471-1784; fax (512) 471-1798; f. 1969; Dir Prof. SHEILA S. WALKER; publs working papers and reprint series (irregular).

African Development Foundation: 1400 Eye St, NW, 10th Floor, Washington, DC 20005; tel. (202) 673-3916; telex 6711367; fax (202) 673-3810; an independent agency of the US federal govt; Pres. GREGORY ROBESON SMITH.

African Studies and Research Program: Dept of African Studies, Howard University, Washington, DC 20059; tel. (202) 806-7115; fax (202) 806-4425; f. 1959; Chair. Dr SULAYMAN S. NYANG; publs include monographs and occasional papers.

African Studies Association of the US: Credit Union Bldg, Emory University, Atlanta, GA 30322; tel. (404) 329-6410; fax (404) 329-6433; e-mail africa@emory.edu; f. 1957; 2,700 mems; collects and publishes information on Africa; Pres. Prof. IRIS BERGER; Dir Dr CHRISTOPHER P. KOCH; publs *African Studies Review, Issue, ASA News, History in Africa.*

African Studies Center: Boston University, 270 Bay State Rd, Boston, MA 02215; tel. (617) 353-7308; fax (617) 353-4975; f. 1953; research and teaching on archaeology, African languages, anthropology, economics, history, geography and political science of Africa; library of 125,000 vols and document titles, 1,000 periodicals and an extensive collection of non-current newspapers and periodicals; Dir Dr JAMES MCCANN; publs include *International Journal of African Historical Studies* (3 a year), working papers, discussion papers.

African Studies Center: 100 Center for International Programs, Michigan State University, Flint, MI 48502; tel. (517) 353-1700; fax (517) 336-1209; e-mail africa@msu.edu; f. 1960; Dir Dr DAVID WILEY; offers instruction in 25 African languages; library of over 200,000 vols; publs include *African Rural and Urban Studies* (3 a year), *Northeast African Studies* (3 a year).

African Studies Program: Ohio University, 56 East Union St, Athens, OH 45701; tel. (614) 593-1834; fax (614) 593-1837; African politics, education, economics, geography, anthropology, languages, literature, philosophy and history; Dir (vacant).

African Studies Program: University of Wisconsin–Madison, 205 Ingraham Hall, 1155 Observatory Drive, Madison, WI 53706; tel. (608) 262-2380; fax (608) 265-5851; study courses; library of over 220,000 vols; Chair. Prof. THOMAS SPEAR; publs include *News and Notes* (bi-annually), *African Economic History* (annually), occasional papers and African texts and grammars.

Africare: 440 R St, NW, Washington, DC 20001; tel. (202) 462-3614; telex 64239; f. 1971; aims to improve basic health services, water resource devt and food production in rural Africa; maintains African resource information centre and personnel data bank available to orgs interested in Africa; 2,300 mems; library of c. 3,300 vols; Pres. Dir C. PAYNE LUCAS; publs include *Newsletter* (2 a year).

American Committee on Africa: 17 John St, 12th Floor, New York, NY 10038; tel. (212) 962-1210; fax (212) 964-8570; f. 1953; Pres. WILLIAM H. BOOTH; Dir JENNIFER DAVIS; publ. *ACOA Action News.*

Association of African Studies Programs: Dept of African and African–American Studies, 236 Grange Bldg, Penn State University, University Park, PA 16802; tel. (814) 863-4243; mems represent more than 40 centres of African studies at US colleges and univs; publ. *Newsletter* (2 a year).

Berkeley/Stanford Joint Center for African Studies: Littlefield Center 14, Stanford University, Stanford, CA 94305-5013; tel. (415) 723-0295; fax (415) 725-6119; f. 1979; African languages, society, culture, foreign policy and social and behavioural sciences; holds research confs; offers jt degree in African studies for students enrolled in professional schools; Co-Chair. ROBERT PRICE, RICHARD ROBERTS; Assoc. Dir MARTHA E. SAAVEDRA; publ. *Newsletter* (3 a year).

Brookings Institution: 1775 Massachusetts Ave, NW, Washington, DC 20036; tel. (202) 797-6000; fax (202) 797-6004; f. 1916; research, education, and publishing in economics, govt and foreign policy; organizes confs and seminars; library of c.

95,000 vols; Pres. MICHAEL H. ARMACOST; publs include *The Brookings Review* (quarterly), *National Newsletter* (quarterly), *Brookings Papers on Economic Activity* (3 a year), *Media Guide* (annually), *Annual Report*.

Center for African Studies: 427 Grinter Hall, University of Florida, Gainesville, FL 32611; tel. (352) 392-2183; telex 568757; fax (352) 392-2435; encourages research projects and sponsors lectures, exhbns and confs; library of 50,000 vols, 500 periodical titles, 40,000 maps; Dir MICHAEL CHEGE.

Center for African Studies: University of Illinois at Urbana-Champaign, 210 International Studies Bldg, 910 South Fifth St, Champaign, IL 61820; tel. (217) 333-6335.

Center for International Studies: Massachusetts Institute of Technology, Bldg E38, Room 648, Cambridge, MA 02139; tel. (617) 253-8093; fax (617) 253-9330; f. 1951; Dir Dr KENNETH OYE.

Center of International Studies: Princeton University, Princeton, NJ 08544-1022; tel. (609) 258-4851; fax (609) 258-3988; Dir Prof. MICHAEL DOYLE.

Council on Foreign Relations, Inc: 58 East 68th St, New York, NY 10021; tel. (212) 734-0400; fax (212) 861-1789; f. 1921; 3,010 mems; library of 5,000 vols, 221 periodicals, clippings files and data bases; Pres. LESLIE H. GELB; publs include *Foreign Affairs* (quarterly).

Council on Regional Studies: 218 Palmer Hall, Princeton University, Princeton, NJ 08544; tel. (609) 258-4720; f. 1961; Dir GILBERT ROZMAN.

Human Rights Watch/Africa: 485 Fifth Ave, 3rd Floor, New York, NY 10017; tel. (212) 972-8400; fax (212) 972-0905; also office in Washington, DC.

Institute of African Affairs: Duquesne University, 600 Forbes Ave, Pittsburgh, PA 15282; tel. (412) 434-6000; fax (412) 434-5146; f. 1957; research into uncommon languages of sub-Saharan Africa; library of 9,000 vols; Dir Rev. JOSEPH L. VARGA; publ. *African Reprint Series*.

Institute of African Studies: Columbia University School of International and Public Affairs, 420 West 118th St, New York, NY 10027; tel. (212) 854-4633; fax (212) 854-4639; Dir GEORGE C. BOND.

Institute of World Affairs (IWA): 1321 Pennsylvania Ave, SE, Washington, DC 20003-2027; f. 1924; tel. (860) 824-5135; fax (860) 544-4141; f. 1924; conducts seminars on international issues; Dir BRADFORD P. JOHNSON; publ. *IWA International* (6 a year).

James S. Coleman African Studies Center: University of California, Los Angeles, CA 90095-1310; tel. (310) 825-3686; fax (310) 206-2250; f. 1959; centre for co-ordination of and research on Africa in the social sciences, the arts, humanities, the sciences and public health; and for multi-disciplinary graduate training in African studies; Dir Dr EDMOND J. KELLER; publs include *African Arts* (quarterly), *Studies in African Linguistics* (quarterly), *Ufahamu: Journal of the African Activists Association* (3 a year), *African Studies Centre Newsletter* (2 a year).

Library of International Relations: Chicago-Kent College of Law, Illinois Institute of Technology, 565 West Adams St, Chicago, IL 60661; tel. (312) 906-5622; fax (312) 906-5685; f. 1932; financed by voluntary contributions; stimulates interest and research in international problems; conducts seminars and offers special services to businesses and academic institutions; library of 500,000 items; Pres. HOKEN SEKI; Dir MICKIE A. VOGES.

Program of African and Asian Languages: Northwestern University, 1859 Sheridan Rd, Evanston, IL 60208-2209; tel. (847) 491-5288 fax (847) 467-1097; f. 1973; languages offered include Arabic and Swahili; Dir RICHARD LEPINE.

Program of African Studies: Northwestern University, 620 Library Place, Evanston, IL 60208-4110; tel. (847) 491-7323; fax (847) 491-3739; f. 1948; supported by various private and govt grants for research in Africa and the USA, as well as by university; awards undergraduate minor and graduate certificate of African studies and sponsors fellowship awards for African students pursuing doctoral studies; Dir Prof. JANE I. GUYER; publs include *PAS Newsletter*, conference proceedings.

School of Advanced International Studies: Johns Hopkins University, 1740 Massachusetts Ave, NW, Washington, DC 20036-1983; tel. (202) 663-5600; fax (202) 663-5683; Dean PAUL WOLFOWITZ; Dir of African Studies I. WILLIAM ZARTMAN; publs *SAIS Studies on Africa, SAIS African Library*.

TransAfrica/TransAfrica Forum: 1744 R St, NW, Washington, DC 20009-2410; tel. (202) 797-2301; fax (202) 797-2382; e-mail transforum@igc.org; Pres. RANDALL ROBINSON; publs include *TransAfrica Forum Update*.

Woodrow Wilson School of Public and International Affairs (African Studies Program): Bendheim Hall, Princeton University, Princeton, NJ 08540; tel. (609) 258-5633; fax (609) 258-5974; e-mail herbst@princeton.edu; Program Dir Prof. JEFFREY HERBST.

SELECT BIBLIOGRAPHY (PERIODICALS)

The ACP–EU Courier. Commission of the European Communities, 200 rue de la Loi, 1049 Brussels, Belgium; tel. (2) 299-30-12; telex 21877; fax (2) 299-30-02; affairs of the African, Caribbean and Pacific countries and the European Union; English and French edns; Editor Simon Horner; 6 a year.

Actividade Economica de Angola. Fundo de Comercializacao, CP 1338, Luanda, Angola; tel. and fax (2) 330420; f. 1935; Dir Mario Alberto Adauta de Sousa; quarterly.

AFRE (African Trade Review). German Perez Carrasco 63, 28027 Madrid, Spain; tel. (1) 267-2403; fax (1) 408-7837; Editor Ed. Arsenio Pardo Rodriguez; monthly.

Africa. Istituto Italo-Africano per l'Africa e l'Oriente, Via Ulisse Aldrovandi 16, 00197 Rome, Italy; tel. (6) 3222323; fax (6) 3225348; f. 1946; Dir Prof. Gian Luigi Rossi; in English, French and Italian; quarterly.

Africa. Edinburgh University Press, 22 George Sq., Edinburgh, EH8 9LF, Scotland; tel. (131) 650-4218; telex 727442; fax (131) 662-0053; Editor Dr Murray Last; quarterly; also annual bibliography.

Africa Analysis. 107-111 Fleet St, London, EC4A 2AB, England; tel. (171) 353-1117; fax (171) 353-1516; e-mail 10031.24@compuserve.com; f. 1986; Editor Ahmed Rajab; fortnightly.

Africa Confidential. 73 Farringdon Rd, London, EC1M 3JB, England; tel. (171) 831-3511; fax (171) 831-6778; f. 1960; political news and analysis; Editor Patrick Smith; fortnightly.

Africa Contemporary Record. Africana Publishing Co, Holmes & Meier Publishers, Inc, 160 Broadway, East Bldg, New York, NY 10038, USA; tel. (212) 374-0100; fax (212) 374-1313; annual documents, country surveys, special essays, indices.

Africa Development. Council for the Development of Social Science Research in Africa (CODESRIA), BP 3304, Dakar, Senegal; tel. 259822; fax 241289; f. 1976; in French and English; Editor Tade Akin Aina; quarterly.

Africa Economic Digest. 26–32 Whistler St, London, N5 1NH, England; tel. (171) 359-5335; telex 262505; fax (171) 359-9409; e-mail aed@compuserve.com; f. 1980; Editor Jon Offei-Ansah (acting); fortnightly.

Africa Energy and Mining. 10 rue de Sentier, 75002 Paris, France; tel. 1-44-88-26-10; fax 1-44-88-26-15; f. 1983; French and English edns; Editor Maurice Botbol; 48 a year.

Africa Fund News. 17 John St, 12th Floor, New York, NY 10038-4010, USA; tel. (212) 962-1210; fax (212) 964-8570; Editor Michael Fleshman; 2 a year.

Africa Health. Vine House, Fair Green, Reach, Cambridge, CB5 0JD, England; tel. (1638) 743633; fax (1638) 743998; e-mail iuf@fsg.co.uk; f. 1978; Editor Paul Chinnock; 6 a year.

Africa Insider. Matthews Associates, POB 53398, Temple Heights Station, Washington, DC 20009, USA; tel. (301) 309-6632; f. 1984; Editor Dan Matthews; fortnightly.

Africa Insight. Africa Institute, POB 630, Pretoria 0001, South Africa; tel. (12) 328-6970; fax (12) 323-8153; f. 1971; Editor Madeline Lass; quarterly.

Africa International. BP 172, 75523 Paris Cedex, France; tel. 1-44-93-85-95; fax 1-44-93-74-68; f. 1958; political, economic and social development in francophone Africa; Editor Marie-Roger Biloa; monthly.

Africa Museum. Africa-Museum Tervuren, Leuvensesteenweg 13, 3080 Tervuren, Belgium; tel. (2) 769-52-11; fax (2) 767-02-42; f. 1993; ethnology, history and archaeology of Africa; quarterly.

Africa Quarterly. Indian Council for Cultural Relations, Azad Bhavan, Indraprastha Estate, New Delhi 110 002, India; tel. (11) 3319309; telex 3166004; fax (11) 3318647; Editor Dr T. G. Ramamurthi.

Africa Recovery. Rm S-931, United Nations, New York, NY 10017, USA; tel. (212) 963-6857; fax (212) 963-4556; Editor-in-Chief Salim Lone; in English and French; quarterly.

Africa Research Bulletin. Africa Research Ltd, c/o Blackwell Publishers, 108 Cowley Rd, Oxford, OX4 1JF, England; tel. (1865) 791100; fax (1865) 791347; e-mail jnlinfo@blackwellpublishers.co.uk; f. 1964; bulletins on political and economic topics; Editor Pita Adams; monthly.

Africa Review. Kogan Page Ltd, 120 Pentonville Rd, London, N1 9JN, England; tel. (171) 278-0433; fax (171) 837-6348; f. 1977; Gen. Editor Tony Axon; annually.

Africa Today. Africa Today Associates, Graduate School of International Studies, University of Denver, Denver, CO 80208, USA; tel. (303) 871-3678; fax (303) 871-2456; f. 1954; Editor Angelique Haugerud; quarterly.

Africa 2000. Centro Cultural Hispano-Guineano, Apdo 180, Malabo, Equatorial Guinea; tel. 27-20; f. 1985; Equato-Guinean social and cultural review; Spanish; Editor Donato Ndongo-Bidyogo; quarterly.

African Administrative Studies. Centre africain de formation et de recherche administratives pour le développement (CAFRAD), BP 310, Tangier, 90001 Morocco; tel. (9) 942652; fax (9) 941415; English, French and Arabic; 2 a year.

African Affairs. Royal African Society, School of African and Oriental Studies, Thornhaugh St, Russell Sq., London, WC1H 0XB, England; tel. (171) 323-6253; f. 1901; social sciences and history; Editors David Killingray, Peter Woodward; quarterly.

African Agenda. TWN Africa Secretariat, POB 8604, Accra North, Ghana; tel. (23) 224069; fax (21) 231687; f. 1995; Editor Yao Graham; 6 a year.

African Archaeological Review. Plenum Publishing Corpn, 233 Spring St, New York, NY 10013-1578, USA; tel. (212) 620-8000; fax (212) 463-0742; quarterly.

African Arts. James S. Coleman African Studies Center, University of California, Los Angeles, CA 90095-1310, USA; tel. (310) 825-1218; fax (310) 206-2250; Editors Donald J. Cosentino, Doran H. Ross; quarterly.

African Book Publishing Record. Hans Zell Publishers, 11 Richmond Rd, POB 56, Oxford, OX1 2SJ, England; tel. (1865) 511428; fax (1865) 311534; e-mail hzell@dial.pipex.com; f. 1975; bibliographic listings, book reviews, articles and information on book trade activities in Africa; Editor Hans M. Zell; quarterly.

African Business. 7 Coldbath Sq., London, EC1R 4LQ, England; tel. (171) 713-7711; telex 8811757; fax (171) 713-7970; f. 1966; economics, business, commerce and finance; Editor Anver Versi; monthly.

African Concord International. 26–32 Whistler St, London, N5 1NH, England; tel. (171) 359-5335; telex 262505; fax (171) 359-9173; African and international current affairs; Nigerian and international edns; Editor Soji Omotunde; weekly.

African Crusader. Pacific Printers Ltd, 38 Commercial Ave, Yaba, Nigeria; f. 1978; social, political and economic issues; monthly.

African Environment. BP 3370, Dakar, Senegal; tel. 22-42-29; telex 456; f. 1975; environmental issues; English and French edns; quarterly.

African Farming and Food Processing. Alain Charles Publishing Ltd, 27 Wilfred St, London, SW1E 6PR, England; tel. (171) 834-7676; fax (171) 973-0076; Editor Jonquil L. Phelan; 6 a year.

African Journal of Health Sciences. African Forum for Health Sciences, POB 54840, Nairobi, Kenya; f. 1994; tel. (2) 722541; fax (2) 720030; e-mail kemrilib@ken.healthnet.org; Editor Dr D. Koech; quarterly.

African Journal of International Affairs & Development. POB 30678, Ibadan, Nigeria; fax (2) 8101963; Editors Jide Owoeye, Adebayo Olukoshi; 2 a year.

African Peoples Review. 34–36 Crown St, Reading, Berks, RG1 2SE, England; tel. (1734) 391010; fax (1734) 594442; f. 1992; reviews of publications and creative arts; Editor Herbert Ekwe-Ekwe; 3 a year.

African Publishing Review. POB 4209, Harare, Zimbabwe; tel. (4) 739681; fax (4) 751202; Editor Lesley Humphrey; English and French edns; 6 a year.

African Recorder. A-126 Niti Bagh, POB 595, New Delhi 110 049, India; tel. (11) 665405; f. 1962; news digest; Editor A. K. B. Menon; fortnightly.

African Review. Dept of Political Science and Public Administration, University of Dar es Salaam, POB 35042, Dar es Salaam, Tanzania; tel. (51) 43130; fax (51) 43395; f. 1971; Editor Charles Gasarasi; 2 a year.

African Review of Business and Technology. Alain Charles Publishing Ltd, 27 Wilfred St, London, SW1E 6PR, England; tel. (171) 834-7676; fax (171) 973-0076; Editor Jonquil L. Phelan; 11 a year.

African Security Review. Institute for Defence Policy, POB 4167, Halfway House 1685, South Africa; tel. (11) 315-7096; fax (11) 315-7099; e-mail idp@cis.co.za; security and related issues; Editor Eunice Reyneke; 6 a year.

African Studies. Carfax Publishing Ltd, POB 25, Abingdon, Oxfordshire, OX14 3UE, England; tel. (1235) 401000; fax (1235) 401550; f. 1921; social and cultural studies of southern Africa; Editor D. James; 2 a year.

African Studies Abstracts. Hans Zell Publishers, 11 Richmond Rd, POB 56, Oxford, OX1 2SJ, England; tel. (1865) 511428; fax (1865) 311534; e-mail hzell@dial.pipex.com; abstracting journal of the African Studies Centre, Leiden, The Netherlands; quarterly.

African Studies Review. African Studies Association, Emory University, Credit Union Bldg, Atlanta, GA 30322, USA; tel. (404) 329-6410; e-mail africa@emory.edu; Editor Mark DeLancey; 3 a year.

African Textiles. Alain Charles Publishing Co, 27 Wilfred St, London, SW1E 6PR, England; tel. (171) 834-7676; fax (171) 973-0076; Editor Zsa Tebbit; 6 a year.

Africana Bulletin. Institute of Developing Countries, Faculty of Geography and Regional Studies, University of Warsaw, Krakowskie Przedmieścіe 26/28, 00-325 Warsaw 64, Poland; tel. (22) 269871; telex 815439; fax (22) 261965; f. 1964; articles in English or French; Editor Prof. Dr Bogodar Winid; irregular.

Africana Marburgensia. Philipps-Universität Marburg, Fachgebiet Religionsgeschichte, Fachbereich 05, Marburg, Am Plan 3, Germany; tel. (6421) 283930; f. 1968; religion, law, economics; in English, French and German; Editors Christoph Elsos, Reiner Mahlke, Hans H. Münkner; 2 a year.

Africanus. Unisa Press, Periodicals, POB 392, Pretoria 0001, South Africa; tel. (12) 429-3111; fax (12) 429-3221; e-mail unisapress@unisa.ac.za; f. 1972; development issues; 2 a year.

Afrika. Afrika-Verlag, 85276 Pfaffenhofen, Raiffeisenstrasse 24, Germany; tel. 8441-8690; fax 8441-76582; f. 1960; edns in German and French; Editors Inga Krugman-Randolf, Ursula Bell; 6 a year.

Afrika Spectrum. Institut für Afrika-Kunde, 20354 Hamburg, Neuer Jungfernstieg 21, Germany; tel. (40) 3562523; fax (40) 3562511; mostly in German, but with contributions and summaries in English and French; 3 a year.

Afrika Sud. Informationsstelle Südliches Afrika eV, 53227 Bonn, Königswintererstrasse 116, Germany; tel. (228) 464369; fax (228) 468177; politics, economics, social and military affairs of southern Africa and German relations with the area; 6 a year.

Afrika und Übersee, Sprachen–Kulturen. c/o Dietrich Reimer Verlag, 12203 Berlin, Unter den Eichen 57, Germany; tel. (30) 8314081; fax (30) 8316323; f. 1910; African linguistics and cultures; in German, English and French; Editors E. Dammann, L. Gerhardt, E. Kähler-Meyer, H. Meyer-Bahlburg, J. Zwernemann, L. S. Uhlig; 2 a year.

Afrique Agriculture. 6 rue du Dr Solomon, 60119 Henonville, France; tel. 1-34-35-00-26; fax 1-30-32-04-83; f. 1975; Editor Alain Zolty; monthly.

Afrique Expansion. 17 rue d'Uzes, 75002 Paris, France; tel. 1-40-13-30-30; fax 1-40-41-94-95; building and construction; Editor Michel Levron.

Afrique Contemporaine. La Documentation française, 29–31 quai Voltaire, 75340 Paris Cedex 07, France; tel. 1-40-15-70-00; telex 204826; fax 1-40-15-72-30; f. 1962; political, economic and sociological studies; Editor-in-Chief Michel Gaud; quarterly.

Afrique Entreprise. IC Publications, 10 rue Vineuse, 75784 Paris, France; tel. 1-44-30-81-00; fax 1-44-30-81-11; 22 a year.

Afrique Médicale. BP 1826, Dakar, Senegal; f. 1960; tel. (221) 234880; telex 1300; fax (221) 225630; f. 1960; medical review; Editor, Prof. Paul Correa; 11 a year.

Afryka, Azja, Ameryka Łacińska. Instytut Krajow Rozwijajcych Sie, 02-089 Warsaw, Zwirki i Wigury 93, Poland; tel. (2) 223051; f. 1974; in Polish, with English and French summaries; Editor Prof. Władysław Kubiak; irregular.

Aktueller Informationsdienst Afrika. Spiegel der afrikanischen Presse, Institut für Afrika-Kunde, 20354 Hamburg, Neuer Jungfernstieg 21, Germany; tel. (40) 3562523; fax (40) 3562511; press digest from African publs; English, French and Portuguese; fortnightly.

Botswana Notes and Records. The Botswana Society, POB 71, Gaborone, Botswana; tel. 351500; fax 359321; f. 1969; Editor Doreen Nteta; annually.

Bulletin of the School of Oriental and African Studies. School of Oriental and African Studies, Thornhaugh St, Russell Sq., London, WC1H 0XG, England; tel. (171) 637-2388; telex 291829; fax (171) 436-3844; f. 1917; 3 a year.

Business Africa. Goldcity Communications Ltd, Shakespeare Business Centre, Suite F11, 245A Coldharbour Lane, London, SW9 8RR, England; tel. (171) 737-5933; fax (171) 738-3613; bi-monthly.

CAFRAD News. Centre africain de formation et de recherche administratives pour le développement, (CAFRAD), BP 310, Tangier, 90001 Morocco; tel. (9) 942652; fax (9) 941415; English, French and Arabic; 2 a year.

Cahiers d'Etudes Africaines. Ecole des hautes études en sciences sociales, 131 blvd St-Michel, 75005 Paris, France; tel. 1-40-46-70-80; fax 1-44-07-08-89; e-mail cahiers-afr@chess.fr; f. 1960; Editor J.-L. Amselle; in French and English; quarterly.

Canadian Journal of African Studies. Canadian Association of African Studies, c/o Barry Riddell, Dept of Geography, Queen's University, Kingston, ON K7L 3N6, Canada; tel. (613) 545-6037; fax (613) 545-6122; e-mail riddellb@qsilver.queensu.ca; Editors Barry Riddell, Dennis Cordell; 3 a year.

Communications Africa. Alain Charles Publishing Ltd, 27 Wilfred St, London, SW1E 6PR, England; tel. (171) 834-7676; fax (171) 973-0076; f. 1991; telecommunications, broadcasting and information technology; in French and English; Editor P. Northam; 6 a year.

Development Policy Review. Overseas Development Institute, Portland House, Stag Place, London, SW1 5DP, England; tel. (171) 393-1600; fax (171) 393-1699; f. 1982; Editor Sheila Page; quarterly.

Development and Socio-Economic Progress. Afro-Asian People's Solidarity Organization, 89 Abdel Aziz al-Saoud St, Manial El-Roda, Cairo, Egypt; tel. (2) 845495; English, Arabic and French edns; Editor-in-Chief Nouri Abdel Razzak; quarterly.

Dokumentationsdienst Afrika. Ausgewählte neuere Literatur, Deutsches Übersee-Institut, Übersee-Dokumentation, Referat Afrika (AFDOK), 20354 Hamburg, Neuer Jungfernstieg 21, Germany; tel. (40) 3562598; fax (40) 3562512; e-mail dueidok@hwwa.uni-hamburg.de; current bibliography; quarterly.

East Africa Journal. POB 3209, Dar es Salaam, Tanzania; tel. 724711; f. 1964; Editor B. A. Ogot; monthly.

East African Studies. Makerere Institute of Social Research, Makerere University, POB 16022, Kampala, Uganda; irregular.

Economia de Moçambique: Companhia Editoria de Moçambique, CP 81, Beira, Mozambique; Editor Antonia de Almeida.

Economic Bulletin of Ghana. Economic Society of Ghana, POB 22, Legon, Accra, Ghana; tel. (1) 775381; Editor J. C. Degraft-Johnson; quarterly.

English Studies in Africa. c/o Dept of English, University of the Witwatersrand, 1 Jan Smuts Ave, PO Wits, 2050 Johannesburg, South Africa; tel. (11) 716-2848; fax (11) 403-7309; f. 1959; journal of the humanities; Editor Dr V. H. Houliston; bi-annually.

Ethiopian Register. POB 159, Avon, MN 56310-0159, USA, tel. (320) 845-7770; fax (320) 845-4993; f. 1994; monthly.

Ethiopian Review. POB 98499, Atlanta, GA 30539, USA; tel. and fax (404) 325-8411; Editor Elias Kifle; monthly.

Heritage of Zimbabwe. History Society of Zimbabwe, POB 8268, Causeway, Zimbabwe; tel. (4) 39175; f. 1956; history of Zimbabwe and adjoining territories; Editor Michael J. Kimberley; annually.

Horn of Africa Bulletin. Life and Peace Institute, 75170 Uppsala, Sweden; tel. (18) 169500; fax (18) 693059; Editor Susanne Thurfjell Lundén; bi-monthly.

Indian Ocean Newsletter. 10 rue du Sentier, 75002 Paris, France; tel. 1-44-88-26-10; fax 1-44-88-26-15; f. 1981; French and English edns; Editor Maurice Botbol; 48 a year.

International African Bibliography. Hans Zell Publishers, 11 Richmond Rd, POB 56, Oxford, OX1 2SJ, England; tel. (1865) 511428; fax (1865) 311534; e-mail hzell@dial.pipex.com; bibliographic listings; Editor David Hall; quarterly.

International Journal of African Historical Studies. African Studies Center, Boston University, 270 Bay State Rd, Boston, MA 02215, USA; tel. (617) 353-7306; fax (617) 353-4975; f. 1968; Editor Norman R. Bennett; 3 a year.

Jeune Afrique. JAPRESS, 57 bis d'Auteuil, 75016 Paris, France; tel. 1-44-30-19-60; telex 651105; fax 1-45-20-08-22; f. 1960; Editor-in-Chief Béchir ben Yahmed; weekly.

Journal of African Economies. 21 Winchester Rd, Oxford, OX2 6NA, England; tel. (1865) 56767; telex 837330; fax (1865) 267773; f. 1992; Man. Editors Paul Collier, J. W. Gunning, Benno Ndulu, Ademola Oyejide; 3 a year.

Journal des Africanistes. Société des Africanistes, Musée de l'Homme, Palais de Chaillot, 17 place du Trocadéro, 75116 Paris, France; tel. 1-47-27-72-55; f. 1931; some articles in English; 2 a year.

Journal of African History. School of Oriental and African Studies, Thornhaugh St, Russell Sq., London, WC1H 0XG, England; tel. (171) 637-2388; telex 291829; fax (171) 436-3844; f. 1960; Editors Bill Nasson, Louis Brenner, Thomas Spear, Phyllis Martin; 3 a year.

Journal of Asian and African Studies. Dept of Sociology, Vari Hall 2106, York University, 4700 Keele St, Downsview, ON M3J 1P3, Canada; tel. (416) 441-6343; Editor K. Ishwaran.

Journal of Development Studies. Frank Cass and Co Ltd, Newbury House, 890-900 Eastern Ave, Newbury Park, London, IG2 7HH, England; tel. (181) 599-8866; fax (181) 599-0984; f. 1964; Editors Christopher Colclough, Colin Kirkpatrick, David Booth; 6 a year.

Journal of Ethiopian Studies. Institute of Ethiopian Studies, Addis Ababa University, POB 1176, Addis Ababa, Ethiopia; tel. (1) 119469; telex 21205; fax (1) 552688; f. 1963; social and cultural anthropology, literature, history, linguistics, political science, economics; Editors Bahru Zewde, Shiferaw Bekele, Taddesse Tamrat; Man. Editor Amanuel Gebru; 2 a year.

Journal of Imperial and Commonwealth History. Frank Cass and Co Ltd, Newbury House, 890-900 Eastern Ave, Newbury Park, London, IG2 7HH, England; tel. (181) 599-8866; fax (181) 599-0984; f. 1972; Editors A. J. Stockwell, Peter Burroughs; 3 a year.

Journal of Modern African Studies. Cambridge University Press, The Edinburgh Bldg, Shaftesbury Rd, Cambridge, CB2 2RU, England; tel. (1223) 312393; fax (1223) 315052; politics and economics; Editor Prof. Christopher Clapham; quarterly.

Journal of Peasant Studies. Frank Cass and Co Ltd, Newbury House, 890-900 Eastern Ave, Newbury Park, London, IG2 7HH, England; tel. (181) 530-4226; fax (181) 530-7795; f. 1973; Editors Terry Byres, Henry Bernstein, Tom Brass; quarterly.

Journal of Religion in Africa. Dept of Theology and Religious Studies, University of Leeds, Leeds, West Yorkshire, LS2 9JT, England; tel. (113) 2333640; fax (113) 2333654; e-mail i.lawrie@leeds.ac.uk; f. 1967; Editor Adrian Hastings; quarterly.

Journal of Southern African Studies. c/o Colin Stoneman, Centre for Southern African Studies, University of York, Heslington, York, North Yorkshire, YO1 5DD, England; tel. (1904) 433698; telex 57933; fax (1904) 433433; f. 1974; Editors Saul Dubow, Liz Gunner, Debby Potts; quarterly.

Journal of the Third World Spectrum: POB 44843, Washington, DC 20026-4843, USA; tel. (202) 806-7649; f. 1989; Editor Feraidoon Shams; 2 a year.

Leeds Africa. African Studies Unit, University of Leeds, Leeds, West Yorkshire, LS2 9JT, England; tel. (113) 2335069; annually.

La Lettre d'Afrique Expansion. 17 rue d'Uzès, 75002 Paris, France; tel. 1-40-13-33-81; fax 1-40-41-94-95; f. 1984; business affairs; Editor Hassan Ziady; weekly.

La Lettre du Continent. 10 rue de Sentier, 75002 Paris, France; tel. 1-44-88-26-10; fax 1-44-88-26-15; f. 1985; Editor Maurice Botbol; fortnightly.

Marchés Tropicaux et Mediterranéens. 190 blvd Haussmann, 75008 Paris, France; tel. 1-95-99-50; telex 290131; fax 1-53-90-16; f. 1945; current affairs, mainly economics; Editor Serge Marpaud; weekly.

New African. 7 Coldbath Sq., London, EC1R 4LQ, England; tel. (171) 713-7711; fax (171) 713-7970; f. 1966; politics and general interest; Editor-in-Chief Alan Rake; monthly.

Newslink Africa. 7-11 Kensington High St, London, W8 5NP, England; tel. (171) 411-3111; fax (171) 938-4168; e-mail adlink-internat-newslinkafrica@compuserve.com; business and development issues; Editor Shamlal Puri; weekly.

Nigrizia–Il Mensile dell'Africa e del Mondo Nero. Vicolo Pozzo 1, 37129 Verona, Italy; tel. (45) 596238; fax (45) 8031455; fax (45) 8001737; f. 1883; Dir Pier Maria Mazzola; monthly.

Nouveaux Cahiers de l'IUED. 24 rue Rothschild, CP 136, 1211 Geneva 21, Switzerland; tel. (22) 9065940; fax (22) 7385797; Editor (vacant); 2 a year.

Nouvelles du CAFRAD. Centre africain de Formation et de Recherche administratives pour le Développement (CAFRAD), BP 310, Tangier, 90001 Morocco; tel. (9) 942652; fax (9) 941415; Arabic, English, French; monthly.

Odu. A Journal of West African Studies, New Series (1969–). Obafemi Awolowo University Press, Periodicals Dept, Ile-Ife, Nigeria; tel. (36) 230284; Editor Biadun Adediren; 2 a year.

Opportunity Africa. Westoning House, 2nd Floor, East Central Markets, 1 Lindsey St, London, EC4A 9HP, England; tel. (171) 216-4900; fax (171) 236-0744; f. 1994; Editor Mark Dorman; quarterly.

Optima. POB 61587, 2107 Marshalltown, South Africa; tel. (11) 638-5125; telex 487167; fax (11) 638-3771; f. 1951; political, economic, social, cultural and scientific aspects of South and southern African development; circulated mainly to shareholders of Anglo American Corpn of South Africa, De Beers Consolidated Mines and to educational institutions; Editor Mark Irvine; 2 a year.

Peuples Noirs–Peuples Africains. 82 ave de la Porte-des-Champs, 76000 Rouen, France; tel. 2-35-89-31-97; f. 1978; 6 a year.

Politique Africaine. Editions Karthala, 22–24 blvd Arago, 75013 Paris, France; tel. 1-43-31-15-59; fax 1-45-35-27-05; f. 1981; political science and international relations; Editor-in-Chief Alain Ricard; quarterly.

Red Cross, Red Crescent. BP 372, 1211 Geneva 19, Switzerland; English, French and Spanish edns; tel. (22) 7304222; telex 412133; fax (22) 7530395; e-mail geary@ifrc.org; Editors Barbara Geary, Christina Grisewood; 3 a year.

Research in African Literatures. University of Indiana Press, 601 North Morton St, Bloomington, IN 47404, USA; tel. (812) 855-9449; fax (812) 855-8507; Editor Abiola Irele; quarterly.

Research Review. Institute of African Studies, POB 73, University of Ghana, Legon, Ghana; tel. (21) 775512; telex 2556; f. 1965; Editor K. Arhin; 3 a year.

Review of African Political Economy. Carfax Publishing Ltd, POB 25, Abingdon, Oxfordshire, OX14 3UE, England; tel. (1235) 401000; fax (1235) 401550; f. 1974; Editors Jan Burgess, Chris Allen; quarterly.

Revista Internacional de Estudos Africanos. Instituto de Investigação Cientifica Tropical, Ministério da Ciência e da Tecnologia, Rua de Junqueira 86-1°, 1300 Lisbon, Portugal; tel. (1) 3622621; fax (1) 3631460; 2 a year.

Revue diplomatique de l'Ocean Indien. rue H. Rabesahala, BP 46, Antsakaviro, 101 Antananarivo, Madagascar; tel. 22536; telex 22225; fax 34534; f. 1982; Editor Georges Ranaivasoa; quarterly.

Revue Française d'Etudes Politiques Africaines. Société Africaine d'Edition, BP 1877, Dakar, Senegal; f. 1966; political; Editors Pierre Biarnès, Philippe Decraene; monthly.

Sierra Leone Review. POB 65231, Washington, DC 20035, USA; f. 1992; Editor Sorie Musa; quarterly.

SIMNOW. SIM Media Dept, 10 Huntingdale Blvd, Scarborough, ON M1W 2S5, Canada; tel. (416) 497-2424; fax (416) 497-2444; f. 1958; edns also publ. in Australia, NZ, Southern Africa, Singapore, Switzerland and UK; French, German, Italian and Chinese edns; Editorial Dir David W. Fuller; quarterly.

South Africa Survey. South African Institute of Race Relations, POB 31044, Braamfontein 2017, South Africa; tel. (11) 403-3600; fax (11) 403-3671; Dir J. S. Kane-Berman; annually.

Southern Africa Exclusive. Ludgate House, Suite 71, 107-111 Fleet St, London, EC4A 2AB, England; tel. (171) 353-1117; fax (171) 353-1516; f. 1992; Editor Terry Bell; monthly.

Southern Africa Monthly Regional Bulletin–MRB. POB 724, London, N16 5RZ, England; tel. (171) 923-1467; fax (171) 923-2545; f. 1992; Publr David Coetzee.

Southern Africa Report. POB 261579, Excom 2023, South Africa; tel. (11) 646-8790; fax (11) 646-2596; e-mail alouw@wn.apc.org; f. 1983; current affairs and financial newsletter; Publr and Editor Raymond Louw; 50 a year.

SouthScan. POB 724, London, N16 5RZ, England; tel. (171) 923-1467; fax (171) 923-2545; f. 1986; political and economic affairs in southern Africa; Publr David Coetzee; weekly.

Strategy African Defence. 64–78 Kingsway, Suite 141, London, WC2B 6GB, England; tel. (171) 404-8847; fax (171) 404-8852; aerospace and defence; Editor Brian Walters.

Strategy Southern Africa. 64–78 Kingsway, Suite 141, London, WC2B 6BG, England; tel. (171) 404-8847; fax (171) 404-8852; finance and business; Editor Robert Anderson.

Sudan Democratic Gazette. POB 2295, London, W14 0ND, England; tel. (171) 602-4401; fax (171) 602-0106; f. 1990; Publr and Editor Bona Malwal.

Sudanow. POB 2651, 7 Gamhouria Ave, Khartoum, Sudan; tel. and fax (11) 77915; f. 1976.

Third World Quarterly. 188 Copse Hill, London, SW20 0SP, England; tel. (181) 947-1043; fax (181) 947-1043; Editor Shahid Qadir.

Tiers Monde. 14 ave du Bois-de-l'Epine, BP 90, 91003 Evry Cedex, France; tel. 1-60-79-20-45; telex 600474; fax 1-60-79-20-45; f. 1960; development issues; Editor Maxine Haubert; quarterly.

Uganda Confidential. POB 9948, Kampala, Uganda; fax (41) 245580; Editors Gerald Mwaita, John Kateeba; weekly.

Vostok (Oriens). Afro-Aziatskiye Obtchestva: Istoria i Sovremenost, Institut Vostokovedeniya, Institut Afriki, Rossiyskaya Akad. Nauk, 30/1 Spiridonovka St, Moscow 103001, Russia; tel. (095) 2026650; f. 1955; text in Russian, summaries in English; Editor-in-Chief Dr L. B. Alayev; 6 a year.

Washington Report on Africa. 1413 K St, NW, Suite 1400, Washington, DC 20005, USA; tel. (202) 371-0555; telex 281409; fax (202) 408-9369; Editor John Justin Ford; fortnightly.

West Africa. West Africa Publishing Co Ltd, 43–45 Coldharbour Lane, London, SE5 9NR, England; tel. (171) 737-2946; fax (171) 978-8334; f. 1917; Editor Maxwell Nwagboso; weekly.

West African Journal of Archaeology: Ibadan University Press, University of Ibadan, Ibadan, Nigeria; f. 1961; annually.

PART TWO
Regional Organizations

THE UNITED NATIONS IN AFRICA

Address: United Nations Plaza, New York, NY 10017, USA.

Telephone: (212) 963-1234; **fax:** (212) 963-2180.

The United Nations (UN) was founded on 24 October 1945. The organization aims to maintain international peace and security, and to develop international co-operation in economic, social, cultural and humanitarian problems. The principal organs of the UN are the General Assembly, the Security Council, the Economic and Social Council (ECOSOC), the International Court of Justice and the Secretariat. The General Assembly, which meets for three months each year, comprises representatives of all UN member states. The Security Council investigates disputes between member countries, and may recommend ways and means of peaceful settlement: it comprises five permanent members (the People's Republic of China, France, Russia, the United Kingdom and the USA) and 10 other members elected by the General Assembly for a two-year period. The Economic and Social Council comprises representatives of 54 member states, elected by the General Assembly for a three-year period: it promotes co-operation on economic, social, cultural and humanitarian matters, acting as a central policy-making body and co-ordinating the activities of the UN's specialized agencies. The International Court of Justice comprises 15 judges of different nationalities, elected for nine-year terms by the General Assembly and the Security Council: it adjudicates in legal disputes between UN member states.

Secretary-General of the United Nations: KOFI ANNAN (Ghana) (1997–2001).

MEMBER STATES IN AFRICA SOUTH OF THE SAHARA

(with assessments for percentage contributions to UN budget for 1996, and year of admission)

Angola	0.01	1976
Benin	0.01	1960
Botswana	0.01	1966
Burkina Faso	0.01	1960
Burundi	0.01	1962
Cameroon	0.01	1960
Cape Verde	0.01	1975
Central African Republic	0.01	1960
Chad	0.01	1960
Comoros	0.01	1975
Congo, Democratic Republic*	0.01	1960
Congo, Republic	0.01	1960
Côte d'Ivoire	0.01	1960
Djibouti	0.01	1977
Equatorial Guinea	0.01	1968
Eritrea	0.01	1993
Ethiopia	0.01	1945
Gabon	0.01	1960
The Gambia	0.01	1965
Ghana	0.01	1957
Guinea	0.01	1958
Guinea-Bissau	0.01	1974
Kenya	0.01	1963
Lesotho	0.01	1966
Liberia	0.01	1945
Madagascar	0.01	1960
Malawi	0.01	1964
Mali	0.01	1960
Mauritania	0.01	1961
Mauritius	0.01	1968
Mozambique	0.01	1975
Namibia	0.01	1990
Niger	0.01	1960
Nigeria	0.11	1960
Rwanda	0.01	1962
São Tomé and Príncipe	0.01	1975
Senegal	0.01	1960
Seychelles	0.01	1976
Sierra Leone	0.01	1961
Somalia	0.01	1960
South Africa	0.32	1945
Sudan	0.01	1956
Swaziland	0.01	1968
Tanzania†	0.01	1961
Togo	0.01	1960
Uganda	0.01	1962
Zambia	0.01	1964
Zimbabwe	0.01	1980

* Formerly Zaire; renamed the Democratic Republic of the Congo in 1997.

† Tanganyika was a member of the United Nations from December 1961 and Zanzibar was a member from December 1963. From April 1964 the United Republic of Tanganyika and Zanzibar continued as a single member, changing its name to United Republic of Tanzania in November 1964.

AFRICAN PERMANENT MISSIONS TO THE UNITED NATIONS

(with Permanent Representatives—July 1997)

Angola: 125 East 73rd St, New York, NY 10021; tel. (212) 861-5656; fax (212) 861-9295; AFONSO VAN DÚNEM (MBINDA).

Benin: 4 East 73rd St, New York, NY 10021; tel. (212) 249-6014; fax (212) 734-4735; FASSASSI YACOUBOU.

Botswana: 103 East 37th St, New York, NY 10016; tel. (212) 889-2277; fax (212) 725-5061; LEGWAILA JOSEPH LEGWAILA.

Burkina Faso: 115 East 73rd St, New York, NY 10021; tel. (212) 288-7515; fax (212) 772-3562; GAËTAN RIMWANGUIYA OUÉDRAOGO.

Burundi: 336 East 45th St, 12th Floor, New York, NY 10017; tel. (212) 499-0001; fax (212) 499-0006; NJANZE TERENCE.

Cameroon: 22 East 73rd St, New York, NY 10021; tel. (212) 794-2295; fax (212) 249-0533; Chargé d'affaires a.i.: JEAN-MARC MPAY.

Cape Verde: 27 East 69th St, New York, NY 10021; tel. (212) 472-0333; fax (212) 794-1398; JOSÉ LUIS BARBOSA LEÃO MONTEIRO.

Central African Republic: 386 Park Ave South, Suite 1614, New York, NY 10016; tel. (212) 679-8089; fax (212) 689-6741; HENRY KOBA.

Chad: 211 East 43rd St, Suite 1703, New York, NY 10017; tel. (212) 986-0980; fax (212) 986-0152; AHMAT MAHAMAT-SALEH.

Comoros: 336 East 45th St, 2nd Floor, New York, NY 10017; tel. (212) 972-8010; fax (212) 983-4712; (vacant).

Congo, Democratic Republic: 2 Henry Ave, North Caldwell, NJ 07006; tel. (201) 812-1636; fax (201) 812-2177; (vacant).

Congo, Republic: 14 East 65th St, New York, NY 10021; tel. (212) 744-7840; fax (212) 744-7975; DANIEL ABIBI.

Côte d'Ivoire: 46 East 74th St, New York, NY 10021; tel. (212) 717-5555; fax (212) 717-4492; YOUSSOUFOU BAMBA.

Djibouti: 866 United Nations Plaza, Suite 4011, New York, NY 10017; tel. (212) 753-3163; fax (212) 223-1276; ROBLE OLHAYE.

Equatorial Guinea: 10 East 39th St, Rm 1124, New York, NY 10016; tel. (212) 683-5295; fax (212) 683-5791; Pastor MICHA ONDO BILE.

Eritrea: 211 East 43rd St, Suite 2203, New York, NY 10017; tel. (212) 687-3390; fax (212) 687-3138; AMDEMICAEL KAHSAI.

Ethiopia: 866 United Nations Plaza, Suite 560, New York, NY 10017; tel. (212) 421-1830; fax (212) 754-0360; Dr DURI MOHAMMED.

Gabon: 18 East 41st St, 9th Floor, New York, NY 10017; tel. (212) 686-9720; fax (212) 689-5769; DENIS DANGUE RÉWAKA.

The Gambia: 820 Second Ave, 9th Floor, New York, NY 10017; tel. (212) 949-6640; fax (212) 808-4975; MOMODOU KEBBA JALLOW.

Ghana: 19 East 47th St, New York, NY 10017; tel. (212) 832-1300; fax (212) 751-6743; JACOB BOTWE WILMOT.

Guinea: 140 East 39th St, New York, NY 10016; tel. (212) 687-8115; fax (212) 687-8248; MAHAWA BANGOURA CAMARA.

Guinea-Bissau: 211 East 43rd St, Suite 704, New York, NY 10017; tel. (212) 338-9380; fax (212) 573-6094; ALFREDO LOPES CABRAL.

Kenya: 866 United Nations Plaza, Suite 486, New York, NY 10017; tel. (212) 421-4740; fax (212) 486-1985; NJUGUNA M. MAHUGA.

Lesotho: 204 East 39th St, New York, NY 10016; tel. (212) 661-1690; fax (212) 682-4388; PERCY METSING MANGOAELA.

Liberia: 820 Second Ave, 13th Floor, New York, NY 10017; tel. (212) 687-1033; fax (212) 687-1035; WILLIAM BULL.

Madagascar: 801 Second Ave, Suite 404, New York, NY 10017; tel. (212) 986-9491; fax (212) 986-6271; JOCELYNE LINGAYA.

Malawi: 600 Third Ave, 30th Floor, New York, NY 10016; tel. (212) 949-0180; fax (212) 599-5021; Prof. DAVID RUBADIRI.

Mali: 111 East 69th St, New York, NY 10021; tel. (212) 737-4150; fax (212) 472-3778; MOCTAR OUANE.

Mauritania: 211 East 43rd St, Suite 2000, New York, NY 10017; tel. (212) 986-7963; fax (212) 986-8419; MAHFOUDH OULD DEDDACH.

Mauritius: 211 East 43rd St, 15th Floor, New York, NY 10017; tel. (212) 949-0190; fax (212) 697-3829; (vacant).

Mozambique: 70 East 79th St, New York, NY 10021; tel. (212) 517-4550; fax (212) 734-3083; CARLOS DOS SANTOS.

Namibia: 135 East 36th St, New York, NY 10016; tel. (212) 685-2003; fax (212) 685-1561; MARTIN ANDJABA.

Niger: 417 East 50th St, New York, NY 10022; tel. (212) 421-3260; fax (212) 753-6931; JOSEPH DIATTA.

Nigeria: 828 Second Ave, New York, NY 10017; tel. (212) 953-9130; fax (212) 697-1970; Prof. IBRAHIM AGOOLA GAMBARI.

Rwanda: 336 East 45th St, New York, NY 10017; tel. (212) 808-9149; fax (212) 808-0975; GIDÉON KAYINAMURA.

São Tomé and Príncipe: 122 East 42nd St, Suite 1604, New York, NY 10017; tel. (212) 697-4211; fax (212) 687-8389; (vacant).

Senegal: 238 East 68th St, New York, NY 10021; tel. (212) 517-9030; fax (212) 517-3032; IBRA DEGUÈNE KA.

Seychelles: 820 Second Ave, Suite 900F, New York, NY 10017; tel. (212) 972-1785; fax (212) 972-1786; (vacant).

Sierra Leone: 245 East 49th St, New York, NY 10017; tel. (212) 688-1656; fax (212) 688-4924; JAMES O. JONAH.

Somalia: 425 East 61st St, Suite 703, New York, NY 10021; tel. (212) 688-9140; fax (212) 759-0651; (vacant).

South Africa: 333 East 38th St, 9th Floor, New York, NY 10016; tel. (212) 213-5583; fax (212) 692-2498; KHIPHUSIZI J. JELE.

Sudan: 655 Third Ave, Suite 500-510, New York, NY 10017; tel. (212) 573-6033; fax (212) 573-6160; ELFATIH MOHAMED AHMED ERWA.

Swaziland: 408 East 50th St, New York, NY 10022; tel. (212) 371-8910; fax (212) 754-2755; MOSES MATHENDELE DLAMINI.

Tanzania: 205 East 42nd St, 13th Floor, New York, NY 10017; tel. (212) 972-9160; fax (212) 682-5232; DAUDI NGELAUTWA MWAKAWAGO.

Togo: 112 East 40th St, New York, NY 10016; tel. (212) 490-3455; fax (212) 983-6684; ROLAND Y. KPOTSRA.

Uganda: 336 East 45th St, New York, NY 10017; tel. (212) 949-0110; fax (212) 687-4517; Prof. MATIA M. SEMAKULA KIWANUKA.

Zambia: 800 Second Ave, 9th Floor, New York, NY 10017; tel. (212) 972-7200; fax (212) 972-7360; PETER LESA KASANDA.

Zimbabwe: 128 East 56th St, New York, NY 10022; tel. (212) 980-9511; fax (212) 755-4188; MACHIVENYIKA TOBIAS MAPURANGA.

Observers

Asian-African Legal Consultative Committee: 404 East 66th St, Apt 12C, New York, NY 10021; tel. (212) 734-7608; e-mail 19077.27512@compuserve.com; K. BHAGWAT-SINGH.

Commonwealth Secretariat: 820 Second Ave, Suite 800A, New York, NY 10017; tel. (212) 599-6190; fax (212) 972-3970; e-mail chogrm@aol.com.

International Committee of the Red Cross: 801 Second Ave, 18th Floor, New York, NY 10017; tel. (212) 599-6021; fax (212) 599-6009; e-mail mail@icrc.delnyc.org; PETER KÜNG.

International Federation of Red Cross and Red Crescent Societies: 630 Third Ave, Suite 2104, New York, NY 10017; tel. (212) 338-0161; fax (212) 338-9832; e-mail ifrcay@nygate.undp.org; EIGIL PEDERSEN.

Organization of African Unity: 346 East 50th St, New York, NY 10022; tel. (212) 319-5490; fax (212) 319-7135; IBRAHIMA SY.

Organization of the Islamic Conference: 130 East 40th St, 5th Floor, New York, NY 10016; tel. (212) 883-0140; fax (212) 883-0143.

Several other intergovernmental organizations, including the African, Caribbean and Pacific Group of States and the African Development Bank (q.v.), have standing invitations to participate in the work of the General Assembly, but do not maintain permanent offices in New York.

GENERAL ASSEMBLY BODY CONCERNED WITH AFRICA SOUTH OF THE SAHARA

Advisory Committee on the UN Educational and Training Programme for Southern Africa: f. 1968; 13 mems.

Economic Commission for Africa—ECA

Address: Africa Hall, POB 3005, Addis Ababa, Ethiopia.

Telephone: (1) 517200; **telex:** 21029; **fax:** (1) 514416; **e-mail:** ecainfo@un.org.

The UN Economic Commission for Africa was founded in 1958 by a resolution of ECOSOC to initiate and take part in measures for facilitating Africa's economic development.

MEMBERS

Algeria	Eritrea	Niger
Angola	Ethiopia	Nigeria
Benin	Gabon	Rwanda
Botswana	The Gambia	São Tomé and Príncipe
Burkina Faso	Ghana	Senegal
Burundi	Guinea	Seychelles
Cameroon	Guinea-Bissau	Sierra Leone
Cape Verde	Kenya	Somalia
Central African Republic	Lesotho	South Africa
Chad	Liberia	Sudan
Comoros	Libya	Swaziland
Congo, Democratic Republic	Madagascar	Tanzania
Congo, Republic	Malawi	Togo
Côte d'Ivoire	Mali	Tunisia
Djibouti	Mauritania	Uganda
Egypt	Mauritius	Zambia
Equatorial Guinea	Morocco	Zimbabwe
	Mozambique	
	Namibia	

Organization

(July 1997)

COMMISSION

The Commission may only act with the agreement of the government of the country concerned. It is also empowered to make recommendations on any matter within its competence directly to the government of the member or associate member concerned, to governments admitted in a consultative capacity, and to the UN Specialized Agencies. The Commission is required to submit for prior consideration by ECOSOC any of its proposals for actions that would be likely to have important effects on the international economy.

CONFERENCE OF MINISTERS

The Conference, which meets annually, is attended by ministers responsible for economic or financial affairs, planning and development of governments of member states, and is the main deliberative body of the Commission. A Technical Preparatory Committee of the Whole, representing all member states, was established in 1979 to deal with matters submitted for the consideration of the Conference.

The Commission's responsibility to promote concerted action for the economic and social development of Africa is vested primarily in the Conference, which considers matters of general policy and the priorities to be assigned to the Commission's programmes, considers inter-African and international economic policy, and makes recommendations to member states in connection with such matters. It reviews the course of programmes being implemented in the preceding year and examines and approves the programmes proposed for the next.

OTHER POLICY-MAKING BODIES

Conference of African Ministers of Economic Planning and Social Development.

Conference of African Ministers of Finance.

Conference of African Ministers of Industry.

Conference of African Ministers of Social Affairs.

Conference of African Ministers of Trade.

Conference of African Ministers of Transport, Communications and Planning.

Conference of Ministers of Finance.

Conference of Ministers Responsible for Human Resources Planning, Development and Utilization.

Councils of Ministers of the MULPOCs (see below).

SECRETARIAT

The Secretariat provides the services necessary for the meeting of the Conference of Ministers and the meetings of the Commission's subsidiary bodies, carries out the resolutions and implements the programmes adopted there.

Executive Secretary: KINGSLEY Y. AMOAKO (Ghana).

Subsidiary Bodies

Conference of Ministers of African Least-Developed Countries.

Follow-up Committee on Industrialization in Africa.

Intergovernmental Committee of Experts of African Least-Developed Countries.

Intergovernmental Committee of Experts for Science and Technology Development.

Intergovernmental Regional Committee on Human Settlements and Environment.

Joint Conference of African Planners, Statisticians and Demographers.

Regional Operational Centres

Multinational Programming and Operational Centres (MULPOC) act as 'field agents' for the implementation of regional development programmes. The Centres are located in Yaoundé, Cameroon (serving central Africa), Gisenyi, Rwanda (Great Lakes Community), Lusaka, Zambia (east and southern Africa), Niamey, Niger (west Africa) and Tangier, Morocco (north Africa). Each centre holds regular ministerial meetings. In May 1997 the Commission decided to transform the MULPOCs into Subregional Development Centres.

African Institute for Economic Development and Planning: POB 3186, Addis Ababa, Ethiopia; tel. (1) 22577; Dir JEGGAN C. SENGHOR.

Activities

The Commission's activities are designed to encourage sustainable socio-economic development in Africa and to increase economic co-operation among African countries and between Africa and other parts of the world. The Secretariat is guided in its efforts by major regional strategies including the Abuja Treaty establishing the African Economic Community signed under the aegis of the Organization of African Unity and the UN New Agenda for the Development of Africa covering the period 1991–2000. ECA's main programme areas for the period 1996–2001 were based on an Agenda for Action, which was announced by the OAU Council of Ministers in March 1995 and adopted by African heads of state in June, with the stated aim of 'relaunching Africa's economic and social development'. The five overall objectives were to facilitate economic and social policy analysis and implementation; to ensure food security and sustainable development; to strengthen development management; to harness information for development; and to promote regional co-operation and integration.

AGRICULTURE

ECA provides support in the areas of development of livestock; inter-state co-operation; reduction or prevention of food losses; monitoring and evaluation of agricultural and rural development projects; conservation, expansion and rational utilization of natural resources, particularly land and forests; and preparation of related technical publications or reports. In the mid-1990s ECA's principal objective in the agricultural sector was the promotion of food security in African countries.

ENERGY

ECA's Energy Programme provides assistance to member states in the development of indigenous energy resources and the formulation of energy policies to extricate member states from continued energy crises. The ECA Secretariat supports the African Regional Centre for Solar Energy, based at Bujumbura, Burundi.

ENVIRONMENT AND DEVELOPMENT

During 1991–92 reports were compiled on the development, implementation and sound management of environmental programmes at national, sub-regional and regional levels. ECA members adopted a common African position for the UN Conference on Environment and Development, held in June 1992. In 1995 ECA published its first comprehensive report and statistical survey of human development issues in African countries. The *Human Development in Africa Report*, which was to be published every two years, aimed to demonstrate levels of development attained, particularly in the education and child health sectors, to identify areas of concern and to encourage further action by policy-makers and development experts.

INDUSTRY

Following the failure to implement many of the proposals under the UN Industrial Development Decade for Africa (IDDA, 1980–90) and the UN Programme of Action for African Economic Recovery and Development (1986–90), a second IDDA was adopted by the Conference of African Ministers of Industry in July 1991. The main objectives of the second IDDA include the consolidation and rehabilitation of existing industries, the expansion of new investments, and the promotion of small-scale industries and technological capabilities. Various technical publications were to be produced, including a directory of project profiles in the field of entrepreneurship in small-scale industries.

INFORMATION

The Pan-African Documentation and Information Service (PADIS) was established in 1980. The main objectives of PADIS are: to provide access to numerical and other information on African social, economic, scientific and technological development issues; to assist African countries in their efforts to develop national information handling capabilities through advisory services and training; to establish a data communication network to facilitate the timely use of information on development; and to design sound technical specifications, norms and standards to minimize technical barriers in the exchange of information. ECA is promoting the use of electronic systems to disseminate information throughout the region, under its commitment for the period 1996–2001 to harness information for development purposes. In addition, ECA aims to encourage member governments to liberalize the telecommunications sector and stimulate imports of computers in order to enable the expansion of the information infrastructure.

INTERNATIONAL TRADE AND FINANCE

ECA assists African countries in expanding trade among themselves and with other regions of the world and in promoting financial and monetary co-operation. ECA attempts to ensure that African countries participate effectively in international negotiations. To this end, assistance has been provided to member states in negotiations under UNCTAD and GATT; in the annual conferences of the IMF and the World Bank; in negotiations with the EU; and in meetings related to economic co-operation among developing countries. Studies have been prepared on problems and prospects likely to arise for the African region from the implementation of the Common Fund for Commodities and the Generalized System of Trade Preferences (both supervised by UNCTAD); the impacts of exchange-rate fluctuations on the economies of African countries; and on the long-term implications of different debt arrangements for African economies. ECA assists individual member states by undertaking studies on domestic trade, expansion of inter-African trade, transnational corporations, integration of women in trade and development, and strengthening the capacities of state-trading organizations. ECA aims to assist countries to manage effectively trade issues arising from the conclusion of the Uruguay Round of GATT negotiations and its implementation under the World Trade Organization.

The expansion of trade within Africa is constrained by the low level of industrial production, and by the strong emphasis on commodity trade. ECA encourages the diversification of production, the liberalization of cross-border trade and the expansion of domestic trade structures, within regional economic groupings. ECA helps to organize regional and 'All-Africa' trade fairs.

In 1992 ECA, in co-ordination with the OAU and the African Development Bank (q.v.), embarked on a series of meetings with western governments and financial institutions in an attempt to persuade them to cancel, partially or completely, debts owed by African countries, and to encourage them to invest in the region. In March/April 1997 the Conference of African Ministers of Finance, meeting in Addis Ababa, reviewed a new initiative of the World Bank and IMF to assist the world's 41 most heavily indebted poor countries, of which 33 were identified as being in Africa. While the Conference recognized the importance of the involvement of multilateral institutions in assisting African economies to achieve a sustainable level of development, it criticized aspects of the structural adjustment programmes imposed by the institutions and advocated more flexible criteria to determine eligibility for the new initiative.

NATURAL RESOURCES

The Fourth Regional Conference on the Development and Utilization of Mineral Resources in Africa, held in March 1991, adopted an action plan that included the formulation of national mineral exploitation policies; and the promotion of the gemstone industry, small-scale mining and the iron and steel industry. ECA supports the Southern African Mineral Resources Development Centre in Dar-es-Salaam, Tanzania, and the Central African Mineral Development Centre in Brazzaville, Congo, which provide advisory and laboratory services to their respective member states.

ECA sponsors the two leading institutions in the field of cartography and remote-sensing. The Regional Centre for Services in Surveying, Mapping and Remote-Sensing is based in Nairobi, Kenya; it is currently establishing a satellite receiving station for processing remotely-sensed data for use by member states. The Regional Centre for Training in Aerospace Surveys, base in Ile Ife, Nigeria, provides training in cartography and remote-sensing.

ECA assists member states in the assessment and use of water resources and the development of river and lake basins common to more than one country. The annual information bulletin on water resources in Africa, *Maji,* disseminates technical information to African governments, and inter-governmental and non-governmental organizations. In the field of marine affairs, ECA extends advisory services to member states on the opportunities and challenges provided by the UN Convention on the Law of the Sea.

POLICY AND PROGRAMME CO-ORDINATION

Policy and programme co-ordination is one of the tasks of the Executive Direction and Management office. The office provides guidance in the formulation of policies towards the achievement of Africa's development objectives to the policy-making organs of the UN and OAU. It contributes to the work of the General Assembly and other specialized agencies by providing an African perspective in the preparation of development strategies. In March 1996 the UN announced a system-wide Special Initiative on Africa to mobilize resources and to implement a series of political and economic development objectives over a 10-year period. ECA's Executive Secretary is the Co-Chair, with the Administrator of the UNDP, of the Steering Committee for the Initiative.

POPULATION

ECA assists its member states in (i) population data collection and data processing, which is carried out by the Statistics Division of the Commission (q.v.); (ii) analysis of demographic data obtained from censuses or surveys: this assistance is given by the Population Division; (iii) training demographers at the Regional Institute for Population Studies (RIPS) in Accra (Ghana) and at the Institut de formation et de recherche démographiques (IFORD) in Yaoundé (Cameroon); (iv) formulation of population policies and integrating population variables in development planning, through advisory missions and through the organization of national seminars on population and development; and (v) dissemination of information through its *Newsletter, Demographic Handbook for Africa,* the *African Population Studies* series and other publications. The strengthening of national population policies was an important element of ECA's objective of ensuring food security in African countries. The Ninth Joint Conference of African Planners, Statisticians and Demographers was held in March 1996, in Addis Ababa, Ethiopia.

PUBLIC ADMINISTRATION, HUMAN RESOURCES AND SOCIAL DEVELOPMENT

The Division aims to assist governments, public corporations, universities and the private sector in improving their financial management; strengthening policy-making and analytical capacities; adopting measures to redress skill shortages; enhance human resources development and utilization; and promote social development through programmes focusing on youth, people with disabilities and the elderly. The Division conducts training workshops, seminars and conferences at national, sub-regional and regional levels for ministers, public administrators, senior policy-makers as well as for private and non-governmental organizations.

SCIENCE AND TECHNOLOGY

The Commission's activities in the field of science and technology focus on three areas: the development of policies and institutions; the training and effective utilization of the work-force; and the promotion of regional and inter-regional co-operation. ECA provides technical support to the African Regional Centre for Technology and the African Regional Organization for Standardization.

SOCIO-ECONOMIC RESEARCH AND PLANNING

Monitoring economic and social trends in the African region and studying the development problems concerning it are among the fundamental tasks of the Commission. Every year the Commission publishes the *Survey of Economic and Social Conditions in Africa* and the *Economic Report on Africa*.

The Commission gives assistance to governments in general economic analysis, in fiscal, financial and monetary issues and in planning. The ECA's work on economic planning has been recently broadened, in order to give more emphasis to macro-economic management in a mixed economy approach: a project is being undertaken to develop short-term forecasting and policy models to support economic management. The Commission has also started a major study on the informal sector in African countries. Special assistance is given to least-developed, land-locked and island countries which have a much lower income level than other countries and which are faced with heavier constraints than others. Studies are also undertaken to assist longer-term planning.

The Conference of African Planners, Statisticians and Demographers is held every two years (see above) and provides an opportunity for African governments to exchange views and experiences, and to keep abreast of new policy approaches.

In 1989 ECA published a report entitled *African Alternative Framework to Structural Adjustment Programmes for SocioEconomic Recovery and Transformation,* which argued that programmes of strict economic reform, as imposed by the International Monetary Fund and the World Bank, had not resulted in sustained economic growth in Africa over the past decade. In July 1991 ECA proposed a series of measures which countries might adopt, in a more flexible approach to long-term development. These proposals were subsequently published under the title *Selected Policy Instruments* and included multiple exchange rates (as opposed to generalized currency devaluation), differential interest rates and subsidies to agricultural producers.

In May 1994 ECA ministers of economic and social development and of planning, meeting in Addis Ababa, adopted a *Framework Agenda for Building and Utilizing Critical Capacities in Africa*. The agenda aimed to identify new priority areas to stimulate development, for example, by strengthening management structures, more efficient use of a country's physical infrastructure and by expanding processing or manufacturing facilities. The agenda proposed the establishment of a new regional committee, under ECA leadership, to co-ordinate these initiatives.

In June 1996 a conference, organized by ECA, was held in Accra, Ghana, with the aim of reviving private investment in Africa in order to stimulate the private sector and promote future economic development. The conference established a forum for African political leaders and business executives to discuss the development of capital markets in the region and to co-ordinate efforts in sectoral training and research.

STATISTICS

The Statistics Division of ECA, which comprises two sections (Statistical Development and Economic Statistics) promotes the development and co-ordination of national statistical services in the region and the improvement and comparability of statistical data. It prepares documents to assist in the improvement of statistical methodology and undertakes the collection, evaluation and dissemination of statistical information. A plan of action for statistical development in Africa in the 1990s has been formulated and a Co-ordinating Committee on African Statistical Development (CASD) has been established. ECA's work in the field of statistics has been concentrated in five main areas: the African Household Survey Capability Programme, which aims to assist in the collection and analysis of demographic, social and economic data on households; the Statistical Training Programme for Africa, which aims to make the region self-sufficient in statistical personnel at all levels; the Technical Support Services, which provides technical advisory services for population censuses, demographic surveys and civil registration; the National Accounts Capability Programme, which aims at improving economic statistics generally by building up a capability in each country for the collection, processing and analysis of economic data; and the ECA-Regional Statistical Data Base, part of PADIS (see above), which provides on-line statistical information to users.

TRANSPORT AND COMMUNICATIONS

The ECA was appointed lead agency for the second United Nations Transport and Communications Decade in Africa (UNTACDA II), comprising the period 1991–2000. The principal aim of UNTACDA II is the establishment of an efficient, integrated transport and communications system in Africa. The specific objectives of the programme include: (i) the removal of physical and non-physical barriers to intra-African trade and travel, and improvement in the road transport sector; (ii) improvement in the efficiency and financial viability of railways; (iii) development of Africa's shipping capacity and improvement in the performance of Africa's ports; (iv) development of integrated transport systems for each lake and river basin; (v) improvement of integration of all modes of transport in order to carry cargo in one chain of transport smoothly; (vi) integration of African airlines, and restructuring of civil aviation and airport management authorities; (vii) improvement in the quality and availability of transport in urban areas; (viii) development of integrated regional telecommunications networks; (ix) development of broadcasting services, with the aim of supporting socio-economic development; and (x) expansion of Africa's postal network.

ECA is the co-ordinator, with the World Bank, of a regional Road Maintenance Initiative, which was launched in 1988. By early 1996 13 African countries were receiving assistance under the initiative, which sought to encourage a partnership between the public and private sectors to manage and maintain road infrastructure more efficiently and thus to improve country-wide communications and transportation activities.

BUDGET

For the two-year period 1994–95 ECA's regular budget, an appropriation from the UN budget, was US $78m.

PUBLICATIONS

ECA Annual Report.

Africa Index (3 a year).

African Compendium on Environmental Statistics (irregular).

African Directory of Demographers (irregular).
African Population Newsletter (2 a year).
African Population Studies Series (irregular).
African Socio-Economic Indicators (annually).
African Statistical Yearbook.
African Trade Bulletin (2 a year).
Bulletin of ECA-sponsored Institutions (irregular).
Demographic Handbook for Africa (irregular).
Devindex Africa (quarterly).
Directory of African Statisticians (every 2 years).
ECA Environment Newsletter (3 a year).
Flash on Trade Opportunities (quarterly).
Focus on African Industry (2 a year).
Foreign Trade Statistics for Africa series.
Direction of Trade (quarterly).
Summary Table (annually).
Human Development in Africa Report (every two years).
Maji Water Resources Bulletin (annually).
PADIS Newsletter (quarterly).
Report of the Executive Secretary (every 2 years).
Rural Progress (2 a year).
Statistical Newsletter (2 a year).
Survey on Economic and Social Conditions in Africa (annually).

Information on ECA can be accessed on the Internet at http://www.un.orgs.Depts/eca.

United Nations Development Programme—UNDP

Address: One United Nations Plaza, New York, NY 10017, USA.
Telephone: (212) 906-5000; **fax:** (212) 826-2057.

The Programme was established in 1965 by the UN General Assembly. Its central mission is to help countries eradicate poverty and achieve a sustainable level of human development.

Organization

(July 1997)

UNDP is responsible to the UN General Assembly, to which it reports through the UN Economic and Social Council.

EXECUTIVE BOARD

The 36-member Executive Board is responsible for providing intergovernmental support to and supervision of the activities of UNDP and the UN Population Fund (UNFPA, of which UNDP is the governing body).

SECRETARIAT

Administrator: JAMES GUSTAVE (GUS) SPETH (USA).

REGIONAL OFFICES

Headed by assistant administrators, the regional bureaux share the responsibility for implementing the programme with the Administrator's office. Within certain limitations, large-scale projects may be approved and funding allocated by the Administrator, and smaller-scale projects by the Resident Representatives (see below).

Five regional bureaux, all at the Secretariat in New York, cover: Africa; Asia and the Pacific; the Arab states; and Latin America and the Caribbean; and Europe and the Commonwealth of Independent States.

Assistant Administrator and Director, Regional Bureau for Africa: TREVOR GORDON SOMERS (acting).

FIELD OFFICES

There are 132 UNDP country offices, each headed by the UNDP Resident Representative, who advises the Government on formulating the country programme, sees that field activities are carried out, and acts as the leader of the UN team of experts working in the country. Resident Representatives are normally designated as co-ordinators for all UN operational development activities; the field offices function as the primary presence of the UN in most developing countries.

OFFICES OF UNDP REPRESENTATIVES IN AFRICA SOUTH OF THE SAHARA

Angola: Rua Major Kanhangulo 197, CP 910, Luanda; tel. (2) 334986; fax (2) 335609.

Benin: Lot 3, Zone Residentielle, BP 506, Cotonou; tel. 31-30-45; fax 31-57-86.

Botswana: Barclays House, Khama Crescent, POB 54, Gaborone; tel. 351680; fax 356093; e-mail fo.bwa@undp.org.

Burkina Faso: Immeuble SONAR, Quartier Ex-Koulouba, Secteur 4, 01 BP 575, Ouagadougou 01; tel. (3) 30-67-65; fax (3) 31-04-70.

Burundi: 3 rue du Marché, BP 1490, Bujumbura; tel. (2) 223135; fax (2) 225850.

Cameroon: rue Giscard d'Estaing, BP 836, Yaoundé; tel. 22-17-79; fax 22-43-69.

Cape Verde: Casa Moeda, Ave Andrade Corvo, CP 62, Praia; tel. 61-57-40; fax 61-43-70; e-mail fo.cpv@undp.org.

Central African Republic: ave de l'Indépendance, BP 872, Bangui; tel. 61-12-07; fax 61-17-32.

Chad: ave Colonel D'Ornano, BP 906, N'Djamena; tel. 51-41-00; fax 51-63-30.

Comoros: Hamramba, BP 648, Moroni; tel. 73-10-70; fax 73-15-77.

Congo, Democratic Republic: Immeuble Royal, blvd du 30 juin, BP 7248, Kinshasa; tel. (12) 33431; fax (871) 1503261.

Congo, Republic: ave du Maréchal Foch, BP 465, Brazzaville; tel. 83-59-53; fax 83-39-87.

Côte d'Ivoire: angle rue Gourgas et ave Marchand, Abidjan-Plateau, 01 BP 1747, Abidjan 01; tel. 21-29-95; fax 21-13-67; e-mail fo.civa@undp.org.

Djibouti: blvd Maréchal Joffre, Plâteau du Serpent, BP 2001, Djibouti; tel. 351361; fax 350587.

Equatorial Guinea: CP 399, Esquina Calle de Kenia con Calle Rey Boncoro, Malabo; tel. (9) 3269; fax (871) 383-138168.

Eritrea: 5 Andinet St, Airport Rd, POB 5366, Asmara; tel. (1) 182166; telex 150-7652; fax (1) 181081.

Ethiopia: Africa Hall, Old ECA Bldg, 7th Floor, Menelik II Ave, POB 5580, Addis Ababa; tel. (1) 511025; fax (1) 514599.

Gabon: Immeuble Africa No 1, Boulevard Triomphal Omar Bongo entre Ministère des Affaires Etrangères et Hypermarché Mbolo, BP 2183, Libreville; tel. 74-52-35; fax 74-34-99; e-mail fo.gab@undp.org.

The Gambia: ave Ann Marie Javouhey, POB 553, Banjul; tel. (2) 28722; fax (2) 28921.

Ghana: Ring Rd Dual Carriage, nr Police HQ, POB 1423, Accra; tel. (21) 777831; fax (21) 773899.

Guinea: Immeuble Union, ave de la République, BP 222, Conakry; tel. 41-36-22; fax 41-24-85.

Guinea-Bissau: Rua Rui Djassi, 72 A/B, POB 1011, Bissau; tel. 201368; fax 201753.

Kenya: Kenyatta International Conference Center, Harambee Ave, POB 30218, Nairobi; tel. (2) 228776; fax (2) 211226; e-mail fo.ken@undp.org.

Lesotho: Corner Hilton and Nightingale Rds, POB 301, Maseru 100; tel. 313944; fax 310042.

Liberia: Daher Apt, UN Drive, Mamba Point, POB 10-0274, Monrovia 10; tel. 226188; fax (874) 150-5746.

Madagascar: Rue Rainitovo, Antsahavola, BP 1348, Antananarivo 101; tel. (2) 21907; fax (2) 33315.

Malawi: Plot No 7, Area 40, POB 30135, Lilongwe 3; tel. 782278; fax 783637.

Mali: Immeuble Me Hamaciré N'Douré, Badalabougou-Est, BP 120, Bamako; tel. 22-20-52; fax 22-62-98.

Mauritania: Lot K, Lots No. 159–161, BP 620, Nouakchott; tel. (2) 56900; fax (2) 52616; e-mail fo.mrt@undp.org.

Mauritius: Anglo-Mauritius House, Intendance St, POB 253, Port Louis; tel. 208-8691; fax 208-4871; e-mail 100075.3612@compuserve.com.

Mozambique: Avda Kenneth Kaunda, 921/931, POB 4595, Maputo; tel. (1) 491475; fax (1) 491691; e-mail fo.moz@undp.org.

Namibia: Sanlam Centre, 154 Independence St, Private Bag 13329, Windhoek 9000; tel. (61) 229220; fax (61) 229084.

Niger: Maison de l'Afrique, BP 11207, Niamey; tel. 72-34-90; fax 72-36-30; e-mail fo.ner@undp.org.

Nigeria: 11 Oyinkan Abayomi Drive, Ikoyi, POB 2075, Lagos; tel. (1) 269-1722; fax (1) 269-3397; e-mail fo.nga@undp.org.

Rwanda: ave de l'Armée 12, BP 445, Kigali; tel. 77822; fax 76263; e-mail fo.rwa@undp.org.

São Tomé and Príncipe: Avda das Naçoes Unidas, CP 109, São Tomé; tel. 22562; fax 22198.

Senegal: Immeuble Faycal, 19 rue Parchappe, BP 154, Dakar; tel. 23-60-12; fax 23-55-00; e-mail fo.sen@undp.org.

Seychelles: covered by office in Mauritius.

Sierra Leone: United Nations House, 43 Siaka Stevens St, POB 1011, Freetown; tel. (22) 225346; fax (22) 228720.

Somalia: covered by office in Kenya.

South Africa: Metropark Bldg, 9th and 10th Floors, 351 Schoeman St, POB 6541, Pretoria 0001; tel. (12) 320-4360; fax (12) 320-4353.

Sudan: House No 7, Block 5, R.F.E., Gama'a Ave, POB 913, Khartoum; tel. (11) 783755; fax (873) 151-6741.

Swaziland: SRIC Bldg, Gilfillan St, Mbabane; tel. 42305; fax 45341; e-mail fo.swa@undp.org.

Tanzania: Matasalamat Mansions, 2nd Floor, Zanaki St, POB 9182, Dar es Salaam; tel. (51) 113270; fax (51) 113272; e-mail fo.tza@undp.org.

Togo: 40 ave des Nations Unies, 1ère étage, BP 911, Lomé; tel. 21-20-22; fax 21-16-41; e-mail fo.tgo@undp.org.

Uganda: UN House, 15 Clement Hill Rd, POB 7184, Kampala; tel. (41) 233440; fax (41) 244801; e-mail undp@mukla.gn.apc.org.

Zambia: Plot No. 11867, Alick Nkhata Ave, Longacres, POB 31966, Lusaka; tel. (1) 254417; fax (1) 253805; e-mail fo.zmb@undp.org.

Zimbabwe: Takura House, 9th Floor, 67-69 Union Ave, POB 4775, Harare; tel. (4) 792681; fax (4) 728695; e-mail fo.zwe@undp.org.

Activities

As the world's largest source of grant technical assistance in developing countries, UNDP works with more than 150 governments and 40 international agencies in efforts to achieve faster economic growth and better standards of living throughout the world. Most of the work is undertaken in the field by the various United Nations agencies, or by the government of the country concerned. UNDP is committed to allocating some 87% of its core resources to low-income countries with an annual income per caput of less than US $750, while 60% of resources are allocated to the world's least-developed countries.

Assistance is mostly non-monetary, comprising the provision of experts' services, consultancies, equipment, and fellowships for advanced study abroad. In 1996 35% of spending on projects was for the services of experts, 25% was for subcontracts, 18% was for equipment, 16% was for training, and the remainder was for other costs, such as technical support. Most UNDP projects incorporate training for local workers. Developing countries themselves provide 50% or more of the total project costs in terms of personnel, facilities, equipment and supplies. In 1996 UNDP expenditure on projects in Africa amounted to US $256.5m., or 21% of the total field programme expenditure.

In June 1994 the Executive Board adopted a programme for change which focused on UNDP's role in achieving sustainable human development, an approach to economic growth that encompasses individual well-being and choice, equitable distribution of the benefits of development and conservation of the environment. Within this framework there were to be four priority objectives: poverty elimination; the expansion of employment opportunities; environmental regeneration; and the advancement and empowerment of women. A new Office of Evaluation and Strategic Planning was established to facilitate the restructuring required by these changes, while an Office of UN System Support and Services has been created to assist in unifying various UN agencies around the new framework for sustainable human development. The allocation of programming resources since 1994 has reflected UNDP's new agenda, with 39% of core funding directed towards poverty eradication and livelihoods for the poor, 32% to capacity-building and governance, and 21% to projects concerned with the environment and natural resources. Some 20% of total resources are allocated to promoting gender equality in all UNDP activities.

UNDP aims to help governments to reassess their development priorities and to design initiatives for sustainable development at a country-specific level. UNDP country offices support the formulation of national human development reports (NHDRs), which aim to facilitate activities such as policy-making, the allocation of resources, and monitoring progress towards poverty eradication and sustainable development. By 1996 11 African countries (Benin, Botswana, Cameroon, Central African Republic, Ghana, Mali, Mauritania, Namibia, Sierra Leone, Togo and Uganda) had produced NHDRs. In addition, the preparation of Advisory Notes and Country Co-operation Frameworks help to highlight country-specific aspects of poverty eradication and national strategic priorities. From 1990 UNDP has published an annual *Human Development Report* incorporating a Human Development Index, which ranked countries in terms of human development, using three key indicators: life expectancy, adult literacy and basic income required for a decent standard of living.

In 1994 the Executive Board determined that UNDP should assume a more active and integrative role within the UN development system. This approach has been implemented by UNDP Resident Representatives who aim to co-ordinate UN policies, in consultation with other agencies, in particular UNEP, FAO and UNHCR. In 1997 UNDP planned to allocate more resources to training and skill-sharing programmes in order to promote this co-ordinating role. UNDP is a co-sponsor, jointly with WHO, the World Bank, UNICEF, UNESCO and UNFPA, of a Joint UN Programme on HIV and AIDS, which became operational on 1 January 1996.

UNDP supports the Africa Project Development Facility (APDF) which is administered by the International Finance Corporation (q.v.), and which aims to encourage private investment in the region. In March 1966 the UN Secretary-General inaugurated the Special Initiative on Africa, which was envisaged as a collaborative effort between the principal UN bodies and major regional organizations to secure a set of development objectives for Africa. The cost of the initiative was estimated at US $25,000m. over a 10-year period. UNDP's Africa bureau was initially to provide a secretariat for the programme, while UNDP's mandated involvement was in the areas of conflict prevention, strengthening democracy and enhancing public management in African countries. The other priorities of the Initiative were to achieve improvements in basic education, health and hygiene, food and water security and the expansion of South-South co-operation. UNDP was also to develop its role in co-ordinating activities following global UN conferences. In March 1995 government representatives attending the World Summit for Social Development, that was held in Copenhagen, Denmark, adopted the Copenhagen Declaration and a Programme of Action, which included initiatives to promote the eradication of poverty, to increase and reallocate official development assistance to basic social programmes and to promote equal access to education. With particular reference to UNDP, the Programme of Action advocated that UNDP support the implementation of social development programmes, co-ordinate these efforts through its field offices and organize efforts on the part of the UN system to stimulate capacity-building at local, national and regional levels. By 1996 a new poverty strategy initiative was being implemented in more than 60 countries, while other activities were directed towards strengthening the private sectors in developing countries, in particular through the provision of financing for micro-enterprises, and creating the capacity for sound economic management and good governance. Following the UN Fourth World Conference on Women, held in Beijing, People's Republic of China, in September 1995, UNDP has led inter-agency efforts to ensure the full participation of women in all economic, political and professional activities and assisted with further situation analysis and training activities.

In January 1996 UNDP organized a regional conference, held in Ouagadougou, Burkina Faso, and attended by its Resident Representatives, the ministers of economy and finance of 45 African countries, as well as representatives of other regional organizations, in order to review UNDP's development activities in Africa and to consider a new UN initiative for the region. UNDP's Africa regional bureau presented its three-year programme, for the period 1997–99, which was to concentrate on the enhancement of governance in African countries, strengthening their capacities for economic management, furthering regional trade and economic integration and development of the private sector, in particular at the grass-roots level.

In the mid-1990s UNDP expanded its role in countries in crisis and with special circumstances, working in collaboration with other UN agencies to bridge relief and development efforts. In particular, UNDP was concerned to achieve reconciliation, reintegration and reconstruction in affected countries, as well as to support emergency interventions and manage the delivery of programme aid. In 1996 20 new special development initiatives were undertaken, including the demobilization and reintegration of soldiers in Angola and Mali; environmental rehabilitation to resettle displaced populations in the Horn of Africa; and government capacity-building for programme planning and monitoring in Rwanda. In addition, UNDP extended its Disaster Management Training Programme, in part to help countries to meet the objectives of the International Decade for Natural Disaster Reduction (announced in 1990). During 1996 UNDP organized successful meetings of donor governments, multilateral institutions and private sector organizations, which generated funding commitments of US $900m. for the Congo, $617m. for rehabilitation and development programmes in Rwanda, and $231m. for Sierra Leone.

During 1996 UNDP implemented its first corporate communications and advocacy strategy, which aimed to generate public awareness of the activities of the UN system, to promote debate on development issues and to mobilize resources by increasing public and donor appreciation of UNDP. A series of national and regional workshops was held, while media activities focused on the launch of the annual *Human Development Report* and the International Day for the Eradication of Poverty, held on 17 October. UNDP aims to use the developments in information technology to advance its communications strategy and to disseminate guidelines and technical support throughout its country office network.

FINANCE

UNDP is financed by the voluntary contributions of members of the United Nations and the Programme's participating agencies as well as by cost-sharing by recipient governments and third-party donors. In 1996 total income received amounted to US $1,972.9m. In that year core expenditure on field programme activities totalled $1,231.0m.

PUBLICATIONS

Annual Report.

Choices (quarterly).

Human Development Report (annually).

Co-operation South (2 a year).

Information on UNDP can be accessed on the Internet at http://www.undp.org.

Associated Funds and Programmes

UNDP is the central funding, planning and co-ordinating body for technical co-operation within the UN. Associated funds and programmes, financed separately by means of voluntary contributions, provide specific services through the UNDP network. Total expenditure of these funds and programmes amounted to an estimated US $263.3m. in 1996.

CAPACITY 21

UNDP initiated Capacity 21 at the UN Conference on Environment and Development, which was held in June 1992, to support developing countries in preparing and implementing policies for sustainable development (i.e. the objectives of Agenda 21, which was adopted by the Conference). Capacity 21 promotes new approaches to development, through national development strategies, community-based management and training programmes. Programme expenditure totalled US £7.4m. in 1996.

GLOBAL ENVIRONMENT FACILITY—GEF

The GEF, which is managed jointly by UNDP, the World Bank and UNEP, began operations in 1991, with funding of US $1,500m. over a three-year period. Its aim is to support projects for the prevention of climate change, conserving biological diversity, protecting international waters, and reducing the depletion of the ozone layer in the atmosphere. UNDP is responsible for capacity-building, targeted research, pre-investment activities and technical assistance. UNDP also administers the Small Grants Programme of the GEF, which supports community-based activities by local non-governmental organizations. During the initial phase of the GEF, in the period 1991–94, $242.5m. in funding was approved for 55 UNDP projects; by mid-1996 53 of these were being implemented. In March 1994 representatives of 87 countries agreed to provide $2,000m. to replenish GEF funds for a further three-year period from July of that year. Programme expenditure in 1996 totalled $50.4m.

UNITED NATIONS CAPITAL DEVELOPMENT FUND—UNCDF

The Fund was established in 1966 and became fully operational in 1974. It invests in poor communities in least-developed countries by providing economic and social infrastructure, credit for both agricultural and small-scale entrepreneurial activities, and local development funds which encourage people's participation as well as that of local government in the planning and implementation of projects. UNCDF aims to promote the interests of women in community projects and to enhance their earning capacities. In 1995 new programmes were implemented in Cambodia and Togo and eight evaluations of Fund projects were undertaken. UNCDF programme expenditure totalled US $41.1m. in 1996. In that year income from voluntary contributions amounted to $34.8m.

Executive-Secretary: Poul Grosen.

UNITED NATIONS DEVELOPMENT FUND FOR WOMEN—UNIFEM

UNIFEM is the UN's lead agency in addressing the issues relating to women in development and promoting the rights of women worldwide. The Fund provides direct financial and technical support to enable low-income women in developing countries to increase earnings, gain access to labour-saving technologies and otherwise improve the quality of their lives. It also funds activities that include women in decision-making related to mainstream development projects. UNIFEM has supported the preparation of national reports in 30 countries and used the priorities identified in these reports and in other regional initiatives to formulate a Women's Development Agenda for the 21st century. Through these efforts, UNIFEM played an active role in the preparation for the UN Fourth World Conference on Women, which was held in Beijing, China, in September 1995. Programme expenditure in 1996 amounted to US $11m.

Director: Noeleen Heyzer (Singapore).

OFFICE TO COMBAT DESERTIFICATION AND DROUGHT—UNSO

The Office was established following the conclusion, in October 1994, of the UN Convention to Combat Desertification in Those Countries Experiencing Serious Drought and/or Desertification, Particularly in Africa. In replaced the former UN Sudano–Sahelian Office (UNSO), while retaining the same acronym. UNSO is responsible for UNDP's role in desertification control and dryland management. Special emphasis is given to strengthening the environmental planning and management capacities of national institutions. During 1996 UNSO, in collaboration with other international partners, supported the implementation of the UN Convention in 43 designated countries. Programme expenditure in that year totalled US $6.1m.

Director: Samuel Nyambi.

UNITED NATIONS VOLUNTEERS—UNV

The United Nations Volunteers is an important source of middle-level skills for the UN development system, supplied at modest cost, particularly in the least-developed countries. Volunteers expand the scope of UNDP project activities by supplementing the work of international and host-country experts and by extending the influence of projects to local community levels. The UN Short-term Advisory Programme, which is the private-sector development branch of UNV, has increasingly focused its attention on countries in the process of economic transition. The programme completed 124 assignments in 18 countries in 1995. In addition to development activities, UNV has been increasingly involved in areas such as election and human-rights monitoring, peace-building and community-based programmes concerned with environmental management and protection. UNV is also engaged in a variety of activities to increase youth participation in development and to promote the involvement of domestic development services. In 1995 a total of 3,263 UNV specialists and field workers from 134 nations served in 139 countries. In 1996 programme expenditure totalled US $14.9m.

Executive Co-ordinator: Brenda McSweeney.

Headquarters: Haus Carstanje, Bonn, Germany.

United Nations Environment Programme—UNEP

Address: POB 30552, Nairobi, Kenya.

Telephone: (2) 621234; **telex:** 22068; **fax:** (2) 226890.

The United Nations Environment Programme was established in 1972 by the UN General Assembly, following recommendations of the 1972 UN Conference on the Human Environment, in tockholm, Sweden, to encourage international co-operation in matters relating to the human environment.

Organization

(July 1997)

GOVERNING COUNCIL

The main function of the Governing Council, which meets every two years, is to provide general policy guidelines for the direction and co-ordination of environmental programmes within the UN system. It comprises representatives of 58 states, elected by the UN General Assembly on a rotating basis.

SECRETARIAT

The Secretariat serves as a focal point for environmental action within the UN system.

Executive Director: Elizabeth Dowdeswell (Canada).

AFRICA REGIONAL OFFICE

POB 30552, Nairobi, Kenya; tel. (2) 624283; fax (2) 623928.

OTHER OFFICES

Convention on International Trade in Endangered Species of Wild Fauna and Flora (CITES): 15 chemin des Anémones, CP 456, 1219 Châtelaine, Geneva, Switzerland; tel. (22) 9799139; telex 415391; fax (22) 7973417; Sec.-Gen. Izgrev Topkov.

Harmonization of Environmental Measurement (HEM): c/o GSF, 85758 Oberschleissheim, Neuherberg, Postfach 1129, Germany; tel. (89) 31874418; fax (89) 31873325; Dir Dr Hartmut Keune.

International Register of Potentially Toxic Chemicals (IRPTC): 15 chemin des Anémones, CP 356, 1219 Châtelaine, Geneva, Switzerland; tel. (22) 9799111; fax (22) 7973460; e-mail irptc@unep.ch; Dir James B. Willis.

UNEP Industry and Environment: Tour Mirabeau, 39–43, Quai André Citroen, 75739 Paris Cedex 15, France; tel. 1-44-37-14-50; fax 1-44-37-14-74; Dir Jacqueline Aloisi de Larderel.

UNEP International Environmental Technology Centre: 2-110 Ryokuchi koen, Tsurmi-ku, Osaka 530, Japan; tel. (6) 915-4580; fax (6) 915-0304; Dir Richard Meganck.

UNEP Ozone Secretariat: POB 30552, Nairobi, Kenya; tel. (2) 623885; telex 22068; fax (2) 623913; Exec. Sec. K. Madhava Sarma.

UNEP Secretariat of the Basel Convention: 15 chemin des Anémones, CP 356, 1219 Châtelaine, Geneva, Switzerland; tel. (22) 9799111; telex 415465; fax (22) 7973454; Co-ordinator Dr I. Rummel-Bulska.

UNEP Secretariat for the UN Scientific Committee on the Effects of Atomic Radiation: Vienna International Centre, Postfach 500, 1100 Vienna, Austria; tel. (1) 21131-4330; telex 135612; fax (1) 237608; Sec. B. Bennet.

UNEP/CMS (Convention on the Conservation of Migratory Species of Wild Animals) **Secretariat:** Martin-Luther-King-Str 8, 53175 Bonn, Germany; tel. (228) 8152401; fax (228) 8152449; e-mail cms@unep.de; Co-ordinator Arnulf Müller-Helmbrecht.

Secretariat of the Convention on Biological Diversity: World Trade Centre, 393 rue St Jacques, Bureau 300, Montréal, PQ HR7 1N9, Canada; tel. (514) 288-2220; fax (514) 288-6588; e-mail biodiv@mtl.net; Exec. Sec. Calestous Juma.

Secretariat for the Multilateral Fund for the Implementation of the Montreal Protocol: 1800 Ave McGill College, 27e étage, Montréal, PQ H3A 3J6, Canada; tel. (514) 282-1122; fax (514) 282-0068; Chief Dr Omar El-Arini.

Activities

UNEP aims to maintain a constant watch on the changing state of the environment; to analyse the trends; to assess the problems using a wide range of data and techniques; and to promote projects leading to environmentally sound development. It plays a catalytic and co-ordinating role within and beyond the UN system. Many UNEP projects are implemented in co-operation with other UN agencies, particularly UNDP, the World Bank group, FAO, UNESCO and WHO. About 45 intergovernmental organizations outside the UN system and 60 international non-governmental organizations have official observer status on UNEP's Governing Council, and, through the Environment Liaison Centre in Nairobi, UNEP is linked to more than 6,000 non-governmental bodies concerned with the environment. In September 1996 staff at UNEP headquarters numbered 648, and 276 at regional and other offices.

UNEP played a significant role in preparing for and conducting the UN Conference on Environment and Development (UNCED, or the 'Earth Summit'), which was held in Rio de Janeiro, Brazil, in June 1992. Agenda 21, a programme of activities to promote sustainable development, which was adopted at UNCED, reaffirmed UNEP's mandate and gave its Governing Council an enhanced role in the areas of policy guidance and development. The two-year 1994–95 programme was considered to be a transitional period for UNEP, during which its role and effectiveness as the UN's agency for environmental issues was re-evaluated. In May 1995 the Governing Council adopted a new programme of activities for the two-year period 1996–97, on the basis of a report of the Executive Director. The programme aimed to incorporate the demands of Agenda 21 and achieve a more integrated approach to addressing environmental issues. UNEP's 12 previous sectoral subprogrammes were redesigned into the five main interdisciplinary areas of work listed below. Approaches to assessment and monitoring, formulation and evaluation of environment policy and management of environmental intitiatives (defined as priority actions by Agenda 21) were to be applied in all programme activities, in order to increase the efficacy of UNEP's work. The Governing Council resolved that UNEP should strengthen its co-operation partnerships with other UN agencies and regional, national and local institutions in order to benefit from their expertise and to address varying regional environmental concerns.

SUSTAINABLE MANAGEMENT AND USE OF NATURAL RESOURCES

UNEP aims to promote the sustainable use of natural resources, in order to prevent degradation of the environment and natural ecosystems that results from intensified demands on land, water, marine and coastal resources.

UNEP estimates that one-third of the world's population will suffer chronic water shortages by 2025, owing to rising demand for drinking water as a result of growing populations, decreasing quality of water because of pollution, and increasing requirements of industries and agriculture. Efforts to address these problems include conducting a range of studies and assessments of river basins and regional seas. In addition, UNEP provides scientific, technical and administrative support to facilitate the implementation and co-ordination of regional seas conventions and plans of action. UNEP promotes greater international co-operation in the management of river basins and coastal areas and for the development of tools and guidelines to achieve the sustainable management of freshwater and coastal resources. In particular, UNEP aims to control land-based activities, principally pollution, which affect freshwater resources, marine biodiversity and the coastal ecosystems of small-island developing states. In November 1995 110 governments adopted a Global Programme of Action for the Protection of the Marine Environment from Land-based Activities. UNEP was to manage the Programme's Secretariat. In March 1997 the first meeting was held of parties to the Convention for the Protection, Management and Development of the Marine and Coastal Environment of the Eastern African Region (the Nairobi Convention), where the establishment of a Regional Co-ordinating Unit was approved.

UNEP supports the sound management and conservation of biological resources, in order to maintain biological diversity and to achieve sustainable development. UNEP was instrumental in the drafting of a Convention on Biological Diversity (CBD), which was adopted by UNCED in order to preserve the immense variety of plant and animal species, in particular those threatened with extinction. The Convention entered into force at the end of 1993; the first conference of parties to the Convention was convened in November/December 1994, in Nassau, the Bahamas, and was attended by representatives of some 130 countries. UNEP provides administrative and technical support to the CBD, as well as to other regional and international conventions, including the Convention on the Conservation of Migratory Species, the Convention on International Trade in Endangered Species of Wild Fauna and Flora (CITES) and the Lusaka Agreement on Co-operative Enforcement Operations Directed at Illegal Trade in Wild Fauna and Flora. UNEP supports co-operation for biodiversity assessment and management in selected developing regions and for the development of strategies for the conservation and sustainable exploitation of individual threatened species (e.g. the Global Tiger Action Plan). UNEP also provides assistance for the preparation of individual country studies and strategies to strengthen national biodiversity management and research. In November 1995 UNEP published a Global Diversity Assessment, which was presented as the first comprehensive study on biodiversity throughout the world. In 1996–97 UNEP was to undertake analyses of the impact on biological resources of development, trade liberalization and international trade policies. In June 1997 representatives of 136 countries party to the CITES accord, meeting in Harare, Zimbabwe, approved an initiative, proposed by Bostwana, Namibia and Zimbabwe, to permit the resumption of sales of ivory from those countries to Japan by transferring elephants from Appendix I of the Convention (which forbids international trade) to Appendix II (permitting controlled sales) with effect from 1999.

In October 1994 87 countries, meeting under UN auspices, signed a Convention to Combat Desertification in Those Countries Experiencing Serious Drought and/or Desertification, Particularly in Africa, which aimed to provide a legal framework to counter the degradation of drylands. An estimated 75% of all drylands has suffered some land degradation, affecting approximately 1,000m. people in 110 countries. UNEP continues to support the implementation of the Convention, as part of its efforts to protect land resources. UNEP also aims to improve the assessment of dryland degradation and desertification in co-operation with governments and other international bodies, as well as identifying the causes of degradation and measures to overcome these.

In 1996–97 UNEP aimed to develop and strengthen national and international mechanisms of processing and exchanging information, in order to facilitate decision-making and the formulation of plans of action. Under a programme of supporting Environment and Natural Resource Information Networks (ENRIN), UNEP envisages a functioning information network in every developing region, including eastern Europe, each comprising 10 cross-sectoral information datasets.

SUSTAINABLE PRODUCTION AND CONSUMPTION

The use of inappropriate industrial technologies and the widespread adoption of unsustainable production and consumption patterns have been identified as being inefficient in the use of renewable resources and wasteful, in particular, in the use of energy. UNEP aims to develop new policy and management tools for governments and industry and to encourage the use of environmentally-sound technologies, in order to reduce pollution and the unsustainable use of natural resources. UNEP organizes conferences and training workshops to promote sustainable production practices and disseminates relevant information through the International Cleaner Production Information Clearing House. In 1996–97 UNEP was to undertake case study reports in Latin America, Asia, Africa and countries with economies in transition to identify and assess industrial practices. In addition, UNEP planned to expand on its existing APELL programme (Awareness and Preparedness for Emergencies at the Local Level) and to enhance accident prevention and emergency preparedness capabilities, in relation to the industrial sector, in all developing and transitional countries.

UNEP provides institutional servicing to the Vienna Convention for the Protection of the Ozone Layer (1985) and its 1987 Montreal Protocol, which provided for a 50% reduction in the production of chlorofluorocarbons (CFCs) by 2000. (An amendment to the Protocol was adopted in 1990, which required complete cessation of the production of CFCs by 2000 in industrialized countries and by 2010 in developing countries; these deadlines were advanced to 1996 and 2006 respectively, in November 1992.) Similar support is given to the Basel Convention on the Control of Transboundary Movements of Hazardous Wastes and their Disposal, which was adopted in 1989 with the aim of preventing the disposal of wastes from industrialized countries in countries that have no processing facilities. (In March 1994 the second meeting of parties to the Convention agreed to ban exportation of hazardous wastes between OECD and non-OECD countries by the end of 1997.)

UNEP encourages the development of alternative and renewable sources of energy. To achieve this, UNEP is supporting the establishment of a network of centres to research and exchange information of environmentally-sound energy technology resources. UNEP assists countries to prepare projects for the reduction of so-called 'greenhouse gas' emissions (i.e. carbon dioxide and other gases that have a warming effect on the atmosphere) for submission to the Global Environment Facility (GEF—see also World Bank) for funding. UNEP provides administrative support for the Framework Convention on Climate Change (FCCC), which was adopted at UNCED and entered into force in March 1994. The FCCC commits countries to submitting reports on measures being taken to reduce the emission of 'greenhouse gases'. The Convention recommends stabilizing these emissions at 1990 levels by 2000; however, this is not legally binding. In July 1996, at a meeting of parties to the FCCC (held in Geneva), ministers declared their willingness to commit to legally-binding objectives for emission limitations and significant overall reductions in a specified timetable, details of which were to be determined finally at a full meeting of parties to the Convention, scheduled to be held in Kyoto, Japan, in December 1997. At the end of September 1996 132 countries had ratified the FCCC, while eight countries had approved or accepted the Convention and 14 had acceded to it.

The realignment of UNEP activities, undertaken for the work programme 1996–97, addressed the concerns that unsustainable patterns of consumption and production, in particular in industrialized countries, were major contributing factors to the deterioration of the global environment. UNEP aims to adjust this situation by stimulating understanding and awareness of the relationship between production and consumption, and promoting dialogue among developed countries to attain an agreement on more sustainable forms of production.

A BETTER ENVIRONMENT FOR HUMAN HEALTH AND WELL-BEING

A guiding principle of Agenda 21 was that human beings were at the centre of concerns for sustainable development and that they were entitled to a healthy and productive life. The new UNEP sub-programme integrated its previous activities relating to health, human settlement and welfare with those concerned with toxic wastes and chemicals. UNEP continues to maintain the International Register of Potentially Toxic Chemicals (IRPTC). UNEP aims to facilitate access to data on chemicals and hazardous wastes, in order to assess and control health and environmental risks, by using the IRPTC as a clearing house facility of relevant information and by publishing information and technical reports on the impact of the use of chemicals. UNEP is promoting and formulating an international convention on prior informed consent for hazardous chemicals in international trade.

In conjunction with UNCHS (Habitat), UNDP, the World Bank and other regional organizations and institutions, UNEP promotes environmental concerns in urban planning and management through the Sustainable Cities Programme, as well as regional workshops on urban pollution and the impact of transportation systems. In January 1994 UNEP inaugurated an International Environmental Technology Centre in Tokyo, Japan, in order to strengthen the capabilities of developing countries and countries with economies in transition to promote environmentally-sound management of cities and fresh water reservoirs through technology co-operation and partnerships.

In 1996–97 UNEP aimed to reduce the risk to human populations of environmental change and emergencies. A review of existing strategies for forecasting and responding to environmental hazards was to be undertaken. In addition, UNEP planned to organize and convene an international conference on emerging threats to human health resulting from environmental change and practices.

GLOBALIZATION AND THE ENVIRONMENT

With the globalization of the world's economy UNEP has identified a need to enhance the assessment of the environmental impact of trade patterns and policies, at country and regional level, and to undertake legal analyses of the relationship between environmental laws and international trade regimes. UNCED recommended the need to integrate environmental issues into economic priorities as a prerequisite of sustainable development. UNEP operates a system of environmental valuation and environmental impact assessment, which it aims to promote through national guidelines and technical workshops. Other so-called environmental economic tools may be developed through environmental and natural resource accounting and the eco-labelling of country export products (i.e. identifying products with a high environmental quality profile). UNEP aims to promote the exchange of information relevant to this sector and to assist countries to develop additional sources of finance for environmentally sustainable development.

In order to complement the globalization process and the expanded environment agenda, UNEP supports the formulation and implementation of international and national legislation, as environmental management tools. While it supports and helps co-ordinate the activities of the secretariats of international and regional conventions, UNEP is undertaking preliminary efforts to formulate a definitive international legal framework for sustainable development. At a national level UNEP assists governments to prepare environmental legislation and guidelines and to implement existing international conventions. Training workshops in various aspects of environmental law and its application are conducted.

UNEP aims to promote coherent decision-making, in the environment field, through its support for research and information exchange. It promotes the scientific research and review of key environmental issues and conducts workshops to develop policy recommendations. In 1996–97 UNEP aims to integrate environmental concerns in the activities of international financial institutions and to encourage collaboration among these bodies.

GLOBAL AND REGIONAL SERVICING AND SUPPORT

UNEP has a major responsibility to identify and assess environmental issues of common concern, to alert the world community to these issues, to precipitate their resolution through international co-operation and to provide policy guidance for the direction and co-ordination of environmental programmes within the UN system. Under this sub-programme UNEP aims to fulfill its role and to deliver its programme of work through the basic institutional functions of environmental assessment, advisory services, public awareness and provision of information. The first Global Environment Outlook (GEO-1), which UNEP presented as an assessment of the state of the world's environment, was published in January 1997.

Through regional consultations and specialized centres world-wide, UNEP aims to develop and enhance frameworks, methodologies and indicators to achieve integrated environmental assessment and reporting. In particular, UNEP aims to strengthen early-warning mechanisms and region-specific assessment. UNEP is participating in the design of a Global Terrestrial Observing System, which was to be implemented by the GEF.

UNEP promotes and supports regional co-operation initiatives for environmental action by co-operation with regional banks, economic commissions and other organizations. In addition, UNEP provides policy and technical advice to governments in developing countries and countries with economies in transition for the integration of environmental considerations into national development plans.

Education and public awareness are critical for promoting sustainable development and improving the capacity of groups and individuals to address environmental issues. UNEP's public education campaigns and outreach programmes promote community involvement in environmental issues. Further communication of environmental concerns is undertaken through the media, an information centre service and special promotional events, including World Environment Day, photograph competitions and the awarding of the Sasakawa Prize to recognize distinguished service to the environment by individuals and groups.

UNEP's data and information services include a global resource information data-base (GRID), which converts data collected into information usable by decision-makers, and the INFOterra programme, which facilitates the exchange of environmental information through an extensive network of national 'focal points'. In 1996–97 UNEP aimed to integrate all its information resources in order to improve access to information and international environment information exchange. This was to be achieved through the design and implementation of UNEPNET, which was to operate throughout the UN system and be fully accessible through the world-wide information networks.

FINANCE

UNEP derives its finances from the regular budget of the United Nations (from which US $9.8m. was allotted to it for the two-year period 1994–95), and from voluntary contributions to the Environment Fund, which amounted to $58.0m. in 1995. UNEP's estimated budget for 1996–97 amounted to $9.9m. from the UN regular budget and $90m. (with an additional supplementary appropriation of $15m. if or when funds become available) from the Environment Fund.

PUBLICATIONS

Annual Report of the Executive Director.

APELL Newsletter (quarterly).

Bulletin in Environmental Law (2 a year).

Catalogue of Audio-Visual Material (every 2 years).

Catalogue of Publications (every 2 years).

Cleaner Production Newsletter (2 a year).

Connect (UNESCO-UNEP newsletter on environmental degradation, quarterly).

EarthViews (quarterly).

Environmental Law Biannual Bulletin.

Global Environment Outlook.

Industry and Environment Review (quarterly).

INFOterra Bulletin (quarterly).

INFOterra International Directory of Sources.

IRPTC Bulletin (3 a year: on toxic chemicals).

Our Planet (6 a year).

The Pilot, Newsletter of the Marine Mammal Action Plan (quarterly).

The Siren (quarterly, on regional seas programme).

State of the Environment Report (annually).

UNESCO-UNEP Newsletter (quarterly).

Studies, reports, legal texts, technical guidelines, etc.

Information on UNEP can be accessed on the Internet at http://www.unep.org.

United Nations High Commissioner for Refugees—UNHCR

Address: CP 2500, 1211 Geneva 2 dépôt, Switzerland.

Telephone: (22) 7398111; **telex:** 415740; **fax:** (22) 7319546.

The Office of the High Commissioner was established in 1951 to provide international protection for refugees and to seek durable solutions to their problems.

Organization

(July 1997)

HIGH COMMISSIONER

The High Commissioner is elected by the United Nations General Assembly on the nomination of the Secretary-General, and is responsible to the General Assembly and to the UN Economic and Social Council (ECOSOC).

High Commissioner: SADAKO OGATA (Japan).

Deputy High Commissioner: GERALD WALZER (Austria).

EXECUTIVE COMMITTEE

The Executive Committee of the High Commissioner's Programme, established by ECOSOC, gives the High Commissioner policy directives in respect of material assistance programmes and advice in the field of international protection. In addition, it oversees UNHCR's general policies and use of funds. The Committee, which comprises representatives from 53 states, both members and non-members of the UN.

ADMINISTRATION

Headquarters includes the Executive Office, comprising the offices of the High Commissioner, the Deputy High Commissioner and the Assistant High Commissioner. The offices of Internal Oversight and of International Protection report directly to the Executive Office, as do the Secretariat, the Centre for Documentation and Research and the Department of Public Information. Refugee support services are undertaken by the divisions of Operations Support, Financial and Information Services and Human Resource Management. Operations are administered by the five regional bureaux covering Central, East and West Africa, Asia and Oceania, Europe, the Americas and South-West Asia, the Middle East and North Africa. Separate operational divisions—for the Great Lakes region of Africa, Southern Africa and the former Yugoslavia—are headed by field-based Directors. At February 1997 there were 239 UNHCR field offices in 119 countries.

Activities

The competence of the High Commissioner extends to any person who, owing to well-founded fear of being persecuted for reasons of race, religion, nationality or political opinion, is outside the country of his or her nationality and is unable or, owing to such fear or for reasons other than personal convenience, remains unwilling to accept the protection of that country; or who, not having a nationality and being outside the country of former habitual residence, is unable or, owing to such fear or for reasons other than personal convenience, is unwilling to return to it. Refugees who are assisted by other United Nations agencies, or who have the rights or obligations as nationals of their country of residence, are outside the mandate of UNHCR.

In the early 1990s there was a significant shift in UNHCR's focus of activities. Increasingly, UNHCR is called upon to support people who have been displaced within their own country, i.e. people with similar needs to those of refugees but who have not crossed on international border. Operations involving internally displaced populations may be undertaken only at the request of the UN Secretary-General or the General Assembly and with the consent of the country concerned. In addition, UNHCR is providing greater support to refugees who have returned to their country of origin, to assist their reintegration, and is working to enable the local community to support the returnees.

INTERNATIONAL PROTECTION

As laid down in the Statute of the Office, one of the two primary functions of UNHCR is to extend international protection to refugees. In the exercise of this function UNHCR seeks to ensure that refugees and asylum-seekers are protected against *refoulement* (forcible return), that they receive asylum, and that they are treated according to internationally recognized standards. UNHCR pursues these objectives by a variety of means which include promoting the conclusion and ratification by states of international conventions for the protection of refugees, particularly the 1951 UN Convention relating to the Status of Refugees, extended by a Protocol adopted in 1967 (a total of 134 states had acceded to either or both of these instruments by February 1997). The Convention defines the rights and duties of refugees and contains provisions dealing with a variety of matters which affect their day-to-day lives. UNHCR has also continued to encourage further accessions to the 1969 OAU Convention Governing the Specific Aspects of Refuge Problems in Africa (to which 42 states were party at March 1995). UNHCR has given close attention to the problems of military attacks against refugee camps and settlements in southern Africa and elsewhere, in the hope of formulating a set of internationally recognised principles to ensure the safety of refugees.

ASSISTANCE ACTIVITIES

UNHCR assistance activities are divided into General Programmes, which include a Programme Reserve, a General Allocation for Voluntary Repatriation and an Emergency Fund, and Special Programmes. The latter are undertaken at the request of the UN General Assembly, the Secretary-General of the UN or member states, in response to a particular crisis.

The first phase of an assistance operation uses UNHCR's capacity of emergency preparedness and response. This enables UNHCR to address the immediate needs of refugees at short notice, for example, by employing specially trained emergency teams and maintaining stockpiles of basic equipment, medical aid and materials. A significant proportion of UNHCR expenditure is allocated to the next phase of an operation, providing 'care and maintenance' in stable refugee circumstances. This assistance can take various forms, including the provision of food, shelter, medical care and essential supplies. Also often covered are basic services, including education and counselling.

As far as possible, assistance is geared towards the identification and implementation of durable solutions to refugee problems—this being the second statutory responsibility of UNHCR. Such solutions generally take one of three forms: voluntary repatriation, local integration or resettlement in another country. Where voluntary repatriation is feasible, the Office assists refugees to overcome obstacles preventing their return to their country of origin. This may be done through negotiations with governments involved, or by providing funds for the physical movement of refugees or for the rehabilitation of returnees once back in their own country. When voluntary repatriation is not feasible, efforts are made to assist refugees to integrate locally and to become self-supporting in their countries of asylum. In cases where resettlement through emigration is the only viable solution, UNHCR negotiates with governments in an endeavour to obtain suitable resettlement opportunities, to encourage liberalization of admission criteria and to draw up special immigration schemes.

In the early 1990s UNHCR aimed to consolidate efforts to integrate certain priorities into its programme planning and implementation, as a standard discipline in all phases of assistance. The considerations include awareness of specific problems confronting refugee women, the needs of refugee children, the environmental impact of refugee programmes and long-term development objectives. In an effort to improve the effectiveness of its programmes UNHCR has initiated a process of delegating authority, as well as responsibility for operational budgets, to its regional and field representatives, increasing flexibility and accountability. In 1995 a new Inspection and Evaluation Service was established in order to strengthen UNHCR's capacity to review operational effectiveness and efficiency.

REGIONAL ASSISTANCE

During the early 1990s UNHCR provided assistance to refugee populations in many parts of the continent, where civil conflict, violations of human rights, drought, famine or environmental degradation had forced people to flee their countries. The majority of African refugees and returnees are located in countries that are themselves suffering major economic problems and are thus unable to provide the basic requirements of the uprooted people. Furthermore, UNHCR has often failed to receive adequate international financial support to implement effective relief programmes. At the end of 1995 there were 5.4m. refugees in Africa (including North Africa), and a further 3.5m. other persons of concern to UNHCR, including returnees and internally displaced people.

The Horn of Africa, afflicted by famine, separatist violence and ethnic conflict, has experienced large-scale population movements in recent years. In 1992 UNHCR initiated a repatriation programme for the estimated 500,000 Somali and Ethiopian refugees in Kenya, which included assistance with reconstruction projects and a cross-border operation conducted from Kenya to provide food to returnees and displaced persons. The implementation by UNHCR of community-based projects, for example seed distribution, the establishment of a women's bakery co-operative and support for a brick production initiative, served as important instruments of assistance and of bringing stability to areas of returnee settlements. By mid-1996 an estimated 150,000 Somalis had returned from Kenya, with UNHCR assistance, bringing the total returnees to more than 400,000. None the less, the continuing instability in north-western Somalia prevented a completion of the repatriation process, and by February 1997 there were still some 452,000 Somali refugees in neighbouring countries, the majority of whom were in camps in eastern Ethiopia. At that time Ethiopia was sheltering a total of 394,000 refugees. Almost all Ethiopians who had fled the country during the 1980s had returned by the end of 1996, including 36,000 from Djibouti by means of a UNHCR programme of assistance undertaken from September 1994 to April 1996.

From 1992 some 500,000 Eritreans took refuge in Sudan as a result of separatist conflicts; however, by 1995 an estimated 125,000 had returned spontaneously, in particular following Eritrea's accession to independence in May 1993. A UNHCR repatriation programme to assist the remaining refugees, which had been delayed for various political, security and funding considerations, was initiated in November 1994. A further 125,000 refugees were scheduled to return to Eritrea under the programme by the end of 1996. However, its implementation was hindered by a shortfall in donor funding and by differences between Eritrean and Sudanese Governments. At February 1997 Sudan still hosted a total of 405,000 refugees, mainly from Eritrea and Ethiopia. In May UNHCR concluded an agreement with the Sudanese Government enabling the first of some 20,000 Ethiopian refugees to be repatriated. At February there were some 468,000 Sudanese refugees in Uganda, Kenya and Ethiopia, owing to continuing civil unrest. The Ugandan Government, hosting an estimated 230,000 of these refugees, has provided new resettlement sites and has supported refugee efforts to construct homes and cultivate crops in order to achieve some degree of self-sufficiency.

In West Africa the refugee population increased by one-third during 1992 and the first half of 1993, with the addition of new refugees fleeing Togo, Liberia and Senegal. Between February and August 1993 more than 300,000 people fled abuses of human rights in Togo, crossing the borders into Benin and Ghana. With the majority of Togolese being accommodated by individuals in the host countries, UNHCR aimed to strengthen these countries' infrastructures. Political developments in Togo in 1994 were considered to have accounted for a large-scale spontaneous repatriation movement of Togolese refugees. In August 1995 UNHCR signed an accord with Togo providing for the introduction of a programme of voluntary repatriation for some 168,000 Togolese refugees remaining in Ghana and Benin. Under the programme, which commenced in May 1996, returnees received a small financial grant and a three-month supply of food to assist their repatriation. In early 1994 UNHCR initiated an emergency relief effort to assist some 180,000 Ghanaians displaced within the north of that country as a result of ethnic violence. Also at that time some 40,000 Tuareg nomads, who had fled from northern Mali into Burkina Faso, received protection and material assistance from two newly-established UNHCR field offices. During 1995 large numbers of the Malian refugee population (totalling some 175,000) returned spontaneously from camps in Mauritania, Burkina Faso and Algeria, owing to political developments in Mali. An organized repatriation of the remaining refugees was initiated in 1996. In November UNHCR signed an agreement with the Malian and Nigerien Governments establishing the conditions of repatriation of 25,000 Tuareg refugees living in Niger. In May 1997 UNHCR appealed for US $17m. to finance the continuing repatriation and reintegration of Malian refugees, as well as some 20,000 refugees returning to Niger. In accordance with a peace agreement, signed in July 1993, UNHCR was responsible for the repatriation of 700,000 Liberian refugees who had fled to Guinea, Côte d'Ivoire and Sierra Leone during the civil conflict. The voluntary repatriation programme was to include substantial assistance to rebuild Liberia's infrastructure; however, persisting political insecurity prevented large-scale repatriation of Liberian refugees. In April 1996 an outbreak of hostilities in the Liberian capital, Monrovia, prompted a large-scale population movement. Several thousand people crossed neighbouring borders to join existing Liberian refugee settlements in Guinea and Côte d'Ivoire, while some 4,000 others fled the country by sea and were finally granted temporary asylum in Ghana following UNHCR's agreement to supply the refugees with food and shelter.

UNHCR suspended its preparatory activities for a large-scale repatriation and reintegration operation of Liberian refugees owing to the escalation in hostilities. At February 1997 the Liberian refugee population in West Africa totalled 758,000; however, the prospect of a peaceful settlement in Liberia, with preparations underway for a general election to be conducted in July, prompted a movement of refugees returning home, and in April UNHCR initiated an organized repatriation of Liberian refugees from Ghana. Meanwhile, an escalation of civil violence in Sierra Leone in early 1995 displaced some 900,000 people, of whom an estimated 185,000 fled to Guinea and 90,000 to Liberia. The repatriation of Sierra Leonean refugees from Liberia was initiated in February 1997, however, the programme was suspended in May owing to renewed political violence. By early June a further 14,000 refugees from Sierra Leone had registered at camps in Guinea.

Since 1993 the Great Lakes region of central Africa has again experienced massive population displacement, causing immense operational challenges and demands on the resources of international humanitarian and relief agencies. In October of that year a military coup in Burundi prompted some 580,000 people to flee into

Rwanda and Tanzania, although many had returned by early 1994. By May 1994, however, an estimated 860,000 people from Burundi and Rwanda had fled to neighbouring states (following a resurgence of ethnic violence in both countries), including 250,000 mainly Rwandan Tutsi refugees who entered Tanzania over a 24-hour period in late April in the most rapid mass exodus ever witnessed by UNHCR. In May UNHCR began an immediate operation to airlift emergency supplies to the refugees. The scale of the crisis rapidly depleted resources, forcing UNHCR to request large-scale assistance from governments. For the first time in an emergency operation UNHCR organized support to be rendered in the form of eight defined 'service packages', for example, to provide domestic fuel, road servicing and security or sanitation facilities. Despite overcrowding in camps and a high incidence of cholera and dysentery (particularly in camps in eastern Zaire, where many thousands of Rwandan Hutus had sought refuge following the establishment of a new Government in July) large numbers of refugees refused to accept UNHCR-assisted repatriation, owing to fears of reprisal ethnic killings. In late August the Zairean camps were further overburdened by an influx of Rwandan Hutu refugees, following the withdrawal of French troops from a 'safe haven' in south-west Rwanda. In September reports of mass ethnic violence in Rwanda, which were disputed by some UN agencies, continued to disrupt UNHCR's policy of repatriation and to prompt returnees to cross the border back into Zaire. Security in the refugee camps, which was undermined by the presence of military and political elements of the former Rwandan government regime, remained an outstanding concern for UNHCR. Efforts to restore law and order and to prevent the intimidation of refugees, by introducing more security personnel into the camps, were initiated by UNHCR, in co-operation with the Tanzanian and Zairean authorities. A resurgence of violence in Burundi, in February 1995, provoked further mass population movements. However, in March the Tanzanian authorities, reportedly frustrated at the lack of international assistance for the refugees and the environmental degradation resulting from the camps, closed Tanzania's border with Burundi, thus preventing the admission into the country of some 100,000 Rwandan Hutu refugees who were fleeing camps in Burundi. While persisting disturbances in Rwanda disrupted UNHCR's repatriation programme, in April 1995 Rwandan government troops employed intimidation tactics to force some 90,000 internally-displaced Hutus to leave a heavily-populated camp in the south-west of the country; other small camps were closed. Preparations for the resettlement of the population were being undertaken by UNHCR, mainly in the form of community rehabilitation projects. In August the Zairean Government initiated a programme of forcible repatriation of the estimated 1m. Rwandan and 70,000 Burundian Hutu refugees remaining in the country, which prompted as many as 100,000 refugees to flee the camps into the surrounding countryside. Following widespread international condemnation of the forcible repatriation and expressions of concern for the welfare of the remaining refugees, the Zairean Government suspended the programme, having first received an assurance that UNHCR would assume responsibility for the repatriation of all the refugees by the end of 1995 (although in December the Zairean Government accepted that its deadline could not be achieved). In September Rwanda agreed to strengthen its reception facilities and to provide greater security and protection for returnees, in collaboration with UNHCR, in order to prepare for any large-scale repatriation. UNHCR, meanwhile, expanded its information campaign, to promote the return of refugees, and enhanced its facilities at official border entry points. In December UNHCR negotiated an agreement between the Rwandan and Tanzanian authorities concerning the repatriation of the estimated 500,000 Rwandans remaining in camps in Tanzania. UNHCR agreed to establish a separate camp in north-west Tanzania in order to accommodate elements of the refugee population that might disrupt the repatriation programme. The repatriation of Rwandan refugees from all host countries was affected by reports of reprisals against Hutu returnees by the Tutsi-dominated Government in Rwanda. An estimated total of 237,400 refugees returned to Rwanda during 1995 from countries throughout the region. In February 1996 the Zairean Government renewed its efforts to accelerate the repatriation process, owing to concerns that the camps were becoming permanent settlements and that they were being used to train and rearm a Hutu militia. In July the Burundian Government forcibly repatriated 15,000 Rwandan refugees, having announced the closure of all remaining refugee camps. The repatriation programme was condemned by UNHCR and was suspended by the country's new authorities, (installed after a military coup later in that month).

In October 1996 an escalation of hostilities between Zairean government forces, accused by Rwanda of arming the Hutu *Interahamwe* militia, and Zairean (Banyamulenge) Tutsis, who had been the focus of increasingly violent assaults, resulted in an extreme humanitarian crisis. Some 250,000 refugees fled 12 camps in the east of the country, while an estimated 500,000 were left in Muganga camp, west of Goma, with insufficient relief assistance, following the evacuation of international aid workers. UNHCR appealed to all Rwandan Hutu refugees to return home, and issued assurances of the presence of human rights observers in Rwanda to enhance their security. In mid-November, with the apparent withdrawal of *Interahamwe* forces, an estimated 600,000 refugees unexpectedly returned to Rwanda, however, concern remained on the part of the international community for the substantial number of Rwandan Hutu refugees at large in eastern Zaire. Further mass movement of Rwandan refugee populations occurred in December, owing to the threat of forcible repatriation by the Tanzanian Government, which had announced its intention of closing all camps by the end of the year. UNHCR initiated a repatriation programme; however, 200,000 refugees, unwilling to return to Rwanda, fled their camps. In Februry 1997 violence in Zaire escalated, which prompted some 56,000 Zaireans to flee into Tanzania and disrupted the distribution of essential humanitarian supplies to refugees remaining in Zaire. An estimated 170,000 refugees abandoned their temporary encampment at Tingi-Tingi, fearing attacks by the advancing rebel forces of the Tutsi-dominated Alliance des forces démocratiques pour la libération du Congo–Zaïre (AFDL). About 75,000 re-assembled at Ubundu, south of Kisangani, while the fate of the other refugees remained uncertain. In March and April continued reports of attacks on refugee camps by AFDL forces and local Zaireans, resulted in large numbers of people fleeing into the surrounding countryside, with the consequent deaths of many of the most vulnerable members of the refugee population from disease and starvation. At the end of April the leader of the AFDL, Laurent-Désiré Kabila, ordered the repatriation of all Rwandan Hutu refugees by the UN within 60 days. An operation to airlift some 85,000 refugees who had regrouped into temporary settlements was initiated a few days later, at an estimated cost of US $50m. The repatriation process, however, was hindered by administrative and logistical difficulties and lack of co-operation on the part of the AFDL forces. By the end of May some 40,000 Rwandans had been repatriated under the operation; at that time an estimated 300,000 Rwandans were still missing or dispersed throughout the former Zaire (renamed the Democratic Republic of the Congo by the AFDL in May).

PERSONS OF CONCERN TO UNHCR IN AFRICA SOUTH OF THE SAHARA* (31 December 1995, '000s)

Country	Refugees	Returnees	Internally displaced persons	Others of concern†
Angola	10.9	13.0	–	0.1
Benin	23.5	–	–	0.1
Burkina Faso	29.5	–	–	0.3
Burundi	142.7	5.6	216.4	1.5
Cameroon	45.9	–	–	–
Central African Republic	33.8	–	–	–
Congo‡	15.0	–	–	–
Côte d'Ivoire	297.9	–	–	–
Djibouti	25.7	–	–	0.4
Eritrea	1.1	24.2	–	–
Ethiopia	393.5	34.7	–	–
Gambia	7.2	4.4	–	–
Guinea-Bissau	15.3	–	–	–
Kenya	239.5	–	–	4.4
Liberia	120.0	–	320.0	–
Mali	15.6	39.0	3.0	1.2
Mauritania	40.4	–	–	–
Mozambique	0.1	1,734.2	–	0.1
Niger	22.6	–	–	–
Rwanda	7.8	226.8	–	–
Senegal	68.6	–	–	–
Sierra Leone	4.7§	–	654.6	–
Somalia	0.6	0.3	150.0	–
South Africa	91.8	0.1	–	7.7[1]
Sudan	558.2	0.0	–	–
Tanzania	829.7	–	–	–
Togo	11.0	3.0	–	–
Uganda	229.3	–	–	–
Zaire[2]	1,326.5	0.0	–	6.7
Zambia	130.6	–	–	–

* Figures are provided mostly by governments, based on their own records and methods of estimation. Countries with fewer than 10,000 refugees are not listed.

† Mainly people in a 'refugee-like' situation outside their country, not formally recognized as refugees.

‡ Now Republic of Congo.

§ Figure includes only refugees assisted by UNHCR; figure of those not assisted is unknown.

[1] Asylum seekers.

[2] Now the Democratic Republic of the Congo.

In 1994 continuing civil conflict in Angola caused some 303,800 people to leave their home areas. Prior to the signing of a peace settlement in November, UNHCR provided assistance to 112,000 internally-displaced Angolans and returnees, although military activities, which hindered accessibility, undermined the effectiveness of the assistance programme. In mid-1995, following a consolidation of the peace process in Angola, UNHCR appealed for US $44m. to support the voluntary repatriation of some 300,000 Angolan refugees over a two-and-a-half-year operation. By June 1996 implementation of the repatriation programme was delayed, reportedly owing to poor accommodation and other facilities for returnees, limited progress in confining and disarming opposition troops and the continued hazard of landmines throughout the country.

In the early 1990s UNHCR was the principal agency responsible for the channelling of food aid to the large population of Mozambican refugees dispersed throughout southern Africa. In March 1993 UNHCR announced that it was about to undertake an operation to repatriate and reintegrate the refugees, following the signing of a peace agreement in Mozambique, in October 1992. This was to be UNHCR's largest-ever undertaking in Africa, with an estimated cost of US $203m., much of which was to be used to provide returnees with food and seed rations and to rehabilitate the country's infrastructure. A reintegration strategy was formulated in 1994 which identified some 1,386 quick impact projects required in the four priority areas of water, education, health and roads. The voluntary repatriation operation was concluded in June 1995; at 31 December the process was concluded, having registered 1,734,174 Mozambican returnees.

CO-OPERATION WITH OTHER ORGANIZATIONS

UNHCR works closely with other UN agencies, intergovernmental organizations and non-governmental organizations to increase the scope and effectiveness of its emergency operations. Within the UN system UNHCR co-operates, principally, with the World Food Programme in the distribution of food aid and UNICEF and the World Health Organization in the provision of family welfare and child immunization programmes. UNHCR co-operates with the UN Development Programme in development-related activities and has participated in the preparation of guidelines for the continuum of emergency assistance to development programmes. In 1993 UNHCR and the International Council of Voluntary Agencies initiated a programme of Partnership in Action (PARinAC) to broaden dialogue and improve the effectiveness of the collaboration. Following regional consultations, this effort culminated in a world conference of UNHCR and 450 non-governmental organizations, held in Oslo, Norway, in June 1994, at which a Declaration to consolidate the relationship was adopted. In Africa UNHCR has worked with and employed some 104 different organizations in order to improve the efficiency of the provision of aid, as well as to benefit from their local knowledge and skills.

TRAINING

During 1995 three emergency management training programmes were organized by UNHCR, including one in Ghana for English-speaking countries in West Africa. A programme workshop covering French-speaking countries in West Africa was scheduled to be held during 1996, while an emergency training workshop incorporating the countries in the Horn of Africa and East Africa was conducted early in that year in Addis Ababa, Ethiopia. The workshops aimed to formulate guidelines and a co-ordinated strategy for response to an emergency situation. Other training activities conducted in the region during 1995 and 1996 were concerned with the registration and identification of refugees, enhancing 'people-oriented planning', the dissemination of information through the electronic media, security awareness, and stress management.

In June 1996 UNHCR launched an Education Fund for African Refugees to provide scholarships for refugee students at secondary level.

FINANCE

UNHCR administrative expenditure is mostly financed under the United Nations regular budget. General Programmes of material assistance and Special Programmes undertaken by UNHCR are financed from voluntary contributions made by governments, intergovernmental and non-governmental organizations and individuals. In 1995 expenditure from voluntary funds amounted to an estimated US $1,292m., of which $428m. was allocated to General Programmes and $864m. financed Special Programmes. In that year UNHCR expenditure for assistance in Africa south of the Sahara amounted to $482.6m. ($173m. for General Programmes and $309.6m. for Special Programmes).

PUBLICATIONS

Refugees (quarterly, in English, French, German, Italian, Japanese and Spanish).

UNHCR Handbook for Emergencies.

Refugee Survey Quarterly.

The State of the World's Refugees (every 2 years).

Information on UNHCR can be accessed on the Internet at http://www.unhcr.ch.

United Nations Peace-keeping Operations

Address: Department of Peace-keeping Operations, Room S-3727-B, United Nations, New York, NY 10017, USA.

Telephone: (212) 963-5055; **telex:** 420544; **fax:** (212) 963-4879.

United Nations peace-keeping operations have been conceived as instruments of conflict control. Each operation has been established with a specific mandate. The UN has used these operations in various conflicts, with the consent of the parties involved, to maintain peaceful conditions, without prejudice to the positions or claims of parties, in order to facilitate the search for political settlements through peaceful means such as mediation and the good offices of the Secretary-General. United Nations peace-keeping operations fall into two categories: peace-keeping forces and observer missions.

Peace-keeping forces are composed of contingents of lightly-armed troops, made available by member states. These forces assist in preventing the recurrence of fighting, restoring and maintaining peace, and promoting a return to normal conditions. To this end, peace-keeping forces are authorized as necessary to undertake negotiations, persuasion, observation and fact-finding. They run patrols and interpose physically between the opposing parties. Peace-keeping forces are permitted to use their weapons only in self-defence.

Military observer missions are composed of officers (usually unarmed), who are made available, on the Secretary-General's request, by member states. A mission's function is to observe and report to the Secretary-General (who in turn informs the UN Security Council) on the maintenance of a cease-fire, to investigate violations and to do what it can to improve the situation.

Peace-keeping forces and observer missions must at all times maintain complete impartiality and avoid any action that might affect the claims or positions of the parties.

The UN's peace-keeping operations are financed by assessed contributions from member states. During the 1990s a significant expansion in the UN's peace-keeping activities has been accompanied by a perpetual financial crisis within the organization, as a result of the increased financial burden and some member states delaying payment. At May 1997 unpaid contributions to peace-keeping accounts totalled some US $1,600m.

In March 1995 UN troops completed their withdrawal from Somalia and the mandate of the UN Operation in Somalia II (UNOSOM II) was terminated. The operation, which assumed control of the UN and other multinational activities in Somalia in 1993, had been the largest peace-keeping operation ever undertaken by the UN, with an original deployed force of some 28,000 troops. Following the successful conclusion of democratic elections in Mozambique, the UN Operation in Mozambique (ONUMOZ) was terminated. The military contingent of ONUMOZ withdrew by January 1995, while technical elements of the operation remained in the country until March. The mandate of the UN Assistance Mission to Rwanda (UNAMIR), which had been established in October 1993, was terminated, at the request of the Rwandan Government, in March 1996. All military components of the force had left the country by the following month. Meanwhile, the UN's International Criminal Tribunal for Rwanda, which was formally inaugurated in Arusha, Tanzania, in November 1995, continued to investigate allegations made against some 400 individuals, of their involvement in serious violations of human rights committed during the internal conflict in 1994.

UNITED NATIONS OBSERVER MISSION IN ANGOLA—MONUA

Headquarters: Luanda, Angola.

Special Representative of the UN Secretary-General: ALIOUNE BLONDIN BEYE (Mali).

In December 1988 a peace-keeping operation, the United Nations Angola Verification Mission (UNAVEM), was established by the UN Security Council, at the request of the Governments of Angola and Cuba. Having overseen the withdrawal of Cuban troops from Angola, in May 1991 UNAVEM's presence in the country was extended, in order to verify the implementation of the Peace Accords for Angola, initialled by the Angolan Government and the União Nacional para la Independência Total de Angola (UNITA). UNAVEM II (which it then became) was responsible for verifying the monitoring of the cease-fire undertaken jointly by the Government and UNITA, and for monitoring the neutrality of the Angolan police force. In March 1992 the Security Council enlarged UNAVEM II's mandate to include the observation of the general elections which were held in September. In the event, UNAVEM II also assisted the national electoral commission in the registration of voters. Following the resumption of hostilities provoked by the disputed election results, the Secretary-General's Special Representative was active in organizing new rounds of peace talks. Direct talks between the Angolan Government and UNITA commenced in April 1993, under UN auspices, but were adjourned after six weeks. Peace talks recommenced in mid-November, on the basis of a five-point agenda that had been negotiated by the Secretary-General's Special Representative and the three observer countries. A new peace accord, the Lusaka Protocol, was signed by representatives of the Government and UNITA in November 1994. In February 1995 the Security Council authorized an expansion of the mission, with a mandate to supervise and monitor the terms of the Lusaka Protocol, including the demobilization of UNITA forces and the formation of a new army and police force. In addition, the new mission, UNAVEM III, which was to be concluded within a 2-year period, was to assist the reconstruction of Angola, with particular concern to effect a national mine-clearance operation and to restore the country's transport infrastructure. The full deployment of the authorized 7,000 UNAVEM III troops was disrupted by reports of violations of the cease-fire and insecurity in parts of the country, preventing the free movement of people and goods. By September UNAVEM III observers were positioned at 55 control points to verify the movement of troops and trade in armaments. Throughout 1996 the Security Council extended the mission's mandate but expressed concern at the slow progress being achieved in the peace process. In December the Special Representative of the UN Secretary-General confirmed a declaration by UNITA that all its forces, amounting to some 65,692 troops and 4,644 police officers, had been quartered and disarmed; however, some reports indicated that several thousand UNITA soldiers had since left the UN-controlled sites. Nevertheless, the UN insisted that efforts were to be pursued to form a unified Angolan army, while the 15 UNAVEM III confinement areas were to be converted into centres for demobilization. On 11 December the Security Council extended UNAVEM III's mandate for a final term, until 28 February 1997, when the mission's military units were to be withdrawn. However, in February, the mandate was further extended owing to concerns, expressed by the UN Secretary-General, at delays in the implementation of the peace accord, in particular the formation of a new government. In mid-April, following the inauguration of a Government of National Unity, the mission's mandate was extended for a final period, until 30 June 1997, although the phased withdrawal of UNAVEM III troops was initiated with immediate effect. At the end of June the Security Council decided to maintain a UN presence in the country, and authorized the establishment of MONUA. The withdrawal of the estimated 4,000 UNAVEM III troops remaining in Angola was to be completed by November.

MONUA had an authorized strength of 83 military officers and 345 civilian police.

UNITED NATIONS OBSERVER MISSION IN LIBERIA—UNOMIL

Headquarters: Mamba Point, Monrovia, Liberia.

Special Representative of the UN Secretary-General: TULIAMENI KALOMO (Namibia).

Chief Military Observer: Maj.-Gen. SRIKANDER SHAMI (Pakistan).

In September 1993 a Security Council resolution established UNOMIL to facilitate the implementation of the Cotonou Peace Agreement, which had been signed by the conflicting parties in July of that year. The mission was expected to work alongside a monitoring group of the Economic Community of West African States (ECOMOG—see ECOWAS p. 115), and thus constituted the first UN peace-keeping operation to be undertaken in co-operation with a mission of another organization. A Joint-Cease-fire Monitoring Committee, consisting of representatives from the UN, ECOMOG and Liberian parties, had been established to monitor and investigate cease-fire violations between 1 August and the full deployment of UNOMIL and the reinforcement of ECOMOG, which was considered to be essential for a lasting peace. Following the full deployment of both forces by early 1994, the committee was replaced by a Violations Committee, which was chaired by UNOMIL's chief military observer. In February negotiations between the conflicting parties resulted in an agreement to establish a transitional authority, to commence the disarmament process and to conduct a general election. In accordance with the agreement, three demobilization centres became operational in early March. Progress on disarming the conflicting factions remained slow, however, and in June the Security Council stated that the general election, which had been scheduled for early September, could not be conducted until the demobilization process had been completed. In August a UN fact-finding mission assessed that only 3,500 of an estimated 60,000 combatants had been disarmed. Meanwhile, the peace process was seriously jeopardized by continuing factional hostilities. In early September 43 members of UNOMIL were forcibly detained, and UN property was looted. Subsequently, all UNOMIL military observers returned to the capital, Monrovia, leaving no UN presence in the rest of the country. The persisting instability and uncertain commitment of the country's political leaders towards furthering the peace process resulted in the Security Council granting only short-term extensions (generally, three months) to UNOMIL's mandate. In November a UN mission was dispatched to Liberia to assess the future roles of ECOMOG and UNOMIL. In late December the Liberian warring factions concluded a peace agreement, to further a previous accord signed at Akosombo, Ghana, in September. However, disagreements on the implementation of the accord persisted throughout the first half of 1995. In August a new peace accord, the Abuja Agreement, was concluded, providing for a new ceasefire to come into effect and the installation of a transitional Council of State. In the following month the Security Council extended UNOMIL's mandate until 31 January 1996. The Security Council also endorsed the deployment of an additional 42 military observers to monitor the cease-fire and disengagement of forces. In November 1995 the Security Council adopted a resolution adjusting UNOMIL's mandate, on the basis of a report by the UN Secretary-General, in order to define the mission's role in supporting the efforts of ECOWAS and the transitional national government to implement the peace agreement. The mission's mandate was renewed, in January 1996, until the end of May. In April UNOMIL observers evacuated the country following a resumption of hostilities. By May UNOMIL comprised just 20 civilian and five military observers. At the end of May the Security Council extended the mission's mandate for a further three months; however, it emphasized that the continued UN presence in Liberia was dependent on that of ECOMOG, advocated greater co-ordination between the two observer groups and urged ECOMOG to provide security to UNOMIL personnel. In August a meeting of ECOWAS heads of state concluded an initiative to extend the Abuja peace agreement until June 1997 and formulated a revised timetable for its implementation, according to which the cease-fire was to be restored by 31 August, while a general election was to be conducted on 30 May 1997. UNOMIL was to provide support for the implementation of the renewed peace process, in particular monitoring the process of disarming and demobilizing combatants and investigating alleged violations of human rights. The disarmament process was initiated in late-November 1996. By early February 1997 ECOWAS declared that some 91% of the total rebel forces (revised to number 30,000-35,000) had relinquished their weapons. UNOMIL's mandate was extended, in March, until 30 June and subsequently, for a final period until 30 September 1997. In May ECOWAS agreed to reschedule the date for the Liberian general election, which took place on 19 July.

At 31 December 1996 UNOMIL comprised 78 military personnel. The estimated annual cost of UNOMIL to the UN amounted to US $33.6m.

Food and Agriculture Organization—FAO

Address: Viale delle Terme di Caracalla, 00100 Rome, Italy.

Telephone: (6) 52251; **telex:** 625852; **fax:** (6) 5225-3152; **e-mail:** telex-room@fao.org.

FAO, the first specialized agency of the UN to be founded after World War II, was established in Québec, Canada, in October 1945. The Organization combats malnutrition and hunger, and serves as a co-ordinating agency for development programmes in the whole range of food and agriculture, including forestry and fisheries. It helps developing countries to promote educational and training facilities and the creation of appropriate institutions.

Organization

(July 1997)

CONFERENCE

The governing body is the FAO Conference of member nations. It meets every two years, formulates policy, determines the Organization's programme and budget on a biennial basis, and elects new members. It also elects the Director-General of the Secretariat and the Independent Chairman of the Council. Every second year, FAO also holds conferences in each of its five regions (the Near East, Asia and the Pacific, Africa, Latin America and the Caribbean, and Europe).

COUNCIL

The FAO Council is composed of representatives of 49 member nations, elected by the Conference for staggered three-year terms. It is the interim governing body of FAO between sessions of the Conference. The most important standing Committees of the Council are: the Finance and Programme Committees, the Committee on Commodity Problems, the Committee on Fisheries, the Committee on Agriculture and the Committee on Forestry.

SECRETARIAT

The total number of staff at FAO headquarters in April 1996 was 2,606, of whom some 66 were associate experts, while staff in field, regional and country offices numbered 1,689, including 166 associate experts. Work is supervised by the following Departments: Administration and Finance; General Affairs and Information; Economic and Social Policy; Agriculture; Forestry; Fisheries; Sustainable Development; and Technical Co-operation.

Director-General: Jacques Diouf (Senegal).

REGIONAL OFFICES

Regional Office for Africa: UN Agency Bldg, North Maxwell Rd, POB 1628, Accra, Ghana; tel. 666851; telex 2139; fax 233999; Regional Rep. B. F. Dada.

Subregional Office for Southern and Eastern Africa: POB 3730, Harare, Zimbabwe; tel. (4) 791407; telex 26040; fax (4) 795644; e-mail fao-zimbabwe@fao.org; Subregional Rep. Victoria Sekitoleko.

Activities

FAO aims to raise levels of nutrition and standards of living, by improving the production and distribution of food and other commodities derived from farms, fisheries and forests. Under FAO's medium-term plan for 1992–97 its work covers five basic areas: advising governments on policy and planning; training and technical assistance; promotion of sustainable development; enhancing the economic status of women; and promotion of economic and technical co-operation among developing countries. In November 1996 FAO organized the World Food Summit, which was held in Rome and was attended by heads of state and senior government representatives of 186 countries. Participants approved the Rome Declaration on World Food Security and the World Food Summit Plan of Action, with the aim of halving the number of people afflicted by undernutrition, at that time estimated to total 840m. world-wide, no later than 2015.

FAO's total field programme expenditure for 1995 was US $264m., compared with $275m. spent in 1994. An estimated 38% of field projects were in Africa, 25% in Asia and the Pacific, 12% in the Near East, 13% in Latin America and the Caribbean, 4% in Europe, and 8% were inter-regional or global.

AGRICULTURE

FAO's Field Programme provides training and technical assistance to enable small farmers to increase production, by a number of methods, including improved seeds and fertilizer use, soil conservation and reforestation, better water resource management techniques, upgrading storage facilities, and improvements in processing and marketing. FAO promotes the production of under-exploited traditional food crops, such as cassava, yams, breadfruit, sweet potato and plantains. During the 1980s FAO developed 'wheatless bread', which can be made using cassava, sorghum or millet flour, and is intended to reduce dependence on imports of wheat. Governments are advised on the conservation of genetic resources, on improving the supply of seeds and on crop protection: animal and plant gene banks are maintained. In June 1996 representatives of more than 150 governments attending a conference in Leipzig, Germany, organized by FAO, adopted a Global Plan of Action to conserve and improve the use of plant genetic resources, in order to enhance food security throughout the world. The Plan included measures to strengthen the development of plant varieties and to promote the use and availability of local varieties and locally-adapted crops to farmers, in particular following a natural disaster, war or civil conflict. FAO's Special Programme on Food Security, which was initiated in 1994, was designed to assist target countries, i.e. low-income countries with a food deficit, to increase food production and productivity as rapidly as possible. This was to be achieved primarily through the widespread adoption by farmers of available improved production technologies, with emphasis on areas of high potential. At March 1996 82 countries were categorized as 'low-income food-deficit', of which 41 were in Africa.

Plant protection, weed control, and animal health programmes form an important part of FAO's work as farming methods become more intensive, and pests more resistant to control methods. In 1985 the FAO Conference approved an International Code of Conduct on the Distribution and Use of Pesticides and in 1989 the Conference adopted an additional clause concerning 'Prior Informed Consent', whereby international shipments of newly banned or restricted pesticides should not proceed without the agreement of importing countries. In mid-1996 FAO publicized a new initiative that aimed to increase awareness of, and to promote international action on, obsolete and hazardous stocks of pesticides remaining throughout the world. A central concept of FAO's plant protection programme is the Integrated Pest Management (IPM) strategy, which was initiated in 1988 in order to reduce over-reliance on pesticides. IPM principles include biological control methods, such as the introduction of natural predators to avert pests, crop rotation and the use of pest-resistant crop varieties. A 12-month project to implement the IPM strategy in Zimbabwe was initiated in early 1996. FAO's Joint Division with the International Atomic Energy Agency (IAEA), tests controlled-release formulas of pesticides and herbicides that can limit the amount of agrochemicals needed to protect crops. The Joint FAO-IAEA Division is engaged in exploring biotechnologies and in developing non-toxic fertilizers (especially those that are locally available) and improved strains of food crops (especially from indigenous varieties). FAO's Plant Nutrition Programme aims to promote activities for nutrient management based on the recycling of nutrients through crop production and the efficient use of mineral fertilizers.

An Emergency Prevention System for Transboundary Animal and Plant Pests and Diseases (EMPRES) was established in 1994 to strengthen FAO's activities in the prevention, control and, where possible, eradication of highly contagious diseases and pests. EMPRES's initial priorities were locusts and rinderpest. During 1994 EMPRES published guidelines on all aspects of desert locust monitoring, commissioned an evaluation of recent control efforts and prepared a concept paper on desert locust management. FAO has assumed responsibility for technical leadership and co-ordination of the Global Rinderpest Eradication Campaign, which aims to eradicate the disease, endemic in areas of the Horn of Africa, by 2010. In early 1997 EMPRES was involved in intensive surveillance activities in east Africa, following a serious outbreak of rinderpest in eastern and southern Kenya and the border region of Tanzania. In March 1995 FAO initiated an emergency programme to combat bovine pleuro-pneumonia, a disease which had affected livestock in Tanzania and was a potential threat to a further three million cattle in southern Africa, in particular in Zambia and Malawi. The programme included widespread livestock vaccination and restrictions on cattle movement. Following an incidence of African swine fever in Côte d'Ivoire in April 1996, FAO initiated a long-term epidemio-surveillance programme with the Ivorian authorities.

FAO's work on soil conservation includes erosion control and the reclamation of degraded land. In 1993 FAO was involved in a project to control soil erosion in Burundi, by means of building mounds and planting trees, shrubs and grasses. FAO also assists in developing water resources and irrigation.

FISHERIES

FAO's Fisheries Department consists of a multi-disciplinary body of experts who are involved in every aspect of fisheries development from coastal surveys, improved production, processing and storage, to the compilation of statistics, development of computer databases, improvement of fishing gear, institution building and training. In March 1995 a ministerial meeting of fisheries adopted a Rome Consensus on World Fisheries, which identified a need for immediate action to eliminate overfishing and to rebuild and enhance depleting fish stocks. In November the FAO Conference adopted a Code of Conduct for Responsible Fishing, which incorporated many global fisheries and aquaculture issues (including fisheries resource conservation and development, fish catches, seafood and fish processing, commercialization, trade and research) to promote the sustainable development of the sector. FAO promotes aquaculture as a valuable source of animal protein, and as an income-generating activity for rural communities. Other fisheries initiatives in the early 1990s included the protection and restocking of endangered species and programmes aimed at supporting women in the fisheries communities of developing countries. In 1993 FAO's Aquaculture for Local Community Development Program (ALCOM), which assists the 10 member countries of the Southern African Development Community (SADC–q.v.), funded a project to restock some 200 dams in Zimbabwe. ALCOM also co-operated with the Zimbabwe Government to develop community management of fisheries.

FORESTRY

In collaboration with UNDP, the World Bank and the World Resources Unit, FAO has devised the Tropical Forestry Action Programme (TFAP). The Programme aims to improve the lives of rural people, to increase food production, to intensify forestry activities and to establish interdisciplinary national and regional programmes that both safeguard the forest and make rational use of its resources. Another primary concern of the Forestry Department is the critical fuel wood situation in many developing countries. In 1990 FAO estimated that by 2000 more than one-half of the population of the developing world will face fuel wood shortages and will be caught in a cycle of deforestation, fuel wood scarcity, poverty and malnutrition. FAO assists governments to formulate National Forestry Action Programmes, in order to promote the sustainable development of forestry resources. In 1992 FAO helped to establish and develop National Tree Seed Centres in Sahal countries to improve the genetic resources of forests.

PROCESSING AND MARKETING

An estimated 20% of all food harvested is lost before it can be consumed. FAO helps reduce immediate post-harvest losses, with the introduction of improved processing methods and storage systems. It also advises on the distribution and marketing of agricultural produce and on the selection and preparation of foods for optimum nutrition. A Centre for Agricultural Marketing Training in Eastern and Southern Africa has been established with FAO assistance in Harare, Zimbabwe, to serve Kenya, Malawi, Tanzania and Zimbabwe. FAO continues to favour the elimination of export subsidies and related discriminatory practices, in particular those which create unfavourable trading conditions for developing countries dependent on agricultural products as their main source of foreign income. FAO evaluates new market trends and helps to develop improved plant and animal quarantine procedures.

ENVIRONMENT

In April 1991 a Conference on Agriculture and the Environment was held in the Netherlands, organized jointly by FAO and the Netherlands Government. The alleviation of poverty was identified as being a major prerequisite for sustainable agricultural production. At the UN Conference on Environment and Development, held in Rio de Janeiro in June 1992, FAO participated in several working parties and supported the adoption of Agenda 21, a programme of activities to promote sustainable development. FAO was subsequently designated as the UN agency responsible for the chapters of Agenda 21 comprising water resources, forests, fragile mountain ecosystems and sustainable agriculture and rural development.

NUTRITION

In December 1992 an International Conference on Nutrition was held in Rome, administered jointly by FAO and WHO. The Conference approved a World Declaration on Nutrition and a Plan of Action, aimed at promoting efforts to combat malnutrition as a development priority. Since the conference, more than 100 countries have formulated national plans of action for nutrition, many of which were based on existing development plans such as comprehensive food security initiatives, national poverty alleviation programmes and action plans to attain the targets set by the World Summit for Children in September 1990. By October 1995 several projects based on the national plans of action had been implemented in areas such as nutrition education, food quality and safety, micronutrient deficiency alleviation and nutrition surveillance.

FOOD SECURITY

FAO's food security policy aims to encourage the production of adequate food supplies, to maximize stability in the flow of supplies, and to ensure access on the part of those who need them. FAO's Global Information and Early Warning System (GIEWS), which became operational in 1975, monitors the crop and food outlook at global and national levels in order to detect emerging food supply difficulties and disasters. In early 1992 the GIEWS warned of impending famine in southern Africa, owing to prolonged drought and crop devastation, and in mid-1994 the GIEWS again warned of developing drought in that region in advance of the crop harvest. The GIEWS also analyses emergency food aid requests from governments for consideration by FAO and the World Food Programme (WFP, q.v.). In 1995 FAO identified 26 countries, of which more than half were in Africa, that were confronting acute food shortages and required exceptional and/or emergency food assistance. During that year world output of crops and livestock products expanded at an estimated rate of only 0.2%, compared with 2.8% in 1994. At the same time supplies of food aid became more restricted, with the result that many food needs were not satisfied. At mid-1995, according to FAO, an estimated 23m. people in sub-Saharan Africa were confronted with food shortages, the majority of whom were in southern Africa.

FAO was actively involved in the formulation of a Plan of Action on food security, adopted at the World Food Summit in November 1996, and was to be responsible for monitoring and promoting its implementation.

FAO INVESTMENT CENTRE

The Investment Centre was established in 1964 to help countries prepare viable investment projects that would attract external financing. The Centre focuses its evaluation of projects on two fundamental concerns: the promotion of sustainable activities for land management, forestry development and environmental protection, and the alleviation of rural poverty. In 1995 31 projects were approved, representing a total investment of some US $3,300m.

EMERGENCY RELIEF

FAO works to rehabilitate agricultural production following natural and man-made disasters by providing emergency seed, tools, and technical and other assistance. In 1995 FAO's Special Relief Operations Service undertook new projects in 27 countries, at a cost of more than US $21m. The Service directed substantial funds towards supporting the rehabilitation of the agricultural sector in Rwanda through the provision of agricultural inputs and the co-ordination of emergency assistance. Jointly with the United Nations, FAO is responsible for WFP (see below), which provides emergency food supplies and food aid in support of development projects.

INFORMATION AND RESEARCH

FAO functions as an information centre, collecting, analysing, interpreting and disseminating information through various media. It issues regular statistical reports, commodity studies, and technical manuals in local languages (see list of publications below). Other materials produced by the FAO include information booklets, reference papers, reports of meetings, training manuals and audiovisuals.

FAO compiles and co-ordinates an extensive range of international databases on agriculture, fisheries, forestry, food and statistics, the most important of these being AGRIS (the International Information System for the Agricultural Sciences and Technology) and CARIS (the Current Agricultural Research Information System). Statistical databases include GLOBEFISH databank and electronic library, FISHDAB (the Fisheries Statistical Database), FORIS (Forest Resources Information System), and GIS (the Geographical Information System). In addition, AGROSTAT PC has been designed to provide access to updated figures in six agriculture-related topics via personal computer. In 1996 FAO established a World Agricultural Information Centre (WAICENT), which offers wide access to agricultural data through the electronic media.

FAO's Research and Technology Development Division helps to co-ordinate members' research. Missions to review and plan agricultural research are sent to member countries.

FAO REGIONAL COMMISSIONS

African Commission on Agricultural Statistics: c/o FAO Regional Office for Africa, POB 1628, Accra, Ghana; f. 1961 to advise member countries on the development and standardization of food and agricultural statistics. Mems: 37 states.

African Forestry and Wildlife Commission: Via delle Terme di Caracalla, 00100 Rome, Italy; f. 1959 to advise on the formulation of forest policy and to review and co-ordinate its implementation on a regional level; to exchange information and advise on technical problems. Mems: 42 states.

Commission on African Animal Trypanosomiasis: Via delle Terme di Caracalla, 00100 Rome, Italy; f. 1979 to develop and implement programmes to combat this pathogen. Mems: 39 states.

Joint FAO/WHO/OAU Regional Food and Nutrition Commission for Africa: c/o FAO Regional Office for Africa, POB 1628, Accra, Ghana; f. 1962 to provide liaison in matters concerning food and nutrition, and to review food and nutritional problems in Africa. Mems: 43 states.

FINANCE

FAO's Regular Programme, which is financed by contributions from member governments, covers the cost of the FAO's Secretariat, its Technical Co-operation Programme (TCP) and part of the cost of several special action programmes. The budget for the two years 1996–97 amounted to US $650m., compared with $673m. for the previous biennium. Much of FAO's Field Programme of technical assistance is funded from extra-budgetary sources. The single largest contributor is the United Nations Development Programme (UNDP), which in 1995 accounted for $58.3m., or 22% of Field Programme expenditure. More important are the trust funds that come mainly from donor countries and international financing institutions. In 1995 they totalled $165.1m., or 63% of Field Programme expenditure. FAO's contribution under the TCP (FAO's regular budgetary funds for the Field Programme) was $40.8m., or 15% of field project expenditure.

WORLD FOOD PROGRAMME—WFP

Address: Via Cristoforo Colombo 426, 00145 Rome, Italy.

Telephone: (6) 522821; **telex:** 626675; **fax:** (6) 5960-2348; **e-mail:** wfpinfo@wfp.org.

WFP is a joint UN-FAO effort to stimulate economic and social development through food aid and to provide emergency relief. It became operational in 1963.

WFP provides food aid, primarily to low-income, food-deficit countries, to support economic and social development projects. Through its development activities WFP aims to alleviate poverty in developing countries by promoting self-reliant families and communities. Food is supplied, for example, as an incentive in labour-intensive projects which provide employment and strengthen self-help capacity. WFP supports activities to boost agricultural production, to rehabilitate and improve local infrastructure, particularly transport systems, and to encourage education, training and health programmes. Priority is given to vulnerable groups such as pregnant women and children. Some WFP projects are intended to alleviate the effects of structural adjustment programmes (particularly programmes which involve reductions in public expenditure and in subsidies for basic foods). At the end of 1995 WFP was supporting 204 development projects in 81 countries, with total commitments valued at US $2,281m.

In the early 1990s there was a substantial shift in the balance between emergency and development assistance provided by WFP, owing to the growing needs of victims of drought and other natural disasters, refugees and displaced persons. WFP provides food supplies mainly from the International Emergency Food Reserve, which it manages. In 1995 the main focus of WFP's relief activities continued to be sub-Saharan Africa, which accounted for US $422.8m., or 69%, of total relief operational expenditure in that year. Emergency food relief reached more than 15m. people in 28 countries in the region. The main populations of concern throughout 1995 and 1996 were those in Rwanda, Burundi, Liberia and Sierra Leone, affected by civil conflict, and in drought-ridden east Africa. In the first half of 1997 WFP initiated emergency operations to assist displaced populations in northern Uganda and to distribute food to some 476,000 Kenyans and 360,000 most vulnerable people in Somalia affected by the ongoing drought in that region and the consequent crop failure and population displacement.

Following a comprehensive evaluation of its activities, WFP is increasingly focused on linking its relief and development activities to provide a continuum between short-term relief and longer-term rehabilitation and development. In order to achieve this objective, WFP aims to integrate elements that strengthen disaster mitigation into development projects, including soil conservation, reforestation, irrigation infrastructure and transport construction and rehabilitation and to promote capacity-building elements within relief operations, e.g. training, income-generating activities and environmental protection measures. In 1995 WFP was able to commit more resources to this approach, owing to the cessation of hostilities in many affected countries. Food aid was used, for example, as salary substitutes to teachers and health care staff returning to work in Rwanda and Somalia, to support the demobilization process in Angola and Mozambique, and for the resettlement and reintegration of refugees and internally displaced persons in many countries, including Angola and Zambia. In 1995 WFP approved 19 new 'protracted refugee and displaced persons operations', where the emphasis was on fostering stability, rehabilitation and long-term development after an emergency. In all these operations, which are undertaken in collaboration with UNHCR and other international agencies, WFP is responsible for mobilizing basic food commodities and for related transport, handling and storage costs. The single largest protracted operation was in Liberia, where WFP committed $97.6m. to assist some 2.6m. refugees and displaced persons. In early 1997 WFP committed $19.4m. to assist the repatriation and rehabilitation of some 775,000 refugees from Sierra Leone, as well as relief to those remaining in camps in Guinea.

WFP Executive Director: CATHERINE A. BERTINI (USA).

FAO PUBLICATIONS

Animal Health Yearbook.

Commodity Review and Outlook (annually).

Environment and Energy Bulletin.

Fertilizer Yearbook.

Food Outlook (monthly).

Plant Protection Bulletin (quarterly).

Production Yearbook (in English, French and Spanish).

Quarterly Bulletin of Statistics.

The State of Food and Agriculture (annually).

The State of World Fisheries and Aquaculture (annually).

The State of the World's Forests.

Technical Co-operation Among Developing Countries Newsletter (in English only).

Trade Yearbook.

Unasylva (quarterly).

Yearbook of Fishery Statistics (in English, French and Spanish).

Yearbook of Forest Products (in English, French and Spanish).

World Watch List for Domestic Animal Diversity.

Commodity reviews; studies; manuals.

Information on FAO activities can be accessed on the Internet at http://www.fao.org, and on WFP at http://www.unicc.org/wfp.

International Bank for Reconstruction and Development—IBRD—and International Development Association—IDA (World Bank)

Address: 1818 H St, NW, Washington, DC 20433, USA.

Telephone: (202) 477-1234; **telex:** 248423; **fax:** (202) 477-6391.

The IBRD was established on 27 December 1945. Initially it was concerned with post-war reconstruction in Europe; since then its aim has been to assist the economic development of member nations by making loans where private capital is not available on reasonable terms to finance productive investments. Loans are made either direct to governments, or to private enterprises with the guarantee of their governments. The World Bank, as it is commonly known, comprises the IBRD and the International Development Association (IDA), which was founded in 1960. The affiliated group of institutions, comprising the IBRD, the IDA, the International Finance Corporation (IFC, q.v.), the Multilateral Investment Guarantee Agency (MIGA, q.v.) and the International Centre for Settlement of Investment Disputes (ICSID, see below), is now referred to as the World Bank Group. Only members of the International Monetary Fund (IMF, q.v.) may be considered for membership in the Bank. Subscriptions to the capital stock of the Bank are based on each member's quota in the IMF, which is designed to reflect the country's relative economic strength. Voting rights are related to shareholdings.

Organization

(July 1997)

Officers and staff of the IBRD serve concurrently as officers and staff in the IDA. The World Bank has offices in New York, Paris, Brussels, London and Tokyo; regional missions in Nairobi (for eastern Africa), Abidjan (for western Africa), Bangkok (in Thailand) and Riga (in Latvia); and resident missions in 72 countries.

BOARD OF GOVERNORS

The Board of Governors consists of one Governor appointed by each member nation. Typically, a Governor is the country's finance minister, central bank governor, or a minister or an official of comparable rank. The Board normally meets once a year.

EXECUTIVE DIRECTORS

The general operations of the World Bank are conducted by a Board of 24 Executive Directors. Five Directors are appointed by the five members having the largest number of shares of capital stock, and the rest are elected by the Governors representing the other members. The President of the Bank is Chairman of the Board.

OFFICERS

President and Chairman of Executive Directors: JAMES WOLFENSOHN (USA).

Vice-Presidents, Africa Regional Office: CALLISTO E. MADAVO, JEAN-LOUIS SARBIB.

REGIONAL OFFICES

Regional Mission in Eastern Africa: POB 30577, Hill Park Bldg, Upper Hill, Nairobi, Kenya; tel. (2) 260441; telex 22022; fax (2) 260380; Chief HAROLD E. WACKMAN.

Regional Mission in Western Africa: Booker Washington/Jacques Aka Cocody, BP 1850, Abidjan 01, Côte d'Ivoire; tel. 44-32-44; telex 28132; fax 44-16-87; Chief SHIGEO KATSU.

Activities

FINANCIAL OPERATIONS

The World Bank's primary objectives are the achievement of sustainable economic growth, and the reduction of poverty in developing countries. In mid-1994 the World Bank Group published a review of its role and activities and identified the following five major development issues on which it intended to focus in the future: the pursuit of economic reforms; investment in people, in particular through education, health, nutrition and family-planning programmes; the protection of the environment; stimulation of the private sector; and reorientation of government, in order to enhance the private sector by reforming and strengthening the public sector. The Bank compiles country-specific assessments and formulates country-assistance strategies to ensure that the Bank's own projects support and complement the programmes of the country concerned.

Since 1987 the World Bank has accorded greater importance to the protection of the environment and in 1989/90 systematic 'screening' of all new projects was introduced, in order to assess their environmental impact. The Bank also supports individual countries to prepare and implement national environmental action plans (NEAPs) and to strengthen their institutional capacity for environmental planning and management.

IBRD loans are usually for a period of 20 years or less. Loans are made to governments, or must be guaranteed by the government concerned. IDA assistance is aimed at the poorer developing countries (i.e. mainly those with a GNP per caput of less than US $765 in 1995 dollars), and the majority of the countries of sub-Saharan Africa are eligible to receive it. Under IDA lending conditions, credits can be extended to countries whose balance of payments could not sustain the burden of repayment required for IBRD loans. Terms are more favourable than those provided by the IBRD; credits are for a period of 35–40 years, with a 'grace' period of 10 years, and carry no interest charges.

The IBRD's capital is derived from members' subscriptions to capital shares, the calculation of which is based on their quotas in the IMF. In April 1988 the Board of Governors approved an increase of about 80% in the IBRD's authorized capital, to US $171,000m. At 30 June 1996 the total subscribed capital of the IBRD was $180,630m., of which the paid-in portion was $10,994m. (6.1%); the remainder is subject to call if required. Most of the IBRD's lendable funds come from its borrowing in world capital markets, and also from its retained earnings and the flow of repayments on its loans. Bank loans carry a variable interest rate, rather than a rate fixed at the time of borrowing.

IDA's development resources, consisting of members' subscriptions and supplementary resources (additional subscriptions and contributions) are replenished periodically by contributions from the more affluent member countries. In March 1996 representatives of more than 30 donor countries concluded negotiations for the 11th replenishment of IDA funds (and for a one-year interim fund), to finance the period July 1996–June 1999. New contributions over the three-year period were to amount to US $11,000m., while total funds available for lending, including past donor contributions, repayments of IDA credits and the World Bank's contributions, were to amount to $22,000m.

During the year ending 30 June 1996 53 operations were approved for Africa south of the Sahara amounting to US $2,740.1m. (12.7% of World Bank assistance in that year), all of which was in the form of IDA credits.

Some 45% of the population in sub-Saharan Africa are estimated to be living in poverty. The Bank's poverty reduction strategy for Africa involves projects that aim to alleviate the adverse effects of structural adjustment programmes; that assist governments to assess and monitor poverty; and that increase food security. In 1993 a task force was established to consider measures to reduce poverty in sub-Saharan Africa, in consultation with local and national experts, non-governmental organizations and government officials. The task force published its assessment of the situation in December 1996 and recommended that the Bank revise its lending strategy to emphasize poverty reduction objectives and strengthen systematic monitoring of the poverty situation in all sub-Saharan African countries receiving World Bank assistance. In 1994/95 the Bank helped to prepare and finance Emergency Recovery Programmes for Burundi and Rwanda, in response to the adverse political, social and economic situations in those countries arising from a period of civil conflict. The Programmes assessed priority needs in the health, education, agricultural and private sectors and generated international donor support to assist rehabilitation activities. In July 1996 the Bank established a 'war-to-peace' transition team in order to respond effectively to countries needing assistance for post-conflict economic and social reconstruction.

In July 1985 a Special Facility for sub-Saharan Africa became effective for a three-year period, with funds of US $1,250m., to finance structural adjustment, sectoral reform programmes and rehabilitation. A 'Special Programme of Assistance' (SPA) for sub-Saharan Africa, available from 1988, aimed to increase concessional lending to heavily-indebted and impoverished African countries, mainly by the co-ordination of international aid contributions and to co-financing mechanisms. Only IDA member countries implementing a policy adjustment programme, with a debt-service ration of more than 30%, were to be eligible for SPA funds (numbering 31 countries at the end of 1995). Funds amounting to $6,700m. were pledged for the third phase of the programme covering the three-year period 1994–96. In 1991 the African Capacity Building Foundation was established by the World Bank, the African Development Bank and UNDP, with the aim of encouraging indigenous research and managerial capabilities, by supporting or creating institutions for training, research and analysis.

In March 1996 a new programme to co-ordinate development efforts in Africa was announced by the UN Secretary-General. The World Bank was to facilitate the mobilization of the estimated US $25,000m. required to achieve the objectives of the Special Initiative over a 10-year period. In addition, the Bank was to provide technical assistance to enable countries to devise economic plans (in particular following a period of civil conflict), agricultural development programmes and a common strategy for African countries to strengthen the management capacities of the public sector.

In September 1996 the World Bank/IMF Development Committee endorsed a joint initiative to assist heavily indebted poor countries (HIPCs) to reduce their debt burden to a sustainable level, in order to make more resources available for poverty reduction and economic growth. A new Trust Fund was established by the World Bank in November to finance the initiative. The Fund, consisting of an initial allocation of US $500m. from the IBRD surplus and other contributions from multilateral creditors, was to be administered by IDA. Of the 41 HIPCs identified by the Bank, 33 were in sub-Saharan Africa. In the majority of cases a sustainable level of debt was targetted at 200%–250% of the net present value of the debt in relation to total annual exports. Other countries with a lower debt-to-export ratio were to be eligible for assistance under the initiative providing that their export earnings were more than 40% of GDP and government revenue at least 20% of GDP. In April 1997 the World Bank and the IMF announced that Uganda was to be the first beneficiary of the initiative, enabling the Ugandan Government to reduce its external debt by some 20%, or an estimated $338m. The Bank's approved loan of $160m. was to be disbursed in April 1998, conditional on other official creditors and multinational institutions contributing their share of the debt relief and on Uganda pursuing its programme of economic and social development reforms. A grant of $75m. was to be available to the Ugandan authorities in the interim year.

TECHNICAL ASSISTANCE

The provision of technical assistance to member countries is a major component of Bank activities. The economic, sector and project analysis undertaken by the Bank in the normal course of its operations is the vehicle for considerable technical assistance. In addition, project loans and credits may include funds designated specifically for feasibility studies, resource surveys, management or planning advice, and training. In 1975 a Project Preparation Facility (PPF) was established to provide cash advances to prepare projects that may be financed by the Bank. During 1995 122 PPF grants, with a total value of US $96m., were approved, the majority of which were to countries in sub-Saharan Africa.

In 1992 the Bank established an Institutional Development Fund (IDF), which became operational on 1 July; the purpose of the Fund was to provide rapid, small-scale financial assistance, to a maximum value of US $500,000, for capacity-building proposals. During 1995 105 IDF grants were approved, amounting to $24.2m., to 61 countries.

ECONOMIC RESEARCH AND STUDIES

In the 1990s the World Bank's research, conducted by its own research staff, was increasingly concerned with providing information to reinforce the Bank's expanding advisory role to developing countries. Consequently the principal areas of current research focus on issues such as maintaining sustainable growth while protecting the environment and the poorest sectors of society, encouraging the development of the private sector, and reducing and decentralizing government activities. The Bank chairs the Consultative Group on International Agricultural Research (CGIAR), which was formed in 1971 to raise financial support for research on improving crops and animal production in developing countries. The Group supports 16 research centres.

CO-OPERATION WITH OTHER ORGANIZATIONS

The World Bank co-operates closely with other UN bodies through consultations, meetings, and joint activities, particularly in response to the economic crisis in Africa south of the Sahara, where co-operation with UNDP and WHO is especially important. It collaborates with the IMF in implementing economic adjustment programmes in developing countries. The Bank holds regular consultations with the European Community and OECD on development issues, and the Bank-NGO Committee provides an annual forum for discussion with non-governmental organizations (NGO). The Bank chairs meetings of donor governments and organizations for the co-ordination of aid to particular countries. The Bank also conducts co-financing and aid co-ordination projects with official aid agencies, export credit institutions and commercial banks. In April 1997 the World Bank signed a co-operation agreement with the World Trade Organization, in order to co-ordinate efforts to integrate developing countries into the global economy.

The World Bank administers the Global Environment Facility (GEF), which was established in 1990, in conjunction with UNDP and UNEP. The aim of the GEF, which became operational in 1991 for an initial three-year period,was to assist developing countries in implementing policies that benefit the global environment. In March 1994 87 countries participating in the Facility agreed to restructure and replenish the GEF for a further three-year period from July of that year. Funds amounting to US $2,000m. were to be made available by 26 donor countries which would enable the GEF to act as the financial mechanism for the conventions on climate changes and biological diversity that were signed at the UN Conference on Environment and Development in June 1992. At 30 June 1996 the GEF portfolio comprised 56 projects, with financing of almost $500m., covering the following areas: biodiversity; climate change; the phase-out of ozone-depleting substances; and international waters.

In June 1995 the World Bank joined other international donors (including regional development banks, other UN bodies, Canada, France, the Netherlands and the USA) in establishing a Consultative Group to Assist the Poorest (CGAP), which was to channel funds to the most needy through grass-roots agencies. An initial credit of approximately US $200m. was committed by the donors. The Bank manages the CGAP Secretariat, which is responsible for the administration of external funding and for the evaluation and approval of project financing. In addition, the CGAP provides training and information services on microfinance for policy-makers and practitioners.

EVALUATION

The World Bank's Operations Evaluation Department studies and publishes the results of projects after a loan has been fully disbursed, so as to identify problems and possible improvements in future activities. Internal auditing is also carried out, to monitor the effectiveness of the Bank's operations and management.

In September 1993 the Bank's Board of Executive Directors agreed to establish an Independent Inspection Panel, consistent with the Bank's objective of improving project implementation and accountability. The Panel, which became operational in September 1994, was to conduct independent investigations and report on complaints concerning the design, appraisal and implementation of development projects supported by the Bank.

IBRD INSTITUTIONS

Economic Development Institute—EDI: founded in 1955. Training is provided for government officials at the middle and upper levels of responsibility who are concerned with development programmes and projects. The majority of courses are in economic and sector management and 'training of trainers', which aim to build up local capability to conduct projects courses in future. The Institute also produces training materials, and administers a fellowships scheme and the World Bank graduate scholarship programme (funded by the Government of Japan). In the year ending 30 June 1996 EDI conducted 358 conferences, seminars and workshops. During 1995/96 the EDI curriculum covered the following four broad areas: macroeconomic management and policy; environment and natural resources, in particular the management and valuation of natural assets; human resources and poverty, with an emphasis on the education of girls and on reproductive health; and regulatory reform of private and public sectors. In that year EDI conducted seminars on post-conflict reconstruction in Angola and in the Gaza Strip and West Bank areas of Palestine, and undertook preparations for a similar programme for Bosnia and Herzegovina. Dir AMNON GOLAN.

International Centre for Settlement of Investment Disputes—ICSID: founded in 1966 under the Convention of the Settlement of Investment Disputes between States and Nationals of Other States. The Convention was designed to encourage the growth of private foreign investment for economic development, by creating the possibility, always subject to the consent of both parties, for a Contracting State and a foreign investor who is a national of another Contracting State to settle any legal dispute that might arise out of such an investment by conciliation and/or arbitration before an impartial, international forum. The governing body of the Centre is its Administrative Council, composed of one representative of each Contracting State, all of whom have equal voting power. The President of the World Bank is (ex officio) the non-voting Chairman of the Administrative Council.

At mid-1996 126 states had ratified the Convention to become ICSID member countries, with a further 13 states having signed the Convention. At that time 10 cases were pending before the Centre. Sec.-Gen. IBRAHIM F. I. SHIHATA.

PUBLICATIONS

Abstracts of Current Studies: The World Bank Research Program (annually).

Annual Report on Portfolio Performance.

Global Development Finance (annually).

Global Economic Prospects and Developing Countries (annually).

Research News (quarterly).

Staff Working Papers.

Trends in Developing Economies (annually).

World Bank Annual Report.

World Bank Atlas (annually).

World Bank Economic Review (3 a year).

The World Bank and the Environment (annually).

World Bank News (2 a month).

World Bank Research Observer (2 a year).

World Development Indicators (annually).

World Development Report (annually).

World Tables (annually).

Information on the World Bank can be accessed on the Internet at http://www.worldbank.org.

WORLD BANK OPERATIONS IN AFRICA SOUTH OF THE SAHARA

IDA Credits Approved, 1 July 1995–30 June 1996
(US $ million)

Country	Purpose	Amount
Angola	Social development project	24.0
Cameroon	Privatization technical assistance	12.6
	Road rehabilitation and maintenance	60.7
	Structural adjustment	150.0
	Structural adjustment	30.3*
Cape Verde	Private sector development	11.4
Chad	Structural adjustment	30.0
	Economic management	9.5
Congo	Public sector capacity building	9.0
Côte d'Ivoire	Health services development	40.0
	Private sector development	180.0
	Railways rehabilitation	20.0
	Agricultural reform	223.6†
Eritrea	Community development	17.5
Ethiopia	Social Rehabilitation and Development Fund	120.0
	Water supply development	35.7
Ghana	Basic education	50.0
	Public sector reform and privatization	26.5
	Road construction, rehabilitation and maintenance	100.0
	Urban environmental sanitation	71.0
	Private sector adjustment	4.8*
	Financial sector development	23.9
Guinea	Mining sector investment promotion	12.2
	Agricultural services	35.0
	Higher education management	6.6
Kenya	Structural adjustment	126.8†
	Rehabilitation of Nairobi-Mombasa highway	50.0
	Urban transport infrastructure	115.0
	Arid lands resource management	22.0
Lesotho	Road rehabilitation and maintenance	40.0
Madagascar	Electricity supply and energy sector reforms	46.0
	Poverty reduction	40.0
Malawi	Social Action Fund	56.0
	Macroeconomic reform	106.4†
	Primary education	22.5
Mali	Economic management	60.0
	Rehabilitation of Selingue hydroelectric power plant	27.3
	Vocational education and training	13.4
Mauritania	Public resource management	20.0
	Urban infrastructure	14.0
	Private sector development	0.8*
Mozambique	Health sector development	98.7
Niger	Natural resources management	26.7
Senegal	Higher education	26.5
	Female literacy (pilot project)	12.6
	Agricultural sector adjustment	2.8*
Sierra Leone	Transport sector	35.0
	Basic health services	20.0
	Structural adjustment	0.3*
Tanzania	Urban rehabilitation	105.0
	Financial sector development	10.9
Togo	Economic recovery and adjustment	50.0
Uganda	Agricultural sector management	17.9
	Private sector competitiveness	12.3
	Environmental management	11.8
Zambia	Macroeconomic reform	152.1†
	Implementation of public sector reform programme	23.0
Zimbabwe	Economic development	70.0
Total		2,740.1

* Supplements to existing operations.
† Two credits for one project.
Source: *World Bank Annual Report 1996.*

International Finance Corporation—IFC

Address: 1850 I St, NW, Washington, DC 20433, USA.

Telephone: (202) 473-1234; **telex:** 248423; **fax:** (202) 676-0365.

IFC was founded in 1956 as an affiliate of the World Bank to encourage the growth of productive private enterprise in its member countries, particularly in the less-developed areas.

Organization

(July 1997)

IFC is a separate legal entity in the World Bank Group. Executive Directors of the World Bank also serve as Directors of IFC. The President of the World Bank is, ex officio, Chairman of the IFC Board of Directors, which has appointed him President of IFC. Subject to his overall supervision, the day-to-day operations of IFC are conducted by its staff under the direction of the Executive Vice-President.

PRINCIPAL OFFICERS

President: JAMES WOLFENSOHN (USA).

Executive Vice-President: JANNIK LINDBAEK (Norway).

REGIONAL MISSIONS

East Africa: PO Box 30577, Hill Park Bldg, Upper Hill Rd, Nairobi, Kenya; tel. (2) 714141; fax (2) 720604; Regional Rep. MICHAEL HOOPER.

Southern Africa: 101 Union Ave, 7th Floor, POB 2960, Harare, Zimbabwe; tel. (4) 794860; fax (4) 793805; Regional Rep. MWAGHAZI MWACHOFI.

West and Central Africa: angle rues Booker Washington/Jacques Aka Cocody, BP 1850, Abidjan 01, Côte d'Ivoire; tel. 44-32-44; telex 28132; fax 44-44-83; Regional Rep. (vacant).

Activities

IFC provides financial support and advice for private sector ventures and projects, and assists governments to create conditions that stimulate the flow of domestic and foreign private savings and investment. Increasingly IFC has worked to mobilize additional capital from other financial institutions. In all its activities IFC is guided by three major principles:

(i) The catalytic principle. IFC should seek above all to be a catalyst in helping private investors and markets to make good investments.

(ii) The business principle. IFC should function like a business in partnership with the private sector and take the same commercial risks, so that its funds, although backed by public sources, are transferred under market disciplines.

(iii) The principle of the special contribution. IFC should participate in an investment only when it makes a special contribution that supplements or complements the role of market operators.

IFC's authorized capital is US $2,450m. The World Bank is the principal source of borrowed funds, but IFC also borrows from private capital markets. At 30 June 1996 paid-in capital was $2,076m. In that financial year total investments approved amounted to $8,118m. for 264 projects, compared with $5,467m. for 213 projects in the previous year. Of the total approved, $3,248m. was for IFC's own account, while $4,876m. was used in loan syndications and underwriting of securities issues and investment funds.

In 1995/96 IFC approved 71 projects (including those under the Africa Enterprise Fund—see below) in 21 countries in sub-Saharan Africa, with two regional projects. These included projects concerned with coffee production in Tanzania; hotel refurbishment in Angola, Kenya and Zimbabwe; fishing operations in Côte d'Ivoire, Ghana (seafood processing), Mauritania, Mozambique, Namibia, Senegal and the Seychelles; flower farming in Nigeria, South Africa, Tanzania, Uganda and Zambia; hospital construction in Malawi; and the financial sector in Côte d'Ivoire, Ghana, Mauritius, Mozambique, Senegal, South Africa, Tanzania, Uganda and Zimbabwe.

In April 1989 IFC (with UNDP and the African Development Bank—ADB) initiated the African Management Services Company (AMSCo): its aim is to help find qualified senior executives from around the world to work with African companies, assist in the training of local managers, and provide supporting services. At 31 December 1995 AMSCo had management contracts with 33 companies in 16 countries. The IFC's Africa Enterprise Fund (AEF), which began operations in 1988, provides financial assistance to small and medium-sized enterprises, typically in the tourism, agribusiness and small-scale manufacturing sectors. In 1995/96 AEF financed 42 projects at a total cost of US $28m. In 1995 IFC initiated the Enterprise Support Service for Africa (ESSA) in order to provide post-investment operational advice, including the development and strengthening of management information systems and technical capacity, to small- and medium-sized enterprises in the sub-Saharan region. ESSA commenced operation, on a pilot basis, in Ghana, in February 1996.

The Foreign Investment Advisory Service (FIAS), established in 1986, is operated jointly by IFC and the IBRD, and provides advice to governments on attracting foreign investment. During 1995/96 FIAS completed 27 advisory projects in 25 countries, including the development of a strategic plan for the promotion of foreign direct investment in Ghana and the formulation of recommendations for short-term improvement of the investment environment in Mauritania, Mozambique and Namibia.

AFRICA PROJECT DEVELOPMENT FACILITY (APDF)

APDF was established by IFC, UNDP and the ADB in 1986, to provide technical assistance to entrepreneurs in sub-Saharan Africa, with IFC as the executing agency. The Facility advises entrepreneurs seeking to start businesses or expand existing ones, and helps them identify and prepare viable projects. APDF does not finance projects, but assists entrepreneurs in obtaining debt and equity financing and identifying business partners, both foreign and domestic. Typically, projects assisted by APDF are small, with costs ranging from US $250,000 to $7m. APDF is funded by IFC, UNDP, the ADB and 15 industrialized countries. In addition Brazil, India and Israel make technical experts available to APDF for short-term assignments. During the year to 31 December 1995 APDF assisted the funding of 40 projects in 13 countries. Since its foundation APDF has helped to raise $232m. for 242 projects, which are estimated to have created about 19,000 jobs.

Headquarters: 1801 K St, NW, Rm K-5197, Washington, DC 20433, USA; tel. (202) 473-0606; fax (202) 676-0387; Co-ordinator Macodou N' Daw.

East Africa: International House, 6th Floor, Mama Ngina St, POB 46534, Nairobi, Kenya; tel. (2) 217370; telex 25303; fax (2) 339121; Regional Man. Mishek Ngatunga.

Southern Africa: Southampton House, 5th Floor, 68-70 Union Ave, Box UA 400, Harare, Zimbabwe; tel. (4) 730967; telex 22350; fax (4) 730959; Regional Man. Kalada Harry.

West Africa: Immeuble CCIA, 17e étage, 01 BP 8669, Abidjan 01, Côte d'Ivoire; tel. 21-96-97; fax 21-61-51; Regional Man. Macodou N'Daw.

PUBLICATIONS

Annual Report.

Emerging Stock Markets Factbook (annually).

Global Agribusiness (series of industry reports).

Lessons of Experience series.

Information on IFC can be accessed on the Internet at http://www.ifc.org.

Multilateral Investment Guarantee Agency—MIGA

Address: 1818 H Street, NW, Washington, DC 20433, USA.

Telephone: (202) 477-1234; **telex:** 248423; **fax:** (202) 477-6391.

MIGA was founded in 1988 as an affiliate of the World Bank, to encourage the flow of investments for productive purposes among its member countries, especially developing countries, through the mitigation of non-commercial barriers to investment (especially political risk).

MEMBERS

By mid-1997 MIGA had 141 member countries. Membership is open to all countries that are members of the World Bank.

Organization

(July 1997)

MIGA is legally and financially separate from the World Bank. It is supervised by a Board of Directors.

President: James Wolfensohn (USA).

Executive Vice-President: Akira Iida (Japan).

Activities

The convention establishing MIGA took effect in April 1988. Authorized capital was US $1,082m.

MIGA's purpose is to guarantee eligible investments against losses resulting from non-commercial risks, under four main categories:

transfer risk resulting from host government restrictions on currency conversion and transfer;

risk of loss resulting from legislative or administrative actions of the host government;

repudiation by the host government of contracts with investors in cases in which the investor has no access to a competent forum;

the risk of armed conflict and civil unrest.

Before guaranteeing any investment, MIGA must ensure that it is commercially viable, contributes to the development process and is not harmful to the environment.

During the year ending 30 June 1996 MIGA issued 68 investment insurance contracts. The amount of direct investment associated with the contracts totalled approximately US $6,600m. and generated an estimated 9,200 jobs in 27 developing member countries.

MIGA also provides policy and advisory services to promote foreign investment in developing countries and in transitional economies, and to disseminate information on investment opportunities. Since 1993 MIGA has organized an annual conference to promote investment in the mining sector in Africa. In October 1995 MIGA established a new network on investment opportunities, which connected investment promotion agencies (IPAs) throughout the world on an electronic information network. The so-called IPA*net* aimed to encourage further investments among developing countries, to provide access to comprehensive information on investment laws and conditions and to strengthen communications between governmental, business and financial associations and investors.

International Fund for Agricultural Development—IFAD

Address: Via del Serafico 107, 00142 Rome, Italy.

Telephone: (6) 54591; **telex:** 620330; **fax:** (6) 5043463; **e-mail:** ifad@ifad.org.

Following a decision by the 1974 UN World Food Conference, IFAD was established in 1977 to fund rural development programmes specifically aimed at the poorest of the world's people. It began operations in January 1978.

Organization

(July 1997)

GOVERNING COUNCIL

Each member state is represented in the Governing Council by a Governor and an Alternate. Sessions are held annually, with special sessions convened as required. The Governing Council elects the President of the Fund (who also chairs the Executive Board) by a two-thirds majority for a four-year term. The President is eligible for re-election.

In January 1995 the Governing Council approved the report and recommendations of a Special Committee, which had been established to review IFAD's resource requirements and governance issues. Accordingly, the existing three-category system of membership (which ensured equal voting rights for industrialized countries, or OECD members, petroleum-exporting developing countries, OPEC members, both of which contributed to the Fund's resources, and to recipient developing countries) was to be abolished, with effect from completion of the fourth replenishment of the Fund. Agreement on the replenishment was concluded in February 1997. Under the new voting system the 1,800 votes in the Governing Council and the Executive Board were to be distributed to reflect the size of the financial contribution of each donor country.

EXECUTIVE BOARD

The Board consists of 18 members and 17 alternates, elected by the Governing Council, who serve a three year term. The Executive Board is responsible for the conduct and general operation of IFAD and approves loans and grants for projects; it holds three regular sessions each year.

President and Chairman of Executive Board: FAWZI HAMAD AL-SULTAN (Kuwait).

Vice-President: JIM MOODY (USA).

Activities

The Fund's objective is to mobilize additional resources to be made available on concessional terms for agricultural development in developing member states. IFAD provides financing primarily for projects and programmes specifically designed to introduce, expand or improve food production systems and to strengthen related policies, services and institutions within the framework of national priorities and strategies. In allocating resources IFAD is guided by: the need to increase food production in the poorest food-deficit countries; the potential for increasing food production in other developing countries; and the importance of improving the nutritional level of the poorest people in developing countries and the conditions of their lives. All projects focus on those who often do not benefit from other development programmes: small farmers, artisanal fishermen, nomadic pastoralists, women, and the rural landless.

IFAD is empowered to make both grants and loans. Under its Agreement, grants are limited to 5% of the resources committed in any one financial year. Loans are available on highly concessional, intermediate or ordinary terms. In 1995 all the loans approved for sub-Saharan Africa were awarded on highly concessional terms, i.e. with no interest charges (although bearing an annual service charge of 0.75%) and a repayment period of 40 years. To avoid duplication of work, the administration of loans, for the purpose of disbursements and supervision of project implementation, is entrusted to competent international financial institutions, with the Fund retaining an active interest. During 1995 IFAD provided financing for more than 40% of the costs of projects approved during that year, while the remainder was contributed by external donors, multilateral institutions and the recipient countries.

PROJECTS IN AFRICA SOUTH OF THE SAHARA APPROVED IN 1995

Country	Purpose	Loan amount (SDRm.)
Benin	Income-generating	8.05
The Gambia	Agricultural development	3.40
Ghana	Agricultural development	6.75
Guinea	Small-holder development project	10.20
Niger	Special country programme	9.55*
Senegal	Rural micro-enterprise	5.00†
Togo	Village organization and development	5.10
Angola	Foodcrops development	9.00‡
Madagascar	Upper Mandrare Basin development	4.65§
Tanzania	Farmers' initiative project	9.65
Zambia	Irrigation and water use	4.30
Zimbabwe	Dry areas project	7.15
Total		82.80

* Includes SDR 1.60m. from the Special Programme for Africa (SPA).
† Includes SDR 2.50m. from the SPA.
‡ Includes SDR 2.30m. from the SPA.
§ Includes SDR 1.10m. from the SPA.

IFAD's development projects usually include a number of components, such as infrastructure (e.g. improvement of water supplies, small-scale irrigation and road construction); input supply (e.g. improved seeds, fertilizers and pesticides); institutional support (e.g. research, training and extension services); and producer incentives (e.g. pricing and marketing improvements). IFAD also attempts to enable the landless to acquire income-generating assets: by increasing the provision of credit for the rural poor, it seeks to free them from dependence on the unorganized and exploitative capital market and to generate productive activities. The fund supports projects that are concerned with environmental conservation, in an effort to alleviate poverty that results from the deterioration of natural resources. The fund extends environmental assessment grants to review the environmental consequences of projects under preparation.

IFAD is a leading repository of knowledge, resources and expertise in the field of rural hunger and poverty alleviation. During 1995 a team established to review IFAD's activities focused on IFAD's role as an innovator, emphasizing the importance of pioneering practices and strategies that can be replicated, and of making its knowledge available to relevant agencies and governments. Through its technical assistance grants, IFAD aims to promote research and capacity-building in the agricultural sector. IFAD has supported the research on accelerated diffusion of rice technology, conducted by the West African Rice Development Association (WARDA, q.v.) and efforts to identify the technological and socio-economic aspects to sericulture- and apiculture-based farming practices in rural Africa, undertaken by the International Centre for Insect Physiology and Ecology (ICIPE). In 1995 IFAD's Executive Board approved financing for the second phase of its Agricultural Management Training Programme for Africa.

In 1986 IFAD inaugurated a Special Programme for sub-Saharan African Countries Affected by Drought and Desertification (SPA) in response to the critical failure of agricultural and economic systems during a severe drought in the region in the mid-1980s. The SPA aims to improve sustainable food-crop production through soil and water conservation (with emphasis on traditional techniques), small-scale irrigation and local forestry development. In the second phase of the Programme, which began in 1992, the SPA extended its lending criteria to cover off-farm activities and to promote economic diversification. At the same time the number of countries eligible for assistance increased from 22 to 27. During 1995 IFAD approved four projects totalling SDR 7.5m. under the SPA, bringing the cumulative total to 47 projects, costing SDR 283.4m., since 1986. (The average value of the SDR—Special Drawing Right—in 1995 was US $1.51695.) In September 1995 the Executive Board decided the SPA would be terminated and its resources be integrated into the regular programmes as of 1 January 1996.

During 1995 IFAD approved a total of 12 projects in Africa (including those under the SPA), involving loans of SDR 82.8m. The amount approved represented some 32% of IFAD's total loans for that year.

FINANCE

IFAD's programme of work for 1996 envisaged loans and grants totalling SDR 304.3m., while the budget for administrative expenses amounted to $52.5m. In February 1997 the Governing Council concluded an agreement on the fourth replenishment of the Fund's resources, amounting to $485m. over a three-year period.

PUBLICATIONS

Annual Report.
IFAD Update (3 a year).
Staff Working Papers (series).
The State of World Rural Poverty.
Information on IFAD can be accessed on the Internet at http://www.unic.org/ifad.

International Monetary Fund—IMF

Address: 700 19th St, NW, Washington, DC 20431, USA.

Telephone: (202) 623-7430; **telex:** 64111; **fax:** (202) 623-6701.

The IMF was established at the same time as the World Bank (IBRD) in 1945.

Organization

(July 1997)

BOARD OF GOVERNORS

The highest authority of the Fund is exercised by the Board of Governors, on which each member country is represented by a Governor and an Alternate Governor. The Board normally meets annually, and an Interim Committee meets twice a year. The voting power of each country is related to its quota in the Fund.

BOARD OF EXECUTIVE DIRECTORS

The 24-member Board of Executive Directors is responsible for the day-to-day operations of the Fund. The USA, the United Kingdom, Germany, France and Japan each appoint one Executive Director, while 16 of the remainder are elected by groups of member countries sharing similar interests; there is also one Executive Director each from the People's Republic of China, Russia and Saudi Arabia.

OFFICERS

Managing Director: MICHEL CAMDESSUS (France).

Deputy Managing Directors: STANLEY FISCHER (USA); ALASSANE D. OUATTARA (Côte d'Ivoire); SHIGEMITSU SUGISAKI (Japan).

Director, African Department: EVANGELOS CALAMITSIS.

Activities

The purposes of the IMF, as defined in the Articles of Agreement, are:

(i) To promote international monetary co-operation through a permanent institution which provides the machinery for consultation and collaboration on monetary problems;

(ii) To facilitate the expansion and balanced growth of international trade, and to contribute thereby to the promotion and maintenance of high levels of employment and real income and to the development of members' productive resources;

(iii) To promote exchange stability, to maintain orderly exchange arrangements among members, and to avoid competitive exchange depreciation;

(iv) To assist in the establishment of a multilateral system of payments in respect of current transactions between members and in the elimination of foreign exchange restrictions which hamper the growth of trade;

(v) To give confidence to members by making the general resources of the Fund temporarily available to them, under adequate safeguards, thus providing them with the opportunity to correct maladjustments in their balance of payments, without resorting to measures destructive of national or international prosperity; and

(vi) In accordance with the above, to shorten the duration of and lessen the degree of disequilibrium in the international balances of payments of members.

In joining the Fund, each country agrees to co-operate with the above objectives, and the Fund monitors members' compliance by holding an annual consultation with each country, in order to survey the country's exchange rate policies and determine its need for assistance.

In accordance with its objective of facilitating the expansion of international trade, the IMF encourages its members to accept the obligations of Article VIII, Sections two, three and four, of the IMF Articles of Agreement. Members that accept Article VIII undertake to refrain from imposing restrictions on the making of payments and transfers for current international transactions and from engaging in discriminatory currency arrangements or multiple currency practices without IMF approval. At 30 June 1997 140 members had accepted Article VIII status.

RESOURCES

Members' subscriptions form the basic resource of the IMF. They are supplemented by borrowing. Under the General Arrangements to Borrow (GAB), established in 1962, the 'Group of Ten' industrialized nations (Belgium, Canada, France, Germany, Italy, Japan, the Netherlands, Sweden, the United Kingdom and the USA) and Switzerland (which became a member of the IMF in 1992, but which had been a full participant in the GAB from 1984) undertake to lend the Fund up to SDR 17,000m. in their own currencies, so as to help fulfill the balance-of-payments requirements of any member of the group, or to meet requests to the Fund from countries with balance-of-payments problems that could threaten the stability of the international monetary system. In May 1996 GAB participants concluded an agreement in principle to expand the resources available for borrowing to SDR 34,000m., by securing the support of other countries with the financial capacity to support the international monetary system. The so-called New Arrangements to Borrow (NAB) was endorsed in September and approved by the Executive Board in January 1997; it was to enter into force, for an initial five-year period, as soon as the five largest potential creditors (of the anticipated 25 member countries and institutions participating in NAB) had approved the initiative and the total credit arrangement of participants endorsing the scheme had reached at least SDR 28,900m. While the GAB credit arrangement was to remain in effect, the NAB was expected to be the first facility to be activated in the event of the Fund requiring supplementary resources.

DRAWING ARRANGEMENTS

Exchange transactions within the Fund take the form of members' purchases (i.e. drawings) from the Fund of the currencies of other members for the equivalent amounts of their own currencies. Fund resources are available to eligible members on an essentially short-term and revolving basis to provide members with temporary assistance to contribute to the solution of their payments problems. Before making a purchase, a member must show that its balance of payments or reserve position make the purchase necessary. Apart from this requirement, reserve tranche purchases (i.e. purchases that do not bring the Fund's holdings of the member's currency to a level above its quota) are permitted unconditionally.

With further purchases, however, the Fund's policy of 'conditionality' means that a member requesting assistance must agree to adjust its economic policies, as stipulated by the IMF. All requests other than for use of the reserve tranche are examined by the Executive Board to determine whether the proposed use would be consistent with the Fund's policies, and a member must discuss its proposed adjustment programme (including fiscal, monetary, exchange and trade policies) with IMF staff. Purchases outside the reserve tranche are made in four credit tranches, each equivalent to 25% of the member's quota; a member must reverse the transaction by repurchasing its own currency (with SDR or currencies specified by the Fund) within a specified time. A credit tranche purchase is usually made under a 'stand-by arrangement' with the Fund, or under the extended Fund facility. A stand-by arrangement is normally of one or two years' duration, and the amount is made available in instalments, subject to the member's observance of 'performance criteria'; repurchases must be made within three-and-a-quarter to five years. An extended arrangement is normally of three years' duration, and the member must submit detailed econ-

MEMBERSHIP AND QUOTAS IN AFRICA SOUTH OF THE SAHARA (million SDR)*

Country	August 1996
Angola	207.3
Benin	45.3
Botswana	36.6
Burkina Faso	44.2
Burundi	57.2
Cameroon	135.1
Cape Verde	7.0
Central African Republic	41.2
Chad	41.3
Comoros	6.5
Congo[1]	57.9
Côte d'Ivoire	238.2
Djibouti	11.5
Equatorial Guinea	24.3
Eritrea	11.5
Ethiopia	98.3
Gabon	110.3
The Gambia	22.9
Ghana	274.0
Guinea	78.7
Guinea-Bissau	10.5
Kenya	199.4
Lesotho	23.9
Liberia†	(96.2) 71.3
Madagascar	90.4
Malawi	50.9
Mali	68.9
Mauritania	47.5
Mauritius	73.3
Mozambique	84.0
Namibia	99.6
Niger	48.3
Nigeria	1,281.6
Rwanda	59.5
São Tomé and Príncipe	5.5
Senegal	118.9
Seychelles	6.0
Sierra Leone	77.2
Somalia†	(60.9) 44.2
South Africa	1,365.4
Sudan†	(233.1) 169.7
Swaziland	36.5
Tanzania	146.9
Togo	54.3
Uganda	133.9
Zaire†[2]	(394.8) 291.0
Zambia	363.5
Zimbabwe	261.3

* The Special Drawing Right (SDR) was introduced in 1970 as a substitute for gold in international payments, and is intended eventually to become the principal reserve asset in the international monetary system. Its value (which was US $1.38814 at 30 June 1997 and averaged $1.45176 in 1996) is based on the currencies of the five largest exporting countries. Each member is assigned a quota related to its national income, monetary reserves, trade balance and other economic indicators; the quota approximately determines a member's voting power and the amount of foreign exchange it may purchase from the Fund. A member's subscription is equal to its quota. Under the Ninth General Review of Quotas, which was completed in June 1990, an increase of about 50% in total quotas (from SDR 90,035m. to SDR 135,200m.) was authorized. The increase entered into effect in November 1992; with additional contributions from countries that joined the IMF subsequent to June 1990, by 30 April 1996 total quotas amounted to SDR 145,318.8m. The Tenth General Review of Quotas concluded, in December 1994, that no further increase of quotas was necessary; the Eleventh General Review was expected to be completed by March 1998.

† As of 15 August 1996, these members had not yet paid for their quota increases under the Ninth General Review. The quotas listed are those determined under the Eighth General Review, and the figures in parentheses are the proposed Ninth Review quotas.

[1] Now Republic of Congo.

[2] Now the Democratic Republic of the Congo.

omic programmes and progress reports for each year; repurchases must be made within four-and-a-half to 10 years. A member whose payments imbalance is large in relation to its quota may make use of temporary facilities established by the Fund using borrowed resources, namely the 'enlarged access policy' established in 1981, which helps to finance stand-by and extended arrangements for such a member, up to a limit of between 90% and 110% of the member's quota annually. In October 1994 the Executive Board agreed to increase, for three years, the annual access limit under IMF regular tranche drawings, stand-by arrangements and extended Fund facility credits from 68% to 100% of a member's quota. In exceptional circumstances the access limit may be extended further.

In addition, there are special-purpose arrangements, all of which are subject to the member's co-operation with the Fund to find an appropriate solution to its difficulties. The buffer stock financing facility (BSFF, established in 1969) enables members to pay their contributions to the buffer stocks which are intended to stabilize primary commodity markets by drawing as much as 45% of their quota. The BSFF has not been used since 1984. In August 1988 the Fund established the compensatory and contingency financing facility (CCFF), which replaced and expanded the former compensatory financing facility, established in 1963. The CCFF provides compensation to members whose export earnings are reduced owing to circumstances beyond their control, or who are affected by excess costs of cereal imports. Contingency financing is provided to help members maintain their efforts at economic adjustment even when affected by a sharp increase in interest rates or other externally-derived difficulties. Under the BSFF and CCFF repurchases are made within three-and-a-quarter to five years.

The structural adjustment facility (SAF) was established in 1986 to support medium-term macroeconomic adjustment and structural reforms in low-income developing countries on concessionary terms. Following the adoption of the enlarged enhanced structural adjustment facility (ESAF—see below) it was agreed that no further resources would be made available for SAF arrangements. However, an exceptional SAF arrangement was approved during 1993/94 for Sierra Leone and resources were retained for a previously agreed arrangement for Zambia.

The ESAF, established in 1987, was to provide new resources to assist the adjustment efforts of, in particular, heavily indebted countries. Eligible members must develop a three-year adjustment programme (with assistance given jointly by staff of the Fund and of the World Bank) to strengthen the balance-of-payments situation and foster sustainable economic growth. ESAF loans carry an

NEW ESAF ARRANGEMENTS AGREED FOR COUNTRIES IN AFRICA SOUTH OF THE SAHARA

Country	1 May 1995–30 April 1996 Loan (million SDR)
Chad	49.56
Ghana	164.40
Kenya	149.55
Malawi	45.81
Mali	62.01
Zambia	181.75*
	701.68

Country	1 May 1996–30 April 1997 Loan (million SDR)
Benin	27.18
Burkina Faso	39.78
Congo†	69.48
Ethiopia	88.47
Guinea	70.80
Madagascar	81.36
Mozambique	75.60
Niger	57.96
Tanzania	161.59

* Final SAF arrangement.

† Now Republic of Congo.

PURCHASES OF CURRENCIES AND SPECIAL DRAWING RIGHTS FROM THE IMF BY MEMBERS IN AFRICA SOUTH OF THE SAHARA

1 May 1995–30 April 1996		1 May 1996–30 April 1997	
Member	Total purchases (million SDR)	Member	Total purchases (million SDR)
Cameroon	28.2	Gabon	22.1
Djibouti	2.9		
Gabon	22.1		

interest rate of 0.5% per year and are repayable within 10 years, including a five-and-a-half-year grace period. Maximum access is set at 190% (255% in exceptional circumstances) of the member's quota. Originally 34 African countries were eligible for ESAF loans; in April 1992 Angola, Côte d'Ivoire, Nigeria and Zimbabwe were granted eligibility for the first time. In February 1994 a new period of operations of the ESAF became effective, following an agreement to enlarge the ESAF Trust (the funding source for ESAF arrangements). The terms and conditions of the new facility remain the same as those of the original ESAF, but the list of countries eligible for assistance was enlarged by six, of which Cameroon was the only African country, to 78. (In January 1995 Eritrea became the 79th member eligible for ESAF assistance.) The new commitment period for lending from the ESAF Trust was to expire on 31 December 1996, while disbursements were to be made until 31 December 1999. In September 1996 the Interim Committee of the Board of Governors endorsed measures to finance the ESAF for a further five-year period, 2000–2004, after which the facility was to become self-sustaining. The interim period of the ESAF was to be funded mainly from bilateral contributions, but drawing on the Fund's additional resources as necessary. The ESAF was to support, through long-maturity loans and grants, IMF participation in a joint initiative, with the World Bank, to assist heavily indebted poor countries (HIPCs) to achieve a sustainable level of debt management. Of the 41 HIPCs identified under the initiative, 33 were in sub-Saharan Africa. The initiative was formally approved at the September meeting of the Interim Committee, having received the support of the 'Paris Club' of international creditors which agreed to increase the relief on official debt from 67% to 80%. In April 1997 the World Bank and the IMF announced that Uganda was to be the first beneficiary of the initiative. The IMF's share of the anticipated debt relief of US $338m. was to total $69m., effective from April 1998. (See also the World Bank, p. 92). At the end of July 1997 the IMF suspended disbursement from Kenya's SDR 150m. ESAF arrangement, owing to the failure of the Kenyan Government to implement adequate measures to counter corruption in that country.

At 30 April 1996 one SAF arrangement and 28 ESAF arrangements were in effect. In 1995/96 SAF and ESAF disbursements amounted to SDR 1,477m., while cumulative disbursements to the end of April 1996 totalled SDR 6,466m.

SURVEILLANCE

Under its Articles of Agreement, the Fund is mandated to oversee the effective functioning of the international monetary system and to review the policies of individual member countries to ensure the stability of the exchange rate system. The Fund's main tools of surveillance are regular consultations, conducted by IMF staff with officials from member countries, and World Economic Outlook discussions, held, normally twice a year, by the Executive Board to assess policy implications from a multilateral perspective and to monitor global developments. Following a rapid decline in the value of the Mexican peso in late 1994 and the ensuing financial crisis in that country, the IMF resolved to strengthen its surveillance activities. During 1995/96 these efforts focused on measures to ensure more continuous surveillance, to strengthen the focus of surveillance, in particular on countries or regions deemed to be at risk, and to encourage the full and timely provision of data by member countries. With respect to the latter objective, in April 1996 the IMF adopted the Special Data Dissemination Standard, which was intended to improve access to reliable economic statistical information.

TECHNICAL ASSISTANCE

Technical assistance is provided by special missions or resident representatives who advise members on every aspect of economic management. Assistance is provided by the IMF's various specialized departments and is becoming an increasingly important aspect of the Fund's relationship with its member countries. In particular, the expansion of the Fund's technical assistance activities during the early 1990s resulted from the increase in countries undergoing economic and systemic transformations. The IMF Institute, founded in 1964, trains officials from member countries in financial analysis and policy, balance-of-payments methodology and public finance; it also gives assistance to national and regional training centres. The IMF is co-sponsor of the Joint Vienna Institute, which was opened in the Austrian capital in October 1992 and which trains officials from former centrally-planned economies in various aspects of economic management and public administration. During 1995/96 1,265 people attended training courses or seminars at the IMF Institute or the Joint Vienna Institute, while a further 1,115 senior officials participated in overseas training courses.

PUBLICATIONS

Annual Report.

International Financial Statistics (monthly and annually).

Balance of Payments Statistics Yearbook.

Government Finance Statistics Yearbook.

Direction of Trade Statistics (quarterly and annually).

IMF Survey (2 a month).

Finance and Development (quarterly, issued jointly with the World Bank).

Staff Papers (4 a year).

World Economic Outlook (2 a year).

Occasional papers, books and pamphlets.

Information on the IMF can be accessed on the Internet at http://www.imf.org.

World Health Organization—WHO

Address: ave Appia, 1211 Geneva 27, Switzerland.

Telephone: (22) 7912111; **telex:** 415416; **fax:** (22) 7910746.

WHO was established in 1948 as the central agency directing international health work. Of its many activities, the most important single aspect is technical co-operation with national health administrations, particularly in the developing countries.

Organization

(August 1997)

WORLD HEALTH ASSEMBLY

The Assembly meets annually in Geneva; it is responsible for policy making, and the biennial programme and budget; it appoints the Director-General, admits new members and reviews budget contributions.

EXECUTIVE BOARD

The Board is composed of 32 health experts designated by, but not representing, their governments; they serve for three years, and the World Health Assembly elects 10 or 11 member states each year to the Board. It meets at least twice a year to review the Director-General's programme, which it forwards to the Assembly with any recommendations that seem necessary. It advises on questions referred to it by the Assembly and is responsible for putting into effect the decisions and policies of the Assembly. It is also empowered to take emergency measures in case of epidemics or disasters.

SECRETARIAT

Director-General: Dr Hiroshi Nakajima (Japan).

Assistant Directors-General: Dr Hu Ching-Li (People's Republic of China), Dr Ralph H. Henderson (USA), Dr Nikolai P. Napalkov (Russia), Denis G. Aitken (UK), Dr Fernando S. Antezana (Bolivia), Dr Aissatou Kone-Diabi (Senegal), Dr Françoise Varet (France).

Regional Office in Africa: BP 6, Brazzaville, Republic of Congo; tel. 83-91-11; telex 5217; fax 83-94-00; Dir Dr Ebrahim Malick Samba.

Sub-regional offices were established in Bamako, Mali, and Harare, Zimbabwe, in 1985.

Activities

WHO's objective is stated in the constitution as 'the attainment by all peoples of the highest possible level of health'.

It acts as the central authority directing international health work, and establishes relations with professional groups and government health authorities on that basis.

It supports, on request from member states, programmes to prevent and control health problems, control or eradicate disease, train health workers best suited to local needs and strengthen national health systems. Aid is provided in emergencies and natural disasters.

A global programme of collaborative research and exchange of scientific information is carried out in co-operation with about 1,000 leading national institutions. Particular stress is laid on the widespread communicable diseases of the tropics, and the countries directly concerned are assisted in developing their research capabilities.

It keeps diseases and other health problems under constant surveillance, formulates health regulations for international travel, and sets standards for the quality control of drugs, vaccines and other substances affecting health.

It collects and disseminates health data and carries out statistical analyses and comparative studies in such diseases as cancer, heart disease and mental illness.

It promotes improved environmental conditions, including housing, sanitation and working conditions. All available information on effects on human health of the pollutants in the environment is critically reviewed and published.

Co-operation among scientists and professional groups is encouraged, and WHO may propose international conventions and agreements. It assists in developing an informed public opinion on matters of health.

Strengthening of the national health services has been one of WHO's primary tasks in Africa south of the Sahara. Integrated health systems are being developed to provide services related to medical care, rehabilitation, family health, communicable disease control, environmental health, health education, and health statistics. By providing educators and fellowships and by organizing training courses, support is given to national programmes aimed at preparing health workers best suited to local needs and resources. Specialists and advisory services are provided to assist in planning the health sector, which in most African countries forms an integral part of the overall plan for socio-economic development.

WHO promotes national, regional and global strategies for the attainment of the main target of member states: 'Health for all by the year 2000', or the attainment by all citizens of the world of a level of health that will permit them to lead a socially and economically productive life. In May 1981 the World Health Assembly adopted a Global Strategy in support of this aim. Primary health care was considered to be the key to 'Health for all', with the following as minimum requirements:

(i) safe water in the home or within 15 minutes' walking distance, and adequate sanitary facilities in the home or immediate vicinity;

(ii) immunization against diphtheria, pertussis, tetanus, poliomyelitis, measles and tuberculosis;

(iii) local health care, including availability of at least 20 essential drugs, within one hour's travel; and

(iv) trained personnel to attend childbirth, and to care for pregnant mothers and children up to at least one year old.

DISEASE PREVENTION AND CONTROL

One of WHO's major achievements was the eradication of smallpox. Following a massive international campaign of vaccination and surveillance, begun in 1958 and intensified in 1967, the last case was detected in 1977 and the eradication of the disease was declared in 1980. However, in February 1997, an increase in cases of monkeypox was reported in the former Zaire, possibly due to the discontinuation of immunization programmes against smallpox in the late 1970s. In May 1996 the World Health Assembly resolved that, pending a final endorsement, all remaining stocks of smallpox were to be destroyed on 30 June 1999, though 500,000 doses of smallpox vaccine, also effective against monkeypox were to remain, along with a supply of the smallpox vaccine seed virus, in order to ensure a further supply of the vaccine could be made available if required. In 1988 the World Health Assembly declared its commitment to the eradication of poliomyelitis by the year 2000; and in 1990 the Assembly resolved to eliminate iodine deficiency disorders (causing mental handicap) by 2000.

The objective of providing immunization for all children by 1990 was adopted by the World Health Assembly in 1977. Six diseases (measles, whooping cough, tetanus, poliomyelitis, tuberculosis and diphtheria) became the target of the Expanded Programme on Immunization (EPI) in which WHO, UNICEF and many other organizations collaborated. As a result of massive international and national efforts, the global immunization coverage increased from 20% in the early 1980s to the targeted rate of 80% by the end of 1990. This coverage signified that more than 100m. children in the developing world under the age of one had been successfully vaccinated against the targeted diseases, the lives of about 3m. children had been saved every year, and 500,000 annual cases of paralysis as a result of polio had been prevented. In 1992 the Assembly resolved to reach a new target of 90% immunization coverage with the six EPI vaccines, to introduce hepatitis B as a seventh vaccine and to introduce the yellow fever vaccine in areas where it occurs endemically. In 1996 WHO, UNICEF, Rotary International and other national and international partners initiated a campaign to 'kick polio out of Africa' through the immunization of more than 100m. children in 46 countries over a three-year period. In September 1991 the Children's Vaccine Initiative (CVI) was launched, jointly sponsored by the Rockefeller Foundation, UNDP, UNICEF, WHO and the World Bank, to facilitate the development and provision of children's vaccines. The CVI has as its ultimate goal the development of a single oral immunization shortly after birth that will protect against all major childhood diseases.

WHO's Division of Diarrhoeal and Acute Respiratory Disease Control encourages national programmes aimed at reducing the estimated 3.5m. yearly childhood deaths as a result of diarrhoea, particularly through the use of oral rehydration therapy, and preventive measures. The Division is also seeking to reduce deaths from pneumonia in infants through the use of a simple case-management strategy involving the recognition of danger signs and treatment with an appropriate antibiotic. In keeping with the priority given by WHO to integrated disease control, an integrated approach to management to the sick child is being developed by the Division in collaboration with other relevant WHO programmes and with UNICEF.

In 1995 WHO established the Division of Emerging, Viral and Bacterial Diseases Surveillance and Control to strengthen the national and international capability to respond to the threats to public health from communicable diseases. The Division was to promote the development of national and international infrastructure and resources to recognize, monitor, prevent and control communicable diseases and emerging health problems, including antibiotic resistance. The Division was particularly concerned with identifying and controlling the emergence of haemorrhagic fevers in localized areas of sub-Saharan Africa and planned to co-ordinate a structure of medical teams able to respond rapidly to a reported outbreak of a disease. The Division also aimed to promote applied research on the diagnosis, epidemiology, prevention and control of communicable diseases and emerging health problems. In July 1996 WHO launched an interagency initiative to control an outbreak of cerebrospinal meningitis in Africa, which had caused some 15,000 deaths in the first half of that year. WHO was to provide technical assistance to enable countries to identify and control any outbreaks of the disease and by November 16 African countries had declared their commitment to national action plans for the control of meningitis. In January 1997, as part of the WHO initiative, an international co-ordinating group (ICG) was established to ensure the optimum use and rapid provision of the 14m. doses of vaccine available for epidemic control in 1997, following the previous year's enormous demand.

The Division of Control of Tropical Diseases addresses malaria, dracunculiasis, Chagas disease, schistosomiasis, filariasis (lymphatic filariasis and onchocerciasis), leishmaniasis, dengue, dengue haemorrhagic fever and sleeping sickness. It provides active support for planning and implementing control programmes (based on global strategies for integrated tropical disease control) at regional, subregional and national levels. It takes part in mobilizing resources for disease control where needed, and co-ordinating national and international participation as appropriate. The Division promotes research and training that are directly relevant to control needs and promotes the monitoring and evaluation of control measures. In January 1996 a new initiative to eliminate onchocerciasis became operational, with funding from the World Bank and with WHO as its executing agency. The African Programme for Onchocerciasis Control (APOC) aimed to benefit some 15m. people infected with the disease, which may cause blindness, in 16 participating African countries. APOC was to complement an existing control programme, initiated in 1974, which has eliminated onchocerciasis as a major public health risk in 11 west African countries. WHO's Special Programme for Research and Training in Tropical Diseases, sponsored jointly by WHO, UNDP and the World Bank, was established in 1975, and comprises a world-wide network of about 5,000 scientists working on the development of vaccines, new drugs, diagnostic kits, preventive measures, and applied field research on practical community issues affecting the target diseases. The programme aims to strengthen research institutions in developing countries, and to encourage participation by scientists from the countries most affected by tropical diseases. A Ministerial Conference on Malaria, organized by WHO in October 1992, adopted a global strategy specifying requirements for effective control of the disease, which kills about 1.5m. people every year, with 90% of the deaths occurring in tropical Africa. WHO increased its commitment to control of the disease in sub-Saharan Africa, and by the end of 1995 38 countries in the region had developed plans of action in line with the global strategy.

In December 1995 WHO's Global Programme on AIDS, which began in 1987, was concluded and, on 1 January 1996, a new Joint UN Programme on HIV/AIDS (UNAIDS) became operational, sponsored jointly by WHO, the World Bank, UNICEF, UNDP, UNESCO and UNFPA. WHO established an Office of HIV/AIDS and Sexually-Transmitted Diseases in order to ensure continuity of its global response to the problem, which included support for national control and education plans, improving the safety of blood supplies and improving the care and support of AIDS patients. In addition, the Office was to liaise with UNAIDS and to make available WHO's research and technical expertise.

In 1995 WHO established a Global Tuberculosis Programme to address the emerging challenges of the TB epidemic. According to WHO estimates, one-third of the world's population is infected with TB and more than 3m. people die from the disease each year, prompting WHO to declare TB a global emergency. WHO provides technical support to all member countries, with special attention being given to those with high TB prevalence, to establish effective national tuberculosis control programmes. WHO's strategy for TB control includes the use of DOTS (directly observed treatment, short-course), standardized treatment guidelines, and result accountability through routine evaluation of treatment outcomes. Simultaneously, WHO is encouraging research with the aim of further disseminating DOTS, adapting DOTS for wider use, developing new tools for prevention, diagnosis and treatment, and containing new threats such as the HIV/TB co-epidemic. In March 1997 WHO reported that even limited use of DOTS, which in 1996 had been employed in approximately 10% of cases worldwide, was resulting in the stabilization of the TB epidemic, and it was predicted that an increased use of DOTS would prevent 10m. deaths within 10 years.

WHO's Programme for the Promotion of Environmental Health undertakes a wide range of initiatives to tackle the increasing threats to health and well-being from a changing environment, especially in relation to air pollution, water quality, sanitation, protection against radiation, management of hazardous waste, chemical safety and housing hygiene. The major part of WHO's technical co-operation in environmental health in developing countries is concerned with community water supply and sanitation. In sub-Saharan Africa, where conditions are considered to be the worst in the world, WHO estimated that, at early 1996, more than half of people in the region were lacking safe drinking water, and some 70% were living without adequate sanitation. In March 1994 WHO called for an international partnership between national and international organizations involved in water and sanitation programmes in sub-Saharan countries, where the poor conditions contribute to the problems of endemic malnutrition and diarrhoeal diseases. In May 1997, WHO and UNICEF announced the adoption of a joint strategy for the provision of water and improvement of sanitation systems. To contribute to the solution of environmental health problems associated with the rapid urbanization of cities in the developing world, the Programme was promoting globally in the early 1990s the Healthy City approach that had been initiated in Europe.

WHO's programmes for diabetes mellitus, chronic rheumatic diseases and asthma assist with the development of national programmes, based upon goals and targets for the improvement of early detection, care and reduction of long-term complications. They also monitor the global epidemiological situation and co-ordinate multinational research activities concerned with the prevention and care of non-communicable diseases. 'Inter-Health', a programme to combat non-communicable diseases (such as those arising from an unhealthy diet) was initiated in 1990, with the particular aim of preventing an increase in the incidence of such diseases in developing countries.

FOOD AND NUTRITION

WHO collaborates with FAO, WFP, UNICEF and other UN agencies in pursuing its objectives relating to nutrition and food safety. In December 1992 an International Conference on Nutrition, co-sponsored by FAO and WHO, adopted a World Declaration on Nutrition and a Plan of Action designed to make the fight against malnutrition a development priority. In pursuing the objectives of the Declaration WHO promotes the elaboration of national plans of action for nutrition and aims to identify and support countries with high levels of malnutrition, which includes protein energy deficiencies, and deficiencies of iron, vitamin A and iodine. By January 1996 98 countries had formulated a national plan of action on nutrition. In collaboration with other international agencies, WHO is implementing a comprehensive strategy for promoting appropriate infant, young-child and maternal nutrition, and for dealing effectively with nutritional emergencies in large populations. Areas of emphasis include promoting health-care practices that enhance successful breast-feeding; appropriate complementary feeding; refining the use and interpretation of body measurements for assessing nutritional status; relevant information, education and training; and action to give effect to the International Code of Marketing of Breast-milk Substitutes. WHO's Food Safety Programme aims to eliminate risks, such as biological or chemical contaminants in foods which are a major cause of diarrhoea and malnutrition in children. WHO, together with FAO, establishes food standards (through the work of the Codex Alimentarius Commission) and evaluates food additives, pesticide residues and other contaminants and their implications for health. The Programme provides expert advice on such issues as food-borne pathogens (e.g. listeria), production methods (e.g. aquaculture) and food biotechnology (e.g. genetic modification).

DRUGS

The WHO Action Programme on Essential Drugs aims to prevent the inappropriate and excessive prescription of drugs and to ensure the availability of a selected number of safe and effective drugs and vaccines of acceptable quality and at low cost, in support of primary health care. WHO maintains and regularly revises a Model List of Essential Drugs, which is complemented by information on the prescription of medications. WHO's Division of Drug Management and Policies provides information on international standards for the manufacture of pharmaceutical products in international trade, and advises national health agencies on the safety and efficacy of drugs, with particular regard to counterfeit and substandard products. WHO is also active in monitoring drug abuse and in developing effective approaches to the management of health problems resulting from drug abuse. In 1996 WHO published its first report on the tobacco situation worldwide. According to WHO, about one-third of the world's population aged over 15 years smoke tobacco, which causes approximately 3m. deaths each year (through lung cancer, heart disease, chronic bronchitis and other effects). The World Health Assembly, in May, approved a new five-year plan for the Programme on Tobacco or Health, including expansion of its public information activities and international research, and advocated that all member countries implement comprehensive tobacco control strategies.

WHO's Programme on Traditional Medicine encourages the incorporation of traditional health practices that have been evaluated as safe and effective into primary health care systems.

HEALTH PROMOTION

A Division of Health Promotion, Education and Communication was established in May 1994 to implement the priority assigned to health promotion in the Ninth General Programme of Work. The Division promotes decentralized and community-based health programmes and is concerned with the challenge of population ageing and encouraging healthy life-styles and self-care. Several projects have been undertaken by WHO regional and country offices in collaboration with other relevant organizations, including: the Global School Health Initiative, to bridge the sectors of health and education and to promote the health of school-age children; the Global Strategy for Occupational Health, to promote the health of the working population and the control of occupational health risks; Community-based Rehabilitation, which aimed to provide a more enabling environment for people with disabilities; and a communication strategy to provide training and support for health communications personnel and initiatives.

WHO's Division of Strengthening Health Services assists countries to expand and improve the functioning of their health infrastructure in order to ensure wider access to care, hospital services and health education. It works with countries to ensure continuity and quality of care at all levels, from well-trained health personnel. Under the UN's Special Initiative on Africa, launched in March 1996, WHO was mandated to co-ordinate international efforts to secure improvements in basic health care and to strengthen the management of health services and resources.

In March 1996 WHO's Centre for Health Development opened at Kobe, Japan. The Centre was to research health developments and other determinants to strengthen policy decision-making within the health sector.

EMERGENCY RELIEF

Through its Division of Emergency and Humanitarian Action, WHO acts as the 'health arm' of disaster relief undertaken by the UN system. It works in close co-operation with the UNHCR, UNDP, the UN's Department of Humanitarian Affairs/UNDRO and UNICEF. Its emergency preparedness activities include co-ordination, policy making and planning, awareness-building, technical advice, training, publication of standards and guidelines, and research. Its emergency relief activities include organizational support, the provision of emergency drugs and supplies, and conducting technical emergency assessment missions. The Division's objective is to build the capacity of disaster-vulnerable member states to reduce the adverse health consequences of disasters. In responding to emergency situations, WHO always tries to develop projects and activities that will assist the national authorities concerned in rebuilding or strengthening their own capacity to handle the impact of such situations. In mid-1995 WHO's rapid response to an outbreak of Ebola haemorrhage fever in Kikwit, Zaire, helped to ensure that the epidemic was quickly contained. During that year WHO was also a major participant in other international relief efforts, including in Burundi, to treat an outbreak of cholera, and, in Liberia, to control an outbreak of yellow fever. Subsequently, in late-November, WHO undertook a three-month campaign in Liberia, which successfully vaccinated 1m. people against yellow fever. In April 1996 WHO dispatched emergency medical supplies to the Liberian capital, Monrovia, following renewed civil hostilities, while in early 1997 WHO sent medical experts and essential supplies to the former Zaire, in response to outbreaks of cholera and meningitis among refugees.

FINANCE

WHO's regular budget is provided by assessment of member states and associate members. An additional fund for specific projects is provided by voluntary contributions from members and other sources. Funds are received from the UN Development Programme for particular projects and from UNFPA for population programmes. The two-year budget for 1996–97 amounted to US $842.7m., of which $154.3m., or 18.3% was allocated to Africa. Extra-budgetary funds were expected to amount to $993.7m. during this period.

PUBLICATIONS

Full catalogue of publications supplied free on request.
World Health (6 a year in English, French, Russian and Spanish; quarterly in Arabic and Farsi).
Environmental Health Criteria.
Bulletin of WHO (6 a year in English and French).
Weekly Epidemiological Record.
World Health Statistics Quarterly.
World Health Statistics Annual.
International Digest of Health Legislation (quarterly).
International Statistical Classification of Diseases and Related Health Problems, Tenth Revision, 1992–94.
World Health Forum (quarterly, several languages).
WHO Drug Information (quarterly).
Series of technical reports.
Information on WHO can be accessed on the Internet at http://www.who.ch.

Other UN Organizations active in Africa

UNITED NATIONS CENTRE FOR HUMAN SETTLEMENTS—UNCHS (Habitat)

Address: POB 30030, Nairobi, Kenya.

Telephone: (2) 621234; **telex:** 22996; **fax:** (2) 624266.

The Centre was established in 1978 to service the inter-governmental Commission on Human Settlements, and to serve as a focus for human settlements activities in the UN system.

Assistant Secretary-General: Dr WALLY N'DOW (The Gambia).

UNITED NATIONS CHILDREN'S FUND—UNICEF

Address: 3 United Nations Plaza, New York, NY 10017, USA.

Telephone: (212) 326-7000; **telex:** 49620199; **fax:** (212) 888-7465.

UNICEF was established in 1946 by the UN General Assembly as the UN International Children's Emergency Fund, to meet the emergency needs of children in post-war Europe and China. In 1950 its mandate was changed to emphasize programmes giving long-term benefits to children everywhere, particularly those in developing countries who are in the greatest need.

Executive Director: CAROL BELLAMY (USA).

Regional Office for Central and West Africa: BP 443, Abidjan 04, Côte d'Ivoire; tel. 213131; telex 23340.

Regional Office for Eastern and Southern Africa: POB 44145, Nairobi, Kenya; tel. (2) 520671; telex 25130.

UNITED NATIONS CONFERENCE ON TRADE AND DEVELOPMENT—UNCTAD

Address: Palais des Nations, 1211 Geneva 10, Switzerland.

Telephone: (22) 9071234; **telex:** 412962; **fax:** (22) 9070057.

UNCTAD was established in 1964. Its role is to promote international trade, particularly that of developing countries, with a view to accelerating economic development. It is the principal instrument of the UN General Assembly for deliberation and negotiation in the field of international trade and related issues of international economic co-operation, including commodity agreements.

Secretary-General: RUBENS RICÚPERO (Brazil).

UNITED NATIONS INTERNATIONAL DRUG CONTROL PROGRAMME—UNDCP

Address: Vienna International Centre, Postfach 500, 1400 Vienna, Austria.

Telephone: (1) 213450; **telex:** 135612; **fax:** (1) 21345-5866; **e-mail:** undcp-hq@undcp.un.or.at.

UNDCP was established in 1991, following a decision by the UN General Assembly, in order to enhance the effectiveness of the UN system for drug control and to provide leadership in the international control of drugs.

Executive Director: PINO ARLACCHI (Italy).

UNITED NATIONS POPULATION FUND—UNFPA

Address: 220 East 42nd St, New York, NY 10017, USA.

Telephone: (212) 297-5000; **telex:** 7607883; **fax:** (212) 370-0201.

Created in 1967 as the Trust Fund for Population Activities, the UN Fund for Population Activities (UNFPA) was established as a Fund of the UN General Assembly in 1972 and was made a subsidiary organ of the UN General Assembly in 1979, with the UNDP Governing Council designated as its governing body. In 1987 UNFPA's name was changed to the United Nations Population Fund (retaining the same acronym).

Executive Director: Dr NAFIS SADIK (Pakistan).

UN Specialized Agencies

INTERNATIONAL ATOMIC ENERGY AGENCY—IAEA

Address: Wagramerstrasse 5, Postfach 100, 1400 Vienna, Austria.

Telephone: (1) 20600; **telex:** 1-12645; **fax:** (1) 20607.

The Agency was founded in 1957 with the aim of enlarging the contribution of atomic energy to peace, health and prosperity throughout the world, through technical co-operation (assisting research on and practical application of atomic energy for peaceful uses) and safeguards (ensuring that materials and services provided by the Agency are not used for any military purpose).

Director-General: Dr HANS BLIX (Sweden).

INTERNATIONAL CIVIL AVIATION ORGANIZATION—ICAO

Address: 999 rue Université, Montréal, PQ H5C 5H7, Canada.

Telephone: (514) 954-8219; **telex:** 05-24513; **fax:** (514) 954-6077.

ICAO was founded in 1947 to develop the techniques of international air navigation and to help in the planning and improvement of international air transport. It is based on the Convention on International Civil Aviation, signed in Chicago, in 1944.

Secretary-General: RENATO CLÁUDIO COSTA PEREIRA (Brazil).

Regional Office for Western and Central Africa: BP 2356, Dakar, Senegal; tel. 23-54-52; telex 61348; fax 23-69-26.

Regional Office for Eastern and Southern Africa: POB 46294, Nairobi, Kenya; tel. 333930; telex 25295; fax 520199.

INTERNATIONAL LABOUR ORGANIZATION—ILO

Address: 4 route des Morillons, 1211 Geneva 22, Switzerland.

Telephone: (22) 7996111; **telex:** 415647; **fax:** (22) 7988685.

ILO was founded in 1919 to work for social justice as a basis for lasting peace. It carries out this mandate by promoting decent living standards, satisfactory conditions of work and pay and adequate employment opportunities. Methods of action include the creation of international labour standards; the provision of technical co-operation services; and research and publications on social and labour matters.

Director-General: MICHEL HANSENNE (Belgium).

Regional Office for Africa: 01 BP 3960, Abidjan 01, Côte d'Ivoire; tel. 32-27-16.

INTERNATIONAL MARITIME ORGANIZATION—IMO

Address: 4 Albert Embankment, London, SE1 7SR, England.

Telephone: (171) 735-7611; **telex:** 23588; **fax:** (171) 587-3210.

The Inter-Governmental Maritime Consultative Organization (IMCO) began operations in 1959, as a specialized agency of the UN to facilitate co-operation among governments on technical matters affecting international shipping. Its main functions are the achievement of safe and efficient navigation, and the control of pollution caused by ships and craft operating in the marine environment. IMCO became IMO in 1982.

Secretary-General: WILLIAM A. O'NEILL (Canada).

INTERNATIONAL TELECOMMUNICATION UNION—ITU

Address: Place des Nations, 1211 Geneva 20, Switzerland.

Telephone: (22) 7305111; **telex:** 421000; **fax:** (22) 7337256. **e-mail:** itumail@itu.int.

Founded in 1865, ITU became a specialized agency of the UN in 1947. It acts to encourage world co-operation in the use of telecommunication, to promote technical development and to harmonize national policies in the field.

Secretary-General: Dr PEKKA TARJANNE (Finland).

UNITED NATIONS EDUCATIONAL, SCIENTIFIC AND CULTURAL ORGANIZATION—UNESCO

Address: 7 place de Fontenoy, 75352 Paris, France.

Telephone: 1-45-68-10-00; **telex:** 204461; **fax:** 1-45-67-16-90.

UNESCO was established in 1946 'for the purpose of advancing, through the educational, scientific and cultural relations of the peoples of the world, the objectives of international peace and the common welfare of mankind'. UNESCO's main programme activities are concerned with education, science, social sciences, culture and communication, information and informatics.

Director-General: FEDERICO MAYOR (Spain).

Regional Office for Education in Africa: BP 3311, Dakar, Senegal; tel. 23-50-82; telex 410; fax 23-83-93.

Regional Office for Science and Technology for Africa: POB 30592, Nairobi, Kenya; tel. (2) 621234; telex 22275; fax (2) 215991.

UNITED NATIONS INDUSTRIAL DEVELOPMENT ORGANIZATION—UNIDO

Address: Postfach 300, 1400 Vienna, Austria.

Telephone: (1) 211310; **telex:** 135612; **fax:** (1) 232156.

UNIDO began operations in 1967, following a resolution of the UN General Assembly, to assist in the industrialization of the developing countries through direct assistance and mobilization of national and international resources.

Director-General: MAURICIO DE MARÍA Y CAMPOS (Mexico).

UNIVERSAL POSTAL UNION—UPU

Address: Case postale, 3000 Berne 15, Switzerland.

Telephone: (31) 3503111; **telex:** 912761; **fax:** (31) 3503110.

The General Postal Union was founded by the Treaty of Berne (1874), begining operations in July 1875. Three years later its name was changed to the Universal Postal Union. In 1948 UPU became a specialized agency of the UN. It aims to develop and unify the international postal service, to study problems and to provide training.

Director-General: THOMAS E. LEAVEY (USA).

WORLD INTELLECTUAL PROPERTY ORGANIZATION—WIPO

Address: 34 chemin des Colombettes, 1211 Geneva 20, Switzerland.

Telephone: (22) 3389111; **telex:** 412912; **fax:** (22) 7335428.

WIPO was established in 1970. It became a specialized agency of the UN in 1974. WIPO aims to promote the protection of intellectual property (e.g. industrial and technical patents and literary copyrights) throughout the world through co-operation among states and, where appropriate, with other international organizations. It also centralizes the administration of the Unions which deal with legal and technical aspects of intellectual property. Each Union is founded on a multilateral treaty.

Director-General: Dr ARPAD BOGSCH (USA).

WORLD METEOROLOGICAL ORGANIZATION—WMO

Address: 41 ave Giuseppe Motta, CP 2300, 1211 Geneva 2, Switzerland.

Telephone: (22) 7308111; **telex:** 414199; **fax:** (22) 7342326.

WMO started its activities in 1951, aiming to improve the exchange of weather information and its applications.

Secretary-General: Prof. G. O. P. OBASI (Nigeria).

Regional Office for Africa: BP 605, Bujumbura, Burundi; tel. (2) 25237; telex 5027; fax (2) 22990.

United Nations Information Centres

Burkina Faso: BP 135, ave Georges Konseiga, Secteur no 4, Ouagadougou; tel. (3) 306076; telex 5302; fax (3) 311322. (Also covers Chad, Mali and Niger.)

Burundi: BP 2160, 117 ave de la Révolution, Bujumbura; tel. (2) 25018; telex 5078; fax (2) 25850.

Cameroon: Immeuble Kamden, rue Joseph Clère, BP 836, Yaoundé; tel. 22-50-43; telex 978-8304; fax 23-51-73. (Also covers the Central African Republic and Gabon.)

Congo, Democratic Republic: Bâtiment Deuxième République, blvd du 30 juin, BP 7248, Kinshasa; tel. (12) 33431; fax (871) 150-3261.

Congo, Republic: ave Foch, Case ORTF 15, BNP 13210, Brazzaville; tel. 835090; telex 5399; fax 836140.

Ethiopia: Africa Hall, POB 3001, Addis Ababa; tel. (1) 510172; telex 976-21029; fax (1) 516027.

Ghana: Gamel Abdul Nasser/Liberia Rds, POB 2239, Accra; tel. (21) 666851; telex 0942452; fax (21) 665578. (Also covers Sierra Leone.)

Kenya: United Nations Office, POB 30552, Gigiri, Nairobi; tel. (2) 333930; telex 963-22447; fax (2) 623927. (Also covers Seychelles and Uganda.)

Lesotho: Letsie Rd, Food Aid Compound, behind Hotel Victoria, POB 301, Maseru 100; tel. 312496; telex 342; fax 310042.

Madagascar: 22 rue Rainitovo, Antasahavola, BP 1348, Antananarivo; tel. (2) 24115; telex 983-22345; fax (2) 33315.

Namibia: 372 Independence Ave, Windhoek; tel. (61) 233034; fax (61) 233036.

Nigeria: 17 Kingsway Rd, POB 1068, Ikoyi, Lagos; tel. (1) 269-4886; telex 22857; fax (1) 269-1934.

Senegal: 12 ave Roume, BP 154, Immeuble UNESCO, Dakar; tel. 233070; telex 51450; fax 222679. (Also covers Cape Verde, Côte d'Ivoire, The Gambia, Guinea, Guinea-Bissau and Mauritania.)

South Africa: POB 12677, Metro Park Bldg, 351 Schoeman St, Pretoria; tel. (12) 320-1110; fax (12) 320-1122.

Sudan: United Nations Compound, University Ave, POB 913, Khartoum; tel. (11) 777816; telex 970214; fax (871) 151-6741. (Also covers Somalia.)

Tanzania: Old Boma Bldg, Marogoro Rd/Sokoine Drive, POB 9224, Dar es Salaam; tel. (51) 112923; telex 41284; fax (51) 113272; e-mail fo.tza@undp.org.

Togo: 107 blvd de 13 janvier, BP 911, Lomé; tel. and fax 212306; telex 986-5261. (Also covers Benin.)

Zambia: POB 32905, Lusaka 10101; tel. (1) 228487; telex 45930; fax (1) 222958. (Also covers Botswana, Malawi and Swaziland.)

Zimbabwe: Zimre Centre, 3rd Floor, L. Takawira St/Union Ave, POB 4408, Harare; tel. (4) 79-15-21; telex 22601; fax (4) 75-04-76.

AFRICAN DEVELOPMENT BANK—ADB

Address: 01 BP 1387, Abidjan 01, Côte d'Ivoire.

Telephone: 20-44-44; **telex:** 22202; **fax:** 20-49-09.

Established in 1964, the Bank began operations in July 1966, with the aim of financing economic and social development in African countries.

AFRICAN MEMBERS

Algeria	Eritrea	Niger
Angola	Ethiopia	Nigeria
Benin	Gabon	Rwanda
Botswana	The Gambia	São Tomé and Príncipe
Burkina Faso	Ghana	Senegal
Burundi	Guinea	Seychelles
Cameroon	Guinea-Bissau	Sierra Leone
Cape Verde	Kenya	Somalia
Central African Republic	Lesotho	South Africa
Chad	Liberia	Sudan
Comoros	Libya	Swaziland
Congo, Democratic Republic	Madagascar	Tanzania
Congo, Republic	Malawi	Togo
Côte d'Ivoire	Mali	Tunisia
Djibouti	Mauritania	Uganda
Egypt	Mauritius	Zambia
Equatorial Guinea	Morocco	Zimbabwe
	Mozambique	
	Namibia	

There are also 24 non-African members.

Organization

(July 1997)

BOARD OF GOVERNORS

The highest policy-making body of the Bank. Each member country nominates one Governor, usually its Minister of Finance and Economic Affairs, and an alternate Governor or the Governor of its Central Bank. The Board meets once a year. It elects the Board of Directors and the President.

BOARD OF DIRECTORS

The Board consists of 18 members (of whom six are non-African and hold 33.33% of the voting power), elected by the Board of Governors for a term of three years; it is responsible for the general operations of the Bank. The Board meets on a weekly basis.

OFFICERS

The President is responsible for the organization and the day-to-day operations of the Bank under guidance of the Board of Directors. The President is elected for a five-year term and serves as the Chairman of the Board of Directors. Under a restructuring programme, which was approved by the Bank's Governors in January 1995, the number of Vice-Presidents was reduced from five to three.

The Bank's activities are divided into five sections (for northern, southern, eastern, western and central Africa) and there is a separate department for disbursements.

Executive President and Chairman of Board of Directors: Omar Kabbaj (Morocco).

Secretary-General: Cheikh I. Fall.

FINANCIAL STRUCTURE

The ADB Group of development financing institutions comprises the African Development Fund (ADF) and the Nigeria Trust Fund (NTF), which provide concessionary loans, and the African Development Bank itself. The group uses a unit of account (UA), which, in 1996, was valued at US $1.43796.

The capital stock of the Bank was at first exclusively open for subscription by African countries, with each member's subscription consisting of an equal number of paid-up and callable shares. In 1978, however, the Governors agreed to open the capital stock of the Bank to subscription by non-regional states on the basis of nine principles aimed at maintaining the African character of the institution. The decision was finally ratified in May 1982, and the participation of non-regional countries became effective on 30 December. It was agreed that African members should still hold two-thirds of the share capital, that all loan operations should be restricted to African members, and that the Bank's President should always be an African national. In 1996 the ADB's authorized capital was US $23,295m. At the end of 1996 subscribed capital was $22,835m. (of which the paid-up portion was $2,792m.).

Activities

At the end of 1996 total loan and grant approvals by the ADB Group since the beginning of its operations amounted to US $30,749m. Of that amount the public utilities sector received the largest proportion of assistance (24.0%), while industry received 23.2%, agriculture 19.7%, transport 15.4%, multi-sector activities 12.4%, and education and health projects 5.3%. In 1996 the group approved 31 loans and grants amounting to $803m.

A new credit policy, adopted in May 1995, effectively disqualified 39 low-income regional members, deemed to be non-creditworthy, from receiving non-concessional ADB financing, in an attempt to reduce the accumulation of arrears. The ADB Group estimated that its capital requirements for the period 1997–2001 would amount to US $46,500m. to allow for greater flexibility in its lending. During 1996 the Bank supported international efforts to address the problem of Africa's 33 heavily indebted poor countries, and was to participate in a six-year initiative which aimed to encourage economic prospects while reducing outstanding debt and preventing its recurrence.

The ADB contributed funds for the establishment in 1986 of the Africa Project Development Facility, which assists the private sector in Africa by providing advisory services and finance for entrepreneurs: it is managed by the International Finance Corporation (IFC—q.v.). In 1989 the ADB, in co-ordination with IFC and UNDP, created the African Management Services Company (AMSCo) which provides management support and training to private companies in Africa.

The Bank also provides technical assistance to regional member countries in the form of experts' services, pre-investment feasibility studies, and staff training; much of this assistance is financed through bilateral aid funds contributed by non-African member states. The Bank's African Development Institute provides training for officials of regional member countries in order to enhance the management of Bank-financed projects and, more broadly, to strengthen national capacities for promoting sustainable development. In 1990 the ADB established the African Business Round Table (ABR), which is composed of the chief executives of Africa's leading corporations. The ABR aims to strengthen Africa's private sector, promote intra-African trade and investment, and attract foreign investment to Africa. The ABR is chaired by the ADB's Executive President. At its fourth annual meeting, held in Arusha, Tanzania, in March 1994, the ABR resolved to establish an African Investment Bank, in co-operation with the ADB, which was to provide financial services to African companies.

In 1990 a Memorandum of Understanding for the Reinforcement of Co-operation between the Organization of African Unity (OAU—q.v.), the UN's Economic Commission for Africa (q.v.) and the ADB was signed by the three organizations. A joint secretariat supports co-operation activities between the organizations.

AFRICAN DEVELOPMENT BANK (ADB)

The Bank makes loans at a variable annual interest rate (7.5% in 1990), plus a commitment fee of 1%. Loan approvals amounted to US $508.2m. for 11 loans in 1996.

ADB Loan and Grant Approvals by Region, 1995–96
(millions of UA)

Country	1995	%	1996	%
Central Africa	53.00	11.80	2.60	0.50
Gabon	53.00		—	
São Tomé and Príncipe	—		2.60	
East Africa	1.01	0.20	71.50	12.80
Eritrea	—		14.03	
Ethiopia	—		19.50	
Kenya	—		15.94	
Seychelles	1.01		—	
Uganda	—		22.03	
North Africa	386.15	85.90	354.46	63.40
Algeria	25.75		250.00	
Mauritania	—		16.70	
Morocco	150.00		60.41	
Sudan	1.55		—	
Tunisia	208.85		27.35	
Southern Africa	9.04	2.00	57.36	10.30
Malawi	—		5.00	
Mozambique	—		24.36	
Zambia	7.29		15.00	
Zimbabwe	1.75		13.00	
West Africa	0.55	0.10	72.62	13.00
Benin	—		18.00	
Côte d'Ivoire	—		29.00	
Gambia	—		4.00	
Ghana	—		7.53	
Nigeria	—		2.09	
Senegal	0.55		12.00	
Total	449.74	100.00	558.54	100.00

AFRICAN DEVELOPMENT FUND (ADF)

The Fund commenced operations in 1974. It grants interest-free loans to African countries for projects with repayment over 50 years (including a 10-year grace period) and with a service charge of 0.75% per annum. Grants for project feasibility studies are made to the poorest countries.

In 1987 donor countries agreed on a fifth replenishment of the Fund's resources, amounting to US $2,800m. for 1988–90. In future 85% of available resources was to be reserved for the poorest countries (those with annual GDP per caput of less than $510, at 1985 prices). In 1991 a sixth replenishment of the Fund's resources amounting to $3,340m. was approved for 1991–93. Negotiations for the seventh replenishment of the Fund's resources commenced in May 1993. However, in May 1994, donor countries withheld any new funds owing to dissatisfaction with the Bank's governance. In May 1996, following the implementation of various institutional reforms to strengthen the Bank's financial management and decision-making capabilities and to reduce its administrative costs, an agreement was concluded on the seventh replenishment of the ADF. Donor countries pledged some $2,690m. for the period 1996–98. An additional allocation of $420m. was endorsed at a special donors' meeting held in Osaka, Japan, in June. Since the seventh replenishment came into effect in September 1996 the ADF has funded 19 projects in 14 countries, and aims to offer concessional assistance to 42 African countries over the period 1996–98.

NIGERIA TRUST FUND (NTF)

The Agreement establishing the Nigeria Trust Fund was signed in February 1976 by the Bank and the Government of Nigeria. The Fund is administered by the Bank and its loans are granted for up to 25 years, including grace periods of up to five years, and carry 0.75% commitment charges and 4% interest charges. The loans are intended to provide financing for projects in co-operation with other lending institutions. The Fund also aims to promote the private sector and trade between African countries by providing information on African and international financial institutions able to finance African trade.

In 1996 the fund approved one loan amounting to US $8.63m., bringing the total amount committed since operations began to $320.27m. for 58 loans.

Summary of Bank Group Activities (US $ million)

	1995	1996	Cumulative total*
ADB loans			
Number	11	11	725
Amount approved	668.53	508.18	19,941.39
Disbursements	1,058.37	1,007.94	13,308.52
ADF loans and grants			
Number	—	19	1,183
Amount approved	—	286.36	10,487.22
Disbursements	615.91	626.45	6,955.57
NTF loans			
Number	—	1	58
Amount approved	—	8.63	320.27
Disbursements	3.70	7.18	205.65
Group total			
Number	11	31	1,966
Amount approved	668.53	803.16	30,748.88
Disbursements	1,677.98	1,641.57	20,479.74

* Since the initial operations of the three institutions (1967 for ADB, 1974 for ADF and 1976 for NTF).

ASSOCIATED INSTITUTIONS

The ADB actively participated in the establishment of five associated institutions:

Africa Reinsurance Corporation—Africa-Re: Reinsurance House, 46 Marina, PMB 12765, Lagos, Nigeria; tel. (1) 66-52-82; telex 22647; fax (1) 66-88-02; f. 1977; started operations in 1978; its purpose is to foster the development of the insurance and reinsurance industry in Africa and to promote the growth of national and regional underwriting capacities. Africa-Re has an auth. cap. of US $30m., of which the ADB holds 10%. There are 12 directors, one appointed by the Bank. Mems: 41 countries and the ADB. Sec.-Gen. Bakary Kamara.

African Export-Import Bank—Afreximbank: World Trade Centre Building, POB 404 Gezira, 1191 Corniche el-Nil, Cairo, Egypt 11451; tel. (2) 5780282; telex 20003; fax (2) 5780277; f. 1993; aims to increase the volume of African exports and to expand intra-African trade by financing exporters and importers directly and indirectly through trade finance institutions, such as commercial banks; auth. cap. US $750m., subscribed cap. $495m. (at May 1994). Pres. Christopher Edordu (Nigeria); Exec. Sec. J. W. T. Otieno.

Association of African Development Finance Institutions—AADFI: c/o ADB, 01 BP 1387, Abidjan 01, Côte d'Ivoire; tel. 20-40-90; telex 23717; fax 22-73-44; f. 1975; aims to promote co-operation among the development banks of the region in matters relating to development ideas, project design and financing. Mems: 77 mems in 40 African and non-African countries. Sec.-Gen. J. A. Hammond.

Shelter-Afrique (Société pour l'habitat et le logement territorial en Afrique): Mamlaka Rd, POB 41479, Nairobi, Kenya; tel. (2) 722305; telex 25355; fax (2) 722024; f. 1982 to finance housing in ADB mem. countries. Share capital is US $300m., held by 28 African countries, the ADB, Africa-Re and the Commonwealth Development Corpn. Sec.-Gen. Dr T. Ramdin.

Société internationale financière pour les investissements et le développement en Afrique—SIFIDA: 22 rue François-Perréard, BP 310, 1225 Chêne-Bourg/Génève, Switzerland; tel. (22) 8692000; telex 418647; fax (22) 8692001; f. 1970 by 120 financial and industrial institutions, including the ADB and the IFC. Following a restructuring at the end of 1995, the main shareholders are now Banque Nationale de Paris (BNP), SFOM (itself owned by BNP, Banque Bruxelles Lambert and Dresdner Bank) and the six banking affiliates of BNP/SFOM in West and Central Africa. SIFIDA is active in the fields of project and trade finance in Africa and also provides financial advisory services, notably in the context of privatizations and debt conversion; auth. cap. US $75m., subscribed cap. $7.5m. Chair. Vivien Lévy-Garboua; Man. Dir Philippe Séchaud. Publ. *African Banking Directory* (annually).

PUBLICATIONS

Annual Report.

ADB Today (every 2 months).

African Development Report.

African Development Review.

Basic Information (annually).

Economic Research Papers.

Quarterly Operational Summary.

Statistical Handbook (annually).

Summaries of operations in each member country and various background documents.

COMMON MARKET FOR EASTERN AND SOUTHERN AFRICA—COMESA

Address: Lotti House, Cairo Rd, POB 30051, Lusaka, Zambia.

Telephone: (1) 229726; **telex:** 40127; **fax:** (1) 225107; **e-mail:** comesa@comesa.zm.

Founded in 1993 as a successor to the Preferential Trade Area for Eastern and Southern Africa (PTA), which was established in 1981.

MEMBERS

Angola	Mauritius*
Burundi*	Mozambique†
Comoros*	Namibia
Congo, Democratic Republic	Rwanda*
Eritrea*	Sudan*
Ethiopia*	Swaziland
Kenya*	Tanzania*
Lesotho†	Uganda*
Madagascar*	Zambia*
Malawi*	Zimbabwe*

* Signatory states that have also ratified the COMESA treaty.
† Membership voluntarily suspended.

Organization

(July 1997)

AUTHORITY

The Authority of the Common Market is the supreme policy organ of COMESA, comprising Heads of State or of Government of member countries. The inaugural meeting of the Authority took place in Lilongwe, Malawi, in December 1994.

COUNCIL OF MINISTERS

Each member government appoints a minister to participate in the Council. The Council monitors COMESA activities, including supervision of the Secretariat, recommends policy direction and development, and reports to the Authority.

A Committee of Governors of Central Banks advises the Authority and the Council of Ministers on monetary and financial matters.

SECRETARIAT

Secretary-General: JOEL ERASTUS MWENCHA (Kenya) (acting).

Activities

The COMESA treaty was signed by member states of the PTA in November 1993 and was scheduled to come into effect on being ratified by 10 countries. COMESA formally succeeded the PTA in December 1994 (by which time it had received 12 ratifications), with the aim of strengthening the process of regional economic integration that had been initiated under the PTA, in order to help member states achieve sustainable economic growth.

COMESA aims to establish a free trade area by 2000, requiring full liberalization of trading practices, including the elimination of non-tariff barriers, to ensure the free movement of goods, services and capital within the Common Market. In April 1997 COMESA Heads of State agreed that a common external tariff would be implemented by 2004, to strengthen the establishment of a regional customs union, with a zero tariff on products originated from within the Common Market. COMESA aimed to formulate a common investment procedure to promote domestic, cross-border and direct foreign investment by ensuring the free movement of capital, services and labour.

The PTA aimed to facilitate intra-regional trade by establishing a clearing house to deal with credit arrangements and balance of payments issues. The clearing house became operational in February 1984 using the unit of account of the PTA (UAPTA) as its currency. (The UAPTA was valued at the rate of the IMF special drawing rights.) The clearing house, based in Harare, Zimbabwe, remained an integral part of the COMESA infrastructure. In April 1997 the Authority endorsed a proposal to replace UAPTA with a COMESA dollar, to be equivalent to the value of the US currency. An Automated System of Customs Data (ASYCUDA) has been established to facilitate customs administration in all COMESA member states. Through support for capacity-building activities and the establishment of other specialized institutions (see below) COMESA aims to reinforce its objectives of regional integration. The COMESA treaty envisaged the establishment of a sub-regional Court of Justice, to replace the PTA Tribunal; however, this had yet to be implemented at mid-1997.

Co-operation programmes have been implemented by COMESA in the industrial, agricultural, energy and transport and communications sectors. A regional food security programme aimed to ensure adequate food supplies at all times. In 1997 COMESA Heads of State advocated that the food sector be supported by the immediate implementation of an irrigation action plan for the region. Other initiatives include a road customs declaration document, a regional customs bond guarantee scheme, third party motor vehicle insurance scheme and travellers cheques in the UAPTA unit of currency. A Trade Information Network, established under the PTA to disseminate information on the production and marketing of goods manufactured and traded in the region, was scheduled to be transformed into the COMESA Information Network (COMNET).

Since its establishment there have been concerns on the part of member states, as well as other regional non-member countries, in particular South Africa, of adverse rivalry between COMESA and the Southern African Development Community (SADC, q.v.) and of a duplication of roles. In December 1996 and January 1997 respectively, Lesotho and Mozambique suspended their membership of COMESA and announced their intention to withdraw from the organization owing to concerns that their continued participation in COMESA was incompatible with their SADC membership.

FINANCE

COMESA is financed by member states. Its administrative budget for 1996 amounted to US 4m. In April 1997 COMESA Heads of State concluded that the organization's activities were being undermined by lack of resources, and determined to expel countries which fail to pay membership dues over a five-year period.

COMESA INSTITUTIONS

COMESA Association of Commercial Banks: 101 Union Ave, POB 2940, Harare, Zimbabwe; tel. (4) 793911; telex 26166; fax (4) 730819; aims to strengthen co-operation between banks in the region; organizes training activities; conducts studies to harmonize banking laws and operations. Mems: commercial banking orgs in Burundi, Kenya, Malawi, Sudan, Tanzania, Uganda.

COMESA Leather and Leather Products Institute: POB 5538, Addis Ababa, Ethiopia; tel (1) 510361; fax (1) 512799; f. 1990 as the PTA Leather Institute. Mems: Govts of 16 COMESA mem. states.

COMESA Metallurgical Technology Centre: c/o 101 Union Ave, Harare, Zimbabwe; tel. (1) 793911; telex 26166; fax (1) 730819; conducts research, testing and evaluation of raw materials, training and the exchange of appropriate technologies in order to promote the local mineral resources sectors.

Compagnie de réassurance de la Zone d'échanges préférentiels—Zep-re (COMESA Reinsurance Co): Anniversary Towers, University Way, POB 42769, Nairobi, Kenya; tel. (2) 212792; fax (2) 224102; f. 1993; provides local reinsurance services and training to personnel in the insurance industry; auth. cap. 20m. UAPTA; Man. Dir S. M. LUBASI.

Eastern and Southern African Trade and Development Bank: NSSF Bldg, Bishop's Rd, POB 48596, Nairobi, Kenya; tel. (2) 712260; fax (2) 711510; f. 1983 as PTA Development Bank; aims to mobilize resources and finance COMSA activities to foster regional integration; promotes investment and co-financing within the region; shareholders 15 COMESA mem. states and the African Development Bank; cap. p.u. US $82.9m. (Dec. 1995); Pres. MARTIN OGANG.

Federation of National Associations of Women in Business—FEMCOM; c/o COMESA Secretariat; f. 1993 to provide links between female business executives throughout the region and to promote greater awareness of relevant issues at policy level. FEMCOM was to be supported by a Revolving Fund for Women in Business.

PUBLICATIONS

COMESA Journal.
COMESA Trade Directory (annually).
COMESA Trade Information Newsletter (monthly).
Demand/supply surveys and reports.

THE COMMONWEALTH

Address: Commonwealth Secretariat, Marlborough House, Pall Mall, London, SW1Y 5HX, England.

Telephone: (171) 839-3411; **telex:** 27678; **fax:** (171) 930-0827; **e-mail:** info@commonwealth.int.

The Commonwealth is a voluntary association of 53 independent states (at mid-1997), comprising nearly one-quarter of the world's population. It includes the United Kingdom and most of its former dependencies, and former dependencies of Australia and New Zealand (themselves Commonwealth countries). All Commonwealth countries accept Queen Elizabeth II as the symbol of the free association of the independent member nations and as such the Head of the Commonwealth.

MEMBERS IN AFRICA SOUTH OF THE SAHARA

Botswana	Mauritius	Swaziland
Cameroon	Mozambique	Tanzania
The Gambia	Namibia	Uganda
Ghana	Nigeria*	Zambia
Kenya	Seychelles	Zimbabwe
Lesotho	Sierra Leone†	
Malawi	South Africa	

Dependencies

British Indian Ocean Territory
St Helena
  Ascension
  Tristan da Cunha

* Membership suspended in November 1995.
† Participation in meetings of the Commonwealth suspended in July 1997.

Organization

(July 1997)

The Commonwealth is not a federation: there is no central government nor are there any rigid contractual obligations such as bind members of the United Nations.

The Commonwealth has no written constitution but its members subscribe to the ideals of the Declaration of Commonwealth Principles (see below) unanimously approved by a meeting of heads of government in Singapore in 1971. Members also approved the 1977 statement on apartheid in sport (the Gleneagles Agreement); the 1979 Lusaka Declaration on Racism and Racial Prejudice (see below); the 1981 Melbourne Declaration on relations between developed and developing countries; the 1983 New Delhi Statement on Economic Action; the 1983 Goa Declaration on International Security; the 1985 Nassau Declaration on World Order; the Commonwealth Accord on Southern Africa (1985); the 1987 Vancouver Declaration on World Trade; the Okanagan Statement and Programme of Action on Southern Africa (1987); the Langkawi Declaration on the Environment (1989); the Kuala Lumpur Statement on Southern Africa (1989); the Harare Commonwealth Declaration (1991) (see below); the Ottawa Declaration on Women and Structural Adjustment (1991); the Limassol Statement on the Uruguay Round of multilateral trade negotiations (1993); and the Millbrook Commonwealth Action Programme on the Harare Declaration (1995).

MEETINGS OF HEADS OF GOVERNMENT

Meetings are private and informal and operate not by voting but by consensus. The emphasis is on consultation and exchange of views for co-operation. A communiqué is issued at the end of every meeting. Meetings are held every two years in different capitals in the Commonwealth. The 1995 meeting was held in Auckland, New Zealand, in November, and the 1997 meeting was to be held in Edinburgh, the United Kingdom, in October.

OTHER CONSULTATIONS

Meetings at ministerial and official level are also held regularly. Since 1959 finance ministers have met in a Commonwealth country in the week prior to the annual meetings of the IMF and the World Bank. Meetings on education, legal, women's and youth affairs are held at ministerial level every three years. Ministers of health hold annual meetings, with major meetings every three years, and ministers of agriculture meet every two years. Ministers of trade, labour and employment, industry, science and the environment also hold periodic meetings.

Senior officials—cabinet secretaries, permanent secretaries to heads of government and others—meet regularly in the year between meetings of heads of government to provide continuity and to exchange views on various developments.

COMMONWEALTH SECRETARIAT

The Secretariat, established by Commonwealth heads of government in 1965, operates as an international organization at the service of all Commonwealth countries. It organizes consultations between governments and runs programmes of co-operation. Meetings of heads of government, ministers and senior officials decide these programmes and provide overall direction.

The Secretariat is headed by a secretary-general (elected by heads of government), assisted by three deputy secretaries-general. One deputy is responsible for political affairs, one for economic and social affairs, and one for development co-operation (including the Commonwealth Fund for Technical Co-operation—see below). The Secretariat comprises 13 Divisions in the fields of political affairs; legal and constitutional affairs; information and public affairs; administration; economic affairs; human resource development; women's and youth affairs; science and technology; economic and legal advisory services; export and industrial development; management and training services; general technical assistance services; and strategic planning and evaluation.

Secretary-General: Chief E. CHUKWUEMEKA (EMEKA) ANYAOKU (Nigeria).

Deputy Secretary-General (Political): KRISHNAN SRINIVASAN (India).

Deputy Secretary-General (Economic and Social): Sir HUMPHREY MAUD (United Kingdom).

Deputy Secretary-General (Development Co-operation): EWAN (NICK) HARE (Canada).

BUDGET

The Secretariat's budget for 1995/96 was £9.68m.; a budget of £10.4m. was approved for 1996/97. Member governments meet the cost of the Secretariat through subscriptions on a scale related to income and population, similar to the scale for contributions to the United Nations.

Activities

INTERNATIONAL AFFAIRS

In 1977 Commonwealth heads of government reached an agreement on discouraging sporting links with South Africa, The Gleneagles Agreement on Sporting Contacts with South Africa, which was designed to express their abhorrence of that country's policy of apartheid. At their 1979 meeting in Lusaka, Zambia, the heads of government endorsed a nine-point plan to direct Zimbabwe-Rhodesia towards internationally recognized independence. The leaders also issued the Lusaka Declaration on Racism and Racial Prejudice as a formal expression of their abhorrence of all forms of racist policy.

In October 1985 heads of government, meeting at Nassau, Bahamas, issued the Nassau Declaration on World Order, reaffirming Commonwealth commitment to the United Nations, to international co-operation for development and to the eventual elimination of nuclear weapons. The same meeting issued the Commonwealth Accord on Southern Africa, calling on the South African authorities to dismantle apartheid and open dialogue with a view to establishing a representative government. The meeting also established a Commonwealth 'Eminent Persons Group'. It visited South Africa in February and March 1986 and attempted unsuccessfully to establish a dialogue between the South African Government and opposition leaders. In August the heads of government of seven Commonwealth countries (Australia, the Bahamas, Canada, India, the United Kingdom, Zambia and Zimbabwe) met to consider the Group's report, and (with the exception of the United Kingdom) agreed to adopt a series of measures to exert economic pressure on the South African Government, and to encourage other countries to adopt such measures.

In October 1987 heads of government, meeting at Vancouver, Canada, issued the Okanagan Statement and Programme of Action on Southern Africa, to strengthen the Commonwealth effort to end apartheid in South Africa. They also established the Commonwealth Committee of Foreign Ministers on Southern Africa, comprising the ministers of foreign affairs of Australia, Canada, Guyana, India, Nigeria, Tanzania, Zambia and Zimbabwe (and, subsequently, of Malaysia). The Committee was to provide impetus and guidance in furtherance of the objectives of the Statement. The Vancouver meeting also issued the Vancouver Declaration on World Trade, condemning protectionism and reaffirming the leaders' commitment to work for a durable and just world trading system.

In October 1989 heads of government, meeting in Kuala Lumpur, Malaysia, issued the Langkawi Declaration on the Environment, a 16-point joint programme of action to combat environmental degradation and ensure sustainable development.

In October 1991 heads of government, meeting in Harare, Zimbabwe, issued the Harare Commonwealth Declaration, in which they reaffirmed their commitment to the Commonwealth Principles declared in 1971, and stressed the need to promote sustainable development and the alleviation of poverty. The Declaration placed emphasis on the promotion of democracy and respect for human rights and resolved to strengthen the Commonwealth's capacity to assist countries in entrenching democratic practices. The meeting also welcomed the political reforms introduced by the South African Government and urged all South African political parties to commence negotiations on a new constitution as soon as possible. The meeting endorsed measures on the phased removal of sanctions against South Africa. 'People-to-people' sanctions (including consular and visa restrictions, cultural and scientific boycotts and restrictions on tourism promotion) were removed immediately, with economic sanctions to remain in place until a constitution for a new democratic, non-racial state had been agreed. The sports boycott would continue to be repealed on a sport-by-sport basis, as each sport in South Africa became integrated and non-racial. The embargo on the supply of armaments would remain in place until a post-apartheid, democratic regime had been firmly established in South Africa. At the request of the heads of government in Harare, the Commonwealth Secretary-General went to South Africa in November and held discussions with the Government and the major political parties. In late December a group of six eminent Commonwealth citizens was dispatched to observe multi-party negotiations on the future of South Africa and to assist the process where possible. In mid-October 1992, in a fresh attempt to assist the South African peace process, a Commonwealth team of 18 observers was sent to monitor political violence in the country. A second phase of the Commonwealth Mission to South Africa (COMSA) began in February 1993, comprising 10 observers from nine countries with backgrounds in policing, the law, politics and public life. COMSA issued a report in May in which it urged a concerted effort to build a culture of political tolerance in South Africa. In a report on its third phase, issued in December 1993, COMSA appealed strongly to all political parties to participate in the transitional arrangements leading to democratic elections.

In October 1993 the Commonwealth heads of government, meeting in Limassol, Cyprus, agreed that a democratic and non-racial South Africa would be invited to join the organization; a Commonwealth team of experts was to monitor the South African elections, to be held in April 1994. The heads of government endorsed the removal of all economic sanctions against South Africa, but agreed to retain the arms embargo until a post-apartheid, democratic government had been established. The summit meeting's communiqué urged a speedy withdrawal from Cyprus of all Turkish forces and settlers: this was the first time that the Commonwealth had taken sides so explicitly in the dispute over Cyprus. As an expression of the Commonwealth's collective support for the Uruguay Round of negotiations under GATT, the heads of government established a five-nation task force, which, in November, met with representatives of the Governments of France, Belgium, Germany, Switzerland, the United Kingdom, the USA and Japan to emphasize the importance of a successful and balanced conclusion to the Round.

In September 1994 the Commonwealth Secretary-General visited Bangladesh to consider the confrontational political situation in that country and formulated a proposal for negotiations to assist political dialogue and the consolidation of democracy. A 12-member Commonwealth group visited Bangladesh to observe the conduct of a general election, held in June 1996.

In November 1995 Commonwealth heads of government, convened, in New Zealand, for their biennial meeting, formulated and adopted the Millbrook Commonwealth Action Programme on the Harare Declaration, to promote adherence by member countries to the fundamental principles of democracy and human rights (as proclaimed in the 1991 Declaration). The Programme incorporated a framework of measures, including the establishment of a standing action group, to respond to unlawful activities by member governments and to assist their return to democratic governance. On the basis of this Programme, the leaders suspended Nigeria from the Commonwealth with immediate effect, following the execution by that country's military Government of nine environmental and human rights protesters and a series of other violations of human rights. The meeting determined to expel Nigeria from the Commonwealth if no 'demonstrable progress' had been made towards the establishment of a democratic authority by the time of the next summit meeting. In addition, the Programme formulated measures to promote sustainable development in member countries, which was considered to be an important element in sustaining democracy, and to facilitate consensus-building within the international community. Earlier in the meeting a statement was issued declaring the 'overwhelming majority' of Commonwealth governments to be opposed to nuclear-testing programmes being undertaken in the South Pacific region. However, in view of events in Nigeria, the issue of nuclear testing and disagreement among member countries did not assume the significance anticipated.

In December 1995 the Commonwealth Ministerial Action Group on the Harare Declaration (CMAG), which had been mandated under the Millbrook Action Programme, convened for its inaugural meeting in London. The Group, comprising the Ministers of Foreign Affairs of Canada, Ghana, Jamaica, Malaysia, New Zealand, South Africa, the United Kingdom and Zimbabwe, commenced by considering efforts to restore democratic government in the three Commonwealth countries under military regimes, i.e. The Gambia, Nigeria and Sierra Leone. At the second meeting of the Group, in April 1996, ministers commended the conduct of presidential and parliamentary elections in Sierra Leone and the announcement by The Gambia's military leaders to proceed with a transition to civilian rule. In June a three-member CMAG delegation visited The Gambia to assess the transition process and preparations for the forthcoming elections. While presidential and legislative elections took place as planned, in September 1996 and January 1997 respectively, CMAG criticized the fact that those involved in political life prior to the military takeover were prohibited from contesting. In February CMAG called for an end to the exclusion of pre-coup parties and advised that an investigation be carried out, to determine how the Commonwealth could further aid the transition process. In April 1997 it was noted that the human rights situation in Nigeria had continued to deteriorate. CMAG, having pursued unsuccessful efforts to conduct negotiations with the Nigerian authorities, recommended that member countries adopt a series of punitive and restrictive measures (including visa restrictions on members of the administration, a cessation of sporting contacts and an embargo on the export of armaments) to exert further pressure for reform in Nigeria. In June a delegation of the Nigerian Government met CMAG in London and discussed the country's programme for democracy. The Group agreed to postpone the implementation of the sanctions, pending progress on the dialogue. (Canada, however, determined, unilaterally, to impose the measures with immediate effect.) A proposed ministerial fact-finding visit to Nigeria was postponed in August, owing to restrictions imposed by the military authorities on access to political dissidents and human rights campaigners in that country. In September the Group agreed to proceed with the investigation and to delay further a decision on the implementation of sanction measures. A high-level mission visited Nigeria in November, and in February 1997 CMAG met in London to discuss its findings. Commentators suggested that CMAG was divided over the issue, with some African members claiming that progress had been made towards the restoration of democracy in Nigeria. The Group insisted that it was unified, and called for additional information to be provided by human rights groups and civilian organizations for discussion at a further meeting in July, before deciding upon the measures to be taken. In March, however, Canada suspended diplomatic relations with Nigeria, reportedly owing to frustration at the perceived inaction of CMAG. CMAG met as planned in July to prepare recommendations for review by the Commonwealth heads of government in October, when relations with The Gambia and Sierra Leone were also to be discussed. In addition CMAG suspended Sierra Leone from Commonwealth meetings, following a military coup in May.

Political Affairs Division: assists consultation among member governments on international and Commonwealth matters of common interest. In association with host governments, it organizes the meetings of heads of government and senior officials. The Division services committees and special groups set up by heads of government dealing with political matters. The Secretariat has observer status at the United Nations, and the Division manages an office in New York to enable small states, which would otherwise be unable to afford facilities there, to maintain a presence at the United Nations. The Division monitors political developments in the Commonwealth and international progress in such matters as disarmament, the concerns of small states, dismantling of apartheid and the Law of the Sea. It also undertakes research on matters of common interest to member governments, and reports back to them. The Division is involved in diplomatic training and consular co-operation.

In 1990 Commonwealth Heads of Government mandated the Division to support the promotion of democracy by monitoring the preparations for and conduct of elections in member countries. By mid-1997 21 observer missions had been sent to monitor parliamentary, presidential or other elections at the request of the national governments, the last time being in May, when an observer group was sent to Cameroon (which joined the Commonwealth in 1995) to oversee legislative elections. The mission to South Africa (the Commonwealth Observer Group to South Africa—COGSA), deployed in April 1994, constituted the largest ever monitoring undertaking by the Commonwealth. COGSA numbered some 160 members, including COMSA observers and experts providing technical advice. In June 1995 the first meeting of a Commonwealth Election Management Programme was held in Namibia, attended by 32 officials from 14 countries. The meeting agreed to initiate a regular training programme on the conduct and management of elections.

LAW

Legal and Constitutional Affairs Division: promotes and facilitates co-operation and the exchange of information among member governments on legal matters. It administers a training programme for legislative draftsmen, promotes the establishment of regional law development units and assists governments to reform national laws to meet the obligations of international conventions. The Division initiated four Commonwealth schemes for co-operation on extradition, the protection of material cultural heritage, mutual assistance in criminal matters and the transfer of convicted offenders within the Commonwealth. It liaises with the Commonwealth Magistrates' Association, the Commonwealth Legal Education Association, the Commonwealth Lawyers' Association, the Commonwealth Association of Legislative Counsel, and with other international organizations. It also provides in-house legal advice for the Secretariat, and helps to prepare the triennial Commonwealth Law Conference for the practising profession. An annual 'colloquium' of chief justices is also held. The quarterly *Commonwealth Law Bulletin* reports on legal developments in and beyond the Commonwealth.

The Division's Commercial Crime Unit assists member countries to combat financial and organized crime, in particular transborder criminal activities. A Human Rights Unit aims to assist governments to strengthen national institutions and other mechanisms for the protection for human rights. It also organizes training workshops and promotes the exchange of relevant information among member countries.

ECONOMIC CO-OPERATION

Economic Affairs Division: organizes and services the annual meetings of Commonwealth ministers of finance, and periodic meetings of ministers of labour and employment, and assists in servicing the biennial meetings of heads of government. It engages in research and analysis on economic issues of interest to member governments and organizes seminars and conferences of government officials and experts. The Division initiated a major programme of technical assistance to enable developing Commonwealth countries to participate in the Uruguay Round of multilateral trade negotiations. It continues to help developing countries to strengthen their links with international capital markets and foreign investors. The Division also services groups of experts on economic affairs commissioned by governments. Such groups have reported on, among other things, protectionism; obstacles to the North-South negotiating process; reform of the international financial and trading system; the debt crisis; management of technological change; the special needs of small states; the impact of change on the development process; environmental issues; women and structural adjustment; and youth unemployment. The Division co-ordinates the Secretariat's environmental work. The Division undertook preparatory work for the establishment of a Commonwealth Equity Fund, initiated in September 1990, to allow developing member countries to improve their access to private institutional investment, and promoted a Caribbean Investment Fund.

The Division has supported the establishment of a Commonwealth Private Investment Initiative (CPII) to mobilize capital, on a regional basis, for investment in newly-privatized companies and in small- and medium-sized businesses in the private sector. The CPII was endorsed by Commonwealth heads of state, meeting in Auckland, New Zealand, in November 1995, and the first regional fund under the CPII was launched in July 1996. The Commonwealth Africa Investment Fund (Comafin), which was to be operated jointly with the United Kingdom's official development institution, the Commonwealth Development Corporation, was to assist businesses in 19 countries in sub-Saharan Africa, with initial resources of US $52.5m.

HUMAN RESOURCES

Human Resource Development Division: consists of two departments concerned with education and health. The Division co-operates with member countries in devising strategies for human resource development.

The **Education Department** arranges specialist seminars and co-operative projects and commissions studies in areas identified by ministers of education, whose three-yearly meetings it also services. Its present areas of emphasis include improving the quality of and access to science, technology and mathematics education, in particular expanding the participation of girls in these disciplines, strengthening the capabilities of ministers of education in relevant concerns, and teacher quality. The Secretariat is the lead agency for the Development of African Education Working Group on the region's teaching profession. The Department established a Commonwealth Higher Education Support Scheme, which aims to enhance the quality of tertiary level education in developing countries and to promote the participation of women in managerial roles in higher education.

The **Health Department** organizes ministerial, technical and expert group meetings and workshops, to promote co-operation on health matters, and provides professional and technical advice to member countries. It supports the work of regional health organizations and is currently helping to establish regional training programmes.

Management and Training Services Division: comprises the Management Advisory Unit, the Institutional Development and Training Unit and Programme Support and Special Projects Unit. With CFTC funds, the Division provides approximately 3,000 training awards each year, mostly for managerial and technical staff in government offices and large enterprises. Most training is provided in developing countries, in the form of courses, workshops, training attachments and study visits. A new programme of training in administration and technical services, to enable black South Africans to occupy positions in public administration and business in a non-racial South Africa, was devised in 1991. The Division provided assistance for the establishment of a Commonwealth Local Government Forum, launched in March 1994, which was to promote local democracy and participatory government by providing a network for national local government associations.

Women's and Youth Affairs Division: consists of the Women's Affairs Department and the Youth Affairs Department.

The **Women's Affairs Department** aims to enhance the interests of women towards full and equal political, economic and legal rights and protection from violence, and co-ordinates Commonwealth activities on gender issues. It conducts workshops and undertakes consultancy work on issues such as the participation of women in political and managerial decision-making, women and the environment, and the implementation of international legal instruments affecting the rights of women.

The **Youth Affairs Department** administers the Commonwealth Youth Programme (CYP), funded through separate voluntary contributions from governments, which seeks to promote the involvement of young people in the economic and social development of their countries. The CYP was awarded a budget of £2.1m. for 1996/97. It provides policy advice for governments and operates regional training programmes for youth workers and policy-makers through its centres in Africa, Asia, the Caribbean and the Pacific. It conducts a Youth Study Fellowship scheme, a Youth Project Fund, a Youth Exchange Programme (in the Caribbean), and a Youth Service Awards Scheme, holds conferences and seminars, carries out research and disseminates information. In May 1995 a Commonwealth Youth Credit Initiative was launched, in order to provide funds, training and advice to young entrepreneurs.

SCIENCE

Science and Technology Division: is funded and governed by the Commonwealth Science Council, consisting of 36 governments, which aims to enhance the scientific and technological capabilities of member countries, through co-operative research, training and the exchange of information. Current priority areas of work are concerned with the promotion of sustainable development and cover biological diversity and genetic resources, water resources, and renewable energy.

TECHNICAL CO-OPERATION

Commonwealth Fund for Technical Co-operation (CFTC): financed by voluntary subscriptions from all member governments, funds the development co-operation activities of the Secretariat. Among these activities the Secretariat provides technical assistance to developing Commonwealth countries, including consultancy and advisory services to individual member governments (administered under the Economic and Legal Advisory Services Division), assigns experts to work in member countries (under the General Technical Assistance Services Division), and finances specialized training (under the Management and Training Services Division). The CFTC also funds the work of the Export and Industrial Development Division (see below) and administers the Langkawi awards for the study of environmental issues, which is funded by the Canadian Government. CFTC expenditure during 1995/96 was £23.2m., while a budget of £25m. was approved for 1996/97. During 1993–95 there were 336 experts on long-term assignments under the CFTC. Some 40 countries use the CFTC's computerized debt package.

Export and Industrial Development Division: assists governments in the development and implementation of industrial projects; assistance includes investment planning and project design, entrepreneurial development, transfer of technology, advice on environmental protection, and upgrading enterprises. It also assists governments to improve foreign-exchange earnings through identification and exploration of export markets, using trade promotion events such as export business intensification programmes, buyer-seller meetings, integrated marketing programmes and contact promotion programmes. The Division includes an agricultural development unit.

The Secretariat also includes an Administration Division, a Strategic Planning and Evaluation Unit, and an Information and Public Affairs Division, which produces information publications, and radio and television programmes, about Commonwealth co-operation and consultation activities.

SELECTED PUBLICATIONS

Commonwealth Currents (quarterly).

Commonwealth Declarations 1971–91.

Commonwealth Organisations (directory).

The Commonwealth Today.

In Common (quarterly newsletter of the Youth Programme).

International Development Policies (quarterly).

Link In (quarterly newsletter of the Women and Development Programme).

Notes on the Commonwealth (series of reference leaflets).

Report of the Commonwealth Secretary-General (every 2 years).

The Commonwealth Yearbook.

Numerous reports, studies and papers (catalogue available).

Information on the Commonwealth can be accessed on the Internet at http://www.thecommonwealth.org.

Commonwealth Organizations

(In the United Kingdom, unless otherwise stated)

AGRICULTURE AND FORESTRY

CAB INTERNATIONAL (CABI): Wallingford, Oxon, OX10 8DE; tel. (1491) 832111; telex 847964; fax (1491) 833508; e-mail C.Ogbourne@cabi.org; f. 1928; fmrly Commonwealth Agricultural Bureaux; an intergovernmental organization with 40 mem. countries, which aims to improve human welfare world-wide through the generation, dissemination and application of scientific knowledge in support of sustainable development. It places particular emphasis on agriculture, forestry, human health and the management of natural resources, with priority given to the needs of developing countries.

CABI compiles and publishes extensive information (in the form of abstract journals, newsletters, books, bibliographic and non-bibliographic data bases and maps) on aspects of agriculture, forestry, veterinary medicine, the environment and natural resources, Third World rural development, leisure, recreation and tourism, human nutrition, and human health. CABI's main data bases, CAB ABSTRACTS and CAB HEALTH may be accessed electronically on diskette, CD-ROM and magnetic tape. CABI undertakes research and development in innovative information systems, offers training in information management and other advice and practical assistance in the design and implementation of science-based information systems. CABI has regional offices in Kenya, Malaysia and Trinidad and Tobago. Dir-Gen. J. GILMORE.

Asia Regional Office: 19-21-1 Jalan SR 8/1, off Jalan Serdang Raya 43300 Seri Kembangan, Selangor DE, Malaysia; tel. (3) 9433641; fax (3) 9436400; Rep. Dr A. ZAMZAM MOHAMED.

The following are the four CABI scientific institutions:

International Institute of Biological Control: Silwood Park, Buckhurst Rd, Ascot, Berks, SL5 7TA; tel. (1334) 872999; telex 93121-02255; fax (1334) 875007; f. 1927; since 1983 its main research and admin. centre has been in the United Kingdom, with field stations in Kenya, Malaysia, Pakistan, Switzerland and Trinidad; its purpose is the promotion of biological means of pest control and their integration into sustainable pest-management systems through co-operative research, training and information, with an emphasis on the need of the developing world. Dir Dr J. K. WAAGE. Publ. *Biocontrol News and Information* (quarterly).

International Institute of Entomology: 56 Queen's Gate, London, SW7 5JR; tel. (171) 584-0067; fax (171) 581-1676; f. 1913; undertakes research, training and development activities on insects and mites, relating to agriculture, horticulture and forestry; current emphasis on initiatives relevant to biodiversity and environmental change; undertakes identifications of insects and mites; conducts an extensive training programme. Dir Prof. VALERIE K. BROWN. Publs *Bulletin of Entomological Research* (quarterly), *Distribution Maps of Pests* (18 a year), bibliographies and monographs.

International Institute of Parasitology: 395A Hatfield Rd, St Albans, Herts, AL4 0XU; tel. (1727) 833151; telex 93121-02254; fax (1727) 868721; e-mail cabi-iip@cabi.org; f. 1929; conducts taxonomic and applied research on helminths (parasitic worms), particularly those of economic and medical importance, and on plant parasitic nematodes; provides advisory services and training. Dir Dr W. HOMINICK.

International Mycological Institute: Bakeham Lane, Egham, Surrey, TW20 9TY; tel. (1784) 470111; fax (1784) 470909; e-mail imi@cabi.org; f. 1920 for the collection and dissemination of information on the fungal, bacterial, virus and physiological disorders of plants; on opportunistic fungal diseases of man and animals; and on the taxonomy of fungi; undertakes identifications of fungi and plant pathogenic bacteria from all over the world; incorporates major collection of fungus cultures and a biodeterioration, industrial and environmental services centre; specializes in the areas of biodiversity, crop protection and industrial and environmental development; consultancy services, especially in industrial and environmental mycology, food spoilage by fungi, bacteria and yeasts, and surveys of plant diseases; holds training courses in the United Kingdom and in other countries. Dir Prof. D. L. HAWKSWORTH. Publs *Index of Fungi* (2 a year), *Mycological Papers* (4 or 5 a year), *Phytopathological Papers* (irregular), *Descriptions of Fungi and Bacteria* (4 sets a year), *Bibliography of Systematic Mycology* (2 a year), *Systema Ascomycetum* (2 a year), books on mycology and plant pathology.

Commonwealth Forestry Association: c/o Oxford Forestry Institute, South Parks Rd, Oxford, OX1 3RB; tel. (1865) 275072; fax (1865) 275074; f. 1921; produces, collects and circulates information relating to world forestry and the utilization of forest products and services and provides a means of communication in the Commonwealth and other interested countries. Mems: 1,500. Chair. Dr J. S. MAINI. Publs *Commonwealth Forestry Review* (quarterly), *Commonwealth Forestry Handbook.*

Standing Committee on Commonwealth Forestry: Forestry Commission, 231 Corstorphine Rd, Edinburgh, EH12 7AT; tel. (131) 314-6137; fax (131) 334-0442; e-mail libby.jones@forestry.gov.uk; f. 1923 to provide continuity between Confs, and to provide a forum for discussion on any forestry matters of common interest to mem. govts which may be brought to the Cttee's notice by any member country or organization; c. 50 mems. 1997 Conference: Victoria Falls, Zimbabwe. Sec. LIBBY JONES. Publ. *Newsletter* (quarterly).

COMMONWEALTH STUDIES

Institute of Commonwealth Studies: 28 Russell Sq., London, WC1B 5DS; tel. (171) 580-5876; fax (171) 255-2160; e-mail rowenak@sas.ac.uk; f. 1949 to promote advanced study of the Commonwealth; provides a library and meeting place for postgraduate students and academic staff engaged in research in this field; offers postgraduate teaching. Incorporates the Sir Robert Menzies Centre for Australian Studies. Dir Prof. JAMES MANOR; (from 1 January 1998) PAT CAPLIN; Publs *Annual Report, Collected Seminar Papers, Newsletter, Theses in Progress in Commonwealth Studies.*

COMMUNICATIONS

Commonwealth Telecommunications Organization: Clareville House, 26–27 Oxendon St, London, SW1Y 4EL; tel. (171) 930-5516; telex 27328; fax (171) 930-4248; e-mail info@cto.int; f. 1967; aims to enhance the development of telecommunications in Commonwealth countries and contribute to the communications infrastructure required for economic and social devt, through a devt and training programme. Exec. Dir Dr DAVID SOUTER. Publ. *CTO Briefing* (quarterly).

EDUCATION AND CULTURE

Association of Commonwealth Universities (ACU): John Foster House, 36 Gordon Sq., London, WC1H 0PF; tel. (171) 387-8572; fax (171) 387-2655; e-mail pubinf@acu.ac.uk; f. 1913; holds major meetings of Commonwealth universities and their representatives; publishes factual information about Commonwealth universities and access to them; acts as a general information centre and provides an appointments service; hosts a management consultancy service; supplies secretariats for the Commonwealth Scholarship Comm. in the United Kingdom and the Marshall Aid Commemoration Comm.; administers various other fellowship and scholarship programmes. Mems: 452 universities in 36 Commonwealth countries or regions. Sec.-Gen. Prof. MICHAEL GIBBONS. Publs include: *Commonwealth Universities Yearbook, Checklist of University Institutions in the Commonwealth, ACU Bulletin of Current Documentation* (5 a year), *ACU: What it is and what it does* (annually), *Report of the Council of the ACU* (annually), *Quinquennial Report of the Secretary General to the Commonwealth Universities Congress, Awards for University Teachers and Research Workers* (every 2 years), *Awards for Postgraduate Study at Commonwealth Universities* (every 2 years), *Awards for First Degree Study at Commonwealth Universities* (every 2 years), *Awards for University Administrators and Librarians* (every 2 years), *Who's Who of Commonwealth University Vice-Chancellors, Presidents and Rectors of Commonwealth Universities, Appointments in Commonwealth Universities*, Student Information Papers (study abroad series).

Commonwealth Association for Education in Journalism and Communication—CAEJAC: c/o Faculty of Law, University of Western Ontario, London N6A 3K7, Canada; tel. (519) 6613348; fax (519) 6613790; e-mail caejc@julian.uwo.ca; f. 1985; aims to foster high standards of journalism and communication education and research in Commonwealth countries and to promote co-operation among institutions and professions. c. 700 mems in 32 Commonwealth countries. Pres. Prof. SYED ARABI IDID (Malaysia); Sec. Prof. ROBERT MARTIN. Publ. *CAEJAC Journal* (annually).

Commonwealth Association of Science, Technology and Mathematics Educators—CASTME: c/o Education Dept, Human Resource Development Division, Commonwealth Secretariat, Marlborough House, Pall Mall, London, SW1Y 5HX; tel. (171) 747-6282; telex 27678; fax (171) 747-6287; f. 1974; special emphasis is given to the social significance of education in these subjects. Organizes an Awards Scheme to promote effective teaching and learning in these subjects, and biennial regional seminars. Pres. (vacant); Hon. Sec. Dr VED GOEL. Publ. *CASTME Journal* (quarterly).

Commonwealth Council for Educational Administration: c/o International Educational Leadership and Management Centre, School of Management, Lincoln University Campus, Brayford Pool, Lincoln, LN6 7TS; tel. (1522) 886071; fax (1522) 886023; f. 1970; aims to foster quality in professional development and links among educational administrators; holds nat. and regional confs, as well as visits and seminars. Mems: 60 affiliated groups representing 7,000 persons. Pres. Prof. ANGELA THODY. Publs *Newsletter* (quarterly), *International Directions in Education* (3 a year), *International Studies in Educational Administration* (2 a year).

Commonwealth Institute: Kensington High St, London, W8 6NQ; tel. (171) 603-4535; fax (171) 602-7374; e-mail info@commonwealth.org.uk; f. 1893 as the Imperial Institute; the centre for Commonwealth education and culture in the United Kingdom, the Inst. houses an Education Centre, a Commonwealth Resource and Literature Library and a Conference and Events Centre; organizes visual arts exhbns; 'Commonwealth Experience' opened in 1997. Dir-Gen. DAVID FRENCH.

Commonwealth Music Association: temporarily suspended.

League for the Exchange of Commonwealth Teachers: 7 Lion Yard, Tremadoc Rd, London, SW4 7NQ; tel. (171) 498-1101; fax (171) 720-5403; f. 1901; promotes educational exchanges for a period of one year between teachers in Australia, the Bahamas, Barbados, Bermuda, Canada, Guyana, India, Jamaica, Kenya, Malawi, New Zealand, Pakistan, South Africa and Trinidad and Tobago. Dir PATRICIA SWAIN. Publs *Annual Report, Exchange Teacher* (annually), *Commonwealth Times* (2 a year).

HEALTH

Commonwealth Medical Association: BMA House, Tavistock Sq., London, WC1H 9JP; tel. (171) 383-6095; fax (171) 383-6195; e-mail 72242.3544@compuserve.com; f. 1962 for the exchange of information; provision of tech. co-operation and advice; formulation and maintenance of a code of ethics; provision of continuing medical education; devt and promotion of health education programmes; and liaison with WHO and the UN on health issues; meetings of its Council are held every three years. Mems: medical asscns in Commonwealth countries. Dir MARIANNE HASLEGRAVE; Sec. Dr J. D. J. HAVARD. Publ. *CommonHealth* (quarterly bulletin).

Commonwealth Pharmaceutical Association: 1 Lambeth High St, London, SE1 7JN; tel. (171) 735-9141; telex 93121131542; fax (171) 582-3401; f. 1970 to promote the interests of pharmaceutical sciences and the profession of pharmacy in the Commonwealth; to maintain high professional standards, encourage links between members and the creation of nat. asscns; and to facilitate the dissemination of information. Holds confs (every four years) and regional meetings. Mems: 39 pharmaceutical asscns. Sec. PHILIP E. GREEN. Publ. *Quarterly Newsletter*.

Commonwealth Society for the Deaf: 134 Buckingham Palace Rd, London, SW1W 9SA; tel. (171) 259-0200; fax (171) 259-0300; promotes the health, education and general welfare of the deaf in developing Commonwealth countries; encourages and assists the development of educational facilities, the training of teachers of the deaf, and the provision of support for parents of deaf children; organizes visits by volunteer specialists to developing countries; provides audiological equipment and organises the training of audiological maintenance technicians; conducts research into the causes and prevention of deafness. CEO Brig. J. A. Davis. Publ. *Annual Report*.

Sight Savers International (Royal Commonwealth Society for the Blind): Grosvenor Hall, Bolnore Rd, Haywards Heath, West Sussex, RH16 4BX; tel. (1444) 412424; fax (1444) 415866; e-mail information@sightsaversint.org.uk; f. 1950 to prevent blindness and restore sight in developing countries, and to provide education and community-based training for incurably blind people; operates in collaboration with local partners, with high priority given to training local staff; Chair. DAVID THOMPSON; Dir RICHARD PORTER. Publ. *Horizons* (newsletter, 3 a year).

INFORMATION AND THE MEDIA

Commonwealth Broadcasting Association: Rm 312, BBC Yalding House, 152-156 Great Portland St, London, W1N 6AJ; tel. (171) 765-5151; fax (171) 765-5152; e-mail cba@bbc.co.uk; f. 1945; gen. confs are held every two years. Mems: 63 nat. public service broadcasting orgs in 53 Commonwealth countries. Pres. Dato' JAAGAR KAMIN; Sec.-Gen. ELIZABETH SMITH. Publs *COMBROAD* (quarterly), *Who's Who in Public Service Broadcasting in the Commonwealth—the Handbook of the CBA* (annually).

Commonwealth Institute: see under Education.

Commonwealth Journalists' Association: 17 Nottingham St, London, W1M 3RD; tel. (171) 486-3844; fax (171) 486-3822; f. 1978 to promote co-operation between journalists in Commonwealth countries, organize training facilities and confs, and foster understanding among Commonwealth peoples. Pres. MURRAY BURT; Exec. Dir LAWRIE BREEN.

Commonwealth Press Union (Association of Commonwealth Newspapers, News Agencies and Periodicals): 17 Fleet St, London, EC4Y 1AA; tel. (171) 583-7733; fax (171) 583-6868; e-mail 106156.3331@compuserve.com; f. 1950; promotes the welfare of the Commonwealth press by defending its freedom and providing training for journalists; organizes biennial confs. Mems: c. 1,000 newspapers, news agencies, periodicals in 42 Commonwealth countries. Pres. Sir DAVID ENGLISH; Dir ROBIN MACKICHAN. Publs *CPU News, Annual Report*.

LAW

Commonwealth Lawyers' Association: c/o The Law Society, 114 Chancery Lane, London, WC2A 1PL; tel. (171) 242-1222; telex 261203; fax (171) 831-0057; e-mail karen.brewer@lawsociety.org.uk; f. 1983 (fmrly the Commonwealth Legal Bureau); seeks to maintain and promote the rule of law throughout the Commonwealth, by ensuring that the people of the Commonwealth are served by an independent and efficient legal profession; upholds professional standards and promotes the availability of legal services; assists in organizing the triennial Commonwealth law confs. Pres. RODNEY HANSEN; Exec. Sec. JONATHAN GOLDSMITH. Publs. *The Commonwealth Lawyer*.

Commonwealth Legal Advisory Service: c/o British Institute of International and Comparative Law, Charles Clore House, 17 Russell Sq., London, WC1B 5DR; tel. (171) 636-5802; fax (171) 323-2016; e-mail bicl@dial.pipex.com; financed by the British Institute and by contributions from Commonwealth govts; provides research facilities for Commonwealth govts and law reform commissions. Legal Sec. Dr DEREK OBADINA.

Commonwealth Legal Education Association: Legal Division, Commonwealth Secretariat, Marlborough House, Pall Mall, London, SW1Y 5HX; tel. (171) 747-6410; fax (171) 930-0827; e-mail biicl@bbcnc.org.uk; f. 1971 to promote contacts and exchanges and to provide information. Gen. Sec. JOHN HATCHARD. Publs *Commonwealth Legal Education Association Newsletter* (2 a year), *Directory of Commonwealth Law Schools* (annually).

Commonwealth Magistrates' and Judges' Association: 10 Duke St, London, W1M 5AA; tel. (171) 487-2886; fax (171) 487-4386; f. 1970 to advance the administration of the law by promoting the independence of the judiciary, to further education in law and crime prevention and to disseminate information; confs and study tours; corporate membership for asscns of the judiciary or courts of limited jurisdiction; assoc. membership for individuals. Pres. Chief Justice KIPLING DOUGLAS; Sec.-Gen.VIVIENNE CHIN. Publ. *Commonwealth Judicial Journal* (2 a year).

PARLIAMENTARY AFFAIRS

Commonwealth Parliamentary Association: Suite 700, Westminster House, 7 Millbank, London, SW1P 3JA; tel. (171) 799-1460; fax (171) 222-6073; e-mail hq.sec@comparlas.co.uk; f. 1911 to promote understanding and co-operation between Commonwealth parliamentarians; organization: Exec. Cttee of 32 MPs responsible to annual Gen. Assembly; 139 brs throughout the Commonwealth; holds annual Commonwealth Parliamentary Confs and seminars; also regional confs and seminars; Sec.-Gen. ARTHUR DONAHOE. Publ. *The Parliamentarian* (quarterly).

PROFESSIONAL AND INDUSTRIAL RELATIONS

Commonwealth Association of Architects: 66 Portland Place, London, W1N 4AD; tel. (171) 636-8276; fax (171) 636-5472; f. 1964; an asscn of 39 socs of architects in various Commonwealth countries. Objects: to facilitate the reciprocal recognition of professional qualifications; to provide a clearing house for information on architectural practice, and to encourage collaboration. Plenary confs every three years; regional confs are also held. Exec. Dir GEORGE WILSON. Publs *Handbook, Objectives and Procedures: CAA Schools Visiting Boards, Architectural Education in the Commonwealth* (annotated bibliography of research), *CAA Newsnet* (3 a year), a survey and list of schools of architecture.

Commonwealth Association for Public Administration and Management—CAPAM: 1075 Bay St, Suite 402, Toronto, M5S 2B1, Canada; tel. (416) 920-3337; fax (416) 920-6574; e-mail 103350.3543@compuserve.com; f. 1994; aims to promote sound management of the public sector in Commonwealth countries and to assist those countries undergoing political or financial reforms. An awards scheme to reward innovation within the public sector was to be established in 1997. Pres. AHMAD SARJI (Malaysia); Exec. Dir ART STEVENSON (Canada).

Commonwealth Foundation: Marlborough House, Pall Mall, London, SW1Y 5HY; tel. (171) 930-3783; telex 27678; fax (171) 839-8157; f. 1966 to serve, support and link the 'unofficial' Commonwealth. The Foundation encourages development, knowledge, linkage and exchange within the Commonwealth, through the provision of grants to groups and individuals in the non-governmental, professional and cultural sectors. Awards an annual Commonwealth Writers' Prize. Funds are provided by Commonwealth govts. Chair. DONALD O. MILLS (Jamaica); Dir Dr HUMAYUN KHAN (Pakistan).

Commonwealth Trade Union Council: Congress House, 23–28 Great Russell St, London, WC1B 3LS; tel. (171) 631-0728; fax (171) 436-0301; e-mail ctuc-london@geo2.poptel.org.uk; f. 1979 to promote the interests of workers in the Commonwealth and encourage the development of trades unions in developing countries of the Commonwealth; provides assistance for training. Dir ARTHUR J. JOHNSTONE (United Kingdom). Publ. *Annual Report*.

SCIENCE AND TECHNOLOGY

Commonwealth Engineers' Council: c/o Institution of Civil Engineers, 1–7 Great George St, London, SW1P 3AA; tel. (171) 222-7722; fax (171) 222-7500; f. 1946; the Conf. meets every two years to provide an opportunity for engineering institutions of Commonwealth countries to exchange views on collaboration; there is a standing cttee on engineering education and training; organizes seminars on related topics. Sec. J. A. WHITWELL.

Commonwealth Geological Surveys Consultative Group: c/o Commonwealth Science Council, CSC Earth Sciences Programme, Marlborough House, Pall Mall, London, SW1Y 5HX; tel. (171) 839-3411; telex 27678; fax (171) 930-0827; f. 1948 to promote collaboration in geological, geochemical, geophysical and remote sensing techniques and the exchange of information. Geological Programme Officer Dr SIYAN MALOMO; Publ. *Earth Sciences Newsletter*.

Commonwealth Partnership for Technology Management—CPTM: 14 Queen Anne's Gate, London, SW1H 9AA; tel. (171) 222–3773; fax (171) 930–1543; e-mail 100740.1652@compuserve.com; f. 1995 to succeed the Commonwealth Consultative Group on Technology Management; provides a forum for greater co-operation and partnerships between the private and public sectors, in order to strengthen national capabilities in the management and use of technology; provides advisory services to mem. govts; Chair. Dr OMAR ABDUL RAHMAN.

SPORT

Commonwealth Games Federation: Walkden House, 3–10 Melton St, London, NW1 2EB; tel. (171) 383-5596; telex 9199156; fax (171) 383-5506; the Games were first held in 1930 and are now held every four years; participation is limited to competitors representing the mem. countries of the Commonwealth; held in Victoria, Canada, in 1994 and to be held in Kuala Lumpur, Malaysia, in 1998. Mems: 68 affiliated bodies. Chair. MICHAEL FENNELL; Hon. Sec. DAVID DIXON.

YOUTH

Commonwealth Youth Exchange Council: 7 Lion Yard, Tremadoc Rd, London, SW4 7NQ; tel. (171) 498-6151; fax (171) 720-5403; f. 1970; promotes contact between groups of young people of the United Kingdom and other Commonwealth countries by means of educational exchange visits, provides information for organizers and allocates grants; 198 mem. orgs. Dir V. S. G. CRAGGS. Publs *Contact* (handbook), *Exchange* (newsletter), *Safety and Welfare* (guidelines for Commonwealth Youth Exchange groups).

Duke of Edinburgh's Award International Association: Award House, 7-11 St Matthew St, London, SW1P 2JT; tel. (171) 222-4242; fax (171) 222-4141; e-mail sect@intaward.org; f. 1956; offers a programme of leisure activities for young people, comprising service, expeditions, sport and skills; operates in more than 90 countries (not confined to the Commonwealth). International Sec.-Gen. PAUL ARENGO-JONES. Publs *Award World* (2 a year), *Annual Report*, handbooks and guides.

MISCELLANEOUS

British Commonwealth Ex-Services League: 48 Pall Mall, London, SW1Y 5JG; tel. (171) 973-7263; fax (171) 973-7308; links the ex-service organizations in the Commonwealth, assists ex-servicemen of the Crown and their dependants who are resident abroad; holds triennial confs. Grand Pres. HRH The Duke of EDINBURGH; Sec.-Gen. Lt-Col S. POPE.. Publ. *Annual Report*.

Commonwealth Countries League: 14 Thistleworth Close, Isleworth, Middlesex, TW7 4QQ; tel. (181) 737-3572; fax (181) 568-2495; f. 1925 to secure equal opportunities and status between men and women in the Commonwealth, to act as a link between Commonwealth women's orgs, and to promote and finance secondary education of disadvantaged girls of high ability in their own countries, through the CCL Educational Fund; holds meetings with speakers and an annual Conf., organizes the annual Commonwealth Fair for fund-raising; individual mems and affiliated socs in the Commonwealth. Sec.-Gen. SHEILA O'REILLY. Publ. *CCL Newsletter* (3 a year).

Commonwealth War Graves Commission: 2 Marlow Rd, Maidenhead, Berks, SL6 7DX; tel. (1628) 34221; telex 847526; fax (1628) 771208; f. 1917 (as Imperial War Graves Commission); provides for the marking and permanent care of the graves of Commonwealth Forces casualties in the wars of 1914–18 and 1939–45; maintains over 1.5m. graves in 147 countries and commemorates by name on memorials more than 760,000 who have no known grave or who were cremated. Mems: Australia, Canada, India, New Zealand, South Africa, United Kingdom. Pres. HRH The Duke of KENT; Dir-Gen. D. KENNEDY.

Joint Commonwealth Societies' Council: c/o Royal Commonwealth Society, 18 Northumberland Ave, London, WC2N 5BJ; tel. (171) 930-6733; fax (171) 930-9705; e-mail 106167.365@compuserve.com; f. 1947; provides a forum for the exchange of information regarding activities of mem. orgs which promote understanding among countries of the Commonwealth; co-ordinates the distribution of the Commonwealth Day message by Queen Elizabeth; produces educational materials about the Commonwealth; mems: 16 unofficial Commonwealth organizations and four official bodies. Chair. Sir PETER MARSHALL; Sec. HELEN TRIDGELL.

Royal Commonwealth Society: 18 Northumberland Ave, London, WC2N 5BJ; tel. (171) 930-6733; fax (171) 930-9705; e-mail 106167.371@compuserve.com; f. 1868; to promote international understanding of the Commonwealth and its people; information service; library housed by Cambridge University Library. Chair. Sir MICHAEL MCWILLIAM; Sec.-Gen. Sir DAVID THORNE. Publs *Annual Report, Newsletter* (3 a year).

Royal Over-Seas League: Over-Seas House, Park Place, St James's St, London, SW1A 1LR; tel. (171) 408-0214; telex 268995; fax (171) 499-6738; f. 1910 to promote friendship and understanding in the Commonwealth; club houses in London and Edinburgh; membership is open to all British subjects and Commonwealth citizens. Chair. Sir GEOFFREY ELLERTON; Dir-Gen. ROBERT F. NEWELL. Publ. *Overseas* (quarterly).

Victoria League for Commonwealth Friendship: 55 Leinster Square, London W2 4PW; tel. (171) 243-2633; fax (171) 229-2994; f. 1901; aims to further personal friendship among Commonwealth peoples and to provide hospitality for visitors; maintains Student House, providing accommodation for students from Commonwealth countries; has brs elsewhere in the UK and abroad. Pres. HRH Princess MARGARET, Countess of SNOWDON; Chair. COLIN WEBBER; Gen. Sec. JOHN ALLAN. Publ. *Annual Report*.

Declaration of Commonwealth Principles

Agreed by the Commonwealth Heads of Government Meeting at Singapore, 22 January 1971.

The Commonwealth of Nations is a voluntary association of independent sovereign states, each responsible for its own policies, consulting and co-operating in the common interests of their peoples and in the promotion of international understanding and world peace.

Members of the Commonwealth come from territories in the six continents and five oceans, include peoples of different races, languages and religions, and display every stage of economic development from poor developing nations to wealthy industrialized nations. They encompass a rich variety of cultures, traditions and institutions.

Membership of the Commonwealth is compatible with the freedom of member-governments to be non-aligned or to belong to any other grouping, association or alliance. Within this diversity all members of the Commonwealth hold certain principles in common. It is by pursuing these principles that the Commonwealth can continue to influence international society for the benefit of mankind.

We believe that international peace and order are essential to the security and prosperity of mankind; we therefore support the United Nations and seek to strengthen its influence for peace in the world, and its efforts to remove the causes of tension between nations.

We believe in the liberty of the individual, in equal rights for all citizens regardless of race, colour, creed or political belief, and in their inalienable right to participate by means of free and democratic political processes in framing the society in which they live. We therefore strive to promote in each of our countries those representative institutions and guarantees for personal freedom under the law that are our common heritage.

We recognize racial prejudice as a dangerous sickness threatening the healthy development of the human race and racial discrimination as an unmitigated evil of society. Each of us will vigorously combat this evil within our own nation.

No country will afford to regimes which practise racial discrimination assistance which in its own judgment directly contributes to the pursuit or consolidation of this evil policy. We oppose all forms of colonial domination and racial oppression and are committed to the principles of human dignity and equality.

We will therefore use all our efforts to foster human equality and dignity everywhere, and to further the principles of self-determination and non-racialism.

We believe that the wide disparities in wealth now existing between different sections of mankind are too great to be tolerated. They also create world tensions. Our aim is their progressive removal. We therefore seek to use our efforts to overcome poverty, ignorance and disease, in raising standards of life and achieving a more equitable international society.

To this end our aim is to achieve the freest possible flow of international trade on terms fair and equitable to all, taking into account the special requirements of the developing countries, and to encourage the flow of adequate resources, including governmental and private resources, to the developing countries, bearing in mind the importance of doing this in a true spirit of partnership and of establishing for this purpose in the developing countries conditions which are conducive to sustained investment and growth.

We believe that international co-operation is essential to remove the causes of war, promote tolerance, combat injustice, and secure development among the peoples of the world. We are convinced that the Commonwealth is one of the most fruitful associations for these purposes.

In pursuing these principles the members of the Commonwealth believe that they can provide a constructive example of the multi-national approach which is vital to peace and progress in the modern world. The association is based on consultation, discussion and co-operation.

In rejecting coercion as an instrument of policy they recognize that the security of each member state from external aggression is a matter of concern to all members. It provides many channels for continuing exchanges of knowledge and views on professional, cultural, economic, legal and political issues among member states.

These relationships we intend to foster and extend, for we believe that our multi-national association can expand human understanding and understanding among nations, assist in the elimination of discrimination based on differences of race, colour or creed, maintain and strengthen personal liberty, contribute to the enrichment of life for all, and provide a powerful influence for peace among nations.

The Lusaka Declaration on Racism and Racial Prejudice

The Declaration, adopted by Heads of Government in 1979, includes the following statements:

United in our desire to rid the world of the evils of racism and racial prejudice, we proclaim our faith in the inherent dignity and worth of the human person and declare that:

(i) the peoples of the Commonwealth have the right to live freely in dignity and equality, without any distinction or exclusion based on race, colour, sex, descent, or national or ethnic origin;

(ii) while everyone is free to retain diversity in his or her culture and lifestyle this diversity does not justify the perpetuation of racial prejudice or racially discriminatory practices;

(iii) everyone has the right to equality before the law and equal justice under the law; and

(iv) everyone has the right to effective remedies and protection against any form of discrimination based on the grounds of race, colour, sex, descent, or national or ethnic origin.

We reject as inhuman and intolerable all policies designed to perpetuate apartheid, racial segregation or other policies based on theories that racial groups are or may be inherently superior or inferior.

We reaffirm that it is the duty of all the peoples of the Commonwealth to work together for the total eradication of the infamous policy of apartheid which is internationally recognized as a crime against the conscience and dignity of mankind and the very existence of which is an affront to humanity.

We agree that everyone has the right to protection against acts of incitement to racial hatred and discrimination, whether committed by individuals, groups or other organizations. . . .

Inspired by the principles of freedom and equality which characterise our association, we accept the solemn duty of working together to eliminate racism and racial prejudice. This duty involves the acceptance of the principle that positive measures may be required to advance the elimination of racism, including assistance to those struggling to rid themselves and their environment of the practice.

Being aware that legislation alone cannot eliminate racism and racial prejudice, we endorse the need to initiate public information and education policies designed to promote understanding, tolerance, respect and friendship among peoples and racial groups. . . .

We note that racism and racial prejudice, wherever they occur, are significant factors contributing to tension between nations and thus inhibit peaceful progress and development. We believe that the goal of the eradication of racism stands as a critical priority for governments of the Commonwealth committed as they are to the promotion of the ideals of peaceful and happy lives for their people.

Harare Commonwealth Declaration

The following are the major points of the Declaration adopted by Heads of Government at the meeting held in Harare, Zimbabwe, in 1991:

Having reaffirmed the principles to which the Commonwealth is committed, and reviewed the problems and challenges which the world, and the Commonwealth as part of it, face, we pledge the Commonwealth and our countries to work with renewed vigour, concentrating especially in the following areas: the protection and promotion of the fundamental political values of the Commonwealth; equality for women, so that they may exercise their full and equal rights; provision of universal access to education for the population of our countries; continuing action to bring about the end of apartheid and the establishment of a free, democratic, non-racial and prosperous South Africa; the promotion of sustainable development and the alleviation of poverty in the countries of the Commonwealth; extending the benefits of development within a framework of respect for human rights; the protection of the environment through respect for the principles of sustainable development which we enunciated at Langkawi; action to combat drugs trafficking and abuse and communicable diseases; help for small Commonwealth states in tackling their particular economic and security problems; and support of the United Nations and other international institutions in the world's search for peace, disarmament and effective arms control; and in the promotion of international consensus on major global political, economic and social issues.

To give weight and effectiveness to our commitments we intend to focus and improve Commonwealth co-operation in these areas. This would include strengthening the capacity of the Commonwealth to respond to requests from members for assistance in entrenching the practices of democracy, accountable administration and the rule of law.

In reaffirming the principles of the Commonwealth and in committing ourselves to pursue them in policy and action in response to the challenges of the 1990s, in areas where we believe that the Commonwealth has a distinctive contribution to offer, we the Heads of Government express our determination to renew and enhance the value and importance of the Commonwealth as an institution which can and should strengthen and enrich the lives not only of its own members and their peoples but also of the wider community of peoples of which they are a part.

ECONOMIC COMMUNITY OF WEST AFRICAN STATES—ECOWAS

Address: Secretariat Bldg, Asokoro, Abuja, Nigeria.

Telephone: (9) 5231858; **fax:** (9) 2637052.

The Treaty of Lagos, establishing ECOWAS, was signed in May 1975 by 15 states, with the object of promoting trade, co-operation and self-reliance in West Africa. Outstanding protocols bringing certain key features of the Treaty into effect were ratified in November 1976. Cape Verde joined in 1977. A revised ECOWAS treaty, designed to accelerate economic integration and to increase political co-operation, was drafted in 1991–92, and was signed in July 1993 (see below).

MEMBERS

Benin	Guinea	Niger
Burkina Faso	Guinea-Bissau	Nigeria
Cape Verde	Liberia	Senegal
Côte d'Ivoire	Mali	Sierra Leone
The Gambia	Mauritania	Togo
Ghana		

Organization

(July 1997)

CONFERENCE OF HEADS OF STATE AND GOVERNMENT

The Conference, the highest authority of ECOWAS, meets once a year. The Chairman is drawn from the member states in turn.

COUNCIL OF MINISTERS

The Council consists of two representatives from each country; a chairman is drawn from each country in turn. It meets twice a year, and is responsible for the running of the Community.

TRIBUNAL

The treaty provides for a Community Tribunal, whose composition and competence are determined by the Authority of Heads of State and Government; it interprets the provisions of the treaty and settles disputes between member states that are referred to it.

EXECUTIVE SECRETARIAT

The Executive Secretary is elected for a four-year term, which may be renewed once only.

Executive Secretary: EDOUARD E. BENJAMIN (Guinea).

SPECIALIZED COMMISSIONS

There are six commissions:

(i) Trade, Customs, Immigration, Monetary and Payments;
(ii) Industry, Agriculture and Natural Resources;
(iii) Transport, Communications and Energy;
(iv) Social and Cultural Affairs;
(v) Administration and finance;
(vi) Information.

ECOWAS FUND FOR CO-OPERATION, COMPENSATION AND DEVELOPMENT

Address: BP 2704, blvd du 13 Janvier, Lomé, Togo.

Telephone: 216864; **telex:** 5339; **fax:** 218684.

The Fund is administered by a Board of Directors. The chief executive of the Fund is the Managing Director, who holds office for a renewable term of four years. There is a staff of 100. The authorized capital of the Fund is US $500m., of which $100m. has been called up, and $68.5m. is paid up (Oct. 1994). In 1988 agreements were reached with the African Development Bank and the Islamic Development Bank on the co-financing of projects and joint training of staff. Efforts are currently being undertaken to enhance the Fund's financial resources, by opening its capital to non-regional participants.

Managing Director: SAMUEL KYE APEA (Ghana).

Activities

ECOWAS aims to promote co-operation and development in economic, social and cultural activity, particularly in the fields for which specialized commissions (see above) are appointed, to raise the standard of living of the people of the member countries, increase and maintain economic stability, improve relations among member countries and contribute to the progress and development of Africa.

The treaty provides for compensation for states whose import duties are reduced through trade liberalization and contains a clause permitting safeguard measures in favour of any country affected by economic disturbances through the application of the treaty.

The treaty also contains a commitment to abolish all obstacles to the free movement of people, services and capital, and to promote: harmonization of agricultural policies; common projects in marketing, research and the agriculturally based industries; joint development of economic and industrial policies and elimination of disparities in levels of development; and common monetary policies.

Lack of success in many of ECOWAS' aims has been attributed to the existence of numerous other intergovernmental organizations in the region (in particular the francophone Communauté économique de l'Afrique de l'ouest, replaced by the Union économique et monétaire ouest-africaine in 1994, q.v.) and to member governments' lack of commitment, shown by their reluctance to implement policies at the national level, their failure to provide the agreed financial resources (arrears in contributions were reported to total US $53m. at July 1996), and the absence of national links with the Secretariat. During the 1990s ECOWAS activities were increasingly dominated by its efforts to secure peace in Liberia (see below).

A revised treaty for the Community was drawn up by an ECOWAS Committee of Eminent Persons in 1991–92, and was signed at the ECOWAS summit conference that took place in Cotonou, Benin, in July 1993. The treaty, which was to extend economic and political co-operation among member states, designates the achievement of a common market and a single currency as economic objectives, while in the political sphere it envisages the establishment of a West African parliament, an economic and social council and an ECOWAS court of justice to replace the existing Tribunal and enforce Community decisions. The treaty also formally assigned the Community with the responsibility of preventing and settling regional conflicts. At the summit meeting, held in Abuja, Nigeria, in August 1994, ECOWAS heads of state and government signed a protocol agreement for the establishment of a regional parliament; however, no timetable was specified for this to be achieved. The meeting also adopted a Convention on Extradition of non-political offenders.

The 1995 summit meeting was held in Accra, Ghana, in late July. The final communiqué of the meeting recognized the efforts by member states to pursue sound economic management and structural adjustment policies and supported any further harmonization of the economies of member states. In particular, the meeting expressed concern at the civil conflicts in Liberia and Sierra Leone and their potentially adverse effect on peace and stability in the ECOWAS region. At the end of July the new ECOWAS treaty was reported to have entered into effect, having received the required number of ratifications.

TRADE AND MONETARY UNION

Elimination of tariffs and other obstructions to trade among member states, and the establishment of a common external tariff, were planned over a transitional period of 15 years. At the 1978 Conference of Heads of State and Government it was decided that from 28 May 1979 no member state might increase its customs tariff on goods from another member. This was regarded as the first step towards the abolition of customs duties within the Community. During the first two years import duties on intra-community trade were to be maintained, and then eliminated in phases over the next eight years. Quotas and other restrictions of equivalent effect were to be abolished in the first 10 years. In the remaining five years all differences between external customs tariffs were to be abolished.

The 1980 Conference of Heads of State and Government decided to establish a free trade area for unprocessed agricultural products and handicrafts from May 1981. Tariffs on industrial products made by specified community enterprises were also to be abolished from that date, but implementation was delayed by difficulties in defining the enterprises. From 1 January 1990 tariffs were lifted from 25 listed items manufactured in ECOWAS member states: by mid-1991 the number had increased to 90. Over the ensuing decade, tariffs on other industrial products were to be eliminated as follows: the 'most-developed' countries of ECOWAS (Côte d'Ivoire, Ghana, Nigeria and Senegal) were to abolish tariffs on 'priority' products within four years and on 'non-priority' products within six years; the second group (Benin, Guinea, Liberia, Sierra Leone and Togo) were to abolish tariffs on 'priority' products within six years, and on 'non-priority' products within eight years; and the 'least-developed' members (Burkina Faso, Cape Verde, The Gambia, Guinea-Bissau, Mali, Mauritania and Niger) were to abolish tariffs on 'priority' products within eight years and on 'non-priority' products within 10 years.

In 1990 the Conference of Heads of State and Government agreed to adopt measures that would create a single monetary zone and remove barriers to trade in goods that originated in the Community. ECOWAS regards monetary union as necessary to encourage investment in the region, since it would greatly facilitate capital transactions with foreign countries. In September 1992 it was announced that, as part of efforts to enhance monetary co-operation and financial harmonization in the region, the West African Clearing House (q.v.) was to be restructured as the West African Monetary Agency (WAMA). As a specialized agency of ECOWAS, WAMA was to be responsible for administering an ECOWAS exchange rate system (EERS) and for establishing the single monetary zone. A credit guarantee scheme and travellers' cheque system were to be established in association with the EERS. The agreement establishing WAMA was signed by the Governors of the central banks of ECOWAS member states, meeting in Banjul, The Gambia, in March 1996. In July, the heads of state or government of member countries agreed to impose a common value-added tax (VAT) on consumer goods, in order to rationalize indirect taxation and to stimulate greater intra-Community trade.

In December 1992 ECOWAS ministers agreed on the institutionalization of an ECOWAS trade fair, in order to promote trade liberalization and intra-Community trade. The first trade fair, which was held in Dakar, Senegal in May/June 1995, was attended by some 400 private businesses from the 16 member states. A second trade fair was scheduled to be held in Accra, Ghana, in February/March 1999.

TRAVEL, TRANSPORT AND COMMUNICATIONS

At the 1979 Conference of Heads of State a Protocol was signed relating to free circulation of the region's citizens and to rights of residence and establishment of commercial enterprises. The first provision (the right of entry without a visa) came into force in 1980. The second provision, allowing unlimited rights of residence, was signed in 1986 (although Nigeria indicated that unskilled workers and certain categories of professionals would not be allowed to stay for an indefinite period) and came into force in 1989. The third provision, concerning the right to establish a commercial enterprise in another member state was signed in 1990. In July 1992 the ECOWAS meeting of heads of state and government formulated a Minimum Agenda for Action for the implementation of Community agreements regarding the free movement of goods and people. Measures to be undertaken included removal of non-tariff barriers, the simplification of customs and transit procedures and a reduction in the number of control posts on international roads. By mid-1996 the ECOWAS summit meeting observed that few measures had been adopted by member states to implement the Minimum Agenda, and emphasized that it remained a central element of the Community's integration process. In April 1997 the Gambian and Senegalese finance and trade officials concluded an agreement on measures to facilitate the export of goods via Senegal to neighbouring countries, in accordance with ECOWAS protocols relating to inter-state road transit arrangements.

In August 1996 a programme to improve regional telecommunications was completed. Some US $35m. had been granted for project financing in eight ECOWAS countries.

A programme for the development of an integrated regional road network was adopted by the 1980 Conference. Under the programme two major trans-regional roads were to be completed: the Trans-Coastal Highway, linking Lagos, Nigeria, with Nouackchott, Mauritania (4,767 km); and the Trans-Sahelian Highway, linking Dakar, Senegal with N'Djamena, Chad (4,633 km). By mid-1993 about 88% of the trans-coastal route was complete, and about 78% of the trans-Sahelian route.

ECONOMIC AND INDUSTRIAL DEVELOPMENT

In November 1984 ECOWAS heads of state and government approved the establishment of a private regional investment bank, to be known as Ecobank Transnational Inc. The bank, which was based in Lomé, Togo, opened in March 1988. ECOWAS has a 10% share in the bank. By mid-1997 Ecobank affiliates were operating in Benin, Burkina Faso, Côte d'Ivoire, Ghana, Nigeria and Togo.

The West African Industrial Forum, sponsored by ECOWAS, is held every two years to promote regional industrial investment. The Secretariat is formulating a West African Industrial Master Plan. The first phase involved the compilation of an inventory of industrial enterprises, while the second phase was to comprise study of important industrial sub-sectors, prior to the drawing up of the Master Plan.

In September 1995 Nigeria, Ghana, Togo and Benin signed an agreement for the construction of a 400-km gas pipeline to connect Nigerian gas supplies to the other countries. The pipeline was expected to be completed in three years, under the management of a West African Pipeline Company.

DEFENCE

At the third Conference of Heads of State and Government a protocol of non-aggression was signed. Thirteen members signed a protocol on mutual defence assistance at the 1981 Conference. Member states reaffirmed their commitment to refrain from aggression against one another at a summit conference in 1991. In 1990 a Standing Mediation Committee was formed to mediate in disputes between member states. The revised ECOWAS treaty, signed in July 1993, incorporates a separate provision for regional security, requiring member states to work towards the maintenance of peace, stability and security.

In July 1990 ECOWAS ministers attempted to mediate in civil conflict in Liberia. In August an ECOWAS Cease-fire Monitoring Group (ECOMOG—initially comprising about 4,000 troops from The Gambia, Ghana, Guinea, Nigeria and Sierra Leone) was dispatched to Liberia in an attempt to enforce a cease-fire between the rival factions there, to restore public order, and to establish an interim government, until elections could be held. In November a temporary cease-fire was agreed by the protagonists in Liberia, and an interim president was installed by ECOMOG. Following the signature of a new cease-fire agreement a national conference, organized by ECOWAS in March 1991, established a temporary government, pending elections to be held in early 1992. In June 1991 ECOWAS established a five-member committee to co-ordinate the peace negotiations. In September, at a meeting in Yamoussoukro, Côte d'Ivoire, held under the aegis of the five-nation committee, two of the rival factions in Liberia agreed to encamp their troops in designated areas and to disarm under ECOMOG supervision. During the period preceding the proposed elections (due to take place in May 1992), ECOMOG was to occupy Liberian air and sea ports, and create a 'buffer zone' along the country's border with Sierra Leone. By September 1992, however, ECOMOG had been unable either to effect the disarmament of two of the principal military factions, the National Patriotic Front of Liberia (NPFL) and the United Liberation Movement of Liberia for Democracy (ULIMO), or to occupy positions in substantial areas of the country, as a result of resistance on the part of the NPFL. The proposed elections were consequently postponed indefinitely.

In October 1992 ECOMOG began offensive action against NPFL positions, with a campaign of aerial bombardment. In November ECOWAS imposed sanctions on the NPFL's territory, comprising a land, sea and air blockade, in response to the Front's refusal to comply with the Yamoussoukro accord of October 1991. In April 1993 ECOMOG announced that the disarmament of ULIMO had been completed, amid widespread accusations that ECOMOG had supported ULIMO against the NPFL, and was no longer a neutral force. An ECOWAS-brokered cease-fire agreement was signed in Cotonou, Benin, in late July, and took effect on 1 August. Under the agreement a neutral transitional government was to be formed, and there was to be a disarming of troops prior to the holding of fair and free elections, scheduled to take place in February 1994. In addition, ECOMOG was to be expanded. In September 1993 a 300-member UN observer mission (UNOMIL, q.v.) was established in Liberia to work alongside ECOMOG in monitoring the disarmament process, as well as to verify the impartiality of ECOMOG. In March 1994 a transitional executive council was installed (elections now were to be conducted in September); however, continued fighting prevented ECOMOG conducting its principal functions of disarming and demobilizing the conflicting parties, and made the prospect of conducting elections increasingly untenable.

In mid-September 1994 leaders of the country's main military factions, having negotiated with representatives of ECOWAS, the Organization of African Unity (OAU, q.v.) and the UN, signed an amendment to the Cotonou Agreement in Akosombo, Ghana. The agreement provided for a new five-member Council of State, in the context of a cease-fire, as a replacement to the expired interim executive authority, and established a new timetable for democratic elections. Also in mid-September a coup attempt by a dissident faction of the Armed Forces of Liberia (AFL) was thwarted by ECOMOG forces, which attacked the group occupying the Presidential Mansion and arrested several of its members. Negotiations for a peace settlement recommenced in November, in order to pursue the Akosombo agreement, with delegates from Liberia's six main armed factions, the OAU, the UN and African countries constituting ECOWAS' Ministerial Committee of Nine. The meeting was convened by the serving Chairman of ECOWAS, President Jerry Rawlings of Ghana, who insisted that it was a final effort on the part of the international community to secure peace in Liberia. In late December a new peace accord was signed by the main conflicting parties in Accra, Ghana. However, in early 1995 peace negotiations, conducted under ECOWAS auspices, collapsed, owing to disagreement on the composition of a new Council of State. In May, in an attempt to ease the political deadlock, ECOWAS heads of state and of government met leaders of the six main warring factions. The meeting, which was convened in Abuja, Nigeria, resolved that a greater commitment to the cease-fire and disarmament process needed to be demonstrated by all parties before the Council of State could be established. Under continuing pressure from the international community, the leaders of the Liberian factions signed a new peace accord, in Abuja, in August. This political development led to renewed efforts on the part of ECOWAS countries to strengthen ECOMOG. In September Burkina Faso agreed to send troops to join ECOMOG, and in October Nigeria, Ghana and Guinea pledged troop contributions to increase the force strength from 7,268 to 12,000. In accordance with the peace agreement, ECOMOG forces, with UNOMIL, were to be deployed throughout Liberia and along its borders to prevent the flow of arms into the country and to monitor the disarmament of the warring parties, estimated to total 60,000 troops. In December an attack on ECOMOG troops, by a dissident ULIMO faction, disrupted the deployment of the multinational forces and the disarmament process, which was scheduled to commence in mid-January 1996. At least 16 members of the peace-keeping force were killed in the fighting that ensued. Clashes between ECOMOG and the ULIMO–J forces continued in the west of the country in late December 1995 and early January 1996, during which time 130 Nigerian members of ECOMOG were held hostage. In April, following a series of violations of the cease-fire, serious hostilities erupted in the Liberian capital, Monrovia, between government forces and dissident troops (see chapter on Liberia). An initial agreement to end the fighting, negotiated under ECOWAS auspices, was unsuccessful; however, it secured the release of several civilians and soldiers who had been taken hostage during the civil disruption. Later in April a further cease-fire agreement was concluded, under the aegis of the US Government, the UN and ECOWAS. In May ministers of foreign affairs of the countries constituting the ECOWAS Committee of Nine on Liberia convened, in Accra, to consider the future of the peace process in Liberia. The Committee advocated that all armed factions be withdrawn from Monrovia and that ECOMOG troops be deployed throughout the capital in order to re-establish the city's 'safe-haven' status. According to the Committee's demands, all property, armaments and equipment seized unlawfully from civilians, ECOMOG and other international organizations during the fighting were to be returned, while efforts to disarm the warring factions and to pursue the restoration of democracy in the country were to be resumed. At the end of May the deployment of ECOMOG troops was initiated. In August a new cease-fire accord was signed by the leaders of the principal factions in Liberia, having been negotiated by the newly-appointed ECOWAS Chairman, President Abacha of Nigeria. The revised Abuja agreement envisaged the completion of the disarmament process by the end of January 1997, with elections to be held in May. However, there was a persisting concern, on the part of the UN and the ECOMOG commander, Victor Halu (who replaced Gen. John Inienger in July 1996), that a peace agreement could not be implemented without substantial assistance from the international community to strengthen the ECOMOG force. The disarmament process began in late November, and by the end of January 1997 the ECOMOG commander stated that 23,000 of the targeted 30,000-35,000 soldiers had been disarmed (the original estimate of 60,000 troops having been revised, disputed by both faction leaders and ECOMOG officials once movement between factions was taken into account). The deadline for disarmament was extended by seven days, during which time a further 1,500 soldiers were reported to have been disarmed. However, vigilante attacks by remaining armed faction fighters continued and were condemned by the ECOMOG commander. In February, at the end of a meeting of the Committee of Nine, it was announced that presidential and legislative elections would be held on 30 May. Chief Tom Ikimi, the Chairman of the Committee, stated that ECOMOG would withdraw from Liberia six months after the election date, until which time it had proposed to offer security for the incoming government and to provide training for a new unified Liberian army, which would assume ECOMOG's duties on its departure. The Committee also agreed, in consultation with the Council of State, to replace the existing Electoral Commission with a new Commission comprising seven members, to reflect all aspects of Liberian society. Four members were to be civilians while the remaining members were to represent the three main factions: the NPFL, the Liberia Peace Council (LPC) and ULIMO. The Chairman would be selected from among the seven, in consultation with ECOWAS, which along with the UN and the OAU, would act as a 'technical adviser' to the Commission. In May elections were rescheduled to be held on 19 July, in order to allow sufficient time for planning, and for the repatriation of refugees wishing to vote and the registration of voters. ECOMOG stated at the same time that following the deployment of additional troops and the provision of strengthened logistical support from the international community, it was envisaged that the July elections could be held in the necessary conditions of security.

On 25 May 1997 the democratically elected Sierra Leonean leader, President Ahmed Tejan Kabbah, was overthrown by a military coup involving officers of the national army and Revolutionary United Front (RUF) rebels. Nigerian forces based in Sierra Leone as part of a bilateral defence pact attempted to restore constitutional order. Their numbers were strengthened by the arrival of more than 700 Nigerian soldiers and two naval vessels which had been serving under the ECOMOG mandate in neighbouring Liberia. While the Nigerian Government insisted that the additional troops were acting as part of an ECOMOG operation, many commentators criticized the involvement of ECOMOG personnel in a Nigerian unilateral initiative, which they alleged had contradicted the humanitarian nature of the force's mandate. In early June the intervention of ECOMOG was supported by the UN and the OAU as well as the deposed President of Sierra Leone. On 2 June a naval bombardment of Freetown was launched from Nigerian naval vessels. At the end of that month ECOWAS ministers of foreign affairs convened in Conakry, Guinea, in an extraordinary meeting to consider the developments in Sierra Leone. The ministers agreed to pursue the objective of restoring a democratic government in Sierra Leone through dialogue, the imposition of economic sanctions, and, if necessary, by the use of military measures.

RURAL WATER RESOURCES

The ECOWAS programme for the development of village and pastoral water resources involves the creation of 3,200 water points throughout the region: 200 water points per member state. During the first phase of the programme (1992–96) attention was to be concentrated on the needs of the 10 member states most seriously affected or threatened by drought and desertification (Burkina Faso, Cape Verde, Guinea, Guinea Bissau, Mali, Mauritania, Niger, Nigeria, Senegal and Togo). By mid-1992 preparatory missions had been conducted in all of these member states. The first phase of the programme was expected to cost US $40.7m., with international donors to provide the necessary resources.

AGRICULTURE AND FISHING

An Agricultural Development Strategy was adopted in 1982, aiming at sub-regional self-sufficiency by the year 2000. The strategy included plans for selecting seeds and cattle species, and called for solidarity among member states during international commodity negotiations. Seven seed selection and multiplication centres and eight livestock-breeding centres were designated in 1984.

In February 1993 ECOWAS signed an agreement with the EC concerning a grant of US $9.6m. to help with the development of the fishing industry in the ECOWAS region over a five-year period.

In November 1995 an agro-industrial forum, jointly organized by ECOWAS and the European Union, was held in Dakar, Senegal. The forum aimed to facilitate co-operation between companies in the two regions, to develop the agro-industrial sector in west Africa and to promote business opportunities.

SOCIAL PROGRAMME

Four organizations have been established within ECOWAS by the Executive Secretariat: the Organization of Trade Unions of West Africa, which held its first meeting in 1984; the West African Youth Association; the West African Universities' Association; and the West Africa Women's Association (whose statutes were approved by a meeting of ministers of social affairs in May 1987). Regional sports competitions are held annually. In 1987 ECOWAS member states agreed to establish a West African Health Organization.

INFORMATION AND MEDIA

In March 1990 ECOWAS ministers of information formulated a policy on the dissemination of information about ECOWAS throughout the region and the appraisal of attitudes of its population towards the Community. The ministers established a new information commission. In November 1991 a conference on press communication and African integration, organized by ECOWAS, recommended the creation of an ECOWAS press card, judicial safeguards to protect journalists, training programmes for journalists and the establishment of a regional documentation centre and data bank. In November 1994 the commission of social and cultural affairs, meeting in Lagos, Nigeria, endorsed a series of measures to promote west African integration. These included special radio, television and newspaper features, sporting events and other competitions or rallies.

FINANCE

ECOWAS is financed by contributions from member states, although there is a poor record of punctual payment of dues, which has hampered the work of the Secretariat. Under the revised treaty,

ECOWAS was to receive revenue from a community tax, based on the total value of imports from member countries. In July 1996 the summit meeting approved a protocol on a community levy, providing for the imposition of a 0.5% tax on the value of imports from a third country. Member states were requested to ratify the protocol, in order to enable its application with effect from 1 January 1997.

The 1993 budget amounted to 4,135m. francs CFA (approximately US $14.9m.).

EUROPEAN UNION—THE LOMÉ CONVENTION

The European Union (EU) as a whole provides emergency humanitarian assistance for developing and other non-EU countries, amounting to ECU 211.4m. to African countries in 1995. However, the principal means of co-operation between the Community and developing countries is the Lomé Convention, concluded by the EU and African, Caribbean and Pacific (ACP) countries.

The First Lomé Convention (Lomé I), which came into force on 1 April 1976, replaced the Yaoundé Conventions and the Arusha Agreement, and was designed to provide a new framework of co-operation, taking into account the varying needs of developing countries. Lomé II was concluded at Lomé, Togo, in October 1979, and came into force on 1 January 1981. Lomé III was signed in December 1984, and came into force on 1 March 1985 (trade provisions) and 1 May 1986 (aid). The Fourth Lomé Convention, which had a 10-year commitment period, was signed in December 1989: its trade provisions entered into force on 1 March 1990, and the remainder followed in September 1991, while mid-term revisions were made in 1995. In mid-1997 71 ACP states were parties to the Convention including South Africa, which attained partial membership in April 1997.

SIGNATORY STATES

The European Union

Austria; Belgium; Denmark; Finland; France; Germany; Greece; Ireland; Italy; Luxembourg; Netherlands; Portugal; Spain; Sweden; United Kingdom.

African states adhering to the Convention

Angola; Benin; Botswana; Burkina Faso; Burundi; Cameroon; Cape Verde; Central African Republic; Chad; Comoros; The Democratic Republic of the Congo*; the Republic of Congo; Côte d'Ivoire; Djibouti; Equatorial Guinea; Eritrea; Ethiopia; Gabon; The Gambia; Ghana; Guinea; Guinea-Bissau; Kenya; Lesotho; Liberia; Madagascar; Malawi; Mali; Mauritania; Mauritius; Mozambique; Namibia; Niger; Nigeria; Rwanda; São Tomé and Príncipe; Senegal; Seychelles; Sierra Leone; Somalia†; South Africa‡; Sudan; Swaziland; Tanzania; Togo; Uganda; Zambia; Zimbabwe. There are also 15 Caribbean and eight Pacific signatories.

* Formerly known as Zaire.
† Has not ratified Lomé IV.
‡ Partial membership (see below).

Organization

ACP–EU INSTITUTIONS

Council of Ministers: one minister from each signatory state; one co-chairman from each of the two groups; meets annually; under the revised Lomé IV Convention the Council was to conduct an enlarged political dialogue.

Committee of Ambassadors: one ambassador from each signatory state; chairmanship alternates between the two groups; meets at least every six months.

Joint Assembly: EU and ACP are equally represented; attended by parliamentary delegates from each of the ACP countries and an equal number of members of the European Parliament; one co-chairman from each group; meets twice a year.

Centre for the Development of Industry—CDI: 52 ave Herrmann Debroux, 1160 Brussels, Belgium; tel. (2) 679-18-11; fax (2) 675-26-03; f. 1977 to encourage investment in the ACP states by providing contacts and advice, holding promotion meetings, and helping to finance feasibility studies; under the revised Lomé IV Convention, the CDI was to assist in the formulation of country-specific support programmes for industrial and private-sector development; Dir SURENDRA SHARMA.

Technical Centre for Agricultural and Rural Co-operation: Postbus 380, 6700 AJ Wageningen, Netherlands; tel. (317) 467100; telex 30169; fax (317) 460067; f. 1983 to provide ACP states with better access to information, research, training and innovations in agricultural development and extension; Dir Dr R. D. COOKE.

ACP INSTITUTIONS

ACP Council of Ministers.

ACP Committee of Ambassadors.

ACP Secretariat: ACP House, 451 ave Georges Henri, 1200 Brussels, Belgium; tel. (2) 743-06-00; telex 26558; fax (2) 735-55-73; Sec.-Gen. NG'ANDU PETER MAGANDE.

DELEGATIONS AND OFFICES OF THE EUROPEAN COMMISSION IN AFRICA SOUTH OF THE SAHARA

Angola: Rua Rainha Jinga 6, CP 6, Luanda; tel. (2) 303038; telex 3397; fax (2) 392531.

Benin: ave Roune, Bâtiment administratif, BP 910, Cotonou; tel. 31-26-84; telex 5257; fax 31-53-28.

Botswana: North Ring Rd, POB 1253, Gaborone; tel. 314455; telex 2403; fax 313626.

Burkina Faso: BP 352, Ouagadougou; tel. 30-37-85; telex 5242; fax 30-89-66.

Burundi: ave du 13 octobre, BP 103, Bujumbura; tel. (2) 23426; telex 5031; fax (2) 24612.

Cameroon: 105 rue 1770, quartier Bastos, BP 847, Yaoundé; tel. 20-13-87; fax 20-21-49.

Cape Verde: Achada de Santo António, CP 22, Praia, Santiago; tel. 61-55-71; telex 6071; fax 61-55-70.

Central African Republic: rue de Flandre, BP 1298, Bangui; tel. 61-30-53; telex 5231.

Chad: route de Farcha, BP 552, N'Djamena; tel. 52-89-77; telex 5245; fax 52-71-05.

Comoros: blvd de la Corniche, BP 559, Moroni; tel. (73) 2306; telex 212; fax (73) 2494.

Congo, Democratic Republic: 71 ave des trois Z, BP 2000, Kinshasa; tel. and fax (871) 1546221.

Congo, Republic: ave Lyautey, opposite Embassy of Italy, BP 2149, Brazzaville; tel. 83-38-78; fax 83-60-74.

Côte d'Ivoire: 18 rue de Dr Crozet, BP 1821, Abidjan 01; tel. 21-24-28; telex 23729; fax 21-40-89.

Djibouti: 11 blvd de Maréchal Joffre, BP 2477, Dibouti; tel. 352615; telex 5894; fax 350036.

Equatorial Guinea: Route de l'Aéroport, BP 779, Malabo; tel. 29-44; telex 5402; fax 32-75.

Eritrea: 1 Gainer St, POB 5710, Asmara; tel. 126566; fax 126578.

Ethiopia: POB 5570, Addis Ababa; tel. (1) 612511; telex 21738; fax (1) 612877.

Gabon: Lotissement des Cocotiers, BP 321, Libreville; tel. 73-22-50; telex 5511; fax 73-65-54.

Gambia: 10 Nelson Mandela St, POB 512, Banjul; tel. 227777; fax 226219.

Ghana: The Round House, 65 Cantonments Rd, POB 9505, Kotoka International Airport, Accra; tel. (21) 774201; telex 2069; fax (21) 774154.

Guinea-Bissau: Bairro da Penha, CP 359, 1113 Bissau; tel. 251027; fax 251044.

Kenya: Union Insurance Bldg, Ratati Rd, POB 45119, Nairobi; tel. (2) 713020; telex 22483.

Lesotho: 167 Constitution Rd, POB MS 518, Maseru; tel. 313726; fax 310193.

Liberia: EC Aid Co-ordination Office, UN Drive, Mamba Point, Monrovia; tel. 266273; fax 266274.

Madagascar: Immeuble Ny Havana, 67 Ha., BP 746, Antananarivo; tel. (2) 24216; telex 22327; fax (2) 32169.

Malawi: Europa House, POB 30102, Capital City, Lilongwe 3; tel. 783199; telex 44260; fax 783534.

Mali: ave de l'OUA, Badalabougou est, BP 115, Bamako; tel. 22-23-56; telex 2526; fax 22-36-70.

Mauritania: Ilot V, Lot 24, BP 213, Nouakchott; tel. 527-24; telex 5549; fax 535-24.

Mauritius: BP 1148, Port Louis; tel. 211-6295; fax 211-6624; e-mail europe@bow. intnet.mu.

Mozambique: Avda do Zimbabwe 1214, CP 1306, Maputo; tel. (1) 490266; telex 6146; fax (1) 491866.

Namibia: Sanlam Bldg, 4th Floor, 154 Independence Ave, Windhoek; tel. (61) 220099; telex 419; fax (61) 235135.

Niger: BP 10388, Niamey; tel. 73-23-60; telex 5267; fax 73-23-22.

Nigeria: Knorr House, Ozumba Mbadiwe Ave, opp. 1004 Flats, Victoria Island, PMB 12767, Lagos; tel. (1) 2617852; fax (1) 2617248; e-mail ecnig@infoweb.abs.net.

Rwanda: 14 ave Député Kamuzinzi, BP 515, Kigali; tel. 75586; telex 22515; fax 74313.

São Tomé and Príncipe: CP 132, São Tomé; tel. 21780; fax 22683.

Senegal: 12 ave Albert Sarraut, BP 3345, Dakar; tel. 23-13-14; fax 23-68-85.

Seychelles: POB 530, Victoria; tel. 323940; fax 323890.

Sierra Leone: Wesley House, 4 George St, POB 1399, Freetown; tel. (22) 223975; fax (22) 225212.

Somalia: EC Somalia Unit, Union Insurance House, 1st Floor, Ragati Rd, Nairobi, Kenya; tel. (2) 712830; fax (2) 710997.

Sudan: AAAID Bldg, 3rd Floor, Osman Digna Ave, POB 2363, Khartoum; tel. (11) 775054; telex 23096; fax (11) 775393.

Swaziland: Dhlan'Hbeka Bldg, 3rd Floor, cnr Walker and Tin Sts, POB A36, Mbabane; tel. 42908; telex 2133; fax 46729.

Tanzania: 38 Mirambo St, POB 9514, Dar es Salaam; tel. (51) 117473; telex 41353; fax (51) 113277.

Togo: 37 ave Nicolas Grunitzky, BP 1657, Lomé; tel. 21-36-62; fax 21-13-00.

Uganda: Rwenzori House, 1 Lumumba Ave, POB 52447, Kampala; tel. (41) 233303; telex 61139; fax (41) 233708.

Zambia: Plot 4899, Los Angeles Blvd, POB 34871, Lusaka; tel. (1) 250711; telex 40440; fax (1) 250906.

Zimbabwe: Construction House, 6th Floor, 110 Leopold Takawira St, POB 4252, Harare; tel. (4) 707120; telex 24811; fax (4) 725360.

Activities

Under the first Lomé Convention (Lomé I), the Community committed 3,052.4m. European Currency Units (ECU) for aid and investment in developing countries, through the European Development Fund (EDF) and the European Investment Bank (EIB). Provision was made for over 99% of ACP (mainly agricultural) exports to enter the EC market duty free, while certain products which compete directly with Community agriculture, such as sugar, were given preferential treatment but not free access. The Stabex (Stabilization of Export Earnings) scheme was designed to help developing countries to withstand fluctuations in the price of their agricultural products, by paying compensation for reduced export earnings.

The second Lomé Convention envisaged Community expenditure of ECU 5,530m.; it extended some of the provisions of Lomé I, and introduced new fields of co-operation. One of the most important innovations was a scheme, Sysmin, similar to Stabex, to safeguard exports of minerals. Lomé III provided a total of ECU 8,500m. (about US $6,000m. at 30 January 1985) in assistance to the ACP states over the five years from March 1985, representing little or no increase, in real terms, over the amount provided by Lomé II.

The fourth Lomé Convention covers the 10-year period 1990–99. The financial protocol for 1990–95 made commitments of ECU 12,000m. (US $13,700m.), of which ECU 10,800m. was from the EDF (including ECU 1,500m. for Stabex and ECU 480m. for Sysmin) and ECU 1,200m. from the EIB. Under the fourth Convention the obligation of most of the ACP states to contribute to the replenishment of Stabex resources, including the repayment of transfers made under the first three Conventions, was removed. In addition, special loans made to ACP member countries were to be cancelled, except in the case of profit-orientated businesses. Other innovations included the provision of assistance for structural adjustment programmes, measures to avoid increasing the recipient countries' indebtedness (e.g. by providing Stabex and Sysmin assistance in the form of grants, rather than loans), and increased support for the private sector, environmental protection, and control of growth in population.

In late June 1993 the European Community (EC, as the EU was previously entitled) introduced a regime concerning the import of bananas into the Community, which was designed to protect the banana industries of ACP countries (mostly in the Caribbean), which were threatened by cheaper bananas produced by countries in Latin America. The new regime, which was opposed by the low-cost producing countries and by Germany (the largest EU consumer of bananas), placed a quota of 2m. metric tons of bananas imported from Latin America, which would incur a uniform duty of 20%, while imports above this level were to be subject to a tariff of ECU 850 per ton. In February 1994 a dispute panel of the General Agreement on Tariffs and Trade (GATT) upheld a complaint brought by five Latin American countries that the EU import regime, which reserved 30% of its market for production of member states and ACP countries, was in contravention of free trade. An agreement was subsequently reached in March under which the EU increased the quota for Latin American banana imports to 2.1m. tons from October 1994 and 2.2m. tons in 1995. In February 1996 the USA, supported by four Latin American countries, submitted a formal complaint about the import regime to the World Trade Organization (WTO). The final ruling of the WTO, issued in May 1997, concluded that the EU banana import regime violated 19 free-trade rules. The President of the European Commission, Jacques Santer, noted that WTO regulations allowed for a right of appeal while reaffirming the EU's concern for the economies of the ACP countries affected.

In early September 1993 the Community announced plans to revise and strengthen its relations with the ACP countries under the Lomé Convention. In May 1994 a mid-term review of the Lomé IV Convention was initiated, amid concern on the part of ACP signatory states regarding the future of the Convention. In February 1995 a joint EU-ACP ministerial council, which was scheduled to conclude the negotiations, was adjourned, owing to significant disagreement among EU member states concerning reimbursement of the EDF for the period 1995–2000. In June EU heads of government reached an agreement, which was subsequently endorsed by an EU-ACP ministerial group. The accord was to provide ECU 14,625m. for the second phase of the Lomé IV Convention, of which ECU 12,967m. was to be allocated from the EDF and ECU 1,658m. for loans from the EIB. Agreement was also reached on revision of the country-of-origin rules for manufactured goods; expansion of the preferential system of trade for ACP products; a new protocol on the sustainable management of forest resources; and a joint declaration on support for the banana industry. The revised Convention was signed in November, in Mauritius. The new agreement included a reference to the observance of human rights and respect for democracy and the rule of law as essential elements of the preferential trading arrangement accorded under the Convention. Financial resources were to be made available to support institutional and administrative reforms to strengthen these principles in contracting states.

During 1996 Sysmin assistance totalling ECU 33.8m. was approved in order to finance a copper and nickel mining project in Botswana. In 1996 19 ACP states were eligible for 21 Stabex transfers amounting to ECU 76.2m. In March 1997 the European Commission proposed the provision of debt relief assistance worth ECU 25m. per year for the period 1997–2000 to the 11 heavily indebted poor countries (as identified by the World Bank and IMF) which form part of the ACP Group. This funding would support international efforts to reduce outstanding debt and encourage economic prospects.

In June 1995 negotiations which aimed to conclude a free trade agreement between the EU and South Africa, which was not a signatory of the Lomé Convention, were initiated. In March 1996 the EU-ACP Joint Assembly, convened in Namibia, endorsed a resolution advocating that the trading accord with South Africa be closely compatible with the Lomé IV arrangements. The revised Lomé Convention provided for simplified procedural arrangements to enable South Africa's partial accession to the treaty under a Special Protocol. In March 1997 the European Commission approved the draft protocol for South Africa's accession, and in April South Africa attained partial membership of the Lomé Convention. Full membership was withheld as South Africa was considered to be too developed for access to aid provisions to be warranted. An ECU 375m. programme for reconstruction and development co-operation between the EU and South Africa was signed in May, bringing the total sum committed by the EU for the period 1994–1999 to ECU 740m. A special provision was also introduced into the revised Lomé Convention which would allow Somalia to accede should constitutional government be established prior to theexpiry of the Convention.

In November 1996, with the Lomé Convention due to expire in February 2000, a report considering the options for future ACP-EU relations was published by the European Commission in advance of talks to consider the renewal of the Convention, scheduled for mid–1998. The report concentrated on the areas of trade, aid and politics. On the subject of trade, the Commission suggested adapting to WTO regulations, expanding ACP market access to the EU and encouraging competitiveness. Aid operations would aim to reduce poverty by encouraging faster economic growth in ACP countries, to support private sector investment and to offer increased assistance for structural adjustment. The report also suggested abolishing or altering both Stabex and Sysmin, and questioned whether the ACP countries should remain within their current grouping for the purpose of economic agreements with the EU, or whether alternative options, such as the division of the ACP Group into regions should be considered. Politically, the EU would aim to enhance democracy and the respect of human rights, the objective being for the EU and the ACP states to exist as equal partners.

COMMITMENTS MADE UNDER THE LOMÉ CONVENTION (ECU million)

	1995	1996*
Trade promotion	57.6	8.7
Cultural and social development	163.8	69.5
Education and training	40.7	38.6
Water engineering and urban infrastructure	65.8	22.7
Health	57.3	8.1
Economic infrastructure (transport and communications)	236.8	104.3
Development of production	471.2	122.9
Rural production	93.4	24.6
Industrialization	286.3	51.7
Campaigns on specific themes[1]	91.5	46.5
Exceptional aid, Stabex	334.2	121.3
Rehabilitation	161.0	47.2
Disasters	33.7	–9.7
Stabex	131.1	78.8
AIDS	9.6	3.9
Refugees and returnees	–1.2	1.0
Other[2]	256.4	170.0
Total	1,520.0	596.7

* Provisional figures.

[1] Including desertification and drought, disasters, major endemic and epidemic diseases, hygiene and basic health, endemic cattle diseases, energy-saving research, sectoral import programmes and long-term operations.

[2] Including information and documentation, seminars, programmes and general technical co-operation, general studies, multisectoral programmes, delegations, public buildings and corresponding multisectoral technical cooperation on all projects.

Source: European Commission, *General Report* (1996).

THE FRANC ZONE

Address: Direction Générale des Services Etrangers (Service de la Zone Franc), Banque de France, 39 rue Croix-des-Petits-Champs, 75049, Paris Cédex 01, France.

Telephone: 1-42-92-31-46; **telex:** 220932; **fax:** 1-42-92-39-88.

MEMBERS

Benin	Equatorial Guinea
Burkina Faso	French Republic*
Cameroon	Gabon
Central African Republic	Guinea-Bissau
Chad	Mali
The Comoros	Niger
Republic of Congo	Senegal
Côte d'Ivoire	Togo

* Metropolitan France, Mayotte, St Pierre and Miquelon and the Overseas Departments and Territories.

The Franc Zone embraces all those countries and groups of countries whose currencies are linked with the French franc at a fixed rate of exchange and who agree to hold their reserves mainly in the form of French francs and to effect their exchange on the Paris market. Each of these countries or groups of countries has its own central issuing bank and its currency is freely convertible into French francs. This monetary union is based on agreements concluded between France and each country or group of countries.

Apart from Guinea and Mauritania, all of the countries that formerly comprised French West and Equatorial Africa are members of the Franc Zone. The former West and Equatorial African territories are still grouped within the currency areas that existed before independence, each group having its own currency issued by a central bank.

A number of states left the Franc Zone during the period 1958–73: Guinea, Tunisia, Morocco, Algeria, Mauritania and Madagascar.

The Comoros, formerly a French Overseas Territory, did not join the Franc Zone following its unilateral declaration of independence in 1975. However, francs CFA were used as the currency of the new state and the Institut d'émission des Comores continued to function as a Franc Zone organization. In 1976 the Comoros formally assumed membership. In July 1981 the Banque centrale des Comores replaced the Institut d'émission des Comores, establishing its own currency, the Comoros franc. The island of Mayotte, however, has remained under French administration as an Overseas Collectivité Territoriale, using the French franc as its unit of currency.

Equatorial Guinea, a former Spanish possession, joined the Franc Zone in January 1985.

During the late 1980s and early 1990s the economies of the African Franc Zone countries were adversely affected by increasing foreign debt and by a decline in the prices paid for their principal export commodities. The French Government, however, refused to devalue the franc CFA, as recommended by the IMF. In 1990 the Franc Zone governments agreed to develop economic union, with integrated public finances and common commercial legislation. In April 1992, at a meeting of Franc Zone ministers, a treaty was signed on the insurance industry whereby a regulatory body for the industry was to be established: the Conférence Intrafricaine des Marchés d'Assurances (CIMA). Under the treaty, which was to be effective from 31 December 1992, a council of Franc Zone ministers responsible for the insurance industry was also to be established with its secretariat in Libreville, Gabon. (A code of conduct for members of CIMA came into effect in early 1995.) At the meeting held in April 1992 ministers also agreed that a further council of ministers was to be created with the task of monitoring the social security systems in Franc Zone countries. A programme drawn up by Franc Zone finance ministers concerning the harmonization of commercial legislation in member states through the establishment of l'Organisation pour l'Harmonisation du Droit des Affaires en Afrique (OHADA), was approved by the Franco-African summit in October. A treaty to align corporate and investment regulations was signed by 11 member countries at the annual meeting with France in October 1993. Devaluations of the franc CFA and the Comoros franc were agreed by CFA central banks in January 1994 (see below). Following the devaluation the CFA countries embarked on programmes of economic adjustment, including restrictive fiscal and wage policies and other monetary, structural and social measures, designed to stimulate growth and to ensure eligibility for development assistance from international financial institutions. France established a special development fund of FFr 300m. to alleviate the immediate social consequences of the devaluation, and announced substantial debt cancellations. In April the French Government announced assistance amounting to FFr 10,000m. over three years to Franc Zone countries undertaking structural adjustment programmes. The IMF, which had strongly advocated a devaluation of the franc CFA, and the World Bank approved immediate soft-credit loans, technical assistance and cancellations or rescheduling of debts. In June 1994 Heads of State (or representatives) of African Franc Zone countries convened in Libreville, Gabon, to review the effects of the currency realignment. The final communiqué of the meeting urged further international support for the countries' economic development efforts. In April 1995 Franc Zone finance ministers, meeting in Paris, recognized the positive impact of the devaluation on agricultural export sectors, in particular in west African countries, though central African countries, it was noted, were still afflicted by serious economic difficulties. In September 1995 the Franc Zone member countries and the French Government agreed to establish a research and training institution, Afristat, which was to support national statistical organizations in order to strengthen economic management capabilities in participating states. In April 1997 finance ministers met to review the economies of member states. Capital entries (private investment and public development aid) along with tax and wage policies and an increase in exports were found to have contributed to economic growth. Improvements were continuing within a programme supported by the IMF and the World Bank, though ministers stated that economic development efforts were not sufficiently supported by the private sector, with the average rate of investment remaining at 10% of GDP. The adoption of a charter to encourage private investors was discussed, but postponed pending an investigation into proposals made by UEMOA and CEMAC. The co-operation agreement permitting Guinea-Bissau's membership of the Franc Zone, which would come into effect on 2 May, was also signed. In the same month delegates from OHADA met donors in Guinea-Bissau, aiming to raise funds worth US $50m. over a 12-year period, to allow them to train commercial court judges, provide information for businesses and cover administration costs.

EXCHANGE REGULATIONS

Currencies of the Franc Zone are freely convertible into the French franc at a fixed rate, through 'operations accounts' established by agreements concluded between the French Treasury and the individual issuing banks. It is backed fully by the French Treasury, which also provides the issuing banks with overdraft facilities.

The monetary reserves of the CFA countries are normally held in French francs in the French Treasury. However, the Banque centrale des états de l'Afrique de l'ouest (BCEAO) and the Banque des états de l'Afrique centrale (BEAC) are authorized to hold up to 35% of their foreign exchange holdings in currencies other than the franc. Exchange is effected on the Paris market. Part of the reserves earned by richer members can be used to offset the deficits incurred by poorer countries.

Regulations drawn up in 1967 provided for the free convertibility of currency with that of countries outside the Franc Zone. Restrictions were removed on the import and export of CFA banknotes, although some capital transfers are subject to approval by the governments concerned.

When the French Government instituted exchange control to protect the French franc in May 1968, other Franc Zone countries were obliged to take similar action in order to maintain free convertibility within the Franc Zone. The franc CFA was devalued following devaluation of the French franc in August 1969. Since March 1973 the French authorities have ceased to maintain the franc-US dollar rate within previously agreed margins, and, as a result, the value of the franc CFA has fluctuated on foreign exchange markets in line with the French franc.

In August 1993, as a result of the financial turmoil regarding the European exchange rate mechanism and the continuing weakness of the French franc, the BCEAO and the BEAC decided to suspend repurchasing of francs CFA outside the Franc Zone. Effectively this signified the withdrawal of guaranteed convertibility of the franc CFA with the French franc. In January 1994 the franc CFA was devalued by 50%, and the Comoros franc by 33.3%.

CURRENCIES OF THE FRANC ZONE

French franc (= 100 centimes): used in Metropolitan France, in the Overseas Departments of Guadeloupe, French Guiana, Martinique, Réunion, and in the Overseas Collectivités Territoriales of Mayotte and St Pierre and Miquelon.

1 franc CFA=1 French centime. CFA stands for Communauté financière africaine in the West African area and for Coopération financière en Afrique centrale in the Central African area. Used in the monetary areas of West and Central Africa respectively.

1 Comoros franc=1.333 French centimes. Used in the Comoros, where it replaced the franc CFA in 1981.

1 franc CFP=5.5 French centimes. CFP stands for Comptoirs français du Pacifique. Used in New Caledonia, French Polynesia and the Wallis and Futuna Islands.

WEST AFRICA

Union économique et monétaire ouest-africaine—UEMOA: Ouagadougou, Burkina Faso; f. 1994; replaced the Communauté économique de l'Afrique de l'ouest–CEAO; promotes regional monetary and economic convergence, and aims to improve regional trade by facilitating the movement of labour and capital between member states; the first meeting of heads of state of UEMOA member countries, held in May 1996, in Ouagadougou, agreed to establish a customs union with effect from 1 January 1998; a preferential tariff scheme, eliminating duties on most local products and reducing by 30% import duties on many Community-produced industrial goods, became operational on 1 July 1996; in addition, from 1 July, a community solidarity tax of 0.5% was imposed on all goods from third countries sold within the Community, in order to strengthen UEMOA's capacity to promote economic integration. Mems: Benin, Burkina Faso, Côte d'Ivoire, Guinea-Bissau, Mali, Niger, Senegal and Togo. Chair. Blaise Compaoré (Burkina Faso).

Union monétaire ouest-africaine—UMOA (West African Monetary Union): established by Treaty of November 1973, entered into force 1974; in 1990 the UMOA Banking Commission was established, which is responsible for supervising the activities of banks and financial institutions in the region, with the authority to prohibit the operation of a banking institution. UMOA constitutes an integral part of UEMOA.

Banque centrale des états de l'Afrique de l'ouest—BCEAO: ave Abdoulaye Fadiga, BP 3108, Dakar, Senegal; tel. 23-16-15; telex 21815; fax 23-93-35; f. 1962 by Benin, Burkina Faso, Côte d'Ivoire, Mali, Niger, Senegal and Togo (in co-operation with France) in order to manage the franc CFA; central bank of issue for the mems of UEMOA; cap. and res 657,592m. francs CFA (Dec. 1995). Gov. Charles Konan Banny (Côte d'Ivoire); Sec.-Gen. Michel K. Klousseh (Togo). Publs *Annual Report, Notes d'Information et Statistiques* (monthly), *Annuaire des banques, Bilan des banques et établissements financiers* (annual).

Banque ouest-africaine de développement—BOAD: 68 ave de la Libération, BP 1172, Lomé, Togo; tel. 21-42-44; telex 5289; fax 21-52-67; f. 1973 to promote the balanced development of mem. states and the economic integration of West Africa; cap. 18,100m. francs CFA (Dec. 1995). A Guarantee Fund for Private Investment in west Africa, established jtly by BOAD and the European Investment Bank, was inaugurated in Dec. 1994. The Fund, which had an initial capital of 8,615.5m. francs CFA, aimed to guarantee medium- and long-term credits to private sector businesses in the region. Mems: Benin, Burkina Faso, Côte d'Ivoire, Guinea-Bissau, Mali, Niger, Senegal, Togo. Chair. Boni Yayi (Benin); Vice-Chair. Alpha Touré. Publ. *Rapport Annuel, BOAD-INFO* (every 3 months).

CENTRAL AFRICA

Union douanière et économique de l'Afrique centrale—UDEAC (Customs and Economic Union of Central Africa): BP 969, Bangui, Central African Republic; tel. 61-09-22; telex 5254; fax 61-21-35; f. 1966 by the Brazzaville Treaty of 1964 (revised in 1974); forms customs union, with free trade between mems and a common external tariff for imports from other countries. UDEAC has a common code for investment policy and a Solidarity Fund to counteract regional disparities of wealth and economic development. UDEAC priority areas are transport and communication, agriculture, food and environment, industry, and research. In 1992 the UDEAC General Secretariat was restructured owing to a financial crisis within the organization. It now comprises six technical depts and one admin. dept, with 85 employees. Mems: Cameroon, Central African Republic, Chad, Republic of Congo, Equatorial Guinea, Gabon. Sec.-Gen. Thomas Dakayi Kamga (Cameroon).

At a summit meeting in December 1981, UDEAC leaders agreed in principle to form an economic community of Central African states (Communauté économique des états d'Afrique centrale—CEEAC), to include UDEAC members and Burundi, Rwanda, São Tomé and Príncipe and Zaire (now Democratic Republic of the Congo). CEEAC (q.v.) began operations in 1985.

In March 1994 UDEAC leaders signed a treaty for the establishment of a Communauté économique et monétaire en Afrique centrale (CEMAC), which was to promote the process of sub-regional integration within the framework of an economic union and a monetary union. In August 1996 a meeting of CEMAC heads of state, scheduled to be held in Pointe-Noire, Congo, was cancelled.

Banque de développement des états de l'Afrique centrale (BDEAC): place du Gouvernement, BP 1177, Brazzaville, Republic of Congo; tel. 83-02-12; telex 5306; fax 83-02-66; f. 1975; cap. 19,735m. francs CFA (June 1996); shareholders: Cameroon, Central African Republic, Chad, Republic of Congo, Gabon, Equatorial Guinea, ADB, BEAC, France, Germany and Kuwait; Dir-Gen. JEAN-MARIE MBIOKA.

Banque des états de l'Afrique centrale (BEAC): ave Mgr François Xavier Vogt, BP 1917, Yaoundé, Cameroon; tel. 23-40-30; telex 8343; fax 23-33-29; f. 1973 as the central bank of issue of Cameroon, the Central African Republic, Chad, Republic of Congo, Equatorial Guinea and Gabon; a monetary market, incorporating all national financial institutions of the BEAC countries, came into effect on 1 July 1994; cap. and res 204,933m. francs CFA (Dec. 1995). Gov. JEAN-FÉLIX MAMALEPOT, Publs *Rapport annuel, Etudes et statistiques* (monthly).

CENTRAL ISSUING BANKS

Banque centrale des Comores: BP 405, Moroni, Comoros; tel. (73) 1002; telex 213; f. 1981; Dir-Gen. SAÏD AHMED SAÏD ALI.

Banque centrale des états de l'Afrique de l'ouest: see above.

Banque des états de l'Afrique centrale: see above.

Banque de France: 39 rue Croix-des-Petits-Champs, BP 140-01, 75049 Paris, France; tel. 1-42-92-42-92; telex 220932; fax 1-42-96-04-23; f. 1800; bank of issue for Metropolitan France; Gov. JEAN-CLAUDE TRICHET; Dep. Govs DENIS FERMAN, HERVÉ HANNOUN.

Institut d'émission des départements d'outre-mer: Cité du Retiro, 35/37 rue Boissy d'Anglas, 75379 Paris Cedex 08, France; tel. 1-40-06-41-41; issuing authority for the French Overseas Departments and the French Overseas Collectivité Territoriale of St Pierre and Miquelon; Pres. DENIS FERMAN; Dir-Gen. ANTOINE POUILLIEUTE; Dir GILLES AUDREN.

Institut d'émission d'outre-mer: Cité du Retiro, 35/37 rue Boissy d'Anglas, 75379 Paris Cedex 08, France; tel. 1-40-06-41-41; issuing authority for the French Overseas Territories and the French Overseas Collectivité Territoriale of Mayotte; Pres. DENIS FERMAN; Dir-Gen. ANTOINE POUILLIEUTE; Dir GILLES AUDREN.

FRENCH ECONOMIC AID

France's connection with the African Franc Zone countries involves not only monetary arrangements, but also includes comprehensive French assistance in the forms of budget support, foreign aid, technical assistance and subsidies on commodity exports.

Official French financial aid and technical assistance to developing countries is administered by the following agencies:

Caisse française de développement—CFD (fmrly the Caisse centrale de coopération économique—CCCE): Cité du Retiro, 35/37 rue Boissy d'Anglas, 75379 Paris Cedex 08, France; tel. 1-40-06-31-31; telex 212632; f. 1941. French development bank which lends money to member states and former member states of the Franc Zone and several other states, and executes the financial operations of the FAC (see below). Following the devaluation of the franc CFA in January 1994, the French Government cancelled some 25,000m. French francs in debt arrears owed by member states to the CFD. The CFD established a Special Fund for Development and the Exceptional Facility for Short-term Financing to help alleviate the immediate difficulties resulting from the devaluation. A total of FFr 4,600m. of financial assistance was awarded to Franc Zone countries in 1994. In early 1994 the CFD made available funds totalling 2,420m. francs CFA to assist the establishment of CEMAC (see above); Dir-Gen. ANTOINE POUILLIEUTE.

Fonds d'aide et de coopération—FAC: 20 rue Monsieur, 75007 Paris, France; tel. 1-53-69-00-00; fax 1-53-69-43-82; in 1959 FAC took over from FIDES (Fonds d'investissement pour le développement économique et social) the administration of subsidies and loans from the French Government to the former French African states. FAC is administered by the Ministry of Co-operation, which allocates budgetary funds to it.

ISLAMIC DEVELOPMENT BANK

Address: POB 5925, Jeddah 21432, Saudi Arabia.

Telephone: (2) 6361400; **telex:** 601137; **fax:** (2) 6366871.

The Bank is an international financial institution that was established following a conference of Ministers of Finance of member countries of the Organization of the Islamic Conference (OIC, q.v.), held in Jeddah in December 1973. Its aim is to encourage the economic development and social progress of member countries and of Muslim communities in non-member countries, in accordance with the principles of the Islamic Shari'a (sacred law). The Bank formally opened in October 1975.

MEMBERS

There are 51 members.

Organization

(August 1997)

BOARD OF GOVERNORS

Each member country is represented by a governor, usually its Minister of Finance, and an alternate. The Board of Governors is the supreme authority of the Bank, and meets annually.

BOARD OF EXECUTIVE DIRECTORS

The Board consists of 11 members, five of whom are appointed by the five largest subscribers to the capital stock of the Bank; the remaining six are elected by Governors representing the other subscribers. Members of the Board of Executive Directors are elected for three-year terms. The Board is responsible for the direction of the general operations of the Bank.

President of the Bank and Chairman of the Board of Executive Directors: Dr AHMED MOHAMED ALI.

Bank Secretary: Dr ABDERRAHIM OMRANA.

FINANCIAL STRUCTURE

The authorized capital of the Bank is 6,000m. Islamic Dinars (divided into 600,000 shares, having a value of 10,000 Islamic Dinars each). The Islamic Dinar (ID) is the Bank's unit of account and is equivalent to the value of one Special Drawing Right of the IMF (SDR 1 = US $1.38814 at 30 June 1997).

Subscribed capital amounts to ID 4,000m.

Activities

The Bank adheres to the Islamic principle forbidding usury, and does not grant loans or credits for interest. Instead, its methods of financing are: provision of interest-free loans (with a service fee), mainly for infrastructural projects which are expected to have a marked impact on long-term socio-economic development; provision

SUBSCRIPTIONS (million Islamic Dinars, as at 17 May 1996)

Afghanistan	5.00	Malaysia	79.56
Albania	2.50	Maldives	2.50
Algeria	124.26	Mali	4.92
Azerbaijan	4.92	Mauritania	4.92
Bahrain	7.00	Morocco	24.81
Bangladesh	49.29	Mozambique	2.50
Benin	4.92	Niger	12.41
Brunei	12.41	Oman	13.78
Burkina Faso	12.41	Pakistan	124.26
Cameroon	12.41	Palestine Liberation Organization	9.85
Chad	4.92	Qatar	49.23
Comoros	2.50	Saudi Arabia	997.17
Djibouti	2.50	Senegal	12.42
Egypt	49.23	Sierra Leone	2.50
Gabon	14.77	Somalia	2.50
The Gambia	2.50	Sudan	19.69
Guinea	12.41	Syria	5.00
Guinea-Bissau	2.50	Tunisia	9.85
Indonesia	124.26	Turkey	315.47
Iran	349.97	Turkmenistan	2.50
Iraq	13.05	Uganda	12.41
Jordan	19.89	United Arab Emirates	283.03
Kuwait	496.64	Yemen	24.81
Kyrgyzstan	2.50	**Total**	3,753.77
Lebanon	4.92		
Libya	400.00		

of technical assistance (e.g. for feasibility studies); equity participation in industrial and agricultural projects; leasing operations, involving the leasing of equipment such as ships, and instalment sale financing; and profit-sharing operations. Funds not immediately needed for projects are used for foreign trade financing, particularly for importing commodities to be used in development (i.e. raw materials and intermediate industrial goods, rather than consumer goods); priority is given to the import of goods from other member countries (see table). The Longer-term Trade Financing Scheme, introduced in 1987/88, provides financing for the export of non-traditional and capital goods. In addition, the Special Assistance Account provides emergency aid and other assistance, with particular emphasis on education in Islamic communities in non-member countries.

By 17 May 1996 the Bank had approved a total of ID 3,025.56m. for project financing and technical assistance, a total of ID 8,559.57m. for foreign trade financing, and ID 364.81m. for special assistance operations, excluding amounts for cancelled operations. During the Islamic year AH 1416 (30 May 1995 to 17 May 1996) the Bank approved a total of ID 979.36m., for 180 operations.

The Bank approved 26 loans in the year ending 17 May 1996, amounting to ID 79.16m. (compared with 16 loans, totalling ID 57.51m., in the previous year). These loans supported projects concerned with infrastructural improvements, for example of roads, canals, water-supply and rural electrification, the construction of schools and health centres, and agricultural developments.

During the year 72% of loan financing was directed to least-developed member countries under a Special Account, providing concessionary terms. Loans financed by this Account are charged an annual service fee of 0.75%, compared with 2.5% for ordinary loans, and have a repayment period of 25–30 years, compared with 15–25 years.

During AH 1416 the Bank approved nine technical assistance operations for eight countries in the form of grants and loans, amounting to ID 1.9m.

Import trade financing approved during the Islamic year 1416 amounted to ID 395m. for 54 operations in 9 member countries. By the end of that year cumulative import trade financing amounted to ID 8,560m., of which 42.1% was for imports of crude petroleum, 28% for intermediate industrial goods, 9% for vegetable oil and 6.1% for refined petroleum products. Financing approved under the Longer-term Trade Financing Scheme amounted to ID 59.88m. for 13 operations in six countries in AH 1416. In the same year the Bank's Portfolio for Investment and Development, established in AH 1407 (1986–87), approved 10 operations amounting to US $248.5m. Since its introduction, the Portfolio has approved 75 net financing operations in 17 member countries, amounting to US $1,129m.

Under the Bank's Special Assistance Account, 37 operations were approved during the year, amounting to ID 7.77m., providing assistance primarily in the education and health sectors; of the total financing, 32 operations provided for Muslim communities in non-member countries. The Bank's scholarships programme sponsored 283 students from 38 countries during the year to 17 May 1996. The Merit Scholarship Programme, initiated in AH 1411 (1990–91), aims to develop scientific, technological and research capacities in member countries through advanced studies and/or research. Since the beginning of the programme 93 scholars have been placed in academic centres of excellence in Australia, Europe and the USA. The Bank's Programme for Technical Co-operation aims to mobilize technical capabilities among member countries and to promote the exchange of expertise, experience and skills. During AH 1416 60 projects were implemented under the programme. The Bank also undertakes the distribution of meat sacrificed by Muslim pilgrims: during the year meat from 430,560 head of sheep and 7,022 head of cattle and of camels was distributed to the needy in 27 member countries.

Disbursements during the year ending 17 May 1996 totalled ID 418m., bringing the total cumulative disbursements since the Bank began operations to ID 8,518m.

Operations approved, Islamic year 1416 (30 May 1995–17 May 1996)

Type of operation	Number of operations	Total amount (million Islamic Dinars)
Ordinary operations	66	344.01
Project financing	57	342.12
Technical assistance	9	1.89
Trade financing operations*	77	627.59
Special assistance operations	37	7.77
Total†	180	979.36

* Including import trade financing, the Longer-term Trade Financing Scheme, and the Islamic Bank's Portfolio.

† Excluding cancelled operations.

Project financing and technical assistance by sector, Islamic year 1416

Sector	Number of Operations	Amount (million (Islamic Dinars)	%
Agriculture and agro-industry	13	64.03	18.6
Industry and mining	4	28.34	8.2
Transport and communications	10	70.30	20.4
Public utilities	18	113.67	33.0
Social sectors	18	65.52	19.0
Other*	3	2.16	0.6
Total†	66	344.01	100.0

* Mainly approved amounts for Islamic banks.

† Excluding cancelled operations.

The Bank's Unit Investment Fund became operational in 1990, with the aim of mobilizing additional resources and providing a profitable channel for investments conforming to Shari'a. The initial issue of the Fund was US $100m., with a minimum subscription of $100,000. An additional issue of $100m. became effective on 1 January 1994; the first tranche of an additional issue of $300m. was launched in early 1995, bringing the Fund's subscribed capital to $275m. at 31 December 1995. The Fund finances mainly private-sector industrial projects in middle-income countries.

SUBSIDIARY ORGANS

Islamic Corporation for the Insurance of Investment and Export Credit—ICIEC: POB 15722, Jeddah 21454, Saudi Arabia; tel. (2) 6361400; telex 607509; fax (2) 6379504; e-mail kgazzah@isdb.org.sa; f. 1994; aims to promote trade and the flow of investments among member countries of the OIC; auth. cap. ID 100m., subscribed cap. ID 76.5m. (May 1996). Man. Dr ABDEL RAHMAN A. TAHA. Mems: 15 OIC member states.

Islamic Research and Training Institute: POB 9201, Jeddah 21413, Saudi Arabia; tel. (2) 6361400; telex 601137; fax (2) 6378927; f. 1982 for research enabling economic, financial and banking activities to conform to Islamic law, and to provide training for staff involved in development activities in the Bank's member countries. During the Islamic year 1416 the Institute undertook 10 research studies on economic, financial and general development issues relevant to the Bank's member states. The Institute also organized seminars and workshops, and held training courses aimed at furthering the expertise of government and financial officials in Islamic developing countries. Dir Dr MABID ALI AL-JARHI. Publs *Annual Report*, *Islamic Economic Studies*.

PUBLICATION

Annual Report.

ORGANIZATION OF AFRICAN UNITY—OAU

Address: POB 3243, Addis Ababa, Ethiopia.

Telephone: (1) 517700; **telex:** 21046; **fax:** (1) 513036.

The Organization was founded in 1963 to promote unity and solidarity among African states.

FORMATION

There were various attempts at establishing an inter-African organization before the OAU Charter was drawn up. In November 1958 Ghana and Guinea (later joined by Mali) drafted a Charter which was to form the basis of a Union of African States. In January 1961 a conference was held at Casablanca, attended by the heads of state of Ghana, Guinea, Mali, Morocco, and representatives of Libya and of the provisional government of the Algerian Republic (GPRA). Tunisia, Nigeria, Liberia and Togo declined the invitation to attend. An African Charter was adopted and it was decided to set up an African Military Command and an African Common Market.

Between October 1960 and March 1961 three conferences were held by French-speaking African countries, at Abidjan, Brazzaville and Yaoundé. None of the 12 countries which attended these meetings had been present at the Casablanca Conference. These conferences led eventually to the signing in September 1961, at Tananarive, of a charter establishing the Union africaine et malgache, later the Organisation commune africaine et mauricienne (OCAM).

In May 1961 a conference was held at Monrovia, Liberia, attended by the heads of state or representatives of 19 countries: Cameroon, Central African Republic, Chad, Congo Republic (ex-French), Côte d'Ivoire, Dahomey, Ethiopia, Gabon, Liberia, Madagascar, Mauritania, Niger, Nigeria, Senegal, Sierra Leone, Somalia, Togo, Tunisia and Upper Volta. They met again (with the exception of Tunisia and with the addition of the ex-Belgian Congo Republic) in January 1962 at Lagos, Nigeria, and set up a permanent secretariat and a standing committee of finance ministers, and accepted a draft charter for an Organization of Inter-African and Malagasy States.

It was the Conference of Addis Ababa, held in 1963, which finally brought together African states despite the regional, political and linguistic differences which divided them. The foreign ministers of 32 African states attended the Preparatory Meeting held in May: Algeria, Burundi, Cameroon, Central African Republic, Chad, Congo (Brazzaville) (now Republic of Congo), Congo (Léopoldville) (now the Democratic Republic of the Congo), Côte d'Ivoire, Dahomey (now Benin), Ethiopia, Gabon, Ghana, Guinea, Liberia, Libya, Madagascar, Mali, Mauritania, Morocco, Niger, Nigeria, Rwanda, Senegal, Sierra Leone, Somalia, Sudan, Tanganyika (now Tanzania), Togo, Tunisia, Uganda, the United Arab Republic (Egypt) and Upper Volta (now Burkina Faso).

The topics discussed by the meeting were: (i) creation of the Organization of African States; (ii) co-operation among African states in the following fields: economic and social; education, culture and science; collective defence; (iii) decolonization; (iv) apartheid and racial discrimination; (v) effects of economic grouping on the economic development of Africa; (vi) disarmament; (vii) creation of a Permanent Conciliation Commission; and (viii) Africa and the United Nations.

The Heads of State Conference which opened on 23 May drew up the Charter of the Organization of African Unity, which was then signed by the heads of 30 states on 25 May 1963. The Charter was essentially functional and reflected a compromise between the concept of a loose association of states favoured by the Monrovia Group and the federal idea supported by the Casablanca Group, and in particular by Ghana.

SUMMARY OF OAU CHARTER

Article I. Establishment of the Organization of African Unity. The Organization to include continental African states, Madagascar, and other islands surrounding Africa.

Article II. Aims of the OAU:

1. To promote unity and solidarity among African states.

2. To intensify and co-ordinate efforts to improve living standards in Africa.

3. To defend sovereignty, territorial integrity and independence of African states.

4. To eradicate all forms of colonialism from Africa.

5. To promote international co-operation in keeping with the Charter of the United Nations.

Article III. Member states adhere to the principles of sovereignty, non-interference in internal affairs of member states, respect for territorial integrity, peaceful settlement of disputes, condemnation of political subversion, dedication to the emancipation of dependent African territories, and international non-alignment.

Article IV. Each independent sovereign African state shall be entitled to become a member of the Organization.

Article V. All member states shall have equal rights and duties.

Article VI. All member states shall observe scrupulously the principles laid down in Article III.

Article VII. Establishment of the Assembly of Heads of State and Government, the Council of Ministers, the General Secretariat, and the Commission of Mediation, Conciliation and Arbitration.

Articles VIII–XI. The Assembly of Heads of State and Government co-ordinates policies and reviews the structure of the Organization.

Articles XII–XV. The Council of Ministers shall prepare conferences of the Assembly, and co-ordinate inter-African co-operation. All resolutions shall be by simple majority.

Articles XVI–XVIII. The General Secretariat. The Administrative Secretary-General and his staff shall not seek or receive instructions from any government or other authority external to the Organization. They are international officials responsible only to the Organization.

Article XIX. Commission of Mediation, Conciliation and Arbitration. A separate protocol concerning the composition and nature of this Commission shall be regarded as an integral part of the Charter.

Articles XX–XXII. Specialized Commissions shall be established, composed of Ministers or other officials designated by Member Governments. Their regulations shall be laid down by the Council of Ministers.

Article XXIII. The Budget shall be prepared by the Secretary-General and approved by the Council of Ministers. Contributions shall be in accordance with the scale of assessment of the United Nations. No Member shall pay more than 20% of the total yearly amount.

Article XXIV. Texts of the Charter in African languages, English and French shall be equally authentic. Instruments of ratification shall be deposited with the Government of Ethiopia.

Article XXV. The Charter shall come into force on receipt by the Government of Ethiopia of the instruments of ratification of two-thirds of the signatory states.

Article XXVI. The Charter shall be registered with the Secretariat of the United Nations.

Article XXVII. Questions of interpretation shall be settled by a two-thirds majority vote in the Assembly of Heads of State and Government.

Article XXVIII. Admission of new independent African states to the Organization shall be decided by a simple majority of the Member States.

Articles XXIX–XXXIII. The working languages of the Organization shall be African languages, English, French, Arabic and Portuguese. The Secretary-General may accept gifts and bequests to the Organization, subject to the approval of the Council of Ministers. The Council of Ministers shall establish privileges and immunities to be accorded to the personnel of the Secretariat in the territories of Member States. A State wishing to withdraw from the Organization must give a year's written notice to the Secretariat. The Charter may only be amended after consideration by all Member States and by a two-thirds majority vote of the Assembly of Heads of State and Government. Such amendments will come into force one year after submission.

MEMBERS*

Algeria	Eritrea	Nigeria
Angola	Ethiopia	Rwanda
Benin	Gabon	São Tomé and Príncipe
Botswana	The Gambia	Senegal
Burkina Faso	Ghana	Seychelles
Burundi	Guinea	Sierra Leone
Cameroon	Guinea-Bissau	Somalia
Cape Verde	Kenya	South Africa
Central African Republic	Lesotho	Sudan
Chad	Liberia	Swaziland
The Comoros	Libya	Tanzania
Congo, Democratic Republic†	Madagascar	Togo
Congo, Republic	Malawi	Tunisia
Côte d'Ivoire	Mali	Uganda
Djibouti	Mauritania	Zambia
Egypt	Mauritius	Zimbabwe
Equatorial Guinea	Mozambique	
	Namibia	
	Niger	

* The Sahrawi Arab Democratic Republic (SADR–Western Sahara) was admitted to the OAU in February 1982, following recognition by 26 of the 50 members, but its membership was disputed by Morocco and other states which claimed that a two-thirds majority was needed to admit a state whose existence was in question. Morocco withdrew from the OAU with effect from November 1985.

† Formerly known as Zaire.

Organization

(July 1997)

ASSEMBLY OF HEADS OF STATE

The Assembly of Heads of State and Government meets annually to co-ordinate policies of African states. Resolutions are passed by a two-thirds majority, procedural matters by a simple majority. A chairman is elected at each meeting from among the members, to hold office for one year.

Chairman (1997/98): ROBERT MUGABE (Zimbabwe).

COUNCIL OF MINISTERS

Consists of ministers of foreign affairs and others and meets twice a year, with provision for extraordinary sessions. Each session elects its own Chairman. Prepares meetings of, and is responsible to, the Assembly of Heads of State.

GENERAL SECRETARIAT

The permanent headquarters of the organization. It carries out functions assigned to it in the Charter of the OAU and by other agreements and treaties made between member states. Departments: Political; Finance; Education, Science, Culture and Social Affairs; Economic Development and Co-operation; Administration and Conferences. The Secretary-General is elected for a four-year term by the Assembly of Heads of State.

Secretary-General: SALIM AHMED SALIM (Tanzania).

ARBITRATION COMMISSION

Commission of Mediation, Conciliation and Arbitration: Addis Ababa; f. 1964; consists of 21 members elected by the Assembly of Heads of State for a five-year term; no state may have more than one member; has a Bureau consisting of a President and two Vice-Presidents, who shall not be eligible for re-election. Its task is to hear and settle disputes between member states by peaceful means.

SPECIALIZED COMMISSIONS

There are specialized commissions for economic, social, transport and communications affairs; education, science, culture and health; defence; human rights; and labour.

BUDGET

Member states contribute in accordance with their United Nations assessment. No member state is assessed for an amount exceeding 20% of the yearly regular budget of the Organization. The biennial budget for 1996-98 was US $61.45m. At July 1996 member states owed some $53m. in outstanding contributions.

Principal Events, 1987–97

1987

July — The 23rd Assembly of Heads of State reiterated its demands that Western countries should impose economic sanctions against South Africa. It renewed the mandate of the special OAU committee which had been attempting to resolve the dispute between Chad and Libya. It also discussed the spread of the disease AIDS in Africa; and approved the establishment of an African Commission on Human and People's Rights (q.v.), now that the African Charter on Human and People's Rights (approved in 1981) had been ratified by a majority of member states.

Nov. — A summit meeting on the subject of Africa's substantial external debt (then estimated to total US $200,000m.) was held in Addis Ababa (but was attended by only 10 heads of state and government). The meeting issued a statement requesting the conversion of past bilateral loans into grants, a 10-year suspension of debt-service payments, reduction of interest rates and the lengthening of debt-maturity periods. It asked that creditors should observe the principle that debt-servicing should not exceed a 'reasonable and bearable' percentage of the debtor country's export earnings. A 'contact group' was established to enlist support for an international conference on African debt.

1988

May — The Assembly of Heads of State recognized that no conference on debt was likely to be held in 1988, owing to the reluctance of creditors to participate. It condemned the links with South Africa still maintained by some African countries, and protested at the recently-reported unauthorized disposal of toxic waste in Africa by industrial companies from outside the continent.

Aug. — The OAU organized an international conference in Oslo, Norway, on refugees and displaced persons in southern Africa.

1989

Jan. — A meeting on apartheid, organized by the OAU, resulted in the formation of an African Anti-Apartheid Committee.

May — The OAU Chairman, President Traoré of Mali, undertook a mission of mediation between the governments of Mauritania and Senegal, following ethnic conflict between the citizens of the two countries.

July — The Assembly of Heads of State discussed the Namibian independence process, and urged that the UN should ensure that the forthcoming elections there would be fairly conducted. They again requested that an international conference on Africa's debts should be held.

Sept.–Dec. — The newly-elected OAU Chairman, Hosni Mubarak, and the newly-appointed OAU Secretary-General, Salim Ahmed Salim, attempted to mediate in the dispute between Mauritania and Senegal. In November a mediation committee, comprising representatives of six countries, visited Mauritania and Senegal.

1990

March — A monitoring group was formed by the OAU to report on events in South Africa. The OAU urged the international community to continue imposing economic sanctions on South Africa.

July — The Assembly of Heads of State reviewed the implications for Africa of recent socio-economic and political changes in Eastern Europe, and of the European Community's progress towards monetary and political union.

1991

June — The Assembly of Heads of State signed the treaty on the creation of an African Economic Community (AEC). The treaty was to enter into force after ratification by two-thirds of OAU member states. The Community was to be established by 2025, beginning with a five-year stage during which measures would be taken to strengthen existing economic groupings. The meeting also established a committee of heads of state to assist national reconciliation in Ethiopia; and gave a mandate to the OAU Secretary-General to undertake a mission to assist in restoring political stability in Somalia.

1992

Feb.–March — The OAU was involved, together with the UN and the Organization of the Islamic Conference (OIC, q.v.), in mediation between the warring factions in Mogadishu, Somalia. The OAU subsequently continued to assist in efforts to achieve a peace settlement in Somalia.

May — An OAU mission was dispatched to South Africa to monitor the continued violence in that country.

June–July — Proposals were advanced at the Assembly of Heads of State, held in Dakar, Senegal, for a mechanism to be established within the OAU for 'conflict management, prevention and resolution'. These proposals were accepted in principle, but operational details were to be elaborated at a later stage.

Oct. The Ad Hoc Committee on Southern Africa met in Gaborone, Botswana, to discuss a report compiled by a team of OAU experts on practical steps to be taken towards the democratization of South Africa. Plans to send a mission to monitor the Mozambican peace accord were announced.

Nov. An International Conference on Assistance to African Children, which was organized by the OAU with assistance from UNICEF, was held in Dakar, Senegal. The Conference aimed to focus awareness on the plight of many of Africa's children and to encourage African countries to honour commitments made at the UN World Summit for Children in 1991, whereby governments were to allocate greater resources to programmes benefiting children.

1993

Feb. A session of the Council of Ministers discussed the OAU's serious financial crisis. The meeting agreed to allocate US $250,000 to the creation of a conflict prevention bureau, and a further $250,000 for the purposes of monitoring elections.

May A Pan-African Conference on Reparations for the suffering caused by colonialism in Africa, organized by the OAU together with the Nigerian Government, was held in Abuja. The Conference appealed to those countries which had benefited from the colonization of Africa and the use of Africans as slaves (particularly European countries and the USA) to make reparations to Africans and their descendants, either in the form of capital transfers, or cancellation of debt.

June Eritrea was admitted as the 52nd member of the OAU. The 29th Assembly of Heads of State resolved to establish a mechanism for conflict prevention and resolution. The mechanism's primary objective was to be anticipation and prevention of conflict. In cases where conflicts had already occurred, the OAU was to undertake peace-making and peace-building activities, including the deployment of civilian or military monitoring missions. However, in the case of a conflict seriously degenerating, assistance would be sought from the United Nations.

July A seminar on the AEC was held in Addis Ababa, Ethiopia, concerned with the popularization of the treaty establishing the Community. Lack of resources emerged as one of the main barriers to the actual creation of the Community.

Sept. The OAU announced the immediate removal of economic sanctions against South Africa, following the approval by that country's Parliament of a bill to establish a transitional executive council prior to the democratic elections, scheduled to be conducted in April 1994.

Oct. The OAU Secretary-General condemned an attempted military coup in Burundi, in which the President and six Cabinet ministers were killed, and the subsequent civil unrest.

Nov. A summit conference of African ministers of foreign affairs, conducted in Addis Ababa, resolved to establish an OAU protection and observation mission to Burundi, consisting of 180 military personnel and 20 civilians, and appealed for international financial and material support to assist the mission. The ministers approved the principles for the establishment of a mechanism for conflict prevention, management and resolution. The meeting suggested that 5% of the OAU budget, but not less than US $1m., be allocated for an OAU Peace Fund to finance the mechanism, and that $0.5m. be made available for 1993.

Dec. A meeting of 11 African Heads of State approved the establishment of the Peace Fund and called for contributions from the international community. A draft statement of the mechanism for conflict prevention, management and resolution, issued by the OAU Secretary-General, expressed support for the efforts to resolve the conflict in Somalia and emphasized the need to promote national reconciliation.

1994

Feb. The Council of Ministers, at its 59th ordinary session, reaffirmed its support for the results of elections in Burundi, which were conducted in 1993, and endorsed the establishment of an OAU mission to promote dialogue and national reconciliation in that country. The Council condemned anti-government forces for the escalation of violence in Angola.

April The OAU mission to South Africa participated as observers of the electoral process. An OAU delegation visited Nigeria and Cameroon to investigate the border dispute between the two countries.

May South Africa was admitted as the 53rd member of the OAU.

June Consultations with each of the conflicting parties in Rwanda were conducted by the OAU. The Assembly of Heads of State, meeting in Tunis, approved a code of conduct for inter-African relations, in order to strengthen political consultation and co-operation for the promotion of security and stability in the region. Nine countries were nominated to serve on the central committee (organ) of the mechanism for conflict prevention, management and resolution, which was to implement an early-warning system for identifying potential conflicts and introduce measures to manage and resolve conflicts. The military component of the OAU mission in Burundi was now deployed in that country, and its mandate was extended until mid-September. (The mission has subsequently been granted three-monthly extensions of its mandate.)

Nov. The Secretary-General, noting the Organization's serious financial situation, warned that most activities of the regular budget for 1994/95 would have to be suspended. Certain sanctions were to be imposed on any country that had not paid its contribution in full by 1 June 1995.

1995

March An extraordinary session of the Council of Ministers, held in Cairo, Egypt, adopted an Agenda for Action, which aimed to stimulate African economic and social development. The document emphasized the importance of peace, democratic government and stability in achieving development targets. It also assessed Africa's role in the world economy and the need for structural reforms of countries' economies, in particular in view of agreements reached under the GATT Uruguay Round of trade negotiations. The OAU, together with representatives of the UN and the Commonwealth secretariat, dispatched a special mission to Sierra Leone, in order to assess means of facilitating the peace process in that country.

April A meeting of the conflict mechanism's central organ, held in Tunis, Tunisia, reviewed OAU peace initiatives. The meeting urged OAU member states to offer humanitarian aid to consolidate the peace process in Angola and for further OAU assistance for the rehabilitation and reconstruction of Somalia. A seminar, organized jointly by the OAU and the International Committee of the Red Cross, assembled military and civil experts in Yaoundé, Cameroon, to discuss the issue of land-mines.

May An 81-member OAU observer group was deployed to monitor a general election in Ethiopia. The group confirmed that the electoral process had been 'free and fair'.

June Faced with the threat of sanctions, which included a prohibition on full participation in the forthcoming summit and on the election of a country's nationals to key positions in the Organization, member states paid some US $20m. in owed contributions during the month (leaving an estimated total deficit of $38m.). At the 31st Assembly of Heads of State, held in Addis Ababa, Ethiopia, later in the month, the Secretary-General observed that the OAU's peace-keeping role had been severely affected by the failure of member states to pay their contributions. Sanctions were to be imposed on those countries which had failed to pay 25% of their arrears by the end of June. (Liberia and Somalia were exempted from this deadline.) The meeting endorsed a proposal to establish a conflict management centre, provisionally in Cairo, Egypt, to strengthen the OAU's role in conflict prevention. The situation in warring African countries was discussed, as well as the problem of large-scale refugee and displaced populations in the region. In addition, member states urged the international community to end the application of sanctions against Libya.

Sept. An extraordinary meeting of the conflict mechanism's central organ condemned the attempted assassination of Egypt's President Mubarak prior to the 31st Heads of State meeting in June. The committee censured Sudan for protecting the alleged perpetrators of the attack and for supporting other terrorist elements in the country.

Oct. OAU observers monitored the conduct of elections in Zanzibar and attempted to mediate between the parties when the vote failed to secure a decisive result.

Nov. Ten member states (Angola, Central African Republic, Chad, Comoros, Equatorial Guinea, Guinea-Bissau, Niger, São Tomé and Príncipe, Seychelles and Sierra Leone) lost their full rights to participate in the organization, having failed to pay, in full or part, their accumulated contribution arrears, amounting to US $16.5m. A 50-member OAU observer group was deployed to monitor elections in Algeria, as part of an international team.

1996

Feb. The Council of Ministers reiterated the OAU's readiness to promote and support dialogue and reconciliation in Burundi. However, the meeting did not support military intervention in that country, despite a UN report proposing international co-operation with the OAU to establish a stand-by force for Burundi.

March The UN Secretary-General launched a system-wide Special Initiative on Africa, which was based on the development objectives outlined in the OAU Agenda for Action (see above). Funds were to be allocated under the Initiative to strengthen the OAU's capacity for conflict prevention, management and resolution.

May-June The OAU assisted the International Peace Academy to conduct a meeting of international organizations, in Cape Town, South Africa, to promote the OAU's conflict mechanism, under the theme of 'Civil Society and Conflict Management in Africa'.

July The 32nd Assembly of Heads of State agreed to support a plan, formulated earlier that month by the Governments of Tanzania, Uganda and Ethiopia, to send troops to Burundi in a peace-keeping capacity. The Assembly requested logistical and financial support from the international community for the initiative. In a separate declaration OAU leaders expressed their support for Boutros Boutros-Ghali's candidacy for a second term as the UN Secretary-General. The endorsement was opposed by the President of Rwanda, Pasteur Bizimungu, who condemned the lack of UN protection afforded to his country during the civil unrest in 1994. At the end of the meeting it was announced that member states still owing contributions to the organization were to be exempt from sanctions measures until the end of the year, provided that they pay 30% of their arrears by 31 July. (Burundi, Liberia, Sierra Leone and Somalia were to be exempt until March 1997.) At the end of July, following a military coup in Burundi, the OAU endorsed a decision of seven east and central African states to impose economic sanctions against the new regime.

Aug. The US Government granted US $2.9m. to the OAU Peace Fund, in support of conflict prevention and resolution.

Oct. The OAU Secretary-General cautiously endorsed a US proposal to establish an African military force for the protection of civilian populations in areas of conflict. A regional committee of the OAU declared its support for the continuation of the economic embargo against Burundi.

Nov. An OAU delegation, meeting with the heads of state of eight African countries in Nairobi, Kenya, supported the establishment of an international humanitarian force, to be sent to Zaire (although this was never deployed).

Dec. The OAU President, in an attempt to overcome the impasse reached regarding the election of a new UN Secretary-General (owing to US opposition to Boutros-Ghali), confirmed that African nations should propose alternative candidates for the position.

1997

Jan. The UN and the OAU appointed Muhamed Sahnoun as a joint Special Representative for the Great Lakes Region.

Feb. The 65th session of the Council of Ministers, meeting in Libya, expressed its support of that country in the face of sanctions imposed upon it by the international community. The OAU welcomed the newly-elected Secretary-General of the UN, the Ghanaian, Kofi Annan. The situation in Zaire was discussed and an extraordinary summit of the OAU's conflict management mechanism was scheduled for March. Further donations to the OAU Peace Fund were requested.

March A special summit of the OAU Organ on conflict management and resolution, which was attended by delegations from both the Zairean Government and the rebel Alliance des Forces démocratiques pour la Libération du Congo-Zaïre, called for an immediate cease-fire and concluded a provisional agreement for negotiations between the two sides based on a five-point plan that had been formulated by Sahnoun and approved by the UN Security Council in February.

June The Assembly of Heads of State, meeting in Harare, Zimbabwe, condemned the military coup in Sierra Leone, which took place in May, and endorsed the intervention of ECOMOG troops in order to restore a democratic government in that country. The OAU stated that future coups in the continent would not be tolerated, and the importance of universal human rights to be established across Africa was reiterated throughout the meeting. The inaugural meeting of the African Economic Community also took place.

July The UN Development Programme donated US $3m. to the OAU conflict management mechanism.

Specialized Agencies

African Accounting Council: POB 11223, Kinshasa, Zaire; f. 1979; provides assistance to institutions in member countries on standardization of accounting; promotes education, further training and research in accountancy and related areas of study.

African Bureau for Educational Sciences: 29 ave de la Justice, BP 1764, Kinshasa I, Zaire; tel. (12) 22006; telex 21166; f. 1973 to conduct educational research. Publs *Bulletin d'Information* (quarterly), *Revue africaine des sciences de l'éducation* (2 a year), *Répertoire africain des institutions de recherche* (annually).

African Civil Aviation Commission—AFCAC: 15 blvd de la République, BP 2356, Dakar, Senegal; tel. 23-20-30; telex 61182; fax 23-26-61; f. 1969 to encourage co-operation in all civil aviation activities; promotes co-ordination and better utilization and development of African air transport systems and the standardization of aircraft, flight equipment and training programmes for pilots and mechanics; organizes working groups and seminars, and compiles statistics. Pres. Capt. SHETTIMA ABBA-GANA (Nigeria); Sec. A. CHEIFFOU (acting).

Pan-African News Agency—PANA: BP 4650, Dakar, Senegal; tel. 24-14-10; fax 24-13-90; regional headquarters in Khartoum, Sudan; Lusaka, Zambia; Kinshasa, the Democratic Republic of the Congo; Lagos, Nigeria; Tripoli, Libya; began operations in May 1983; receives information from national news agencies and circulates news in English and French. Following financial problems, plans to restructure the agency at a cost of US $4.7m., in order to allow shares to be held by the private sector, were announced in June 1997. Capital was to be increased by 25,000 shares, while the agency was to be renamed PANA Presse. Co-ordinator BABACAR FALL. Publ. *PANA Review*.

Pan-African Postal Union—PAPU: POB 6026, Arusha, Tanzania; tel. (57) 8603; telex 42096; fax (57) 8606; f. 1980 to extend members' co-operation in the improvement of postal services. Sec.-Gen. GEZAHEGNE GEBREWOLD (Ethiopia). Publ. *PAPU Bulletin*.

Pan-African Railways Union: BP 687, Kinshasa, Zaire; tel. (12) 23861; telex 21258; f. 1972 to standardize, expand, co-ordinate and improve members' railway services; the ultimate aim is to link all systems; main organs: Gen. Assembly, Exec. Bd, Gen. Secr., five tech. cttees. Mems in 30 African countries. Pres. TOM MMARI; Sec.-Gen. ROBERT GEBE NKANA (Malawi).

Pan-African Telecommunications Union: POB 7248, Kinshasa, Zaire; f. 1977; co-ordinates devt of telecommunications networks and services in Africa.

Supreme Council for Sports in Africa: BP 1363, Yaoundé, Cameroon; tel. and fax 23-95-80; telex 8295. Sec.-Gen. Dr AWOTURE ELEYAE (Nigeria). Publ. *SCSA News* (6 a year).

ORGANIZATION OF THE ISLAMIC CONFERENCE—OIC

Address: Kilo 6, Mecca Rd, POB 178, Jeddah 21411, Saudi Arabia.

Telephone: (2) 680-0800; **telex:** 601366; **fax:** (2) 687-3568.

The Organization was formally established in May 1971, when its Secretariat became operational, following a summit meeting of Muslim heads of state at Rabat, Morocco, in September 1969, and the Islamic Foreign Ministers' Conference in Jeddah in March 1970, and in Karachi, Pakistan, in December 1970.

MEMBERS

Afghanistan	Iran	Qatar
Albania	Iraq	Saudi Arabia
Algeria	Jordan	Senegal
Azerbaijan	Kazakhstan	Sierra Leone
Bahrain	Kuwait	Somalia
Bangladesh	Kyrgyzstan	Sudan
Benin	Lebanon	Suriname
Brunei	Libya	Syria
Burkina Faso	Malaysia	Tajikistan
Cameroon	Maldives	Tunisia
Chad	Mali	Turkey
The Comoros	Mauritania	Turkmenistan
Djibouti	Morocco	Uganda
Egypt	Mozambique	United Arab Emirates
Gabon	Niger	Uzbekistan
The Gambia	Nigeria*	Yemen
Guinea	Oman	
Guinea-Bissau	Pakistan	
Indonesia	Palestine	

* Nigeria renounced its membership of the OIC in May 1991; however, the OIC has not formally recognized this decision.

Note: Observer status has been granted to Bosnia and Herzegovina, the Central African Republic, Guyana, Togo, the Muslim community of the 'Turkish Republic of Northern Cyprus', the Moro National Liberation Front (MNLF) of the southern Philippines, the United Nations, the Non-Aligned Movement, the League of Arab States, the Organization of African Unity, the Economic Co-operation Organization, the Union of the Arab Maghreb and the Co-operation Council for the Arab States of the Gulf.

Organization

(August 1997)

SUMMIT CONFERENCES

The supreme body of the Organization is the Conference of Heads of State, which met in 1969 at Rabat, Morocco, in 1974 at Lahore, Pakistan, and in January 1981 at Mecca, Saudi Arabia, when it was decided that summit conferences would be held every three years in future. Sixth Conference: Dakar, Senegal, December 1991; seventh Conference: Casablanca, Morocco, December 1994. The eighth Conference was to be held in Teheran, Iran, in December 1997.

CONFERENCE OF MINISTERS OF FOREIGN AFFAIRS

Conferences take place annually, to consider the means for implementing the general policy of the Organization, although they may also be convened for extraordinary sessions.

SECRETARIAT

The executive organ of the Organization, headed by a Secretary-General (who is elected by the Conference of Ministers of Foreign Affairs for a four-year term, renewable only once) and four Assistant Secretaries-General (similarly appointed).

Secretary-General: Azeddine Laraki (Morocco).

At the summit conference in January 1981 it was decided that an International Islamic Court of Justice should be established to adjudicate in disputes between Muslim countries. Experts met in January 1983 to draw up a constitution for the court, but by 1997 it was not yet in operation.

SPECIALIZED COMMITTEES

Al-Quds Committee: f. 1975 to implement the resolutions of the Islamic Conference on the status of Jerusalem (Al-Quds); it meets at the level of foreign ministers; maintains the Al-Quds Fund; Chair. King Hassan II of Morocco.

Standing Committee for Economic and Commercial Co-operation (COMCEC): f. 1981; Chair. Süleyman Demirel (Pres. of Turkey).

Standing Committee for Information and Cultural Affairs (COMIAC): f. 1981; Chair. Abdou Diouf (Pres. of Senegal).

Standing Committee for Scientific and Technological Co-operation (COMSTECH): f. 1981; Chair. Farooq A. Leghari (Pres. of Pakistan).

Islamic Commission for Economic, Cultural and Social Affairs: f. 1976.

Permanent Finance Committee.

Other committees comprise the Committee of Islamic Solidarity with the Peoples of the Sahel, the Six-Member Committee on the Situation of Muslims in the Philippines, the Six-Member Committee on Palestine, the *ad hoc* Committee on Afghanistan, the OIC contact group on Bosnia and Herzegovina, and the OIC contact group on Jammu and Kashmir.

Activities

The Organization's aims, as proclaimed in the Charter that was adopted in 1972, are:

(i) To promote Islamic solidarity among member states;

(ii) To consolidate co-operation among member states in the economic, social, cultural, scientific and other vital fields, and to arrange consultations among member states belonging to international organizations;

(iii) To endeavour to eliminate racial segregation and discrimination and to eradicate colonialism in all its forms;

(iv) To take necessary measures to support international peace and security founded on justice;

(v) To co-ordinate all efforts for the safeguard of the Holy Places and support of the struggle of the people of Palestine, and help them to regain their rights and liberate their land;

(vi) To strengthen the struggle of all Muslim people with a view to safeguarding their dignity, independence and national rights; and

(vii) To create a suitable atmosphere for the promotion of co-operation and understanding among member states and other countries.

The first summit conference of Islamic leaders (representing 24 states) took place in 1969 following the burning of the Al Aqsa Mosque in Jerusalem. At this conference it was decided that Islamic governments should 'consult together with a view to promoting close co-operation and mutual assistance in the economic, scientific, cultural and spiritual fields, inspired by the immortal teachings of Islam'. Thereafter the foreign ministers of the countries concerned met annually, and adopted the Charter of the Organization of the Islamic Conference in 1972.

At the second Islamic summit conference (Lahore, Pakistan, 1974), the Islamic Solidarity Fund was established, together with a committee of representatives which later evolved into the Islamic Commission for Economic, Cultural and Social Affairs. Subsequently, numerous other subsidiary bodies have been set up (see below).

ECONOMIC CO-OPERATION

A general agreement for economic, technical and commercial co-operation came into force in 1981, providing for the establishment of joint investment projects and trade co-ordination. This was followed by an agreement on promotion, protection and guarantee of investments among member states. A plan of action to strengthen economic co-operation was adopted at the third Islamic summit conference in 1981, aiming to promote collective self-reliance and the development of joint ventures in all sectors. In May 1993 the OIC committee for economic and commercial co-operation, meeting in Istanbul, agreed to review and update the 1981 plan of action.

A meeting of ministers of industry was held in February 1982, and agreed to promote industrial co-operation, including joint ventures in agricultural machinery, engineering and other basic industries. The fifth summit conference, held in 1987, approved proposals for joint development of modern technology, and for improving scientific and technical skills in the less developed Islamic countries. In December 1988 it was announced that a committee of experts, established by the OIC, was to draw up a 10-year programme of assistance to developing countries (mainly in Africa) in science and technology.

CULTURAL CO-OPERATION

The Organization supports education in Muslim communities throughout the world, and was instrumental in the establishment of Islamic universities in Niger and Uganda (see below). It organizes seminars on various aspects of Islam, and encourages dialogue with the other monotheistic religions. Support is given to publications on Islam both in Muslim and Western countries.

In March 1989 the Conference of Ministers of Foreign Affairs denounced as an apostate the author of the controversial novel *The Satanic Verses* (Salman Rushdie), demanded the withdrawal of the book from circulation, and urged member states to boycott publishing houses that refused to comply.

HUMANITARIAN ASSISTANCE

Assistance is given to Muslim communities affected by wars and natural disasters, in co-operation with UN organizations, particularly UNHCR. The countries of the Sahel region (Burkina Faso, Cape Verde, Chad, The Gambia, Guinea, Guinea-Bissau, Mali, Mauritania, Niger and Senegal) receive particular attention as victims of drought. In April 1993 member states pledged US $80m. in emergency assistance for Muslims affected by the war in Bosnia and Herzegovina (see below for details of subsequent assistance).

POLITICAL CO-OPERATION

The Organization is also active at a political level. From the beginning it called for vacation of Arab territories by Israel, recognition of the rights of Palestinians and of the Palestine Liberation Organization (PLO) as their sole legitimate representative, and the restoration of Jerusalem to Arab rule. The 1981 summit conference called for a *jihad* (holy war—though not necessarily in a military sense) 'for the liberation of Jerusalem and the occupied territories'; this was to include an Islamic economic boycott of Israel. In 1982 Islamic ministers of foreign affairs decided to establish Islamic offices for boycotting Israel and for military co-operation with the PLO. The 1984 summit conference agreed to reinstate Egypt (suspended following the peace treaty signed with Israel in 1979) as a member of the OIC, although the resolution was opposed by seven states.

The fifth summit conference, held in January 1987, discussed the continuing Iran–Iraq war, and agreed that the Islamic Peace Committee should attempt to prevent the sale of military equipment to the parties in the conflict. The conference also discussed the conflicts in Chad and Lebanon, and requested the holding of a United Nations conference to define international terrorism, as opposed to legitimate fighting for freedom.

In August 1990 a majority of ministers of foreign affairs condemned Iraq's recent invasion of Kuwait, and demanded the withdrawal of Iraqi forces. In August 1991 the Conference of Ministers of Foreign Affairs obstructed Iraq's attempt to propose a resolution demanding the repeal of economic sanctions against the country. The sixth summit conference, held in Senegal in December 1991, reflected the divisions in the Arab world that resulted from Iraq's invasion of Kuwait and the ensuing war. Twelve heads of state did not attend, sending representatives, reportedly to register protest at the presence of Jordan and the PLO at the conference, both of which had given support to Iraq. Disagreement also arose between the PLO and the majority of other OIC members when it was proposed to cease the OIC's support for the PLO's *jihad* in the Arab territories occupied by Israel. The proposal, which was adopted, represented an attempt to further the Middle East peace negotiations.

In August 1992 the UN General Assembly approved a non-binding resolution, introduced by the OIC, that requested the UN Security Council to take increased action, including the use of force, in order to defend the non-Serbian population of Bosnia and Herzegovina (some 43% of Bosnians being Muslims) from Serbian aggression, and to restore its 'territorial integrity'. The OIC Conference of Ministers of Foreign Affairs, which was held in Jeddah, Saudi Arabia, in early December, demanded anew that the UN Security Council take all necessary measures against Serbia and Montenegro, including military intervention, in accordance with Article 42 of the UN Charter, in order to protect the Bosnian Muslims. In early February 1993 the OIC appealed to the Security Council to remove the embargo on armaments to Bosnia and Herzegovina with regard to the Bosnian Muslims, to allow them to defend themselves from the Bosnian Serbs, who were far better armed.

A report by an OIC fact-finding mission, which in February 1993 visited Azad Kashmir while investigating allegations of repression of the largely Muslim population of the Indian state of Jammu and Kashmir by the Indian armed forces, was presented to the 1993 Conference. The meeting urged member states to take the necessary measures to persuade India to cease the 'massive human rights violations' in Jammu and Kashmir and to allow the Indian Kashmiris to 'exercise their inalienable right to self-determination'. In September 1994 ministers of foreign affairs, meeting in Islamabad, Pakistan, urged the Indian Government to grant permission for an OIC fact-finding mission, and for other human rights groups, to visit Jammu and Kashmir (which it had continually refused to do) and to refrain from human rights violations of the Kashmiri people. The ministers agreed to establish a contact group on Jammu and Kashmir, which was to provide a mechanism for promoting international awareness of the situation in that region and for seeking a peaceful solution to the dispute. In December OIC heads of state approved a resolution condemning reported human rights abuses by Indian security forces in Kashmir.

In July 1994 the OIC Secretary-General visited Afghanistan and proposed the establishment of a preparatory mechanism to promote national reconciliation in that country. In mid-1995 Saudi Arabia, acting as a representative of the OIC, pursued a peace initiative for Afghanistan and issued an invitation for leaders of the different factions to hold negotiations in Jeddah.

A special ministerial meeting on Bosnia and Herzegovina was held in July 1993, at which seven OIC countries committed themselves to making available up to 17,000 troops to serve in the UN Protection Force in the former Yugoslavia (UNPROFOR), to assist the United Nations in providing adequate protection and relief to the victims of war in Bosnia and Herzegovina. The meeting also decided to dispatch immediately a ministerial mission to persuade influential governments to support the OIC's demands for the removal of the arms embargo on Bosnian Muslims and the convening of a restructured international conference to bring about a political solution to the conflict. At the end of September 1994 ministers of foreign affairs of nine countries constituting the OIC contact group on Bosnia and Herzegovina, meeting in New York, resolved to prepare an assessment document on the issue, and to establish an alliance with its Western counterpart (comprising France, Germany, Russia, the United Kingdom and the USA). The two groups met in Geneva, Switzerland, in January 1995. In December 1994 OIC heads of state, convened in Morocco, proclaimed that the UN arms embargo on Bosnia and Herzegovina could not be applied to the Muslim authorities of that Republic, and requested the support of the international community for the continued presence of a UN force in the area. The Conference also resolved to review economic relations between OIC member states and any country that supported Serbian activities. An aid fund was established, to which member states were requested to contribute between US $500,000 and $5m., in order to provide further humanitarian and economic assistance to Bosnian Muslims. In relation to wider concerns the conference adopted a Code of Conduct for Combating International Terrorism, in an attempt to control Muslim extremist groups. The code commits states to ensuring that militant groups do not use their territory for planning or executing terrorist activity against other states, in addition to states refraining from direct support or participation in acts of terrorism. In a further resolution the OIC supported the decision by Iraq to recognize Kuwait, but advocated that Iraq comply with all UN Security Council decisions.

In July 1995 the OIC contact group on Bosnia and Herzegovina (at that time comprising Egypt, Iran, Malaysia, Morocco, Pakistan, Saudi Arabia, Senegal and Turkey), meeting in Geneva, declared the UN arms embargo against Bosnia and Herzegovina to be 'invalid'. Several Governments, including that of Malaysia, subsequently announced their willingness officially to supply weapons and other military assistance to the Bosnian Muslim forces. In September a meeting of all OIC ministers of defence and foreign affairs endorsed the establishment of an 'assistance mobilization group' which was to supply military, economic, legal and other assistance to Bosnia and Herzegovina. In a joint declaration the ministers also demanded the return of all territory seized by Bosnian Serb forces, the continued NATO bombing of Serb military targets, and that the city of Sarajevo be preserved under a Muslim-led Bosnian Government. In November the OIC Secretary-General endorsed the peace accord for the former Yugoslavia, which was signed, in Dayton, USA, by leaders of all the conflicting factions, and reaffirmed the commitment of Islamic states to participate in efforts to implement the accord. In the following month the OIC Conference of Ministers of Foreign Affairs, convened in Conakry, Guinea, requested the full support of the international community to reconstruct Bosnia and Herzegovina through humanitarian aid as well as economic and technical co-operation. Ministers declared that Palestine and the establishment of fully-autonomous Palestinian control of Jerusalem were issues of central importance for the Muslim world. The Conference urged the removal of all aspects of occupation and the cessation of the construction of Israeli settlements in the occupied territories. In addition, the final statement of the meeting condemned Armenian aggression against Azerbaijan, registered concern at the persisting civil conflict in Afghanistan, demanded the elimination of all weapons of mass destruction and pledged support for Libya (affected by the US trade embargo).

In December 1996 OIC ministers of foreign affairs, meeting in Jakarta, Indonesia, urged the international community to apply pressure on Israel in order to ensure its implementation of the terms of the Middle East peace process. The ministers reaffirmed the importance of ensuring that the provisions of the Dayton Peace Agreement for the former Yugoslavia were fully implemented, called for a peaceful settlement of the Kashmir issue, demanded that Iraq fulfil its obligations for the establishment of security, peace and stability in the region and proposed that an international conference on peace and national reconciliation in Somalia be convened. In addition, the meeting appealed for the cessation of the conflicts in Afghanistan and between Armenia and Azerbaijan. The ministers elected a new Secretary-General, Azeddine Laraki, who confirmed that the organization would continue to develop its role as an international mediator. In March 1997, at an extraordinary summit held in Pakistan, OIC heads of state and of government reiterated the organization's desire to increase international pressure upon Israel to ensure the full implementation of the terms of the Middle East peace process. An 'Islamabad Declaration' was also adopted, which pledged to increase co-operation between members of the OIC. In June, both the OIC and the Islamic World League condemned the decision by the US House of Representatives to recognize Jerusalem as the Israeli capital. The Secretary-General of the OIC issued a statement rejecting the US decision as counter to the role of the US as sponsor of the Middle East peace plan, while stating that peace could not be restored without a return to Palestinian sovereignty.

SUBSIDIARY ORGANS

International Commission for the Preservation of Islamic Cultural Heritage (ICPICH): POB 24, 80692 Beşiktaş, Istanbul, Turkey; tel. (212) 2591742; telex 26484; fax (212) 2584365; f. 1982. Sec. Prof. Dr Ekmeleddin İhsanoğlu (Turkey).

Islamic Centre for the Development of Trade: Complexe Commerciale des Habous, ave des FAR, BP 13545, Casablanca, Morocco; tel. (2) 314974; telex 46296; fax (2) 310110; e-mail icdt.org; f. 1983 to encourage regular commercial contacts, harmonize policies and promote investments among OIC mems. Dir Badre Eddine Allali. Publs *Tijaris: International and Inter-Islamic Trade Magazine* (quarterly), *Inter-Islamic Trade Report* (annual).

Islamic Institute of Technology: GPO Box 3003, Board Bazar, Gazipur, Dhaka, Bangladesh; tel. (2) 980-0960; telex 642739; fax (2) 980-0970; f. 1981 to develop human resources in OIC mem. states, with special reference to engineering, technology, tech. and vocational education and research; capacity of 90 full-time and 51 part-time staff and 1,000 students; library of 18,000 vols. Dir-Gen. Prof. A. M. Patwari. Publs *News Bulletin* (annually), reports, human resources development series.

Islamic Jurisprudence Academy: Jeddah, Saudi Arabia; f. 1982. Sec.-Gen. Sheikh Mohamed Habib Belkhojah.

Islamic Solidarity Fund: c/o OIC Secretariat, POB 178, Jeddah 21411, Saudi Arabia; tel. (2) 680-0800; fax (2) 687-3568; f. 1974 to meet the needs of Islamic communities by providing emergency aid and the finance to build mosques, Islamic centres, hospitals, schools and universities. Chair. Sheikh Nasir Abdullah bin Hamdan; Exec. Dir Abdullah Hersi.

Islamic University of Niger: BP 11507, Niamey; tel. 723903; fax 733796; f. 1984; provides courses of study in *Shar'ia* (Islamic law) and Arabic language and literature; also offers courses in pedagogy and teacher training; receives grants from Islamic Solidarity Fund and contributions from OIC member states; Rector Prof. Abdelali Oudhriri.

Islamic University in Uganda: POB 2555, Mbale; tel. (45) 33417; fax (45) 3034; Kampala Liaison Officer: POB 7689, Kampala; tel. (41) 236874; fax (41) 254576; f. 1988 to meet the educational needs of Muslim populations in English-speaking Africa; financed by OIC. Prin. Officer Prof. Mahdi Adamu.

Research Centre for Islamic History, Art and Culture (IRCICA): POB 24, Beşiktaş 80692, Istanbul, Turkey; tel. (212) 2591742; telex 26484; fax (212) 2584365; f. 1980; library of 50,000 vols. Dir-Gen. Prof. Dr Ekmeleddin İhsanoğlu. Publ. *Newsletter* (3 a year).

Statistical, Economic and Social Research and Training Centre for the Islamic Countries: Attar Sok 4, GOP, Ankara, Turkey; tel. (312) 4686172; telex 18944838; fax (312) 4673458; f. 1978. Dir-Gen. Dr Şadi Cindoruk.

SPECIALIZED INSTITUTIONS

International Islamic News Agency (IINA): King Khalid Palace, Madinah Rd, POB 5054, Jeddah, Saudi Arabia; tel. (2) 665-8561; telex 601090; fax (2) 665-9358; f. 1972. Dir-Gen. Abdulwahab Kashif.

Islamic Development Bank: see p. 122.

Islamic Educational, Scientific and Cultural Organization (ISESCO): Hay Ryad, BP 2275, Rabat 10104, Morocco; tel. (7) 772433; telex 32645; fax (7) 777459; f. 1982. Dir-Gen. Dr Abdulaziz bin Othman al-Twaijri. Publs *ISESCO Bulletin* (quarterly), *Islam Today* (2 a year), *ISESCO Triennial*.

Islamic States Broadcasting Organization (ISBO): POB 6351, Jeddah 21442, Saudi Arabia; tel. (2) 672-1121; telex 601442; fax (2) 672-2600. Sec.-Gen. Hussein al-Askary.

AFFILIATED INSTITUTIONS

International Association of Islamic Banks (IAIB): Queen's Bldg, 23rd Floor, Al-Balad Dist, POB 23425, Jeddah 21426, Saudi Arabia; tel. (2) 643-1276; fax (2) 644-7239; f. 1977 to link financial institutions operating on Islamic banking principles; activities include training and research; mems: 192 banks and other financial institutions in 34 countries. Sec.-Gen. Samir A. Shaikh.

Islamic Chamber of Commerce and Industry: POB 3831, Clifton, Karachi 75600, Pakistan; tel. (21) 5874756; telex 27272; fax (21) 5870765; f. 1979 to promote trade and industry among member states; comprises nat. chambers or feds of chambers of commerce and industry. Sec.-Gen. Aqeel Ahmad al-Jassim.

Islamic Committee for the International Crescent: c/o OIC, Kilo 6, Mecca Rd, POB 178, Jeddah 21411, Saudi Arabia; tel. (2) 680-0800; telex 601366; fax (2) 687-3568; f. 1979 to attempt to alleviate the suffering caused by natural disasters and war. Sec.-Gen. Dr Ahmad Abdallah Cherif.

Islamic Solidarity Sports Federation: POB 6040, Riyadh 11442, Saudi Arabia; tel. and fax (1) 482-2145; telex 404760; f. 1981. Sec.-Gen. Dr Mohamed Saleh Gazdar.

Organization of Islamic Capitals and Cities (OICC): POB 13621, Jeddah 21414, Saudi Arabia; tel. (2) 698-6651; fax (2) 698-1053; f. 1980 to promote and develop co-operation among OICC mems, to preserve their character and heritage, to implement planning guidelines for the growth of Islamic cities and to upgrade standards of public services and utilities in those cities. Sec.-Gen. Abdulqadir Hamzak Koshak.

Organization of the Islamic Shipowners' Association: POB 14900, Jeddah 21434, Saudi Arabia; tel. (2) 665-3379; telex 607303; fax (2) 660-4920; f. 1981 to promote co-operation among maritime cos in Islamic countries. Sec.-Gen. Dr Abdullatif A. Sultan.

SOUTHERN AFRICAN DEVELOPMENT COMMUNITY—SADC

Address: SADC Bldg, Private Bag 0095, Gaborone, Botswana.

Telephone: 351863; **telex:** 2555; **fax:** 372848.

The first Southern African Development Co-ordination Conference (SADCC) was held at Arusha, Tanzania, in July 1979, to harmonize development plans and to reduce the region's economic dependence on South Africa. On 17 August 1992 the 10 member countries of the SADCC signed a treaty establishing the Southern African Development Community (SADC), which replaced the SADCC. The treaty places binding obligations on member countries, with the aim of promoting economic integration towards a fully developed common market. A tribunal was to be established to arbitrate in the case of disputes between member states arising from the treaty. By September 1993 all of the member states had ratified the treaty; it came into effect on 5 October. South Africa and Mauritius have subsequently become members of the SADC.

MEMBERS

Angola	Mauritius	Swaziland
Botswana	Mozambique	Tanzania
Lesotho	Namibia	Zambia
Malawi	South Africa	Zimbabwe

TREATY ESTABLISHING THE SADC

The Treaty declares the following aims:

(i) deeper economic co-operation and integration, on the basis of balance, equality and mutual benefit, providing for cross-border investment and trade, and freer movement of factors of production, goods and services across national boundaries;

(ii) common economic, political and social values and systems, enhancing enterprise competitiveness, democracy and good governance, respect for the rule of law and human rights, popular participation, and the alleviation of poverty; and

(iii) strengthened regional solidarity, peace and security, in order for the people of the region to live and work in harmony.

Organization

(July 1997)

SUMMIT MEETING

The meeting is held annually and is attended by Heads of State and Government or their representatives. It is the supreme policy-making organ of the SADC.

COUNCIL OF MINISTERS

Representatives of SADC member countries at ministerial level meet at least twice a year; in addition, special meetings are held to co-ordinate regional policy in a particular field by, for example, ministers of energy and ministers of transport.

CONFERENCES ON CO-OPERATION

A conference with the SADC's 'international co-operating partners' (donor governments and international agencies) is held annually to review progress in the various sectors of the SADC programme and to present new projects requiring assistance.

SECRETARIAT

Executive Secretary: KAIRE MBUENDE (Namibia).

SECTORAL CO-ORDINATION OFFICES

Agricultural and Natural Resources Research and Training: Private Bag 0033, Gaborone, Botswana; tel. 328780; telex 2752; fax 328965.

Culture and Information: Ministry of Information, Avda Francisco Orlando Magumbwe 750, Maputo, Mozambique; tel. (1) 493423; telex 6487; fax (1) 493427.

Employment and Labour: POB 32186, Lusaka, Zambia; tel. (1) 223154; telex 40686; fax (1) 227251.

Energy: rua Gil Vicente No. 2, Luanda, Angola; tel. 345288; telex 4090; fax 343003.

Environment and Land Management: Ministry of Agriculture, Co-operatives and Marketing, POB 24, Maseru 100, Lesotho; tel. 312158; telex 4414; fax 310190.

Finance and Investment: Private Bag X115, Pretoria, 0001, South Africa; tel. (12) 3155693; fax (12) 219580.

Food, Agriculture and Natural Resources: 88 Rezende St, POB 4046, Harare, Zimbabwe; tel. (4) 736051; telex 22440; fax (4) 795345.

Human Resources Development: Dept of Economic Planning and Statistics, POB 602, Mbabane, Swaziland; tel. 46344; telex 3020; fax 46407.

Industry and Trade: POB 9491, Dar es Salaam, Tanzania; tel. (51) 31455; telex 41686; fax (51) 46919.

Inland Fisheries, Wildlife and Forestry: Ministry of Forestry and Natural Resources, Private Bag 350, Lilongwe 3, Malawi; tel. 782600; telex 44465; fax 780260.

Livestock Production and Animal Disease Control: Private Bag 0032, Gaborone, Botswana; tel. 350620; telex 2543; fax 303744.

Marine Fisheries and Resources: Private Bag 13355, Windhoek, Namibia; tel. (61) 2053911; fax (61) 224566.

Mining: Ministry of Mines and Mineral Development, POB 31969, Lusaka, Zambia; tel. (1) 251719; telex 40539; fax (1) 252095; e-mail sadc-mcu@zamnet.zm.

Southern African Centre for Co-operation in Agricultural Research (SACCAR): Private Bag 00108, Gaborone, Botswana; tel. 328847; telex 2752; fax 328806; Dir Dr BRUNO NDUNGURU.

Southern African Transport and Communications Commission (SATCC): CP 2677, Maputo, Mozambique; tel. (1) 420246; telex 6606; fax (1) 420213; Dir SEVENIN KAOMBWE (acting).

Tourism: Ministry of Tourism, Sports and Culture, POB 52, Maseru 100, Lesotho; tel. 313034; telex 4228; fax 310194.

Activities

In July 1979 the first Southern African Development Co-ordination Conference was attended by delegations from Angola, Botswana, Mozambique, Tanzania and Zambia, with representatives from donor governments and international agencies; the group was later joined by Lesotho, Malawi, Swaziland and Zimbabwe, and Namibia became a member in 1990.

In April 1980 a regional economic summit conference was held in Lusaka, Zambia, and the Lusaka Declaration, a statement of strategy entitled 'Southern Africa: Towards Economic Liberation', was approved, together with a programme of action allotting specific studies and tasks to member governments (see list of co-ordinating offices, above). The members aimed to reduce their dependence on South Africa for rail and air links and port facilities, imports of raw materials and manufactured goods, and the supply of electric power. In 1985, however, an SADCC report noted that since 1980 the region had become still more dependent on South Africa for its trade outlets, and the 1986 summit meeting, although it recommended the adoption of economic sanctions against South Africa, failed to establish a timetable for doing so.

In January 1992 a meeting of the SADCC Council of Ministers approved proposals to transform the organization into a fully integrated economic community, and in mid-August the treaty establishing the SADC (see above) was signed. South Africa became a member of the SADC in August 1994, thus strengthening the objective of regional co-operation and economic integration.

A possible merger between the SADC and the Preferential Trade Area for Eastern and Southern African States (PTA), which consisted of all the members of the SADC apart from Botswana and had similar aims of enhancing economic co-operation, was rejected by the SADC's Executive Secretary in January 1993. He denied that the two organizations were duplicating each other's work, as had been suggested. In August 1994 SADC heads of state, meeting in Gaborone, Botswana, advocated that, in order to minimize any duplication of activities, the PTA be divided into two sections: a southern region, incorporating all SADC members, and a northern region. It was emphasized that there would not be a merger between the two groupings. Concerns of regional rivalry with the PTA's successor, the Common Market for Eastern and Southern Africa (COMESA, q.v.), were ongoing in 1995. In July SADC heads of state and government agreed to hold a joint SADC/COMESA summit meeting on the future of the two organizations. In August 1986 an SADC–COMESA ministeral meeting advocated the continued separate functioning of the two organizations.

In September 1994 the first meeting of ministers of foreign affairs of the SADC and the European Union (EU) was held in Berlin, Germany. The two sides agreed to establish working groups to promote closer trade, political, regional and economic co-operation. In particular, a declaration issued from the meeting specified joint objectives, including a reduction of exports of weapons to southern Africa and of the arms trade within the region, promotion of investment in the region's manufacturing sector and support for democracy at all levels. A consultative meeting between representatives of the SADC and EU was held in February 1995, in Lilongwe, Malawi, at which both groupings resolved to strengthen security in the southern African region. The meeting proposed initiating mechanisms to prevent conflicts and to maintain peace, and agreed to organize a conference to address the problems of drug-trafficking and cross-border crime in the region. A second SADC–EU ministerial meeting, held in Namibia in October 1996, endorsed a Regional Indicative Programme to enhance co-operation between the two organizations over the next five years.

In April 1997 the SADC announced the establishment of a Parliamentary Forum in order to promote democracy, human rights and good governance throughout the region. Membership was to be open to national parliaments of all SADC countries, and was to offer fair representation for women. Representatives were to serve for a period of five years. The Parliamentary Forum, with its headquarters in Windhoek, Namibia, was to receive funds from member parliaments, governments and charitable and international organizations.

REGIONAL SECURITY

In November 1994 SADC ministers of defence, meeting in Arusha, Tanzania, approved the establishment of a regional rapid-deployment peace-keeping force, which could be used to contain regional conflicts or civil unrest in member states.

In June 1996 SADC heads of state and government, meeting in Gaborone, Botswana, inaugurated a new Organ on Politics, Defence and Security, which was expected to enhance co-ordination of national policies and activities in these areas. The objectives of the new body were, *inter alia,* to safeguard the people and development of the region against instability arising from civil disorder, inter-state conflict and external aggression; to undertake conflict prevention, management and resolution activities, by mediating in inter-state and intra-state disputes and conflicts, pre-empting conflicts through an early-warning system and using diplomacy and peace-keeping to achieve sustainable peace; to promote the development of a common foreign policy, in areas of mutual interest, and the evolution of common political institutions; to develop close co-operation between the police and security services of the region; and to encourage the observance of universal human rights, as provided for in the charters of the UN and OAU. The summit meeting elected the Zimbabwean President, Robert Mugabe, to chair the Organ in its first year. The Zambian President, Frederick Chiluba, failed to attend the meeting, owing to his Government's concern that the new body was empowered to interfere in the country's internal affairs. In October the Organ convened, at summit level, to consider measures to promote the peace process in Angola.

In April 1997 a newly-formed peace-keeping force commenced a training programme which aimed to inform troops from nine SADC countries of UN peace-keeping doctrines, procedures and strategies. The exercise, which took place in Zimbabwe, cost US $900,000 and was funded by the British Government and the Zimbabwe National Army. Also in April representatives from each SADC country, meeting in Harare, established a regional co-ordination committee to pursue the objectives of an intergovernmental campaign to conclude a worldwide ban on the use of anti-personnel landmines, and to eliminate all existing landmines from the southern Africa region.

TRANSPORT AND COMMUNICATIONS

At the SADC's inception transport was seen as the most important area to be developed, on the grounds that, as the Lusaka Declaration noted, without the establishment of an adequate regional transport and communications system, other areas of co-operation become impractical. Priority was to be given to the improvement of road and railway services into Mozambique, so that the landlocked countries of the region could transport their goods through Mozambican ports instead of South African ones. The Southern African Transport and Communications Commission (SATCC) was established, in Maputo, Mozambique, in order to undertake SADC's activities in this sector. The successful distribution of emergency supplies in 1992/93, following a severe drought in the region, was reliant on improvements made to the region's infrastructure in recent years. The facilities of 12 ports in southern Africa, including South Africa, were used to import some 11.5m. metric tons of drought-related commodities, and the SADC co-ordinated six transport corridors to ensure unobstructed movement of food and other supplies. In 1997 Namibia announced plans, supported by the SADC, to establish a rail link with Angola in order to form a trade route similar to that created in Mozambique, on the western side of southern Africa.

In 1993/94 208 of the SADC's 446 development projects were in the transport and communications sector, amounting to US $6,934.1m., or 81% of total project financing. These projects aimed to address missing links and over-stretched sections of the regional network, as well as to improve efficiency, operational co-ordination and human resource development, such as management training projects. Other sectoral objectives were to ensure the compatibility of technical systems within the region and to promote the harmonization of regulations relating to intra-regional traffic and trade.

Port rehabilitation projects in 1993/94 were centred on Maputo and Nacala ports, in Mozambique, and Lobito, in Angola. The SADC promotes greater co-operation in the civil aviation sector, in order to improve efficiency and to reverse a steady decline in the region's airline industries. Within the telecommunications sector efforts have been made to increase the capacity of direct exchange lines and international subscriber dialling (ISD) services. An SADC Expedited Mail Service operates in the postal services sector. The SATCC's Technical Unit oversees the region's meteorological services and issues a regular *Drought-Watch for Southern Africa* bulletin, a monthly *Drought Overview* bulletin and forewarnings of impending natural disasters.

During 1995 the SATCC undertook a study of regional transport and communications to provide a comprehensive framework and strategy for future courses of action. The study was compiled using analysis and data of existing infrastructure, their viability and trading use. A task force was also established to identify measures to simplify procedures at border crossings throughout southern Africa.

FOOD, AGRICULTURE AND NATURAL RESOURCES

The food, agriculture and natural resources sector covers eight sub-sectors: agricultural research and training; inland fisheries; forestry; wildlife; marine fisheries and resources; food security; livestock production and animal disease control; and environment and land management. At July 1994 funding required for 101 projects in this sector was US $658.8m., of which $354.0m. had been secured. The importance of this sector is evident in the fact that, according to SADC figures, agriculture contributes one-third of the region's GNP, accounts for 26% of total earnings of foreign exchange and employs some 80% of the labour force. A new integrated strategy for the sector was prepared in 1992 and was adopted by ministers of agriculture and natural resources in January 1993. The sector's principal objectives are regional food security, agricultural development and natural resource development.

The Southern African Centre for Co-operation in Agricultural Research (SACCAR), in Gaborone, Botswana, which began operations in 1985, co-ordinates SADC efforts in this field of activity. It aims to strengthen national agricultural research systems, in order to improve management, increase productivity, promote the development and transfer of technology to assist local farmers, and improve training. Examples of activity include: a sorghum and millet improvement programme; a land and water management research programme; a root crop research network; agroforestry research, implemented in Malawi, Tanzania, Zambia and Zimbabwe; and a grain legume improvement programme, comprising separate research units for groundnuts, beans and cowpeas. The SADC's Plant Genetic Resources Centre was established in 1988, near Lusaka, Zambia, to collect, conserve and utilize indigenous and exotic plant genetic resources and to develop appropriate management practices.

The sector aims to promote inland and marine fisheries as an important, sustainable source of animal protein. Marine fisheries are also considered to be a potential source of income of foreign exchange. In May 1993 the first formal meeting of SADC ministers of marine fisheries convened in Namibia, and it was agreed to hold annual meetings. The development of fresh water fisheries is focused on aquaculture projects, and their integration into rural community activities. In 1995 efforts were initiated for regional fisheries capacity-building and for the management of shared water bodies. The environment and land management sub-sector is concerned with sustainability as an essential quality of development. Following the severe drought in the region in 1991/92, the need for water resources development has become a priority. The sector also undertakes projects for the conservation and sustainable development of forestry and wildlife, the control of animal diseases and the improvement of livestock production.

Under the food security programme, the Harare-based Regional Early Warning System aims to anticipate and prevent food shortages through the provision of information relating to the food security situation in member states. As a result of the drought crisis experience, SADC member states have agreed to inform the food security sector of their food and non-food requirements on a regular basis, in order to assess the needs of the region as a whole. A regional food reserve project was also to be developed. In June 1995 the SADC appealed for US $270m. of aid from western countries in order to combat the effects of drought, which had afflicted food production in the region. The Regional Early Warning System predicted that the region's total maize output would decrease by 41% in 1995, from the level of the previous year's harvest, to only 12m. metric tons, leaving a basic food requirement deficit of 3.5m. tons. By 1997 the situation had greatly improved and the SADC Food Security Bulletin announced that sufficient cereal was available for both normal consumption and the reserve fund, leaving a surplus of 1.33m. tons.

ENERGY

Areas of activity in the energy sector include: joint petroleum exploration, training programmes for the petroleum sector and studies for strategic fuel storage facilities; promotion of the use of coal; development of hydroelectric power and the co-ordination of SADC generation and transmission capacities; new and renewable sources of energy, including pilot projects in solar energy; assessment of the environmental and socio-economic impact of wood-fuel scarcity and relevant education programmes; and energy conservation. In July 1995 SADC energy ministers approved the establishment of a Southern African Power Pool, an arrangement whereby all member states were to be linked into a single electricity grid. (Several grids are already integrated and others are being rehabilitated.) At the same time, ministers endorsed a Protocol to promote greater co-operation in energy development within the SADC. On receiving final approval and signature by member states, the Protocol was to replace the energy sector with an Energy Commission, responsible for 'demand-side' management, pricing, ensuring private-sector involvement and competition, training and research, collecting information, etc.

TRADE, INDUSTRY AND MINING

Under the treaty establishing the SADC, efforts were to be undertaken to achieve regional economic integration. The trade and industry sector aims to facilitate this by the creation of an enabling investment and trade environment in SADC countries, the establishment of a single regional market, by progressively removing barriers to the movement of goods, services and people, and the promotion of cross-border investment. The sector supports programmes for industrial research and development and standardization and quality assurance. A new sector of finance and investment has been established to mobilize industrial investment resources and to co-ordinate economic policies and the development of the financial sector. During 1995 work was proceeding on the preparation of two Protocols on trade co-operation and finance and investment, which were to provide the legal framework for integration. In August 1996 SADC member states (except Angola) signed a Protocol providing for the establishment of a free-trade area, through the gradual elimination of tariff barriers over an eight-year period, at a summit meeting held in Lesotho. The Protocol was to come into effect following its ratification by two-thirds of member states.

In January 1992 a new five-year strategy for the promotion of mining in the region was approved, with the principal objective of stimulating local and foreign investment in the sector to maximize benefits from the region's mineral resources. In December 1994 the SADC held a mining forum, jointly with the EU, in Lusaka, Zambia, with the aim of demonstrating to potential investors and promoters the possibilities of mining exploration in the region. Other objectives of the mining sector are the improvement of industry training, increasing the contribution of small-scale mining, reducing the illicit trade in gemstones and gold, increasing co-operation in mineral exploration and processing, and minimizing the adverse impact of mining operations on the environment. Of the 31 mining projects planned at July 1994 (amounting to US $30.9m.), 11 were for overall co-ordination of the industry and five for environmental protection.

HUMAN RESOURCES DEVELOPMENT

The SADC helps to supply the region's requirements in skilled manpower by providing training in the following categories: high-level managerial personnel; agricultural managers; high- and medium-level technicians; artisans; and instructors. The sector aims to harmonize and strengthen the education and training systems in the SADC through initiatives such as the determination of active labour market information systems and institutions in the region, improving education policy analysis and formulation, the standardization of curricula and examinations and addressing issues of teaching and learning materials in the region. It has also initiated a programme of distance education to enable greater access to education, and operates the SADC's scholarship and training awards programme.

CULTURE AND INFORMATION

A new culture and information sector was established in 1990, and is co-ordinated by Mozambique. Following the ratification of the new treaty establishing the Community, the sector was expected to emphasize regional socio-cultural development as part of the process of greater integration. The SADC Press Trust was established, in Harare, Zimbabwe, to disseminate information about the SADC and to articulate the concerns and priorities of the region. Public education initiatives have commenced to encourage the involvement of people in the process of regional integration and development, as well as to promote democratic and human rights' values. A four-year programme, entitled the SADC Festival on Arts and Culture, was initiated in 1994. The following events were to be held: a music festival, in Zimbabwe, in 1995; a theatre festival, in Mozambique, in 1996; an arts and crafts regional exposition, in Namibia, in 1997; and a dance festival, in Tanzania, in 1998.

TOURISM

The sector's current programme is to promote tourism within the context of national and regional socio-economic development objectives. It comprises four components: tourism product development; tourism marketing and research; tourism services; and human resources development and training. The SADC has promoted tourism for the region at trade fairs in Europe, and has initiated a project to provide a range of promotional material. By September 1993 a project to design a standard grading classification system for tourist accommodation in the region was completed, with the assistance of the World Tourism Organization, and the Council approved its implementation. The sector also aims to stimulate and assess the potential of intra-regional tourism, which is considered to be a major element of regional integration. In an attempt to further promote tourism in the region, SADC ministers have approved the establishment of a new tourism body, to be administered jointly by SADC officials and private-sector operators. The Regional Tourism Organization for Southern Africa (RETOSA) was to assist member states to formulate tourism promotion policies and strategies. In June 1996 SADC ministers of tourism, meeting in Maputo, Mozambique, agreed on funding to assist the establishment of RETOSA.

FINANCE

SADC PROJECT FINANCING BY SECTOR (July 1994)

Sector	Number of projects	Total cost (US $ million)	Funding secured (US $ million)*
Culture and information	6	14.30	4.44
Energy	60	820.22	673.63
Food, agriculture and natural resources			
Agricultural research and training	16	126.92	79.91
Inland fisheries	12	69.18	33.19
Food security	10	63.17	18.27
Forestry	16	117.29	50.40
Wildlife	11	68.15	53.74
Livestock production and animal disease control	18	126.65	85.54
Environment and land management	12	80.06	32.80
Marine fisheries and resources	6	7.38	0.15
Industry and trade	11	12.63	2.84
Human resources development	21	45.23	17.11
Mining	31	30.91	14.75
Tourism	8	4.67	1.96
Transport and communications	208	6,934.10	3,238.10
Total	446	8,520.86	4,306.83

* Includes both local and foreign resources.

PUBLICATIONS

SACCAR Newsletter (quarterly).
SADC Annual Report.
SADC Energy Bulletin.
SATCC Bulletin (quarterly).
SKILLS.
SPLASH.

OTHER REGIONAL ORGANIZATIONS

These organizations are arranged under the following categories:

Agriculture, Food, Forestry and Fisheries
Arts and Culture
Commodities
Development and Economic Co-operation
Education
Economics and Finance
Government and Politics
Industrial and Professional Relations
Law
Medicine and Public Health
Press, Radio and Telecommunications
Religion
Science and Technology
Social Sciences, Social Welfare and Human Rights
Trade and Industry
Transport and Tourism

AGRICULTURE, FOOD, FORESTRY AND FISHERIES

African Feed Resources Network—AFRNET: c/o International Livestock Research Institute (ILRI), POB 30709, Nairobi, Kenya; tel. (2) 630743; fax (2) 631499; f. 1991 by merger of two African livestock fodder and one animal nutrition research networks; aims to assist farmers in finding effective ways to feed their livestock; Co-ordinator Dr JOHN NDIKUMAMA. Publ. *AFRNET Newsletter* (quarterly).

African Timber Organization: BP 1077, Libreville, Gabon; tel. 73-29-28; telex 5620; fax 734030; f. 1976 to enable mems to study and co-ordinate ways of ensuring the optimum utilization and conservation of their forests. Mems: Angola, Cameroon, Central African Republic, the Dem. Repub. of the Congo, Repub. of Congo, Côte d'Ivoire, Equatorial Guinea, Gabon, Ghana, Liberia, Nigeria, São Tomé and Príncipe, Tanzania. Tech. Dir PHILEMON SELEBANGUE; Sec.-Gen. MOHAMMED LAWAL GARBA. Publs *ATO-Information* (every 2 months), *Annual Report*.

Association for the Advancement of Agricultural Science in Africa—AAASA: POB 30087, Addis Ababa, Ethiopia; tel. (1) 44-3536; f. 1968 to promote the development and application of agricultural sciences and the exchange of ideas; to encourage Africans to enter training; holds several seminars each year in different African countries. Mems: individual agricultural scientists, research insts in 63 countries. Sec.-Gen. Prof. M. EL-FOULQ (acting). Publs *Journal* (2 a year), *Newsletter* (quarterly).

Desert Locust Control Organization for Eastern Africa: POB 30023, Nairobi, Kenya; tel. (2) 501704; telex 25510; fax (2) 505137; f. 1962 to promote most effective control of desert locust in the region and to carry out research into the locust's environment and behaviour; conducts pesticides residue analysis; assists mem. states in the monitoring and extermination of other migratory pests such as the quelea-quelea (grain-eating birds), the army worm and the tsetse fly; bases at Asmara (Eritrea), Dire Dawa (Ethiopia), Mogadishu and Hargeisa (Somalia), Nairobi (Kenya), Khartoum (Sudan), Arusha (Tanzania), Kampala (Uganda) and Djibouti. Mems: Djibouti, Eritrea, Ethiopia, Kenya, Somalia, Sudan, Tanzania and Uganda. Dir Dr KARRAR; Co-ordinator C. K. MUINAMIA. Publs *Desert Locust Situation Reports* (monthly), *Annual Report*, technical reports.

International Crops Research Institute for the Semi-Arid Tropics (ICRISAT) West and Central Africa Regional Office: BP 12404, Niamey, Niger; tel. 722529; telex 5406; fax 73-43-29; ICRISAT f. 1972 as world centre for genetic improvement of sorghum, millet, pigeon-pea, chick-pea and groundnut and for research and training on the management of resources in the world's semi-arid tropics; receives support from the Consultative Group on International Agricultural Research (q.v.).

International Institute of Tropical Agriculture—IITA: Oyo Rd, PMB 5320, Ibadan, Nigeria; tel. (2) 2412626; telex 31417; fax (874) 177-2276; e-mail iita@cgnet.com; f. 1967; principal financing arranged by the Consultative Group on International Agricultural Research (CGIAR, q.v.), an informal group of donor countries, development banks, foundations and agencies, co-ordinated by the World Bank. Three main research programmes: crop improvement (chiefly cassava, maize, plantain/banana, yam and soybean); plant health management; and resource and crop management. The international co-operation programme comprises large-scale research projects with nat. programmes and a training programme for scientists and technicians in tropical agriculture. The information services programme produces publs on research results and has a library of 75,000 vols and data-base of 95,500 records; it also maintains six agro-ecological research stations. Dir-Gen. Dr LUKAS BRADER. Publs *Annual Report, IITA Research*.

International Livestock Research Institute—ILRI: POB 30709, Nairobi, Kenya; tel. (2) 630743; telex 22040; fax (2) 631499; f. 1995, to replace the International Laboratory for Research on Animal Diseases and the International Livestock Centre for Africa; conducts laboratory and field research on animal health (in particular, animal trypanosomiasis and theileriosis), the conservation of genetic resources, production systems analysis, natural resource management, livestock policy analysis and strengthening national research capacities; undertakes training programmes for scientists and technicians; specialized science library. Dir Dr HANK FITZHUGH. Publs *Annual Report, Annual Scientific Report, Livestock Research for Development Newsletter* (2 a year).

International Red Locust Control Organization for Central and Southern Africa: POB 240252, Ndola, Zambia; tel. (2) 615684; telex 30072; fax (2) 614285; f. 1971; controls locusts in eastern, central and southern Africa, and assists in the control of African army-worm and quelea-quelea. Mems: nine countries. Dir E. K. BYARUHANGA. Publs *Annual Report, Monthly Report* and scientific reports.

International Scientific Council for Trypanosomiasis Research and Control: PM Bag 2359, Lagos, Nigeria; tel. (1) 633289; telex 22199; fax (1) 2636093; f. 1949 to review the work on tsetse and trypanosomiasis problems carried out by organizations and workers concerned in laboratories and in the field; to stimulate further research and discussion and to promote co-ordination between research workers and organizations in the different countries in Africa, and to provide a regular opportunity for the discussion of particular problems and for the exposition of new experiments and discoveries.

Joint Organization for Control of Desert Locust and Bird Pests (Organisation commune de lutte antiacridienne et de lutte antiaviaire—OCLALAV): route des Pères Maristes, BP 1066, Dakar, Senegal; tel. 32-32-80; fax 32-04-87; f. 1965 to eradicate the desert locust and grain-eating birds, in particular the quelea-quelea, and to sponsor related research projects. Mems: Benin, Burkina Faso, Cameroon, Chad, Côte d'Ivoire, The Gambia, Mali, Mauritania, Niger, Senegal. Dir-Gen. ABDULLAHI OULD SOUEID AHMED. Publ. *Bulletin* (monthly).

ARTS AND CULTURE

African Cultural Institute (Institut culturel africain): 13 ave du Président Bourguiba, BP 01, Dakar, Senegal; tel. 24-78-82; telex 61334; f. 1971 to promote scientific and cultural development; established (1976) the Centre régional d'action culturelle, Lomé, Togo, (1977) the Centre Inter-Etats pour la promotion de l'artisanat et du tourisme culturel, Abomey, Benin, and (1978) the Centre régional de recherche et de documentation pour le développement culturel, Dakar, Senegal. Annual budget: 400m. francs CFA. Mems: 18 African states. Dir-Gen. B. T. KOSSU. Publ. *ICA-Information* (quarterly).

Afro-Asian Writers' Association: 'Al Ahram', Al Gala's St, Cairo, Egypt; tel. (2) 5747011; telex 20185; fax (2) 5747023; f. 1958. Mems: writers' orgs in 51 countries. Sec.-Gen. LOTFI EL-KHOLY. Publs *Lotus Magazine of Afro-Asian Writings* (quarterly in English, French and Arabic), *Afro-Asian Literature Series* (in English, French and Arabic).

Pan-African Writers' Association—PAWA: POB C450, Cantonments, Accra, Ghana; tel. 773062; fax 773042; f. 1989; awards the African Prize for Literature; in 1993 launched a US $10m. fund to encourage African writers; organizes an International African Writers' Day. Sec.-Gen. ATUKWEI OKAI (Ghana).

Society of African Culture (Société africaine de culture): 25 bis rue des Ecoles, 75005 Paris, France; tel. 1-43-54-15-88; fax 1-43-25-96-67; f. 1956 to create unity and friendship among black scholars in Africa, the Caribbean, Europe and America for the encouragement of their own cultures. Mems from 45 countries. Pres. AIMÉ CÉSAIRE; Sec.-Gen. CHRISTIANE YANDÉ DIOP. Publ. *La Revue Présence Africaine* (2 a year).

COMMODITIES

African Groundnut Council: Trade Fair Complex, Badagry Expressway Km 15, POB 3025—Marina, Lagos, Nigeria; tel. (1) 880982; telex 21366; fax (1) 880982; f. 1964 to advise producing countries on marketing policies; administers compensation fund. Mems: The Gambia, Mali, Niger, Nigeria, Senegal, Sudan. Chair. TUKUR MANI (Nigeria); Exec. Sec. Alhaji MOUR MAMADOU SAMB (Senegal). Publs *Groundnut Review, Newsletter* (French and English).

African Oil Palm Development Association—AFOPDA: 15 BP 341, Abidjan 15, Côte d'Ivoire; tel. 25-15-18; f. 1985; seeks to increase production of and investment in palm oil. Mems: Benin, Cameroon, the Dem. Repub. of the Congo, Côte d'Ivoire, Ghana, Guinea, Nigeria, Togo. Exec. Sec. BAUDELAIRE SOUROU.

African Petroleum Producers' Association—APPA: BP 1097, Brazzaville, Congo; tel. 83-64-38; telex 5552; fax 83-67-99; f. 1987 by African petroleum-producing countries to reinforce co-operation among regional producers and to stabilize prices; council of ministers responsible for the hydrocarbons sector of each country meets twice a year. Mems: Algeria, Angola, Benin, Cameroon, the Dem. Repub. of the Congo, Repub. of Congo, Côte d'Ivoire, Egypt, Equatorial Guinea, Gabon, Nigeria. Presidency rotates. Publ. *APPA Bulletin* (2 a year).

Association of Coffee Producing Countries—ACPC: 7–10 Old Park Lane, 5th Floor, Suite B, London, W1Y 3LJ, England; tel. (171) 493-4790; fax (171) 355-1690; f. 1993; aims to co-ordinate policies of coffee production and to co-ordinate the efforts of producer countries to achieve stability in the world coffee market. Mems: 29 African, Asian and Latin American countries. Pres. RUBENS BARBOSA; Sec.-Gen. ROBÉRIO OLIVEIRA SILVA.

Cocoa Producers' Alliance: POB 1718, Western House, 8–10 Broad St, Lagos, Nigeria; tel. (1) 2635574; telex 28288; fax (1) 2635684; f. 1962 to exchange scientific and tech. information; to discuss problems of mutual concern to producers; to ensure adequate supplies at remunerative prices; to promote consumption. Mems: Brazil, Cameroon, Côte d'Ivoire, Dominican Republic, Ecuador, Gabon, Ghana, Malaysia, Nigeria, São Tomé and Príncipe, Togo and Trinidad and Tobago. Sec.-Gen. DJEUMO SILAS KAMGA.

Inter-African Coffee Organization—IACO: BP V210, Abidjan, Côte d'Ivoire; tel. 21-61-31; telex 22406; fax 21-62-12; f. 1960 to adopt a united policy on the marketing of coffee. General Assembly meets annually; Bd of Dirs holds quarterly meetings to direct policy; the financial contribution of mem. countries is based on the volume of their exports; mem. countries account for about 97% of African coffee exports. Aims to foster greater collaboration in research techniques, in particular through the establishment of the African Coffee Research Network, and improve quality of exports. Mems: Angola, Benin, Burundi, Cameroon, Central African Repub., the Dem. Repub. of the Congo, Repub. of Congo, Côte d'Ivoire, Equatorial Guinea, Ethiopia, Gabon, Ghana, Guinea, Kenya, Liberia, Madagascar, Malawi, Nigeria, Rwanda, Sierra Leone, Tanzania, Togo, Uganda, Zambia and Zimbabwe. Pres. GUY-ALAIN GAUZE (Côte d'Ivoire); Sec.-Gen. AREGA WORKU (Ethiopia). Publs *African Coffee* (quarterly), *Directory of African Exporters* (every 2 years).

International Cocoa Organization—ICCO: 22 Berners St, London, W1P 3DB, England; tel. (171) 637-3211; telex 28173; fax (171) 631-0114; f. 1973 under the first International Cocoa Agreement, 1972 (renewed in 1975, 1980, 1986 and the fifth ICA entered into force in Feb. 1994). ICCO supervises the implementation of the agreement, and provides member governments with conference facilities and up-to-date information on the world cocoa economy and the operation of the agreement. Mems: 16 exporting countries which account for about three-quarters of world cocoa exports, and 21 importing countries which account for about 55% of world cocoa imports. (The USA is not a member.) Chair. GUY-ALAIN GAUZE (until end Sept. 1997); Exec. Dir EDOUARD KOUAMÉ (Côte d'Ivoire). Publs *Quarterly Bulletin of Cocoa Statistics, Annual Report, The World Cocoa Directory, Cocoa Newsletter, The World Cocoa Market to the Year 2000.*

International Coffee Organization: 22 Berners St, London, W1P 4DD, England; tel. (171) 580-8591; telex 267659; fax (171) 580-6129; e-mail library@intercaf.win.uk.net; f. 1963 under the International Coffee Agreement, 1962, which was renegotiated in 1968, 1976, 1983 and 1994; aims to achieve a reasonable balance between supply and demand on a basis which will assure adequate supplies at fair prices to consumers and expanding markets at remunerative prices to producers; system of export quotas, to stabilize prices, was abandoned in July 1989. Mems: (1994 Agreement, at April 1997) 44 exporting countries and 18 importing countries. Exec. Dir CELSIUS A. LODDER (Brazil).

International Grains Council: 1 Canada Sq., Canary Wharf, London, E14 5AE, England; tel. (171) 513-1122; fax (171) 513-0630; f. 1949 as International Wheat Council, present name adopted in 1995; responsible for the admin. of the Grains Trade Convention of the International Grains Agreement, 1995; aims to further international co-operation in all aspects of trade in grains, to promote international trade in grains, and to secure the freest possible flow of this trade in the interests of mems, particularly developing mem. countries; and to contribute to the stability of the international grain market; acts as forum for consultations between mems, and provides comprehensive information on the international grain market and factors affecting it. Mems: 32 countries and the EU. Exec. Dir. G. DENIS. Publs *World Grain Statistics* (annually). *Wheat and Coarse Grain Shipments* (annually), *Report for the Fiscal Year* (annually), *Grain Market Report* Monthly.

International Tea Promotion Association: POB 20064, Tea Board of Kenya, Nairobi, Kenya; tel. (2) 220241; telex 987-22190; fax (2) 331650; f. 1979. Mems: eight countries (Bangladesh, Indonesia, Kenya, Malawi, Mauritius, Mozambique, Tanzania, and Uganda), accounting for about 35% of world exports of black tea. Chair. GEORGE M. KIMANI; Liaison Officer NGOIMA WA MWAURA. Publ. *International Tea Journal* (2 a year).

International Tobacco Growers' Association: POB 125, East Grinstead, West Sussex, RH18 5FA, England; tel. (1342) 823549; fax (1342) 825502; f. 1984 to provide a forum for the exchange of information of concern to tobacco producers and to provide information relating to tobacco production; mems collectively produce more than 80% of the world's internationally traded tobacco. Mems: 17 countries. Chair. ALBERT JOHNSON (USA); CEO DAVID WALDER (United Kingdom).

International Tropical Timber Organization—ITTO: International Organizations Center, 5th Floor, Pacifico-Yokohama, 1-1-1, Minato-Mirai, Nishi-ku, Yokohama 220, Japan; tel. (45) 223-1110; fax (45) 223-1111; f. 1985 under the International Tropical Timber Agreement 1983; a new treaty, ITTA 1994, was expected to enter into force in 1997; aims to promote the conservation of tropical forest resources through sustainable management; conducts research and development in marketing and economics, and reforestation and forest management; and provides a forum for consultation and co-operation between producers and consumers, as well as non-governmental organizations; facilitates progress towards the 'Year 2000' objective (by which year all trade in tropical timber is to be derived from sustainably managed resources). Mems: 26 producing and 26 consuming countries, and the EU. Exec. Dir FREEZAILAH BIN CHE YEOM (Malaysia).

West Africa Rice Development Association—WARDA: 01 BP 2551, Bouaké 01, Côte d'Ivoire; tel. 63-45-14; telex 69138; fax 63-47-14; f. 1971; undertakes research to improve rice production in West Africa; maintains research stations in Côte d'Ivoire, Nigeria and Senegal; major research projects undertaken through four continuing programmes, the Rainfed Rice Programme, Policy Support Programme, Information and Technology Transfer Programme (based in M'be, Côte d'Ivoire) and the Irrigated Rice Programme (based in St Louis, Senegal); WARDA is a member of the network of agricultural research centres supported by the Consultative Group on International Agricultural Research (CGIAR, q.v.); provides training and consulting services; revenue US $9.4m. (1996). Mems: Benin, Burkina Faso, Cameroon, Chad, Côte d'Ivoire, The Gambia, Ghana, Guinea, Guinea-Bissau, Liberia, Mali, Mauritania, Niger, Nigeria, Senegal, Sierra Leone, Togo. Dir-Gen. KANAYO NWANSE (Nigeria). Publs *Annual Report, Directory of Rice Scientists in West Africa, Current Contents at WARDA* (monthly).

DEVELOPMENT AND ECONOMIC CO-OPERATION

African Capacity Building Foundation: POB 1562, Harare, Zimbabwe; tel. (4) 702931; fax (4) 702915; f. 1991 by the World Bank, UNDP and the African Development Bank and bilateral donors; assists African countries to strengthen local skills and institutions in economic policy analysis and dev. man.; a fund of US $100m. was to be provided over the first four years of operations. Mems: 12 countries. Exec. Sec. ABEL L. THOAHLANE.

Afro-Asian Rural Reconstruction Organization—AARRO: Plot No. 2, State Guest Houses Complex, nr Telephone Exchange, Chanakyapuri, New Delhi 110021, India; tel. (11) 600475; telex 72326; fax (11) 4672045; e-mail aarrohg@hub.nic.in; f. 1962 to act as a catalyst for co-operative restructuring of rural life in Africa and Asia and to explore, collectively, opportunities for co-ordination of efforts to promote welfare and eradicate malnutrition, disease, illiteracy and poverty among rural people. Activities include collaborative research on development issues; training; assistance in forming orgs of farmers and other rural people; the exchange of information; international confs and seminars; and awarding 100 individual training fellowships at nine insts in Egypt, India, Japan, the Repub. of Korea, Malaysia and Taiwan. Mems: 11 African, 13 Asian, and one African assoc. Sec.-Gen. AHMED ABDELWAHED KHALIL. Publs *Annual Report, Rural Reconstruction* (2 a year), *AARRO Newsletter* (quarterly), *PATAP News* (quarterly), conference and committee reports.

Agence de coopération culturelle et technique: 13 quai André Citroën, 75015 Paris, France; tel. 1-44-37-33-00; telex 201916; fax 1-45-79-14-98; f. 1970; promotes co-operation among French-speaking countries in the areas of education, culture, science and technology; tech. and financial assistance has been given to projects in every mem. country, mainly to aid rural people. Mems: 37 countries, mainly African; Sec.-Gen. JEAN-LOUIS ROY (Canada). Publs *Lettre de la Francophonie* (monthly), *AGECOP Liaison* (6 a year).

Arab Bank for Economic Development in Africa (Banque arabe pour le développement économique en Afrique—BADEA): Sayed Abdar-Rahman el-Mahdi Ave, POB 2640, Khartoum, Sudan; tel. (11) 773646; telex 22248; fax (11) 770600; f. 1973 by Arab League; provides loans and grants to sub-Saharan African countries to finance development projects; paid-up cap. US $1,145.8m. (Dec.

1996); BADEA financing activities totalled $1,630.6m. over the period 1975–1996. These included 226 devt projects, 13 lines of credit, 14 special operations (as part of an emergency aid programme) as well as 755 tech. assistance operations for feasibility studies and institutional support. Chair. AHMAD ABDALLAH AL-AKEIL (Saudi Arabia); Dir-Gen. MEDHAT SAMI LOTFY (Egypt). Publs *Annual Report, Co-operation for Development,* Studies on Afro-Arab co-operation.

Centre africain de formation et de recherches administratives pour le développement—CAFRAD (African Training and Research Centre in Administration for Development): ave Mohamed V, BP 310, Tangier, 90001 Morocco; tel. (9) 942652; telex 33664; fax (9) 941415; e-mail cafradt@mail.sis.net.ma; f. 1964 by agreement between Morocco and UNESCO; undertakes research into administrative problems in Africa, documentation of results, provision of a consultative service for govts and orgs; holds frequent seminars; aided by national and international orgs. Mems: 27 African countries. Pres. MESSAOUD MANSOURI; Dir-Gen. Dr M. A. WALI. Publs include *Cahiers Africains d'Administration Publique* (2 a year), *African Administrative Studies* (2 a year), *CAFRAD News* (2 a year, in English, French and Arabic), *Collection: Etudes et Documents, Répertoire des Consultants*.

Centre on Integrated Rural Development for Africa—CIRDAfrica: POB 6115, Arusha, Tanzania; tel. (57) 2576; telex 42053; fax (57) 8532; f. 1979 (operational 1982) to promote integrated rural development through a network of nat. institutions; to improve the production, income and living conditions of small-scale farmers and other rural groups; to provide tech. support; and to foster the exchange of ideas and experience; financed by mem. states and donor agencies. Mems: 17 African countries. Dir Dr ABDELMONEIM M. ELSHEIKH. Publ. *CIRDafrica Rural Tribune* (2 a year).

Club du Sahel (Club of the Sahel): c/o OECD, 2 rue André Pascal, 75775 Paris, France; tel. 1-45-24-82-00; telex 640048; fax 1-45-24-90-31; f. 1976; an informal forum of donor countries and member states of the Permanent Inter-State Committee on Drought Control in the Sahel—CILSS (q.v.), for promoting the co-ordination of long-term policies and programmes in key development sectors affecting food production and drought control in the nine mem. countries of the CILSS; formed by the CILSS in assocn with the OECD. The Club collects information, conducts studies and helps to mobilize resources for the development of the Sahel region in agriculture, livestock, cereals pricing policy, ecology, forestry and village water supplies.

Communauté économique des états de l'Afrique centrale—CEEAC: BP 2112, Libreville, Gabon; tel. 73-35-47; telex 5780; f. 1983; operational since 1985; aims to promote co-operation between member states by abolishing trade restrictions, establishing a common external customs tariff, linking commercial banks, and setting up a development fund, over a period of 12 years; budget (1993) US $3.5m. Membership comprises the states belonging to UDEAC (q.v.), those belonging to the Economic Community of the Great Lakes Countries (q.v.) and São Tomé and Príncipe. Sec.-Gen. KASASA MUTATI CHINYATA (Democratic Republic of the Congo).

Comunidade dos Países de Língua Portuguesa (Community of Portuguese-Speaking Countries): rua S. Caetano 32, 1200 Lisbon, Portugal; tel. (1) 392-8560; fax (1) 392-8588; f. July 1996; aims to promote close political, economic, diplomatic and cultural links between Portuguese-speaking countries and to strengthen the influence of the Lusophone commonwealth within the international community; Mems: Angola, Brazil, Cape Verde, Guinea-Bissau, Mozambique, Portugal and São Tomé and Príncipe. Exec. Sec. MARCOLINO MOCO (Angola).

Conseil de l'Entente (Entente Council): 01 BP 3734, Abidjan 01, Côte d'Ivoire; tel. 33-28-35; telex 23558; fax 33-11-49; f. 1959; aims to promote economic development in the region. The Council's Mutual Aid and Loan Guarantee Fund (Fonds d'Entraide et de Garantie des Emprunts) finances development projects, including agricultural projects, vocational training centres, research into new sources of energy and building of hotels to encourage tourism. Fund budget (1992): 1,746m. francs CFA. Mems: Benin, Burkina Faso, Côte d'Ivoire, Niger, Togo. Admin. Sec. of Fund PAUL KAYA. Publs *Entente africaine* (quarterly), *Rapport d'activité* (annually).

Communauté économique du bétail et de la viande du Conseil de l'Entente (Livestock and Meat Economic Community of the Entente Council): BP 638, Ouagadougou, Burkina Faso; tel. (3) 30-62-66; telex 5329; f. 1970 to promote the production, processing and marketing of livestock and meat; negotiates between members and with third countries on tech. and financial co-operation and co-ordinated legislation; attempts to co-ordinate measures to combat drought and cattle disease. Mems: states belonging to the Conseil de l'Entente. Sec. Dr ELIE LADIKPO.

Eastern and Southern African Mineral Resources Development Centre: POB 9573, Dar es Salaam, Tanzania; tel. (51) 47021; telex 41401; fax (51) 46096; f. 1975, sponsored by the ECA (q.v.); provides advisory and consultancy services in exploration geology, geophysics, geochemistry, mining and mineral processing; organizes training courses; operates specialized laboratory services. Mems: Angola, Comoros, Ethiopia, Mozambique, Tanzania, Uganda. Dir-Gen. T. K. MWASHA.

Economic Community of the Great Lakes Countries (Communauté économique des pays des Grands Lacs—CEPGL): BP 58, Gisenyi, Rwanda; tel. 40228; telex 602; fax 40785; f. 1976; main organs: annual conf. of heads of state, council of ministers, perm. exec. secr., consultative comm., Security Commission, three Specialized Tech. Comms. There are three specialized agencies: the Banque de Développement des Etats des Grands Lacs (BDEGL, BP 3355, Goma, Dem. Republic of the Congo); the Organisation de la CEPGL pour l'Energie (BP 1912, Bujumbura, Burundi); the Institut de Recherche Agronomique et Zoologique (BP 91, Gitega, Burundi); and four jt enterprises, producing electric power, glass bottles, cement and hoes. Two extraordinary summit meetings were held in 1994 to discuss security concerns in the region and efforts to revive economic co-operation activities. Mems: Dem. Repub. of the Congo, Burundi, Rwanda. Publs *Grands Lacs* (quarterly review), *Journal* (annually).

Gambia River Basin Development Organization (Organisation pour la mise en valeur du fleuve Gambie—OMVG): 13 passage Le Blanc, BP 2353, Dakar, Senegal; tel. 22-31-59; telex 51487; fax 22-59-26; f. 1978 by Senegal and The Gambia; Guinea joined in 1981 and Guinea-Bissau in 1983. Plans include the construction of a bridge over the River Gambia (feasibility studies were concluded in early 1997); a hydraulic development plan of the River Gambia (commenced in 1996); and an agro-sylvo pastoral project (pending funding); maintains documentation centre. Administrative budget (1997): 135m. francs CFA. Exec. Sec. MAMADOU NASSIROU DIALLO.

Indian Ocean Commission—IOC: Q4, ave Sir Guy Forget, BP 7, Quatre Bornes, Mauritius; tel. 425-9564; fax 425-1209; f. 1982 to promote regional co-operation, particularly in economic devt; prin. projects under way in the early 1990s (at a cost of 11.6m. francs CFA) comprised tuna-fishing and regional tourism development and the protection and management of environmental resources, reinforcement of meteorological services; with assistance principally from the European Community; tariff reduction is also envisaged. Perm. tech. cttees cover: tuna-fishing; regional industrial co-operation; regional commerce; tourism; environment; maritime transport; handicrafts; sports. The IOC organizes an annual regional trade fair (1994: Madagascar). Mems: Comoros, France (representing the French Overseas Department of Réunion), Madagascar, Mauritius and Seychelles. Sec.-Gen. (vacant). Publ. *Guide Import/Export*.

Indian Ocean Rim Association for Regional Co-operation—IORARC: Mauritius; the first intergovernmental meeting of countries in the region to promote an Indian Ocean Rim initiative was convened in March 1995; charter to establish the Asscn signed at a ministerial meeting in March 1997; aims to promote regional economic co-operation through trade, investment, infrastructure, tourism, science and technology. Mems Australia, India, Indonesia, Kenya, Madagascar, Malaysia, Mauritius, Mozambique, Oman, Singapore, South Africa, Sri Lanka, Tanzania and Yemen. Interim Chair. PAUL RAYMOND BÉRENGER (Mauritius).

Intergovernmental Authority on Development—IGAD: BP 2653, Djibouti; tel. 354050; fax 356994; e-mail IGAD@intnet.dj; f. 1986 (as Intergovernmental Authority on Drought and Development—present name adopted in March 1996) to co-ordinate measures to combat the effects of drought and desertification; programmes of action include food security, desertification control, environmental protection, agricultural research, water resources management, fisheries, early warning and remote-sensing for food security and manpower devt; in March 1996 heads of state and government of mem. states agreed to amend the Authority's charter and expand its mandate to cover issues of economic co-operation, regional integration and other political and social concerns, including conflict prevention and resolution. Mems: Djibouti, Eritrea, Ethiopia, Kenya, Sudan, Uganda. Exec.-Gen. Dr TEKESTE GHEBRAY (Eritrea). Publs *IGAD News* (2 a year), *Annual Report, Food Situation Report* (quarterly), *Agromet Bulletin* (quarterly).

Lake Chad Basin Commission—LCBC: BP 727, N'Djamena, Chad; tel. 52-41-45; telex 5251; fax 51-41-37; e-mail lake!-lcbc@sdntcd.undp.org; f. 1964 to encourage co-operation in developing the Lake Chad region and in regulating and controlling the use of water and other natural resources in the basin; maintains relations with donor agencies and other international orgs in order to attract financial and tech. assistance; during 1988–92 a border demarcation exercise concerning all mem. states was conducted; a work programme, adopted by heads of state in March 1994, emphasizes protection and sound environmental management and development of Lake Chad and incorporates 36 projects relating to water resources, agriculture, forestry, biodiversity management, livestock and fishery developments within the basin. Budget 400m. francs CFA. Mems: Cameroon, Central African Republic, Chad, Niger, Nigeria. Exec. Sec. ABUBAKAR B. JAURO.

Liptako-Gourma Integrated Development Authority (Autorité de développement intégré de la région du Liptako-Gourma): BP 619, ave M. Thevenond, Ouagadougou, Burkina Faso; tel. 30-61-48; telex 5247; f. 1972; scope of activities includes water infrastructure, telecommunications and construction of roads and railways; in 1986 undertook study on development of water resources in the basin of the Niger river (for hydroelectricity and irrigation). Budget (1996) 400m. francs CFA. Mems: Burkina Faso, Mali, Niger. Dir-Gen. GISANGA DEMBÉLÉ (Mali).

Mano River Union: Mail Bag 133, Freetown, Sierra Leone; tel. (22) 226883; f. 1973 to establish a customs and economic union between mem. states, in order to accelerate development by means of integration. A common external tariff was instituted in April 1977; intra-union free trade was officially introduced on 1 May 1981, as the first stage in progress towards a customs union. An industrial development unit was set up in 1980 to identify projects and encourage investment. Construction of the Monrovia-Freetown–Monrovia highway was partially completed by 1991, and other road projects were also being undertaken in 1991. The Union was inactive for three years until mid-1994, owing to disagreements regarding funding. In January 1995 a Mano River Union Centre for Peace and Development was established, which was to be temporarily based in London, the United Kingdom. The Centre aimed to provide a permanent mechanism for conflict prevention and resolution, monitoring of human rights violations and to promote sustainable peace and development in the region following a peaceful resolution of the civil conflicts. Decisions are taken at meetings of a joint ministerial council. Mems: Guinea, Liberia, Sierra Leone. Dir Dr KABINEH KOROMAH (Sierra Leone).

Niger Basin Authority (Autorité du bassin du Niger): BP 729, Niamey, Niger; tel. 72-31-02; fax 73-53-10; f. 1964 to harmonize national programmes concerned with the River Niger Basin and to execute an integrated development plan; activities comprise: statistics; navigation regulation; hydrological forecasting; environmental control; infrastructure and agro-pastoral development; and arranging assistance for these projects. Mems: Benin, Burkina Faso, Cameroon, Chad, Côte d'Ivoire, Guinea, Mali, Niger, Nigeria. Exec. Sec. OTHMAN MUSTAPHA (Nigeria). Publs *Bulletin, Bibliographical Index.*

Organization for the Development of the Senegal River (Organisation pour la mise en valeur du fleuve Sénégal—OMVS): 46 rue Carnot, BP 3152, Dakar, Senegal; tel. 22-36-79; telex 51670; fax 23-47-62; f. 1972 to use the Senegal river for hydroelectricity, irrigation and navigation. The Djama dam in Senegal (completed in 1986) provides a barrage to prevent salt water from moving upstream, and the Manantali dam in Mali (completed in 1988) is intended to provide a reservoir for irrigation of about 400,000 ha of land and (eventually) for production of hydroelectricity and provision of year-round navigation for ocean-going vessels. In 1991 an agreement was signed whereby a company, l'Agence de gestion pour les ouvrages communs (AGOC), was formed; the mem. states were to hold 75% of the capital and private shareholders 25%. Work was to begin in 1996 on a hydro-electric power station on the Senegal River: international donors were to provide US $520m. for the project which was due for completion in 1999. Mems: Mali, Mauritania, Senegal; Guinea has held observer status since 1987; Chair. ALPHA OUMAR KONARÉ (Mali).

Organization for the Management and Development of the Kagera River Basin (Organisation pour l'aménagement et le développement du bassin de la rivière Kagera): BP 297, Kigali, Rwanda; tel. (7) 84665; telex 0909 22567; fax (7) 82172; f. 1978; envisages jt devt and management of resources, incl. the construction of a 61.5-MW hydroelectric dam at Rusumo Falls, on the Rwanda-Tanzania border, a 2,000-km railway network between the four mem. countries; road construction (914 km); agricultural projects; river transport; and a polytechnic inst. Budget (1992): US $2m. Mems: Burundi, Rwanda, Tanzania, Uganda. Exec. Sec. JEAN-BOSCO BALINDA.

Pan-African Institute for Development—PAID: BP 4056, Douala, Cameroon; tel. 42-10-61; telex 6048; fax 42-43-35; f. 1964 to train rural development officers from Africa (47 countries in 1995), chiefly at an intermediate level but also some higher specialists, in devt questions; emphasis in education is given to: involvement of local populations in development; women in devt; promotion of small- and medium-scale enterprises; implementation of regional projects for training development staff; preparation of projects for regional co-operation; applied research, consultation and project support. Four regional insts in Africa, two anglophone (POB 133, Buéa, Cameroon; POB 80448, Kabwe, Zambia), two francophone (BP 4078, Douala, Cameroon; BP 1756, Ouagadougou, Burkina Faso). Sec.-Gen. FAYA KONDIANO. Publs *Newsletter* (2 a year), *PAID Report* (quarterly), *Annual Progress Report.*

Permanent Inter-State Committee on Drought Control in the Sahel (Comité permanent inter-états de lutte contre la sécheresse dans le Sahel—CILSS): BP 7049, Ouagadougou, Burkina Faso; tel. 30-67-58; telex 5263; fax 30-67-57; f. 1973; works in co-operation with UN Sudano-Sahelian Office (UNSO, q.v.); aims to combat the effects of chronic drought in the Sahel region, where the deficit in grain production was estimated at 1.7m. metric tons for 1988, by improving irrigation and food production, halting deforestation and creating food reserves. Maintains Institut du Sahel at Bamako (Mali) and centre at Niamey (Niger). Budget (1995): 318.5m. francs CFA. Mems: Burkina Faso, Cape Verde, Chad, The Gambia, Guinea-Bissau, Mali, Mauritania, Niger, Senegal. Exec. Sec. CISSÉ MARIAM K. SIDIBE.

Permanent Tripartite Commission for East African Co-operation: International Conference Centre, Arusha, Tanzania; f. 1993 by agreement between the heads of state of Kenya, Tanzania and Uganda to promote greater regional co-operation (previously pursued under the East African Community, f. 1967; dissolved 1977); agreement to establish a secretariat was signed in Nov. 1994; initial areas for co-operation were to be trade and industry, security, immigration and promotion of investment; further objectives were the elimination of trade barriers and ensuring the free movement of people and capital within the grouping; secretariat inaugurated in March 1996. Exec. Sec. FRANCIS KIRIMI MUTHAURA.

United Nations African Institute for Economic Development and Planning (Institut africain de développement économique et de planification—IDEP): BP 3186, Dakar, Senegal; tel. 23-10-20; telex 51579; fax 21-21-85; f. 1963 by ECA (q.v.) to train economic development planners, conduct research and provide advisory services; has library of books, journals and documents. Dir Dr JEGGAN C. SENGHOR.

EDUCATION

African Association for Literacy and Adult Education: Finance House, 6th Floor, Loita St, POB 50768, Nairobi, Kenya; tel. (2) 222391; telex 22096; fax (2) 340849; f. 1984, combining the fmr African Adult Education Asscn and the AFROLIT Society (both f. 1968); aims to promote adult education and literacy in Africa, to study the problems involved, and to allow the exchange of information; programmes are developed and implemented by 'networks' of educators; holds assembly every three years. Mems: 28 nat. education asscns and 300 institutions in 33 countries. Chair. Dr ANTHONY SETSABI (Lesotho); Sec.-Gen. PAUL WANGOOLA (Uganda). Publs. *The Spider Newsletter* (quarterly, French and English), *Regional Conference Report* (every 3 years), *Journal* (2 a year).

Association of African Universities (Association des universités africaines): POB 5744, Accra North, Ghana; tel. (21) 774495; telex 2284; fax (21) 774821; f. 1967 to promote exchanges, contacts and co-operation between African university institutions; to study and make known educational and related needs in Africa, and to co-ordinate arrangements to meet these needs, to collect, classify and disseminate information on higher education and research, particularly in Africa. Mems: 132 univs in 39 African countries. Sec.-Gen. Prof. NARCISO MATOS (Mozambique). Publs include *Newsletter* (3 a year), *Handbook of African Universities* (every 2 years).

International Association for the Development of Documentation, Libraries and Archives in Africa: BP 375, Dakar, Senegal; tel. 24-09-54; f. 1957 to organize and develop documentation and archives in all African countries. Sec.-Gen. ZACHEUS SUNDAY ALI (Nigeria); Perm. Sec. EMMANUEL K. W. DADZIE (Togo).

International Congress of African Studies: c/o International African Institute, Thornhaugh St, London, WC1H 0XG, England; tel. (171) 323-6035; fax (171) 323-6118; f. 1962 to encourage co-operation and research in African studies; Congress convened approx. every five years (1990: in Khartoum, Sudan). Publ. *Proceedings.*

West African Examinations Council—WAEC (Conseil des examens de l'Afrique orientale): Examination Loop, POB 125, Accra, Ghana; tel. (21) 221511; telex 2934; fax (21) 222905; f. 1952; administers prescribed examinations in mem. countries; aims to harmonize examinations procedures and standards. Offices in each mem. country and in London, the United Kingdom. Mems: The Gambia, Ghana, Liberia, Nigeria, Sierra Leone; Chair. Dr YAHAYA HAMZA; Registrar SYLVIA AWO MANSAH BOYE.

ECONOMICS AND FINANCE

African Centre for Monetary Studies: 15 blvd F. Roosevelt, BP 1791, Dakar, Senegal; tel. 23-38-21; telex 61256; fax 23-77-60; f. 1978 as an organ of the Association of African Central Banks (AACB, see below) as a result of a decision by the OAU Heads of State and Government; aims to promote better understanding of banking and monetary matters; to study monetary problems of African countries and the effect on them of international monetary devts; seeks to enable African countries to co-ordinate strategies in international monetary affairs. Mems: all mems of AACB. Dir. JEAN-MARIE GANKOU. Publs *Financial Journal* (2 a year), *Annual Report.*

African Insurance Organization: BP 5860, Douala, Cameroon; tel. 42-47-58; fax 43-20-08; f. 1972 to promote the expansion of the insurance and reinsurance industry in Africa, and to increase regional co-operation; has established African insurance 'pools' for aviation, petroleum and fire risks; holds annual conference, and arranges meetings for reinsurers, brokers, consultants and supervisory authorities in Africa; has created the African Insurance Educators' Agency, the Asscn of African Insurance Brokers and the Asscn of African Insurance Supervisory Authorities. Mems: insurers, reinsurers, brokers and supervisory authorities in 42 African countries. Sec.-Gen. Y. ASEFFA.

Association of African Central Banks—AACB: 15 blvd F. Roosevelt, BP 1791, Dakar, Senegal; tel. 23-38-21; telex 61256; fax 23-77-60; f. 1968 to promote co-operation among mem. central banks in monetary and banking policy, and to provide a forum for views and information on matters of interest to monetary and financial stability on the African continent. Mems: 36 African central banks, representing 47 countries. Chair. SABER MOHAMED HASSAN (Sudan).

Association of African Tax Administrators: POB 13255, Yaoundé, Cameroon; tel. 22-41-57; fax 22-41-51; f. 1980 to promote co-operation among African countries in the fields of taxation policy, legislation and admin. Mems: 20 states. Chair. JAMES A. H. SCOTT; Sec.-Gen. OWONA PASCAL-BAYLON.

East African Development Bank: 4 Nile Ave, POB 7128, Kampala, Uganda; tel. (41) 230021; telex 61074; fax (41) 259763; f. 1967 by the fmr East African Community, to promote development within Kenya, Tanzania and Uganda, which each hold 25.78% of the equity capital; cap. SDR 25.4m. (Dec. 1995). Dir-Gen. F. R. TIBEITA.

Fonds Africain de Garantie et de Co-opération Economique—FAGACE (African Guarantee and Economic Co-operation Fund): BP 2045, Cotonou, Benin; tel. 300376; telex 5024; fax 300284; commenced operations in 1981; guarantees loans for development projects, provides loans and grants for specific operations and supports national and regional enterprises. Cap. 7,750m. francs CFA. Mems Benin, Burkina Faso, Central African Republic, Côte d'Ivoire, Mali, Niger, Rwanda, Senegal, Togo. Dir-Gen. SOULEYMANE GADO.

Union africaine des banques pour le développement: BP 2045, Cotonou, Benin; tel. 30-15-00; telex 5024; fax 30-02-84; f. 1962 to promote devt through exchanges, training and co-operation by regional banks. Mems: National or central banks of 12 countries. Exec. Sec. KOUANVI TIGOUE (Togo).

West African Bankers' Association: 22 Wilberforce St, PMB 1012, Freetown, Sierra Leone; fax (22) 229024; f. 1981; aims to strengthen links between banks in West Africa, to enable exchange of information, and to contribute to regional economic development; holds annual general assembly. Mems: 135 commercial banks in 14 countries. Publ. *West African Banking Almanac.*

West African Clearing House—WACH: PMB 218, Freetown, Sierra Leone; tel. (22) 224485; telex 3368; fax (22) 223943; f. 1975, began operating in 1976; administers payments among its 10 mem. central banks in order to promote the use of local currencies for sub-regional trade and monetary co-operation, thus effecting savings in mems' foreign reserves. (See under ECOWAS for restructuring as the West African Monetary Agency.) Mems: Banque centrale des états de l'Afrique de l'ouest (serving Benin, Burkina Faso, Côte d'Ivoire, Mali, Niger, Senegal and Togo: see under Franc Zone) and the central banks of Cape Verde, The Gambia, Ghana, Guinea, Guinea-Bissau, Liberia, Mauritania, Nigeria and Sierra Leone. Exec. Sec. CHEIKH S. B. DIAO (Mauritania). Publ. *Annual Report.*

GOVERNMENT AND POLITICS

African Association for Public Administration and Management: POB 48677, Nairobi, Kenya; tel. (2) 52-19-44; fax (2) 52-18-45; f. 1971 to provide senior officials with a forum for the exchange of ideas and experience, to promote the study of professional techniques and encourage research in particular African admin. problems. Mems: 500 individual, 50 corporate. Pres. WILLIAM N. WAMALWA; Sec.-Gen. Prof. A. D. YAHAYA. Publs include *Newsletter* (quarterly), annual seminar reports.

Afro-Asian Peoples' Solidarity Organization—AAPSO: 89 Abdel Aziz Al-Saoud St, POB 11559-61 Manial El-Roda, Cairo, Egypt; tel. (2) 3636081; telex 92627; fax (2) 3637361; f. 1957; acts among and for the peoples of Africa and Asia in their struggle for genuine independence, sovereignty, socio-economic devt., peace and disarmament; congress held every four years (1992: Lebanon). Mems: 82 nat. cttees from African and Asian countries, and 10 European orgs as assoc. mems. Pres. Dr MORAD GHALEB; Sec.-Gen. NOURI ABDEL RAZZAK (Iraq). Publ. *Development and Socio-Economic Progress* (quarterly).

Pan-African Youth Movement: 19 rue Debbih Cherif, BP 72, Didouch Morad, 16000 Algiers, Algeria; tel. and fax (2) 71-64-71; telex 61244; f. 1962; promotes participation of African youth in socio-economic and political development; organizes confs, seminars and festivals. Mems: over 50 orgs and independence movements in African countries. Publ. *MPJ News* (quarterly).

Sommet francophone (la Francophonie): c/o Agence de co-opération culturelle et technique, 13 quai André-Citroën, 75015 Paris, France; tel. 1-44-37-33-00; fax 1-45-79-14-98; conference of Heads of State convened every two years to promote co-operation throughout the French-speaking world (1995: Cotonou, Benin; 1997: Hanoi, Viet Nam). Mems: Governments of 49 countries.

Union of African Parliaments: BP V314, Abidjan 01, Côte d'Ivoire; tel. 21-37-57; telex 22338; fax 22-20-87; f. 1976; holds annual conf. Mems: 31 states. Sec.-Gen. HENRI ADOU SESS.

INDUSTRIAL AND PROFESSIONAL RELATIONS

International Confederation of Free Trade Unions—African Regional Organization (ICFTU—AFRO): POB 67273, Ambank House, 14th Floor, University Way, Nairobi, Kenya; tel. (2) 221357; telex 25792; fax (2) 215072; f. 1957. Mems: 5m. workers in 36 African countries; Gen. Sec. ANDREW KAILEMBO (Tanzania).

Organisation of African Trade Union Unity—OATUU: POB M386, Accra, Ghana; tel. 772574; telex 2673; fax 772621; f. 1973 as a single continental trade union org, independent of international trade union organizations; has affiliates from all African trade unions. Congress, composed of four delegates from all affiliated trade union centres, meets at least every four years as supreme policy-making body; General Council, composed of one representative from all affiliated trade unions, meets annually to implement Congress decisions and to approve annual budget. Mems: trade union movements in 52 independent African countries. Sec.-Gen. HASSAN SUNMONU (Nigeria). Publ. *Voice of African Workers.*

Pan-African Employers' Confederation: c/o Federation of Kenya Employers, POB 48311, Nairobi, Kenya; tel. (2) 721929; telex 22642; fax (2) 721990; f. 1986 to link African employers' orgs, and to represent them at the UN, the International Labour Organisation and the OAU. Pres. HEDI JILIANI (Tunisia); Sec.-Gen. TOM DIJU OWUOR (Kenya).

LAW

African Bar Association: POB 3451, 29 La Tebu St, East Cantonments, Accra, Ghana; f. 1971; aims to uphold the rule of law, to maintain the independence of the judiciary, and to improve legal services. Pres. CHARLES IDEHEN (Nigeria).

African Society of International and Comparative Law: Kairaba Ave, Private Bag 520, Banjul, The Gambia; tel. 375476; fax 375469; f. 1986; promotes public education on law and civil liberties; aims to provide a legal aid and advice system in each African country, and to facilitate the exchange of information on civil liberties in Africa; seeks to promote the Rule of Law by the publ. of legal texts and org. of confs. Pres. MOHAMMED BEDJAOUI; Sec. EMILE YAKPO. Publs *African Journal of International and Comparative Law* (quarterly in French and English), *Reportings of the Annual Conferences of the African Society of International and Comparative Law* (annually in French and English), *Report of the African Commission on Human and People's Rights* (biennially in French, English and Arabic).

Asian-African Legal Consultative Committee: 27 Ring Rd, Lajpat Nagar IV, New Delhi 110024, India; tel. (11) 6414265; fax (11) 6221344; f. 1956 to consider legal problems referred to it by mem. countries and to be a forum for Afro-Asian co-operation in international law and economic relations; provides background material for confs, prepares standard/model contract forms suited to the needs of the region; promotes arbitration as a means of settling international commercial disputes; trains officers of mem. states; has perm. UN observer status. Mems: 44 states. Pres. Dr M. JAVAD ZARIF (Iran); Sec.-Gen. TANG CHENGYAN (China).

Inter-African Union of Lawyers: 12 rue du Prince Moulay Abdullah, Casablanca, Morocco; tel. (2) 271017; fax (2) 204686; f. 1980; holds congress every three years. Pres. ABDELAZIZ BENZAKOUR (Morocco); Sec.-Gen. FRANÇOIS XAVIER AGONDJO-OKAWE (Gabon). Publ. *L'avocat africain* (2 a year).

MEDICINE AND PUBLIC HEALTH

International Federation of Red Cross and Red Crescent Societies—IFRC: 17 chemin des Crêts, Petit-Saconnex, CP 372, 1211 Geneva 19, Switzerland; tel. (22) 7304222; telex 412133; fax (22) 7330395; e-mail secretariat@ifrc.org; f. 1919 to prevent and alleviate human suffering, and to promote humanitarian activities by nat. Red Cross and Red Crescent socs; conducts relief operations for refugees and victims of disasters, co-ordinates relief supplies and assists in disaster prevention; Pres. Dr MARIO VILLARROEL LANDER (Venezuela); Sec.-Gen. GEORGE WEBBER (Canada). Publs *Annual Report, Red Cross Red Crescent* (quarterly), *Weekly News, World Disasters Report, Emergency Appeal.*

Médecins sans frontières: rue de la Tourelle, 1040 Brussels, Belgium; tel. (2) 280-18-81; fax (2) 280-01-73; f. 1971; undertakes emergency humanitarian missions, provides medical treatment in refugee camps, and supports long-term field operations in countries with inadequate health facilities. Publs *Annual Report, MSF International Newsletter.*

Organisation panafricaine de lutte contre le SIDA—OPALS: 15/21 rue de L'Ecole de Médecine, 75006 Paris, France; tel. 1-43-26-72-28; fax 1-43-29-70-93; f. 1988; disseminates information relating to the treatment and prevention of AIDS; provides training of medical personnel; promotes co-operation between African medical centres and specialized centres in the USA and Europe. Publ. *OPALS Liaison.*

Organization for Co-ordination and Co-operation in the Struggle against Endemic Diseases (Organisation de coordination et de coopération pour la lutte contre les grandes endémies—OCCGE): 01 BP 153, Bobo-Dioulasso 01, Burkina Faso; tel. 97-01-55; fax 97-00-99; e-mail SG@pegase.OCCGE.BF; f. 1960; conducts research, provides training and maintains a documentation centre and computer information system; in 1990 announced intention to merge with anglophone West African Health Community (q.v.) to form West African Health Organization. Mems: Govts of Benin, Burkina Faso, Côte d'Ivoire, Mali, Mauritania, Niger, Senegal, Togo. Sec.-Gen. Prof. ABDOULAYE RHALY. Publs *OCCGE Info* (3 a year), *Rapport annuel, Bulletin Bibliographique* (quarterly). Centres of the OCCGE are:

Centre de recherches sur les méningites et les schistosomiases: BP 10887, Niamey, Niger; tel. 75-20-45; fax 75-31-80; f. 1979.

Centre Muraz: 01 BP 153, Bobo-Dioulasso 01, Burkina Faso; tel. 97-01-02; telex 8260; fax 97-04-57; multi-discipline medical research centre with special interest in biology and epidemiology of tropical diseases and training of health workers. Dir Prof. PHILIPPE VANDEPERRE.

Institut Marchoux: BP 251, Bamako, Mali; tel. 22-51-31; telex 1200; fax 22-28-45; f. 1935; staff of seven doctors; research on leprosy, epidemiology, training. Dir Dr PIERRE BOBIN.

Institut d'ophtalmologie tropicale africaine—IOTA: BP 248, Bamako, Mali; tel. 22-34-21; fax 22-51-86; f. 1952; undertakes training, research and specialized care in ophthalmology. Dir Dr PIERRE HUGUET.

Institut Pierre Richet: 01 BP 1500, Côte d'Ivoire; tel. 63-37-46; fax 63-27-38; research on malaria, trypanosomiasis and impregnated mosquito nets; Dir Dr PIERRE CARNEVALE.

Office de recherches sur l'alimentation et la nutrition africaine—ORANA: BP 2098, Dakar, Senegal; tel. 22-58-92; f. 1956. Dir Dr A. M. NDIAYE.

Offices are also based in Cotonou, Benin (entomology), Lomé, Togo (nutrition), Nouakchott, Mauritania (tuberculosis), and Bafoulabé, Mali (leprosy).

Organization for Co-ordination of the Control of Endemic Diseases in Central Africa (Organisation de coordination pour la lutte contre les endémies en Afrique centrale—OCEAC): BP 288, Yaoundé, Cameroon; tel. 23-22-32; fax 23-00-61; f. 1965 to standardize methods of fighting endemic diseases, to co-ordinate national action, and to negotiate programmes of assistance on a regional scale. Mems: Cameroon, Central African Republic, Chad, Rep. of Congo, Equatorial Guinea, Gabon. Pres. J. R. PENDY BOUYIKI (Cameroon); Sec.-Gen. Dr BILONGO MANENE. Publs *Rapport Final des Conférences Techniques* (every 2 years), *Rapport annuel, Bulletin de liaison et de documentation* (quarterly), *EPI–Notes OCEAC* (quarterly).

West African Health Community: PMB 2023, Yaba, Lagos, Nigeria; tel. and fax (1) 862324; telex 27896; f. 1972 to promote higher medical and allied professional education, disseminate tech. health information, establish special agencies and programmes and collaborate with other medical orgs in mem. states and elsewhere; Ministers of Health meet annually. Three specialized agencies have been formed: the West African Postgraduate Medical College, the West African Pharmaceutical Federation and the West African College of Nursing. Mems: The Gambia, Ghana, Liberia, Nigeria and Sierra Leone; in 1990 announced intention to merge with francophone Organization for Co-ordination and Co-operation in the Struggle against Endemic Diseases (q.v.) to form the West African Health Organization, covering all the mem. states of ECOWAS (subject to ratification by mem. states). Exec. Dir Dr KABBA T. JOINER. Publ. *West African Journal of Medicine, West African Journal of Nursing, West African Pharmacy Journal.*

PRESS, RADIO AND TELECOMMUNICATIONS

African Postal and Telecommunications Union: ave Patrice Lumumba, BP 44, Brazzaville, Republic of Congo; tel. 83-27-78; telex 5212; f. 1961 to improve postal and telecommunication services between mem. administrations; consists of three Commissions: Post and Financial Services, Telecommunications, Administrative and Budget Affairs. Mems: Benin, Burkina Faso, Central African Republic, Chad, Repub. of Congo, Côte d'Ivoire, Mali, Mauritania, Niger, Rwanda, Senegal, Togo. Sec.-Gen. MAHMOUDOU SAMOURA.

Regional African Satellite Communications System—RASCOM: c/o International Telecommunication Union, place des Nations, 1211 Geneva 20, Switzerland; tel. (22) 7305111; telex 421000; fax (22) 7337256; f. 1992 to launch Africa's first satellite into space within five years. Mems: 42 countries.

Union of National Radio and Television Organizations of Africa—URTNA (Union des radiodiffusions et télévisions nationales d'Afrique): BP 3237, 101 rue Carnot, Dakar, Senegal; tel. 21-59-70; telex 650; fax 22-51-13; f. 1962; co-ordinates radio and television services, including monitoring and frequency allocation, the exchange of information and coverage of national and international events, among African countries; maintains programme exchange centre (Nairobi, Kenya), tech. centre (Bamako, Mali) and a centre for rural radio studies (Ouagadougou, Burkina Faso); AFROVISION co-ordinating centre for the exchange of television news in Algiers, Algeria. Budget (1993): US $1.8m. There are 49 active, two supplementary active and nine assoc. mem. orgs. Sec.-Gen. EFOE ADODO MENSAH (Togo). Publs *URTNA Review* (2 a year in English and French).

West African Journalists' Association: BP 849, 20 rue Mohammad V, Dakar, Senegal; tel. 22-36-25; fax 22-17-61; e-mail sysop@endakak.gn.apc.org; f. 1986; defends journalists and the freedom of the press, and promotes links between journalists' asscns. Mems: journalists' asscns in the mem. states of ECOWAS.

RELIGION

All Africa Conference of Churches: POB 14205, Waiyaki Way, Nairobi, Kenya; tel. (2) 441483; telex 22175; fax (2) 443241; f. 1958; promotes co-operation and fellowship among Protestant, Orthodox and independent Churches and Christian Councils in Africa; last assembly Harare, Zimbabwe, 1992. Mems: 147 churches and associated councils in 39 African countries. Pres. Most Rev. DESMOND TUTU (South Africa); Gen. Sec. Rev. JOSÉ CHIPENDA (Angola). Publs *ACLCA News, Tam Tam.*

World Council of Churches: BP 2100, 150 route de Ferney, 1211 Geneva 2, Switzerland; tel. (22) 7916111; telex 415730; fax (22) 7910361; f. 1948 to promote co-operation between Christian churches; conducts programmes related to Christian unity, mission, international affairs, development, inter-church aid, refugees, education, youth and women. The programme to combat racism (PCR) is responsible for working out WCC policies and programmes on combating racism; giving expression to solidarity with the racially oppressed; assisting churches in education for racial justice; studying the causes and effects of all forms of racism, especially white racism; organizing action-orientated research; and operating the Special Fund to Combat Racism for movements of the racially oppressed. Gen. Sec. Rev. Dr KONRAD RAISER (Germany). Publs *Ecumenical Review* (quarterly), *International Review of Mission* (quarterly).

SCIENCE AND TECHNOLOGY

African Organization of Cartography and Remote Sensing: BP 3, 16040 Hussein Dey, Algiers, Algeria; tel. (2) 77-79-34; telex 65474; fax (2) 77-79-34; f. 1988 by amalgamation of African Association of Cartography and African Council for Remote Sensing; aims to encourage the development of cartography and of remote-sensing by satellites; organizes confs and other meetings, promotes establishment of training inst; maintains regional training centres in Burkina Faso, Kenya, Nigeria and Tunisia. Mems: national cartographic institutions of 24 countries. Sec.-Gen. UNIS MUFTAH.

African Regional Centre for Technology: Immeuble FAHD, 17e étage, blvd Djily Mbaye, BP 2435, Dakar, Senegal; tel. 23-77-12; telex 61282; fax 23-77-13; f. 1980 to encourage the devt of indigenous tech. and to improve the terms of access to imported tech.; assists the establishment of nat. centres. Dir Dr OUSMANE KANE. Publs include *African Technodevelopment, Alert Africa, Infonet.*

Association for the Taxonomic Study of the Tropical African Flora: National Botanic Garden of Belgium, Domein von Bouchout, B-1860 Meise, Belgium; tel. (2) 2693905; fax (2) 2701567; e-mail J.Rammeloo@br.fgov.be; f. 1950 to facilitate co-operation and liaison between botanists engaged in the study of the flora of tropical Africa; maintains a library. Mems: c. 800 botanists in 63 countries. Sec.-Gen. Prof. J. RAMMELOO. Publs *AETFAT Bulletin* (annually), *Proceedings.*

Inter-African Committee for Hydraulic Studies (Comité interafricain d'études hydrauliques—CIEH): 01 BP 369, Ouagadougou, Burkina Faso; tel. 30-71-12; telex 5277; fax 36-24-41; f. 1960 to ensure co-operation in hydrology, hydrogeology, climatology, urban sanitation and other water sciences; co-ordination of research and other projects. Mems: 14 African countries. Sec.-Gen. AMADOU CISSÉ. Publs scientific and technical research studies, *Bulletin de liaison technique* (quarterly).

Pan-African Union of Science and Technology: BP 2339, Brazzaville, Republic of Congo; tel. 83-22-65; telex 5511; fax 83-21-85; f.

1987 to promote the use of science and tech. in furthering the devt of Africa; membership open to any scientific or tech. inst. or asscn in Africa. Pres. Prof. EDWARD AYENSU (Ghana); Sec.-Gen. Prof. LÉVY MAKANY.

Regional Centre for Services in Surveying, Mapping and Remote Sensing: POB 18118, Nairobi, Kenya; tel. (2) 803320; telex 25285; fax (2) 802767; f. 1975 to provide services in the professional techniques of map-making and the application of satellite and remote sensing data in resource analysis and devt planning; undertakes training and research and provides advisory services to African govts. Mems: 15 signatory and nine non-signatory states. Dir-Gen. Prof. SIMON NDYETABULA.

Regional Centre for Training in Aerospace Surveys (RECTAS): PMB 5545, Ile-Ife, Nigeria; tel. (36) 230050; telex 34262; fax (36) 230481; f. 1972 to provide training, research and advisory services in aerial surveying; administered by the ECA (q.v.). Mems: Benin, Burkina Faso, Cameroon, Ghana, Mali, Niger, Nigeria, Senegal. Dir J. A. OGUNLAMI. Publ. *RECTAS Newsletter* (annually).

Scientific, Technical and Research Commission—STRC: Nigerian Ports Authority Bldg, PMB 2359, Marina, Lagos, Nigeria; tel. (1) 2633289; fax (1) 2636093; f. 1965 to succeed the Commission for Technical Co-operation in Africa (f. 1954). Supervises the Inter-African Bureau for Animal Resources (Nairobi, Kenya), the Inter-African Bureau for Soils (Lagos, Nigeria) and the Inter-African Phytosanitary Commission (Yaoundé, Cameroon) and several joint research projects. The Commission provides training in agricultural man., and conducts pest control programmes. Exec. Sec. Prof. JOHNSON A. EKPERE.

United Nations University Institute for Natural Resources in Africa (UNU/INRA): ISSER Bldg Complex, Nasia Rd, University of Ghana, Legon; Private Mail Bag, Kotoka International Airport, Accra, Ghana; tel. (21) 500396; telex 2195; fax (21) 500792; e-mail unuinra@ncs.com.gh; f. 1986 as a research and training centre of the United Nations University (Tokyo, Japan); operational since 1990; aims at human resource development and institutional capacity building through co-ordination with African universities and associated research institutes in advanced research, training and dissemination of knowledge and information on the conservation and management of Africa's natural resources and their rational utilization for sustainable devt. Dir. Prof. A. UZO MORWUNYE. INRA has a mineral resources unit (MRU) at the University of Zambia in Lusaka. MRU Co-ordinator Prof. MUTALE W. CHANDA.

SOCIAL SCIENCES, SOCIAL WELFARE AND HUMAN RIGHTS

African Centre for Applied Research and Training in Social Development—ACARTSOD: Africa Centre, Wahda Quarter, Zawia Rd, POB 80606, Tripoli, Libya; tel. (21) 833640; fax (21) 832357; f. 1977 under the jt auspices of the ECA and OAU to promote and co-ordinate applied research and training in social devt, and to assist in formulating nat. development strategies. Officer-in-Charge LAMIS GABSI.

African Commission on Human and People's Rights: Kairaba Ave, POB 673, Banjul, The Gambia; tel. 96042; telex 2346; f. 1987; meets twice a year for two weeks in March and Oct.; The Commission comprises 15 members. Its mandate is to monitor compliance with the African Charter on Human and People's Rights (ratified in 1986), and it investigates claims of human rights abuses perpetrated by govts that have ratified the Charter. Claims may be brought by other African govts, the victims themselves, or by a third party. Pres. ISAAC NGUEMA; Sec. GERMAIN BARICAKO (Burundi).

African Social and Environmental Studies Programme: Box 44777, Nairobi, Kenya; tel. (2) 747960; fax (2) 740817; f. 1968; develops and disseminates educational material on social environmental studies, and education for all in eastern and southern Africa. Mems: 18 African countries. Chair. Prof. WILLIAM SEMTEZA KAJUBI; Exec. Dir Prof. PETER MUYANDA MUTEBI. Publs *African Social Studies Forum* (2 a year), teaching guides.

Association of Social Work Education in Africa: Addis Ababa University, POB 1176, Addis Ababa, Ethiopia; tel. (1) 126827; f. 1971 to promote teaching and research in social devt, to improve standards of institutions in this field, to exchange information and experience. Mems: schools of social work, community development training centres, other institutions and centres; 55 training institutions and 150 social work educators in 33 African countries; 22 non-African assoc. mems in Europe and North America. Sec.-Gen. Dr SEYOUM G. SELASSIE. Publ. *Journal for Social Work Education in Africa*.

Council for the Development of Social Science Research in Africa—CODESRIA: ave Cheikh Anta Diop, Angle Canal IV, BP 3304, Dakar, Senegal; tel. 25-98-22; telex 61339; fax 24-12-89; f. 1973; promotes research, provides confs, working groups and information services. Mems: research insts and university faculties in African countries. Exec. Sec. (vacant). Publs *Africa Development / Afrique et Développement* (quarterly), *CODESRIA Bulletin* (quarterly), *Index of African Social Science Periodical Articles* (annually).

Third World Forum: 39 Dokki St, POB 43, Orman, Cairo, Egypt; f. 1973 to link social scientists and others from the developing countries, to discuss alternative devt policies and encourage research. Regional offices in Mexico, Senegal and Sri Lanka. Mems: individuals in more than 50 countries. Chair. ISMAIL-SABRI ABDALLA. Publ. *TWF Newsletter*.

TRADE AND INDUSTRY

African Regional Industrial Property Organization—ARIPO: POB 4228, Harare, Zimbabwe; tel. (4) 794338; telex 26726; fax (4) 704025; e-mail aripo@harare.iafrica.com; f. 1976 to grant patents, register industrial designs and marks and to promote devt and harmonization of laws concerning industrial property. Mems: Botswana, The Gambia, Ghana, Kenya, Lesotho, Malawi, Sierra Leone, Somalia, Sudan, Swaziland, Tanzania, Uganda, Zambia and Zimbabwe. Dir.-Gen. MZONDI H. CHIRAMBO.

African Regional Organization for Standardization: POB 57363, Nairobi, Kenya; tel. (2) 224561; fax (2) 794338; f. 1977 to promote standardization, quality control, certification and metrology in the continent, to formulate regional standards to promote the exchange of information on standards, tech. regulations and related subjects and to co-ordinate participation in international standardization activities. Mems: 24 states. Sec.-Gen. ZAWDU FELLEKE. Publs *News Bulletin* (2 a year).

Association of African Trade Promotion Organizations—AATPO: Pavillon International, BP 23, Tangier, Morocco; tel. (9) 41687; telex 33695; f. 1974 under the auspices of the ECA and OAU to encourage regular trade contact between African states and to assist in the harmonization of their commercial policies in order to promote intra-African trade. Mems: 26 states. Sec.-Gen. Prof. ADEYINKA W. ORIMALADE. Publs include *FLASH: African Trade* (monthly), *Directory of Trade Promotion Institutions in Africa, Directory of State Trading Organizations, Directory of Exporters and Importers of Food Products in Africa, Calendar of Major Trade Events in Africa, African Trade Perspective* (on individual countries).

Federation of African Chambers of Commerce: c/o ECA, POB 3001, Addis Ababa, Ethiopia; tel. (1) 517200; telex 21029; fax (1) 514416; f. 1983. Dir Dr B. W. MUTHAUKA.

Organization of the Petroleum Exporting Countries—OPEC: 1020 Vienna, Obere Donaustrasse 93, Austria; tel. (1) 211-12-0; telex 134474; fax (1) 216-43-20; f. 1960 to unify and co-ordinate members' petroleum policies and to safeguard their interests generally: holds regular confs of mem. countries to set prices and production levels; conducts research in energy studies, economics and finance; provides data services and news agency covering petroleum and energy issues. Mems: Algeria, Indonesia, Iran, Iraq, Kuwait, Libya, Nigeria, Qatar, Saudi Arabia, United Arab Emirates, Venezuela. Sec.-Gen. Dr. RILWANU LUKMAN (Nigeria). Publs *Opec News Agency* (daily), *OPEC Bulletin* (monthly), *OPEC Review* (quarterly), *Annual Report, Annual Statistical Bulletin*.

OPEC Fund for International Development: Postfach 995, 1011 Vienna, Austria; tel. (1) 515-64-0; telex 131734; fax (1) 513-92-38; f. 1976 by mem. countries of OPEC, to provide financial co-operation and assistance for developing countries; in 1995 commitments amounted to US $196.8m., 40.9% of project loans approved in 1995 was for countries in Africa south of the Sahara. Dir-Gen. Y. SEYYID ABDULAI (Nigeria). Publs *Annual Report, OPEC Fund Newsletter* (3 a year).

Southern African Customs Union: no permanent headquarters; f. 1969; provides common pool of customs, excise and sales duties, according to the relative volume of trade and production in each country; goods are traded within the union free of duty and quotas, subject to certain protective measures for less developed mems; the South African rand is legal tender in Lesotho and Swaziland. The Customs Union Commission meets annually in each of the mems' capital cities in turn. Mems: Botswana, Lesotho, Namibia, South Africa, Swaziland.

Union of African Water Suppliers: 01 BP 1843, Abidjan 01, Côte d'Ivoire; tel. 24-14-43; telex 43398; fax 24-26-29; f. 1980; facilitates co-operation between public and private bodies concerned with water supply and sewage management in Africa; promotes the study of economic, technical and scientific matters relating to the industry; congress held every two years (1997 congress scheduled to be held in Casablanca, Morocco). Mems in 33 countries.

Union of Producers, Conveyors and Distributors of Electric Power in Africa—UPDEA: 01 BP 1345, Abidjan 01, Côte d'Ivoire; tel. 32-64-33; telex 23483; fax 33-12-10; f. 1970 to study tech. matters and to promote efficient devt of enterprises in this sector; operates training school in Côte d'Ivoire. Mems: 22 nat. electricity authorities in Africa. Sec.-Gen. LIONEL KELLER. Publs *AFRIQUELEC* (periodical), technical papers.

TRANSPORT AND TOURISM

African Airlines Association: POB 20116, Nairobi, Kenya; tel. (2) 502645; fax (2) 502504; f. 1968 to give African air cos expert advice in tech., financial, juridical and market matters; to improve communications in Africa; to represent African airlines; and to develop manpower resources; published first continent-wide timetable in 1988. Mems: 35 nat. carriers. Pres. (1996/97) Group Capt. PETER GANA (Nigeria).

Agency for the Safety of Air Navigation in Africa and Madagascar—ASECNA (Agence pour la sécurité de la navigation aérienne en Afrique et Madagascar): BP 8132, Dakar, Senegal; tel. 20-07-80; telex 31519; fax 20-06-00; f. 1959; organizes air-traffic communications in mem. states; co-ordinates meteorological forecasts; provides training for air-traffic controllers, meteorologists and airport fire-fighters. ASECNA is under the authority of a cttee comprising Ministers of Civil Aviation of mem. states. Mems: Benin, Burkina Faso, Cameroon, Central African Republic, Chad, Repub. of Congo, Côte d'Ivoire, France, Gabon, Madagascar, Mali, Mauritania, Niger, Senegal, Togo. Dir-Gen. MAURICE RAJAOFETRA (Madagascar).

Southern African Regional Tourism Council: POB 564 Blantyre, Malawi; tel. 624888; fax 634339; f. 1973 for the devt and marketing of tourism in southern African countries. Mems public and private representatives in 22 countries world-wide.

INDEX OF REGIONAL ORGANIZATIONS

(Main references only)

PART THREE
Country Surveys

ANGOLA

Physical and Social Geography

RENÉ PÉLISSIER

Revised for this edition by JOÃO GOMES CRAVINHO

PHYSICAL FEATURES

The Republic of Angola, covering an area of 1,246,700 sq km (481,354 sq miles), is the largest Portuguese-speaking state in Africa. It is composed of 18 provinces, one of which, Cabinda (formerly known as Portuguese Congo), is separated from the others by the oceanic outlet of the Democratic Republic of the Congo (DRC—formerly Zaire) and the River Congo. On its landward side Cabinda is surrounded by the DRC and the Republic of the Congo. Greater Angola is bordered to the north and east by the DRC, to the east by Zambia and to the south by Namibia. Excluding the Cabinda exclave, Angola extends 1,277 km from the northern to the southern border, and 1,236 km from the mouth of the Cunene river to the Zambian border.

Two-thirds of Angola is a plateau. The average elevation is 1,050–1,350 m above sea-level, with higher ranges and massifs reaching above 2,000 m. The highest point of Angola is Mt Moco (2,620 m) in the Huambo province. Through the central part of the inland plateau runs the watershed of Angola's rivers. The coastal plain on the Atlantic is separated from this plateau by a sub-plateau zone which varies in breadth from about 160 km in the north to about 25–40 km in the centre and south. The Namib desert occupies the coastal plain at a considerable height above Namibe. Towards the Cuango (Kwango) basin, in the Zaire province, a sedimentary hollow forms the Cassange depression, in which cotton is cultivated. The north-western section of the Angolan plateau has jungle-covered mountains which are suitable for the cultivation of coffee. The Mayombe range in Cabinda is covered by equatorial jungle.

Except for the Cuanza (Kwanza) river, which is navigable up to Dondo (193 km upstream), Angolan rivers do not provide easy access to the interior from the coast. On the other hand, they are harnessed for the production of electricity and for irrigation. The main rivers are, above the Cuanza, the Chiloango (Cabinda), the Congo, the M'bridge, the Loge, the Dange and the Bengo. The Cassai (Kasai), Cuilo (Kwilu) and Cuango rivers are known more for their importance to the DRC than for their upper reaches in Angola, although many tributaries of the Kasai intersect the Angolan plateau, exposing rich diamond fields in the Lunda provinces.

Angola has a tropical climate, locally tempered by altitude. The Benguela current, along the coast, influences and reduces rainfall in that part of the country which is arid or semi-arid. The interior uplands in the Bié, Huambo and Huíla provinces enjoy an equable climate. On the other hand, along the Cuanza river, in the north-west and north-east, and in the eastern and southern provinces, high temperatures and heavy seasonal rainfall discouraged European colonization wherever there were no economic incentives, such as coffee in the provinces of Zaire and Uíge, and diamonds in Lunda.

POPULATION

Angola is an underpopulated country, with only 5,646,166 inhabitants enumerated at the 1970 census, when the population density was 4.5 persons per sq km. By mid-1995, when the population was officially estimated at 11,561,000, the density had risen to 9.3 persons per sq km. Angola is overwhelmingly rural and has considerable ethnic diversity, although all indigenous groups, of which the Ovimbundu (1.7m. in 1960) and Mbundu (1m.) are the largest, are of Bantu stock. An important characteristic of the population is its youth, as 45% are under 15 years old and only 5% are over 60. According to UN estimates, the average life expectancy at birth in 1990–95 was 46.5 years. In 1990–95 Angola's population increased at an average annual rate of 3.2%.

Since the onset of civil strife in the mid-1970s, Angola has experienced considerable economic dislocation, accompanied by a widespread regrouping of African populations, brought about by insecurity and massacres. There has also been general movement from cities to rural areas. In the late 1980s less than 25% of the population were believed to be residing in urban centres of more than 2,000 inhabitants. The population is predominantly engaged in food-crop farming and, in the south, in cattle-raising. Only in areas where coffee, cotton and maize are cultivated are Africans engaged to any extent in commercial agriculture. Some 70% of the economically active population are believed to be engaged in the farming and cattle-raising sectors. Since the mid-1980s, government-controlled towns and villages have, over large parts of the country, co-existed with regroupings of guerrilla-controlled populations sheltered in shifting villages: this has applied mostly to the south-east, east and north-east. Serious food shortages and periods of famine have periodically beset central and southern Angola during the years of post-independence strife. The war has also created problems of 'internal' refugees (estimated to number up to 1.2m. people), while in the late 1980s it was estimated that more than 500,000 Angolans had fled to neighbouring countries.

The population of the capital, Luanda (which was 480,613 at the 1970 census), was estimated to have risen to 1.3m. by 1986. Outside the capital, most urban centres are operating at a reduced level, some having been partially destroyed or looted. Benguela and Lobito (the outlet of the Benguela railway, which has been effectively out of operation since 1975) have felt the impact of war, and Lobito harbour is still suffering from the disruption of traffic with the DRC and Zambia. The rehabilitation of the Lobito corridor, which will benefit both cities, was to be expedited following the conclusion of the Lusaka peace accord and formation of a government of national unity and reconciliation in early 1997. Huambo, formerly an important centre for rail traffic to the eastern regions, and to the DRC and Zambia, and for road traffic to Luanda and Namibia, should again become a focal point of economic activity. Other centres, such as Namibe, Lubango, Kuito and Luena, have also suffered from the war and local disorder. The city of Cabinda has benefited from the exploitation of offshore petroleum resources, while pioneer towns such as Menongue and Saurimo may eventually assume new importance as regional centres.

Recent History

JOÃO GOMES CRAVINHO

Based on an earlier article by MILES SMITH-MORRIS

INDEPENDENCE AND CIVIL WAR

In Angola, uniquely among the former Portuguese-ruled African territories, the colonial power was not confronted by a unified nationalist movement, but instead by three rival groups: the Movimento Popular de Libertação de Angola (MPLA), founded in 1956; the União das Populações de Angola/Frente Nacional de Libertação de Angola (UPA/FNLA), founded in 1962; and the União Nacional para a Independência Total de Angola (UNITA), founded in 1966. This fragmentation was attributable to ethnic divisions, rivalries among the leaderships, as well as by profound ideological differences. Each of the groups engaged in armed activity, mainly in areas bordering Zambia and Zaire (now the Democratic Republic of the Congo—DRC): the MPLA was probably the most effective, partly because of an increase in support from the Organization of African Unity (OAU) from 1967 onwards. However, the nationalists' effectiveness was reduced by conflicts within and between the movements. The three groups vied for external support, both from governments and from non-governmental organizations. The major Western powers initially supported the Portuguese, while the USSR and its allies were the principal sponsors of the MPLA.

Following a military coup in Portugal in April 1974, the new Portuguese government, under Gen. António Spínola, did not favour rapid decolonization. Within Angola, intermittent fighting occurred between nationalists and the Portuguese armed forces, while random attacks were also made on Africans by extremist right-wing Portuguese settlers. In September a new Portuguese government, under Gen. Francisco da Costa Gomes, expressed its determination to end the fighting and to expedite independence for the African territories, overriding the interests of the white settlers.

In 1974 the MPLA, the least cohesive of the nationalist movements, agreed upon a formal internal structure, appointing Dr Agostinho Neto as president. Later in the year, pacts were made between the FNLA and UNITA, and between the MPLA and UNITA, and in January 1975 the three groups formulated a common political programme. In the same month agreement was reached with the Portuguese government, establishing the date of Angola's independence as 11 November 1975: until then Angola would be governed by a transitional administration, comprising representatives of the three independence movements and a Portuguese high commissioner. A constituent assembly was to be elected, comprising only candidates who had been endorsed by the three movements.

During the first half of 1975 fighting broke out on several occasions between the MPLA and the FNLA, despite their January agreements. Another co-operation pact, adopted by the three movements in June also proved unsuccessful. In July the MPLA ejected the FNLA from the Angolan capital, Luanda, and UNITA was drawn into the fighting. By October the MPLA controlled 12 of the country's 16 provincial capitals. Considerable financial and military aid was received by the MPLA from Eastern bloc countries, and by the FNLA and UNITA from the USA and its allies. In October South African forces entered Angola, in support of UNITA and the FNLA, and in November Cuban troops arrived to assist the MPLA. Independence was declared on 11 November, as originally planned, by the MPLA in Luanda, by UNITA in Huambo, and by the FNLA in Carmona and Ambriz. In January 1976 the MPLA decisively defeated the FNLA, and at the end of the month South African forces withdrew. In February the MPLA expelled UNITA from Huambo, and on the same day the OAU recognized Angola as a member state. Cuban forces remained in the country.

Despite its military successes, the MPLA government was confronted by considerable difficulties: Angola's infrastructure had been damaged by war, most of the Portuguese population (who had dominated the modern sector of the economy) had fled abroad, and there were large numbers of refugees requiring support. Neto's administration refused to contemplate sharing power with the FNLA and UNITA, and during 1976 it acted to quell its opponents both within and outside the MPLA. An attempt in the following year by rebellious army units to seize power was quickly suppressed, and there ensued a purge of the country's mass organizations (the trade union federation, and women's and young people's organizations), the provincial administrations, and the armed forces. In December 1977 the Neto regime introduced a rigorous Marxist-Leninist programme for the MPLA, changing its name to the MPLA—Partido do Trabalho (Party of Labour) (MPLA—PT). In December 1978 Neto's power was further reinforced by a reorganization of the government and of the party structure. Following Neto's death in September 1979, the party effected a smooth transfer of power to José Eduardo dos Santos, previously the minister of planning, and reiterated its commitment to the policies that had been formulated under Neto's leadership. In 1980 there were further changes in the political structure, which confirmed the MPLA—PT's greater sense of self-confidence. The central committee had decided in 1976 that elections could be held only when MPLA structures were sufficiently strong, and by 1980 it was felt that they were. In August the central committee initiated a series of constitutional changes, to create a people's assembly and a number of provincial assemblies. These bodies were elected through an electoral college system, and the candidates at every level were vetted by the MPLA—PT or the mass organizations. A new people's assembly was inaugurated in November.

The cornerstone of Angolan foreign policy after 1976 was a close relationship with the Eastern bloc countries, especially Cuba, the USSR and, to some extent, the German Democratic Republic. Although a treaty of friendship and co-operation was signed with the USSR in 1976, the Angolan regime vigorously denied that the country was a Soviet client state, and actively pursued other diplomatic initiatives aimed at achieving commercial and aid agreements that would assist the country's development. The MPLA also cultivated improved relations with Angola's immediate neighbours, as a result of which Zambia undertook to expel UNITA forces operating from its territory. However, relations with Zaire remained difficult and, despite an attempt at conciliation in 1976, deteriorated considerably during 1977 and 1978, as a result of two incursions from Angola into the Shaba province of Zaire by forces of the Zairean anti-government Front National pour la Libération du Congo. In addition, the Angola government had, in 1977, claimed knowledge of an invasion plot ('Operation Cobra'), in which Zaire was alleged to be implicated. Whatever the involvement of some Western interests in plots against Angola, one effect of the Second Shaba Crisis (see Recent History of the Democratic Republic of the Congo) was Western insistence that Zaire should reach an accommodation with Angola. This was duly achieved in 1978, and brought its greatest benefit to Angola in 1979, when President Mobutu ordered the deportation from Zaire of the leaders of anti-MPLA—PT groups.

Relations with Portugal were strained following independence, and diplomatic links were not formalized until 1976. These relations were not particularly cordial until 1978 when the two countries resolved most of their remaining differences. The United Kingdom opened an embassy in Angola in 1977. Full diplomatic relations were established with France and the Federal Republic of Germany in 1979, and in the same year Angola introduced legislation offering attractive investment incentives to foreign companies. The most significant example of successful co-operation between Angola and Western multinational corporations has been in the petroleum industry, whose contributions to Angola's balance of payments and to government revenue have been of crucial importance.

CONFLICT WITH SOUTH AFRICA AND THE RESURGENCE OF UNITA

From early 1981, national life came to be increasingly dominated by the damaging effects of Angola's undeclared war with South Africa. The origins of this conflict lay in South Africa's refusal to concede independence to Namibia and in its unremitting campaign against the South West Africa People's Organisation of Namibia (SWAPO), the principal nationalist group conducting an armed struggle against South African rule in the territory. From 1978 onwards, South African troops made periodic incursions into Angolan territory, and from 1981 these attacks intensified and were directed as much against Angolan as against SWAPO targets. The most notable escalation was 'Operation Protea' in August 1981, in which several thousand South African troops advanced at least 120 km into Angola.

Armed incursions by South Africa were accompanied by an escalation in the activities of UNITA, which assumed a more prominent military role, expanding its operations in eastern Angola while the government deployed its main forces in the west against 'Operation Protea'. Throughout 1982 and 1983, South Africa and UNITA together intensified their activities in Angola, with the South Africans occupying large sections of Cunene province, while UNITA launched attacks on a wide variety of targets. In August 1983 the conflict sharply escalated when a large UNITA force captured the strategic town of Cangamba, in Moxico province, with the aid of intense aerial bombardment by the South African air force. This type of operation was increasingly difficult to justify as a 'hot-pursuit' action against SWAPO, and was clearly aimed at destabilizing the MPLA government. UNITA continued to conduct operations throughout 1984.

The Angolan government countered these challenges with new policy initiatives. While maintaining good relations with its Eastern bloc allies, it continued to diversify its international contacts, establishing formal relations with the People's Republic of China in 1983, and moving towards a relationship with the European Community (EC, now the European Union—EU). The petroleum industry, the country's economic mainstay, continued to prosper. At least 50% of the government's revenue from the petroleum sector was used for expenditure on defence and security, including the purchase of increasingly sophisticated military equipment. In July 1983 regional military councils were established in all areas affected by the fighting, concentrating all state power in the hands of military officers directly responsible to the president. Counter-attacks against UNITA by the government forces, the Forças Armadas Populares de Libertação de Angola (FAPLA), achieved some success in 1982 and 1983.

In January 1984, South Africa abruptly changed course, and proposed to withdraw its troops in exchange for Angola's restraining the activities of SWAPO guerrillas. By the terms of this proposal, formulated in February as the Lusaka Accord, South Africa was to withdraw from Angola, whose government was to control the activities of SWAPO. The agreement, however, was conditional on South Africa's proceeding towards Namibian independence in accordance with the UN Security Council's Resolution 435. As these developments ran almost concurrently with the Nkomati Accord between South Africa and Mozambique, they engendered considerable confidence in certain circles when perhaps scepticism would have been more appropriate: as stipulated by the Lusaka Accord, South Africa officially withdrew its troops from Angola in April 1985, only to have a unit of its special forces captured in the following month while engaged in operations against petroleum installations in Cabinda. 'Hot-pursuit' operations into Angola were resumed in June 1985, after which South Africa periodically deployed troops in Angola until August 1988 (see below).

Despite differences within each of the governments of the USA, South Africa and Angola on the appropriate course of action to follow, the position of the three main protagonists became clearer in the period following the Lusaka Accord. In US policy-making circles the view that the Angolan government must be weakened sufficiently in order to force the withdrawal of the Cubans clearly came to prevail over the view that Angola's legitimate security needs were better served by a resolution of the Namibian issue. Protracted negotiations, usually involving the USA as well as Angola and South Africa, collapsed because of a failure to agree on the question of 'linkage', i.e. the withdrawal of the Cubans as a *quid pro quo* for South African withdrawal from Angola and the creation of an independent Namibia.

From the mid-1980s, Angolan relations with the USA deteriorated, largely as a result of the reverse in US policy towards UNITA. In July 1985 the US congress repealed legislation which since 1976 had prohibited US military support for UNITA. In September 1985, as a result of the military situation, a South African delegation visited Washington to seek US aid for UNITA. This was followed in January 1986 by a visit to the USA by UNITA's leader, Dr Jonas Savimbi. His reception there was comparable to that for a head of state, and included well-publicized meetings with President Reagan and leading members of the administration who openly expressed their support for UNITA. The US congress subsequently agreed to provide UNITA with armaments, and these began to arrive in Angola during the second half of the year. In April President dos Santos had complained to the UN secretary-general of the US government's escalating support for UNITA, and requested the UN to terminate the role of the USA as primary mediator in negotiations over Namibia. In August, however, the Angolan government approached the US government, with a view to improving relations. The Reagan administration was not receptive to these overtures, and in October the US congress approved legislation prohibiting the purchase of Angolan petroleum and petroleum products by the US department of defense. Savimbi attempted to improve UNITA's international standing in October, when he accepted an invitation by centrist and right-wing members to visit the European parliament. However, his trip was largely unsuccessful; the European parliament refused to grant him official recognition and proceeded to condemn US support for UNITA and to propose the imposition of compulsory and comprehensive sanctions against South Africa. In March 1987 UNITA continued to seek international recognition in a move which some observers believe to have been prompted by the US central intelligence agency: UNITA offered to allow non-military traffic to operate on the Benguela railway, which had been effectively closed since 1975, owing to persistent sabotage by the rebels. In April 1987 Angola, Zaire, Zambia and Zimbabwe discussed the possible reopening of the railway line, which provides the shortest west coast route from Zambia and Zaire. However, UNITA's sincerity with regard to ceasing its sabotage activities became questionable in June, when it launched an attack on the railway.

By mid-1987 it was apparent that South African security forces were becoming increasingly active inside Angola and Namibia, and in October South Africa confirmed, for the first time, that it was maintaining a 'limited presence' inside Angola. In the following month South Africa confirmed that it was providing military support to UNITA, and announced that it had engaged in direct action against Soviet and Cuban forces. UNITA, however, denied that South Africa was providing military reinforcements to the rebels. South Africa's intensification of aggression against Angola was widely condemned, and in late November the UN Security Council demanded the unconditional withdrawal of South African troops from Angola within two weeks. Having eventually agreed to comply with this demand, South Africa nevertheless remained militarily active in Angola in the first half of 1988 (see below).

In April 1987 Angola and the USA resumed talks aimed at achieving a negotiated settlement over Namibia and Angola. The Angolan government made considerable efforts to secure diplomatic recognition from the USA, despite the announcement by the US administration, in June, of its intentions to continue to provide covert military aid to UNITA in both 1987 and 1988. By July 1987 the Namibia talks had failed to produce agreement, but negotiations were resumed in September. Angola's readiness to establish good relations with the USA was reflected in the change in the direction of the government's economic policy, indicated in August by the announcement of Angola's application for membership of the International Monetary Fund (IMF). In the following month the president made visits to several European capitals, including Paris and Lisbon, aimed at securing economic and, in some cases, military aid, and at obtaining support for Angola's proposed membership of the IMF.

Negotiations relating to a regional peace agreement were resumed in January 1988 between the USA and Angola, without success. In March, when it appeared that, in spite of a sharp escalation in the armed conflict in late 1987 and early 1988, a deadlock had again been reached between the two sides, renewed attempts to settle the guerrilla war by means of negotiation were made by the parties involved. In that month, representatives of Angola, Cuba and the USA held a meeting in Luanda, at which Angola and Cuba presented a peace plan, which included a new proposal for the evacuation of Cuban forces from southern Angola. The Angolan government also indicated that it was prepared to be flexible regarding the timetable for this evacuation. However, South Africa viewed the provisions of these peace proposals as too vague. Discussions were also held in March between the South African government and UNITA, and between the USA and the USSR. In April South African forces sustained a serious defeat at Cuito Cuanarale by the combined Cuban and FAPLA forces whose newly-acquired Russian anti-aircraft artillery denied South Africa its former superiority in the air. The extent of the South African losses and the change in the balance of military advantage were believed to have made a negotiated settlement considerably more urgent for South Africa.

TOWARDS A REGIONAL ACCORD

One of the main obstacles to progress towards a regional peace settlement had been South Africa's reluctance to commit itself to a comprehensive withdrawal from Angola and to the implementation of an independence settlement for Namibia. Following the changes on the military front, in May 1988 Cuba and Angola held 'exploratory talks' with South Africa in London, with the USA as mediator. At talks between Angola and South Africa, held nine days later, modest progress was reportedly made towards reaching a compromise. Later in May, at a meeting in Lisbon, the USA and the USSR discussed an outline peace plan for Angola, involving the withdrawal of both the Cuban and South African troops from Angola within one year. During a summit meeting between the USSR and the USA, held in Moscow in late May and early June, a target date of 29 September 1988 was set for reaching a settlement on the Angolan and Namibian conflicts. However, South Africa indicated that it regarded this deadline as unrealistic. At this time, the security situation worsened considerably; it was suggested by observers that UNITA and South Africa were intensifying their offensive in order to precipitate a peace agreement by Angola. Cuba, meanwhile, was reported to have increased its military forces from 35,000 to 50,000 troops. UNITA, which was excluded from the London meeting and subsequent consultations, initiated a diplomatic campaign in major Western capitals to advance its terms for an Angolan settlement. Discussions between representatives of the governments of Angola, Cuba, South Africa and the USA, held in July, resulted in a mutually agreed 'statement of principle', encompassing a programme that the US negotiator described as 'containing the essential elements of a peaceful settlement in south-western Africa'. Its provisions included the termination of US support for UNITA, South African assent to independence for Namibia on terms and conditions acceptable to the UN, and the simultaneous withdrawal of Cuban and South African troops from Angola. No timetable, however, was agreed for the start of the proposed withdrawals.

In early August 1988 discussions in Geneva resulted in an agreement on a 'sequence of steps' towards a regional peace settlement, whereby a cease-fire was to commence on 8 August, pending the withdrawal of all South African troops from Angola by 1 September, and the agreement, by that date, of a timetable for the evacuation of all Cuban forces from Angola; the implementation of the UN Security Council's Resolution 435 for Namibian independence was to commence on 1 November. However, although the cease-fire was observed and it was reported that all South African troops had duly departed by the end of August, agreement on a timetable for the Cuban withdrawal was not concluded. As a result, implementation of the Namibian independence process was postponed. Following further negotiations on an exact schedule for the Cuban withdrawal, an agreement in principle was eventually reached in mid-November, although the signing of a formal protocol was delayed until mid-December, owing to South African dissatisfaction over verification procedures for the Cuban troop departures.

On 22 December 1988 the participants in the negotiations met in New York, where a bilateral agreement was signed by Angola and Cuba, and a tripartite accord by Angola, Cuba and South Africa: under these agreements, 1 April 1989 was designated as the implementation date for the Namibian independence process, which was to culminate in elections to a constituent assembly from 1 November 1989, and Cuba undertook to complete a phased withdrawal of its estimated 50,000 troops from Angola by July 1991. Angola, Cuba and South Africa were to establish a joint commission, in which the USA and the USSR would be present as observers. All prisoners of war were to be exchanged, and the signatories of the tripartite accord were to refrain from supporting forces intent on undermining each other's governments. The latter clause necessitated both the curtailment of South African aid to UNITA and the departure from Angola of an estimated 6,000 members of the African National Congress of South Africa (ANC). In accordance with the agreements, the UN Security Council authorized the creation of a UN Angola Verification Mission (UNAVEM) to monitor the redeployment and withdrawal of Cuban troops. UNAVEM commenced operations in January 1989. Its mandate was for a period of 31 months.

Following the signing of the New York accords, the new Bush administration reassured UNITA of continued US support. The Angolan government remained intransigent towards appeals by UNITA for a cease-fire, but in early February 1989 it offered a 12-month amnesty to members of the rebel organization, reaffirming the regime's aim of re-assimilating defectors from UNITA into society. However, UNITA, restating its own aim of negotiating a settlement with the government which would lay the foundations for a multi-party democracy in Angola, reacted to the government's amnesty by launching a major offensive against FAPLA targets. This was abandoned shortly afterwards, owing to the intercession of President Houphouët-Boigny of Côte d'Ivoire. In the following month, both the government and UNITA showed a new willingness to end the civil war, and in early March President dos Santos announced that he was ready to attend a regional 'summit' conference to advance a resolution of the conflict. Shortly afterwards, Dr Savimbi announced that UNITA would honour a unilateral moratorium on offensive military operations until mid-July, during which time he hoped that African leaders would mediate an internal settlement. In addition, Savimbi offered to exclude himself from any peace negotiations, in order that this might make them more palatable to the dos Santos government. In mid-May eight African heads of state attended a conference in Luanda, at which President dos Santos presented a peace plan. He did not appear to have altered his terms for a peaceful solution to the Angolan civil war, demanding the cessation of US aid to UNITA and offering rebels reintegration into society.

In June 1989, however, dos Santos and Savimbi attended a further conference, held at Gbadolite, in Zaire, under the auspices of President Mobutu, at which 18 African leaders were present. Dos Santos agreed to hold direct negotiations with Savimbi, as a result of which a cease-fire was signed between UNITA and the Angolan government, with effect from midnight on 23 June. It was decided that the presidents of the Congo, Gabon and Zaire would oversee a commission responsible for monitoring the implementation of the peace agreement. The full terms of the accord were not, however, made public at that time, and it soon became clear that these were interpreted differently by each party: claims by the Angolan government that Savimbi had agreed to go into temporary exile and that members of UNITA were to be absorbed into existing Angolan institutions and to respect the existing constitution were strongly denied by the rebels. Within one week each side had accused the other of violating the cease-fire. In late August Savimbi announced a resumption of hostilities.

In September 1989, after boycotting a conference of eight African heads of state at Kinshasa, Zaire, at which the Gbadolite Accord had been redrafted, Savimbi announced a series of counter-proposals, envisaging the creation of an African peace-keeping force to supervise a renewed cease-fire, and the commencement of direct negotiations between UNITA and the government, with the objective of agreeing a settlement which could lay the foundation of a multi-party democracy in Angola. In early October, following a meeting with US President Bush, Savimbi agreed to resume peace talks with the Angolan government, with President Mobutu of Zaire acting as mediator: the US government announced during that month, however, that it would continue to support UNITA until 'national reconciliation' was achieved. Indirect negotiations between Savimbi and the government, mediated by Mobutu, took place in mid-October. In late December dos Santos proposed an eight-point peace plan which envisaged some political reform but did not compromise on the issue of a one-party state; the plan was rejected by UNITA. In mid-January 1990 Cuba temporarily suspended its troop withdrawal, following an attack by UNITA forces which resulted in the deaths of four Cuban soldiers. In early February a summit of four African heads of state took place in Zaire; although he had been invited, dos Santos did not attend the meeting. During that month fighting intensified between FAPLA and UNITA forces in the Mavinga region of southern Angola, a UNITA stronghold. In early March UNITA, admitting that the government troops had made substantial advances, agreed to accept an immediate cease-fire on condition that FAPLA forces withdraw from Mavinga.

THE ESTORIL PEACE AGREEMENT

In early April 1990, following a further summit meeting of four African heads of state, held in São Tomé and Príncipe and this time including the Angolan president, dos Santos reaffirmed his commitment to achieving a peace settlement. Shortly afterwards, UNITA agreed to an immediate cease-fire and requested direct talks with the government, abandoning its demand for the withdrawal of FAPLA troops from Mavinga. The government agreed to renew negotiations, and exploratory talks between representatives of UNITA and the government were held in Portugal later in that month, under Portuguese government auspices. Six further rounds of negotiations took place before May 1991 (see below). In May 1990 the government announced that it was withdrawing its forces from Mavinga, and in June FAPLA withdrew its troops from south-eastern Angola, as a 'gesture of goodwill'.

The government and UNITA both made significant political concessions during 1990. In early May UNITA announced that it would recognize dos Santos as head of state, and in October the rebel organization announced its acceptance of the MPLA—PT government as an interim administration, pending elections. During an historic meeting of the central committee of the MPLA—PT in late June and early July, it was decided that the country would 'evolve towards a multi-party political system', thus conceding one of UNITA's principal demands. In late October the MPLA's central committee proposed a general programme of reforms, including the replacement of the party's Marxist-Leninist ideology with a commitment to 'democratic socialism', the introduction of a market economy, the legalization of political parties (after which UNITA would be recognized as a legitimate political force), the transformation of the army from a party to a state institution, a revision of the constitution and the holding of multi-party elections in 1994, following a population census. The decisions of the central committee were formally approved by the party's third congress in December. However, the government and UNITA continued to disagree over the timing of elections and the interim status of UNITA. UNITA insisted on immediate political recognition as a precondition for a cease-fire, and elections by the end of 1991.

In March 1991 legislative approval was granted for the formation of political parties. On 1 May, as a result of the rounds of talks which commenced in April 1990, the government and UNITA concluded a peace agreement in Estoril, Portugal. The agreement provided for a cease-fire from midnight on 15 May, to be monitored by a joint political and military committee, comprising representatives from the MPLA—PT, UNITA, the UN, Portugal, the USA and the USSR. Immediately following the cease-fire, aid from abroad to the government and UNITA would cease, and a new national army was to be established, composed of equal numbers of FAPLA and UNITA soldiers. Free and democratic elections were to be held by the end of 1992. In early May 1991 the government approved legislation giving all exiles one year in which to return to Angola. The cease-fire took effect, according to plan, on 15 May, despite an intensification of FAPLA and UNITA activities prior to that date. On 31 May the government and UNITA formally ratified the Estoril peace agreement. The joint political and military committee held its first meeting in June.

The legalization of opposition parties in March 1991 prompted the emergence of numerous political groups. Among the most influential of these were the Associação Cívica Angolana, which was expected to deflect votes from the MPLA—PT (which had lost popularity following the implementation of economic austerity measures in late 1990 and early 1991), and the Fórum Democrático Angolano, which was viewed particularly as a rival to UNITA for electoral support. In early 1991 UNITA began the process of obtaining registration as a legal political movement. Legislation approved by the national people's assembly in May stipulated that political parties must enjoy support in at least 14 of Angola's 18 provinces, in order to discourage the emergence of ethnically-based political movements. This measure operated to the disadvantage of the Frente de Libertação do Enclave de Cabinda (FLEC), a secessionist movement seeking independence for the Cabinda province.

The USA and the USSR were both influential in bringing about the Estoril peace agreement. In September 1990 both powers joined the negotiations between UNITA and the government. In the following month the US congress agreed to provide UNITA with assistance worth US $60m. in 1991, but voted to cancel such payment if the government respected a cease-fire and promised to hold multi-party elections within two years of the cease-fire. However, in mid-June 1991, following the conclusion of the Estoril peace agreement (in which these conditions were fulfilled) in May, the US congress agreed to continue supplying aid to UNITA, at a reduced level of $20m.

Implementation of the Estoril peace accord was subject to considerable delay in its initial stages. In September 1991 UNITA briefly withdrew from participation in the joint political and military commission, demanding that the government proceed more rapidly with the confinement of its forces to assembly points and with agreeing on an electoral timetable. UNITA agreed to return to the commission following a meeting between Savimbi and the US vice-president, Dan Quayle. At the end of September Savimbi returned to Luanda for the first time since the civil war began in 1975; UNITA headquarters were transferred to the capital from Jamba in October.

Multi-party Politics and the 1992 Elections

In November 1991 dos Santos announced a provisional date for general elections. Voting was to take place in the second half of September, subject to consultations with political parties and to the extension of state administration to areas still under UNITA control. The arrangements were also contingent on the confinement of all UNITA forces to assembly points by mid-December. A step towards the creation of a unified national army was taken in January 1992, with the appointment of Gen. João de Matos, commander of FAPLA's ground forces, and Gen. Ahilo Camalata Numa, commander of UNITA's northern front, as joint supreme commanders of the armed forces.

In January 1992, on the recommendation of the joint political and military commission, a monitoring task group was established to expedite the implementation of the Estoril peace accord. The creation of the group, which was to include members of the government, UNITA and UNAVEM, followed growing concern over the reported decline in the number of government and UNITA troops in confinement areas and the reoccupation of territory by UNITA forces; troops from both armies, abandoning confinement areas, were blamed for rising levels of criminal activity. Concern about the security situation was heightened in the same month by the murder of four British tourists near a UNITA base in Huíla province.

Representatives of the government and 26 political parties met in Luanda in the second half of January 1992 to discuss the transition to multi-party democracy; the government rejected demands to convene a national conference to formulate the transition arrangements. UNITA declined to attend the meeting, but in February it held talks with the government, at which agreement was reached on various points of electoral procedure. It was agreed that the elections would be organized on the basis of proportional representation, with the president elected for a five-year term, renewable for three terms. The legislative assembly would be elected for a four-year term. On 2 April dos Santos announced that the elections would be held on 29–30 September. Two days after this announcement, the people's assembly adopted electoral legislation providing for an assembly of 223 members (90 to be elected in 18 provincial constituencies and the remainder from national lists). Provision was also made for the creation of a national electoral council to supervise the elections. The members of the council were appointed in early May.

Evidence of serious divisions within UNITA became apparent in early March 1992, with the announcement that two leading members, Gen. Miguel N'Zau Puna (the movement's spokesman on internal affairs) and Gen. Tony da Costa Fernandes (the spokesman for foreign affairs), had resigned. Both men were from Cabinda and were stated by UNITA to have resigned because of differences over the future of the petroleum-producing enclave, whose secession from Angola they were alleged to support. In February the two men had secretly left Angola for Paris, France, from where they issued statements denouncing Savimbi as a dictator and claiming that he was maintaining a clandestine force of some 2,000 troops near the Namibian border. Puna and Fernandes, however, subsequently returned to Angola and formed a 'Democratic Breakaway Tendency' to attract disaffected elements of UNITA.

The demobilization of FAPLA and UNITA forces began on 31 March 1992 and was to be completed by the end of July. According to the joint military and political commission, by the end of March 94% of UNITA's forces and 64% of those of FAPLA had gathered at the assembly points. There were reports, however, that both sides planned to keep some forces in reserve, and there were fears that the demobilization process, and the creation of a unified national army, would fall behind schedule.

The Partido Renovador Democrático, regarded as the third largest of the 30 or more political parties that had been formed since the introduction of a multi-party system, held its first congress in late April 1992, and immediately afterwards divided into two factions. The party's former honorary president, Joaquim Pinto de Andrade, and his supporters resigned from the party, alleging that the election of the party president, Luís dos Passos, and a new party executive during the congress had been the result of electoral malpractice. The MPLA—PT held an extraordinary congress in early May to prepare for the forthcoming elections. The 600 delegates voted to enlarge the membership of the central committee from 140 to 193, to allow the inclusion of prominent dissidents who had returned to the party. Among those who were readmitted to the party at the congress was Daniel Chipenda, a leading figure in the struggle for independence, who had left the MPLA in 1975, in protest at its alliance with the USSR, and had lived in exile until 1986. A meeting of the new central committee elected Chipenda to the political bureau. The suffix 'Partido do Trabalho' was deleted from the party's official name.

Dos Santos, Savimbi, Chipenda and the president of the FNLA, Holden Roberto, were among 12 candidates who had registered by the end of July 1992 for the presidential election. Chipenda, who was proposed by the Partido Nacional Democrata de Angola (PNDA), had earlier resigned as the election organizer of the MPLA. Despite concerns about delays in voter registration, some 4.8m. Angolans had been registered to vote in the elections by the deadline on 10 August (following a 10-day extension).

In August 1992 a constitutional revision took effect, removing the remnants of the country's former Marxist ideology, and deleting the worlds 'People's' and 'Popular' from the constitution and from the names of official institutions. The name of the country was changed from the People's Republic of Angola to the Republic of Angola.

On 27 September 1992 FAPLA and the UNITA forces were formally disbanded, and the new national army, the Forças Armadas de Angola (FAA), was officially established. However, the process of training and incorporating FAPLA and UNITA troops into the new 50,000-strong national army had been hindered by delays in the demobilization programme. By 28 September fewer than 10,000 soldiers were ready to be inducted into the FAA. Tens of thousands of government troops were reported to be awaiting demobilization or to have abandoned confinement areas, owing to poor conditions and non-payment of wages. It became evident that only a small percentage of UNITA soldiers had been demobilized, and that UNITA retained a heavily-armed and disciplined force. UNITA had deliberately slowed the process of demobilizing its soldiers, in protest at the formation of a new government paramilitary unit, the 'emergency police', recruited from the MPLA's own special forces.

Increased tension and outbreaks of violence prior to the general elections seriously threatened to disrupt the electoral process. Nevertheless, presidential and legislative elections took place, as scheduled, on 29–30 September 1992. Some 800 foreign observers, one-half of them provided by the UN, monitored the voting at nearly 6,000 polling stations. Despite fears of violence or intimidation, the level of participation was high, averaging almost 90% of the electorate, although a low turnout was reported from Cabinda, where FLEC had urged its supporters to boycott the elections. International observers reported that the conduct of the elections had been free and fair, but, when preliminary results indicated that the MPLA had obtained a majority of seats in the new national assembly, Savimbi accused the government of electoral fraud and demanded the suspension of the official announcement of the election results, pending an inquiry into the alleged electoral irregularities. On 5 October UNITA withdrew from the FAA. Rioting by UNITA supporters broke out in Luanda on 11 October, and similar incidents were reported in Malanje, Huambo and Huíla provinces.

According to the official election results, published on 17 October 1992, dos Santos received 49.57% of the total votes cast in the presidential election, just short of the 50% required to avoid a second round against Savimbi, who secured 40.07% of the votes. However, the MPLA had achieved a clear majority in the legislative elections, winning 129 of the 220 seats in the national assembly, compared with 70 for UNITA. Ten other parties won between one and six seats each. Three seats reserved for Angolans abroad were not filled, by mutual agreement among the parties. UNITA's share of the total vote was 34.1%, compared with the MPLA's 53.7%.

Savimbi, who had withdrawn to the UNITA-dominated province of Huambo, had agreed to participate in a second round of presidential elections on the condition that it be conducted by the UN, while the government insisted that the election should not take place until UNITA had conformed to the rules of the Estoril peace agreement by transferring its troops to assembly points and by returning to the FAA.

RESUMPTION OF CIVIL STRIFE

Following the announcement of the official election results, however, violence erupted between MPLA and UNITA supporters in various cities, including Luanda and Huambo, as UNITA launched a new offensive. By the end of October 1992 hostilities had spread throughout Angola, with the majority of UNITA's demobilized soldiers returning to arms. Serious fighting took place in Luanda and the central and southern towns of Benguela, Huambo, Lobito and Lubango in the first week of November, despite UN attempts to arrange a cease-fire. A number of senior UNITA officials were among an estimated 1,000 people killed in the renewed conflict. Reports that South Africa and Zaire had been providing logistical support to UNITA led to a deterioration in relations with these states.

On 6 November 1992 the UN under-secretary-general for peace-keeping operations, Marrack Goulding, arrived in Angola. Following discussions with Goulding and the UN special representative, Margaret Anstee, on 17 November, Savimbi announced that he would abide by the election results, although he maintained that the ballot had been fraudulent, and stated that he would participate in the second round of presidential elections, expected to take place in December 1992 or January 1993. Despite assurances that it would attend, UNITA was absent from multi-party talks convened by the government on 21 November. The national assembly convened on 26 November, without the 70 elected UNITA delegates, who claimed that to convene the assembly in the absence of an elected president was illegal. Fernando José França van-Dúnem, a former prime minister, was elected president of the assembly. On the following day, dos Santos appointed Marcolino José Carlos Moco, the secretary-general of the MPLA, as prime minister. Savimbi, meanwhile, continued to negotiate with the government and the UN while his forces remained on the offensive outside the capital. On 27 November, after direct talks between dos Santos and Savimbi, the two leaders issued a declaration reaffirming their commitment to the Estoril peace agreement, and committing themselves to the implementation of a cease-fire and a continuing UN presence in Angola. Shortly afterwards, UNITA launched an offensive in the north, capturing Uíge and an air base at Negage. By the end of November UNITA was reported to be in control of about two-thirds of the country.

The composition of a council of ministers was announced on 2 December 1992. The majority of the posts were assigned to members of the MPLA, with four smaller parties also represented. One full and four deputy ministerial posts (including that of deputy defence minister) were allocated to UNITA, along with the positions of armed forces deputy chief of the general staff and chief of army general staff. The names of their appointees were announced by UNITA and accepted by Moco, although he stipulated that their appointment would be dependent upon the full implementation of the peace accords. Relations with South Africa deteriorated further with the announcement by the South African government that it was withdrawing its diplomatic representation from Luanda; earlier the Angolan government had announced that it had detained the crew of a South African aircraft that had made an emergency landing on Angolan soil, an incident which it cited as further evidence of South African support for UNITA.

International pressure on the warring parties to reach a negotiated solution continued with the visit of the US deputy assistant secretary of state for African affairs, Jeffrey Davidow, in the second half of December 1992 for meetings with both leaders. As a result of the talks, UNITA withdrew its forces from Uíge and Negage, but fighting nevertheless intensified in late December, as the government launched an offensive. The offensive had some success, driving UNITA out of most major towns, but at the cost of heavy casualties, particularly in southern Angola. A fierce battle began for control of Huambo in the central highlands, the country's second largest city and traditionally a UNITA stronghold. In early 1993 UNITA captured the petroleum producing centre of Soyo, on the Zaire border. UNITA appeared, however, to have been deterred from attacking the petroleum installations of the Cabinda enclave, many of them operated by US companies, by a direct warning from the US representative in Angola, Edmund De Jarnette.

From late January 1993 diplomatic efforts to end the hostilities centred on peace talks convened by the UN in Addis Ababa, Ethiopia, with Portugal, Russia and the USA attending as observers. A first round began on 27 January, with discussions reported to be focusing on four issues: the establishment of a cease-fire; the implementation of the Estoril peace agreement; the definition of the UN's role in a cease-fire and the second round of the presidential elections; and the release of prisoners. A second round of talks, due to begin on 7 February, was repeatedly delayed by the failure of the UNITA delegation to attend and was finally cancelled on 1 March, amid sharp criticism of UNITA by the observers.

In early March 1993 the government confirmed that it had lifted its two-month siege on Huambo, in which some 10,000 people were thought to have died. On 12 March the UN Security Council adopted a resolution condemning UNITA's violations of the peace accords and requesting the UN secretary-general, Dr Boutros Boutros-Ghali, to arrange a meeting between the combatants. The government claimed military successes during March, recapturing Soyo and M'banza-Congo, in the north, and Caxito, north-east of Luanda, and repelling a UNITA assault on Cubal, west of Huambo. Meanwhile, UNITA besieged the government garrison in the central city of Kuito, capital of Bié province. Peace talks resumed, under UN auspices, in Abidjan, Côte d'Ivoire, on 12 April, but, despite some signs of progress on the issue of power-sharing, were hampered by UNITA's intransigence in its demand for the deployment of a UN peace-keeping force to precede negotiation of a formal cease-fire. By early May most issues appeared to have been resolved, although UNITA maintained its refusal to withdraw from areas that its forces had occupied since the elections. After an adjournment while both delegations returned to Angola for consultations, the talks resumed on 14 May, with the government delegation announcing that it accepted the entire 47-point memorandum of understanding that had been drafted during the negotiations. UNITA, however, continued to raise objections, refusing to evacuate captured territory until government troops had been confined to barracks and UN peace-keeping forces deployed. The talks were finally suspended indefinitely on 21 May.

UNITA's actions appeared by this stage to have lost it the sympathy of even its former supporters. In May 1993 South Africa reopened its representative office in Luanda (closed since November 1992), with the South African government promising to suppress any assistance being provided to Savimbi from private sources in South Africa. However, South Africa did not grant full recognition to the Angolan government, stating that this would occur only when a 'fully representative' administration was in power. UNITA's refusal to sign the Abidjan agreement proved to be a deciding factor for the USA, and in mid-May President Clinton announced that the USA was to recognize the Angolan government. Meanwhile, Zambia announced that it was stationing troops on its north-western border with Angola, to counter any threat of attack by UNITA.

In June 1993, in a move reflecting a further improvement in their diplomatic relations, Angola and South Africa agreed to raise their mutual diplomatic missions to ambassadorial level. In the same month a US embassy was opened in Luanda, and a Malian diplomat, Alioune Blondin Beye, replaced Margaret Anstee as the UN secretary-general's special representative in Angola. Prior to relinquishing the post, Anstee made an urgent appeal for humanitarian aid at a conference in Geneva, Switzerland. Donor countries were informed that in excess of US $227m. would be required to help some 2m. people affected by the civil war. On 15 July the UN Security Council extended the mandate of the UN Angola Verification Mission (UNAVEM II) for a further two months and warned that an embargo would be enforced against UNITA unless an effective cease-fire had been established by 15 September.

Fighting escalated during August 1993, with government forces launching air raids on the UNITA stronghold of Huambo, and UNITA intensifying its attacks on the besieged city of Kuito. On 9 August, in recognition of the government's 'legitimate right of self-defence', the United Kingdom ended its arms embargo against the Angolan government (which had been in force since independence in 1975). Later in the month the government signed an agreement with the World Food Programme, providing for a six-month emergency food operation, which was intended to reach almost 2m. people.

On 14 September 1993 UNITA announced that it would implement a unilateral cease-fire, to begin on 20 September, thus prompting the UN Security Council to delay its deadline for imposing an embargo against UNITA until 25 September. However, despite UNITA's claims that it was observing the cease-fire, diplomatic sources reported an intensification of UNITA activity beyond the UN deadline. Consequently, on 26 September the UN imposed an arms and petroleum embargo against UNITA. Observers calculated, however, that clandestine supplies of arms and petroleum from Zaire, in addition to UNITA's existing stockpiles of arms, would ensure that the rebels' military capacity would be sustained for some years, despite the embargo. Further UN sanctions, including the expulsion of UNITA representatives from foreign capitals and the freezing of the rebels' assets abroad, were to be imposed on 1 November should UNITA fail to cease hostilities.

Optimism about a resumption of the peace talks increased in October 1993 after apparent concessions by UNITA in discussions with the UN and the three international observers of the peace process, Portugal, Russia and the USA. UNITA announced that it was prepared to accept the results of the September 1992 elections, although still declaring them to have been 'fraudulent', and accepted the validity of the May 1991 peace accord, but added that the agreement needed revision. UNITA also agreed to co-operate with the UN and to maintain the cease-fire declared on 20 September. After talks between the UN, UNITA and the observers in Lusaka, Zambia in late October there were suggestions that direct talks between the rebels and the government were imminent. On 1 November, Beye informed the UN Security Council that UNITA had agreed to withdraw its forces to UN-monitored confinement areas. In response the UN agreed to delay the imposition of further sanctions against UNITA until 15 December, provided the rebels comply with their undertakings.

Direct talks between UNITA and the government resumed in Lusaka on 16 November 1993. The talks, which had been adjourned in May, were to be conducted, at Beye's insistence and despite objections from UNITA, in conformity with the provisions of the May 1991 peace accords. Following three days of discussions a five-point agenda for the talks was agreed: a cease-fire, the mandate of UNAVEM II, the police, the armed forces, and national reconciliation. By 10 December agreement had reportedly been reached on issues concerning the demobilization and confinement of UNITA troops, the surrender of UNITA weapons to the UN, and the integration of UNITA generals into the FAA. On 13 December UNITA temporarily withdrew from the talks, alleging that a premeditated attempt had been made by the government to assassinate Savimbi. A UN enquiry found nothing to support the allegations and UNITA subsequently agreed to resume talks. On 15 December the UN Security Council extended the mandate of UNAVEM II for a further three months and agreed to a further postponement of additional sanctions against UNITA.

The Lusaka talks resumed on 6 January 1994, focusing on issues concerning the police force. On 30 January an agreement was announced on the formation of a national police force of 26,700 members, of which UNITA was to provide 5,500, to be formed under UN supervision. The force would be open to legal challenge in court and detention without trial would be outlawed. Talks continued during February, concentrating on the issue of national reconciliation, culminating in the signing of a document on 17 February enshrining five fundamental principles. Acceptance of the September 1992 election results by both sides was also reaffirmed.

The resignation of the minister of finance prompted a wider reorganization of the cabinet in mid-March 1994, including the creation of a new ministry, of economic planning. On 16 March the UN Security Council extended the mandate of UNAVEM II until 31 May. Progress at the Lusaka peace talks slowed as discussions moved on to the issue of the participation of UNITA in central and local government. Negotiations on the distribution of cabinet posts appeared to have reached an impasse in mid-March, and Beye announced at the end of the month that negotiations would instead move on to discuss the conclusion of the electoral process: the second round of presidential elections. On 20 April it was announced that agreement had been reached on four principles to ensure the free and fair conduct of the second-round elections. These concerned the reinstatement of the state administration throughout the country, guarantees of security, freedom of expression, and the resumption of air and ground communications nationwide to ensure free movement of people and goods. The UN was to be responsible for monitoring and declaring whether the conditions for conducting the elections had been met. It was agreed, in late April, that once the UN had made this declaration, the national assembly would select a date for the election. It was also agreed that a timetable for the implementation of the conditions would be formulated in early May.

On 5 May 1994 agreement was officially confirmed regarding the provisions for the second round of presidential elections, although some related issues remained to be discussed, including the role of the independent observers. Further talks, concerning the issues of UNITA's representation in the cabinet and the status of Savimbi, reached an impasse in May. The talks took place against a background of intensified hostilities, particularly in Kuito and Malanje. On 31 May the UN Security Council extended the mandate of UNAVEM II until 30 June, when it said it would reconsider the role of the UN if a peace accord had not been reached. The Security Council emphasized that its decision would take into account the extent to which the two sides demonstrated their political will to achieve a lasting peace. In mid-June agreement was reached on the extension of the state administration throughout the entire national territory. Talks continued in Lusaka in late June, culminating in the signing of an 18-point document on national reconciliation. At the same time, government forces were reported to have gained complete control of Kuito, ending an 18-month siege of the city by UNITA forces.

In early July 1994, at the instigation of President Mandela of South Africa, the presidents of Angola, Mozambique and Zaire met in Pretoria. Their discussions concentrated on allegations of Zairean support for UNITA, and resulted in the re-establishment of a joint defence and security commission between Angola and Zaire, with the aim of curbing the supply of armaments to the rebels. In early August UNITA acceded to government insistence that its officials be permitted to participate in government institutions only after the full demilitarization of the movement. An 11-point procedural accord, enabling discussions on full reconciliation, was signed on 9 August. In mid-August UNITA officially acknowledged that it had lost control of the diamond-mining centre of Kafunfo (in the north-east of the country), an important source of funds for UNITA. Government troops were also reported to have captured the strategic diamond-producing town of Catoca, close to the border with Zaire, during a campaign to expel UNITA from Lunda-Norte province.

Throughout July and August 1994 the question of the governorship of Huambo continued to constitute the main obstacle to the progress of the peace talks. However, in early September, in what was widely considered to be a bid to avert further UN sanctions, UNITA announced that it would abandon its demand for the governorship of Huambo, on condition that it had the power to veto the appointment made by the government. The proposal was rejected by dos Santos. On 8 September Savimbi was reported to have accepted a proposal by mediators for the allocation to UNITA of 170 posts in central and local administration, excluding the governorship of Huambo. On 9 September the UN Security Council announced that the sanctions imposed on UNITA would not be extended. In mid-September the government and UNITA agreed on the general principles governing the mandate of a new UN Angola Verification Mission (UNAVEM III). At the end of September, following successive extensions since July, the UN Security Council further extended the mandate of UNAVEM II until 31 October and urged both sides to sign a peace accord by 15 October. However, talks continued throughout October, concentrating on the replacement of the joint political and military commission with a new joint commission—under the chairmanship of Beye and comprising representatives of the government and UNITA and observers from the USA, Russia and Portugal—and the issue of Savimbi's security. A peace accord was provisionally agreed on 31 October, and was to be signed by dos Santos and Savimbi in Lusaka on 15 November. However, an intensified military campaign by the government, which resulted in the seizure in early November of Soyo and the UNITA stronghold of Huambo, threatened to jeopardize the accord, and UNITA indicated that it was no longer disposed to sign the treaty. On 15 November, following mediation by the president of South Africa, government and UNITA generals signed a truce in Lusaka, which was to operate until 22 November, when a permanent cease-fire was to come into force. The formal signing of the peace accord was postponed until 20 November, to allow outstanding issues to be discussed. Despite the absence of Savimbi, the formal signing of the Lusaka accord took place on the designated date, with the secretary-general of UNITA, Eugênio Antonino Ngolo Manuvakola, signing on behalf of the rebels, and the minister of foreign affairs, Dr Venâncio da Silva Moura, signing for the government. However, hostilities persisted beyond 22 November, notably in Huambo and in Bié province, and each side accused the other of violations of the cease-fire.

In December 1994 the UN Security Council extended the mandate of UNAVEM II until 8 February 1995, when it was to be superseded by UNAVEM III, providing the cease-fire was observed. In January 1995, in the light of continuing hostilities, a meeting took place at Chipipa, in Huambo province, between the chief of general staff of the FAA, Gen. João Baptista de Matos, and his UNITA counterpart, Gen. Arlindo Chenda Isaac Pena Ben-Ben, at which agreement was reached on an immediate cessation of hostilities nation-wide, the disengagement of troops (particularly in sensitive areas such as Huambo and Uíge), the release of prisoners of war and the creation of conditions to allow the free movement of people and goods. Despite these undertakings hostilities continued.

In early February 1995 the UN Security Council adopted Resolution 976 creating UNAVEM III. The new mission, the initial mandate of which was to expire on 8 August, was to comprise a military peace-keeping force of some 7,000 troops, in addition to 350 military observers, 260 police observers and some 350 civilian staff. The annual cost of the mission, which was expected to conclude in early 1997, was estimated at US $383m. However, the deployment of UNAVEM III remained conditional on the cessation of hostilities and the disengagement of government and UNITA forces. Early in the same month the UN conducted an appeal for humanitarian aid in excess of $200m. to provide emergency assistance for more than 3m. people, to support the demobilization and reintegration of former combatants, and to finance a programme to clear the country of an estimated 10m. land mines. At a meeting held later that month in Geneva, donor countries were reported to have pledged approximately US $170m. in aid.

At UNITA's party congress, held at Bailundo, in Huambo province, in February 1995, agreement was reached to accept the terms of the Lusaka accord and to endorse a proposed meeting between Savimbi and dos Santos. However, reports of division within the party concerning the commitment to the peace process were supported in late February by the testimony of Col Isaac Zabarra, secretary to UNITA's military council, who, having surrendered to the FAA, alleged that Savimbi had privately rejected the peace accord and intended to launch a major offensive. Furthermore, according to Zabarra, several important UNITA members active in the pursuit of the peace process had been placed in detention by the rebel leadership.

In March 1995 both the government and UNITA were the subject of criticism in a report to the UN Security Council by Dr Boutros Boutros-Ghali, who accused the two sides of a lack of good will in implementing the peace process, and reiterated the conditions for the deployment of UNAVEM III, which required strict observance of the cease-fire. The report followed continued and widespread violations of the truce including clashes in Cabinda and Uíge, and set a deadline of 25 March for the two sides to demonstrate a commitment to the peace process. It also appealed for preparations to be expedited to enable the prompt transfer of UNITA troops into the FAA. On 28 March, following a meeting of the joint commission, Beye announced that the initial stage of troop disengagement had been completed, allowing arrangements to continue for the deployment of UNAVEM III. In the same month dos Santos conducted a minor reshuffle of the council of ministers which included the appointment of Fernando Faustino Muteka to the position of minister without portfolio and head of the government delegation to the joint commission.

In April 1995 the governor of the Banco Nacional de Angola, Generoso Hermenegildo Gaspar de Almeida, was dismissed following the discovery that the bank had been defrauded of 3,700m. new kwanza by corrupt officials of the ministry of the interior and the national treasury directorate. In that month Beye confirmed that the majority of UNAVEM III personnel would begin arriving in early May. In late April the joint commission reported a significant reduction in violations of the cease-fire and a concomitant increase in the free movement of people and goods. However, that month Dr Boutros-Ghali indicated that the fragility of the cease-fire and reports of military preparations, including acquisition of arms from abroad, remained serious causes of concern.

In early May 1995, in an important development in the peace process, dos Santos and Savimbi met in Lusaka for direct talks. These discussions, which had been achieved as the result of mediation by Beye, concluded with a reaffirmation by both sides of their commitment to the implementation of the Lusaka peace accord. Notably, Savimbi accepted dos Santos as president of Angola, addressing him as such, and pledged his full co-operation in national reconstruction. At the meeting the two leaders agreed to accelerate the consolidation of the cease-fire, create conditions for the deployment of UNAVEM III, expedite the integration of UNITA troops into the FAA, and establish a government of unity based on the provisions of the Lusaka accord (following the demobilization of the UNITA forces). Dos Santos requested that Savimbi nominate immediately the UNITA appointees to the new government, in which UNITA members were to assume the portfolios of geology and mines, trade, health, and hotels and tourism.

In June 1995 the MPLA announced its decision to propose a revision of the constitution to create two new posts of vice-president, of which one was to be offered to Savimbi, conditional upon the prior disbanding of UNITA forces. The remaining vice-presidency was to be assumed by the then president of the national assembly, Fernando José França van-Dúnem. Later that month Savimbi, who had publicly expressed his intention to accept the vice-presidency, declared the war in Angola to be at an end and appealed to neighbouring nations to prevent the traffic of arms to the country. In July the national assembly approved the reform of the constitution providing for the creation of the two new vice-presidential positions, and Dr Boutros-Ghali announced that the deployment of UNAVEM III personnel, which had fallen seriously behind schedule, would be completed by the end of August. In late July, at continuing discussions between delegations of the government and UNITA concerning the implementation of military aspects of the Lusaka accord, it was agreed that the FAA should be expanded to 90,000 troops. Other issues under discussion included the formation of a fourth, non-combatant branch of the FAA, which would carry out public works projects.

Direct talks between dos Santos and Savimbi resumed in August 1995 in Franceville, Gabon. At the meeting Savimbi agreed in principle to accept the vice-presidency but requested that the offer be formally extended to UNITA. The government duly complied. Earlier in August the UN Security Council had extended the mandate of UNAVEM III until February 1996. In September the joint commission expressed concern at continuing violations of the cease-fire. However, in the following month, figures issued by UNAVEM III revealed that recorded cease-fire violations had decreased by approximately 50% between July and September. In late September the government signed a four-month cease-fire agreement with FLEC–Renovada (FLEC–R), a faction of the FLEC insurgent group in Cabinda province. It was anticipated that the agreement, which followed an offensive by FLEC–R on Cabinda City in the previous month, would facilitate the negotiation, between the government and all factions of FLEC, of a pact aimed at national reconciliation. Discussions concerning the implementation of the military aspects of the Lusaka accord continued in October and November.

In late September 1995 dos Santos and Savimbi met for direct talks in Brussels, Belgium, immediately prior to the convention there of an international donors' conference on Angola. It was reported that the two leaders discussed the presentation of an appeal for assistance totalling some US $650m. towards Angola's national rehabilitation and reconciliation programme. However, at the conference donors exceeded the requested sum, pledging a total of $997.5m., of which $200m. was to be allocated to emergency humanitarian assistance. The cantonment of UNITA forces began officially in late November 1995. However, continued hostilities were reported that month, including confrontations in the diamond-producing areas of the north-east and in the Cabinda exclave. In early December, following concerted military operations by government forces aimed at occupying UNITA-controlled territory in Zaire province, UNITA suspended the confinement of its troops. In the light of this setback, and in an effort to promote confidence in the peace process in advance of discussions, to be conducted that month with US President Clinton, dos Santos promptly introduced a number of conciliatory measures, including the withdrawal of government troops from positions seized in Zaire province and the confinement, which began the following month, of the paramilitary Rapid Intervention Force. In addition, dos Santos cancelled the government's contract with Executive Outcomes, a South African company ostensibly providing military advisers to give logistical support to the FAA, but condemned by UNITA as mercenaries in active service, in direct contravention of the Lusaka accord, which forbids mercenary support for either side. In early January 1996 Executive Outcomes confirmed that it had departed from Angola. Later that month UNITA resumed the process of confining its troops. However, that month the US ambassador to the UN, Madeleine Albright, warned that further delay would prompt the international community to withdraw its support for the peace process. In response, Savimbi pledged to confine a total of 16,500 UNITA troops by 8 February, when the UN Security Council was to review the mandate of UNAVEM III. By that date, however, UNITA had succeeded in confining only some 8,200 troops, prompting the UN Security Council to renew the mandate of UNAVEM III for a reduced term of only three months. In late January, following discussions conducted in Brazzaville, the Congo, the government and FLEC–R agreed to extend the cease-fire accord secured in September 1995. Discussions were to continue in pursuit of a definitive cease-fire agreement.

In March 1996 discussions between dos Santos and Savimbi, held in Libreville, Gabon, resulted in agreement on the establishment of a government of national unity and reconciliation, in accordance with the provisions of the Lusaka accord, by the end of July. Savimbi presented dos Santos with a proposal listing the UNITA nominees who would participate in such a government, while dos Santos in turn presented Savimbi with a formal invitation to assume the vice-presidency. (Later that month, however, Savimbi demanded the inclusion of other opposition parties in the government of national unity and reconciliation, presenting as a condition to his own participation the inclusion in the new administration of the president of the FNLA, Holden Roberto.) Agreement was also reached in Libreville on the formation of the unified national army, which was to be concluded in June. In subsequent talks conducted that month between representatives of the government and UNITA it was agreed that 18 UNITA generals would be appointed to command posts in the new unified FAA, of which nine would be in the army and nine in the non-combatant 'fourth branch'. It was also established that 26,300 of UNITA's total force of some 62,000 would be integrated into the FAA. In late March the government began the phased withdrawal to barracks of its troops.

On 8 May 1996, in the light of further delays in the peace process, the UN Security Council extended the mandate of UNAVEM III by just two months. Also in May, the national assembly approved an amnesty law pardoning all crimes against internal state security committed since the signing of the Estoril peace agreement. In mid-May Savimbi gave assurances to Beye that 50,000 UNITA troops would be confined by 15 July. In late May, following negotiations between the government and UNITA, agreement was reached on a programme to integrate UNITA troops into the FAA. Selection of UNITA personnel was to begin on 1 June. During May Savimbi introduced further conditions for his acceptance of the vice-presidency and expressed his intention to retain control of diamond-producing areas in north-eastern Angola. In mid-May the government and one of the Cabinda secessionist factions, FLEC–Forças Armadas Cabindesas (FLEC–FAC), signed an agreement outlining the principles of a cease-fire. However, following renewed fighting later that month between government troops and the secessionists, the leader of FLEC–FAC, Henrique N'zita Tiago, declared that a definitive cease-fire would only follow the withdrawal of the FAA from Cabinda.

In mid-1996 public protest at deteriorating economic conditions and at the high level of corruption within the state apparatus placed increasing political pressure on dos Santos, who responded in early June with the replacement of Moco as prime minister by the president of the national assembly, and former prime minister, Fernando José França van-Dúnem. In addition the governor of the Banco Nacional de Angola was dismissed and succeeded by Sebastião Bastos Lavrador (who had himself been removed from this post in 1992.) A new government was sworn in on 8 June with only four changes to the previous administration, at the ministries of economic planning, finance, industry and education.

In July 1996 the UN Security Council extended the mandate of UNAVEM III for a further three months. In August, following its party congress, UNITA issued a communiqué declining the appointment of Savimbi to the position of national vice-president. UNITA did not propose the appointment of another of its officials to the post, and in September Beye confirmed that the offer of the vice-presidency had become void. In October the UN Security Council, dissatisfied with delays in the implementation by UNITA of the provisions of the Lusaka accord, threatened to impose sanctions against the movement unless it completed a series of military tasks by 20 November, including the surrender of weapons and the designation of those UNITA troops to be integrated into the FAA. In mid-November the national assembly adopted a constitutional revision extending its mandate, which was due to expire that month, for a period of between two and four years, pending the establishment of suitable conditions for the conduct of free and fair elections. On 11 December the UN Security Council extended the mandate of UNAVEM III until 28 February 1997, when the peace-keeping force was due to begin withdrawing from Angola. In December 1996 UNAVEM III reported that a total of 70,336 UNITA troops and police had entered confinement areas since the cantonment process began, but that, of these, 15,705 had deserted. In addition the peace-keepers expressed concern that certain UNITA command posts remained operational. That month UN sources reported the existence of a residual UNITA force of some 15,000 well-armed troops in central and north-eastern Angola.

In mid-January 1997 dos Santos confirmed his acceptance of UNITA's nominees to the new government of national unity and reconciliation. However, following the failure of the UNITA deputies to join the national assembly in mid-January, the inauguration of the new government, which had been scheduled for 25 January, was postponed. A key issue obstructing the full implementation of the Lusaka accord was the question of the special status to be accorded to Savimbi in the light of his rejection of the vice-presidency. A proposal by UNITA that he be appointed chief adviser to dos Santos was dismissed by the government in February. In that month UNITA announced that it would not send its deputies or government nominees to Luanda until the government agreed to negotiate a draft programme for the government of national unity and reconciliation. The government initially rejected this proviso but in mid-March conceded to UNITA's demand. Agreement was reached on a basic programme later that month.

In March 1997 UN officials reported the involvement of both government and UNITA troops in the civil war in Zaire. UNITA, which relied on Zaire as a conduit for exporting diamonds and importing arms, reportedly sent some 2,000 troops to support its ally and maintain supply lines, while the Angolan government supported the rebels of Laurent-Désiré Kabila. The subsequent capture of Kamina, a Zairean military base of considerable strategic importance to UNITA, by Kabila's forces was believed to have ended any possibility of Savimbi resuming military action against the Angolan government, and consequently appeared to remove any remaining obstacles to UNITA fully implementing the provisions of the Lusaka accord. In early April agreement was reached concerning the special status to be conferred on Savimbi, who was to be accorded the official title of 'leader of the opposition'. Following the arrival of the full contingent of UNITA deputies and government nominees in Luanda, on 11 April the new government of national unity and reconciliation was inaugurated at a ceremony attended by 13 foreign heads of state, but conducted in the absence of Savimbi who maintained that his personal security could not be guaranteed. UNITA assumed the ministerial portfolios of geology and mines, health, trade and hotels and tourism, and a further seven deputy ministerial posts. A further 10 minor political parties were represented in the 87-member government.

In May 1997 the government officially recognized the new government of the Democratic Republic of the Congo (formerly Zaire), while, independently, the MPLA welcomed Kabila's victory. In that month there were reports of an FAA offensive on the north-eastern provinces of Lunda Sul and Lunda Norte, diamond-producing areas mainly under UNITA control. UNITA claimed that the FAA was contravening the Lusaka accord by attempting to restore control of the areas by force. In early 1997 Savimbi had reiterated his assertion that UNITA would not relinquish control of these diamond-producing regions, which industry sources estimated to have earned UNITA some US $2,000m. since 1992. Reports of hostilities in the area were continuing in July.

On 30 June 1997 the UN Security Council voted unanimously to approve the secretary-general's recommendations that UNAVEM III be discontinued and replaced by a scaled-down observer mission, the United Nations Observer Mission in Angola (MONUA), with a seven-month mandate to oversee the implementation of the remaining tasks of the Lusaka accord, including the reinstatement of state administration throughout the country. MONUA, which comprised a 193-strong military contingent, 86 military observers, 345 civilian police monitors and 310 civilian staff, began operating on 1 July. The remaining UNAVEM III personnel were to be withdrawn gradually.

Economy

JOÃO GOMES CRAVINHO

INTRODUCTION

Prior to independence in 1975, Angola enjoyed a high-output economy, with a rapidly expanding manufacturing sector, near self-sufficiency in agriculture, with crop surpluses for export, and abundant natural resources, such as petroleum and iron ore. The petroleum sector continues to prosper, but almost all other sectors of the economy are operating at a fraction of pre-independence levels. The civil war that began in 1975, and only reached a definitive resolution in April 1997, disrupted output, made transport and distribution increasingly difficult and led to the displacement of a large part of the population. Resources were diverted towards defence; in the late 1980s defence spending absorbed as much as 48% of the government's total budget expenditure, and following the resumption of hostilities in 1992, the purchase of arms was estimated to have surpassed the levels of the 1980s, with some analysts estimating government expenditure on arms (including unofficial spending) to amount to some 80% of total expenditure.

Assessments of output are uncertain, although, according to estimates by the UN, Angola's gross domestic product (GDP) increased, in real terms, by an average of 1.4% per year in 1975–80, by 3.1% per year in 1980–85, by 0.9% in 1985–95, by 7.7% in 1994 and by 12.5% in 1995. These figures should be regarded with great caution, however, and it must be remembered that the economy has experienced severe disruption since 1975. Petroleum has become the mainstay of the economy, accounting for 97% of export earnings in 1993. Mining, of which petroleum is by far the largest component, provided 51.2% of GDP in 1994. It is estimated, however, that some 70% of the economically active population are dependent on the depressed agricultural sector.

Following independence, the government implemented economic policies based on its Marxist-Leninist ideology. During 1987, however, President dos Santos announced that the government intended to implement major reforms of the economy, aimed at reducing reliance on the state sector, and increasing productivity, purchasing power and consumption levels. In August 1987 dos Santos announced that Angola would seek membership of the International Monetary Fund (IMF) in order to take advantage of Western financial assistance for a programme of economic reform. This economic and financial restructuring programme, the Saneamento Econômico e Financeiro (SEF), was instituted on 1 January 1988. The main elements included: a restructuring of state enterprises, allowing for much greater managerial and financial autonomy; redeployment of civil servants to more productive enterprises; improvements in the supply and distribution systems; and more price incentives for smaller enterprises. External financial support was needed for the success of the programme, and the government actively encouraged joint ventures between foreign and Angolan enterprises. In 1988 the government introduced a new law relating to foreign investment, offering tax concessions and permitting the repatriation of profits. Angola was admitted to the IMF in September 1989, thus enhancing prospects for a rescheduling of payments on Angola's external debt, which was estimated at US $11,482m. at the end of 1995, of which $9,533m. was long-term public debt. In that year the cost of debt-servicing was equivalent to 12.5% of the value of exports of goods and services. The largest creditor is the former Soviet Union, owed some $4,000m. for military purchases. In September 1990 the kwanza was replaced, at par, by a new kwanza. With effect from October 1990, the new kwanza was devalued by more than 50%, with the exchange rate adjusted to US $1 = 60 new kwanza. Despite intense popular opposition to this measure, a further devaluation took place in March 1991. In late October the central committee of the ruling MPLA—PT proposed the introduction of a market economy. In April 1991 the government announced that 100 companies which were nationalized after independence would be returned to their original owners, and that some state-owned enterprises, including the national airline and the state diamond company, Empresa Nacional de Diamantes de Angola (ENDIAMA), would sell as much as 49% of their equity to the private sector.

A programme of radical economic reforms was announced in November 1991, as part of the government's commitment to move towards a market economy. The measures included: a 33.3% devaluation of the currency, bringing the exchange rate of US $1 = 90 new kwanza; reductions in personal income taxes and consumer taxes; the abolition of price 'ceilings' on all except a few basic commodities; salary increases for public-sector workers, to compensate for the withdrawal of ration cards, and a national minimum wage of 12,000 kwanza per month. A further 50% devaluation, with the exchange rate adjusted to US $1 = 180 new kwanza, was announced in December, followed by a devaluation of 67% (to US $1 = 550 new kwanza) in April 1992. A heavy devaluation of the currency, to US $1 = 7,000 new kwanza, was announced on 1 February 1993. This measure, which brought the official exchange rate closer to the 'black market' rate of approximately 10,000 new kwanza per US dollar, was unfavourably received by the legislature and the local business community. In late February the minister of finance, Salomão Xirimbimbi, and Sebastião Bastos Lavrador, the governor of the central bank, were dismissed, on the grounds that they had exceeded their powers in authorizing the devaluation. In mid-April the exchange rate was adjusted to US $1 = 4,000 new kwanza.

The state budget for 1993, envisaging expenditure of 1,300,000m. new kwanza, was announced in early April and included subsidies of some 150,000m. new kwanza for a fund to assist in mitigating the effects of sharply rising unemployment. A tripling of the budgetary deficit in the previous year, due to unplanned (largely military) spending, had contributed to a rise in inflation to an annual rate of some 500%. In conjunction with the budget statement, the government announced an emergency programme to combat inflation and the effects of devaluation, including measures to control prices and the award of increases in salaries for civil servants.

In October 1993 the new kwanza was devalued by 39.5% to US $1 = 6,500 new kwanza, compared with a free market rate of US $1 = 50,000 new kwanza. A series of devaluations of the currency followed, taking the official rate to US $1 = 35,000 new kwanza at the end of March 1994, when it compared with a free market rate of US $1 = 135,000 new kwanza. In April the government introduced a new method of fixing exchange rates through agreement between the central bank and the commercial banks, with the effect that the currency underwent an effective devaluation, decreasing to US $1 = 68,297 kwanza in that month. The new policy sought to provide for an end to the system of multiple exchange rates.

The state budget for 1994 was announced in March 1994. The main feature of the budget, which totalled the equivalent of US $1,700m., was a policy to guarantee the prices of basic commodities, although defence remained the sector with the largest allocation of funds. Successive devaluations of the currency between April and December resulted in an exchange rate of US $1 = 1,320,000 new kwanza at 30 December 1994. In January 1995 the currency underwent a further devaluation of 63%. Legislation providing for the creation of a new currency, the 'readjusted' kwanza, with a value equivalent to 1,000 new kwanza, was approved in June and entered circulation in the following month.

The state budget for 1995 was approved in April 1995 with envisaged expenditure of 4,793,863,326.3m. new kwanza and estimated revenue of 3,880,103,863.2m. new kwanza. The government's Social and Economic Programme, approved concurrently with the budget, aimed to create the conditions for a 5% increase in gross national product (GNP), concentrating on infrastructural reconstruction, the rehabilitation of agriculture and monetary and administrative reform.

The erosion of the value of the currency continued throughout 1995 and early 1996. In March 1996 the readjusted kwanza underwent a devaluation of some 80%, to US $1 = 31,784 readjusted kwanza. By June the rate had declined further, to US $1 = 55,000 readjusted kwanza, while the free market rate stood at about US $1 = 240,000 readjusted kwanza. The state budget for 1996 was approved in February 1996 and envisaged expenditure of 178,000,000m. readjusted kwanza.

In July 1996 the government introduced a reform programme known as *Nova Vida* ('New Life') which resulted in lowering the inflation rate by about 13% per month and decreasing the differential between the official and parallel exchange rates to around 10%. In October the IMF announced that it was to provide US $75m. in a three-year emergency programme under an enhanced structural adjustment facility. The announcement was expected to facilitate further bilateral and multilateral assistance and debt relief.

In March 1997 the national assembly approved the state budget for 1997 and the economic and social plan for the year. The two documents focus on restoring economic and financial stability and promoting economic production. Some 38% of the US $890m. budget were allocated to state operating costs while the remainder was to be spent on economic reconstruction and stabilization programmes, including plans to reduce foreign debt, programmes for the promotion of rural trade, health, education, agricultural development and the stabilization of the diamond mining sector. The budget also sought to support private sector development through fiscal, customs and financial incentives for productive investment.

During 1996 and 1997 the banking sector exhibited signs of vitality. In September 1996 the central bank ceased all commercial activities in order to focus on the monetary system. The Banco de Crédito Comercial e Industrial assumed the commercial responsibilities of the central bank. In November the African Investment Bank opened a branch in Luanda, with the Angolan government holding a 39% share in the US $35m. joint capital stock. In 1997 various foreign investors declared an interest in the privatization of the Banco de Comércio e Indústria, which was founded in 1991 in order to support international business activities in Angola.

MAJOR CROPS

Only about 3% of Angola's total area is cultivated as arable or permanent crop land. Reliable statistics have not yet revealed the true magnitude of the deterioration of modern agriculture caused by the departure of Portuguese settlers in 1974–75. The main cash crop is coffee. Prior to independence, annual production of green coffee was more than 200,000 metric tons, with the USA as the main export customer. In the mid-1970s Angola was the second largest African coffee producer and the world's main supplier of *robusta* coffee, cultivated mainly in the Uíge, Cuanza Norte, Cuanza Sul and Luanda provinces. Coffee was cultivated on a variety of Portuguese plantations (*fazendas*), ranging from substantial commercial holdings, employing thousands of labourers, down to family plantations with only a score of workers, where the owner combined agriculture with minor trade with local Africans. However, the subsequent departure of the Portuguese, neglect of the plantations (which were nationalized following independence), drought, insufficient transport, excessive bureaucracy and the continuing armed conflict have all contributed to the decline, reducing production to about one-fiftieth of pre-independence levels. Output was estimated at about 5,000 tons in 1993, declining to just 1,560 tons in 1994, before increasing to 2,880 tons in 1995 and to 4,980 tons in 1996. The impact of the decline in agricultural production has been aggravated by reductions in world prices for *robusta* coffee, following the collapse in 1989 of the International Coffee Organization's export quota systems, by increasing competition from Asian producers of *robusta* and by a shift in Western consumer demand to *arabica* varieties. Export earnings from coffee fell from US $80m. in 1984 to an estimated $6m. in 1995. In 1983 the government established the Empresa de Rebenefício e Exportação do Café de Angola (CAFANGOL), a state-controlled coffee-processing and trading organization. Plans to sell all 33 state-owned coffee plantations were announced in 1991. Foreign investment in the plantations would be welcomed, but overall foreign ownership was to be limited to 30% or 40%; the British-based Lonrho company and a Portuguese group, Espírito Santo, were among those bidding for the plantations. According to government estimates issued in 1995, about $20m. would be required for the rehabilitation of 60,000 ha of family plantations and 30,000 ha of private estates. However, the potential revenue from coffee production was estimated to be as high as $15m. per annum. According to government sources, coffee production was expected to advance strongly in the late 1990s owing to renewed access to coffee-producing land, increased yields and considerable interest from foreign investors.

Sisal exports reached 66,719 tons in 1974, when Angola was Africa's second most important producer. Production has since fallen sharply; according to FAO estimates, output amounted to only 1,000 tons per year during the period 1987–94. An estimated 500 tons were produced annually in 1995 and 1996. In the intervening years the crop was adversely affected by a slump in world prices and by the transition from private ownership to state enterprise. The main producing regions were the Benguela plateau, Huíla, Cuanza Norte and Malanje provinces. Maize formerly ranked fifth or sixth among Angola's agricultural exports, with a harvest of 700,000 tons in 1973. However, by 1975 the country's output of cereals was declining, and from that year Angola has been a recipient of food aid. Maize output was reduced to some 300,000 tons in 1980, and had fallen further, to an estimated 250,000 tons, in 1985. Output increased to 300,000 tons in 1987, falling to 180,000 tons in 1990, before rising again, to an estimated 369,000 tons in 1992. The resumption of hostilities led to a renewed decline in production, with output of 274,000 tons in 1993 and 201,000 tons in 1994, increasing slightly to 235,000 tons in 1995. By 1996 maize production had increased to 398,000 tons.

Cotton was formerly one of the most promising products of Angola, and was both a concessionary and an African cultivation. At independence, the main areas of cultivation were the Baixa de Cassange, in the Malanje province, and the region east of Luanda. Organized planters in the Cuanza Sul province were responsible for a large increase in mechanized production, and an increasing part of production was processed in Angola by three textile mills. The breakdown of activities in most European-owned plantations reduced production of seed (unginned) cotton from 104,000 tons in 1974 to an estimated 33,000 tons annually during the 1980s, according to the FAO. Advisers from the USSR were unable to revive this activity and, for the first time in Angola's history, cotton was imported in 1983. The first exports of cotton since independence resumed on a small scale in 1995.

Prior to independence, sugar production was controlled by three Portuguese companies, and output of raw sugar was about 85,000 tons per year from annual sugar cane production of just under 1,000,000 tons. Following independence, the main sugar cane plantations were reorganized as workers' co-operatives, with Cuban management and assistance. Production of raw sugar subsequently declined sharply, and nearly all sugar for domestic consumption is imported. The withdrawal of Cuban personnel by mid-1991 led to further deterioration in the sector, with sugar cane production declining to 220,000 tons per annum between 1993–95. However, production increased in 1996 to 330,000 tons.

Cassava is the main Angolan crop in terms of volume produced, and is the staple food of the majority of the population. Production was an estimated 2.5m. tons in 1996, and most of the crop is consumed domestically, with no transaction above the local market level. The cultivation of bananas is being increased in the lower reaches of the rivers north of Luanda and of the Cuvo river. Estimated output was 295,000 tons in 1996.

OTHER CROPS

Exports of palm oil totalled 4,410 tons in 1973. From the 1980s onwards estimated annual production was 12,000 tons of palm kernels and 40,000 tons of palm oil, rising to an estimated 15,600 tons of palm kernels and 52,000 tons of palm oil in 1995. Tobacco grows well on the formerly white-owned farms in the central and southern provinces of Benguela, Huíla and Namibe, with an estimated annual output of 4,000 tons between 1993–95.

Other commodities (such as rice, millet, sorghum, beans, tropical and temperate fruit, cocoa and groundnuts) are testimony to the agricultural potential of Angola, provided that investment capital and expertise can be deployed for this sector.

Because of its large area and variety of climate, Angola is one of the most promising agricultural countries of southern Africa. However, owing to civil unrest, transport problems, the lack of proper marketing facilities and incentives, and drought, shortages have been prevalent and famine has been a frequent occurrence. By early 1984 malnutrition affected some 15% of Luanda's population, and physical survival had become the prime objective of more than 50% of Angola's rural population. By early 1991 it was estimated that food shortages threatened 1.8m. people. In recent years less than one-half of the country's cereal requirements have been produced locally, and high levels of cereal imports have been required. According to the UN Special Relief Programme for Angola, the cereal deficit for 1990 was 565,000 tons. Some 236,000 tons of cereals were not covered by commercial imports, and were therefore required as food aid. The resumption of the civil war in late 1992 represented a considerable reverse to efforts to effect a recovery in agricultural production. By February 1993 the UN World Food Programme (WFP) was warning that as many as 3m. people were threatened with hunger and disease, with harvests in many areas destroyed or disrupted by the hostilities. In April the WFP appealed for 350,000 tons of emergency food supplies for nearly 2m. Angolans. Those in need of assistance included 344,000 people displaced from their homes, 122,000 former refugees who had returned from Zambia and Zaire, and 256,000 affected by drought in the south-western provinces of Huíla, Cunene and Namibe. In 1994 there was an estimated shortfall on the country's maize requirements of 1.3m. tons.

One of the most serious impediments to increasing the level of agricultural production is the vast number of anti-personnel mines which remain concealed about the countryside as a result of the war. It is estimated that there are some 10m. unexploded mines in Angola, and around 70,000 civilians have suffered casualties necessitating the amputation of limbs as a result of accidentally detonating mines; this is the highest proportion of casualties among the civilian population of any country in the world. UNICEF, UNHCR and other international organizations have joined forces with UNAVEM in conducting demining operations and in supporting the UNAVEM Central Mine Action Training School, established to instruct demobilized soldiers from both the government and UNITA forces.

LIVESTOCK, FORESTRY AND FISHERIES

Livestock raising is concentrated in southern and central Angola, owing to the prevalence of the tsetse fly and the poor quality of the natural pastures in the north of the country. Some two-thirds of all cattle are found in Huíla province alone. The modern ranching sector, established by the Portuguese, was nationalized following independence, and has subsequently been adversely affected by civil war and drought. Meat shortages are prevalent in all cities, and imports of meat are indispensable. In 1973 Angola had only about 4.4m. head of cattle, 2m. goats, 1.4m. pigs and 350,000 sheep. In 1996 cattle numbers were estimated by the FAO at 3.3m., pigs at 810,000, sheep at 245,000 and goats at 1.47m. (These figures appear to be inflated: the full extent of damage to the livestock industry in the civil war may not have been taken into account.)

Angola possesses important forestry resources, especially in the Cabinda, Moxico, Luanda and Kwanza-Norte provinces. Cabinda, in particular, has some valuable indigenous species, such as African sandalwood, rosewood and ebony. Softwood plantations of eucalyptus and cypress are used for fuel and grow along the Benguela railway and near Benguela, where they are used for wood pulp and paper manufacture. Exports of timber however, ceased at independence. As in other sectors, output of logs fell sharply after independence, from over 550,000 cu m in 1973 to 39,750 cu m in 1981. Although this activity was especially sensitive to guerrilla actions, output of logs recovered to 116,000 cu m in 1984, and to 134,000 cu m in 1985. However, production was estimated at only 66,000 cu m per annum between 1990–95.

Fisheries are mainly in and off Namibe, Tombua and Benguela. However, of a total of 263 Angolan trawlers in 1981, only 87 were operational, owing to lack of maintenance. In that year the government formed a fisheries enterprise, in an attempt to restore the industry, and Angola was granted a loan of US $10m. from the Arab Bank for Economic Development in Africa (BADEA) for the rehabilitation of fishing facilities. A further grant of ECU 6.76m. was made to the fishing sector by the EC in 1984. Foreign trawlers operate off the coast and have significantly depleted the fish reserves in Angolan waters. In February 1988 the USSR agreed to strengthen co-operation in the fisheries sector, with the possibility of the establishment of a joint fisheries venture and the construction of a fishing port in Namibe province. The total catch declined from an annual average of 450,000 tons in the early 1970s to 191,000 tons in 1985. According to FAO figures, the total catch had declined to 71,981 tons by 1995.

MINERALS

Angola is believed to be one of the richest countries in mineral reserves of southern Africa. Two minerals, petroleum and diamonds, are of paramount importance to the Angolan economy, and Angola is the second largest exporter of hydrocarbons in sub-Saharan Africa, after Nigeria.

Angola's kimberlite pipes, first discovered in 1911, are believed to rank among the world's five richest deposits of embedded diamonds. Since 1986, full control of this sector has been exercised by the state enterprise, ENDIAMA, which instigated a new national diamond policy, whereby mining was to be divided into blocks, to be exploited under production-sharing agreements with foreign concessionaires. In October 1986 ENDIAMA signed an agreement with Roan Selection Trust International to operate at Kafunfo in the Cuango province. Angola's total output of diamonds was 2.4m. carats in 1974, falling to about 300,000 carats in 1976, following independence. Annual production remained below 1m. carats until 1989, when it achieved 1.3m. carats. In 1992 output was estimated to have risen to 2.7m. carats, but in 1993 production fell back to around 1m. carats, recovering to 1.4m. carats in 1994 and 1.9m. carats in 1995. Official sales of diamonds, which are subject to a marketing agreement between ENDIAMA and the De Beers group (see below), earned US $190m. in 1991 and $250m. in 1992, but fell back to $63m. in 1993. However, figures of diamond output are deceptive, since a significant proportion (perhaps one-half) of the real production has been mined and smuggled by UNITA, whose leader, Dr Jonas Savimbi, has admitted that his movement has derived a significant share of its resources from the diamond-producing area, which remained partially under his control during the civil war. In mid-1992 the director-general of ENDIAMA stated that illegal excavation and smuggling were depriving the government of $200m.–$300m. per year in revenue. Following the resumption of the civil war in late 1992, diamond mining areas again came under UNITA control. Losses incurred by ENDIAMA due to illegal excavation and smuggling (mainly into Zaire) in 1994 were estimated at between $300m.–$500m. Following the recapture of Kafunfo and Catoca by the government forces in mid-1994, however, diamond smuggling activities have declined, although it is believed that the bulk of Angola's diamond output continues to be smuggled out of the country to Antwerp, Belgium, and to Israel, mainly via Zaire. In November 1996 ENDIAMA granted permission for UNITA representatives to begin negotiations with foreign corporations concerning the exploration and mining of diamond reserves in areas under *de facto* UNITA control. At the same time ENDIAMA announced plans to increase diamond production, over a period of three to four years, to more than 2m. carats per year.

In December 1987 Angola and the USSR signed a co-operation agreement, covering the mining of diamonds and quartz. De Beers Consolidated Mines lost exclusive marketing rights over ENDIAMA diamonds in 1985; however, in May 1989 ENDIAMA and De Beers signed a 'declaration of intent' to enter into co-operation in diamond prospecting, mining and marketing, and in 1991 an agreement was signed to market all production from the Cuango area through De Beers' Central Selling Organisation. Since 1995, De Beers has been active in exploration both for alluvial and kimberlite diamonds in five areas of the country. South African, Canadian, Brazilian, Portuguese and Russian interests are also currently involved in exploration activities.

The Russian diamond corporation, Almazy Rossii-Sakha, has announced that it will open a processing mill at the Catoca diamond field in north-eastern Angola, with an investment of some US $13m. Covering an area of more than 660 ha, the Catoca kimberlite has been estimated to contain potential diamond reserves of up to 200m. carats, which would establish it as one of the world's largest deposits of diamonds. In April 1991 the government announced that ENDIAMA was to sell as much as 49% of its equity to the private sector.

In September 1995 the government introduced a programme aimed at curbing the activities of the many thousands of illegal diamond prospectors and traders operating in areas under its control. In 1996 the dispute between the government and UNITA concerning the control of Angola's diamond mines was being formally conducted in negotiations mediated by a subsidiary of De Beers, namely De Beers Angolan Prospecting Ltd. In early 1995 ENDIAMA and De Beers reached an agreement providing the latter with a prospecting contract which committed it to an investment of US $40m. in the short term, increasing to $500m. in the medium term, provided that peace was sustained. The objective was to increase output to around 4m.–5m. carats per annum, and to end illegal prospecting. Under the terms of this agreement De Beers began prospecting in the area of Maringa, Cuando-Cubango province, in May 1997. UNITA was also party to an agreement signed between ENDIAMA and a Brazilian company, Odebrecht, for a vast diamond concession in the Lunda provinces. By mid-1997 UNITA had come under increasing pressure to reach a definitive profit-sharing agreement covering the mining areas still under its control. Following the fall, in May, of UNITA's ally, Mobutu Sese Seko of Zaire, the government launched several military offensives against UNITA-controlled mines, recovering about 10% of UNITA's productive areas. Meanwhile, UNITA has set up its own legal mining company, Sociedade Geral das Minas, which was awarded two prospecting concessions in late May, one in Cuando-Cubango province, the other near the central UNITA-held town of Andulo. UNITA has also been offered a share in a consortium comprising Ashton Mining (Australia), Odebrecht (Brazil) and Endiama, which has been awarded the extremely important Cuango Valley concession.

The Canadian mining company DiamondWorks announced that it would begin commercial production in its concessions in the province of Lunda Norte by mid-1997. Two further investments were announced for Lunda Norte in March 1997: the Namibian Minerals Corporation announced plans to invest US $2.5m. to develop three diamond concessions; and the Canadian company SouthernEra Resources announced that it would invest $5m. over the next five years in the development of a major kimberlite pipe.

The petroleum industry is the principal economic mainstay of the government, with petroleum extraction, refining and distribution constituting Angola's most important economic activity. Hydrocarbons generally accounted for more than 90% of total exports during the 1980s. The petroleum sector accounts for more than 50% of state revenues and for about 30% of GDP. Total estimated proven recoverable reserves of crude petroleum totalled 2,074m. barrels in 1990; in 1995 these reserves had been raised to 5,412m. barrels.

In 1955 a Belgian-owned company, Petrofina, discovered petroleum in the Cuanza valley. A petroleum company, Fina Petróleos de Angola (PETRANGOL), was subsequently established, under the joint ownership of the Angola government and Petrofina interests. PETRANGOL constructed a refinery in the suburbs of Luanda. The greatest impetus to expansion came from the Cabinda Gulf Oil Co (Cabgoc), which discovered petroleum offshore at Cabinda in 1966. In 1976 a national oil company, the Sociedade Nacional de Combustíveis de Angola (SONANGOL), was established to manage all fuel production and distribution. In 1978 SONANGOL was authorized to acquire a 51% interest in all petroleum companies operating in Angola, although the management of operations was to remain under the control of foreign companies. In the late 1970s the government initiated a campaign to attract foreign oil companies. In 1978–79 SONANGOL divided the Angolan coast, excluding Cabinda, into 13 exploration blocks, which were leased to foreign companies under production-sharing agreements. Although Cabgoc's Cabinda offshore fields (which are operated by the US Chevron Corpn) remain the core of the Angolan petroleum industry (accounting for about two-thirds of total output), production is buoyant at other concessions, held by Agip, Elf Aquitaine, Conoco and Texaco. In addition SONANGOL itself operates a production block in association with Petrobrás Internacional (BRASPETRO) of Brazil and Petrofina. In 1992 Elf took a 10% interest in Cabgoc, reducing SONANGOL's share to 41%, with Chevron holding 39.2% and Agip 9.8%. Onshore, Petrofina remained the operator. SONANGOL took a 51% interest in Petrofina's original Cuanza valley operations, including the Luanda refinery, whose capacity meets most domestic requirements. SONANGOL also had a 51% interest in an onshore venture by Petrofina in the River Congo estuary area, in which Texaco held a 16.33% share. Onshore production in 1991 was estimated at 30,000 barrels per day (b/d); however, with recoverable petroleum reserves almost exhausted and activities vulnerable to UNITA attack, production declined and in 1993 Petrofina suspended onshore operations near the port of Soyo, in northern Angola near the Zaire border. Production was resumed, however, in February 1996, when an output of 5,000 b/d was quickly restored. It was forecast that production would advance to 12,000 b/d by early 1997.

Despite the uncertain security situation in the Cabinda enclave, exploration licences for three onshore blocks were awarded in October 1992. The principal operators for the three concessions, Cabinda North, Central and South, were to be Occidental of the USA, British Petroleum and Petrofina respectively. In 1994 Chevron announced the discovery of four new offshore fields. It estimated that production would increase from 320,000 b/d in 1994 to 390,000 b/d in 1995 as the development of deep-water areas continued under its five-year programme. In 1995 Chevron announced a US $5,100m. capital and exploratory expenditure programme for that year, an increase of 5% on 1994. In 1997 Chevron announced its intention to invest $700m. a year until 2000 and envisaged increasing its output to 600,000 b/d. In late 1994 Texaco announced a five-year investment programme for petroleum exploration and production totalling $600m.; the programme aimed to increase Texaco's output in the country by 50%. In September 1996 SONANGOL signed new production sharing agreements with six international petroleum companies: Shell Exploration Angola, Amoco Angola, Eagle (Nigeria), Petro Inett Corpn (South Africa), Mobil and Texaco.

Output of petroleum expanded rapidly during the 1980s, reflecting continued investment in the sector. It was estimated that total investment in Angola by oil companies for the period 1987–90 would reach US $2,050m. Total Angolan production averaged 155,000 b/d in late 1982, rising to about 285,000 b/d in 1986, to 358,000 b/d, in 1987 and to 450,000 b/d in 1988 and 1989. Output rose to 475,000 b/d in 1990, 491,000 b/d in 1991, and 549,000 b/d in 1992. Production declined to 505,000 b/d in 1993 but increased to 556,000 b/d in 1994, to 637,000 b/d in 1995 and to 700,000 b/d in 1996. Output was projected to increase to 780,000 b/d by 1998, of which 450,000 b/d would be produced by Chevron in Cabinda's offshore fields alone, and to 1m. b/d by 2000. In April 1997 Chevron announced the discovery of a further new oil field off the coast of Cabinda which was thought capable of producing an additional 20,000 b/d. In May, following another significant deep-water discovery, production began in the remote North N'Dola oil field, which was expected to yield up to 20,000 b/d by the end of 1997. In that year the law governing the exploitation of petroleum was under revision with a view to facilitating further foreign investment. Petroleum production appeared to be relatively unaffected by the resumption of hostilities in late 1992, and the main installations in Cabinda escaped attack by UNITA or the regional separatist organization, FLEC. Before withdrawing from Soyo in late 1994 UNITA destroyed the onshore installations. However, in March 1995 the government announced that production would resume, although at a reduced rate of 5,000 b/d.

The major portion of Angola's petroleum is exported to the USA in its crude form, although Angola refines about 35,000 b/d and exports lubricating oil, bunkering oils and heavy fuels. Plans to build a new petroleum refinery were announced in August 1992, but depended on obtaining as much as $2,000m. to finance the project. In 1994 the country's annual refinery capacity was 1,598,000 tons.

Angola's export earnings from petroleum increased after 1982, following the rise in production, and reached $1,191m. in 1985. With the sharp fall in the price of petroleum, export earnings declined to $1,140m. in the following year, but recovered to $2,100m. in 1987, $2,250m. in 1988, $2,700m. in 1989 and—helped by increased production and a period of higher prices, due to the Gulf crisis—an estimated $3,580m. in 1990. In 1991 petroleum export earnings stood at $3,217m., increasing to $3,556m. in 1992 before declining to $2,813m. in 1993. In 1995 estimated earnings from petroleum exports stood at $5,000m. As Angola is not a member of OPEC, the country is not constrained by production quotas, enabling it to stabilize the value of its petroleum exports during the late 1980s, when world prices remained depressed, by increasing output.

Iron mining began in 1956 and production averaged 700,000–800,000 tons annually in the 1960s from mines in the Huambo and Bié provinces. However, the Cassinga mines in the Huíla province, which have proven reserves of more than 1,000m. tons of high-grade haematite, were the decisive factor in increasing production. A railway spur was built to link the mines with the Namibe–Menongue railway, and a new harbour built to the north of Namibe. Ore output was about 6m. tons (60%–65% iron) in 1973. However, in 1975 the Cassinga mines were partially destroyed in the fighting, and they have since remained inoperative. Angola holds considerable ore production stockpiles, which await the eventual rehabilitation of rail links to the coast. In 1981 a state-owned iron company, the Empresa Nacional de Ferro de Angola (FERRANGOL), was created.

Other minerals abound. Reserves of copper have been identified in the Uíge province, and other deposits are known to exist in the Namibe, Huíla and Moxico provinces. Important deposits of feldspar have been found in the southern province of Huíla. Manganese ore was mined in the Malanje province, with 4,682 tons exported in 1973. Unexploited reserves of phosphate rock exist in the Zaire and Cabinda provinces, and deposits of uranium have been found along the border with Namibia. In 1991 a new secretariat of geology and mines was established to co-ordinate mining activity and to formulate mineral policy in preparation for the restoration of civil order.

POWER

Angola's power potential exceeds its needs. Most of Angola's energy output is of hydroelectric origin, and there is an impressive dam on the Cuanza at Cambambe, constructed and operated by a Brazilian company, which produced 370.7m. kWh in 1972, and whose generating capacity stood at 450MW in 1989. Luanda's industries are the main beneficiaries of Cambambe power. In 1996 a US $64m. project was under way to renovate the transmission lines from Cambambe to Luanda, with funding of $35.5m. from the World Bank and $20m. from the African Development Bank. A 520-MW power station is being constructed at Kapunda, on the Cuanza river, with assistance from Brazilian and former Soviet contractors. The US $1,230m. project, described by the World Bank as the key to Angola's post-war reconstruction, would increase the country's generating capacity by almost 100%. The first two Russian-built turbines were scheduled to be installed in 1993, but in early 1992 the project's future appeared to be in some doubt, pending agreement on the repayment of Angola's military debt to the former Soviet Union. An attack on the dam site by UNITA in November 1992 was reported to have caused damage amounting to $40m., delaying completion by as much as one year. Further south, Lobito and Benguela were provided with electricity by two privately-owned dams, the Lomaum and the Biópio, both on the Catumbela river. Production exceeded 206m. kWh in 1973. Destruction of the Lomaum dam reportedly reduced the power resources of Lobito and Benguela. In late 1987 it was announced that a Portuguese banking consortium was providing $11m. towards the first stage of a scheme to rehabilitate the Lomaum dam, and earlier in the year the Portuguese government granted a credit of $140m. towards the scheme. Still further south, the Matala dam serves Lubango, Namibe and Cassinga. However, this project is only a very small part of the grandiose Angolan-Namibian scheme for damming the Cunene river, thus providing Namibia, which is deficient in power and water, with cheap electricity and a permanent water supply. The Gove dam, in the Huambo course of the Cunene river, was completed with South African capital. The construction of a major power station at the Ruacaná Falls, where the Cunene river reaches the Namibian border, has been impeded by the military and political instability in the region, although the first stage became operational in 1977. The potential annual output of the scheme is provisionally assessed at 1,000m. kWh. At a meeting in October 1991, President dos Santos and Namibia's President Sam Nujoma, agreed to pursue feasibility studies for construction of a hydro-electric dam on the Cunene, although its location remained to be decided.

INDUSTRY

Angola's industrial activity is centred on construction materials, petroleum refining, food processing, textiles, equipment for the petroleum industry, steel, chemicals, electrical goods and vehicle assembly. Output from Angola's industrial sector has dwindled to a fraction of pre-independence levels. Following the withdrawal of Portuguese owners, many enterprises were brought under state control and ownership, and by the mid-1980s about 80% of the industrial work-force was employed in state-owned companies. Under the SEF, introduced in January 1988 (see above), legislation was to be reformed, granting state enterprises autonomous control of management. The continuing civil unrest, shortages of raw materials, unreliability of power supplies and disruption of the transport infrastructure have all since contributed to the sharp reduction in industrial output. Official figures showed manufacturing output in 1985 to be only 54% of its 1973 level, and the sector suffered more in the ensuing three years, when a decline in earnings from petroleum exports, caused by the sharp fall in the price of petroleum, reduced the supply of foreign exchange needed for industrial raw materials and imports of capital goods. However, the allocation of foreign exchange for this purpose was more than doubled in 1990.

Angola's manufacturing sector has considerable potential, in view of the country's abundance of raw materials, such as petroleum and iron ore. During 1962–70, manufacturing output expanded at an average rate of 19% per year. The food-processing, brewing and tobacco industries were the most developed. The textile industry flourished after the ban on the creation of industries competing against metropolitan manufacturers was repealed in 1966. Cotton is the principal fibre used, and in 1973 textile industries occupied second place in Angola. In 1979 French industrialists built a new textile complex at Lobito, with a capacity of 16m. metres of cloth per year, and a second was planned in Luanda, with a capacity of 18m. metres per year. In 1987 production of textile fabrics was equivalent to only one-third of its 1973 level. A steel plant, built in Luanda in 1972–73, was reopened in 1984. Production of steel bars was 6,589 metric tons in 1986, compared with 26,572 tons in 1973.

Most branches of the manufacturing sector continued to contract during the 1980s. However, there are a few exceptions to the general depressed state of the sector. A yard for the construction of oil equipment was built at Ambriz in 1984/85. In mid-1987 a loan was approved by the African Development Bank for the construction of three pharmaceutical plants, and construction work on one of these commenced in February 1989. In September 1987 the government signed a contract with a Dutch company for the import and assembly of trucks at a plant in Luanda. In 1988 a new foreign investment code was introduced, which aimed to increase the rights of foreign companies regarding operation, transfer of profits, taxation, etc., while, in return, foreign investors were expected to expand transfer of technical and managerial skills to Angolan industrial personnel. Under the new code, however, many sectors remained closed to foreign investment: these included the postal and telecommunications sectors, the news media, air transport and shipping, defence and security and state banking. The approval in April 1994 of a US export credit guarantee protocol, under which US investors were to be insured against political upheaval and have access to loans, was expected to stimulate investment from the USA. In mid-1994 the government introduced proposals to parliament for new regulations regarding foreign investment and privatization aimed at attracting foreign capital, increasing private investment in national economic activity and reducing state participation.

After independence, the building trade came to a standstill, except for the reconstruction of some of the 130 bridges destroyed in the conflict (by 1978 more than 60 had been rebuilt). Major housing programmes have been initiated in large cities. Acute shortages of building materials have limited construction, for the most part, to shanty buildings, resulting in unzoned urban growth. However, the construction sector has been helped by the rehabilitation of the main cement works, operated by the Empresa de Cimento de Angola (CIMANGOLA), in Luanda, and the sector is expected to benefit greatly from the Kapunda dam project. Output of cement was estimated at 370,000 metric tons in 1992.

In May 1997 Coca-Cola and Indol International (a subsidiary of South African Breweries) announced plans to construct a US $20m. bottling plant at Bom Jesus, some 60 km from Luanda.

TRANSPORT AND TRADE

Angola's colonial administration made a considerable effort to improve the communications network. In 1974 there were 8,317 km of tarred roads in a total road network of 72,323 km. In 1973 there were 127,271 passenger cars, 26,221 lorries and 20,029 motor cycles in use. However, most lorries and cars were taken back to Portugal by their owners, and others were destroyed or left without spare parts. It is now theoretically possible to drive on tarred roads from Quimbele (Uíge province) to the Namibian border, and from Luanda to Lumbala (Moxico province), close to the Zambian frontier. Bus transportation was fairly developed following independence, carrying some 22.4m. passengers in 1978, but has since suffered from shortages of imported spare parts. In 1995 Angola had 72,626 km of roads, of which about 25% were paved. However, since the early 1980s guerrilla warfare has dramatically curtailed most road transportation.

Railways serve a dual purpose, to open the interior and to provide export channels for Zambia and the land-locked province of Shaba in the Democratic Republic of the Congo (formerly Zaire), which export large volumes of minerals. Hence, all railway lines run towards the coast. The Luanda railway, chiefly for local goods traffic and passengers, was the only line functioning with a degree of regularity during the late 1980s, albeit at a low level of activity, transporting only 63,000 metric tons of freight in 1985. In mid-1995 the Luanda railway remained closed between Dondo and Malanje due to the destruction by UNITA of bridges prior to the signing of the May 1991 peace agreement. The Namibe railway, in the south, was assuming a new importance as a carrier of iron ore from Cassinga before the security situation resulted in the closure of the mines. This railway transported 196,000 tons of freight in 1985. The Benguela railway was of international importance and was the strategic outlet for exports of copper and zinc from Zaire and Zambia, bypassing South Africa and providing the most direct link to the west coast. However, UNITA guerrilla attacks caused the suspension of all cross-border traffic after 1975. In April 1987 a declaration of intent to restore these services was signed by the governments of Angola, Zambia and Zaire. For the most part the domestic Lobito–Huambo section of the railway was maintained in operation, although at a reduced level; it transported 262,000 tons of freight along the coastal tracks during 1985. The Amboim railway was of local importance, but is not currently operational. The volume of freight handled on Angolan railways was 9,272,883 tons in 1973, but the annual total had declined to 443,200 tons by 1990.

Internal air transport is well developed, with a network of good airports and rural landing strips, and has become the only moderately safe means of transportation, owing to the insecurity on road and rail routes: 198,667 passengers were carried by air in 1973, with the total increasing to 927,000 in 1985, but falling to 334,000 in 1993 before increasing to 519,000 in 1994. Angola's main harbours are Lobito, Luanda and Namibe. Cabinda has become the principal loading port, with 7,552,652 tons (mostly petroleum) handled in 1973. In 1985 Lobito handled 522,000 tons of cargo, compared with 2.5m. tons in 1973; Luanda handled more than 942,000 tons in 1985, compared with 2.3m. tons in 1973. Namibe's traffic declined from 6,379,000 tons in 1973 to 171,000 tons in 1985. As the country exports very little except petroleum, unloaded goods account for about 85% of traffic south of Cabinda. Passenger traffic is now almost negligible. A state-owned shipping company is in operation.

In 1988 an emergency programme was launched to rehabilitate the transport infrastructure. Under the programme, which was to cost a total of US $340m., $142m. was allocated to the rehabilitation of roads and $121m. to the rehabilitation of the Luanda and Namibe railways. The programme was also to include work on the ports of Luanda and Namibe, and on Saurino and Luena airports. In February 1992 a Portuguese consortium, led by the state railway authority (Caminhos de Ferro de Portugal), signed an $11.5m. agreement to repair port and railway installations that had been damaged during the civil war. In 1995 the cost of rehabilitating the Namibe railway and corresponding port facilities was estimated at $272m. In 1997 the state-owned road construction and maintenance company, the Instituto de Estradas de Angola, declared that 80% of the country's road network was in disrepair and estimated the total cost of rebuilding roads and bridges destroyed during the civil conflict at $4,000m.

In January 1989 international donors pledged most of the US $94m. required to finance the first phase of a 10-year programme initiated by the Southern African Development Coordination Conference (SADCC, now the Southern African Development Community—SADC) for the development of the Lobito corridor: the programme was to include the rehabilitation of the ports of Lobito and Benguela, while the rehabilitation of the Benguela railway (see above) was also to come under its auspices. An emergency plan to restore services on the Benguela railway between Lobito and Kuito was announced, following the May 1991 cease-fire between the government and UNITA. Estimated to cost US $17m., the project aimed to restore full services to Kuito by 1995. Discussions were to be held with the World Bank in late 1992 on rehabilitation of the line from Kuito to the Zaire border, following the completion of a new study of the Lobito corridor. The World Bank subsequently released $21m. in funds for the redevelopment of the Benguela railway. In 1997 an Italian company, Tor di Vale, began a $450m. programme of repairs to the Benguela railway. Minimum repairs allowing the resumption of freight traffic were expected to take three years to complete, to be followed by further modernization including the reconstruction of 22 passenger stations. Finance for the project was to come from the harvest and export of 37,000 ha of eucalyptus plantations belonging to the Benguela Railway Co, which were expected to generate revenue of as much as $500m. In April 1997 work was completed on the reconstruction of the 180 km rail link between Luanda and Dondo, in Cuanza-Norte province, which had been closed for seven years owing to the hostilities. It was expected that the rail link between Dondo and Malanje would be completed by the end of 1997.

Angola's telephone communications network, which was badly damaged during the years of war, was due to benefit from considerable investment in the late 1990s. After inter-state communications were re-established with Menongue in March 1997, only three provincial capitals remained without inter-state communications: namely, Ndalatando, Mbanza-Kongo and Malanje. The first step in Angola Telecom's plans for improving and extending services is the recovery of some US $18m. in service payments owed by government agencies. The next step will be to begin an $80m. infrastructure investment plan, focusing initially on the cities of Luanda and Benguela. Angola Telecom's infrastructure investment aims for compatibility with Africa One, the $1,600m. fibre-optic cable system that will serve the African continent.

Angola's trade balance during the last years of the Portuguese presence was traditionally positive. In 1974 the country exported goods to the value of 30,996m. escudos and imported 15,836m. escudos' worth. Portugal was the chief supplier of Angolan imports, providing products worth 3,481m. escudos. In 1974 the USA was the main market for Angolan exports, buying goods valued at 11,772m. escudos, compared with Portugal's 8,419m. escudos.

It is estimated that more than one-half of the country's food requirements are now imported, and Angola survives as a result of external purchases and assistance, mostly from Western Europe and the UN organizations. In March 1997 the UN launched its 1997 Consolidated Inter-Agency Appeal for Angola, requesting US $228.4m. for the transition from emergency assistance to national rehabilitation and reconstruction. The World

Food Programme pledged to provide some $68m. in food assistance during 1997. The principal exported commodities in 1993 were: mineral fuels and lubricants (97.0%); diamonds (2.2%). In 1994 the value of exports was $3,002m., and the value of imports was $1,633m., leaving a trade surplus of $1,369m. There was a deficit of $872m. on the current account of the balance of payments in that year. In 1994 the USA remained Angola's principal customer (taking 64.0% of total exports), followed by Belgium (7.5%), China (5.0%) and Portugal (4.0%). The main sources of imports in 1994 were Portugal (53.0%), the USA (9.0%), Spain (7.0%) and France (5.0%). Economic relations with Portugal have developed renewed momentum since the conclusion of the Estoril peace agreement. In February 1992 Portugal agreed to lend $325m. to enable Angola to import Portuguese goods. At the same time, it was agreed that Portugal would increase its purchases of petroleum from Angola, and that four Portuguese banks were to open branches in Angola.

Angola's inclusion in the African, Caribbean and Pacific group of signatories of the third and fourth Lomé Conventions should, in addition to making more EC funds available, increase both the range and volume of its trading operations. Angola participates fully in the SADC, and has special responsibility for the co-ordination of energy development and conservation.

Statistical Survey

Source (unless otherwise stated): Instituto Nacional de Estatística, Luanda.

Area and Population

AREA, POPULATION AND DENSITY

Area (sq km)	1,246,700*
Population (census results)	
30 December 1960	4,480,719
15 December 1970	
Males	2,943,974
Females	2,702,192
Total	5,646,166
Population (official estimates at mid-year)	
1993	10,916,000
1994	11,233,000
1995	11,561,000
Density (per sq km) at mid-1995	9.3

* 481,354 sq miles.

DISTRIBUTION OF POPULATION BY DISTRICT
(provisional estimates, mid-1995)

	Area (sq km)	Population	Density (per sq km)
Luanda	2,418	2,002,000	828.0
Huambo	34,274	1,687,000	49.2
Bié	70,314	1,246,000	17.7
Malanje	87,246	975,000	11.2
Huíla	75,002	948,000	12.6
Uíge	58,698	948,000	16.2
Benguela	31,788	702,000	22.1
Cuanza-Sul	55,660	688,000	12.4
Cuanza-Norte	24,110	412,000	17.1
Moxico	223,023	349,000	1.6
Lunda-Norte	102,783	311,000	3.0
Zaire	40,130	247,000	6.2
Cunene	88,342	245,000	2.8
Cabinda	7,270	185,000	25.4
Bengo	31,371	184,000	5.9
Lunda-Sul	56,985	160,000	2.8
Cuando-Cubango	199,049	137,000	0.7
Namibe	58,137	135,000	2.3
Total	1,246,600	11,561,000	9.3

PRINCIPAL TOWNS (population at 1970 census)

Luanda (capital)	480,613*	Benguela	40,996
Huambo (Nova Lisboa)	61,885	Lubango (Sá da Bandeira)	31,674
Lobito	59,258	Malanje	31,559

* 1982 estimate: 1,200,000.

Source: Direcção dos Serviços de Estatística, Luanda.

BIRTHS AND DEATHS (UN estimates, annual averages)

	1980–85	1985–90	1990–95
Birth rate (per 1,000)	50.8	51.3	51.3
Death rate (per 1,000)	22.8	21.3	19.2

Expectation of life (UN estimates, years at birth, 1990–95): 46.5 (males 44.9; females 48.1).

Source: UN, *World Population Prospects: The 1994 Revision.*

ECONOMICALLY ACTIVE POPULATION
(estimates, '000 persons, 1991)

	Males	Females	Total
Agriculture, etc.	1,518	1,374	2,892
Industry	405	33	438
Services	644	192	836
Total labour force	2,567	1,599	4,166

Source: UN Economic Commission for Africa, *African Statistical Yearbook.*

Mid-1995 (estimates in '000): Agriculture, etc. 3,784; Total (incl. others) 5,125. Source: FAO, *Production Yearbook.*

Agriculture

PRINCIPAL CROPS ('000 metric tons)

	1993	1994	1995
Wheat†	3	3	5
Rice (paddy)*	18	18	19
Maize	274†	201	235†
Millet and sorghum†	40	53	62
Potatoes*	41	42	43
Sweet potatoes*	185	200	200
Cassava (Manioc)	1,861†	1,600*	1,700*
Dry beans*	36	34	34
Groundnuts (in shell)*	17	17	17
Sunflower seed*	10	11	10
Cottonseed†	8	8	8
Cotton (lint)†	4	4	4
Palm kernels*	15	16	16
Palm oil*	50	52	52
Vegetables*	249	249	249
Citrus fruit*	78	79	79
Pineapples*	34	34	34
Bananas*	280	275	275
Other fruits*	28	29	29
Sugar cane*	220	220	220
Coffee (green)	5	2†	3†
Tobacco (leaves)*	4	4	4
Sisal	1†	1*	1*

* FAO estimate(s). † Unofficial figure(s).

Source: FAO, *Production Yearbook*.

LIVESTOCK (FAO estimates, '000 head, year ending September)

	1993	1994	1995
Cattle	3,250	3,280	3,280
Pigs	810	805	800
Sheep	255	255	255
Goats	1,570	1,570	1,570

Poultry (FAO estimates, million): 6 in 1993; 6 in 1994; 6 in 1995.

Source: FAO, *Production Yearbook*.

LIVESTOCK PRODUCTS (FAO estimates, '000 metric tons)

	1993	1994	1995
Beef and veal	56	56	56
Goat meat	4	4	4
Pig meat	22	23	23
Poultry meat	7	7	7
Other meat	7	7	7
Cows' milk	159	160	160
Butter and ghee	0.4	0.4	0.4
Cheese	1.0	1.0	1.0
Poultry eggs	3.9	3.9	3.9
Honey	21	21	21
Cattle hides	8.6	8.7	8.7

Source: FAO, *Production Yearbook*.

Forestry

ROUNDWOOD REMOVALS
(FAO estimates, '000 cubic metres, excluding bark)

	1992	1993	1994
Sawlogs, veneer logs and logs for sleepers*	66	66	66
Other industrial wood	832	865	898
Fuel wood	5,480	5,652	5,830
Total	6,378	6,583	6,794

* Annual output assumed to be unchanged since 1990.

Source: FAO, *Yearbook of Forest Products*.

SAWNWOOD PRODUCTION
(FAO estimates, '000 cubic metres, including railway sleepers)

	1992	1993	1994
Total	5	5	5

Source: FAO, *Yearbook of Forest Products*.

Fishing

('000 metric tons, live weight)

	1992	1993	1994
Freshwater fishes	7.0	7.0	7.0
Cunene horse mackerel	31.5	44.0	29.5
Sardinellas	14.7	12.4	19.7
Other marine fishes (incl. unspecified)	19.5	15.7	19.6
Total fish	72.7	79.0	75.8
Crustaceans and molluscs	1.8	1.7	2.1
Total catch	74.5	80.7	77.9

Source: FAO, *Yearbook of Fishery Statistics*.

Mining

('000 metric tons, unless otherwise indicated)

	1992	1993	1994
Crude petroleum	26,000	25,200	25,250*
Natural gas (petajoules)*	7	7	7
Salt (unrefined)†	20	30	30
Diamonds ('000 carats):†			
Industrial	80	15	30
Gem	1,100	130	270
Gypsum (crude)†	57	50	50

* Estimate(s).
† Data from the US Bureau of Mines.

Source: UN, *Industrial Commodity Statistics Yearbook*.

Industry

SELECTED PRODUCTS
('000 metric tons, unless otherwise indicated)

	1992	1993	1994
Raw sugar	33*	20*	20†
Cigarettes (million)‡	2,400	n.a.	n.a.
Plywood ('000 cubic metres)*§	10	10	10
Chemical wood pulp*§	15	15	15
Jet fuels§	160	162	160
Motor spirit (petrol)§	110	110	105
Kerosene§	50	52	50
Distillate fuel oils§	330	325	320
Residual fuel oils§	650	645	640
Cement‖	370	n.a.	n.a.
Crude steel‖	10	9	9
Electric energy (million kWh)§	1,855	1,855	1,865

* Data from the FAO.
† Data from the International Sugar Organization (London).
‡ Data from the US Department of Agriculture.
§ Estimates.
‖ Data from the US Bureau of Mines.

Source: UN, *Industrial Commodity Statistics Yearbook*.

Finance

CURRENCY AND EXCHANGE RATES

Monetary Units

100 lwei = 1 readjusted kwanza.

Sterling and Dollar Equivalents (31 December 1996)

£1 sterling = 332,000 readjusted kwanza;
US $1 = 194,000 readjusted kwanza;
1,000,000 readjusted kwanza = £3.012 = $5.155.

Average Exchange Rate (new kwanza per US $)

1992	457
1993	4,832
1994	175,672

Note: An official exchange rate of US $1 = 29.62 kwanza was introduced in 1976 and remained in force until September 1990. In that month the kwanza was replaced, at par, by the new kwanza. At the same time, it was announced that the currency was to be devalued by more than 50%, with the exchange rate adjusted to US $1 = 60 new kwanza, with effect from 1 October 1990. This rate remained in force until 18 November 1991, when a basic rate of US $1 = 90 new kwanza was established. The currency underwent further devaluation, by 50% in December 1991, and by more than 67% on 15 April 1992, when a basic rate of US $1 = 550 new kwanza was established. In February 1993 the currency was again devalued, when a basic rate of US $1 = 7,000 new kwanza was established. In April 1993 this was adjusted to US $1 = 4,000 new kwanza, and in October to US $1 = 6,500 new kwanza, a devaluation of 38.5%. Following a series of four devaluations in February and March 1994, a rate of US $1 = 35,000 new kwanza was established in late March. In April 1994 the introduction of a new method of setting exchange rates resulted in an effective devaluation, to US $1 = 68,297 new kwanza, and provided for an end to the system of multiple exchange rates. Further substantial devaluations followed, and in July 1995 a 'readjusted' kwanza, equivalent to 1,000 new kwanza, was introduced. The currency, however, continued to depreciate.

BUDGET ('000 million new kwanza)

Revenue	1992	1993*	1994*
Tax revenue	924.4	10,300	256,800
Income tax	606.3	6,800	187,400
Petroleum corporate tax	265.5	2,900	75,600
Petroleum transaction tax	292.5	3,900	106,600
Tax on goods and services	173.1	2,100	54,500
Petroleum sector	150.0	1,800	49,700
Diamond sector	12.7	100	200
Taxes on foreign trade	130.3	700	11,200
Other taxes	14.7	700	3,600
Stamp tax	14.1	300	2,500
Total (incl. others)	941.0	10,500	260,900

* Figures are rounded.

Expenditure*	1992	1993	1994
Defence	230	4,700	150,600
Public order	205	2,500	90,500
Education	155	1,000	10,900
Health	80	800	14,600
Social security	200	900	6,100
Foreign relations	—	200	8,400
General administration	195	3,300	124,000
Total (incl. others)	2,445	16,400	427,100

* Figures are rounded.

Source: IMF, *Angola—Recent Economic Developments* (December 1995).

1995 (estimates, million new kwanza): Total revenue 3,880,103,863.2; Total expenditure 4,793,863,326.3.

COST OF LIVING

(Consumer Price Index for Luanda; base: 1991 = 100)

	1992	1993	1994
Food	408.9	6,856.0	70,425
Clothing	224.5	n.a.	n.a.
Rent, fuel and light	298.5	n.a.	n.a.
All items (incl. others)	399.1	5,904.5	61,982

Source: ILO, *Yearbook of Labour Statistics*.

NATIONAL ACCOUNTS

Composition of the Gross National Product (US $ million)

	1987	1988	1989
Gross domestic product (GDP) at factor cost	6,482	6,877	7,682
Indirect taxes	94	95	117
Less Subsidies	189	122	93
GDP in purchasers' values	6,386	6,850	7,706
Net factor income from abroad	−402	−938	−1,079
Gross national product	5,984	5,912	6,627

Gross Domestic Product by Economic Activity
(million kwanza at current prices)

	1992	1993	1994
Agriculture, forestry and fishing	1,086.6	9,075.3	122,480.0
Mining	1,381.6	11,360.8	367,085.0
Processing industry	120.9	983.2	16,877.0
Electricity and water	1.8	16.9	239.0
Construction	86.3	550.9	10,504.0
Trade	380.2	3,460.3	57,332.0
Transport and communications	89.5	832.8	13,466.0
Financial services	312.0	2,952.3	95,497.0
Other services	529.7	3,375.2	33,969.0
Sub-total	3,988.6	32,607.7	717,449.0
Import duties	130.3	683.2	10,916.0
GDP in purchasers' values	4,118.9	33,290.9	728,365.0

BALANCE OF PAYMENTS (US $ million)

	1992	1993	1994*
Exports of goods f.o.b.	3,833	2,900	3,002
Imports of goods f.o.b.	−1,988	−1,463	−1,633
Trade balance	1,845	1,437	1,369
Services (net)	−2,302	−1,874	−1,860
Balance on goods and services	−457	−437	−491
Interest payments (net)	−504	−583	−549
Unrequited transfers (net)	102	166	169
Current balance	−859	−854	−872
Direct investment abroad	−385	−549	−576
Direct investment from abroad	673	851	902
Other long-term capital (net)	−604	−783	−450
Short-term capital (net) } Net errors and omissions }	−165	−383	−326
Overall balance	−1,340	−1,718	−1,321

* Estimates.

Source: IMF, *Angola—Recent Economic Developments* (December 1995).

External Trade

SELECTED COMMODITIES

Imports (million kwanza)	1983	1984	1985
Animal products	1,315	1,226	1,084
Vegetable products	2,158	3,099	2,284
Fats and oils	946	1,006	1,196
Food and beverages	2,400	1,949	1,892
Industrial chemical products	1,859	1,419	1,702
Plastic materials	431	704	454
Paper products	376	380	411
Textiles	1,612	1,816	1,451
Base metals	1,985	3,730	2,385
Electrical equipment	3,296	2,879	2,571
Transport equipment	2,762	2,240	3,123
Total (incl. others)	20,197	21,370	19,694

Total Imports (million kwanza): 18,691 in 1986; 13,372 in 1987; 29,845 in 1988; 34,392 in 1989 (Source: UN, *Monthly Bulletin of Statistics*).

Exports (US $ million)	1991	1992	1993
Crude petroleum	3,161	3,490	2,750
Refined petroleum products	56	66	63
Diamonds	190	250	63
Total (incl. others)	3,449	3,833	2,900

Source: IMF, *Angola—Recent Economic Developments* (December 1995).

PRINCIPAL TRADING PARTNERS (US $ million)

Imports c.i.f.	1987	1988	1989
Belgium-Luxembourg	17.9	22.9	99.9
Brazil	55.8	119.2	104.0
France	63.3	8.8	114.1
German Dem. Repub.	35.2	34.7	41.9
Germany, Fed. Repub.	51.0	149.0	178.4
Italy	19.0	19.3	35.2
Japan	8.1	39.7	34.5
Netherlands	20.6	148.3	160.5
Portugal	51.4	171.4	206.8
Spain	4.8	53.2	55.6
United Arab Emirates	70.5	25.1	23.1
United Kingdom	9.1	26.7	32.9
Total (incl. others)	442.6	987.9	1,139.6

Total Imports (US $ million): 1,139.5 in 1990; 457.9 in 1991; 728.7 in 1992.

Exports f.o.b.	1990	1991	1992
Austria	62.8	—	—
Belgium-Luxembourg	231.9	45.9	106.0
Brazil	80.0	210.2	46.0
Canada	28.1	37.1	—
Chile	76.7	22.2	—
China, People's Republic	—	—	63.0
France	456.3	290.4	300.0
Germany	40.4	21.0	—
Gibraltar	72.8	12.5	—
Italy	143.9	82.6	37.0
Netherlands	414.0	206.2	167.1
Portugal	88.8	87.8	75.5
Singapore	—	—	49.0
Spain	2.5	40.5	50.1
United Kingdom	21.5	144.3	316.0
USA	2,067.6	2,094.6	2,460.0
Yugoslavia	—	62.2	—
Total (incl. others)	3,910.3	3,409.7	3,697.5

Source: UN, *International Trade Statistics Yearbook*.

Transport

GOODS TRANSPORT ('000 metric tons)

	1988	1989	1990
Road	1,056.7	690.1	867.3
Railway	580.9	510.3	443.2
Water	780.8	608.6	812.1
Air	24.6	10.5	28.3
Total	2,443.0	1,819.5	2,150.9

Sources: Instituto Nacional de Estatística; Ministério de Transporte e Comunicações.

PASSENGER TRANSPORT ('000 journeys)

	1988	1989	1990
Road	12,699.2	32,658.7	48,796.1
Railway	6,659.7	6,951.2	6,455.8
Water	151.8	163.2	223.8
Air	608.9	618.4	615.9
Total	20,119.6	40,391.5	56,091.6

Sources: Instituto Nacional de Estatística; Ministério de Transporte e Comunicações, Luanda.

ROAD TRAFFIC (estimates, motor vehicles in use at 31 December)

	1993	1994	1995
Passenger cars	174,000	180,000	197,000
Lorries and vans	30,900	32,100	26,000
Total	204,900	212,100	223,000

Source: IRF, *World Road Statistics*.

SHIPPING

Merchant Fleet (registered at 31 December)

	1994	1995	1996
Number of vessels	112	112	113
Total displacement (grt)	89,591	89,594	81,856

Source: Lloyd's Register of Shipping, *World Fleet Statistics*.

International Sea-borne Freight Traffic
(estimates, '000 metric tons)

	1989	1990	1991
Goods loaded	19,980	21,102	23,288
Goods unloaded	1,235	1,242	1,261

Source: UN Economic Commission for Africa, *African Statistical Yearbook*.

CIVIL AVIATION (traffic on scheduled services)

	1992	1993	1994
Kilometres flown (million)	10	9	13
Passengers carried ('000)	440	334	519
Passenger-km (million)	1,196	948	1,594
Total ton-km (million)	147	113	197

Source: UN, *Statistical Yearbook*.

Tourism

	1992	1993	1994
Tourist arrivals ('000)	40	21	11
Tourist receipts (US $ million)	n.a.	20	13

Source: UN, *Statistical Yearbook*.

Communications Media

	1992	1993	1994
Radio receivers ('000 in use)	282	295	320
Television receivers ('000 in use)	62	68	70
Telephones ('000 main lines in use)	49	53	n.a.

Book production: 47 titles (books 35, pamphlets 12) and 419,000 copies (books 338,000, pamphlets 81,000) in 1985; 14 titles (all books) and 130,000 copies in 1986.

Daily newspapers: 4 (estimated circulation 115,000) in 1990; 4 (estimated circulation 116,000) in 1992; 4 (estimated circulation 117,000) in 1994.

Sources: UNESCO, *Statistical Yearbook*; UN, *Statistical Yearbook*.

Education

(1991/92)

	Teachers	Pupils
Pre-primary	n.a.	214,867
Primary	31,062*	989,443
Secondary:		
general	5,138†	196,099
teacher training	280‡	10,772
vocational	286†	12,116
Higher	787	6,331

* Figure for school year 1990/91.

† Figure for school year 1989/90.

‡ Figure for school year 1987/88.

Source: mainly UNESCO, *Statistical Yearbook*.

Directory

The Constitution

The MPLA regime adopted an independence Constitution for Angola in November 1975. It was amended in October 1976, September 1980, March 1991, April and August 1992, and November 1996. The main provisions of the Constitution, as amended, are summarized below:

BASIC PRINCIPLES

The Republic of Angola shall be a sovereign and independent state whose prime objective shall be to build a free and democratic society of peace, justice and social progress. It shall be a democratic state based on the rule of law, founded on national unity, the dignity of human beings, pluralism of expression and political organization, respecting and guaranteeing the basic rights and freedoms of persons, whether as individuals or as members of organized social groups. Sovereignty shall be vested in the people, which shall exercise political power through periodic universal suffrage.

The Republic of Angola shall be a unitary and indivisible state. Economic, social and cultural solidarity shall be promoted between all the Republic's regions for the common development of the entire nation and the elimination of regionalism and tribalism.

Religion

The Republic shall be a secular state and there shall be complete separation of the State and religious institutions. All religions shall be respected.

The Economy

The economic system shall be based on the coexistence of diverse forms of property—public, private, mixed, co-operative and family—and all shall enjoy equal protection. The State shall protect foreign investment and foreign property, in accordance with the law. The fiscal system shall aim to satisfy the economic, social and administrative needs of the State and to ensure a fair distribution of income and wealth. Taxes may be created and abolished only by law, which shall determine applicability, rates, tax benefits and guarantees for taxpayers.

Education

The Republic shall vigorously combat illiteracy and obscurantism and shall promote the development of education and of a true national culture.

FUNDAMENTAL RIGHTS AND DUTIES

The State shall respect and protect the human person and human dignity. All citizens shall be equal before the law. They shall be subject to the same duties, without any distinction based on colour, race, ethnic group, sex, place of birth, religion, level of education, or economic or social status.

All citizens aged 18 years and over, other than those legally deprived of political and civil rights, shall have the right and duty to take an active part in public life, to vote and be elected to any state organ, and to discharge their mandates with full dedication to the cause of the Angolan nation. The law shall establish limitations in respect of non-political allegiance of soldiers on active service, judges and police forces, as well as the electoral incapacity of soldiers on active service and police forces.

Freedom of expression, of assembly, of demonstration, of association and of all other forms of expression shall be guaranteed. Groupings whose aims or activities are contrary to the constitutional order and penal laws, or that, even indirectly, pursue political objectives through organizations of a military, paramilitary or militarized nature shall be forbidden. Every citizen has the right to a defence if accused of a crime. Individual freedoms are guaranteed. Freedom of conscience and belief shall be inviolable. Work shall be the right and duty of all citizens. The State shall promote measures necessary to ensure the right of citizens to medical and health care, as well as assistance in childhood, motherhood, disability, old age, etc. It shall also promote access to education, culture and sports for all citizens.

STATE ORGANS

President of the Republic

The President of the Republic shall be the Head of State, Head of Government and Commander-in-Chief of the Angolan armed forces. The President of the Republic shall be elected directly by a secret universal ballot and shall have the following powers:

to appoint and dismiss the Prime Minister, Ministers and other government officials determined by law;

to appoint the judges of the Supreme Court;

to preside over the Council of Ministers;

to declare war and make peace, following authorization by the National Assembly;

to sign, promulgate and publish the laws of the National Assembly, government decrees and statutory decrees;

to preside over the National Defence Council;

to decree a state of siege or state of emergency;

to announce the holding of general elections;

to issue pardons and commute sentences;

to perform all other duties provided for in the Constitution.

National Assembly

The National Assembly is the supreme state legislative body, to which the Government is responsible. The National Assembly shall be composed of 223 deputies, elected for a term of four years. The National Assembly shall convene in ordinary session twice yearly and in special session on the initiative of the President of the National Assembly, the Standing Commission of the National Assembly or of no less than one-third of its deputies. The Standing Commission shall be the organ of the National Assembly that represents and assumes its powers between sessions.

Government

The Government shall comprise the President of the Republic, the ministers and the secretaries of state, and other members whom the law shall indicate, and shall have the following functions:

to organize and direct the implementation of state domestic and foreign policy, in accordance with decision of the National Assembly and its Standing Commission;

to ensure national defence, the maintenance of internal order and security, and the protection of the rights of citizens;

to prepare the draft National Plan and General State Budget for approval by the National Assembly, and to organize, direct and control their execution;

The Council of Ministers shall be answerable to the National Assembly. In the exercise of its powers, the Council of Ministers shall issue decrees and resolutions.

Judiciary

The organization, composition and competence of the courts shall be established by law. Judges shall be independent in the discharge of their functions.

Local State Organs

The organs of state power at provincial level shall be the Provincial Assemblies and their executive bodies. The Provincial Assemblies shall work in close co-operation with social organizations and rely on the initiative and broad participation of citizens. The Provincial Assemblies shall elect commissions of deputies to perform permanent or specific tasks. The executive organs of Provincial Assemblies shall be the Provincial Governments, which shall be led by the Provincial Governors. The Provincial Governors shall be answerable to the President of the Republic, the Council of Ministers and the Provincial Assemblies.

National Defence

The State shall ensure national defence. The National Defence Council shall be presided over by the President of the Republic, and its composition shall be determined by law. The Angolan armed forces, as a state institution, shall be permanent, regular and non-partisan. Defence of the country shall be the right and the highest indeclinable duty of every citizen. Military service shall be compulsory. The forms in which it is fulfilled shall be defined by the law.

Note: In accordance with the terms of the Lusaka peace accord of November 1994, in April 1997 a new government of national unity and reconciliation was inaugurated in which UNITA held four portfolios. In November 1996 the National Assembly adopted a constitutional revision extending the mandate of parliament, which was due to expire that month, for a period of between two and four years in order to allow for the establishment of suitable conditions for the conduct of elections.

The Government

HEAD OF STATE

President: José Eduardo dos Santos (assumed office 21 September 1979).

COUNCIL OF MINISTERS
(July 1997)

Prime Minister: Fernando José França van-Dúnem.

Minister of Defence: Gen. Pedro Sebastião.

Minister of the Interior: Santana André Pitra Petroff.

Minister of Foreign Affairs: Dr Venâncio da Silva Moura.

Minister of Territorial Administration: Fernando Faustino Muteka.

Minister of Finance: Mário de Alcantara Monteiro.

Minister of Economic Planning: Emanuel Moreira Carneiro.

Minister of Petroleum: Albina Faria de Assis Pereira Africano.

Minister of Industry: Manuel Diamantino Borges Duque.

Minister of Agriculture and Rural Development: Carlos António Fernandes.

Minister of Fisheries: Maria de Fátima Monteiro Jardim.

Minister of Geology and Mines: Marcos Samondo.

Minister of Public Works and Urbanization: Pedro de Castro van-Dúnem Loy.

Minister of Transport: André Luís Brandão.

Minister of Trade: Victorino Domingos Hossi.

Minister of Health: Anastacio Ruben Sikatu.

Minister of Education: António Burity da Silva Neto.

Minister of Assistance and Social Reintegration: Albino Malungo.

Minister of Culture: Ana Maria de Oliveira.

Minister of Youth and Sports: José da Rocha Sardinha de Castro.

Minister of Justice: Dr Paulo Tchipilica.

Minister of Public Administration, Employment and Social Welfare: Dr António Domingos Pitra Costa Neto.

Minister of Information: Dr Pedro Hendrik Vaal Neto.

Minister of Science and Technology: Francisco Mubengai.

Minister of Post and Telecommunications: Licínio Tavares Ribeiro.

Minister of Women's Affairs: Dra Joana Lima Ramos Baptista Cristiano.

Minister of War Veterans: Pedro José van-Dúnem.

Minister of Hotels and Tourism: Jorge Alicerces Valentim.

Minister of Energy and Water: João Moreira Pinto Saraiva.

SECRETARY OF STATE
(June 1997)

Secretary of State for Coffee: Gilberto Buta Lutukuta.

MINISTRIES

Office of the President: Luanda; telex 3072.

Ministry of Agriculture and Rural Development: Avda Norton de Matos 2, Luanda; telex 3322.

Ministry of Assistance and Social Reintegration: Luanda.

Ministry of Culture: Luanda.

Ministry of Defence: Rua Silva Carvalho ex Quartel General, Luanda; telex 3138.

Ministry of Economic Planning: Luanda.

Ministry of Education: Avda Comandante Jika, CP 1281, Luanda; tel. (2) 321592; telex 4121; fax (2) 321592.

Ministry of Energy ad Water: Luanda.

Ministry of Finance: Avda 4 de Fevereiro, Luanda; tel. (2) 344628; telex 3363.

Ministry of Fisheries: Avda 4 de Fevereiro 25, Predio Atlântico, Luanda; tel. (2) 392782; telex 3273.

Ministry of Foreign Affairs: Avda Comandante Jika, Luanda; telex 3127.

Ministry of Geology and Mines: Luanda.

Ministry of Health: Rua Diogo Cão, Luanda.

Ministry of Hotels and Tourism: Luanda.

Ministry of Industry: Luanda.

Ministry of Information: Luanda.

Ministry of the Interior: Avda 4 de Fevereiro, Luanda.

Ministry of Justice: Largo do Palácio, Luanda.

Ministry of Petroleum: Avda 4 de Fevereiro 105, CP 1279, Luanda; tel. (2) 337448; telex 3300.

Ministry of Post and Telecommunications: Luanda.

Ministry of Public Administration, Employment and Social Welfare: Rua 17 de Setembro 32, CP 1986, Luanda; tel. (2) 339656; telex 4147; fax (2) 339054.

Ministry of Public Works and Urbanization: Luanda.

Ministry of Science and Technology: Luanda.

Ministry of Territorial Administration: Luanda.

Ministry of Trade: Largo Kinaxixi 14, Luanda; tel. (2) 344525; telex 3282.

Ministry of Transport: Avda 4 de Fevereiro 42, CP 1250-C, Luanda; tel. (2) 370061; telex 3108.

Ministry of War Veterans: Luanda.

Ministry of Women's Affairs: Luanda.

Ministry of Youth and Sports: Luanda.

PROVINCIAL GOVERNORS*

Bengo: Ezelino Mendes.

Benguela: Dumilde das Chagas Simões Rangel.

Bié: Luís Paulino dos Santos.

Cabinda: José Amaro Tati.

Cuando-Cubango: Manuel Gama.

Cuanza-Norte: Manuel Pedro Pacavira.

Cuanza-Sul: Francisco José Ramos da Cruz.

Cunene: Pedro Mutinde.

Huambo: Paulo Kassoma.

Huíla: Kundi Paihama.

Luanda: José Aníbal Lopes Rocha.

Lunda-Norte: Manuel Francisco Gomes Maiato.

Lunda-Sul: Gonçalves Manuel Manvumbra.

Malanje: Flavio Fernandes.

Moxico: João Ernesto dos Santos (Liberdade).

Namibe: Joaquim da Silva Matias.

Uíge: Kananito Alexandre.

Zaire: Ludi Kissassunda.

*All Governors are ex-officio members of the Government.

President and Legislature

PRESIDENT*

Presidential Election, 29 and 30 September 1992

	Votes	% of votes
José Eduardo dos Santos (MPLA)	1,953,335	49.57
Dr Jonas Malheiro Savimbi (UNITA)	1,579,298	40.07
António Alberto Neto (PDA)	85,249	2.16
Holden Roberto (FNLA)	83,135	2.11
Honorato Lando (PDLA)	75,789	1.92
Luís dos Passos (PRD)	59,121	1.47
Bengui Pedro João (PSD)	38,243	0.97
Simão Cacete (FPD)	26,385	0.67
Daniel Júlio Chipenda (Independent)	20,646	0.52
Anália de Victória Pereira (PLD)	11,475	0.29
Rui de Victória Pereira (PRA)	9,208	0.23
Total	3,940,884	100.00

NATIONAL ASSEMBLY

President: Roberto de Almeida.

Legislative Election, 29 and 30 September 1992

	Votes	% of votes	Seats†
MPLA	2,124,126	53.74	129
UNITA	1,347,636	34.10	70
FNLA	94,742	2.40	5
PLD	94,269	2.39	3
PRS	89,875	2.27	6
PRD	35,293	0.89	1
AD Coalition	34,166	0.86	1
PSD	33,088	0.84	1
PAJOCA	13,924	0.35	1
FDA	12,038	0.30	1
PDP—ANA	10,620	0.27	1
PNDA	10,281	0.26	1
CNDA	10,237	0.26	—
PSDA	19,217	0.26	—
PAI	9,007	0.23	—
PDLA	8,025	0.20	—
PDA	8,014	0.20	—
PRA	6,719	0.17	—
Total	3,952,277	100.00	220

* Under the terms of the electoral law, a second round of presidential elections was required to take place in order to determine which of the two leading candidates from the first round would be elected. However, a resumption of hostilities between UNITA and government forces prevented a second round of presidential elections from taking place. The electoral process was to resume only when the provisions of the Estoril peace agreement, concluded in May 1991, had been fulfilled. However, provision in the Lusaka peace accord of November 1994 for the second round of presidential elections was not pursued.

† According to the Constitution, the total number of seats in the National Assembly is 223. On the decision of the National Electoral Council, however, elections to fill three seats reserved for Angolans abroad were abandoned.

Political Organizations

Aliança Democrática de Angola: Leader Simba da Costa.

Angolan Alliance and Hamista Party.

Angolan Democratic Coalition (AD Coalition): Pres. Evidor Quiela (acting).

Angolan Democratic Confederation: f. 1994; Chair. Gaspar Neto.

Angolan Democratic Unification: Leader Eduardo Milton Sivi.

Associação Cívica Angolana (ACA): f. 1990; Leader Joaquim Pinto de Andrade.

Centro Democrático Social (CDS): Pres. Mateus José; Sec.-Gen. Delfina Francisco Capciel.

Christian Democratic Convention: Leader Gaspar Neto.

Democratic Civilian Opposition: f. 1994; opposition alliance including:

Convenção Nacional Democrata de Angola (CNDA): Leader Paulino Pinto João.

Frente Nacional de Libertação de Angola (FNLA): f. 1962; Pres. Holden Roberto.

Frente para a Democracia (FPD): Leader Nelso Pestana; Sec.-Gen. Filomeno Vieira Lopes.

Movimento de Defesa dos Interesses de Angola—Partido de Consciência Nacional: Leader Isidoro Klala.

National Ecological Party of Angola: Leader Sukawa Dizizeko Ricardo.

National Union for Democracy: Leader Sebastião Rogerio Suzama.

Partido Renovador Social (PRS):

Party of Solidarity and the Conscience of Angola: Leader Fernando Dombassi Quiesse.

Fórum Democrático Angolano (FDA): Leader Jorge Rebelo Pinto Chicoti.

Frente de Libertação do Enclave de Cabinda (FLEC): f. 1963; comprises several factions, claiming total forces of c. 5,000 guerrillas, seeking the secession of Cabinda province; mem. groups include:

Frente Democrática de Cabinda (FDC).

Frente de Libertação do Enclave de Cabinda–Forças Armadas Cabindesas (FLEC–FAC): Chair. Henrique Tiago N'Zita; Chief-of-Staff (FAC) Commdr Estanislau Miguel Bomba.

Frente de Libertação do Enclave de Cabinda–Renovada (FLEC–R): Pres. António Bento Bembe.

Movimento Amplo para a Democracia: Leader Francisco Viana.

Movimento Popular de Libertação de Angola (MPLA) (People's Movement for the Liberation of Angola): Luanda; telex 3369; f. 1956; in 1961–74, as MPLA, conducted guerrilla operations against Portuguese rule; governing party since 1975; known as Movimento Popular de Libertação de Angola—Partido do Trabalho (MPLA—PT) (People's Movement for the Liberation of Angola—Workers' Party) 1977–92; in Dec. 1990 replaced Marxist-Leninist ideology with commitment to 'democratic socialism'; Chair. José Eduardo dos Santos; Sec.-Gen. Lopo Fortunato Ferreira do Nascimento.

Movimento de Unidade Democrática para a Reconstrução (Mudar): Leader Manuel dos Santos Lima.

National Union for the Light of Democracy and Development of Angola: Pres. Miguel Muendo; Sec.-Gen. Domingos Chizela.

Partido de Aliança de Juventude, Operários e Camponêses de Angola (PAJOCA) (Angolan Youth, Workers' and Peasants' Alliance Party): Leader Miguel João Sebastião.

Partido para a Aliança Popular: Leader Campos Neto.

Partido Angolano Independente (PAI): Leader Adriano Parreira.

Partido Democrático Angolano (PDA): Leader António Alberto Neto.

Partido Liberal Democrata (PLD): Leader Anália de Victória Pereira.

Partido Nacional Democrata de Angola (PNDA): Sec.-Gen. Pedro João António.

Partido Reformador de Angola (PRA): Leader Rui de Victória Pereira.

Partido Renovador Democrático (PRD): Leader Luís dos Passos.

Partido Republicano Conservador de Angola (PRCA): Leader Martinho Mateus.

Partido Social Democrata (PSD): Leader Bengui Pedro João.

Partido do Trabalho de Angola (PTA): Leader Agostinho Paldo.

Patriotic Front: f. 1995; opposition alliance including:

Partido Angolano Liberal (PAL): Leader Manuel Francisco Lulo (acting).

Partido Democrático Liberal de Angola (PDLA): Leader Honorato Lando.

Partido Democrático para o Progresso—Alliança Nacional de Angola (PDP—ANA): Leader Mfufumpinga Nlandu Victor.

Partido Social Democrata de Angola (PSDA): Leader André Milton Kilandonoco.

Peaceful Democratic Party of Angola: Leader António Kunzolako.

Unangola: Leader André Franco de Sousa.

União Nacional para a Independência Total de Angola (UNITA): f. 1966 to secure independence from Portugal; later received Portuguese support to oppose the MPLA; UNITA and the Frente Nacional de Libertação de Angola conducted guerrilla campaign against the MPLA Govt with aid from some Western nations, 1975–76; supported by South Africa until 1984 and in 1987–88, and by USA after 1986; support drawn mainly from Ovimbundu ethnic group; Pres. Dr Jonas Malheiro Savimbi; Sec.-Gen. Paulo Lukamba 'Gato'.

United Front for the Salvation of Angola: Leader José Augusto da Silva Coelho.

Vofangola: Leader Lomby Zuendoki.

Diplomatic Representation

EMBASSIES IN ANGOLA

Algeria: Luanda; Ambassador: Hanafi Oussedik.

Belgium: Avda 4 de Fevereiro, CP 1203, Luanda; tel. (2) 372368; telex 3356; Ambassador: Guido Vansina.

Brazil: Rua Houari Boumedienne 132, CP 5428, Luanda; tel. (2) 344848; telex 3365; Ambassador: Paulo Dyrceu Pinheiro.

Bulgaria: Rua Fernão Mendes Pinto 35, CP 2260, Luanda; tel. (2) 321010; telex 2189; Chargé d'affaires a.i.: Lilo Tochev.

Cape Verde: Rua Alexandre Peres 29, Luanda; tel. (2) 333211; telex 3247; Ambassador: José Luís Jesus.

China, People's Republic: Rua Houari Boumedienne 196, Luanda; tel. (2) 344185; Ambassador: Zhang Baosheng.

Congo, Democratic Republic: Rua Cesario Verde 24, Luanda; tel. (2) 361953; Ambassador: Mundindi Didi Kilengo.

Congo, Republic: Rua 4 de Fevereiro 3, Luanda; Ambassador: Anatole Khondo.

Côte d'Ivoire: Rua Karl Marx 43, Luanda; tel. (2) 390150; Ambassador: Jean-Marie Kacou Gervais.

Cuba: Rua Che Guevara 42, Luanda; tel. (2) 339165; telex 3236; Ambassador: Narcisco Martín Mora.

Czech Republic: Rua Amílcar Cabral 5, CP 2691, Luanda; tel. (2) 334456.

Egypt: Rua Comandante Stona 247, Luanda; tel. (2) 321590; telex 3380; Ambassador: Anwar Dakroury.

France: Rua Reverendo Pedro Agostinho Neto 31–33, Luanda; tel. (2) 334335; fax (2) 391949; Ambassador: André Cira.

Gabon: Avda 4 de Fevereiro 95, Luanda; tel. (2) 372614; telex 3263; Ambassador: Raphaël Nkassa-Nzogho.

Germany: Avda 4 de Fevereiro 120, CP 1295, Luanda; tel. (2) 334516; telex 2096; fax (2) 334516; Ambassador: Helmut Van Edig.

Ghana: Rua Cirilo da Conceição e Silva 5, CP 1012, Luanda; tel. (2) 339222; telex 2051; fax (2) 338235; Chargé d'affaires a.i.: E. Obeng Kufuor.

Guinea: Luanda; telex 3177.

Holy See: Rua Luther King 123, CP 1030, Luanda (Apostolic Delegation); tel. (2) 336289; fax (2) 332378; Apostolic Delegate: Most Rev. Aldo Cavalli, Titular Archbishop of Vibo Valentia.

Hungary: Rua Comandante Stona 226-228, Luanda; tel. (2) 32313; telex 3084; fax (2) 322448; Ambassador: Dr Gábor Tóth.

India: Prédio dos Armazens Carrapas 81, 1°, D, 6040, Luanda; tel. (2) 345398; telex 3233; fax (2) 342061; Ambassador: Baldev Raj Ghuliani.

Italy: Edif. Importang 7°, Rua Kinaxixi, Luanda; tel. (2) 393533; telex 3265; Ambassador: Francesco Lanata.

Korea, Democratic People's Republic: Rua Cabral Moncada 116–118, CP 599, Luanda; tel. (2) 323037; Ambassador: Hyon Sok.

Morocco: Largo 4 de Fevereiro 3, Luanda; tel. (2) 338847.

Mozambique: Luanda; tel. (2) 330811; Ambassador: M. Salessio.

Namibia: Rua dos Coqueiros, Luanda; tel. (2) 396281; fax (2) 339234.

Netherlands: Edif. Secil, Avda 4 de Fevereiro 42, CP 3624, Luanda; tel. (2) 333544; telex 3051; fax (2) 333699; Ambassador: Mr Wolfswinkel.

Nigeria: Rua Houari Boumedienne 120, CP 479, Luanda; tel. (2) 340084; telex 3014; Ambassador: Gabriel Sam Akumafor.

Poland: Rua Comandante N'zaji 21–23, CP 1340, Luanda; tel. (2) 323086; telex 3222; Ambassador: Jan Bojko.

Portugal: Rua Karl Marx 50, CP 1346, Luanda; tel. (2) 333027; telex 3370; Ambassador: Ramalho Ortigão.

Romania: Ramalho Ortigão 30, Alvalade, Luanda; tel. and fax (2) 321076; telex 2085; Ambassador: Marin Iliescu.

Russia: Rua Houari Boumedienne 170, CP 3141, Luanda; tel. (2) 345028; Ambassador: Yurii Kapralov.

São Tomé and Príncipe: Rua Armindo de Andrade 173–175, Luanda; tel. (2) 345677; Ambassador: Ariosto Castelo David.

Slovakia: Rua Amílcar Cabral 5, CP 2691, Luanda; tel. (2) 334456.

South Africa: Rua Manuel Fernandes Caldeira 6B, CP 6212 Luanda; tel. (2) 397301; fax (2) 396788; Chargé d'affaires a.i.: Roger Ballard-Tremeer.

Spain: Avda 4 de Fevereiro 95, 1°, CP 3061, Luanda; tel. (2) 391187; telex 2621; fax (2) 391188; Ambassador: Rafael Fernández-Pita y González.

Sweden: Rua Garcia Neto 9, Luanda; tel. (2) 340424; telex 3126; Ambassador: Lena Sund.

Switzerland: Avda 4 de Fevereiro 129, 2°, CP 3163, Luanda; tel. (2) 338314; fax (2) 336878; Chargé d'affaires a.i.: Arnoldo Lardi.

Tanzania: Rua Joaquim Kapango 57–63, Luanda; tel. (2) 330536.

United Kingdom: Rua Diogo Cão 4, CP 1244, Luanda; tel. (2) 392991; telex 3130; fax (2) 333331; Ambassador: Roger D. Hart.

USA: Rua Houari Boumedienne 32, Miramar, CP 6468, Luanda; tel. (2) 346418; Ambassador: Bill Richardson.

Viet Nam: Rua Comandante N'zaji 66–68, CP 75, Luanda; tel. (2) 323388; telex 3226; Ambassador: Nguyen Huy Loi.

Yugoslavia: Rua Houari Boumedienne 142, Luanda; tel. (2) 343792; telex 3234; Ambassador: Pavle Živković.

Zambia: Rua Rei Katyavala 106–108, CP 1496, Luanda; tel. (2) 331145; telex 3439; Ambassador: Boniface Zulu.

Zimbabwe: Edif. do Ministério de Transportes e Comunicações, Avda 4 de Fevereiro 42, CP 428, Luanda; tel. (2) 332338; telex 3275; fax (2) 332339; Ambassador: B. G. Chidyausiku.

Judicial System

There is a Supreme Court and Court of Appeal in Luanda. There are also civil, criminal and military courts.

Chief Justice of the Supreme Court: João Felizardo.

Religion

Much of the population follows traditional African beliefs, although a majority profess to be Christians, mainly Roman Catholics.

CHRISTIANITY

Conselho de Igrejas Cristãs em Angola (Council of Christian Churches in Angola): Rua Amílcar Cabral 182, 1° andar, CP 1659, Luanda; tel. (2) 330415; fax (2) 393746; f. 1977; 14 mem. churches; five assoc. mems; one observer; Pres. Rev. Alvaro Rodrigues; Gen. Sec. Rev. Augusto Chipesse.

Protestant Churches

Evangelical Congregational Church in Angola (Igreja Evangélica Congregacional em Angola: CP 551, Huambo; tel. 3087; 100,000 mems; Gen. Sec. Rev. Júlio Francisco.

Evangelical Pentecostal Church of Angola (Missão Evangélica Pentecostal de Angola): CP 219, Porto Amboim; 13,600 mems; Sec. Rev. José Domingos Caetano.

United Evangelical Church of Angola (Igreja Evangélica Unida de Angola): CP 122, Uíge; 11,000 mems; Gen. Sec. Rev. A. L. Domingos.

Other active denominations include the African Apostolic Church, the Church of Apostolic Faith in Angola, the Church of Our Lord Jesus Christ in the World, the Evangelical Baptist Church, the Evangelical Church in Angola, the Evangelical Church of the Apostles of Jerusalem, the Evangelical Reformed Church of Angola, the Kimbanguist Church in Angola and the United Methodist Church.

The Roman Catholic Church

Angola comprises three archdioceses and 12 dioceses. At 31 December 1995 an estimated 44.7% of the total population were adherents.

Bishops' Conference: Conferência Episcopal de Angola e São Tomé, CP 3579, Luanda; tel. (2) 343686; fax (2) 345504; f. 1967; Pres. Cardinal Alexandre do Nascimento, Archbishop of Luanda.

Archbishop of Huambo: Most Rev. Francisco Viti, Arcebispado, CP 10, Huambo; tel. 2371.

Archbishop of Luanda: Cardinal Alexandre do Nascimento, Arcebispado, CP 87, 1230-C, Luanda; tel. (2) 334640; fax (2) 334433.

Archbishop of Lubango: Most Rev. Manuel Franklin da Costa, Arcebispado, CP 231, Lubango; tel. 20405; fax 23547.

The Press

The press was nationalized in 1976.

DAILIES

Diário da República: CP 1306, Luanda; official govt bulletin.

O Jornal de Angola: Rua Rainha Ginga 18–24, CP 1312, Luanda; tel. (2) 338947; telex 3341; fax (2) 333342; f. 1923; Dir-Gen. Adelino Marques de Almeida; mornings and Sun.; circ. 41,000.

Newspapers are also published in several regional towns.

PERIODICALS

Angola Norte: CP 97, Malanje; weekly.

A Célula: Luanda; political journal of MPLA; monthly.

Comércio Actualidade: Rua da Missão 85, CP 6375, Luanda; tel. (2) 334060; fax (2) 392216.

Correio da Semana: Rua Rainha Ginga 18–24, CP 1213, Luanda; f. 1992; owned by *O Jornal de Angola*; weekly. Editor-in-Chief MANUEL DIONISIO.

Jornal de Benguela: CP 17, Benguela; 2 a week.

Lavra & Oficina: CP 2767-C, Luanda; tel. (2) 322155; f. 1975; journal of the Union of Angolan Writers; monthly; circ. 5,000.

M: Luanda; f. 1996; MPLA publ.

Militar: Luanda; f. 1993; Editor-in-Chief CARMO NETO.

Novembro: CP 3947, Luanda; tel. (2) 331660; monthly; Dir ROBERTO DE ALMEIDA.

O Planalto: CP 96, Huambo; 2 a week.

A Voz do Trabalhador: Avda 4 de Fevereiro 210, CP 28, Luanda; telex 3387; journal of União Nacional de Trabalhadores Angolanos (National Union of Angolan Workers); monthly.

NEWS AGENCIES

ANGOP: Rua Rei Katiavala 120, Luanda; tel. (2) 334595; telex 4162; Dir-Gen. and Editor-in-Chief AVELINO MIGUEL.

Foreign Bureaux

Agence France-Presse (AFP): Prédio Mutamba, CP 2357, Luanda; tel. (2) 334939; telex 3334; Bureau Chief MANUELA TEIXEIRA.

Allgemeiner Deutscher Nachrichtendienst (ADN) (Germany): CP 3193, Luanda; telex 3323; Correspondent GUDRUN GROSS.

Informatsionnoye Telegrafnoye Agentstvo Rossii—Telegrafnoye Agentstvo Suverennykh Stran (ITAR—TASS) (Russia): Rua Marechal Tito 75, CP 3209, Luanda; tel. (2) 342524; telex 3244; Correspondent VLADIMIR BORISOVICH BUYANOV.

Inter Press Service (IPS) (Italy): c/o Centro de Imprensa Anibal de Melo, Rua Cequeira Lukoki 124, Luanda; tel. (2) 334895; fax: (2) 393445; Correspondent CHRIS SIMPSON.

Prensa Latina (Cuba): Rua D. Miguel de Melo 92-2, Luanda; tel. (2) 336804; telex 3253; Chief Correspondent LUÍS MANUEL SÁEZ.

Reuters (UK): c/o Centro de Imprensa Anibal de Melo, Rua Cequeira Lukoki 124, Luanda; tel. (2) 334895; fax (2) 393445; Correspondent CRISTINA MULLER.

Rossiyskoye Informatsionnoye Agentstvo—Novosti (RIA—Novosti) (Russia): Luanda; Chief Officer VLADISLAV Z. KOMAROV.

Xinhua (New China) News Agency (People's Republic of China): Rua Karl Marx 57-3, andar E, Bairro das Ingombotas, Zona 4, Luanda; tel. (2) 332415; telex 4054; Correspondent ZHAO XIAOZHONG.

Publishers

Empresa Distribuidora Livreira (EDIL), UEE: Rua da Missão 107, CP 1245, Luanda; tel. (2) 334034.

Neográfica, SARL: CP 6518, Luanda; publ. *Novembro*.

Nova Editorial Angolana, SARL: CP 1225, Luanda; f. 1935; general and educational; Man. Dir POMBO FERNANDES.

Offsetográfica Gráfica Industrial Lda: CP 911, Benguela; tel. 32568; f. 1966; Man. FERNANDO MARTINS.

Government Publishing House

Imprensa Nacional, UEE: CP 1306, Luanda; f. 1845; Gen. Man. Dr ANTÓNIO DUARTE DE ALMEIDA E CARMO.

Radio and Television

In 1994 there were an estimated 320,000 radio receivers and 70,000 television receivers in use.

RADIO

Rádio Nacional de Angola: Rua Comandante Jika, CP 1329, Luanda; tel. (2) 320192; telex 3066; fax (2) 324647; broadcasts in Portuguese, English, French, Spanish and vernacular languages (Chokwe, Kikongo, Kimbundu, Kwanyama, Fiote, Ngangela, Luvale, Songu, Umbundu); Dir-Gen. AGOSTINHO VIEIRA LOPES.

Luanda Antena Comercial (LAC): Praceta Luther King 5, Luanda; tel. (2) 396229.

TELEVISION

Televisão Popular de Angola (TPA): Rua Ho Chi Minh, CP 2604, Luanda; tel. (2) 320025; telex 3238; fax (2) 391091; f. 1975; state-controlled; Man. Dir CARLOS CUNHA.

Finance

(cap. = capital; res = reserves; dep. = deposits; m. = million; brs = branches; amounts in old kwanza)

BANKING

All banks were nationalized in 1975. In 1995 the Government authorized the creation of private banks.

Central Bank

Banco Nacional de Angola: Avda 4 de Fevereiro 151, CP 1298, Luanda; tel. (2) 399141; telex 3005; fax (2) 393179; f. 1976 to replace Banco de Angola; bank of issue; cap. and res 7,657m.; dep. 111,975m. (1983); Gov. SEBASTIÃO BASTOS LAVRADOR.

Commercial Banks

Banco de Crédito Comercial e Industrial: CP 1395, Luanda.

Banco de Poupança e Crédito (BPC): Largo Saydi Mingas, CP 1343, Luanda; tel. (2) 339158; telex 4149; fax (2) 393790; cap. 10,000m. (Dec. 1992); Chair. AMILCAR S. AZEVEDO SILVA; brs throughout Angola.

Caixa de Crédito Agro-Pecuario e Pescas (CCAPP): f. 1991; assumed commercial operations of Banco Nacional de Angola in 1996.

Development Bank

Banco de Comércio e Indústria: Avda 4 de Fevereiro 86, CP 1395, Luanda; tel. (2) 333684; telex 2009; fax (2) 333823; f. 1991; provides loans to businesses in all sectors; cap. 1,000m., dep. 424,591.3m. (1992); Chair. PEDRO MAIANGALA PUNA; 2 brs.

Investment Bank

African Investment Bank: Luanda; f. 1996; Govt of Angola holds 39% share of US $35m. joint capital stock.

Foreign Banks

Banco Espírito Santo e Comercial de Lisboa SA: 5-3°, Rua Cirilo da Conceição Silva, CP 1471, Luanda; tel. (2) 392287; telex 3400; fax (2) 391484; Rep. JOSÉ RIBEIRO DA SILVA.

Banco de Fomento e Exterior SA: Edifício BPC, 7° andar, Rua Dr Alfredo Troni, Luanda; Man. TERESA MATEUS.

Banco Totta e Açores SA: Avda 4 de Fevereiro 99, CP 1231, Luanda; tel. (2) 334257; telex 2015; fax (2) 333233; Gen. Man. Dr MÁRIO NELSON MAXIMINO.

INSURANCE

Empresa Nacional de Seguros e Resseguros de Angola (ENSA), UEE: Avda 4 de Fevereiro 93, CP 5778, Luanda; tel. (2) 332991; telex 3087.

Trade and Industry

SUPERVISORY BODY

National Supplies Commission: Luanda; f. 1977 to combat sabotage and negligence.

CHAMBERS OF COMMERCE

Angolan Chamber of Commerce and Industry: Largo do Kinaxixi 14, 1° andar, CP 92, Luanda; tel. (2) 344506; telex 3283.

Associação Comercial de Luanda: Edifício Palácio de Comércio, 1° andar, CP 1275, Luanda; tel. (2) 322453.

STATE TRADING ORGANIZATIONS

Angomédica, UEE: Rua Dr Américo Boavida 85/87, CP 2698, Luanda; tel. (2) 332945; telex 4195; f. 1981 to import pharmaceutical goods; Gen. Dir Dr A. PITRA.

Direcção dos Serviços de Comércio (Dept of Trade): Largo Diogo Cão, CP 1337, Luanda; f. 1970; brs throughout Angola.

Epmel, UEE: Rua Karl Marx 35–37, Luanda; tel. (2) 330943; industrial agricultural machinery.

Exportang, UEE: Rua dos Enganos 1A, CP 1000, Luanda; tel. (2) 332363; telex 3318; co-ordinates exports.

Importang, UEE: Calçada do Município 10, CP 1003, Luanda; tel. (2) 337994; telex 3169; f. 1977; co-ordinates majority of imports; Dir-Gen. SIMÃO DIOGO DA CRUZ.

Maquimport, UEE: Rua Rainha Ginga 152, CP 2975, Luanda; tel. (2) 339044; telex 4175; f. 1981 to import office equipment.

Mecanang, UEE: Rua dos Enganos, 1°–7° andar, CP 1347, Luanda; tel. (2) 390644; telex 4021; f. 1981 to import agricultural and construction machinery, tools and spare parts.

STATE INDUSTRIAL ENTERPRISES

Companhia do Açúcar de Angola: 77 Rua Direita, Luanda; production of sugar.

Companhia Geral dos Algodões de Angola (COTONANG): Avda da Boavista, Luanda; production of cotton textiles.

Empresa Abastecimento Técnico Material (EMATEC), UEE: Largo Rainha Ginga 3, CP 2952, Luanda; tel. (2) 338891; telex 3349; technical and material suppliers to the Ministry of Defence.

Empresa Açucareira Centro (OSUKA), UEE: Estrada Principal do Lobito, CP 37, Catumbela; tel. 24681; telex 08268; sugar industry.

Empresa Açucareira Norte (ACUNOR), UEE: Rua Robert Shilds, Caxito, Bengo; tel. 71720; sugar production.

Empresa Angolana de Embalagens (METANGOL), UEE: Rua Estrada do Cacuaco, CP 151, Luanda; tel. (2) 370680; production of non-specified metal goods.

Empresa de Cimento de Angola (CIMANGOLA), UEE: Avda 4 de Fevereiro 42, Luanda; tel. (2) 371190; telex 3142; f. 1954; 69% state-owned; cement production; exports to several African countries.

Empresa de Construção de Edificações (CONSTROI), UEE: Rua Alexandre Peres, CP 2566, Luanda; tel. (2) 333930; telex 3165; construction.

Empresa de Pesca de Angola (PESCANGOLA), UEE: Luanda; f. 1981; state fishing enterprise, responsible to Ministry of Fisheries.

Empresa de Rebenefício e Exportação do Café de Angola (CAFANGOL), UEE: Avda 4 de Fevereiro 107, CP 342, Luanda; tel. (2) 337916; telex 2137; f. 1983; nat. coffee-processing and trade org.

Empresa de Tecidos de Angola (TEXTANG), UEE: Rua N'gola Kiluanji-Kazenga, CP 5404, Luanda; tel. (2) 381134; telex 4062; production of textiles.

Empresa Nacional de Cimento (ENCIME), UEE: CP 157, Lobito; tel. (711) 2325; cement production.

Empresa Nacional de Comercialização e Distribuição de Produtos Agrícolas (ENCODIPA): Luanda; central marketing agency for agricultural produce; numerous brs throughout Angola.

Empresa Nacional de Construções Eléctricas (ENCEL), UEE: Rua Comandante Che Guevara 185/7, Luanda; tel. (2) 391630; fax (2) 331411; f. 1982; electric energy.

Empresa Nacional de Diamantes de Angola (ENDIAMA), UEE: Rua Major Kanhangulo 100, Luanda; tel. (2) 392336; telex 3046; fax (2) 337276; f. 1981 as the sole diamond-mining concession; commenced operations 1986; Dir-Gen. AUGUSTO PAULINO ALMEIDA NETO.

Empresa Nacional de Electricidade (ENE), UEE: Edifício Geominas, 6°–7° andar, CP 772, Luanda; tel. (2) 326582; telex 3170; fax (2) 323382; f. 1980; production and distribution of electricity; Dir-Gen. Eng. MARIO FERNANDO PONTES MOREIRA FONTES.

Empresa Nacional de Ferro de Angola (FERRANGOL): Rua João de Barros 26, CP 2692, Luanda; tel. (2) 373800; iron production; Dir ARMANDO DE SOUSA (MACHADINHO).

Empresa Nacional de Manutenção (MANUTECNICA), UEE: Rua 7, Avda do Cazenga 10, CP 3508, Luanda; tel. (2) 383646; assembly of machines and specialized equipment for industry.

Empresa Publica de Telecomunicações (EPTEL), UEE: Rua I Congresso 26, CP 625, Luanda; tel. (2) 392285; telex 3012; fax (2) 391688; international telecommunications.

Empresa Texteis de Angola (ENTEX), UEE: Avda Comandante Kima Kienda, CP 5720, Luanda; tel. (2) 336182; telex 3086; weaving and tissue finishing.

Fina Petróleos de Angola SARL: CP 1320, Luanda; tel. (2) 336855; telex 3246; fax (2) 391031; f. 1957; petroleum production, refining and exploration; operates Luanda petroleum refinery, Petrangol, with capacity of 32,000 b/d; also operates Quinfuquena terminal; Man. Dir CARLOS ALVES.

Siderurgia Nacional, UEE: CP Zona Industrial do Forel das Lagostas, Luanda; tel. (2) 373028; telex 3178; f. 1963, nationalized 1980; steelworks and rolling mill plant.

Sociedade Nacional de Combustíveis de Angola (SONANGOL): Rua I Congresso do MPLA, CP 1318, Luanda; tel. (2) 331690; telex 3148; f. 1976 for exploration, production and refining of crude petroleum, and marketing and distribution of petroleum products; sole concessionary in Angola, supervises on- and offshore operations of foreign petroleum cos; holds majority interest in jt ventures with Cabinda Gulf Oil Co (Cabgoc), Fina Petróleos de Angola and Texaco Petróleos de Angola; Dir-Gen. JOAQUIM DAVID.

Sociedade Unificada de Tabacos de Angola, Lda (SUT): Rua Deolinda Rodrigues 530/537, CP 1263, Luanda; tel. (2) 360180; telex 3237; fax (2) 362138; f. 1919; tobacco products; Gen. Man. Dr MANUEL LAMAS.

MAJOR INDUSTRIAL COMPANY

Cabinda Gulf Oil Co (Cabgoc): CP 2950, Luanda; tel. (2) 392646; telex 3167; wholly-owned subsidiary of Chevron Corpn (USA): undertakes exploration and production of petroleum in Cabinda province, in assen with SONANGOL, which holds a 51% interest in these jt ventures; other partners incl. Elf Petroleum (Angola) (10%) and Agip Angola Ltd (9.8%); Dir M. PUCKETT.

TRADE UNIONS

Angolan General Independent and Free Trade Union Confederation: Chair. MANUEL DIFUILA.

União Nacional de Trabalhadores Angolanos (UNTA) (National Union of Angolan Workers): Avda 4 de Fevereiro 210, CP 28, Luanda; telex 3387; f. 1960; Sec.-Gen. PASCOAL LUVUALU; 600,000 mems.

Transport

The transport infrastructure has been severely dislocated by the civil war.

RAILWAYS

The total length of track operated was 2,952 km in 1987. There are plans to extend the Namibe line beyond Menongue and to construct north–south rail links.

Caminhos de Ferro de Angola: Avda 4 de Fevereiro 42, CP 1250-C, Luanda; tel. (2) 339794; telex 3224; fax (2) 339976; f. 1975; nat. network operating four fmrly independent systems covering 2,952 track-km; Nat. Dir R. M. DA CONCEIÇÃO JUNIOR.

Amboim Railway: Porto Amboim; f. 1922; 123 track-km; Dir A. GUIA.

Benguela Railway (Companhia do Caminho de Ferro de Benguela): Rua Praça 11 Novembro 3, CP 32, Lobito; tel. (711) 22645; telex 2922; fax (711) 22865; f. 1903, line completed 1928; owned 90% by Tank Consolidated Investments (a subsidiary of Société Générale de Belgique), 10% by Govt of Angola; line carrying passenger and freight traffic from the port of Lobito across Angola, via Huambo and Luena, to the border of the Democratic Republic of the Congo (fmrly Zaire) where it connects with that country's railway system, which, in turn, links with Zambia Railways, thus providing the shortest west coast route for central African trade; 1,394 track-km; guerrilla operations by UNITA suspended all international traffic from 1975, with only irregular services from Lobito to Huambo being operated; a declaration of intent to reopen the cross-border lines was signed in April 1987 by Angola, Zambia and Zaire, and the rehabilitation of the railway was a priority of a 10-year programme, planned by the SADCC (now SADC), to develop the 'Lobito corridor'; In 1997 an Italian company, Tor di Vale, began a US $450m. programme of repairs to the railway. Minimum repairs allowing the resumption of freight traffic were expected to take three years to complete, to be followed by further modernization, including the reconstruction of 22 passenger stations; Dir-Gen. LUKOKI SEBASTIÃO.

Luanda Railway (Empresa de Caminho de Ferro de Luanda, UEE): CP 1250-C, Luanda; tel. (2) 370061; telex 3108; f. 1886; serves an iron, cotton and sisal-producing region between Luanda and Malanje; reconstruction of Luanda-Dombo rail link completed April 1997, rehabilitation of Dombo-Malanje section due for completion end 1997; 536 track-km; Man. A. ALVARO AGANTE.

Namibe Railway: CP 130, Lubango; f. 1905; main line from Namibe to Menongue, via Lubango; br. lines to Chibia and iron ore mines at Cassinga; 899 track-km; Gen. Man. J. SALVADOR.

ROADS

In 1995 Angola had 72,626 km of roads, of which 7,955 km were main roads and 15,571 km were secondary roads. About 25% of roads were paved. In 1997 the state-owned road construction and maintenance company, the Instituto de Estradas de Angola, reported that 80% of the country's road network was in disrepair and that the cost of rebuilding the roads and bridges damaged during the civil conflict would total some US $4,000m.

SHIPPING

The main harbours are at Lobito, Luanda and Namibe; the commercial port of Porto Amboim, in Cuanza-Sul province, has been closed for repairs since 1984. The expansion of port facilities in Cabinda was due to begin in late 1995 and was expected to be completed within two years. In May 1983 a regular shipping service began to operate between Luanda and Maputo (Mozambique). Under the emergency transport programme launched in 1988, refurbishment work was to be undertaken on the ports of Luanda and Namibe. The first phase of a 10-year SADCC (now SADC) programme to develop the 'Lobito corridor', for which funds were pledged in January 1989, was to include the rehabilitation of the ports of Lobito and Benguela.

Angonave—Linhas Marítimas de Angola, UEE: Rua Serqueira 31, CP 5953, Luanda; tel. (2) 330144; telex 3313; national shipping line; Dir-Gen. FRANCISCO VENÂNCIO.

Cabotang—Cabotagem Nacional Angolana, UEE: Avda 4 de Fevereiro 83A, Luanda; tel. (2) 373133; telex 3007; operates off the coasts of Angola and Mozambique; Dir-Gen. JOÃO OCTAVIO VAN-DÚNEM.

Empresa Portuaria do Lobito, UEE: Avda da Independência, CP 16, Lobito; tel. (711) 2710; telex 8233; long-distance sea transport.

Empresa Portuaria de Moçâmedes—Namibe, UEE: Rua Pedro Benje 10A and 10C, CP 49, Namibe; tel. (64) 60643; long-distance sea transport; Dir HUMBERTO DE ATAIDE DIAS.

Linhas Marítimas de Angola, UEE: Rua Serqueira 31, CP 5953, Luanda; tel. (2) 30144; telex 3313.

Secil Marítima SARL, UEE: Avda 4 de Fevereiro 42, 1° andar, CP 5910, Luanda; tel. (2) 335230; telex 3060.

CIVIL AVIATION

Air Nacoia: Rua Comandante Che Guevara 67, 1° andar, Luanda; tel. and fax (2) 395477; f. 1993; Pres. SALVADOR SILVA.

TAAG—Linhas Aéreas de Angola: Rua da Missão 123, CP 79, Luanda; tel. (2) 332485; telex 3442; fax (2) 393548; f. 1939; internal scheduled passenger and cargo services, and services from Luanda to destinations within Africa and to Europe, South America and the Caribbean; Chair. JÚLIO SAMPAIO ALMEIDA; Gen. Dir ABEL ANTÓNIO LOPES.

Angola Air Charter: Aeroporto Internacional 4 de Fevereiro, CP 3010, Luanda; tel. (2) 330994; fax (2) 392229; subsidiary of TAAG.

Transafrik International: Rua Joaquim Kapango, CP 2839, Luanda; tel. (2) 352141; telex 4159; fax (2) 351723; f. 1986; operates contract cargo services mainly within Africa; Man. Dir ERICH F. KOCH; Gen. Man. PIMENTAL ARAUJO.

Tourism

National Tourist Agency: Palácio de Vidro, CP 1240, Luanda; tel. (2) 372750.

Defence

In December 1990 the governing party, the Movimento Popular de Libertação de Angola—Partido do Trabalho (MPLA—PT), agreed to terminate its direct link with the armed forces. In accordance with the peace agreement concluded by the government and the União Nacional para a Independência Total de Angola (UNITA) in May 1991 (see Recent History), a new 50,000-strong national army, the Forças Armadas de Angola (FAA), was to be established, comprising equal numbers of government forces, the Forças Armadas Populares de Libertação de Angola (FAPLA), and UNITA soldiers. The formation of the FAA was to coincide with the holding of a general election in late September 1992. Pending the general election, a cease-fire between FAPLA and UNITA forces, which commenced in mid-May 1991, was monitored by a joint political and military commission, comprising representatives of the MPLA—PT, UNITA, the UN, Portugal, the USA and the USSR. This commission was to oversee the withdrawal of FAPLA and UNITA forces to specific confinement areas, to await demobilization. Although not all troops had entered the confinement areas, demobilization began in late March 1992. Military advisers from Portugal, France and the United Kingdom were to assist with the formation of the new national army. However, the demobilization process and the formation of the FAA fell behind schedule and were only partially completed by the end of September and the holding of the general election. Following the election, UNITA withdrew its troops from the FAA, alleging electoral fraud on the part of the MPLA, and hostilities resumed. Following the signing of the Lusaka peace accord in November 1994, preparations for the confinement and demobilization of troops, and the integration of the UNITA contingent into the FAA, resumed. In mid-1995 agreement was reached between the government and UNITA on the enlargement of the FAA to comprise a total of 90,000 troops, and discussions began concerning the potential formation of a fourth, non-combatant branch of the FAA, which would engage in public works projects. The internment of UNITA forces began in November 1995. In March 1996 agreement was reached that the unified FAA would include 26,300 UNITA troops. In mid-1997, following the inauguration of the government of national unity and reconciliation in April, the demobilization of government and UNITA troops and the integration of a UNITA contingent into the FAA were proceeding.

In August 1996 the FAA, which at that time was composed almost entirely of government forces, had an estimated total strength of 97,000: army 90,000, navy 1,500 and air force 5,500. In addition, there was a paramilitary force numbering an estimated 9,400. UNITA forces totalled an estimated 62,000.

Defence Expenditure: Budgeted at US $225m. for 1996.

Chief of General Staff of the Armed Forces: Gen. JOÃO BAPTISTA DE MATOS.

Education

Education is officially compulsory for eight years, between seven and 15 years of age, and is provided free of charge by the government. Primary education begins at the age of six and lasts for four years. Secondary education, beginning at the age of 10, lasts for up to seven years, comprising a first cycle of four years and a second of three years. As a proportion of the school-age population, the total enrolment at primary and secondary schools was 45% in 1991. Enrolment at primary schools stood at 989,443 in 1991/92, and that at secondary schools (including students receiving vocational instruction and teacher training) totalled 218,987. There is one university, at Luanda, with 5,736 students in 1986/87. In 1991 the government approved legislation permitting the foundation of private educational establishments.

At independence the adult illiteracy rate was over 85%, and Angola's independent economic development continues to be hampered by the widespread lack of basic skills. A national literacy campaign was launched in 1976, since when almost 1m. adults have received instruction in reading, writing and basic arithmetic. The average rate of adult illiteracy in 1990 was estimated by UNESCO to be 58.3% (males 44.4%, females 71.5%).

Bibliography

Adams, I. *The War: Its Impact and Transformation in Angola*. Bellville, South Africa, Centre for Southern African Studies, University of the Western Cape, 1996.

Bhagavan, M. R. *Angola's Political Economy: 1975–1985*. Uppsala, Scandinavian Institute of African Studies, 1986.

Birmingham, D. *Frontline Nationalism in Angola and Mozambique*. London, Currey; Trenton, NJ, Africa World Press, 1992.

Bridgland, F. *Jonas Savimbi: A Key to Africa*. Edinburgh, Mainstream, 1986.

Broadhead, S. H. *Historical Dictionary of Angola*. 3rd Edn. Metuchen, NJ, Scarecrow Press, 1992. (First edition by P. M. Martin, published 1980.)

Conçalves, J. *Economics and Politics of the Angolan Conflict: the Transition Re-Negotiated*. Bellville, South Africa, Centre for Southern Africa Studies, University of the Western Cape, 1995.

Crocker, C. A. *High Noon in Southern Africa: Making Peace in a Rough Neighbourhood*. New York, W. W. Norton, 1992.

Davidson, B. *In the Eye of the Storm: Angola's People*. London, Longman, 1972.

Ekwe-Ekwe, H. *Conflict and Intervention in Africa: Nigeria, Angola and Zaire*. London, Macmillan, 1990.

Estermann, C. *Ethnographie du sud-ouest de l'Angola*. 2 vols. Paris, Académie des Sciences d'Outre-mer, 1984.

Hart, K., and Lewis, J. (Eds). *Why Angola Matters*. London, James Currey Publishers, 1995.

Henderson, L. W. *Angola: Five Centuries of Conflict*. Ithaca, NY, Cornell University Press, 1979.

Hodges, T. *Angola to 2000: Prospects For Recovery*. London, Economist Intelligence Unit, 1993.

Konczacki, Z. A., Parpart, J. L., and Shaw, T. M. (Eds). *Studies in the Economic History of Southern Africa*. Vol. I. London, Cass, 1990.

Martin, J. W. *Political History of the Civil War in Angola, 1974–90*. New Brunswick, NJ, Transaction Publishers, 1991.

McCormick, S. H. *The Angolan Economy: Prospects for Growth in a Postwar Environment*. Washington DC, CSIS, 1994.

Minter, W. *Apartheid's Contras: An Inquiry into the Roots of War in Angola and Mozambique*. London, Zed Press, 1994.

Mohanty, S. *Political Development and Ethnic Indentity in Africa: a Study of Angola since 1960*. London, Sangham, 1992.

Nunez, B. *Dictionary of Portuguese-African Civilization*. Vol. I. London, Hans Zell, 1995.

Pélissier, R. *Explorar: Voyages en Angola*. Orgeval, Editions Pélissier, 1980.

Sogge, D. *Sustainable Peace: Angola's Recovery*. Harare, Southern African Resource and Documentation Centre, 1992.

Somerville, K. *Angola: Politics, Economics and Society*. London, Frances Pinter; Boulder, CO, Lynne Riener, 1986.

Spikes, D. *Angola and the Politics of Intervention*. Jefferson, NC, McFarland Publishers, 1993.

Steenkamp, W. *South Africa's Border War, 1966–1989*. Gibraltar, Ashanti Publishers, 1989.

United Nations. *The United Nations and the Situation in Angola, May 1991–February 1995*. New York, United Nations, 1995.

Venter, A. J. *War in Angola*. Hong Kong: Concord Publications, 1992.

Vincenti, S. *Angola e Africa do Sul*. Luanda, Eclicas do Autor, 1994.

Virmani, K. K. (Ed.) *Angola and the Super Powers*. Delhi, University of Delhi, 1989.

Wheeler, D. L., and Pélissier, R. *Angola*. London, Greenwood Press, 1978.

Wolfers, M., and Bergerol, J. *Angola in the Front Line*. London, Zed Press, 1983.

World Bank. *Angola: An Introductory Economic Review*. Washington, DC, International Bank for Reconstruction and Development, 1990.

BENIN

Physical and Social Geography

R. J. HARRISON CHURCH

The Republic of Benin, bordered on the west by Nigeria, on the east by Togo and to the north by Burkina Faso and Niger, covers an area of 112,622 sq km (43,484 sq miles). From a coastline of some 100 km on the Gulf of Guinea, the republic extends inland about 650 km to the Niger river. The population was 4,915,555 at the census of February 1992, rising to 5,561,000 at mid-1995 (according to official estimates—giving an average population density of 49.4 inhabitants per sq km). The population of Cotonou, the political capital and major port, was enumerated at 536,827 at the 1992 census, and that of Porto-Novo, the official capital, at 179,138.

The coast is a straight sand-bar, pounded by heavy surf on the seaward side and backed by one or more lagoons and former shorelines on the landward side. Rivers flow into these lagoons, Lakes Ahémé and Nokoué being estuaries of two rivers whose seaward exits are obstructed by the sand-bar. A lagoon waterway is navigable for barges to Lagos, in Nigeria.

North of Lake Nokoué the Ouémé river has a wide marshy delta, with considerable agricultural potential. Elsewhere the lagoons are backed northward by the Terre de Barre, a fertile and intensively farmed region of clay soils. North again is the seasonally flooded Lama swamp. Beyond are areas comparable with the Terre de Barre, and the realm of the pre-colonial kingdom of Dahomey.

Most of the rest of the country is underlain by Pre-Cambrian rocks, with occasional bare domes, laterite cappings on level surfaces, and poor soils. In the north-west are the Atacora mountains, whose soils, although less poor, are much eroded. On the northern borders are Primary and other sandstones, extremely infertile and short of water.

Deposits of low-grade iron ores, chromium, rutile, phosphates, kaolin and gold occur in the north of the country, but to date the lack of infrastructure has inhibited both their exploitation and a fuller investigation of Benin's potential mineral resources. The small Sémé oilfield, offshore from Cotonou, entered production in 1982. Reserves of natural gas, estimated to total 4,000m. cu m, were being evaluated in the mid-1990s. Limestone and marble are currently mined.

Southern Benin has an equatorial climate, most typical along the coast, although with a low rainfall of some 1,300 mm. Away from the coast the dry months increase until a tropical climate prevails over the northern half of the country. There a dry season alternates with a wet one, the latter being of seven months in the centre and four months in the north; the rainfall nevertheless averages 1,300 mm per year.

In the colonial period the Fon and Yoruba of the south enjoyed educational advantages and were prominent in administration throughout French West Africa. After independence many were expelled to Benin, where there is great unemployment or under-employment of literates. The northern peoples, such as the Somba and Bariba, are less Westernized.

Recent History

PIERRE ENGLEBERT

Revised for this edition by the Editor

Benin (then known as Dahomey) was formerly part of French West Africa. It became a self-governing republic within the French Community in December 1958 and an independent state on 1 August 1960. Political life in the republic was extremely unstable following independence, as regionally-based interests contended for power. Hubert Maga, a northerner, became the republic's first president following elections held in December 1960, but in October 1963 he was deposed by an army *coup d'état*, led by Col (later Gen.) Christophe Soglo. In January 1964 Soglo installed a coalition government led by Sourou-Migan Apithy, a south-easterner who had been vice-president under Maga, with Justin Ahomadegbé, who represented the interests of the south-western region, as prime minister. Intense opposition from the north, however, led to a series of political crises which resulted in army intervention and the return to power of Soglo in December 1965. A further military coup in December 1967, led by Maj. (later Lt-Col) Maurice Kouandété, installed Lt-Col Alphonse Alley as head of state. During 1967–70 three successive army-supported regimes each failed to resolve regional rivalries, and in May 1970 the army installed a civilian triumvirate comprising Ahomadegbé, Apithy and Maga.

KÉRÉKOU TAKES POWER

In October 1972 a junta, led by Maj. (later Brig.-Gen.) Mathieu Kérékou, seized power. Kérékou, a northener, established a ruling military council, comprising equal numbers of army officers from each of the three main regions, and introduced Marxism-Leninism as the national ideology. In December 1975 the country was renamed the People's Republic of Benin. Meanwhile, banking, insurance and important industrial sectors were nationalized. From 1975 Kérékou endeavoured to reform Benin's organs of state. A new ruling party, the Parti de la révolution populaire du Bénin (PRPB), was formed. A *loi fondamentale*, adopted in August 1977, defined the structure of government. The regime was 'civilianized' in November 1979, when a single list of PRPB candidates for a new Assemblée nationale révolutionnaire (ANR) was overwhelmingly endorsed by the electorate. Kérékou was himself unanimously elected president of the republic by the ANR in February 1980.

During the 1980s a more pragmatic approach to Benin's economic needs began to supplant the government's socialist philosophy. Western private investment was encouraged, and, beginning in 1982, the government undertook a reform of the largely corrupt and inefficient parastatal sector. Meanwhile, Maga, Apithy and Ahomadegbé, who had been detained in the aftermath of the October 1972 coup, were released from house arrest in 1981. Kérékou sought also to assert his personal authority over the various rival factions within the ruling élite, demoting or removing during 1982 several extreme leftist government ministers. The consolidation process continued in 1984, with the election of a new ANR. Candidates who had been proposed at public meetings were subjected to a selection process, based by the PRPB on complex socio-professional quotas within which there was undoubtedly further selection by region and ethnic background. The final list was submitted in June to the electorate, whose choice was limited to accepting or rejecting the entire list, and was approved by almost 98% of voters. In July the ANR re-elected Kérékou to the presidency for a five-year term. A presidential amnesty followed for most political prisoners (notably excluding those implicated in a raid on Cotonou by mercenaries in January 1977).

The limited economic and political liberalization of the early 1980s was accompanied by a reorientation of Benin's foreign policy at the expense of the communist bloc, aid contributions from which had declined considerably. Conversely, relations with France, Benin's principal trading partner and provider of development aid, improved following the election of François Mitterrand to the French presidency in 1981.

ECONOMIC PROBLEMS AND INTERNAL UNREST

In an attempt to reduce smuggling, Nigeria closed its border with Benin between April 1984 and March 1986, bringing recession to Benin and causing a sharp deterioration in relations between the two countries. The worsening economic crisis prompted Benin to move increasingly towards the Western bloc and the IMF, seeking increased aid and the rescheduling of Benin's external debts. France had by now replaced the USSR as the principal supplier of military equipment, while also remaining predominant in other forms of co-operation. The Kérékou regime also solicited financial support from some of the more conservative African countries, including Côte d'Ivoire, Cameroon and Gabon. Student unrest followed the announcement, in April 1985, that university graduates could no longer be guaranteed jobs by the state. Classes at the national university were suspended, and student activists were arrested. Following the release, in 1986, of 50 of those implicated in the student riots, Kérékou asserted that there remained no political prisoners in Benin, although in March 1987 a students' demonstration prompted a statement by the PRPB of its intention to suppress any 'subversive elements' within the university. Economic problems, meanwhile, exacerbated social tensions and ethnic rivalries, and Kérékou's confidence in the continuance of his regime resulted from a much-strengthened internal security network.

Kérékou resigned from the army in January 1987 to become a civilian head of state, and made efforts to restore equilibrium in both north-south and military-civilian representation. However, ensuing tensions between the government and the army culminated in an attempted *coup d'état* in March 1988. More than 150 army members were arrested in connection with the plot, which had been instigated by disaffected southerners, among them the chief of staff of the paramilitary forces. There was a further attempt to overthrow the government in June, while Kérékou was attending a regional conference in neighbouring Togo.

'CIVILIAN COUP'

A period of repression in the aftermath of the coup attempts, in conjunction with popular dissatisfaction at the government's austerity measures (imposed in accordance with the IMF stipulations), engendered an atmosphere of increased social tension and instability. In early 1989 public-sector workers took strike action in protest against protracted delays in the payment of salaries, while students boycotted classes, demanding the disbursement of delayed grants and scholarships. There was, moreover, evidence of corruption within the government and in the banking sector, as well as allegations that the government had agreed to accept shipments of hazardous waste from Western countries. None the less, at elections to the ANR in June 1989, a single list of 206 candidates was approved by almost 90% of the votes cast. In August the ANR re-elected Kérékou to the presidency for a further five-year term. A reorganized government comprised relatively fewer military officers and PRPB members; several incoming ministers were known to have expressed support for multi-party politics. In August the government announced a partial payment of salaries owed to public-sector employees. In the same month an amnesty was announced for some 200 dissidents, among them Dr Emile-Derlin Zinsou (who had been installed as president by the military in July 1968, only to be deposed in December 1969), who was now leading an opposition movement based in France. Fifty of those detained in the aftermath of the 1985 student unrest had been released in April 1989.

Although academic staff and students agreed to resume classes in October 1989, persistent social and political difficulties—including the decision by the sole official labour organization, the Union nationale des syndicats des travailleurs du Bénin (UNSTB), to sever its links with the PRPB—continued to undermine Kérékou's authority. In December, as the government's failure to pay the salaries of public-sector employees caused further disruption, the Kérékou regime yielded to demands made by the Beninois population and by the country's external creditors (notably France), announcing the abandonment of Marxism-Leninism as the state ideology. Benin's external creditors subsequently agreed to a partial funding of outstanding salaries.

A national conference of the 'active forces of the nation' was convened in Cotonou in February 1990, attended by 488 delegates representing more than 50 political organizations (including the PRPB and opposition movements, which, while still officially banned, had become increasingly active in anticipation of political change). The conference declared itself sovereign and voted to abolish the 1977 *loi fondamentale* and institutions. Pending national elections to a new legislature, the functions of the ANR were to be assumed by an interim Haut conseil de la république (HCR), which was to include the principal opposition leaders. The president of the republic was for the first time to be elected by universal suffrage, with a five-year mandate, renewable only once. The conference also designated Nicéphore Soglo, a former official of the World Bank, as interim prime minister. Kérékou was obliged to relinquish the defence portfolio to Soglo, and also to accept the conference's resolution to change the country's name to the Republic of Benin. In March 1990 an amnesty was announced for all dissidents, and a human rights commission was established. In the same month the HCR was inaugurated, and Soglo named his transitional, civilian government. In May the military prefects of Benin's six provinces were replaced by civilians, and in June the transitional government undertook an extensive restructuring of the armed forces. In August legislation was promulgated to permit the registration of political parties. Restrictions on the press were relaxed, and independent journals flourished.

Benin was thus the first sub-Saharan African country to experience a 'civilian coup': a single-party regime, dominated by the armed forces, that had assumed power following a *coup d'état*, was obliged by popular pressure to accept a return to multi-party democracy.

A draft constitution was published in May 1990, and, after some delay, was submitted to a national referendum in December. Voters were asked to choose between two versions of the constitution, one of which incorporated a clause stipulating upper and lower age-limits for presidential candidates (thereby automatically disqualifying ex-presidents Ahomadegbé, Maga and Zinsou). In all, 95.8% of those who voted gave their assent to one or other of the versions, with 79.7% of voters endorsing the document in full.

Some 24 political parties participated in the legislative election, which took place on 17 February 1991. No party or group of parties won an overall majority of the 64 seats in the national assembly, although a pro-Soglo alliance secured the greatest number of seats (12) in the new legislature. The successor party to the PRPB, the Union des forces du progrès, failed to win any seats.

The first round of the presidential election, on 10 March 1991, was contested by 13 candidates. The distribution of votes between the two leading candidates largely reflected regional ethnic divisions: Soglo, who secured 36.2% of the total, received his greatest support in the south of the country, while Kérékou, who was reported to have the support of more than 80% of voters in the north, took 27.3% of the overall vote. Soglo and Kérékou proceeded to a second round of voting, which was conducted on 24 March amid allegations of electoral malpractice, as well as violence involving supporters of the rival candidates. Despite continuing support for Kérékou in the north, Soglo (supported by most of the candidates eliminated at the first round) was elected president, securing 67.7% of the total votes cast. Before its dissolution, in late March, the HCR granted

Kérékou immunity from any legal proceedings connected with actions committed since October 1972.

THE SOGLO PRESIDENCY, 1991–96

Soglo was inaugurated as president on 4 April 1991. He subsequently relinquished the defence portfolio to his brother-in-law, Désiré Vieyra. In July the leader of the Parti du renouveau démocratique (PRD), Adrien Houngbédji, who had also contested the presidency earlier in the year, was elected speaker of the national assembly; Soglo had been known to favour a different candidate. Also in July Vieyra was promoted to the rank of senior minister, secretary-general at the office of the president of the republic.

The Soglo administration intensified efforts at economic liberalization, and also began criminal proceedings against corrupt former state officials (among them erstwhile close associates of Kérékou). During 1991–92, none the less, civil servants, resenting that salary arrears accumulated in the final years of the Kérékou regime remained unpaid, undertook intermittent industrial action.

In May 1992 several soldiers were arrested in suspicious circumstances near the presidential palace in Cotonou, accused of plotting a coup. Among those detained was Capt. Pascal Tawes, a former deputy commander of Kérékou's (now-disbanded) presidential guard. Tawes and some of his associates subsequently escaped from custody, and in August he gained control of an army base in the north; however, the rebels failed to win support from other northern garrisons, and the rebellion collapsed when the government dispatched élite paratroops to recover the captured base. One rebel was killed and about 45 mutineers were detained, although Tawes himself evaded arrest. In September 1994 Tawes and 15 others were sentenced *in absentia* to life imprisonment with hard labour, convicted of plotting to overthrow the government. Eight of those present at the trial received lesser sentences, and three defendants were acquitted.

Coalition Alliances

Although broad groupings of parties evolved, the absence of a majority party or coalition in the national assembly tended to delay the passage of legislation, a situation exacerbated by the legislature's apparent determination to assert its independence from the executive, most notably in areas of economic policy. However, the president's position was strengthened by the formation in June 1992 of Le Renouveau, a pro-Soglo majority group comprising 34 deputies from 10 parliamentary parties.

Despite the existence of legislation guaranteeing press freedom, libel proceedings were instigated during 1992–93 against several journalists who had criticized Soglo and his associates. None the less, Soglo sought to consolidate popular support for his administration, and made particular efforts to develop contacts in the north. He also displayed a conciliatory attitude towards practitioners of traditional *vodoun* religious rites, which had been discouraged under the Kérékou regime. Social unrest persisted in Cotonou, however, with government proposals for a 10% reduction in civil servants' salaries (in accordance with the economic adjustment programme) provoking a three-day strike in February 1993.

In March 1993 more than 100 prisoners escaped from detention in the south-western town of Ouidah; among them were several soldiers who were suspected of involvement in the previous year's alleged coup plot. The subsequent dismissal of the armed forces chief of staff and of other senior members of the security forces prompted the resignation of the government minister responsible for defence, who protested that Soglo had acted unconstitutionally by making new appointments without consulting him. In September Soglo announced a reorganization of the government. Vieyra (as minister of state, in charge of national defence) remained the most senior cabinet member. Members of the national assembly, who believed that Soglo had acted discourteously in leaving Benin for a private visit to Europe without first having presented the new government list to parliament, delayed the official publication of the cabinet changes for several days. In October 1993 Soglo lost his majority support in parliament after 15 members of Le Renouveau, including the group's chairman, withdrew from the coalition, alleging that the president was consistently excluding the legislature from the decision-making process. In July, meanwhile, Soglo, who had previously asserted his political neutrality, made public his membership of the (Parti de la) Renaissance du Bénin (RB), formed by his wife, Rosine, in the previous year; he was appointed leader of the RB in July 1994.

Social unrest was exacerbated by the 50% devaluation, in January 1994, of the CFA franc. Following several weeks of severe labour unrest, in March the government announced salary increases of 10% for all state employees, as well as the reintroduction of housing allowances (abolished in 1986) and an end to the eight-year 'freeze' on promotions within the civil service. The government's attempts to limit increases in spending obligations arising from the currency devaluation were threatened in July 1994, when the national assembly approved increases in wages and student grants that were in excess of those envisaged in the government's draft budget. Stating that the imbalanced budget thereby arising was not only unconstitutional, but would also, if implemented, result in the loss of funding and debt-relief already agreed with external creditors, Soglo announced that he was to impose the government's draft budget by decree. The national assembly referred the matter to the constitutional court for adjudication, and the court ruled that the presidential ordinances relating to the budget were invalid; however, it was the court's judgment that presidential recourse to the relevant article of the constitution was discretionary, and could not therefore be subject to legal control. A subsequent court ruling was that the formulation of policies relating to matters such as wage indexation was solely within the government's competence, and parliamentary amendments to the budget were thereby inferred to be unconstitutional. The payment of salary arrears from 1983–91 began in November 1994.

Electoral Tensions

Preparations for elections to the national assembly, scheduled for February 1995, were the cause of further friction between the executive and legislature. In November 1994 parliament voted to establish an independent body Commission électorale nationale autonome (CENA) to oversee the elections: the creation of such a body, which Soglo was known to oppose, was subsequently approved by the constitutional court. Soglo also opposed the planned increase in the number of parliamentary deputies from 64 to 83. Organizational difficulties twice necessitated the postponement of the legislative elections, which finally took place on 28 March. Some 31 political organizations had been authorized to participate, and a total of 5,580 candidates contested seats in the enlarged assembly. Although observers concluded that the elections had generally been conducted fairly, irregularities were apparent in several constituencies in Atlantique province, in the south, where the CENA accused polling agents of sabotage, and in the Bourgou region in the north. Provisional results indicated that, although the RB had won the largest number of seats in the legislature, opposition parties were likely, in alliance, to outnumber the president's supporters. Of the opposition parties, Houngbédji's PRD emerged as the strongest, while supporters of ex-president Kérékou, mainly representing the Front d'action pour le renouveau et le développement–Alafia (FARD–Alafia), enjoyed particular success in the north, although Kérékou himself had not actively campaigned in the elections. In mid-April the constitutional court annulled the results of voting for nine seats in Cotonou (part of the Atlantique province) and for four seats in the Bourgou region. Among those who were obliged to rerun were Rosine Soglo, who had (controversially) headed the RB list and had been elected as a deputy for Cotonou. At by-elections in May representatives of the RB (among them Rosine Soglo) were elected to five of the seats being contested in Cotonou, although one of these was immediately disqualified by the constitutional court, on the grounds that he failed to fulfil residency criteria. In June, in response to a letter in which the president of the constitutional court, Elisabeth Kayissan Pognon, had criticized the RB for organizing a demonstration in Cotonou to protest against the annulment of the by-election result, Soglo accused her of 'incitement to riot and rebellion'.

Following the elections, the RB thus held 20 seats in the national assembly, and other supporters of Soglo a total of 13. Opposition parties held a total of 49 seats, the most prominent organizations being the PRD, with 19 seats, and FARD–Alafia, with 10. Bruno Amoussou, the leader of the opposition Parti social-démocrate, was elected speaker of the legislature: Soglo's supporters had voted for Amoussou in preference to Houngbédji, who was regarded as potentially a strong challenger in the 1996 presidential election.

A new government was announced in late June 1995. Two nominated ministers did not take up their posts: one, a member of the Parti communiste du Bénin, reportedly refused to serve in a government that included the incumbent minister of the interior, security and territorial development, Antoine Gbegan, while the other, a member of the Alliance pour la démocratie et le progrès (and the sole opposition representative to be invited to join the coalition), had made his acceptance of ministerial office dependent on certain guarantees, including what he termed 'respect for the institutions of the republic' by Soglo.

From October 1995 rumours circulated of a coup plot and of attempts to sabotage a conference of heads of state and government of the Conseil permanent de la francophonie, which was due to take place in Cotonou, under the chairmanship of ex-president Zinsou, at the beginning of December. The government denied suggestions that a destabilization plot had been discovered, attributing such rumours, together with reports that Soglo was in poor health and also that Algerian fundamentalist organizations had threatened to disrupt the francophone conference, to those wishing to discredit the Soglo regime in advance of the summit and thus undermine his prospects at the forthcoming presidential election. None the less, it was confirmed that members of the military had been among several people arrested in security operations. Tensions escalated in November, following a rocket attack on the newly-built conference centre at which the francophone summit was to take place. Although the authorities dismissed the attack as a minor act of sabotage, it was announced shortly afterwards that one person had been killed and seven arrested, and that munitions stolen during a raid on the Ouidah barracks in early 1994 had been recovered, as part of operations to apprehend the perpetrators of the rocket attack. Later in November 1995 Soulé Dankoro, a former government minister under Kérékou, was arrested (together with a business executive who had earlier served a prison sentence in connection with violence in northern Benin at the time of the 1991 presidential election), accused of assisting in the preparation of the attack.

Presidential Candidacies

Despite Kérékou's effective withdrawal from active politics following his defeat in 1991, the success of his supporters at the 1995 parliamentary elections prompted speculation that he might again contest the presidency in 1996. While Soglo's economic policies had earned him the respect of the international financial community, there was disquiet within Benin that strong growth had been achieved at the expense of social concerns; moreover, criticism was increasingly levelled at what was termed the regime's 'authoritarian drift' and alleged nepotism. Tribute was paid, meanwhile, to what was regarded as Kérékou's dignified acceptance of the decisions of the 1990 national conference and of his 1991 electoral defeat. By the time Kérékou officially announced, in January 1996, that he was again to contest the presidency, promising greater emphasis on social issues, it was widely accepted that his would be the most powerful challenge to Soglo. Amoussou and Houngbédji were among those who had already announced their candidatures. In February Soglo formally announced that he would seek a second mandate, asserting that the economic successes now attained would henceforth permit his administration to concentrate on addressing unemployment and other social problems exacerbated by the adjustment policies of the first half of the decade.

Renewed institutional conflict followed the national assembly's decision, in late December 1995, to delay ratification of the third phase of the country's structural adjustment programme, a particularly contentious element of which was the planned restructuring of Sonacop, the state company responsible for the distribution of petroleum products. Soglo warned that failure to ratify the programme could result in the suspension of co-operation by the Bretton Woods institutions and in the loss of much-needed bilateral development assistance, and potentially also hinder preparations for the presidential election. None the less, deputies twice subsequently rejected ratification of a modified programme, and also rejected the government's draft budget for 1996, causing Soglo to announce that, in the national interest, he was to implement the budget and adjustment programme by decree.

The first round of the presidential election, on 3 March 1996, was contested by seven candidates. As had been expected, Soglo and Kérékou emerged as the leading candidates, although Soglo's supporters alleged widespread vote-rigging. Some 22.8% of the votes cast were subsequently invalidated by the constitutional court prior to the announcement, five days after the poll, of the official results. Soglo secured 35.7% of the valid votes and Kérékou 33.9%, followed by Houngbédji (19.7%) and Amoussou (7.8%). The rate of participation by voters was high, at 86.9%. Most of the defeated candidates quickly expressed their support for Kérékou, among them Houngbédji (who had in 1975 been sentenced to death *in absentia* for his part in a plot to overthrow Kérékou's military regime). A government decision to delay the second round of voting by four days, to 21 March (owing to the late proclamation of the results of the first poll), was overturned by the constitutional court following an appeal by Kérékou's supporters, and the vote was set for 18 March. Soglo's supporters asserted that indications of a clear victory for Kérékou at this round were based on incomplete results and attributable to 'massive fraud', and Soglo himself spoke of an international plot to end democracy in Benin. Kérékou's supporters denounced delays in the publication of the official results: although collated by the national statistical service, it appeared that the results of voting had not been transmitted to the CENA, while a senior official of the statistical service was arrested on suspicion of 'issuing false documents and incitement to rebellion'. International monitors, meanwhile, stated that any irregularities in the conduct of voting in no way affected the overall credibility of the result.

Prior to the official announcement of the second-round results, a gun attack was reported on the home of a member of the constitutional court. (Earlier in the month members of the court had received intimidatory letters, signed by 'southerners in rebellion', accusing them of plotting against democracy.) Soglo meanwhile dismissed Vieyra and the presidential chief of staff. On 24 March 1996 the constitutional court announced that Kérékou had received the support of 52.5% of voters. Some 78.1% of those eligible had voted, and less than 3% of the votes had been invalidated. Kérékou had won the support of a majority of voters in four of the country's six provinces, and had secured more than 90% of the votes in his home province of Atakora; Soglo had won some 80% of the votes in his native Zou province, in central Benin, and (despite a high rate of unemployment) had also performed strongly in Atlantique province. Soglo, who continued to claim victory, announced that he was contesting the outcome on several counts. A statement issued by the constitutional court in late March, denouncing pressure brought to bear on its members by Soglo and his associates, was rejected by Soglo's aides as a deliberate attempt to tarnish the president's reputation. On 1 April the court announced that it had rejected all appeals against the outcome of the election, and accordingly confirmed Kérékou's victory; Soglo conceded defeat the following day.

THE RETURN OF KÉRÉKOU

At his inauguration, on 4 April 1996 (which was not attended by Soglo), Kérékou undertook to strive for national reconciliation. Having sought authorization by the constitutional court for the appointment of a prime minister (provision for such a post is not stipulated in the constitution), he named Houngbédji as premier in a government mostly composed of representatives of those parties that had supported his presidential campaign; a former associate of Soglo, Moïse Mensah, was named minister of finance. Kérékou assumed personal responsibility for defence. The government's stated priorities were to be to strengthen the rule of law, economic revival and social development. Despite Kérékou's campaign pledges to halt privatization, a new funding arrangement was approved by the IMF in the following month.

Seven of those detained in late 1995, including Soulé Dankoro, were released on bail in late April 1996. The authorities stated, none the less, that no political pressure had been exerted to secure their release, and it was emphasized that applications for bail made by five other defendants had been rejected. In September four defendants were convicted of involvement in the rocket attack: three were sentenced to five years' enforced labour, and the fourth to a year's imprisonment. A fifth defendant was sentenced *in absentia* to 15 years' imprisonment.

Soglo returned to Benin in early August 1996, having spent the previous four months in the USA and France. Speaking in Washington, DC, in mid-June, he had expressed his desire to lead Benin's opposition. In an article written for *The Washington Post,* moreover, Soglo subsequently indicated his recognition of the legitimacy of Kérékou's election to the presidency.

A national economic conference took place in mid-December 1996, with the aim of identifying, and ensuring consensus regarding, Benin's economic aims. The six-day meeting was attended by some 500 delegates from all sectors, including representatives of commerce, industry, trade unions and political organizations. Addressing the conference, Kérékou expressed his belief that the further development of the private sector was essential to Benin's future economic prosperity. He also emphasized his commitment to eliminating corruption.

EXTERNAL AFFAIRS

Benin's international standing was enhanced following the introduction of democratic reforms, and the success of the Soglo regime's economic liberalization measures in promoting strong growth earned the respect of the international financial community. In the course of his numerous regional and overseas official visits, Soglo repeatedly appealed to Western donors to provide financial support for those African countries undergoing the transition to political pluralism. Soglo's relations with France under Presidents François Mitterrand and (subsequently) Jacques Chirac were generally close. Visiting France in June 1995, Soglo was received by Chirac, and in July Soglo travelled to Yamoussoukro, in Côte d'Ivoire, as part of a delegation of regional heads of state that met Chirac during his first visit to sub-Saharan Africa since his election to the presidency. France provided some 30m. French francs for the construction of Cotonou's new conference centre, in preparation for the 1995 summit meeting of the Conseil permanent de la francophonie. However, the 'northern countries' accused by Soglo of influencing his defeat in the 1996 presidential elections apparently included France and other countries that had seemingly supported his regime.

Following Kérékou's election to the presidency in March 1996, there was initial uncertainty regarding his government's likely conduct of external political and economic relations. While he had undoubtedly abandoned his former commitment to Marxist economic theory, Kérékou's campaign pledges to halt privatization and devote increased resources to social and welfare projects raised doubts as to the future conduct of relations with the IMF (which stipulated continued spending restraint as a precondition for assistance) and thus with other creditors. None the less, the conclusion of the new agreement with the IMF in August indicated a pragmatic approach to international economic relations. France was swift to acknowledge the legitimacy of Kérékou's election. Kérékou made an official visit to that country in October, during which he was received by President Jacques Chirac, by the prime minister, Alain Juppé, and by other senior state officials. During the visit, Kérékou asked for French assistance in transferring the economic capital from Cotonou to the administrative capital, Porto-Novo. Houngbédji visited France in December, and in February 1997 the French minister-delegate responsible for co-operation, Jacques Godfrain, visited Benin, pledging assistance for the economic priorities identified at the recent national economic conference.

The new regime also sought to foster close regional relations. Kérékou led a government delegation to Togo in September 1996; he and the Togolese president, Gnassingbe Eyadéma, discussed issues of mutual concern, including efforts to combat the proliferation of organized crime and banditry in the sub-region. Benin, Burkina Faso and Togo conducted joint military exercises in March 1997. As part of its stated policy of countering violent crime in Benin, the Kérékou administration expelled some 700 foreign nationals in mid-October 1996. In August the governments of Benin and Nigeria had agreed to review the demarcation of disputed areas of their joint border.

Recognition of the 'Sahrawi Arab Democratic Republic', accorded by the military regime in 1976, was withdrawn in March 1997. The new Kérékou administration appeared at this time to be developing close relations with Morocco.

Economy

EDITH HODGKINSON

The dominant characteristics of the economy of Benin are its dualism and its dependence on Nigeria. There is an official, documented sector covering government and relatively modern industry and agriculture, and an unofficial, largely unrecorded sector consisting of basic food production and cross-border trade with Nigeria. Changes in the rate of economic growth are largely determined by trends in Nigeria. Overall economic growth has been slow, with the annual increase in Benin's gross domestic product (GDP) averaging only 2.0%, in real terms, in 1980–90. During this period the performance of the Beninois economy fluctuated fairly widely. Beginning in 1985 Benin suffered a period of economic depression, caused by the closure of the border with Nigeria (which was in force between April 1984 and March 1986), by the continuing economic recession in Nigeria and by the decline in international prices for Benin's major export commodities, cotton and petroleum, while the strengthening of the CFA franc in relation to the US dollar reduced the proceeds from these commodities in local currency terms. The 1990s have seen an improvement in economic performance, with GDP growth averaging 4.7 per year in 1991–96. This has owed much to good harvests in almost every year, but a significant contribution was also made by the complete reversal in economic policy in 1990–91 under the new civilian regime (see Recent History), which aimed to enhance the role of the private sector and to reduce government participation in production. Bolstered by the significant rescheduling of debt that was agreed by bilateral official creditors in December 1991 (see below) and an enhanced structural adjustment facility at the IMF for the period 1993–95, the administration of Nicéphore Soglo aimed to set Benin on the path to sustainable economic growth, with a target of annual GDP growth of 4% during this period. The domestic political acceptability of the programme of reform was improved by the IMF's agreement to redundancy payments for civil servants and parastatal workers, as well as the rehabilitation of the social infrastructure.

However, the context for the programme was fundamentally modified by the devaluation, by 50%, of the CFA franc in January 1994. This had severe short-term costs, in the form of a sudden increase in the rate of inflation which the government was not fully able to counter by the imposition of price controls. Inflation accelerated from an almost negligible rate in 1993 to an average of 38.5% in 1994. Moreover, the domestic manufacturing sector, which is heavily dependent on foreign supplies of raw materials and intermediates, was adversely affected by the overnight doubling of import costs. None the less, the devaluation had some positive effects—stimulating export growth (since producers of export goods, in particular agricultural commodities, command more in local currency terms) and demand for local products, notably foodstuffs. With increased inflows of foreign aid to allow the maintenance of imports that are essential for the economy's expansion, in conjunction with particularly good cotton crops, GDP growth increased from 3.2% in 1994 (slightly below target) to 6.3% in 1995. However, the reduction in household income that devaluation entailed—even if the erosion was less marked in 1995, when average inflation declined to 14.5%—had alienated popular support for the Soglo regime, and it was the urban areas (traditionally a stronghold for the president) that had borne the brunt of the adjustment. Devaluation thus had a high political cost, which was paid by President Soglo when he was defeated in the 1966 election. Contrary to some expectations the new Kérékou administration is far from reverting to the Marxist economic policies of the past. Liberalization is now well entrenched in many sectors, and, in view of the country's dependence on foreign assistance and the need to generate sustainable, long-term growth so as to fulfil its promises of improved living standards and more jobs, the government has been anxious to maintain a co-operative relationship with the IMF. Within months of Kérékou taking power, the terms were agreed for an Enhanced Structural Adjustment Facility (ESAF) to replace that which had expired in the final months of the Soglo regime. The programme the funding supports aims at a steady improvement in economic growth, from 5.8% in 1996 to 6.2% in 1999, with inflation in the low single digits and both fiscal and current-account deficits falling as a ratio of GDP.

POPULATION AND EMPLOYMENT

Despite its relative lack of urbanization in previous decades, Benin has for some time had a high standard of education; the existence of a large élite—for whom employment cannot easily be found in an underdeveloped, slowly-growing economy—was at the root of Benin's unstable political situation in the years after independence. Another contributory factor, again exacerbated by the unsatisfactory economic situation, is the rift between three clearly-defined regions: Parakou and the north, Abomey and the centre-south, and the narrow coastal zone around Cotonou (the main port) and Porto-Novo (the official capital). Almost three-quarters of the country's inhabitants—the population was estimated to total 5.70m. at mid-1996—reside in the southern regions, giving a population density there of more than 120 per sq km—one of the highest in western Africa. Recent years have seen a pronounced movement to the towns. About 40% of the inhabitants are urban, and the population of Cotonou was 533,000 at the 1992 census. While agriculture, livestock and fishing engage an estimated 70% of the work-force, the public sector has also been a significant source of employment, accounting for about one-half of wage and salary earners. This proportion will have been declining under the privatization and fiscal stabilization programmes implemented by the Soglo administration and continued by its successor.

AGRICULTURE

The economy is dependent on the agricultural sector, which accounts for about two-fifths of GDP and occupied some 56% of the working population at the time of the 1992 census. Output of the major food crops has been rising strongly since the drought of 1981–83, reflecting both improved climatic conditions and a transfer of emphasis from cash crops to the cultivation of staple foods. Production levels since 1987/88 have been 50%–100% higher than 1983/84 figures. In 1994/95 output of cassava was 1,145,800 metric tons, yams 1,250,500, maize 491,500 and millet and sorghum 137,600 tons. With the area under food crops increasing substantially in 1995/96, in response to the impact of devaluation, production of both traditional and non-traditional food crops—notably rice (to substitute for imports), tomatoes, beans and onions—were likely to have risen. Benin, which is already self-sufficient in staple foods, is thus expanding its exports of foodstuffs, particularly to Nigeria.

In the past the major cash crop was oil palm, which remains the principal tree crop. Output of palm products, which was formerly based on natural plantations covering 400,000 ha, benefited in the 1970s from intensive cultivation on some 30,000 ha of industrial plantations, partly financed by France's Fonds d'aide et de coopération and by the European Development Fund (EDF). Production of palm kernels was estimated at 70,000 tons in 1976, and palm oil at more than 23,000 tons. However, output has since fallen, owing to low producer prices, with marketed production of palm kernels declining to an average of only about 3,000 tons per year by the early 1990s, while output of palm oil was last recorded in 1987/88, at 12,500 tons. In both cases the figures for marketed production were distorted by the incidence of smuggling from Nigeria (in order to secure payment in the 'hard currency' CFA franc, rather than in the unstable naira).

The most valuable commercial crop is cotton, the production of which expanded rapidly in the mid- and late 1980s, and which now constitutes by far the most important export commodity. Benin's annual output of unginned (seed) cotton increased from 9,000 tons in 1966/67 to 50,000 tons in 1972/73, as cultivation was established in the northern areas, supported by funds from the World Bank. Output declined in subsequent years, to an annual average of around 14,000 tons in the late 1970s and early 1980s. The overall decline in cotton production was partly the result of the departure of a French cotton company and partly the result of poor marketing organization and smuggling to neighbouring countries, because of low producer prices locally. However, with new investment in this sector, output tripled between 1983/84 and 1986/87, reaching 131,262 tons in the latter year. After a brief downturn in 1987/88, in response to the fall in international prices, the crop resumed its expansion in subsequent years, reaching 277,303 tons in 1993/94. This result was attributable to favourable weather conditions, which consolidated the benefits of an increase in the area under cultivation, while higher producer prices sustained output in 1994/95 and generated another rise in 1995/96, to a record 365,000 tons.

Whereas cotton is grown mainly in the north, other cash crops are produced in the south, where there are two rainy seasons. These include coffee, cocoa, groundnuts and shea-nuts (karité nuts). Marketed production of cocoa and coffee tends to vary widely, since most of the recorded production is normally not from Benin but originates in Nigeria. Production of cash crops was in decline because official purchase prices did not keep pace with the rise in the cost of living, prompting farmers to switch to subsistence food crops, or to sell their output outside official channels, on the local 'black market' or across the border in Nigeria. This situation has to some extent been remedied by the 1994 devaluation, whose doubling of the local-currency value of foreign earnings has benefited producers.

Exploitation of timber resources (mainly for fuel) is still limited, though rising, with annual roundwood removals increasing from 2.05m. cu m in 1970 to an estimated 5.5m. cu m in 1993. A reafforestation programme, which was inaugurated in 1985 to counter desertification, is concentrating on fast-growing species around populated areas. Livestock farming is practised in its traditional form in the north. In 1994 cattle herds numbered 1.2m., sheep and goats were estimated by the FAO at 2.1m., and pigs (kept mainly in the south) numbered 555,000. The EDF has provided finance to develop animal husbandry, including a cattle-farming project in Borgou province in the south. Food supply is also supplemented by fishing (according to the FAO, the total annual catch has, in recent years, averaged some 40,000 tons). The more advanced sector of fishing should grow rapidly as new investment comes into effect: two deep-sea fishing boats have been bought for the national fishing company. Meanwhile, the traditional sector is in decline, owing to salination of the lagoons from the development of the port of Cotonou.

MINING AND POWER

Although phosphates, kaolin, chromium, rutile, gold and iron ore have been located in the north, the only minerals so far exploited are limestone, marble, petroleum and natural gas. Production of petroleum in Benin began in the Sémé oilfield, 15 km offshore from Cotonou, in late 1982, with initial output averaging 4,000 barrels per day (b/d). Production reached a peak of 9,000 b/d in 1985, with the entry into operation of a third well and of water-injection facilities. Meanwhile, five new wells were drilled, and gas reserves evaluated. However, the transfer of the service contracts from the Norwegian developer in 1985 failed to realize the expected increase in output, and production was reduced to 3,000 b/d by mid-1988. Remedial work by a new service contractor, Ashland Exploration of the USA, briefly expanded output to 4,500 b/d, but it had fallen to 2,600 b/d by 1991. An enhanced recovery programme was then implemented, involving the deepening of three existing wells and the drilling of a further three, supported by funds from the International Development Association (IDA). Output increased to an average of 3,000 b/d in 1993 and 1994, but has since run at only 2,000 b/d.

Supply of electricity (259.2m. kWh in 1994) was formerly almost wholly from the Akosombo hydroelectric dam in Ghana. At the beginning of 1988, however, operations began at the 62-MW hydroelectric installation on the frontier with Togo at Nangbeto, on the River Mono. This will eventually produce 150,000 kWh and thus substantially reduce Benin's reliance on imported energy. The scheme was aided by a number of foreign agencies, including the African Development Fund, the IDA, and the Kuwaiti Fund for African Economic Development, as well as France and Canada. A second dam, with 104 MW capacity, is planned downstream, at Adjarala, with the aim of achieving self-sufficiency in power for both Benin and Togo.

MANUFACTURING

Manufacturing activity is still small-scale and, apart from the construction materials industry, is confined to the processing of primary products for export (cotton ginning, oil palm processing), or import substitution of simple consumer goods. The sector accounted for about 7% of GDP in 1994. Oil palm processing capacity, of 215,000 metric tons, is currently grossly under-utilized, but the sector is being restructured with a view to privatization. Conversely, cotton ginning capacity (at 78,000 tons) was inadequate during much of the 1980s; however, additional ginning plants have come into operation since 1989, including three new ginneries in a joint venture between the cotton marketing agency, the Société nationale pour la promotion agricole (Sonapra) and a French company in 1995/96, which means that the entire national crop can now be processed domestically. In addition, other agricultural processing plants—for maize, cashew-nuts and vegetables—have been rehabilitated to supply the stronger domestic and foreign markets.

Two joint ventures with Nigeria came into operation in the early 1980s, but have proved unprofitable. The cement plant at Onigbolo began production in 1982. Plans to sell one-half of the scheduled annual output of 600,000 tons to Nigeria failed to materialize, because of the downturn in its economy and the overcapacity that has developed in cement production in west Africa. The plant has been operating at only about one-half of its capacity. Meanwhile, the other joint venture with Nigeria, a sugar complex at Savé, with an annual capacity of 45,000 tons, operated only intermittently following its commissioning in 1983. Production reached 7,000 tons in 1985/86, from 4,400 ha planted: it was hoped to extend cultivation to the targeted area of 5,200 ha in the 1986/87 season. However, with world sugar prices still much lower than the project's production costs, the complex remained unprofitable, and it ceased operation in 1991. These two projects are among those that the Soglo government aimed to dispose of as part of its privatization programme. This represented a complete reversal of the policies pursued by Kérékou's military regime in its early years: during the 1970s there had been an increasing emphasis on state participation in industry, exemplified by the nationalization of a number of private enterprises. However, the worsening in budget finances, as the economy contracted, forced the government to reconsider the desirability of maintaining the parastatal organizations (which cover a wide range of services as well as products). Through the privatization, rehabilitation or liquidation of these organizations, the number of parastatals was reduced from a high point of 120 to only about 40 at the time of Soglo's accession to power. The process was continued, but slowed after 1993, as it became increasingly difficult to attract offers at acceptable prices for the 27 enterprises remaining to be sold at the end of that year. Meanwhile, the debts accumulated at the Onigbolo cement plant and the Savé sugar complex delayed the privatization agreed in principle by the two governments. The future of the whole privatization programme was thrown into doubt by the outcome of the March 1996 presidential election. The new Kérékou administration initially expressed its opposition to any further disposals of state assets, essentially because of the job losses this often entails, but one of the commitments made by the new regime to secure another ESAF was a continuation of the privatization programme. Thus disposals planned by the Soglo administration—of the Sonacop petroleum products distribution chain and the cotton marketing company are proceeding. However, it is intended that divestment be of minority stakes only, with 25% instead of the scheduled 75% in the case of Sonacop, and not necessarily by way of bloc sales to foreign interests.

TRANSPORT INFRASTRUCTURE

The country's transport infrastructure is comparatively good. Most internal transportation uses the country's road network, which extends over some 8,500 km (of which about 2,700 km are paved). A number of major road construction schemes, including the upgrading of the 222-km Dassa–Parakou link of the Cotonou–Niger highway, have been implemented, with financial support from the European Community (now European Union—EU), the African Development Bank and the Arab Bank for Economic Development in Africa. By the construction of new roads and the upgrading of existing routes, it is hoped to develop the country's status as an entrepôt for regional trade. Feeder roads are also being built for the marketing of agricultural products. Benin's foreign earnings benefit from the transit trade from Niger via the 579-km Benin–Niger railway; in 1987 the network handled 444,000 tons, of which approximately three-quarters was for Niger. There have long been plans to extend the line from Parakou to Niamey, but, given the country's economic circumstances and strained budget resources, the project's implementation is now only a remote possibility. France provided the funding for a programme, undertaken in 1987–91, to rehabilitate rolling stock and to overhaul 440 km of track between Cotonou and Parakou, as well as to restructure the rail company's finances. The port of Cotonou has a capacity of 2m. metric tons of merchandise. Of the 1,482,350 tons handled at the port in 1991, some 438,738 tons was in transit. During the 1980s there had been a general decline in the volume handled, since congestion had eased at Nigerian ports and some transit trade from Burkina Faso and Nigeria had been transferred to Lomé, in Togo. However, the political upheaval in Togo from 1991 resulted in the transfer to Benin of a significant part of its import-export activity, and Cotonou port was operating close to capacity by 1993. A rehabilitation programme for the port, projected to cost 3,300m. francs CFA (at the pre-1994 parity), has received pledges of aid from multilateral and French agencies. Among infrastructural projects currently planned is the construction of a 425-km road from Savalou (in the centre of the country) to Djougou (in the north-east), which would improve communications with Burkina Faso and Mali, the reconstruction of the Parakou–Djougou–Natitingou road (as the first stage of the Benin–Burkina Faso–Togo highway) and an expressway linking Cotonou, Sémé and Porto Novo. External finance has been obtained for these projects.

FINANCE

For over a decade now the government has been struggling to reduce the chronic deficit on its budget. Government finances had come under pressure in the mid-1980s as the result of the impact on revenues of economic recession in Nigeria and of the temporary closure of the border (customs duties account for the greater part of budgetary revenue), while spending was inflated by the cost of operating the parastatal companies. After the budget deficit had reached a peak of 7.3% of GDP (after grants equivalent to 2.5% of GDP) in 1986, a wide-ranging austerity programme was implemented in 1987, with the aim of reducing current expenditure. Public enterprises were transferred to private ownership, liquidated or rehabilitated, and public-sector salaries were initially 'frozen' (in 1987) and subsequently reduced (in 1988). Further retrenchment was planned for 1989, with reductions both in personnel and salaries in the civil service, together with measures to improve the collection of taxes. However, the political turmoil of late 1989 and early 1990 meant that revenue from taxation virtually ceased, and it was the accumulation of salary arrears that precipitated the downfall of the Kérékou regime. The budget deficit surged to 10.7% of GDP in 1989. The Soglo administration succeeded in reducing the deficit, which was equivalent to only 3.1% of GDP (after grants) in 1993. (Before grants, the deficit was a less impressive 4.7%.) This was due to several factors: higher revenues (as the rate of economic growth improved, and port trade was displaced from Togo to Benin), privatization (which both generates immediate funds and, in the case of loss-making operations, relieves a drain on budget resources), and a reduction in interest payments (as a result of the rescheduling of foreign debt by the 'Paris Club' of official creditors in 1991). The devaluation of the CFA franc put pressure on the spending side of the budget, as the government was obliged to concede an overall increase of 21% in public-sector salaries, to compensate for the surge in consumer prices, while interest payments on the external debt doubled in local currency terms. Consequently, the deficit (excluding grants) rose to an estimated 6.6% of GDP in 1994. Although the deficit rose again in 1995, there were some significant structural improvements, with a higher proportion of total spending going to the capital programme and a lower proportion to salaries, as the public sector pay-roll was reduced. The combination of a higher deficit and higher capital spending was maintained through 1996, while the 1997 budget is considerably more expansionary, with a rise of one third in the deficit, largely due to a surge in current spending as new jobs were created in the public sector. This departure from orthodoxy leaves a deficit considerably higher than the target 6% of GDP set at the agreement on the ESAF, but it has apparently been sanctioned by the IMF. The new jobs answer a political need, since the president had campaigned on a pledge to provide an extra 20,000 jobs a year, but they are to be concentrated in health and education services in the poorer areas. As in the past, external grants, notably from France, will be a signficant source of budget funding.

Benin's fiscal difficulties were compounded by the breakdown of the banking system in 1988, when the state-owned Banque Commerciale du Bénin (the country's sole commercial bank, created in 1974 following the nationalization of all banks) collapsed as a result of protracted mismanagement and corruption. In 1989 the Banque Béninoise de Développement was obliged to close, and the Caisse Nationale de Crédit Agricole was finally wound up in 1990. This left the state with a debt of 57,000m. francs CFA to the regional central bank, the Banque centrale des états de l'Afrique de l'ouest. An important component of the structural adjustment programme adopted in 1989 was the rehabilitation of the banking system, with the aid of a loan of 5,000m. francs CFA from France. The state's monopoly over the sector has thus been ended; four new, foreign-owned banks have been established, and Crédit Lyonnais of France opened a subsidiary in Cotonou in 1993. However, losses on its Benin operations caused the bank to withdraw from the country at the end of 1995.

FOREIGN TRADE AND PAYMENTS

Benin has traditionally maintained a very substantial external trade deficit, with import spending usually some 50% more than the level of export receipts. During the 1980s export earnings were adversely affected by the recession in Nigeria, and by the closure of the border between the two countries during 1984–86, as well as by the impact of drought upon palm products, cocoa and coffee in 1981–83, and the decline in international cotton prices in 1986 and 1987 (cotton being the leading export). Exports fell by around one-half in 1989, to US $214m., as political unrest paralysed the economy. The decline was almost fully reversed by 1992, as the economy recovered under the new administration. However, the gap between exports and imports remained massive, since the resumption in economic growth prompted an increase in the level of imports, and the trade deficit widened from $132m. in 1988 to $198m. in 1993. This was reversed in 1994, when the realignment of the currency resulted in a decline by one-third in imports (in US dollar terms), while exports declined by around one-tenth. The trade gap thus narrowed to only $67m. Faster economic growth brought with it a recovery in import spending in 1995, to close to pre-devaluation levels which outpaced the upturn in export earnings owing to higher cotton prices, bringing a widening in the trade gap to $145m. With the record cotton crop boosting export supply in 1996 and import growth easing off, the gap narrowed sharply once more in 1996, to around the 1994 figure.

The deficit on foreign trade is partly met by remittances from Beninois overseas (equivalent to around one-half of export earnings) and, more significantly, by aid inflows. Disbursements of development aid by non-communist countries and agencies, which averaged some US $84m. per year in the early 1980s, increased in the second half of that decade, to reach $285m. in 1990, boosted by French aid for the programme for the restructuring of the banking sector. Aid flows were increasing through 1991 to 1993, in support of the new democratic regime, to reach $317m. in the latter year, almost matching the country's earnings from merchandise exports ($341m.). They have since broadly maintained this level. In the 1970s loans from governments and multilateral agencies accounted for the major part of the external public debt ($158.4m. out of $192.2m. at the end of 1979), as Benin's radical economic policies tended to deter foreign private capital. Commercial borrowing then increased sharply in the early 1980s, to finance the oil development programme, and at the end of 1987 42% of the long-term debt was owed to private creditors. The situation was reversed again as a result of the 1989 debt-relief agreement (see below), and at the end of 1994 virtually all of Benin's medium- and long-term debt was owed to official creditors (multilateral and bilateral), with some 85% on concessionary terms.

Reflecting the high concessionary element in official flows of aid, service payments on the external public debt in 1979 amounted to only 5.1% of total earnings from exports of goods and services in that year. This very manageable ratio deteriorated markedly with the rise in borrowing from private sources, at much higher interest rates, which caused debt-servicing payments to increase more than 10-fold by 1986, when they reached US $62m. (equivalent to 13.6% of export earnings in that year). However, this represented only one half of the debt-servicing payments that were due in 1986, and arrears on interest continued to accrue during the following two years, to total $88m. (on the long-term debt) by the end of 1988. Arrears on repayments were also accumulating, and had reached $321m. by the end of 1988. Benin was one of the 22 sub-Saharan African countries identified by the World Bank as 'debt-distressed' (those countries whose debt-service ratio would exceed 30% in 1988–90 on the basis of existing commitments), and therefore became eligible for new assistance schemes at the IMF. However, access to such funding was dependent upon Benin's compliance with a structural adjustment programme agreed with, and monitored by, that body. In June 1989 the IMF approved a three-year (1989–92) structural adjustment facility of SDR 21.9m. in support of such a programme. The 'Paris Club' thereupon agreed to the rescheduling, on concessionary terms, of debt amounting to $193m. in principal and interest due to July 1990. Additionally, Benin's debt to both France and the US government were cancelled. The burden of debt, while still considerable, was thus eased during 1989, when debt-servicing payments declined to $26m., while arrears on interest payments were reduced to $23m. Further debt-relief was accorded in December 1991, when the 'Paris Club', recognizing the efforts of the new government to resolve the country's public-financing difficulties, undertook to reduce the debt-service burden by one-half. Creditors would either cancel 30% of outstanding debt, rescheduling the balance over 23 years (including six years' grace), or reduce interest rates so as to halve the net payments. There was a further rescheduling, on similar terms, in June 1993, after Benin was accorded access to the IMF's Enhanced Structural Adjustment Facility (ESAF). Such concessions, which affect only one-quarter of the total debt, did not solve Benin's debt problem, but did relieve pressure on government finances at a time when the economic adjustment programme would otherwise have had even greater consequences for employment and income within the country. At the end of 1993 Benin's total foreign debt was $1,479m. (equivalent to 71% of gross national product—GNP), and debt-servicing was equivalent to only 5.4% of the value of exports of goods and services.

Immediately upon the devaluation of the CFA franc, in January 1994, the burden on the Beninois economy of servicing foreign debt (the value of which had thereby doubled in local currency terms) was greatly increased. Supplementary assistance was therefore arranged (for the entire Franc Zone in Africa) by the IMF, the World Bank and the EU, and France accorded debt waivers. In the case of Benin, 600m. French francs (equivalent to US $109m.) was cancelled with immediate effect. However, the increase in borrowing, particularly from multilateral institutions (which is not eligible for rescheduling), pushed up Benin's debt by 11% by the end of 1995, to $1,646m., which—at the new exchange parity—was equivalent to almost 110% of GNP. With a regression in the debt-servicing ratio to 10.2% of export earnings, and with remittances from expatriate Beninois likely to have declined markedly in 1996 (owing to uncertainty regarding the consequences of Kérékou's return to power), there was increased urgency for the new administration to agree terms with the IMF for an ESAF. The agreement was signed in August, opening the way for a fourth round of debt rescheduling by the country's bilateral official creditors. Some $208m. in non-concessionary debt was restructured on the highly concessionary 'Naples' terms. Under these terms, creditors either write off two-thirds of the liability (both principal and interest) and reschedule the balance over 23 years at market rates, or they reduce interest rates, with repayment over 33 years (effectively reducing the debt by two-thirds). This relaxation in the foreign debt burden, while welcome, is relatively modest in Benin's case. The bulk of its debt is to multinational institutions, and is thus not amenable to restructuring. Keeping economic policy on the track delineated by its multilateral creditors will therefore remain a priority.

Statistical Survey

Source (unless otherwise stated): Institut National de la Statistique et de l'Analyse Economique, BP 323, Cotonou; tel. 31-40-81.

Area and Population

AREA, POPULATION AND DENSITY

Area (sq km)	112,622*
Population (census results)	
20–30 March 1979	
Total	3,331,210
15–29 February 1992	
Males	2,390,336
Females	2,525,219
Total	4,915,555
Population (official estimates at mid-year)	
1993	5,215,000
1994	5,387,000
1995	5,561,000
Density (per sq km) at mid-1995	49.4

* 43,484 sq miles.

ETHNIC GROUPS

1979 census (percentages): Fon 39.2; Yoruba 11.9; Adja 11.0; Bariba 8.5; Houeda 8.5; Peulh 5.6; Djougou 3.0; Dendi 2.1; Non-Africans 6.5; Others 1.2; Unknown 2.4.

POPULATION BY PROVINCE (1992 census, provisional)

Atakora	648,330
Atlantique	1,060,310
Borgou	816,278
Mono	646,954
Ouémé	869,492
Zou	813,985
Total	4,855,349

PRINCIPAL TOWNS (population at 1992 census)

Cotonou	536,827	Djougou	134,099
Porto-Novo (capital)	179,138	Parakou	103,577

BIRTHS AND DEATHS (UN estimates, annual averages)

	1980–85	1985–90	1990–95
Birth rate (per 1,000)	49.3	49.0	48.7
Death rate (per 1,000)	20.8	19.1	17.8

Expectation of life (UN estimates, years at birth, 1990–95): 47.6 (males 45.9; females 49.3).
Source: UN, *World Population Prospects: The 1994 Revision.*

1994 (official estimates): Death rate (per 1,000) 14.3; Expectation of life (years at birth) 54.3

ECONOMICALLY ACTIVE POPULATION
(persons aged 10 years and over, 1992 census)

	Males	Females	Total
Agriculture, hunting, forestry and fishing	780,469	367,277	1,147,746
Mining and quarrying	609	52	661
Manufacturing	93,157	67,249	160,406
Electricity, gas and water	1,152	24	1,176
Construction	50,959	696	51,655
Trade, restaurants and hotels	36,672	395,829	432,501
Transport, storage and communications	52,228	609	52,837
Finance, insurance, real estate and business services	2,705	401	3,106
Community, social and personal services	126,122	38,422	164,544
Activities not adequately defined	25,579	12,917	38,496
Total employed	1,169,652	883,476	2,053,128
Unemployed	26,475	5,843	32,318
Total labour force	1,196,127	889,319	2,085,446

Source: ILO, *Yearbook of Labour Statistics.*

Mid-1995 (estimates in '000): Agriculture, etc. 1,463; Total 2,450 (Source: FAO, *Production Yearbook*).

Agriculture

PRINCIPAL CROPS ('000 metric tons)

	1993	1994	1995*
Rice (paddy)	10	14	14
Maize	483	492	492
Millet	24	25	25
Sorghum	106	113	113
Sweet potatoes	41	50	47
Cassava (Manioc)	1,040*	1,146	1,146
Yams	1,150*	1,250	1,250
Taro (Coco yam)	3*	4	4
Dry beans	58	63	63
Groundnuts (in shell)	74	83	83
Cottonseed	140*	132	132
Cotton (lint)	116†	103	103
Coconuts*	20	20	20
Palm kernels	13.3	13.3	13.3
Tomatoes	73	85	85
Green peppers*	12	12	12
Oranges*	12	12	12
Mangoes*	12	12	12
Bananas*	13	13	13
Pineapples*	3	3	3

* FAO estimate(s) † Unofficial figure.

Source: FAO, *Production Yearbook.*

LIVESTOCK ('000 head, year ending September)

	1993*	1994	1995*
Horses*	6	6	6
Asses*	1	1	1
Cattle	1,100	1,223	1,223
Pigs	550	555	555
Sheep*	940	940	940
Goats*	1,180	1,180	1,180

Poultry (million): 26* in 1993; 20 in 1994; 20 in 1995.

* FAO estimate(s). † Unofficial figure.

Source: FAO, *Production Yearbook*.

LIVESTOCK PRODUCTS (FAO estimates, '000 metric tons)

	1993	1994	1995
Beef and veal	16	16	16
Mutton and lamb	3	3	3
Goat meat	3	4	4
Pig meat	6	6	6
Poultry meat	32	32	32
Other meat	5	5	5
Cows' milk	16	16	16
Goats' milk	6	6	6
Poultry eggs	18.7	18.7	18.7

Source: FAO, *Production Yearbook*.

Forestry

ROUNDWOOD REMOVALS
(FAO estimates, '000 cubic metres, excl. bark)

	1992	1993	1994
Sawlogs, veneer logs and logs for sleepers	50	50	50
Other industrial wood	247	254	262
Fuel wood	5,087	5,246	5,414
Total	5,384	5,550	5,726

Source: FAO, *Yearbook of Forest Products*.

SAWNWOOD PRODUCTION
('000 cubic metres, incl. railway sleepers)

	1992	1993	1994
Total	24	24*	24*

* FAO estimate.

Source: FAO, *Yearbook of Forest Products*.

Fishing

(FAO estimates, '000 metric tons, live weight)

	1992	1993	1994
Cichlids	7.8	7.9	8.1
Black catfishes	1.0	1.1	1.1
Torpedo-shaped catfishes	1.8	1.8	1.9
Other freshwater fishes	7.9	8.0	8.1
Groupers and seabasses	1.5	1.6	1.6
Threadfins and tasselfishes	1.0	1.1	1.1
Sardinellas	1.5	1.6	1.7
Bonga shad	2.1	2.1	2.2
Other marine fishes	4.1	4.2	4.4
Total fish	28.8	29.4	30.0
Freshwater crustaceans	3.5	3.6	3.6
Marine crustaceans	3.2	3.3	3.3
Total catch	35.5	36.3	37.0

Note: Figures exclude catches by Beninois canoes operating from outside the country.

Source: FAO, *Yearbook of Fishery Statistics*.

Mining

(provisional or estimated figures, '000 metric tons)

	1992	1993	1994
Crude petroleum	298	302	310

Source: UN, *Industrial Commodity Statistics Yearbook*.

Industry

SELECTED PRODUCTS ('000 metric tons, unless otherwise indicated)

	1992	1993	1994
Salted, dried or smoked fish*	2.0	n.a.	n.a.
Cement†	370	380	380
Electric energy (million kWh)‡	5	5	6

* Data from the FAO.
† Data from the US Bureau of Mines.
‡ Provisional or estimates figures.

Source: UN, *Industrial Commodity Statistics Yearbook*.

Palm oil and palm kernel oil ('000 metric tons): 9.9 in 1992; 10.8 in 1993; 10.3 in 1994; 5.4 in 1995 (Source: IMF, *Benin—Recent Economic Developments,* October 1996).

Finance

CURRENCY AND EXCHANGE RATES

Monetary Units

100 centimes = 1 franc de la Communauté financière africaine (CFA).

French Franc, Sterling and Dollar Equivalents (31 March 1997)

1 French franc = 100 francs CFA;
£1 sterling = 924.20 francs CFA;
US $1 = 562.85 francs CFA;
1,000 francs CFA = £1.082 = $1.777.

Average Exchange Rate (francs CFA per US $)

1994 555.20
1995 499.15
1996 511.55

Note: An exchange rate of 1 French franc = 50 francs CFA, established in 1948, remained in force until January 1994, when the CFA franc was devalued by 50%, with the exchange rate adjusted to 1 French franc = 100 francs CFA.

BUDGET ('000 million francs CFA)

Revenue	1993	1994	1995*
Tax revenue	65.8	91.6†	123.0
Taxes on income and profits	18.1	30.5	40.2
Individual	6.3	7.1	8.8
Corporate	8.5	20.7	25.9
Domestic taxes on goods and services	12.8	15.6	19.2
Turnover taxes	7.8	11.4	10.4
Excises	3.4	2.0	1.8
Arrears of taxes on goods and services	0.6	0.6	5.2
Taxes on international trade and transactions	32.7	42.1	60.3
Import duties	30.0	38.5	56.4
Non-tax revenue	11.8	14.5	26.1
From non-financial public enterprises	2.3	3.1	10.7
Contribution to government employees' pension fund	5.0	5.5	7.3
Repayment on on-lending	2.5	4.2	4.8
Total	77.7	106.2	149.1

Expenditure‡	1993	1994	1995*
Primary expenditure§	64.7	88.3	126.0
Salaries	37.7	45.7	53.9
Pensions and scholarships	8.9	10.4	11.5
Other current expenditure (incl. current transfers)	15.2	27.9	47.5
Budgetary contribution to investment	3.0	4.3	13.2
Interest due	15.9	26.2	27.9
Domestic debt	4.6	3.7	2.7
External debt	11.3	22.5	25.2
Investment expenditure (financed from abroad)	25.5	49.9	65.0
Total	106.1	164.4	218.9

* Estimates.

† Including adjustment.

‡ Excluding net lending ('000 million francs CFA): 3.0 (estimate) in 1995.

§ Excluding foreign-financed investment.

Note: Excluding official grants, the overall budget deficit on a commitment basis (in '000 million francs CFA) was: 28.4 in 1993; 58.3 in 1994; 72.7 (estimate) in 1995. After adjusting for changes in domestic arrears, the deficit on a cash basis (in '000 million francs CFA) was: 37.9 in 1993; 68.9 in 1994; 89.7 (estimate) in 1995.

Source: IMF, *Benin—Recent Economic Developments* (October 1996).

1996 (revised draft budget, '000 million francs CFA): Revenue 168.7; Expenditure 251.9.

INTERNATIONAL RESERVES (US $ million at 31 December)

	1994	1995	1996
Gold*	4.2	4.3	4.2
IMF special drawing rights	—	0.1	0.3
Reserve position in IMF	3.1	3.2	3.1
Foreign exchange	255.1	194.7	183.1
Total	262.3	202.2	190.7

* Valued at market-related prices.

Source: IMF, *International Financial Statistics*.

MONEY SUPPLY ('000 million francs CFA at 31 December)

	1993	1994	1995
Currency outside banks	25.52	77.34	50.65
Demand deposit at deposit money banks	84.59	106.32	107.80
Checking deposits at post office	0.64	2.04	2.84
Total money (incl. others)	111.34	186.22	161.73

Source: IMF, *International Financial Statistics*.

COST OF LIVING
(Consumer price index; base: December 1991 = 100)

	1994	1995	1996
All items	144.7	165.7	173.8

Source: IMF, *International Financial Statistics*.

NATIONAL ACCOUNTS
('000 million francs CFA at current prices)

Expenditure on the Gross Domestic Product

	1993	1994	1995*
Government final consumption expenditure	71.2	91.1	107.5
Private final consumption expenditure	501.2	674.1	832.2
Increase in stocks	2.3	2.0	24.0
Gross fixed capital formation	87.4	131.5	172.6
Total domestic expenditure	662.1	898.7	1,136.3
Exports of goods and services	135.5	228.3	265.0
Less Imports of goods and services	195.8	279.3	365.5
GDP in purchasers' values	601.7	847.7	1,035.8
GDP at constant 1992 prices	592.0	617.7	647.2

* Estimates.

Gross Domestic Product by Economic Activity

	1993	1994*	1995*
Agriculture, livestock, forestry and fishing	215.3	292.2	351.5
Mining and petroleum	3.7	6.6	7.2
Manufacturing and handicrafts	47.1	64.5	83.7
Water, gas and electricity	5.3	6.1	6.8
Construction and public works	21.3	37.6	49.6
Trade	103.6	164.4	215.6
Transport and other marketable services	47.8	67.6	78.0
Public administration	55.1	72.4	79.8
Other non-marketable services	72.9	93.6	103.6
GDP at factor cost	572.1	804.9	975.8
Indirect taxes, *less* subsidies	29.7	42.8	60.0
GDP in purchasers' values	601.7	847.7	1,035.8

* Estimates.

Source: IMF, *Benin—Recent Economic Developments* (October 1996).

BALANCE OF PAYMENTS (US $ million)

	1992	1993	1994
Exports of goods f.o.b.	371.4	341.1	301.0
Imports of goods f.o.b.	−560.6	−538.9	−365.8
Trade balance	−189.2	−197.8	−64.8
Exports of services	142.8	137.4	103.9
Imports of services	−158.7	−152.6	−111.1
Balance on goods and services	−205.1	−213.0	−72.0
Other income paid	−61.6	−39.9	−40.5
Balance on goods, services and income	−266.7	−252.9	−112.6
Current transfers received	244.1	257.8	159.6
Current transfers paid	−16.6	−19.1	−10.6
Current balance	−39.2	−14.1	36.4
Investment assets	−21.9	−4.9	−70.8
Investment liabilities	−18.0	35.4	36.4
Net errors and omissions	1.6	−56.4	54.0
Overall balance	−77.5	−40.1	56.0

Source: IMF, *International Financial Statistics*.

External Trade

Source: Banque centrale des états de l'Afrique de l'ouest.

PRINCIPAL COMMODITIES (million francs CFA)

Imports c.i.f.*	1988	1989	1990
Food products	25,743	12,814	17,863
Food products of animal origin	2,856	2,040	1,300
Food products of plant origin	19,655	8,579	15,020
Rice	13,523	4,753	9,110
Wheat	2,170	1,769	3,562
Processed foodstuffs	3,222	2,195	1,543
Beverages and tobacco	4,643	4,688	5,268
Alcoholic beverages	1,863	1,199	2,241
Manufactured tobacco products	2,760	3,482	2,983
Energy products	13,343	10,113	10,393
Refined petroleum products	9,355	5,795	6,158
Other raw materials (inedible)	4,500	2,449	2,410
Machinery and transport equipment	13,302	9,593	7,860
Non-electrical machinery	5,478	3,486	n.a.
Electrical machinery	4,239	2,251	n.a.
Road transport equipment	3,454	3,812	n.a.
Other industrial products	34,774	25,036	28,026
Chemical products	7,726	4,710	7,235
Fertilizers	866	3	1,533
Miscellaneous manufactured articles	27,048	20,326	20,791
Cotton yarn and fabrics	14,988	11,160	7,715
Total (incl. others)	97,257	66,132	72,192

Exports f.o.b.†	1988	1989	1990
Food products	517	228	266
Energy products	6,388	6,636	7,765
Crude petroleum	6,314	6,636	7,765
Other raw materials (inedible)	8,772	20,007	18,734
Cottonseed	717	1,119	68
Cotton (ginned)	7,725	18,681	16,792
Oils and fats	2,243	1,951	1,191
Palm and palm-kernel oil	1,586	1,437	1,181
Machinery and transport equipment	1,278	613	460
Other industrial products	1,756	1,505	4,833
Miscellaneous manufactured articles	1,337	1,378	4,704
Cotton yarn and fabrics	189	1,008	4,021
Total (incl. others)	20,995	31,090	33,254

* Excluding imports for re-export.
† Excluding re-exports.

PRINCIPAL TRADING PARTNERS (million francs CFA)

Domestic imports	1987	1988	1989
Belgium-Luxembourg	2,002	1,345	856
Brazil	798	1,066	481
China, People's Repub.	4,253	3,667	2,498
Côte d'Ivoire	2,481	4,487	3,814
Czechoslovakia	809	1,240	1,401
France	18,493	18,786	12,357
German Democratic Repub.	226	1,183	165
Germany, Fed. Repub.	3,924	2,739	2,507
Ghana	3,449	4,245	4,390
Ireland	188	66	1,526
Italy	3,707	2,198	8
Japan	5,894	2,265	1,806
Netherlands	7,427	5,223	5,895
Nigeria	1,851	4,296	3,181
Senegal	1,013	1,517	692
Spain	1,372	1,138	801
Thailand	14,766	11,649	3,958
Togo	1,375	2,688	2,359
USSR	526	2,352	181
United Kingdom	4,897	4,012	2,902
USA	4,124	5,117	4,804
Total (incl. others)	104,980	97,257	66,132

Domestic exports	1987	1988	1989
Belgium-Luxembourg	364	131	551
China, People's Repub.	1,983	36	3,581
France	1,298	1,536	453
Germany, Fed. Repub.	1,044	356	278
Italy	4,742	443	1,785
Morocco	298	105	668
Netherlands	480	159	720
Niger	207	315	460
Nigeria	2,505	2,692	1,928
Portugal	7,189	2,889	3,800
Spain	864	289	367
Switzerland	260	337	368
Taiwan	1,910	—	878
Togo	212	1,048	684
United Kingdom	1,080	991	469
USA	5,742	6,328	6,636
Total (incl. others)	34,266	20,995	31,090

Transport

RAILWAYS (traffic)

	1993*	1994	1995
Passenger-km (million)	75.8	107.0	116.0
Freight ton-km (million)	225.3	253.0	388.4

* Estimates.

Source: IMF, *Benin—Recent Economic Developments* (October 1996).

ROAD TRAFFIC (estimates, '000 motor vehicles in use)

	1993	1994	1995
Passenger cars	32.1	33.6	35.6
Lorries and vans	16.8	18.8	19.3

Source: IRF, *World Road Statistics*.

SHIPPING

Merchant Fleet (registered at 31 December)

	1992	1993	1994
Total displacement ('000 grt)	2	1	1

Source: Lloyd's Register of Shipping.

International Sea-borne Freight Traffic
(at Cotonou, including goods in transit, '000 metric tons)

	1993*	1994	1995
Goods loaded	236.9	373.5	338.5
Goods unloaded	1,680.3	1,611.2	1,738.4

* Estimates.

Source: IMF, *Benin—Recent Economic Developments* (October 1996).

CIVIL AVIATION (traffic on scheduled services)*

	1992	1993	1994
Kilometres flown (million)	2	2	2
Passengers carried ('000)	66	68	69
Passenger-km (million)	201	207	215
Total ton-km (million)	33	33	33

* Including an apportionment of the traffic of Air Afrique.

Source: UN, *Statistical Yearbook*.

Tourism

	1992	1993	1994
Tourist arrivals ('000)	130	140	142
Tourist receipts (US $ million)	32	38	55

Source: UN, *Statistical Yearbook*.

Communications Media

	1992	1993	1994
Radio receivers ('000 in use)	442	461	480
Television receivers ('000 in use)	25	28	29
Telephones ('000 main lines in use)	16	20	24
Daily newspapers			
Number	1	n.a.	1
Average circulation ('000 copies)	12	n.a.	12
Book production*			
Titles	647†	n.a.	84
Copies ('000)	874†	n.a.	42

* First editions. † Excluding pamphlets.

Sources: UNESCO, *Statistical Yearbook*; UN, *Statistical Yearbook*.

Education

(1993/94)

	Institutions	Teachers	Students		
			Males	Females	Total
Pre-primary	282	n.a.	7,528	6,299	13,827
Primary	2,889	12,343	392,748	209,321	602,069
Secondary					
General	145	2,384	70,831	27,649	97,480
Vocational	14	283	3,553	1,320	4,873
Higher	16	602	8,330	1,634	9,964

Source: Ministère de l'Education Nationale, Cotonou.

Directory

The Constitution

A new Constitution was approved in a national referendum on 2 December 1990.

The Constitution of the Republic of Benin guarantees the basic rights and freedoms of citizens. The functions of the principal organs of state are delineated therein.

The President of the Republic, who is Head of State and Head of Government, is directly elected, by universal adult suffrage, for a period of five years, renewable only once. The executive is responsible to the legislature—the 83-member Assemblée nationale—which is elected, also by direct universal suffrage, for a period of four years.

The Constitution upholds the principle of an independent judiciary, and provides for the creation of a Constitutional Court, an Economic and Social Council and an authority regulating the media, all of which are intended to counterbalance executive authority.

The Government

HEAD OF STATE

President: Gen. (retd) Mathieu Kérékou (took office 4 April 1996).

COUNCIL OF MINISTERS
(July 1997)

President and Minister of Defence: Gen. (retd) Mathieu Kérékou.

Prime Minister: Adrien Houngbédji.

Minister-delegate, responsible for Defence: Sévérin Adjovi.

Minister of Foreign Affairs and Co-operation: Pierre Otcho.

Minister of Justice: Ismael Djani-Cerpos.

Minister of Finance: Moïse Mensah.

Minister of the Interior: Théophile Nda.

Minister of Planning and Employment Promotion: Albert Tévoédjré.

Minister of Rural Development: Jérôme-Désiré Sakassina.

Minister of Industry, Tourism and Handicrafts: Delphin Houngbédji.

Minister of Energy and Water Resources: Emmanuel Golou.

Minister of Public Works and Transport: Oumarou Fassassi.

Minister of the Environment and Housing: Saidou Binadé Dango.

Minister of the Civil Service: Yacoubou Assouma.

Minister of National Education: Djidjofon Léonard Kpadonou.

Minister of Health: Marina d'Almeida.

Minister of Communications, Culture and Information: Timothée Zanou.

Minister of Youth and Sports: Zinsou Damien Alahata.

MINISTRIES

Office of the President: BP 1288, Cotonou; tel. 30-02-28; telex 5222.

Ministry of the Civil Service : BP 907, Cotonou; tel. 31-26-18.

Ministry of Communications, Culture and Information: BP 120, Cotonou; tel. 31-59-31; telex 5266.

Ministry of Defence: BP 2493, Cotonou; tel. 30-08-90.

Ministry of Energy and Water Resources: BP 363, Cotonou; tel. 31-45-20; fax 31-08-90.

Ministry of the Environment and Housing: BP 01-3621, Cotonou; tel. 31-21-00.

Ministry of Finance: BP 342, Cotonou; tel. 30-10-20; fax 30-18-51.

Ministry of Foreign Affairs and Co-operation: BP 318, Cotonou; tel. 30-04-00; telex 5200.

Ministry of Health: BP 882, Cotonou; tel. 33-08-70.

Ministry of Industry, Tourism and Handicrafts: BP 363, Cotonou; tel. 30-16-46; telex 5252.

Ministry of the Interior: BP 925, Cotonou; tel. 30-10-06; telex 5065.

Ministry of Justice: BP 967, Cotonou; tel. 31-31-46.

Ministry of National Education: BP 348, Cotonou; tel. 30-06-81; fax 30-18-48.

Ministry of Planning and Employment Promotion: BP 342, Cotonou; tel. 30-05-41; telex 5118.

Ministry of Public Works and Transport: BP 351, Cotonou; tel. 31-56-96; telex 5289.

Ministry of Rural Development: BP 03-2900, Cotonou; tel. 30-19-55; fax 30-03-26.

Ministry of Youth and Sports: BP 03-2103, Cotonou; tel. 31-46-00; telex 5036.

President and Legislature

PRESIDENT

Presidential Election, First Ballot, 3 March 1996

Candidate	% of votes
Nicéphore Soglo	35.69
Mathieu Kérékou	33.94
Adrien Houngbédji	19.71
Bruno Amoussou	7.76
Pascal Fantondji	1.08
Léandre Djagoue	0.92
Jacques Lionel Agbo	0.90
Total	100.00

Second Ballot, 18 March 1996

Candidate	Votes	% of votes
Mathieu Kérékou	999,453	52.49
Nicéphore Soglo	904,626	47.51
Total	1,904,079	100.00

ASSEMBLÉE NATIONALE

Speaker: Bruno Amoussou (PSD).

Elections, 28 March and 28 May 1995*

Party	Seats
RB	20
PRD	19
FARD–Alafia	10
PSD	8
UDS	5
IPD	3
NCC	3
RDL–Vivoten	3
NG	2
AC	1
ADD	1
ADP	1
ASD	1
MNDD†	1
PCB	1
RAP	1
RDP	1
UNDP	1
Total	82

* The results of voting for 13 seats at the March 1995 general election were subsequently annulled by the Constitutional Court, and by-elections for these seats were held on 28 May. The result of one by-election was itself invalidated by the Court, and the seat was to remain vacant: the electoral code stipulates that supplementary elections may not be organized unless the number of vacant seats in the Assemblée nationale is equivalent to one-fifth of the overall membership.

† The Mouvement national pour la démocratie et le développement subsequently merged with the RB.

Advisory Councils

Cour Constitutionnelle: BP 2050, Cotonou; tel. 31-59-92; fax 31-37-12; f. 1990, inaug. 1993; seven mems (four appointed by the Assemblée nationale, three by the President of the Republic); determines the constitutionality of legislation, oversees national elections and referendums, responsible for protection of individual and public rights and obligations, charged with regulating functions of organs of state and authorities: Pres. Elisabeth Kayissan Pognon; Sec.-Gen. Jean-Baptiste Monsi.

Conseil Economique et Social (ECOSOC): Cotonou; f. 1994; 30 mems, representing the executive, legislature and 'all sections of the nation'; competent to advise on proposed economic and social legislation, as well as to recommend economic and social reforms; Pres. Valentin Agbo.

Haute Autorité de l'Audiovisuel et de la Communication (HAAC): Cotonou; f. in accordance with the 1990 Constitution to act as the highest authority for the media; Pres. René M. Dossa.

Political Organizations

The registration of political parties commenced in August 1990. Of the 88 parties holding legal status, 31 contested the 1995 legislative elections. The following secured seats in the Assemblée nationale:

The **Alliance caméléon (AC)**; the **Alliance pour la démocratie et le développement (ADD):** Leader Karim Dramane; the **Alliance pour la démocratie et le progrès (ADP):** Leader Adekpedjou S. Akindes; the **Alliance pour la social-démocratie (ASD):** Leader Robert Dossou; The **Front d'action pour le renouveau et le développement–Alafia (FARD–Alafia):** Leader Saka Kina; **Impulsion au progrès et à la démocratie (IPD)**; Leader Bertin Borna; **Notre cause commune (NCC):** Leader François Odjo Tankpinon; **Nouvelle génération pour la République (NGR):** Leader Paul Dossou; the **Parti communiste du Bénin (PCB):** Leader Pascal Fantondji; the **Parti du renouveau démocratique (PRD):** Leader Adrien Houngbédji; the **Parti social-démocrate (PSD):** Leader Bruno Amoussou; the **Rassemblement africain pour le progrès et la solidarité (RAP)**; the **Rassemblement des démocrates libéraux pour la reconstruction nationale–Vivoten (RDL–Vivoten):** Leader Sévérin Adjovi; the **Rassemblement pour la démocratie et le progrès (RDP)**; the **(Parti de la) Renaissance du Bénin (RB):** Leader Nicéphore Soglo; the **Union pour la démocratie et la solidarité nationale (UDS):** Leader Adamou N'Diaye Mama; the **Union nationale pour la démocratie et le progrès (UNDP):** Leader Dr Emile Derlin Zinsou; the **Union nationale pour la solidarité et le progrès (UNSP):** Leader Wallis M. Zoumarou.

Diplomatic Representation

EMBASSIES IN BENIN

Chad: BP 080359, Cotonou; tel. 33-08-51; Chargé d'affaires a.i.: Darkou Ahmat Kalabassou.

China, People's Republic: BP 196, Cotonou; tel. 30-12-92; Ambassador: Zhao Huimin.

Cuba: BP 948, Cotonou; tel. 31-52-97; telex 5277; Ambassador: Evangelio Montero Hernández.

Denmark: BP 04-1223, Cotonou; tel. 30-38-62; telex 5078; fax 30-38-60; Chargé d'affaires a.i.: Flemming Nichols.

Egypt: BP 1215, Cotonou; tel. 30-08-42; telex 5274; Ambassador: Mohamed Mahmoud Aguib.

France: route de l'Aviation, BP 966, Cotonou; tel. 30-08-24; telex 5209; Ambassador: Cathérine Boivineau.

Germany: 7 ave Jean-Paul II, BP 504, Recette Principale, Cotonou; tel. 31-29-67; telex 5224; fax 31-29-62; Ambassador: Volker Seitz.

Ghana: Les Cocotiers, BP 488, Cotonou; tel. 30-07-46; Ambassador: Christian T. K. Quarshie.

Korea, Democratic People's Republic: Cotonou; tel. 30-10-97; Ambassador: Pak Song Il.

Libya: Les Cocotiers, BP 405, Cotonou; tel. 30-04-52; telex 5254; People's Bureau Representative: Sanoussi Awad Abdallah.

Niger: derrière Hôtel de la Plage, BP 352, Cotonou; tel. 31-56-65; Chargé d'affaires a.i.: Soumana Aminata.

Nigeria: blvd de France Marina, BP 2019, Cotonou; tel. 30-11-42; telex 5247; Chargé d'affaires a.i.: Abdul Kader Ibrahim.

Russia: BP 2013, Cotonou; tel. 31-28-34; telex 9725008; fax 31-28-35; Ambassador: Yurii Tchepik.

USA: rue Caporal Anani Bernard, BP 2012, Cotonou; tel. 30-06-50; fax 30-14-39; e-mail usis.cotonou@bow.intnet.bj; Ambassador: John M. Yates.

Zaire: BP 130, Cotonou; Ambassador: Tatu Longwa.

Judicial System

The Constitution of December 1990 establishes the judiciary as an organ of state whose authority acts as a counterbalance to that of the executive and of the legislature. There is provision for a Constitutional Court (see Advisory Councils, above), a High Court of Justice and a Supreme Court.

President of the Supreme Court: Abraham Zinzindohoue.

Attorney-General: Lucien Degeno.

Religion

Some 60% of the population hold animist beliefs; more than 20% are Christians (mainly Roman Catholics) and the remainder mostly Muslims. Religious and spiritual cults, which were discouraged under Kérékou's military regime, re-emerged as a prominent force in Beninois society during the early 1990s.

CHRISTIANITY

The Roman Catholic Church

Benin comprises one archdiocese and eight dioceses. At 31 December 1995 there were an estimated 1.2m. Roman Catholics (about 20.4% of the population), mainly in the south of the country.

Bishops' Conference: Conférence Episcopale du Bénin, Archevêché, BP 491, Cotonou; tel. 31-31-45; fax 30-07-07; Pres. Rt Rev. LUCIEN MONSI-AGBOKA, Bishop of Abomey.

Archbishop of Cotonou: Most Rev. ISIDORE DE SOUZA, Archevêché, BP 491, Cotonou; tel. 30-01-45; fax 30-07-07.

Protestant Church

There are 257 Protestant mission centres, with a personnel of about 120.

Eglise protestante méthodiste en République du Bénin: 54 ave Mgr Steinmetz, BP 34, Cotonou; tel. 31-11-42; fax 31-25-20; f. 1843; Pres. Rev. Dr MOÏSE SAGBOHAN; Sec. Rev. MATHIEU D. OLODO; 95,827 mems (1996).

VODOUN

The origins of the traditional *vodoun* religion can be traced to the 14th century. Its influence is particularly notable in spiritual religions of Latin America and the Caribbean, owing to the shipment of slaves from the West African region to the Americas in the 18th and 19th centuries.

Grand conseil de la réligion vodoun du Bénin: Ouidah; Supreme Chief DAAGBO HOUNON HOUNA.

The Press

In the mid-1990s some 50 newspapers and magazines were being published in Benin.

La Croix du Bénin: BP 105, Cotonou; tel. and fax 32-11-19; f. 1946; fortnightly; Roman Catholic; Dir BARTHÉLEMY ASSOGBA CAKPO.

FLASH-HEBDO: BP 120, Cotonou; tel. 30-18-57; weekly; Dir PASCAL ADISSODA.

Le Forum de la Semaine: BP 04-0391, Cotonou; tel. 30-03-40; weekly; Dir BRUNO SODEHOU.

La Gazette du Golfe: Carré 961 'J' Etoile Rouge, BP 03-1624, Cotonou; tel. 31-35-58; telex 5053; fax 30-01-99; f. 1987; weekly; Dir ISMAËL Y. SOUMANOU; Editor KARIM OKANLA; circ. 18,000 (nat. edn), 5,000 (international edn).

Initiatives: BP 2093, Cotonou; tel. 31-44-47; six a year; Dir THÉOPHILE CAPO-CHICHI.

Journal Officiel de la République du Bénin: BP 59, Porto-Novo; tel. 21-39-77; f. 1890; official govt bulletin; fortnightly; Dir AFIZE D. ADAMON.

La Lumière de l'Islam: BP 08-0430, Cotonou; tel. 31-34-59; fortnightly; Dir MOHAMED BACHIR SOUMANOU.

Le Matin: Cotonou; f. 1994; daily; Dir SAID SAHNOUN.

La Nation: BP 1210, Cotonou; tel. 30-08-75; f. 1990; official newspaper; daily; Dir AKUETE ASSCOI.

L'Observateur: Cotonou; fortnightly; Dir FRANÇOIS COMLAN.

Le Patriote: BP 2093, Cotonou; tel. 31-44-47; monthly; Dir CALIXTE DA SILVA.

Le Pays: BP 06-2170, Cotonou; tel. 33-10-09; fortnightly; Dir ENOCK YAKA.

La Récade: BP 08-0086, Cotonou; tel. 33-11-15; monthly; Dir TITOMAS MEGNASSAN.

La Sentinelle: BP 34, Cotonou; tel. 31-25-20; monthly; Dir MICHÉE D. AHOUANDJINOU.

Le Soleil: Cotonou; tel. 30-14-90; fortnightly; Dir EDGARD KAHO.

Tam-Tam-Express: BP 2302, Cotonou; tel. 30-12-05; fax 30-39-75; f. 1988; fortnightly; Dir DENIS HODONOU; circ. 8,000.

L'Union: Cotonou; tel. 31-55-05; fortnightly; Dir PAUL HERVÉ D'ALMEIDA.

NEWS AGENCIES

Agence Bénin-Presse (ABP): BP 72, Cotonou; tel. 31-26-55; telex 5221; f. 1961; national news agency; section of the Ministry of Communications, Culture and Information; Dir BONIFACE AGUEH.

Foreign Bureaux

Agence France-Presse (AFP): BP 06-1382, Cotonou; tel. 33-24-02; Correspondent VIRGILE C. AHISSOU.

Reuters (UK) is also represented in Benin.

Publishers

Les Editions du Flamboyant: 08 BP 271, Cotonou; tel. and fax 31-02-20; f. 1985.

Government Publishing House

Office National d'Edition, de Presse et d'Imprimerie (ONEPI): BP 1210, Cotonou; tel. 30-08-75; f. 1975; Dir-Gen. BONI ZIMÉ MAKO.

Radio and Television

In 1994, according to UNESCO, there were an estimated 480,000 radio receivers and 29,000 television receivers in use.

Office de Radiodiffusion et de Télévision du Bénin: BP 366, Cotonou; tel. 30-10-96; telex 5132; state-owned; radio programmes broadcast from Cotonou and Parakou in French, English and 18 local languages; TV transmissions 25 hours weekly; Dir-Gen. JACQUES PHILIPPE DA MATHA; Dir of Radio PELU DIOGO; Dir of TV CLÉMENT HOUENONTIN.

Radio Parakou: BP 128, Parakou; tel. 61-07-73; Dir DIEUDONNÉ METOZOUNVÉ.

Finance

(cap. = capital; res = reserves; m. = million; br. = branch; amounts in francs CFA)

BANKING

Central Bank

Banque Centrale des Etats de l'Afrique de l'Ouest (BCEAO): ave d'Ornano, route Inter-Etat no 11, Zone portuaire, BP 325, Cotonou; tel. 31-24-66; telex 5211; fax 31-24-65; headquarters in Dakar, Senegal; f. 1962; bank of issue for the member states of the Union économique et monétaire ouest-africaine (UEMOA); cap. and res 657,592m. (Dec. 1995); Gov. CHARLES KONAN BANNY; Dir in Benin PAULIN COSSI; br. at Parakou.

Commercial Banks

Bank of Africa–Bénin: blvd Jean-Paul II, BP 08-0879, Cotonou; tel. 31-32-28; telex 5079; fax 31-31-17; f. 1990; 27% owned by African Financial Holding; cap. and res 7,200m. (Dec. 1995); Pres. FRANÇOIS TANKPINOU; Man. Dir PAUL DERREUMAUX.

Banque Internationale du Bénin (BIBE): carrefour des Trois Banques, ave Giran, BP 03-2098, Jericho, Cotonou; tel. 31-55-49; telex 5075; fax 31-23-65; f. 1989; 49% owned by Nigerian commercial banks; cap. and res 1,978m. (Dec. 1995); Pres. Chief JOSEPH OLADÉLÉ SANUSI; Man. Dir RANSOME OLADÉLÉ ADEBOLU; 4 brs.

Continental Bank–Bénin: ave Jean-Paul II, carrefour des Trois Banques, 01 BP 2020, Cotonou 01; tel. 31-24-24; telex 5151; fax 31-51-77; f. 1995 to assume activities of Crédit Lyonnais Bénin; cap. 3,600m.; Pres. EMMANUEL KOUTON; Man. Dir MOUSSIBAOU ADJIBI.

Ecobank–Bénin SA: rue du Gouverneur Bayol, BP 1280, Cotonou; tel. 31-40-33; telex 5394; fax 31-33-85; f. 1989; 72% owned by Ecobank Transnational Inc (operating under the auspices of the Economic Community of West African States); cap. and res 2,441.8m. (Dec. 1995); Pres. ISSA DIOP; Man. Dir RIZWAN HAIDER; 1 br.

Financial Bank: Immeuble Adjibi, rue du Commandant Decoeur, BP 2700, Cotonou; tel. 31-31-00; telex 5280; fax 31-31-02; f. 1988; 91% owned by Financial BC (Switzerland); cap. and res 282.6m. (Dec. 1995); Pres. RÉMY BAYSSET; Man. Dir THOMAS WIELEZYNSKI; 3 brs.

Financial Institution

Caisse Autonome d'Amortissement du Bénin: BP 59, Cotonou; tel. 31-47-81; telex 5289; fax 31-53-56; manages state funds; Man. Dir IBRAHIM PEDRO BONI.

STOCK EXCHANGE

Côte d'Ivoire's Bourse des Valeurs d'Abidjan was scheduled to become a regional stock exchange, serving the member states of the UEMOA.

INSURANCE

Union Béninoise d'Assurance-Vie: Cotonou; f. 1994 as Benin's first private insurance co; cap. 400m.; 51% owned by Union Africaine Vie (Côte d'Ivoire).

Trade and Industry

DEVELOPMENT ORGANIZATIONS

Caisse Française de Développement (CFD): blvd Jean-Paul II, BP 38, Cotonou; tel. 31-35-80; telex 5082; fax 31-20-18; fmrly Caisse Centrale de Coopération Economique; Dir HENRI PHILIPPE DE CLERCQ.

Mission de Coopération et d'Action Culturelle (Mission Française d'Aide et de Coopération): BP 476, Cotonou; tel. 30-08-24; telex 5209; administers bilateral aid from France according to the cooperation agreement of 1975; Dir BERNARD HADJADJ.

STATE MARKETING BOARDS AND ENTERPRISES

Office National du Bois (ONAB): BP 1238, Recette Principale, Cotonou; tel. 33-16-32; fax 33-19-56; f. 1983; forest development and management, manufacture and marketing of wood products; cap. 300m. francs CFA; transfer of industrial activities to private ownership pending in 1996; Man. Dir Pascal Patinvoh.

Société Béninoise d'Electricité et d'Eau (SBEE): BP 123, Cotonou; tel. 31-21-45; fax 31-50-28; f. 1973; cap. 10,000m. francs CFA; state-owned; production and distribution of electricity and water; Man. Dir Godefroy Chekete.

Société des Ciments d'Onigbolo (SCO): Onigbolo; f. 1975; cap. 10,000m. francs CFA; 51% state-owned; transfer pending to majority private ownership; produces and markets cement; Pres. Justin Gnidehou; Man. Dir Jean-Marie Octave Roko.

Société Nationale pour l'Industrie des Corps Gras (SONICOG): BP 312, Cotonou; tel. 33-07-01; telex 5205; fax 33-15-20; f. 1962; cap. 2,555m. francs CFA; state-owned; processes shea-nuts (karité nuts), palm kernels and cottonseed; Man. Dir Joseph Gabin Dossou.

Société Nationale pour la Promotion Agricole (SONAPRA): BP 933, Cotonou; tel. 33-08-20; telex 5248; fax 33-19-48; f. 1983; cap. 500m. francs CFA; state-owned; manages five cotton-ginning plants and one fertilizer plant; distributes fertilizers and markets agricultural products; Pres. Imorou Salley; Man. Dir Michel Dassi.

CHAMBER OF COMMERCE

Chambre de Commerce, d'Agriculture et d'Industrie de la République du Bénin (CCIB): ave du Général de Gaulle, BP 31, Cotonou; tel. 31-32-99; Pres. Raffet Loko; Sec.-Gen. N. A. Viadenou.

EMPLOYERS' ORGANIZATIONS

Association des Syndicats du Bénin (ASYNBA): Cotonou; Pres. Pierre Fourn.

Conseil Nationale des Chargeurs du Bénin (CNCB): carré no 114, Zone Industrielle d'Akpakpa PK3, BP 06-2528, Cotonou; tel. 33-13-71; telex 5023; fax 33-18-49; Pres. Fidelia Azodogbehou.

Groupement Interprofessionnel des Entreprises du Bénin (GIBA): BP 6, Cotonou; Pres. A. Jeukens.

Syndicat des Commerçants Importateurs et Exportateurs du Bénin: BP 6, Cotonou; Pres. M. Benchimol.

Syndicat Interprofessionnel des Entreprises Industrielles du Bénin: Cotonou; Pres. M. Doucet.

Syndicat National des Commerçants et Industriels Africains du Bénin (SYNACIB): BP 367, Cotonou; Pres. Urbain da Silva.

Syndicat des Transporteurs Routiers du Bénin: Cotonou; Pres. Pascal Zenon.

MAJOR INDUSTRIAL COMPANIES

The following are among the largest companies in terms of either capital investment or employment.

Bio-Benin: BP 04-1227; Cotonou; tel. 30-16-81; fax 30-12-76; f. 1982; cap. 300m. francs CFA; mfrs and wholesalers of pharmaceutical preparations; Dir Ali Assani.

CFAO Bénin: ave Pierre Delorme, BP 7, Cotonou; tel. 31-34-61; fax 31-34-63; f. 1973; cap. 963.4m. francs CFA; import-export co, mfrs of bicycles and mopeds; Pres. and Man. Dir Emmanuel Kouton.

CIMBENIN SA: BP 1124, Cotonou; tel. 30-03-30; telex 5322; fax 33-02-45; f. 1991; cap. 1,950m. francs CFA; mfrs of cement and wholesalers of bldg materials; Man. Dir Hans Fredrik Myklesto.

Communauté Electrique de Bénin (CEB): BP 385, Cotonou; see under Togo.

Complexe Textile du Bénin SA (COTEB): BP 231, Parakou; tel. 61-09-49; fax 61-11-99; production of textiles and garments; Dir-Gen. D. Lenaerts.

Grands Moulins du Bénin (GMB): Zone Industrielle d'Akpakpa, BP 949, Cotonou; tel. 33-08-17; telex 5267; f. 1971; cap. 438m. francs CFA; Lebanese shareholders hold majority interest; wheat-milling; Man. Dir Gilbert Chagoury-Ramez.

Société Béninoise de Brasserie (SOBEBRA): route de Porto-Novo, BP 135, Cotonou; tel. 33-10-61; telex 5275; fax 33-01-48; f. 1957, nationalized 1975–91 (as Société Nationale de Boissons); cap. 3,200m. francs CFA; production and marketing of beer, soft drinks and ice; Pres. Barnabé Bidouzo; Man. Dir André Fontana.

Société Béninoise de Sidérurgie (SBS): Cotonou; f. 1989; operates a wire and steel mill; Chair. John Moore.

Société Béninoise des Tabacs et Allumettes du Bénin (SOBETA): BP 07, Ouidah; tel. 34-13-04; fax 34-13-23; f. 1984 as Manufacture de Cigarettes et d'Allumettes de Ouidah; owned by Rothmans International PLC (UK); mfrs of tobacco products and matches; Pres. Séfou Fagbohoun; Man. Dir Eric Pacitti.

Société Béninoise des Textiles (SOBETEX): BP 208, Cotonou; tel. 33-09-16; telex 5239; f. 1968; cap. 500m. francs CFA; 49% state-owned; bleaching, printing and dyeing of imported fabrics; Pres. François Vrinat; Man. Dir Albert Chambost.

TRADE UNIONS

Confédération Générale du Travail (CGT): Leader: Pascal Todjenou.

Confédération des Syndicats Autonomes du Bénin (CSAB): Cotonou; First Sec. Albert Gougan.

Union Nationale des Syndicats de Travailleurs du Bénin (UNSTB): 1 blvd Saint-Michel, BP 69, Cotonou; tel. and fax 30-36-13; sole officially-recognized trade union 1974–90; Sec.-Gen. Amidou Lawani.

Other autonomous labour organizations include the **Collectif des Syndicats Indépendants**, the **Confédération Générale des Travailleurs du Bénin** and the **Confédération des Syndicats des Travailleurs du Bénin**.

Transport

In October 1996 the World Bank approved a credit of US $40m., to be issued through the International Development Association, in support of a major programme of investment in Benin's transport network. The integrated programme aimed to enhance Benin's status as an entrepôt for regional trade, and also to boost domestic employment and, by improving the infrastructure and reducing transport costs, agricultural and manufacturing output.

RAILWAYS

In 1995 the network handled 388,000 metric tons of goods. Plans for a 650-km extension, linking Parakou to Niamey (Niger), via Gaya, were postponed in the late 1980s, owing to lack of finance.

Organisation Commune Bénin-Niger des Chemins de Fer et des Transports (OCBN): BP 16, Cotonou; tel. 31-33-80; telex 5210; fax 31-41-50; f. 1959; 50% owned by Govt of Benin, 50% by Govt of Niger; total of 579 track-km; main line runs for 438 km from Cotonou to Parakou in the interior; br. line runs westward via Ouidah to Segboroué (34 km); also line of 107 km from Cotonou via Porto-Novo to Pobé (near the Nigerian border); Man. Dir Isaac Enidé Kilanyossi.

ROADS

In 1995 there were an estimated 8,460 km of roads, including 3,440 km of main roads and 2,640 km of secondary roads. About 2,700 km of the network were paved. Road construction or rehabilitation projects in progress at this time were intended primarily to enhance Benin's regional trading links.

Compagnie de Transit et de Consignation du Bénin (CTCB Express): route de l'Aéroport, BP 7079, Cotonou; f. 1986; Pres. Souléman Koura Zoumarou.

SHIPPING

The main port is at Cotonou. In 1995 the port handled some 2,076,900 metric tons of goods, of which 210,100 tons were in transit. The rehabilitation and expansion of facilities at the port of Cotonou is in progress, with financial assistance from the Netherlands.

Port Autonome de Cotonou: BP 927, Cotonou; tel. 31-28-90; telex 5004; fax 31-28-91; f. 1965; state-owned port authority; Man. Dir Issa Badarou-Soulé.

Association pour la Défense des Intérêts du Port de Cotonou (AIPC) (Communauté Portuaire du Bénin): BP 927, Cotonou; tel. 31-17-26; telex 5004; fax 31-28-91; f. 1993; promotes, develops and co-ordinates of port activities at Cotonou; Pres. Issa Badarou-Soulé; Sec.-Gen. Camille Médégan.

Association des Professionnels Agréés en Douanes du Bénin (APRAD): BP 2141, Cotonou; tel. 31-55-05; telex 5355; Chair. Gatien Houngbédji.

Cie Béninoise de Navigation Maritime (COBENAM): 01 BP 2032, Recette Principale, Cotonou; tel. 31-32-87; telex 5225; fax 31-09-78; f. 1974; 51% state-owned, 49% by Govt of Algeria; Pres. Abdel Kader Allal; Man. Dir Cocou Théophile Hounkponou.

SDV Bénin: route du Collège de l'Union, BP 433, Cotonou; tel. 33-11-78; fax 33-06-11; f. 1986; fmrly Delmas–Bénin; Pres. J. F. Mignonneau; Dir F. Lebrat.

Société Béninoise des Manutentions Portuaires (SOBEMAP): place des Martyrs, BP 35, Cotonou; tel. 31-39-83; telex 5135; state-owned; Pres. Georges Sekloka; Man. Dir Théodore Ahouménou Ahouassou.

CIVIL AVIATION

The international airport at Cotonou (Cotonou-Cadjehoun) has a 2.4-km runway, and there are secondary airports at Parakou, Natitingou, Kandi and Abomey.

Air Afrique: ave du Gouverneur Ballot, BP 200, Cotonou; tel. 31-21-07; fax 31-53-41; see under Côte d'Ivoire; Dir in Benin JOSEPH KANZA.

Bénin Inter-Régional: Cotonou; f. 1991 as a jt venture by private Beninois interests and Aeroflot (then the state airline of the USSR); operates domestic and regional flights.

Tourism

Benin's national parks and game reserves are its principal tourist attractions. About 142,000 tourists visited Benin in 1994, when receipts from tourism were estimated at US $55m.

Conseil National du Tourisme: Cotonou; f. 1993.

Defence

In August 1996 the Beninois Armed Forces numbered some 4,800 active personnel (land army 4,500, navy about 150, air force 150). Paramilitary forces comprised a 2,500-strong gendarmerie. Military service is by selective conscription, and lasts for 18 months.

Defence Expenditure: Estimated at US $24.0m. in 1996.

Chief of Defence Staff: Col GANDONOU KODJA.

Chief of Staff of the Army: Col FÉLICIEN DOS SANTOS.

Chief of Staff of the Navy: Lt-Col PROSPER TIANDO.

Education

Primary education, which is officially compulsory, begins at six years of age and lasts for six years. Secondary education, beginning at 12 years of age, lasts for up to seven years, comprising a first cycle of four years and a second of three years. In 1991 only 53% of children in the relevant age-group were enrolled at primary schools (71% of boys; 35% of girls). Enrolment at secondary schools in that year was equivalent to only 12% of the appropriate age-group (17% of boys; 7% of girls). The Government's economic adjustment programme for the second half of the 1990s was to include, with assistance both from multilateral and bilateral donors, schemes to extend the provision of primary and vocational education facilities. Higher education facilities include the University of Benin, founded at Cotonou in 1970. In 1993/94 9,964 students were enrolled at tertiary institutions. At the time of the 1992 census the average rate of adult illiteracy was 72.5% (males 59.9%; females 83.2%); UNESCO estimated an illiterate adult population of 63.0% (males 51.3%; females 74.2%) in 1995.

Consolidated budget estimates for 1990 allocated 14,839m. francs CFA to the education sector (12.8% of central government expenditure).

Bibliography

Adamon, A. D. *Renouvea démocratique au Bénin: La Conférence nationale des forces vives et la période de transition.* Paris, L'Harmattan, 1995.

Allen, C., Radu, M. S., and Somerville, K., (Eds). *Benin, The Congo, Burkina Faso: Economics, Politics and Society.* New York and London, Pinter Publishers, Marxist Regimes Series, 1989.

Cornevin, R. *La République populaire du Bénin, des Origines dahoméennes à nos jours.* Paris, Académie des Sciences d'Outre-mer, 1984.

Le Dahomey. Paris, Presses universitaires de France, 1965.

Histoire du Dahomey. Paris, Berger-Levrault, 1962; new edn as *Histoire du Bénin.* Paris, Maisonneuve et Larose.

Decalo, S. *Historical Dictionary of Dahomey.* Metuchen, NJ, Scarecrow Press, 1975; new edn as *Historical Dictionary of Benin*, 1988.

Dunn, J. (Ed.). *West African States: Failure and Promise.* Cambridge University Press, 1978.

Egharevba, J. *A Short History of Benin (1900–1933).* Oxford, ABC, Ibadan University Press, 1991.

Garcia, L. *Le royaume du Dahomé face à la pénétration coloniale.* Paris, Editions Karthala, 1988.

Harrison Church, R. J. *West Africa.* 8th Edn, London, Longman, 1979.

Journaux, A., Pélissier, P., and Parisse, R. *Géographie du Dahomey.* Caen, Imprimerie Ozanne, 1962.

Lusignan, G. de. *French-Speaking Africa since Independence.* London, Pall Mall, 1969.

Manning, P. *Slavery, Colonialism and Economic Growth in Dahomey, 1640–1960.* Cambridge, Cambridge University Press, 1982.

Medeiros, F. de. *Peuples du golfe du Bénin (Aja-Ewé).* Paris, Editions Karthala, 1984.

Ogbemudia, S. O. *Years of Challenge.* Oxford, Heineman Educational Books (Nigeria), 1991.

Rimmer, D. *The Economies of West Africa.* London, Weidenfeld and Nicolson, 1984.

BOTSWANA

Physical and Social Geography

A. MacGREGOR HUTCHESON

PHYSICAL FEATURES

The Republic of Botswana is a land-locked country, bordered by Namibia to the west and north, by the latter's Caprivi Strip to the north, by Zimbabwe to the north-east, and by South Africa to the south and south-east. Botswana occupies 581,730 sq km (224,607 sq miles) of the downwarped Kalahari Basin of the great southern African plateau, which has here an average altitude of 900 m above sea-level. Gentle undulations to flat surfaces, consisting of Kalahari sands overlying Archean rocks, are characteristic of most of the country but the east is more hilly and broken. Most of southern Botswana is without surface drainage and, apart from the bordering Limpopo and Chobe rivers, the rest of the country's drainage is interior and does not reach the sea. Flowing into the north-west from the Angolan highlands, the perennial Okavango river is Botswana's major system. The Okavango drains into a depression in the plateau, 145 km from the border, to form the Okavango swamps and the ephemeral Lake Ngami. From this vast marsh covering 16,000 sq km there is a seasonal flow of water eastwards along the Botletle river 260 km to Lake Xau and thence into the Makarakari salt pan. Most of the water brought into Botswana by the Okavango is lost through evaporation and transpiration in the swamps.

The Kalahari Desert dominates southern and western Botswana. From the near-desert conditions of the extreme south-west with an average annual rainfall around 130 mm, there is a gradual increase in precipitation towards the north (635 mm) and east (380–500 mm). There is an associated transition in the natural vegetation from the sparse thornveld of the Kalahari Desert to the dry woodland savannah of the north and east, and the infertile sands give way eastwards to better soils developed on granitic and sedimentary rocks.

POPULATION AND RESOURCES

The eastern strip, the best-endowed and most developed region of Botswana, possesses about 80% of the population, which was estimated to be 1,456,000 in mid-August 1995. Seven of the eight Batswana tribes, and most of the Europeans and Asians, are concentrated in the east. A substantial number of Batswana (the figure is unrecorded but estimated to be at least 50,000) are employed in South Africa, many of them (an estimated 12,746 in 1995) in mining. The absence of these workers helps to ease pressure on resources and contributes to the country's income through deferred pay and remittances sent home to their families. However, as a result of the rapid population growth, and since a large proportion of the population is less than 15 years of age, there is a pressing need for improvements in agricultural productivity and in other sectors of the economy to provide work for the growing number of young people who are entering the labour market.

Shortage of water, resulting from the low annual rainfall and aggravated by considerable fluctuations in the monthly distribution and total seasonal rainfall, is the main hindrance to the development of Botswana's natural resources, although a number of projects have improved water supply to the main centres of economic activity. Limitations imposed by rainfall make much of the country more suitable for the rearing of livestock, especially cattle, but it has been estimated that in eastern Botswana 4.45m. ha are suitable for cultivation, of which only about 10% is actually cultivated. Although in the east the irrigation potential is limited, the Okavango-Chobe swamps offer substantial scope for irrigation (as much as an estimated 600,000 ha).

In recent years Botswana's economic base has been considerably widened. Exploitable deposits of diamonds (of which Botswana is now the world's third largest producer), gold, silver, uranium, copper, nickel, coal, manganese, asbestos, common salt, potash, soda ash and sodium sulphate have been identified, and some of these minerals are currently being mined. In particular, the major developments of diamond mining at Orapa, Letlhakane and Jwaneng, and copper-nickel mining focused on Selebi-Phikwe, with their attendant infrastructural improvements, are helping to diversify the predominantly agricultural economy.

Recent History

RICHARD BROWN

Revised for this edition by the Editor

COLONIAL RULE TO THE KHAMA PERIOD, 1885–1980

The political history of Botswana (known as Bechuanaland until its independence in 1966) has been influenced by three main factors: the country's geographical position, adjoining the formerly white-ruled South Africa, Namibia and Zimbabwe; the absence of a significant African nationalist movement before independence; and the strong allegiances between the eight main tribal groups.

In 1885 the British government declared Bechuanaland a protectorate, at the request of local rulers who wished to deter encroachment by Boers from the Transvaal. The British assumed that Bechuanaland would eventually be absorbed into the Union of South Africa, but this was resolutely opposed by the indigenous population, particularly after the introduction of apartheid by South Africa in 1948. In 1950 the British administration approved the formation of a joint advisory council, and elections to a legislative council took place in 1961: Bechuanaland's 3,200 white inhabitants were represented by 10 elected members, while a further 10 were indirectly elected to represent the 317,000 Africans.

In 1960 the Bechuanaland People's Party (BPP) was founded, maintaining close links with the African National Congress of South Africa (ANC). The BPP soon split into two factions, which later became the Botswana Independence Party (BIP) and the more important Botswana People's Party (BPP). In 1961 Seretse (later Sir Seretse) Khama, the former heir to the chieftainship of the important Bamangwato tribe (who had been forced to renounce the chieftainship in 1956, by pressure from the British, South African and Southern Rhodesian governments, after he had married a white woman), gained a seat on the legislative council, and was also appointed to the territory's executive council. In 1962 Khama formed the Bechuanaland Democratic Party (BDP), securing the support of 10 of the African members of the legislative council. Many whites also gave their support to the BDP, in preference to the more militant BPP. In the territory's first direct election, held in March 1965 (in accordance with a pre-independence constitution which granted internal self-government), the BDP won 28 of the 31 seats in a new legislative assembly, chosen by universal adult suffrage. Khama duly became prime minister. Independence was achieved on 30 September 1966, when Bechuanaland became the Republic of Botswana, with Khama as president.

During the years following independence, the BDP (restyled the Botswana Democratic Party) was challenged by the BPP (particularly in urban areas) and by a new Marxist-orientated party, the Botswana National Front (BNF), both of which won small numbers of parliamentary seats in the 1969, 1974 and 1979 general elections. The BDP nevertheless retained by far the largest majority in the legislature. The BPP significantly reduced the powers of the tribal chiefs, including their traditional rights to allocate land and to control mineral concessions.

Following the unilateral declaration of independence by Rhodesia (now Zimbabwe) in 1965, President Khama denounced the illegal regime; however, he was unable to enforce strict economic sanctions against Rhodesia, owing to Botswana's dependence on the Rhodesian-owned railways for its economic survival. During the 1970s Botswana, with the other 'front-line' states (Angola, Mozambique, Tanzania and Zambia), declared support for the nationalist Patriotic Front in Rhodesia, and allowed sanctuary and passage for nationalist guerrillas, although they were not permitted to establish military bases in Botswana. Zimbabwe's achievement of independence in April 1980 brought considerable economic benefits to Botswana. Botswana was a founder member of the Southern African Development Co-ordination Conference (SADCC), formed in 1979, with the aim of encouraging regional development and reducing members' economic dependence on South Africa. (The SADCC was superseded by the Southern African Development Community—SADC—in 1992.)

BOTSWANA UNDER MASIRE

Internal Developments

Khama died in July 1980, and was succeeded as president by Dr Quett Ketumile Masire, a founder of the BDP and hitherto the vice-president. Masire had previously served for several years as minister of finance and development planning, and had played a pivotal role in the country's economic development.

Masire's presidency was renewed in September 1984, when, in a general election to the national assembly, the BDP again won a decisive victory, originally gaining 29 of the 34 elective seats in an enlarged chamber. The election was contested by the six registered political parties, and 78% of the electorate voted. The BNF originally won four of the elective seats; the party's leader, Kenneth Koma, initially failed to gain a seat, losing to the vice-president, Peter Mmusi, by a narrow margin. However, this result was challenged by the BNF, and was invalidated by the high court in October, following the discovery of an unopened ballot box. Mmusi had to relinquish the vice-presidency, but retained his position as minister of finance and development planning. His position in the cabinet appeared to be in jeopardy after he was defeated by Koma in a re-contest, held in December. However, following the resignation of an MP during that month, Mmusi was appointed to the vacant seat and was subsequently reinstated as vice-president.

Although the BDP's success in the parliamentary elections consolidated its position, popular discontent at the country's high level of unemployment was reflected in the outcome of the local government elections (held on the same day as the parliamentary elections), in which the BDP lost control of all the town councils except that of Selebi-Phikwe. The BDP's strength was also undermined by the defection, in November 1985, of two prominent party members to the BNF.

Tension between the BDP and the BNF continued to grow in early 1987. In May some members of the BDP alleged that youthful elements within the BNF were being trained in insurgency techniques by Libya and the USSR. The government, however, dissociated itself from these allegations. In September 1987 a referendum was held on constitutional amendments concerning the electoral system; a large majority reportedly voted in favour of endorsing the reforms, although the BNF boycotted the referendum.

At parliamentary elections held in October 1989, the BDP strengthened its position by winning 31 of the 34 elective seats, receiving 65% of all votes cast. The BNF, weakened by internal dissension, won only three seats, although it obtained 27% of the total votes. As in 1984, the BNF challenged the results in a number of constituencies. The BPP lost its only seat, and four other parties also failed to secure representation. In October the new national assembly elected Masire for a third term as president. He subsequently threatened that his government would take action against workers involved in illegal strikes, as a measure to suppress widespread unrest among bank employees, mineworkers and primary school teachers.

In 1990 the BNF and the BPP formed an opposition alliance, agreeing to nominate a single candidate in each constituency at future elections. However, the BNF candidate failed to win a by-election at Mochudi in June (caused by a high court ruling upholding BNF charges of irregularities at the 1989 elections). Some BNF leaders subsequently claimed that the party had become a national liberation movement, an assertion which disrupted the harmony of the opposition coalition. Despite the high court ruling on the Mochudi election result, the president later accused the opposition parties of bringing Botswana's democratic system into disrepute by persistently challenging election results. In late 1991 the government dismissed some 12,000 striking workers from public-sector unions, who had demanded wage increases.

In early March 1992 the vice-president, Peter Mmusi, and the minister of agriculture, Daniel Kwelagobe, resigned, having been implicated by a commission of inquiry in a corruption scandal involving the illegal transfer of land. Festus Mogae, the minister of finance and development planning, was appointed vice-president and also allocated the portfolio of local government and lands; a new minister of agriculture was also appointed. In June Mmusi and Kwelagobe were suspended from the central committee of the BDP, but were re-elected at the party's congress in July 1993. As leaders of one of the two main factions into which the BDP was increasingly divided, Mmusi and Kwelagobe opposed the government's economic liberalization policy, as well as seeking to overturn the findings of the commission on illegal land dealings. A corruption scandal in 1993, involving the Botswana Housing Corpn, led to the resignation of two other government ministers. The government's reputation was also undermined by the revelation that seven ministers were among the debtors of the National Development Bank, which was found to be in financial difficulties. Uncertainty about the future leadership of the BDP (President Masire is over 70 years of age) and the president's silence on this matter added to the divisions within the ruling party both before and after the general election, held in October 1994.

Meanwhile, the opposition BNF's demands, made in May 1993, for the appointment of an independent electoral commission and for the reduction of the voting age (to 18 years) were rejected by the government. In spite of this, the BNF abandoned its threat to boycott elections and sought, instead, to mobilize popular support on the issues of government corruption and the recession in Botswana's economy. The success of this strategy was demonstrated when the party fared unexpectedly well in the general election of 15 October 1994, winning 37.7% of votes and increasing its representation to 13 of the 40 elective seats. The BNF performed particularly strongly in urban areas, and for the first time an opposition party emerged from an election in a position to offer a serious challenge to the ruling party. The BDP, however, with 53.1% of the vote, retained its dominance in rural constituencies, winning a total of 26 of the elective seats. The election was conducted peacefully, with over 70% of the electorate turning out to vote. Only three ministers (including Mogae) retained their portfolios in the new cabinet. The national assembly re-elected Masire to the presidency, on 17 October. One week later four additional deputies were elected to the national assembly, including two new cabinet ministers. The new cabinet included Daniel Kwelagobe as minister of works, transport and communications (Kwelagobe had been acquitted by the high court of charges relating to corruption allegations made in 1992—see above).

The months following the election were marked by sporadic unrest, triggered by the release of three people who had been detained in connection with the ritual killing of a schoolgirl, but also reflecting a more generalized social and political discontent. Rioting, which had begun in Mochudi, north of Gaborone, in late January 1995, spread to the capital in mid-February, when demonstrators (mainly students and unemployed youths) were prevented by the security forces from entering the parliament buildings; the protesters subsequently erected barricades outside the university. Three days of violent clashes and looting followed, during which one person was killed. The BNF denied government allegations that it had promoted the unrest, which it claimed to be a reaction to the country's high rate of unemployment and other social problems. The government rejected allegations of excessive violence by the security forces in their suppression of the demonstrations.

In June 1995 the governor of the central bank expressed his view that a new economic strategy was needed to address the country's socio-economic problems. In July the opposition BNF unsuccessfully sought to obtain a parliamentary majority for a vote of 'no confidence' in the government, on the grounds of its failure to redress the country's social problems and the alleged involvement of government officials in financial irregularities at the National Development Bank. In the same month Ponatshego Kedikilwe, the minister of presidential affairs and public administration, was appointed chairman of the BDP (a post which had remained vacant since the death of Peter Mmusi in October 1994).

In November 1995 it was proposed that Botswana's constitution be amended in order to limit presidential tenure to a maximum of two five-year terms. It was emphasized, however, that the amendment, which was to take effect from the 1999 elections, was not to apply retrospectively, and would not therefore debar Masire from seeking a fifth term as president. The imposition of a limit on presidential terms had consistently been a major demand of opposition parties. The approval of the amendment, at an all-party conference held in May 1996, followed an earlier concession, in April, to reduce the minimum voting age from 21 to 18 years. Also accepted at the meeting were government proposals for the establishment of an independent electoral commission, to be headed by a High Court judge: opposition parties had hitherto been critical of the prevailing system, whereby the election supervisor was an appointee of the president's office. Agreement in principle was also reached on changes to the method of selecting local councils (including the abolition of the nomination of councillors by the minister of local government, lands and housing), and on the introduction of proxy votes for Batswana resident abroad. A plebiscite on the proposed reforms was expected to take place in October 1997, following the conclusion of a national consultative exercise.

External Relations

During the 1980s, relations with South Africa remained strained, and Botswana was not immune to South Africa's general destabilizing pressures on its black-ruled neighbours. Revelations in mid-1980 that the South African armed forces had been recruiting Basarwa (Bushmen) from Botswana to serve in Namibia against guerrillas of the South West Africa People's Organisation of Namibia (SWAPO) caused alarm, and President Masire promised that the government would conduct an investigation. During 1981 tensions developed with South Africa over the supply of Soviet military equipment for the Botswana Defence Force (BDF). Masire defended the purchases on financial grounds and reiterated Botswana's adherence to its policy of non-alignment, stating that the instructors who accompanied the weapons had all left the country. By expanding the capabilities of the BDF, Botswana sought to achieve a more extensive and effective surveillance of its borders, thereby preventing insurgents from crossing into South Africa, and so removing any South African excuse for mounting punitive raids into Botswana. At the same time, it remained Botswana's policy to accommodate South African refugees, while not allowing them to use the country as a base for attacks on South Africa.

Several incidents, including, in April 1982, an exchange of fire over the border between Botswana and South African troops, led to increased tensions. In May 1984 Masire accused South Africa of attempting to coerce Botswana into signing a non-aggression pact similar to that negotiated by the Pretoria government with Lesotho. The president claimed that South Africa had hinted that, if Botswana refused to sign, it might position troops along the frontier between the two countries and cause disruptions of cross-border traffic. However, in late February 1985 South Africa reportedly abandoned its insistence that Botswana sign a formal joint security pact. Relations deteriorated once again in June, following a raid on alleged ANC bases in Gaborone by South African forces, in which at least 15 people were killed.

In early 1986 the United Kingdom and the USA pledged military aid to help Botswana to deter South African attacks and terrorist infiltration. In February Botswana's government reiterated its undertaking that the country was not to be used as a base for attacks by terrorists, and in March ANC representatives were expelled. The improvement in relations was short-lived: in May 1986, in conjunction with attacks on Zambia and Zimbabwe, South African troops launched land and air attacks on targets near Gaborone, causing one death. South Africa again claimed that its action was aimed at ANC bases. Although Botswana fully sympathized with the renewed international condemnation of apartheid, the vulnerability of the country's position, both geographically and economically, prevented the government from committing itself to the imposition of economic sanctions against South Africa, which was recommended by the SADCC in August.

With the approach of the South African general election in May 1987, tension increased as South Africa warned Botswana and other 'front-line' states that it would launch attacks against them in order to pre-empt disruption of the election by the ANC. Such an attack was alleged to have taken place in April, when four people were killed in a bomb explosion in Gaborone. In March 1988 South Africa openly admitted responsibility for a commando raid on a house in Gaborone, in which four alleged members of the ANC were killed. In June Masire announced the capture of two members of a South African defence force unit which had allegedly opened fire on Botswana security forces while engaged in a commando raid. South Africa claimed that the unit had been on an intelligence mission. South African armed incursions continued in subsequent months, and in March 1989 nine South Africans were expelled from Botswana for 'security reasons'. The relaxation of the political climate within South Africa from 1990 onwards, however, led to a gradual improvement in relations between the two countries. Full diplomatic relations were established in June 1994.

Relations between Botswana and Zimbabwe (whose ideologies are far apart) have been correct rather than friendly. Although Masire made an official visit to Harare in 1982, tension subsequently increased as a large number of former guerrillas of the Zimbabwe African People's Union (ZAPU), supporters of Joshua Nkomo (viewed as insurgents by the Zimbabwe government), crossed the border and entered refugee camps. A sharp deterioration in Botswana-Zimbabwe relations occurred in March 1983, when, with serious unrest in Zimbabwe's Matabeleland province, Nkomo fled to Botswana. Zimbabwe had already claimed that Botswana was providing a base for pro-Nkomo insurgents. To the considerable relief of the Botswana government, Nkomo left for London after only a few days in the country.

The presence of Zimbabwean refugees in Botswana persistently beset relations between the two countries throughout the 1980s. In 1983 allegations that armed dissidents from Zimbabwe were being sheltered among the 3,000–4,000 Zimbabwean refugees encamped in Botswana led the Botswana government to agree to impose stricter controls on the refugees. In May 1983 Botswana and Zimbabwe established full diplomatic relations. In August Robert Mugabe, the prime minister (later president) of Zimbabwe, visited Botswana for discussions, and it was announced that a joint trade agreement was being drafted. However, the recurrence of incidents on the Botswana–Zimbabwe border between members of the BDF and armed men wearing Zimbabwean military uniforms created further tension, and led to security talks between the two countries in late 1983. In July 1984 the Zimbabwe government stated that Botswana had repatriated more than 1,200 Zimbabwean refugees, including more than 300 alleged guerrillas. However, following the July 1985 general election in Zimbabwe, a new influx of refugees threatened to disrupt relations once again. In May 1988 Masire expressed confidence that the remaining Zimbabwean exiles would return to their country voluntarily as a result of an apparent improvement in the political climate in Zimbabwe. At the end of April 1989 the Botswana government announced that refugee status for Zimbabwean nationals in the country was to be revoked, and by September almost all Zimbabwean refugees were reported to have left Botswana. In the mid-1990s, however, the government expressed concern at the growing number of illegal immigrants in the country, the majority of whom were from Zimbabwe; of more than 40,000 illegal immigrants repatriated during 1995, more than 14,000 were Zimbabwean.

Following the achievement of independence by Namibia in March 1990, presidential visits were exchanged by Botswana and Namibia and steps were taken to ensure bilateral co-operation. However, in 1992 a border dispute developed between the two countries regarding their rival territorial claims over a small island in the Chobe river. In early 1995 Botswana and Namibia agreed to present the case for arbitration at the International Court of Justice; and in February 1996 the two countries signed an agreement committing themselves in advance to the court's eventual judgement. Meanwhile, Namibia appealed to Botswana to remove its troops—stated by the Botswana authorities to be anti-poaching patrols—and national flag from the island. In the following month it was announced that Botswana and Namibia were to establish joint sub-committees at posts along the frontier in order to control illegal border crossings and smuggling. None the less, what were perceived as attempts by Botswana to extend the role and capabilities of its armed forces (most notably the completion of a new air base in 1995 and efforts during 1996–97 to procure military tanks) remained a source of friction between the two countries, although Botswana emphasized that a principal aim of such expansion was to enable its military to fulfil a wider regional and international peace-keeping role. Namibia's decision to construct a pipeline to take water from the Okavango river created further tension in 1996. (The river feeds the Okavango delta, an important habitat for Botswana's varied wildlife.) In early 1997 it was reported that Namibia had been angered by Botswana's erection of a fence along Namibia's Caprivi Strip, which separates the two countries to the north; Botswana insisted, however, that the fence was simply a measure to control the spread of livestock diseases. In August 1996 it was announced that a three-year programme for the repatriation of some 1,000 Herero refugees to Namibia was almost complete.

Botswana is a member of the OAU, the UN and the Commonwealth. It is also a non-aligned nation and its principled stands over issues such as apartheid, coupled with general moderation of approach, have given Botswana an effective voice in many international deliberations. In mid-1993 several hundred Botswana troops were deployed in UN operations.

Economy

LINDA VAN BUREN

Diamonds have transformed the Botswana economy. At independence in 1966, Botswana was one of the 20 poorest countries in the world, with minimal infrastructural development and a predominantly subsistence economy. Government revenues were critically dependent on foreign aid and the remittances of Batswana males employed in South Africa. The average life expectancy at birth was 50 years. Dominated by a few large-scale, mainly expatriate, farms, the commercial livestock sector was the largest contributor to gross domestic product (GDP) and export earnings. During the 1980s, however, Botswana's economic performance exceeded that of all other non-petroleum producing countries in Africa. GDP rose, in real terms, by an annual average of 10.3% in 1980–90, giving Botswana one of the world's highest economic growth rates, and by an average of 4.4% yearly in 1990–94. This exceptional record was partly due to the rapid expansion of the beef industry, although the principal cause was the discovery and development of valuable mineral resources, especially diamonds. Apart from transforming the export base, the development of the mining sector has also helped to stimulate and finance the development of Botswana's infrastructure, manufacturing sector and social services. In the 1990s Botswana became an 'upper middle income' country under World Bank definitions and, unusually for an African country, a contributor to Bank funds. In 1996 the average life expectancy was 67 years.

The rise in the mineral sector is reflected in changes in the economic structure after 1966. The contribution of agriculture to GDP fell dramatically, exacerbated by prolonged periods of drought during 1981–87, from almost 40% of the total at independence to an average of 4.3% between 1990/91 and 1994/95. The contribution of mining increased from 0% to an average of 35.0% during 1990/91—1994/95, having reached an exceptional 49.8% in 1988/89. Growth in manufacturing, transport and communications, and the financial and social services sectors was also impressive, if less dramatic. A similar situation has prevailed in exports, with beef sales falling from over 90% of merchandise earnings in 1966 to an estimated 4.5% in 1993. Visible export earnings from diamonds rose from 0% in 1966 to an estimated 67.2% of the total in 1995. When combined with exports of copper-nickel matte, minerals accounted for about 72.5% of total export earnings in that year.

Growth based on such narrow foundations is vulnerable and difficult to sustain in the long term. The sixth National Development Plan (1984/85–1989/90) was predicated on a substantial diminution in growth rates, to an average of 4.8% per year, through a stabilization of diamond and beef output and the lack of alternative means to sustain high growth levels, particularly in the mining sector. However, higher than anticipated diamond production and price levels rendered the projections for the Plan too pessimistic; GDP increased, in real terms, by an annual average of 12.0% in 1985/86—1987/88. During 1989/90—1991/92 growth in GDP slowed to an average annual rate of 7.5%. Nevertheless, it is of concern that growth in GDP during the late 1980s and early 1990s was also greatly assisted by a rapid increase in government expenditure, which cannot be sustained indefinitely. The government plans to encourage the short-term development of the manufacturing and tourism sectors in order to combat lower diamond and beef sales and to stimulate future growth. The seventh National Development Plan (1990/91–1996/97) aimed to increase earnings from the mining sector sufficiently to support a doubling of government expenditure, and envisaged an expanded role for the private sector in economic development. In 1993 the Plan's targets were reviewed and scaled down, the shortage of skilled manpower being identified as the major constraint on faster progress. Botswana's economic performance was adversely affected during the early 1990s by the international economic recession, and real GDP, which declined by 0.1% in 1992/93, dropped below the rate of population growth for the first time since independence. The recovery in the diamond market in late 1993 was the principal cause of GDP growth of 4.1% in 1993/94. A further mining downturn brought GDP growth back down to 3.1% in 1994/95. In 1995/96, however, an upturn in the mining sector lifted GDP growth to 7.0%. In February 1997 the government forecast real GDP growth of 6.8% for 1996/97. Also in that month the eighth National Development Plan (1997/98—2002/03) was introduced with the theme 'Sustainable Economic Diversification'. The Plan laid emphasis on encouraging the growth of the private sector and intensifying diversification efforts. During the same period, under a scheme called 'Vision 2016', Botswana's populace is to be invited to participate in the debate on developmental issues that affect its future.

AGRICULTURE

Despite recent rapid urbanization, 25.7% of the employed labour force were engaged in agriculture in 1991. According to FAO estimates, 39.3% of the economically active population were engaged in the sector in mid–1995. Composed partly of semi-desert and partly of a savannah area with highly erratic rainfall and relatively poor soils, Botswana is more suited to grazing than to arable production (only about 5% of Botswana's land is arable). There have been some recent attempts to compensate for this through development of the country's irrigation potential, but agriculture remains dominated by the livestock sector generally, and the cattle industry in particular, which is the main activity of rural Botswana, and which contributes over 80% of agricultural GDP. The GDP of the agricultural sector increased at an average rate of 7.1% per year over the period 1989/90–1994/95.

The national herd increased dramatically after independence, from 1.4m. head in 1965 to a peak of almost 3m. in 1981, stimulated by improved beef export prices, the expansion of available grazing through drilling of new boreholes, and the establishment of effective disease control, based on a system of cordon fences and vaccination, which has kept the country free of foot-and-mouth disease since 1981. The cordon system opened up the lucrative market within the European Union (EU), which offered preferential terms and handsome price subsidies (in Botswana's case, a 92% levy rebate) to Lomé Convention signatories able to satisfy the stringent disease-control criteria, but it also involved the government in international controversy over the impact of the cordon system on wildlife. The criticism was intensified by the fact that the economic benefit of beef exports largely accrued to the 5% of households who were estimated to own more than one-half of the national herd, with about 20% of the total held by 360 large-scale commercial farms. Approximately 50% of rural households neither own nor have access to cattle. However, the General Agreement on Tariffs and Trade (GATT), renegotiated in December 1993, proposed to end the beef subsidies previously enjoyed by Botswana and other eligible countries under the beef protocol of the Lomé Convention. The eighth round of GATT talks in Punta del Este, Uruguay (known as the 'Uruguay Round'), lasted seven years and concluded on 15 December 1993 with a new trade-liberalization agreement signed by 117 countries. Under that agreement, the name of the Geneva-based GATT was changed to the World Trade Organization (WTO).

The recurrence of drought from 1981 until 1986/87 had a severe impact on cattle numbers, reducing the national herd by an estimated 25%, to 2.3m. The end of the drought in the 1987/88 rainy season allowed the replenishment of stocks to an estimated 2.7m. head in 1990. An exceptionally severe drought in 1991/92, however, reduced the national herd drastically, although by 1994 the herd had again been increased to 2.8m. For the beef industry, recurrent drought caused a decline in cattle weight, and the Botswana Meat Commission (BMC) was able to fulfil no more than 70% of its annual EU quota of 18,910 metric tons of beef after 1985. Nevertheless, Europe remained its single most important market, taking more than 50% of total exports. Although previously profitable, the BMC made a loss in 1990/91. In 1991/92 the severe drought conditions resulted in a 35.4% increase in the number of cattle slaughtered and a corresponding improvement in the BMC's profitability, to P39.6m. in the year to 30 September 1994. It had ample slaughtering capacity, following the opening in 1989 of a new abattoir in Francistown, which complemented existing BMC facilities at Lobatse and Maun. In 1994 neighbouring South Africa raised its beef prices by 30%–40%, with mixed results for Botswana. Although legal beef exports to South Africa were more profitable, some cattle-owners opted to smuggle their cattle across the border, dodging both the BMC and the Botswana tax authorities. The BMC sought a tax ruling from the Botswana government that would have enabled it to raise its own cattle prices to farmers; the decision did not come in time to prevent three months of cattle-smuggling, which hitherto had been a relatively rare occurrence in Botswana. In 1996/97 the beef sector was beset by two new problems, one domestic and one international. An outbreak of cattle lung disease in Ngamiland resulted in the destruction of some 300,000 head of cattle, and led to the closure of the Maun abattoir in September 1996. In previous years the abattoir had contributed 25% of the raw material for the meat-canning industry and 15% for the hides industry. In addition, veld fires in the Chobe area, and locust infestation in the North East District, also had a negative effect on the cattle sector. Internationally, the scare precipitated by fears over the prevalence in the UK of the cattle disease Bovine Spongiform Encephalitis (BSE), also known as 'mad cow disease', caused a collapse in global beef consumption (down by 30% in the UK, by 60% in Germany, and by 98% in Greece). Surplus beef stocks reached unprecedented levels, and the international real market price of beef declined by 25%. By February 1997 a programme to restock Ngamiland's cattle herd was well under way, the ministry of agriculture had purchased 49,000 of the 70,000 head required from cattle farmers in other areas of Botswana.

In contrast to cattle, sheep and goat numbers have withstood the periodic droughts reasonably well. Predominantly a subsistence sector resource, they increased from 776,000 head in 1982 to an estimated 2.15m. in 1995. The main commercial development outside beef has been in urban poultry farming. Efforts have also been made to improve the availability of eggs and chickens in rural areas, and to improve local production of milk and fish. Diversification efforts in 1996 were focused on ostrich farming and fish farming, and on improving the infrastructure for the marketing of fresh milk. Ostrich farming has become a promising new industry, with a view to marketing this low-cholesterol meat in European markets. Progress could be inhibited, however, in the absence of government financial assistance in meeting the high start-up costs involved.

In the arable sector, as in beef, commercial farmers provide a disproportionate amount of crop production: official figures indicate that just 100 commercial farms account for 37% of total output of sorghum, maize, millet, beans and pulses. Of the 85% of small-scale farms producing crops, almost one-third cover less than 3 ha, and only 6.8% more than the 10 ha minimum necessary for household self-sufficiency, even in years of reasonable rains. As a result, two-thirds of rural households are reported to depend for as much as 40% of their income on members employed in the formal, predominantly commercial, agricultural sector. In 1992 a commission of inquiry uncovered widespread corruption in the sale and distribution of land. In February 1997 a new fresh-produce horticultural market was opened in Lobatse, and a similar facility, due to open in 1998, was to be built in Francistown.

As a result of the 1991/92 drought (the worst this century), the total area planted with food crops was reduced by 70%–80%; even prior to this, however, the government had abandoned its former aim of achieving national self-sufficiency in cereals. In accordance with the seventh National Development Plan (1990/91–1996/97), shortfalls in cereal production were to be offset by imports, and efforts were made to improve household incomes, in order to reduce reliance on subsidies. In 1993 Boswana imported some 133,000 metric tons of cereals. An official drought was declared for the fourth consecutive year in April 1995, with the output of both maize and sorghum being expected to drop by about two-thirds. The government has allocated P131m. for the drought relief programme in the year to 30 June 1996. Good rains in late 1995 and early 1996 led Vice-President F. G. Mogae to state in his budget speech of February 1996 that drought relief in 1996/97 should be rendered unnecessary. Rains in the 1996/97 growing season were good and led to an overall cereal surplus.

In the mid-1980s land under irrigation totalled only 1,000 ha, the majority consisting of privately-owned farms producing primarily cotton, citrus fruits and tobacco. Botswana is considered to have substantial irrigated potential, however, particularly in the Okavango Delta and Chobe areas. In view of the unique and fragile nature of the Okavango, especially, there are also significant possible environmental risks in realizing this potential, which have been the subject of considerable study in recent years. Some experimentation, utilizing flood-recession irrigation, has been initiated at Molapo, on the eastern fringe of the Okavango. Pending the final outcome of environmental studies on the project, it is planned to proceed with a scheme, costing P180m., to develop between 5,000–10,000 ha of high-yielding crops by improving water- and crop-management systems. Other projects are currently being studied under the government's 'accelerated water resource development programme'.

MINERALS AND MINING

Botswana is now Africa's third largest mineral producer by value, but it was not until after independence in 1966 that the country was found to have abundant reserves of diamonds, coal, copper-nickel, soda ash, potash and sodium sulphate. Substantial deposits of salts and plutonium, as well as smaller reserves of gold, silver and a variety of industrial minerals, were also identified. In real terms, the GDP of the mining sector increased at an average rate of 3.6% per year between 1985/86 and 1994/95.

Large-scale mineral exploitation began in 1971, when the Orapa diamond mine began production, and Botswana now has a relatively diverse mining sector, with three major diamond mines, coal and copper-nickel mines, as well as small-scale mining of gold, industrial minerals and semi-precious stones. The diamond mines are owned and operated by the Debswana Diamond Co (Pty), a joint venture owned equally by the Botswana government and De Beers Consolidated Mines of South Africa. De Beers began diamond exploration in 1955, but it was not until 1969 that the 117-ha Orapa kimberlite pipe, the world's second largest in terms of size, was discovered. Mining at Orapa, which commenced in 1971, was followed in 1977 by the inauguration of production at the adjacent Letlhakane pipe, and in 1982 a major new mine at Jwaneng, 125 km west of Gaborone, was brought into production. A 20% expansion at Jwaneng in 1995 was expected to raise GDP growth by a full percentage point. This expansion of plant capacity, known as Jwaneng Fourth Stream, did indeed contribute in large measure to the doubling of Botswana's real GDP growth rate in 1995/96. The GDP of the mining sector grew by 9.9% in that year. In 1996 the combined output of Debswana's diamond-mining operations totalled 17.7m. carats, compared with 16.8m. carats in 1995 and 15.6m. carats in 1994. Although all current mining operations are conducted by Debswana, a number of other companies have become involved in diamond exploration. Prominent among these is Challenger Mining International (CMI) which, through its operating subsidiary, Kalahari Resources, has carried out extensive ground surveys and has reported the identification of four kimberlite pipes under the desert sands.

Since the mid-1980s, the diamond industry has continued to strengthen its role as the mainstay of Botswana's vigorous economic performance. In 1987 earnings from the export of diamonds more than doubled, although this increase was attributable to two exceptional factors: a 10% increase in the diamond price in October, and the sale in that year by Debswana of its stockpile to De Beers. The sale, valued at some US $600m., formed part of an agreement giving Debswana a 5.27% shareholding in De Beers. For the government, this meant an effective 2.6% interest, entitling it to appoint two directors both to the main De Beers board and to that of its London-based Diamond Trading Co subsidiary, in reflection of Botswana's increasing importance in production by the group. For the Botswana government, the agreement was not only a long-term investment, but also a means of gaining access to decision-making on the diamond market. By early 1997 diamonds accounted for an estimated 70% of Botswana's exports, more than 45% of government revenue and some 30% of GDP. The government has recently encouraged the development of two diamond-cutting and -polishing ventures. Debswana employed a work-force of more than 6,000 workers in 1997. Capacity at the Orapa diamond mine was to be expanded with the building of a P1,400m. additional treatment plant. The construction work, which was to begin in 1997, with completion due by the year 2000, was to create 1,500 new jobs, and the plant itself was to create 300 permanent jobs. Continuous operation at Jwaneng was increased from six days a week to seven in 1997, despite earlier objections by trade unions.

Production of copper-nickel matte at Selebi-Phikwe began in 1974, and output rose steadily, reaching around 50,000 tons per year by the late 1980s. However, the value of sales of matte per ton declined consistently during the 1980s, owing to depressed international prices for nickel and copper. This created acute financial problems for the operating company, BCL, and its parent group, Botswana Roan Selection Trust (BRST), in which the Botswana government held 15%, with Anglo American Corpn of South Africa and Amax Corpn of the USA holding the remainder. To address these problems, a series of financial restructurings and debt-reschedulings was undertaken, while the resurgence of prices for base metals after mid-1987 led to a considerable improvement in BCL's financial position. This was advantageous to the economy as a whole: the company had a work-force of 5,000, and was an important source of foreign exchange, accounting for up to 10% of Botswana's total export earnings. The improvement in prices also enabled two new copper-nickel mines to be brought into production. In July 1988 BCL announced plans to bring the high-grade Selebi North mine into production, to replace deteriorating ore bodies at its other two mines. Work on the project started in early 1989, with a view to reaching full capacity of about 1,500 tons of ore per day by mid-1990. Nevertheless, in 1993 the prevailing low level in international copper prices rendered BCL unable to cover its operating costs. The government subsequently warned that BCL would need a substantial level of new capital investment, together with stringent restraints on wages if the mine were to survive as a viable operation. Copper export earnings fell to $99m. in 1994. The other copper-nickel mine (at Selkirk, east of Francistown) was brought into production at the end of 1988 by a consortium of Swiss and British investors. At full capacity, output was expected to reach 60,000 tons of high-grade ore per year; BCL was to undertake refining of the output on a toll basis. There were also plans to develop the adjacent, and larger, Phoenix deposit.

Plans to exploit Botswana's coal reserves have been restricted by the low level of international prices and the great distance to principal coal markets. Some 17,000m. tons of steam coal suitable for power-plant use have been identified in the east, and coal is extracted at the Morupule colliery, whose output rose from 579,400 tons in 1987 to 901,500 tons in 1992. Most of the coal is for electricity generation to service the mining industry and the new soda ash plant. The government is also encouraging domestic coal use, in order to conserve fuel wood. In 1995 imports of mineral fuels accounted for an estimated 5.1% of the value of total imports.

Following independence, there were several attempts to exploit brine deposits at Sua Pan, in central Botswana, by establishing a soda ash/salt plant (soda ash is used by the glass-, paper-, steel- and detergent-making industries). In 1986 South African interests began talks with British Petroleum to acquire its subsidiary, Soda Ash Botswana, with Botswana government participation in a project to build a plant at Makgadikgadi, with forecast annual output of some 300,000 tons of soda ash and 650,000 tons of salt. Agreement to undertake the project was completed in 1988, and production began, on schedule, in early 1991. However, output of 63,154 tons of soda ash in 1991 was considerably below expectations, owing initially to technical problems. Subsequently, the lack of demand and increased competition in the South African market have also restricted output, which remains at a level well below profitable operation.

Botswana's dependence on South African support to implement the soda ash project has raised domestic and regional concern that the government is increasing the country's vulnerability to political pressure. Similar concerns have surrounded exploration work on plutonium deposits being carried out in the south by two South African firms, Gold Fields of South Africa (GFSA) and Southern Prospecting. GFSA holds three prospecting licences, through its Gold Fields of Botswana subsidiary, for a 3,000 sq km concession north of the Molopo river adjacent to its existing concession in South Africa's Bushveld igneous complex, which contains substantial reserves of platinum and chromium. Botswana's reserves are, however, thought to be of lower grade and far less substantial, and in 1992 platinum exploration in the Molopo area was suspended.

For many years gold has been mined, on a small scale, in Botswana. In 1987 a joint venture, Shashe Mines, was formed by the Botswana government and private US and Canadian interests, to explore gold deposits at Map Nora near Francistown, and exploitation of the mineral commenced in 1989. Botswana's total output of gold reached 67 kg in 1989, but by the early 1990s had dwindled to only 40 kg annually.

In May 1996 government officials held a meeting with representatives of the mining industry to discuss draft proposals for changes to the Mines and Minerals Act, aimed at making Botswana's mining sector more attractive to investors.

MANUFACTURING AND CONSTRUCTION

Although manufacturing contributed only 4.6% of GDP in 1995/96, according to provisional figures, and has been constrained by a small domestic market, limited export outlets, weak infrastructure, import dependence and shortage of skilled manpower, it has emerged since the late 1970s as one of Botswana's most dynamic economic sectors. Manufacturing GDP increased by an annual average of 10.0% over the period 1985/86–1994/95, and, increased by 6.5% in 1995/96, according to provisional figures. The 1995 budget reduced the rate of company tax from 35% to 15% to encourage the sector (see below), and a White Paper on the new Industrial Policy was due in late 1996. Formal employment in manufacturing increased from 4,400 in August 1978 to 27,548 in March 1991. This expansion did much to reduce the parastatal BMC's domination of the sector, with its share of industrial employment declining from 36% to 18% over the period 1979–84. It also represented a considerable diversification of Botswana's manufacturing base, with textiles, beverages, chemicals, paper, metals, plastics, vegetable oils and electrical products experiencing the highest rates of expansion. The sector's strong performance was attributable to a number of government policies, based on a financial assistance programme (FAP), inaugurated in 1982, which provides a wide range of subsidies to potential entrepreneurs, particularly in the small-scale sector, and a highly attractive foreign investment code. The government's current diversification programme also places a priority on the country's need to develop manufacturing, and a preferential tax rate was introduced for the sector from July 1995 (see below).

The parastatal Botswana Development Corpn (BDC) has been a major promoter of industrial development, identifying projects and potential joint-venture partners, and establishing industrial sites for smaller firms to rent. BDC's interests include brewing, sugar packaging, furniture and clothing manufacturing, tourism, milling and concrete products. In 1984 BDC established the Setshaba Investment Trust Co as a vehicle for offering shares in its subsidiaries to the public. Since 1986, Botswana's strong foreign exchange position has proved an increasing attraction for foreign companies, mainly from South Africa, but also from the United Kingdom and the USA, have made investments since 1988. The government is currently promoting textile production as part of its diversification programme, partly because Botswana has a less skilled work-force than South Africa, the dominant industrial power in the region. In April 1997 the government launched a three-year Local Procurement Programme, aimed at obtaining more of the central government's purchases from local suppliers.

The construction sector developed rapidly during the 1980s, particularly from 1988 (registering growth of 30% in 1988/89). In the early 1990s, however, growth in the sector slowed, reflecting both the general downturn in economic performance and the management crisis at the Botswana Housing Corpn (see Recent History). From July 1995, the government increased the wage rate from P4.50 to P6.00 per day for workers on the Drought Labour-Intensive Public Works Programme.

ENERGY AND WATER DEVELOPMENT

Rapid growth in the economy and in the population resulted in an equally rapid expansion in demand for energy and water. Shortfalls in supply were offset by imports from South Africa, although these were sufficient to satisfy only 8.5% of total demand in 1987/88. The principal consumers of energy are urban areas, including industrial consumers, and the mines. The Botswana Power Corpn (BPC) has been implementing a continuing programme of capacity expansion, of which a major project was the Morupule power station. Using coal mined at Morupule, the station became the focus of a new national grid system linking the existing northern and southern networks, based on Selebi-Phikwe and Gaborone power stations. The first phase of the power station, comprising three 30-MW units, was commissioned in 1987, and work on a fourth 30-MW unit was completed in 1989. Units five and six entered service in the early 1990s, and as many as 14 units could be operational by the year 2000, if demand increases as predicted. A project to link Botswana into the Zambian and Zimbabwean grids was completed in 1991. Apart from the further work at Morupule, the main short-term focus of the electricity programme will be the extension of the rural catchment area of the national grid, with the aim of conserving fuelwood and reducing oil demand. The BPC, following the political changes in South Africa in 1994, undertook a major shift in its policy from self-sufficiency to the supplementation of local supply through imports, in order to take advantage of the cheaper power available south of the border. In so doing, the BPC was able to reduce its tariffs by 10% in October 1995. The BPC's previously controversially high connection charges were also reduced. In rural collective schemes, consumers who once had to save up to pay 40% of the cost of connection now have to pay only 10% 'up front'. For major consumers, the 100% deposit fell to 25%. In 1996/97 the BPC was able to declare a financial dividend and became the third parastatal enterprise, after the BDC and the Botswana Telecommunications Corpn, to achieve profitability. Although oil imports have not imposed as heavy a burden on foreign exchange as in many other African countries, they accounted for some 6.2% of total imports in 1992: the mining industry is the major consumer.

Botswana's vast coal reserves and the substantial surplus power generated in neighbouring countries has made it relatively easy to satisfy the rising energy demand, when compared with the problem of the increasing domestic and livestock requirements for water. There are only minimal surface water supplies outside the remote Okavango and Chobe areas, and 80% of national demand is met from groundwater sources, with livestock the largest single user, consuming about one-third, followed by mining, urban areas and rural areas and villages. Although not fully assessed, groundwater supplies are not expected to exceed 4,000m. cu m per year, and intense competition for water resources has emerged in the main urban-mining areas in the east, leading to the postponement of plans for the development of industrial sites, particularly in Gaborone. The situation has been further exacerbated by recurrent drought. Aid from overseas is currently being used to develop water resources. In addition, an 'accelerated water resource development programme' commenced in 1989: this was to provide more dams, in an attempt to fulfil the projected requirements of the 1990s. A project to provide water for the southern Okavango region was suspended in early 1991, following pressure from local and international environmentalists. A pipeline from a proposed dam on the Motlontse river was to be built at an estimated cost of P1,200m. to enhance the water supply in the capital and in adjacent districts of eastern Botswana; construction was due for completion by March 1998. A project to construct a 360 km-long pipeline to carry water from the Sashe river in the north-east to the south-eastern region of the country commenced in May 1996.

FOREIGN TRADE AND BALANCE OF PAYMENTS

Diamonds have been Botswana's principal export (accounting for as much as 88% of total earnings and for 30%–35% of government revenue) since the mid-1970s. Other exports include vehicles and parts (which contributed an estimated 16.1% of export earnings in 1995), copper-nickel matte (an estimated 5.4%), beef and textiles. The four main categories of imports in 1995 were vehicles and transport equipment (18.6%), food, beverages and tobacco (15.9%), machinery and electrical equipment (15.7%), and chemical and rubber products (9.2%). Europe provides the largest export market (73.6% in 1995) and the Southern African Customs Union (SACU) the main source of imports (73.9%). A persistent deficit on the merchandise trade account was replaced by a small trade surplus, of P27m., in 1983. With the recovery of world diamond prices in 1985, the surplus rapidly escalated, reaching P459m. in 1986. In 1987 it surged by almost 170%, to P1,230.5m., reflecting the impact of the sale of Debswana's diamond stockpile to De Beers (see above). The merchandise trade account thereafter remained in surplus in spite of the recession and the diamond sales quota: in 1995 the surplus amounted to $585.7m., or 4.7% of GDP.

Botswana operates an open economy, with combined import and export values exceeding GDP, making both the domestic economy and the external account vulnerable to fluctuations in the terms of trade and exchange rates. The government has operated a flexible, trade-orientated exchange rate policy since the pula was established in 1976 as the national currency. It was initially tied to the US dollar exchange rates, but the appreciation of the South African rand against the dollar forced several revaluations in the following four years, in order to contain import costs and domestic inflation. In June 1980 the pula was linked to a trade-weighted 'basket' of currencies, in order to minimize such disruptions. However, after 1982 the relationship between the US dollar and the South African rand began to reverse, while the pula strengthened in relation to the rand as the annual rate of domestic inflation fell from 12.7% in 1982 to 5.5%, considerably below the South African rate, at the end of 1984. The result was a series of trade-orientated devaluations during 1982–85. Throughout the 1980s and 1990s, Botswana's exchange controls have been liberal by African standards, and more liberal than those of South Africa. In January 1995 a major liberalization of controls was introduced by the Bank of Botswana (the central bank). Following these relaxations, the Bank of Botswana monitored foreign-currency transactions closely to assess the effects of the reforms. They were found to be sufficiently favourable to foreshadow further liberalizations for 1996, which were to include the removal of limits on current-account transactions. In 1996 the pula depreciated against most major currencies, ranging from a 29.1% decline against sterling to a decline of 12.8% against the Japanese yen. The exchange rate of the pula declined by 10% against the Zimbabwean dollar and by 0.8% against the South African rand. A number of companies reported that the reforms significantly reduced their commercial overheads in Botswana. Domestic inflation rose to 10% in 1985 and averaged 11.4% per year in 1988–95. In 1996, however, inflation dropped to just under 10%.

Apart from maintaining trade competitiveness, the exchange rate adjustments have also ameliorated the effect on the balance of payments of the steady deterioration in the country's terms of trade. Since 1976 Botswana has generally enjoyed a secure balance-of-payments position, with the current account in surplus in every year since 1982. Net transfers, including Botswana's share of revenue from SACU, and capital inflows of private investment and foreign aid more than offset the continuing deficit on both the invisible and overall trade account. During the 1980s the healthy balance-of-payments position was assured by the expansion of export earnings, particularly from diamonds, which, apart from pushing the trade account into surplus, underpinned a rapid growth in the overall surplus. This reached P936m. in 1987, a record created by the sale of the Debswana stockpile. The overall balance averaged nearly P800m. in subsequent years, and amounted to P591m. in 1995, and to P848m. in 1996.

The most obvious effect of Botswana's strong balance-of-payments position has been the increase in official reserves of foreign exchange. These were sufficient to cover 5.5 months of imports in 1980. In December 1996 the reserves stood at P18,322m., or enough to cover 29 months of imports of goods and services. The government views the high level of reserves as essential to sustain Botswana's future economic development as diamond earnings level out, with no single source of export revenue to replace them. The rapid escalation in reserves after 1985 was paralleled, however, by increasing criticism of the government's concern with long-term financial security. According to the critics, the government's conservative fiscal policies were depressing productive investment, particularly by the private sector, and were subsequently hindering job-creation.

Botswana's balance-of-payments situation has also been helped by its low debt burden. The total external public debt was US $682.1m. at the end of 1995, with the cost of debt-servicing at 3.2% of the total value of exports of goods and services. In 1996 the total of all debts guaranteed by the government amounted to less than 10% of its foreign reserves.

GOVERNMENT FINANCE

At independence about one-half of Botswana's public expenditure was financed directly by the government of the United Kingdom. This extreme level of reliance on external support was altered by Botswana's accession to SACU in 1969, and the country had become financially independent of the UK by 1972/73. From 1977/78 until 1982/83 customs revenue constituted the principal component of government income, but since then this source has been overtaken by mineral revenue, which now accounts for an estimated 50% of the total, compared with about 15% for customs revenue. Non-tax revenue, excluding grants, accounted for 24.6% of government income in 1995/96. Following the unexpected fall in diamond revenues in 1981/82, the government adopted a generally cautious approach to expenditure, which was reflected in a succession of budget surpluses. The financial surplus that was generated by the sale of the Debswana stockpile led the government, in December 1987, to adopt a more positively expansionary approach, based on increases in public spending. Additional recurrent and development expenditure was approved, but the government continued to exercise caution, warning that any levelling out of revenues from the diamond industry would quickly lead to the return of an overall deficit, as had happened in 1981/82. Although deficits were anticipated in 1992/93 and 1993/94, later figures indicated surpluses of P881.3m. and P878.3m. respectively. The 1994/95 budget estimated a deficit of P237m., which by 1996 was acknowledged to have been a surplus of P195.6m. In 1995 a budgetary deficit of P229m. was forecast for 1995/96. In 1996 this figure was revised to a deficit of P270m. In February 1997 however, it was announced that 1995/96 had produced a budgetary surplus of P269.9m. In a dramatic move, the budget reduced the corporate tax rate from 35% to 25% and by a further 10% to 15% for manufacturing firms (including the BMC). Personal income tax was also reduced, but changes in sales tax, including an extension of the tax to canned and processed foodstuffs, raised the level of indirect taxation. These changes followed tax reductions and simplified foreign exchange procedures introduced in the previous budget, which similarly aimed to increase Botswana's international competitiveness and to attract greater foreign investment. The 1996 budget speech projected total revenue for 1996/97 of P5,421m. and total expenditure of P6,177m. (comprising P4,329m. as recurrent expenditure and P1,848m. as development expenditure), leaving a projected budget deficit of P756m. In February 1997 it was forecast that revenue in 1996/97 would increase to P6,933m., with expenditure rising by 5.0%, to P6,491m., revising the 1996/97 budgetary balance from a deficit of P756m. to a surplus of P442m. The official forecast for 1997/98 was for a balanced budget, with both revenue and expenditure projected at P7,815m. Income from mining was forecast to account for 45% of total revenue.

EMPLOYMENT AND WAGES

Botswana's population growth rate accelerated significantly during the 1980s, and the population increased by an average of 3.0% per year during 1985–95. As a result, the total population increased from 941,027 at the census of August 1981 to 1,326,796 at the August 1991 census. Current figures indicate an estimated population of 1.5m. in 1996 and a projected population of 1.8m. in 2000. As a result of the high growth rate, the net addition to the labour force of people aged 15–64 years has been in the region of 20,000 per year, many of them joining the 53% of the working-age population who were estimated in 1985/86 to be unemployed or in school. Only around 20% of the labour force are employed in the formal sector, while about 10% are self-employed. The strong economic growth rates since 1979 have led to a significant expansion in job-creation, with formal-sector employment rising from 65,500 to 231,100 during 1978–94. The main sectors of employment growth have been manufacturing, finance and business services, construction, transport and communications and social services. From the beginning of 1988 government employment expanded significantly. In 1996/97 the civil service wage bill was budgeted to account for 35.5% of all recurrent expenditure. Despite the rate of economic growth exceeding that of population growth, formal-sector employment in terms of absolute numbers was unable to absorb the increase in the labour force during the early 1980s. This situation was exacerbated by a decline in the number of

Batswana working abroad, from a peak of 25,500 in 1976 to 18,800 in 1983. During the late 1980s the increase in employment opportunities began to exceed the growth rate of the labour force, causing unemployment to fall temporarily. Nevertheless, an estimated 21% of the labour force were unemployed in April 1996. In the year to 31 March 1996 formal-sector employment grew by only 0.8%, owing in part to the restructuring of parastatal enterprises. In 1995 the number of Batswana employed in South African mines had fallen to 12,746.

Job creation has become a major political issue and the main priority in government planning. Another priority is to increase the country's pool of trained labour. In 1996 the government was considering the adoption of a strategy to stimulate employment by promoting small-scale and informal-sector enterprises.

Statistical Survey

Source (unless otherwise stated): Central Statistics Office, Private Bag 0024, Gaborone; tel. 352200; fax 352201.

Area and Population

AREA, POPULATION AND DENSITY

Area (sq km)	581,730*
Population (census results)	
16 August 1981	941,027†
21 August 1991	
Males	634,400
Females	692,396
Total	1,326,796
Population (official estimates at 19 August)	
1994	1,423,000
1995	1,456,000
Density (per sq km) at August 1995	2.5

* 224,607 sq miles.

† Excluding 42,069 citizens absent from the country during enumeration.

POPULATION BY CENSUS DISTRICT (August 1991 census)

Barolong	18,400	Kweneng	170,437
Central	412,970	Lobatse	26,052
Chobe	14,126	Ngamiland	94,534
Francistown	65,244	Ngwaketse	128,989
Gaborone	133,468	North-East	43,354
Ghanzi	24,719	Orapa	8,827
Jwaneng	11,188	Selebi-Phikwe	39,772
Kgalagadi	31,134	South-East	43,584
Kgatleng	57,770	Sowa	2,228

PRINCIPAL TOWNS (August 1988 estimates)

Gaborone (capital)	110,973	Kanye	26,300
Francistown	49,396	Mahalapye	26,239
Selebi-Phikwe	46,490	Lobatse	25,689
Molepolole	29,212	Maun	18,470
Serowe	28,267	Ramotswa	17,961
Mochudi	26,320		

August 1991 (census results): Gaborone 133,468; Francistown 65,244; Selebi-Phikwe 39,772; Lobatse 26,052.

BIRTHS AND DEATHS (UN estimates, annual averages)

	1980–85	1985–90	1990–95
Birth rate (per 1,000)	42.8	39.4	37.1
Death rate (per 1,000)	9.4	7.7	6.6

Expectation of life (UN estimates, years at birth, 1990–95): 64.9 (males 63.0; females 66.7).

Source: UN, *World Population Prospects: The 1994 Revision.*

ECONOMICALLY ACTIVE POPULATION
(persons aged 12 years and over, 1991 census*)

	Males	Females	Total
Agriculture, hunting, forestry and fishing	70,439	27,187	97,626
Mining and quarrying	12,556	779	13,335
Manufacturing	13,751	13,797	27,548
Electricity, gas and water	5,637	778	6,415
Construction	50,347	7,701	58,048
Trade, restaurants and hotels	13,802	21,392	35,194
Transport, storage and communications	9,651	1,844	11,495
Financing, insurance, real estate and business services	8,743	4,624	13,367
Community, social and personal services	48,616	58,046	106,662
Activities not adequately defined	6,031	4,217	10,248
Total employed	239,573	140,365	379,938
Unemployed	31,852	29,413	61,265
Total labour force	271,425	169,778	441,203

* Excluding members of the armed forces.

Source: ILO, *Yearbook of Labour Statistics.*

Mid-1995 (estimates, '000 persons): Agriculture, etc. 258; Total labour force 657. (Source: FAO, *Production Yearbook*).

Agriculture

PRINCIPAL CROPS ('000 metric tons)

	1993	1994	1995
Wheat*	1	1	1
Maize	6	11	5†
Millet	2	2	2†
Sorghum	38	37	38†
Roots and tubers*	9	9	9
Pulses*	14	16	12
Cottonseed*	2	2	2
Cotton (lint)*	1	1	1
Vegetables*	16	16	13
Fruit*	11	11	10

* FAO estimate(s). † Unofficial figure(s).

Source: FAO, *Production Yearbook.*

LIVESTOCK (FAO estimates, '000 head, year ending September)

	1993	1994	1995
Cattle	2,700	2,800	2,800
Horses	31	31	32
Asses	220	231	235
Sheep	270	238	250
Goats	1,950	1,850	1,900
Pigs	15	16	16

Chickens (FAO estimates, million): 2 in 1993; 2 in 1994; 2 in 1995.

Source: FAO, *Production Yearbook.*

LIVESTOCK PRODUCTS (FAO estimates, '000 metric tons)

	1993	1994	1995
Beef and veal	47	52	49
Goat meat	5	5	5
Poultry meat	5	5	5
Other meat	10	8	8
Cows' milk	114	117	117
Goats' milk	6	6	6
Cheese	2.7	1.5	1.5
Butter and ghee	1.5	1.5	1.5
Hen eggs	1.9	1.9	1.9
Cattle hides	6.3	6.5	6.5

Source: FAO, *Production Yearbook*.

Forestry

ROUNDWOOD REMOVALS (FAO estimates, '000 cubic metres)

	1992	1993	1994
Industrial wood	89	92	95
Fuel wood	1,358	1,400	1,443
Total	1,447	1,492	1,538

Source: FAO, *Yearbook of Forest Products*.

Fishing

(FAO estimates, metric tons, live weight)

	1992	1993	1994
Total catch	1,900	2,000	2,000

Source: FAO, *Yearbook of Fishery Statistics*.

Mining

(metric tons, unless otherwise indicated)

	1993	1994	1995
Coal	890,497	900,298	816,724
Copper ore*	21,621	22,780	21,029
Nickel ore*	20,132	19,041	18,672
Cobalt ore*	205	n.a.	200†
Gold ore (kilograms)*	192	n.a.	n.a.
Diamonds ('000 carats)	14,731	15,540	16,674
Soda ash	126,000	174,222	201,641
Salt	98,000	185,986	392,258

* Figures refer to the metal content of ores.

† Data from the US Bureau of Mines.

Sources: Central Statistics Office, Gaborone, and UN, *Industrial Commodity Statistics Yearbook*.

Industry

SELECTED PRODUCTS

	1991	1992	1993
Beer ('000 hectolitres)	1,283	1,290	1,374
Soft drinks ('000 hectolitres)	274	317	276
Electric energy (million kWh)*	910	910	910

Electric energy (million kWh): 1,011* in 1994.

* Provisional or estimated figure(s).

Source: UN, *Industrial Commodity Statistics Yearbook*.

Finance

CURRENCY AND EXCHANGE RATES

Monetary Units

100 thebe = 1 pula (P).

Sterling and Dollar Equivalents (31 March 1997)

£1 sterling = 5.816 pula;
US $1 = 3.542 pula;
100 pula = £17.19 = $28.23.

Average Exchange Rate (pula per US $)

1994	2.6846
1995	2.7722
1996	3.3241

BUDGET (million pula, year ending 31 March)

Revenue*	1994/95	1995/96	1996/97†
Taxation	3,632.7	3,857.3	4,017.6
Mineral revenues	2,349.4	2,513.1	2,568.9
Customs pool revenues	711.8	832.9	897.3
Non-mineral income tax	386.9	300.0	330.0
General sales tax	169.2	185.7	192.9
Other current revenue	764.1	1,259.0	1,335.1
Interest	200.5	165.7	248.2
Other property income	452.5	978.8	965.0
Fees, charges, etc.	92.7	96.9	103.7
Sales of fixed assets and land	18.4	17.6	18.3
Total	4,396.8	5,116.3	5,352.7

* Excluding grants received (million pula): 75.66 in 1994/95; 28.33 in 1995/96; 68.57 in 1996/97.

† Forecasts.

Expenditure*	1994/95	1995/96	1996/97†
General administration	659.2	801.6	907.0
Public order and safety	161.7	185.7	234.7
Defence	452.5	491.4	445.2
Education	937.5	1,196.3	1,545.5
Health	227.5	268.6	303.6
Food and social welfare programme	47.6	79.9	50.5
Housing, urban and regional development	416.3	447.3	501.1
Other community and social services	68.2	85.2	109.8
Economic services	826.4	1,325.3	1,346.6
Agriculture, forestry and fishing	252.9	309.2	292.1
Mining	89.4	282.6	66.6
Electricity and water supply	124.4	321.4	469.0
Roads	211.3	242.7	288.5
Promotion of commerce and industry	73.3	97.0	116.8
Interest on public debt	84.5	97.5	112.2
Deficit grants to local authorities	359.2	395.3	462.1
Other grants	36.2	40.0	40.0
Total	4,276.8	5,414.2	6,057.3

* Figures refer to recurrent and development expenditure, including net lending (million pula): –112.2 in 1994/95; –15.8 in 1995/96; 30.0 in 1996/97.

† Forecasts.

INTERNATIONAL RESERVES (US $ million at 31 December)

	1994	1995	1996
IMF special drawing rights	37.07	40.22	41.28
Reserve position in IMF	23.86	28.66	28.63
Foreign exchange	4,401.47	4,695.48	5,027.66
Total	4,462.40	4,764.36	5,097.57

Source: IMF, *International Financial Statistics*.

MONEY SUPPLY (million pula at 31 December)

	1994	1995	1996
Currency outside banks	194.9	222.7	247.1
Demand deposits at commercial banks	578.8	606.6	702.8
Total money	773.7	829.3	949.9

Source: IMF, *International Financial Statistics.*

COST OF LIVING (Consumer Price Index; base: 1990 = 100)

	1993	1994	1995
Food	150.9	165.0	182.9
Clothing	157.4	179.1	198.0
All items (incl. others)	148.5	164.2	181.4

Source: ILO, *Yearbook of Labour Statistics.*

1996 (low-income group): Food 207.0; All items 199.8 (Source: UN, *Monthly Bulletin of Statistics*).

NATIONAL ACCOUNTS
(million pula at current prices, year ending 30 June)

National Income and Product

	1985/86	1986/87	1987/88
Compensation of employees	700.7	849.6	1,051.6
Operating surplus	1,216.7	1,312.3	1,936.3
Domestic factor incomes	1,917.4	2,161.9	2,987.9
Consumption of fixed capital	349.8	432.4	575.6
Gross domestic product (GDP) at factor cost	2,267.2	2,594.3	3,563.5
Indirect taxes	160.4	226.2	251.2
Less Subsidies	7.0	10.7	19.1
GDP in purchasers' values	2,420.6	2,809.8	3,795.6
Factor income received from abroad	173.0	225.9	308.7
Less Factor income paid abroad	495.8	477.9	773.8
Gross national product	2,097.8	2,557.8	3,330.5
Less Consumption of fixed capital	349.8	432.4	575.6
National income in market prices	1,748.0	2,125.4	2,754.9
Other current transfers from abroad	141.5	123.2	115.1
Less Other current transfers paid abroad	68.5	78.6	233.3
National disposable income	1,821.0	2,169.9	2,636.7

Source: UN, *National Accounts Statistics.*

Expenditure on the Gross Domestic Product

	1993/94	1994/95	1995/96*
Government final consumption expenditure	3,186.8	3,618.5	4,233.6
Private final consumption expenditure	3,637.1	4,130.0	4,155.6
Gross capital formation	2,731.0	3,053.4	3,522.8
Total domestic expenditure	9,554.9	10,801.9	11,912.0
Exports of goods and services	5,413.6	5,980.1	7,486.7
Less Imports of goods and services	3,853.5	4,251.6	4,767.7
GDP in purchasers' values	11,115.0	12,530.3	14,631.0
GDP at constant 1985/86 prices	4,700.5	4,847.5	5,184.8

* Provisional figures.

Source: Bank of Botswana, Gaborone, and Central Statistics Office, Gaborone.

Gross Domestic Product by Economic Activity

	1993/94	1994/95	1995/96*
Agriculture, hunting, forestry and fishing	495.2	520.6	563.1
Mining and quarrying	3,932.3	4,086.3	4,859.0
Manufacturing	499.5	593.9	693.2
Water and electricity	239.4	269.5	270.6
Construction	694.5	757.1	858.4
Trade, restaurants and hotels	1,706.7	2,093.7	2,489.1
Transport	363.1	437.4	504.2
Finance, insurance and business services	1,148.6	1,397.8	1,613.3
Government services	1,846.7	2,159.0	2,544.5
Social and personal services	479.3	550.9	622.3
Sub-total	11,405.3	12,866.2	15,017.7
Less Imputed bank service charge	290.3	335.9	386.7
GDP in purchasers' values	11,115.0	12,530.3	14,631.0

* Provisional figures.

Source: Bank of Botswana, Gaborone, and Central Statistics Office, Gaborone.

BALANCE OF PAYMENTS (US $ million)

	1993	1994	1995
Exports of goods f.o.b.	1,722.2	1,878.4	2,164.4
Imports of goods f.o.b.	−1,455.4	−1,350.0	−1,578.7
Trade balance	266.8	528.4	585.7
Exports of services	191.3	186.1	260.4
Imports of services	−325.6	−322.0	−444.2
Balance on goods and services	132.5	392.6	401.8
Other income received	554.5	230.8	483.2
Other income paid	−260.9	−455.0	−515.6
Balance on goods, services and income	426.1	168.4	369.4
Current transfers received	352.3	370.0	342.3
Current transfers paid	−275.1	−295.1	−369.5
Current balance	503.3	243.3	342.1
Capital account (net)	8.5	6.0	2.9
Direct investment abroad	−9.5	−9.5	−40.9
Direct investment from abroad	−286.9	−14.3	70.4
Portfolio investment assets	—	—	−36.4
Portfolio investment liabilities	0.2	−0.1	5.8
Other investment assets	63.4	15.8	−88.7
Other investment liabilities	192.5	49.2	55.9
Net errors and omissions	−74.5	−151.1	−104.6
Overall balance	397.0	139.3	206.6

Source: IMF, *International Financial Statistics.*

External Trade

PRINCIPAL COMMODITIES (million pula)

Imports c.i.f.	1993	1994	1995*
Food, beverages and tobacco	764.1	775.0	844.0
Fuels	273.2	262.6	270.6
Chemicals and rubber products	394.6	425.7	490.6
Wood and paper products	233.7	256.1	401.8
Textiles and footwear	309.0	391.0	399.8
Metals and metal products	434.6	411.6	461.0
Machinery and electrical equipment	743.2	774.0	831.4
Vehicles and transport equipment	568.3	528.4	988.7
Total (incl. others)	4,285.0	4,398.1	5,304.8

Exports f.o.b.	1993	1994	1995*
Meat and meat products	160.6	181.8	179.2
Diamonds	3,340.2	3,717.8	3,983.7
Copper-nickel matte	219.8	258.8	319.2
Textiles	95.0	177.4	146.3
Vehicles and parts	91.0	300.6	957.2
Total (incl. others)	4,312.1	4,965.0	5,931.5

* Provisional figures.

PRINCIPAL TRADING PARTNERS (million pula)

Imports c.i.f.	1993	1994	1995*
SACU†	3,541.0	3,437.4	3,922.7
Zimbabwe	196.2	258.9	293.0
United Kingdom	112.1	109.9	134.7
Other Europe	192.3	259.9	319.3
Korea, Republic	—	91.7	377.5
USA	140.8	82.9	107.4
Total (incl. others)	4,285.0	4,407.3	5,304.8

Exports f.o.b.	1993	1994	1995*
SACU†	379.5	691.4	1,277.6
Zimbabwe	135.2	134.1	176.4
Other Africa	57.4	49.1	49.3
United Kingdom	639.4	1,245.4	2,223.0
Other Europe	3,082.9	2,800.6	2,143.1
USA	14.3	34.8	51.6
Total (incl. others)	4,312.1	4,965.0	5,931.5

* Provisional figures.

† Southern African Customs Union, of which Botswana is a member; also including Lesotho, Namibia, South Africa and Swaziland.

Transport

RAILWAYS

	1993	1994	1995
Passengers carried	344,066	420,070	614,579
Freight (net ton-km)	450,482	568,996	687,012

ROAD TRAFFIC (vehicles registered at 31 December)

	1993	1994	1995
Passenger cars	26,320	27,058	30,517
Lorries and vans	51,352	57,235	59,710
Others	16,938	17,153	17,448
Total	94,610	101,446	107,675

CIVIL AVIATION (traffic on scheduled services)

	1992	1993	1994
Kilometres flown (million)	3	3	2
Passengers carried ('000)	111	123	101
Passenger-km (million)	76	75	58
Total ton-km (million)	8	8	6

Source: UN, *Statistical Yearbook*.

Tourism

FOREIGN TOURIST ARRIVALS (incl. same-day visitors)

Country of origin	1993	1994*	1995*
South Africa and Namibia	498,574	513,687	529,238
United Kingdom and Ireland	38,651	39,823	41,029
Zambia	31,978	32,947	33,944
Zimbabwe	308,018	317,355	326,962
Total (incl. others)	961,844	991,000	1,021,000

* Estimated figures.

Receipts from tourism (US $million): 24 in 1992; 31 in 1993; 35 in 1994 (Source: UN, *Statistical Yearbook*).

Communications Media

	1990	1991	1992
Radio receivers ('000 in use)	150	155	160
Television receivers ('000 in use)	20	21	22
Book production: titles*	n.a.	158	n.a.
Daily newspapers:			
Number	1	n.a.	1
Average circulation ('000 copies)	18	n.a.	40
Non-daily newspapers:			
Number	n.a.	n.a.	4
Average circulation ('000 copies)	n.a.	n.a.	61
Other periodicals:			
Number	n.a.	n.a.	14
Average circulation ('000 copies)	n.a.	n.a.	177

* Figures refer to first editions only and include pamphlets (61 titles in 1991).

Radio receivers ('000 in use): 167 in 1993; 180 in 1994.
Television receivers ('000 in use): 23 in 1993; 24 in 1994.
Daily newspapers: 1 in 1994 (average circulation 35,000 copies).

Source: UNESCO, *Statistical Yearbook*.

Telephones ('000 main lines in use, year ending 31 March): 36 in 1992/93; 43 in 1993/94; 50 in 1994/95 (Source: UN, *Statistical Yearbook*).

Education

(1994)

	Institutions	Teachers	Students
Primary	670	11,731	310,128
Secondary	188	4,712	86,684
Brigades*	19	218	2,118
Teacher training	6	295	2,363
Technical education	7	544	3,544
University	1	507	5,062

* Semi-autonomous units providing craft and practical training.

Directory

The Constitution

The Constitution of the Republic of Botswana took effect at independence on 30 September 1966.

EXECUTIVE

President

Executive power lies with the President of Botswana, who is also Commander-in-Chief of the armed forces. Election for the office of President is linked with the election of members of the National Assembly*. Presidential candidates must be over 30 years of age and receive at least 1,000 nominations. If there is more than one candidate for the Presidency, each candidate for office in the Assembly must declare support for a presidential candidate. The candidate for President who commands the votes of more than one-half of the elected members of the Assembly will be declared President. If the Presidency falls vacant the members of the National Assembly will themselves elect a new President. The President, who is an *ex-officio* member of the National Assembly, holds office for the duration of Parliament. The President chooses four members of the National Assembly.

* The Constitution was to be amended to restrict the President to two terms of office, with effect from the 1999 elections.

Cabinet

There is also a Vice-President, whose office is ministerial. The Vice-President is appointed by the President and deputizes in the absence of the President. The Cabinet consists of the President, the Vice-President and 14 other Ministers, including four Assistant Ministers, appointed by the President. The Cabinet is responsible to the National Assembly.

LEGISLATURE

Legislative power is vested in Parliament, consisting of the President and the National Assembly, acting after consultation in certain cases with the House of Chiefs. The President may withhold assent to a Bill passed by the National Assembly. If the same Bill is again presented after six months, the President is required to assent to it or to dissolve Parliament within 21 days.

House of Chiefs

The House of Chiefs comprises the Chiefs of the eight principal tribes of Botswana as *ex-officio* members, four members elected by sub-chiefs from their own number, and three members elected by the other 12 members of the House. Bills and motions relating to chieftaincy matters and alterations of the Constitution must be referred to the House, which may also deliberate and make representations on any matter.

National Assembly

The National Assembly consists of 40 members directly elected by universal adult suffrage, together with four members who are elected by the National Assembly from a list of candidates submitted by the President; the President and the Attorney-General are also *ex-officio* members of the Assembly. The life of the Assembly is five years.

The Constitution contains a code of human rights, enforceable by the High Court.

The Government

HEAD OF STATE

President: Sir Ketumile Masire (took office as Acting President 29 June 1980; elected President 18 July 1980; re-elected 10 September 1984, 10 October 1989 and 17 October 1994).

CABINET
(July 1997)

President: Sir Ketumile Masire.

Vice-President and Minister of Finance and Development Planning: Festus G. Mogae.

Minister of Health: Chapson Butale.

Minister of Agriculture: Roy Blackbeard.

Minister of Foreign Affairs: Lt-Gen. Mompati Merafhe.

Minister of Mineral Resources and Water Affairs: David Magang.

Minister of Commerce and Industry: George Kgoroba.

Minister of Local Government, Lands and Housing: Patrick Balopi.

Minister of Works, Transport and Communications: Daniel Kwelagobe.

Minister of Presidential Affairs and Public Administration: Ponatshego Kedikilwe.

Minister of Education: Gaositwe Chiepe.

Minister of Labour and Home Affairs: Bahiti Temane.

There are also four assistant ministers.

MINISTRIES

Office of the President: Private Bag 001, Gaborone; tel. 350800; telex 2414.

Ministry of Agriculture: Private Bag 003, Gaborone; tel. 350581; telex 2543; fax 356027.

Ministry of Commerce and Industry: Private Bag 004, Gaborone; tel. 3601200; telex 2674; fax 371539.

Ministry of Education: Private Bag 005, Gaborone; tel. 3600400; fax 3600458.

Ministry of Finance and Development Planning: Private Bag 008, Gaborone; tel. 350100; telex 2401; fax 356086.

Ministry of Foreign Affairs: Private Bag 00368, Gaborone; tel. 3600700; telex 2414; fax 313366.

Ministry of Health: Private Bag 0038, Gaborone; tel. 352000; telex 2959.

Ministry of Labour and Home Affairs: Private Bag 002, Gaborone; tel. 3601000.

Ministry of Local Government, Lands and Housing: Private Bag 006, Gaborone; tel. 354100.

Ministry of Mineral Resources and Water Affairs: Private Bag 0018, Gaborone; tel. 352454; telex 2503; fax 372738.

Ministry of Works, Transport and Communications: Private Bag 007, Gaborone; tel. 358500; telex 2743; fax 358500.

Legislature

HOUSE OF CHIEFS

The House has a total of 15 members.

Chairman: Chief Seepapitso IV.

NATIONAL ASSEMBLY

Speaker: M. P. K. Nwako.

General Election, 15 October 1994

Party	Votes	%	Seats
Botswana Democratic Party	138,826	53.1	26
Botswana National Front	98,427	37.7	13
Botswana People's Party	12,052	4.6	—
Independence Freedom Party	7,685	2.9	—
Botswana Progressive Union	3,016	1.2	—
Others	1,225	0.5	—
Total	261,231	100.0	39*

* Polling in one constituency was delayed, owing to the death of a candidate. Four additional members were subsequently elected by the National Assembly. The President and the Attorney-General are also *ex-officio* members of the National Assembly.

Political Organizations

Botswana Democratic Party (BDP): Gaborone; f. 1962; Pres. Sir Ketumile Masire; Chair. Ponatshego Kedikilwe; Sec.-Gen. Daniel K. Kwelagobe.

Botswana Labour Party: f. 1989; Pres. Lenyeletse Koma.

Botswana Liberal Party (BLP): Gaborone.

Botswana National Front (BNF): POB 42, Mahalapye; f. 1967; Pres. Dr Kenneth Koma; Sec.-Gen. James Pilane.

Botswana People's Party (BPP): POB 159, Francistown; f. 1960; Pres. Dr Knight Maripe; Chair. Kenneth Mkhwa; Sec.-Gen. Matlhomola Modise.

Botswana Progressive Union (BPU): POB 10229, Francistown; f. 1982; Pres. Tabulawa Mokgethi; Sec.-Gen. R. K. Monyatsiwa.

Botswana Workers' Front (BWF): Gaborone.

Independence Freedom Party (IFP): POB 3, Maun; f. 1996 by merger of Botswana Freedom Party and Botswana Independence Party; Pres. MOTSAMAI K. MPHO.

Lesedi La Botswana (LLB): Gaborone.

Social Democratic Party (SDP): Gaborone.

United Socialist Party (USP): Gaborone.

Diplomatic Representation

EMBASSIES AND HIGH COMMISSIONS IN BOTSWANA

Angola: Private Bag 111, Phala Crescent, Gaborone; tel. 300204; telex 2361; fax 375089; Ambassador: PEDRO F. MAVUNZA.

China, People's Republic: POB 1031, Gaborone; tel. 352209; telex 2428; fax 300156; Ambassador: ZHANG SHIHUA.

Germany: Professional House, Broadhurst, Segodithsane Way, POB 315, Gaborone; tel. 353143; telex 2225; fax 353038; Ambassador: ALBERT JOSEF GISY.

India: Private Bag 249, 4th Floor, Tirelo House, The Mall, Gaborone; tel. 372676; telex 2622; fax 374636; e-mail hicomind@cis.co.za; High Commissioner: CHERRY GEORGE.

Libya: POB 180, Gaborone; tel. 352481; telex 2501; Ambassador: TAHER ETTOUMI.

Namibia: POB 987, Gaborone; tel. 302181; fax 302248; High Commissioner: Dr JOSEPH HOEBEB.

Nigeria: POB 274, Gaborone; tel. 313561; telex 2415; fax 313738; High Commissioner: ALABA OGUNSANWO.

Russia: POB 81, Gaborone; tel. 353389; telex 22595; Ambassador: VLADIMIR UKHIN.

South Africa: Private Bag 00402, Kopanyo House, Plot 5131, Nelson Mandela Rd, Gaborone; tel. 304800; fax 305502; High Commissioner: O. R. W. MOKOU.

Sweden: Private Bag 0017, Gaborone; tel. 353912; telex 2421; fax 353942; Ambassador: (vacant).

United Kingdom: Private Bag 0023, Gaborone; tel. 352841; fax 356105; High Commissioner: DAVID C. B. BEAUMONT.

USA: POB 90, Gaborone; tel. 353982; telex 2554; fax 356947; Ambassador: ROBERT C. KRUEGER.

Zambia: POB 362, Gaborone; tel. 351951; telex 2416; fax 353952; High Commissioner: J. PHIRI.

Zimbabwe: POB 1232, Gaborone; tel. 314495; telex 2701; High Commissioner: LUCIA MUVINGI.

Judicial System

There is a High Court at Lobatse and a branch at Francistown, and Magistrates' Courts in each district. Appeals lie to the Court of Appeal of Botswana.

High Court: Private Bag 1, Lobatse; tel. 330607; telex 2758; fax 332317.

Chief Justice: (vacant).

President of the Court of Appeal: A. N. E. AMMISSAH.

Justices of Appeal: T. A. AGUDA, G. BIZOS, W. H. R. SCHREINER, D. R. DOYLE.

Puisne Judges: I. R. ABOADYE, K. J. GYEKE-DAKO.

Attorney-General: PHANDU SKELEMANI.

Religion

The majority of the population hold animist beliefs; an estimated 30% are thought to be Christians. There are Islamic mosques in Gaborone and Lobatse. The Bahá'í Faith is also represented.

CHRISTIANITY

Lekgotla la Sekeresete la Botswana (Botswana Christian Council): POB 355, Gaborone; tel. 351981; f. 1966; comprises 25 churches and organizations; Pres. Rev. JOSEPH MATSHENG; Gen. Sec. CHURCHILL M. GAPE.

The Anglican Communion

Anglicans are adherents of the Church of the Province of Central Africa, comprising 12 dioceses and covering Botswana, Malawi, Zambia and Zimbabwe. The Province was established in 1955, and the diocese of Botswana was formed in 1972.

Archbishop of the Province of Central Africa and Bishop of Botswana: Most Rev. WALTER PAUL KHOTSO MAKHULU, POB 769, Gaborone; fax 313015.

Protestant Churches

African Methodist Episcopal Church: POB 141, Lobatse; Rev. L. M. MBULAWA.

Evangelical Lutheran Church in Botswana: POB 1976, Gaborone; tel. 352227; fax 313966; Bishop Rev. PHILIP ROBINSON; 16,305 mems.

Evangelical Lutheran Church in Southern Africa (Botswana Diocese): POB 400, Gaborone; tel. 353976; Bishop Rev. M. NTUPING.

Methodist Church in Botswana: POB 260, Gaborone; Dist. Supt Rev. Z. S. M. MOSAI.

United Congregational Church of Southern Africa (Synod of Botswana): POB 1263, Gaborone; tel. 352491; Synod status since 1980; Chair. Rev. D. T. MAPITSE; Sec. Rev. M. P. P. DIBEELA; 24,000 mems.

Other denominations active in Botswana include the Church of God in Christ, the Dutch Reformed Church, the United Methodist Church and the Seventh-day Adventists.

The Roman Catholic Church

Botswana comprises a single diocese. The metropolitan see is Bloemfontein, South Africa. The church was established in Botswana in 1928, and had an estimated 54,854 adherents in the country at 31 December 1995. The Bishop participates in the Southern African Catholic Bishops' Conference, currently based in Pretoria, South Africa.

Bishop of Gaborone: Rt Rev. BONIFACE TSHOSA SETLALEKGOSI, POB 218, Bishop's House, Gaborone; tel. 312958; fax 356970.

The Press

DAILY NEWSPAPER

Dikgang tsa Gompieno (Daily News): Private Bag 0060, Gaborone; tel. 352541; telex 2409; f. 1964; publ. by Dept of Information and Broadcasting; Setswana and English; Mon.–Fri.; Editor L. LESHAGA; circ. 50,000.

PERIODICALS

Agrinews: Private Bag 003, Gaborone; f. 1971; monthly; agriculture and rural development; circ. 6,000.

Botswana Advertiser: POB 130, 5647 Nakedi Rd, Broadhurst, Gaborone; tel. 312844; telex 2351; weekly.

The Botswana Gazette: POB 1605, Gaborone; tel. 312833; fax 312833; weekly; circ. 16,000.

Botswana Guardian: POB 1641, Gaborone; tel. 314937; telex 2692; fax 374381; f. 1982; weekly; Editor JOEL SEBONEGO; circ. 18,700.

Government Gazette: Private Bag 0081, Gaborone; tel. 314441; fax 312001.

Kutlwano: Private Bag 0060, Gaborone; tel. 352541; telex 2409; monthly; Setswana and English; publ. by Dept of Information and Broadcasting; circ. 24,000.

The Midweek Sun: Private Bag 00153, Gaborone; tel. 352085; fax 374381; f. 1989; weekly; circ. 16,445.

Mmegi/The Reporter: Private Bag BR50, Gaborone; tel. 374784; fax 305508; f. 1984; weekly; Setswana and English; publ. by Dikgang Publishing Co; circ. 19,000.

Northern Advertiser: POB 402, Francistown; tel. 212265; fax 213769; f. 1985; weekly; advertisements, local interest, sport; Editor GRACE FISH; circ. 5,500.

The Zebra's Voice: Private Bag 00114, Gaborone; f. 1982; quarterly; cultural affairs; circ. 7,000.

NEWS AGENCIES

Botswana Press Agency (BOPA): Private Bag 0060, Gaborone; tel. 313601; telex 2284; f. 1981.

Foreign Bureaux

Deutsche Presse-Agentur (Germany) and **Reuters** (UK) are represented in Botswana.

Publishers

A.C. Braby (Botswana) (Pty) Ltd: POB 1549, Gaborone; tel. 371444; fax 373462; telephone directories.

Department of Information and Broadcasting: Private Bag 0060, Gaborone; tel. 352541; telex 2409; fax 357138.

Heinemann Educational Boleswa (Pty) Ltd: Plot 10223, Mokolwane Rd, Gaborone; tel. 372305; telex 2378; fax 371832.

Longman Botswana (Pty) Ltd: POB 1083, Gaborone; tel. 322969; fax 322682; f. 1981; educational; Gen. Man. K. RAKHUDU.

Macmillan Botswana Publishing Co (Pty) Ltd: POB 1155, Gaborone; tel. 314379; telex 2841; fax 374326.

Magnum Press (Pty) Ltd: Gaborone; tel. 372852; fax 374558.

Printing and Publishing Co (Botswana) (Pty) Ltd: POB 130, 5647 Nakedi Rd, Broadhurst, Gaborone; tel. 312844; telex 2351.

Government Publishing House

Department of Government Printing and Publishing Services: Private Bag 0081, Gaborone; tel. 314441; fax 312001.

Radio and Television

According to UNESCO, there were an estimated 180,000 radio receivers and 24,000 television receivers in use in 1994.

RADIO

Radio Botswana: Private Bag 0060, Gaborone; tel. 352541; telex 2633; fax 357138; broadcasts in Setswana and English; f. 1965; Dir TED MAKGEKENENE.

Radio Botswana II: Private Bag 0060, Gaborone; tel. 352541; telex 2409; f. 1992; commercial radio network.

TELEVISION

Gaborone Television Corporation: Private Bag 0060, Gaborone; tel. 352541; fax 357138; limited service; Dep. Dir BATATU TAFA.

TV Association of Botswana: Gaborone; relays SABC-TV and BOP-TV programmes from South Africa; plans for a national TV service are under consideration.

Finance

(cap. = capital; res = reserves; dep. = deposits; m. = million; brs = branches; amounts in pula)

BANKING

Central Bank

Bank of Botswana: Private Bag 154, Khama Crescent, Plot 1863, Gaborone; tel. 3606000; telex 2448; fax 372984; f. 1975; bank of issue; cap. and res 3,319.7m., dep. 8,558.8m. (Dec. 1995); Gov. H. C. L. HERMANS.

Commercial Banks

Barclays Bank of Botswana Ltd: POB 478, Barclays House, Khama Crescent, Gaborone; tel. 352041; telex 2417; fax 313672; f. 1975; 74.9% owned by Barclays Bank PLC (UK); cap. and res 116.2m., dep. 985.0m. (Dec. 1995); Chair. B. GAOLATHE; Man. Dir C. J. MIDDLETON; 48 brs, etc.

First National Bank of Botswana: POB 1552, Finance House, 5th Floor, Plot 8843, Khama Crescent, Gaborone; tel. 311669; telex 2520; fax 306130; f. 1991; 70% owned by First National Bank Holdings Botswana Ltd; cap. and res 100.6m., dep. 755.7m. (Dec. 1996); Chair. P. C. H. THOMPSON; Man. Dir J. K. MACASKILL; 13 brs.

Stanbic Bank Botswana Ltd: Private Bag 00168, Travaglini House, Old Lobatse Rd, Gaborone; tel. 301600; telex 2562; fax 300171; f. 1992, following the merger of ANZ Grindlays PLC and UnionBank Botswana; subsidiary of Standard Bank Investment Corpn Africa Holdings Ltd; cap. and res 32.5m., dep 250.6m. (Sept. 1996); Chair. G. C. BELL; Man. Dir J. N. MCLEMAN; 5 brs.

Standard Chartered Bank Botswana Ltd: POB 496, Standard House, 5th Floor, The Mall, Gaborone; tel. 353111; telex 2422; fax 372933; f. 1975; 75% owned by Standard Chartered Bank Africa PLC, London; cap. and res 85.5m., dep. 743.9m. (Dec. 1994); Chair. P. L. STEENKAMP; Man. Dir L. S. GIBSON; 15 brs.

Other Banks

Botswana Savings Bank: POB 1150, Gaborone; tel. 312555; telex 2401; fax 352608; Chair. F. MODISE; Man. Dir E. B. MATHE.

National Development Bank: POB 225, Development House, The Mall, Gaborone; tel. 352801; telex 2553; fax 374446; f. 1964; cap. and res 89.2m., dep 20.5m. (March 1995); priority given to agricultural credit for Botswana farmers, and co-operative credit and loans for local business ventures; Chair. F. MODISE; Gen. Man. J. HOWELL; 6 brs.

STOCK EXCHANGE

Botswana Stock Exchange: Private Bag 00417, Barclays House, Ground Floor, Khama Crescent, Gaborone; tel. 357900; fax 357901; e-mail bse@info.bw; f. 1989 as Stockbrokers Botswana; formally inaugurated as a stock exchange in Nov. 1995; CEO ALAN D. NORRIE.

INSURANCE

Botswana Co-operative Insurance Co Ltd: POB 199, Gaborone; tel. 313654; fax 313654.

Botswana Eagle Insurance Co Ltd: POB 1221, 501 Botsalano House, Gaborone; tel. 212392; telex 2259; fax 213745; Gen. Man. JOHN MAIN.

Botswana Insurance Co (Pty) Ltd: POB 336, BIC House, Gaborone; tel. 351791; telex 2359; fax 313290; Gen. Man. P. B. SUMMER.

Sedgwick James Insurance Brokers (Pty) Ltd: POB 103, Plot 730, The Mall, Botswana Rd, Gaborone; tel. 314241; fax 373120.

Tshireletso Insurance Brokers: POB 1967, Gaborone; tel. 357064; telex 2916; fax 371558.

Trade and Industry

PUBLIC CORPORATIONS

Botswana Housing Corporation: POB 412, Gaborone; tel. 353341; telex 2729; fax 352070; f. 1971; provides housing for central govt and local authority needs and assists with private-sector housing schemes; Chair. Z. P. PITSO; Gen. Man. (vacant); 900 employees.

Botswana Meat Commission (BMC): Private Bag 4, Lobatse; tel. 330321; telex 2420; fax 330530; f. 1966; slaughter of livestock, export of hides and skins, carcasses, frozen and chilled boneless beef; operates tannery and beef products cannery; Exec. Chair. Dr MARTIN M. MANNATHOKO.

Botswana Posts and Telecommunications Corporation: POB 700, Gaborone; tel. 358000; f. 1980; CEO M. T. CURRY.

Botswana Power Corporation: POB 48, Motlakase House, Macheng Way, Gaborone; tel. 360300; telex 2431; fax 373563; f. 1971; operates power stations at Selebi-Phikwe (capacity 65 MW) and Moropule (132 MW); Chair. the Dep. Perm. Sec., Ministry of Mineral Resources and Water Affairs; CEO K. SITHOLE.

Water Utilities Corporation: Private Bag 00276, Gaborone; tel. 360400; telex 2545; fax 373852; f. 1970; public water supply undertaking for principal townships; Chair. the Perm. Sec., Ministry of Mineral Resources and Water Affairs; CEO B. MPHO.

CHAMBER OF COMMERCE

Botswana National Chamber of Commerce and Industry: POB 20344, Gaborone; tel. 52677.

MARKETING BOARD

Botswana Agricultural Marketing Board (BAMB): Private Bag 0053, 1227 Haile Selassie Rd, Gaborone; tel. 351341; fax 352926; Chair. the Perm. Sec., Ministry of Agriculture; Gen. Man. S. B. TAUKOBONG.

DEVELOPMENT ORGANIZATIONS

Botswana Development Corporation Ltd: Private Bag 160, Moedi, Plot 50380, Gaborone International Showgrounds, Off Machel Drive, Gaborone; tel. 351811; telex 2251; fax 303105; f. 1970; Chair. O. K. MATAMBO; Man. Dir M. O. MOLEFANE.

Botswana Livestock Development Corporation (Pty) Ltd: POB 455, Gaborone; tel. 351949; fax 357251; f.1977; Chair. M. M. MANNATHOKO; Gen. Man. S. M. R. BURNETT.

Department of Trade and Investment Promotion (TIPA), Ministry of Commerce and Industry: Private Bag 00367, Gaborone; tel. 351790; telex 2674; fax 305375; promotes industrial and commercial investment, diversification and expansion; offers consultancy, liaison and information services; participates in int. trade fairs and trade and investment missions; Dir D. TSHEKO.

Financial Services Co of Botswana (Pty) Ltd: POB 1129, Finance House, Khama Crescent, Gaborone; tel. 351363; telex 2207; fax 357815; f. 1974; hire purchase, mortgages, industrial leasing and debt factoring; Chair. M. E. HOPKINS; Man. Dir R. A. PAWSON.

Integrated Field Services: Private Bag 004, Ministry of Commerce and Industry, Gaborone; tel. 353024; telex 2674; fax 371539; promotes industrialization and rural development; Dir B. T. TIBONE.

Trade and Investment Promotion Agency (TIPA): Gaborone; promotion of trade; operates as part of the Ministry of Commerce and Industry.

EMPLOYERS' ASSOCIATION

Botswana Confederation of Commerce, Industry and Manpower (BOCCIM): POB 432, BOCCIM House, Gaborone; f. 1971; Chair. D. N. MOROKA; Dir MODIRI J. MBAAKANYI; 1,478 affiliated mems.

MAJOR INDUSTRIAL COMPANIES

The following are among the leading companies in Botswana in terms of capital investment and employment.

Botswana RST Ltd (Botrest): POB 3, Selebi-Phikwe; tel. 810211; telex 2219; fax 810441; f. 1967 as Botswana Roan Selection Trust Ltd; holding co with 85% shareholding in copper-nickel producers, BCL Ltd; Chair. Dr D. J. Hudson; Man. Dir Dr B. V. Stewart.

Debswana Diamond Co (Pty) Ltd: Debswana House, The Mall, POB 329, Gaborone; tel. 351131; telex 2410; fax 356110; sole diamond-mining interest in Botswana; owned equally by De Beers Centenary AG and the Botswana Govt; CEO Baledzi Gaolathe.

Gold Fields Botswana (Pty) Ltd: BCC Bldg, 1st Floor, Lobatse Rd, Box 271, Gaborone; tel. and fax 312760; telex 2706; holds prospecting licences covering an area of 4,180 sq km.

TRADE UNIONS

Botswana Federation of Trade Unions: POB 440, Gaborone; tel. and fax 352534; f. 1977; Gen. Sec. Maranyane Kebitsang.

Affiliated Unions

Air Botswana Employees' Union: POB 92, Gaborone; Gen. Sec. Daniel Motsumi.

Barclays Management Staff Union: POB 478, Gaborone; Gen. Sec. Tefo Lionjanga.

BCL Senior Staff Union: POB 383, Selebi-Phikwe; Gen. Sec. Kabelo Matthews.

Botswana Agricultural Marketing Board Workers' Union: Private Bag 0053, Gaborone; Gen. Sec. M. E. Semathane.

Botswana Bank Employees' Union: POB 111, Gaborone; Gen. Sec. Keolopile Gaborone.

Botswana Beverages and Allied Workers' Union: POB 41358, Gaborone; Gen. Sec. S. Senwelo.

Botswana Brigade Teachers' Union: Private Bag 007, Molepolole; Gen. Sec. Sadike Kgokong.

Botswana Commercial and General Workers' Union: POB 62, Gaborone; Gen. Sec. Kediretse Mpetang.

Botswana Construction Workers' Union: POB 1508, Gaborone; Gen. Sec. Joshua Kesiilwe.

Botswana Diamond Sorters-Valuators' Union: POB 1186, Gaborone; Gen. Sec. Felix T. Lesetedi.

Botswana Housing Corporation Staff Union: POB 412, Gaborone; Gen. Sec. Gorata Dingalo.

Botswana Meat Industry Workers' Union: POB 181, Lobatse; Gen. Sec. Johnson Bojosi.

Botswana Mining Workers' Union: Gaborone; Gen. Sec. Balekamang S. Ganasiane.

Botswana Postal Services Workers' Union: POB 87, Gaborone; Gen. Sec. Aaron Mosweu.

Botswana Power Corporation Workers' Union: Private Bag 0053, Gaborone; Gen. Sec. Molefe Modise.

Botswana Railways and Artisan Employees' Union: POB 1486, Gaborone; Gen. Sec. Patrick Magowe.

Botswana Railways Senior Staff Union: POB 449, Mahalapye; Gen. Sec. Lentswe Letsweletse.

Botswana Railways Workers' Union: POB 181, Gaborone; Gen. Sec. Ernest T. G. Mohutsiwa.

Botswana Telecommunications Employees' Union: Gaborone; Gen. Sec. Sedibana Robert.

Botswana Vaccine Institute Staff Union: Private Bag 0031, Gaborone; Gen. Sec. Elliot Modise.

Central Bank Union: POB 712, Gaborone; Gen. Sec. Godfrey Ngidi.

National Amalgamated Local and Central Government, Parastatal, Statutory Body and Manual Workers' Union: POB 374, Gaborone; Gen. Sec. Dickson Kelatlhegetswe.

National Development Bank Employees' Union: POB 225, Gaborone; Sec.-Gen. Matshediso Fologang.

Non-Academic Staff Union: Private Bag 0022, Gaborone; Gen. Sec. Isaac Thothe.

CO-OPERATIVES

Department of Co-operative Development: POB 86, Gaborone; f. 1964; promotes marketing and supply, consumer, dairy, horticultural and fisheries co-operatives, thrift and loan societies, credit societies, a co-operative union and a co-operative bank.

Botswana Co-operative Union: Gaborone; telex 2298; f. 1970; Dir Aaron Ramosako.

TRADE FAIR

Botswana International Trade Fair: c/o Dept of Trade and Investment Promotion, Private Bag 00367, Gaborone; tel. 351790; telex 2674; fax 305375.

Transport

RAILWAYS

The 960-km railway line from Mafikeng, South Africa, to Bulawayo, Zimbabwe, passes through Botswana. In 1994 there were 888 km of 1,067-mm-gauge track within Botswana, including three branches serving the Selebi-Phikwe mining complex (56 km), the Morupule colliery (16 km) and the Sua Pan soda ash deposits (175 km). The entire main railway line in Botswana is to be rehabilitated under an SADC project, estimated to cost US $114m.

Botswana Railways (BR): Private Bag 0052, Mahalapye; tel. 411375; telex 2980; fax 411385; Gen. Man. A. Ramji.

ROADS

In 1995 there were an estimated 11,800 km of roads, of which some 14.2% were bituminized (including a main road from Gaborone, via Francistown, to Kazungula, where the borders of Botswana, Namibia, Zambia and Zimbabwe meet). The construction of a 340-km road between Nata and Maun is currently under way. Construction of the Trans-Kalahari road, from Jwaneng to the port of Walvis Bay on the Namibian coast, commenced in 1990 and was scheduled for completion in 1998. A car-ferry service operates from Kazungula across the Zambezi river into Zambia.

CIVIL AVIATION

The main international airport is at Gaborone. A second major airport, at Kasane in the Chobe area of northern Botswana, opened in 1992. There are airfields at Francistown, Maun and at other population centres, and there are numerous airstrips throughout the country. Scheduled services of Air Botswana are supplemented by an active charter and business sector.

Air Botswana: POB 92, Head Office Bldg, Sir Seretse Khama Airport, Gaborone; tel. 352812; telex 2413; fax 375408; f. 1972; govt-owned; domestic services and regional services to most countries in eastern and southern Africa; Chair. A. V. Lionjanga; Gen. Man. J. B. Galeforolwe.

Tourism

There are five game reserves and three national parks, including Chobe, near Victoria Falls, on the Zambia–Zimbabwe border. Efforts to expand the tourist industry include plans for the construction of new hotels and the rehabilitation of existing hotel facilities. In 1995 tourist arrivals (including same-day visitors) totalled an estimated 1,021,000, and in 1994 receipts from tourism amounted to US $35m.

Department of Tourism: Ministry of Commerce and Industry, Private Bag 0047, Koh-I-Noor House, Main Mall, Gaborone; tel. 353024; telex 2674; fax 308675; Dir Gaylard Kombani.

Department of Wildlife and National Parks: POB 131, Gaborone; tel. 371405; Dir. G. Seeletso.

Defence

Military service is voluntary. Botswana established a permanent defence force in 1977. In August 1996 the total strength of the Botswana Defence Force was some 7,500, comprising an army of 7,000 and an air force of 500. In addition, there was a paramilitary police force of 1,000. There are plans to enlarge the strength of the army to 10,000 men.

Defence Expenditure: Budgeted at P445.2m. in 1996/97.

Defence Force Commander: Lt-Gen. Ian Khama.

Education

Although education is not compulsory, enrolment ratios are high. Primary education, which is provided free of charge, begins at seven years of age and lasts for up to seven years. Secondary education, beginning at the age of 14, lasts for a further five years, comprising a first cycle of two years and a second of three years. As a proportion of the school-age population, the total enrolment at primary and secondary schools increased from 52% in 1975 to the equivalent of 92% (boys 91%; girls 93%) in 1994.

Enrolment at primary schools in 1993 included 96% of children in the relevant age-group (boys 93%; girls 99%), while the comparable ratio for secondary enrolment in 1994 was equivalent to 56% (boys 54%; girls 58%). The government aims to provide universal access to nine years of basic education by the late 1990s. Botswana has the highest teacher-pupil ratio in Africa, but continues to rely heavily on expatriate secondary school teachers.

A National Literacy Programme was initiated in 1980, and 9,473 people were enrolled under the programme in 1991. According to estimates by UNESCO, the average rate of adult illiteracy in 1995 was 30.2% (males 19.5%; females 40.1%). Education was allocated some 10% of total projected expenditure under the National Development Plan for 1991–97. Budget estimates for 1996/97 allocated P1,545.5m. to education (representing 25.5% of total forecast expenditure by the central government).

Bibliography

Benson, M. *Tshekedi Khama*. London, Faber and Faber, 1960.

Bhuiyan, M. N. (Ed.). *Selected Papers on the Botswana Economy*. Gaborone, Bank of Botswana, 1987.

Botswana Society. *Settlement in Botswana*. London, Heinemann Educational, 1982.

Chipasula, J. C., and Miti, K. *Botswana in Southern Africa*. Delhi, Ajanta, 1989.

Colclough, C., and McCarthy, S. *The Political Economy of Botswana: A Study of Growth and Distribution*. London, Oxford University Press, 1980.

Dale, R. *Botswana's Search for Autonomy in Southern Africa*. Westport, CT, Greenwood Press, 1995.

Du Toit, P. *State Building and Democracy in Southern Africa: Botswana, Zimbabwe and South Africa*. Washington, DC, US Institute of Peace Press, 1995.

Hailey, Lord. *The Republic of South Africa and the High Commission Territories*. London, Oxford University Press, 1963.

Halpern, J. *South Africa's Hostages, Basutoland, Bechuanaland and Swaziland*. Harmondsworth, Penguin Books, 1965.

Hartland-Thunberg, P. *Botswana: An African Growth Economy*. Boulder, CO, Westview Press, 1978.

Harvey, C. (Ed.). *Papers on the Economy of Botswana*. London, Heinemann Educational, 1981.

Harvey, C., and Lewis, S. R. *Policy Choice and Development Performance in Botswana*. Basingstoke, Macmillan, 1990.

Hayward, M. F. *Elections in Independent Africa*. Boulder, CO, Westview Press, 1987.

Jones, D. *Aid and Development in Southern Africa*. London, Croom Helm/Overseas Development Institute, 1977.

Konzacki, Z.A., Parpart, J. L., and Shaw, T. M. (Eds). *Studies in the Economic History of Southern Africa*. Vol. 1. London, Cass, 1990.

Landau, P. S. *The Realm of the Word: Language, Gender and Christianity in a Southern African Kingdom*. London, James Currey Publishers, 1996.

Lipton, M. *Employment and Labour Use in Botswana*. Gaborone, Botswana Government Printer, 1978.

Mazonde, I. N. *Ranching and Enterprise in Eastern Botswana: A Case Study of Black and White Farmers*. London, Edinburgh University Press, 1994.

Molomo, M. G., and Mokopakgosi, B. T. *Multi-Party Democracy in Botswana*. Harare, SAPES Trust, 1991.

Morton, F., et al. *Historical Dictionary of Botswana*. 2nd Edn, Methuen, NJ, Scarecrow Press, 1989. (First edn by R. P. Stevens published in 1975.)

Oden, B. *The Macroeconomic Position of Botswana*. Uppsala, Scandinavian Institute of African Studies, 1981.

Oommen, M. A., et al. *Botswana Economy since Independence*. New Delhi, Tate/McGraw-Hill, 1983.

Parson, J. D. *Botswana: Liberal Democracy and Labour Reserve in Southern Africa*. Aldershot, Gower Publishers; Boulder CO, Westview Press, 1984.

Picard, L. A. *The Politics of Development in Botswana: A Model For Success*. Boulder, CO, Lynne Rienner Publishers, 1987.

Picard, L. A. (Ed.). *The Evolution of Modern Botswana*. London, Rex Collings, 1988.

Politics and Rural Development in Southern Africa: The Evolution of Modern Botswana. London, Rex Collings, 1985.

Schapera, I., et al. *Ethnographic Survey of Africa: The Tswana*. London, International African Institute, 1953.

Seidman, J. *In Our Own Image*. Gaborone Foundation for Education with Production 1990.

Seisa, S., and Youngman, F. (Eds). *Education For All in Botswana*. Gaborone, Macmillan Botswana, 1995.

Sillery, A. *Botswana, A Short Political History*. London, Methuen, 1974.

Stedman, S. J. *Botswana: The Political Economy of Democratic Development*. Boulder, CO, Lynne Rienner Publishers, 1993.

Tlou, T., and Campbell, A. *History of Botswana*. Gaborone, Macmillan Botswana, 1984.

Tlou, T., et al. *Seretse Khama, 1921–1980*. Johannesburg, Macmillan, 1995.

Tsie, B. *The Political Economy of Botswana in SADCC*. Harare, Southern Africa Printing and Publishing House, 1995.

Wylie D. A. *Little God: the Twilight of Patriarchy in a Southern African Chiefdom*. Johannesburg, Witwatersrand University Press, 1990.

BURKINA FASO

Physical and Social Geography

R. J. HARRISON CHURCH

Like Niger and Mali, the Republic of Burkina Faso (formerly Upper Volta) is a land-locked state of west Africa and is situated north of Côte d'Ivoire, Ghana and Togo. Burkina has an area of 274,200 sq km (105,870 sq miles). The December 1985 census recorded a total population of 7,964,705, giving an average density of 29 inhabitants per sq km. According to official estimates, the population had risen to 10,200,000 at mid-1995 (37 per sq km). In recent years there has been large-scale emigration to neighbouring Côte d'Ivoire and Ghana by people seeking work on farms, in industries and the service trades, although economic difficulties in these host countries have prompted the return of large numbers of migrant workers to Burkina. The main ethnic groups are the Bobo in the south-west, and the Mossi and Gourma in the north and east respectively. Along the northern border are the semi-nomadic Fulani, who are also present in the east of the country.

Towards the south-western border with Mali there are Primary sandstones, terminating eastward in the Banfora escarpment. As in Guinea, Mali and Ghana, where there are also great expanses of these rocks, their residual soils are poor and water percolates deeply within them. Although most of the rest of the country is underlain by granite, gneisses and schists, there is much loose sand or bare laterite; consequently, there are extensive infertile areas. Moreover, annual rainfall is only some 635–1,145 mm, and comes in a rainy season of at the most five months. Water is scarce except by the rivers or in the Gourma swampy area; by the former the simulium fly, whose bite leads to blindness, can still occur despite extensive eradication projects, while in the latter the tsetse, a fly which can cause sleeping-sickness, is found. Given the grim physical environment, the density of population in the north-central Mossi area is remarkable. The area is, in fact, one of the oldest indigenous kingdoms of west Africa, dating back to the 11th century. Islam first penetrated the area during the 14th–16th centuries. At the end of the 18th century it was adopted by some local rulers, notably the leader of the Mossi, but traditional religious practices among the population remained strong. Islam's expansion was facilitated by the circumstances of French rule but more than one-half of the population retain their traditional beliefs.

Burkina Faso has potentially valuable deposits of gold, manganese and zinc, industrial exploitation of which is in progress or is planned. Deposits of silver, nickel, lead, phosphates and vanadium have also been identified.

Recent History

PIERRE ENGLEBERT

Revised for this edition by the Editor

Burkina Faso (then Upper Volta) became a self-governing republic within the French Community in December 1958. Full independence followed on 5 August 1960, with Maurice Yaméogo, the leader of the Union démocratique voltaïque (UDV), as president of the new republic. Support for the UDV was centred on the Mossi, the country's dominant ethnic group, constituting about 50% of the population.

Yaméogo's administration was autocratic in style. Opposition parties were banned, and popular support for the government receded as the country's economic condition worsened. Following a prolonged period of economic crisis and social unrest, Yaméogo was deposed in an army coup in January 1966. The new head of state, Lt-Col Sangoulé Lamizana, suspended the constitution and introduced austerity measures which led to improved economic conditions. In December 1970 the military regime assented to the formation of an elected civilian administration under the premiership of Gérard Ouédraogo, the president of the UDV. Several new parties emerged, among them the Mouvement de libération nationale (MLN), an urban-supported radical group led by Prof. Joseph Ki-Zerbo, the Mouvement national pour le renouveau, a short-lived national unity movement formed by President Lamizana, and the Union nationale pour la défense de la démocratie (UNDD), led by Herman Yaméogo, son of the former president. The UDV itself began to experience factional strain, while the MLN allied itself with other elements to form the Union progressiste voltaïque (UPV).

For much of the 1970s Upper Volta was ravaged by the Sahelian drought, which disrupted the economy and caused severe food shortages in rural areas. In 1974 a long-standing dispute with Mali regarding sovereignty of the 'Agacher Strip', a well-irrigated and reputedly mineral-rich border region, suddenly escalated when Malian troops were sent in to occupy the area. Mediation by the Organization of African Unity (OAU) failed to resolve the issue, which was to continue to strain relations for more than a decade.

In 1977 Lamizana promulgated a new constitution, and, following presidential and legislative elections in May 1978, a mainly civilian government, dominated by the UDV, took office. All political parties except the UDV, the UNDD and the UPV were suppressed.

ARMY REGIMES, 1980–83

In November 1980, following a period of renewed economic difficulty and popular unrest, Lamizana was overthrown in a bloodless military coup led by Col Saye Zerbo, who suspended the constitution and formed a governing Comité militaire de redressement pour le progrès national (CMRPN). Although the trade unions initially supported the coup, they soon became discontented with a total ban on political activity. Relations between government and unions deteriorated after Zerbo announced in 1981 that priority was to be given to the rural sector and emphasized the need for restraint by urban workers. Meanwhile, serious rifts began to appear in the CMRPN, and the resignation, in April 1982, of the populist Capt. Thomas Sankara from the information ministry was perceived to be indicative of dissatisfaction in some quarters of the military.

Ouédraogo and the CSP

In November 1982 a group of NCOs seized power, accusing Zerbo of corruption, suppression of liberties and arrests of workers and students. A military Conseil du salut du peuple (CSP) was formed, with Surgeon-Maj. Jean-Baptiste Ouédraogo as chairman, head of state and minister of defence. The chief of staff of the army, Col Gabriel Somé, and some of Zerbo's government ministers remained in their posts. Sankara's rumoured involvement was seemingly confirmed in January 1983, when he was appointed prime minister.

The CSP adopted a radical stance in favour of the unions and the right to strike. Ouédraogo also repeatedly promised that there would be a return to civilian rule in 1984, and that a major restructuring of the armed forces would take place. By mid-1983, however, it had become apparent that Ouédraogo was presiding over an increasingly divided regime, as the compromise between traditionalists in the army (led by Somé) and the radicals (led by Sankara) degenerated into open conflict in May. Angered that Sankara had personally invited the Libyan leader, Col Qaddafi, to visit Upper Volta, Ouédraogo ordered the arrest of Sankara and his supporters in the CSP; Sankara was accused of 'dangerously threatening national unity'. Members of his commando unit in Pô, near the border with Ghana, immediately rebelled. Led by Capt. Blaise Compaoré, they took control of the town and refused orders from the capital. Ouédraogo twice released Sankara to negotiate with the mutineers, but was unwilling to accede to the rebels' demand for the dismissal of Somé (now responsible for national defence), whom they suspected of having orchestrated Sankara's arrest. Although Sankara was freed unconditionally in June, the mutiny spread, and in August Sankara deposed Ouédraogo in a military coup. Ouédraogo was placed under house arrest, and Somé was killed shortly afterwards in a skirmish involving the opposing factions.

Sankara installed a Conseil national de la révolution (CNR) and formed a new government, with himself as head of state and Compaoré as minister of state at the presidency. The CNR, composed of junior officers and NCOs, was supported by left-wing civilians grouped in the previously clandestine Ligue patriotique pour le développement (LIPAD).

SANKARA: REVOLUTION AND REFORM, 1983–87

Sankara encouraged the establishment of Comités pour la défense de la révolution (CDR) throughout the country, and purged the army of 'reactionary' elements. In its first months in power the CNR reorganized the administrative regions of the country, deprived the country's traditional chiefs of their privileges and influence, and installed what was termed 'revolutionary people's tribunals' to try former public officials charged with political crimes and embezzlement. The first politician to be tried when the tribunals began work in January 1984 was Lamizana, who was acquitted on charges of misusing official funds. However, several former senior figures were convicted of embezzlement and subsequently imprisoned, among them Zerbo and Gérard Ouédraogo, and other erstwhile officials were fined.

In March 1984 schoolteachers took strike action in protest against the arrest of three of their leaders. Internal discord was also burgeoning, as LIPAD's attempts to gain full control of the CNR met with resistance from other elements. A prominent LIPAD member was dismissed from the government in May, and in June seven army officers, accused of plotting a coup, were executed; other alleged conspirators received sentences of hard labour ranging from 15 years to life.

To symbolize the political changes that were taking place, and as an expression of 'decolonization', Sankara changed the name of the country to Burkina Faso ('Land of the Incorruptible Men') in August 1984. Later in the month Sankara dismissed his entire government, as a prelude to a complete break with LIPAD. Sankara's closest advisers remained Compaoré, as minister of state, Maj. Jean-Baptiste Boukary Lingani, the minister of defence, and Capt. Henri Zongo, who became minister of economic promotion. In October several LIPAD members were arrested, and 19 junior army officers and lower-ranking military personnel were dismissed, accused of 'subversive attitudes'. In January 1985 the general secretary of the Confédération syndicale burkinabè and a prominent member of LIPAD, Soumane Touré, was detained, and several other trade unionists were removed from office.

The momentum for change was maintained by a thorough reform of the judicial and education systems, and through economic austerity measures. Sankara's revolution was now generally seen to be less identified with Marxist forces, and as seeking to accommodate a wider cross-section of society. The extended role of the CDR in imposing government policy and organizing local affairs helped to consolidate Sankara's power. Sankara's growing confidence in his own authority was manifested during 1986 with the release from detention of all his significant political opponents.

The dispute with Mali over the Agacher strip erupted into six days of armed conflict in December 1985. Fifty people were estimated to have died in the conflict, during which Mali, with its superior forces and armaments, inflicted considerable damage inside Burkinabè territory. The regional defence grouping, Accord de non-agression et d'assistance en matière de défense, negotiated a cease-fire and dispatched peace-keeping forces, and in January 1986 Sankara and President Moussa Traoré of Mali agreed to a reconciliation. Both countries subsequently withdrew their troops from the disputed area, and in June ambassadors were exchanged for the first time in 12 years. In December the International Court of Justice, to which the dispute had been referred in 1983, ruled that the territory be divided equally between the two countries, with Burkina gaining sovereignty over the eastern district of Beli.

Sankara established close relations with Ghana's head of state, Flt-Lt Jerry Rawlings, in both military and political spheres, and arrangements were discussed for an eventual union of the two countries. However, other neighbouring states, particularly Togo and Côte d'Ivoire, opposed such an alliance, and Togo accused Burkina and Ghana of acting to promote a coup attempt in Lomé in September 1986. Relations with France were generally close, and France and other Western governments encouraged the distancing of the Sankara regime from both Libya and the USSR.

The Fall of Sankara

During 1987 divisions between Sankara and the other leaders of the CNR, Compaoré, Boukary Lingani and Zongo, became increasingly evident. In particular, Compaoré opposed Sankara's attitude to the trade unions, which was exemplified, in May, by the renewed imprisonment of Soumane Touré. Divisions were equally apparent between two of the semi-official political organizations participating in the CNR: the generally pro-Sankara Union des luttes communistes reconstruite (ULCR) and the Union des communistes burkinabè (UCB), which was closely associated with Compaoré. A split in the ULCR undermined Sankara's principal base of civilian support, and forced him to dismiss two of the three ULCR ministers in August. A proposal by Sankara that a single party be formed to embrace all existing political organizations (in an attempt to forestall his further marginalization in the CNR) was vehemently opposed by his former allies. On 15 October a commando unit loyal to Compaoré opened fire on Sankara, killing him and 13 of his associates. A Front populaire (FP) was proclaimed as successor to the CNR, and Compaoré, the chairman of the FP, became head of state. Sankara was denounced as a traitor and a renegade, and many of his relatives and former ministers were arrested.

THE FRONT POPULAIRE

While the FP pledged a continuation of the CNR's revolutionary process, a new phase, to be known as 'rectification', was announced. This concept embraced both economic liberalization (including attempts to foster private enterprise, as well as the instigation of negotiations with the IMF and the World Bank) and the removal from positions of influence of Sankara loyalists. The CDR were abolished in March 1988 and replaced by Comités révolutionnaires (CR); however, attempts at recruitment to these attracted little popular interest. The FP allowed Sankara's widow to seek asylum in Gabon in mid-1988, and released several of those arrested in the aftermath of the coup. In April 1989 the formation was announced of a new political group, the Organisation pour la démocratie populaire/Mouvement du travail (ODP/MT), under the leadership of the former head of the UCB, Clément Oumarou Ouédraogo. Prominent members of groups that had refused to affiliate to the ODP/MT were swiftly removed from political office, while Ouédraogo was appointed to the newly-created government post of minister-delegate to the co-ordinating committee of the FP.

The only remaining 'orthodox' elements of the 1983 revolution were eliminated in September 1989, when Zongo and Boukary Lingani were summarily executed, together with two others, following the alleged discovery of a coup plot. Compaoré subsequently assumed the defence and security portfolio (previously held by Boukary Lingani). None the less, the continuing 'revolutionary' dogma of the ODP/MT, in contrast with Compaoré's increasingly moderate orientation, remained a potential source of instability within the FP, and in December it was announced that a further conspiracy had been foiled.

The first congress of the FP, convened in March 1990, was attended by representatives of seven political organizations. Delegates appointed a commission to draft a new constitution that would define a process of 'democratization'. A reorganization of the executive committee of the FP included the appointment of the 'moderate' Herman Yaméogo. (Three months later, however, Yaméogo and his supporters were expelled from the FP.) In April Clément Oumarou Ouédraogo, accused of having deviated from the organization's political doctrine, was dismissed from its leadership and subsequently removed from the government. Roch Marc Christian Kaboré, whose political orientation was closer to that of Compaoré, assumed both the leadership of the ODP/MT and the post of secretary for political affairs within the FP's executive committee. Kaboré was promoted to the rank of minister of state in September.

The constitutional commission, which began work in May 1990, was not given plenary powers, suggesting that the FP intended to exercise close supervision over the process of democratization. The first draft of the constitution, published in October, provided for a multi-party political system in what was to be designated the fourth republic. Among the main provisions of the final document was a clause denying legitimacy to any regime that might take power as the result of a *coup d'état*. Presidential and legislative elections were to be by universal adult suffrage: the seven-year mandate of the head of state would be renewable only once, while elections to the Assemblée des députés populaires (ADP) would be held every five years. It was envisaged that a second, consultative chamber, to be composed of the 'active forces of the nation', would eventually be established.

In March 1991 a congress of the ODP/MT adopted Compaoré as the party's official candidate to contest the forthcoming presidential election, and at the same time replaced its Marxist-Leninist ideology with a commitment to policies of free enterprise. In April an official amnesty was proclaimed for the alleged perpetrators of the December 1989 coup attempt; the rehabilitation was announced, in May 1991, of Maurice Yaméogo, and an appeal was made to political exiles to return to Burkina. In June plans were announced for the construction of a memorial honouring Sankara, and in August Compaoré declared an amnesty for all political 'crimes' committed since independence.

THE FOURTH REPUBLIC

The draft constitution was submitted for approval in a national referendum on 2 June 1991: it was reported that 93% of those who voted (about one-half of the electorate) endorsed the document. The constitution took effect on 11 June, whereupon the functions of the (restructured) FP were separated from the organs of state. The council of ministers was dissolved and a transitional administration appointed. Compaoré remained head of state on an interim basis, pending the presidential election. The most senior member of the new cabinet was Kaboré (as minister of state, in charge of the co-ordination of government action), and its composition was notable for the appointment of a civilian as minister of popular defence and security. Many political parties criticized the dominant role of the ODP/MT, and several nominated government members declined to accept their appointments. A reorganized government, appointed in July, included several opposition figures (among them Herman Yaméogo, himself a presidential contender, who, following his expulsion from the FP, had formed the Alliance pour la démocratie et la fédération–ADF).

Compaoré's refusal to accede to persistent opposition demands that a sovereign national conference be convened in advance of the presidential and legislative elections was a source of considerable political tension. In August 1991 Yaméogo and two other ADF members resigned their government posts, in protest against proposed electoral procedures. In the following month opposition parties established a Coordination des forces démocratiques (CFD), to which about 20 political organizations had affiliated by the end of the year. The seven remaining opposition members resigned from the transitional government later in September, as Compaoré again failed to agree to a national conference. In October, furthermore, five CFD representatives who had previously declared their intention to contest the presidency withdrew their candidatures.

Compaoré (who had resigned his army commission in order to contest the presidency as a civilian) was thus the sole candidate in the presidential election, which took place, as scheduled, on 1 December 1991, despite appeals from Burkinabè human rights and religious leaders for a postponement of the poll. He secured the support of 90.4% of those who voted, but an appeal by the CFD for a boycott of the poll had been widely heeded, and an abstention rate of 74.7% was recorded. Shortly afterwards Clément Oumarou Ouédraogo was assassinated while leaving a CFD meeting. Although the government and the ODP/MT condemned the attacks, opposition leaders accused the Compaoré administration of seeking to eliminate those who held evidence of its earlier misdeeds. Two days after Ouédraogo's death the government announced the indefinite postponement of the legislative elections. (The CFD had for some weeks been advocating a boycott of the elections to the ADP, and few parties had registered their intention to submit candidates. Compaoré was sworn in as president of the fourth republic on 24 December. In January 1992 the rehabilitation was announced of some 4,000 people who had been punished for political or trade union activity since 1983.

In an apparent attempt to restore a national consensus, Compaoré proposed a 'national reconciliation forum', embracing diverse political and social groups, to discuss the democratic process, human rights and development issues. The agenda of the reconciliation forum (which was convened in February 1992 and attended by some 380 delegates) was, however, restricted by Compaoré, and the conference was suspended within two weeks. In late February, none the less, the government was reorganized again to include Herman Yaméogo and three other opposition members.

In all, 27 parties contested the elections to the ADP, which finally took place on 24 May 1992. Although international observers declared that the poll had been conducted in a 'satisfactory' manner, Compaoré's opponents alleged widespread malpractice. The ODP/MT won 78 of the new legislature's 107 seats; Pierre Tapsoba's Convention nationale des patriotes progressistes–Parti social-démocrate (CNPP–PSD) obtained 12 seats, while the ADF secured four. An abstention rate of 64.8% was recorded. The ADP was inaugurated on 15 June. On the following day Compaoré appointed a young economist, Youssouf Ouédraogo, to the premiership. Ouédraogo's council of ministers included representatives of seven political organizations, although the ODP/MT retained control of most strategic ministries. Herman Yaméogo remained in the government as minister of state without portfolio, and Kaboré became minister of state, with responsibility for finance and planning.

In December 1992 the government, trade unions and representatives of the private sector began a series of negotiations, with a view to defining a 'social charter'. During late 1992 and early 1993, none the less, there was evidence of social tensions, mainly linked to the government's adoption of austerity measures (in the context of its structural adjustment programme), with some labour unrest and disruption in the education sector. A 'freeze' in public-sector salaries, in force since 1987, was ended in January 1993; however, workers' representatives judged a new salary structure to be unfavourable in real terms. In April the Confédération générale du travail burkinabè (CGTB) withdrew from the 'social charter' negotiations, protesting at the government's dilatory attitude towards addressing workers' grievances.

The ODP/MT's predominance in the legislature was enhanced following a split in the CNPP–PSD in May 1993, as a result of which six of the party's parliamentary members joined Joseph Ki-Zerbo's newly-formed Parti pour la démocratie et le progrès (PDP). Two of the CNPP–PSD's members left the government in September, as part of a reshuffle whereby Kaboré was redesignated minister of state, with responsibility for relations with the organs of state. Further government changes in January 1994 included the appointment of new ministers of defence and of justice.

Following the 50% devaluation of the CFA franc, in January 1994, the government introduced emergency measures (including controls on the prices of essential commodities and tax adjustments) in an attempt to offset the immediate adverse effects of the currency's depreciation. However, trade unions denounced such measures as inadequate, demanding compensatory salary increases of 40%–50%. Negotiations between the government and trade unions failed to reach a compromise, and in March Youssouf Ouédraogo resigned. Kaboré was appointed prime minister; his administration, dominated by the ODP/MT and its associates, included a new minister of the economy, finance and planning. Herman Yaméogo was designated minister of state, with responsibility for African integration and solidarity. The new government upheld Compaoré's desire to enforce austerity measures necessitated by the devaluation and the structural adjustment programme. A dialogue was sought with trade union leaders, but proposed salary increases of 6%–10%, as well as other concessions designed to mitigate the effects of the ending of price controls, failed to prevent a three-day general strike by members of the CGTB in April.

At municipal elections in February 1995 the ODP/MT won control of 26 of the country's 33 major towns. Representatives of 19 parties contested the elections (some opposition parties had refused to participate, protesting at what they claimed to be inadequate preparations for the elections). Fewer than 10% of those eligible were reported to have registered to vote. A government reorganization in June included the appointment of Col Badaye Fayama as minister of defence: Fayama was succeeded as chief of the general staff of the armed forces and army chief of staff by Lt-Col Ibrahim Traoré (hitherto minister of youth and sports). In August 1995 Ernest Nongma Ouédraogo, the secretary-general of the Bloc socialiste burkinabè (BSB), was convicted of insulting the head of state and sentenced to six months' imprisonment: in an article published in an independent journal, *Observateur Paalga*, Ouédraogo had alleged that Compaoré had fraudulently amassed a personal fortune.

In early February 1996 Kadré Désiré Ouédraogo, hitherto deputy governor of the Banque centrale des états de l'Afrique de l'ouest, was appointed to succeed Kaboré as prime minister. Kaboré was designated special adviser to the presidency and also first vice-president of a new, pro-Compaoré political party, the Congrès pour la démocratie et le progrès (CDP). The CDP, termed a social-democratic party, grouped the ODP/MT and some 10 other parties (among them the CNPP–PSD); its president was a long-time ally of Compaoré, Arsène Bognessan Yè, the president of the ADP and the former head of the ODP/MT.

Ouédraogo claimed no party political affiliation. He stated that his government's priority would be to strengthen and revitalize economic development, with particular emphasis on the agro-pastoral sector, employment, the stable management of public finances and on environmental protection. Most of the members of the outgoing administration were reappointed to the new prime minister's first council of ministers. Ouédraogo assumed personal responsibility for the economy and finance in a government reshuffle in early September 1996. Zéphirin Diabré, who had held the economy portfolio since 1994, subsequently became president of the advisory economic and social council.

With a reported 87 parliamentary deputies belonging to the CDP, the new party was expected to be a powerful political force at the legislative elections due the following year. A further significant development was the enlargement of Ki-Zerbo's PDP, in late March 1996, to include three other organizations.

In early October 1996 the government confirmed newspaper reports of the arrest of several members of the presidential security services. It emerged that those detained (numbering about 25) were close associates of Chief Warrant Officer Hyacinthe Kafando, hitherto responsible for the head of state's security, who had been ordered to return from a period of training in Morocco but who was reportedly seeking asylum at the French embassy in Abidjan, Côte d'Ivoire. Rumours circulated, in particular, of animosity between Kafando and Capt. Gilbert Diendéré, Compaoré's personal chief of staff. It was reported that the recent closure of the élite commando training centre from which members of the presidential guard were recruited had been a source of dissatisfaction within the service, and Compaoré's sudden cancellation, in late September, of an official visit to Libya had been attributed to what were termed security difficulties by some observers. Other sources, meanwhile, asserted that the arrests reflected the authorities' desire to restore discipline within the guard prior to the Franco-African summit meeting that was to take place in Ouagadougou in December. The government denied press speculation that a coup attempt had been foiled, emphasizing that there was no 'political connotation' to the arrests. Representatives of the national human rights organization, the Mouvement burkinabè des droits de l'homme et du peuple (MBDHP), visited the detainees, and subsequently confirmed that two relations of Kafando (one a civilian) were among those arrested. The MBDHP was, meanwhile, informed by Diendéré that Kafando had left the French embassy in Abidjan, and that his whereabouts were unknown.

Constitutional amendments and a new electoral code were approved by the ADP in January 1997: among the changes were the removal of restrictions on the renewal of the presidential mandate, as well as an increase (with effect from the forthcoming elections) in the number of parliamentary seats to 111. The national motto, hitherto 'fatherland or death, we shall conquer', was changed to 'unity, progress, justice', and parts of the national anthem were modified. In February the ADP approved proposals for a national commission for the organization of elections. The government's original proposals, adopted in November 1996, had provoked considerable criticism by the opposition, particularly since the commission would have no remit to scrutinize the compilation and revision of voters' lists (processes that were to remain under the control of the ministry of territorial administration and security). The new commission was denounced by the PDP as 'non-independent and non-permanent'.

The general election to the enlarged ADP took place on 11 May 1997, contested by some 569 candidates from 13 political parties. As had been expected, the CDP won resounding victory. In mid-May the supreme court annulled the results of voting for four seats, all of which had been won by the CDP; these were retained by the party at a further round of voting in the relevant constituencies in mid-June. The CDP thus preserved its overwhelming majority in the legislature, with its total of 101 seats augmented by two seats held by the ADF. The opposition was represented by the PDP, with six seats, and the Rassemblement démocratique africain, which returned two deputies. A new government, again led by Ouédraogo, was appointed in mid-June. Herman Yaméogo left the cabinet, while Arsène Bognessan Yè was named minister of state at the presidency of the republic. Maurice Mélégué Traoré, hitherto minister of secondary and higher education and scientific research, had been elected president of the ADP earlier in the month.

FOREIGN RELATIONS

During the 1990s Compaoré has increasingly assumed a role as a regional mediator. Some Western governments have, none the less, expressed concern at Burkina's maintenance of close links with Libya, and Compaoré's role in the Liberian conflict has frequently been a focus of regional and international scrutiny.

Following the escalation of the civil conflict in Liberia after early 1990, Burkina's relations with some members of the Economic Community of West African States (ECOWAS) deteriorated as a result of the Compaoré government's open support for Charles Taylor's rebel National Patriotic Front of Liberia (NPFL) and refusal to contribute members of the Burkinabè military to the ECOWAS monitoring group (ECOMOG) that was sent to Liberia in mid-1990. Allegations that the government of Burkina was aiding the NPFL were renewed in 1991, when in May a Burkinabè-chartered vessel was intercepted by ECOMOG forces outside the Liberian port of Buchanan: the ship was apparently transporting rubber from NPFL-controlled plantations, allegedly to Libya, where it was to be exchanged for a shipment of arms. Shortly afterwards two Burkinabè soldiers were captured in Sierra Leone, where they were said to have been aiding NPFL troops. In September Compaoré admitted that some 700 Burkinabè troops had been assisting the NPFL in Liberia. However, Compaoré's assertion that his country's involvement in Liberia had ended contrasted with reports in late 1991 that a pro-NPFL mercenary force, comprising Liberian, Burkinabè, Ivorian and Guinean nationals, was being trained at the Pô military base. In November 1992 the US government recalled its ambassador to Burkina, and announced that the recently-appointed Burkinabè ambassador to Washington would not be welcome in the USA, owing to Burkina's alleged role in transporting arms from Libya to the NPFL. Shortly afterwards, however, Compaoré expressed willingness in principle to contribute a military contingent to the ECOWAS force, on condition that ECOMOG's role be confined to that of a neutral peace-keeping body. Although allegations persisted that, in facilitating the supply of weapons to the NPFL, Burkina was undermining attempts to achieve a negotiated settlement to the Liberian conflict, in July 1994 the Compaoré government denied assertions by the Liberian transitional authorities that some 3,000 Burkinabè mercenaries were assisting the NPFL. In the following month, moreover, Burkina refuted claims, made by the ECOMOG chief of staff, of Burkinabè collusion in the transfer of weaponry to Taylor's forces. In September 1995, following the signing of a new peace agreement in Abuja, Nigeria, in the previous month, the Compaoré administration, stating that it regarded the new accord as more 'credible' than previous peace settlements for Liberia, announced that (subject to parliamentary approval) Burkina would contribute troops to ECOMOG. The ADP endorsed legislation authorizing participation in the monitoring group, in preparation for the forthcoming elections in Liberia, in February 1997.

Since 1990 the conflict between Tuareg rebels and government forces in Mali and Niger, and the attendant issues of refugee movements and border insecurity, have dominated Burkina's relations with these two countries. The influx of refugees from Mali has, in particular, been a cause of concern to both the Burkinabè and Malian authorities and to representatives of the UN High Commissioner for Refugees: at mid-1995 there were reported to be some 50,000 Malian refugees sheltering in Burkina, although the return of peace in Mali was expected to facilitate the repatriation of refugees from Burkina. During 1994 Compaoré hosted negotiations between the Nigerian government and Tuareg leaders.

In December 1988 Compaoré attended the Franco-African summit, held in Morocco (the first occasion on which the country had been represented since 1983); subsequent meetings of this bloc have also been attended. Compaoré's first official visit to France, in June 1993, was widely interpreted as a recognition by the French authorities of his legitimacy following the installation of elected organs of state; he made further visits in April and November 1994 (on the last occasion attending the Franco-African summit meeting in Biarritz). Burkina swiftly forged close relations with Jacques Chirac following his election to the French presidency in May 1995. Compaoré travelled to meet President Chirac in Yamoussoukro, Côte d'Ivoire, in July 1995, and was received by Chirac in Paris in November. He again visited France in June 1996, and the 19th Franco-African summit took place in Ouagadougou in December of that year. Compaoré subsequently participated in a regional mediation effort, conceived at the meeting, to resolve the political crisis in the Central African Republic. The ADP authorized the contribution of a Burkinabè military contingent to the surveillance mission for that country in February 1997.

Diplomatic relations with Israel (severed in 1973) were re-established in October 1993, and, following the restoration of links with Taiwan (also suspended in 1973) in February 1994, the Taiwanese government formally announced a comprehensive programme of assistance. The People's Republic of China terminated relations with Burkina shortly afterwards. Diplomatic relations were established with South Africa in May 1994. Recognition of the 'Sahrawi Arab Democratic Republic', accorded by the Sankara regime in 1984, was withdrawn in June 1996.

Economy

EDITH HODGKINSON

A land-locked country in the savannah lands of the west African Sahel, Burkina Faso has been continually challenged in its efforts to ensure the survival of its agricultural and pastoral economy, and has had only limited prospects for modernization, whether through industrialization or the expansion of the country's external trade. The population (estimated at 10.2m. in mid-1995) is largely rural, depending on traditional farming methods for subsistence and receiving modest earnings from the sale of cash crops, fruit, vegetables, livestock or firewood. The climate is arid, and the rivers mostly seasonal, so supplies of water can run low during the long dry period, and the economy is very vulnerable to weather conditions.

Burkina is also highly dependent on the maintenance of good economic and political relations with its six neighbours. Large numbers of Burkinabè work in Côte d'Ivoire, some seasonally and some permanently. There is also seasonal migration to Ghana. In all, an estimated 2m. Burkinabè work abroad. This migration of workers reinforces Burkina's commercial contacts with its southern neighbours, where many consumer goods are purchased for resale in Burkina, and these links form a possible basis for more substantial intra-regional trade and integration in the future. Workers' remittances also contribute substantially to the national balance of payments, helping to offset the country's chronic trade deficit.

Manufacturing activity is restricted to small units, established principally in Bobo-Dioulasso and, to a lesser extent, in the capital, Ouagadougou. It takes the form of import substitution and the processing of local products (cotton, leather and sugar), and, apart from cotton ginning, the manufacturing sector makes little contribution to exports. Small-scale artisanal production serves regional and tourist markets, with the active informal sector representing an important source of jobs and income. Burkina's mineral resources are only just beginning to be exploited on a significant basis, and there is considerable optimism regarding the country's deposits of gold (which has been mined in small quantities for centuries), zinc and manganese.

The economy's dependence on agriculture—and hence the weather—and on workers' remittances means that its performance can fluctuate widely from year to year. Overall, however, growth in gross domestic product (GDP) has only just kept pace with the increase in population, averaging 2.6% per year in 1986–90 and 2.9% in 1991–96. None the less, the rate has been strengthening since 1995, with GDP growth officially estimated at 5.7% in 1996 and forecast at just less than 6% for 1997. This improvement can be attributed to the structural adjustment programme initiated in 1991, and to the enhancement of export earnings generated by the 50% devaluation of the CFA franc in January 1994. The devaluation has reinforced Burkina's trading relations with its immediate neighbours, as traders and industrialists have sought the cheapest sources of supply.

Reversing the nationalization policy pursued by the Sankara regime (1983–87), a major aspect of structural adjustment is a divestment programme designed to enhance the role of the private sector. Although the programme has attracted some interest from both domestic and foreign private investors, the domestic private sector is itself limited in size and influence—having had little opportunity to develop in a previously state-controlled environment—while foreign investors have in general been reluctant to locate in African members of the franc zone, especially prior to the currency devaluation. Burkina's best prospects for modernization and economic growth would appear to lie in the development of the mining sector, small-scale, resource-based manufacturing, increased exports of horticultural products to Europe and in a modest expansion of the tourism industry.

AGRICULTURE

Agriculture and livestock—which accounted for some 33% of Burkina's GDP and employed about 90% of the total labour force in 1995—is largely at subsistence level. In those years when conditions are favourable, the country rebuilds its food stocks to last through periods of unfavourable climatic conditions, when severe shortages have been experienced. In 1994/95 (a good year) production of millet and sorghum was put at 2,064,000 metric tons, while that of maize was 350,000 tons and rice 61,000 tons. However, poor levels of rainfall in the second half of 1995 resulted in a shortfall in cereals supply of 69,000 tons in 1995/96 (from total output of some 2.31m. tons). An improvement was registered in the overall cereals harvest in 1996/97, to 2.48m. tons, largely as a consequence of increased output of rice. While this represents a theoretical return to surplus of about 69,400 tons, transport and storage inadequacies mean that some areas will still have suffered a deficit.

The country's cash crops were formerly the surplus of subsistence cultivation, mainly shea-nuts (karité nuts), marketed production of which was 70,100 tons in 1994/95, and sesame seeds (10,600 tons). In recent years, however, there has been considerable government investment in cotton, groundnuts, sugar, cashew nuts and market gardening, with financial aid from, among others, the European Development Fund. The most important cash crop (and principal source of export earnings—an estimated 42% of the total in 1995, according to IMF calculations) is cotton, output of which more than doubled in the decade to 1985. After a low point of 145,898 tons in 1988/89, production of cottonseed recovered to 189,543 tons in 1990/91, but declined to only about 117,000 tons in 1993/94. Increased prices paid to producers following the currency devaluation, in conjunction with a more favourable international market, led to an improvement in 1995/96, to 151,000 tons. A major investment programme for the cotton sector, announced in 1996, aims to increase output by the state-owned processing and marketing company, Société burkinabè des fibres textiles (SOFITEX), to more than 300,000 tons by 1999/2000. Through investment of some 25,200m. francs CFA, SOFITEX facilities are to be updated, the area under cultivation is to be expanded by about one-half, and average yields are to be raised. This programme, together with good rains, allowed an even more marked rise in production, to 206,000 tons (well above the official forecast), in 1996/97.

As many farmers switched production to cotton, output of (less profitable) groundnuts declined. However, there has been a good recovery in the present decade: marketed production increased from an average of 132,000 tons per year in 1989/90–1990/91 to almost 200,000 tons in 1993/94. Output of sugar, which began in 1974/75, has recently amounted to 30,000–40,000 tons (refined) annually.

The livestock sector (including livestock and livestock products, hides and skins) accounts for about one-tenth of the country's export earnings—and significantly more if unrecorded shipments are taken into account. Stock-rearing is practised by the semi-nomadic Fulani in the thinly-populated area of the north and east, although a large-scale programme is redeveloping livestock production in the west of the country. A west African regional development project, supported by the FAO, for those areas affected by trypanosomiasis (usually sleeping-sickness), includes Burkina Faso. In 1995 there were an estimated 4.35m. cattle, 5.8m. sheep and 7.24m. goats. Livestock exports were boosted during 1994 by the currency devaluation: numbers exported increased from 152,000 in 1993 to 321,000 in 1994, with Côte d'Ivoire constituting the principal market. The small fish catch (some 7,000–8,000 tons per year) is consumed locally. Timber production is insignificant, despite the large area under forest (almost one-quarter of the total); however, foreign agencies are now funding timber development projects in the Kompienga and Bagre dam regions.

MINING AND POWER

A priority of the Compaoré administration is the exploitation of Burkina's mineral resources, which include gold, manganese, zinc and silver. Industrial gold-mining output, mainly at Poura in western-central Burkina, reached a peak of 3,572 kg in 1990, but declined steadily thereafter, owing to production difficulties at Poura, to 1,275 kg in 1994. To bring in new capital to enhance production at this mine, and as part of the wider programme to attract foreign investment in mining, the government has sold part of its stake in the company involved in its development, the Société de recherches et d'exploitations minières du Burkina (SOREMIB), in order to attract new capital to the mine, which had production of 3,461 kg in 1990, before it switched production from open-pit to underground operations. In 1995 International Gold Resources of Canada reached agreement to acquire a majority interest in the operation. The liberalization of the mining code and the boost of currency devaluation have combined to attract other mining companies, from Australia and South Africa, including BHP and Randgold Resources. Investment in Burkina's mining sector by foreign companies amounted to 20,000m. francs CFA by November 1996, mainly in gold, and 153 prospecting licences had been taken up by that date. Significant quantities of gold are also produced on an artisanal basis (an estimated average of 1.6 tons per year in 1989–92), with much escaping documentation and smuggled out of the country. However, after reforms to the Comptoir burkinabè des métaux précieux—the state authority responsible for the purchase of all gold production—and a 60% increase in the price paid to informal-sector gold producers, a greater share of output is now going through official channels.

Trial exploitation of manganese deposits at Tambao, in the north-east, was begun by Interstar of Canada during 1993. The deposits are estimated at almost 18m. tons of ore, containing 51% manganese, and the aim is to produce 30,000–80,000 tons per year in the initial phase of development. Production was forecast at 35,000 tons in 1995. However, the project is hampered by the lack of a rail connection to the port of Abidjan, in Côte d'Ivoire. The government's railway extension project has been completed between Ouagadougou and Kaya, but this is more than 200 km short of the mining area, a distance which in the first phase will be served by road transport.

The potential for zinc mining operations at Perkoa (in central Burkina), which would be well served by the existing railway through Koudougou, has been under investigation by Boliden International of Sweden since 1990. Proven reserves are 5.6m. tons, and total deposits may be as high as 17.4m. tons. However, transport difficulties and low world prices prompted Boliden to abandon the project, and a new deal to develop the Perkoa deposit was agreed with Gencor, of South Africa, in March 1997. Burkina's other mineral prospects include titanium, vanadium, nickel, bauxite, lead and phosphates, although none of these is considered to be commercially viable at present. A more immediate development prospect is for the quarrying of limestone deposits at Tin Hrassan, near Tambao, which can be developed for cement production. Exploration for petroleum and diamonds is also envisaged.

A considerable expansion of electricity generation has been in progress, and output reached 216m. kWh in 1995. The bulk of output (143m. kWh) is thermal, with the remainder provided by two hydroelectric stations, on the Kompienga and Bagre rivers, with a combined capacity of 31 MW. A 60-MW scheme is planned at Noumbiel, on the Mouhoun (formerly Black Volta) river, at a cost of some US $300m. (Under normal circumstances, however, none of these hydroelectric installations is likely to operate at full capacity, because of the low level of rainfall.) There are plans for electricity interconnection with Côte d'Ivoire and Ghana; France and the European Investment Bank (EIB) are to finance the cost (21,100m. francs CFA) of the latter scheme.

MANUFACTURING

Manufacturing activity is still rudimentary but has been expanding, and its share of GDP increased from 8% in 1960 to 15%–20% in the mid-1990s. Growth has been modest because of the small size of the domestic market, the lack of indigenous raw materials, and shortages of finance and management skills. Moreover, while investment is no longer deterred by political uncertainty, depressed local demand following the devaluation of the CFA franc precluded significant recovery in the manufacturing sector. Production takes the form of agricultural processing and the substitution of consumer goods imports. The first industrial plant of any significance was the textile plant at Koudougou, which entered production in 1970. Cotton-ginning capacity was increased in 1989 with the expansion of the SOFITEX complex in Bobo-Dioulasso; further expansion is planned (see above).

During the period of political revolution under Sankara, the Société des brasseries du Burkina Faso (BRAKINA) brewery operation was one of the few major industries to retain a substantial private holding. Under the 1986–90 development plan a total of 35 new industrial enterprises was envisaged, but the state was unable to raise the finance required for the wide range of activities identified. Only a few of the projects were completed, including a tomato-concentrate plant, a cottonseed oil and shea-butter plant, and companies involved in the manufacture of medical solutions and animal feeds. Other projects outside the scope of the development plan were pursued, but by 1990 the manufacturing sector was suffering from several general difficulties, including competition from imported (often smuggled) products from neighbouring countries. Industries that have hitherto remained viable include the Société industrielle du Faso (SIFA), which produces motor cycles and bicycles (important methods of transport in this predominantly rural country). Part of the state's holding in SIFA (47.5% since 1985) was sold to private Burkinabè interests in 1993, in accordance with the government's programme to reduce its equity stake in individual concerns to a maximum 25%. Under the first phase of the privatization programme (1994–96) 22 parastatals were identified for sale, and all but three were subsequently disposed of. Legislation was adopted in mid-1994 authorizing the privatization of a further 19 organizations, among them the Caisse de stabilisation des prix des produits agricoles du Burkina (CSPPAB), the Société Sucrière de la Comoé (SOSUCO) and the Société Faso-Fani textiles concern. Only slow progress has been made on these sales, with valuations still being carried out in mid-1997.

TRANSPORT INFRASTRUCTURE

An important transport artery is the railway line from the border with Côte d'Ivoire through Bobo-Dioulasso, Koudougou and Ouagadougou to Kaya. However, the track, vehicles and services have been in need of maintenance and further investment. The extension of the main line to Tambao is dependent upon the provision of external financing (see above). Following the withdrawal, in 1987, of Côte d'Ivoire from the joint rail partnership, Burkina and Côte d'Ivoire established separate rail companies, and in 1993 issued a joint tender for the transfer to private ownership of services on the line. SITARAIL, a consortium of French, Belgian, Ivorian and Burkinabè interests, assumed management of operations in 1995. Financing for the attendant investment programme was provided by the International Development Association, the Caisse française de développement, the EIB, the West African Development Bank and the Belgian government. In 1995 there were 12,506 km of classified roads, of which 5,610 km were main roads. Funding is being sought for the upgrading of the road between Bobo-Dioulasso and the Malian border, which will complete the Burkinabè section of the Trans-Sahelian highway linking Dakar (Senegal) and N'Djamena (Chad). The runways of the country's two international airports (at Ouagadougou and Bobo-Dioulasso) were extended during the 1980s to accommodate large cargo aircraft; infrastructure at Ouagadougou airport is to be updated, with financial assistance from France. In 1991 almost 194,000 passengers and 8,000 tons of freight passed through Ouagadougou airport.

FINANCE

Since the early 1970s, when expenditure was held down and small budget surpluses were achieved, there has been a history of fiscal deficit. Expenditure on development, which reached a peak of 7,800m. francs CFA (one-sixth of total budget expenditure) in 1981, was reduced in subsequent years, in order to restrict the rise in budget spending. There was, however, a noticeable change in direction in 1985, with spending forecast to rise by one-fifth, as development expenditure more than doubled, reflecting work on the Kompienga and Bagre dams and on the Tambao rail link. The budget deficit was, none the less, almost eliminated, as the Sankara government introduced new taxes. There were further increases in taxation in both 1986 and 1987; however, the budget deficit rose dramatically, reaching the equivalent of about 13% of GDP in 1987, as a result of even higher increases in government current and capital outlays.

The Compaoré government initially relaxed the unpopular austerity measures that had been introduced under Sankara. None the less, the structural adjustment programme for 1991–93, agreed with the World Bank and the IMF in late 1990, again made rigorous control of government finances a priority. The programme included measures to widen the tax base and reform customs duties, while aiming to stabilize expenditure on wages and channel funds into such areas as primary education and health. However, the government was unable to achieve the improvement it sought, owing to the stagnation of the economy in 1992–93 (when GDP rose by only 1.2% overall), with the result that, despite the introduction of value-added tax (VAT) in 1993, the oveall deficit was still some 84,700m. francs CFA in that year, equivalent to 10.4% of GDP.

Reducing the budget deficit remained the aim under the terms of the enhanced structural adjustment facility accorded in 1993 and again in 1996 (1996–98). Some progress has been made, through controls on spending (which fell in both 1995 and 1996) and enhanced revenue from taxation, including higher VAT rates from September 1996. Burkina is unlikely to attain the balanced budget by 1997 that it had promised the Bretton Woods institutions. None the less, at a projected 25,400m. francs CFA for that year, the deficit represents a significantly lower proportion of GDP (in the region of 2%); before grants, the shortfall is likely to be just under 9% of GDP. Neither the Burkinabè government nor its creditors are looking to eliminate the latter deficit, which reflects external grant support for the government's capital spending programme.

FOREIGN TRADE AND PAYMENTS

Burkina suffers a chronic and substantial trade deficit. Its export capacity is highly vulnerable to weather conditions and trends in international prices for cotton, while the import bill reflects a range of factors: the domestic food balance, international prices for petroleum and the level of investment spending, both public and private. Annual fluctuations in the size of the deficit have therefore been substantial. Over time it has tended to rise in nominal terms, registering a peak of US $367m. in 1993 (calculated in balance-of-payments terms, which exclude the cost of transportation—a significant item for this remote, land-locked country). Coverage by export earnings of the import bill has rarely exceeded one-third. The immediate impact of the devaluation of the CFA franc in 1994 was a 43% fall in import spending in US dollar terms (in local currency there was a rise of 12%) and an 18% decline in dollar export receipts (representing a 60% rise in CFA franc values). The trade deficit consequently fell to only $139m. (in payments terms), while import cover improved to an unprecedented 62%. The trade gap widened once more in 1995, as demand for imports revived, although the trade gap remained relatively low, at $181m., and import cover was unchanged.

This still represents a large outflow on the current account, compounded by the substantial debit represented by transport costs. It is in part—and in some years wholly—offset by remittances from emigrants and aid inflows. Workers' remittances raised private transfers to an average of US $97m. (net) per year in 1980–85. These remittances were equivalent to more than two-thirds of export earnings and more than one-half of official aid in that period. Net private transfers totalled $159.6m. in 1986, but declined steadily thereafter, to only $97.5m. in 1989, owing to economic problems in the countries to which Burkinabè workers have traditionally migrated. With some year-on-year fluctuation, they have averaged only just above the 1989 level. Meanwhile, net inflows of official development assistance from OECD and OPEC countries and multilateral institutions averaged $432m. per year in 1990–95, with grants (which appear on the current account of the balance of payments) averaging $333m. The major sources of bilateral aid are generally France, Germany, Italy, Canada and the Netherlands.

Given this significant inflow of concessional funds, Burkina's external debt remained comparatively low—only $511m. at the end of 1985, according to the World Bank—and its debt-servicing burden moderate (equivalent to 9.9% of exports of goods and services in that year). By 1988 total external debt had increased by 65%, to $845m, although the level of debt-servicing declined to 9.3%, owing to the increasing proportion of loans from official sources (governments and multilateral agencies) on concessionary terms. At the end of 1988 almost three-quarters of the country's borrowing was on concessionary terms. However, since Burkina still had difficulties in meeting debt-servicing payments, its bilateral creditors agreed, in 1991 and again in 1993, to rescheduling. Further concessions were made after the devaluation of the CFA franc, which had the effect of doubling the external debt denominated in local currency. The application of so-called Naples terms to $70m. in non-concessional debt (which effectively annul two-thirds of the liability) was agreed in June 1996; in the same month France cancelled 60,300m. francs CFA in concessional debt. The share of bilateral debt has thus fallen, leaving almost 78% of debt owed to multilateral institutions and therefore not open to rescheduling or cancellation. Therefore, while the country's debt ratios are theoretically not excessive—with total debt at the end of 1995, at $1,267m., equivalent to 55% of gross national product and debt-service at 13.2% of the country's foreign earnings—in practice, given the fragility of the economy, Burkina has very limited scope to increase its call on foreign funds other than on extremely concessionary terms. None the less, in recognition of its commitment to structural adjustment and a debt burden classified as 'unsustainable', Burkina is likely to be a beneficiary of a special debt-reduction under the terms of the heavily indebted poor countries (HIPC) initiative, introduced by the World Bank and the IMF in 1997.

Statistical Survey

Source (except where otherwise stated): Institut National de la Statistique et de la Démographie, BP 374, Ouagadougou; tel. 33-55-37.

Area and Population

AREA, POPULATION AND DENSITY

Area (sq km)	274,200*
Population (census results)	
1–7 December 1975	5,638,203
10–20 December 1985	
Males	3,833,237
Females	4,131,468
Total	7,964,705
Population (official estimates at mid-year)	
1993	9,682,000
1994	9,889,000
1995	10,200,000
Density (per sq km) at mid-1995	37.2

* 105,870 sq miles.

POPULATION BY PROVINCE (at 1985 census)

Province	Population	Capital
Bam	162,575	Kongoussi
Bazèga	303,941	Kombissiri
Bougouriba	220,895	Diébougou
Boulougou	402,236	Tenkodogo
Boulkiemdé	365,223	Koudougou
Comoé	249,967	Banfora
Ganzourgou	195,452	Zorgo
Gnagna	229,152	Bogandé
Gourma	294,235	Fada-Ngourma
Houet	581,722	Bobo-Dioulasso
Kadiogo	459,826	Ouagadougou
Kénédougou	139,973	Orodara
Kossi	332,960	Nounga
Kouritenga	198,486	Koupéla
Mouhoun	288,735	Dédougou
Nahouri	105,509	Pô
Namentenga	198,890	Boulsa
Oubritenga	304,265	Ziniaré
Oudalan	106,194	Gorom-Gorom
Passoré	223,830	Yako
Poni	235,480	Gaoua
Sangouié	217,277	Réo
Sanmatenga	367,724	Kaya
Séno	228,875	Dori
Sissili	244,919	Léo
Soum	186,812	Djibo
Sourou	268,108	Tougan
Tapoa	158,859	Diapaga
Yatenga	536,578	Ouahigouya
Zoundwéogo	156,007	Manga
Total	7,964,705	

Sources: UN, *Demographic Yearbook*; Secrétariat du Comité de la Zone Franc *La Zone Franc—Rapport 1994*.

Note: In early 1997 the number of provinces was increased from 30 to 45.

PRINCIPAL TOWNS (population at 1985 census)

Ouagadougou (capital)	441,514	Ouahigouya	38,902
Bobo-Dioulasso	228,668	Banfora	35,319
Koudougou	51,926	Kaya	25,814

1991 (official estimates at mid-year): Ouagadougou 634,479; Bobo-Dioulasso 268,926.

BIRTHS AND DEATHS (UN estimates, annual averages)

	1980–85	1985–90	1990–95
Birth rate (per 1,000)	47.2	47.1	46.8
Death rate (per 1,000)	19.8	18.6	18.2

Expectation of life (UN estimates, years at birth, 1990–95): 47.4 (males 45.8; females 49.0).

Source: UN, *World Population Prospects: The 1994 Revision.*

ECONOMICALLY ACTIVE POPULATION
(sample survey, persons aged 10 years and over, 1991)

	Males	Females	Total
Agriculture, hunting, forestry and fishing	2,162,759	2,131,025	4,293,784
Mining and quarrying	2,286	304	2,590
Manufacturing	26,996	24,698	51,694
Electricity, gas and water	3,038	806	3,844
Construction	10,988	28	11,016
Trade, restaurants and hotels	48,117	72,197	120,314
Transport, storage and communications	14,620	421	15,041
Finance, insurance, real estate and business services	1,650	425	2,075
Community, social and personal services	84,136	27,420	111,556
Activities not adequately defined	8,355	9,105	17,460
Total employed	2,362,945	2,266,429	4,629,374
Unemployed	38,515	11,304	49,819
Total labour force	2,401,460	2,277,733	4,679,193

Source: ILO, *Yearbook of Labour Statistics.*

Mid-1995 (estimates in '000): Agriculture, etc. 5,004; Total 5,414 (Source: FAO, *Production Yearbook).*

Agriculture

PRINCIPAL CROPS ('000 metric tons)

	1993	1994	1995*
Maize	271	350	350
Millet	899	831	831
Sorghum	1,310	1,232	1,232
Rice (paddy)	54	61	61
Sweet potatoes	20*	11	20
Yams	42	38	38
Other roots and tubers	21*	17	17
Vegetables*	254	254	254
Fruit*	73	73	73
Pulses	80	74	62
Groundnuts (in shell)	206	203	203
Cottonseed*	94	94	94
Cotton (lint)	64†	67	67
Sesame seed	8	2	2
Tobacco (leaves)*	1	1	1
Sugar cane*	400	400	400

* FAO estimate(s). † Unofficial figure.

Source: FAO, *Production Yearbook.*

LIVESTOCK ('000 head, year ending September)

	1993	1994	1995*
Cattle	4,178	4,261	4,350
Sheep	5,520	5,686	5,800
Goats	7,060	7,242†	7,242
Pigs	540	551	560
Horses	23	23†	23
Asses	436*	445†	455
Camels*	12*	12†	12

Poultry (million): 18 in 1992; 18 in 1993; 19† in 1994; 19* in 1995.

* FAO estimate(s). † Unofficial figure.

Source: FAO, *Production Yearbook.*

LIVESTOCK PRODUCTS (FAO estimates, '000 metric tons)

	1993	1994	1995
Beef and veal	40	40	40
Mutton and lamb	11	11	11
Goat meat	19	19	19
Pig meat	6	6	6
Poultry meat	20	20	20
Cows' milk	121	121	121
Goats' milk	21	21	21
Butter	0.9	0.9	0.9
Hen eggs	16.5	16.5	16.5
Cattle hides	6.5	6.5	6.5
Sheepskins	2.8	2.8	2.8
Goatskins	5.0	5.0	5.0

Source: FAO, *Production Yearbook.*

Forestry

ROUNDWOOD REMOVALS
(FAO estimates, '000 cubic metres, excluding bark)

	1992	1993	1994
Sawlogs, veneer logs and logs for sleepers*	1	1	1
Other industrial wood	417	428	440
Fuel wood	8,823	9,075	9,330
Total	9,241	9,504	9,771

* Estimated to be unchanged since 1985.

Source: FAO, *Yearbook of Forest Products.*

Fishing

('000 metric tons, live weight)

	1992	1993	1994
Total catch	7.5	7.0	8.0

Source: FAO, *Yearbook of Fishery Statistics.*

Mining

(mineral content of ore, metric tons)

	1994	1995	1996
Gold	3.0	2.7	2.5

Source: Gold Fields Mineral Services Ltd, *Gold 1997.*

Industry

SELECTED PRODUCTS

	1993	1994	1995
Edible oils (metric tons)	8,906	6,412	4,286
Shea (karité) butter (metric tons)	1,758	574	296
Flour (metric tons)	27,555	26,235	31,046
Pasta (metric tons)	1,175	633	788
Sugar (metric tons)	34,955	54,824	47,107
Beer ('000 hl)	334	287	172
Soft drinks ('000 hl)	106	86	115
Cigarettes (million packets)	47	44	47
Printed fabric ('000 sq metres)	4,618	5,957	5,297
Soap (metric tons)	14,056	6,526	5,787
Matches (cartons)	14,587	n.a.	n.a.
Bicycles (units)	24,464	18,321	11,150
Mopeds (units)	12,857	5,423	8,673
Tyres ('000)	294	23	1,738
Inner tubes ('000)	1,924	165	2,660
Electric energy ('000 kWh)	215,517	216,006	n.a.

Source: IMF, *Burkina Faso—Statistical Tables* (March 1997).

Finance

CURRENCY AND EXCHANGE RATES

Monetary Units

100 centimes = 1 franc de la Communauté financière africaine (CFA).

French Franc, Sterling and Dollar Equivalents (31 March 1997)

1 French franc = 100 francs CFA;
£1 sterling = 924.20 francs CFA;
US $1 = 562.85 francs CFA;
1,000 francs CFA = £1.082 = $1.777

Average Exchange Rate (francs CFA per US $)

1994 555.20
1995 499.15
1996 511.55

Note: An exchange rate of 1 French franc = 50 francs CFA, established in 1948, remained in force until January 1994, when the CFA franc was devalued by 50%, with the exchange rate adjusted to 1 French franc = 100 francs CFA.

BUDGET ('000 million francs CFA)

Revenue	1993	1994	1995
Current revenue	99.4	113.3	138.5
Tax revenue	72.6	104.0	127.8
Income and profits	18.9	21.2	29.7
Domestic goods and services	14.8	19.4	23.3
International trade	36.4	61.2	71.9
Other tax revenue	2.5	2.1	2.9
Other current revenue	26.8	9.4	10.7
Capital revenue	0.6	—	—
Total	100.0	113.3	138.5

Expenditure and net lending	1993	1994	1995
Domestic expenditure and net lending	124.6	137.2	140.6
Wages and salaries	52.2	58.2	61.6
Goods and services	19.3	26.6	24.8
Interest payments	12.4	15.0	16.4
Current transfers	34.3	31.2	29.1
Other current expenditure	—	—	9.7
Budgetary contribution to investment	8.8	9.2	11.6
Net lending*	−2.5	−3.0	−3.0
Foreign-financed government investment	54.6	62.5	97.5
On-lending	0.9	—	—
Restructuring operations	2.2	27.3	7.6
Total	182.4	227.0	245.8

*Including proceeds from privatization, which are excluded from revenue and are treated as a deduction from expenditure.

Source: IMF, *Burkina Faso—Statistical Tables* (March 1997).

INTERNATIONAL RESERVES (US $ million at 31 December)

	1994	1995	1996
Gold*	4.1	4.3	4.2
IMF special drawing rights	8.1	8.2	2.6
Reserve position in IMF	10.5	10.7	10.4
Foreign exchange	218.6	328.4	305.8
Total	241.3	351.7	322.9

* Valued at market-related prices.

Source: IMF, *International Financial Statistics*.

MONEY SUPPLY ('000 million francs CFA at 31 December)

	1993	1994	1995
Currency outside banks	78.48	94.90	123.49
Demand deposits at deposit money banks*	42.00	69.84	81.54
Checking deposits at post office	1.61	2.37	2.68
Total money (incl. others)	122.61	170.32	213.70

* Excluding the deposits of public establishments of an administrative or social nature.

Source: IMF, *International Financial Statistics*.

COST OF LIVING (Consumer Price Index for African households in Ouagadougou; base: 1990 = 100)

	1993	1994	1995
Food	95.6	112.6	125.9
All items	101.1	126.0	135.9

Source: ILO, *Yearbook of Labour Statistics*.

NATIONAL ACCOUNTS

(estimates, '000 million francs CFA at current prices)

Expenditure on the Gross Domestic Product

	1993	1994	1995
Government final consumption expenditure	121.0	160.2	165.1
Private final consumption expenditure	635.2	806.0	916.4
Increase in stocks	8.4	−18.3	−20.6
Gross fixed capital formation	149.0	216.5	279.1
Total domestic expenditure	913.7	1,164.5	1,340.0
Exports of goods and services	92.2	135.6	155.6
Less Imports of goods and services	209.8	270.7	332.6
GDP in purchasers' values	796.1	1,029.4	1,163.0
GDP at constant 1985 prices	814.7	824.5	856.4

Gross Domestic Product by Economic Activity

	1993	1994	1995
Agriculture, livestock, forestry and fishing	270.2	335.0	367.1
Mining and manufacturing	120.2	198.3	232.3
Electricity, gas and water	7.4	9.0	10.6
Construction and public works	42.4	55.7	62.4
Trade	102.8	122.7	140.4
Transport	33.5	39.0	44.7
Non-marketable services	93.1	102.7	112.1
Other services	102.6	119.0	136.1
Sub-total	774.0*	981.5	1,105.8
Import taxes and duties	32.9	58.7	68.0
Less Imputed bank service charge	−10.8	−10.8	−10.8
GDP in purchasers' values	796.1	1,029.4	1,163.0

* Including adjustment.

Source: IMF, *Burkina Faso—Statistical Tables* (March 1997).

BALANCE OF PAYMENTS (US $ million)

	1992	1993	1994
Exports of goods f.o.b.	237.2	226.1	215.6
Imports of goods f.o.b.	–458.9	–469.1	–344.3
Trade balance	–221.7	–243.0	–128.7
Exports of services	64.5	64.6	56.3
Imports of services	–207.7	–209.0	–138.3
Balance on goods and services	–364.9	–387.4	–210.7
Other income received	21.7	21.5	8.7
Other income paid	–19.1	–28.6	–38.1
Balance on goods, services and income	–362.3	–394.5	–240.1
Current transfers received	419.2	389.6	308.0
Current transfers paid	–79.9	–66.3	–53.0
Current balance	–23.0	–71.1	14.9
Investment assets	–45.2	24.2	–139.2
Investment liabilities	79.9	44.9	125.3
Net errors and omissions	8.3	4.6	–8.3
Overall balance	20.0	2.5	–7.3

Source: IMF, *International Financial Statistics.*

External Trade

Source: Banque centrale des états de l'Afrique de l'ouest.

PRINCIPAL COMMODITIES (million francs CFA)

Imports c.i.f.	1989	1990	1991
Food products	29,222	26,522	29,186
Food products of animal origin	4,810	5,928	6,218
Dairy products	3,326	4,743	5,155
Food products of plant origin	20,402	15,534	18,730
Cereals	15,413	9,375	10,832
Processed foodstuffs	4,010	5,060	4,238
Beverages and tobacco	2,775	2,911	3,251
Refined petroleum products	10,801	16,344	17,383
Other raw materials (inedible)	2,744	3,104	2,841
Oils and fats	1,253	2,115	3,199
Machinery and transport equipment	32,178	35,166	31,321
Non-electrical machinery	13,569	13,220	12,506
Electrical machinery	6,653	9,017	7,972
Road transport equipment	11,549	12,554	10,799
Other industrial products	46,379	59,671	63,073
Chemical products	15,252	20,912	27,779
Miscellaneous manufactured articles	31,127	38,759	35,294
Hydraulic cement	5,877	7,461	6,560
Total (incl. others)	125,352	145,833	150,255

Exports f.o.b.	1989	1990	1991
Food products	3,072	3,766	3,826
Food products of animal origin	1,681	2,738	2,993
Cattle, beef and veal	1,142	1,938	2,147
Food products of plant origin	812	855	667
Vegetables	519	654	519
Other raw materials (inedible)	17,727	27,437	20,792
Shea-nuts (karité nuts)	111	630	158
Hides and skins	2,809	3,071	1,449
Cotton (ginned)	14,356	23,415	18,754
Machinery and transport equipment	1,048	325	286
Other industrial products	8,301	9,586	4,487
Miscellaneous manufactured articles	8,236	9,539	4,455
Unworked gold	6,893	8,104	2,452
Total (incl. others)	30,269	41,282	29,892

PRINCIPAL TRADING PARTNERS (million francs CFA)

Imports	1989	1990	1991
Belgium-Luxembourg	1,969	2,728	3,305
Cameroon	416	1,392	931
Canada	968	1,975	1,405
Denmark	747	1,449	1,236
China, People's Repub.	1,482	1,320	2,298
Côte d'Ivoire	18,209	23,971	29,130
France	36,145	40,099	36,644
Germany, Fed. Repub.	5,933	6,949	6,020
Italy	5,312	5,057	3,970
Japan	5,931	6,181	6,334
Netherlands	4,314	4,949	4,100
Nigeria	1,839	3,252	4,157
Senegal	1,445	3,172	2,444
Spain	2,273	1,729	1,987
Taiwan	1,414	1,575	3,823
Thailand	11,595	2,561	3,455
Togo	3,611	4,816	3,943
United Kingdom	2,929	2,652	2,584
USA	5,649	9,198	7,395
Total (incl. others)	125,352	145,833	150,255

Exports	1989	1990	1991
Belgium-Luxembourg	1,555	623	115
China, People's Repub.	342	3,218	808
Côte d'Ivoire	3,797	4,676	3,351
Denmark	351	246	150
France	8,848	9,535	4,107
Germany, Fed. Repub.	671	19	173
Italy	1,783	3,136	3,007
Japan	483	542	551
Mali	235	232	366
Nigeria	5	391	425
Portugal	836	1,624	2,793
Spain	986	1,008	455
Switzerland	161	4,392	6,067
Taiwan	5,112	3,113	1,845
Thailand	—	1,891	2,495
Togo	1,846	1,283	853
Tunisia	87	1,986	—
United Kingdom	375	935	104
Total (incl. others)	30,269	41,282	29,892

Transport

RAILWAYS (traffic)

	1991	1992	1993
Passenger-km (million)	340	360	403
Freight ton-km (million)	177	184	180

Source: UN Economic Commission for Africa, *African Statistical Yearbook.*

ROAD TRAFFIC (motor vehicles in use)

	1993	1994	1995
Passenger cars	29,855	32,224	35,460
Buses and coaches	1,760	1,939	2,237
Lorries and vans	13,945	14,439	14,985
Road tractors	1,977	2,087	2,251
Motor cycles and mopeds	93,150	97,900	100,591

Source: IRF, *World Road Statistics.*

CIVIL AVIATION (traffic on scheduled services)*

	1992	1993	1994
Kilometres flown (million)	3	3	3
Passengers carried ('000)	127	128	130
Passenger-km (million)	233	239	247
Total ton-km (million)	37	37	37

* Including an apportionment of the traffic of Air Afrique.

Source: UN, *Statistical Yearbook.*

Tourism

	1991	1992	1993
Tourist arrivals	110,327	128,107	154,937
Tourist receipts (million francs CFA)	6,208	8,650	8,895

Source: Direction de l'Administration Touristique et Hôtelière, Ouagadougou.

Communications Media

	1992	1993	1994
Radio receivers ('000 in use)	255	265	280
Television receivers ('000 in use)	50	54	55
Telephones ('000 main lines in use)	20	22	26
Daily newspapers			
Number	1	n.a.	1
Average circulation ('000 copies)	3	n.a.	3

Non-daily newspapers (1990): 10; average circulation 14,000 copies.

Book production (1985): 9 titles.

Sources: UNESCO, *Statistical Yearbook*; UN, *Statistical Yearbook.*

Education

(1993/94, unless otherwise indicated)

	Institu-tions	Teachers	Students		
			Males	Females	Total
Pre-primary*	95	259†	3,744	3,911	7,655
Primary	2,971	10,300	366,226	233,806	600,032
Secondary					
General	n.a.	3,346	76,482	39,551	116,033
Vocational	n.a.	639	4,473	4,335	8,808
Teacher training‡	n.a.	n.a.	220	130	350
Tertiary	n.a.	571	6,684	2,131	8,815

* 1989/90 figures.

† State education only.

‡ 1992/93 estimates.

Source: UNESCO, *Statistical Yearbook.*

Directory

The Constitution

The present Constitution was approved in a national referendum on 2 June 1991, and was formally adopted on 11 June. The following are its main provisions:

The Constitution of the 'revolutionary, democratic, unitary and secular' Fourth Republic of Burkina Faso guarantees the collective and individual political and social rights of Burkinabè citizens, and delineates the powers of the executive, legislature and judiciary.

Executive power is vested in the President, who is Head of State, and in the Government, which is appointed by the President upon the recommendation of the Prime Minister. The President is elected, by universal suffrage, for a seven-year term; as amended in January 1997, there are no restrictions on the renewal of the presidential mandate.

Legislative power is exercised by the multi-party Assemblée des députés populaires (ADP). Delegates to the ADP are elected, by universal suffrage, for a five-year term. An increase in the number of deputies, from 107 to 111, was provided for by constitutional amendment in January 1997. The President is empowered to appoint a Prime Minister; however, the ADP has the right to veto any such appointment. Provision is also made for the creation of a second, consultative chamber: the Chambre des représentants is to comprise 120 members, nominated for a three-year term of office.

Both the Government and the ADP may initiate legislation.

The judiciary is independent. Judges are to be accountable to a Higher Council, under the chairmanship of the Head of State.

The Constitution denies legitimacy to any regime that might take power as the result of a *coup d'état.*

The Government

HEAD OF STATE

President: BLAISE COMPAORÉ (assumed power as Chairman of the Front populaire 15 October 1987; elected President 1 December 1991).

COUNCIL OF MINISTERS

(August 1997)

President: BLAISE COMPAORÉ.

Prime Minister and Minister of the Economy and Finance: KADRÉ DÉSIRÉ OUÉDRAOGO.

Minister of State, with responsibility for the Environment and Water Resources: SALIF DIALLO.

Minister of State at the Presidency of the Republic: ARSÈNE BOGESSAN YÈ.

Minister of the Economy and Finance, Spokesperson for the Government: TERTIUS ZONGO.

Minister of External Relations: ABLASSE OUÉDRAOGO.

Minister of Defence: ALBERT D. MILOGO.

Minister of Justice and Keeper of the Seals: YARGA LARBA.

Minister of Territorial Administration and Security: YERO BOLI.

Minister of Trade, Industry and Crafts: IDRISSA ZAMPALIGRÉ KAFANDO.

Minister of Energy and Mines: ELIE OUÉDRAOGO.

Minister of Secondary and Higher Education and Scientific Research: CHRISTOPHE DABIRÉ.

Minister of Primary Education and Mass Literacy: SEYDOU BAWORO SANOU.

Minister of Public Works, Housing and Town Planning: JOSEPH KABORÉ.

Minister of the Civil Service and Administrative Modernization: JULIETTE BONKOUNGOU.

Minister of Employment, Labour and Social Security: ELIE SARE.

Minister of Agriculture: MICHEL KOUTABA.

Minister of Regional Integration: VIVIANE YOLANDE COMPAORÉ.

Minister with responsibility for Relations with Parliament: CYRIL GOUNGOUNGA.

Minister of Communications and Culture: MAHAMADOU OUÉDRAOGO.
Minister of Health: LUDOVIC ALAN TOU.
Minister of Youth and Sports: JOSEPH ANDRÉ TIENDRÉBÉOGO.
Minister of Transport and Tourism: BEDOUMA ALAIN YODA.
Minister of Social Welfare and the Family: BANA OUANDAOGO.
Minister of Animal Resources: ALASSANE SERE.
Minister of Women's Promotion: ALICE TIENDRÉBÉOGO.

There are, in addition, ministers-delegate responsible for the Budget, Finance, Water Resources, Housing and Town Planning and Employment Promotion.

MINISTRIES

Office of the President: Ouagadougou.

Office of the Prime Minister: Ouagadougou.

Ministry of Agriculture and Animal Resources: BP 7005, Ouagadougou.

Ministry of the Civil Service and Administrative Modernization: Ouagadougou.

Ministry of Communications and Culture: 01 BP 2507, Ouagadougou 01; tel. 30-70-52; telex 5237; fax 30-70-56.

Ministry of Defence: BP 496, Ouagadougou; telex 5297.

Ministry of the Economy and Finance: 01 BP 6444, Ouagadougou 01; tel. 30-67-21; fax 31-23-04.

Ministry of Employment, Labour and Social Security: BP 7006, Ouagadougou.

Ministry of Energy and Mines: Ouagadougou.

Ministry of the Environment and Water Resources: BP 7044, Ouagadougou; tel. 33-41-65; telex 5555.

Ministry of External Relations: BP 7038, Ouagadougou; telex 5222.

Ministry of Health: Ouagadougou; tel. 33-28-68; telex 5555.

Ministry of Justice: BP 526, Ouagadougou.

Ministry of Primary Education and Mass Literacy: 01 BP 1179, Ouagadougou 01; tel. 30-12-94.

Ministry of Public Works, Housing and Town Planning: Ouagadougou; tel. 31-53-84; fax 31-53-83.

Ministry of Regional Integration: Ouagadougou.

Ministry of Secondary and Higher Education and Scientific Research: 03 BP 7130, Ouagadougou 03; tel. 31-29-11; telex 5555; fax 31-41-41.

Ministry of Social Welfare and the Family: c/o World Bank Resident Mission, BP 622, Ouagadougou; tel. 30-62-37; telex 5265; fax 30-86-49.

Ministry of Territorial Administration and Security: BP 7034, Ouagadougou.

Ministry of Trade, Industry and Crafts: BP 365, Ouagadougou.

Ministry of Transport and Tourism: BP 177, Ouagadougou.

Ministry of Women's Promotion: Ouagadougou.

Ministry of Youth and Sports: BP 7035, Ouagadougou.

Legislature

ASSEMBLÉE DES DÉPUTÉS POPULAIRES

President: MAURICE MÉLÉGUÉ TRAORÉ.

General Election, 11 May 1997

Party	Seats
Congrés pour la démocratie et le progrès	97
Parti pour la démocratie et le progrès	6
Alliance pour la démocratie et la fédération	2
Rassemblement démocratique africain	2
Total	107*

* Results of voting in four constituencies were cancelled by the Supreme Court. All four seats were won by the CDP at a further round of voting on 18 June.

CHAMBRE DES REPRÉSENTANTS

The 1991 Constitution provides for the establishment of a second chamber, with advisory functions, whose 120 members are to be nominated for a three-year term.

Advisory Council

Conseil Economique et Social: 01 BP 6162, Ouagadougou 01; tel. 32-40-90; fax 31-06-54; f. 1985 as Conseil Révolutionnaire Economique et Social, present name adopted in 1992; 90 mems; Pres. ZÉPHIRIN DIABRÉ.

Political Organizations

The 1997 legislative elections were contested by 13 of the country's 46 registered political organizations. The following parties secured parliamentary representation:

Alliance pour la démocratie et la fédération (ADF): 01 BP 2061 Ouagadougou 01; tel. 31-15-15; f. 1990; mem. of presidential 'group'; Leader HERMAN YAMÉOGO.

Congrès pour la démocratie et le progrès (CDP): f. 1996, by merger of more than 10 parties, to succeed the Organisation pour la démocratie populaire/Mouvement du travail as the prin. political org. supporting Pres. Compaoré; social-democratic; Pres. Dr ARSÈNE BOGNESSAN YÉ; First Vice-Pres. ROCH MARC CHRISTIAN KABORÉ.

Parti pour la démocratie et le progrès (PDP): f. 1993, expanded in 1996 to include three other parties; Pres. JOSEPH KI-ZERBO.

Rassemblement démocratique africain (RDA): pre-independence party; Leader GÉRARD KANGO OUÉDRAOGO.

Diplomatic Representation

EMBASSIES IN BURKINA FASO

Algeria: BP 3893, Ouagadougou; telex 5359.

China (Taiwan): 01 BP 5563, Ouagadougou 01; tel. 31-61-95.

Cuba: BP 3422, Ouagadougou; telex 5360; Ambassador: REME REMIGIO RUIZ.

Denmark: rue Agostino Neto, 01 BP 1760, Ouagadougou 01; tel. 31-31-92; telex 5230; fax 31-31-89; Chargé d'affaires: HANS HENRIK LILJEBORG.

Egypt: Ouagadougou; telex 5289; Ambassador: Dr MOHAMAD ALEY EL-KORDY.

France: 902 ave de l'Indépendance, 01 BP 504, Ouagadougou 01; tel. 30-67-70; telex 5211; Ambassador: FRANÇOIS COUSIN.

Germany: 01 BP 600, Ouagadougou 01; tel. 30-67-31; telex 5217; fax 31-39-91; Ambassador: DORETTA LOSCHELDER.

Ghana: 01 BP 212, Ouagadougou 01; tel. 30-76-35; Ambassador: (vacant).

Libya: BP 1601, Ouagadougou; telex 5311; Secretary of People's Bureau: (vacant).

Netherlands: 415 ave du Dr KWAMÉ N'KRUMAH, 01 BP 1302, Ouagadougou 01; tel. 30-61-34; telex 5303; fax 30-76-95; Ambassador: BEATRIX E. A. AMBAGS.

Nigeria: BP 132, Ouagadougou; tel. 33-42-41; telex 5236; Chargé d'affaires a.i.: A. K. ALLI ASSAYOUTI.

USA: 01 BP 35, Ouagadougou 01; tel. 30-67-23; telex 5290; fax 31-23-68; Ambassador: SHARON P. WILKINSON.

Judicial System

The Constitution of 2 June 1991 provides for the independence of the judiciary. Judges are to be accountable to a Higher Council, under the chairmanship of the President of the Republic.

Religion

More than 50% of the population follow animist beliefs.

ISLAM

At 31 December 1986 there were an estimated 2,514,261 Muslims in Burkina Faso.

CHRISTIANITY

The Roman Catholic Church

Burkina comprises one archdiocese and eight dioceses. At 31 December 1995 there were an estimated 1,053,000 adherents.

Bishops' Conference: Conférence des Evêques de Burkina Faso et du Niger, BP 1195, Ouagadougou; tel. 30-60-26; f. 1966, legally recognized 1978; Pres. Rt Rev. JEAN-NAPTISTE SOMÉ, Bishop of Diébougou.

Archbishop of Ouagadougou: Most Rev. JEAN-MARIE UNTAANI COMPAORÉ, 01 BP 1472, Ouagadougou 01; tel. 30-67-04; fax 30-72-75.

Protestant Churches

At 31 December 1986 there were an estimated 106,467 adherents.

The Press

Direction de la presse écrite: Ouagadougou; govt body responsible for press direction.

DAILIES

Le Journal du Soir: Ouagadougou; Dir ISSA TAPSOBA.

Observateur Paalga (New Observer): 01 BP 584, Ouagadougou 01; tel. 33-27-05; fax 31-45-79; f. 1974; Dir EDOUARD OUÉDRAOGO; circ. 8,000.

Le Pays: 01 BP 4577, Ouagadougou 01; tel. 31-35-46; fax 31-45-50; f. 1991; Dir SIGUÉ JÉRÉMIE BOUREIMA; circ. 4,000.

Sidwaya (Truth): 5 rue du Marché, 01 BP 507, Ouagadougou 01; tel. and fax 31-03-62; f. 1984; state-owned; Mossi; Editor-in-Chief ISSAKA SOURWEMA; circ. 3,000.

PERIODICALS

Bendré: Ouagadougou; weekly; Dir CHERIFF SY.

Le Berger: Zone commerciale, ave Binger, BP 2581, Bobo-Dioulasso; f. 1992; weekly; Dir KOULIGA BLAISE YAMÉOGO.

Bulletin de l'Agence d'Information du Burkina: 01 BP 2507, Ouagadougou 01; tel. 30-70-52; telex 5327; fax 30-70-56; 2 a week; Editor-in-Chief JAMES DABIRÉ; circ. 200.

La Clef: 01 BP 6113, Ouagadougou 01; tel. 31-38-27; f. 1992; weekly; Dir KY SATURNIN; circ. 3,000.

L'Indépendant: Ouagadougou; weekly; Dir NORBERT ZONGO.

L'Intrus: 01 BP 2009, Ouagadougou 01; f. 1985; weekly; satirical; Dir JEAN HUBERT BAZIÉ; circ. 3,000.

Le Journal du Jeudi: 01 BP 3654, Ouagadougou 01; tel. 31-41-08; fax 31-17-12; f. 1991; weekly; Dir BOUBACAR DIALLO; circ. 8,000.

Le Matin: Bobo-Dioulasso; tel. 97-16-93; f. 1992; weekly; Dir DOFINITA FLAURENT BONZI.

Nekr Wagati: Ouagadougou; six a year; Dir SIMON COMPAORÉ.

La Nouvelle Tribune: Ouagadougou; weekly; Dir KYALBABOUÊ BAYILI.

L'Ouragan: Ouagadougou; weekly; Dir LOHÉ ISSA KONATÉ.

Regard: Ouagadougou; weekly; Dir CHRIS VALÉA.

Sidwaya Magazine: 5 rue du Marché, 01 BP 507, Ouagadougou 01; state-owned; Mossi; monthly; Editor-in-Chief BONIFACE COULIBALY; circ. 2,500.

Yeelen (Light): Ouagadougou; monthly; pro-Govt.

NEWS AGENCIES

Agence d'Information du Burkina (AIB): 01 BP 2507, Ouagadougou 01; tel. 30-70-52; telex 5327; fax 30-70-56; f. 1963; fmrly Agence Burkinabè de Presse; state-controlled; Dir JAMES DABIRÉ.

Foreign Bureaux

Agence France-Presse (AFP): BP 391, Ouagadougou; tel. 33-56-56; telex 5204; Bureau Chief KIDA TAPSOBA.

Reuters (UK) is also represented in Burkina Faso.

Publishers

Presses Africaines SA: BP 1471, Ouagadougou; tel. 33-43-07; telex 5344; general fiction, religion, primary and secondary textbooks; Man. Dir A. WININGA.

Société Nationale d'Edition et de Presse (SONEPRESS): BP 810, Ouagadougou; f. 1972; general, periodicals; Pres. MARTIAL OUÉDRAOGO.

Government Publishing House

Imprimerie Nationale du Burkina Faso (INBF): route de l'Hôpital Yalgado, BP 7040, Ouagadougou; tel. 33-52-92; f. 1963; Dir LATY SOULEYMANE TRAORÉ.

Radio and Television

In 1994, according to UNESCO, there were an estimated 280,000 radio receivers and 55,000 television receivers in use.

RADIO

Radiodiffusion Nationale du Burkina: 03 BP 7029, Ouagadougou 03; tel. 32-40-55; fax 31-04-41; f. 1959; state radio service; Dir RODRIGUE BARRY.

Radio Bobo-Dioulasso: BP 392, Bobo-Dioulasso; tel. 97-14-13; daily programmes in French and vernacular languages; Dir of Programmes SITA KAM.

Radio Horizon FM: 01 BP 2714, Ouagadougou 01; tel. 31-28-58; fax 31-39-34; private commercial station; broadcasts in French, English and eight vernacular languages; Dir MOUSTAPHA LAABLI THIOMBIANO.

TELEVISION

Télévision Nationale du Burkina: 29 blvd de la Révolution, 01 BP 2530, Ouagadougou 01; tel. 31-01-35; telex 5327; f. 1963; Dir AINE KOALA.

Finance

(cap. = capital; res = reserves; m. = million; brs = branches; amounts in francs CFA)

BANKING

Central Bank

Banque Centrale des Etats de l'Afrique de l'Ouest (BCEAO): ave Gamal-Abdel-Nasser, BP 356, Ouagadougou; tel. 30-60-15; telex 5205; fax 31-01-22; headquarters in Dakar, Senegal; f. 1962; bank of issue for the member states of the Union économique et monétaire ouest-africaine (UEMOA); cap. and res 657,592m. (Dec. 1995); Gov. CHARLES KONAN BANNY; Dir in Burkina Faso MOUSSA KONÉ; br. in Bobo-Dioulasso.

Other Banks

Banque Commerciale du Burkina (BCB): ave Nelson Mandela, 01 BP 1336, Ouagadougou 01; tel. 30-78-78; telex 5501; fax 31-06-28; f. 1987 as Banque Arabe-Libyenne-Burkinabè pour le Commerce et le Développement; 50% state-owned, 50% owned by Libyan Arab Foreign Bank; cap. and res 881m. (Dec. 1995); Pres. GUÉBRILA OUÉDRAOGO; Man. Dir IBRAHIM K. HELLAWI.

Banque Internationale du Burkina: rue de la Chance, angle rue Patrice Lumumba, 01 BP 362, Ouagadougou 01; tel. 30-61-69; telex 5210; fax 31-00-94; f. 1974; 25% owned by Banque Belgolaise SA (Belgium), 23% state-owned; cap. and res 4,834m. (Dec. 1995); Pres. and Man. Dir GASPARD OUÉDRAOGO; 14 brs.

Banque Internationale pour le Commerce, l'Industrie et l'Agriculture du Burkina (BICIA–B): ave Dr Kwamé N'Krumah, 01 BP 8, Ouagadougou 01; tel. 30-62-26; telex 5203; fax 31-19-55; f. 1973; 25% state-owned, 22.5% owned by Société Financière pour les Pays d'Outre-Mer; cap. and res 5,774m. (Dec. 1995); Pres. AMADOU TRAORÉ; Man. Dir HAMADÉ OUÉDRAOGO; 11 brs.

Caisse Nationale de Crédit Agricole du Burkina (CNCAB): 2 ave Gamal-Abdel-Nasser, 01 BP 1644, Ouagadougou 01; tel. 30-24-88; telex 5443; fax 31-43-52; f. 1979; 26% state-owned; cap. and res 5,868m. (Dec. 1995); Pres. TIBILA KABORÉ; Man. Dir NOËL KABORÉ; 4 brs.

Ecobank–Burkina SA: Ouagadougou; operations commenced 1997; 80% owned by Ecobank Transnational Inc (operating under the auspices of the Economic Community of West African States); cap. 1,250m.; Man. Dir OLAYEMI AKAPO.

Groupe BFCIB-UREBA-CAI: 01 BP 585, Ouagadougou 01; tel. 30-60-35; telex 5269; fax 31-05-61; est. in progress, entailing merger of Banque pour le Financement du Commerce et des Investissements du Burkina (BFCIB), Union Révolutionnaire de Banques (UREBA) and Caisse Autonome d'Investissements (CAI); proposed cap. 1,600m.; Dir DER AUGUSTIN SOMDA (provisional).

STOCK EXCHANGE

Côte d'Ivoire's Bourse des Valeurs d'Abidjan was scheduled to become a regional stock exchange, serving the member states of the UEMOA.

INSURANCE

Fonci-Assurances (FONCIAS): ave Léo Frobénius, 01 BP 398, Ouagadougou 01; tel. 30-62-04; telex 5323; fax 31-01-53; f. 1978; 51% owned by Athena Afrique (France), 20% state-owned; cap. 140m.; Pres. El Hadj OUMAROU KANAZOE; Man. Dir GÉRARD G. MANTOUX.

Société Nationale d'Assurances et de Réassurances (SONAR): 01 BP 406, Ouagadougou 01; tel. 30-62-43; telex 5294; f. 1973; 25% state-owned; cap. 240m.; Man. Dir AUGUSTIN N. TRAORÉ.

Union des Assurances du Burkina (UAB): 08 BP 11041, Ouagadougou 08; tel. 31-26-15; fax 31-26-20; f. 1991; 80% owned by private Burkinabè interests, 20% by l'Union Africaine–IARD (Côte d'Ivoire); cap. 270m.; Maj. Dir. J. V. ALFRED YARÉOGO.

Trade and Industry

DEVELOPMENT AGENCIES

Caisse Française de Développement (CFD): ave Binger, BP 529, Ouagadougou; tel. 30-68-26; telex 5271; fmrly Caisse Centrale de Coopération Economique, named changed 1992; Dir M. GLEIZES.

Mission Française de Coopération: 01 BP 510, Ouagadougou 01; tel. 30-67-71; telex 5211; fax 30-89-00; centre for administering bilateral aid from France under co-operation agreements signed in 1961; Dir PIERRE JACQUEMOT.

GOVERNMENT REGULATORY BODIES AND ENTERPRISES

Bureau des Mines et de la Géologie du Burkina (BUMIGEB): 01 BP 601, Ouagadougou 01; tel. 30-01-94; fax 30-01-87; f. 1978; research into geological and mineral resources; Pres. MODESTE DABIRA; Man. Dir JEAN-LÉONARD COMPAORÉ.

Caisse de Stabilisation des Prix des Produits Agricoles du Burkina (CSPPAB): 01 BP 1453, Ouagadougou 01; tel. 30-62-17; telex 5202; fax 31-06-14; f. 1964; responsible for purchase and marketing of shea-nuts (karité nuts), sesame seeds, cashew nuts and groundnuts; transfer pending to private ownership; Admin. DIANGO CHARLY HEBIE (acting); br. at Bobo-Dioulasso, representation at Boromo, Fada N'Gourma and Gaoua.

Comptoir Burkinabè des Métaux Précieux (CBMP): Ouagadougou; responsible for purchase of all gold production.

Office National d'Aménagement des Terroirs (ONAT): 01 BP 524, Ouagadougou 01; tel. 30-61-10; fax 30-61-12; f. 1974; fmrly Autorité des Aménagements des Vallées des Voltas; integrated rural development, including economic and social planning; Man. Dir ZACHARIE OUÉDRAOGO.

Office National du Commerce Exterieur (ONAC): ave Léo Frobénius, 01 BP 389, Ouagadougou 01; tel. 31-13-00; telex 5258; fax 31-14-69; f. 1974; promotes and supervises external trade; Man. Dir SÉRIBA OUATTARA (acting).

Office National de l'Eau et de l'Assainissement (ONEA): 01 BP 170, Ouagadougou 01; tel. 30-60-73; fax 30-33-60; f. 1977; storage, purification and distribution of water; Dir ALY CONGO.

Société Nationale Burkinabè d'Electricité (SONABEL): ave Nelson Mandela, BP 54, Ouagadougou; tel. 33-62-05; telex 5208; f. 1968; cap. 963m. francs CFA; production and distribution of electricity; Dir-Gen. M. BARRO.

CHAMBER OF COMMERCE

Chambre de Commerce, d'Industrie et d'Artisanat du Burkina: ave Nelson Mandela, 01 BP 502, Ouagadougou 01; tel. 30-61-14; telex 5268; fax 30-61-16; f. 1948; Pres. El Hadj OUMAROU KANAZOÉ; Sec.-Gen. SALIF LAMOUSSA KABORÉ; br. in Bobo-Dioulasso.

EMPLOYERS' ORGANIZATIONS

Association Professionnelle des Banques et Établissements Financiers (APBEF): Ouagadougou; Pres. HAMADÉ OUÉDRAOGO.

Conseil National du Patronat Burkinabè: Ouagadougou; Pres. BRUNO ILBOUDO.

Groupement Professionnel des Industriels: BP 810, Ouagadougou; tel. 30-28-19; f. 1974; Pres. MARTIAL OUÉDRAOGO.

Syndicat des Commerçants Importateurs et Exportateurs (SCIMPEX): 01 BP 552, Ouagadougou 01; tel. 31-18-70; fax 31-30-36; Pres. PATRICK LEYDET.

CO-OPERATIVES

Société de Commercialisation du Burkina 'Faso Yaar': ave du Loudun, BP 531, Ouagadougou; tel. 30-61-28; telex 5274; f. 1967; 99% state-owned; transfer to private ownership pending; import-export and domestic trade; Pres. Minister of Trade, Industry and Crafts.

Union des Coopératives Agricoles et Maraîchères du Burkina (UCOBAM): 01 BP 277, Ouagadougou 01; tel. 30-65-27; telex 5287; f. 1968; comprises 8 regional co-operative unions (20,000 mems); production and marketing of fruit and vegetables.

MAJOR INDUSTRIAL COMPANIES

The following are some of the largest companies in terms of either capital investment or employment.

CIMAT–Ciments du Burkina: 01 BP 1930, Ouagadougou 01; tel. 30-59-21; fax 30-59-23; cap. 2,103m. francs CFA; cement production, clinker crushing; Man. Dir DIDIER BONHOMME; 150 employees.

Compagnie Burkinabè pour la Transformation des Métaux (CBTM): BP 235, Bobo-Dioulasso; tel. 99-01-60; telex 8209; f. 1973; cap. 120m. francs CFA; mfrs of aluminium household goods; Pres. SIDI MADATALI; Man. Dir JEAN-PIERRE JOYEUX.

Compagnie des Mines d'Or de Kieré (COMIDOK): Kiéré; f. 1993; exploitation and exploration of gold deposits.

Compagnie Minière de Tambao (COMITAM): 01 BP 12, Ouagadougou 01; tel. 30-67-47; fax 31-27-58; f. 1975; cap. 200m. francs CFA; 65% owned by Interstar Mining Group Inc (Canada), 35% state-owned; exploitation of manganese deposits at Tambao; Pres. S. DONALD MOORE; Man. Dir K. H. E. REICHER.

Grands Moulins du Burkina (GMB): BP 64, Banfora; tel. 88-00-57; telex 8238; f. 1970; cap. 865m. francs CFA; flour-millers and mfrs of animal feed; Man. Dir JOSEPH ADAMA SOMBIE.

Groupe Aliz: Bobo-Dioulasso; processing and export of animal hides and skins; 2m. hides and skins processed, 600,000 raw hides exported annually.

Manufacture Burkinabè de Cigarettes (MABUCIG): BP 94, Bobo-Dioulasso; tel. 97-01-22; telex 8205; fax 97-21-62; f. 1966; cap. 935m. francs CFA; cigarette production of 1,000 metric tons per year; Pres. PIERRE IMBERT; Man. Dir MICHEL BLONDE.

Société Africaine de Pneumatiques (SAP): BP 389, Bobo-Dioulasso; tel. 98-15-69; telex 8207; f. 1972; cap. 1,005m. francs CFA; tyres and inner tubes; Pres. and Man. Dir K. LAZARE SORE.

Société des Brasseries du Burkina Faso (BRAKINA): BP 519, Ouagadougou; tel. 30-13-55; telex 5331; fax 30-08-37; f. 1960; cap. 2,530m. francs CFA; brewers and mfrs of soft-drinks and ice; Pres. JEAN-CLAUDE PALU; Man. Dir MARC BEAUQUESNE.

Société Burkinabè des Fibres Textiles (SOFITEX): BP 147, Bobo-Dioulasso; tel. 98-22-03; telex 8208; fax 98-14-05; f. 1979; cap. 4,400m. francs CFA; 65% state-owned; development and processing of fibrous plants; Pres. DIEUDONNÉ YAMÉOGO; Man. Dir GUY SOMÉ.

Société de Construction et de Gestion Immobilière du Burkina (SOCOGIB): BP 148, Ouagadougou; tel. 30-01-97; f. 1961; cap. 1,843m. francs CFA; 36% state-owned; housing development; Man. Dir ANATOLE BELEMSAGHA.

Société de Fabrication des Piles du Faso (SOFAPIL): Zone Industrielle, BP 266, Bobo-Dioulasso; tel. 98-04-97; telex 8220; fax 98-21-54; f. 1971; cap. 683m. francs CFA; mfrs of batteries; Pres. SALIF OUÉDRAOGO; Man. Dir PATRICK LEYDET.

Société Faso-Fani: BP 105, Koudougou; tel. 44-01-33; telex 5250; f. 1965 as Société Voltaïque des Textiles; cap. 1,223m. francs CFA; 56% state-owned; transfer to private ownership pending; weaving, spinning, dyeing and printing of textiles; Man. Dir DOMINIQUE KAFANDO.

Société des Huiles et Savons du Burkina (SHSB CITEC HUILERIE): 01 BP 338, Bobo-Dioulasso 01; tel. 97-04-70; telex 8203; fax 97-04-39; f. 1967; cap. 1,500m. francs CFA; production of groundnut oil; mfrs of shea (karité) butter, soap and animal feed; Pres. GUY SOMÉ; Man. Dir ABDOULAYE KADER OUÉDRAOGO.

Société Industrielle du Faso (SIFA): Bobo-Dioulasso; affiliate of Cie française de l'Afrique Occidentale; mfrs of motor cycles and bicycles.

Société Nationale d'Exploitation et de Distribution Cinématographique du Burkina (SONACIB): BP 206, Ouagadougou; tel. 33-55-04; cap. 128m. francs CFA; 95% state-owned; Man. JUSTIN KAREMBEGA.

Société des Plastiques du Faso (FASOPLAST): Zone Industrielle de Gounghin, 01 BP 534, Ouagadougou 01; tel. 30-20-76; fax 34-20-67; f. 1986; cap. 681m. francs CFA; mfrs of plastics; Man. Dir MAMADY SANOH; 150 employees.

Société de Recherches et d'Exploitations Minières du Burkina (SOREMIB): BP 5562, Ouagadougou; tel. 30-62-35; telex 5412; f. 1961; cap. 4,000m. francs CFA; 60% state-owned, transfer to private ownership of part of state holding pending; mineral exploration and exploitation; Pres. DIEUDONNÉ YAMÉOGO; Man. Dir JOSEPH OUÉDRAOGO.

Société Sucrière de la Comoé (SOSUCO): BP 13, Banfora; tel. 88-00-18; telex 8212; f. 1969; fmrly Société Sucrière du Burkina Faso; cap. 6,031m. francs CFA; 69% state-owned; transfer to private ownership pending; sugar refining; Man. Dir FULGENCE TOE.

TRADE UNIONS

There are more than 20 autonomous trade unions. The five trade union syndicates are:

Confédération Générale du Travail Burkinabè (CGTB): Ouagadougou; f. 1988; confed. of several autonomous trade unions; Sec.-Gen. TOLE SAGNON.

Confédération Nationale des Travailleurs Burkinabè (CNTB): BP 445, Ouagadougou; f. 1972; Leader of Governing Directorate ABDOULAYE BÂ.

Confédération Syndicale Burkinabè (CSB): BP 299, Ouagadougou; f. 1974; mainly public service unions; Sec.-Gen. YACINTHE OUÉDRAOGO.

Organisation Nationale des Syndicats Libres (ONSL): BP 99, Ouagadougou; f. 1960; 6,000 mems (1983).

Union Syndicale des Travailleurs Burkinabè (USTB): BP 381, Ouagadougou; f. 1958; Sec.-Gen. BONIFACE SOMDAH; 35,000 mems in 45 affiliated orgs.

Transport

RAILWAY

At the end of 1991 there were some 622 km of track in Burkina Faso. A 105-km extension from Donsin to Ouagadougou was inaugurated in December of that year. Plans exist for the construction of an extension to the manganese deposits at Tambao: in 1989 the cost of the project was estimated at 12,000m. francs CFA. Responsibility for operations on the railway line linking Abidjan (Côte d'Ivoire) and Kaya, via Ouagadougou, was transferred to SITARAIL (a consortium of French, Belgian, Ivorian and Burkinabè interests) in May 1995.

Société des Chemins de Fer du Burkina (SCFB): 01 BP 192, Ouagadougou 01; tel. 30-60-50; telex 5433; fax 30-77-49; f. 1989 to operate the Burkinabè railway network that was fmrly managed by the Régie du Chemin de Fer Abidjan–Niger; services privatized in May 1995 (see above); Pres. SIDIKI SIDIBE; Man. Dir ANDRÉ EMMANUEL YAMÉOGO.

ROADS

In 1995 there were 12,506 km of roads, including 5,610 km of main roads and 2,982 km of secondary roads; about 16% of the road network was paved. A major aim of current projects for the construction or upgrading of roads, as part of the Government's 1991–96 infrastructure development programme (funded by the Arab Bank for Economic Development in Africa, the Islamic Development Bank, the OPEC Fund for International Development and the Governments of Kuwait and Saudi Arabia), was to improve transport links with other countries of the region.

Régie X9: 01 BP 2991, Ouagadougou 01; tel. 30-42-96; telex 5313; f. 1984; urban, national and international public transport co; Dir FRANÇOIS KONSEIBO.

CIVIL AVIATION

There are international airports at Ouagadougou and Bobo-Dioulasso, 49 small airfields and 13 private airstrips. Ouagadougou airport handled 193,773 passengers and 7,986 metric tons of freight in 1991. In late 1995 France agreed funding of 13,500m. francs CFA for improvements to the airport infrastructure at Ouagadougou.

Air Afrique: BP 141, Ouagadougou; tel. 30-60-20; telex 5292; see under Côte d'Ivoire.

Air Burkina: ave Loudun, 01 BP 1459, Ouagadougou 01; tel. 30-76-76; fax 31-48-80; f. 1967 as Air Volta, name changed 1984; 25% state-owned; operates domestic and regional services; Man. Dir MATHIEU BOUDA.

Air Inter-Burkina: Ouagadougou; f. 1994; operates domestic passenger and postal services.

Tourism

Among the principal tourist activities is big game hunting in the east and south-west, and along the banks of the Mouhoun (Black Volta) river. There is a wide variety of wild animals in the game reserves. Important cultural events, notably the pan-African film festival held bienially in Ouagadougou, attract many visitors. In 1993 there were 154,937 tourist arrivals, and receipts from tourism totalled 8,895m. francs CFA.

Direction de l'Administration Touristique et Hôtelière: 01 BP 624, Ouagadougou 01; tel. 30-63-96; telex 5555; Dir-Gen. MOUSSA DIALLO.

Office National du Tourisme Burkinabè: BP 1318, Ouagadougou; tel. 3-19-59; telex 5202; fax 31-44-34; Dir-Gen. ABDOULAYE SANKARA.

Defence

National service is voluntary, and lasts for two years on a part-time basis. In August 1996 the armed forces numbered 10,000 (army 5,600, air force 200, gendarmerie 4,200). There was also a 'security company' of 250 and a part-time people's militia of 45,000.

Defence Expenditure: Estimated at US $68m. in 1996

Chief of the General Staff of the Armed Forces and Chief of Staff of the Army: Lt-Col IBRAHIM TRAORÉ.

Chief of Staff of the National Gendarmerie: Maj. MAMADOU TRAORÉ.

Education

Education is provided free of charge, and is officially compulsory for six years between the ages of seven and 14. Primary education begins at seven years of age and lasts for six years. Secondary education, beginning at the age of 13, lasts for a further seven years, comprising a first cycle of four years and a second of three years. In 1993 primary enrolment included only 32% of children in the relevant age-group (males 39%; females 25%). Secondary enrolment in the same year included only 7% of the appropriate age-group (males 10%; females 5%). There is a university in Ouagadougou; the number of students registered at university-level institutions in 1992/93 was 8,276, compared with 1,520 in 1980. A rural radio service has been established to further general and technical education in rural areas. In 1995, according to UNESCO estimates, adult illiteracy averaged 80.8% (males 70.5%; females 90.8%). Central government expenditure on education in 1994 was 36,315m. francs CFA, representing some 11.1% of total government spending in that year).

Bibliography

Allen, C., Radu, M. S., and Somerville, K. (Eds). *Benin, The Congo, Burkina Faso: Economics, Politics and Society*. New York and London, Pinter Publishers, 1989.

Anderson, S. (Ed. and Trans.). *Thomas Sankara Speaks: The Burkina Faso Revolution 1983–87*. New York and London, Pathfinder Press, 1988.

Andrimirado, S. *Sankara le rebelle*. Paris, Jeune Afrique Livres, 1987.

Il s'appelait Sankara: Chronique d'une mort violente. Paris, Jeune Afrique Livres, 1988.

Audouin, J., and Deniel, R. *L'Islam en Haute-Volta à l'epoque coloniale*. Paris, L'Harmattan, 1979.

Cruise O'Brien, D. B., Dunn, J., and Rathbone, R. (Eds). *Contemporary West African States*. Cambridge, Cambridge University Press, 1989.

Duval, M. *Un totalitarisme sans Etat—essai d'anthropologie politique à partir d'un village burkinabè*. Paris, L'Harmattan, 1985.

Englebert, P. *Burkina Faso: Unsteady Statehood in West Africa*. Boulder, CO, Westview Press, 1996.

Guion, J. R. *Blaise Compaoré: Réalisme et intégrité*. Paris, Mondes en devenir, 1991.

Harrison Church, R. J. *West Africa*. 8th Edn. London, Longman, 1979.

Izard, M. *Le Yatenga précolonial*. Paris, Editions Karthala, 1985.

Kargoubou, S. *Géographie de la Haute-Volta*. Ouagadougou, Ecole nationale d'administration.

Kayeba-Muase, C. *Syndicalisme et démocratie en Afrique noire. L'expérience de Burkina*. Paris, Editions Karthala, 1989.

Kiéthéga, J.-B. *L'or de la Volta noire*. Paris, Editions Karthala, 1983.

Labazée, P. *Entreprises et entrepreneurs du Burkina Faso*. Paris, Editions Karthala, 1988.

McFarland, D. M. *Historical Dictionary of Upper Volta*. Metuchen, NJ, Scarecrow Press, 1978.

Obinwa Nnaji, B. *Blaise Compaoré: The Architect of Burkina Faso Revolution*. Ibadan, Spectrum Books, 1989.

Rimmer, D. *The Economies of West Africa*. London, Weidenfeld and Nicolson, 1984.

Savadogo, K., and Wetta, C. *The Impact of Self-Imposed Adjustment: The Case of Burkina Faso 1983–1989*. Florence, Spedale degli Innocenti, 1991.

Savonnet-Guyot, C. *Etat et sociétés au Burkina: essai sur le politique africain*. Paris, Karthala, 1986.

Ye, B. A. *Profil politique de la Haute Volta coloniale et néo-coloniale ou les origines du Burkina Faso révolutionnaire*. Ouagadougou, Imprimerie Nouvelle du Centre, 1986.

Ziegler, J. *Sankara, Un nouveau pouvoir africain*. Lausanne, Pierre-Marcel Favre/ABC, 1986.

BURUNDI

Physical and Social Geography

The Republic of Burundi, like its neighbour Rwanda, is exceptionally small in area, comprising 27,834 sq km (10,747 sq miles), but with a relatively large population of 6,090,000 (official estimate for mid-1996). The result is a high density of 218.8 persons per sq km. The principal towns are the capital, Bujumbura (population 235,440 at the 1990 census), and Gitega (population 15,943 in 1978).

Burundi is bordered by Rwanda to the north, by the Democratic Republic of the Congo (DRC) to the west and by Tanzania to the south and east. The natural divide between Burundi and the DRC is formed by Lake Tanganyika and the Ruzizi river on the floor of the western rift-valley system. To the east, the land rises sharply to elevations of around 1,800 m above sea-level in a range that stretches north into the much higher, and volcanic, mountains of Rwanda. Away from the edge of the rift valley, elevations are lower, and most of Burundi consists of plateaux of 1,400–1,800 m. Here the average temperature is 20°C and annual rainfall 1,200 mm. In the valley the temperature averages 23°C, while rainfall is much lower at 750 mm.

Population has concentrated on the fertile, volcanic soils at 1,500–1,800 m above sea-level, away from the arid and hot floor and margins of the rift valley. The consequent pressure on the land, together with recurrent outbreaks of intense internal unrest, has resulted in extensive migration, mainly to Tanzania, the DRC and Uganda. The ethnic composition of the population is much the same as that of Rwanda: about 85% Hutu, 14% Tutsi (later arrivals in the country and, until recently, unchallenged as the dominant group) and less than 1% Twa, pygmoid hunters. Historically, the kingdoms of Urundi and Ruanda had a strong adversarial tradition, and rivalry between the successor republics remains strong. Thus the assimilation of their related languages, Kirundi and Kinyarwanda, has yet to be achieved.

Recent History

FILIP REYNTJENS

Revised for this edition by GREGORY MTHEMBU-SALTER

Unlike most African states, Burundi and its northern neighbour Rwanda were not an artificial creation of colonial rule. When they were absorbed by German East Africa in 1899, they had been organized kingdoms for centuries, belatedly forced to open their borders to European intrusion. When, in 1916, Belgium occupied Ruanda-Urundi (as the League of Nations mandated territory encompassing both Rwanda and Burundi was designated), it continued the system of 'indirect rule' operated by the Germans. This choice of colonial policy had a particular impact, since an ethnic minority, the Tutsi (comprising about 14% of the population), had long been dominant over the majority Hutu (85%) and a pygmoid group, the Twa (1%). Unlike the situation in Rwanda, however, the potential for conflict between Hutu and Tutsi was contained by the existence of the ganwa, an intermediate princely class between the mwami (king) and the populace. The mwami and ganwa were Tutsi, standing apart from the Tutsi masses, who, in turn, comprised two main groups, the Banyaruguru and the Bahima. Relations between the ordinary Tutsi and the Hutu were on an equal footing, and intermarriage was common.

The exercise of its perceived duties under the League of Nations mandate led to arbitrary and disruptive intervention by Belgium in Burundi's social and political system. However, to fulfil the criteria imposed by the UN Trusteeship Council after 1948, the Belgian administration was moved towards some degree of democratization. Two main parties came to the fore. The Union pour le progrès national (UPRONA), led by Prince Louis Rwagasore (the eldest son of the mwami), was a progressive nationalist movement, aiming to unite all groups and interests. The rival Parti démocrate chrétien (PDC) was more conservative and maintained cordial links with the Belgian administration. At legislative elections held in September 1961, prior to the granting of internal self-government in January 1962, UPRONA won 58 of the 64 seats in the new national assembly. Rwagasore, who became prime minister after the elections, was assassinated in October 1961 by agents of the PDC. His death was to prove a crucial event in the subsequent history of Burundi; the absence of his unifying influence was to lead to the division of UPRONA and to the emergence of open conflict between Hutu and Tutsi.

MICOMBERO AND BAGAZA

UPRONA was unable to contain the ethnic tensions that followed the attainment of independence on 1 July 1962. The monarchy emerged as the only significant institution to synthesize the interests of both Hutu and Tutsi populations. In order to consolidate his own position, the mwami, Mwambutsa IV, sought to ensure a balance of ethnic interests in government. Four governments held office during 1963–65, each comprising almost equal proportions of Hutu and Tutsi. Tensions were exacerbated when the Hutu prime minister, Pierre Ngendandumwe, was assassinated in January 1965, only a week after taking office. The ensuing political crisis was resolved by a decisive Hutu victory at parliamentary elections held in May. Mwambutsa nevertheless appointed a Tutsi prince as the new prime minister. Incensed by this and by other actions taken by the mwami, a faction of the Hutu-dominated gendarmerie attempted to seize power in October. The repression of this abortive coup was extremely violent: virtually the entire Hutu political establishment was massacred, together with thousands of rurally-based Hutu who had supported the revolt. These events effectively ended any significant participation by the Hutu in Burundi's political life for many years.

In July 1966 Mwambutsa was deposed by his son, who took the title of Ntare V. He appointed Capt. (later Lt-Gen.) Michel Micombero as prime minister. In November Ntare was himself deposed by Micombero, who declared Burundi a republic. With the abolition of the monarchy, the keystone of the political system was removed, and subsequent purges of Hutu officers and politicians further consolidated Tutsi supremacy. Following an abortive coup attempt in April 1972, massacres of unprecedented magnitude and brutality were carried out. It was estimated that 100,000–200,000 Hutu were killed, and that a further 200,000 fled the country, mainly to Zaire, Tanzania and Rwanda. All Hutu elements were eliminated from the armed forces.

In November 1976 Col Jean-Baptiste Bagaza, like Micombero a Tutsi-Hima from Rutovu, in the south, seized power in a bloodless coup. The new regime made strenuous efforts to encourage national reconciliation and integration. Under agrarian reforms introduced in the mid-1970s, former Tutsi overlords were compelled to cede much of their titular land to Hutu peasants, and refugees were encouraged to return. More significantly, the archaic system of land tenure was abolished, along with the requirement for peasants to render onerous services to their landlords, and proprietary rights over the land were vested in the hands of the peasantry. None the less, patron-client ties have persisted in various forms, with Tutsi elements generally in the role of patron.

Although the army remained a significant force, attempts were made by the Bagaza regime to increase democratic participation in government. A new constitution, adopted by national referendum in November 1981, provided for a national assembly to be elected by universal adult suffrage, and the first elections were held in October 1982. Having been re-elected president of UPRONA at the party's second national congress in July 1984, Bagaza was elected head of state in August, for the first time by direct suffrage; he was the sole candidate in both elections.

During the period 1984–87 there was a sharp deterioration in the government's observance of human rights. This was particularly marked in relation to religious freedom, and led Bagaza's regime into intense conflict with several Christian denominations. The number of political prisoners, which rose considerably during this period, included critics of government restrictions on religious activities, as well as people suspected of involvement in Hutu opposition groups. Many detainees were reported to have been subjected to torture. This intensification of authoritarian rule led to strained relations with a number of donor countries, which sought to bring pressure on Bagaza by withholding development aid.

THE BUYOYA REGIME, 1987-93

In September 1987, during a visit abroad, Bagaza was deposed by an army-led *coup d'état*, instigated by Maj. Pierre Buyoya, a close associate who accused the former president of corruption and formed a Military Committee for National Salvation (CMSN), comprising 31 army officers. UPRONA was dissolved and the 1981 constitution was suspended. On 2 October Buyoya was sworn in as president, at the head of a new 20-member government. Bagaza subsequently went into exile in Libya.

Apart from its adoption of a more liberal approach to the issue of religious freedoms, the new regime did not differ significantly from that of Bagaza. It remained dependent upon the support of a small Tutsi-Hima élite, prevalent in the army, the civil service, the judiciary and educational institutions. Although Buyoya emphasized a desire for *rapprochement* and released hundreds of political prisoners, it was clear that the major problem facing the new leadership, as had been the case with Bagaza's regime, was the claim by the Hutu majority for fuller participation in public life.

Hutu-Tutsi Tensions

In August 1988 tribal tensions erupted in the north of the country when groups of Hutu, claiming Tutsi provocation, slaughtered hundreds of Tutsi in the towns of Ntega and Marangara. The Tutsi-dominated army was immediately dispatched to the region to restore order, and in the subsequent week, large-scale tribal massacres, similar to those of 1972, occurred. More than 60,000 refugees, mainly Hutu, fled to neighbouring Rwanda, as the death toll rose to an estimated 20,000. In the aftermath of the killings, a group of Hutu intellectuals were arrested for protesting against the army's actions and for demanding the establishment of an independent commission of inquiry into the massacres. In October 1988, however, Buyoya announced changes to the council of ministers, including the appointment of a Hutu, Adrien Sibomana, to the post of prime minister. Significantly, the council comprised an equal number of Tutsi and Hutu representatives. In the same month a commission for national unity (again comprising an equal number of Tutsi and Hutu) was established to investigate the massacres and to make recommendations for national reconciliation.

The political situation remained tense during the first half of 1989. There were several attempted coups by hard-line Tutsi activists and by supporters of ex-president Bagaza. Following the publication, in April, of the report of the commission for national unity, Buyoya announced plans to combat all forms of discrimination against the Hutu and to introduce new regulations to ensure equal opportunities in education, employment and in the armed forces. Inter-ethnic tensions continued to fester, however, and in August 1991 the detention, by security forces, of several Hutus thought to be members of the Parti de libération du peuple Hutu (PALIPEHUTU), the principal Hutu opposition party, for alleged 'incitement to massacre', was denounced by the human rights organization, Amnesty International. In November violent confrontations occurred in Bujumbura and the north and north-west of the country between Hutus and Tutsis, involving armed men and civilians on both sides. In January 1992 the minister of the interior stated that order had been restored and announced an official total of 551 deaths resulting from the November disturbances. Unofficial sources, however, estimated that as many as 3,000 had been murdered, many of them Hutus killed by government security forces in reprisal attacks. In late April 1992 further violent disturbances were reported in the north-west of the country, along the border with Rwanda. The government attributed responsibility for the unrest to an insurgency by PALIPEHUTU activists, whom they alleged had been trained and armed in Rwanda. Despite a bilateral undertaking, agreed in August 1992, to implement increased border security and to co-operate more fully in attempts to repatriate refugees, border tension persisted into late 1992 and early 1993.

Constitutional Transition

In April 1990 the commission for national unity produced a draft charter, which, as with the 1989 report, was submitted to extensive national debate. Public discussion, however, was closely directed and monitored by UPRONA, and did little to satisfy the demands of internal (clandestine) and external opposition groups. Political tensions were renewed in August, when the exiled leader of PALIPEHUTU died in prison in Tanzania, and the leader of a smaller dissident group was killed in a motor accident in Rwanda. Opponents of UPRONA alleged that both men had been assassinated by agents of Buyoya. Later in the same month, army barracks at Mabanda, in southern Burundi, were attacked by an armed group of exiled Hutu who had crossed the frontier from Tanzania.

In December 1990 UPRONA abolished the CMSN and transferred its functions to an 80-member central committee of UPRONA, with a Hutu, Nicolas Mayugi, as its secretary-general. The draft charter on national unity, duly approved at a referendum held in February 1991 by an electoral margin of 89.2% to 10.2%, was rejected by PALIPEHUTU and other opposition groups. Later in the same month the implementation of a cabinet reshuffle, whereby Hutus were appointed to 12 of the 23 government portfolios, was viewed with scepticism by political opponents. In March a commission was established to prepare a report on the 'democratization' of national institutions and political structures, in preparation for the drafting of a new constitution. President Buyoya insisted that transfer to a multiparty system of government was not implicit in the adoption of a new constitution, although both Buyoya and Sibomana subsequently expressed hopes that a new constitution, providing for a more democratic system of government, would be approved by referendum in early 1992 and would take effect from March of that year.

In September 1991 Buyoya presented the report of the constitutional commission on 'national democratization'. Among its recommendations were the establishment of a parliamentary forum to operate in conjunction with a presidential system of government, a renewable five-year presidential mandate, the introduction of proportional representation, freedom of the press, guarantees of human rights, and a system of 'controlled multipartyism' whereby political groupings seeking legal recognition would be required to comply with certain requirements, including acceptance of the charter on national unity.

In February 1992 the government announced that a referendum was to be held on 9 March to ascertain support for the constitutional reform proposals. It was stated that electoral endorsement of the draft constitution would be followed by legislative elections, and by a presidential poll in 1993. A swiftly-suppressed coup attempt, only days before the referendum, failed to disrupt the proceedings, and the proposals received the support of more than 90% of voters. The new constitution was promulgated on 13 March. At the beginning of April, in an extensive ministerial reshuffle, seven ministers left the government, and Hutus were appointed to 15 of the 25 portfolios. In April Buyoya approved legislation relating to the creation of new political parties in accordance with the provisions of the new constitution. Under the terms of this legislation, new political parties were required to demonstrate impartiality with regard to ethnic or regional origin, gender and religion, and to support national unity. By October eight political parties had received legal recognition. Later in that month, the president announced the creation of the National Electoral Preparatory Commission (NEPC), a 33-member body comprising representatives of the eight recognized political parties, together with administrative, judicial, religious and military officials. The NEPC, which was responsible for co-ordinating the process of democratization, met for the first time at the end of November. Earlier that month Buyoya had rejected the demands of five political parties to participate in a transitional government to oversee preparations for the forthcoming legislative elections (tentatively scheduled for March 1993). In response, however, the president announced the creation of a national consultative commission on democratization, to function in a purely advisory capacity. By early December 1992 Buyoya had appointed a new 12-member technical commission, charged with drafting an electoral code and a communal law.

In February 1993 President Buyoya announced that presidential and legislative elections would take place in June, with elections for local government officials to follow in November. The presidential poll, conducted on 1 June, was won, with 64.8% of votes cast, by Melchior Ndadaye, the candidate of the Front pour la démocratie au Burundi (FRODEBU), with the support of the Rassemblement du peuple burundien (RPB), the Parti du peuple (PP) and the Parti liberal (PL). Buyoya, the UPRONA candidate, received 32.4% of the votes, with support from the Rassemblement pour la démocratie et le développement économique et social (RADDES) and the Parti social démocrate (PSD). Legislative elections for 81 seats in the new legislative body were held on 29 June. Once again, FRODEBU emerged as the leading party, with 71% of the votes and 65 of the 81 seats in the new legislature. UPRONA, with 21.4% of the votes, secured the remaining 16 seats. The Parti de réconciliation du peuple (PRP), the PP, the RADDES and the PRB all failed to attract the minimum 5% of votes needed for representation in the legislature. The elections, however, were followed in early July by an attempted coup by army officers, which was swiftly suppressed. Ndadaye assumed the presidency on 10 July, thus becoming Burundi's first ever Hutu head of state. A new 23-member council of ministers was subsequently announced. The new prime minister, Sylvie Kinigi, was one of seven newly-appointed Tutsi ministers.

NDADAYE, NTARYAMIRA AND THE RESURGENCE OF ETHNIC UNREST

On 21 October 1993 more than 100 army paratroopers, supported by armoured vehicles, overwhelmed supporters of the government, and occupied the presidential palace and the headquarters of the national broadcasting company. Several prominent Hutu politicians and officials, including President Ndadaye, were detained and subsequently killed by the insurgents, who later proclaimed François Ngeze, one of the few prominent Hutu members of UPRONA, and a minister in the government of ex-president Buyoya, as head of a national committee for public salvation (CPSN). While members of the government sought refuge abroad and in the offices of foreign diplomatic missions in Bujumbura, the armed forces declared a state of emergency, closing national borders and the capital's airport. However, immediate and unanimous international condemnation of the coup, together with the scale and ferocity of renewed tribal violence (exacerbated by reports of massacres of Hutu intellectuals by Tutsi-dominated army units), undermined support for the insurgents from within the armed forces, and precipitated the collapse of the CPSN, which was disbanded on 25 October. The prime minister, Sylvie Kinigi, who had earlier refused to accept the insurgents' offer of surrender in exchange for amnesty, remained in hiding, and urged the international community to send an international force to Burundi to protect the civilian government. Communications were restored on 27 October, and on the following day the UN confirmed that the government had reassumed control of the country. Ngeze and 10 coup leaders were placed under arrest, although about 40 other insurgents were thought to have fled to Zaire. Although the coup was widely interpreted as an attempt by the Tutsi military élite to check the political advancement of Hutus, there was some speculation that supporters of ex-president Bagaza were responsible for the uprising, which may have been precipitated by suggestions that Ndadaye was attempting to establish an alternative, Hutu-dominated presidential gendarmerie. In early December a 27-member commission of judicial inquiry was created to investigate the insurgency.

Meanwhile, in early November 1993, several members of the government, including the prime minister, had left the French embassy (where they had remained throughout the uprising) with a small escort of French troops, and on 8 November Kinigi convened a meeting of the surviving government ministers in an attempt to address the humanitarian crisis arising from the massacre and displacement of thousands of Burundians (see below) provoked by the failed coup. On the same day the constitutional court officially recognized the presidential vacancy resulting from the murder of both Ndadaye and his constitutional successor, Giles Bimazubute, the speaker of the national assembly, and directed that presidential powers should pass to the council of ministers, acting in a collegiate capacity, pending fresh presidential elections, to be conducted within three months. However, the minister of external relations and co-operation, Sylvestre Ntibantunganya (who had succeeded Ndadaye as leader of FRODEBU), rejected these arrangements, asserting that elections should await the resolution of internal security difficulties and the initiation of a comprehensive programme for the repatriation of refugees. Ntibantunganya was subsequently elected speaker of the national assembly, and relinquished the foreign affairs portfolio, which was assumed by Jean-Marie Ngendahayo, minister of communications and government spokesman.

In early January 1994 the FRODEBU deputies in the national assembly approved a draft amendment to the constitution, whereby henceforth a president of the republic could be elected by the national assembly, in the event of a presidential vacancy having been recognized by the constitutional court. UPRONA deputies, who had boycotted the vote, challenged the constitutionality of the amendment, and expressed concern that such a procedure represented election by indirect suffrage, in direct contravention of the terms of the constitution. Although the continued boycott of the national assembly by UPRONA deputies, together with procedural impediments to the immediate ratification of the amendment, forced the postponement, on 10 January, of an attempt by FRODEBU deputies to elect their presidential candidate, the minister of agriculture and livestock, Cyprien Ntaryamira. However, three days later, following the successful negotiation of a political truce with opposition parties, Ntaryamira was elected president by the national assembly (with 78 of the 79 votes cast), and assumed office on 5 February. A UPRONA prime minister, Anatole Kanyenkiko, was appointed two days later, while the composition of a new multi-party council of ministers was finally agreed in mid-February.

In November 1993, following repeated requests by the government for an international contribution to the protection of government ministers in Burundi, the OAU agreed to the deployment of a 200-strong protection force (MIPROBU), to be composed of civilian and military personnel, for a period of six months. In December opposition parties, including UPRONA and the RADDES, organized demonstrations in protest at the arrival of the military contingent of 180, scheduled for late January 1994, claiming that Burundi's sovereignty and territorial integrity were being compromised.

Although a degree of commitment to establishing political stability was demonstrated by the representation of the main opposition parties in the new government (ministerial posts were occupied by members of UPRONA, RADDES, Inkinzo and the Parti indépendent des travailleurs—parties which had also secured a guaranteed percentage of future diplomatic, security and civil service posts), the impunity of those responsible for the failed October coup and for reprisal attacks against Tutsis, perpetuated the volatile security situation. On 11 February 1994 an international commission of inquiry, established by a number of human rights organizations, concluded that a majority of members of the armed forces had been directly or indirectly involved in the October coup attempt. It was estimated that 25,000–50,000 Burundians had died as a result of the violence arising from the insurrection. (A UN-sponsored fact-finding mission to investigate the incident arrived in Burundi in March.)

During February 1994 ethnic tension mounted as extremist factions of both Hutu and Tutsi groups attempted to establish territorial strongholds within the country. Reports that both sides had amassed considerable supplies of armaments aroused fears of a severe escalation of the conflict. (The minister of the interior, Léonard Nyangoma, claimed that the armed forces had been distributing weapons to Tutsi extremists since 1973, whereas Burundian Hutu refugees in Rwanda were thought to have received arms and military training from the Rwandan armed forces and the *Interahamwe* Hutu militia operating in Rwanda.) Fighting in the capital in early February resulted in the deaths of around 100 Burundians, prompting a delay in the deployment of MIPROBU. (In mid-March the government persuaded the OAU to reduce the MIPROBU military contingent from 180 to 47.) Attempts by the armed forces to disable Hutu strongholds in and around the capital resulted in the imposition of a *de facto* curfew in Bujumbura in late March, exaggerating existing divisions between FRODEBU's moderate faction, headed by President Ntaryamira (who, anxious to sustain cordial relations with the armed forces, advocated a programme of forced disarmament of militia groups on both sides), and Nyangoma's hardline faction, which opposed further military action against the militias. However, Ntaryamira's insistence that several senior army personnel and the chief of the national gendarmerie should be replaced for having failed to address the security crisis, and that the armed forces should not overlook its own ranks in the enforcement of the pacification programme, provoked sections of the security forces to embark on a campaign of violent destruction in the capital, resulting in dozens of civilian deaths. Following the incident Nyangoma described the state of the capital as one of 'total confusion', and estimated that as many as 1,000 civilians had been killed by the errant soliders, claims which were denied by the government spokesman, Cyriaque Simbizi, (who estimated a death toll of around 400), prompting accusations that Nyangoma was exaggerating the security crisis in order to precipitate a large-scale civil confrontation.

POLITICAL MANOEUVRES AND COALITION GOVERNMENT

On 6 April 1994, returning from a regional summit meeting in Dar es Salaam, Tanzania, President Ntaryamira was killed (together with the ministers of development, planning and reconstruction, and communications) when the aircraft of Rwandan President Juvénal Habyarimana, in which he was travelling at Habyarimana's invitation, was the target of a rocket attack above Kigali airport, and crashed on landing. Habyarimana was also killed in the crash, and was widely-acknowledged to have been the intended victim of the attack. In contrast to the violent political and tribal chaos which erupted in Rwanda in the aftermath of the death of Habyarimana, Burundians responded positively to appeals for calm issued by Sylvestre Ntibantunganya, the speaker of the national assembly, who, on 8 April, was confirmed (in accordance with the constitution) as interim president for a three-month period, following which a presidential election would be held. Although considered to be a less compromising FRODEBU member than Ntaryamira, Ntibantunganya had demonstrated no affinity with Nyangoma's radical supporters. Nevertheless, Ntibantunganya's statesmanship was immediately tested by several army dissidents, who attempted to organize a coup but were swiftly apprehended by loyalist troops on 25 April.

Meanwhile, sporadic violent exchanges between Hutu extremist rebels and factions of the armed forces continued to claim casualties (on 21 April 1994 the attorney-general was killed during an exchange of gunfire). In late April, hoping to ease tensions within the lower ranks of the armed forces, and to assert his leadership over dissident factions of FRODEBU, the president issued an ultimatum to the warring militias, that all illegal arms should be surrendered by 1 May. Following unsuccessful attempts to negotiate the disarmament of the Kamenge 'people's army', the armed forces were authorized to bombard the district with mortar shells, forcing the withdrawal and surrender of many of the rebels. Relations between the government and the armed forces improved considerably as a result, prompting the president to indicate that the contentious reform of the armed forces would not be achieved through the imposition of ethnic quotas. The government and the military were further reconciled following a statement, issued by the prime minister in early May, that Nyangoma had forfeited his position in the council of ministers, having failed to return from government business abroad. During May UPRONA elected a Hutu, Charles Mukasi, a newspaper editor, as its new leader. In the same month, ex-president Bagaza resumed political activity, at the head of a new party, the Parti pour le redressement national (PARENA).

Having discounted the possibility of organizing a general election, owing to security considerations, in June 1994 all major political parties engaged in lengthy negotiations to establish a procedure for the restoration of an elected presidency. The mandate of the interim president was extended for three months by the constitutional court in July, and by the end of August it had been decided that a new president would be elected by a broadly representative commission, with a composition yet to be decided. A new agreement on power-sharing, in addition to a tentative agreement concluded in mid-July, was announced on 10 September. This convention of government, which detailed the terms of government for a four-year transitional period (including the allocation of 45% of cabinet posts to opposition parties), was incorporated into the constitution on 22 September. The convention also provided for the creation of a national security council (formally inaugurated on 10 October) to address the national security crisis. On 30 September the convention elected Ntibantunganya to the presidency from a list of six candidates including Charles Mukasi, the UPRONA leader. Ntibantunganya's appointment was endorsed immediately by the national assembly, and he was formally inaugurated on 1 October 1994. Anatole Kanyenkiko was reappointed as prime minister on 3 October, and two days later a coalition government was announced, with a composition reflecting the terms of the September convention. In December, however, UPRONA announced its intention to withdraw from the government and from the legislature, following the election, in early December, of Jean Minani (a prominent FRODEBU member) to the post of speaker of the national assembly. UPRONA members accused Minani of having incited Hutu attacks against Tutsis in the aftermath of the October 1993 attempted coup. In early January 1995 the political crisis was averted by agreement on a compromise FRODEBU candidate, Léonce Nyendakumana. Minani subsequently assumed the FRODEBU party leadership, and by mid-January UPRONA had declared its willingness to rejoin the government. Later in the month, however, Kanyenkiko resisted attempts by the UPRONA leadership to expel him from the party for having failed to comply with party demands for the withdrawal from the government of all party members over the Minani affair. Two UPRONA ministers were subsequently dismissed from the council of ministers, in apparent retaliation, prompting the UPRONA leader, Charles Mukasi, to demand the resignation of the prime minister, and to declare an indefinite general strike in support of this demand, in mid-February. Increased political opposition to Kanyenkiko forced the prime minister to acknowledge that he no longer enjoyed the necessary mandate to continue in office, and on 22 February Antoine Nduwayo, a UPRONA candidate selected in consultation with other opposition parties, amid allegations of extremist Tutsi militia intimidation, was appointed prime minister by presidential decree. A new coalition council of ministers was announced on 1 March, but political stability was undermined immediately by the murder, in early March, of the Hutu minister of energy and mines, Ernest Kabushemeye. (Another member of the RPB, Emmanuel Sindayigaya, was subsequently appointed to the post.)

Ethnic tension persisted in the second half of 1994, exacerbated by the scale and proximity of the violence in Rwanda (see above), and by the presence in Burundi of an estimated 200,000 Rwandan Hutu refugees, who had fled the advancing FPR in Rwanda. While nationwide civil confrontation was largely contained in Burundi, ethnically-motivated atrocities became a daily occurrence in parts of the country (several prominent politicians and government officials were murdered), resulting in the imposition of a partial curfew in the capital in December. Fears that the security crisis in Burundi would develop into civil war were agitated, in late 1994, by reports that the allegedly 30,000-strong Force pour la défense de la démocratie (FDD), the armed wing of Nyangoma's extremist Conseil national pour la défense de la démocratie (CNDD), were making preparations for an armed struggle against the armed forces in Burundi. In early November the national security council had urged all political and civilian groups to dissociate themselves from Nyangoma, who was believed to be co-ordinating party activities from Zaire. An escalation in the scale and frequency of incidents of politically- and ethnically-motivated violence during 1995 prompted renewed concern that the security crisis would precipitate a large-scale campaign of ethnic massacres similar to that witnessed in Rwanda during 1994. Government-sponsored military initiatives were concentrated in Hutu-dominated suburbs of Bujumbura (particularly Kamenge) and in the north-east, where an aggressive campaign was waged against the alleged insurgent activities of PALIPEHUTU members, resulting in the deaths of hundreds of Hutu civilians. The government accused Hutu extremist militiamen of conducting an intimidating and violent programme of recruitment of Hutu males in the region.

In May 1995 humanitarian organizations suspended their activities in Burundi for one week in order to draw international attention to the security situation and the increasingly dangerous position of relief workers in the area. Anti-insurgency operations were intensified in June in several suburbs of the capital, where an estimated 2,000 heavily-armed troops sought to apprehend members of the FDD. It was reported that as many as 130 civilians were killed (many of them women and children) in the ensuing hostilities, which also forced thousands of Hutus to flee into the surrounding countryside. (In October the armed forces claimed to have destroyed the FDD headquarters.) Also in June, a report published by Amnesty International claimed that national security forces in Burundi had collaborated with extremist Tutsi factions in the murder of thousands of Hutus since 1993. A number of increased security measures, announced by the president in the same month, included restrictions on a number of civil liberties (a curfew was imposed, demonstrations were proscribed and the media and the movement of civilians in urban areas were to be severely regulated) and the regrouping of many communes into administrative sectors to be administered jointly by civilian and military personnel. A request by the president to be granted the power to rule by decree until the next legislative session, scheduled for October 1995, was subsequently rejected by the national assembly which considered such a move to be incompatible with the spirit of the convention of government.

Notwithstanding the latest security initiative, in late June 1995 the minister of state in charge of external relations and co-operation, Jean-Marie Ngendahayo, announced his resignation, in expression of his dissatisfaction at the government's inability to guarantee the safety and basic rights of the population. Later in the month, a meeting of the OAU, convened in Addis Ababa, concluded that some degree of military intervention in Burundi would be necessary should ethnic violence continue to escalate. (In April the Burundian government had declined an OAU offer of military intervention in favour of increasing the number of MIPROBU personnel to 67.) In early July Paul Munyembari was appointed to the external relations portfolio. Vedaste Ngendanganya was appointed minister of posts and telecommunications in early September, in place of Innocent Nimpagariste, who had resigned from the post in August amidst concern for his safety, following a number of unsuccessful assassination attempts. Further changes to the council of ministers were announced in October, in response to a division within the governing coalition arising from remarks made by prominent members of the government (most notably the UPRONA minister of the interior, Gabriel Sinarinzi), which were highly critical of the attitude to the country's security crisis demonstrated by the US ambassador to Burundi. Sinarinzi was among seven ministers replaced in the reshuffle.

In September 1995 the composition of a UN-sponsored, five-member commission of inquiry into events leading to the assassination of President Ndadaye in October 1993 was announced by the UN secretary-general, Dr Boutros Boutros-Ghali. The announcement followed a visit to Burundi which was undertaken by the UN secretary-general in mid-July. In December Boutros Boutros-Ghali appointed Marc Faguy of Canada to be his new special representative in Burundi.

ETHNIC CONFRONTATION

By early 1996 reports of atrocities perpetrated against both Hutu and Tutsi civilians by rogue elements of the Tutsi-led armed forces (including militias known as the *Sans Echecs),* and by extremist Hutu rebel groups had become almost commonplace in rural areas. It was estimated that the capital had been effectively purged of any significant Hutu presence by the end of 1995. In late December the UN secretary-general had petitioned the Security Council to sanction some form of international military intervention in Burundi to address rapidly worsening security conditions, and in February these efforts were renewed following a report made by the UN special *rapporteur* on human rights which concluded that no discernible improvement had been made in the protection of human rights since mid-1995 and that a state of near civil war existed in many areas of the country. However, the Burundian government (and the weight of Tutsi political opinion in Burundi) remained fiercely opposed to a foreign military presence, claiming that reports of the severity of the security crisis had been exaggerated, and persuading the UN Security Council that a negotiated settlement to the conflict was still attainable. Reports delivered by representatives of the US Agency for International Development and the Humanitarian Office of the European Union (EU) following an official visit to Burundi, undertaken in early April, were severely critical of the administration's failure to reconcile the country's various ethnic and political interests within government, and expressed doubts that effective power-sharing could be achieved within the terms of the 1994 convention of government and under the leadership of a Tutsi premier with considerable executive power. The USA and the EU announced the immediate suspension of aid to Burundi.

Despite an undertaking by President Ntibantunganya in late April 1996 that a human rights commission was to be established and a comprehensive reform of the security forces and the judiciary was to be carried out, violence continued to escalate, prompting the suspension of French military co-operation with Burundi at the end of May. (Aid workers reported a number of atrocities perpetrated by units of the armed forces against Hutu civilians — including separate incidents in which some 235 villagers in Buhoro and an estimated 375 villagers in Kivyuka were massacred — during May.) In early June the International Committee of the Red Cross (ICRC) suspended all activities in Burundi following the murder of three ICRC employees in the north-west of the country. Other aid agencies announced that future operations would be restricted to the capital. All ICRC staff were subsequently withdrawn from Burundi.

At a meeting of the member nations of the Economic Community of the Great Lakes Countries, convened in Cairo, Egypt in November 1995 at the request of the UN secretary-general, the presidents of Burundi, Rwanda, Uganda and Zaire, and a Tanzanian presidential representative, announced a sub-regional initiative for a negotiated peace in Burundi, involving mediation by eminent African statesmen, including (most prominently) the former president of Tanzania, Julius Nyerere. Nyerere's role as principal mediator in the conflict was endorsed at a meeting between representatives of more than 20 African states and European and UN diplomats in Addis Ababa, Ethiopia at the end of February 1996. Representatives of some 13 political parties (including FRODEBU and UPRONA) participated in inter-party discussions conducted in Mwanza, Tanzania, with Nyerere as mediator, in April. A second round of discussions, scheduled for May, was subsequently postponed. While a reluctance to further interrupt the work of the current legislative session in Burundi was offered as an official explanation for the stalling of negotiations, unofficial reports indicated that UPRONA representatives had objected to the possible participation of the CNDD. A second round of talks was conducted in Mwanza in early June, again with mediation by Nyerere, but political polarization appeared to have been intensified by the talks. UPRONA leader Charles Mukasi, with support from an informal coalition of seven smaller, predominantly Tutsi parties (the Rassemblement unitaire), accused FRODEBU deputies of seeking to abrogate the convention of government, a charge which was strenuously denied by FRODEBU spokesmen following the talks. At a conference of regional powers in Arusha, Tanzania, in late June 1996, the Burundian president and prime minister requested foreign intervention to protect politicians, civil servants and crucial installations. By early July a regional technical commission to examine the request for 'security assistance' (comprising regional defence ministers, but not representatives of the Burundian armed forces) had convened in Arusha and had reached preliminary agreement, with the support of the UN, for an intervention force to be composed of units of the Ugandan and Tanzanian armed forces and police officers from Kenya. Meanwhile, significant differences of interpretation, with regard to the purpose and mandate of such a force, had emerged between Ntibantunganya and Nduwayo (who suggested that the president was attempting to neutralize the country's military capability). At a mass rally of Tutsi-dominated opposition parties, organized in the capital on 5 July, the prime minister joined political leaders, including Charles Mukasi, in rejecting foreign military intervention and criticizing Ntibantunganya's alleged encouragement of external interference in domestic affairs. Some days later, however, full endorsement of the Arusha proposal for intervention was recorded by member nations of the OAU at a summit meeting convened in Yaoundé, Cameroon.

Political and ethnic tensions intensified still further when reports of a massacre of more than 300 Tutsi civilians at Bugendana, allegedly committed by Hutu extremists including heavily-armed Rwandan Hutu refugees, emerged just hours after the UN accused the Burundian authorities of collaborating with the Rwandan administration in a new initiative of (largely enforced) repatriation of Rwandan refugees in Burundi (see below). While FRODEBU members made un urgent appeal for foreign military intervention to contain the increasingly violent civil and military reaction to these events, ex-president Bagaza urged civil resistance to foreign intervention and advocated a general strike in the capital, which was partially observed. Meanwhile students (with the support of the political opposition) began a second week of protests against regional military intervention, and demonstrated in support of demands for the removal of the country's leadership. On 23 July 1996 Ntibantunganya was forced to abandon an attempt to attend the funeral of the victims of the Bugendana massacre following the pelting with missiles of the presidential helicopter by enraged mourners. On the following day, amid strong indications that UPRONA intended to join a number of smaller opposition parties which had already withdrawn from the convention of government, it was reported that Ntibantunganya had sought refuge in the US embassy. Several government ministers and the speaker of the national assembly withdrew to the German embassy compound, while the FRODEBU chairman, Jean Minani, fled the country.

THE RETURN OF BUYOYA

On 25 July 1996, in a bloodless military coup, the armed forces were extensively deployed in the capital. An announcement made by the minister of national defence, Lt-Col Firmin Sinzoyiheba, criticized the failure of the administration to safeguard national security and announced the suspension of the national assembly and all political activity, the imposition of a nationwide curfew and the closure of national borders and the airport at Bujumbura. Former president Buyoya was declared to be the new interim president of a transitional republic. In an address to the nation, delivered on the same day, Buyoya defined his immediate aim as the restoration of peace and national security, and sought to reassure former ministers and government officials that their safety would be guaranteed by the new regime. While Ntibantunganya conveyed his refusal to relinquish office, Nduwayo immediately resigned. In response to widespread condemnation of the coup, Buyoya announced that a largely civilian, broadly-based government of national unity would be promptly installed, and that future negotiations with all Hutu groups would be considered. The forced repatriation of Rwandan Hutu refugees was halted immediately. Despite the appointment of Pascal-Firmin Ndimira, a Hutu member of UPRONA, as prime minister, and an urgent attempt by Buyoya to obtain support from East African countries, a summit meeting of regional powers, convened in Arusha on 31 July, declared its intention to impose severe economic sanctions against the new regime, failing the immediate restoration of constitutional government. Western countries, which had until this point strongly supported regional initiatives in Burundi, were unwilling to carry out the imposition of sanctions. In early August the composition of a new 23-member, multi-ethnic cabinet was announced. In mid-August Buyoya announced that an expanded transitional national assembly, incorporating existing elected deputies, would be inaugurated during September for a three-year period. A consultative council of elders was also to be established to oversee a period of broad political debate, during which time formal political activity would remain proscribed. Meanwhile, reports emerged that the armed forces were launching indiscriminate attacks against Hutus (thousands have been killed since the coup) in an attempt to safeguard rural and border regions for Tutsi communities, and Hutu militia were also indiscriminately attacking Tutsi civilians. In mid-August, following the publication of a report by the UN on events preceding the 1993 coup, Buyoya dismissed the army chief-of-staff, Col Jean Bikomagu, and the commander of the *gendarmerie*, Col Pascal Simbanduko, both of whom were found by the UN to be involved in plotting the coup.

In the months following August 1996, military action in eastern Zaire (now the DRC), destroyed most of the FDD operations in the area, and prompted the repatriation of at least 30,000 Burundians. Most militia activists appear to have crossed into Tanzania, from where they have since made incursions into Burundi's southern provinces, attacking both military targets and unarmed civilians. However, the loss of their freedom of movement in Zaire has weakened their fighting capacity.

The shift in the balance of power in eastern Zaire weakened the regional sanctions initiative, and has enabled some Burundian exports to be transported via Goma and a limited amount of imports from east Africa to enter Burundi. However, the bulk of Burundi's trade passes through countries which are party to the sanctions agreement, and the availability of the same range of products in Burundi as before the embargo (albeit at higher prices), has demonstrated widespread violations of sanctions by these countries. In August 1996 Buyoya met Nyerere in Tanzania, in an unsuccessful attempt to obtain a relaxation of the sanctions. In the following month the Regional Sanctions Co-ordinating Committee (RSCC) held its first meeting, at which it agreed to ease restrictions on the importation of emergency relief supplies; however, it emphasized that economic sanctions would remain in force until the national assembly was restored, political parties legalized and unconditional negotiations opened with Hutu militias, including the FDD. Concurrently, the leader of the CNDD, Léonard Nyangoma, announced that he had assumed leadership of FRODEBU, a claim promptly disputed by Jean Minani (who was believed to have tacit support from Nyerere and the RSCC), although most of the exiled FRODEBU members of the national assembly appeared to prefer Nyangoma.

On 12 September 1996 Buyoya announced that political parties that made a 'positive contribution' to national life would be permitted to operate. The powers of the national assembly were restored, with the proviso that it could not dismiss the government. Exiled members of the national assembly were invited to return to the country. The response of the NSCC was to invite Buyoya to a meeting of regional heads of state, but as a factional leader and not as president. Neither Buyoya nor Nyangoma, who was also approached by the RSCC, attended the conference. No further concessions were forthcoming from the RSCC, which imposed a deadline of 31 October for the commencement of negotiations between the Burundi government and Hutu militias. Buyoya informed the RSCC that he was unwilling to enter into negotiations until economic sanctions were eased.

The RSCC granted further exemptions for aid agencies in October 1996, and in December there were further discussions in Arusha, at which Nyerere unsuccessfully sought to bring together the government, FRODEBU, the CNDD and UPRONA. A further meeting of the regional heads of state also took place, at which it was agreed to retain economic sanctions pending the opening of negotiations by the contending forces.

Towards the end of 1996, the government instituted a policy of 'regroupment' in a number of provinces. This involved the transfer of the population of villages in areas affected by violence to guarded camps from which agricultural activity had to be carried out under military supervision. Most of the villagers affected were Hutu, as the majority of rural Tutsi have been in 'displacement' camps for some time. The 'regroupment' policy has severely curtailed the country's agricultural production.

Successive reports by the UN High Commission, published in December and in January 1997, alleged widespread human rights abuses, carried out both by Hutu militias and the army. The reports were rejected by the government, with the threat to expel UN human rights observers if their 'unfounded' allegations continued. In January legal proceedings were commenced against the speaker of the national assembly, Leonce Ngendakumana, for his alleged complicity in massacres of Tutsi people following the October 1993 coup.

By February 1997, when Buyoya declared his willingness to negotiate prior to the lifting of economic sanctions, most major commodities were widely available in Burundi, with sufficient supplies of fuel entering the country from illicit suppliers in Tanzania and Rwanda. The economic embargo had, however, led to increased unemployment, particularly in the capital, and had thus been the cause of serious unemployment and a general decline in living standards.

Most members of the national executive of PARENA were taken into custody in mid-March, following an allegation by Buyoya that the security forces had uncovered a coup conspiracy. Ex-president Bagaza, the party leader, had been under house arrest since January.

A further meeting of regional heads of state was convened in mid-April at Arusha; on this occasion, Buyoya was invited to attend as president rather than faction leader. Recognizing the effective collapse of the sanctions policy, the heads of state agreed to permit the import of food, agricultural inputs, educational and construction materials and medicines; imports of fuel, however, remained at the discretion of the aid agencies, and the export of goods through countries participating in the sanctions programme was to remain prohibited. The CNDD, which initially denounced the relaxation of sanctions, subsequently abandoned its objections and intensified its armed attacks.

It was disclosed by Buyoya in May 1997 that contacts had taken place in Rome, Italy, between the government and the CNDD, but that no substantive peace negotiations were immediately contemplated. This announcement prompted violent protests by university students (who are almost exclusively Tutsi), and were denounced by the UPRONA leadership, although some sections of the party expressed cautious support for a peace initiative.

REFUGEE AND AID CONCERNS

The cross-border movement of vast numbers of refugees, provoked by regional ethnic and political violence, has dominated recent relations with Rwanda, Tanzania and the DRC, and has long been a matter of considerable concern to the international aid community. In October and November 1993, following an abortive coup by factions of the Tutsi-dominated armed forces (see above), ethnic violence erupted on a massive scale throughout the country, claiming an estimated 50,000 lives and leaving an estimated 800,000 displaced persons, including 500,000 who had fled into neighbouring Tanzania, Rwanda and the DRC. Limited relief resources were overburdened in April 1994 by the exodus of thousands of Rwandans, and by the repatriation of most Burundian refugees from camps in Rwanda, as a result of the political violence and accompanying massacres perpetrated by the presidential guard and Hutu militias, following the death of President Habyarimana. In mid-July 1995 the UN High Commissioner for Refugees (UNHCR) estimated that some 50,000 Rwandan refugees had been repatriated since the beginning of the year. Estimates compiled by the UN in June 1997 suggest that over 600,000 Burundians, more than 10% of the population, are internally displaced, including at least 275,00 who have been 'regrouped'. The number of external refugees has fallen considerably since 1994. Only 40,000 are thought to be left in the Democratic Republic of the Congo, where they are in a terrible condition and allegedly subject to constant harrassment and attack from the AFDL. There are only 7,000 refugees in Rwanda, as most were repatriated shortly after the July 1996 coup. However, there are 275,000 refugees in Tanzania. The UNHCR is no longer advocating the repatriation of refugees to Burundi, in view of the unstable internal security situation, and the persistent allegations of attacks on returnees by the Burundian army.

Economy

FRANÇOIS MISSER

In terms of average income, Burundi is one of the poorest countries in the world, and its economic performance is heavily dependent on international prices for coffee. In 1995, according to estimates by the World Bank, Burundi's gross national product (GNP), measured at average 1993–95 prices, was US $984m., equivalent to $160 per head. During 1985–95, in the context of a high rate of population growth (3.0% annually), GNP per head decreased, in real terms, at an average annual rate of 1.3%. However, overall GNP declined dramatically in 1993 owing to a decline in world coffee prices and the civil disturbances arising from the assassination of President Melchior Ndadaye. The recovery of coffee markets in 1994, however, failed to reverse the economy's downward trend, and a decline in all sectors contributed to a 16.7% reduction in per-capita GNP. Overall gross domestic product (GDP) increased, in real terms, at an average rate of 7.1% per year during 1965–80, and by an annual average of 3.2% in 1987–92. Real GDP rose by 3.5% in 1990, 5.0% in 1991 and 2.3% in 1992, but decreased by an estimated 5.7% in 1993, 6.6% in 1994 and 3.7% in 1995. According to Burundian government estimates, by February 1996 more than 60% of the population were living in conditions of extreme poverty, compared with 30% before October 1993. Other social indicators such as primary school enrolment have also deteriorated during this period and the rate of childhood malnutrition has doubled, to 12%, since 1993. The annual rate of inflation averaged 6.8% in 1985–93. The rate averaged 9.0% in 1991, declined to 4.5% in 1992, and increased again to 9.7% in 1993, 14.7% in 1994 and 19.0% in 1995. Burundi is among the 30 African states designated by the fourth Lomé Convention as least developed and therefore qualifying for special treatment under that Convention's scheme to stabilize export earnings (Stabex) for products sold to the European Union (EU). At mid-1996 Burundi had a population density of 218.8 persons per sq km, the second highest in mainland Africa. Before 1993 efforts were being made to move people from the over-populated hilly areas to the Ruzizi valley. Burundi's population density has been subject to significant fluctuation since mid-1993 as a result of the cross-border movement of vast numbers of refugees. Large numbers of Burundians have also been relocated under government plans aimed at removing them from areas of conflict. In April 1997, UN officials reported that this large scale movement, combined with the shortage of food aid has led to widespread childhood malnutrition in the regroupment camps. This in turn provoked more cross-border movement as did the attacks by Congolese and Rwandan troops in October 1996.

AGRICULTURE AND TRADE

At mid-1994 an estimated 91% of the labour force were engaged in agriculture (including forestry and fishing), mainly at subsistence level, and the sector provided about 56% of GDP in 1995. During 1985–94 agricultural production declined, in real terms, by an annual average of 0.8%. Burundi's dominant cash crop and economic mainstay is coffee. However, the overwhelming dependence on coffee, which provided 81% of total export earnings in 1995, has had an adverse effect on the balance of payments in times of declining world coffee prices. The Stabex scheme, introduced in 1975 under the first Lomé Convention and retained in the three subsequent Conventions, has helped to ease this difficulty. Additionally, in the early 1990s the government acted to attract private-sector investment in the coffee industry. The state monopoly on coffee exports was relaxed, and a restructuring of the two factories that process Burundi's entire coffee crop was undertaken. Although exports of coffee were valued at a record 17,057m. Burundian francs in 1986, the pattern of earnings from this source has been erratic, declining to 7,891m. francs in 1987 before recovering to 16,010m. francs in 1988. Revenue from coffee exports declined to 9,502m. francs in 1989 and totalled 9,567m. francs in 1990, reflecting downward trends in world coffee prices. In 1991, however, the value of exports of coffee improved to 13,482m. francs, a figure which represented US $73m., according to World Bank statistics. But in 1992, coffee exports amounted to just $51m., owing to a 35% decrease in coffee prices on the world market. In 1993 continuing depression in world coffee prices and a reduction in the volume of production as a result of civil unrest contributed to a further decline, to just $47m., in the value of coffee exports. A spectacular recovery in world prices prompted a significant rise in the value of exports in 1994, with revenues exceeding $100m. The value of coffee exports remained encouraging, at $94m., in 1995, although it fell to $41m. in 1996.

Despite civil and political disturbances during 1993 and 1994, the mid-year crop amounted to 29,526 metric tons (a 42% increase in production compared to the previous mid-year crop), owing to favourable climatic conditions. From mid-1994, however, the military operations of extremist guerrilla groups, based principally in Zaire (now the Democratic Republic of the Congo, DRC), and the armed response to such incursions, by the Burundian army, created a climate of extreme insecurity which was reflected in a 13.1% decrease in the mid-year crop for 1995 (24,773 metric tons). The mid-1996 crop also decreased, to 22,600 metric tons, due to the destruction of eight washing stations and the increased insecurity. According to the central bank, just over half this total could be exported before the embargo came into force. A small increase in output is expected in 1997, and despite the embargo, Burundi managed to export the remainder of the 1996 crop by air, with the assistance of private airlines. The Burundian government considers the embargo (which does not have UN endorsement) illegal and is considering taking legal action. Following a report from the international medical relief charity, Médecins sans frontières, in January 1997 that 50% of Burundian child mortality is caused by malnutrition, some restrictions on medicine and food aid were lifted in April.

Burundi's total export earnings amounted to US $116m. in 1995 and $124m. in 1994 (owing to improved world coffee prices), compared with $75m. per year in 1993 and 1992. Estimates for 1996 show a significant drop to $50–55m. Meanwhile, the cost of imports declined from $236m. in 1990 to $205m. in 1993, only to increase again, to $239m. in 1994 and $246m. in 1995. The principal imports are refined petroleum products (including gasoline and gas oils), general industrial machinery, road vehicles, basic metal manufactures, cereals and cereal preparations (especially malt) and cement. While imports have greatly decreased as a result of the embargo imposed by neighbouring countries, it has not been entirely effective, as products are still being smuggled in from Tanzania and Rwanda. The EU countries (in particular Belgium-Luxembourg, France and Germany), together with the USA, Switzerland, Kenya and Japan, are Burundi's main trading partners.

The credibility of a free export zone, established in 1992, was seriously undermined in August 1993, when the new administration withdrew the financial advantages being offered to a Belgian gold dealer and refiner under the scheme, having calculated that the company's use of the zone was depriving the state of US $12m. per year in taxes. In 1994, however, these advantages were once again extended to the company. An estimated 9.6 metric tons of gold were exported from Burundi in 1994. Almost 80% of this total was believed to have originated in Zaire, with the remainder proceeding from Tanzania and Uganda, and only an insignificant share mined locally. (In 1994 the Zairean minister of mines commented on the re-exportation through Burundi of some 10 metric tons of gold smuggled from Zaire.) Import statistics from the Belgian office of foreign trade suggest that in 1992 Burundi exported precious stones and metals worth 1,100m. Belgian francs to Belgium. In 1993 the value of these exports increased to 1,500m. Belgian francs but declined to 784m. Belgian francs (around US $23m.) in 1994. However, despite official claims that such transactions involve 'goods in transit', the failure of official export statistics in Burundi to reflect the importance of the trade in gold has prompted concern as to the accuracy of official export figures in general. As a result of the embargo, the trade in gold has fallen considerably since the end of July 1996. This prompted the Belgian gold dealer to look at other locations for a gold refining plant, in Rwanda or the DRC.

Officially, tea is now Burundi's second most important export commodity, and had steadily increased its share of export earnings until the recovery of world coffee prices in late 1993. Exports of tea accounted for 14.6% of total export earnings in 1993, compared with 5.3% in 1985. In 1994 and 1995, however, export revenues from tea represented 7.2% and 7.7% of total exports, respectively. Exports of tea fell again in 1996, amounting to 4,668m. Burundian francs. During the early 1990s five tea plantations were undergoing development and expansion, with financial assistance from the Caisse française de développement and the European Development Fund (EDF). The 1994 crop of 6,862 metric tons represented a 24.3% increase over output of 5,520 metric tons for 1993. A further 1.7% increase in production (to 6,982 metric tons) was recorded in 1995. However, in 1996 production fell to 5,716 metric tons due to the destruction of the Teza tea factory.

In 1987 cotton became a significant export, accounting for 5.7% of total export receipts. Production has subsequently declined sharply, following heavy rains which destroyed some 600 ha of plantations. In 1993 revenue from cotton exports accounted for just 4% of total export earnings and in 1994 production declined to 4,915 metric tons, almost half of that for 1993. Production continued to decline in 1995, to 4,593 metric tons, and this trend continued in 1996, with a decline to 2,065 metric tons owing to worker migration as a result of violent confrontation between the armed forces and guerrilla troops on the Imbo plain. Mainly grown in the plain of Ruzizi, the cotton crop is nearly all sold to Belgium.

Burundi has obtained foreign assistance for the development of other crops. On the Imbo plain, land is being reclaimed for the cultivation of cotton and rice in an integrated rural development scheme which is assisted by the UN Development Programme and the FAO. However, rice development projects have also been interrupted by fighting in the region and many fields have been abandoned, road maintenance has deteriorated and pumping stations have been sabotaged. The extent of the security crisis has also inclined the majority of aid workers from bilateral and multilateral agencies to leave the country or to remain in the capital. Until recently, irrigated rice cultivation was also being encouraged in the Mosso region. Plans to establish an integrated sugar scheme in the south-east of this region, with finance provided mainly by the African Development Bank, the OPEC Fund and the Arab Bank for Economic Development in Africa (BADEA), are proceeding. Plantations of sugar cane have been established on the Mosso plain, near Bujumbura, in association with a refinery, which was projected to satisfy 90% of Burundi's demand for sugar by the early 1990s, with further potential for exports. However, both civil unrest and the inadequate size of the cultivated areas have prevented Burundi from becoming self-sufficient in cane. Cassava, sweet potatoes, bananas, pulses, maize and sorghum are other important, but mainly subsistence, crops.

Although potentially self-sufficient in food production, recent civil disturbances have tended to disrupt the country's infrastructure and have prevented supplies from reaching urban centres. In September 1994 there was an estimated food deficit of 200,000 metric tons.

The development of livestock is hindered by the social system, which encourages the maintenance of cattle herds that are both too large and too little exploited. However, the sale of hides has increased, and in the early 1990s was among the most valuable source of export earnings (641m. Burundian francs in 1994). However, as with other sub-sectors, livestock-rearing has been adversely affected by civil unrest, and in 1995 and early 1996 cattle rustlers removed entire herds (some cattle have been used by rebel groups to explode mines around army barracks). Some fishing is practised in the waters of Lake Tanganyika, but this activity was banned by the government in April 1996 following reports that the lake was being used as a transit point by extremist insurgents from Zaire and Tanzania.

MINERALS

Small quantities of bastnaesite and cassiterite have been exploited by the Karongo Mining Co (SOMIKA). In 1995 the government was considering extending the financial advantages of the free-trade zone to a private company seeking to export cassiterite. Tungsten and columbo-tantalite are mined in small quantities. A small amount of alluvial gold is also produced but production could increase significantly if negotiations to exploit the Muyinga reserves, initiated in 1994 between the Canadian corporation, AMTEC, and the government-owned Burundi Mining Corpn (BUMINCO), are successful. Important deposits of vanadium (estimated at some 14m. metric tons) and uranium are being surveyed. Petroleum has been detected beneath Lake Tanganyika and in the Ruzizi valley, for which test drillings were carried out in the late 1980s by US petroleum interests, in association with the Burundian government. In 1973 a UN survey discovered large nickel deposits, then estimated at 5% of world reserves, near Musongati. Subsequent surveys estimated Burundi's nickel deposits to be about 300m. metric tons. A three-year exploration agreement for the southern part of the area was signed in 1993 with a subsidiary of the British company, Rio Tinto-Zinc, whereas the Australian BHP corporation has demonstrated interest in a similar project for the northern area of Musongati. Should the reserves eventually prove to have commercial potential, the processing of this ore could include the recovery of copper, cobalt and platinum-group metals, as well as nickel. An evaluation of the economic feasibility of exploiting identified deposits of phosphate rock in the Matongo region was under way in 1991. (With estimated reserves of 15m. metric tons, Burundi has the potential to fulfil the demands of the domestic market for inputs.) Sufficient reserves of carbonatite (7.3m. metric tons) to satisfy the domestic demand for cement have also been identified, near Gatara; Burundi is currently 100% dependent on imports of cement. However, the continuing deterioration of the security situation in 1995 and 1996 has deterred foreign companies from bringing these projects to fruition.

INDUSTRY AND TRANSPORT

There is little industrial activity in Burundi, apart from the processing of agricultural products, e.g. cotton, coffee, tea and vegetable oil extraction, and small-scale wood mills. Industry, comprising mining, manufacturing, construction and utilities, provided an estimated 17.9% of GDP in 1995. The manufacturing sector accounted for some 12% of GDP in 1994 and 6% of exports in 1995. During 1980–93 industrial GDP increased by an annual average of 3.0%. However, the sector's GDP decreased by 9.9% in 1994 and by 8.2% in 1995, as a result of civil unrest. Problems with the electricity supply, due to sabotage, and a lack of imported raw materials owing to the economic embargo continued to depress Burundi's GDP in 1996. Only 2.3% of the working population were employed in industrial activities in 1979, and this ratio had not increased by 1992. The Five-Year Plans for 1978–82 and 1983–87 aimed to revitalize the stagnant economy by increasing and diversifying production, both for export and for import-substitution, and by encouraging businesses in unfavourable areas. By the mid-1980s several small enterprises, including cement, footwear, insecticide factories, a flour mill and a brewery, had been established. (The Brarudi brewery, 60%-owned by Heineken and 40%-owned by the government of Burundi was reported to have provided almost 40% of total government tax receipts in 1996.) A textile industry was also developed, with aid from the People's Republic of China, which exported fabrics to the neighbouring states of Rwanda and Zaire until the end of 1995 when, as with most industry in Bujumbura, this textile plant was closed temporarily after the sabotage of electricity pylons which left the capital without electric power for several weeks. However, the government demonstrated its determination to keep the sector operational and the installations were repaired and placed in the custody of the army. In January 1996, as a safeguard against similar inconveniences in the future, the government purchased a US $3.5m. thermic power station (comprising four generators with a total capacity of 5.2 MW) from an Anglo-Belgian company.

During 1994, within the framework of the Preferential Trade Area for Eastern and Southern African States, Burundi and Zimbabwe initiated a series of trade negotiations at which Burundi hoped to secure greater access to the textile market in Zimbabwe in exchange for a commitment from the Burundian government to purchase 50% of its malt requirements from Zimbabwe. (Almost all of the malt used in breweries in Burundi is currently imported from Europe.) Meanwhile a Franco-Belgian textile concern has expressed interest in purchasing cotton fabrics produced by the state textile company, COTEBU, and the export of banana powder to Germany for use in the production of ice-creams and fruit juices is also under negotiation.

The International Development Association (IDA) is helping to finance a long-term programme to develop basic forestry services, and to promote tree-planting to supply wood for fuel, building-poles and timber. The project will benefit an estimated 60,000 rural families. The Irish Peat Development Authority has been assisting Burundi to exploit peat bogs as an alternative fuel source. An estimated 12,000 metric tons of peat were extracted in 1992.

Industrial development is hampered by Burundi's distance from the sea (about 1,400 km to Dar es Salaam and 2,000 km to Mombasa), which means that only manufactures capable of absorbing the high costs of transport can be developed.

The network of roads is dense, but few of the 6,300 km of routes are made up with asphalt, and these are the roads that connect Bujumbura with Gitega, Kayanza and Nyanza-Lac. In February 1992 the government revealed that 600 km of roads had been rehabilitated during the previous three years, and announced a four-year programme of future road improvements covering a further 1,000 km. A new crossing of the Ruzizi river, the Bridge of Concord (Burundi's longest bridge), was inaugurated in early 1992. However, recent improvements to Tanzania's road network, the reopening in July 1994 of the Rwanda-Uganda border (facilitating road access to Mombasa) and competition between Burundian private road transport concerns and Tanzanian railways for the movement of goods from Burundi, have all contributed to a reduction in transportation costs.

Lake Tanganyika (about 8% of which is the sovereign responsibility of Burundi) is a crucial component in Burundi's transport system, since most of the country's external trade is conducted along the lake between Bujumbura and Tanzania and the DRC. This trade has become more difficult in 1996 due to the embargo and also to guerrilla attacks on shipping. Plans to construct a railway linking Burundi with Uganda, Rwanda and Tanzania were announced in 1987. The proposed line would connect with the Kigoma–Dar es Salaam line in Tanzania, substantially improving Burundi's isolated trade position. However, the civil unrest in Burundi has since caused these plans to be postponed. There is an international airport at Bujumbura.

FOREIGN AID AND DEVELOPMENT PLANNING

Burundi is severely dependent on foreign assistance, not only for capital projects but also for budgetary support. Before early 1996 the main bilateral donors of aid and technical assistance were Belgium, France, Japan and Germany. The multilateral agencies, such as the IDA and the EDF, have been involved in schemes to increase Burundi's production of coffee, and BADEA has also been a substantial source of development loans. Burundi has also been a considerable beneficiary of aid from the European Union (EU) through the Lomé Conventions. The main focus of EU development aid has been the rural sector, while Stabex transfers have been of pivotal importance to the coffee, tea and cotton industries. Under the current Lomé agreement, the EDF has allocated ECU 126m. for projects in Burundi during the period 1990–95, of which ECU 112m. is in grants and the balance in venture capital. However, the lack of regional security has prompted many donors (who have already withdrawn aid workers to the capital and even to their own countries) to 'freeze' disbursements and to stall projects. A meeting between Prime Minister Nduwayo, EU officials and the Belgian prime minister, Jean-Luc Dehaene, in Brussels in February 1996, has so far proved fruitless. Although European and Belgian officials were sympathetic to Burundi's plight, their commitments were restricted to further consideration of new initiatives to assist Burundi's economic survival in the event of an improved security situation.

In 1977 Burundi, Rwanda and Tanzania established the Organization for the Management and Development of the Kagera River Basin, which was formed to continue projects started in 1971 to develop irrigation, electric power, navigation and mining in the basin. The Kagera river basin project, combined with a hydroelectric power station already completed at Mugere and another, of 18 MW, at Rwegura, which was inaugurated in 1986 and was expected to provide about one-third of Burundi's electricity requirements, will eventually free Burundi from dependence on electricity from outside sources, mainly the DRC. Eventual self-sufficiency in power should also promote mineral production.

In 1976 Burundi, Rwanda and Zaire established the Economic Community of the Great Lakes Countries (CEPGL). The energy directorate of CEPGL was established in Bujumbura in 1981, and a large joint hydroelectric scheme to benefit the three member-countries (the Ruzizi II project) was commissioned in 1987. Confronted by continued export shortfalls, however, the government has been forced to restrict infrastructural investment, raising the question of whether Burundi can make a significant contribution to regional integration schemes. Burundi became a full member of the Preferential Trade Area for Eastern and Southern African States (PTA) in 1985, and provides the headquarters for the organization's trade and development bank. (In 1993 the PTA was superseded by the Common Market for Eastern and Southern Africa—COMESA.)

In November 1983 the Burundian franc, whose exchange rate had hitherto been fixed in relation to the US dollar, was effectively devalued by 23% when it was linked instead to the IMF's special drawing right (SDR). Burundi is currently one of the largest recipients per caput of low-interest loans from the World Bank, and, to satisfy criteria imposed by the Bank, the first of a series of devaluations of the Burundian franc took place in July 1986, when the currency was devalued by 15% as part of a structural adjustment programme (SAP) which was agreed with the IMF and the World Bank as a counter to Burundi's over-reliance on coffee export earnings, and to address the decline in economic growth and the rapid increase in external indebtedness. This programme, which operated during 1986–89, sought to encourage diversification from coffee production, to improve the rate of economic growth, to reduce domestic inflation, to strengthen the balance of payments and to increase Burundi's reserves of foreign exchange. In February 1988 the Burundian franc was devalued by 9%, the first stage in a phased devaluation of 35%. In August the exchange rate was stabilized at SDR 1 = 201 Burundian francs. This remained in force until December 1989, when a rate of SDR 1 = 232.14 Burundian francs was established. By 1990, however, few of the programme's specific objectives had been achieved. Burundi remained dependent upon foreign resources to finance its external account deficits, no significant diversification of its productive base had taken place, and coffee remained the dominant export commodity. In August 1991 the Burundian franc was devalued by about 15%, and in November the World Bank agreed to extend the SAP arrangements. The currency's direct link with the SDR ended in May 1992, since when the value of the Burundian franc has been determined in relation to a 'basket' of the currencies of the country's principal trading partners. An open general licensing system (OGL) was also introduced in May 1992 to liberalize current account transactions, a measure designed to facilitate imports, stimulate diversification of exports and to promote non-traditional exports. An export-processing zone was established in 1993 but operations are currently suspended (except for the processing of gold) owing to political and civil instability. In 1993 the Burundian government declared its aim to achieve economic growth averaging at least 4% annually during 1991–94 and to reduce the average annual rate of inflation to 4% over the same period.

During 1992, according to IMF estimates, Burundi's GDP rose by about 2.3%, and the annual rate of inflation fell to 4.5% from 9% in 1991. In 1993, however, the rate increased again, to 9.7%, whereas GDP decreased by 12.9%. Consumer prices increased by 14.9% in 1994 and by 19.2% in 1995, reflecting food shortages and a rapid expansion in money supply, whereas real GDP declined by an estimated 3.7% in 1995. In 1993 the budgetary deficit was estimated to be equivalent to 13.4% of GDP, compared with 14% of GDP in 1992 and 9% of GDP in 1991, largely owing to increased defence spending. The overall fiscal deficit for 1994 and for 1995 was equivalent to 7% of GDP, a percentage lower than had been predicted, largely owing to the government's appropriation of the surplus of the Coffee Stabilization Fund. World Bank forecasts of economic growth for 1993 and the following years were expected to be undermined by increased ethnic and political instability in late 1993 and early 1994, and by the financial burden of repatriating and accommodating hundreds of thousands of refugees and displaced persons, in the aftermath of tribal violence arising from the failed coup of October 1993. In such a climate, it seemed unlikely that the successful implementation of plans to privatize one-half of all public enterprises and establish private management contracts for the remainder, by the end of 1995, would be achieved. (By mid-1992 some 24 of Burundi's 84 state-operated companies had been transferred to private ownership.) Foreign debt remains a major cause of economic concern. Burundi's external debt at the end of 1995 was $1,157m., of which $1,095m. was long-term public debt, although both France and Belgium cancelled repayment obligations amounting to some 13% of Burundi's total debt in 1991. By the end of 1995, three-quarters of Burundi's outstanding debt was owed to multilateral organizations, and was not reschedulable. In 1994 the cost of debt-servicing was equivalent to 25.2% of revenue from exports of goods and services.

Burundi's structural adjustment programme (SAP) was interrupted by political and civil instability and was terminated in June 1995. Despite the introduction of adjustments including a new labour code, a new banking law and central bank statutes, the promotion of exports, a duty drawback scheme and transport subsidies for exports, the government failed to reduce the role of the state in the economy and to redirect public resources to support development or improve the efficiency, transparency and accountability of public sector management. Military expenditure and subsidies for inefficient parastatals remained high and, in the view of the Bretton Woods institutions, adequate state divestment was not achieved.

Major economic reconstruction is needed. In late 1994 it was reported that production of food staples had declined by 20%, the financial sector was in crisis with unpaid debts amounting to 514m. Burundian francs, and rehabilitation of the education infrastructure was expected to cost some 550m. Burundian francs. While assistance from the international donor community resumed in mid-1995 with a US $21.3m. loan from the IDA for the reconstruction of the health infrastructure, in September 1994 a meeting of potential donors, conducted in Paris under the auspices of the World Bank, had insisted that national reconciliation and the respect of human rights and democracy would be preconditions to the resumption of a comprehensive programme of financial assistance for Burundi. The World Bank has identified a number of key areas with potential for economic growth, given a swift resolution of the security crisis. These include improvements in productivity of traditional crops, the introduction of new export crops (flowers, fruits, vegetables, medicines and ornamental plants), artisanal mining (cassiterite, gold, columbo-tantalite), light manufacturing, industrial mining and the services sector. However, political and civil instability continued to deteriorate during 1995. Development projects outside of the capital became increasingly difficult to implement and foreign financial assistance dwindled while public investment declined by more than 50%.

Statistical Survey

Area and Population

AREA, POPULATION AND DENSITY

Area (sq km)	27,834*
Population (census results)†	
15–16 August 1979	4,028,420
16–30 August 1990	
Males	2,473,599
Females	2,665,474
Total	5,139,073
Population (official estimates at mid-year)	
1994	5,870,000
1995	5,980,000
1996	6,090,000
Density (per sq km) at mid-1996	218.8

* 10,747 sq miles.
† Excluding adjustment for underenumeration.

PRINCIPAL TOWNS

Bujumbura (capital), population 235,440 (census result, August 1990); Gitega 15,943 (1978).

Source: Banque de la République du Burundi.

BIRTHS AND DEATHS (UN estimates, annual averages)

	1980–85	1985–90	1990–95
Birth rate (per 1,000)	46.1	46.6	46.0
Death rate (per 1,000)	17.6	16.7	15.7

Expectation of life (UN estimates, years at birth, 1990–95): 50.2 (males 48.4; females 51.9).

Source: UN, *World Population Prospects: The 1994 Revision.*

ECONOMICALLY ACTIVE POPULATION
(persons aged 10 years and over, 1990 census)

	Males	Females	Total
Agriculture, hunting, forestry and fishing	1,153,890	1,420,553	2,574,443
Mining and quarrying	1,146	39	1,185
Manufacturing	24,120	9,747	33,867
Electricity, gas and water	1,847	74	1,921
Construction	19,447	290	19,737
Trade, restaurants and hotels	19,667	6,155	25,822
Transport, storage and communications	8,193	311	8,504
Financing, insurance, real estate and business services	1,387	618	2,005
Community, social and personal services	68,905	16,286	85,191
Activities not adequately defined	8,653	4,617	13,270
Total labour force	1,307,255	1,458,690	2,765,945

Source: UN, *Demographic Yearbook.*

Agriculture

PRINCIPAL CROPS ('000 metric tons)

	1993	1994	1995
Wheat	9*	8*	9*
Maize	172*	123*	153*
Millet	13*	11*	14*
Sorghum	66*	45*	66*
Rice	39*	38*	27*
Potatoes	45*	32*	42*
Sweet potatoes	680*	601*	674*
Cassava (Manioc)	584*	527*	501*
Yams	8*	8*	8*
Taro (Coco yam)	132*	94*	102*
Dry beans	337*	232*	319*
Dry peas	37*	24*	37*
Palm kernels†	1.5	1.3	1.4
Groundnuts (in shell)	14†	10†	13*
Cottonseed	5*	3*	3†
Cotton (lint)	4	2	2*
Sugar cane	146	121	138†
Coffee (green)	23	41	26*
Tea (made)	6	7	7†
Tobacco (leaves)†	4	2	3†
Bananas and plantains	1,585*	1,487*	1,421*

* Unofficial figure. † FAO estimate(s).

Source: FAO, *Production Yearbook.*

LIVESTOCK (FAO estimates, '000 head, year ending September)

	1993	1994	1995
Cattle	442	420	420
Sheep	370	350	350
Goats	950	920	920
Pigs	87	80	80

Poultry (FAO estimates, million): 4 in 1993; 4 in 1994; 4 in 1995.

Source: FAO, *Production Yearbook.*

LIVESTOCK PRODUCTS (FAO estimates, '000 metric tons)

	1993	1994	1995
Beef and veal	12	10	10
Mutton and lamb	1	1	1
Goat meat	3	3	3
Pig meat	5	5	5
Cows' milk	34	32	32
Goats' milk	8	7	7
Poultry eggs	3.2	2.9	2.9

Source: FAO, *Production Yearbook.*

Forestry

ROUNDWOOD REMOVALS ('000 cubic metres)

	1992	1993	1994
Sawlogs, veneer logs and logs for sleepers	6*	46	45
Other industrial wood*	47	51	62
Fuel wood*	4,448	4,588	4,724
Total	4,501	4,685	4,831

* FAO estimate(s).

Source: FAO, *Yearbook of Forest Products.*

Fishing

('000 metric tons, live weight)

	1992	1993	1994
Dagaas	19.0	18.4	19.2
Freshwater perches	2.9	2.5	2.7
Others	1.2	1.2	1.2
Total catch	23.0	22.0	23.1

Source: FAO, *Yearbook of Fishery Statistics*.

Mining

	1992	1993	1994
Gold (kilograms)*†	32	20	20
Tin ore (metric tons)*†	110	50	50
Kaolin ('000 metric tons)*	10	5†	5†
Peat ('000 metric tons)	12	11	n.a.

* Data from US Bureau of Mines.

† Estimate(s).

Source: UN, *Industrial Commodity Statistics Yearbook*.

Industry

SELECTED PRODUCTS ('000 metric tons, unless otherwise indicated)

	1992	1993	1994*
Beer ('000 hectolitres)	1,161.6	1,188.6	1,382.7
Soft drinks ('000 hectolitres)	159.9	179.3	201.4
Cottonseed oil ('000 hectolitres)	3.4	3.3	2.8
Sugar	17.3	13.9	12.3
Cigarettes (million)†	453	517	n.a.
Paint	1.0	0.8	0.6
Insecticides	2.0	2.7	3.9
Soap	3.0	5.2	5.7
Bottles	5.3	3.5	5.1
Blankets (units)	196.2	242.7	248.4
Footwear ('000 pairs)	450.6	405.2	74.9
Fibro-cement products	0.3	1.9	0.8
Corrugated metal sheets	1.9	1.2	0.6
Steel rods	0.2	0.4	0.3
Batteries ('000 cartons)‡	36.2	35.0	28.9
Electric energy (million kWh)†	107	140*	149

* Estimate(s)

† Source: UN, *Industrial Commodity Statistics Yearbook*.

‡ Cartons of 240 batteries.

Source: Banque de la République du Burundi.

Finance

CURRENCY AND EXCHANGE RATES

Monetary Units

100 centimes = 1 Burundian franc.

Sterling and Dollar Equivalents (31 March 1997)

£1 sterling = 556.9 francs;
US $1 = 339.2 francs;
1,000 Burundian francs = £1.796 = $2.948.

Average Exchange Rate (Burundian francs per US dollar)

1994	252.66
1995	249.76
1996	302.75

Note: In November 1983 the Burundian franc was linked to the IMF's special drawing right (SDR), with the mid-point exchange rate initially fixed at SDR 1 = 122.7 francs. This remained in force until July 1986, after which the rate was frequently adjusted. A rate of SDR 1 = 232.14 francs was established in December 1989. This was in operation until August 1991, when the currency was devalued by about 15%, with the new rate set at SDR 1 = 273.07 francs. This arrangement ended in May 1992, when the Burundian franc was linked to a 'basket' of the currencies of the country's principal trading partners.

BUDGET ('000 million Burundian francs)

Revenue*	1993	1994†	1995†
Tax revenue	34.0	38.9	47.2
Income tax	10.6	8.4	9.6
Transaction tax	6.8	6.7	7.3
Excise tax	6.3	10.7	11.3
Import duties	7.7	6.9	7.9
Export tax	0.4	5.4	10.4
Coffee	0.3	5.3	10.2
Other foreign trade tax	0.1	0.1	0.2
Other tax revenue	1.7	0.1	0.1
Non-tax revenue	5.8	3.3	2.7
Total	39.8	42.2	49.9

Expenditure and net lending	1993	1994†	1995†
Current expenditure	39.1	41.9	45.2
Salaries	16.3	17.4	19.0
Military	5.1	5.9	6.4
Goods and services	8.4	10.4	12.7
Military	4.1	4.2	4.1
Transfers and subsidies	5.2	5.8	6.7
Public administrations	3.9	4.3	4.4
International organizations	0.3	0.2	0.3
Households	1.0	1.3	2.0
Interest payments	3.7	3.6	4.4
Foreign	2.9	2.9	3.6
Domestic	0.8	0.7	0.8
Extrabudgetary/exceptional expenditure	5.6	4.7	2.4
Capital expenditure	29.9	19.8	24.7
Domestic resources	5.6	4.1	7.0
Project lending	11.4	11.1	11.7
Capital grants	12.8	4.6	6.0
Net lending	0.4	−2.1	−0.9
Total	69.4	59.5	69.1

* Excluding grants received ('000 million Burundian francs): 20.7 in 1993; 5.7 in 1994; 9.7 in 1995.

† Estimates.

Source: IMF, *Burundi—Statistical Annex* (May 1996).

CENTRAL BANK RESERVES (US $ million at 31 December)

	1994	1995	1996
Gold*	6.59	6.66	6.36
IMF special drawing rights	0.21	0.07	0.11
Reserve position in IMF	8.56	8.71	8.43
Foreign exchange	195.94	200.67	131.06
Total	211.30	216.11	145.96

* Valued at market-related prices.

Source: IMF, *International Financial Statistics*.

MONEY SUPPLY (million Burundian francs at 31 December)

	1994	1995	1996
Currency outside banks	19,075	n.a.	n.a.
Non-financial public enterprise deposits	649	577	371
Demand deposits at commercial banks	19,095	18,730	18,088
Demand deposits at other monetary institutions	1,329	n.a.	n.a.
Total money	40,147	n.a.	n.a.

Source: IMF, *International Financial Statistics.*

COST OF LIVING
(Consumer Price Index for Bujumbura; base: January 1991 = 100)

	1993	1994	1995
Food	113.5	133.7	159.8
Clothing	135.3	136.0	155.6
Housing, heating and light	105.1	119.2	145.6
Transport	100.5	101.4	102.0
All items (incl. others)	111.7	128.2	152.0

Source: IMF, *Burundi—Statistical Annex* (May 1996).

NATIONAL ACCOUNTS (million Burundian francs at current prices)
Composition of the Gross National Product

	1993	1994	1995
GDP in purchasers' values	261,952	286,548	308,314
Net factor income from abroad	−2,674	−3,291	−4,619
Gross national product	259,278	283,257	303,695

Expenditure on the Gross Domestic Product

	1994	1995	1996
Government final consumption expenditure	45,680	54,553	47,302
Private final consumption expenditure	243,328	262,134	268,043
Increase in stocks	53	−199	−481
Gross fixed capital formation	27,985	28,406	27,942
Total domestic expenditure	322,057	344,894	342,806
Exports of goods and services	35,314	28,725	13,914
Less Imports of goods and services	65,813	63,666	46,248
GDP in purchasers' values	286,548	309,953	310,472

Source: IMF, *International Financial Statistics.*

Gross Domestic Product by Economic Activity*

	1993	1994	1995
Agriculture, hunting, forestry and fishing	111,027	116,156	126,664
Mining and quarrying Electricity, gas and water }	1,532	1,374	1,296
Manufacturing	18,346	19,858	19,756
Construction	10,041	10,303	11,436
Trade, restaurants and hotels	9,362	10,368	8,709
Transport, storage and communications	7,709	9,963	8,892
Government services	33,826	37,025	37,866
Other services	4,295	5,529	4,648
GDP at factor cost	196,138	210,575	219,268
Indirect taxes, *less* subsidies	23,235	26,495	37,623
GDP in purchasers' values	219,373	237,070	256,891

* Figures are estimates, and exclude the GDP of the artisan branch (million francs): 8,855 in 1993; 8,291 in 1994; 8,099 in 1995.

Source: IMF, *Burundi—Statistical Annex* (May 1996).

BALANCE OF PAYMENTS (US $ million)

	1993	1994	1995
Exports of goods f.o.b.	73.9	80.7	112.5
Imports of goods f.o.b.	−172.8	−172.6	−175.6
Trade balance	−99.0	−91.9	−63.1
Exports of services	14.2	14.6	16.6
Imports of services	−115.5	−95.0	−101.8
Balance on goods and services	−200.2	−172.3	−148.3
Other income received	11.2	8.1	10.4
Other income paid	−22.2	−19.5	−19.7
Balance on goods, services and income	−211.2	−183.7	−157.6
Current transfers received	183.8	167.0	153.3
Current transfers paid	−1.8	−1.6	−2.1
Current balance	−29.2	−18.3	−6.5
Capital account (net)	−1.2	−0.2	−0.8
Direct investment abroad	−0.1	−0.1	−0.6
Direct investment from abroad	0.5	—	2.0
Other investment assets	−1.5	−1.6	7.3
Other investment liabilities	53.6	32.9	18.3
Net errors and omissions	−6.1	23.0	16.1
Overall balance	16.0	35.7	35.8

Source: IMF, *International Financial Statistics.*

External Trade

PRINCIPAL COMMODITIES (distribution by SITC, US $ '000)

Imports c.i.f.	1991	1992	1993
Food and live animals	22,675	19,706	20,312
Cereals and cereal preparations	14,424	12,520	13,341
Cereal preparations, etc.	6,447	7,116	7,480
Malt (including malt flour)	6,290	6,962	7,365
Crude materials (inedible) except fuels	8,081	4,915	5,478
Mineral fuels, lubricants, etc.	31,183	27,992	25,387
Petroleum and petroleum products	31,044	27,888	25,346
Petroleum products, refined	29,603	27,248	24,538
Motor spirit (gasoline) and other light oils	12,511	10,570	8,630
Gas oils	9,893	8,966	7,993
Chemicals and related products	33,890	32,475	28,807
Medicinal and pharmaceutical products	10,289	11,554	8,523
Fertilizers, manufactured	3,228	4,865	4,562
Plastic materials, etc.	4,774	4,721	5,401
Basic manufactures	52,433	48,948	42,868
Rubber manufactures	6,641	5,383	7,077
Rubber tyres, tubes, etc.	5,334	4,059	5,215
Paper, paperboard and manufactures	6,062	5,777	5,556
Non-metallic mineral manufactures	13,512	12,898	9,445
Lime, cement, building products	11,093	10,896	7,145
Cement	10,481	10,226	6,820
Manufactures of metal	22,187	20,991	17,641
Machinery and transport equipment	70,144	63,206	43,603
General industrial machinery	29,926	23,147	20,484
Electrical machinery, apparatus and appliances	10,695	12,355	1,677
Road vehicles	26,388	23,999	18,265
Passenger motor cars (excl. buses)	9,687	8,202	5,350
Motor vehicles for the transport of goods or materials	9,557	7,530	5,984
Motor vehicle parts and accessories	4,326	5,543	4,194

Imports c.i.f.	1991	1992	1993
Miscellaneous manufactured articles	12,105	16,798	8,188
Photographic apparatus, equipment and supplies and optical goods	6,725	10,154	4,182
Special transactions and commodities not classified according to kind	14,291	13,406	19,877
Total (incl. others)	247,087	229,508	204,525

Exports f.o.b.	1991	1992	1993
Food and live animals	82,477	59,065	52,300
Coffee, tea, cocoa, spices, and manufactures thereof	82,477	59,065	51,936
Coffee (incl. husks and skins) and substitutes containing coffee	74,149	49,665	43,262
Tea and maté	8,328	9,400	8,674
Tea	—	9,400	8,674
Crude materials (inedible) except fuels	2,384	1,676	4,089
Hides and skins (except furskins), raw	2,384	1,676	844
Textile fibres and waste	—	—	3,245
Cotton	—	—	3,245
Raw cotton (excl. linters)	—	—	3,245
Basic manufactures	2,464	4,413	4,402
Textile yarn, fabrics, etc.	1,340	1,679	2,442
Cotton fabrics (woven)	1,340	1,679	2,442
Non-metallic mineral manufactures	1,051	2,417	1,909
Bottles etc. of glass	1,002	2,390	1,729
Special transactions and commodities not classified according to kind	4,150	8,795	4,826
Total (incl. others)	91,536	74,701	68,703

Source: UN, *International Trade Statistics Yearbook*.

1994 (estimates, US $ million): *Imports c.i.f.*: Capital goods 56.1; Intermediate goods 72.0; Consumption goods 111.2; Total imports 239.3. *Exports f.o.b.*: Coffee 99.7; Tea 8.9; Cotton 5.4; Hides and skins 1.3; Other primary products 2.9; Manufactured products 5.5 Total exports 123.6.
1995 (estimates, US $ million): *Imports c.i.f.*: Capital goods 61.7; Intermediate goods 79.3; Consumption goods 105.0; Total imports 246.1. *Exports f.o.b.*: Coffee 98.6; Tea 9.1; Cotton 1.8; Hides and skins 1.4; Other primary products 2.7; Manufactured products 7.5; Total exports 116.0. Source: IMF, *Burundi—Statistical Annex* (May 1996).

PRINCIPAL TRADING PARTNERS

Imports c.i.f. (US $ '000)	1991	1992	1993
Belgium-Luxembourg	35,781	34,108	33,809
China, People's Repub.	14,562	8,371	8,176
France	24,145	25,493	23,676
Germany	18,695	17,614	13,865
Iran	—	7,520	12,578
Italy	8,773	8,053	9,246
Japan	20,876	18,585	18,754
Kenya	6,999	7,520	6,590
Netherlands	5,728	6,305	6,319
Tanzania	4,024	20,538	11,752
United Arab Emirates	1,553	3,093	2,068
United Kingdom	4,118	5,289	3,459
USA	4,346	9,801	3,638
Zambia	7,676	6,648	5,015
Zimbabwe	4,789	2,151	2,237
Total (incl. others)	247,087	229,508	204,525

Exports (million Burundian Francs)	1989	1990	1991
Belgium-Luxembourg	169.9	99.8	238.6
France	790.0	1,246.1	818.6
Germany	1,876.4	1,760.0	2,905.5
Italy	275.0	302.5	164.0
Netherlands	119.6	180.9	561.9
United Kingdom	280.0	808.2	410.3
USA	887.7	1,508.8	3,207.1
Others	7,905.8	6,878.0	8,338.9
Total	12,304.4	12,783.6	16,644.9

Total exports f.o.b. (revised figure, million Burundian francs): 16,698 in 1991.

Source: Banque de la République du Burundi.

1992: Total imports c.i.f. (million Burundian francs): 46,106; Total exports f.o.b. (million Burundian francs): 15,355.
1993: Total imports c.i.f. (million Burundian francs): 47,434; Total exports f.o.b. (million Burundian francs): 15,019.
1994: Total imports c.i.f. (million Burundian francs): 56,468; Total exports f.o.b. (million Burundian francs): 26,500.
1995: Total imports c.i.f. (million Burundian francs): 58,200; Total exports f.o.b. 26,591. (Source IMF, *International Financial Statistics*).

Transport

ROAD TRAFFIC (estimates, '000 motor vehicles in use)

	1992	1993	1994
Passenger cars	17.5	18.5	17.5
Commercial vehicles	11.8	12.3	10.2

Source: UN, *Statistical Yearbook*.

LAKE TRAFFIC (Bujumbura—'000 metric tons)

	1989	1990	1991
Goods:			
Arrivals	150.4	152.9	188.4
Departures	33.0	32.5	35.1

Source: Banque de la République du Burundi.

CIVIL AVIATION (traffic on scheduled services)

	1992	1993	1994
Passengers carried ('000)	9	9	9
Passengers — km (million)	2	2	2

Source: UN, *Statistical Yearbook*.

Tourism

	1992	1993	1994
Tourist arrivals ('000)	86	75	29
Tourist receipts (US $ million)	3	3	3

Source: UN, *Statistical Yearbook*.

Communications Media

	1992	1993	1994
Radio receivers ('000 in use)	360	375	400
Television receivers ('000 in use)	5	9	9
Telephones ('000 main lines in use)	13	16	16
Daily newspapers:			
Number	1	n.a.	1
Circulation ('000 copies)	20	n.a.	20

Source: UNESCO, *Statistical Yearbook*.

Education

(1992/93)

	Teachers	Pupils
Pre-primary*	49	2,381
Primary	10,400	651,086
Secondary:		
General†	n.a.	46,381
Teacher training	n.a.	2,470
Vocational	502	6,862
Higher	556	4,256

* Figures refer to 1988/89 (Source: Ministry of Primary and Secondary Education).

† Including first cycle of teacher training.

Source: UNESCO, *Statistical Yearbook*.

Directory

The Constitution

The Constitution was promulgated on 13 March 1992 and provided for the establishment of a plural political system. The Constitution seeks to guarantee human rights and basic freedoms for all citizens, together with the freedom of the press. Executive powers are vested in the President, who (under normal circumstances—see below) is elected directly, by universal adult suffrage, for a five-year term, renewable only once. Statutory power is shared with the Prime Minister, who appoints a Council of Ministers. Legislative power is exercised by a National Assembly, whose members are elected directly, by universal adult suffrage, for a five-year renewable mandate. In September 1994 a Convention of Government was agreed among the country's major political parties. The Convention, which defines the terms of government for a four-year transitional period, provides for the establishment of a National Security Council of 10 members, including the President, the Prime Minister and the Ministers of State with responsibility for External Affairs, Interior and Public Security, and National Defence. The Convention was incorporated into the Constitution on 22 September 1994. However, the Convention disintegrated in July 1996, prompting the military coup which returned Maj. Pierre Buyoya to power.

The Government

HEAD OF STATE

President: Maj. PIERRE BUYOYA (assumed power 25 July 1996).

COUNCIL OF MINISTERS
(June 1997)

Prime Minister: PASCAL-FIRMIN NDIMIRA.

Minister of Foreign Affairs: LUC RUKINGAMA.

Minister of the Interior and Public Security: Lt.-Col EPITACE BAYAGANAKANDI.

Minister of Justice: TERENCE SINUNGURUZA.

Minister of Defence: Col FIRMIN SINZOYIHEBA.

Minister of Development Planning and Reconstruction: EVARISTE MINANI.

Minister of Communal Development: PIERRE BAMBASI.

Minister of Relocation and Resettlement of Displaced Persons and Refugees: PASCAL NKURUNZIZA.

Minister of Territorial Management and Environment: SAMUEL BIGAWA.

Minister of Agriculture and Livestock: DAMAS NYIRANGIWANGIRA.

Minister of Finance: GÉRARD NIYIBIGIRA.

Minister of Commerce, Industry and Tourism: GREGOIRE BARANYIZIGIYE.

Minister of Labour, Handicrafts and Professional Training: BARNABÉ MUKERAGIRANWA.

Minister of Public Service: Mme MONIQUE NDAKOZI.

Minister for Basic Education and Adult Literacy: JOSEPH NDAYISABA.

Minister of Secondary and Higher Education and Scientific Research: LOGATIEN NDORICIMPA.

Minister of Human Rights, Social Action and Women's Affairs: Mme CHRISTINE RUHAZA.

Minister of Culture, Youth and Sport: BONAVENTURE GASUTWA.

Minister of Health: JUMA KARIBURIJO.

Minister of Communications: PIERRE-CLAVER NDAYISHARYE.

Minister of Public Works and Equipment: VITAL NZOBONIMPA.

Minister of Transport, Posts and Telecommunications: VENERAND NZOHABONAYO.

Minister of Energy and Mines: BERNARD BARANDEREKA.

Minister of Institutional Reforms: EUGÈNE NINDORERA.

There are also two Secretaries of State.

MINISTRIES

Office of the President: Bujumbura; tel. (2) 26063; telex 5049.

Ministry of Agriculture and Livestock: Bujumbura; tel. (2) 22087.

Ministry of Commerce, Industry and Tourism: Bujumbura; tel. (2) 25330.

Ministry of Communal Development: Bujumbura.

Ministry of Communications: Bujumbura.

Ministry of Culture, Youth and Sport: Bujumbura; tel. (2) 26822.

Ministry of Development, Planning and Reconstruction: BP 1830, Bujumbura; tel. (2) 23988; telex 5135.

Ministry of Energy and Mines: BP 745, Bujumbura; tel. (2) 25909; telex 5182; fax (2) 23337.

Ministry of External Relations and Co-operation: Bujumbura; tel. (2) 22150; telex 5065.

Ministry of Finance: BP 1830, Bujumbura; tel. (2) 25142; telex 5135; fax (2) 23128.

Ministry of Human Rights, Social Action and Women's Affairs: Bujumbura; tel. (2) 25039.

Ministry of the Interior: Bujumbura.

Ministry of Justice: Bujumbura; tel. (2) 22148.

Ministry of Labour, Handicrafts and Professional Training: Bujumbura.

Ministry of National Defence: Bujumbura.

Ministry of National Education: Bujumbura.

Ministry of Public Health: Bujumbura; tel. (2) 26020.

Ministry of Public Security: Bujumbura.

Ministry of the Public Service: BP 1480, Bujumbura; tel. (2) 23514; fax (2) 28715.

Ministry of Public Works and Equipment: BP 1860, Bujumbura; tel. (2) 26841; telex 5048; fax (2) 26840.

Ministry of Relocation and Resettlement of Displaced Persons and Refugees: Bujumbura.

Ministry of Territorial Management and Environment: Bujumbura.

Ministry of Transport, Posts and Telecommunications: BP 2000, Bujumbura; tel. (2) 22923; telex 5103; fax (2) 26900.

President and Legislature

PRESIDENT

Following the assassination of President Melchior Ndadaye and his constitutional successor in October 1993, a constitutional amendment was adopted whereby a successor was to be elected by the National Assembly. On 13 January 1994 Cyprien Ntaryamira, a member of FRODEBU, was elected President by 78 of the 79 votes cast by the National Assembly. Following Ntaryamira's death in April 1994, the Speaker of the National Assembly, Sylvestre Ntibantunganya, assumed the presidency for an interim, three-month period (subsequently extended for a further three months), in accordance with the Constitution. Ntibantunganya was subsequently appointed to the presidency for a four-year transitional term, by broad consensus in accordance with the Convention of Government adopted in September 1994. In July 1996 Ntibantunganya was deposed by a military coup and replaced by Maj. Pierre Buyoya; the National Assembly was immediately suspended, but was reconvened in October.

NATIONAL ASSEMBLY

Speaker: LÉONCE NGENDAKUMANA (FRODEBU).

Legislative elections, 29 June 1993

Party	Votes cast	% of votes cast	Seats
FRODEBU	1,532,107	71.04	65
UPRONA	462,324	21.44	16
RPB	35,932	1.67	—
PRP	29,966	1.39	—
RADDES	26,631	1.23	—
PP	24,372	1.13	—
Independents	853	0.04	—
Invalid votes	44,474	2.06	—
Total	2,156,659	100.00	81

PROVINCIAL GOVERNORS
(June 1997)

Bubanza: (vacant).

Bujumbura (Rural): ALOYS HAKIZIMANA.

Bururi: ANDRÉ NDAYIZAMBA.

Cankuzo: HENRI TUZAGI.

Cibitoke: Lt-Col ANTOINE NIMBESHA.

Gitega: Lt-Col LOUIS MURENGERA.

Karuzi: Lt-Col GABRIEL GUNUNGU.

Kayanza: Lt-Col DANIEL MENGERI.

Kirundo: DEOGRATIAS BIZIMANA.

Makamba: JEAN-BAPTISTE GAHIMBARE.

Muramvya: NESTOR NIYUNGEKO.

Muyinga: Col ALEXIS BANUMA.

Ngozi: ASCENSION TWAGIRAMUNGU.

Rutana: LÉONIDAS HAKIZIMANA.

Ruyigi: HENRI BUKUMBANYA.

Political Organizations

Although the March 1992 Constitution provided for the establishment of a multi-party system, political parties are required to demonstrate firm commitment to national unity, and impartiality with regard to ethnic or regional origin, gender and religion, in order to receive legal recognition.

Alliance burundaise-africaine pour le salut (ABASA): Bujumbura.

Alliance nationale pour les droits et le développement (ANADDE): Bujumbura; f. 1992.

Front pour la démocratie au Burundi (FRODEBU): Bujumbura; f. 1992; Leader JEAN MINANI.

Inkinzo y'Ijambo Ry'abarundi (Inkinzo) (Guarantor of Freedom of Speech in Burundi): Bujumbura; f. 1993; Pres. Dr ALPHONSE RUGAMBARARA.

Parti indépendant des travailleurs (PIT): Bujumbura.

Parti libéral (PL): Bujumbura; f. 1992.

Parti du peuple (PP): Bujumbura; f. 1992; Leader SHADRAK NIYONKURU.

Parti de réconciliation du peuple (PRP): Bujumbura; f. 1992; Leader MATHIAS HITIMANA

Parti pour le redressement national (PARENA): Bujumbura; f. 1994; Leader JEAN-BAPTISTE BAGAZA.

Parti social démocrate (PSD): Bujumbura; f. 1993.

Rassemblement pour le démocratie et le développement économique et social (RADDES): Bujumbura; f. 1992; Chair. CYRILLE SIGEJEJE.

Rassemblement du peuple burundien (RPB): Bujumbura; f. 1992.

Union pour le progrès national (UPRONA): BP 1810, Bujumbura; tel. (2) 25028; telex 5057; f. 1958; following the 1961 elections, the numerous small parties which had been defeated merged with UPRONA, which became the sole legal political party in 1966; party activities were suspended following the coup of Sept. 1987, but resumed in 1989; Leader CHARLES MUKASI.

The constitutional reforms, which exclude political organizations advocating 'tribalism, divisionalism or violence' and require party leaderships to be equally representative of Hutu and Tutsi ethnic groups, have been opposed by some externally-based opposition parties. These include the **Parti de libération du peuple hutu (PALIPEHUTU**, f. 1980 and based in Tanzania), which seeks to advance the interests of the Hutu ethnic group. An armed dissident wing of PALIPEHUTU, known as the **Force nationale de libération (FNL)**, led by KABORA KHOSSAN, is based in southern Rwanda. Another grouping representing the interests of Hutu extremists, the **Conseil national pour la défense de la démocratie (CNDD)** is led by LÉONARD NYANGOMA, in exile in the Democratic Republic of the Congo. The CNDD claims a 30,000-strong armed wing, the **Force pour la défence de la démocratie (FDD)**.

Diplomatic Representation

EMBASSIES IN BURUNDI

Belgium: 9 ave de l'Industrie, BP 1920, Bujumbura; tel. (2) 23676; telex 5033; Ambassador: DENIS BANNEEL.

China, People's Republic: BP 2550, Bujumbura; tel. (2) 24307; Ambassador: ZHANG LONGBAO.

Congo, Democratic Republic: 5 ave Olsen, BP 872, Bujumbura; tel. (2) 23492; Ambassador: (vacant).

Egypt: 31 ave de la Liberté, BP 1520, Bujumbura; tel. (2) 23161; telex 5040; Ambassador: MUHAMMAD MOUSA.

France: 31 ave de l'UPRONA, BP 1740, Bujumbura; tel. (2) 26767; fax (2) 27443; Ambassador: JEAN-PIERRE LAJAUNIE.

Germany: 22 rue 18 septembre, BP 480, Bujumbura; tel. (2) 26412; telex 5068; Ambassador: KARL FLITTNER.

Holy See: 46 chaussée Prince Louis-Rwagasore, BP 1068, Bujumbura (Apostolic Nunciature); tel. (2) 22326; fax (2) 23176; Apostolic Nuncio: Most Rev. EMIL PAUL TSCHERRIG, Titular Archbishop of Voli.

Korea, Democratic People's Republic: BP 1620, Bujumbura; tel. (2) 22881; Ambassador: PAE SOK JUN.

Romania: rue Pierre Ngendandumwe, BP 2770, Bujumbura; tel. (2) 24135; Chargé d'affaires a.i.: ALEXANDRA ANDREI.

Russia: 78 blvd de l'UPRONA, BP 1034, Bujumbura; tel. (2) 26098; telex 5164; fax (2) 22984; Ambassador: IGOR S. LIAKIN-FROLOV.

Rwanda: 24 ave du Zaïre, BP 400, Bujumbura; tel. (2) 23140; telex 5032; Ambassador: SYLVESTRE UWIBAJIJE.

Tanzania: BP 1653, Bujumbura; Ambassador: NICHOLAS J. MARO.

USA: ave des Etats-Unis, BP 1720, Bujumbura; tel. (2) 23454; fax (2) 22926; Ambassador: MORRIS N. HUGHES.

Judicial System

The 1981 Constitution prescribed a judicial system wherein the judges were subject to the decisions of UPRONA. Under a programme of legal reform, announced in 1986, provincial courts were to be replaced by a dual system of courts of civil and criminal jurisdiction. A network of mediation and conciliation courts was to be established to arbitrate in minor disputes arising among the rural population. Substantial reforms of the legal system were expected to follow the implementation of the 1992 Constitution.

Supreme Court: BP 1460, Bujumbura; tel. (2) 22571; fax (2) 22148. Court of final instance; four divisions: ordinary, cassation, constitutional and administrative.

Courts of Appeal: Bujumbura, Gitega and Ngozi.

Tribunals of First Instance: There are 17 provincial tribunals and 123 smaller resident tribunals in other areas.

Tribunal of Trade: Bujumbura.

Tribunals of Labour: Bujumbura and Gitega.

Administrative Courts: Bujumbura and Gitega.

Religion

More than 65% of the population are Christians, the majority of whom (an estimated 61%) are Roman Catholics. Anglicans number about 60,000. There are about 200,000 Protestants, of whom some 160,000 are Pentecostalists. Fewer than 40% of the population adhere to traditional beliefs, which include the worship of the God 'Imana'. About 1% of the population are Muslims. The Bahá'í Faith is also active in Burundi.

CHRISTIANITY

Conseil National des Eglises protestantes du Burundi (CNEB): BP 17, Bujumbura; tel. (2) 24216; fax (2) 27941; f. 1970; five mem. churches; Pres. Rt. Rev. Jean Nduwayo (Anglican Bishop of Gitega); Gen. Sec. Rev. Osias Habingabwa.

The Anglican Communion

The Church of the Province of Burundi, established in 1992, comprises four dioceses.

Archbishop of Burundi and Bishop of Matana: Most Rev. Samuel Sindamuka, BP 1300, Bujumbura; tel. (2) 24389; telex 5127; fax (2) 29129.

Provincial Secretary: Rev. Bernard Ntahoturi, BP 2098, Bujumbura.

The Roman Catholic Church

Burundi comprises one archdiocese and six dioceses. At 31 December 1995 there were an estimated 3,594,127 adherents.

Bishops' Conference: Conférence des Evêques Catholiques du Burundi, 5 blvd de l'UPRONA, BP 1390, Bujumbura; tel. (2) 23263; fax (2) 23270; f. 1980; Pres. Rt Rev. Bernard Bududira, Bishop of Bururi.

Archbishop of Gitega: (vacant), Archevêché, BP 118, Gitega; tel. (40) 2160; fax (40) 2547.

Other Christian Churches

Union of Baptist Churches of Burundi: Rubura, DS 117, Bujumbura 1; Pres. Paul Baruhenamwo.

Other denominations active in the country include the Evangelical Christian Brotherhood of Burundi, the Free Methodist Church of Burundi and the United Methodist Church of Burundi.

BAHÁ'Í FAITH

National Spiritual Assembly: BP 1578, Bujumbura.

The Press

NEWSPAPERS

Burundi chrétien: BP 232, Bujumbura; Roman Catholic weekly; French.

Le Renouveau du Burundi: BP 2870, Bujumbura; f. 1978; publ. by UPRONA; daily; French; circ. 20,000; Dir Jean Nzeyimana.

Ubumwe: BP 1400, Bujumbura; tel. (2) 23929; f. 1971; weekly; Kirundi; circ. 20,000.

PERIODICALS

Au Coeur de l'Afrique: Association des conférences des ordinaires du Rwanda et Burundi, BP 1390, Bujumbura; bimonthly; education; circ. 1,000.

Bulletin économique et financier: BP 482, Bujumbura; bimonthly.

Bulletin mensuel: Banque de la République du Burundi, Service des études, BP 705, Bujumbura; tel. (2) 25142; telex 5071; monthly.

Bulletin officiel du Burundi: Bujumbura; monthly.

Le Burundi en Images: BP 1400, Bujumbura; f. 1979; monthly.

Culture et Sociétés: BP 1400, Bujumbura; f. 1978; quarterly.

Ndongozi Y'uburundi: Catholic Mission, BP 690, Bujumbura; tel. (2) 22762; fax (2) 28907; fortnightly; Kirundi.

Revue administration et juridique: Association d'études administratives et juridiques du Burundi, BP 1613, Bujumbura; quarterly; French.

PRESS ASSOCIATION

Burundian Association of Journalists (BAJ): Bujumbura; Pres. François Sendazirasa.

NEWS AGENCY

Agence burundaise de Presse (ABP): 6 ave de la Poste, BP 2870, Bujumbura; tel. (2) 25417; telex 5056; publ. daily bulletin.

Publishers

BURSTA: BP 1908, Bujumbura; tel. (2) 31796; fax (2) 32842; f. 1986; Dir Richard Kashirahamwe.

Editions Intore: 7 chaussée Prince Louis-Rwagasore, BP 525, Bujumbura; tel. (2) 20603.

GRAVIMPORT: BP 156, Bujumbura; tel. (2) 22285; fax (2) 26953.

IMPARUDI: BP 3010, Bujumbura.

Imprimerie la Licorne: 29 ave de la Mission, BP 2942, Bujumbura; tel. (2) 23503; fax (2) 27225; f. 1991.

Imprimerie MAHI: BP 673, Bujumbura.

MICROBU: BP 645, Bujumbura.

Mister Minute Service: 3 ave d'Angola, BP 1536, Bujumbura; tel. (2) 29398; fax (2) 20643.

Imprimerie Moderne: BP 2555, Bujumbura.

Imprimerie du Parti: BP 1810, Bujumbura.

Les Presses Lavigerie: 5 ave de l'UPRONA, BP 1640, Bujumbura; tel. (2) 22368; fax (2) 20318.

Régie de Productions Pédagogiques: BP 3118, Bujumbura.

SASCO: BP 204, Bujumbura.

Government Publishing House

Imprimerie nationale du Burundi (INABU): BP 991, Bujumbura; tel. (2) 24046; fax (2) 25399; f. 1978; Dir Nicolas Nijimbere.

Radio and Television

In 1993 there were 375,000 radio receivers and some 9,000 television receivers in use.

Radio Democracy/Radio Rutomorangingo ('the radio that tells the truth'): promotes the interests of extremist Hutu groups; broadcasts in French, Kirundi and Swahili.

Radio Hope/Radio Umwizero: Bujumbura; f. 1996; EU-funded, private station promoting national reconciliation and peace; broadcasts four hours daily in Kirundi, Swahili and French; Dir. Hubert Vieille.

Voix de la Révolution/La Radiodiffusion et Télévision Nationale du Burundi (RTNB): BP 1900, Bujumbura; tel. (2) 23742; telex 5119; fax (2) 26547; f. 1960; govt-controlled; television service and daily radio broadcasts in Kirundi, Swahili, French and English; Dir-Gen. Charles Ndayiziga; Dir (Radio) Gérard Mfuranzima; Dir (Television) Bonaventure Barizira.

Finance

(cap. = capital; res = reserves; dep. = deposits; m. = million; brs = branches; amounts in Burundian francs)

BANKING

Central Bank

Banque de la République du Burundi (BRB): BP 705, Bujumbura; tel. (2) 25142; telex 5071; fax (2) 23128; f. 1964 as Banque du Royaume du Burundi; state-owned; bank of issue; cap. and res 9,015.4m., dep. 11,008.5m. (Dec. 1994); Gov. Mathias Sinamenye; Vice-Gov. Emmanuel Ndayiragije.

Commercial Banks

Banque Burundaise pour le Commerce et l'Investissement SARL (BBCI): blvd du 1 Novembre, BP 2320, Bujumbura; tel. (2) 23328; telex 5012; fax (2) 23339; f. 1988; cap. 330m. (Dec. 1995); Pres. Charles Kaburahe; Vice-Pres. Gabriel Baziruwisabiye.

Banque Commerciale du Burundi SARL (BANCOBU): 84 chaussée Prince Louis-Rwagasore, BP 990, Bujumbura; tel. (2) 22317; telex 5051; fax (2) 21018; f. 1988 by merger; cap. and res 945m., dep. 11,848m. (Dec. 1994); Pres. Jacques van Eetvelde; Dir-Gen. Libère Ndabakwaje.

Banque de Crédit de Bujumbura SARL (BCB): ave Patrice Emery Lumumba, BP 300, Bujumbura; tel. (2) 22091; telex 5063; fax (2) 23007; f. 1964; cap. and res 1,850m., dep. 15,605m. (Dec. 1994); Pres. Thacien Nzeyimana; Man. Athanase Gahungu; 7 brs.

Banque Populaire du Burundi (BPB): 10 ave du 18 Septembre, BP 1780; Bujumbura; tel. (2) 21255; telex 5174; fax (2) 21256; cap. 285m.

Development Banks

Banque de Gestion et de Financement: Immeuble Ucar II, chaussée du Peuple Murundi, BP 1035, Bujumbura; tel. (2) 21352; fax (2) 21351; f. 1992; cap. 399.7m. (Dec. 1995); Pres. Didace Nzohabonayo; Dir-Gen. Mathias Ndikumana.

Banque Nationale pour le Développement Economique SARL (BNDE): 3 rue du Marché, BP 1620, Bujumbura; tel. (2) 22888; telex 5091; fax (2) 23775; f. 1966; cap. and res 2,363m., dep. 6,459m. (Dec. 1995); Pres. GASPARD SINDIYIGAYA; Gen. Sec. FRANÇOIS BARWENDERE.

Caisse de Mobilisation et de Financement (CAMOFI): 4 ave de la J.R.R., BP 8, Bujumbura; tel. (2) 25106; telex 5081; fax (2) 29589; f. 1979; 50% state-owned; finances public-sector development projects; scheduled for privatization; cap. 200m. (Dec. 1994); Dir-Gen. GÉRARD NIYIBIGIRA.

Meridien BIAO Bank Burundi SARL: 1 blvd de la liberté, BP 45, Bujumbura; tel. (2) 25712; telex 5151; fax (2) 25794; f. 1992 by merger; 30% owned by Meridien International Bank (Bahamas); all operations assumed by central bank in May 1995; cap. 800m. (Dec. 1992); Pres. and Chair. M. DONATIEN BIHUTE; Man. Dir KEVIN HUGH CAIN; 4 brs.

Société Burundaise de Financement SARL (SBF): 6 rue de la Science, BP 270, Bujumbura; tel. (2) 22126; telex 5080; fax (2) 25437; f. 1981; cap. 860m. (Dec. 1993); Dir-Gen. CYPRIEN SINZOBAHAMVYA.

Co-operative Bank

Banque Coopérative d'Epargne et de Crédit Mutuel (BCM): BP 1340, Bujumbura; operating licence granted in April 1995.

INSURANCE

Burundi Insurance Corporation (BICOR): BP 2377, Bujumbura.

Société d'Assurances du Burundi (SOCABU): 14–18 rue de l'Amitié, BP 2440, Bujumbura; tel. (2) 26520; telex 5113; fax (2) 26803; f. 1977; partly state-owned; cap. 180m.; Chair. EGIDE NDAHIBESHE; Man. SÉRAPHINE RUVAHAFI.

Société Générale d'Assurances et de Réassurance (SOGEAR): BP 2432, Bujumbura; tel. (2) 22345; fax (2) 29338; f. 1991.

Union Commerciale d'Assurances et de Réassurance (UCAR): BP 3012, Bujumbura; tel. (2) 23638; telex 5162; fax (2) 23695; f. 1986; cap. 150m. (June 1990); Chair. Lt-Col EDOUARD NZAMBIMANA; Man. Dir HENRY TARMO.

Trade and Industry

STATE TRADE ORGANIZATION

Office National du Commerce (ONC): Bujumbura; f. 1973; supervises international commercial operations between the Govt of Burundi and other states or private orgs; also organizes the import of essential materials; subsidiary offices in each province.

DEVELOPMENT ORGANIZATIONS

Compagnie de Gérance du Coton (COGERCO): BP 2571, Bujumbura; tel. (2) 22208; telex 5112; fax (2) 25323; f. 1947; promotion and development of cotton industry; Dir THÉRENCE NIYONDAGARA.

Institut des Sciences Agronomiques du Burundi (ISABU): BP 795, Bujumbura; tel. (2) 23384; f. 1962 for the scientific development of agriculture and livestock.

Office de la Tourbe du Burundi (ONATOUR): BP 2360, Bujumbura; tel. (2) 26480; telex 48; f. 1977 to promote the exploitation of peat deposits.

Office des Cultures Industrielles du Burundi (Office du Café du Burundi) (OCIBU): BP 450, Bujumbura; tel. (2) 26031; fax (2) 25532; supervises coffee plantations and coffee exports.

Office du Thé du Burundi (OTB): 52 blvd de l'UPRONA, Bujumbura; tel. (2) 24228; telex 5069; fax (2) 24657; f. 1979 supervises production and marketing of tea; Dir REMY NIBIGARA.

Office National du Logement (ONL): BP 2480, Bujumbura; tel. (2) 26074; telex 48; f. 1974 to supervise housing construction.

Société d'Exploitation du Quinquina du Burundi (SOKINABU): 16 blvd Mwezi Gisabo, BP 1783, Bujumbura; tel. (2) 23469; telex 81; f. 1975 to develop and exploit cinchona trees, the source of quinine; Dir RAPHAËL REMEZO.

Société Sucrière du Mosso (SOSUMO): BP 835, Bujumbura; tel. (2) 26576; telex 5035; fax (2) 23028; f. 1982 to develop and manage sugar cane plantations.

CHAMBER OF COMMERCE

Chambre de Commerce et de l'Industrie du Burundi: BP 313, Bujumbura; tel. (2) 22280; f. 1923; Chair. DONATIEN BIHUTE; 130 mems.

MAJOR INDUSTRIAL COMPANY

Complexe Textile de Bujumbura (COTEBU): BP 2899, Bujumbura; tel. (2) 31900; telex 5061; fax (2) 31750; textile mfrs; Dirs JEAN KABURA, DÉO NDABANEZE, ANICET NDAYISABA.

TRADE UNIONS

Confédération des Syndicats du Burundi (COSIBU): Bujumbura; Chair. CHARLES NDAMIRAWE.

Union des Travailleurs du Burundi (UTB): BP 1340, Bujumbura; tel. (2) 23884; telex 57; f. 1967 by merger of all existing unions; closely allied with UPRONA; sole authorized trade union prior to 1994, with 18 affiliated nat. professional feds; Sec.-Gen. MARIUS RURAHENYE.

Transport

RAILWAYS

There are no railways in Burundi. Plans have been under consideration since 1987 for the construction of a line passing through Uganda, Rwanda and Burundi, to connect with the Kigoma–Dar es Salaam line in Tanzania. This rail link would relieve Burundi's isolated trade position.

ROADS

The road network is very dense and in 1992 there was a total of 14,473 km of roads, of which 1,950 km were national highways and 2,523 km secondary roads. A new crossing of the Ruzizi River, the Bridge of Concord (Burundi's longest bridge), was opened in early 1992. In February 1992 the Government revealed that 600 km of roads had been rehabilitated during the previous three years, and announced a four-year programme of future road improvements covering a further 1,000 km.

INLAND WATERWAYS

Bujumbura is the principal port for both passenger and freight traffic on Lake Tanganyika, and the greater part of Burundi's external trade is dependent on the shipping services between Bujumbura and lake ports in Tanzania, Zambia and the Democratic Republic of the Congo.

CIVIL AVIATION

There is an international airport at Bujumbura, equipped to take large jet-engined aircraft.

Air Burundi: 40 ave du Commerce, BP 2460, Bujumbura; tel. (2) 24,609; telex 5080; fax (2) 23452; f. 1971 as Société de Transports Aériens du Burundi; state-owned; operates charter and scheduled passenger services to destinations throughout central Africa; Man. Dir Maj. ISAAC GAFURERO.

Tourism

Tourism is relatively undeveloped. Tourist arrivals were estimated at 75,000 in 1993, with receipts amounting to US $3m.

Office National du Tourisme (ONT): 2 ave des Euphorbes, BP 902, Bujumbura; tel. (2) 24208; telex 5081; fax (2) 29390; f. 1972; responsible for the promotion and supervision of tourism; Dir HERMENEGILDE NIMBONA (acting).

Defence

Total armed strength in August 1996 was estimated at 22,000, comprising an army of 18,500, and a paramilitary force of 3,500 gendarmes (including a 50-strong marine police force).

Defence Expenditure: Budgeted at 10,200m. Burundian francs for 1996.

Chief of Staff of the Army: Lt-Col VINCENT NIYUNGEKO.

Chief of Staff of the Gendarmerie: Col. GEORGES MUKURAKO.

Education

Education is provided free of charge. Kirundi is the language of instruction in primary schools, while French is used in secondary schools. Primary education, which is officially compulsory, begins at seven years of age and lasts for six years. Secondary education, which is not compulsory, begins at the age of 13 and lasts for up to seven years, comprising a first cycle of four years and a second of three years. In 1992 the total enrolment at primary schools included 51% of students in the relevant age-group (males 56%; females 47%). Enrolment at primary schools increased from 175,856 in 1980 to 651,086 in 1992. Enrolment at secondary schools, including pupils receiving vocational instruction and teacher training, rose from 19,013 in 1980 to 55,713 in 1992. However, the latter total included only 5% of students in the secondary age-group. There is one university, in Bujumbura, with 2,749 students in 1988/89. According to UNESCO estimates, the average rate of illiteracy among the population aged 15 years and over was 64.7% (Males 50.7%; females 77.5%) in 1995. Expenditure on education was estimated at 11.9% of total government spending in 1992.

Bibliography

Chrétien, J.-P. 'La société du Burundi: Des mythes aux réalités', in *Revue Française d'Etudes Politiques Africaines,* July-August 1979, Nos. 163–4, pp. 94–118.

Histoire rurale de l'Afrique des Grands Lacs. Paris, Editions Karthala.

Chrétien, J.-P., Guichaoua, A., and Le Jeune, G. *La crise d'août 1988 au Burundi.* Paris, Editions Karthala.

Gahama, J. *Le Burundi sous administration belge.* Paris, Editions Karthala, 1983.

Guichaoua, A. (Ed.). *Les crises politiques au Burundi et au Rwanda (1993–1994).* Paris, Editions Karthala, 1995.

Guillet, C., and Ndayishinguje, P. *Légendes historiques du Burundi.* Paris, Editions Karthala, 1987.

Hausner, K.-H., and Jezic, B. *Rwanda et Burundi.* Bonn, Kurt Schroeder, 1968.

Lambert, M. Y. *Enquête démographique Burundi* (1970–1971). Bujumbura, Ministère du Plan, 1972.

Lemarchand, R. *Rwanda and Burundi.* London, Pall Mall, 1970.

Selective Genocide in Burundi. 1974.

African Kingships in Perspective. 1974.

Ethnocide as Discourse and Practice. Woodrow Wilson Center Press and Cambridge University Press, 1994.

Mpozagara, G. *La République du Burundi.* Paris, Berger-Levrault, 1971.

Mworoha, E. *Histoire du Burundi.* Paris, Hatier, 1987.

Nsanzé, T. *Le Burundi au carrefour de l'Afrique.* Brussels, Remarques africaines, 1970.

L'Edification de la République du Burundi. Brussels, 1970.

Ntahombaye, P. *Des noms et des hommes. Aspects du nom au Burundi.* Paris, Editions Karthala, 1983.

République du Burundi. *Plan quinquennal de développement économique et social du Burundi (1978–82).* Bujumbura.

Reyntjens, F. *Burundi 1972–1988. Continuité et changement.* Brussels, Centre d'étude et de documentation africaines (CEDAF–ASDOC), 1989.

United States Committee for Refugees. *From Coup to Coup: Thirty Years of Death, Fear and Displacement in Burundi.* Washington, DC, USCR, 1996.

University of Burundi. *Questions sur la paysannerie au Burundi. Actes de la table ronde: Sciences sociales, humaines et développement rural.* Bujumbura, 1985.

Vasina, J. *La légende du passé, traditions orales du Burundi.* Tervuren, Musée royale de l'Afrique centrale, 1972.

Weinstein, W. *Historical Dictionary of Burundi.* Metuchen, NJ, Scarecrow Press, 1976.

World Bank. *Farming Systems in Africa: The Great Lakes Highlands of Zaire, Rwanda and Burundi.* Washington, DC, International Bank for Reconstruction and Development, 1984.

CAMEROON

Physical and Social Geography

JOHN I. CLARKE

PHYSICAL FEATURES

The Republic of Cameroon covers an area of 475,442 sq km (183,569 sq miles), and contains exceptionally diverse physical environments. The country occupies a fairly central position within the African continent, with the additional advantage of a 200-km coastline. Its environmental diversity arises from various factors, including the country's position astride the volcanic belt along the hinge between west and central Africa, together with its intermediate location between the great basins of the Congo, the Niger and Lake Chad, its latitudinal extent between 2° and 13°N, its altitudinal range from sea-level to more than 4,000 m, and its spread from coastal mangrove swamp to remote continental interior.

In the south and centre of the country a large undulating and broken plateau surface of granites, schists and gneisses rises northwards away from the Congo basin to the Adamawa plateau (900–1,520 m above sea-level). North of the steep Adamawa escarpment, which effectively divides northern from southern Cameroon, lies the basin of the Benue river, a tributary of the Niger, which is floored by sedimentary rocks, interspersed with inselbergs and buttes. In the west of the country a long line of rounded volcanic mountains and hills extends from Mt Cameroun (4,095 m), the highest mountain in west and central Africa, north-eastwards along the former boundary between East and West Cameroon and then along the Nigerian border. Volcanic soils derived from these mountains are more fertile than most others in the country and have permitted much higher rural population densities than elsewhere.

Cameroon has a marked south-north gradation of climates, from a seasonal equatorial climate in the south (with two rainy seasons and two moderately dry seasons of unequal length), to southern savannah and savannah climates (with one dry and one wet season), to a hotter drier climate of the Sahel type in the far north. Rainfall thus varies from more than 5,000 mm in the south-west to around 610 mm near Lake Chad. Corresponding to this climatic zonation is a south-north gradation of vegetal landscapes: dense rain forest, Guinea savannah, Sudan savannah and thorn steppe, while Mt Cameroun incorporates a vertical series of sharply divided vegetation zones.

POPULATION

The population of Cameroon was enumerated at 10,493,655 at the census of April 1987, and was officially estimated to have risen to 13,277,000 in mid-1995. Population growth has been rapid (by an average of 2.8% per year in 1985–94) and the composition and distribution are extremely diverse. In the southern forest regions Bantu peoples prevail, although there are also pygmy groups in some of the more remote areas. North of the Bantu tribes live many semi-Bantu peoples including the ubiquitous Bamiléké. Further north the diversity increases, with Sudanese Negroes, Hamitic Fulani (or Foulbe) and Arab Choa.

The population has a very uneven distribution, with concentrations in the west, the south-central region and the Sudan savannah zone of the north. An important religious and social divide lies across the country. While the peoples of the south and west have been profoundly influenced by Christianity and by the European introduction of an externally orientated colonial-type economy, the peoples of the north are either Muslim or animist and have largely retained their traditional modes of life. Consequently, the population of the south and west is much more developed, economically and socially, than that of the north, although the government has made efforts to reduce this regional disparity.

One aspect of this disparity is the southern location of the capital, Yaoundé (estimated population 800,000 in 1992), and the main port of Douala (1,200,000), as well as most of the other towns. Much of their growth results from rural-urban migration; many of the migrants come from overcrowded mountain massifs in the west, and the Bamiléké constitute more than one-third of the inhabitants of Douala. Nevertheless, about two-thirds of all Cameroonians remain rural village-dwellers.

One other major contrast in the social geography of Cameroon is between anglophone north-west and south-west Cameroon, with less than one-tenth of the area and just over one-fifth of the population, and the much larger, more populous francophone area of former East Cameroon. The contrasting influences of British and French rule are still evident in education, commerce, law and in many other ways, although unification of the civil services since 1972, official bilingualism and the integration of transport networks and economies have helped to reduce the disparities between the two zones.

Recent History

PIERRE ENGLEBERT

Revised for this edition by the Editor

European interest in the Cameroon coast, spanning the area between Mt Cameroun and the Río Muni (now the mainland component of the Republic of Equatorial Guinea), dates from the arrival of Portuguese explorers in about 1472. For the next 300 years, Portuguese, Spanish, English, French, German and subsequently US traders and slavers operated along the Cameroon coast, until the establishment of the German protectorate of Kamerun in 1884. In 1916 the German administration was overthrown by combined French-British-Belgian military operations during the First World War.

MANDATES, TRUSTEESHIP AND INDEPENDENCE

In 1919, following the military occupation of the Kamerun protectorate during the First World War, the territory was divided into British and French spheres of influence. In 1922 both zones became subject to mandates of the League of Nations, which allocated four-fifths of the territory to French administration as French Cameroun, and the other one-fifth, comprising two long, non-contiguous areas along the eastern Nigerian border, to British administration as the Northern and Southern Cameroons.

In 1946 the mandates were converted into UN trust territories, still under their respective French and British administrations. However, growing anti-colonial sentiment made it difficult for France and Britain to resist the UN Charter's promise of eventual self-determination for all inhabitants of trust territories. Between 1948–60 more than 100 political associations were established in French Cameroun, including the Union des populations camerounaises (UPC), which was formed in 1948 by trade unionists and demanded the reunification of French Cameroun and the British Cameroons, and independence from France. By May 1955, unable to gain power legally, the UPC instigated an unsuccessful revolt and subsequently commenced a guerrilla insurgency. In 1957 French Cameroun became an autonomous state within the French Community. With the joint impetus of domestic and international pressure, the territory progressed toward independence. On 1 January 1960 the Republic of Cameroon was established. Ahmadou Ahidjo, the leader of the Union camerounaise who had served as prime minister since 1958, was elected as the country's first president.

Political developments in the British Cameroons, which was attached for administrative purposes to neighbouring Nigeria, progressed more slowly. In 1955 the Kamerun National Democratic Party (KNDP) was formed by John Foncha, with a programme of complete secession from Nigeria and unification with French Cameroun. Following the elections in 1959, Foncha became premier. After discussions at the UN it was agreed that a plebiscite would be held in both parts of the trust territory to determine their future. In February 1961 the electorate in the Southern Cameroons voted in favour of union with the Republic of Cameroon (which took place on 1 October), while northern Cameroon voters chose to merge with Nigeria (becoming the province of Sardauna). The new Federal Republic of Cameroon comprised two states: the former French zone became East Cameroon, while the former British portion became West Cameroon. Shortly afterwards, Ahidjo and Foncha assumed, respectively, the presidency and vice-presidency of the federation.

After federation, Cameroon moved towards increasing political, economic and social integration. By 1966 most of the states' areas of jurisdiction were under central control. In the same year the dominant parties in the two states, the UC and the KNDP, along with four minor parties, merged to form the Union nationale camerounaise (UNC). In 1968 Foncha was replaced as premier by Salomon Tandeng Muna, a strong supporter of Ahidjo. In 1970 Ahidjo was re-elected president, while Muna became vice-president.

In May 1972 the electorate decisively endorsed a new constitution, which abolished all the separate state institutions, as well as the office of federal vice-president, and provided for a strong executive president, a national executive council of ministers responsible to the president, a unicameral national assembly and a fully centralized administration. In June the country was officially renamed the United Republic of Cameroon. Ahidjo retained the presidency and in May 1973 Muna became president of the newly-elected national assembly.

The United Republic of Cameroon adopted a non-aligned foreign policy and sought to reduce its dependence on France and its Western allies. The UNC assumed full supervision of Cameroon's organized political and social affairs. In April 1975 Ahidjo was re-elected unopposed by more than 99% of registered voters. In June, Paul Biya, the former secretary-general in the president's office, was appointed to the new post of prime minister and a new cabinet was formed.

Despite dissatisfaction in some quarters with the single-party system and discontent among English-speaking politicians about their relatively low representation in government, the single list of candidates for the second national assembly chosen by the UNC was overwhelmingly approved by the electorate in May 1978. An increase in activity by clandestine opposition groups dissatisfied with Ahidjo's autocratic rule became evident in 1979, notably in the English-speaking south-western region of the country. In April 1980, however, Ahidjo was again re-elected as sole candidate for a further five-year term.

THE BIYA PRESIDENCY

In November 1982 Ahidjo resigned on the grounds of ill-health, and transferred the presidency to Biya, who was expected to continue Ahidjo's policies of national unity and non-alignment. The appointment of Bello Bouba Maigari, a northerner, as prime minister in the subsequent cabinet reshuffle confirmed the continuity of the new regime, in which Ahidjo retained the chairmanship of the UNC. In April 1983, however, four prominent ministers were dismissed in an unexpected cabinet reshuffle. Following a further reorganization in June, rumours began to emerge of divisions between Ahidjo and Biya.

Tensions and Coup Attempts

On 22 August 1983 Biya announced that a plot to overthrow the government had been discovered, and that two close military advisers of Ahidjo had been arrested. Maigari and the minister for the armed forces—both northern Muslims—were subsequently dismissed and, in an administrative reorganization, the number of the country's provinces was increased from seven to 10. On 27 August it was announced that Ahidjo had resigned the chairmanship of the UNC. Biya was elected to the post at a special UNC congress in September; Ahidjo left the country, and remained in exile in France and Senegal until his death in November 1989. In January 1984 Biya was re-elected president, as sole candidate, with 99.98% of the vote. The national assembly subsequently approved a constitutional amendment restoring the country's original official name, the Republic of Cameroon.

In February 1984 Ahidjo and his two military advisers were tried (Ahidjo *in absentia*) for their alleged complicity in the 1983 coup attempt. All three men received death sentences, which were subsequently commuted to terms of life imprisonment. An attempt by the élite republican guard to overthrow the government in April 1984 was suppressed by forces loyal to Biya, after intense fighting, in which a large number of people were reported to have been killed. In contrast to the February trials, the alleged instigators of the coup attempt were swiftly tried by a military court, and 46 of the defendants were subsequently executed.

Reassertion of Presidential Power

The 1984 coup attempt had a destabilizing effect on the Biya government. In the following months, however, Biya was able to maintain control, and confidence in the government was gradually restored. Further trials of those allegedly involved in the conspiracy took place, but always in conditions of secrecy. Members of the government whose allegiance remained in doubt were gradually removed from office, most of the major public enterprises experienced a change of leadership, and in May the UNC central committee dismissed seven of the 12 members of its political bureau. At a party congress, held in March 1985, the UNC was renamed the Rassemblement démocratique du peuple camerounais (RDPC).

From January to March 1986 elections took place for members of RDPC bodies on all levels; the choice of candidates for the first time since the creation of the party indicated that a measure of democratization was emerging. New candidates were elected to more than 50% of the posts, with the proportion rising to 70% at the lower levels of office. The gradual appointment to the administration, often to posts in the parastatal bodies, of a further number of the formerly influential functionaries of the Ahidjo period also indicated Biya's increasing confidence in the stability of his government. The return to Cameroon, from Ghana, of 55 former political dissidents in February 1986 was followed in August by the release of 14 supporters of the UPC, who had been detained since late 1985 on charges of organizing clandestine meetings and distributing tracts.

Elections to the national assembly were held in April 1988, together with a presidential election (brought forward from January 1989 for reasons of economy). Voters in the legislative elections were presented with a choice of RDPC-approved candidates; however, the abstention rate was estimated at 9.9% (compared with 0.8% at the previous general election, in May 1983). Biya, the sole candidate for the presidency, obtained 98.75% of the votes cast. In May 1988 24 ministers were dismissed, and several ministries were merged or abolished. In subsequent months the president's relations with the press became increasingly strained, and journalists who were critical of the government were detained. The ensuing appointment of a reputable journalist as minister of information was intended to reduce tensions between the government and the media. In a government reorganization in April 1989, an additional secretary of state for finance was appointed to assist in negotiations for the rescheduling of Cameroon's external debt, following the adoption of an IMF-approved structural adjustment programme (see Economy).

Opposition and the Pro-Democracy Movement

In February 1990 a number of people were arrested and tried for subversion, as a result of their alleged involvement in an unofficial opposition organization, the Social Democratic Front (SDF). Twelve of the 18 defendants were imprisoned. Later that month, in an apparent attempt to strengthen national unity in the aftermath of the convictions, it was announced that an estimated 100 prisoners who had been detained following the April 1984 coup attempt were to be released.

Biya continued to oppose the establishment of a multi-party system, stating that such a fundamental political change would undermine attempts to resolve the prevailing economic crisis. From March 1990 a series of demonstrations in support of the RDPC took place. In May six deaths were reported, after security forces violently suppressed a demonstration organized by the SDF, which took place in Bamenda (in the English-speaking north-west of the country) and was attended by at least 20,000 people. The SDF, led by John Fru Ndi, received the support of many prominent writers and lawyers (and was alleged by the government to be receiving financial support from Nigeria).

In late June 1990 a congress of the RDPC re-elected Biya as president of the party and carried out a major reorganization of the central committee. In response to continued civil unrest, Biya stated that the future adoption of a multi-party system was envisaged, and subsequently announced a series of reforms, including the abolition of laws governing subversion, the relaxation of restraints on the press, and the reform of legislation prohibiting political associations. In the same month a committee was established to formulate legislation on human rights. In August several political prisoners were released. In early September Biya effected an extensive reorganization of the cabinet, and created a new ministry to oversee the country's programme for economic stabilization. Later in September the vice-president of the RDPC resigned, in protest at alleged corruption and violations of human rights by the government.

In December 1990 the national assembly approved a constitutional amendment providing for the establishment of a multi-party system. Under the new arrangements, the government was required to grant (or refuse) registration within three months to any political association seeking legal recognition. In addition, registered parties were to receive state support during election campaigns. However, the recruitment of party activists on a regional or ethnic basis and the financing of political parties from external sources was prohibited. A large number of political associations subsequently emerged.

During 1991 pressure for political reform intensified. In January anti-government demonstrators protested at Biya's failure (despite previous undertakings) to grant an amnesty to prisoners implicated in the April 1984 coup attempt. In the same month the trial of two journalists, who had published an article critical of Biya in an independent periodical, provoked violent rioting. Meanwhile, opposition leaders renewed their demands for the convening of a national conference to formulate a timetable for multi-party elections. In April Biya's continued opposition to the holding of such a conference provoked a series of demonstrations and widespread riots, which were violently suppressed by security forces; by the end of that month more than 100 people were reported to have been killed. Later in April in response to increasing pressure for constitutional reform, the national assembly formally granted a general amnesty to all political prisoners, and reintroduced the post of prime minister. Sadou Hayatou, hitherto secretary-general to the presidency, was appointed to the position. Hayatou subsequently formed a 32-member transitional government, which principally comprised members of the former cabinet.

In late April 1991 a newly-established alliance of 11 leading opposition groups, the National Co-ordination Committee of Opposition Parties (NCCOP), demanded an unconditional amnesty for all political prisoners (the existing arrangements for an amnesty excluded an estimated 400 political prisoners jailed ostensibly for non-political offences), and the convening of a national conference before 10 May. In early May the University of Yaoundé was closed, after security forces suppressed demonstrations by students. The continuing reluctance of the government to set a date for the national conference prompted the NCCOP to initiate a campaign of civil disobedience, initially comprising one-day strikes and demonstrations. Opposition leaders also demanded the resignation of Hayatou and his cabinet as a precondition to multi-party elections. Later that month seven of Cameroon's 10 provinces were placed under military rule, and in June the government prohibited meetings of opposition parties. In June the NCCOP intensified the campaign of civil disobedience, and orchestrated a general strike, which halted economic activity in most towns. In an attempt to end the campaign, the government prohibited opposition gatherings, and, following continued civil disturbances, banned the NCCOP, on the grounds that it was fomenting terrorist activity. Leaders of the opposition alliance announced that the campaign of civil disobedience was to continue. (However, the effect of the general strike declined in subsequent months.) In September several opposition leaders were temporarily detained, following further violent demonstrations, during which several hundred people were reportedly arrested.

In October 1991 Biya announced that legislative elections were to take place in February 1992, and that a prime minister was to be appointed from the party that secured a majority in the national assembly. He also invited opposition leaders to meet Hayatou to discuss the proposed establishment of a new electoral code. Tripartite negotiations between the government, the opposition parties and independent officials commenced at the end of October, but were delayed by procedural disputes, owing to opposition demands that the agenda of the meeting be extended to include a review of the constitution. In mid-November, however, the government and about 40 of the 47 registered opposition parties signed an agreement providing for the establishment of a 10-member committee to draft constitutional reforms. The opposition pledged to suspend the campaign of civil disobedience, while the government agreed to end the ban on opposition meetings and to release all prisoners who had been arrested during the demonstrations earlier that year. However, several parties within the NCCOP, including the SDF, subsequently rejected the agreement, resulting in further division within the opposition. Later in November the government revoked the ban on opposition gatherings, and, in December, ended the military rule which had been imposed in seven of the provinces. In the same month the national assembly approved a new electoral code. In January 1992 the government announced that legislative elections were to take place on 1 March, following demands from opposition leaders that elections be postponed in order to allow additional time for preparation. However, a number of opposition groups, including two of the four principal parties, the SDF and the Union démocratique du Cameroun (UDC), refused to participate in the elections, claiming that the scheduled date was too early and that the electoral code was biased in favour of the RDPC.

In February 1992 the opposition parties that had not accepted the tripartite agreement in November 1991 formed a political association, the Alliance pour le redressement du Cameroun (ARC), which was to boycott the elections. Later in February the former prime minister, Bello Bouba Maigari, was elected as chairman of one of the principal opposition movements, the Union nationale pour la démocratie et le progrès (UNDP); the UNDP subsequently announced that it would contest the elections.

At the legislative elections on 1 March 1992, which were contested by 32 political parties, the RDPC won 88 of the 180 seats in the national assembly, while the UNDP secured 68, the Union des populations camerounaises (UPC) 18, and the Mouvement pour la défense de la République (MDR) six seats. An estimated 61% of registered voters took part in the elections, although the proportion was only 10% in regions affected by the general strike. Following discussions between Biya and the leader of the MDR, Dakole Daissala, after the elections, the RDPC formed an alliance with the MDR, thereby securing an absolute majority in the national assembly. Biya subsequently appointed Joseph-Charles Doumbu as secretary-general of the RDPC, replacing Ebénézer Njoh Mouelle, who had failed to be re-elected to the national assembly. Later in March a francophone member of the RDPC, Djibril Cavayé Yeguie, was elected as president of the newly-established national assembly. On 9 April Biya formed a new 25-member cabinet, which, however, retained the majority of ministers from the previous government. Five members of the MDR, including Dakole Daissala, also received portfolios. Simon Achidi Achu, an anglophone member of the RDPC who had served in the Ahidjo administration, was appointed as prime minister.

In August Biya announced that the forthcoming presidential election, due to take place in May 1993, was to be brought forward to October 1992. This measure was widely believed to benefit the government, following the failure of a large number of opposition supporters to register earlier that year, as a result of the SDF boycott of the legislative elections. Later in August the minister of the civil service and administrative reform, who had been relieved of certain duties after his discovery of financial malpractice perpetrated by a number of civil servants, resigned. In September three independent publications, including *Le Messager,* were banned. Later that month the government introduced legislation regulating the election of the president, which prohibited political parties from forming electoral alliances, and stipulated that, contrary to the system in operation in the majority of francophone countries, the election was to comprise a single round of voting. Despite protracted negotiations, the opposition subsequently failed to select a single candidate to contest the presidential election, as planned; however, two of the seven opposition members who had presented their candidacy withdrew in favour of the leader of the SDF, John Fru Ndi, who received the support of the ARC alliance.

At the presidential election, which took place on 11 October 1992, Biya was re-elected by 39.9% of votes cast, while Fru Ndi secured 35.9%, and Maigari, the candidate of the UNDP, 19.2% of the vote. However, Fru Ndi disputed the official results, and claimed that he had won the election. A number of violent demonstrations, particularly in the north-west and in Douala, were subsequently staged by opposition supporters in protest at the alleged electoral irregularities by the government; several hundred people were reported to have been arrested in Bamenda, in the North-West Province. Later in October, however, the supreme court ruled against an appeal by Fru Ndi that the results of the election be declared invalid, despite confirmation from a US monitoring organization that it had detected widespread electoral irregularities. At the end of October, in response to continued unrest, the government placed Fru Ndi and a number of his supporters under house arrest, and declared a state of emergency in the North-West Province for a period of three months.

Pressure for Constitutional Reform

Biya was inaugurated for a third term as president in November 1992. Although he undertook to carry out further constitutional reforms, international criticism of the government increased, resulting in the suspension of economic aid by the USA and Germany in protest at the government's suppression of opposition activity and the continued enforcement of the state of emergency. At the end of November Biya appointed a new 30-member cabinet, which included, for the first time, representatives of the UPC, the UNDP and the Parti national du progrès (PNP). In December order was restored in the North-West Province, and at the end of that month, the state of emergency was lifted, although Fru Ndi claimed that a number of troops remained in the region. In January 1993 the government granted amnesty to a number of political prisoners, who had been arrested in October 1992.

In March 1993 the Union pour le changement, an alliance of opposition parties, which included the SDF, co-ordinated a campaign of demonstrations and a boycott of French consumer goods (in protest at the French government's continuing support for Biya), to reinforce demands that a new presidential election take place. The government accused the Union pour le changement of attempting to incite civil disorder in order to destabilize the country. In the same month, however, in response to international pressure, the government announced that a national debate on constitutional reform was to take place by the end of May. In early April, following SDF demands that a revised constitution be submitted for approval at a national referendum by a stipulated date, Fru Ndi stated that he was to convene a national conference to determine the political future of Cameroon. In the same month a meeting organized by the Cameroon Anglophone Movement (CAM), which took place in Buéa, the capital of the South-West Province, issued demands for the restoration of a federal system of government, in response to the dominance of the French-speaking section of the population in the country. (The SDF, however, opposed the proposed establishment of a federal state.) Later in April reports of division within the SDF emerged, after a prominent party official, Bernard Muna, declared his support for SDF participation in the national debate that was to be organized by the government; Muna was subsequently dismissed from his post in the SDF.

Following a meeting with the French president, François Mitterrand, in early May 1993, Biya announced that the planned debate on the revision of the constitution was to take place in early June. Instead of the envisaged national conference, however, a technical commission was established to prepare recommendations based on proposals from all sectors of the population. Later in May the government promulgated draft constitutional amendments, which provided for a democratic system of government, including the establishment of an upper legislative chamber, a council of supreme judiciary affairs, a council of state, and a high authority to govern the civil service. The constitutional provisions also restricted the powers of the president, whose tenure was to be limited to two five-year terms of office. Elections were to comprise two rounds of voting (a system more favourable to the opposition). The draft legislation retained a unitary state, but, in recognition of demands by supporters of federalism, introduced a more decentralized system of government. The constitutional proposals were subject to amendment, following the recommendations of the technical commission. However, three representatives of the English-speaking community subsequently resigned from the technical commission, in protest at the government's alleged control of the constitutional debate.

At a party congress, which took place in July 1993, the SDF adopted a draft constitution that provided for a decentralized federal state. At the end of August a two-day strike, which was organized by the SDF as part of its anti-government campaign, failed to attract the support of other prominent opposition parties, and was only partially observed; however, rioting by opposition supporters was reported in Bamenda. In September a number of opposition activists were arrested, in an effort by the government to pre-empt further strikes. Later that month, however, the Union pour le changement announced plans to organize a new series of demonstrations in support of its demands. In early November security forces prevented Fru Ndi from conducting a press conference in Yaoundé on the occasion of the first anniversary of Biya's re-election, while about 30 SDF members were arrested; Fru Ndi briefly took refuge at the Netherlands embassy. The SDF detainees were subsequently released, following the intervention of the French government.

In February 1994 six principal opposition parties (excluding the SDF) formed an electoral coalition, the Front démocratique et patriotique, to contest municipal elections which were due to take place later that year. In April the authorities banned a conference by supporters of the CAM, which, nevertheless, took place at Bamenda. In July, in accordance with the government's aim of promoting economic recovery, a new ministry with responsibility for the economy and finance was created as part of an extensive reconstruction of the cabinet. At the end of that month about eight people were killed in clashes in the northern town of Maroua, following agitation within the UNDP, which subsequently led to a split in the party, over the decision by its vice-chairman, Hamadou Moustapha, to accept a cabinet portfolio without obtaining the party's prior consent.

In September 1994 it was reported that a former prominent member of the security forces had confessed to conspiring to assassinate Biya at a public ceremony in May. Later that month an informal alliance of 16 opposition movements, the Front des alliés pour le changement (FAC), was established under the leadership of Fru Ndi (effectively replacing the Union pour le changement); the FAC criticized alleged human rights violations on the part of the authorities, together with the indefinite postponement of the municipal elections and the proposed transfer of state-owned enterprises to the private sector. Two of the most prominent opposition parties, the UNDP and the UDC refused to join the alliance, however, on the grounds that it was dominated by the SDF. In October the SDF organized a one-day strike, which was observed principally in anglophone regions. In early November Biya announced that discussions on the revision of the constitution were to resume, following the establishment of a 'consultative constitutional review committee' and that the municipal elections were to take place in 1995. Later that month the SDF accused the French ambassador in Yaoundé of discrediting the movement at meetings with traditional leaders. Also in November UNDP deputies boycotted parliamentary sessions in support of demands for the release of a number of party members who had been detained following the factional clashes in July.

Constitutional discussions commenced in mid-December 1994, but were boycotted by the opposition, which cited limitations in the agenda of the debate; the UDC (the only opposition movement to attend the discussions) withdrew after two days. In early 1995, however, revised constitutional amendments were submitted to Biya for consideration. In February the leader of the Mouvement pour la démocratie et le progrès, Samuel Eboua, were elected president of the FAC, replacing Fru Ndi. In the same month the UNDP expelled Moustapha and another member of government from the party; Moustapha subsequently established a breakaway faction. In April Biya announced the creation of 64 new local government districts, in preparation for the forthcoming municipal elections. Following reports of division within the SDF, seven members of the executive committee were refused admission to the party congress, which took place in May; a breakaway group, the Social Democratic Movement, was subsequently formed under the leadership of the former secretary-general of the SDF, Siga Asanga.

In early July 1995 members of a newly-emerged anglophone organization, the Southern Cameroons National Council (SCNC, which demanded that the former portion of the British Cameroons that had amalgamated with the republic of Cameroon in 1961 be granted autonomy), staged a demonstration in Bamenda, subsequently clashing with security forces. Later that month English-speaking representatives of the government criticized the demands for the establishment of an anglophone republic (which would be known as Southern Cameroons); the SCNC apparently intended to proclaim formally the independence of Southern Cameroons on 1 October 1996, following the adoption of a separate constitution for the new republic. In early August the SCNC was prohibited from staging a demonstration. In the same month representatives of anglophone movements, including the SCNC and the CAM, officially presented their demands for the establishment of an independent republic of Southern Cameroons at the UN, and urged the international community to assist in resolving the issue in order to avert civil conflict in Cameroon; the organizations claimed that the plebiscite of 1961, whereby the former southern portion of British Cameroons had voted to merge with the Republic of Cameroon on terms of equal status, had been rendered invalid by subsequent francophone domination.

In October 1995 a special congress of the RDPC re-elected Biya as leader of the party for a further term of five years. Meanwhile, Cameroon's pending application for membership of the Commonwealth (see below) prompted further controversy; opposition movements urged the Commonwealth to refuse admission to Cameroon on the grounds that no progress had been achieved with regard to Commonwealth stipulations on human rights and the democratic process, while the SCNC submitted a rival application for membership on behalf of the proposed independent republic of Southern Cameroons. (Nevertheless, following a visit by Commonwealth officials in mid-1995, Cameroon was admitted to the organization in November.) In the same month Biya announced that the municipal elections were to take place in January 1996 (although both opposition movements and parties belonging to the government coalition had demanded that the elections be preceded by constitutional reform and the establishment of an independent electoral commission). In December 1995 the national assembly formally adopted the revised constitutional amendments, submitted by Biya earlier that month, which increased the presidential mandate from five to seven years (while restricting the maximum tenure of office to two terms).

Some 38 political parties participated in the municipal elections, which took place relatively peacefully in January 1996 (although the SDF had urged its supporters to disrupt voting in constituencies where the movement had been refused authorization to present candidates). The RDPC (which was the only party to contest the elections in 45 constituencies) retained about 55% of the 336 local government areas, while the SDF secured 27%, principally in the west of the country. In March the SDF and the UNDP (which had also achieved some success in the municipal elections, principally in the north) urged a campaign of civil disobedience in protest at the government's appointment by decree of representatives to replace the elected mayors in principal towns. At the beginning of that month about two people were killed in a demonstration which had been organized by the SDF in the south-western town of Limbe as part of the campaign. Later in March the supreme court annulled the results of municipal elections in two constituencies, which had been secured by the RDPC, owing to alleged irregularities. In the same month eight UNDP activists were imprisoned for their involvement in an attack on the vehicle of a UNDP deputy minister in July 1994 (during violence that had been prompted by the factional division within the party). In April the government imposed a total ban on all media reports of the SDF and UNDP campaign of civil disobedience.

In May 1996, following increasing division within the UPC apparently resulting from its lack of success in the municipal elections, the secretary-general, Augustin Frédéric Kodock (who held the ministerial portfolio of agriculture), was dismissed from the party, and subsequently formed a breakaway faction. In the same month a two-day general strike, organized by the SDF and the UNDP in protest at the appointment of the government delegates in towns, was principally observed in western and northern regions, where the parties received popular support. The two parties announced a further general strike in June, which was, however, supported only in the west of the country.

In August 1996 Fru Ndi criticized SCNC activists for urging supporters of anglophone movements to boycott the registration process for the forthcoming elections. (A number of SDF members were believed to also belong to the SCNC.) In September Biya appointed Peter Mafany Musonge, hitherto the manager of the Cameroon Development Corpn, to the office of prime minister, replacing Achidi Achu; the cabinet was subsequently reorganized. In October the editor of *Le Messager*, Pius Njawe, and another journalist were imprisoned, after publishing material critical of Biya. (Following an appeal by Njawe, however, the supreme court ordered his release in November.) In December Biya was nominated by an RDPC congress as the party candidate in the presidential election (which was due to take place in October 1997). At the end of January 1997 the government announced that the legislative elections, which had been scheduled to take place in early March, were to be postponed owing to organizational difficulties, following opposition complaints that its supporters had been allowed insufficient time for registration. (However, Biya's failure to extend the mandate of the incumbent national assembly, which expired in early March, subsequently prompted criticism from opposition deputies.) Also in January Fru Ndi stated that the opposition would not stage demonstrations in support of demands that the government establish an independent electoral commission, in order to avert unrest prior to the elections. At the end of March, however, about 10 people were killed when unidentified armed groups staged attacks against government and security buildings in Bamenda and other towns in the North-West Province; a curfew was imposed in the province and a number of people were subsequently detained in connection with the violence, which was generally attributed to members of the SCNC. In April the government announced that the legislative elections were to take place on 17 May.

In May 1997 about five people were killed in pre-election violence, which prompted the imposition of increased security measures, including the closure of the country's borders. The government ordered an inquiry into clashes which took place in the northern town of Rey Bouba between supporters of a UNDP candidate and followers of the local traditional leader (an RDPC member). The legislative elections, which were contested on 17 May by 46 political parties, were monitored by a 13-member Commonwealth observer mission; the poll was extended in parts of northern Cameroon, where voting had been delayed as a result of logistical difficulties. The announcement later that month of provisional election results (which attributed a large majority of seats to the RDPC) prompted claims from the opposition parties of widespread electoral malpractice. (However, the Commonwealth observer group expressed general satisfaction with the election process.) Three people were killed in clashes between RDPC and SDF members in the South-West Province, where the election result was disputed by the two parties. In early June the supreme court (which had rejected most opposition appeals against RDPC victories) announced the official election results: the RDPC had secured 109 of the 180 seats in the legislature, while the SDF had obtained 43, the UNDP 13 and the UDC five seats. On 3 August further polls were conducted in seven constituencies, where the results had been annulled owing to alleged irregularities; the RDPC won all of the seats. In mid-June the SDF announced that it had abandoned an initial decision to boycott the national assembly. In July it was reported that the former minister of public health, Titus Edzoa, who in April had resigned from the cabinet in order to contest the presidential election later that year, had been arrested and charged with embezzlement.

EXTERNAL RELATIONS

During 1989–91 President Biya pursued initiatives with the ultimate aim of securing Cameroon's admission to the Commonwealth. It was widely suggested that Biya's motives for joining that organization reflected both a wish to appease the English-speaking population at a time of increasing participation in the activities of francophone associations, and a means of obtaining additional development aid. (Cameroon continued to receive French support, as well as significant assistance from the USA.) In 1993 an application by Cameroon for membership of the Commonwealth was accepted, in principle, subject to the government complying with certain democratic conditions. In November 1995 Cameroon was formally admitted to the Commonwealth.

In June 1991 the Nigerian government claimed that Cameroon had annexed nine Nigerian fishing settlements, following a long-standing border dispute, based on a 1913 agreement between Germany and the United Kingdom that ceded the Bakassi peninsula in the Gulf of Guinea (a region of strategic significance) to Cameroon. Subsequent attempts to negotiate the dispute achieved little progress, and further incursions by Cameroon were reported in November. In early January 1994 it was reported that members of the Cameroonian security forces had entered Nigeria and raided villages, killing several Nigerian nationals. Some 500 Nigerian troops subsequently occupied the two nominally Cameroonian islands of Diamant and Jabane in the Gulf of Guinea. Cameroon also dispatched troops to the region, while the two nations agreed to resume bilateral negotiations in an effort to resolve the dispute. In February the Cameroonian government announced that it was to submit the dispute for adjudication by the UN Security Council, the Organization of African Unity (OAU) and the International Court of Justice (ICJ). However, subsequent clashes between Nigerian and Cameroonian forces in the disputed region prompted fears of a full-scale conflict between the two nations. Shortly afterwards, a French diplomatic and military mission arrived in Cameroon, in response to a request for military assistance from the Cameroonian government in the context of the defence agreements between the two countries. Nevertheless, bilateral negotiations continued: in late March a proposal by the Nigerian government that a referendum be conducted in the contested areas was rejected by the Cameroon government. In the same month the OAU urged the withdrawal of troops from the disputed region; however Cameroon failed to obtain an official condemnation of Nigeria, and both governments indicated dissatisfaction with the resolution. In May two members of the Nigerian armed forces were killed in further clashes in the region. Later that month negotiations between the two nations, which were mediated by the Togolese government, resumed in Yaoundé. In September 10 members of the Cameroonian armed forces were killed in further confrontations.

In February 1996 renewed hostilities between Nigerian and Cameroonian forces in the Bakassi peninsula resulted in several casualties. Later that month, however, Cameroon and Nigeria agreed to refrain from further military action, and delegations from the two countries resumed discussions, with mediation by the Togolese president, in an attempt to resolve the dispute. In March the ICJ ruled that Cameroon had failed to provide sufficient evidence to substantiate its contention that Nigeria had instigated the border dispute, and ordered both nations to cease military operations in the region, to withdraw troops to former positions, and to co-operate with a UN investigative mission, which was to be dispatched to the area. In April, however, clashes continued, with each government accusing the other of initiating the attacks. Claims by Nigeria that the Cameroonian forces were supported by troops from France were denied by the French government. Diplomatic efforts to avoid further conflict increased; in May a Cameroonian delegation visited Nigeria, while the Nigerian president accepted an invitation to attend an OAU summit meeting (which was convened in Yaoundé in July). However, tension between the two countries increased prior to the OAU summit meeting, after the Nigerian government accused Cameroon of reinforcing its contingent in the Bakassi peninsula. In September both governments assured the UN investigative mission of their commitment to a peaceful settlement of the dispute. In December, however, the Nigerian authorities claimed that Cameroonian troops had resumed attacks in the region. In May 1997 the Cameroonian government denied further Nigerian claims that it had initiated attacks. In the same month the UN requested that the Togolese government continue efforts to mediate in the dispute.

Economy

EDITH HODGKINSON

Revised for this edition by ANDREW MANLEY

In contrast to a number of countries in the region, post-independent governments in Cameroon have pursued moderate, centrist economic policies, aiming at a diversification of international relations and allowing a cautious growth in state intervention. However, the economic crisis (which emerged during the late 1980s following the decline in the price of petroleum in 1986) prompted radical changes in government policy, in accordance with the mainstream of IMF-guided programmes of economic restructuring and liberalization. However, Cameroon has frequently reneged on its commitments.

During the 1960s and 1970s Cameroon demonstrated a significant level of economic growth, which was based on a variety of agricultural exports and the development of self-sufficiency in food, and increased in the late 1970s, owing to the development of the petroleum sector. By 1980 petroleum had become the country's principal export commodity, shielding the economy from fluctuations in earnings from export crops. In the first half of the 1980s economic growth averaged 7%–8% annually (more than double the annual average in the previous two decades). Following a sharp decline in the international price for petroleum in 1986, however, the economy deteriorated, although the effects were initially limited by the government's policy of drawing on accumulated revenue from sales of petroleum in order to sustain the level of investment expenditure and imports. Nevertheless, owing to sustained weaknesses in international prices for petroleum and for the country's major cash crops, these funds were depleted by the end of the decade, and the Biya government was obliged to introduce austerity programmes, involving reductions in both current and capital expenditure. Consequently, the economy contracted sharply, with the rate of decline in real gross domestic product (GDP) reaching 10.4% in the year ending 30 June 1988, but easing to about 2% per year in 1988/89 and 1989/90. In this situation, and with the support of loans from the World Bank, the African Development Bank (ADB) and France, Cameroon undertook an extensive, five-year programme of economic restructuring in 1989/90. This entailed the reform of the country's parastatal organizations (through the liquidation of unprofitable enterprises and the transfer to private ownership of others) and of the cumbersome and inefficient administrative structure. Specifically, the role of the national agricultural marketing board, the Office national de commercialisation des produits de base (ONCPB), was reduced, and responsibility for marketing was gradually transferred to the private sector.

The implementation of reforms was, however, impeded by an opposition campaign of civil disobedience, which was initiated in 1991 (see Recent History). Political instability, in conjunction with widespread corruption within the civil service and increasing external debt, contributed to the deterioration in the economy. The decline was halted by the devaluation of the CFA franc in January 1994, which doubled the local currency value of petroleum and other commodity exports, stimulating an increase in supply. Buoyant soft commodity prices on the international market provided a further boost. Real GDP expanded by 3.3% in 1994/95, with official estimates of 5% real growth in 1995/96. However, the economy's dependence on export crops has intensified, owing to the adverse effects on the manufacturing and services sectors of the sharp reduction in real income following devaluation, and to the continuing decline in petroleum output. Cameroon's prospects for sustained recovery in the long term are therefore reliant on continuing structural reform, to improve resource allocation.

AGRICULTURE

In the early 1980s, as the petroleum industry increased in importance, the contribution of agriculture, forestry and fishing to Cameroon's GDP declined, from 32% in the year 1978/79 to 21% in 1984/85. While petroleum production declined, the contribution of agriculture again increased, to an estimated 28.6% in 1994. It remains the dominant sector of the economy, employing an estimated 70% of the labour force and accounting for 40% of total export earnings. The government provides incentives in the form of subsidies on fertilizers and pesticides. Small-scale farmers dominate agricultural export production with the exception of rubber and palm oil. Despite efforts to develop Cameroonian participation, timber production remains dominated by large foreign firms.

Coffee is cultivated on some 400,000 ha, predominantly in the west and south. Four-fifths of the coffee crop is robusta, the remainder being arabica. Output has fluctuated widely in recent years, in response to climatic and vegetative circumstances and trends in producer prices. Thus, the dramatic reduction in the robusta price in 1989/90 prompted a decline in its production from 121,857 tons in 1988/89 to 76,000 tons. After recovering in subsequent years, it fell to a low of 48,000 tons in 1992/93. By 1994/95 output had recovered slightly, to an estimated 57,000 tons. Output of cocoa, grown on around 350,000 ha, has similarly demonstrated an overall, if less marked, decline since the producer price was reduced in 1989/90, with production at 111,000 tons in 1993/94, nearly one-fifth less than the 1988/89 level. Both coffee and cocoa yields have suffered as a result of the failure of replanting programmes to keep pace with the ageing of plantations. The liberalization of marketing and the abandonment of the producer price system, in conjunction with improved world prices, was expected to stimulate higher production in the mid-1990s. However, individual producers had little incentive to reinvest, while private-sector buyers tended to form cartels to force prices down; these problems were exacerbated by the smuggling of poor quality cocoa to Nigeria. In October 1996 the European Union (EU) opened a Stabilization of Export Earnings (Stabex) credit line to support the cocoa marketing system. Following devaluation cocoa output rose in both 1994/95, to 109,000 tons, and in 1995/96, to 130,000 tons. The annual production of bananas declined from more than 100,000 tons in the early 1960s to about two-thirds of this level in the early 1980s. Following a major restructuring of the sector, which began in 1987, and the transfer to the private sector of the state-owned enterprise, Organisation camerounaise de banane, output increased dramatically, reaching an estimated 200,000 tons in 1994/95. Bananas have consequently become a leading agricultural export, although there is concern that the sector could suffer as a result of future disputes between European and US-supported signatories to the World Trade Organization.

Cotton production, which is concentrated in the north, recovered from the drought of the late 1970s and early 1980s, and reached a record 165,400 metric tons of unginned (seed) cotton in 1988/89. Production declined in subsequent years, owing in part to the 32% reduction in producer prices in 1989/90 and their subsequent stagnation. However, devaluation, which permitted a 44% increase in the producer price for the 1994/95 crop, stimulated a rise in output, to 165,000 tons. Production in 1995/96 increased further, to 195,000 tons, with higher yields per hectare. Output of palm oil has recently fluctuated between 100,000 tons and 120,000 tons per year, about twice the level of the late 1970s, but the product is not competitive on world markets. Rubber, however, has good prospects, with yields competing with those of the major Asian producers. After a decline in the early 1990s, output exceeded the previous high of 1989/90, at an estimated 55,500 tons in 1994/95, and was projected at 87,000 tons in 1996/97.

Cameroon's food production has been advancing at a higher rate than population growth, and the country is generally self-sufficient. In 1994 output of millet and sorghum reached an estimated 460,000 metric tons, while maize production amounted to some 430,000 tons. The annual harvest of paddy rice, which is grown under both traditional and modern methods, had increased dramatically, from only 15,000 tons in 1979/80 to 107,400 tons in 1984/85, reflecting the government's priority of achieving self-sufficiency in this cereal. Output declined in subsequent years, to only 61,050 tons in 1988/89, but in the early 1990s averaged some 95,000 tons per year. The long-term target for annual rice production remains 280,000 tons. Commercial production of sugar began in 1966 and averaged some 60,000 tons per year in the early 1990s. Livestock makes a significant contribution to the food supply. In 1995 the national herds were assessed at 4.9m. cattle, 7.6m. sheep and goats, and 1.4m. pigs, while commercial poultry farms had an estimated 20m. birds. The development of the fisheries industry has been constrained by the relatively small area available for exploitation (because of boundary disputes and the presence of the offshore island of Bioko, part of Equatorial Guinea) and the poor level of fish stocks in these waters. By the late 1980s the number of industrial fishing vessels was reduced, and the total fishing catch had declined substantially; in 1994 the total catch was estimated at 66,000 tons. The industrial catch is less than one-tenth of the total.

Almost half of the country is covered by forest, but an inadequate transport system has impeded the development of this sector. After declining during the early 1980s (reflecting the recession in world timber prices), production recovered to almost 2.1m. cu m in 1984/85 and 1985/86, while revenue from exports of logs and wood products totalled some 30,000m. francs CFA in 1986. Forestry has been a priority under structural adjustment efforts since 1989, and by 1994/95 production was estimated at 3m. cu m. However, recorded exports reflected less than one-third of this total; in the first nine months of 1996 exports amounted to 980,000 cu m.

MINING AND POWER

In 1976 Elf, the French oil company, established a commercial oilfield in shallow water near the Nigerian border, and four fields came on stream in 1977–78. Production of crude petroleum reached 9.16m. tons in 1985, but then declined in each subsequent year, to an estimated 4.7m. tons in 1995. Exploration has remained limited, although new permits were granted in 1991 and a new field came on stream in that year. In 1995 improved incentives were introduced for the development of marginal fields, prompting Elf to invest in a production platform at Kole. Production commenced there and at some other marginal fields in 1997, stimulating hopes that the decline in overall oil production would be halted. Total recoverable oil reserves were estimated at 298m. barrels (equivalent to the output of 7.4 years at current production levels). It was therefore possible that Cameroon would cease to be a significant exporter of petroleum by the year 2000. A consortium led by the US company, Exxon, planned to construct a 1,000-km pipeline to transport oil from the Doba basin in southern Chad to the southern Cameroonian port of Kribi. Royalties from the pipeline, which was scheduled to be operational by the year 2000, were expected partially to offset the decline in direct revenue from petroleum. Natural gas reserves, estimated at 110,000m. cu m, have been located offshore near the Nigerian border and off Kribi.

Bauxite deposits have hitherto remained unexploited. However, following the signing of an agreement with the Chinese government in early 1997, it was announced that the Chinese Gansu Corpn for Techno-Economic Co-operation was to mine bauxite from three deposits (which were estimated to contain reserves of 2,000 metric tons). Development of these deposits would enable the Edéa smelter, which was dependent on imports of bauxite from Guinea, to be supplied locally. Deposits of iron ore near Kribi remain unexploited, and uranium reserves totalling up to 10,000 tons have been identified, but not developed, owing to low international prices. Large-scale limestone deposits near Garoua supply clinker and cement plants.

Hydroelectricity meets 95% of the country's electricity demand, which was 2,374 kWh in 1992/93: heavy industry is the major consumer, with the aluminium plant taking nearly 50% of the total generation. The chief installations are at Edéa (total capacity 263 MW) and at Song-Loulou (total capacity 384 MW). These stations supply the network linking Yaoundé, Edéa, Douala and the west. The other major network supplies the north and draws principally on the 72-MW hydroelectric station at Lagdo. A 210-MW hydroelectric installation is planned at the Nachtigal Falls on the Sanaga river and feasibility studies were completed in 1991, but the contraction in the economy in the early 1990s reduced the pressure for expansion in capacity.

MANUFACTURING

In 1994/95 manufacturing accounted for 11.3% of GDP. This sector is dominated by the processing of raw materials, and the assembly of imported raw materials and components. It is therefore not deeply integrated into the economic structure and has limited linkage effects.

The bulk of manufacturing industry is of post-independence origin. The government gave priority to industrial development aimed at national and regional markets as a means of accelerating growth. To this end, extensive tax and financing incentives were made available, while the state took substantial shareholdings in major ventures, held through the Société nationale d'investissement du Cameroun (SNI). During the economic crisis in the 1980s a major restructuring programme was announced. However, its implementation was slow and little progress was made until late 1990, when 15 companies were transferred to the private sector. Other parastatal enterprises were liquidated, and those remaining under the aegis of the state, such as the electricity corporation, SONEL, were obliged to sign performance contracts with the government as part of the overall structural adjustment programme. Privatization continued in subsequent years, although the programme was constantly behind target (for example, only five out of fifteen enterprises were transferred to the private sector, as scheduled, in 1994), owing, in part, to the poor financial situation of the enterprises. Following renewed pressure from its multilateral creditors, the government has expanded the programme since mid-1994; another 15 enterprises were designated for the privatization list, in both the services and the manufacturing sector. In early 1997 the privatization of the state water company, Société nationale des eaux du Cameroun, the state railway and the state telecommunications enterprise, which was scheduled for completion, was still pending. However, the successful privatization of the rubber producer, Hévéa-Cameroun, and the shipping line was welcomed by multilateral creditors.

Under the fourth Five-Year Plan (1976–81), linkages between the raw material base and manufacturing were increased by the development of an integrated pulp and paper mill, a tyre factory based on local rubber, the expansion of cement production (quadrupling to 516,000 tons in 1981), the increase in aluminium production capacity, and the installation of a petroleum refinery. The Edéa pulp and paper plant began operations in 1981 but closed after only a year, following heavy financial losses, and was liquidated in 1986. A petroleum refinery began production at Cap Limboh in 1981. Its initial annual capacity was increased to 2m. tons, but output declined to 883,000 tons, owing to competition from illicit imports from Nigeria. An industrial free zone, which offers concessions for energy-intensive operations, was established on 300 ha in Douala in 1991, but interest remained limited, owing to the country's economic and political crisis. Local manufacturing in general has been adversely affected by the widespread illicit trade in Nigerian goods, resulting from the strong CFA franc; the currency devaluation of 1994 was expected to remedy this problem, at least in the short term.

TRANSPORT

The rail network, totalling some 1,104 km, is the most important element of the transport infrastructure. The main line is the 885-km 'Transcameroon', from Douala to Ngaoundéré. There are plans to connect the line with the proposed new port at Grand Batanga (see below) and, in the long term, to construct a 1,000 km-line from Kribi to the Central African Republic (CAR).

The road network totalled some 34,300 km in 1995, of which 4,288 km were paved. Roads in the north have been improved to give access to the Ngaoundéré rail-head, and there are long-term plans to upgrade the east-west road linking Nigeria with the CAR. In recent years, however, development has been impeded by the economic crisis.

Cameroon has seaports at Douala-Bonabéri, Kribi and Limbe-Tiko (although the latter is now almost completely unuseable). Total traffic handled by Doula-Bonabéri in 1995 was an estimated 4.2m. tons, accounting for about 95% of all port activity. Feasibility studies have been conducted for deep-water ports at Cap Limboh (near Limbe and the oil refinery) and Grand Batanga, south of the existing port handling wood and minerals at Kribi. The latter is dependent on the exploitation of the offshore gas reserve and iron ore reserves, neither of which seems likely in the near future.

The poor state of the road network has encouraged the development of internal air travel and of small domestic airports. Cameroon Airlines—75% owned by the government and 25% by Air France—has provided domestic flights and services to Africa and Europe since Cameroon's withdrawal from Air Afrique in 1971; the company has, however, encountered severe financial difficulties. There are international airports at Douala, Garoua and Yaoundé.

FINANCE

Revenue from petroleum production profoundly changed the country's fiscal position, and allowed a rapid rise in both current and capital spending during the early 1980s. However, the decline in world petroleum prices during 1986 and the consequent fall in oil royalties resulted in reduced expenditure, in real terms, compared with 1985/86. It was not until 1991/92, however, that spending was curtailed in nominal terms, by as much as 24%, with a further cut of 10% in 1992/93. The reduction affected the capital budget, which declined by more than 50% in the two-year period, undermining the government's investment programme. However, revenue also failed to meet projections, as a result of both the general contraction in the economy and a politically-motivated refusal to pay taxes, with the result that the budget deficit, which had been halved between 1990/91 and 1992/93, in both nominal and real terms (from the equivalent of 13.4% of GDP to 6.5%), again increased in 1993/94, to 9% of GDP. A modest improvement was registered in 1994/95, however, as current expenditure was curtailed through a reduction in the salary bill and in funds for health and education, to allow a small recovery in capital expenditure. More significant was the increase in revenue from the reintroduction of export taxes on agro-industrial products and an extended and increased sales tax. The budget deficit was reported to have been contained at the equivalent of 7%–8% of GDP, still far above the target of 4.5%. The government aimed to reduce the deficit further, to 1.5% of GDP in 1995/96, and intensified efforts to restrict expenditure, and to increase revenue by imposing additional levies and improving customs collection. Expenditure was to be contained by the programme to reduce the public sector bill further, and an associated programme of privatizations and liquidations of parastatal companies; however, only about 4,300 civil servants had been dismissed by mid-1996. The 1996/97 budget was projected to achieve a surplus of 1,110m. francs CFA. (including external debt-servicing payments totalling 548,000m. francs CFA).

The financial sector is relatively sophisticated; however, the economic crisis of the late 1980s affected the sector rapidly and severely, as the government withdrew its reserves with the commercial banks and private companies supplying the public sector suffered from accumulating arrears. By mid-1987 most commercial banks were technically insolvent. An important element of the structural adjustment programme was a restructuring of the financial sector, with banks being liquidated or, in a few cases, merging. Debts owed to the country's banks were believed to total US $1,130m. in late 1995. In early 1997 the Banque internationale pour le commerce et l'industrie du Cameroun was restructured, prior to its privatization by the year 2000.

FOREIGN TRADE AND AID

Following a deterioration in Cameroon's foreign trade position in the 1970s, the emergence of petroleum as the leading export (crude petroleum accounted for 55% of export earnings in 1985) resulted in a considerable and growing surplus, despite significant increases in the level of import spending. Although petroleum earnings declined sharply in the late 1980s, trade remained in surplus, sustained by earnings from agricultural exports. However, the trade position, as measured by export coverage of imports, deteriorated from the figure of more than 200% recorded in 1985; in 1990–93 it averaged 127%. Following the currency devaluation, exports were stimulated and imports reduced, restoring the ratio to 185% in 1995/96, according to provisional government figures.

The high level of earnings from the petroleum sector during the early 1980s enabled development expenditure to be financed without a substantial increase in the foreign debt. Servicing of the foreign debt was thus manageable, representing about 15% of export earnings in most years during the first half of the decade. From 1986, however, there was a marked deterioration, owing to the sharp decline in revenue from the petroleum sector, while debt rose by over a quarter in that year. The combination of increasing debt and slowing export growth resulted in a debt-servicing ratio of as much as 31% by 1988, which was, however, sharply reduced through debt-rescheduling by the 'Paris Club' of Western official creditors. In May 1989, following the negotiation of agreements with the IMF on stand-by and compensatory credits, and in the context of continuing budgetary restraint, Cameroon obtained rescheduling over a period of ten years of US $535m. in liabilities to official creditors. The debt-servicing ratio was consequently reduced to 16.3% in 1989, and subsequently remained at around this level, with further rescheduling in 1992, and again in 1994 following the devaluation of the CFA franc, which immediately doubled the local currency value of the foreign debt. Despite a 50% reduction in Cameroon's debt to France, total indebtedness had increased to $9,350m. by the end of 1995 (including combined principal and interest arrears of $1,020m.). Cameroon's payments commitments of $780m. in 1996 (excluding arrears reduction) were highly unlikely to have been met. The debt-exports ratio stood at 338% at the end of 1995.

In view of the high level of debt and the urgent necessity of restricting debt-servicing payments Cameroon has been obliged to maintain good relations with the IMF and World Bank, to ensure continuing accommodation by its bilateral official creditors. Relations have, however, proved difficult. Both the 1989 agreement with the IMF and a US $150m. structural adjustment loan (SAL) from the World Bank were suspended in 1990, when the government failed to comply with performance requirements. Debt-servicing arrears to the World Bank prompted that institution to suspend disbursements again in December 1992, and the French government was obliged to provide funds in 1993 for payment of the arrears. Shortly after the currency devaluation in January 1994, the IMF and the World Bank approved a further programme, but within three months the IMF had suspended payments as a result of the government's failure to meet performance criteria. A further standby credit, agreed with the IMF in September 1995, was rapidly converted to a non-disbursing IMF-monitored programme, after the government again failed to meet targets; a concomitant 'Paris Club' rescheduling agreement and a World Bank loan were also suspended. Relations with the international financial instutions remained poor in 1997, despite efforts by the ministry of economy and finance to reach an agreement on a three-year enhanced structural adjustment facility.

Statistical Survey

Source (unless otherwise stated): Direction de la Statistique et de la Comptabilité Nationale, BP 25, Yaoundé; tel. 22-07-88; telex 8203.

Area and Population

AREA, POPULATION AND DENSITY

Area (sq km)	475,442*
Population (census results)	
9 April 1976†	
Males	3,754,991
Females	3,908,255
Total	7,663,246
April 1987	10,493,655
Population (official estimates at mid-year)	
1987	10,821,746
1989‡	11,540,000
1995‡	13,277,000
Density (per sq km) at mid-1995	27.9

* 183,569 sq miles.

† Including an adjustment for underenumeration, estimated at 7.4%. The enumerated total was 7,090,115 (males 3,472,786; females 3,617,329).

‡ Official mid-year estimates for 1988 and 1990–94 are not available.

PROVINCES (population at 1976 census)

	Urban	Rural	Total
Centre-South	498,290	993,655	1,491,945
Littoral	702,578	232,588	935,166
West	232,315	803,282	1,035,597
South-West	200,322	420,193	620,515
North-West	146,327	834,204	980,531
North	328,925	1,904,332	2,233,257
East	75,458	290,750	366,235
Total	2,184,242	5,479,004	7,663,246

Note: In August 1983 the number of provinces was increased to 10. Centre-South province became two separate provinces, Centre and South. The northern province was split into three: Far North, North and Adamoua.

PRINCIPAL TOWNS (population at 1976 census)

Douala	458,426	Bafoussam	62,239
Yaoundé (capital)	313,706	Bamenda	48,111
Nkongsamba	71,298	Kumba	44,175
Maroua	67,187	Limbe	27,016
Garoua	63,900		

1992 (estimated population, '000): Douala 1,200; Yaoundé 800; Garoua 160; Maroua 140; Bafoussam 120 (Source: *La Zone Franc—Rapport 1992*).

BIRTHS AND DEATHS (UN estimates, annual averages)

	1980–85	1985–90	1990–95
Birth rate (per 1,000)	43.9	42.0	40.7
Death rate (per 1,000)	15.7	13.8	12.2

Expectation of life (UN estimates, years at birth, 1990–95): 56.0 (males 54.5; females 57.5).

Source: UN, *World Population Prospects: The 1994 Revision*.

ECONOMICALLY ACTIVE POPULATION
(official estimates, persons aged six years and over, mid-1985)

	Males	Females	Total
Agriculture, hunting, forestry and fishing	1,574,946	1,325,925	2,900,871
Mining and quarrying	1,693	100	1,793
Manufacturing	137,671	36,827	174,498
Electricity, gas and water	3,373	149	3,522
Construction	65,666	1,018	66,684
Trade, restaurants and hotels	115,269	38,745	154,014
Transport, storage and communications	50,664	1,024	51,688
Financing, insurance, real estate and business services	7,447	562	8,009
Community, social and personal services	255,076	37,846	292,922
Activities not adequately defined	18,515	17,444	35,959
Total in employment	2,230,320	1,459,640	3,689,960
Unemployed	180,016	47,659	227,675
Total labour force	2,410,336	1,507,299	3,917,635

Source: ILO, *Yearbook of Labour Statistics*.

Mid-1995 (estimates in '000): Agriculture, etc. 3,651; Total 5,372 (Source: FAO, *Production Yearbook*).

Agriculture

PRINCIPAL CROPS ('000 metric tons)

	1993	1994	1995
Rice (paddy)*	90	70	80
Maize	430*	450*	654†
Millet and sorghum	460*	400*	526†
Potatoes*	40	40	40
Sweet potatoes*	180	180	180
Cassava (Manioc)*	1,550	1,600	1,300
Yams*	110	110	110
Other roots and tubers*	530	450	450
Dry beans*	70	72	72
Groundnuts (in shell)*	110	110	110
Sesame seed*	15	16	16
Cottonseed	66†	71†	71*
Cotton lint	52	48†	48*
Palm kernels*	55	55	55
Sugar cane*	1,350	1,350	1,350
Vegetables*	465	467	467
Avocados*	42	44	45
Pineapples*	40	42	44
Bananas*	900	950	980
Plantains*	930	950	970
Coffee (green)*	41	60	70
Cocoa beans	98†	100†	100*
Tobacco (leaves)*	2	2	2
Natural rubber	50†	54†	54*

* FAO estimate(s). † Unofficial figure(s).

Source: FAO, *Production Yearbook*.

LIVESTOCK (FAO estimates, '000 head, year ending September)

	1993	1994	1995
Cattle	4,850	4,870	4,900
Pigs	1,390	1,400	1,410
Sheep	3,770	3,780	3,800
Goats	3,760	3,770	3,800

Poultry (FAO estimates, million): 20 in 1993; 20 in 1994; 20 in 1995.

Source: FAO, *Production Yearbook*.

LIVESTOCK PRODUCTS (FAO estimates, '000 metric tons)

	1993	1994	1995
Beef and veal	74	75	75
Mutton and lamb	16	16	16
Goat meat	14	14	14
Pig meat	17	17	18
Poultry meat	20	20	20
Other meat	47	47	47
Cows' milk	120	123	125
Poultry eggs	12.6	13.0	13.0
Cattle hides	10.8	11.0	11.2
Sheepskins	2.7	2.7	2.7
Goatskins	1.4	1.4	1.4

Source: FAO, *Production Yearbook*.

Forestry

ROUNDWOOD REMOVALS ('000 cubic metres)

	1992	1993*	1994*
Sawlogs, veneer logs and logs for sleepers	2,111	2,111	2,111
Other industrial wood*	821	844	867
Fuel wood*	11,472	11,762	12,062
Total	14,404	14,717	15,040

* FAO estimates.

Source: FAO, *Yearbook of Forest Products*.

SAWNWOOD PRODUCTION
(FAO estimates '000 cubic metres, incl. railway sleepers)

	1992	1993	1994
Total	489	465	465

Source: FAO, *Yearbook of Forest Products*.

Fishing

('000 metric tons, live weight)

	1992	1993	1994*
Freshwater fishes	22.0	23.0	23.0
Croakers and drums	10.3	3.3	3.7
Threadfins and tasselfishes	2.7	2.2	2.4
Sardinellas	16.0	16.0	16.0
Bonga shad	16.0	16.0	16.0
Other marine fishes (incl. unspecified)	4.4	4.3	4.4
Total fish	71.4	64.8	65.4
Crustaceans and molluscs	0.5	0.5	0.6
Total catch	72.0	65.3	66.0

* FAO estimates.

Source: FAO, *Yearbook of Fishery Statistics*.

Mining

	1992	1993	1994
Crude petroleum ('000 metric tons)	6,790	6,210	5,477

Source: UN, *Industrial Commodity Statistics Yearbook*.

Tin (estimated metal content of ore, metric tons): 5 in 1991; 5 in 1992; 5 in 1993 (Source: UNCTAD, *International Tin Statistics*).

1995 ('000 metric tons): Crude petroleum 5,040.

Source: UN, *Monthly Bulletin of Statistics*.

Industry

SELECTED PRODUCTS ('000 metric tons, unless otherwise indicated)

	1992	1993	1994
Raw sugar	65	57	65
Cigarettes (million)*	5,000	n.a.	n.a.
Jet fuels	9	9	9
Motor spirit (petrol)	294*	294*	296
Kerosene	242*	243*	245
Distillate fuel oils	284*	283*	287
Residual fuel oils	152	150	152
Lubricating oils	35	37	38
Aluminium (unwrought)†	82.5	86.5	81.1
Electric energy (million kWh)*	2,726	2,731	2,740

* Provisional or estimated figures.

† Using alumina imported from Guinea.

Source: UN, *Industrial Commodity Statistics Yearbook*.

Finance

CURRENCY AND EXCHANGE RATES

Monetary Units

100 centimes = 1 franc de la Coopération financière en Afrique central (CFA).

French Franc, Sterling and Dollar Equivalents (31 March 1997)

1 French franc = 100 francs CFA;
£1 sterling = 924.20 francs CFA;
US $1 = 562.85 francs CFA;
1,000 francs CFA = £1.082 = $1.777.

Average Exchange Rate (francs CFA per US $)

1994 555.20
1995 499.15
1996 511.5

Note: An exchange rate of 1 French franc = 50 francs CFA, established in 1948, remained in force until January 1994, when the CFA franc was devalued by 50%, with the exchange rate adjusted to 1 French franc = 100 francs CFA.

BUDGET ('000 million francs CFA, year ending 30 June)

Revenue	1990/91	1991/92*	1992/93*
Taxation	327.46	311.66	300.13
Taxes on income, profits, etc.	87.38	90.50	89.15
General income tax	31.26	37.94	47.20
Corporate tax on profits	56.12	52.56	41.95
Social security contributions	30.01	—	—
Domestic taxes on goods and services	96.66	86.92	89.16
Sales taxes	57.11	49.19	53.43
Excises	39.55	36.98	33.40
Taxes on international trade and transactions	67.71	91.80	87.64
Import duties	64.07	87.77	83.29
Export duties	3.64	4.03	4.35
Other current revenue	190.10	172.30	135.25
Entrepreneurial and property income	163.16	131.73	86.78
Unclassified current revenue	23.05	11.95	12.76
Capital revenue	7.29	2.56	0.27
Total	547.90	498.47	448.41

Expenditure†	1990/91	1991/92*	1992/93*
Current expenditure	545.92	464.80	442.62
Expenditure on goods and services	376.51	346.01	324.79
Wages and salaries	286.48	282.34	274.91
Other purchases of goods and services	90.03	63.67	49.88
Interest payments	43.05	39.40	57.88
Subsidies and other current transfers	126.36	79.39	59.95
Capital expenditure	151.45	101.39	47.53
Acquisition of fixed capital assets	151.45	101.39	47.53
Adjustment to cash basis	22.39	12.24	11.00
Total	719.76	578.43	501.15

* Excluding national social security funds.

† Excluding net lending ('000 million francs CFA, year ending 30 June): 3.02 in 1990/91; 1.20 in 1991/92; 2.00 in 1992/93.

Source: IMF, *Government Finance Statistics Yearbook*.

INTERNATIONAL RESERVES
(US $ million, excluding gold, at 31 December)

	1993	1994	1995
Gold*	11.91	11.33	11.56
IMF special drawing rights	0.09	0.05	0.04
Reserve position in IMF	0.47	0.49	0.53
Foreign exchange	1.90	1.72	3.22
Total	14.36	13.59	15.35

* Valued at market-related prices.

Source: IMF, *International Financial Statistics*.

MONEY SUPPLY ('000 million francs CFA at 31 December)

	1993	1994	1995
Currency outside banks	116.13	136.33	102.29
Demand deposits at deposit money banks	150.06	223.09	213.97
Total money (incl. others)	267.46	361.29	319.24

Source: IMF, *International Financial Statistics*.

COST OF LIVING
(Consumer Price Index for Africans in Yaoundé; base: 1990 = 100)

	1993	1994	1995
All items	96.8	130.8	149.0

Source: IMF, *International Financial Statistics*.

NATIONAL ACCOUNTS

('000 million francs CFA at current prices, year ending 30 June)

National Income and Product

	1986/87	1987/88	1988/89
Compensation of employees	1,142.4	1,091.2	1,055.1
Operating surplus	2,197.7	2,003.0	1,934.5
Domestic factor incomes	3,340.1	3,094.2	2,989.6
Consumption of fixed capital	190.8	232.6	230.4
Gross domestic product (GDP) at factor cost	3,530.9	3,326.8	3,220.0
Indirect taxes	430.2	337.9	299.3
Less Subsidies	39.2	20.2	6.3
GDP in purchasers' values	3,921.9	3,644.5	3,513.0
Factor income received from abroad	5.3	3.4	–121.0
Less Factor income paid abroad	88.1	103.5	
Gross national product	3,839.1	3,544.5	3,392.0
Less Consumption of fixed capital	190.8	232.6	230.4
National income in market prices	3,648.4	3,311.9	3,161.6
Other current transfers received from abroad	13.1	8.9	–60.0
Less Other current transfers paid abroad	57.0	82.8	
National disposable income	3,604.5	3,238.0	3,101.6

Source: UN, *National Accounts Statistics*.

Expenditure on the Gross Domestic Product

	1991/92	1992/93	1993/94
Government final consumption expenditure	409	405	340
Private final consumption expenditure	2,179	2,198	2,464
Increase in stocks	–27	30	—
Gross fixed capital formation	457	493	524
Total domestic expenditure	3,018	3,126	3,328
Exports of goods and services	646	535	754
Less Imports of goods and services	469	505	666
GDP in purchasers' values	3,195	3,155	3,416
GDP at constant 1989/90 prices	3,128	3,029	2,954

Source: IMF, *Cameroon—Selected Issues and Statistical Appendix* (November 1996).

Gross Domestic Product by Economic Activity

	1991/92	1992/93	1993/94
Agriculture, hunting, forestry and fishing	849	861	1,322
Mining and quarrying	219	179	314
Manufacturing	445	420	331
Electricity, gas and water	54	55	58
Construction	84	105	82
Government services	335	541	427
Other services	1,128	922	807
GDP at factor cost	3,114	3,082	3,341
Indirect taxes, *less* subsidies	81	73	75
GDP in purchasers' values	3,195	3,155	3,416

Source: IMF, *Cameroon—Selected Issues and Statistical Appendix* (November 1996).

BALANCE OF PAYMENTS (US $ million)

	1991	1992	1993
Exports of goods f.o.b.	1,957.5	1,934.1	1,507.7
Imports of goods f.o.b.	–1,173.1	–983.3	–1,005.3
Trade balance	784.3	950.8	502.4
Exports of services	406.0	407.5	390.9
Imports of services	–1,122.3	–907.3	–741.1
Balance on goods and services	68.0	450.9	152.2
Other income received	18.3	41.8	17.0
Other income paid	–442.7	–823.9	–669.5
Balance on goods, services and income	–356.4	–331.2	–500.3
Current transfers received	57.0	141.0	65.2
Current transfers paid	–105.4	–148.3	–130.2
Current balance	–404.8	–338.5	–565.4
Capital account (net)	7.9	17.0	6.3
Direct investment abroad	–21.5	–33.1	–22.1
Direct investment from abroad	–14.5	29.2	5.1
Portfolio investment from abroad	–2.2	–46.5	–106.3
Other investment assets	–112.3	16.8	105.5
Other investment liabilities	–211.7	–312.9	–286.7
Net errors and omissions	26.9	–640.7	–16.2
Overall balance	–732.3	–1,308.7	–879.9

Source: IMF, *International Financial Statistics*.

External Trade

PRINCIPAL COMMODITIES (distribution by SITC, US $ million)

Imports c.i.f.	1989	1990	1991
Food and live animals	179.6	269.4	314.3
Fish, crustaceans, molluscs and preparations	46.9	55.2	58.7
Fresh, chilled or frozen fish	41.2	47.8	51.1
Cereals and cereal preparations	76.8	137.9	171.1
Malt (incl. malt flour)	27.9	38.6	37.3
Beverages and tobacco	21.0	31.8	27.5
Crude materials (inedible) except fuels	47.9	65.6	162.6
Metalliferous ores and metal scrap	35.7	49.7	129.7
Alumina (aluminium oxide)	34.7	48.4	128.3
Chemicals and related products	193.9	233.1	339.6
Medicinal and pharmaceutical products	67.2	88.9	68.8
Medicaments (incl. veterinary medicaments)	62.2	84.3	64.6
Artificial resins, plastic materials, etc.	30.2	30.7	55.4
Disinfectants, insecticides, fungicides, etc.	24.0	19.5	25.4
Basic manufactures	292.8	366.6	554.3
Paper, paperboard and manufactures	36.3	54.1	81.5
Paper and paperboard	26.7	38.4	67.3
Textile yarn, fabrics, etc.	41.0	58.6	80.4
Woven fabrics of jute, etc.	9.7	20.0	0.5
Non-metallic mineral manufactures	49.0	51.5	69.7
Lime, cement, etc.	28.1	24.4	40.8
Cement	24.2	21.0	37.4
Iron and steel	41.9	59.3	106.0
Machinery and transport equipment	391.9	460.1	625.8
Power-generating machinery and equipment	20.3	19.9	26.4
Machinery specialized for particular industries	62.9	57.2	98.5
Civil engineering and contractors' plant and equipment	30.6	25.0	34.4
General industrial machinery, equipment and parts	87.0	81.3	146.5
Telecommunications and sound equipment	13.2	54.6	44.8

Imports c.i.f. — *continued*	1989	1990	1991
Other electrical machinery, apparatus, etc.	34.2	62.6	125.4
Road vehicles and parts*	100.8	121.4	125.8
Passenger motor cars (excl. buses)	43.2	51.2	44.1
Motor vehicles for the transport of goods, etc.	28.4	25.5	39.8
Goods vehicles (lorries and trucks)	25.9	22.0	29.9
Other transport equipment*	57.7	43.3	31.0
Ships, boats and floating structures	38.8	32.3	21.5
Tugs, special purpose vessels and floating structures	30.6	31.1	8.4
Miscellaneous manufactured articles	109.0	198.8	171.3
Printed matter	30.1	108.4	25.5
Total (incl. others)	1,273.3	1,656.2	2,306.2

* Excluding tyres, engines and electrical parts.

Exports f.o.b.	1989	1990	1991
Food and live animals	434.9	400.5	546.9
Coffee, tea, cocoa and spices	412.1	351.1	450.0
Coffee and coffee substitutes	214.7	174.6	86.5
Unroasted coffee and coffee husks and skins	214.1	173.4	86.5
Cocoa	196.2	168.5	361.3
Cocoa beans (raw or roasted)	168.7	142.0	327.2
Cocoa butter and cocoa paste	27.4	25.7	32.9
Crude materials (inedible) except fuels	245.6	301.2	404.3
Cork and wood	141.3	190.2	231.1
Rough or roughly squared wood (excl. fuel wood and pulpwood)	107.1	132.7	156.6
Non-coniferous sawlogs and veneer logs	107.1	132.7	153.3
Simply worked wood and railway sleepers	34.2	57.4	74.6
Shaped non-coniferous wood	32.8	56.2	74.0
Textile fibres and waste	68.7	69.5	110.5
Raw cotton (excl. linters)	68.6	69.5	110.0
Mineral fuels, lubricants, etc.	230.9	1,037.5	1,374.0
Petroleum, petroleum products, etc.	230.9	1,037.5	1,374.0
Crude petroleum oils, etc.	229.6	1,034.8	1,371.9
Basic manufactures	243.5	231.1	237.1
Non-metallic mineral manufactures	40.3	34.3	33.2
Lime, cement, etc.	36.5	29.9	25.7
Cement	36.5	29.9	25.7
Non-ferrous metals	144.6	139.8	108.3
Aluminium and aluminium alloys	144.5	139.7	108.7
Unwrought aluminium and alloys	126.1	125.6	87.6
Machinery and transport equipment	66.8	47.0	217.3
Transport equipment (excl. tyres, engines and electrical parts)	43.0	13.6	63.4
Ships, boats and floating structures	27.6	3.1	34.7
Tugs, special purpose vessels and floating structures	20.5	2.5	8.0
Total (incl. others)	1,281.6	2,080.7	2,892.5

Source: UN, *International Trade Statistics Yearbook*.

1992 (million francs CFA): Total imports c.i.f. 307,790; Total exports f.o.b. 487,130.

1993 (million francs CFA): Total imports c.i.f. 311,960; Total exports f.o.b. 533,250.

1994 (million francs CFA): Total imports c.i.f. 404,280; Total exports f.o.b. 754,889.

Source (for 1992–94): UN, *Monthly Bulletin of Statistics*.

PRINCIPAL TRADING PARTNERS (US $ million)

Imports c.i.f.	1989	1990	1991
Bangladesh	11.0	21.1	4.2
Belgium-Luxembourg	39.9	78.3	117.4
Brazil	25.8	34.8	82.2
Canada	49.0	15.4	36.0
Denmark	—	4.4	18.3
France	464.7	624.3	628.8
Germany, Fed. Repub.	71.6	149.8	199.4*
Guinea	34.7	41.5	108.6
Italy	38.5	72.9	106.1
Japan	72.6	77.8	68.0
Korea, Repub.	8.4	12.2	16.5
Netherlands	116.4	52.7	69.5
Pakistan	8.6	15.6	9.4
Panama	5.0	26.4	—
Senegal	15.9	24.8	20.2
Spain	19.9	33.7	87.3
Switzerland	17.5	20.6	20.7
Tunisia	10.4	14.2	21.9
United Kingdom	7.0	42.5	77.7
USA	64.3	73.7	151.6
Total (incl. others)	1,273.3	1,656.2	2,306.2

* Including the former German Democratic Republic.

Exports f.o.b.	1989	1990	1991
Belgium-Luxembourg	246.9	30.8	36.0
Central African Repub.	22.8	29.3	35.8
Chad	6.4	11.4	27.6
Congo	17.3	15.6	19.6
Côte d'Ivoire	17.4	3.7	2.6
Equatorial Guinea	35.5	30.2	81.8
France	301.3	844.1	485.1
Gabon	30.1	30.6	100.3
Germany, Fed. Repub.	113.4	61.6	59.7*
Italy	18.0	146.2	230.3
Japan	18.8	6.4	9.9
Netherlands	81.5	314.9	717.9
Nigeria	30.3	34.9	66.9
Portugal	16.1	30.2	32.0
Spain	64.0	143.8	181.5
USSR	6.6	5.4	7.2
USA	128.1	156.8	12.5
Total (incl. others)	1,281.6	2,080.7	2,892.5

* Including the former German Democratic Republic.

Source: UN, *International Trade Statistics Yearbook*.

Transport

RAILWAYS (traffic, year ending 30 June)

	1985/86	1986/87	1987/88
Passengers carried ('000)	2,079	2,267	2,413
Passenger-km (million)	412	444	469
Freight carried ('000 tons)	1,791	1,411	1,375
Freight ton-km (million)	871	675	594

Source: the former Ministère des Travaux Publics et des Transports, Yaoundé.

Net ton-km (million): 679 in 1991; 613 in 1992; 653 in 1993.

Passenger-km (million): 530 in 1991; 445 in 1992; 352 in 1993.

Source: UN, *Statistical Yearbook*.

ROAD TRAFFIC (estimates, motor vehicles in use at 31 December)

	1993	1994	1995
Passenger cars	82,600	89,000	92,200
Goods vehicles	52,200	56,600	60,000
Total	135,000	146,000	153,000

Source: International Road Federation, *World Road Statistics*.

SHIPPING

Merchant Fleet (registered at 31 December)

	1994	1995	1996
Number of vessels	50	50	50
Total displacement ('000 grt)	36	37	37

Source: Lloyd's Register of Shipping.

International Sea-borne Freight Traffic
(estimates, '000 metric tons)

	1988	1989	1990
Goods loaded	9,760	9,565	10,081
Goods unloaded	3,100	3,298	3,396

Source: UN, *Monthly Bulletin of Statistics*.

1991 (freight traffic at Douala, '000 metric tons): Goods loaded 1,185; Goods unloaded 2,413.
1992 (freight traffic at Douala, '000 metric tons): Goods loaded 1,257; Goods unloaded 2,337.
1993 (freight traffic at Douala, '000 metric tons): Goods loaded 1,453; Goods unloaded 2,147.

Source: Banque des états de l'Afrique centrale, *Etudes et Statistiques*.

CIVIL AVIATION (traffic on scheduled services)

	1992	1993	1994
Kilometres flown (million)	5	5	6
Passengers carried ('000)	363	275	295
Passenger-km (million)	477	402	436
Total ton-km (million)	53	58	64

Source: UN, *Statistical Yearbook*.

Tourism

	1992	1993	1994
Tourist arrivals ('000)	62	81	84
Tourist receipts (US $ million)	59	47	49

Source: UN, *African Statistical Yearbook*.

Communications Media

	1992	1993	1994
Radio receivers ('000 in use)	1,775	1,830	1,900
Television receivers ('000 in use)	288	307	309
Telephones ('000 main lines in use)	55	57	n.a.

Daily newspapers (1994): 1 (average circulation 50,000 copies).

Non-daily newspapers (1988): 25 (average circulation 315,000 copies).

Sources: UNESCO, *Statistical Yearbook*; UN, *African Statistical Yearbook*.

Education

(1994/95, unless otherwise indicated)

	Institutions	Teachers	Students
Pre-primary	1,061	3,778	91,242
Primary	6,801	40,970	1,896,722
Secondary			
General	n.a.	14,917	459,068
Teacher training	183*	123†	435†
Vocational	n.a.	5,885	91,779
Higher‡	n.a.	1,086	33,177
Universities‡	n.a.	761	31,360

* 1986/87 figure. † 1993/94 figure. ‡ 1990/91 figures.

Source: mainly UNESCO, *Statistical Yearbook*.

Directory

The Constitution*

The Republic of Cameroon is a multi-party state. The main provisions of the 1972 Constitution, as amended, are summarized below:

The Constitution declares that the human being, without distinction as to race, religion, sex or belief, possesses inalienable and sacred rights. It affirms its attachment to the fundamental freedoms embodied in the Universal Declaration of Human Rights and the UN Charter. The State guarantees to all citizens of either sex the rights and freedoms set out in the preamble of the Constitution.

SOVEREIGNTY

1. The Republic of Cameroon shall be one and indivisible, democratic, secular and dedicated to social service. It shall ensure the equality before the law of all its citizens. Provisions that the official languages be French and English, for the motto, flag, national anthem and seal, that the capital be Yaoundé.

2–3. Sovereignty shall be vested in the people who shall exercise it either through the President of the Republic and the members returned by it to the National Assembly or by means of referendum. Elections are by universal suffrage, direct or indirect, by every citizen aged 21 or over in a secret ballot. Political parties or groups may take part in elections subject to the law and the principles of democracy and of national sovereignty and unity.

4. State authority shall be exercised by the President of the Republic and the National Assembly.

THE PRESIDENT OF THE REPUBLIC

5. The President of the Republic, as Head of State and Head of the Government, shall be responsible for the conduct of the affairs of the Republic. He shall define national policy and may charge the members of the Government with the implementation of this policy in certain spheres.

6–7. Candidates for the office of President must hold civic and political rights, be at least 35 years old and have resided in Cameroon for a minimum of 12 consecutive months, and may not hold any other elective office or professional activity. The President is elected for seven years, by a majority of votes cast by the people, and may serve a maximum of two terms. Provisions are made for the continuity of office in the case of the President's resignation.

8–9. The Ministers and Vice-Ministers are appointed by the President to whom they are responsible, and they may hold no other appointment. The President is also head of the armed forces, he negotiates and ratifies treaties, may exercise clemency after consultation with the Higher Judicial Council, promulgates and is responsible for the enforcement of laws, is responsible for internal and external security, makes civil and military appointments, provides for necessary administrative services.

10. The President, by reference to the Supreme Court, ensures that all laws passed are constitutional.

11. Provisions whereby the President may declare a state of emergency or state of siege.

THE NATIONAL ASSEMBLY

12. The National Assembly shall be renewed every five years, though it may at the instance of the President of the Republic legislate to extend or shorten its term of office. It shall be composed of 180 members elected by universal suffrage.

13–14. Laws shall normally be passed by a simple majority of those present, but if a bill is read a second time at the request of the President of the Republic a majority of the National Assembly as a whole is required.

15–16. The National Assembly shall meet twice a year, each session to last not more than 30 days; in one session it shall approve the budget. It may be recalled to an extraordinary session of not more than 15 days.

17–18. Elections and suitability of candidates and sitting members shall be governed by law.

RELATIONS BETWEEN THE EXECUTIVE AND THE LEGISLATURE

19. Bills may be introduced either by the President of the Republic or by any member of the National Assembly.

20. Reserved to the legislature are: the fundamental rights and duties of the citizen; the law of persons and property; the political, administrative and judicial system in respect of elections to the National Assembly, general regulation of national defence, authorization of penalties and criminal and civil procedure etc., and the organization of the local authorities; currency, the budget, dues and taxes, legislation on public property; economic and social policy; the education system.

21. The National Assembly may empower the President of the Republic to legislate by way of ordinance for a limited period and for given purposes.

22–26. Other matters of procedure, including the right of the President of the Republic to address the Assembly and of the Ministers and Vice-Ministers to take part in debates.

27–29. The composition and conduct of the Assembly's programme of business. Provisions whereby the Assembly may inquire into governmental activity. The obligation of the President of the Republic to promulgate laws, which shall be published in both languages of the Republic.

30. Provisions whereby the President of the Republic, after consultation with the National Assembly, may submit to referendum certain reform bills liable to have profound repercussions on the future of the nation and national institutions.

THE JUDICIARY

31. Justice is administered in the name of the people. The President of the Republic shall ensure the independence of the judiciary and shall make appointments with the assistance of the Higher Judicial Council.

THE SUPREME COURT

32–33. The Supreme Court has powers to uphold the Constitution in such cases as the death or incapacity of the President and the admissibility of laws, to give final judgments on appeals on the Judgment of the Court of Appeal and to decide complaints against administrative acts. It may be assisted by experts appointed by the President of the Republic.

IMPEACHMENT

34. There shall be a Court of Impeachment with jurisdiction to try the President of the Republic for high treason and the Ministers and Vice-Ministers for conspiracy against the security of the State.

THE ECONOMIC AND SOCIAL COUNCIL

35. There shall be an Economic and Social Council, regulated by the law.

AMENDMENT OF THE CONSTITUTION

36–37. Bills to amend the Constitution may be introduced either by the President of the Republic or the National Assembly. The President may decide to submit any amendment to the people by way of a referendum. No procedure to amend the Constitution may be accepted if it tends to impair the republican character, unity or territorial integrity of the State, or the democratic principles by which the Republic is governed.

* In December 1995 the National Assembly formally adopted constitutional amendments that provided for a democratic system of government, with the establishment of an upper legislative chamber (to be known as the Senate), a Council of Supreme Judiciary Affairs, a Council of State, and a Civil Service High Authority, and restricted the power vested in the President, who was to serve a maximum of two seven-year terms. The restoration of decentralized local government areas was also envisaged.

The Government

HEAD OF STATE

President: PAUL BIYA (took office 6 November 1982; elected 14 January 1984; re-elected 24 April 1988 and 11 October 1992).

CABINET
(July 1997)

A coalition of the Rassemblement démocratique du peuple camerounais (RDPC), the Mouvement pour la défense de la République (MDR), the Union des populations camerounaises (UPC), and the Parti national du progrès (PNP).

Prime Minister: PETER MAFANY MUSONGE.

Deputy Prime Minister in charge of Territorial Administration: GILBERT ANDZE TSOUNGUI.

Deputy Prime Minister in charge of Housing and Town Planning: HAMADOU MOUSTAPHA.

Minister of State in charge of Posts and Telecommunications: DAKOLE DAISSALA.

Minister of State in charge of Communications: Prof. AUGUSTIN KONTCHOU KOUOMEGNI.

Minister of State in charge of Agriculture: AUGUSTIN FRÉDÉRIC KODOCK.

Minister of State in charge of the Economy and Finance: EDOUARD AKAME MFOUMOU.

Minister of Foreign Affairs: FERDINAND LEOPOLD OYONO.

Minister of Justice and Keeper of the Seals: LAURENT ESSO.

Minister of Livestock, Fisheries and Animal Husbandry: HAMADJODA ADJOUDJI.

Minister of Higher Education: Prof. PETER AGBOR-TABI.

Minister of Public Health: CHARLES ETOUNDI.

Minister of Labour and Social Security: SIMON MBILA.

Minister of Industrial and Commercial Development: JUSTIN NDIORO.

Minister of Public Service and Administrative Reform: SALI DAIROU.

Minister of Social Affairs and Women's Affairs: YAOU AISSATOU.

Minister of Public Works: JEAN-BAPTISTE BOKAM.

Minister of Scientific and Technical Research: Dr BAVA DJINGOER.

Minister of Tourism: PIERRE SOUMAN.

Minister of the Environment and Forests: Prof. JOSEPH MBEDE.

Minister of Youth and Sports: SAMUEL MAKON.

Minister of National Education: Dr ROBERT MBELLA MBAPPE.

Minister of Mines, Water and Energy: ANDRÉ BELLO MBELE.

Minister of Transport: JOSEPH TSANGA ABANDA.

Minister of Culture: ISAIE CHARLES TOKO MANGAN.

Ministers in charge of Missions: AMADOU BABA, JOHN EBONG NGOLLE, PETER ABETTY.

Minister in charge of Special Duties at the Presidency: MARTIN ARISTIDE LEOPOLD OKOUDOU.

Minister Delegate at the Ministry of Economy and Finance in charge of the Budget: ROGER MELINGUI.

Minister Delegate at the Ministry of Economy and Finance: JEAN MARIE GANKOU.

Minister Delegate at the Presidency in charge of Defence: PHILIPPE MENYE ME MVE.

Minister Delegate at the Ministry of Foreign Affairs: FRANCIS NKWAIN.

Minister Delegate for State Control: Prof. JOSEPH OWONA.

There are also six Secretaries of State.

MINISTRIES

Correspondence to ministries not holding post boxes should generally be addressed c/o the Central Post Office, Yaoundé.

Office of the President: Yaoundé; tel. 23-40-25; telex 8207.

Office of the Prime Minister: Yaoundé.

Ministry of Agriculture: Yaoundé; tel. 23-40-85; telex 8325.

Ministry of Communications: BP 1588, Yaoundé; tel. 22-31-55; telex 8215.

Ministry of Culture: Yaoundé.

Ministry of Defence: Yaoundé; tel. 23-40-55; telex 8261.

Ministry of Economy and Finance: BP 18, Yaoundé; tel. 23-40-40; telex 8260; fax 23-21-50.

Ministry of the Environment and Forests: Yaoundé.

Ministry of Foreign Affairs: Yaoundé; tel. 22-01-33; telex 8252.

Ministry of Higher Education: Yaoundé; telex 8418.

Ministry of Housing and Town Planning: Yaoundé; tel. 23-22-82; telex 8560.

Ministry of Industrial and Commercial Development: Yaoundé; tel. 23-40-40; telex 8638; fax 22-27-04.

Ministry of Justice: Yaoundé; tel. 22-01-97; telex 8566.

Ministry of Labour and Social Security: Yaoundé; tel. 22-01-86.

Ministry of Livestock, Fisheries and Animal Husbandry: Yaoundé; tel. 22-33-11.

Ministry of Mines, Water and Energy: Yaoundé; tel. 23-34-04; telex 8504.

Ministry of National Education: Yaoundé; tel. 23-40-50; telex 8551.

Ministry of Planning and Regional Development: Yaoundé; telex 8268.

Ministry of Posts and Telecommunications: Yaoundé; tel. 23-06-15; telex 8582; fax 23-31-59.

Ministry of Public Health: Yaoundé; tel. 22-29-01; telex 8565.

Ministry of the Public Service and Administrative Reform: Yaoundé; fax 23-08-00.

Ministry of Public Works: Yaoundé; tel. and fax 22-01-56; telex 8653.

Ministry of Scientific and Technical Research: Yaoundé.

Ministry of Social Affairs and Women's Affairs: Yaoundé; tel. 22-41-48.

Ministry of Territorial Administration: Yaoundé; tel. 23-40-90; telex 8503.

Ministry of Tourism: BP 266, Yaoundé; tel. 22-44-11; telex 8318; fax 22-12-95.

Ministry of Transport: Yaoundé.

Ministry of Youth and Sports: Yaoundé; tel. 23-32-57; telex 8568.

President and Legislature

PRESIDENT

Election, 11 October 1992

Candidate	Votes (%)
Paul Biya (RDPC)	39.9
John Fru Ndi (SDF)	35.9
Bello Bouba Maigari (UNDP)	19.2
Adamou Ndam Njoya (UDC)	3.6
Jean-Jacques Ekindi (MP)	0.5
Ema Otou (RFP)	0.4

ASSEMBLÉE NATIONALE

President: Djibril Cavaye Yeguie.

General Election, 17 May 1997

Party	Seats
Rassemblement démocratique du peuple camerounais	109
Social Democratic Front	43
Union nationale pour la démocratie et le progrès	13
Union démocratique du Cameroun	5
Mouvement pour la défense de la République	1
Mouvement pour la jeunesse du Cameroun	1
Union des populations camerounaises (K)	1
Total*	180

* On 3 August 1997 further elections took place in seven constituencies, where the results had been annulled; all the seats were won by the RDPC.

Political Organizations

The Rassemblement démocratique du peuple camerounais (RDPC) was the sole legal party (initially as the Union nationale camerounaise) between 1972 and December 1990, when the Constitution was amended to permit the formation of other political associations. In January 1997 some 133 political parties were in existence. The most important of these are listed below:

Alliance pour la démocratie et le développement (ADD): Sec.-Gen. Garga Haman Adji.

Alliance démocratique pour le progrès du Cameroun (ADPC): Garoua; f. 1991.

Alliance pour le progrès et l'émancipation des dépossédés (APED): Yaoundé; f. 1991; Leader Bohin Bohin.

Alliance pour le redressement du Cameroun (ARC): f. 1992 by a number of opposition movements.

Association social-démocrate du Cameroun (ASDC): Maroua; f. 1991.

Cameroon Anglophone Movement (CAM): advocates a federal system of govt.

Congrès panafricain du Cameroun (CPC): Douala; f. 1991.

Convention libérale (CL): f. 1991; Leader Pierre-Flambeau Ngayap.

Démocratie intégrale au Cameroun (DIC): Douala; f. 1991; Leader Gustave Essaka.

Front des alliés pour le changement (FAC): Douala; f. 1994; alliance of 16 opposition movements; Leader Samuel Eboua.

Front démocratique et patriotique (FDP): f. 1994; alliance of six opposition parties.

Liberal Democratic Alliance (LDA): Buéa; Pres. Henri Fossung.

Mouvement pour la démocratie et le progrès (MDP): Leader Samuel Eboua.

Mouvement pour la défense de la République (MDR): f. 1991; Leader Dakole Daissala.

Mouvement pour la jeunesse du Cameroun (MLJC): Leader Marcel Yondo.

Mouvement progressif (MP): f. 1991; Leader Jean-Jacques Ekindi.

Mouvement social pour la nouvelle démocratie (MSND): Leader Yondo Black.

Parti de l'action du peuple (PAP): Leader Victor Mukuelle Ngoh.

Parti de l'alliance libérale (PAL): Leader Céléstin Bedzigui.

Parti des démocrates camerounais (PDC): Yaoundé; f. 1991; Leader Louis-Tobie Mbida.

Parti libéral-democrate (PLD): f. 1991; Leader Njoh Litumbe.

Parti national du progrès (PNP): Leader Antar Gassagay.

Parti ouvrier unifié du Cameroun (POUC): Leader Dieudonné Bizole.

Parti républicain du peuple camerounais (PRPC): Bertoua; f. 1991; Leader Ateba Ngoua.

Parti socialiste camerounais (PSC): Leader Jean-Pierre Dembele.

Parti socialiste démocratique (PSD): Douala; f. 1991; Leader Ernest Koum Bin Biltik.

Parti socialiste démocratique du Cameroun (PSDC): Leader Jean Michel Tekam.

Rassemblement camerounais pour la République (RCR): Leader Samuel Wouaffo.

Rassemblement démocratique du peuple camerounais (RDPC): BP 867, Yaoundé; tel. 23-27-40; telex 8624; f. 1966 as Union nationale camerounaise by merger of the Union camerounaise, the Kamerun National Democratic Party and four opposition parties; adopted present name in 1985; sole legal party 1972–90; Pres. Paul Biya; Sec.-Gen. Joseph-Charles Doumba.

Rassemblement des forces patriotiques (RFP): Leader Ema Otou.

Rassemblement pour l'unité nationale (RUN): Yaoundé; f. 1991.

Social Democratic Front (SDF): Bamenda; f. 1990; Leader John Fru Ndi.

Social Democratic Movement (SDM): f. 1995; breakaway faction of the Social Democratic Front; Leader Siga Asanga.

Southern Cameroons National Council (SCNC): f. 1995; supports the establishment of an independent republic in anglophone Cameroon; Chair. Sam Ekontang Elad.

Union démocratique du Cameroun (UDC): f. 1991; Leader Adamou Ndam Njoya.

Union des forces démocratiques du Cameroun (UFDC): Yaoundé; f. 1991; Leader Victorin Hameni Bieleu.

Union nationale pour la démocratie et le progrès (UNDP): f. 1991; split in 1995; Chair. Bello Bouba Maigari.

Union des populations camerounaises (UPC): Douala; f. 1948; divided into two main factions in 1996: UPC (N), led by NDEH NTUMAZAH and UPC (K), led by AUGUSTIN FRÉDÉRIC KODOCK.

Union des républicains du Cameroun (URC): Douala; f. 1991.

Union pour le changement (UPC): coalition of opposition parties; Leader JOHN FRU NDI.

Union sociale démocratique (USD): Yaoundé; f. 1991.

Diplomatic Representation

EMBASSIES AND HIGH COMMISSIONS IN CAMEROON

Algeria: Yaoundé; Ambassador: M'HAMED ACHACHE.

Belgium: BP 816, Yaoundé; tel. 22-27-88; telex 8314; Ambassador: BAUDOUIN VANDERHULST.

Brazil: BP 348, Yaoundé; tel. 21-45-67; telex 8587; Chargé d'affaires a.i.: BASSUL ATHUIL NETTO.

Canada: Immeuble Stamatiades, BP 572, Yaoundé; tel. 23-02-03; telex 8209; High Commissioner: PIERRE GIGUERE.

Central African Republic: BP 396, Yaoundé; tel. 22-51-55; Ambassador: JEAN POLOKO.

Chad: BP 506, Yaoundé; tel. 22-06-24; telex 8352; Ambassador: HOMSALA OUANGMOTCHING.

China, People's Republic: BP 1307, Yaoundé; tel. 23-00-83; Ambassador: ZHU YOUROUNG.

Congo, Democratic Republic: BP 632, Yaoundé; tel. 22-51-03; telex 8317; Ambassador: (vacant).

Congo, Republic: BP 1422, Yaoundé; tel. 23-24-58; telex 8379; Chargé d'affaires a.i.: SAMUEL KOUAHI.

Egypt: BP 809, Yaoundé; tel. 22-39-22; telex 8360; fax 20-26-47; Ambassador: NOFAL IBRAHIM EL-SAYED.

Equatorial Guinea: BP 277, Yaoundé; tel. 22-41-49; Ambassador: SANTIAGO ENEME OVONO.

France: Plateau Atémengué, BP 1631, Yaoundé; tel. 23-40-13; telex 8233; fax 23-50-43; Ambassador: PHILIPPE SELZ.

Gabon: BP 4130, Yaoundé; tel. 22-29-66; telex 8265; Ambassador: NORBERT SINGATADY.

Germany: rue Charles de Gaulle, BP 1160, Yaoundé; tel. 20-05-66; telex 88238; fax 20-73-13; Ambassador: KLAUS HOLDERBAUM.

Greece: BP 82, Yaoundé; tel. 22-39-36; telex 8364; Ambassador: VASSILIS COUZOPOULOS.

Holy See: rue du Vatican, BP 210, Yaoundé (Apostolic Nunciature); tel. 20-04-75; fax 20-75-13; Apostolic Pro-Nuncio: Most Rev. FÉLIX DEL BLANCO PRIETO, Titular Archbishop of Vannida.

Israel: BP 5934, Yaoundé; tel. 20-16-44; telex 8632; fax 21-08-23; Ambassador: MOSHE LIBA.

Italy: Quartier Bastos, BP 827, Yaoundé; tel. 20-33-76; telex 88305; fax 21-52-50; Ambassador: PIETRO LONARDO.

Japan: Yaoundé; Ambassador: TAKERU SASAGUCHI.

Korea, Republic: BP 301, Yaoundé; Ambassador: DAE-TAEK LIM.

Liberia: Ekoudou, Quartier Bastos, BP 1185, Yaoundé; tel. 23-12-96; telex 8227; Ambassador: CARLTON ALEXWYN KARPEH.

Morocco: BP 1629, Yaoundé; tel. 20-50-92; telex 8347; fax 20-37-93; Ambassador: MOHAMED BENOMAR.

Netherlands: Immeuble Desamp 1067, rue 1750, Nouvelle Route Bastos, BP 310, Yaoundé; tel. 20-05-44; telex 8237; fax 20-47-04; Ambassador: ANNA ELISABETH DE BIJLL NACHENIUS.

Nigeria: BP 448, Yaoundé; tel. 22-34-55; telex 8267; High Commissioner: MAHMUD GEORGE BELLO.

Romania: Quartier Bastos, BP 6212, Yaoundé; tel. 23-39-86; telex 8417; Chargé d'affaires a.i.: ION MOGOS.

Russia: BP 488, Yaoundé; tel. 20-17-14; telex 8859; fax 20-78-91; Ambassador: YEVGENII UTKIN.

Saudi Arabia: BP 1602, Yaoundé; tel. 22-39-22; telex 8336; Ambassador: HAMAD AL-TOAIMI.

Spain: BP 877, Yaoundé; tel. 20-41-89; telex 8287; fax 20-64-91; Chargé d'affaires a.i.: JOSÉ JAVIER NAGORE SAN MARTÍN.

Tunisia: rue de Rotary, BP 6074, Yaoundé; tel. 22-33-68; telex 8370; Chargé d'affaires: MOHAMED ABDEL SMAOUI.

United Kingdom: ave Winston Churchill, BP 547, Yaoundé; tel. 22-05-45; fax 22-01-48; High Commissioner: NICHOLAS MCCARTHY.

USA: rue Nachtigal, BP 817, Yaoundé; tel. 23-40-14; telex 8223; Ambassador: CHARLES TWINING.

Judicial System

Supreme Court: Yaoundé; consists of a president, nine titular and substitute judges, a procureur général, an avocat général, deputies to the procureur général, a registrar and clerks.

President of the Supreme Court: ALEXIS DIPANDA MOUELLE.

High Court of Justice: Yaoundé; consists of 9 titular judges and 6 substitute judges, all elected by the National Assembly.

Attorney-General: RISSOUCK A MOULONG MARTIN.

Religion

It is estimated that 53% of the population are Christians (mainly Roman Catholics), 25% adhere to traditional religious beliefs and 22% are Muslims.

CHRISTIANITY

Protestant Churches

There are about 1m. Protestants in Cameroon, with about 3,000 church and mission workers, and four theological schools.

Fédération des Eglises et missions évangéliques du Cameroun (FEMEC): BP 491, Yaoundé; tel. 22-30-78; f. 1968; 10 mem. churches; Pres. Rev. Dr JEAN KOTTO (Evangelical Church of Cameroon); Admin. Sec. Rev. Dr GRÉGOIRE AMBADIANG DE MENDENG (Presbyterian Church of Cameroon).

Eglise évangélique du Cameroun (Evangelical Church of Cameroon): BP 89, Douala; tel. 42-36-11; fax 42-40-11; f. 1957; 500,000 mems (1992); Pres. Rev. CHARLES E. NJIKE; Sec. Rev. HANS EDJENGUELE.

Eglise presbytérienne camerounaise (Presbyterian Church of Cameroon): BP 519, Yaoundé; tel. 32-42-36; independent since 1957; comprises four synods and 16 presbyteries; 200,000 mems (1985); Gen. Sec. Rev. GRÉGOIRE AMBADIANG DE MENDENG.

Eglise protestante africaine (African Protestant Church): BP 26, Lolodorf; f. 1934; 8,400 mems (1985); Dir-Gen. Rev. MARNIA WOUNGLY-MASSAGA.

Presbyterian Church in Cameroon: BP 19, Buéa; tel. 32-23-36; telex 5310; 250,000 mems (1990); 211 ministers; Moderator Rev. HENRY ANYE AWASOM.

Union des Eglises baptistes au Cameroun (Union of Baptist Churches of Cameroon): BP 6007, New Bell, Douala; tel. 42-41-06; autonomous since 1957; 37,000 mems (1985); Gen. Sec. Rev. EMMANUEL MBENDA.

Other Protestant churches active in Cameroon include the Cameroon Baptist Church, the Cameroon Baptist Convention, the Church of the Lutheran Brethren of Cameroon, the Evangelical Lutheran Church of Cameroon, the Presbyterian Church in West Cameroon and the Union of Evangelical Churches of North Cameroon.

The Roman Catholic Church

Cameroon comprises five archdioceses and 17 dioceses. At 31 December 1995 there were an estimated 3,431,074 adherents. There are several active missionary orders, and four major seminaries for African priests.

Bishops' Conference: Conférence Episcopale Nationale du Cameroun, BP 807, Yaoundé; tel. 27-13-53; f. 1981; Pres. Rt Rev. ANDRÉ WOUKING, Bishop of Bafoussam.

Archbishop of Bamenda: Most Rev. PAUL VERDZEKOV, Archbishop's House, BP 82, Bamenda; tel. 36-12-41; fax 36-34-87.

Archbishop of Bertoua: Most Rev. LAMBERTUS JOHANNES VAN HEYGEN, Archevêché, BP 40, Bertoua; tel. 24-17-48; fax 24-25-85.

Archbishop of Douala: Cardinal CHRISTIAN WIYGHAN TUMI, Archevêché, BP 179, Douala; tel. 42-37-14; fax 42-18-37.

Archbishop of Garoua: Most Rev. ANTOINE NTALOU, Archevêché, BP 272, Garoua; tel. 27-13-53; fax 27-29-42.

Archbishop of Yaoundé: Most Rev. JEAN ZOA, Archevêché, BP 185, Yaoundé; tel. 22-24-89; telex 8681; fax 23-50-58.

BAHÁ'Í FAITH

National Spiritual Assembly: BP 145, Limbe; tel. 33-21-46; mems in 1,744 localities.

The Press

Restrictions on the press have been in force since 1966. In 1993 there were about 40 newspapers and other periodical publications.

DAILY

Cameroon Tribune: BP 1218, Yaoundé; tel. 30-40-12; telex 8311; fax 30-43-62; f. 1974; govt-controlled; French and English; Dir PAUL C. NDEMBIYEMBE; Editor-in-Chief EBOKEM FOMENKY; circ. 20,000.

PERIODICALS

Afrique en Dossiers: BP 1715; Yaoundé; f. 1970; French and English; Dir EBONGUE SOELLE.

Cameroon Outlook: BP 124, Limbe; f. 1969; 3 a week; independent; English; Editor JEROME F. GWELLEM; circ. 20,000.

Cameroon Panorama: BP 46, Buéa; tel. 32-22-40; f. 1962; monthly; English; Roman Catholic; Editor Sister MERCY HORGAN; circ. 2,000.

Cameroon Post: Yaoundé; weekly; English; independent; Publr PADDY MBAWA; Editor JULIUS WAMEY; circ. 50,000.

Cameroon Review: BP 408, Limbe; monthly; Editor-in-Chief JEROME F. GWELLEM; circ. 70,000.

Cameroon Times: BP 408, Limbe; f. 1960; weekly; English; Editor-in-Chief JEROME F. GWELLEM; circ. 12,000.

Challenge Hebdo: BP 13088, Douala; Editor BENJAMIN ZEBAZE.

Le Combattant: Yaoundé; weekly; independent; Editor BENYIMBE JOSEPH; circ. 21,000.

Courrier Sportif du Bénin: BP 17, Douala; weekly; Dir HENRI JONG.

Dikalo: BP 12656, Douala; independent; weekly; Dir EMMANUEL NOUBISSIE NGANKAM.

La Gazette: BP 5485, Douala; 2 a week; Editor ABODEL KARIMOU; circ. 35,000.

The Herald: BP 3659, Yaoundé; tel. 31-55-22; fax 31-81-61; weekly; English; Dir Dr BONIFACE FORBIN; circ. 8,000.

Le Jeune Observateur: Yaoundé; f. 1991; Editor JULES KOUM.

Journal Officiel de la République du Cameroun: BP 1603, Yaoundé; tel. 23-12-77; telex 8403; fortnightly; official govt notices; circ. 4,000.

Le Messager: 266 blvd de la Liberté, BP 5925, Douala; tel. 42-04-39; fax 42-02-14; f. 1979; 2 a week; independent; Man. Editor PIUS NJAWE; circ. 24,000.

The Messenger: BP 15043, Douala; English edn of Le Messager; Editor HILARY FOKUM.

Nleb Ensemble: Imprimerie Saint-Paul, BP 763, Yaoundé; tel. 23-97-73; fax 23-50-58; f. 1935; fortnightly; Ewondo; Dir Most Rev. JEAN ZOA; Editor JOSEPH BEFE ATEBA; circ. 6,000.

La Nouvelle Expression: BP 15333, Douala; independent; weekly; Man. Editor SÉVERIN TCHOUNKOU.

Presbyterian Newsletter: BP 19, Buéa; telex 5613; quarterly.

Recherches et Études Camerounaises: BP 193, Yaoundé; monthly; publ. by Office National de Recherches Scientifiques du Cameroun.

Le Serviteur: BP 1405, Yaoundé; monthly; Protestant; Dir Pastor DANIEL AKO'O; circ. 3,000.

Le Travailleur/The Worker: BP 1610, Yaoundé; tel. 22-33-15; f. 1972; monthly; French and English; journal of Organisation Syndicale des Travailleurs du Cameroun/Cameroon Trade Union Congress; Sec.-Gen. LOUIS SOMBES; circ. 10,000.

L'Unité: BP 867, Yaoundé; weekly; French and English.

Weekly Post: Obili, Yaoundé; Publr Chief BISONG ETAHOBEN.

NEWS AGENCIES

CAMNEWS: c/o SOPECAM, BP 1218, Yaoundé; Dir JEAN NGANDJEU.

Foreign Bureaux

Agence France-Presse (AFP): Villa Kamdem-Kamga, BP 229, Elig-Essono, Yaoundé; telex 8218; Correspondent RENÉ-JACQUES LIGUE.

Xinhua (New China) News Agency (People's Republic of China): ave Joseph Omgba, BP 1583, Yaoundé; tel. 20-25-72; telex 8294; Chief Correspondent SUN XINGWEN.

Reuters (UK) and ITAR—TASS (Russia) are also represented in Cameroon.

Publishers

Cameroon Review Publications: Boyo Bldg, Halfmile, BP 408, Limbe; f. 1983; periodicals, maps, books and pamphlets; Dir and Editor-in-Chief JEROME F. GWELLEM.

Editions Buma Kor: BP 727, Yaoundé; tel. 23-13-30; fax 23-07-68; f. 1977; general, children's, educational and Christian; English and French; Man. Dir B. D. BUMA KOR.

Editions Clé: BP 1501, Yaoundé; tel. 22-35-54; fax 23-27-09; f. 1963; African and Christian literature and studies; school textbooks; Gen. Man. COMLAN PROSPER DEH.

Editions Le Flambeau: BP 113, Yaoundé; tel. 22-36-72; f. 1977; general; Man. Dir JOSEPH NDZIE.

Editions Semences Africaines: BP 5329, Yaoundé-Nlongkak; f. 1974; fiction, history, religion, textbooks; Man. Dir PHILIPPE-LOUIS OMBEDE.

Government Publishing Houses

Centre d'Edition et de Production pour l'Enseignement et la Recherche (CEPER): BP 808, Yaoundé; tel. 22-13-23; telex 8338; f. 1977; transfer to private ownership pending in 1996; general non-fiction, science and technology, tertiary, secondary and primary textbooks; Man. Dir JEAN CLAUDE FOUTH.

Imprimerie Nationale: BP 1603, Yaoundé; tel. 23-12-77; telex 8403; transfer to private ownership pending in 1996; Dir AMADOU VAMOULKE.

Société de Presse et d'Editions du Cameroun (SOPECAM): BP 1218, Yaoundé; tel. 30-40-12; telex 8311; fax 30-43-62; f. 1977; under the supervision of the Ministry of Communications; Dir-Gen. PAUL CÉLESTIN NDEMBIYEMBE; Man. Editor PIERRE ESSAMA ESSOMBA.

Radio and Television

In 1994 there were an estimated 1.9m. radio receivers and 309,000 television receivers in use. In 1989 a total of 32 television transmitters were in service. Television programmes from France were broadcast by the Office de Radiodiffusion—Télévision Camerounaise from early 1990.

Office de Radiodiffusion-Télévision Camerounaise (CRTV): BP 1634, Yaoundé; tel. 21-40-88; telex 8888; fax 20-43-40; f. 1987 by merger; broadcasts in French and English; Pres. HENRI BANDOLO; Dir-Gen. GERVAIS MENDO ZE.

Radio Buéa: POB 86, Buéa; tel. 32-26-15; programmes in English, French and 15 vernacular languages; Man. PETERSON CHIA YUH; Head of Station GIDEON MULU TAKA.

Radio Douala: BP 986, Douala; tel. 42-60-60; programmes in French, English, Douala, Bassa, Ewondo, Bakoko and Bamiléké; Dir BRUNO DJEM; Head of Station LINUS ONANA MVONDO.

Radio Garoua: BP 103, Garoua; tel. 27-11-67; programmes in French, Hausa, English, Foulfouldé, Arabic and Choa; Dir BELLO MALGANA; Head of Station MOUSSA EPOPA.

There are also provincial radio stations at Abong Mbang, Bafoussam, Bamenda, Bertoua, Ebolowa, Maroua and Ngaoundéré, and a local radio station serving Yaoundé.

Finance

(cap. = capital; res = reserves; dep. = deposits; m. = million; brs = branches; amounts in francs CFA)

BANKING

Central Bank

Banque des Etats de l'Afrique Centrale (BEAC): BP 1917, Yaoundé; tel. 23-40-30; telex 8343; fax 23-33-29; f. 1973 as the central bank of issue for mem. states of the Customs and Economic Union of Central Africa (UDEAC); 6 brs in Cameroon; cap. and res 204,933m. (Dec. 1995); Gov. JEAN-FÉLIX MAMALEPOT; Dir in Cameroon SADOU HAYATOU.

Commercial Banks

Amity Bank Cameroon SA: place Joss, BP 2705, Douala; tel. 43-20-49; telex 5639; fax 43-20-46; f. 1991; cap. 1,000m. (1996), dep. 3,760m. (1994); Pres. LAWRENCE LOWEH TASHA; 3 brs.

Banque Internationale du Cameroun pour l'Epargne et le Commerce (BICEC): ave du Général de Gaulle, BP 4070, Douala; tel. 42-29-65; telex 55046; fax 42-41-16; f. 1962 as the Banque Internationale pour le Commerce et l'Industrie du Cameroun; 54% state-owned; cap. 6,000m. (June 1996); Pres. JEAN BAPTISTE BOKAM; Gen. Man. MICHEL TORIELLI; 34 brs.

Highland Corporation Bank SA: Immeuble Hotel Hilton, blvd du 20 mai, BP 10039, Yaoundé; tel. 23-92-87; telex 8439; fax 23-92-91; f. 1995; cap. 600m. (Dec. 1996); Pres PAUL ATANGA NJI.

Société Commerciale de Banque—Crédit Lyonnais Cameroun (SCB—CLC): 220 ave Monseigneur Vogt, BP 700, Yaoundé; tel. 23-40-05; telex 8213; fax 22-41-32; f. 1989; 35% state-owned; cap. 6,000m. (June 1995); Pres. MARTIN OKOUDA; Dir-Gen. MICHEL TRICAUD; 18 brs.

Société Générale de Banques au Cameroun (SGBC): 10 rue Joss, BP 4042, Douala; tel. 42-70-10; telex 5646; fax 42-87-72; f. 1963; 26.7% state-owned; cap. 4,900m. (June 1996); Pres. AMADOU MOULIOM NJIFENJOU; Gen. Man. GASTON NGUENTI; 29 brs.

Standard Chartered Bank Cameroon SA: 57 blvd de la Liberté, BP 1784, Douala; tel. 42-36-12; telex 5858; fax 42-27-89; f. 1980; 34% state-owned; cap. 1,000m. (June 1993); Chair. EPHRAIM INONI; Man. Dir JOHN SPINK TAYLOR; 5 brs.

Development Banks

Banque de Développement des États de l'Afrique Centrale: (see Franc Zone, p. 120).

Crédit Agricole du Cameroun: ave du Maréchal Foch, BP 11801, Yaoundé; tel. 23-23-60; telex 8332; fax 22-53-74; f. 1987; 41% state-owned; cap. 4,850m. (June 1994); agricultural development bank; transfer of state-owned shares to private ownership pending in 1997; Chair. GILBERT ANDZE TSOUNGUI; Dir-Gen. HUBERT RAUCH.

Crédit Foncier du Cameroun (CFC): BP 1531, Yaoundé; tel. 23-52-14; telex 8368; fax 23-52-15; f. 1977; 70% state-owned; cap. 6,000m. (June 1995); provides financial assistance for low-cost housing; Chair. GEORGES NGANGO; Dir-Gen. SYLVESTRE NAAH ONDOA.

Société Nationale d'Investissement du Cameroun (SNI): place de la Poste, BP 423, Yaoundé; tel. 22-44-22; telex 8205; fax 22-39-64; f. 1964; state-owned investment and credit agency; cap. 11,500m. (June 1995); Chair. VICTOR AYISSI MVODO; Dir-Gen. ESTHER BELIB DANG.

Financial Institutions

Caisse Autonome d'Amortissement du Cameroun: BP 7167, Yaoundé; tel. 22-01-87; telex 8858; fax 22-01-29; Dir-Gen. ISAAC NJIEMOUN.

Caisse Commune d'Epargne et d'Investissement (CCEI): place de l'Hôtel de Ville, BP 11834, Yaoundé; tel. 22-58-37; telex 8907; fax 22-17-85; cap. 1,505m. (June 1995); Pres. Dr PAUL KANMOGNE FOKAM; Dir-Gen. JACQUES NZEALE.

Fonds d'Aide et de Garantie des Crédits aux Petites et Moyennes Entreprises (FOGAPE): BP 1591, Yaoundé; tel. 23-38-59; telex 8395; fax 23-12-21; Pres. BERNARD BIDIAS NGON; Dir JACQUES MVUH LAMERO.

INSURANCE

State-owned Companies*

Assurances Mutuelles Agricoles du Cameroun (AMACAM): BP 962, Yaoundé; tel. 22-49-66; telex 8300; f. 1965; cap. 100m.; Pres. SAMUEL NGBWA NGUELE; Dir-Gen. LUC CLAUDE NANFA.

Caisse Nationale de Réassurances (CNR): ave Foch, BP 4180, Yaoundé; tel. 22-37-99; telex 8262; fax 23-36-80; f. 1965; all classes of reinsurance; cap. 1,000m.; Pres. JEAN KEUTCHA; Man. Dir ANTOINE NTSIMI.

Société Camerounaise d'Assurances et de Réassurances (SOCAR): 1-450 blvd de la Liberté, BP 280, Douala; tel. 42-55-84; telex 5504; fax 42-13-35; f. 1973; cap. 800m.; Chair. J. YONTA; Man. Dir R. BIOUELE.

*In 1996 the Government announced plans to liquidate AMACAM and SOCAR, and to transfer CNR to the private sector.

Privately-owned Companies

Compagnie Camerounaise d'Assurances et de Réassurances (CCAR): 11 rue Franqueville, BP 4068, Douala; tel. 42-31-59; telex 5341; fax 42-64-53; f. 1974; cap. 499.5m.; Pres. YVETTE CHASSAGNE; Dir Gen. CHRISTIAN LE GOFF.

Compagnie Nationale d'Assurances (CNA): BP 12125, Douala; tel. 42-44-46; telex 5100; fax 42-47-27; f. 1986; all classes of insurance; cap. 600m.; Chair. THÉODORE EBOBO; Man. Dir. PROTAIS AYANGMA AMANG.

General and Equitable Assurance Cameroon Ltd (GEACAM): 56 blvd de la Liberté, BP 426, Douala; tel. 42-59-85; telex 5690; fax 42-71-03; cap. 300m.; Pres. V. A. NGU; Man. Dir J. CHEBAUT.

Société Nouvelle d'Assurances du Cameroun (SNAC): rue Manga Bell, BP 105, Douala; tel. and fax 42-92-03; telex 5745; f. 1974; all classes of insurance; cap. 700m.; Dir-Gen. JEAN CHEBAUT.

Trade and Industry

ADVISORY BODY

Economic and Social Council: BP 1058, Yaoundé; tel. 23-24-74; telex 8275; advises the Govt on economic and social problems; comprises 150 mems and a perm. secr.; mems serve a five-year term; Pres. LUC AYANG; Sec.-Gen. FRANÇOIS EYOK.

PRINCIPAL DEVELOPMENT ORGANIZATIONS

Caisse Française de Développement (CFD): BP 46, Yaoundé; tel. 22-23-24; telex 8301; fax 23-57-07; Dir DOMINIQUE DORDAIN.

Cameroon Development Corporation (CAMDEV): Bota, Limbe; tel. 33-22-51; telex 5242; fax 33-26-54; f. 1947, reorg. 1982; cap. 15,626m. francs CFA; state-owned; statutory corpn established to acquire and develop plantations of tropical crops; transfer to private ownership pending 1996; operates two oil mills, six banana packing stations, three tea and seven rubber factories; transfer to private ownership pending in 1997; Chair. NERIUS NAMASO MBILE.

Direction Générale des Grands Travaux du Cameroun (DGTC): BP 6604, Yaoundé; tel. 22-18-03; telex 8952; fax 22-13-00; f. 1988; commissioning, implementation and supervision of public works contracts; Chair. JEAN FOUMAN AKAME; Man. Dir MICHEL KOWALZICK.

Hévéa-Cameroun (HEVECAM): BP 1298, Douala and BP 174, Kribi; tel. 42-75-64; telex 5880; f. 1975; cap. 16,518m. francs CFA; state-owned; development of 15,000 ha rubber plantation; 4,500 employees; transferred to private ownership in 1997; Pres. NYOKWEDI MALONGA; Man. Dir JEAN REMY.

Mission d'Aménagement et d'Equipement des Terrains Urbains et Ruraux (MAETUR): BP 1248, Yaoundé; tel. 22-31-13; telex 8571; f. 1977; Pres. LÉOPOLD FERDINAND OYONO; Dir-Gen. ANDRÉ MAMA FOUDA.

Mission de Développement de la Province du Nord-Ouest (MIDENO): BP 442, Bamenda; telex 5842; Dir ANDREW WAINDIM NDONYI.

Mission Française de Coopération et d'Action Culturelle: BP 1616, Yaoundé; tel. 22-44-43; telex 8392; fax 22-33-96; administers bilateral aid from France; Dir JEAN BOULOGNE.

Office Céréalier dans la Province du Nord: BP 298, Garoua; tel. 27-14-38; telex 7603; f. 1975 to combat effects of drought in northern Cameroon and stabilize cereal prices; Pres. Alhadji MAHAMAT; Dir-Gen. GILBERT GOURLEMOND.

Société de Développement du Cacao (SODECAO): BP 1651, Yaoundé; tel. and fax 30-33-95; f. 1974, reorg. 1980; cap. 425m. francs CFA; development of cocoa, coffee and food crop production in the Littoral, Centre and South provinces; Pres. JOSEPH-CHARLES NDOUMBA; Dir-Gen. JOSEPH INGWAT II.

Société de Développement de l'Elevage (SODEVA): BP 50, Kousseri; cap. 50m. francs CFA; Dir Alhadji OUMAROU BAKARY.

Société de Développement et d'Exploitation des Productions Animales (SODEPA): BP 1410, Yaoundé; tel. 22-24-28; f. 1974; cap. 375m. francs CFA; development of livestock and livestock products; Man. Dir ETIENNE ENGUELEGUELE.

Société de Développement de la Haute-Vallée du Noun (UNVDA): BP 25, N'Dop, North-West Province, f. 1970; cap. 1,380m. francs CFA; rice, maize and soya bean cultivation; Dir-Gen. SAMUEL BAWE CHI WANKI.

Société d'Expansion et de Modernisation de la Riziculture de Yagoua (SEMRY): BP 46, Yagoua; tel. 29-62-13; telex 7655; f. 1971; cap. 4,580m. francs CFA; commercialization of rice products and expansion of rice-growing in areas where irrigation is possible; Pres. ALBERT EKONO; Dir-Gen. LIMANGANA TORI.

Société Immobilière du Cameroun (SIC): BP 387, Yaoundé; tel. 23-34-11; telex 8577; fax 22-51-19; f. 1952; cap. 1,000m. francs CFA; housing construction and development; Pres. ENOCH KWAYEB; Dir-Gen. GILLES-ROGER BELINGA.

CHAMBERS OF COMMERCE

Chambre d'Agriculture, d'Elevage et des Forêts du Cameroun: Parc Repiquet, BP 287, Yaoundé; tel. 23-14-96; telex 8243; f. 1955; 120 mems; Pres. RENÉ GOBÉ; Sec.-Gen. SOLOMON NFOR GWEI; other chambers at Yaoundé, Ebolowa, Bertoua, Douala, Ngaoundéré, Garoua, Maroua, Buéa, Bumenda and Bafoussam.

Chambre de Commerce, d'Industrie et des Mines du Cameroun: BP 4011, Douala; tel. 42-36-90; telex 5948; fax 42-55-96; f. 1963; also at BP 12206, Douala; BP 36, Yaoundé; BP 211, Limbe; BP 59, Garoua; BP 944, Bafoussam; BP 551, Bamenda; 138 mems; Pres. PIERRE TCHANQUÉ; Sec.-Gen. SAÏDOU ABDOULAYE BOBBOY.

EMPLOYERS' ASSOCIATIONS

Groupement des Femmes d'Affaires du Cameroun (GFAC): BP 1940, Douala; tel. 42-4-64; telex 6100; Pres. FRANÇOISE FONING.

Groupement Interpatronal du Cameroun (GICAM): ave Konrad Adenauer, BP 1134, Yaoundé; tel. 20-27-22; fax 20-96-94; also at BP 829, Douala; tel. and fax 42-31-41; f. 1957; Pres. ANDRÉ SIAKA; Sec.-Gen. GÉRARD KOSOSSEY.

Syndicat des Commerçants Importateurs-Exportateurs du Cameroun (SCIEC): 16 rue Quillien, BP 562, Douala; tel. 42-03-04; Sec.-Gen. G. TOSCANO.

Syndicat des Industriels du Cameroun (SYNDUSTRICAM): 17 blvd de Liberté, BP 673, Douala; tel. 42-30-58; fax 42-56-16; f. 1953; Pres. SAMUEL KONDO EBELLÉ.

Syndicat des Producteurs et Exportateurs de Bois du Cameroun: BP 570, Yaoundé; tel. 20-27-22; telex 8998; fax 20-96-94; Pres. CARLO ORIANI.

Syndicat Professionnel des Entreprises du Bâtiment, des Travaux Publics et des Activités Annexes: BP 1134, Yaoundé; also at BP 660, Douala; tel. and fax 20-27-22; Pres. PAUL SOPPO-PRISO.

Syndicats Professionnels Forestiers et Activités connexes du Cameroun: BP 100, Douala.

Union des Syndicats Professionnels du Cameroun (USPC): BP 829, Douala; Pres. MOUKOKO KINGUE.

West Cameroon Employers' Association (WCEA): BP 97, Tiko.

PRINCIPAL CO-OPERATIVE ORGANIZATIONS

Bakweri Co-operative Union of Farmers Ltd: Dibanda, Tiko; produce marketing co-operative for bananas, cocoa and coffee; 14 socs, 2,000 mems; Pres. Dr E. M. L. ENDELEY.

Cameroon Co-operative Exporters Ltd: BP 19, Kumba; f. 1953; mems: 8 socs; cen. agency for marketing of mems' coffee, cocoa and palm kernels; Man. A. B. ENYONG; Sec. M. M. EYOH (acting).

Centre National de Développement des Entreprises Coopératives (CENADEC): Yaoundé; f. 1970; promotes and organizes the co-operative movement; bureaux at BP 43, Kumba and BP 26, Bamenda; Dir JACQUES SANGUE.

North-West Co-operative Association Ltd (NWCA): BP 41, Bamenda; tel. 36-12-12; telex 5842; Pres. SIMON ACHIDI ACHU; Dir Dr ROBERT GHOGOMU TAPISI.

Union Centrale des Coopératives Agricoles de l'Ouest (UCCAO): ave Samuel Wonko, BP 1002, Bafoussam; tel. 44-14-39; telex 7005; fax 44-11-01; f. 1957; marketing of cocoa and coffee; 110,000 mems; Pres. VICTOR GNIMPIEBA; Dir-Gen. PIERRE NZEFA TSACHOUA.

West Cameroon Co-operative Association Ltd: BP 135, Kumba; founded as cen. financing body of the co-operative movement; provides short-term credits and agricultural services to mem. socs; policy-making body for the co-operative movement in West Cameroon; 142 mem. unions and socs with total membership of c. 45,000; Pres. Chief T. E. NJEA; Sec. M. M. QUAN.

There are 83 co-operatives for the harvesting and sale of bananas and coffee and for providing mutual credit.

MAJOR INDUSTRIAL COMPANIES

The following are some of the largest companies in terms of either capital investment or employment:

ALUCAM, Camerounaise de l'Aluminium: BP 54, Edéa; tel. 46-43-11; telex 5223; fax 42-47-74; f. 1954; cap. 17,388m. francs CFA; 39% state-owned; manufacture of aluminium by electrolysis using imported alumina; Pres. MAURICE LAPARRA; Man. Dir M. MALONG.

British American Tobacco Cameroun (BAT Cameroun): BP 94, Yaoundé; tel. 21-08-75; telex 8282; fax 20-04-00; f. 1946; cap. 2,394.8m. francs CFA; 99.5% owned by British American Tobacco; production of tobacco and manufacture of cigarettes; Pres. JOHAN MATHIJS; Man. Dir J. L. CERVESATO.

Cameroon Sugar Co, Inc (CAMSUCO): BP 1462, Yaoundé; tel. 23-09-56; telex 8309; f. 1975; cap. 10,691m. francs CFA; sugar plantations, refining and marketing; transfer to private ownership pending in 1997; Pres. SALOMON ELOGO METOMO; Gen. Man. JOSEPH ZAMBO.

Céramiques Industrielles du Cameroun (CERICAM): BP 2033, Douala; tel. 42-37-71; telex 5637; f. 1969; cap. 1,200m. francs CFA; 20% state-owned; production of ceramic tiles, enamelled mosaics, etc.; Dir-Gen. MICHELANGELO BALDUCCI.

Cimenteries du Cameroun (CIMENCAM): BP 1323, Douala; tel. 39-11-19; telex 5325; fax 39-09-84; f. 1965; cap. 5,600m. francs CFA; cement works at Figuil and clinker-crushing plant at Douala-Bonabéri; Pres. ADAMA MODI; Dir-Gen. PIERRE REGENET.

Contreplaqués du Cameroun (COCAM): BP 154, Mbalmayo; tel. 28-11-20; telex 8242; fax 28-14-20; f. 1966; cap. 2,489m. francs CFA; 89% state-owned, of which 49% by Société nationale d'investissement du Cameroun; development of forest resources, production of plywood and slatted panels; Pres. PATRICE MANDENG; Dir-Gen. RAYMOND VINCENT ATAGANA ABENA.

Cotonnière Industrielle du Cameroun (CICAM): BP 7012, Douala-Bassa; tel. 42-62-15; telex 5253; fax 42-28-30; f. 1965; cap. 2,137m. francs CFA; factory for bleaching, printing and dyeing of cotton at Douala; Pres. ESTHER DANG; Dir-Gen. MICHEL VIALLET; 1,000 employees.

Dumez Camindustrie: BP 3476, Douala; tel. 42-79-24; telex 5883; f. 1982; cap. 1,250m. francs CFA; mfrs of construction materials; Pres. ANDRÉ KAMEL.

Les Grandes Huileries Camerounaises: Zone Industrielle de Bassa, Douala; f. 1982; cap. 1,400m. francs CFA; 50% state-owned; Pres. Alhadji BACHIROU; Man. Dir ERIC JACOBSEN.

Guinness Cameroun SA: BP 1213, Douala; tel. 40-27-58; telex 55327; fax 40-71-82; f. 1967; cap. 6,410m. francs CFA; production and marketing of beers; Man. Dir C.R. FREER; 927 employees.

International Brasseries (IB): BP 4237, Douala; cap. 2,400m. francs CFA; 34% owned by Heineken (Netherlands); mfrs of beer; Dir-Gen. PHILIPPE MATHIEU.

Nouvelles Brasseries Africaines (NOBRA): BP 2280, Douala; tel. 42-85-03; telex 5291; f. 1979; cap. 7,000m. francs CFA; mfrs of soft drinks; Pres. PIERRE TCHANQUE; Dir-Gen. ANDERS ANDERSEN.

Société Africaine Forestière et Agricole du Cameroun (SAFACAM): BP 100, Douala; tel. 42-97-58; fax 42-75-12; f. 1897; cap. 1,820m. francs CFA; plantation of natural rubber and production of rubber and latex; rubber and palm plantations at Dizangué; Pres. JACQUES ROULAND; Man. Dir GILBERT SUJET; 1,900 employees.

Société Anonyme des Brasseries du Cameroun (SABC): BP 4036, Douala; tel. 42-91-33; telex 5305; fax 42-79-45; f. 1948; cap. 10,102m. francs CFA; production of beer and soft drinks; Dir Gen. ANDRÉ SIAKA; 2,631 employees.

Société Bernabe Cameroun SARL: BP 529, Douala; tel. 42-96-22; telex 5350; fax 42-50-33; f. 1950; cap. 1,276m. francs CFA; mfrs of metal goods, hardware and construction materials; Pres. ANDRÉ NICOLAS; Man. Dir GÉRARD BOUYER.

Société Camerounaise des Dépôts Pétroliers (SCDP): rue de la Cité Chardy, BP 2271, Douala; tel. 40-54-45; telex 5609; fax 40-47-96; f. 1978; cap. 3,500m. francs CFA; storage and distribution of Cameroon petroleum; Pres. BERNARD MOUDIO; Dir JEAN-BAPTISTE NGUINI EFFA.

Société Camerounaise de Fabrication de Piles Electriques (PILCAM): BP 1916, Douala; tel. 42-26-28; telex 5712; f. 1970; cap. 1,472m. francs CFA; Pres. VICTOR FOTSO; Dir ANDRÉ FONTANA; 745 employees.

Société Camerounaise de Métallurgie (SCDM): BP 706, Douala; tel. 42-42-56; telex 5316; fax 42-01-85; f. 1984; cap. 1,475m. francs CFA; steel processors and mfrs of metal products; Man. Dir ALAIN GILBERT-DESVALLONS.

Société Camerounaise de Palmeraies (SOCAPALM): blvd Leclerc, BP 691, Douala; tel. 42-81-38; telex 5576; f. 1968; cap. 9,470m. francs CFA; 68.1% state-owned; management of palm plantations and production of palm oil and manufactured products; transfer to private ownership pending in 1997; Chair. JEAN-BAPTISTE YONKEU; Gen. Man. ROBERT MBELLA MBAPPE.

Société Camerounaise de Sacherie (SCS): Zone Industrielle de Bassa, BP 398, Douala; tel. 42-31-04; telex 5608; f. 1971; cap. 2,075m. francs CFA; 39% owned by ONCPB; production of sacks; Pres. GUILLAUME NSEKE; Dir THOMAS DAKAYI KAMGA.

Société Camerounaise des Tabacs (SCT): rue Joseph-Clerc, BP 29, Yaoundé; tel. 22-14-88; telex 8567; f. 1964; cap. 1,750m. francs CFA; tobacco cultivation and curing; Pres. PHILÉMON ADJIBOLO; Man. Dir LUCIEN KINGUE EBONGUE.

Société Camerounaise de Transformation de l'Aluminium (SOCATRAL): BP 291, Edéa; tel. 46-40-24; telex 5223; fax 46-47-74; f. 1960; cap. 750m. francs CFA; 49% owned by ALUCAM (q.v.); production of corrugated sheets, aluminium strips and rolled discs; Pres. M. CHARDON; Dir-Gen. M. NDIORO.

Société Camerounaise de Verrerie (SOCAVER): BP 1456, Douala; tel. 40-05-06; fax 40-64-03; f. 1966; cap. 1,100m. francs CFA; 47% owned by SABC (q.v.); mfrs of glassware; Pres. MICHEL PALU; Man. Dir CHRISTIAN BOULON.

Société de Développement du Coton au Cameroun (SODECOTON): BP 302, Garoua; tel. 27-10-80; telex 7617; f. 1974; cap. 4,529m. francs CFA; 70% state-owned; cotton ginning and production of cottonseed oil; transfer to private ownership pending in 1997; Pres. Alhadji MAHAMAT; Man. Dir MOHAMED IYA.

Société ELF de Recherches et d'Exploitation des Pétroles du Cameroun (ELF–SEREPCA): 83 blvd de la Liberté, BP 2214, Douala-Bassa; tel. 42-17-85; telex 5299; fax 42-13-66; f. 1951; cap. 1,000m. francs CFA; 20% state-owned; prospecting and exploitation of offshore petroleum; Pres. JEAN LOUIS VERMEULEN; Dir-Gen. MICHEL CHARLES.

Société Forestière et Industrielle de Belabo (SOFIBEL): BP 1762, Yaoundé; tel. 23-26-57; telex 5834; f. 1975; cap. 1,902m. francs CFA; 39% state-owned; sawmill; mfrs of plywood; Pres. SADOU DAOUDOU; Man. Dir DENIS KEEDI ATOK.

Société Générale des Travaux Métalliques (GETRAM): BP 3693, Douala; tel. 42-80-68; telex 5206; fax 42-77-61; f. 1980; cap. 1,200m. francs CFA; Pres. BERNARD MOUNDIO; Dir-Gen. OLIVIER BOUYGUES.

Société Industrielle Camerounaise des Cacaos (SIC CACAOS): BP 570, Douala; tel. 40-37-95; telex 5201; f. 1949; cap. 1,147.5m. francs CFA; production of cocoa and cocoa butter; Pres. JEAN-MARC DIEUDONNÉ OYONO; Man. Dir YVES SCHMUCK.

Société Industrielle des Tabacs du Cameroun (SITABAC): BP 1105, Douala; tel. 42-49-19; telex 6147; fax 42-59-49; cap. 4,556.6m. francs CFA; manufacture and sale of cigarettes; Pres. and Dir-Gen. JAMES ONOBIONO.

La Société les Minotiers du Cameroun: BP 785, Douala; tel. 37-75-01; telex 5573; fax 37-17-61; f. 1986; cap. 1,010m. francs CFA; flour mill; Pres. BABA AHMADOU; Dir-Gen. ANDRÉ NGANDEU.

Société Nationale des Eaux du Cameroun (SNEC): BP 157, Douala; tel. 42-87-11; telex 5265; fax 42-29-45; f. 1967; cap. 6,500m. francs CFA; 73% state-owned, 22% by Société Nationale d'Electricité du Cameroun; production, storage and distribution of drinking water; transfer to private ownership pending in 1997; Pres. AMADOU ALI; Dir-Gen. CLÉMENT OBOUH FEGUE; 2,340 employees.

Société Nationale d'Electricité du Cameroun (SONEL): 63 ave du Général de Gaulle, BP 4077, Douala; tel. 42-54-44; telex 5551; fax 42-22-47; f. 1974; 93.1% state-owned, 6.9% held by Caisse Française de Developpement; cap. 30,000m.; transfer to private ownership pending in 1997; Pres. JEAN FALMAN AKAME; Dir-Gen. MARCEL NIAT NJIFENJI.

Société Nationale des Hydrocarbures (SNH): BP 955, Yaoundé; tel. 22-19-10; telex 8514; fax 20-46-51; f. 1980; cap. 8,000m. francs CFA; national petroleum co; Pres. AMADOU ALI; Dir-Gen. ADOLPHE MOUDIKI.

Société Nationale de Raffinage (SONARA): BP 365, Cap Limboh, Limbé; tel. 42-38-15; fax 42-34-44; f. 1976; cap. 17,800m. francs CFA; 66% state-owned; establishment and operation of petroleum refinery at Cap Limboh; Chair. JOHN EBONG NGOLE; Gen. Man. BERNARD EDING; 548 employees.

Société de Palmeraies de la Ferme Suisse (SPFS): BP 06, Edéa-Ongué; tel. 42-34-18; telex 5745; f. 1976; cap. 1,525m. francs CFA; cultivation of products for industrial processing, operates factory for processing palm oil and palm kernels; Pres. and Man. Dir PHILIPPE PIECHAUD; Man. YVON LE FLOCH (acting).

Société Shell du Cameroun: BP 4082, Douala; tel. 42-24-15; telex 5221; fax 42-60-31; f. 1954; cap. 1,600m. francs CFA; import and distribution of petroleum products; Pres. and Dir-Gen. OLIVIER DE TINGUY.

Société Sucrière du Cameroun (SOSUCAM): BP 857, Yaoundé; tel. 22-07-99; telex 8323; f. 1965; cap. 2,500m. francs CFA; 24% state-owned; sugar refinery at M'bandjock; Man. Dir. LOUIS YINDA.

Société Textile du Cameroun pour le Linge de Maison (SOLICAM): BP 2413, Douala; tel. 42-97-20; telex 6024; f. 1979; cap. 3,000m. francs CFA; textile complex; Pres. SIMON NGANNYON; Dir-Gen. MICHEL VIALLET.

Total Cameroun: rue de la Cité Chardy, BP 4048, Douala; tel. 42-63-41; telex 5264; f. 1947; cap. 1,646m. francs CFA; exploration for, exploitation and distribution of petroleum reserves; Pres. J. GOUBEAU; Dir P. THIBAUD.

TRADE UNION FEDERATION

Confederation of Cameroon Trade Unions (CCTU): BP 1610, Yaoundé; tel. 22-33-15; f. 1985; fmrly the Union National des Travailleurs du Cameroun (UNTC); Pres. EMMANUEL BAKOD; Sec.-Gen. LOUIS SOMBES.

Transport

RAILWAYS

There are some 1,104 km of track, the West Line running from Douala to Nkongsamba (166 km) with a branch line leading south-west from Mbanga to Kumba (29 km), and the Transcameroon railway which runs from Douala to Ngaoundéré (885 km), with a branch line from Ngoumou to Mbalmayo (30 km).

Office du Chemin de Fer Transcamerounais: BP 625, Yaoundé; tel. 22-44-33; telex 8293; supervises the laying of new railway lines and improvements to existing lines, and undertakes relevant research; Dir-Gen. LUC TOWA FOTSO.

Régie Nationale des Chemins de Fer du Cameroun (REGIFERCAM): BP 304, Douala; tel. 40-60-45; telex 5607; fax 42-32-05; f. 1947; transfer to private ownership pending in 1997; Chair. SAMUEL EBOUA; Man. Dir SAMUEL MINKO.

ROADS

In 1995 there were an estimated 34,300 km of roads of which about 4,288 km were paved. In 1991 the African Development Bank approved a loan of $125m. towards the construction of a further 136 km of tarred roads.

SHIPPING

There are seaports at Kribi and Limbe-Tiko, a river port at Garoua, and an estuary port at Douala-Bonabéri, the principal port and main outlet, which has 2,510 m of quays and a minimum depth of 5.8 m in the channels and 8.5 m at the quays. In 1995 the port handled 4.16m. metric tons of cargo. Total handling capacity is 7m. metric tons annually. Plans are under way to increase the annual capacity of the container terminal.

Office National des Ports/National Ports Authority: Centre des Affaires Maritimes, 18 rue Joffre, BP 4020, Douala; tel. 42-01-33; telex 5270; fax 42-67-97; f. 1971; Chair. JOSEPH TSANGA ABANDA (Minister of Transport); Gen. Man. TCHOUTA MOUSSA.

Cameroon Shipping Lines SA (CAMSHIP): Centre des Affaires Maritimes, 18 rue Joffre, BP 4054, Douala; tel. 42-00-38; telex 5615; fax 42-01-14; f. 1975; transferred to private ownership in 1997; 6 vessels trading with western Europe, USA, Far East and Africa; Chair. FRANÇOIS SENGAT KUO; Man. Dir RENÉ MBAYEN.

Compagnie Maritime Camerounaise SA (CMC): Douala.

Conseil National des Chargeurs du Cameroun (CNCC): BP 1588, Douala; tel. 42-32-06; telex 5669; fax 42-89-01; f. 1986; promotion of the maritime sector; Gen. Man. EMMANUEL EDOU.

Delmas Cameroun: rue Kitchener, BP 263, Douala; tel. 42-47-50; telex 5222; fax 42-88-51; f. 1977; Pres. JEAN-GUY LE FLOCH; Dir-Gen. DANY CHUTAUX.

Société Africaine de Transit et d'Affrètement (SATA): Vallée Tokoto, BP 546, Douala; tel. 42-82-09; telex 5239; f. 1950; Man. Dir RAYMOND PARIZOT.

Société Agence Maritime de l'Ouest Africain Cameroun (SAMOA): 5 blvd de la Liberté, BP 1127, Douala; tel. 42-16-80; telex 5256; f. 1953; shipping agents; Dir JEAN PERRIER.

Société Camerounaise de Manutention et d'Acconage (SOCAMAC): BP 284, Douala; tel. 42-40-51; telex 5537; f. 1976; freight handling; Pres. MOHAMADOU TALBA; Dir-Gen. HARRY J. GHOOS.

Société Camerounaise de Transport et d'Affrètement (SCTA): BP 974, Douala; tel. 42-17-24; telex 6181; f. 1951; Pres. JACQUES VIAULT; Dir-Gen. GONTRAN FRAUCIEL.

Société Ouest-Africaine d'Entreprises Maritimes—Cameroun (SOAEM—Cameroon): 5 blvd de la Liberté, BP 4057, Douala; tel. 42-52-69; telex 5220; fax 42-05-18; f. 1959; Pres. JACQUES COLOMBANI; Man. Dir JEAN-LOUIS GRECIET.

Société de Transports Urbains du Cameroun (SOTUC): BP 1697, Yaoundé; tel. 21-38-07; telex 8330; fax 20-77-84; f. 1973; 58% owned by Société Nationale d'Investissement du Cameroun; operates urban transport services in Yaoundé and Douala; Dir-Gen. MARCEL YONDO; Mans JEAN-VICTOR OUM (Yaoundé), GABRIEL VASSEUR (Douala).

SOCOPAO (Cameroun): BP 215, Douala; tel. 42-64-64; telex 5252; f. 1951; shipping agents; Pres. VINCENT BOLLORE; Man. Dir E. DUPUY.

Transcap Cameroun: BP 4059, Douala; tel. 42-72-14; telex 5247; f. 1960; Pres. RENÉ DUPRAZ; Man. Dir MICHEL BARDOU.

CIVIL AVIATION

There are international airports at Douala, Garoua and Yaoundé.

Cameroon Airlines (CAM-AIR): 3 ave du Général de Gaulle, BP 4092, Douala; tel. 42-25-25; telex 5345; fax 42-34-59; f. 1971; domestic flights and services to Africa and Europe; transfer to private ownership pending in 1997; Chair. JOSEPH BELIBI; CEO SAMUEL MINKO.

Tourism

Tourists are attracted by the cultural diversity of local customs, and by the national parks, game reserves, sandy beaches and dinosaur sites. In 1994 an estimated 84,000 tourists visited Cameroon. In that year receipts from tourism totalled some US $49m.

Ministère du Tourisme: BP 266, Yaoundé; tel. 22-44-11; telex 8318; fax 22-12-95.

Defence

In August 1996 Cameroon's armed forces totalled 22,100 men, including 9,000 in paramilitary forces. The army numbered 11,500, the navy about 1,300 and the air force 300. Cameroon has a bilateral defence agreement with France.

Defence Expenditure: Estimated at 51,000m. francs CFA in 1995.

Commander-in-Chief of the Armed Forces: PAUL BIYA.

Education

Since independence, Cameroon has achieved one of the highest rates of school attendance in Africa, but provision of educational facilities varies according to region. Education, which is bilingual, is provided by the government, missionary societies and private concerns. Education in state schools is available free of charge, and the government provides financial assistance for other schools.

Primary education begins at six years of age. It lasts for six years in Eastern Cameroon (where it is officially compulsory), and for seven years in Western Cameroon. Secondary education, beginning at the age of 12 or 13, lasts for a further seven years, comprising two cycles of four years and three years in Eastern Cameroon, and of five years and two years in Western Cameroon. In 1994 primary enrolment was equivalent to 89% of children in the appropriate age-group (males 93%; females 84%), while secondary enrolment in that year was equivalent to only 27% (males 32%; females 22%). In 1995 according to estimates by UNESCO, the average rate of adult illiteracy was 36.6% (males 25.0%; females 47.9%). The State University at Yaoundé, which was established in 1962, has been decentralized, and consists of five regional campuses, each devoted to a different field of study. In the budget for 1991/92 education was allocated 70,770m. francs CFA (22.7% of total projected current expenditure).

Bibliography

Bandolo, H. *La flamme et la fumée*. Yaoundé, Editions SOPECAM, 1988.

Bayart, J.-F. *L'Etat au Cameroun*. Paris, Presses de la Fondation Nationale des Sciences Politiques, 1985.

Belinga, E. *Cameroun: La Révolution pacifique du 20 mai*. Yaoundé, 1976.

Beti, M. *Lutte ouverte aux camerounais*. Rouen, Editions des Peuples Noirs, 1986.

Biya, P. *Communal Liberalism*. London, Macmillan, 1987.

Biyita bi Essam, J.-P. *Cameroun: Complots et Bruits de Bottes*. Paris, Harmattan, 1984.

Bjornson, R. *The African Quest for Freedom and Identity: Cameroonian Writing and the National Experience*. Bloomington, Indiana University Press, 1994.

Bouchaud, J. *La Côte du Cameroun dans l'histoire et la cartographie des origins à l'annexation allemande*. Yaoundé, Centre IFAN, 1952.

Cruise O'Brien, D. B., Dunn, J., and Rathbone, R. *Contemporary West African States*. Cambridge University Press, 1989.

De Lancey, M. W. *Cameroon: Dependence and Independence*. Boulder, CO, Westview Press, 1989.

De Lancey, M. W., and Schrader, P.J. *Cameroon*. Oxford, Clio, 1986.

Donnat, G. *Afin que nul l'oublie*. Paris, Editions L'Harmattan, 1986.

Epale, S. J. *Plantations and Development in Western Cameroon 1875-1975: A Study in Agrarian Capitalism*. New York, Vantage Press, 1985.

Eyinga, A. *Introduction à la politique camerounaise*. Paris, Harmattan, 1984.

Gabriel, R. *L'Administration publique camerounaise*. Paris, Librairie Générale de Droit et de Jurisprudence, 1986.

Gaillard, P. *Le Cameroun*. Paris, Editions L'Harmattan, 1989.

Hugon, P. *Analyse du sous-développement en Afrique noire: L'exemple de l'économie du Cameroun*. Paris, Presses Universitaires de France, 1968.

Joseph, R. A. *Radical Nationalism in Cameroon*. London, Oxford University Press, 1977.

Koenig, E. L., Chia, E., and Povey, J. (Eds). *A Socio-Linquistic Profile of Urban Centers in Cameroon*. Los Angeles, UCLA (Crossroads Press), 1983.

Konings, P. *Gender and Class in the Tea Estates of Cameroon*. Brookfield, VT, Ashgate Publishing, 1996.

Konings, P. *Labour Resistance in Cameroon*. London, James Currey Publishers, 1993.

Le Vine, V. T., and Nye, R.P. *Historical Dictionary of the Republic of Cameroon*. 2nd Edn, Metuchen, NJ., Scarecrow Press, 1990.

Marc, A. *La Politique économique de l'état britannique dans la région du sud-Cameroun, 1920-60*. Paris, 1985.

Mbembe, J. A. *Ruben Um Nyobe: Le Problème national kamerunais*. Paris, Editions L'Harmattan, 1984.

Mehler, A. *Kamerun in der Ära Biya: Bedingungen, erste Schritte und Blockaden einer demokratischen Transition*. Hamburg, Institut für Afrika-Kunde, 1993. (Hamburger Beiträge zur Afrika-Kunde; 42).

Ndongko, W.A., and ViveKananda, F. *Economic Development of Cameroon*. Stockholm, Bethany Books, 1990.

Ngoh, V.J. *Cameroon 1884-1985: A Hundred Years of History*. Yaoundé, Imprimerie Nationale, 1988.

Ngongo, L. *Histoire des forces religieuses au Cameroun*. Paris, Editions Karthala, 1982.

Ngwa, J.A. *A New Geography of Cameroon*. 2nd Edn, London, Longman, 1979.

Previtali, S. *Le Cameroun par les ponts et par les routes*. Paris, Editions Karthala, 1988.

Schatzberg, M. G., and Zartman, W. *The Political Economy of Cameroon*. New York, Praeger, 1986.

Stoecker, H. (Ed.). *German Imperialism in Africa*. London, Hurst Humanities, 1986.

Zeltner, J.-C., and Torneux, H. *L'arabe dans le bassin du Tchad*. Paris, Editions Karthala, 1986.

CAPE VERDE

Physical and Social Geography

RENÉ PÉLISSIER

The island Republic of Cape Verde, comprising 10 islands, of which nine are inhabited, and five islets, lies in the Atlantic Ocean, about 500 km west of Dakar, Senegal. The archipelago comprises the windward islands of Santo Antão (754 sq km), São Vicente (228 sq km), Santa Luzia (34 sq km), São Nicolau (342 sq km), Boa Vista (622 sq km), and Sal (215 sq km) to the north, while to the south lie the leeward islands of Maio (267 sq km), Santiago (992 sq km), Fogo (477 sq km) and Brava (65 sq km).

The total area is 4,033 sq km (1,557 sq miles) and the administrative capital is Cidade de Praia (population of 62,000 at 1990 census) on Santiago Island. The other main centre of population is Mindelo (São Vicente), with 47,000 inhabitants in 1990, which is the foremost port and, with Praia, the economic centre of the archipelago. The 1990 census recorded a total population of 341,491 (84.7 inhabitants per sq km). According to UN estimates, the population numbered 392,000 at mid-1995. Santiago is the most populous of the inhabited islands, with a population of 175,000 in 1990, followed by São Vicente (51,000), Santo Antão (44,000) and Fogo (34,000). Santa Luzia has no permanent inhabitants.

Except for the low-lying islands of Sal, Boa Vista and Maio, the archipelago is mountainous, craggy and deeply furrowed by erosion and volcanic activity. The highest point is Mt Fogo (2,829 m), an active volcano. Located in the semi-arid belt, the islands have an anaemic hydrography, and suffer from chronic shortages of rainfall, which, coupled with high temperatures (yearly average 22°–26° C at Praia), cause catastrophic droughts which have periodically devastated the islands and necessitated heavy dependence on international food aid, which provide most of Cape Verde's food requirements. A desalination plant in São Vicente serves the needs of Mindelo, which is otherwise without drinkable water.

Ethnically, about 71% of the inhabitants are of mixed descent, except on Santiago, where the majority is of pure African stock. Whites represent about 1% of the population. The vernacular is a creole Portuguese (*Crioulo*), which is influenced by African vocabulary, syntax and pronunciation. Illiteracy is still prevalent. In 1990 the average life expectancy at birth was 63.5 years for men and 71.3 years for women.

Since independence, a significant number of islanders have emigrated, principally to the USA, the Netherlands, Italy and Portugal, where Cape Verdeans have replaced Portuguese migrants to other countries of the European Union. An estimated 700,000 Cape Verdeans live outside the country, and their remittances to the country provide an important source of development capital.

Recent History

JONATHAN GREPNE

The Cape Verde islands were colonized by Portugal in the 15th century. In the movement during the 1950s for independence from Portuguese rule, Cape Verde aligned itself with the mainland territory of Portuguese Guinea (now Guinea-Bissau) in a unified nationalist movement, the Partido Africano da Independência do Guiné e Cabo Verde (PAIGC). At Guinea-Bissau's independence in September 1974, however, the PAIGC leadership in Cape Verde decided to pursue its claims separately, rather than to seek an immediate federation with Guinea-Bissau, with which there were few unifying factors other than a common colonial heritage. In December 1974 the Portuguese government and representatives of the islands' PAIGC formed a transitional administration, from which members of other political parties were excluded. Elections to a national people's assembly took place in June 1975, with independence, as the Republic of Cape Verde, following on 5 July. Aristides Pereira, the secretary-general of the PAIGC, became the republic's first president. In 1980 the PAIGC was constitutionally established as the sole legal party, and in November of the same year prospects of unification with Guinea-Bissau were extinguished when Luiz Cabral, the president of Guinea-Bissau (and himself a Cape Verdean), was removed in a *coup d'état*. At the beginning of 1981 the Cape Verdean branch of the PAIGC held a special congress at which the party renamed itself the Partido Africano da Independência de Cabo Verde (PAICV).

PEREIRA AND THE PAIGC, 1975–91

Cape Verde's political affairs have long been secondary to the islands' struggle for physical survival amid geographical and economic pressures that are perhaps unequalled in intensity anywhere else in the world. Substantial infusions of foreign aid (from sources including the European Union (EU), the USA, certain Arab states and, until the late 1980s, the former Eastern bloc countries) have been augmented by remittances from Cape Verdeans resident overseas (whose numbers greatly exceed those living in the country). Owing to the rugged terrain of most of the islands, only some 10% of the land area is suitable for farming, and this hindrance is exacerbated by the country's constant vulnerability to drought. Further difficulties were brought about by the system of tenure, under which the vast majority of the land was owned by absentee landlords, allowing tenant farmers no security of tenure and therefore no incentive to improve their land. In 1983 the government began the redistribution of land under the provisions of legislation introduced in 1981. The reforms, however, elicited considerable opposition and even public disorder, as the farmers viewed them as an attempt by the PAICV regime to exert even greater control over them. Simultaneously an ambitious programme of dike-construction and tree-planting was implemented, to enhance the islands' capacity for water-retention.

Following the publication, in 1985, of forecasts that the population of Cape Verde would reach 500,000 by the year 2000, the government made the promotion of birth control a priority of its second National Development Plan (1986–90), in which it aimed to reduce the average number of children per family from 6.3 to 4.7 by the year 2000. In 1987 the national assembly approved legislation to legalize abortion, despite concerted opposition by the Roman Catholic Church. Tension developed, and 16 people were arrested following public demonstrations. In January 1993 the government announced that a referendum would be held that year on whether to revoke the legislation on abortion, but later withdrew the decision. Two proposals to revoke the legislation, introduced by a small inter-party group of legislators, were unsuccessful in that year.

Although Cape Verde was, until September 1990, a one-party state (see below), government policies were generally pragmatic and sensitive, and in the mid-1980s non-PAICV members began to take an increasingly prominent role in public and political life. Central control of the economy was eased, to allow a greater degree of private economic initiative, and in 1989 the government introduced legislation to encourage Cape Verdeans abroad to become involved in the process of development.

Moves towards a relaxation of the PAICV's political monopoly began to emerge in early 1990, as Cape Verde became affected both by political changes in west Africa and by those overtaking the Eastern bloc. In February 1990, in an apparent response to increasing pressure from church and academic circles, the PAICV announced the convening of an emergency congress to discuss the possible abolition of the constitutional provision which guaranteed its political monopoly. Two months later, a newly-formed opposition group, the Movimento para a Democracia (MPD), issued a manifesto in Paris, France, which demanded the immediate introduction of a multi-party system. Pereira subsequently announced that the next presidential election, which was planned for December 1990, would be held, for the first time, on the basis of universal adult suffrage.

The tempo of opposition activity on the islands increased in May 1990, with the presentation of a petition to the president of the national people's assembly, appealing for an immediate introduction of a multi-party system. Later in the month, Pereira announced that he would retire as secretary-general of the PAICV at the party congress in July, in preparation for his own political campaigning in a future multi-party system. At the first public meeting of the MPD, held in Praia in June, the movement's co-ordinator, Carlos Veiga, stated that the MPD was prepared to negotiate with the PAICV for a transition to political plurality. The party was also to seek immediate constitutional reform, the disbanding of the political police, the separation of the army from the PAICV and the holding of legislative elections prior to the presidential election.

Some of the opposition's demands were met in the following month. In July 1990 Pereira announced that legislative elections would be held on a multi-party basis before the end of the year. In September Cape Verde officially became a multi-party state, with the approval by the national people's assembly of the constitutional amendment abolishing the PAICV's monopoly of power. No limit was placed on the number of parties that could be registered, although it was stipulated that they should not be based on religious affiliation or purely regional interests. Legislative elections were scheduled for January 1991, with the presidential election to follow before the end of February. Although the MPD duly obtained registration, an application made by the União Caboverdiana Independente e Democrática (UCID), led by John Wahnon, was rejected. The UCID, founded in 1974 and subsequently active mainly abroad (particularly among Cape Verdeans resident in the USA, Portugal and the Netherlands), subsequently announced that it was to co-operate with the MPD in the forthcoming elections. The MPD held its first congress in Praia in November 1990, at which Veiga was elected party chairman. The MPD subsequently declared its support for the candidacy of António Manuel Mascarenhas Gomes Monteiro, a former supreme court judge, in the forthcoming presidential election. In November Pereira confirmed that he would seek re-election as president.

VEIGA AND THE MPD

The legislative elections held in January 1991 resulted in a clear victory for the MPD, which secured 56 of the 79 seats in the national assembly. The PAICV held the remaining 23 seats. The PAICV government resigned, and the party declared its intention to adopt a constructive role in parliamentary opposition. In late January Veiga was sworn in as prime minister at the head of an interim government, mostly comprising members of the MPD, pending the result of the presidential election. This took place in February, and resulted in a decisive victory for Mascarenhas, who secured 73.5% of the votes cast. The new president took office in March, and a new government was formed in April. In his initial statements of the new government's policies, Veiga promised to limit public spending and to improve the poor living conditions which affect the majority of the population. Cape Verde would maintain a non-aligned foreign policy. In the economic sphere, Veiga cited fishing, tourism and service industries as areas of priority for development.

The new government announced plans to redraft the constitution to include provision for fundamental human rights and a market economy, and it also established a commission to prepare a new national anthem and national flag. The first multi-party local elections, held in December 1991, brought another decisive victory for the MPD, which gained control of 10 of the 14 local councils, including that of the capital, Praia. The PAICV secured control of three councils, and an independent group, which was supported by the UCID, won control of one council.

In January 1992 Veiga restructured the cabinet and created three new ministries, of infrastructure and transport, culture and communication, and tourism, industry and commerce. In accordance with Veiga's stated intention to enhance the influence of the national assembly, a new ministry, for public administration and parliamentary affairs, was also created under the charge of a newly appointed minister. This measure received the support of the opposition PAICV. A new constitution, enshrining the democratic basis of the 'Second Republic', took effect in September, when a new national flag and emblem were adopted.

In March 1993 the council of ministers was reorganized, and the number of ministries increased from 11 to 12. The functions of the former ministries of finance and planning were consolidated under the ministry of finance, while a new ministry, of economic co-ordination, was created. The posts of secretary of state for finance, fisheries, and tourism, industry and commerce were abolished, while the position of secretary of state for internal administration was upgraded to the status of minister. During 1993 the government reversed, to considerable public satisfaction, the Pereira government's agrarian reform law of 1981.

At its annual national congress in August 1993 the PAICV elected Aristides Lima to the post of secretary-general of the party, replacing Gen. Pedro Pires, a former prime minister and Pereira's successor as secretary-general, who became party president. At the annual national conference of the UCID, held in the same month, Celso Celestino replaced Antero Barros as party president, with support from radical elements in the party. Celestino subsequently announced that, should the UCID obtain office in the 1996 elections, he would reverse the privatization policies of the MPD. In February 1994, John Wahnon, the former leader, left the UCID. The development, meanwhile, of dissent within the MPD prompted Veiga to announce in late 1993 that a special convention of the party would take place in February 1994. In December 1993 the minister for health, Rui Alberto Figueiredo Soares, left the government, and in the same month the minister of justice and labour, Eurico Correia Monteiro, was dismissed following his announcement that he would seek the leadership of the MPD at the forthcoming convention. The minister of public administration and parliamentary affairs, Alfredo Gonçalves Teixeira, was also dismissed.

At the party convention held in February 1994, Veiga was re-elected to the MPD presidency. However, increasing internal dissent prompted about 15 senior members of the party, led by Eurico Monteiro and a former minister of foreign affairs, Jorge Carlos Almeida Fonseca, to leave the MPD and form a new opposition group, the Partido da Convergência Democrática (PCD).

In March 1994 Veiga again reshuffled the council of ministers. Pedro Monteiro Freire de Andrade was appointed minister of justice and João Baptista Medina became minister of health. In addition, José António Mendes dos Reis was appointed minister of a newly created ministry, of employment, youth and social promotion. In May a motion of confidence in the government was debated by the legislature. It was carried in the government's favour by a narrow margin of 41 votes to 38.

In December 1994 Veiga extensively restructured the cabinet, reducing the number of ministerial portfolios to 11 and that of secretaryships to three. The ministry of tourism, industry and commerce was dissolved and its functions transferred to the ministry of economic co-ordination. The ministries of culture and communications, cabinet affairs, and public administration and parliamentary affairs were also abolished. The ministry of fisheries, agriculture and rural activity was divided into two separate ministries, of agriculture and of the sea.

At legislative elections held in December 1995 the MPD obtained an absolute majority, taking 50 seats in a smaller national assembly (reduced from 79 seats to 72 under legislation approved in 1994); the PAICV gained 21 seats and the PCD won the remaining seat. Two other parties, the UCID and the Partido Socialista Democrático (PSD), attracted little support, placing their continued existence in question. At local elections which took place in January 1996 the MPD won control of eight of the islands' 16 municipal councils, while the PAICV secured four, with the remainder gained by independents. At the presidential election which followed in February, Mascarenhas was re-elected unopposed. However, despite appeals for the electorate to demonstrate its support for Mascarenhas' second term of office, the turnout of voters was low, at only 45%. Veiga, meanwhile, expressed his intention to continue the policies of liberal economic and social reform of his previous term in office, and to introduce further constitutional amendments in 1997.

In March 1996 Veiga announced a further reorganization of the cabinet. The ministry of employment, youth and social promotion, headed by José António Reis, was disbanded, and Reis was appointed assistant minister to the prime minister, with responsibility for public administration, labour, employment and training, social communication, youth and sports. New ministers were appointed to portfolios of foreign affairs and communities, education, science and culture, and justice and internal administration, and the number of secretaryships was increased from three to six. In April the minister of infrastructure and transport was replaced. In June 1997 Reis assumed the additional portfolio of social promotion.

External Affairs and Foreign Aid

Since taking office in 1991, the MPD government has successfully sought to extend Cape Verde's range of international contacts, with special emphasis on potential new sources of development aid: substantial assistance has been received from both Israel and the Gulf states. The MPD government has extended the scope of Cape Verde's diplomatic contacts, establishing embassies in South Africa and Sweden, as well as diplomatic presences in Hong Kong, Spain, Singapore, the United Kingdom and the USA. In January 1997 the government announced that it was to open an embassy in the People's Republic of China. Promotional trips overseas by the president and the prime minister have included visits to Belgium, Luxembourg, the Netherlands, the People's Republic of China, Italy, Germany, Portugal, Switzerland and the USA. Cape Verde has particularly good relations with Portugal, exemplified by official visits made by the then Portuguese prime minister, Aníbal Cavaco Silva, who visited Cape Verde in November 1994 to promote trade and investment in the islands, and by the president of Portugal, Jorge Sampaio, in May 1996. In February 1997 the Portuguese prime minister, António Guterres, made an official trip to Cape Verde accompanied by several of his ministers and a large delegation of Portuguese business representatives. The country, which remains militarily non-aligned, has continued to maintain particularly close relations with Portugal and Brazil, and with other former lusophone African colonies—Angola, Guinea-Bissau, Mozambique and São Tomé and Príncipe, known collectively, with Cape Verde, as the Países Africanos da Língua Oficial Portuguesa (PALOP). Cape Verde is regularly represented at meetings of PALOP, whose principal aid donors include the EU, the IMF, the World Bank and the African Development Bank. In July 1996 a 'lusophone commonwealth', known as the Comunidade dos Países de Língua Portuguesa (CPLP), comprising the five PALOP countries together with Portugal and Brazil, was formed with the intention of benefiting each member state through joint co-operation on technical, cultural and social matters. In December 1996 Cape Verde became a full member of the Sommet francophone, a francophone commonwealth comprising all the French-speaking nations of the world, and benefits in turn from membership of this body's Agence de coopération culturelle et technique, an agency which promotes cultural and technical co-operation among francophone countries. Although a lusophone nation, Cape Verde has been an observer at annual meetings of the Sommet francophone since 1977. Cape Verde is a member of the Organization of African Unity (OAU), the Economic Community of West African States (ECOWAS), the UN, and is a signatory to the Lomé Convention, which promotes co-operation between the European Union (EU) and African, Caribbean and Pacific (ACP) nations.

Economy

JONATHAN GREPNE

In 1995, according to estimates by the World Bank, Cape Verde's gross national product (GNP), measured at average 1993–95 prices, was US $366m., equivalent to $960 per head. During 1985–95, it was estimated, GNP per head increased, in real terms, by 2.1% per year. Poverty, which affects some 40% of the population, remains the dominant theme in this largely subsistence economy. In 1995, unemployment was estimated to affect about 25% of the labour force, with a further 26% underemployed. The Cape Verde archipelago is situated in the Sahelian climatic zone and thus suffers from severe periodic droughts. In the absence of the necessary infrastructure to combat the effects of these droughts, it is not possible to achieve self-sufficiency in food production. Only some 10% (39,000 ha) of Cape Verde's total surface area is cultivable (one half of this is on Santiago) with cultivation actually taking place on 34,000 ha, of which only 3,000 ha are irrigated.

Despite the country's physical disadvantages, the economy has grown fairly steadily since independence in 1975, benefiting from the considerable provision of official aid, on very favourable terms, and the substantial remittances of Cape Verdean emigrés, whose number is almost double that of those actually living on the islands. Cape Verde's gross domestic product (GDP) increased, in real terms, by an annual average of 7% between 1975–82, and by 4.3% between 1986–91. According to the IMF, in 1992 GDP growth slowed to 3.3%, before increasing to an estimated 4.2% in 1993, falling to an estimated 3.8% in 1994 and rising again to an estimated 4.7% in 1995. According to official figures GDP growth stood at 4.1% in 1996. During 1985–95 the population increased by an annual average of 2.0%. The annual rate of inflation was 10% in 1991, falling to 2.7% in 1992, before increasing to 10.6% in 1993. Inflation averaged 2.4% in 1994, increased to 7.8% in 1995, and was, according to government figures, at 6% in 1996.

AGRICULTURE AND FISHERIES

Agriculture (including forestry and fishing) remains an important source of employment, despite adverse climatic conditions and a severe limitation on cultivable land, employing 27.4% of the labour force in 1995. However, agriculture contributed just 20.7% of GDP in 1993, and on average provides only about 15% of Cape Verde's domestic food requirements. About 54% of farms are smaller than 1 ha and fewer than 3% exceed 5 ha. In the late 1970s the Partido Africano da Independência de Cabo Verde (PAICV) government nationalized a few large irrigated properties, mainly banana plantations (predominantly white-owned), and in 1981 it enacted an agrarian reform law to distribute to their peasant cultivators landholdings over 5 ha (1 ha if irrigated) that were not directly farmed by their owners. However, in 1993, the Movimento para a Democracia (MPD) government revoked the agrarian reform law, which had been widely condemned by farmers who saw it as an attempt by the former single-party regime of the PAICV to exercise further control over them. In 1996 the MPD government was concentrating on the introduction of new agricultural methods aimed at maximizing the use of scarce water resources.

A 10-year drought eased in 1978, but in 1979, 1981 and 1983 the drought was so severe that almost all crops were lost. In 1984 heavy rainfall caused catastrophic floods, which were followed by drought in 1985, 1986, 1989, 1990, 1991 and 1994. In 1996 the worst drought for nearly 50 years again resulted in an almost total loss of crops. A reafforestation plan has been put into effect with assistance from the Food and Agriculture Organization (FAO). Some 2.8m. drought-resistant trees (American acacias) were planted during 1978–81, and a further 1.5m. were planted in 1982/83, bringing the total to 9m. by 1986. In that year a further 3m. trees were planted, and the government aimed to continue planting 3m. trees annually to ensure self-sufficiency in firewood by the year 2000. In 1987 Cape Verde received US $10.8m. in aid from the Netherlands to finance a major land and water conservation project on Santo Antão, and a loan of $6.7m. from the African Development Fund (ADF) to finance an agricultural rehabilitation programme. In the same year, the US Agency for International Development (USAID) provided $1m. for a three-year programme of water conservation projects, and a locust-control programme. A five-year programme of soil conservation began in 1990, with the aim of planting a further 2m. trees on three islands for which finance totalling $3.5m. was provided by the EC (European Community, now the European Union—EU). In 1991 some 16% of the total surface area of the archipelago was forested. The FAO estimated in 1995 that it had granted some $50m. in aid for some 114 agricultural projects in Cape Verde over the previous 20 years. Estimates suggest that the total potentially exploitable groundwater and surface water resources of Cape Verde are around 150m. cubic metres per year; enough to irrigate around 8,600 ha, compared with the present area under irrigation of around 3,000 ha. About 7,200 rainwater dikes have been built, and well-sinking is a high priority in the government's programme, which aims to irrigate a further 5,600 ha by the end of the century. Since 1994 a new, more efficient system of irrigation has been adopted. This system is expected to be introduced at an average of 50 ha per year, to cover 300 ha by the year 2000. At that point the water saved is expected to be sufficient to irrigate a further 150 ha.

Santiago is the main agricultural producer, followed by Santo Antão, Fogo and São Nicolau. Cash crops, such as bananas (production 6,000 tons in 1995, according to FAO estimates), arabica coffee, groundnuts, castor beans and pineapples, are encouraged, but poor inter-island communications, low educational attainment, the shortage of government funds, the lack of suitable available land and adverse climatic conditions militate against the development of a thriving agriculture. Cape Verde's food crops are maize, beans, cassava and sweet potatoes, supplemented (wherever soils, terrain and rainfall permit) with bananas, vegetables, sugar cane, fruits, etc. The main staples are beans and maize, which are intercropped. As the result of drought and damage by locusts, production of maize declined to 16,000 tons in 1988/89 and to 7,300 tons in 1990/91. Production declined further to 2,500 tons in 1991, before increasing to 5,000 tons in 1992, and to 12,000 tons in 1993, but declined to 6,000 tons in 1994 following another year of drought. Production improved to 10,000 tons, owing to better rainfall levels, in 1995, but was estimated to be almost negligible following severe drought in 1996. More than one-half of Cape Verde's total irrigated land is under sugar cane (production 18,000 tons in 1995, according to FAO estimates), most of which is used in the production of a popular alcoholic beverage for local consumption. The government is seeking to reallocate this land to staple and cash crops by encouraging the manufacture (and future export) of an alternative liquor using imported molasses.

International food aid has been required since independence in 1975. In 1986 and 1987 these requirements amounted to 70,000 tons and 56,000 tons respectively. These requirements were reduced to 28,000 tons in 1988/89, following two years of good harvests. Poor harvests occurred in 1989, 1990 and 1991, resulting in an import requirement of 65,000 tons of cereal in 1992, of which 58,000 tons were anticipated food aid and only 7,000 tons were commercial imports. In January 1995 Cape Verde appealed for further emergency food aid following a particularly poor harvest in the previous year. In 1996, following an exceptionally severe drought, the appeal for emergency food aid included a request for some 82,000 tons of cereal. The only crop that the islands export to any significant extent is that of bananas (2,054 tons in 1992, and 864 tons in 1993). These were mainly shipped to Portugal, with a small amount going to Germany. However, strict quality restrictions imposed by the EU on banana imports from ACP countries have halted almost all banana exports from Cape Verde to the EU since 1994. The EU granted funding of US $700,000 in 1995 and a further $390,000 in 1996 towards the improvement of banana production, packaging and delivery in order that Cape Verdean bananas may meet the quality requirements. Cape Verde has a 4,800 ton banana quota with the EU which, if fulfilled, could produce valuable export earnings. According to IMF estimates Cape Verde's banana exports totalled 90 tons in 1994 and 78 tons in 1995. A rather exotic commodity, locally known as *purgueira (Jatropha curcas),* which grows wild, is also exported (for soap-making). In the past, Cape Verde exported coffee, castor beans and tomatoes, but quantities were minimal, owing to the prevailing climatic conditions.

Livestock herds have been reduced to one-quarter, or even one-tenth, of their pre-drought level, but are slowly recovering. In 1995, according to FAO estimates, about 19,000 cattle, 130,000 goats, 4,000 sheep and 450,000 pigs were raised for food and milk. Following the poor rains in 1990, the government announced emergency measures to maintain stocks of cattle fodder. About 14,000 horses, asses and mules provide the main form of transport in rural areas.

Fishing offers great development potential, and modern appliances and boats are being slowly introduced to the sector. Fishing exports consist primarily of tuna and lobster. In the long term Cape Verde should be able to reduce its dependency on high levels of food aid by developing its fishing resources. Cape Verde's exclusive economic zone comprises 734,265 sq km and contains one of the last significantly underused fishing grounds in the world. However, fishing remains very much a small-scale industry, employing about 7,000 local fishermen in 1993, representing some 6% of the economically active population. The sector is still largely in the hands of artisanal fishermen who catch only a small percentage of the total sustainable yield, estimated at about 45,000 tons per year. Productivity is low for both artisanal and commercial fishermen, who together contribute no more than 4% of GDP. This is mainly the result of inadequate training, the lack of modern equipment and technology, and the shortage of available finance. Of some 1,400 fishing boats only around 40% are motorized, and of some 95 larger vessels used for industrial fishing, only 64 are fully operational. A five-year US $28m. project to rehabilitate and develop the fishing industry was approved in 1994; it was to be supported by loans from the ADB ($8.9m.), BADEA ($7.15m.), the Norwegian Development Fund ($3.7m.), the Icelandic Development Agency ($2.8m.) and the Cape Verde government ($4.15m.). In 1993 a fishing vessel worth US $5.6m. was donated by Japan, which country is also financing the construction of fishing quays at Praia and Mindelo. The MPD government, which has privatized the state-owned fishing company, the Empresa Caboverdiana de Pescas (PESCAVE), aims to encourage private operators by means of credit facilities, training and research. A fishing agreement was signed with the EC for the first time in 1990. The agreement initially ran for three years and was subsequently renewed for a further two-year period, establishing quotas for catches by boats from EC countries in Cape Verdean waters, in exchange for which the EC agreed to pay Cape Verde $1.2m. per year, in addition to the revenue from the sale of fishing licences. In 1994 the European Investment Bank granted a loan of $2.5m. to help finance the construction of an anchovy canning plant in Mindelo by a Spanish/Italian consortium, Fishpackers Lda, which announced in 1996 its intention to open another factory which will can mackerel and tuna, caught in Cape Verdean waters, for export, principally to Europe and the USA. The government aimed to increase annual production in the fishing sector, which stood at 7,100 tons in 1995, to around 21,000 tons in 1996, and to increase exports from 1,763 tons in 1993 to 6,000 tons in 1996. It also intended to increase annual production of canned fish products to 1,400 tons by 1997.

TRANSPORT AND TOURISM

Cape Verde is strategically located between Africa, Europe and America. International maritime and air transport, including transhipment, have been identified as an important source of foreign exchange by both the PAICV and MPD governments. The main port of the islands is Porto Grande at Mindelo on São Vicente, where a new ship-building and repair yard was opened in 1983. Work began in 1995 on a project, estimated to cost US $13.2m., to increase capacity and modernize the container storage terminal at Porto Grande to contend with an increase in trade from local light industrial activities. The port of Praia was recently completely modernized to handle 550,000 tons of cargo per year and offers refrigerator and container storage. In January 1997 the government formed two companies in strategic partnership with a US ship manufacturer and operator, Skaarup, and with local investors; Seainvest builds and charters cargo vessels, while CS Line leases the same vessels to operate shipping services to Europe. Under this venture two new vessels were being built during 1997 at a total cost of US $24m. In March 1993 a World Bank programme was approved for the upgrading and maintenance of the archipelago's infrastructure. The Programme for Infrastructure and Transport was to include the upgrading of Porto Grande (see above) and of the port of Vale de Cavaleiros on Fogo Island, as well as the construction and maintenance of roads. The programme, which was expected to take four years to implement, at a cost of $87m., was to be financed by donors including the World Bank ($12.5m.), the ADF ($11.3m.), BADEA ($7m.) and the European Investment Bank ($5.6m.). In 1988 the Cape Verdean government rejected an offer of $65m. from a consortium of Western industrialized countries, including the USA and Australia, to dispose of their toxic waste.

The Amílcar Cabral international airport on Sal Island has a capacity of 1m. passengers per year and can accommodate aircraft of up to 50 tons. In 1991 Portugal granted a loan of US $8m. to finance the construction of a new terminal at the airport. Its facilities have been used as a strategic refuelling point, chiefly by the airlines of South Africa, Portugal, the USSR, Cuba, Guinea-Bissau and Angola. Between 1987–91 Cape Verde suffered a loss of about $6m. in revenue as a result of the curtailment by the US government of flights by South African Airways (SAA) to the USA. These transatlantic flights, which had previously comprised 90% of air traffic through Sal, declined from 38 to only six per month. Cape Verde attempted to attract other airlines to Sal: in early 1988 discussions were held with Italian, Zambian and Botswana airlines concerning the introduction of stop-over flights to the USA. However, following the repeal of US sanctions in late 1991, South African air traffic was resumed. In 1993 other African nations, located on a more direct flight path, ended their ban on SAA flights, thus substantially reducing the importance of Sal as a refuelling point. In early 1996, nevertheless, SAA announced that it would be increasing the number of its flights from Johannesburg and New York using Sal as a stop-over from four to seven per week between July and November. In 1994 some 300,000 passengers passed through the airport, when cargo lines between Europe and South America accounted for around 30% of all landings. The national airline, Transportes Aéreos de Cabo Verde (TACV), operates a regular inter-island service as well as scheduled international flights to Amsterdam, Banjul, Bissau, Boston (USA), Conakry, Dakar, Frankfurt (Germany), Lisbon, Milan (Italy) and Paris. A new international airport is under construction at Praia, funded by the African Development Bank ($22.5m.), and is due for completion in late 1999. The airport is designed to accommodate Airbus 310 aircraft and will be able to receive flights from Europe and the USA.

Tourism has been identified as the area with the most potential for economic development. Cape Verde benefits from its proximity to the European market, enjoys a favourable climate for most of the year, and offers white sandy beaches and some spectacular mountain scenery. At present the industry contributes only around 3.5% of GDP, but legislation, introduced since 1991, has aimed to provide increased incentives and guarantees to investors. Tourism has been the sector to gain the greatest benefit from foreign investment, and several new hotel developments began operating during 1996 on Sal, Santiago, São Vicente and Boa Vista. The successful development of tourism on Santiago is envisaged with the opening of the new international airport at Praia, and the construction of a major hotel development at the Baia de São Francisco by British developers. Currently there are four hotels of international standard on Sal, one on Boa Vista, two on São Vicente and three on Santiago. In 1996 around 37,000 tourists visited Cape Verde, mainly from Portugal (35%), France (12%), Germany (11%), the Netherlands (8%), Italy, Belgium and Spain. In that year earnings from tourism totalled US $11m. It was estimated that tourist numbers would increase to 65,000 in 1999, with earnings of $20m. envisaged. Foreign investment totalling some $38m. was expected to increase the number of hotel beds from 2,500 in mid-1997 to 4,350 by the end of 1998.

MANUFACTURING

The manufacturing sector is still largely undeveloped, accounting for only 6.5% of GDP and employing about 5% of the total labour force in 1993. It consists primarily of fish canning, textiles, footwear, rum distilling and bottling plants. Cape Verde currently has around 120 small- and medium-sized industrial enterprises, mostly privately-owned. The larger enterprises were mainly formed under the PAICV government and have, since 1991, been privatized, restructured, liquidated or identified for future privatization. In October 1993 the free-zone enterprise law was enacted permitting enterprises producing goods and services exclusively for export to benefit from exemptions on tax and customs duties. It was intended that the new legislation would attract foreign investment and promote the expansion of Cape Verde's industrial exports. Further incentives to foreign investment in the manufacturing sector are the country's geographical location, available work-force, low wage costs and beneficial trade agreements with the countries of the Economic Community of West African States (ECOWAS), as well as the EU and the USA. Since early 1994 the manufacturing sector has attracted some US $35m. in foreign investment, most of which originates from Portugal; Confecções Porto Grande, established in Mindelo on São Vicente in 1995 by Portuguese investors, produces clothing for export to Europe, while footwear manufacturer Growela, another example of Portuguese investment, manufactures shoes for export directly to the United Kingdom. Mining is of little significance, representing less than 1% of GDP in 1993, with pozzolana, a volcanic ash used in cement manufacture (10,000 tons per year in 1981–90, according to estimates by the US Bureau of Mines and the UN), and salt (an estimated 4,000 tons in 1994) being the main products. A consortium led by a Portuguese enterprise, CIMPOR, announced in 1995 that it was to establish a company on Maio for the manufacture of cement, involving a total investment of some US $45m., to date the largest individual foreign investment project proposed in Cape Verde. The plant, in which a Chinese cement producer and local investors will have a stake, is to open in 2000, with an annual capacity of 200,000 tons.

AID AND INVESTMENT

Government policy in recent years has sought to attract private foreign investment, particularly towards the tourism, fishing and light manufacturing sectors. In 1989 legislation was introduced to open the economy to private external investment, mainly from the Cape Verdean immigrant community. In 1993 an external investment law opened the economy to all foreign investment. Between January 1995 and July 1997 Cape Verde attracted some US $102m. in foreign investment, creating about 2,000 new jobs. In 1996 the export earnings of companies formed with foreign investment totalled some $18m. Some two-thirds of all foreign investment originated from Portugal. The main area for public investment, accounting for about one-third of total government expenditure, is that of infrastructure, in particular telecommunications, port facilities, and the provision of water and electricity. In 1990 the World Bank provided a loan of $8m. for a programme to promote export industries, aiming to exploit Cape Verde's strategic location and establish the country as an international trading centre, based on light manufacturing, transhipping and financial services. A free-enterprise law passed in 1993 offered exemptions on tax and import duties for a period of 10 years as an incentive to exporting companies to establish themselves in Cape Verde. Industrial parks at Praia and Mindelo have been constructed with funding from the EU. On completion of the new international airport at Praia the smaller existing airport is to be transformed into an international trade fair centre. In December 1995 40% of the state telecommunications company, Cabo Verde Telecom (CVT), was sold to Portugal Telecom International for $20m. In 1997 a further 25% of CVT was divested; 15% to nationals resident in Cape Verde, 5% to Cape Verdean emigrés and 5% to CVT employees. Some $90m. will be invested by the Portuguese company before the year 2000 to modernize and expand the current network from 21,500 to 55,000 subscribers. In 1995 Austria and the OPEC Development Fund granted financing of $12m. for the installation of a fibre optic telecommunication line linking Santiago, Sal, São Nicolau and São Vicente. The line, which will be in operation by mid-1997, will offer on-line data communications and video-conferencing and will eventually be linked to a transatlantic network. Improved telecommunications will, potentially, enable the government to transform Cape Verde into an off-shore banking centre. In 1997 investors from the USA, Saudi Arabia and Pakistan established an international ship registration agency in Mindelo, establishing the Cape Verdean flag as a 'flag of convenience.'

Foreign aid is indispensable to Cape Verde, which receives one of the highest levels of aid per capita in the world ($320). According to the Organisation for Economic Co-operation and Development, total official development assistance reached $124.2m. in 1992, $119.7m. in 1993, $121.6m. in 1994, and $111.5m. in 1995 (of which 63% derived from Europe). Grants account for 85% of international aid, and loans for the remaining 15%. In 1995 bilateral aid totalled $71.6m. The principal donors were Portugal ($12.2m.), Germany ($10.7m.), the Netherlands ($10.4m.), France ($8.6m.), Austria ($6.4m.) and the USA ($6m.). In that year, of the $39.9m. in multilateral aid, the EU provided $10.9m., the World Food Programme $9.2m., the ADF $6.1m. and the International Development Association (IDA) $5.9m. Cape Verde receives aid from the EU under the Lomé Conventions, and was allocated $28.1m. for its 1986–90 development programme, $38m. for 1991–95, and $42.2m. for 1996–2000. The EU aid programme is primarily directed at improving the provision of water, electricity and sanitation, particularly in Praia and Mindelo. In 1993 the EU granted $6m. for a project to provide a network of water pipelines connecting suburban water wells and a reservoir to Praia by the end of 1996. A more comprehensive government scheme estimated to cost some $82m., to be funded by major foreign donors, was announced in September 1993. The project aimed to provide access to drinking water for the entire population by 2005. In 1995 Israeli technology was being used to install desalination units in Praia, with finance provided by the EU. In 1994 a project funded by the EU ($6m.), to provide wind-powered electricity generators at Praia, Mindelo and on Sal Island was completed. On average the new generators provide about 10% of local residential electricity requirements. In early 1993 the European Investment Bank agreed to lend more than $6m. towards the extension of the power plant at Mindelo. In 1995 the IDA approved a credit of $11.5m. for a programme aimed at achieving 100% enrolment in primary education by 1999. The project also included plans to adapt vocational training to the requirements of the local employment market. Furthermore, the IDA has agreed finance of $13.2m. for a programme to address poverty and improve public health. Funding of $6m. was agreed by the ADF in 1995 for a programme to improve secondary education.

A point worth noting is the low level of Cape Verde's debt-servicing costs, which the budget-conscious government has kept to a minimum. Cape Verde's total external debt at the end of 1995 was $216.3m., of which $185.2m. was long-term debt. As a proportion of the value of exports of goods and services, the debt-service ratio was 3.2% in that year.

A fourth National Development Plan (NDP) was adopted in 1997 outlining the government's plans for economic development up to 2001. The key aim of the NDP was to alleviate poverty, which affects some 40% of the population. This was to be achieved principally by the creation of jobs and wealth by means of the development of the private sector, particularly the light-manufacturing and service-sector industries. In addition, control over infrastructure development and social promotion programmes was to be devolved to local government bodies which were deemed better qualified to decide the needs of those living in poverty. The NDP received support from all its major international development partners, both bilateral and multilateral. The key service-sector industries targetted for development were tourism, fishing, maritime services (including transhipping), air-traffic and re-exporting.

In August 1992 the IDA agreed to provide a $4.7m. loan to finance technical assistance in preparation for privatization and private-sector economic development programmes. In 1996 the World Bank took over, from USAID, the funding of the Centro de Promoção Turística, do Investimento Externo e das Exportações (PROMEX), a body under partial government control, established in 1991 to promote exports and foreign investment in Cape Verde. In 1996 the IDA agreed financing of $11.4m., of which $5.6m. was allocated to PROMEX for the period 1996–1998, and $4.6m. was for a vocational training programme designed to modernize the running of financial institutions. By mid-1997 the government had divested a 65% share of Cabo Verde Telecom (see above) and 90% of the fuel retailer Empresa Nacional de Combustíveis. Several public companies have been liquidated and others have been re-structured or undergone partial privatization. The Banco Comercial do Atlântico, the Caixa Económica de Cabo Verde, Hotel-Mar (a hotel holding company) and the national airline, TACV, have all been identified for divestment in 1997/98. A stock exchange was due to open in Praia in April 1998.

TRADE, FINANCE AND PLANNING

Cape Verde's principal merchandise exports are canned tuna and mackerel, frozen fish, lobster and manufactured textile goods (mainly clothing and footwear). Small amounts of salt and pozzolana are exported. Large scale exports of bananas, interrupted in 1994 owing to quality restrictions imposed by the EU, were expected to resume in 1998. Exports of processed fish and light-manufactured goods are expected to increase substantially in the future as new freezing and canning plants come into operation, as well as industrial parks at Praia and Mindelo. Merchandise exports increased from US $4.9m. in 1994 to $8.4m. in 1995, and to more than $13m. in 1996. Cape Verde traditionally operates a substantial trade deficit which stems from the need to import 85% of its food requirements (although most of this is provided free under aid schemes), as well as manufactured goods, fuel and other essential goods. Since 1991 imports have risen significantly thus widening the trade deficit further. This has been due partly to the MPD government's open market policies; notably, the liberalization of previous restrictions on almost all imported goods, and the introduction of measures enabling local firms to borrow from domestic banks in order to purchase imported materials. In 1989 imports stood at $112m., with exports covering around 6.1% of imports. However, the value of imports more than doubled to $232m. in 1995, when exports covered only 3.6% of imports. In 1996 and 1997 the government imposed import restrictions and tariffs on certain non-essential goods in order to reduce the trade deficit. In 1996 imports were reduced marginally to $219m., while exports increased to more than $13m., covering 5.9% of imports. In recent years Portugal has significantly increased its trading with Cape Verde. In 1989 Portugal exported goods worth $34m. (32% of imports) to Cape Verde, but this reached about $105m. (45% of imports) in 1995. Other important sources of imports in 1995 were the Netherlands (7.5%), Côte d'Ivoire (6%), France (4%) and Denmark (3.5%). Portugal is also the principal market for exports, accounting for an estimated 82.8% of the total in 1995. Other major recipients were Spain and France. Of income from the export of goods and services, the latter typically accounted for some 90% of the total between 1989–94, providing average annual receipts of $50m. It was envisaged that export earnings from the services sector would increase significantly in the near future, particularly from tourism, transhipment and the refuelling and servicing of aircraft belonging to foreign airlines.

In July 1993 the first commercial and development bank was established, the Banco Comercial do Atlântico (BCA). Despite the fact that its capital was raised solely from state funds provided by the Banco de Cabo Verde, the BCA enjoys relative independence from the central bank and has a high degree of autonomy in its administration and management. The Banco de Cabo Verde now functions solely as a central bank. New legislation introduced in 1993 provides for the creation of financial institutions to offer loans and credit to small- and medium-sized entrepreneurs. According to the ministry for economic co-ordination, during 1994 some 67% of requests for loans by small- to medium-sized businesses were successful in securing loans from the BCA and the Caixa Económica de Cabo Verde. A Portuguese bank, Banco Totta e Açores (BTA), opened a branch in Praia in December 1995. A further branch was expected to open in Mindelo in 1996. A second Portuguese bank, the Banco Nacional Ultramarino, opened an office in Praia in October 1995 which was expected to be upgraded to branch status, and in late 1996 a third Portuguese bank, Banco Mello, also opened an office in Praia. The establishment of these foreign banks in Cape Verde was expected to raise the level of available credit lines through Portugal, and subsequently the level of investment and imports from that country. Cape Verde's first venture capital company, Promotora, began operating in December 1995 and will support the development of the private sector by offering local businessmen an opportunity to enter into joint ventures with foreign partners.

Measures were adopted in 1993 to reduce by 50% the size of the civil service, estimated at 12,000, by means of a voluntary redundancy scheme. Restructuring of the public administration is being implemented to introduce greater bureaucratic efficiency and to reduce public expenditure. In early 1994 the IDA approved a credit of US $8.1m. to help finance a $9m. public sector reform and capacity building project which was due for completion in 1999.

Revenue from fiscal sources has increased following the broadening of the scope of liability for income tax and modernization of the tax collection system. The budget for 1997 envisaged total government expenditure of 23,400m. escudos.

Statistical Survey

Source (unless otherwise stated): Statistical Service, Banco de Cabo Verde, Av. Amílcar Cabral, Santiago; tel. 61-31-53; telex 99350.

AREA AND POPULATION

Area: 4,033 sq km (1,557 sq miles).

Population: 272,571 at census of 15 December 1970; 295,703 (males 135,695; females 160,008) at census of 2 June 1980; 341,491 (males 161,494; females 179,997) at census of 23 June 1990; 392,000 at mid-1995 (UN estimate). *By island* (1990 census, figures rounded to nearest '00): Boa Vista 3,500, Brava 7,000, Fogo 34,000, Maio 5,000, Sal 7,700, Santo Antão 44,000, São Nicolau 14,000, Santiago 175,000, São Vicente 51,000.

Density (mid-1995): 97.2 per sq. km.

Principal Town: Cidade de Praia (capital), population 61,644 at 1990 census.

Births and Deaths (1992): Registered live births 9,671 (birth rate 26.9 per 1,000); Registered deaths 2,843 (death rate 7.9 per 1,000). Source: UN, *Population and Vital Statistics Report*.

Expectation of Life (years at birth, 1990): males 63.53; females 71.33. Source: UN, *Demographic Yearbook*.

Economically Active Population (persons aged 10 years and over, 1990 census): Agriculture, hunting, forestry and fishing 29,876; Mining and quarrying 410; Manufacturing 5,520; Electricity, gas and water 883; Construction 22,722; Trade, restaurants and hotels 12,747; Transport, storage and communications 6,138; Financing, insurance, real estate and business services 821; Community, social and personal services 17,358; Activities not adequately defined 24,090; Total labour force 120,565 (males 75,786; females 44,779), including 31,049 unemployed persons (males 19,712; females 11,337). Source: International Labour Office, *Yearbook of Labour Statistics*.

AGRICULTURE, ETC.

Principal Crops (FAO estimates, '000 metric tons, 1995): Maize 10; Potatoes 2; Cassava 3; Sweet potatoes 4 (1994); Pulses 1 (1992); Coconuts 5; Dates 2 (1992); Sugar cane 18; Bananas 6. Source: FAO, *Production Yearbook*.

Livestock ('000 head, year ending September 1995): Cattle 19; Pigs 450; Sheep 4 (FAO estimate); Goats 130 (FAO estimate); Asses 11 (FAO estimate). Source: FAO, *Production Yearbook*.

Fishing ('000 metric tons, live weight): Total catch 7.2 in 1993; 7.2 in 1994; 7.1 in 1995. Source: FAO, *Yearbook of Fishery Statistics*.

MINING

Production (metric tons): Salt (unrefined) 4,000 (1994 estimate, Source: US Bureau of Mines—Washington D.C.); Pozzolana 10,000 (1990, Source: UN Economic Commission for Africa, *African Statistical Yearbook*).

INDUSTRY

Production (metric tons, unless otherwise indicated, 1994): Biscuits 348 (1990 figure); Bread 3,926 (1991 figure); Canned fish 273; Frozen fish 2,700 (1992 FAO estimate); Manufactured tobacco 94 (1992 figure); Beer 4,162,033 litres; Soft drinks 932,154 litres; Paint 492; Shoes 120,524 pairs; Electric energy 63.6m. kWh. Sources: UN, *Industrial Commodity Statistics Yearbook;* IMF, *Cape Verde—Recent Economic Developments* (October 1996).

FINANCE

Currency and Exchange Rates: 100 centavos = 1 Cape Verde escudo; 1,000 escudos are known as a conto. *Sterling and Dollar Equivalents* (31 March 1997): £1 sterling = 150.563 escudos; US $1 = 91.695 escudos; 1,000 Cape Verde escudos = £6.642 = $10.906. *Average Exchange Rate* (escudos per US dollar): 81.891 in 1994; 76.853 in 1995; 82.591 in 1996.

Budget (preliminary, million escudos, 1995): *Revenue:* Taxation 6,407 (Taxes on income and profits 2,131, Municipal taxes 103, Taxes on international trade 3,757, Stamp tax 416); Other revenue 1,997 (Licences and miscellaneous fees 256, Property income 487, Transfers 425, Reimbursement of debt principal by public enterprises 101, Sales of fixed assets and services 190, Autonomous revenue 530); Total 8,404, excl. external grants (5,303) and domestic capital participation (761). *Expenditure:* Recurrent 9,284; Capital 9,844; Total 19,128. Source: IMF, *Cape Verde—Recent Economic Developments* (October 1996).

International Reserves (US $ million at 31 December 1996): IMF special drawing rights 0.06; Foreign exchange 40.28; Total 40.35. Source: IMF, *International Financial Statistics*.

Money Supply (million escudos at 31 December 1996): Currency outside banks 4,638.0; Demand deposits at commercial banks 9,948.7; Total money 14,586.7. Source: IMF, *International Financial Statistics*.

Cost of Living (Consumer Price Index for Praia; base: 1990 = 100): 125 in 1993; 128 in 1994; 138 in 1995. Source: IMF, *International Financial Statistics*.

Expenditure on the Gross Domestic Product (million escudos at current purchasers' values, 1993): Government final consumption expenditure 5,099; Private final consumption expenditure 22,199; Increase in stocks 811; Gross fixed capital formation 9,404; *Total domestic expenditure* 37,513; Exports of goods and services 3,981; *Less* Imports of goods and services 14,343; *GDP in purchasers' values* 27,151. Source: UN Economic Commission for Africa, *African Statistical Yearbook*.

Gross Domestic Product by Economic Activity (million escudos at current prices, 1993): Agriculture, forestry and fishing 4,878; Mining and quarrying 67; Manufacturing 1,515; Electricity, gas and water 698; Construction 4,814; Trade, restaurants and hotels 5,634; Transport and communications 2,898; Finance, insurance, real estate and business services 939; Government services 1,936; Other community, social and personal services 221; *GDP at factor cost* 23,600; Indirect taxes, *less* Subsidies 3,551; *GDP in purchasers' values* 27,151. Source: UN, Economic Commission for Africa, *African Statistical Yearbook*.

Balance of Payments (preliminary, million escudos, 1995): Exports of goods f.o.b. 646.5; Imports of goods f.o.b. −17,849.1; *Trade balance* −17,202.6; Services (net) 1,679.9; *Balance on goods and services* −15,522.7; Other income (net) −408.4; *Balance on goods,* *services and income* −15,931.1; Current transfers (net) 11,351.6; *Current balance* −4,579.6; Capital and financial account (net) 5,312.8; Net errors and omissions −151.4; *Overall balance* 581.8. Source: IMF, *Cape Verde—Recent Economic Developments* (October 1996).

EXTERNAL TRADE

Principal Commodities (million escudos, 1993): *Imports c.i.f.:* Live animals and animal products 596 (Milk 408); Vegetable products 1,414 (Maize 329, Rice 414); Edible oils and fats 358; Food and beverage products 1,916 (Sugar 416); Mineral products 1,272 (Cement 588, Petroleum, petroleum products, etc. 492); Chemical products 717; Plastics and rubber 452; Wood products 329; Paper and paper products 261; Textiles 322; Stone and glass products 285; Metal and metal products 906; Machinery and electrical equipment 1,417; Transport equipment 1,645; Total (incl. others) 12,387. *Exports f.o.b.:* Bananas 36.3; Fish 76.4; Crustaceans 118.4; Total (incl. others) 311.4. Source: IMF, *Cape Verde—Recent Economic Developments* (October 1996).

Principal Trading Partners (US $ '000, 1992): *Imports c.i.f.:* Brazil 10,252; Belgium and Luxembourg 4,676; Côte d'Ivoire 4,500; Denmark 3,058; France 6,475; Germany 6,665; Italy 7,734; Japan 8,993; Netherlands 18,706; Portugal 57,916; Romania 4,856; Spain 3,777; Sweden 3,957; Switzerland 3,058; USA 10,072; Total (incl. others) 179,864. *Exports f.o.b.:* Netherlands 462; Portugal 3,909; Spain 327; Total (incl. others) 4,808.

TRANSPORT

Road Traffic (motor vehicles in use, estimates, December, 1995): Passenger cars 2,860; Lorries and vans 870. Source: IRF, *World Road Statistics*.

Shipping: Merchant fleet (registered at 31 December 1996): Number of vessels 27, total displacement ('000 grt) 14.9 (Source: Lloyd's Register of Shipping, *World Fleet Statistics*); International freight traffic (estimates, '000 metric tons, 1993): Goods loaded 144, goods unloaded 299 (Source: UN, Economic Commission for Africa, *African Statistical Yearbook*).

Civil Aviation (traffic on scheduled services, 1994): Kilometres flown 3,000,000; passengers carried 118,000; passenger-km 173,000,000; total ton-km 17,000,000. Source: UN, *Statistical Yearbook*.

TOURISM

Tourist Arrivals (1996): 37,000.

Tourist Receipts (1996): US $11m.

COMMUNICATIONS MEDIA

Radio Receivers (1994): 67,000 in use (estimate). Source: UNESCO, *Statistical Yearbook*.

Television Receivers (1994): 1,000 in use (estimate). Source: UNESCO, *Statistical Yearbook*.

Telephones (1995): 21,500 in use. Source: Cabo Verde Telecom.

Newspapers (1995): 2 titles (average circulation 5,000 copies).

Periodicals (1995): 7 titles.

Book Production (1989): 10 titles. Source: UNESCO, *Statistical Yearbook*.

EDUCATION

Pre-primary (1986/87): 58 schools; 136 teachers; 4,523 pupils.

Primary (1993/94): 370 schools (1990/91); 2,657 teachers; 78,173 pupils.

Total Secondary: 268 teachers (1987/88); 14,097 pupils (1993/94).

General Secondary (1993/94): 438 teachers; 11,808 pupils.

Teacher Training: 25 teachers (1987/88); 889 pupils (1993/94).

Vocational Schools (1993/94): 94 teachers; 1,400 pupils.

Source: UNESCO, *Statistical Yearbook*.

Directory

The Constitution

A new Constitution of the Republic of Cape Verde ('the Second Republic') came into force on 25 September 1992. The Constitution defines Cape Verde as a sovereign, unitary and democratic republic, guaranteeing respect for human dignity and recognizing the inviolable and inalienable rights of man as a fundament of humanity, peace and justice. It recognizes the equality of all citizens before the law, without distinction of social origin, social condition, economic status, race, sex, religion, political convictions or ideologies and promises transparency for all citizens in the practising of fundamental liberties. The Constitution gives assent to popular will, and has a fundamental objective in the realization of economic, political, social and cultural democracy and the construction of a society which is free, just and in solidarity. The Republic of Cape Verde will create, progressively, the necessary conditions for the removal of all obstacles which impede the development of mankind and limit the equality of citizens and their effective participation in the political, economic, social and cultural organizations of the State and of Cape Verdean society.

The Head of State is the President of the Republic, who is elected by universal adult suffrage and must obtain two-thirds of the votes cast to win in the first round of the election. If no candidate secures the requisite majority, a new election is held within 21 days and contested by the two candidates who received the highest number of votes in the first round. Voting is conducted by secret ballot. Legislative power is vested in the Assembléia Nacional, which is also elected by universal adult suffrage. The Prime Minister is nominated by the Assembléia Nacional, to which he is responsible. On the recommendation of the Prime Minister, the President appoints the Council of Ministers, whose members must be elected deputies of the Assembléia Nacional. There are 17 local government councils, elected by universal suffrage for a period of five years.

The Government

HEAD OF STATE

President: António Manuel Mascarenhas Gomes Monteiro (took office 22 March 1991; re-elected 18 February 1996).

COUNCIL OF MINISTERS
(July 1997)

Prime Minister: Dr Carlos Alberto Wahnon de Carvalho Veiga.

Assistant Minister to the Prime Minister, with responsibility for Public Administration, Labour, Employment and Training, Social Communication, Youth and Sports and Social Promotion: Dr José António Mendes dos Reis.

Minister of Foreign Affairs and Communities: Dr Amílcar Spencer Lopes.

Minister of Economic Co-ordination: Dr António Gualberto do Rosário.

Minister in the Office of the President of the Council of Ministers and of Defence: Dr Ulpio Napoleão Fernandes.

Minister of Agriculture, Food and the Environment: Dr José António Pinto Monteiro.

Minister of the Sea: Dra Helena Nobre de Morais Semedo.

Minister of Education, Science and Culture: Eng. José Luís Livramento.

Minister of Justice and Internal Administration: Dr Simão Monteiro Rodrigues.

Minister of Health: Dr João Baptista Medina.

Minister of Infrastructure and Transport: Eng. Armindo Ferreira.

Secretary of State for Finance: Dr José Ulisses de Pina Correia e Silva.

Secretary of State for Foreign Affairs and Co-operation: Dr José Luís Jesus.

Secretary of State for Sports and Youth: Dr Victor Osório.

Secretary of State for Culture: António José Delgado.

Secretary of State for Public Administration: Dra Paula Almeida.

Secretary of State for Decentralisation: Dr César Almeida.

Secretary of State for the Fight Against Poverty: Dra Manuela Silva.

Secretary of State for Tourism, Industry and Commerce: Dr Alexandre Monteiro.

MINISTRIES

Office of the President: Presidência da República, Praia, Santiago; tel. 61-26-69; telex 6051.

Office of the Prime Minister: Palácio do Governo, Várzea CP 16, Praia, Santiago; tel. 61-04-05; telex 6054; fax 61-30-99.

Ministry of Agriculture, Food and the Environment: Ponta Belém, Praia, Santiago; tel. 61-57-17; telex 6072; fax 61-40-54.

Ministry of Decentralisation: Praia, Santiago.

Ministry of Economic Co-ordination: 107 Avda Amílcar Cabral, CP 30, Praia, Santiago; tel. 61-58-46; telex 6058; fax 61-38-97.

Ministry of Education, Science and Culture: Palácio do Governo, Várzea, Praia, Santiago; tel. 61-05-07; telex 6057.

Ministry of the Fight Against Poverty: Praia, Santiago.

Ministry of Foreign Affairs and Communities: Praça Dr Lorena, Praia, Santiago; tel. 61-57-27; telex 6070; fax 61-39-52.

Ministry of Health: Palácio do Governo, Várzea, Praia, Santiago; tel. 61-05-01; telex 6059.

Ministry of Infrastructure and Transport: Ponta Belém, Praia, Santiago; tel. 61-57-09; telex 6060; fax 61-56-99.

Ministry of Justice and Internal Administration: Rua Serpa Pinto, Praia, Santiago; tel. 61-56-91; telex 6025; fax 61-56-78.

Ministry of National Defence: Palácio do Governo, Várzea, Praia, Santiago; tel. 61-35-91; telex 6077; fax 61-30-99.

Ministry of Public Administration, Labour, Employment and Training, Social Communication, Youth and Sports and Social Promotion: Praia, Santiago.

Ministry of the Sea: Ponta Belém, Praia, Santiago; tel. 61-57-17; telex 6072; fax 61-40-54.

Ministry of Tourism, Industry and Commerce: Praia, Santiago.

President and Legislature

PRESIDENT

At a presidential election conducted on 18 February 1996 the incumbent President, ANTÓNIO MANUEL MASCARENHAS GOMES MONTEIRO, was the sole candidate and was duly re-elected.

ASSEMBLÉIA NACIONAL (AN)

Legislative Election, 17 December 1995

Party	Votes	% of votes	Seats
Movimento para a Democracia (MPD)	93,249	61.3	50
Partido Africano da Independência de Cabo Verde (PAICV)	45,263	29.8	21
Partido da Convergência Democrática (PCD)	10,211	6.7	1
Other parties	3,399	2.2	—
Total	152,122	100.0	72

Political Organizations

Movimento para a Democracia (MPD): Achada Santo António, CP 90A, Praia, Santiago; tel. 61-40-82; fax 61-41-22; f. 1990; advocates administrative decentralization; governing party since Jan. 1991; Chair. Dr CARLOS ALBERTO WAHNON DE CARVALHO VEIGA.

Partido Africano da Independência de Cabo Verde (PAICV): CP 22, Praia, Santiago; telex 6022; fax 61-16-09; f. 1956 as the Partido Africano da Independência do Guiné e Cabo Verde (PAIGC); name changed in 1981, following the 1980 coup in Guinea-Bissau; sole authorized political party 1975–90; Pres. Gen. PEDRO VERONA RODRIGUES PIRES; Sec.-Gen. ARISTIDES LIMA.

Partido da Convergência Democrática (PCD): Praia, Santiago; f. 1994 by fmr mems of the MPD; Pres. Dr EURICO CORREIA MONTEIRO.

Partido Socialista Democrático (PSD): Praia, Santiago; f. 1992; Sec.-Gen. JOÃO ALÉM.

União Caboverdiana Independente e Democrática (UCID): Praia, Santiago; f. 1974 by emigrants opposed to the PAICV; obtained legal recognition in 1991; Pres. CELSO CELESTINO.

Diplomatic Representation

EMBASSIES IN CAPE VERDE

Brazil: Chã de Areia, CP 93, Praia, Santiago; tel. 61-56-07; telex 6075; fax 61-56-09; Ambassador: ROMEO ZERO.

China, People's Republic: Achada de Santo António, Praia, Santiago; tel. 61-55-86; Ambassador: YANG YUANDE THIANG.

Cuba: Prainha, Praia, Santiago; tel. 61-55-97; telex 6087; fax 61-55-90; Ambassador: PABLO REYES.

France: CP 192, Praia, Santiago; tel. 61-55-89; telex 6064; fax 61-55-90; Ambassador: ANDRÉ BARBE.

Portugal: Achada de Santo António, CP 160, Praia, Santiago; tel. 61-56-02; telex 6055; fax 61-40-58; Ambassador: EUGÉNIO ANACORETA CORREIA.

Russia: Achada de Santo António, CP 31, Praia, Santiago; tel. 61-21-32; telex 6016; Ambassador: VLADIMIR PETUKHOV.

Senegal: Prainha, Praia, Santiago; tel. 61-56-21; Ambassador: AMADOU MOUSTAPHA DIOP.

USA: Rua Hoji Ya Yenna 81, CP 201, Praia, Santiago; tel. 61-56-16; telex 6068; fax 61-13-55; Ambassador: LAWRENCE NEAL BENEDICT.

Judicial System

Supremo Tribunal da Justiça: Praça Alexandre de Albuquerque, Platô, Praia, Santiago; tel. 61-58-10; telex 6025; fax 61-17-51; established 1975; the highest court.

President: Dr OSCAR GOMES.

Attorney-General: Dr HENRIQUE MONTEIRO.

Religion

CHRISTIANITY

At 31 December 1995 there were an estimated 389,680 adherents of the Roman Catholic Church, representing 96.3% of the total population. Protestant churches, among which the Church of the Nazarene is prominent, represent about 1% of the population.

The Roman Catholic Church

Cape Verde comprises the single diocese of Santiago de Cabo Verde, directly responsible to the Holy See. The Bishop participates in the Episcopal Conference of Senegal, Mauritania, Cape Verde and Guinea-Bissau, currently based in Senegal.

Bishop of Santiago de Cabo Verde: Rt Rev. PAULINO DO LIVRAMENTO EVORA, Avda Amílcar Cabral, Largo 5 de Outubro, CP 46, Praia, Santiago; tel. 61-11-19; fax 61-45-99.

The Anglican Communion

Cape Verde forms part of the diocese of The Gambia, within the Church of the Province of West Africa. The Bishop is resident in Banjul, The Gambia.

The Press

Agaviva: Mindelo, São Vicente; tel. 31-21-21; f. 1991; monthly; Editor GERMANO ALMEIDA; circ. 4,000.

Boletim Informativo: CP 126, Praia, Santiago; f. 1976; weekly; publ. by the Ministry of Foreign Affairs; circ. 1,500.

Boletim Oficial da República de Cabo Verde: Imprensa Nacional, CP 113, Praia, Santiago; tel. 61-41-50; weekly; official.

Contacto: CP 89C, Praia, Santiago; tel. 61-57-52; fax 61-14-42; f. 1993; quarterly; economic bulletin produced by Centro de Promoção Turística, do Investimento e das Exportações (PROMEX); circ. 1,500.

Novo Jornal Cabo Verde: Largo do Hospital Dr Agostinho Neto, CP 118, Praia, Santiago; tel. 61-39-89; fax 61-38-29; f. 1993; two a week; Editor LÚCIA DIAS; circ. 5,000.

Perspectiva: Achada de Santo António, CP 89C, Praia, Santiago; tel. 62-27-41; fax 62-27-37; f. 1995; annual; economic bulletin produced by Centro de Promoção Turística, do Investimento e das Exportações; Editor Dr AGUINALDO MARÇAL; circ. 5,000.

Raízes: CP 98, Praia, Santiago; tel. 319; f. 1977; quarterly; cultural review; Editor ARNALDO FRANÇA; circ. 1,500.

A Semana: CP 36C, Avda Cidade de Lisboa, Praia, Santiago; tel. 61-39-50; fax 63-22-71; weekly; independent; Editor FILOMENA SILVA; circ. 5,000.

Terra Nova: CP 166, São Vicente; tel. 32-24-42; fax 32-14-75; f. 1975; monthly; Roman Catholic; Editor P. FIDALGO BARROS; circ. 3,000.

NEWS AGENCIES

Cabopress: Achada de Santo António, CP 40/A, Praia, Santiago; tel. 61-55-57; telex 6044; fax 61-55-55; f. 1991.

Foreign Bureaux

Agence France-Presse (AFP): CP 26/118 Praia, Santiago; tel. 61-38-89; telex 52; Rep. Fátima Azevedo.

Agência Portuguesa de Noticias (LUSA): Prainha, Praia, Santiago; tel. 61-35-19.

Inter Press Service (IPS) (Italy): CP 14, Mindelo, São Vicente; tel. 31-45-50; Rep. Juan A. Coloma.

Publisher

Government Publishing House

Imprensa Nacional: CP 113, Praia, Santiago; tel. 61-42-09; Admin. João de Pina.

Radio and Television

There were an estimated 67,000 radio receivers and 1,000 television receivers in use in 1994.

Rádio Televisão de Cabo Verde (RTC): Praça Albuquerque, CP 26, Praia, Santiago; tel. 61-57-55; fax 61-57-54; govt-controlled; five radio transmitters and five solar relay radio transmitters; FM transmission only; radio broadcasts in Portuguese and Creole for 18 hours daily; one television transmitter and seven relay television transmitters; television broadcasts in Portuguese and Creole for eight hours daily with co-operation of RTPI (Portugal); Dir Manuela Fonseca Soares.

Rádio Educativa de Cabo Verde: Achada de Santo António, Praia, Santiago; tel. 61-11-61.

Voz de São Vicente: CP 29, Mindelo, São Vicente; fax 31-10-06; f. 1974; govt-controlled; Dir José Fonseca Soares.

Finance

(cap. = capital; res = reserves; m. = million; dep. = deposits; brs = branches; amounts in Cape Verde escudos)

BANKING

Central Bank

Banco de Cabo Verde (BCV): 117 Avda Amílcar Cabral, CP 101, Praia, Santiago; tel. 61-31-53; telex 99350; fax 61-44-47; f. 1976; bank of issue; cap. and res 1,796.2m., dep. 3,790.4m. (1984); Gov. Amaro Alexandre da Luz.

Other Banks

Banco Comercial do Atlântico (BCA): 117 Avda Amílcar Cabral, Praia, Santiago; tel. 61-55-29; telex 99350; f. 1993; commercial and development bank; Gov. Amélia Figueiredo; 17 brs.

Banco Totta e Açores (BTA) (Portugal): 1 Rua Justinho Lopes, Praia, Santiago; tel. 61-26-65; fax 63-18-46; Cape Verde branch f. 1995; Gen. Man. Antão da Luz.

Caixa de Crédito Rural: Praia, Santiago; f. 1995; rural credit bank.

Caixa Económica de Cabo Verde (CECV): Avda Cidade de Lisboa, CP 199, Praia, Santiago; tel. 61-55-61; telex 6097; fax 61-55-60; f. 1928; commercial and development bank; cap. 348m. (Aug. 1993).

The **Fundo de Solidariedade Nacional** is the main savings institution; the **Fundo de Desenvolvimento Nacional** channels public investment resources; and the **Instituto Caboverdiano** administers international aid.

STOCK EXCHANGE

Plans were announced in 1996 for the establishment of a stock exchange at Praia.

INSURANCE

Companhia Caboverdiana de Seguros (IMPAR): Avda Amílcar Cabral, CP 469, Praia, Santiago; tel. 61-14-05; fax 61-37-65; f. 1991; Pres. Dr Corsino Fortes.

Garantia Companhia de Seguros: CP 138, Praia, Santiago; tel. 61-35-32; fax 61-25-55; f. 1991.

Trade and Industry

CHAMBERS OF COMMERCE

Associação Comercial Industrial e Agrícola de Barlavento (ACIAB): CP 62, Mindelo, São Vicente; tel. 31-32-81; fax 32-36-58; f. 1918.

Associação Comercial de Sotavento (ACAS): Rua Serpa Pinto 23, 1°, CP 78, Praia, Santiago; tel. 61-29-91; telex 6005; fax 61-29-64.

Centro de Promoção Turística, do Investimento Externo e das Exportações (PROMEX): CP 89c, Achada de Santo António, Praia, Santiago; tel. 62-27-41; fax 62-27-37; f. 1990; promotes tourism, foreign investment and exports; Chair. Dr Sá Nogueira.

Instituto Nacional das Cooperativas: Fazenda, CP 218, Praia, Santiago; tel. 61-41-12; fax 61-39-59; central co-operative organization.

STATE INDUSTRIAL ENTERPRISES

Correios de Cabo Verde, SARL: Direcção-Geral, Praia, Santiago; tel. 61-55-79; telex 6087.

Empresa de Comercialização de Produtos do Mar—INTERBASE, EP: CP 59, Mindelo, São Vicente; tel. 31-46-68; fax 31-39-40; supervises marketing of seafood; shipping agency and ship chandler.

Empresa Nacional de Administração dos Portos, EP (ENAPOR): Avda Marginal, CP 82, Mindelo, São Vicente; tel. 31-44-14; telex 3049; fax 31-46-61.

Empresa Nacional de Aeroportos e Segurança Aérea, EP (ASA): Aeroporto Amílcar Cabral, CP 58, Ilha do Sal; tel. 41-13-94; telex 4036; fax 41-15-70; airports and aircraft security.

Empresa Nacional de Avicultura, EP (ENAVI): CP 135, Praia, Santiago; tel. 61-56-51; telex 6072; fax 61-12-92; f. 1979; poultry farming.

Empresa Nacional de Conservação e Reparação de Equipamentos (SONACOR): Praia, Santiago; tel. 61-25-57; telex 6080.

Empresa Nacional de Produtos Farmacêuticos (EMPROFAC): CP 59, Praia, Santiago; tel. 61-56-36; telex 6024; fax 61-58-72; f. 1979; state monopoly of pharmaceuticals and medical imports.

Empresa Pública de Abastecimento (EMPA): CP 107, Praia, Santiago; tel. 61-56-27; telex 6054; fax 61-37-37; f. 1975; state provisioning enterprise, supervising imports, exports and domestic distribution; Dir-Gen. Nasolino Silva dos Santos.

Empresa Pública de Electricidad e Agua (ELECTRA): 10 Avda Unidade Africana, CP 137, Mindelo, São Vicente; tel. 31-44-48; telex 3045.

MAJOR INDUSTRIAL COMPANIES

Companhia da Pozolana de Cabo Verde: Porto Novo, Ilha de Santo Antão; pozzolan industry.

Companhia Fomento de Cabo Verde: Santa Maria, Ilha do Sal; salt industry.

Confecções Morabeza, SARL: CP 18, Mindelo, São Vicente; tel. 31-21-44; telex 3048; fax 31-28-19; f. 1978; textiles; 55% state-owned; exports to Africa, Europe and Canada; Man. Dir Cesário J. G. Lopes.

Empresa Nacional de Combustíveis, EP (ENACOL): CP 1, Mindelo, São Vicente; tel. 31-31-49; telex 3086; fax 31-48-73; f. 1979; supervises import and distribution of petroleum; Dir Dr Mário A. Rodrigues.

Salins du Cap Vert: Pedra Lume, Ilha do Sal; salt industry.

SOCAL: Sociedade Industrial de Calçado, SARL: CP 92, Mindelo, São Vicente; tel. 31-50-59; telex 3089; fax 31-20-61; industrial shoe factory.

TRADE UNIONS

Confederação Cabo-Verdiana dos Sindicatos Livres (CCSL): Rua Dr Júlio Abreau, Praia, Santiago; tel. 61-63-41.

Sindicato da Indústria, Agricultura e Pesca (SIAP): Plateau, Praia, Santiago; tel. 61-63-19.

Sindicato dos Transportes, Comunicações e Turismo (STCT): Praia, Santiago; tel. 61-63-38.

União Nacional dos Trabalhadores de Cabo Verde—Central Sindical (UNTC—CS): Estrada do Aeroporto, Praia, Santiago; tel. 61-43-05; fax 61-36-29; f. 1978; Chair. Julio Ascensão Silva.

Transport

ROADS

In 1995 there were an estimated 1,100 km of roads, of which 858 km were paved.

SHIPPING

Cargo-passenger ships call regularly at Porto Grande, Mindelo, on São Vicente, and Praia, on Santiago. In 1993 plans were announced for the upgrading of Porto Grande, at a cost of US $13.2m., and for the re-establishment of the port of Vale dos Cavaleiros, on Fogo island, at a cost of $10.6m. There are small ports on the other islands.

Comissão de Gestão dos Transportes Marítimos de Cabo Verde: CP 153, São Vicente; tel. 31-49-79; fax 31-20-55; telex 3031.

Companhia Cabo-Verdiana de Transportes Marítimos: CP 150, Praia, Santiago; tel. 61-22-84; fax 61-60-95.

Companhia Nacional de Navegação Arca Verde: Rua 5 de Julho, CP 41, Praia, Santiago; tel. 61-10-60; telex 6067; fax 61-54-96; f. 1975.

Companhia de Navegação Estrela Negra: Avda 5 de Julho 17, CP 91, São Vicente; tel. 31-54-23; telex 3030; fax 31-53-82.

Companhia Nacional de Navegação Portuguesa: Agent in Santiago: João Benoliel de Carvalho, Lda, CP 56, Praia, Santiago.

Companhia Portuguesa de Transportes Marítimos: Agent in Santiago: João Benoliel de Carvalho, Lda, CP 56, Praia, Santiago.

CS Line: Praia, Santiago.

Linhas Marítimas (LINMAC): Dr João Battista Ferreira Medina, Praia, Santiago; tel. 61-40-99.

Mare Verde: Mindelo, São Vicente.

Seage Agência de Navegação de Cabo Verde: Avda Cidade de Lisboa, CP 232, Praia, Santiago; tel. 61-57-58; telex 6033; fax 61-25-24; Chair. CESAR MANUEL SEMEDO LOPES.

CIVIL AVIATION

The Amílcar Cabral international airport is at Espargos, on Sal Island, with capacity for aircraft of up to 50 tons and 1m. passengers per year. Expansion of the airport's facilities began in 1987, with EC and Italian aid. There is also a small airport on each of the other inhabited islands. A second international airport, under construction on Santiago, was due for completion in late 1999. The new airport was to be capable of accommodating Airbus 310 aircraft.

CABOVIMO: 32 Avda Unidade Guiné-Cabo Verde, Praia, Santiago; tel. 61-33-14; fax 61-55-59; f. 1992; internal flights; Gen. Man. JORGE DANIEL SPENCER LIMA.

Transportes Aéreos de Cabo Verde (TACV): Avda Amílcar Cabral, CP 1, Praia, Santiago; tel. 61-58-13; telex 6065; fax 61-35-85; f. 1958; internal services connecting the nine inhabited islands; also operates regional services to Senegal, Guinea, the Gambia and Guinea-Bissau, and long-distance services to Europe and the USA; Dir ALFREDO CARVALHO.

Tourism

The islands of Santiago, Santo Antão, Fogo and Brava offer attractive mountain scenery, and Santiago combines this with white sandy beaches. There are also extensive beaches on the islands of Sal, Boa Vista and Maio. There are four hotels on Sal, one on Boa Vista, one on São Vicente, and three in Praia. Some 37,000 tourists visited Cape Verde during 1996, mainly from Portugal (35%), France (12%), Germany (11%), the Netherlands (8%), Italy, Belgium and Spain. In that year tourism receipts totalled US $11m. In 1993 a 15-year National Tourism Development Plan was adopted providing for a projected increase in tourist arrivals to some 400,000 annually by 2008.

Centro de Promocão Turística, do Investimento Externo e das Exportações (PROMEX): CP 89c, Achada de Santo António, Praia, Santiago; tel. 62-27-41; fax 62-27-37; f. 1990; promotes tourism, foreign investment and exports; Dir of Tourism AIDA DUARTE SILVA.

Defence

The armed forces numbered about 1,100 (army 1,000, air force less than 100) in August 1996. There is also a police force, the Police for Public Order, which is organized by the local municipal councils. National service is by selective conscription.

Defence Expenditure: Budgeted at 310m. Cape Verde escudos (US $4m.) in 1996.

Education

Primary education, beginning at seven years of age and lasting for six years, comprises a first cycle of four years, which is compulsory, and a second cycle of two years. Secondary education, beginning at 13 years of age, is also divided into two cycles, the first comprising a three-year general course, the second a three-year pre-university course. There are three teacher-training units and two industrial and commercial schools of further education. In 1993 the total enrolment at primary and secondary schools was equivalent to 83% of all school-age children (males 85%; females 81%). In 1986/87 there were 4,523 children enrolled at pre-primary schools. In 1993/94 78,173 pupils attended primary schools, and 11,808 attended general secondary schools. Primary enrolment in 1993 included 100% of children in the relevant age-group. In that year secondary enrolment was equivalent to 22% of children in the relevant age-group. In 1996/97 there were 1,660 Cape Verdean students studying at overseas universities. A university was to be established in Praia in 1998 with assistance from Portugal. In 1995, according to estimates by UNESCO, the average rate of illiteracy among the population aged 15 years and over was 28.4% (males 18.6%; females 36.2%).

Bibliography

A.G.U. *Cabo Verde.* Lisbon, 1966.

Amaral, I. d. *Santiago de Cabo Verde.* Lisbon, 1964.

Cabral, N. E. *Le Moulin et le Pilon, les îles du Cap-Vert.* Paris, 1980.

Cape Verde Government Publication. *República de Cabo Verde: 5 Anos de Independência (1975–80).* Lisbon, 1980.

Carreira, A. *Cabo Verde, Formação e Extinção de uma Sociedade Escravocrata.* Bissau, 1972.

Migrações nas Ilhas de Cabo Verde. Lisbon, Universidade Nova, 1977.

Cabo Verde: Classes sociais, estructura familiar, migrações. Lisbon, Ulmeiro, 1977.

The People of the Cape Verde Islands: Exploitation and Emigration (trans. and edited by C. Fyfe). London, Hurst, and Hamden, CT, Archon Books, 1983.

Davidson, B. *No Fist is Big Enough to Hide the Sky: The Liberation of Guinea-Bissau and Cape Verde.* 2nd Edn. London, Zed Press, 1984.

The Fortunate Isles: A Study of Cape Verde. London, Hutchinson, and Trenton, NJ, World Press, 1989.

de Pina, M.-P. *Les îles du Cap-Vert.* Paris, Karthala, 1987.

Foy, C. *Cape Verde: Politics, Economics and Society.* London, Printer Publishers, Marxist Regimes Series, 1988.

Lobban, R. *Historical Dictionary of Cape Verde.* 3rd Edn. Metuchen, NJ, Scarecrow Press, 1995.

May, S. *Tourismus in der Dritten Welt: Das Beispiel Kapverde.* Frankfurt am Main, Campus Verlag, 1985.

Meintel, D. *Race, Culture and Portuguese Colonialism in Cabo Verde.* Syracuse, NY, Syracuse University Press, 1985.

Nunez, B. *Dictionary of Portuguese-African Civilization.* Vol. I. London, Hans Zell, 1995.

Promex–Centre for Export and Investment Promotion, *Cape Verde–Guide for Investors.* Praia, 1994.

World Bank Report. *Poverty in Cape Verde–A Summary Assessment and a Strategy for its Alleviation.* Africa Region, 1994.

THE CENTRAL AFRICAN REPUBLIC

Physical and Social Geography

DAVID HILLING

PHYSICAL FEATURES

Geographically, the Central African Republic forms a link between the Sudano-Sahelian zone and the Congo basin. The country consists mainly of plateau surfaces at 600–900 m above sea-level, which provide the watershed between drainage northwards to Lake Chad and southwards to the Oubangui/Congo river system. In the Bongo massif of the north-east, altitudes of 1,400 m are attained. There are numerous rivers, and during the main rainy season (July–October) much of the south-east of the country becomes inaccessible as a result of extensive inundation. The Oubangui river to the south of Bangui provides near-year-round commercial navigation and is the country's main outlet for external trade. However, development of the country is inhibited by its land-locked location and the great distance (1,815 km) to the sea by way of the fluvial route from Bangui to Brazzaville, in the Republic of the Congo, and thence by rail to Pointe-Noire.

POPULATION AND RESOURCES

The Central African Republic covers an area of 622,984 sq km (240,535 sq miles). At the census of December 1988 the population was 2,463,616, an average density of only 4.0 inhabitants per sq km. The greatest concentration of population is in the western part of the country, while large areas in the east are virtually uninhabited. There are numerous ethnic groups, but the Banda and Baya together comprise more than 50% of the population. Sango, a lingua franca, has been adopted as the national language.

Only in the south-west of the country is the rainfall sufficient (1,250 mm) to sustain a forest vegetation. The south-western Lobaye region is a source of coffee (the main cash crop), cocoa, rubber, palm produce and timber. Cotton, also an important cash crop, is cultivated in a belt beyond the forest. This area could benefit substantially from a proposed rail link with the Transcameroon railway.

Alluvial deposits of diamonds occur widely and are exploited, but uranium is potentially of much greater economic importance. The exploitation of ore-rich deposits at Bakouma, 480 km east of Bangui, which has been inhibited by inadequate access routes and by technical problems, now awaits a recovery in the present level of world uranium prices.

Recent History

PIERRE ENGLEBERT

Revised for this Edition by the Editor

The former French territory of Oubangui-Chari became the Central African Republic (CAR) on achieving internal self-government in 1958. Barthélemy Boganda, the first prime minister, died in 1959, and was succeeded by David Dacko, who became the CAR's first president at independence on 13 August 1960. The ruling Mouvement d'évolution sociale de l'Afrique noire (MESAN) was declared the sole legal party in December 1962. In December 1965–January 1966 the commander-in-chief of the armed forces, Col Jean-Bédel Bokassa, staged a *coup d'état*, placing Dacko, his cousin, under house arrest. Bokassa's power was virtually absolute, and he involved himself in every aspect of national life. However, he was unpredictable and despotic, and the country suffered from frequent changes in policy and an inefficient and corrupt administration. Relations with France were turbulent. Little open opposition to Bokassa emerged, but twice, in 1969 and 1973, senior ministers were implicated in alleged coup attempts. Bokassa declared himself president for life in 1972 and a marshal of the republic in 1974. In September 1976 the council of ministers was replaced by the Council for the Central African Revolution (CRC), with Ange-Félix Patassé as prime minister and Dacko as personal adviser to Bokassa. Two months later Bokassa dissolved the CRC, and announced the foundation of the Central African Empire. His coronation as emperor took place in December 1977, at a cost estimated to have absorbed one-quarter of the country's annual foreign earnings. Following his coronation, Bokassa increasingly withdrew from public view.

Open opposition to Bokassa's rule mounted from the beginning of 1979, when student demonstrations in Bangui escalated into pitched battles between police and protesters. Unrest was intensified in May, following reports that a number of children had been killed by the police. Several opposition groups were formed in exile, including the Mouvement pour la libération du peuple centrafricain (MLPC), led by Patassé (who had been dismissed as prime minister in 1978 and had subsequently sought asylum in France), and in July these groups formed a common front. On the night of 20 September, while Bokassa was in Libya, he was deposed in a bloodless coup by Dacko, supported by a contingent of French troops flown in from Gabon. Dacko proclaimed the country once again a republic and himself its president. Bokassa initially sought refuge in France, but was granted asylum in Côte d'Ivoire. The government appointed by Dacko, which retained many of Bokassa's ministers, quickly became plagued by internal dissension and public opposition. A new multi-party constitution was approved by referendum in February 1981 and a presidential election followed in March. Dacko was elected with 50% of the votes cast, while his main opponent, Patassé, received 38%, although all the opposition candidates challenged the result and protested about alleged electoral irregularities. Opposition to Dacko's rule increased during 1981; legislative elections were cancelled, and the government suppressed the opposition parties, in breach of its commitment to political pluralism. Deprived of French support by the change of government in Paris, Dacko was persuaded to transfer power to a military government. In September Gen. André Kolingba, the army chief of staff, was declared head of state. All party-political activity was suspended.

KOLINGBA'S RULE, 1981–93

On the first anniversary of his assumption of power, Kolingba announced a programme of economic recovery covering the period to 1985, and said that a one-party system would be envisaged thereafter. However, disenchantment with the military regime had begun to spread. In March 1982 an unsuccessful coup attempt was staged by Patassé, who subsequently took refuge in the French embassy. A crisis in the two countries' relations followed when the French, despite consistent support for the Kolingba administration, insisted that Patassé be granted safe passage to exile in Togo. Kolingba, whose government remained dependent on French economic support, had little option but to comply, against his stated intention to bring Patassé to trial. Relations between the two countries improved following an official visit by Kolingba to Paris in October.

In August 1982 Abel Goumba, the leader of the opposition Front patriotique oubanguien–Parti du travail (FPO–PT), was arrested, with another leading member of the party, on charges of plotting against the government. Following intense but discreet French pressure, they were released in September 1983, together with some of the prisoners who had been arrested in the 1982 coup attempt. Other members of the FPO–PT, meanwhile, had appointed a new leadership which was committed to armed struggle. The two other political parties fell into a similar state of fragmentation: part of the membership of the MLPC rejected the leadership of Patassé; and sections of the Mouvement centrafricain pour la libération nationale (MCLN) rejected their leader, Dr Iddi Lala. Some elements of the three parties agreed in August 1983 to form a united front, named the Parti révolutionnaire centrafricain. The government appeared to be less alarmed by this development, however, than by Bokassa's attempt, in November, to return from exile in Côte d'Ivoire. His departure was prevented by the Ivorian authorities, who then expelled him to France, where he was reluctantly allowed to take up residence.

In early 1984 several civilian politicians, including Goumba and Henri Maidou, a former vice-president, were arrested for violating the ban on political parties. At a trial held in July, sentences of up to 10 years' imprisonment were passed on those implicated in the 1982 coup attempt. Some of these were reduced by Kolingba in December 1984, when both Goumba and Maidou were also released. In that month several opposition leaders formed a 'government-in-exile' in Libya, a development which appeared to cause some anxiety to Kolingba. Former Brig.-Gen. Alphonse Mbaikoua, the 'president', and former Brig.-Gen. François Bozize, the 'vice-president', had previously supported Kolingba, before helping to organize the 1982 coup attempt. In July 1986 the MLPC and the FPO–PT announced the formation of a Front uni (FU), which was to campaign for a democratic system of government.

In September 1985 Kolingba dissolved the cabinet and formed a new administration, in which civilians were not only appointed ministers for the first time since the military take-over, but also held the majority of portfolios. Nevertheless, military personnel held the major posts. At a referendum held in November 1986 some 91.17% of voters granted a further six-year mandate to Kolingba as president and approved a draft constitution which provided for wide-ranging powers for the head of state, with the legislature occupying a mainly advisory role. In December a government reshuffle took place, in which Kolingba assumed the defence portfolio. In February 1987, at the constitutive assembly of the Rassemblement démocratique centrafricain (RDC), the sole political party stipulated in the new constitution, a clear separation was defined between party and state, and membership of the party was made voluntary. In July the country's first legislative elections for 20 years were held, at which all 142 candidates contesting the 52 seats in the national assembly were nominated by the RDC. It is conjectural whether an electoral boycott by the FU was responsible for an electoral turnout of only 50%.

In October 1986, with the economy under scrutiny from the IMF and moves towards an ostensibly more democratic regime in progress, the government was highly embarrassed when Bokassa suddenly returned to the CAR. He was arrested upon his arrival at Bangui airport. Reluctant to carry out the death sentence imposed on him in his absence for charges ranging from embezzlement to murder and cannibalism, the government ordered a new trial, to be held in public in the presence of international observers.

The reasons for Bokassa's return were unclear. He had reportedly been led to suppose that he would be reinstated as emperor by popular acclaim. During his retrial, represented by French defence lawyers, he argued that he had returned of his own free will to clear his name. However, he subsequently accepted an element of responsibility for some of his actions. The prosecution was poorly organized, with several of its witnesses themselves being arrested after giving evidence, and the trial lasted for six months. In June 1987 Bokassa was found guilty of four of the 14 charges brought against him, and was sentenced to death. An appeal was lodged, but was rejected by the supreme court in November. In February 1988, however, Kolingba commuted the sentence to one of imprisonment for life. In August 1989 it was announced that all remaining death sentences were to be similarly commuted; however, the remission excluded those who had been sentenced to death *in absentia*. In September 1991 Bokassa's life sentence was commuted to 20 years' imprisonment and in December 1992 the length of the sentence was further reduced, to 10 years.

After the Bokassa trial, Kolingba resumed his earlier attempts at democratization and national reconciliation. The first municipal elections were held in May 1988, at which voters were offered a choice of RDC-approved candidates. A government reshuffle followed in July. Kolingba sought a *rapprochement* with former opponents of his regime by inviting Brig.-Gen. Bozize to return from exile. (Bozize chose to remain in Benin, where he had founded an opposition movement, the Rassemblement populaire pour la reconstruction de la Centrafrique.) In addition, Kolingba appointed Maidou to an influential banking position. Members of Patassé's MLPC were also rehabilitated during 1988, although Patassé himself remained in exile in Togo. However, in July 1989 12 opponents of the Kolingba regime, including members of the FPO–PT and Brig.-Gen. Bozize, were arrested in Benin, and subsequently extradited to the CAR and imprisoned.

In May 1990 the RDC ruled that the establishment of a multi-party system in the CAR would be 'incompatible' with the country's political and economic development. However, this ruling was immediately contested in the form of a petition for a national conference on the future of the country, signed by 253 prominent citizens. The petition claimed that society in the CAR was 'corrupted by tribal discrimination, nepotism, fraud and injustice'. In October there was an outbreak of rioting in Bangui when the police attempted to disperse a public meeting of opposition supporters; several people were detained, including Dacko, Maidou and Goumba.

From late 1990 the government's unpopularity intensified, owing to the implementation of further economic austerity measures. Public servants were unpaid for several months in 1990, and in December the trade union movement, the Union syndicale des travailleurs de la Centrafrique (USTC), appealed for a general strike. The RDC eventually agreed to pay the workers one-quarter of the arrears owed to them, as well as promising to re-establish the post of prime minister and to undertake a fundamental review of the constitution. In March 1991 most of those who had been detained after the riots of October 1990 were released. The new post of prime minister was created in March 1991, with Edouard Franck, a former minister of state at the presidency, as the first occupant.

During April–July 1991 sporadic strikes plagued the government, as the political opposition conducted its operations from within the USTC. In early July, following the arrests of at least 10 union leaders on charges of convening an illegal political assembly, the government finally conceded the restoration of a multi-party political system and the imminent legalization of political parties. Kolingba conceded that the reforms were being made to meet the wishes of the international donor community. However, public meetings remained illegal, opposition parties were prevented access to the state-controlled media and civil service unions were banned by decree until the end of October. In early August the USTC called a 48-hour general strike in protest at the arrests of its leaders, and at the suppression of civil service unions. In August Kolingba relinquished the presidency of the RDC.

At the end of October 1991 the government agreed to convene a national debate, comprising representatives of the government and opposition movements. Throughout the next few months negotiations on the reform process took place between the government and the opposition; the latter advocated the replacement of the planned national debate by a national conference, which would have sovereign powers to overrule the president's recommendations and to introduce reforms itself. Meanwhile, Kolingba continued to oscillate between repression and compromise. In December he pardoned Bozize for his involvement in the attempted coup of March 1982, although in May 1992 an opposition politician was sentenced to six months' imprisonment for criticizing a speech by the president.

The negotiations on reform collapsed in early May 1992. Nevertheless, the government continued to make preparations for a national debate. Divisions emerged within the opposition at this time, as five centrist parties formed the Conseil de l'entente des partis modérés, which appeared more inclined towards compromise than the main opposition grouping, the Concertation des forces démocratiques (CFD).

In August 1992 Kolingba opened the 'grand national debate'. Boycotted by the CFD and the Roman Catholic Church, it was dominated by pro-Kolingba nominees from the RDC and local government. The opening of the debate coincided with the killing of a leading member of the CFD by the security forces during an anti-government protest: this incident provoked condemnation from Amnesty International and the US ambassador.

At the end of August 1992, the national assembly approved legislation in accordance with decisions taken by the grand national debate: constitutional amendments were introduced which provided for the strict separation of executive, legislative and judicial powers and for direct multi-party presidential and legislative elections. Kolingba was granted temporary powers to rule by decree pending the election of a multi-party legislature. In early September Kolingba announced that presidential and parliamentary elections would be held in the following month. The elections commenced in late October, but were suspended by decree of the president (himself a candidate at the presidential election) and subsequently annulled by the supreme court, owing to alleged electoral irregularities. Three other candidates (ex-president David Dacko, former premier Ange-Félix Patassé and Enoch Derant Lakoué, the leader of the Parti social-démocrate—PSD) supported the annullment, although it was opposed by Dr Abel Goumba, the CFD candidate and leader of the Front patriotique pour le progrès (FPP). The CFD eventually accepted the postponement, suggesting that the elections should be restaged in February 1993. All sides accepted this proposal, and Kolingba appointed Gen. Timothée Malendoma as prime minister of a transitional government. Malendoma's Forum civique had broken ranks with the CFD by participating in the grand national debate, but Malendoma nevertheless retained the support of the opposition, having been one of the founders of the campaign for democracy. However, the CFD chose not to participate in his government.

In January 1993 Malendoma was dismissed after complaining that Kolingba had curtailed his powers as prime minister. The elections were again postponed, and in May the new prime minister, Enoch Durant Lakoué, announced that polling would take place in October. However, after strong opposition protest and severe pressure exerted by the French government, Kolingba brought the elections forward to August. At the first round of the presidential election on 22 August, Patassé received 37.31% of the votes cast, followed by Goumba with 21.68%, and Dacko with 20.1%. Kolingba received just 12.1%. At the elections to the legislature, held concurrently, of the 31 seats won outright, 15 were secured by the MLPC (led by Patassé), four seats by supporters of Dacko, four by the RDC and eight by smaller parties, some of which were grouped in the CFD. Kolingba initially sought to prevent the publication of the first-round results by issuing decrees which modified the electoral code and altered the composition of the supreme court. However, strong pressure from France, including the threat to suspend all forms of bilateral co-operation, forced him to reverse his decision. Some 2,000 supporters of David Dacko also demonstrated in Bangui in September to demand the invalidation of the results of the first round. Two days later, however, Dacko officially accepted the results, thereby acknowledging his defeat.

DEMOCRATIC TRANSITION

Patassé won the second round of the ballot on 19 September 1993, receiving 52.47% of votes cast (Goumba received 45.62%), and was declared president by the supreme court on 27 September. After the second round of voting for seats in the national assembly the MLPC held a total of 34 seats (nine seats short of an absolute majority), the RDC had 13 seats, the FPP and the Parti libéral démocratique (PLD) had seven seats each, and the Alliance pour la démocratie et le progrès (ADP) and supporters of Dacko, had six seats each. The remaining 12 seats were shared among seven minor parties and independents.

Former president Bokassa was freed by Kolingba in September 1993, three years before the end of his sentence, in a general amnesty for prisoners declared ostensibly in celebration of the 12th anniversary of Kolingba's accession to power, but nevertheless widely interpreted to have been an attempt by the president to disrupt the elections and remain in power. After his release Bokassa declared that he was still 'the emperor' and that he would return to power if public opinion supported him; the government, however, banned him for life from participating in elections and deprived him of the rank of marshal. (Bokassa died of natural causes in November 1996.)

Patassé was sworn in as president on 22 October 1993. In his inaugural address he stressed that his administration would aim to promote the decentralization of government. He also pledged to address the outstanding problem of unpaid salaries for civil servants. In late October Patassé appointed Jean-Luc Mandaba, a former minister of health under Kolingba and vice-president of the MLPC, as prime minister. After appointing a 19-member cabinet at the end of October, which included three ministers from the outgoing administration, Mandaba emphasized the primacy of economic policy in his reform programme. In addition to the MLPC, the new government included representatives of the PLD, the ADP and supporters of David Dacko, giving the coalition government a working majority of 53 seats in the national assembly. On 27 October, Patassé appointed Gen. Jean-Roger Lako as chief of staff of the armed forces.

In December 1993 Dacko launched a new party, the Mouvement pour la démocratie et le développement (MDD), whose stated objectives were to consolidate and safeguard national unity, and to promote the equitable distribution of wealth. At the end of 1993 the government announced the establishment of a commission of enquiry (including an audit of the former administration's finances) which would investigate Kolingba's conduct during his tenure as president. In March 1994, following the arrest for seditious activities of two senior members of the RDC, accused Kolingba was deprived of his army rank.

In August 1994 several committees of specialists, appointed by the government, began to draft a new constitution. The completed document included provisions empowering the president to nominate senior military, civil service and judicial officials, and requiring the prime minister to implement policies decided by the president. In addition, provision was made for the creation of directly-elected regional assemblies, to enable the decentralization of government, and for the establishment of an advisory state council, which was to deliberate on administrative issues. Despite opposition from a number of groups in the governing coalition (notably the MDD), which expressed concern at the level of power afforded to the president in the draft constitution, 82% of those who participated in a national referendum in late December voted in favour of the draft Constitution. (The turnout at the referendum was, however, estimated at only 45% of the electorate.) The new constitution was duly adopted on 7 January 1995.

In early April 1995 Mandaba resigned as prime minister, pre-empting a threatened vote of no confidence in his government (initiated by his own party), following accusations against the administration of corruption and incompetence. On the following day Patassé appointed Gabriel Koyambounou, a former civil servant, as the new prime minister. Koyambounou subsequently nominated a new cabinet, with an enlarged membership.

At the end of August 1995 supporters of Kolingba's RDC staged a peaceful demonstration in protest at perceived abuses of power by the government, including the imposition of a two-year term of imprisonment on the editor of the RDC newspaper, who had been convicted of treason following the publication of an article which criticized the head of state. In December several opposition movements (including the ADP and MDD, but excluding the RDC) united to form the Conseil démocratique des partis politiques de l'opposition (CODEPO), which aimed to campaign against alleged corruption and political and economic mismanagement by the Patassé regime.

ARMY DISCONTENT

In the mid-1990s the government repeatedly failed to pay the salaries of public-sector employees and members of the security forces, prompting frequent strikes and mounting political unrest. In mid-April 1996 CODEPO staged an anti-government rally in Bangui. Shortly afterwards part of the national army mutinied in the capital and demanded the immediate settlement of all salary arrears. Patassé promised that part of the overdue salaries would be paid and that the mutineers would not be subject to prosecution. Faced with the presence of French troops (the Eléments français d'assistance opérationelle—EFAO) in Bangui, with a mandate to secure the safety of foreign nationals and (in accordance with a bilateral military accord) to protect the presidential palace and other key installations, the rebellion swiftly collapsed. About nine people, including civilians, were reported to have died in the uprising. In late April Patassé appointed a new chief of staff of the armed forces, Col Maurice Regonessa, and banned all public demonstrations. In mid-May, however, discontent again resurfaced and CODEPO organized another rally in Bangui, at which it demanded the resignation of the government. Patassé defended the record of his administration by blaming the country's economic crisis on his predecessors. Soon afterwards, in an attempt to tighten his hold on power, the president ordered that control of the national armoury should be transferred from the regular army to the traditionally loyal presidential guard. However, adverse reaction to this move within the ranks of the armed forces rapidly escalated into a second, more determined insurrection. Once again EFAO troops were deployed to protect the Patassé administration; some 500 reinforcements were brought in from Chad and Gabon to consolidate the resident French military presence (numbering 1,400). Five hostages were taken by the mutineers, including Col Regonessa, together with a cabinet minister and the president of the national assembly. After five days of fierce fighting between dissident and loyalist troops, the French forces intervened to suppress the rebellion. France's military action (which allegedly resulted in civilian deaths) prompted intense scrutiny of the role of the former colonial power, and precipitated large pro- and anti-French demonstrations in Bangui. In all, 11 soliders and 32 civilians were reported to have been killed in the second army mutiny. Following extended negotiations between the mutineers and government representatives, the two sides eventually signed an accord, providing for an amnesty for the rebels (who were to return to barracks under EFAO guard), the immediate release of hostages (upon Col Regonessa's release he was promoted to the rank of general), and the installation of a new government of national unity. The political opposition now became active in the debate, rejecting the proposed government of national unity and demanding instead a transitional government leading to fresh legislative and presidential elections. The opposition also requested a revision of the constitution to remove some executive powers from the president and enhance the role of the prime minister.

In early June 1996 a protocol was signed by the government and the opposition, which provided for the establishment of a government of national unity under the leadership of a civilian prime minister with no official party ties. Although the constitution was not to be amended to alter the balance of power between the president and the prime minister, Patassé agreed to permit 'some room for manoeuvre'. In addition, national defence and economic conferences were to be organized and the new government was to finalize a pending economic agreement with the IMF as a matter of priority. Meanwhile, France agreed to assist the CAR authorities with the payment of salary arrears still owed to public-sector employees and members of the security forces. Following the publication of the protocol, Koyambounou's government resigned. Jean-Paul Ngoupandé, hitherto ambassador to France and with no official political affiliation (although previously secretary-general of the RDC in the late 1980s), was appointed as the new prime minister; Ngoupandé immediately nominated a new cabinet. National co-operation, however, remained elusive. CODEPO, dissatisfied with the level of its representation in the council of ministers, immediately withdrew from the government of national unity. Moreover, it was reported that there was a growing animosity between Patassé and Ngoupandé, with the former refusing to transfer any effective power to the latter.

At a conference on national defence held in late August and early September 1996, several resolutions were adopted regarding restructuring and improving conditions within the army. In late October, however, it was reported that troops who had been involved in the insurrections of April and May were refusing to be transferred from their barracks in the capital to a more remote location; Patassé insisted that their departure would take place none the less. However, in mid-November a further mutiny erupted among these troops, shortly after the withdrawal from CODEPO of four opposition parties, including the ADP and the MDD. A substantial part of Bangui was occupied by the rebels, and a number of hostages were taken. The latest uprising appeared to have a strong tribal and political motivation: the mutineers, who were demanding the resignation of Patassé, belonged to the Yakoma ethnic group of Kolingba. Maj. Guy Kolingba, son of the former president, was reportedly arrested soon after the outbreak of the violence. EFAO troops were deployed once again, ostensibly to maintain order and protect foreign residents; however, by guarding key installations and government buildings they also effectively prevented the overthrow of the Patassé administration. More than 100 people were killed in the unrest during late November and early December, including a former (Yakoma) cabinet minister under Kolingba, who was abducted and murdered, allegedly by troops loyal to the government.

In December 1996 the presidents of Burkina Faso, Chad, Gabon and Mali negotiated a 15-day truce, which was supervised by the former transitional president of Mali, Brig.-Gen. Amadou Toumani Touré; a one-month extension to the cease-fire was subsequently agreed. In January 1997, following the killing of two French soldiers in Bangui (reportedly by mutineers), EFAO troops retaliated by killing at least 10 members of the rebel forces; French military involvement in the CAR was condemned by prominent opposition parties, including the ADP, the MDD and the RDC, which also sought (without success) to initiate a parliamentary vote to bring impeachment proceedings aganst Patassé. Subsequent to the renewal of violence, Touré again came to Bangui as mediator and assisted in the establishment of a cross-party Committee of Consultation and Dialogue. The 'Bangui accords', drawn up by this committee, were signed towards the end of January; these, as well as offering an amnesty to the mutineers, agreed upon the formation of a new government of national unity and on the replacement of the EFAO troops patrolling Bangui by peace-keeping forces from African nations. The opposition at first threatened to boycott the new government, voicing its discontent with the appointment at the end of January of Michel Gbezera-Bria (hitherto the minister of foreign affairs) as prime minister, who, as a close associate of Patassé, was considered unlikely to mitigate the exercise of presidential power. However, with the creation of new ministerial posts for opposition politicians, a 'Government of Action' (which did not include Ngoupandé) was formed on 18 February; soon afterwards, Bozize replaced Regonessa as chief of staff of the armed forces.

Meanwhile, on 12 February 1997 responsibility for peace-keeping operations had been transferred from EFAO to forces of the newly formed Mission interafricaine de surveillance des accords de Bangui (MISAB), comprising some 700 soldiers from Burkina Faso, Chad, Gabon, Mali, Senegal and Togo (with logistical support from 50 French military personnel). MISAB soldiers were also to assist in disarming the former mutineers; however, when in late March they attempted to do so, fighting broke out in which some 20 MISAB soldiers were killed. A spokesman for the rebels, Capt. Anicet Saulet, claimed that the lack of representation of the former mutineers in the new government constituted a breach of the 'Bangui accords'; following a meeting between Saulet and Patassé in early April, the council of ministers was expanded to include two military officers as representatives of the rebels. On 18 April several hundred of the former mutineers attended a ceremony marking their reintegration into the regular armed forces.

In mid-April 1997 a dusk-to-dawn curfew was imposed on Bangui, following serious escalations in violent crime, much of which was allegedly perpetrated by groups of former mutineers. In early May, following the deaths in police custody of three former rebels suspected of criminal activities, members of the G11 group of opposition parties, including the ADP, the FPP, the MDD and the RDC (shortly followed by the two representatives of the former mutineers), announced that they were suspending their participation in the government. Gbezera-Bria chose to interpret this as a total withdrawal from his administration, but he did not fill the nine (subsequently 11) ministerial posts which he deemed to have been vacated.

On 20 June 1997 there were further violent clashes between MISAB forces and former mutineers, after a MISAB soldier was killed, reportedly as he was trying to prevent a crime. On the following day a grenade landed in the French embassy compound and exploded, wounding several members of the diplomatic staff. Despite calls from Saulet for an immediate ceasefire, the violence continued, and several hundred EFAO troops were redeployed on the streets of Bangui. On 23 June, following further rebel attacks on the French embassy, MISAB forces launched a major offensive, capturing most of the rebel-controlled districts of the capital. This assault led to the arrest of more than 80 former mutineers, but also to some 100 deaths, both of soldiers and of civilians, whilst numerous homes and business premises were destroyed. On 25 June some 500 demonstrators gathered outside the French embassy compound in protest at alleged human rights abuses by MISAB troops; MISAB officials claimed that criminals were impersonating their soldiers in order to perpetrate atrocities. On the same day Touré arrived once again in Bangui in his capacity as chairman of MISAB, and negotiated a four-day truce, which took effect on 29 June, followed by a 10-day cease-fire agreement, signed on 2 July: all of the former mutineers were to be reintegrated into the regular armed forces, and their safety and that of the people living in the districts under their control was guaranteed; the rebels, for their part, were to relinquish the remainder of their heavy weaponry, much of which they had already handed over on 30 June.

EXTERNAL RELATIONS

The CAR's relations with France, the former colonial power, have remained important. France is still the principal source of foreign aid, and French advisers oversee the CAR's security services, while providing a buttress against Libyan adventurism. Indeed, the French military presence in the CAR is a vital element of France's strategy in the region, notably with regard to Chad. France's repeated military interventions during 1996 to protect the democratically-elected administration of President Patassé prompted intense debate within the CAR regarding the rightful boundaries of French influence over its former colonies.

In January 1989, shortly after the CAR had recognized the declaration, by the Palestine Liberation Organization, of an independent state of Palestine, it was announced that diplomatic relations were to be re-established with Israel. In May, however, diplomatic relations with Sudan were suspended, and the border with that country closed, when Sudan, in accordance with the boycott by the Arab states of all links with Israel, refused to allow the aircraft in which President Kolingba was travelling on an official visit to Israel to cross its airspace. Kolingba's visit was postponed until July, when he travelled to Israel via Zaire and Europe. Diplomatic relations between the CAR and Sudan were resumed in September. In 1991 the government appealed to the international donor community for relief aid for an estimated 20,000 refugees from Sudan. In early 1994, the government denied rumours that it was aiding the Sudanese army in its operations against the Sudan People's Liberation Army (SPLA) by allowing weapons to cross its territory.

In July 1991 the CAR established diplomatic relations with Taiwan, and those with the People's Republic of China were suspended. Diplomatic relations with South Africa were restored by Kolingba prior to his departure from office in October 1993. In December 1993 a CAR government delegation held discussions with President Mobutu of Zaire on cross-border issues. In February 1994 the Patassé administration sponsored peace negotiations in Bangui between the government of Chad and rebel factions. At the end of 1994 the CAR and Chad agreed to establish a bilateral security structure to ensure mutual border security. Attacks on Chadian nationals resident in Bangui and on the Chadian contingent of the MISAB forces in late 1996 and early 1997 (carried out apparently by members of the security forces and of the general public, as well as by mutineers), led the Chadian government to issue a *communiqué* in March 1997 warning that further incidences of such aggression would not be tolerated. In May 1997 it was reported that considerable numbers of Rwandan Hutus (many of whom had previously served in that country's army when it was implicated in acts of genocide) were seeking asylum in the CAR; later in that month the CAR recognized the administration of Laurent Kabila in the Democratic Republic of the Congo (formerly Zaire). However heavily armed soldiers of what had been the Zairean army were reportedly fleeing troops loyal to Kabila and crossing the Oubangui river into the CAR.

In March 1994 the CAR was admitted as the fifth member of the Lake Chad Basin Commission, in acknowledgement that the country is the main watershed for two major rivers flowing north to Lake Chad.

Economy

DIANA HUBBARD

Revised for this edition by ANDREW MANLEY

From independence in 1960 until 1965, under the first government of President Dacko, the economy of the Central African Republic (CAR) stagnated and, in particular, showed a severe decline in the output of cotton. In 1966 the new military government, under Jean-Bédel Bokassa, introduced measures to revive agricultural production and to encourage rural development. These measures had some considerable success up to 1970; however, during the early 1970s economic stagnation and recession recurred, and these problems (which continue to beset the CAR) became increasingly severe during the three years of the 'Central African Empire' (1976–79). The country's economic plight was a prime factor in the military take-over in September 1981. Faced with declining output and worsening budgetary and balance-of-payments deficits, the new government of Gen. Kolingba concluded an agreement with the International Monetary Fund (IMF) for a stand-by loan, which had already been partly negotiated by the second Dacko regime. Severe cuts in public expenditure formed part of an austerity plan implemented in early 1982. This, in turn, led to political strains which prompted a coup attempt in March 1982. Fear of further unrest led the Kolingba government in late 1983 to break budgetary promises that had been made to the IMF. The stand-by facility and the allied rescheduling of the foreign debt were consequently suspended, and by the end of 1983 the country's financial position was precarious. The government yielded to the economic circumstances and revised its budget and investment targets to comply with IMF requirements. Stand-by credits were resumed, allowing for debt rescheduling. In mid-1987 the CAR introduced a three-year structural adjustment programme, which aimed to liberalize the economy, to foster private enterprise and to improve public finances, primarily through policies of retrenchment in the civil service and the liquidation or privatization of parastatal organizations. Considerable progress was made, and in May 1990 a new structural adjustment facility was agreed with the IMF, to cover the period mid-1991–mid-1992. During the early 1990s, however, a decline in international prices for coffee and cotton and a sharp increase in illicit cross-border diamond trading resulted in depressed foreign currency earnings and tax and customs revenue; a severe disruption in economic growth ensued, accompanied by a sharp deterioration in public finances. During the mid-1990s, despite some improvement in economic conditions, the Patassé administration became unable to meet its salary obligations to public-sector employees and to members of the armed forces, resulting in serious political instability. In mid-1996, however, France agreed to assist with the payment of salary arrears; discussions with the IMF on the introduction of an economic rehabilitation and development programme were suspended, following renewed violence late in 1996.

Since the mid-1980s growth in real gross domestic product (GDP) has been erratic, generally reflecting the effect of climatic factors and fluctuations in world market prices on, respectively, the supply of and receipts from the CAR's major exports, as well as the increase in diamond smuggling (see above). An exceptional rate of growth in GDP in 1986, amounting to 5.2% in real terms, was reversed in 1987 with a decline of 2.5%. Three years of steady real growth followed in 1988–90. However, real GDP increased by only 0.1% in 1991 and registered a decline of 2.6% in both 1992 and 1993. In 1994 real GDP growth of 7.4% was recorded, consolidated by an increase of 4.8% in 1995, reflecting an improvement in international prices for the CAR's agricultural exports. In 1995, according to estimates by the World Bank, the CAR's gross national product, measured at average 1993–95 prices, was US $1,123m., equivalent to $340 per head.

AGRICULTURE

In 1995 agriculture, hunting, forestry and fishing, contributed an estimated 53.4% of GDP, while about 80.2% of the working population were engaged in the sector in that year. Agriculture is concentrated in the tropical rain-forest area of the south-west and the savannah lands in the central region and north-west. The food crops (mainly cassava, maize, millet, sorghum, groundnuts and rice) are grown principally for domestic consumption. The rise in agricultural production has failed to keep pace with population growth, partly owing to drought. In recent years, food has accounted for around one-tenth of import spending, with a deficit in domestic production of one-fifth of total consumption. As a result, the government has placed a greater emphasis on food production in its regional development programmes, and the cultivation of rice is being encouraged. Meanwhile, agricultural diversification is being promoted, mainly to substitute imports. A US $20m. palm oil complex is in operation at Bossongo, with an oil mill with an annual capacity of 7,500 tons, servicing 2,500 ha of plantations. In 1988 production began at a sugar refinery, supplied from 1,300 ha of new plantations (see below). The government has also encouraged the cultivation of vegetables for export to the European market: peppers and green beans are being increasingly cultivated in an area within easy reach of the country's international airport at Bangui.

Coffee is the CAR's major export crop (contributing an estimated 19.0% of export earnings in 1995). It was formerly produced on large, European-owned plantations, but, since the late 1970s, small-holder production has become increasingly important and now accounts for more than 75% of total output. The crop is cultivated mainly in the south-western and central-southern regions of the country, and more than 90% is of the *robusta* variety. The level of production varies widely and is influenced by drought and trends in international prices for coffee. The Agence de développement de la zone caféière (ADECAF) is the parastatal organization responsible for the purchase, transportation and marketing of this commodity. Yields were raised to 935 kg per ha in 1994, which is relatively high by world standards. Output stood at 9,100 tons in the year ending 30 September 1994, rising to 14,500 tons in 1994/95 before declining to 5,600 tons in 1995/96.

Cotton, the most widely-grown cash crop after coffee, is cultivated by an estimated 280,000 small-holder farmers. Yields—generally below 500 kg per ha—are among the lowest in Africa. The sharp fall in world cotton prices in 1986 led the government to respond to World Bank prompting and to cut back subsidies to cotton farmers and close down three of the CAR's seven cotton ginning complexes, while concentrating planting on the most productive areas. Nevertheless, the importance of cotton cultivation as a source of employment and to the economy of the northern area prompted the government, in 1988, to halt the reduction of the area under cultivation, and to maintain the level of producer prices. However, owing to reduced demand much raw cotton remained unsold in subsequent years, and producers responded by planting significantly less. Output totalled 7,000 tons in 1993, before rising to an estimated 12,000 tons in 1994 and to 13,000 tons in 1995. The longer-term outlook for the CAR's cotton crop is favourable, particularly as it is less vulnerable to drought than some other crops.

Since 1950 efforts have been made to develop the livestock industry, and the number of cattle has increased substantially, despite the problems provided by droughts, the limitations of available fodder and the prevalence of the tsetse fly. The herd has also grown as a result of migration from Chad and Sudan. In 1994 there were an estimated 2.8m. head of cattle and 1.3m. goats. Nevertheless, domestic meat production fails to satisfy demand, and around 100,000 head of cattle are imported annually, mainly from Chad and Sudan. Efforts are being made to improve marketing, and to encourage the sedentary raising of cattle to allow for treatment against disease. Abattoirs and factories to utilize the products of the animal industries are also being promoted.

The CAR's large forest resources (an estimated 35m. ha of tropical rain-forest in the south-west of the country) are at present under-exploited commercially, largely as a result of a lack of adequate roads and low-cost means of transportation to the coast. Only about 10% of the forest area is accessible to river transport. In addition, large areas are held as private hunting reserves. Nevertheless, timber exploitation expanded considerably from the late 1960s, following the formation of new companies geared to export and the establishment of new sawmills. Fellings of industrial roundwood reached a peak of 846,000 cu m in 1974, but fell back sharply in subsequent years, owing partly to low water levels on the traditional transport route along the Congo river. Moreover, the rise in the value of the CFA franc in relation to the currencies of the major Asian producers reduced the price competitiveness of the CAR product. Log production, which averaged some 330,000 cu m annually in 1980–85, declined to 152,000 cu m in 1988. Output has subsequently been erratic, registering 217,000 cu m and 168,000 cu m in 1992 and 1993 respectively, and 231,000 cu m in 1994. The overall decline appears to reflect a decrease in the area under forest, owing to the absence of a timber conservation programme during the 1980s and in response to the demands of agriculture and pasture. In 1995 exports of wood and wood products accounted for an estimated 15.8% of the total value of exports. In 1990 the IDA announced a loan of US $19m. to support a new forestry policy, which included the preparation of an inventory of forests and tree types and a substantial forest management programme. In addition, a national park was to be established to protect part of the rain-forest. Logging controls imposed in 1994 obliged companies to part-process at least 85% of logs before export. Following devaluation, this rule was relaxed slightly in 1996.

MINING

Mining contributed only an estimated 6.2% of the CAR's GDP in 1995, although this may underestimate the sector's true importance. Diamonds are the main mineral deposit, and are found in alluvial deposits, mainly in the south-west and west of the country. Until 1960 production was wholly in the hands of expatriate companies but by 1970 individual African prospectors had taken over the whole of production. The decline in recorded output since the late 1960s, from a peak of 609,000 carats in 1968 to an average of 480,000 carats per year in 1992–95, is partly attributable to smuggling to the Congo, a concomitant of which has been a decline in the quality of officially traded stones, in addition to substantial reductions in government revenue. Smuggled, unofficial output is thought to be double the official total. In the mid-1980s the government attempted to discourage smuggling by increasing customs surveillance and by reducing the relatively high export tax. Subsequently there was some improvement in recorded diamond exports. However, a sharp increase in smuggling was reported in the early 1990s. Recorded production was 494,900 carats in 1993 and 532,000 carats in 1994 (of which 436,000 carats were of gem quality and 96,000 carats were industrial diamonds). Recorded output in 1995 amounted to 484,300 carats (practically all of which was exported, at an estimated value of 37,600m. francs CFA). The government aims to encourage the development of local cutting and polishing industries; by the mid-1990s, however, there was still only one diamond cutting centre, and exports of diamonds remained almost entirely in uncut form.

Gold is also mined, although production levels have fluctuated sharply, from a peak of 538 kg in 1980 to 97.9 kg in 1995. The government plans to establish a gold-processing plant. Uranium has been discovered near Bakouma, 480 km east of Bangui. Reserves are estimated at 20,000 tons, with a concentration ratio of some 50%. The weakening in international prices for uranium has obstructed development of the deposits, which would also necessitate the construction of a road from Bakouma to the border with Cameroon.

It was reported in early 1995 that the government was reviewing mining investment codes and compiling a comprehensive geological database in order to attract interest from international mining companies. Plans to seek assistance from the European Union (EU—see p. 118) in developing and regularizing the sector were set back by the violent upheavals of 1996–97.

MANUFACTURING AND POWER

The industrial sector is little developed, and contributed only an estimated 14.3% of GDP in 1995. Manufacturing, which contributed 8.8% of GDP in 1995, is based upon the processing of primary products. The destruction wrought by successive mutinies in Bangui in 1996–97 severely damaged the sector. The country's second largest employer, the Société Centrafricaine de Cigarettes, reportedly ceased production in 1996, following the destruction of its premises, whilst the Motte-Cordonnier-Afrique brewery, the CAR's largest industrial concern, suffered losses amounting to almost 4,000m. francs CFA. Companies escaping material damage were none the less severely affected by a dramatic decrease in consumer spending. In 1990 the major activities, measured by gross value of output, were the processing of foods, beverages and tobacco, and the processing of wood and cotton to make furniture, fixtures, paper and textiles. A vehicle-assembly plant opened in 1981, but output levels were very low and operations were virtually suspended in 1986.

Following independence, the textile and leather industries constituted the chief industrial sector. By the mid-1970s, however, the sector was in decline. A textile complex, undertaking spinning, weaving and dyeing, which formed the CAR's largest single industrial enterprise, was acquired by the state when it was on the point of liquidation in 1976. Following its closure in 1980, the European Investment Bank and the French government agreed in 1983 to provide loans of 4,600m. francs CFA to rehabilitate the project, at a capacity of 4.4m. metres of cloth per year. However, the complex has never functioned satisfactorily. Cotton ginning takes place at four factories (compared with 21 in 1970). An oil mill has been built at the Bossongo oil palm plantation (see above), with funding from the African Development Bank, France and the African Development Fund. A sugar-processing plant was opened at Ouaka in 1987 and is the first in the CAR, with cane supplied from 1,100 ha of new plantations.

The CAR is heavily dependent on imported petroleum as an energy source (70% of commercial supply). The remainder is provided by local hydroelectricity: the two Boali stations at the M'Bali falls supply about 80% of total electricity output, with about 10 smaller thermal stations accounting for the remainder. Plans are under way to construct a new hydroelectric plant at Kembe. In 1995 total output of electric energy was 102m. kWh, of which hydroelectricity accounted for the largest proportion. Plans to privatize the state power utility (ENERCA) and the petroleum distribution monopoly (PETROCA) were delayed by the violence of 1996–97.

TRANSPORT

The transport infrastructure is badly underdeveloped and a major constraint on the country's economic development. There is an extensive network of roads (23,810 km in 1995), but only about 1.8% of the system is paved. The road network suffered serious deterioration over the 1977–81 period, owing to lack of maintenance. In recent years, however, international development organizations and bilateral donors have extended funds for road rehabilitation projects. The CAR section of the Trans-african highway from Lagos to Mombasa was completed in 1984, providing a link with Cameroon. There is no railway, but there are long-standing plans to extend the Transcameroon line to Bangui and also to link the CAR with the rail systems in Sudan and Gabon. For the foreseeable future any development in the land transport network will be in the form of roads rather than rail. A much larger volume of freight is carried by river; of a total of 7,000 km of inland waterways, some 2,800 km are navigable, most importantly the Oubangui river south of Bangui, which is the country's main outlet for external trade, and the Sangha and Lobaye rivers. Port facilities are being improved, with French and EU assistance.

The principal route for the import and export trade is the trans-equatorial route which involves 1,800 km by river from Bangui to Brazzaville, in the Congo and then rail from Brazzaville to Pointe-Noire. This route also handles traffic for Chad. It was formerly operated by a public corporation, jointly owned by the countries of the Union douanière et économique de l'Afrique centrale (UDEAC), but this was dissolved, and the CAR subsequently operated its own river transport authority. In 1980 river transport operations were transferred to private-sector control. During the 1980s river traffic declined, as importers and exporters increasingly used the new land route through Cameroon.

There is an international airport at Bangui–M'Poko, and there are 37 small airports. Internal services are, however, irregular and dependent on the availability of fuel.

A five-year programme for the modernization of the existing transport infrastructure, at a total projected cost of US $139m. (to be financed by bilateral and multilateral donors), was announced in 1990.

PUBLIC FINANCE

The CAR's fiscal position is weak, with a narrow tax base which is vulnerable to adverse trends in international prices for coffee and cotton and prone to erosion as a result of smuggling, while bearing the burden of losses incurred by the parastatal organizations and of personnel expenditure for the cumbersome civil service. Consequently, substantial deficits have been incurred. France provided budgetary aid to the new Dacko government in December 1979, but the budget deficit continued to increase (reaching 8,200m. francs CFA in 1982). As part of its agreement with the IMF for payments support, the government implemented measures in 1982 to reduce the numbers of the 27,000-strong civil service and to cut the salaries of those remaining by 28%. Despite the partial success of this policy, a deficit of 7,500m. francs CFA was recorded in 1983, and France extended direct budgetary aid. In 1984 the government was obliged by the country's difficult payments situation to agree to another stabilization programme guided by the IMF. This provided for an increase in tax revenues and a restructuring of the parastatal organizations to lessen the drain on budget resources. The deficit was subsequently almost eliminated in 1985, but rose again in 1989, as revenue stagnated while expenditure continued to rise, despite the partial success of a civil service redundancy programme. The deficit had fallen to 49,700m. francs CFA by 1993, but in 1994 rose sharply to 70,800m. francs CFA. A reduction in the deficit to an estimated 64,100m. francs CFA in 1995 was only achieved through the non-payment of salary arrears. However, the resulting unrest significantly damaged the revenue base, thus in 1997 one of Jean-Paul Ngoupandé's priorities as prime minister was to negotiate a new agreement on economic reform with the IMF. His removal from the council of ministers, followed by the outbreak of further fighting, dispelled hopes of any such assistance in the short term.

TRADE, AID AND THE BALANCE OF PAYMENTS

The CAR's foreign trade accounts show a persistent deficit. While imports have tended to increase, export receipts have fluctuated widely, in response to trends in international prices for diamonds, coffee, timber and cotton. Diamonds remain the principal source of export earnings, accounting for about 44% of total export revenue in 1995 followed by coffee, wood and wood products and cotton.

With a large net outflow on services, partly offset by transfer payments (i.e. official grants), the CAR has shown a substantial deficit on the current account of the balance of payments in recent years, totalling US $83.1m. in 1992, $13.0m. in 1993 and $24.7m. in 1994.

Since independence, France has continued to be the major source of aid. Substantial funding has also been provided by the EDF through support for export earnings (under the Stabex provisions of the Lomé Conventions), aid to improve productivity and diversify the economy, and technical assistance. Net annual official development assistance averaged just over $170m. in 1991–95, with France remaining the dominant bilateral lender, accounting for two-thirds of net bilateral flows. Japan has built up a solid aid presence, with net aid of $50m. Multilateral lending has been dominated by the IDA and the EU's European Development Fund. Grants accounted for 83% of assistance, on average, in 1991–95, but this level of funding has not been sufficient to resolve the country's balance-of-payments difficulties, and the CAR has repeatedly sought stand-by credits from the IMF. In 1994 the IMF approved a stand-by credit of $23m. to support economic reform policies, but conditionalities were repeatedly breached and the arrangement was not renewed. Attempts to secure a more advantageous ESAF agreement, met with little success, as the fiscal and political situation deteriorated. The total external debt increased rapidly throughout the 1980s, rising from $185m. in 1980 to $943.9m. at the end of 1995, in which year the cost of debt-servicing was equivalent to 6.8% of the value of exports of goods and services (compared with 13.0% in 1994—this apparent reduction resulting, however, from the non-payment of scheduled arrears). In 1995 90% of the total external debt was owed to official creditors; concessionary terms with long maturity periods had been arranged for 80% of the total external debt. Beginning in 1989 the CAR was to benefit from debt relief under the terms of the June 1988 'Toronto Agreement', and the country's public debt to France was cancelled with effect from January 1990. A further rescheduling, covering only $30m. in debt, was agreed in 1994.

ECONOMIC REFORM

The first Development Plan, covering the four-year period 1967–70, placed particular emphasis upon rural development and education. The second Development Plan covered the five-year period 1971–75. The development of productive capacity absorbed rather more than 50% of planned expenditure, economic infrastructure about 25% and social infrastructure about 15%. The CAR's third Development Plan, for 1976–80, was abandoned in 1978, with only one-sixth of the total investments realized. In early 1980 the CAR adopted, with IMF approval, an austerity plan aimed at limiting the payments deficit and budgetary disequilibrium by concentrating resources on promoting agricultural production, and by monitoring public transfers more carefully. This short-term (1980–81) Rehabilitation Plan was to cover investments of 45,000m. francs CFA but, partly due to political uncertainties, barely 25% were realized.

A Recovery Plan for 1983–86, prepared within the framework of the IMF proposals for economic stabilization, envisaged total expenditure of 169,000m. francs CFA. A Development Plan, involving expenditure of 280,000m. francs CFA, was prepared for the period 1986–90, but later was formally superseded by the objectives of the 1987–89 structural adjustment programme. In May 1990 a new structural adjustment facility was agreed with the IMF. However, growing political instability during 1990 and 1991 hindered the Kolingba government's progress in pursuing economic adjustment targets. The new administration of President Patassé, which came to power during 1993, was confronted by an urgent need to rehabilitate government finances and to eliminate the primary budget deficit. The Patassé regime was, however, initially unable to meet preconditions imposed by the IMF as a requirement for the disbursement of assistance. The implementation of a three-year Economic Policy Document (1996–98), designed to stabilize public finances by reforming the taxation system, controlling state expenditure and gradually reducing arrears on the national debt, to restructure public enterprises and the unwieldy civil service, and to implement measures to stimulate private-sector activity (including a revision of the regulatory framework for investment) was cast into doubt by the unrest of 1996–97: the IMF postponed discussions concerning an ESAF agreement, whilst much of Bangui's tax base was destroyed. There were, none the less, intermittent signs of meaningful reform, especially with the planned privatization of PETROCA.

In January 1994 the CAR and the other member countries of the CFA franc zone adopted a comprehensive macroeconomic strategy which included devaluation of the CFA franc against the French franc by 50%. Consumer prices in the CAR declined at an average rate of 2.5% per year during 1985–93, but increased by an average of 19.2% in 1995.

PROBLEMS AND PROSPECTS

In addition to its vulnerability to adverse climatic conditions and to unfavourable movements in world prices for its agricultural exports, the inadequacy of the CAR's transport facilities has been a severe handicap to sustained economic growth. The development of these facilities would benefit economic development in all sectors, particularly forestry. In the second part of the 1960s the country made determined efforts to address its economic problems, but during the 1970s, the economy lost its momentum, an outcome for which domestic policies and their administration must bear a large responsibility, although adverse climatic factors also played a part. Agricultural production declined, and marketing difficulties were experienced with domestic food crops. The diamond industry's lack of probity added to the government's own financial problems. Industry and commerce stagnated, an outcome to which the payments difficulties of the treasury contributed both directly and indirectly. To these various problems were added the damaging effects of high energy prices and the world economic recessions of the early 1980s and early 1990s. If significant economic recovery is to be achieved following the unrest of 1996–97, there will be a need for both continued foreign technical and financial assistance at high levels and for fundamental domestic economic, financial and administrative reforms.

Statistical Survey

Source (unless otherwise stated): Division des Statistiques et des Etudes Economiques, Ministère de l'Economie, des Finances et du Plan, Bangui.

Area and Population

AREA, POPULATION AND DENSITY

Area (sq km)	622,984*
Population (census results)	
8 December 1975	2,054,610
8 December 1988	
Males	1,210,735
Females	1,252,881
Total	2,463,616
Density (per sq km) at 8 December 1988	4.0

* 240,535 sq miles.

PRINCIPAL TOWNS (population, 1988 census)

Bangui (capital)	451,690	Bambari	38,633
Berbérati	41,891	Bossangoa	31,502
Bouar	39,676	Carnot	31,324

BIRTHS AND DEATHS (UN estimates, annual averages)

	1980–85	1985–90	1990–95
Birth rate (per 1,000)	41.5	41.4	41.5
Death rate (per 1,000)	18.6	17.4	16.7

Expectation of life (UN estimates, years at birth, 1990–95): 49.4 (males 46.9; females 51.9).

Source: UN, *World Population Prospects: The 1994 Revision*.

ECONOMICALLY ACTIVE POPULATION
(persons aged 6 years and over, 1988 census)

	Males	Females	Total
Agriculture, hunting, forestry and fishing	417,630	463,007	880,637
Mining and quarrying	11,823	586	12,409
Manufacturing	16,096	1,250	17,346
Electricity, gas and water	751	58	809
Construction	5,583	49	5,632
Trade, restaurants and hotels	37,435	54,563	91,998
Transport, storage and communications	6,601	150	6,751
Financing, insurance, real estate and business services	505	147	652
Community, social and personal services	61,764	8,537	70,301
Activities not adequately defined	7,042	4,627	11,669
Total employed	565,230	532,974	1,098,204
Unemployed	66,624	22,144	88,768
Total labour force	631,854	555,118	1,186,972

Source: International Labour Office, *Yearbook of Labour Statistics*.

Mid-1995 (estimates in '000): Agriculture, etc. 1,154; Total 1,439 (Source: FAO, *Production Yearbook*).

Agriculture

PRINCIPAL CROPS ('000 metric tons)

	1993	1994	1995
Rice (paddy)	8	8	9
Maize	58	63	71
Millet*	8	9	10
Sorghum*	20	21	23
Cassava (Manioc)	575	518	402
Yams†	250	250	250
Taro (Coco yam)†	60	65	65
Groundnuts (in shell)	72	84	86
Sesame seed	25	27	29
Cottonseed	9	16*	19*
Palm kernels†	4.9	5.0	5.0
Palm oil	6.6	6.7	6.7
Pumpkins, squash and gourds	13	15*	16
Other vegetables (incl. melons)	50	50	50
Oranges†	17	18	20
Mangoes†	9	9	9
Bananas†	96	98	100
Plantains†	74	76	78
Coffee (green)	9	15	9
Cotton (lint)	7	12*	13*

* Unofficial figure(s). † FAO estimate(s).

Source: FAO, *Production Yearbook*.

LIVESTOCK ('000 head, year ending September)

	1993	1994	1995
Cattle	2,674	2,735	2,797
Goats	1,340	1,340*	1,350*
Sheep	156	164	172
Pigs	502	524	547

* FAO estimate.

Poultry (million): 3 in 1993; 3 in 1994; 3 in 1995.

Source: FAO, *Production Yearbook*.

LIVESTOCK PRODUCTS ('000 metric tons)

	1993	1994*	1995*
Beef and veal*	45	45	45
Mutton and lamb*	1	1	1
Goat meat*	5	5	6
Pig meat*	8	9	9
Poultry meat*	3	3	3
Other meat*	7	7	7
Cows' milk	49	50	50
Cattle hides (fresh)*	7.0	7.2	7.3
Hen eggs*	1.4	1.4	1.4
Honey	9.7	10.0	10.5

* FAO estimates.

Source: FAO, *Production Yearbook*.

Forestry

ROUNDWOOD REMOVALS ('000 cubic metres, excluding bark)

	1992	1993	1994
Sawlogs, veneer logs and logs for sleepers	217	168	231
Other industrial wood*	267	274	281
Fuel wood*	3,250	3,250	3,250*
Total	3,734	3,692	3,762

* FAO estimate(s).

Source: FAO, *Yearbook of Forest Products.*

SAWNWOOD PRODUCTION ('000 cubic metres)

	1992	1993	1994
Total	68	60*	73

* FAO estimate.

Source: FAO, *Yearbook of Forest Products.*

Fishing

('000 metric tons, live weight)

	1992	1993*	1994*
Total catch (freshwater fish)	13.3	13.5	13.0

* FAO estimates.

Source: FAO, *Yearbook of Fishery Statistics.*

Mining

	1992	1993	1994
Gold (kg, metal content of ore)	154.7	170.6	138.2
Gem diamonds ('000 carats)	328.9	390.1	436.0
Industrial diamonds ('000 carats)	85.4	104.8	96.0

1995: Gold (kg) 97.9; Diamonds ('000 carats, uncut) 484.3 (Source: IMF, *Central African Republic—Recent Economic Developments,* April 1997).

Industry

SELECTED PRODUCTS

	1993	1994	1995*
Beer ('000 hectolitres)	123.8	249.6	268.9
Soft drinks and syrups ('000 hectolitres)	20.9	39.4	58.8
Cigarettes (million packets)	11.5	20.7	29.7
Sugar ('000 metric tons)	10.8	15.1	n.a.
Palm oil ('000 metric tons)	2.8	3.6	3.3
Motor cycles (number)	413	914	412
Bicycles (number)	388	477	647
Electric energy (million kWh)†	93.7	96.9	101.6

* Estimates. † Net production.

Source: IMF, *Central African Republic—Recent Economic Developments* (April 1997).

Finance

CURRENCY AND EXCHANGE RATES

Monetary Units

100 centimes = 1 franc de la Coopération financière en Afrique centrale (CFA).

French Franc, Sterling and Dollar Equivalents (31 March 1997)

1 French franc = 100 francs CFA;
£1 sterling = 924.2 francs CFA;
US $1 = 562.85 francs CFA;
1,000 francs CFA = £1.082 = $1.777.

Average Exchange Rate (francs CFA per US $)

1994 555.20
1995 499.15
1996 511.55

Note: The exchange rate of 1 French franc = 50 francs CFA, established in 1948, remained in force until January 1994, when the CFA franc was devalued by 50%, with the exchange rate adjusted to 1 French franc = 100 francs CFA.

BUDGET (Central Government, million francs CFA)

Revenue	1993	1994	1995*
Tax revenue	26,500	32,100	49,300
Income and profits	6,500	8,600	10,600
Domestic goods and services	10,600	12,000	16,800
International trade	9,400	11,500	21,900
Other receipts	1,900	3,200	2,200
Total	28,400	35,400	51,500

Expenditure	1993	1994	1995*
Current expenditure	46,000	57,400	57,700
Wages and salaries	23,000	25,700	26,000
Goods and services	9,000	12,800	11,500
Interest payments	7,700	11,500	13,100
Capital expenditure	32,000	48,800	57,900
Total	78,100	106,200	115,600

* Estimates.

Source: IMF, *CAR—Recent Economic Developments* (April 1997).

INTERNATIONAL RESERVES (US $ million at 31 December)

	1993	1994	1995
Gold*	4.42	4.21	4.29
IMF special drawing rights	0.04	0.01	0.02
Reserve position in IMF	0.13	0.14	0.14
Foreign exchange	111.81	209.86	233.48
Total	116.40	214.22	237.93

* National valuation.

Source: IMF, *International Financial Statistics.*

MONEY SUPPLY ('000 million francs CFA at 31 December)

	1993	1994	1995
Currency outside banks	52.16	88.53	98.97
Demand deposits at commercial and development banks	7.26	14.86	12.27
Total money	59.42	103.40	111.24

Source: IMF, *International Financial Statistics.*

COST OF LIVING

(Consumer Price Index for Bangui; base: 1981 = 100)

	1993	1994	1995
Food	117.5	146.3	179.9
Fuel and light	136.0	147.6	151.5
Clothing	153.7	217.2	238.7
All items (incl. others)*	126.3	157.3	187.5

* Excluding rent.

Source: IMF, *CAR—Recent Economic Developments* (April 1997).

NATIONAL ACCOUNTS
(IMF estimates, million francs CFA at current prices)

Gross Domestic Product by Economic Activity

	1993	1994	1995
Agriculture, hunting, forestry and fishing	166,400	237,800	282,900
Mining and quarrying	17,400	36,500	32,700
Manufacturing	36,000	43,800	46,600
Electricity, gas and water	3,100	3,800	4,300
Construction	14,900	21,700	25,000
Trade, restaurants and hotels; Transport, storage and communications	75,500	85,900	97,300
Government services	23,300	45,700	41,000
Sub-total (incl. others)	336,600	475,100	529,800
Import duties	20,000	23,500	38,700
GDP in purchasers' values	356,600	498,600	568,500

Source: IMF, *CAR—Recent Economic Developments* (April 1997).

Expenditure on the Gross Domestic Product

	1993	1994	1995
Government final consumption expenditure	42,300	72,600	66,900
Private final consumption expenditure	302,900	380,800	462,100
Increase in stocks	1,800	4,000	5,300
Gross fixed capital formation	39,900	61,900	76,300
Total domestic expenditure	386,900	519,300	610,600
Exports of goods and services	51,400	112,100	116,800
Less Imports of goods and services	81,800	132,800	159,000
GDP in purchasers' values	356,600	498,600	568,500
GDP at constant 1985 prices	368,900	397,300	406,900

Source: IMF, *CAR—Recent Economic Developments* (April 1997).

BALANCE OF PAYMENTS (US $ million)

	1992	1993	1994
Exports of goods	115.9	132.5	145.9
Imports of goods	-189.0	-158.1	-130.6
Trade balance	-73.2	-25.7	15.3
Exports of services	45.1	49.3	33.1
Imports of services	-152.7	-131.9	-113.8
Balance on goods and services	-180.7	-108.3	-65.4
Other income received	6.4	4.5	—
Other income paid	-22.2	-23.2	-22.7
Balance on goods, services and income	-196.5	-127.1	-88.1
Current transfers received	-151.0	152.4	92.6
Current transfers paid	-37.6	-38.3	-29.2
Current balance	-83.1	-13.0	-24.7
Direct investment abroad	-5.9	-5.3	-7.2
Other investment assets	-33.2	-18.2	8.1
Investment liabilities	68.4	34.8	48.3
Net errors and omissions	26.2	6.3	-15.0
Overall balance	-38.2	-5.3	13.1

Source: IMF, *International Financial Statistics.*

External Trade

PRINCIPAL COMMODITIES (distribution by SITC, US $'000)

Imports c.i.f.	1989
Food and live animals	22,768
Cereals and cereal preparations	8,192
Wheat flour	4,320
Sugar, sugar preparations and honey	6,232
Sugar and honey	5,959
Refined sugars	5,945
Beverages and tobacco	5,706
Tobacco and tobacco manufactures	3,715
Mineral fuels, lubricants, etc	10,658
Petroleum and petroleum products	10,390
Refined petroleum products	10,273
Gas oils (distillate fuels)	3,358
Chemicals and related products	22,239
Medicinal and pharmaceutical products	10,333
Medicaments	6,705
Essential oils, perfume materials and cleansing preparations	3,009
Pesticides, disinfectants, etc.	3,104
Basic manufactures	28,364
Paper, paperboard and manufactures	3,325
Textile yarn, fabrics, etc.	5,737
Non-metallic mineral manufactures	6,780
Lime, cement, etc.	5,288
Cement	5,244
Machinery and transport equipment	52,876
Machinery specialized for particular industries	7,605
Civil engineering and contractors' plant and equipment	3,094
General industrial machinery, equipment and parts	7,712
Electrical machinery, apparatus, etc.	8,061
Road vehicles and parts (excl. tyres, engines and electrical parts)	23,638
Passenger motor cars (excl. buses)	5,510
Motor vehicles for goods transport and special purposes	7,395
Goods vehicles (lorries and trucks)	4,969
Parts and accessories for motor vehicles	6,625
Miscellaneous manufactured articles	11,722
Total (incl. others)	159,124

Source: UN, *International Trade Statistics Yearbook.*

Total imports (c.i.f., million francs CFA): 42,050 in 1990; 50,400 in 1991; 43,211 in 1992; 35,559 in 1993; 73,263 in 1994; 94,203 in 1995 (Sources: IMF, *International Financial Statistics*; Ministry of the Economy, Finance and Planning).

Exports f.o.b.	1989
Food and live animals	40,341
Coffee, tea, cocoa and spices	40,204
Coffee (green and roasted)	40,204
Crude materials (inedible) except fuels	34,999
Cork and wood	18,204
Sawlogs and veneer logs	12,712
Sawn lumber	5,102
Textile fibres and waste	12,608
Cotton	12,608
Basic manufactures	59,232
Non-metallic mineral manufactures	58,972
Diamonds (non-industrial)	58,970
Total (incl. others)	140,287

Source: UN, *International Trade Statistics Yearbook.*

Total exports (million francs CFA): 32,770 in 1990; 35,440 in 1991; 28,328 in 1992; 31,073 in 1993; 79,541 in 1994; 93,524 in 1995 (Sources: IMF, *International Financial Statistics*; Ministry of the Economy, Finance and Planning).

PRINCIPAL TRADING PARTNERS (US $'000)

Imports c.i.f.	1989
Belgium/Luxembourg	4,032
Cameroon	14,514
Chad	1,701
China	4,211
Congo	5,111
France	67,631
Gabon	2,469
Italy	2,681
Japan	12,043
Netherlands	3,338
United Kingdom	1,988
USA	2,037
Zaire	5,715
Total (incl. others)	159,124

Exports f.o.b.*	1989
Belgium/Luxembourg	71,353
France	48,242
Spain	2,482
Sudan	3,320
Switzerland	6,967
Total (incl. others)	137,903

* Excluding exports of gold (US $'000): 2,384 in 1989.

Source: UN, *International Trade Statistics Yearbook.*

Transport

ROAD TRAFFIC (motor vehicles in use)

	1993	1994	1995*
Passenger cars	1,042	1,172	1,200
Buses and coaches	52	66	4
Lorries and vans	387	202	185
Road tractors	11	15	7
Motorcycles and mopeds	1,643	1,254	990

* Estimates.

Source: IRF, *World Road Statistics.*

INLAND WATERWAYS TRAFFIC—INTERNATIONAL SHIPPING (metric tons)

	1986	1987	1988
Freight unloaded at Bangui	152,000	113,300	126,300
Freight loaded at Bangui	75,500	57,200	53,100
Total	227,500	170,500	179,400

CIVIL AVIATION (traffic on scheduled services)*

	1992	1993	1994
Kilometres flown (million)	3	3	3
Passengers carried ('000)	120	122	122
Passenger-km (million)	213	219	219
Total ton-km (million)	35	35	35

*Including an apportionment of the traffic of Air Afrique.

Source: UN, *Statistical Yearbook.*

Tourism

	1992	1993	1994
Tourist arrivals ('000)	6	6	6
Tourist receipts (US $ million)	3	6	6

Source: UN, *Statistical Yearbook.*

Communications Media

	1992	1993	1994
Radio receivers	220,000	227,000	235,000
Television receivers	14,000	15,000	16,000

Daily newspapers: 1 (estimated circulation 2,000 copies) in 1994.

Source: UNESCO, *Statistical Yearbook.*

Telephones: 5,712 in use in 1991.

Education

(1990/91)

	Schools	Teachers	Pupils
Pre-primary	n.a.	10	n.a.
Primary	930	4,004	308,409
Secondary			
General	46*	1,005	46,989
Vocational	n.a.		1,862
Higher	n.a.	136	2,823

* State-funded general secondary schools..

Directory

The Constitution

A new Constitution was adopted on 7 January 1995, following approval by a national referendum held on 28 December 1994. It replaced the 1986 Constitution and all subsequent amendments. The new Constitution provided for decentralization, through the election of regional assemblies by direct universal adult suffrage, and the establishment of a Constitutional Court (whose officials were to be appointed by the President), and it redefined the separation of sovereign and executive powers between the President and the Prime Minister.

THE PRESIDENCY

The President of the Republic is Head of State and Commander-in-Chief of the national armed forces. The President is elected for a six-year term by direct universal suffrage and may serve for a maximum of two consecutive terms*. Election of the President is determined by an absolute majority of votes cast. If such is not obtained at the first ballot, a second ballot is to take place, contested by the two candidates gaining the largest number of votes in the first ballot. The election of the new President is to take place not less than 20 days and not more than 40 days before the expiration of the mandate of the President in office. However, the President may choose to hold a referendum to determine whether or not his mandate is to be renewed. Should the electorate reject the proposal, the President is to resign and a new presidential election is to be held two weeks after the publication of the results of the referendum. The Presidency is to become vacant only in the event of the President's death, resignation, condemnation by the High Court of Justice or permanent physical incapacitation, as certified by a Special Committee comprising the presidents of the National Assembly, the Economic and Regional Council and the Supreme Court (see below). The election of a new President must take place not less than 20 days and not more than 40 days following the occurrence of a vacancy, during which time the president of the National Assembly is to act as interim President, with limited powers.

The President appoints the Prime Minister, who presides over the Council of Ministers. The President promulgates laws adopted by the National Assembly or by the Congress and has the power to dissolve the National Assembly, in which event legislative elections must take place not less than 20 and not more than 40 days following its dissolution.

PARLIAMENT

This is composed of the National Assembly, the Economic and Regional Council and the State Council, which, when sitting together, are to be known as the Congress. The primary function of the Congress is to pass organic laws in implementation of the Constitution, whenever these are not submitted to a referendum.

The National Assembly

The National Assembly is composed of 85 deputies elected by direct universal suffrage for a five-year term. Its president is designated by, and from within, its bureau. Legislation may be introduced either by the President of the Republic or by a consensus of one-third of the members of the Assembly. Provisions are made for the rendering inadmissible of any law providing for the execution of projects carrying a financial cost to the State which exceeds their potential value. The National Assembly holds two ordinary sessions per year of 60 days each, at the summons of the President of the Republic, who may also summon it to hold extraordinary sessions with a pre-determined agenda. Sessions of the National Assembly are opened and closed by presidential decree.

The Economic and Regional Council

The Economic and Regional Council is composed of representatives from the principal sectors of economic and social activity. One-half of its members are appointed by the President, and the remaining half are elected by the National Assembly on the nomination of that body's president. It acts as an advisory body in all legislative proposals of an economic and social nature.

The State Council

The State Council is an advisory body which deliberates on administrative matters that are referred to it by the president of the National Assembly.

The Congress

The Congress has the same president and bureau as the National Assembly. An absolute majority of its members is needed to pass organic laws, as well as laws pertaining to the amendment of the Constitution which have not been submitted to a referendum. It defines development priorities and may meet, at the summons of the President, to ratify treaties or to declare a state of war.

* A special clause was incorporated in the 1995 Constitution, whereby the incumbent President, Ange-Félix Patassé, was to be permitted to remain in office, if re-elected, for three consecutive terms.

The Government

HEAD OF STATE

President: ANGE-FÉLIX PATASSÉ (inaugurated 22 October 1993).

COUNCIL OF MINISTERS
(June 1997)

A coalition 'Government of action' incorporating the Mouvement pour la libération du peuple centrafricain (MLPC), the Convention nationale (CN), the Parti Libéral-démocrate (PLD), the Mouvement d'évolution sociale de l'Afrique noire (MESAN), the Rassemblement démocratique centrafricain (RDC), the Front patriotique pour le progrès (FPP), the Mouvement pour la démocratie et le développement (MDD), the Mouvement démocratique pour la renaissance et l'évolution de la République Centrafricaine (MDRERC), the Alliance pour la démocratie et le progrès (ADP), the Parti social-démocrate (PSD) and three independents.

Prime Minister: MICHEL GBEZERA-BRIA (Independent).

Minister of Foreign Affairs: JEAN METTE-YAPENDE (MLPC).

Minister of National Defence, War Veterans and War Victims: Dr PASCAL KADO (MLPC).

Minister of Territorial Administration and Public Security: Gen. N'DJDDER FRANÇOIS BEDAYA (MLPC).

Minister of Justice: MARCEL METEFARA (MLPC).

Minister of Finance and the Budget: ANICET GEORGES DOLOGUELE (MLPC).

Minister of Economic Reform Planning and International Co-operation: CHRISTOPHE MBREMAIDOU (CN).

Minister of Public Works and Road Infrastructure: JACQUESSON MAZETTE (MLPC).

Minister of Human Rights and Promotion of Democratic Culture: LAURENT GOMINA-PAMPALI (RDC).*

Minister of National Education: ALBERT MBERYO (MLPC).

Minister of Higher Education, Scientific and Technological Research: THÉOPHILE TOUBA (RDC).*

Minister of Public Health and Population: Dr FERNANDE DJENGBO (Independent).

Minister of Civil Service, Labour and Professional Training: JEAN-CLAUDE GOUANDJA (FPP).*

Minister of Mines and Energy: JOSEPH AGBO (MLPC).

Minister of Transport and Civil Aviation: ANDRÉ GOMBAKO (FPP).*

Minister of Commerce, Industry, Small and Medium-Scale Enterprises, and Small and Medium-Scale Industries: SIMOM BONGOLAPKE (MDD).*

Minister of Communications: THIERRY VAN DEN BOSS YONIFOLO (PLD).

Minister of Tourism, Arts and Culture: GASTON BEINA NGABANDI (MLPC).

Minister of Family Promotion, Social Welfare and National Solidarity: ÉLIANE MOKODOKPO (MESAN).

Minister of Environment, Water, Forest Resources, Hunting and Fishery: JOSEPH GNOMBA (MDRERC).

Minister of Housing and Town Planning: CLÉMENT BELIBANGA (ADP).*

Minister of Posts and Telecommunications: MECHEL BINDO (RDC).*

Minister of Youth and Sports Promotion: BEERTIN BEYA (MDD).*

Minister of Relations with Parliament: CHARLES ARMEL DOUBANE (ADP).*

Secretary of State for Territorial Administration: GILBERT MOUSSA LABE (Independent).

Secretary of State for National Solidarity: ALBERTINE BISSA (PSD).

There are, in addition, two Ministers-Delegate responsible for security and civilian disarmament, and the reorganization of the army.

* Participation in government suspended in May 1997. Despite an announcement by the prime minister that he considered this to amount to resignation, no re-allocation of ministerial posts has taken place.

MINISTRIES

Office of the President: Palais de la Renaissance, Bangui; tel. 61-03-23; telex 5253.

Ministry of the Civil Service, Labour and Professional Training: Bangui; tel. 61-01-44.

Ministry of Communications: BP 1290, Bangui; telex 5301.

Ministry of Finance and the Budget: BP 734, Bangui; tel. 61-44-88; telex 5280; fax 61-21-82.

Ministry of Foreign Affairs: Bangui; tel. 61-15-74; telex 5213.

Ministry of Justice: Bangui; tel. 61-16-44.

Ministry of Mines and Energy: Bangui; telex 5243; fax 61-6076.

Ministry of National Defence, War Veterans and War Victims: Bangui; tel. 61-46-11; telex 5298.

Ministry of National Education: BP 791, Bangui; telex 5333.

Ministry of Public Health and Population: Bangui; tel. 61-29-01.

Ministry of Transport and Civil Aviation: BP 941, Bangui; tel. 61-23-07; telex 5335; fax 61-15-52.

Ministry of Youth, Sport and the Arts: BP 573, Bangui; tel. 61-39-69; fax 61-75-38.

President and Legislature

PRESIDENT

Presidential election, First Ballot, 22 August 1993

Candidate	Votes	% of votes
ANGE-FÉLIX PATASSÉ (MLPC)	302,004	37.31
Dr ABEL GOUMBA (CFD)	175,467	21.68
DAVID DACKO (Independent)	162,721	20.10
Gen. ANDRÉ KOLINGBA (RDC)	97,942	12.10
ENOCH DERANT LAKOUÉ (PSD)	19,368	2.39
Gen. TIMOTHÉE MALENDOMA (FC)	16,400	2.03
Brig.-Gen. FRANÇOIS BOZIZE (RPRC)	12,169	1.50
RUTH ROLLAND JEANNE MARIE (PRC)	8,068	1.00
Invalid votes	15,317	1.89
Total	809,456	100.00

Second Ballot, 19 September 1993

Candidate	% of votes
ANGE-FÉLIX PATASSÉ (MLPC)	52.47
Dr ABEL GOUMBA (CFD)	45.62
Invalid votes	1.91
Total	100.00

ASSEMBLÉE NATIONALE

Legislative power is vested in the Congress, which comprises the National Assembly and the advisory Economic and Regional Council and State Council.

President: HUGUES DOBOZENDI.

General election, 27 August and 19 September 1993

	Seats
MLPC	34
RDC	13
FPP	7
PLD	7
ADP	6
Supporters of David Dacko*	6
CN	3
PSD	3
MESAN	1
FC	1
PRC	1
MDRERC	1
Independents	2
Total	85

* Formed the Mouvement pour la démocratie et le développement in December 1993.

Political Organizations

The Rassemblement démocratique centrafrican (RDC) was the sole legal political party between 1987–91, when the Constitution was amended to enable the establishment of a plural political system.

Alliance pour la démocratie et le progrès (ADP): Bangui; f. 1991; Leader FRANÇOIS PEHOUA; Nat. Sec. TCHAPKA BRÉDÉ.

Conseil démocratique des partis politiques de l'opposition (CODEPO): Bangui; f. 1995; political alliance led by AUGUSTE BOUKANGA; comprises the following parties:

> **Mouvement démocratique pour la renaissance et l'évolution de la République Centrafricaine (MDRERC):** Bangui; Chair. JOSEPH BENDOUNGA; Sec.-Gen. LÉON SEBOU.
>
> **Parti républicain centrafricain (PRC):** Bangui.

Convention nationale (CN): Bangui; f. 1991; Leader DAVID GALIAMBO.

Forum civique (FC): Bangui; Leader Gen. TIMOTHÉE MALENDOMA.

Front patriotique pour le progrès (FPP): BP 259, Bangui; tel. 61-37-91; fax 61-52-23; f. 1972; aims to promote political education and debate; Leader Dr ABEL GOUMBA.

Front pour la libération centrafricaine: based in Brazzaville, Republic of the Congo; f. 1996 to combat French military and political intervention; Leaders Dr JEAN PAUL MANDAKOUZOU, Maj. LÉOPOLD ADETO.

G11: Bangui; f. 1997; alliance of 11 opposition parties led by Dr ABEL GOUMBA; prin. mems: ADP, FPP, MDD and RDC.

Mouvement centrafricain pour la libération nationale (MCLN): Lagos, Nigeria; Leader Dr IDDI LALA.

Mouvement d'évolution sociale de l'Afrique noire (MESAN): f. 1949; now comprises two factions, led respectively by PROSPER LAVODRAMA and JOSEPH NGBANGADIBO.

Mouvement pour la démocratie et le développement (MDD): Bangui; f. 1993; aims to safeguard national unity and the equitable distribution of national wealth; Leader DAVID DACKO.

Mouvement pour la libération du peuple centrafricain (MLPC): f. 1979; Pres. ANGE-FÉLIX PATASSÉ; Vice-Pres. JEAN-LUC MANDABA.

Mouvement pour la libération de la République Centrafricaine: Bangui; Leader HUGUES DOBOZENDI.

Mouvement socialiste centrafricaine: Bangui.

Parti libéral-démocrate (PLD): Bangui; Leader NESTOR KOMBO-NAGUEMON.

Parti social-démocrate (PSD): Bangui; Leader ENOCH DERANT LAKOUÉ.

Rassemblement démocratique centrafricain (RDC): BP 503, Bangui; tel. 61-53-75; f. 1987; sole legal political party 1987–91; Sec.-Gen. PIERRE LAKOUTINI.

Rassemblement populaire pour la reconstruction de la Centrafrique (RPRC): Leader Brig.-Gen. FRANÇOIS BOZIZE.

Union populaire pour le développement économique et social: Bangui; Leader HUBERT KATOSSI SIMANI.

Diplomatic Representation

EMBASSIES IN THE CENTRAL AFRICAN REPUBLIC

Cameroon: BP 935, Bangui; telex 5249; Ambassador: CHRISTOPHER NSAHLAI.

Chad: BP 461, Bangui; telex 5220; Ambassador: El Hadj MOULI SEID.

China (Taiwan): BP 1058, Bangui; tel. 61-36-28; Ambassador: LIU HSIANG-PU.

Congo: BP 1414, Bangui; telex 5292; Chargé d'affaires a.i.: ANTOINE DELICA.

Egypt: BP 1422, Bangui; telex 5284; Ambassador: SAMEH SAMY DARWICHE.

France: blvd du Général de Gaulle, BP 884, Bangui; tel. 61-30-00; telex 5218; fax 61-74-04; Ambassador: JEAN-MARC SIMON.

Gabon: BP 1570, Bangui; tel. 61-29-97; telex 5234; Ambassador: FRANÇOIS DE PAULE MOULENGUI.

Germany: ave G. A. Nasser, BP 901, Bangui; tel. 61-47-65; telex 5219; fax 61-19-89; Ambassador: REINHARD BUCHHOLZ.

Holy See: ave Boganda, BP 1447, Bangui; tel. 61-26-54; fax 61-03-71; Apostolic Nuncio: Most Rev. DIEGO CAUSERO, Titular Archbishop of Meta.

Iraq: Bangui; telex 5287; Chargé d'affaires a.i.: ABDUL KARIM ASWAD.

Japan: ave G. A. Nasser, BP 1367, Bangui; tel. 61-06-68; telex 5204; Ambassador: YOICHI HAYASHI.

Libya: Bangui; telex 5317; Head of Mission: EL-SENUSE ABDALLAH.

Nigeria: BP 1010, Bangui; tel. 61-40-97; telex 5269; fax 61-12-79; Chargé d'affaires: AYODELE J. BAKARE.

Romania: BP 1435, Bangui; Chargé d'affaires a.i.: MIHAI GAFTONIUC.

Russia: Bangui; Ambassador: YURII BALABANOV.

Sudan: Bangui; Ambassador: TIJANI SALIH FADAYL.

USA: blvd David Dacko, BP 924, Bangui; tel. 61-02-00; fax 61-44-94; Ambassador: MOSINA H. JORDAN.

Zaire: BP 989, Bangui; telex 5232; Ambassador: EMBE ISEA MBAMBE.

Judicial System

Supreme Court: BP 926, Bangui; tel. 61-41-33; highest judicial organ; acts as a Court of Cassation in civil and penal cases and as Court of Appeal in administrative cases; comprises four chambers: constitutional, judicial, administrative and financial.

President of the Supreme Court: EDOUARD FRANCK.

There is also a Court of Appeal, a Criminal Court, 16 tribunaux de grande instance, 37 tribunaux d'instance, six labour tribunals and a permanent military tribunal. A High Court of Justice was established under the 1986 Constitution, with jurisdiction in all cases of crimes against state security, including high treason by the President of the Republic.

In August 1992 constitutional amendments were introduced which provided for the strict separation of executive, legislative and judicial powers.

The 1995 Constitution provides for the establishment of a Constitutional Court, the judges of which were to be appointed by the President.

Religion

An estimated 60% of the population hold animist beliefs, 35% are Christians and 5% are Muslims; Roman Catholics comprise about 17% of the total population.

CHRISTIANITY

The Roman Catholic Church

The Central African Republic comprises one archdiocese and six dioceses. There were an estimated 621,571 adherents at 31 December 1995.

Bishops' Conference: Conférence Episcopale Centrafricaine, BP 798, Bangui; tel. 61-31-48; fax 61-46-92; f. 1982; Pres. Most Rev. JOACHIM N'DAYEN, Archbishop of Bangui.

Archbishop of Bangui: Most Rev. JOACHIM N'DAYEN, Archevêché, BP 1518, Bangui; tel. 61-31-48; fax 61-46-92.

Protestant Church

Eglise Protestante de Bangui: Bangui.

The Press

DAILIES

E Le Songo: Bangui; Sango; circ. 2,000.

Le Novateur: Bangui; independent; Publr MARCEL MOKWAPI.

PERIODICALS

Bangui Match: Bangui; monthly.

Le Courrier Rural: BP 850, Bangui; publ. by Chambre d'Agriculture.

Le Delit d'Opinion: Bangui; independent.

Journal Officiel de la République Centrafricaine: BP 739, Bangui; f. 1974; fortnightly; economic data; Dir-Gen. GABRIEL AGBA.

Le Rassemblement: Bangui; organ of the RDC; Editor-in-Chief MATHIAS GONEVO REAPOGO.

Renouveau Centrafricain: Bangui; weekly.

Ta Tene (The Truth): BP 1290, Bangui; monthly.

Terre Africaine: BP 373, Bangui; weekly.

NEWS AGENCIES

Agence Centrafricaine de Presse (ACAP): BP 40, Bangui; tel. 61-10-88; telex 5299; f. 1974; Gen. Man. VICTOR DETO TETEYA.

Informatsionnoye Telegrafnoye Agentstvo Rossii—Telegrafnoye Agentstvo Suverennykh Stran (ITAR—TASS) (Russia) and Agence France-Presse are the only foreign press agencies represented in the CAR.

Publisher

Government Publishing House

Imprimerie Centrafricaine: BP 329, Bangui; tel. 61-00-33; f. 1974; Dir-Gen. PIERRE SALAMATE-KOILET.

Radio and Television

There were an estimated 235,000 radio receivers in use in 1994. A 100-kW transmitter came into service at Bimbo in 1970, and two 50-kW transmitters were introduced in 1984. Television broadcasting began in 1983. An estimated 16,000 television receivers were in use in 1994.

Radiodiffusion-Télévision Centrafrique: BP 940, Bangui; tel. 61-25-88; telex 2355; f. 1958 as Radiodiffusion Nationale Centrafricaine; govt-controlled; radio programmes in French and Sango; Man. Dir PAUL SERVICE.

Finance

(cap. = capital; res = reserves; dep. = deposits; m. = million; amounts in francs CFA)

BANKING

Central Bank

Banque des Etats de l'Afrique Centrale (BEAC): BP 851, Bangui; tel. 61-24-00; telex 5636; fax 61-19-95, headquarters in Yaoundé, Cameroon; f. 1973 as the central bank of issue for mem. states of the Customs and Economic Union of Central Africa (UDEAC), comprising Cameroon, the Central African Republic, Chad, the Congo, Equatorial Guinea and Gabon; cap. and res 204,933m. (Dec. 1995); Gov. JEAN-FÉLIX MAMALEPOT; Dir in CAR AUGUSTE TENÉ-KOYZOA.

Commercial Banks

Banque de Crédit Agricole et de Développement (BCAD): 1 place de la République, BP 801, Bangui; tel. 61-32-00; telex 5207; f. 1984; 50% owned by BPP Holding (Luxembourg), 33.33% state-owned, 8.33% owned by Caisse Nationale de Crédit Agricole and 8.33% owned by Pacfinancial Consultants Ltd; Pres. MICHEL M. CHAUTARD; Gen. Man. RENÉ JAULIN.

Banque Meridien BIAO Centrafrique SA: place de la République, BP 910, Bangui; tel. 61-36-33; telex 5233; fax 61-61-36; f. 1980; takeover pending by Banque Belgolaise SA; cap. 700m., dep. 17,318m. (Dec. 1994); Pres. RAOUL KONTCHOU; Gen. Man. TADI WANTWADI; 1 br.

Banque Populaire Maroco-Centrafricaine (BPMC): rue Guerillot, BP 844, Bangui; tel. 61-12-90; telex 5244; fax 61-62-30; f. 1991; 50% owned by Banque Centrale Populaire (Morocco), 12.5% owned by Banque Marocaine du Commerce Extérieur and 37.5% state-owned; cap. 842m., total assets 4,520m. (Dec. 1995); Pres. ABDELLATIF LARAKI; Gen. Man. AHMED IRAQI HOUSSAINI.

Union Bancaire en Afrique Centrale: rue de Brazza, BP 59, Bangui; tel. 61-29-90; telex 5225; fax 61-34-54; f. 1962; 85% state-owned and 15% owned by Crédit Lyonnais (France); cap. 1,000m. (Dec. 1995), res 789m., dep. 10,869 (Dec. 1993), total assets 19,383m. (Dec. 1995); Pres. JEAN-SERGE WAFIO; Gen. Man. ETIENNE DJIMARIM; 1 br.

Development Bank

Banque de Developpement des Etats de l'Afrique Centrale: (see Franc Zone, p. 174).

Investment Bank

Banque Centrafricaine d'Investissement (BCI): BP 933, Bangui; tel. 61-00-64; telex 5317; f. 1976; 34.8% state-owned; cap. 1,000m.; Pres. ALPHONSE KONGOLO; Man. Dir GÉRARD SAMBO.

Financial Institutions

Caisse Autonome d'Amortissement des Dettes de la République Centrafricaine: Bangui; fax 61-21-82; management of state funds; Dir-Gen. JOSEPH PINGAMA.

Caisse Nationale d'Epargne (CNE): Bangui; tel. 61-22-96; telex 5202; fax 61-78-80; Pres. ETIENNE GOYEMIDE: Dir-Gen. ANDRÉ NDOMONDJI.

Development Agencies

Caisse Française de Développement: BP 817, Bangui; tel. 61-36-34; telex 5291; Dir NILS ROBIN.

Mission Française de Coopération et d'Action Culturelle: BP 934, Bangui; tel. 61-53-63; fax 61-28-24; administers bilateral aid from France; Dir ALAIN MOREL.

INSURANCE

Agence Centrafricaine d'Assurances (ACA): BP 512, Bangui; tel. 61-06-23; f. 1956; Dir Mme R. Cerbellaud.

Assureurs Conseils Centrafricains Faugère et Jutheau: rue de la Kouanga, BP 743, Bangui; tel. 61-19-33; telex 5331; fax 61-44-70; f. 1968; Dir Jean Claude Roy.

Entreprise d'Etat d'Assurances et de Réassurances (SIRIRI): Bangui; tel. 61-36-55; telex 5306; f. 1972; Pres. Emmanuel Dokouna; Dir-Gen. Jean-Marie Yollot.

Legendre, A. & Cie: rue de la Victoire, BP 896, Bangui; Pres. and Dir-Gen. André Legendre.

Trade and Industry

CHAMBERS OF COMMERCE

Chambre d'Agriculture, d'Elevage, des Eaux, Forêts, Chasses, Pêches et Tourisme: BP 850, Bangui; tel. 61-09-33; f. 1964; Pres. François T. Beyélé; Sec.-Gen. Moïse Denissio.

Chambre de Commerce, d'Industrie, des Mines et de l'Artisanat (CCIMA): BP 813, Bangui; tel. 61-16-68; telex 5261; Pres. Rigobert Yombo; Sec. Gertrude Zouta-Yamandja.

PRINCIPAL DEVELOPMENT ORGANIZATIONS

Agence de Développement de la Zone Caféière (ADECAF): BP 1935, Bangui; tel. 61-47-30; coffee producers' asscn; assists coffee marketing co-operatives; Dir-Gen. J. J. Nimiziambi.

Caisse de Stabilisation et de Pérequation des Produits Agricoles (CAISTAB): BP 76, Bangui; tel. 61-08-00; telex 5278; supervises pricing and marketing of agricultural products; Dir-Gen. M. Bounandele-Koumba.

Comptoir National du Diamant (CND): blvd B. Boganda, BP 1011, Bangui; tel. 61-07-02; telex 5262; f. 1964; 50% state-owned, 50% owned by Diamond Distributors (USA): mining and marketing of diamonds; Dir-Gen. M. Vassos.

Office National des Forêts (ONF): BP 915, Bangui; tel. 61-38-27; f. 1969; reafforestation, development of forest resources; Dir-Gen. C. D. Songuet.

Société Centrafricaine de Développement Agricole (SOCADA): ave David Dacko, BP 997, Bangui; tel. 61-30-33; telex 5212; f. 1964; reorg. 1980; 75% state-owned, 25% Cie Française pour le Développement des Fibres Textiles (France); purchasing, transport and marketing of cotton, cotton-ginning, production of cottonseed oil and groundnut oil; Pres. Maurice Methot.

Société Centrafricaine des Palmiers (CENTRAPALM): BP 1355, Bangui; tel. 61-49-40; fax 61-38-75; f. 1975; state-owned; production and marketing of palm oil; operates the Bossongo agro-industrial complex; Pres. Mathieu-Francis Nganawara; Gen. Man. Dr Joël Beassem.

Société Énergie de Centrafrique (ENERCA): Bangui; state-owned, scheduled for privatization; production of electric energy.

Société Nationale des Eaux (SNE): BP 1838, Bangui; tel. 61-20-28; telex 5306; state-owned water co; Dir-Gen. François Farra-Frond.

Société Petrolière de Centrafrique (PETROCA): Bangui; state-owned, scheduled for privatization in 1997; import and marketing of petroleum products; Dir-Gen. Dogone Jibe.

MAJOR INDUSTRIAL COMPANIES

The following are among the largest companies in terms of either capital investment or employment.

Bata SA Centrafricaine: BP 364, Bangui; tel. 61-45-79; telex 5257; f. 1969; cap. 150m. francs CFA; footwear mfrs; Dir Victor de Rycke.

Centrafrique-Roumano-Bois (CAROMBOIS): BP 1159, Bangui; telex 5264; f. 1974; cap. 673m. francs CFA; 60% owned by FOREXIM (Romania); Dir-Gen. Victor Ionescu; 306 employees.

COLALU: rue Chavannes, BP 1326, Bangui; tel. 61-20-42; telex 5248; f. 1969; cap. 69m. francs CFA; 57% owned by ALUCAM (Cameroon); mfrs of household articles and sheet aluminium; Pres. Claude Millet; Dir-Gen. M. Kappes.

Compagnie Industrielle d'Ouvrages en Textiles (CIOT): BP 190, Bangui; tel. 61-36-22; telex 5238; f. 1949; cap. 250m. francs CFA; mfrs of clothing and hosiery; Dir-Gen. Michel Robert.

Entreprise Forestière des Bois Africains Centrafrique (EFBACA): BP 205, Bangui; tel. 61-25-33; telex 5265; f. 1969; cap. 259m. francs CFA; 12% state-owned; exploitation of forests and wood processing; Pres. Victor Balet; Dir Jean Quennoz.

Huilerie Savonnerie Centrafricaine (HUSACA): BP 1020, Bangui; tel. 61-58-54; telex 5234; fax 61-68-11; mfrs of soap, edible oil and animal feed; Dir B. Abdallah.

Industrie Centrafricaine du Textile (ICAT): BP 981, Bangui; tel. 61-40-00; telex 5215; f. 1965; cap. 586m. francs CFA; state-owned; textile complex; Man. Dir M. Ngoundoukoua.

Industries Forestières de Batalimo (IFB): BP 517, Bangui; f. 1970; cap. 100m. francs CFA; Dir Jacques Gaden.

Manufacture Centrafricaine de Cigares (MANUCACIG): Bangui; tel. 61-23-14; f. 1976; cap. 163m. francs CFA; 13% state-owned; processes locally-grown tobacco leaf; capacity 10m. cigars per annum; Pres. Albert Goffi; Dir Jean-Marie Decourchelle; 130 employees.

Motte-Cordonnier-Afrique (MOCAF): BP 806, Bangui; tel. 61-04-77; telex 5224; f. 1951; cap. 1,123m. francs CFA; production of beer, soft drinks and ice; Pres. Bertrand Motte; Dir-Gen. Philippe Magnaval.

Société Centrafricaine de Cigarettes (SOCACIG): BP 728, Bangui; tel. 61-03-00; fax 61-51-30; f. 1970; cap. 698.4m. francs CFA; cigarette mfrs; Pres. Pierre Imbert; Dir in Bangui Alain Perreard.

Société Centrafricaine des Cuirs (CENTRA-CUIRS): Bangui; f. 1975; cap. 75m. francs CFA; 20% state-owned; mfrs of leather goods.

Société Centrafricaine de Déroulage (SCAD): BP 1607, Bangui; tel. 61-18-05; telex 5226; fax 61-56-60; f. 1972; cap. 700m. francs CFA; exploitation of forests, mfrs of plywood; also operates a sawmill; Dir-Gen. J. Kamach; 392 employees.

Société Centrafricaine du Diamant (SODIAM): BP 1016, Bangui; tel. 61-03-79; telex 5210; cap. 100m. francs CFA; export of diamonds; Dir Dimitri Anagnostellis.

Société Centrafricaine d'Exploitation Forestière et Industrielle (SOCEFI): BP 3, M'Bata-Bangui; f. 1947, nationalized 1974; cap. 880m. francs CFA; sawmill; timber exports, mfrs of prefabricated dwellings; Man. Dir Pierre Opanzoyen.

Société Centrafricaine des Gaz Industriels (SOCAGI): blvd du Général de Gaulle, BP 905, Bangui; tel. 61-19-11; telex 5205; f. 1965; cap. 53m. francs CFA; manufacture and sale of industrial and medical gases; Pres. and Dir-Gen. Paul Lalague.

Société d'Exploitation et d'Industrialisation Forestière en RCA (SLOVENIA-BOIS): BP 1571, Bangui; tel. 61-44-35; telex 5266; f. 1970; cap. 250m. francs CFA; partly Slovenian-owned; sawmill; Dir Franc Benković.

Société Industrielle Centrafricaine (SICA): BP 1325, Bangui; tel. 61-44-99; telex 5251; f. 1967; cap. 200m. francs CFA; sawmill at M'baiki in the Lobaye area, annual capacity 18,000 cu m; Dir Charles Sylvain.

Société Industrielle Forestière en Afrique Centrale (SIFAC): BP 156, Bangui; telex 5272; f. 1970; cap. 95m. francs CFA; sawmill and joinery; Dir Jacques Gaden.

Société de Plantations d'Hévéas et de Caféiers (SPHC): BP 1384, Bangui; f. 1974; cap. 160m. francs CFA; rubber and coffee plantations.

Total Centrafricaine de Gestion (TOCAGES): BP 724, Bangui; tel. 61-05-88; telex 5243; f. 1950; cap. 200m. francs CFA; 51% state-owned; storage, retailing and transport of petroleum products; Dir Christian-Dimanche Songuet.

EMPLOYERS' ASSOCIATION

Union Nationale du Patronat Centrafricain (UNPC): Bangui; Pres. Rigobert Yombo.

TRADE UNION

Union Syndicale des Travailleurs de la Centrafrique (USTC): Bangui; Sec.-Gen. Théophile Sonny Kolle.

Transport

A five-year programme for the modernization of the CAR's transport infrastructure, at a projected cost of US $139m. (to be funded by bilateral and multilateral creditors), was announced in 1990.

RAILWAYS

There are no railways at present. There are long-term plans to connect Bangui to the Transcameroon railway. A line linking Sudan's Darfur region with the CAR's Vakaga province is also planned.

ROADS

In 1995 there were about 23,810 km of roads, including 4,700 km of main roads and 3,910 km of secondary roads. Only about 1.8% of the total network is paved. Eight main routes serve Bangui, and those that are surfaced are toll roads. Both the total road length and the condition of the roads are inadequate for current requirements. A major project of road rehabilitation and construction is being assisted by France, the EU and Japan. The CAR is linked with Cameroon by the Transafrican Lagos–Mombasa highway.

Bureau d'Affrètement Routier Centrafricain (BARC): BP 523, Bangui; tel. 61-20-55; telex 5336; Dir-Gen. J. M. Laguerema-Yadinguin.

Compagnie Nationale des Transports Routiers (CNTR): Bangui; tel. 61-46-44; state-owned; Dir-Gen. GEORGES YABADA.

Compagnie de Transports Routiers de l'Oubangui Degrain & Cie (CTRO): Bangui; f. 1940; Man. NICOLE DEGRAIN.

INLAND WATERWAYS

There are some 2,800 km of navigable waterways along two main water courses. The first, formed by the Congo and Oubangui rivers can accommodate convoys of barges (of up to 800 metric tons load) between Bangui, Brazzaville and Pointe-Noire, except during the dry season, when the route is impassable. The second is the river Sangha, a tributary of the Oubangui, on which traffic is also seasonal. There are two ports, at Bangui and Salo, on the rivers Oubangui and Sangha respectively. Efforts are being made to develop the stretch of river upstream from Salo to increase the transportation of timber from this area, and to develop Nola as a timber port. The 1990–95 transport development programme aimed to improve the navigability of the Oubangui river.

Agence Centrafricaine des Communications Fluviales (ACCF): BP 822, Bangui; tel. 61-02-11; telex 5256; f. 1969; state-owned; development of inland waterways transport system; Man. Dir JUSTIN NDJAPOU.

Société Centrafricaine de Transports Fluviaux (SOCATRAF): BP 1445, Bangui; tel. and fax 61-43-15; telex 5256; f. 1980; 51%-owned by ACCF; Man. Dir FRANÇOIS TOUSSAINT.

CIVIL AVIATION

The international airport is at Bangui-M'Poko. There are also 37 small airports for internal services.

Air Afrique: BP 875, Bangui; tel. 61-46-60; telex 5281; see under Côte d'Ivoire; Dir in Bangui ALBERT BAGNERES.

Tourism

The main tourist attractions are the waterfalls, forests and wildlife. There are excellent hunting and fishing opportunities. There were an estimated 1,599 tourist arrivals in 1990.

Office National Centrafricain du Tourisme (OCATOUR): BP 655, Bangui; tel. 61-45-66.

Defence

In August 1996 the armed forces numbered about 2,650 men (army 2,500; air force 150), with a further 2,300 men in paramilitary forces. Military service is selective and lasts for two years. France maintains a force of 1,800 troops in the CAR, 1,200 based in Bangui and 600 at Bouar.

Defence Expenditure: Estimated at 12,000m. francs CFA in 1995.

Chief of Staff of the Armed Forces: Gen. FRANÇOIS BOZIZE.

Education

Education is officially compulsory for eight years between six and 14 years of age. Primary education begins at the age of six and lasts for six years. Secondary education begins at the age of 12 and lasts for up to seven years, comprising a first cycle of four years and a second of three years. In 1989 an estimated 58% of children in the relevant age-group (71% of boys; 46% of girls) attended primary schools, while secondary enrolment was equivalent to only 12% (boys 17%; girls 6%). According to estimates by UNESCO, the adult illiteracy rate in 1995 averaged 40% (males 31.5%; females 47.6%). Government expenditure on education totalled 9,862m. francs CFA in 1990, equivalent to 2.8% of gross national product. The provision of state-funded education was severely disrupted during the early 1990s, owing to the government's inadequate resources.

Bibliography

Bigo, D. *Pouvoir et obéissance en Centrafrique.* Paris, Editions Karthala, 1989.

Carter, G. M. (Ed.). *National Unity and Regionalism in Eight African States.* Ithaca, NY, Cornell University Press, 1966.

de Dreux Brezé, J. *Le Problème du regroupement en Afrique équatoriale.* Paris, Librairie Gale de Droit et de Jurisprudence, 1968.

Hance, W. A. 'Middle Africa from Chad to Congo (Brazzaville)', in *The Geography of Modern Africa.* New York and London, Columbia University Press, 1964.

O'Toole, T. *The Central African Republic. The Continent's Hidden Heart.* Boulder, CO, Westview Press, 1986.

Historical Dictionary of the Central African Republic. 2nd Edn. Metuchen, NJ, Scarecrow Press, 1992.

Robson, P. 'Economic Integration in Equatorial Africa', in *Economic Integration in Africa.* London, Allen and Unwin, 1968.

UDEAC. *Bulletin des Statistiques Générales de l'UDEAC.* Bangui, Secrétariat-Général de l'UDEAC, 1976.

CHAD

Physical and Social Geography

DAVID HILLING

The Republic of Chad is bordered to the north by Libya, to the south by the Central African Republic, to the west by Niger and Cameroon and to the east by Sudan. The northernmost of the four independent states which emerged from French Equatorial Africa, Chad is, with an area of 1,284,000 sq km (495,800 sq miles), the largest in terms of size and population (enumerated at 6,158,992 at the census of April 1993, and officially estimated at 6,214,000 in mid-1994). Traditionally a focal point for equatorial and Saharan trade routes, the country's vast size, land-locked location and great distance from the coast create problems for economic development.

The relief is relatively simple. From 240 m in the Lake Chad depression in the south-west, the land rises northwards through the Guéra massif at 1,800 m to the mountainous Saharan region of Tibesti at 3,350 m. Eastwards, heights of 1,500 m are attained in the Ouaddai massif. In the south the watershed area between the Chari and Congo rivers is of subdued relief and only slight elevation. The only rivers of importance, both for irrigation and seasonal navigation, are the Chari and Logone, which traverse the south-west of the country and join at N'Djamena, before flowing into Lake Chad.

Extending across more than 16° of latitude, Chad has three well-defined zones of climate, natural vegetation and associated economic activity. The southern third of the country has annual rainfall in excess of 744 mm (increasing to 1,200 mm in the extreme south), and has a savannah woodland vegetation. This is the country's principal agricultural zone, providing the two main cash crops, cotton and groundnuts, and a variety of local food crops (especially rice). Northwards, with rainfall of 250–500 mm per year, there is a more open grassland, where there is emphasis on pastoral activity, limited cultivation of groundnuts and local grains, and some collection of gum arabic. This marginal Sahel zone was adversely affected by drought during most of the 1970s and 1980s, and the cattle herds were greatly reduced in number. The northern third of the country has negligible rainfall and a sparse scrub vegetation, which grades north into pure desert with little apparent economic potential, although the 'Aozou strip', a region of 114,000 sq km in the extreme north, formerly claimed by Libya but returned to Chad in 1994, is believed to contain significant reserves of uranium and other minerals.

Chad's total population is relatively small in relation to its large area, and is markedly concentrated in the southern half of the country. Religious and ethnic tensions between the people of the north and south have traditionally dominated the history of Chad. The population of the north is predominantly Islamic, of a nomadic or semi-nomadic character, and is largely engaged in farming and in breeding livestock. Rivalry between ethnic groups is strong. By contrast, the inhabitants of the south are settled farmers, who largely follow animistic beliefs. The Sara tribes, some 10 ethnic groups with related languages and cultural links, comprise a large section of the population of the south. Since the end of the Second World War, the population of the south has inclined towards a modern, Western culture; the rate of literacy has increased rapidly, and Christian churches have attracted a number of adherents. The population of the north, however, forms a traditional, Islamic society, and is largely unaffected by modern education. As a result, the majority of administrators and civil servants who were recruited after independence originated from the south. The state is secular and exercises neutrality in relation to religious affiliations. French and Arabic are the official languages, but local languages (Karembou, Ouadi, Teda, Daza, Djonkor) are also spoken.

Recent History

BERNARD LANNE

Revised for this edition by the Editor

Formerly a province of French Equatorial Africa, Chad became an autonomous state within the French Community in November 1958. François Tombalbaye, a southerner and leader of the Parti progressiste tchadien (PPT), was elected prime minister in March 1959. Chad proceeded to independence on 11 August 1960, with Tombalbaye as president. However, the Saharan territory of the north, Borkou-Ennedi-Tibesti (BET), remained under French military administration until 1964. In 1962 Tombalbaye dissolved all political parties except the PPT. In 1963 the PPT was declared the sole legal party, and its executive body, the Bureau politique national (BPN), became Chad's supreme political organ. Although the BPN was composed equally of Muslims and southerners, it came increasingly under the domination of Tombalbaye.

THE EMERGENCE OF FROLINAT

The political monopoly of the PPT was opposed by certain northern politicians who had been influential prior to independence, and in September 1963 civil disturbances occurred in the capital, Fort-Lamy (now N'Djamena). In 1964 mismanagement and corruption on the part of government officials intensified this discontent, and in 1965 a serious rebellion broke out, focused mainly in the north. The Front de libération nationale du Tchad (FROLINAT), which was established in Sudan in 1966, later assumed leadership of the revolt. In August 1968 French troops intervened in support of the government; French reinforcements subsequently launched a number of successful military offensives against the rebels.

Despite various initiatives by the government to satisfy the political aspirations of FROLINAT supporters, the rebellion in the north of the country continued. In August 1971 Tombalbaye suspended diplomatic relations with Libya, which he accused of complicity in an attempted coup at Fort-Lamy. The Libyan leader, Col Muammar al-Qaddafi, subsequently transferred support to FROLINAT. As a result of the French military intervention, however, the rebellion was contained (although FROLINAT remained undefeated), and in 1972 the French reinforcements left the country. (In 1972 and 1973 diplomatic relations between Chad and France deteriorated, after Tombalbaye accused the French government of interference in Chad's internal affairs.) In November 1972, in an apparent attempt to isolate the rebels, Tombalbaye severed diplomatic relations with

Israel, and signed a pact of friendship with Libya. However, FROLINAT continued to receive military assistance from Libya, which, in 1973, annexed the 'Aozou strip' in northern Chad; the Libyan claim to sovereignty over the region was based on an unratified treaty, which was signed by France and Italy in 1935.

In 1973 several prominent members of the government, including the army chief of staff, Gen. Felix Malloum, were imprisoned on conspiracy charges. In August of that year the PPT was reconstituted as the Mouvement national pour la révolution culturelle et sociale (MNRCS), and its executive council, which was composed equally of Muslims and southerners, was proclaimed the supreme political organ. Under the influence of President Mobutu of Zaire, Tombalbaye adopted the policy of 'authenticity', changing his first name from François to Ngarta, and ordering the abandonment of all Christian first names. Ritual initiation, known as *ndo* among the Sara, was reintroduced, and execution was decreed for those who refused to undergo the ordeal. (Muslims however, were exempted from the new policies.)

MALLOUM TAKES POWER

In April 1975 Tombalbaye was killed in a military coup, which was organized by army officers originating from the south. Malloum was subsequently released, and became president of a supreme military council. The national assembly and the MNRCS were dissolved, and a provisional government was formed. Despite initial popular support, the new government soon encountered difficulties. Following a disagreement with France over the continued detention of a French hostage by rebel forces, the French garrison at N'Djamena was closed in October; however, new co-operation agreements were signed with France in March 1976. Although the government appealed for national reconciliation, a number of rebel groups, including FROLINAT, remained in opposition. However, divisions subsequently emerged within FROLINAT, and its leader, Hissène Habré, who opposed the Libyan annexation of the 'Aozou strip', was replaced by Goukouni Oueddei. (Habré continued, however, to lead a faction within FROLINAT.)

Following a deterioration in relations between Chad and Libya concerning the annexation of the 'Aozou strip', the Libyan government increased military aid to FROLINAT, which launched renewed offensives in 1977. In January 1978 an agreement was signed between Malloum and Habré, in an attempt to secure a cease-fire. However, FROLINAT unified its command under a revolutionary council, which was led by Goukouni, and continued to overrun large areas of territory. The government successfully sought French assistance, and in mid-1978 French reinforcements halted the advance of FROLINAT.

CIVIL CONFLICT AND LIBYAN INTERVENTION

In August 1978, following negotiations between Malloum and Habré, a *charte fondamentale,* which provided for Habré's appointment to the post of prime minister, was promulgated, and a civilian government replaced the military council. However, disagreements soon arose between Malloum and Habré, and in February 1979 fighting broke out in N'Djamena between government forces (Forces armées tchadiennes—FAT) and Habré's troops, known as the Forces armées du nord (FAN). Members of the FAN seized control of the capital, with the support of the French government (which, however, officially pursued a policy of neutrality), while rebels, under the leadership of Goukouni, known as the Forces armées populaires (FAP), gained territory in the north. Subsequent massacres of southerners in the north of the country, and of Muslims in the south, reflected the increasing division between the two communities. In March Malloum resigned and fled the country, after appointing the former commander of the gendarmerie, Lt-Col (later Gen.) Wadal Abdelkader Kamougue, as his successor.

In April 1979, following the failure of attempts to reach a *rapprochement,* a provisional government (Gouvernement d'union nationale de transition—GUNT) was formed by FROLINAT, the FAN, the Mouvement populaire pour la libération du Tchad (MPLT), and the FAT. The leader of the MPLT, Lol Mahamat Choua, was appointed president, while Goukouni and Habré received ministerial portfolios. However, the southern factions rejected the authority of the new government, and a committee, under the presidency of Kamougue, was established at Moundou to govern the south. Attempts to capture the prefecture of Mayo-Kebbi from Kamougue's forces failed, and the GUNT became increasingly isolated by governments of neighbouring countries. In August a further conference resulted in the creation of a second GUNT, under the presidency of Goukouni, with Kamougue as vice-president. In November a council of ministers, which represented the various groupings, was appointed. However, the fragmentation of the northern factions increased, while Goukouni's authority was undermined by continued disagreement with Habré.

In March 1980 fighting between the FAP and the FAN resumed in N'Djamena. Numerous attempts at mediation failed, and in April the GUNT dismissed Habré from his post as minister of state for defence. In accordance with the French government's policy of neutrality, its troops were withdrawn from Chad in May. In June a treaty of friendship and co-operation was signed in Tripoli between Libya and a representative of Goukouni, without the prior consent of the GUNT. In October Libyan forces intervened in the hostilities, resulting in the defeat of Habré and the retreat of the FAN from N'Djamena by the end of that year. A Libyan contingent, numbering some 15,000 men, subsequently entered the country.

In January 1981 Goukouni signed a further agreement in Tripoli, which provided for a gradual political union of Chad and Libya. However, the French government strongly opposed the proposed union, and French military personnel in the Central African Republic (CAR) were reinforced. In April the intervention of Libyan troops in skirmishes between members of Goukouni's FAP and the Conseil démocratique révolutionnaire (CDR), one of the breakaway factions of FROLINAT, at Abéché, the capital of the prefecture of Ouaddai, resulted in numerous casualties. Goukouni subsequently negotiated the withdrawal of Libyan forces stationed at N'Djamena airport. In September, at a meeting between Goukouni and the French president, François Mitterrand, in Paris, France affirmed its support for the GUNT; the French government subsequently hastened the departure of the Libyan troops by urging the president of the OAU to send a peace-keeping force to Chad. In November, at the request of the council of ministers, Libyan troops were withdrawn, and an Inter-African Force (IAF) was subsequently installed under the auspices of the OAU.

Following the departure of the Libyan troops, the FAN renewed its offensive, and by mid-January 1982 had gained control of several towns in northern Chad. In February, however, the OAU adopted a resolution, whereby a cease-fire was to be imposed later that month, elections were to take place under OAU supervision before 30 June and the IAF was subsequently to withdraw. The resolution, which was effectively a political victory for the FAN, was rejected by Goukouni, and hostilities intensified. In subsequent months the FAN continued to advance, and finally captured N'Djamena in early June. Goukouni fled to Algeria, while the coalition of factions that constituted the GUNT began to fragment.

HABRÉ'S RETURN TO POWER

In mid-June 1982, following the capture of N'Djamena, the formation of a provisional council of state, with Habré as head of state, was announced. By the end of that month the IAF had withdrawn fully from Chad. A provisional constitution, the *acte fondamental*, was promulgated in September. In the following month Habré was inaugurated as president and formed a new government, which included former members of the Tombalbaye and Goukouni administrations, with southerners receiving a large proportion of ministerial portfolios. However, Goukouni's troops regained control of the greater part of the BET, with Libyan support, and in October Goukouni announced the formation of a rival 'government of national salvation' at Bardai. Habré's government, however, obtained international recognition, occupying Chad's seat at the UN and gaining the support of the majority of African states. By early 1983, however, Habré's forces had suffered defeats in the north, while tribal differences had caused divisions within the FAN. In January of that year a number of members of Kamougue's FAT joined the FAN to form the Forces armées nationales tchadiennes (FANT).

FRENCH INTERVENTION

In March 1983 negotiations took place between Habré and the Libyan government; however, Habré rejected Libyan demands for the recognition of Chad's Islamic character and of the annexation of the 'Aozou strip', and the signing of a treaty of alliance. In June Goukouni's rebel troops, with assistance from Libya, captured the northern administrative centre of Faya-Largeau, and, in early July, occupied the entire BET region, subsequently advancing to Abéché. Following Habré's appeals for aid to counter Libyan intrusions, Zaire responded by sending a paratroop contingent, while the USA supplied armaments. The French government, however, refused Habré's request for direct intervention. After a successful counter-offensive by the FANT at the end of July, Goukouni's forces, with Libyan air support, recaptured Faya-Largeau, and again advanced southwards. In early August, as a result of pressure from francophone African heads of state, France dispatched some 3,000 troops to Chad. The French forces subsequently imposed an 'interdiction line' from Salal to Arada, preventing Goukouni's troops and their Libyan allies from advancing further south; by mid-September all fighting between the Chadian factions had ceased.

In January 1984 a meeting of all factions, which took place at Addis Ababa, Ethiopia, under the aegis of the OAU, was abandoned. Later that month following an offensive against the post of Zigueï in the north of Kanem, Goukouni's troops were attacked by French military aircraft, one of which was destroyed. The French subsequently decided to extend the limit of the exclusion zone to the 16th parallel (the 'Koro Toro–Oum Chalouba line').

THE FORMATION OF UNIR AND REORGANIZATION OF THE OPPOSITION

During early 1984 it became increasingly evident that Habré needed to regain support in southern Chad in order to consolidate political power. At a conference of *préfets* in April, the army's treatment of civilians and its interference in administrative and judicial affairs were criticized, and in May several senior members of the security forces were removed from office. In June Habré dissolved the FROLINAT–FAN faction, and created a new official party, the Union nationale pour l'indépendance et la révolution (UNIR). Six of the 15 members of UNIR's executive bureau were southerners, but former FAN officials maintained a prominent role in the new party. The formation of UNIR was, however, regarded as a move towards national reconciliation and the creation of a democratic, unified government. In a government reshuffle, which took place in July, one-half of the ministerial posts (including the foreign affairs portfolio) were allocated to southerners.

In late August 1984 the guerrilla commandos (*commandos rouges,* or *codos*), led by Col Alphonse Kotiga, suspended negotiations with the government, and resumed hostilities. The entire region of southern Chad, apart from Mayo-Kebbi, returned to civil war. The subsequent repression of the rebellion by government forces inflicted considerable suffering on the civilian population, and about 25,000 refugees fled to the CAR. The conduct of government forces effectively intensified religious and ethnic rivalries, and negated any political advantages that had been gained by the formation of UNIR.

Meanwhile, increasing dissension among anti-Habré forces emerged, resulting in the formation by GUNT factions of new 'splinter groups' and an anti-Goukouni movement. At a meeting of GUNT factions, which took place in August 1985, a Conseil suprême de la révolution (CSR), comprising seven anti-government groupings, under the presidency of Goukouni, was formed. Later that year, however, several former opposition factions declared support for the Habré regime, including the Front démocratique du Tchad (FDT) and the Comité d'action et de concertation (CAC–CDR), which had broken away from the pro-Goukouni CDR.

In November 1984, following offers of financial remuneration by Habré, some 1,200 *codos* joined government forces; by the end of the year hostilities had ceased.

FRENCH WITHDRAWAL AND LIBYAN INCURSIONS

Negotiations between France and Libya resulted in an agreement, which was signed in September 1984, providing for the simultaneous withdrawal from Chad of French and Libyan forces. The evacuation of French forces was completed in early November, but Libyan troops remained, in contravention of the agreement. Following unsuccessful representations to Qaddafi, the French government conceded that it had been misled, and that it would not enforce Libyan withdrawal from northern Chad, but would intervene if Libyan forces advanced towards N'Djamena. President Mitterrand recognized Chad's claim to the 'Aozou strip', while criticizing Habré for jeopardizing national unity, in favour of territorial gain. A national reconciliation conference, held in October 1984, ended in failure.

From October 1985 Libya began to reinforce its military presence in the north of Chad, assembling an estimated 4,000 troops. In November President Mitterrand reiterated that France would respond to any Libyan military action in Chad. In February 1986, however, GUNT forces initiated Libyan-supported attacks on government positions to the south of the 16th parallel. The offensive was repelled by the FANT, and Habré appealed to France for increased military aid. Shortly afterwards French military aircraft, operating from the CAR, bombed a Libyan-built airstrip at Ouadi Doum, north-east of Faya-Largeau. A retaliatory air strike on N'Djamena airport caused minor damage. France subsequently established an air strike force at N'Djamena to counteract any further Libyan attack (an intervention which was known as *'Opération Epervier'*), while the USA provided supplementary military aid to Habré's forces. Further incursions across the interdiction line in March were repelled by FANT ground forces. Later that month hostilities ceased temporarily, following the capture by government forces of a rebel base at Chicha.

HABRÉ'S RECAPTURE OF THE NORTH

In March 1986 Habré appointed several former opponents to the council of ministers. Meanwhile, divisions within the GUNT increased; Goukouni's refusal to attend OAU-convened reconciliation talks prompted the resignation in June of the vice-president of the GUNT, Col Kamougue, who transferred his support to Habré in February 1987 and joined the government in August of that year. In August 1986 Acheikh Ibn Oumar's CDR withdrew its support for Goukouni, leaving the latter virtually isolated. Later that month clashes between FAP and CDR troops occurred in the Tibesti region. By October Goukouni had indicated his willingness to negotiate with Habré, amid indications that the FAP had decided to join Habré's FANT. Goukouni was subsequently wounded during an alleged attempt at abduction by Libyan troops in Tripoli, and in mid-November, with Libyan support, Oumar assumed the presidency of a reconstituted GUNT coalition, comprising seven of the original 11 factions, including the Mouvement révolutionnaire du peuple (MRP), formerly led by Kamougue.

In December 1986 clashes took place in the Tibesti region between Libyan forces and the now pro-Habré FAP. In January 1987 FANT troops recaptured a number of strategic targets in the north of the country. Following a Libyan offensive on the southern town of Arada, France launched a retaliatory air attack against the airbase of Ouadi Doum; in March Ouadi Doum was recaptured by the FANT. Libyan forces subsequently began to retreat, evacuating Faya-Largeau, and by May Habré's troops had regained control of northern Chad, with Libya occupying only the Aozou region. In August the FANT seized control of the town of Aozou, the administrative centre of the region, but later had to withdraw to positions in Tibesti, following a series of Libyan air attacks on Chadian targets. In September Habré's forces entered south-eastern Libya, where they attacked and occupied the military base of Maaten-es-Sarra. A Libyan military aircraft was subsequently shot down over N'Djamena by the French defensive force, and French positions at Abéché were bombed. (In protest at this offensive, the French government suspended supplies of arms to Chad until December.) In September a cease-fire, which had been mediated by the OAU, took effect. However, the Chadian government claimed that Libyan aircraft continued to infringe Chadian airspace, and that members of a Libyan-supported 'Islamic Legion' had clashed with members of the FANT near the Sudanese border. There was also a considerable reinforcement of the Libyan bases in the Aozou region and in Toummo (in Niger). Military engagements took place in November 1987, near Goz Beïda, and in March 1988, to the east of Ennedi.

RECONCILIATION WITH LIBYA

A meeting between the heads of state of Chad and Libya, under the aegis of the OAU *ad hoc* committee (which had been established in 1977 to debate the question of the sovereignty of the Aozou region) was scheduled for May 1988. Shortly before the summit it was announced that Qaddafi (who had repeatedly boycotted meetings of the *ad hoc* committee) would not be attending, in protest at Chad's treatment of prisoners of war. However, Qaddafi subsequently announced his willingness to recognize the Habré régime, invited Habré and Goukouni to meet in Libya for discussions concerning reconciliation and offered to provide financial aid for the reconstruction of bombed towns in northern Chad. Habré reacted with caution to Qaddafi's proposals, but in early June announced that his government was prepared to restore diplomatic relations with Libya, which had been suspended in 1982. Following discussions between the ministers of foreign affairs of the two countries, which took place in Gabon in July 1988, both Chad and Libya agreed, in principle, to the restoration of diplomatic relations, although the questions of the fate of Libyan prisoners of war in Chad, the disputed sovereignty of the Aozou region and the future security of common borders remained unresolved. In October, following mediation by Togo, Chad and Libya issued a joint communiqué expressing their willingness to seek a peaceful solution to the territorial dispute, and to co-operate with the OAU committee appointed for that purpose. The cease-fire was reaffirmed, diplomatic relations were resumed, and the two countries exchanged ambassadors in November.

INTERNAL DEVELOPMENTS

In July 1987 reconciliation talks between Habré and Goukouni (who had been resident in Algiers since February) ended in failure. Following a ministerial reshuffle in August, both Kamougue and the former leader of the *codos,* Col Kotiga Guerina, joined the government. In February 1988 a number of former opposition parties, including the FAP and the CAC–CDR, merged with UNIR. In March the GUNT was reconstituted under Goukouni, following a dispute with Oumar regarding the leadership. In November, following the conclusion of a peace agreement in Iraq, forces led by Oumar declared support for Habré, and subsequently returned to Chad. In January 1989 it was announced that the GUNT was willing to resume negotiations with the Habré government.

Despite a semblance of unity, which was exemplified in March 1989 by the appointment of Oumar as minister of foreign affairs, political tensions persisted. In early April the minister of the interior and territorial administration, Ibrahim Mahamat Itno, was arrested, following the discovery of an alleged plot to overthrow the Habré government. The c-in-c of the armed forces, Hassan Djamous, and his predecessor in that post, Idriss Deby (who were both implicated in the conspiracy), fled to Sudan with their supporters. FANT troops were dispatched to quell the mutiny, during which Djamous was killed. Meanwhile, Deby escaped to Libya (with Sudanese assistance), and in June formed a new opposition movement, the 'Action du 1 avril' in Sudan. In July the unity of GUNT was undermined, when a number of factions announced their withdrawal from the coalition. A reorganization of the council of ministers took place in October, following the death of the minister of planning and co-operation, Soumaila Mahamat. (Mahamat was among 171 people who were killed when a French airliner exploded in September, shortly after leaving N'Djamena.) In February 1990 two ministers were dismissed from the government.

In July 1988 a presidential decree established a committee to formulate a new constitution. Constitutional proposals were submitted to Habré in June 1989, and a draft document was approved in a national referendum on 10 December (reportedly receiving the support of 99.94% of votes cast). The new constitution, which was promulgated on 20 December, endorsed Habré as president for a further seven-year term, upheld the principle of a sole ruling party, and envisaged the creation of a legislative body, the national assembly, which was to be elected, with a five-year mandate, by direct universal suffrage. At legislative elections, which took place in July 1990, 436 candidates (many of whom were members of UNIR) contested 123 seats; 56% of the registered electorate voted. However, several prominent members of UNIR failed to secure seats in the new legislature.

DIPLOMATIC ACTIVITY

Although a Libyan delegation attended the second UNIR congress in November 1988, relations between the two countries remained strained. Chad continued to accuse Libya of repeated violations of the cease-fire agreement, and in December clashes between Chadian and pro-Libyan forces near the border with Sudan were reported. Relations between the two countries deteriorated further in mid-1989, when Habré accused Qaddafi of preparing a further military offensive against Chad (with the support of the al-Mahdi regime in Sudan). Subsequent negotiations between Habré and Qaddafi were inconclusive, owing to Habré's rejection of proposals made by President Chadli of Algeria, which envisaged the withdrawal of the *'Opération Epervier'* force from Chad. At the end of August, however, Oumar and the Libyan minister of foreign affairs, Jadellah Azouz at-Tali, signed a draft agreement (*accord cadre*), which envisaged the peaceful resolution of the dispute: if a political settlement were not achieved within one year, the issue would be submitted to arbitration by the International Court of Justice (ICJ). Provision was made for all armed forces to be withdrawn from the Aozou region, under the supervision of non-partisan African observers, and for the release of all prisoners of war. Chad and Libya reaffirmed their commitment to the principles of the September 1987 cease-fire agreement, and declared a policy of mutual non-interference in each other's internal affairs: hostile radio broadcasts and financial or military support for dissidents were to cease. In September, however, the first session of a Chad-Libya joint commission, which was to oversee the implementation of the agreement, broke down over arrangements for the release of Libyan prisoners of war. Later that year the agreement was further undermined by the resumption of hostilities between the FANT and pro-Libyan forces along Chad's border with Sudan.

In March 1990 Deby and his supporters, the Forces patriotiques du salut (subsequently known as the Mouvement patriotique du salut, MPS), invaded eastern Chad from bases in Sudan. France dispatched military equipment and personnel to reinforce *'Opération Epervier'* at Abéché: although the French contingent did not participate in the military engagements, its presence undoubtedly induced the rebel forces to retreat. In late March discussions between Oumar and Libyan officials, which took place in Gabon, were undermined by a statement issued by the Chad government, alleging Libyan and Sudanese support for the MPS; the accusations were denied by the leaders of both countries. In May the fifth session of the Chad-Libya joint commission was compromised by the seizure, by Chadian forces, of 10 Libyan vehicles on Sudanese territory; Libya subsequently protested to the UN and the OAU at this offensive against what were claimed to be civilian vehicles. Following an emergency session of the executive bureau of UNIR in late July, the Chad government alleged that Libya and Sudan were massing forces in Sudan's Darfur region, in preparation for a major offensive against Chad. Subsequent discussions between Chadian and Libyan delegates failed to secure agreement. In late August, however, shortly before the agreed deadline for a settlement, apparently successful negotiations between Habré and Qaddafi took place in Morocco. Both governments subsequently agreed to refer the territorial dispute for adjudication by the ICJ.

DEBY TAKES POWER

On 10 November 1990 forces led by Deby, which were believed to number some 2,000, again invaded Chad from Sudan, and launched an attack on positions held by Chadian government forces at Tiné, to the north-east of Abéché. The governments of Libya and Sudan again denied accusations of complicity in the offensive. The FANT initially forced the rebels to retreat to Sudan; however, the attacks were soon resumed, and by mid-November the MPS was reported to have captured Tiné. Despite an appeal by Habré to the French government for military assistance, the *'Opération Epervier'* contingent, which had been reinforced to protect French interests in the region, took no part in the military engagements. The MPS continued to consolidate its position in eastern Chad, and many FANT units reportedly transferred their allegiance to Deby. Negotiations concerning the sovereignty of the Aozou region, which had been scheduled for late November, were suspended by Qaddafi, who claimed that recent Chadian allegations of Libyan involvement in the rebel invasion had undermined conditions for the discussions. Although the US government declared its full support for Habré, France maintained its policy of non-intervention in Chad's internal affairs. (It was widely believed that France's lack of support for the incumbent regime reflected Habré's failure to initiate a transition towards multi-party democracy.)

On 29 November 1990 the MPS seized control of Abéché. On the following day, Habré, together with members of his family and of the council of ministers, fled to Maroua, in eastern Cameroon. Deby arrived in N'Djamena two days later. A curfew was immediately imposed, in an attempt to suppress the rioting and looting that had followed Habré's flight from the capital. Deby subsequently declared his commitment to the creation of a democratic multi-party political system. In December the national assembly was dissolved, and the constitution suspended. Shortly afterwards a provisional council of state was established, and Deby assumed power as interim head of state. The new 33-member council of state mainly comprised members of the MPS and allied parties; however, Oumar (hitherto the minister of foreign affairs in the Habré government), was appointed special adviser to the head of state. A number of political organizations that had opposed Habré subsequently declared their support for the MPS. Goukouni Oueddei declared his willingness to begin political discussions with the new government, despite persistent reports that he was massing forces in northern Chad. Also in December a report, compiled by the MPS, accused Habré of violations of human rights and of corruption. Deby subsequently sought Habré's extradition from Senegal (where he had been granted political asylum) so that he might be tried on criminal charges. Later that month the curfew was removed, and the government announced that the FANT was to be restructured to form a smaller republican army, to be known as the Armées nationales tchadiennes (ANT), and that a national gendarmerie was to replace the military police.

Following the accession to power of the MPS, it was announced that aid and co-operation agreements between France and the Habré government would be honoured, and that new accords would be formulated. The USA, however, refused to extend formal recognition to the new regime, on the grounds of Deby's allegedly close links with Libya, although it affirmed its commitment to honouring existing aid agreements. The Libyan and Sudanese governments declared support for the new regime and undertook not to allow forces hostile to Deby to operate in their territory. However, relations between Chad and Libya were temporarily strained, following the airlift, apparently organized by the USA and France, of an estimated 600 Libyan detainees, who had allegedly been trained by the USA to undertake military action against Qaddafi. A visit to Libya by Deby in February 1991 consolidated relations between the two countries; however, Deby refused to abandon Chad's claim to the sovereignty of the Aozou region, which remained under consideration by the ICJ.

On 1 March 1991 a national charter, which had been submitted by the executive committee of the MPS, was adopted for a 30-month transitional period, at the end of which a referendum was to be held to determine Chad's constitutional future. The charter confirmed Deby's appointment as president, head of state and chairman of the MPS, and required the government to institute measures to prepare for the implementation of a multi-party system. Under the terms of the charter, a new council of ministers and a 31-member legislative body, to be known as the council of the republic, were to replace the provisional council of state. On 4 March Deby was formally inaugurated as president. On the following day the council of state was dissolved, and the former president of the national assembly, Dr Jean Alingue Bawoyeu, was appointed prime minister in a new 29-member government, which included 16 new ministers. A number of influential portfolios were allocated to southerners. Later in March two political organizations which had opposed the Habré government amalgamated with the MPS.

POLITICAL REFORM

In early May 1991 an informal alliance of five principal opposition movements, led by Goukouni, demanded that the registration of political associations be immediately authorized, and that a national conference be convened to determine a programme for the transition to a multi-party system. Later that month Deby announced that a national conference, scheduled for May 1992, would prepare a new constitution to provide for the introduction of a multi-party system, and would be followed by legislative elections. Constitutional amendments permitting the registration of opposition movements would enter into force in January 1992; a commission would be established to draft legislation governing the future activity of political associations. Goukouni, who visited Chad (from Algeria) for the first time in nine years, subsequently met Deby to discuss the proposals for the introduction of a pluralist system. In early June a commission, which consisted of members of the council of the republic, was to submit recommendations concerning the authorization of political associations within 60 days. In July a minor reshuffle of the council of ministers was carried out.

On 1 October 1991 the council of ministers adopted the commission's recommendations, which stipulated conditions for the authorization of political associations. Under the new legislation, each political party was required to have a minimum of 30 founder members, three each from 10 of Chad's 14 prefectures; the formation of parties on an ethnic or regional basis was prohibited. The minister of the interior was obliged to approve the authorization of associations within three months of registration. However, the MPS was exempted from the conditions of registration, and opposition groups declared the legislation to be biased in its favour. In subsequent months a number of political organizations applied for legal recognition.

OPPOSITION TO THE DEBY GOVERNMENT

In September 1991 rebels attacked military garrisons in Tibesti, in northern Chad, killing 50 people. Deby alleged that the offensive was instigated by troops loyal to Habré, who had fled to Niger in December 1990. In October troops attacked an arsenal at N'Djamena airport in an attempt to seize power; some 40 people were killed in the ensuing fighting. Several officials, including the minister of the interior, Maldoum Bada Abbas, were arrested on charges connected with the incident. Although the government asserted that Abbas had been motivated by personal ambition, there was speculation that the coup attempt had been provoked by discontent within his ethnic group, the Hadjerai, who were under-represented in the council of ministers. The French government reaffirmed its support for the MPS, and announced that the *'Opération Epervier'* contingent would be reinforced by an additional 300 troops. Following the coup attempt, the Chad government abrogated a co-operation agreement with Libya which Abbas had negotiated in September, on the grounds that the sovereignty of the Aozou region remained in dispute. In December the government was extensively reshuffled and later that month a national commission was established to determine the composition and agenda of the national conference.

In late December 1991 some 3,000 troops loyal to Habré attacked several towns in the region of Lake Chad, in the west of the country. The rebels were reported to be members of the Mouvement pour la démocratie et le développement (MDD), an opposition group based in Libya, led by Goukouni Guët, a former supporter of Habré. Government forces, which launched a counter-offensive, initially suffered heavy losses. By early January 1992 the rebels had captured the towns of Liwa and Bol, and were advancing towards N'Djamena. The French government dispatched some 450 troops to reinforce the *'Opération Epervier'* force (which numbered about 1,100), ostensibly to protect French citizens in the area. Shortly afterwards the government claimed that the rebels had been defeated, and that the ANT had recaptured Liwa and Bol.

Following the failure of the insurrection, a number of prominent members of the opposition and former ministers of the Habré government, who were suspected of complicity in the rebellion, were arrested; several of these were reported to have been executed. The French government condemned the violence in N'Djamena, and warned that its continued support for Deby was dependent on the implementation of political reforms. Later in January 1992 the government reaffirmed its commitment to the process of democratization, and declared an amnesty for political prisoners (which also applied to those implicated in the coup attempt in October 1991, including Maldoum Bada Abbas). In February 1992 Abbas was appointed as president of a new provisional council of the republic. However, ethnic factions within the ANT continued to carry out acts of violence against civilians in the capital, particularly against southerners; in mid-February a prominent member of the human rights organization, the Ligue tchadienne des droits des hommes (LTDH), was killed, reportedly by soldiers loyal to Deby. The LTDH and other opposition groups subsequently organized demonstrations and a two-day strike in support of its demands for the resignation of the government.

In February 1992 government forces suppressed an alleged coup attempt, when a group of disaffected soldiers, reported to be members of the Comité de sursaut national pour la paix et la démocratie (CSNPD), attacked a police station in N'Djamena. The LTDH and other opposition groups claimed that the incident had been fabricated by the government, in an attempt to divert attention from the generally disorderly conduct of troops stationed in N'Djamena. In March four French citizens stated to have been involved in the incident were expelled from Chad. In early April the French government announced that the role of *'Opération Epervier'* as a defensive air-strike force was to cease, although French troops were to remain in the country to assist in the restructuring of the ANT. This change in policy was widely interpreted as a warning to Deby to end the human rights violations perpetrated against opponents of the government, and to continue with the implementation of democratic reform. In the same month the MDD claimed that more than 40 of its members, including Goukouni Guët, had been arrested in Nigeria in February, extradited to Chad, and subsequently imprisoned or executed. Later in April soldiers belonging predominantly to the Zaghawa ethnic group surrounded the presidential palace in protest at government plans to demilitarize N'Djamena and to reduce the number of personnel in the ANT, which, it was feared, would restrict the influence of the Zaghawa ethnic group in the armed forces. After mediation by the minister of state for public works and transport, Abbas Koti (himself a Zaghawa), the troops agreed to withdraw.

In May 1992 the national conference, which had been envisaged as the next stage in the process towards democracy, was postponed, on the grounds that the preparatory commission had not completed its work; it was indicated that the conference would take place in September of that year. During May a number of amendments to the national charter were adopted, in accordance with recommendations by the council of the republic. Under the revised charter, the prime minister was permitted to assume the interim presidency, in the absence of the president. In late May Joseph Yodoyman, a member of the Alliance nationale pour la démocratie et le développement (ANDD), replaced Bawoyeu as prime minister. Deby formed a new council of ministers, which included, for the first time, five members of the opposition. However, it was reported that other opposition leaders had refused to join the government, while the influence of southerners in the council of ministers was also reduced. By the end of May some 10 political parties had been granted legal recognition, including the Union pour la démocratie et la République (UDR), led by Bawoyeu.

In late May 1992 rebels affiliated to the MDD launched a further attack in the region of Lake Chad, which was reported to have been led by a former minister in the GUNT, Moussa Medela. Government forces subsequently counter-attacked from Nigerian territory. In mid-June an agreement between the government and the CSNPD, which was led by Lt (later Col) Moise Nodji Kette, provided for the release of members of the CSNPD in detention. Later that month the government announced that it had pre-empted a coup attempt, led by Abbas Koti. Shortly afterwards supporters of Koti, known as the Conseil de redressement du Tchad (CNRT), attacked government forces in the region of Lake Chad; fighting was also reported at Chicha, near Faya-Largeau. At the end of June an agreement, which was signed in Libreville, Gabon, between the government and the MDD, provided for a cessation of hostilities and the immediate release of those imprisoned for their membership of the MDD. In July, however, government forces were reported to have launched renewed attacks against MDD troops in the region of Lake Chad.

In July 1992 the trade union federation, the Union syndicats du Tchad (UST), organized a series of strikes, in protest at government plans to reduce salaries and to increase taxes. Later that month Yodoyman was expelled from the ANDD for allegedly failing to support the process of democratic reform. Shortly afterwards the minister of the civil service and labour, Nabia Ndali (who was a member of the ANDD), resigned from the government. In early August three representatives of human rights organizations serving in the government, including a member of the LTDH, also resigned, in protest at the continued violent acts by security forces in N'Djamena. The council of ministers was subsequently reorganized. In the same month clashes between CSNPD forces and government troops were reported from Doba, in southern Chad. In September the government signed further peace agreements with the MDD, the CSNPD and an opposition movement based in Sudan, the Front national du Tchad (FNT).

In October 1992 public-sector workers staged a one-month general strike, which was organized by the UST, in support of demands for higher salaries and the convening of the national conference (which had been postponed since May). Two members of the opposition who held ministerial portfolios resigned in protest at the subsequent ban imposed by the government on the activities of the UST; a minor reorganization of the council of ministers followed. In mid-October, in response to increasing public pressure, the government announced that the national conference was to take place in January 1993. Later in October 1992 MDD forces launched a further offensive against the ANT at Bagassola, in the region of Lake Chad. At the end of October the MDD claimed that the government had received armaments from Libya, in preparation for the resumption of hostilities, and renounced the peace agreement, signed in September. In November a number of prominent members of the UST were arrested, after the general strike was extended for a further month. Later in November the government ended the ban that had been imposed on the UST, but suspended the civil servants who continued to observe the general strike. In December renewed clashes between government forces and members of the MDD occurred near Lake Chad. In that month a co-operation agreement, signed by the governments of Chad and Libya, was criticized by opposition parties. In early January 1993 the government withdrew the sanctions that had been imposed on a number of civil servants, and the general strike effectively ended. Later that month FROLINAT announced that three of its long-standing leaders, including Goukouni Oueddei, had been removed, and party organs dissolved.

CONSTITUTIONAL TRANSITION AND CIVIL UNREST

In mid-January 1993 some 800 delegates (representing, among others, the organs of state and 30 political organizations, together with trade unions and other professional associations) attended the opening of the national conference, which was to prepare for the establishment of a democratic system of government. However, following disputes over a motion confirming the sovereign status of the conference, proceedings were temporarily delayed. In the same month it was reported that members of the CSNPD had attacked government forces at Gore, in the south. Later in January an abortive coup attempt was mounted by troops loyal to Habré during a visit by Deby to Paris. In February government troops, in conflict with the MDD in the region of Lake Chad, clashed with members of the Nigerien armed forces, after attacking rebel bases in Niger. In the same month, following renewed military engagements between government troops and the CSNPD in southern Chad, opposition groups claimed that members of the ANT had conducted massacres of civilians in the region of Gore, prompting increased tension between the population of the north and south. By March some 15,000 civilians had fled from southern Chad to the CAR, following atrocities committed by government forces. In the same month it was reported that Koti (who had been arrested in Cameroon in December 1992) had escaped from detention.

MOUNGAR'S TRANSITIONAL GOVERNMENTS

The progress of the national conference was impeded by controversy over demands for the extension of the use of Arabic for official communications; in April 1993, however, the conference adopted a transitional charter, elected Dr Fidèle Moungar, the minister of national and higher education, to be prime minister, and established a 57-member interim legislature, the conseil supérieur de la transition (CST). The leader of the Rassemblement pour la démocratie et le progrès (RDP), ex-president Choua, was elected chairman of the CST. Under the terms of the transitional charter, Deby was to remain in office as head of state and c-in-c of the armed forces for a period of one year (with provision for one extension), while a transitional government, under the supervision of the CST, was to implement economic, political and social programmes, drafted by the conference; multi-party elections were to take place at the end of this period. Later in April Moungar appointed a transitional government, which retained only four members of the former council of ministers and included representatives of a number of opposition parties.

In early May 1993, following a report by a commission of inquiry, the transitional government confirmed that members of the ANT had carried out a number of massacres of civilians in southern Chad earlier that year, apparently in reprisal for hostilities initiated by the CSNPD. Moungar announced that officials implicated in the violence had been arrested, that military units in the region were to be replaced, and that a judicial investigation was to take place. In the same month, in compliance with the resolutions of the national conference, Deby dissolved the government intelligence service, which had attracted criticism from opposition and human rights groups. Later in May a human rights organization, Chad Non-Violence, withdrew its representative from the CST, in protest at the violence perpetrated by members of the ATN, and at the alleged failure of the government to observe the decisions of the national conference. In June the CST refused to ratify the co-operation agreement that had been signed with Libya in November 1992, in view of the unresolved dispute over the sovereignty of the Aozou region (which was to be reviewed at the ICJ later that month). In late June 1993 Moungar announced the formation of a new transitional government, in which the number of members were reduced from 30 to 17. In the same month widespread concern at the increasing incidence of violent crime emerged, following the assassination of the director of the soldiers' reintegration committee by troops in N'Djamena. In an attempt to restore civil order, the transitional government subsequently introduced a number of new security measures, and in early July announced that the ANT and the security forces were to be reorganized. Violent crime continued throughout the country, however, and in early July a one-day general strike, organized by opposition parties, was staged in protest at the continuing civil disorder.

In early August 1993 some 82 civilians were killed in the region of Chokoyam, in Ouaddai, apparently as a result of ethnic differences. Shortly afterwards it was reported that some 41 people had been killed when a demonstration, staged by residents of N'Djamena (originating from Ouaddai) in protest at the massacre, was violently suppressed by the republican guard. The CST accused the government of exceeding its powers by deploying the republican guard to disperse the demonstration, and by imposing a national curfew in response to the unrest. In mid-August Koti (who had denied allegations by the government that CNRT troops had carried out the massacre in Ouaddai) returned to Chad, after a peace agreement was reached by the CNRT and the Chadian authorities. In September, despite efforts by the government to allay discontent in the south, the CSNPD threatened to impede plans to exploit petroleum reserves in the region of Doba, in southern Chad (which were considered to be essential to future prospects of economic development), unless the government met its demands for the establishment of a federal state. In mid-October Koti signed a further agreement with the government, whereby the CNRT was to be granted legal status as a political party and its forces were to be integrated into the ANT. However, Koti was subsequently killed by security forces while allegedly resisting arrest on charges of involvement in a conspiracy to overthrow the government. The CNRT rejected claims by the authorities that documents, signed by Koti, detailing plans to stage an armed coup had been discovered, and announced that hostilities with government forces would be resumed. (Koti's brother, Hissène, subsequently assumed leadership of the CNRT.)

KOUMAKOYE AND OPPOSITION PRESSURE

In September 1993 increasing disagreement between Deby and Moungar concerning government policy intensified, after Deby dismissed the minister of finance and computer sciences, Robert Roingam, without consulting Moungar. Although relations between Deby and Moungar appeared to improve following the appointment of a successor to Roingam, in October a motion expressing 'no confidence' in the Moungar administration, apparently initiated by supporters of Deby, was approved in the CST by 45 of the 56 votes cast. Moungar subsequently resigned and his government was dissolved. In early November the CST elected Delwa Kassire Koumakoye, hitherto the minister of justice and keeper of the seals, as prime minister. Later that month a new 16-member transitional government, which included 10 members of the former administration, was appointed.

In December 1993 a 17-member 'institutional committee' was established to prepare a draft constitution, an electoral code and legislation governing the registration of political organizations; the committee, which included representatives of the transitional organs and a number of political parties, was to submit recommendations within a period of two months. However, industrial action by public sector workers (particularly by teachers) in protest at the government's continued failure to pay arrears in salaries resumed, and in January 1994 the government banned an opposition demonstration and threatened to implement sanctions against striking civil servants. Later that month the transitional government was reshuffled. Meanwhile, opposition activity continued: the MDD and the Union nationale pour la démocratie et le socialisme announced that they were to unite against government forces, while members of the FNT, who apparently were to have been integrated into the army following a peace agreement, attacked a military garrison at Abéché. (It was subsequently reported that more than 200 people had been killed in ensuing clashes between the FNT and government forces.) Also in January Cameroon claimed that members of the CNRT, who were allegedly planning to launch an attack on N'Djamena, had killed members of the Cameroonian security forces in the north of that country. In February negotiations between the government and the CSNPD, which were mediated by the government of the CAR, resulted in a cease-fire agreement; the discussions subsequently ended in failure, however, and further clashes between government and CSNPD forces took place in the south of the country at the end of March.

THE RETURN OF THE AOZOU REGION

In February 1994 the ICJ ruled in favour of Chad in the dispute over the sovereignty of the Aozou region, thereby upholding the provisions of a treaty that had been signed in 1955 by the governments of France and Libya. Later that month, however, Chad claimed that Libya had deployed additional troops in the region. In March discussions between the governments of Chad and Libya to establish a timetable for the withdrawal of Libyan troops resulted in little progress, apparently owing to Libyan insistence on adherence to the agreement that had been reached in 1989, providing for repatriation of Libyan prisoners of war. Nevertheless, the Libyan government maintained that it would comply with the ICJ ruling, and in April agreed to commence the withdrawal of troops from the region, in an operation that was to be monitored by UN observers and officials from both countries. At the end of May 1994 Libya and Chad issued a joint statement confirming that the withdrawal of Libyan troops had been completed as scheduled. In June the two governments signed a co-operation agreement.

CONSTITUTIONAL PROPOSALS

In March 1994 the institutional committee presented recommendations for a draft constitution, which included provisions for the election of a president for a term of five years, the installation of a bicameral legislature and a constitutional court, and the establishment of a decentralized administrative structure. In April, in accordance with demands by the opposition, the CST extended the transitional period for one year, on the grounds that the government had achieved little progress in the preparation for democratic elections. A new electoral timetable was adopted, whereby the government was obliged to provide funds for the organization of the elections and reach an agreement with the UST in order to end industrial unrest. The government also agreed to implement further preparatory measures by June, which included the adoption of an electoral code, the establishment of a national reconciliation council (which was to negotiate a peace settlement with rebel movements) and the appointment of electoral and human rights commissions. The constitutional recommendations were to be submitted for approval at a national referendum in December; in the event that the new constitution was adopted by the electorate, legislative elections would take place in January 1995, followed by a presidential election in March.

Subsequent government efforts to negotiate a settlement with the UST in accordance with the stipulations of the new electoral timetable were impeded by further strike action, which was initiated by public sector workers at the end of April, in support of demands for an increase in salaries to compensate for the effects of the devaluation of the CFA franc in January 1994. Despite the promulgation of a presidential decree at the beginning of May declaring the strike to be illegal, industrial action continued throughout that month. Also in May, despite apparent opposition from Deby, the government established a 12-member national reconciliation council, which was to initiate negotiations with the opposition engaged in hostilities. Later that month Deby announced an extensive government reorganization, in which nine ministers were removed. However, one of the newly-appointed ministers, Salomon Ngarbaye Tombalbaye, the son of the former president and leader of the Mouvement pour la démocratie et le socialisme du Tchad, refused to serve in the government, on the grounds of its continued failure to address social and economic hardship in the country. In June the CSNPD denied claims by the Chad authorities that a number of its members had joined government forces. (Following the failure of the peace negotiations in March, the government of the CAR had prohibited the CSNPD from conducting military operations from CAR territory.) In early July the government and the UST reached a negotiated settlement, which provided for a limited increase in salaries and the payment of arrears.

TRANSITIONAL POLITICS

In August 1994, following the resumption of negotiations between the Chadian authorities and the CSNPD (with mediation by the government of the CAR), the two sides signed a cease-fire agreement, which provided for the recognition of the CSNPD as a legal political organization, and the integration of its forces into the ANT; the implementation of the agreement was to be supervised by a committee, comprising representatives of the UN and the governments of the CAR, France and Gabon. Later that month, however, it was reported that government troops had killed some 26 civilians in southern Chad, in reprisal for attacks by members of another rebel faction, known as the Forces armées pour la République fédérale (FARF). In mid-August the government convened a four-day national conference to allow the proposal of amendments to the draft constitution; dissent was reported between government and opposition participants in the debate, particularly concerning the extent of the executive powers vested in the constitutional president. The draft constitution was to be reviewed by the government with regard to the recommendations of the conference, and subsequently to be submitted for approval at a national referendum. In September, following discussions between Koumakoye and the Sudanese head of state regarding the occupation (in August) by Sudanese troops of Chadian villages near the border with Sudan; a co-operation agreement was signed, which provided for a new demarcation of the Chad–Sudan frontier.

In September 1994 it was reported that the minister of mines and energy, Lt-Col Mahamat Garfa (who had apparently opposed his recent dismissal from the post of chief of army staff), had fled N'djamena with substantial government funds, and, together with some 600 members of the ANT, had joined CNRT forces in eastern Chad. In October Choua (who had previously been re-elected twice as chairman of the CST) was replaced by a member of the MPS, Mahamat Bachar Ghadaia. Choua susequently accused the government of perpetrating violations of human rights, including the assassination of two prominent members of the RDP, after several RDP activists were arrested, apparently on the grounds that they were supporters of the MDD. Also in October the government and the FNT negotiated a peace agreement, which was, however, subsequently repudiated by the leader of the FNT. Despite minor impediments in the implementation of the agreement that had been signed by the government and the CSNPD, in November a number of former members of the CSNPD were integrated into the ANT, including the leader of the movement, Col Moise Nodji Kette. Later in November Deby officially announced that the process of democratic transition would end on 9 April 1995, following presidential and legislative elections. (A number of opposition alliances had been established in preparation for the forthcoming elections, including a coalition led by Moungar, the Collectif des partis pour le changement.)

In early December 1994 Deby announced a general amnesty for political prisoners and opposition members in exile (excluding Habré); a number of political detainees were subsequently released. Nevertheless, the LTDH continued to accuse Deby of violations of human rights, in view of reprisals undertaken by the ANT for rebel activity. Later in December a minor reshuffle of the transitional government took place. In January 1995 the CST adopted a new electoral code, after the French government expressed concern at delays in the preparation for democratic elections. In the same month an independent national electoral commission was established. Later in January the CST approved the draft constitution, which had been amended in accordance with recommendations reached by consensus at the national conference; the constitution was to be submitted for ratification at a national referendum. In February the CSNPD claimed that the Chadian government had violated the cease-fire agreement reached in August. In the same month a loose grouping of the opposition movements, known as the Concertation des partis politiques (CPP), demanded that the transitional organs of government be dissolved and a new administration installed by the stipulated date in April.

In February and early March 1995 the government conducted a population census with the aim of revising the electoral register; following reports of widespread irregularities, however, opposition parties accused the MPS of attempted electoral malpractice and demanded that a new census be organized. On 30 March the CST extended the transitional period for a further year and amended the national charter to the effect that the incumbent prime minister was henceforth prohibited from contesting the forthcoming presidential election or from belonging to a political party. These measures prompted strong criticism from opposition parties, which subsequently instituted a legal challenge to the extension of the transitional period at the court of appeal. In early April the CST voted in favour of Koumakoye's removal from the office of prime minister, after criticizing him for the government's lack of progress in the organization of democratic elections. (Koumakoye opposed his dismissal, which he declared to be unconstitutional.) On 8 April the CST elected Djimasta Koibla, a prominent member of the Union pour la démocratie et la République (UDR), as prime minister. A new transitional government was subsequently formed; despite the CSNPD's condemnation of the extension of the transitional period, Kette joined the cabinet as minister of the environment and tourism. In the same month the results of the population census were annulled by the court of appeal on grounds of procedural irregularities. (A new census was to be conducted with financial assistance from the French government and the European Union.) In early May the national electoral commission scheduled the constitutional referendum for November 1995; the presidential election was to take place on 11 February 1996 (with a possible second round on 3 March), while legislative elections were to follow on 28 April and 11 May.

In May 1995 Amnesty International and the LTDH claimed that members of the ANT had perpetrated human rights' violations against civilians in retaliation for rebel attacks. In June members of the armed forces raided the premises of an independent newspaper, N'Djamena-Hebdo, which had reportedly published an article criticizing the activities of the ANT. Deby subsequently announced an inquiry into the incident, in response to ensuing widespread protests. Later that month the authorities banned a demonstration which had been planned by the opposition in protest at the government's continued failure to adopt democratic conditions. In July a unilateral government declaration of a national cease-fire was received with caution by the rebel movements. Later that month Koumakoye announced that he was to contest the forthcoming presidential election. Also in July the Chad government claimed that Nigerian troops had occupied a number of islands in the region of Lake Chad (which were under the sovereignty of Chad).

In August 1995 the chairman and other members of the executive bureau of the CST resigned, following accusations regarding the misappropriation of funds; a new chairman was subsequently elected. At the end of the month security forces raided the private residence of Saleh Kebzabo, the leader of an opposition movement, the Union nationale pour le développement et le renouveau (UNDR). The CPP subsequently announced that its member organizations were to suspend participation in the CST and the national reconciliation council, in protest at the raid, and demanded the resignation of the head of security forces. In September, however, Kebzabo was arrested and charged with endangering state security by associating with rebel groups, prompting further protests from the CPP, which urged his release. (Kebzabo was released on bail later that month.) In early November Deby announced that Gabon was to act as a mediator in reconciliation discussions between the government and political organizations and armed opposition groups, which were to be convened in December. However, a number of rebel movements subsequently presented preconditions to participation in the negotiations, including the dissolution of the national security agency. Later that month the government and the MDD signed a peace agreement providing for a cease-fire (which would take effect at the end of November), an exchange of prisoners and the integration of a number of MDD troops into the ANT. Also in November the independent national electoral commission promulgated a further timetable whereby a constitutional referendum was to take place at the end of March 1996, followed by a presidential election in early June and legislative elections later that year. A further population census commenced in December 1995. In the same month a minor reorganization of the transitional government was effected. The reconciliation discussions between the government and rebel movements were convened in Franceville, Gabon, in early January 1996, with mediation by the governments of Gabon, the CAR and Niger. However, a number of delegates from the rebel groups immediately objected that Deby had failed to invite representatives from all the opposition parties to the negotiations, and demanded his resignation. In March, following protracted negotiations, the government and 13 opposition parties signed an agreement providing for the imposition of a cease-fire and the establishment of a special security force to maintain order during the electoral period, while it was requested that the French troops stationed in the country provide additional assistance. It was reported, however, that the majority of armed movements had rejected the agreement.

PRESIDENTIAL AND LEGISLATIVE ELECTIONS

The conclusion of the Franceville agreement allowed the electoral timetable to proceed as scheduled. However, a number of opposition parties, particularly the southern-based organizations that supported the adoption of a federal system of government, urged their members to reject the draft constitution (which enshrined a unitary state) at the national referendum. Despite consequent opposition from the south of the country, the new constitution was adopted by 63.5% of votes cast at the referendum, which took place on 31 March 1996. It was subsequently announced that the multi-party presidential election was to take place in June, as planned. By April 15 presidential candidates, including Deby, had emerged; a further five potential candidates (including Moungar) had been rejected on the grounds that they failed to meet electoral regulations concerning residency in the country. In the same month a minor government reorganization was carried out after two ministers, who had announced their candidature, resigned their portfolios. Meanwhile, Koumakoye, who in March had been jailed for three months for the illegal possession of arms, was released shortly before the election. In the first round of voting, which took place on 2 June, Deby secured 43.8% of votes cast, while Kamougue (who had contested the election on behalf of the Union pour le renouveau et la démocratie—URD) obtained the second-highest number of votes, with 12.4%. Opposition parties subsequently claimed that the French government had supported efforts by the Chad authorities to perpetrate electoral fraud, while the majority of the candidates who had been eliminated urged a boycott of the second round. However, Kebzabo, who had contested the first round on behalf of the UNDR and had obtained the third-highest number of votes, agreed to transfer support to Deby. In early July the government suspended the activities of the UST, after it attempted to organize a boycott of the election; the ban was repealed at the end of that month.

The second round of the presidential election took place on 3 July 1996: according to official results, Deby was elected by 69.1% of votes cast (while Kamougue secured 30.9% of votes). Deby was officially inaugurated as president on 8 August, and subsequently reappointed Koibla to the office of prime minister. Later that month Koibla announced the formation of a new government, which included several opposition members, notably Kebzabo (who, in exchange for his support for Deby in the second round, received the portfolio of foreign affairs).

In early August 1996 the CNRT merged with another dissident faction, the Front d'action pour l'installation de la démocratie au Tchad (FAIDT), to form the Congrès pour le renouveau et la démocratie. Later that month the government and elements of the FARF signed a peace agreement, which provided for the imposition of a cease-fire and an amnesty for members of the faction, which was to be reconstituted as a legal political organization, the Front patriotique pour la démocratie. (The remaining rebel faction of the FARF, led by Laokein Barde, subsequently signed a peace accord with the government in April 1997; the accord included a stipulation that a political debate be initiated on whether Chad should be a unitary or a federal state.) In mid-September a further rebel movement, the Front national du Tchad renové (FNTR), threatened to abandon plans for peace negotiations with the Chadian authorities, after claiming that government forces had launched attacks against FNTR positions in eastern Chad. The government and a faction of the MDD signed a peace agreement in Niger at the end of September, which provided for a cease-fire and an amnesty for all members; a further peace accord was signed in December with a separate MDD faction. In the following month Deby announced that he had dispatched an adviser to meet representatives of other dissident factions, in an attempt to initiate peace negotiations.

In early October 1996 Amnesty International published a report accusing France of complicity in alleged violations of human rights in Chad; the allegations were denied by the French government. Deby appeared to concede that problems existed (and, in particular, that further training of the security forces might be necessary), but insisted that French training of Chadian troops had, in effect, improved human rights. In the same month the French minister of defence announced that, as a result of Chad's improved relations with neighbouring states, the mission of the *Epervier* force was to be redefined, but with no reduction in the number of troops deployed. In December Deby participated in a regional effort to mediate in the political crisis in the CAR and, in the following month, Chadian troops joined an African peace-keeping force which was to replace the French military presence in that country. Meanwhile Chad condemned Cameroon's expulsion of some 1,000 Chadian nationals following an incident on the border between the Cameroonian authorities and a group of armed individuals. In January human rights organizations, including the LTDH, severely criticized a decree sanctioning the summary execution of alleged criminals, which had resulted in dozens of shootings since its promulgation in November 1996. The decree was finally revoked as a result of international pressure, which included a condemnation of Chad by the European Union for serious violations of human rights.

Legislative elections, which had already been postponed in October 1996, were delayed further in November, and eventually took place on 5 January and 23 February 1997. A total of 658 candidates representing some 49 political parties contested the elections. Voting was reported to have been conducted relatively peacefully, however, a number of opposition activists, including two RDP candidates, were arrested for apparently disrupting the electoral process in N'Djamena. In early March preliminary results for a number of constituencies were challenged by both the MPS and opposition parties. Later that month the court of appeal announced the final results, allocating a further eight seats to the MPS, which thus secured an absolute majority with a total of 63 seats, while the URD won 29 seats, the UNDR 15, the UDR four, the Parti pour la liberté et le développement three, with nine seats shared by six other opposition parties. The national assembly was installed on 4 April, although by-elections were still to be held in two constituencies where the results of the first round of voting had been annulled. Kamougue was elected president of the national assembly by a large majority on 9 May, following an accord between his party (the URD), the MPS and the UNDR. Later that month Nassour Ouado (hitherto secretary-general at the president's office) was appointed prime minister and formed a new government, which included representatives from a range of political parties, although the MPS retained the most senior ministerial portfolios.

In August 1997 it was disclosed that Chad was to establish diplomatic relations with Taiwan; the People's Republic of China consequently announced the severance of its ties with Chad.

Economy

EDITH HODGKINSON

Chad is one of the poorest and least developed countries of continental Africa, and its geographical isolation, climate and meagre natural resources have resulted in an economy of very narrow range. The agricultural sector has traditionally dominated the economy, accounting for an estimated 40.3% of Chad's gross domestic product (GDP), and employing an estimated 80.8% of the labour force in 1995. The industrial and commercial sectors are small, and virtually all production facilities of the modern sector are installed in the south or in N'Djamena, the capital. Much economic activity is illicit, and very few statistics are published. There are hardly any all-weather roads and no railways. The country is land-locked and its major economic centres are situated 1,400–2,800 km from the sea. Its structural problems of economic development, which are immense in any circumstances, have been rendered still more acute by civil conflict and by drought.

The country's recent economic performance has thus been poor. GDP contracted by one-quarter in 1977–81, recovered slightly overall in the 1980s (with wide fluctuations from year to year) and then declined by nearly one-fifth in 1989-1993. The devaluation of the CFA franc in January 1994 stimulated the economy, benefiting both cotton and livestock production, and GDP increased by 7.1% in that year. The rate of growth slowed in 1995 (to an estimated 2.6%) because of a poor cereal harvest, but, with a surge in earnings from cotton, GDP growth was estimated at some 5% in 1996. While economic performance remains vulnerable to climatic conditions, and to world prices for a single commodity, the planned construction of a pipeline linking the oilfields in southern Chad to the Cameroonian port of Kribi should give a new impetus to economic growth in the final years of this decade, and offers the prospect of considerably higher income from the year 2000 (when petroleum production is due to commence). Meanwhile, GDP per head remained among the lowest in the world, at some US $165 in 1995.

AGRICULTURE

The main area of crop production is situated in the south of the country, with cattle production prevailing in the more arid northern zones. In the extreme north camel and sheep rearing, and date orchards are predominant. Subsistence agriculture accounts for three-quarters of annual crop production. The principal food crops are sorghum, millet and groundnuts. Cassava, rice, dates and maize are also grown for domestic consumption. As a result of drought, production of cereals in the 1984/85 crop year declined to 289,800 metric tons (the lowest for twenty years), and a severe famine ensued. Following the return of adequate rainfall, production recovered to 570,000–680,000 tons in the late 1980s. Despite adverse climatic conditions and serious food shortages in some parts of the country in 1990, grain production continued to increase and in 1995/96 a record crop of 908,000 tons of cereals came close to meeting the country's annual requirement of 1.1m. tons. The following year output decreased slightly, to some 840,000 tons. Some progress has been made in the cultivation of rice by modern methods. Rural development schemes, which have been implemented in southern Chad, with assistance from France, the EU, Canada and the World Bank, aim to increase production of cereals and livestock. However, major problems remain in the area of distribution and marketing, which have resulted in some localized scarcity.

Cotton is the dominant crop and principal export commodity. Production of cotton has been widely encouraged since the 1920s, and the crop was grown on some 210,000 ha in 1995/96, in the south of the country. Annual yields fluctuate widely, mainly reflecting rainfall patterns. Owing to civil conflict in the south in late 1984 and early 1985, and the decline in international prices for cotton in the following years, production declined to 89,500 metric tons in 1986/87, contributing to the substantial losses already incurred by the marketing monopoly, the Société cotonnière du Tchad (COTONTCHAD), largely as a result of mismanagement and corruption. This agency, which is 75% state-owned, is responsible for the provision of inputs and the purchasing, transportation, ginning and marketing of the crop, and the manufacture of cottonseed oil. In response to the near bankruptcy of COTONTCHAD in 1986, the country's donors contributed funds for its restructuring. The programme involved the closure of half of the cotton-ginning mills and the elimination of the subsidies on fertilizers and pesticides for farmers. Following the introduction of new pricing policies to provide greater incentives for production, seed cotton output increased to 174,500 tons in 1991/92. There was a sharp decline in output in the following two years, with only 94,900 tons recorded in 1993/94, as international prices weakened. However, the devaluation of the CFA franc in January 1994 was followed by a 50% increase in the producer price, which generated an immediate increase in output, to 135,000 tons in 1994/95. With world cotton prices rising strongly, producer prices were increased in each of the following two years, prompting more extensive planting (to cover a forecast 265,000 ha in 1996/97) and increased fertilizer and insecticide use. COTONTCHAD expected marketed production to reach an all-time record level of 204,600 tons in 1996/97.

Gum arabic, which is harvested from traditional plantations in the north, is a minor export product. Output has been adversely affected by drought and the unstable political situation: in the late 1980s annual production averaged 200 metric tons (compared with the record level of 1,100 tons produced in 1969). However, as with cotton, currency devaluation stimulated exports, which were reported to have quadrupled in value, to $26m., in 1994.

Livestock production has a significant role in the Chadian economy, accounting for 13% of GDP, and engaging about 40% of the labour force. It generally yields more in terms of cash income than the cotton industry, but much of this is not officially registered. Cattle raising is concentrated in the central part of the country, but as a result of drought cattle have moved southwards into the mainly-crop producing prefectures of Moyen Chari and Mayo-Kebbi. Livestock is often exported illicitly, without payment of taxes, and mainly to Nigeria where it is sold or bartered for consumer goods. In 1995, according to the

FAO, there were 4.5m. cattle and 5.5m. sheep and goats. In the long term there is considerable potential for livestock production in Chad, but its realization would require the upgrading of the herds and improvements in marketing arrangements. A large slaughterhouse has been constructed near N'Djamena, intended as the centre of an export-orientated meat industry. Fishing was an important economic activity in the Lake Chad region, but effectively ceased during the drought period in the early 1980s. However, the sector subsequently showed signs of recovery; in 1994, according to the FAO, the total catch amounted to 80,000 metric tons.

MINING, MANUFACTURING AND POWER

Exploitation of proven deposits of petroleum has been inhibited by the high cost of importing plant and machinery long distances with poor or non-existent transport facilities. In response to the increase in the international price of petroleum during the 1970s, however, Conoco, in conjunction with Shell, began petroleum extraction in the Sedigi region, to the north of Lake Chad, in 1977. Amounts available during 1979/80 were small—about 1,500 barrels per day (b/d)—but the precarious security situation resulted in the suspension of even this small output. In 1988 an agreement was signed with a consortium led by Exxon, Shell and Chevron, providing for the establishment of a petroleum refinery to exploit the reserves in the Sedigi region, estimated at 70m. tons. (In 1992 Elf Aquitaine replaced Chevron in the consortium.) The project was abandoned in 1993, but in the same year exploration in the Doba Basin (in southern Chad) revealed reserves of petroleum, which were initially estimated at 150m.–200m. barrels, but were subsequently revised upwards to 900m. barrels. The consortium of Exxon, Shell and Elf plans to develop 300 wells and install a processing facility, and begin production in the year 2000 at a rate of 200,000 b/d. An agreement was signed in January 1995 with the governments of Chad and Cameroon for the construction and operation of a 1,050-km pipeline to transport petroleum to the Cameroon port of Kribi. A protocol between the government of Chad and the three oil companies, signed in November 1996, also provided for the development of the Sedigi field, with the construction of a pipeline to supply a refinery in the capital. The Chad–Cameroon pipeline was estimated to cost some US $1,000m., and the entire project, including the oilfield development, some $4,000m. Sources of financing being explored in mid-1997 included the World Bank (through the International Development Association and the International Finance Corpn) and the African Development Bank.

Natron, found in pans on the northern edge of Lake Chad, is at present the only mineral of importance exploited in Chad. It is used as salt, for human and animal consumption, in the preservation of meats and hides and in soap production, and has been exported to Nigeria via the Logone river from N'Djamena. Evidence of other minerals—notably tin, uranium, bauxite and gold in the north—offers prospects for the future, but none has so far been exploited on a commercial scale.

Manufacturing (which accounted for 14.9% of GDP in 1995) is centred in N'Djamena and Moundou, and is mainly devoted to the processing of agricultural products. The processing of cotton is the principal industry; however, the importance of this sector declined during the 1980s, with the closure of one-half of COTONTCHAD's ginning mills (by the late 1980s annual ginning capacity was only 120,000 tons, compared with 184,000 tons at the beginning of the decade). The recovery in cotton production during the mid-1990s (see above) prompted COTONTCHAD to increase capacity at its eight mills in 1996/97. Cotton thread and cloth were produced by the Société textile du Tchad (STT) in Sarh; by 1989, however, production had declined by 45% to 8.5m. metres of cloth, largely a result of illicit imports from Nigeria (following the decline in the value of the naira). In 1992 the STT suspended operations; following the positive effects of devaluation, however, production was resumed. Despite increases in sugar production, which reached 47,000 tons in 1990, sales were adversely affected by illicit imports of low-priced sugar from Nigeria and Cameroon. However, the government planned to raise capacity to meet domestic demand. There is a wide range of small-scale enterprises operating outside the recorded sector, including crafts and the production of agricultural implements, which make a significant contribution to employment and overall production.

Electricity in Chad is generated by two oil-powered plants operated by a public corporation, Société tchadienne d'eau et d'électricité (STEE); installed capacity is 29 MW. The annual output of electricity increased rapidly until the mid-1970s, but has since stagnated, as a result of the difficulties in importing petroleum. The utility has also been severely affected by persistent non-payment of bills, notably by other public sector enterprises.

TRANSPORT

Transportation within Chad is inadequate and expensive. Communications with the outside world are difficult, slow and costly because of the great distance from the sea, the character of the trade, and poor facilities in neighbouring countries. The total length of the road network in 1995 was an estimated 32,700 km, but only some 500 km are paved. Transport limitations are a major obstacle to the country's economic development, and efforts are being made to improve the internal transport system (with help from the World Bank, the EDF and the USA), including the rehabilitation and construction of an ancillary road network as part of rural development in the south. Some 250 km of tarred road between Abéché and N'Djamena has been completed, in a project funded by French aid and the construction of a road linking N'Djamena to Mao is also under way. Transport infrastructural improvements in adjacent countries, especially in Cameroon, were expected to benefit Chad; however, plans to extend the Transcameroon railway from N'Gaoundéré to Sarh, in southern Chad, have been indefinitely postponed. Inland waterways are significant, with 2,000 km of the Chari and Logone rivers navigable in all seasons. The international airport at N'Djamena is served by Air Afrique, in which Chad is a participant, and there are regular services to Sudan and northern Nigeria.

PUBLIC FINANCE

Economic decline and civil strife have exacerbated Chad's severe public-finance difficulties, which can be relieved only by substantial contributions from both international agencies and the country's allies, notably France and the USA. The deterioration in the political situation in the 1970s effectively halted development expenditure, while spending on defence accounted for one-quarter of the total budget. (However, much military expenditure was extra-budgetary, and was covered by grants from France and the USA.) Since 1983, when a budget was adopted after an interval of five years, there has been a substantial deficit each year, with expenditure three to four times as high as the level of revenue. Foreign aid has therefore been required to maintain basic government services. Since the mid-1980s, with the support of the IMF, the World Bank and the major bilateral donors (France and the USA), the government has attempted to increase revenue receipts (through increased taxes on petroleum products and luxury goods) and to reduce spending (for example, on subsidies for cotton production and on civil service employment). The deficit remained high, however, reaching 79,300m. francs CFA in 1991, equivalent to 21.3% of GDP; after grants it was 32,600m. francs CFA, or 8.7% of GDP. An austerity budget was announced in 1992, with a programme to restructure the civil service and to transfer a number of banks and state-owned enterprises to the private sector. Later in 1992, in accordance with recommendations by the IMF, the government announced plans to increase taxes and to reduce the salaries of civil servant staff, prompting a protracted strike in the public sector. However, the budget outturn was hardly affected in either 1992 or 1993, with after-grant deficits of 41,500m. francs CFA and 34,600m. francs CFA respectively, since revenues were depressed by falling customs receipts (the principal source of revenue), largely as the result of an increase in illicit trade across the Nigerian and Cameroonian borders. Revenue losses from illicit trade with Nigeria were expected to ease somewhat after the January 1994 devaluation of the CFA franc. In March of that year the government introduced a structural adjustment programme, supported by credits from the IMF ($74m. over three years) and the World Bank ($40m.), which aimed to reduce the deficit on the primary budget (the balance before interest payments) from 6% in 1994 to 2.25% in

1995 and to produce a modest surplus of 1.25% by 1998. The funds from the World Bank were to be used, in part, for severance payments in the continued reduction in members of the armed forces since 1992. Only limited progress was made in 1994 and 1995, because any improvement in customs collection is difficult to achieve, while spending was under pressure from the sharp inflationary impact of devaluation. The government was expecting to register a surplus as early as 1996, and its programme received new backing from the enhanced structural adjustment facility accorded by the IMF in September 1995. This again laid emphasis on improving the rate of revenue collection, as well as introducing a single turnover tax from the beginning of 1997. Spending was to be controlled through reform of the large state enterprises (in cotton, sugar and electricity), retrenchment in the civil service and a further reduction in military personnel. It was hoped that the budget including interest payments (which were some 7,300m. francs CFA in 1995) would be in balance in 1997.

FOREIGN TRADE, AID AND PAYMENTS

While exports and imports have fluctuated widely as a result of the civil war, Chad's foreign trade has, almost without exception, shown a very large deficit, owing to the low level of production in the economy and the high cost of transport. The principal imports are food products (accounting for 17% of the cost of total imports in 1991) and petroleum. Cotton is the principal export commodity (contributing 43% of total export earnings in 1995), followed by meat and live animals (19% in 1994). In the late 1980s the decline in international prices for cotton resulted in a significant reduction in export revenue, while imports increased sharply, resulting in a substantial rise in the trade deficit to 35,000m. francs CFA in 1987, more than the total value of exports in that year. The rise in output of cotton and the improvement in international prices generated an increase in export earnings in 1990, and the trade deficit remained between 16,000m. and 20,000m. francs CFA for most of the early 1990s. The devaluation of the CFA franc in 1994 failed to reduce the imbalance, because, while export earnings more than doubled in CFA franc terms in that year, import spending rose by almost the same rate as a result of the economy's high dependence on imports. The strong performance of cotton exports did, however, produce a modest surplus on foreign trade in 1995, of 16,880m. francs CFA, and this was likely to have been sustained through 1996. The current account has been persistently in deficit, however, owing to the very high outflows on services, largely reflecting transport costs.

To offset the deficit Chad has relied heavily on foreign assistance, which has also been needed to fund basic budgetary requirements and any development expenditure, as well as the episodes of military activity. France has remained the principal supplier of aid, including direct budgetary assistance (63% of the bilateral aid disbursed in 1990–95 was of French origin). EC and multilateral agencies and, more recently, Arab countries also provide substantial help, principally for agricultural and infrastructure projects. Net inflows of aid funds increased during the second half of the 1980s, to US $317m. in 1990, subsequently declining, prior to a dramatic rise in multilateral aid following the currency devaluation. Net multilateral aid is now approximately equal to bilateral flows, accounting for $112m. in 1995 out of a total of $239m. A large proportion of this aid is in the form of grants (78% in 1995). The current programme of national reconstruction has received considerable support from the EDF (through funds to restore the road network and to reconstruct N'Djamena), France (both civil and military) and the USA (for road rehabilitation).

Most of Chad's borrowing has been from government and other official sources, on highly concessionary terms. Consequently, while external debt has increased significantly, from US $285.3m. in 1980 to $908.4m. at the end of 1995, debt-servicing has remained very low, equivalent to 5.9% of earnings from exports of goods and services in that year, helped by unusually good cotton export earnings. This modest level has also been due to failure to pay liabilities as they fall due (arrears on repayment were $32.6m. at the end of 1995, double the total debt service paid in that year), as well as debt relief accorded by France. The CFA franc's devaluation—which represented an immediate increase in the cost of debt-servicing—was followed by the cancellation of Chad's official debt to France. Moreover, in February 1995 Chad was granted enhanced relief on its debt to official bilateral creditors under the 'Naples' terms (which apply to countries with a high debt to export ratio or particularly low GNP per head). However, as the greater part of Chad's foreign debt is to multilateral institutions (78% of the total at the end of 1995), and hence not eligible for debt relief, there is little scope for a reduction in the already low burden of debt service. Also, while petroleum development holds out the prospect of much improved foreign earnings in the next decade, that is still to be realized, and could be affected by political developments. Meanwhile, the reconstruction task remains substantial.

Statistical Survey

Source (unless otherwise stated): Direction de la Statistique, des Etudes Economiques et Démographiques, BP 453, N'Djamena.

Area and Population

AREA, POPULATION AND DENSITY

Area (sq km)	
Land	1,259,200
Inland waters	24,800
Total	1,284,000*
Population (sample survey)	
December 1963–August 1964	3,254,000†
Population (census result)	
8 April 1993‡	
Males	2,950,415
Females	3,208,577
Total	6,158,992
Population (official estimate at mid-year)	
1994	6,214,000§
Density (per sq km) at mid-1994	4.9§

* 495,800 sq miles.

† Including areas not covered by the survey.

‡ Figures are provisional. The revised total, including an adjustment for underenumeration (estimated at 1.4%), is 6,279,931.

§ Not revised to take account of the 1993 census result (see above).

PREFECTURES (official estimates, mid-1988)

	Area (sq km)	Population	Density (per sq km)
Batha	88,800	431,000	4.9
Biltine	46,850	216,000	4.6
Borkou-Ennedi-Tibesti (BET)	600,350	109,000	0.2
Chari-Baguirmi	82,910	844,000	10.2
Guera	58,950	254,000	4.3
Kanem	114,520	245,000	2.1
Lac	22,320	165,000	7.4
Logone Occidental	8,695	365,000	42.0
Logone Oriental	28,035	377,000	13.4
Mayo-Kebbi	30,105	852,000	28.3
Moyen Chari	45,180	646,000	14.3
Ouaddaï	76,240	422,000	5.5
Salamat	63,000	131,000	2.1
Tandjilé	18,045	371,000	20.6
Total	1,284,000	5,428,000	4.2

PRINCIPAL TOWNS (officially-estimated population in 1988)

N'Djamena (capital)	594,000	Moundou	102,000
Sarh	113,400	Abéché	83,000

BIRTHS AND DEATHS (UN estimates, annual averages)

	1980–85	1985–90	1990–95
Birth rate (per 1,000)	44.2	43.9	43.7
Death rate (per 1,000)	21.4	19.5	18.0

Expectation of life (UN estimates, years at birth, 1990–95): 47.5 (males 45.9; females 49.1).

Source: UN, *World Population Prospects: The 1994 Revision.*

ECONOMICALLY ACTIVE POPULATION
(ILO estimates, '000 persons at mid-1980)

	Males	Females	Total
Agriculture, etc.	1,043	318	1,361
Industry	72	4	76
Services	154	44	197
Total labour force	1,269	366	1,635

Source: ILO, *Economically Active Population Estimates and Projections, 1950–2025.*

Mid-1988 (official estimates, persons aged 10 years and over): Total labour force 2,032,401 (males 1,547,626; females 484,775) (Source: ILO, *Yearbook of Labour Statistics*).

Mid-1995 (estimates in '000): Agriculture 2,494; Total 3,086 (Source: FAO, *Production Yearbook*).

Agriculture

PRINCIPAL CROPS ('000 metric tons)

	1993	1994	1995*
Wheat	5	2	2
Rice (paddy)	32	90	90
Maize	100	94	94
Millet	234	307	307
Sorghum	306	379	379
Other cereals	70	91	91
Potatoes	20	8	8
Sweet potatoes*	47	47	47
Cassava (Manioc)	220*	195	195
Yams*	210	240	240
Taro (Coco yam)	35*	38	38
Dry beans	11	12	12
Other pulses	22	22	22
Groundnuts (in shell)	190	207	207
Sesame seed	16	13	13
Cottonseed	101	134	134
Cotton (lint)	40*	45†	45
Dry onions	14	14*	14
Other vegetables	60	60*	60
Dates	18	18	18
Mangoes*	32	32	32
Other fruit	50	50	50
Sugar cane	400*	308	308

* FAO estimate(s). † Unofficial figure.

Source: FAO, *Production Yearbook.*

LIVESTOCK ('000 head, year ending September)

	1993	1994	1995
Cattle	4,517	4,621	4,539
Goats	3,086	3,178	3,271
Sheep	2,089	2,152	2,219
Pigs	16	17	18
Horses	210	214	218*
Asses	248	253	252*
Camels	578	593	600*

* FAO estimate.

Poultry (FAO estimates, million): 4 in 1993; 4 in 1994; 4 in 1995.

Source: FAO, *Production Yearbook.*

LIVESTOCK PRODUCTS (FAO estimates,'000 metric tons)

	1993	1994	1995
Total meat	96	98	98
Beef and veal	67	68	68
Mutton and lamb	10	10	10
Goat meat	11	11	11
Poultry meat	4	4	4
Cows' milk	123	123	123
Sheep's milk	9	9	9
Goats' milk	16	16	16
Butter	0.3	0.3	0.3
Hen eggs	3.9	4.0	4.0
Cattle hides	9.5	9.7	9.7
Sheep skins	1.6	1.7	1.7
Goat skins	2.0	2.1	2.1

Source: FAO, *Production Yearbook.*

Forestry

ROUNDWOOD REMOVALS
('000 cubic metres, excluding bark)

	1991	1992	1993
Sawlogs, veneer logs and logs for sleepers	5	8	14
Other industrial wood*	570	585	602
Fuel wood*	3,472	3,568	3,667
Total	4,047	4,161	4,283

* FAO estimates.

Source: FAO, *Yearbook of Forest Products.*

Fishing

('000 metric tons, live weight)

	1992	1993	1994
Total catch (freshwater fishes)	80.0	87.3	80.0

Source: FAO, *Yearbook of Fishery Statistics.*

Industry

SELECTED PRODUCTS

('000 metric tons, unless otherwise indicated)

	1992	1993	1994
Salted, dried or smoked fish	15.0	15.0	15.0
Edible oil ('000 hectolitres)	87.9	70.2	86.9
Raw sugar	26	25	27
Beer ('000 hectolitres)	129.4	117.1	107.7
Soft drinks ('000 hectolitres)	35	35	26
Cigarettes (million)	415	499	508
Woven cotton fabrics (million metres)	—	—	0.2
Radio receivers ('000)	7	—	—
Electric energy (million kWh)	84	86	85

Source: mainly UN, *Industrial Commodity Statistics Yearbook.*

1995 (estimates): Edible oil ('000 hectolitres) 117.0; Beer ('000 hectolitres) 95.0; Refined sugar ('000 metric tons) 26.0.

Source: IMF, *Chad—Recent Economic Developments.*

Finance

CURRENCY AND EXCHANGE RATES

Monetary Units

100 centimes = 1 franc de la Coopération financière en Afrique centrale (CFA).

French Franc, Sterling and Dollar Equivalents (31 March 1997)

1 French franc = 100 francs CFA;
£1 sterling = 924.20 francs CFA;
US $1 = 562.85 francs CFA;
1,000 francs CFA = £1.082 = $1.777.

Average Exchange Rate (francs CFA per US $)

1994 555.20
1995 499.15
1996 511.55

Note: The exchange rate of 1 French franc = 50 francs CFA, established in 1948, remained in force until January 1994, when the CFA franc was devalued by 50%, with the exchange rate adjusted to 1 French franc = 100 francs CFA.

BUDGET (million francs CFA)

Revenue*	1993	1994	1995
Tax revenue	18,733	25,779	39,699
Taxes on income and profits	6,372	8,695	16,630
Companies	1,469	3,073	8,395
Individuals	4,130	4,614	7,189
Employers' payroll tax	773	1,009	1,046
Taxes on goods and services	6,771	8,337	6,578
Turnover tax	1,826	3,080	1,728
Tax on petroleum products	2,451	2,254	2,046
Single tax	1,866	2,519	2,015
Taxes on international trade	3,962	6,199	12,166
Import taxes	3,280	4,944	9,600
Export taxes	473	1,049	1,432
Other tax revenues	1,138	2,071	1,270
Other revenue	6,543	5,387	5,135
Property income	704	350	1,246
Total	25,276	31,166	44,834

Expenditure	1993	1994	1995
Current expenditure	51,948	65,481	64,684
Primary current expenditure	44,930	56,545	56,923
Wages and salaries	22,713	25,968	30,109
Materials and supplies	8,783	12,664	11,851
Transfers	2,349	5,015	4,963
Defence	11,085	12,333	10,000
Salaries	9,340	8,996	7,100
Materials and supplies	1,745	3,337	2,900
Interest	4,836	7,634	7,261
External	4,236	6,503	6,301
Investment expenditure	29,633	59,229	61,799
Foreign-financed	28,333	58,030	61,479
Total	83,781	124,710	126,482

* Excluding grants received (million francs CFA): 15,384 in 1993; 44,231 in 1994; 37,273 in 1995.

Note: Figures include the operations of the extrabudgetary Caisse Autonome d'Amortissement.

Source: IMF, *Chad—Recent Economic Developments* (July 1996).

INTERNATIONAL RESERVES

(US $ million, at 31 December)

	1993	1994	1995
Gold*	4.42	n.a.	n.a.
IMF special drawing rights	0.01	—	0.03
Reserve position in IMF	0.38	0.41	0.42
Foreign exchange	38.54	75.60	142.07
Total	43.36	n.a.	n.a.

* Valued at market-related prices.

1996 (US $ million, at 31 December): IMF special drawing rights 0.24; Reserve position in IMF 0.40.

Source: IMF, *International Financial Statistics.*

MONEY SUPPLY ('000 million francs CFA at 31 December)

	1993	1994	1995
Currency outside banks	35.84	39.69	61.98
Demand deposits at commercial and development banks	9.19	18.73	20.68
Total money (incl. others)	45.47	59.79	85.33

Source: IMF, *International Financial Statistics.*

COST OF LIVING (Consumer Price Index for African households in N'Djamena; base: 1990 = 100)

	1993	1994	1995
All items	93.8	131.7	143.6

Source: IMF, *International Financial Statistics.*

NATIONAL ACCOUNTS

Expenditure on the Gross Domestic Product ('000 million francs CFA at current prices)

	1992	1993	1994
Government final consumption expenditure	66.5	58.7	65.7
Private final consumption expenditure	322.5	262.5	397.1
Gross fixed capital formation	29.9	36.8	73.7
Total domestic expenditure	419.0	357.9	536.5
Exports of goods and services	55.3	55.2	100.4
Less Imports of goods and services	123.6	121.5	178.0
GDP in purchasers' values	350.6	291.7	458.9
GDP at constant 1977 prices	231.5	195.2	215.1

Source: IMF, *Chad—Recent Economic Developments* (July 1996).

Gross Domestic Product by Economic Activity (estimates, million francs CFA at current prices)

	1989	1990	1991
Agriculture, hunting, forestry and fishing	133,458	135,150	134,609
Mining and quarrying	1,073	1,398	1,411
Manufacturing	52,712	30,950	27,886
Electricity, gas and water	2,223	1,908	1,990
Construction	5,214	5,270	5,808
Wholesale and retail trade, restaurants and hotels	90,970	91,220	91,311
Transport and communications	7,027	5,697	5,499
Finance, insurance, real estate and business services	2,447	2,500	2,522
Public administration and defence	30,480	29,695	31,674
Other community, social and personal services	2,311	2,600	2,912
GDP at factor cost	327,915	306,388	305,622
Indirect taxes, *less* subsidies	17,655	16,409	16,853
GDP in purchasers' values	345,570	322,797	322,475

Source: UN Economic Commission for Africa, *African Statistical Yearbook*.

BALANCE OF PAYMENTS (US $ million)

	1992	1993	1994
Exports of goods f.o.b.	182.3	151.8	135.3
Imports of goods f.o.b.	-243.0	-215.2	-212.1
Trade balance	-60.7	-63.5	-76.8
Exports of services	26.7	47.1	54.8
Imports of services	-224.1	-235.1	-199.4
Balance on goods and services	-258.1	-251.4	-221.4
Other income received	17.5	4.3	5.0
Other income paid	-14.9	-15.7	-12.4
Balance on goods services and income	-255.5	-262.9	-228.7
Current transfers received	222.3	192.4	209.4
Current transfers paid	-52.5	-46.2	-18.4
Current balance	-85.7	-116.6	-37.7
Direct investment abroad	-13.8	-10.9	-0.6
Direct investment from abroad	2.0	15.2	27.1
Other investment assets	3.9	42.1	0.6
Other investment liabilities	41.6	22.5	49.2
Net errors and omissions	9.2	-0.1	-33.0
Overall balance	-42.8	-47.9	5.5

Source: IMF, *International Financial Statistics*.

External Trade

PRINCIPAL COMMODITIES (million francs CFA)

Imports	1983
Beverages	71.7
Cereal products	2,272.1
Sugar, confectionery, chocolate	292.7
Petroleum products	2,280.5
Textiles, clothing, etc.	392.1
Pharmaceuticals, chemicals	1,561.9
Minerals and metals	311.2
Machinery	843.2
Transport equipment	987.6
Electrical equipment	773.3
Total (incl. others)	13,539.6

Total imports (million francs CFA): 74,708 in 1985; 73,437 in 1986; 67,894 in 1987; 68,000 in 1988; 75,100 in 1989; 77,742 in 1990; 70,500 in 1991; 64,320 in 1992; 56,910 in 1993; 102,820 in 1994. (Source: Banque des Etats de l'Afrique Centrale).

Exports	1983
Live cattle	49.5
Meat	23.5
Fish	2.0
Oil-cake	8.1
Natron	8.1
Gums and resins	0.4
Hides and skins	16.6
Raw cotton	3,753.7
Total (incl. others)	4,120.0

Total exports (million francs CFA): 27,781 in 1985; 34,145 in 1986; 32,892 in 1987; 42,900 in 1988; 49,570 in 1989; 51,202 in 1990; 54,600 in 1991; 48,250 in 1992; 37,330 in 1993; 86,870 in 1994. (Source: Banque des Etats de l'Afrique Centrale).

Cotton exports ('000 million francs CFA): 26.8 in 1991; 25.3 in 1992.

PRINCIPAL TRADING PARTNERS (million francs CFA)

Imports	1984	1985	1986
Belgium/Luxembourg	435	520	1,712
Cameroon	3,461	12,371	8,777
China, People's Republic	n.a.	39	896
Congo	417	519	395
France	22,132	14,439	21,772
Germany, Fed. Republic	1,322	1,562	2,876
Italy	3,133	2,874	3,263
Netherlands	777	1,950	2,017
Nigeria	4,817	4,368	5,673
USA	4,095	9,247	7,670
Total (incl. others)	45,759	51,520	58,831

Exports	1984	1985	1986
Cameroon	929	1,711	2,661
Central African Republic	64	1,219	321
France	6,950	1,432	1,774
Nigeria	113	1,981	425
Sudan	8	47	101
Zaire	125	5	n.a.
Total (incl. others)	8,231	6,446	5,374

Transport

ROAD TRAFFIC (motor vehicles in use at 31 December)

	1993	1994	1995*
Passenger cars	7,817	8,720	9,630
Buses and coaches	657	708	760
Lorries and vans	11,772	12,650	13,600
Tractors	1,337	1,413	1,490
Motorcycles and mopeds	987	1,855	2,730

* Estimates.

Source: International Road Federation, *World Road Statistics*.

CIVIL AVIATION (traffic on scheduled services*)

	1992	1993	1994
Kilometres flown (million)	2	2	2
Passengers carried ('000)	83	85	86
Passengers-km (million)	208	214	222
Total ton-km (million)	35	34	35

* Including an apportionment of the traffic of Air Afrique.

Source: UN, *Statistical Yearbook*.

Tourism

	1992	1993	1994
Tourist arrivals ('000)	17*	21*	19
Tourist receipts (US $ million)	21	23	36

* Including same-day visitors.

Source: UN, *Statistical Yearbook*.

Tourist arrivals ('000): 57 in 1995 (Source: Ministère de l'environnement et du tourisme).

Communications Media

	1992	1993	1994
Radio receivers ('000 in use)	1,425	1,470	1,520
Television receivers ('000 in use)	8	8	9
Telephones ('000 main lines in use)	4	5	5

Daily newspapers: 1 in 1994 (average circulation 2,000).

Non-daily newspapers: 1 in 1988 (average circulation 1,000).

Sources: UNESCO, *Statistical Yearbook*, and UN, *Statistical Yearbook*.

Education

(1993/94)

	Institutions	Teachers	Pupils
Primary	2,739*	8,826†	547,695†
Secondary:			
General	48‡	1,893	69,784
Teacher training	18‡	54§	635
Vocational	7‡	231§	3,247
Higher	4‡	187*	2,941

* Figure refers to 1992/93.

† Figure refers to 1994/95.

‡ Figure refers to 1987.

§ Figure refers to 1988.

Source: UNESCO, *Statistical Yearbook*, and Ministry of National Education.

Directory

The Constitution

The Constitution of the Republic of Chad, which was adopted by national referendum on 31 March 1996, enshrines a unitary state. The President is elected for a term of five years by direct universal adult suffrage, and is restricted to two terms in office. The Prime Minister, who is appointed by the President, nominates the Council of Ministers. The bicameral legislature comprises the 125-member National Assembly, which is elected by direct universal suffrage for a term of four years, and the Senate, which has a six-year mandate (with one-third of members renewed every two years). The Constitution provides for an independent judicial system, with a High Court of Justice, and the establishment of a Constitutional Court and a High Council for Communication.

The Government

HEAD OF STATE

President and Commander-in-Chief of the Armed Forces: IDRISS DEBY (assumed office 4 December 1990; elected President 11 July 1996).

GOVERNMENT

(July 1997)

Prime Minister: NASSOUR OUADO.

Minister of State for Public Works, Transport, Housing and Town Planning: SALEH KEBZABO.

Minister of Justice and Keeper of the Seals: NADJITA BEASSOUMAL.

Minister of Foreign Affairs and Co-operation: MAHAMAT SALEH ANNADIF.

Minister of the Interior and Security: ABDRAMAN SALLAH.

Minister of Finance, the Economy, Planning and Territorial Development: BICHARA CHERIF DAOUSSA.

Minister of the Civil Service: OUSMANE DJIDDA.

Minister of Defence: MAHAMAT NIMIR HAMATA.

Minister of Mines, Energy and Petroleum: PASCAL YOADIMNADJI.

Minister of Agriculture: MAHAMAT ZENE ALI FADEL.

Minister of Public Health: KEDELLAH YOUNOUSS.

Minister of Primary, Secondary and Adult Education: ABDERAHIM BREME.

Minister of Livestock: MAHAMAT NOURI.

Minister of Higher Education and Scientific Research: Dr ADOUM GOUDJA.

Minister of Social Welfare and Family Support: MONIQUE NGARLBAYE.

Minister of Commercial Development and Cottage Industry: PADACKE ALBERT PAHIMI.

Minister of Posts and Telecommunications: MAHAMAT AHMAT KARAMBAL.

Minister of the Environment and Water Resources: EDGAR NGARBAROUM.

Minister of Culture, Youth and Sports Promotion: NASSINGAR MASSOUNGARAL.

Minister of Tourism Development: OUMAR KADJALAMI.

Minister of Communications and Government Spokesman: SALIBOU GARBA.

Minister, Secretary-General of the Government; MARIAM MAHAMAT NOUR.

Secretary of State for Finance: CHETIMA ALI.

Secretary of State for Foreign Affairs: LAOUANE GILBERT.

Secretary of State for the Interior and Security: Alhadj ZENE MAHAMAT YAYA.

Secretary of State for the Civil Service: HASSAN DINGAMADJI.

Deputy Secretary-General of the Government: NGARE MAHAMAT ABBA.

MINISTRIES

Office of the President: N'Djamena; tel. 51-44-37; telex 5201.

Office of the Prime Minister: N'Djamena.

Ministry of Agriculture: N'Djamena.

Ministry of the Civil Service: BP 437, N'Djamena; tel. and fax 52-21-98.

Ministry of Commercial Development and Cottage Industry: N'Djamena.

Ministry of Communications: BP 154, N'Djamena; tel. 51-41-64; telex 5254; fax 51-60-94.

Ministry of Culture, Youth and Sports Promotion: N'Djamena.

Ministry of Defence: N'Djamena; tel. 51-58-89.

Ministry of the Environment and Water Resources: N'Djamena.

Ministry of Finance, the Economy, Planning and Territorial Development: BP 144, N'Djamena; tel. 52-21-61; telex 5257.

Ministry of Foreign Affairs and Co-operation: N'Djamena; tel. 51-50-82; telex 5238.

Ministry of Higher Education and Scientific Research: N'Djamena.

Ministry of the Interior and Security: N'Djamena.

Ministry of Justice: N'Djamena; tel. 51-56-56.

Ministry of Livestock: N'Djamena; tel. 51-59-07.

Ministry of Mines, Energy and Petroleum: N'Djamena; tel. 51-56-03; fax 51-25-65.

Ministry of Posts and Telecommunications: N'Djamena.

Ministry of Primary, Secondary and Adult Education: N'Djamena.

Ministry of Public Health: N'Djamena; tel. 51-39-60.

Ministry of Public Works, Transport, Housing and Town Planning: BP 436, N'Djamena; tel. 51-20-96.

Ministry of Social Welfare and Family Support: N'Djamena.

Ministry of Tourism Development: N'Djamena.

President and Legislature

PRESIDENT

In a first round of voting, which took place on 2 June 1996, none of the 15 candidates secured the requisite 50% of total votes cast. A second round of voting took place on 3 July: the incumbent, President IDRISS DEBY, was elected by 69.1% of the votes, while the other candidate, Gen. WADAL ABDELKADER KAMOUGUE, received 30.9%.

ASSEMBLÉE NATIONALE

President: Gen. WADAL ABDELKADER KAMOUGUE.

General Election, 5 January and 23 February 1997

Party	Seats
Movement patriotique du salut	63
Union pour le renouveau et la démocratie	29
Union nationale pour le développement et le renouveau	15
Union pour la démocratie et la République	4
Parti pour la liberté et le développement	3
Rassemblement pour la démocratie et le progrès	3
Other opposition parties	6
Total*	125

* By-elections were to be held in two constituencies where the results of the first round of voting had been annulled.

Note: By mid-1997 the upper house of the legislature, the Senate, had not yet been established.

Political Organizations

Legislation permitting the operation of political associations, subject to official registration, took effect in October 1991. In mid-1997 about 60 political organizations were in existence, of which the most important are listed below.

Action pour l'unité et le socialisme (ACTUS): N'Djamena; f. 1992; Leader Dr FIDÈLE MOUNGAR.

Action du peuple pour l'unité et le développement (APUD): N'Djamena; f. 1996; Chair. BESHIR DISCO HAMAT.

Alliance nationale pour la démocratie et le développement (ANDD): BP 4066, N'Djamena; tel. 51-46-72; f. 1992; Leader SALIBOU GARBA.

Alliance nationale pour la démocratie et le renouveau (ANDR): N'Djamena; f. 1993.

Alliance nationale pour le progrès et le développement (ANT): N'Djamena; f. 1992.

Alliance des partis politiques pour la démocratie (APD): f. 1994; opposition coalition comprising:

Forte alliance démocratique (FAD): Leader NDJIRAWE FATIKAREMON.

Parti démocratique tchadien (PDT): Leader Dr ABDOULAYE DJIDA.

Parti pour le renouveau du Tchad (PRT): Leader MAHAMAT KANASSO AKIM.

Parti pour l'unité et la reconstruction (PUR): Leader MAHAMAT SALEH MATIB.

Rassemblement démocratique et culturel pour la paix et le travail (RDCPT): Leader MONGOUNKOU HARAMA.

Rassemblement des forces démocratiques tchadiennes (RFDT): Leader BERNARD MBANGADOU.

Union nationale pour la démocratie et le progrès (UNDP): Leader ABDELKADER YASSINE BAKIT.

Union du peuple tchadien pour la reconstruction nationale (UPTRN): Leader ABAKAR MOUSSA.

Collectif des partis pour le changement (COPAC): f. 1994; alliance of eight opposition parties: Leader Dr FIDÈLE MOUNGAR.

Comité de sursaut national pour la paix et la démocratie (CSNPD): fmr dissident faction; obtained legal recognition in Sept. 1994; Leader Col MOÏSE NODJI KETTE.

Concertation nationale pour la démocratie sociale (CNDS): N'Djamena; Leader ADOUM MOUSSA SEIF.

Concertation des partis politiques (CPP): f. 1995; informal grouping comprising all opposition parties; Chair. ABDERAHMANE DJASNABAYE.

Concertation social-démocrate tchadien (CSDT): N'Djamena; Pres. YOUNOUS IBEDOU.

Convention de l'opposition démocratique (CODE): f. 1996; alliance of 23 opposition parties; Leader KASSIRE DELWA KOUMAKOYE.

Front des forces d'action pour la République: Leader YORONGAR LEMOHIBAN.

Front patriotique pour la démocratie (FPD): f. 1996 by elements of a fmr dissident faction; Nat. Co-ordinator MICHEL MBAILAMA.

Front républicain: f. 1996; alliance of 27 parties supporting President Idriss Deby.

Mouvement patriotique du salut (MPS): N'Djamena; f. 1990 as a coalition of several opposition movements, incl. the Action du 1 avril, the Mouvement pour le salut national du Tchad and the Forces armées tchadiennes; other opposition groups joined during the Nov. 1990 offensive against the Govt of Hissène Habré, and following the movement's accession to power in Dec. 1990; Chair. MALDOM BADA ABBAS; Exec. Sec. NADJITA BEASSOUMAL.

Mouvement pour la démocratie et le socialisme du Tchad (MDST): N'Djamena; Leader Dr SALOMON NGARBAYE TOMBALBAYE.

Mouvement pour la démocratie du Tchad (MPDT): N'Djamena; Leader MAHAMAT ABDOULAYE.

Mouvement socialiste pour la démocratie du Tchad (MSTD): N'Djamena; Leader ALBERT MBAINAIDO DJOMIA.

Mouvement pour l'unité et la démocratie du Tchad (MUDT): f. 1992; Leader JULIEN MARABAYE.

Parti africain pour le progrès et la justice sociale (PAPJS): Leader NEATOBEI DIDIER VALENTIN.

Parti pour la liberté et le développement (PLD): N'Djamena; f. 1993; Leader IBN OUMAR MAHAMAT SALEH.

Parti social-démocrate tchadien (PSDT): Moundou; Leader NIABE ROMAIN.

Rassemblement pour la démocratie et le progrès (RDP): N'Djamena; f. 1992; Leader LOL MAHAMAT CHOUA.

Rassemblement démocratique du Tchad (RDT): N'Djamena; f. 1992.

Rassemblement pour le développement et le progrès: f. 1992; Leader MAMADOU BISSO.

Rassemblement national pour la démocratie et le progrès (RNDP): N'Djamena; f. 1992; Pres. KASSIRE DELWA KOUMAKOYE.

Rassemblement des nationalistes tchadiennes (RNT): N'Djamena; f. 1992.

Rassemblement du peuple du Tchad (RPT): N'Djamena; f. 1992; Leader DANGBE LAOBELE DAMAYE.

Union pour la démocratie et la République (UDR): N'Djamena; f. 1992; Leader Dr JEAN ALINGUE BAWOYEU.

Union démocratique pour le progrès du Tchad (UDPT): 17 rue de kélo, Kabalaye, POB 1071, N'Djamena; tel. 51-24-34; f. 1992; Pres. ELIE ROMBA.

Union démocratique tchadienne (UDT): N'Djamena; Leader ABDERAHMANE KOULAMALLAH.

Union des forces démocratiques (UFD): N'Djamena; f. 1992; Sec.-Gen. Dr NAHOR MAHAMOUT.

Union des forces démocratiques—Parti républicain (UFD—PR): f. 1992; Leader GALI GATTA NGOTHE.

Union nationale: f. 1992; Leader ABDOULAYE LAMANA.

Union nationale pour le changement du Tchad (UNCT): N'Djamena; f. 1995; Pres. ADOUM HASSAN ISSA.

Union nationale pour le développement et le renouveau (UNDR): Leader SALEH KEBZABO.

Union du peuple tchadien pour la reconstruction nationale (UPTRN): N'Djamena; f. 1992; Leader HAPPA KAROUMA.

Union pour le renouveau et la démocratie (URD): N'Djamena; f. 1992; Leader Gen. WADAL ABDELKADER KAMOUGUE.

A number of dissident factions (some based overseas) are also active. These include the **Concertation nationale pour l'unité et la paix,** led by Maj. ADOUM YACOUB; the **Congrès pour le renouveau et la démocratie,** f. 1996 by merger of the Conseil national de redressement du Tchad and the Front d'action pour l'installation de la démocratie au Tchad; the **Front de libération nationale du Tchad (FROLINAT)**, led by GOUKOUNI OUEDDEI; the **Front national du Tchad (FNT)**, based in Sudan and led by Dr FARIS BACHAR; **Front national du Tchad renové (FNTR)**, led by Maj. ADAM HAMAT; the **Mouvement pour la démocratie et le développement (MDD)**, led by MOUSSA MEDELLA MAHAMAT; and the **Union nationale pour la démocratie et le socialisme (UNDS)**, led by YOUSSOU SOUGOUDI.

Diplomatic Representation

EMBASSIES IN CHAD

Algeria: N'Djamena; tel. 51-38-15; telex 5216; Ambassador: MOHAMED CHELLALI KHOURI.

Central African Republic: BP 115, N'Djamena; tel. 51-32-06; Ambassador: DAVID NGUINDO.

Congo, Democratic Republic: ave du 20 août, BP 910, N'Djamena; tel. 51-59-35; telex 5322; Ambassador: (vacant).

Egypt: BP 1094, N'Djamena; tel. 51-36-60; telex 5216; Ambassador: AZIZ M. NOUR EL-DIN.

France: BP 431, N'Djamena; tel. 52-25-75; telex 5202; fax 52-28-55; Ambassador: ALAIN DU BOISPÉAN.

Germany: ave Félix Eboué, BP 893, N'Djamena; tel. 51-62-02; telex 5246; fax 51-48-00; Chargé d'affaires a.i.: DIETER FREUND.

Libya: N'Djamena; Ambassador: IDRIS SANDRIL.

Nigeria: 35 ave Charles de Gaulle, BP 752, N'Djamena; tel. 51-24-98; telex 5242; Chargé d'affaires a.i.: A. M. ALIYU BIU.

Sudan: BP 45, N'Djamena; tel. 51-34-97; telex 5235; Ambassador: TAHA MAKKAWI.

USA: ave Félix Eboué, BP 413, N'Djamena; tel. 51-40-09; telex 5203; fax 51-33-72; Ambassador: LAURENCE POPE.

Judicial System

The highest judicial authority is the Supreme Court, which includes a constitutional chamber. The legal structure also comprises the Court of Appeal, and Magistrate and Criminal Courts. Under the terms of the Constitution that was introduced in 1996, a High Court of Justice was to be established.

Religion

It is estimated that some 50% of the population are Muslims and about 30% Christians. Most of the remainder follow animist beliefs.

ISLAM

Conseil Suprème des Affaires Islamiques: POB 1101, N'Djamena; tel. 51-81-80; telex 5248; fax 52-58-84.

Head of the Islamic Community: Imam MOUSSA IBRAHIM.

CHRISTIANITY

The Roman Catholic Church

Chad comprises one archdiocese and four dioceses. At 31 December 1995 the estimated number of adherents represented about 7.6% of the total population.

Bishops' Conference: Conférence Episcopale du Tchad, BP 456, N'Djamena; tel. 51-74-44; fax 52-28-60; Pres. Most Rev. CHARLES VANDAME, Archbishop of N'Djamena.

Archbishop of N'Djamena: Most Rev. CHARLES VANDAME, Archevêché, BP 456, N'Djamena; tel. 51-74-44; fax 52-28-60.

Protestant Church

Entente des Eglises et Missions Evangéliques au Tchad: BP 2006, N'Djamena; tel. and fax 51-53-93; an asscn of churches and missions working in Chad; includes Eglise évangélique au Tchad, Assemblées chrétiennes, Eglise fraternelle Luthérienne and Eglise évangélique des frères.

BAHÁ'Í FAITH

National Spiritual Assembly: BP 181, N'Djamena; tel. 51-47-05; mems in 1,125 localities.

The Press

Al-Watan: BP 407, N'Djamena; tel. 51-57-96; weekly; Editor-in-Chief MOUSSA NDORKOÏ.

Bulletin Mensuel de Statistiques du Tchad: BP 453, N'Djamena; monthly.

Comnat: BP 731, N'Djamena; tel. 51-46-75; fax 51-46-71; publ. by Commission Nationale Tchadienne for UNESCO.

Contact: N'Djamena; f. 1989; current affairs; Dir KOULAMALO SOURADJ.

Info-Tchad: BP 670, N'Djamena; daily news bulletin issued by Agence Tchadienne de Presse; French.

Informations Economiques: BP 458, N'Djamena; publ. by the Chambre de Commerce, d'Agriculture et d'Industrie; weekly.

NEWS AGENCIES

Agence Tchadienne de Presse (ATP): BP 670, N'Djamena; tel. 51-58-67; telex 5240.

Foreign Bureaux

Agence France-Presse (AFP): N'Djamena; tel. 51-54-71; telex 5248; Correspondent ALDOM NADJI TITO.

Reuters (United Kingdom): BP 206, N'Djamena; tel. 51-56-57; Correspondent ABAKAR ASSIDIC.

Publisher

Government Publishing House: BP 453, N'Djamena.

Radio and Television

In 1994, according to UNESCO, there were an estimated 1,520,000 radio receivers and 9,000 television receivers in use.

RADIO

Radiodiffusion Nationale Tchadienne: BP 892, N'Djamena; tel. 51-60-71; state-controlled; programmes in French, Arabic and eight vernacular languages; there are four transmitters; Dir KHAMIS TOGOÏ.

Radio Abéché: BP 105, Abéché; tel. 69-81-49; Dir SANOUSSI SAÏD.

Radio Moundou: BP 122, Moundou; tel. 69-13-22; daily programmes in French, Sara and Arabic; Dir DIMANANGAR DJAÏNTA.

Radio Sarh: BP 270, Sarh; daily programmes in French, Sara and Arabic; Dir BIANA FOUDA NACTOUANDI.

TELEVISION

Télé-Chad: Commission for Information and Culture, BP 748, N'Djamena; tel. 51-29-23; state-controlled; broadcasts c. 12 hours per week in French and Arabic; Dir IDRISS AMANE MAHAMAT; Programme Man. MACLAOU NDILDOUM.

Finance

(cap. = capital; res = reserves; m. = million; br. = branch; amounts in francs CFA)

BANKING

Central Bank

Banque des Etats de l'Afrique Centrale (BEAC): BP 50, N'Djamena; tel. 52-41-76; telex 5220; fax 52-44-87; headquarters in Yaoundé, Cameroon; f. 1973 as central bank of issue for mem. states of the Customs and Economic Union of Central Africa (UDEAC), comprising Cameroon, the Central African Republic, Chad, the Congo Republic, Equatorial Guinea and Gabon; cap. and res 214,492m. (June 1996); Gov. JEAN-FÉLIX MAMALEPOT; Dir in Chad TAHIR SOULEYMAN HAGGAR; 2 brs.

Other Banks

Banque de Développement du Tchad (BDT): rue Capitaine Ohrel, BP 19, N'Djamena; tel. 52-28-29; telex 5375; fax 52-33-18; f. 1962; 25.9% state-owned; cap. 1,581.9m. (Dec. 1995); Pres. NAGOUM YAMASOUM; Dir-Gen. NADJILENGAR NGARDINGA.

Banque Méridien BIAO Tchad: ave Charles de Gaulle, BP 87, N'Djamena; tel. 52-43-14; telex 5228; fax 52-23-45; f. 1980; 19.7% state-owned; cap. and res 1,495.5m., dep. 16,083.3m. (Dec. 1993); Pres. RAOUL KONTCHOU; Dir-Gen. MICHEL LE BLANC.

Banque Tchadienne de Crédit et de Dépôts (BTCD): 2–6 rue Robert Lévy, BP 461, N'Djamena; tel. 52-41-90; telex 5212; fax 52-17-13; f. 1963; 75% state-owned; cap. 1,100m. (Dec. 1996); Pres. KOUMTOG LAOTEGUELNODJI; Dir-Gen. CHEMI KOGRIMI; br. at Moundou.

Financial Bank Tchad: ave Charles de Gaulle, BP 804; tel. 52-33-89; telex 5380; fax 52-29-05; f. 1992; cap. 1,000m. (Dec. 1995); Pres. RÉMY BAYSSET; Dir-Gen. PATRICK LELONG.

Bankers' Organizations

Association Professionnelle des Banques au Tchad: 2–6 rue Robert Lévy, BP 461, N'Djamena; tel. 52-41-90; telex 5212; fax 52-17-13; Pres. CHEMI KOGRIMI.

Conseil National de Crédit: N'Djamena; f. 1965 to formulate a national credit policy and to organize the banking profession.

INSURANCE

Assureurs Conseils Tchadiens Faugère et Jutheau et Cie: BP 139, N'Djamena; tel. 51-21-15; telex 5235; Dir PHILIPPE GARDYE.

Société de Représentation d'Assurances et de Réassurances Africaines (SORARAF): N'Djamena; Dir Mme FOURNIER.

Société Tchadienne d'Assurances et de Réassurances (STAR): BP 914, N'Djamena; tel. 51-56-77; telex 5268; Dir PHILIPPE SABIT.

Trade and Industry

CHAMBER OF COMMERCE

Chambre Consulaire: BP 458, N'Djamena; tel. 51-52-64; f. 1938; Pres. ELIE ROMBA; Sec.-Gen. SALEH MAHAMAT RAHMA; brs at Sarh, Moundou, Bol and Abéché.

DEVELOPMENT ORGANIZATIONS

Caisse Française de Développement: BP 478, N'Djamena; tel. 51-40-71; fax 51-28-31; Dir JACBIE BATHANY.

Mission Française de Coopération et d'Action Culturelle: BP 898, N'Djamena; tel. 52-42-87; telex 5340; fax 52-44-38; administers bilateral aid from France; Dir EDOUARD LAPORTE.

Office National de Développement Rural (ONDR): BP 896, N'Djamena; tel. 51-48-64; f. 1968; Dir MICKAEL DJIBRAEL.

Société pour le Développement de la Région du Lac (SODELAC): BP 782, N'Djamena; tel. 51-35-03; telex 5248; f. 1967; cap. 180m. francs CFA; Pres. CHERIF ABDELWAHAB; Dir-Gen. MAHAMAT MOCTAR ALI.

TRADE

Office National des Céréales (ONC): BP 21, N'Djamena; tel. 51-37-31; f. 1978; production and marketing of cereals; Dir YBRAHIM MAHAMAT TIDEI; 11 regional offices.

Société Nationale de Commercialisation du Tchad (SONACOT): N'Djamena; telex 5227; f. 1965; cap. 150m. francs CFA; 76% state-owned; nat. marketing, distribution and import-export co; Man. Dir MARBROUCK NATROUD.

MAJOR INDUSTRIAL COMPANIES

The following are some of the largest private and state-owned companies in terms of capital investment or employment.

Boissons et Glacières du Tchad (BT): BP 656, N'Djamena; tel. 51-31-71; telex 5315; f. 1972; cap. 110m. francs CFA; production of mineral water, Coca-Cola, squashes and ice; Pres. MARCEL ILLE; Dir GASTON BONLEUX.

Brasseries du Logone: ave du Gouverneur Général Félix Eboué, BP 170, Moundou; telex 7204; f. 1962; cap. 800m. francs CFA; brewery; Man. Dir BRUNO DELORME; 145 employees.

Les Grands Moulins du Tchad: BP 173, N'Djamena; f. 1963; cap. 158.25m. francs CFA; milling of flour; mfrs of pasta, biscuits and cattle feed; Pres. EMILE MIMRAN; Man. Dir in N'Djamena JEAN-PAUL BAILLEUX.

Manufacture de Cigarettes du Tchad: BP 572, N'Djamena; tel. 51-21-45; telex 5278; f. 1968; cap. 340m. francs CFA; 15% state-owned; mfrs of cigarettes at Moundou; Pres. PIERRE IMBERT; Man. Dir XAVIER LAMBERT.

Shell Tchad: route de Farcha, BP 110, N'Djamena; tel. 51-24-90; telex 5221; fax 51-22-67; f. 1971; cap. 205m. francs CFA; Pres. DAVID LAWSON LOUGHMAN; Dir-Gen. JEAN-RENÉ MBIANDJEU.

Société Cotonnière du Tchad (COTONTCHAD): rue du Capitaine d'Abzac, BP 1116, N'Djamena; tel. 51-41-32; telex 5229; fax 51-31-71; f. 1971; cap. 4,256m. francs CFA; 75% state-owned; buying, ginning and marketing of cotton; owns eight cotton gins and one cottonseed oil mill; Pres. NGARNAYAL MBAILEMDANA; Dir-Gen. HAROUN KABADI.

Société Nationale Sucrière du Tchad (SONASUT): BP 37, N'Djamena; tel. 51-32-70; telex 5263; f. 1963, 53% state-owned; cap. 5,871m. francs CFA; refining of sugar; mfrs of lump sugar and confectionery; Pres. YOUSSOUF SIDI SOUGOUNI; Dir-Gen. NOUSSA KADAM.

Société Tchadienne d'Eau et d'Electricité (STEE): 11 rue du Colonel Largeau, BP 44, N'Djamena; tel. 51-28-81; telex 5226; fax 51-21-34; f. 1968; cap. 4,989m. francs CFA; production and distribution of electricity and water; Pres. GOMON MAWATA WAKAG; Dir-Gen. ISMAEL MAHAMAT ADOUM.

Société des Télécommunications Internationales du Tchad (TIT): BP 1132, N'Djamena; tel. 51-57-82; telex 5200; fax 51-50-66; cap. 150m. francs CFA; 52% state-owned; study and development of international communications systems; Man. Dir KHALIL D'ABZAC.

TRADE UNION

Union Syndicats du Tchad (UST): BP 1143, N'Djamena; tel. 51-42-75; telex 5248; f. 1988 by merger; Pres. DOMBAL DJIMBAGUE; Sec.-Gen. DJIBRINE ASSALI HAMDALLAH.

Transport

RAILWAYS

There are no railways in Chad. In 1962 the Governments of Chad and Cameroon signed an agreement to extend the Transcameroon railway from N'Gaoundéré to Sarh, a distance of 500 km. Although the Transcameroon reached N'Gaoundéré in 1974, its proposed extension into Chad remains indefinitely postponed.

ROADS

The total length of the road network in 1995 was an estimated 32,700 km, of which 7,730 km were principal roads and 5,270 km were secondary roads. There are also some 20,000 km of tracks suitable for motor traffic during the October–July dry season. In July 1986 the World Bank provided a loan of US $21m. towards a major programme to rehabilitate 2,000 km of roads. In 1988 the International Development Association (IDA) granted $47m. to support the final stage of the programme: the rehabilitation of the 30-km N'Djamena–Djermaya road and the 146-km N'Djamena–Guelengdeng road. In the following year the IDA approved a further credit of $60m. for the rehabilitation of more than 1,800 km of main roads. The EU is contributing to the construction of a highway connecting N'Djamena with Sarh and Lere, on the Cameroon border.

Coopérative des Transportateurs Tchadiens (CTT): BP 336, N'Djamena; tel. 51-43-55; telex 5225; road haulage; Pres. SALEH KHALIFA; brs at Sarh, Moundou, Bangui (Central African Repub.), Douala and N'Gaoundéré (Cameroon).

INLAND WATERWAYS

The Chari and Logone rivers, which converge a short distance south of N'Djamena, are navigable. These waterways connect Sarh with N'Djamena on the Chari and Bongor and Moundou with N'Djamena on the Logone.

CIVIL AVIATION

The international airport at N'Djamena opened in 1967: an improvement programme was completed in 1987. The renewal of the runway at Abéché, with French aid, began in 1988, and the upgrading of facilities at Faya-Largeau, also with assistance from France, began in 1990. There are more than 40 smaller airfields.

Air Afrique: BP 466, N'Djamena; tel. 51-40-20; see under Côte d'Ivoire.

Air Tchad: 27 ave du Président Tombalbaye, BP 168, N'Djamena; tel. 51-50-90; telex 5345; f. 1966; 98% govt-owned; international charters and domestic passenger, freight and charter services; Pres. DJIBANGAR MADJIREBAYE; Dir-Gen. MAHAMAT NOURI.

Tourism

Chad's potential attractions for tourists include a variety of scenery from the dense forests of the south to the deserts of the north. Receipts from tourism in 1994 totalled an estimated US $36m. According to official estimates, about 57,000 tourists visited Chad in 1995.

Délégation Régionale au Tourisme: tel. 68-13-54; f. 1962; Delegate DJASSINRA NINGADOUM.

Direction du Tourisme et de l'Hôtellerie: BP 86, N'Djamena; tel. 52-23-03; telex 5358; fax 52-43-97 Dir ZAKARIA HOSKI.

Defence

In August 1996 the Armée nationale tchadienne (ANT) was estimated to number some 25,350 (army approximately 25,000, air force 350). In addition, there were paramilitary forces of as many as 4,500 and a 5,000-strong Republican Guard. In September of that year the government announced that the army was to be restructured and the number of troops reduced, with financial support from the World Bank and the French government; in April 1997 it was reported that the number of soldiers in the ANT had been reduced to some 20,000. Military service is by conscription for three years. Under defence agreements with France, the army receives technical and other aid: in mid-1996 France deployed an estimated 800 troops in Chad.

Defence Expenditure: Budgeted at an estimated 20,000m. francs CFA in 1996.

Commander-in-Chief of the Armed Forces: IDRISS DEBY.

Chief of Army Staff: Col BACHAR MOUSSA.
Chief of Naval Staff: Lt MORNADJI MBAISSANEBE.
Chief of Air Force: (vacant).

Education

Education is officially compulsory for eight years between six and 14 years of age. Primary education begins at the age of six and lasts for six years. Secondary education, from the age of 12, lasts for a further seven years, comprising a first cycle of four years and a second cycle of three years. In 1994 primary enrolment was equivalent to 55% of children in the relevant age-group (75% of boys; 36% of girls), while the comparable ratio for secondary enrolment in 1993 was only 8% (13% of boys; 3% of girls). The Université du Tchad was opened at N'Djamena in 1971. In addition, there are several technical colleges. In 1989 the African Development Bank approved a loan of more than 3,500m. francs CFA for the construction of 40 primary schools. Total government expenditure on education in 1994 was 10,796m. francs CFA. In 1995, according to estimates by UNESCO, the average rate of adult illiteracy was 51.9% (males 37.9%; females 65.3%).

Bibliography

Buijtenhuijs, R. *Le Frolinat et les révoltes populaires du Tchad (1965–1976).* The Hague, 1978.

Le Frolinat et les guerres civiles du Tchad (1977–1984). Paris, Editions Karthala, 1987.

Cruise O'Brien, D. B., Dunn, J., and Rathbone R. (Eds). *Contemporary West African States.* Cambridge, Cambridge University Press, 1989.

Decalo, S. *Historical Dictionary of Chad.* Metuchen, NJ, Scarecrow Press, 1977; new edn 1987.

Desjardins, T. *Avec les otages du Tchad.* Paris, 1975.

Foltz, W. J. 'Chad's Third Republic: Strengths, Problems and Prospects', in *CSIS Africa Notes,* Briefing Paper No. 77. Washington, DC, Center for Strategic and International Studies, 1987.

Hugo, P. *Le Tchad.* Paris, Nouvelles Editions Latines, 1965.

Lanne, B. *Tchad-Libye. La querelle des frontières.* Paris, Editions Karthala, 1982.

Le Cornec, J. *Histoire politique du Tchad de 1900 à 1962.* Paris, Librairie générale de Droit et Jurisprudence, 1963.

Le Rouvreur, A. *Sahariens et Sahéliens du Tchad.* Paris, Berger-Levrault, 1962.

Magnant, J.-P. (Ed.). *L'Islam au Tchad.* Talence Cedex, IEP, 1992.

Mbaïosso, A. *L'éducation au Tchad.* Paris, Editions Karthala, 1990.

N'Gangbet, M. *Peut-on encore sauver le Tchad?* Paris, Editions Karthala, 1984.

N'Gansop, G.-J. *Tchad: Vingt ans de crise.* Paris, Harmattan, 1986.

Sikes, S. *Lake Chad.* London, 1972.

Whiteman, K. *Chad.* London, Minority Rights Group (Report No. 80), 1988.

Zeltner, J.-C., and Tourneux, H. *L'arabe dans le bassin du Tchad.* Paris, Editions Karthala, 1986.

THE COMOROS*

Physical and Social Geography

R. J. HARRISON CHURCH

The Comoro Islands, an archipelago of four small islands, together with numerous islets and coral reefs, lie between the east African coast and the north-western coast of Madagascar. The four islands cover a total land area of only 2,236 sq km (863 sq miles) and are scattered along a NW – SE axis, a distance of 300 km separating the towns of Moroni in the west and Dzaoudzi in the east. The French names for the islands, Grande-Comore (on which the capital, Moroni, is situated), Anjouan, Mohéli and Mayotte were changed in May 1977 to Njazidja, Nzwani, Mwali and Mahoré respectively, although the former names are still widely used. The islands are volcanic in structure, and Mt Karthala (rising to 2,440 m above sea-level) on Njazidja is still active; its last significant eruption was in 1991. Climate, rainfall and vegetation all vary greatly from island to island. There are similar divergences in soil characteristics, although in this instance natural causes have been reinforced by human actions, notably in deforestation and exhaustion of the soil.

The ethnic composition of the population (officially enumerated at 446,817, excluding Mayotte, at the census of September 1991) is complex. The first settlers were probably Melano-Polynesian peoples who came to the islands from the Far East by the sixth century AD. Immigrants from the coast of Africa, Indonesia, Madagascar and Persia, as well as Arabs, had all arrived by about 1600, when the Comoros were becoming established as a port of call on European trade routes to India and the Indonesian archipelago. The Portuguese, the Dutch and the French further enriched the ethnic pattern, the latter introducing into the islands Chinese (who have since left) and Indians. In Mayotte and Mwali Arabic features are less evident, mainly because the two islands were settled by immigrants from the African coast and Madagascar. In fact, while Arab characteristics are strong in the islands generally, in particular in the coastal towns, the African is predominant in the territory as a whole. Islam is the predominant religion of the islands. The official languages are Comorian (a mixture of Swahili and Arabic), French and Arabic. Average population density (excluding Mayotte) was 240 inhabitants per sq km at the census of September 1991, and is increasing rapidly in conjunction with growing pressure on the available land.

Recent History

Revised for this edition by ANDREW MANLEY

The Comoros, acquired as a French possession during 1841–1909, became a French Overseas Territory in 1947. The islands attained internal autonomy in December 1961, although substantial powers remained with a French resident commissioner. Local administration was carried out by an elected chamber of deputies and a government council.

A movement for full independence from France (while retaining French financial co-operation and support) gained momentum in the early 1970s and led to a referendum in December 1974, in which there was a 96% vote in favour of independence. This was strongly opposed, however, by the Mouvement populaire mahorais, which sought the status of a French overseas department for the island of Mayotte (Mahoré), where there was a 64% vote against independence. France sought to persuade the Comoran government to draft a constitution for the islands which would allow a large measure of decentralization and thus satisfy the population of Mayotte. It was also proposed by France that any constitutional proposals should be ratified by referendum in each island separately before independence could be granted. These proposals were rejected by the Comoran chamber of deputies, and on 6 July 1975 the chamber approved a unilateral declaration of independence, designated Ahmed Abdallah, president of the government council, as president of the republic and head of state, and reconstituted itself as the national assembly. Although France made no attempt to intervene, it retained control of Mayotte.

In August 1975 Abdallah was removed from office and the assembly was abolished. A national executive council, led by Prince Saïd Mohammed Jaffar, was established. Jaffar, leader of the Front national uni, a grouping of parties in favour of a more conciliatory policy towards Mayotte, was himself replaced as president in January 1976 by Ali Soilih, who obtained increased powers under the terms of a new constitution. In February Mayotte voted overwhelmingly to retain its links with France. (For further information on Mayotte, see p. 326).

Preparations for the 1976 referendum in Mayotte were accompanied by a deterioration in relations between France and the Comoros: the Comoran government nationalized all French administrative property and expelled French officials. On 31 December 1975 France formally recognized the independence of Grande-Comore (Njazidja), Anjouan (Nzwani) and Mohéli (Mwali), but all relations between the two governments, together with aid and technical assistance programmes, were effectively suspended.

The Soilih regime initiated a revolutionary programme, blending Maoist and Islamic philosophies, aimed at creating an economically self-sufficient and ideologically progressive state. The excesses of Soilih's methods aroused widespread resentment among traditional elements of society, and his economic reforms failed. Four unsuccessful coup attempts were staged during the period of the Soilih administration.

PRESIDENTIAL GOVERNMENT

The Second Abdallah Presidency, 1978–89

In May 1978 Soilih was finally overthrown in an unopposed coup, accomplished by about 50 European mercenaries, led by a Frenchman, Col Robert Denard, on behalf of the exiled ex-president, Ahmed Abdallah. Soilih was killed a fortnight later, allegedly while trying to escape from house arrest. Power was assumed by a 'politico-military directory', with Abdallah and his former deputy, Muhammed Ahmed, as co-presidents; the new administration pledged to adopt a constitution and conduct

* Most of the information contained in this chapter relates to the whole Comoran archipelago, which the Comoros claims as its national territory and has styled 'The Federal Islamic Republic of the Comoros'. The island of Mayotte, however, is administered by France as an Overseas Collectivité Territoriale, and is treated separately at the end of this chapter (p. 326).

elections, while Abdallah announced his intention of restoring good relations with members of the Arab League. Neighbouring African countries were, however, concerned by the role of mercenaries in effecting the coup, and the Comoros delegation was expelled from the ministerial council of the Organization of African Unity (OAU). The presence of Denard and his associates became increasingly embarrassing, and at the end of September they were asked to leave. Diplomatic relations with France were, however, restored shortly after the coup, and the French government, while it denied having given any official encouragement to the mercenaries, was clearly willing to support the new regime as being favourable to its strategic interests in the Indian Ocean. The resumption of French economic, cultural and military co-operation was accompanied by assistance from Arab countries (including Saudi Arabia, Kuwait and Iraq), the European Community (EC, now the European Union—EU) and the African Development Fund. In February 1979 the Comoran delegation was readmitted to the OAU.

Meanwhile, at a referendum held in October 1978, a new constitution creating a Federal Islamic Republic (in which each island was to be granted some degree of autonomy under an elected governor) was adopted by more than 99% of votes cast. Abdallah was elected president for a term of six years, and in December elections to a 38-member federal assembly (comprising 18 representatives of Njazidja, 15 of Nzwani and five of Mwali) took place. Although the new constitution provided for the free activity of all political parties, the federal assembly voted in January 1979 to establish a single-party system for a period of 12 years. The Union comorienne pour le progrès (Udzima) became the sole legal party in February 1982.

Under the terms of the 1978 constitution, it was envisaged that the island of Mayotte would rejoin the Comoran state at some future date, although Mayotte continued to demand the status of a French overseas department. The Mayotte issue was not mentioned in five agreements which were signed with France in November; both governments were apparently willing to defer making a definite decision on the future of Mayotte and to give priority to the resumption of French aid to the other islands of the archipelago.

A federal balance in the Comoran government proved difficult to establish, with the people of Mwali, for example, complaining that they were under-represented in major posts. There were reports of political repression: Amnesty International and other groups expressed concern at the alleged ill-treatment of political prisoners. In February 1981 about 150 people were arrested, following reports (which were officially denied) of an attempted coup. The detainees were released in May, together with 31 of the 40 political prisoners who had been convicted of involvement in the coup in 1978. A number of unofficial opposition groups, which were based mainly in France, were established.

In January 1982, following allegations of government corruption and financial mismanagement, Abdallah dissolved the federal assembly and appointed a new prime minister, Ali Mroudjae, formerly minister of foreign affairs and co-operation. A new council of ministers, which was to implement the government's policy of economic revival, was appointed. Elections to a new federal assembly took place in March and it was announced that the civil service was to be reduced in size by one-third. Constitutional amendments, approved in October, increased the power of the president, while reducing that of the governors of the four islands; each governor was henceforth to be appointed by the president and no longer directly elected. In addition, the federal government became responsible for controlling the islands' economic resources.

At a presidential election, which took place in September 1984, Abdallah (who was the sole candidate) was re-elected for a further six-year term by 99.4% of votes cast. Despite appeals by opposition groups for voters to boycott the election, some 98% of the electorate participated. In January 1985, following the adoption of constitutional amendments, the post of prime minister was abolished, and President Abdallah assumed the powers of head of government. In March an attempt by members of the presidential guard to overthrow Abdallah (who was absent on a private visit to France) was thwarted. In November 17 people, including Mustapha Saïd Cheikh, the secretary-general of the Front démocratique (FD), a banned opposition movement, were sentenced to forced labour for life and 50 others were imprisoned for their part in the coup attempt. In December, however, 30 political prisoners, many of whom were members of the FD, were granted amnesty, and in May 1986 a further 15 detainees were released.

In February 1987 the government announced that elections to the federal assembly would take place in March. Although Abdallah had indicated that all political groups would be permitted to participate, opposition candidates were allowed to contest seats only on Njazidja, where they obtained more than 35% of votes cast; Udzima retained full control of the legislature. In July 1987 Abdallah reinstated all the civil servants who had been dismissed or suspended following the coup attempt in 1985, in an apparent effort to gain favour with the traditional Comoran élite, which dominated the civil service. In November 1987, during Abdallah's absence in France, the Comoran authorities suppressed an attempted coup by a left-wing group. In April the president's son, Nassuf Abdallah, formed the pro-government Union régionale pour la défense de la politique du Président Ahmed Abdallah, which was based on Njazidja.

In mid-1987 it was reported that Abdallah intended to secure a third elected term as president, following the expiry of his mandate in 1990, and that the constitution, which limited presidential tenure to two six-year terms, was to be revised accordingly. In November 1989 the constitutional amendment permitting Abdallah to serve a third six-year term as president was approved by 92.5% of votes cast in a popular referendum. However, this result was challenged by the president's opponents, and violent demonstrations ensued.

Mercenary Intervention

On the night of 26–27 November 1989 President Abdallah was assassinated in an attack on the presidential palace by members of the presidential guard (which included a number of European advisers), under the command of Col Denard. As stipulated in the constitution, the president of the supreme court, Saïd Mohamed Djohar, took office as interim head of state, pending a presidential election. Denard and his supporters however, staged a coup, in which 27 members of the security forces were reportedly killed. This effective seizure of power by Denard prompted immediate international condemnation; France and South Africa suspended aid to the islands, despite denials by Denard of any complicity in Abdallah's death. France despatched a naval task force to Mayotte, with the stated aim of evacuating French citizens from the Comoros. In mid-December Denard agreed to withdraw peacefully from the islands, and, following the arrival of French paratroops in Moroni, was flown to South Africa with 25 other mercenaries. It was subsequently agreed that a French military presence would remain on the islands for up to two years in order to train local security forces.

The Djohar Presidency, 1990–96

At the end of December 1989 the main political groups agreed to form a provisional government of national unity. A general amnesty was granted to all political prisoners, and an inquiry was initiated into the assassination of President Abdallah. In January 1990 demonstrations were staged in protest at the postponement of the presidential election, due to be held that month, until February. The election duly took place on 18 February, but voting was abandoned, amid opposition allegations of widespread fraud. Balloting eventually took place on 4 and 11 March; after an inconclusive first round, Djohar, who was supported by Udzima, obtained 55.3% of the total votes cast, while Mohamed Taki, the leader of the Union nationale pour la démocratie aux Comores (UNDC), secured 44.7% of the vote. In late March Djohar appointed a new government, which included two of his minor opponents in the presidential election: Prince Saïd Ali Kemal (grandson of the last sultan of the Comoros), a former diplomat and the founder of the opposition Islands' Fraternity and Unity Party (CHUMA), and Ali Mroudjae, a former prime minister and the leader of the Parti comorien pour la démocratie et le progrès (PCDP). In April Djohar accused Taki, who was temporarily abroad, of attempting to destabilize the government, and threatened reprisals against him. In the same month Djohar announced plans for the formal constitutional restoration of a multi-party political system, and indicated that extensive economic reforms were to be undertaken.

On 18–19 August 1990 a coup was attempted by armed rebels, who attacked various French installations on Njazidja. Two Comorans who were detained in connection with the plot were alleged to be supporters of Taki. The revolt was apparently organized by a small group of European mercenaries, who intended to bring about Djohar's downfall through the enforced removal of French forces from the islands. In September the minister of the interior and administrative reform, Ibrahim Halidi, was accused of involvement in the conspiracy and dismissed from office. By mid-September more than 20 people had been detained in connection with the insurgency. It was reported in October that the leader of the conspirators, Max Veillard, had been killed by Comoran security forces.

A ministerial reshuffle, which took place in October 1990, was followed by a period of dissension within the leadership of Udzima. By December an unofficial contest for the chairmanship of the party had emerged between the minister of foreign affairs, Mtara Maecha, and two former ministers from the Abdallah administration, Saïd Ahmed Saïd Ali (Sharif) and Omar Tamou.

In March 1991 the government announced that a conference, comprising three representatives of each political association, was to be convened to discuss constitutional reform. The conference took place in May, but several principal opposition parties, which objected to arrangements whereby Djohar reserved the right to modify the conference's recommendations, refused to attend. However, the conference presented draft constitutional amendments, which were to be submitted for endorsement by a national referendum.

On 3 August 1991 the president of the supreme court, Ibrahim Ahmed Halidi, announced the dismissal of Djohar, on the grounds of negligence, with the support of the court, and proclaimed himself interim president. Opposition leaders declared the seizure of power to be legitimate under the terms of the constitution. The government, however, ordered the arrests of Halidi and several other members of the supreme court. A state of emergency was imposed, and remained in force until early September. In August the government banned all public demonstrations, following violent clashes between pro-government demonstrators and members of the opposition.

Djohar subsequently formed a new coalition government, which included two members of the FD. In an attempt to appease increasing discontent on the island of Mwali, which had repeatedly demanded greater autonomy, two members of Mwalian opposition groups were appointed to the government. However, the two dominant parties in the coalition, Udzima and the PCDP, objected to the ministerial changes, and accused Djohar of attempting to reduce their influence. Shortly afterwards the PCDP and Udzima left the government.

In November 1991 Udzima condemned the proposed constitutional amendments and joined the opposition. Opposition leaders demanded the dissolution of the federal assembly, which they declared to be illegitimate on the grounds that it had been elected under the former one-party system, and the formation of a government of national unity. Later in November, however, Djohar reached an agreement with the principal opposition leaders to initiate a process of national reconciliation, which would include the formation of a government of national unity and the convening of a new constitutional conference. The agreement also recognized the legitimacy of Djohar's election as president.

In January 1992 a new transitional government of national unity was formed, under the leadership of Taki, who was designated as its co-ordinator. Later in January a national conference, comprising representatives of political associations supporting Djohar and of opposition parties, was convened to draft a new constitution, which was subsequently to be submitted for approval by public referendum. However, the conference was boycotted by representatives of Mwali (which in late 1991 had announced plans to conduct a referendum on self-determination for the island). In April 1992 the conference submitted a number of constitutional reform proposals.

In May 1992 18 opposition parties demanded the resignation of Djohar's son-in-law, Mohamed M'Changama, as minister of finance, following allegations of irregularities in negotiating government contracts. Djohar subsequently redesignated Taki as prime minister and formed a new interim cabinet, in which, however, M'Changama retained his portfolio. The constitutional referendum was postponed from late May until 7 June, when, despite concerted opposition by eight parties, led by Udzima and the FD, the reform proposals were accepted by 74.25% of those voting. The new constitutional provisions, which limited presidential tenure to a maximum of two five-year terms, also provided for a bicameral legislature, comprising a federal assembly, together with a 15-member senate, comprising five representatives from each island to be chosen by an electoral college. Elections at national and local level were to take place later in 1992. In early July the president dismissed Taki from the cabinet, on the grounds that he had allegedly appointed a former associate of Col Denard to a financial advisory post in the government. Later that month a new government was formed.

In mid-1992 social and economic conditions on the Comoros deteriorated, following renewed strikes in a number of sectors, in protest at economic austerity measures undertaken by the government in conjunction with the IMF and World Bank. In early September Djohar announced that legislative elections were to begin in late October, but opposition parties claimed that the schedule provided insufficient time for preparation, and threatened to boycott the elections. Later that month a demonstration, organized by Udzima, the UNDC and the FD, in support of demands for Djohar's resignation, was forcibly suppressed.

In late September 1992, during a visit by Djohar to Paris, a coup attempt was mounted by disaffected members of the armed forces, who seized the radio station at Moroni and announced that the government had been overthrown. A number of the rebels, including two sons of ex-president Abdallah were subsequently arrested, and, in October, were charged with involvement in the insurgency. In mid-October rebel troops, led by a former member of Abdallah's presidential guard, attacked the military garrison of Kandani, in an attempt to release the detainees. Shortly afterwards, government forces attacked the rebels at Mbeni, to the north-east of Moroni; fighting was also reported on Nzwani. Later in October a demonstration was staged in protest at the French government's support of Djohar. By the end of October some 25 people had been killed in clashes between rebels and government troops in Moroni.

In October 1992 Djohar agreed to delay the legislative elections until late November, although opposition parties demanded a further postponement, and Udzima and the UNDC continued to support a boycott of the elections. The first round of the elections, which took place on 22 November, was marred by widespread violence and electoral irregularities. Several of the 21 political parties that had contested the election demanded that the results be declared invalid, and joined the boycott implemented by Udzima and the UNDC. Results in six constituencies were subsequently annulled, while the second round of voting, on 29 November, took place in only 34 of the 42 constituencies. Following partial elections on 13 and 30 December, reports indicated that candidates supporting the president, including seven members of the Union des démocrates pour le développement (UDD), had secured a narrow majority in the federal assembly. The leader of the UDD, Ibrahim Abdérémane Halidi, was appointed prime minister on 1 January 1993, and formed a new council of ministers. Later in January, in response to pressure from the Mwalian deputies in the federal assembly, one of their number, Amir Attoumane, was elected speaker. Shortly after the new government took office, divisions began to emerge between Djohar and Halidi, while the political parties supporting Djohar, which commanded a majority in the federal assembly, fragmented into three dissenting factions. A reshuffle in late February failed to resolve their grievances over the allocation of portfolios.

In April 1993 nine people, including the two sons of ex-president Abdallah and two prominent members of Udzima, were convicted on charges of involvement with the coup attempt in September 1992, and sentenced to death. After domestic and international pressure the sentences were commuted. In May 1993 the government announced that local government elections were to take place in September. Later in May eight supporters of M'Changama, allied with a number of opposition deputies, proposed a motion of censure against the government (apparently with the tacit support of Djohar), contesting Halidi's competence as prime minister. Following the approval of the motion by 23 of the 42 deputies in the federal assembly, Djohar replaced Halidi with an associate of M'Changama, Saïd Ali Mohamed. Mohamed subsequently formed a new council of ministers, which, however, received the support of only 13 of the 42 members of the federal assembly. In mid-June 19 parliamentary deputies affiliated to Halidi, who had established an informal alliance, known as the Rassemblement pour le triomphe et la démocratie, proposed a motion of censure against the new government, on the grounds that the prime minister had not been appointed from a party that commanded a majority in the federal assembly. However, Djohar declared the motion unconstitutional, dissolved the federal assembly, and announced legislative elections. Shortly afterwards, he appointed a former presidential adviser, Ahmed Ben Cheikh Attoumane, as prime minister. A new council of ministers was subsequently formed (although two of the newly-appointed ministers immediately resigned).

Following the dissolution of the federal assembly, opposition parties declared Djohar unfit to hold office, in view of the increasing political confusion, and demanded that legislative elections take place within the period of 40 days stipulated in the constitution. In early July, however, Djohar announced that the elections were to be postponed until October, and requested that the 24 registered political parties form themselves into three main groupings. Despite pressure from the French government, Djohar failed to honour earlier pledges to grant amnesties to those imprisoned following the coup attempt in September 1992. Later in July 1993 opposition parties organized a widely-observed one-day general strike as a prelude to a campaign of civil disobedience designed to force Djohar to bring forward the legislative elections or to resign. Opposition members who had allegedly participated in the campaign of civil disobedience were temporarily detained.

In early September 1993 a number of opposition movements, led by Udzima and the UNDC, established an informal electoral alliance, known as the Union pour la République et le progrès. The FD, the PCDP, CHUMA and the Mouvement pour la démocratie et le progrès (MDP) also announced that they would present joint candidates. Later in September Djohar postponed the legislative elections until November, officially on the grounds that the government had inadequate resources to conduct them. There was, however, widespread speculation that Djohar was seeking to gain time to organize his supporters into a united alliance to contest the elections. In the same month security forces closed a private radio station owned by Abbas Djoussouf, the leader of the MDP.

Having failed to obtain party political support for an electoral alliance, (owing to hostility towards M'Changama) Djohar announced in October 1993 the formation of a new party, the Rassemblement pour la démocratie et le renouveau (RDR), mainly comprising supporters of M'Changama and including several prominent members of the government. Later that month 16 political parties, including several organizations that supported Djohar, threatened to boycott the elections unless the government repealed legislation that redrew constituency boundaries and appointed a new electoral commission. Opposition supporters subsequently prevented government candidates from convening political gatherings. In November the legislative elections were rescheduled for 12 and 19 December, and local government elections were postponed indefinitely. Later in November Djohar reshuffled the council of ministers, and established a new electoral commission, in compliance with the demands of the opposition.

In the first round of the legislative elections, which took place on 12 December 1993, four opposition candidates secured seats in the federal assembly, apparently provoking official concern. However, in the second round of polling, it was reported that three people had been killed in violent incidents on Nzwani, where the authorities had taken over supervision of the polling stations. The electoral commission subsequently invalidated results in eight constituencies. Partial elections subsequently took place in these constituencies and at Moroni, where the second round of voting had been postponed at the demand of two government candidates; however, opposition candidates refused to participate on the grounds that voting was again to be conducted under government supervision rather than that of the electoral commission. The RDR consequently secured all 10 contested seats in the partial elections, and 22 seats overall, thereby gaining a narrow majority in the federal assembly. In early January 1994 Djohar appointed the secretary-general of the RDR, Mohamed Abdou Madi, as prime minister. The new council of ministers included several supporters of M'Changama, who was elected speaker of the federal assembly.

Following the installation of the new government, 12 prominent opposition parties adopted a joint resolution claiming that the RDR had obtained power illegally, and established a new alliance, known as the Forum pour le redressement national (FRN), led by Djoussouf. Later in January 1994 three opposition leaders, including Djoussouf, were temporarily prevented from leaving the Comoros. In February security forces seized the transmitters of a private radio station, owned by Udzima, which had broadcast independent news coverage. In March the Comoros protested to the French government, after a French periodical published an article claiming that M'Changama was implicated in a number of fraudulent business transactions. At a religious ceremony later that month, attended by Djohar, a former bodyguard of an RDR candidate was arrested by the security forces and stated to be in possession of a firearm. A former governor of Njazidja and member of the FRN, Mohamed Abdérémane, was subsequently arrested and temporarily detained, on suspicion of involvement in an assassination attempt against Djohar. Djoussouf and Mroudjae (who was also a prominent member of the FRN) were also questioned.

In April 1994 pressure increased from both the Comoran opposition and the French government in favour of an amnesty for political prisoners. In the same month disagreements emerged between M'Changama and Abdou Madi over the appointments of a number of senior officials. At the end of May teachers initiated strike action (which was later joined by health workers) in support of higher salaries and the reorganization of the public sector. In early June a motion of censure against Abdou Madi, proposed by supporters of the FRN in the federal assembly, was rejected. In mid-June five people were killed on Mwali, following an opposition demonstration in support of the strike, which was violently suppressed by the security forces.

An agreement by the government to sell the state-owned airline, Air Comores, to an international financier, known as Rowland Ashley, was rescinded in June 1994, following protests from both opposition and government supporters in the federal assembly. As a compromise, Ashley's privately-owned company was granted management of the airline's operations. In August, however, Ashley's credentials were shown to be fraudulent; he subsequently alleged that prominent members of the government had accepted bribes in connection with the proposed sale. Later that month the political management committee of the RDR, which was headed by M'Changama, criticized Abdou Madi's involvement in the affair.

In early September 1994 public-sector workers carried out further strikes; union officials refused to enter into negotiations with the authorities while Abdou Madi's government remained in power. In mid-September the government suspended the salaries of workers joining the general strike. In the same month the French national airline, Air France, threatened to suspend flights to the Comoros, in protest at debts incurred by Air Comores under Ashley's management. Despite previous expressions of support for Abdou Madi, in October Djohar dismissed him as prime minister (apparently over the Air Comores affair), and appointed Halifa Houmadi to the post. The resultant new council of ministers included only two members of the former administration.

In November 1994 negotiations between the government and union officials, which were initiated by Houmadi, ended in failure. In December Djohar denied a request by the federal assembly to grant amnesty to political prisoners who had been implicated in the coup attempt in September 1992. In January 1995 public-sector workers suspended strike action, after the government agreed to a number of union demands. In the same month Djohar condemned a decision by the French government to reimpose visa requirements for Comoran nationals entering Mayotte; the French authorities were responding to concerns over illegal economic migration by Comorans. Threats were reportedly issued against French residents. Later in January divisions emerged within the RDR, after the party chairman and secretary-general (Abdou Madi) both criticized the government's failure to contain the hostility towards French citizens. At an

RDR congress in early February the two officials were removed from the party, and Houmadi took over the chairmanship. In the same month the government announced that elections to the regional councils would take place in April, to be followed by the establishment of a senate and a constitutional council (in accordance with the terms of the constitution). The opposition, however, accused Djohar of resorting to unconstitutional tactics and electoral manipulation. In March Djohar announced that forthcoming elections to the regional councils were to be rescheduled for July 1996, ostensibly for financial reasons.

In April 1995 reports emerged of disagreements between Djohar and Houmadi, following accusations by Houmadi of financial corruption by Djohar and M'Changama. Djohar subsequently replaced Houmadi as prime minister with a former minister of finance, Mohamed Caabi El Yachroutu, who brought with him a reputation as a reformist, technocratic administrator, with good relations with the IMF and World Bank. A 13-member cabinet, including only five members of the previous administration, was formed. In May three former prime ministers, Mohamed, Abdou Madi and Houmadi, urged the removal of M'Changama (who, they claimed, exerted undue influence over Djohar) and the dissolution of the federal assembly. In July further tension developed within the cabinet over an agreement whereby Air Comores was to be jointly managed by an airline based in the United Arab Emirates, Menon Airways: M'Changama and the minister of transport and tourism, Ahmed Saïd Issilame, claimed that the agreement was technically invalid, having been signed by Djohar before legislation providing for the privatization of Air Comores had been approved in the federal assembly. Meanwhile, it was feared that the further postponement of elections to the regional councils would delay the presidential election. To facilitate the organization of the presidential poll, the government introduced minor constitutional amendments, including the relaxation of regulations governing the registration of political candidates and a provision allowing the prime minister to act as interim head of state. At the end of July Djohar removed Issilame and a further three associates of M'Changama from the council of ministers.

Invasion and Intervention

In late September 1995 about 30 European mercenaries, led by Denard, staged an armed coup, seizing control of the garrison at Kandani and capturing Djohar. The mercenaries, joined by some 300 members of the Comoran armed forces, released a number of prisoners (including those detained for involvement in the September 1992 coup attempt), and installed a former associate of Denard, Capt. Ayouba Combo, as a leader of a transitional military committee. The French government denounced the coup and suspended economic aid to the Comoros, but initially refused to intervene, despite requests for assistance from El Yachroutu, who had taken refuge in the French embassy. In early October Combo announced that he had transferred authority to Mohamed Taki and the leader of CHUMA, Saïd Ali Kemal (both of whom had welcomed the coup), as joint civilian presidents, apparently in an attempt to avert military action by the French government. The FRN, however, rejected the new leadership and entered into negotiations with El Yachroutu. Following a further appeal for intervention from El Yachroutu, who invoked a defence co-operation agreement that had been established between the two countries in 1978, some 900 French military personnel landed on the Comoros. Shortly afterwards, Denard and his associates, together with the disaffected members of the Comoran armed forces, surrendered to the French troops. (The mercenaries were subsequently placed under arrest and transported to France.)

Following the French military intervention, El Yachroutu declared himself interim president in accordance with the constitution and announced the formation of a government of national unity, which included members of the constituent parties of the FRN. Djohar (who had been transported to Réunion by the French in order to receive medical treatment) rejected El Yachroutu's assumption of power and announced the reappointment of Saïd Ali Mohamed as prime minister. Later in October a national reconciliation conference decided that El Yachroutu would remain interim president, pending the forthcoming election, which was provisionally scheduled for early 1996. The interim administration, which was supported by the armed forces, refused to recognize Djohar's appointments and announced that he would be prohibited from re-entering the country. At the end of October El Yachroutu granted an amnesty to all Comorans involved in the coup attempt and appointed representatives of the UNDC and Udzima (which had supported the coup) to the new council of ministers. In early November both governments simultaneously convened cabinet meetings and held rival political rallies in the capital, and it was reported that separatist movements had become active on Nzwani and Mwali. Representatives of the OAU, who visited the Comoros and Réunion in mid-November in an effort to resolve the situation, unofficially advised their organization that only El Yachroutu's administration was capable of governing. It was also widely believed that the French government had tacitly encouraged Djohar's removal from power. Later in November, however, supporters of Djohar, including M'Changama, organized a political gathering to demand the resignation of El Yachroutu's administration. Meanwhile, political leaders on Mwali rejected the authority of both rival governments, urged a campaign of civil disobedience and established a 'citizens' committee' to govern the island; discontent with the central administration also emerged on Nzwani.

The Taki Presidency

In December 1995 a decision by El Yachroutu's government to schedule the presidential election for the end of January 1996 was opposed by a number of political leaders (including Taki, Kemal and M'Changama), who demanded a postponement until March, ostensibly on the grounds that the stipulated date would coincide with the Islamic festival of Ramadan. In January 1996 the government agreed to reschedule the presidential election for March. (Some 15 presidential candidates subsequently emerged.) Later that month Djohar returned to the Comoros, after apparently signing an agreement stipulating that he would retain only symbolic presidential powers.

In the first round of the presidential election, which took place on 6 March 1996, Taki and the leader of the MDP, Abbas Djoussouf, secured the highest number of votes; it was subsequently reported that 12 of the 13 unsuccessful candidates had transferred their support to Taki in the second round of the election. Taki was duly elected to the presidency on 16 March, obtaining 64% of the vote. International observers, including delegates from the UN and OAU, were satisfied with the electoral process; officials reported that 62% of the electorate had participated in the second round. The new head of state was sworn in on 25 March. Taki appointed a new council of ministers, headed by Tadjidine Ben Saïd Massoundi, which included five of the presidential candidates who had given him their support in the second round of the election.

In early April 1996 Taki dissolved the federal assembly and announced that legislative elections would take place on 6 October, despite the constitutional requirement that elections be held within a period of 40 days following a dissolution. New governors, all belonging to the UNDC, were appointed to each of the three islands. In mid-June, during a visit to France, discussions took place between Taki and the French president, Jacques Chirac. Taki requested financial aid to enable him to liquidate the wage arrears owed to civil servants, and confirmed his wish for French troops to remain on the Comoros. It was subsequently announced that Chirac had agreed to these requests and, in addition, had offered French assistance in the reorganization of public finance, education, public health and the judicial system.

In a government reorganization in late August 1996, Saïd Ali Kemal and a representative of the Forces pour l'action républicaine were dismissed, following their parties' refusal to disband in order to join the single pro-presidential party which Taki intended to establish. A consultative committee on the constitution, established in September, considered requests from Taki for the reinforcement of presidential powers, including the president's right to choose governors for each island, and an end to the two-term limit on presidential office. Other proposals included a more visibly Islamist orientation of the state, with the names of Allah and the Prophet Muhammad to be inscribed on the national flag. Taki also promised a return to sharia-based lawgiving (public executions for murder were instituted in September). The constitutional committee was boycotted by the FRN and other opposition parties. The referendum on the constitutional reforms, held on 20 October, attracted a reported 64% turnout, 85% of whom voted in favour of the new constitution. It was then announced that the first round of the proposed legislative elections would be postponed until 1 December. Meanwhile, Taki had succeeded in building a single-party ruling group to back his presidency. On 5 October delegates from the UNDC, RDR, Udzima, and 20 other pro-government parties merged, as the Rassemblement national pour le développement (RND). This prompted Abbas Djoussouf and other anti-Taki politicians to form the Collectif de l'opposition and announce, on 13 November, a boycott of the legislative elections. On 30 November a number of government opponents, including former prime ministers Ali Mroudjae and Mohammed Abdou Madi, were arrested on arson charges, as the boycott campaign continued. They were released on 2 December. Results from the polls held on 1 December gave the RND 32 seats out of a total of 43 in the federal assembly. There were widespread reports of irregularities. The second round awarded a further four seats to the RND, giving it 36 seats, with the Islamist Front national pour la justice obtaining three seats, and independent candidates four.

Following the elections, the prime minister, Tadjidine Ben Saïd Massoundi, resigned. A new government was appointed on 27 December 1996, under Ahmed Abdou. It included such veteran politicians as Ibrahim Halidi and Mouazoir Abdallah. The government quickly came into conflict with opposition politicians and public servants. On 1 January 1997 workers went on strike in protest against salary arrears of up to 10 months. Opposition politicians, including Djoussouf, were detained on several occasions in January, and 30 people were injured during a demonstration in Moroni late in the month when strikers clashed with the security forces. There was further unrest and isolated incidents of arson in February. Meanwhile, tensions rose further on Nzwani and Mwali. On Nzwani there were serious clashes between workers and the security forces in mid-March, as up to 3,000 people erected barricades in the streets of the main town, Mutsamudu. Up to four people were reported to have been killed. Taki replaced the senior members of the Nzwani island administration and carried out a minor cabinet reshuffle. By that time, informal contacts had been taking place with Djoussouf and other opposition leaders and in May it was reported that, in an attempt to resolve the crisis, Taki and Djoussouf had agreed to establish a joint commission to define terms for a proposed accord on the participation of the FRN in formulating national policy. Two people were killed on Nzwani in mid-July in skirmishes between the security forces and separatists who had raised the French flag and blocked roads around Mutsamudu during a demonstration.

EXTERNAL RELATIONS

Diplomatic relations between the Comoros and France, suspended in December 1975, were restored in July 1978; in November of that year the two countries signed agreements on military and economic co-operation, apparently deferring any decision on the future of Mayotte. In subsequent years, however, member countries of the UN general assembly repeatedly voted in favour of a resolution affirming the Comoros' sovereignty over Mayotte, with only France dissenting. Following Djohar's accession to power, diplomatic relations were established with the USA in June 1990. In September of that year the Comoros and South Africa signed a bilateral agreement providing for a series of South African loans towards the development of infrastructure in the Comoros. In September 1993 the League of Arab States (Arab League) accepted an application for membership from the Comoros. In November 1994 the government signed an agreement with Israel that provided for the establishment of diplomatic relations between the two countries, prompting protests from the Arab League and from Islamic leaders in the Comoros. Djohar subsequently announced that the implementation of the agreement was to be postponed, pending a satisfactory resolution to the conflict in the Middle East. Since his election in 1996 Taki has cultivated closer relations with the president of Gabon, Omar Bongo, and with the People's Republic of China.

Economy

Revised for this edition by ANDREW MANLEY

The Comoros, with few natural resources, a chronic shortage of cultivable land, a narrow base of agricultural crops and a high density of population, is among the poorest countries of sub-Saharan Africa, and is highly dependent on external trade and assistance. In 1995, according to estimates by the World Bank, the gross national product (GNP) of the Comoros (excluding Mayotte), measured at average 1993–95 prices, was US $237m., equivalent to $470 per head. During 1985–95, it was estimated, GNP per head declined, in real terms, at an average annual rate of 1.4%. Over the same period, the population increased by an annual average of 2.8%. The Comoros' gross domestic product (GDP) increased, in real terms, by an annual average of 0.6% in 1985–95; GDP declined by 2.3% in 1994, and again in 1995, according to the World Bank.

Agriculture is the dominant economic activity in the Comoros (contributing an estimated 38.7% of GDP and employing about 75.2% of the labour force in 1995). At the census of September 1991, despite large-scale emigration to neighbouring countries, overall population density was 240 inhabitants per sq km (excluding Mayotte), with a density of 445.6 on the island of Nzwani (Anjouan). The problem of overpopulation on the three independent islands has worsened since the break with Mayotte, which has the largest area of unexploited cultivable land in the archipelago. Settlers from Nzwani and Njazidja (Grande-Comore) have been compelled to leave Mayotte and return to their already overpopulated native islands, where the potential for agricultural development is very limited.

Local subsistence farming, using primitive implements and techniques, is inadequate to maintain the population. Yields are poor, storage facilities lacking, and much of the best land is reserved for export cash-crop production. Cassava, sweet potatoes, rice, maize, pulses, coconuts and bananas are also cultivated. Almost all meat and vegetables are imported, as is most of the rice consumed on the islands.

The major export crops are vanilla, ylang-ylang and cloves. Prices for vanilla, of which the islands are the world's second largest producer (with an estimated average output of 180-200 tons per year), have been affected in recent years by competition from low-cost producers, notably Indonesia, and by synthetic substitutes. France accounts for about one-third of the Comoros' vanilla exports. Adverse conditions in the market for cloves have prevailed since the mid-1980s; only 474 metric tons were exported in 1992 (compared with 2,750 tons in 1991). In 1994, however, 2,755 tons of cloves were exported, and in early 1995 the authorities signed export contracts providing for the purchase of the Comoros' total annual harvest of cloves, although only 483 tons of exports were recorded in that year. The Comoros is the world's main supplier of ylang-ylang, for which prices have been favourable in recent years. Ageing plantations and inadequate processing equipment, however, have prevented this export from achieving its full potential, and output declined from 72 metric tons in 1989 to an estimated 44 tons in 1995. Shortfalls in foreign exchange revenue from these three commodities have been met by funds, under the Stabex (Stabilization of Export Earnings) scheme provided for in the Lomé Conventions. The commercial exploitation of copra, formerly a significant export crop, has virtually ceased, owing to lack of demand from the domestic and international market. Agricultural GDP increased by an annual average of 3.3% in 1985–90, and by 0.3% in 1992–95.

The manufacturing sector contributed an estimated 5.3% of GDP in 1995. The sector consists primarily of the processing of agricultural produce, particularly of vanilla and essential oils, and a few factories supplying the domestic market. Manufacturing GDP increased by an annual average of 4.6% in 1985–90 and by 2.8% in 1992–95.

Fishing is practised on a small scale, with a total catch of about 13,500 metric tons in 1994, according to the FAO. According to recent studies, the Comoros has a potential annual catch of 25,000–30,000 tons of tuna, which could provide the basis for a processing industry. A two-year project, aiming to provide an infrastructure for a Comoran fishing industry, has been initiated. The Comoros' fishing industry has received substantial aid from Japan. In October 1987 the Comoros and the European Community (EC, now the European Union—EU) signed a fishing agreement which permitted 40 tuna-fishing vessels from EC countries to operate in Comoran waters for three years and allowed the implementation of a scientific programme; the agreement was renewed in early 1995, with effect until July 1997.

The Comoros has a developing tourist industry. In 1991 16,942 tourists visited the islands (compared with 7,627 in 1990), of which 9,584 were European. In 1993 the number of tourists increased to an estimated 24,000, while receipts from tourism totalled US $8m. The devaluation of the Comoros franc by 33% (in relation to the French franc) in January 1994 was thought to have improved the sector's competitiveness, and receipts increased considerably, mostly due to the change in the exchange rate; the number of tourists increased to 27,000 in that year. Unrest in the wake of the attempted mercenary coup of September 1995 has, however, inhibited subsequent growth. The majority of tourists are from France and South Africa. In the late 1980s the government, with financial support from South Africa, implemented a number of hotel development projects; in 1991 hotel capacity increased fom 112 to 294 rooms, with another 90 rooms available in small family guest-houses.

Economic development in the Comoros is impeded by poor infrastructure, with a shortage of electricity, a very limited road system and a lack of reliable transportation between the islands and with the outside world. In the early 1990s, however, public investment laid emphasis on infrastructural development, with the initiation of a programme, financed by the EC, to construct a port at Fomboni, on Mwali, to improve shipping access to the island, and the expansion of the road network on all three islands. In January 1996 the EU pledged just over US $7m. for repairs to one of the major roads on Nzwani. The country's air carrier, Air Comores, has been inactive since privatization arrangements collapsed in 1994 (see below). Charter operations have taken its place, providing long-haul air links with Dubai, Paris and Johannesburg

France represents the main source of economic support (see below), while the other member states of the EU, Japan (see above), Saudi Arabia, Kuwait and the United Arab Emirates also provide financial assistance. The government's development priorities for the 1980s were: increased production of basic foodstuffs and energy; an improvement in inter-island communications, water supply, and housing and regional development; and the creation of more efficient public health and training facilities. The Comoros' first international aid donors' conference took place in Moroni in 1984: discussion focused on the Comoros Development Plan 1983–86, which aimed to achieve self-sufficiency in food, improved supplies of water and electricity, better health care, urban planning and housing, and a controlled rate of population growth. Donors pledged some US $114m. of project finance, of which $15.25m. was allocated for the construction of a hydroelectric power plant on Nzwani. In 1985 the EC announced that it would channel 7,065m. Comoros francs into aid for the agricultural sector over the period 1986–90. In 1988 the European Development Fund approved loans to develop the port at Moroni; the project was completed in mid-1991. France, the Comoros' major bilateral donor, provided 29.5m. French francs in budgetary aid in 1988 and 30m. French francs in 1989. In 1990 the French government cancelled Comoran debt totalling 229m. French francs, and waived repayment of a state loan of a further 9m. French francs. In 1991 the Comoros government received substantial budgetary aid from France, which facilitated the repayment of about $14m. of debt arrears owed to the African Development Bank (ADB), allowing the resumption of suspended disbursements. In 1992 France pledged some 60m. French francs towards co-operation projects, and budgetary aid totalling 20m. French francs. Following the devaluation of the Comoros franc in January 1994, the French government agreed to cancel outstanding debt arrears. In 1993 budgetary assistance from France contributed to the payment of civil servants' salaries, while French aid in 1994 was again expected to allow the repayment of arrears owed to the ADB, as a precondition to the resumption of credit from that organization. French aid to the Comoros reached 155.5m. French francs in 1995 (increasing to an estimated 168.9m. French francs in 1996). At the end of 1994, however, France suspended budgetary assistance (which had totalled 24m. French francs in 1994) to the Comoros, in response to the Comoran government's failure to agree a structural adjustment programme with the International Monetary Fund (IMF) and the World Bank. In May 1996 a French trade mission visited Moroni to discuss possible projects. However, the French government reiterated its insistence that the Comoros reach an accommodation with the World Bank and the IMF before budgetary assistance could be renewed, but agreed to continue to provide aid for projects in the social sector and education. Finance in the latter area was also to be forthcoming from the United Nations Development Programme, the World Bank and UNICEF. In February 1997 the government finalized a six-month surveillance programme with the IMF (see below). In May the French government sent a number of technical advisers to assist with financial administration in the Comoros.

The Comoros' foreign trade accounts have shown a persistent deficit; imports have tended to increase, while export receipts have fluctuated widely, in response to trends in international prices for vanilla, cloves and ylang-ylang. After two particularly difficult years in 1987–88, by 1989 the visible trade deficit had declined to US $17.6m., while there was a surplus of $2.9m. on the current account of the balance of payments. In 1990, however, the visible trade deficit increased to $27.3m., and there was a deficit of $9.3m. on the current account of the balance of payments. Following a current account deficit of $1.4m. in 1991, the trade gap widened to $36.7m. in 1992, giving a current account deficit of $14.4m. There was a modest improvement in 1993, largely due to compressed demand for imports, but exports collapsed to $11m. in 1994 and 1995, leading to reported trade deficits exceeding $30m. in both years. The current account deficit stood at $19m. in 1995 and at an estimated $16m. in 1996. Principal export destinations in 1995 were France, the USA and Germany. The principal source of imports was France, followed by South Africa and Kenya. Vanilla and ylang-ylang accounted for virtually all exports; imports were dominated by rice and petroleum products.

In 1990, in an attempt to curtail increasing deficits in the budget and external current account, the government initiated measures to improve tax collection and reduce expenditure. Although these reforms were, in part, successful, domestic and external arrears remained high. In 1991, however, the budgetary deficit increased to the equivalent of 20% of GDP (compared with a level of 18% of GDP in 1990). As a result, the government suffered difficulties in meeting wage and other payment obligations. In 1993 the budget (after external grants) was in surplus by 2,012m. Comoros francs, but the following years saw heavy deficits: of 5,887m. Comoros francs in 1994, and an estimated 6,085m. Comoros francs in 1995. During 1985–94 prices of all goods and services produced in the economy increased at an average rate of 3.5% per year; however, consumer prices increased by an average of 10% in 1994 itself, due to the impact of the devaluation of the Comoros franc.

At the end of 1995 the Comoros' external public debt totalled US $203.3m. (of which $186.7m. was long-term public debt), while the cost of debt-servicing was equivalent to 0.9% of the value of exports of goods and services, due to the highly concessionary nature of the debt and accumulated interest arrears. Following negotiations with the IMF, a three-year structural adjustment programme for the period 1991–93 was agreed, providing facilities totalling almost $135m., whereby the Comoros government undertook to diversify exports, reduce public expenditure, promote export-orientated industries and transfer state-owned enterprises to private-sector ownership. Measures subsequently implemented under the programme included the abolishment of levies on export crops, the liberalization of imports of a number of commodities, the initiation of environmental projects to control soil erosion (particularly on Nzwani), the 'privatization' of a number of state-owned hotels, the liquidation of the state-owned meat-marketing company, the Société comorienne des viandes (SOCOVIA), and the dismissal of a number of civil servants. However, the restructure of the public sector prompted widespread strikes, which caused severe economic disruption. In 1992 it appeared that insufficient progress had been achieved under the programme, and in September of that year it was announced that IMF and World Bank delegations were to visit the Comoros to discuss new reform objectives. In early 1993 the World Bank and IMF agreed to continue disbursements, following the approval of government plans, which included further privatization measures and reduction in civil service personnel. However, the continuing volubility of internal political conditions impeded the implementation of the structural adjustment programme, and, despite some success in reducing fiscal imbalances, economic prospects have remained unfavourable.

In January 1994 the devaluation of the Comoros franc led to a sharp increase in the price of imported goods, prompting strike action in the education and health sectors in support of higher salaries. In March, however, following the adoption of an economic reform programme for the period 1994–96, the IMF approved a one-year structural adjustment facility, equivalent to US $1.9m., while the World Bank also agreed to further credit. The programme laid emphasis on the continuation of the restructuring of the public sector and the reduction of price controls; the government aimed to achieve economic growth of 4%, to restrict the rate of inflation to 4%, and to reduce the current account deficit (excluding official transfers) to less than 15% of GDP by 1996. In early 1995, however, plans to privatize state-owned enterprises such as the national airline, Air Comores, and the public utilities enterprise, Electricité et Eau des Comores (EEDC), in conjunction with the structural adjustment programme were impeded by inter-government dissension. At the end of that year it was announced that Air Comores was to be liquidated, with a view to establishing a new airline. Privatization plans were further delayed in 1996, initially because of the presidential elections and subsequently because of differing views within the new government as to techniques of implementation. By mid-1997 it had been agreed that EEDC would pass into private management by the French company SOGEA, with finance provided by the Caisse française de développement (see p. 122).

In mid-1995, in response to a further deterioration in the fiscal situation, the government introduced a number of measures to limit budgetary expenditure under a public finance recovery programme, including tax increases and a reduction in civil servants' salaries. However, political instability continued to impede economic progress; following a coup attempt in September (see Recent History), a new interim government initiated emergency financial measures, which included the payment of debts outstanding to the World Bank in order to qualify for agreements with international institutions. In early 1996 the government failed to adopt a budget for that year, and interim financial procedures were instigated, with the resultant confusion contributing to a further decline in the economy. During April 1996, following the election of President Mohamed Taki, various international aid-donors visited the Comoros to assess the new government's stance on economic reform, principally in relation to privatization. In the same month the World Bank outlined measures that needed to be taken by the Comoros to improve the economy: greater control of the wage bill, a reduction in public-sector staff, increased customs and fiscal revenues and the privatization of state-owned companies. In February 1997 an IMF-supervised six-month austerity programme was agreed. The government hoped this would lead to the approval of an enhanced structural adjustment facility.

Statistical Survey

Source (unless otherwise stated): Ministry of Finance, the Budget and the Economy, BP 324, Moroni; tel. 2767; telex 219.

Note: Unless otherwise indicated, figures in this Statistical Survey exclude data for Mayotte.

AREA AND POPULATION

Area: 1,862 sq km (719 sq miles) *By island:* Njazidja (Grande-Comore) 1,146 sq km, Nzwani (Anjouan) 424 sq km, Mwali (Mohéli) 290 sq km.

Population: 335,150 (males 167,089; females 168,061), excluding Mayotte (estimated population 50,740), at census of 15 September 1980; 484,000 (official estimate), including Mayotte, at 31 December 1986; 446,817 (males 221,152; females 225,665), excluding Mayotte, at census of 15 September 1991. *By island* (1991 census): Njazidja (Grande-Comore) 233,533, Nzwani (Anjouan) 188,953, Mwali (Mohéli) 24,331.

Principal Towns (population at 1980 census): Moroni (capital) 17,267; Mutsamudu 13,000; Fomboni 5,400.

Births and Deaths (including figures for Mayotte, UN estimates): Average annual birth rate 48.5 per 1,000 in 1980–85, 48.5 per 1,000 in 1985–90, 48.5 per 1,000 in 1990–95; average annual death rate 14.4 per 1,000 in 1980–85, 13.0 per 1,000 in 1985–90, 11.7 per 1,000 in 1990–95. Source: UN, *World Population Prospects: The 1994 Revision*.

Economically Active Population (ILO estimates, '000 persons at mid-1980, including figures for Mayotte): Agriculture, forestry and fishing 150; Industry 10; Services 20; Total 181 (males 104, females 77). Source: ILO, *Economically Active Population Estimates and Projections, 1950–2025.*

AGRICULTURE, ETC.

Principal Crops (FAO estimates, '000 metric tons, 1995): Rice (paddy) 17, Maize 4, Cassava (Manioc) 52, Sweet potatoes 14, Pulses 8, Coconuts 52, Bananas 58. Source: FAO, *Production Yearbook*.

Livestock (FAO estimates, '000 head, year ending September 1995): Asses 5, Cattle 50, Sheep 15, Goats 128. Source: FAO, *Production Yearbook*.

Livestock Products (FAO estimates, '000 metric tons, 1995): Meat 2 (beef and veal 1); Cows' milk 4. Source: FAO, *Production Yearbook*.

Fishing ('000 metric tons, live weight): Total catch 11.9 in 1992; 12.0 in 1993; 13.5 in 1994. Source: FAO, *Yearbook of Fishery Statistics*.

INDUSTRY

Electric energy (production by public utilities): 17 million kWh in 1994. Source: UN, *Industrial Commodity Statistics Yearbook*.

FINANCE

Currency and Exchange Rates: 100 centimes = 1 Comoros franc. *Sterling and Dollar Equivalents* (31 March 1997): £1 sterling = 693.15 Comoros francs; US $1 = 422.14 Comoros francs; 1,000 Comoros francs = £1.443 = $2.369. *Average Exchange Rate* (Comoros francs per US $): 416.40 in 1994; 374.36 in 1995; 383.66 in 1996. Note: The Comoros franc was introduced in 1981, replacing (at par) the CFA franc. The fixed link to French currency was retained, with the exchange rate set at 1 French franc = 50 Comoros francs. This remained in effect until January 1994, when the Comoros franc was devalued by 33.3%, with the exchange rate adjusted to 1 French franc = 75 Comoros francs.

Budget (million Comoros francs, 1994): *Revenue:* Tax revenue 9,799 (Taxes on income and profits 1,399; Taxes on goods and services 929; Taxes on international trade 4,045; Unified tax on petroleum products and rice 3,132); Other revenue 1,268 (Proceeds from services 525); Total 11,067, excluding grants received (12,833). *Expenditure:* Budgetary current expenditure 14,783 (Wages and salaries 6,871; Goods and services 6,008; Transfers 1,048; Interest payments 857); Current expenditure under technical assistance programmes 5,300; Budgetary capital expenditure 638; Capital expenditure financed with external resources 7,582; Total 28,303, excluding net lending (393) and civil service action plan (1,091). Source: IMF, *Comoros—Recent Economic Developments* (October 1996).

International Reserves (US $ million at 31 December 1995): Gold 0.22; IMF special drawing rights 0.11; Reserve position in IMF 0.80; Foreign exchange 43.58; Total 44.71. Source: IMF, *International Financial Statistics*.

Money Supply (million Comoros francs at 31 December 1995): Currency outside deposit money banks 5,672; Demand deposits at deposit money banks 4,170; Total money (incl. others) 11,916. Source: IMF, *International Financial Statistics*.

Expenditure on the Gross Domestic Product (million Comoros francs at current prices, 1993): Government final consumption expenditure 15,033; Private final consumption expenditure 57,347; Gross fixed capital formation 10,497; Change in stocks 2,721; *Total domestic expenditure* 85,598; Exports of goods and services 11,247; *Less* Imports of goods and services 22,583; *GDP in purchasers' values* 74,261. Source: IMF, *Comoros—Recent Economic Developments* (October 1996).

Gross Domestic Product by Economic Activity (million Comoros francs at current prices, 1993): Agriculture, hunting, forestry and fishing 29,044; Manufacturing 3,340; Electricity, gas and water 889; Construction 4,652; Trade, restaurants and hotels 21,547; Transport and communications 3,190; Finance, insurance, real estate and business services 3,452; Government services 9,669; Other services 400; *Sub-total* 76,183; *Less* Imputed bank service charge 1,922; *GDP in purchasers' values* 74,261. Source: IMF, *Comoros—Recent Economic Developments* (October 1996).

Balance of Payments (US $ million, 1994): Exports of goods f.o.b. 10.8; Imports of goods f.o.b. -44.9; *Trade balance* -34.1; Services and other income (net) -15.7. *Balance on goods, services and income* -49.7; Current transfers (net) 39.0; *Current balance* -10.7; Capital account (net) -0.6; *Overall balance* -11.3. Source: IMF, *Comoros—Recent Economic Developments* (October 1996).

EXTERNAL TRADE

Principal Commodities (million Comoros francs, 1995): *Imports c.i.f.:* Rice 5,252; Meat 1,617; Petroleum products 2,897; Cement 1,652; Iron and steel 887; Total (incl. others) 25,411. *Exports f.o.b.:* Vanilla 2,320; Clove buds 133; Ylang-ylang 855; Total (incl. others) 4,236. Source: IMF, *Comoros—Recent Economic Developments* (October 1996).

Principal Trading Partners (US $'000, 1993): *Imports:* Total 67,755. *Exports:* France 10,450; Germany 2,105; USA 11,553; Total Source: UNESCO, *Statistical Yearbook*.

(incl. others) 25,058. Source: UN, *International Trade Statistics Yearbook*. **1995** (percentage of trade): *Imports:* France 32.2%; Japan 1.3%; Kenya 4.3%; Madagascar 1.1%; Mauritius 1.3%; Réunion 3.3%; South Africa 6.7%. *Exports:* France 36.5%; Germany 8.0%; USA 28.4%. Source: IMF, *Comoros—Recent Economic Developments* (October 1996).

TRANSPORT

Road Traffic (estimates, motor vehicles in use, 1995): Passenger cars 7,080; Lorries and vans 4,870. Source: International Road Federation, *World Road Statistics*.

International Shipping (estimated sea-borne freight traffic, '000 metric tons, 1991): Goods loaded 12; Goods unloaded 107. Source: UN Economic Commission for Africa, *African Statistical Yearbook*.

Civil Aviation (traffic on scheduled services, 1994): Passengers carried ('000) 26; Passenger-km (million) 3. Source: UN, *Statistical Yearbook*.

TOURISM

Tourist Arrivals ('000): 19 in 1992; 24 in 1993; 27 in 1994.

Receipts from Tourism (US $ million): 8 in 1992; 8 in 1993; 9 in 1994.

Source: UN, *Statistical Yearbook*.

COMMUNICATIONS MEDIA

Radio receivers (1994): 81,000 in use. Source: UNESCO, *Statistical Yearbook*.

Television receivers (1994): 200 in use. Source: UNESCO, *Statistical Yearbook*.

Telephones (1994): 4,000 main lines in use. Source: UN, *Statistical Yearbook*.

EDUCATION

Pre-Primary (1980/81): 600 teachers; 17,778 pupils.

Primary (1993/94): 275 schools; 1,737 teachers; 77,837 pupils.

Secondary (1980/81): 449 (1991/92) teachers (general education 613; teacher training 11; vocational 9). (1993/94): 17,637 secondary pupils (general education 17,474; teacher training 37; vocational 126).

Higher (1992/93): 32 teachers (1989/90); 229 pupils.

Source: UNESCO, *Statistical Yearbook*.

Directory

The Constitution

The Constitution of the Federal Republic of the Comoros was approved by popular referendum on 20 October 1996. The following is a summary of the main provisions:

PREAMBLE

The preamble affirms the will of the Comoran people to derive from the state religion, Islam, inspiration for the principles and laws that the State and its institutions govern, to adhere to the principles laid down by the Charters of the UN, the Organization of African Unity and the Organization of the Islamic Conference and by the Treaty of the League of Arab States, and to guarantee the rights of all citizens, without discrimination, in accordance with the UN Declaration of Human Rights and the African Charter of Human Rights.

GENERAL PROVISIONS

The Comoros archipelago constitutes a federal Islamic republic. Sovereignty belongs to the people, and is exercised through their elected representatives or by the process of referendum. There is universal secret suffrage, which can be direct or indirect, for all citizens who are over the age of 18 and in full possession of their civil and political rights. Political parties and groups operate freely, respecting national sovereignty, democracy and territorial integrity. However, political parties which are not represented by at least two deputies from each island, as a result of the first legislative election to follow the adoption of the Constitution, will be dissolved, unless those parties merge with others which are legitimately represented in the Federal Assembly. If only one political party has representation in the Federal Assembly, the party which has obtained the second highest number of votes will continue to operate freely. Only political parties and groups active throughout the Republic may participate in national elections. Political parties must be democratic both in their internal structure and their activities.

PRESIDENT OF THE REPUBLIC

The President is the Head of State and is elected by direct universal suffrage for a six-year term, which is renewable for an unrestricted number of mandates. He is also Head of the Armed Forces and ensures the legitimate functioning of public powers and the continuation of the State. He is the guarantor of national independence, the unity of the Republic, the autonomy of the islands, territorial integrity and adherence to international agreements. Candidates for the presidency must be aged between 40 and 75 years, of Comoran nationality by birth, and resident in the archipelago for at least 12 consecutive months prior to elections. The President presides over the Council of Ministers. He is empowered to ask the Federal Assembly to reconsider a Bill. The President can, having consulted with the Prime Minister and the Presidents of the Federal Assembly and the High Council of the Republic in writing, dissolve the Federal Assembly. The President determines and implements the Republic's foreign policy.

THE GOVERNMENT

The President appoints the Prime Minister, and on his recommendations, the other members of the Government. Under the authority of the President of the Republic, the Council of Ministers determines and implements domestic policy.

LEGISLATIVE POWER

Legislative power is vested in the Federal Assembly, which represents the Comoran nation. Deputies in the Federal Assembly are elected for five years by direct suffrage. Legislative elections take place between 30 and 90 days after the expiry of the mandate of the incumbent Federal Assembly. The electoral law dictates the number of members of the Federal Assembly, but there is a minimum of five deputies from each island. The deputies elect the President of the Federal Assembly at the beginning of their mandate. The Federal Assembly sits for two sessions each year and, if necessary, for extraordinary sessions. Matters covered by federal legislation include constitutional institutions, defence, posts and telecommunications, transport, civil and penal law, public finance, external trade, federal taxation, long-term economic planning, education and health.

JUDICIAL POWER

Judicial power is independent of executive and legislative power. The President is the guarantor of the independence of the judicial system and chairs the Higher Council of the Magistracy (Conseil Supérieur de la Magistrature), of which the Minister of Justice is Vice-President.

HIGH COUNCIL OF THE REPUBLIC

The High Council of the Republic considers constitutional matters and the control of public finance, and acts as a High Court of Justice. It has a renewable mandate of seven years and is composed of four members appointed by the President, three members elected by the Federal Assembly and one member elected by the Council of each island. The High Council oversees and proclaims the results of presidential and legislative elections and referendums.

COUNCIL OF THE ULÉMAS

The Council of the Ulémas offers opinions on projects for laws, ordinances and decrees. The President of the Republic, the Prime Minister, the President of the Federal Assembly, the Presidents of the Councils and the Governors of the islands may consult the Council of the Ulémas on any religious issue. The Council of the Ulémas may submit recommendations to the Federal Assembly, the Government or the Governors of the islands if it considers legislation to be in contravention of the principles of Islam.

ISLAND INSTITUTIONS

While respecting the unity of the Republic, each island is an autonomous territorial entity which freely controls its own administration through a Governor and a Council. The Governor of each island is appointed by the President of the Republic, from three candidates proposed by the Council of the island. The Council of each island is composed of the mayors of the communes and sits for not more than 15 days at a time, in March and December, and, if necessary, for extraordinary sessions. The Council is responsible for such matters as the budget of the island, taxes, culture, health, primary education and the environment.

REVISION OF THE CONSTITUTION

The power to initiate constitutional revision is vested in the President of the Republic. However, one-third of the members of the Federal Assembly may propose amendments to the President. Constitutional revision must be approved by a majority of two-thirds of the deputies in the Federal Assembly, and is subject to approval by national referendum. However, the President of the Republic may decide to promulgate a constitutional project, without submitting it to a referendum, if it has been adopted at a congress of deputies and the councillors of the islands, by a majority of two-thirds. The Republican and Islamic nature of the State cannot be revised.

The Government

HEAD OF STATE

President: MOHAMED TAKI ABDOULKARIM (elected President by popular vote 16 March 1996; took office 25 March 1996).

COUNCIL OF MINISTERS*

(June 1997)

Prime Minister: AHMED ABDOU.

Minister of National Education, Culture and Scientific Research: MOUZAOIR ABDALLAH.

Minister of Foreign Affairs, Co-operation and Francophone Affairs: MOUHTARE AHMED CHARIF.

Minister of Transport, Tourism, Posts and Telecommunications: IBRAHIM HALIDI.

Minister of Finance, the Budget and Planning: MOHAMED ALI SOILIHI.

Minister of Administrative Reform, Decentralization, Labour and Relations with the Federal Assembly: NIDHOIM ATTOUMANE.

Minster of the Economy, Domestic and External Trade and Energy: HARIMIA AHMED.

Minister of the Interior: ACHIRAFI SAÏD HACHIM.

Minister of Justice and Prison Administration, Guardian of the Seals: ALI HASSANALY.

Minister of Territorial Administration, Urban Affairs and Housing: ABDOULHAMID AFFRAITANE.

Minister of Agricultural Production, Fisheries and the Environment: ISSAMIDINE ADAINE.

Minister of Public Health and Population: NOURDINE BOURHANE.

* See Late Information.

MINISTRIES

Office of the Prime Minister: BP 421, Moroni; tel. (73) 2413; telex 233.

Ministry of Administrative Reform, Decentralization, Labour and Relations with the Federal Assembly: Moroni.

Ministry of Agricultural Production, Fisheries and the Environment: Moroni.

Ministry of the Economy, Domestic and External Trade and Energy: Moroni; tel. (73) 2767; telex 219.

Ministry of Finance, the Budget and Planning: BP 324, Moroni; telex 245.

Ministry of Foreign Affairs, Co-operation and Francophone Affairs: BP 482, Moroni; tel. (73) 2306; telex 219; fax (73) 2108.

Ministry of the Interior: Moroni.

Ministry of Justice and Prison Administration: Moroni.

Ministry of National Education, Culture and Scientific Research: BP 421, Moroni; telex 219.

Ministry of Public Health and Population: BP 42, Moroni; tel. (73) 2277; telex 219.

Ministry of Territorial Administration, Urban Affairs and Housing: Moroni.

Ministry of Transport, Tourism, Posts and Telecommunications: Moroni; tel. (73) 2098; telex 244.

President and Legislature

PRESIDENT

In the first round of voting, which took place on 6 March 1996, none of the 15 candidates received 50% of the total votes cast. A second round of voting took place on 16 March, when voters chose between the two leading candidates. MOHAMED TAKI ABDOULKARIM received 64.3% of the votes, while ABBAS DJOUSSOUF obtained 35.7%.

ASSEMBLÉE FÉDÉRALE

Chairman: SALIM DJABIR.

General Election, 1 and 8 December 1996

	Seats
Rassemblement national pour le développement	36
Front national pour la justice	3
Independent	4
Total	43

Political Organizations

The Union comorienne pour le progrès (Udzima) was the sole legal party between 1982 and December 1989, when formal restrictions on multi-party activity were ended. Under the terms of a new Constitution, which was adopted in October 1996, however, existing political parties that failed to fulfil certain conditions, were to be dissolved; following legislative elections, held in December, the only legal political organizations were:

Front national pour la justice (FNJ): Islamic fundamentalist orientation; Leader AHMED ABDALLAH MOHAMED.

Rassemblement national pour le développement (RND): f. 1996 by 24 parties supporting President Taki; Chair. ALI BAZI SELIM; Sec. Gen. ABDOULHAMID AFFRAITANE.

The following opposition groups were active in mid-1997:

CHUMA (Islands' Fraternity and Unity Party): Moroni; Leader Prince SAÏD ALI KEMAL.

Collectif de l'opposition: f. 1996; alliance of opposition parties.

Forces pour l'action républicaine (FAR): Leader Maj. ABDURAZAK.

Forum pour le redressement national (FRN): f. 1994; alliance of 12 opposition parties; Leader ABBAS DJOUSSOUF.

Front démocratique (FD): BP 758, Moroni; tel. (73) 2939; f. 1982; Leader MOUSTAPHA SAÏD CHEIKH.

Front populaire comorien (FPC): Mwali; Leader MOHAMED HASSANALY.

Mouvement pour la démocratie et le progrès (MDP): Moroni; Leader ABBAS DJOUSSOUF.

Mouvement pour la rénovation et l'action démocratique (MOURAD): Moroni; f. 1990; aims to promote economic and financial rehabilitation; Leader ABDOY ISSA.

Nguzo: Moroni; Leader TAKI MBOREHA.

Parti comorien pour la démocratie et le progrès (PCDP): Route Djivani, BP 179, Moroni; tel. (73) 1733; fax (73) 0650; Leader ALI MROUDJAE.

Parti socialiste des Comores (PASOCO): POB 720, Moroni; tel. (73) 1328; Leader ALI IDAROUSSE.

Parti du salut national (PSN): f. 1993; breakaway faction of PCDP; Islamic orientation; Leader SAÏD ALI MOHAMED.

Diplomatic Representation

EMBASSIES IN THE COMOROS

China, People's Republic: Moroni; tel. (73) 2721; Ambassador: XU DAIJIE.

France: blvd de Strasbourg, BP 465, Moroni; tel. (73) 0753; telex 220; Ambassador: GASTON LE PAUDERT.

Korea, Democratic People's Republic: Moroni; Ambassador: KIM RYONG YONG.

Libya: Moroni.

Mauritius: Moroni.

Seychelles: Moroni.

Judicial System

Under the terms of the Constitution of October 1996, the President is the guarantor of the independence of the judicial system, and chairs the Higher Council of the Magistracy (Conseil Supérieur de la Magistrature), of which the Minister of Justice is Vice-President. The High Council of the Republic, which comprises four members appointed by the President, three members elected by the Federal Assembly and one member elected by the Council of each island, acts as a High Court of Justice.

Religion

The majority of the population are Muslims. At 31 December 1995 there were an estimated 5,000 adherents of the Roman Catholic Church, equivalent to 1.0% of the total population.

CHRISTIANITY

The Roman Catholic Church

Office of Apostolic Administrator of the Comoros: Mission Catholique, BP 46, Moroni; tel. and fax (73) 0570; Apostolic Pro-Admin. Fr GABRIEL FRANCO NICOLAI.

The Press

Al Watwan: Nagoudjou, BP 984, Moroni; tel. (73) 2861; f. 1985; weekly; state-owned; Dir LAITH BEU ALI; Editor-in-Chief AMAD MDAHOMA; circ. 1,500.

L'Archipel: Moroni; f. 1988; weekly; independent; Publrs ABOUBACAR MCHANGAMA, SAINDOU KAMAL.

NEWS AGENCIES

Agence Comores Presse (ACP): Moroni.

Foreign Bureau

Agence France-Presse (AFP): BP 1327, Moroni; telex 242; Rep. ABOUBACAR MICHANGAMA.

Radio and Television

In 1994 there were an estimated 81,000 radio receivers and 200 television receivers in use. Transmissions to the Comoros from Radio France Internationale commenced in early 1994.

Radio-Comoros: BP 250, Moroni; tel. (73) 0531; telex 241; govt-controlled; domestic service in Comoran and French; international services in Swahili, Arabic and French; Tech. Dir KOMBO SOULAIMANA.

Finance

BANKING

(cap. = capital; res = reserves; dep. = deposits; m. = million; brs = branches; amounts in Comoros francs)

Central Bank

Banque Centrale des Comores: BP 405, Moroni; tel. (73) 1002; telex 213; f. 1981; bank of issue; cap. and res 2,202.8m. (Dec. 1989); Dir-Gen. SAÏD AHMED SAÏD ALI.

Commercial Bank

Banque pour l'Industrie et le Commerce—Comores (BIC): place de France, BP 175, Moroni; tel. (73) 0243; telex 242; fax (73) 1229; f. 1990; 51% owned by Banque Nationale de Paris–Internationale; 34% state-owned; cap. and res 1,138.1m., dep. 10,494.3m. (Dec. 1993); Pres. MOHAMED MOUMINI; Dir-Gen. JEAN-PIERRE BAJON-ARNAL; 6 brs.

Development Bank

Banque de Développement des Comores: place de France, BP 298, Moroni; tel. (73) 0818; telex 213; fax (73) 0397; f. 1982; provides loans, guarantees and equity participation for small and medium-scale projects; 50% state-owned; cap. 300m. (Dec. 1992); Pres. AHMED EL-HARIF HAMIDI; Dir. Gen. AZALI AMBARI DAROUECHE.

Trade and Industry

CHAMBER OF COMMERCE

Chambre de Commerce, d'Industrie et d'Agriculture: BP 763, Moroni; privatized in 1995.

DEVELOPMENT ORGANIZATIONS

CEFADER: a rural design, co-ordination and support centre, with brs on each island.

Mission Permanente de Coopération: Moroni; centre for administering bilateral aid from France; Dir GABRIEL COURCELLE.

Office National du Commerce: Moroni, Njazidja; state-operated agency for the promotion and development of domestic and external trade.

Société de Développement de la Pêche Artisanale des Comores (SODEPAC): state-operated agency overseeing fisheries development programme.

STATE ENTERPRISES

Electricité et Eau des Comores (EEDC): Moroni; telex 251; production and distribution of electricity and water; transfer to private management pending in 1997.

Société Comorienne des Hydrocarbures (SCH): POB 28, Moroni; tel. (73) 0486; telex 226; fax (73) 1883; imports petroleum products; transfer to private management pending in 1997; Gen. Man. Col JEAN MRADABI.

Société Nationale des Postes et des Télécommunications: Moroni; operates posts and telecommunications services.

TRADE UNION

Union des Travailleurs des Comores: Moroni.

Transport

ROADS

In 1995 there were an estimated 875 km of classified roads, of which 430 km were principal roads and 225 km secondary roads. About 76.5% of the network was paved. A major road-improvement scheme was launched in 1979, with foreign assistance, and by 1990 about 170 km of roads on Njazidja and Nzwani had been resurfaced. In January 1996 the EU granted over US $7m. to finance urgent repairs on a major road on Nzwani.

SHIPPING

The port of Mutsamudu, on Njazidja, can accommodate vessels of up to 11 m draught. Goods from Europe are routed via Madagascar, and coastal vessels connect the Comoros with the east coast of Africa. The development of the port of Moroni, with EC support, was completed in mid-1991. In 1993 the EC pledged US $4m. to finance the construction of a port at Fomboni, on Mwali, to improve shipping access to the island.

Société Comorienne de Navigation: Moroni; services to Madagascar.

CIVIL AVIATION

The international airport is at Moroni-Hahaya on Njazidja. Each of the three other islands has a small airfield. At the end of 1995 it was announced that Air Comores, the national airline, was to be liquidated. In 1996 the Government was considering the establishment of a new airline, with the majority of shares to be held by the private sector.

Tourism

The principal tourist attractions are the beaches, underwater fishing and mountain scenery. In 1994 an estimated 27,000 tourists visited the Comoros, and receipts from tourism totalled US $9m. In 1991 hotel capacity increased from 112 to 294 rooms, following the implementation of a number of hotel development projects, which resulted in a considerable increase in tourism receipts that year.

Société Comorienne de Tourisme et d'Hôtellerie (COMOTEL): Itsandra Hotel, Njazidja; tel. (73) 2365; national tourist agency.

Defence

The national army, the Force comorienne de défense (FCD), comprised 520 men in early 1995. In December 1996 an agreement was ratified with France, which provided for the permanent presence of a French military contingent in the Comoros.

Defence Expenditure: Budgeted at 910.8m. Comoros francs in 1987.

Chief of Staff of the Comoran Armed Forces: Commdr ASSOUMANI AZZALY.

Education

Education is officially compulsory for nine years between seven and 16 years of age. Primary education begins at the age of six and lasts for six years. Secondary education, beginning at 12 years of age, lasts for a further seven years, comprising a first cycle of four years and a second of three years. In 1993 enrolment at primary schools included an estimated 51% of children in the relevant age-group (boys 55%; girls 46%). Children may also receive a basic education through traditional Koranic schools, which are staffed by Comoran teachers. In 1993 enrolment at secondary schools was equivalent to 19% of children in the relevant age-group (males 21%; females 17%). Expenditure by the central government on education in 1992 was 2,829m. Comoros francs, representing 25.1% of total spending. In 1995, according to estimates by UNESCO, the average rate of adult illiteracy was 42.7% (males 35.8%, females 49.6%).

MAYOTTE

Since the Comoros unilaterally declared independence in July 1975, Mayotte (Mahoré) has been administered separately by France. The independent Comoran state claims Mayotte as part of its territory and officially represents it in international organizations, including the UN. In December 1976, following a referendum in April (in which the population voted to renounce the status of an overseas territory), France introduced the special status of *collectivité territoriale* for the island. The French government is represented on Mayotte by an appointed prefect. There is a general council, with 19 members, who are elected by universal adult suffrage. Mayotte has one representative in the national assembly in Paris, and one in the senate.

Following the coup in the Comoros in May 1978, Mayotte rejected the new government's proposal that it should rejoin the other islands under a federal system, and reaffirmed its intention of remaining linked to France. The main political party on Mayotte, the Mouvement populaire mahorais (MPM), demands full departmental status for the island, but France has been reluctant to grant this, in view of Mayotte's underdeveloped condition. In December 1979 the French national assembly approved legislation to prolong Mayotte's special status for another five years, during which period a referendum was to be conducted on the island. In October 1984, however, the national assembly further extended Mayotte's status, and the referendum on the island's future was postponed indefinitely. The UN general assembly has adopted several resolutions reaffirming the sovereignty of the Comoros over the island, and urging France to reach an agreement with the Comoran government as soon as possible. The Organization of African Unity (OAU) has endorsed this view.

Following elections to the French national assembly in March 1986, Henry Jean-Baptiste, representing an alliance of the Centre des démocrates sociaux and the Union pour la démocratie française (UDF), was elected as deputy for Mayotte. In October Jacques Chirac became the first French prime minister to visit Mayotte, where he assured the islanders that they would remain French citizens for as long as they wished. However, relations between the MPM and the French government rapidly deteriorated following the Franco-African summit in November 1987, when Chirac expressed his reservations to the Comoran president concerning the elevation of Mayotte to the status of a full overseas department (despite his announcement, in early 1986, that he endorsed the MPM's aim to upgrade the status of Mayotte.)

In the first round of the 1988 French presidential election, which took place on 24 April, the islanders demonstrated their response to Chirac's stance on Mayotte's constitutional future by favouring the candidacy of Raymond Barre to that of Chirac. The second round of the election, held on 10 May, was contested by Chirac and François Mitterrand, the incumbent president and candidate of the Parti socialiste (PS); a substantial proportion of votes on Mayotte was transferred to Mitterrand, who received 50.3% of votes cast on Mayotte, defeating Chirac. At elections to the French national assembly, which took place in June, Jean-Baptiste retained his seat. (Later that month he joined the newly-formed centrist group in the French national assembly, the Union du centre.) In elections to the general council in September and October, the MPM retained a majority of seats.

In November 1989 the general council demanded that the French government introduce measures to curb immigration to Mayotte from neighbouring islands, particularly from the Comoros. In January 1990 pressure by a group from the town of Mamoudzou resulted in increasing tension over the presence of Comoran refugees on the island. Later that month there was a demonstration in protest against illegal immigration to the island. A paramilitary organization, 'Caiman' (which demanded the expulsion of illegal immigrants), was subsequently formed. In May the Comoran president, Saïd Mohamed Djohar, undertook to pursue peaceful dialogue to resolve the question of Mayotte's sovereignty, and issued a formal appeal to France to reconsider the island's status. Mayotte was used as a strategic military base in late 1990, in preparation for French troop participation in multinational operations during the 1991 Gulf War.

In late June 1991 a demonstration on the adjacent islet of Pamandzi, in protest at the relocation of a number of people as a result of the expansion of the airfield, prevented an aircraft from Réunion from landing. Unrest among young people on Pamandzi escalated in early July; the mayor fled after demonstrators attempted to set fire to the town hall. Clashes took place between demonstrators and security forces, and the prefect requested that police reinforcements be dispatched from Réunion to restore order. An organization of young people, l'Association des jeunes pour le développement de Pamandzi (AJDP), accused the mayor of maladministration and demanded his resignation. The demonstrations, which threatened to destabilize the MPM, were generally viewed as a manifestation of general discontent among young people on Mayotte (who comprised about 60% of the population). Later in July five members of the AJDP, who had taken part in the demonstration at the airfield in June, received prison sentences.

In June 1992 increasing tension resulted in further attacks against Comoran immigrants resident in Mayotte. In early September representatives of the MPM met the French prime minister, Pierre Bérégovoy, to request the reintroduction of entry visas in order to restrict immigration from the Comoros. Later that month the MPM organized a boycott (which was widely observed) of Mayotte's participation in the French referendum on the Treaty on European Union, in protest at the French government's refusal to introduce entry visas. In December legal proceedings were taken against the prefect of Mayotte, Jean-Paul Costes, and a number of other prominent officials, in connection with the deaths of several people in domestic fires that had been caused by poor quality fuel imported from Bahrain. In February 1993 a general strike, staged in support of wage increases, culminated in violent rioting; security forces were subsequently dispatched from Réunion and mainland France to restore order. At the end of February Costes was replaced as prefect by Jean-Jacques Debacq.

At elections to the French national assembly, which took place in March 1993, Jean-Baptiste was returned by 53.4% of votes cast, while Mansour Kamardine, the secretary-general of the local branch of the right-wing French mainland party, the Rassemblement pour la République (RPR), obtained 44.3% of the vote. Kamardine subsequently accused Jean-Baptiste of illegally claiming the support of an electoral alliance of the RPR and the UDF, known as the Union pour la France (UPF), by forging the signatures of the secretary-general of the RPR and his UDF counterpart on a document. However, Jean-Baptiste denied the allegations, and, in turn, began legal proceedings against Kamardine for alleged forgery and defamation. Elections to the general council (which was enlarged from 17 to 19 members) took place in March 1994; the MPM secured 12 seats, the local branch of the RPR four seats, and independent candidates three seats. During an official visit to Mayotte in November, the French prime minister, Edouard Balladur, announced the reintroduction of entry visas as a requirement for Comoran nationals and the adoption of a number of security measures, in an effort to reduce illegal immigration. He also indicated that a referendum to determine the future of Mayotte would be conducted by the year 2000. In the first round of the French presidential election, which took place in April 1995, Balladur received the highest number of votes on Mayotte (although Chirac subsequently won the election).

Following a further coup attempt in September 1995 by mercenaries in the Comoros, the French government dispatched additional troops to Mayotte, prior to carrying out a military intervention. In elections to the French senate held in that month, the incumbent MPM representative, Marcel Henry, was returned by a large majority. During a visit to Mayotte in October, the French minister of overseas departments and territories pledged that a referendum on the future status of the island would be conducted by 1999. In October 1996 he confirmed that two commissions, operating from Paris and Dzaoudzi, were preparing a consultation document, which would be presented in late 1997, and announced that the proposed referendum would take place before the end of the decade.

Partial elections to fill nine seats in the general council were held in March 1997; the MPM secured three seats (losing two which it had previously held), the local branch of the RPR won three seats, the local PS one seat, and independent right-wing candidates two seats. In elections to the French national assembly Jean-Baptiste, representing the UDF/Force démocrate (FD, formerly the CDS) alliance, defeated Kamardine, securing 51.7% of votes cast in the second round of voting, which took place at the beginning of June.

Mayotte's gross domestic product (GDP) per head was estimated at 4,050 French francs in 1991. Between the censuses of 1985 and 1991 the population of Mayotte increased by an annual average of 5.8%. The economy of Mayotte is based almost entirely on agriculture. Rice, cassava and maize are cultivated for domestic consumption, and vanilla, ylang-ylang (an ingredient of perfume), coffee and copra are the main export products. Construction is the sole industrial sector. There are no mineral resources on the island. Imports of mineral products comprised 4.4% of the cost of total imports in 1988.

In 1992 France was the principal source of imports (74%), and the principal market for exports (70%). Other major trading partners were South Africa, Singapore, Thailand, the Comoros, and Réunion. Owing to its reliance on imports, Mayotte operates a substantial trade deficit, which totalled 437.8m. French francs in 1992. In 1988 the principal imports were foodstuffs (22%), machinery and transport equipment (20.7%) and metals (10.5%), and the main exports were oil of ylang-ylang (78%) and vanilla (21%). In 1986 Mayotte's external assets totalled 203.8m. francs.

In 1991 Mayotte's budget expenditure was an estimated 365m. francs. Official debt totalled 435.7m. francs at 31 December 1995. It was estimated that 38% of the labour force were unemployed in 1991.

A five-year Development Plan (1986 – 91) included measures to improve infrastructure and to increase investment in public works. (The Plan was subsequently extended to the end of 1993.) In 1995 the Caisse française de développement (see p. 122) granted a loan of 80m. French francs, as part of a 153m. francs programme, to further develop infrastructure on the island. Substantial aid from France during the period 1987–92 was designed to stimulate the development of tourism on the island through the construction of a deep-water port at Longoni and the expansion of the airfield at Dzaoudzi. Mayotte's remote location, however, remains an obstacle to the development of tourism. In 1994 it was reported that the value of exports had declined, owing, in part, to strong regional competition in the agricultural sector, in conjunction with an increase in the cost of labour on the island. In April 1995 an economic and social programme was agreed with the French government for the period 1995–99. Later in that year Mayotte received credit from France to finance further investment in infrastructure, particularly in the road network. The adjustment of the minimum wage, which increased by 10.3% in 1994, sustained economic activity, resulting in higher consumer spending and imports. In 1996 construction began on a plant to produce Coca-Cola products in the industrial zone around Longoni; construction costs were estimated at 16m.–18m. francs.

The principal towns are the capital, Dzaoudzi (estimated population 8,300 in 1991), Mamoudzou and Pamandzi-Labattoir. France is responsible for the defence of the island: in August 1996 there were 4,000 French troops stationed on Mayotte and Réunion.

Statistical Survey

Source: mainly Office of the Prefect, Government Commissioner, Dzaoudzi.

AREA AND POPULATION

Area: 374 sq km (144 sq miles).

Population: 67,167 (census of August 1985); 94,410 (census of August 1991). *Principal towns* (population at 1985 census): Dzaoudzi (capital) 5,865, Mamoudzou 12,026, Pamandzi-Labattoir 4,106. *Dzaoudzi* (estimated population at 1991 census): 8,300. Source: INSEE, *Annuaire Statistique de la France 1991–92*.

Births and Deaths (1985–90): Birth rate 35.6 per 1,000; Death rate 6.2 per 1,000. Source: Institut National de la Statistique et des Etudes Economiques, *L'Economie de la Réunion*.

AGRICULTURE, ETC.

Livestock (1990): Cattle 12,000; Sheep 3,000; Goats 15,000. Source: Secrétariat du Comité Monétaire de la Zone Franc, *La Zone Franc, Rapport 1990.*

Fishing (metric tons, 1989): Total catch 1,700. Source: Ministère des Départements et Territoires d'Outre-Mer.

FINANCE

Currency and Exchange Rates: 100 centimes = 1 French franc. *Sterling and Dollar Equivalents* (31 March 1997): £1 sterling = 9.2420 francs; US $1 = 5.6285 francs; 1,000 French francs = £108.20 = $177.67. *Average Exchange Rate* (French francs per US dollar): 5.5520 in 1994; 4.9915 in 1995; 5.1155 in 1996.

Budget (estimates, million francs): Total expenditure 371.6 (current 197.2, capital 174.4) in 1989; 338 (current 236, capital 102) in 1990; 365 in 1991.

Money Supply (million French francs at 31 December 1994): Currency outside banks 942; Demand deposits 171; Total money 1,113.

Source: Secrétariat du Comité Monétaire de la Zone Franc, *La Zone Franc, Rapport 1994.*

EXTERNAL TRADE

Principal Commodities ('000 francs, 1988): *Imports:* Foodstuffs 65,014; Machinery and appliances 61,097; Metals and metal products 31,061; Transport equipment 50,097; Total (incl. others) 294,981. *Exports:* Oil of ylang-ylang 8,188; Vanilla 1,810; Coffee (green) 178; Total (incl. others) 10,189. Figures exclude re-exports (42.9 million francs in 1988). **1989** (million francs): Total imports 338.1; Total exports 35.5. **1990** (million francs): Total imports 327.7; Total exports 37.6.

Principal Trading Partners ('000 francs): *Imports* (1988): France 193,984; Singapore 9,507; South Africa 26,854; Thailand 12,617; Total (incl. others) 294,981. *Exports* (1983): France 4,405.
Source: Secrétariat du Comité Monétaire de la Zone Franc, *La Zone Franc, Rapport 1988.*

TRANSPORT

Roads (1984): 93 km of main roads, of which 72 km are tarred, 137 km of local roads, of which 40 km are tarred, and 54 km of tracks unusable in the rainy season; 1,528 vehicles.

Civil Aviation (1984): *Arrivals:* 7,747 passengers, 120 metric tons of freight; *Departures:* 7,970 passengers, 41 metric tons of freight.

EDUCATION

Primary (1986): 28 schools; 366 teachers; 15,632 pupils (20,836 in 1990).

Secondary (1990): 6 schools; 65 teachers (1986); 2,957 pupils.

Directory

The Constitution

Under the status of Collectivité Territoriale, which was adopted in December 1976, Mayotte has an elected General Council, comprising 19 members, which assists the Prefect in the administration of the island. In 1984 a referendum on the future of Mayotte was postponed indefinitely.

The Government

Représentation du Gouvernement, Dzaoudzi, 97610 Mayotte; tel. 60-10-54.

(June 1997)

Prefect: PHILIPPE BOISADAM.

Secretary-General: JEAN-PIERRE LAFLAQUIÈRE.

Deputy to the French National Assembly: HENRY JEAN-BAPTISTE (UDF–FD).

Representative to the French Senate: MARCEL HENRY (MPM).

GENERAL COUNCIL

Conseil Général, Mamoudzou, 97600 Mayotte; tel. 61-12-33.

The General Council comprises 19 members. At elections in March 1994, the Mouvement Populaire Mahorais (MPM) secured 12 seats, the Fédération de Mayotte du Rassemblement pour la République four seats, and independent candidates three seats. As a result of by-elections held in March 1997, the MPM hold eight seats, the Fédération de Mayotte du Rassemblement pour la République five seats, independent right-wing candidates five seats, and the Parti Socialiste one seat.

President of the General Council: YOUNOUSSA BAMANA.

Political Organizations

Fédération de Mayotte du Rassemblement pour la République: Dzaoudzi, 97610 Mayotte; local branch of the French (Gaullist) Rassemblement pour la République (RPR); Sec.-Gen. MANSOUR KAMARDINE.

Mouvement Populaire Mahorais (MPM): Dzaoudzi, 97610 Mayotte; seeks departmental status for Mayotte; Leader YOUNOUSSA BAMANA.

Parti pour le Rassemblement Démocratique des Mahorais (PRDM): Dzaoudzi, 97610 Mayotte; f. 1978; seeks unification with the Federal Islamic Republic of the Comoros; Leader DAROUÈCHE MAOULIDA.

Parti Socialiste: Dzaoudzi; local branch of the French party of the same name.

In 1990 the two major French right-wing political parties, the **Rassemblement pour la République (RPR)** and the **Union pour la Démocratie Française (UDF)**, formed an electoral alliance, the **Union pour la France (UPF)**.

Judicial System

Tribunal Supérieur d'Appel: Mamoudzou, 97600 Mayotte; tel. 61-12-65; fax 61-19-63; Pres. JEAN-BAPTISTE FLORI.

Procureur de la République: PATRICK BROSSIER.

Tribunal de Première Instance: Pres. ARLETTE MEALLONNIER-DUGUE.

Religion

Muslims comprise about 98% of the population. Most of the remainder are Christians, mainly Roman Catholics.

CHRISTIANITY

The Roman Catholic Church

Mayotte is within the jurisdiction of the Apostolic Administrator of the Comoros.

The Press

Le Journal de Mayotte: BP 181, Mamoudzou, 97600 Mayotte; tel. 61-16-95; fax 61-03-88; f. 1983; weekly; circ. 15,000.

Radio and Television

In 1995 there were an estimated 50,000 radio receivers and 3,500 television receivers in use.

Société Nationale de Radio-Télévision Française d'Outre-Mer (RFO)—Mayotte: BP 103, Dzaoudzi, 97610 Mayotte; tel. 60-10-17; telex 915822; fax 60-18-52; f. 1977; govt-owned; radio broadcasts in French and Mahorian; television transmissions began in 1986; Regional Dir JOSEPH EDERN; Technical Dir SERGE SULPICE-TIMOTHÉE; Station Dir ROBERT XAVIER.

Finance

BANKS

Institut d'Emission d'Outre-Mer: BP 500, Mamoudzou, 97600 Mayotte; tel. 61-05-05; telex 915804; fax 61-05-02.

Banque Française Commerciale: Mamoudzou, 97600 Mayotte; br. at Dzaoudzi.

Transport

ROADS

The main road network totals approximately 93 km, of which 72 km are bituminized. There are 137 km of local roads, of which 40 km are tarred, and 54 km of minor tracks which are unusable during the rainy season.

SHIPPING

Coastal shipping is provided by locally-owned small craft. A deep-water port is under construction at Longoni.

CIVIL AVIATION

There is an airfield at Dzaoudzi, serving four-times weekly commercial flights to Réunion and twice-weekly services to Njazidja, Nzwani and Mwali. The expansion of the airfield commenced in 1991, and was completed in 1994.

Tourism

Tropical scenery provides the main tourist attraction. In 1985 the island had six hotels, providing a total of approximately 100 beds. Mayotte received 16,272 tourists in 1992.

Comité Territorial du Tourisme de Mayotte: rue de la Pompe, BP 1169, Mamoudzou, 97600 Mayotte; tel. 61-09-09; fax 61-03-46.

Bibliography

Bourde, A. 'The Comoro Islands: problems of a microcosm', in *Journal of Modern African Studies*, No. 3, 1965.

Cornu, H. *Paris et Bourbon, La politique française dans l'Océan indien*. Paris, Académie des Sciences d'Outre-mer, 1984.

Dubins, B. 'The Comoro Islands: A Bibliographical Essay', in *African Studies Bulletin*, No. 12, 1969.

Mantoux, T. 'Notes socio-économiques sur l'archipel des Comores', in *Revue française d'études politiques africaines*, No. 100, 1974.

Marquardt, W. *Seychellen, Komoren und Maskarenen*. Munich, 1976.

Newitt, M. *The Comoros Islands: Struggle against Dependency in the Indian Ocean*. Aldershot, Gower, 1985.

Perri, P. *Les nouveaux mercenaires*. Paris, L'Harmattan, 1994.

Salesse, Y. *Mayotte: L'illusion de la France, propositions pour une décolonisation*. Paris, L'Harmattan, 1995.

Weinberg, S. *Last of the Pirates: The Search for Bob Denard*. London, Jonathan Cape, 1994.

World Bank. *Comoros: Current Economic Situation and Prospects*. Washington, DC, International Bank for Reconstruction and Development, 1983.

THE DEMOCRATIC REPUBLIC OF THE CONGO

Physical and Social Geography

PIERRE GOUROU

PHYSICAL FEATURES

Covering an area of 2,344,885 sq km (905,365 sq miles) and sharing borders with eight other countries, the Democratic Republic of the Congo (DRC—formerly Zaire) is, after Sudan, the largest country of sub-Saharan Africa. Despite its vast size, it lacks any particularly noteworthy points of relief, affording it a considerable natural advantage. Lying across the Equator, the DRC has an equatorial climate in the whole of the central region. Average temperatures range from 26°C in the coastal and basin areas to 18°C in the mountainous regions. Rainfall is plentiful in all seasons. In the north (Uele) the winter of the northern hemisphere is a dry season; in the south (Shaba) the winter of the southern hemisphere is dry. The only arid region (less than 800 mm of rain per annum) is an extremely small area on the bank of the lower Congo.

The basin of the River Congo forms the country's dominant geographical feature. This basin had a deep tectonic origin; the continental shelf of Africa had given way to form an immense hollow, which drew towards it the waters from the north (Ubangi), from the east (Uele, Arruwimi), and from the south (Lualaba—that is the upper branch of the River Congo, Kasaï, Kwango). The crystalline continental shelf levels out at the periphery into plateaux in Shaba (formerly Katanga) and the Congo-Nile ridge. The most broken-up parts of this periphery can be found in the west, in Bas-Zaïre, where the river cuts the folds of a Pre-Cambrian chain by a 'powerful breach', and above all in the east. Here, as a result of the volcanic overflow from the Virunga, they are varied by an upheaval of the rift valleys (where Lakes Tanganyika, Kivu, Edward and Albert are located).

The climate is generally favourable for agriculture and wood-forestry. Evergreen equatorial forest covers approximately 1m. sq km in the equatorial and sub-equatorial regions. In the north as in the south of this evergreen forest, tropical vegetation appears, with many trees that lose their leaves in the dry season. Vast stretches from the north to the south are, probably as a result of frequent fires, covered by sparse forest land, where trees grow alongside grasses (*biombo* from east Africa), and savannah dotted with shrubs.

Although favourable on account of its warmth and rainfall, the climate has a few unfortunate indirect effects. There are vast stretches of the DRC where the soil is leached of its soluble elements by the heavy, warm rainfall. In addition, the microbes and carriers of malaria, sleeping sickness, filariasis, bilharziasis, ankylostomiasis and haemorrhagic fevers flourish in a warm, rainy climate.

The natural resources of the DRC are immense: its climate is favourable to profitable agriculture; the forests, if rationally exploited, could yield excellent results; the abundance of water should eventually be useful to industry and agriculture; and finally, there is considerable mineral wealth. The network of waterways is naturally navigable. The River Congo carries the second largest volume of water in the world. With the average flow to the mouth being 40,000 cu m per second, there are enormous possibilities for power generation, some of which are being realized at Inga. Indeed, the hydroelectric resources are considerable in the whole of the Congo basin.

The major exports of the DRC derive from the exploitation of its mineral resources. Copper is mined in upper Shaba, as are other metals—tin, silver, uranium, cobalt, manganese and tungsten. Diamonds are found in Kasaï, and tin, columbite, etc. in the east, around Maniema. In addition, many other mineral resources (such as iron ore and bauxite) await exploitation.

POPULATION

The DRC's population comprises numerous ethnic groups, which the external boundaries separate. The Kongo people are divided between the DRC, the Republic of Congo, and Angola; the Zande between the DRC and Sudan; the Chokwe between the DRC and Angola; the Bemba between the DRC and Zambia; and the Alur between the DRC and Uganda. Even within its frontiers, the ethnic and linguistic geography of the DRC is highly diverse. The most numerous people are the Kongo; the people of Kwangu-Kwilu, who are related to them; the Mongo with their many subdivisions, who inhabit the Great Forest; the Luba, with their related groups the Lulua and Songe; the Bwaka; and the Zande. The majority speak Bantu languages, of which there is a great diversity. However, the north of the DRC belongs linguistically to Sudan. The extreme linguistic variety of the DRC is maintained to some extent by the ability of the people to speak several languages, by the existence of 'intermediary' languages (a Kongo dialect, a Luba dialect, Swahili and Lingala) and by the use of French.

About 80% of the population (officially estimated at 36.7m. at mid-1991) live in rural areas. The average density of population is low (15.6 per sq km in 1991), and the population is unevenly distributed. The population density in the Great Forest is only about one-half of the national average, with stretches of several tens of thousands of sq km virtually deserted, although this is not because the area cannot accommodate more people. However, it is clear that the population (with the exception of some pygmies) cannot increase in density as long as the forest is preserved. Indeed, certain areas belonging to the forest belt but partly cleared for cultivation, although they have no particular natural advantages, have higher than average densities. At the northern edge of the Great Forest the population density increases up to 20 people per sq km, and is then reduced to one or two in the extreme north of the country. Certain parts of Mayombé (Bas-Zaïre) have 100 people per sq km, but the south of the republic is sparsely populated (1–3 people per sq km). The capital, Kinshasa, had 2,653,558 inhabitants at the 1984 census and is the principal urban centre. Other major centres of population are Lubumbashi, with 543,268 inhabitants at the 1984 census; Mbuji-Mayi (423,363); Kananga (290,898) and Kisangani (282,650).

Recent History

JACQUES VANDERLINDEN

Revised for this edition by Gill Tudor

Belgian interest in the area now comprising the Democratic Republic of the Congo (DRC—formerly Zaire) dates from 1876, when the Association internationale du Congo, under the control of King Léopold II of Belgium, began to establish a chain of trading stations along the River Congo. Economic exploitation of the territory expanded rapidly with the increasing demand for wild rubber, following the development of rubber tyres. However, the methods used in the collection of rubber frequently involved the infliction of atrocities on the indigenous population, and in 1908, as a result of British and US diplomatic pressure, responsibility for the administration of the territory was transferred from the king to the Belgian government, and the Congo became a Belgian colony.

African political development was not encouraged, and it was not until shortly before the Second World War that a consultative body was established, on which African interests were represented mainly by civil servants or missionaries. In the absence of a forum for political expression, radical Africans organized in 'cultural associations', which included the Alliance des Ba-Kongo (ABAKO), led by Joseph Kasavubu. The Belgian authorities established elected councils in the main urban areas, intending to allow gradual progress towards self-government over an extended period.

This process was abruptly accelerated following a demonstration organized by ABAKO in January 1959, during which some 50 Africans were killed. Within one year, at a conference held in Brussels, it was agreed that the Congo was to accede to full sovereignty after six months: during this period the Belgian legislature was to prepare a constitution (*loi fondamentale*) for the new state. The Belgian government favoured the creation of a unitary state, based on the centralized pattern of the colonial system. However, ABAKO and most other Congolese political groups were ethnically based and (with the exception of Patrice Lumumba's Mouvement national congolais–MNC) favoured the creation of a federal state. The *loi fondamentale* that eventually emerged represented a compromise, affirming the unitary character of the state, but allowing each province to have its own government and legislature, and equal representation in a national senate.

Throughout the colonial period the Belgians had restricted Africans to the lower ranks of the civil service, and there were no African officers in the armed forces. The Belgian government assumed that, following independence, Belgian personnel would remain in *de facto* control.

THE FIRST REPUBLIC

The independence of the Republic of the Congo was proclaimed on 30 June 1960. Kasavubu became president and Lumumba prime minister. Five days later the armed forces mutinied. Their demands were partly satisfied by the replacement of the Belgian chief of staff by Col (later Marshal) Joseph-Désiré Mobutu who was aligned with Lumumba's MNC. At the same time, a number of non-commissioned officers were also promoted to the officer corps. Belgian civil servants rapidly left the country. Belgian troops intervened to protect their nationals, and at the same time the provinces of Katanga (subsequently Shaba) and South Kasaï resolved to secede. Lumumba requested help from the United Nations. Disagreement over Lumumba's response to the secession led to his dismissal by Kasavubu in September. This was challenged by Lumumba, who asked the legislature to remove Kasavubu. The political deadlock was resolved by the intervention of the armed forces. On 14 September Col Mobutu announced the temporary suspension of all political institutions and assumed control of the country, ruling with the assistance of a collège des commissaires généraux (CCG), under the chairmanship of Justin-Marie Bomboko of the Union Mongo (UNIMO), previously Lumumba's minister of foreign affairs. The CCG governed the Congo for one year, but failed to control the north-eastern region, where some of Lumumba's former ministers had established a rival government in Stanleyville (later Kisangani).

Mobutu restored power to President Kasavubu in February 1961. A few days later Lumumba was murdered. The forceful reactions to this development by African governments and the UN prompted negotiations between Kasavubu and the MNC, and in August a new government was formed, with Cyrille Adoula as prime minister. The new administration received the support of most political groups (with the exception of Katanga separatists, led by Moïse Tshombe), and it was hoped that it would progressively re-establish national unity. In April 1962 a constitutional amendment was approved, allowing the creation of new provinces. A new constitution entered into force on 1 August 1964, establishing a presidential system of government and a federalist structure.

Meanwhile, the movement for the secession of Katanga had collapsed in January 1963, when its leader, Tshombe, went into exile. In January 1964 a rebellion began in the Kwilu region, led by Pierre Mulele, formerly a minister in Lumumba's government, who failed, however, to attract much support beyond the limits of his own ethnic group. In April a second rebellion began in southern Kivu and northern Katanga provinces. Within a few months the rebels controlled the east and north-east of the country, and had established their capital at Stanleyville. In July Kasavubu invited Tshombe to become interim prime minister, pending legislative elections. In the following month the country was renamed the Democratic Republic of the Congo. In early 1965 the rebellion was defeated by the army, assisted by Belgian troops and by mercenaries.

In March and April 1965 the Tshombe government organized legislative elections, in accordance with the 1964 constitution. The coalition led by Tshombe, the Convention nationale congolaise (CONACO), won 122 of the 167 seats in the chamber of deputies. However, an opposition bloc, the Front démocratique congolais (FDC), soon emerged. Kasavubu dismissed the Tshombe administration and appointed Evariste Kimba as prime minister, but Kimba was unable to secure majority support in the CONACO-dominated assembly. The president, instead of seeking a new prime minister, reappointed Kimba, creating a deadlock between Kasavubu, supported by the FDC, and Tshombe's CONACO. The army, led by Mobutu, again intervened, and on 24 November 1965 Mobutu assumed full executive powers and declared himself the head of the 'Second Republic'. A close associate, Col (later Gen.) Léonard Mulamba, was appointed prime minister. The government sought and obtained a parliamentary mandate. The legislature thereupon requested its own suspension, as a result of which Mobutu was constitutionally empowered to legislate by decree.

Moving decisively to consolidate his power, Mobutu imposed a five-year ban on party politics, and in 1966 founded the Mouvement populaire de la révolution (MPR), whose organization was superimposed on the existing administrative structures. The MPR political bureau held responsibility for policy formulation and political guidance. Power was progressively concentrated in the office of the president, who became the sole legislator, and the functions of prime minister were merged with those of the head of state. The number of provinces was successively reduced, from 21 to eight, and provincial institutions were supplanted by appointed governors, who were responsible to the president. European place names were indigenized, the capital, Léopoldville, becoming Kinshasa.

'PRESIDENTIALISM' AND THE PARTY-STATE

After Mobutu's assumption of power, Kasavubu retired from political life, and Tshombe went into exile: both men died in 1969. A number of former ministers, however, were accused of plotting against Mobutu, and were executed in June 1966.

Congolese students, although they had initially supported the new regime, soon began to criticize Mobutu's authoritarian style of rule: a students' strike was suppressed in early 1967. Labour organizations were deprived of their right to strike, but the government's dynamic policy against Belgian economic interests in the country secured the support of the three main trade unions, which were amalgamated in 1967 to form the Union nationale des travailleurs congolais (UNTC). In June a new constitution was approved by referendum, establishing a presidential regime, with a new legislature to be elected at a date to be determined by the president. The constitution provided for a maximum of two legally-authorized political parties. The claims of existing political groups to official recognition were ignored, however, while former senior politicians were appointed to overseas diplomatic posts; they were subsequently accused of plotting against the president, and dismissed or arrested. By 1970 no senior politicians remained as potential rivals to Mobutu.

Presidential and legislative elections took place in late 1970. Mobutu, as sole candidate, was duly elected president, and members of the national legislative council were elected from a list of candidates presented by the MPR. The constitution was amended so that the government, the legislature and the judiciary all became institutions of the MPR, and all citizens automatically became party members. In October 1971 the country was renamed the Republic of Zaire. In 1972 the president took the name Mobutu Sese Seko Kuku Ngbendu Wa Za Banga, as part of a national policy of 'authenticity'. During the period 1970–77 the discovery of several anti-government plots was announced, including, in 1975, one which was allegedly instigated by the US government.

From the 1960s onwards one of the rival factions fighting for independence in the neighbouring Portuguese colony of Angola, the Frente Nacional de Libertação de Angola (FNLA), was permitted to maintain guerrilla bases and refugee camps along the border in Bas-Zaïre. However, in 1976, after a rival faction, the Movimento Popular de Libertação de Angola (MPLA) had won the struggle for decolonization, there was an apparent reconciliation between Mobutu and President Neto of Angola. It was agreed that Angolan refugees in Zaire would be repatriated, and that Angola would return to Zaire several thousand Katangese soldiers, who had been members of Tshombe's forces at the time of the secession of Katanga. In March 1977 some of the latter, distrusting Mobutu's promises of an amnesty, invaded the Zairean province of Shaba from Angola, receiving support from many of the disaffected inhabitants. Mobutu obtained military assistance from France and Morocco, and by May the 'First Shaba War' was over. Apparently in response to the prompting of his French and Moroccan allies, Mobutu announced the holding, not only of a scheduled presidential election, but also of a legislative election (not due until 1980), and a partial election of the MPR political bureau. The legislative election took place in October 1977, and Mobutu was re-elected, unopposed, in December to a further term of office.

In July 1977 Mobutu created the office of first state commissioner, equivalent to that of prime minister. In August the commissioner for foreign affairs, Nguza Karl-I-Bond, was dismissed and sentenced to death for alleged treason: the sentence was later commuted to life imprisonment, and in March 1979 Nguza Karl-I-Bond was reinstated to his former post (becoming first state commissioner in 1980). The military establishment was purged in 1978, when a number of senior officers and civilians were executed or imprisoned after the alleged discovery of a coup plot.

In Shaba province, retribution by the army against those who had failed to support the government after the 1977 invasion caused resentment, and this helped to provoke the 'Second Shaba War': in early May 1978 several thousand men, originating from Angola, crossed the Zambian border and entered Shaba, occupying Kolwezi, a major mining centre. French paratroops intervened to assist the Zairean forces in recapturing the town, and in June a Pan-African peace-keeping force arrived in Shaba, remaining there for more than a year.

THE ONSET OF OPPOSITION

In January 1980, as part of a declared purge on official corruption, Mobutu extensively reorganized the national executive council, dismissing 13 of the 22 commissioners. In a further series of political changes in August, the new post of chairman of the MPR (to be held by Mobutu in addition to the presidency of the party), became the focal point of decision-making and control of the MPR's activities. In September Mobutu appointed a 114-member central committee to become the MPR's second most important organ, after the congress. The party's executive committee became the executive secretariat and, in a ministerial reshuffle, the outgoing first state commissioner, Bo-Boliko Lokonga, was appointed executive secretary. In April 1981 Nguza Karl-I-Bond, who had survived the successive changes to remain first state commissioner, abruptly went into self-imposed exile in Belgium. He was replaced by N'Singa Udjuu Ongwakebi Untube, who was additionally appointed executive secretary of the MPR.

During 1982 opponents of Zaire's one-party system of government attempted to establish a new party, the Union pour la démocratie et le progrès social (UDPS). Mobutu responded to this challenge by imprisoning 13 members of the national legislative council. In October, however, Nguza Karl-I-Bond emerged as the spokesman for a new coalition of opposition opinion, the Front congolais pour le rétablissement de la démocratie (FCD). In the following month Mobutu appointed Kengo Wa Dondo first state commissioner.

In May 1983, following the publication of a highly critical report on Zaire by the human rights organization, Amnesty International, Mobutu offered an amnesty to all political exiles who returned to Zaire by 30 June. A number of exiles accepted the offer, but a substantial opposition movement remained active in Belgium. Internal opposition to Mobutu's regime continued to manifest itself during 1984. In January and March a number of bombs exploded in Kinshasa, causing loss of life, and a rebel force occupied the town of Moba, in Shaba province, for two days in November, before it was retaken by Zairean troops. Zaire accused Belgium of harbouring the groups responsible for these insurgencies, and claimed that the rebels had crossed into Zaire from neighbouring Tanzania. However, the main opposition groups in Belgium denied any involvement in the occupation of Moba, and suggested that mutinous Zairean troops had been responsible. It was widely believed that the violent opposition in Zaire had been co-ordinated in order to disrupt the proceedings for the election and inauguration of the president. However, Mobutu was re-elected unopposed in July.

Ministerial reshuffles in February, April and July 1985, and a further round of changes in the structure of the MPR (separating party and governmental functions), reinforced Mobutu's personal position. In July 1985 the return from exile of Nguza Karl-I-Bond (who was appointed ambassador to the USA in July 1986, a post which he held until March 1988), and the lifting of restrictions on seven members of the banned UDPS under the terms of another amnesty for political opponents, appeared to provide further evidence of the president's confidence in his position. In October, however, two UDPS members were arrested, being subsequently tried and imprisoned for 'insulting the head of state'. The post of first state commissioner was abolished in late 1985, but was revived in January 1987, and allocated to Mabi Mulumba, previously state commissioner for finance. In March 1988 Mobutu again reconstructed the government, appointing Sambwa Pida Nbagui to replace Mabi Mulumba as first state commissioner. In November, in the fourth ministerial reshuffle of the year, Mobutu replaced about one-third of the members of the national executive council and reinstated Kengo Wa Dondo as first state commissioner.

In March 1986 Amnesty International published a further report condemning Zaire for abuses of human rights, specifically accusing the Mobutu regime of the illegal arrest, torture or murder of UDPS supporters in late 1985. In October 1986 Mobutu responded to the allegations in the report by appointing a state commissioner for citizens' rights, and announcing the disbandment of the military state security agency.

Regional and municipal elections were held in May and June 1987, but the results were annulled because of alleged electoral malpractice. The elections were rescheduled for March 1988, but were subsequently postponed until March 1989, for 'budgetary reasons' and to ensure their conduct in a democratic and harmonious manner. Elections to the 210 seats in the national legislative council (reduced from 310) took place in September

1987. In the same month several opposition groups announced that they had united to form a government-in-exile.

In June 1987 several members of the UDPS, including Etienne Tshisekedi Wa Mulumba (its secretary-general and a former minister of the interior), availed themselves of an amnesty offered by Mobutu. In October four other former UDPS leaders were admitted to the central committee of the MPR, and other reconciled opponents of the government were appointed to senior posts in state-owned enterprises. In January 1988, however, Tshisekedi was arrested after he attempted to organize an unauthorized public meeting, and subsequently placed under house arrest. In April he was rearrested after advocating a boycott of the partial legislative elections scheduled to take place in Kinshasa on 10 April. In September Tshisekedi withdrew from political activity, although this did not prevent his arrest in March 1989 for alleged involvement in student disturbances which broke out in Kinshasa and Lubumbashi at the end of February, in which an estimated 37 people were killed.

In February 1990 the UDPS organized demonstrations in Kinshasa and three other towns to commemorate the 29th anniversary of the assassination of Lumumba. Further unrest followed in April, when students staged protests in Kinshasa to demand larger study grants and the removal of Mobutu from power. In what was seen by many observers as an attempt to defuse the growing tension, Mobutu announced in late April that a multi-party political system, initially comprising three parties (including the MPR), would be introduced after a transitional period of one year. At the same time Mobutu declared the inauguration of the 'Third Republic' and announced his resignation as chairman of the MPR and state commissioner for national defence. However, he retained the office of president. The national executive council was dissolved, and Prof. Lunda Bululu, the secretary-general of the Economic Community of Central African States (CEEAC) and formerly a legal adviser to Mobutu, replaced Kengo Wa Dondo as first state commissioner.

In early May 1990 a new transitional government was formed. Mobutu announced that a special commission would draft a new constitution by the end of April 1991, and that presidential elections would be held before December of that year, with legislative elections to follow in 1992. He also announced the imminent 'depoliticization of the armed forces, the gendarmerie, the civil guard, the security services and the administration in general'. Additionally, legislation permitting the operation of political parties and of free trade unions was to be prepared. In late April 1990 Tshisekedi was released from house arrest.

Further unrest occurred in early May 1990, when students at Lubumbashi University staged anti-government demonstrations. It was reported that between 50–150 students were massacred by members of the presidential guard, acting on Mobutu's orders. Strong condemnation was voiced by many humanitarian organizations, and the Belgian government announced the immediate suspension of all official bilateral assistance to Zaire. After some procrastination and strenuous denial of the reports, Mobutu authorized an official parliamentary inquiry, as a result of which a provincial governor and other senior local officials were arrested and charged with having organized the killing of one student and the injury of 13 others. However, Mobutu refused to allow an independent international board of inquiry to enter Zaire, despite Belgium's insistence, to investigate the case further. By late June it appeared inevitable that relations between the two countries would enter another crisis (see below), following the expulsion from Zaire of about 700 Belgian technical assistants and the closure by Mobutu of all but one of Belgium's consular offices in Zaire.

As part of the continuing process of political reform, in late June 1990 the legislature adopted amendments to the constitution, whereby presidential control over the national executive council and over foreign policy was ended. At the same time, the establishment of independent trade unions was authorized. In early October Mobutu announced that a full multi-party political system would be established, and in November the necessary enabling legislation was adopted. In the same month, however, the USA announced that it was to terminate all military and economic aid to Zaire. This development followed renewed allegations of abuses of human rights in Zaire, and also reflected speculation that for many years Mobutu had been systematically misappropriating foreign economic aid. Popular unrest re-emerged in late 1990: in November an anti-government rally in Kinshasa, organized by the UDPS, was violently suppressed, and in the following months anti-government demonstrations took place in Kinshasa and Matadi.

In early February 1991 the UNTC organized a three-day general strike, supported by hundreds of thousands of workers, civil servants and public service employees, to protest against working and living conditions and to demand the resignation of the government. Later in the same month 20,000 people attended an anti-government rally, in Kinshasa, organized by the UDPS.

NATIONAL CONFERENCE

The announcement of a timetable for the restoration of multi-party politics led to a proliferation of political parties. Prominent among these was the Union des fédéralistes et républicains indépendants (UFERI), led by Nguza Karl-I-Bond. In March 1991 a new and enlarged transitional government was appointed, in which Lunda Bululu was replaced as first state commissioner by Prof. Mulumba Lukoji, an economist who had served in previous administrations. Several minor political parties were represented in the transitional government, although more influential opposition parties refused to participate. In April Mobutu announced that a national conference would convene at the end of the month, at which members of the government and opposition organizations would discuss the drafting of a new constitution, which would then be submitted for approval in a national referendum. The response of the major opposition parties was to reject the call for a national conference unless Mobutu relinquished power. Widespread anti-government demonstrations followed this announcement, and in mid-April 42 people were reported to have been killed and many others wounded when security forces opened fire on demonstrators in the town of Mbuji-Mayi, in central Zaire. Mobutu reacted to these developments initially by suspending and then reconvening the national conference for 31 July.

In response to these initiatives, three of the more influential opposition parties, the Parti démocrate et social chrétien (PDSC), the UDPS and the UFERI, formed the Union sacrée de l'opposition radicale (USOR), which urged a general boycott of the national conference. By the end of July 1991 the USOR had expanded to include 130 parties. It then decided that its growing influence and the weakening of Mobutu's power justified its participation in the national conference. On 22 July Mobutu requested the resignation of the Lukoji administration, and under increasing pressure from the USOR, offered the premiership to Tshisekedi of the UDPS. However, this overture was rejected by Tshisekedi, under pressure from his party, and Lukoji's government was reinstated.

The national conference opened on 7 August 1991, with 2,850 delegates, including 900 representing opposition political parties. The opposition delegates, however, immediately threatened to withdraw unless its demands were met in full. The election of Isaac Kalonji Mutambay, a protestant pastor, as president of the conference was rejected by the opposition delegates, and by late September the conference, from which representatives of the influential Roman Catholic Church had withdrawn, had become overshadowed by a worsening internal crisis.

On 2 September 1991 violent clashes took place between opposition supporters and the security forces, with heavy casualties. The demonstrations represented growing popular frustration with the national conference, massive inflation and aggravated hardship. By late September the disorders had developed into widespread rioting and looting, which was initiated by the military and then spread to the civilian population. Massive destruction of properties and business premises took place and a large number of deaths were reported. French and Belgian troops were dispatched, ostensibly to evacuate foreigners, and suppressed the rioting.

In the wake of these riots France, Belgium and the USA put pressure on Mobutu to appoint a new government, as a result of which Tshisekedi returned as first state commissioner on 2 October 1991. However, he remained in this post for only 12 days, when he was dismissed by Mobutu and a 'government of crisis' sworn in: Tshisekedi's departure had been hastened by his refusal to swear an oath of allegiance to the president, and by his public denunciation of Mobutu as a 'human monster'.

Four posts in the 'government of crisis' were awarded to the MPR. Bernardin Mungul Diaka, the leader of the Rassemblement démocratique pour la République (RDR), was appointed first state commissioner. Although the RDR was part of the USOR, Mungul Diaka had formerly been a close political associate of Mobutu.

It rapidly became evident that the 'government of crisis' lacked acceptance both within Zaire and among the Western powers. A new initiative was undertaken by President Diouf of Senegal to break the impasse. Diouf's proposals committed both Mobutu and opposition supporters to the convening of a sovereign national conference, which would have legislative power, and a first state commissioner drawn from the opposition. With an agreement signed on 22 November 1991, a new government was sworn in on 28 November, with Nguza Karl-I-Bond, the leader of the UFERI, as first state commissioner. Various political factions were present in this government, but the USOR was largely excluded and key portfolios retained by Mobutu's allies, who received eight ministerial posts, including defence and security, external relations and international co-operation. The national conference was resumed in December under the presidency of the Roman Catholic archbishop of Kisangani, Laurent Monsengwo Pasinya. Joseph Ileo (also known as Ileo Nsongo Amba), who had been prime minister in 1960–61 and was now the leader of the PDSC, was selected as vice-president.

Serious divisions soon arose within the national conference. The UFERI, once a central force within the USOR, became instrumental in setting up a new political coalition, the Alliance of Patriotic Forces, grouping 30 political parties which declared themselves opposed to 'extremist measures' in obtaining political reform. Nguza Karl-I-Bond, following consultations with Mobutu, suspended the national conference in January 1992, citing its cost and its alleged responsibility for exacerbating ethnic tensions. Violence soon followed; on 14 January the Rassemblement des démocrates libéraux (RDL), which had close links with the UFERI, claimed that seven of its supporters had been killed in clashes with another political party in Kasaï Oriental (a stronghold of the USOR). Similarly Nguza Karl-I-Bond announced eight deaths following clashes between the Lunda (his ethnic group) and the Luba (Tshisekedi's ethnic group). Nguza Karl-I-Bond proposed that each party should only have one representative at the national conference from any ethnic group. Mobutu endorsed this view, accusing the conference of being unrepresentative, and asserting that 45% of the delegates originated from the two Kasaï provinces.

During January and February 1992 violence intensified as the USOR and Christian churches attempted to mobilize demonstrations against the suspension of the conference. On 16 February over 30 people were killed by security forces in mass protests in Kinshasa. These incidents further impaired Mobutu's international standing with France, Belgium and the USA, leading to pressure from donor countries for the national conference to be reinstated, and to a further suspension of aid. On 22–23 January troops briefly seized the national radio station, urging the removal of the government and resumption of the national conference. A number of strikes broke out in February demanding both better wages and resumption of the political conference. At the end of March, two government ministers resigned in protest at government policies.

Increasingly isolated and under pressure at home and abroad, Mobutu, against the wishes of Nguza Karl-I-Bond, agreed to reconvene the conference on 6 April 1992. On 17 April the conference declared itself 'sovereign', with power to take binding legislative and executive decisions, thus undermining the role of the government. In return for accepting this ruling, Mobutu was permitted by the conference to remain as head of state. The main role of the conference was now to define a draft constitution, which would be put to a referendum, and to establish a timetable for legislative and presidential elections. In June a 65-member special commission was set up to examine arrangements for a transitional multi-party government. In the same month it was also announced that a transitional government would be established in July, and that an electoral college was to be formed.

As the conference began debating the choice of a first state commissioner, in mid-June 1992, Mobutu warned that the conference had the power only to draw up a draft constitution, not to adopt it, and threatened to 'call the conference to order', as he had done in the past. However, by late July, Mobutu appeared to have conceded to the conference's demands. On 23 July, it was announced that it had been mutually agreed that the conference would elect a transitional first state commissioner, who would appoint a government. It was reported that Mobutu had also agreed to the establishment of a high council of the republic, to oversee the implementation of the conference's decisions, and to place the gendarmerie and civil guard under the control of the transitional government. Mobutu, however, was to retain control of the army.

On 15 August 1992 the conference overwhelmingly elected Tshisekedi as the transitional prime minister, replacing Nguza Karl-I-Bond, who had not stood for re-election. A 'transition act', adopted by the conference in early August, granted Tshisekedi a 24-month mandate, pending the promulgation of a new constitution which would curtail the powers of the president. On 30 August Tshisekedi, whose election was widely welcomed as a victory for pro-democratic forces, appointed a 'transitional government of national union' which included opponents of Mobutu.

The political interests of Tshisekedi and Mobutu clashed almost immediately, following an announcement by the president of his intention to promote the adoption of a 'semi-presidential constitution', in opposition to the parliamentary system favoured by the conference. In October 1992 attacks on opposition leaders and the offices of newspapers critical of Mobutu became increasingly frequent in Kinshasa, while Shaba was beset by ethnic violence. On 14 November the national conference (without the participation of Mobutu's supporters) adopted a draft constitution providing for the establishment of a 'Federal Republic of the Congo', the introduction of a bicameral legislature and the election, by universal suffrage, of a non-executive president to fulfil largely ceremonial functions. (Executive and military power was to be exercised by the prime minister.) The draft document was vigorously opposed by Mobutu who, having failed to persuade Tshisekedi to reorganize his government in order to accommodate the president's own supporters, unsuccessfully attempted in early December to declare the Tshisekedi government dissolved.

HIGH COUNCIL OF THE REPUBLIC

On 6 December 1992 the national conference dissolved itself and was succeeded by a 453-member high council of the republic (HCR), retaining Archbishop Monsengwo as its president. As the supreme interim executive and legislative authority, the HCR was empowered to amend and adopt the new constitution and to organize legislative and presidential elections. Monsengwo announced that the report of a special commission, established by the conference in order to examine allegations of corruption brought against the president and his associates, would be considered by the high council. In response to this effective seizure of his powers, Mobutu ordered the suspension of the HCR and the government, and decreed that civil servants should usurp ministers in the supervision of government ministries (a demand which they refused). Attempts by the presidential guard to obstruct the convening of the high council ended following the organization of a public demonstration in Kinshasa, organized by the HCR, in protest at the actions of the armed forces. The HCR received the support of the USA, Belgium and France, in its declaration of Tshisekedi as head of Zaire's government.

In mid-January 1993 the HCR declared Mobutu to be guilty of treason and threatened impeachment proceedings unless he recognized the legitimacy of the transitional government. A brief general strike and campaign of civil disobedience, organized by the USOR, resulted in five fatalities and numerous injuries. At the end of the month several units of the army rioted in protest at an attempt by the president to pay them with discredited banknotes. Order was eventually restored, but only after the deaths of some 65 people (including the French ambassador to Zaire), and the intervention of French troops.

Rival Governments

In early March 1993, in an attempt to reassert his political authority, Mobutu convened a special 'conclave' of political forces to debate the country's future. The HCR and the USOR declined to participate. In mid-March the 'conclave' appointed Faustin Birindwa, a former UDPS member and adviser to Tshisekedi, as prime minister, charged with the formation of a 'government of national salvation'. Mobutu also reconvened the dormant national assembly as a rival to the HCR. In early April Birindwa appointed a cabinet which included Nguza Karl-I-Bond (as first deputy prime minister in charge of defence), and three members of the USOR, who were immediately expelled from that organization. While the Birindwa administration was denied official recognition by Belgium, France, the USA and the European Union (EU), Tshisekedi became increasingly frustrated at the impotence of his own government and increasing internal instability (during April the army embarked upon a campaign of intimidation of opposition members, while tribal warfare re-emerged in Shaba and also erupted in the north-eastern province of Kivu), and sought the intervention of the UN. In July the secretary-general of the UN appointed Lakhdar Brahimi, a former minister of foreign affairs in Algeria, as his special envoy to Zaire and mediator there. Meanwhile, in late June, six of Birindwa's ministers, all former activists in the USOR, had announced the formation of the Union sacrée rénovée (USR), claiming that the USOR had abandoned its original political objectives in the pursuit of radical policies. Mobutu was widely perceived to be fostering divisions in the opposition through the extensive use of his personal patronage: he had direct access to much of the country's capital and assets. A series of pre-negotiations, conducted during August between representatives of the 'conclave', the USOR and the HCR, failed to conclude a significant initiative for future consensus. In early September, in response to a declaration made by Mobutu scheduling a constitutional referendum for October and presidential elections for December, Tshisekedi announced the formation of a new opposition grouping, the Forces démocratiques de Congo-Kinshasa. The new party, led by Tshisekedi, was to take no part in any future negotiations with the presidential 'conclave', and accepted the exclusive right of the HCR to formulate electoral arrangements.

In late September 1993, following almost three weeks of negotiations, an agreement was reached between representatives of Mobutu and the principal opposition groups, providing for the adoption of a single constitutional text for the transitional period, which would be subject to approval by a national referendum. Under the provisions of the agreement, transitional institutions would include the president of the republic, a reorganized transitional parliament, together with the transitional government and the national judiciary. As already agreed, the organization of presidential and legislative elections would provide for the establishment of a new republic in January 1995. During October 1993, however, attempts to finalize the terms of the agreement were complicated by the insistence of Tshisekedi's supporters that he should continue in the office of prime minister, despite the objections of Mobutu's representatives that Tshisekedi's mandate, proceeding from the national conference, had been superseded by the September agreement. The opposing positions of the principal political parties (largely polarized as the supporters of Tshisekedi in the USOR and the pro-Mobutu Forces politiques du conclave–FPC) became more firmly entrenched during the closing weeks of 1993.

In December 1993, at a rally in Kolwezi attended by Nguza Karl-I-Bond, the governor of Shaba declared the autonomy of the province (reverting to the name of Katanga). While Nguza Karl-I-Bond denied that his presence had in any way endorsed the declaration, the (separatist) UFERI welcomed the development and encouraged provincial political committees to pursue the establishment of greater regional autonomy. Mobutu's subdued response to the Shaba declaration was attributed to his reluctance to engender further political opposition during negotiations that might dictate his political future.

EMERGENCE OF THE HCR–PT

An ultimatum, issued to all political parties by Mobutu in early January 1994, in an attempt to end the political impasse, led to an agreement to form a government of national reconciliation, signed by all major constituent parties of the FPC and the USOR (with the notable exception of Tshisekedi's UDPS). Encouraged by the unexpected level of political support for the initiative, on 14 January Mobutu announced the dissolution of the HCR and the national legislative council, the dismissal of the Birindwa government, and a contest for the premiership between two contestants, Tshisekedi and Molumba Lukoji, to be decided by a transitional legislature (to be known as the haut conseil de la république–parlement de transition—HCR–PT) within 15 days of its inauguration, provisionally scheduled for 17 January. Despite widespread opposition condemnation of Mobutu's procedural circumvention of the authority of the HCR, and a well-supported 24-hour strike organized in Kinshasa, the HCR–PT was convened on 23 January under the presidency of Archbishop Monsengwo. The HCR–PT immediately rejected Mobutu's procedure for the selection of a new prime minister, but its subsequent attempts to formulate a new procedure were frustrated by the increasingly divergent interests of the member parties of the USOR, and by Tshisekedi's insistence of his legitimate claim to the office.

On 8 April 1994 the HCR–PT endorsed a new transitional constitution act, reiterating the provisions of previous accords for the organization of a constitutional referendum and presidential and legislative elections, and defining the functions of and relationship between the president of the republic, the transitional government and the HCR–PT, during a 15-month transitional period. The government, to be accountable to the HCR–PT, was to assume some relinquished powers of the president, including the control of the central bank and the security forces and the nomination of candidates for senior posts in the civil service. A new prime minister was to be appointed from opposition candidates, to be nominated within 10 days of the president's promulgation of the act. Despite the initial indignation of Tshisekedi's supporters at the declaration of a prime-ministerial vacancy that they did not recognize, by late April Tshisekedi was reported to have agreed to be considered for the post. Widening divisions within the USOR frustrated attempts to unite the opposition behind Tshisekedi as sole candidate, prompting the expulsion, in May, of 10 dissident parties from the USOR (including the Union pour la république et la démocratie–URD, whose members occupied several ministerial posts in the transitional government).

In June 1994 the HCR–PT ratified the candidature of seven opposition representatives for the premiership, rejecting that of Tshisekedi on the grounds that he had described his position as 'prime minister awaiting rehabilitation', rather than candidate for the office. On 14 June it was reported that Léon Kengo Wa Dondo, described as a moderate opposition leader, had been elected prime minister by 322 votes to 133 in the HCR–PT. However, Kengo Wa Dondo's election was immediately rejected as void, under the terms of the April constitution act, by opposition spokesmen and by the president of the HCR–PT (who refused to endorse the actions of the legislature). A new transitional government, announced on 6 July, was similarly rejected by the radical opposition, despite the offer of two cabinet posts to the UDPS. On 11 July, during a motion of confidence, the government received overwhelming support from the HCR–PT. The new prime minister swiftly sought to restore the confidence of the international donor community by committing the new administration to the implementation of political change (general elections were promised to take place before the end of July 1995) and economic adjustment (more financial control was to be exerted over the armed forces, and the central bank was to be granted greater autonomy). In mid-1994, the international standing of the new government was further enhanced by its support for French and US initiatives to address the humanitarian crisis presented by the flight to Zaire of more than 2m. Rwandan refugees seeking to escape the violent aftermath of the death of President Habyarimana.

Zaire's already formidable economic difficulties were compounded in September 1994 by the circulation throughout the country of some 30 tons of counterfeit Zairean currency notes. Government initiatives for economic retrenchment included the announcement, in the same month, of the closure of more than half of its 64 diplomatic missions abroad and the president's statement of intent to privatize the state mining corporation, GÉCAMINES. It had been reported in March that some 300,000 civil servants (around one-half of the total number) were to be dismissed as part of a programme to rationalize the public sector and reduce public expenditure. Later in the month, widespread industrial action was organized by public sector workers in protest at this decision and in support of demands for the payment of substantial amounts of salary arrears. In early December the prime minister had announced an economic austerity plan for 1995 which aimed to reduce inflation massively, to just 20%. By the end of December it was reported that national financial reserves were virtually exhausted.

In October 1994 an expanded radical opposition grouping (the Union sacrée de l'opposition radicale et ses alliés–USORAL) resumed its participation in the HCR–PT, having boycotted proceedings since the election of Kengo Wa Dondo in June. By early November a reformist wing of the UDPS, led by Joseph Ruhana Mirindi, had agreed to join the government, and the subsequent reallocation of portfolios included the appointment of two ministers and two deputy ministers who were (or had previously been) members of the UDPS.

Despite the successful adoption, in May 1995, of the electoral law establishing the national electoral commission, a lack of government funds and the logistical problems presented by the presence in Zaire of as many as 2.5m. refugees forced the extension of the 15-month period of transitional government beyond the 9 July deadline. In late June political consensus was achieved between the FPC and the USORAL, resulting in the HCR–PT's adoption of a constitutional amendment (approved by Mobutu) whereby the period of national transition was to be extended by two years. On 1 July deputies from both groups had voted to relieve Archbishop Monsengwo of the presidency of the transitional legislature, prompting concern that the concerted political strength of the FPC and the USORAL would be sufficient to oust the prime minister. Meanwhile, Monsengwo's protest at the unconstitutional nature of his dismissal received cautious support from the French and Belgian governments. Further political manoeuvring in July suggested that the FPC and the radical opposition were seeking to replace Kengo Wa Dondo with Tshisekedi. Meanwhile, Mobutu made no obvious attempt to resolve the political crisis, prompting suggestions that such political divisions could only serve to strengthen his own position. In late July, however, Kengo Wa Dondo announced a reallocation of cabinet portfolios which appeared to consolidate his own position and to restore, to some extent, the confidence of the international community in the stability of his administration.

Meanwhile, opposition frustration at the government's failure to finalize an electoral timetable continued to escalate. In late July 1995, at an anti-government demonstration organized in the capital, some 2,000 supporters of the Parti lumumbiste unifié (PALU—an organization which supports the aims of the late prime minister, Patrice Lumumba) clashed with the security forces, resulting in the deaths of nine civilians and one police officer. A subsequent protest in Kinshasa, organized by the USORAL in early August, denounced international endorsement of the prime minister and urged his removal. The demonstration, which was conducted peacefully, was attended by an estimated 5,000 of Tshisekedi's supporters. In early December opposition groups voiced a unanimous rejection of a government offer to participate in a national coalition government, and reiterated their demands for the prompt announcement of a timetable for multi-party elections. At the end of December the HCR–PT formalized the establishment of the national electoral commission (NEC), to be composed of 44 members (22 from both of the major political groupings), and headed by Bayona Bameya, a close political associate of Mobutu. A comprehensive reorganization of the cabinet was effected in late February 1996, and in early April the NEC was formally installed.

In mid-April 1996 it was announced that multi-party presidential and legislative elections would take place in May 1997. Regional and municipal elections would be organized for June and July of the same year. All elections would be preceded by a referendum on a new constitution, to be conducted in December 1996. Mobutu immediately announced his intention to contest the presidential poll. (However, neither the elections nor the referendum took place, as the security situation in the country rapidly worsened—see below.) A draft of the new constitution, which provided for a federal state with a semi-presidential parliamentary system of government, was adopted by the government in late May, and by the HCR–PT in October. Meanwhile, by late 1995 tensions within the UDPS appeared to be intensifying, with support divided between Tshisekedi and the USORAL president, Frédéric Kibassa Maliba. Divisions were exacerbated in April 1996 by Tshisekedi's attempt to expel 60 prominent members who refused to support his demands for his return to the premiership prior to the organization of elections. In early May a meeting of representatives of some 215 opposition interests within the USORAL voted to remove Tshisekedi from the leadership. Kibassa Maliba was re-elected to the USORAL presidency. Supporters of Tshisekedi within the UDPS, however, pressed demands that he replace Kengo Wa Dondo as prime minister.

A further delay in the electoral timetable was announced in July 1996. The constitutional referendum, due to take place in December, was to be postponed to February 1997, although no alteration was proposed for the completion of the transitional period by July. Nguza Karl-I-Bond, who had been in poor health since 1993, returned to active politics in July 1996, with his resumption of the chairmanship of the FPC. In the following month it was announced that Mobutu had left for Switzerland to receive treatment for a serious form of cancer.

THE FALL OF MOBUTU

Mobutu's illness, combined with the political and military legacy of the 1994 Rwandan refugee crisis, proved to be the turning-point in his rule. The president remained in Europe for four months, undergoing surgery in Switzerland and later moving to his villa in the south of France for convalescence. Kengo Wa Dondo's government, meanwhile, was left to confront a rapid escalation of violence in the eastern provinces of North and South Kivu. Rwandan Hutu militiamen and former soldiers who had fled their own country in 1994, fearing Tutsi retribution, had been allowed to mingle freely with civilian refugees, and had turned the refugee camps into bases for rearmament. From mid-1996 Rwandan Hutu militias actively began trying to carve out a strategic territory for themselves in eastern Zaire with the support of locally-based Hutus and members of the Zairean armed forces (FAZ), killing and expelling local Tutsis and other ethnic groups. The picture was complicated by historical rivalries in the area, including widespread resentment of Tutsis resident in South Kivu (known locally as the Banyamulenge), and a long-running dispute over their Zairean citizenship. The conflict soon spread further south, and in early October the deputy governor of South Kivu ordered the Banyamulenge to leave the country within a week. Although the order was subsequently suspended, it provoked the mobilization of a powerful Tutsi backlash. Tutsi militias, with, according to many reports, covert support from the Tutsi-dominated Rwandan government and its close regional ally, Uganda, made rapid advances against the combined forces of the Hutus and the poorly trained, ill-disciplined FAZ. What initially appeared to be a regional movement seeking to defend the Tutsi population and to disempower extremist Hutus soon gathered momentum and emerged as a national rebellion aiming to overthrow the Mobutu regime. Tutsi rebels were joined by dissidents of diverse ethnic origin (including Shaba and Kasaï secessionists, and local Mai-Mai warriors) to form the Alliance des forces démocratiques pour la libération du Congo-Zaïre (AFDL), led by Laurent-Désiré Kabila, a ministerial aid under Lumumba and an active opponent of the Mobutu regime since the 1960s. By early November AFDL forces controlled a substantial area adjoining the border with Rwanda, Burundi and parts of Uganda, including the key towns of Goma and Bukavu. Mobutu's absence, and uncertainties as to the state of his health, contributed to the poor co-ordination of the Zairean government's response to the AFDL, which by the end of November was in control of most of Kivu.

The rebels' success in the east exacerbated anti-Tutsi sentiment in Kinshasa. In November 1996 the HCR–PT urged the expulsion of all Tutsis from Zairean territory; following attacks on Tutsis and their property, many Tutsi residents of Kinshasa fled to Brazzaville (Republic of the Congo). In the same month repeated public demonstrations demanded the resignation of Kengo (himself, part-Tutsi in origin) for having failed to respond effectively to the insurrection. Mobutu flew back to Kinshasa on 17 December and promptly appointed Gen. Mahele Lieko Bokungu as chief of staff of the joint armed forces. Kengo Wa Dondo remained prime minister, but Mobutu ordered the formation of a crisis government which included some opposition members, although it excluded both main factions of the UDPS and was not approved by the HCR–PT. The continued exclusion of Tshisekedi from the government prompted his supporters to mount a campaign of civil disobedience, and in January 1997 his faction of the UDPS announced its support for the AFDL. In February, following a highly effective general strike in Kinshasa, Mobutu banned all demonstrations and industrial action.

In late January 1997 a counter-offensive by Zairean troops, reportedly assisted by foreign mercenaries, failed to make any significant territorial gains. In February the AFDL captured the towns of Shabunda, Kalemie and Kindu; in the same month the Zairean air force began an aerial bombardment of several AFDL-controlled towns. In March, after a brief battle, the AFDL entered the strategically-important northern town of Kisangani (which had served as the centre of military operations for the government), and in early April Mbuji-Mayi fell to the rebels. Nguza Karl-I-Bond called on his followers (for the most part Shaba secessionists) to support the AFDL. According to international media reports, AFDL troops entering Zaire's 'second city', Lubumbashi, on 9 April were cheered by crowds and greeted as liberators, as government troops withdrew from the city. The Zairean government continued to make allegations that the AFDL offensive was being supported by government troops from Rwanda, Uganda, Burundi and Angola, while the AFDL, in turn, claimed that the Zairean army was being supplemented by white mercenary soldiers and by forces of UNITA. Several attempts at mediation between the two sides, undertaken by various foreign governments (most notably South Africa) and international organizations, during February-April, failed to halt the escalation of the conflict. With control of all of the country's main productive resources, Kabila was in a commanding position to resist domestic and international calls for compromise.

In March 1997, following the capture of Kisangani, the HCR–PT, although technically inquorate, voted to dismiss Kengo Wa Dondo, who tendered his resignation as prime minister towards the end of the month. He was replaced at the beginning of April by Tshisekedi, who, having offered government posts to members of AFDL (which they refused), announced that he was dissolving the HCR–PT. Parliament, in turn, voted to dismiss Tshisekedi, whose supporters organized a demonstration of support in Kinshasa, only to come under attack from the security forces. On 8 April Mobutu declared a national state of emergency, dismissing the government and ordering the deployment of security forces throughout Kinshasa. Gen. Likulia Bolongo was appointed prime minister at the head of a new 28-member national salvation government, in which the USORAL refused to participate. On 14 and 15 April supporters of the UDPS organized a further two-day 'ghost city' general strike in Kinshasa, which was widely observed. An arrest warrant was subsequently issued for Kengo Wa Dondo, who was alleged to have fled to Switzerland with funds from the national treasury.

Following inconclusive peace talks between Mobutu and Kabila, mediated by the South African president, Nelson Mandela, and conducted on board a South African naval supply vessel off the coast of the Republic of the Congo in early May 1997, Mobutu refused to resign (despite intense international pressure to do so and thereby avoid a violent battle for Kinshasa) and Kabila reiterated his intention to seize the capital by force. A further reorganization of the government was carried out by Mobutu in the same month. A hastily-assembled regional initiative to transfer interim executive power to Monsengwo Pasinya (recently re-elected speaker of the HCR–PT) was rejected by the rebels, and was widely dismissed as a procedural device designed to afford Mobutu a dignified withdrawal from office.

TRANSFER OF POWER

On 16 May 1997 Mobutu left Kinshasa (travelling to Togo, and then to Morocco), while many of his supporters and family fled across the border to Brazzaville, in the Republic of Congo. On the night of 16 May Mahele Bokungu, the chief of the general staff, was murdered by elements of the presidential guard (reportedly led by Mobutu's son, Kongolo) who suspected him of attempting to negotiate a peaceful transfer of power to the rebels. On 17 May AFDL troops entered Kinshasa (encountering no resistance) and Kabila, speaking from Lubumbashi, declared himself president of the Democratic Republic of the Congo (DRC—the name used between 1964 and 1971), which swiftly gained international recognition. He immediately announced plans to form a provisional government within 72 hours and a constituent assembly within 60 days; presidential and parliamentary elections were to be held in April 1999. On 20 May Kabila arrived in Kinshasa, and on 22 May AFDL forces captured Matadi, giving the AFDL control of most of the country. On 23 May Kabila announced the formation of a government, which, while dominated by members of the AFDL, also included members of the UDPS and of the Front patriotique, and avoided a potentially unpopular preponderance of ethnic Tutsis. No prime minister was appointed, and Tshisekedi was not offered a cabinet post; he refused to recognize the new government, and advocated public protest against the administration, but failed to raise the mass support that he had previously enjoyed. Following several demonstrations, including one in Uvira in which a number of people were reportedly killed by the security forces, on 26 May Kabila issued a decree banning all political parties and public demonstrations. An illegal gathering on 28 May in support of Tshisekedi was dispersed by the army.

On 28 May 1997 Kabila issued a constitutional decree, to remain in force until the adoption of a new constitution. The international community expressed concern that the decree allowed the president to wield near-absolute power, since it accorded him legislative and executive power as well as control over the armed forces and the treasury. Of the previously existing institutions, only the judiciary was not disbanded. On 29 May, at a ceremony attended by the presidents of Uganda, Rwanda, Angola, Burundi and Zambia, Kabila was sworn in as president of the DRC. Despite the concerns of a number of humanitarian organizations regarding the new administration's treatment of refugees (see below), Kabila's assumption of power was widely welcomed by the international community. In early June seven additional cabinet ministers were appointed. Soon afterwards it was announced that a number of high-ranking officials from the Mobutu period, including the secretary-general of the MPR and the governor of the central bank, had been arrested, whilst the directors of all parastatal companies had been suspended, pending further investigations. Later in the month, the detention overnight of Tshisekedi, following a political address to students, prompted renewed scepticism regarding the Kabila government's commitment to future political pluralism.

FOREIGN RELATIONS

During the early 1980s, a period of intense superpower rivalry in southern Africa, the Mobutu regime was an important ally of the USA, France and Belgium, receiving large amounts of aid. The Kamina air base in southern Shaba was alleged to have been used by the USA to support the insurgent União Nacional para a Independência Total de Angola (UNITA) in its campaign against the government of Angola. Mobutu was, however, also instrumental in negotiating the June 1989 *rapprochement* between the Angolan government and UNITA. The ending of superpower conflicts at the end of the 1980s and the increasing prominence being given in aid policies to the issues of democracy and human rights led, however, to a distancing of the relationship between Mobutu and his Western allies. In November 1988 a serious dispute arose between Zaire and Belgium, following Belgian press reports criticizing the public corruption in Zaire and alleged misappropriation of funds by Mobutu. This led to a major rift between the two countries which was resolved in March 1990 with a treaty of co-operation, the cancellation of one-third of Zaire's state-guaranteed commercial debt and restoration of normal corporate and banking relations between the two countries. But relations deteriorated again in May 1990 following Belgium's reaction to the killings of students at Lubumbashi. Increasing internal repression and violence drew further criticism and condemnation of the Mobutu regime by Belgium, France and the USA, and pressure for Mobutu to relinquish power. They openly blamed Mobutu for the deteriorating internal economy and for political repression, and refused to renew aid to Zaire. In November 1991 a francophone summit due to be held in Kinshasa was relocated in

Paris, and France declared that Mobutu would not be welcome. On 22 January 1992 the EC (European Community, now the European Union–EU) announced the suspension of all aid, except humanitarian relief, to Zaire. After the outbreak of rioting in September 1991, when French and Belgian troops intervened to evacuate foreigners and restore order, France, Belgium and the USA became more interventionist, maintaining pressure on Mobutu to reconvene the national conference and to transfer power. The USA insisted that Mobutu must concede power to an interim government and relinquish control over national finances and defence; although it negotiated for Mobutu to remain as titular head of state, owing to concerns that his sudden removal might lead to a rapid breakdown of control over the military apparatus and to anarchy and turmoil.

Zaire's relations with Belgium, France, the USA and the EU improved considerably following the inauguration of Prime Minister Kengo Wa Dondo and his new government in July 1994. Zaire's willingness to co-operate with international initiatives to address the refugee crisis arising from the flight across the Zairean border of more than 2m. Rwandan refugees in 1994–95 resulted in 1996 in the limited resumption of development aid from France and the USA, channelled through non-governmental organizations. By 1996 relations with France had thawed considerably, as Mobutu came to be seen as representative of francophone interests in Africa, interests which had diminished with the establishment of new anglocentric regimes in Rwanda and Burundi. Most international and regional powers, with the notable exception of France, cautiously welcomed the AFDL's victory. Paris, however, which was widely seen as having made a grave policy miscalculation by backing Mobutu against the AFDL, said that it deplored the forcible take-over and called for early elections.

In late July 1994 President Mobutu met President Bizimungu of Rwanda and concluded an agreement for the disarmament and gradual repatriation of Rwandan refugees. By mid-August 1995, however, the security situation in refugee camps along the Zairean border had deteriorated to such an extent that the Zairean government initiated a programme of forcible repatriation. Some 15,000 Rwandans were deported in a number of days, prompting widespread international concern for their welfare. Later in the month in Geneva, at a meeting with the UN High Commissioner for Refugees (UNHCR), Kengo Wa Dondo agreed to entrust the repatriation process to UNHCR officials until the end of the year, after which time the Zairean government would resume the forcible return of all remaining refugees. In early September a formal agreement was concluded between UNHCR and the Zairean government for a more regulated and bilateral approach to the refugee crisis, and later in the month, following a further meeting of representatives of UNHCR, Rwanda and Zaire in Geneva, further commitments were made by both governments to improve security conditions on both sides of the border. At a conference of the Great Lakes Countries, convened in Cairo in late November, and attended by the presidents of Burundi, Rwanda, Uganda and Zaire and by a Tanzanian presidential envoy, the member nations recognized the need to disarm and demilitarize displaced groups within their borders which threatened the security of neighbouring nations. Mobutu also indicated (and in December confirmed) that the forcible return of remaining refugees in early 1996 was no longer a realistic objective.

By October 1996, despite reports that large numbers of refugees were beginning to return to Rwanda from Burundi and Tanzania, little progress had been made in repatriating displaced Rwandans in Zaire. In that month UNHCR warned that the distribution of food to the refugees was being prevented by the prevailing instability in eastern Zaire. Hundreds of thousands of Rwandan Hutus fled in advance of the arrival of AFDL troops (see above), who, in early November, declared a cease-fire for returning refugees, and later in the month announced the creation of a humanitarian corridor to the Rwandan border, in the hope that the estimated 700,000 Rwandan refugees now seeking shelter at the Mugunga camp, west of Goma, would return to Rwanda. (An additional 300,000 refugees were believed to have scattered into the surrounding hills.) However, the large-scale return of refugees was finally prompted by an AFDL attack on extremist Hutu units operating from the camp. In mid-November UNHCR reported the return of some 400,000 refugees in recent weeks, which did much to reassure the international aid community that the immediate humanitarian crisis had abated (a number of initiatives for multinational intervention were cancelled), but failed to allay continuing concern as to the whereabouts and welfare of a vast number of refugees who could not be accounted for. As the AFDL advance continued as far west as Kisangani, reports began to emerge that relief supplies for the estimated 200,000 remaining refugees were being intercepted by the rebels, who were also accused of forcing refugees to flee nearby camps, and of refusing to allow aid workers and journalists to enter the camps. In late April 1997 the AFDL leader, Laurent Kabila, demanded that the UN complete full repatriation of the refugees within 60 days, after which time their return would be undertaken unilaterally by the rebels. By early May the AFDL had initiated an organized repatriation programme which encountered almost immediate condemnation from the UN, owing to the overcrowded conditions in which the refugees were being transported. (More than 90 refugees were killed in a stampede arising from overcrowding in a railway carriage in Kisangani early in the month.) Allegations continued to emerge during 1997 that elements of the AFDL had committed massacres of Hutu refugees, and in May Emma Bonino, the EU commissioner for humanitarian affairs, accused the AFDL of complicity in the death of refugees from disease and starvation. In the same month the UN Security Council urged the immediate cessation of violence against refugees in the DRC. In July serious differences arose between the government and UNHCR concerning the imminent arrival in the DRC of a UN inquiry mission charged with the investigation of allegations of human rights abuses against refugees: the Kabila administration objected to one of the members of the mission, as well as demanding that the inquiry should concern an extended period of time, on the basis that massacres imputed to AFDL forces might have been committed by the FAZ or by Hutu militiamen. However, this official hindrance of the investigation was widely condemned, and a growing number of reports were cited in the international press from alleged witnesses to massacres committed by the AFDL, the occurrence of which the Kabila administration consistently and categorically denied.

The country's relationship with its neighbours has been complicated by the presence in border areas of rebels opposed to regional governments. In May 1986 Zaire's relations with a number of southern African countries deteriorated, owing to allegations that the USA was covertly supplying weapons, through Zaire, to the South African-supported UNITA, which was in conflict with the Angolan government. Although the Zairean government denied these allegations and, in July, Mobutu visited Angola and declared his support for the Angolan government, reports that military equipment was reaching UNITA through Zaire nevertheless continued until the overthrow of Mobuto in May 1997.

In 1992 relations with the Republic of Congo deteriorated, with the repatriation of Zairean refugees from the Congo. In June 1997 civil war erupted in the Republic of Congo, and several shells exploded in Kinshasa that had been fired from Brazzaville. Border clashes with Uganda occurred in 1992, when Zairean troops claimed that they had entered Uganda to attack guerrillas planning to overthrow Mobutu. (The presence of rebels in Kivu opposed to the Ugandan government was cited as a reason for that country's support for the AFDL.)

As relations with the West came under increasing strain, Mobutu attempted to improve links with Arab countries, which deteriorated after 1982, when Zaire restored diplomatic relations with Israel. Relations with Morocco remained good, Zaire being one of the few OAU countries to support its annexation of Western Sahara; with the establishment of the DRC, however, a policy reversal was marked in June 1997 by the arrival of the self-styled Western Saharan 'president', Muhammad Abd al-Aziz, in Kinshasa. In July 1983 Zaire sent 3,000 troops to Chad to support the French-backed government of President Habré. In July 1985 a military co-operation agreement was signed between the two countries.

The success of the AFDL, with support from Rwanda, Uganda and Burundi, among others, has radically changed the pattern of political and economic ties in central Africa. First, the DRC, like Rwanda before it, has shifted firmly away from France and into the anglophone sphere of influence, notably that of the USA. Moreover, the AFDL's regional alliances and Kabila's links with post-independence pan-Africanist leaders such as Tanzania's former president, Julius Nyerere, have given rise to talk of a swathe of like-minded 'New African' governments, reaching from Kinshasa to as far as Eritrea, which challenge Western models of democracy while embracing pragmatic market economics.

Economy

FRANÇOIS MISSER

MINING AND PETROLEUM

Although the Democratic Republic of the Congo (DRC—formerly Zaire) commands enormous economic potential and is richly endowed with a wide range of resources, the mining sector dominates the economy. In 1990 mining, mineral processing and petroleum extraction accounted for about 17% of gross domestic product (GDP) and around 75% of total export earnings (rising to 92% in 1993 and declining to 60% in 1994, before recovering again to 92% in 1995). In 1995 mining contributed an estimated 4.4% of GDP. The country possesses an abundance of mineral resources, the most important being copper, diamonds, cobalt and zinc; there are also deposits of gold, cassiterite, manganese, cadmium, silver, wolframite and columbo-tantalite, most of which are exploited only on a small-scale industrial or artisanal basis. Copper, cobalt, zinc and germanium are found mainly in the south-eastern Shaba province, adjoining the Zambian Copperbelt; diamonds are located mainly in Kasaï province, particularly around the towns of Mbuji-Mayi and Tshikapa, although some mining activity is conducted in Bandundu and Haut-Zaïre regions. Cassiterite, wolframite, gold and columbo-tantalite are exploited mainly in the Kivu region in the east.

The state-owned mining corporation, the Générale des Carrières et des Mines (GÉCAMINES), was the dominant producer in the 1980s, accounting for more than 90% of copper output, and all production of cobalt, zinc and coal. The much smaller-scale, state-owned enterprise, the Société de Développement Industriel et Minier du Zaïre (SODIMIZA), originally a Japanese venture, merged with GÉCAMINES in 1990. Production of copper ore remained static in the mid-1980s, consistently totalling around 500,000 tons per year, equivalent to about 6% of world output. However, production took a downward trend from 1988 onwards. The international copper market is generally volatile and, as world technology advances, substitute materials, such as aluminium and optical fibres (in telecommunications), are being increasingly used. In addition, other world producers, such as Chile, have established new open-cast, lower-cost mines. Consequently, GÉCAMINES has pursued a policy of vertical integration and increased value added, as opposed to the accelerated production of ore. In the period 1990–93 production was further hampered by strikes, the theft of equipment and concentrate, technical problems (particularly a cave-in at the Kamoto mine in 1990) and the worsening political situation. These factors led GÉCAMINES to declare, in early May 1991, a partial *force majeure* on its contracts to deliver copper to foreign clients. From total output of 471,500 tons in 1985, production fell steadily to 291,500 tons in 1991, virtually half the average for the first half of the 1980s, and then plunged to just 33,700 tons in 1994, following looting that led GÉCAMINES to close a number of mines and factories. A modest improvement followed in 1995, with output rising to almost 34,000 tons, and in 1996, with the production of 42,425 tons.

Cobalt is mined mainly in association with copper, and world prices have been among the most volatile of all minerals—ranging from US $7.50 per lb in December 1989 to $33 in January 1992. GÉCAMINES produced 3,631 tons of cobalt in 1994, 4,100 tons in 1995 and 4,210 tons in 1996. Zinc output has declined sharply in recent years. In 1985 GÉCAMINES produced 64,000 tons, but output then declined steadily to 2,515 tons in 1994, before recovering to 4,510 tons in 1995. New equipment, installed by GÉCAMINES in that year, was expected to boost production of copper and cobalt considerably by the end of 1998; however, zinc production in 1996 stood at 3,159 tons. Intense international pressure to privatize GÉCAMINES prompted the government to attempt to reduce operating costs by merging the three branches of the company in 1995. Subsequent negotiations with a Swiss-based joint venture, Swiss Procurement Co. (SWIPCO), regarding the privatization of GÉCAMINES foundered, after doubts were raised concerning the transparency of the tendering process.

With the capture of Lubumbashi early in April 1997, Shaba's mining concerns passed into the hands of the Alliance des forces démocratiques pour la libération du Congo-Zaïre (AFDL), led by Laurent-Désiré Kabila, who agreed to honour existing contracts. It was estimated that full rehabilitation of GÉCAMINES would require investment amounting to US $1,000m. A controversial framework agreement was signed in April 1997 between the AFDL and American Mineral Fields International (AMFI), awarding AMFI exclusive rights to conduct feasibility studies for the rehabilitation of the mine and facilities at Kipushi; if these are positive, the DRC's zinc output could rise considerably in the next few years. Prior to its closure in 1993, the mine also produced copper, gold, silver, cadmium, germanium and cobalt. AMFI was also awarded the Kolwezi project, with a maximum annual production of 50,000 tons of copper and 6,000 tons of cobalt. In May 1997 the Australian group Broken Hill Pty, together with ISCOR and GENCOR of South Africa and a Swedish- and Canadian-owned company, Lundin, concluded a joint-venture agreement with GÉCAMINES for the exploitation of the Tenké-Fungurumé mine in Shaba. This mine has estimated exploitable reserves of 200,000 tons of copper and 6,000 tons of cobalt. A further contract was signed in June, between the Belgian group, Forrest International, the US OM Group and GÉCAMINES, for the processing of tailings in Lubumbashi, with a projected annual output of 5,000 tons of cobalt, 3,500 tons of copper and 15,000 tons of zinc by mid-1999.

Until 1986, when it was overtaken by Australia, Zaire was the world's leading producer of industrial diamonds. Although about 98% of the country's production, from Eastern Kasaï, is of industrial diamonds, gem stones are also found, and since 1993 the country's combined output of industrial and gem diamonds has exceeded that of Botswana. Official production figures tend to fluctuate and do not give an accurate picture, as there are extensive and elaborate smuggling networks. A report obtained by the Zairean media in early 1993 estimated the value of diamonds smuggled every year at US $300m. The only large-scale producer is the Société Minière de Bakwanga (MIBA), which produced 8.2m. carats in 1987. Output stood at 4.8m. in 1994, 5.6m. carats in 1995 and 6.5m. carats in 1996. The remainder of the diamond output is accounted for by artisan diggers (whose share of total output increased from 59% to 69% between 1987 and 1994). Artisan diggers are responsible for the majority of smuggling. Combined with MIBA's output, the total official production for 1996 was 21.9m. carats (compared with 19.7m. carats in 1987), although the real output was higher. According to estimates from the Bank of Zaire, diamonds became Zaire's principal source of foreign exchange in 1993 ($532m.), ahead of GÉCAMINES products ($225m.) and crude petroleum ($137m.). Diamonds retained this distinction in 1994, although foreign exchange proceeding from the sale of coffee increased considerably in that year. De Beers, which marketed all production by MIBA, valued its 1995 output at $400m. In March 1997 the AFDL decided to end this monopoly, allowing American Diamond Buyers, a company associated with AMFI, to open a buying office in Kisangani. De Beers' local subsidiary, SEDIZA, continues to purchase diamonds from artisan diggers. It was reported in July that the DRC had carried out independent diamond sales on the Brussels market. Gold output in 1996 was an estimated 977.3 kg, valued at about $17m., compared with 2,200 kg, worth $40m., in 1986. Rehabilitation work commenced in 1989 at the main gold mine, the Office des Mines d'Or de Kilo-Moto (OKIMO). In 1990 two foreign companies in the Belgo-Canadian MINDEV consortium were given management contracts for OKIMO, and output was expected to increase steadily during the decade (despite recurrent labour unrest). The closure of the border with Burundi in May 1996 was expected to limit considerably the persistent problem of large-scale smuggling. In February 1997 Affimet initiated negotiations with the AFDL to transfer its gold-refining activities from Burundi to Kivu region, whilst the Ugandan company, Caleb International, has expressed an interest in obtaining gold concessions in the region. However, the Fédération des Entreprises du Congo (FEC) protested in March against the continuing smuggling of gold towards Rwanda and Uganda.

Zaire became a producer of offshore petroleum in 1975, operating from fields on the Atlantic coast and at the mouth of the River Congo. Output averaged around 30,000 barrels a day (b/d) during the second half of the 1980s, with output in 1988 totalling 10.7m. barrels. Output stood at 8.9m. barrels in 1994, 10m. barrels in 1995 and 10.7m. barrels in 1996. The reserves in the Atlantic fields, operated by Zaire Gulf Oil, have declined, but the Belgian–Zairean consortium ZAIREP, operating in the mouth of the River Congo, slightly increased output in 1990. Current campaigns of prospecting, undertaken by both companies, have been hampered by political instability, and only began to benefit the sector in 1996.

In the face of the prolonged economic recession, the country's petroleum output has been broadly equivalent to domestic demand, although the DRC cannot consume its own production as the local refinery is not equipped to treat this exceptionally heavy petroleum. In the longer term, however, unless current onshore exploration near the border with Uganda and Tanzania proves successful, current oil reserves (estimated at around 187m. barrels in 1993) will be exhausted and, in all probability, the DRC will have to continue to import its petroleum requirements.

AGRICULTURE AND FORESTRY

The DRC's wide range of geography and climate produces an equally wide range of both food and cash crops. The main food crops are cassava, maize, rice and plantains, grown mainly by small-scale subsistence farmers. Cash crops include coffee, palm oil and palm kernels, rubber, cotton, sugar, tea and cocoa, many of which are grown on large plantations. The DRC has the potential to be not only self-sufficient in food but also to be a net exporter. In addition, with the exception of some parts of Kivu and Katanga, it has escaped the droughts which have caused such great damage in other parts of Africa in the last 20 years. The share of agriculture's contribution to GDP remained almost constant throughout the 1980s, standing at 32% in 1981, 33% in 1985 and 32% in 1989. However, the decline of the mining sector (excluding diamonds) contributed to an increase to 59% in the contribution of agriculture to GDP in 1995. In 1995 the agricultural sector employed approximately 66% of the active work-force.

However, the economic condition of agriculture in the DRC has been adversely affected both by the widespread expropriations of privately-owned plantations in the early 1970s and the subsequent decline in output and from poor government funding (only 1% of GDP). The trend has improved since the end of the 1980s, with a strong growth in production of food crops. However, the efficient supply of food to urban population centres is hampered by one of the economy's most damaging structural deficiencies: lack of infrastructure for the transportation of agricultural produce. For example, demand for the staple food, cassava, from the inhabitants of Kinshasa is simply too great to be satisfied by output from the nearby regions of Bas-Zaïre and Bandundu, and yet the inadequate road network hinders transport of foodstuffs grown in more distant areas. This situation has had serious repercussions in the capital, where it was estimated by the World Bank that child malnutrition had doubled during 1991–94. In June 1994 maize crops were reported to be rotting in northern Shaba, while fuel shortages prevented their transportation to the regional capital, Lubumbashi, where widespread food shortages were occurring. Estimates of food imports vary widely, ranging from official figures of 157,000 tons in 1985 to unofficial estimates of 393,000 tons. Wheat and flour imports, for example, were stated to be 220,000 tons in 1990. There have been indications of an improvement in production of local food crops, but this is difficult to assess accurately as a large proportion are subsistence crops and do not enter the money economy. Official figures suggest that 712,000 tons of locally-produced maize and 453,000 tons of locally-produced rice were traded in 1988. More recent developments present a mixed outlook. Since the beginning of the 1990s, in most urban centres, an increasing number of inhabitants are growing their own food, either in their own gardens or in public open spaces. In 1995 the European Union agreed to finance an ECU 90m. programme to support agricultural rehabilitation. The programme is to focus mainly on the renewal of 4,000 km of local roads and 600 km of national roads connecting the rural areas of Northern and Southern Kivu and of Eastern and Western Kasaï with the main cities of these regions in order to provide outlets for the land-locked hinterlands. This programme will particularly benefit Kivu, formerly the principal food-producing area of the DRC, where the economy has been seriously disrupted by massive influxes of refugees from Burundi and Rwanda since 1994, and by local inter-ethnic violence. Nearly three-quarters of the cattle herds there have been destroyed, while any marketable surpluses of beans and potatoes (grown without fertilizers in conditions of extreme shortages) cannot easily be taken to markets in Kisangani and Kinshasa because of unusable roads. Export earnings from agriculture, which accounted for approximately 40% of total revenue in 1960, had fallen to only 12.5% by 1994. This decline has been caused in part by the smuggling of coffee (the major agricultural export); it has been estimated that quantities of smuggled coffee are approximately equal to official production figures. An estimated 92,800 tons of robusta were grown in 1988, of which 59,800 tons were exported, together with a further 8,200 tons of arabica. In early 1990 it was reported that the coffee crop was being seriously threatened by tracheomycose, a fungal disease, and production declined to 59,800 tons in 1993. In 1994, however, increased prices for coffee on world markets encouraged growers to intensify their harvesting efforts, and output reached 76,864 tons, accounting for 34.9% of total export earnings (compared with just 10.6% in 1993). Output retreated to 56,685 tons in 1995, owing to a combination of lower world prices, internal transport difficulties and the lack of foreign exchange needed to purchase fertilizers and pesticides to fight tracheomycose, especially in the east of the country. However, while the production of robusta declined by 18% in volume, the arabica output nearly doubled and represented in 1995 about one-quarter of the total production, compared with 14% the previous year. This improvement in arabica output was in part a result of the closure of the Rwandan border through which an estimated 4,000 tons are smuggled annually. In 1995 the Office Zaïrois du Café (OZACAF) drew attention to the continuation of smuggling to Uganda, albeit at a lower level (about 2,000 tons). Production in 1996 fell substantially, with the destruction of numerous plantations in Northern Kivu during the civil war. Palm oil production averaged 85,000 tons per year between 1981–86 and was estimated at 95,000 tons in 1988, but only a small percentage is exported. The cost of transporting a ton of palm oil down river from Haut-Zaïre to Matadi is equivalent to that of a Malaysian producer shipping the same quantity of palm oil to the end market in Europe—and thus local producers find they are unable to export at competitive prices. In 1995 palm oil production was 18,076 tons, against 17,052 tons in 1994. In the colonial period Zaire had been a sizeable rubber producer. In 1991 it still produced 10,644 tons of rubber but by 1993 production had collapsed to 3,516 tons. Output was less than 3,000 tons in 1995.

During September 1996–May 1997 the agricultural sector was severely disrupted by the ongoing civil war. Traffic on the river Congo was paralysed for several months, and consequently the prices of essential commodities soared in Kinshasa. In Haut-Zaïre, looting prevented much agricultural produce (particularly plantains) from reaching its markets, whilst the movement of hundreds of thousands of refugees from Kivu region towards the interior of the country also affected production. Moreover, according to the FEC, substantial quantities of coffee were once again being smuggled from Kivu into Uganda and Rwanda.

More than 1m. sq km of the DRC's land area is covered by forest (an estimated 6% of the world's woodlands), representing a potential annual production of 6m. cu m. However, only a small proportion of this resource is currently exploited. Canada provided considerable technical assistance for the sector during the 1980s, including the preparation of an exhaustive inventory of forest resources. About 416,500 cu m of logs were felled in 1988, and 107,700 cu m were exported. Following a decline in production, output stood at 168,844 cu m in 1994, rising to 163,695 cu m in 1995 and to an estimated 187,000 cu m in 1996. Government measures in recent years have been aimed at increasing local value added in the sector, as activity has so far been mainly limited to sawing the wood, with only minimal production of veneer and plywood. A substantial proportion of logging and sawing activity is carried out by SIFORZAL, a subsidiary of the German Danzer Group, with concessions of 2.6m. ha, although in 1996 a Malaysian enterprise was examining the possibility of seeking logging concessions covering 1.5m. ha in Haut-Zaïre and Equateur regions. An improvement in security conditions would eventually permit an expansion in the forestry sector. However, the scarcity of foreign exchange and the lack of alternative means of revenue for the local inhabitants has given rise to fears that excessive logging may be undertaken, devastating the forest environment. In 1996 SIFORZAL expressed concern over the government's failure to allocate taxes imposed on logging towards reafforestation programmes.

INDUSTRY AND MANUFACTURING

Heavy industrial activity is concentrated in the mining sector and in GÉCAMINES refineries in Shaba province. Prior to the decline in copper production of the late 1980s and early 1990s, the Shituru refinery processed about 225,000 tons of copper ore per year and a similar volume was refined 'on toll' in Belgium. In 1990 GÉCAMINES completed a large-scale five-year investment plan to improve copper-mining equipment and related infrastructure. However, GÉCAMINES' copper operation in Shaba suffered severe damage during regional unrest in 1992–93, and rehabilitation costs were estimated at US $1,000m. In addition, according to World Bank estimates at the end of 1994, private investors would be required to absorb debts exceeding $2,000m. The GÉCAMINES recovery programme 1996-2000 includes projects to modernize the Shituru plant, to process tailings at Lubumbashi and Kipushi, and to build a new cobalt processing unit at Kakanda. In the course of 1996 GÉCAMINES signed agreements with a number of foreign companies, concerning in particular the extraction and production of cobalt. A steel mill was set up at Maluku in 1972, during the era of high commodity prices, but it proved to be unprofitable and was closed down in 1986. A refinery at Muanda for the processing of imported light crude petroleum has an installed capacity of 847,000 tons per year but, in 1986, processed less than 90,000 tons. This low level of activity was attributable both to the sharp fall in world oil prices, which meant that it was often cheaper to import refined products, and also to the Zairean government's own liquidity problems, and thus the shortage of funds to pay for crude imports. Extensive studies have been made on the conversion of the refinery to treat the DRC's own rather heavy crude, and external funding for the project is being sought.

The manufacturing sector is dominated by textiles, cement, engineering and agro-industries producing consumer goods. In 1995 manufacturing contributed an estimated 6.5% of GDP. The sector has been consistently held back on three fronts; firstly, by the lack of foreign exchange to import badly needed spare parts, secondly, by the continuing decline in domestic purchasing power and finally, by chronic electricity cuts. It is estimated that throughout most of the 1980s, manufacturers were operating at just 30% of installed capacity levels. During 1980–90 manufacturing production increased by an annual average of 2.3%. In 1993, however, manufacturing production was estimated to have declined considerably, with production of cement alone thought to have declined by 28% compared with the previous year. A slight recovery was recorded in 1994 and 1995, with the country's three main cement factories increasing sales to 166,000 tons and 182,051 tons respectively (compared with 150,000 tons in 1993). Small quantities of cement are exported to the Central African Republic and to the Republic of Congo. In 1995 1.7m. hl of beer were produced in Zaire. A new brewery near Mbuji-Mayi, with an annual production capacity of 96m. litres, came on stream late in that year.

One of the most important areas of expansion in the sector in the 1990s has been informal light industry, especially in the shipyards at Kinshasa and in furniture manufacture.

ENERGY

The DRC's potential for producing hydroelectric power is rivalled on the African continent only by that of Cameroon. Total potential is considered to be 100,000 MW, while the state electricity board SNEL estimated installed capacity in 1987 as 2,486 MW. The country's most ambitious infrastructure project to date (and one which is estimated to account for a substantial proportion of the DRC's foreign indebtedness) is the Inga hydroelectric power project based close to the port of Matadi at the mouth of the River Congo in the west. This comprises two hydroelectric stations, which in 1986 produced 3,100m. kWh, and a 1,725-km high-voltage power line extending almost the entire length of the country from Inga to Kolwezi in the heart of the mining region. Inga produces some of the cheapest power in the world, but the ZOFI industrial free zone set up beside the power stations with the hope of attracting major heavy industry projects (and in particular an aluminium smelter) has proved unsuccessful, so far attracting only a small number of small-scale industrial operations. In early 1990 a project, funded by France and the African Development Bank (ADB), and worth 390m. French francs, was under way to double the capacity of the high-voltage power line over the section from Inga to Kinshasa. The project also included a new transformer post and the reinforcement of the Inga-2 and Lingwala stations. Other components involve a line linking the urban centres of Kolwezi (in Shaba region), Mbuji-Mayi and Kananga as part of an integrated electricity network. Ironically, numerous small towns and villages situated directly along the path of the power line have no access to electricity supplies. However, there are plans for further low-voltage links. While some grandiose plans, including one to transport power as far as Egypt, are unlikely to be realized, the Inga plant already supplies some power to neighbouring Congo. SNEL is also linked to the grid of the Zambian Electricity Supply Corpn (ZESCO) and the South African company ESKOM has carried out joint studies to optimise this connection with those companies and the Zimbabwe Electricity Supply Authority (ZESA). One of ESKOM's strategic objectives is the creation of a southern African grid which could benefit from the energy of the Inga dam. There are supply agreements between the DRC, Zambia and Zimbabwe, and ESKOM provides regular training courses to the technicians and engineers of these three companies. In 1996 ESKOM, SNEL, the Angolan power company ENE and NAMPOWER of Namibia initiated a study to interconnect their national electricity grids to utilize the potential of the Inga dam. In late 1989, a small hydroelectric power station was inaugurated at Mobayi–Mbongo in Equateur region, on the border with the Central African Republic (CAR). In July 1995 discussions were under way between SNEL and the China Machine Building Corpn to increase the capacity of the Mobayi-Mbongo power station (which exports about 2MW to the CAR) and to construct new lines between Businga and the towns of Gemena and Lisala, at an estimated total cost of US $33m. In March 1994, construction began on a 15 MW power plant at Katende on the Lulua river, in Western Kasai province. This project and the construction of the Lubilanji II plant in the neighbouring Eastern Kasaï region are also expected to cost some $33m. A power line was completed early in 1997 that interconnects the power grids of the CAR and SNEL for the provision of supplies from the CAR to Zongo, in the Equateur region of the DRC.

TRANSPORT AND COMMUNICATIONS

Poor transport and communications infrastructure has proved a major handicap to the DRC's economic development. With a small strip of coastline of just 40 km, the DRC has no deep-water port and depends on the port of Matadi, close to the mouth of the River Congo, for its maritime traffic. Plans to construct a deep-water port at Banana, on the Atlantic coast, were closely connected with the aluminium smelter project, both of which have been suspended. In 1989 Matadi handled 273,300 tons of mineral exports, compared with 53,000 tons sent via the Tanzanian port of Dar es Salaam and 160,000 tons by the 'southern route' through South Africa. However, in recent years, inadequate maintenance and dredging of the port, coupled with extremely high charges, have contributed to a transfer of activity to the port of Pointe-Noire (Repub. of Congo). The port of Matadi handled 267,250 tons of exports and 639,880 tons of imports in 1994. In 1995 the figures rose to 299,464 tons and 812,972 tons, respectively.

Owing to the civil war in Angola, the Benguela railway to the Angolan Atlantic port of Lobito (1,348 km), which offers the shortest rail route to the sea remains closed. Until recently, the country's main transport route was the Voie Nationale, which runs from Matadi to Shaba. It comprises a tortuous circuit of railway from Matadi to Kinshasa, then river transport from Kinshasa to Ilebo, where goods are loaded once more on to the railway. Use of this route has dwindled in recent years owing to poor maintenance, fuel shortages and increased regional insecurity. Communications between Kasaï, Shaba and southern Africa, and also in the eastern DRC, improved somewhat as a result of a management contract signed in 1995 between the national railways company (Société Nationale des chemins de fer Zaïrois–SNCZ) and a joint Belgian–South African company, Sizarail, for the management of two SNCZ subsidiaries with a total rail network of 4,121 km. In 1996 traffic on the Sizarail network increased to 409,000 tons from 259,000 tons in 1995. However, in May 1997 the incoming administration nationalized Sizarail, and transferred its assets, without compensation, to the national railways company (renamed the Société Nationale des Chemins de Fer du Congo – SNCC). These assets included 14 locomotives and 100 wagons of the South African railway operator Spoornet (a member of the Sizarail consortium); moreover, the SNCC defaulted on debts of some $22m. owed to Spoornet and of $3.3m. owed to Zambia Railways. In protest, rail traffic via the Zambian border was suspended for several weeks. Transport to the north and north-east is possible along the River Congo, and river traffic is probably the single most important means of transport in the country; the national transport office ONATRA is responsible for almost 14,000 km of waterways. Passenger and freight services operate between Kinshasa and Kisangani, but the vessels are mainly old and poorly maintained and the journey can take weeks. ONATRA has begun to encounter increasing competition from small private shipowners. Proposals, announced in August 1996, for the privatization of ONATRA, and of the railway line linking Kinshasa with Matadi, on a five-year franchise basis, were jeopardized by foreign investors' anger at the nationalization of Sizarail.

The road network is wholly inadequate for a country of the DRC's size: of the estimated 145,000 km of roads, of which some 68,000 km are main roads, only about 2,500 km are surfaced, and most of the road network is in a very poor state of repair. A plan to build a road bridge across the River Congo to link Kinshasa with Brazzaville, the capital of the Republic of Congo, has frequently been raised and the EU has sponsored feasibility studies. Domestic air services deteriorated rapidly during the 1980s, as a result of Zaire's economic crisis. Some relief has been provided by a private carrier, Scibe Airlift Cargo, which began operations in 1982. Scibe operates services between the DRC's regional capitals and major towns and by 1985 was carrying more domestic passengers than Air Zaïre. In 1994 the Zaire government was joined by the Belgian national carrier Sabena in establishing Zaire Express. Under Belgian management, the service provided passenger and cargo services to various regional points. Scibe, together with a smaller operator, Shabair, undertook services to Europe and South Africa. In addition, some 40 smaller carriers were providing freight and passenger services in 1995. In late 1996 Zaire Express and Shabair merged to form Zaire Airlines (renamed Alliance Airlines in April 1997). Safety conditions are poor at the DRC's airports, and accidents have become commonplace. In September 1996 a Belgian construction company, Besix, won a contract to rehabilitate the Kinshasa airport at Ndjili. Telecommunications facilities within the DRC, operated by the state telecommunications concern, the Office Congolais des Postes et des Télécommunications (OCPT – previously known as the ONPTZ), are among the worst in Africa and international lines, apart from those to Brussels and Paris, are erratic. In 1980, when Zaire had an estimated 30,000 telephone lines, the ratio to the population was less than one line per 1,000 inhabitants. By 1995 many prominent businessmen and government ministers were using the satellite communications networks provided by two private companies, Telecel and Comcell. In September 1996, it was estimated that the ONPTZ network had shrunk to some 13,000 lines, with the private companies operating an additional 10,000 lines. However, Telecel, the largest private operator, suffered severe losses in 1996-97 during inter-ethnic riots: Telecel's director is a Banyamulenge Tutsi. Government estimates in the mid-1990s indicated that investment of US $200m. would be necessary to rehabilitate the telecommunications infrastructure; SAIT Holland and Inforindus, a Congolese company, subsequently undertook to repair, and temporarily to manage, the network of the OCPT.

EXTERNAL TRADE

In common with most commodity-producing developing countries, throughout the 1980s Zaire experienced a steady deterioration in its terms of trade, as world market prices for most of its exports failed to keep pace with import price rises. Added to this, the 1980s also brought a massive acceleration in external debt-servicing requirements, making the country's external position even more parlous. Many of the problems now faced by the DRC have their origins in the early 1970s, when commodity prices were relatively high. At that time, following OPEC's first initiative in raising petroleum prices, the international banks found themselves with substantial deposits of 'petro-dollars' and were eager to utilize the funds as loans to developing countries from which they could obtain high rates of interest. With money flowing into the country to support grandiose development projects, such as the Inga hydroelectric station and the steelworks in Maluku, Zaire's import bill rose sharply (US $1,579m. in 1974) and a recurrent trade deficit began to accrue, although for several years this was offset to some extent by external borrowing and inflows of foreign aid.

Cushioned by these inflows of funds, the government made little serious effort to regulate the economic situation until the early 1980s. But, as the flow of aid and, in particular, commercial loans began to decrease, the import bill had, perforce, to be cut. Export earnings remained more or less stagnant throughout the 1980s, totalling US $2,269m. in 1980, falling back to $1,853m. in 1985 and recovering to $2,138m. in 1990. A decline in copper production (generated by a long period of under-investment and repeated incidents of looting since late 1991), however, resulted in export earnings of just $988m. for 1993. Export earnings in 1994, however, were assisted by higher prices for coffee and an increase in exports of crude petroleum, and totalled $1,272m. In 1995 and 1996 exports rose to $1,453m. and $1,541m. respectively, in the wake of increased mineral (except copper) and petroleum output; coffee exports dropped substantially in 1996. The trend in imports has been similar, with a bill of $1,519m. in 1980, $1,247m. in 1985 and $1,539m. in 1990, again at current prices. The cost of imports in 1993 was estimated to have declined to $610m. Despite the reduction in the volume of trade, Zaire still recorded a surplus of $378m. in 1993. In 1994 imports rose slightly, to $629m., increasing sharply in 1995 to $924m. and reaching an estimated $1,002m. in 1996.

Until the 1990s, the composition of exports remained fairly constant, with minerals accounting for about 80%, of which GÉCAMINES produced more than half (diamonds between 10% and 15%, according to world prices, crude oil about 10% and gold about 1%). By 1993, however, diamonds accounted for more than half of total exports (53.8%), while all GÉCAMINES products represented only 22.7% of the total, and in 1994 these percentages were 34.9% and 12.2% respectively. Before 1994, agricultural exports were in decline. Cotton, which was an important source of revenue before independence, is no longer exported, and such output as still exists is used locally. Coffee is the only sizeable agricultural export but its share in export revenue has fluctuated widely in recent years, along with the world coffee market. In 1985 it contributed 9% of export revenue. In the following year it contributed 25%, declining to 9% in

1987 and accounting for only 4.2% of export income in 1990. An increase in world coffee prices in 1994, however, helped to increase the share of coffee in export earnings to almost 40%. An analysis of Zaire's export revenue in 1990 by the World Bank showed copper earning US $1,001m., diamonds $240m., petroleum $227m. and coffee $120m. In 1994 the structure of exports had changed dramatically, with diamonds and coffee exports accounting for $432m. each, ahead of GÉCAMINES products ($151m.) and petroleum ($138m.). The DRC's principal imports comprise equipment and spare parts, food and beverages, as well as a substantial amount of luxury goods for resident expatriates and the affluent Congolese business community, and crude oil (when the local refinery is operating) or, more often, petroleum products.

As the former colonial power, Belgium has traditionally been the DRC's main trading partner. Approximately 60% of Zaire's exports went directly to Belgium, but this figure included the substantial amount of blister copper refined in Belgium, most of which was subsequently re-exported. Faltering relations between the two countries since 1988 have intermittently halted the flow of trade and assistance. Between 1991–93 the value of Zairean exports to Belgium decreased from 26,400m. Belgian francs to 14,400m., representing slightly more than 40% of the sale of Zairean goods abroad. Over the same period, the value of imports from Belgium also decreased from 6,500m. to 4,400m. Belgian francs, equivalent to just 20.4% of Zaire's total import bill. In 1994–1996, however, Zaire's exports to Belgium increased again (to 21,700m. Belgian francs in 1994, to 22,110m. francs in 1995 and to 23,250m. francs in 1996), largely as a result of a 72% increase in the value of diamond exports. Belgian exports to Zaire remained modest at 4,600m. Belgian francs in 1994, before rising to 5,880m. francs in 1995 and to 6,520m. francs in 1996. A 'freeze' on foreign aid and export insurance guarantees, imposed by Belgium and many other Western countries, made Zaire increasingly reliant on trade with South Africa. In 1993 South Africa became Zaire's second largest supplier (South African imports amounted to some US $100m.), while Zaire became South Africa's fifth largest African market. The USA is an important trading partner. Its percentage share of exports fluctuates, but can reach 30% or more in years when the US administration replenishes strategic stocks such as cobalt. However, the recent reduction in GÉCAMINES' production capacity, unless righted, may turn the USA towards other suppliers, such as Zambia.

BALANCE OF PAYMENTS AND EXTERNAL DEBT

During the 1980s the government's extensive deficit spending of the 1970s generated recurrent deficits on the balance-of-payments current account as new sources of external funding evaporated and service payments on debts incurred in earlier years fell due. In 1984, for example, a trade surplus of US $742m. was wholly absorbed by outflows on the services account of $1,292m. (more than the country's entire merchandise import bill), against which inflows on services were just $141m., resulting in a deficit of $409m. on goods and services, a current account deficit of $325m. and an overall balance-of-payments deficit of $549m. Net transfers to Zaire were negative between 1984–86, at a total of –$75m. but, following vigorous protests by President Mobutu, a Consultative Group meeting of Western donors in 1987 acted as a catalyst for net transfers totalling $1,092m. between 1987–89, of which $326m. came from the World Bank group, with the African Development Bank, the EU, the USA and Japan also providing balance-of-payments support. Net inward transfers totalled $136m. in 1990. However, the deficit on the current account of the balance of payments still continued to grow, from –$585m. before official transfers in 1985 (and –$399m. net of official transfers) to figures of –$860m. and –$643m. net respectively in 1990. In 1993 the deficit on the current account of the balance of payments was estimated at –$779m. (and –$770m. net of official transfers).

Faced with this rate of economic deterioration and with no local remedies available, Mobutu became, in 1982, one of the first African leaders to submit his country to an IMF-prescribed austerity programme. In 1983, following IMF and World Bank advice, the Zaire currency was devalued by a massive 77.5%. Subsequent visits by the state commissioner for finance to the 'Paris Club' of official creditors to request reschedulings of the official portion of external debt (accruing to Western governments and Japan) became virtually an annual event, and 'Paris Club' rescheduling agreements were negotiated in each of the years from 1983–86.

Initially, the Zairean government's apparent enthusiasm to fulfil IMF performance targets was favourably received by creditors. By 1986, however, following five years of economic austerity, there were few tangible positive results. There was little, if any, real growth in the economy and no improvement in the balance of payments. Net outflows of foreign exchange from Zaire now exceeded inflows into the country and the proportion of export earnings devoted to servicing the external debt was more than 25%. In late October 1986 Mobutu announced restrictions on the level of debt-servicing, freezing repayments in some cases, and declared his intention to return to a system of fixed parity for the zaire against the Special Drawing Right (SDR) of the IMF. These proposals were not, in the event, fully implemented, although the IMF, concerned not to set a precedent for other beleaguered African debtors, agreed, after lengthy negotiations, to revise performance criteria (many of which had been based on the Fund's own over-optimistic estimates of world commodity prices and potential export earnings). In May 1987 a new agreement was signed with the IMF, under which Zaire obtained a 12-month stand-by arrangement of SDR 100m., to be disbursed in four instalments against financial performance criteria; a three-year Structural Adjustment Facility (SAF) of SDR 136.8m., with immediate access to a first tranche of SDR 58.2m.; and a compensatory financing facility of SDR 45.3m. to cover the shortfall in foreign exchange earnings until the end of March 1987. This agreement opened the way to a new debt-rescheduling agreement with the 'Paris Club', also in May, under which approximately US $880m. of official debt service was rescheduled. In June 1987 the World Bank granted Zaire a Structural Adjustment Loan (SAL) of SDR 134.4m.

Despite the IMF programme of May 1987, the economy continued to deteriorate. From early 1988 onwards, the slow depreciation in the value of the zaire gathered momentum, and between January and May it fell by 26% against the US dollar. Disbursement of the IMF funds was also suspended because Fund officials would not accept the projected deficit in the national budget. By June, Mobutu was, once again, threatening to suspend debt repayments. Failure to reach an agreement with the IMF also made impossible a new debt-rescheduling arrangement with the 'Paris Club', the previous agreement having expired in May 1988. The economic stalemate continued into the autumn, but in early November, with inflation almost at an annual rate of 100%, Mobutu announced a further devaluation of the currency and a rise in the retail price of petrol, both measures having been prescribed by the IMF.

In early 1989 the zaire was devalued by a further 8.2% and negotiations were reopened with the IMF for the resumption of the SAF first proposed in 1987. As negotiations continued, the EU postponed the disbursement of an ECU 30m. loan to fund vital imports for manufacturers and the agro-industry sector. The World Bank also delayed a credit of US $75m. for a major transport rehabilitation project. By early May 1989, relations with the IMF had improved distinctly, although a major obstacle remained in the form of growing arrears on earlier IMF credits. At the end of the month, there was an unexpected announcement that the government had liquidated these arrears, reportedly by means of a short-term credit of $120m. from a Belgian commercial bank. This opened the way to the release in June of the second tranche of the 1987 three-year facility and a new 12-month stand-by arrangement of SDR 116.4m. Accommodation with the IMF encouraged further loans from other donors and from the 'Paris Club' and the World Bank released the second $82.5m. tranche of the June 1987 essential import loan. The EU also disbursed its ECU 30m. loan. IMF performance criteria were met at the end of June and the end of September.

In June 1989 a 'Paris Club' meeting agreed to a rescheduling of debt worth US $1,530m. on the 'Toronto Terms' accorded to the poorest countries, while a meeting of the 'London Club' of commercial creditors, also in June, agreed to reschedule $61m. of commercial debt totalling about $627m. The political and social deterioration from late 1991 brought all negotiations with the IMF to a halt. As a result all rescheduling talks also ceased. No funds will flow into Zaire for the purpose of structural adjustment or balance-of-payments support until a satisfactory settlement of Zaire's internal crisis has been achieved. At the end of 1995, Zaire's total external debt stood at $13,137m., equivalent to about 255% of GNP. In 1992 Zaire suspended virtually all payments on its foreign debt: of total debt service due of $3,450m., only $79m. was paid. In February 1994 the World Bank closed its office in Kinshasa, and in June 1994 Zaire was suspended from the IMF. Since the civil disturbances of 1991 private investment has virtually ceased, the country having been declared 'a dangerous if not prohibitive risk' for exporters, investors and bankers by all country risk analysis and export credit guarantee insurance organizations of the OECD countries. Various donors, including Belgium, made it clear that suspension from the IMF could only be ended by the installation of a credible government with a feasible economic adjustment programme and plans to exert greater control over the armed forces and increase the efficiency of the central bank. Hopes for a prompt end to the suspension were encouraged by the announcement in July 1994 of the intention of the new prime minister, Kengo Wa Dondo, to regulate treasury disbursements to available resources, and to consider granting autonomous status to the central bank. However, following the visit of an IMF mission to Kinshasa at the end of 1994, the organization concluded that Zaire's draft budget for 1995 did not correspond to its own projections, with expenditure exceeding revenues by some 106,000m. new zaires (approximately $30m.). The control of inflation and the stabilization of the exchange rate were awaited as the concrete signs of recovery upon which donors were prepared to build a support programme. By September 1995, however, there were few signs that Kengo Wa Dondo's government had managed to reduce inflation; indeed, in the space of 12 months the exchange rate against the US dollar had decreased from NZ 1,400=$1 to NZ 7,000=$1. Despite Zaire's inability to fulfil the minimum requirements of the Bretton Woods institutions (Zaire reimbursed just $2m. per month during the first nine months of 1995, whereas the country's total debt to the IMF amounted to $336m. at that time), its strategic position in Central Africa and Kengo Wa Dondo's apparent efforts to sponsor a transition process and avert a humanitarian crisis prompted the EU to consider the resumption of aid in the autumn of 1995. An ECU 90m. rehabilitation project, aimed at restoring basic infrastructures and at stimulating food production, was subsequently adopted by the EU. A meeting between Kengo Wa Dondo and the IMF managing director took place in mid-1996. However, the outbreak of civil war in September 1996 caused the inflation rate to rise once again, reaching 741% at the end of the year. The need to finance the war effort also prompted the government to cease the repayment of debt arrears to the IMF altogether.

By freezing the issue of new banknotes in May 1997, the new administration prevented the further deterioration of the exchange rate; it also meant, however, that money was not available to pay salary arrears. In July plans were announced (for which foreign assistance would be necessary) to introduce a new Congolese franc as the national currency. However, negotiations with foreign donors were hampered both by what was seen as a lack of transparency in the management of public resources (with the nationalization of Sizarail and with mining contracts being granted without the holding of public tenders), and by the government's refusal to allow an official United Nations investigation into the treatment of Rwandan Hutu refugees in the eastern DRC.

THE DOMESTIC ECONOMY

During 1968–74, Zaire's real GDP expanded at an average annual rate of 7%, assisted in large part by strong world commodity prices. During the period 1975–80, however, the trend sharply reversed under falling prices for copper, coffee and diamonds, and the impact of Mobutu's 1973 'Zairianization' programme, under which hundreds of industrial, manufacturing and agricultural concerns were expropriated and put under the control of often inexperienced nationals, began to affect GDP performance.

Real growth in 1975 was −6.8%, followed by only marginally better results of −4.7%, −2.3% and −3.0% in 1976, 1977 and 1978 respectively. In 1977, when earlier stabilization programmes elaborated with the IMF showed poor results, Mobutu launched his own proposals for economic recovery. These economic plans, however, were eclipsed by political considerations during the Shaba invasions of 1977 and 1978. By 1981 there were indications of an improvement in the economy and a real growth rate of 2%, although this was more than offset by annual population growth of 2.7%. In December 1982 the decision was taken to embrace fully measures prescribed by the IMF, including the massive devaluation of the zaire in September 1983. Public spending was sharply reduced and by 1984 the budget deficit was down to 3.4% of GDP from 10.5% in 1982. After the 100% inflation rate of 1983, the annual rate had settled at 20% by 1985. Yet, while some basic economic indicators certainly improved, the programme gave rise to a long succession of austerity measures, placing many basic foodstuffs, such as manioc, beyond the reach of the average Zairean. Industry was left working at an average 30% of capacity, hampered by ageing equipment and shortages of spare parts for which no corporate funds existed. Mobutu's decision in May 1986 to raise public sector salaries by 40%, was followed by his announcement in October that he would restrict debt-servicing payments to the IMF. Over the whole year, real growth was a minimal 0.5%. In 1987 there was considerable improvement, with real growth of 2.7%, followed again in 1988 by 0.5%. However, in 1989 it again began to decline with negative growth of 1.3% followed by a real fall of 2.6% in 1990. The unrest of 1991–93 resulted in disastrous growth performance, with GDP estimated to have contracted by at least 20% between 1989–92, by 14% in 1993 and by 7.2% in 1994. Real GDP contracted by only 0.7% in 1995, and was estimated to have risen by 1.3% in 1996.

The last budget to balance was that for 1989. Estimates for 1993 revealed total revenues of US $300m., accounting for less than half of primary expenditure ($664m.). However, since inflation, and the economy in general, had become seemingly uncontrollable after 1990, the draft budget exercise had become somewhat academic. In November 1993 the government introduced a new currency, the new zaire (each new unit being equivalent to 3m. old zaires), in an attempt at monetary reform. Nevertheless, in the absence of comprehensive adjustment and stabilization programmes, the measure was unable to stem the erosion of the national currency. The unequal allocation of primary expenditure between the executive and the public sector, and between ministries, was singled out as one major reason for the deterioration of the situation. As a result of a lack of budgetary discipline and of a widespread lack of confidence in the new currency, the value of the new zaire collapsed in a matter of months. Between November 1993 and the end of August 1995, the exchange rate against the US dollar decreased from NZ 3 = US $1 to NZ 7,000 = US $1. Annual inflation averaged 401.2% in 1985–93. In 1994 consumer prices increased by an average of 23,773.1%, then settled to the comparatively stable rate of 542% in 1995, increasing slightly to 659% in 1996.

ECONOMIC DEVELOPMENT

Unlike the majority of francophone African countries, Zaire never pursued conventional five-year economic development plans. The 'Mobutu Plan' of 1977 was somewhat vague in conception and was never published in full. Substantial effort and money were, however, expended on the preparation of a Five-Year Plan which was to run from 1986–90. This was published in many volumes and provided for continued economic growth as well as new infrastructure and industry, such as the aluminium smelter and fertilizer plant in the Inga Free Zone and the deep-water port at Banana. However, prevailing economic conditions hampered its realization. Although the Plan was not officially abandoned, economic policy in the second half of the 1980s was almost entirely devoted to reducing budget deficits and the level of inflation. In November 1989 a paper presented to the legislature stated that expenditure under the plan to date had only been at an implementation rate of 49%, and referred to the 'ambitious and costly five-year plan and the restrictive programme of structural adjustment'. With the collapse of the giant state mining corporation GÉCAMINES, the progressive substitution of copper by other materials in world industry (and with Chile having opened one of the world's largest and lowest-cost copper mines in 1990), economic activity in Zaire must clearly become more diversified.

There is vast potential both to rehabilitate and expand the agricultural sector, and to tap the country's huge forestry resources. The DRC's population (estimated at 36.7m. in 1991) represents a potentially large consumer base and offers great incentives for developing industry and manufacturing. One of the most immediate obstacles to development remains the lack of infrastructure of all categories—road, rail and river transport and telecommunications. It is to be hoped, also, that the implementation of constitutional and political reform will clear the way for the eradication of endemic financial corruption that has long been an inhibiting factor in the country's economic betterment. The appointment of new managers at the country's nationalized industries, the payment of some civil service arrears in June 1997 and plans to reorganize public administration may be the first steps in this direction.

Statistical Survey

Sources (unless otherwise stated): Département de l'Economie Nationale, Kinshasa; Institut National de la Statistique, Office Nationale de la Recherche et du Développement, BP 20, Kinshasa; tel. (12) 31401.

Area and Population

AREA, POPULATION AND DENSITY

Area (sq km)	2,344,885*
Population (census result)	
1 July 1984	
Males	14,593,370
Females	15,078,037
Total	29,671,407
Population (official estimates at mid-year)	
1989	34,491,000
1990	35,562,000
1991	36,672,000
Density (per sq km) at mid-1991	15.6

* 905,365 sq miles.

REGIONS*

	Area (sq km)	Population (31 Dec. 1985)†
Bandundu	295,658	4,644,758
Bas-Zaïre	53,920	2,158,595
Equateur	403,293	3,960,187
Haut-Zaïre	503,239	5,119,750
Kasaï Occidental	156,967	3,465,756
Kasaï Oriental	168,216	2,859,220
Kivu	256,662	5,232,442
Shaba (formerly Katanga)	496,965	4,452,618
Kinshasa (city)‡	9,965	2,778,281
Total	2,344,885	34,671,607

* In mid-1997 proposals to change the names of some regions were under consideration.

† Provisional. ‡ Including the commune of Maluku.

Source: Département de l'Administration du Territoire.

PRINCIPAL TOWNS (population at census of July 1984)

Kinshasa	2,653,558
Lubumbashi	543,268
Mbuji-Mayi	423,363
Kananga	290,898
Kisangani	282,650
Kolwezi	201,382
Likasi	194,465
Bukavu	171,064
Matadi	144,742
Mbandaka	125,263

Source: UN, *Demographic Yearbook*.

BIRTHS AND DEATHS (UN estimates, annual averages)

	1980–85	1985–90	1990–95
Birth rate (per 1,000)	48.3	47.8	47.5
Death rate (per 1,000)	16.2	15.0	14.5

Expectation of life (UN estimates, years at birth, 1990–95): 52.0 (males 50.4; females 53.7).

Source: UN, *World Population Prospects: The 1994 Revision*.

ECONOMICALLY ACTIVE POPULATION

Mid-1995 (estimates in '000): Agriculture, etc. 12,174; Total 18,421 (Source: FAO, *Production Yearbook*).

Agriculture

PRINCIPAL CROPS ('000 metric tons)

	1993	1994	1995
Rice (paddy)	458	414	425
Maize	1,201*	1,198	1,170
Millet	32†	35†	39
Sorghum†	53	55	55
Potatoes†	35	35	35
Sweet potatoes	385†	385†	407
Cassava (Manioc)	20,835	18,051	17,500†
Yams†	315	315	315
Taro (Coco yam)†	41	41	41
Dry beans†	123	124	125
Dry peas†	64	65	66
Groundnuts (in shell)	604	547	581
Cottonseed†	50	50	50
Palm kernels†	72	72	72
Cabbages†	30	30	30
Tomatoes†	41	41	41
Onions (dry)†	32	32	32
Pumpkins†	44	44	44
Sugar cane†	1,350	1,350	1,350
Oranges†	156	156	156
Grapefruit†	14	14	14
Avocados†	47	47	47
Mangoes†	212	212	212
Pineapples†	145	145	145
Bananas†	408	410	412
Plantains	2,291	2,424	2,262
Papayas†	210	210	210
Coffee (green)*	54	77	76
Cocoa beans†	7	7	7
Tea (made)†	3	3	3
Tobacco (leaves)†	3	3	3
Cotton (lint)†	26	26	26
Natural rubber (dry weight)	10*	12*	12†

* Unofficial figure(s). † FAO estimate(s).

Source: FAO, *Production Yearbook*.

LIVESTOCK ('000 head, year ending September)

	1993*	1994	1995*
Cattle	1,470	1,475	1,480
Sheep	1,000	1,047	1,050
Goats	4,180	4,212	4,220
Pigs	1,160	1,192	1,200

Poultry (FAO estimates, million): 35 in 1993; 35 in 1994; 36 in 1995.

* FAO estimates.

Source: FAO, *Production Yearbook*.

LIVESTOCK PRODUCTS (FAO estimates, '000 metric tons)

	1993	1994	1995
Cows' milk	8	8	8
Beef and veal	28	28	28
Mutton and lamb	3	3	3
Goat meat	10	10	10
Pig meat	42	43	43
Poultry meat	30	30	30
Other meat	124	127	130
Hen eggs	8.9	9.0	9.0

Source: FAO, *Production Yearbook*.

Forestry

ROUNDWOOD REMOVALS
(FAO estimates, '000 cubic metres, excl. bark)

	1992	1993	1994
Sawlogs, veneer logs and logs for sleepers	391	391	391
Other industrial wood	2,763	2,853	2,944
Fuel wood	40,152	41,352	42,592
Total	43,306	44,596	45,927

Sawnwood production (FAO estimates, '000 cubic metres, incl. railway sleepers): 105 in 1992; 105 in 1993; 105 in 1994.

Source: FAO, *Yearbook of Forest Products*.

Fishing

('000 metric tons, live weight)

	1992	1993	1994*
Inland waters	184.8	193.3	190.0
Atlantic Ocean	3.8	4.2	4.0
Total catch	188.6	197.5	194.0

* FAO estimates.

Source: FAO, *Yearbook of Fishery Statistics*.

Mining

('000 metric tons, unless otherwise indicated)

	1992	1993	1994
Copper	147.3	48.3	33.6
Cobalt	6.4	2.2	3.6
Zinc (bullion)	18.8	4.2	2.5
Gold (kg)	2.5	1.5	0.8
Cassiterite	1.0	1.0	0.9
Crude petroleum ('000 barrels)	8,211.6	8,307.9	8,971.5
Diamonds ('000 carats)	13,501	15,150	16,259

Source: IMF, *Zaire—Background Information and Statistical Data* (April 1996).

Industry

SELECTED PRODUCTS
('000 metric tons, unless otherwise indicated)

	1992	1993	1994
Maize flour	13.0	12.8	10.3
Sugar	81.7	82.3	79.0
Butter	816.0	1,120.0	947.0
Cigarettes ('000 cartons)	2,682.1	2,472.5	2,535.0
Beer (million litres)	165.4	148.8	160.7
Soft drinks (million litres)	85.3	71.1	75.9
Steel	1,029.0	941.0	961.0
Non-ferrous metal	8.0	12.0	15.0
Hollow-ware	447.0	244.0	303.0
Explosives	4,819.9	634.8	575.3
Soaps	38.7	38.6	37.4
Acetylene	39.2	54.3	62.0
Tyres	41.0	26.0	35.6
Cement	208.0	161.7	165.7
Glassware	10.9	12.5	12.9
Diesel and gas oil	52.6	30.7	20.7
Fuel oil	34.3	32.8	9.1
Jet fuel and kerosene	31.4	31.2	1.1
Butane	0.1	10.2	0.2
Premium gasoline	28.3	30.8	8.3
Cotton fabrics ('000 sq metres)	20,510.0	15,099.0	17,804.0
Printed fabrics ('000 sq metres)	30,994.0	28,400.0	25,900.0
Shoes ('000 pairs)	934.0	1,661.0	1,061.0
Blankets ('000 units)	54.0	177.0	94.0
Metallic furniture ('000 pieces)	9.0	6.0	7.5
Matchets ('000 pieces)	26.0	136.0	150.0
Shovels and spades ('000 pieces)	1.0	21.0	20.0
Sheet metal ('000 pieces)	144.6	163.4	151.0
Motor cars (units)	131	150	140
Electric energy (million kWh)	5,883.0	5,3516.0	5,006.0

Source: IMF, *Zaire—Background Information and Statistical Data* (April 1996).

Finance

CURRENCY AND EXCHANGE RATES

Monetary Units

100 new makuta (singular: likuta) = 1 new zaire (NZ).

Sterling and Dollar Equivalents (30 September 1996)

£1 sterling = 104,138 new zaires;
US $1 = 66,610 new zaires;
1,000,000 new zaires = £9.603 = $15.013.

Average Exchange Rate (new zaires per US $)

1993 2.5
1994 1,194.1
1995 7,024

Note: The new zaire (NZ), equivalent to 3m. old zaires, was introduced in October 1993. Some of the figures in this Survey are still in terms of old zaires.

BUDGET ('000 million new zaires, unless otherwise indicated)

Revenue*	1993†	1993	1995
Taxation	934	184	1,955
Taxes on income, profits, etc.	282	34	700
Social security contributions	17	—	—
Taxes on payroll and workforce	7	3	27
Turnover tax	16	19	109
Excises	245	29	286
Other domestic taxes on goods and services	4	—	1
Import duties	218	71	642
Export duties	114	20	50
Other tax revenue	31	7	140
Administrative fees and charges, etc.	25	13	48
Other current revenue	256	11	117
Total	1,216	208	2,120

Expenditure‡	1993†	1994	1995
General public services§	2,616	205	1,646
Defence	1,258	11	122
Education	8	2	27
Health	2	2	25
Social security and welfare	55	n.a.	n.a.
Housing and community amenities	2	9	1
Recreational, cultural and religious affairs and services	1	—	19
Economic affairs and services	307	59	1,194
Agriculture, forestry and fishing	33	18	1,183
Mining, manufacturing and construction	4	2	1
Electricity, gas and water	11	—	8
Transport and communications	259	39	2
Other purposes	582	43	255
Interest payments	304	43	21
Total	4,831	331‖	3,289‖

* Excluding grants: 30m. new zaires in 1993; 17,000m. new zaires in 1994; 1,177,000m. new zaires in 1995.

† Figures in million new zaires.

‡ Excluding lending minus repayments (new zaires): 109m. in 1993; 17,000m. in 1994; none in 1995.

§ Including public order and safety.

‖ Excluding social security operations.

Source: IMF, *Government Finance Statistics Yearbook.*

INTERNATIONAL RESERVES (US $ million at 31 December)

	1993	1994	1995
Gold	8.59	10.71	10.83
Foreign exchange	46.20	120.69	146.60
Total	54.79	131.40	158.43

1996: Foreign exchange US $ 82.50m.

Source: IMF, *International Financial Statistics.*

MONEY SUPPLY (million new zaires at 31 December)

	1993	1994	1995
Currency outside banks	4,693	277,000	1,684,000
Demand deposits at deposit money banks	1,618	92,000	187,000
Total money (incl. others)	6,495	373,000	1,889,000

Source: IMF, *International Financial Statistics.*

COST OF LIVING

(Consumer Price Index for Kinshasa; base: 1988 = 100)

	1990	1991	1992
Food	785.2	33,900	1,002,187
Rent	771.6	29,658	973,432
Health	1,046.7	50,004	1,881,696
Clothing	488.1	21,019	689,652
Transport and other	930.7	44,134	797,283
All items	782.4	33,867	958,367

All items (base: 1990 = 0.01): 47,501 in 1994; 304,915 in 1995; 2,313,781 in 1996. (Source: IMF, *International Financial Statistics.*)

NATIONAL ACCOUNTS

Expenditure on the Gross Domestic Product

('000 million old zaires at current prices, unless otherwise indicated)

	1993	1994*	1995*†
Government final consumption expenditure	12,462,186	522.2	3,356.1
Private final consumption expenditure	64,305,274	5,417.7	31,924.1
Gross capital formation	1,817,933	162.1	982.4
Total domestic expenditure	78,585,393	6,102.0	36,262.6
Exports of goods and services	10,648,434	825.6	5,527.2
Less Imports of goods and services	8,462,269	627.7	5,167.5
GDP in purchasers' values	80,771,558	6,300.0	36,622.3

* Figures in '000 million new zaires (1 new zaire = 3m. old zaires).

† Estimates.

Source: IMF, *Zaire—Background Information and Statistical Data* (April 1996).

Gross Domestic Product by Economic Activity

('000 million old zaires at current prices, unless otherwise indicated)

	1993	1994*	1995*†
Agriculture, forestry, livestock, hunting, and fishing	41,443,328	3,631.2	21,247.6
Mining‡	5,111,950	296.1	1,590.7
Manufacturing	5,523,985	338.6	2,364.8
Construction and public works	797,646	126.2	845.1
Electricity and water	1,793,098	100.8	603.6
Transportation and telecommunications	2,833,538	176.0	1,022.6
Trade and commerce	17,074,694	1,021.9	6,114.4
Public administration	2,743,993	195.4	482.9
Other services	2,796,040	349.5	2,038.1
GDP at factor cost	80,118,272	6,241.7	36,309.8
Import duties	653,286	58.3	312.5
GDP at market prices	80,771,558	6,300.0	36,622.3

* Figures in '000 million new zaires (1 new zaire = 3m. old zaires).

† Estimates.

‡ Including processing.

Source: IMF, *Zaire—Background Information and Statistical Data* (April 1996).

BALANCE OF PAYMENTS (US $ million)

	1988	1989	1990
Exports of goods f.o.b.	2,178	2,201	2,138
Imports of goods f.o.b.	−1,645	−1,683	−1,539
Trade balance	533	518	599
Exports of services	150	137	157
Imports of services	−895	−921	−907
Balance on goods and services	−212	−266	−151
Other income received	36	28	14
Other income paid	−563	−539	−642
Balance on goods, services and income	−739	−777	−779
Current transfers received	226	276	217
Current transfers paid	−67	−109	−81
Current balance	−580	−610	−643
Investment assets	−54	86	111
Investment liabilities	43	−146	−331
Net errors and omissions	−133	111	102
Overall balance	−724	−559	−761

Source: IMF, *International Financial Statistics.*

External Trade

PRINCIPAL COMMODITIES (UN estimates, million old zaires)

Imports c.i.f.	1989	1990	1991
Food and live animals	63,380	121,824	2,172,956
Beverages and tobacco	3,436	6,605	117,812
Crude materials (inedible) except fuels	9,545	18,347	327,252
Mineral fuels, lubricants, etc.	24,436	46,968	837,761
Chemicals	33,217	63,848	1,138,847
Basic manufactures	68,343	131,365	2,343,137
Machinery and transport equipment	102,706	197,414	3,521,243
Miscellaneous manufactured articles	16,418	31,557	562,877
Other commodities and transactions	2,673	5,137	91,628
Total	324,154	623,066	11,113,531

Exports f.o.b.	1989	1990	1991
Food and live animals	93,541	148,201	2,535,635
Beverages and tobacco	5,071	8,035	137,474
Crude materials (inedible) except fuels	14,087	22,319	381,865
Mineral fuels, lubricants, etc.	36,064	57,138	977,599
Chemicals	49,024	77,672	1,328,924
Basic manufactures	100,866	159,807	2,734,207
Machinery and transport equipment	151,581	240,157	4,108,950
Miscellaneous manufactured articles	24,230	38,389	656,814
Other commodities and transactions	3,944	6,249	106,917
Total	478,409	757,967	12,968,384

Source: UN Economic Commission for Africa, *African Statistical Yearbook*.

1994 (US $ million): *Imports c.i.f.:* Mineral fuels 45.4; Total 628.8. *Exports f.o.b.:* Copper 42.8; Cobalt 140.3; Zinc 0.5; Diamonds 293.6; Crude petroleum 123.5; Coffee 158.6; Total 1,271.6. (Source: IMF, *Zaire—Background Information and Statistical Data* (April 1996).

SELECTED TRADING PARTNERS (US $'000)

Imports c.i.f.	1982	1984*	1985
Belgium-Luxembourg	156,600	116,994	240,918
Brazil	n.a.	87,031	157,716
France	53,400	52,293	118,834
Japan	7,400	20,704	50,147
Netherlands	7,700	31,152	46,107
United Kingdom	29,500	24,339	59,164
USA	60,800	73,600	134,457
Total (incl. others)	475,600	658,741	1,299,282

* Figures for 1983 are not available.

1986 (US $'000): Belgium-Luxembourg 243,929; Brazil 75,238; France 125,981; Japan 47,165; Netherlands 76,275; United Kingdom 49,809; USA 108,143; *Total* (incl. others) 1,331,531.

Exports f.o.b.	1981	1982	1985*
Belgium-Luxembourg	521,300	385,100	165,784
France	25,500	68,100	42,018
Italy	400	200	57,676
Netherlands	2,100	1,500	44,579
Switzerland	71,500	60,500	32,971
United Kingdom	13,700	10,700	21,444
USA	10,900	20,100	228,391
Total (incl. others)	685,200	585,700	796,905

* Figures for 1983 and 1984 are not available.

Source: UN, *International Trade Statistics Yearbook*.

Transport

RAILWAYS (Total traffic, million)*

	1986	1988†	1990†
Passenger-km	330	200	260
Freight (net ton-km)	1,785	1,901	1,732

* Figures are for services operated by the Société Nationale des Chemins de Fer Zaïrois (SNCZ), which controls 4,772 km of railway line out of the country's total facility of 5,252 km.

† Figures for 1987 and 1989 are not available.

Source: *Railway Directory: A Railway Gazette Yearbook*.

ROAD TRAFFIC (motor vehicles in use at 31 December)

	1992	1993	1994
Passenger cars	665,853	693,974	698,672
Buses and coaches	44,357	46,265	51,578
Lorries and vans	399,222	416,385	464,205
Total vehicles	1,109,432	1,156,624	1,214,455

Source: IRF, *World Road Statistics*.

SHIPPING

Merchant Fleet (registered at 31 December)

	1994	1995	1996
Number of vessels	27	27	27
Total displacement ('000 grt)	15	15	15

Source: Lloyd's Register of Shipping, *World Fleet Statistics*.

International Sea-borne Freight Traffic
(estimates, '000 metric tons)

	1988	1989	1990
Goods loaded	2,500	2,440	2,395
Goods unloaded	1,400	1,483	1,453

Source: UN, *Monthly Bulletin of Statistics*.

CIVIL AVIATION (traffic on scheduled services)

	1992	1993	1994
Kilometres flown (million)	4	4	6
Passengers carried ('000)	116	84	178
Passenger-km (million)	295	218	480
Total ton-km (million)	56	42	87

Source: UN, *Statistical Yearbook*.

Tourism

	1992	1993	1994
Tourist arrivals ('000)	22	22	18
Tourist receipts (US $ million)	7	6	5

Source: UN, *Statistical Yearbook*.

Communications Media

	1992	1993	1994
Radio receivers ('000 in use)	3,870	4,000	4,150
Television receivers ('000 in use)	55	62	63
Telephones ('000 main lines in use)	36	36	36
Daily newspapers	9	n.a.	9

Sources: UNESCO, *Statistical Yearbook*; UN Economic Commission for Africa, *African Statistical Yearbook*.

Education

	Institutions	Teachers	Students
Pre-primary (1992)	429	768	33,235
Primary (1993)	12,987	112,041	4,939,297
Secondary (1993)	n.a.	59,325	1,341,446
Higher (1988)	n.a.	3,873	61,422

Source: UNESCO, *Statistical Yearbook*.

Directory

Note: Following the proclamation of the Democratic Republic of the Congo in May 1997 it was assumed that the names of public- and private-sector businesses and organizations would be revised to reflect this change in the country's designation. Some entries in this section have been revised in anticipation of this development.

The Constitution

Following the proclamation of the Democratic Republic of the Congo, a 15-point constitutional decree was promulgated on 28 May 1997, which abrogated all previous constitutional dispositions. The decree declared the institutions of the Republic to be the President, the Government and the courts and tribunals; all institutions of the previous regime were suspended, except for the judiciary. All power was to be vested in the Head of State, until the adoption of a constitution by a constituent assembly.

EXECUTIVE POWER

The President of the Republic exercises legislative power by decree, following consultation with the Cabinet; he is chief of the executive and of the armed forces and has the authority to issue currency; he has the power to appoint and dismiss members of the Government, ambassadors, provincial governors, senior army officers, senior civil servants and magistrates.

POLITICAL PARTIES

A decree of 26 May 1997 banned all political parties.

REGIONAL GOVERNMENTS

Local government in each region is administered by a regional governor and deputy governor, who are appointed and dismissed by the President.

The Government

HEAD OF STATE

President: Laurent-Désiré Kabila (assumed power 17 May 1997; inaugurated 29 May 1997).

CABINET
(July 1997)

President and Minister of Defence: Laurent-Désiré Kabila.

Minister of Agriculture: Paul Bandoma.

Minister of the Civil Service: Justine Mpoyo Kasavubu.

Minister of Economy, Industry and Trade: Pierre-Victor Mpoyo.

Minister of Education: Kamara wa Kahikara.

Minister of Energy: Pierre Lokombe Kitete.

Minister of Environment and Tourism: Eddy Angulu.

Minister of Finance: Ferdinand Mawapanga Mwana Nanga.

Minister of Foreign Affairs: Bizima Karaha.

Minister of Health: Dr Jean-Baptiste Sondji.

Minister of Information: Raphael Ghenda.

Minister of Internal Affairs: Kongolo Mwenze.

Minister of International Co-operation: Thomas Kanza.

Minister of Justice: Céléstin Luangi.

Minister of Mines: Matukulo Kambale.

Minister of Planning and Development: Dr Babi Mbayi.

Minister of Posts and Telecommunications: Kinkela Vinkasi.

Minister of Public Works: Tshubaka Bisikuabo.

Minister of Reconstruction and Emergency Works: Etienne Mbaya.

Minister of Transport: Henri Mova Sakani.

Minister of Youth and Sports: Tshibal Mutombo.

MINISTRIES

All ministries are in Kinshasa.

Office of the President: Hotel du Conseil Exécutif, ave des 3Z, Kinshasa-Gombe; tel. (12) 30892.

Ministry of Agriculture: Building SOZACOM, 3rd floor, blvd du 30 juin, BP 8722 KIN I, Kinshasa-Gombe; tel. (12) 31821.

Ministry of the Civil Service: ave des Ambassadeurs, BP 3, Kinshasa-Gombe.

Ministry of Defence: Kinshasa-Gombe.

Ministry of Economy, Industry and Trade: Building ONATRA, blvd du 30 juin, BP 8500 KIN I, Kinshasa-Gombe.

Ministry of Education: Enceinte de l'Institut de la Gombe, BP 3163, Kinshasa-Gombe; tel. (12) 30098; telex 21460.

Ministry of Energy: Building SNEL, 239 ave de la Justice, BP 5137 KIN I, Kinshasa-Gombe.

Ministry of Environment and Tourism: 15 ave des Cliniques, BP 12348 KIN I, Kinshasa-Gombe.

Ministry of Finance: blvd du 30 juin, BP 12998 KIN I, Kinshasa-Gombe; tel. (12) 31197; telex 21161.

Ministry of Foreign Affairs: place de l'Indépendance, BP 7100, Kinshasa-Gombe; tel. (12) 32450; telex 21364.

Ministry of Health: blvd du 30 juin, BP 3088 KIN I, Kinshasa-Gombe; tel. (12) 31750.

Ministry of Information and Cultural Affairs: ave du 24 novembre, BP 3171 KIN I, Kinshasa-Kabinda; tel. (12) 23171.

Ministry of Internal Affairs: Kinshasa-Gombe.

Ministry of International Co-operation: Enceinte SNEL, ave de la Justice, Kinshasa-Gombe.

Ministry of Justice: 228 ave des 3Z, BP 3137, Kinshasa-Gombe; tel. (12) 32432.

Ministry of Mines: Building SNEL, 239 ave de la Justice, BP 5137 KIN I, Kinshasa-Gombe.

Ministry of Planning and Development: 4155 ave des Côteaux, BP 9378 KIN I, Kinshasa-Gombe 1; tel. (12) 31346; telex 21781.

Ministry of Posts and Telecommunications: Building KILOU, 4484 ave des Huiles, BP 800 KIN I, Kinshasa-Gombe; tel. (12) 24854; telex 21403.

Ministry of Public Works: Building TRAVAUX PUBLICS, Kinshasa-Gombe.

Ministry of Reconstruction and Emergency Works: Building TRAVAUX PUBLICS, blvd Colonel Tshatshi, BP 26, Kinshasa-Gombe.

Ministry of Transport: Building ONATRA, blvd du 30 juin, BP 3304, Kinshasa-Gombe; tel. (12) 23660; telex 21404.

Ministry of Youth and Sports: 77 ave de la Justice, BP 8541 KIN I, Kinshasa-Gombe.

President

Laurent-Désiré Kabila declared himself President on 17 May 1997, and was inaugurated on 29 May 1997.

Legislature

The Head of State legislates by decree.

Political Organizations

Alliance des forces démocratiques pour la libération du Congo-Zaïre (AFDL): Kinshasa; f. 1996; asscn of parties formed originally to overthrow Mobutu Govt; Leader LAURENT-DÉSIRÉ KABILA; Sec.-Gen. DEOGRATIAS BUGERA.

Front patriotique: Kinshasa; joined AFDL in July 1997; Leaders JEAN-BAPTISTE SONDJI, KINKELA VINKASI.

All political parties except the AFDL were banned on 26 May 1997. These organizations include:

Alliance des nationalistes africains (ANA): Kinshasa; f. 1994; agricultural manifesto; Chair. THÉOPHANE KINGOMBO MULULA.

Alliance des républicains pour le développement et le progrès (ARDP): Kinshasa; f. 1994; Chair. JOHN MILALA MBONO-MBUE; Sec.-Gen. MATAMO KUAKA.

Fédération des libéraux du Zaïre (FLZ): Kinshasa; f. 1994; asscn of 10 liberal political groups.

Forces novatrices pour l'union et la solidarité (FONUS): Kinshasa; advocates political pluralism; Leader JOSEPH OLENGHAKOY.

Forces politiques du conclave (FPC): Kinshasa; f. 1993; alliance of pro-Mobutu groups, incl the UFERI, led by MPR; Chair. NGUZA KARL-I-BOND.

Front Lumumba pour l'unité et la paix en Afrique (FLUPA): Kinshasa; f. 1963, obtained legal recognition 1994; supports aims of fmr prime minister, Patrice Lumumba.

Front national pour la libération du Katanga: Johannesburg, South Africa; f. 1997; seeks autonomy for province of Shaba (fmrly Katanga); Leader Gen. KPAMA BARAMOTO KATA.

Front populaire de résistance armée: Paris, France; f. 1997; advocates armed resistance to Kabila regime; Leader JACQUES MATANDA MA MBOYO.

Katanga Gendarmes: based in Angola; guerrilla group which aims to win independence for the province of Shaba (fmrly Katanga).

Mouvement national du Congo–Lumumba (MNC–Lumumba): Kinshasa; f. 1994; coalition of seven parties, incl. the Parti lumumbiste unifié (PALU), led by ANTOINE GIZENGA; supports the aims of the fmr Prime Minister, Patrice Lumumba; Co-ordinating Cttee PASCAL TABU, MBALO MEKA, OTOKO OKITASOMBO.

Mouvement populaire de la révolution (MPR): Palais du Peuple, angle ave des Huileries et ave Kasa-Vubu, Kinshasa; tel. (12) 22541; f. 1966; sole legal political party until Nov. 1990; advocates national unity and opposes tribalism; Leader (vacant); Sec.-Gen. KITHIMA BIN RAMAZANI.

Parti démocrate et social chrétien (PDSC): 32B ave Tombalbaye, Kinshasa-Gombe; tel. (12) 21211; f. 1990; centrist; seeks political change; Pres. ANDRÉ BO-BOLIKO; Sec. Gen. TUYABA LEWULA.

Parti démocrate et social chrétien national (PDSCN): Kinshasa; f. 1994; centrist.

Parti des nationalistes pour le développement integral (PANADI): Kinshasa; f. 1994; Leader BALTAZAR HOUNGANGERA.

Parti ouvrier et paysan du Congo (POP): f. 1986; Marxist-Leninist.

Rassemblement des démocrates libéraux: Kinshasa; Leader MWAMBA MULANDA.

Sacré alliance pour le dialogue (SAD): Kinshasa; f. 1993; alliance of 10 political groups; Leader Gen. NATHANIEL MBUMBA.

Union des fédéralistes et républicains indépendants (UFERI): Kinshasa; f. 1990; seeks autonomy for province of Shaba (fmrly Katanga); dominant party in the USOR; Pres. NGUZA KARL-I-BOND; Leader KOUYOUMBA MUCHULI MULEMBE.

Union pour la démocratie et le progrès social (UDPS): Twelfth St, Limete Zone, Kinshasa; f. 1982; Leader ETIENNE TSHISEKEDI WA MULUMBA; Sec.-Gen. Dr ADRIEN PHONGO KUNDA.

Union pour la démocratie et le progrès social national: Kinshasa; f. 1994; Chair. CHARLES DEOUNKIN ANDEL.

Union pour la République et la démocratie (URD): Kinshasa; centrist; expelled from USOR in May 1994; Chair. GÉRARD KAMANDA WA KAMANDA.

Union sacrée de l'opposition radicale (USOR): Kinshasa; f. July 1991; comprised c. 130 movements and factions opposed to Pres. Mobutu; led by the UDPS. The existence, within the transitional legislature, of an umbrella radical opposition grouping, known as the **Union sacrée de l'opposition radicale et ses alliés (USORAL)**, was announced in late 1994. In May 1996 FRÉDÉRIC KIBASSA MALIBA was re-elected President of the USORAL.

Union sacrée rénovée (USR): Kinshasa; f. 1993 by several ministers in Govt of Nat. Salvation; Leader KIRO KIMATE.

Diplomatic Representation

EMBASSIES IN THE DEMOCRATIC REPUBLIC OF THE CONGO

Algeria: 50/52 ave Colonel Ebeya, BP 12798, Kinshasa; tel. (12) 22470; Chargé d'affaires a.i.: HOCINE MEGHLAOUI.

Angola: 4413–4429 blvd du 30 juin, BP 8625, Kinshasa; tel. (12) 32415; Ambassador: MIGUEL GASPARD NETO.

Argentina: 181 blvd du 30 juin, BP 16798, Kinshasa; tel. (12) 25485; Ambassador: WERNER ROBERTO JUSTO BURGHARDT.

Austria: 39 ave Lubefu, BP 16399, Kinshasa-Gombe; tel. (12) 22150; telex 21310; Ambassador: Dr HANS KOGLER.

Belgium: Immeuble Le Cinquantenaire, place du 27 octobre, BP 899, Kinshasa; tel. (12) 20110; telex 21114; fax 22120; Ambassador: JOHAN VAN DESSEL.

Benin: 3990 ave des Cliniques, BP 3265, Kinshasa-Gombe; tel. (12) 33156; Ambassador: PIERRE DÉSIRÉ SADELER.

Brazil: 190 ave Basoko, BP 13296, Kinshasa; tel. (12) 21781; telex 21515; Ambassador: AYRTON G. DIEGUEZ.

Burundi: 17 ave de la Gombe, BP 1483, Kinshasa; tel. (12) 31588; telex 21655; Ambassador: LONGIN KANUMA.

Cameroon: 171 blvd du 30 juin, BP 10998, Kinshasa; tel. (12) 34787; Chargé d'affaires a.i.: DOMINIQUE AWONO ESSAMA.

Canada: BP 8341, Kinshasa 1; tel. (12) 21801; telex 21303; Ambassador: CLAUDE LAVERDURE.

Central African Republic: 11 ave Pumbu, BP 7769, Kinshasa; tel. (12) 30417; Ambassador: J.-G. MAMADOU.

Chad: 67–69 ave du Cercle, BP 9097, Kinshasa; tel. (12) 22358; Ambassador: MAITINE DJOUMBE.

China, People's Republic: 49 ave du Commerce, BP 9098, Kinshasa; tel. 23972; Ambassador: AN GUOZHENG.

Congo, Republic: 179 blvd du 30 juin, BP 9516, Kinshasa; tel. (12) 30220; Ambassador: MAURICE OGNAMY.

Côte d'Ivoire: 68 ave de la Justice, BP 9197, Kinshasa; tel. (12) 30440; telex 21214; Ambassador: GASTON ALLOUKO FIANKAN.

Cuba: 4660 ave Cateam, BP 10699, Kinshasa; telex 21158; Ambassador: ENRIQUE MONTERO.

Czech Republic: 54 ave Colonel Tshatshi, BP 8242, Kinshasa-Gombe; tel. (12) 34610; telex 21183.

Egypt: 519 ave de l'Ouganda, BP 8838, Kinshasa; tel. (12) 30296; Ambassador: AZIZ ABDEL HAMID HAMZA.

Ethiopia: BP 8435, Kinshasa; tel. (12) 23327; Ambassador: Col LEGESSE WOLDE-MARIAM.

France: 97 ave de la République du Tchad, BP 3093, Kinshasa; tel. (12) 30513; telex 21074; Ambassador: MICHEL ROUGAGNOU.

Gabon: ave du 24 novembre, BP 9592, Kinshasa; tel. (12) 68325; telex 21455; Ambassador: JOSEPH KOUMBA MOUNGUENGUI.

Germany: 82 ave des 3Z, BP 8400, Kinshasa-Gombe; tel. (12) 21529; telex 21110; fax (12) 21527; Ambassador: KLAUS BÖNNEMANN.

Ghana: 206 ave du 24 novembre, BP 8446, Kinshasa; tel. (12) 31766; Ambassador: KWAKU ADU BEDIAKO.

Greece: 72 ave des 3Z, BP 478, Kinshasa; tel. (12) 33169; Ambassador: STELIO VALSAMAS-RHALLIS.

Guinea: 7–9 ave Lubefu, BP 9899, Kinshasa; tel. (12) 30864; Ambassador: FÉLIX FABER.

Holy See: 81 ave Goma, BP 3091, Kinshasa; tel. (12) 33128; telex 21527; fax (12) 33346; Apostolic Nuncio: Mgr FAUSTINO SAINZ MUÑOZ, Titular Archbishop of Novaliciana.

India: 188 ave des Batétéla, BP 1026, Kinshasa; tel. (12) 33368; telex 21179; Ambassador: ARUN KUMAR.

Iran: 76 blvd du 30 juin, BP 16599, Kinshasa; tel. (12) 31052; telex 21429.

Israel: 12 ave des Aviateurs, BP 8343, Kinshasa; tel. (12) 21955; Ambassador: SHLOMO AVITAL.

Italy: 8 ave de la Mongala, BP 1000, Kinshasa; tel. (12) 23416; telex 21560; Ambassador: VITTORIO AMEDEO FARINELLI.

Japan: Immeuble Marsavco, 2e étage, ave Colonel Lusaka, BP 1810, Kinshasa; tel. (12) 22118; telex 21227; Ambassador: KYOICHI OMURA.

Kenya: 5002 ave de l'Ouganda, BP 9667, Kinshasa; tel. (12) 30117; telex 21359; Ambassador: MWABILI KISAKA.

Korea, Democratic People's Republic: 168 ave de l'Ouganda, BP 16597, Kinshasa; tel. (12) 31566; Ambassador: KIM PONG HUI.

Korea, Republic: 2A ave des Orangers, BP 628, Kinshasa; tel. (12) 31022; Ambassador: CHUN SOON-KYU.

Kuwait: Suite 232, Intercontinental Hotel, Kinshasa.

Lebanon: 3 ave de l'Ouganda, Kinshasa; tel. (12) 32682; telex 21423; Ambassador: MUSTAFA HOREIBE.

Liberia: 3 ave de l'Okapi, BP 8940, Kinshasa; tel. (12) 82289; telex 21205; Ambassador: JALLA D. LANSANAH.

Libya: BP 9198, Kinshasa.

Mauritania: BP 16397, Kinshasa; tel. (12) 59575; telex 21380; Ambassador: Lt-Col M'BARECK OULD BOUNA MOKHTAR.

Morocco: 4497 ave Lubefu, BP 912, Kinshasa; tel. (12) 30255; Ambassador: ABOUBKEUR CHERKAOUI.

Netherlands: 11 ave Zongo Ntolo, BP 10299, Kinshasa; tel (12) 30733; Chargé d'affaires a.i.: J. G. WILBRENNINCK.

Nigeria: 141 blvd du 30 juin, BP 1700, Kinshasa; tel. (12) 43272; Ambassador: DAG S. CLAUDE-WILCOX.

Pakistan: Kinshasa; Chargé d'affaires a.i.: SHAFQAT ALI SHAIKH.

Poland: 63 ave de la Justice, BP 8553, Kinshasa; tel. (12) 33349; telex 21057; Ambassador: ANDRZEJ M. LUPINA.

Portugal: 270 ave des Aviateurs, BP 7775, Kinshasa; tel. (12) 24010; telex 221328; Ambassador: LUÍS DE VASCONCELOS PIMENTEL QUARTIN BASTOS.

Romania: 5 ave de l'Ouganda, BP 2242, Kinshasa; tel. (12) 33127; telex 21316; Ambassador: EMINESCU DRAGOMIR.

Russia: 80 ave de la Justice, BP 1143, Kinshasa 1; tel. (12) 33157; telex 21690; fax (12) 45575; Ambassador: YURII SPIRINE.

Rwanda: 50 ave de la Justice, BP 967, Kinshasa; tel. (12) 30327; telex 21612; Ambassador: ANTOINE NYILINKINDI.

South Africa: 17 ave Pumbu, BP 7829, Kinshasa-Gombe; tel. (12) 34676; fax (satellite) 1-212-3723510; Ambassador: J. W. J. VAN DEVENTER.

Spain: Immeuble de la Communauté Hellénique, 4e étage, blvd du 30 juin, BP 8036, Kinshasa; tel. (12) 21881; fax (12) 24388; Ambassador: ANTONIO LÓPEZ MARTÍNEZ.

Sudan: 83 ave des Treis, BP 7347, Kinshasa; Ambassador: MUBARAK ADAM HADI.

Sweden: 89 ave des 3Z, BP 11096, Kinshasa; tel. (12) 33201; Chargé d'affaires a.i.: L. EKSTRÖM.

Switzerland: 654 ave Colonel Tshatshi, BP 8724, Kinshasa 1; tel. (12) 34243; fax (12) 34246; Ambassador: WILHELM SCHMID.

Togo: 3 ave de la Vallée, BP 10197, Kinshasa; tel. (12) 30666; telex 21388; Ambassador: MAMA GNOFAM.

Tunisia: ave du Cercle, BP 1498, Kinshasa; tel. (12) 31632; telex 21171; Ambassador: ABDEL KRIM MOUSSA.

Turkey: 18 ave Pumbu, BP 7817, Kinshasa; tel. (12) 33774; Ambassador: HİKMET SENGENÇ.

Uganda: 177 ave Tombalbaye, BP 1086, Kinshasa; tel. (12) 22740; telex 21618; Ambassador: Dr AJEAN.

United Kingdom: ave des 3Z, BP 8049, Kinshasa; tel. (12) 34775; fax (satellite) 871-144-5470; Ambassador: MARCUS HOPE.

USA: 310 ave des Aviateurs, BP 697, Kinshasa; tel. (12) 21532; telex 21405; fax 21232; Ambassador: DANIEL SIMPSON.

Yugoslavia: 112 quai de l'Etoile, BP 619, Kinshasa; tel. (12) 32325; Ambassador: (vacant).

Zambia: 54–58 ave de l'Ecole, BP 1144, Kinshasa; tel. (12) 23038; telex 21209; Ambassador: C. K. C. KAMWANA.

Judicial System

A Justice Department, under the control of the Minister of Justice, is responsible for the organization and definition of competence of the judiciary; civil, penal and commercial law and civil and penal procedures; the status of persons and property; the system of obligations and questions pertaining to nationality; international private law; status of magistrates; organization of the legal profession, counsels for the defence, notaries and of judicial auxiliaries; supervision of cemeteries, non-profit-making organizations, cults and institutions working in the public interest; the operation of prisons; confiscated property.

There is a Supreme Court in Kinshasa, and there are also nine Courts of Appeal and 36 County Courts.

The Head of State is empowered to appoint and dismiss magistrates.

President of the Supreme Court: GÉRARD KAMANDA WA KAMANDA.

Procurator-General of the Republic: MONGULU T'APANGANE.

Courts of Appeal

Bandundu: Pres. MUNONA NTAMBAMBILANJI.

Bukavu: Pres. TINKAMANYIRE BIN NDIGEBA.

Kananga: Pres. MATONDO BWENTA.

Kinshasa: Pres. KALONDA KELE OMA.

Kisangani: Pres. MBANGAMA KABUNDI.

Lubumbashi: Pres. BOKONGA W'ANZANDE.

Matadi: Pres. TSHIOVO LUMAMBI.

Mbandaka: Pres. MAKUNZA WA MAKUNZA.

Mbuji-Mayi: Pres. LUAMBA BINDU.

Religion

Many of the country's inhabitants follow traditional beliefs, which are mostly animistic. A large proportion of the population is Christian, predominantly Roman Catholic.

In 1971 new national laws officially recognized the Roman Catholic Church, the Protestant (ECC) Church and the Kimbanguist Church. The Muslim and Jewish faiths and the Greek Orthodox Church were granted official recognition in 1972.

CHRISTIANITY

The Roman Catholic Church

The Democratic Republic of the Congo comprises six archdioceses and 41 dioceses. An estimated 50% of the population are Roman Catholics.

Bishops' Conference: Conférence Episcopale du Congo, BP 3258, Kinshasa-Gombe; tel. (12) 30082; telex 21571; f. 1981; Pres. Rt Rev. FAUSTIN NGABU, Bishop of Goma.

Archbishop of Bukavu: (vacant), Archevêché, BP 3324, Bukavu; tel. 2707; fax (16) 82060067.

Archbishop of Kananga: Most Rev. MARTIN-LÉONARD BAKOLE WA ILUNGA, Archevêché, BP 70, Kananga; tel. 2477.

Archbishop of Kinshasa: Cardinal FRÉDÉRIC ETSOU-NZABI-BAMUNGWABI, Archevêché, ave de l'Université, BP 8431, Kinshasa 1; tel. (12) 3723-546.

Archbishop of Kisangani: Most Rev. LAURENT MONSENGWO PASINYA, Archevêché, ave Mpolo 10B, BP 505, Kisangani; tel. 3132-897; fax 3132-898.

Archbishop of Lubumbashi: Most Rev. EUGÈNE KABANGA SONGASONGA, Archevêché, BP 72, Lubumbashi; tel. (2) 34-1442.

Archbishop of Mbandaka-Bikoro: JOSEPH KUMUONDALA MBIMBA, Archevêché, BP 1064, Mbandaka; tel. 2234.

The Anglican Communion

The Church of the Province of Zaire comprises six dioceses.

Archbishop of the Province of Zaire and Bishop of Boga-Zaïre: Most Rev. PATRICE BYANKYA NJOJO, c/o POB 21285, Nairobi, Kenya.

Bishop of Bukavu: Rt Rev. FIDÈLE BALUFUGA DIROKPA, BP 2876, Bukavu.

Bishop of Kindu-Maniema: Rt Rev. ZACHARIA MASIMANGE KATANDA, c/o BP 53435, Nairobi, Kenya.

Bishop of Kisangani: Rt Rev. SYLVESTRE TIBAFA MUGERA, BP 861, Kisangani.

Bishop of Nord Kivu: Rt Rev. METHUSELA MUNZENDA MUSUBAHO, BP 322, Butembo.

Bishop of Shaba: Rt Rev. EMMANUEL KOLINI MBONA, c/o United Methodist Church, POB 22037, Kitwe, Zambia.

Kimbanguist

Eglise de Jésus Christ sur la Terre par le Prophète Simon Kimbangu: BP 7069, Kinshasa; tel. (12) 68944; telex 21315; f. 1921 (officially est. 1959); c. 5m. mems (1985); Spiritual Head HE DIANGIENDA KUNTIMA; Sec.-Gen. Rev. LUNTADILLA.

Protestant Churches

Eglise du Christ au Congo (ECC): ave de la Justice (face no. 75), BP 4938, Kinshasa-Gombe; f. 1902; a co-ordinating agency for all the Protestant churches, with the exception of the Kimbanguist Church; 62 mem. communities and a regional org. in each admin. region; c. 10m. mems (1982); Pres. Bishop BOKELEALE ITOFO; includes:

Communauté Baptiste du Congo-Ouest: BP 4728, Kinshasa 2; f. 1970; 450 parishes; 170,000 mems (1985); Gen. Sec. Rev. LUSAKWENO-VANGU.

Communauté des Disciples du Christ: BP 178, Mbandaka; tel. 31062; telex 21742; f. 1964; 250 parishes; 650,000 mems (1985); Gen. Sec. Rev. Dr ELONDA EFEFE.

Communauté Episcopale Baptiste en Afrique: 2 ave Jason Sendwe, BP 3866, Lubumbashi 1; tel. (2) 24724; f. 1956; 1,300 episcopal communions and parishes; 150,000 mems (1993); Pres. Bishop KITOBO KABWEKA-LEZA.

Communauté Evangélique: BP 36, Luozi; f. 1961; 50 parishes; 33,750 mems (1985); Pres. Rev. K. LUKOMBO NTONTOLO.

Communauté Lumière: BP 10498, Kinshasa 1; f. 1931; 150 parishes; 220,000 mems (1985); Patriarch KAYUWA TSHIBUMBU WA KAHINGA.

Communauté Mennonite: BP 18, Tshikapa; f. 1960; 40,000 mems (1985); Gen. Sec. Rev. KABANGY DJEKE SHAPASA.

Communauté Presbytérienne: BP 117, Kananga; f. 1959; 150,000 mems (1985); Gen. Sec. Dr M. L. TSHIHAMBA.

Eglise Missionaire Apostolique: BP 15859, Kinshasa 1, f. 1986; 3 parishes; 1,000 mems.; Apostle for Africa L. A. NANANDANA.

The Press

DAILIES

L'Analyste: 129 ave du Bas-Zaïre, BP 91, Kinshasa-Gombe; tel. (12) 80987; Dir and Editor-in-Chief BONGOMA KONI BOTAHE.

Boyoma: 31 blvd Mobutu, BP 982, Kisangani, Haut-Zaïre; Dir and Editor BADRIYO ROVA ROVATU.

Elima: 1 ave de la Révolution, BP 11498, Kinshasa; tel. (12) 77332; f. 1928; evening; operations suspended by Govt in Nov. 1993; Dir and Editor-in-Chief ESSOLOMWA NKOY EA LINGANGA.

Mjumbe: BP 2474, Lubumbashi, Shaba; tel. (2) 25348; f. 1963; Dir and Editor TSHIMANGA KOYA KAKONA.

Le Palmarès: Kinshasa; supports Union pour la démocratie et le progrès social; Editor MICHEL LADELUYA.

La Référence Plus: Kinshasa; Dir ANDRÉ IPAKALA.

Salongo: 143 10e rue Limete, BP 601, Kinshasa/Limete; tel. (12) 77367; morning; operations suspended by Govt in Nov. 1993; Dir and Editor BONDO-NSAMA; circ. 10,000.

PERIODICALS

Allo Kinshasa: 3 rue Kayange, BP 20271, Kinshasa-Lemba; monthly; Editor MBUYU WA KABILA.

Annales Aequatoria: Centre Aequatoria, BP 276, Mbandaka; f. 1980; central African culture, history and language; annually; Editor HONORÉ VINCK; circ. 400.

BEA Magazine de la Femme: 2 ave Masimanimba, BP 113380, Kinshasa 1; every 2 weeks; Editor MUTINGA MUTWISHAYI.

Beto na Beto: 75 ave Tatamena, BP 757, Matadi; weekly; Dir-Gen. and Editor BIA ZANDA NE NANGA.

Bibi: 33 ave Victoria, Kinshasa; f. 1972; French; general interest; monthly.

Bingwa: ave du 30 juin, zone Lubumbashi no 4334, Shaba; weekly; sport; Dir and Editor MATEKE WA MULAMBA.

Cahiers Economiques et Sociaux: BP 257, Kinshasa XI, (National University of the Congo); sociological, political and economic review; quarterly; Dir Prof. NDONGALA TADI LEWA; circ. 2,000.

Cahiers des Religions Africaines: Faculté de Théologie Catholique de Kinshasa, BP 712, Kinshasa/Limete; tel. (12) 78476; f. 1967; English and French; religion; 2 a year; circ. 1,000.

Le Canard Libre: Kinshasa; f. 1991; Editor JOSEPH CASTRO MULEBE.

Circulaire d'Information: Association Nationale des Entreprises du Congo, 10 ave des Aviateurs, BP 7247, Kinshasa I; tel. (12) 22565; f. 1959; French; legal and statutory texts for the business community; monthly; circ. (variable).

La Colombe: 32B ave Tombalbaye, Kinshasa-Gombe; tel. (12) 21211; organ of parti démocrate et social chrétien; circ. 5,000.

Congo-Afrique: Centre d'Etudes pour l'Action Sociale, 9 ave Père Boka, BP 3375, Kinshasa-Gombe; tel. (12) 34682; f. 1961; economic, social and cultural; monthly; Editors KIKASSA MWANALESSA, RENÉ BEECKMANS; circ. 4,500.

Conseiller Comptable: Immeuble SNCC, 17 ave du Port, BP 308, Kinshasa; f. 1974; French; public finance and taxation; quarterly; circ. 1,000.

Dionga: Immeuble Amassio, 2 rue Dirna, BP 8031, Kinshasa; monthly.

Documentation et Informations Africaines (DIA): BP 2598, Kinshasa 1; tel. (12) 33197; fax (12) 33196; Roman Catholic news agency reports; 3 a week; Dir Rev. Père VATA DIAMBANZA.

Documentation et Informations Protestantes (DIP): Eglise du Christ au Zaïre, BP 4938, Kinshasa-Gombe; French and English; religion.

L'Entrepreneur Flash: Association Nationale des Entreprises du Congo, 10 ave des Aviateurs, BP 7247, Kinshasa I; tel. (12) 22565; f. 1978; French; business news; monthly; circ. 1,000.

Etudes d'Histoire Africaine: National University of the Congo, BP 1825, Lubumbashi; f. 1970; French and English; history; annually; circ. 1,000.

Horizons 80: Société Congolaise d'Edition et d'Information, BP 9839, Kinshasa; economy; weekly.

JUA: BP 1613, Bukavu, Kivu; weekly; Dir and Editor MUTIRI WA BASHARA.

Les Kasaï: 161 9e rue, BP 575, Kinshasa/Limete; weekly; Editor NSENGA NDOMBA.

Kin-Média: BP 15808, Kinshasa 1; monthly; Editor ILUNGA KASAMBAY.

KYA: 24 ave de l'Equateur, BP 7853, Kinshasa-Gombe; tel. (12) 27502; f. 1984; weekly for Bas-Zaïre; Editor SASSA KASSA YI KIBOBA.

Libération: Kinshasa; f. 1997; French; politics; pro-AFDL; weekly; Man. NGOYI KABUYA DIKATETA M'MIANA.

Maadini: Générale des Carrières et des Mines, BP 450, Lubumbashi; quarterly.

Mambenga 2000: BP 477, Mbandaka; Editor BOSANGE YEMA BOF.

Ngabu: Société Nationale d'Assurances, Immeuble Sonas Sankuru, blvd du 30 juin, BP 3443, Kinshasa-Gombe; tel. (12) 23051; f. 1973; insurance news; quarterly.

Njanja: Société Nationale des Chemins de Fer Congolais, 115 place de la Gare, BP 297, Lubumbashi; tel. (2) 23430; telex 41056; fax (2) 61321; railways and transportation; annually; circ. 10,000.

NUKTA: 14 chaussée de Kasenga, BP 3805, Lubumbashi; weekly; agriculture; Editor NGOY BUNDUKI.

L'Opinion: BP 15394, Kinshasa; weekly; Editor SABLE FWAMBA KIEPENDA.

Presse et Information Kimbanguiste (PIK): ave Bongolo, Kinshasa-Kalamu.

Promoteur Congolais: Centre du Commerce International du Congo, 119 ave Colonel Tshatshi, BP 13, Kinshasa; f. 1979; French; international trade news; six a year.

La Revue Juridique du Congo: Société d'Etudes Juridiques du Congo, Université de Lubumbashi, BP 510, Lubumbashi; f. 1924; 3 a year.

Sciences, Techniques, Informations: Centre de Recherches Industrielles en Afrique Centrale (CRIAC), BP 54, Lubumbashi.

Le Sport Africain: 13è niveau Tour adm., Cité de la Voix du Congo, BP 3356, Kinshasa-Gombe; monthly; Pres. TSHIMPUMPU WA TSHIMPUMPU.

Taifa: 536 ave Lubumba, BP 884, Lubumbashi; weekly; Editor LWAMBWA MILAMBU.

Telema: 7–9 ave Père Boka, BP 3277, Kinshasa-Gombe; f. 1974; religious; quarterly; Editor BOKA DI MPASI LONDI; circ. 3,000.

Umoja: Kinshasa; weekly.

NEWS AGENCIES

Congolese News Agency (CNA): 44–48 ave Tombalbaye, BP 1595, Kinshasa 1; tel. (12) 22035; telex 21096; f. 1957; state-controlled; Dir-Gen. ALI KALONGA.

Documentation et Informations Africaines (DIA): BP 2598, Kinshasa I; tel. (12) 34528; telex 2108; f. 1957; Roman Catholic news agency; Dir Rev. Père VATA DIAMBANZA.

Foreign Bureaux

Agence France-Presse (AFP): Immeuble Wenge 3227, ave Wenge, Zone de la Gombe, BP 726, Kinshasa 1; tel. (12) 27009; telex 21648; Bureau Chief JEAN-PIERRE REJETTE.

Agencia EFE (Spain): BP 2653, Lubumbashi; Correspondent KANKU SANGA.

Agência Lusa de Informação (Portugal): BP 4941, Kinshasa; tel. (12) 24437; telex 21605.

Agenzia Nazionale Stampa Associata (ANSA) (Italy): BP 2790, Kinshasa 15; tel. (12) 30315; Bureau Chief (vacant).

Pan-African News Agency (PANA) (Senegal): BP 1400, Kinshasa; tel. (12) 23290; telex 21475; f. 1983; Bureau Chief ADRIEN HONORÉ MBEYET.

Xinhua (New China) News Agency (People's Republic of China): 293 ave Mfumu Lutunu, BP 8939, Kinshasa; tel. (12) 25647; telex 21259; Correspondent CHEN WEIBIN.

PRESS ASSOCIATIONS

Médias Libres—Médias pour Tous: Kinshasa; org. representing Kinshasa newspapers.

Union de la Presse du Congo: BP 4941, Kinshasa 1; tel. (12) 24437; telex 21605.

Publishers

Centre Protestant d'Editions et de Diffusion (CEDI): 209 ave Kalémie, BP 11398, Kinshasa 1; tel. (12) 22202; fax (12) 26730; f. 1935; fiction, poetry, biography, religious, juvenile; Christian tracts, works in French, Lingala, Kikongo, etc.; Dir-Gen. HENRY DIRKS.

Maison d'Editions 'Jeunes pour Jeunes': BP 9624, Kinshasa 1; youth interest.

MEDIASPAUL: BP 127 Limete, Kinshasa; tel. (12) 40531; religion, education, literature; Dir LUIGI BOFFELLI.

Le Potentiel: Kinshasa; Chair. LUNGA MUTUSHA.

Les Presses Africaines: place du 27 Octobre, BP 12924, Kinshasa 1; general non-fiction, poetry; Man. Dir MWAMBA DI MBUYI.

Presses Universitaires du Congo (PUC): 290 rue d'Aketi, BP 1682, Kinshasa 1; tel. (12) 30652; telex 21394; f. 1972; scientific pubs; Dir Prof. MUMBANZA MWA BAWELE.

Radio and Television

According to estimates by UNESCO, there were 4,150,000 radio receivers and 63,000 television receivers in use in 1994. Several private radio and television broadcasters operate in Kinshasa.

Radio-Télévision Nationale Congolaise (RTNC): tel. (12) 23171; telex 21583; state radio and terrestrial and satellite television broadcasts; Dir-Gen. JOSE KAJANGUA.

Télévision Congolaise: BP 3171, Kinshasa-Gombe; tel. (12) 23171; telex 21583; govt commercial station; broadcasts for 5 hours daily on weekdays and 10 hours daily at weekends.

La Voix du Congo: Station Nationale, BP 3164, Kinshasa-Gombe; tel. (12) 23175; telex 21583; state-controlled; home service broadcasts in French, Swahili, Lingala, Tshiluba, Kikongo; regional stations at Kisangani, Lubumbashi, Bukavu, Bandundu, Kananga, Mbuji-Mayi, Matadi, Mbandaka and Bunia.

Tele Kin Malebo (TKM): Kinshasa; private television station; nationalization announced 1997; Dir-Gen. NGONGO LUWOWO.

Voice of the People: Centre d'Animation et de Diffusion Pédagogique, BP 373, Bunia; state-controlled.

Finance

(cap. = capital; res = reserves; dep. = deposits; m. = million; brs = branches; amounts in old zaires unless otherwise indicated)

BANKING

Central Bank

Banque du Congo: blvd Colonel Tshatshi au nord, BP 2697, Kinshasa; tel. (12) 20701; telex 21365; f. 1964; cap. and res 50,088.4m. (Dec. 1988); 8 brs, 34 agencies.

Commercial Banks

Banque Commerciale Congolaise SARL: blvd du 30 juin, BP 2798, Kinshasa; tel. (12) 23772; telex 21127; f. 1909 as Banque du Congo Belge, name changed 1997; cap. NZ 36.6m., res NZ 166,358.7m., dep. NZ 221,416.7m. (Dec. 1994); Gen. Man. KASONGO TAIBU; 29 brs.

Banque Continentale Africaine (Congo) SCARL: 4 ave de la Justice, BP 7613, Kinshasa-Gombe; tel. (12) 28006; telex 21508; fax (12) 25243; f. 1983; total assets 28,786.5m. (Dec. 1994); Chair. PAUL LENOIR.

Banque de Crédit Agricole: angle ave Kasa-Vubu et ave M'Polo, BP 8837, Kinshasa-Gombe; tel. (12) 21800; telex 21383; fax (12) 27221; f. 1982 to expand and modernize enterprises in agriculture, livestock and fishing, and generally to improve the quality of rural life; state-owned; cap. 5m. (Dec. 1991); Pres. MOLOTO MWA LOPANZA.

Banque Internationale de Crédit SCARL (BIC): 191 ave de l'Equateur, BP 1299, Kinshasa 1; tel. (12) 20342; telex 21113; fax (12) 123769600; f. 1994; cap. NZ 5,473.7m., res NZ 2,881.7m., dep. NZ 21,973.4m. (Dec. 1995); Pres. PASCAL KINDUELO LUMBU; Man. Dir THARCISSE K. M. MILEMBWE.

Banque Paribas Congo: Immeuble Unibra, ave Colonel Ebeya, BP 1600, Kinshasa 1; tel. (12) 24747; telex 21020; f. 1954; cap. and res 1.4m. (Dec. 1980).

Banque Congolaise du Commerce Extérieur SARL: blvd du 30 juin, BP 400, Kinshasa 1; tel. (12) 20393; telex 21108; fax (12) 27947; f. 1947, reorg. 1987; state-owned; cap. NZ 133.0m., res NZ 19,170.1m., dep. NZ 27,419.9m. (Dec. 1994); Chair. and Gen. Man. GBENDO NDEWA TETE; Dirs MAKUMA NDESEKE, ZIKONDOLO BIWABEKI; 31 brs.

Caisse Générale d'Epargne du Congo: 38 ave de la Caisse d'Epargne, BP 8147, Kinshasa-Gombe; tel. (12) 33701; telex 21384; f. 1950; state-owned; Chair. and Man. Dir NSIMBA M'VUEDI; 45 brs.

Caisse Nationale d'Epargne et de Crédit Immobilier: BP 11196, Kinshasa; f. 1971; state-owned; cap. 2m. (Dec. 1983); Dir-Gen. BIANGALA ELONGA MBAÜ.

Citibank (Congo) SARL: Immeuble Citibank Congo, angle aves Col Lukusa et Ngongo Lutete, BP 9999, Kinshasa 1; tel. (12) 20554; telex 21622; fax (12) 21064; f. 1971; cap. and res 152,120.0m., dep. 1,613,301.9m. (Dec. 1991); Chair. SHAUKAT AZIZ; Man. Dir MICHEL ACCAD; 1 br.

Compagnie Immobilière du Congo: BP 332, Kinshasa; f. 1962; cap. 150m. (Dec. 1983); Chair. A. S. GERARD; Man. Dir M. HERALY.

Crédit Foncier de l'Afrique Centrale: BP 1198, Kinshasa; f. 1961; cap. 40,000 (Dec. 1983).

Fransabank (Congo) SARL: Immeuble Congo-Shell 14/16, ave du Port, BP 9497, Kinshasa 1; tel. (12) 20119; telex 21430; fax (12) 27864; f. 1989; cap. 300m. (1993); Pres. ADNAN WAFIC KASSAR.

Nouvelle Banque de Kinshasa: 1 place du Marché, BP 8033, Kinshasa 1; tel. (12) 26361; telex 21304; fax (12) 20587; f. 1969 as Banque de Kinshasa; nationalized 1975; control assumed by National Union of Congolese Workers in 1989; cap NZ 2,000, res NZ 92,179.4m., dep. NZ 25,396.8m. (Dec. 1994); Pres. MANTOMINA KIALA; 14 brs.

Société de Crédit aux Classes Moyennes et à l'Industrie: BP 3165, Kinshasa-Kauna; f. 1947; cap. 500,000 (Dec. 1983).

Société Financière de Développement SCARL (SOFIDE): Immeuble SOFIDE, 9–11 angle aves Ngabu et Kisangani, BP 1148, Kinshasa 1; tel. (12) 20676; telex 21476; fax (12) 20788; f. 1970; partly state-owned; provides tech. and financial aid, primarily for agricultural development; cap. and res NZ 16,303.3m. (Dec. 1995); Pres. and Dir-Gen. KIYANGA KI-N'LOMBI; 4 brs.

Stanbic Bank (Congo) SCARL: 12 ave de Mongala, BP 16297, Kinshasa 1; tel. (12) 20074; telex 21507; fax (12) 46216; f. 1973 as Grindlays Bank; acquired by Standard Bank Investment Corpn (South Africa) in 1992; adopted current name in 1997; cap. NZ 358.0m. (April 1996), res NZ 2,698.2m., dep. NZ 32,587.7m. (Dec. 1994); Chair. A. D. B. WRIGHT; Man. Dir JOHN CALLAGHAN; 1 br.

Union Congolaise de Banques SARL: angle ave de la Nation et ave des Aviateurs 19, BP 197, Kinshasa 1; tel. (12) 25180; telex 21026; fax (12) 25527; f. 1929, renamed in 1997; cap. NZ 34,497.0m. (Dec. 1995), res 3,077,897m., dep. 2,975,182,180m. (Dec. 1993); Pres. RAOUL ISUNGU KY-MAKA; 12 brs.

INSURANCE

Société Nationale d'Assurances (SONAS): 3473 blvd du 30 juin, Kinshasa-Gombe; tel. (12) 23051; telex 21653; f. 1966; state-owned; cap. 23m.; 9 brs.

Trade and Industry

At November 1994 the Government's portfolio of state enterprises numbered 116, of which 56 were wholly owned by the Government. The heads of all state-owned enterprises were suspended by decree in June 1997.

DEVELOPMENT ORGANIZATIONS

Caisse de Stabilisation Cotonnière (CSCo): BP 3058, Kinshasa-Gombe; tel. (12) 31206; telex 21174; f. 1978 to replace Office National des Fibres Textiles; acts as an intermediary between the Govt, cotton ginners and textile factories, and co-ordinates international financing of cotton sector.

La Générale des Carrières et des Mines (GÉCAMINES): BP 450, Lubumbashi; tel. (2) 13039; telex 41034; f. 1967 as state holding co to acquire assets of Union Minière du Haut-Katanga; privatization announced in 1994; subsequently delayed; Man. Dir MBAKA KAWAYA SWANA; operates the following three enterprises which were merged in 1995:

GÉCAMINES—Commercial: marketing of mineral products.

GÉCAMINES—Développement: operates agricultural and stockfarming ventures in Shaba region.

GÉCAMINES—Exploitation: mining operations.

Institut National pour l'Etude et la Recherche Agronomiques: BP 1513, Kisangani, Haut-Zaïre; f. 1933; agricultural research.

Office Congolais du Café: ave Général Bobozo, BP 8931, Kinshasa I; tel. (12) 77144; telex 20062; f. 1979; state agency for coffee and also cocoa, tea, quinquina and pyrethrum.

Pêcherie Maritime Congolaise: Kinshasa; the only sea-fishing enterprise.

PetroCongo: 1513 blvd du 30 juin, BP 7617, Kinshasa 1; tel. (12) 25356; telex 21066; f. 1974; state-owned; petroleum refining, processing, stocking and transporting.

TRADE ASSOCIATIONS

Association Nationale des Entreprises du Congo: 10 ave des Aviateurs, BP 7247, Kinshasa; tel. (12) 24623; telex 21071; f. 1972; represents business interests for both domestic and foreign institutions; Man. Dir EDOUARD LUBOYA DIYOKA; Gen. Sec. ATHANASE MATENDA KYELU.

Chambre de Commerce, d'Industrie et d'Agriculture du Congo: 10 ave des Aviateurs, BP 7247, Kinshasa 1; tel. (12) 22286; telex 21071.

TRADE FAIR

FIKIN—Foire Internationale de Kinshasa (Kinshasa International Trade Fair): BP 1397, Kinshasa; tel. (12) 77506; telex 20145; f. 1968; state-sponsored; held annually in July; Pres. TOGBA MATA BOBOY.

MAJOR INDUSTRIAL COMPANIES

The following are some of the largest companies in terms either of capital investment or employment.

Manufacturing and Trading

BAT Congo SARL: 973 ave Gen. Bobozo, Kingabwa, BP 621, Kinshasa I; tel. (12) 20289; telex 20073; fax (satellite) 871-682-340868; f. 1950; wholly-owned subsidiary of British American Tobacco Co Ltd, London; mfrs of tobacco products; Chair. and Man. Dir B. MAVAMBU ZOYA.

Brasseries, Limonaderies et Malteries du Congo (BRALIMA): 912 ave du Flambeau, BP 7246, Kinshasa; tel. (12) 22141; telex 21662; f. 1923; production of beer, soft drinks and ice; Gen. Man. J. L. HOME.

Britmond: BP 8853, Kinshasa; British-Zaire Diamond Distributors; exporters of rough diamonds.

Compagnie des Margarines, Savons et Cosmétiques au Congo SARL (MARSAVCO CONGO): 1 ave Kalemie, BP 8914, Kinshasa; tel. (12) 24821; telex 21100; f. 1922; subsidiary of Unilever NV; mfrs of detergents, foods and cosmetics; Pres. C. GODDE; 1,100 employees.

Compagnie Sucrière: 1963 ave de Général Bobozo, BP 8816, Kinshasa, and BP 10, Kwilu Ngongo, Bas-Zaïre; tel. (12) 20476; telex 21085; f. 1925; mfrs of sugar, alcohol, acetylene, oxygen and carbon dioxide; Man. Dir B. MICHEL; Gen. Man. NKAZI BASISULULA; Dir M. LUVIYZ.

Cultures et Elevages du Congo (CELCO) SARL: BP 16796, Kinshasa I; interests in cattle ranches, abattoirs, coffee, cocoa, rubber, oil palm, quinquina plantations and associated processing plants.

IBM World Trade Corporation (Congo): 6 ave du Port, BP 7563, Kinshasa 1; tel. (12) 23358; telex 21298; fax (12) 24029; f. 1954; sale and maintenance of computers and business machines and associated materials; Gen. Man. MUKADI KABUMBU.

Industries Congolaises des Bois (ICB): 23 ave de l'Ouganda, BP 10399, Kinshasa; state forestry and sawmilling enterprise.

Plantations Lever au Congo: 16 ave Colonel Lukusa, BP 8611, Kinshasa I; telex 21053; f. 1911; subsidiary of Unilever NV; plantations of oil palm, rubber, cocoa and tea; Man. Dir A. J. RITCHIE.

NOVATEX: 29B 16ème rue, BP 8456, Kinshasa; principal producer of synthetic fibres.

Société BATA Congolaise: 33 ave Général Bobozo, BP 598, Kinshasa I; tel. (12) 27414; telex 21208; f. 1946; principal shoe mfr in DCR; Man. Dir JEAN-LOUIS ANTZ; 100 employees.

Société Commerciale et Minière du Congo SA: BP 499, Kinshasa; subsidiary of Lonrho Ltd; engineering, motor trade, insurance, assembly and sale of earth-moving equipment.

Société Générale d'Alimentation (SGA): BP 15898, Kinshasa; state enterprise; import, processing and distribution of foodstuffs; largest chain of distributors in DCR.

Société Congo-Suisse de Produits Chimiques SARL: BP 14096, Kinshasa 1; tel. (12) 24707; telex 21463; sales agent for Ciba-Geigy pharmaceutical products.

TABAZAIRE: blvd du 30 juin, BP 42, Kinshasa; cigarette mfrs.

Minerals

Office des Mines d'Or de Kilo-Moto (OKIMO): BP 219–220, Bunia; state-owned; operates gold mines; Pres. ISSIAKA TABU; Sec.-Gen. ISSIKATA TABU.

Société de Développement Industriel et Minier du Congo (SODIMICO): 4219 ave de l'Ouganda, BP 7064, Kinshasa; tel. (12) 32511; telex 21370; fmrly SODIMIZA; subsidiary of GÉCAMINES (see Development Organizations); copper-mining consortium exploiting mines of Musoshi and Kinsenda in Shaba.

Société Minière de Bakwanga (MIBA): BP 377, Mbujmayi, Kasaï Oriental; f. 1961; cap. 27m. zaires; 80% state-owned; industrial diamond mining (produces 9m. carats per year); Gen. Man. ANDRÉ CASTIAUX.

Société Minière du Tenke-Fungurume: Immeuble UCB Centre, 5ème étage, BP 1279, Kinshasa; f. 1970 by international consortium comprising Charter Consolidated of London, govt of Zaire, Mitsui (Japan), Bureau de Recherches Géologiques et Minières de France, Léon Tempelsman and Son (USA) and COGEMA (France); copper and cobalt mining; Dir B. L. MORGAN.

Société de Recherche et d'Exploitation des Pétroles au Congo (ZAÏREP): BP 15596, Kinshasa; tel. (12) 26565; telex 21528; fax (12) 20468; exploitation of petroleum; Gen. Man. C. KETELS.

Société Congo Gulf Oil: blvd du 30 juin, BP 7189, Kinshasa I; tel. (12) 23111; telex 21462; international mining consortium exploiting offshore petroleum at Muanda.

Société Congo Shell: 1513 blvd du 30 juin, BP 2799, Kinshasa; tel. (12) 21368; telex 21271; fax (12) 21550; f. 1978; marketing of petroleum products; Dir-Gen. F. H. KOOL; 2,000 employees.

Société Congo-Italienne de Raffinage (SOCIR): BP 1478, Kinshasa I; tel. (12) 22683; telex 21119; f. 1963; cap. 11,400m. zaires; oil refinery; Pres. LESSEDJINA IKWAME IPU'OZIA; Dir-Gen. VIERO COGNIGNI; 579 employees.

Congoétain: ave Mutombo Katshi, BP 7129, Kinshasa; tin producer.

TRADE UNIONS

The Union Nationale des Travailleurs was founded in 1967 as the sole trade union organization. In mid-1990 the establishment of independent trade unions was legalized, and in early 1991 there were 12 officially recognized trade union organizations.

Union Nationale des Travailleurs du Congo: BP 8814, Kinshasa; f. 1967; embraces 16 unions; Pres. KATALAY MOLELI SANGOL.

Transport

Office National des Transports (ONATRA): BP 98, Kinshasa 1; tel. (12) 24761; fax (12) 24892; operates 12,174 km of waterways, 366 km of railways and road and air transport; administers ports of Kinshasa, Matadi, Boma and Banana; Dir-Gen. I. BANGONDA LOOLA.

RAILWAYS

The main line runs from Lubumbashi to Ilebo. International connections run to Dar es Salaam (Tanzania) and Lobito (Angola), and also connect with the Zambian, Zimbabwean, Mozambican and South African systems. In March 1994 an agreement was concluded with the South African Government for the provision of locomotives, rolling stock and fuel, to help rehabilitate the rail system. In May 1997 the railway network and its assets were nationalized.

Kinshasa–Matadi Railway: BP 98, Kinshasa 1; 366 km operated by ONATRA; Pres. K. WA NDAYI MULEDI.

Société Nationale des Chemins de Fer du Congo (SNCC): 115 place de la Gare, BP 297, Lubumbashi; tel. (2) 23430; telex 41056; f. 1974; 4,772 km (including 858 km electrified); administers all internal railway sections as well as river transport and transport on Lakes Tanganyika and Kivu; man. contract concluded with a Belgian-South African corpn, Sizarail, in 1995 for the man. of the Office des Chemins de Fer du Sud (OCS) and the Société des Chemins de Fer de l'Est (SFE) subsidiaries, with rail networks of 2,835 km and 1,286 km respectively; assets of Sizarail nationalized and returned to SNCC control in May 1997; Dir-Gen. TSHISOLA KANGOA.

ROADS

In 1994 there were approximately 145,000 km of roads, of which some 68,000 km were main roads. In general road conditions are poor, owing to inadequate maintenance.

INLAND WATERWAYS

The River Congo is navigable for over 1,600 km. Above the Stanley Falls the Congo becomes the Lualaba, and is navigable along a 965-km stretch from Bubundu to Kindu and Kongolo to Bukama. The River Kasai, a tributary of the River Congo, is navigable by shipping as far as Ilebo, at which the line from Lubumbashi terminates. The total length of inland waterways is 13,700 km.

Régie des voies fluviales: 109 ave Lumpungu, Kinshasa-Gombe, BP 11697, Kinshasa 1; administers river navigation; Gen. Man. MONDOMBO SISA EBAMBE.

Société Congolaise des Chemins de Fer des Grands Lacs: River Lualaba services: Bubundu–Kindu and Kongolo–Malemba N'kula; Lake Tanganyika services: Kamina–Kigoma–Kalundu–Moba–Mpulungu.

SHIPPING

The principal seaports are Matadi, Boma and Banana on the lower Congo (Zaire). The port of Matadi has more than 1.6 km of quays and can accommodate up to 10 deep-water vessels. Matadi is linked by rail with Kinshasa. The country's merchant fleet numbered 27 vessels and amounted to 14,917 gross registered tons at 31 December 1996.

Compagnie Maritime Congolaise SARL: Immeuble CMC (AMIZA), place de la Poste, BP 9496, Kinshasa; tel. (12) 25816; telex 21626; fax (12) 26234; f. 1946; services: North Africa, Europe, North America and Asia to West Africa, East Africa to North Africa; Chair. MAYILUKILA LUSIASIA.

CIVIL AVIATION

International airports are located at Ndjili (for Kinshasa), Luano (for Lubumbashi), Bukavu, Goma and Kisangani. There are smaller airports and airstrips dispersed throughout the country.

Air Charter Service: Place Salongo, BP 5371, Kinshasa 10; tel. (12) 27891; telex 21573; passenger and cargo charter services; Dir TSHIMBOMBO MAKUNA; Gen. Man. N. MCKANDOLO.

Alliance Airlines: 210 bis 6e rue, Limete-Kinshasa, BP 12847, Kinshasa; tel. (12) 43862; fax (12) 372-3156; f. 1996 as Zaire Airlines in merger of Zaire Express and Shabair, name changed 1997; regional and domestic scheduled services for passengers and cargo; Pres. JOSE ENDUNO; CEO STAVROS PAPAIOANNOU.

Blue Airlines: BP 1115, Kinshasa 1; tel. (12) 20455; f. 1991; regional and domestic charter services for passengers and cargo; Man. T. MAYANI.

Congolese Airlines: 3555-3560 blvd du 30 Juin, BP 2111, Kinshasa; tel. (12) 24624; telex 21525; international, regional and domestic services for passengers and cargo; f. 1981; Dir-Gen. ALFRED SOMMERAUER.

Eastern Congo Airlines: Bukavu; f. 1997; Chair. Chief NAKAZIBA CIMANYE.

Express City: BP 12847, Kinshasa; tel. (12) 275748; regional and domestic passenger and cargo services.

Filair: BP 14671, Kinshasa; tel. (88) 45702; fax (USA) 1-212-3769367; f. 1987; regional and domestic charter services; Pres. DANY PHILEMOTTE.

Scibe Airlift: BP 614, Kinshasa; tel. (12) 26237; fax (12) 24386; f. 1979; domestic and international passenger and cargo charter services between Kinshasa, Lubumbashi, Bujumbura (Burundi) and Brussels; Pres. BEMBA SAOLONA; Dir-Gen. BEMBA GOMBO.

Local charter services are also provided by Trans Service Airlift, Transair Cargo and Wetrafa Airlift.

Tourism

The Democratic Republic of the Congo has extensive lake and mountain scenery. Tourist arrivals totalled about 18,000 in 1994, generating some US $5m. in revenue.

Office National du Tourisme: 2A/2B ave des Orangers, BP 9502, Kinshasa-Gombe; tel. (12) 30070; f. 1959; Man. Dir BOTOLO MAGOZA.

Société Congolaise de l'Hôtellerie: Immeuble Memling, BP 1076, Kinshasa; tel. (12) 23260; Man. N'JOLI BALANGA.

Defence

Military service is compulsory. In August 1996 the Zairean armed forces totalled 28,100, of whom 25,000 were in the army, 1,800 in the air force and 1,300 in the navy. There is also a paramilitary force, the Gendarmerie, of about 21,000. A Civil Guard, numbering 10,000, created in 1984, was responsible for security and anti-terrorist operations. Composition of the armed forces of the Democratic Republic of the Congo is not yet known.

Defence Expenditure: Estimated at 122,000m. new zaires in 1995.

Commander-in-Chief: LAURENT-DÉSIRÉ KABILA.

Chief of Staff of the Armed Forces: Gen. MASASU NEDAGA.

Education

Primary education, beginning at six years of age and lasting for six years, is officially compulsory. Secondary education, which is not compulsory, begins at 12 years of age and lasts for up to six years, comprising a first cycle of two years and a second of four years. In 1993, according to UNESCO, the total enrolment at primary and secondary schools was equivalent to 49% of the school-age population (males 58%; females 39%); primary enrolment was equivalent to 68% of the school-age population (boys 78%; girls 58%), whilst secondary enrolment was 24% (boys 33%; girls 15%). There are four universities in the DRC, situated at Kinshasa, Kinshasa/Limete, Kisangani and Lubumbashi. According to estimates by UNESCO, the average rate of adult illiteracy in 1995 was 22.7% (males 13.4%; females 32.3%). In the budget for 1989 a total of 24,291.5m. zaires (6.7% of total expenditure by the central government) was allocated to education. In the budget for 1995 education received an estimated 27,000m. new zaires (less than 1% of central government expenditure).

Bibliography

Abi-Saab, G. *The United Nations Operations in the Congo 1960–64*. London, Oxford University Press, 1978.

Asch, S. *L'Eglise du Prophète Kimbangu*. Paris, Editions Karthala, 1983.

Bezy, F., Peemans, J. P., and Wantelet, J. M. *Accumulation et sous-développement au Zaïre 1960–1980*. Louvain-la-Neuve, Presses universitaires de Louvain, 1981.

Bontinck, F. *L'évangélisation du Zaïre*. Kinshasa, Saint Paul Afrique, 1980.

Cornevin, R. *Le Zaïre*. Paris, Presses universitaires de France, 1977.

Ekpebu, L. B. *Zaire and the African Revolution*. Ibadan, Ibadan University Press, 1989.

Ekwe-Ekwe, H. *Conflict and Intervention in Africa: Nigeria, Angola and Zaire*. London, Macmillan, 1990.

Gérard-Libois, J. *Katanga Secession*, (trans. by Rebecca Young). Madison and London, University of Wisconsin Press, 1966.

Gourou, P. *La Population du Congo*. Paris, Hachette, 1966.

Hayward, M. F. *Elections in Independent Africa*. Boulder, CO, Westview Press, 1987.

Huybrechts, A. *Transports et structures de développement au Congo. Etude de progrès économique de 1900 à 1970*. Paris and The Hague, Editions Mouton, 1970.

Jewsiewicki, B. (Ed.). *Etat indépendant du Congo, Congo belge, République démocratique du Congo, République du Zaïre?* Sainte-Foy, Québec, SAFI Press, 1984.

Kamitatu-Massamba, C. *Zaïre, le pouvoir à la portée du peuple*. Paris, Editions de l'Harmattan, 1977.

Kanza, T. *Conflict in the Congo. The Rise and Fall of Lumumba*. Harmondsworth, Penguin, 1972.

Kelly, S. *America's Tyrant: The CIA (Central Intelligence Agency) and Mobutu of Zaire*. Lanham, MD, University of America Press, 1993.

Kronsten, G. *Zaire to the 1990s: Will Retrenchment Work?* London, Economist Intelligence Unit (Economic Prospects Series), 1986.

Leslie, W. J. *Zaire: Continuity and Political Change in an Oppressive State*. Boulder, CO, Westview Press, 1993.

Louis, W. R., and Stengers, J. *E. D. Morel's History of the Congo Reform Association*. Oxford, Clarendon Press, 1968.

Lumumba, P. *Congo My Country*. London, Praeger, 1963.

MacGaffey, J. *The Real Economy of Zaire: An Anthropological Study*. London, James Currey, 1991.

MacGaffey, J., and Mukohya, V. *The Real Economy of Zaire: The Contribution of Smuggling and Other Unofficial Activities to National Wealth*. London, James Currey, 1991.

Mbaya, K. (Ed.). *Zaire: What Destiny?* Dakar, CODESRIA, 1993.

Mokoli, M. M. *State Against Development: The Experience of Post-1965 Zaire*. Westport, CT, Greenwood Press, 1992.

Sanqmpam, S. N. *Pseudocapitalism and the Overpolitical State: Reconciling Politics and Anthropology in Zaire*. Brookfield, VT, Ashgate Press, 1994.

Schatzberg, M. G. *The Dialectics of Oppression in Zaire*. Bloomington, IN, Indiana University Press, 1988.

Shapiro, D. and Tollens, E. *The Agricultural Development of Zaire*. Aldershot, Avebury, 1992.

Vanderlinden, Huybrechts, Mudimbe, Peeters, Van Der Steen and Verhaegen. (Eds). *Du Congo au Zaïre, 1960–1980, essai de bilan*. Brussels, Etudes du CRISP, 1980.

Vanderlinden, J. *La crise congolaise*. Brussels, Complexe, 1985.

Willame, J. C. *Eléments pour une lecture du contentieux Belgo-Zaïrois*. Les Cahiers du CEDAF, Vol. VI. Brussels, Centre d'etude et de documentation africaines, 1988.

Patrice Lumumba—La crise congolaise revisitée. Paris, Editions Karthala, 1990.

Young, M. C. *Politics in the Congo: Decolonization and Independence*. Princeton, Princeton University Press, 1965.

Young, M. C., and Turner, T. *The Rise and Decline of the Zairean State*. Madison, WI, University of Wisconsin Press, 1985.

For a detailed study of recent Zairean history, see the annual collection of documents, together with the commentary, published by the Centre de recherche et d'information socio-politique (CRISP), Brussels, starting with *Congo*, 1959.

REPUBLIC OF CONGO

Physical and Social Geography

DAVID HILLING

POPULATION

The Congo river forms approximately 1,000 km of the eastern boundary of the Republic of Congo, the remainder of which is provided by the Oubangui river from just south of the point at which the Equator bisects the country. Across these rivers lies the Democratic Republic of the Congo. To the north, the republic is bounded by the Central African Republic and Cameroon. Gabon lies to the west, and the Cabinda exclave of Angola to the south, adjoining the short Atlantic coastline. Covering an area of 342,000 sq km (132,047 sq miles) the country supported a population of 1,843,421 at the census of 1984. The population was estimated by the UN to have increased to 2,590,000 at mid-1995, giving an average density of only 7.6 inhabitants per sq km. About one-third of the population are dependent on agriculture, mainly of the bush-fallowing type, but this is supplemented where possible by fishing, hunting and gathering. The main ethnic groups are the Vili on the coast, the Kongo (centred on Brazzaville), and the Téké, M'Bochi and Sanga of the plateaux in the centre and north of the country. At the 1984 census the principal centres of urban population were the capital, Brazzaville (population 596,200), and the main port of Pointe-Noire (population 298,014).

PHYSICAL FEATURES AND RESOURCES

Substantial deposits of petroleum have been found offshore, and their exploitation by US, French and Italian companies represents a major sector of the economy. The immediate coastal zone is sandy in the north, more swampy south of Kouilou, and in the vicinity of Pointe-Indienne yields small amounts of petroleum. A narrow coastal plain does not rise above 100 m, and the cool coastal waters modify the climate, giving low rainfall and a grassland vegetation. Rising abruptly from the coastal plain are the high-rainfall forested ridges of the Mayombé range, parallel to the coast and achieving a height of 800 m, in which gorges, incised by rivers such as the Kouilou, provide potential hydroelectric power sites. At Hollé, near the Congo-Océan railway and at the western foot of the range, there are considerable phosphate deposits. Mayombé also provides an important export commodity, timber, of which the main commercial species are okoumé, limba and sapele.

Inland, the south-western Niari valley has lower elevation, soils that are good by tropical African standards and a grassland vegetation which makes agricultural development easier. A variety of agricultural products such as groundnuts, maize, vegetables, palm oil, coffee, cocoa, sugar and tobacco, is obtained from large plantations, smaller commercial farms and also peasant holdings. These products provide the support for a more concentrated rural population and the basis for some industrial development.

A further forested mountainous region, the Chaillu massif, is the Congo basin's western watershed, and this gives way north-eastwards to a series of drier plateaux, the Batéké region and, east of the Likoula river, a zone of Congo riverine land. Here are numerous watercourses, with seasonal inundation, and dense forest vegetation, which supports some production of forest products, although the full potential has yet to be realized. The rivers Congo and Oubangui, with tributaries, provide more than 6,500 km of navigable waterway, which are particularly important, owing to the lack of a developed network of roads.

Recent History

PIERRE ENGLEBERT

Revised for this edition by the Editor

The Republic of the Congo, now known as the Republic of Congo, became autonomous within the French Community in November 1958, with Abbé Fulbert Youlou as prime minister. Full independence followed on 15 August 1960; in March 1961 Youlou was elected president, and a new constitution was adopted, giving the president extensive executive powers. Youlou's domestic policies exacerbated ethnic tensions, and his attempt, in August 1963, to curtail trade union activity led to a general strike and the declaration of a state of emergency. In mid-August Youlou resigned, and a provisional government was formed under the premiership of Alphonse Massamba-Débat. In December a new constitution was approved by referendum, and Massamba-Débat was elected president. In 1964 the Mouvement national de la révolution (MNR) was established, on Marxist-Leninist principles, as the sole political party. In the following years, tension developed between the MNR and the army. This period saw the emergence of the paratroop commander, Capt. Marien Ngouabi, as the dominant figure in Congolese politics. In August 1968, following a series of confrontations between Massamba-Débat and the MNR, Ngouabi took power in a military coup. In January 1969 he became president. In December a new Marxist-Leninist party, the Parti congolais du travail (PCT), replaced the MNR, and in the following month the country was renamed the People's Republic of the Congo.

Unsuccessful attempts to overthrow the government took place in February and May 1972 and in February 1973. The adoption of a new constitution in June 1973 was followed by elections to a new national assembly and the formation of a new government in August, with Henri Lopes as prime minister. Ethnic tensions, added to disagreements over political ideology and power struggles within the political élite, contributed to a continuing atmosphere of national instability. In December 1975 Ngouabi dismissed both the PCT's political bureau and the government, and appointed Maj. (later Gen.) Louis-Sylvain Goma, formerly the chief of staff of the armed forces, as prime minister. After several attempts on his life, Ngouabi was assassinated in March 1977 during an attempted coup by supporters of Massamba-Débat, who was arrested, tried and executed. In April Col (later Brig.-Gen.) Jacques-Joachim Yhombi-Opango, a former chief of staff of the armed forces, was appointed head of state. Yhombi-Opango improved relations with the USA and France, but his regime inherited severe economic problems and came into conflict with the left wing of the PCT. In February 1979, faced with a collapse in support, Yhombi-Opango surrendered his powers to a provisional committee appointed by the PCT. In the following month the president of the committee, Col (later Gen.) Denis Sassou-Nguesso, was appointed president of the republic and chairman of the PCT's central committee. A new council of ministers, led by Goma, was announced in April.

THE SASSOU-NGUESSO REGIME

In July 1979 elections were held for a national people's assembly and for regional councils, and a socialist constitution was overwhelmingly approved in a referendum. In the following month, Sassou-Nguesso agreed to release a number of political prisoners, including those implicated in the assassination of Ngouabi. The president also announced that Congolese living abroad who were opposed to the regime could return to their country without fear of repression. A number of those implicated in the coup plot of February 1973 were later rehabilitated.

The revolutionary stance of the Sassou-Nguesso regime was belied by an increasingly pro-Western foreign policy, a correspondingly liberal economic policy, and the relative marginalization of some left-wing factions within the PCT. At the PCT congress in July 1984 Sassou-Nguesso was re-elected chairman of the party central committee and president of the republic for a further five-year term. The congress also adopted a constitutional amendment, by which the head of state assumed additional powers as the head of the government. The pro-Western faction and Sassou-Nguesso's personal supporters obtained considerable representation in the new politburo and central committee, and in the government. However, the main branch of the radical wing of the PCT, M-22, retained its influence, both within the party and the government. Sassou-Nguesso further consolidated his position by assuming the post of minister of defence and security. Legislative elections were held in September.

Persistent ethnic rivalries, together with disillusionment with the government's response to the country's worsening economic problems, resulted in an increase in opposition to the Sassou-Nguesso regime during the late 1980s. In July 1987 20 army officers were arrested on suspicion of undermining state security. They were mostly members of the northern Kouyou ethnic group (prominent members of which have included Ngouabi and Yhombi-Opango: Sassou-Nguesso is from a different northern group, the Mboshi). A commission of enquiry, established by the government, identified the affair as a coup attempt. Although the plot had apparently been instigated by a right-wing army group, it appeared to have some links with M-22. The findings of the enquiry also implicated Yhombi-Opango and his former colleague, Pierre Anga, both of whom were being held under house arrest. Yhombi-Opango, who agreed to appear before the commission of enquiry, was transferred to prison; Anga, however, responded by inciting an armed uprising in his native town of Owando, during which up to 60 people were reported to have been killed. Under the terms of the Franco-Congolese military co-operation treaty, a French aircraft was dispatched from Gabon to transport troops to Owando; Anga, however, evaded arrest, and remained at large until July 1988, when he was killed by Congolese security forces.

At the PCT congress in July 1989 Sassou-Nguesso was re-elected chairman of the party and president of the republic for a further five-year term. In August Alphonse Mouissou Poaty-Souchalaty, elected to the politburo of the ruling party in the previous month, was appointed prime minister, and a new government was announced. At legislative elections, held in September, the single list of 133 candidates was approved by 99.19% of those who used their vote. For the first time the list included candidates who were not members of the PCT. In November Sassou-Nguesso announced a series of extensive reforms, aiming to achieve a liberalization of the economy: state intervention was to be reduced, while private enterprise was to be fostered. In the following month it was reported that more than 40 prisoners, who had been detained without charge since July 1987, had been released.

POLITICAL TRANSITION

In February 1990 a committee was appointed to examine the implications for the Congo of the political changes taking place in Eastern Europe. In July the PCT announced that an extraordinary congress would be held in 1991 to introduce a multi-party system and that the PCT's role in mass and social organizations was to be reduced.

In mid-August 1990, on the occasion of the 30th anniversary of the country's independence, Sassou-Nguesso announced the release of several political prisoners, including Yhombi-Opango. In September the Confederation of Congolese Trade Unions (CSC) was refused permission by the government to disaffiliate itself from the PCT. The CSC had also demanded an immediate transition to a multi-party political system and increased salaries for workers in the public sector. However, in response to a general strike, called in protest by the CSC, the government agreed to permit free elections to the leadership of the trade union organization, and in late September the central committee of the PCT resolved to permit the immediate registration of new political parties, and the assumption of power in early 1991 by a transitional government, in preparation for the convocation of a national conference on the country's constitutional future.

In December 1990 Alphonse Poaty-Souchalaty resigned as prime minister over a 'conflict of views' within the party on finding a solution to the national crisis. In the same month a hastily convened extraordinary congress of the PCT abandoned Marxism-Leninism and legalized the formation of a multi-party system, with effect from January 1991. A new central committee, politburo and secretary-general were elected, although Sassou-Nguesso remained as chairman of the central committee.

From early January 1991 the army was instructed to dissociate itself from the PCT, and to remain neutral in its support of democracy. In early January Gen. Goma was appointed prime minister, and shortly afterwards an interim government was installed.

The national conference, convened in February 1991, was immediately adjourned until mid-March, owing to a dispute over the number and representation of the participant organizations. In a settlement to the dispute opposition movements were allocated seven of 11 seats on the conference's governing body and were represented by 700 of the 1,100 delegates; the Roman Catholic bishop of Owando, Ernest N'Kombo, was elected chairman. The conference voted itself a sovereign body whose decisions were to be binding and not subject to government approval. In April the conference announced that the constitution was to be abrogated and that the national people's assembly and other national and regional institutions were to be dissolved. In June a 153-member legislative higher council of the republic was established under N'Kombo's chairmanship, in order to supervise the implementation of these measures, pending the adoption of a new constitution and the holding of elections. In the same month the prime minister replaced Sassou-Nguesso as head of government, and the country reverted to the name Republic of the Congo. André Milongo, a former World Bank official without formal political affiliation, succeeded Goma as prime minister. Independent trade unions were also legalized.

In December 1991 the higher council of the republic adopted a draft constitution, which provided for legislative power to be vested in an elected national assembly and senate and for executive power to be held by an elected president. A reshuffle of cabinet posts was announced at the end of December.

In mid-January 1992, following a reorganization of senior army posts by the prime minister, members of the army, who were reported to be supporters of Sassou-Nguesso, occupied strategic positions in Brazzaville and demanded the reinstatement of military personnel who had allegedly been dismissed because of their ethnic affiliations, the removal of the newly appointed secretary of state for defence and payment of overdue salaries. The government rejected these demands, whereupon the mutinous soldiers demanded Milongo's resignation as prime minister. Armed clashes in Brazzaville at that time between government supporters and mutinous troops resulted in at least five civilian deaths. The crisis was resolved when the secretary of state for defence resigned, and Milongo agreed to reorganize the council of ministers, substantially reducing it in size and appointing a candidate preferred by the army as minister of defence. Milongo appointed himself supreme chief of the armed forces.

Electoral Discord

The draft constitution was approved by 96.3% of those who voted at a referendum in March 1992. In late May Milongo appointed a new cabinet, whose membership was drawn from each of the country's regions, in order to avoid domination by any one ethnic group. Elections to the new national assembly took place in late June and mid-July. The Union panafricaine pour la démocratie sociale (UPADS) became the majority party, winning 39 of the 125 contested seats, followed by the Mouvement congolais pour la démocratie et le développement intégral (MCDDI), with 29 seats, and the PCT (18 seats). At elections to the senate, held on 26 July, the UPADS again won a majority (23) of the contested seats (60), followed by the MCDDI, with 13 seats. In August, Pascal Lissouba, the leader of the UPADS and a former prime minister, won 36% and 61% of the votes respectively at two rounds of presidential elections, defeating Bernard Kolelas, the leader of the MCDDI, and President Sassou-Nguesso. Lissouba, whose election campaign had promised the devolution of power from Brazzaville to the regions and the continued implementation of economic reforms, was inaugurated as president at the end of August. At the beginning of September he appointed Maurice-Stéphane Bongho-Nouarra (a member of the UPADS) as prime minister, with a mandate to form a coalition government based on a UPADS–PCT parliamentary alliance. However, shortly after a new cabinet had been named, the PCT terminated the pact, on the grounds that Lissouba had not given it as many ministerial posts as he had promised. The PCT then formed an alliance with the Union pour le renouveau démocratique (URD), a new grouping of seven parties, including the MCDDI. The URD–PCT alliance, which now had a majority of seats in parliament, demanded the right to form a new administration and, at the end of October, won a vote of no confidence in the government. In mid-November Bongho-Nouarra announced the resignation of his government. Soon afterwards President Lissouba, in defiance of demands by the URD–PCT, dissolved the national assembly and announced that new legislative elections would be held in 1993. In response, the URD–PCT coalition commenced a protest campaign of civil disobedience. In early December the chief of staff of the armed forces intervened and, with the barely veiled threat of a military take-over in the background, demanded that the two sides form a transitional government, pending the holding of the fresh parliamentary elections. Claude Antoine Dacosta, a former FAO and World Bank official, was appointed prime minister of the new transitional administration.

INTERNAL CONFRONTATION

At the first round of legislative elections, which took place in early May 1993, the Mouvance présidentielle, comprising the UPADS and its allies, won 62 of the 125 seats in the national assembly, while the URD–PCT coalition secured 49. Protesting that serious electoral irregularities had occurred, the URD–PCT refused to contest the second round of elections in early June (for seats where a clear majority had not been achieved in the first round) and demanded that some of the first-round polls should be repeated. At the second round the Mouvance présidentielle secured an absolute majority (69) of seats in the national assembly. In late June Lissouba appointed a new cabinet, with ex-president Yhombi-Opango as prime minister. During June Bernard Kolelas, the MCDDI leader and chairman of the URD–PCT coalition, nominated a rival cabinet and urged his supporters to force the government to call new elections by means of a campaign of civil disobedience. However, the political crisis soon precipitated violent conflict between armed militias, representing party political and ethnic interests, and the security forces (many of whom were themselves affiliated to the various militias). At the end of June the supreme court ruled that electoral irregularities had occurred at the first round of elections. In mid-July Lissouba declared a state of emergency. In late July the government and the opposition negotiated a truce, and in early August, following mediation by the OAU, France and President Bongo of Gabon, the two sides agreed that the disputed first-round election results should be examined by a committee of impartial international arbitrators and that the second round of elections should be restaged. (The second round already held was consequently annulled by the supreme court). The state of emergency was revoked in mid-August.

Following the repeated second round of legislative elections, which took place at the beginning of October 1993, the Mouvance présidentielle, which secured 65 seats, retained its overall majority in the national assembly. (Therefore the cabinet that had been appointed in June, with Yhombi-Opango as prime minister, remained unchanged.) The URD–PCT, which had amassed 57 seats, agreed to participate in the new assembly. In November, however, confrontations between armed militias, affiliated to political parties, and the security forces erupted once again. During the second half of 1993 activities by militias resulted in serious social and economic disruption and, reportedly, at least 2,000 deaths. A cease-fire was eventually agreed by the Mouvance présidentielle and the opposition at the end of January 1994, although fighting continued to erupt sporadically throughout 1994 and 1995.

In February 1994 the committee of international arbitrators, which had been investigating the conduct of the first round of legislative elections held in May 1993, ruled that the results in eight constituencies were unlawful. In September six opposition parties, including Sassou-Nguesso's PCT, formed an alliance, the Forces démocratiques unies (FDU), under the chairmanship of Sassou-Nguesso. The alliance, which was affiliated with the URD, comprised about 15 members of the national assembly, who, it was reported, came mainly from the north of the country, where Sassou-Nguesso enjoyed greatest support. In November, following mounting anti-government protests by both trade union members and students (owing to arrears in payments of, respectively, salaries and scholarships), Lissouba accused unnamed neighbouring countries of attempting to foment unrest in the Congo—a comment widely believed to refer to Zaire.

Coalition Politics

In early December 1994 the government announced its intention to re-form as a coalition administration, including members of the opposition, in the near future. At the end of the month, following the holding of reconciliation talks between the government and the opposition under the auspices of a Central African forum for culture and peace, a co-ordinating body was established to oversee the disarmament of the opposition militias and the restoration of judicial authority. Meanwhile, Lissouba and the two main opposition leaders—Sassou-Nguesso and Kolelas—signed an agreement which sought an end to hostilities between their respective supporters. In early January 1995 the chairman of the national defence committee, Gen. Raymond Ngollo, announced that 2,000 places would be allocated in the national army for opposition militia, as soon as their units (reported to number at least 3,000 personnel) were finally disbanded. In mid-January the government resigned and, later in that month, a new coalition council of ministers was appointed, including members of the MCDDI and headed by Yhombi-Opango. The FDU, however, refused to participate in the new administration. Some 12 parliamentary deputies defected from the majority UPADS in protest at the lack of representation for south-western Congolese in the newly-appointed council of ministers; they subsequently established a new party, the Union pour la République, which remained affiliated to the Mouvance présidentielle.

During early 1995 by-elections were contested for seven seats in the national assembly (outstanding since the partially annulled elections of May 1993): five were won by opposition parties and two by the UPADS. In March 1995 the government announced the introduction of measures to restrain state expenditure, including significant reductions in the salaries of government members and a substantial decrease in the number of civil service personnel, in order to secure assistance from the IMF. The Lissouba administration banned all public demonstrations in August, in order to restrict anti-government protest activities by trade unions. In the following month the national assembly approved legislation which curtailed the freedom of the press, providing for a five-year term of imprisonment for journalists, printing houses and newspaper distributers convicted of libel, and prohibiting media coverage of libel cases, except where permission had previously been granted by the ministry of justice.

In October 1995 the government announced the impending restructuring of the armed forces with the stated aim of achieving a more balanced representation of ethnic and regional interests. In late December political parties from the Mouvance présidentielle and opposition groupings signed a peace pact which required the imminent disarmament of all party militias and the integration into the national security forces of 1,200 former militia members. In February 1996 about 100 soldiers who had previously belonged to militias staged a short-lived mutiny, in order to demand improved pay and conditions; five people were reportedly killed during the unrest. Later in that month the FDU suspended the integration of its militia associates into the national armed forces, claiming that the pact agreed in December 1995 favoured pro-government militias, while under-representing those affiliated to opposition organizations. In mid-March 1996 the government agreed to increase the quota of opposition recruits into the security forces and, consequently, the integration of FDU-affiliated militia members resumed. However, activities by armed militia groups continued to be reported. In August, following a local political dispute, some 200 armed militia men professing allegiance to the FDU occupied a small town in central Congo for several days.

In early May 1996 Lissouba inaugurated a national census commission, comprising representatives of the government and political organizations, as well as members of the general public and foreign advisers, which was to draw up the electoral rolls for the next presidential elections, scheduled to take place in July and August 1997. The URD declined to be represented on the commission, protesting that the body was insufficiently independent of government interests. In July 1996 the national assembly approved legislation which required all independent newspaper and periodical publishers to obtain a commercial licence. A government decree was issued in August banning all as yet unlicensed publications. In late August Yhombi-Opango resigned as prime minister; he was replaced shortly afterwards by David Charles Ganao, the leader of the Union des forces démocratiques and a former minister of foreign affairs. In early September Ganao appointed an expanded council of ministers, including representatives of the URD. The Ganao administration undertook to continue with the implementation of an economic reform programme which had been agreed with the IMF in June. In early October elections were held for 23 of the 60 seats in the senate. The Mouvance présidentielle retained its majority, winning 12 of the seats, while opposition organizations took 10 seats and one seat was secured by an independent candidate.

In January 1997 Sassou-Nguesso returned to the Congo for the first time since 1995; it was widely assumed that he was complying with the requirement that prospective presidential candidates be present in the country at the beginning of February; he did not, however, formally declare his candidature until 5 June. The government's decentralization programme suffered a set-back in February, when the supreme court ruled that the *de facto* establishment of almost 100 community councils was unconstitutional, on the grounds that they had only limited autonomy, their members being appointed and dismissed by central government officials rather than being elected by universal suffrage; however, the court suspended the implementation of the decision to dissolve the councils, with the stated wish of avoiding government embarrassment and the risk of social unrest.

During 1994–96 some 4,000 militia members had been integrated into the defence and security forces. In early 1997 divisions remained apparent, as a number of mutinies and protests erupted, predominantly among newly recruited military personnel affiliated to the Mouvance présidentielle. In February former militiamen blockaded the Congo-Océan railway for several days, and disconnected regional electricity supplies. Their demands, for immediate integration into the regular army at the rank of sergeant and for the dismissal of the commander of their training camp, were subsequently met by Lissouba; the mutineers themselves went unpunished. Opposition politicians accused Lissouba of political and ethnic favouritism, when, in April and May, he likewise acceded to the demands of further groups of protestors, by dismissing several high-ranking officers (northerners installed during the Sassou-Nguesso period), including the commander of the Congolese navy.

Factional Violence

In a memorandum dated February 1997, 19 opposition parties (including the PCT and the MCDDI) called for the expedited establishment of republican institutions, the free movement of people and goods, and a more balanced access to the media and to public funds; in the short term, they also requested, as matters of urgency, the establishment of an independent electoral commission, the disarmament of civilians, and the deployment of a multinational peace-keeping force, on the basis that the continued existence of armed militias was otherwise likely to lead to violence on the scale of that of 1993–94. The government met none of these demands. In March 1997 a multinational force of about 1,000 troops was stationed in Brazzaville, to provide if necessary for the evacuation of foreign nationals from Kinshasa (Zaire); following the largely bloodless capture of that city in May by forces supporting Laurent-Désiré Kabila, the force was disbanded, although about 300 French troops remained in Brazzaville.

In May 1997 skirmishes in the northern towns of Owando and Oyo between supporters of Sassou-Nguesso and Yhombi-Opango resulted in a number of deaths; on 5 June security forces sent to arrest those responsible for the violence surrounded the residence of Sassou-Nguesso, and shots were fired. On 31 May a code of conduct had been generally adopted prior to the forthcoming elections (the first round of which was scheduled for 27 July). None the less, localized exchanges of fire (which each side alleged that the other had instigated) swiftly developed into a widespread conflict along ethnic and political lines between militia groups and opposing factions within the regular armed forces. Barricades were erected in Brazzaville, and the city was split effectively into three zones: those districts (primarily in the north) controlled by supporters of Sassou-Nguesso, districts (mostly in the south) controlled by supporters of Lissouba, and the riverside suburb of Bacongo, controlled by militiamen loyal to Kolelas. Despite efforts to mediate led by Kolelas at a national level and, on behalf of the international community, by Omar Bongo, the president of Gabon, and Muhammad Sahnoun, the joint UN-OAU special representative to the Great Lakes region, none of the numerous cease-fires signed in June led to more than a brief lull in hostilities. It was reported that both sides were systematically killing civilians assumed to belong to rival ethnic groups, allegations that both sides denied. French troops (substantially reinforced) meanwhile assisted in the evacuation of foreign residents from Brazzaville; in mid-June they themselves departed, despite mediators' requests that they remain to protect the civilian population and to try to prevent futher hostilities.

On 19 June 1997 Lissouba established a constitutional council, apparently in order to have it extend by 90 days his presidential mandate, which had been due to expire on 31 August. On 23 June troops loyal to Sassou-Nguesso directed artillery fire towards the national assembly building, where the constitutional council was due to be sworn in; Lissouba subsequently petitioned the constitutional court to postpone elections and extend his presidential mandate.

On 13 July 1997 a cease-fire was signed which failed to prevent sporadic violence from continuing; however, on 16 July an accord was reached between Lissouba and Sassou-Nguesso, and it was reported that fighting had generally ceased. On the following day, representatives of the two sides arrived in Libreville (Gabon) for further talks. Between 1,000 and 3,000 people were estimated to have been killed during June and early July 1997, while many more left their homes for the relative sanctuary of Bacongo, or fled the capital altogether.

FOREIGN RELATIONS

France, the former colonial power, is the source of more than one-half of total assistance to the Republic of Congo, the major supplier of imports and the primary business partner in the extraction of petroleum. After the mid-1970s the Congo moved away from the sphere of influence of the former USSR, fostering links with France, with neighbouring francophone countries, and also with the USA and the People's Republic of China. Nevertheless, Cuban troops were stationed in the Congo from 1977 until April 1991. In 1988 the Congo mediated in negotiations between Angola, Cuba, South Africa and the USA, which resulted in the signing, in December, of the Brazzaville accord, regarding the withdrawal of Cuban troops from Angola and progress towards Namibian independence. Diplomatic relations with the Republic of Korea (severed in 1964) were restored in

June 1990, and relations with Israel (broken off in 1973) were resumed in August 1991. The Congo established diplomatic relations with South Africa in March 1993. Relations with the Democratic Republic of the Congo came under strain in June 1997, when a number of shells fired from Brazzaville exploded in Kinshasa.

Economy

EDITH HODGKINSON

For several years after independence in 1960 a systematic policy of state participation in productive enterprise was pursued, but the private sector was permitted to continue its activities, especially in mining, forestry and transport. During the early 1970s, however, President Ngouabi introduced the policy of 'scientific socialism'. All public services and transport systems were nationalized and more government control introduced throughout the economy. Upon becoming head of state in 1977, Joachim Yhombi-Opango emphasized that the Congo needed a 'mixed' economy and would benefit from the expertise which private investment could provide. Under his successor, Sassou-Nguesso, who ousted him two years later, foreign management consortia were introduced to restructure seriously inefficient nationalized companies, while the petroleum sector was further opened to private foreign investment. In 1989, formally acknowledging the failure of the public sector to stimulate economic growth, the government of Sassou-Nguesso implemented a new policy of economic liberalization, including revised taxation procedures intended to foster private-sector activity (notably through the even application of value-added tax). However, economic restructuring was only undertaken on a sustained basis under the Lissouba government, following the devaluation of the CFA franc and reconciliation with the opposition; in May 1994 President Lissouba's government and the IMF agreed on a programme of economic restructuring and retrenchment: this envisaged the privatization of the major public-sector industries (including rail, air and water transport, electricity, the petroleum industry and postal services) and a substantial reduction in the number of civil service personnel. The transformation in government policy was reflected in a statement by the prime minister in July 1995 that the role of the state should be only regulatory, allowing maximum freedom for private-sector activity. Moreover, in the disposal of public-sector enterprises, whose failure was explicitly recognized, Congolese and foreign investors were to compete on equal terms. Substantial implementation of the programme began early in 1995, with reductions in public salaries and redundancies in the civil service (which was reduced in size from 85,000 to some 70,000 by 1996). On the basis of both intentions stated and actual progress achieved on economic liberalization and budgetary stabilization, the Congo received approval from the IMF for an enhanced structural adjustment facility (ESAF), providing concessionary funding over the medium term, in June 1996. However, further restructuring of the civil service was jeopardized by renewed political violence in mid-1997.

Partly as a result of Brazzaville's former position as the capital of French Equatorial Africa, and partly because the Congo and Oubangui rivers have long provided the main access to the Central African Republic (CAR) and Chad, the Republic of Congo's economic structure has evolved rather differently from that of most countries of comparable levels of economic development; transport, services and administration in particular have been significantly more important. These sectors accounted for 43.3% of gross domestic product (GDP) in 1994, while close to 60% of the population reside in urban areas, principally in Brazzaville. The next most significant sector is mining (mainly petroleum, which is the country's principal export commodity): the sector, which was of negligible importance at independence, accounted for around one-quarter of GDP in 1993. The petroleum sector accounted for 34.5% of GDP in 1994. About one-third of the country's inhabitants are dependent on agriculture and forestry. Despite the development of commercial agriculture, this sector contributed only 10.8% to GDP in 1994. Manufacturing developed relatively well at an early stage, partly to serve the markets of the CAR and Chad. Subsequently, however, its performance has been disappointing, to which inefficient management in the public sector, increased competition for industry among the member countries of the Union douanière et économique de l'Afrique centrale (UDEAC), and ill-advised investments have all contributed. The manufacturing sector accounted for only 6.4% of GDP in 1994.

Economic growth has fluctuated widely in the recent past. The mid- and late 1970s saw overall stagnation, and decline in some sectors, as output of petroleum fell and production of potash ceased altogether. However, improved output of petroleum, from 1979 onwards, coincided with increases in international prices for that commodity, thus stimulating very high rates of investment by both the public sector and the petroleum companies, as well as strong GDP growth. The collapse of world petroleum prices in 1986 had severe repercussions throughout the economy, initially most acutely felt in major cuts in government spending. GDP initially fell (by 6.8% in 1986) and only slowly recovered over the next few years, with the rise in most years below the rate of population growth. Political turmoil led to a 1% fall in GDP in 1993, and the decline deepened in 1994, to 5.5%, because of the impact on domestic demand of the 50% devaluation of the CFA franc in January of that year. The record was slightly better in 1995, when GDP was estimated to have risen by 0.9%. Provisional government figures for 1996 put GDP growth at 6.8%; this positive trend may well have been undermined by destruction and looting in Brazzaville in mid-1997, although the petroleum sector, based at Pointe-Noire, was substantially unaffected.

Over the longer term, the devaluation of the CFA franc was expected to enhance export competitiveness, particularly for primary products, and also to stimulate domestic import-substitution, particularly in the manufacturing sector, as a result of the substantial rise in import costs. However, the price competitiveness of the country's petroleum exports has not been enhanced by the devaluation, as petroleum prices are denominated in US dollars and determined in the international market. Government estimates of an increase in the GDP growth rate of some 6.8% in 1996 were based largely on the 17% rise in oil production brought about by the Nkossa field coming on stream.

AGRICULTURE AND FORESTRY

Since the early 1970s the agricultural sector has suffered from relative neglect, hasty nationalizations and the abandonment of farmwork in favour of salaried employment in the towns. Cash crops are much less important as exports than minerals or timber, and the country is far from self-sufficient in food. With the exception of palm products, sugar and tobacco, which are grown on modern plantations (particularly in the south-western Niari valley), most agricultural crops are grown by families on small farms. In 1971 'Operation Manioc' was launched, which aimed to make the country self-sufficient in cassava, its staple food crop; 9,000 ha were cultivated on state farms, but most of these were poorly managed and required subsidy; many have now been sold to the private sector. During 1995–97 some 20 white South African farmers settled in the Niari valley as employees of the Niari Valley Industrial and Agricultural Co (SAIVN), which had been created in 1995 by the South African Development Co in partnership with the Congolese state. The farmers were to use their agricultural expertise in working the 80,000 ha of arable land and pastures in the valley owned by bankrupt parastatals. However, much of this land had not yet been transferred to SAIVN by 1997, reportedly because of local animosity towards the South Africans, and because the land could not be sold at a price that enabled redundancy payments to be made to former employees. In 1995, according to estimates from the FAO, output of cassava reached 630,000 metric tons and that of maize totalled an estimated 26,000 tons. Secondary food crops are plantains, yams and sweet potatoes. According to the FAO, total food crop production in 1995 was 5.9% higher than the average level in 1989–91; however, food crop production per head decreased by 8.8% during the same period.

Export crops contribute very little to foreign earnings. Sugar cane and tobacco have traditionally been the most important cash crops, with exports going almost wholly to other UDEAC countries. In 1978 the sugar industry was put under the control of a state corporation, the Sucrerie du Congo (SUCO). This enterprise had a troubled history, and was replaced in 1991 by a joint venture between the government and a French company. Plantations were reorganized and re-equipped, allowing them to satisfy domestic demand. According to the International Sugar Organization, production of raw sugar increased steadily from 20,000 tons in 1991 to 29,000 tons in 1995. In 1995 plans were announced to revive tobacco production, which had almost ceased during the 1980s; it was hoped that an annual output of 100 tons would be achieved by 2000.

Other export crops include cocoa, coffee and oil palm. Both cocoa and coffee output have been in decline in recent years, the former falling from 2,305 tons in 1987/88 to only around 300 tons per year in 1991/92 and 1992/93, and the latter declining from an annual average of some 2,300 tons in the 1980s to only 632 tons in 1992/93. Both crops were adversely affected by the closure of the government marketing agency, but higher local currency prices consequent on the January 1994 devaluation of the CFA franc, in a liberalized environment, and the rise in world prices brought a sharp improvement in coffee production in 1994/95, at some 1,200 tons, with the prospect of another rise in 1995/96. Palm oil output increased from only 1,093 tons in 1984 to an estimated 17,000 tons in 1991, as the area under cultivation in state-owned plantations expanded. Plans were announced in 1994 for rubber cultivation, both on large industrial plantations and on small farms around villages; output of some 20,000 tons per year was envisaged.

Animal husbandry has developed slowly, owing to the prevalence of the tsetse fly and the importance of the forestry sector, which has restricted the availability of pasture. Although numbers of livestock are increasing, the country is not self-sufficient in meat and dairy products. Fishing is not well developed but is carried out commercially on a small scale, especially for tuna. The total fish catch was about 37,000 tons in 1994.

Forestry

Forests cover about 55% of the Congo's total area and are a significant natural resource. Forestry is a major economic activity and timber was the main export until it was superseded by petroleum in the mid-1970s. Exploitation began at the coast and penetrated inland following the line of the Congo-Océan railway. There is further activity in the Congo basin from where rough timber is floated out. Until 1987 the purchase and sale of logs was a monopoly of the state-owned Office Congolaise des Bois, although 95% of production was carried out by the private sector, with foreign companies accounting for 58% of the total in 1984. The exploitation by foreign investors of forest resources in the north of the country is being encouraged, while the more accessible but heavily depleted southern forests have been reserved for local interests. It is hoped that the ending of the state monopoly over the marketing of timber, the inauguration of new concessions in the north and improvements in the transport infrastructure will eventually stimulate further increases in both production and exports of timber. The principal woods exploited are okoumé, limba and sapele.

Output of timber averaged about 393,000 cu m in the late 1980s, but declined during the early 1990s, to some 167,000 cu m in 1993. The fall in production reflected adverse developments in the export market, notably pressure from environmentalists in western Europe against the use of rainforest timber. Exports in 1993, at some 168,000 cu m, were less than one-half of the 1988 level. There was a marked improvement in both output and exports (to some 225,000 cu m) in 1994, reflecting the boost to competitiveness derived from the devaluation of the CFA franc in January of that year. Meanwhile, a forestry conservation programme is being supported by aid from the World Bank and the UNDP. The government is attempting to relieve the pressure on virgin forest by requiring forestry companies to replant and by increasing plantation production, in part to serve local demand for fuel wood. There are substantial plantations of eucalyptus in the south-west of the country, with the Unité d'afforestation industrielle du Congo alone owning some 25,000 ha.

MINING AND ENERGY

Until the 1970s mining was of little significance, with mineral exports accounting for less than 5% of total exports in 1969. By 1984, however, mineral sales provided 90% of export earnings and mining contributed 43% of GDP, reflecting the development of the hydrocarbons sector, which is the only significant mining activity. Although the petroleum sector's contribution to GDP has since declined, it still dominates export earnings, accounting for 85.3% of the total in 1994.

Production of petroleum has fluctuated since onshore deposits were discovered, at Pointe-Indienne, in 1957. In 1971, when these deposits were almost exhausted, new offshore oilfields were discovered, and their subsequent development has maintained production levels. The Emeraude field went into production in 1972, Loango in 1977, Likouala in 1980, Sendji Marine in 1981, Yanga in 1982, Tchibouela in 1987, Zatchi Marine in 1988 and Nkossa in 1996. Development of the offshore fields has been carried out by Elf Congo and AGIP Recherches Congo, which together account for 98% of the Congo's petroleum production. Annual output increased from 2m.–3m. tons in the late 1970s to 7.04m. tons in 1988, and to 9.04m. tons in 1994. Expansion is likely to be maintained throughout the 1990s, with output of 13m. tons forecast for 2000, with operations due to commence at AGIP's Kitina field in 1997 and at Elf's Tchibouela Est field by 1999. These projections do not take into account the potential exploitation of some 600m. tons of heavy viscous oil at the Emeraude field, which would require expensive recovery procedures. In 1996 the Congo had about 140m. tons of proven reserves of heavy viscous oil, of which 55m. tons were at Nkossa.

In accordance with its continuing programme of privatization, the government has been reducing its stake in the petroleum industry. In 1990 the monopoly of the state-owned Société nationale de recherches et d'exploitation pétrolière (HYDRO-CONGO) over the distribution of petroleum products in the Congo was ended. In 1995 the government sold its 25% share in Elf Congo to the French company Elf Aquitaine, which previously held 75% of the share capital and its 20% share in AGIP Recherches Congo to the majority shareholder, Italy's AGIP. Similarly HYDRO-CONGO's 60% stake in the 1m.-ton capacity petroleum refinery at Pointe-Noire, a joint venture with Elf, is due to be taken over by Elf and Shell, as are the state company's distribution activities, under an agreement signed in late 1996. Deposits of natural gas are exploited at Pointe-Indienne. Production reached 15m. cu m in 1977, but production is almost all flared.

Lead, zinc, gold and copper are produced in small quantities, and deposits of phosphate and bauxite are known. In 1985 the Congo and Gabon signed an agreement for joint exploitation of the High Ivingo iron ore deposits (estimated at about 1,000m. tons), but the implementation of this scheme will require substantial external funds, together with an improvement in the international market for iron ore.

Production and distribution of electricity have been in the hands of a state-owned corporation, the Société Nationale d'Electricité, since 1967, but this is due to be transferred to a private concession. Total generating capacity was 149 MW in 1990, mainly from the hydroelectric stations on the Bouenza (74 MW) and Djoué (15 MW). A major hydroelectric plant is planned at the confluence of the Kouillou and Niari rivers, with a projected capacity of 1,000 MW.

MANUFACTURING

Manufacturing is concerned mainly with the processing of agricultural and forest products and most of the industry is in Brazzaville, Pointe-Noire and N'Kayi. Many of the larger manufacturing companies are state-owned. However, several have been transferred to private ownership, or closed down, in accordance with the country's pledges to the IMF.

The industrial development of the 1970s and 1980s had little success. A cement plant was established at Loutété in 1968, reached its peak output in 1971, but subsequently showed a sharp fall in production, despite strong demand from construction programmes. The plant closed in 1985, reopened, and then ceased production again in 1987, because of cash-flow problems. In 1988 the company's assets were transferred to a new, partly Norwegian-owned, concern.

The textile industry is represented by two operations, a textile complex at Kinsoundi, which was established in 1968, and a textile printing works, using both local and imported cloth, which was inaugurated in Brazzaville in 1975. A long-standing project for the construction of a plant to produce paper pulp, with an annual production capacity of 290,000 tons, was abandoned because of a lack of foreign finance, and newly-developed eucalyptus plantations have been used instead to supply a telegraph-pole and charcoal factory, production at which commenced in 1988. A French company bought a 25% stake in the factory in 1990, and as the area under eucalyptus is being expanded, there is a possibility that the original plan will be revived.

TRANSPORT

The Congo plays an important role in the trans-equatorial transport system (formerly operated on an inter-state basis) which links Chad, the CAR and parts of Cameroon and Gabon with the Atlantic coast; all of the rail and much of the river portion of the system is located in the Congo. The deep-water port at Pointe-Noire is the terminus of this network, and is central Africa's second most important gateway, after Douala in Cameroon. In 1986 it handled 9.5m. tons of freight, including 5.4m. tons of petroleum, some 552,100 tons of timber (most of this extracted in the CAR and floated downstream to the smaller port of Brazzaville, from which it is transported by rail to Pointe-Noire), and about 2.46m. tons of manganese ore from Gabon; transportation of Gabonese manganese ore has now ceased. The river system (in all some 5,000 km is navigable) is also of great significance as a transport artery throughout the country, reaching areas that would otherwise be isolated (particularly in the north).

Some 60%–70% of the traffic on the 515-km Congo-Océan railway (which links Pointe-Noire and Brazzaville, where it connects with transport services on the Congo river) is of an international nature. In the 1970s the saturation of the existing railway capacity and the constraint that this represented on the further development of timber exports prompted a major scheme to increase capacity by two-fifths. Work on realignment was completed in 1985. With the acquisition of new rolling stock, the railway increased its freight handling to 1.4m. tons (excluding manganese) in 1986, compared with 1.15m. tons in 1984. Congo-Océan Railways is scheduled for privatization.

Other transport facilities, and especially the road network, are little developed, owing to the great distances and dense equatorial forest. Large areas in the north of the country have no road access. Only about 10% of the total 12,745 km of roads and tracks are asphalted. During the 1980s a project was initiated to construct a long-distance all-weather road from Ouesso, in the north, to Port Rousset and Brazzaville, crossed by another road between Belinga, in Gabon, and Bangui, in the CAR, but pressure from environmental groups may deter donors from financing any future road improvement projects in the north of the country. In general, poor communications continue to constitute a major obstacle to economic development. There are international airports at Brazzaville and Pointe-Noire, as well as 37 smaller airfields.

DEVELOPMENT PLANNING

For two decades, from 1964 on, the government organized its capital spending under successive five-year development plans, drawing heavily on rising oil income to finance projects in infrastructure, agriculture and the state industrial sector. Consequently, the plunge in petroleum prices in the final year of the 1982–86 plan precipitated a budgetary crisis (see below) and forced the government to turn to the IMF. As part of the structural adjustment plan designed to restore balance to public finances, the launch of the next five-year plan was postponed, while an 'interim investment programme' (envisaging reduced levels of expenditure) was formulated for 1987 and 1988. Only in 1989 was the government able to draw up a further medium-term development plan, covering the period 1990–94. The plan emphasized the reduction of the economy's dependence on petroleum and the public sector, by stimulating primary production (farming, forestry and fishing) and the reform of the parastatal organizations. However, the political unrest of 1990–93 severely disrupted the programme's implementation. The resolution of the political turmoil in early 1994, coinciding with the devaluation of the CFA franc, formed the background to a new economic and social recovery plan, which restated the objectives of the earlier programme, and which was supported by the IMF through an ESAF awarded in June 1996.

The rise in petroleum taxes and royalties from 1978 onwards (at some 110,000m. francs CFA, they constituted 70% of budget revenue in 1981) stimulated a sharp rise in budget development spending at the beginning of the 1980s. This increased seventeenfold between 1979–83, and formed the basis of the rapid growth in the economy at the beginning of the 1980s. The fall in petroleum revenues in 1986 threatened almost to double the budget deficit, which was bloated by recent rises in the public sector payroll as a result of the oil boom and by the losses incurred by state-owned enterprises. As a result, both current and capital spending were severely cut back. The reduction in current spending was to be achieved by means of a wide range of measures, including a 'freeze' on government salaries (the payroll had been increasing steadily during the early 1980s) and the rationalization (including sale to private interests) of several state-owned companies, whose losses had depleted budget resources. In 1987 further substantial reductions were made in current and capital spending, with the latter totalling less than one-half of its level in 1984. However, the deficit continued to rise in both 1987 and 1988, owing to the contraction in the economy and despite further reductions in capital spending. Some progress was achieved in 1989, when the deficit was reduced by around one-third.

The sharp rise in petroleum revenues in 1990 (owing to the rise in international prices which followed the invasion and annexation of Kuwait by Iraq in that year) allowed a further narrowing of the deficit and enabled the government to repay some of its substantial debt arrears. Under the stabilization programme agreed with the IMF in 1990, the government was to reduce the deficit by imposing further restrictions on both current and capital spending, and by selling its interests in all but seven parastatal bodies (classified as strategic) and closing those for which there were no buyers. But with tax receipts adversely affected by political unrest and generally weaker oil prices, and debt-service costs continuing to rise, government finances remained highly dependent on foreign aid and the non-payment of liabilities. Indeed, budget deficits calculated on commitment and cash bases show quite different trends, according to the IMF. On a commitment basis (before grants), the deficit stood at 96,000m. francs CPA in 1993, rising to 140,400m. francs CFA in 1994, before decreasing to 97,300m. francs CFA in 1995. In 1993 the budget deficit on a cash basis (before grants) stood at 58,100m. francs CFA. Some progress was made in 1994, when the government managed to reduce the salary bill, and, in the wake of the CFA franc devaluation, France provided supplementary budgetary assistance. Cuts in both numbers on the public payroll and salaries resulted in a further decline in the fiscal deficit in 1995 (to an estimated 25,300m. francs CFA, from 45,400m. francs CFA in 1994). The government's plans for 1996 envisaged a further fall in the deficit; the public-sector salary bill was expected to fall again, while budget income was due to rise, owing to improved tax administration, proceeds from the start of production at the Nkossa oilfield and amendments in petroleum production-sharing agreements, which increased the government's take from 17.5% to 31%. On this basis, together with indications of a much greater commitment by the government to privatization, the Congo and the IMF were able to reach agreement on an enhanced structural adjustment facility (ESAF) during 1996. This aimed to bring the budget into surplus in 1997, through higher oil revenues, a wider tax base (with the introduction of value-added tax at 18%) and tighter controls on the public sector wage bill. Following criticisms voiced by the IMF in November 1996 regarding the continuing burden of wage payments on public finances, the budget for 1997 aimed to dismiss civil servants with falsified qualifications (an estimated 14% of public employees) and to impose systematic retirement at the age of 55, as well as increasing the repayment of debt arrears.

FOREIGN TRADE AND PAYMENTS

Whereas the Congo's foreign trade was in chronic deficit during the 1960s and 1970s, the expansion of the petroleum sector which began in the late 1970s transformed the situation. In 1978 the Congo recorded a foreign trade deficit of 24,090m. francs CFA, and in 1979 a surplus of 46,150m. With export receipts increasing from only 34,200m. francs CFA in 1978 to 552,600m. in 1984, the surplus reached 282,600m. francs CFA in that year. The fall in petroleum prices in 1986 resulted in a reduction in export earnings of more than 50%, and, although imports declined as a result of budget austerity, the trade surplus narrowed to only 50,100m. francs CFA. This, in conjunction with higher interest payments on the rapidly-escalating foreign debt, prompted a sharp deterioration in the current account of the balance of payments, from a surplus of US $210m. in 1984 to a deficit of $601m. in 1986. The current account has since remained in deficit, with movements largely reflecting trends on the merchandise account. A good level of petroleum earnings, and the impact of austerity measures on the demand for imports, combined to narrow the deficit to $85m. in 1989, but the trend began to deteriorate in 1992, with the current account registering a deficit of $793m. in 1994. In that year there was, however, some improvement in the overall balance of payments position, owing to inflows of official funds in the aftermath of the CFA franc devaluation. This led to some recovery in foreign exchange reserves; these stood at $49.63m. at the end of 1994, compared with $0.68m. at the end of 1993. In 1995, aided by the improvement in the trade balance, the current account deficit fell to $570m., whilst foreign exchange reserves rose to $58.52m.

In recent years the Congo has received considerable amounts of foreign aid. Net inflows of official development assistance from OECD countries and multilateral agencies averaged US $179m. per year in 1990–95. France has been by far the most important source, with an annual average of $129.7m., boosted by exceptional disbursements in 1990 (net $169.3m.) and again in 1994 ($227.2m.). While borrowing (as distinct from grants) from official creditors (multilateral and bilateral) expanded only slowly in the early 1980s, borrowing from private creditors rose sharply, mainly reflecting the expansion in imports, and exceeded that from official sources, to give an external debt of $3,031m. at the end of 1985. This was equivalent to 157% of the country's gross national product (GNP) in that year. The cost of servicing the debt was equivalent to one quarter of the country's foreign earnings in both 1983 and 1984, and to one-third in 1985—a very substantial burden, which necessitated a rescheduling of the debt. This was accorded after the Congo received IMF approval in 1986 for its structural adjustment programme designed to remedy the budgetary crisis. Debt liabilities falling due in 1985–87 were rescheduled over a 10-year period. Further reschedulings gave relief for 1988 and 1989. However, the external debt had risen to $4,095m. by the end of 1988, or 215% of GNP, making the Congo the most heavily indebted African nation (on a per caput basis). The debt-service ratio was 45%, a dangerously high level in view of the government's practice of borrowing against future petroleum earnings. Further debt relief and additional funds were essential. In order to secure such concessions, the Congo entered negotiations for a new structural adjustment programme with the IMF and the World Bank in 1989. Although finalization was delayed by slow progress in reducing the fiscal deficit (as previously agreed), and hence by the need for additional foreign assistance, a programme of support by external donors, led by France, was operational by mid-1990. These funds enabled the Congo to pay off some of its debt arrears, notably to the World Bank, permitting a resumption of lending. However, debt service payments increased once more, to a total of $531m. in 1990. Foreign indebtedness fluctuated slightly in the following three years, before reaching a new high of $6,032m. in 1995, equivalent to almost four times the country's GNP (at the new US $: CFA franc parity). After the massive debt relief accorded in the wake of the CFA franc devaluation (a total of $989m. was rescheduled), debt-service payments were reduced to $181m. in 1995, representing a debt-service to exports ratio of 14.4%, compared with $557m. (54.2%) in 1994. But this apparent improvement was largely the consequence of the non-payment of liabilities: arrears at the end of 1995 had increased to $1,141m. from $1,075m. at the end of 1994. With the Congo clearly unable to sustain its debt burden, and, following the devaluation of the CFA franc, with the World Bank having accorded least developed status to the country, a new round of debt relief was extended in 1996, subsequent to IMF approval of an ESAF. Bilateral official creditors granted 'Naples terms' on all liabilities incurred before 1986 (involving write-offs, interest rate reductions and reschedulings equivalent, in all, to a two-thirds reduction in debt). In addition, debts incurred by the Lissouba government to a US petroleum company through the advance payment of oil revenue (a device to which the previous administration had often had recourse) was settled, although there remained some $560m. in petroleum-secured debt to be cleared.

Statistical Survey

Source (unless otherwise stated): Centre National de la Statistique et des Etudes Economiques, Ministère de l'Economie, du Plan et des Finances, BP 2093, Brazzaville; tel. 81-06-20; telex 5210.

Area and Population

AREA, POPULATION AND DENSITY

Area (sq km)	342,000*
Population (census results)	
7 February 1974	1,319,790
22 December 1984	1,843,421
Population (UN estimates at mid-year)†	
1993	2,443,000
1994	2,516,000
1995	2,590,000
Density (per sq km) at mid-1995	7.6

* 132,047 sq miles.

† Source: UN, *World Population Prospects: The 1994 Revision.*

REGIONS (estimated population at 1 January 1983)*

Brazzaville	456,383	Kouilou	78,738
Pool	219,329	Lékoumou	67,568
Pointe-Noire	214,466	Sangha	42,106
Bouenza	135,999	Nkayi	40,419
Cuvette	127,558	Likouala	34,302
Niari	114,229	Loubomo	33,591
Plateaux	110,379	**Total**	1,675,067

* Figures have not been revised to take account of the 1984 census results.

PRINCIPAL TOWNS (population at 1984 census)

Brazzaville (capital)	596,200
Pointe-Noire	298,014

BIRTHS AND DEATHS (UN estimates, annual averages)

	1980–85	1985–90	1990–95
Birth rate (per 1,000) . . .	43.9	44.3	44.7
Death rate (per 1,000) . . .	15.6	14.7	14.9

Expectation of life (UN estimates, years at birth, 1990-95): 51.3 (males 48.9; females 53.8).
Source: UN, *World Population Prospects: The 1994 Revision*.

EMPLOYMENT ('000 persons at 1984 census)

	Males	Females	Total
Agriculture, etc.	105	186	291
Industry	61	8	69
Services	123	60	183
Total	289	254	543

Mid-1995 (FAO estimates, '000 persons): Agriculture, etc. 480; Total labour force 1,077 (Source: FAO, *Production Yearbook*).

Agriculture

PRINCIPAL CROPS ('000 metric tons)

	1993	1994*	1995*
Maize*	26	26	26
Sugar cane*	320	370	440
Sweet potatoes*	22	23	24
Cassava (Manioc)	632	630	630
Yams*	14	15	16
Other roots and tubers* . . .	37	39	40
Dry beans*	5	5	5
Tomatoes*	10	10	10
Other vegetables (incl. melons)*	34	34	34
Avocados*	24	25	25
Pineapples*	12	12	12
Bananas*	43	44	44
Plantains*	90	95	95
Palm kernels*	2.7	2.7	2.7
Palm oil*	14.5	14.5	14.5
Groundnuts (in shell)* . . .	25	25	25
Coffee (green)*	1	1	1
Cocoa beans*	1	1	1
Natural rubber*	2	2	2

* FAO estimates.

Source: FAO, *Production Yearbook*.

LIVESTOCK (FAO estimates, '000 head, year ending September)

	1993	1994	1995
Cattle	67	68	68
Pigs	56	56	56
Sheep	111	111	111
Goats	305	305	305

Poultry (FAO estimates, million): 2 in 1993; 2 in 1994; 2 in 1995.

Source: FAO, *Production Yearbook*.

LIVESTOCK PRODUCTS (FAO estimates, '000 metric tons)

	1993	1994	1995
Beef and veal	2	2	2
Pig meat	3	3	3
Poultry meat	6	6	6
Other meat	12	12	12
Cows' milk	1	1	1
Hen eggs	1.2	1.2	1.2

Source: FAO, *Production Yearbook*.

Forestry

ROUNDWOOD REMOVALS ('000 cubic metres, excluding bark)

	1992	1993*	1994*
Sawlogs, veneer logs and logs for sleepers	635	635	635
Pulpwood	391	391	391
Other industrial wood* . . .	306	315	325
Fuel wood	2,156	2,222	2,288
Total	3,488	3,563	3,639

* FAO estimates.

Source: FAO, *Yearbook of Forest Products*.

SAWNWOOD PRODUCTION
('000 cubic metres, including railway sleepers)

	1992	1993	1994
Total	52	52*	52*

* FAO estimate.

Source: FAO, *Yearbook of Forest Products*.

Fishing

('000 metric tons, live weight)

	1992	1993	1994
Freshwater fishes	21.1	19.3	19.0
Common sole*	0.8	0.8	0.6
Sea catfishes*	0.7	0.6	0.5
Boe drum*	0.9	0.9	0.7
West African croakers* . . .	2.2	2.1	1.7
Sardinellas	9.5*	8.8*	10.9
Other marine fishes (incl. unspecified)*	4.4	4.1	3.3
Crustaceans*	0.4	0.3	0.3
Total catch	40.0	36.9	37.0

* FAO estimate(s).

Source: FAO, *Yearbook of Fishery Statistics*.

Mining

('000 metric tons, unless otherwise indicated)

	1992	1993*	1994*
Crude petroleum	8,654	8,710	9,158
Gold (kg)†	5	5	5

* Provisional or estimated figures.
† Data from the US Bureau of Mines, referring to the metal content of ores.

Source: UN, *Industrial Commodity Statistics Yearbook*.

Crude petroleum ('000 metric tons): 8,448 in 1995. (Source: UN, *Monthly Bulletin of Statistics*.)

Industry

SELECTED PRODUCTS ('000 metric tons, unless otherwise indicated)

	1992	1993	1994
Raw sugar	27	28	29*
Beer ('000 hectolitres)	708	759	n.a.
Soft drinks ('000 hectolitres)	294	300	n.a.
Cigarettes (metric tons)	431	n.a.	n.a.
Veneer sheets ('000 cu metres)	35	35†	35†
Soap	3.2	1.5	n.a.
Jet fuels‡	14	15	15
Motor spirit (petrol)	53	55	58‡
Kerosene	49	50‡	52‡
Distillate fuel oils	90	92†	95‡
Residual fuel oils	267	285‡	288‡
Cement	124	95	n.a.
Electric energy (million kWh)	428	431‡	435‡

* Data from the International Sugar Organization.
† Data from the FAO.
‡ Provisional figure(s).
Source: UN, *Industrial Commodity Statistics Yearbook*.

Finance

CURRENCY AND EXCHANGE RATES

Monetary Units

100 centimes = 1 franc de la Coopération financière en Afrique centrale (CFA).

French Franc, Sterling and Dollar Equivalents (31 March 1997)

1 French franc = 100 francs CFA;
£1 sterling = 924.20 francs CFA;
US $1 = 562.85 francs CFA;
1,000 francs CFA = £1.082 = $1.777.

Average Exchange Rate (francs CFA per US $)

1994 555.20
1995 499.15
1996 511.55

Note: The exchange rate of 1 French franc = 50 francs CFA, established in 1948, remained in force until January 1994, when the CFA franc was devalued by 50%, with the exchange rate adjusted to 1 French franc = 100 francs CFA.

BUDGET ('000 million francs CFA)

Revenue*	1993	1994	1995†
Petroleum revenue	93.9	138.9	131.0
Royalties	44.1	74.4	78.5
Profits tax	0.8	0.2	13.1
Dividends	49.0	64.3	39.4
Tax revenue	83.8	77.8	116.9
Taxes on income and profits	31.8	34.1	31.4
Excise duty	36.6	30.6	47.8
Domestic petroleum tax	0.1	10.3	13.0
Other indirect taxes	15.3	2.8	24.7
Other revenue	5.4	3.4	1.5
Total	183.1	220.1	249.4

Expenditure	1993	1994	1995†
Current expenditure	266.4	333.3	315.0
Wages and salaries	136.2	130.8	111.1
Local authority subsidies	7.3	11.1	4.4
Interest payments	56.1	119.0	148.9
Other current expenditure	66.8	72.3	50.6
Capital expenditure	12.7	27.3	31.6
Sub-total	279.1	360.6	346.6
Less Adjustment for payment arrears	37.9	95.1	71.9
Total (cash basis)	241.2	265.5	274.7

* Excluding grants received ('000 million francs CFA): 0.1 in 1993; 10.4 in 1994; 10.7 in 1995.
† Provisional figures.
Source: IMF, *Republic of Congo—Statistical Annex* (August 1996).

CENTRAL BANK RESERVES (US $ million at 31 December)

	1993	1994	1995
Gold*	4.42	4.21	4.29
IMF special drawing rights	0.02	0.05	0.03
Reserve position in IMF	0.64	0.68	0.75
Foreign exchange	0.68	49.63	58.52
Total	5.76	54.57	63.59

* National valuation.
Source: IMF, *International Financial Statistics*.

MONEY SUPPLY ('000 million francs CFA at 31 December)

	1993	1994	1995
Currency outside banks	53.71	69.49	81.58
Demand deposits at commercial and development banks	41.94	60.57	49.16

Source: IMF, *International Financial Statistics*.

COST OF LIVING
(Consumer Price Index for Africans in Brazzaville; base: 1964 = 100)

	1993	1994	1995
Food	179.6	265.1	282.9
Fuel and light	181.6	207.4	229.6
Clothing	276.6	357.6	430.6
Rent (incl. construction)	247.7	321.5	355.9
Healthcare	210.7	330.4	377.2
Transportation and leisure	267.7	375.1	422.6
All items	206.2	293.7	320.1

Source: IMF, *Republic of Congo—Statistical Annex* (August 1996).

NATIONAL ACCOUNTS (million francs CFA at current prices)
National Income and Product

	1986	1987	1988
Compensation of employees	264,296	253,198	245,033
Operating surplus	133,347	183,843	188,612
Domestic factor incomes	397,643	437,041	433,645
Consumption of fixed capital	156,074	164,360	144,647
Gross domestic product (GDP) at factor cost	553,717	601,401	578,292
Indirect taxes	91,444	90,790	82,358
Less Subsidies	4,754	1,668	1,686
GDP in purchasers' values	640,407	690,523	658,964
Factor income from abroad	2,781	9,333	3,112
Less Factor income paid abroad	44,717	86,030	93,328
Gross national product	598,471	613,826	568,748
Less Consumption of fixed capital	156,074	164,360	144,647
National income in market prices	442,397	449,466	424,101
Other current transfers from abroad	17,470	25,403	24,100
Less Other current transfers paid abroad	25,512	36,255	36,264
National disposable income	434,355	438,614	411,937

Source: UN, *National Accounts Statistics*.

Expenditure on the Gross Domestic Product

	1993	1994	1995*
Government final consumption expenditure	210,000	213,600	165,200
Private final consumption expenditure	391,300	531,700	586,300
Increase in stocks	400	13,800	—
Gross fixed capital formation	220,000	480,000	293,600
Total domestic expenditure	821,700	1,239,100	1,045,100
Exports of goods and services	336,900	619,400	669,000
Less Imports of goods and services	398,500	894,100	710,100
GDP in purchasers' values	760,100	964,400	1,003,900
GDP at constant 1990 prices	792,800	749,200	755,800

* Provisional figures.

Source: IMF, *Republic of Congo—Statistical Annex* (August 1996).

Gross Domestic Product by Economic Activity

	1993	1994	1995*
Agriculture, hunting, forestry and fishing	85,500	101,300	107,800
Mining and quarrying† } Manufacturing† }	245,400	397,900	410,900
Electricity, gas and water	14,900	14,200	14,800
Construction	8,000	16,800	16,100
Trade, restaurants and hotels	104,300	113,000	119,000
Transport, storage and communication	71,300	76,900	87,300
Government services	133,800	135,000	130,300
Other services	68,200	80,300	78,700
Sub-total	731,400	935,400	964,900
Import duties	28,700	29,000	39,100
GDP in purchasers' values	760,100	964,400	1,003,900

* Provisional figures.

† Includes petroleum sector (million francs CFA): 184,700 in 1993; 322,400 in 1994; 329,400 (provisional figure) in 1995.

Source: IMF, *Republic of Congo—Statistical Annex* (August 1996).

BALANCE OF PAYMENTS (US $ million)

	1993	1994	1995
Exports of goods f.o.b.	1,119.1	958.9	1,172.6
Imports of goods f.o.b.	-500.1	-612.7	-650.1
Trade balance	619.1	346.2	522.5
Exports of services	56.2	67.0	76.3
Imports of services	-845.5	-995.8	-775.1
Balance on goods and services	-170.2	-582.7	-176.3
Other income received	11.3	2.0	3.0
Other income paid	-384.9	-291.1	-399.5
Balance on goods, services and income	-543.9	-871.8	-572.8
Current transfers received	50.5	111.3	40.9
Current transfers paid	59.3	-33.0	-38.3
Current balance	-552.7	-793.4	-570.2
Investment assets	-22.6	35.5	-10.4
Investment liabilities	6.0	569.9	-69.9
Net errors and omissions	149.3	33.1	75.7
Overall balance	-420.0	-154.9	-574.8

Source: IMF, *International Financial Statistics.*

External Trade

Note: Figures exclude trade with other states of the Customs and Economic Union of Central Africa (UDEAC).

PRINCIPAL COMMODITIES (US $ '000)

Imports c.i.f.	1988	1989	1990
Fresh meat etc	14,237	9,643	16,098
Fish and fish preparations	19,927	17,806	18,523
Wheat flour	11,410	12,790	12,819
Chemicals and related products	68,114	57,313	76,867
Medicines	35,050	30,089	42,849
Paper and paperboard products	19,249	13,031	14,068
Iron and steel	41,550	34,335	69,304
General industrial machinery	80,088	66,233	107,873
Electrical machinery	41,610	48,355	39,694
Road vehicles	58,855	85,742	53,984
Precision instruments, watches, etc.	16,520	14,916	22,175
Total (incl. others)	543,693	503,340	594,491

Exports f.o.b.	1988	1989	1990
Petroleum and petroleum products	598,123	747,880	830,173
Sawlogs and veneer logs	83,240	96,598	43,901
Veneer sheets etc	21,424	19,475	23,669
Total (incl. others)*	751,109	908,851	977,670

* Including special transactions and commodities not classified according to kind (US $ 000): 24,409 in 1988; 29,422 in 1989; 51,979 in 1990.

Source: UN, *International Trade Statistics Yearbook.*

Exports of petroleum and petroleum products ('000 million francs CFA): 272.9 in 1993; 454.0 in 1994; 527.9* in 1995.
Exports of wood and wood products ('000 million francs CFA): 26.6 in 1993; 48.6 in 1994; 52.3* in 1995.
Total exports ('000 million francs CFA): 316.8 in 1993; 532.4 in 1994; 624.1* in 1995.

* Provisional figure.

Source: IMF, *Republic of Congo—Statistical Annex* (August 1996).

PRINCIPAL TRADING PARTNERS (US $ '000)

Imports c.i.f.	1988	1989	1990
France/Monaco	233,510	246,413	218,645
Germany, Fed. Repub.	24,983	35,471	29,066
Italy	39,831	29,247	62,559
Japan	23,157	19,988	23,877
Netherlands	20,169	19,130	27,175
Spain	14,106	6,484	9,419
USA	35,873	27,262	66,152
Total (incl. others)	543,693	503,340	594,491

Exports f.o.b.	1988	1989	1990
France/Monaco	165,262	175,305	240,506
Italy	33,154	70,128	112,803
Netherlands	79,027	66,474	54,196
Spain	13,525	55,059	23,727
USA	307,186	419,185	354,503
Total (incl. others)	752,000	911,000	976,000

Source: UN, *International Trade Statistics Yearbook.*

Transport

RAILWAYS (traffic)

	1993	1994	1995
Passenger-km (million)	312	227	302
Freight ton-km (million)	259	222	266

Source: *Mostly* IMF, *Republic of Congo—Statistical Annex* (August 1996).

ROAD TRAFFIC (estimates, '000 motor vehicles in use at 31 December)

	1993	1994	1995
Passenger cars	33.4	33.5	36.1
Goods vehicles	15.2	14.5	15.6

Source: IRF, *World Road Statistics.*

SHIPPING

Merchant Fleet (registered at 31 December)

	1994	1995	1996
Number of vessels	23	24	20
Total displacement ('000 grt)	9.2	12.1	6.3

Source: Lloyd's Register of Shipping, *World Fleet Statistics.*

International Sea-borne Freight Traffic ('000 metric tons)

	1988	1989	1990
Goods loaded	9,400	9,295	8,987
Goods unloaded	686	707	736

Source: UN, *Monthly Bulletin of Statistics.*

Inland Waterways (freight traffic, '000 metric tons)

Port of Brazzaville	1985	1986	1987
Goods loaded	77	77	62
Goods unloaded	407	309	331

CIVIL AVIATION (traffic on scheduled services)*

	1992	1993	1994
Kilometres flown (million)	3	3	3
Passengers carried ('000)	229	231	232
Passenger-km (million)	250	256	264
Total ton-km (million)	39	38	40

* Including an apportionment of the traffic of Air Afrique.

Source: UN, *Statistical Yearbook.*

Tourism

	1992	1993	1994
Foreign tourist arrivals	36,072	34,027	30,338
Tourist receipts (US $ million)	7	6	3

Source: UN, *Statistical Yearbook.*

Communications Media

	1992	1993	1994
Radio receivers ('000 in use)	270	280	290
Television receivers ('000 in use)	14	17	18
Telephones ('000 main lines in use)	18	19	21
Daily newspapers	6	n.a.	6

Sources: UNESCO, *Statistical Yearbook*; UN, *Statistical Yearbook.*

Education

(1996)

	Teachers	Pupils
Primary	6,926	489,546
Secondary		
General	5,466	190,409
Vocational	1,746	23,606
Higher*	1,341	16,602

* 1995 figures.

Directory

The Constitution

The Constitution, which was approved by a national referendum in March 1992, provides for legislative power to be exercised by a directly-elected National Assembly and Senate and for executive power to be held by a directly-elected President, who is also the Supreme Chief of the Armed Forces. The President appoints a Prime Minister from the political party with the majority of parliamentary seats. The President, acting on the advice of the Prime Minister, also appoints a Council of Ministers. Elections to the presidency and the 125-member National Assembly are to take place every five years, and elections to the 60-member Senate are to be held every six years. There is universal adult franchise. Further provisions guarantee an independent judiciary and the freedom of the media.

The Government

HEAD OF STATE

President: PASCAL LISSOUBA (took office 31 August 1992).

COUNCIL OF MINISTERS
(July 1997)

A coalition of the Union panafricaine pour la démocratie sociale (UPADS) and allied parties, together with the Union pour le renouveau démocratique (URD).

Prime Minister: DAVID CHARLES GANAO.

Minister of State for Decentralization, Communications, Urban Development and Housing: MARTIN M'BERI.

Minister of State for the Interior in charge of Security: Col PHILIPPE BIKINKITA.

Minister of State for Transport and Civil Aviation: VICTOR TAMBA-TAMBA.

Minister of National Defence: Brig.-Gen. FRANÇOIS AYAYEN.

Minister of the Economy, Planning and Finance: N'GUILA MOUNGOUNGA NKOMBO.

Minister of Foreign Affairs and Co-operation, in charge of Francophone Affairs: DESTIN-ARSENE TSATSY M'BOUNGOU.

Minister of Energy: JEAN ITADI.

Minister of Justice and Keeper of the Seals: JOSEPH OUABARI.

Minister of Equipment and Public Works: LAMBERT NGALIBALI.

Minister of the Civil Service and Territorial Administration, in charge of Administration Reform: MARIUS MOUAMBENGA.

Minister of Scientific Research: ANACLET TSOMAMBET.

Minister of Hydrocarbons and Mines: BENOÎT KOUKÉBÉNÉ.

Minister of Agriculture, Animal Husbandry, Water and Forest Resources and Fisheries: JEAN-PROSPER KOYO.

Minister of Labour and Vocational Training: THÉOPHILE OBENGA.

Minister of Commerce, Consumer Affairs and Small- and Medium-sized Enterprises: JOSEPH HONDJUILA MIOKONO.

Minister of Industrial Development: RAYMOND OMBAKA-EKORI.

Minister of Posts and Telecommunications: ALPHONSE NKOUA.

Minister of Public Health: GASTON BIKANDOU.

Minister of Primary and Secondary Education: SYLVAIN MAKOSSO-MAKOSSO.

Minister of Higher and Technical Education: MARTIAL VINCENT DE PAUL IKOUNGA.

Minister of Youth and Sports: HENRI OKEMBA.

Minister in charge of Women's Integration in Development: MARIE-THÉRÈSE AVEMEKA.

Minister of Tourism and the Environment: GABRIEL MATSIONA.

Minister of Culture and the Arts: MARÈME NDEBEKI.

MINISTRIES

All ministries are in Brazzaville.

Office of the President: Palais du Peuple, Brazzaville; telex 5210.

Ministry of the Economy, Planning and Finance: Centre Administratif, Quartier Plateau, BP 2093, Brazzaville; tel. 81-06-20; telex 5210.

Ministry of Education: BP 169, Brazzaville; tel. 83-24-60; telex 5210.

Ministry of Foreign Affairs and Co-operation: BP 2070, Brazzaville; tel. 83-20-28; telex 5210.

Ministry of Industrial Development: Brazzaville; tel. 83-18-27; telex 5210.

Ministry of Public Health: Palais du Peuple, Brazzaville; tel. 83-29-35; telex 5210.

President and Legislature

PRESIDENT

Presidential Election, First Ballot, 2 August 1992

Candidate	% of votes
PASCAL LISSOUBA	35.89
BERNARD KOLELAS	22.89
Gen. DENIS SASSOU-NGUESSO	16.87
ANDRÉ MILONGO	10.18
Others (12 candidates)	14.17
Total	100.00

Second Ballot, 16 August 1992

Candidate	% of votes
PASCAL LISSOUBA	61.32
BERNARD KOLELAS	38.68
Total	100.00

SÉNAT*

Speaker: AUGUSTIN POIGNET.

General Election, 26 July 1992*

Party	Seats
UPADS	23
MCDDI	13
RDD	8
RDPS	5
PCT	3
UDR	1
Independents	7
Total	60

* On 6 October 1996 elections were held for 23 of the seats in the Senate. The 'Presidential Group' of parties won 12 of the seats, retaining its majority, while opposition organizations took 10 seats and one seat was secured by an independent candidate.

ASSEMBLÉE NATIONALE*

Speaker: ANDRÉ MILONGO.

General Election, 2 May 1993 and 3 October 1993*

Party	Seats
UPADS	47
MCDDI	28
PCT	15
RDPS	10
RDD	6
UFD	3
Other parties	14
Independents	2
Total	125

* In January 1994 an independent electoral committee annulled the results in eight constituencies where there was found to be evidence of electoral fraud; three of the seats were held by supporters of the Government, and the remaining five by opposition members. At by-elections in seven of the constituencies, which took place in early 1995, three seats were won by the PCT, two by the MCDDI and two by the UPADS.

Political Organizations

Coordination des partis indépendants: Brazzaville; f. 1997 as an alliance of 25 parties to contest presidential elections; Chair. MBIKI DENA MITELAGNON.

Forces démocratiques unies (FDU): Brazzaville; f. 1994 as an alliance of six political parties; Leader Gen. DENIS SASSOU-NGUESSO; Deputy Leader PIERRE NZE.

Convention pour l'alternative démocratique: Leader ALFRED OPIMBA.

Parti congolais du travail (PCT): Brazzaville; telex 5335; f. 1969; sole legal political party 1969–90; socialist orientation; Pres. Gen. DENIS SASSOU-NGUESSO; Sec.-Gen. AMBROISE NOUMAZALAY.

Parti libéral républicain: Leader NICÉPHORE FYLA.

Union nationale pour la démocratie et le progrès (UNDP): f. 1990; Leader PIERRE NZE.

Union patriotique pour la réconstruction nationale: Leader MATHIAS DZON.

Union pour le renouveau nationale: Leader GABRIEL BOKILO.

Front uni des républicains congolais (FURC): f. 1994, regd 1995; promotes national development on a non-ethnic and non-regional basis; Chair. RAYMOND TIMOTHÉE MAKITA.

Mouvance présidentielle: Brazzaville; f. 1992 as alliance of c. 80 political parties supporting Lissouba's candidature for presidency; Leader JACQUES-JOACHIM YHOMBI-OPANGO.

Union pour la démocratie et la République–Mouinda (UDR—Mouinda): f. 1992; Leader ANDRÉ MILONGO.

Union des forces démocratiques (UFD): Leader DAVID CHARLES GANAO.

Union panafricaine pour la démocratie sociale (UPADS): Pres. PASCAL LISSOUBA; Sec.-Gen. CHRISTOPHE MOUKOUEKE.

Mouvement africain pour la réconstruction sociale: Leader JEAN ITADI.

Mouvement pour l'unité et la réconstruction: f. 1997 as an alliance of three political parties; mems:

Mouvement pour la démocratie et la solidarité (MDS): Pres. PAUL KAYA.

Rassemblement pour la démocratie et le progrès social (RDPS): f. 1990; Pres. JEAN-PIERRE THYSTÈRE-TCHICAYA; Sec.-Gen. JEAN-FELIX DEMBA TELO.

Union pour la République (UR): Brazzaville; f. 1995 by breakaway faction of UPADS; Leader BENJAMIN BOUNKOULOU.

Mouvement patriotique du Congo (MPC): Paris, France.

Mouvement pour la réconciliation congolaise: Paris, France; f. 1996; Leader Gen. JEAN-MARIE MICHEL MOKOKO.

Parti africain des pauvres: f. 1996; Leader ANGÈLE BANDOU.

Parti congolais pour la réconstruction (PCR): Brazzaville.

Parti libéral congolais: f. 1990; Gen. Sec. MARCEL MAKON.

Parti du renouvellement et du progrès: Leader HENRI MARCEL DOUMANGUELE.

Parti social-démocrate congolais (PSDC): f. 1990; Pres. CLÉMENT MIERASSA.

Parti du travail: f. 1991; Leader Dr AUGUSTE MAYANZA.

Parti pour l'unité, le travail et le progrès (PUTP): f. 1995 by defectors from the MCDDI; Leader DIDIER SENGHA.

Programe national de la jeunesse unie: f. 1996; Chair. LUDOVIC MIYOUNA.

Rassemblement pour la démocratie et le développement (RDD): f. 1990; advocates a mixed economy; Chair. SATURNIN OKABE.

Rassemblement démocratique et populaire du Congo: Leader JEAN-MARIE TASSOUA.

Rassemblement pour la République et la démocratie (RRD): f. 1996; Leader Maj.-Gen. RAYMOND DAMASSE NGOLLO.

Union du centre: Leader OKANA MPAN.

Union pour la démocratie congolaise (UDC): f. 1989; advocates economic liberalization; Chair. FÉLIX MAKOSSO.

Union pour la démocratie et le progrès social (UDPS): f. 1994 by merger of the Union pour le développement et le progrès social and the Parti populaire pour la démocratie sociale et la défense de la République; Leader JEAN-MICHEL BOUKAMBA-YANGOUMA.

Union patriotique pour la démocratie et le progrès: Sec.-Gen. CÉLESTIN NKOUA.

Union pour le progrès: Pres. JEAN-MARTIN M'BEMBA.

Union pour le progrès du peuple congolais: f. 1991; advocates democracy and national unity; Leader ALPHONSE NBIHOULA.

Union pour le progrès social et la démocratie (UPSD): Brazzaville; f. 1991; Pres. ANGE-EDOUARD POUNGUI.

Union pour le renouveau démocratique (URD): f. 1992 as an alliance of seven political parties; Chair. BERNARD KOLELAS; prin. mems:

Mouvement congolais pour la démocratie et le développement intégral (MCDDI): Brazzaville; f. 1990; mainly Kongo support; Leader BERNARD KOLELAS.

Rassemblement pour la démocratie et le progrès social (RDPS): see under Mouvement pour l'unité et la réconstruction.

Diplomatic Representation

EMBASSIES IN THE CONGO

Algeria: BP 2100, Brazzaville; tel. 83-39-15; telex 5303; Ambassador: MOHAMED NACER ADJALI.

Angola: BP 388, Brazzaville; tel. 81-14-71; telex 5321; Ambassador: JOSÉ AGOSTINHO NETO.

Belgium: BP 225, Brazzaville; tel. 83-29-63; telex 5216; fax 83-71-18; Ambassador: ERNEST STAES.

Cameroon: BP 2136, Brazzaville; tel. 83-34-04; telex 5242; Ambassador: JEAN-HILAIRE MBEA MBEA.

Central African Republic: BP 10, Brazzaville; tel. 83-40-14; Ambassador: CHARLES GUEREBANGBI.

Chad: BP 386, Brazzaville; tel. 81-22-22; Chargé d'affaires a.i.: NEATOBEI BIDI.

China, People's Republic: BP 213, Brazzaville; tel. 83-11-20; Ambassador: YE HONGLIANG.

Congo, Democratic Republic: 130 ave de l'Indépendance, BP 2450, Brazzaville; tel. 83-29-38; Ambassador: (vacant).

Cuba: BP 80, Brazzaville; tel. 81-29-80; telex 5308; Ambassador: JUAN CÉSAR DÍAZ.

Czech Republic: Brazzaville; tel. 82-08-37.

Egypt: BP 917, Brazzaville; tel. 83-44-28; telex 5248; Ambassador: MOHAMED ABDEL RAHMAN DIAB.

France: rue Alfassa, BP 2089, Brazzaville; tel. 83-14-23; telex 5239; Ambassador: RAYMOND CÉSAIRE.

Gabon: ave Fourneau, BP 2033, Brazzaville; tel. 81-05-90; telex 5225; Ambassador: CONSTANT TSOUMOU.

Germany: place de la Mairie, BP 2022, Brazzaville; tel. 83-29-90; telex 5235; Ambassador: ADOLF EDERER.

Guinea: BP 2477, Brazzaville; tel. 81-24-66; Ambassador: BONATA DIENG.

Holy See: rue Colonel Brisset, BP 1168, Brazzaville; tel. 83-15-46; fax 83-65-39; Apostolic Nuncio: Most Rev. DIEGO CAUSERO, Titular Archbishop of Meta.

Italy: 2-3 blvd Lyauté, BP 2484, Brazzaville; tel. 83-40-47; telex 5251; Ambassador: TIBOR HOOR TEMPIS LIVI.

Korea, Democratic People's Republic: BP 2032, Brazzaville; tel. 83-41-98; Ambassador: KIM PONG HU.

Libya: BP 920, Brazzaville; Secretary of People's Bureau: (vacant).

Nigeria: BP 790, Brazzaville; tel. 83-13-16; telex 5263; Ambassador: LAWRENCE OLUFOLAHAN OLADEJO OYELAKIN.

Romania: BP 2413, Brazzaville; tel. 81-32-79; telex 5259; Chargé d'affaires a.i.: DIACONESCO MILCEA.

Russia: BP 2132, Brazzaville; tel. 83-44-39; telex 5455; fax 83-69-17; Ambassador: ANATOLII SAFRONOVICH ZAITSEV.

USA: ave Amílcar Cabral, BP 1015, Brazzaville; tel. 83-20-70; telex 5367; fax 83-63-38; Ambassador: AUBREY HOOKS.

Viet Nam: BP 988, Brazzaville; tel. 83-26-21; Ambassador: BUI VAN THANH.

Judicial System

Supreme Court: Brazzaville; telex 5298; acts as a cour de cassation; Pres. GASTON MAMBOUANA.

Religion

At least one-half of the population follow traditional animist beliefs. Most of the remainder are Christians (mainly Roman Catholics).

CHRISTIANITY

The Roman Catholic Church

The Congo comprises one archdiocese and five dioceses. At 31 December 1995 there were an estimated 1.3m. adherents (about 45% of the total population).

Bishops' Conference: Conférence Episcopale du Congo, BP 200, Brazzaville; tel. 83-06-29; fax 83-79-08; f. 1967; Pres. Rt Rev. BERNARD NSAYI, Bishop of Nkayi.

Archbishop of Brazzaville: Most Rev. BARTHÉLÉMY BATANTU, Archevêché, BP 2301, Brazzaville; tel. and fax 83-17-93.

Protestant Church

Eglise Evangélique du Congo: BP 3205, Bacongo-Brazzaville; tel. 83-43-64; fax 83-77-33; f. 1909; autonomous since 1961; 135,811 mems (1993); Pres. Rev. ALPHONSE MBAMA.

ISLAM

In 1991 there were an estimated 25,000 Muslims and 49 mosques in the Congo.

Comité Islamique du Congo: 77 Makotipoko Moungali, BP 55, Brazzaville; tel. 82-87-45; f. 1988; Leaders HABIBOU SOUMARE, BACHIR GATSONGO, BOUILLA GUIBIDANESI.

The Press

In 1995 the National Assembly approved legislation providing for a five-year term of imprisonment for journalists, printing houses and newspaper distributors convicted of libel, and prohibiting media coverage of libel cases, except where permission had previously been granted by the Ministry of Justice. In July 1996 legislation was approved which required all independent newspaper and periodical publishers to obtain a commercial licence. In August the Government issued a decree banning several unlicensed publications.

DAILIES

ACI: BP 2144, Brazzaville; tel. 83-05-91; telex 5285; daily news bulletin publ. by Agence Congolaise d'Information; circ. 1,000.

Aujourd'hui: BP 1171, Brazzaville; tel. and fax 83-77-44; f. 1991; Man. Dir and Chief Editor FYLLA DI FUA DI SASSA.

L'Eveil de Pointe-Noire: BP 66, Pointe-Noire.

Mweti: BP 991, Brazzaville; tel. 81-10-87; national news; Dir MATONGO AVELEY; Chief Editor HUBERT MADOUABA; circ. 7,000.

PERIODICALS

Bakento Ya Congo: BP 309, Brazzaville; tel. 83-27-44; quarterly; Dir MARIE LOUISE MAGANGA; Chief Editor CHARLOTTE BOUSSE; circ. 3,000.

Bulletin Mensuel de la Chambre de Commerce de Brazzaville: BP 92, Brazzaville; monthly.

Bulletin de Statistique: Centre Nationale de la Statistique et des Etudes Economiques, BP 2031, Brazzaville; tel. 83-36-94; f. 1977; quarterly; Dir-Gen. JEAN-PAUL TOTO.

Le Choc: Brazzaville; fortnightly; satirical; Chief Editor: JEAN-BAPTISTE BAKOUVOUKA.

Combattant Rouge: Brazzaville; tel. 83-02-53; monthly; Dir SYLVIO GEORGES ONKA; Chief Editor GILLES OMER BOUSSI.

Congo-Magazine: BP 114, Brazzaville; tel. 83-43-81; monthly; Dir GASPARD MPAN; Chief Editor THÉODORE KIAMOSSI; circ. 3,000.

Effort: BP 64, Brazzaville; monthly.

Etumba: Brazzaville; weekly; circ. 8,000.

Le Forum: Brazzaville.

Le Guardien: Brazzaville.

Jeunesse et Révolution: BP 885, Brazzaville; tel. 83-44-13; weekly; Dir JEAN-ENOCH GOMA-KENGUE; Chief Editor PIERRE MAKITA.

Le Madukutsekele: Brazzaville; f. 1991; weekly; satirical; Editor MATHIEU BAKIMA-BALIELE; circ. 5,000.

Le Pays: f. 1991; weekly; Dir ANTOINE MALONGA.

La Rue Meurt: Brazzaville.

La Semaine: Brazzaville; weekly; circ. 7,000.

La Semaine Africaine: BP 2080, Brazzaville; tel. 81-03-28; f. 1952; weekly; general information and social action; circulates widely in francophone equatorial Africa; Dir JEAN-PIERRE GALLET; Chief Editor JOACHIM MBANZA; circ. 6,500.

Le Soleil: f. 1991; weekly; organ of the Rassemblement pour la démocratie et le développement.

Le Stade: BP 114, Brazzaville; tel. 81-47-18; telex 5285; f. 1985; weekly; sports; Dir HUBERT-TRÉSOR MADOUABA-NTOUALANI; Chief Editor LELAS PAUL NZOLANI; circ. 6,500.

Voix de la Classe Ouvrière (Voco): BP 2311, Brazzaville; tel. 83-36-66; six a year; Dir MICHEL JOSEPH MAYOUNGOU; Chief Editor MARIE-JOSEPH TSENGOU; circ. 4,500.

NEWS AGENCIES

Agence Congolaise d'Information (ACI): BP 2144, Brazzaville; tel. 83-46-76; telex 5285; f. 1961; Dir RIGOBERT DOUNIAMA-ETOUA.

Foreign Bureaux

Agence France-Presse (AFP): c/o Agence Congolaise d'Information, BP 2144, Brazzaville; tel. 83-46-76; telex 5285; Correspondent JOSEPH GOUALA.

Associated Press (AP) (USA): BP 2144, Brazzaville; telex 5477; Correspondent ARMAND BERNARD MASSAMBA.

Informatsionnoye Telegrafnoye Agentstvo Rossii—Telegrafnoye Agentstvo Suverennykh Stran (ITAR—TASS) (Russia): BP 379, Brazzaville; tel. 83-44-33; telex 5203; Correspondent MAKSIM YEVGENIEVICH KORSHUNOV.

Inter Press Service (IPS) (Italy): POB 964, Brazzaville; tel. 810565; telex 5285.

Pan-African News Agency (PANA) (Senegal): BP 2144, Brazzaville; tel. 83-11-40; telex 5285; fax 83-70-15.

Reuters (United Kingdom): BP 2144, Brazzaville; telex 5477; Correspondent ANTOINE MOUYAMBALA.

Rossiyskoye Informatsionnoye Agentstvo—Novosti (RIA—Novosti) (Russia): BP 170, Brazzaville; tel. 83-43-44; telex 5227; Bureau Chief DMITRI AMVROSIEV.

Xinhua (New China) News Agency (People's Republic of China): 40 ave Maréchal Lyauté, BP 373, Brazzaville; tel. 83-44-01; telex 5230; Chief Correspondent XU ZHENQIANG.

Publishers

Imprimerie Centrale d'Afrique (ICA): BP 162, Pointe-Noire; f. 1949; Man. Dir M. SCHNEIDER.

Société Congolaise Hachette: Brazzaville; telex 5291; general fiction, literature, education, juvenile, textbooks.

Government Publishing House

Imprimerie Nationale: BP 58, Brazzaville; Man. KIALA MATOUBA.

Radio and Television

In 1993 there were an estimated 290,000 radio sets and 18,000 television receivers in use.

Radio Congo Liberté: Brazzaville; f. 1997; operated by supporters of fmr pres. Sassou-Nguesso.

Radiodiffusion-Télévision Congolaise: BP 2241, Brazzaville; tel. 81-24-73; telex 5299; Dir JEAN-FRANÇOIS SYLVESTRE SOUKA.

Radio Congo: BP 2241, Brazzaville; tel. 83-03-83; radio programmes in French, Lingala, Kikongo, Subia, English and Portuguese; transmitters at Brazzaville and Pointe-Noire; Dir of Broadcasting THÉOPHILE MIETE LIKIBI.

Télévision Nationale Congolaise: BP 2241, Brazzaville; tel. 81-51-52; began transmission in 1963; operates for 46 hours per week, with most programmes in French but some in Lingala and Kikongo; Dir JEAN-GILBERT FOUTOU.

Finance

(cap. = capital; res = reserves; m. = million; dep. = deposits; br. = branch;amounts in francs CFA)

BANKING

Central Bank

Banque des Etats de l'Afrique Centrale (BEAC): BP 126, Brazzaville; tel. 83-28-14; telex 5200; fax 83-63-42; headquarters in Yaoundé, Cameroon; f. 1973 as the central bank of issue for mem. states of the Customs and Economic Union of Central Africa (UDEAC), comprising Cameroon, the Central African Republic, Chad, Republic of Congo, Equatorial Guinea and Gabon; cap. and res 204,933m. (Dec. 1995); Gov. JEAN-FÉLIX MAMALEPOT; Dir in Repub. of Congo ANGE-EDOUARD POUNGUI; br. at Pointe-Noire.

Commercial Banks

Banque Internationale du Congo (BIDC): ave Amílcar Cabral, BP 33, Brazzaville; tel. 83-03-08; telex 5339; fax 83-53-82; f. 1983; 62% state-owned; privatization pending in 1997; cap. and res 2,454.8m., dep. 37,301.8m. (Dec. 1992); Pres. and Chair. EDOUARD EBOUKA BABACKAS; Gen. Man. FRANÇOIS BITA; 1 br.

Crédit Rural du Congo: BP 2889, Brazzaville; tel. 83-53-50; telex 5532; fax 83-53-52; 50% state-owned; Chair. EDOUARD EBOUKA-BABACKAS; Man. Dir DELPHINE MBOUNGOU.

Financial Bank Congo: BP 602, Pointe-Noire; tel. and fax 94-16-30; f. 1994; cap. 1,110m. (1994); Dir-Gen. JEAN-LOUIS CHAPUIS.

Union Congolaise de Banques SA (UCB): ave Amílcar Cabral, BP 147, Brazzaville; tel. 83-30-00; telex 5206; fax 83-68-45; f. 1974; state-owned, privatization pending; cap. and res 3,212.1m. (Dec. 1995); Pres. JOSEPH KOMBO KINTOMBO; Man. Dir GUY VALERO; 8 brs.

Co-operative Banking Institution

Mutuelles Congolaises de l'Epargne et du Crédit: Brazzaville; f. 1994; Dir. SERGE BAGETA.

Development Bank

Banque de Développement des États de l'Afrique Centrale: (see Franc Zone, p. 176).

Financial Institution

Caisse Congolaise d'Amortissement: 410 allée du Chaillu, BP 2090, Brazzaville; tel. 83-32-41; telex 5294; fax 83-63-42; f. 1971; management of state funds; Dir-Gen. EMMANUEL NGONO.

INSURANCE

Assurances et Réassurances du Congo (ARC): ave Amílcar Cabral, BP 977, Brazzaville; tel. 83-01-71; telex 5236; f. 1973 to acquire the businesses of all insurance cos operating in the Congo; 50% state-owned; Dir-Gen. RAYMOND IBATA; brs at Pointe-Noire, Loubomo and Ouesso.

Trade and Industry

DEVELOPMENT AGENCIES

Caisse Française de Développement: BP 96, Brazzaville; tel. 83-15-95; telex 5202; French fund for economic co-operation; Dir JACQUES BENIER.

Mission Française de Coopération: BP 2175, Brazzaville; tel. 83-15-03; f. 1959; administers bilateral aid from France; Dir JEAN-BERNARD THIANT.

Office des Cultures Vivrières (OCV): BP 894, Brazzaville; tel. 82-11-03; f. 1979; state-owned; food-crop development; Dir-Gen. GILBERT PANA.

STATE MARKETING BOARDS

Office du Café et du Cacao (OCC): BP 2488, Brazzaville; tel. 83-19-03; telex 5273; f. 1978; marketing and export of coffee and cocoa; Man. Dir PAUL YORA.

Office Congolais des Bois (OCB): 2 ave Moe Vangoula, BP 1229, Pointe-Noire; tel. 94-22-38; telex 8248; f. 1974; purchase and marketing of timber products; Man. Dir ALEXANDRE DENGUET-ATTIKI.

Office National de Commercialisation des Produits Agricoles (ONCPA): Brazzaville; tel. 83-24-01; telex 5273; f. 1964; marketing of all agricultural products except sugar; promotion of rural co-operatives; Dir JEAN-PAUL BOCKONDAS.

Office National du Commerce (OFNACOM): BP 2305, Brazzaville; tel. 83-43-99; telex 5309; f. 1964; importer and distributor of general merchandise; monopoly importer of salted and dried fish, cooking salt, rice, tomato purée, buckets, enamelled goods and blankets; Dir-Gen. VALENTIN ENOUSSA NCONGO.

CHAMBERS OF COMMERCE

Chambre de Commerce, d'Agriculture et d'Industrie de Brazzaville: BP 92, Brazzaville; tel. 83-21-15; Pres. MAURICE OGNAOY; Sec.-Gen. FRANÇOIS DILOU-YOULOU.

Chambre de Commerce, d'Agriculture et d'Industrie de Loubomo: BP 78, Loubomo.

Chambre de Commerce, d'Industrie et d'Agriculture du Kouilou: 8 ave Charles de Gaulle, BP 665, Pointe-Noire; tel. 94-12-80; f. 1948; Chair. FRANÇOIS-LUC MACOSSO; Sec.-Gen. JEAN-BAPTISTE SOUMBOU.

PROFESSIONAL ORGANIZATION

Union Patronale et Interprofessionnelle du Congo (UNICONGO): BP 42, Brazzaville; tel. 83-33-73; fax 83-68-16; f. 1960; employers' union; Pres. E. HANNA; Sec.-Gen. J. FUMEY.

NATIONALIZED INDUSTRIES

Minoterie, Aliments de Bétail, Boulangerie (MAB): BP 789, Pointe-Noire; tel. 94-19-09; telex 8283; f. 1978; monopoly importer of cereals; production of flour and animal feed; Man. Dir DENIS TEMPERE.

Régie Nationale des Palmeraies du Congo (RNPC): BP 8, Brazzaville; tel. 83-08-25; f. 1966; production of palm oil; Man. Dir RENÉ MACOSSO.

Société Nationale de Construction (SONACO): Brazzaville; tel. 83-06-54; f. 1979; building works; Man. Dir DENIS M'BOMO.

Société Nationale de Distribution d'Eau (SNDE): rue du Sergent Malamine, BP 229 and 365, Brazzaville; tel. 83-73-26; telex 5272; fax 83-38-91; f. 1967; proposals for transfer to private-sector ownership pending; water supply and sewerage; holds monopoly over wells and import of mineral water; Chair. and Man. Dir S. MPINOU.

Société Nationale d'Elevage (SONEL): BP 81, Loutété, Massangui; f. 1964; development of semi-intensive stock-rearing; exploitation of by-products; Man. Dir THÉOPHILE BIKAWA.

Société Nationale d'Exploitation des Bois (SNEB): Pointe-Noire; tel. 94-02-09; f. 1970; production of timber; Pres. RIGOBERT NGOULOU; Man. Dir ROBERT ZINGA KANZA.

Société Nationale de Recherches et d'Exploitation Pétrolières (HYDRO-CONGO): Cnr ave Paul Doumer and ave du Camp, BP 2008, Brazzaville; tel. 83-40-22; telex 5300; fax 83-12-38; f. 1973; transfer to private-sector ownership pending; research into and production of petroleum resources; operates petroleum refinery at Pointe-Noire; also mfrs of lubricants; Dir-Gen. BERNARD OKIORIMA.

Société des Verreries du Congo (SOVERCO): BP 1241, Pointe-Noire; tel. 94-19-19; telex 8288; f. 1977; mfrs of glassware; Chair. A. E. NOUMAZALAYE; Man. Dir NGOYOT IBARRA.

Unité d'Afforestation Industrielle du Congo (UAIC): BP 1120, Pointe-Noire; tel. 94-04-17; telex 8308; f. 1978; transfer pending of 65% interest to Shell; production of wood-pulp for export from eucalyptus plantations; Dir ROLAND JAFFRÉ.

MAJOR INDUSTRIAL COMPANIES

The following are some of the largest companies in terms of either capital investment or employment.

AGIP Recherches Congo: BP 2047, Brazzaville; tel. 83-11-52; telex 6010; f. 1969; cap. US $7m.; wholly-owned by AGIP (Italy); exploration and exploitation of petroleum resources; Chair. PIETRO CAVANNA; Man. Dir ANTONIO ROSSANI.

BATA SA Congolaise: ave du Général de Gaulle, BP 32, Pointe-Noire; tel. 94-03-26; telex 8232; f. 1965; cap. 250m. francs CFA; mfrs of footwear; Pres. GEORGES MAREINE; Man. Dir MICHEL DUMOULIN.

Boissons Africaines de Brazzaville (BAB): BP 2193, Brazzaville; tel. 83-20-06; telex 5266; f. 1964; cap. 350m. francs CFA; mfrs and markets carbonated drinks and syrups; Man. Dir J. SERVAIS.

Brasseries du Congo: 55 ave du Nouveau Port, BP 105, Brazzaville; tel. 83-85-81; telex 5305; fax 83-25-64; mfrs and markets beer and soft drinks, fruit juices, soda, ice and carbon dioxide; Pres. J. L. HOME; Man. Dir G. J. BOUR; 570 employees.

La Congolaise des Bois Impregnés (CBI): BP 820, Pointe-Noire; f. 1986; cap. 800m. francs CFA; 49% owned by UAIC (see Nationalized Industries); production of electricity poles from eucalyptus trees; Pres. AMBROISE NOUMAZALAY; Man. Dir JOHN F. BRIDGES.

Elf Congo: BP 761, Pointe-Noire; tel. 94-60-00; telex 8239; also at BP 405, Brazzaville; tel. 83-02-40; f. 1969; cap. US $17.2m.; wholly-owned by Elf Aquitaine; exploration and exploitation of petroleum resources; Dir-Gen. (at Brazzaville) PIERRE OFFANT; Dir at Pointe-Noire EMMANUEL YOKA.

Impressions de Textiles de la République du Congo (IMPRECO): BP 188, Brazzaville; tel. 81-02-74; telex 5218; fax 83-01-96; f. 1973; cap. 720m. francs CFA; 30% state-owned; textile printing; Chair. FRANÇOIS VRINAT; Man. Dir LOUIS DEFFOND.

PLACONGO SA: BP 717, Pointe-Noire; tel. 94-02-79; telex 8224; f. 1965 as Société des Placages du Congo; cap. 4,400m. francs CFA; 36% state-owned; rotary peeling of logs; Pres. Dr DOUNIAM OSSEBI; Man. Dir DOMINIQUE TOURANCHET.

Savonnerie du Congo (SAVCONGO): Brazzaville; tel. 83-10-17; telex 5221; f. 1958; cap. 1,100m. francs CFA; mfrs of soap and domestic cleaning products; Pres. PIERRE OTTO MBONGO; Dir JUSTIN ELENGA.

Société Cimentière du Congo (SOCICO): BP 72, Loutété; tel. 92-61-26; telex 5244; f. 1968 as Cimenterie Domaniale de Loutété (CIDOULOU); 50% owned by Scancem (Norway); cap. 900m. francs CFA; Man. Dir OLE KULSETH.

Société Congolaise des Bois (SOCOBOIS): BP 300, Loubomo; tel. 91-02-04; telex 8257; f. 1964; cap. 400m. francs CFA; timber mills; Dir OTTO SCHLUMBOHM.

Société Congolaise Industrielle des Bois (CIB): BP 145, Brazzaville; tel. 83-11-31; fax 83-33-79; cap. 2,070m. francs CFA; logs and timber production; Pres. Dr HEINRICH LÜDER STOLL; Dir-Gen. JEAN-MARIE MEVELLEC.

Société Congolaise Industrielle des Bois d'Ouesso: Ouesso; f. 1981; cap. 2,500m. francs CFA; 51% state-owned; forestry production.

Société Congolaise de Pêches Maritimes (COPEMAR): Pointe-Noire; tel. 94-20-32; telex 8322; f. 1981; cap. 860m. francs CFA; processing of fish products; Man. Dir PASCAL ISSANGA.

Société Forestière Algéro-Congolaise (SFAC): BP 5109, Brazzaville; tel. 83-46-40; telex 5420; f. 1983; cap. 3,000m. francs CFA; timber production and marketing; Dir-Gen. ARMAND BIENVENU VOUIDIBIO.

Société des Huiles du Congo (HUILCA SA): BP 103, N'Kayi; tel. 92-11-60; telex 5565; f. 1988; cap. 700m. francs CFA; 40% state-owned; production of oils and fats, vegetable oil refinery at Brazzaville; Pres. ANTOINE TABET; Man. Dir EMMANUEL PAMBOU.

Société Industrielle et Agricole du Tabac Tropical (SIAT): BP 50, Brazzaville; tel. 83-16-15; telex 5211; fax 83-16-72; f. 1945; cap. 1,550m. francs CFA; mfrs of cigarettes; Dir-Gen. BERNARD PUILLET.

Société Industrielle des Bois de Mossendjo (SIBOM): Pointe-Noire; f. 1984; cap. 1,782m. francs CFA; 35% state-owned.

Société Industrielle de Déroulage et de Tranchage (SIDETRA): BP 1202, Pointe-Noire; tel. 94-20-07; telex 8206; f. 1966; cap. 950m. francs CFA; 35% state-owned; forestry, production of sawn wood and veneers; Pres. JACQUES SERVAIS; Dir-Gen. MARIE-ALPHONSE ONGAGOU-DATCHOU; 650 employees.

Société Mixte Bulgaro-Congolaise de Recherche et d'Exploitation des Phosphates (SOPHOSCO): Brazzaville; f. 1976; cap. 250m. francs CFA; 51% state-owned, 49% by govt of Bulgaria; mining of phosphate.

Société d'Economie Mixte de Construction (SEMICO): BP 13022, Brazzaville; f. 1983; cap. 1,050m. francs CFA; 25% state-owned; construction.

Société des Silos à Ciment du Congo (SIACIC): Pointe-Noire; cap. 600m. francs CFA; Dir Lt-Col FLORENT TSIBA.

Société des Textiles du Congo (SOTEXCO): BP 3222, Brazzaville; tel. 83-33-83; f. 1966; cap. 1,700m. francs CFA; operates cotton-spinning mills, dyeing and weaving plants in Kinsoundi; Man. Dir M. KOMBO-KITOMBO.

TRADE UNIONS

Independent trade unions were legalized in 1991.

Confédération Générale des Travailleurs du Congo (CGTC): Brazzaville; f. 1995; Chair. PAUL DOUNA.

Confédération Nationale des Syndicats Libres (CNASYL): Brazzaville; f. 1994; Sec.-Gen. MICHEL KABOUL MAOUTA.

Confédération Syndicale Congolaise (CSC): BP 2311, Brazzaville; tel. 83-19-23; telex 5304; f. 1964; 80,000 mems.

Confédération Syndicale des Travailleurs Congolais (CSTC): Brazzaville; f. 1993; fed. of 13 trade unions; Sec.-Gen. LOUIS GOUNDOU; 40,000 mems.

Transport

Agence Transcongolaise des Communications (ATC): BP 711, Pointe-Noire; tel. 94-15-32; telex 8345; f. 1969; transfer to private-sector ownership pending; three divisions: Congo-Océan Railways, inland waterways and Brazzaville inland port, and the Atlantic port of Pointe-Noire; Man. Dir Col JEAN-FÉLIX ONGOUYA.

RAILWAYS

There are 515 km of track from Brazzaville to Pointe-Noire. A 286-km section of privately-owned line links the manganese mines at Moanda (in Gabon), via a cableway to the Congo border at M'Binda, with the main line to Pointe-Noire.

ATC—Chemin de Fer Congo-Océan (CFCO): BP 651, Pointe-Noire; tel. 94-11-84; telex 8231; fax 94-12-30; transfer to private ownership pending; Dir DÉSIRÉ GOMA.

INLAND WATERWAYS

The Congo and Oubangui rivers form two axes of a highly developed inland waterway system. The Congo river and seven tributaries in the Congo basin provide 2,300 km of navigable river, and the Oubangui river, developed in co-operation with the Central African Republic, an additional 2,085 km.

ATC—Direction des Voies Navigables, Ports et Transports Fluviaux: BP 2048, Brazzaville; tel. 83-06-27; waterways authority; Dir MÉDARD OKOUMOU.

Compagnie Congolaise de Transports: BP 37, Loubomo; f. 1960; Pres. and Dir-Gen. ROBERT BARBIER.

Société Congolaise de Transports (SOCOTRANS): BP 617, Pointe-Noire; tel. 94-23-31; f. 1977; Man YVES CRIQUET.

Transcap-Congo: BP 1154, Pointe-Noire; tel. 94-01-46; telex 8218; f. 1962; Chair. J. DROUAULT.

SHIPPING

The deep-water Atlantic seaport at Pointe-Noire is the major port and Brazzaville is the principal port on the Congo river. A major expansion programme, undertaken during the 1980s, aimed to establish Brazzaville port as a container traffic centre for several central African countries. In 1989 Congolese seaports handled 10m. metric tons of goods for international transport.

ATC—Direction du Port de Brazzaville: BP 2048, Brazzaville; tel. 83-00-42; port authority; Dir JEAN-PAUL BOCKONDAS.

ATC—Direction du Port de Pointe-Noire: BP 711, Pointe-Noire; tel. 94-00-52; telex 8318; fax 94-20-42; port authority; Dir DOMINIQUE BEMBA.

La Congolaise de Transport Maritime (COTRAM): f. 1984; national shipping co; state-owned.

ROADS

In 1995 there were an estimated 12,760 km of roads and tracks, including 3,430 km of main roads and 4,140 km of secondary roads. Only about 9.7% of the total network was paved. The principal routes link Brazzaville with Pointe-Noire, in the south, and with Ouesso, in the north.

Régie Nationale des Transports et des Travaux Publics: BP 2073, Brazzaville; tel. 83-35-58; f. 1965; civil engineering, maintenance of roads and public works; Man. Dir HECTOR BIENVENU OUAMBA.

CIVIL AVIATION

There are international airports at Brazzaville (Maya-Maya) and Pointe-Noire. There are airports at six regional capitals, as well as 37 smaller airfields. In 1994 the state monopoly on internal flights was terminated.

Air Afrique: BP 1126, Pointe-Noire; tel. 94-17-00; telex 8342; see under Côte d'Ivoire; Dir at Pointe-Noire JEAN-CLAUDE NDIAYE; Dir at Brazzaville I. CISSÉ DEMBA.

Congo-Aviation: Brazzaville; f. 1994.

Lina Congo (Lignes Nationales Aériennes Congolaises): ave Amílcar Cabral, BP 2203, Brazzaville; tel. 81-30-65; telex 5243; fax 82-80-34; f. 1965; 33% state-owned; operates an extensive internal network; Man. Dir JEAN-JACQUES ONTSA-ONTSA.

Trans Air Congo: Brazzaville; f. 1994; private airline operating internal flights.

Tourism

Brazzaville has three international hotels. There is a shortage of accommodation in Pointe-Noire, owing to the requirements of the petroleum and business sectors. A regional hotel chain is to be established to cater for travellers in the provinces. Tourist visitors numbered 37,182 in 1992, when earnings from this sector were estimated at US $8m. Tourism earnings declined to an estimated $2m. in 1993.

Direction Générale du Tourisme et des Loisirs: BP 456, Brazzaville; tel. 83-09-53; telex 5210; f. 1980; Dir-Gen. ANTOINE KOUNKOU-KIBOUILOU.

Defence

In August 1996 the army numbered 8,000, the navy about 800 and the air force 1,200. There were 5,000 men in paramilitary forces. National service is voluntary for men and women, and lasts for two years.

Defence Expenditure: Estimated at 24,000m. francs CFA for 1995.

Supreme Commander of the Armed Forces: PASCAL LISSOUBA.

Chief of General Staff of the National People's Army: Col. GASPARD LOUNDOU.

Education

Education is officially compulsory for 10 years between six and 16 years of age. Primary education begins at the age of six and lasts for six years. Secondary education, from 12 years of age, lasts for seven years, comprising a first cycle of four years and a second of three years. Private education was legalized in 1990. In 1996 there were 489,546 pupils enrolled at primary schools, while 190,409 pupils were receiving general secondary education. In addition, there were 23,606 secondary students attending vocational institutions. The Marien Ngouabi University, at Brazzaville, was founded in 1971. In 1995 there were 16,602 students at university level. Some Congolese students attend further education establishments in France and Russia. In 1995, according to estimates by UNESCO, the average rate of adult illiteracy was 25.1% (males 16.9%, females 32.8%), one of the lowest in Africa. Expenditure on education by the central government was about 57,092m. francs CFA in 1991.

Bibliography

Allen, C., Radu, M. S., Somerville, K., et al. *Benin, The Congo, Burkina Faso: Economics, Politics and Society*. New York, Columbia University Press, 1989.

Amin, S., and Coquery-Vidrovitch, C. *Histoire économique du Congo 1880–1968*. Paris, Anthropos, 1969.

Asch, S. *L'Eglise du Prophète Kimbangu*. Paris, Editions Karthala, 1983.

Balliff, N. *Le Congo*. Paris, Karthala, 1993.

Bertrand, H. *Le Congo*. Paris, Maspero, 1975.

Coquery-Vidrovitch, C. *Le Congo au temps des grandes compagnies concessionnaires, 1898–1930*. Paris, Mouton, 1972.

Decalo, S., Thompson, V., and Adloff, R. *Historical Dictionary of the People's Republic of the Congo*. 3rd Edn. Lanham, MD, Scarecrow Press, 1996.

Ekondy, A. *Le Congo-Brazzaville: essai d'analyse et d'explication sociologiques selon la méthode pluraliste*. Berne, Lang, 1983.

Gakosso, G-F. *La réalité congolaise*. Paris, La Pensée Universelle, 1983.

Gauze, R. *The Politics of Congo Brazzaville*. Stanford, CA, 1973.

Gide, A. *Voyage au Congo*. 1926.

Lissouba, P. *Conscience du développement et démocratie*. Dakar, 1975.

M'Kaloulou, B. *Dynamique paysanne et développement rural au Congo*. Paris, L'Harmattan, 1984.

Rabut, E. *Brazza, commissaire général. Le Congo français (1886 – 1897)*. Paris, Editions de l'école des hautes études en sciences sociales, 1989.

Rey, P. P. *Colonialisme, néo-colonialisme et transition au capitalisme. Exemple de la Comilog au Congo-Brazzaville*. Paris, 1971.

Soret, M. *Les Kongo nord occidentaux*. Paris, Presses universitaires de France, 1959.

Histoire du Congo. Paris, Berger-Levrault, 1978.

Wagret, J.-M. *Histoire et sociologie politiques du Congo*. Paris, Librairie générale de droit et de jurisprudence, 1963.

West, R. *Brazza of the Congo*. Newton Abbot, 1973.

CÔTE D'IVOIRE

Physical and Social Geography

R. J. HARRISON CHURCH

The Republic of Côte d'Ivoire is situated on the west coast of Africa, between Ghana to the east and Liberia to the west, with Guinea, Mali and Burkina Faso to the north. Côte d'Ivoire is economically the most important of the states of sub-Saharan francophone Africa. The country has an area of 322,462 sq km (124,503 sq miles), and at the 1988 census the population was 10,815,694, rising to an estimated 14,230,000 in mid-1995 (giving an average population density of 44.1 inhabitants per sq km). There is a diversity of peoples, with the Agni and Baoulé having cultural and other affinities with the Ashanti of Ghana.

From the border with Liberia eastwards to Fresco, the coast has cliffs, rocky promontories and sandy bays. East of Fresco the rest of the coast is a straight sandbar, backed, as in Benin, by lagoons. None of the seaward river exits is navigable, and a canal was opened from the sea into the Ebrié lagoon at Abidjan only in 1950, after half a century's battle with nature.

Although Tertiary sands and clays fringe the northern edge of the lagoons, they give place almost immediately to Archaean and Pre-Cambrian rocks, which underlie the rest of the country. Diamonds are obtained from gravels south of Korhogo, and near Séguéla, while gold is mined at Ity, in the west, and at Aniuri, in the south-east. The Man mountains and the Guinea highlands on the border with Liberia and Guinea are the only areas of vigorous relief in the country. Substantial deposits of haematite iron ore may be developed near Man for export through the country's second deep-water port of San Pedro. There is considerable commercial potential for large offshore deposits of petroleum and also of natural gas, exploitation of which began in 1995: Côte d'Ivoire aims to become self-sufficient in (and in the medium-term a net exporter of) hydrocarbons. Plans for the development of nickel reserves are proceeding.

Except for the north-western fifth of Côte d'Ivoire, the country has an equatorial climate. This occurs most typically in the south, which receives annual rainfall of 1,250 mm–2,400 mm, with two maxima, and where the relative humidity is high. Much valuable rain forest survives in the south-west, but elsewhere it has been extensively planted with coffee, cocoa, bananas, pineapple, rubber and oil palm. Tropical climatic conditions prevail in the north-west, with a single rainy season of five to seven months, and 1,250 mm–1,500 mm of rain annually. Guinea savannah occurs here, as well as in the centre of the country, and projects southwards around Bouaké.

Recent History

PIERRE ENGLEBERT

Revised for this edition by the Editor

By independence in 1960 the Parti démocratique de la Côte d'Ivoire (PDCI) had achieved a virtual monopoly of political life in Côte d'Ivoire. As party leader and a representative of the PDCI in the French national assembly, Dr Félix Houphouët-Boigny dominated the grouping known as the Rassemblement démocratique africain, which had affiliates in other francophone countries. Throughout the 1950s Houphouët-Boigny supported French colonial rule and strongly opposed the formation of an independent West African federation. When, in 1960, it became clear that most colonies would be granted independence, Houphouët-Boigny pre-empted negotiations on federation by declaring unilateral independence on 7 August. He was the sole candidate for the presidency at every election until 1990, and (despite constitutional provision for the operation of a multi-party system) his party, as the name Parti démocratique de la Côte d'Ivoire–Rassemblement démocratique africain (PDCI–RDA), was the only legal political party until the same year.

THE HOUPHOUËT-BOIGNY ERA

President Houphouët-Boigny dictated the course of Ivorian politics from independence until his death—officially at 88 years of age—in December 1993, guiding the economic and political evolution of the country without any effective challenge to his rule. Sporadic political unrest was usually without cohesion, and Houphouët-Boigny's response to public discontent was generally to hold 'dialogues'—bringing together different strands of opinion to allow grievances to be aired. Prominent personalities were periodically removed from positions of influence, but most eventually returned to office or were rehabilitated by means of patronage. Political opponents were at times awarded government posts as a means of defusing potential unrest. Several destabilization plots were disclosed in the early years of Houphouët-Boigny's presidency, and a number of prominent political figures were detained. However, Houphouët-Boigny later admitted that the plots had been fabricated in an effort to strengthen his regime and eliminate potential rivals. Student unrest in 1968 and 1969 coincided with the beginning of an attempt to 'Ivorianize' public administration and the economy. None the less, France has remained influential in Côte d'Ivoire's political and economic life, and French investment has been favoured, creating a sizeable French community (of about 20,000 in the mid-1990s. Although the number of French advisers working in the country has been reduced in recent years, many important sectors of the economy are French-managed, and French financial backing, together with membership of the Franc Zone, has been of major influence in Côte d'Ivoire's economic development. A principal guarantee of the security of the state has, moreover, been in the form of a French military base and joint French-Ivorian military exercises.

Speculation about the succession to Houphouët-Boigny accompanied each electoral campaign from the 1960s. Following Houphouët-Boigny's re-election for a fourth five-year term in 1975, the constitution was amended to allow the president of the national assembly (then Philippe Yacé), to succeed as executive head of state in the event of the president's death, resignation or incapacity. Yacé lost presidential favour after 1978, when he was accused of manipulating mayoral elections; their results were annulled and Yacé did not appear in public for several months.

Houphouët-Boigny supervised wide-ranging economic and political changes in 1980, following a period of economic and social *malaise* and rumours of a coup plot. Prior to presidential and legislative elections held, respectively, in October and November, the order of succession was again revised with a further constitutional amendment allowing the president to nominate a vice-president who would automatically succeed him. At the elections voters were for the first time presented with a choice of candidates for the national assembly. Yacé had, in September, been removed from political prominence by the abolition of his post as secretary-general of the PDCI–RDA, and his influence was further diminished when Henri Konan Bédié—a former ambassador to the USA and finance minister, who was being increasingly mentioned as a likely successor to the presidency—was named president of the incoming national assembly. However, Houphouët-Boigny refrained from designating a vice-president and delayed appointing a new government until February 1981.

The growing economic problems of the early 1980s, as the decline in international prices for Côte d'Ivoire's main agricultural exports reversed the prosperity engendered by the so-called post-independence 'Ivorian miracle', were accompanied by evidence of social discontent. None the less, the rule of Houphouët-Boigny and the PDCI–RDA remained largely unchallenged. The succession issue re-emerged prior to the October 1985 presidential election, with the abolition of the unfilled post of vice-president in a constitutional amendment which allowed only for the president of the legislature to succeed to the presidency on an interim basis. The reported result of the presidential election was a 100% vote for Houphouët-Boigny, although at legislative elections in the following month, in which 546 candidates (all PDCI–RDA members) contested the assembly's 175 seats, only 64 of the incumbent deputies were returned. In January 1986 Bédié was re-elected president of the national assembly, and in February Yacé's apparent rehabilitation was confirmed by his election as president of the economic and social council, the country's third most senior political post. In April it was announced that the country wished to be known internationally by its official French name of Côte d'Ivoire, rather than having the name translated.

By the end of the 1980s Houphouët-Boigny's disinclination to designate a successor, and the absence of any clear indication of his willingness to retire, continued to suppress open political debate, while engendering considerable rivalry among would-be successors. An opportunity for the airing of grievances was provided by the 'days of national dialogue': in September 1989 Houphouët-Boigny convened meetings attended by representatives of the government and PDCI–RDA, armed forces and representatives of trade unions and professional organizations. None the less, the president rejected appeals to activate constitutional provisions permitting a multi-party system, on the grounds that political pluralism would impede progress towards national unity.

In early 1990 Côte d'Ivoire experienced unprecedented political upheaval, doubtless influenced by events elsewhere in the region and compounded by the unresolved succession issue and the prospect of economic austerity that was a precondition for assistance granted by international creditors in 1989. Demonstrations involving students and workers centred on the government's austerity policies, in particular the announcement in March of cuts in salaries of as much as 40% for public servants and the imposition of a new tax on private-sector incomes. Persistent anti-government unrest led to the deployment of troops in Abidjan, and in April, following the death of a student when troops intervened to disperse demonstrators, all educational establishments were closed and the 1989/90 academic year was declared invalid. Aware that to proceed with the levies on income entailed too great a political risk and, moreover, would generate only a small proportion of Côte d'Ivoire's revenue requirements, Houphouët-Boigny appointed Alassane Ouattara, the governor of the Banque centrale des états de l'Afrique de l'ouest, to head a commission whose function would be to formulate adjustment measures both more economically effective and more politically acceptable. In May Houphouët-Boigny, on the recommendation of the PDCI–RDA political bureau, agreed to the establishment of a plural political system. The authorities adopted a conciliatory attitude towards further instances of unrest, including a mutiny by army conscripts later in May. At the end of the month a less stringent programme of austerity measures was announced, in accordance with the recommendations of the Ouattara commission.

In accordance with the newly-sanctioned multi-party system, opposition groups that had previously operated unofficially acquired legal status, and numerous new parties were quickly formed. However, prior to the presidential and legislative elections, due in late 1990, opposition leaders accused the incumbent regime of impeding the reform process, as Houphouët-Boigny refused to accede to demands for a transitional government and for a national conference to discuss Côte d'Ivoire's political future. Security forces intervened at several rallies organized by the opposition, and in September Houphouët-Boigny accused his opponents of complicity in an alleged plot to assassinate Pope John Paul II at the time of his visit to Côte d'Ivoire. (During his visit the Pope consecrated a basilica in Yamoussoukro, Houphouët-Boigny's birthplace, constructed—officially at Houphouët-Boigny's own expense—at a cost of some 40,000m. francs CFA.)

Côte d'Ivoire's first contested presidential election took place on 28 October 1990. Houphouët-Boigny was challenged by Laurent Gbagbo, the candidate of the Front populaire ivoirien (FPI). The incumbent was, none the less, elected for a seventh term of office, having, by the official count, received the support of 81.7% of those who voted (69.2% of the electorate). The FPI and its allies, claiming that Gbagbo was the victor, appealed unsuccessfully to the supreme court to invalidate the election. In November the national assembly approved two constitutional amendments. The first (an amendment to Article 11) effectively strengthened Bédié's position by providing for the president of the national assembly to assume the functions of the president of the republic, should this office become vacant, until the expiry of the mandate of the previous incumbent. The second allowed for the appointment of a prime minister, a post subsequently awarded to Alassane Ouattara.

Almost 500 candidates, representing some 17 parties, contested the parliamentary elections on 25 November 1990. According to the official results, the PDCI–RDA secured 163 seats in the new legislature, while the FPI won nine (Gbagbo was among the successful FPI candidates). Francis Wodié, the leader of the Parti ivoirien des travailleurs (PIT), was also elected, as were two independent candidates. Bédié was subsequently reconfirmed as president of the national assembly.

In a reorganization of the council of ministers, announced following the legislative elections, Ouattara took the economy and finance portfolio in addition to the premiership, and several long-serving government members left office. Administrative changes instituted in the first half of 1991 included policies of retrenchment in the public sector and the replacement of senior civil servants with younger technocrats. In April an extraordinary session of the PDCI–RDA appointed Laurent Dona-Fologo, a former government minister who had failed to secure a parliamentary seat in the 1990 elections, to the revived post of party secretary-general.

DISSENSION, REPRESSION AND SUCCESSION

The greatest source of overt opposition to the new administration was the education sector. In May 1991 security forces used violent methods to disperse a students' meeting at the University of Abidjan, reportedly arresting about 180 people. Students and academic staff staged demonstrations in protest against the forces' brutality, prompting further intervention by the security forces. The situation deteriorated in June, when members of the Fédération estudiantine et scolaire de Côte d'Ivoire (FESCI), attacked and killed a student who had defied an order to boycott classes. The government ordered that the students' association be disbanded, and deployed security forces on the campus. University lecturers began an indefinite strike, and in July the arrest of 11 students on suspicion of involvement in the death of their fellow-student prompted further protests. Tensions were temporarily dispelled in August, when the government withdrew troops from the campus, suspended legal proceedings against FESCI activists, and restored the right of 'non-academic assembly' at the university (although the ban on FESCI remained). However, the political and social climate again deteriorated following the publication, in January 1992, of the findings of a commission of inquiry appointed by Houphouët-Boigny to investigate the security forces' actions at the university. Although the commission found the chief of the general staff of the armed forces, Gen. Robert Gueï, directly responsible for the acts of violence committed by his troops, Houphouët-Boigny expressed his support for Gueï, and emphasized that neither he nor any of those incriminated in the commission's report would be subject to disciplinary proceedings. Violent demonstrations by FESCI supporters immediately erupted on the university campus, and opposition parties demanded sanctions against Gueï and called on the government to resign. In February 16 FESCI leaders, including the union's secretary-general, were arrested. Shortly afterwards a 20,000 strong demonstration, organized by the FPI, degenerated into violence, and more than 100 protesters were arrested following clashes with the security forces. Among those detained were Gbagbo and René Degny-Segui, the president of the Ligue ivoirienne des droits de l'homme (LIDHO). It was announced that they and other opposition leaders would be prosecuted under the term of a new presidential ordinance that rendered political leaders responsible for acts of violence committed by their supporters. This ordinance had, according to the government, been signed by Houphouët-Boigny (who had been in Europe since early February) on the eve of the demonstration, but was rumoured among the opposition to have been introduced retrospectively. In late February the FESCI leader was fined and sentenced to three years' imprisonment, after having been convicted of reconstituting a banned organization and of responsibility for acts of vandalism committed by students earlier in the month. In March Gbagbo, Degny-Segui and seven others were each fined and sentenced to two-year prison terms; three others received lesser sentences, and the trials of opposition supporters continued in the following weeks. FPI deputies began a boycott of the national assembly in April, in protest against the imprisonment of Gbagbo and another FPI member of parliament, and in the following month Wodié similarly withdrew from the legislature.

Houphouët-Boigny returned to Côte d'Ivoire in June 1992, after an absence (spent mainly in France) of almost five months. In July he declared an amnesty for all those convicted of political offences since the time of the 1990 disturbances. The amnesty was approved by PDCI–RDA deputies in the national assembly, in the continued absence of opposition deputies, who protested that the amnesty not only prevented detainees from pursuing the right of appeal, but also exempted members of the security forces from charges relating to offences allegedly committed during the period covered by the measure.

The abolition of free public transport for students in higher education prompted violent protests in Abidjan in September 1992, and in November security forces were reported to have used tear gas to disperse university students who were refusing to sit examinations. There was further student unrest in April and May 1993, after a gathering of some 3,000 students at the University of Abidjan, organized by radical members of FESCI, was dispersed by security forces. In August students staged a two-week hunger strike outside the cathedral in Abidjan, following rumours that university accommodation was to be privatized and to demand the payment of grant arrears.

Members of the élite presidential guard, demanding salary increases, mutinied twice in March and April 1993; on both occasions they returned to barracks only after direct negotiations with Houphouët-Boigny. These incidents were cited by Ouattara's opponents (including, within the PDCI–RDA, supporters of Bédié) as evidence of the prime minister's inability to reconcile the demands of economic austerity with the need to maintain domestic harmony. In March, moreover, following criticism that some state holdings had been undervalued prior to their sale, the legislature had voted effectively to deprive the prime minister of control of the proceeds of privatization, recommending that a parliamentary committee be established to scrutinize the government's divestment programme.

Houphouët-Boigny left Côte d'Ivoire in May 1993, and subsequently spent six months receiving medical treatment in France and Switzerland. As it became increasingly evident that the president's health was failing, controversy arose concerning the issue of succession. Ouattara and Gbagbo (both of whom were known to have presidential ambitions) were among prominent politicians who denounced the process defined in the constitution. It was alleged that Article 11 effectively endorsed an hereditary presidency—Bédié, like Houphouët-Boigny, was a member of the Baoulé ethnic group from a family of chiefs and cocoa-planters—and demands were made for a further revision of the constitution to permit the president of the legislature to assume the post of president of the republic on an interim basis only.

President Houphouët-Boigny died in Yamoussoukro on 7 December 1993. Later the same day Henri Konan Bédié made a television broadcast announcing that he was assuming the duties of president of the republic, with immediate effect, in accordance with the constitution. France assumed what was widely regarded as a decisive role in the matter, promptly acknowledging Bédié's legitimacy as president and conveying official condolences to him in his capacity as the new head of state. Ouattara, who had initially refused to recognize Bédié's right of succession, resigned the premiership two days after Houphouët-Boigny's death. The supreme court confirmed Bédié as president on 10 December. Daniel Kablan Duncan, formerly minister-delegate, responsible for the economy, finance and planning, was appointed prime minister; his government retained senior members of the previous administration in charge of defence, foreign affairs, the interior and raw materials, and included two close associates of Bédié, Laurent Dona-Fologo and Timothée N'Guetta Ahoua, as ministers of state. Lamine Fadika, who had been removed from the government in 1987, amid rumours of a coup plot, was appointed minister of mines and energy. In January 1994 Charles Donwahi was elected president of the national assembly; a prominent member of the PDCI–RDA, he had been vice-president of the legislature since 1991. Thus during the two-month period of official mourning that followed Houphouët-Boigny's death, Bédié conducted an effective purge of Ouattara sympathizers, appointing his own supporters to positions of influence in government agencies, the judiciary and in the state-owned media. Ouattara was, moreover, the subject of virulent attacks in the official daily newspaper, *Fraternité Matin*, which emphasized both his Muslim and Burkinabè origins.

THE BÉDIÉ PRESIDENCY

Several months of sporadic labour unrest were brought to an end by Houphouët-Boigny's death, and, largely owing to the period of national mourning, reactions to the 50% devaluation, in January 1994, of the CFA franc were generally more muted in Côte d'Ivoire than in other countries of the region. Opposition leaders did, none the less, condemn the measure, and trade unions denounced salary increases of 5%–15%, together with compensatory tax reductions and price controls, as insufficient to offset the adverse effects of the currency's depreciation. In May and June, moreover, a new campaign of action by students, in an attempt to secure the payment of grant arrears, resulted in numerous arrests. Despite Bédié's earlier criticism of Ouattara's economic policies, notably the dismantling of the state-owned sector, the new president and prime minister confirmed their commitment to adjustment measures initiated under Ouattara, and accelerated privatization was a major element of financial programmes agreed with international creditors in the mid-1990s.

Bédié was elected chairman of the PDCI–RDA in April 1994. His position as head of state was further strengthened by Ouattara's appointment, in May, to the post of deputy managing director of the IMF, based in Washington, DC. However, that Bédié did not command the support of the whole of his party was confirmed in June, when a group of Ouattara loyalists left the PDCI–RDA to form what they termed a moderate, centrist organization, the Rassemblement des républicains (RPR). By the end of the year nine former PDCI–RDA deputies in the national assembly were reported to have joined the new party, which had, moreover, supplanted the FPI as the principal parliamentary opposition, following the defection of two FPI members to the presidential majority. Ouattara officially announced his membership of the RDR in early 1995.

The new regime used far-reaching legislation (introduced under Houphouët-Boigny) governing the press to prosecute several journalists who were deemed to have been disrespectful to Bédié or to other state officials. Among those prosecuted was the head of an influential news publishing group, Abou Drahamane Sangaré (also the deputy leader of the FPI). In his capacity as director of the daily *La Voie*, Sangaré was (together with other journalists of his newspaper) imprisoned in April 1994, but was released in December, in accordance with a presidential amnesty for some 2,000 detainees. In June 1995 there was widespread outrage after Sangaré was severely beaten by security forces at the office of the minister of security, Gaston Ouassénan Koné, following the publication of remarks in a satirical review owned by Sangaré's publishing group that were interpreted by Koné as insulting to him and his family. Although Bédié unequivocally condemned the beating, he did not submit to the FPI's demands that Koné be dismissed.

The increase in violent crime in Côte d'Ivoire was of particular concern to the Bédié government, and in June 1995 the national assembly approved proposals for legislation permitting the extension of the death penalty (already in existence for murder convictions, although there was no record of its implementation since independence) to cases of robbery with violence. New security operations accompanying the government's anti-crime measures, which frequently targeted non-Ivorian groups, were denounced by Bédié's opponents as indicative of the regime's xenophobic tendencies.

Considerable controversy was caused by the adoption, in December 1994, of a new electoral code, in preparation for presidential and legislative elections scheduled for October and November 1995. Opposition parties denounced clauses imposing restrictions on eligibility for public office, in particular requirements that candidates be of direct Ivorian descent and have been continuously resident in Côte d'Ivoire for five years prior to seeking election, both of which were interpreted as being directly aimed at preventing Ouattara from contesting the presidency. The RDR, the FPI and the Union des forces démocratiques (a coalition of opposition parties including the PIT), allied in a Front républicain (FR), organized several mass demonstrations in Abidjan in mid-1995 to demand the reform of the electoral code and the establishment of an independent electoral commission (the latter to reduce government influence over the electoral process). In June an FPI congress formally adopted Gbagbo as its candidate for the presidency, and in July the RDR invited Ouattara to stand as its presidential candidate. (The two parties were already reported to have agreed to present a single candidate in the event of a second round of presidential voting.) In August, however, Ouattara announced that, although he wished to contest the presidency, he would not attempt to do so in violation of the law. Also in August the PDCI–RDA officially adopted Bédié as the party's presidential candidate. The FR persisted in its efforts to seek a revision of the electoral code, together with guarantees regarding the autonomy of the electoral commission and the revision of voters' lists. In September, citing the need to ensure the continuation of economic activity, the government imposed a three-month ban on political demonstrations. Opposition groups protested that this was in violation of constitutional recognition of the right to demonstrate, and clashes between demonstrators and security forces continued in Abidjan and elsewhere. At the end of the month six opposition supporters who had participated in a protest on the day of the announcement of the ban were each fined and sentenced to one year's imprisonment.

The deadline for the submission of candidates for the presidential election was reached at the beginning of October 1995. Both the FPI and the RDR (whose secretary-general, Djény Kobina, had been expected to replace Ouattara as the party's candidate) stated that they would not be contesting the election as long as the conditions were not 'clear and open'; however, Wodié intended to contest the presidency as the candidate of the PIT. An eruption of violence in Abidjan and in other major towns coincided with the opening of an international investment forum in Abidjan. At a (prearranged) meeting between Bédié and representatives of almost 90 political parties, the president reiterated his administration's refusal to submit to opposition demands for the withdrawal of the electoral code, for the postponement of the elections, and for the formation of a transitional government of national unity. Shortly afterwards the constitutional council announced that, of the six prospective candidates for the presidency, two—Bédié and Wodié—had fulfilled the necessary criteria to contest the election. Negotiations involving Bédié, the FPI and other opposition groups took place in subsequent days; however, the RDR (which was later involved in separate talks with the authorities) claimed that it was being isolated from those discussions. No effective progress was made, and the FR warned that further protests and disturbances would be organized during the week preceding the presidential election, refusing to accept a government offer to include opposition representatives on the commission responsible for scrutinizing voters' lists and the results of the elections as sufficient guarantee of the commission's autonomy. For its part, the government rejected the opposition's demand that the elections be postponed, and, more specifically, emphasized that one of the principal grounds for the FR's proposed boycott of the presidential election—that the stipulation regarding continuous residency was directly aimed at preventing Ouattara's candidature—was invalid, since this did not apply to individuals selected by the government to serve abroad. Meanwhile, nine further opposition activists were fined and sentenced to one-year prison terms, convicted of involvement in disturbances.

The 1995 Elections

The presidential election took place, as scheduled, on 22 October 1995, following a week of violent incidents in several towns. The FR claimed that its call for an 'active boycott' of the poll had been largely successful (despite appeals by Wodié for the opposition vote), while the government claimed that voters had participated both peacefully and in large numbers. Troops were deployed, ostensibly to prevent the disruption of voting by the opposition, although it was reported that polling had proceeded in only one of 60 designated centres in the FPI stronghold of Gagnoa, in the Centre-Ouest region. The official results of the presidential election were announced by the constitutional council five days after the poll. As had been expected, Bédié, with 95.2% of the valid votes cast, secured an overwhelming victory. While most areas remained generally calm following the election, the apparent persecution of Baoulé around Gagnoa by members of the local majority Bété ethnic group became a cause of considerable concern, as large numbers of Baoulé converged on the town of Gagnoa from surrounding areas. In early November the government announced the establishment of a commission of inquiry to investigate the situation. At this time official reports stated that there had been some 25 deaths in the region (although it later transpired that only one death had resulted from the unrest); more than 3,500 people, mainly Baoulé, had been displaced, and numerous settlements had been destroyed.

Efforts were intensified to reach an accommodation between the government and opposition prior to the legislative elections, which were scheduled for 26 November 1995. Following a series of discussions, in early November it was announced that the FR had agreed to abandon its threatened boycott of the elections, in return for government concessions regarding the revision of voters' lists; representatives of both the FPI and the RDR were subsequently appointed to the electoral commission. The two principal opposition parties were, however, unable to agree terms for the presentation of a single list of candidates for the national assembly, and submitted separate lists for approval. The opposition suffered a further reverse when the authorities announced that voting in three of Gagnoa's four constituencies, including the constituency that was to have been contested by Gbagbo, was to be postponed, owing to the disruption arising from the recent disturbances; moreover, Kobina's candidacy (in Abidjan's Adjamé constituency) was disallowed, on the grounds that he had been unable to prove direct Ivorian descent. Voting for the legislature was reported to have proceeded generally without incident, and the earliest indications were that the PDCI–RDA had retained a decisive majority. There was evidence of strong ethno-geographical trends in the distribution of votes, with a notable loss of support for the PDCI–RDA in the Nord region, in favour of the RDR. The FPI, as expected, secured strong representation in the Centre-Ouest region, while the PDCI–RDA secured overwhelming victories in the Centre, Ouest and Sud-Ouest regions, and had strong support in Abidjan and other major towns. (It was expected that the FPI would retain control of the seats in Gagnoa where voting had yet to take place.) Wodié, contesting the Cocody district of Abidjan, failed to secure re-election to the Assemblée nationale. In late December the constitutional council annulled the results of the elections in three constituencies, including the one seat in

Gagnoa for which voting had been permitted. The PDCI–RDA thus held 146 seats, the RDR 14, and the FPI nine. In that month Donwahi was re-elected president of the national assembly.

In October 1995, shortly before the presidential election, Gen. Gueï was appointed to the government as minister of employment and the civil service. He was replaced in his armed forces command by his former deputy, Cdre Lassana Timité. Duncan reshuffled his government in January 1996. Léon Konan Koffi was transferred from the post of minister of defence to that of minister of state, responsible for religious affairs and dialogue with the opposition, while Gueï became minister of sports. Also appointed to the new government were a resident minister for Yamoussoukro and two regional high commissioners. At local elections in February the governing party won control of 158 communes (of a total of 195); the RDR secured 19 (mainly northern) communes, and the FPI 13 (principally in the west). The rate of participation by voters was low, and voting was reported to have proceeded generally without incident.

Undercurrents of Unrest

Reports emerged in the independent press in May 1996 of a coup attempt by disaffected members of the armed forces at the time of the civil unrest that preceded the 1995 presidential election: one newspaper, *Le Jour*, published the text of a letter purportedly written to Bédié by 11 detained soliders, of various ranks, denying involvement in any destabilization plot. Gueï's appointment to a relatively minor government post was now interpreted as a reaction to unrest in the forces under his command. Apparently in response to these rumours the minister of defence, Bandama N'Gatta, made a televised statement that members of the military high command had recently sought an audience with Bédié, at which they had affirmed their loyalty to the head of state and demanded that 'exemplary sanctions' be taken against armed forces personnel involved in 'disloyal' actions in September and October 1995. Later in May 1996 the Ivorian authorities denounced a report by a prominent human rights organization, Amnesty International, in which it was alleged that opposition members in Côte d'Ivoire were, notably since the 1995 election campaign, the target of systematic repression: particular concern was expressed regarding the detention of opposition activists (many of whom had yet to be tried) under anti-riot legislation. Bédié and his ministers responded to the report with assertions of Côte d'Ivoire's respect for human rights and for correct judicial procedure, emphasizing that all those in detention had been convicted of, or were awaiting trial for, specific violations of the country's laws. In the following month *La Voie* reported the release, on appeal, of several opposition members who had been detained during pre-election unrest and subsequently convicted in unpublicized trials. The release on bail of a further 39 detainees was reported by the same newspaper in late October. *La Voie* also drew attention to the death in custody of several opposition activists who had been arrested in connection with the so-called 'active boycott'. (In an interview published by the French journal, *Jeune Afrique*, in mid-1997, Gbagbo stated that, of some 450 opposition activists questioned in connection with election violence, 70 remained in detention without trial.)

Meanwhile, the issue of press censorship was again brought to the fore by the imprisonment, in late 1995 and early 1996, of journalists linked to the opposition. Most notably, Sangaré was, together with two other journalists of *La Voie*, sentenced to two years' imprisonment for publishing an article deemed insulting to the head of state; in addition, publication of the newspaper was suspended for three months. In August 1996 it was announced that the three *La Voie* journalists had refused to submit to preconditions for their release under a presidential amnesty (announced by Bédié to commemorate the country's national day), whereby they would be required to write directly to the head of state seeking a pardon and renouncing any appeal against sentence: in June the court of appeal had confirmed their convictions, and a higher appeal was rejected by the supreme court in late November. None the less, Bédié announced a pardon for the three journalists at the end of December.

A reorganization of government portfolios in mid-August 1996 appeared to reflect both Bédié's desire to remove from positions of influence figures connected with the insecurity prior to the 1995 elections and his concern to strengthen national security. Thus, among those to leave the government were Koffi, Koné and Gueï; in addition, a new minister of justice and public freedom was appointed, and the secretary-general of the country's new national security council (which had been established in late July 1996 to co-ordinate all issues of national security) took the rank of minister-delegate to the presidency. Gueï personally denied a subsequent announcement by a foreign news agency that he was under house arrest, and refused to comment on reports that he was to be questioned by a military commission appointed to investigate cases of indiscipline in the armed forces in 1995. In early September LIDHO wrote to N'Gatta, expressing concern at the continued detention, in an unknown location, of several members of the armed forces on charges of plotting an armed insurrection. In mid-November the government announced the dismissal of seven members of the armed forces (six of them commissioned officers) and the suspension of several other members of the military, in accordance with the investigations into what was now apparently confirmed as a destabilization plot. In late January 1997, moreover, Gueï was dismissed from the army: a government communiqué stated that the investigative commission had found that the then armed forces chief had committed 'serious disciplinary offences' in the discharge of his duties. At the end of March it was announced that Bédié had instructed N'Gatta to effect the release from custody of members of the military detained in connection with the events of late 1995.

At a congress of the PDCI–RDA held in late October 1996, Bédié was re-elected party chairman, and Laurent Dona-Fologo its secretary-general. Bédié, opening the congress, had urged a campaign against corruption. The president additionally advocated the opening of government to the parliamentary and non-parliamentary opposition. The RDR and the FPI did not exclude the possibility of participating in a government of national reconciliation; however, the former stipulated that advance agreement be reached on the allocation of ministerial portfolios and on the government's programme, while the latter indicated that it would require, in particular, amendment of Article 11 of the constitution (concerning the presidential succession) and revision of the electoral code. A commission of inquiry into the 1995 pre-election unrest was inaugurated in early December 1996. The RDR and the FPI refused to take up their allotted seats, however, protesting that the opposition had been judged responsible in advance of the inquiry. Rumours of an imminent government reorganization, to include opposition parties in the cabinet, circulated in subsequent months.

By-elections for eight parliamentary seats (including those for which voting did not take place or was cancelled in 1995) took place in late December 1996: the FPI won five seats, and the PDCI–RDA three. In mid-January 1997 the government approved changes to the names of Côte d'Ivoire's administrative regions.

After a period of relative calm, there was severe disruption in the higher education sector from late 1996. In mid-December students in Abidjan began a protest against the late payment of grants and to demand a modified examinations system. Four members of the outlawed FESCI were arrested after, according to official reports, causing a disturbance outside the ministry of security. In early January 1997 three of the students were fined and sentenced to two years' imprisonment, provoking outrage at the university. Later in the month a student died while fleeing police who disrupted a FESCI meeting, and shortly afterwards, on the eve of a planned 72-hour boycott of classes, two students were seriously injured in clashes with security forces at the Yopougon campus; officials denied allegations that police had fired bullets on demonstrators. The arrest of several leading members of FESCI, including the organization's secretary-general, in early February prompted further protests, but tensions were temporarily defused at the end of the month, when Bédié issued a decree pardoning the three students who had been sentenced in January (after they had abandoned their appeal against sentence) and ordering the release of all detained student activists. The establishment was additionally announced of a permanent committee, chaired by the president of the University of Cocody, to mediate or arbitrate in future disputes. In early April, none the less, disturbances at the University of Bouaké resulted in considerable material damage, and it was reported that some students had been attacked by groups of activists, in an effort to prevent their sitting examinations. In response, the government announced the closure of the University of Bouaké and its halls of residence. FESCI, adding the reopening of the university to its demands regarding improvements in conditions of study and accommodation and in the allocation and disbursement of scholarships, gave notice of a five-day boycott of classes. In early May the authorities ordered the closure of university residences in Abidjan, in view of the persistent disruptions there; lectures were to continue, none the less, and the resumption of classes at Bouaké was announced at the end of the month. Stating that it had achieved some progress in its demands, FESCI announced a return to classes in mid-June, but immediately urged a renewed boycott after the government denied having made any concessions; two students were subsequently severely injured in clashes on the Cocody campus.

In mid-March 1997 Bédié announced the rehabilitation of Ernest Boka. The first president of independent Côte d'Ivoire's supreme court, Boka had been detained in 1963 at the time of the so-called 'youth plot', and was subsequently said to have committed suicide while in custody. The impending publication of a book entitled *Les faux complots d'Houphouët-Boigny,* written by another former political detainee, Samba Diarra, had recently prompted considerable coverage in the Ivorian media of the time of the 'false plots', and had raised questions regarding the human rights record of the Houphouët-Boigny regime.

FOREIGN RELATIONS AND REGIONAL CONCERNS

Throughout his presidency Houphouët-Boigny was active in regional and international affairs, assisting in the peace process in Angola and, despite strong criticism by the Organization of African Unity, favouring black African dialogue with the apartheid regime in South Africa. Both prime minister Vorster and President Botha of South Africa visited Côte d'Ivoire while in office, and President de Klerk had also been received by Houphouët-Boigny before the dismantling of apartheid legislation began. South African financial assistance was granted for the Ivorian gold-mining, agricultural and agro-industrial sectors following a visit by de Klerk in December 1989. In April 1992 Côte d'Ivoire became the first black African country to establish diplomatic relations with South Africa. Speaking in Côte d'Ivoire in March 1996, President Nelson Mandela stated that Houphouët-Boigny's support for the anti-apartheid cause in South Africa had been of great importance to the movement's eventual success.

In regional affairs, Côte d'Ivoire under Houphouët-Boigny exerted a strong conservative influence, and tended to favour the maintenance of close links with the West, although Houphouët-Boigny was particularly critical in the final years of his regime of what he regarded as attempts by 'Anglo-Saxon' countries to depress the prices of Africa's major commodities. Relations with France were generally close, despite the apparent support of the socialist regime of François Mitterrand for Gbagbo and the FPI. Links remained cordial following Bédié's accession to the presidency, and were apparently enhanced by the election of Jacques Chirac as French president in May 1995. Chirac began his first presidential visit to sub-Saharan Africa in Côte d'Ivoire in July of that year, and the presidents of Benin, Burkina Faso, Niger and Togo travelled to Yamoussoukro for informal discussions with the new French leader. Support for Bédié and the PDCI–RDA was evident within the Chirac administration prior to the Ivorian presidential and legislative elections in late 1995 (the Ivorian ruling party has long been close to the Gaullist Rassemblement pour la République), and it was believed that France had exerted influence over Ouattara not to disrupt the electoral process in Côte d'Ivoire by seeking to contest the presidency in defiance of the law. During late 1995 and 1996 the Bédié administration sought assurances from France that its programme of armed forces restructuring would not entail any reduction of the French military presence in Côte d'Ivoire. It was anticipated that the new socialist government under prime minister Lionel Jospin, elected in mid-1997, would proceed with plans to reduce French military commitments in west Africa, although it was thought likely that a base would be maintained in Abidjan. Relations with the USA were expected to remain close, while Bédié also expressed a wish to forge stronger links with other countries of the European Union and in the Far East.

In late 1989 the government of Liberia alleged that rebel forces, who were involved in an attempt to overthrow the incumbent regime, had entered the country through Côte d'Ivoire. Despite evidence to the contrary, Houphouët-Boigny consistently denied that his government was supporting Charles Taylor's National Patriotic Front of Liberia (NPFL), which was instrumental in the overthrow of President Doe in mid-1990. During 1991 Côte d'Ivoire assumed a prominent role in attempts to achieve a peaceful dialogue between opposing forces in Liberia. A series of negotiations involving the rival factions was initiated in Yamoussoukro in the second half of the year. In December, none the less, the Liberian interim president, Dr Amos Sawyer, accused Côte d'Ivoire of providing the NPFL with arms and training facilities. Although Côte d'Ivoire did not at this time contribute troops to the ECOMOG military observer group that was dispatched to Liberia by the Economic Community of West African States (ECOWAS) in August 1990, Houphouët-Boigny attended the ECOWAS summit meeting, convened in November 1992 in Abuja, Nigeria, to discuss the Liberian issue, and supported a communiqué proposing that ECOMOG be extended to all ECOWAS member states and appealing for UN intervention in the peace process.

Relations with other ECOWAS members deteriorated in February 1993, when (following recent allegations that NPFL units were operating from Ivorian territory) aircraft under ECOMOG command bombed the Ivorian border region of Danané. Côte d'Ivoire formally protested to ECOWAS, which expressed its regret at the incident, claiming that the area attacked had been mistaken for Liberian territory. Rumours persisted that Ivorian authorities were violating the international economic and military blockade of Liberia by (either actively or passively) allowing the NPFL access to the sea via the port of San Pedro in southwestern Côte d'Ivoire, and there were reports that several of Taylor's close and influential associates had taken up residence in Abidjan. In May Côte d'Ivoire protested that ECOMOG jets had again bombed territory in the Danané region, although this was denied by the ECOMOG command.

The presence in Côte d'Ivoire of large numbers of refugees from Liberia (variously estimated at 300,000–400,000 in mid-1996) has been increasingly cited by the Ivorian authorities as a cause of the perceived escalation in insecurity in the country, and periodic incursions onto Ivorian territory by members of armed factions in the Liberian conflict provoked considerable disquiet. In September 1994, shortly after an attempted coup in Liberia had caused a renewed influx of refugees, four people, including two Ivorian civilians, were killed following an attack, attributed to NPFL rebels (which was suppressed by the Ivorian armed forces), on a village in the Danané region. Clashes around Taï between partisans of the Liberia Peace Council (LPC) faction and the NPFL in June 1995, as a result of which some 32 people, including 10 Ivorians, were killed, prompted a major security operation by Côte d'Ivoire's armed forces to regain control of border areas where infiltration by Liberian fighters was frequent.

In July 1995 Côte d'Ivoire, which has tended to promote the full integration of refugees into Ivorian society (a process facilitated by the common ethnic origin of communities on both sides of the Côte d'Ivoire–Liberia border), announced the establishment of the first reception centre for Liberian refugees at Guiglo, and stated that further camps would also be established. An agreement was signed in Abidjan in January 1996 regarding a major programme of assistance (valued at about US $100m.), to be co-ordinated by the office of the UN High Commissioner for Refugees and the World Food Programme, for refugees from the conflicts in Liberia and Sierra Leone displaced in those countries and in Côte d'Ivoire and Guinea. It was, however, increasingly suspected that Liberian militias operating near the border with Côte d'Ivoire were, either by looting or by registering as refugees, exploiting humanitarian assistance schemes in operation in Côte d'Ivoire. In February 1996 a suspected looting raid, attributed to LPC fighters, on an oil-palm plantation near the border resulted in the deaths of five civilians, and in June some 14 deaths were reported following a cross-border attack in the Toulépleu area by suspected NPFL rebels. The Ivorian authorities announced that security measures were to be increased in the west (in an effort to prevent further rebel incursions and the infiltration of refugee groups by Liberian fighters. In late July the government proclaimed western Côte d'Ivoire to be a military 'operational zone', extending the powers of the armed forces to act in response to rebel activity.

The reinforcement of security and military operations in western Côte d'Ivoire additionally followed a period of concern regarding the integrity of the border with Guinea (the demarcation of part of which had long been disputed by the latter). Bilateral relations had been strained in August 1995, after Guinea established a border post in an area assumed to be part of Ivorian territory, claiming the need to prevent incursions into Guinea by Liberian rebels. Despite an announcement in September that the two countries were to co-operate in resolving this and other joint border issues, it was reported in March 1996 that Guinean soldiers had occupied a village in the Sipilou sub-prefecture. Ivorian troops in the region were mobilized in preparation for a military response, although Côte d'Ivoire's minister of defence reaffirmed his government's desire to resolve such border disputes through dialogue.

Economy

EDITH HODGKINSON

For some 20 years following its independence, Côte d'Ivoire was remarkable for its very high rate of economic growth: gross domestic product (GDP) increased, in real terms, by an annual average of 11% in 1960–70 and 6%–7% in 1970–80, bringing it into the ranks of middle-income developing countries. During the 1980s, however, the economy entered a period of decline, owing mainly to a weakening in international prices for the country's major export commodities (coffee and cocoa) and the serious drought of 1982–84. GDP fell in 1982–84. Economic growth was resumed in 1985, with record harvests of cocoa and cotton and a recovery in coffee output (owing to the ending of the drought), and higher world prices for most export commodities. However, the economy's sensitivity to developments in international markets for cocoa and coffee was revealed when the sharp fall in export prices for both commodities in 1987 (to below Ivorian production costs), for cocoa in subsequent years and for coffee after 1989 resulted in a decline or stagnation in GDP for seven consecutive years (1987–93). Gross national product (GNP), converted from estimates in CFA francs, was US $5,445m. in 1994, equivalent to $397 per head. GDP in 1993 was US $10,406m. (converted from CFA francs at the prevailing exchange rate), equivalent to $780 per head. The devaluation of the CFA frank in 1994 cut the per head figure to $545 in that year. Previously classified as a lower-middle-income country, Côte d'Ivoire is now listed by the World Bank as a low-income country.

A new phase in the development of the Ivorian economy began in 1991 with the implementation of a far-reaching programme of structural reform, involving the acceptance by Côte d'Ivoire of an IMF/World Bank programme of fiscal austerity and market liberalization (including the disengagement of the state from both production and service sectors). The 'Plan Ouattara' had ambitious targets: an increase of 5% in GDP by 1995 and the achievement of an average annual growth rate of 3.2% in 1992–95; a doubling in the rate of investment growth, and a reduction by more than one-half in the deficit on the current account of the balance of payments. However, even with financial support from foreign donors and creditors, none of these targets had been achieved by the time Alassane Ouattara relinquished the premiership at the end of 1993. By late 1994, however, a marked recovery was in progress, with GDP growth for the whole year reaching 1.8%, then accelerating to 7% in 1995 and an estimated 6.8% in 1996. The significant factor was the 50% devaluation of the CFA franc in January 1994, which improved the competitiveness, in price terms, of Côte d'Ivoire's timber and non-traditional exports such as fish and rubber at a time when a boom in international prices for coffee was coming to an end. With the programme of structural adjustment well entrenched, and the Bédié administration's very positive attitude towards foreign investment, GDP growth is expected to maintain a robust pace for the remainder of the decade.

A return to strong and sustained economic growth is all the more needed given the very high rate of population growth. At about 3.6% per year since 1985, this is one of the fastest in the world (bringing the total population to an estimated level of 14.7m. by mid-1996). The rate of urbanization has been rapid (one-half again the overall rate of population growth), with some 44% of the population residing in urban areas in 1995—more than double the proportion in 1960. Abidjan's population was recorded as 1.9m. at the 1988 census, more than double its level at the 1975 census, and urban unemployment (registered at 22.4%—excluding foreigners—in 1988) is a growing problem. This pressure on Abidjan was a significant factor in the designation of Yamoussoukro as the country's future political capital, although Abidjan will remain the major centre for economic activity. A major factor in population growth has been immigration from less prosperous neighbouring countries, particularly Burkina Faso, Guinea and Mali, and immigrants now constitute almost 40% of the population, providing vital manpower for plantations and urban services.

AGRICULTURE, FORESTRY AND FISHING

Although the Ivorian economy is relatively diversified, it remains dependent on agriculture, which contributes about one-third of GDP and employs some 60%–80% of the economically active population. Agriculture provides about three-quarters of export earnings, and the sector's rapid growth was the basis for the economic expansion of the 1960s and 1970s.

The principal cash crops are coffee and cocoa. The cultivation and processing of coffee is the main source of income for about one-half of all Ivorians, and it employs more than 2.5m. people. Côte d'Ivoire is now the largest African producer. The record crop of 366,838 metric tons was registered in 1980/81, and was grown on about 280,000 small, family-owned plantations covering some 1m. ha. Output has since been in overall decline, and averaged only some 166,000 tons per year in 1991–95, when three-quarters of the country's coffee plants had passed their most productive age. Thus, the surge in international coffee prices in 1993–94 and the leeway provided by the currency devaluation, which allowed increases in the price paid to producers, elicited a relatively modest response in terms of Ivorian output: the crop in 1995/96 was 175,000 tons. By 1996/97, however, the strength of prices had stimulated a sharp improvement in output, to an estimated 230,000 tons. Government plans provide for extensive replanting of the old robusta plantations with a cross between robusta and arabica varieties: the total area under cultivation is projected to increase by 270,000 ha to 1.3m. ha by the end of the century, and production is expected to consolidate at 300,000 tons per year.

Production of cocoa beans doubled between 1970 and 1979, making Côte d'Ivoire the largest exporter in the world. The country has been the world's largest cocoa producer since 1977/78, when its level of production overtook that of Ghana. Overall output continued to rise, with some fluctuations, reaching a record 1.1m. tons in 1995/96 (in the previous four years the crop had averaged 750,000 tons per year) and an estimated 1m. tons in 1996/97. This increase in the cocoa harvest owes much to a major replanting programme implemented by the government in the 1980s, aimed at eliminating ageing cultivation in the traditional cocoa belt, in the south-east, and developing it in the west, where rainfall is abundant. The expansion in cocoa production was also attributable to the transfer to the cultivation of cocoa by many former coffee producers: until 1989 the two crops attracted virtually the same producer price, although the latter was more heavily taxed and is more difficult to grow.

A state marketing agency, the Caisse de stabilisation et de soutien des prix des productions agricoles (Caistab), traditionally purchased all cocoa and coffee production, and during the boom years of 1975–77 this agency bought the crops from producers at prices that were significantly below world market levels, so providing a surplus for investment in other sectors of the economy. However, the subsequent weakening in world prices meant that the government was unable to maintain the real income of producers, and for the four years until 1983/84 and again in 1986/87–1987/88 purchase prices were 'frozen'. From early 1988 the government attempted to bring about an increase in international prices by stockpiling cocoa, pursuing a policy of bulk sales to major buyers. This was abandoned in late 1989, by which time the collapse of international prices for cocoa, in conjunction with pressure from the IMF to end the drain on budget resources that Caistab's operations represented, had obliged the Ivorian government to impose very steep reductions in the official prices payable to producers of cocoa. Producer prices for the 1989/90 season were thus halved, to 200 francs CFA per kg for cocoa—their lowest level since 1978—to 100 francs CFA per kg for coffee. There was a significant new development in the 1991/92 season, with the abolition of export quotas for cocoa and coffee, while the liberalization of the sector was completed when Caistab was opened to participation by private interests and its quality-control function was eliminated. The agency now operates essentially as a consultative body, with the prices it sets at the beginning of each season serving as no more than a guide-line. The diminution in its role reflected concerted pressure from the IMF and the World Bank institutions, whose support has been critical to the economy's recovery in the mid-1990s. Producer prices for both cocoa and coffee were increased immediately after the January 1994 devaluation, although not to the full extent of the depreciation in the currency's value: the cocoa price was set at 240 francs CFA per kg for the 1993/94 season and 315 francs CFA for 1994/95, while prices for coffee were initially raised to 200 francs CFA per kg and then, with a series of further increases, to 695 francs CFA per kg for 1995/96—thus ending the comparative advantage of cocoa production over coffee.

With about one-half of Côte d'Ivoire's total export earnings provided by sales of these two crops, both highly vulnerable to international market trends, the government has sought to diversify agricultural production. Since the 1960s Côte d'Ivoire has become a major producer of palm oil, and local processing of palm products has developed. A series of replanting programmes has been supported by the World Bank, the European Community (now European Union—EU), France and the United Kingdom. The current programme, which began in 1986, aimed, initially, to clear and replant 65,000 ha, and to construct two processing mills: the target was to make Côte d'Ivoire the world's leading producer of palm oil. The steep fall in world prices in 1987 prompted the government to reduce the planting target and to postpone the construction of one of the mills. However, output reached some 309,700 tons in 1993, and exports in 1994 were 189,000 tons.

Cotton cultivation has done particularly well in recent decades. Production had increased only slowly until the mid-1970s, when the government embarked on a deliberate policy of helping the farmers in the north of the country. In recent years output has averaged about 250,000 tons per year, and Côte d'Ivoire vies with Sudan, Mali and Benin for the position as Africa's second largest cotton producer (after Egypt). Most of the cotton is processed locally in eight ginning complexes (total capacity 300,000 tons per year), both for export (some 80% of total production) and for the local textile industry.

The rubber industry has also shown growth since the mid-1980s (when output was some 50,000 tons per year), registering an average 75,000 tons per year in 1990–94, as the government pursues plans for Côte d'Ivoire to become Africa's leading rubber producer by the end of the century. The country is also a significant producer of pineapples and bananas, with exports (149,500 tons and 181,700 tons, respectively, in 1995) directed principally at the European market.

In recent years the government stressed the need to increase output of basic food crops, in which Côte d'Ivoire was not self-sufficient. The country is normally self-sufficient in maize, cassava, yams and plantains; however, the government is targeting the production of rice, large quantities of which are imported. Farmers in the traditional cocoa belt are increasingly engaged in food production, while two of the country's sugar complexes have been converted to rice cultivation. By the mid-1980s the rice development programme was showing an effect, and output of white rice reached 536,000 tons (paddy) in 1995. None the less, output still fails to fulfil domestic demand, which is rising rapidly as the population moving from rural areas to towns tends to switch its grain preference to rice: imports in 1995 reached 398,000 tons.

A deficiency in sugar supply and the need to save foreign exchange on sugar imports led the government to initiate a sugar programme in the 1970s. Production began at the first complex in 1977, and by 1980 the two schemes in operation could supply most of internal demand, then estimated at 80,000 tons of raw sugar per year. However, the cost of sugar production in the local complexes proved to be unexpectedly high, and was at least double the world market price at the beginning of 1980. This situation, in conjunction with the need to reduce foreign borrowing, led to the cancellation of six more planned complexes and the reduction of planned areas of sugar cane plantations on those areas already sanctioned, resulting in a decline in sugar production from the 186,000 tons recorded in 1982/83 to an average of 130,000 tons in recent years, still sufficient to fulfil domestic demand as well as small quotas in the US and EU markets.

Forestry has always been a significant source of export earnings, from both logs and sawn timber, and, boosted by enhanced price competitiveness, these have displaced both coffee and petroleum products to come second to cocoa since 1994. Most production is carried out by large integrated firms, many of which are foreign-owned. The area of exploitable timber had fallen to only about 1m. ha in 1987, compared with some 15.6m. ha at independence, because of inadequate reafforestation and the encroachment of agriculture on forest areas. In an attempt to conserve resources, the government therefore restricted commercial production to 3m. cu m per year. With domestic demand rising, the volume available for export declined, with exports falling from 3.1m. cu m (logs) in 1980 to only 29,000 cu m (and 521,000 cu m of sawn timber) in 1992. Export volume has since recovered to a total of 1.3m. cu m in 1994, under the stimulus of much higher earnings in local currency terms. Meanwhile, the World Bank and other external agencies are supporting a reafforestation programme, which includes replanting on 22,000 ha, with a production target of 6.6m. cu m over 35 years. Progress has, however, been disappointing (replanting has recently averaged only 5,000 ha per year), and the government has committed itself to a ban on exports of timber once the country's foreign payments position has improved.

Livestock herds are small: in 1995 there were some 1.3m. cattle, 2.2m. sheep and goats and 414,000 pigs—and meat production satisfies only one-third of national demand. Fishing is a significant activity (Abidjan is the largest tuna-fishing port in Africa, with an annual catch of more than 90,000 tons). However, most of the catch is made by foreign ships and merely transits through the port. Ivorian participation in this sector is still low, with Côte d'Ivoire's own fishing fleet numbering only 38 vessels and most traditional fishing being undertaken by non-Ivorians. Domestic production currently meets only about 40% of local demand.

MANUFACTURING AND MINING

The manufacturing sector, which accounted for about 13% of GDP in the early 1990s, is dominated by agro-industrial activities—such as the processing of cocoa, coffee, cotton, oil palm, pineapples and fish. It was stimulated, immediately after independence, by the need to replace goods traditionally imported from Senegal, the manufacturing centre for colonial French West Africa, and it formed one of the most dynamic areas of the economy during this period. In 1965–74 Côte d'Ivoire's manufacturing output expanded, in real terms, at an average rate of 8.9% per year, with growth easing to 5.4% per year in the following decade, after the main industrial opportunities had been exploited. However, this sector continued to be sustained by the high rate of growth in domestic demand, arising from the rapid increase in the country's population, and it was given a sharp boost by the 1994 devaluation, which greatly enhanced the competitiveness of the local product. Industrial output was rising by 10% in 1995, from 2%–3% in the preceding two years; while this largely reflected the entry into production of the Lion oilfield (see below), the pace was maintained in 1996, when a 16% year-on-year rise was registered in the first eight months. Meanwhile, since the late 1980s the emphasis of government policy has shifted from import substitution to export promotion, with a higher proportion of local processing—particularly of cocoa, where the government's target is for one-half of the crop to be processed locally by 2000.

In the past a significant strand in government policy was the attempt to 'Ivorianize' both equity and management. Ivorian-held equity in industrial firms, virtually nil in 1960, had reached almost two-thirds of the total by 1982. However, this was almost entirely held by the government (51.5%), while the private-sector Ivorian share was very small (13.6%). This reflected the development of parastatal organizations during the 1970s as a means of restructuring and diversifying the economy. However, the financial losses being incurred by the parastatal companies became so serious that in 1980 the government reversed its policy regarding these organizations and began to dispose of its interests through outright sale, leasing, or the creation of autonomous co-operatives. An important element of the stabilization programme introduced by Alassane Ouattara in 1990 was an acceleration of the privatization process. Several major companies had been sold off by the end of 1992, including the electricity and water utilities. In all, the government aimed to dispose of 80 of a total of about 140 public companies by the end of 1995. Despite some public disquiet regarding the programme, the Bédié administration has maintained the pace, aiming to privatize, or part-privatize, 60 state-owned companies by mid-1997. Among the disposals that had been realized by early 1997 were the state-owned telecommunications company (CI-Telecom) and the palm oil company (Palmindustrie).

The only significant activity in the mining sector (apart from hydrocarbons) is the extraction of diamonds and gold. Output from the two diamond mines, at Tortiya and Séguéla, is some 15,000 carats annually, but very much larger quantities are produced in illicit operations. Total output was put at 84,300 carats in 1994. The exploitation of deposits of gold-bearing rock at Ity began in 1991, in a joint venture with the Cie française des mines; production reached 1,300 kg in 1995. A second gold mine, at Aniuri, began operations in 1993, in a joint venture between Eden Roc of Canada and the state mining company. Gold-concession agreements have been signed with other French and Canadian companies and with Australian and South African interests. There is considerable potential for nickel mining: in late 1996 Falconbridge of Canada signed an agreement with the government to invest US $500m. over five years in the development of reserves at Biankouma-Touba, estimated at 169m. tons of ore.

ENERGY

Electricity generating capacity rose very rapidly, from only 41 MW in 1962 to 675 MW in the early 1980s, as the result of the development of hydroelectric capacity. However, the focus of development switched after the 1982–84 drought severely reduced the contribution of hydroelectric generation, from 90% at the beginning of the decade to only 23% in 1994. Although its share has since recovered to about 60%, government policy is now to develop thermal capacity. Long-discussed plans for a thermal plant at Vridi, utilizing offshore reserves of natural gas, finally came to realization in 1994. A consortium led by United Meridian of the USA is developing the Panthère gas field, with production beginning in October 1995 at a rate of 15m. cu ft per day initially and due to reach 50m. cu ft per day to supply the 100-MW power facilities at Vridi. There were plans for three additional turbines to enter operation by 1997, to supply neighbouring countries.

Côte d'Ivoire has experienced mixed success in the development of its petroleum reserves. Offshore petroleum was discovered in 1975, with reserves at the Bélier field, located 15 km south of Grand Bassam, estimated at 75m. tons. A larger discovery was made in the Espoir field (also offshore) in 1980, but production failed to meet expectations. Output from Bélier attained a maximum of 457,000 tons in 1982, and that from Espoir reached a peak of 771,000 tons in 1984, to give a record total output of 1.1m. tons in that year. However, output declined in subsequent years; operations at the Espoir field were suspended in early 1989, and those at the Bélier field ceased one year later. In addition, offshore exploration for petroleum had virtually ceased by 1984; the Ivorian continental shelf had proved difficult to drill, and its hydrocarbon reserves were found to be dispersed in small pockets. However, a new round of exploration undertaken in the early 1990s proved successful, with a major discovery of offshore petroleum, near Jacqueville and Grand-Lahou, in 1994. A joint venture by United Meridian and the state-owned Société nationale d'opérations pétrolières de la Côte d'Ivoire (PETROCI) began production at the Lion field in April 1995: output increased from an initial level of 10,000 barrels per day (b/d) to 20,000 b/d by the end of the year. Additional development contracts were signed in late 1996 between PETROCI and a consortium including Shell for a nearby offshore block, the Entente field. Production here was expected to reach 19,000 b/d in early 1997. With other foreign companies showing interest in Côte d'Ivoire's offshore reserves, the government is hoping that self-sufficiency in petroleum will be achieved by 2000, with the prospect of exports thereafter.

TRANSPORT

The most important transport facility is the deep-water port of Abidjan, rivalled in francophone West Africa only by the iron ore-handling port of Nouadhibou in Mauritania. During the late 1980s and early 1990s Abidjan handled an average of about 10m. tons of freight per year, including shipments to and from Burkina Faso and Mali. This represents a recovery to near the levels recorded in 1980, after several years during which the volume of traffic fell, mainly because of a decline in timber exports and oil imports. Major improvements have been carried out, including the installation of large-scale container-handling facilities, and there are plans to double capacity by 1999. Another port has been developed since 1971 at San Pedro, mainly for timber and cocoa exports; this handled total traffic of more than 1m. tons in 1994.

Côte d'Ivoire has about 68,000 km of classified roads. In all, some 6,000 km of roads are now paved, almost six times the extent in 1970. A four year (1994–97) programme for the repair and extension of the road network, estimated to cost 147,000m. francs CFA, has been supported by the World Bank, the African Development Bank, the West African Development Bank and the governments of Germany and Japan. In 1995 France announced funding of 15,000m. francs CFA, in support of a project to rehabilitate more than 2,000 km of roads in northern regions. In addition, tolls were being introduced on some roads in the mid-1990s, to assist in funding the maintenance of the network. A railway line links Abidjan to Ouagadougou, with 638 km of line in Côte d'Ivoire. The line was managed by a single authority, the Régie du chemin de fer Abidjan–Niger (RAN), but experienced financial and technical difficulties, with both freight and passenger traffic in decline. As a result, RAN was liquidated in 1989, and its Ivorian activities were assumed by the Société ivoirienne des chemins de fer. Management responsibility has since been transferred to SITARAIL, a consortium of French, Belgian, Ivorian and Burkinabè investors. Côte d'Ivoire has international airports at Abidjan, Bouaké and Yamoussoukro, and there are several regional airports.

TOURISM

Tourism developed strongly in the 1970s, with a newly-created ministry stimulating diversification in location (away from the Abidjan area) and in type of visitor (away from business travellers, who previously accounted for almost two-thirds of arrivals). Special tax incentives and government guarantees on loans were offered for hotel construction. By late 1984 the number of hotels was 452, five times the level in 1970. The number of tourists increased from some 93,000 in 1974 to 198,900 in 1979, with business visitors accounting for 40% of arrivals. Since then visitor arrivals have fluctuated in the range 200,000–290,000 per year, broadly reflecting trends in world tourism. The government's target is 500,000 arrivals annually by 2000.

PUBLIC FINANCE

Budget spending has risen in parallel with economic growth, with current spending in the past covered from internal sources and investment spending largely financed by foreign borrowing. The deterioration in the economy during the early 1980s, and the associated fall in tax receipts, threatened serious disequilibrium. In response, a series of austerity budgets was adopted, with total spending declining, in real terms, each year from 1982 onwards. Reductions were initially limited to the investment budget, which had been halved, in real terms, by 1985. In 1986 current spending declined, in real terms, for the first time, with restrictions being applied to recruitment to the civil service and reductions in salaries for staff in parastatal bodies. These austerity measures transformed the budget balance from a record deficit of 361,000m. francs CFA (equivalent to 13% of GDP) in 1982 to a small surplus (83,000m. francs CFA) in 1985. However, the sharp fall in the late 1980s in international prices for Côte d'Ivoire's principal agricultural commodities, and the consequent increase in compensatory transfers to the marketing board, meant that the deficit had risen to 17.1% of GDP by 1989, despite overall reductions in both current and capital spending. Far more rigorous cuts in expenditure, particularly in agricultural price support, gradually lowered the deficit to 9.9% of GDP in 1992: for the first time in more than a decade the primary budget (i.e. excluding interest payments on the debt) recorded a modest surplus. After some deterioration in 1993, largely attributable to the impact on tax revenue of reductions in import tariffs, the budget balance was assisted by the reinstatement of export taxes on cocoa and coffee in 1994, allowed by the impact of currency devaluation, as well as by cuts in the public-sector payroll. The primary budget recorded a surplus, of 217,900m. francs CFA, equivalent to 5.2% of GDP. With the economy in strong recovery in both 1995 and 1996, revenue increased sufficiently to allow the government to raise the level of its capital spending while maintaining a surplus on the primary budget (of 161,000m. francs CFA in 1995). The government has thus been able to pay off some arrears on its domestic debt. None the less, the budget remains in overall deficit because of the massive burden of interest payments on the foreign debt, representing around 30% of total current spending.

FOREIGN TRADE AND PAYMENTS

Despite its very rapid economic growth during the period 1950–75, Côte d'Ivoire had, in the past, fewer problems with the balance of payments than most comparable African economies. Exports have increased at a faster rate than gross national product (GNP), and they remain the main factor contributing to economic growth.

Côte d'Ivoire's balance of trade has always been in surplus because of the strength of its exports, which have largely been determined by the level of earnings from sales of coffee and cocoa. With the recovery in coffee and cocoa output after the 1982–84 drought, the surplus increased more than fivefold in 1984, to 525,700m. francs CFA, and reached a new record level of 545,100m. francs CFA in 1985, despite a relaxation of the import restraints that had been imposed to offset the decline in commodity earnings. The surplus was halved by 1988 (to 289,000m. francs CFA), owing to the severe decline in international prices for cocoa and coffee, and in spite of the reduction in expenditure on imports (because of the contraction in the economy). The surplus remained around this level in the years immediately subsequent, with import spending adjusted to reflect trends in receipts from exports. However, the balance improved markedly in 1994, in both US dollar and local currency terms, as the consequence of the devaluation of the CFA franc. This enhanced the profitability of producing exports the prices of which were set in dollars, as well as the price competitiveness of those denominated in local currency. At the same time demand for imports was depressed by their higher cost. The surplus on merchandise trade thus reached $1,304m. in 1994, compared with $748m. in 1993. Despite pressure on the import bill as a result of the economic recovery in 1995 and 1996, the surplus rose further as earnings from sales of commodities expanded in response to greater supply (boosted by the improvement in producer prices) and still higher international prices. A surplus of $731m. was recorded in 1995, followed by a surplus of an estimated $1,900m. in 1996.

This improvement in merchandise trade, and the debt relief that followed currency devaluation (see below), brought an end to almost 10 years of deficits on the current account of the balance of payments. 1994 saw a surplus of US $368m.—the first surplus since 1985 (when a positive $64m. was recorded). Current payments deteriorated markedly in the following three years, reflecting the diminishing trade surplus and the heavy burden of interest payments, owing to earlier, very substantial, foreign borrowing (particularly in the late 1970s), as high prices for cocoa and coffee stimulated ambitious capital investment programmes by the government, and particularly by the state corporations. The deficit stabilized at an average of just over $1,000m. in 1989–93, with some improvement in the final years because of reduced interest payments as the result of debt relief, to register $916m. in 1993. After a brief return to deficit in 1995 ($447m.), the current account was again in surplus in 1996, at an estimated $150m. One of the major aims of the stabilization programme has therefore been achieved.

Reflecting the difficulties of the 1980s, the external debt has escalated sharply since the beginning of that decade, and at the end of 1993 was more than twice the level of 1980, at US $19,071m. This was equivalent to 243% of GNP in that year, while the debt-service ratio had been about 35% of the value of exports of goods and services in almost every year since 1981. Both are unmanageable proportions, and by the end of 1993 Côte d'Ivoire's arrears on its long term debt totalled $3,973m. These arrears had accumulated despite a series of debt-reschedulings—of both commercial and official liabilities— facilitated by Côte d'Ivoire's compliance with economic retrenchment programmes agreed with the IMF. The devaluation of the CFA franc in January 1994 threatened to precipitate a crisis, since it doubled the external debt in local currency terms overnight. In common with other Franc Zone countries in Africa, Côte d'Ivoire was the beneficiary of special measures of compensation and relief. The 'Paris Club' of official creditors agreed a new round of debt-reschedulings and cancellation, the exact form of relief varying between donor countries: France, Germany and Canada opted for a cancellation of 50% of debt, while the USA rescheduled debt over 25 years. In all, some $800m. of debt was cancelled (representing 4% of the country's indebtedness at the end of 1993), and a further 5%–6% was rescheduled. Total debt was thus reduced to $17,395m. by the end of 1994. However, arrears were still at very substantial levels—some $3,646m. at the end of 1994 and $3,800m. by the end of 1995. In that year the foreign debt was back up to $18,952m., equivalent to 252% of GNP (at the new dollar/CFA franc rate). Côte d'Ivoire thus remained highly dependent on further debt rescheduling both by official and commercial creditors, as well as on sustained inflows of aid. The 1994 devaluation had prompted new pledges of aid. France announced, among other commitments, structural adjustment credits totalling 600m. French francs, repayable over 22 years. Disbursements of net official development assistance subsequently increased markedly, to $1,594m. in 1994 and $1,212m. in 1995, from an annual average of $711m. in 1990–93. A significant form of development assistance in the recent past has been structural adjustment loans from the World Bank and sectoral loans in support of the adjustment programme. The support of the Bretton Woods institutions has become even more important since the devaluation, with the World Bank's concessionary lending agency, the International Development Association, disbursing a net $448m. in 1994 and $226m. in 1995, while the IMF accorded a three-year enhanced structural adjustment facility in 1994. These are critical to Côte d'Ivoire's obtaining further debt relief and new funding from both official bilateral and commercial donors, and hence its ability to secure the capital necessary for its economic development. In 1997 the country secured agreement from the 'London Club' of commercial donors to restructure debts of $7,200m., and further relief was expected to be agreed by the 'Paris Club'. Debt-servicing will, none the less, remain a heavy burden (for 1996 it was officially estimated at equivalent to almost one-quarter of export revenue), and, despite the expansion in export capacity arising from the devaluation, Côte d'Ivoire's payments situation will remain fragile for some years to come.

Statistical Survey

Source (unless otherwise stated): Institut National de la Statistique, BP V55, Abidjan; tel. 21-05-38.

Area and Population

AREA, POPULATION AND DENSITY

Area (sq km)	322,462*
Population (census results)	
30 April 1975	6,702,866
1 March 1988	
Males	5,527,343
Females	5,288,351
Total	10,815,694
Population (official estimates at mid-year)	
1993	13,175,000
1994	13,695,000
1995	14,230,000
Density (per sq km) at mid-1995	44.1

* 124,503 sq miles.

POPULATION BY ETHNIC GROUP (1988 census)

Ethnic group	Number	%
Akan	3,251,227	30.1
Voltaïque	1,266,235	11.7
Mane Nord	1,236,129	11.4
Krou	1,136,291	10.5
Mane Sud	831,840	7.7
Naturalized Ivorians	51,146	0.5
Others	3,039,035	28.1
Unknown	3,791	0.0
Total	10,815,694	100.0

Source: UN, *Demographic Yearbook*.

POPULATION BY REGION (1988 census)

Region	Population
Centre	815,664
Centre-Est	300,407
Centre-Nord	915,269
Centre-Ouest	1,542,945
Nord	745,816
Nord-Est	514,134
Nord-Ouest	522,247
Ouest	968,267
Sud	3,843,249
Sud-Ouest	647,696
Total	10,815,694

Source: UN, *Demographic Yearbook*.

Note: In January 1997 the Government adopted legislation whereby Côte d'Ivoire's regions were to be renamed. The new regions (with their regional capitals) were to be: Lagoon (Abidjan), Upper Sassandra (Daloa), Savannah (Korhogo), Bandama Valley (Bouaké), Lakes (Yamoussoukro), Middle Comoé (Abengourou), Moutains (Man), Zanzan (Bondoukou), Lower Cavally (San Pedro), Denguélé (Odienné), Marahoué (Bouaflé), Nzi Comoé (Dimbroko), South Comoé (Aboisso), Worodougou (Seguéla), South Bandama (Divo), Agneby (Agboville).

PRINCIPAL TOWNS (population at 1988 census)

Abidjan*	1,929,079	Korhogo	109,445
Bouaké	329,850	Yamoussoukro*	106,786
Daloa	121,842		

* The process of transferring the official capital from Abidjan to Yamoussoukro began in 1983.

Source: UN, *Demographic Yearbook*.

BIRTHS AND DEATHS (UN estimates, annual averages)

	1980–85	1985–90	1990–95
Birth rate (per 1,000)	50.2	49.9	49.9
Death rate (per 1,000)	15.8	14.8	15.1

Expectation of life (UN estimates, years at birth, 1990–95): 51.0 (males 49.7; females 52.4).

Source: UN, *World Population Prospects: The 1994 Revision.*

ECONOMICALLY ACTIVE POPULATION

Mid-1995 (estimates in '000): Agriculture, etc. 2,967; Total 5,194. (Source: FAO, *Production Yearbook*).

Agriculture

PRINCIPAL CROPS ('000 metric tons)

	1993	1994	1995
Maize	529	517	517*
Millet	80	81	81*
Sorghum	31	31	31*
Rice (paddy)	890	988	1,045
Sweet potatoes	36	36	36*
Cassava (Manioc)	1,535*	1,564	1,564*
Yams	2,850*	2,824	2,824*
Taro (Coco yam)	315*	337	337*
Pulses*	8	8	8
Tree nuts*	15	15	15
Sugar cane	1,450*	1,318	1,300*
Palm kernels	34.5	31.9	31.5
Groundnuts (in shell)	151	138	147*
Cottonseed	124	133	109
Coconuts	225	213	213*
Copra*	37	34	34
Tomatoes	80*	129	129*
Aubergines (Eggplants)*	40	40	40
Green peppers*	20	20	20
Other vegetables*	343	343	343
Oranges*	28	28	28
Other citrus fruit*	28	28	28
Bananas	192	173	185
Plantains*	1,300	1,300	1,300
Mangoes*	14	14	14
Pineapples	191	205	206
Other fruit*	12	12	12
Coffee (green)	139	148	194
Cocoa beans	804	809	860
Tobacco (leaves)*	10	10	10
Cotton (lint)	111	116	93
Natural rubber (dry weight)	90	70	68

* FAO estimate(s).

Source: FAO, *Production Yearbook*.

LIVESTOCK ('000 head, year ending September)

	1993	1994	1995
Cattle	1,205	1,231	1,258
Pigs	392	403	414
Sheep	1,219	1,251	1,282
Goats	954	978	1,002

Poultry (million): 26 in 1993; 27 in 1994; 27 in 1995.

Source: FAO, *Production Yearbook*.

LIVESTOCK PRODUCTS
(FAO estimates unless otherwise indicated, '000 metric tons)

	1993	1994	1995
Beef and veal	34	40	38
Mutton and lamb	5	5	5
Goat meat	4	4	4
Pig meat	16	16	16
Poultry meat	48	48	48
Other meat	28	29	29
Cows' milk*	21	22	22
Poultry eggs*	16.2	16.0	16.1
Cattle hides	4.5	5.2	5.0
Sheepskins	1.2	1.3	1.3
Goatskins	1.1	1.1	1.1

* Official figures.

Source: FAO, *Production Yearbook*.

Forestry

ROUNDWOOD REMOVALS ('000 cubic metres)

	1992	1993	1994
Sawlogs, veneer logs and logs for sleepers	1,994	1,961	2,416
Other industrial wood*	811	840	869
Fuel wood*	10,453	10,824	11,202
Total	13,258	13,625	14,487

* FAO estimates.

Source: FAO, *Yearbook of Forest Products*.

SAWNWOOD PRODUCTION
('000 cubic metres, including railway sleepers)

	1992	1993	1994
Total	623	587	708

Source: FAO, *Yearbook of Forest Products*.

Fishing

('000 metric tons, live weight)

	1992	1993	1994
Freshwater fishes	13.8	14.7	11.2
Bigeye grunt	4.3	5.0	5.0
Sardinellas	17.3	16.3	16.4
Bonga shad	9.5	10.0	10.1
Other marine fishes (incl. unspecified)	24.1	26.9	27.2
Total fish	69.0	72.9	69.8
Crustaceans	1.2	1.2	0.7
Total catch	70.2	74.1	70.5
Inland waters	14.8	15.7	11.7
Atlantic Ocean	55.3	58.4	58.9

Source: FAO, *Yearbook of Fishery Statistics*.

Mining

	1992	1993	1994
Gold (kg)	1,665.1	1,714.9	1,859.5
Diamonds ('000 carats)	117.3	98.4	84.3

Crude petroleum (estimates, '000 metric tons): 325 in 1992; 324 in 1993; 335 in 1994 (Source: UN, *Industrial Commodity Statistics Yearbook*).

Industry

SELECTED PRODUCTS ('000 metric tons, unless otherwise indicated)

	1992	1993	1994
Salted, dried or smoked fish*	15.2	n.a.	n.a.
Tinned fish*	41.4	49.9	n.a.
Raw sugar	155*	130*	141‡
Cigarettes (million)§	4,500	n.a.	n.a.
Plywood ('000 cubic metres)	39	41	41
Jet fuel†	58	59	59
Motor gasolene (Petrol)	472	414	420†
Kerosene	670	484	672†
Gas-diesel (Distillate fuel) oils	847	665	695†
Residual fuel oils	468	410†	454†
Cement†	510	500	500

Palm and palm kernel oil ('000 metric tons): 218† in 1991.
Cocoa powder (exports, '000 metric tons): 22.1*† in 1988.
Cocoa butter (exports, '000 metric tons): 28.2*† in 1988.
Cotton yarn (pure and mixed, '000 metric tons): 24.7† in 1989.

* Data from the FAO.
† Provisional or estimated figures.
‡ Data from the International Sugar Organization.
§ Data from the US Department of Agriculture.

Source: UN, *Industrial Commodity Statistics Yearbook*.

Electric energy (million kWh): 1,811 in 1991; 1,847 in 1992; 2,252 in 1993; 2,368 in 1994; 2,915 in 1995 (Source: IMF, *Côte d'Ivoire—Statistical Annex*, December 1996).

Finance

CURRENCY AND EXCHANGE RATES

Monetary Units
100 centimes = 1 franc de la Communauté financière africaine (CFA).

French Franc, Sterling and Dollar Equivalents (31 March 1997)
1 French franc = 100 francs CFA;
£1 sterling = 924.20 francs CFA;
US $1 = 562.85 francs CFA;
1,000 francs CFA = £1.082 = $1.777.

Average Exchange Rate (francs CFA per US $)
1994 555.20
1995 499.15
1996 511.55

Note: An exchange rate of 1 French franc = 50 francs CFA, established in 1948, remained in force until January 1994, when the CFA franc was devalued by 50%, with the exchange rate adjusted to 1 French franc = 100 francs CFA.

BUDGET (estimates, '000 million francs CFA)

Revenue*	1993	1994	1995
Tax revenue	435.3	678.6	897.4
Direct taxes	100.6	126.4	202.1
Taxes on profits	19.4	33.9	91.2
Individual income taxes	49.7	58.0	68.8
Employers' contributions	13.6	16.3	17.0
Taxes on petroleum products	81.9	90.8	98.9
Excise taxes	57.1	63.2	59.2
Value-added tax (VAT)	23.3	23.5	23.5
Other indirect taxes	116.6	131.0	167.3
VAT	53.1	53.3	62.2
Prepayment levy for various taxes	21.3	29.6	45.5
Turnover tax on services	9.2	11.5	15.6
Excise taxes on alcohol and tobacco	10.5	9.7	12.0
Registration and stamp taxes	13.1	15.9	20.6
Other taxes on imports	130.4	189.8	251.7
Customs, fiscal and statistical duties	62.5	84.0	116.9
Other import charges	11.2	19.0	21.6
VAT	56.7	86.8	113.3
Taxes on exports	5.7	140.5	177.4
Coffee and cocoa	—	126.2	162.7
Other revenue	82.7	168.4	205.9
Price equalization fund surplus	11.2	2.3	0.0
Stabilization fund surplus	18.1	112.7	135.9
Social security contributions	37.6	42.6	52.2
Total	518.0	846.9	1,103.3

Expenditure	1993	1994	1995
Wages and salaries	314.6	328.0	346.3
Social security benefits	39.8	51.3	65.2
Subsidies and other current transfers	26.2	42.3	51.7
Other current expenditure	156.6	201.2	236.1
Investment expenditure	90.8	195.0	280.1
Interest due on public debt	255.9	334.2	343.2
Total	883.9	1,152.0	1,322.6

* Excluding grants received (estimates, '000 million francs CFA): 15.0 in 1993; 29.7 in 1994; 35.0 in 1995.

Source: IMF, *Côte d'Ivoire—Statistical Annex* (December 1996).

1996 (draft budget, '000 million francs CFA): Current expenditure 625.2; Investment expenditure 356.3.

1997 (draft budget, '000 million francs CFA): Current expenditure 1,356.1; Investment expenditure 430.0.

INTERNATIONAL RESERVES (US $ million at 31 December)

	1994	1995	1996
Gold*	16.6	17.1	16.7
IMF special drawing rights	0.2	1.8	1.2
Reserve position in IMF	0.1	0.1	0.2
Foreign exchange	204.0	527.0	604.4
Total	220.9	546.1	622.5

* Valued at market-related prices.

Source: IMF, *International Financial Statistics*.

MONEY SUPPLY ('000 million francs CFA at 31 December)

	1993	1994	1995
Currency outside banks	272.5	392.6	451.4
Demand deposits at deposit money banks*	219.2	403.3	490.7
Checking deposits at post office	1.7	2.1	1.5
Total money (incl. others)	494.0	798.8	944.5

* Excluding the deposits of public establishments of an administrative or social nature.

Source: IMF, *International Financial Statistics*.

COST OF LIVING (Consumer Price Index for African households in Abidjan; base: 1990 = 100)

	1994	1995	1996
All items	136.5	156.0	159.9

Source: IMF, *International Financial Statistics*.

NATIONAL ACCOUNTS ('000 million francs CFA at current prices)

Expenditure on the Gross Domestic Product

	1993	1994	1995
Government final consumption expenditure	484.1	543.7	598.3
Private final consumption expenditure	2,184.9	2,678.0	3,453.5
Increase in stocks	13.6	41.8	33.6
Gross fixed capital formation	231.4	454.9	630.5
Total domestic expenditure	2,914.0	3,718.4	4,716.0
Exports of goods and services	846.0	1,803.4	2,165.8
Less Imports of goods and services	814.0	1,385.6	1,850.4
GDP in purchasers' values	2,946.0	4,136.2	5,031.4

Gross Domestic Product by Economic Activity

	1993	1994	1995
Agriculture, livestock-rearing, forestry and fishing	1,028.0	1,274.9	1,572.9
Mining and quarrying Manufacturing Electricity, gas and water	550.0	771.1	876.8
Construction and public works	59.0	78.2	99.1
Transport, storage and communications	266.0	324.9	362.9
Trade	275.0	742.3	1,024.6
Other marketable services	235.0	328.1	395.9
Public administration	381.0	426.7	442.2
Sub-total	2,794.0	3,946.2	4,774.4
Import duties and taxes	152.0	190.0	257.0
GDP in purchasers' values	2,946.0	4,136.2	5,031.4

Source: IMF, *Côte d'Ivoire—Statistical Annex* (December 1996).

BALANCE OF PAYMENTS (US $ million)

	1993	1994	1995
Exports of goods f.o.b.	2,518.7	2,811.4	3,819.7
Imports of goods f.o.b.	−1,770.4	−1,507.4	−2,474.4
Trade balance	748.3	1,304.0	1,345.3
Exports of services	675.9	560.7	730.6
Imports of services	−1,331.7	−1,233.3	−1,396.0
Balance on goods and services	92.5	631.4	680.0
Other income received	97.8	85.6	32.1
Other income paid	−887.8	−706.4	−862.5
Balance on goods, services and income	−697.5	10.5	−150.4
Current transfers received	270.9	774.3	255.8
Current transfers paid	−465.1	−416.6	−552.1
Current balance	−891.7	368.2	−446.7
Direct investment from abroad	87.9	26.8	19.4
Portfolio investment assets	7.4	28.8	—
Portfolio investment liabilities	—	−0.7	—
Other investment assets	51.9	−168.4	−44.9
Other investment liabilities	−503.2	−459.2	239.2
Net errors and omissions	11.1	−107.8	−21.3
Overall balance	−1,236.6	−312.7	−254.2

Source: IMF, *International Financial Statistics*.

External Trade

PRINCIPAL COMMODITIES (million francs CFA)

Imports c.i.f.	1992	1993	1994
Rice	23,011	28,497	44,002
Wheat	8,592	8,156	18,112
Dairy products and birds' eggs	14,959	16,484	14,854
Fish, crustaceans and molluscs	26,676	30,119	54,312
Pharmaceutical products	34,253	33,064	43,707
Petroleum products	135,082	130,085	203,661
Chemical products	15,815	13,748	28,175
Electrical plant	11,063	18,836	40,866
Non-electrical machinery and apparatus	41,380	34,753	67,930
Base metals	20,148	14,797	29,925
Paper and paperboard	26,282	15,382	29,135
Industrial parachemical products	18,555	16,604	23,709
Passenger cars, coaches, lorries and vans	26,851	18,288	35,985
Total	615,149	561,321	1,018,171

Exports f.o.b.	1992	1993	1994
Fresh pineapples	11,820	11,313	18,992
Fresh bananas	14,108	18,333	30,803
Green coffee	41,156	48,859	78,001
Instant coffee	17,335	12,156	32,715
Cocoa beans	186,426	222,656	424,905
Cocoa paste	14,930	13,384	27,200
Cocoa butter	26,782	21,434	38,612
Natural rubber	15,897	15,411	38,159
Sawlogs	8,711	11,683	28,052
Sawnwood	42,307	41,736	113,117
Veneer sheets and plywood	15,513	14,798	27,166
Palm oil	18,358	21,035	32,965
Cotton fabrics	10,508	9,335	16,791
Raw (unginned) cotton	29,523	30,666	64,254
Tinned fish	26,220	20,084	64,923
Total (incl. others)	791,322	747,282	1,530,361

PRINCIPAL TRADING PARTNERS (percentage of trade)

Imports	1993	1994	1995
Belgium-Luxembourg	2.6	3.2	2.5
Brazil	1.3	1.7	1.0
China, People's Repub.	2.6	1.0	1.7
France	30.4	27.7	32.0
Germany	2.4	3.3	3.9
Ghana	3.9	4.9	4.0
Italy	3.8	3.1	3.8
Japan	2.7	2.6	3.2
Mauritania	1.3	1.5	1.3
Netherlands	3.4	2.8	2.7
Nigeria	24.3	26.5	19.6
Spain	2.7	1.4	2.5
United Kingdom	2.5	1.6	2.7
USA	4.3	5.7	5.9

Exports	1993	1994	1995
Belgium-Luxembourg	4.8	4.8	4.7
Burkina Faso	4.9	5.0	5.0
France	16.4	15.8	18.1
Germany	8.6	9.7	7.8
Italy	7.0	7.0	7.6
Mali	5.8	5.9	5.9
Netherlands	7.3	8.8	8.3
Niger	1.3	1.3	1.3
Nigeria	1.3	1.1	1.0
Spain	3.7	4.0	4.5
Togo	1.7	1.7	1.7
United Kingdom	2.9	1.9	3.2
USA	5.7	5.0	4.6

Source: IMF, *Direction of Trade Statistics*.

Transport

RAILWAYS (traffic)

	1991	1992	1993
Passengers ('000)	926	820	744
Passenger-km (million)	199	189	173
Freight ('000 metric tons)	488	484	292
Freight (million net ton-km)	272	266	168

Source: Société Ivoirienne des Chemins de Fer, Abidjan.

ROAD TRAFFIC (estimates, '000 motor vehicles in use)

	1991	1992	1993
Passenger cars	185	187	188
Commercial vehicles	97	97	98

Source: UN Economic Commission for Africa, *African Statistical Yearbook*.

SHIPPING

Merchant Fleet (registered at 31 December)

	1994	1995	1996
Number of vessels	50	46	45
Total displacement ('000 grt)	61.5	40.0	12.7

Source: Lloyd's Register of Shipping, *World Fleet Statistics*.

International Sea-Borne Freight Traffic
(freight traffic at Abidjan, '000 metric tons)

	1993	1994	1995
Goods loaded	3,882.4	3,702.3	4,172.9
Goods unloaded	5,936.4	6,183.9	7,227.8

Freight traffic at San Pedro ('000 metric tons, 1994): Goods loaded 883.8; Goods unloaded 184.9.

Source: Banque centrale des états de l'Afrique de l'ouest.

CIVIL AVIATION (traffic on scheduled services)*

	1992	1993	1994
Kilometres flown (million)	4	4	3
Passengers carried ('000)	195	186	157
Passenger-km (million)	297	295	282
Total ton-km (million)	43	41	40

* Including an apportionment of the traffic of Air Afrique.

Source: UN, *Statistical Yearbook*.

Tourism

	1994
Tourist arrivals ('000)	200
Tourist receipts (US $ million)	66

* Estimates.

Source: Haut Commissariat au Tourisme, Abidjan.

Communications Media

	1992	1993	1994
Radio receivers ('000 in use)	1,835	1,905	1,975
Television receivers ('000 in use)	765	805	822
Telephones ('000 main lines in use)	86	94	108
Daily newspapers			
Number	1	n.a.	1
Average circulation ('000 copies)	90	n.a.	90

Sources: UNESCO, *Statistical Yearbook*; UN, *Statistical Yearbook*.

Education

(1993/94)

	Institutions	Teachers	Students		
			Males	Females	Total
Pre-primary	128	39,691*	11,507*	10,951*	22,458*
Primary	7,249		902,932	650,608	1,553,540
Secondary					
General	395	10,378	294,951	150,554	445,505
Teacher training	13	538	n.a.	n.a.	2,821
Vocational	48	1,388	6,301	2,581	8,882

* Data refer only to schools attached to the Ministry of National Education.

Source: the former Ministère de l'Education nationale, Abidjan.

1994/95: *Students:* Pre-primary 25,638 (males 13,315; females 12,323). Primary 1,612,417 (males 919,233; females 693,184).

University level (1988/89): 15,501 students (males 12,600; females 2,901) (Source: UNESCO, *Statistical Yearbook*).

Directory

The Constitution

The Constitution was promulgated on 31 October 1960. It was amended in June 1971, October 1975, August 1980, November 1980, October 1985, January 1986 and November 1990.

PREAMBLE

The Republic of Côte d'Ivoire is one and indivisible. It is secular, democratic and social. Sovereignty belongs to the people who exercise it through their representatives or through referendums. There is universal, equal and secret suffrage. French is the official language.

HEAD OF STATE

The President is elected for a five-year term by direct universal suffrage and is eligible for re-election. He is Head of the Administration and the Armed Forces and has power to ask the Assemblée nationale to reconsider a Bill, which must then be passed by two-thirds of the members of the legislature; he may also have a Bill submitted to a referendum. In case of the death or incapacitation of the President of the Republic, the functions of the Head of State are assumed by the President of the Assemblée nationale, until the expiry of the previous incumbent's mandate.

EXECUTIVE POWER

Executive power is vested in the President. He appoints the Prime Minister, who, in turn, appoints the Council of Ministers. Any member of the Assemblée nationale appointed minister must renounce his seat in the legislature, but may regain it on leaving the Government.

LEGISLATIVE POWER

Legislative power is vested in the 175-member Assemblée nationale, elected for a five-year term of office. Legislation may be introduced either by the President or by a member of the National Assembly.

JUDICIAL POWER

The independence of the judiciary is guaranteed by the President, assisted by the High Council of Judiciary.

ECONOMIC AND SOCIAL COUNCIL

This is an advisory commission of 120 members, appointed by the President because of their specialist knowledge or experience.

POLITICAL ORGANIZATIONS

Article 7 of the Constitution stipulates that political organizations can be formed and can exercise their activities freely, provided that they respect the principles of national sovereignty and democracy and the laws of the Republic.

The Government

HEAD OF STATE

President: AIMÉ HENRI KONAN BÉDIÉ (took office 7 December 1993; elected President 22 October 1995).

COUNCIL OF MINISTERS

(August 1997)

Prime Minister and Minister of Planning and Industrial Development: DANIEL KABLAN DUNCAN.

Minister of State, with responsibility for Relations with the Organs of State: TIMOTHÉE N'GUETTA AHOUA.

Minister of State, with responsibility for National Solidarity: LAURENT DONA-FOLOGO.

Minister of Foreign Affairs: AMARA ESSY.

Minister of the Interior and National Integration: EMILE CONSTANT BOMBET.

Minister of Defence: BANDAMA N'GATTA.

Minister of Justice and Public Freedom, Keeper of the Seals: BROU KACOU.

Minister in charge of Presidential Affairs: Me FAUSTIN KOUAMÉ.

Minister of Agriculture and Animal Resources: LAMBERT KOUASSI KONAN.

Minister with responsibility for Raw Materials: GUY-ALAIN EMMANUEL GAUZE.

Minister of the Economy and Finance: N'GORAN NIAMIEN.

Minister of Economic Infrastructure: EZAN AKELE.

Minister of Higher Education, Scientific Research and Technological Innovation: SALIOU TOURÉ.

Minister of National Education and Basic Training: PIERRE KIPRE.

Minister of Technical Education and Professional Training: KOMENAN ZAKPA.

Minister of Security: MARCEL DIBONAN KONÉ.

Minister of Public Health: MAURICE KAKOU GUIKAHUE.

Minister of Mines and Petroleum Resources: LAMINE FADIKA.

Minister of Employment, the Civil Service and Social Welfare: PIERRE ACHI ATSAIN.

Minister of Trade: NICOLAS KOUASSI AKON.

Minister of Housing, Living Conditions and the Environment: ALBERT KAKOU TIAPANI.

Minister of Communications and Spokesperson for the Government: DANIÈLE BONI-CLAVERIE.

Minister of Culture: BERNARD ZADI ZAHOUROU.

Minister of the Family and Women's Promotion: ALBERTINE GNANAZAN HEPIE.

Minister of Youth Promotion and Civil Education: VLAMI BI DOU.

Minister of Sports: SITUIDÉ SOUMAHORO.

Minister of Handicrafts Development: LANCINÉ GON COULIBALY.

Resident Minister for the Autonomous District of Yamoussoukro: JEAN KONAN BANNY.

High Commissioner for the Development of the Savannah Regions of the North and Centre: TIMITÉ AMADOU.

High Commissioner for the Integrated Development of the Semi-mountainous Region of the West: TCHÉRÉ SEKA.

High Commissioner for Water Resources: TOURÉ SEKOU.

High Commissioner for Tourism: EUGÈNE KINDO BOUADI.

There are Ministers-delegate responsible for Planning and Industrial Development, the Promotion of Young Farmers and for Energy and Transport; the Secretary-General of the National Security Council also holds the rank of Minister-delegate.

MINISTRIES AND HIGH COMMISSIONS

Office of the President: Abidjan.

Office of the Prime Minister: Abidjan.

Office of the High Commissioner for the Development of the Savanna Regions of the North and Centre: Abidjan.

Office of the High Commissioner for the Integrated Development of the Semi-mountainous Region of the West: Abidjan.

Office of the High Commissioner for Tourism: Immeuble EECI, place de la Republique, 01 BP 8538, Abidjan 01; tel. 20-65-00; fax 22-59-24.

Office of the High Commissioner for Water Resources: Abidjan.

Ministry of Agriculture and Animal Resources: BP V82, Abidjan; tel. 21-08-33; telex 23612; fax 21-46-18.

Ministry of Communications: BP V138, Abidjan; telex 23501.

Ministry of Culture: Abidjan.

Ministry of Defence: BP V11, Abidjan; telex 22855.

Ministry of the Economy, Finance, Planning and Industrial Development: Immeuble SCIAM, ave Marchand, BP V163, Abidjan; tel. 21-05-66; telex 23747.

Ministry of Employment, the Civil Service and Social Welfare: BP V93, Abidjan 01; tel. 21-04-00.

Ministry of the Family and Women's Promotion: Abidjan.

Ministry of Foreign Affairs: BP V109, Abidjan; telex 23752.

Ministry of Handicrafts Development: Abidjan.

Ministry of Higher Education, Scientific Research and Technological Innovation: BP V151, Abidjan.

Ministry of Housing, Living Conditions and the Environment: ave Jean Paul II, BP V6, Abidjan 01; tel. 29-13-67; telex 22108.

Ministry of the Interior and National Integration: BP V241, Abidjan; telex 22296.

Ministry of Justice and Public Freedom: BP V107, Abidjan.

Ministry of Mines and Petroleum Resources: BP V50, Abidjan; tel. 21-66-17; fax 21-53-20.

Ministry of National Education and Basic Training: BP V120, Abidjan; tel. 21-12-31.

Ministry of Public Health: Cité Administrative, Tour C, 16e étage, BP V4, Abidjan; tel. 21-08-71; telex 22597; fax 21-10-85.

Ministry of Raw Materials: Abidjan.

Ministry of Security: Abidjan.

Ministry of Sports: Abidjan.

Ministry of Trade: Abidjan.

Ministry of Youth Promotion and Civil Education: BP V136, Abidjan; telex 22719; fax 22-48-21.

Office of the Resident Ministers for Yamoussoukro: Yamoussoukro.

President and Legislature

PRESIDENT

Presidential Election, 22 October 1995

Candidate	Votes	% of votes
AIMÉ HENRI KONAN BÉDIÉ	1,640,635	95.25
ROMAIN FRANCIS WODIÉ	65,486	3.80
Abstentions	16,385	0.95
Total	1,722,506	100.00

ASSEMBLÉE NATIONALE

President: CHARLES BAUZA DONWAHI.

General Election, 26 November 1995

Party	Seats
PDCI–RDA	146
RDR	14
FPI	9
Total	169*

* Voting for three further seats was postponed prior to the election, and the results of voting in three constituencies was annulled by the Constitutional Court in December 1995. By-elections for these and for two other seats took place in December 1996: the FPI won five seats and the PDCI–RDA three.

Advisory Councils

Conseil Constitutionnel: Abidjan; f. 1994; Pres. NOËL NÉMIN.

Conseil Economique et Social: 04 BP 301, Abidjan 04; tel. 21-14-54; Pres. PHILIPPE GRÉGOIRE YACÉ; Vice-Pres BEDA YAO, GLADYS ANOMA, AUGUSTE DAUBREY, MARTIN KOUAKOU KOUADIO, BERNARD ANO BOA; 120 mems.

Political Organizations

Despite constitutional provision for the existence of more than one political organization, President Houphouët-Boigny's Parti démocratique de la Côte d'Ivoire–Rassemblement démocratique africain (PDCI–RDA) was the sole legal party until May 1990. By mid-1996 there were some 90 registered political organizations. The following parties are represented in the Assemblée nationale:

Front populaire ivoirien (FPI): 22 BP 302, Abidjan 22; f. 1982 in France; Chair. LAURENT KOUDOU GBAGBO; Sec.-Gen. ABOU DRAHAMANE SANGARÉ.

Parti démocratique de la Côte d'Ivoire–Rassemblement démocratique africain (PDCI–RDA): Maison du Parti, Abidjan; f. 1946 as the local section of the Rassemblement démocratique africain; Chair. AIMÉ HENRI KONAN BÉDIÉ; Sec.-Gen. LAURENT DONA-FOLOGO.

Rassemblement des républicains (RDR): Abidjan; f. 1994, following split from PDCI–RDA; Pres. HYACINTHE LEROUX; Sec.-Gen. DJÉNY KOBINA.

Other registered parties include:

The **Congrès démocrate national (CDN):** Nat. Exec. Sec. MOCTAR HAIDARA; the **Front ivoirien du salut (FIS):** Sec.-Gen. N'TAKPE AUCHORET MONNON'GBA; the **Front de redressement national (FRN):** Sec.-Gen. VICTOR ATSEPI; the **Groupement pour la solidarité (GPS):** Pres. ACHI KOMAN; the **Mouvement démocratique et social (MDS):** First Nat. Sec.-Gen. SIAKA TOURÉ; the **Mouvement indépendantistes ivoirien (MII):** Pres. ADOU YAPI; the **Mouvement progressiste de Côte d'Ivoire (MPCI):** Sec.-Gen. AUGUSTIN NANGONE BI DOUA; the **Organisation populaire de la jeunesse (OPJ):** Sec.-Gen. DENIS LATTA; the **Parti africain pour la renaissance ivoirienne (PARI):** Sec.-Gen. DANIEL ANIKPO; the **Parti communiste ivoirien (PCI):** Sec.-Gen. DENIS GUEU DRO; the **Parti fraternel des planteurs, des parents d'élèves et industriels ivoiriens (PFPPEI):** Pres. ERNEST AMESSAN; the **Parti ivoirien pour la démocratie (PID):** Sec.-Gen. FAUSTIN BOTOKO LÉKA; the **Parti ivoirien des travailleurs (PIT):** First Nat. Sec. ROMAIN FRANCIS WODIÉ; the **Parti ivoirien de justice et de solidarité (PIJS):** Pres. KEKONGO N'DIEN; the **Parti libéral de Côte d'Ivoire (PLCI):** Sec.-Gen. YADY SOUMAH; the **Parti pour la libération totale de la Côte d'Ivoire (PLTCI):** Sec.-Gen. ELISE ALLOUFOU NIAMIEN; the **Parti pour les libertés et la démocratie (PLD):** Pres. JEAN-PIERRE OUYA; the **Parti national socialiste (PNS):** Pres. RAPHAËL YAPI BEDA; the **Parti ouvrier et paysan de Côte d'Ivoire**

(POPCI): Exec. Pres. KOUASSI ADOLPHE BLOKON; the **Parti pour le progrès et la solidarité (PPS):** Sec.-Gen. BAMBA MORIFÉRÉ; the **Parti progressiste ivoirien (PPI):** Pres. SOUMAHORO KASSINDOU; the **Parti pour la protection de l'environnement (PPE):** Sec.-Gen. DIOBA COULIBALY; the **Parti du rassemblement du peuple pour la jeunesse de Côte d'Ivoire (PRJCI):** Sec.-Gen. PHILIPPE ESSIS KHOL; the **Parti pour la reconstruction nationale et la démocratie (PRND):** Pres. MARC JOSEPH BEHED; the **Parti réformiste démocratique ivoirien (PRDI):** Sec.-Gen. RAPHAËL BEUGRÉ KOAMÉ; the **Parti pour la réhabilitation ivoirienne du social et de l'économie (PRISE):** Exec. Pres. GEORGES GRAHOU; the **Parti républicain de Côte d'Ivoire (PRCI):** Sec.-Gen. ROBERT GBAI TAGRO; the **Parti socialiste ivoirien (PSI):** First Nat. Sec. MANDOUADJOA KOUAKOU; the **Rassemblement des forces démocratiques (RFD):** Pres. FAKOUROU TOURÉ; the **Rassemblement pour le progrès social (RPS):** Pres. MAMADOU KONÉ; the **Rassemblement pour la République (RPR):** Sec.-Gen. BLAISE BONOUA KODJO; the **Rassemblement des sociaux-démocrates (RSD):** Sec.-Gen. MAHI GUINA; the **Union des libéraux pour la République (ULR):** Pres. CÉLESTIN AMON; the **Union nationale des démocrates (UND):** Sec.-Gen. AMADOU KONÉ; the **Union des paysans, des ouvriers et des salariés de Côte d'Ivoire (UPOSCI):** Sec.-Gen. COA KIÉMOKO; the **Union pour le progrès social (UPS):** Sec.-Gen. ALBERT SÉHÉ; and the **Union des sociaux-démocrates (USD):** Sec.-Gen. BERNARD ZADI ZAOUROU.

Note: In April 1995 the **FPI**, the **RDR** and the **Union des forces démocratiques** (a coalition of parties including the PPS, the PIT, the PLCI and the UND) formed an opposition **Front républicain**.

Diplomatic Representation

EMBASSIES IN CÔTE D'IVOIRE

Algeria: 53 blvd Clozel, 01 BP 1015, Abidjan 01; tel. 21-23-40; telex 23243; Ambassador: MOHAMED SENOUSSI.

Angola: Lot 19, Cocody-les-Deux-Plateaux, derrière l'Ecole Nationale d'Administration, 16 BP 1734, Abidjan 16; tel. 41-38-79; telex 27187; fax 41-28-89; Ambassador: SIMEÃO ADÃO MANUEL KAFUXI.

Austria: Immeuble N'Zarama, blvd Lagunaire-Charles de Gaulle, Plateau, 01 BP 1837, Abidjan 01; tel. 21-25-00; telex 22664; fax 22-19-23; Ambassador: Dr EWALD JÄGER.

Belgium: Immeuble Alliance, ave Terrasson de Fougères, 01 BP 1800, Abidjan 01; tel. 21-00-88; telex 23633; Ambassador: PIERRE COLOT.

Benin: rue des Jardins, 09 BP 238, Abidjan 09; tel. 41-44-14; telex 27103; Ambassador: (vacant).

Brazil: Immeuble Alpha 2000, rue Gourgas, 01 BP 3820, Abidjan 01; tel. 22-23-41; telex 23443; Chargé d'affaires a.i.: FERNANDO JABLONSKI.

Burkina Faso: 2 ave Terrasson de Fougères, 01 BP 908, Abidjan 01; tel. 32-13-55; telex 23453; fax 32-66-41; Ambassador: LÉANDRE BASSOLE.

Cameroon: 01 BP 2886, Abidjan 01; tel. 32-33-31; Ambassador: PAUL KAMGA NJIKE.

Canada: Immeuble Trade Centre, 01 BP 4104, Abidjan 01; tel. 21-20-09; telex 23593; fax 21-77-28; Ambassador: SUZANNE LAPORTE.

Central African Republic: 7 rue des Jasmins, Cocody Danga, Abidjan; tel. 44-86-29; Ambassador: EMMANUEL BONGOPASSI.

China, People's Republic: 01 BP 3691, Abidjan 01; tel. 44-59-00; telex 22104; fax 44-67-81; Ambassador: LIU LIDE.

Colombia: 01 BP 3874, Abidjan 01; tel. 33-12-44; fax 32-47-31; Ambassador: MARÍA EUGENIA CORREA OLARTE.

Congo, Democratic Republic: 29 blvd Clozel, 01 BP 3961, Abidjan 01; tel. 22-20-80; telex 23795; Ambassador: BAMBI MAVUNGU.

Czech Republic: Immeuble Tropique III, 01 BP 1349, Abidjan 01; tel. 21-20-30; fax 22-19-06; Chargé d'affaires a.i.: ZDENEK MRKLOVSKY.

Egypt: Immeuble El Nasr, ave du Général de Gaulle, 01 BP 2104, Abidjan 01; tel. 32-79-25; telex 23537; Ambassador: ABEDLMONEIM ABDELAZIZ SEOUDY.

Ethiopia: Immeuble Nour Al-Hayat, ave Chardy, Plateau, 01 BP 3712, Abidjan 01; tel. 21-33-65; fax 21-37-09; Ambassador: WESSEN BESHAH.

France: rue Lecoeur, quartier du Plateau, 17 BP 175, Abidjan 17; tel. 20-04-04; telex 23699; fax 22-42-54; Ambassador: CHRISTIAN DUTHEIL DE LA ROCHÈRE.

Gabon: Cocody Danga Nord, derrière la Direction de la Géologie, 01 BP 3765, Abidjan 01; tel. 41-51-54; telex 27188; fax 44-75-05; Ambassador: VICTOR MAGNAGNA.

Germany: Immeuble Le Mans, angle blvd Botreau Roussel et ave Nogues, 01 BP 1900, Abidjan 01; tel. 21-47-27; telex 23642; fax 32-47-29; Ambassador: HANS-ALBRECHT SCHRAEPLER.

Ghana: Résidence de la Corniche, blvd du Général de Gaulle, 01 BP 1871, Abidjan 01; tel. 33-11-24; Ambassador: AKUMFI AMEYAW MUNIFIE.

Guinea: Immeuble Crosson Duplessis, 08 BP 2280, Abidjan 08; tel. 32-86-00; telex 22865; Ambassador: DOMINIQUE KOLY.

Holy See: 08 BP 1347, Abidjan 08 (Apostolic Nunciature); tel. 44-38-35; fax 44-72-40; Apostolic Nuncio: Most Rev. LUIGI VENTURA, Titular Archbishop of Equilio.

India: Lot 36, impasse Ablaha Pokou, Cocody, Danga Nord, 06 BP 318, Abidjan 06; tel. 44-52-31; telex 28103; fax 44-01-11; Ambassador: PRADEEP K. GUPTA.

Israel: Immeuble Nour Al-Hayat, ave Chardy, Plateau, 01 BP 1877, Abidjan 01; tel. 21-49-53; fax 21-87-04; Ambassador: JAACOV REVAH.

Italy: 16 rue de la Canebière, Cocody, 01 BP 1905, Abidjan 01; tel. 44-61-70; telex 26123; fax 44-35-87; Ambassador: RAFFAELE CAMPANELLA.

Japan: ave Chardy, 01 BP 1329, Abidjan 01; tel. 21-28-63; telex 23400; fax 21-30-51; Ambassador: HIROMI SATO.

Korea, Republic: Immeuble Le Général, 01 BP 3950, Abidjan 01; tel. 32-22-90; telex 23638; Ambassador: BAE SANG-KIL.

Lebanon: 01 BP 2227, Abidjan 01; tel. 33-28-24; telex 22245; Ambassador: MOHAMED DAHER.

Liberia: Immeuble Taleb, 20 ave Delafosse, Abidjan; tel. 32-39-73; telex 23535; Chargé d'affaires a.i.: TIAHKWEE JOHNSON.

Libya: Immeuble Shell, 48 ave Lamblin, 01 BP 5725, Abidjan 01; tel. 22-01-27; Chargé d'affaires a.i.: BADREDDIN M. RABIE.

Mali: Maison du Mali, rue du Commerce, 01 BP 2746, Abidjan 01; tel. 32-31-47; telex 23429; Ambassador: LASSANA KEITA.

Mauritania: blvd Latrille, rue de la Paroisse St Jacques, Cocody-les-Deux-Plateaux, 01 BP 2275, Abidjan 01; tel. 44-16-43; telex 27181; fax 41-05-77; Ambassador: Dr DIAGANA YOUSSOUF.

Morocco: 24 rue de la Canebière, Cocody, 01 BP 146, Abidjan 01; tel. 44-58-78; telex 26147; Ambassador: AHMED ASSOULI.

Netherlands: Immeuble Les Harmonies, 2e étage angle blvd Carde et ave Dr Jamot, Plateau, 01 BP 1086, Abidjan 01; tel. 22-77-12; telex 22694; fax 21-17-61; Ambassador: W. O. SERVATIUS.

Niger: 01 BP 2743, Abidjan 01; tel. 26-28-14; telex 43185; Ambassador: MADI KONATÉ.

Nigeria: 35 blvd de la République, 01 BP 1906, Abidjan 01; tel. 21-38-17; telex 23532; Ambassador: JONATHAN OLUWOLE COKER.

Norway: Immeuble N'Zarama, blvd du Général de Gaulle, 01 BP 607, Abidjan 01; tel. 22-25-34; telex 23355; fax 21-91-99; Ambassador: JAN NAERBY.

Poland: 04 BP 308, Abidjan 04; tel. 44-12-25; telex 26114; Chargé d'affaires a.i.: PIOTR MYSLIWIEC.

Russia: Riviera SQ-1 Sud, 01 BP 7646, Abidjan 01; tel. 43-09-59; Ambassador: MIKHAIL V. MAIOROV.

Senegal: Résidence Nabil, blvd du Général de Gaulle, 08 BP 2165, Abidjan 08; tel. 32-28-76; telex 23897; Ambassador: OUSMANE CAMARA.

South Africa: Villa Marc André, rue Mgr René Kouassi, Cocody, 08 BP 1806, Abidjan 08; tel. 44-59-63; fax 44-74-50; Ambassador: S. NGOMBANE.

Spain: impasse Ablaha Pokou, Cocody, Danga Nord, 08 BP 876, Abidjan 08; tel. 44-48-50; fax 44-71-22; Ambassador: ALMUDENA MAZARRASA ALVEAR.

Sweden: Immeuble N'Zarama, 4e étage, blvd Lagunaire, 04 BP 992, Abidjan 04; tel. 21-24-10; telex 23293; fax 21-21-07; Ambassador: BO WILÉN.

Switzerland: Immeuble Alpha 2000, rue Gourgas, 01 BP 1914, Abidjan 01; tel. 21-17-21; telex 23492; fax 21-27-70; Ambassador: PIERRE DE GRAFFENRIED.

Tunisia: Immeuble Pelieu, 6e étage, ave Delafosse, Abidjan 01; tel. 22-61-22; Ambassador: MONCEF LARBI.

United Kingdom: Immeuble Les Harmonies, 3e étage, angle blvd Carde et ave Dr Jamot, Plateau, 01 BP 2581, Abidjan 01; tel. 22-68-50; fax 22-32-21; Ambassador: MARGARET ROTHWELL.

USA: 5 rue Jesse Owens, 01 BP 1712, Abidjan 01; tel. 21-09-79; telex 23660; fax 22-32-59; Ambassador: LANNON WALKER.

Judicial System

Since 1964 all civil, criminal, commercial and administrative cases have come under the jurisdiction of the Tribunaux de première instance (magistrates' courts), the assize courts and the Court of Appeal, with the Supreme Court as highest court of appeal.

The Supreme Court: rue Gourgas, BP V30, Abidjan; has four chambers: constitutional, judicial, administrative and auditing; Pres. MICHEL KOUI MAMADOU.

Courts of Appeal: Abidjan and Bouaké; hear appeals from courts of first instance; Abidjan: First Pres. (vacant), Attorney-Gen. LOUIS

FOLQUET; Bouaké: First Pres. AHIOUA MOULARE, Attorney-Gen. ANOMAN OGUIE.

The High Court of Justice: composed of Deputies elected from and by the National Assembly; has jurisdiction to impeach the President or other member of the Government.

Courts of First Instance: Abidjan, Pres. ANTOINETTE MARSOUIN; Bouaké: Pres. KABLAN AKA EDOUKOU; Daloa: Pres. WOUNE BLEKA; there are a further 25 courts in the principal centres.

Religion

At the time of the 1988 census some 39% of the population were Muslims and 26% Christians (mainly Roman Catholics); about 17% followed traditional animist beliefs.

ISLAM

Conseil National Islamique (CNI): f. 1993; Chair. El Hadj IDRISS KOUDOUSS KONÉ.

Conseil Supérieur Islamique (CSI): f. 1978; Chair. El Hadj MOUSTAPHA DIABY.

CHRISTIANITY

The Roman Catholic Church

Côte d'Ivoire comprises four archdioceses and 10 dioceses. At 31 December 1995 Roman Catholics comprised about 15% of the total population.

Bishops' Conference: Conférence Episcopale de la Côte d'Ivoire, 01 BP 1287, Abidjan 01; tel. 33-22-56; f. 1973; Pres. Most Rev. AUGUSTE NOBOU, Archbishop of Korhogo.

Archbishop of Abidjan: Most Rev. BERNARD AGRÉ, Archevêché, ave Jean Paul II, 01 BP 1287, Abidjan 01; tel. 21-12-46; fax 21-40-22.

Archbishop of Bouaké: Most Rev. VITAL KOMENAN YAO, Archevêché, 01 BP 649, Bouaké 01; tel. and fax 63-24-59.

Archbishop of Gagnoa: Most Rev. NOËL KOKORA-TEKRY, Archevêché, BP 527, Gagnoa; tel. 77-25-68; fax 77-20-96.

Archbishop of Korhogo: Most Rev. AUGUSTE NOBOU, Archevêché, BP 12, Korhogo; tel. 86-01-18; fax 86-05-26.

Protestant Churches

Assemblée de Dieu: 04 BP 266, Abidjan 04; Pres. ADAMO OUÉDRAOGO.

CB International: BP 109, Korhogo; tel. 86-01-07; fax 86-11-50; f. 1947; fmrly Conservative Baptist Foreign Mission Society; active in evangelism, medical work, translation, literacy and theological education in the northern area and in Abidjan.

Christian and Missionary Alliance: BP 585, Bouaké 01; tel. 63-23-12; fax 63-54-12; f. 1929; 13 mission stations; Dir Rev. DAVID W. ARNOLD.

Eglise du Nazaréen (Church of the Nazarene): 22 BP 623, Abidjan 22; tel. 41-07-80; fax 41-07-81; f. 1988; active in evangelism, ministerial training and medical work; Dir JOHN SEAMAN.

Eglise Protestante Baptiste Oeuvres et Mission: 03 BP 1032, Abidjan 03; tel. 45-20-18; fax 45-56-41; f. 1975; active in evangelism, teaching and social work; medical centre, 664 places of worship, 285 missionaries and 97,000 mems; Pres. YAYÉ ROBERT DION.

Eglise Protestante Méthodiste de Côte d'Ivoire: 41 blvd de la République, 01 BP 1282, Abidjan 01; tel. 21-17-97; fax 22-52-03; c. 650,000 mems; Pres. LAMBERT AKOSSI N'CHO.

Mission Baptiste Méridionale: 01 BP 3722, Abidjan 01.

Mission Evangélique de l'Afrique Occidentale: BP 822, Bouaflé; tel. 68-93-70; fax 44-58-17; f. 1934; 11 mission centres, 59 missionaries; Field Dirs LINDA NAGEL, MARRY SCHOTTE; affiliated church: Alliance des Eglises Evangéliques de Côte d'Ivoire; 254 churches, 50 full-time pastors; Pres. BOAN BI ZRÈ EMMANUEL.

Mission Evangélique Luthérienne en Côte d'Ivoire (MELCI): BP 196, Touba; tel. and fax 70-71-78; f. 1984; active in evangelism and social work; Dir JOHANNES REDSE.

Union des Eglises Evangéliques du Sud-Ouest de la Côte d'Ivoire and **Mission Biblique:** 08 BP 20, Abidjan 08; f. 1927; c. 250 places of worship.

The Press

DAILIES

Le Démocrate: Maison du Parti à Treichville, 01 BP 1212, Abidjan 01; tel. 24-25-61; organ of the PDCI–RDA; Dir JEANE-PIERRE AYE.

Fraternité-Matin: blvd du Général de Gaulle, 01 BP 1807, Abidjan 01; tel. 37-06-66; telex 23718; f. 1964; organ of the PDCI–RDA; Man. Dir MICHEL KOUAMÉ; circ. 80,000.

Ivoir 'Soir: blvd du Général de Gaulle, 01 BP 1807, Abidjan 01; tel. 37-06-66; telex 23718; f. 1987; organ of the PDCI–RDA; social, cultural and sporting activities; Man. Dir MICHEL KOUAMÉ; circ. 50,000.

Le Jour: 26 ave Chardy, Plateau, 01 BP 2432, Abidjan 01; tel. 21-95-78; fax 21-95-80; e-mail lejour@africaonline.co.ci; f. 1994; Dirs DIEGOU BAILLY, ABDOULAYE SANGARÉ; circ. 16,000.

Nouvelle République: face Théâtre de la Cité, Cocody, 09 BP 960, Abidjan 09; tel. 44-90-96; fax 44-97-10.

L'Oeil du Peuple: 220 Logements, escalier P, porte 160, rez-de-chaussée, blvd du Général de Gaulle, Adjamé, 23 BP 1093, Abidjan 23; tel. 37-98-09.

Le Populaire: 19 blvd Angoulvand, résidence Neuilly, Plateau, 01 BP 5496, Abidjan 01; tel. 22-79-69.

Le Républicain: zone 3, rue des Carrossiers, 01 BP 1942, Abidjan 01; tel. 25-55-43; fax 25-49-80.

Le Réveil Hebdo: face Théâtre de la Cité, Cocody, 09 BP 960, Abidjan 09; tel. 44-90-96; fax 44-97-10.

Soir Info: derrière IBIS Marcory, 10 BP 2462, Abidjan 10; tel. 25-32-77.

La Voie: face Institut Marie-Thérèse Houphouët-Boigny, 17 BP 656, Abidjan 17; tel. 37-68-23; fax 37-74-76; organ of the FPI; Dir ABOU DRAHAMANE SANGARÉ; Man. MAURICE LURIGNAN.

PERIODICALS

Alif: Cité Fairmont, 20 BP 575, Abidjan 20; tel. 37-20-90; weekly.

Le Bélier: Immeuble Roum, 2e étage, blvd Roum, Plateau, 16 BP 465, Abidjan 16; tel. 22-68-12; weekly.

Bol Kotch: face Institut Marie-Thérèse Houphouët-Boigny, Adjamé, 17 BP 656, Abidjan 17; tel. 37-68-23; weekly.

Le Changement: Immeuble Ghadar, blvd Giscard d'Estaing, 16 BP 10, Abidjan 16; tel. 25-52-52; f. 1991; weekly; Dir GOGBÉ DELIWA DAVID; circ. 10,000.

Le Combat: Yopougon, 23 BP 2044, Abidjan 23; tel. 45-85-16; weekly.

L'Essentiel: Cocody St Jean, 08 BP 1163, Abidjan 08; tel. 44-96-11; weekly.

Journal Officiel de la Côte d'Ivoire: Service Autonome des Journaux Officiels, BP V70, Abidjan; tel. 22-67-76; weekly; circ. 1,000.

La Lettre de l'Afrique de l'Ouest: rue des Jardins, Cocody-les-Deux-Plateaux, 01 BP 8534, Abidjan 01; tel. 41-04-76; fax 41-04-15; f. 1995; publ. by Centre Africain de Presse et d'Edition; six a year; politics, economics, regional integration; Editors JUSTIN VIEYRA, JÉRÔME CARLOS.

Mousso: zone 4, prolongement blvd du 7 décembre, après Carrefour rue Paul Laugevin, à 100 m de La Pharmacie St Joseph, 16 BP 522, Abidjan 16; tel. 25-19-06; weekly.

Notre chance: Immeuble SICOGI, 1er étage, porte escalier E, blvd du Gabon (Marcory), 10 BP 654, Abidjan 10; tel. 26-44-28; weekly.

Nouvel Elan: rue des Banques, Plateau, 18 BP 577, Abidjan 18; weekly.

Le Nouvel Horizon: 220 Logements, blvd du Général de Gaulle, Adjamé, 17 BP 656, Abidjan 17; tel. 37-68-23; f. 1990; organ of the FPI; weekly; Dir ABOU DRAHAMANE SANGARÉ; circ. 15,000.

La Nouvelle Presse: Cocody-les-deux-Plateaux, rue des Jardins, 01 BP 8534, Abidjan 01; tel. 41-04-76; fax 41-04-15; f. 1992; publ. by Centre Africain de Presse et d'Edition; weekly; current affairs; Editors JUSTIN VIEYRA, JÉRÔME CARLOS; circ. 25,000.

Plume Libre: Petite Mosquée Riviera, 08 BP 2464, Abidjan 08; tel. 43-47-58; weekly; Dir DEMBÉLÉ FOUSSENI; Editor KÉMÉ BRAHMA.

Revue Ivoirienne de Droit: BP 3811, Abidjan; f. 1969; publ. by the Centre ivoirien de recherches et d'études juridiques; legal affairs; circ. 1,500.

Star Magazine: Immeuble SIAM, Plateau, 17 BP 464, Abidjan 17; tel. 22-73-76; fax 35-85-66; weekly.

Téré: 220 Logements, blvd du Général de Gaulle, Adjamé, 20 BP 43, Abidjan 20; tel. 37-79-42; organ of the PIT; weekly; Dir ANGÈLE GNONSOA.

L'Union: 04 BP 2295, Abidjan 04; tel. 22-49-59; weekly; Dir YACOUBA BALLO.

La Voix d'Afrique: Cocody-les-Deux-Plateaux, rue des Jardins, 01 BP 8534, Abidjan 01; tel. 41-04-76; fax 41-04-15; publ. by Centre Africain de Presse et d'Edition; monthly; Editor-in-Chief GAOUSSOU KAMISSOKO.

NEWS AGENCIES

Agence Ivoirienne de Presse (AIP): 04 BP 312, Abidjan 04; telex 23781; f. 1961; Dir KONÉ SEMGUÉ SAMBA.

Foreign Bureaux

Agence France-Presse (AFP): 18 ave du Docteur Crozet, 01 BP 726, Abidjan 01; tel. 21-90-17; telex 22481; fax 21-10-36; Dir FRANÇOIS-XAVIER HARISPE.

Associated Press (AP) (USA): 01 BP 5843, Abidjan 01; tel. 41-37-49; telex 28129; Correspondent ROBERT WELLER.

Reuters West Africa (United Kingdom): Résidence Les Acacias, 2e étage, appt 203–205, 20 blvd Clozel, 01 BP 2338, Abidjan 01; tel. 21-12-22; telex 23921; fax 21-30-77; West Africa Man. MICHAEL CLEMENT; Bureau Chief NICHOLAS PHYTHIAN.

Xinhua (New China) News Agency (People's Republic of China): Cocody Danga Nord Lot 46, 08 BP 1212, Abidjan 08; tel. 44-01-24; Chief Correspondent XIONG SHANWU.

Central News Agency (Taiwan) is also represented in Abidjan.

PRESS ASSOCIATION

Association de la Presse Démocratique Ivoirienne (APDI): Abidjan; f. 1994; Chair. JEAN-BAPTISTE AKROU.

Publishers

Centre Africain de Presse et d'Edition (CAPE): rue des Jardins, Cocody-les-Deux-Plateaux, 01 BP 8534, Abidjan 01; tel. 41-04-76; fax 41-04-15; Man. JUSTIN VIEYRA.

Centre d'Edition et de Diffusion Africaines (CEDA): square Aristide Briand, 04 BP 541, Abidjan 04; tel. 22-22-42; telex 22451; fax 32-72-62; f. 1961; general non-fiction; Chair. and Man. Dir VENANCE KACOU.

Centre de Publications Evangéliques: 08 BP 900, Abidjan 08; tel. 44-48-05; fax 44-58-17; f. 1970; religious; Dir JULES OUOBA.

Nouvelles Editions Ivoiriennes: 01 BP 1818, Abidjan 01; tel. 32-12-51; telex 22564; f. 1972; literature, criticism, essays, drama, religion, art, history; Dir K. L. LIGUER-LAUBHOUET.

Université Nationale de Côte d'Ivoire: 01 BP V34, Abidjan 01; tel. 44-08-59; telex 26138; f. 1964; academic and general non-fiction and periodicals; Publications Dir GILLES VILASCO.

Government Publishing House

Imprimerie Nationale: BP V87, Abidjan; tel. 21-76-11; telex 23868; fax 21-68-68.

Radio and Television

In 1994, according to UNESCO, there were an estimated 1.98m. radio receivers and 822,000 television receivers in use.

Legislation to end the state monopoly of the broadcast media was enacted in late 1991. A private television channel, operated by Canal Horizon, a subsidiary of Canal Plus (France), commenced broadcasts from Abidjan in 1994: the channel had some 15,000 subscribers in mid-1995. Broadcasts from Abidjan by BBC Afrique, the British Broadcasting Corporation's first FM station outside Europe, began in April 1994. By 1995 five new FM broadcasting licences had been issued.

Broadcasting facilities were expected to be enhanced following the inauguration, scheduled for mid-1995, of Côte d'Ivoire's Comsat satellite communications project. A television licence fee was introduced in February of that year.

Radiodiffusion-Télévision Ivoirienne (RTI): Dir OUATTARA GNONZIE:

Radiodiffusion Ivoirienne: BP V191, Abidjan 01; tel. 21-48-00; telex 22635; f. 1962; govt radio station broadcasting in French, English and local languages; MW station at Abidjan, relay at Bouaké; VHF transmitters at Abidjan, Bouaflé, Man and Koun-Abbrosso; Dir MAMADOU BERTÉ.

Télévision Ivoirienne: 08 BP 883, Abidjan 08; tel. 43-90-39; telex 22293; f. 1963; broadcasts in French; two channels; stations at Abidjan, Bouaflé, Bouaké, Binao, Digo, Dimbokro, Koun, Man, Niangbo, Niangué, Séguéla, Tiémé and Touba; Man. (vacant).

Radio Espoir: 12 BP 27, Abidjan 12; tel. 27-60-01; fax 27-69-70; f. 1990; radio broadcasts from Port-Bouët.

Radio Nostalgie: Abidjan; f. 1993; subsidiary of Radio Nostalgie (France); FM station; Dirs HAMED BAKAYOKO, YVES ZOGBO, Jr.

Finance

(br. = branch; cap. = capital; res = reserves; dep. = deposits; m. = million; amounts in francs CFA)

BANKING

Central Bank

Banque Centrale des Etats de l'Afrique de l'Ouest (BCEAO): angle blvd Botreau Roussel et ave Delafosse, 01 BP 1769, Abidjan 01; tel. 21-04-66; telex 23474; fax 22-28-52; headquarters in Dakar, Senegal; bank of issue and central bank for the member states of the Union économique et monétaire ouest-africaine (UEMOA), f. 1962; cap. and res 657,592m. (Dec. 1995); Gov. CHARLES KONAN BANNY; Dir in Côte d'Ivoire TIÉMOKO MEYLIET KONÉ; 5 brs.

Other Banks

Bank of Africa–Côte d'Ivoire (BOA–CI): Immeuble ex-BNDA, rue Joseph Anoma, 01 BP 4132, Abidjan 01; tel. 33-15-36; telex 22321; fax 32-89-93; 52% owned by Groupe African Financial Holding; cap. and res 1,470m. (Dec. 1996); Chair. PAUL DERREUMAUX; Man. Dir FRANCIS SUEUR.

Banque Atlantique–Côte d'Ivoire: Immeuble El Nasr, ave du Général de Gaulle, Plateau, 04 BP 1036, Abidjan 04; tel. 21-82-18; telex 23834; fax 21-68-52; f. 1978; cap. and res 4,867m. (Dec. 1995); Chair. DOSSONGUI KONÉ; Man. Dir PAUL PEETERS.

Banque de l'Habitat de Côte d'Ivoire (BHCI): 22 ave Joseph Anoma, 01 BP 2325, Abidjan 01, tel. 22-60-00; telex 22544; fax 22-58-18; f. 1993 to finance housing projects, operations commenced 1994; cap. and res 736m. (Dec. 1995); Chair. and Man. Dir KONÉ KAFONGO.

Banque Internationale pour le Commerce et l'Industrie de la Côte d'Ivoire SA (BICICI): Tour BICICI, ave Franchet d'Espérey, 01 BP 1298, Abidjan 01; tel. 20-16-00; telex 23651; fax 20-17-00; f. 1962; 28% owned by Société Financière pour les Pays d'Outre-Mer, 21% by Banque Nationale de Paris, 20% state-owned; cap. and res 24,293m. (Dec. 1995); Chair. JOACHIM RICHMOND; Man. Dir PATRICK MATHIEU; 39 brs.

Banque Paribas Côte d'Ivoire (PARIBAS CI): Immeuble Alliance, 6e étage, 17 ave Terrasson de Fougères, 17 BP 09, Abidjan 17; tel. 21-86-86; telex 22870; fax 21-88-23; f. 1984; 84% owned by Banque Paribas (France); cap. and res 1,172m. (Dec. 1995); Chair. DANIEL BÉDIN; Man. Dir CHRISTIAN ARLOT.

BIAO–Côte d'Ivoire SA: 8–10 ave Joseph Anoma, 01 BP 1274, Abidjan 01; tel. 20-07-20; telex 23641; fax 20-07-00; f. 1980; 100% state-owned; transfer to private ownership pending; cap. and res 7,951m. (Dec. 1995); Chair. NICOLAS KOUASSI AKON YAO; Man. Dir MARC DEMEULENAERE; 37 brs.

BICI Bail de Côte d'Ivoire: Tour BICICI, 5e étage, ave Franchet d'Espérey, 01 BP 6495, Abidjan 01; tel. 22-24-31; telex 23870; fax 20-17-00; 75% owned by BICICI; cap. and res 1,510m. (Dec. 1995); Chair JOACHIM RICHMOND; Man. Dir PATRICK MATHIEU.

Compagnie Financière de la Côte d'Ivoire (COFINCI): Tour BICICI, 15e étage, ave Franchet d'Espérey, 01 BP 1566, Abidjan 01; tel. 21-27-32; telex 22228; fax 20-17-00; f. 1974; 72% owned by BICICI; cap. and res 1,937m. (Dec. 1995); Chair. and Man. Dir JOACHIM RICHMOND.

Ecobank–Côte d'Ivoire: Immeuble Alliance, 17 ave Terrasson de Fougères, 01 BP 4107, Abidjan 01; tel. 21-10-41; telex 23266; fax 21-88-16; f. 1989; 93% owned by Ecobank Transnational Inc (operating under the auspices of the Economic Community of West African States); cap. 3,226m. (Jan. 1997); Chair. ABDOULAYE KONÉ; Man. Dir LOUIS NALLET; 1 br.

Société Générale de Banques en Côte d'Ivoire SA (SGBCI): 5–7 ave Joseph Anoma, Plateau, 01 BP 1355, Abidjan 01; tel. 20-12-34; telex 23741; fax 20-14-82; f. 1962; 39% owned by Société Générale (France); cap. and res 23,186m. (Dec. 1995); Chair. TIÉMOKO YADÉ COULIBALY; Man. Dir LUC BARAS; 55 brs.

Société Générale de Banques de Financement et de Participations en Côte d'Ivoire (SOGEFINANCE): 5–7 ave Joseph Anoma, 01 BP 3904, Abidjan 01; tel. 22-55-30; telex 23502; fax 32-67-60; f. 1978; 58% owned by SGBCI; cap. and res 1,661m. (Dec. 1995); Chair. and Man. Dir TIÉMOKO YADÉ COULIBALY; Man. Dir ANTOINE CASSAIGNAN.

Société Ivoirienne de Banque (SIB): Immeuble Alpha 2000, 34 blvd de la République, 01 BP 1300, Abidjan 01; tel. 20-00-00; telex 22283; fax 21-97-41; f. 1962; 51% owned by Crédit Lyonnais (France); 49% state-owned; cap. and res 4,241m. (Dec. 1995); Man. Dir JEAN-PIERRE GREYFIE DE BELLECOMBE; 35 brs.

Financial Institution

Caisse Autonome d'Amortissement: Immeuble SCIAM, ave Marchand, 01 BP 670, Abidjan 01; tel. 21-06-11; telex 23798; fax 21-35-78; f. 1959; management of state funds; Chair. ABDOULAYE KONÉ; Man. Dir VICTOR KOUAMÉ.

Bankers' Association

Association Professionnelle des Banques et Etablissements Financiers de Côte d'Ivoire (APBEFCI): 01 BP 3810, Abidjan 01; tel. 21-20-08; Pres. JEAN-PIERRE MEYER.

STOCK EXCHANGE

Bourse des Valeurs d'Abidjan (BVA): Immeuble BVA, ave Joseph Anoma, 01 BP 1878, Abidjan 01; tel. 21-57-42; telex 22221; fax 22-16-57; f. 1976; Pres. LÉON NAKA.

The BVA was scheduled to become a regional stock exchange, serving the member states of the UEMOA.

INSURANCE

Assurances Générales de Côte d'Ivoire (AGCI): Immeuble AGCI, ave Noguès, 01 BP 4092, Abidjan 01; tel. 33-11-31; telex 22502; fax 33-25-79; f. 1979; cap. 3,750m.; Chair. JEAN KACOU DIAGOU; Man. Dir GILBERT HIS.

Assurances Générales de Côte d'Ivoire—Vie (AGCI—Vie): Immeuble AGCI, ave Nogues, 01 BP 4092, Abidjan 01; tel. 33-11-31; telex 22502; fax 33-25-79; f. 1988; cap. 300m.; life; Chair. JEAN KACOU DIAGOU; Man. Dir GILBERT HIS.

Colina SA: Immeuble Colina, blvd Roume, 01 BP 3832, Abidjan 01; tel. 21-65-05; telex 23570; fax 22-59-05; f. 1980; cap. 600m.; Chair. MICHEL PHARAON; Dir-Gen. RAYMOND FARHAT.

Mutuelle Universelle de Garantie (UNIWARRANT): 01 BP 301, Abidjan 01; tel. 32-76-32; telex 22120; fax 32-55-36; f. 1970; cap. 400m.; Chair. and Man. Dir FATIMA SYLLA.

La Nationale d'Assurances (CNA): 30 ave du Général de Gaulle, 01 BP 1333, Abidjan 01; tel. 22-08-00; telex 22176; fax 22-49-06; f. 1972; cap. 400m.; insurance and reinsurance; Chair. SOUNKALO DJIBO; Man. Dir RICHARD COULIBALY.

La Sécurité Ivoirienne: Immeuble La Sécurité Ivoirienne, blvd Roume, 01 BP 569, Abidjan 01; tel. 21-50-63; telex 23817; fax 21-05-67; f. 1971; cap. 300m.; general; Chair. DIA HOUPHOUËT-BOIGNY; Dir-Gen. JACQUES BARDOUX.

Société Africaine d'Assurances et de Réassurances en République de Côte d'Ivoire (SAFARRIV): Immeuble SAFARRIV, 2 blvd Roume, 01 BP 1741, Abidjan 01; tel. 21-91-57; telex 22159; fax 21-82-72; f. 1975; cap. 700m.; Pres. TIÉMOKO YADÉ COULIBALY; Man. Dir CHRISTIAN ARRAULT.

Société Ivoirienne d'Assurances Mutuelles—Mutuelle d'Assurances Transports (SIDAM—MAT): Immeuble SIDAM, ave Houdaille, 01 BP 1217, Abidjan 01; tel. 21-97-82; telex 22670; fax 32-94-39; f. 1970; cap. 150m.; Chair. ABOU DOUMBIA; Dir-Gen. SOULEYMANE MEITE.

L'Union Africaine-IARD (UA): ave de la Fosse Prolongée, 01 BP 378, Abidjan 01; tel. 21-73-81; telex 23568; fax 22-12-42; f. 1981; cap. 2,175m.; insurance and reinsurance; Chair. JOACHIM RICHMOND; Dir MAURICE GIBOUDOT.

Union Africaine Vie: ave Houdaille, 01 BP 2016, Abidjan 01; tel. 22-25-15; telex 22200; fax 22-37-60; f. 1985; cap. 825m.; life assurance; Chair. ERNEST AMOS DJORO; Dir JEAN-KACOU DIAGOU.

Trade and Industry

DEVELOPMENT AGENCIES

Caisse Française de Développement: 01 BP 1814, Abidjan 01; tel. 44-53-05; telex 28113; fmrly Caisse Centrale de Coopération Economique, name changed 1992; Dir in Côte d'Ivoire ANTOINE BAUX.

Mission Française de Coopération: 01 BP 1839, Abidjan 01; tel. 21-60-45; administers bilateral aid from France.

STATE COMPANIES

Bureau Nationale d'Etudes Techniques et de Développement (BNETD): ancien hôtel le Relais, blvd de la Corniche, Cocody, 04 BP 945, Abidjan 04; tel. 44-28-05; telex 26193; fax 44-56-66; f. 1978 as Direction et Controle des Grands Travaux; cap. 2,000m. francs CFA; management and supervision of major public works projects; Man. Dir TIDJANE THIAM.

Caisse de Stabilisation et de Soutien des Prix des Productions Agricoles (Caistab): BP V132, Abidjan; tel. 20-27-00; telex 23712; fax 21-89-94; f. 1964; cap. 4,000m. francs CFA; fmrly controlled price, quality and export of agricultural products; role reduced 1995; offices in Paris, London and New York; Man. Dir RENÉ AMANI.

Compagnie Ivoirienne pour le Développement des Cultures Vivrières (CIDV): 01 BP 2049, Abidjan 01; tel. 21-00-79; telex 23612; f. 1988; production of food crops; Man. Dir BENOÎT N'DRI BROU.

Société pour le Développement Minier de la Côte d'Ivoire (SODEMI): 31 blvd André Latrille, 01 BP 2816, Abidjan 01; tel. 44-29-94; telex 26162; fax 44-08-21; f. 1962; cap. 600m. francs CFA; geological and mineral research; Pres. NICOLAS KOUANDI ANGBA; Man. Dir JOSEPH N'ZI.

Société pour le Développement des Plantations de Canne à Sucre, l'Industrialisation et la Commercialisation du Sucre (SODESUCRE): 16 ave du Docteur Crozet, 01 BP 2164, Abidjan 01; tel. 21-04-79; telex 23451; fax 21-07-75; f. 1971; cap. 30,500m. francs CFA; transfer to private ownership pending; management of sugar plantations, refining, marketing and export of sugar and by-products; Chair. and Man. Dir JOSEPH KOUAMÉ KRA.

Société de Développement des Plantations Forestières (SODEFOR): blvd François Mitterrand, 01 BP 3770, Abidjan 01; tel. 44-46-16; telex 26156; fax 44-02-40; f. 1966; cap. 50m. francs CFA; establishment and management of tree plantations, management of state forests, marketing of timber products; Pres. Minister of Agriculture and Animal Resources; Man. Dir DENIS KOKAN KONAN.

Société pour le Développement des Productions Animales (SODEPRA): Immeuble Les Harmonies, angle blvd Carde et ave Dr Jamot, 01 BP 1249, Abidjan 01; tel. 21-13-10; telex 22123; f. 1970; cap. 404m. francs CFA; rearing of livestock; Chair. CHARLES DONWAHI; Man. Dir PAUL LAMIZANA.

Société Nationale d'Opérations Pétrolières de la Côte d'Ivoire (PETROCI): Immeuble les Hévéas, BP V194, Abidjan 01; tel. 21-40-58; telex 22135; fax 21-68-24; f. 1975; transfer to private ownership pending in 1996; cap. 20,000m. francs CFA; all aspects of petroleum development; Pres. and Man. Dir (vacant).

STATE PRIVATIZATION AUTHORITY

Comité de Privatisation: 6 blvd de L'Indénié, 01 BP 1141, Abidjan 01; tel. 22-22-31; fax 22-22-35.

CHAMBERS OF COMMERCE

Chambre d'Agriculture de la Côte d'Ivoire: 11 ave Lamblin, 01 BP 1291, Abidjan 01; tel. 32-92-13; fax 32-92-20; Sec.-Gen. GAUTHIER N'ZI.

Chambre de Commerce et d'Industrie de Côte d'Ivoire: 6 ave Joseph Anoma, 01 BP 1399, Abidjan 01; tel. 33-16-00; telex 23224; fax 32-39-46; f.1992; Pres. SEYDOU DIARRA; Dir-Gen. KONAN KOFFI.

EMPLOYERS' ASSOCIATIONS

Fédération Maritime de la Côte d'Ivoire (FEDERMAR): 04 BP 723, Abidjan 04; tel. 21-25-83; Sec.-Gen. VACABA DE MOVALY TOURÉ.

Fédération Nationale des Industries de la Côte d'Ivoire: 01 BP 1340, Abidjan 01; tel. 35-71-42; f. 1993; Pres. PIERRE MAGNE; Sec.-Gen. PHILIPPE MEYER; 150 mems.

Groupement Interprofessionnel de l'Automobile (GIPA): Immeuble Jean Lefèbvre, 14 blvd de Marseille, 01 BP 1340, Abidjan 01; tel. 35-71-42; telex 42380; f. 1953; 30 mems; Pres. DANIEL DUBOIS; Sec.-Gen. PHILIPPE MEYER.

Syndicat des Commerçants Importateurs, Exportateurs et Distributeurs de la Côte d'Ivoire (SCIMPEX): 01 BP 3792, Abidjan 01; tel. 21-54-27; Pres. JACQUES ROSSIGNOL; Sec.-Gen. M. KOFFI.

Syndicat des Entrepreneurs et des Industriels de la Côte d'Ivoire (SEICI): Immeuble Jean Lefèbvre, 14 blvd de Marseille, 01 BP 464, Abidjan 01; tel. 21-83-85; f. 1934; Pres. ABDEL AZIZ THIAM.

Syndicat des Exportateurs et Négociants en Bois de Côte d'Ivoire: Immeuble CCIA, 11e étage, 01 BP 1979, Abidjan 01; tel. 21-12-39; fax 21-26-42; Pres. JEAN-CLAUDE BERNARD.

Syndicat des Producteurs Industriels du Bois (SPIB): Immeuble CCIA, 11e étage, 01 BP 318, Abidjan 01; tel. 21-12-39; fax 21-26-42; f. 1973; Pres. BRUNO FINOCCHIARO.

Union des Entreprises Agricoles et Forestières: Immeuble CCIA, 11e étage, 01 BP 2300, Abidjan 01; tel. 21-12-39; fax 21-26-42; f. 1952; Pres. FULGENCE KOFFY.

MAJOR INDUSTRIAL COMPANIES

The following are some of the largest companies in terms of either capital investment or employment.

Blohorn SA: 01 BP 1751, Abidjan 01; tel. 24-90-60; telex 42279; fax 25-11-05; f. 1960; cap. 6,040m. francs CFA; 80% owned by Unilever Group; management of industrial complex for processing oil-seeds; production of palm oil and its derivatives, incl. soap, margarine and glycerine; Chair. PIERRE BONNEIL; Vice-Chair. MARTIN RUSHWORTH; 1,000 employees.

Bois Transformés d'Afrique (BTA): 01 BP 958, Abidjan 01; tel. 22-33-04; fax 22-74-69; f. 1972; cap. 233.5m. francs CFA; sawmills, plywood factory at Zagné; Dir M. DEKEULENEER.

Carnaud Metalbox SIEM: blvd Giscard d'Estaing, 01 BP 1242, Abidjan 01; tel. 35-89-74; telex 634000; fax 35-03-94; f. 1954; subsidiary of Carnaud Metalbox (France); cap. 1,889m. francs CFA; mfrs of cans; Chair. BRIAN APPLEYARD; Man. Dir PHILIPPE EYMARD.

Compagnie des Caoutchoucs du Pakidie (CCP): 01 BP 1191, Abidjan 01; tel. 37-15-38; telex 23605; fax 37-15-40; f. 1960; cap. 856m. francs CFA; rubber plantations and factory; Chair. FULGENCE KOFFY.

Compagnie Ivoirienne pour le Développement des Textiles (CIDT): route de Béoumi, 01 BP 622, Bouaké 01; tel. 63-30-13; telex 69121; fax 63-41-67; f. 1974; cap. 7,200m. francs CFA; 70% state-owned; transfer to private ownership pending; development of cotton production, cotton ginning; Man. Dir COULIBALY SAMBA; 1,713 employees.

Compagnie Ivoirienne d'Electricité (CIE): 01 BP 6932, Abidjan 01; f. 1990 to assume electricity distribution network fmrly operated by Energie Electrique de la Côte d'Ivoire; 20% state-owned, 51% controlled by Société Bouygues group (France) and Electricité de France; Pres. MARCEL ZADI KESSY; Man. Dir GÉRARD THEURIAU.

Compagnie Ivoirienne de Production d'Electricité (CIPREL): Tour Cidam, 12e étage, ave Houdaille, 01 BP 4039, Abidjan 01; tel. 22-60-97; operates national electricity production network.

Eveready Côte d'Ivoire SA: Zone Industrielle de Vridi, 15 BP 611, Abidjan 15; tel. 27-33-84; telex 43390; f. 1969; cap. 894m. francs CFA; wholly-owned subsidiary of Eveready Battery Co (USA); mfrs of batteries; Dir A. CORVEZ.

Ets R. Gonfreville (ERG): route de l'Aéroport, BP 584, Bouaké; tel. 63-32-13; telex 69105; fax 63-46-65; f. 1921; cap. 2,999m. francs CFA; 10.5% state-owned; transfer to private ownership of state holding pending; spinning, weaving, dyeing and printing of cotton textiles; clothing mfrs; Chair. SOUNKALO DJIBO; Man. Dir CLAUDE TRESCOL; 2,452 employees.

Ficelleries de Bouaké-Sociéte Industrielle Ivoirienne d'Emballage (FIBAKO–IVOIREMBAL): BP 117, Bouaké; tel. 63-32-12; telex 69115; fax 63-18-92; f. 1946; cap. 300m. francs CFA; spinning, mfrs of sacking and plastic packaging; expansion programme in progress in 1996; Man. Dir JEAN DUTRUGE.

Filatures, Tissages, Sacs–Côte d'Ivoire SA (FILTISAC): Km 8, route d'Adzopé, 01 BP 3962, Abidjan 01; tel. 37-13-02; telex 23273; fax 37-09-67; f. 1965; cap. 2,644m. francs CFA; mfrs of polypropylene and jute bags and other packaging; Pres. SIDI MADATALI; 1,500 employees.

Grands Moulins d'Abidjan (GMA): Quai 1, Zone Portuaire, 01 BP 1743, Abidjan 01; tel. 21-28-33; telex 23740; f. 1963; cap. 2,000m. francs CFA; flour milling and production of animal feed; Dir KOUASSI KOUADIO.

Industrie de Transformation des Produits Agricoles (API): Zone Industrielle de Vridi, 15 BP 431, Abidjan 15; tel. 35-20-09; telex 43159; f. 1968; cap. 900m. francs CFA; wholly owned by Cacao Barry Group (France); marketing of cocoa products, processing of cocoa beans; Man. Dir HONORÉ AKPANGNI.

Mobil Oil-Côte d'Ivoire: impasse Paris-Village, 01 BP 1777, Abidjan 01; tel. 21-73-20; telex 23779; f. 1974; cap. 2,000m. francs CFA; distribution of petroleum products; Chair. MICHEL BONNET; Dir J. LABAUNE.

Nandjelait: Zone Industrielle de Vridi, 01 BP 2149, Abidjan 01; f. 1986; cap. 600m. francs CFA; production, packaging and sale of dairy products and by-products; Chair. and Man. Dir ROGER ABINADER.

National Electric-Côte d'Ivoire (NELCI): 16 BP 131, Abidjan 16; f. 1983; cap. 1,000m. francs CFA; assembly of radio and television receivers; Chair. TAMADA TAKASHI.

Nestlé Côte d'Ivoire: rue du Lycée Technique, 01 BP 1840, Abidjan 01; tel. 44-44-44; telex 27194; fax 44-43-43; f. 1959; cap. 5,518m. francs CFA; subsidiary of Nestlé SA (Switzerland); production of coffee and cocoa products, manufacture and sale of food products; Chair. GEORGES N'DIA KOFFI; Man. Dir FRANÇOIS PRÉVOT.

Omnium Chimique et Cosmétique (COSMIVOIRE): Zone Industrielle de Vridi, 01 BP 3576, Abidjan 01; tel. 27-57-32; telex 43223; fax 27-28-13; f. 1974; cap. 702m. francs CFA; mfrs of soaps, cosmetics, oils, margarine, butter and alcohol; Pres. ALAIN YACOUBA BAMBARA; Man. Dir YAO KOFFI NOËL.

Palmindustrie: Pointe des Fumeurs, 01 BP V239, Abidjan 01; tel. 27-00-70; telex 43100; fax 25-47-00; f. 1969; cap. 34,000m. francs CFA; transferred to private ownership in 1996; development of palm, coconut and copra products; Man. Dir BONIFACE BRITO.

Société Africaine de Cacao (SACO): rue Pierre et Marie Curie, 01 BP 1045, Abidjan 01; tel. 35-44-10; telex 43293; f. 1956; cap. 1,733m. francs CFA; 65% owned by Cacao Barry Group (France), 35% state-owned; sale of state holding pending in 1996; mfrs of cocoa powder, chocolate products, cocoa butter and oil-cake; expansion programme in progress in 1996; Pres. and Man. Dir SEYDOU DIARRA; 670 employees.

Société Africaine de Plantations d'Hévéas (SAPH): 14 blvd Carde, 01 BP 1322, Abidjan 01; tel. 21-18-91; fax 22-18-67; f. 1956; cap. 10,249m. francs CFA; 38.7% owned by Octide Finance, 30.9% by Société Internationale des Plantations d'Hévéas (France); production of rubber on 17,000 ha of plantations; Pres. and Man. Dir YVES ROLAND.

Société des Caoutchoucs de Grand-Béréby (SOGB): 17 BP 18, Abidjan 17; tel. 21-99-47; telex 23888; fax 33-25-80; f. 1979; cap. 21,602m. francs CFA; 60% owned by Befin (Belgium), 35% state-owned; rubber plantations and processing; Pres. FULGENCE KOFFI; Gen. Man. MARC MUTSAARS; 4,400 employees.

Société des Ciments d'Abidjan (SCA): 01 BP 3751, Abidjan 01; tel. 21-32-63; telex 23610; f. 1965; cap. 2,000m. francs CFA; 40% state-owned; cement mfrs; Chair. and Man. Dir PIERRE AMIDA.

Société de Conserves de Côte d'Ivoire (SCODI): Quai de Pêche, Zone Industrielle de Vridi, 01 BP 677, Abidjan 01; tel. 25-66-74; telex 43254; fax 27-05-52; f. 1960; cap. 908m. francs CFA; tuna canning; Chair. PAUL ANTONIETTI; Gen. Man. YVON RIVA.

Société de Construction et d'Exploitation d'Installations Frigorifiques (SOCEF): Port de Pêche, 04 BP 154, Abidjan 04; tel. 35-54-42; f. 1962; cap. 900m. francs CFA; mfrs of refrigeration units; Dir GÉRARD CLEMENT.

Société Cotonnière Ivoirienne (COTIVO): BP 244, Agboville; tel. 51-70-01; telex 51002; fax 51-73-34; f. 1972; cap. 3,600m. francs CFA; textile complex; Pres. MICHEL HEMONNOT; Man. Dir MICHEL DUTRONC.

Société de Distribution d'Eau de la Côte d'Ivoire (SODECI): 1 ave Christiani-Treichville, 01 BP 1843, Abidjan 01; tel. 23-30-00; fax 24-20-33; f. 1959; cap. 2,000m. francs CFA; production, treatment and distribution of drinking water; Chair. MARCEL ZADI KESSY; Man. Dir PIERRE LE TAREAU; 1,330 employees.

Société de Galvanisation de Tôles en Côte d'Ivoire (TOLES-IVOIRE): 15 BP 144, Abidjan 15; tel. 27-53-38; telex 43184; f. 1969; cap. 975m. francs CFA; mfrs of galvanized corrugated sheets and other roofing materials; Chair. SIDI MADATALI; Man. Dir PHILIPPE GODIN.

Société Ivoirienne de Béton Manufacturé (SIBM): 12 rue Thomas Edison, 01 BP 902, Abidjan 01; tel. 35-52-71; fax 35-82-27; f. 1978; cap. 800m. francs CFA; mem. of Société Africaine de Béton Manufacturé group; mfrs of concrete; Man. Dir DANIEL PAUL.

Société Ivoirienne de Câbles (SICABLE): Zone Industrielle de Vridi, 15 BP 35, Abidjan 15; tel. 27-57-35; fax 27-12-34; f. 1975; cap. 740m. francs CFA; 51% owned by Câbles Pirelli; mfrs of electricity cables; Chair. ANDRÉ BOURG; Man. Dir HERVÉ JACOTOT.

Société Ivoirienne de Ciments et Matériaux (SICM-SOCIMAT): blvd du Port, 01 BP 887, Abidjan 01; tel. 24-17-34; telex 42382; fax 24-27-21; f. 1962; cap. 507m. francs CFA; clinker-crushing plant; Chair. KURT WEGMANN; Man. Dir O. RONIN.

Société Ivoirienne de Construction et de Gestion Immobilière (SICOGI): 01 BP 1856, Abidjan 01; tel. 37-03-40; telex 24122; f. 1962; cap. 2,000m. francs CFA; 54% state-owned; planning and construction; Man. Dir KONÉ BANGA.

Société Ivoirienne d'Oxygène et d'Acetylène (SIVOA): 131 blvd de Marseille, 01 BP 1753, Abidjan 01; tel. 35-44-71; telex 43394; fax 35-80-96; f. 1962; cap. 873m. francs CFA; 20% state-owned, 72% by Air Liquide (France); mfrs of industrial and medical gases; Dir JEAN-PIERRE DESSALLES; 120 employees

Société Ivoirienne de Raffinage (SIR): route de Vridi, blvd de Petit-Bassam, 01 BP 1269, Abidjan 01; tel. 27-01-60; telex 43442; fax 21-17-98; f. 1962; cap. 26,000m. francs CFA; 47% owned by PETROCI; transfer to private ownership of state holding pending; operates petroleum refinery at Abidjan; Man. Dir JEAN-PIERRE JANIN; 736 employees.

Société Ivoirienne des Tabacs (SITAB): Zone Industrielle, 01 BP 607, Bouaké 01; tel. 63-35-31; telex 61116; f. 1971; cap. 4,449m. francs CFA; mfrs of cigarettes; Chair. FRANÇOISE AIDARA; Vice-Chair. and Man. Dir PIERRE MAGNE; 849 employees.

Société Ivoirienne de Trituration de Graines Oléagineuses et de Raffinage d'Huiles Végétales (TRITURAF): 15 BP 324, Abidjan 15; tel. 24-90-58; telex 42279; fax 24-68-14; f. 1973; cap. 1,300m. francs CFA; 75% owned by Blohorn SA; Chair. PIERRE BONNEIL; Man. Dir GEORGES BROU KOUASSI.

Société de Limonaderies et Brasseries d'Afrique (SOLIBRA): 27 rue du Canal, 01 BP 1304, Abidjan; tel. 24-91-33; fax 35-97-91; f. 1955; absorbed Société des Brasseries de la Côte d'Ivoire in 1994; cap. 4,100m. francs CFA; mfrs of beer, lemonade and ice at Abidjan, Bouaflé and Yopougon; Chair. PIERRE CASTEL; Man. Dir JACQUES GOCHELY.

Société des Mines d'Afema (SOMIAF): Abidjan; jt venture by Eden Roc Mineral Corpn (Canada) (68%) and SODEMI (32%); exploitation of gold deposits at Aniuri.

Société des Mines d'Ity (SMI): Ity; regd office 08 BP 872, Abidjan 08; f. 1989; cap. 600m. francs CFA; 60% owned by SODEMI, 40% by Mine-Or SA; development of gold reserves at Ity; Pres. ABDOULAYE KONÉ; Man. Dir M. PALANQUE.

Société Multinationale de Bitumes (SMB): blvd de Petit-Bassam, Zone Industrielle de Vridi, 12 BP 622, Abidjan 12; tel. 27-01-60; telex 42539; fax 27-05-18; f. 1976; cap. 1,218m. francs CFA; 53% owned by SIR, 20% of state holding transferred to private ownership in 1996; Chair. and Man. Dir MOUSSA TOURÉ; 50 employees.

Société Nationale Ivoirienne de Travaux (SONITRA): route d'Anyama, 01 BP 2609, Abidjan 01; tel. 37-13-68; telex 24105; f.

1963; cap. 2,273m. francs CFA; 55% state-owned; building and construction; Chair. FERNAND KONAN KOUADIO; Man. Dir AMOS SALOMON; 1,393 employees.

Société Nouvelle Abidjanaise de Carton Ondulé (SONACO): Zone Industrielle de Yopougon, 01 BP 1119, Abidjan; tel. 46-49-70; telex 29164; fax 46-45-06; f. 1964; cap. 1,200m. francs CFA; mfrs of paper goods and corrugated cardboard; Chair. DANIEL FORGET; Man. Dir FÉLIX DADIE; 406 employees.

Société Nouvelle Sifca: rue des Galions, 01 BP 1289, Abidjan 01; tel. 24-26-52; telex 43453; fax 24-07-90; f. 1964; cap. 2,000m. francs CFA; export of cocoa and coffee, cultivation and processing of rice; Pres. and Man. Dir YVES LAMBELIN; 235 employees.

Société Shell-Côte d'Ivoire: Zone Industrielle de Vridi, 15 BP 378, Abidjan 15; tel. 27-00-18; telex 43362; fax 27-24-99; f. 1928; cap. 1,800m. francs CFA; 50% holding by PETROCI; transferred to 80% private ownership in 1995; distribution of petroleum products; Pres. and Man. Dir EDOUARD ETTE.

Société de Stockage de Côte d'Ivoire (STOCACI): rue des Thoniers, Zone Portuaire, 01 BP 1798, Abidjan 01; f. 1980; cap. 1,000m. francs CFA; treatment and storage of cocoa and other products; Chair. JEAN ABILE GAL; Vice-Chair. and Man. Dir MADELEINE TCHICAYA.

Société de Tubes d'Acier et Aluminium en Côte d'Ivoire (SOTACI): Zone Industrielle de Yopougon, 01 BP 2747, Abidjan 01; tel. 45-39-22; telex 29110; fax 45-39-25; f. 1978; cap. 1,029m. francs CFA; mfrs of steel and aluminium tubing and pipes; Chair. and Man. Dir MOUSTAPHA KHALIL; Dir JOSÉ HURTADO.

Star Auto: rue Pierre et Marie Curie, 01 BP 4054, Abidjan 01; tel. 25-43-06; telex 43324; fax 25-44-15; f. 1983; cap. 1,400m. francs CFA; subsidiary of Mercedes-Benz AG (Germany); mfrs and distributors of motor vehicles; Chair. H. UTESS; Gen. Man. GÉRARD FAU.

Union Industrielle Textile de Côte d'Ivoire (UTEXI): Zone Industrielle de Vridi, 15 BP 414, Abidjan 15; tel. 27-44-81; telex 43264; fax 27-16-16; f. 1972; cap. 3,700m. francs CFA; 12.75% state-owned; spinning and weaving mill at Dimbokro; Chair. JACQUES ROSSIGNOL; Man. Dir NOBOYUKI YOSHIDA.

Union Ivoirienne de Traitement de Cacao (UNICAO): 15 BP 406, Abidjan 15; tel. 27-14-49; telex 42343; fax 27-56-82; cap. 1,100m. francs CFA; processing of cocoa beans; Chair. YVES LAMBELIN; Man. Dir HENRI KORNER.

UNIWAX: Zone Industrielle de Yopougon, 01 BP 3994, Abidjan 01; tel. 46-64-15; fax 46-69-42; f. 1967; cap. 1,000m. francs CFA; mfrs of batik fabrics; Chair. PIERRE BONNEIL; Man. Dir JEAN-LOUIS MENUDIER; 538 employees.

Usine de Traitement de Produits Agricoles (UTPA): rue des Thonniers, Zone Portuaire, 01 BP 1798, Abidjan 01; tel. 21-16-55; telex 23657; f. 1977; cap. 2,000m. francs CFA; coffee packaging at Abengourou, Kotobi and Daloa; Chair. EMILE ABILE-GAL; Man. Dir ALAIN PERILLAUD.

TRADE UNIONS

Union Générale des Travailleurs de Côte d'Ivoire (UGTCI): 05 BP 1203, Abidjan 05; tel. 21-26-65; f. 1962; Sec.-Gen. HYACINTHE ADIKO NIAMKEY; 100,000 individual mems; 190 affiliated unions.

There are also several independent trade unions, the most prominent independent federations being the **Fédération des Syndicats Autonomes de la Côte d'Ivoire**, which grouped 19 workers' organizations in early 1995, and **Dignité**.

Transport

RAILWAYS

Société Ivoirienne des Chemins de Fer (SICF): 01 BP 1551, Abidjan 01; tel. 21-02-45; telex 23564; fax 21-39-62; f. 1989, following dissolution of Régie du Chemin de Fer Abidjan–Niger (a jt venture with the Govt of Burkina Faso); 660 km of track; Pres. and Man. Dir ABDEL AZIZ THIAM.

SITARAIL: Immeuble SAGA-CI, rond-point du Nouveau Port, 16 BP 1216, Abidjan 16; tel. 23-23-23; fax 24-22-11; consortium of French, Belgian, Ivorian and Burkinabè interests managing rail line linking Abidjan with Kaya (Burkina Faso).

ROADS

There are about 68,000 km of roads, of which some 6,000 km are paved. A four year (1994–97) programme for the repair and extension of the road network, valued at its outset at 147,000m. francs CFA, was supported by the World Bank, the African Development Bank, the Banque ouest-africaine de développement and the Governments of Germany and Japan. In late 1995 France announced funding of 15,000m. francs CFA, in support of a project (costing 18,000m. francs CFA) to rehabilitate more than 2,000 km of roads in northern regions. Tolls were being introduced on some roads in the mid-1990s, to assist in funding the maintenance of the network.

Société des Transports Abidjanais (SOTRA): 01 BP 2009, Abidjan 01; tel. 24-90-80; telex 43101; fax 25-97-21; f. 1960; 60% state-owned; urban transport; Man. Dir PASCAL YÉBOUÉ-KOUAMÉ.

SHIPPING

Côte d'Ivoire has two major ports, Abidjan and San Pedro, both of which are industrial and commercial establishments with financial autonomy. Abidjan, which handled 11.4m. metric tons of goods in 1995, is the largest container and trading port in west Africa. Access to the port is via the 2.7-km Vridi Canal. The port at San Pedro, which handled 1.1m. tons of goods in 1994, remains the main gateway to the south-western region of Côte d'Ivoire. Construction of a new fishing port at San Pedro, financed by a grant of US $14m. from the Japanese Government, was scheduled for completion in mid-1996.

Port Autonome d'Abidjan (PAA): BP V85, Abidjan; tel. 24-26-40; telex 42318; fax 24-23-28; f. 1950; public undertaking supervised by the Govt; Man. Dir JEAN-MICHEL MOULOD.

Port Autonome de San Pedro (PASP): BP 339/340, San Pedro; tel. 71-20-80; telex 99102; fax 71-27-85; f. 1971; Man. Dir OGOU ATTEMENE.

Compagnie Maritime Africaine-Côte d'Ivoire (COMAF-CI): rond-point du Nouveau Port, 08 BP 867, Abidjan 08; tel. 32-40-77; telex 23357; f. 1973; navigation and management of ships; Dir FRANCO BERNARDINI.

Nouvelle SITRAM: rue des Pétroliers, 01 BP 1546, Abidjan 01; tel. 36-92-00; telex 42254; fax 35-73-93; f. 1967, nationalized in 1976; returned to private ownership in 1995; services between Europe and west Africa and the USA; Chair. BONIFACE PEGAWAGNABA; Dir Commdt FAKO KONÉ.

SAGA–CI: Immeuble SAGA—CI, rond-point du Nouveau Port, 01 BP 1727, Abidjan 01; tel. 23-23-23; telex 43312; fax 24-25-06; merchandise handling, transit and storage; Chair. CHARLES BENITAL; Dir DANIEL CHARRIER.

Société Agence Maritime de l'Ouest Africain—Côte d'Ivoire (SAMOA–CI): rue des Gallions, 01 BP 1611, Abidjan 01; tel. 21-29-65; telex 23765; f. 1955; shipping agents; Man. Dir CLAUDE PERDRIAUD.

Société Ivoirienne de Navigation Maritime (SIVOMAR): 5 rue Charpentier, zone 2b, Treichville, 01 BP 1395, Abidjan 01; tel. 21-73-23; telex 22226; fax 32-38-53; f. 1977; shipments to ports in Africa, the Mediterranean and the Far East; Dir SIMPLISSE DE MESSE ZINSOU.

Société Ouest-Africaine d'Entreprises Maritimes en Côte d'Ivoire (SOAEM–CI): 01 BP 1727, Abidjan 01; tel. 21-59-69; telex 23654; fax 32-24-67; f. 1978; merchandise handling, transit and storage; Chair. JACQUES PELTIER; Dir JACQUES COLOMBANI.

SOCOPAO–Côte d'Ivoire: km 1 blvd de Marseille, 01 BP 1297, Abidjan 01; tel. 24-13-14; telex 43261; fax 24-21-30; shipping agents; Shipping Dir OLIVIER RANJARD.

CIVIL AVIATION

There are three international airports: Abidjan—Félix Houphouët-Boigny, Bouaké and Yamoussoukro. In addition, there are smaller airports at Bouna, Korhogo, Man, Odienné and San Pedro.

Air Afrique (Société Aérienne Africaine Multinationale): 3 ave Joseph Anoma, 01 BP 3927, Abidjan 01; tel. 20-30-00; telex 23785; f. 1961; 70.4% owned jtly by the Govts of Benin, Burkina Faso, the Central African Republic, Chad, the Congo, Côte d'Ivoire, Mali, Mauritania, Niger, Senegal and Togo; extensive regional flights and services to Europe, North America and the Middle East; Dir-Gen. Sir HARRY TIRVENGADUM.

Air Ivoire: 13 ave Barthe, 01 BP 1027, Abidjan 01; tel. 20-66-66; fax 33-26-26; f. 1960; state-owned since 1976, transfer to private ownership pending; internal flights and services within west Africa; Man. Dir NICOLAS ADOM.

Tourism

The game reserves, forests, lagoons, coastal resorts, rich tribal folklore and the lively city of Abidjan are tourist attractions; Côte d'Ivoire also has well-developed facilities for business visitors, including golfing centres. An estimated 200,000 tourists visited Côte d'Ivoire in 1994; receipts from tourism in that year totalled some US $66m. The Government aims to increase visitor arrivals to 500,000 annually by 2000.

Office Ivoirien du Tourisme et de l'Hôtellerie: Immeuble EECI, place de la République, 01 BP 8538, Abidjan 01; tel. 20-65-00; fax 22-59-24; f. 1992; Dir EUGÈNE KINDO BOUADI.

Defence

In August 1996 Côte d'Ivoire's active armed forces comprised an army of 6,800 men, a navy of about 900, an air force of 700, a paramilitary presidential guard of 1,100 and a gendarmerie of 4,400. There were also reserve forces of 12,000 men. Military service is by selective conscription and lasts for six months. France supplies equipment and training, and maintains a military presence in Côte d'Ivoire (520-strong in 1997).

Defence Expenditure: Budgeted at US $96m. in 1996.

Chief of General Staff of the Armed Forces: Cdre LASSANA TIMITÉ.

Chief of Staff of the Army: Maj.-Gen. MARIUS TAUTHUI.

Education

At the time of the 1988 census adult illiteracy averaged 65.9% (males 55.6%; females 76.6%); UNESCO estimated the average to be 59.9% in 1995 (males 50.1%; females 70.0%). Education at all levels is available free of charge. Primary education, which is officially compulsory, usually begins at seven years of age and lasts for six years. Total enrolment at primary schools in 1994/95 was equivalent to 68% of the relevant age-group (78% of boys; 59% of girls). The Ivorian authorities anticipated that the rate of attendance at primary schools would have reached 90% by 2000. Secondary education, usually beginning at the age of 13, lasts for up to seven years, comprising a first cycle of four years and a second cycle of three years. In 1993/94 the total enrolment in the first cycle was equivalent to 20.7% of children in the relevant age-group, while that in the second cycle was equivalent to 15.5%. The National University at Abidjan has six faculties, and in 1993/94 had 40,000–50,000 enrolled students. University-level facilities have been constructed in Yamoussoukro. Expenditure on education in 1995 was an estimated 241,100m. francs CFA, equivalent to 24.6% of total government expenditure (excluding spending on the public debt).

Bibliography

Affou, Y. S. *La relève paysanne en Côte d'Ivoire.* Paris, Editions Karthala, 1990.

Amin, S. *Le développement du capitalisme en Côte d'Ivoire.* Paris, 1966.

Amondji, M. *Félix Houphouët-Boigny et La Côte d'Ivoire.* Paris, Editions Karthala, 1984.

Avenard, J.-M. *Le milieu naturel de la Côte d'Ivoire.* Bondy, France, ORSTOM, 1972.

Cowan, L. G. 'Côte d'Ivoire at 27'. *CSIS Africa Notes,* Briefing Paper No. 71. Washington, DC, Center for Strategic and International Studies, 1987.

Cruise O'Brien, D. B., Dunn, J., and Rathbone, R. (Eds.). *Contemporary West African States.* Cambridge, Cambridge University Press, 1989.

David, P. *Côte d'Ivoire.* Paris, Editions Karthala, 1986.

Domergue-Cloarec. *La Santé en Côte d'Ivoire.* 2 vols. Paris, Académie des Sciences d'Outre-Mer, 1987.

Dozon, J.-P. *La Société bété en Côte d'Ivoire.* Paris, Editions Karthala, 1983.

Duruflé, G. *L'ajustement structurel en Afrique (Sénégal, Côte d'Ivoire, Madagascar).* Paris, Editions Karthala, 1987.

Fauré, Y. A., and Médard, J.-F. *Etat et bourgeoisie en Côte d'Ivoire.* Paris, Editions Karthala, 1983.

Foster, P., and Zolberg, A. R. (Eds). *Ghana and the Ivory Coast, Perspectives and Modernization.* University of Chicago Press, 1972.

Gombeaud, J.-L., Moutout, C., and Smith, S. *La Guerre du cacao, histoire secrète d'un embargo.* Paris, Calmann-Lévy, 1990.

Harrison Church, R. J. *West Africa.* 8th Edn. London, Longman, 1979.

Lisette, G. *Le Combat du Rassemblement Démocratique Africain.* Paris, Présence Africaine, 1983.

Loucou, J.-N. *Histoire de la Côte d'Ivoire.* Paris, Editions Karthala.

Rapley, J. *Ivorien Capitalism: African Entrepreneurs in Côte d'Ivoire.* London, Lynne Rienner, 1993.

Rimmer, D. *The Economies of West Africa.* London, Weidenfeld and Nicolson, 1984.

Rougerie, G. *La Côte d'Ivoire.* Paris, Presses universitaires de France, 1964.

Siriex, P. H. *Félix Houphouët-Boigny: L'homme de la paix.* Paris, Seghers, 1975.

Sy, M. S. *Recherches sur l'exercice du pouvoir politique en Afrique noir (Côte d'Ivoire, Guinée, Mali).* Paris, 1965.

Touré, A. *La Civilisation quotidienne en Côte d'Ivoire.* Paris, Editions Karthala, 1983.

Verdier, I. (Ed.) *Côte d'Ivoire: 100 Hommes de Pouvoir.* Paris, Indigo Publications, 1996.

de Wilde, J., et al. *Agricultural Development in Tropical Africa.* Baltimore, MD, Johns Hopkins Press, 1967.

World Bank. *Côte d'Ivoire Living Standards Survey: Design and Implementation.* Washington, DC, International Bank for Reconstruction and Development, 1986.

Zartman, I. W. *The Political Economy of the Ivory Coast.* New York, Praeger, 1984.

DJIBOUTI

Physical and Social Geography

I. M. LEWIS

The Republic of Djibouti is situated at the southern entrance to the Red Sea. It is bounded on the far north by Eritrea, on the west and south by Ethiopia, and on the south-east by Somalia. Djibouti covers an area of 23,200 sq km (8,958 sq miles), consisting mostly of volcanic rock-strewn desert wastes, with occasional patches of arable land, and spectacular salt lakes and pans. The climate is torrid, with high tropical temperatures and humidity during the monsoon season. The average annual rainfall is less than 125 mm. Only in the upper part of the basaltic range north of the Gulf of Tadjourah, where the altitude exceeds 1,200 m above sea-level, is there continuous annual vegetation.

At 31 December 1990 the population was officially estimated at 519,900, including refugees and other resident non-nationals. In 1981 the capital town, Djibouti (whose port and railhead dominate the territory's economy), had a population of about 200,000. The indigenous population is almost evenly divided between the Issa (who are of Somali origin) and the Afar, the former having a slight predominance. Both are Muslim Cushitic-speaking peoples with a traditionally nomadic economy and close cultural affinities, despite frequent local rivalry. The Afar inhabit the northern part of the country, the Issa the southern, and both groups span the artificial frontiers separating the Republic of Djibouti from Ethiopia, Eritrea and Somalia.

Since the development of the port of Djibouti in the early 1900s, the indigenous Issas have been joined by immigrants from the adjoining regions of Somalia. The Afar generally follow more restricted patterns of nomadic movement than the Issa, and a more hierarchical traditional political organization. While they formed a number of small polities, these were linked by the pervasive cleavage running throughout the Afar population between the 'noble' Asaimara (or 'red') clans and the less prestigious Asdoimara (or 'white') clans. There is also a long-established Arab trading community. European expatriates are mainly French, mostly in government employment, commerce and the armed forces.

Recent History

THOMAS OFCANSKY

French involvement in the territory that now comprises the Republic of Djibouti dates from the mid-19th century, and was stimulated by subsequent Anglo-French rivalry for control of the entrance to the Red Sea. During 1897–1917 a Franco-Ethiopian railway was constructed to carry Ethiopia's trade through the French port.

The territory's indigenous inhabitants, the Afar and the Issa, have strong connections with Ethiopia and Somalia respectively. Until the 1960s, ethnic divisions were not marked; subsequently, however, conflicting international interests in the Horn of Africa, together with France's policy of favouring the minority Afar community, combined to create tensions in the territory, then known as French Somaliland (renamed the French Territory of the Afars and the Issas in 1967).

Demands for independence were led by the Issa community, while numbers of Afars, who favoured maintenance of the French connection, were significantly enlarged in the mid-1970s by immigration from Somalia. Support by the Organization of African Unity for the granting of full independence to Djibouti added to the pressures on France, which sought to improve relations between the two ethnic groups. A unified political movement, the Ligue populaire africaine pour l'indépendance (LPAI), was formed, and, following an overwhelming vote favouring independence at a referendum held in May 1977, the territory became independent on 27 June. Hassan Gouled Aptidon, a senior Issa politician and leader of the LPAI, became the first president of the Republic of Djibouti.

Initial intentions to maintain a careful ethnic balance in government were not sustained. In March 1979 Gouled replaced the LPAI with a new political party, the Rassemblement populaire pour le progrès (RPP), whose leadership and policies were to be determined by himself. The two principal Afar-dominated pre-independence parties responded by merging into a clandestine opposition movement, the Front démocratique pour la libération de Djibouti (FDLD).

POLITICAL DISCONTENT

In June 1981 the first presidential election was held; Gouled, as the sole candidate, received 84% of the popular vote and was thus elected for a further six-year term. The FDLD rejected the results of the presidential election and, from its base in Addis Ababa, demanded a return to democracy and the release of political prisoners. Soon afterwards, a new opposition party, the Parti populaire djiboutien (PPD), was formed under the leadership of a former premier, Ahmed Dini. The leadership was arrested in September and the party banned, but in October, following the adoption of legislation to establish a one-party state, the PPD leaders were released.

At legislative elections held in May 1982, 90% of the electorate endorsed the single list of candidates presented by the RPP. A new government, formed in June, differed little from its predecessor, and Gourad Hamadou continued in the post of prime minister. One potential source of dissent was removed when, in September, members of the FDLD returned from exile in Ethiopia, under the terms of an amnesty.

Until the mid-1980s, there was little overt opposition to the RPP under Gouled's leadership. In January 1986 a bomb was exploded at the headquarters of the RPP, killing two people. The bombing and the subsequent assassination of a prominent local businessman were followed by intensive security operations, in which more than 1,000 people were arrested. Evidence of open opposition to Gouled attracted wider international attention in May 1986, when Aden Robleh Awalleh, a former cabinet minister, was charged with conducting 'massive propaganda campaigns' against the RPP, and was expelled from the party. Aden Robleh Awalleh fled to Ethiopia, where he announced the formation of a new opposition group, the Mouvement national djiboutien pour l'instauration de la démocratie (MNDID), with the stated aim of restoring a multi-party parliamentary democracy.

At the presidential election held in April 1987 Gouled, the sole candidate, received just over 90% of the votes cast. Concurrently, a single list of candidates for the chamber of deputies was endorsed by 87% of those voting. In November Gouled dissolved the government and appointed an enlarged council of ministers comprising 16 members. In February 1988 an attack on the border town of Balho was attributed to the Mouvement populaire de libération, an opposition group based in Ethiopia, and was widely seen as a sign of increasing ethnic tensions.

In April 1989 inter-ethnic hostilities erupted in the capital and the Afar town of Tadjourah. Tension increased in Afar-inhabited areas in May, and in October violent clashes again occurred between members of rival clans in the capital. Security forces subsequently arrested several hundred people, some of whom were stated to have been deported to Gesdir, a remote border region between Djibouti, Ethiopia and Somalia. Sizeable numbers of these deportees were later reported to have been killed by the insurgent Somali National Movement and Issa militia men.

In January 1990 the FDLD, the MNDID and independent members of the opposition merged to form a new opposition party, the Union des mouvements démocratiques (UMD). The group's declaired aim was to 'unite all the ethnic groups and different political persuasions' and to resolve 'the chaotic situation' existing in the country. In May inter-ethnic strife erupted between the Issa and the Gadabursi communities in the capital. In June units of the Djibouti armed forces raided the town of Tadjourah and arrested Afars who were suspected of involvement in the UMD.

In November 1990 the president reshuffled his council of ministers, introducing one new member and reallocating several portfolios. In so doing, he was believed to have strengthened his position in the ministry of finance, and to have reduced the influence of the former minister of finance and national economy, Mohamed Djama Elabe, who was regarded as a potential successor to Gouled.

In early January 1991 Ali Aref Bourhan, who had led the council of ministers in the period prior to independence, was detained, together with about 100 Afar dissidents, on suspicion of having conspired to assassinate political leaders and senior army officers. Bourhan was subsequently charged with murder, attempted murder and with plotting to destabilize the country. Stricter security measures were applied against disaffection among the Afar community, but the government denied allegations that some Afars who had been arrested had been tortured.

At the fifth RPP congress, held in March 1991, the party resolved that it would remain Djibouti's sole legal political organization. This rejection of political pluralism was widely interpreted as a sign of its increasing insecurity in response to mounting discontent among Djibouti's various clans and clan branches—especially the Afar—at their exclusion from political power.

In April 1991 a former presidential adviser, Mohamed Moussa Kahin, was arrested on suspicion of involvement with the proscribed Mouvement pour l'unité et pour la démocratie (MUD), and in the following month Gouled dismissed two ministers from the government.

CIVIL INSURRECTION

A serious challenge to Gouled's authority appeared in April 1991 with the formation of a new and powerful armed opposition group, the Front pour la restauration de l'unité et de la démocratie (FRUD), which comprised three militant Afar groups, the Front pour la restauration des droits et de la legalité, the Front pour la résistance patriotique djiboutienne and the Action pour la révision de l'ordre à Djibouti. In mid-November the FRUD, with a force of about 3,000 men, launched a full-scale insurrection, and by the end of the month controlled many towns and villages in the north of the country, and was besieging the northern cities of Tadjourah and Obock, which were held by the national army. The government conscripted all men between 18 and 25 years of age, and requested military assistance from France (see below) to repel what it described as external aggression by soldiers loyal to the deposed President Mengistu of Ethiopia. The FRUD denied that it constituted a foreign aggressor (although many of its officers had received training in Ethiopian military camps), claiming that its aim was to achieve political parity for all ethnic groups.

In December 1991 Gouled stated that a national referendum regarding proposed changes in the system of government would be held, but only when the 'external aggressors' had been expelled from the country. At the end of the month, 14 Afar deputies resigned from the RPP (and, therefore, from the chamber of deputies), claiming that its leaders were seeking to protect their privileges rather than the national interest. In January 1992 two ministers resigned, in protest at the government's policy of continuing the war, and subsequently formed the nucleus of a new political movement. In the same month, Gouled appointed a committee to draft a new constitution, intended to provide for a plural political system. Following a meeting in January with senior French officials, the FRUD agreed to open a dialogue with the government, based on an immediate bilateral cease-fire and progress on the promised democratic reforms. The government, however, continued to insist that the FRUD was controlled by foreign interests, describing its military activities as an 'invasion' and responded to French mediation attempts with complaints that France had failed to honour its defence agreement. By the end of January the government had lost control of most of northern Djibouti, with its garrisons in Tadjourah and Obock kept supplied from the sea.

Attempts by France at achieving a *rapprochement* appeared to improve in late February 1992, when, following meetings with the FRUD and the Djibouti government it was announced that the FRUD would declare a cease-fire, that France would deploy troops from its Djibouti garrison as a peace-keeping force in the north and that the government would release the FRUD's spokesman in the capital, Abbate Ebo Adou, who had been arrested in December 1991. However, initial hopes that the agreement would facilitate a negotiated settlement were soon disappointed, despite sustained diplomatic efforts by France. In late March 1992 the FRUD announced that it was ending its cease-fire, stating that the deployment of the French peace-keeping forces, which it had initially agreed to, was merely protecting a 'blood-stained dictatorship'. In April Adou was re-arrested, ostensibly for contravening the terms of his release.

Constitutional Manoeuvres

The presidential commission on constitutional reform submitted its report in late March 1992 and on 4 April the president announced his plans for reform, which, while conceding the principle of political pluralism, proposed few other changes and retained a strong executive presidency. The proposals were rejected as inadequate by the opposition, which demanded the holding of a national constitutional conference, and by the FRUD, although cautiously welcomed by France. The president announced that the reforms would be determined in a national referendum in mid-June, and that legislative elections would follow in July. The mandate of the chamber of deputies, which had been due to expire at the end of May, was later extended for a further five years. The election timetable that the president announced was quickly dismissed as unrealistic, especially since large areas of the country were not within government control. In late June Gouled announced that the referendum would be held on 4 September, followed by the introduction of a multi-party system on 20 September. Legislative elections would then take place on 20 November.

In early July 1992 Gouled granted pardons to a number of opposition figures, including Aden Robleh Awalleh, the exiled leader of the Parti national démocratique (PND), and the leader of the Front des forces démocratiques, Omar Elmi Khaireh. However, in the same month Ali Aref Bourhan and five others (who had been arrested for treason in January 1991) were sentenced to 10 years' imprisonment. Others among the 47 accused received prison sentences of up to six years. The government sustained another defection in August with the announcement that Elaf Orbiss Ali, an Afar, had resigned as minister of labour, in protest against the continuing civil war and deteriorating economic situation, and was joining the Front uni de l'opposition djiboutienne (FUOD), a coalition of opposition parties, including the FRUD.

The draft constitution that the president prepared was approved by referendum on 4 September 1992, with 96.84%

voting in favour, according to the ministry of the interior, which claimed a turnout of 75.16% of the 120,000 eligible voters. A proposition to restrict the number of political parties to four was approved by 96.79% of those who voted. However, with two-thirds of the country controlled by the FRUD, which had urged its supporters to boycott the referendum, and no independent observers present, the voting figures were received with some scepticism, notably by France, which refused to endorse the results. The referendum nevertheless facilitated the registration of political parties and the holding of multi-party elections, which, it was announced in mid-October, would take place on 18 December. Applications for registration were initially accepted from only the ruling RPP and the Parti pour le renouveau démocratique (PRD), led by Elabe (a former minister), which had split from the FUOD in September. Applications from the FRUD and the FUOD were rejected. The application from the PND, which had withdrawn from the FUOD following the pardon and return from exile of Aden Robleh Awalleh, was initially rejected, but subsequently allowed in mid-October.

Attempts by France to foster negotiations between the government and the FRUD appeared to have achieved success following the announcement in November 1992 that representatives of the two sides were to meet for the first time, under French auspices. However, the meeting was cancelled at short notice by the government, which claimed that the FRUD had failed to honour preconditions, including the release of prisoners of war. In late November France withdrew its troops from northern Djibouti, where they had acted as a buffer between government and rebel forces.

With the opposition largely excluded from the process, the elections held on 18 December 1992, which were monitored by observers from France, the OAU and the Arab League, provided an easy victory for the RPP, which won all 65 seats in the chamber of deputies and 76.71% of the popular votes. Only the PRD contested the elections (taking one-third of the votes cast in the capital), Awalleh having withdrawn the PND after protesting about irregularities and demanding a postponement of the elections. More than 51% of the electorate abstained from voting in the elections, leading to charges from the PND that the chamber was unrepresentative. Renewed fighting was reported in January 1993, with dozens of people said to have been killed in what appeared to be a new government offensive against the FRUD in the Tadjourah area. The army claimed a series of successes during February and March, recapturing the FRUD strongholds in the south of the country and severing the rebels' supply routes to the sea. Nevertheless, the FRUD achieved a propaganda victory with its first guerrilla attack on the capital in mid-March.

Gouled reshuffled the cabinet in early February 1993, preserving a careful ethnic balance, with Issa ministers receiving eight portfolios, and Afar representatives seven (including the foreign affairs and economy and commerce portfolios), with one portfolio each held by representatives of three other minorities. However, other changes suggested no relaxation of the government's policy, with the transfer of the former minister of the interior, Ahmed Bulaleh Barreh (an opponent of negotiations with the FRUD), to the ministry of defence. The former minister of foreign affairs, Moumin Bahdon Farah, was appointed minister of justice and Islamic affairs, but retained his post as secretary-general of the RPP. Five candidates stood in Djibouti's first contested presidential election, which was held on 7 May: Gouled himself, Elabe (for the PRD), Awalleh (PND) and two independents, Mohamed Moussa Ali 'Tourtour' (actually of the still proscribed MUD, but not representing his party) and Ahmed Ibrahim Abdi. The level of electoral participation was low (at 49.9% of those registered to vote), suggesting an Afar boycott. Official results indicated that Gouled received 60.76% of the votes cast, compared with 22.03% for Elabe and 12.25% for Awalleh, while 'Tourtour' and Abdi won 2.99% and 1.97% of the votes cast respectively. The opposition alleged that there had been widespread electoral fraud.

Military and Political Initiatives

Following his re-election as president, Gouled appealed to the FRUD to negotiate with the government. His appeal was rejected, as he proposed that discussions should take place in Djibouti itself, while the FRUD insisted that it would only meet the government abroad, in the presence of foreign mediators. In early July 1993 the army launched a full-scale offensive on the FRUD positions in the centre and north of the country. The campaign was successful, and within a week the army had captured the FRUD's headquarters on the plateau of Asa Gayla, as well as other towns and areas held by the rebel group. As a result of the hostilities, thousands of the inhabitants of these largely Afar-populated areas fled towards the Ethiopian border. Many of the rebels were reported to have retreated into the mountains in the far north of the country. The FRUD continued its struggle, however, and in mid-July it launched armed attacks on government forces, including an assault on the army's camp at Tadjourah. Under sustained pressure from the French government, Gouled agreed in December to an exchange of prisoners with the FRUD, and this was followed later in the month by the release of Bourhan and his immediate associates in the alleged coup conspiracy of January 1991.

Relations with France came under further strain in early 1993 as the result of threats by the French government to withhold financial aid, in an attempt to persuade Gouled to negotiate with the FRUD. Counter-insurgency operations were intensified, with the result that, by July, an estimated 80,000 civilians had been displaced by the fighting. In September the Djibouti government was strongly criticized by Amnesty International for abuses of human rights, inflicted by the army.

The extent of the military reverses inflicted on the FRUD was reflected in the intensification of political activity during late 1993. In October the PRD and the FRUD issued joint proposals for a cease-fire, to be followed by negotiations aimed at forming a transition 'government of national unity' to supervise the implementation of democratic reforms. These objectives were also defined by two new parties formed in the same month: the Organisation des masses Afars and the Parti centriste et des reformes démocratiques (PCRD). The PCRD, whose leadership comprised former members of the FRUD, announced that it was to seek legal recognition. In December the PRD and the PND launched a co-ordinated campaign to persuade the government to agree to new parliamentary elections under the supervision of an independent electoral commission.

In early 1994, again under economic pressure from France, the government agreed to reduce the scale of its military expenditure, although operations against the FRUD continued in February. During March, however, a split developed within the FRUD leadership, several of whose members, led by Ougoureh Kifleh Ahmed, began to seek support within the movement for a negotiated political settlement of the conflict. In May, Kifleh Ahmed was expelled from the FRUD executive committee, but re-emerged in the following month, with the claimed support of the majority of FRUD members, as the party's secretary-general. Ali Mohamed Daoud was declared to be president of the FRUD. The new leaders, who were stated to hold office on a 'provisional' basis, continued to be opposed by several senior FRUD activists, including the party's former president, Ahmed Dini, based in Addis Ababa, who subsequently formed his own faction favouring a continuation of military operations. In late June, Kifleh Ahmed and the Djibouti government agreed terms for an immediate cease-fire, and formal negotiations for a peace settlement began in July.

On 26 December 1994 the two sides signed a peace agreement which envisaged the establishment of a coalition government, the implementation of a power-sharing arrangement based on a quota system, and a devolution of power to the regions. In June 1995 Gouled made a significant contribution to the fulfilment of the terms of the agreement by reorganizing his cabinet and appointing Mohamed Daoud and Kifleh Ahmed as ministers of health and agriculture respectively. In addition, the agreement offered an amnesty to FRUD insurgents for actions committed before 12 June 1994. In exchange, the FRUD undertook to abandon its military struggle against the Gouled regime and to engage in peaceful political competition. The Djibouti government also pledged to integrate some FRUD insurgents into the armed forces; indeed, in early 1995, 300 former FRUD insurgents joined the national army. One of the most controversial clauses of the peace agreement concerned a demobilization plan to reduce the size of the army,which had increased from some 2,500 troops before the war to approximately 20,000 at the height of the conflict. The successful implementation of the agreement was hampered further by factionalism within the FRUD. FRUD rebels continued to launch small-scale attacks against government targets in late 1995, and in January 1996 FRUD guerrillas fired ammunition at a French military helicopter in the Medeho region in northern Djibouti, slightly injuring the pilot. Nevertheless, in March 1996 the government announced that it had granted legal recognition to the FRUD, which became the country's fourth and largest political party. However, at approximately the same time, Ibrahim Chehem Daoud, a former FRUD deputy secretary-general for communications, rejected the reconciliation between the government and the FRUD, and formed a new group called FRUD-Renaissance.

By March 1994 reports of widespread military atrocities against civilians in the north had ended. Nevertheless, the security forces continued to mistreat Afar civilians by ordering extrajudicial killings in the northern region and by suppressing anti-government demonstrations in the capital. However, during 1994 and 1995 the authorities allowed increased freedom of speech and of the press and eased travel restrictions in the north. In addition, the government allowed the International Committee of the Red Cross, UN representatives, and diplomats resident in Djibouti access to prisoners and to military operational areas. By the end of 1994 the Gouled regime claimed to have released all political or security detainees.

In early September 1995 trade unions organized a widely-observed one-day general strike in protest at the government's economic austerity measures. Several trade union leaders were arrested. In some sectors, work stoppages continued until mid-September, when the unions recommended a return to work. In late October a demonstration organized by members of the PND resulted in the arrest of several protesters, including the PND leader, Awalleh. In November he was released, but subsequently was reported to have begun a hunger strike in support of other demonstrators who remained in prison. In January 1996, after demonstrations organized by school teachers against the economic reforms, some 500 protesters were reported to have been arrested. They were released later in the month, and further strikes were staged in April and May. Also in May 34 people were arrested and one person was reported to have been killed during clashes between the security forces and supporters of the former paymaster-general, Nouh Omar Miguil, who had been detained by the police. Miguil had been dismissed from his post in October 1995 on suspicion of embezzlement, although his followers alleged that he had been the victim of a political power struggle.

In December 1995 Gouled received medical treatment in France, where he remained in convalescence until early March 1996. His prolonged absence from Djibouti prompted a succession crisis within the RPP, between the president's nephew and chief minister, Ismael Omar Gelleh, and his private secretary, Ismael Gedi Hared. In February 1996 a prison riot in the capital (which resulted in two deaths and 29 injuries) provoked a confrontation between the minister of justice and Islamic affairs, Moumin Bahdon Farah (who suggested that the incident had occurred because the cost of maintaining a sizeable army had resulted in poor staffing levels at the prison), and the minister of the interior, Idris Harbi Farah, who attributed the uprising to inadequate prison food supplies. Bahdon Farah's remarks reflected his opposition to Gelleh (whom Harbi Farah supported), who was known to favour a large standing army. In late March Bahdon Farah was dismissed from the council of ministers, together with Ahmed Bulaleh Barreh, the minister of defence. Both ministers had openly opposed the December 1994 peace agreement with the FRUD, on the grounds that it strengthened the position of Gelleh and his followers. In April Bahdon Farah established a splinter group of the RPP, the Groupe pour la démocratie de la république (RPP–GDR), which included 13 of the 65 members of the chamber of deputies. The president of the chamber subsequently claimed that the RPP–GDR would remain illegal while Bahdon Farah continued to hold his position as secretary-general of the RPP. In May, in an apparent attempt to settle the succession dispute, Gouled expelled Gedi Hared from the RPP's executive committee, together with Bahdon Farah and former ministers Barreh and Ali Mahamade Houmed, all of whom opposed Gelleh. In June Gedi Hared formed a new opposition alliance, the Coordination de l'opposition djiboutienne, embracing the PND, the FUOD and the RPP–GDR. In August Gedi Hared, Bahdon Farah and Barreh were among five people sentenced to six months' imprisonment, and the suspension of their civil rights for five years, for 'insulting the head of state'. The accused reportedly signed a document in late May alleging that President Gouled ruled by force and terror. Although the detainees were released from prison in early January 1997 (following a presidential pardon) their civil rights were not restored.

In September 1996 an internal dispute arose in the RPP when Ismael Omar Gelleh began a discreet campaign against the holding of several positions concurrently, which was aimed at the prime minister and deputy chairman of the RPP, Barkad Gourad Hamadou. In an apparent attempt to end these internecine disputes, Gouled declared his intention to remain as head of state until the expiry of his term in office in 1999, and as president of the RPP until March 1997. Moreover, later in September it was announced that a new RPP executive committee had been appointed, and that thenceforth Gouled (as president of the party) would be assisted by three deputies, namely Hamadou, Ahmed Hassan Liban and Gelleh. Mohamed Ali Mohamed, the minister of finance and the economy, was appointed as the RPP's secretary-general. At the RPP party congress in March 1997 President Gouled was re-elected as president of the RPP and 125 central committee members were selected. In April the pro-government faction of the FRUD convened its first party congress and announced its intention to participate in legislative elections which were scheduled to be held later in the year. According to FRUD president, Ali Mohamed Daoud, the party hoped to form an alliance with the RPP and to present joint electoral lists in the legislative elections. At a PRD congress in May Abdillahi Hamareiteh was elected as the party's president, to succeed Mohamed Djama Elabe, who died in November 1996. Later in May the authorities banned two meetings by a rival faction of the PRD, led by Kaireh Allaleh Hared and Mohamed Ahmed Kassim. The government argued that the PRD congress served the interests of all its members and insisted that the rival faction should accept Hamareiteh's leadership. The Gouled administration was believed to favour the new leader in preference to the rival faction which had welcomed several officials who had defected from the RPP.

It was reported that in May 1997 more than 200 troops demonstrated in front of the military headquarters in the capital to protest the fact that they had not been paid for more than three months. In addition, there was concern that several hundred demobilized soldiers had received severance payments from the authorities that were considerably lower than anticipated. Meanwhile, the US government criticized Djibouti's record on human rights during 1996, claiming that the security forces had carried out a number of extrajudicial executions, had maltreated detainees, and had denied medical treatment to prisoners. Political dissidents were reported to have been arrested arbitrarily and frequently detained beyond the 48 hours permitted by law.

REFUGEES AND EXTERNAL RELATIONS

A source of international discontent has been the substantial flow of refugees from the Eritrean and Ogaden conflicts in Ethiopia (see below), which has greatly added to Djibouti's economic problems. In April 1984 a new scheme for repatriating Ethiopian refugees (estimated to number 35,000), under the aegis of the UN High Commissioner for Refugees (UNHCR), was begun. By December an estimated 16,000 had returned to Ethiopia. However, the recurrence of drought and the political situation in Ethiopia caused some refugees to return, and by June 1987 the number of 'official' refugees in Djibouti was 17,200. In August 1986 a new repatriation programme was announced by the Djibouti government in consultation with the Ethiopian government and UNHCR. According to sources within Djibouti, the number of voluntary repatriations under this programme had reached 2,000 by the end of March 1987. The burden that 'official' refugees have imposed on the economy has been exacerbated by an influx of illegal immigrants from Somalia and Ethiopia, and in June 1987 the government announced tighter controls on border crossings and identity papers. Following discussion in February 1988, Djibouti and Ethiopia agreed to control movements across their common border and to curb the influx of refugees into Djibouti. In

January 1989, President Gouled announced that measures were to be taken against illegal refugees, who, he claimed, were not only an economic burden on the country, but also a source of instability. In early June 1991 there were an estimated 35,000 Somali and 5,000 Ethiopian official refugees in Djibouti. By August about 4,000 of the Ethiopians had registered to return, under a repatriation scheme administered by UNHCR. By early 1993, it was estimated, the number of Somali refugees in Djibouti had reached 120,000 and UNHCR was investigating ways to repatriate the majority of them to the north of Somalia, to the self-declared 'Republic of Somaliland' (formed by insurgent forces in northern Somalia in April 1991). There has been considerable disagreement as to the number of refugees in Djibouti. In 1994, the Djibouti government maintained that there were as many as 150,000 refugees in the country, most of whom had settled in the capital despite the official requirement that all refugees should remain in designated camps. However, UNHCR claimed that those who lived in the capital were economic migrants and only acknowledged the presence of some 45,000 genuine refugees, most of whom were from Ethiopia and Somalia. These refugees lived in four UNHCR-recognized refugee camps in the southern part of the country. In September 1994 UNHCR began a repatriation programme for Ethiopian refugees, and an estimated 15,000 returned home between mid-October 1994 and mid-March 1995. According to the US Committee for Refugees, in early 1996 there were some 20,000 Somali and 5,000 Ethiopian refugees in Djibouti. In March 1996 the Djibouti government announced a programme to repatriate Ethiopian refugees. According to UNHCR, some 35,000 Ethiopians had returned voluntarily to their homes between early 1995 and April 1996. Fighting between government forces and the FRUD forced about 10,000 Djiboutians to seek refuge in Ethiopia, and caused another 50,000 to become internally displaced.

Because of its geographical position, the maintenance of peaceful relations with both Ethiopia and Somalia has been a vital consideration in Djibouti's foreign policy. The key economic goal of maintaining its share in the rail and sea transport of Ethiopian trade, which was intermittently disrupted by guerrilla action and regional unrest during the late 1970s, was partially realized in 1985 when the governments of Ethiopia and Djibouti agreed to create an independent railway company.

During 1979 Djibouti concluded agreements with both Ethiopia and Somalia for closer co-operation in transport, communications and trade. Regular meetings of frontier boundary commissioners were proposed with Ethiopia in that year, and official visits to Djibouti by high-ranking Ethiopian delegations took place in 1980 and again in 1983. In May 1985 the two countries concluded a trade and development co-operation agreement, although relations became clouded in the following year when Ethiopia granted asylum to Awalleh and the MNDID. However, since the removal of Ethiopia's President Mengistu Haile Mariam in May 1991, Djibouti has maintained good relations with the successor transitional government in that country. In early 1994 the two nations concluded a 16-point co-operation agreement covering a number of subjects, including agriculture, industry, border patrols, use of port facilities, movement of commercial goods and trade subsidies. In August Djibouti and Ethiopia signed a judicial affairs agreement which guaranteed the equality of citizens before one another's courts. The accord also provided for the extradition of criminals. In October Ethiopian President Meles Zenawi made an official visit to Djibouti, his first since he took power in 1991. Meles and Gouled explored ways to improve bilateral relations and reviewed several regional issues and projects being undertaken by the Intergovernmental Authority on Drought and Development (IGADD, now the Intergovernmental Authority on Development, IGAD). Later in the month Djibouti and Ethiopia issued a joint communiqué which pledged both countries to improving economic, transportation, and telecommunications co-operation. Additionally, Gouled and Meles undertook to work for peace and stability throughout the Horn of Africa. In December 1995 Ethiopia announced plans to increase trade with Djibouti, which would be facilitated by the rehabilitation of the Djibouti-Addis Ababa railway. In September 1996 Djibouti and Ethiopia concluded a series of agreements, the most important of which concerned a joint pledge to combat al-Ittihad al-Islam (the Islamic Union Party), a radical group active in western Somalia and eastern Ethiopia. The two countries also promised to increase economic and social co-operation, easing access rules into Djibouti for Ethiopian passenger and freight transport, granting customs exemptions to Ethiopia for imports of salt and fish products from Djibouti, and providing scholarships to Djibouti students studying in Ethiopia. In March 1997 the two countries pledged to fight against smuggling, drugs-trafficking, and other cross-border crimes along their common frontier. During a visit to Addis Ababa in May, President Gouled held discussions with Prime Minister Meles Zenawi on increasing co-operation between IGAD members and on the effect of Djibouti's demobilization programme on Ethiopia's Ogaden region. It was feared that a massive influx of Issa mercenaries from Djibouti could destabilize the region further.

As a result of Gouled's wish to reconcile the vying factions in the Horn of Africa, Djibouti was instrumental in promoting the creation in 1985 of the six-nation IGADD, with a permanent secretariat in Djibouti. IGADD's first summit meeting, in January 1986, brought both the Ethiopian and Somali heads of state to Djibouti, marking a significant step towards an eventual settlement of regional conflicts. In April 1988, following a further meeting in Djibouti, between the two leaders, Ethiopia and Somalia agreed to re-establish diplomatic relations, to withdraw troops from their common border and to exchange prisoners of war.

Relations with Somalia deteriorated following an attack by the Somali National Movement (SNM) on border posts along the Somali-Djibouti border in May 1989. The Somali government had always regarded with suspicion Djibouti's declared neutrality in respect of the Somali-Ethiopian conflict. Following the outbreak of armed insurgency in northern Somalia, Somalia accused the Djibouti government of openly supporting the SNM, whose opposition to the Siad Barre regime had many sympathizers among Issa and Isaaq clansmen in Djibouti. In March 1990, when inter-tribal conflict erupted into heavy fighting in Loya Adde and Zeila on the Somali side of the border with Ethiopia, Somalia accused Djibouti of waging armed aggression in its territory. A denial by the Djibouti government did not prevent a further deterioration in relations, and the maritime border between Djibouti and Somalia was closed in October.

In June 1991 Djibouti provided the venue for a preliminary conference of groups from southern Somalia, aimed at forming a transitional Somali government. In October the land borders between Djibouti and Somalia were reopened for the first time since May 1989. Relations between Djibouti and the government of 'Somaliland' deteriorated sharply in early 1992 following contacts between the 'Somaliland' authorities and the FRUD. Tensions involving the presence of refugee Issas in the border area were reported in July 1994. In September Djibouti reopened the border post of Loyada, which had been closed for four months because of clashes with armed units from the 'Republic of Somaliland'. Relations deteriorated in August 1995, when there were reports of clashes along the border, which, some suggested, had occurred as a result of the involvement of local militia groups in Djibouti in an armed conflict between 'Somaliland' troops and the rebel United Somali Front, which was suspected of receiving clandestine support from Djibouti. In addition, during 1995 Somali pirates reportedly attacked at least 15 vessels in international waters off Djibouti, prompting fears that trade between Djibouti and other countries might be jeopardized. In June 1996, however, Djibouti and 'Somaliland' concluded a 10-point agreement, which included provisions for co-operation on border security and the establishment of trade relations. In September President Gouled was reported to have met Ali Mahdi Mohamed, the leader of the Somali Salvation Alliance, to discuss the possibility of convening a conference in Yemen on Somali reconciliation. A further meeting between Gouled and Ali Mahdi took place in Djibouti in June 1997.

In December 1987 President Mitterrand visited Djibouti: the first visit by a French president since 1977. President Gouled made an official visit to France in June 1989, during which he described relations with France as of an 'exceptional quality' and praised the stabilizing influence of the French military presence in Djibouti. However, the French military presence became more controversial following Iraq's invasion of Kuwait in August 1990 and the onset of the 'Gulf crisis'. French troops in Djibouti were reinforced and Djibouti became the operational base for France's participation in the multinational force deployed in Saudi Arabia. By supporting the UN resolutions which were formulated against Iraq, Djibouti jeopardized its future relations with that country, which was emerging as an important supplier of economic and military aid. However, Djibouti's stance during the Gulf War of January–February 1991 strengthened its ties with France, and in February the two countries signed two defence treaties which extended military co-operation. In January 1992, however, there was serious disagreement between France and Djibouti over France's refusal to intervene militarily in the conflict between government forces and the FRUD. Relations between the two countries remained tense during 1992 and 1993, with France using the threat of withholding its aid, in an attempt to persuade the government to negotiate with the rebels, and showing dissatisfaction with the pace and extent of Gouled's political reforms. A meeting betweeen the two presidents in November 1992 led to the release of French budgetary aid, but France later made clear its irritation at the government's failure to attend a planned meeting with the FRUD. From December Djibouti became the operational centre for French troops participating in multinational (and subsequently United Nations) operations in Somalia. The facilities of Djibouti airport were also made available for US troop transport. In March 1994 the Franco–Djibouti joint co-operation commission met, for the first time in more than four years, in Djibouti. As a result, the Gouled regime re-established its line of credit with the French government, which had been interrupted because of the war with FRUD insurgents.

France repeatedly sought to end the conflict between the Djibouti government and FRUD insurgents, and in December 1994 a number of influential French parliamentarians expressed the opinion that, if the conflict continued, France should reassess its military commitment to Djibouti, and subsequently urged the French national assembly's foreign affairs commission to examine the utility of France's military presence in Djibouti. As a result of the peace accord signed on 26 December, relations with France improved. However, tensions remained, primarily concerning French aid to Djibouti. Although in January 1996 the French minister of defence pledged to maintain a military presence in Djibouti, in March he indicated that the French military contingent would probably be reduced by about one-fifth. (Meanwhile, in April a French judge issued warrants for the arrest of the chairman of the PND, Aden Robleh Awalleh, and his wife, both of whom were suspected of involvement in a grenade attack on a cafeteria in Djibouti in 1990, during which a French child was killed and 15 others were injured.)

Djibouti became a member of the UN Security Council, for a two-year period, on 1 January 1993. In February the Egyptian minister of foreign affairs visited Djibouti, and ties were strengthened with the signing of an agreement on co-operation in economic, technical, cultural, religious and trade sectors. Since 1991 Djibouti has maintained diplomatic relations with Eritrea, which became a *de facto* independent state (breaking away from Ethiopia) in that year. In May 1993 Gouled attended celebrations in Eritrea on the occasion of that country's official transition to independence. In November 1995 the Eritrean minister of foreign affairs, Petros Solomon, held talks with President Gouled in Djibouti. The two countries stressed the importance of revitalizing IGADD, and pledged to enhance bilateral relations, particularly in the areas of transport, telecommunications, trade, fishing, tourism, and information and culture. It was agreed that a joint ministerial commission would be established to foster co-operation. In December allegations made in a Yemeni newspaper that Eritrean military forces had launched a cross-border raid into the Moulhoule area of north-east Djibouti were vehemently denied by Eritrea. Relations between the two countries were strained in April 1996, when President Gouled rejected a map of Eritrea submitted by Solomon, which reportedly included a 20-km strip of territory belonging to Djibouti. At the same time reports emerged of exchanges of artillery fire at a frontier post in northern Djibouti. Eritrea denied the incident, which some observers attributed to a misinformation campaign by Yemen.

Djibouti has sought to maintain close relations with several nations in the Middle East. In August 1995 Djibouti and Yemen concluded a defence agreement to conduct joint surveillance of the southern approaches to the strategically important Bab al-Mandab strait. A further security agreement was concluded in May 1996. In September 1995 Djibouti's minister of foreign affairs, Muhammad Musa Chehem, held talks with his Israeli counterpart, Shimon Peres. As a result, Chehem announced that representatives of the chambers of commerce from both countries would meet on a regular basis, with the aim of opening liaison offices in the countries' capitals, prior to the eventual establishment of full diplomatic relations. In October the ministers of the interior of Djibouti and Saudi Arabia held a meeting to discuss development projects and security co-operation. During 1995 Djibouti also strengthened commercial ties with Japan and China. President Gouled visited Egypt, Saudi Arabia and Yemen in May 1997 in an attempt to consolidate bilateral relations.

Economy

THOMAS OFCANSKY

Based on an earlier article by MILES SMITH-MORRIS

The economy is based on trade through the international port of Djibouti, and its developing service sector, which accounted for 76.6% of the country's gross domestic product (GDP) in 1995. In addition to the port, there is a railway, which links Djibouti to Addis Ababa in Ethiopia, and a modern airport that can be used by large jet-engined aircraft. The financial sector is growing in importance, aided by the stable and freely convertible Djibouti franc and the absence of exchange controls. A substantial share of the country's receipts derive from the provision of services to the French military garrison (with about 3,900 men in mid-1996) and other expatriates.

There is little arable farming in Djibouti, as the land is mainly volcanic desert, one of the least hospitable and most unproductive terrains in Africa, and the country is able to produce only about 3% of its food requirements. More than one-half of the population are pastoral nomads, herding goats, sheep and camels. Agriculture (including hunting, forestry and fishing) provided only 3.4% of GDP in 1995, although an estimated 75.2% of the labour force were employed in this sector in 1991. A 10-year programme to develop fishing was started in 1980, supported by the International Fund for Agricultural Development, and in 1990 the Islamic Development Bank (IDB) agreed to finance the construction of a fish-canning factory with an annual capacity of 1,500 metric tons.

The development of underground water supplies for irrigation is being studied, and deep-water wells have been sunk in an attempt to alleviate the effects of periodic drought. A loan was received in 1987 from the African Development Bank (ADB) to finance a project to supply water to the towns of Djibouti, Ali-Sabieh, Tadjourah and Obock. Relief assistance during periods of periodic drought and flooding has been forthcoming from the European Community (EC, now the European Union—EU) France, Japan, Saudi Arabia, and Germany.

Industry is limited to a few small-scale concerns. Regional political uncertainties and high labour costs have discouraged the creation of new industries, despite the existence of a free zone and the major liberalization of investment legislation in 1984, and almost all consumer goods have to be imported. Industry (comprising manufacturing, construction and utilities) provided 19.9% of GDP in 1995 and engaged 11.0% of the employed labour force in 1991. A power station supplying a mineral-water bottling factory at Tadjourah, the first major industrial project outside the capital, was commissioned in 1981, and a dairy plant (on the outskirts of Djibouti town), a government printing press and an extension to the Boulaos power station were all opened in 1984–85. Plans to privatize the Tadjourah mineral water plant were announced in 1991, but the plant later sustained damage in fighting between government and rebel forces. Djibouti opened its first pharmaceutical factory in 1996, at a cost of US $3m. The company planned to manufacture five generic drugs for the national and regional markets.

Work began in 1986 on a major geothermal exploration project, in the Hanle Gaggade area. Conditions there proved to be unsuitable for the development of this form of energy, but more favourable results were reported from tests carried out in the Goubet-Lac-Assal region in 1987. The object of this scheme is to make Djibouti self-sufficient in energy, and possibly able to export gas to neighbouring countries. This remains a distant goal, however, and in the mid-1990s Djibouti relied on imported fuels for 90% of its energy requirements. Italy has donated US $22m. towards the purchase of equipment for the first phase of the project, whose total cost has been estimated at $38m. France is also participating in the project, which is co-financed by the World Bank, OPEC and the UN Development Programme. In mid-1986 Saudi Arabia granted Djibouti $21.4m. for the purchase and installation of three electricity generators, with a combined capacity of 15 MW. Total electricity generating capacity rose from 40 MW to 80 MW in 1988, when the second part of the Boulaos power station became operative.

Work on Djibouti's first petroleum refinery at Dorale, began in 1990, with Saudi Arabian private-sector assistance. The US $533m. refinery was expected to produce 100,000 barrels per day of petrol, kerosene and liquefied gas. The project, which was reported to have been delayed by the conflict between the government and the insurgent Front pour la restauration de l'unité et de la démocratie (FRUD), resumed in 1996. In February 1996 private investors in Djibouti established the Compagnie des Gaz de la Mer Rouge to take over the assets of Air Liquide, a subsidiary of a larger French company. The former, with French technical assistance, sought to manufacture and market industrial gases and to import and export industrial and medical gases.

Djibouti's establishment as a free port, in 1981, has helped to arrest a relative decline in total port business, which, affected by competition from rising Arab ports nearby, was virtually stagnant until the completion, in 1985, of a deep-water container terminal, with 'roll-on, roll-off' facilities and a refrigerated warehouse, capable of handling 40,000 tons. The rehabilitation of the port's berth facilities, together with dredging and reclamation work, has been proceeding. In 1992 France agreed to lend US $8m. towards continuing modernization of the port facilities, including internal transport and management. As Djibouti has good bunkering and watering facilities and is well placed for transhipment, it was hoped that the addition of these facilities would help the port to regain some of the business that it lost during the closure of the Suez Canal (1967–75), and to increase its competitiveness with the expanding Arab ports. The Gulf crisis of 1990–91 acted as a major stimulus to the port, with total traffic rising to nearly 1.5m. tons in 1990, compared with only 870,000 tons in the previous year. In 1992 Djibouti established a 'flag of convenience' registry, with the aim of attracting international shipowners seeking such facilities. Tax incentives were also being offered to shipping companies reinvesting their profits in Djibouti. It was hoped that the port would benefit from an expected increase in Ethiopian traffic, following the independence in 1992 of Eritrea, whose facilities at Assab and Massawa are less developed than those available in Djibouti. In early 1996 Djibouti sought to increase the country's earnings by implementing new tariffs for port services and taxes, including a revised tariff for transit goods and a new fee schedule for exports, imports and transhipments. Activity at Djibouti's port was reported to have declined by 40% in 1995, primarily because business was being diverted to the Eritrean port of Assab and the Somali port of Berbera. However, an administrative reform programme, funded by France and supervised by the port authority of Nantes–Saint-Nazaire, enhanced the port's operations and reputation. The programme aimed to streamline port tariffs, foster closer co-operation between customs and transport officials, and overhaul labour practices. In February 1997 two quays were reopened following a $32m. renovation, which had been financed by the Japanese government. The French Development Agency subsequently granted loans for the purchase of a tug boat and for the renovation of the port. During 1996 the volume of cargo handled by the port exceeded 1,500m. tons, an increase of 35% compared with the previous year. The increase was attributable primarily to the fact that the US Navy had resumed using Djibouti as a refuelling port. Of the 892 ships that docked at Djibouti port in 1996, just over one-third were container vessels, accounting for one-half of the total gross registered tonnage of 7.78m. tons.

Several other developments in communications infrastructure in the 1980s enhanced Djibouti's competitiveness on trading routes. These included the inauguration, in 1985, of a second earth station, linking Djibouti to the telecommunications network of the Arab Satellite Communication Organization, and the laying of an undersea telecommunications cable to Saudi Arabia. In early 1997 the Société de Télécommunications Internationales de Djibouti (STID, a subsidiary of France Cable et Radio) launched a cellular telephone network enabling the country to have Internet services. The STID planned to make Djibouti a regional and international transit centre for communications links between Africa and Asia by using submarine optic cables and building a satellite communications station.

For many years, the Djibouti government was anxious about its lack of control over the railway linking Djibouti town with Addis Ababa; 660 km of the line's 781 km pass through the territory of Ethiopia, which employs more than three-quarters of the railway staff. The signing of a new railway agreement with Ethiopia in 1981 brought some improvement, which was further enhanced in July 1985, when a joint ministerial meeting between the two countries decided to grant autonomous status to the railway company (the Chemin de Fer Djibouti–Ethiopien—CDE), with the aim of increasing its profitability. A major programme for the replacement of rolling stock and the rehabilitation of track was begun in 1986, with funding from the EU. Further financial assistance from this source was received in 1993. During 1994 and 1995 Djibouti and Ethiopia sought to improve the deteriorating capabilities of the railway, which has been beset by operational problems such as derailments and mechanical failures. In addition, the line has suffered because of inadequate maintenance of the track, track bed and damaged bridges. The lack of spare parts and a poor telecommunications system has also hampered the smooth operation of the railway. The amount of cargo carried by rail between Djibouti and Ethiopia has declined from some 60% of total cargo to around 7% in recent years. There has been a similar decline in passenger traffic. Djibouti has largely relied on the international community to resolve these problems. In December 1994 the French Development Agency agreed to extend 55m. French francs in aid for track repair and technical assistance. The World Bank has also funded short-term technical aid and a programme to improve the railway's spare parts inventory and its telecommunications system. Additionally, the German government, the Kuwait Fund for Arab Economic Development (KFAED) and the IDB have expressed an interest in helping to rehabilitate the railway. In September 1995 the EU pledged US $100m.–$200m., and the French Development Agency agreed to provide 40m. French francs for the rehabilitation project. However, the project was hampered by the persistent theft of railway fittings, and by an incident in mid-1996 when a freight train hit a landmine in Ethiopia, resulting in the death of one passenger. In December 1996 the CDE announced its intention to purchase four new locomotives with a $9.6m. grant from France, significantly reducing the travelling time between Djibouti and Addis Ababa. Meanwhile, interest was reported to have been expressed by the EU, the KFAED, the World Bank, France, Germany and Switzerland in financing a project to replace the CDE's obsolete rail and communications equipment. In February 1997 Djibouti and Ethiopia agreed to grant the CDE autonomous management, thereby opening the way for the participation of private operators in some of the railway's activities. In March Ethiopia revealed that the railway was incurring monthly losses of some $3,000.

The government's first Development Plan (1982–84) was undertaken to channel foreign aid into a cohesive development strategy. Potential has been constrained, however, by the lack of infrastructure, of trained labour and of natural resources. Nevertheless, a highly successful conference of aid donors was held in Djibouti in 1983, when most of the funds that the country needed for its 1984–89 Development Plan (which envisaged total expenditure of US $570m.) were raised, including more than $100m. from Arab sources. Development projects that had already started included the construction by a Yugoslav contractor of a 114-km 'unity' highway linking Djibouti to Tadjourah. There are also plans for an improved road through Loyada into northern Somalia.

Djibouti remains heavily dependent on foreign assistance, which, because of the country's strategic position, is readily forthcoming. The main donors are the EU, France and Saudi Arabia. The Saudi Fund for Development was to provide funds for the renovation of Djibouti's port facilities, and was also to finance housing and educational projects and road construction. Djibouti is a member of the ADB, the IMF, the IDB, the World Bank and its affiliate, the International Finance Corporation, and also receives considerable financial support from these organizations. After some years of declining levels of foreign aid, which combined with stagnating government receipts to create serious financial problems, aid disbursements to Djibouti rose sharply in 1990 to US $129.1m., an increase of 57% on 1989 levels. France provided 45% of the total, but there was a marked increase in aid from Arab countries. In 1992 Djibouti's primary bilateral donors included France ($43.5m.) and Italy ($38m.). Multilateral donors included the African Development Fund ($8.1m.) and the EU ($4.7m.).

In 1993, according to estimates by the World Bank, Djibouti's gross national product, measured at average 1991–93 prices, was US $448m., equivalent to $780 per head. In 1991, according to UN estimates, Djibouti's GDP, measured at current purchasers' values, was 67,078m. Djibouti francs, equivalent to 149,062 Djibouti francs per head. Djibouti's GDP expanded, in real terms, at an average annual rate of 1.2% in 1980–85 and 2.0% in 1985–89, reversing an average annual decline of 2.7% in 1977–79. However, as a result of rapid population increase, GDP per head declined, in real terms, during 1980–86. According to estimates by the IMF, GDP declined, in real terms, in each of the four years 1992–95. Real GDP fell by 3.9% in 1993, by 2.9% in 1994 and by 4.0% in 1995. During 1985–94 the population increased by an annual average of 4.1% (according to World Bank estimates), owing partly to the influx of refugees from Ethiopia and Somalia.

Djibouti's external debt was estimated to total US $260.2m. at the end of 1995, of which $218.0m. was long-term public debt. Debt-servicing has remained at manageable levels, representing 7.1% of exports of goods and services in 1987, declining steadily to 2.6% in 1995. The annual rate of inflation averaged 5.5% during 1989–94 and was 6.1% in the year to October 1995.

The 1990 budget fixed ordinary government expenditure at 25,200m. Djibouti francs, while total revenue was fixed at 24,000m. Djibouti francs. The 1991 budget was projected to balance at 26,000m. Djibouti francs. The IMF has, since 1992, repeatedly warned the government about the seriousness of its growing budget and balance-of-payments deficits. In 1993 ordinary expenditure was forecast at 28,321m. Djibouti francs, and expenditure in 1994 was estimated to reach 32,500m. Djibouti francs. Djibouti's overall budget deficit for 1994 was 5,328m. Djibouti francs (equivalent to 6.2% of GDP).

In 1995 Djibouti recorded a visible trade deficit of US $171.5m., and there was a deficit of $23.0m. on the current account of the balance of payments. In 1994 the principal sources of imports were Thailand (13.8%), France (13.7%) and Saudi Arabia (12.4%). The principal markets for exports in that year were Somalia (39.0%), Ethiopia (34.2%) and the Republic of Yemen (20.8%). The principal imports were food and beverages, qat (a narcotic leaf), machinery and electrical appliances, clothing and footwear, petroleum and chemical products, and vehicles and transport equipment. Most exports are unclassified.

Since early 1986 the Djibouti franc has fluctuated in value, along with the US dollar, to which it is linked. During that year inflation emerged as a problem for the first time since Djibouti's independence, reaching 22.5% in the 12 months ending June 1986. Current budgetary aid for 1989 totalling 37.5m. French francs was promised by the French government. The aid was provided under the terms of an agreement, signed in 1980, which expired in 1989. In that year, France indicated a change of policy with regard to budgetary aid to Djibouti: aid would no longer extend over a 10-year period, but would be fixed annually. At the same time, the French government requested Djibouti to reduce its public expenditure and to intensify its revenue-raising efforts. During the period of military insurgency by the FRUD (which commenced in late 1991) France used its aid as a lever in persuading the government to negotiate with the insurgents: budgetary aid of 23.5m. French francs for 1992 was not disbursed until November of that year. In March 1994 an allocation of 11.5m. French francs for rebuilding war-damaged infrastructure was added to a budgetary aid allocation of 8.5m. French francs.

It was initially feared that the crisis in the Persian (Arabian) Gulf region, which began in August 1990 following Iraq's invasion and annexation of Kuwait, would imperil the economy of Djibouti. Development projects which had been funded by Iraq and Kuwait, for instance, were immediately suspended. However, Djibouti's decision to support the UN's efforts to liberate Kuwait ensured that its relations with its three principal benefactors, France, Saudi Arabia and Kuwait, were unharmed. Moreover, the ensuing war in the Gulf region emphasized Djibouti's strategic importance to the USA, from whose Economic Support Fund Djibouti receives some US $3m. annually.

In September 1990 the government estimated that losses resulting from the crisis in the Gulf would amount (in 1990) to US $218m. This estimate took into account increases in the price of imports (especially petroleum), which were expected to average 15%; increases in transport expenses; and the postponement of investments pledged by Kuwait, Saudi Arabia and Iraq. Losses of state revenues in 1990 were forecast at $23m. There was, however, a doubling of official revenues from Djibouti port, deriving from the war-related traffic. Djibouti's role as a service centre was also enhanced by the Western military intervention in Somalia in 1992.

It was planned to increase substantially public investment in 1990. A total of 10,788m. Djibouti francs was to be invested in projects in the communications, agricultural and fisheries sectors, and in social, environmental and urban improvement schemes. Almost 40% of total expenditure on public projects (about twice the level of 1989) was allocated to projects in the communications sector. It was also proposed to invest 2,058m. Djibouti francs in agriculture and fisheries. Capital expenditure in 1991 was fixed at 13,850m. Djibouti francs, most of which would, again, be directed towards the communications sector; the total budget was projected to balance at 26,000m. Djibouti francs. Internal civil unrest has since had a noticeable impact on investment, with capital spending allocated only 540m. Djibouti francs out of total expenditure of 28,320m. Djibouti francs in the 1993 budget. Capital spending was forecast to account for only 3% of the 1994 budget. Serious flooding in November 1994 caused extensive damage to Djibouti's infrastructure and necessitated emergency relief aid (notably from France) to provide temporary shelters throughout the country, and to assist in the reconstruction of the capital's sewage system.

Djibouti remains reliant on France for budgetary aid. However, despite repeated encouragement from the French government, in early 1995 Djibouti announced that it would not apply to the IMF for assistance with its 1995 budget deficit, estimated at some 225m. French francs. Instead, the Gouled administration hoped to secure new bank loans and financial aid from Arab nations. In addition, Djibouti planned to plead its case before IMF donors at a meeting in Geneva, scheduled for April 1995; however, the conference was subsequently postponed until October 1995. The international financial community responded to Djibouti's budget strategy by insisting that the country, if it hoped to maintain its credit rating with lending banks, would have to honour its loan repayments to the Banque pour le Commerce et l'Industrie—Mer Rouge, a subsidiary of France's Banque Nationale de Paris, although to do so would increase the country's budget deficit. The Djibouti government would also be expected to pay those civil servants with three and four weeks' salary arrears, in order to avoid civil unrest. In pursuit of these goals, the Gouled administration suspended payments to all other creditors and to many of its suppliers. As an incentive to Arab donors, the authorities closed more than 80 establishments serving alcoholic beverages in the capital in order to court the favour of many increasingly Islamist regimes. However, the failure of this attempt to end reliance on IMF donors to produce any significant gain prompted the Djibouti government to reassess its policy in this area. In late April 1995 the council of ministers announced a reduction in budget expenditure of 26.6m. French francs (from 1 July) and launched an initiative to increase public revenues. (Measures which reflected recommendations made by an IMF team which had visited Djibouti earlier in the month.) In July the IMF demanded a budget cut of more than US $37m., and in October insisted on an additional $11.2m. cut in civil service salaries. Moreover, in December the IMF informed the Djibouti government that it would have to settle its debts with France before entering a structural adjustment programme, and demanded a comprehensive survey by 31 March 1996 of crossed debts incurred by state-owned companies and the Djibouti government. The IMF stipulated that Djibouti's debt to France (estimated at 2,400m. Djibouti francs) would have to be rescheduled before September 1996. The government's subsequent announcement, in August 1995, of reductions in salaries for government employees and increases in taxes on incomes was fiercely opposed by trade union leaders, who organized a widely-observed one-day general strike in early September. In late December the chamber of deputies adopted the 1996 budget, which sought to placate the public as well as the IMF and the World Bank. The budget amended many of the unpopular measures that led to the general strike. Plans to increase income tax from 10% to 15% were abandoned, as were taxes of 60% on civil servants' bonuses and indemnities. Consumer taxes on a range of products were reduced, although civil servants' wages were also curtailed.

In April 1996, after months of negotiation, the government and the IMF concluded an agreement for Djibouti's first stand-by credit, equivalent to US $6.7m. Djibouti agreed to implement a range of austerity measures, including the reform of the civil service, a demobilization programme and the restructuring of the country's port, airport, electricity, water, and telecommunications companies. (Under the terms of a $24.2m. agreement concluded with the World Bank in December 1995, Djibouti was to demobilize 10,000 soldiers and police over a five-year period.) Domestic opposition to the negotiations with the IMF continued, and in early 1996 teachers protested at proposed reforms, resulting in numerous arrests (see Recent History). It was estimated that in 1996 unemployment in Djibouti had reached 58%.

In September 1996 a delegation from the IMF visited Djibouti, and decided to postpone the disbursement of a second tranche of financial aid as it was dissatisfied with Djibouti's progress in undertaking fiscal reforms. In April 1997 Djibouti's minister of finance and the economy, Mohamed Ali Mohamed, led a delegation to the IMF headquarters in Washington, DC, as a result of which the IMF agreed to the disbursal of some US $6.4m. In May, moreover, the IMF agreed to extend Djibouti's stand-by programme until March 1998, and approved $2.8m. in credits. Meanwhile, in late 1996 the EU pledged ECU 22m. to Djibouti to improve transportation links between Djibouti and Ethiopia, increase available drinking water supplies, and provide additional support for the country's health and education sectors. In January 1997 the International Development Association granted Djibouti credit of $6.5m. to finance technical assistance for the economic reform programme.

Djibouti's agreement with the IMF in April 1996 led to an improvement in the government's relations with France, which had refused to provide concessionary financing to Djibouti until it had reached an understanding with the IMF. Funds were subsequently released by France for a variety of projects in Djibouti, primarily in the sectors of health and education. French aid to Djibouti for 1996 amounted to 162.5m. French francs. In October 1996 France agreed to furnish 53m. French francs in aid to Djibouti (primarily for budgetary assistance and debt relief), and in November it granted Djibouti a structural adjustment subsidy (worth 28m. Franch francs) which was to be disbursed in two tranches.

In January 1997 the French government announced that it might reconsider its military commitments in Africa, leading to a possible reduction of French forces in the region. It was feared that a withdrawal of troops from Djibouti would have a significant detrimental effect on the country as French troops contributed an estimated US $53m. to the local economy in 1996.

Statistical Survey

Source (unless otherwise stated): Ministère de l'Economie et du Commerce, BP 1846, Djibouti; tel. 351682; telex 5871.

AREA AND POPULATION

Area: 23,200 sq km (8,958 sq miles).

Population: 220,000 (1976 estimate), including Afars 70,000, Issas and other Somalis 80,000, Arabs 12,000, Europeans 15,000, other foreigners 40,000; 519,900 (including refugees and resident foreigners) at 31 December 1990 (official estimate).

Density (1990): 22.4 per sq km.

Principal Towns: Djibouti (capital), population 200,000 (1981); Dikhil; Ali-Sabieh; Tadjourah; Obock.

Births and Deaths (UN estimates, 1990–95): Average annual birth rate 38.1 per 1,000; Average annual death rate 16.1 per 1,000. Source: UN, *World Population Prospects: The 1994 Revision*.

Expectation of life (years at birth, 1990–95): 48.3 (males 46.7; females 50.0). Source: UN, *World Population Prospects: The 1994 Revision*.

Economically Active Population (estimates, '000 persons, 1991): Agriculture, etc. 212; Industries 31; Services 39; *Total* 282 (males 167, females 115). Source: UN Economic Commission for Africa, *African Statistical Yearbook*.

AGRICULTURE, ETC.

Principal Crops (FAO estimate, '000 metric tons, 1995): Vegetables 22. Source: FAO, *Production Yearbook*.

Livestock (FAO estimates, '000 head, year ending September 1995): Cattle 190, Sheep 470, Goats 507, Asses 8, Camels 62. Source: FAO, *Production Yearbook*.

Livestock Products: (FAO estimates, metric tons, 1995): Beef and veal 3,000; Mutton and lamb 2,000; Goat meat 2,000; Cows' milk 7,000; Cattle hides 540; Sheepskins 420; Goat-skins 464. Source: FAO, *Production Yearbook*.

Fishing (FAO estimates, metric tons, live weight): Total catch 275 in 1992; 300 in 1993; 320 in 1994. Source: FAO, *Yearbook of Fishery Statistics*.

INDUSTRY

Electric energy (million kWh): 180 in 1992; 182 in 1993; 185 in 1994. Source: UN, *Industrial Commodity Statistics Yearbook*.

FINANCE

Currency and Exchange Rates: 100 centimes = 1 Djibouti franc. *Sterling and Dollar Equivalents* (31 March 1997): £1 sterling = 291.82 Djibouti francs; US $1 = 177.72 Djibouti francs; 1,000 Djibouti francs = £3.427 = $5.627. *Exchange Rate:* Fixed at US $1 = 177.721 Djibouti francs since February 1973.

Budget (million Djibouti francs, 1994): *Revenue:* Tax revenue 24,320 (Taxes on incomes and profits 5,186, Other direct taxes 4,659, Indirect taxes 13,101; Registration fees, etc. 1,376); Other revenue (incl. property sales) 1,271; Total 25,591, excl. grants received from abroad (4,314). *Expenditure:* Treasury current expenditure 31,467 (General administration 10,905, Defence 4,648, Mobilization and demobilization 5,553, Education 2,615, Health 1,894, Economic services 1,758, Transfers 2,110); Other current expenditure 942; Capital expenditure 4,808; Sub-total 37,217; *Less* Payment arrears 1,984; Total 35,233. Source: IMF, *Djibouti—Statistical Annex* (June 1996).

International Reserves (US $ million at 31 December 1996): IMF special drawing rights 0.15; Foreign exchange 76.82; Total 76.97. Source: IMF, *International Financial Statistics*.

Money Supply (million Djibouti francs at 31 December 1996): Currency outside banks 9,686; Demand deposits at commercial banks 18,738; Total money (incl. others) 35,925. Source: IMF, *International Financial Statistics*.

Cost of Living: (Consumer Price Index for expatriates; base: 1989 = 100): All items 117.6 in 1992, 122.8 in 1993, 130.8 in 1994. Source: IMF, *Djibouti—Statistical Annex* (June 1996).

Expenditure on the Gross Domestic Product (million Djibouti francs at current purchasers' values, 1995): Government final consumption expenditure 30,108; Private final consumption expenditure 62,581; Gross capital formation 10,556; *Total domestic expenditure* 103,246; Exports of goods and services 36,670; *Less* Imports of goods and services 51,992; *GDP in purchasers' values* 87,994. Source: IMF, *Djibouti—Statistical Annex* (June 1996).

Gross Domestic Product by Economic Activity (million Djibouti francs at current factor cost, 1995): Agriculture, hunting, forestry and fishing 2,668; Manufacturing 4,105; Electricity, gas and water 6,967; Construction 4,440; Trade, restaurants and hotels 13,637; Transport, storage and communications 13,362; Finance, insurance, real estate and business services 8,197; Public administration 20,600; Other services 3,857; *GDP at factor cost* 77,835; Indirect taxes *less* subsidies 10,159; *GDP in purchasers' values* 87,994. Source: IMF, *Djibouti—Statistical Annex* (June 1996).

Balance of Payments (US $ million, 1995): Exports of goods f.o.b. 33.5; Imports of goods f.o.b. –205.0; *Trade balance* –171.5; Exports of services 151.4; Imports of services –87.2; *Balance on goods and services* –107.3; Other income received 25.9; Other income paid –8.7; *Balance on goods, services and income* –90.0; Current transfers received 85.4; Current transfers paid –18.4; *Current balance* –23.0; Direct investment from abroad 3.2; Other investment liabilities –5.4; Net errors and omissions 0.7; *Overall balance* –24.5. Source: IMF, *International Financial Statistics*.

EXTERNAL TRADE

Principal Commodities: *Imports c.i.f.* (million Djibouti francs, 1994): Food and beverages 9,733; Qat 4,823; Petroleum products 2,778; Chemical products 2,449; Clothing and footwear 3,530; Metals and metal products 1,673; Machinery and electrical appliances 4,212; Vehicles and transport equipment 2,566; Total (incl. others) 37,966. Note: figures refer only to imports for domestic use. Source: IMF, *Djibouti—Statistical Annex* (June 1996). *Exports f.o.b.* (distribution by SITC, US $'000, 1992): Food and live animals 3,393 (Rice 726, Coffee and coffee substitutes 1,773); Crude materials (inedible) except fuels 715; Basic manufactures 833; Machinery and transport equipment 1,260 (Road vehicles and parts 585, Other transport equipment 501); Commodities not classified according to kind 9,487; Total (incl. others) 15,919. Source: UN, *International Trade Statistics Yearbook*.

Principal Trading Partners (US $'000, 1992): *Imports c.i.f.:* People's Republic of China 6,724; Ethiopia 17,157; France (incl. Monaco) 58,003; Italy 12,064; Japan 14,810; Netherlands 7,771; Saudi Arabia 8,750; Thailand 6,207; United Kingdom 6,955; USA 6,764; Total (incl. others) 219,926. *Exports f.o.b.:* Ethiopia 523; France (incl. Monaco) 9,144; Saudi Arabia 1,587; Somalia 664; Yemen 686; Total (incl. others) 15,919. Source: UN, *International Trade Statistics Yearbook*.

TRANSPORT

Railways (Djibouti-Ethiopian Railway, 1990): Freight traffic ('000 metric tons): 301.9; Passengers 957,000.

Road Traffic ('000 motor vehicles, 1992): Passenger cars 13; Commercial vehicles 3. Source: UN, *Statistical Yearbook*.

Shipping: *Merchant Fleet* (registered at 31 December 1996): 11 vessels (displacement 3,784 grt): *International Freight Traffic* ('000 metric tons, Djibouti port, 1990): Goods loaded 414; Goods unloaded 958. Source: UN, *Monthly Bulletin of Statistics*.

Civil Aviation (Djibouti airport, 1990): Freight loaded 1,145 metric tons; Freight unloaded 6,381 metric tons; Passenger arrivals 61,727; Passenger departures 62,494.

TOURISM

Tourist arrivals: 27,624 in 1992; 24,715 in 1993; 46,595 in 1994. Source: IMF, *Djibouti—Statistical Annex* (June 1996).

COMMUNICATIONS MEDIA

Newspapers (1988): 2 non-dailies (estimated combined circulation 7,000).

Periodicals (1989): 7 (estimated combined circulation 6,000).

Radio Receivers (1994): 46,000 in use.

Television Receivers (1994): 25,000 in use.

Telephones (1994): 7,436 main lines in use.

Source: mainly UNESCO, *Statistical Yearbook*.

EDUCATION

Pre-Primary (1994/95): 2 schools; 259 pupils.

Primary (1994/95): 81 schools; 35,024 pupils; 932 teachers.

Secondary (1994/95): 11,562 pupils (general 9,755, teacher-training 110, vocational 1,697); 385 teachers.

Higher (1992/93): 61 students.

Source: UNESCO, *Statistical Yearbook*.

Directory

The Constitution

In February 1981 the National Assembly approved the first constitutional laws controlling the election and terms of office of the President, who is elected by universal adult suffrage for six years and may serve for no more than two terms. Candidates for the presidency must be presented by a regularly constituted political party and represented by at least 25 members of the Chamber of Deputies. The Chamber, comprising 65 members, is elected for a five-year term.

In October 1984 a new constitutional law was proposed, specifying that, when the office of President falls vacant, the President of the Supreme Court will assume the power of Head of State for a minimum of 20 days and a maximum of 35 days, during which period a new President shall be elected.

Laws approving the establishment of a single-party system were adopted in October 1981. A new Constitution, providing for the establishment of a maximum of four political parties, was approved by national referendum on 4 September 1992 and entered into force on 15 September.

The Government

HEAD OF STATE

President and Commander-in-Chief of the Armed Forces: HASSAN GOULED APTIDON (took office 27 June 1977; re-elected June 1981, April 1987 and May 1993).

COUNCIL OF MINISTERS
(July 1997)

Prime Minister and Minister of Planning: BARKAD GOURAD HAMADOU.

Minister of Justice and Islamic Affairs: HASSAN FARAH MIGUIL.

Minister of the Interior and Extension of Regional Administration: IDRIS HARBI FARAH.

Minister of Defence: ABDALLAH CHERWA DJIBRILL.

Minister of Foreign Affairs and Co-operation: MUHAMMAD MUSA CHEHEM.

Minister of Finance and the Economy: MOHAMED ALI MOHAMED.

Minister of Transport and Communications: SALEH OMAR HILDID.

Minister of Education: AHMED GIREH WABERI.

Minister of Labour and Manpower Training: OUGOUREH ROBLEH DAHACH.

Minister of the Civil Service and Administrative Reform: MOHAMED BARKAT ABDILLAHI.

Minister of Health and Social Affairs: ALI MOHAMED DAOUD.

Minister of Public Works, Housing and Construction: MOHAMED DINI FARAH.

Minister of Agriculture and Water Resources: OUGOUREH KIFLEH AHMED.

Minister of Industry, Energy and Minerals: ALI ABDI FARAH.

Minister of Youth, Sports and Culture: MOHAMED BOLOK ABDOU.

Minister of Trade and Tourism: RIFKI ABDULKADER.

MINISTRIES

Office of the Prime Minister: BP 2086, Djibouti; tel. 351494; telex 5871; fax 355049.

Ministry of Agriculture and Water Resources: BP 453, Djibouti; tel. 351297; telex 5871.

Ministry of the Civil Service and Administrative Reform: BP 155, Djibouti; tel. 351464; telex 5871.

Ministry of Defence: BP 42, Djibouti; tel. 352034; telex 5871.

Ministry of Education: BP 2102, Djibouti; tel. 350850; telex 5871.

Ministry of Finance and the Economy: BP 13, Djibouti; tel. 350297; telex 5871; fax 35601.

Ministry of Foreign Affairs and Co-operation: BP 1863, Djibouti; tel. 352471; telex 5871.

Ministry of Health and Social Affairs: BP 296, Djibouti; tel. 353331; telex 5871.

Ministry of Industry, Energy and Minerals: BP 175, Djibouti; tel. 350340; telex 5871.

Ministry of the Interior and Extension of Regional Administration: BP 33, Djibouti; tel. 350791; telex 5990.

Ministry of Justice and Islamic Affairs: BP 12, Djibouti; tel. 351506; telex 5871; fax 354012.

Ministry of Labour and Manpower Training: BP 170, Djibouti; tel. 350497; telex 5871.

Ministry of Planning: Djibouti.

Ministry of Public Works, Housing and Construction: BP 11, Djibouti; tel. 350006; telex 5871.

Ministry of Trade and Tourism: BP 1846, Djibouti; tel. 351682; telex 5871.

Ministry of Transport and Communications: Djibouti; tel. 350971; telex 5871.

Ministry of Youth, Sports and Culture: Djibouti.

President and Legislature

PRESIDENT

Presidential Election, 7 May 1993

Candidates	Votes	%
Hassan Gouled Aptidon (RPP)	45,470	60.76
Mohamed Djama Elabe (PRD)	16,485	22.03
Aden Robleh Awalleh (PND)	9,170	12.25
Mohamed Moussa Ali 'Tourtour' (Independent)	2,239	2.99
Ahmed Ibrahim Abdi (Independent)	1,474	1.97
Total	74,838	100.00

CHAMBRE DES DÉPUTÉS

Elections for the 65-seat Chamber of Deputies were held on 18 December 1992. The election was contested by the governing Rassemblement populaire pour le progrès (RPP) and the opposition Parti du renouveau démocratique (PRD). All 65 seats were won by the RPP.

President of the Chamber: Said Ibrahim Badoul.

Political Organizations

Constitutional reforms permitting a maximum of four political parties took effect in September 1992. By mid-1997 the following parties were legally recognized:

Front pour la restauration de l'unité et de la démocratie (FRUD): f. 1991 by merger of three militant Afar groups; advocates fair representation in government of Djibouti's different ethnic groups; commenced armed insurgency in Nov. 1991; split into two factions in March 1994; the dissident group, which negotiated a settlement with the Govt, obtained legal recognition in March 1996 and recognizes the following leaders: Pres. Ali Mohamed Daoud; Sec.-Gen. Ougoureh Kifleh Ahmed; the faction favouring a continuation of mil. operations is led by Ahmed Dini Ahmed; a dissident group, FRUD–Renaissance, led by Ibrahim Chehem Daoud was formed in 1996.

Parti national démocratique (PND): f. 1992; seeks formation of a 'govt of national unity' to supervise implementation of democratic reforms; Chair. Aden Robleh Awalleh.

Parti du renouveau démocratique (PRD): BP 2198, Djibouti; tel. 356235; fax 351474; f. 1992; seeks to establish democratic parliamentary govt; Pres. Abdillahi Hamareiteh; Sec.-Gen. Maki Houmed Gaba.

Rassemblement populaire pour le progrès (RPP): Djibouti; f. 1979; sole legal party 1981–92; Pres. Hassan Gouled Aptidon; Sec.-Gen. Mohamed Ali Mohamed.

The following organizations are banned:

Coordination de l'opposition djiboutienne: f. 1996; alliance of PND, FUOD and RPP–GDR; Leader Ismael Gedi Hared.

Front des forces démocratiques (FFD): Leader Omar Elmi Khaireh.

Front de libération de la côte des Somalis (FLCS): f. 1963; Issa-supported; has operated from Somalia; Chair. Abdallah Waberi Khalif; Vice-Chair. Omar Osman Rabeh.

Front uni de l'opposition djiboutienne (FUOD): f. 1992; based in Ethiopia; united front of internal opposition groups, incl. some fmr mems of the RPP; Leader Mohamed Ahmed Issa ('Cheiko').

Groupe pour la démocratie de la république (RPP–GDR): f. 1996 by a dissident faction of the RPP; Leader Moumin Bahdon Farah.

Mouvement de la jeunesse djiboutienne (MJD): Leader Abdoulkarim Ali Amarkak.

Mouvement pour l'unité et la démocratie (MUD): advocates political pluralism; Leader Mohamed Moussa Ali ('Tourtour').

Organisation des masses Afar (OMA): f. 1993 by mems of the fmr Mouvement populaire de libération; Chair. Ahmed Malco.

Parti centriste et des reformes démocratiques (PCRD): f. 1993 in Addis Ababa, Ethiopia, by a breakaway faction of the FRUD; seeks official registration as an opposition party; Chair. Hassan Abdallah Watta.

Parti populaire djiboutien (PPD): f. 1981; mainly Afar-supported; Leader Moussa Ahmed Idris.

Union des démocrates djiboutiens (UDD): affiliated to FUOD; Chair. Mahdi Ibrahim Ahmed.

Union démocratique pour le progrès (UDP): f. 1992; advocates democratic reforms; Leader Farah Waberi.

Union des mouvements démocratiques (UMD): f. 1990 by merger of two militant external opposition groups; Pres. Mohamed Adoyta.

Diplomatic Representation

EMBASSIES IN DJIBOUTI

China, People's Republic: Djibouti; tel. 352246; telex 5926; Ambassador: Sun Zhirong.

Egypt: BP 1989, Djibouti; tel. 351231; telex 5880; Ambassador: Ibrahim Elchoumi.

Eritrea: Djibouti; Ambassador: Daniel Yohannes Hagdu.

Ethiopia: BP 230, Djibouti; tel. 350718; fax 354803; Ambassador: Berhanu Dinka.

France: 45 blvd du Maréchal Foch, BP 2039, Djibouti; tel. 350963; telex 5861; Ambassador: Bernard Le Tourneau.

Iraq: BP 1983, Djibouti; tel. 353469; telex 5877; Ambassador: Abdel Aziz al-Gailani.

Libya: BP 2073, Djibouti; tel. 350202; telex 5874; Ambassador: Kamel al-Hadi Almarash.

Oman: BP 1996, Djibouti; tel. 350852; telex 5876; Ambassador: Saoud Salem Hassan al-Ansi.

Russia: BP 1913, Djibouti; tel. 352051; telex 5906; fax 355990; Ambassador: Mikhail Tsvigoun.

Saudi Arabia: BP 1921, Djibouti; tel. 351645; telex 5865; fax 352284; Chargé d'affaires a.i.: Mowaffak al-Doligane.

Somalia: BP 549, Djibouti; tel. 353521; telex 5815; Ambassador: Mohamed Shek Mohamed Malingur.

Sudan: BP 4259, Djibouti; tel. 351404; fax 356662; Ambassador: Sayed Sharif Ahmed Sharif.

USA: Villa Plateau du Serpent, blvd du Maréchal Joffre, BP 185, Djibouti; tel. 353995; fax 353940; Chargé d'affaires a.i.: Terri Robl.

Yemen: BP 194, Djibouti; tel. 352975; Ambassador: Muhammad Abdoul Wassi Hamid.

Judicial System

The Supreme Court was established in 1979. There is a high court of appeal and a court of first instance in Djibouti; each of the five administrative districts has a 'tribunal coutumier'.

President of the Court of Appeal: Kadidja Abeba.

Religion

ISLAM

Almost the entire population are Muslims.

Qadi of Djibouti: Mogue Hassan Dirir, BP 168, Djibouti; tel. 352669.

CHRISTIANITY

The Roman Catholic Church

Djibouti comprises a single diocese, directly responsible to the Holy See. There were an estimated 8,000 adherents in the country at 31 December 1995.

Bishop of Djibouti: Rt Rev. Georges Perron, Evêché, blvd de la République, BP 94, Djibouti; tel. 350140; fax 354831.

The Anglican Communion

Within the Episcopal Church in Jerusalem and the Middle East, Djibouti lies within the jurisdiction of the Bishop in Egypt.

Other Christian Churches

Eglise Protestante: blvd de la République, BP 416, Djibouti; tel. 351820; fax 350706; f. 1957; Pastor Philippe Girardet.

Greek Orthodox Church: blvd de la République, Djibouti; tel. 351325; c. 350 adherents; Archimandrite Stavros Georganas.

The Ethiopian Orthodox Church is also represented in Djibouti.

The Press

L'Atout: Palais du peuple, Djibouti; twice a year; publ. by the Centre National de la Promotion Culturelle et Artistique.

Carrefour Africain: BP 393, Djibouti; fax 354916; fortnightly; publ. by the Roman Catholic mission; circ. 500.

La Nation de Djibouti: place du 27 juin, BP 32, Djibouti; tel. 352201; fax 353937; weekly; Dir Ismael H. Tani; circ. 4,300.

Le Progrès: Djibouti; weekly; publ. by the RPP; Publr Ali Mohamed Humad.

Revue de l'ISERT: BP 486, Djibouti; tel. 352795; telex 5811; twice a year; publ. by the Inst. Supérieur d'Etudes et de Recherches Scientifiques et Techniques (ISERT).

NEWS AGENCIES

Agence Djiboutienne d'Information (ADJI): place du 27 juin, BP 32, Djibouti; tel. 355672; fax 353957.

Foreign Bureau

Agence France-Presse (AFP): BP 97, Djibouti; tel. 352294; telex 5863; Correspondent Khalid Haidar Abdallah.

Radio and Television

There were an estimated 46,000 radio receivers and 25,000 television receivers in use in 1994. In 1980 Djibouti became a member of the Arab Satellite Communication Organization, and opened an earth station for radio, television and telecommunications; a second earth station opened in June 1985.

Radiodiffusion-Télévision de Djibouti (RTD): BP 97, Djibouti; tel. 352294; telex 5863; fax 356502; f. 1957; state-controlled; programmes in French, Afar, Somali and Arabic; 17 hours radio and 5 hours television daily; Dir-Gen. Mohamed Djama Aden.

Finance

(cap. = capital; res = reserves; dep. = deposits; m. = million; br. = branch; amounts in Djibouti francs)

BANKING

Central Bank

Banque Nationale de Djibouti: BP 2118, Djibouti; tel. 352751; telex 5838; fax 356288; f. 1977; bank of issue; Gov. Djama M. Haid.

Commercial Banks

Banque al-Baraka Djibouti: ave Pierre Pascal, BP 2607, Djibouti; tel. 355046; telex 5739; fax 355038; f. 1991; cap. and res 627.8m., dep. 4,692.1m. (Dec. 1995); Chair. Tarek Osman Alkasaby; Dir-Gen. Mustapha Boodhoo.

Banque Indosuez Mer Rouge: 10 place Lagarde, BP 88, Djibouti; tel. 353016; telex 5829; fax 351638; f. 1908; owned by Banque Indosuez (France); cap. and res 1,650m.; dep. 20,679.5m. (Dec. 1995); Chair. and CEO Bernard Pardigon.

Banque pour le Commerce et l'Industrie-Mer Rouge (BCIMR): place Lagarde, BP 2122, Djibouti; tel. 350857; telex 5821; fax 354260; f. 1977; 51% owned by Banque Nationale de Paris Intercontinentale; cap. and res 4,440m., dep. 27,531.7m. (Dec. 1995); Pres. Mohamed Aden; Vice-Pres. Vincent de Roux; Gen. Man. Joseph Detraux; 8 brs.

Development Bank

Banque de Développement de Djibouti: angle ave Georges Clemenceau et rue Pierre Curie, BP 520, Djibouti; tel. 353391; telex 5717; fax 355022; f. 1983; 39.2% govt-owned; cap. 1,557m. (Dec. 1993); Dir-Gen. Osman Walieh Samatar.

Banking Association

Association Professionnelle des Banques: c/o Banque pour le Commerce et l'Industrie (Mer Rouge), place Lagarde, BP 2122, Djibouti; tel. 350857; telex 5821; fax 354260; Pres. Mohamed Aden.

INSURANCE

Ets Marill 'La Prudence': 8 rue Marchand, BP 57, Djibouti; tel. 351150; fax 355623; f.1896.

Trade and Industry

CHAMBER OF COMMERCE

Chambre Internationale de Commerce et d'Industrie: place Lagarde, BP 84, Djibouti; tel. 351070; telex 5957; f. 1906; 24 mems; 12 assoc. mems; Pres. Said Ali Coubeche; First Vice-Pres. Mohamed Aden.

TRADE ORGANIZATION

Office National d'Approvisionnement et de Commercialisation (ONAC): BP 75, Djibouti; tel. 350327; telex 5933.

TRADE UNION

Union Générale du Travail: Djibouti; f. 1992 to succeed Union Générale des Travailleurs de Djibouti; confed. of 22 unions; Chair. Ahmed Djama Egueh (Oboley); Sec.-Gen. Aden Mohamed Ardou.

Transport

RAILWAYS

Chemin de Fer Djibouti-Ethiopien (CDE): BP 2116, Djibouti; tel. 350280; telex 5953; fax 351256; POB 1051, Addis Ababa; tel. 517250; telex 21414; fax 513533; f. 1908, adopted present name in 1981; jtly-owned by Govts of Djibouti and Ethiopia; plans to grant autonomous status were announced in 1985; 781 km of track (100 km in Djibouti) linking Djibouti with Addis Ababa; Pres. W. Guemachou; Commercial Dir A. Douale Absie.

ROADS

In 1991 there were 2,879 km of roads, comprising 1,081 km of main roads and 1,798 km of regional roads; 12% of the roads were paved. Of the remainder, 1,000 km are serviceable throughout the year, the rest only during the dry season. About one-half of the roads are usable only by heavy vehicles. In 1981 the 40-km Grand Bara road was opened, linking the capital with the south. In 1986 the Djibouti–Tadjourah road, the construction of which was financed by Saudi Arabia, was opened, linking the capital with the north. In mid-1996 the Islamic Development Bank granted Djibouti a loan of US $3.6m. to finance road construction projects.

SHIPPING

Djibouti, which was established as a free port in 1981, handled 1.7m. metric tons of freight in 1991.

Port Autonome International de Djibouti: BP 2107, Djibouti; tel. 352331; telex 5836; fax 356187; Dir Aden Ahmed Douale.

Maritime and Transit Service: rue de Marseille, BP 680, Djibouti; tel. 353204; telex 5845; fax 354149.

Principal Shipping Agents

Almis Shipping Line & Transport Co: BP 85, Djibouti; tel. 356996; telex 5958; fax 356998; Man. Dir Mohamed Noor.

Compagnie Générale Maritime: 3 rue Marchand, BP 182, Djibouti; tel. 353825; telex 5817; fax 354778; agents for Mitsui OSK, CGM, CGM-SUD, SNC, Capricorne, WAKL, Hapaglloyd, Sea Consortium, Total Transport and others; Gen. Man. Henri Ferrand.

Compagnie Maritime et de Manutention de Djibouti: ave des Messageries Maritimes, BP 89, Djibouti; tel. 351028; telex 5825; fax 350466; agents for Wec Lines, Zim Line, Mitsui Osk Line, Western Bulk Carriers, Metalink, Portserv; also stevedores and freight forwarders; Man. Dir Ali A. Hettam.

Inchcape Shipping Services & Co (Djibouti) SA: 9–11 rue de Genève, BP 81, Djibouti; tel. 353844; telex 3856; fax 353294; f. 1942; agents for Lloyds and DHL; shipping agents for Nippon Yusen Kaisha, Waterman Steamship Co, Harrison Lines, Ellerman Lines, Shell, Mobil, and others; Dir-Gen. JOHN MCCAULEY.

J. J. Kothari & Co Ltd: rue d'Athens, BP 171, Djibouti; tel. 350219; telex 5860; fax 351778; agents for Shipping Corpn of India, Pacific International Lines, Shipping Corpn of Saudi Arabia, Egyptian Navigation, Sealift NV, India Shipping Co, Mediterranean Shipping Co, and others; also ship managers, stevedores, freight forwarders; Dirs S. J. KOTHARI, NALIN KOTHARI.

Mitchell Cotts Djibouti SARL: blvd de la République, BP 85, Djibouti; tel. 351204; telex 5812; fax 355851; agents for Central Gulf, Cunard Ellerman, Dry Tank/Piraeus, Harrison, Khan Shipping, Mobil/Fairfax/London, Scan-Shipping/Denmark and others; Dir FAHMY SAID CASSIM.

Société Maritime L. Savon et Ries: blvd Cheikh Osman, BP 2125, Djibouti; tel. 352351; telex 5823; fax 351103; agents for DRML, Conti Lines, SUDGARCO, Lloyd Triestino, Messina, Polish Ocean Lines and others; Gen. Man. J. P. DELARUE.

CIVIL AVIATION

The international airport is at Ambouli, 6 km from Djibouti, and there are six other airports providing domestic services.

Air Djibouti (Red Sea Airlines): BP 505, rue Marchand, Djibouti; tel. 352651; telex 5820; fax 354363; f. 1971; the Djibouti Govt holds 62.5% of shares, and Air France 32.3%; in liquidation since 1991; internal flights and international services to points in the Middle East and Europe; Gen. Man. PAUL BOTBOL.

Daallo Airlines: BP 1954, Djibouti; tel. 353401; fax 351765; f. 1992; regional carrier operating services to Somalia, Saudi Arabia and the United Arab Emirates; Man. Dir MOHAMED I. YASSIN.

Tourism

Djibouti offers desert scenery in its interior and watersport facilities on its coast. In addition, a casino opened in the capital in January 1997. In 1994 there were 46,595 tourist arrivals.

Office National du Tourisme et de l'Artisanat (ONTA): place du 27 juin, BP 1938, Djibouti; tel. 353790; telex 5938; fax 356322; Dir ALI MOHAMED ABDALLAH.

Defence

Arrangements for military co-operation exist between Djibouti and France, and in August 1996 there were about 3,900 French military personnel stationed in Djibouti. The total armed forces of Djibouti itself, in which all services form part of the army, numbered 8,400 (including 200 naval and 200 air force personnel). There were also paramilitary forces numbering 1,200 gendarmes, as well as a 3,000-strong national security force. Conscription of all men between 18 and 25 years of age was introduced in 1992.

Defence Expenditure: Budgeted at 3,700m. Djibouti francs in 1996.

Commander-in-Chief of the Armed Forces: Pres. HASSAN GOULED APTIDON.

Chief of Staff of the Army: Gen. FATHI AHMED HUSSEIN.

Education

The government has overall responsibility for education. Primary education generally begins at six years of age and lasts for six years. Secondary education, usually starting at the age of 12, lasts for seven years, comprising a first cycle of four years and a second of three years. In 1994 the total enrolment at primary and secondary schools was equivalent to 26% of the school-age population (30% of boys; 22% of girls), while primary enrolment included 32% of pupils in the relevant age-group (36% of boys; 28% of girls). Budgetary current expenditure on education in 1994 was 2,615m. Djibouti francs, equivalent to 7.4% of total government expenditure. In 1994 there were 35,024 primary school pupils and 11,562 pupils receiving general secondary and vocational education (including teacher training). As Djibouti has no university, students seeking further education travel abroad to study, mainly to France. In 1995, according to UNESCO estimates, the rate of illiteracy among the population aged 15 years and over was 53.8% (males 39.7%; females 67.3%).

Bibliography

Coubba, A. *Djibouti: line nation en otage*. Paris, L'Harmattan, 1993.

Koburger, C. W. *Naval Strategy East of Suez: the Role of Djibouti*. New York, Praeger, 1992.

Laudouze, A. *Djibouti, Nation carrefour*. Paris, Editions Karthala, 1982.

Martineau, A. *Djibouti*. Boulogne-Billancourt, Editions Delroisse, 1977.

Oberle, P., and Hugot, P. *Histoire de Djibouti: des origines à la république*. Paris, Editions Présence Africaine, 1985.

Schrader, P. J. *Djibouti*. Oxford, Clio Press, 1991.

'Ethnic Politics in Djibouti: From the "Eye of the Hurricane" to "Boiling Cauldron", in *African Affairs*, Vol. 92, No. 367 (April 1993), pp 203–221.

Tholomier, R. *Djibouti: Pawn of the Horn of Africa*. Metuchen, NJ, Scarecrow Press, 1981.

Thompson, V., and Adloff, R. *Djibouti and the Horn of Africa*. London, Oxford University Press, 1968.

Tramport, J. *Djibouti Hier: de 1887 à 1939*. Paris, Hatier, 1990.

Weiss, E. *Djibouti: Évasion*. Paris, Editions du Fer a Marquer, 1990.

EQUATORIAL GUINEA

Physical and Social Geography

RENÉ PÉLISSIER

The Republic of Equatorial Guinea occupies an area of 28,051 sq km (10,831 sq miles). Geographically, the main components of the republic are the islands of Bioko (formerly known as Fernando Póo), covering 2,017 sq km, and Annobón (also known as Pagalu), 17 sq km; and, on the African mainland, bordered to the north by Cameroon, to the south and east by Gabon and westwards by the Gulf of Guinea, lies the province of Río Muni (also formerly known as Mbini), 26,017 sq km, including three coastal islets, Corisco (15 sq km), and the Great and Little Elobeys (2.5 sq km).

Bioko is a parallelogram-shaped island, 72 km by 35 km, formed from three extinct volcanoes. To the north lies the Pico de Basilé (rising to 3,007 m above sea-level), with an easy access. In the centre of the island are the Moka heights, while, further south, the Gran Caldera forms the remotest and least developed part of the island. The coast is steep to the south. Malabo is the only natural harbour. Crop fertility is high, owing to the combination of volcanic soils and plentiful rainfall. At the southern extremity of the Guinean archipelago lies the remote island of Annobón, south of the island of São Tomé.

Mainland Río Muni is a jungle enclave, from which a coastal plain rises steeply toward the Gabonese frontier. Its main orographic complexes are the spurs of the Monts de Cristal of Gabon. The highest peaks are Piedra de Nzas, Monte Mitra and Monte Chime, all rising to 1,200 m. The main river is the Mbini (formerly known as the Río Benito), non-navigable except for a 20-km stretch, which bisects the mainland province. On the Cameroon border is the Río Campo; its tributary, the Kye, is the *de facto* eastern border with Gabon. The coast is a long beach, with low cliffs towards Cogo. There is no natural harbour.

The country has an equatorial climate with heavy rainfall, especially in Bioko. The average temperature of Malabo is 25°C and the average rainfall is in excess of 2,000 mm. Humidity is high throughout the island, except on the Moka heights. Río Muni has less debilitating climatic conditions.

According to the 1983 census, which recorded a total population of 300,000, there were 240,804 inhabitants in Río Muni, 57,190 on Bioko and 2,006 on Annobón. The population was estimated by the UN to be 400,000 at mid-1995. The main city is Malabo (with 15,253 inhabitants at the July 1983 census), the capital of Bioko and of the republic, as well as the main economic, educational and religious centre. The other town of note is Luba. Bubi villages are scattered in the eastern and western parts of the island. On the mainland the only urban centre is the port of Bata, which had a population of 24,100 in 1983. Other ports are Mbini and Cogo. Inland, Mikomeseng, Nkumekie, Ebebiyín and Evinayong are small market and administrative centres. The country is divided into seven administrative provinces: Bioko Norte, Bioko Sur and Annobón for the two main islands; Centro-Sur, Kié-Ntem, Litoral and Wele-Nzas for the mainland and its adjacent islets.

The ethnic composition of Equatorial Guinea is unusually complex for so small a political unit. The Fang are the dominant group in Río Muni, where they are believed to comprise 80%–90% of the population. North of the Mbini river are the Ntumu Fang, and to the south of it the Okak Fang. Coastal tribes—notably the Kombe, Balengue and Bujeba—have been pushed towards the sea by Fang pressure. Both Fang and coastal peoples are of Bantu origin. Since independence in 1968, many inhabitants of Río Muni have emigrated to Bioko, where they have come to dominate the civil and military services. The Bubi, who are the original inhabitants of Bioko, may now number about 15,000. The Fernandino, of whom there are a few thousand, are the descendants of former slaves liberated by the British, mingled with long-settled immigrants from coastal west Africa. The working population of Annobón are mainly fishermen and seafarers.

The official language is Spanish. In Río Muni the Fang language is spoken, as well as those of coastal tribes. On Bioko the principal local language is Bubi, although pidgin English and Ibo are widely understood.

Recent History

MARISÉ CASTRO

The Republic of Equatorial Guinea, comprising the region of Río Muni, on the African mainland, and the islands of Bioko (Fernando Póo), Annobón, Corisco and the Elobeys, was granted independence on 12 October 1968, after 190 years of Spanish colonial rule. Francisco Macías Nguema, a mainland Fang from the Esangui clan, took office as president of the new republic, following multi-party elections in which he had received the support of a moderate coalition grouping.

In office, Macías Nguema moved swiftly to suppress opposition, and to assert his absolute power through a 'reign of terror'. In 1970 all political parties were fused into a single party, which came to be known as the Partido Unico Nacional de los Trabajadores (PUNT). The brutal and increasingly capricious nature of the regime led to the flight of as many as one-third of the total population, including nearly all of the skilled and educated elements of Equato-Guinean society. Macías Nguema obtained much of his economic and military aid from Eastern bloc countries; relations with Spain deteriorated, and serious quarrels arose regionally with Gabon and Nigeria. The country's economy, centred on cocoa plantations on Bioko and relying on imported African labour, was devastated by the excesses of Macías Nguema's regime.

OBIANG NGUEMA'S PRESIDENCY

On 3 August 1979 Lt-Col (now Gen.) Teodoro Obiang Nguema Mbasogo, the commander of the national guard and a nephew of the president, staged a successful *coup d'état*. Macías, who fled from the capital, was eventually captured, tried and executed on 29 September. Obiang Nguema announced the restoration of the rule of law, but banned all political parties and ruled through a supreme military council (SMC), which continued to be dominated by the Esangui clan. An alleged attempt to depose the new regime in April 1981 was followed by some 150 arrests and reports of brutality. However, sustained pressure from exiled opposition groups, together with the government's need to secure foreign economic assistance, compelled Obiang Nguema to grant political concessions. In December 1981 the first civilians were appointed to the SMC, and in August 1982 a new constitution was submitted to a referendum, being approved by 95% of voters. Provisions for the protection of human rights and for a limited form of popular representation were incorporated in the constitution, and Obiang Nguema was appointed to a seven-year term as president. In May 1983 a coup attempt involving military personnel close to the president was foiled, and in August elections were held. An estimated 50,000 voters balloted for 41 candidates, nominated by the president, to serve for a term of five years in a unicameral legislature, with virtually no independent legislative powers.

In 1986 there was a third attempted coup, promoted by the minister of defence, Lt-Col Fructuoso Mba Onaña Nchama, an uncle of the president. Obiang Nguema responded in the following year by creating a 'governmental party', the Partido Democrático de Guinea Ecuatorial (PDGE), while still resisting demands for multi-party democracy. The higher ranks of the civil service and armed forces remained firmly in the hands of the president's Esangui clan, and elections continued to be overtly manipulated by the government. At legislative elections held in July 1988, all of the PDGE candidates were returned, receiving 99.2% of the votes cast. Numerous arrests followed a fourth unsuccessful coup attempt in August.

The first presidential election since 1968 took place in June 1989, with Obiang Nguema, the sole candidate, receiving 99% of the votes cast. The election was not conducted by secret ballot. An amnesty for political detainees was proclaimed in August. However, the international human rights organization Amnesty International has since reiterated long-standing accusations against the government of detaining and mistreating its political opponents. The Roman Catholic church, which claims the allegiance of the majority of the population, has also been active in criticizing the regime's human rights abuses.

Opposition Pressures

Under growing internal and international pressure, Obiang Nguema eventually conceded the principle of political plurality in July 1991. A new constitution containing such provisions was approved by referendum in mid-November; however, the few human rights safeguards contained in the 1982 constitution were removed. In early January 1992 a number of new laws were promulgated, which included legislation on political parties and on freedom of assembly and demonstration. This was followed, in mid-January, by the formation of a new transitional government and the implementation of a general amnesty which included all political exiles. However, these reform measures failed to meet the opposition's expectations. Provisions of the new constitution exempted Obiang Nguema from any judicial procedures arising from his tenure, while Equato-Guinean citizens who also hold foreign passports and persons not continuously resident in Equatorial Guinea for 10 years were barred from standing as election candidates. This measure thus effectively excluded virtually all exiled political opponents from participation in national political life. In addition, the legislation on political parties required each organization to submit a deposit of 30m. francs CFA as a condition of registration, and prohibited the use of funds from abroad for this purpose. The president indicated that legislative and presidential elections would not be held until the current mandates of the legislature and of the president had expired, in 1993 and 1996 respectively. The transitional government included only PDGE members, although the party's 'liberal' wing was represented, notably by the new foreign minister, Benjamín Mba Ekua. The first two opposition parties, the Unión Popular and Partido Liberal, were legalized in June 1992, and in September an alliance of opposition organizations, the Plataforma de Oposición Conjunta (POC), was created.

During January 1992 the UN published a report that criticized the human rights record of the Equato-Guinean authorities and some of the provisions incorporated in the new constitution, and appointed a 'Special Rapporteur for Equatorial Guinea'. Throughout 1992 the security forces continued to arrest members of opposition parties. In early November two Spanish businessmen were charged with plotting against the government; they were found guilty in late November, sentenced to 12 years' imprisonment, and simultaneously pardoned. In mid-December about 100 anti-government protesters were arrested in Malabo; however, they were released soon afterwards.

In January 1993, following the promulgation of an electoral law, further arrests of opposition members took place. In early February the UN published another report alleging a serious disregard for human rights by the Obiang Nguema regime. During February and March the government and several opposition organizations negotiated a national pact that established conditions for the conduct of the forthcoming legislative elections; these included the freedom to organize political activity and equal access by all parties to the media. However, the government was soon accused of violating the pact. In late May five opposition members were arrested while attending a political meeting, and in August further arrests took place of political opponents accused of attempting to overthrow the government; one detainee died, reportedly as a result of torture. During August violent clashes occurred on the island of Annobón between anti-government demonstrators and security forces. Accusations by the Equato-Guinean authorities that Spain had incited the unrest were strenuously denied by the Spanish government.

Multi-party legislative elections took place in mid-November 1993. They were, however, boycotted by most of the parties in the POC alliance, in protest at Obiang Nguema's refusal to review contentious clauses of the electoral law or to permit international observers to inspect the electoral register. Although OAU representatives attended as observers, the UN declined a request by the Equato-Guinean authorities to monitor the elections, asserting that correct procedures were evidently not being implemented. Following a turn-out variously estimated at between 30%-50% of the electorate, the PDGE won 68 of the 80 seats in the house of representatives; of the six opposition parties which presented candidates, the Convención Socialdemocrática Popular won six seats, the Unión Democrática y Social de Guinea Ecuatorial secured five seats and the Convención Liberal Democrática obtained one seat. Prior to the elections, opposition politicians were reported to have been harassed by the security forces and during the polling irregularities in procedures were allegedly widespread. In early December the government announced that henceforth all party political gatherings would be subject to prior official authorization. In mid-December Silvestre Siale Bileka, prime minister in the interim government, became prime minister of the new administration. His council of ministers included no opposition representatives.

In June 1994, in response to pressure from international aid donors, the government agreed to modify the electoral law. In September, however, the authorities began to compile a full population census, instead of preparing for local elections, which had been scheduled for November. The census was boycotted by opposition parties, and there were numerous arrests in ensuing clashes with the security forces. The local elections were postponed. During late November and early December the Convergencia para la Democracia Social held the first congress of an opposition political party to take place within Equatorial Guinea.

In early 1995 the constitution and electoral law were amended to reduce the minimum time required for candidates to be resident in Equatorial Guinea from 10 to five years. In April several leaders of the opposition Partido del Progreso de Guinea Ecuatorial (PPGE), including its president, Severo Moto Nsa, were sentenced to terms of imprisonment, having been convicted of treason by a military court. (Moto Nsa received a sentence of 28 years.) These proceedings were widely condemned by the international community, and in August, following representations by President Chirac of France on behalf of Moto Nsa, Obiang Nguema unexpectedly pardoned all the convicted PPGE members. In the previous month Amnesty International had issued a report detailing alleged human rights violations in Equatorial Guinea from mid-1994 to mid-1995.

Local elections (which had been postponed in 1994—see above) were eventually held in mid-September 1995. Contested by 14 parties, they were the first truly representative multi-party elections to take place since independence. The electoral roll had been drafted with assistance from the UN, and the elections were monitored by a team of 27 international observers; observers representing the government and opposition parties were also present at polling stations. The six member parties of the POC presented a united front, fielding a single candidate in each constituency. Although no major problems were reported during the election campaigns, the ruling PDGE was accused of electoral fraud and harassment once polling was under way. The initial results indicated that opposition parties had won an overwhelming victory; however, the official results credited the ruling party with a majority of the votes cast in two-thirds of local administrations. Judicial appeals by the opposition against the outcome, supported by the team of international observers, were rejected.

At the presidential election, which was held at short notice in late February 1996 (having initially been scheduled for the following June), Obiang Nguema was returned to office for a third term, securing more than 90% of the votes cast. The election was boycotted by influential opposition leaders, in protest at alleged electoral irregularities and official intimidation. The electoral roll drawn up by the UN in 1995 was discarded in favour of an allegedly fraudulent list produced by the government, and the conduct of the elections was severely criticized by foreign observers. In late March Obiang Nguema appointed a new prime minister, Angel Serafin Seriche Dougan, hitherto a vice-minister; a new, enlarged council of ministers was announced in early April. Representatives of the major opposition parties had declined a presidential invitation to participate in the new administration.

In early 1996 internal friction within the POC led to the withdrawal of two parties from the alliance. The government attempted to capitalize on the disunity by issuing a decree in March that effected the organization's immediate dissolution. In August Obiang Nguema issued a decree awarding himself the rank of general. In November a military court found 11 army officers guilty of conspiring to overthrow the government; all were sentenced to terms of imprisonment.

In February 1997 Obiang Nguema conceded that human rights violations (particularly in Río Muni) were damaging his government's international reputation. Measures, reportedly being taken by the government to prevent official torture and to punish those responsible, were dismissed by human rights organizations and opposition politicians as an empty gesture designed to appease potential foreign donors; complaints continued of acts of violence and intimidation allegedly carried out by members of the security forces. In the same month some 500 people held a demonstration in Malabo, the first in more than five years, to protest against the continuing demolition of houses in furtherance of an officially designated slum clearance programme.

In April 1997 a new national pact was signed by representatives of the government and of 14 opposition parties, following two months of negotiations; however, the Convergencia para la Democracia Social (CPDS), a leading opposition party instrumental in the establishment of the POC, was excluded from the talks. In May Moto Nsa was arrested by the Angolan authorities, having been discovered on board a boat carrying a consignment of arms, which, Moto Nsa subsequently admitted, had been intended for use in a planned *coup d'état* in Equatorial Guinea. Moto Nsa was released in June and subsequently sought refuge in Spain, from where he announced that he continued to advocate the use of force to overthrow Obiang Nguema. The government responded by announcing its intention to ban the PPGE; it was however, widely viewed as unlikely that this threat would be carried out, following Moto Nsa's dismissal from the leadership of the PPGE by members of the party with closer links to the government.

In June 1997 Obiang Nguema unexpectedly dismissed two cabinet ministers, one of whom, Santos Pascual Bikomo Nanguande, the minister of information, was subsequently arrested by the Spanish authorities on charges of drugs smuggling.

Equato-Guinean exiles have reacted cautiously to Obiang Nguema's efforts to encourage their return. His regime's authoritarian ethos, together with reports of persistent human rights abuses, corruption and economic stagnation, have tended to discourage the great majority of emigrés. During the Macías period, the most influential exiled opposition party had been the Alianza Nacional para la Restauración Democrática de Guinea Ecuatorial (ANRDGE). Based in Geneva, Switzerland, it achieved a semi-representative, if unofficial, standing with UN bodies. Following Obiang Nguema's accession to power, however, ANRDGE's influence declined, and the exiled opposition split into numerous small and shifting groups, many of which were based in Spain. The PPGE, founded in 1983, emerged as a particularly influential opposition platform during the 1980s. Severo Moto Nsa, the PPGE's leader, was appointed secretary-general of the Junta Coordinadora de las Fuerzas de Oposición Democrática, which was formed in Zaragoza, Spain, in 1983, as a co-ordinating body for exiled opposition groups. Moto Nsa did not return to Equatorial Guinea until late 1992. Smaller concentrations of exiled politicians continue to operate from France and Portugal and political liberalization in Gabon led during 1990 to the emergence of Libreville as a new centre of activity for the Equato-Guinean opposition in exile. The most significant of these groups was the Unión para la Democracia y el Desarollo Social (UDDS), founded in September 1990 and led by Antonio Sibacha Bueicheku. A coalition of parties dominated by the UDDS was formed in Libreville, Gabon, in April 1991, under the title of Coordinación Democrática de los Partidos de Oposición de Guinea Ecuatorial. Following the government's amnesty for political exiles in January 1992 and the enactment of legislation in that month legalizing a multi-party political system, the opposition began to prepare for the legislative elections due to take place in 1993 (see above). The POC was formed in 1992, grouping several opposition organizations, the most significant and active of which was the Convergencia pora la Democracia Social (CPDS), led by Plácido Mikó Abogo; the POC was dissolved in March 1996. In November 1993 members of the Bubi ethnic group founded the Movimento para la Autodeterminación de la Isla de Bioko (MAIB), which demanded independence for Bioko.

Foreign Relations

Equatorial Guinea's relations with Spain, the former colonial power (which has traditionally provided substantial economic aid), have been consistently strained in recent years by reports of internal corruption, the misuse of aid funds and abuses of human rights. In December 1993 the Spanish consul in Bata was expelled 'for interference in the country's internal affairs', following an alleged meeting between the consul and members of opposition parties. The Spanish government recalled its ambassador and reduced aid to the country by 50%, excluding humanitarian assistance, from the beginning of January 1994. The ban was extended to all forms of aid at the end of the month. The European Union has also withdrawn financial assistance and the United Nations Development Programme has suspended a number of projects. In early 1994 negotiations commenced between the Equato-Guinean and Spanish governments, with a view to the resumption of full Spanish financial assistance. In June aid donors met representatives of the Obiang Nguema administration and opposition parties; it was agreed that assistance would be resumed gradually, on condition that improvements were made in both the human rights situation and the democratization process. Relations with Spain improved considerably in 1996, with the installation of a new Spanish government; in 1997 negotiations recommenced between the two countries concerning the resumption of economic co-operation and aid. Opposition politicians expressed dismay at the *rapprochement,* which they believed would reduce international pressures on the Obiang Nguema government to install a truly democratic political system in Equatorial Guinea.

In the early 1980s Obiang Nguema attempted to move the country away from Spanish influence and into France's economic sphere. In December 1983 Equatorial Guinea became a member of the Union douanière et économique de l'Afrique centrale (UDEAC), and in August 1984 it joined the Banque des états de l'Afrique centrale (BEAC). Full entry to the Franc Zone followed in January 1985, when the CFA franc replaced the epkwele as the national currency. The increasing level of French economic influence was reflected in the president's regular attendance at Franco-African summit meetings, and in an extended curriculum of French-language classes in Equato-Guinean schools. During the late 1980s France became increasingly impatient with the economic and political shortcomings of the Obiang Nguema regime. Obiang Nguema has also sought to establish amicable relations with China and the Democratic People's Republic of Korea. In September 1996 an agreement on economic co-operation was signed with China. Military aid from Morocco, which replaced that from Cuba after 1979, has remained crucial to the maintenance of his regime. Some military aid has also been received from the USA.

Regionally, Equatorial Guinea's relations with Nigeria deteriorated when, in 1988, Nigeria threatened to invade Bioko to eject South African personnel, who were alleged to be installing a satellite-tracking station and extending Malabo airport, in preparation for a military assault on the Niger delta oilfields. The affair was eventually resolved in 1990 by reciprocal state visits by the two heads of state. In mid-1994, following a visit to Nigeria by Obiang Nguema, the two countries agreed to co-operate in the establishment of an international commission to demarcate maritime borders in the Gulf of Guinea. Cameroon and São Tomé and Príncipe were also expected to become members. During 1996–97 these negotiations between Equatorial Guinea and Nigeria continued, although complicated by the presence of substantial reserves of petroleum in the disputed offshore areas. Relations with Gabon have come under strain, as the result of unresolved frontier disputes, revived by petroleum exploration activity in southern Mbini. In May 1993 Equatorial Guinea and South Africa established diplomatic relations, and in January 1994 diplomatic relations with Israel were re-established. As part of a programme of cost-saving measures, the US government closed its diplomatic mission in Malabo in 1996.

Economy

MARISÉ CASTRO

With revisions by the Editor

The economy of Equatorial Guinea has traditionally been based on agriculture and forestry, the principal products being timber, cocoa, coffee, palm oil, bananas and cassava. The petroleum sector, however, has become increasingly important during the 1990s. In 1994, according to estimates by the World Bank, Equatorial Guinea's gross national product (GNP), measured at average 1993–95 prices, was US $152m., equivalent to $380 per head. During 1985–95, it was estimated, GNP per head increased, in real terms, at an average annual rate of 1.9%. In 1985–95 the population increased by an annual average of 2.5%. According to estimates by the World Bank, Equatorial Guinea's gross domestic product (GDP) increased, in real terms, by an annual average of 2.4% in 1985–90. GDP per head totalled $391, at current prices, in 1989. According to the IMF, real GDP decreased by 1.1% in 1991, then soared by 14.0% in 1992, and increases of 7.1% and 6.8% were recorded in 1993 and 1994 respectively. According to the World Bank, real GDP increased by 11.2% in 1995; a rise of some 15% was expected in 1996. Recent growth in GDP is substantially a result of increasing petroleum production, which has significantly improved Equatorial Guinea's economic prospects.

AGRICULTURE, FORESTRY AND FISHING

Agriculture, including forestry and fishing, contributed 47.4% of GDP in 1994 and an estimated 46.2% of GDP in 1995, in which year it employed 73.1% of the active population. Timber from the mainland province of Río Muni accounted for 41.6% of export revenue in 1995. There are some 1.3m. ha of timber estimated to be suitable for lumbering operations, of which only 597,000 ha had been conceded to timber production in 1993. However, timber output was stimulated by the devaluation of the national currency, the CFA franc, in January 1994, and concessions had been granted to more than 1m. ha of land in 1995. This massive growth in the forestry sector has called into question its sustainability. The environmental impact on easily accessible areas close to the coast or to navigable waterways has already been devastating. According to the IMF, at the current rate of extraction, available resources would be exhausted by the year 2012. The principal exploited species of wood are *okoumé* and *akoga*. In 1967, the year before independence, production by Spanish concessionaires reached nearly 340,000 metric tons. Output subsequently declined sharply, and amounted to a mere 1,000 tons in 1978. Production and exports recovered quickly after the overthrow of Macías Nguema in 1979, although annual production remained considerably below the level of 300,000 cu m until 1992, when it soared to 613,000 cu m.; in 1993 and 1994 output rose further, to 638,000 cu m and 714,000 cu m. respectively. Exports totalled 216,559 cu m. in 1994 and an estimated 281,000 cu m in 1995. The government's wish to increase the proportion of processed to unprocessed exports has largely failed to materialize, despite the construction in 1982, with Italian aid, of a sawmill with an annual capacity of 20,000 cu m. Exploitation rights to sizeable areas of forest were granted by Obiang Nguema to foreign (mainly French and Spanish) concessionaires. Following many years of stagnation, the sector grew rapidly throughout the mid-1990s. By the end of 1995 there were 38 timber concessions, as compared with 15 at the end of 1993. This is attributable, not only to the devaluation of 1994, but also to an increased demand for *okoumé* and reportedly to the failure to enforce cultivation guidelines, which has allowed concessionaires to fell trees officially set aside for conservation. In 1990 the government had adopted a forestry action plan, which aimed to revitalize timber production and emphasized the necessity of implementing reafforestation measures.

Cocoa, which provided 10.3% of export earnings in 1990, is the main crop of Bioko, where its cultivation accounts for about 90% of the country's total output. Production of cocoa fell sharply from about 38,000 tons annually before independence to less than 7,000 tons by the early 1980s; output has subsequently stagnated, totalling an estimated 4,000 tons in 1995. Prior to independence an area in excess of 41,000 ha was under cocoa cultivation, underpinned by high guaranteed prices on the Spanish domestic market. More than 800 plantations belonged to Africans, but most of the land and production was controlled by Europeans. Nationalized under Macías Nguema, the cocoa plantations were intially offered back to their former owners after the coup of 1979. However, many plantations remained unclaimed and others were subsequently re-confiscated; most are now owned by members of the presidential entourage, and are managed by two Spanish companies. They are worked on a share-cropping basis by local small farmers. Only about one-third of the land that was cultivated before independence is now exploited, and most of the trees are old and poorly tended. The main problem remains that of labour, as Nigerian plantation workers who were repatriated during the mid-1970s have not wished to return, while forced labourers who were brought from mainland Río Muni were sent home after 1979. A five-year cocoa rehabilitation project for 7,550 ha, initiated in 1985 by the World Bank and supported by a variety of donors, achieved little success. In 1991 the World Bank initiated a 10-year cocoa rehabilitation scheme, under which strictly commercial criteria were to be applied, to preclude any accusations of uneconomic subsidies. Under the programme, it was hoped that yields would be increased through replanting and the control of plant pests and diseases. The programme also provides for a gradual expansion in the areas under cultivation, with the promotion of diversification into other crops in areas of marginal cocoa production. The cocoa rehabilitation scheme is part of a wider agricultural project, which has attracted a pledge of US $18m. from the World Bank and lesser sums from other donors. The government is carrying out a survey of land tenure on Bioko, and has promised to follow this up with a land reform programme. Although the immediate outlook for cocoa remains dubious, the prospect of at least a short-term recovery in export earnings arose after the devaluation of the CFA franc in January 1994, which enabled Equatorial Guinea's cocoa exports to become more cost-competitive in relation to those of South-East Asian producers, who were aggressively expanding their share of the market.

Coffee is the third most important export commodity, but it lags far behind timber and cocoa. The Spanish administration encouraged smallholder cultivation in Río Muni for the Spanish market during the 1940s. In 1968, the year of independence, exports stood at just under 8,500 metric tons, part of which represented coffee from Gabon and Cameroon (smuggled over the frontier to benefit from higher Spanish prices). By 1979–80, exports had dwindled to just over 100 tons. Production recovered to about 7,000 tons per year by the end of the 1980s, and was estimated at 7,000 tons in 1994. However, it is believed that about two-thirds of the harvest is smuggled into Gabon to benefit from that country's higher producer prices. In 1988 it was estimated that there were nearly 20,000 ha planted with coffee, divided among some 25,000 households. The quality is poor and the yields are extremely low, as the bushes are mainly old and ill-tended. However, France and the European Union (EU) are currently financing a project to rejuvenate coffee smallholdings in Río Muni.

France and the EU are also encouraging the growth of food production as part of their rural development aid programme, aimed at enhancing production of cassava, cocoyam, plantain, bananas, rice, maize, palm oil, and eggs for the domestic market. There are also eventual prospects of substantial food exports to Gabon, which is persistently short of foodstuffs and which already imports about 3,000 tons of plantain a year from Río Muni.

Livestock raising almost disappeared from the country during the Macías Nguema period. In 1986 the African Development Bank (ADB) provided a loan of US $12.6m. to revive cattle-rearing on the high pastures of Moka, in Bioko, to a level comparable to that prevailing prior to independence, when the island was self-sufficient in beef and dairy products. The cattle herd was estimated at 5,000 head in 1994, and a slaughterhouse was in operation. In Río Muni the emphasis has been on poultry raising, again with ADB support, and by the end of the 1980s Río Muni was again well supplied with chickens and eggs.

At independence, some 5,000 people worked in the fishing industry, and those of Annobón (Pagalu) were renowned as skilled fishermen. Tuna from Annobón waters and shellfish from Bioko were processed locally and exported. Under Macías Nguema, the fishing industry collapsed, and the former USSR was granted a fishing monopoly. This was terminated in January 1980, and replaced by agreements with Spain in 1980, with Nigeria in 1982 (renewed in 1991), and with the European Community (EC, now the European Union—EU) in 1983 (renewed in 1986 and 1989). In 1989 the EC paid 6m. European Currency Units (ECU) for an agreed monthly tonnage catch by European fishing vessels, mainly Spanish and French. The agreement expired in 1992, and was renewed in 1994. The EU has also financed research and training schemes to improve Equatorial Guinea's own artisanal fishing operations. The overall catch rose from around 1,000 tons in 1981–82 to an estimated 3,800 tons in 1993, of which a negligible proportion came from artisanal fisherman. Shellfish constituted nearly one-half of the total catch. A tuna-processing factory at the port of Luba on Bioko, which was financed by Spanish aid, was due to begin production in the early 1990s; it was hoped that the plant would stimulate local involvement in the fishing industry.

INDUSTRY, MINING, POWER AND COMMUNICATIONS

In 1984 the offshore Alba gas and condensate field was discovered by Spain's Repsol on behalf of Empresa Guineano-Española de Petroleos (Gepsa), a joint venture between the government and Repsol. However, Gepsa was dissolved in 1990, and the concession was taken over, on a production-sharing basis, by a consortium of US independent operators, led by Walter International. Production began in late 1991, at a rate of 1,200 barrels per day (b/d), and was shipped to a storage complex near Malabo. The first consignment of condensates left Bioko in early 1992. Output rose to full capacity, at 6,700 b/d, in 1995, and was expected to last a further 10–15 years. Walter International carried out further successful exploration work in neighbouring blocs near Bioko, and between April 1992 and March 1993 it was reported that the company had exported some 1.2m. barrels of high-grade petroleum valued at $23m. In 1995 the Northern Michigan Electric Company (NOMECO) took over the operation of the Alba wells. Petroleum production has greatly increased since October 1995, when Mobil Oil Corpn's Zafiro field came on stream; Mobil, which is investing US $130m. in the country, began to produce 40,000 b/d from Zafiro in August 1996. Output was expected to double by late 1997. Test drilling is now under way in the Topacio prospect, also controlled by Mobil, in which United Meridien International Corpn (UMIC) has a 25% stake. The Topacio prospect could potentially yield a further 40,000 b/d. UMIC is the majority shareholder and operator for blocs A, C and D, to the north of Bioko, where test drilling was scheduled to commence in late 1996. The French company Elf Aquitaine has been exploring offshore concessions near Río Muni, and in 1996 was planning to set up several Equato-Guinean–Gabonese joint ventures in order to circumvent a territorial dispute between Equatorial Guinea and Gabon regarding offshore fields in the vicinity of the islands of Corisco and the Great and Little Elobeys. The Equato-Guinean petroleum fields also contain considerable reserves of natural gas, most of which, however, is currently flared; the lack of infrastructure in Equatorial Guinea hinders the commercial viability of production for domestic consumption. However, the construction of a liquefied petroleum gas (LPG) transformation facility by NOMECO was expected to increase the condensate output of the Alba fields by up to 3,000 b/d by early 1997. Equatorial Guinea has reserves of gold, iron, manganese, tantalum and uranium, but these have yet to be exploited.

On Bioko the existing electricity distribution system supplies only the towns of Malabo and Riaba. In 1987 funding was finalized for the construction of a 3.6-MW hydroelectric power station on the Riaba river (Bioko), at a total cost of US $32.1m., and the project was officially opened in 1989. There have been commissioning problems with the power station, and disputes over electricity tariffs with a French company, Saur-Afrique, which manages the distribution of electricity on the island. During the dry season the Malabo diesel plant supplements output from Riaba. A further 3.6-MW power station, constructed with aid from the People's Republic of China, at Bikomo, near Bata, supplies 90% of Río Muni's energy requirements.

Before independence, there was a diversified and flourishing light industrial sector, centred in Malabo; this infrastructure was effectively ruined by Macías Nguema and has yet to be fully restored. The manufacturing sector contributed only 1.2% of GDP in 1994. Two sawmills in Bata currently account for most of the country's industrial activity; the town also has a small cement works and a bleach factory. Food-processing and soap production are carried out on a small scale. Cocoa fermenting and drying is the only manufacturing industry on Bioko.

Since independence the entire Equato-Guinean road network has fallen into disrepair. During the early 1990s Spain allocated much of its economic aid towards the repair of roads on Bioko, in order to allow the cocoa plantations in the Luba and Riaba areas to re-enter production. A group of international donors are providing assistance for the upgrading of road access from Río Muni to Cogo on the Gabonese frontier, much of which is currently impassable in the rainy season; it is hoped that this will stimulate exports of foodstuffs to Gabon. 'Food for work' programmes are also being introduced, in order to maintain the network of feeder roads. There are no railways.

The harbour which handles by far the largest volume of exports is Bata, in Río Muni; the port is used by the timber companies, and handled nearly 125,990 metric tons of exports in 1990. The Italian government provided some US $5m. for the rehabilitation of the port in 1987, on condition that the facility be operated by a joint Italo-Equato-Guinean company. The initial aim is to increase the handling capacity of Bata to 500,000 tons per year, and eventually to 1m. tons. There have, however, been long delays in implementing this project. Malabo has an excellent natural harbour (formed by a sunken volcanic crater), which has been rehabilitated by a French company. There are regular shipping services to Europe, but maritime communications between Malabo, Bata and Annobón are erratic, and there is little maritime traffic with neighbouring mainland states.

There is an international airport at Malabo. A larger international airport at Bata, constructed with Italian aid, was completed in 1995. France has provided funds to upgrade facilities at Malabo airport. Attempts to form a national airline have been bedevilled by mismanagement and alleged corruption. Aerolíneas Guinea Ecuatorial, founded in 1982, had collapsed by 1985. Its successor, the Compañía Ecuato-Guineana de Aviación, was established in 1986 as a partnership between the government and Air Inter-Gabon. After incurring heavy losses, the company went into liquidation in 1990, but has continued to operate limited domestic services. During the mid-1990s the only scheduled international services were provided by IBERIA, between Malabo and Madrid, Cameroon Airlines (Cam-Air), operating a passenger service between Malabo and Douala and air freight facilities to destinations in the EU and the USA, and Air Gabon, providing a weekly service connecting Malabo, Bata, Douala and Libreville.

AID, FINANCE AND DEVELOPMENT

The economy continues to rely to a great extent on good relations with Spain, which supplied aid totalling 17,000m. pesetas over the period 1979–86. In addition to aid of 2,000m. Spanish pesetas in 1989, Spain also cancelled repayment of one-third of Equatorial Guinea's debt of 5,000m. pesetas, with the remaining two-thirds to be repaid over 14 years, with eight years' grace. In February 1990 Spain signed an agreement to provide a further US $100m. of aid, to be disbursed over four years, covering education, health, administrative reform and economic infrastructure. The Spanish government stated that this involved expenditure amounting to 11 times as much per caput as for any of the other hispanophone countries which receive Spanish assistance. In 1991 Spain waived a further one-third of the country's debt.

During the early 1990s Spanish assistance to Equatorial Guinea totalled about 350m. pesetas annually. However, in January 1994 Spain suspended one-half of its aid following a diplomatic contretemps. A tentative agreement for the gradual resumption of full assistance was made in mid-1994, and further negotiations were expected to take place in 1997. France is the second main provider of aid; French assistance rose sharply after Equatorial Guinea joined the various French-sponsored regional economic associations for Central Africa in 1983–85.

In January 1985 Equatorial Guinea entered the Franc Zone. The Banco de Guinea Ecuatorial (the former central bank and bank of issue) ceased operation, and the epkwele, which had been linked to the Spanish peseta, was replaced by the franc CFA at a rate of 4 bipkwele = 1 franc CFA. It was hoped that Equatorial Guinea's entry into the Franc Zone would bring the country out of isolation by encouraging foreign trade and investment. In July 1985 the 'Paris Club' of Western creditor governments granted a rescheduling, over 10 years, of 246m. French francs of debt, with a five-year period of grace. According to the World Bank, Equatorial Guinea's total external debt reached $293.0m. at the end of 1995, almost 200% of GNP, imposing a heavy burden on such an underdeveloped economy. According to the IMF, during 1991–95 total scheduled external debt servicing amounted to an annual average of 89% of GDP; however, total cash payments on the external debt (including payments on arrears) averaged some 14% of domestic revenue over the same period.

France has been displeased by Equatorial Guinea's inability to fulfil IMF loan conditions (see below) and by a persistent tendency for it to draw too heavily on the resources of the Franc Zone's regional central bank, the Banque des Etats de l'Afrique Centrale (BEAC), without providing adequate national accounts.

Loans and grants have come from a variety of other Western and Middle Eastern sources, as well as from China and Nigeria, but none on the scale of those provided by Spain and France. An international aid conference, held in Geneva in April 1982, aimed to provide $140m. for development projects. In November 1988 a second international aid conference pledged a total of US $63m. in support of Equatorial Guinea's medium-term investment programme (1989–91). In December 1988 the IMF granted a structural adjustment facility (SAF) of SDR 11.7m. (Equatorial Guinea had received its first IMF stand-by credit, totalling SDR 9.2m., in July 1985.) However, in February 1990 the IMF refused to make any further payments, and shortly afterwards a World Bank mission announced that it was not prepared to make any recommendation for the implementation of a structural adjustment programme. Both multilateral agencies declared themselves particularly dissatisfied with the government's failure to eradicate the budgetary deficit, which stood, according to BEAC estimates, at 2,512m. francs CFA in 1989. In 1990, when the budget deficit fell to an estimated 585m. francs CFA, the government adopted measures to reduce the deficit further which included liberalizing import prices, stimulating private investment and raising the tariffs charged by public utilities. By 1994 the budget, according to an optimistic estimate by the BEAC, showed a surplus of 1,169m. francs CFA; the surplus was estimated to have narrowed to 142m. francs CFA in 1995. However, figures from the IMF present a very different picture: in 1994 the overall budget deficit (including grants) stood at 3,950m. francs CFA on a commitment basis, and at 2,090m. francs CFA on a cash basis, whilst in 1995 the deficit was estimated at 4,595m. francs CFA on a commitment basis and at 9,689m. francs CFA on a cash basis (following substantial arrears payments brought about by the devaluation of the CFA franc). The multilateral agencies also expressed concern at the continuing deficit on the current account of the balance of payments, which stood at $24.66m. in 1991, although this has been offset, to some extent, by inflows of foreign aid.

The commencement of petroleum exports was expected to generate a significant improvement in both the balance of payments and budgetary deficits during the 1990s. As a result of this projected amelioration in the economic situation, the IMF agreed to unblock the disbursement of SAF funds in December 1991. The government introduced an economic programme for 1994–96, supported by an SDR 12.9m. three-year enhanced structural adjustment facility (ESAF) from the IMF, which aimed to accelerate the diversification of the economy and the reform of the public sector, and to restructure the financial sector. Under the programme it was expected that the real rate of economic growth could be increased while containing inflation at 35% and reducing the current account deficit. However, while petroleum exports had a significant effect on the deficit on the current account of the balance of payments, which decreased, according to the IMF, from US $45.5m. in 1991 to only $0.6m. in 1994, the sector had little direct impact on the budgetary deficit. In early 1997 there was still no agreement on how much tax was to be paid on oil revenue, and consequently none had ever been received by the government. Meanwhile, non-oil tax revenue was seriously eroded by a deteriorating customs administration, and by systematic tax evasion within the timber industry. While non-tax revenue from the petroleum sector did increase during 1992–95, it only amounted on average to some 10% of export earnings, which is low by regional standards.

The devaluation of the CFA franc has had a limited positive impact on Equatorial Guinea's economic prospects, although it has been found necessary to impose price restraints on bread, medicines and petroleum to protect vulnerable sections of the population from economic hardship brought about by the reduction in their consumer purchasing power. Products for export have been rendered more competitive on the international market and inflationary pressures have been successfully contained, with consumer prices increasing, according to estimates from the IMF, by only 11.4% in 1995, after a rise of 38.9% in 1994. However, recent improvements in the trade balance are in part the result of a decreased purchasing power brought about by reductions in foreign aid; the re-establishment of good relations with the international donor community remains a priority, especially given the reliance of the export base on timber and petroleum, and the finite nature of the reserves of these commodities. Greater public accountability in the use of government funds is also much to be desired, especially given frequent allegations of widespread corruption.

Statistical Survey

Source (unless otherwise stated): Dirección Técnica de Estadística, Secretaría de Estado para el Plan de Desarrollo Económico, Malabo.

AREA AND POPULATION

Area: 28,051 sq km: Río Muni 26,017 sq km, Bioko 2,017 sq km, Annobón 17 sq km.

Population: 246,941 (Río Muni 200,106, Bioko 44,820, Annobón 2,015) at December 1965 census; 300,000 (Río Muni 240,804, Bioko 57,190, Annobón 2,006), comprising 144,268 males and 155,732 females, at census of 4–17 July 1983. Source: Ministerio de Asuntos Exteriores, Madrid. 400,000 (UN estimate) at mid-1995.

Provinces (population, census of July 1983): Kié-Ntem 70,202, Litoral 66,370, Centro-Sur 52,393, Wele-Nzas 51,839, Bioko Norte 46,221, Bioko Sur 10,969, Annobón 2,006.

Principal towns (population at 1983 census): Malabo (capital) 15,253, Bata 24,100.

Births and Deaths (UN estimates, annual averages): Birth rate 43.8 per 1,000 in 1985–90, 43.5 in 1990–95; Death rate 19.6 per 1,000 in 1985–90, 18.0 in 1990–95. Source: UN, *World Population Prospects: The 1994 Revision*.

Expectation of life (UN estimates, years at birth, 1990–95): 48.0 (males 46.4; females 49.6) (Source: UN, *Demographic Yearbook*.)

Economically Active Population (persons aged 6 years and over, 1983 census): Agriculture, hunting, forestry and fishing 59,390; Mining and quarrying 126; Manufacturing 1,490; Electricity, gas and water 224; Construction 1,929; Trade, restaurants and hotels 3,059; Transport, storage and communications 1,752; Financing, insurance, real estate and business services 409; Community, social and personal services 8,377; Activities not adequately defined 984; Total employed 77,740 (males 47,893, females 29,847); Unemployed 24,825 (males 18,040, females 6,785); Total labour force 102,565 (males 65,933, females 36,632). Note: Figures are based on unadjusted census data, indicating a total population of 261,779. The adjusted total is 300,000. Source: International Labour Office, *Yearbook of Labour Statistics*.

AGRICULTURE, ETC.

Principal Crops (FAO estimates, '000 metric tons, 1995): Sweet potatoes 35; Cassava 47; Coconuts 8; Palm kernels 3; Bananas and plantains 17; Cocoa beans (unofficial estimate) 4; Green coffee 7. Source: FAO, *Production Yearbook*.

Livestock (FAO estimates, '000 head, year ending September 1994): Cattle 5; Pigs 5; Sheep 36; Goats 8. Source: FAO, *Production Yearbook*.

Forestry (1994): Roundwood removals (FAO estimates, '000 cu m): Fuel wood 447 (assumed to be unchanged since 1983); Sawlogs, veneer logs and logs for sleepers 267; Total 714. Source: FAO, *Yearbook of Forest Products*.

Fishing (FAO estimates, metric tons, live weight): Total catch 3,800 in 1993; 3,700 in 1994; 3,800 in 1995. Source: FAO, *Yearbook of Fishery Statistics*.

INDUSTRY

Palm oil (FAO estimates, '000 metric tons): 5.0 in 1993; 5.0 in 1994; 5.0 in 1995. Source: FAO, *Production Yearbook*.

Veneer sheets ('000 cubic metres): 7 in 1992; 8 in 1993; 8 in 1994. Source: FAO, *Yearbook of Forest Products*.

Electric energy (million kWh): 19 in 1992; 19 in 1993; 20 in 1994. Source: UN, *Industrial Commodity Statistics Yearbook*.

FINANCE

Currency and Exchange Rates: 100 centimes = 1 franc de la Coopération financière en Afrique centrale (CFA). *French Franc, Sterling and Dollar Equivalents* (31 March 1997): 1 French franc = 100 francs CFA; £1 sterling = 924.20 francs CFA; US $1 = 562.85 francs CFA; 1,000 francs CFA = £1.082 = $1.777. *Average Exchange Rate* (francs CFA per US dollar): 555.20 in 1994; 499.15 in 1995; 511.55 in 1996. *Note:* An exchange rate of 1 French franc = 50 francs CFA, established in 1948, remained in force until January 1994, when the CFA franc was devalued by 50%, with the exchange rate adjusted to 1 French franc = 100 francs CFA.

Budget (million francs CFA, 1995): *Revenue:* Petroleum sector 2,260; Taxation 8,395 (Taxes on income and profits 373; Taxes on domestic goods and services 3,223; Taxes on international trade 3,960; Other taxes 839); Other revenue 2,753; Total revenue 13,408, excl. grants from abroad (2,134). *Expenditure:* Current expenditure 14,396 (Wages and salaries 3,609; Other goods and services 5,068; Subsidies and transfers 893; Interest payments 4,826); Capital expenditure 3,628; Unclassified expenditure 2,114; Total expenditure 20,138. Source: IMF, *Equatorial Guinea—Recent Economic Developments* (December 1996).

International Reserves (US $ million at 31 December 1995): IMF special drawing rights 0.01; Foreign exchange 0.03; Total 0.04. Source: IMF, *International Financial Statistics*.

Money Supply ('000 million francs CFA at 31 December 1995): Currency outside deposit money banks 6.78; Demand deposits at deposit money banks 2.73; Total money 9.50. Source: IMF, *International Financial Statistics*.

Cost of Living (Consumer price index for Africans in Malabo; base: 1990 = 100): 96.84 in 1991; 89.90 in 1992; 93.49 in 1993. Source: IMF, *International Financial Statistics*.

Expenditure on the Gross Domestic Product (million francs CFA at current prices, 1994): Government final consumption expenditure 11,600; Private final consumption expenditure 42,700; Gross capital formation 17,300; *Total domestic expenditure* 71,600; Exports of goods and services 39,100; *Less* Imports of goods and services 39,200; *GDP in purchasers' values* 71,500; GDP at constant 1985 prices 49,237. Source: IMF, *Equatorial Guinea—Recent Economic Developments* (December 1996).

Gross Domestic Product by Economic Activity (million francs CFA at current prices, 1994): Agriculture, hunting, forestry and fishing 33,893; Petroleum sector 14,446; Manufacturing 835; Electricity, gas and water 2,452; Construction 3,391; Trade, restaurants and hotels 6,567; Transport and communications 1,452; Finance, insurance, real estate and business services 1,497; Government services 3,472; Other services 2,170; *Sub-total* 70,175; Import duties 1,330; *GDP in purchasers' values* 71,507. Source: IMF, *Equatorial Guinea—Recent Economic Developments* (December 1996).

Balance of Payments (US $ million, 1991): Exports of goods f.o.b. 35.75; Imports of goods f.o.b. −59.56; *Trade balance* −23.81; Exports of services 6.19; Imports of services −43.03; *Balance on goods and services* −60.65; Other income paid −9.41; *Balance on goods, services and income* −70.06. Current transfers received 63.35. Current transfers paid −17.94; *Current balance* −24.66; Direct investment abroad −0.11; Direct investment from abroad 42.26; Other investment assets −1.49; Other investment liabilities −8.48; Net errors and omissions −30.72; *Overall balance* −23.19. Source: IMF, *International Financial Statistics*.

EXTERNAL TRADE

Principal Commodities (distribution by SITC, US $ '000, 1990): *Imports c.i.f.:* Food and live animals 4,340; Beverages and tobacco 3,198, (Alcoholic beverages 2,393); Crude materials (inedible) except fuels 2,589 (Crude fertilizers and crude minerals 2,102); Petroleum and petroleum products 4,738; Chemicals and related products 2,378; Basic manufactures 3,931; Machinery and transport equipment 35,880 (Road vehicles and parts 3,764, Ships, boats and floating structures 24,715); Miscellaneous manufactured articles 2,725; Total (incl. others) 61,601. *Exports f.o.b.:* Food and live animals 6,742 (Cocoa 6,372); Beverages and tobacco 3,217 (Tobacco and tobacco manufactures 2,321); Crude materials (inedible) except fuels 20,017 (Sawlogs and veneer logs 12,839, Textile fibres and waste 7,078); Machinery and transport equipment 24,574 (Ships, boats and floating structures 23,852); Total (incl. others) 61,705. Source: UN, *International Trade Statistics Yearbook*.

1995: (US $ '000): Imports c.i.f. 75,900; Exports f.o.b. 86,440. Source: IMF, *Equatorial Guinea—Recent Economic Developments* (December 1996).

Principal Trading Partners (US $'000, 1991): *Imports c.i.f.:* Cameroon 29,141; France 5,915; Italy 3,001; Liberia 22,032; Spain 11,640; USA 33,366; Total (incl. others) 113,545. *Exports f.o.b.:* Cameroon 47,212; Gabon 2,389; Netherlands 2,103; Nigeria 8,955; São Tomé and Príncipe 1,952; Spain 11,645; Total (incl. others) 86,151. Source: UN, *International Trade Statistics Yearbook*.

TRANSPORT

Shipping: *Merchant Fleet* (displacement, '000 grt at 31 December 1996): 20.6. Source: Lloyd's, *World Fleet Statistics*. International Sea-borne Freight Traffic ('000 metric tons, 1990): Goods loaded 110; Goods unloaded 64. Source: UN, *Monthly Bulletin of Statistics*.

Civil Aviation (traffic on scheduled services, 1994): Passengers carried ('000) 14; Passenger-km (million) 7. Source: UN, *Statistical Yearbook*.

COMMUNICATIONS MEDIA

1994: 165,000 radio receivers in use; 4,000 television receivers in use; 3,000 main telephone lines in use (Source: UN, *Statistical Yearbook*); 1 daily newspaper (estimated circulation 1,000); Book production 17 titles (1988). Source: UNESCO, *Statistical Yearbook*.

EDUCATION

Primary (1993/94): Schools 781; Teachers 1,381; Pupils 75,751.
Secondary and Further (1993/94): Teachers 588; Pupils 16,616.
Higher (1990/91): Teachers 58; Pupils 578.
Source: UNESCO, *Statistical Yearbook*.

Directory

The Constitution

The present Constitution was approved by a national referendum on 16 November 1991 and amended in January 1995. It provided for the introduction of multi-party democracy and for the establishment of an 80-member legislative House of Representatives. The term of office of the President is seven years, renewable on an indefinite number of occasions. The President is immune from prosecution for offences committed before, during or after his tenure of the post. The House of Representatives serves for a term of five years. Both the President and the House of Representatives are directly elected by universal adult suffrage. The President appoints a Council of Ministers, headed by a Prime Minister, from among the members of the House of Representatives.

The Government

HEAD OF STATE

President and Supreme Commander of the Armed Forces: Gen. (TEODORO) OBIANG NGUEMA MBASOGO (assumed office 25 August 1979; elected President 25 June 1989; re-elected 25 February 1996).

COUNCIL OF MINISTERS
(July 1997)

Prime Minister and Head of Government: ANGEL SERAFIN SERICHE DOUGAN.

Deputy Prime Minister and Minister of Civil Service and Administrative Reform: FRANCISCO JAVIER NGOMO MBENGONO.

Minister of State for Missions: ALEJANDRO EVUNA OWONO ASANGONO.

Minister of State for Foreign Affairs and Co-operation: MIGUEL OYONO NDONG MIFUMU.

Minister of State for the Interior and Local Communities: JULIO NDONG ELA MANGUE.

Minister of State for Youth and Sports: (vacant).

Minister of State for Labour and Social Security: CARMELO MODU AKUNE.

Minister of State for Planning and Economic Resources: (vacant).

Secretary-General of the Presidency: SALOMON NGUEMA OWONO.

Minister of Parliamentary Relations and Legislative Co-ordination: ANTONIO PASCUAL OKO EBOBO.

Minister of Transport and Communications: FRANCISCO ABAGA NDONG.

Minister of Justice: IGNACIO MINLANE NTANG.

Minister of Education and Science: RICARDO MANGUE OBAMA NFUE.

Minister of Health: DARÍO TADEO NDONG OLOMO.

Minister of Mines and Energy: JUAN OLO MBA NSENG.

Minister of Public Works, Housing and Town Planning: PEDRO NZE OBAMA ANGONO.

Minister of Agriculture and Livestock: VIDAL DJONI BECOBA.

Minister of Information: FRANCISCO PASCUAL EYEGUE OBAMA ASUE.

Minister of Industry and Small- and Medium-sized Enterprises: CONSTANTINO EKONG ZUE.

Minister of Culture and Francophone Affairs: PEDRO CRISTINO BUERIBERI.

Minister of Social Affairs and Women's Affairs: MARGARITA ALENE MBA.

Minister of the Economy and Finance: MARCELINO OYONO NTUTUMU.

MINISTRIES

All ministries are in Malabo.

Ministry of Agriculture and Livestock: Apdo 504, Malabo.

Ministry of the Economy and Finance: Malabo; tel. (9) 31-05; fax (9) 32-05.

Ministry of Foreign Affairs and Co-operation: Malabo; tel. (9) 32-20.

Ministry of Mines and Energy: Calle 12 de Octobre s/n, Malabo; tel. (9) 35-67; fax (9) 33-53.

Legislature

CÁMARA DE REPRESENTANTES DEL PUEBLO
(House of Representatives)

Speaker: (vacant).

General Election, 21 November 1993

Party	Seats
Partido Democrático de Guinea Ecuatorial (PDGE)	68
Convención Socialdemocrática Popular (CSDP)	6
Unión Democrática y Social de Guinea Ecuatorial (UDS)	5
Convención Liberal Democrática (CLD)	1
Total	80

Political Organizations

A plural political system has operated since 1992.

Accion Popular (AP): Pres. MIGUEL ESONO.

Alianza Democratica Progresista (ADP): Pres. VICTORINO BOLEKIA.

Alianza Nacional para la Restauración Democrática de Guinea Ecuatorial (ANRDGE): 95 Ruperto Chapi, 28100 Madrid, Spain; tel. (1) 663-60-13; f. 1974; Sec.-Gen. LUIS ONDO AYANG.

Convención Liberal Democrática (CLD): Pres. ALFONSO NSUE MIFUMU.

Convención Socialdemocrática Popular (CSDP): Leader SECUNDINO OYONO.

Convergencia para la Democracia Social (CPDS): Pres. SANTIAGO OBAMA; Sec.-Gen. PLÁCIDO MIKÓ ABOGO.

Coordinación Democrática de los Partidos de Oposición de Guinea Ecuatorial: based in Libreville, Gabon; f. 1991; coalition of the following groups:

- **Frente Democrático para la Reforma:** Sec.-Gen. BIYONGO BITUNG.
- **Movimento Nacional para la Nueva Liberación de Guinea Ecuatorial.**
- **Partido Republicano.**
- **Partido de Reunificación (PR).**
- **Unión para la Democracia y el Desarrollo Social (UDDS):** f. 1990; Sec.-Gen. ANTONIO SIBACHA BUEICHEKU.

Foro Democrático de Guinea Ecuatorial (FODEGE): seeks co-operation with PDGE; Sec.-Gen. JOAQUIN ELEMA BORENGUE.

Fuerza Demócrata Republicana: f. 1995; Leader FELIPE ONDO OBIANG.

Movimento para la Autodeterminación de la Isla de Bioko (MAIB): f. 1993 by Bubi interests seeking independence of Bioko; Spokesman JOAQUIN MAHO.

Partido de la Convergencia Social Demócrata (PCSD): Pres. BUENAVENTURA MOSUY.

Partido Democrático de Guinea Ecuatorial (PDGE): Malabo; f. 1987; sole legal party 1987–92; Chair. Gen. (TEODORO) OBIANG NGUEMA MBASOGO.

Partido Social Demócrata (PSD): Pres. BENJAMÍN BALINGA.

Partido Socialista (PS): Pres. TOMÁS MACHEBA.

Partido del Progreso de Guinea Ecuatorial (PPGE): f. 1983; Leaders BASILIO AVA EWORO and DOMINGO ABUY.

Unión Democrática Nacional (UDEMA): Pres. JOSÉ MECHEBA.

Unión Democrática y Social de Guinea Ecuatorial (UDS): Pres. CARMELO MODÚ AKUNE.

Unión Popular (UP): f. 1992; Leader ANDRÉS MOISÉS MBA.

Diplomatic Representation

EMBASSIES IN EQUATORIAL GUINEA

Cameroon: 37 Calle Rey Boncore, Apdo 292, Malabo; tel. and fax (9) 23-64; Ambassador: JOHN NCHOTU AKUM.

China, People's Republic: Malabo; Ambassador: XU SHAOHAI.

France: Carreterra del Aeropuerto, Malabo; tel. (9) 20-05; Ambassador: GÉRARD BRUNET.

Gabon: Apdo 648, Douala, Malabo; tel. (9) 420; telex 1125; Ambassador: JEAN-BAPTISTE MBATCHI.

Korea, Democratic People's Republic: Malabo; Ambassador: RYOM THAE RYUL.

Nigeria: 4 Paseo de los Cocoteros, Apdo 78, Malabo; tel. (9) 23-86; Ambassador: JOHN SHINKAME.

Russia: Malabo; Ambassador: LEV ALEKSANDROVICH VAKHRAMEYEV.

Spain: Parque de las Avenidas de Africa, Malabo; tel. (9) 20-20; fax (9) 26-11; Ambassador: JOSÉ MARÍA OTERO DE LEÓN.

Judicial System

The structure of Judicial Administration was established in 1981. The Supreme Tribunal in Malabo, consisting of a President of the Supreme Tribunal, the Presidents of the three chambers (civil, criminal and administrative), and two magistrates from each chamber, is the highest court of appeal, There are Territorial High Courts in Malabo and Bata, which also sit as courts of appeal. Courts of first instance sit in Malabo and Bata, and may be convened in the other provincial capitals. Local courts may be convened when necessary.

President of the Supreme Tribunal: ALFREDO KING TOMÁS.

Religion

An estimated 90% of the population are adherents of the Roman Catholic Church. Traditional forms of worship are also followed.

CHRISTIANITY

The Roman Catholic Church

Equatorial Guinea comprises one archdiocese and two dioceses. There were an estimated 364,411 adherents in the country at 31 December 1995.

Bishops' Conference: Arzobispado, Apdo 106, Malabo; tel. (9) 24-16; f. 1984; Pres. Rt Rev. ANACLETO SIMA NGUA, Bishop of Bata.

Archbishop of Malabo: Most Rev. ILDEFONSO OBAMA OBONO, Arzobispado, Apdo 106, Malabo; tel. (9) 29-09; fax (9) 21-76.

Protestant Church

Iglesia Reformada Evangélica de Guinea Ecuatorial (Evangelical Church of Equatorial Guinea): Apdo 195, Malabo; f. 1960; c. 8,000 mems; Sec.-Gen. Rev. JAIME SIPOTO.

The Press

El Patio: Apdo 180, Malabo; tel. (9) 27-20; fax (9) 29-32; Spanish; cultural review; quarterly; publ. by Centro Cultural Hispano-Guineano; Editor DONATO NDONGO-BIDYOGO.

El Sol: 24 Calle Camerún, Apdo 944, Malabo; f. 1994; Spanish; weekly; Chief Editor NVO MBOMIO AVOMO; circ. 3,500.

Hoja Parroquial: Malabo; weekly.

La Gaceta: Malabo; f. 1996; bi-weekly.

La Verdad: Malabo; opposition monthly; publ. by the Convergencia para la Democracia Social; Editor PLÁCIDO MIKÓ ABOGO.

Voz del Pueblo: Malabo; publ. by the Partido Democrático de Guinea Ecuatorial.

FOREIGN NEWS BUREAU

Agencia EFE (Spain): 50 Calle del Presidente Nasser, Malabo; tel. (9) 31-65; Bureau Chief DONATO NDONGO-BIDYOGO.

Publisher

Centro Cultural Hispano-Guineano: Apdo 180, Malabo; tel. (9) 27-20; fax (9) 29-32.

Radio and Television

There were an estimated 165,000 radio receivers and 4,000 television receivers in use in 1994.

RADIO

Radio Africa and Radio East Africa: Apdo 851, Malabo; e-mail pabcomain@aol.com; commercial station; owned by Pan American Broadcasting; music and religious programmes in English.

Radio Nacional de Guinea Ecuatorial: Apdo 749, Barrio Comandachina, Bata; tel. (8) 83-82; fax (8) 20-93; and Apdo 195, 90 ave 30 de Agostó, Malabo; tel. (9) 22-60; fax (9) 20-97; govt-controlled; commercial station; programmes in Spanish, French and vernacular languages; Dir (Bata) SEBASTIAN ELÓ ASEKO; Dir (Malabo) JUAN EYENE OPKUA NGUEMA.

TELEVISION

Television Nacional: Malabo; Dir ANTONIO NKULU OYE.

Finance

(cap. = capital; p.u. = paid up; res = reserves; m. = million; br. = branch; amounts in francs CFA)

BANKING

Central Bank

Banque des Etats de l'Afrique Centrale (BEAC): Apdo 510 Malabo; tel. (9) 20–10; telex 5407; fax (9) 20–06; headquarters in Yaoundé, Cameroon; f. 1973 as the bank of issue for mem. states of the Customs and Economic Union of Central Africa (UDEAC), comprising Cameroon, the Central African Republic, Chad, the Congo, Equatorial Guinea and Gabon; cap. and res 204,933m. (Dec. 1995); Gov. JEAN-FÉLIX MAMALEPOT; Dir in Equatorial Guinea MARTÍN-CRISANTO EBE MBA.

Commercial Banks

Banco Meridien BIAO Guinea Ecuatorial (BMB-GE): 6 Calle de Argelia, Apdo 686, Malabo; tel. (9) 28-87; telex 5403; fax (9) 27-42; f. 1986; cap. p.u. 300m. (Dec. 1993); Pres. CASTRO NVONO AKELE; Gen. Man. CHARLES SANLAVILLE; brs in Bata and Malabo.

Caisse Commune d'Epargne et d'Investissement Guinea Ecuatorial (CCEI): Malabo; f. 1995.

Development Bank

Banque de Développement des Etats de l'Afrique Centrale (see Franc Zone, p. 120).

Financial Institution

Caja Autónoma de Amortización de la Deuda Pública: Ministry of the Economy and Finance, Malabo; tel. (9) 31-05; fax (9) 32-05; management of state funds; Dir PATRICIO EKA NGUEMA.

Trade and Industry

Cámara de Comercio, Agrícola y Forestal de Malabo: Apdo 51, Malabo; tel. (9) 151.

Cámaras Oficiales Agrícolas de Guinea: Bioko and Bata; purchase of cocoa and coffee from indigenous planters, who are partially grouped in co-operatives.

Empresa General de Industria y Comercio (EGISCA): Malabo; f. 1986; parastatal body jtly operated with the French Société pour l'Organisation, l'Aménagement et le Développement des Industries Alimentaires et Agricoles (SOMDIA); import-export agency.

INPROCAO: Malabo; production, marketing and distribution of cocoa.

Oficina para la Cooperación con Guinea Ecuatorial (OCGE): Malabo; f. 1981; administers bilateral aid from Spain.

Sociedad Anónima de Desarrollo del Comercio (SOADECO-Guinée): Malabo; f. 1986; parastatal body jtly operated with the French Société pour l'Organisation, l'Aménagement et le Développement des Industries Alimentaires et Agricoles (SOMDIA); development of commerce.

Total Ecuatoguineana de Gestion (GE-Total): Malabo; f. 1984; 50% state-owned, 50% by CFP-Total (France); petroleum marketing and distribution; Chair. of Bd of Dirs Minister of Public Works, Housing and Town Planning.

TRADE UNIONS

A law permitting the establishment of trade unions was passed in 1992.

Transport

RAILWAYS

There are no railways in Equatorial Guinea.

ROADS

In 1995 there were an estimated 2,820 km of roads and tracks.

Bioko: a semi-circular tarred road serves the northern part of the island from Malabo down to Batete in the west and from Malabo to Bacake Grande in the east, with a feeder road from Luba to Moka and Bahía de la Concepción.

Río Muni: a tarred road links Bata with the town of Mbini (Río Benito) in the west; another road, partly tarred, links Bata with the frontier post of Ebebiyín in the east and then continues into Gabon; other earth roads join Acurenam, Mongomo and Anisok.

SHIPPING

The main ports are Bata (general cargo and most of the country's export timber), Malabo (general), Luba (bananas, timber), Mbini and Cogo (timber). A regular monthly service is operated by the Spanish Compañía Transmediterránea from Barcelona, calling at Malabo and Bata, and by other carriers.

CIVIL AVIATION

There is an international airport at Malabo. A larger international airport at Bata, constructed with Italian aid, was to be completed in the mid-1990s. The national carrier, Compañia Ecuato-Guineana de Aviación (which has been in liquidation since 1990), continues to provide limited regional and domestic services. During the mid-1990s scheduled services between Malabo and Madrid were being operated by IBERIA, Líneas Aéreas de España, while Cameroon Airlines (Cam-Air) carried passengers between Malabo and Douala (Cameroon) and provided air freight facilities linking Malabo with destinations in the EU and the USA. Air Gabon operates weekly services between Malabo, Bata, Douala and Libreville (Gabon).

EGA-Ecuato Guineana (Ecuato-Guineana de Aviación): Apdo 665, Malabo; tel. (9) 23-25; fax (9) 33-13; regional and domestic passenger and cargo services.

Tourism

Few foreigners visit Equatorial Guinea, and tourism remains undeveloped.

Defence

In August 1996 there were 1,100 men in the army, 120 in the navy and 100 in the air force. There was also a paramilitary force of 200–400 men, referred to both as 'Antorchas' and 'Ninjas', which was trained by French military personnel. Military service is voluntary. Spain and Morocco have provided military advisers and training since 1979. Military aid has also been received from the USA.

Defence Expenditure: Estimated at 1,200m. francs CFA in 1996.

Supreme Commander of the Armed Forces: Gen. (TEODORO) OBIANG NGUEMA MBASOGO.

Education

Education, which is provided free of charge, is officially compulsory for five years between the ages of six and 11 years. Primary education starts at six years of age and normally lasts for five years. Secondary education, beginning at the age of 11, spans a seven-year period, comprising a first cycle of four years and a second cycle of three years. In 1982 the total enrolment at primary and secondary schools was equivalent to 81% of the school-age population. In 1993/94 primary education in nine grades was provided for 75,751 pupils in 781 schools with 1,381 teachers. More advanced education for 16,616 pupils was provided in that year, with 588 teachers. In 1990 there were 578 students in higher education, the majority enrolled at distance-learning institutions.

Since 1979, assistance in the development of the educational system has been provided by Spain, which had 100 teaching staff working in Equatorial Guinea in 1986. Two higher education centres, at Bata and Malabo, are administered by the Spanish Universidad Nacional de Educación a Distancia. The French government also provides considerable financial assistance, and French was expected to become a compulsory subject in Equato-Guinean schools during the 1990s. In 1995, according to UNESCO estimates, the average rate of adult illiteracy was 21.5% (males 10.4%; females 31.9%). In 1993 expenditure on education by the government amounted to 734m. francs CFA (5.6% of total public expenditure).

Bibliography

Agencia Española de Cooperación Internacional. *Segundo plano marco de cooperación entre el Reino de España y la República de Guinea Ecuatorial.* Madrid, AECI, 1990.

Castro A., Mariano, and de la Calle Muñoz, M. L. *Geografía de Guinea Ecuatorial.* Madrid, Programa de Colaboración Educativa con Guinea Ecuatorial, 1985.

Castroviejo Bolívar, Javier, Juste Balleste, Javier, and Castelo Alvarez, Ramón. *Investigación y conservación de la naturaleza en Guinea Ecuatorial.* Madrid, Oficina de Cooperación con Guinea Ecuatorial, 1986.

Cohen, R. (Ed.) *African Islands and Enclaves.* London, Sage Publications, 1983.

Cronjé, S. *Equatorial Guinea: The Forgotten Dictatorship.* London, 1976.

Economist Intelligence Unit. *Gabon, Equatorial Guinea, Country Profile.* London, annual.

Eman, A. *Equatorial Guinea during the Macías Nguema régime.* Washington DC, 1983.

Fegley, R. *Equatorial Guinea: An African tragedy.* New York, Peter Lang, 1989.

González-Echegaray, C. *Estudios Guineos: Filología.* Madrid, IDEA, 1964.

Estudios Guineos: Etnología. Madrid, IDEA, 1964.

Jakobeit, C. 'Äquatorialguinea' in Hanisch, R. and Jakobeit, C. (Eds). *Der Kakaoweltmarkt,* Vol. 2. Hamburg, Deutsches Übersee-institut, 1991.

Klitgaard, R. *Tropical Gangsters.* London, I. B. Tauris, 1990.

Liniger-Goumaz, M. *Guinea Ecuatorial: Bibliografía General.* 5 vols. Berne and Geneva, 1976–85.

Equatorial Guinea: An African Historical Dictionary. Metuchen, NJ, Scarecrow Press, 1979.

De la Guinée équatoriale nguemiste. Eléments pour le dossier de l'afro-fascisme. Geneva, Editions du Temps, 1983.

Statistics of Nguemist Equatorial Guinea. Geneva, Editions du Temps, 1986.

Small is not always Beautiful: The Story of Equatorial Guinea. London, Hurst, 1988.

Martín de Molino, A. *Los Bubis, ritos y creencias.* Malabo, Centro Cultural Hispano-Guineano, 1989.

Miranda Díaz, M. *España en el continente africano.* Madrid, IDEA, 1963.

Ndongo Bidyogo, D. *Historia y Tragedia de Guinea Ecuatorial.* Madrid, Cambio, 1977.

Nguema-Obam, P. *Aspects de la religion fang.* Paris, Editions Karthala, 1984.

Pélissier, R. *Los Territorios Españoles de Africa.* Madrid, 1964.

Africana. Bibliographies sur l'Afrique luso-hispanophone (1800–1980). Orgeval, Editions Pélissier, 1981.

Sundiata, I. K. *Equatorial Guinea.* Boulder, CO, Westview Press, 1990.

de Unzueta y Yuste, A. *Islas del Golfo de Guinea (Elobeyes, Corisco, Annobón, Príncipe y Santo Tomé).* Madrid, Institito de Estudios Políticos, 1945.

Historia geográfica de Fernando Póo. Madrid, IDEA, 1947.

ERITREA

Physical and Social Geography

MILES SMITH-MORRIS

The State of Eritrea, which formally acceded to independence on 24 May 1993, covers an area of 121,144 sq km (46,774 sq miles). Its territory includes the Dahlak islands, a low-lying coralline archipelago offshore from Massawa. Eritrea, which has a coastline on the Red Sea extending for almost 1,000 km, is bounded to the north-west by Sudan, to the south and west by Ethiopia, and to the south-east by Djibouti. The terrain comprises the northern end of the Ethiopian plateau (rising to more than 2,000 m above sea-level), where most cultivation takes place, and a low-lying semi-desert coastal strip, much of which supports only pastoralism. Lowland areas have less than 500 mm of rainfall per year, compared with 1,000 mm in the highlands. Average annual temperatures range from 17°C in the highlands to 30°C in Massawa. The Danakil depression in the south-east descends to more than 130 m below sea-level and experiences some of the highest temperatures recorded on earth, frequently exceeding 50°C. Much of the coniferous forest that formerly covered the slopes of the highlands has been destroyed by settlement and cultivation; soil erosion is a severe problem.

The extent of Eritrea's natural resources awaits fuller exploration and evaluation. Copper ores and gold were mined from the Eritrean plateau in prehistoric times and there has been some extraction of iron ore, but the study and exploitation of the country's mineral resources were halted by the war for independence. The Dallol depression, south of Massawa, is known to have valuable potash deposits. Some exploration for petroleum has taken place in Red Sea coastal areas; oil seepages and offshore natural gas finds have been recorded.

The population of Eritrea was enumerated at just over 2.7m. in the Ethiopian census of 1984, but the war for independence resulted in large-scale population movements. Some 500,000 refugees fled to neighbouring Sudan and a significant, but unquantified, number of Eritreans have remained in Ethiopia. At mid-1991, according to official Ethiopian sources, the population of the Eritrean territory was estimated at 3,435,500. A total of 1.2m. people registered to vote in the April 1993 referendum, 860,000 of them within Eritrea, leading to estimates of a domestic population of about 2m. At mid-1995, according to UN estimates, Eritrea's population totalled 3,531,000. The population is fairly evenly divided between Tigrinya-speaking Christians, the traditional inhabitants of the highlands, and the Muslim communities of the western lowlands, northern highlands and east coast.

Recent History

ALAN RAKE

Modern Eritrea dates from the establishment of an Italian colony at the end of the 19th century. From a small concession gained near Assab in 1869, the Italians extended their control to Massawa in 1885 and to most of Eritrea by 1889. In the same year the Ethiopian emperor, Menelik, and the Italian government signed the Treaty of Uccialli, which effectively recognized Italian control over Eritrea (and from which Italy derived its subsequent claim to a protectorate over Ethiopia). The Eritrea colony was formed in an area where, at times in the past, the peoples had had varying and discontinuous tributary relations with Ethiopian empires to the south, the Ottoman empire and Egypt on the Red Sea coast and various Sudanic empires to the west and north-west. Eritrea's entanglement with these different neighbouring political units prior to colonial rule brought forth highly contested versions of pre-colonial history, the most contentious of which was the Ethiopian claim that all of Eritrea had been an integral part of historic Ethiopia. This claim for sovereignty was as spurious as the claim that Eritrea had previously constituted a distinct entity. There were and are religious beliefs and practices common to Ethiopian and Eritrean Orthodox Christians, and Tigrinya, an Ethiopian language, is spoken both in highland Eritrea and in the most northerly Ethiopian province of Tigre. These cultural and religious ties, however, do not extend to other communities in Ethiopia. Similarly, large parts of Eritrea, notably the north and west, have had, at most, no more than minimal historic and cultural links to Ethiopia. Nevertheless, history provided the setting for the subsequent political and military struggle between Eritrean nationalists and Ethiopia.

The period of Italian rule (1889–1941) and the subsequent years under British military administration (1941–52) created a society, economy and polity more advanced than in the semi-feudal Ethiopian empire. Under Italian rule the rudiments of an urban social and economic order were founded, and in the British period political parties and trade unions were permitted and a free press was established as, successively, the victorious Allied powers and the UN discussed the future of the former Italian colony. Ethiopia pressed its territorial claims and mobilized support for political union largely among the Christian highlanders. The strategic interests of the USA and its influence in the newly-founded UN resulted in a compromise, in the form of a federation between Eritrea and Ethiopia. There was, however, no provision for proper federal institutions. Emperor Haile Selassie, an autocratic ruler, set about stifling Eritrean autonomy until, in 1962, its status was reduced to that of an Ethiopian province.

THE LIBERATION STRUGGLE

The dissolution of the federation brought forth a more militant Eritrean nationalism, whose political roots had been established during the process of consultation for the disposal of the Italian colony in the latter part of the period of British rule. The Eritrean Liberation Movement, founded in 1958, was succeeded by the Eritrean Liberation Front (ELF), which began an armed struggle in September 1961. Organizational and ideological differences erupted into violence within the ELF in the mid-1960s, as the result of demands for reform from the increasing numbers of educated guerrilla fighters, particularly those from the Christian highlands and the Muslim eastern lowland towns. A reformist group separated from the ELF and formed the Popular Liberation Forces (renamed the Eritrean People's Liberation Front—EPLF, in 1977). A major consequence of the split was the civil war of 1972–74. Some reformists, however, remained within the ELF, although most of these eventually left in two stages, the first group breaking away in 1977–78 and the second (the Sagem group joining the EPLF) in 1985, following a second civil war. These desertions destroyed the

ELF as a coherent military organization, although a number of disaffected factions remained loyal to it and suspicious of the EPLF. The most influential groups remaining outside the EPLF have been those associated with Ahmed Nasser, leader of the ELF–Revolutionary Council (ELF–RC), and an Islamic movement which emerged during the 1980s among refugees in Sudan. The EPLF leadership consolidated a highly centralized and disciplined political and military organization, in contrast to the more loosely organized and factionalized ELF.

The course of the 1974 revolution in Ethiopia and its violent aftermath brought thousands of new recruits into the resistance groups. Even greater numbers of recruits joined the EPLF after the Mengistu regime launched its 'red terror' campaign in Asmara, and following its capture of smaller cities such as Keren and Decamhare in 1977. The retreat from the cities and liberated highland areas in 1978 brought with it thousands of young peasants, both male and female. From 1978 onwards the EPLF consolidated the defence of its base area in the north. Through the 1980s the EPLF pushed back the Ethiopian forces on all fronts, capturing large quantities of heavy artillery and tanks, and transforming itself from a guerrilla force into a regular army. Ethiopian defeats gave the EPLF control of the north, the west (formerly the ELF's heartland) and, finally, the east coast with the capture of Massawa port in 1990. The EPLF broke through the Decamhare front in May 1991 and entered Asmara, the capital. The retreating Ethiopian forces left the city largely undamaged. The discipline of the Eritrean People's Liberation Army (EPLA) and the extensive network of secret cells in the capital helped to ensure a smooth transition from liberation movement to government.

Concurrent with the liberation of Asmara in 1991 was the London Conference under the chairmanship of the US assistant secretary of state for Africa. Representatives of the EPLF attended in a delegation separate from the Ethiopian People's Revolutionary Democratic Front, now in control of Ethiopia and sympathetic to Eritrean nationalist aspirations. Both the USA and the Ethiopian delegation accepted the EPLF as the provisional government, and the latter agreed to hold a referendum on independence in 1993. Ethiopian assent to this process played an important role in the international legitimation of Eritrea's path to independence. In advance of the referendum, the EPLF formed a government and established ministries, most of whose key personnel were drawn from the EPLF. Although the international and regional political context was favourable for the transition to independence, the international economic context, prolonged warfare, drought and the legacy of neglect and destruction left by the Ethiopian forces placed the new government in straitened circumstances; 80% of the population were still dependent on food aid and urban economic activity had virtually ceased. Over and above these domestic problems was the task of attracting back and reintegrating around 750,000 refugees. Of these, there were about 500,000 in neighbouring Sudan, 90% of whom would require extensive financial assistance to return. An additional legacy of war was the scale of fatalities, which have been estimated at 60,000–75,000.

In the absence of any significant sources of domestic revenue for reconstruction, the task of rebuilding fell largely on the 75,000-strong EPLA, the members of which received a small stipend for their work. Administrative and technical cadres have taken government positions, skilled fighter-workers have been used to reconstruct manufacturing industry and many ordinary fighters have been drafted to undertake the arduous work of road and other infrastructural repair. Finance for reconstruction has come largely from contributions by Eritreans abroad and from assistance by foreign governments and non-governmental organizations. Without full legal sovereignty, access to loans and assistance from international financial institutions was limited, but in 1993 this formal constraint was removed. During 23–25 April a UN-supervised referendum took place in an atmosphere of national celebration. Of the 1,102,410 Eritreans who voted, 99.8% endorsed national independence. The anniversary of the liberation of Asmara, 24 May, was proclaimed Independence Day, and on 28 May the State of Eritrea formally attained international recognition.

INDEPENDENCE AND TRANSITIONAL GOVERNMENT

Following Eritrea's accession to independence, a four-year transitional period was declared, during which preparations were to proceed for establishing a constitutional and pluralist political system. At the apex of the transitional government were three state institutions: the consultative council (the executive authority formed from the ministers, provincial governors and heads of government commissions); the national assembly (the legislative authority formed from the central committee of the EPLF together with 30 members from the provincial assemblies and an additional 30 individuals selected by the central committee); and the judiciary. One of the national assembly's first acts was the election of a head of state. To little surprise, Issaias Afewerki, the secretary-general of the EPLF, was elected, by a margin of 99 votes to five.

Internal Politics

President Afewerki appointed a new state council in early June 1993, comprising 14 ministers (all members of the EPLF politburo) and 10 regional governors. Ramadan Muhammad Nur was removed from the politically sensitive post of governor of Danakil province (where he had successfully contained Afar nationalism) and was appointed minister of local government. Another prominent EPLF member, Petros Solomon, was allocated the defence portfolio. The third congress of the EPLF was convened at Nakfa, in Sahel province, in February 1994. There the EPLF effected the formal transformation from a military front to a national movement for peace and democracy (the People's Front for Democracy and Justice–PFDJ), hoping to embrace all Eritreans (with the exception of those accused of collaboration during the liberation struggle). The party congress also confirmed its support for a plural political system which was to be included in the final draft of a new constitution, which (together with legislation to regulate the formation of political parties) was to be submitted for approval by a national referendum. Afewerki was elected chairman of an 18-member executive committee (while remaining head of state, and leader of the PFDJ). A 75-member PFDJ central committee was also elected (an additional 75 members were to be elected by PFDJ regional committees).

In March 1994 the national assembly adopted a series of resolutions whereby the former executive body, the consultative council, was formally superseded by a 16-member state council. (Former government authorities with responsibility for transport and tourism were to be upgraded to ministerial level.) Other measures adopted by resolutions of the assembly included the creation of a 50-member constitutional commision, and the establishment of a committee charged with the reorganization of the country's administrative divisions. It was also decided that the national assembly would henceforth comprise 75 members of the PFDJ central committee, and 75 directly elected members. However, no mechanism was announced for their election, and in the interim period membership of the assembly remained unchanged. All but eight of the 50-member constitutional commission were government appointees, and there was no provision for any opposition participation in the interim system. Later in the month Afewerki carried out a ministerial reshuffle. The reorganization was, however, widely interpreted as an attempt to formalize a separation of the functions of the government and the PFDJ executive. Ramadan Muhammad Nur left the government, together with Amin Muhammad Sa'ïd, the minister of information and culture, following his nomination as secretary-general of the PFDJ. One of the first actions of the new state council was to draft legislation governing investment, which aimed to achieve a significant liberalization of trade.

International conferences on the draft constitution were held in the capital in July 1994 and in January 1995. The symposia were presided over by Dr Berekhet Habteselassie, the chairman of the draft constitutional commission. Many foreign constitutional experts were invited to attend and discuss the draft document, and there was extensive popular consultation, with more than 1,000 meetings throughout the country, attended by some 500,000 Eritreans. However, no opposition parties or opponents of the regime were invited to contribute. A third stage of consultation was begun in October 1995, when former soldiers of the EPLF armed forces were invited to discuss the draft law. The new constitution was scheduled to be adopted in mid-1996, to be followed by presidential and parliamentary elections in 1997.

In April 1995 the minister of defence, Mesfin Hagos, was replaced by Sebhat Ephrem (promoted to the rank of general in April 1996), previously the minister of health. Reports suggested that Hagos had been demoted because his popularity with the armed forces posed a threat to Afewerki, with whom he had recently contested a number of sensitive issues. In May Afewerki announced that the 30,000-strong civil service was to be reduced by one-third. All ministries (with the exceptions of interior and defence) would be subject to the rationalization programme, and 6,500 civil servants who had not been combatant members of the EPLF were made redundant immediately. In the same month the national assembly approved a law reducing the previous 10 administrative regions to six, each with regional, sub-regional and village administrations. In November the assembly approved new names for the regions, unrelated to the ethnic groups which inhabit them, and finalized details of their exact boundaries and sub-divisions. In the same month the assembly approved a new structure for the government, which now included 17 ministers and two commissioners.

The Eritrean Orthodox Church was a notable casualty of the Ethiopian occupation of the country at the time of the liberation war. Several monasteries were occupied by Ethiopian soliders and many of the religious instructors and their students were killed. Much church land was confiscated and was never returned by the Ethiopian government. The present Eritrean government, in an attempt to raise revenue, is seeking to sell the land back to the church at arbitrary prices. These events provoked considerable dissatisfaction within the church, and a movement promoting secession from the Ethiopian church gained widespread support. In June 1994 Eritrea sent five abbots from Eritrean monasteries to the headquarters of the Coptic church in Cairo, where they were inducted as bishops by Shenouda III, the Coptic Orthodox pontiff. In September the first bishops of the Eritrean Orthodox Church were consecrated at a ceremony conducted in Cairo. These consecrations signified the formal separation of the Eritrean Orthodox Church from the Ethiopian Orthodox Church as an independent body.

The ban on political organizations continued, and the ELF opposition claimed that hundreds of political prisoners remained incarcerated in a number of provincial towns. In April 1994 26 members of the more radical ELF–RC faction were detained in Ethiopia; other ELF–RC members were reported to have been forcibly repatriated to Eritrea. Meanwhile, the country's Jehovah's Witnesses encountered alleged discrimination as a result of their refusal to recognize the state of Eritrea. Jehovah's Witnesses had elected not to fight in the war of secession, vote in the 1993 referendum, or fulfil military service obligations. Consequently they were denied Eritrean citizenship, a number were imprisoned in December 1994, and some were reported to have been evicted from state-owned housing.

Major demobilization of freedom fighters began following the 1993 referendum, and in May 1994 compulsory military service was introduced to compensate for the contraction of the armed forces. All Eritreans between 18 and 40 years of age (with certain exceptions) were obliged to undertake six months' military training and 12 months' service; some 250,000 young men were due to be trained in the following five years. Some observers suggested that government strategy was to reduce the power of troublesome veteran freedom fighters, while introducing a malleable younger element into the armed forces. High-ranking officers were also reorganized, with the objective of removing political agitators and those who were not members of the PFDJ from the armed forces. In July disillusioned war veterans took hostage the director of the rehabilitation centre at Mai Habar and demanded to meet the president to discuss the meagre rehabilitation benefits. Moreover, in December fighting erupted when government officials attempted to take by force hundreds of Eritreans (recently deported to Massawa from Saudi Arabia) to the military training camp at Sawa in order to undertake national service. In July 1995 further clashes were reported between government troops and groups of young men refusing to report for national service. By mid-1995 the membership of the armed forces had been reduced from 95,000 to 55,000, and plans were in place for a further cut of 20,000 men. The USA reportedly pledged funds and training for Eritrea's military after Afewerki's visit to the USA in January 1995. By mid-1995 there were 30 US military advisers present in Keren. In April 1996 ranks were introduced into the armed forces for the first time. Several senior officers were promoted to the rank of general, including the minister of defence, Sebhat Ephrem.

December 1996 was marked by a number of assassinations, including the former commanding officer of the ELF, Abubekar Al-Hussein, and a recently-promoted colonel. Meanwhile, numerous people were wounded in a bomb attack in Habero. A former military commander of the radical religious opposition group, the Eritrean Islamic Jihad (EIJ), was also killed in December. The government blamed most of these violent incidents on the EIJ, although some analysts suggested that they were perpetrated by pro-government elements involved in internal disputes. Others linked the killings to an anti-corruption investigation which started in December. During the investigation PFDJ members responsible for the party's Red Sea Trading Corpn were found guilty (by a closed tribunal) of involvement in a smuggling operation with customs officials and sentenced to lengthy terms of imprisonment.

In February 1997 President Afewerki carried out a discreet but extensive reshuffle of the state council. Petros Solomon was transferred from the ministry of foreign affairs to the ministry of marine resources. Haile Wolde Tensae was moved from the finance ministry to the ministry of foreign affairs, and Gebre Selassie Yosef, the former director of macro-economic budget policy in the president's office, was appointed in his place. Worku Tesfay Mikael, hitherto the minister of tourism, was relieved of his portfolio and appointed as head of the Eritrean Refugee Commission. Notably, no public announcement was made of the government reshuffle.

In early 1997 a constituent assembly was established to discuss and ratify the draft constitution. The constituent assembly comprised 527 members, of whom 150 were from the national assembly, and the remainder were selected from representatives of Eritreans residing abroad or elected by regional assemblies (adhering to a 30% quota for women). On 23 May the constituent assembly unanimously adopted the constitution, instituting a presidential regime, with a president elected for a maximum of two five-year terms. According to the constitution, the president, as head of state, was empowered to appoint the prime minister and judges of the supreme court, although his mandate could be revoked should two-thirds of the members of the national assembly so demand. 'Conditional' political pluralism was authorized. Following the adoption of the constitution, the constituent assembly was disbanded, having empowered a transitional national assembly (comprising the 75 members of the PFDJ, 60 members of the constituent assembly and 15 representatives of Eritreans residing abroad) to act as the legislative body until the holding of national elections. It was anticipated that elections to the new assembly would be held before mid-1998.

Regional Concerns

Eritrea gradually increased its international contacts during 1993. Diplomatic ties were established with Sudan, Ethiopia, Israel, Australia and Pakistan, and several international organizations, shortly after independence. Relations with Ethiopia improved considerably during 1993. An agreement for the joint use of the ports of Assab and Massawa was signed in July, while in August it was reported that 90,000 Ethiopian prisoners of war had been released by the Eritrean government. In September the first meeting of the Ethiopian-Eritrean joint ministerial commission was held in Asmara, during which agreement was reached on measures to allow the free movement of nationals between each country, and on co-operation regarding foreign affairs and economic policy. However, cordial relations with several Arab states deteriorated following the publication and dissemination of articles critical of the Afewerki administration by the militant Islamic fundamentalist organization, Jihad Islamiyya, based in Sudan.

Relations between the transitional government and Sudan, which had supported the EPLF during the war, deteriorated in December 1993, following an incursion by members of an Islamist group into Eritrea from Sudan. In a clash with Eritrean forces, all the members of the group, and an Eritrean commander, were killed. In response to the incident, the Eritrean president stressed the links between the EIJ and the Sudanese National Islamic Front, led by Dr Hassan at-Turabi, implying that the latter had prior knowledge of the incursion. However, following a swift denial by the Sudanese government that it would ever interfere in the affairs of neighbouring states, the Eritrean president reaffirmed his support for the Sudanese authorities and his commitment to improving bilateral relations. In August 1993 it was reported that the EIJ had split between its political wing, led by Sheikh Mohamed Arafa, and a military wing, the former having been accused by the latter of inefficiency and of establishing contacts with the government.

In August 1994 Eritrea and Sudan signed an agreement concerning borders, security and the repatriation of refugees, and in October Eritrea, Sudan and the UN High Commissioner for Refugees issued a joint statement giving details of a repatriation programme for Eritrean refugees currently in Sudan. The repatriation programme began in November. By June 1995 some 24,000 refugees had returned to Eritrea, but an estimated 100,000 remained in Sudan. A further phase in the repatriation process began in October.

Relations between Eritrea and Sudan again deteriorated in November 1994, when the Eritrean government accused the Sudanese government of training 400 terrorists since August. Sudan accused Eritrea of training some 3,000 Sudanese rebels in camps within Eritrea. In early December Eritrea severed diplomatic relations with Sudan, alleging hostile behaviour by the Sudanese government and that it had hindered members of the Eritrean diplomatic mission in Khartoum in performing their diplomatic duties. The Sudanese government expressed deep regret over Eritrea's decision and denied all the allegations made. President Ali Abdullah Saleh of Yemen subsequently agreed to mediate in the dispute, but Sudanese-Eritrean talks, held in Yemen at the end of December, ended in failure. Further destabilization followed in early 1995 after attacks and infiltration in Barka Province by commandos of the military wing of the EIJ. The insurgents deployed land-mines on border roads, and a number of schools, dispensaries and buses were destroyed. The Eritrean government subsequently identified six alleged terrorist training camps on the Sudanese side of the border, and protested to the UN secretary-general, Dr Boutros Boutros-Ghali, that the Sudanese government was continuing to promote instability in the region. The Eritrean government also claimed that large numbers of Eritrean refugees living in Sudan had been arrested by the Sudanese authorities. Sudan responded by proposing Eritrea's suspension from the Intergovernmental Authority on Drought and Development (IGADD, now the Intergovernmental Authority on Development–IGAD), which had been attempting to mediate in Sudan's civil war. The Sudanese government strongly criticized Eritrea for hosting a series of conferences in Asmara for Sudan's opposition grouping, the National Democratic Alliance (NDA), in December 1994, June 1995 and January 1996. The Sudanese minister of foreign affairs, Ali Uthman Muhammad Taha, complained that Eritrea was deliberately encouraging military activity against Sudan. In February 1996 the Eritrean government granted Sudanese opposition leaders permission to use Sudan's embassy in Asmara as their headquarters. In addition, the insurgents were allowed to make daily four-hour radio transmissions to Sudan. In January the EIJ had threatened to increase its military operations against the Eritrean government, in response to Eritrea's occupation of the disputed island of Greater Hanish (see below). Several attacks on government vehicles in Eritrea in April were claimed by the EIJ.

Relations with Sudan remained hostile throughout 1996. In March the Eritrean authorities refused a request by Sudan that they extradite three Iranians who had hijacked a Sudan Airways aircraft to Asmara, and in April relations deteriorated further when Col John Garang, the leader of the Sudan People's Liberation Army, visited Eritrea. In July the Eritrean authorities denied reports in the Sudanese media that its troops had attacked Sudanese forces across the border. The Sudanese government was becoming increasingly convinced that Eritrea, Ethiopia, Uganda and Kenya formed part of a US-backed anti-Sudanese alliance. This was of considerable concern to Eritrean Muslims who constituted approximately one-half of the country's population.

In January 1997 the NDA launched an attack from Eritrea on Sudanese forces in the border region, resulting in numerous casualties. Sudan, however, blamed the incident on Eritrea's armed forces. Meanwhile, Eritrea claimed that the EIJ was training more than 4,000 Eritrean Muslims in Sudan to launch attacks against the Eritrean authorities from Sudanese bases in Eritrea. In June Eritrea's minister of foreign affairs, Haile Wolde Tensae, announced that in May the security forces had thwarted a plot by the Sudanese government to assassinate Afewerki.

In November 1995 there were reports that Eritrean troops had attempted to land on the Red Sea island of Greater Hanish, one of three islands (the others being Lesser Hanish and Zuqar) claimed by both Eritrea and Yemen. The attempted invasion had apparently been prompted by Yemen's announced intention to develop Greater Hanish as a tourist resort, and its subsequent refusal to comply with an Eritrean demand that the island be evacuated. The disputed islands had been used by Eritrea (with apparent Yemeni approval) during its struggle for independence from Ethiopia. Yemen had subsequently resumed its claims to the islands, because of both their strategic importance (located close to a principal shipping lane) and the possibility of discovering lucrative petroleum reserves in their surrounding waters. Negotiations in Eritrea and Yemen in late November and early December failed to defuse the crisis, and on 15 December fighting broke out between the two sides, resulting in the deaths of six Eritrean and three Yemeni soldiers. Although Eritrea and Yemen agreed to a cease-fire on 17 December, fighting was renewed on the following day, and Eritrean forces succeeded in occupying Greater Hanish. The cease-fire was adhered to thenceforth, and some 180 Yemeni soldiers (captured during the fighting) were released at the end of the month. Attempts by the Ethiopian and Egyptian governments to broker an agreement between the two sides proved unsuccessful. In January 1996 France assumed the mediatory role. In May representatives of Eritrea and Yemen signed an arbitration accord in Paris, France, whereby the two sides agreed to submit the dispute to an international tribunal. France subsequently undertook to observe and supervise military movements in the area around the disputed islands. In mid-August, despite the accord, Eritrean troops occupied Lesser Hanish; however, later in the month Eritrea withdrew its soldiers after mediation by France and a UN Security Council edict to evacuate the island forthwith. In October representatives of Eritrea and Yemen signed an agreement in Paris to establish the international tribunal. A five judge arbitration court was established in the United Kingdom and started work in April 1997. Meanwhile, forecasts of petroleum deposits in areas adjacent to the islands threatened to complicate the dispute further.

In November 1995 Eritrea's minister of foreign affairs, Petros Solomon, held talks with President Gouled in Djibouti. As a result, both countries pledged to enhance bilateral co-operation. Allegations made in a Yemeni newspaper in December that Eritrean troops had made an incursion into north-east Djibouti were vehemently denied by Eritrea. In April 1996 Gouled reportedly rejected a map (produced in Italy in 1935) submitted by Solomon, which apparently indicated that a 20-km strip of land currently claimed by Djibouti was, in fact, Eritrean territory. Concurrently, reports emerged of the attempted occupation of a border post in Djibouti (within the disputed territory) by Eritrean troops. The Eritrean authorities again denied the incident, claiming that it was part of a misinformation campaign by Yemen. Some observers suggested that the alleged attack could have been retaliation either for Djibouti's apparent support for Yemen in Eritrea's dispute over the Red Sea islands, or for Djibouti's refusal to return to Eritrea naval vessels which had taken refuge there in 1991, after the collapse of the Mengistu Haile Mariam regime in Ethiopia.

In early May 1994, following a three-day official visit to France (the first such visit undertaken to a Western nation since independence), President Afewerki announced that financial commitments amounting to some 20m. French francs had been secured, from the French government, for the rehabilitation of the airport and the water-supply system in Asmara.

In November 1996 a Chinese military delegation visited Asmara, indicating China's support for Eritrea's policy in the region. In December President Afewerki and Tewolde Woldemichael (the head of Eritrea's privatization agency) visited Italy, the United Kingdom and the USA in an attempt to promote investment in Eritrea.

Economy

ALAN RAKE

There is little statistical information available on the Eritrean economy. However, according to estimates by the IMF, Eritrea's gross domestic product (GDP) was 3,381m. birr in 1994, with a real growth rate of 9.8%. In 1995 GDP was estimated to be 3,905m. birr, with a real growth rate of 3.9%. It is estimated that Eritrea is one of the poorest countries in Africa, with an annual income of US $75–$150 per head. Although Eritrea has the distinction of being one of the very few non-debtor states in Africa, many of its people are without even a basic subsistence income; at the end of the war in 1991 it was estimated that more than 85% of the population were surviving on international relief. The need for the government to redevelop the economy was, therefore, the greatest challenge facing the country. In 1993 it was estimated that it would cost some $3,000m. to begin the reconstruction of the economy and infrastructure. However, in 1992, according to the government relief co-ordination office, Eritrea received less than $32m. in overseas aid. It was estimated that by 1995 Eritrea's budget deficit had risen significantly, to about 21% of GDP in that year.

AGRICULTURE

By far the most important sector of the economy is agriculture, which, despite a reduction in food production of roughly 40% over the period 1980–90, still sustains 90% of the population. In 1995 agricultural production (including forestry and fishing) accounted for an estimated 12.0% of GDP. Most sedentary agriculture is practised in the highlands, where rainfall is sufficient to cultivate the main crops: teff (an indigenous grain), maize, wheat, sorghum and millet. In 1992, which was described as a satisfactory year in agricultural terms, some 315,000 ha of land were cultivated, and the harvest was good enough to satisfy an estimated 54% of Eritrea's food requirements. The grain harvest increased from some 70,000 metric tons in 1991 to between 250,000 and 300,000 tons in 1992, but 1993 was a disastrous year, following the almost complete failure of the rains and persistent problems caused by crop pests. There was a substantial cereal deficit, and much of the country required the distribution of emergency food aid. In June 1993 the World Food Programme announced the launch of a six-month emergency food operation (including several food-for-work projects) to assist more than 500,000 Eritreans suffering serious food shortages. The 1994 harvest was considerably better than in the previous few years, owing to high levels of rainfall and an extensive government programme of rehabilitation of communications and irrigation systems. Crop production declined in 1995 (despite good rainfall), owing to a severe locust infestation. In 1996 a small enterprise was established in Eritrea to export cut flowers and fruit, initially to the Netherlands, Germany and Israel. The number of livestock in Eritrea (severely depleted during the war) has increased since 1992, primarily as a result of improved animal husbandry and access to veterinary services, and has led to the export of live animals.

Land reform legislation was promulgated in 1994, whereby the government was to maintain ownership of all land, but farmers would be allowed a life-time lease on currently held land. In addition, every Eritrean citizen would automatically qualify for the right to use a specific plot throughout their life. The government initiated agricultural resettlement projects for demobilized soldiers and introduced a special credit scheme for ex-combatants to facilitate the establishment of new farms and co-operatives. In January 1995 two loans for agricultural development were granted: US $12.7m. from the International Fund for Agricultural Development (IFAD) and $5.3m. from the joint IFAD-Belgium Survival Fund Programme. In February 1996 Japan pledged aid worth $3m. to assist in the development of the agricultural sector.

Serious environmental degradation, caused directly and indirectly by the war, presents a huge problem. Owing to the difficulties resulting from water scarcity and unreliable rainfall, careful water management and conservation are essential. In 1992, 17 water reservoirs and 20 small dams were built as part of an effort to improve water harvesting. In an attempt to prevent soil erosion, more than 40,000 km of badly eroded hillsides have been terraced and 22m. new trees planted. In mid-1994 the European Development Fund committed ECU 3.6m. (US $4m.) for the construction of five small-scale irrigation dams. In mid-1977 the African Development Bank (ADB) granted a loan worth $11.6m. to finance an irrigated horticulture development project, repayable over a 50-year period, which included 10 years' grace.

Fisheries are a potential growth area for the Eritrean economy. Fishing of sardines, anchovies, tuna, shark and mackerel is practised in the waters of the Red Sea. An FAO-sponsored conference was held in Massawa in March 1993 to discuss measures to develop Eritrea's marine fishery resources. UN fishery experts have estimated that Eritrea has the potential to achieve annual yields of around 70,000 metric tons. Although fishing activity is on a very small scale, the total catch has increased considerably in recent years, amounting to 7,921 tons in 1996. In the past, government price controls and a poor transport infrastructure discouraged the development of a domestic market, with the result that much of the catch was smuggled abroad. In May 1994 the China State Construction and Engineering Co was awarded a 3.7m. birr contract to build a new fishing centre at the port of Massawa. A US $5.4m. project, funded by the UN, to build a fisheries complex was nearing completion in late 1995, and the fishing industry was experiencing rapid growth in spite of competition from foreign fishing fleets operating illegally in Eritrean waters. By early 1996 fishing fleets from Saudi Arabia, the United Kingdom, Greece, the Netherlands and Israel were licensed to operate in the area, and were exporting sardines, tuna, shrimps and lobsters. The companies have been building cold storage and processing facilities in Massawa. In March 1997 it was announced that France was assisting Eritrea with a three-month programme to evaluate the fishing potential of Eritrean waters, and to help develop a suitable fisheries monitoring organization.

INDUSTRY

Eritrea's industrial base traditionally centred on the production of glass, cement, footwear and canned goods. Although some of the 42 public-sector factories—producing textiles, footwear, beverages and other light industrial goods—were operating in 1991, they were doing so at only one-third of capacity. By 1995 production had increased considerably, mostly as a result of substantial aid from the government, which provided raw materials and new machinery. The government has calculated that the cost of industrial recovery would be US $20m. for the private sector and $66m. for the state sector. In 1995 industrial production (comprising mining, manufacturing, construction and utilities) accounted for an estimated 24.6% of GDP.

The manufacturing sector provided an estimated 16.2% of GDP in 1995. In June 1994 there were 43 public enterprises in the industrial sector, with a total of 10,464 employees. All public enterprises in the sector are currently scheduled for divestment or liquidation, following the initiation of a programme of privatization in 1995. Since independence several small manufacturing companies have been established, including a contact lens factory that exports to countries in Europe, Africa and Asia. Imported petroleum is processed at the Assab refinery, whose entire output of petroleum products is delivered to Ethiopia. Eritrea purchases its own petroleum requirements from Ethiopia under a quota arrangement.

MINING AND POWER

Eritrea's mineral resources are believed to be of significant potential value, although in 1995 mining and quarrying accounted for less than 0.1% of GDP. Of particular importance, in view of Eritrea's acute energy shortage, is the possibility of large reserves of petroleum and natural gas beneath the Red Sea. In early 1993 the government made petroleum exploration regulations more stringent, and British Petroleum, which had signed a contract for petroleum exploration with the former Ethiopian regime, had its exploration rights invalidated. A US petroleum company, Amoco, and the International Petroleum Corpn of Canada are the only two remaining companies with concessions. The latter has operating rights in the 31,000 sq km Danakil block along the Eritrean coast, where there are believed to be good prospects for petroleum and gas discoveries. However, the two companies are still waiting for the legal status of their contracts, signed under the Mengistu regime, to be determined. In November 1993 a new code of practice regulating the petroleum sector was promulgated, allowing companies a 25-year licence, renewal periods of 10 years and fiscal advantages. Several prominent petroleum companies, including Amoco, Anadarko, Total, Chevron, Mobil and Shell expressed an interest in exploration and distribution. A local company, Prima, backed by expatriate Eritrean shareholders and Shell-Eritrea, was expected to handle internal distribution. In October 1995 the government signed an agreement with Anadarko of the USA for a seven-year prospecting contract, worth US $28.5m. Anadarko began its seismic studies for petroleum in the Zula block (near the Hanish islands) in November 1996. It announced that it planned to commence test-drilling before 1998.

Gold-bearing seams exist in many of the igneous rocks forming the highlands of Eritrea. There are at least 15 gold-mines and a large number of prospects close to Asmara, and the potential for new discoveries in the area is considered good. There are two regions of widespread gold mineralization in the western lowlands, at Tokombia and Barentu. Other mineral resources include potash, zinc, magnesium, copper, iron ore and marble. In April 1995 a new mining law was promulgated. The law emphasized that all mineral resources in Eritrea were a public asset and that the state would oversee the conservation and development of mineral resources for the benefit of the people. However, it recognized that this could not be achieved without extensive private investment. Investor companies would enjoy a concessionary tax regime, pay royalties of 2%–5% and would encounter no restriction on repatriating profits. The government retained the right to acquire a 10% share in any mining undertaking. In December applications to explore for gold and base metals were received from numerous foreign companies, including Anglo American Corpn of South Africa, Western Mining of Australia and Ashanti Goldfields of Ghana. Particular interest was expressed in the old Eritrean mines that had been exploited until the early 1940s. In March 1996 Canada's Reese Mining Co signed two agreements with Eritrea for the exploration of gold and copper reserves. In the following month the government signed exploration agreements with Western Mining and Ashanti Goldfields. In late 1996 Golden Star Resources of Canada, and its subsidiary, Pan African Resources, began drilling for diamonds in the Adi Rassi area.

Eritrea's economic performance is hampered by its lack of capacity to produce energy. Most electric energy is provided by the four thermal power stations, largely dependent on fuel imported from Ethiopia. However, electricity is provided to only some 10% of the population, the remainder relying on fuel wood and animal products. Attempts are being made to harness the plentiful and clear sunlight for solar energy. By mid-1994, 37 schools and three hospitals had been purpose-built to operate on solar power. With an increase in the use of solar power, it is hoped that the demand for wood for fuel (from the rapidly diminishing forests, already severely denuded by the liberation war) will diminish. In September 1994 the Kuwait Fund for Arab Economic Development allocated US $158m. for a project to upgrade the production and distribution of electricity in Eritrea. In March 1996 the government announced plans to construct a barrage, at a cost of $45m., at Toker, some 50 km from Asmara. The barrage was expected to increase water reserves for Asmara, although no immediate plans were announced for its use in generating electricity. In mid-1997 Korean contractors were scheduled to commence work on the construction of a $114m. power station (Hirgigo) at Massawa Port. The station was to have an initial output of 80 MW produced by four 20 MW diesel generators, and was to be financed primarily by Arab and Italian donors. Meanwhile, in late 1996, work commenced on the construction of a 2,000-metric ton gas depot at Massawa (funded by public and private capital) to provide additional storage facilities.

RECOVERY AND REHABILITATION PROGRAMME

In March 1993 the International Development Association (IDA), part of the World Bank, approved a credit of SDR 18.1m. (US $25m.) to support Eritrea's two-year Recovery and Rehabilitation Programme (involving total investment of $147m.), which was to be funded by a series of loans on concessionary terms. The second largest contributor was Italy, which pledged $24.3m. Contributions were also promised by a number of other European countries, the European Union (EU) and the UN Development Programme. The main components of the programme were: agricultural and industrial input, equipment for infrastructural development, mechanical, electrical and telecommunications spare parts, construction materials for social utilities and cottage industries, and support for administration and economic planning. In 1994 the Paris Club of official creditors granted Eritrea a long-term loan of $250m. to fund rehabilitation and development programmes.

FOREIGN TRADE AND PAYMENTS

In 1993, according to estimates by the IMF, Eritrea recorded a trade deficit of US $239m. However, owing mainly to private transfers (mostly remittances from Eritreans working abroad), the current account showed a surplus of $97m. The trade deficit increased to an estimated $331m. in 1994 (with a current account surplus of $98m.) and to $323m. in 1995, in which year the current account surplus declined to $12m. In 1994 the principal sources of non-petroleum imports were Italy (accounting for 21.6% of the total) and Saudi Arabia (16.5%). Exports in that year were mostly to Ethiopia (52.3%) and Sudan (14.6%). The principal exports to these countries were food and live animals, salt and basic manufactures. In 1994 the main non-petroleum imports were machinery and transport equipment (45.2% of the total), basic manufactures and food and live animals.

In 1993 it was estimated that Eritrea's budget deficit reached 153m. birr, equivalent to some 6.0% of GDP. By 1995, it was estimated, the budget deficit had increased to 820.9m. birr, equivalent to 21.0% of GDP. There are no overall price indices for Eritrea, but statistics for Asmara showed that prices rose by 9.6% in the year to December 1993, compared with 8.8% in the previous 12 months. Consumer prices in Asmara rose by 6.8% in 1994, and by 10.9% in 1995. Unemployment and under-employment are estimated to affect as many as 50% of the labour force.

In May 1993 Eritrea was admitted to the group of African, Caribbean and Pacific countries party to the Lomé Convention. In September an IMF delegation visited Asmara and held talks with the government regarding Eritrea's application to join the Fund, and in July 1994 Eritrea became the 179th member of the IMF, with an initial quota of SDR 11.5m. Eritrea is eager to show the international donor community its commitment to implementing a liberal trade and exchange regime and developing an export-orientated domestic economy. As early as January 1992 Eritrea and Ethiopia signed an agreement whereby the port of Assab became a free port for Ethiopia, and which provided for tax-free trade between the two countries, using the Ethiopian birr as currency. In October 1994 Eritrea and Ethiopia signed a further agreement to allow the free movement of goods between the two countries without payment of customs dues. A tariff agreement which provides for a free-trade zone and the basis for future economic union between the two countries was announced by the Ethiopian government in May 1995.

In late 1996 President Afewerki and a trade delegation visited Italy, the United Kingdom and the USA in an attempt to promote investment in Eritrea. In mid-1996 28 US companies operating in Eritrea had established an American Business Council to protect their interests and to assist local Eritrean businesses involved in promoting or selling US merchandise.

CONSTRUCTION, TRANSPORT AND TOURISM

Since 1993 construction projects in Eritrea have been supported by the Recovery and Rehabilitation Programme. Public enterprises, particularly cement, metalworks and limestone factories, have been undergoing rehabilitation, while emphasis has also been placed on the rebuilding of government offices, commercial and residential buildings and the reconstruction of roads and infrastructure. In early 1995 a Republic of Korea company started work on Eritrea's biggest housing project; the US $70m.-project will provide accommodation for some 1,300 families in the outskirts of Asmara.

Construction work on a new airport in Massawa began in April 1996. In 1993 the government announced plans for the rehabilitation of the Asmara–Massawa railway line, which had been severely damaged during the war. The government initially sought estimates for the repair work from foreign companies, but in 1995 decided that the rehabilitation should be undertaken locally. In early 1997 the line was formally inaugurated.

Significant progress has been made in rehabilitating the port of Massawa, which was heavily bombed by Ethiopia during the war. The port was obstructed by shipwrecked vessels, and much of the city was reduced to rubble. By late 1994 the harbour had been cleared by the US navy, and port activity has since accelerated. In 1991 104 small ships visited the port; however, in 1996 some 445 vessels docked at the port (a further 676 vessels docked at Assab). The government announced a long-term project to build a container terminal at the port, as well as a liquefied petroleum gas terminal. Finance for both projects was to be sought from foreign investors. In mid-1996 Italy and the IDA pledged loans of US $21m. and $18m., respectively, to fund the repair and refurbishment of the port, including the construction of the container terminal, the extension of quays and the development of customs facilities. It was anticipated that finance would also be sought to improve facilities at Assab port (which handles the majority of Ethiopia's external trade) as difficulties had been reported by the Ethiopian authorities in verifying loading and unloading at the port.

Tourism in Eritrea remains undeveloped. However, new construction activity in Massawa has resulted in the rehabilitation of three hotels with a combined capacity of 160 beds, and the government remains optimistic that the number of tourist arrivals will gradually increase. In 1995 a US company had expressed interest in building a US $200m. casino and hotel complex (and desalination plant) on the Dahlak islands. A Chinese company had also begun rehabilitation work on a hotel in Massawa, using local financing. In late 1996 it was announced that an Italian company had won a contract to build Eritrea's first five star hotel. It was estimated that the 200-room hotel would cost $17.5m. to construct. The divestment of state-owned hotels is integral to the government's privatization programme.

ECONOMIC POLICY AND AID

In August 1994 the national assembly approved a long-awaited programme of economic reforms governing investment, land tenure, monetary and fiscal policy and trade. The programme represented a major change from a wartime command economy to a liberal market economy, designed for peace. Private investment was to be liberalized, and government involvement reduced to a regulatory capacity (with the exception of the provision of assistance for depressed regions). Private and foreign investors were to be treated equally, and remission of capital and profits was to be unrestricted, but employment for Eritrean nationals would be prioritized. The 43 state enterprises were scheduled for privatization, and 11 state-owned hotels were also expected to be sold. Nearly 45,000 houses, nationalized during the Ethiopian occupation, were to be returned to their owners. It was announced that small export-orientated businesses would qualify for competitive exchange rates and loans under the Recovery and Rehabilitation Programme (see above). The Ethiopian birr was to remain legal tender, although in 1995 the government announced plans to introduce a separate national currency, the nakfa. In July 1997 a decree was promulgated, announcing the issuance of the nakfa as Eritrea's legal currency and abolishing the use of the Ethiopian birr in Eritrea. Some criticism was levelled at the revised land tenure law, as the government had declared itself to be the owner of all land, with Eritreans and foreign investors receiving usufructuary rights for farming, development and housing. In October 1994 a new tariff regime was adopted; it was hoped that this measure would curb inflation but encourage trade and investment. Capital goods and raw materials were subject to minimal tariffs of less than 3%, whereas tariffs on some luxury goods were fixed as high as 50%.

Since independence the government has allocated considerable expenditure to financing the demobilization and reintegration of ex-combatants. During 1993–96 the demobilization programme was estimated to have cost 300m. birr. The government remains committed to restructuring the public administration and reforming taxation policy in order to reduce the widening budget deficit. In March 1997 the National Agency for the Supervision and Privatization of Public Enterprises requested that bids be submitted for several state-owned industries; bids for other public enterprises were invited in May. Although interest was expressed by France, Italy, the Republic of Korea and the USA, many of the enterprises offered for sale had few assets and were in need of considerable investment.

Pledges of financial aid from international organizations became more frequent in 1994. The EU promised US $4.1m., under the Lomé agreement, for diverse projects such as the demobilization of the army and the provision of health equipment, veterinary services and pharmaceutical supplies. A further ECU 20m. was allocated in November for the upgrading of the Asmara–Massawa road, for drilling wells and for establishing schools and health centres. In addition, the European Investment Bank pledged $10m. to upgrade telecommunication networks in Massawa and Keren. (The number of telephone subscribers had increased from 12,000 at the time of independence to 40,000 by November 1994.) In late 1996, it was announced that Norway was to provide an additional $7m. in aid to improve the telecommunications service.

Eritrea's first donor conference was convened by the World Bank in Paris in December 1994. Donors pledged US $250m. in international aid for 1995. The World Bank promised $25m., the ADB $50m., Kuwait $20m., and Saudi Arabia $50m. The EU, which had already pledged $200m. since 1992, offered a further $30m. for 1995. However, an economic memorandum, prepared by the World Bank, expressed concern regarding the Eritrean government's ability to provide counterpart funds to discharge the substantial range of international commitments. It also stressed the acute shortage of skilled manpower in key sectors, and the absence of essential statistics, necessary for effective economic planning. In late 1995 the IDA announced that it would fund community-based micro-projects in the areas of health and irrigation, to the value of $25m., as well as a $20m. project aimed at rehabilitating and expanding capacity in Eritrea's ports. The World Bank was approached for assistance with the re-equipment of a cement and a glass factory in Asmara. In early 1997 the Arab Bank for Economic Development in Africa allocated Eritrea $10m. to finance improvements to the drinking water network. In April the World Bank approved a $6.3m. credit to finance feasibility and engineering studies in the construction and transport sectors.

During late 1996 the government imposed severe restrictions on non-governmental organizations (NGO) operating in Eritrea. Thenceforth NGO would be permitted to operate only in the education and health sectors, and expatriate personnel would be required to pay income tax at 38%. Many NGO expressed concern that the restrictions would prevent them from continuing their work in Eritrea.

Statistical Survey

Area and Population

AREA, POPULATION AND DENSITY*

Area (sq km)	121,144†
Population (census results)	
9 May 1984	
Males	1,374,452
Females	1,373,852
Total	2,748,304
Population (official estimates at mid-year)	
1989	3,239,400
1990	3,329,600
1991	3,435,500
Density (per sq km) at mid-1991	28.4

* Including the Assab district.

† 46,774 sq miles.

Note: In 1993 the domestic population was estimated to be about 2m., based on the total of 1.2m. people who registered to vote in the April 1993 referendum, 860,000 of whom lived in Eritrea.

PRINCIPAL TOWN (estimated population at mid-1990)

Asmara (capital) . . . 358,100

Source: UN, *Demographic Yearbook*.

BIRTHS AND DEATHS (UN estimates, annual averages)

	1980–85	1985–90	1990–95
Birth rate (per 1,000)	45.2	44.6	43.0
Death rate (per 1,000)	20.3	17.0	15.2

Expectation of life (UN estimates, years at birth, 1990–95): 50.4 (males 48.9; females 52.1).

Source: UN, *World Population Prospects: The 1994 Revision*.

Agriculture

PRINCIPAL CROPS ('000 metric tons)

	1993	1994	1995
Wheat	3*	16	9*
Barley	4*	41	29*
Maize	6*	22	8*
Millet	8*	73	30†
Sorghum	51*	127	68*
Potatoes†	39	39	39
Other roots and tubers†	70	70	70
Pulses	25†	38	45†
Groundnuts (in shell)†	1	1	1
Sesame seed	4†	7	7†
Linseed†	3	3	3
Vegetables†	20	34	35
Fruits and berries†	3	5	5

* Unofficial figure. † FAO estimate(s).

Source: FAO, *Production Yearbook*.

LIVESTOCK ('000 head, year ending September)

	1993	1994	1995
Cattle*	1,269	1,290	1,312
Sheep†	1,510	1,520	1,530
Goats†	1,400	1,400	1,400
Camels†	69	69	69

Poultry† (million): 4 in 1993; 4 in 1994; 4 in 1995.

* Unofficial figures.

† FAO estimates.

Source: FAO, *Production Yearbook*.

LIVESTOCK PRODUCTS (FAO estimates, '000 metric tons)

	1993	1994	1995
Beef and veal	9	10	10
Mutton and lamb	5	5	5
Goat meat	5	5	5
Poultry meat	5	6	6
Edible offals	5	5	5
Cows' milk	29	30	31
Goats' milk	7	7	7
Sheep's milk	4	4	4
Butter	0.4	0.4	0.4
Cheese	0.2	0.2	0.2
Hen eggs	5.9	5.9	5.9
Wool:			
greasy	0.8	0.8	0.8
clean	0.4	0.4	0.4
Cattle hides	1.9	1.9	1.9
Sheepskins	0.5	0.5	0.5
Goatskins	0.5	0.5	0.5

Source: FAO, *Production Yearbook* and *Quarterly Bulletin of Statistics*.

Fishing

(metric tons, live weight)

	1993	1994
Inland waters	1	1
Indian Ocean	416	2,960
Total catch	417	2,961

Source: FAO, *Yearbook of Fishery Statistics*.

Total catch (metric tons, live weight): 3,773 in 1995; 7,921 in 1996 (Source: IMF, *Eritrea—Recent Economic Developments* (1996)).

Finance

CURRENCY AND EXCHANGE RATES

Monetary Units

100 cents = 1 birr.

Sterling and Dollar Equivalents (31 December 1996)

£1 sterling = 10.997 birr;
US $1 = 6.426 birr;
1,000 birr = £90.94 = $155.62.

Note: Following its secession from Ethiopia in May 1993, Eritrea retained the Ethiopian currency. An exchange rate of US $1 = 5.000 birr was introduced in October 1992 and remained in force until April 1994, when it was adjusted to $1 = 5.130 birr. Further adjustments were made subsequently. In addition to the official exchange rate, the Bank of Eritrea applies a marginal auction rate (determined at fortnightly auctions of foreign exchange, conducted by the National Bank of Ethiopia) to aid-funded imports and to most transactions in services. A more depreciated preferential rate applies to remittances of foreign exchange by Eritreans abroad, to proceeds from exports and to most payments for imports. In July 1997 the Government announced the introduction of a separate national currency, the nakfa, replacing (and initially at par with) the Ethiopian birr.

BUDGET (provisional, million birr)

Revenue*	1993	1994	1995
Tax revenue	517.6	657.5	715.6
Direct taxes	179.3	315.8	339.7
Taxes on personal income	37.0	79.1	74.2
Taxes on business profits	95.1	160.7	185.0
Rehabilitation tax	40.9	73.0	73.2
Domestic sales tax (incl. stamp duties)	143.6	142.8	151.0
Import duties and taxes	180.7	187.1	224.9
Export tax	14.0	11.8	—
Port fees and charges	244.5	152.9	233.5
Other current revenue	131.1	180.5	396.1
Capital revenue	—	35.6	—
Total	893.2	1,026.5	1,345.2

Expenditure	1993	1994	1995
Current expenditure	1,103.7	1,551.8	2,131.3
General services	649.8	635.9	1,090.3
Internal affairs	33.9	38.0	110.7
Regional administration	21.8	32.7	48.6
Foreign affairs	25.0	54.0	71.5
Defence	539.2	438.7	770.5†
Economic services	103.3	185.0	235.1
Agriculture and natural resources	17.1	18.0	30.1
Construction and urban development	24.4	57.7	88.5
Transport and communications	52.7	98.5	97.6
Social services	94.5	135.4	226.9
Education and training	46.3	64.9	97.6
Health	18.2	35.1	75.3
Demobilization of ex-combatants	99.0	153.6	41.8
Capital expenditure	455.3	453.9	525.8
General services	41.7	17.3	31.5
Economic development	372.5	339.4	410.4
Agriculture and natural resources	244.3	130.8	272.5
Trade, industry and tourism	58.1	69.7	25.1
Construction, transport and communications	60.2	55.4	93.8
Social development	41.1	73.4	83.9
Education	19.3	9.3	15.5
Health	18.1	13.5	35.5
Total	1,559.0	2,005.7	2,657.1

* Excluding grants received (million birr): 507.0 (current 142.4, capital 364.6) in 1993; 626.0 (current 456.3, capital 169.7) in 1994; 491.0 (current 170.6, capital 320.4) in 1995.

† Including some demobilization costs.

Source: IMF, *Eritrea—Recent Economic Developments* (1996).

MONEY SUPPLY (million birr at 31 December)

	1993	1994	1995
Demand deposits at banks	866.8	1,258.4	1,295.8

Source: IMF, *Eritrea—Recent Economic Developments* (1996).

COST OF LIVING*
(price index for Asmara at December; base: January 1992 = 100)

	1993	1994	1995
All items	119.3	127.4	141.3

* The index has been constructed using estimated weights for various categories of commodity prices, compiled by the Ministry of Trade and Industry.

Source: IMF, *Eritrea—Recent Economic Developments* (1996).

NATIONAL ACCOUNTS (estimates, million birr at current prices)

Gross Domestic Product by Economic Activity

	1993	1994	1995
Agriculture, forestry and fishing	277.4	489.1	390.9
Mining and quarrying	1.0	1.5	2.1
Manufacturing*	301.6	372.5	571.3
Electricity and water	31.6	39.0	59.8
Construction	117.0	166.0	235.6
Wholesale and retail trade	589.6	857.5	921.9
Transport and communications	362.9	416.1	453.4
Financial services	37.6	39.8	57.8
Dwellings and domestic services	54.0	65.3	79.0
Public administration and defence	304.6	457.0	558.0
Social services	65.0	93.5	156.2
Other services	40.5	41.7	43.0
GDP at factor cost	2,182.7	3,039.1	3,528.9
Indirect taxes, *less* subsidies	338.3	341.7	375.9
GDP in purchasers' values	2,521.0	3,380.8	3,904.8

* Including handicrafts and small-scale industry.

Source: IMF, *Eritrea—Recent Economic Developments* (1996).

BALANCE OF PAYMENTS (provisional, US $ million)

	1993	1994	1995
Exports of goods f.o.b.	36	64	81
Imports of goods c.i.f.	–275	–396	–404
Trade balance	–239	–331	–323
Exports of services*	103	80	99
Imports of services*	–1	–7	–44
Balance on goods, services and income	–137	–258	–268
Private unrequited transfers (net)	165	276	215
Official unrequited transfers (net)	69	80	73
Current balance	97	98	20
Official long-term capital (net)	—	25	24
Short-term capital (net) and Net errors and omissions	17	–45	–108
Overall balance	115	79	–65

* Including other income.

Source: IMF, *Eritrea—Recent Economic Developments* (1996).

External Trade

PRINCIPAL COMMODITIES (million birr)

Imports c.i.f.*	1993	1994	1995
Food and live animals	166.4	426.2	446.9
Beverages and tobacco	35.9	43.3	12.4
Crude materials (inedible) except fuels	31.3	49.1	64.7
Chemicals and related products	56.4	120.3	157.0
Basic manufactures	222.2	320.5	499.3
Machinery and transport equipment	381.9	752.6	1,178.4
Miscellaneous manufactured articles	111.2	234.9	169.2
Total (incl. others)	1,022.8	1,993.1	2,608.5

* Figures exclude imports of petroleum. The data also exclude aid-related imports.

Exports f.o.b.	1993	1994	1995
Food and live animals	27.8	117.7	138.5
Beverages and tobacco	8.7	9.2	20.2
Crude materials (inedible) except fuels	76.6	132.1	157.7
Chemicals and related products	6.2	7.5	13.1
Basic manufactures	52.9	67.8	102.4
Miscellaneous manufactured articles	33.5	51.1	75.8
Total (incl. others)	209.2	397.2	529.5

Source: IMF, *Eritrea—Recent Economic Developments* (1996).

PRINCIPAL TRADING PARTNERS (million birr)

Imports c.i.f. (excl. petroleum)	1992*	1993*	1994
Djibouti	13.0	11.3	29.8
Ethiopia	61.9	66.3	90.8
Germany	7.0	79.3	147.4
Italy	27.8	136.8	431.0
Netherlands	6.7	22.0	n.a.
Saudi Arabia	136.1	282.5	328.0
Sudan	2.1	53.4	51.7
Sweden	2.1	25.9	n.a.
United Arab Emirates	35.8	96.6	178.6
United Kingdom	4.7	29.7	79.1
USA	1.3	11.4	35.3
Yemen	7.1	12.5	20.5
Total (incl. others)	367.1	1,024.4	1,993.2

Exports f.o.b.	1992	1993	1994
Ethiopia	40.0	130.5	207.5
Italy	3.4	5.4	10.2
Saudi Arabia	0.1	3.6	50.3
Sudan	—	46.5	57.9
Sweden	1.2	0.6	n.a.
United Kingdom	0.3	—	10.2
Yemen	0.2	—	18.4
Total (incl. others)	46.1	209.9	397.1

* Excluding aid-related imports.

Source: IMF, *Eritrea—Recent Economic Developments* (1996).

Transport

SHIPPING

Merchant Fleet (registered at 31 December)

	1994	1995	1996
Number of vessels	1	5	4
Displacement (grt)	104	12,403	830

Communications Media

	1993	1994
Radio receivers ('000 in use)	n.a.	300
Television receivers ('000 in use)	n.a.	1
Telephones ('000 main lines in use)	13	15

Book production: 106 titles in 1993 (including 23 pamphlets) and 420,000 copies.

Source: UNESCO, *Statistical Yearbook*; UN, *Statistical Yearbook*.

Education

(1994/95)

	Institutions	Teachers	Pupils
Pre-primary	80	256	8,032
Primary	507	5,583	224,287
Secondary:			
General	n.a.	2,029	71,723
Teacher-training	n.a.	44	427
Vocational	n.a.	89	819
University level	n.a.	136	3,081
Other higher	n.a.	n.a.	56

Source: UNESCO, *Statistical Yearbook*.

Directory

The Constitution

On 23 May 1997 the Constituent Assembly unanimously adopted the Eritrean Constitution. A presidential regime was instituted, with the President elected for a maximum of two five-year terms. The President, as Head of State, has extensive powers and appoints the Prime Minister and the judges of the Supreme Court, although his mandate can be revoked if two-thirds of the members of the National Assembly (the Legislature) so demand. 'Conditional' political pluralism is authorized. Elections to the National Assembly were scheduled to be held before mid-1988; in the interim period the Transitional National Assembly was empowered to act as the legislature.

The Government

HEAD OF STATE

President: ISSAIAS AFEWERKI (assumed power May 1991; elected President by National Assembly 8 June 1993).

STATE COUNCIL
(July 1997)

President: ISSAIAS AFEWERKI.

Minister of Defence: Gen. SEBHAT EPHREM.

Minister of Justice: FAWZIYYAH HASHIM.

Minister of Foreign Affairs: HAILE WOLDE TENSAE.

Minister of Information and Culture: BARAKI GEBRE SELASSIE.

Minister of Finance and Development: GEBRE SELASSIE YOSEF.

Minister of Trade and Industry: ALI SAYYID ABDULLAH.

Minister of Agriculture: AREFAYNE BERHE.

Minister of Local Government: MAHMOUD AHMED MAHMOUD.

Minister of Labour and Social Security: OQBE ABRAHA.

Minister of Marine Resources: PETROS SOLOMON.

Minister of Construction: ABRAHA ASFAHA.

Minister of Energy and Mining: TESFAY GEBRE SELASSIE.

Minister of Education: OSMAN SALIH MUHAMMAD.

Minister of Health: Dr SALIH MEKKI.

Minister of Transport and Communications: SALEH KEKIA.

Minister of Tourism: AHMED HAJI ALI.

Minister of Land, Water and the Environment: Dr TESFAY GHIRMAZION.

MINISTRIES AND COMMISSIONS

Ministry of Agriculture: POB 1024, Asmara; tel. (1) 181499; fax (1) 181415.

Ministry of Construction: POB 841, Asmara; tel. (1) 119077.

Ministry of Defence: POB 629, Asmara; tel. (1) 113349; fax (1) 114920.

Ministry of Education: POB 5610, Asmara; tel. (1) 113044; fax (1) 113866.

Ministry of Energy and Mining: POB 5285, Asmara; tel. (1) 116872; fax (1) 127652.

Ministry of Finance and Development: POB 896, Asmara; tel. (1) 113633; fax (1) 117947.

Ministry of Foreign Affairs: POB 190, Asmara; tel. (1) 113811; fax (1) 123788.

Ministry of Health: POB 212, Asmara; tel. (1) 112877; fax (1) 112899.

Ministry of Information and Culture: POB 242, Asmara; tel. (1) 115171; fax (1) 119847.

Ministry of Internal Affairs: POB 250, Asmara; tel. (1) 119299; fax (1) 114920.

Ministry of Justice: POB 241, Asmara; tel. (1) 111822.

Ministry of Labour and Social Security: Asmara.

Ministry of Land, Water and the Environment: Asmara.

Ministry of Local Government: POB 225, Asmara; tel. (1) 113006.

Ministry of Marine Resources: POB 923, Asmara; tel. (1) 114271; fax (1) 112185.

Ministry of Tourism: POB 1010, Asmara; tel. (1) 126997; fax (1) 126949.

Ministry of Trade and Industry: POB 1844, Asmara; tel. (1) 113910; fax (1) 120586.

Ministry of Transport and Communications: POB 204, Asmara; tel. (1) 110444; fax (1) 127048.

Commission for Relief and Refugee Affairs: POB 198, Asmara; tel. (1) 112495; fax (1) 112861.

Land and Housing Commission: POB 348, Asmara; tel. (1) 117400.

Provincial Administrators

In May 1995 the National Assembly adopted legislation reducing the country's 10 administrative regions to six, each with regional, sub-regional and village administrations.

Anseba Province: ALAMIN SHEIKH SALIH.

Debub Province: MESFIN HAGOS.

Debubawi Keyih Province: HAMID MUHAMMAD KARIKAREH.

Gash-Barka Province: MUSTAFA NUR HUSSEIN.

Maakel Province: WELDENKIEL ABRAHA.

Semenawi Keyih Bahri Province: IBRAHIM IDRIS TOTIL.

Legislature

NATIONAL ASSEMBLY

In accordance with transitional arrangements formulated in Decree No. 37 of May 1993, the National Assembly consists of the Central Committee of the People's Front for Democracy and Justice (PFDJ) and 60 other members: 30 from the Provincial Assemblies and an additional 30 members, including a minimum of 10 women, to be nominated by the PFDJ Central Committee. The legislative body 'outlines the internal and external policies of the government, regulates their implementation, approves the budget and elects a president for the country'. The National Assembly is to hold regular sessions every six months under the chairmanship of the President. In his role as Head of the Government and Commander-in-Chief of the Army, the President nominates individuals to head the various government departments. These nominations are ratified by the legislative body. In March 1994 the National Assembly voted to alter its composition: it would henceforth comprise the 75 members of the Central Committee of the PFDJ and 75 directly elected members. In May 1997, following the adoption of the Constitution, the Constituent Assembly empowered a Transitional National Assembly (comprising the 75 members of the PFDJ, 60 members of the Constituent Assembly and 15 representatives of Eritreans residing abroad) to act as the legislature until elections were held for a new National Assembly. Elections to the National Assembly were scheduled to be held before mid-1998.

Chairman of the Transitional National Assembly: ISSAIAS AFEWERKI.

Political Organizations

At independence in May 1993, many of the rival political organizations to the Eritrean People's Liberation Front (now the People's Front for Democracy and Justice) declared their support for the transitional Government.

Democratic Movement for the Liberation of Eritrea: opposition group; Leader HAMID TURKY.

Eritrean Islamic Jihad (EIJ): radical opposition group; in Aug. 1993 split into a mil. wing and a political wing, led by Sheikh MOHAMED ARAFA.

Eritrean Liberation Front (ELF): f. 1958; commenced armed struggle against Ethiopia in 1961; subsequently split into numerous factions (see below); mainly Muslim support; opposes the PFDJ; principal factions:

Eritrean Liberation Front–Central Command (ELF–CC): f. 1982; Chair. ABDALLAH IDRISS.

Eritrean Liberation Front–National Council (ELF–NC): Leader ABDULKADER JAILANY.

Eritrean Liberation Front–Revolutionary Council (ELF–RC): Leader AHMED NASSER.

People's Front for Democracy and Justice (PFDJ): Asmara; f. 1970 as the Eritrean Popular Liberation Forces, following a split in the Eritrean Liberation Front; renamed the Eritrean People's Liberation Front in 1977; adopted present name in Feb. 1994;

Christian and Muslim support; in May 1991 took control of Eritrea and formed provisional Govt; formed transitional Govt in May 1993; Chair. ISSAIAS AFEWERKI; Sec.-Gen. AMIN MUHAMMAD SA'ID.

Diplomatic Representation

EMBASSIES IN ERITREA

China, People's Republic: POB 204, Asmara; tel. (1) 116988; Ambassador: SHI YONGJIU.

Denmark: Asmara; Ambassador: PETER TRUELSEN.

Djibouti: POB 5589, Asmara; tel. (1) 114189; Chargé d'affaires a.i.: DJAMA OMER IDLEH.

Egypt: POB 5577, Asmara; tel. (1) 119935; Ambassador: HUSSEIN ALI AL-ZEQBI.

Ethiopia: Franklin D. Roosevelt St, Asmara; tel. (1) 116365; fax (1) 116144; Ambassador: AWALOM WOLDU.

France: POB 209, Asmara; tel. (1) 126599; fax (1) 121036; Ambassador: LOUIS LE VERT.

Germany: Saba Development Bldg, Airport Rd, POB 4974, Asmara; tel. (1) 182670; fax (1) 182900; Ambassador: WOLFGANG RINGE.

Israel: POB 5600, Asmara; tel. (1) 120137; fax (1) 120187; Ambassador: RAPHAEL WALDEN.

Italy: Wedajo Ali St, POB 220, Asmara; tel. (1) 120914; fax (1) 121115; Ambassador: CLAUDIO BAY ROSSI.

Russia: POB 6557, Asmara; tel. (1) 182112; fax (1) 182033; Ambassador: RACHID IBRAGIMOV.

Saudi Arabia: POB 5599, Asmara; tel. (1) 120171; fax (1) 121027; Ambassador: ABDUL R. IBRAHIM AL-TOELMI.

USA: POB 211, Asmara; tel. (1) 123410; fax (1) 117584; Ambassador: JOHN HICKS.

Yemen: POB 5566, Asmara; tel. (1) 114434; fax (1) 127921; Chargé d'affaires a.i.: AHMED HASSEN BIN HASSEN.

Judicial System

In 1994 the judicial system comprised the Supreme Court, 10 provincial courts and 29 district courts. At present the legal system incorporates laws adopted by the Eritrean People's Liberation Front prior to and following liberation, together with elements of customary law and Islamic law. Decree No. 37, issued in May 1993, directed the Eritrean courts 'to perform their duties according to the law and independently of the legislative and executive bodies of the Eritrean Government, and to safeguard the rights, interests and freedoms of the Government, associations and individuals, which are stated by the law.' According to the Constitution adopted in May 1997, the President appoints the judges of the Supreme Court.

Religion

Eritrea is almost equally divided between Muslims and Christians. Most Christians are adherents of the Orthodox Church, although there are Protestant and Roman Catholic communities. A small number of the population follow traditional beliefs.

CHRISTIANITY

The Eritrean Orthodox Church

In September 1993 the separation of the Eritrean Orthodox Church from the Ethiopian Orthodox Church was agreed by the respective church leaderships. The Eritrean Orthodox Church announced plans to appoint a bishop for each of the country's then 10 provinces. The first five bishops of the Eritrean Orthodox Church were consecrated in Cairo in September 1994. These consecrations signified the formal establishment of the Eritrean Orthodox Church as an independent body.

Leader: Bishop PHILIPPOS.

The Roman Catholic Church

At 31 December 1995 there were an estimated 125,564 adherents in the country.

Bishop of Asmara: Rt Rev. ZEKARIAS YOHANNES, 19 Gonder St, POB 244, Asmara; tel. (1) 120206; fax (1) 126519.

Bishop of Barentu: Rt Rev. LUCA MILESI, c/o 107 National Ave, POB 224, Asmara; tel. (1) 120631; fax (1) 122322.

Bishop of Keren: Rt Rev. TESFAMARIAN BEDHO, POB 460, Keren; tel. 401604.

The Anglican Communion

Within the Episcopal Church in Jerusalem and the Middle East, Eritrea lies within the jurisdiction of the Bishop in Egypt.

Leader: ASFAHA MAHARY.

ISLAM

There are substantial Muslim communities in the western lowlands, the northern highlands and the eastern coastal region.

Leader: Sheikh AL-AMIN OSMAN AL-AMIN.

The Press

Chamber News: POB 856, Asmara; tel. (1) 121388; fax (1) 120138; Tigrinya and English; publ. by Asmara Chamber of Commerce.

Eritrea Profile: POB 247, Asmara; f. 1994; weekly; English; publ. by the Ministry of Information and Culture.

Hadas Eritra (New Eritrea): Asmara; f. 1991; twice a week; in English, Tigrinya and Arabic; govt publ.; Editor YITBAREK ZEROM; circ. 25,000.

Trade and Development Bulletin: POB 856, Asmara; tel. (1) 121388; telex 42079; fax (1) 120138; monthly; Tigrinya and English; publ. by Asmara Chamber of Commerce (publication temporarily suspended in 1994); Editor TAAME FOTO.

Radio and Television

There were an estimated 300,000 radio receivers and 1,000 television receivers in use in 1993.

Communications and Postal Authority: POB 4918, Asmara; tel. (1) 112966; fax (1) 115847; Dir ESTIFANOS AFEWERKI.

RADIO

Voice of the Broad Masses of Eritrea (Dimseehafash): Ministry of Information, Radio Division, POB 872, Asmara; govt-controlled; programmes in Arabic, Tigrinya, Tigre, Amharic, Afar and Kunama.

TELEVISION

ERI-TV: Asmara: f. 1992; govt station providing educational, tech. and information service; broadcasting began in Jan. 1993 in Arabic and Tigrinya; transmissions limited to Asmara and surrounding areas.

Finance

(cap. = capital; brs = branches; amounts in Ethiopian birr)

Until mid-1997 the unit of currency in Eritrea was the Ethiopian birr. In July 1997 a decree was promulgated announcing the introduction of a new currency, the nakfa, to replace the birr.

BANKING

Bank of Eritrea: POB 849, Asmara; tel. (1) 123036; telex 42065; fax (1) 123162; f. 1993; state central bank; Gov. TEKIE BEYENE.

Commercial Bank of Eritrea: Asmara; dep. 5,100m. (Dec. 1996); Gen. Man. YAMANE TESFAI; 12 brs.

Housing and Commerce Bank of Eritrea: POB 235, Asmara; tel. (1) 120350; fax (1) 120401; f. 1994; cap. 5m.; finances residential and commercial construction projects; Gen. Man. and CEO Dr ARAIA TSEGGAI; 2 brs.

Trade and Industry

During the war of independence much of Eritrea's industrial base was either destroyed or dismantled and removed to Ethiopia. The transitional Government has estimated the initial cost of industrial regeneration to be US $20m. for the private sector and $66m. for the public sector. As part of its commitment to a free-market economy, the Government plans to divest itself of some 42 public enterprises which have resumed production, although at limited capacity. The greatest challenge facing Eritrean industry remains the acute shortage of energy. Offshore petroleum deposits beneath the Red Sea and substantial natural gas reserves in the Danakil depression await commercial exploitation.

CHAMBER OF COMMERCE

Asmara Chamber of Commerce: POB 856, Asmara; tel. (1) 121388; fax (1) 120138.

TRADE ORGANIZATION

Red Sea Trading Corpn: 29/31 Ras Alula St, POB 332, Asmara; tel. (1) 127846; fax (1) 124353; import and export services; operated by the PFDJ.

Transport

Eritrea's transport infrastructure was severely damaged during the three decades of war. As part of the Government's Recovery and Rehabilitation Programme, US $27m. has been allocated to road reconstruction and $10.2m. to improving port facilities.

Ministry of Transport: POB 204, Asmara; tel. (1) 110444; fax (1) 127048.

RAILWAYS

The 344-km railway connection between Agordat, Asmara and the port of Massawa was severely damaged during the war and ceased operation in 1978. In early 1997 the Asmara–Massawa line became operational (a short section of the railway had been reopened in 1994).

ROADS

Most of Eritrea's road system is unpaved. Roads that are paved require considerable repair, as do many of the bridges across seasonal water courses destroyed in the war. Road construction between Asmara and the port of Massawa is being given particular priority in the Recovery and Rehabilitation Programme.

SHIPPING

Eritrea has two major seaports: Massawa, which sustained heavy war damage in 1990, and Assab, which has principally served Addis Ababa, in Ethiopia. Under an agreement signed between the Ethiopian and Eritrean Governments in 1993, the two countries will share the facilities of both ports. Since the end of the war, activity in Massawa has increased substantially. In mid-1996 Italy and the World Bank approved funding for a major programme of investment at both ports. In 1996 a total of 445 vessels docked at Massawa, handling 813,126 metric tons of goods; 676 vessels docked at Assab, which handled 2,982,654 tons of goods.

Department of Maritime Transport: POB 6, Massawa; tel. 552992; fax 552157; Dir-Gen. MOKONEN HABTETSION.

Port and Maritime Transport Authority: POB 851, Asmara; tel. (1) 111399; fax (1) 113647; Dir WELDE MIKAEL ABRAHAM.

Eritrean Shipping Lines: 80 Semaetat Ave, POB 1110, Asmara; tel. (1) 120359; fax (1) 120331; f. 1992; provides shipping services in Red Sea and Persian (Arabian) Gulf areas and owns and operates four cargo ships; Gen. Man. TEWELDE KELATI.

CIVIL AVIATION

The international airport is at Asmara.

Civil Aviation Authority (Eritrean Airlines): POB 252, Asmara; tel. (1) 181822; fax (1) 181255; handles freight and passenger traffic for six scheduled carriers which use Asmara airport; Dir-Gen. ESTIFANOS AFEWERKI.

Tourism

With Eritrea's transport infrastructure still requiring massive repair, tourism remains undeveloped. However, the country possesses many areas of scenic and scientific interest, including the Dahlak Islands (a coralline archipelago rich in marine life), off the coast from Massawa, and the massive escarpment rising up from the coastal plain and supporting a unique ecosystem. In late 1993 the transitional Government inaugurated a programme of privatization of state-operated hotels in Asmara, Massawa, Keren and Assab. The Ministry of Tourism oversees the development of this sector. During 1995 some 315,000 tourists visited Eritrea.

Eritrean Tourism Service Corpn: Asmara; operates govt-owned hotels.

Defence

By mid-1995 some 64,000 combatants of the former Eritrean People's Liberation Front (which dominated the government formed at independence) had been demobilized, leaving an estimated strength of 55,000. Following independence, the Eritrean authorities assumed control of the Ethiopian navy, based in the ports of Massawa and Assab. National service is compulsory for all Eritreans between 18 and 40 years of age (with certain exceptions), for a period of 18 months, including six months of military training. The defence budget for 1996 was estimated at US $60m.

Education

Education is provided free of charge in government schools and at the University of Asmara. There are also some fee-paying private schools. Education is officially compulsory for children between seven and 13 years of age. Primary education begins at the age of seven and lasts for five years. Secondary education, beginning at 12 years of age, lasts for as much as six years, comprising a first cycle of two years and a second of four years. In 1994 the total enrolment at primary and secondary schools was equivalent to 32% of the school-age population (37% of boys; 28% of girls). In that year primary enrolment included 27% of children in the relevant age-group (males 28%; females 25%), while the comparable ratio for secondary enrolment was only 12% (males 13%; females 11%). Government expenditure on education and training in 1995 was estimated at 113.1m. birr (4.3% of total spending). By mid-1994 Eritrea had about 600 schools, almost three times as many as in 1991. In 1994 there were 3,081 students enrolled at the University of Asmara or at equivalent level institutions.

Bibliography

Cliffe, L., and Davidson, B. (Eds). *The Long Struggle of Eritrea for Independence and Constructive Peace*. Nottingham, Spokesman, 1988.

Connell, D. *Against All Odds: A Chronicle of the Eritrean Revolution*. Trenton, NJ, Red Sea Press, 1993.

Constitutional Commission of Eritrea. *Constitutional Proposals for Public Debate*. Asmara, Adulis Printing Press, 1995.

Doornbos, M., Cliffe, L., and Markakis, J. (Eds). *Beyond Conflict in the Horn: The Prospects of Peace and Development in Ethiopia, Somalia, Eritrea and Sudan*. Lawrenceville, KS, Red Sea Press, 1992.

Duffield, M., and Prendergast, J. *Without Troops and Tanks: Humanitarian Intervention in Ethiopia and Eritrea*. Lawrenceville, KS, Red Sea Press, 1995.

Ellingson, L. *The Emergence of Eritrea, 1958–1992*. London, James Currey Publishers, 1993.

Erlich, H. *The Struggle over Eritrea 1962–78*. Stanford, CA, Hoover Institution, 1983.

Firebrace, J., and Holland, S. *Never Kneel Down*. Trenton, NJ, Red Sea Press, 1985.

Fukui, K., and Markakis, J. (Eds). *Ethnicity and Conflict in the Horn of Africa*. London, James Currey, 1994.

Gebregergis, T. *Eritrea: An Account of an Eritrean Political Exile on his Visit to Liberated Eritrea: December 1991–March 1992*. Amsterdam, Liberation Books, 1993.

Gebre-Medhin, J. *Peasants and Nationalism in Eritrea*. Trenton, NJ, Red Sea Press, 1989.

Ghebre-Ab, H. (Ed.). *Ethiopia and Eritrea: A Documentary Study*. Trenton, NJ, Red Sea Press, 1993.

Gorke, I., Klingebiel, S., et al. *Promoting the Reintegration of Former Female and Male Combatants in Eritrea*. Berlin, German Development Institute, 1995.

Iyob, R. *The Eritrean Struggle for Independence: Domination, Resistance, Nationalism 1941–93*. Cambridge, Cambridge University Press, 1995.

Kibreab, G. *Ready and Willing . . . But Still Waiting: Eritrean Refugees in Sudan and the Dilemmas of Return*. Uppsala, Life and Peace Institute, 1996.

Legum, C., and Lee, B. *Conflict in the Horn of Africa*. London, Rex Collings, 1977.

Lewis, I. M. (Ed.). *Nationalism in the Horn of Africa*. London, Ithaca Press, 1983.

Machida, R. *Eritrea: The Struggle for Independence*. Trenton, NJ, Red Sea Press, 1987.

Markakis, J. *National and Class Conflict in the Horn of Africa*. Cambridge, Cambridge University Press (African Studies Series No. 55), 1988.

Medhanie, T. *Eritrea: The Dynamics of a National Question*. Amsterdam, B. R. Grunner, 1986.

Eritrea and Neighbours in the 'New World Order': Geopolitics, Democracy and 'Islamic Fundamentalism'. Munster, LIT, 1994.

Mesghenna, Y. *Italian Colonialism: A Case Study of Eritrea 1869–1934.* Lund, University of Lund, 1989.

Negash, T. *Italian Colonialism in Eritrea, 1882–1941: Policies, Praxis and Impact.* Uppsala, Almqvist and Wiksell International, 1987.

No Medicine for the Bite of a White Snake: Notes on Nationalism and Resistance in Eritrea 1890–1940. Uppsala, University Press, 1987.

Eritrea and Ethiopia: The Federal Experience. New Brunswick, NJ, Transaction Publishers, 1997.

Papstein, R. *Eritrea: A Tourist Guide.* Lawrenceville, KS, Red Sea Press, 1995.

Pateman, R. *Eritrea: Even the Stones are Burning.* Trenton, NJ, Red Sea Press, 1990.

Eritrea: Revolution at Dusk. Trenton, NJ, Red Sea Press, 1991.

Prouty, C., and Rosenfeld, E. *Historical Dictionary of Ethiopia and Eritrea.* 2nd Edn. Lanham MD, and London, Scarecrow Press, 1994.

Sherman, R. *Eritrea: The Unfinished Revolution.* New York, Praeger, 1980.

Tekle, A. (Ed.). *Eritrea and Ethiopia: From Conflict to Co-operation.* Lawrenceville, KS, Red Sea Press, 1994.

Tesfagiorgis, G. H. (Ed.). *Emergent Eritrea: Challenges of Economic Development.* Lawrenceville, KS, Red Sea Press, 1993.

Trevaskis, G. K. *Eritrea: A Colony in Transition.* London, Oxford University Press, 1960.

With, P. *Politics and Liberation: the Eritrean Struggle, 1961–1986.* Aarhus, Denmark, University of Aarhus, 1987.

Wolde-Yesus, A. *Eritrea: Root Causes of War and Refugees.* Baghdad, Sinbad, 1992.

ETHIOPIA

Physical and Social Geography

G. C. LAST

The Federal Democratic Republic of Ethiopia is a land-locked country in the Horn of Africa. Its boundaries stretch from latitude 3°N to 15°N and from longitude 33°E to 48°E, enclosing an area of 1,133,380 sq km (437,600 sq miles). Ethiopia's western neighbour is Sudan; to the south it shares a border with Kenya; and to the east and south-east lie the Republic of Djibouti and Somalia. To the north and north-east lies the State of Eritrea.

PHYSICAL FEATURES

Elevations range from around 100 m below sea-level in the Dallol Depression (Kobar Sink), on the north-eastern border with Eritrea, to a number of mountain peaks in excess of 4,000 m above sea-level, which dominate the plateaux and of which the highest is Ras Dashen, rising to 4,620 m.

The southern half of Ethiopia is bisected by the rift valley, ranging between 40–60 km in width and containing a number of lakes. In the latitude of Addis Ababa, the western wall of the rift turns north and runs parallel to the west coast of Arabia, leaving a wide plain between the escarpment and the Red Sea coast of Eritrea. The eastern wall of the rift turns to the east in the latitude of Addis Ababa, forming an escarpment looking north over the Afar plains. The escarpments are nearly always abrupt, and are broken at only one point near Addis Ababa where the Awash river descends from the rim of the plateau.

The plateaux to the west of the rift system dip gently towards the west and are drained by right bank tributaries of the Nile system, which have carved deep and spectacular gorges. The plateaux to the north of Lake Tana are drained by the Tekeze and Angareb rivers, headwaters of the Atbara. The central plateaux are drained by the Abbai (Blue Nile) river and its tributaries. The Abbai rises in Lake Tana and is known as the Blue Nile in Sudan. Much of the flood water in the Blue Nile system comes from the left-bank tributaries, which rise in the high rainfall region of south-west Ethiopia. This southern region is also drained by the Akobo, Gilo and Baro rivers which form the headwaters of the Sobat river. The only river of significance to the west of the rift valley which is not part of the Nile system is the Omo, which drains southwards into Lake Turkana and is known in its upper course as the Gibie. The lower trough of the Omo has, in recent years, been the site of interesting archaeological discoveries of early human occupation, pre-dating the early remains at Olduvai in Tanzania. The rift valley itself contains a number of closed river basins, including the largest, the Awash, which flows north from the rift valley proper into the Afar plain and terminates in Lake Abe. It is in the middle and lower Awash regions of the rift valley that even earlier remains of man have been discovered, in the locality of Hadow, below the escarpment to the east of Dessie. The highlands to the east of the rift are drained south-eastwards by the headstreams of the Webi-Shebelli and Juba river systems.

The location of Ethiopia across a series of major fault lines and its association with earth movements, particularly in the Afar plains, which are related to the continuing drift of the African continent away from the Asian blocks, makes it highly susceptible to minor earth tremors.

CLIMATE, VEGETATION AND NATURAL RESOURCES

Ethiopia lies within the tropics but the wide range of altitude produces considerable variations in temperature conditions which are reflected in the traditional zones of the *dega* (the temperate plateaux), the *kolla* (hot lowlands) and the intermediate frost-free zone of the *woina dega*. The boundaries between these three zones lie at approximately 2,400 m and 1,700 m above sea-level. Average annual temperature in the *dega* is about 16°C, in the *woina dega* about 22°C and in the *kolla* at least 26°C. A main rainy season covers most of the country during June, July and August, when moist equatorial air is drawn in from the south and west.

Ethiopia is extremely vulnerable to drought conditions, particularly in the low-lying pastoral areas, and along the eastern escarpment where there is a widespread dependence upon the spring rains (*belg*). The development of cultivation in areas of marginal rainfall has accentuated this problem.

Despite the significant variations in local climates and in the distribution of rainfall, Ethiopia's climatic conditions can be described generally in terms of well-watered highlands and uplands, mostly receiving at least 1,000 mm of rain a year with the exception of the Tigrean plateau, and dry lowlands, generally having less than 500 mm of rain, with the significant exception of the Baro and Akobo river plains in the south-west, which lie in the path of summer rain-bearing winds.

The natural vegetation of the plateaux and highlands above 1,800 m is coniferous forest (notably *zigba* and *tid)*, but these forests have now largely disappeared and are found today only in the more inaccessible regions of the country. In the south-west higher rainfall with lower elevations and higher temperatures has produced extensive broad-leafed rain forests with a variety of species including abundant *karraro*. Although there has been a steady encroachment by shifting cultivators, these forested areas in the former Illubabor and Kaffa Administrative Regions of the south-west are relatively remote and have not yet been subjected to extensive commercial exploitation.

Above the tree line on the plateaux are wide expanses of mountain grassland. The highlands are the site of settled agriculture in which approximately 4m. farmers produce a variety of grain crops. Unfortunately, the growth of population and the depletion of resources in forest cover and soil has led to the practice of farming in areas which are very marginal and unreliable in rainfall, particularly along the eastern escarpment. This has exacerbated the drought and famine conditions which have developed in the period since 1973. In the lowlands, dependent on rainfall conditions, there is a range of dry-zone vegetation. The extensive natural range-lands, particularly in the Borena and Ogaden plains in the south, are an important natural resource in Ethiopia, a fact which is responsible for the country's estimated cattle population of around 29.8m. head.

However, the drought conditions, which began in 1972–73, in association with abnormal conditions affecting the whole Sahel region of Africa, have completely disrupted the pastoral economy in many areas. There has been a high mortality rate both of humans and livestock, while the vegetation cover has sustained a long-term set-back.

Although the exploitation of gold and copper ores on the Eritrean plateau dates from prehistoric times, relatively little is known of the potential mineral resources of Ethiopia; by the mid-1990s only about one-quarter of the country had been geologically mapped. There are alluvial gold workings in the Adola area of the Sidamo region, and platinum deposits near Yubdo in the Wollega region. Probably the area with the highest mineral potential lies in the west and south-west (in the Wollega, Illubabor and Kaffa regions). However, this region is largely inaccessible and much of it is covered by rain forest. Potentially valuable deposits of potash have been located in the Dallol Depression. Their exploitation, however, awaits the development of other infrastructure in this desolate region.

Exploration for petroleum was carried out for some years in the Ogaden region without success. More recently, however, attention has been diverted to the southern borders of Ethiopia. In the Bale region between the rivers Web and Webi-Shebelli, it has been reported that petroleum reserves have been identified. The geothermal power potential of extensive sources in the Afar plain region is being evaluated.

Ethiopia commands excellent potential for the generation of hydroelectric power. A number of plants are already in operation along the course of the Awash river, south of Addis Ababa. Along the Blue Nile river basin, numerous sites have been identified at which power production could be coupled with irrigation schemes.

POPULATION

There has never been a full population census in Ethiopia, but a census that was conducted in May 1984 was estimated to have reached 85% of the population. The results showed the total population (excluding Eritrea, but including an estimate for areas not covered by the census) to be 39,868,501 (males 20,062,453, females 19,806,048). Based on these figures, the country's estimated total population was 56,677,100 at mid-1995. The average annual population growth rate for Ethiopia in 1985–94 was 2.9%. The large percentage of the population aged 19 years or less, coupled with the early age of marriage in Ethiopia, contributed to the rapidly increasing population growth rate during the 1980s. However, the annual population growth rate during 1990–95 declined to 1.9%.

At the 1984 census the capital, Addis Ababa, was the largest city (with a population of 1,412,577), followed by Asmara (now the capital of Eritrea—275,385) and Dire Dawa (98,104). There were also nine towns with between 50,000 and 90,000 inhabitants each. Mid-1993 population estimates (excluding Eritrea) suggested that the population of the capital had increased to 2,200,186, while a further eight towns each had more than 100,000 inhabitants. The growth rates in these larger urban settlements are high. Overall density of population at mid-1995 was 50.0 per sq km. However, this average conceals a very wide variation among the regions, as might be expected from the multiplicity of natural environments.

Generally speaking, the distribution of population reflects the pattern of relief. The highlands, having a plentiful rainfall, are the home of settled agriculture and contain nearly all of the major settlements. Land more than 2,000 m above sea-level is free of the malarial mosquito, a factor contributing to the non-occupation of lowlands which are suitable for farming. It would not be unreasonable to assume that 10% of the population live below 1,000 m, 20% at 1,000 m–1,800 m and 70% above the 1,800 m contour line. The distribution of population has been affected by recurrent droughts since the mid-1980s, which have forced many people to leave their traditional areas in search of emergency aid; and by the erstwhile government's policy of resettling famine victims from the former Tigre and Wollo Administrative Regions in newly-established villages in the lowlands of the south-west; additionally, the civil war, which intensified between 1989 and its resolution in 1991, caused the displacement of large numbers of the population.

Recent History

PATRICK GILKES

THE ETHIOPIAN EMPIRE

Ethiopia's history as an organized and independent polity dates from about 100 BC with a kingdom at Axum. The Axumite empire, as it later became, covered the northern part of the present state and included part of Eritrea down to the coast around Massawa. It was converted to Christianity in the fourth century AD. In the fourth and sixth centuries, it extended across the Red Sea, but its core lay in the northern Ethiopian highlands. When Axum collapsed in the eighth century, power shifted south to Lasta, and later to Shoa. In the 16th century, 50 years of conflict with the Muslim sultanate of Adal exhausted both; they fell an easy prey to the Oromos, a pastoral people who expanded out of a small area to the south. Adal was reduced to the city of Harar; the Ethiopian rulers removed to Gondar in the north-west.

In the late 18th century, as the monarchy weakened, central government broke down, although the position of emperor, however enfeebled, and the Ethiopian Orthodox (Coptic) Church, provided an element of continuity. Real power was in the hands of provincial nobles from the highlands, Tigrean, Oromo and Amhara, who fought for control of the throne, although none seized it until 1855. Tewodros, a minor noble from Gondar, and then Yohannes IV from the northern Tigre region, tried to restore imperial power. Yohannes spent most of his reign fending off Egyptians, Italians and Dervishes: he died in battle with the Dervishes in 1889. His successor, Menelik of Shoa, reunited and expanded the empire to the east, south and west of Shoa. These largely Oromo-inhabited areas provided virtually all Ethiopia's resources, in particular coffee, gold, ivory and slaves. Menelik's successes coincided with the arrival of the European colonial powers. He defeated the Italians at the battle of Adua in 1896, but under the subsequent treaty Italy retained control of Eritrea, which it had formally colonized in 1890.

Menelik's conquests shifted the balance of the empire south again; in the 1880s he founded a new capital, Addis Ababa, where the first bank, hospital, modern school and printing press were established in the 1900s. A railway, from Djibouti, reached Dire Dawa in 1902 and Addis Ababa in 1918. In 1907, also as part of his programme of modernization and unification, Menelik established a cabinet, although it was largely disregarded following his death in 1911, when his grandson, Lij Yasu, assumed imperial control. Suspicious of the Christian Amhara nobility of Shoa, he tried to put together an alternative coalition of support, composed of Oromos (the ethnic group of his father) and Muslims; and, in the hope of gaining access to the sea (cut off by the Italian colony of Eritrea), he looked for support to Germany and Turkey as enemies of France, Britain and Italy. Still uncrowned, Lij Yasu was deposed in 1916, following an alleged conversion to Islam. Zauditu, a daughter of Menelik, became empress while Ras Teferi, later Emperor Haile Selassie, became regent and heir. As regent he obtained Ethiopia's entry into the League of Nations and issued the first anti-slavery decrees. Once emperor (1930), Haile Selassie began the process of wresting power from the nobility and turning Ethiopia into a modern autocracy. His efforts were interrupted in 1935 by the Italian invasion. Mussolini had imperial ambitions and sought revenge for the defeat of Adua. In May 1936 with his armies defeated, partly because of Italy's use of poison gas, Haile Selassie left Ethiopia to appeal to the League of Nations. On his departure the Italian army entered Addis Ababa and a five-year period under Italian fascist occupation began. The liberation of Ethiopia was facilitated by the Second World War, with Haile Selassie's cause becoming part of the Allies' campaign against Germany and Italy. In May 1941, following its capture by South African troops, Haile Selassie re-entered his capital. The Italians left little behind except an extensive road network, although their administrative divisions, ethnically based, influenced post-war attitudes.

After 1941, Haile Selassie continued his largely successful policy of centralization, playing off the United Kingdom, which came close to occupying Ethiopia after 1941 (it only withdrew from the Ogaden in 1948 and the Reserved Haud area in 1954), against the USA. In 1952, after protracted discussions, Eritrea, which had been made a UN mandated territory after the war, was federated with Ethiopia. Almost immediately Haile Selassie set about dismantling its institutions, including the press, the trade unions and the elected parliament, all anathema to his own highly centralized system of government. In 1962 Eritrea became a province of Ethiopia: a development that ignited the Eritrean struggle for independence. Originally led by the Eritrean Liberation Front (ELF) which drew most of its support from Muslim pastoralists from the lowland areas, it was joined in the early 1970s by the Eritrean People's Liberation Front (EPLF), which was more representative of the Christian highland agriculturalists.

Haile Selassie provided the trappings of a modern state, including, in 1955, a constitution with parliament elected by universal adult suffrage; but it had no power. Similarly, he made no real attempt to effect necessary changes in land policy, or adjust the hierarchies of administrative power to lessen the dominance of Christian Amharas (who constituted no more than 35% of the population). Ethiopia remained essentially feudal, with small Amhara-dominated modern sectors in the bureaucracy and in industry. These provided the impetus for the outbreak of opposition among non-Amhara nationalities, in Tigre region in 1943, among Oromos and Somalis in Bale in 1963–70, and from 1961 in Eritrea. Haile Selassie himself dismissed the revolt of his own bodyguard in 1960 as no more than a minor problem, and remained bemused by annual student demonstrations which took place from 1965 onwards. He preferred to concentrate on international affairs, securing Addis Ababa as the headquarters of the Organization of African Unity (OAU), and of the UN Economic Commission for Africa. His main ally was the USA, with Ethiopia being the principal recipient of US aid in Africa in the 1950s and 1960s and providing the USA with a major communications base at Kagnew, near Asmara. Haile Selassie failed, however, to quell Somali irredentism or to prevent Sudan assisting the Eritrean rebels, even though he helped negotiate the settlement of 1972 between Northern and Southern Sudan.

The long-term weaknesses of the regime included the growing agrarian crisis, inequitable distribution of land, and lack of development. More immediately, the costs of revolts in Bale and Eritrea, drought and famine in Wollo in 1972–74 (when 200,000 people died) and, by 1973, Haile Selassie's own near-incapacity (owing to old age) and his failure to designate an heir, fuelled the grievances of the military, students (with no employment prospects) and workers. A series of mutinies in the army started in January 1974, paralleled by civilian strikes. A new prime minister was appointed, with a mandate to introduce real constitutional change. Matters seemed to settle briefly; but behind the scenes more radical political groups and elements within the armed forces were gaining prominence. By June, when it was clear that reform was stagnating, a newly-formed co-ordinating committee of the armed forces, police and territorial army took action, arresting leading aristocrats and political figures, including the emperor's closest associates and advisers. After a series of revelations concerning financial manipulation, Haile Selassie was deposed in September, with hardly a murmur of dissent. In March 1975 the constitution was abrogated, parliament dissolved and the monarchy was formally abolished.

REVOLUTION AND MILITARY RULE

The imperial regime was replaced by the co-ordinating committee, as a provisional military administrative council (PMAC), known as the Dergue. A popular soldier, Lt-Gen. Aman Andom, was drafted in as head of state and chairman of the Dergue, but the Dergue itself, a group of 109 soldiers up to the rank of major, held the real power. Internal disputes over whether to take a hard line against the ongoing Eritrean revolt (Gen. Aman was himself Eritrean) led to the deaths of Aman and two other Dergue members in November 1974. At the same time 57 former high-ranking military and civilian officials were summarily shot without trial, including two former prime ministers and 17 generals. A new head of state was appointed, Brig.-Gen. Teferi Banti, who also became the nominal chairman of the Dergue. His two vice-chairmen were Maj. (later Lt-Col) Mengistu Haile Mariam and Lt-Col Atnafu Abate.

The PMAC began to see itself as the vanguard of the revolution, and under the influence of left-wing intellectuals returning from abroad, opted for a socialist model of government. In December 1974, Ethiopia was declared a socialist state, and a programme of revolutionary reforms called *Ethiopia Tikdem* ('Ethiopia First') was initiated. Most of the major reforms were implemented in early 1975. More than 100 companies were nationalized or partly taken over by the state. Rural land was nationalized in March, and urban land four months later. Thousands of students were dispatched to the countryside as part of a national campaign for development, designed to provide education in health, literacy and to organize the land reform. (Later, in 1979, an impressive and highly successful national literacy campaign was launched.) More than 30,000 local, electively-led peasant associations were created with responsibility for their own tax collection, judicial affairs and administration. Similar associations, *kebeles*, were established in towns, with pyramids of higher level organizations, district, regional and national. In December 1975 a new trade union organization was created, the All-Ethiopia Trade Union.

It was not until April 1976, however, that the theory of the revolution was outlined in the 'national democratic revolution programme'. This was essentially the work of a Marxist-Leninist group, the All-Ethiopia Socialist Movement (MEISON) which wanted a Soviet-style communist party, and, more important, was prepared to accept the need for military rule for the time being. It was therefore allowed to operate through a political office and an ideological school, both established in May. Its rival was the Ethiopian People's Revolutionary Party (EPRP), another and more popular Marxist-Leninist grouping, which argued for the immediate creation of a civilian government, and also supported the Eritrean struggle. Both groups had supporters within the Dergue; both were involved in the struggle to control the new institutions. Their disputes intensified into urban terrorism and spilt over into the Dergue. Lt-Col Mengistu (who in 1975 had emerged as the most influential member of the Dergue) came under threat in December 1976 when the structure of the Dergue was reorganized. Six weeks later Mengistu retaliated: in February 1977 Gen. Teferi Banti and five other leading members of the Dergue were executed and Mengistu took over as head of state and chairman of the PMAC. He subsequently launched, originally on behalf of his ally MEISON, the 'red terror' campaign, aimed at eliminating the EPRP. Tens of thousands of people were killed or tortured, particularly in urban areas. MEISON did not benefit; in mid-1977 Mengistu turned against it. By late 1978 both organizations had been virtually eliminated.

These ideological and power struggles were intensified by the deteriorating military situation in both Eritrea in the north and in the south and south-east where Somalia was also attempting to take advantage of the weakness of the central administration and of the Ethopian army, whose structure and effectiveness had been virtually destroyed by the revolution. In Eritrea the collapse of the government position was first apparent in January 1975 when a joint attack by the ELF and the EPLF on Asmara, the Eritrean capital, nearly succeeded in capturing the city. The government response was substantial and brutal, and for the first time many Tigrean Christians in Eritrea joined the liberation fronts. In 1976 the Dergue made its first effort to raise a 'people's army', organizing a force of some 20,000 ill-armed and untrained peasants who were easily defeated by the Eritreans. It quickly learnt from the disaster: Cuba, persuaded of Ethopia's revolutionary authenticity by Mengistu, trained more than 300,000 men in six months in 1977.

The new units proved to be necessary. By the end of 1977 only five garrisons remained in Eritrea—in Adi Caieh, Asmara, Barentu, Massawa, and Assab far to the south. Some of the new militia were moved in to hold these five towns; most had to be rushed down to the south-east where guerrilla operations were reinforced by a Somali invasion in July 1977. Somalia claimed the Somali-inhabited area of the Ogaden, arguing that it had been colonized by the Ethiopians in the late 19th century. For Ethiopia, the issue was simply one of an undefined border. There was a brief undeclared war in 1964, followed by an OAU cease-fire, but as Ethiopia's internal security weakened in 1975–76, Somalia reorganized the Western Somali Liberation Front (WSLF), and increased arms supplies and training. Cuba made an unsuccessful effort to mediate between the two states in March 1977. In July Somali forces crossed the border, and by November the city of Harar was under attack. However the overstretched Somali army ran out of supplies, just as Ethiopia received a massive influx of Soviet weapons, including hundreds of tanks, and fighter aircraft. Somalia, until then a close ally of the USSR (which had tried to remain on good terms with both countries), expelled Soviet military advisers and severed relations with Cuba, correctly convinced that the USSR had decided for Ethiopia. (In early 1977 Mengistu had formally broken with the USA after criticisms of Ethiopia's human rights record and its failure to supply the arms he needed.) With its new weaponry and some 16,000 Cuban troops, the Ethiopian army went on the offensive in February 1978. In early March the Somali army was forced to withdraw.

In June 1978 a revitalized Ethiopian army moved back into Eritrea. Within three months, it had recaptured most of the towns and reopened the roads south. By the end of the year the ELF, largely subdued, had reverted to guerrilla operations, while the EPLF had withdrawn to the far north to the proximity of the remote town of Nakfa. There, however, advancing Ethiopian forces lost their momentum, and over several years accumulated severe losses in a series of unsuccessful offensives. The largest, undertaken as part of 'Operation Red Star', was personally commanded by Mengistu. Launched when a government campaign to mollify discontent in Eritrea had had some effect, the operation was to have combined military and development activity and was designed to achieve the full integration of Eritrea with Ethiopia. It was, however, another failure (resulting in 30,000 casualties) despite the continuing religious, ethnic and ideological differences among the Eritrean movements which had erupted into civil war in 1981. (The EPLF, in alliance with the Tigre People's Liberation Front (TPLF) from neighbouring Tigre region, forced the ELF into Sudan in 1982, where they were disarmed and later fragmented.)

THE NATIONALITIES ISSUE

The successes of 1978 allowed Mengistu to turn his attention to organizing a political party of government. The removal of MEISON left several small Marxist-Leninist political organizations, but disputes among them and within the PMAC led Lt-Col Mengistu to opt for a party of individuals. The Commission for Organizing the Party of the Working People of Ethiopia was established in 1979. The composition of its central committee was 70% military. Loyalty rather than ideology became the prime criterion for membership. Revolutionary women's and youth movements were founded in 1980, and the All-Ethiopia Peasant Association and the All-Ethiopia Trade Union were restructured in 1982. In September 1984, the Workers' Party of Ethiopia (WPE) was formally inaugurated; for the first time representatives from the workers', peasants' and local organizations were included in the central committee. The WPE failed to attract either support or loyalty from the general population, being seen, rightly, as a vehicle for the regime's control. Nor did it have the desired effect on the PMAC's major problem in the 1970s: the continued failure to solve the nationality issue.

From the beginning the rhetoric of the revolution raised expectations among various nationalities, particularly Oromos, Somalis, Afars and Tigreans. (Eritrea, with nine nationalities, was seen less as a nationalist issue by the EPLF than as a colonial issue, a more acceptable reason for independence to the international community.) The government had one partial success, the Afars. The Afar Liberation Front was founded in 1975 after an unsuccessful revolt by the traditional ruler, Sultan Ali Mirreh; but a 'progressive' Afar National Liberation Movement (ANLM) appeared, which was prepared to accept the PMAC's version of regional autonomy. A successful Afar congress was held in Gewane in April 1977. Subsequently ANLM members were appointed local administrators, but the speed of progress towards autonomy satisfied no one. No advance was made in autonomy for Somalis or Oromos. The Somalis, despite the defeat of Somalia in 1978, had the great advantage of an open border, and the Somali government continued its support for the WSLF and the Somali Abo Liberation Front (which operated in Bale and Sidamo regions) until the mid-1980s when both movements, suffering from internal splits, virtually collapsed. The Ethiopian government, similarly, backed Somali opposition groups, holding two Somali villages in 1982–88. Relations between the two governments improved in 1986 as a result of Italian and Djiboutian mediation; and in 1988, faced by a desperate need for extra troops in Eritrea, Mengistu abandoned his insistence on border demarcation as a precondition to the cessation of hostilities with Somalia.

By the early 1980s, the Oromo Liberation Front (OLF), which advocates self-determination for the Oromo people and emphasizes the use of Oromo culture and language, was gaining support from peasants critical of government efforts to establish co-operatives. Prior to this the regime's greatest area of support had been among Oromo peasantry who had benefited from the land reforms of 1975. Government responses to Oromo opposition included widespread arrests of Oromos in Addis Ababa and other towns, but the OLF remained militarily small, operating along the Sudan border of western Wollega, and in an area south-west of Harar.

Most serious for the government was the growth of the TPLF. Established in 1975, it gained the support of the EPLF, from which it received training and arms. The TPLF had other opponents besides the central government: the Ethiopian Democratic Union, a group operating in exile which included members of the former aristocracy, and the EPRP, which had taken up armed struggle in Tigre in 1975. The TPLF drove them out in 1977–78, and later gained considerable support from the effects of the 'red terror' campaign, and from its calls for Tigrean self-determination. It became increasingly left wing, setting up the Marxist-Leninist League of Tigre in the mid-1980s. Like the Eritreans and Oromos, the TPLF gained substantially from using the border with Sudan. Throughout the 1980s Ethio-Sudanese relations were poor, with each country supporting the other's dissidents. The regime's response to the growth of the nationality movements and their guerrilla operations was at first military, though operations against the TPLF and other groups always took second place to those in Eritrea. A political response finally came in a constitution endorsed by referendum in February 1987. This provided for an 835-seat elected legislature, the national shengo, and in September the People's Democratic Republic of Ethiopia was proclaimed with Mengistu as president, chief executive, c-in-c of the armed forces, and chairman of the council of ministers, the defence council and the state council. Ethiopia was declared a unified socialist state under the democratic centralism of the WPE. A new administrative structure allowed for five autonomous regions, of which four were based on ethnicity: Tigre for the Tigrean people; Dire Dawa for the Issa Somalis; the Ogaden region for all other Somalis; Assab for the Afars; and Eritrea (with nine different nationalities). The EPLF and the TPLF at once rejected the new structure. By then both were determined to depose Mengistu, regarding his removal as a prerequisite for achievement of their aims.

Political failure was paralleled by economic and military disasters. Efforts to mobilize production after 1979 made some progress, but the state farms proved extremely inefficient, and the catastrophic drought of 1984–85 eradicated any gains. The international community's response to the disaster was slow, partly because of Ethiopia's degree of commitment to the USSR, which in total, provided the regime with some US $8,000m. of military equipment. The numbers of those who died are unknown. The government, as part of its relief measures, moved about 600,000 people into the south and west in a highly unpopular resettlement campaign, while the TPLF (Tigre was the most badly affected area) moved 200,000 into Sudan. The resettlement scheme, ill-prepared and less than voluntary, was terminated in 1986 as a result of international criticism. Another major famine threatened in 1989–90, following the highly unpopular villagization policy, bringing together several villages as single units for security and political reasons. Agricultural production slumped, while provision of aid was complicated by the conflicts, with both sides using food as a weapon.

OVERTHROW OF MENGISTU'S REGIME

The military situation deteriorated steadily after 1988, with defeats in Eritrea followed by the loss to the TPLF of all Tigre region in the following year. Disillusionment grew in the army, which previously had been prepared to accept Mengistu because of his determination to keep Eritrea and his commitment to a united Ethiopia; but by 1989 his refusal to contemplate a political solution was regarded as a liability. In May most senior army officers took part in an attempted *coup d'état*. Its failure led to sweeping changes in the command structure. The appointment of unqualified commanders, coupled with a series of defeats, further demoralized the army. Within weeks of the attempted coup, Mengistu agreed to more talks with the EPLF, which itself only accepted under heavy international pressure, since meetings held in 1982–85 had been fruitless. In 1989, utilizing the provisions of the 1987 constitution, the government offered autonomy to the regions, whereby regional assemblies, with control over health, education, development, finance and taxation, would be elected. This was not enough for the leaders of the EPLF, nor did they trust Mengistu. Neither side was prepared to compromise on the issue of Eritrean independence. Talks with the TPLF made equally little progress.

Once in control of Tigre in 1989, the TPLF established a united front, the Ethiopian People's Revolutionary Democratic Front (EPRDF), with the Ethiopian People's Democratic Movement, an Amhara organization created by the TPLF as a surrogate group to fight in non-Tigrean areas. This group subsequently became the Amhara National Democratic Movement (ANDM). As the EPRDF advanced further south, it created other bodies: the Oromo People's Democratic Organization (OPDO), after the OLF refused to join the EPRDF, and a short-lived officers' movement (EDORM). The TPLF remained the major element in the front, but its own original demands for self-determination were replaced by its commitment to the removal of Mengistu and the establishment of a democratic government in Addis Ababa. By November 1989, the EPRDF had reached within 160 km of Addis Ababa. For a time it looked as if Mengistu might be able to obtain Israel's support in return for allowing Falashas to leave (13,000 had been flown from Sudan to Israel in a secret airlift in 1984). Relations were restored in November, and Israel provided Ethiopia with cluster bombs and anti-guerrilla training; but, under strong US pressure, this support was stopped. (In May 1991, with government consent, the Israelis took control of Addis Ababa airport for 36 hours to evacuate the remaining Falasha population, numbering about 14,000.)

By February 1990, when the EPLF captured Massawa (severing supply lines for the Ethiopian army in Eritrea), Mengistu made further concessions. Ethiopian socialism was abandoned; opposition groups were invited to participate in a unity party; free market principles replaced economic planning; and peasants were allowed to bequeath land to their children. It was too late. The economy was collapsing as rapidly as the military and political situation. The price of coffee was falling, and supplies of low-cost Soviet petroleum had ceased in May 1989. The revolution in Eastern Europe precipitated a complete collapse of Ethiopia's overseas alliances and the loss of critically necessary arms supplies. In January 1991, the EPRDF produced a new political programme which did not mention Marxism and was moderate and democratic enough to be acceptable to the USA. As the guerrillas closed in on Addis Ababa, Mengistu's armies ceased to fight. On 21 May, Mengistu fled to Zimbabwe, where he was granted political asylum. The USA presided over peace talks in London in an attempt to provide an orderly transfer of power from the government. The government delegation could not even surrender before the USA, fearing a collapse of law and order in Addis Ababa, invited the EPRDF to form a government, a move which the OLF regarded as premature. The EPLF attended the conference but as observers only, to mark Eritrea's *de facto* independence. On 28 May the EPRDF entered the capital and subsequently established an interim government. The EPLF likewise established a provisional government in Eritrea, pending the holding of a referendum on the issue of independence. This was successfully conducted in April 1993, when 99.8% of voters demonstrated overwhelming support for independence. Full independence was achieved in May 1993 and relations with Ethiopia improved considerably following a series of agreements covering defence, security, trade and economy. A joint venture between the two countries' national airlines was concluded in November 1994, and agreement was also reached on the joint use of Assab—its status as a free port being of particular importance to Ethiopia, which had become the world's most populous land-locked state.

THE EPRDF AND ETHNIC POLITICS

In July 1991 the EPRDF convened a national conference attended by representatives of some 20 political organizations to discuss Ethiopia's political future and establish a transitional government. It was carefully organized, with the EPRDF preparing the agenda, drafting a national charter providing for an 87-seat council of representatives to govern during a two-year transition period, creating some of the political groups which attended, and organizing seat allocations. The chairman of the EPRDF, Meles Zenawi, was elected head of state; the vice-chairman of the EPRDF, Tamirat Layne, became prime minister. Some 32 political organizations were subsequently represented on the council, with the EPRDF's component parts occupying 32 of the 87 seats. The next largest group on the council was the OLF with 12 seats. The Oromos were allocated a total of 27 seats but they were divided between five different organizations. The portfolios of the council of ministers were similarly distributed with 17 ministers from seven different organizations being appointed.

From the outset, the EPRDF made it clear it would support Eritrean independence, and emphasized self-determination for Ethiopia's nationalities within a federal system as the answer to the political problem of a multi-ethnic state. The EPRDF originally established 12 self-governing regions with two chartered cities. After changes including the merger of four regions in the south west, the new constitution of 1994 created the states of Tigre, Afar, Amhara, Oromia, Benishangul-Gumuz, Southern Peoples, Gambela, and Harar, together with Addis Ababa and the administrative area of Dire Dawa. The basis of the new states is ethnicity and language , although equally they reflect political power. Tigre region, the home of the TPLF, lost a large area of desert, and gained the rich farming lands of Setit Humera along the Sudanese border. The Oromo region brought together most of four former regions, while nationalities that were widely spread, like the Amhara and the Gurage, and those who sought a centralized state, were not favoured by the new system.

The first stage of implementation of the new policies was the organization of local administrative elections, conducted in 1992, followed by regional nationality elections. By mid-1993 the elected regional assemblies were functioning to a greater or lesser extent. Regions were expected, in theory at least, to raise their own funding after 1993, but this has proved difficult. The bulk of revenue still comes from central government sources. In 1994 there was a significant decline in agricultural production, and the threat of large-scale famine was only averted with substantial imports. Agricultural production subsequently improved, and the government claimed to have achieved self-sufficiency in food in 1996–97; but distribution of resources remained a subject of controversy.

Numerous political parties emerged, mostly ethnically based. More than 100 parties had appeared by early 1993, although the May 1995 elections were contested by only 49. As Tigreans constitute no more than 7% of the population, the EPRDF created surrogate parties or 'democratic organizations' with which it could form alliances and which it intended should eventually join the EPRDF, though only one has actually done so since the EPRDF's takeover—the Southern Ethiopian People's Democratic Union (SEPDU), established in 1992. This approach has complicated the political process. The existence of the EPRDF's OPDO was a major reason for the breakdown in relations with the OLF, despite the OLF's position in government. In the months preceding the 1992 elections, there were numerous clashes as the two organizations manoeuvred for position in the Oromo regions. Both also sought to remove other nationalities from their areas. Just before the elections, the OLF and several other groups pulled out, and the OLF also withdrew from the government. Its criticisms of the election were supported by international observers who reported harassment, intimidation, failures to deliver registration and voting cards or to organize election committees. The EPRDF and its supporting parties did extremely well in almost every region, and even in Addis Ababa it won a surprising 81 of 84 regional seats. Elections were briefly postponed in Afar and Somali regions, where EPRDF support was less well organized. After its withdrawal from government, the OLF attempted to revive guerrilla activity. Most of its fighters were quickly apprehended but small groups were still operating across large areas of Oromia in 1997. Western diplomats and former US president Jimmy Carter made a number of unsuccessful attempts to reconcile the OLF and the EPRDF.

In June 1994 elections were conducted for a constituent assembly to ratify a draft constitution already approved by the council of representatives. The election was much better organized than in 1992 and there were no reports of obvious intimidation. The EPRDF again triumphed decisively, demonstrating that it had become a disciplined, tightly organized and highly centralized front using government resources to great effect, while the main opposition groups boycotted the election. In December the constituent assembly ratified the draft constitution (including controversial articles on the right to self-determination and secession, and state ownership of land) with little change, although recognition of *Shari'a* law for Muslims was included, following a major demonstration in Addis Ababa.

The final stage in the creation of the Federal Democratic Republic of Ethiopia came in May 1995 with elections to the federal parliamentary assembly (the council of people's representatives) and to the regional state councils, which elect representatives to the upper house (the council of the federation). Executive power lies with a prime minister, chosen by the majority party in the federal assembly. The EPRDF and its allies won an overwhelming victory, and Meles Zenawi, as chairman of the EPRDF, and of the TPLF which is still the dominant element in the EPRDF, became prime minister in August 1995; Dr Negasso Gidada of the OPDO was elected president. The election was considered by foreign observers to have been well organized and fairly conducted on the day, although the turnout was smaller than in previous elections. In Tigre region the TPLF took all seats for both the federal and state assemblies; EPRDF parties were equally successful in Amhara and Oromia regions. Despite Addis Ababa's reputation as a centre for opposition, the EPRDF won all 92 local assembly seats; independents took only two of the city's 23 federal assembly seats. In Afar and Somali regions, after postponements, pro-EPRDF parties won narrow victories; in neither case did this stop guerrilla activities by opposition parties seeking greater autonomy or secession. Overall the election results were seriously undermined by the decision of most opposition parties to boycott, as in 1992 and 1994. A US congressional task force sought to encourage participation, organizing talks in Washington, DC, between the EPRDF and opposition parties in early 1995. They were attended by the OLF, the All-Amhara People's Organization (AAPO), the Coalition of Ethiopian Democratic Forces, and the Coalition of Alternative Forces for Peace and Democracy in Ethiopia (CAFPDE), all of which claimed insufficient access to media, extensive arrest and harassment of their officials and closure of party offices.

EPRDF control of the political process and of the political debate left the opposition fractured and in disarray. CAFPDE, which brings together some 30 groups, was established in 1993 following conferences in March in Paris and in December in Addis Ababa. The second meeting was disrupted by the arrest of seven leading participants on arrival, prompting strong international criticism. Under the chairmanship of Dr Beyene Petros (who also heads the SEPDU), CAFPDE includes ethnic and non-ethnic parties and professional bodies, and, in theory, some exile-based organizations. It finally achieved official registration in July 1996, and has been a major critic of EPRDF policies on land, rents and leases, the economy and human rights. However, EPRDF pressure and its control of the media, coupled with CAFPDE's own divisions, have limited its impact. Individual parties in CAFPDE have also been targeted by the EPRDF. AAPO's chairman, Prof. Asrat Woldyes, was accused of inciting violence, and jailed for a total of five years after a series of trials; numerous other AAPO officials have been detained. AAPO has always rejected violence but has been outspoken over concern that EPRDF policies, together with Eritrean independence, could lead to Ethiopia's fragmentation. In January 1993 a student died in a protest against UN support for Eritrean independence, and in April 41 university staff were dismissed or refused new contracts. Dismissals from the civil service and state companies were seen as ethnically motivated. The majority were Amhara, giving rise to suspicions that the EPRDF was trying to silence Amhara opposition to Eritrean independence. In fact, this occurred without incident, and was generally, if reluctantly, accepted.

Armed opposition has appeared in several regions, including the Afar and Benishangul-Gumuz, as well as from the externally based OLF and the Ogaden National Liberation Front (ONLF), a Somali region party which split in 1995 allowing the pro-government Ethiopian Somali Democratic League (ESDL) to win the election. The OLF and the ONLF, which signed a military co-operation agreement in July 1996, demand greater autonomy and firmer commitments to possible independence. They claim the EPRDF has no intention of allowing secession, deliberately making the process lengthy and difficult — secession would require a two-thirds' majority in the regional legislature, a majority vote in a federally organized referendum, and an agreed transfer of power over a three-year period. Another Somali organization, the Islamic Union Party (al-Ittihad al-Islam), is fighting for an Islamic state. Al-Ittihad claimed responsibility for bomb explosions in hotels in Addis Ababa and Dire Dawa in early 1996, and for the attempted assassination in July of the minister of transport, a Somali and the chairman of the ESDL, though not for explosions in Harar in February 1997, and in Addis Ababa and Dire Dawa in April. The EPRDF retaliated with attacks against al-Ittihad bases in Somalia. Ethiopian troops crossed the border three times in 1996 and again in January and June 1997, seizing several towns and villages and claiming to kill hundreds of al-Ittihad fighters.

In late 1996 corruption appeared to be becoming endemic in Ethiopia. In October the deputy prime minister and minister of defence, Tamirat Layne, was dismissed for corruption; his trial opened six months later. (He was also ejected from the central committee of the ANDM and removed from the position of secretary-general.) In the Oromo region more than 300 OPDO officials were arrested or dismissed; and EPRDF-organized peace, democracy and development conferences in the Benishangul-Gumuz, Afar and Somali states and in the Dire Dawa administration led to significant changes in government and administration with numerous dismissals. In the Amhara region there were complaints over redivision of land in early 1997. Peasants from Gojjam who protested in Addis Ababa were supported by a university student demonstration. In Addis Ababa sharp rent increases prompted considerable opposition; a number of arrests were made following public rallies and demonstrations. Meanwhile, in June the minister of justice resigned; Werede Woldu Wolde assumed the portfolio.

The EPRDF also encountered opposition to its regional linguistic education policy from the Ethiopian Teachers Association (ETA) which claimed it threatened the status of Amharic as a national language. Numerous members of the ETA were dismissed or detained. Its secretary-general was arrested on return from Europe in May 1996; by mid-1997 he had still not been brought to trial. Another leading ETA member was shot and killed by police in May 1997. The Confederation of Ethiopian Labour Unions opposed the EPRDF's privatization policies and the IMF stabilization programme. Three of its leaders fled the country in April. In both cases the EPRDF created alternative organizations. There was trouble, too, in the Ethiopian Orthodox Church with opposition against the patriarch, Abune Paulos, a Tigrean appointed in 1992 after his predecessor, an appointee of the previous government, was retired on grounds of ill-health. The Patriarch's critics accused him of maladministration and nepotism. In January 1997 a monk was shot and killed in church while apparently trying to assassinate the Patriarch, underlining the dissension within the church.

The EPRDF's decision to continue state ownership of land, although coupled with security of usage, was widely resented, but other policies were more popular. By the end of 1994 more than 30,000 (mostly Tigrean) fighters had been demobilized, and recuitment was later widened to provide for a more national and professional army, under US prompting.

Human rights has emerged as a contentious issue, with international and local human rights organizations making serious criticisms. In 1992 the EPRDF approved a press law which was subsequently invoked to arrest or detain dozens of editors, owners and journalists, largely, it appeared, on the basis of criticism or questioning of government policy. Ethiopia has subsequently detained more journalists than any other country in Africa; of 15 in detention in February 1997 only three had been tried. A series of reports from the Ethiopian Human Rights Council, over the period 1992–97, alleged extrajudicial killings, disappearances and numerous cases of arbitrary arrest and imprisonment. The majority of the 20,000 Oromos detained in 1992 on suspicion of guerrilla activity were released by late 1994, and detention camps closed; nearly 300 were brought to trial in 1995. However, there have been a number of reports that hundreds of executions and disappearances have taken place in Oromo areas from 1993 onwards. Amnesty International also condemned detentions without trial, disappearances and the use of torture. The long delays in bringing senior officials of the former regime to trial also raised comment, although few disagreed with the special prosecutor's intention to charge them with crimes against humanity. In February 1994 Ethiopia requested the extradition of the former leader, Col Mengistu, but the Zimbabwe government has consistently refused. The trial of 69 former senior officials (23 *in absentia*, including Mengistu) on charges of crimes against humanity and war crimes began in December 1994, although proceedings have been adjourned on numerous occasions. In February 1997 the special prosecutor's office announced it was going to put another 5,198 people on trial on charges of genocide and war crimes, nearly 3,000 of them *in absentia*. Ethiopia remains one of only two African countries not to have ratified the African Charter on Human and Peoples' Rights; the other is Eritrea.

Internationally, the EPRDF continued to maintain good relations with the USA and with European powers (President Meles visited the USA in 1994, and attended the Franco-African summit as an observer in November of the same year). He visited France in January 1996, receiving the president of Germany in the same month and the Chinese president in May. Despite doubts over the EPRDF's commitment to pluralism and human rights, neither this nor concern over EPRDF economic policies has prevented the 'Paris Club' of official creditors and international agencies from providing generous amounts of loans and grants. The USA regards Ethiopia as crucial to stability in the Horn of Africa and in containing Sudan and 'radical' Islam. Relations with Sudan deteriorated sharply in 1995, following the apparent Sudanese complicity in the attempted assassination of President Mubarak of Egypt in Addis Ababa in June. Ethiopia, together with Uganda and Eritrea, has backed Sudanese opposition forces, providing arms, training and, in 1996, artillery support. Although during 1996 and early 1997 Sudan protested at alleged border incursions by Ethiopian troops, in July 1997 the two countries reportedly agreed to 'normalize' relations. On the Somali border, Ethiopian troops invaded five times in 1996–97, the latest occasion in June, to strike at Islamist bases. Relations with Eritrea remain extremely cordial; both support the possibility of wider co-operation in the Horn of Africa and would like to see the Djibouti-based Intergovernmental Authority on Development (IGAD–formerly the Intergovernmental Authority on Drought and Development–IGADD) assume a more political role. The Authority (which includes Djibouti, Eritrea, Ethiopia, Kenya, Somalia, Sudan and Uganda) is viewed by the USA as a useful medium for economic and political activity in the region.

Meles has adopted an assertive regional role, heading OAU efforts to foster a peace settlement in Somalia, hosting reconciliation conferences in Addis Ababa in 1993 and the Sodere conference of 26 Somali factions which agreed on a process to establish a transitional government in January 1997. In 1994 Ethiopia provided a battalion of troops for UN peace-keeping operations in Rwanda, and in 1996 offered troops for OAU operations in Burundi; it also expressed support for the US proposals for an African peace-keeping force. President (now Prime Minister) Meles was OAU chairman for 1995–96. Ethiopia, like Eritrea, has established close relations with Israel, and has also formed closer diplomatic links with Saudi Arabia.

Economy

JAMES PICKETT

Successive annual accounts of the Ethiopian economy have told largely the same story. In particular they have focused initially on a few basic—and largely unchanging—characteristics and developed from there. The central features of the economy are such that it would perhaps be unfair to expect major change to be revealed by year-on-year comparisons. Nevertheless, in a growing economy the cumulative impact of annual developments should normally be reflected in significant alterations in economic structure.

The current Ethiopian government has had responsibility for economic policy for more than six years. That said, it has to be recalled that when power changed hands in May 1991 the economy was close to collapse. Recovery was thus a necessary prelude to resumed economic growth. Redressing the damage caused by the civil war and misconceived economic policy became an early priority. Moreover, the process of recovery attracted considerable international support. Although it might be unfair to expect substantial economic progress to have taken place in the period 1991–97, sufficient time should have passed to indicate whether the economy is in recovery.

In this regard, it is convenient to recall briefly the main features of the Ethiopian economy, to consider with equal brevity how that had fared under the two regimes that preceded the current one, and to examine the more recent record.

PRINCIPAL CHARACTERISTICS OF THE ECONOMY

The most significant features of the Ethiopian economy are the depth and spread of its poverty, and the continued dominance of traditional agriculture. Thus, according to recent data, the average annual income per caput is estimated at US $100, and more than one-third of the population earns less than $80 per year. This latter figure, while reflecting the approximate nature of economic measurement in low-productivity, subsistence agriculture economies, none the less conveys an accurate enough picture of widespread and searing poverty. According to the World Bank's rating of 133 economies world-wide, only Mozambique has a lower income per head than Ethiopia.

The gross domestic product (GDP) measures, *inter alia,* the productive capacity of a country. In Ethiopia the problem is that this is so low that it is not yet possible through production and trade to liberate the majority from the near-subsistence living standards that they currently endure. The proximate cause of Ethiopian poverty is the burden of traditional, low-productivity, agriculture on total economic activity. Peasant farms require minimal investment—sickles, hoes, crude wooden ploughs, and machetes are the principal purchases— and there is virtually no systematic training. People and animals meet power needs. Sowing practices have remained unchanged for many years and the crop is harvested by sickle, trampled by oxen, and winnowed by tossing into the wind. The marketable surplus is normally small, and much production is for own consumption.

Low-productivity at the heart of the economy inevitably correlates with other symptoms of poverty. Thus compared to an average expectation of life at birth of 63 years in poor countries, in Ethiopia average current life expectation is 49 years. Data on health, education, energy use and food aid tell a broadly similar story.

More than 50% of total GDP derives from peasant agriculture. Industry, conversely, contributes just over 10% of GDP, and is largely dependent on small-scale, craft-type industries. Services contribute more than 30% of GDP. The sector primarily comprises public administration and household services, which are often very poorly paid.

Ethiopia is particularly prone to drought, which almost inevitably leads to famine. Thus, in 1985 a general failure of the rains, which had cumulated in some regions in successive years, led to food shortages in many parts of the country. Throughout that year 8m. people were in need of emergency relief, and in 1986 there were still 6m. in the same plight. Deaths associated with famine may have reached 1m. in 1985, compared with the estimated 200,000 who died in the 1972–73 famine that played a part in the downfall of Haile Selassie.

The Ethiopian economy has traditionally depended heavily on peasant agriculture. This provides more than 90% of the annual coffee output and most of the highland food grains—barley, wheat, teff, maize and sorghum. Moreover, much of the transport sector is involved in the movement of agricultural commodities. And industry, which is often small-scale and rural, is highly concentrated in the production of food, beverages and textiles. Agricultural goods provide a very high proportion of export earnings. Coffee, which accounts for about one-half of the agricultural value added, normally generates more than 60% of export revenue.

Ethiopia has the largest cattle population in Africa, and ranks about seventh in the world in terms of cattle numbers. Most of the livestock is reared by the peasants. Animals are generally in poor health, and largely untouched by a fledgling veterinary service. Yet they are the most easily realizable of peasant assets, and their utility under conditions of drought is perhaps the best reason for keeping them.

There are more than 8m. peasant households, virtually all of which practice rain-fed agriculture. Production techniques are primitive, and, with the peasant lack of tradable assets, leave rural households vulnerable to the vagaries of the weather, the international economy, the government and pestilential insects. Peasant farming employs more than 80% of the labour force, and it accounts for a significant proportion of export revenue, notably owing to sales of coffee. Manufacturing exports are insignificant, and modern and traditional industry account for some 2% of the labour force.

Although the peasant sector has many of the attributes of a 'closed' economy, international trade is important to Ethiopia, accounting for almost 40% of GDP. Ethiopia's exports largely comprise primary products, while manufactured goods are normally prominent imports. In the last 20 years, however, food has accounted for a growing proportion of total purchases in foreign markets. The balance of trade is usually negative, and in 1995 it amounted to 1.9% of total output.

Ethiopia's population is approaching 60m. Of this number, some 25m. are in the labour force, resulting in a dependency ration of 2.4:1. Between 1980–90 the labour force grew at an average annual rate of 2.9%, and in the period 1990–95 the corresponding annual growth was 2.3%. These are grim statistics, and they give some indication of the magnitude of the challenge confronting those whose aim is to banish poverty from Ethiopia. The challenge becomes apparent when considering the size of the investment needs implicit in the current rate of increase of the labour force, and when examining the current capital-labour ratio. Although peasant agriculture accounts for more than 50% of GDP, it is the residual sector of the economy that has modern activities including manufacturing, transport and communications, public administration, and financial markets. Capital stock in peasant agriculture is limited, and a capital-output ratio of 1.5:1 would almost certainly overestimate that stock.

Modern infrastructure, manufacturing and progressive financial institutions would normally result in much higher ratios than that cited for peasant agriculture. Notwithstanding, the non-agricultural sector does contain many labour-intensive, low-capital activities in which the capital-output ratio can be estimated at 3.5:1. Applying the above ratios to the economy in 1995 would leave the capital stock in that year at US $13,217m. Allocating this across labour employed in the agricultural and non-agricultural sectors would leave the respective capital-labour ratios at $198 and $1,850 per head. By the standards of most other economies the capital available to Ethiopian workers is extremely limited.

Economic progress in Ethiopia must begin within, and for some time be sustained by, the peasant sector. Such progress will necessitate substantial increases in the capital goods available to the labour force. In this regard, average annual incomes of US $750 and $5,000 per worker in the agricultural and non-agricultural sectors respectively would still leave Ethiopia behind other economies. Yet even to achieve this level would require an investment of more than 17% of the 1995 GDP. Moreover, this would be gross investment, with the result that investment per worker would be lower than the ratios given. Although these calculations oversimplify, they serve to confirm that Ethiopia will struggle to achieve sustained and substantial economic growth. In truth, however, Ethiopia is not poor because its agriculture is backward. On the contrary, its agriculture is backward because the country is poor. Ethiopia has long been lacking extensive and sustained commercial and cultural contact with other countries, and has only recently begun to develop the institutions and attitudes that would enable it to emulate the ways of technologically more advanced economies. Indeed it was not until after the Second World War that any sustained effort was made to modernize the economy.

ECONOMIC PERFORMANCE DURING 1960–91

During the period 1960–91 Ethiopia experienced two strikingly different forms of government: the regime of Emperor Haile Selassie, which lasted until 1974, and the subsequent military administration, known as the Dergue. Under Haile Selassie's somewhat feudal style of government, emphasis was placed on market forces. There were, nevertheless, high levels of protection, and three five-year development plans were more or less executed. A fourth plan was prepared, but not implemented.

Between 1960–73 Ethiopia's GDP rose at an average annual rate of 4.3%. As the rate of population growth in this period averaged an annual 2.3%, income per head increased annually by 2%. In the period 1974–91, however, total output registered average annual gains of 1.3%, while the rate of population growth was 2.7%. Average income fell, therefore, at an annual rate of 1.4%. However, this data should be treated with caution. Moreover, those who would defend the Dergue could argue that both the world and the sub-Saharan economies were much less buoyant after 1973. But whereas Ethiopia had fared better economically than a number of African countries in the earlier period, it lagged behind most in the latter. Prior to 1973 a market economy had begun to develop, and, increasingly, attention was given to peasant agriculture. Between 1974 and the late 1980s the market economy was widely suppressed, and peasants were seriously discouraged by the new regime. The attempt to plan peasant farming stretched to coercion—sometimes through the imposition of grain quotas and pricing, sometimes by forced relocation, and sometimes by both. The establishment of state farms and the ill-fated attempt to create producer co-operatives were largely a waste of resources.

As a result, the economic policy of the Dergue had no firm basis. The ill-advised attempt at central planning and the concomitant discouragement of private enterprise led to disaster. Despite the country's reliance on coffee exports, during the Dergue administration local prices paid to coffee growers were so low that many farmers switched to the production of other crops. In addition, state marketing was inefficient, and Ethiopia had difficulty in meeting the quotas allotted to it by the International Coffee Agreement. Meanwhile, expenditure on public administration and defence grew inordinately, the currency was overvalued, foreign economic assistance from the developed market economies largely ceased, and by 1991 the economy was close to collapse.

The Dergue itself must have recognized the failure of its economic policies as in the late 1980s it adopted a more market-orientated stance. However, the new measures were introduced too late, and the economic damage incurred could not be remedied quickly. When the Dergue collapsed in 1991 the economy was in a worse state than it had been in 1973. Public spending, which had been less than 20% of the GDP in 1973, had reached 44%. Much of this rise had been financed from abroad, including the Soviet Union and Eastern Europe. By 1990 external debt totalled some US $8,600m., equivalent to $172 per head. In the domestic economy interest rates were negative, industry had virtually ceased, agriculture was repressed and in disarray, government and export revenues were at their lowest for 16 years, and foreign exchange reserves were lower than they had ever been since 1960.

The failure of economic policy and the alienation of the peasant were reflected in changes in agricultural trade. In 1974 Ethiopia imported 118,000 metric tons of cereals on commercial terms. By 1990 the imports had reached 687,000 tons, an increase of 482%. Imports of food aid increased from 54,000 tons in 1974 to 538,000 tons in 1990, a rise of almost 900%. The ratio of aid to commercial imports also increased, from 46% in 1974 to 78% in 1990.

ECONOMIC POLICY SINCE 1991

Following the overthrow of the Dergue regime in May 1991, and the establishment of a transitional government committed to extending the market economy, a programme of economic reconstruction and rehabilitation was launched with the assistance of the World Bank, the IMF, the African Development Bank and bilateral donors. An ambitious structural adjustment programme is still in progress; to date, the government's attention has focused on the highland economy, where the majority of the population is concentrated and most economic activity takes place. At lower altitudes in the south-west of the country the 'false' banana plant (enset) is a staple crop. It is, moreover, one that has benefited from technical advances, thus helping to sustain dense and growing populations. Much of Ethiopia's coffee is grown in this relatively wet area. At even lower altitudes, and at sea-level, the population is sparse and scattered. The nomads it comprises are mainly pastoralists.

The final stages of the civil war had a strongly adverse effect on the economy and there was a significant decline in real GDP and in agricultural output. By 1993/94, however, real GDP growth of 1.7% was achieved, and in 1994/95 real GDP growth of 4.9% was recorded, in which year agricultural GDP increased by 3.6%.

ECONOMIC POLICY REFORM

The Economic Relief and Rehabilitation Programme (ERRP) has aimed to redress the ravages of war, including the resettlement of Mengistu's disbanded army. The programme aims to create a largely market-driven economy in order to foster the conditions for sustained economic growth. Wide-ranging macroeconomic changes are central to this effort. However, the government will retain responsibility for economic progress, maintain almost direct control of strategic enterprises, and contribute to growth through the provision of public and merit goods. The administrative system has been reorganized to allow regional parliamentary assemblies to exercise legislative, executive and judicial powers within their areas, except for matters such as defence, foreign affairs, economic policy, citizenship and the printing of money, which are reserved for the central government. A central council of representatives determines devolved powers. The second-tier governments are empowered to raise money from domestic lenders and to levy dues and taxes. In general, the decentralized governments must act in concert with central economic and other policies. These arrangements aim to bring economic federalism to Ethiopia. This is, however, normally a less efficient system than a unitary one. The new mode of government will certainly strain the country's stock of skilled manpower and, in particular, will place heavy demands on central government. Considerable skill will be required if it is to co-ordinate spending and borrowing at each level of government in such a way as to bring consistency to its overall economic policy. This task will be eased, but not be made easy, if there is maximum reliance on the market at all levels of government. The demands that will result from the restructuring of government reinforce the importance that attaches to the economic freedom of the peasants.

Substantial progress has been made in restoring a market economy, notably through the devaluations of the national currency, the birr, in October 1992 and in April and May 1994, the introduction in May 1993 of a fortnightly foreign exchange auction, the partial reform of taxation and the elimination of all export taxes (except on coffee), the removal of the capital charge on subsidies to public enterprises and the encouragement of private-sector merchant trading. While it will take time for the full impact of these measures to be felt, the short-term evidence is encouraging. The immediate effect of the 1992 devaluation was an improvement in the real exchange rate. Defined as the nominal rate multiplied by the ratio of domestic to foreign inflation, this is perhaps the most important single factor in the reform programme. It determines the allocation of resources between tradable and non-tradable goods in the domestic economy, and greatly influences the scope for trade. Following a period in which domestic price rises were outpacing inflation elsewhere, devaluation of the nominal rate removes the disability under which the economy had been operating. The longer-term effectiveness of these exchange rate corrections will depend upon the trend in prices in their wake. Thus, the control of inflation is critical. In the short term, however, it is difficult to increase output by the more efficient use of resources as these are switched from lower to higher productivity, even in the favourable conditions created by devaluation. It takes time to organize an increase in exports and to seize the increased opportunity for efficient import substitution. There is, therefore, a danger that inflationary expectations can become entrenched before growth-producing measures are in operation. The annual rate of inflation averaged 7.0% in 1985–95. The rate rose to 35.7% in 1991, but declined to 10.5% in 1992 and to 3.5% in 1993. Consumer prices increased by 7.6% in 1994 and by 10.1% in 1995.

There has been an encouraging increase in output, particularly of cereals. Against this, the early impact of devaluation on exports has been somewhat disappointing. Coffee deliveries in Addis Ababa did rise, but not dramatically. Leather goods earned more foreign exchange than in the pre-devaluation period. Exports of sesame seed and haricot beans, for which floor prices had been set, were disappointing, although a fall in international prices clearly had an impact on their earnings.

Devaluation has had a beneficial impact on Ethiopia's ability to secure external credit. The international financial institutions, the European Community (EC, now the European Union—EU), the UN and other major donors understood Ethiopia's willingness to devalue to be a sign of its commitment to pursuing economic reform, and so deserving of external support. One of the most immediate benefits was the rescheduling of external debt at a meeting of the 'Paris Club' of official creditors in December 1992. Ethiopia's external debt was then US $3,670m. Servicing this in 1992/93 would have necessitated more than $300m., equivalent to some 8% of GDP or 60% of estimated export earnings. Although rescheduling will save the treasury a considerable sum in the short term, it will result in higher debt servicing in later years. Rescheduling grants respite, and will be justified if, as a consequence, the economy is fortified and is more able to carry the burden of earlier debts. At the end of 1995 Ethiopia's total external debt was $5,221m., of which $4,958m. was long-term public debt. In that year the cost of debt servicing was equivalent to an estimated 13.6% of total earnings from the export of goods and services.

There has been a significant deficit in the balance of trade in recent years. This reached its peak in 1991/92, when the effects of the war were greatest, and the inducement to smuggle exports (including coffee) was at its height. In the first quarter of 1992/93 the gap widened to 118.2m. birr. This still did not match the imbalance of 1990/91, when the deficit was 602.2m. birr. The level of exports and imports in 1992/93 were higher than in 1991/92, but still had not recovered to that of the late 1980s and the early 1990s. In the corresponding period of 1988/89, for example, exports and imports were 256.3m. birr and 612.2m. birr respectively. These data compare with exports of 93.1m. birr and imports of 211.3m. birr in the first quarter of 1992/93. In 1994 Ethiopia recorded a visible trade deficit of US $553.7m., an increase of 9.2% compared with 1993; moreover, in 1995 the trade deficit reached $724.9m., a rise of 30.9% compared with the previous year. Nevertheless, coffee exports have recovered significantly, as farmers have taken advantage of renewed stability and higher cash prices. The smuggling of coffee has also declined. Overall, it is still too early to assess the impact of devaluation on the balance of payments, but it is already clear that the restoration of external balance will not be easily achieved.

THE PUBLIC SECTOR

The level and composition of government spending and the ways in which it is financed are central to the economy. If government expenditure is financed by the domestic banking system, the money supply is automatically increased. Thus in 1989/90 and 1990/91 the budget deficits amounted respectively to 17% and 15% of GDP. These were financed by credit from domestic banks, and broad money expanded by some 18% in each of the two years. In 1991/92 money growth slowed to 13% but much of this still derived from government borrowing. In 1992/93 the broad money supply grew by 11% in the first eight months. Unfortunately, indications at the end of that period were that the annual rate could be as high as 16%.

The continuing expansion of the money supply can be attributed largely to an increase in foreign assets. These totalled some 400m. birr in 1991/92, but had risen to about 900m. birr in 1992/93. Growth in government credits was relatively modest, although facilities given to non-government sectors of the economy increased significantly. Therefore, there is excess liquidity in the economy. If this is to be eliminated, the money supply should grow at a rate below that of the nominal GDP.

Hitherto Ethiopia has been financially prudent. Repayment and servicing have been on schedule, and careful control of fiscal deficits has contained inflation, particularly by sub-Saharan standards. In the early 1990s, however, the rate of inflation rose sharply as the needs of a war economy were increasingly met by domestic credit, Interruption of agricultural production also caused the prices of food grains to rise. Delays in the arrival of imports financed by the ERRP and the increase in their price following devaluation have adversely affected the agricultural and industrial sectors, with the result that the economy is working at less than capacity. This has made a decrease in government revenues more manageable since the shortfall in revenue has been offset, to some extent, by below average expenditure. Indeed, by the first quarter of 1992/93 capital and current expenditure were surpassed by income from taxes and grants by some 29m. birr. This contrasts with first quarter deficits in the three previous fiscal years of 60.5m. birr, 180.5m. birr and 143.9m. birr respectively. The surplus could not be sustained, however, and in the second quarter of 1992/93 a deficit of 498m. birr was recorded. The change between the two quarters was due to a marked increase in capital spending. This was not matched by a reduction in current expenditure, which totalled 795.3m. birr in the second quarter, or 36% higher than in the same period of 1991/92. More than two-thirds of the total deficit was financed by domestic bank credit. There must, therefore, be a lingering fear that as the economy expands the fiscal deficit will grow also.

Expenditure on education and health are often targeted in periods of structural adjustment and financial retrenchment. Thus far, this has not been the case in Ethiopia. The 1993/94 budget allocated total expenditure on education and health of 990.3m. birr and 436.4m. birr respectively. The 1994/95 budget allocated the respective amounts of 1,212.2m. birr and 492.0m. birr.

The overall fiscal deficit reached an estimated 9.6% of GDP in 1993/94 (compared with a target of 6.9%); however, reform is proceeding. In 1994/95 it was estimated that the budgetary deficit reached 1,277.5m. birr (equivalent to 3.8% of GDP). As the economy grows revenues will increase, whether it be under a reformed or an unreformed system. Receipts, however, will still be limited, and priorities must be applied resolutely to capital and current spending. Not only must resources be left for private sector development, but public spending has to be supportive of private markets. In order to strengthen the economy, the government will have to develop an efficient network of rural credit, improve the road system, increase and refocus agricultural research and extension services, offer basic health and education provision in all regions, design an agricultural intelligence system, vastly reform financial institutions (including the development of a capital market), and gear the legal system to the sanctity of contract and the inviolability of private property. In addition, a reformed and efficient civil service will be required that, *inter alia,* can manage a rising flow of aid and foreign investment, conduct timely and competent policy analysis to provide the government with well-founded advice, and establish the institutions needed if economic federalism is to be effective. The role of the state in Ethiopian economic affairs has never been as challenging.

RECENT ADVANCES

Given that the current Ethiopian government has adopted more market-encouraging policies than its predecessors, it is interesting to examine any progress that it has made. It may, therefore, be useful to consider the growth of the economy and changes in economic structure. Unfortunately the data on which comprehensive description and analysis could be based are not readily available. However, it is apparent that the government's main achievement has been that of stabilizing the economy, even though much remains to be done.

By 1995 income per head had yet to reach its 1980 level, and peasant agriculture still accounted for 57% of GDP. Moreover, the swollen service sector had hardly shrunk, and in 1995 it was responsible for 33% of production. This compares with 31% in 1980, indicating that the effects of privatization and civil service reform have yet to be felt. Nevertheless, the level of government consumption fell from 14% of GDP in 1980 to 12% in 1995. Over the same period private consumption also declined—from 83% to 81% respectively. This decrease allowed domestic savings and investment to rise, with the result that capital formation increased from 9% of GDP in 1980 to 17% in 1990.

With regard to public finance, total tax revenue accounted for a smaller percentage of GDP in 1995 than in 1980. Receipts for tax collection in 1980 represented 13% of GDP, compared with 12% in 1995. Notwithstanding the relative decrease in the level of taxation, health and educational provision was in important respects better in 1995 than in 1980. Thus the proportion of the population with access to safe water increased from 4% in 1980 to 27% in 1995. Infant mortality declined from 155 per 1,000 live births in 1980 to 112 in 1995. The proportion of the relative age group receiving education sharply declined between 1980 and 1995, but in secondary and tertiary education the numbers rose. It is, perhaps, particularly significant that the share of the age group in secondary schools for girls increased from 6% at the beginning of the period to 11% by 1995.

There can be no doubt that the Ethiopian economy has been more liberal since 1991 than it was, on the whole, in the period 1974–91. In particular, the peasant sector has been permitted to decide what to produce and what to sell. Additionally, market forces have been increasingly allowed to determine the exchange rate, with the result that the international sector has been freer than before. The foreign exchange position has certainly improved. Thus in 1980 reserves offered import cover for four months, and even less by 1991, but in 1995 import coverage had increased to seven months.

As has been noted, the role of the state in the economy has been complicated by the introduction of economic federalism. It remains to be seen how this radical experiment will fare, although there are already some signs of difficulties that could be associated with the decentralization of state power. These include problems in controlling the money supply, in reducing the level of public expenditure, and in privatization and the reform of the public service.

Since Ethiopia has a small, open economy it can be greatly influenced by events elsewhere. Thus it has benefited in 1996 and 1997 from a rise in the international price of coffee, which has led to estimates of overall economic growth of 10% for the fiscal year 1996–97. Such rapid increase in output is, of course, to be welcomed; however, it is unlikely that it can be sustained on the basis of high coffee prices which are largely determined by the size of the coffee crop in Brazil. It would be imprudent to expect Brazil's coffee crop to fail regularly for an extended period.

In mid-1997 the British government stated that one of its priorities was to eliminate poverty by 2025. This raises the intractable question, however, of where the dividing line between poverty and its absence is to be drawn. If the World Bank categories of low-income, lower-middle-income, upper-middle-income and high-income economies is accepted, then it may be argued that the high-income economies are those that can maintain domestic economic growth without seeking substantial assistance from abroad. It may also be argued that such economies are at least better placed than others to tackle residual poverty. At current prices, the minimum annual income per head in the rich economies is some US $10,000. Even if Ethiopian average annual incomes were to grow at 10% a year, it would still take almost 50 years for poverty in the country to be reduced to the level experienced in the United Kingdom. It should be recalled that income per head in Ethiopia has never increased at an annual rate of 10% for any extended period. Nor is there reason to believe that it will do so in the near future. Approximate as it is, therefore, the estimate of 50 years is clearly that of the minimum time needed to escape from substantial and widespread poverty. Moreover, if annual incomes were to increase by 6% a year, rather than by 10%, it would extend the relevant period to 80 years. Ethiopia's economy remains confronted by an extended period of economic challenge.

Statistical Survey

Source (unless otherwise stated): Central Statistical Authority, POB 1143, Addis Ababa; tel. (1) 553010; fax (1) 550334.

Note: Unless otherwise indicated, figures in this Survey refer to the territory of Ethiopia after the secession of Eritrea in May 1993.

Area and Population

AREA, POPULATION AND DENSITY

Area (sq km)	1,133,380*
Population (census of 9 May 1984)†	
Males	20,062,453
Females	19,806,048
Total	39,868,501
Population (official estimates at mid-year)	
1993	53,236,000
1994	54,938,000
1995	56,677,100
Density (per sq km) at mid-1995	50.0

* 437,600 sq miles.

† Including an estimate for areas not covered by the census.

ADMINISTRATIVE REGIONS (census results of October 1994)

Region	Population
1 Tigre	3,136,267
2 Afar	1,106,383*
3 Amhara	13,834,297
4 Oromia	18,732,525
5 Somalia	2,514,399†
6 Metekel, Abosa, Metema	460,459
7–11 Southern Ethiopian Peoples‡	10,377,028
12 Gambela, Agriwak, Nuwar, Mezanger	181,862
13 Harar Town	131,139
14 Addis Ababa	2,112,737

* Population at July 1996.

† Estimated population at mid-1993.

‡ Comprising five separate regions.

Note: A new Constitution, ratified in December 1994, provided for the establishment of a federal government and the division of the country into nine states. The new states were formally instituted in August 1995.

PRINCIPAL TOWNS (census results of October 1994)

Addis Ababa (capital)	2,112,737	Dessie	97,314
Dire Dawa	164,851	Mekele	96,938
Harar	131,139	Bahir Dar	96,140
Nazret	127,842	Jimma	88,867
Gondar (incl. Azeso)	112,249		

BIRTHS AND DEATHS (UN estimates, annual averages)

	1980–85	1985–90	1990–95
Birth rate (per 1,000)	50.1	48.8	48.5
Death rate (per 1,000)	24.1	19.9	18.0

Expectation of life (UN estimates, years at birth, 1990–95): 47.5 (males 45.9; females 49.1).

Source: UN, *World Population Prospects: The 1994 Revision.*

ECONOMICALLY ACTIVE POPULATION (official estimates, ISIC Major Divisions, persons aged 10 years and over, mid-1995)*

	Males	Females	Total
Agriculture, hunting, forestry and fishing	12,681,037	8,924,280	21,605,317
Mining and quarrying	12,114	4,426	16,540
Manufacturing	224,106	160,889	384,995
Electricity, gas and water	14,799	2,267	17,066
Construction	55,906	5,326	61,232
Trade, restaurants and hotels	335,353	600,584	935,937
Transport, storage and communications	87,975	15,179	103,154
Financing, insurance, real estate and business services	14,513	4,938	19,451
Community, social and personal services	777,907	474,317	1,252,224
Total labour force	14,203,710	10,192,206	24,395,916

* The figures exclude persons seeking work for the first time, totalling 210,184 (males 100,790; females 109,394), but include other unemployed persons.

Source: ILO, *Yearbook of Labour Statistics.*

Agriculture

PRINCIPAL CROPS ('000 metric tons)

	1993	1994	1995
Wheat*	897	1,313	1,571
Barley*	996	1,284	1,417
Maize*	1,644	2,011	2,189
Oats*	20	46	52
Millet (Dagusa)*	272	172	248
Sorghum*	1,079	1,125	1,232
Other cereals*	1,998	1,325	1,536
Potatoes*	349	350	350
Sweet potatoes*	154	155	155
Yams*	262	263	263
Other roots and tubers*	1,200	1,250	1,250
Dry beans*	200	270	390
Dry peas*	109	120	150
Dry broad beans*	282	281	281
Chick-peas*	119	122	126
Lentils*	35	34	34
Other pulses*	127	127	127
Sugar cane*	1,700	1,200	1,200
Soybeans*	22	21	21
Groundnuts (in shell)*	54	54	54
Castor beans*	14	14	14
Rapeseed*	82	80	80
Sesame seed*	32	31	31
Linseed*	33	32	32
Safflower seed*	36	35	35
Cottonseed†	30	28	30
Cotton (lint)†	15	14	15
Vegetables and melons*	574	565	565
Bananas*	80	80	80
Other fruit (excl. melons)*	150	147	147
Tree nuts*	65	65	65
Coffee (green)†	180	207	228
Tobacco (leaves)*	4	4	4
Fibre crops (excl. cotton)*	18	17	17

* FAO estimates. † Unofficial figures.

Source: FAO, *Production Yearbook.*

LIVESTOCK (FAO estimates, '000 head, year ending September)

	1993	1994	1995
Cattle	29,450	29,450	29,825
Sheep	21,700	21,700	21,700
Goats	16,700	16,700	16,700
Asses	5,200	5,200	5,200
Horses	2,750	2,750	2,750
Mules	630	630	630
Camels	1,000	1,000	1,000
Pigs	20	20	20

Poultry (FAO estimates, million): 54 in 1993; 54 in 1994; 54 in 1995.

Source: FAO, *Production Yearbook.*

LIVESTOCK PRODUCTS (FAO estimates, '000 metric tons)

	1993	1994	1995
Beef and veal	230	230	231
Mutton and lamb	77	78	78
Goat meat	62	62	62
Pig meat	1	1	1
Poultry meat	72	72	72
Other meat	133	134	134
Edible offals	94	94	94
Cows' milk	738	738	738
Goats' milk	93	93	93
Sheep's milk	54	54	54
Butter	10.4	10.4	10.4
Cheese	4.6	4.6	4.6
Hen eggs	73.4	73.4	73.4
Honey	23.7	23.7	23.7
Wool:			
greasy	11.5	11.5	11.5
clean	6.0	6.0	6.0
Cattle hides	45.9	45.9	46.2
Sheepskins	14.1	14.1	14.1
Goatskins	13.2	13.2	13.2

Source: FAO, *Production Yearbook* and *Quarterly Bulletin of Statistics.*

Forestry

ROUNDWOOD REMOVALS ('000 cubic metres, excl. bark)

	1992*	1993	1994
Sawlogs, etc.	15	26	33
Other industrial wood†	1,693	1,693	1,693
Fuel wood	44,387	45,254	45,254
Total	46,095	46,973	46,980

* Including Eritrea.

† Assumed to be unchanged since 1983.

Source: FAO, *Yearbook of Forest Products.*

SAWNWOOD PRODUCTION
('000 cubic metres, incl. railway sleepers)

	1992*	1993	1994
Total	12	40	33

* Including Eritrea.

Source: FAO, *Yearbook of Forest Products.*

Fishing

('000 metric tons, live weight)

	1993	1994	1995
Total catch (freshwater fishes)	4.2	5.3	6.4

Source: FAO, *Yearbook of Fishery Statistics.*

Mining

('000 metric tons, including Eritrea, unless otherwise indicated)

	1989	1990	1991
Gold (kilograms)*	745	848	2,000†
Salt (unrefined)	188	110	94
Limestone ('000 cu metres)	150	100	85
Sand	775	1,250	1,000
Kaolin	0	1	0

* Figures for 1990 and 1991 exclude Eritrea.

† Provisional figure.

1992: Gold (kilograms) 2,652; Kaolin (provisional, metric tons) 1,000.
1993: Gold (kilograms) 3,404.

Source: US Bureau of Mines, quoted in UN, *Industrial Commodity Statistics Yearbook*.

Industry

SELECTED PRODUCTS
('000 metric tons, unless otherwise indicated; year ending 7 July)

	1992/93*	1993/94	1994/95
Edible oils	4.0	4.2	5.6
Wheat flour	62.3	74.7	116.0
Flour of other cereals	0.3	2.3	1.6
Macaroni and pasta	5.7	11.2	19.1
Raw sugar	136.7	123.3	129.3
Wine ('000 hectolitres)	68.9	57.3	70.9
Beer ('000 hectolitres)	522.3	634.4	723.5
Mineral waters ('000 hectolitres)	159.3	199.3	298.4
Soft drinks ('000 hectolitres)	553.8	546.2	710.5
Cigarettes (million)	1,932.0	1,468.4	1,582.8
Cotton yarn (metric tons)	3,448	5,669	4,934
Woven cotton fabrics ('000 sq metres)	36,423	60,591	50,016
Nylon fabrics ('000 sq metres)	3,840	3,752	4,910
Leather footwear ('000 pairs)	928.8	1,999.2	1,159.4
Canvas and rubber footwear ('000 pairs)	2,030.9	1,609.4	2,196.3
Plastic footwear ('000 pairs)	123.5	62.3	395.7
Paper	—	—	7.1
Soap	17.3	15.0	15.2
Tyres ('000)	99.8	171.3	167.5
Clay building bricks ('000)	19.8	19.5	19.3
Quicklime	3.7	2.7	4.9
Cement	377.1	464.4	609.3

* Including Eritrea.

Finance

CURRENCY AND EXCHANGE RATES

Monetary Units
100 cents = 1 birr.

Sterling and Dollar Equivalents (31 December 1996)
£1 sterling = 10.977 birr;
US $1 = 6.426 birr;
1,000 birr = £90.94 = $155.62.

Exchange Rate
An official rate of US $1 = 2.070 birr was established in February 1973. This remained in force until October 1992, when a rate of $1 = 5.000 birr was introduced. That rate was in effect until April 1994, when it was adjusted to $1 = 5.130 birr. Further adjustments were made subsequently. The average exchange rate (birr per US $) in financial years (12 months ending 7 July) was: 4.2675 in 1992/93; 5.1142 in 1993/94.

GENERAL BUDGET (provisional, million birr, year ending 7 July)
Note: The figures for 1992/93 include Eritrea.

Revenue*	1992/93	1993/94	1994/95
Taxation	2,135.3	3,535.1	3,890.3
Taxes on income and profits	670.5	880.9	1,210.1
Personal income	251.8	266.8	289.2
Business profits	376.8	557.3	848.2
Domestic production, sales and excise taxes†	711.2	816.5	925.6
Alcohol and tobacco	276.3	264.2	316.3
Import duties	697.0	1,774.0	1,472.7
Customs duties	348.8	1,182.0	771.4
Sales and other taxes‡	348.2	592.0	701.3
Export duties§	18.7	16.7	201.4
Customs duties§	11.0	15.1	190.1
Other revenue	956.3‖	833.2	1,948.9
Surplus, capital charges, interest payments and state dividends	437.9	476.8	1,399.3
Reimbursements and property sales	54.7	52.8	118.7
Total	3,091.6	4,368.3	5,839.2

* Excluding grants received from abroad (million birr): 1,067.0 in 1992/93; 1,218.1 in 1993/94; 1,034.9 in 1994/95.
† Sales tax until 1992/93; and excise taxes thereafter.
‡ Sales taxes until 1992/93; sales and excise taxes thereafter.
§ Figures refer to coffee only from December 1992.
‖ Including extraordinary transfer for evacuation of Felashas (Ethiopian Jews).

Expenditure	1992/93	1993/94	1994/95
Current expenditure	3,903.8	4,474.3	5,075.0
General services	1,173.4	1,452.5	1,560.5
Organs of state	80.0	195.3	189.8
Defence	697.0	709.3	672.5
Public order and security	165.1	226.0	289.5
Economic services	329.7	452.9	579.6
Agriculture and natural resources	164.4	261.3	366.0
Social services	876.9	1,224.9	1,520.3
Education and training	583.3	742.0	936.0
Public health	185.8	279.3	354.7
Pension payments	224.3	279.9	287.7
Interest and charges	530.3	951.5	855.2
External assistance (grants)*	600.0	0.0	0.0
Capital expenditure	2,150.4	3,018.0	3,076.6
Economic development	1,509.0	2,217.5	2,192.0
Agriculture, water and natural resources	530.2	732.3	656.5
Mining and industry	311.4	358.8	376.5
Electric power	75.1	115.8	212.4
Roads, transport and communications	532.7	967.0	811.4
Social development	267.9	718.2	593.0
Education	86.8	248.3	276.2
Public health	66.8	157.1	137.3
Community services†	114.3	312.8	179.5
General services and compensation	23.5	82.3	291.6
External assistance (grants)*	350.0	0.0	—
Total	6,054.2	7,492.3	8,151.6

* Imputed value of goods and services provided in kind.

† Including urban development and housing, social security, manpower and training, and sport.

Source: National Bank of Ethiopia.

NATIONAL BANK RESERVES (US $ million, at 31 December)

	1994	1995	1996
Gold*	11.4	11.4	0.4
IMF special drawing rights	0.4	0.3	—
Reserve position in IMF	10.2	10.5	10.1
Foreign exchange	533.6	760.8	722.0
Total	555.6	782.9	732.6

* National valuation.

Source: IMF, *International Financial Statistics*.

MONEY SUPPLY (million birr, at 31 December)

	1993	1994	1995
Currency outside banks	4,776	5,380	5,718
Demand deposits at commercial banks	2,674	3,646	3,562
Total money	7,450	9,027	9,280

Source: IMF, *International Financial Statistics.*

COST OF LIVING (General Index of Retail Prices for Addis Ababa, excluding rent; base: 1990 = 100)

	1993	1994	1995
Food	160.4	176.7	198.6
Fuel, light and soap*	133.1	134.1	n.a.
Clothing	189.9	170.3	n.a.
All items (incl. others)	155.3	167.1	183.9

* Including certain kitchen utensils.

Source: ILO, *Yearbook of Labour Statistics.*

NATIONAL ACCOUNTS
(million birr at current prices; year ending 7 July)

Expenditure on the Gross Domestic Product (excluding Eritrea)

	1992/93	1993/94	1994/95
Government final consumption expenditure	2,819	3,155	3,675
Private final consumption expenditure*	22,209	23,446	27,720
Gross capital formation	3,288	4,189	5,229
Total domestic expenditure	28,316	30,790	36,624
Exports of goods and services	2,223	3,223	4,899
Less Imports of goods and services	4,521	6,091	8,217
GDP in purchasers' values	26,018	27,922	33,306

* Including statistical discrepancies.

Source: National Bank of Ethiopia.

Gross Domestic Product by Economic Activity (at factor cost, including Eritrea)

	1991/92	1992/93	1993/94*
Agriculture, hunting, forestry and fishing	12,507.7	14,832.9	13,754.1
Mining and quarrying	45.5	132.8	85.3
Manufacturing	953.1	1,595.9	1,867.0
Electricity, gas and water	236.5	245.8	254.8
Construction	403.8	552.2	736.0
Trade, hotels and restaurants	1,468.4	2,187.5	2,551.3
Transport, storage and communications	779.3	1,041.0	1,163.5
Finance, insurance and real estate†	840.3	878.0	2,035.2
Public administration and defence	959.0	1,504.0	1,792.7
Education	505.1	617.6	752.5
Health	128.9	168.8	255.7
Domestic and other services	923.9	1,128.4	1,354.2
Subtotal	19,751.5	24,884.9	26,602.3
Less Imputed bank service charge	335.4	348.3	1,287.5
Total	19,416.1	24,536.6	25,314.8

* Figures are provisional.

† Including imputed rents of owner-occupied dwellings.

Source: National Bank of Ethiopia.

BALANCE OF PAYMENTS (US $ million)

	1993*	1994	1995
Exports of goods f.o.b.	198.8	372.0	423.0
Imports of goods f.o.b.	−706.0	−925.7	−1,147.9
Trade balance	−507.1	−553.7	−724.9
Exports of services	277.2	294.6	344.4
Imports of services	−299.0	−310.4	−359.2
Balance on goods and services	−528.9	−569.5	−739.7
Other income received	25.9	42.9	60.7
Other income paid	−78.4	−74.6	−85.6
Balance on goods, services and income	−581.4	−601.1	−764.5
Current transfers received	532.6	728.5	737.3
Current transfers paid	−1.2	−2.0	−1.1
Current balance	−50.0	125.4	−28.3
Investment assets	−31.7	−318.5	67.0
Investment liabilities	129.4	144.6	135.0
Net errors and omissions	−15.2	−13.1	−121.4
Overall balance	32.4	−61.5	52.4

* Excluding transactions between Ethiopia and Eritrea.

Source: IMF, *International Financial Statistics.*

External Trade

PRINCIPAL COMMODITIES (distribution by SITC, US $ '000)

Imports c.i.f.	1991*	1992*	1993
Food and live animals	20,151	83,418	93,928
Cereals and cereal preparations	14,172	76,285	78,942
Wheat and meslin (unmilled)	10,059	69,133	62,576
Mineral fuels, lubricants, etc.	50,196	149,749	166,612
Petroleum, petroleum products, etc.	50,134	149,546	165,633
Crude petroleum oils, etc.	29,148	99,993	71,393
Refined petroleum products	20,543	48,905	92,750
Animal and vegetable oils, fats and waxes	1,371	15,076	25,949
Fixed vegetable oils and fats	583	14,024	20,774
Chemicals and related products	72,735	58,256	106,125
Inorganic chemicals	6,629	8,015	20,813
Medicinal and pharmaceutical products	17,141	23,044	31,595
Medicaments	16,150	22,338	30,987
Manufactured fertilizers	23,613	159	18,736
Basic manufactures	76,327	99,432	124,232
Rubber manufactures	9,250	15,325	17,534
Textile yarn, fabrics, etc.	16,192	35,976	22,589
Iron and steel	15,559	13,913	38,552
Universals, plates and sheets	8,499	9,944	22,491
Machinery and transport equipment	210,482	192,831	208,897
Machinery specialized for particular industries	28,652	43,182	34,382
General industrial machinery, equipment and parts	13,268	7,349	14,344
Telecommunications and sound equipment	13,028	17,720	8,156
Other electrical machinery, apparatus, etc.	9,963	16,716	25,718
Road vehicles and parts†	77,506	96,703	113,440
Passenger motor cars (excl. buses)	26,561	21,283	29,589
Motor vehicles for goods transport, etc.	26,929	35,030	50,587
Goods vehicles (lorries and trucks)	25,906	34,482	48,989
Parts and accessories for cars, buses, lorries, etc.†	16,223	35,154	28,835
Other transport equipment†	54,633	1,127	2,336
Aircraft, etc., and parts†	53,056	630	1,949
Miscellaneous manufactured articles	30,092	43,160	30,421
Total (incl. others)	471,810	656,601	771,584

* Including Eritrea.

† Excluding tyres, engines and electrical parts.

Exports f.o.b.	1991*	1992*	1993
Food and live animals	126,325	113,228	138,541
Vegetables and fruit	6,292	3,609	3,053
Sugar, sugar preparations and honey	1,773	1,622	4,883
Coffee, tea, cocoa and spices	117,169	107,845	129,395
Coffee and coffee substitutes	116,233	107,310	129,177
Crude materials (inedible) except fuels	32,312	45,908	52,754
Raw hides, skins and furskins	25,068	32,288	32,697
Raw hides and skins (excl. furs)	25,068	32,288	32,697
Cattle hides	3,748	3,384	4,567
Goat skins	5,088	4,842	5,413
Sheep skins with the wool on	16,202	23,704	22,517
Mineral fuels, lubricants, etc.	1,836	13,162	8,020
Petroleum, petroleum products, etc.	1,836	13,162	8,020
Non-monetary gold (excl. ores and concentrates)	21,348	20,185	—
Total (incl. others)†	188,609	197,171	201,706

* Including Eritrea.

† Excluding platinum.

Source: UN, *International Trade Statistics Yearbook*.

1994 (US $ million): Imports c.i.f. 1,033; Exports f.o.b. 372.

PRINCIPAL TRADING PARTNERS (million birr)

Imports c.i.f.	1992*	1993	1994
Austria	20.2	10.6	15.1
Belgium-Luxembourg	37.6	103.4	111.5
Canada	38.2	73.1	136.8
China, People's Repub.	5.9	58.6	107.3
Denmark	31.5	70.5	46.9
Djibouti	129.9	172.3	239.5
France	24.6	59.9	134.6
Germany	196.1	407.8	450.7
Greece	5.4	39.9	24.5
India	25.5	53.7	101.0
Italy	143.8	397.8	627.5
Japan	103.9	156.5	296.5
Kenya	67.2	105.0	144.3
Korea, Repub.	8.8	27.4	74.0
Netherlands	98.6	141.7	228.1
Saudi Arabia	342.2	726.1	848.2
Sweden	45.5	93.9	103.6
Switzerland	66.2	61.8	54.6
United Kingdom	139.5	148.8	271.2
USA	106.0	366.3	694.5
Yemen	67.9	116.5	60.8
Total (incl. others)	1,987.8	3,852.3	5,650.8

Exports f.o.b.	1992*	1993	1994
Belgium-Luxembourg	6.6	30.1	37.8
Djibouti	35.8	121.7	153.3
France	25.1	37.0	102.0
Germany	48.9	198.4	654.3
Italy	32.5	76.4	166.8
Japan	108.4	191.7	300.0
Kuwait	—	—	76.4
Malaysia	2.3	8.9	20.8
Netherlands	7.2	21.1	44.1
Saudi Arabia	101.1	99.5	110.2
Sudan	—	13.2	18.3
United Kingdom	82.0	46.4	71.8
USA	19.6	92.1	133.2
Yemen	9.2	19.5	60.8
Total (incl. others)	504.0	1,007.5	2,062.4

* Including Eritrea.

Source: National Bank of Ethiopia.

Transport

RAILWAYS (traffic, year ending 7 July)*

	1992/93	1993/94	1994/95
Addis Ababa–Djibouti:			
Passenger-km (million)	230	187	151
Freight (million net ton-km)	111	102	93

* Including traffic on the section of the Djibouti–Addis Ababa line which runs through the Republic of Djibouti. Data pertaining to freight include service traffic.

Source: Ministry of Transport and Communications.

ROAD TRAFFIC (motor vehicles in use, year ending 7 July)

	1992/93	1993/94	1994/95
Cars	39,292	31,608	45,559
Buses and coaches	2,042	5,633	3,683
Lorries and vans	17,865	16,755	15,525
Motorcycles and mopeds	2,130	3,416	566
Road tractors	3,889	5,440	4,402
Total	65,218	62,852	69,735

Source: Ministry of Transport and Communications.

SHIPPING

Merchant Fleet (registered at 31 December)

	1994	1995	1996
Number of vessels	27	15	15
Displacement (grt)	83,386	79,520	86,009

Source: Lloyd's Register of Shipping, *World Fleet Statistics*.

International Sea-borne Shipping
(estimated freight traffic, including Eritrea, '000 metric tons)

	1989	1990	1991*
Goods loaded	615	520	592
Goods unloaded	3,190	3,014	3,120

* Estimates.

Source: Economic Commission for Africa, *African Statistical Yearbook*.

CIVIL AVIATION (traffic on scheduled services, including Eritrea)

	1992	1993	1994
Kilometres flown (million)	26	23	24
Passengers carried ('000)	756	752	716
Passenger-km (million)	1,725	1,717	1,607
Total ton-km (million)	264	259	267

Source: UN, *Statistical Yearbook*.

Tourism

Note: The figures include Eritrea.

	1992	1993	1994
Tourist arrivals ('000)	83	93	98
Tourist receipts (US $ million)	23	20	23

Source: UN, *Statistical Yearbook*.

Communications Media

Note: Figures for 1992 and 1993 include Eritrea.

	1992	1993	1994
Telephones ('000 main lines in use)	127*	132	138
Radio receivers ('000 in use)	9,900	10,200	10,550
Television receivers ('000 in use)	145	165	230
Daily newspapers:			
Number	4	n.a.	4
Average circulation ('000 copies)	70†	n.a.	81†

* Year ending 30 June.
† Estimate.

Book production: 240 titles (including 93 pamphlets) in 1991.

Non-daily newspapers: 4 in 1990.

Source: mainly UNESCO, *Statistical Yearbook*.

Education

(1993)

	Institutions	Teachers	Students
Pre-primary	652	1,638	66,086
Primary	8,674	75,736	2,283,638
Secondary: general	n.a.	21,598	714,622
Vocational*	n.a.	310	2,589
Universities†	n.a.	1,440	20,948
Other higher†	n.a.	257	5,270

* 1992 figures. † 1991 figures.

Source: UNESCO, *Statistical Yearbook*.

Directory

The Constitution

In July 1991 a national conference elected a transitional Government and approved a charter under the provisions of which the Government was to operate until the holding of democratic elections. The charter provided guarantees for freedom of association and expression, and for self-determination for Ethiopia's different ethnic constituencies. The transitional Government was to be responsible for drafting a new constitution to replace that introduced in 1987. A Constituent Assembly, dominated by representatives of the EPRDF, was elected in June 1994. It ratified the draft Constitution (already approved by the Council of Representatives) in December. The Constitution of the Federal Democratic Republic of Ethiopia provides for the establishment of a federal government and the division of the country into nine states. It also provides for regional autonomy, including the right of secession. Simultaneous elections of deputies to the federal and state parliaments were conducted on 7 May 1995. The new Constitution came into effect on 22 August 1995.

The Government

HEAD OF STATE

President: Dr NEGASSO GIDADA (took office 22 August 1995).

COUNCIL OF MINISTERS
(July 1997)

Prime Minister: MELES ZENAWI.

Deputy Prime Minister and Head of Economic Affairs at the Prime Minister's Office: Dr KASSA YLALA.

Deputy Prime Minister and Minister of Defence: TEFERA WALWA.

Minister of Foreign Affairs: SEYOUM MESFIN.

Minister of Health: ADEM IBRAHIM.

Minister of Energy and Mines: EZEDIN ALI.

Minister of Development and Economic Co-operation: GIRMA BIRU.

Minister of Information and Culture: WOLDE MIKAEL CHAMO.

Minister of Education: GENET ZEWDE.

Minister of Agriculture: SEIFU KEFEMA.

Minister of Commerce and Industry: KASAHUN AYELE.

Minister of Finance: SUFYAN AHMED.

Minister of Justice: WEREDE WOLDU WOLDE.

Minister of Works and Urban Development: HAILE SELASSIE ASEGIDE.

Minister of Transport and Communications: Dr ABDUL-MEJID HUSSEN.

Minister of Labour and Social Affairs: HASAN ABDELA.

Minister of Water Resources: SHIFERAW JARSO.

Minister and Head of the Revenue Collectors Board: DESTA AMARE.

MINISTRIES AND COMMISSIONS

Office of the Prime Minister: POB 1013, Addis Ababa; tel. (1) 123400.

Ministry of Agriculture: POB 62347, Addis Ababa; tel. (1) 518040; fax (1) 512984.

Ministry of Commerce and Industry: POB 704, Addis Ababa; tel. (1) 518025; telex 21514; fax (1) 515411.

Ministry of Defence: POB 125, Addis Ababa; tel. (1) 445555; telex 21261.

Ministry of Development and Economic Co-operation: POB 2559, Addis Ababa; tel. (1) 151066; telex 21320.

Ministry of Education: POB 1367, Addis Ababa; tel. (1) 553133.

Ministry of Energy and Mines: POB 486, Addis Ababa; tel. (1) 448250; telex 21448; fax (1) 517874.

Ministry of Finance: POB 1905, Addis Ababa; tel. (1) 113400; telex 21147.

Ministry of Foreign Affairs: POB 393, Addis Ababa; tel. (1) 447345; telex 21050.

Ministry of Health: POB 1234, Addis Ababa; tel. (1) 516156.

Ministry of Information and Culture: POB 1020, Addis Ababa; tel. (1) 111124.

Ministry of Justice: POB 1370, Addis Ababa; tel. (1) 517390.

Ministry of Labour and Social Affairs: POB 2056, Addis Ababa; tel. (1) 517080.

Ministry of Transport and Communications: POB 1238, Addis Ababa; tel. (1) 516166; telex 21348; fax (1) 515665.

Ministry of Water Resources: POB 1043, Addis Ababa, tel. (1) 510455; fax (1) 513042.

Ministry of Works and Urban Development: POB 3386, Addis Ababa; tel. (1) 150000.

Legislature

FEDERAL PARLIAMENTARY ASSEMBLY

The legislature comprises an upper house, the Council of the Federation, with 117 seats (members are selected by state assemblies and are drawn one each from 22 minority nationalities and one from each professional sector of the remaining nationalities) and a lower house of 548 directly elected members, the Council of People's Representatives.

At elections conducted on 7 May 1995 the EPRDF secured 483 of the 537 confirmed seats, while 46 were won by regional political groupings and eight were won by independent candidates. The Federal Parliamentary Assembly assumed formal legislative power from the transitional Council of Representatives on 21 August 1995.

Speaker of the Council of the Federation: WEIZERO ALMAZ MEKO.

Speaker of the Council of People's Representatives: DAWIT YOHANES.

Political Organizations

Afar People's Democratic Organization (APDO): fmrly Afar Liberation Front (ALF); based in fmr Hararge and Wollo Admin.

Regions; supported the Ethiopian transitional Govt; Leader ALI MIRAH.

Coalition of Alternative Forces for Peace and Democracy in Ethiopia (CAFPDE): f. 1993 as a broadly-based coalition of groups opposing the EPRDF; Chair. Dr BEYENE PETROS.

Coalition of Ethiopian Democratic Forces (COEDF): f. 1991 in USA by the Ethiopian People's Revolutionary Party–EPRP (the principal party involved), a faction of the Ethiopian Democratic Union (EDU) and the Ethiopian Socialist Movement (MEISON); opposes EPRDF; Chair. MERSHA YOSEPH.

Ethiopian Democratic Unity Party (EDUP): Addis Ababa; f. 1984 as Workers' Party of Ethiopia; adopted present name in March 1990, when its adherence to Marxist-Leninist ideology was relaxed and membership opened to non-Marxist and opposition groups; sole legal political party until May 1991; Sec.-Gen. Lt-Gen. TESFAYE GEBRE KIDAN.

Ethiopian National Democratic Party (ENDP): f. 1994 by merger of five pro-Govt orgs with mems in the Council of Representatives; comprises: the Ethiopian Democratic Organization, the Ethiopian Democratic Organization Coalition (EDC), the Gurage People's Democratic Front (GPDF), the Kembata People's Congress (KPC), and the Wolaita People's Democratic Front (WPDF); Chair. FEKADU GEDAMU.

Ethiopian People's Revolutionary Democratic Front (EPRDF): Addis Ababa; f. 1989 by the TPLF as an alliance of insurgent groups seeking regional autonomy and engaged in armed struggle against the EDUP Govt; Leader MELES ZENAWI; in May 1991, with other orgs, formed transitional Govt; alliance comprises:

Amhara National Democratic Movement (ANDM): based in Tigre; represents interests of the Amhara people; fmrly the Ethiopian People's Democratic Movement (EPDM); adopted present name in Jan. 1994. Sec.-Gen. TEFERA WALWA.

Oromo People's Democratic Organization (OPDO): f. 1990 by the TPLF to promote its cause in Oromo areas; based among the Oromo people in the Shoa region; Dep. Sec.-Gen. KUMA DEMEKSA.

Tigre People's Liberation Front (TPLF): f. 1975; the dominant org. within the EPRDF; Leader MELES ZENAWI.

Ethiopian Somali Democratic League (ESDL): f. 1994 by merger of 11 Ethiopian Somali orgs; comprises: Somali Democratic Union Party, the Issa and Gurgura Liberation Front, the Gurgura Independence Front, the Eastern Gabooye Democratic Organization, the Eastern Ethiopian Somali League, the Horyal Democratic Front, the Social Alliance Democratic Organization, the Somali Abo Democratic Union, the Shekhash People's Democratic Movement, the Ethiopian Somalis' Democratic Movement and the Per Barreh Party; Chair. Dr ABDUL-MEJID HUSSEN.

Oromo Liberation Front (OLF): seeks self-determination for the Oromo people; participated in the Ethiopian transitional Govt until June 1992; Sec.-Gen. GELASSA DILBO; Vice Sec.-Gen. LENCHO LETTA.

Somali Abo Liberation Front (SALF): operates in fmr Bale Admin. Region; has received Somali military assistance; Sec.-Gen. MASURAD SHU'ABI IBRAHIM.

Southern Ethiopian People's Democratic Union (SEPDU): f. 1992 as an alliance of 10 ethnically-based political groups from the south of the country; represented in the Council of Representatives, although five of the 10 groups were expelled from the Council in April 1993; Chair. Dr BEYENE PETROS.

Western Somali Liberation Front (WSLF): POB 978, Mogadishu, Somalia; f. 1975; aims to unite the Ogaden region with Somalia; maintains guerrilla forces of c. 3,000 men; has received support from regular Somali forces; Sec.-Gen. ISSA SHAYKH ABDI NASIR ADAN.

The following Oromo organizations are operating in a coalition (f. 1991):

Oromo Abo Liberation Front (OALF): Chair. MOHAMMED SIRAGE.

Oromo People's Democratic Organization (OPDO): see above.

United Oromo Liberation Front: f. 1995 by merger of United Oromo People's Liberation Front and Islamic Front for the Liberation of Oromia; Chair. AHMAD MUHAMMAD SARO.

Other organizations in opposition to the Ethiopian Government include: the **Democratic Unity Party (DUP):** Chair. AHMAD ABD AL-KARIM; the **Ethiopian Medhin Democratic Party:** Leader Col GOSHU WOLDE; the **Ethiopian National Democratic Organization**, the **Ethiopian People's Democratic Unity Organization (EPDUO):** Leader TADESE TILAHUN; the **Ethiopian People's Revolutionary Party (EPRP)**; the monarchist **Moa Ambessa Party** and the **National Democratic Union**.

Other ethnic organizations seeking self-determination for their respective groups include: the **Abugda Ethiopian Democratic Congress**; the **Afar Revolutionary Democratic Unity Front (ARDUF)**; the **All-Amhara People's Organization (AAPO):** Chair. Prof. ASRAT WOLDYES; the **Burji People's Democratic Organization**; the **Daworo People's Democratic Movement**; the **Gedeo People's Democratic Organization (GPDO):** Leader ALESA MENGESHA; the **Hadia People's Democratic Organization**; the **Harer National League**; the Somali-based **Islamic Union Party (al-Ittihad al-Islam)**, seeking self-determination for the Ogaden; the **Jarso Democratic Movement**; the **Kaffa People's Democratic Union (KPDU)**; the **Kefa People's Democratic Movement**; the **Ogaden National Liberation Front (ONLF):** Chair. BASHIR ABDI; the **Sidama Liberation Movement**; and the **Yem Nationality Movement**.

Other political organizations include the **Ethiopian Democratic Action Group:** Chair. EPHREM ZEMIKAEL; and **Forum 84**.

Diplomatic Representation

EMBASSIES IN ETHIOPIA

Algeria: POB 5740, Addis Ababa; tel. (1) 652300; telex 21799 fax (1) 650187; Ambassador: DELMI BOUDJEMAÂ.

Angola: Addis Ababa; Ambassador: TOKO D. SERÃO.

Argentina: Addis Ababa; telex 21172; Ambassador: Dr H. R. M. MOGUES.

Austria: POB 1219, Addis Ababa; tel. (1) 712144; telex 21060; Ambassador: KLAUS DERKOWITSCH.

Belgium: Addis Ababa; Ambassador: ALAIN GENOT.

Bulgaria: POB 987, Addis Ababa; tel. (1) 612971; telex 21450; Chargé d'affaires a.i.: LIBERT POPOV.

Burundi: POB 3641, Addis Ababa; tel. (1) 651300; telex 21069; Ambassador: ANTOINE NAMOBWA.

Cameroon: Bole Rd, POB 1026, Addis Ababa; telex 21121; fax (1) 518116; Ambassador: JEAN-HILAIRE MBÉA MBÉA.

Canada: Old Airport Area, Higher 23, Kebele 12, House No. 122, POB 1130, Addis Ababa; tel. (1) 713022; telex 21053; fax (1) 713033; Ambassador: GABRIEL M. LESSARD.

Chad: Addis Ababa; telex 21419; fax (1) 612050; Charge d'affaires a.i.: MAHAMAT A. KERIM.

China, People's Republic: POB 5643, Addis Ababa; telex 21145; Ambassador: JIANG ZHENGYUN.

Congo, Democratic Republic: Makanisa Rd, POB 2723, Addis Ababa; tel. (1) 204385; telex 21043; Ambassador: (vacant).

Congo, Republic: POB 5571, Addis Ababa; tel. (1) 154331; telex 21406; Ambassador: VICTOR NIMI.

Côte d'Ivoire: POB 3668, Addis Ababa; tel. (1) 711213; telex 21061; Ambassador: ANTOINE KOUADIO-KIRINE.

Cuba: Jimma Road Ave, POB 5623, Addis Ababa; tel. (1) 202010; telex 21306; Ambassador: MARIANO M. L. BETANCOURT.

Czech Republic: POB 3108, Addis Ababa; tel. (1) 516132; fax (1) 513471; Ambassador: ZDENĚK POLAČEK.

Djibouti: POB 1022, Addis Ababa; tel. (1) 613200; telex 21317; fax (1) 612786; Ambassador: DILEITA MOHAMED DILEITA.

Egypt: POB 1611, Addis Ababa; tel. (1) 113077; telex 21254; Ambassador: MUHAMMAD ASIM IBRAHIM.

Equatorial Guinea: POB 246, Addis Ababa; Ambassador: SALVADOR ELA NSENG ABEGUE.

Eritrea: Addis Ababa; Ambassador: GRMAY ASMEROM.

Finland: Tedla Desta Bldg, Bole Rd, POB 1017, Addis Ababa; tel. (1) 513900; telex 21259; Chargé d'affaires a.i.: LAURI KANGAS.

France: Kabana, POB 1464, Addis Ababa; tel. (1) 550066; telex 21040; fax (1) 551180; Ambassador: ALAIN ROUQUIÉ.

Gabon: POB 1256, Addis Ababa; tel. (1) 611090; telex 21208; fax (1) 613700; Ambassador: EMMANUEL MENDOUME-NZE.

Germany: Kabana, POB 660, Addis Ababa; tel. (1) 550433; telex 21015; fax (1) 551311; Ambassador: WITRUD HOLIK.

Ghana: POB 3173, Addis Ababa; tel. (1) 711402; telex 21249; fax (1) 712511; Ambassador: BENJAMIN G. GODWYLL.

Greece: Africa Ave, POB 1168, Addis Ababa; tel. (1) 654912; telex 21092; fax (1) 654883; Ambassador: VASSILIOS N. VASSALOS.

Guinea: POB 1190, Addis Ababa; tel. (1) 651308; Ambassador: MAMADI DIAWARA.

Holy See: POB 588, Addis Ababa (Apostolic Nunciature); tel. (1) 712100; fax (1) 711499; Apostolic Nuncio: Most Rev. SILVANO M. TOMASI, Titular Archbishop of Cercina.

Hungary: Abattoirs Rd, POB 1213, Addis Ababa; tel. (1) 651850; telex 21176; Ambassador: Dr SÁNDOR ROBEL.

India: Kabena, POB 528, Addis Ababa; tel. (1) 552100; telex 21148; fax (1) 552521; Ambassador: GURCHARAN SINGH.

Indonesia: Mekanisa Rd, POB 1004, Addis Ababa; tel. (1) 712014; telex 21264; fax (1) 710877; Ambassador: ROCHSJAD DAHLAN.

Iran: 317/02 Jimma Rd, Old Airport Area, POB 1144, Addis Ababa; tel. (1) 200369; telex 21118; Ambassador: YOUSEF RAJAB.

Ireland: Addis Ababa; Chargé d'affaires a.i.: DAVID BARRY.

Israel: POB 1266, Addis Ababa; tel (1) 610999; fax (1) 612456; Ambassador: AVI A. GRANOT.

Italy: Villa Italia, POB 1105, Addis Ababa; tel. (1) 551565; telex 21342; fax (1) 550218; Ambassador: MAURIZIO MELANI.

Jamaica: National House, Africa Ave, POB 5633, Addis Ababa; tel. (1) 613656; telex 21137; Ambassador: OWEN A. SINGH.

Japan: Sunshine Bldg, Bole Rd, POB 5650, Addis Ababa; tel. (1) 511088; telex 21108; fax (1) 511350; Ambassador: YASUHIRO HAMADA.

Kenya: Fikre Mariam Rd, POB 3301, Addis Ababa; tel. (1) 610303; telex 21103; Ambassador: G. K. MURITHI.

Korea, Democratic People's Republic: POB 2378, Addis Ababa; Ambassador: MUN SONG MO.

Korea, Republic: Jimma Rd, Old Airport Area, POB 2047, Addis Ababa; tel. (1) 444490; telex 21140; Ambassador: DEUK PO KIM.

Lesotho: Addis Ababa; Ambassador: J. T. METSING.

Liberia: POB 3116, Addis Ababa; tel. (1) 513655; telex 21083; Ambassador: MARCUS M. KOFA.

Libya: POB 5728, Addis Ababa; telex 21214; Chargé d'affaires a.i.: OMAR ELHADI SHENSHEN.

Madagascar: Addis Ababa; Ambassador: JEAN DELCROCX BALKONIA-RIVO.

Malawi: POB 2316, Addis Ababa; tel. (1) 712440; telex 21087; fax (1) 710490; Ambassador: Mrs KALINDE.

Mali: Addis Ababa; Ambassador: S. Y. SIDIBE.

Mauritius: Addis Ababa; Ambassador: SAHID MAUDARABOCUS.

Mexico: Tsige Mariam Bldg 292/21, 4th Floor, Churchill Rd, POB 2962, Addis Ababa; tel. (1) 443456; telex 21141; Ambassador: CARLOS FERRER.

Morocco: Addis Ababa; Ambassador: ABD AL-LATIF NASIF.

Mozambique: Addis Ababa; telex 21008; Ambassador: ALEXANDRE ZANDAMELA.

Namibia: Addis Ababa; Ambassador: EDDIE S. AMKNOKO.

Netherlands: Old Airport Area, POB 1241, Addis Ababa; tel. (1) 711100; telex 21049; fax (1) 711577; Ambassador: JONE BOS.

Niger: Debrezenit Rd H-18 K-41 N-057, POB 5791, Addis Ababa; tel. (1) 651175; telex 21284; Ambassador: ASSANE IGODOE.

Nigeria: POB 1019, Addis Ababa; tel. (1) 550644; telex 21028; Ambassador: BROWNSON N. DEDE.

Norway: Addis Ababa; Ambassador: SVEN A. HOLMSEN.

Oman: Addis Ababa.

Poland: Bole Rd, POB 1123, Addis Ababa; tel. (1) 610197; telex 21185; Ambassador: TADEUSZ WUJEK.

Romania: Africa Ave, POB 2478, Addis Ababa; tel. (1) 610156; telex 21168; fax (1) 611191; Chargé d'affaires a.i.: BORIS RANGHET.

Russia: POB 1500, Addis Ababa; tel. (1) 552061; telex 21534; fax (1) 613795; Ambassador: VLADIMIR A. VOLKOV.

Rwanda: Africa House, Higher 17 Kelele 20, POB 5618, Addis Ababa; tel. (1) 610300; telex 21199; fax (1) 610411; Ambassador: CALLIXTE HABAMENSHI.

Saudi Arabia: Old Airport Area, POB 1104, Addis Ababa; tel. (1) 448010; telex 21194; Ambassador: SAOUD A. M. AL-YAHAYA.

Senegal: Africa Ave, POB 2581, Addis Ababa; tel. (1) 611376; telex 21027; Ambassador: PAPA LOUIS FALL.

Sierra Leone: POB 5619, Addis Ababa; tel. (1) 710033; telex 21144; Ambassador: IBRAHIM M. BABA KAMARA.

Somalia: Addis Ababa; Ambassador: ABRAHIM HAJI NUR.

South Africa: POB 1091, Addis Ababa; tel. (1) 713034; fax (1) 711330; Ambassador: W. NHLAPO.

Spain: Entoto St, POB 2312, Addis Ababa; tel. (1) 550222; telex 21107; fax (1) 551131; Ambassador: AURORA BERNÁLDEZ.

Sudan: Kirkos, Kabele, POB 1110, Addis Ababa; telex 21293; Ambassador: OSMAN AS-SAYED.

Sweden: Ras Ababa Aregaye Ave, POB 1029, Addis Ababa; tel. (1) 511255; telex 21039; fax (1) 515830; Ambassador: CARL OLOF CEDERBLAD.

Switzerland: Jimma Rd, Old Airport Area, POB 1106, Addis Ababa; tel. (1) 711107; telex 21123; fax (1) 712177; Ambassador: PAOLO BROGINI.

Tanzania: POB 1077, Addis Ababa; tel. (1) 441064; telex 21268; Ambassador: CHARLES BEHSTEVAN.

Tunisia: Kesetegna 20, Kebele 39, POB 10069, Addis Ababa; Ambassador: BECHIR BEN AISSA.

Turkey: POB 1506, Addis Ababa; tel. (1) 612321; telex 21257; Ambassador: OKAN GEZER.

Uganda: POB 5644, Addis Ababa; tel. (1) 513088; telex 21143; fax (1) 514355; Ambassador: B. W. K. MATOGO.

United Kingdom: Fikre Mariam Abatechan St, POB 858, Addis Ababa; tel. (1) 612354; telex 21299; fax (1) 610588; Ambassador: G. G. WETHERELL.

USA: Entoto St, POB 1014, Addis Ababa; tel. (1) 550666; telex 21282; fax (1) 551166; Ambassador: DAVID SHINN.

Venezuela: Debre Zeit Rd, POB 5584, Addis Ababa; tel. (1) 654790; telex 21102; Chargé d'affaires a.i.: ALFREDO HERNÁNDEZ-ROVATI.

Viet Nam: POB 1288, Addis Ababa; Ambassador: NGUYEN DUY KINH.

Yemen: POB 664, Addis Ababa; telex 21346; Ambassador: MANSUR ABD AL-JALIL ABD AL-RAB.

Yugoslavia: POB 1341; Addis Ababa; tel. (1) 517804; telex 21233; Ambassador: IGOR JOVOVIĆ.

Zambia: POB 1909; Addis Ababa; tel. (1) 711302; telex 21065; Ambassador: SIMATTA AKAPELWA.

Zimbabwe: POB 5624, Addis Ababa; tel. (1) 183872; telex 21351; Ambassador: T. A. G. MAKOMBE.

Judicial System

Special People's Courts were established in 1981 to replace the former military tribunals. Judicial tribunals are elected by members of the urban dwellers' and peasant associations. In 1987 the Supreme Court ceased to be administered by the Ministry of Law and Justice and became an independent body. In October 1993, however, the Council of Representatives approved draft amendments empowering the Ministry of Justice to assume, additionally, the functions of prosecutor; the office of prosecutor was to operate as a division under the Ministry.

The Supreme Court: Addis Ababa; comprises civil, criminal and military sections; in 1987 its jurisdiction (previously confined to hearing appeals from the High Court) was extended to include supervision of all judicial proceedings throughout the country; the Supreme Court is also empowered, when ordered to do so by the Procurator-General or at the request of the President of the Supreme Court, to review cases upon which final rulings have been made by the courts, including the Supreme Court, but where basic judicial errors have occurred; prior to May 1991, judges were elected by the National Shengo (the former national legislature); Pres. ASEFA LIBEN.

The High Court: Addis Ababa; hears appeals from the Provincial and sub-Provincial Courts; has original jurisdiction.

Awraja Courts: Regional courts composed of three judges, criminal and civil.

Warada Courts: Sub-regional; one judge sits alone with very limited jurisdiction, criminal only.

Religion

About 45% of the population are Muslims and about 40% belong to the Ethiopian Orthodox (Tewahido) Church. There are also significant Evangelical Protestant and Roman Catholic communities. The Pentecostal Church and the Society of International Missionaries carry out mission work in Ethiopia. There are also Hindu and Sikh religious institutions. Most of Ethiopia's small Jewish population was evacuated by the Israeli Government in May 1991. An estimated 5%–15% of the population adhere to animist rites and beliefs.

CHRISTIANITY

Ethiopian Orthodox (Tewahido) Church

The Ethiopian Orthodox (Tewahido) Church is one of the five oriental orthodox churches. It was founded in AD 328, and in 1989 had more than 22m. members, 20,000 parishes and 290,000 clergy. The Supreme Body is the Holy Synod and the National Council, under the chairmanship of the Patriarch. The Church comprises 25 archdioceses and dioceses (including those in Jerusalem, Sudan, Djibouti and the Western Hemisphere). There are 32 Archbishops and Bishops. The Church administers 1,139 schools and 12 relief and rehabilitation centres throughout Ethiopia.

Patriarchate Head Office: POB 1283, Addis Ababa; tel. (1) 116507; telex 21489; Patriarch Archbishop ABUNE PAULOS; Gen. Sec. L. M. DEMTSE GEBRE MEDHIN.

The Roman Catholic Church

At 31 December 1995 Ethiopia contained an estimated 66,546 adherents of the Alexandrian-Ethiopian Rite and 279,642 adherents of the Latin Rite.

Bishops' Conference: Ethiopian Episcopal Conference, POB 2454, Addis Ababa; tel. (1) 550300; telex 21381; fax (1) 553113; f. 1966; Pres. Cardinal PAULOS TZADUA, Archbishop of Addis Ababa.

Alexandrian-Ethiopian Rite

Adherents are served by one archdiocese (Addis Ababa) and three dioceses (Adigrat, Asmara, Keren).

Archbishop of Addis Ababa: Cardinal PAULOS TZADUA, Catholic Archbishop's House, POB 21903, Addis Ababa; tel. (1) 111667; fax (1) 553113.

Latin Rite

Aherents are served by the five Apostolic Vicariates of Awasa, Harar, Meki, Nekemte and Soddo-Hosanna, and by the Apostolic Prefecture of Jimma-Bonga.

Other Christian Churches

The Anglican Communion: Within the Episcopal Church in Jerusalem and the Middle East, the Bishop in Egypt has jurisdiction over seven African countries, including Ethiopia.

Armenian Orthodox Church: Deacon VARTKES NALBANDIAN, St George's Armenian Church, POB 116, Addis Ababa; f. 1923.

Ethiopian Evangelical Church (Mekane Yesus): Pres. Rev. YADESA DABA, POB 2087, Addis Ababa; tel. (1) 553280; telex 21528; fax (1) 552966; f. 1959; affiliated to Lutheran World Fed., All Africa Conf. of Churches and World Council of Churches; c. 2.1m. mems (1996).

Greek Orthodox Church: Metropolitan of Axum Most Rev. PETROS GIAKOUMELOS, POB 571, Addis Ababa.

Seventh-day Adventist Church: Pres. Pastor BEKELE BIRI, POB 145, Addis Ababa; tel. (1) 511199; telex 21549; f. 1907; 64,000 mems.

ISLAM

Leader: Haji MOHAMMED AHMAD.

JUDAISM

Following the phased emigration to Israel of about 21,000 Falashas (Ethiopian Jews), during 1984–91, there are now estimated to be fewer than 2,000 Falashas remaining in the country.

The Press

DAILIES

Addis Zemen: POB 30145, Addis Ababa; f. 1941; Amharic; publ. by the Ministry of Information and Culture; Editor-in-Chief MERID BEKELE; circ. 40,000.

Ethiopian Herald: POB 30701, Addis Ababa; tel. (1) 119050; f. 1943; English; publ. by the Ministry of Information and Culture; Editor-in-Chief KIFLOM HADGOI; circ. 37,000.

PERIODICALS

Abyotawit Ethiopia: POB 2549, Addis Ababa; fortnightly; Amharic.

Addis Tribune: Tambek International, POB 2395, Addis Ababa; tel. (1) 129524; fax (1) 552110; e-mail tambek@telcom.net.et; f. 1993; weekly; English; Editor-in-Chief T. BEKELE; circ. 5,000.

Addis Zimit: POB 2395, Addis Ababa; f. 1993; tel. (1) 118613; fax (1) 552110; weekly; Amharic; Editor-in-Chief T. BEKELE; circ. 8,000.

Al-Alem: POB 30232, Addis Ababa; weekly; Arabic; publ. by the Ministry of Information; Editor-in-Chief TELSOM AHMED; circ. 2,500.

Berisa: POB 30232, Addis Ababa; f. 1976; weekly; Oromogna; publ. by the Ministry of Information; Editor BULO SIBA; circ. 3,500.

Birhan Family Magazine: POB 2248, Addis Ababa; monthly; women's magazine.

Birritu: National Bank of Ethiopia, POB 5550, Addis Ababa; tel. (1) 517430; telex 21020; fax (1) 514588; six a year; Amharic and English; business, insurance and financial news; circ. 6,000; Editor-in-Chief TAREKEGN ASSEFA.

Ethiopian Trade Journal: Ethiopian Chamber of Commerce, POB 517, Addis Ababa; tel. (1) 518240; telex 21213; quarterly; English; Editor-in-Chief GETACHEW ZICKE.

Ethiopis Review: Editor-in-Chief TESFERA ASMARE.

Meskerem: Addis Ababa; quarterly; theoretical politics; circ. 100,000.

Negarit Gazzetta: POB 1031, Addis Ababa; irregularly; Amharic and English; official gazette.

Negradas: Ethiopian Chamber of Commerce, POB 517, Addis Ababa; tel. (1) 518240; telex 21213; Amharic.

Nigdina Limat: POB 2458, Addis Ababa; tel. (1) 513882; telex 21213; fax (1) 511479; monthly; Amharic; publ. by the Ethiopian Chamber of Commerce; circ. 6,000.

Tinsae (Resurrection): Addis Ababa; tel. (1) 116507; telex 21489; Amharic and English; publ. by the Ethiopian Orthodox Church.

Tobiya: Addis Ababa; weekly; Gen.-Man. HAILU WOLDETSADIK (acting).

Wetaderna Alamaw: POB 1901, Addis Ababa; fortnightly; Amharic.

Yezareitu Ethiopia (Ethiopia Today): POB 30232, Addis Ababa; weekly; Amharic and English; publ. by the Ministry of Information; Editor-in-Chief IMIRU WORKU; circ. 30,000.

NEWS AGENCIES

Ethiopian News Agency (ENA): Patriots' St, POB 530, Addis Ababa; tel. (1) 120014; telex 21068; Chief AMARE AREGAWI.

Foreign Bureaux

Agence France-Presse (AFP): POB 3537, Addis Ababa; tel. (1) 511006; telex 21031; Chief SABA SEYOUM.

Agenzia Nazionale Stampa Associata (ANSA) (Italy): POB 1001, Addis Ababa; tel. (1) 111007; Chief BRAHAME GHEBREZGHI-ABIHER.

Associated Press (AP): Addis Ababa; tel. (1) 161726; Correspondent ABEBE ANDUALAM.

Deutsche Presse-Agentur (dpa) (Germany): Addis Ababa; tel. (1) 510687; Correspondent GHION HAGOS.

Informatsionnoye Telegrafnoye Agentstvo Rossii—Telegrafnoye Agentstvo Suverennykh Stran (ITAR—TASS) (Russia): POB 998, Addis Ababa; tel. (1) 181255; telex 21091; Bureau Chief GENNADII G. GABRIELYAN.

Prensa Latina (Cuba): Gen. Makonnen Bldg, 5th Floor, nr Ghion Hotel, opp. National Stadium, POB 5690, Addis Ababa; tel. (1) 519899; telex 21151; Chief HUGO RIUS BLEIN.

Reuters (UK): Addis Ababa; tel. (1) 156505; telex 21407; Correspondent TSEGAYE TADESSE.

Rossiyskoye Informatsionnoye Agentstvo—Novosti (RIA—Novosti) (Russia): POB 239, Addis Ababa; telex 21237; Chief VITALII POLIKARPOV.

Xinhua (New China) News Agency (People's Republic of China): POB 2497, Addis Ababa; tel. (1) 515676; telex 21504; fax (1) 514742; Correspondent CHEN CAILIN.

PRESS ASSOCIATION

Ethiopian Journalists' Association: POB 5911, Addis Ababa; tel. (1) 128198; Chair. IMERU WORKU (acting).

Publishers

Addis Ababa University Press: POB 1176, Addis Ababa; tel. (1) 119148; telex 21205; f. 1968; educational and reference works in English; Editor MESSELECH HABTE.

Ethiopia Book Centre: POB 1024, Addis Ababa; tel. (1) 116844; f. 1977; privately-owned; publr, importer, wholesaler and retailer of educational books.

Kuraz Publishing Agency: POB 30933, Addis Ababa; tel. (1) 551688; telex 21512; state-owned.

Government Publishing House

Government Printing Press: Addis Ababa.

Radio and Television

In 1994, according to UNESCO, there were an estimated 10.6m. radio receivers and 230,000 television receivers in use.

Telecommunications Authority of Ethiopia: POB 1047, Addis Ababa; tel. (1) 510500; telex 21000; Gen. Man. FIKRU ASFAW.

RADIO

Radio Ethiopia: POB 1020, Addis Ababa; tel. (1) 121011; f. 1941; Amharic, English, French, Arabic, Afar, Oromifa, Tigre, Tigrinya and Somali; Gen. Man. KASA MILOKO.

Radio Voice of One Free Ethiopia: Amharic; broadcasts twice a week; opposes current govts of Ethiopia and Eritrea.

Torch: Addis Ababa; f. 1994; Amharic; Gen. Man. SEIFU TURE GETACHEW.

Voice of the Tigre Revolution: Mekele; supports Tigre People's Liberation Front.

TELEVISION

Ethiopian Television: POB 5544, Addis Ababa; tel. (1) 116701; telex 21429; f. 1964; state-controlled; commercial advertising is accepted; programmes are transmitted from Addis Ababa to 18 regional stations; Dir-Gen. WOLE GURMU.

Finance

(cap. = capital; dep. = deposits; m. = million; res = reserves; brs = branches; amounts in birr)

BANKING

There are currently three state-owned and three privately-owned banks in Ethiopia.

Central Bank

National Bank of Ethiopia: POB 5550, Addis Ababa; tel. (1) 517430; telex 21020; fax (1) 514588; f. 1964; bank of issue; cap. and res 1,131.5m., dep. 5,253.1m. (Nov. 1996); Gov. DUBALE JALE; Vice-Gov. TEKLEWOLD ATNAFU; 1 br.

Other Banks

Awash Bank: POB 12638, Addis Ababa; tel. and fax (1) 614477; cap. and res 27.2m., dep. 212.5m. (Nov. 1996); Gen. Man. LEIKUN BERHANU; 11 brs.

Bank of Abyssinia: Addis Ababa; f. 1905 (closed 1935 and reopened 1996); commercial banking service; cap. and res 17.7m., dep. 14.3m. (Nov. 1996); CEO TEKALEGNE GEDAMU; 1 br.

Commercial Bank of Ethiopia: Unity Square, POB 255, Addis Ababa; tel. (1) 515004; telex 21037; fax (1) 517822; f. 1964, reorg. 1980; cap. and res 853.4m., dep. 11,868m. (Nov. 1996); Pres. TILAHUN ABBAY; 167 brs.

Construction and Business Bank: Higher 21, Kebele 04, POB 3480, Addis Ababa; tel. (1) 512300; telex 21869; fax (1) 515103; f. 1975 as Housing and Savings Bank; provides credit for construction projects and a range of commercial banking services; cap. and res 55.8m., dep. 447.7m. (Nov. 1996); Gen. Man. ADMASSU TECHANE; 20 brs.

Dashen Bank: POB 12752, Addis Ababa; tel. (1) 650286; telex 654073; cap. and res 14.9m., dep. 201.6m. (Nov. 1996); CEO TEKETEL HAPTE GIORGIS; 14 brs.

Development Bank of Ethiopia: Joseph Broz Tito St, POB 1700, Addis Ababa; tel. (1) 511188; telex 21173; fax (1) 511606; provides development finance for industry and agriculture, technical advice and assistance in project evaluation; cap. and res 371.4m., dep. 8.9m. (June 1993); Gen. Man. MOGES CHEMERE; 19 brs.

INSURANCE

Africa Insurance Co: POB 12941, Addis Ababa; tel. (1) 517861; fax (1) 510376; Gen. Man. ALEM TESFATSION.

Awash Insurance Co: POB 34369, Addis Ababa; tel. (1) 614418; telex 21792; fax (1) 654788; Gen. Man. TSEGAYE KEMAI.

Ethiopian Insurance Corpn: POB 2545, Addis Ababa; tel. (1) 517974; telex 21120; fax (1) 517499; f. 1976; Gen. Man. MICHAEL KUMSA.

National Insurace Co of Ethiopia: POB 12645, Addis Ababa; tel. (1) 652448; fax (1) 650660; Gen. Man. HABTEMARIAM SHUMGIZAW.

Nile Insurance Co: POB 12836, Addis Ababa; tel. (1) 114041; fax (1) 550336; Gen. Man. MAHTSENTU FELEKE.

Nyala Insurance Co: POB 12753, Addis Ababa; tel. (1) 340532; telex 21807; fax (1) 654078; Gen. Man. NAHUSENAY ARAYA.

United Insurance Co: POB 1156, Addis Ababa; tel. (1) 519847; fax (1) 513258; Gen. Man. EYESUSWORK ZAFU.

Trade and Industry

CHAMBER OF COMMERCE

Ethiopian Chamber of Commerce: Mexico Sq., POB 517, Addis Ababa; tel. (1) 518240; telex 21213; f. 1947; city chambers in Addis Ababa, Asella, Awasa, Bahir Dar, Dire Dawa, Nazret, Jimma, Gondar, Dessie and Lekempte; Pres. (vacant); Sec.-Gen. KASSAHUN JEMBERE.

AGRICULTURAL ORGANIZATION

Ethiopia Peasants' Association (EPA): f. 1978 to promote improved agricultural techniques, home industries, education, public health and self-reliance; comprises 30,000 peasant asscns with c. 7m. mems; Chair. (vacant).

TRADE AND INDUSTRIAL ORGANIZATIONS

Ethiopian Beverages Corpn: POB 1285, Addis Ababa; tel. (1) 186185; telex 21373; Gen. Man. MENNA TEWAHEDE.

Ethiopian Cement Corpn: POB 5782, Addis Ababa; tel. (1) 552222; telex 21308; fax (1) 551572; Gen. Man. REDI GEMAL.

Ethiopian Chemical Corpn: POB 5747, Addis Ababa; tel. (1) 184305; telex 21011; Gen. Man. ASNAKE SAHLU.

Ethiopian Coffee Marketing Corpn: POB 2591, Addis Ababa; tel. (1) 515330; telex 21174; fax (1) 510762; f. 1977; Gen. Man. GETACHW HAILE LEUL.

Ethiopian Food Corpn: Higher 21, Kebele 04, Mortgage Bldg, Addis Ababa; tel. (1) 158522; telex 21292; fax (1) 513173; f. 1975; produces and distributes food items including edible oil, ghee substitute, pasta, bread, maize, wheat flour etc.; Gen. Man. BEKELE HAILE.

Ethiopian Fruit and Vegetable Marketing Enterprise: POB 2374, Addis Ababa; tel. (1) 519192; telex 21106; fax (1) 516483; f. 1980; sole wholesale domestic distributor and exporter of fresh and processed fruit and vegetables, and floricultural products; Gen. Man. AGEGENHU SISSAY.

Ethiopian Handicrafts and Small-Scale Industries Development Organization: Addis Ababa; tel. (1) 157366.

Ethiopian Import and Export Corpn (ETIMEX): POB 2313, Addis Ababa; tel. (1) 511112; telex 21235; fax (1) 515411; f. 1975; state trading corpn under the supervision of the Ministry of Commerce and Industry; import of building materials, foodstuffs, stationery and office equipment, textiles, clothing, chemicals, general merchandise, capital goods; Gen. Man. ASCHENAKI G. HIWOT.

Ethiopian Livestock and Meat Corpn: POB 5579, Addis Ababa; tel. (1) 159341; telex 21095; f. 1984; state trading corpn responsible for the development and export of livestock and livestock products; Gen. Man. GELANA KEJELA.

Ethiopian National Metal Works Corpn: Addis Ababa; fax (1) 510714; Gen. Man. ALULA BERHANE.

Ethiopian Oil Seeds and Pulses Export Corpn: POB 5719, Addis Ababa; tel. (1) 550597; telex 21133; fax (1) 553299; f. 1975; Gen. Man. EPHRAIM AMBAYE.

Ethiopian Petroleum Corpn: POB 3375, Addis Ababa; telex 21054; fax (1) 512938; f. 1976; Gen. Man. ZEWDE TEWOLDE.

Ethiopian Pharmaceuticals and Medical Supplies Corpn: POB 21904, Addis Ababa; tel. (1) 134577; telex 21248; fax (1) 752555; f. 1976; manufacture, import, export and distribution of pharmaceuticals, chemicals, dressings, surgical and dental instruments, hospital and laboratory supplies; Gen. Man. BERHANU ZELEKE.

Ethiopian Sugar Corpn: POB 133, Addis Ababa; tel. (1) 519700; telex 21038; fax (1) 513488; Gen. Man. ABATE LEMENGH.

National Leather and Shoe Corpn: POB 2516, Addis Ababa; tel. (1) 514075; telex 21096; fax (1) 513525; f. 1975; produces and sells semi-processed hides and skins, finished leather, leather goods and footwear; Gen. Man. GIRMA W. AREGAI.

National Textiles Corpn: Addis Ababa; tel. (1) 157316; telex 21129; fax (1) 511955; f. 1975; production of yarn, fabrics, knitwear, blankets, bags, etc.; Gen. Man. FIKRE HUGIANE.

Natural Gums Processing and Marketing Enterprise: POB 62322, Addis Ababa; tel. (1) 159930; telex 21336; fax (1) 518110; Gen. Man. ESKINDER TAYE.

TRADE UNIONS

Ethiopian Trade Union (ETU): POB 3653, Addis Ababa; tel. (1) 514366; telex 21618; f. 1975 to replace the Confed. of Ethiopian Labour Unions; comprises nine industrial unions and 22 regional unions with a total membership of 320,000 (1987); Chair. (vacant).

Transport

RAILWAYS

Djibouti-Ethiopian Railway (Chemin de Fer Djibouti-Ethiopien–CDE): POB 1051, Addis Ababa; tel. (1) 517250; telex 21414; fax (1) 513997; f. 1909, adopted present name in 1981; jtly-owned by Govts of Ethiopia and Djibouti; plans to grant autonomous status were announced by the two Govts in 1985; 781 km of track, of which 681 km in Ethiopia, linking Addis Ababa with Djibouti; Pres. AHMED WABERI GEDIE; Vice-Pres. A. BITEWLEGNE.

ROADS

In 1995 the total road network comprised an estimated 28,360 km of primary, secondary and feeder roads and trails, of which 19,400 km were main roads. A highway links Addis Ababa with Nairobi in Kenya, forming part of the Trans-East Africa Highway. In November 1995 a five-year programme of road construction was announced. Some US $200m. was allocated to the programme, mostly financed by loans from the World Bank and the European Union.

Ethiopian Roads Authority: POB 1770, Addis Ababa; tel. (1) 517170; telex 12180; fax (1) 514866; f. 1951; construction and maintenance of roads, bridges and airports; Gen. Man. TESFA MICHAEL NAHUSENAI.

Ethiopian Road Transport Authority: POB 2504, Addis Ababa; tel. (1) 510244; fax (1) 510715; enforcement of road transport regulations, registering of vehicles and issuing of driving licences; Gen. Man. ZEMEDKUN GIRMA.

National Freight Transport Corpn: POB 2538, Addis Ababa; tel. (1) 151841; telex 21238; f. 1974; truck and tanker operations throughout the country; restructured into five autonomous enterprises in 1994 and scheduled for privatization.

Public Transport Corpn: POB 5780, Addis Ababa; tel. (1) 153117; telex 21371; fax (1) 510720; f. 1977; urban bus services in Addis Ababa and Jimma, and services between towns; restructured into three autonomous enterprises in 1994 and scheduled for privatization; Gen. Man. TESFAYE SHENKUTE.

SHIPPING

The formerly Ethiopian-controlled ports of Massawa and Assab now lie within the boundaries of the State of Eritrea (q.v.). There is, however, an agreement between the two Governments allowing Ethiopian access to the two ports. There are regular services by foreign vessels to Massawa and Assab, which can handle more than 1m. metric tons of merchandise annually. Assab, a free port, has a petroleum refinery with an annual capacity of 800,000 metric tons. Much trade passes through Djibouti (in the Republic of Djibouti) to Addis Ababa, and Ethiopia has access to the Kenyan port of Mombasa. At the end of 1996 Ethiopia's registered merchant fleet numbered 15 vessels, with a total displacement of 86,009 grt.

Ethiopian Shipping Lines Corpn: POB 2572, Addis Ababa; tel. (1) 518280; telex 21045; fax (1) 519525; e-mail esl@telecom.net.et; f. 1964; serves Red Sea, Europe, Mediterranean, Gulf and Far East with its own fleet and chartered vessels; Chair. G. TSADKAN GEBRE TENSAY; Gen. Man. AMBACHEW ABRAHA.

Marine Transport Authority: Maritime Dept, POB 1861, Addis Ababa; tel. (1) 158227; telex 21348; fax (1) 515665; f. 1993; regulates maritime transport services; Chair. TESHOME WOLDEGIORGIS.

Maritime and Transit Services Enterprise: POB 1186, Addis Ababa; tel. (1) 510666; telex 21290; fax (1) 514097; f. 1979; handles cargoes for import and export; operates shipping agency service; Chair. DESTA AMARE; Gen. Man. AHMED YASSIN.

CIVIL AVIATION

Ethiopia has two international airports (at Addis Ababa and Dire Dawa) and around 40 airfields. Bole International Airport in the capital handles 95% of international air traffic and 85% of domestic flights. A programme to modernize the airport, at an estimated cost of 819m. birr (US $130m.), was to be undertaken during 1997–2000. Construction of an international airport at Mekele began in November 1995. This airport was scheduled to become operational in 1997.

Civil Aviation Authority: POB 978, Addis Ababa; tel. (1) 610277; telex 21162; fax (1) 612533; constructs and maintains airports; provides air navigational facilities; Gen. Man. MESHESHA BELAYNEH.

Ethiopian Airlines: Bole International Airport, POB 1755, Addis Ababa; tel. (1) 612222; telex 21012; fax (1) 611474; f. 1945; operates regular domestic services and flights to 41 international destinations in Africa, Europe, Middle East and Asia; Chair. SEEYE ABRAHA; Dir-Gen. BISRAT NIGATU.

Tourism

Ethiopia's tourist attractions include the early Christian monuments and churches, the ancient capitals of Gondar and Axum, the Blue Nile Falls and the National Parks of the Semien and Bale Mountains. Tourist arrivals in 1994 totalled some 98,000 and provided an estimated US $23m. in foreign exchange.

Ethiopian Tourism Commission: POB 2183, Addis Ababa; tel. (1) 517470; telex 21067; fax (1) 513899; f. 1964; formulates national tourism policy, publicizes tourist attractions and regulates standards of tourist facilities; Commr YOUSUF ABDULLAHI SUKKAR.

Defence

Following the fall of Mengistu's government and the defeat of his army in May 1991, troops of the Eritrean People's Liberation Front (EPLF) and the Ethiopian People's Revolutionary Democratic Front (EPRDF) were deployed in Eritrea and in Ethiopia respectively. In June 1993 EPRDF forces were estimated at about 100,000. In October 1993 it was announced that preparations were under way to create a 'multi-ethnic defence force'. In 1993 Ethiopian armed forces were estimated to number some 120,000 (the majority of whom being former members of the TPLF and some 10,000–15,000 from the OLF). By December 1995 some 20,000 members of EPRDF forces had been demobilized. In March 1996 the transitional Government announced plans to sell Ethiopia's naval assets.

Defence Expenditure: Budgeted at 700m. birr in 1996.

Education

Education in Ethiopia is available free of charge, and, after a rapid growth in numbers of schools, it became compulsory between the ages of seven and 13 years. Since September 1976 most primary and secondary schools have been controlled by local peasant associations and urban dwellers' associations. Primary education begins at seven years of age and lasts for six years. Secondary education, beginning at 13 years of age, lasts for a further six years, comprising a first cycle of two years and a second of four years. In 1993 total enrolment at primary schools was equivalent to 27% of children in the relevant age-group (33% of boys; 21% of girls); the comparable ratio for secondary enrolment was only 11% (11% of boys; 10% of girls). The 1994–95 budget allocated 14.9% (1,212.2m. birr) of total expenditure to education and training. A major literacy campaign was launched in 1979. By 1990 more than 23m. people had been enrolled for tuition programmes, and the rate of adult illiteracy had reportedly been reduced to 23% (compared with 96% in 1970). The campaign subsequently lost momentum, however, and in 1995, according to UNESCO estimates, the rate of adult illiteracy had risen to 64.5% (males 54.5%; females 74.7%). Ethiopia has two universities. In 1990 some 16,116 students were enrolled at Addis Ababa University. There is an agricultural university at Alemaya and a polytechnic institute at Bahir Dar. There is a considerable shortage of qualified teachers, which is particularly acute in secondary schools, which rely heavily on expatriate staff.

Bibliography

Abegaz, B. (Ed.). *Essays on Ethiopian Economic Development.* Aldershot, Avebury, 1994.

Abir, M. *Ethiopia and the Red Sea: The Rise and Decline of the Solomonic Dynasty and Muslim-European Rivalry in the Region.* London, Frank Cass, 1980.

Abraham, K. *Ethiopia: from Bullets to the Ballot Box: The Bumpy Road to Democracy and the Political Economy of Transition.* Trenton, NJ, Red Sea Press, 1994.

Africa Watch. *Evil Days: 30 Years of War and Famine in Ethiopia.* New York, Human Rights Watch, 1991.

Agyeman-Duah, B. *The United States and Ethiopia: Military Assistance and the Quest for Security 1953–1993.* Lanham, MD, University Press of America, 1994.

Bekele, S. (Ed.). *An Economic History of Ethiopia. Vol.* I: *The Imperial Era, 1941–1974.* Dakar, CODESRIA, 1995.

Clapham, C. *Transformation and Continuity in Revolutionary Ethiopia.* Cambridge, Cambridge University Press, 1988.

Transformation and Continuity in Revolutionary Ethiopia. New York, Cambridge University Press, 1990.

Clarke, J. *Ethiopia's Campaign against Famine.* London, Harney and Jones, 1987.

Connell, D. *Against all Odds: A Chronicle of the Eritrean Revolution.* Trenton, NJ, Red Sea Press, 1993.

Del Boca, A. *The Ethiopian War 1935–1941.* Chicago, University of Chicago Press, 1969.

Dessaleggn, R. *Agrarian Reform in Ethiopia.* Trenton, NJ, Red Sea Press, 1984.

Donham, D., and James, W. (Eds). *The Southern Marches of Imperial Ethiopia.* Cambridge, Cambridge University Press, 1986.

Doornbos, M., Cliffe, L., Ahmed, A.G.M., and Markakis, J. (Eds). *Beyond Conflict in the Horn: The Prospects of Peace and Development in Ethiopia, Somalia, Eritrea and Sudan.* Trenton, NJ, Red Sea Press, 1992.

Dugan, J., and Lafore, L. *Days of Emperor and Clown, The Italo-Ethiopian War 1935–1936.* New York, Doubleday, 1973.

Erlich, H. *Ethiopia and the Middle East*. Boulder, CO, and London, Lynne Rienner Publishers, 1994.

Faye, B. *Eleveurs d'Ethiopie*. Paris, Editions Karthala, 1990.

Fukui, K., and Markakis, J. (Eds). *Ethnicity and Conflict in the Horn of Africa*. London, James Currey, 1994.

Gebre-Medhin, J. *Peasants and Nationalism in Eritrea*. Trenton, NJ, Red Sea Press, 1989.

Ghebre-Ab, H. (Ed.). *Ethiopia and Eritrea: A Documentary Study*. Trenton, NJ, Red Sea Press, 1993.

Gilkes, P. *The Dying Lion: Feudalism and Modernization in Ethiopia*. London, Julian Friedmann, 1974.

Giorgis, D. W. *Red Tears: War, Famine and Revolution in Ethiopia*. Trenton, NJ, Red Sea Press, 1989.

Griffin, K. (Ed.). *The Economy of Ethiopia*. New York, St Martin's Press, 1992.

Gurdon, C. (Ed.). *The Horn of Africa*. London, University College London Press, 1994.

Haile Sellassie I. *The Autobiography of Emperor Haile Sellassie I. 'My Life and Ethiopia's Progress.'* Oxford, Oxford University Press, 1976.

Halliday, F., and Molyneux, M. *The Ethiopian Revolution*. London, Verso Editions, 1981.

Hansson, G. *The Ethiopian Economy 1974–94: Ethiopia Tikdem and After*. London, Routledge, 1995.

Harbeson, J. W. *The Ethiopian Transformation*. Boulder, CO, Westview Press, 1988.

Hassen, M. *The Oromo of Ethiopia: A History 1570–1860*. Trenton, NJ, Red Sea Press, 1994.

Hess, R. L. *The Modernization of Autocracy*. Ithaca, NY, and London, Cornell University Press, 1972.

(Ed.). *Proceedings of the 5th International Conference on Ethiopian Studies: Session B*. Chicago, University of Illinois, 1979.

Iyob, R. *The Eritrean Struggle for Independence: Domination, Resistance, Nationalism 1941–93*. Cambridge, Cambridge University Press, 1995.

Jalata, A, *Oromia and Ethiopia: State Formation and Ethnonational Conflict, 1868–1992*. Boulder, CO, Lynne Rienner Publishers, 1993.

Kapuscinski, R. *The Emperor*. New York, Random House, 1989.

Katsuyoski, F., and Markakis, J. (Eds). *Ethnicity and Conflict in the Horn of Africa*. London, James Currey, 1994.

Kebbede, G. *The State and Development in Ethiopia*. Atlantic Highlands, NJ, Humanities Press, 1992.

Keller, E. J. *Revolutionary Ethiopia: From Empire to People's Republic*. Bloomington, Indiana University Press, 1989.

Kiros, F. G. *The Subsistence Crisis in Africa: The Case of Ethiopia: Root Causes and Challenges of the 1990s and the New Century*. Nairobi, OSSREN, 1993.

Korn, D. A. *Ethiopia, the United States and the Soviet Union 1974–85*. London, Croom Helm, 1986.

Last, G. C. 'Introductory Notes on the Geography of Ethiopia', in *Ethiopia Observer*, Vol. VI, No. 2, 1962.

Levine, D. *Greater Ethiopia: The Evolution of a Multicultural Society*. Chicago, University of Chicago Press, 1974.

McCann, J. *From Poverty to Famine in Northeast Ethiopia*. Philadelphia, University of Pennsylvania Press, 1987.

Marcus, H. G. *Ethiopia, Great Britain and the United States, 1941–1974*. Berkeley, University of California Press, 1983.

A History of Ethiopia. Berkeley, University of California Press, 1994.

(Ed.). *New Trends in Ethiopian Studies: Papers of the 12th International Conference of Ethiopian Studies*. Trenton, NJ, Red Sea Press, 1994.

Markakis, J. *Ethiopia: Anatomy of a Traditional Polity*. London, Oxford University Press, 1974.

National and Class Conflict in the Horn of Africa. Cambridge, Cambridge University Press (African Studies Series, No. 55), 1988.

Markakis, J., and Ayele, N. *Class and Revolution in Ethiopia*. Nottingham, Spokesman, 1978.

Mockler, A. *Haile Selassie's War*. Oxford, Oxford University Press, 1985.

Negash, T. *Rethinking Education in Ethiopia*. New Brunswick NJ, Transaction Publishers, 1996.

Ofcansky, T. B. and Berry, L. (Eds). *Ethiopia: A Country Study*. Washington, DC, USGPO, 1991.

Ottaway, M. *Soviet and American Influence in the Horn of Africa*. New York, Praeger, 1982.

(Ed.). *The Political Economy of Ethiopia*. New York, Praeger, 1990.

Ottaway, M., and Ottaway, D. *Ethiopia: Empire in Revolution*. New York, Africana Publishing, 1978.

OXFAM. *Ethiopia: Breaking New Ground*. Oxford, Oxfam Publishing, 1994.

Pankhurst, A. *Resettlement and Famine in Ethiopia: The Villagers' Experience*. Manchester, Manchester University Press, 1992.

Pankhurst, R. *Economic History of Ethiopia, 1880–1935*. Addis Ababa, 1968.

History of Ethiopian Towns. London, 1982.

Patman, R. G. *The Soviet Union in The Horn of Africa*. Cambridge, Cambridge University Press, 1990.

Pansewang, S., et al. (Eds) *Ethiopia: Rural Development Options*: London, Zed Books, 1990.

Perham, M. F. *The Government of Ethiopia*. Evanston, IL, Northwestern University Press, 1969.

Pickett, J. *Economic Development in Ethiopia: Agriculture, the Market and the State*. Paris, OECD, 1991.

Prouty, C. *Empress Taytu and Menilek II: Ethiopia 1883–1910*. London, Ravens Educational and Development Services, 1986.

Prouty, C. and Rosenfeld, E. *Historical Dictionary of Ethiopia and Eritrea*. 2nd Edn. Lanham, MD, and London, Scarecrow Press, 1994.

Relief Society of Tigray. *Tigray: The Struggle for Development*. Makelle, REST, 1993.

Rubenson, S. *The Survival of Ethiopian Independence*. London, Heinemann, 1976.

Sbacchi, A. *Ethiopia under Mussolini: Fascism and the Colonial Experience*. London, Zed Press, 1985.

Selassie, Z. G. *Yohannes IV of Ethiopia*. Oxford, Oxford University Press, 1975.

Sellassie, H. B. *Conflict and Intervention in the Horn of Africa*. New York and London, Monthly Review Press, 1980.

Tadesse, K. *The Generation: A History of the Ethiopian People's Revolutionary Party*. Trenton, NJ, Red Sea Press, 1993.

Tareke, G. *Ethiopia: Power and Protest*. New York, Cambridge University Press, 1991.

Thompson, B. *Ethiopia: The Country That Cut off Its Head: A Diary of the Revolution*. London, Robson Books, 1975.

Tiruneh, A. *The Ethiopian Revolution 1974–87*. Cambridge, Cambridge University Press, 1993.

Transitional Government of Ethiopia. *Ethiopia's Economic Policy during the Transitional Period: An Official Translation*. Addis Ababa, 1991.

Tubiana, J. (Ed.). *Modern Ethiopia from the Accession of Menelik II to the Present*. Rotterdam, A. A. Balkema. Proceedings of the 5th International Conference of Ethiopian Studies: Session A, 1980.

Ullendorff, E. *The Ethiopians: An Introduction to Country and People*. Oxford, Oxford University Press, 1973.

Wolde, M. M. *A Preliminary Atlas of Ethiopia*. Addis Ababa, 1962.

Wubner, M., and Abate, Y. *Ethiopia: Transition and Development in the Horn of Africa*. Boulder, CO, Westview Press, 1988.

Yakobsen, S. *The Soviet Union and Ethiopia: A Case of Traditional Behavior*. Notre Dame, IN, University of Notre Dame Press, 1965.

Zegeye, A., and Pausewang, S. (Eds). *Ethiopia in Change: Peasantry, Nationalism and Democracy*. London, British Academic Press, 1994.

Zewde, B. *A History of Modern Ethiopia 1855–1974*. London, James Currey, 1991.

GABON

Physical and Social Geography

DAVID HILLING

Lying along the Equator, on the west coast of Africa, the Gabonese Republic covers an area of 267,667 sq km (103,347 sq miles) and comprises the entire drainage basin of the westward-flowing Ogooué river, together with the basins of several smaller coastal rivers such as the Nyanga and Como.

The low-lying coastal zone is narrow in the north and south but broader in the estuary regions of the Ogooué and Gabon. South of the Ogooué numerous lagoons, such as the N'Dogo, M'Goze, and M'Komi, back the coast, and the whole area is floored with Cretaceous sedimentary rocks, which at shallow depth yield oil. The main producing oil fields are in a narrow zone stretching southwards from Port-Gentil, both on- and off-shore. The interior consists of Pre-Cambrian rocks, eroded into a series of plateau surfaces at heights of 450–600 m and dissected by the river system into a number of distinct blocks, such as the Crystal mountains, the Moabi uplands and the Chaillu massif. This area is one of Africa's most mineralized zones, and traditional small-scale mining of gold and diamonds has been replaced in importance by large-scale exploitation of manganese at Moanda and uranium at Mounana. There are also numerous deposits of high-grade iron ore.

Gabon has an equatorial climate, with uniformly high temperatures, high relative humidities and mean annual rainfalls of 1,500–3,000 mm. About three-quarters of the country's surface is covered with forests, and wood from the okoumé tree provided the basis for the country's economy until superseded by minerals in the 1960s. Grassland vegetation is restricted to the coastal sand zone south of Port-Gentil and parts of the valleys of the Nyanga, upper N'Gounié and upper Ogooué.

Agricultural development in the potentially rich forest zone has been limited by the small size of the country's population. According to provisional results of the July 1993 census, the population totalled 1,011,710, giving an average density of only 3.8 inhabitants per sq km. As the population is small in relation to national income, Gabon has the highest level of income per head in mainland sub-Saharan Africa, although many of the country's enterprises depend on labour imported from neighbouring countries. The three main urban concentrations may now account for more than one-half of the population; in 1988 Libreville, the capital, had more than 352,000 inhabitants, Port-Gentil, the centre of the petroleum industry, 164,000, and Franceville/Moanda, the mining centres, 75,000. The major rural concentrations are found in Woleu N'Tem, where coffee and cocoa are the main cash crops, and around Lambaréné, where palm oil and coffee are important. The country's principal ethnic groups are the Fang (30%) and the Eshira (25%). The resident French population is estimated at 20,000.

Recent History

PIERRE ENGLEBERT

Revised for this edition by the Editor

Gabon was granted internal autonomy in November 1958, with Léon M'Ba, leader of the Bloc démocratique gabonais (BDG), as prime minister. The country became fully independent on 17 August 1960 and M'Ba was elected president of the republic in February 1961. Following an unsuccessful military coup attempt in February 1964, M'Ba gradually established Gabon as a *de facto* one-party state: most opposition members of the national assembly joined the BDG, which contested the 1967 elections unopposed. M'Ba died in November 1967 and was succeeded by his appointed vice-president, Albert-Bernard Bongo. In March 1968 Bongo formally instituted a one-party state and a new ruling party, the Parti démocratique gabonais (PDG).

ONE-PARTY GOVERNMENT

Gabon enjoyed relative political stability during the 1970s. Legislative and presidential elections took place in February 1973; all PDG candidates for the national assembly, and Bongo, the sole candidate for the presidency, were elected with 99.56% of the votes cast. In 1975 Bongo abolished the office of vice-president and appointed its holder, Léon Mébiame, to the new post of prime minister. Gabon experienced rapid growth under a liberal economic system which encouraged and protected foreign capital investment; in 1975 Gabon became a full member of the Organization of the Petroleum Exporting Countries (OPEC). In September of that year Bongo converted to Islam, changing his forename to Omar.

In December 1979 Bongo was re-elected for a further seven-year term as president, with 99.96% of the votes cast. Legislative elections in February 1980 were followed by the appointment of several new ministers, although Bongo's most trusted allies retained the most influential positions. In 1981 Bongo transferred his functions as head of government to Mébiame, and relinquished his other ministerial portfolios.

Social and political strains, deriving from the rapid growth of the economy in the mid-1970s and the subsequent decline, became evident in the early 1980s. The Mouvement de redressement national (MORENA), a moderate opposition group which emerged in late 1981, accused Bongo of corruption and personal extravagance and demanded the restoration of a multi-party system. Bongo, while maintaining his commitment to single-party rule, sought to persuade exiles to return to Gabon to participate in democratic debate within the existing political framework.

At elections to an enlarged national assembly in March 1985, PDG candidates received 99.5% of votes cast. In May Bongo repeated his invitation to opposition members to return to Gabon; in August, however, MORENA formed a government-in-exile in Paris. A MORENA candidate contested the presidential election of November 1986, but was prevented from organizing a campaign, and the movement's exiled leadership appealed to voters to boycott the election. Bongo was duly re-elected for a further seven-year term, with 99.97% of the vote. Despite the provision of more than one list of PDG-approved candidates in the local government elections in June 1987, the incumbent officials were re-elected in most cases.

Following a deterioration in the economy, compulsory reductions in salaries for public-sector employees in October 1988 provoked strike action. Bongo's subsequent announcement that economic reforms and austerity measures would, henceforth, be pursued only to the extent that they did not undermine social and political stability had a detrimental effect on the country's negotiations with its external creditors.

MORENA, which had been preoccupied with internal divisions since 1987, resumed its campaign against the government in early 1989. In May, however, the movement's chairman, Fr Paul M'Ba Abessole, visited Gabon and, after a meeting with Bongo, announced that he and many of his supporters would return to the country in the near future. M'Ba Abessole subsequently declared his support for Bongo's regime and in early 1990, following his removal from the leadership of MORENA, formed a new organization, MORENA des bûcherons (renamed Rassemblement national des bûcherons in 1991 to avoid confusion with the rival MORENA–originels).

A number of arrests took place in October 1989, following an alleged conspiracy to overthrow the government. It was claimed that the detainees, who included senior members of the security forces and prominent public officials, had acted in concert with a Paris-based opposition group, the Union du peuple gabonais (UPG). Further arrests followed in November, after the alleged discovery of a second anti-government conspiracy.

CONSTITUTIONAL TRANSITION

A series of strikes and demonstrations by students and workers in early 1990 reflected increasing public discontent with economic conditions. In late February a 'special commission for democracy', established in January by the PDG central committee, submitted a report, which contained an explicit condemnation of the one-party system. On the following day, Bongo announced that immediate and fundamental political reforms would be introduced. However, his proposal to replace the PDG by a Rassemblement social-démocrate gabonais (RSDG), which would cover a diverse ideological spectrum, did little to allay popular discontent.

In March 1990 Bongo announced that legislative elections, scheduled for April, were to be postponed for six months to allow time for the constitution to be amended. It was also proposed that a multi-party system would be introduced, under the supervision of the RSDG, at the end of a five-year transitional period. However, a national conference of some 2,000 delegates, which was convened in late March to formulate a programme for the transfer to a plural democracy, rejected Bongo's proposals, and voted instead for the immediate creation of a multi-party system and the formation of an interim government, to hold office only until the October legislative elections. Bongo acceded to the conference's decisions, and in April, Casimir Oye Mba, the governor of the Banque des états de l'Afrique centrale, was appointed prime minister in a transitional administration, which included several opposition members.

In May 1990 PDG and legislative approval was given to constitutional amendments to facilitate the transition to a multi-party system. The existing presidential mandate (effective until January 1994) was to be respected; thereafter, elections to the presidency would be contested by more than one candidate and the tenure of office would be reduced to five years, renewable only once. At the same time, Bongo resigned as secretary-general of the PDG (claiming that a party political role was now incompatible with his position as head of state), and the post was assumed by Jean Adiahenot. These far-reaching changes, however, were overshadowed by the repercussions of the death, in suspicious circumstances, of Joseph Rendjambe, the secretary-general of an opposition movement, the Parti gabonais du progrès (PGP). Demonstrators, who alleged Bongo's complicity in the death, attacked property belonging to the president and his associates. A country-wide curfew was imposed as unrest spread. French troops were dispatched to Gabon to protect the interests of the 20,000 resident French nationals, and several hundred Europeans were evacuated. The strength of the Gabonese economy was for a time jeopardized by the severe disruption of the petroleum sector resulting from the disorders. A state of emergency was imposed in Port-Gentil and its environs, and at least two deaths were reported after Gabonese security forces intervened to restore order. In early June 1990 it was announced that the French military reinforcements were to be withdrawn. The national curfew was lifted in early July, although the state of emergency remained in force in the area surrounding Port-Gentil.

Legislative Elections

Legislative elections were scheduled for 16 and 23 September 1990; however, only political parties which had registered during the national conference in March were allowed to present candidates. The first round of the elections, on 16 September, was disrupted by violent protests by voters, who claimed that electoral fraud was being practised in favour of the PDG. Following allegations by opposition parties of widespread electoral irregularities, results in 32 constituencies were declared invalid, although the election of 58 candidates (of whom 36 were members of the PDG) was confirmed. The transitional government subsequently conceded that malpractices had occurred, and the second round of the elections was postponed until 21 and 28 October. A commission representing both the PDG and opposition parties was established to supervise polling. At the elections in October, the PDG won an overall majority, with 62 seats, while opposition candidates secured 55 seats.

The formation of a government of national unity was announced on 27 November 1990; Oye Mba, the prime minister of the former interim government, was appointed as prime minister. Sixteen portfolios were allocated to members of the PDG, with the remaining eight distributed among members of five opposition parties. Three other opposition movements refused Bongo's offer of inclusion in the government. A new draft constitution, which was promulgated on 22 December, endorsed reforms included in the transitional constitution introduced in May. Further measures included the proposed establishment of an upper house, to be known as the senate, which was to control the balance and regulation of power. This proposal, however, was strongly opposed by the opposition parties. A constitutional council was also to replace the administrative chamber of the supreme court and a national communications council was to be formed to ensure the impartial treatment of information by the state media.

The final composition of the national assembly was determined in March 1991, when elections took place in five constituencies where the results had been annulled, owing to alleged irregularities. Following the completion of the elections, the PDG secured 66 seats, while the PGP obtained 19, the Rassemblement national des bûcherons (RNB, formerly MORENA des bûcherons) 17, MORENA–originels seven, the Association pour le socialisme au Gabon (APSG) six, the Union socialiste gabonais (USG) three, and two smaller parties one seat each.

Opposition Realignments and Social Unrest

In May 1991 six opposition parties formed an alliance, known as the Coordination de l'opposition démocratique (COD). The COD announced its withdrawal from the national assembly, and demanded the full and immediate implementation of the new constitution, the appointment of a new prime minister, the submission of constitutional proposals for consideration by the national assembly, and access to the state-controlled media. Following a general strike, which was organized by the COD, Bongo dissolved the council of ministers, affirmed his intention fully to implement the new constitution, and announced that, in accordance with the constitution, a constitutional court and a national communications council had been created. In a further attempt to appease public discontent, Bongo pardoned more than 200 political prisoners. However, opposition parties within the COD refused to participate in the new government, of which Oye Mba was appointed as prime minister. Later in June, opposition deputies terminated their boycott of the national assembly and resumed parliamentary duties. On 22 June a new coalition government was formed, which retained 14 members of the previous council of ministers and included representatives of MORENA–originels, the USG and the APSG.

In September 1991 clashes took place between demonstrators supporting the RNB and members of the PDG. In October a minor reshuffle of the council of ministers was carried out. In December two deputies in the national assembly resigned from the PGP, owing to its alleged political links with the PDG. In the same month a vote of censure against the government was defeated in the national assembly. Two prisoners released in December were stated by the government to be the last remaining political detainees. In February 1992 three political associations, MORENA–originels, the Parti socialiste gabonais (PSG) and the USG, formed an alliance, known as the Forum d'action pour le renouveau (FAR). Later in February the government announced that a multi-party presidential election would take place in December 1993, two months before the expiry of Bongo's term of office.

Widespread strikes and demonstrations continued in 1992; in February, following protests by students demanding additional scholarship grants, the university was closed, and a ban on public demonstrations and gatherings was imposed. In the same month a meeting of supporters of the RNB was dispersed by security forces; several injuries were reported. Later in February the COD organized a one-day general strike in Port-Gentil (which was only partially observed), followed by a one-day 'dead city' campaign in Port-Gentil and Libreville. In late February the government reopened the university, and lifted the ban on political gatherings and demonstrations. In March, however, a protester was killed, during a demonstration by teachers in support of improvements in salary and working conditions. The COD subsequently instigated a further one-day 'dead city' campaign in Libreville. In early April, in an attempt to regain public support, the PDG organized a pro-government rally in the capital.

In July 1992 the national assembly adopted a new electoral code (which had been submitted by the government), despite protests by the FAR that the government had failed to comply with the demands presented by the COD in October 1991. Later in July 1992 a motion of censure against the government, proposed by opposition deputies in the national assembly in response to the postponement of local government elections, was defeated. The cabinet was reshuffled in August, and in December three members of the PDG, including a former minister, were expelled from the party, after establishing a faction, known as the Cercle des libéraux réformateurs (CLR).

Social unrest continued during the first half of 1993. In April there were widespread protests and demonstrations in central and southern Gabon at the poor quality of living conditions resulting from the lack of social infrastructure, particularly road facilities and reliable water supplies in rural areas. In the same month Jules Bourdès-Ogouliguendé (who had left the PDG in January) resigned as president of the national assembly, prior to standing as a candidate in the forthcoming presidential election. Pierre-Claver Maganga Moussavou, the leader of the PSD, and Alexandre Sambat, a former ambassador to the USA, subsequently declared their candidacies. In July Bongo reshuffled the council of ministers, following the resignation of the minister with responsibility for labour and employment, Simon Oyono Aba'a, who had been nominated as the presidential candidate of MORENA–originels. In October Bongo formally announced that he was to contest the presidential election; by the end of that month 16 candidates had emerged (of which three subsequently withdrew in favour of Bongo), including M'Ba Abessole, the leader of the PGP, Pierre-Louis Agondjo-Okawé, and a former prime minister, Léon Mébiame.

In early November 1993 five political groups (the PDG, the USG, the APSG, the CLR and the Parti de l'unité du peuple gabonais) agreed to support Bongo's candidacy in the presidential election, while eight opposition candidates established an informal alliance, known as the Convention des forces du changement (CFC). Later that month a number of demonstrations were staged by members of the CFC, in protest at alleged irregularities in the electoral register. Following public disorders in early December, the government agreed to a partial revision of electoral lists, but rejected opposition demands for a postponement of the election.

Presidential Election and Political Retrenchment

At the presidential election, which took place on 5 December 1993, Bongo was re-elected by 51.18% of votes cast, while M'Ba Abessole secured 26.51% of the votes; some 86% of the registered electorate participated. The official announcement of the results provoked rioting by opposition supporters, in which several foreign nationals were attacked (apparently as a result of dissatisfaction with international observers, who declared that the elections had been properly conducted). Security forces intervened, and a national curfew and state of alert (which included a ban on demonstrations) were subsequently imposed. M'Ba Abessole, however, rejected the election results, and established a 'high council of the republic' (HCR), which included the majority of the presidential candidates, as part of a parallel government. Despite generally favourable reports by international observers on the conduct of the elections, the opposition appealed to the constitutional court to annul the results, on the grounds that the government had perpetrated electoral malpractice. In mid-December Bongo strongly denounced the establishment of the HCR, and invited the unsuccessful presidential candidates to take part in a government of national consensus. As a result of the administrative confusion, local government elections, which were due to take place in late December, were postponed until March 1994.

In early January 1994 the Bongo administration was accused by the USA of human rights violations, after three opposition leaders, including two presidential candidates, were prevented from leaving the country. Later that month the constitutional court endorsed the election results, and on 22 January Bongo was inaugurated as president. M'Ba Abessole subsequently redesignated the HCR as the 'high council for resistance', and urged his supporters to refuse to pay taxes and to boycott the local government elections (which were again postponed, to August). In mid-February the national curfew and the state of alert, in force since the previous December, were lifted, only to be reimposed later that month, after a general strike, in support of demands for an increase in salaries to compensate for a devaluation of the CFA franc in January, degenerated into violence. Security forces destroyed the transmitters of Radio Liberté, a radio station owned by the RNB (which had supported the strike), and attacked M'Ba Abessole's private residence, leading to further clashes with protesters. Strike action was suspended after four days, following negotiations between the government and trade unions; nine people had been killed during that period, according to official figures (although the opposition claimed that a total of 38 had died). At the end of February the minister of state control, in charge of parastatal affairs, left the government and the PDG, citing his disagreement with the increasingly authoritarian stance adopted by Bongo.

In March 1994 Oye Mba submitted his resignation and dissolved the council of ministers; later that month he was reappointed as prime minister and, following the opposition's rejection of his offer to participate in a government of national unity, a 38-member administration was formed. The size of the new government, in view of the deterioration in the economy, attracted widespread criticism. In the same month the national assembly approved a constitutional amendment providing for the establishment of a senate (which the opposition had resisted) and repealing legislation that prohibited unsuccessful presidential candidates from participating in the government within a period of 18 months.

In June 1994 opposition parties agreed to a further postponement of the local government elections, to early 1995. In August opposition parties announced that they were prepared to participate in a coalition government, on condition that it was installed on a transitional basis pending new legislative elections. In September negotiations between the government and opposition took place in Paris, under the auspices of the Organization of African Unity (OAU), in order to resolve remaining differences concerning the results of the presidential election and the proposed formation of a government of national unity. In mid-September the RNB, which took part in the discussions, indicated that it would refuse to join a coalition government.

Coalition Problems

At the end of September 1994 an agreement was reached, as a result of the Paris meetings, whereby a transitional coalition government was to be installed, with local government elections scheduled to take place after a period of one year, followed by legislative elections six months later; the electoral code was to be revised and an independent electoral commission established, in an effort to ensure that the elections be conducted fairly. In early October Oye Mba resigned from office and dissolved the council of ministers. Shortly afterwards Bongo appointed Dr Paulin Obame-Nguema, a member of the PDG who had served in former administrations, as prime minister. Obame-Nguema subsequently formed a 27-member council of ministers, which included six opposition members. The composition of the new government was, however, immediately criticized by the opposition, on the grounds that it was entitled to one-third of ministerial portfolios in proportion to the number of opposition deputies in the national assembly; the HCR announced that the opposition would boycott the new administration, which, it claimed, was in violation of the Paris accord. Four opposition members consequently refused to accept the portfolios allocated to them, although two of these finally agreed to join the government. (The portfolios that remained vacant were later assigned to a further two opposition members.) Following the inauguration of the council of ministers in early November, a motion expressing confidence in the new prime minister was adopted by 99 of 118 votes cast in the national assembly. In the same month associates of Bongo established an informal grouping, known as the Mouvement des amis de Bongo.

In January 1995 controversy emerged over the extent of the authority vested in the national assembly, after members of the HCR refused to participate in the drafting of the new electoral code until the Paris agreement was ratified. The constitutional court subsequently ruled that the national assembly was not empowered, under the terms of the constitution, to ratify the agreement. In early February, however, opposition deputies ended a boycott of the national assembly, following a further ruling by the constitutional court that the national assembly was entitled to act as a parliamentary body, pending the installation of a senate after the legislative elections in 1996, but that the constitutional provisions adopted under the terms of the Paris agreement would require endorsement by referendum. Following a pronouncement by the authorities that all illegal immigrants remaining in Gabon by mid-February would be arrested, some 55,000 foreign nationals left the country by the stipulated date. In April Bongo announced that a referendum to endorse the constitutional amendments would take place on 25 June. In the same month, in accordance with the Paris accord, the cabinet approved legislation providing for the release of prisoners detained on charges involving state security. Later in April Gabon withdrew its ambassador from Paris, in protest at reports in the French media containing allegations about the president's private life, and a number of anti-French demonstrations in support of Bongo took place in Libreville. (The national communications council had rejected government efforts to ban two pro-opposition newspapers, which had published French press reports considered to be critical of Bongo.) At the national referendum (which had been postponed until 24 July), the constitutional amendments were approved by 96.48% of votes cast, with 63.45% of the electorate participating. In September 1995, following dissent within the UPG, Sébastien Mamboundou Mouyama, the minister of social affairs and national solidarity, was elected party chairman, replacing Pierre Mamboundou. However, the latter subsequently regained the leadership of the UPG. (Mamboundou Mouyama formed a new political party, the Mouvement alternatif, in August 1996.)

Local and Legislative Elections

During early 1996 opposition parties criticized the government for delaying the implementation of the electoral timetable contained in the Paris accord. At the beginning of May, following a meeting attended by all the officially recognized political parties, Bongo agreed to establish a national electoral commission to formulate a timetable for local, legislative and senatorial elections, in consultation with all the official parties. It was also decided that access to state-controlled media and election funding should be equitably divided. Obame-Nguema's government resigned at the beginning of June, in accordance with the Paris agreement. Bongo, however, rejected the resignation on the grounds that the government should, before leaving office, organize the elections and finalize pending agreements with the International Monetary Fund (IMF) and the World Bank. At the beginning of October the national electoral commission adopted a timetable for legislative elections: the first round was to take place on 17 November, with a second round scheduled for 1 December. HCR representatives denounced the timetable, withdrew their participation from the commission and demanded the postponement of the local and legislative elections. In mid-October Pierre-Claver Maganga Moussavou, the leader of the PSD, was compelled to resign from the government, following his condemnation of the electoral timetable. The chairman of the HCR claimed that the 'dismissal' was a violation of the Paris accord. Later that month a minor reshuffle of the council of ministers was effected. Meanwhile, the government announced the suspension of salary payments for teachers, who had been on strike since 1 October in protest against the government's suspension of their housing allowances. The teacher's unions subsequently announced their intention to seek legal redress.

Organizational problems disrupted the local elections, which were held on 20 October 1996, having been postponed twice previously; according to reports, only 15% of the electorate participated. The PDG gained control of the majority of the municipalities, although the PGP secured victory in Port-Gentil, while the RNB was successful in the north of the country. Elections in Fougamou (where voting had not taken place) and Libreville (where the results had been invalidated) were eventually rescheduled for 24 November, although the RNB demanded the validation of the original results. On 24 November the RNB secured 62 of the 98 seats available in Libreville; M'Ba Abessole was subsequently elected mayor.

Legislative elections were rescheduled on several occasions, owing to the delay in the release of the local election results and the failure to revise electoral registers in time. The first round of the elections took place on 15 December, without major incidents. Later that month it was reported that the PDG had obtained 47 of the 55 seats that were decided in the first round of voting. The opposition disputed the results, and there were demands for protest marches and a boycott of the second round of voting. The PDG secured a substantial majority of the remaining seats in the second round, which was held on 29 December, and in by-elections conducted in January. Of the national assembly's 120 seats, 82 were won by the PDG, 12 by the RNB, eight by the PGP, seven by other parties represented in the HCR, six by independent candidates, three by the CLR and two by the USG. Following the legislative elections, the prime minister and his council of ministers resigned on 24 January 1997, in accordance with the terms of the constitution. Obame-Nguema was reappointed prime minister on 27 January, and a new council of ministers, dominated by members of the PDG, was announced on the following day. The PGP had refused to participate in the new government.

Elections to the new senate took place on 26 January and 9 February, with senators to be elected by members of municipal councils and departmental assemblies. According to the national electoral commission, 71 of the 91 seats were decided in the first round; the PDG won 44 seats and the RNB won 14. Provisional results, released after the second round of voting, allocated 52 seats to the PDG, while the RNB secured 19, the PGP four, the Alliance démocratique et républicaine (ADR) three, the CLR one, and the RDP one, with independent candidates obtaining nine seats. (Results for the remaining two seats were not declared.)

On 18 April, at a congress of deputies and senators, constitutional amendments which extended the presidential term to seven years, provided for the creation of the post of vice-president and formally designated the senate as an upper chamber of a bicameral legislature were adopted, despite the protests of opposition leaders who objected to the creation of a vice-presidency and demanded that a referendum be held. The vice-president was to deputize for the president when required, but was not to have any power of succession. In late May Didjob Divungui-di-N'Dingue, a senior member of the ADR and a candidate in the 1993 presidential election, was appointed to the new position. Although officially part of the HCR, the ADR had signed a number of local electoral agreements with other parties, including the PDG, prior to the legislative elections.

President Bongo has pursued a policy of close co-operation with France in the fields of economic and foreign affairs. In October 1992 Bongo represented the then French president, François Mitterrand, at a Franco-African summit meeting which took place in Libreville. On a visit to Gabon in July 1996, the French president, Jacques Chirac, urged the industrialized countries to continue to give economic aid to the African nations. Relations became strained in March 1997, however, when allegations that Bongo had been a beneficiary in an international fraud emerged, during a French judicial investigation into the affairs of the petroleum company Elf-Aquitaine. The chairman of Elf-Gabon, André Tarallo, was temporarily detained, and bank accounts in Switzerland and the British Virgin Islands, said to contain Gabonese government funds, were blocked. In response, Bongo cancelled a visit to France and reportedly threatened to impose economic sanctions on French oil interests in Gabon. He insisted that the Elf enquiry was a matter for the French judiciary and was not the concern of Gabon.

Bongo has often acted as an intermediary in regional disputes, chairing the OAU *ad hoc* committee seeking to resolve the border dispute between Chad and Libya, and encouraging dialogue between Angola and the USA. In 1997 he intervened in civil conflicts in Zaire (now the Democratic Republic of the Congo) and the Central African Republic, and presided over an international mediation committee attempting to resolve the crisis in the Republic of Congo, still ongoing in mid-August of that year. In July 1997 the government expressed concern at the large numbers of refugees arriving in Gabon and subsequently announced plans for repatriation.

In February 1996 the northern part of Gabon was quarantined in response to an outbreak of Ebola haemorrhage fever, in which at least 13 people died, according to the World Health Organization (WHO). In April it was reported that the World Bank and the World Wide Fund for Nature were seeking to identify areas of equatorial forest for conservation, amid fears that increasing exploitation by logging companies would imperil the survival of indigenous plant and animal species. It was also feared that opening up the forest could lead to another outbreak of the Ebola virus, which is believed to reside in small, forest-dwelling animals. In October a second outbreak claimed 14 lives in the north-east of the country, and by January 1997 a further 40 deaths had been reported.

Economy

EDITH HODGKINSON

The combination of a small population, estimated at 1.32m. in mid-1995 by the UN, and plentiful petroleum resources has given Gabon one of the highest incomes per head in sub-Saharan Africa. In 1993—the year before the devaluation of the CFA franc—its gross domestic product (GDP) per head was equivalent to US $4,325; even after devaluation, the estimated figure in 1996 was a comfortable $3,868. It therefore ranks as an upper-middle-income country. However, reflecting the dominance of the petroleum sector, and hence the vulnerability to trends in world prices for this commodity, the rate of economic growth has tended to fall over time. While GDP growth averaged 9.5% per year in 1965–80, after the collapse in petroleum prices in 1986 the average declined to 0.8% in 1985–90, although the 1990s have seen an improvement to a relatively modest 3.4% per year in 1991–96, because of the development of the Rabi-Kounga oilfield.

The earlier period of rapid growth contained the petroleum boom of the mid-1970s, when the surge in domestic production, prompted by higher world prices, generated government investment spending and borrowing which left the country with a heavy debt burden and increased its vulnerability to adverse trends in the international economy—petroleum prices, interest rates and the value of the US dollar. Consequently, since the mid-1980s, the government has had to undertake a series of economic adjustment programmes, designed to reduce the external current-account deficit while promoting the development of non-petroleum activities. Private enterprise is being encouraged, and a policy of retrenchment in the public sector initiated, including the rationalization of public-sector enterprises. Progress has been very limited in all these areas, and the non-petroleum economy remained very weak; the disbursement of IMF funds has been suspended on occasion, due to lack of compliance with performance criteria. Following the devaluation of the CFA franc by 50% in relation to the French franc in January 1994, the government adopted a programme for economic recovery, supported, as in the past, by IMF funding, in the form of a stand-by credit, and with similar objectives. However, shortcomings in implementation and the Fund's dissatisfaction with public financial transparency delayed the award of an extended Fund facility (EFF) until November 1995. The targets of the 1995–98 programme, supported by this funding, include an improvement in the rate of return on petroleum resources; a thorough reform of the tax revenue system; a reduction in current budget spending (including retrenchment in the payroll); higher implementation of the budget's capital expenditure programme; and privatization of public-sector enterprises. If this programme is carried out as scheduled, the Gabonese economy will enter a period of much-needed modernization. The danger remains that the robust performance of the petroleum sector and, to a lesser extent, the upsurge in timber will allow the government to defer the less politically attractive aspects of structural reform.

AGRICULTURE

Owing to the density of the tropical rain forest, only a small proportion of land area is suitable for agricultural activity, and only 2% is estimated to be under cultivation. With nearly 50% of the population living in towns and a poor road infrastructure, the contribution to GDP of the agriculture, forestry and fishing sector is very modest, at around 7% in the mid-1990s. The country lacks self-sufficiency in staple crops, and over one-half of food requirements have to be imported. Until the late 1980s the focus of public investment was industry and infrastructure, notably the Transgabonais railway, and the sector's growth lagged far behind the expansion of the overall economy. Only in 1988 did a belated attempt begin to rectify the situation and arrest the urban drift which was denuding the rural area of workers. A three-year investment programme allocated one-quarter of its funds to agriculture, compared with under 10% in preceding years. This helped lift the sector's share of GDP slightly, but production remains both low and inefficient. Agricultural GDP increased by an annual average of 1.1% in 1985–90, but declined by 0.2% per year in 1990–95.

The principal cash crops are palm oil, cocoa, coffee and sugar cane. Of these, palm oil is the most important, although export potential is limited, owing to intense competition from producers in the Far East, and by 1990 production of refined palm oil had declined to about one-half of the 1988 level of 10,300 metric tons. A parastatal organization, the Société de développement de l'agriculture au Gabon (AGROGABON), manages plantations covering 7,500 ha. The main agricultural export is cocoa, but with production unofficially estimated at 2,000 tons in the mid-1990s, it makes a minimal contribution to export earnings. Coffee output is even lower, at around 200 tons in the mid-1990s, one-sixth of the level registered in 1988/89. The reason for the decline in production of both cocoa and coffee lies in the fall in producer prices in 1990. Production of refined sugar increased from negligible levels to 20,905 tons in 1989, with the development of a large-scale mechanized sugar complex at Franceville, designed to produce 30,000 tons annually. With internal demand of about 11,000 tons per year, the surplus is exported. In the 1980s the government decided to promote the development of rubber as an export crop and four plantations have been developed by the state-owned Société de développement de l'hévéaculture (HEVEGAB), covering a total area of 12,000 ha. Two of these, at Mitzic, began exporting in 1992; shipments in 1995 reached 4,874 tons.

Animal husbandry was, for many decades, hindered by the prevalence of the tsetse fly. In 1980, however, the first tsetse-resistant cattle were imported from Senegal, The Gambia and Zaire. The Société gabonaise de développement d'élevage (an offshoot of AGROGABON) manages three cattle ranches, covering 14,000 ha. Poultry farming is mainly on a smallholder basis. In 1995 Gabon had 39,000 cattle, 165,000 pigs and 256,000 sheep and goats (FAO estimates).

FORESTRY

Tropical forests cover some 75% of Gabon's total land area. Until the commencement of mineral exploitation in the early 1960s, the economy was dependent upon the timber industry. Okoumé and, to a lesser extent, ozigo are the most important timbers, accounting for 80% of Gabon's timber exports. Gabon's forests contain an estimated 100 other species of commercially exploitable hard and soft woods. Gabon currently ranks as Africa's fourth largest producer of tropical wood, and the world's largest exporter of okoumé wood. About 50 companies are active in the forestry sector, which is dominated by a small number of European enterprises. Gabonese enterprises are involved in small-scale timber production.

For the purpose of granting licences, the government has divided Gabon into three distinct logging regions. With the depletion of forests in the accessible 'first zone' (which is reserved exclusively for Gabonese firms), exploitation has been expanded in the 'second zone', which covers the central part of the country. The completion of the second section of the Transgabonais railway, in 1986, improved the accessibility of the 'third zone'.

Output of timber has fluctuated since independence, mainly in response to international demand and to movements in the value of the US dollar in relation to the CFA franc, which affect the sector's competitiveness as regards suppliers in south-east Asia. Output averaged some 1.6m. cu m a year in 1990–92 and exports 1.4m. cu m, but then increased steadily because of production controls in some Asian countries and the unsettled political climate in several of Gabon's African competitors. Devaluation in 1994 gave a significant additional boost. Production consequently increased to 2.3m. cu m by 1995, when exports reached 2.2m. cu m, bringing in earnings of 172,600m. francs CFA, compared with 61,300m. francs CFA in 1990. The total amount of timber cut is thought to be much higher, and there is concern that expansion may prove unsustainable with the present low level of reforestation. The government has imposed ceilings on production (exceeded in both 1995 and apparently 1996), but a more effective constraint on the ability to meet foreign demand is the inadequacy of the transport infrastructure.

The state-owned Société nationale des bois du Gabon (SNBG) has a monopoly in the marketing and export of okoumé, but sales of other woods have been liberalized as part of the restructuring of this much-criticized parastatal. Gabon, like most African timber producers, exports the vast majority of its wood in the form of raw logs. One of the government's aims is to raise the share of locally processed wood from its present level of about 20%. The state-owned Cie forestière du Gabon (CFG) operates the largest sawmill in the country and is a major producer of plywood, but it has been running at a loss for some time, and little progress has been made in its restructuring.

MINING

The main source of Gabon's considerable economic growth since the 1970s has been the exploitation of the country's mineral wealth, principally petroleum and, to a lesser extent, manganese and uranium. In 1995 petroleum and petroleum products accounted for 80% of total export earnings, while the contribution of manganese was 5% and that of uranium only around 1%. Previously a member of OPEC, Gabon withdrew from the organization in June 1996, after production from the Rabi-Kounga field had raised national output well above the quota set by OPEC—a ceiling that Gabon was not prepared to impose on its industry.

The petroleum industry remains by far the dominant sector of the economy, even as its contribution fluctuates from year to year with trends in world prices and the value of the US dollar. Thus its share of GDP, totalling 40.4% in 1980, fell to a low of 16.5% in 1986, and, following the Gulf crisis and the development of Rabi-Kounga, recovered to 39.0% in 1995.

Exploitation began in 1956, but significant growth only commenced after 1967, with the coming into production of the Gamba-Ivinga deposits and the exploitation of the offshore Anguille deposit. Production was largely offshore until January 1989, when the massive Rabi-Kounga onshore deposit entered production. Output rapidly exceeded projections; by July the field was producing 50,000 barrels per day (b/d), and 135,000 b/d by early 1990. Total domestic production had averaged 202,000 b/d in 1989. National output reached 13.5m. tons in 1990, compared with 7.9m. tons in 1988 and 10.2m. tons in 1989; exports were 12.5. tons in 1990, up from 8.6m. tons in the preceding year. Volumes of both output and exports have increased in most years since, with the former reaching 18.7m. tons (359,000 b/d) in 1996. Gabon ranks as sub-Saharan Africa's third largest petroleum producer. Rabi-Kounga, which accounts for about one-half of total petroleum exports, remains the country's principal oilfield. Government policy is to maintain overall production levels, but no major discoveries have been made in recent years (estimated proven reserves were 183.6m. tons in 1995) and exploration costs are high, although they were reduced by the currency's devaluation in 1994.

The main producer was previously Elf-Gabon (a 25/75 joint venture between the government and Elf-Aquitaine) but it was overtaken in 1993 by Shell-Gabon, which operates the Rabi-Kounga field in association with Elf-Gabon and Amerada-Hess. In 1997 there were 25 producing fields, with a number of other foreign companies participating, including Total, Conoco, Agip, Occidental, Marathon, Amoco, OMV, Santa Fe and Repsol. An important new producer appeared in December 1995, when a South African company, Energy Africa, acquired a 40% interest in three satellite fields of Rabi-Kounga and smaller interests in a number of offshore fields. The joint venture with the government, Energy Africa Gabon, will have the right to purchase up to 40% participation in future petroleum production.

The bulk of production is exported as crude (the country's refining capacity is some 800,000 tons), with the USA, France, Argentina and Brazil as the major markets. Export earnings have mirrored output and price trends, with an increase in most years since 1986, when 244,500m. francs CFA was recorded, to 1,040,300m. francs CFA in 1995 and an estimated 1,198,000m. in 1996. Yielding income to the government in the form of royalties, taxes on company profits, exploration permits and dividends and returns from the 15 fields in which it has equity, petroleum provided 63.4% of budget revenue in 1996.

Since 1962, manganese ore has been mined at Moanda, near Franceville, by the Cie minière de l'Ogooué (COMILOG). Gabon has estimated reserves of 200m. tons, representing around one-quarter of known reserves outside the former Soviet Union and South Africa. Virtually all production is exported (almost wholly in ore form) through the port of Owendo, the opening of which in 1988 stimulated volumes, which reached an all-time peak of 2.4m. tons in the following year. Previously most export ore was transported through the neighbouring Congo to the port of Pointe-Noire. Despite a slight decline in shipments in 1990, to 2.2m. tons, in that year Gabon overtook South Africa as the world's principal exporter of manganese ore. In 1993 the South African group, Gencor, acquired a 15% holding in COMILOG from US Steel; other shareholders are Eramet of France, which took a 47% equity in September 1995, the Société nationale d'investissement and private Gabonese interests. Production had been tending to decrease in 1991–93 but has since recovered, to 1.9m. tons in 1995. Reflecting the foreign corporate involvement, COMILOG has expanded its operations abroad, notably in China, where it signed up to a joint venture with Shaoxing Steel in 1995.

The exploitation of uranium began in 1958. Deposits are exploited at Mounana and the ore is concentrated before export by the Cie des mines d'uranium de Franceville (COMUF), a consortium largely controlled by French interests but with a 26% share held by the Gabonese government. Gabonese uranium is marketed through the French Atomic Energy Commission. Proven reserves are some 35,000 tons, and production averaged 582 tons a year in 1990–95, with wide year-on-year fluctuation, far below the industry's capacity. In 1980 output had been 999 tons. The decline in world demand, as nuclear power programmes are cut back, has brought with it a steep fall in prices; COMUF suffered losses in 1991–93, with output of only 292 tons in the final year. COMUF responded by cutting its workforce by almost two-thirds by 1995. However, with little prospect of any recovery in the industry in the near future, the company plans to cease operations at Mounana by the year 2000.

One of the largest iron-ore deposits in the world, some 850m. tons at Belinga, in the north-east of Gabon, remains economically unviable, in view both of depressed international price levels, and of the government's inability to secure the funds necessary for a 237-km spur to the Transgabonais railway, to transport the ore. Alluvial deposits of gold are exploited on a small scale, with output estimated at 72 kg in 1994. Stimulated by the decline in costs after the 1994 devaluation, foreign companies have since secured exploration licences. Lead, zinc, baryte and phosphate deposits are known to exist. In 1996 the Société minière du Moyen-Ogooué (SOMIMO) decided to go ahead with its plans to develop the Mabounie phosphate deposit. Marble is quarried at Doussé-Oussou.

MANUFACTURING AND POWER

Gabon's manufacturing sector is relatively small, accounting for some 6% of GDP in 1995. A substantial part of this contribution is represented by oil refining and timber processing. Other manufacturing industries include the processing of agricultural products, cement, soap, paint, industrial gas, cigarettes and textiles. Gabon has sought to develop large-scale natural-resource-based industries, but since its own domestic market is very small, these can for the most part be viable only in the context of the Union douanière et économique de l'Afrique centrale (UDEAC), of which Gabon is one of the six member countries. Gabon imports substantial quantities of manufactures from other UDEAC countries, but exports little to its UDEAC partners other than refined petroleum. Cement output totalled 154,000 metric tons in 1995, significantly below annual capacity of 400,000 tons. In addition to competition from suppliers in UDEAC, which is increasing as the movement of goods is liberalized, Gabon's manufacturing industries face a challenge from both smuggled goods and the expanding informal (and untaxed) sector.

Electricity is produced and distributed by the Société d'énergie et d'eau du Gabon (SEEG), a parastatal whose management was taken over by a consortium of Lyonnais des eaux, Electricité de France and Hydro-Quebec in 1993 and which was sold off in March 1997 to a French-Irish joint venture of Cie générale des eaux and Electricity Supply Board International. This was the first major privatization under the programme agreed with the IMF in 1996. Generation is both hydroelectric and thermal (gas-fired), with around three-quarters of total capacity (some 279 MW in 1990) hydroelectric. There is considerable potential for expansion in this sector.

TRANSPORT

Despite substantial investment in the Transgabonais railway and foreign backing for road development in the 1990s, the surface transportation system is inadequate. Until 1979 there were no railways except for the cableway link between the Congo border and the Moanda manganese mine, and the main rivers are navigable only for the last 80–160 km of their course to the Atlantic Ocean. The road network is poorly developed and much of it is unusable during the rainy seasons. In 1995 there were an estimated 7,633 km of roads, of which only some 8% was asphalted. The government's aim is to surface some 1,400 km of the road network by the year 2000, with a target of 3,580 km in the long term.

The Transgabonais railway scheme is among the most prestigious achievements of the Bongo presidency, opening up hitherto inaccessible areas and those more accessible from the Republic of Congo, such as the mineral-rich Franceville area. The 679-km railway required total investment of 800,000m.–900,000m. francs CFA between 1974 and 1986, which is not likely to be paid off, and external donors have been highly critical of the expenditure involved. It proved difficult to find financial backing for even the first 340-km section of the rail line, linking Owendo and Booué; work was completed in January 1983. Work on the 357-km second section of the Transgabonais, from Booué to Franceville, was completed in December 1986. Plans for a third section of 237 km, from Booué to Belinga, intended to enable exploitation of the large iron-ore deposits in the north-east of the country, were suspended, owing to lack of finance, and available resources reallocated to the completion of the Booué–Franceville stretch. By 1989 the line linking Libreville and Franceville was fully operational. The inauguration, in late 1988, of the minerals-handling terminal at Owendo resulted in an increase in revenue for the operator of the railway, the Office du chemin de fer transgabonais (OCTRA). This is one of the major parastatals that is due to be restructured, but where little has been achieved, and in 1996 the government announced plans to privatize the railways. COMILOG, whose entire manganese production is transported by OCTRA, declared an interest in making a bid. In 1995 the Transgabonais carried an estimated total of 3.01m. tons of freight, including 1.75m. tons of manganese and 940,000 tons of hardwood; passenger numbers were 175,800. The government is still hoping to build the spur from Booué to the iron-ore deposits at Belinga, but this development must await better market prospects.

The main port for petroleum exports is Port-Gentil, which also handles logs (floated down the Ogooué river) as does Owendo, the principal mineral port. The construction of a deep-water port at Mayumba is planned.

Air transport plays an extremely important role in the economy, particularly because the dense forest, which covers much of the country, makes other modes of transport impracticable. Libreville's Léon M'Ba international airport was modernized and expanded in the late 1980s, bringing capacity to 1.5m. passengers by 1990. As well as five domestic airports (Libreville, Port-Gentil, Franceville, Lambaréné and Moanda), there are several small airfields owned mainly by large companies working in the region. In 1977, following its withdrawal from Air Afrique, Gabon established its own international air carrier, Air Gabon, in which the state has an 80% interest. It has been running at a substantial loss in recent years, and there are plans to privatize the airline.

FINANCE

In the first period of petroleum exploitation the government budget was sustained by rapidly increasing income, but the investment requirements of the Transgabonais were largely met by borrowing at non-concessionary rates in the late 1970s, resulting in a serious deterioration in the fiscal position, which pushed the budget into deficit by 1983. The situation was gravely exacerbated by the collapse in petroleum prices in 1986, which reduced government revenue from petroleum by one-quarter. In that year the deficit peaked at 186,700m. francs CFA (equivalent to 11.7% of GDP). Despite the completion of the Transgabonais, allowing the government to reduce its investment spending by 74% in 1987, and the surge in petroleum revenue in 1990 and 1991, the budget remained in deficit (on a commitment basis) because of two sets of pressure on current expenditure—debt service and the very high salary bill. The gap was, however, narrowing in 1993–94, and in 1995 a small surplus, of 79,700m. francs CFA (3.1% of GDP), was registered. This was the result of a combination of factors: petroleum production was continuing to rise steadily while the January 1994 devaluation had doubled petroleum operators' incomes in local currency terms; the growth in the salary bill was at last controlled; and the burden of debt service was eased by the major rescheduling of the bilateral debt (see below). The budget continued in surplus (on a commitment basis) through 1996, at an estimated 78,600m. francs CFA, with revenue rising modestly and interest payments declining by 14%, to 173,100m. francs CFA, while capital expenditure increased by 13%, to 154,000m. francs CFA.

FOREIGN TRADE AND PAYMENTS

Gabon has sustained a considerable surplus on its foreign trade, even through periods of quite marked fluctuation in petroleum prices, because the import demand of its small population has remained relatively modest. Exports are normally three times the value of imports, and even though the latter has been augmented by major investment spending, a large proportion of this investment has served to generate rapidly increased earnings, from oil, timber and manganese. Even in the crisis year of 1986, when spending on the Transgabonais was still high and export earnings were halved, the value of imports was still 10% lower than that of exports, at 339,100m. francs CFA against 372,000m. francs CFA. Subsequently this favourable gap widened markedly, to average a surplus of 316,000m. francs CFA per year in 1987–93. It then surged to 903,000m. francs CFA in 1994, 904,000m. francs CFA in 1995 and an officially estimated 1,013,000m. francs CFA in 1996, with the devaluation windfall in petroleum earnings more than matching the increase in expenditure on imports generated by higher local currency costs in an economy with very limited capacity for import substitution. Although less spectacular in US dollar terms, from US $1,481m. in 1993 to $1,593m. in 1994, $1,831m. in 1995 and $1,978m. in 1996, the improvement in the surplus was nevertheless substantial.

Whereas previously the current account had been in modest surplus in most years, the surplus on foreign trade has been exceeded by the deficit on the invisibles side of the account (services and transfers) in nearly every year since 1985. This deficit is the result of high outflows on interest payments on the foreign debt and on remittances of profits and dividends by the petroleum industry. The current-account balance is very sensitive to movements in the oil price. Thus the current-account deficit increased dramatically from US $163m. in 1985 to $1,058m. in 1986, when oil prices collapsed, while the surge in oil prices after the Iraqi invasion of Kuwait in 1990 produced a surplus of $168m. in 1990 and $75m. in 1991. Devaluation generated a surplus on the current account of $320m. in 1994, as spending on imported goods and services was depressed, and, owing to the steady improvement in the merchandise trade balance, the current account remained in surplus in 1995 ($204m.) and in 1996 (an estimated $250m.).

The overall deficit on the balance of payments has been compounded by outflows on the capital account, as the heavy foreign borrowing which characterized the late 1970s and early 1980s came to an end while the debt-repayment burden has been high. 'Exceptional financing' (the postponement of due debt-service payments) has made the most significant contribution in most recent years to covering the payments gap, as Gabon has built up arrears on its foreign debt. That debt reached a peak of US $4,177m. at the end of 1991, equivalent to 86% of GNP; a significant part of the indebtedness was in the form of arrears on the foreign debt ($276m. in interest and $261m. in principal). The situation became worse in 1992–93, by the end of which period arrears had increased to $1,104m., or nearly 30% of the country's total foreign debt of $3,818m. Yet its high GDP per head, and its poor record of compliance with commitments to the IMF, meant that Gabon was not a priority candidate for debt relief. The currency devaluation of January 1994 changed the environment. Against the background of the stand-by agreement with the IMF, both the 'Paris Club' of official bilateral creditors and the 'London Club' of commercial creditors agreed to debt rescheduling. Maturities on the official debt falling due in the period April 1994–March 1995, and all arrears, were rescheduled over 15 years, with a two-year period of grace. The 'London Club' restructured all commercial debt contracted before 1986. The debt situation was alleviated further by France's cancellation in 1994 of 50% of the loans contracted through the Caisse française de développement (CFD) and the cancellation of some $78m. in obligations in July 1996. As a result, the external debt has remained relatively steady in 1994–96, and by the end of 1996 it was estimated to be very close to the 1993 figure, which—given the real expansion in the economy since—represents a lower proportion of GNP.

Despite Gabon's high income levels and the foreign investment its petroleum sector attracts, inflows of foreign aid, while relatively modest, have been significant in underpinning both the budget and the balance of payments. In the period 1990–93 net disbursements of official development assistance averaged US $167m. a year, with two-thirds coming from France, much of it representing support for the overvalued CFA franc. The devaluation of 1994, and the associated external support, brought a sudden surge in inflows, to a net $815m. in that year (of which $504m. came from France) and a still high $443m. in 1995. These levels can be expected to fall back, and Gabon will still have to tackle the underlying problem of its dependence on the export of a very limited range of raw materials and the infrastructural and funding constraints on their growth and the economy's diversification. The task is all the more urgent in that, in the absence of major new oil discoveries on the scale of Rabi-Kounga, Gabon's petroleum production will decline sharply at the beginning of the next century, to around one-half of its current level.

Statistical Survey

Source (unless otherwise stated): Direction Générale de l'Economie, Ministère de la Planification, de l'Economie et de l'Administration Territoriale, Libreville.

Area and Population

AREA, POPULATION AND DENSITY

Area (sq km)	267,667*
Population (census results)	
8 October 1960–May 1961	448,564
31 July 1993 (provisional)	
Males	498,710
Females	513,000
Total	1,011,710
Density (per sq km) at 31 July 1993	3.8

* 103,347 sq miles.

REGIONS (1993 census)

Region	Area (sq km)	Population*	Density (per sq km)	Chief town
Estuaire	20,740	462,086	22.3	Libreville
Haut-Ogooué	36,547	102,387	2.8	Franceville
Moyen-Ogooué	18,535	41,827	2.3	Lambaréné
N'Gounié	37,750	77,871	2.1	Mouila
Nyanga	21,285	39,826	1.9	Tchibanga
Ogooué-Ivindo	46,075	48,847	1.1	Makokou
Ogooué-Lolo	25,380	42,783	2.1	Koula-Moutou
Ogooué-Maritime	22,890	98,299	4.3	Port-Gentil
Woleu-N'Tem	38,465	97,739	2.5	Oyem
Total	267,667	1,011,665	3.8	

* Excluding 45 persons in unspecified regions.

Source: UN, *Demographic Yearbook*.

PRINCIPAL TOWNS (population in 1988)

Libreville (capital)	352,000	Franceville	75,000
Port-Gentil	164,000		

BIRTHS AND DEATHS (UN estimates, annual averages)

	1980–85	1985–90	1990–95
Birth rate (per 1,000)	33.8	36.5	37.3
Death rate (per 1,000)	18.1	16.6	15.5

Expectation of life (UN estimates, years at birth, 1990–95): 53.5 (males 51.9; females 55.2).

Source: UN, *World Population Prospects: The 1994 Revision*.

ECONOMICALLY ACTIVE POPULATION
(estimates, '000 persons, 1991)

	Males	Females	Total
Agriculture, etc.	187	151	338
Industry	62	9	71
Services	69	26	95
Total labour force	318	186	504

Source: UN Economic Commission for Africa, *African Statistical Yearbook*.

Mid-1995 (estimates, '000 persons): Agriculture, etc. 280; Total 616.
Source: FAO, *Production Yearbook*.

Agriculture

PRINCIPAL CROPS ('000 metric tons)

	1993	1994	1995
Maize*	25	26	27
Cassava (Manioc)*	210	230	210
Yams*	110	120	120
Taro (Coco yam)*	62	64	64
Vegetables*	32	32	33
Bananas*	9	9	9
Plantains*	245	250	250
Cocoa beans†	2	2	2
Groundnuts (in shell)*	15	15	15
Sugar cane*	220	210	220

* FAO estimates. † Unofficial figures.

Source: FAO, *Production Yearbook*.

LIVESTOCK ('000 head, year ending September)

	1993	1994	1995
Cattle	37	39*	39*
Pigs*	165	165	165
Sheep*	170	172	172
Goats*	83	84	84

* FAO estimate(s).

Poultry (FAO estimates, million): 3 in 1993; 3 in 1994; 3 in 1995.

Source: FAO, *Production Yearbook*.

LIVESTOCK PRODUCTS

1995 (FAO estimates, '000 metric tons): Meat 28; Hen eggs 1.5.

Source: FAO, *Production Yearbook*.

Forestry

ROUNDWOOD REMOVALS (FAO estimates, '000 cubic metres)

	1992	1993	1994
Sawlogs, veneer logs and logs for sleepers*	1,633	1,633	1,633
Fuel wood	2,657	2,734	2,812
Total	4,290	4,367	4,445

* Annual output assumed to be unchanged since 1990.

Source: FAO, *Yearbook of Forest Products*.

SAWNWOOD PRODUCTION
(FAO estimates, '000 cubic metres, incl. railway sleepers)

	1992	1993	1994
Total	32	32	32

Source: FAO, *Yearbook of Forest Products*.

Fishing

('000 metric tons, live weight)

	1993	1994	1995
Freshwater fishes*	2.5	2.5	2.5
Grunts, sweetlips, etc.	0.7	0.7	1.1
Bobo croaker	0.2	0.9	1.0
West African croakers	3.4	1.6	2.1
Dentex	0.8	0.5	0.8
Lesser African threadfin	1.6	1.0	1.9
Bonga shad	10.0*	10.0	11.8
Other marine fishes (incl. unspecified)	7.4*	6.5	5.8
Total fish	26.5	23.6	27.0
Southern pink shrimp	0.5	0.6	0.9
Other crustaceans and molluscs	0.1	0.1	0.2
Total catch	27.1	24.4	28.0

* FAO estimate(s).

Source: FAO, *Yearbook of Fishery Statistics*.

Mining

('000 metric tons, unless otherwise indicated)

	1992	1993	1994
Crude petroleum	15,368	15,068	15,823
Natural gas (petajoules)*	4	4	3
Uranium ore (metric tons)†	589	556	650
Manganese ore*†‡	718	595	663
Gold (kilograms)†‡	70	120	72

* Provisional or estimated figures.
† Figures refer to the metal content of ores.
‡ Data from the US Bureau of Mines.

Source: UN, *Industrial Commodity Statistics Yearbook*.

Industry

PETROLEUM PRODUCTS ('000 metric tons)

	1992	1993	1994
Liquefied petroleum gas*	7	8	8
Motor spirit (petrol)*	91	93	95
Kerosene*	78	80	85
Jet fuel*	65	68	70
Distillate fuel oils	227	218*	223*
Residual fuel oil	292	294*	295*
Bitumen (asphalt)*	1	1	1

* Provisional or estimated figure(s).

Source: UN, *Industrial Commodity Statistics Yearbook*.

SELECTED OTHER PRODUCTS
('000 metric tons, unless otherwise indicated)

	1990	1991	1992
Palm oil (crude)*†	5	5	n.a.
Flour	29	30	31
Beer ('000 hectolitres)	819	814	785
Soft drinks ('000 hectolitres)	413	439	410
Cement‡	116	117	116
Electric energy (million kWh)*	908	914	919

1993: Cement ('000 metric tons) 132‡; Electric energy (million kWh) 922*.

1994: Cement ('000 metric tons) 126‡; Electric energy (million kWh) 933*.

* Provisional or estimated figure(s).

† Data from the FAO.

‡ Data from the US Bureau of Mines.

Source: UN, *Industrial Commodity Statistics Yearbook*.

Plywood (FAO estimates, '000 cu metres): 80 in 1991; 80 in 1992; 80 in 1993 (Source: FAO, *Yearbook of Forest Products*).

Veneer sheets ('000 cu metres): 60 in 1991 (Unofficial figure); 60 in 1992 (FAO estimate); 60 in 1993 (FAO estimate) (Source: FAO, *Yearbook of Forest Products*).

Finance

CURRENCY AND EXCHANGE RATES

Monetary Units

100 centimes = 1 franc de la Coopération financière en Afrique centrale (CFA).

French Franc, Sterling and Dollar Equivalents (31 March 1997)

1 French franc = 100 francs CFA;
£1 sterling = 924.20 francs CFA;
US $1 = 562.85 francs CFA;
1,000 francs CFA = £1.082 = $1.777.

Average Exchange Rate (francs CFA per US $)

1994	555.20
1995	499.15
1996	511.55

Note: An exchange rate of 1 French franc = 50 francs CFA, established in 1948, remained in force until January 1994, when the CFA franc was devalued by 50%, with the exchange rate adjusted to 1 French franc = 100 francs CFA.

BUDGET ('000 million francs CFA)

Revenue*	1994	1995	1996
Petroleum revenue	324.9	442.4	530.2
Profits tax	151.2	252.1	311.9
Royalties	139.8	155.7	185.5
Production-sharing and assets	23.9	14.6	17.8
Dividends	10.0	20.0	15.0
Non-petroleum revenue	221.2	288.2	306.0
Tax revenue	210.5	277.7	293.9
Direct taxes	58.3	76.8	80.2
Company taxes	25.0	42.7	45.0
Individual taxes	33.4	34.1	35.2
Indirect taxes	58.5	61.7	43.0
Turnover taxes	45.0	51.6	29.4
Taxes on goods and services	13.5	10.1	13.6
Taxes on refined petroleum products	6.2	4.3	—
Taxes on international trade and transactions	87.2	128.7	147.8
Import duties	75.2	110.7	125.2
Export duties	12.0	18.0	22.6
Other revenue	17.2	21.0	35.0
Total	546.1	730.6	836.2

Expenditure	1994	1995	1996
Current expenditure	461.2	514.9	512.0
Wages and salaries	165.1	178.1	184.8
Other goods and services	113.8	112.9	132.4
Transfers and subsidies	26.0	23.0	21.6
Interest payments	156.3	201.0	173.1
Domestic	38.8	n.a.	n.a.
External	117.5	n.a.	n.a.
Capital expenditure	131.2	136.0	154.3
Domestically financed investment	89.9	n.a.	n.a.
Externally financed investment	41.3	n.a.	n.a.
Other expenditure	—	—	10.2
Sub-total	592.4	650.9	676.5
Adjustment for payment arrears	370.3	53.6	125.1
Total (cash basis)	962.7	704.5	801.6

* Excluding grants received ('000 million francs CFA): 8.4 in 1994.

Source: IMF, *Gabon—Statistical Annex* (July 1997).

INTERNATIONAL RESERVES (US $ million at 31 December)

	1993	1994	1995
Gold*	5.11	4.85	4.95
IMF special drawing rights	0.03	0.25	n.a.
Reserve position in IMF	0.07	0.08	0.08
Foreign exchange	0.64	174.86	148.01
Total	5.86	180.04	n.a.

* Valued at market-related prices.

1996 (US $ million at 31 December): IMF special drawing rights 0.03; Reserve position in IMF 0.09.

Source: IMF, *International Financial Statistics*.

MONEY SUPPLY ('000 million francs CFA at 31 December)

	1993	1994	1995
Currency outside banks	50.47	76.93	100.69
Demand deposits at commercial and development banks	86.92	117.96	117.90
Total money (incl. others)	137.44	195.01	219.09

Source: IMF, *International Financial Statistics*.

COST OF LIVING
(Retail Price Index for African families in Libreville; base: 1991 = 100)

	1992	1993	1994
Food	82.4	83.5	109.9
All items	90.9	91.4	124.3

Source: UN, *Monthly Bulletin of Statistics*.

NATIONAL ACCOUNTS ('000 million francs CFA at current prices)
Expenditure on the Gross Domestic Product

	1994	1995	1996*
Government final consumption expenditure	278.9	291.0	317.2
Private final consumption expenditure	994.0	1,188.3	1,343.4
Increase in stocks	18.5	—	—
Gross fixed capital formation	490.3	541.7	587.0
Total domestic expenditure	1,781.7	2,021.1	2,247.7
Exports of goods and services	1,435.0	1,455.4	1,738.5
Less Imports of goods and services	890.0	922.1	1,068.4
GDP in purchasers' values	2,326.8	2,554.4	2,917.8

* Estimates.

Source: IMF, *Gabon—Statistical Annex* (July 1997).

Gross Domestic Product by Economic Activity

	1994	1995	1996*
Agriculture, livestock, hunting and fishing	115.5	118.8	123.4
Forestry	95.9	77.1	75.3
Petroleum exploitation and research	914.3	951.8	1,170.0
Other mining	49.1	47.6	48.9
Manufacturing	114.7	148.3	166.3
Electricity and water	34.2	39.1	40.3
Construction and public works	83.5	91.6	98.9
Trade	264.0	360.3	424.3
Transport	133.6	139.2	147.6
Financial services	14.8	14.2	14.9
Government services	222.1	232.5	245.3
Other services	209.8	223.2	237.5
GDP at factor cost	2,251.6	2,443.6	2,792.8
Import duties	75.2	110.7	125.0
GDP in purchasers' values	2,326.8	2,554.4	2,917.8

* Estimates.

Source: IMF, *Gabon—Statistical Annex* (July 1997).

BALANCE OF PAYMENTS (US $ million)

	1992	1993	1994
Exports of goods f.o.b.	2,259.2	2,326.2	2,349.4
Imports of goods f.o.b.	−886.3	−845.1	−756.5
Trade balance	1,372.9	1,481.1	1,592.9
Exports of services	347.6	311.1	219.6
Imports of services	−924.8	−1,022.7	−812.1
Balance on goods and services	795.6	769.5	1,000.4
Other income received	47.2	32.1	11.9
Other income paid	−868.9	−658.3	−569.0
Balance on goods, services and income	−26.1	143.4	443.3
Current transfers received	51.4	48.0	59.3
Current transfers paid	−193.4	−240.5	−182.8
Current balance	−168.1	−49.1	319.7
Direct investment abroad	−25.7	−2.5	−0.7
Direct investment from abroad	126.9	−113.7	−102.8
Other investment assets	−27.2	−7.8	−258.8
Other investment liabilities	−292.8	−265.2	−144.3
Net errors and omissions	−55.1	−13.6	6.7
Overall balance	−442.0	−451.9	−180.2

Source: IMF, *International Financial Statistics*.

External Trade

PRINCIPAL COMMODITIES ('000 million francs CFA)

Imports	1987	1988	1989
Machinery and apparatus	42.3	48.8	70.6
Transport equipment	31.1	21.2	24.2
Food products	42.1	33.9	31.8
Metals and metal products	24.2	32.8	27.2
Chemical products	8.0	8.9	13.1
Vegetable and animal products (non-food)	4.2	3.3	3.5
Precision instruments	5.7	9.1	14.4
Textiles and textile products	6.2	5.3	4.3
Hygiene and cleaning products	9.5	8.9	10.5
Vehicles	3.9	5.8	6.0
Mineral products	3.5	3.6	3.8
Total (incl. others)	216.7	215.8	241.8

Exports	1994	1995	1996*
Petroleum and petroleum products	1,019.2	1,055.3	1,295.1
Manganese	57.4	66.4	77.6
Timber	194.6	172.6	196.0
Uranium	16.0	15.5	13.2
Total (incl. others)	1,313.2	1,319.1	1,591.7

* Preliminary figures.

Source: IMF, *Gabon—Statistical Annex* (July 1997).

PRINCIPAL TRADING PARTNERS (% of total trade)*

Imports c.i.f.	1992	1993	1994
Belgium/Luxembourg/Netherlands	1.9	2.0	8.3
France	41.7	41.4	35.2
Germany	3.0	2.0	3.2
Italy	2.5	2.3	2.8
Japan	5.3	5.0	3.9
United Kingdom	3.5	3.4	4.9
USA	5.5	5.0	4.8
Total (incl. others)	100.0	100.0	100.0

Exports f.o.b.	1992	1993	1994
France	26.4	18.2	16.3
Germany	2.2	0.3	0.9
Italy	0.8	0.9	1.1
Japan	3.4	15.6	8.3
USA	37.5	41.6	50.0
Total (incl. others)	100.0	100.0	100.0

* Based on data reported by partner countries.

Source: IMF, *Direction of Trade Statistics*.

Transport

RAILWAYS (traffic)

	1993	1994	1995*
Passengers carried ('000)	150.5	180.8	175.8
Freight carried ('000 metric tons)	2,402.8	2,548.1	3,012.9

* Estimates.

Source: IMF, *Gabon—Statistical Annex* (July 1997).

ROAD TRAFFIC (estimates, motor vehicles in use)

	1993	1994	1995
Passenger cars	21,800	22,100	23,800
Lorries and vans	14,300	14,800	15,700

Source: IRF, *World Road Statistics*.

INTERNATIONAL SEA-BORNE SHIPPING
(freight traffic, '000 metric tons)

	1988	1989	1990
Goods loaded	8,890	10,739	12,828
Goods unloaded	610	213	212

Source: UN, *Monthly Bulletin of Statistics*.

CIVIL AVIATION (traffic on scheduled services)

	1992	1993	1994
Kilometres flown (million)	6	6	6
Passengers carried ('000)	471	302	481
Passenger-kilometres (million)	536	570	719
Total ton-kilometres (million)	77	82	96

Source: UN, *Statistical Yearbook*.

Tourism

	1992	1993	1994
Tourist arrivals ('000)	133	115	103
Tourist receipts (US $ million)	5	4	5

Source: UN, *Statistical Yearbook*.

Communications Media

	1992	1993	1994
Radio receivers ('000 in use)	177	183	189
Television receivers ('000 in use)	46	48	49
Telephones ('000 main lines in use)	28	30	31
Daily newspapers:			
Number	1	n.a.	1
Average circulation ('000 copies)	20	n.a.	20*

* Provisional or estimated figure.

Sources: UNESCO, *Statistical Yearbook*; UN, *Statistical Yearbook*.

Education

(1991/92)

	Institutions	Teachers	Pupils		
			Males	Females	Total
Pre-primary	9	37	465	485	950
Primary	1,024	4,782	105,819	104,181	210,000
Secondary:					
General	n.a.	1,356	n.a.	n.a.	42,871
Vocational	n.a.	476	n.a.	n.a.	8,477
Teacher training*	n.a.	37	556	506	1,062
University level	2	299	2,148	852	3,000
Other higher	n.a.	257†	1,033‡	315‡	1,348‡

* 1988/89 figures. † 1983/84 figure. ‡ 1986/87 figure.

Source: UNESCO, *Statistical Yearbook*.

Directory

The Constitution

The Constitution of the Gabonese Republic was adopted on 14 March 1991. The main provisions are summarized below:

PREAMBLE

Upholds the rights of the individual, liberty of conscience and of the person, religious freedom and freedom of education. Sovereignty is vested in the people, who exercise it through their representatives or by means of referenda. There is direct, universal and secret suffrage.

HEAD OF STATE*

The President is elected by direct universal suffrage for a five-year term, renewable only once. The President is Head of State and of the Armed Forces. The President may, after consultation with his ministers and leaders of the National Assembly, order a referendum to be held. The President appoints the Prime Minister, who is Head of Government and who is accountable to the President. The President is the guarantor of national independence and territorial sovereignty.

EXECUTIVE POWER

Executive power is vested in the President and the Council of Ministers, who are appointed by the Prime Minister, in consultation with the President.

LEGISLATIVE POWER

The National Assembly is elected by direct universal suffrage for a five-year term. It may be dissolved or prorogued for up to 18 months by the President, after consultation with the Council of Ministers and President of the Assembly. The President may return a bill to the Assembly for a second reading, when it must be passed by a majority of two-thirds of the members. If the President dissolves the Assembly, elections must take place within 40 days.

The Constitution also provides for the establishment of an upper chamber (the Senate), to control the balance and regulation of power.

POLITICAL ORGANIZATIONS

Article 2 of the Constitution states that 'Political parties and associations contribute to the expression of universal suffrage. They are formed and exercise their activities freely, within the limits delineated by the laws and regulations. They must respect the principles of democracy, national sovereignty, public order and national unity'.

JUDICIAL POWER

The President guarantees the independence of the Judiciary and presides over the Conseil Supérieur de la Magistrature. Supreme judicial power is vested in the Supreme Court.

* A constitutional amendment, adopted by the legislature on 18 April 1997, extended the presidential term to seven years and provided for the creation of the post of Vice-President.

The Government

HEAD OF STATE

President: El Hadj OMAR (ALBERT-BERNARD) BONGO (took office 2 December 1967, elected 25 February 1973, re-elected December 1979, November 1986 and December 1993).

Vice-President: DIDJOB DIVUNGUI-DI-N'DINGUE.

COUNCIL OF MINISTERS

(August 1997)

Prime Minister: Dr PAULIN OBAME-NGUEMA.

Minister of State for Foreign Affairs and Co-operation: CASIMIR OYÉ MBA.

Minister of State for Equipment and Construction: ZACHARIE MYBOTO.

Minister of State for Justice and Keeper of the Seals: MARCEL ELOI RAHANDI CHAMBRIER.

Minister of State for Habitat, Housing, Urban Planning and Territorial Administrationand Welfare: JEAN-FRANÇOIS NTOUTOUME-EMANE.

Minister of State for Labour, Human Resources and Professional Training: JEAN-RÉMY PENDY BOUYIKI.

Minister of State for Agriculture, Livestock and Rural Development: EMMANUEL ONDO METHOGO.

Minister of State for the Interior: ANTOINE MBOUMBOU MIYAKOU.

Minister of State for National Education and Women's Affairs: PAULETTE MISSAMBO.

Minister of Mining, Energy and Oil: PAUL TOUNGUI.

Minister of National Defence, Security and Immigration, in charge of Posts and Telecommunications: Gen. IDRISS NGARI.

Minister of Communications, Culture, the Arts and Mass Education: JACQUES ADIAHÉNOT.

Minister of Finance, the Economy, the Budget and Participation, in charge of Privatization: MARCEL DOUPAMBY MATOKA.

Minister of Commerce, Industry, Small and Medium-sized Enterprises and Industries and Handicrafts: MARTIN FIDÈLE MAGNAGA.

Minister of Water, Forestry and Reafforestation: ANDRÉ DIEUDONNÉ BERRE.

Minister of Planning, the Environment and Tourism: JEAN PING.

Minister of the Civil Service and Administrative Reform: PATRICE ZIENGUI.

Minister of Transport and Civil Aviation: Gen. ALBERT NDJAVÉ-NDJOY.

Minister of Social Affairs, National Solidarity and the Family: PIERRE-CLAVER ZENG EBOME.

Minister of Merchant Marine and Fishing: JOACHIM MAHOTES MAGOUINDI.

Minister of Youth, Sports and Leisure: ALEXANDRE SAMBAT.

Minister of Higher Education and Scientific Research: LAZARE DIGOMBÉ.

Minister of Relations with Parliament and the Assemblies and Spokesperson for the Government: ANDRÉ MBA OBAME.

Minister of Public Health and Population: FAUSTIN BOUKOUBI.

Minister Delegate to the Prime Minister: EMMANUEL AKOGHE MBA.

Minister Delegate to the Minister of State for Equipment and Construction: SENTUREL NGOMA MADOUNGOU.

Minister Delegate to the Minister of State for National Education and Women's Affairs: JEAN-PIERRE MENGWANG-ME-NGIEMA.

Minister Delegate to the Minister of State for Habitat, Housing, Urban Planning and Territorial Administration: ANDRÉ JULES NDJAMBE.

Minister Delegate in charge of the Budget: ANTOINE YALANZELE.

Minister Delegate in charge of Small and Medium-sized Enterprises and Industries: FABIEN OWONO ESSONO.

Minister Delegate to the Minister of Planning, the Environment and Tourism: ALFRED MABIKA.

Minister Delegate to the Minister of Public Health and Population: DANIEL ONA ONDO.

MINISTRIES

Office of the Prime Minister: BP 546, Libreville; telex 5409.

Ministry of Agriculture, Livestock and Rural Development: BP 551, Libreville; tel. 76-29-43; telex 5587.

Ministry of the Civil Service and Administrative Reform: Libreville.

Ministry of Commerce, Industry, Small and Medium-sized Enterprises and Industries and Handicrafts: BP 3906, Libreville; tel. 76-30-55; telex 5347.

Ministry of Communications, Culture, the Arts and Mass Education: Libreville.

Ministry of Equipment and Construction: BP 49, Libreville; tel. 76-38-56; telex 5408; fax 74-80-92.

Ministry of Finance, the Economy, the Budget and Participation: BP 165, Libreville; tel. 72-12-10; telex 5238.

Ministry of Foreign Affairs and Co-operation: BP 2245, Libreville; tel. 76-22-70; telex 5255.

Ministry of Habitat, Housing, Urban Planning and Territorial Administration: Libreville.

Ministry of Higher Education and Scientific Research: Libreville.

Ministry of the Interior: Libreville.

Ministry of Justice: Libreville; tel. 72-26-95.

Ministry of Labour, Human Resources and Professional Training: BP 4577, Libreville; tel. 74-32-18.

Ministry of Merchant Marine and Fishing: Libreville.

Ministry of Mining, Energy and Oil: Libreville; tel. 72-31-96; telex 5629.

Ministry of National Defence, Security and Immigration: Libreville; tel. 76-25-95; telex 5453.

Ministry of National Education and Women's Affairs: BP 6, Libreville; tel. 76-13-01; fax 74-14-48.

Ministry of Planning, the Environment and Tourism: BP 178, Libreville; tel. 76-34-62; telex 5711.

Ministry of Public Health and Population: Libreville; tel. 76-35-90; telex 5385.

Ministry of Relations with Parliament and the Assemblies: Libreville.

Ministry of Social Affairs, National Solidarity and the Family: Libreville.

Ministry of Transport and Civil Aviation: BP 3974, Libreville; tel. 72-11-62; telex 5479; fax 77-33-31.

Ministry of Water, Forestry and Reafforestation: Libreville.

Ministry of Youth, Sports and Leisure: Libreville.

President and Legislature

PRESIDENT

Presidential Election, 5 December 1993

Candidate	% of votes
El Hadj OMAR (ALBERT-BERNARD) BONGO	51.18
Fr PAUL M'BA ABESSOLE	26.51
PIERRE-LOUIS AGONDJO-OKAWÉ	4.78
PIERRE-CLAVER MAGANGA MOUSSAVOU	3.64
JULES BOURDÈS-OGOULIGUENDÉ	3.38
ALEXANDRE SAMBAT	2.59
DIDJOB DIVUNGUI-DI-N'DINGUE	2.20
Prof. LÉON MBOYEBI	1.83
JEAN-PIERRE LEPANDOU	1.38
MARC SATURNIN NAN NGUEMA	0.86
SIMON OYONO ABA'A	0.83
ADRIEN NGUEMA ONDO	0.44
LÉON MÉBIAME	0.38
Total	100.00

ASSEMBLÉE NATIONALE

President: (vacant).

Secretary-General: (vacant).

General Election, 15 and 29 December 1996

Party	Seats
Parti démocratique gabonais	82
Rassemblement national des bûcherons*	12
Parti gabonais du progrès*	8
Independents	6
Cercle des libéraux réformateurs	3
Union socialiste gabonais	2
Alliance démocratique et républicaine*	1
Cercle pour le renouveau et le progrès*	1
Congrès pour la démocratie et la justice*	1
Forum africain pour la reconstruction*	1
Mouvement de redressement national (MORENA—originels)*	1
Rassemblement pour la démocratie et le progrès*	1
Union du peuple gabonais*	1
Total	120

* Contested the election as the High Council of Resistance.

SÉNAT

President: GEORGES RAWIRI.

Election, 26 January and 9 February 1997*

Party	Seats
Parti démocratique gabonais	52
Rassemblement national des bûcherons	19
Independents	9
Parti gabonais du progrès	4
Alliance démocratique et républicaine	3
Cercle des libéraux réformateurs	1
Rassemblement pour la démocratie et le progrès	1
Total†	91

* Provisional results.

† Results for two seats were still to be released.

Political Organizations

Constitutional amendments providing for the introduction of a multi-party system took effect in May 1990. Political associations in existence in mid-1997 included:

Alliance démocratique et républicaine (ADR).

Association pour le socialisme au Gabon (APSG).

Cercle des libéraux réformateurs (CLR): f. 1993 by breakaway faction of the PDG; Leader JEAN-BONIFACE ASSELE.

Cercle pour le renouveau et le progrès (CRP).

Congrès pour la démocratie et la justice.

Convention des forces du changement: f. 1993 as an informal alliance of eight opposition presidential candidates.

Coordination de l'opposition démocratique (COD): f. 1991 as an alliance of eight principal opposition parties; Chair. SÉBASTIEN MAMBOUNDOU MOUYAMA.

Forum d'action pour le renouveau (FAR): f. 1992; a factional alliance within the COD; Leader Prof. LÉON MBOYEBI; comprises three political parties:

Mouvement de redressement national (MORENA-originels): f. 1981 in Paris, France; Leader SIMON OYONO ABA'A.

Parti socialiste gabonais (PSG): f. 1991; Leader Prof. LÉON MBOYEBI.

Union socialiste gabonais (USG): Leader Dr SERGE MBA BEKALE.

Front national (FN): f. 1991; Leader MARTIN EFAYONG.

Mouvement alternatif: f. 1996; Leader SÉBASTIEN MAMBOUNDOU MOUYAMA.

Mouvement pour la démocratie, le développement et la reconciliation nationale (Modern): Libreville; f. 1996; Leader GASTON MOZOGO OVONO.

Parti démocratique gabonais (PDG): BP 268, Libreville; tel. 70-31-21; fax 70-31-46; f. 1968; sole legal party 1968–90; Sec.-Gen. SIMPLICE NGUEDE MANZELA.

Parti gabonais du centre indépendent (PGCI): Leader JEAN-PIERRE LEPANDOU.

Parti gabonais du progrès (PGP): f. 1990; Pres. PIERRE-LOUIS AGONDJO-OKAWÉ; Sec.-Gen. ANSELME NZOGHE.

Parti des libéraux démocrates (PLD): Leader MARC SATURNIN NAN NGUEMA.

Parti social-démocrate (PSD): f. 1991; Leader PIERRE-CLAVER MAGANGA MOUSSAVOU.

Parti de l'unité du peuple gabonais (PUP): Libreville; f. 1991; Leader LOUIS GASTON MAYILA.

Rassemblement des démocrates (RD): f. 1993.

Rassemblement pour la démocratie et le progrès (RDP): Pres. ALEXANDRE SAMBAT.

Rassemblement des Gaubis: Libreville; f. 1994; Leader MAX ANICET KOUMBA-MBADINGA.

Rassemblement national des bûcherons (RNB): f. 1990 as MORENA des bûcherons; Leader Fr PAUL M'BA ABESSOLE; Sec.-Gen. Prof. PIERRE-ANDRÉ KOMBILA.

Union pour la démocratie et le développement Mayumba (UDD).

Union démocratique et sociale (UDS): f. 1996; Leader HERVÉ OUSSAMANE.

Union nationale pour la démocratie et le développement (UNDD): f. 1993; supports President Bongo.

Union du peuple gabonais (UPG): f. 1989 in Paris, France; Leader PIERRE MAMBOUNDOU.

Diplomatic Representation

EMBASSIES IN GABON

Algeria: BP 4008, Libreville; tel. 73-23-18; telex 5313; fax 73-14-03; Ambassador: ABDELHAMID CHEBCHOUB.

Angola: BP 4884, Libreville; tel. 73-04-26; telex 5565; Ambassador: BERNARDO DOMBELE M'BALA.

Argentina: BP 4065, Libreville; tel. 74-05-49; telex 5611; Ambassador: HUGO HURTUBEI.

Belgium: BP 4079, Libreville; tel. 73-29-92; telex 5273; Ambassador: PAUL DE WULF.

Brazil: BP 3899, Libreville; tel. 76-05-35; telex 5492; fax 74-03-43; Ambassador: JAIME VILLA-LOBOS.

Cameroon: BP 14001, Libreville; tel. 73-28-00; telex 5396; Chargé d'affaires a.i.: NYEMB NGUENE.

Canada: BP 4037, Libreville; tel. 74-34-64; telex 5527; Ambassador: JEAN NADEAU.

Central African Republic: Libreville; tel. 72-12-28; telex 5323; Ambassador: FRANÇOIS DIALLO.

China, People's Republic: BP 3914, Libreville; tel. 74-32-07; telex 5376; Ambassador: SUN ZHIRONG.

Congo, Democratic Republic: BP 2257, Libreville; tel. 74-32-54; telex 5335; Ambassador: KABANGI KAUMBU BULA.

Congo, Republic: BP 269, Libreville; tel. 73-29-06; telex 5541; Ambassador: PIERRE OBOU.

Côte d'Ivoire: BP 3861, Libreville; tel. 72-05-96; telex 5317; Ambassador: JEAN-OBEO COULIBALY.

Egypt: BP 4240, Libreville; tel. 73-25-38; telex 5425; fax 73-25-19; Ambassador: SALAH ZAKI.

Equatorial Guinea: BP 14262, Libreville; tel. 76-30-15; Ambassador: CRISANTOS NDONGO ABA MESSIAN.

France: BP 2125, Libreville; tel. 74-04-75; telex 5249; Ambassador: MICHEL LUNVEN.

Germany: blvd de l'Indépendance, BP 299, Libreville; tel. 76-01-88; telex 5248; fax 72-40-12; Ambassador: HORST K. RUDOLF.

Guinea: BP 4046, Libreville; tel. 70-11-46; Chargé d'affaires a.i.: MAMADI KOLY KOUROUMA.

Iran: BP 2158, Libreville; tel. 73-05-33; telex 5502; Ambassador: Dr ABBASSE SAFARIAN.

Italy: Immeuble Personnaz et Gardin, rue de la Mairie, BP 2251, Libreville; tel. 74-28-92; telex 5287; fax 74-80-35; Ambassador: VITTORIO FUMO.

Japan: BP 2259, Libreville; tel. 73-22-97; telex 5428; fax 73-60-60; Ambassador: HIDEO KAKINUMA.

Korea, Republic: BP 2620, Libreville; tel. 73-40-00; telex 5356; fax 73-00-79; Ambassador: PARK CHANG-IL.

Lebanon: BP 3341, Libreville; tel. 73-14-77; telex 5547; Ambassador: MAMLOUK ABDELLATIF.

Mauritania: BP 3917, Libreville; tel. 74-31-65; telex 5570; Ambassador: El Hadj THIAM.

Morocco: BP 3983, Libreville; tel. 77-41-51; telex 5434; fax 77-41-50; Ambassador: MOHAMED GHALI TAZI.

Nigeria: BP 1191, Libreville; tel. 73-22-03; telex 5605; Ambassador: JOE-EFFIONG UDOH EKONG.

Philippines: BP 1198, Libreville; tel. 72-34-80; telex 5279; Chargé d'affaires a.i.: ARCADIO HERRERA.

Russia: BP 3963, Libreville; tel. 72-48-68; telex 5797; fax 72-48-70; Ambassador: YOURI LEYZARENKO.

São Tomé and Príncipe: BP 409, Libreville; tel. 72-15-46; telex 5557; Ambassador: JOSEPH FRET LAU CHONG.

Senegal: BP 3856, Libreville; tel. 73-26-87; telex 5332; Ambassador: OUMAR WELE.

South Africa: Immeuble les Arcades, 142 rue des Chavannes, BP 4063, Libreville; tel. 77-45-30; fax 77-45-36; Ambassador: Dr WILHELM P. STEENKAMP.

Spain: Immeuble Diamant, blvd de l'Indépendance, BP 2105, Libreville; tel. 72-12-64; telex 5258; fax 74-88-73; Ambassador: MIGUEL ANTONIO ARIAS ESTÉVEZ.

Togo: BP 14160, Libreville; tel. 73-29-04; telex 5490; Ambassador: AHLONKO KOFFI AQUEREBURU.

Tunisia: BP 3844, Libreville; tel. 73-28-41; Ambassador: EZZEDINE KERKENI.

USA: blvd de la Mer, BP 4000, Libreville; tel. 76-20-03; telex 5250; Ambassador: ELIZABETH RASPOLIC (designate).

Venezuela: BP 3859, Libreville; tel. 73-31-18; telex 5264; fax 73-30-67; Ambassador: VÍCTOR CROQUER-VEGA.

Yugoslavia: Libreville; tel. 73-30-05; telex 5329; Ambassador: ČEDOMIR STRBAC.

Judicial System

Supreme Court: BP 1043, Libreville; tel. 72-17-00; three chambers: judicial, administrative and accounts; Pres. BENJAMIN PAMBOU-KOMBILA.

Constitutional Court: Libreville; Pres. MARIE MADELEINE BORANSOUO.

Courts of Appeal: Libreville and Franceville.

Court of State Security: Libreville; 13 mems; Pres. FLORENTIN ANGO.

Conseil Supérieur de la Magistrature: Libreville; Pres. El Hadj OMAR BONGO; Vice-Pres. Pres. of the Supreme Court (ex officio).

There are also Tribunaux de Première Instance (County Courts) at Libreville, Franceville, Port-Gentil, Lambaréné, Mouila, Oyem, Koula-Moutou, Makokou and Tchibanga.

Religion

About 60% of Gabon's population are Christians, mainly adherents of the Roman Catholic Church. About 40% are animists, and fewer than 1% are Muslims.

CHRISTIANITY

The Roman Catholic Church

Gabon comprises one archdiocese and three dioceses. At 31 December 1995 the estimated number of adherents in the country was equivalent to 51.6% of the total population.

Bishops' Conference: Conférence Episcopale du Gabon, BP 209, Oyem; tel. 98-63-20; f. 1989; Pres. Rt Rev. BASILE MVÉ ENGONE, Bishop of Oyem.

Archbishop of Libreville: Most Rev. ANDRÉ-FERNAND ANGUILÉ, Archevêché, Sainte-Marie, BP 2146, Libreville; tel. 72-20-73.

Protestant Churches

Christian and Missionary Alliance: active in the south of the country; 16,000 mems.

Eglise Evangélique du Gabon: BP 10080, Libreville; tel. 72-41-92; f. 1842; independent since 1961; 120,000 mems; Pres. Pastor SAMUEL NANG ESSONO; Sec. Rev. EMILE NTETOME.

The Evangelical Church of South Gabon and the Evangelical Pentecostal Church are also active in Gabon.

The Press

Le Bûcheron: BP 6424, Libreville; official publ. of the Rassemblement national des bûcherons; Pres. PIERRE ANDRÉ KOMBILA.

Bulletin Evangélique d'Information et de Presse: BP 80, Libreville; monthly; religious.

Bulletin Mensuel de la Chambre de Commerce, d'Agriculture, d'Industrie et des Mines: BP 2234, Libreville; tel. 72-20-64; telex 5554; fax 74-64-77; monthly.

Bulletin Mensuel de Statistique de la République Gabonaise: BP 179, Libreville; monthly; publ. by Direction Générale de l'Economie.

L'Economiste Gabonais: BP 3906, Libreville; quarterly; publ. by the Centre gabonais du commerce extérieur.

Gabon d'Aujourd'hui: BP 750, Libreville; weekly; publ. by the Ministry of Communications, Posts and Telecommunications.

Gabon Libre: BP 6439, Libreville; tel. 74-42-22; weekly; Dir DZIME EKANG; Editor RENÉ NZOVI.

Gabon-Matin: BP 168, Libreville; daily; publ. by Agence Gabonaise de Presse; Man. HILARION VENDANY; circ. 18,000.

La Griffe: BP 4928, Libreville; tel. 74-73-45; weekly; independent; satirical; Pres. JÉRÔME OKINDA; Editor NDJOUMBA MOUSSOCK.

Journal Officiel de la République Gabonaise: BP 563, Libreville; f. 1959; fortnightly; Man. EMMANUEL OBAMÉ.

Ngondo: BP 168, Libreville; monthly; publ. by Agence Gabonaise de Presse.

Le Progressiste: blvd Léon-M'Ba, Libreville; tel. 74-54-01; Dir BENOÎT MOUITY NZAMBA; Editor JACQUES MOURENDE-TSIOBA.

La Relance: BP 268, Libreville; tel. 70-31-66; weekly; publ. of the Parti démocratique gabonais; Pres. JACQUES ADIAHENOT; Dir RENÉ NDEMEZO'O OBIANG.

Sept Jours: BP 213, Libreville; weekly.

L'Union: BP 3849, Libreville; tel. 73-21-84; telex 5305; fax 73-83-26; f. 1975; 75% state-owned; daily; official govt publication; Man. Dir ALBERT YANGARI; Editor NGOYO MOUSSAVOU; circ. 40,000.

NEWS AGENCIES

Agence Gabonaise de Presse (AGP): BP 168, Libreville; tel. 21-26; telex 5628.

Foreign Bureau

Agence France-Presse (AFP): Immeuble Sogapal, Les Filaos, BP 788, Libreville; tel. 76-14-36; telex 5239; fax 72-45-31; Correspondents LAURENT CHEVALLIER, MICHEL MARTIN.

Publishers

Imprimerie Centrale d'Afrique (IMPRIGA): BP 154, Libreville; tel. 70-22-55; fax 70-05-19; f. 1973; Chair. ROBERT VIAL; Dir FRANCIS BOURQUIN.

Multipress Gabon: blvd Léon-M'Ba, BP 3875, Libreville; tel. 73-22-33; telex 5389; f. 1973; Chair. PAUL BORY.

Société Imprimerie de l'Ogooué (SIMO): BP 342, Port-Gentil; f. 1977; Man. Dir URBAIN NICOUE.

Société Nationale de Presse et d'Edition (SONAPRESSE): BP 3849, Libreville; tel. 73-21-84; telex 5391; f. 1975; Pres. and Man. Dir JOSEPH RENDJAMBE.

Radio and Television

In 1994, according to UNESCO, there were an estimated 189,000 radio receivers and 49,000 television receivers in use.

RADIO

The national network, 'La Voix de la Rénovation', and a provincial network broadcast for 24 hours each day in French and local languages. Plans to construct 13 new FM radio stations were announced in 1986.

Africa No. 1: BP 1, Libreville; tel. 76-00-01; telex 5558; fax 74-21-33; f. 1980; 35% state-controlled; international commercial radio station; broadcasts began in 1981; daily programmes in French and English; Pres. LOUIS BARTHÉLEMY MAPANGOU; Mans MICHEL KOUMBANGOYE, PIERRE DEVOLUY.

Radiodiffusion-Télévision Gabonaise (RTG): BP 150, Libreville; tel. 73-20-25; telex 5342; f. 1959; state-controlled; Dir-Gen. JOHN JOSEPH MBOUROU; Dir of Radio PIERRE-NOËL BOTSIKABOBE.

Radio Fréquence 3: f. 1996.

Radio Génération Nouvelle: f. 1996.

Radio Mandarine: f. 1995.

Radio Soleil: f. 1995; affiliated to Rassemblement national des bûcherons.

Radio Unité: f. 1996.

TELEVISION

Television transmissions can be received as far inland as Kango and Lambaréné; in 1986 proposals were announced for the extension and modernization of the network to cover the whole of Gabon, including the construction of 13 new TV broadcasting stations. Programmes are also transmitted by satellite to other African countries. Colour broadcasts began in 1975.

Radiodiffusion-Télévision Gabonaise (RTG): BP 150, Libreville; tel. 73-21-52; telex 5342; fax 73-21-53; f. 1959; state-controlled; Dir-Gen. JOHN JOSEPH MBOUROU; Dir of Television ROBERT ALOLI.

Télé-Africa: Libreville; tel. 76-20-33; private channel; daily broadcasts in French.

Télédiffusion du Gabon: f. 1995.

Finance

(cap. = capital; res = reserves; dep. = deposits; m. = million; brs = branches; amounts in francs CFA)

BANKING

Central Bank

Banque des Etats de l'Afrique Centrale (BEAC): BP 112, Libreville; tel. 76-13-52; telex 5215; fax 74-45-63; headquarters in Yaoundé, Cameroon; f. 1973 as central bank of issue for mem. states of the Customs and Economic Union of Central Africa (UDEAC); cap. and res 214,492m. (June 1996); Gov. JEAN-FÉLIX MAMALEPOT; Dir in Gabon JEAN-PAUL LEYIMANGOYE; 3 brs.

Commercial Banks

Banque Gabonaise et Française Internationale: blvd de l'Indépendance, BP 2253, Libreville; tel. 76-01-37; telex 5265; fax 74-08-94; f. 1971 as Banque Paribas-Gabon; 39.6% state-owned; cap. and res 25,738.1m., dep. 48,037.7m. (Dec. 1995); Chair. PATRICE OTHA; Dir-Gen. HENRI-CLAUDE OYIMA; br. at Port-Gentil.

Banque Internationale pour le Commerce et l'Industrie du Gabon, SA (BICIG): ave du Colonel Parant, BP 2241, Libreville; tel. 76-26-13; telex 5226; fax 74-64-10; f. 1973; 26.4% state-owned; cap. 7,000m. (Dec. 1994); Pres. GUY-ETIENNE MOUVAGHA-TCHIOBA; Man. Dir EMILE DOUMBA; 9 brs.

Banque Internationale pour le Gabon: Immeuble Concorde, blvd de l'Indépendance, BP 106, Libreville; tel. 76-26-26; telex 5221; fax 76-20-53.

Banque Populaire du Gabon 'La Populaire': blvd d'Indépendance, BP 6663, Libreville; tel. 72-86-88; telex 5264; fax 72-86-91; f. 1996; Pres. JEAN-MARCE EKOHNGYEMA; Dir-Gen. SAMSON NGOMO.

Crédit Foncier du Gabon: blvd de l'Indépendance, BP 3905, Libreville; tel. 72-47-45; telex 3905; fax 76-08-70; 75% state-owned; Pres. HENRI MINKO; Dir-Gen. EMMANUEL NTOUTOUME.

Union Gabonaise de Banque, SA (UGB): ave du Colonel Parant, BP 315, Libreville; tel. 77-70-00; telex 5232; fax 76-46-16; f. 1962; 25% state-owned; cap. and res 15,323.5m., dep. 74,011.9m. (Dec. 1995); Pres. MICHEL ANCHOUEY; Man. Dir JEAN-CLAUDE DUBOIS; 6 brs.

Development Banks

Banque Gabonaise de Développement (BGD): rue Alfred Marche, BP 5, Libreville; tel. 76-24-29; telex 5430; fax 74-26-99;

f. 1960; 69% state-owned; cap. 10,500m. (Dec. 1995); Pres. JEAN-BAPTISTE OBIANG ETOUGHE; Dir-Gen. RICHARD ONOUVIET; 3 brs.

Banque Nationale de Crédit Rural (BNCR): ave Bouet, BP 1120, Libreville; tel. 72-47-42; telex 5830; fax 74-05-07; f. 1986; 74% state-owned; cap. 1,350m. (Dec. 1992); Pres. GÉRARD MEYO M'EMANE; Man. Dir GEORGES ISSEMBE.

Société Gabonaise de Participation et de Développement (SOGAPAR): blvd de l'Indépendance, BP 2253, Libreville; tel. 73-23-26; telex 5265; fax 74-08-94; f. 1971; 38% state-owned; studies and promotes projects conducive to national economic development; cap. 2,063m. (Dec. 1995); Pres. DANIEL BEDIN; Man. Dir HENRI-CLAUDE OYIMA.

Société Nationale d'Investissement du Gabon (SONADIG): BP 479, Libreville; tel. 72-09-22; fax 74-81-70; f. 1968; state-owned; cap. 500m.; Pres. ANTOINE OYIEYE; Dir-Gen. MASSALA TSAMBA.

Financial Institution

Caisse Autonome d'Amortissement du Gabon: BP 912, Libreville; tel. 74-41-43; telex 5537; management of state funds; Dir-Gen. MAURICE EYAMBA TSIMAT.

INSURANCE

Agence Gabonaise d'Assurance et de Réassurance (AGAR): BP 1699, Libreville; tel. 74-02-22; fax 76-59-25; f. 1987; cap. 50m.; Man. Dir LOUIS GASTON MAYILA.

Assurances Générales Gabonaises (AGG): ave du Colonel Parant, BP 2148, Libreville; tel. 76-09-73; telex 5473; f. 1974; cap. 66.5m.; Co-Chair. JEAN DAVIN, JACQUES NOT.

Assureurs Conseils Franco-Africains du Gabon (ACFRA-GABON): BP 1116, Libreville; tel. 72-32-83; telex 5485; cap. 43.4m.; Chair. FRÉDÉRIC MARRON; Dir M. GARNIER.

Assureurs Conseils Gabonais-Faugère et Jutheau & Cie: Immeuble Shell-Gabon, rue de la Mairie, BP 2138, Libreville; tel. 72-04-36; telex 5435; fax 76-04-39; cap. 10m.; represents foreign insurance cos; Dir GÉRARD MILAN.

Groupement Gabonais d'Assurances et de Réassurances (GGAR): Immeuble les Horizons, blvd Triomphal Omar Bongo, BP 3949, Libreville; tel. 74-28-72; telex 5673; f. 1985; cap. 225m.; Chair. RASSAGUIZA AKEREY; Dir-Gen. DENISE OMBAGHO.

Mutuelle Gabonaise d'Assurances: ave du Colonel Parant, BP 2225, Libreville; tel. 72-13-91; telex 5240; Sec.-Gen. M. YENO-OLINGOT.

Omnium Gabonais d'Assurances et de Réassurances (OGAR): blvd Triomphal Omar Bongo, BP 201, Libreville; tel. 76-15-96; telex 5505; fax 76-58-16; f. 1976; 10% state-owned; cap. 340m.; general; Pres. MARCEL DOUPAMBY-MATOKA; Man. Dir EDOUARD VALENTIN.

Société Nationale Gabonaise d'Assurances et de Réassurances (SONAGAR): ave du Colonel Parant, BP 3082, Libreville; tel. 76-28-97; telex 5366; f. 1974; owned by l'Union des Assurances de Paris (France); Dir-Gen. JEAN-LOUIS MESSAN.

SOGERCO-Gabon: BP 2102, Libreville; tel. 76-09-34; telex 5224; f. 1975; cap. 10m.; general; Dir M. RABEAU.

L'Union des Assurances du Gabon (UAG): ave du Colonel Parant, BP 2141, Libreville; tel. 74-34-34; telex 5404; fax 74-14-53; f. 1976; cap. 280.5m.; Chair. ALBERT ALEWINA CHAVIOT; Dir EKOMIE AFENE.

Trade and Industry

GOVERNMENT ADVISORY BODY

Conseil Economique et Social de la République Gabonaise: BP 1075, Libreville; tel. 76-26-68; comprises representatives from salaried workers, employers and Govt; commissions on economic, financial and social affairs and forestry and agriculture; Pres. EDOUARD ALEXIS M'BOUY-BOUTZIT.

CHAMBER OF COMMERCE

Chambre de Commerce, d'Agriculture, d'Industrie et des Mines du Gabon: BP 2234, Libreville; tel. 72-20-64; telex 5554; fax 74-64-77; f. 1935; regional offices at Port-Gentil and Franceville; Pres. JOACHIM BOUSSAMBA-MAPAGA; Sec.-Gen. DOMINIQUE MANDZA.

EMPLOYERS' FEDERATIONS

Confédération Patronale Gabonaise: BP 410, Libreville; tel. 76-02-43; fax 74-86-52; f. 1959; represents the principal industrial, mining, petroleum, public works, forestry, banking, insurance, commercial and shipping concerns; Pres. EMILE DOUMBA; Sec.-Gen. ERIC MESSERSCHMITT.

Conseil National du Patronat Gabonais (CNPG): Libreville; Pres. RAHANDI CHAMBRIER; Sec.-Gen. THOMAS FRANCK EYA'A.

Syndicat des Entreprises Minières du Gabon (SYNDIMINES): BP 260, Libreville; telex 5388; Pres. ANDRÉ BERRE; Sec.-Gen. SERGE GREGOIRE.

Syndicat des Importateurs Exportateurs du Gabon (SIMPEX): BP 1743, Libreville; Pres. ALBERT JEAN; Sec.-Gen. R. TYBERGHEIN.

Syndicat des Producteurs et Industriels du Bois du Gabon: BP 84, Libreville; tel. 72-26-11; Pres. HERVÉ BOZEC.

Syndicat Professionnel des Usines de Sciages et Placages du Gabon: BP 417, Port-Gentil; f. 1956; Pres. PIERRE BERRY.

Union des Représentations Automobiles et Industrielles (URAI): BP 1743, Libreville; Pres. M. MARTINENT; Sec. R. TYBERGHEIN.

Union Nationale du Patronat Syndical des Transports Urbains, Routiers et Fluviaux du Gabon (UNAPASYFTU-ROGA): BP 1025, Libreville; f. 1977; Pres. LAURENT BELLAL BIBANG-BI-EDZO; Sec.-Gen. MARTIN KOMBILA-MOMBO.

PRINCIPAL DEVELOPMENT ORGANIZATIONS

Agence Nationale de Promotion de la Petite et Moyenne Entreprise (PROMO-GABON): BP 3939, Libreville; tel. 74-31-16; telex 000576; f. 1964; state-controlled; promotes and assists small and medium-sized industries; Pres. SIMON BOULAMATARI; Man. Dir JEAN-FIDÈLE OTANDO.

Caisse Française de Développement: BP 64, Libreville; tel. 74-33-74; telex 5362; fax 74-51-25; Dir ANTOINE BAUX.

Centre Gabonais de Commerce Extérieur (CGCE): BP 3906, Libreville; tel. 76-11-67; telex 5347; promotes foreign trade and investment in Gabon; Man. Dir MICHEL LESLIE TEALE.

Commerce et Développement (CODEV): BP 2142, Libreville; tel. 76-06-73; telex 5214; f. 1976; cap. 2,000m. francs CFA; 95% state-owned, proposed transfer to private ownership announced 1986; import and distribution of capital goods and food products; Chair. and Man. Dir JÉRÔME NGOUA-BEKALE.

Mission Française de Coopération: BP 2105, Libreville; tel. 76-10-56; telex 5249; fax 74-55-33; administers bilateral aid from France; Dir JEAN-CLAUDE QUIRIN.

Office Gabonais d'Amélioration et de Production de Viande (OGAPROV): BP 245, Moanda; tel. 66-12-67; f. 1971; development of private cattle farming; manages ranch at Lekedi-Sud; Pres. PAUL KOUNDA KIKI; Dir-Gen. VINCENT EYI-NGUI.

Palmiers et Hévéas du Gabon (PALMEVEAS): BP 75, Libreville; f. 1956; cap. 145m. francs CFA; state-owned; palm-oil development.

Société de Développement de l'Agriculture au Gabon (AGRO-GABON): BP 2248, Libreville; tel. 76-40-82; fax 76-44-72; f. 1976; cap. 2,788m. francs CFA; 92% state-owned; Man. Dir ANDRÉ PAUL-APANDINA.

Société de Développement de l'Hévéaculture (HEVEGAB): BP 316, Libreville; tel. 70-03-43; telex 5615; fax 70-19-89; f. 1981; cap. 5,500m. francs CFA; 99.9% state-owned; development of rubber plantations in the Mitzic, Bitam and Kango regions; Chair. EMMANUEL ONDO-METHOGO; Man. Dir GUY DE ROQUEMAUREL.

Société Gabonaise de Recherches et d'Exploitations Minières (SOGAREM): blvd de Nice, Libreville; state-owned; research and development of gold mining; Chair. ARSÈNE BOUNGUENZA; Man. Dir SERGE GASSITA.

Société Gabonaise de Recherches Pétrolières (GABOREP): BP 564, Libreville; tel. 75-06-40; telex 8268; fax 75-06-47; exploration and exploitation of hydrocarbons; Chair. HUBERT PERRODO; Man. Dir P. F. LECA.

Société Nationale de Développement des Cultures Industrielles (SONADECI): BP 256, Libreville; tel. 76-33-97; telex 5362; f. 1978; cap. 600m. francs CFA; state-owned; agricultural development; Chair. PAUL KOUNDA KIKI; Man. Dir GEORGES BEKALÉ.

MAJOR INDUSTRIAL COMPANIES

The following are some of the largest private and state-owned companies in terms of either capital investment or employment.

L'Auxiliaire du Bâtiment J.-F. Aveyra (ABA): BP 14382, Libreville; tel. 70-44-80; telex 5454; f. 1977; cap. 1,000m. francs CFA; production of construction materials, plastics; Chair. JEAN-FRANÇOIS AVEYRA; Man. Dir G. DUTILH.

Compagnie Forestière du Gabon (CFG): BP 521, Port-Gentil; tel. 55-20-45; telex 8209; fax 55-36-43; f. 1945; cap. 6,785m. francs CFA; 63% state-owned; production of okoumé plywood and veneered quality plywoods; Chair. MICHEL ESSONGHÉ.

Compagnie des Mines d'Uranium de Franceville (COMUF): BP 260, Libreville; tel. 76-43-10; telex 5388; f. 1958; cap. 5,050m. francs CFA; 25% state-owned; uranium mining at Mounana; Man. Dir EGIDE BOUNDONO-SIMANGOYE; 998 employees.

Compagnie Minière de l'Ogooué (COMILOG): BP 27-28, Moanda; tel. 66-10-00; telex 6213; fax 66-11-57; f. 1953; cap.

32,812.5m. francs CFA; 30% owned by private Gabonese interests; manganese mining at Moanda; Pres. CLAUDE VILLAIN; Man. Dir MARCEL ABEKE; 1,405 employees.

Elf-Gabon: BP 525, Port-Gentil; tel. 75-60-00; telex 8210; f. 1934; cap. 22,500m. francs CFA; 25% state-owned, 57% owned by Elf-Aquitaine group; prospecting for and mining of petroleum; Chair. JEAN-FRANÇOIS GAVALDA; Man. Dir MARC COSSÉ; 1,157 employees.

Gabo-Ren: Port-Gentil; f. 1975; cap. 1,600m. francs CFA; 33% state-owned, 32% owned by Elf-Gabon, 35% owned by N'Ren Corpn; mfrs of artificial ammonia and urea.

Leroy-Gabon: BP 69, Libreville; tel. 72-14-14; telex 5252; fax 76-15-94; f. 1976; cap. 2,080m. francs CFA; forestry; Chair. and Man. Dir JEAN LEPRINCE.

Mobil Oil Gabon: Zone Industrielle Sud Owendo, BP 145, Libreville; tel. 70-05-48; telex 5562; fax 70-05-87; f. 1974; cap. 547m. francs CFA; storage and distribution of petroleum products; Chair. MICHEL BONNET; Man. Dir RÉGIS D'HUART.

Rougier Océan Gabon SA (ROG): BP 130, Libreville; tel. 74-31-50; telex 5257; cap. 1,200m. francs CFA; forestry and mfr of plywood; Chair. MAURICE ROUGIER; Dir HERVÉ BOZEC.

Shell Gabon: BP 146, Port-Gentil; tel. 55-26-62; telex 8206; f. 1960; cap. 15,000m. francs CFA; owned 75% by Royal Dutch-Shell group, 25% state-owned; exploration and production of hydrocarbons; Chair. and Man. Dir PAUL H. ROWLANDS.

Société Bernabé Gabon: BP 2084, Libreville; tel. 74-34-32; telex 5351; fax 76-05-21; cap. 1,000m. francs CFA; metallurgical products, construction materials, hardware; Man. Dir J. P. BERGER; Finance Dir J. LE GAL.

Société des Brasseries du Gabon (SOBRAGA): 20 blvd Léon M'Ba, BP 487, Libreville; tel. 73-23-66; telex 5275; fax 73-36-12; f. 1966; cap. 1,500m. francs CFA; mfrs of beer and soft drinks; Chair. and Man. Dir PIERRE CASTEL; Dir M. PALU.

Société des Ciments du Gabon: BP 477, Libreville; tel. 70-20-25; telex 5483; fax 70-27-05; f. 1976; cap. 12,505m. francs CFA; 91.44% state-owned, 8.55% owned by Elf-Gabon; clinker crushing works at N'Toum, Owendo (Libreville) and Franceville; Chair. LÉONARD ANDJEMBE; Man. Dir SERGE LASSENI DUBOZE.

Société d'Exploitation des Produits Oléagineux du Gabon (SEPOGA): BP 1491, Libreville; tel. 76-01-92; telex 5494; fax 74-15-67; f. 1977; cap. 732m. francs CFA; 25% state-owned, 14% owned by Shell Gabon; production and marketing of vegetable oils; Chair. PAUL KOUNDA-KIKI; Man. Dir EDMUND SCHEFFLER.

Société Gabonaise des Ferro-Alliages (SOGAFERRO): BP 2728, Moanda; telex 5218; f. 1974; cap. 1,000m. francs CFA; 10% state-owned; manganese processing; Chair. Dr HERVÉ MOUTSINGA; Man. Dir GILLES DE SEAUVE.

Société Gabonaise de Raffinage (SOGARA): BP 530, Port-Gentil; tel. 55-36-52; telex 8217; f. 1965; cap. 1,200m. francs CFA; 25% state-owned; refines locally-produced crude petroleum; Chair. RENÉ RADEMBINO CONIQUET; Man. Dir JEAN FIDÈLE OTANDO; 455 employees.

Société Gabonaise des Textiles (SOGATEX): f. 1987; 36.5% state-owned; mfrs of garments.

Société de la Haute Mondah (SHM): BP 69, Libreville; tel. 72-22-29; telex 5252; f. 1939; cap. 888m. francs CFA; forestry, plywood and sawmilling; ETIENNE GUY MOUVAGHA-TCHIOBA; Man. Dir M. DEJOIE.

Société Industrielle d'Agriculture et d'Elevage de Boumango (SIAEB): BP 68, Franceville; tel. 67-72-88; telex 3301; f. 1977; cap. 1,740m. francs CFA; 35% state-owned; maize, soya, rice and poultry production; Man. Dir JEAN-JACQUES DUBOIS.

Société Industrielle Textile du Gabon (SOTEGA): blvd Léon M'Ba, BP 2171, Libreville; tel. 72-19-29; telex 5236; f. 1968; cap. 260m. francs CFA; 15% state-owned; textile printing; Chair. RAPHAËL EBOBOCA; Man. Dir M. MARESCAUX.

Société Italo-Gabonaise des Marbres (SIGAMA): BP 3893, Libreville; tel. 72-25-83; telex 5384; f. 1974; cap. 542m. francs CFA; operates a marble quarry and factory at Doussé Oussou; Man. Dir FRANCO MARCHIO.

Société Meunière et Avicole du Gabon (SMAG): BP 462, Libreville; tel. 70-18-76; telex 5298; fax 70-28-12; f. 1968; cap. 910m. francs CFA; partly state-owned; production of eggs, cattle-food, flour, bread; Chair. J. LOUIS VILGRAIN; Dir X. THOMAS; 475 employees.

Société des Mines de Fer de Mekambo (SOMIFER): Libreville; tel. 73-28-58; f. 1960; cap. 900m. francs CFA; 49% state-owned; mineral prospecting and mining; Chair. ADAMA DIALLO; Dir JEAN AUDIBERT.

Société de Mise en Valeur du Bois (SOMIVAB): BP 3893, Libreville; tel. 78-18-27; telex 5384; cap. 1,550m. francs CFA; forestry, sawmill, mfrs of sleepers for Transgabon railway; Chair. HERVÉ MOUTSINGA; Man. Dir FRANCO MARCHIO.

Société Nationale des Bois du Gabon (SNBG): BP 67, Libreville; tel. 76-47-94; telex 5201; f. 1944; cap. 1,000m. francs CFA; 51% state-owned; has a monopoly of marketing all okoumé production; Chair. and Man. Dir MAMADOU DIOP; 500 employees.

Société National de Distribution de Produits Pétroliers (PIZO): BP 4030, Libreville; tel. 72-01-21; telex 5526; f. 1975; cap. 1,500m. francs CFA; 50% state-owned, proposed transfer to private ownership announced 1986; Chair. and Man. Dir JEAN-BERNARD SAULNEROND-MAPANGOU.

Société National Immobilière (SNI): BP 515, Libreville; tel. 76-05-81; f. 1976; cap. 750m. francs CFA; 77% state-owned; development and maintenance of housing; Chair. and Man. Dir GEORGES ISSEMBE.

Société Pizo de Formulation de Lubrifiants (PIZOLUB): BP 699, Port-Gentil; tel. 55-28-40; telex 8299; fax 55-03-82; f. 1978; cap. 500m. francs CFA; 49% state-owned; mfrs of lubricating materials; Chair. MARCEL SANDOUNGOUT; Dir-Gen. PIERRE RIPOLL.

Société Sucrière du Haut-Ogooué (SOSUHO): BP 1180, Libreville; tel. 72-00-51; telex 5298; f. 1974; cap. 500m. francs CFA; sugar production and agro-industrial complex at Ouélé; Chair. L. SABA; Man. Dir P.-Y. LE MAOUT.

Société des Télécommunications Internationales Gabonaises (TIG): BP 2261, Libreville; tel. 78-77-56; telex 5200; fax 74-19-09; f. 1971; cap. 3,000m. francs CFA; 61% state-owned; study and development of international telecommunications systems; Man. Dir A. N'GOUMA MWYUMALA.

TRADE UNIONS

Confédération Gabonaise des Syndicats Libres (CGSL): Libreville; Sec.-Gen. FRANCIS MAYOMBO.

Confédération Syndicale Gabonaise (COSYGA): BP 14017, Libreville; telex 5623; f. 1969, by the Govt, as a specialized organ of the PDG, to organize and educate workers, to contribute to social peace and economic development, and to protect the rights of trade unions; Gen. Sec. MARTIN ALLINI.

Transport

RAILWAYS

The construction of the Transgabonais railway, which comprises a section running from Owendo (the port of Libreville) to Booué (340 km) and a second section from Booué to Franceville (357 km), was completed in December 1986. By 1989 regular services were operating between Libreville and Franceville. More than 3m. metric tons of freight and 175,000 passengers were carried on the network in 1995. Plans to transfer ownership of the railways to the private sector were announced in 1996.

Office du Chemin de Fer Transgabonais (OCTRA): BP 2198, Libreville; tel. 70-24-78; telex 5663; fax 70-27-68; f. 1972; state-owned; Chair. ALEXANDRE AYO BARRO; Dir-Gen. CÉLESTIN NDOLIA-NHAUD.

ROADS

In 1995 there were an estimated 7,633 km of roads, including 3,750 km of main roads and 2,410 km of secondary roads; about 626 km of the road network was paved. In 1992 a seven-year project to surface some 1,400 km of road by the year 2000 was announced. In the same year a programme was initiated to construct a further 1,851 km of roads, at an estimated cost of some US $528m.

INLAND WATERWAYS

The principal river is the Ogooué, navigable from Port-Gentil to Ndjolé (310 km) and serving the towns of Lambaréné, Ndjolé and Sindara.

Compagnie de Navigation Intérieure (CNI): BP 3982, Libreville; tel. 72-39-28; fax 74-04-11; f. 1978; cap. 500m. francs CFA; state-owned; inland waterway transport; agencies at Port-Gentil, Mayumba and Lambaréné; Chair. JEAN-PIERRE MENGWANG ME NGYEMA; Dir-Gen. JEAN LOUIS POUNAH-NDJIMBI.

SHIPPING

The principal deep-water ports are Port-Gentil, which handles mainly petroleum exports, and Owendo, 15 km from Libreville, which services mainly barge traffic. The principal ports for timber are at Owendo, Mayumba and Nyanga, and there is a fishing port at Libreville. The construction of a deep-water port at Mayumba is planned. A new terminal for the export of minerals, at Owendo, was opened in 1988. In 1989 the merchant shipping fleet had a total displacement of 25,000 grt, compared with a displacement of 98,000 grt in 1985.

Compagnie de Manutention et de Chalandage d'Owendo (COMACO): BP 2131, Libreville; tel. 70-26-35; telex 5208; f. 1974; Pres. GEORGES RAWIRI; Dir in Libreville M. RAYMOND.

Office des Ports et Rades du Gabon (OPRAG): BP 1051, Libreville; tel. 70-00-48; telex 5319; fax 70-37-35; f. 1974; state-owned; national port authority; Pres. ALI BONGO; Dir-Gen. PHILIBERT ANDZEMBE.

SAGA Gabon: BP 518, Port-Gentil; tel. 55-54-00; telex 8205; fax 55-21-71; Chair. G. COGNON; Man. Dir J. C. SIMON.

Société Nationale d'Acconage et de Transit (SNAT): BP 3897, Libreville; tel. 70-04-04; telex 5420; fax 70-13-11; f. 1976; 51% state-owned; freight transport; Dir-Gen. CLAUDE AYO-IGUENDHA.

Société Nationale de Transports Maritimes (SONATRAM): BP 3841, Libreville; tel. 74-06-32; telex 5289; fax 74-59-67; f. 1976; relaunched 1995; 51% state-owned; river and ocean cargo transport; Man. Dir RAPHAEL MOARA WALLA.

Société du Port Minéralier d'Owendo: f. 1987; cap. 4,000m. francs CFA; majority holding by COMILOG; management of new terminal for minerals at Owendo.

SOCOPAO–Gabon: BP 4, Libreville; tel. 70-21-40; telex 5212; fax 70-02-76; f. 1963; freight transport and storage; Dir HENRI LECORDIER.

CIVIL AVIATION

There are international airports at Libreville, Port-Gentil and Franceville, 65 other public and 50 private airfields linked mostly with the forestry and petroleum industries.

Air Affaires Gabon: BP 3962, Libreville; tel. 73-25-13; telex 5360; fax 73-49-98; f. 1975; domestic passenger chartered and scheduled flights; Chair. RAYMOND BELLANGER; Dir-Gen. Commdr RENÉ MORVAN.

Air Service Gabon (ASG): BP 2232, Libreville; tel. 73-24-08; telex 5522; fax 73-60-69; f. 1965; charter flights; Chair. JÉRÔME OKINDA; Gen. Man. FRANCIS LASCOMBES.

Compagnie Nationale Air Gabon: BP 2206, Libreville; tel. 73-00-27; telex 5371; fax 73-11-56; f. 1951 as Cie Aérienne Gabonaise; began operating international services in 1977, following Gabon's withdrawal from Air Afrique (see under Côte d'Ivoire); 80% state-owned; internal and international cargo and passenger services; Chair. MARTIN BONGO; Dir-Gen. Commdr RENÉ MORVAN.

Société de Gestion de l'Aéroport de Libreville (ADL): BP 363, Libreville; tel. 73-62-44; fax 73-61-28; f. 1988; 26.5% state-owned; management of airport at Libreville; Pres. CHANTAL LIDJI BADINGA; Dir-Gen. PIERRE ANDRÉ COLLET.

Tourism

Tourist arrivals were estimated at 103,000 in 1994, while receipts from tourism totalled US $5m. The tourist sector is being extensively developed, with new hotels and associated projects and the promotion of national parks. In 1996 there were 74 hotels, with a total of 4,000 rooms.

Centre de Promotion Touristique du Gabon (GABONTOUR): BP 2085, Libreville; tel. 74-67-90; f. 1988; Dir-Gen. JUSTE LAMBERT LOUMBANGOYE.

Office National Gabonais du Tourisme: BP 161, Libreville; tel. 72-21-82.

Defence

In August 1996 the army consisted of 3,200 men, the air force of 1,000 men, and the navy of 500 men. Paramilitary forces numbered 4,800 (including a gendarmerie of 2,000). Military service is voluntary. In mid-1996 France deployed a military detachment of 600 in Gabon.

Defence Expenditure: Estimated at 51,000m. francs CFA in 1996.

Commander-in-Chief of the Armed Forces: Maj.-Gen. ANDRÉ OYINI.

Education

Education is officially compulsory for 10 years between six and 16 years of age: in 1984 an estimated 75% of children in the relevant age-group attended primary and secondary schools (78% of boys; 72% of girls). Primary and secondary education is provided by the state and mission schools. Primary education begins at the age of six and lasts for six years. Secondary education, beginning at 12 years of age, lasts for up to seven years, comprising a first cycle of four years and a second of three years. The Université Omar Bongo, at Libreville, had 2,741 students in 1986. The Université des Sciences et des Techniques de Masuku, at Franceville, was opened in 1986, with an enrolment of 550 students. Many students go to France for university and technical training. In 1995, according to estimates by UNESCO, adult illiteracy averaged 36.8% (males 26.3%; females 46.7%). The 1994 budget allocated 78,850m. francs CFA (19% of total administrative spending) to expenditure on education.

Bibliography

Aicardi de Saint-Paul, M. *Le Gabon du roi Denis à Omar Bongo.* Paris, Editions Albatros, 1987. Trans. (Palmer, A. F., and Palmer, T.) as *Gabon: The Development of a Nation.* New York and London, Routledge, 1989.

Ambouroué-Avaro, J. *Un peuple gabonais à l'aube de la colonisation.* Paris, Editions Karthala, 1983.

Barnes, J. F. *Gabon: Beyond the Colonial Legacy.* Boulder, CO, Westview Press, 1992.

Bongo, O. *El Hadj Omar Bongo par lui-même.* Libreville, Multipress Gabon, 1988.

Bory, P. *The New Gabon.* Monaco, 1978.

Bouquerel, J. *Le Gabon.* Paris, Presses universitaires de France, 1970.

Deschamps, H. *Traditions orales et archives du Gabon.* Paris, Berger-Levrault, 1962.

Fernandez, J. W. *Bwiti.* Princeton, NJ, Princeton University Press, 1982.

Gaulme, F. *Le Pays de Cama Gabon.* Paris, Editions Karthala, 1983.

Le Gabon et son ombre. Paris, Editions Karthala, 1988.

McKay, J. 'West Central Africa', in Mansell Prothero, R. (Ed.), *A Geography of Africa*, London, 1969.

Péan, P. *Affaires africaines.* Paris, Fayard, 1983.

Raponda-Walker, A. *Notes d'histoire du Gabon.* Montpellier, Imprimerie Charité, 1960.

Vennetier, P. 'Problems of port development in Gabon and Congo', in Hoyle, B. S. and Hilling, D. (Eds), *Seaports and Development in Tropical Africa.* London, 1970.

Les Plans de Développement des Pays d'Afrique Noire. 4th Edn, Paris, Ediafric, 1977.

L'Economie Gabonaise. Ediafric, Paris, 1977.

THE GAMBIA

Physical and Social Geography

R. J. HARRISON CHURCH

The Republic of The Gambia occupies an area of 11,295 sq km (4,361 sq miles). Its population (enumerated at 1,025,867 in April 1993, according to provisional census results) is, however, one of the fastest-growing of mainland Africa: the government reported a rate of population growth of 4.2% in 1996. Apart from a very short coastline, The Gambia is a semi-enclave in Senegal, with which it shares some physical and social phenomena, but differs in history, colonial experience and certain economic affiliations.

The Gambia essentially comprises the valley of the navigable Gambia river. Around the estuary (3 km wide at its narrowest point) and the lower river, the state is 50 km wide, and extends eastward either side of the navigable river for 470 km. In most places the country is only 24 km wide with but one or two villages within it on either bank, away from mangrove or marsh. The former extends about 150 km upstream, the limit of the tide in the rainy season, although in the dry season and in drought years the tide penetrates further upstream. Annual rainfall in The Gambia averages 1,150 mm.

Small ocean-going vessels can reach Kaur, 190 km upstream, throughout the year; Georgetown, 283 km upstream, is accessible to some small craft. River vessels regularly call at Fatoto, 464 km upstream, the last of 33 wharf towns served by schooners or river boats. Unfortunately, this fine waterway is underutilized because it is separated from most of its natural hinterland by the nearby frontier with Senegal.

Some mangrove on the landward sides has been removed for swamp rice cultivation. Behind are seasonally flooded marshes with freshwater grasses, and then on the upper slopes of Tertiary sandstone there is woodland with fallow bush and areas cultivated mainly with groundnuts and millet.

The Gambia has no commercially exploitable mineral resources, although reserves of petroleum have been identified.

The principal ethnic groups are the Mandinka, Fula, Wollof, Jola and Serahuli. There is also a small but influential Creole (Aku) community. Each ethnic group has its own vernacular language, although the official language is English.

Recent History

JOHN A. WISEMAN

Although European contact with the region constituting The Gambia dates back to the 15th century, it was not until 1816 that the British founded a settlement at what they named Bathurst (now Banjul). Establishment of control over the whole territory came in the later part of the 19th century, and until 1888 the territory was formally administered from Sierra Leone. For much of the early colonial period an exchange arrangement with France was envisaged, whereby the French would take control of The Gambia and unite it with Senegal, in return for which Britain would be ceded some other French-held territory. However, no such agreement was ever finalized, and The Gambia remained a separate colonial entity.

Under British colonial rule the division of the territory into crown colony (Banjul and adjacent areas) and protectorate (virtually all the rest) had a marked effect on political geography, as it was not until 1960 that the franchise was granted to the latter. The early development of political parties was thus confined to the urban coastal areas, where the United Party (UP), led by a Wollof Banjul lawyer, P. S. N'jie, emerged as the most important. The situation changed in 1959 with the establishment of the Protectorate People's Party (PPP, subsequently the People's Progressive Party), led by Dr (later Sir) Dawda Jawara, a rural Mandinka veterinary officer. Following the extension of the franchise to the rural population, the PPP became the dominant party, winning an overall majority in the 1962 elections. On assuming the premiership, Jawara widened the PPP's support-base by forming alliances with many of the coastal political élites. On 18 February 1965 The Gambia became an independent state, within the Commonwealth, with Jawara as prime minister.

JAWARA AND THE PPP, 1965–94

From independence in 1965 until the successful military *coup d'état* of July 1994, political life and government control were firmly concentrated in the hands of Sir Dawda Jawara and the PPP, and Jawara remained the pivotal figure in Gambian politics. Most of the changes in party formation and political factionalism were based on the making and breaking of alliances between Jawara and other prominent Gambian political figures, a process which was often highly personalized. Successive general elections resulted in firm parliamentary majorities for the PPP, although opposition parties always managed to secure minority representation in the legislature.

In November 1965 a national referendum was organized on the issue of transforming The Gambia into a republic. Although Jawara strongly supported the move to republican status, the proposal failed to gain the necessary two-thirds' majority of the popular vote and was temporarily abandoned. A second referendum on the issue, in April 1970, produced the necessary majority, and the country became a republic on 24 April. As leader of the majority party in parliament, Jawara became president of the republic, replacing the British monarch as head of state. (Separate direct elections for the presidency were not introduced until 1982.) The opposition UP went into steady decline after independence, its representation falling from eight seats (of 32) in the 1966 parliamentary elections to three in 1972. In 1975 a new opposition party, the National Convention Party (NCP), was formed under the leadership of Sherif Dibba, previously a leading figure in the PPP who had served as vice-president before his expulsion from the ruling party. Dibba, like Jawara a Mandinka, was able to build some support on the basis of a strong feeling among many of that ethnic group that, in building wider coalitions, Jawara had neglected the interests of his own people. In the 1977 elections the NCP won five of 34 elective seats in the house of representatives, gaining support not only from the Baddibu Mandinka but also from a more ethnically diverse group of opponents of the PPP in urban areas. The UP, winning just two seats, thereafter ceased to exist as an electoral force. The late 1970s also saw the formation of a number of small Marxist-inclined organizations, among them the Gambia Socialist Revolutionary Party (GSRP) and the Movement for Justice in Africa–The Gambia (MOJA–G), and of several clandestine 'underground' groups, although none of these appeared to have any real political influence.

In July 1981, while Jawara was out of the country, dissident members of the paramilitary field force (the country had no army at this time) allied with some of the small radical groupings to attempt a *coup d'état*. Although the rebels initially gained control of several key buildings in the capital, resistance from members of the field force loyal to Jawara, in co-operation with members of the government, prevented outright victory for the rebels. Jawara secured from Senegal the support of troops to help suppress the coup attempt, and, following a week of fierce fighting in and around Banjul, the rebellion was crushed. At least 1,000 people (possibly double that number) were killed in the conflict: much of the killing involved neither the rebels nor the loyal troops and their Senegalese allies, but resulted from the release and arming of convicts from gaol in Banjul, who conducted a campaign of looting and murder. As the Jawara government was returned to power some 1,000 people were detained, although many were soon released without being brought to trial. Since the Gambian legal system was unable to process the number of detainees, judges and lawyers were brought in from other Commonwealth countries. Among those charged was Sherif Dibba, who was subsequently acquitted and released.

There were two important ramifications of the coup attempt. The first was the establishment of a confederation with Senegal in February 1982. The Senegambian confederation was always more favoured by the Senegalese authorities than it was by the Gambians, and for most of the decade the pattern of relationships was one of the former's trying to establish ever greater unity while the smaller partner perceived the need to preserve its independent sovereignty: fears of Senegalese domination have long been a feature of Gambian political consciousness. The confederal partners' differences of approach produced numerous disagreements and tensions, and in September 1989 the Senegambian confederation was formally dissolved. The second development arising from the coup attempt was the establishment for the first time of a Gambian army. Initially the army was raised as part of a confederal army, which tended to be dominated in terms of finance and leadership by Senegal, but the subsequent dissolution of the confederation left the Gambian national army (GNA) as an independent force. Even before the 1994 coup there were several indications of dissatisfaction within the GNA. In June 1991 Gambian soldiers who had served in Liberia, as members of the ECOMOG force of the Economic Community of West African States (ECOWAS), staged a protest in Banjul over the late payment of allowances and general conditions of service. In February 1992 senior officers managed to contain a similar protest within the confines of the army barracks.

The effects of the 1981 coup attempt on Gambian party politics were less marked, and the PPP continued to dominate. Elections were held on schedule in May 1982. Although Dibba was still in detention at this time, he and the NCP participated in the elections. Jawara was re-elected president, with 72% of the votes, overwhelmingly defeating Dibba. Once again the PPP emerged with a clear majority in parliament, winning 27 seats, compared with three obtained by the NCP and five by independent candidates (most of these in fact PPP members who had had some dispute with their local party organization). In February 1985 apparent normality was restored to Gambian politics with the ending of the state of emergency imposed following the coup attempt. In 1986 two new political parties were created. The Gambia People's Party (GPP) was established and led by Assan Musa Camara, who (like Dibba in the 1970s) had previously been a leading figure in the PPP and national vice-president. Also formed in 1986 was the People's Democratic Organization for Independence and Socialism (PDOIS), led by Halifa Sallah and Sam Sarr—both of whom had been detained briefly in 1981. With a distinctive socialist approach, the PDOIS offered a clear ideological choice to the electorate (in reality, the other major parties differed little in terms of political doctrine). However, at the May 1987 elections neither of the new parties took a single parliamentary seat. The NCP increased its representation in parliament to five elective seats, but all of the remainder were won by the PPP. In the presidential election Jawara took 59% of the votes, defeating Dibba (27%) and Camara (14%). Prior to the April 1992 elections Jawara announced that he wished to retire from politics, but was said to have been persuaded by his party colleagues to seek re-election once more. He proceeded to secure 58% of the popular vote. Dibba (who won 22% of the votes), Camara and two others also contested the presidency. Although the 1992 elections (the last before the imposition of military rule) marked an upturn in support for opposition parties—in the parliamentary elections the NCP won six seats, the GPP two, and independent candidates three—the results did not deviate significantly from the pattern set in all previous post-independence elections, and Jawara and the PPP (whose parliamentary representation had been reduced to 25 members) retained comfortable majorities.

Jawara reshuffled his cabinet following the 1992 elections. One of the more unexpected aspects of this reorganization was the promotion to the vice-presidency of Saihou Sabally, regarded by many as tainted by allegations of corruption, in place of the widely respected Bakary Dabo (who now took the finance portfolio). Sabally's appointment fuelled increasingly outspoken allegations of corruption and mismanagement in public life. In late 1993 leading Christian and Islamic clerics in Banjul publicly accused the government of corruption, embezzlement and lack of financial accountability, which they claimed were causing hardship for the majority of the population and benefiting only a few élite. In January 1994 Jawara announced the establishment of an independent public complaints commission, with the aim of combating corruption in public life. However, while public dissatisfaction with the PPP regime certainly appeared to be increasing in late 1993 and early 1994, there was little indication of the dramatic political change that was shortly to occur.

MILITARY GOVERNMENT

On July 22 1994 Jawara and his government were overthrown by a military *coup d'état*. Although the coup appears to have had little or no advance planning, it took place without bloodshed and met with very little resistance. Soldiers from the GNA seized key installations, including the airport and national radio headquarters, and marched on government buildings in Banjul. Jawara and some of his government colleagues (including vice-president Sabally), boarded a US naval vessel that was anchored off the coast in preparation for scheduled training exercises involving US marines and the GNA. Jawara appealed unsuccessfully for the rebels to return to barracks, and for the US marines to put down the coup, and he and his entourage were disembarked in Senegal. (Jawara subsequently took up residence in the United Kingdom.) In The Gambia, meanwhile, senior members of the army and the police, together with those members of the government who had not escaped, were arrested and placed in detention. That evening radio broadcasts were made announcing that government was now in the hands of an armed forces provisional ruling council (AFPRC), led by Lt (later Capt.) Yahya Jammeh. The other members of the council were Lts Sana Sabally, Sadibou Hydara, Edward Singhateh and Yankuba Touray (all of whom were susequently promoted to the rank of captain). While they were of diverse ethnic background, the common feature of this group was their extreme youth: none was more than 30 years of age at the time of the coup. The AFPRC announced the suspension of the constitution, a ban on all political parties and political activity, the temporary closure of the country's borders and a dusk-to-dawn curfew, and gave warning that they would 'mercilessly crush' any opposition to the take-over. Jammeh's early speeches, justifying the coup by portraying the Jawara regime as corrupt, inefficient and not truly democratic, while promising 'a new era of freedom, progress, democracy and accountability', resembled many post-coup speeches in other African states. The absence of any mention of specific changes to be sought in the country's political or economic system probably reflected the rather precipitate manner in which the coup had occurred. Although not articulated by the new regime, grievances specific to the army—such as the late or non-payment of salaries to soldiers involved in ECOMOG operations in Liberia, poor standards of food and accommodation for troops, and the lack of prospects for promotion caused by the deployment in senior positions in the GNA of officers seconded in accordance with a bilateral defence accord with Nigeria—could also be regarded as motives for the coup. Jammeh announced the formation of a provisional cabinet, comprising both soldiers and civilians. Almost immediately, however, two military members of the cabinet were dismissed and arrested. The frequency of cabinet changes has been a continuous feature of the Jammeh regime. In order to increase the technical competence of the cabinet, Jammeh appointed two ex-PPP ministers: Bakary Dabo resumed the finance portfolio, and Fafa M'bai (a minister of justice in the early 1980s, who had led an anti-corruption campaign but subsequently himself been implicated in allegations of financial impropriety and forced to resign) as minister of justice and attorney-general, but both appointments proved relatively brief. Dabo was dismissed in October 1994 and fled the country in the following month (see below), while M'bai was removed from office in March 1995 and subsequently arrested and charged with corruption.

International reaction to the military take-over, especially from major aid donors such as the USA, the European Union (EU), the United Kingdom and Japan, was generally unfavourable, and, when attempts to persuade the AFPRC to restore the elected regime failed, efforts were concentrated on a fairly rapid return to democratic rule. Arab donor states such as Saudi Arabia and Kuwait agreed, none the less, to continue funding aid projects; relations with Libya improved significantly, and the restoration of full diplomatic relations (severed in 1980) in November 1994 was accompanied by Libyan aid for the regime. Diplomatic links were established with Taiwan in July 1995, whereupon the People's Republic of China (which had maintained aid to The Gambia following the coup) suspended relations.

In September 1994 the AFPRC established several commissions of inquiry to examine allegations of corruption and maladministration in the public sector under Jawara. Commissions examining the assets of public officers, the working of government departments and public corporations, as well as the issue of land allocation, were set up under the guidance of senior legal practitioners, recruited from Sierra Leone and Ghana as well as locally. Many prominent political figures and civil servants from the Jawara period, together with large numbers of business executives (many of whom had strong political connections), were summoned before the commissions to answer for their past actions; cases involving individuals who had fled the country since the coup were examined in their absence. Even allowing for the fact that the commissions were designed, in part, to discredit the previous regime, they were seen to act according to due legal process and without direct interference from the military AFPRC, and they undoubtedly uncovered significant and genuine evidence of widespread, systematic corruption, as well as high levels of bureaucratic confusion and chaos. The commissions continued to operate in 1995–97.

The AFPRC survived an attempted counter-coup from within the military in November 1994. After fierce fighting in the army barracks, the coup leader, Lt Basiru Barrow (the commander of the first infantry battalion), and several other officers of equivalent rank were killed by forces loyal to the government. Allegations of summary executions following the defeat of the coup attempt were denied by the authorities. Several senior PPP figures were arrested but later released. Bakary Dabo fled to Senegal amid unsubstantiated government assertions that he had been involved in the plot. A significant repercussion of this coup attempt was that the British government issued a warning to travellers that The Gambia was unsafe, causing most major tour companies in the United Kingdom to suspend operations in The Gambia. This had a devastating effect on the tourist industry (see Economy).

An even more serious attempt at a coup took place in January 1995, when two of the most senior AFPRC members, vice-chairman Sana Sabally and the minister of the interior, Sadibou Hydara, reportedly attempted to assassinate Jammeh and seize power. The attempt was defeated, and Sabally and Hydara were imprisoned. (In June Hydara died in prison, officially of natural causes.) Edward Singhateh was promoted to the post of AFPRC vice-chairman, while Capts Lamin Bajo and Ebou Jallow were appointed to the council as minister of the interior and AFPRC spokesman, respectively. Official reports of events surrounding the attempted *putsch* were contradicted by persistent rumours in The Gambia (by their nature impossible to substantiate) that Jammeh had fabricated allegations of a coup in order to eliminate those whom he regarded as potential rivals. With their detention, an open campaign of vilification of Sabally and Hydara was undertaken by the remaining members of the AFPRC. In December Sabally was sentenced by court martial to nine years' imprisonment for plotting to overthrow Jammeh.

Unity within the reorganized AFPRC was short-lived. In October 1995 Ebou Jallow fled the country amid accusations that he had embezzled government funds amounting to US $3m. and was conspiring with members of the banned PPP. Jallow denied the theft, and accused Jammeh's regime of tyranny and corruption—producing documentary evidence purportedly relating to the latter. In December two further senior military figures (not AFPRC members) fled the country: these were Capt. Pa Sanneh, head of the Gambian contingent of ECOMOG, and Maj. David Coker, third-in-command of the GNA.

The frequency of arrests of politicians and journalists (and for foreign—mainly Liberian and Sierra Leonean—journalists, deportations), as well as allegations of the harassment of civilians by the military, fuelled accusations of authoritarianism on the part of the Jammeh regime. There was, notably, considerable national shock in June 1995, when the body was discovered of Ousman Koro Ceesay, since March the finance minister (and an 'honorary member' of the AFPRC): although the authorities attributed his death to a motor accident, rumours circulated of more suspicious circumstances. Ceesay was replaced in the government by Bala Garba Jahumpa, who had held the finance portfolio between October 1994 and March 1995. In June the AFPRC established a new police organization, the national intelligence agency, which was given wide powers of surveillance and arrest, and in August the restoration of the death penalty (abolished in 1993) was attributed to an increase in the incidence of murder. A government decree issued in November 1995 accorded the minister of the interior (an AFPRC member) unlimited powers of arrest and detention without charge: the decree appeared to have been frequently used against suspected opponents of the regime, and there were increasingly frequent allegations of the torture of political detainees.

Constitutional Debate

Of paramount importance following the seizure of power by the military was the issue of a return to democratic civilian rule, to which the AFPRC consistently expressed its commitment. Much public debate focused on the timetable for, and manner of, such a restoration. In October the AFPRC announced what it termed its programme of rectification and transition to democratic constitutional rule, which provided for the restitution of elected civilian organs of state in 1998—four years from the seizure of power. This timetable was heavily criticized both within The Gambia and abroad. Gambian trade unions, professional associations, former opposition politicians and journalists united to condemn the length of the proposed transitional period. Internationally, the intended duration of military rule was denounced by the United Kingdom, the USA, the EU and the Commonwealth, as well as by human rights groups and many others. Apparently in response to such generally adverse reactions, Jammeh announced at the end of November 1994 the establishment of a national consultative committee (NCC) to examine the question of the transition, and indicated that he was willing to reconsider the timetable. The NCC consisted of 23 members appointed by the AFPRC: its chairman was Dr Lenrie Peters, a widely respected writer and physician, and it included representatives of trade unions, religious groups, women's organizations, professional associations and leading traditional chiefs. Following nation-wide consultations and meetings with representatives of The Gambia's aid donors, in January 1995 the NCC submitted its recommendation to the AFPRC that the transition period be reduced to two years from the time of the coup, a timetable which had majority support within the country and was more likely to be acceptable to external creditors. Jammeh subsequently announced that he would accept the revised programme, but rejected a further NCC suggestion that an interim civilian government be established while he remained head of state. The reduction in the proposed duration of military rule was generally welcomed in The Gambia and abroad; however, prominent creditors, including the EU and the USA, continued to withhold assistance, stating that they wished to see a shorter period of transition to civilian government.

After some delay, attributed to financial problems, the AFPRC established a constitutional review commission (CRC) in April 1995, under the chairmanship of a Ghanaian lawyer, Justice Gilbert Mensah Quaye. The CRC began a series of public hearings, at which all citizens were invited to make proposals regarding constitutional change. One of the most contentious issues to emerge at the public hearings, and one much discussed in the Gambian press, was the question of what should be the minimum age for presidential candidates. Underlying this debate was the widespread belief that Jammeh was himself planning to contest the presidency in 1996, although Jammeh consistently refused to confirm or deny this. Those suggesting a minimum age of 40 were interpreted as seeking to preclude Jammeh's candidature. There was at this time increasing criticism that Jammeh's tours of the country resembled an election campaign, while civilian politicians were still forbidden by military decree to organize political meetings of any sort. Jammeh's cause was, moreover, now supported by the July 22 Movement: although ostensibly a non-governmental development organization, the movement appeared to be functioning as a quasi-political party.

The CRC submitted its draft document to the AFPRC in November 1995, although none of its findings was made public until March 1996—prompting suspicion in some quarters that in the intervening period the AFPRC had been able to accept, amend, or reject the commission's recommendations without public consultation. In April it was announced that the elections were to be postponed, on the grounds that there was insufficient time to complete preparations, and in May voting was set for September (presidential) and December (legislative); the ban on political parties was to remain in place until after the constitutional referendum, which was to take place in August. Many aspects of the constitution and the new electoral arrangements provoked concern among opponents of the AFPRC, who stated that the transition process had now been manipulated to promote Jammeh's election to the presidency and give political advantage to his supporters. The stipulation that presidential candidates must be aged between 30 and 65 years ensured Jammeh's eligibility for office, while preventing many veteran politicians from participating; there was to be no restriction on the number of times a president might seek re-election. The revised demarcation of constituency boundaries, it was alleged, would unduly favour the incumbent regime, and significant financial obstacles to political organizations seeking elected public office had been presented by raising both the deposit required from candidates and the proportion of the vote necessary to secure the deposit's return. Meanwhile, human rights organizations were critical of effective provision in the proposed constitution for the revocation of political freedoms in the event of a state of public emergency.

In January 1996 Jawara was charged *in absentia* with embezzlement, following investigations into the alleged diversion of proceeds (estimated at more than US $11m.) from the sale of petroleum donated by Nigeria; similarly charged was a Sierra Leonean business executive, now resident in Panama. Moreover, the possible involvement in the affair of a former vice-president of Sierra Leone, Abdulai Conteh, who had been resident in The Gambia since 1993, was also reported to have been investigated during anti-corruption proceedings: Conteh was briefly detained in mid-October 1995 and subsequently ordered to leave the country. During March–April 1996 the confiscation was ordered of the assets in The Gambia of Jawara and 11 former government members. In July the minister of health and social welfare was arrested and charged with the misappropriation of state funds.

The referendum on the constitution took place (one day later than scheduled) on 8 August 1996. The rate of participation was high (more than 85%), and more than 70.4% of voters were reported to have endorsed the new document. A presidential decree was issued on 14 August reauthorizing party political activity. Shortly afterwards, however, it was announced that the PPP, the NCP and the GPP were to be prohibited from contesting the forthcoming elections, as were all holders of executive office in the 30 years prior to the 1994 military takeover; thus, the only pre-coup parties authorized to contest the elections were the PDOIS and the People's Democratic Party. The effective ban on participation in the restoration of elected institutions of all those associated with political life prior to July 1994 provoked strong criticism from the Commonwealth, whose Ministerial Action Group on the Harare Declaration (CMAG) had hitherto made a significant contribution to the transition process. At the same time it was announced that, following consultations between the military authorities and the independent electoral commission (which had expressed concern that political organizations would have insufficient time to campaign for the elections), the presidential poll was to be postponed by two weeks, to 26 September 1996.

ELECTIONS AND BEYOND

As the ban on all political organizations remained in force until only weeks before the presidential election, the formation of parties was a fairly rushed affair. As had been widely anticipated, the July 22 Movement transformed itself into an official political grouping to support Jammeh's campaign for the presidency, styling itself the Alliance for Patriotic Reorientation and Construction (APRC). The PDOIS nominated Sidia Jatta as its presidential candidate. Some of the elements associated with the pre-1994 parliamentary parties formed the United Democratic Party (UDP) under the leadership of a prominent human rights lawyer, Ousainou Darboe, who became the party's candidate. Hamat Bah was to contest the presidency as the candidate of the 'personalist' National Reconciliation Party (NRP). In early September 1996 Jammeh and his AFPRC colleagues formally retired from the GNA: Jammeh was to contest the presidency as a civilian, as required by the constitution.

The short presidential campaign was widely condemned by opponents of the Jammeh regime as having been neither free nor fair, while international observers, including CMAG, expressed doubts as to the credibility of the election. The state-owned media, including the recently established television service, promoted Jammeh while offering minimal coverage of the other candidates' campaigns. Moreover, the APRC enjoyed privileged access to government finance and resources. There were reports of violence and intimidation, often involving military personnel, directed especially at the UDP. As polling proceeded, on 26 September 1996, Ousainou Darboe sought refuge in the Senegalese embassy in Banjul, having received threats to his life; he remained there until the end of the month. The official results of voting, issued on 27 September, gave Jammeh 55.77% of the votes. Darboe polled 35.84%, Bah 5.52% and Jatta 2.87%. A further set of 'leaked' results later indicated a victory for Darboe, but these had limited credibility. The dissolution of the AFPRC was also announced on 27 September: pending the legislative elections, the cabinet was to be the sole provisional governing body. Jammeh was inaugurated as president on 18 October. In early November an unconditional amnesty was proclaimed for more than 40 political detainees, among them former government ministers detained since July 1994.

Following considerable debate among the opposition parties as to whether to participate in the legislative elections, now scheduled (after a further postponement) for 2 January 1997, all decided to present candidates. Only the APRC had the organization and finance to field candidates in all 45 constituencies (in five of these they were unopposed); the UDP was to contest 34 seats, the PDOIS 17, and the NRP five. The APRC again made full use of state resources and media, but violence and intimidation were generally acknowledged as having occurred at a much reduced level. Some opposition activists, including one UDP candidate, were, none the less, detained for all or part of the campaign period. Voting took place as scheduled, and the Gambian authorities, opposition groups and most international observers expressed broad satisfaction at the conduct of the poll. The official results of the elections gave the APRC 28 seats (plus the five unopposed) in the new national assembly, with 52% of the votes cast. The UDP won seven seats, with 34% of the votes, the PDOIS one seat, with 8%, and the NRP two seats, with 2%; two independent candidates also secured seats. Jammeh's presidency thus had the backing of a significant legislative majority. As head of state, Jammeh was empowered by the constitution to nominate four additional members of parliament, from whom the speaker (and deputy speaker) would be chosen. The opening session of the national assembly, held on 16 January, accordingly elected Mustapha Wadda, previously secretary-general of the APRC and secretary at the presidency, as speaker. This session denoted the full entry into force of the constitution and thus the inauguration of the second republic.

In early February 1997 most remaining long-term political detainees, including army and police personnel, were released. Later in the month, none the less, there were new arrests: among those detained were Lt Landing Sanneh, the commander of the state guard, and Maj. Pa Modou Ann, the commander of the newly-established Gambia national guards. In March Isatou Njie-Saidy, secretary of state for health, social welfare and women's affairs, was appointed vice-president, the first woman to hold this position. However, most of the powers and duties hitherto associated with the vice-presidency were transferred to the secretary of state for the office of the president, a post now held by Edward Singhateh (who, at 27, remained too young to hold the office of vice-president). In the national assembly a high proportion of the debate in the legislature's first months was taken up with procedural disputes, as opposition members accused Jammeh of failing to abide by the constitution.

Overall the security situation remained tense. In particular, in November 1996 armed rebels, apparently mercenaries formerly associated with Charles Taylor's National Patriotic Front of Liberia, attacked the GNA barracks at Farafenni; six soldiers were killed and many more wounded. Five rebels who were captured claimed to have been working with Kukoi Samba Sanyang, the exiled leader of the 1981 coup attempt. The detained rebels were charged before an open court in early April 1997, although their trial proceeded in camera. One of the alleged rebels died in detention in May, reportedly as a result of an infection contracted while in custody. A further mercenary suspected of involvement in the Farafenni attack was arrested in mid-April.

Economy

JOHN A. WISEMAN

Apart from the development of a significant tourist industry, the principal features of the Gambian economy have altered relatively little in the post-independence period. The country has remained poor, underdeveloped, and dependent. The often stated goal of transforming the country into the 'Singapore of Africa' would appear to have no foundation in reality. With a small population of little more than 1m. (1,211,067, according to official figures, in 1996), high levels of illiteracy, no significant mineral resources, a poorly-developed infrastructure and an erratic, arid climate, the prospects for dramatic economic development are slight. Official statistics on the economy are not noted for their reliability, partly due to administrative weakness and partly due to a significant (and inherently unmeasurable) informal sector. More positively, there has been a moderate improvement in health and education provision, access to safe drinking water has widened, and life expectancy has increased while infant mortality has declined. Most importantly, the country has, despite widespread poverty, avoided the famine and food insecurity experienced in many other African states.

AGRICULTURE AND FISHING

More than 70% of the Gambian population are directly dependent on agriculture for their livelihood, making this sector overwhelmingly the largest employer of labour, accounting for almost 80% of the labour force in 1995. For the most part, agricultural production is still organized through small-scale peasant units in which kinship predominates: over 90% of agricultural production is derived from this type of farming. Traditional patterns of shifting cultivation are widely used, and the bulk of production is for subsistence purposes. Large-scale plantation agriculture, whether privately-operated or state-run, is minimal. Women play a key role in the agricultural labour force, especially in the cultivation of subsistence crops. Attempts by the Jawara administration to increase capital investment in agriculture, such as by the establishment of the Agricultural Development Bank in 1981, largely failed as a result of corruption and mismanagement. Large loans were made to powerful élites who then defaulted on repayments, causing the bank's collapse. Foreign non-governmental organizations (NGOs) have become the main source of investment capital for small-scale peasant farmers. The most crucial factor affecting agricultural production is the level of rainfall. Since the mid-1960s the country has experienced recurrent drought, of varying severity, which has adversely affected production levels and led to significant environmental degradation, especially the damage caused by the penetration of saline river water.

The predominant cash crop in The Gambia is groundnuts, first introduced from America in the 18th century. About one-half of cultivated land is devoted to groundnuts—although this proportion has been declining slowly since the early 1970s. While the country produces less than 1% of the world's exported groundnuts, the national significance of the crop is immense. Some 20% of groundnut production is for domestic consumption by growers, the rest being grown for export, particularly in a processed form (groundnut-processing constitutes the major industrial activity). The cultivation of groundnuts is almost entirely undertaken by men, who therefore have major control over cash income in rural areas. The government-controlled Gambia Produce Marketing Board (GPMB) had a monopoly over the purchase and export marketing of groundnuts from 1973 until 1990, when this was removed to allow competition from the private sector. In common with other crops, fluctuations in rainfall levels have a major effect on production levels from year to year. Additionally, the relative levels of official prices paid to producers in The Gambia and in neighbouring Senegal are a major determinant in groundnut sales. In years when producer prices are high in Senegal much of the Gambian crop is smuggled across the border into Senegal: estimates suggest, for example, that in 1986/87 some 50%–70% of Gambian groundnuts were sold in Senegal. Official statistics on groundnut production tend to be somewhat misleading. Even allowing for problems of measurements, the 1996/97 groundnut crop was reported to be the worst in living memory. Recorded production of 16,000 metric tons was less than half that of 1995/96 and only about one-tenth of annual crops during the boom years of the 1970s. The dramatic decline was officially attributed to a number of factors, including poor seed varieties, low rainfall, shortage of fertilizers, bureaucratic inefficiency and labour shortages caused by migration to urban areas.

For subsistence purposes, rice is a more important crop than groundnuts. Most of the crop is consumed by producers and their families, although some is sold locally; the country remains a net importer of rice. Traditionally rice has been grown (almost entirely by women) in the swamplands along the edge of the Gambia river, but since independence there have been schemes to expand pump-irrigated rice production. Technical assistance for such schemes was provided from 1966–74 by Taiwan, and in 1975–79 by the People's Republic of China. In 1988 the African Development Bank made a loan of almost US $7m. to support additional rice development projects. While increased rice production would provide the best route to the goal of self-sufficiency in basic foodstuffs, the rate of population growth continues to exceed increases in output. Other important subsistence crops include millet, sorghum and cassava. In recent years there has been some expansion of fruit cultivation (bananas, mangoes, papayas and oranges) and horticulture. Produced mainly for subsistence purposes and local sales, these also provide about 5% of export earnings. Livestock-rearing makes a contribution to subsistence in many parts of the country. Cattle, especially the more disease-resistant N'Dama strain, are an important source of meat, milk and hides. Most peasant farmers raise small numbers of goats, sheep and chickens. Fishing, largely using traditional methods, is an important source of local food, while fish-processing results in this sector's contributing about 8% of exports.

TOURISM

The post-independence development of the tourist industry represents the most important and successful attempt at economic diversification and expansion in The Gambia. Prior to the 1994 *coup d'état* tourism had risen to become the country's largest source of foreign exchange. The industry began in 1965, but it was not until 1972 that its development was seriously undertaken by the government with the creation of 'tourism development areas'. Tourists initially came mainly from Sweden, but these were rapidly overtaken in numbers by British visitors, who came to constitute about two-thirds of tourist arrivals. Despite some diversification, the vast majority of tourists are still from western Europe. Tourism in The Gambia is mostly in the form of 'packages' organized by major western European (especially British) tour operators, whose decisions on whether or not to expand the promotion of tourism to The Gambia have a very major impact on the development of the industry. The independent, 'non-package' tourist sector has remained very small. Largely for climatic reasons the main tourist season runs from October to April, during which time The Gambia has the considerable advantage of warm, dry conditions. Apart from rainfall in May–September, climatic disadvantages in this period include extreme heat and humidity, rendering The Gambia much less attractive to tourists. Attempts to promote off-season tourism have been generally ineffective, and most employees in the sector are thus laid off during these months. The rainy season marks the most active period in farming, but evidence suggests that very few workers in tourism actually return to farming during the tourist low-season. Despite its significant attractions for ornithologists and for those with an interest in African life and culture, The Gambia is mainly perceived by visitors as a 'beach' destination. Hotel development, to international standards, has therefore taken place mainly in the coastal areas and especially in the strip running from Bakau to Kotu Point. Attempts to attract tourists up-river for at least part of their stay have met with little success, apart from short day-trips organized by the hotels and tour companies. In a good year The Gambia might expect to receive more than 100,000 tourists, but actual numbers are sensitive to a number of factors, including economic recession in western Europe and, of late, political uncertainty in The Gambia itself. According to the IMF, about one-third of the formal-sector work-force was employed in the tourist sector in 1992/93; elsewhere, it has been estimated that some 10% of the population are totally dependent on earnings from the industry. A considerable amount of tourist-related employment lies in the informal sector, which is not amenable to statistical measurement. Although there are official, government-recognized tourist guides, there are very many more unofficial guides who make their living by providing a variety of services for tourists. Wood-carvers, silversmiths, potters, tailors, weavers and—especially—taxi drivers receive considerable income from the tourist trade.

Inevitably, the tourist industry is extremely vulnerable to political developments. Tourist arrivals declined following the failed 1981 coup attempt, but the rapid return to political normality meant that this was a temporary downturn. The successful *coup d'état* in 1994 proved far more problematic. European tour operators had emphasized the image of the democratic stability of the country for many years, but this image was negated by the military's seizure of power. Following the November 1994 attempted coup, the British government advised travellers that The Gambia was an 'unsafe' destination, and as a consequence most of the major British tour operators withdrew from the country; the Swedish and Danish governments offered similar warnings. Although the official advice was changed by March 1995, tourist numbers for 1994/95 fell to little more than one-third of the level in 1993/94, causing the closure of many hotels and mass unemployment in the tourist sector. For the 1995/96 season some of the main foreign tour companies chose to recommence operations in The Gambia, but others decided to maintain the suspension until the political situation became clearer. The 1995/96 season was thus better than the previous one, although tourist arrivals remained well below pre-coup levels. To compensate for the decline in arrivals from western Europe the government inaugurated a 'Roots Festival' in May 1996, designed to attract African-American visitors; the success of this venture, in terms of numbers, was relatively slight, although the festival was again held in June 1997. The Gambian government anticipated a full recovery in 1996/97. During that season there was for the first time some success in attracting significant numbers of German tourists.

FINANCE, AID AND TRADE

At independence the Gambian pound replaced the colonial West African Currency Board pound, at parity with sterling. This parity was maintained up to the inauguration of the Central Bank of The Gambia in March 1971. In July of that year the dalasi (divided into 100 bututs) was adopted as the new national currency, with an exchange rate of D5 = £1. With minor adjustments this rate was retained until, as part of the economic recovery programme (ERP—see below), the fixed exchange was abandoned and replaced by a floating rate. In recent years a rate of around D15 = £1 has prevailed, and there has been very little difference between official and informal rates (unlike in many sub-Saharan African countries, the latter is only slightly higher than the former).

The Gambia has since independence been heavily dependent on external funding from a variety of bilateral and multilateral sources. Development assistance has frequently exceeded more than one-half of gross national product. Until the 1994 coup the major foreign donors were the European Union (EU), the USA, the United Kingdom, Canada, the Nordic countries, Japan, Saudi Arabia and the People's Republic of China. Opposition by most of the donor community to the imposition of military rule resulted in significant reductions in disbursements of development aid. The EU, for example, halved financial assistance (from US $20m. to $10m.), and announced that it had no plans to renew its aid programme until elected civilian government had been restored. Most government-to-government bilateral aid programmes were either scaled down or abandoned. In an attempt to compensate for these losses, the Jammeh regime has tried to foster new sources of foreign assistance. Taiwan, notably, agreed to lend some $35m. following the restoration of diplomatic relations (severed in 1974) in July 1995; assistance was also forthcoming for the Gambian army. (The restoration of links with Taiwan led to a corresponding severance of ties with, and thus a loss of co-operation by, the People's Republic of China.) Taiwan announced an increase in its development funding in January 1997. The Gambia was also reported to have received significant financial assistance from Libya upon the restoration of diplomatic relations in November 1994 (after an interval of almost 15 years), and co-operation accords have, additionally, been signed with Cuba and with Iran. The country has continued to receive considerable amounts of aid from a wide variety of (mostly Western) charitable NGOs; such aid is mainly targeted at projects designed to help the rural poor. More than 100 NGOs were operating in The Gambia in the mid-1990s. A further source of external finance is the remittances of Gambians working abroad, mainly in western Europe and the USA, to their families in The Gambia. About one-third of The Gambia's gross domestic product (GDP) is derived from re-exports: goods imported into The Gambia under low import tariffs are then re-exported (not always in a legal manner) to other countries of the region, principally to Senegal but often as far afield as Guinea, Guinea-Bissau and Mali. Some aspects of this trade are politically sensitive, and have periodically led to border problems with Senegal (see below).

ECONOMIC RESTRUCTURING

Having performed relatively strongly in the 10 years after independence, the Gambian economy then entered a decline which by the mid-1980s had reached crisis proportions. The balance of payments was in increasing deficit, leading to an accumulation of external payments' arrears and increased external borrowing. Government expenditure continued to expand, unsupported by a parallel expansion of state revenue. Increased government intervention in the economy through loan-guarantee schemes, extended parastatal activity, subsidized interest rates and exchange and price controls had the effect of distorting the economy, and by 1984 The Gambia was unable to meet its obligations to the IMF, causing the latter to consider a ban on further drawings by the country. In response to this crisis the Jawara administration adopted its ERP in August 1985: drawn up in consultation with, and with support from, the IMF and the World Bank, this represented a significant attempt to restructure the Gambian economy. In common with other similar, IMF-inspired economic adjustment programmes undertaken elsewhere in Africa, the primary goals of the ERP were to restructure the economy by means of a reduction of unprofitable state involvement and a liberalization of economic mechanisms. One of the first measures of the ERP was the floating, in January 1986, of the dalasi by means of the creation of an inter-bank market for foreign exchange, resulting in the devaluation of the national currency. There was a 120% depreciation in the first six months, with further falls in subsequent years until a *de facto* stabilization was achieved by the early 1990s. This policy resulted in the rechannelling of significant amounts of foreign exchange from the informal sector into the official sector. The ERP also entailed considerable retrenchment in the civil service, with the loss of about 20% of jobs in the government sector. Meanwhile, producer prices for groundnuts were increased, and these two measures in combination went some way towards correcting the urban bias in the Gambian economy. The central bank first raised, then decontrolled, interest rates. Parastatal organizations were either privatized or subjected to strict financial discipline through performance contracts. For a time at least efforts were made to combat customs fraud, which led to an increase of one-third in revenue from such duties. The positive medium-term effects of the ERP included fiscal stabilization, significant reductions in inflation and higher rates of GDP growth. The programme for sustained development (PSD), inaugurated in 1990, was essentially a continuation of the economic policies of the ERP. The GPMB and the Gambia Utilities Corpn were privatized under the PSD in 1993.

Although, as noted above, the Gambian economy was damaged by reductions in foreign aid and the (possibly short-lived) collapse of the tourist industry following the military take-over, the Jammeh regime has not pursued any significant reversals of macroeconomic policy, and has consistently pledged its commitment to 'free-market capitalism'. Presenting the budget for the forthcoming financial year in July 1996, the government reported a 3.2% increase in GDP during 1995/96. Although final figures relating to tourist arrivals for the year were not yet available, preliminary estimates suggested an increase of 75% over the—extremely low—total for 1994/95. Currency exchange rates had remained relatively stable in 1995/96, with only minor depreciations against the US dollar and the pound sterling. For 1996/97, additional government revenues were to be derived notably by raising the retail price of petrol and by increasing fees for issuing passports. A 6% increase in public-sector pay was announced, offsetting a projected 5% rate of inflation. GDP growth of 2% was forecast for the year. A budget for the six months to the end of 1997 was presented in June of that year (thereafter, the financial year was to coincide with the calendar year); Domestic revenue was to amount to D841.4m. in the six-month period.

Despite the apparent stabilization of the economy in the post-coup period, there has been criticism in some quarters of the new regime's enthusiasm for ambitious infrastructural and other 'prestige' projects. The government's long-term aim, outlined in its *Vision 2020* document published in September 1996, setting targets for all sectors of the economy, for education, health care, welfare, the environment and public administration, is to achieve the status of a middle-income economy within 25 years. The Jammeh administration hoped, moreover, that the return to government by elected civilian institutions, from early 1997, would prompt a return to the full support by the international economic community that will be essential to the achievement of strong and sustained growth.

RELATIONS WITH SENEGAL

The formal dissolution, in September 1989, of the Senegambia confederation (see Recent History), and subsequent allegations regarding Senegal's economic 'harassment' of The Gambia, raised serious questions regarding future economic relations between the two countries. During 1990 the Senegalese authorities eased restrictions on cross-border traffic, and the conclusion, in January 1991, of a new co-operation treaty confirmed several existing bilateral agreements governing such areas as defence and security, transport and telecommunications, health, trade, fishing, agriculture and energy. None the less, Senegal's closure, in September 1993, of the border between the two countries prompted protests by The Gambia that its overland trading links had been blocked.

Economic relations with Senegal did not improve following the imposition of military rule in The Gambia. Although Jammeh announced that the Senegalese restrictions on cross-border trade were to be revoked following a visit to Senegal in September 1994, this failed to materialize. In retaliation, in April 1995 the Gambian authorities raised the tolls on the Yellitenda–Bambatenda ferry (Senegal's main link with its southern province of Casamance) by 1,000% for Senegalese vehicles, forcing these to use the much longer Tambacounda route; the increase was, however, abandoned in June. In January 1996 the Senegalese and Gambian governments agreed to end restrictions on cross-border trade between the two countries, subject to the implementation of measures designed to prevent smuggling. A further agreement, concluded in April 1997, was to facilitate trans-border movement of goods destined for re-export.

Both countries have also maintained their membership of the sub-regional Gambia River Basin Development Organization, to which Guinea and Guinea-Bissau also belong. This organization is principally concerned with promoting development by means of regional co-operation and the joint exploitation of shared natural resources.

Statistical Survey

Source (unless otherwise stated): the former Directorate of Information and Broadcasting, 14 Hagan St, Banjul; tel. 227230.

Area and Population

AREA, POPULATION AND DENSITY

Area (sq km)	11,295*
Population (census results)	
15 April 1983	
Total	687,817
15 April 1993†	
Males	514,530
Females	511,337
Total	1,025,867
Density (per sq km) at census of 1993	90.8

* 4,361 sq miles. † Provisional.

PRINCIPAL TOWNS (population at 1983 census)

Banjul (capital)	44,188	Farafenni	10,168
Serrekunda	68,433	Sukuta	7,227
Brikama	19,584	Gunjur	7,115
Bakau	19,309		

BIRTHS AND DEATHS (UN estimates, annual averages)

	1980–85	1985–90	1990–95
Birth rate (per 1,000)	48.2	46.5	43.7
Death rate (per 1,000)	23.1	20.7	18.8

Expectation of life (UN estimates, years at birth, 1990–95): 45.0 (males 43.4; females 46.6).

Source: UN, *World Population Prospects: The 1994 Revision*.

ECONOMICALLY ACTIVE POPULATION*
(persons aged 10 years and over, 1983 census)

	Total
Agriculture, hunting, forestry and fishing	239,940
Quarrying	66
Manufacturing	8,144
Electricity, gas and water	1,233
Construction	4,373
Trade, restaurants and hotels	16,551
Transport, storage and communications	8,014
Public administration and defence	8,295
Education	4,737
Medical services	2,668
Personal and domestic services	6,553
Activities not adequately defined	25,044
Total	325,618†

* Figures exclude persons seeking work for the first time.
† Males 174,856; females 150,762.

Mid-1995 (estimates in '000): Agriculture, etc. 450; Total 499 (Source: FAO, *Production Yearbook*).

Agriculture

PRINCIPAL CROPS ('000 metric tons)

	1993	1994	1995
Millet and sorghum	61	62	66
Rice (paddy)	12	20	20
Maize	24	13	22
Cassava (Manioc)*	6	6	6
Pulses*	4	4	4
Palm kernels*	2	2	2
Groundnuts (in shell)	77	81	84
Vegetables*	8	8	8
Fruits*	4	4	4
Seed (unginned) cotton*	5	5	10

* FAO estimates.

Source: FAO, *Production Yearbook*.

LIVESTOCK (FAO estimates, '000 head, year ending September)

	1993	1994	1995
Cattle	400	400	400
Goats	150	150	150
Sheep	121	121	121
Pigs	11	11	11
Asses	30	30	30
Horses	16	16	16

Poultry (FAO estimates, million): 1 in 1993; 1 in 1994; 1 in 1995.

Source: FAO, *Production Yearbook*.

LIVESTOCK PRODUCTS (FAO estimates, '000 metric tons)

	1993	1994	1995
Beef and veal	6	6	6
Poultry meat	1	1	1
Other meat	2	2	2
Cows' milk	7	7	7
Poultry eggs	0.9	0.9	0.9

Source: FAO, *Production Yearbook*.

Forestry

ROUNDWOOD REMOVALS
('000 cubic metres, excluding bark)

	1992*	1993	1994
Sawlogs, veneer logs and logs for sleepers	90	103	106
Other industrial wood	7	7	7
Fuel wood	1,016	1,078	1,096
Total	1,113	1,188	1,209

* FAO estimates.

Source: FAO, *Yearbook of Forest Products*.

Fishing

('000 metric tons, live weight)

	1993	1994	1995
Tilapias	1.1	1.0	1.1
Other freshwater fishes	1.4	1.4	1.5
Tonguefishes	0.2	0.2	0.9
Sea catfishes	0.4	0.3	0.8
Croakers and drums	1.2	0.5	1.4
Bonga shad	14.1	16.9	13.9
Other marine fishes (incl. unspecified)	1.5	1.3	2.6
Total fish	19.8	21.7	22.2
Southern pink shrimp	0.5	0.6	0.4
Other crustaceans and molluscs	0.1	0.1	0.5
Total catch	20.5	22.3	23.1
Inland waters	2.4	2.4	2.5
Atlantic Ocean	18.1	19.9	20.6

Source: FAO, *Yearbook of Fishery Statistics*.

Industry

SELECTED PRODUCTS

	1990	1991	1992
Salted, dried or smoked fish ('000 metric tons)*	0.7	0.5	0.5
Vegetable oils—unrefined ('000 metric tons)†	3	3	n.a.
Electric energy (million kWh)†	70	70	71

Electric energy (million kWh)†: 73 in 1993; 75 in 1994.

* Data from the FAO. † Provisional or estimated figures.

Source: UN, *Industrial Commodity Statistics Yearbook*.

Finance

CURRENCY AND EXCHANGE RATES

Monetary Units

100 butut = 1 dalasi (D).

Sterling and Dollar Equivalents (28 February 1997)

£1 sterling = 16.28 dalasi;
US $1 = 9.98 dalasi;
1,000 dalasi = £61.42 = $100.20.

Average Exchange Rate (dalasi per US $)

1994 9.576
1995 9.546
1996 9.781

BUDGET (million dalasi, year ending 30 June)

Revenue*	1992/93	1993/94	1994/95‡
Tax revenue	704.4	682.9	599.9
Direct taxes	122.9	126.0	135.8
Taxes on personal incomes	40.4	36.4	55.3
Taxes on corporate profits	76.6	80.6	73.7
Indirect taxes	581.5	556.9	464.1
Domestic taxes on goods and services	47.9	57.1	48.7
Domestic sales tax	46.5	54.7	36.8
Taxes on international trade	374.2	306.5	256.2
Customs duties	196.1	156.9	144.7
Sales tax on imports	178.1	149.1	109.8
Petroleum taxes	159.4	193.3	159.2
Duty	136.8	166.8	137.8
Sales tax	22.6	26.5	21.4
Other current revenue	61.9	84.2	65.7
Government services and charges	18.8	22.8	27.0
Interest on property	19.8	10.3	10.0
Central Bank profit	17.7	28.0	25.0
Capital revenue	0.6	4.0	3.7
Total	766.9	771.1	669.3

Expenditure†	1992/93	1993/94	1994/95‡
Current expenditure	570.7	613.3	613.4
Expenditure on goods and services	369.4	414.3	432.5
Personal emoluments, allowances and pensions	161.0	198.6	206.0
Other charges	208.4	215.7	226.5
Goods and services	128.3	133.5	142.5
Maintenance and equipment	49.0	65.0	45.2
Interest payments	117.9	133.9	128.6
Internal	72.7	84.9	77.3
External	45.2	49.2	51.3
Subsidies and current transfers	83.4	65.1	52.4
To non-profit institutions	54.4	44.9	29.7
Development expenditure	253.2	248.6	266.3
Unallocated expenditure	3.4	5.8	22.4
Total	827.3	867.7	902.2

* Excluding grants received (million dalasi): 123.3 in 1992/93; 126.5 in 1993/94; 67.8 in 1994/95.

† Excluding lending minus repayments (million dalasi): 12.1 in 1992/93; –5.7 in 1993/94; –14.7 in 1994/95.

‡ Estimates.

Source: IMF, *The Gambia—Recent Economic Developments* (December 1995).

INTERNATIONAL RESERVES (US $ million at 31 December)

	1994*	1995	1996
IMF special drawing rights	0.26	0.13	0.29
Reserve position in IMF	2.17	2.21	2.14
Foreign exchange	95.59	103.81	99.37
Total	98.02	106.15	101.79

* **1993** (US $ million): IMF special drawing rights 0.31; Reserve position in IMF 2.04. Complete figures for 1993 are not available.

Source: IMF, *International Financial Statistics*.

MONEY SUPPLY (million dalasi at 31 December)

	1994	1995	1996
Currency outside banks	207.36	247.97	255.03
Demand deposits at commercial banks	200.17	223.50	198.46
Total money	407.53	471.47	453.49

Source: IMF, *International Financial Statistics*.

COST OF LIVING
(Consumer Price Index for Banjul and Kombo St Mary; base: 1990 = 100)

	1992	1993	1994
Food	117.6	127.7	126.2
Fuel and light	116.2	119.9	160.1
Clothing*	124.5	122.5	130.9
Rent	198.0	209.2	219.1
All items (incl. others)	118.9	126.6	128.8

* Including household linen.

1995: Food 137.1; All items 137.8 (Source: UN, *Monthly Bulletin of Statistics*).

Source: ILO, *Yearbook of Labour Statistics*.

NATIONAL ACCOUNTS
(million dalasi at current prices, year ending 30 June)

Expenditure on the Gross Domestic Product

	1992/93	1993/94	1994/95*
Government final consumption expenditure	576.1	613.9	615.5
Private final consumption expenditure	2,427.7	2,605.8	2,708.6
Increase in stocks } Gross fixed capital formation	677.9	626.6	557.1
Total domestic expenditure	3,681.7	3,846.3	3,881.2
Exports of goods and services	1,973.0	1,916.9	1,505.6
Less Imports of goods and services	2,426.0	2,352.1	1,949.7
GDP in purchasers' values	3,228.6	3,411.2	3,438.5†
GDP at constant 1976/77 prices	572.2	579.8	556.8

* Estimates.

† Including adjustment.

Gross Domestic Product by Economic Activity

	1991/92	1992/93	1993/94†
Agriculture, hunting, forestry and fishing	663.0	641.9	762.5
Manufacturing	166.4	188.3	191.7
Electricity and water	25.6	31.4	35.7
Construction	148.9	166.1	186.0
Trade, restaurants and hotels	647.0	738.4	635.2
Transport and communications	280.8	335.2	378.6
Business services and housing	171.8	194.9	228.1
Government services	196.9	227.3	262.3
Other services*	110.5	123.5	174.1
GDP at factor cost	2,410.9	2,647.1	2,854.3
Indirect taxes, *Less* Subsidies	536.7	581.5	556.9
GDP in purchasers' values	2,947.6	3,228.6	3,411.2

* Including banking and insurance, net of imputed bank service charges.

† Estimates.

Source: IMF, *The Gambia—Recent Economic Developments* (December 1995).

BALANCE OF PAYMENTS (US $ million, year ending 30 June)

	1993	1994	1995
Exports of goods f.o.b.	157.03	124.97	122.96
Imports of goods f.o.b.	–214.46	–181.62	–162.53
Trade balance	–57.43	–56.65	–39.57
Exports of services	79.57	90.47	53.71
Imports of services	–74.56	–67.04	–69.25
Balance on goods and services	–52.42	–33.22	–55.11
Other income received	5.82	4.87	4.37
Other income paid	–5.11	–5.14	–9.58
Balance on goods, services and income	–51.71	–33.50	–60.32
Current transfers received	49.99	45.85	55.81
Current transfers paid	–3.60	–4.18	–3.68
Current balance	–5.32	8.17	–8.19
Direct investment from abroad	11.07	9.81	7.78
Other investment assets	1.40	3.79	–3.66
Investment liabilities	26.92	19.54	20.65
Net errors and omissions	–22.72	–35.12	–15.63
Overall balance	11.35	6.19	0.95

Source: IMF, *International Financial Statistics*.

External Trade

PRINCIPAL COMMODITIES (SDR '000, year ending 30 June)

Imports c.i.f.	1991/92	1992/93	1993/94
Food and live animals	50,838	45,688	39,594
Beverages and tobacco	7,748	6,527	8,175
Raw materials	1,273	2,117	1,443
Mineral fuels, lubricants, etc.	19,223	14,641	9,618
Animal and vegetable oils	3,456	5,292	3,687
Chemicals	9,400	8,820	8,175
Manufactured goods classified by material	31,018	37,220	40,716
Machinery and transport equipment	26,457	41,101	37,671
Miscellaneous manufactured articles	12,385	13,585	10,099
Total (incl. others)	163,901	176,400	160,300

Exports f.o.b.*	1992/93	1993/94	1994/95†
Groundnuts and groundnut products	8,300	7,579	7,571
Fish and fish products	2,233	1,500	1,633
Cotton products	95	2,800	3,853
Total (incl. others)	13,695	13,962	14,900

* Excluding re-exports (SDR '000): 97,000 in 1992/93; 75,232 in 1993/94; 67,332 in 1994/95.

† Estimates.

Source: IMF, *The Gambia—Recent Economic Developments* (December 1995).

PRINCIPAL TRADING PARTNERS (percentage of trade)

Imports c.i.f.	1992	1993	1994*
Belgium-Luxembourg	5.7	7.9	10.1
China, People's Repub.	14.8	20.3	24.7
France (incl. Monaco)	6.2	7.9	4.2
Germany	4.2	3.9	4.6
Hong Kong	16.0	11.1	7.7
Italy	7.0	3.2	2.2
Japan	3.1	3.7	2.1
Netherlands	4.7	5.8	4.3
Senegal	1.9	2.9	5.4
Spain	1.6	1.1	0.8
Thailand	4.5	4.2	4.9
United Kingdom	10.1	10.3	8.5
USA	2.9	2.9	1.3

Exports f.o.b.	1992	1993	1994*
Belgium-Luxembourg	51.5	51.0	50.4
France (incl. Monaco)	0.5	0.6	2.6
Guinea	3.5	5.7	6.2
Italy	19.7	n.a.	n.a.
Japan	14.3	22.0	21.5
Senegal	n.a.	n.a.	n.a.
Spain	2.2	1.3	2.2
United Kingdom	2.1	5.0	3.6
USA	0.4	5.7	1.3

* Estimates.

Source: IMF, *The Gambia—Recent Economic Developments* (December 1995).

Transport

ROAD TRAFFIC (estimates, '000 motor vehicles in use)

	1991	1992	1993
Private cars	6	7	7
Commercial vehicles	6	6	7

Source: UN Economic Commission for Africa, *African Statistical Yearbook*.

SHIPPING

Merchant Fleet (registered at 31 December)

	1994	1995	1996
Number of vessels	9	6	6
Total displacement (grt)	2,512	1,490	1,490

Source: Lloyd's Register of Shipping, *World Fleet Statistics*.

International Sea-borne Freight Traffic (estimates, '000 metric tons)

	1991	1992	1993
Goods loaded	175	181	185
Goods unloaded	220	230	240

Source: UN Economic Commission for Africa, *African Statistical Yearbook*.

CIVIL AVIATION (traffic on scheduled services)

	1992	1993	1994
Kilometres flown (million)	1	1	1
Passengers carried ('000)	19	19	19
Passenger-km (million)	50	50	50
Total ton-km (million)	5	5	5

Source: UN, *Statistical Yearbook*.

Tourism

TOURIST ARRIVALS (air charter tourists, year ending 30 June)

	1992/93	1993/94	1994/95*
Total	63,940	89,997	38,000

* Estimate.

Source: IMF, *The Gambia—Recent Economic Developments* (December 1995).

Communications Media

	1992	1993	1994
Radio receivers ('000 in use)	155	169	176
Television receivers ('000 in use)	n.a.	n.a.	3
Daily newspapers	2	n.a.	2
Books published (first editions)*			
Titles	n.a.	n.a.	21
Copies ('000)	n.a.	n.a.	20

* Including pamphlets: 5 titles, 9,000 copies in 1994.

Telephones: ('000 main lines in use, excluding public call offices, year ending 31 March): 14 in 1992/93; 16 in 1993/94; 18 in 1994/95.

Sources: UNESCO, *Statistical Yearbook*; UN, *Statistical Yearbook*.

Education

(1992/93, unless otherwise indicated)

	Teachers	Students		
		Males	Females	Total
Pre-primary*	408	n.a.	n.a.	13,118
Primary	3,193	56,948	40,314	97,262
Secondary	1,054	16,916	9,013	25,929

* 1991/92 figures.

Tertiary (1994/95): 155 teachers; 1,591 students (males 1,018, females 573).

Source: UNESCO, *Statistical Yearbook*.

Directory

The Constitution

Following the *coup d'état* of July 1994, the 1970 Constitution was suspended and the presidency and legislature, as defined therein, dissolved. A Constitutional Review Commission was inaugurated in April 1995. Its findings were submitted to the Armed Forces Provisional Ruling Council in November; the amended document was published in March 1996, and approved in a national referendum on 8 August. The new Constitution of the Second Republic of The Gambia entered into full effect on 16 January 1997.

The Constitution provides for the separation of the powers of the executive, legislative and judicial organs of state. The Head of State is the President of the Republic, who is directly elected by universal adult suffrage. No restriction is placed on the number of times a President may seek re-election. Legislative authority is vested in the National Assembly, comprising 45 members elected by direct universal suffrage and four members nominated by the President of the Republic. The Speaker and Deputy Speaker of the Assembly are elected, by the members of the legislature, from among the President's nominees. The Constitution upholds the principle of executive accountability to parliament. Thus, the Head of State appoints government members, but these are responsible both to the President and to the National Assembly. Ministers of cabinet rank take the title of Secretary of State. Committees of the Assembly have powers to inquire into the activities of ministers and of government departments, and into all matters of public importance.

In judicial affairs, the final court of appeal is the Supreme Court. Provision is made for a special criminal court to hear and determine all cases relating to the theft and misappropriation of public funds.

The Constitution provides for an Independent Electoral Commission, an Independent National Audit Office, an Office of the Ombudsman, a Lands Commission and a Public Service Commission, all of which are intended to ensure transparency, accountability and probity in public affairs.

The Constitution guarantees the rights of women, of children and of the disabled. Tribalism and other forms of sectarianism in politics are forbidden. Political activity may be suspended in the event of a state of national insecurity.

The Government

HEAD OF STATE

President: Capt. (retd) YAHYA A. J. J. JAMMEH (proclaimed Head of State 26 July 1994; elected President 26 September 1996).

Vice-President: ISATOU NJIE-SAIDY.

THE CABINET
(August 1997)

President: Capt. (retd) YAHYA A. J. J. JAMMEH.

Vice-President and Secretary of State for Health, Social Welfare and Women's Affairs: ISATOU NJIE-SAIDY.

Secretary of State for the Office of the President, responsible for the National Assembly, the Civil Service, Fisheries and Natural Resources: Capt. (retd) EDWARD SINGHATEH.

Secretary of State for Local Government and Lands: Capt. (retd) YANKUBA TOURAY.

Secretary of State for the Interior and Religious Affairs: Maj. (retd) MOMODOU BOJANG.

Secretary of State for Finance and Economic Affairs: DOMINIC MENDY.

Secretary of State for External Affairs: OMAR NJIE.

Secretary of State for Education: SATANG JAW.

Secretary of State for Tourism and Culture: SUSAN WAFFA-OGOOH.

Secretary of State for Agriculture: MUSA MBENGA.

Secretary of State for Works, Communications and Information: EBRIMA CEESAY.

Secretary of State for Trade, Industry and Employment: FAMARA JATTA.

Secretary of State for Youth and Sports: Capt. (retd) LAMIN BAJO.

MINISTRIES

Office of the President: State House, Banjul; tel. 227208; telex 2204; fax 227034.

Ministry of Agriculture and Natural Resources: The Quadrangle, Banjul; tel. 22147; fax 229546.

Ministry of Defence: Banjul.

Ministry of Education: Bedford Place Bldg, POB 989, Banjul; tel. 228522; telex 2264; fax 225066.

Ministry of External Affairs: 4 Marina Parade, Banjul; tel. 225654; telex 2351; fax 228060.

Ministry of Finance and Economic Affairs: The Quadrangle, Banjul; tel. 227221; fax 227954.

Ministry of Health, Social Welfare and Women's Affairs: The Quadrangle, Banjul; tel. 227872; telex 2357; fax 228505.

Ministry of the Interior: 71 Dobson St, Banjul; tel. 228611.

Ministry of Justice: Marina Parade, Banjul; tel. 228181.

Ministry of Local Government and Lands: The Quadrangle, Banjul; tel. 228291.

Ministry of Tourism and Culture: The Quadrangle, Banjul; tel. 228496; fax 227753.

Ministry of Trade, Industry and Employment: Central Bank Bldg, Banjul; tel. 228229; telex 2293.

Ministry of Works, Communication and Information: Half-Die, Banjul; tel. 228251.

Ministry of Youth and Sports: Bedford Place Bldg, POB 989, Banjul; tel. 228522; telex 2264; fax 225066.

President and Legislature

PRESIDENT

Presidential Election, 26 September 1996

Candidate	Votes	% of votes
YAHYA A. J. J. JAMMEH	220,011	55.77
OUSAINOU DARBOE	141,387	35.84
HAMAT N. K. BAH	21,759	5.52
SIDIA JATTA	11,337	2.87
Total	394,494	100.00

NATIONAL ASSEMBLY

Speaker: MUSTAPHA WADDA.

General Election, 2 January 1997

Party	Seats
Alliance for Patriotic Reorientation and Construction	33*
United Democratic Party	7
National Reconciliation Party	2
People's Democratic Organization for Independence and Socialism	1
Independents	2
Total	45*

* Including five seats taken in constituencies in which the party was unopposed.

† The President of the Republic is empowered by the Constitution to nominate four additional members of parliament.

Political Organizations

The ban on all political activity, imposed following the *coup d'état* of July 1994, was revoked in August 1996.

The following parties were authorized at this time:

Alliance for Patriotic Reorientation and Construction (APRC): Banjul; f. 1996; Chair. President YAHYA A. J. J. JAMMEH.

National Reconciliation Party (NRP): Banjul; f. 1996; Leader HAMAT N. K. BAH.

People's Democratic Organization for Independence and Socialism (PDOIS): Banjul; f. 1986; radical socialist; Leaders HALIFA SALLAH, SAM SARR, SIDIA JATTA.

People's Democratic Party (PDP): Bojang Kunda, Brikama, Kombo Central; tel. 84190; f. 1991; advocates promotion of agricultural self-sufficiency, mass education and infrastructural development; Pres. Dr MOMODOU LAMIN BOJANG; First Sec. JABEL SALLAH.

United Democratic Party (UDP): Banjul; f. 1996; Leader OUSAINOU DARBOE.

Note: The **Gambia People's Party,** of ASSAN MUSA CAMARA, the **National Convention Party,** of SHERIF MUSTAPHA DIBBA, and the **People's Progressive Party,** of fmr Pres. Sir DAWDA KAIRABA JAWARA, were banned from contesting the 1996 presidential election and the 1997 legislative elections.

Diplomatic Representation

EMBASSIES AND HIGH COMMISSIONS IN THE GAMBIA

China (Taiwan): Banjul; Ambassador FRANCIS CHUNG LEE.

Liberia: Banjul; Ambassador: JAMES MOLLY SCOTT.

Nigeria: Garba Jahumpa Ave, Banjul; tel. 95805; High Commissioner: MARK NNABUGWU EZE.

Senegal: 10 Nelson Mandela St, Banjul; tel. 227469; Ambassador: MOKTAR KÉBÉ.

Sierra Leone: 67 Hagan St, Banjul; tel. 228206; High Commissioner: AROUN BOHARE.

United Kingdom: 48 Atlantic Rd, Fajara, POB 507, Banjul; tel. 495133; telex 2211; fax 496134; High Commissioner: JOHN WILDE.

USA: Kairaba Ave, Fajara, POB 19, Banjul; tel. 92858; fax 92475; Ambassador: ANDREW WINTER.

Judicial System

The judicial system of The Gambia is based on English Common Law and legislative enactments of the Republic's Parliament which include an Islamic Law Recognition Ordinance whereby an Islamic Court exercises jurisdiction in certain cases between, or exclusively affecting, Muslims.

The Constitution of the Second Republic guarantees the independence of the judiciary. The Supreme Court is defined as the final court of appeal. Provision is made for a special criminal court to hear and determine all cases relating to theft and misappropriation of public funds.

Supreme Court of The Gambia: Law Courts, Independence Drive, Banjul; tel. 227383; fax 228380; consists of the Chief Justice and puisne judges.

Chief Justice: BRAIMAH AMEN OMOSUN.

The Banjul Magistrates Court, the Kanifing Magistrates Court and the **Divisional Courts** are courts of summary jurisdiction presided over by a magistrate or in his absence by two or more lay justices of the peace. There are resident magistrates in all divisions. The magistrates have limited civil and criminal jurisdiction, and appeal lies from these courts to the Supreme Court.

Islamic Courts have jurisdiction in matters between, or exclusively affecting, Muslim Gambians and relating to civil status, marriage, succession, donations, testaments and guardianship. The Courts administer Islamic (Shari'a) Law. A cadi, or a cadi and two assessors, preside over and constitute an Islamic Court. Assessors of the Islamic Courts are Justices of the Peace of Islamic faith.

District Tribunals have appellate jurisdiction in cases touching on customs and traditions. Each court consists of three district tribunal members, one of whom is selected as president, and other court members from the area over which it has jurisdiction.

Attorney-General: FATOU BENSOUDA.

Religion

About 85% of the population are Muslims. The remainder are mainly Christians, and there are a few animists, mostly of the Jola and Karoninka ethnic groups.

ISLAM

Imam Ratib of Banjul: Alhaji ABDOULIE M. JOBE, King Fahd Bun Abdul Aziz Mosque, 39 Lancaster St, POB 562, Banjul; tel. 228094.

CHRISTIANITY

The Gambia Christian Council: POB 27, Banjul; tel. and fax 392092; telex 2290; f. 1966; six mems (churches and other Christian bodies); Chair. Rt Rev. MICHAEL J. CLEARY (Roman Catholic Bishop of Banjul); Sec.-Gen. HANNAH ACY PETERS.

The Anglican Communion

The diocese of The Gambia, which includes Senegal and Cape Verde, forms part of the Church of the Province of West Africa. The Metropolitan of the Province is the Archbishop of West Africa. There are about 1,500 adherents in The Gambia.

Bishop of The Gambia: Rt Rev. SOLOMON TILEWA JOHNSON, Bishopscourt, POB 51, Banjul; tel. 227405; fax 229495.

The Roman Catholic Church

The Gambia comprises a single diocese (Banjul), directly responsible to the Holy See. At 31 December 1995 there were an estimated 27,200 adherents of the Roman Catholic Church in the country. The diocese administers a development organization (Caritas, The Gambia), and runs 63 schools and training centres. The Bishop of Banjul is a member of the Inter-territorial Catholic Bishops' Conference of The Gambia, Liberia and Sierra Leone (based in Freetown, Sierra Leone).

Bishop of Banjul: Rt Rev. MICHAEL J. CLEARY, Bishop's House, POB 165, Banjul; tel. 393437; fax 390998.

Protestant Church

Methodist Church: POB 288, Banjul; f. 1821; tel. 227425; Chair. and Gen. Supt Rev. K. JOHN A. STEDMAN; Sec. Rev. TITUS K. A. PRATT.

The Press

Publication of newspapers and journals by political organizations was officially suspended following the July 1994 *coup d'état*. All publications were required to re-register in February 1996: those failing to do so were obliged to close.

The Daily Observer: PMB 131, Banjul; tel. 496608; fax 496878; f. 1992; daily; independent; Editor BABA GALLEH JALLOW.

Foroyaa (Freedom): Bundunka Kunda, POB 2306, Serrekunda; publ. by the PDOIS; Editors HALIFA SALLAH, SAM SARR, SIDIA JATTA.

The Gambia Daily: Banjul; Editor MOMODOU MUSA SECKA.

The Gambia Onward: 48 Grant St, Banjul; Editor RUDOLPH ALLEN.

The Gambia Weekly: 14 Hagan St, Banjul; tel. and fax 227230; telex 2204; f. 1943; govt bulletin; Editor A. F. SAGNIA; circ. 500.

The Gambian: 60 Lancaster St, Banjul; Editor NGAING THOMAS.

The Gambian Times: 21 OAU Blvd, POB 698, Banjul; tel. 445; f. 1981; fortnightly; publ. by the PPP; Editor MOMODOU GAYE.

The Nation: People's Press, 3 Boxbar Rd, POB 334, Banjul; fortnightly; Editor W. DIXON-COLLEY.

Newsmonth: Banjul; f. 1993; weekly; Editor BARBUCARR GAYE.

The Point: 2 Garba Jahumpa Rd, Fajara, Banjul; tel. 49-74-41; fax 49-74-42; f. 1991; 2 a week; Man. Editor DEYDA HYDARA; circ. 4,000.

The Toiler: 31 OAU Blvd, POB 698, Banjul; Editor PA MODOU FALL.

The Worker: 6 Albion Place, POB 508, Banjul; publ. by the Gambia Labour Union; Editor M. M. CEESAY.

NEWS AGENCIES

Gambia News Agency (GAMNA): Information Office, 14 Hagan St, Banjul; tel. 226621; telex 2204; fax 227230; Dir EBRIMA SAGNIA.

Foreign Bureau

Agence France-Presse (AFP): Banjul; tel. 228873; Correspondent DEYDA HYDARA.

Associated Press (USA), Inter Press Service (Italy) and Reuters (UK) are also represented in The Gambia.

Publisher

Government Printer: MacCarthy Sq., Banjul; tel. 227399; telex 2204.

Radio and Television

In 1994, according to UNESCO estimates, there were 176,000 radio receivers and 3,000 television receivers in use. The Gambia's first television station began broadcasts in 1996.

Gambia Television and Radio: Mile 7, Banjul; tel. 225060; telex 2204; fax 227230; f. 1962; non-commercial govt service of information, education and entertainment; radio broadcasts in English, Mandinka, Wolof, Fula, Jola, Serer and Serahuli; television broadcasts began in 1996; Dir E. SAGNIA.

Radio 1 FM; Kairaba Ave, Serrekunda; f. 1990; private station broadcasting FM music programmes to the Banjul area; Dirs GEORGE CHRISTENSEN, VICKIE CHRISTENSEN.

Radio Syd: POB 279/280, Banjul; tel. and fax 226490; commercial station broadcasting mainly music; programmes in English, French, Spanish, Wolof, Mandinka, Fula, Jola and Serahuli; also tourist information in Swedish; Dir CONSTANCE WADNER ENHÖRNING.

Finance

(cap. = capital; res = reserves; dep. = deposits; m. = million; brs = branches; amounts in dalasi)

BANKING

Central Bank

Central Bank of The Gambia: 1–2 Buckle St, Banjul; tel. 228103; telex 2218; fax 226969; f. 1971; bank of issue; cap. and res 4.0m., dep. 756.1m. (June 1994); Gov. MOMODOU CLARK BAJO; Gen. Man. J. A. BAYO.

Other Banks

Arab-Gambian Islamic Bank: Banjul; f. 1996, operations commenced 1997; Man. Dir MAMOUR JAGNE.

Continent Bank Ltd: 61 Buckle St, PMB 142, Banjul; tel. 229961; telex 2257; fax 229711; f. 1990; privately-owned; cap. 4m. (June 1996); Chair. Dr MUHAMMAD NADAR BAYZID; Man. Dir Alhaji ALIEU NJIE

Meridien BIAO Bank Gambia Ltd: 3–4 Buckle St, POB 1018, Banjul; tel. 225777; telex 2382; fax 225781; f. 1992; management assumed by Central Bank of The Gambia in 1995; cap. 20m. (Dec. 1994); Man. Dir ANTHONY C. GRANT; 3 brs.

Standard Chartered Bank Gambia Ltd: 8 Ecowas St, POB 259, Banjul; tel. 228681; telex 2210; fax 227714; f. 1978; 75% owned by Standard Chartered Bank Africa PLC (UK); cap. and res 24.8m., dep. 456.2m. (Dec. 1994), cap. 8,950 (Dec. 1995); Chair. Dr PETER JOHN N'DOW; Man. Dir DAVID N. T. KUWANA; 3 brs.

INSURANCE

Capital Insurance Co Ltd: 22 Anglesea St, POB 485, Banjul; tel. 228544; telex 2320; fax 229219; f. 1986; Man. Dir JOSEPH C. FYE.

The Gambia National Insurance Co Ltd: 6 OAU Blvd, POB 750, Banjul; tel. 228412; telex 2268; f. 1979; Man. Dir YAKUBA Y. S. DIBBA.

Greater Alliance Insurance Co: 10 Nelson Mandela St, Banjul; tel. 227839; telex 2245; fax 226687; f. 1989.

Senegambia Insurance Co Ltd: 7 Nelson Mandela St, POB 880, Banjul; tel. 228866; telex 2314; fax 226820; f. 1984; Man. Dir Alhaji BABOU A. M. CEESAY; Gen. Man. PA ALASSAN JAGNE.

Trade and Industry

CHAMBER OF COMMERCE

Gambia Chamber of Commerce and Industry: 78 Wellington St, POB 33, Banjul; tel. 765; f. 1961; Exec. Sec. PIERRE W. F. N'JIE.

GOVERNMENT REGULATORY BODIES

National Environmental Agency (NEA): 5 Fitzgerald St, Banjul; tel. 228056; fax 229701; Dir Ndey-Isatou Njie.

National Investment Promotion Authority (NIPA): Independence Drive, Banjul; tel. 228332; telex 2230; fax 229220; f. 1994 to replace the National Investment Bd; CEO S. M. Mboge.

National Trading Corpn of The Gambia Ltd (NTC): 1–3 Wellington St, POB 61, Banjul; tel. 228395; telex 2252; f. 1973; transfer pending to private-sector ownership; Chair. and Man. Dir Momodou Cham; 15 brs.

EMPLOYERS' ASSOCIATION

Gambia Employers' Association: POB 333, Banjul; f. 1961; Vice-Chair. G. Madi; Sec. P. W. F. N'Jie.

CO-OPERATIVE

The Gambia Co-operative Union (GCU): Banjul; f. 1959; co-operative for groundnut producers; Gen. Man. Lamin Willy Jammeh; 110,000 mems.

MAJOR COMPANIES

Banjul Breweries Ltd: Kanifing Industrial Estate, Kombo St Mary Division, Banjul; tel. 392566; fax 392266; f. 1975; owned by Brauhaase (Germany); Gen. Man. A. F. Huberts; 160 employees.

CFAO (Gambia): 14 Wellington St, POB 297, Banjul; tel. 227473; telex 2281; fax 227472; f.1887; general merchants; Chair. R. P. Couerbe; Man. G. Durand; 100 employees.

K. Chellaram & Sons (Gambia) Ltd: POB 275, Banjul; tel. 392912; fax 392910; importers and general merchants; Man. Dir Nitin Chellaram; 35 employees.

The Gambia Groundnut Corpn (GGC): Banjul; owned by Alimenta SA; Gen. Man. Richard Kettlewell.

Gambia Oilseeds Processing and Marketing Co Ltd: Marina Foreshore, Banjul; tel. 227572; telex 2205; fax 228037; assumed 'core' assets of The Gambia Produce Marketing Board in 1993.

Lenrie Holdings: Banjul; import-export agency; Chair. Lenrie Peters.

S. Madi (Gambia) Ltd: 10c Nelson Mandela St, POB 225/226, Banjul; tel. 227372; telex 2209; fax 226192; general merchants, agents for Lloyd's of London; Man. Dir A. B. Dandeh-N'Njie.

Maurel and Prom: 22 Buckle St Banjul; telex 2309; fax 228942; general merchants; Man. J. Eschenlohr.

The Milky Way: 40 Kanifing Industrial Estate, POB 95, Banjul; tel. 394522; fax 390599; f. 1983; general merchants; Mans Kamal Melki, Nawal Melki, Boundia S. Dibba, Jere Sanyang; also **Elof Trading Co Ltd**; f. 1991.

Utilities Holding Corporation (UHC): NIB Bldg, Independence Drive, POB 609, Banjul; telex 2302; fax 228260; fmrly The Gambia Utilities Corpn, transferred to private ownership in 1993; distributes electricity and water; Man. Dir Shola Joiner; 450 employees.

Zingli Manufacturing Co Ltd: Kanifing Industrial Estate, POB 2402, Serrekunda; tel. 392282; telex 2291; mfrs of corrugated iron and wire.

TRADE UNIONS

Gambia Labour Union: 6 Albion Place, POB 508, Banjul; tel. 641; f. 1935; 25,000 mems; Pres. B. B. Kebbeh; Gen. Sec. Mohamed Ceesay.

Gambia Workers' Confederation: Banjul; f. 1958 as The Gambia Workers' Union, present name adopted in 1985; govt recognition withdrawn 1977–85; Sec.-Gen. Pa Modou Fall.

The Gambia Trades Union Congress: POB 307, Banjul; Sec.-Gen. Sam Thorpe.

Transport

Gambia Public Transport Corporation: Factory St, Kanifing Industrial Estate, POB 801, Kanifing; tel. 392230; telex 2243; fax 392454; f. 1975; operates road transport and ferry services; Chair. Kekoto B. S. Maane; Man. Dir Ismailla Ceesay.

RAILWAYS

There are no railways in The Gambia.

ROADS

In 1995 there were an estimated 2,640 km of roads in The Gambia, of which 835 km were main roads, and 505 km were secondary roads. In that year only 32% of the road network was paved. Some roads are impassable in the rainy season. The expansion and upgrading of the road network is planned, as part of the Jammeh administration's programme to improve The Gambia's transport infrastructure. Among intended schemes is the construction of a motorway along the coast, with the aid of a loan of US $8.5m. from Kuwait.

SHIPPING

The River Gambia is well suited to navigation. A weekly river service is maintained between Banjul and Basse, 390 km above Banjul, and a ferry connects Banjul with Barra. Small ocean-going vessels can reach Kaur, 190 km above Banjul, throughout the year. Facilities at the port pf Banjul have been modernized and expanded during the mid-1990s, with the aim of enhancing The Gambia's potential as a transit point for regional trade.

Gambia Ports Authority: Wellington St, POB 617, Banjul; tel. 227266; telex 2235; fax 227268.

The Gambia River Transport Co Ltd: 61 Wellington St, POB 215, Banjul; tel. 227664; river transport of groundnuts and general cargo; Man. Dir. Lamin Juwara; 200 employees.

The Gambia Shipping Agencies Ltd: Liberation Ave, Banjul; tel. 227518; telex 2202; fax 227929; shipping agents and forwarders; Man. Nils Langgaard Sorensen; 30 employees.

CIVIL AVIATION

Banjul International Airport, at Yundum, 27 km from the capital, handled some 275,000 passengers and 3,000 metric tons of cargo in 1992. Construction of a new terminal, at a cost of some US $10m., was completed in late 1996. Facilities at Yundum have been upgraded by the US National Aeronautics and Space Administration (NASA), to enable the airport to serve as an emergency landing site for space shuttle vehicles.

Gambia International Airlines: Banjul International Airport, PMB, Banjul; tel. 472747; fax 472750; f. 1996; state-owned; sole handling agent at Banjul, sales agent; Man. Dir Lamin K. Manjang.

Tourism

Tourists are attracted by The Gambia's beaches and also by its abundant birdlife. A total of 89,997 air-charter tourists visited The Gambia in 1993/94, of whom 67.9% came from the United Kingdom and 7.5% from Sweden. Gross earnings from the sector were D241.5m. in 1992/93. A major expansion of tourism facilities was under way in the early 1990s. However, the withdrawal from The Gambia of many tour operators in the final months of 1994, in response to fears of political insecurity, resulted in a dramatic fall in tourist arrivals (to an estimated 38,000). Most operators resumed tours to The Gambia for the 1995/96 season, and the Government anticipated a full recovery in the sector by 1996/97. An annual 'Roots Festival' was inaugurated in 1996, with the aim of attracting African-American visitors to The Gambia.

The Gambia National Tourist Office: New Administrative Bldg, The Quadrangle, Banjul; tel. 227881; telex 2204; fax 227753; Dir of Tourism M. B. O. Cham.

Hotel Owners' Association of The Gambia (HOAG): Banjul; Chair. Sammy Lai Mboge.

Defence

In August 1996 the Gambian National Army comprised 800 men, including a marine unit of about 70 men and a presidential guard, in active service. Military service has been mainly voluntary; however, the Constitution of the Second Republic, which entered into full effect in January 1997, makes provision for conscription.

Defence Expenditure: Budgeted at D143m. in 1996/97.

Education

Primary education, beginning at seven years of age, is free but not compulsory and lasts for six years. Secondary education, from 13 years of age, comprises a first cycle of five years and a second, two-year cycle. In 1992/93 some 55% of children in the relevant age-group were enrolled at primary schools (64% of boys; 46% of girls), while secondary enrolment included only 18% of students aged between 13 and 19 (24% of boys; 12% of girls). According to UNESCO estimates, adult illiteracy in 1995 averaged 61.4% (males 47.2%, females 75.1%). The Jammeh administration has, since 1994, embarked on an ambitious project to improve educational facilities and levels of attendance and attainment. A particular aim has been to improve access to schools for pupils in rural areas. Post-secondary education is available in teacher training, agriculture, health and technical subjects. Some 1,591 students were enrolled at tertiary establishments in 1994/95. The new University of The Gambia was scheduled for inauguration in October 1997. In 1977 Koranic studies were introduced at all stages of education, and many children attend Koranic schools (daara). Central government expenditure on education in 1991/92 was D78m. (12.9% of total budget expenditure in that year).

Bibliography

Bridges, R. C. (Ed.). *Senegambia.* Aberdeen University African Studies Group, 1974.

Cooke, D. and Hughes, A. *The Politics of Economic Recovery: The Gambia's Experience of Structural Adjustment, 1985—94*, in The Journal of Commonwealth and Comparative Politics, Vol. 35, No. 1, London, Frank Cass, 1997.

Dieke, P. U. C. *Tourism in The Gambia: Some Issues in Development Policy*, in World Development, Vol. 21, No. 2, Oxford, Pergamon Press, 1993.

Gailey, H. A. *A History of The Gambia.* London, Routledge and Kegan Paul, 1964.

Historical Dictionary of The Gambia. Metuchen, NJ, Scarecrow Press, 1975.

Gamble, D. P. *A General Bibliography of The Gambia.* Boston, G. K. Hall and Co, 1979.

The Gambia, World Bibliographical Series, Vol. 91. Oxford, Clio Press, 1988.

Gray, J. M. *A History of the Gambia.* New York, Barnes and Noble, and London, Cass, 1966.

Harrison Church, R. J. *West Africa.* 8th Edn. London, Longman, 1979.

Hughes, A. 'From Colonialism to Confederation: the Gambian Experience of Independence 1965–1982', in Cohen, R. (Ed.), *African Islands and Enclaves.* London, Sage Publications, 1983.

The Senegambian Confederation, in Contemporary Review, February 1984.

(Ed.). *The Gambia: Studies in Society and Politics.* University of Birmingham Centre of West African Studies, 1991.

The Collapse of the Senegambian Confederation, in The Journal of Commonwealth and Comparative Politics, Vol. 30, No. 2, London, Frank Cass, 1992.

Jarrett, H. R. *A Geography of Sierra Leone and Gambia.* Harlow, Longman, 1981.

People's Progressive Party Special Editorial Commission. *The Voice of the People, the Story of the PPP, 1959–1989.* Banjul, The Gambia Communications Agency and Barou-Ueli Enterprises, 1992.

Quinn, C. A. *Mandingo Kingdoms of the Senegambia.* Evanston, IL, Northwestern University Press, 1972.

Radelet, S. *Reform without Revolt: The Political Economy of Economic Reform in The Gambia*, in World Development, Oxford, Pergamon Press, Vol. 28, No. 8, 1992.

Rice, B. *Enter Gambia: the Birth of an Improbable Nation.* London, Angus and Robertson, 1968.

Rimmer, D. *The Economies of West Africa.* London, Weidenfeld and Nicolson, 1984.

Robson, P. *Integration, Development and Equity: Economic Integration in West Africa.* London, Allen and Unwin, 1983.

Sallah, T. M. *Economics and Politics in The Gambia,* in The Journal of Modern African Studies, Vol. 28, No. 4, 1990.

Tomkinson, M. *Gambia.* London, Michael Tomkinson Publishing, 1987.

Wiseman, J. A. *Democracy in Black Africa: Survival and Revival.* New York, Paragon House, 1990.

Military Rule in The Gambia: An Interim Assessment, in Third World Quarterly, Vol. 17, No. 5, London, 1996.

Wiseman, J. A., and Vidler, E. *The July 1994 Coup d'Etat in The Gambia: The End of an Era*, in The Round Table, No. 333, Abingdon, Carfax, 1995.

Wright, D. R. *The Early History of Niumi.* Ohio University Center for International Studies, 1977.

Yeebo, Z. *State of Fear in Paradise: The Coup in The Gambia and the Prospect for Democracy.* London, African Research and Information Bureau, 1995.

GHANA

Physical and Social Geography

E. A. BOATENG

PHYSICAL FEATURES

Structurally and geologically, the Republic of Ghana exhibits many of the characteristics of sub-Saharan Africa, with its ancient rocks and extensive plateau surfaces marked by prolonged sub-aerial erosion. About half of the surface area is composed of Pre-Cambrian metamorphic and igneous rocks, most of the remainder consisting of a platform of Palaeozoic sediments believed to be resting on the older rocks. These sediments occupy a vast area in the north-central part of the country and form the Voltaic basin. Surrounding this basin on all sides, except along the east, is a highly dissected peneplain of Pre-Cambrian rocks at an average of 150–300 m above sea-level but containing several distinct ranges of up to 600 m. Along the eastern edge of the Voltaic basin and extending right down to the sea near Accra is a narrow zone of highly folded Pre-Cambrian rocks forming the Akwapim-Togo ranges. These ranges rise to 300–900 m above sea-level, and contain the highest points in Ghana. Continuing northwards across Togo and Benin, they form one of west Africa's major relief features, the Togo-Atakora range.

The south-east corner of the country, below the Akwapim-Togo ranges, is occupied by the Accra-Ho-Keta plains, which are underlain by the oldest of the Pre-Cambrian series (known as the Dahomeyan) and contain extensive areas of gneiss, of which the basic varieties weather to form heavy but agriculturally useful soils. Extensive areas of young rocks, formed between the Tertiary and Recent ages, are found only in the broad delta of the Volta in the eastern part of the Accra plains, and in the extreme south-west corner of the country along the Axim coast; while in the intervening littoral zone patches of Devonian sediments combine with the rocks of the Pre-Cambrian peneplain to produce a coastline of sandy bays and rocky promontories.

Most of the country's considerable mineral wealth, consisting mainly of gold, diamonds, manganese and bauxite, is associated with the older Pre-Cambrian rocks, although there are indications that petroleum may be available in commercial quantities in some of the younger sedimentaries. For a brief period in the 1980s actual exploitation, in relatively small quantities, of offshore deposits took place at Saltpond.

The drainage is dominated by the Volta system, which occupies the Voltaic basin and includes the vast artificial lake of 8,502 sq km formed behind the hydroelectric dam at Akosombo. A second dam is sited at Kpong, 8 km downstream from Akosombo. Most of the other rivers in Ghana, such as the Pra, Birim, Densu, Ayensu and Ankobra, flow between the southern Voltaic or Kwahu plateau and the sea. Most are of considerable local importance as sources of drinking water, but are hardly employed for irrigation purposes.

CLIMATE AND VEGETATION

Climatic conditions are determined by the interaction of two principal airstreams: the hot, dry, tropical, continental air mass or harmattan from the north-east, and the moist, relatively cool, maritime air mass or monsoon from the south-west across the Atlantic. In the southern part of the country, where the highest average annual rainfall (of 1,270–2,100 mm) occurs, there are two rainy seasons (April–July and September–November), while in the north, with annual averages of 1,100–1,270 mm, rainfall occurs in only a single season between April and September, followed by a long dry season dominated by the harmattan. There is much greater uniformity as regards mean temperatures, which average 26°–29°C. These temperatures, coupled with the equally high relative humidities, which fall significantly only during the harmattan, tend to produce oppressive conditions, relieved only by the relative drop in temperature at night, especially in the north, and the local incidence of land and sea breezes near the coast.

Vegetation in Ghana is determined mainly by climate and soil conditions. The area of heavy annual rainfall broken by one or two relatively short dry seasons, to be found in the south-west portion of the country and along the Akwapim-Togo ranges, is covered with evergreen forest in the wetter portions and semi-deciduous forest in the drier portions, while the area of rather lower rainfall, occurring in a single peak in the northern two-thirds of the country and the anomalously dry area around Accra, are covered with savannah and scrub. Prolonged farming activities and timber exploitation have reduced the original closed forest vegetation of some 82,000 sq km to about 24,000 sq km, while in the savannah areas prolonged cultivation and bush burning have also caused serious degradation of the vegetation. Truly edaphic vegetation types are found mostly in swampy or estuarine areas and on isolated lateritic hardpans in the savannah zone.

POPULATION

Ghana covers an area of 238,537 sq km (92,100 sq miles). The March 1984 census recorded a population of 12,296,081, giving an approximate density of 51.5 inhabitants per sq km. During 1990–95, according to World Bank estimates, the population increased by an annual average of 2.8%, and in mid-1991, according to official estimates, was 15,400,000, with a density of 64.6 inhabitants per sq km. The high rate of population growth, together with the influx of large numbers—mostly youth from the rural areas into the urban centres—coupled with a virtually stagnant economy and the lack of adequate employment openings, has created serious social and political problems. In view of these demographic trends, the government has initiated a campaign of family planning and population control, and aims to improve living standards through increased economic development. The highest densities occur in the urban and cocoa-farming areas in the southern part of the country, and also in the extreme north-eastern corner, where intensive compound farming is practised.

There are no less than 75 spoken languages and dialects, each more or less associated with a distinct ethnic group. The largest of these groups are the Akan, Mossi, Ewe and the Ga-Adangme, which, according to 1991 estimates, formed respectively 52.4%, 15.8%, 11.9% and 7.8% of the population. Any divisive tendencies which might have arisen from this situation have been absent, largely as a result of governmental policies; however, a distinction can be made between the southern peoples, who have come most directly and longest under the influence of modern European life and the Christian religion, and the northern peoples, whose traditional modes of life and religion have undergone relatively little change, owing mainly to their remoteness from the coast. One of the most potent unifying forces has been the adoption of English as the official national language, although it is augmented by eight major national languages.

Recent History

T. C. McCASKIE

Revised for this edition by the Editor

Longstanding protest within the Gold Coast against British rule, chiefly expressed by the educated professional classes, resulted in the formation in 1947 of the United Gold Coast Convention (UGCC), led by a lawyer, Dr J. B. Danquah. In 1949 the secretary of the UGCC, Dr Kwame Nkrumah, formed the more radical Convention People's Party (CPP), which demanded immediate self-government. In 1950 the British authorities imprisoned Nkrumah, but later that year permitted the drafting of a constitution, which provided for indigenous ministerial government under the British crown. A general election, held in 1951, was won by the CPP, and in the following year Nkrumah became prime minister; subsequent elections in 1954 and 1956 were also won by the CPP. Ghana was formed as the result of a UN-supervised plebiscite in May 1956, when the British-administered section of Togoland, a UN Trust Territory, voted to join the Gold Coast in an independent state. On 6 March 1957 Ghana was granted independence within the Commonwealth, becoming the first British dependency in sub-Saharan Africa to attain independence under majority rule.

NKRUMAH AND THE CPP

Nkrumah (who became prime minister of the new state) espoused 'African socialism' and maintained close relations wih the USSR and its allies, while remaining economically dependent on Western countries. In 1957 the opponents of the CPP merged to form the United Party (UP), led by Dr Kofi Busia, a former university professor. The government responded by assuming powers to imprison opponents without trial. Following a referendum held in 1958, Ghana became a republic on 1 July 1960, with Nkrumah as executive president. In 1964 Ghana officially became a 'socialist single-party state'.

Following widespread discontent at the country's economic difficulties, and at alleged corruption within the CPP, Nkrumah was deposed by a military coup in February 1966. A National Liberation Council (NLC) took power, under the chairmanship of Gen. Joseph Ankrah. (He was replaced in April 1969, following internal disputes, by Brig.—later Lt-Gen.—Akwasi Afrifa.) The NLC declared its intention of restoring civilian rule: it established commissions of inquiry into the alleged crimes of the CPP administration, and formed a constituent assembly to draft a new constitution. A ban on party politics was lifted in May 1969, and a general election took place in August. The Progress Party (PP), led by Busia, secured 105 of the 140 seats in the new national assembly, and Busia assumed office as prime minister on 1 October. A three-man commission, comprising members of the former NLC, held presidential power until August 1970, when Edward Akufo-Addo, a lawyer, took office as a non-executive civilian president.

ACHEAMPONG AND THE NRC

The Busia government proved unable to resolve Ghana's economic problems; increasing hardship prompted renewed discontent, while the PP was also widely perceived as corrupt. In January 1972 the armed forces again seized power, under the leadership of Lt-Col (later Gen.) Ignatius Kutu Acheampong. A National Redemption Council (NRC) assumed control of the country, and political parties were once again banned. The policy of self-reliance encouraged by the NRC subsequently achieved a modest improvement in Ghana's economic situation. The NRC also attempted to decentralize the government. During the NRC's period in power, a number of unsuccessful coup attempts were staged by members of the armed forces or supporters of the banned political parties.

In October 1975 the NRC was succeeded by a reorganized Supreme Military Council (SMC). In 1976 Acheampong proposed the formation of a 'union government' (UNIGOV), which would comprise a tripartite power-sharing arrangement between the armed forces, the police and civilians, without political parties. In July 1977, despite strong public opposition to the plans, and indications of dissent within the armed forces, the SMC announced a timetable for relinquishing power, stating that a referendum on the formation of UNIGOV would be conducted in March 1978 and would be followed by a general election in June 1979. The referendum, which duly took place in March 1978, endorsed the proposed system by 55.6% of votes cast; however, the result was widely believed to have been obtained by malpractice. In April selected opposition groups were proscribed; by May nearly 300 opponents of the government had been placed in preventive detention. In July Lt-Gen. (later Gen.) Frederick Akuffo, the chief of the defence staff, assumed power in a bloodless coup. Akuffo subsequently dismissed all but three members of the SMC, and shortly afterwards, Acheampong was placed under arrest.

THE FIRST RAWLINGS COUP AND THE LIMANN GOVERNMENT

On 1 January 1979 the ban on the formation of political associations was revoked, and 16 parties were registered, in preparation for the general election, which was still scheduled for June. In May, however, junior military officers staged an unsuccessful coup attempt. Flt-Lt Jerry Rawlings, the alleged leader of the conspirators, was imprisoned, but was subsequently released by other officers. On 4 June he and his associates successfully seized power, amid great popular acclaim. They subsequently established an Armed Forces Revolutionary Council (AFRC), headed by Rawlings, and initiated a campaign to eradicate corruption. In the same month Acheampong, Akuffo and other senior officers were convicted of corruption, and executed.

The AFRC indicated that its assumption of power was temporary, and the general election, which took place in June 1979, as scheduled, was contested by five parties: the Action Congress Party (ACP); the People's National Party (PNP); the Popular Front Party (PFP); the Social Democratic Front (SDF); and the United National Convention (UNC). The PNP secured 71 of the 140 seats, and agreed to form a governing coalition with the UNC, which obtained 13 seats. The leader of the PNP, Dr Hilla Limann, was elected to the presidency, and was inaugurated on 24 September.

Almost immediately serious disagreements developed within the ruling coalition and within the PNP itself. In October 1980 the UNC ended the alliance with the PNP, which subsequently retained a majority of only one seat in the legislature. In September 1981 the other parties represented in the legislature (including the UNC) amalgamated to form the All People's Party, electing the leader of the PFP, Victor Owusu, as their leader. Measures implemented by the government in an attempt to stimulate the economy, proved unsuccessful, and public discontent was manifested in widespread strikes and riots over the escalating price of food. In March and May 1980 and February 1981 several attempts to seize power by members of the armed forces were reported. A second coup by Rawlings, who retained enormous personal popularity, was widely anticipated.

THE SECOND RAWLINGS COUP AND THE PNDC

On 31 December 1981 Rawlings seized power for the second time. The constitution was abolished, parliament dissolved, and civilian political parties proscribed. Rawlings assumed chairmanship of a Provisional National Defence Council (PNDC), comprising four military personnel and three civilians. Limann and a number of prominent members of the PNP were imprisoned or placed in preventive detention. The PNDC subsequently appointed a national administration.

In direct contrast to the events of June 1979, Rawlings expressed no intention of restoring power to civilian politicians; instead, the PNDC decided to implement measures to 'democratize' political decision-making and to decentralize power. In

March 1982 city and district councils were replaced by People's Defence Committees (PDC), in an attempt to create mass participation at the local level in the 'revolution' (as the PNDC described the coup), and to create and foster public awareness and vigilance. The PDC were to form the basic structure of the new government.

The 'democratization' of the army led to the creation of factions, and to the consequent threat of constant instability; in March 1982 a number of military personnel staged an abortive coup against the PNDC. By mid-1982 the armed forces were increasingly divided along ethnic lines, with the Ewes supporting Rawlings, and the majority of northerners backing Sgt Alolga Akata-Pore (a member of the PNDC). In November the chief of the defence staff, Brig. Joseph Nunoo-Mensah, resigned, publicly voicing his disagreement with the policies of the PNDC. On the following day soldiers staged a coup attempt, which was suppressed by troops loyal to the PNDC. Akata-Pore was arrested, but other conspirators, together with Chris Bukari-Atim (a member of the PNDC), managed to escape to neighbouring Togo, from where, together with groups based in the United Kingdom, they continued to plan to overthrow Rawlings.

In February and March 1983 there were minor attempts to overthrow the government, and widespread rumours of numerous other minor disturbances. In June Ghanaian military exiles from Togo, led by a former bodyguard to Nunoo-Mensah, infiltrated Accra and briefly seized control of the Ghana Broadcasting Corpn. Troops loyal to Rawlings quickly suppressed the coup, but many of the leading conspirators escaped. In August 1983 the perpetrators of the coup attempts of November 1982 and June 1983 were put on trial (many of them *in absentia*). Of the 20 who were sentenced to death, only five were actually in custody; four of these were executed on 13 August. In March 1984 three of the leading conspirators were apprehended and executed.

The process of 'democratization' also affected Ghana's student community; by May 1983, university students, initially supporters of Rawlings, were engaged in violent protests regarding a number of issues: discontent with the apparent ineffectiveness of the government's economic policies; demands for a return to civilian rule; and resentment at the government's links with Libya and Cuba. Major clashes between workers and students ensued, and the PNDC closed the universities and converted them into training schools for revolutionary cadres. Despite an improvement in the economic situation during 1984, demands by the Trades Union Congress (TUC) for better wages and living standards became more insistent. The universities were reopened in March.

During 1985 elements of the army, with support from groups outside the country, were reported to be conspiring against the PNDC. In February a number of alleged plotters were arrested in Kumasi (Ashanti), and were accused of planning to assassinate Rawlings. Later that month a coup plot was detected in the army, and two majors and three sergeants were subsequently tried in camera. Five conspirators, allegedly linked to dissidents in Togo, were executed in May. In September Maj.-Gen. (later Lt-Gen.) Arnold Quainoo, the c-in-c of the armed forces, and Brig. (later Maj.-Gen.) Winston M. Mensa-Wood, the commandant of the military academy training school, were appointed to the PNDC, which was expanded from eight to 10 members.

INTERNAL AFFAIRS

The PNDC became increasingly preoccupied with domestic security in 1986 and 1987, possibly as a result of the dissident political activity abroad. In March 1986 a number of people were tried for involvement in a conspiracy to overthrow the government by dissident Ghanaians; several executions were subsequently carried out. In August Victor Owusu, the leader of the disbanded PFP, was arrested for alleged subversion. In June 1987 the PNDC announced further arrests in connection with an alleged conspiracy to overthrow the government. Seven further arrests took place in November; on this occasion the detainees included former officials of the PNDC.

Various administrative reforms were introduced by the PNDC from late 1984 to 1988. In December 1984 the PDC were redesignated committees for the defence of the revolution (CDR). In April 1986 there was an extensive review of the judiciary, resulting in the summary retirement of some judges for alleged incompetence and corruption. In December Rawlings announced that the PNDC was to seek a national mandate through district assembly elections, scheduled for mid-1987. It was envisaged that each district assembly would have an elected chairman, while the district secretary would continue to be appointed by the PNDC and would retain responsibility for routine administration. In July 1987, however, district council elections were postponed until the final quarter of 1988, and it was announced that the ban on political parties was to remain in force.

Elections to district assemblies were held in three stages, between December 1988 and February 1989. The PNDC reserved one-third of seats for its own nominees, and retained the power to scrutinize and disqualify individual candidates, although it was envisaged that the elected district assemblies would move towards regional representation, and ultimately form a national body which would supersede the PNDC.

However, the envisaged adoption of democratic reforms continued to be overshadowed by the grave economic situation. In 1988 the three universities were closed for four months, following renewed student unrest. In December of that year the PNDC discontinued free secondary and university education, and in the following month inaugurated a student loan scheme, provoking considerable student discontent. In addition, the PNDC's attempts to implement economic reforms were impeded by widespread mismanagement and corruption in the commercial sector. In 1989 further controls were imposed on the media; in March of that year newspaper and magazine licences became subject to review under new legislation.

In September 1989 an attempted coup took place, led by Maj. Courage Quashigah, a former commander of the military police and a close associate of Rawlings. Quainoo was subsequently dismissed as commander of the armed forces, although he remained a member of the PNDC. (Rawlings himself assumed control of the armed forces until June 1990, when Mensa-Wood was appointed to that post.) Quashigah (who had taken a leading part in suppressing the June 1983 coup attempt) and four other members of the security forces were charged with conspiring to assassinate Rawlings. In November a board of enquiry, which investigated the charges of treason, concluded that most of the conspirators were motivated by personal grievances and ambition. In January 1990 five further arrests were made in connection with the coup attempt. In August the human rights organization, Amnesty International, criticized the continued detention of Quashigah and six other members of the security forces, and claimed that they were imprisoned for political dissent.

CONSTITUTIONAL TRANSITION

In 1990 there were increasing demands for an end to the ban on political activities and associations, and for the abolition of a number of laws, particularly those concerning the detention of suspects. In July of that year, in response to pressure from Western donors to increase democracy in return for a continuation in aid, the PNDC announced that a national commission for democracy (NCD), under the chairmanship of Justice Annah, a member of the PNDC, would organize a series of regional debates, which would review the decentralization process, and consider Ghana's political and economic future. In August, however, a newly-formed political association, the Movement for Freedom and Justice (MFJ), criticized the NCD, claiming that it was too closely associated with the PNDC. In addition, the MFJ demanded the abolition of a number of laws, the release of political prisoners, the end of press censorship, and the imminent restoration of a multi-party system. The PNDC, however, advocated a national consensus, rather than a return to the discredited political system. In September the MFJ accused the PNDC of intimidation, after security forces suppressed its inaugural meeting. Both students and trade unionists voiced support for the MFJ's general objectives. However, the PNDC maintained that it would not permit the emergence of political associations, despite toleration of more generalized political activities.

On 30 December 1990 Rawlings announced proposals for the establishment of a constitution by the end of 1991. The NCD was to present a report on the democratic process with reference to the series of regional debates. The PNDC was to consider the recommendations, and then convene a consultative body to determine constitutional reform. However, the MFJ and other opponents of the PNDC criticized the absence of a timetable for political reform and the lack of information on the composition of the proposed consultative body. The MFJ continued unsuccessfully to demand the immediate restoration of a multi-party system, which the PNDC dismissed as inappropriate, while accusing the MFJ of ignoring the economic constraints on political reform.

In late March 1991 the NCD presented its report, which recommended the election of an executive president for a fixed term, the establishment of a national assembly, and the creation of the post of prime minister. Rawlings announced that the PNDC would consider the report and submit recommendations to the proposed national consultative body, which was to be established in May, and to start work in July. On 10 May, contrary to previous expectations, the PNDC endorsed the restoration of a plural political system, and accepted the NCD's recommendations. It was emphasized, however, that the formation of political associations remained prohibited. The MFJ immediately challenged the veracity of the PNDC's announcement, and the state-controlled press accused the MFJ of planning subversive action. In late May a 260-member consultative assembly was established, which was to review recommendations by a government-appointed committee of constitutional experts. A new constitution was subsequently to be submitted for endorsement by a national referendum.

In June 1991 the government reiterated denials of political detentions, and announced that it had invited Amnesty International to investigate the allegations. In the same month the PNDC announced an amnesty for political exiles, excepting those implicated in acts of subversion against the government. In early August a newly-formed alliance of opposition movements, human rights organizations and trade unions, including the MFJ and the socialist New Democratic Movement (NDM), known as the Co-ordinating Committee of Democratic Forces of Ghana (CCDFG), demanded that a constitutional conference be convened to determine a schedule for the transition to democracy, and that legislation prohibiting political activities be immediately repealed. Later in August the committee submitted a series of recommendations for constitutional reform, which included the establishment of a legislature, a council of state and a national security council. It was proposed that a president, who would also be c-in-c of the armed forces, would be elected by universal suffrage for a four-year term of office; the leader of the party which commanded a legislative majority would be appointed to the post of prime minister. However, the subsequent review of the draft constitution by the consultative assembly was impeded by opposition demands for a boycott, on the grounds that the number of government representatives in the assembly was too high. Two organizations, representing students and the legal profession, refused to attend. In the same month Rawlings announced that presidential and legislative elections would take place in late 1992.

In early December 1991 Rawlings ordered the arrest of the secretary-general of the MFJ, John Ndebugre, for allegedly failing to stand when the national anthem was played. Amnesty International subsequently reiterated claims that a number of prisoners in Ghana were detained for political dissension. In the same month the government announced the establishment of an interim national electoral commission (INEC), which was to assume functions formerly allocated to the NCD: the demarcation of electoral regions, and the supervision of public elections and referenda. In January 1992 the government extended the allocated period for the review of the draft constitution, originally scheduled for completion by the end of 1991, to the end of March 1992, provoking widespread speculation that Rawlings planned to delay the democratic process. In February, however, preparations for the forthcoming multi-party elections commenced; the PNDC subsequently carried out a government reshuffle. In March Rawlings announced a programme for constitutional transition, which was to be completed in January 1993. The new constitution was to be submitted for endorsement by national referendum on 28 April 1992. Legislation permitting the formation of political associations was to be introduced on 18 May, despite opposition demands that a multi-party system be adopted prior to the referendum. A presidential election was to take place on 3 November, and was to be followed by legislative elections on 8 December. Later in March the government granted an amnesty to 17 prisoners, who had been convicted of subversion, including Quashigah.

At the end of March 1992 the consultative assembly endorsed the majority of the constitutional recommendations, which were subsequently presented for approval by the PNDC. However, the proposed creation of the post of prime minister was rejected by the assembly; executive power was to be vested solely in the president, who would appoint a vice-president. In addition, the draft constitution included a provision that members of the government be exempt from prosecution for acts committed during the PNDC's rule; opposition groups subsequently condemned the legislation, on the grounds that it contravened human rights. At the national referendum held on 28 April, however, the adoption of the draft constitution was approved by 92% of votes cast, with 43.7% of the electorate voting.

In May 1992 the government introduced legislation which ended the ban on the formation of political associations imposed in 1981; political parties were required to apply to the INEC for legal recognition. Under the terms of the legislation, however, 21 former political organizations remained proscribed, while emergent parties were not permitted to use the names or slogans of these organizations. Moreover, the permitted amounts of individual financial contributions to parties were restricted. Later in May Komla A. Gbedemah, a former member of the Nkrumah government, and 28 other prominent opposition figures, unsuccessfully applied to the high court to disallow the legislation, which, it was claimed, was biased in favour of the PNDC. At the end of May the government announced that the legislation had been amended to allow the INEC to impose a new limit for individual financial contributions.

In June 1992 a number of political associations emerged, many of which were established by supporters of former politicians; six opposition groups subsequently obtained legal status. In the same month a coalition of pro-government organizations, the National Democratic Congress (NDC), was formed to contest the elections on behalf of the PNDC. However, an existing alliance of supporters of Rawlings, known as the Eagle Club, refused to join the NDC, and formed the Eagle Party of Ghana, subsequently known as the EGLE (Every Ghanaian Living Everywhere) Party. In July Rawlings denied that he was associated with the Eagle Club, and rejected an offer by the EGLE Party to represent it in the presidential election. In August the government promulgated legislation regulating the conducting of the forthcoming elections, which included a stipulation that, if no presidential candidate received more than 50% of votes cast, a second ballot between the two candidates with the highest number of votes would take place within 21 days.

In September 1992, in accordance with the new constitution, Rawlings retired from the armed forces (although he retained the title of c-in-c of the armed forces in his capacity as head of state), and was subsequently nominated as the presidential candidate of the NDC. (The NDC later formed an electoral coalition with the EGLE Party and the National Convention Party–NCP). A member of the NCP, Kow Nkensen Arkaah, became Rawlings' vice-presidential candidate. Four other political associations presented candidates to contest the presidency: the People's Heritage Party (PHP); the National Independence Party (NIP); the People's National Convention (PNC, which nominated a former president, Dr Hilla Limann); and the New Patriotic Party (NPP). Although the establishment of a united opposition to Rawlings was discussed, the parties failed to achieve agreement, owing, in part, to the apparent conviction of the NPP (which was recognized as the strongest of the movements) that its presidential candidate, Prof. A. A. Boahen, could win unaided against Rawlings.

Electoral Discord

In preparation for the November 1992 presidential election, and for the subsequent legislative elections, the INEC divided Ghana into 200 constituencies. Despite controversy over the accuracy of the high number of registered voters, the PNDC, acting through INEC, refused to carry out a revision of the electoral register. However, the INEC did arrange for the forthcoming election to be monitored by Commonwealth observers. During the pre-election period, Rawlings enacted a number of popular measures, which included, in September, the announcement of substantial wage increases for civil servants and other public sector workers, and, in October, the introduction of legislation that restricted (but did not abolish) the PNDC's powers of detention without trial. However, these measures were widely viewed as electoral bribes, and their popular impact was limited. Later in October the high court dismissed an application by the MFJ for an injunction to prevent Rawlings from contesting the presidential election, on the grounds that he was not a Ghanaian national (his father was Scottish), and that he remained accountable for charges in connection with the May 1979 and December 1981 coups. Prior to the election, widespread outbreaks of sporadic violence between NPP and NDC supporters were reported.

Less than 48.3% of the registered electorate voted in the presidential election, which took place, as scheduled, on 3 November 1992. Rawlings secured 58.3% of the vote, while Boahen obtained 30.4%, Limann 6.7%, the NIP candidate, Kwabena Darko, 2.8%, and the PHP candidate, Lt-Gen. (retd) E. A. Erskine, 1.7% of votes cast. Rawlings, with more than 50% of the vote, was declared the winner. The Commonwealth observers subsequently declared that the conducting of the election had been both free and fair. However, the opposition parties, led by the NPP, claimed that widespread electoral irregularities had taken place. A curfew was imposed in Kumasi, in Ashanti, following incidents of violence, and rioting by opposition supporters, in which a NDC ward chairman was killed; in addition, a series of explosive devices were detonated in Accra and Tema. The government subsequently rescheduled the legislative elections for 22 December. Later in November a prominent member of the PHP was detained, together with other opposition supporters, on the grounds of complicity in the bombings.

In early December 1992 Boahen announced that the opposition had direct evidence of electoral fraud perpetrated by the government, and that this would be made public in due course. The opposition parties declared, however, that they would not legally challenge the result of the presidential election, but that they would boycott the forthcoming legislative elections. Accordingly, these elections (which had been postponed until 29 December) were contested only by the NDC and its allies, the EGLE Party and the NCP. On this basis, the NDC obtained 189 of the 200 seats in the parliament, while the NCP secured eight seats, the EGLE Party one seat, and independent candidates two seats. On 7 January 1993 Rawlings was sworn in as president of the Fourth Republic, the PNDC was dissolved and the new parliament was inaugurated.

THE FOURTH REPUBLIC

In early January 1993 a number of the severe economic austerity measures, introduced under the 1993 budget, resulted in an immediate increase in transport and supply costs, and food prices. The NPP, the PNC, the NIP and the PHP subsequently formed an alliance, known as the Inter-Party Co-ordinating Committee (ICC), which strongly criticized the budget (widely believed to have been formulated under the terms of the World Bank and the IMF), and announced that it was to act as an official opposition to the government, despite its lack of representation in the parliament. In March Rawlings submitted nominations for members of the cabinet and other ministers for approval by the parliament. In the same month the two main perpetrators of the bombings in November 1992 were fined and sentenced to 10 years' imprisonment. In early April the NPP published a book, entitled *The Stolen Verdict,* which provided detailed evidence of malpractice perpetrated by the NDC and the INEC in the presidential election. On 14 April elections were held for the 10 regional seats in the council of state, and in May a 17-member cabinet (which included a number of members of the former PNDC administration) was sworn in. International approval of the series of election results was apparently indicated by subsequent pledges of economic assistance for Ghana. However, the member parties of the ICC continued to dispute the results of the presidential election. In June Rawlings urged a boycott of products manufactured by companies that supported the opposition. In the same month the supreme court upheld a claim by the NPP that certain existing legislation was in contravention of the constitution. In August the NPP (which had apparently been adversely affected by discrimination in the allocation of government contracts) announced that it was prepared to recognize the legitimacy of the election results, thereby undermining the solidarity of the ICC. In October the minister of justice, who in his capacity as public prosecutor had failed to win several trials in the supreme court, resigned after a state-controlled newspaper questioned his competence. In November, in accordance with the constitution, a 20-member national security council, chaired by Arkaah, was established. In December the PHP, the NIP and a faction of the PNC (all of which represented supporters of ex-president Nkrumah) merged to form a new organization, known as the People's Convention Party (PCP).

Ethnic Tensions and Security Concerns

In February 1994 long-standing hostility between the Konkomba ethnic group, which originated in former Togoland, and the land-owning Nanumba escalated, following demands by the Konkomba for traditional status that would entitle them to own land; some 500 people were killed in ethnic clashes in the Northern Region. The government subsequently dispatched troops to the Northern Region to restore order and imposed a state of emergency in seven districts for a period of three months; however, skirmishes between a number of ethnic factions continued, and it was reported that some 6,000 Konkomba had fled to Togo. In early March 12 people were killed at Tamale, 420 km north of Accra, when security forces fired on demonstrators belonging to the Dagomba ethnic group, who had allegedly attacked a group of Konkomba.

In March 1994 Rawlings carried out a minor reshuffle of the government. Later that month district assembly elections took place (except in the seven districts where the state of emergency remained in force); although the elections were contested on a non-party basis, it was reported that candidates who were unofficially supported by the NPP had secured the majority of seats in a number of the district assemblies. Negotiations between representatives of the various ethnic groups involved in the conflict in the Northern Region began in April, under government sponsorship. In the same month it was reported that the authorities had discovered a conspiracy to overthrow the government, which apparently involved threats to kill Quashigah (the instigator of the September 1989 coup attempt) and the editors of two private newspapers; the opposition, however, questioned the veracity of these claims. In May 1994 the NPP announced that it was to withdraw from reconciliation discussions between the government and the opposition, owing to lack of progress. In the same month a cabinet reshuffle took place, and the state of emergency in force in the Northern Region (where a total of 1,000 people had been killed, and a further 150,000 displaced) was extended for one month. In early June, however, the seven ethnic factions involved in the fighting signed a peace agreement that provided for the imposition of an immediate cease-fire and renounced violence as a means of settling disputes over land-ownership. The government subsequently announced that troops were to be permanently stationed in the Northern Region in order to pre-empt further conflict, and appointed a negotiating team, which was to attempt to resolve the inter-ethnic differences. The state of emergency was extended for a further month in June, and again in July. In early August, however, the government announced that order had been restored in the region, and ended the state of emergency.

In September 1994 five civilians, who had allegedly conspired to overthrow the government, were charged with treason. In October two men were arrested for allegedly attempting to transport armaments illicitly to the Northern Region; an increase in tension in the region was reflected by further arrests, in connection with violent incidents in which several people had been killed. Following a joint rally of the NPP, the PNC and the PCP in November, the parties announced that they would present a single candidate to contest the presidential election in 1996. Meanwhile, rumours emerged of ill-feeling between Rawlings and Vice-President Arkaah, reflecting increasing division between the NDC and NCP. In January 1995 Arkaah discounted speculation that Rawlings was responsible for allegations, which had appeared in an independent newspaper, of an illicit relationship between Arkaah and a minor, and attributed blame to subversive elements. In the same month, however, the government denied a reported statement by Arkaah that he had refused a request by Rawlings for his resignation.

In March 1995 the government imposed a curfew in the Northern Region in response to renewed ethnic violence, in which about 100 were killed. In April a joint committee, comprising prominent members of the Konkomba and Nanumba ethnic groups, was established in an effort to resolve the conflict. Meanwhile, the imposition, in February, of value-added tax (VAT) under that year's budget prompted widespread protests, while civil servants threatened to initiate strike action if the government failed to increase salaries following the ensuing rise in consumer prices; a series of demonstrations, which was organized by a grouping of opposition leaders, Alliance for Change, culminated in May, when five people were killed in clashes between government supporters and protesters. Later that month the national executive committee of the NCP decided to withdraw the party from the government coalition, claiming that the NDC had dominated the alliance. However, Arkaah (a member of the NCP) subsequently announced that he was to retain the office of vice-president on the grounds that his mandate had not expired. In June the authorities agreed to suspend VAT, and reinstated the sales tax that had previously been in force. In July the long-serving minister of finance, Kwesi Botchwey, resigned, apparently as a result of disagreement with the government's economic policies; a minor reorganization of the council of ministers ensued. At a by-election in the same month, the vacant seat was secured by a joint candidate of the PNC, NPP, NCP and PCP. In October the chairman of the NCP resigned, following dissent within the party. In November a commission of human rights and administrative justice (CHRAJ) commenced investigations into allegations of corruption on the part of government ministers and civil servants.

In January 1996 an alleged incident in which Rawlings assaulted Arkaah during a meeting of the council of ministers prompted further speculation of discord between the president and vice-president; opposition parties subsequently demanded that Rawlings resign. In February three journalists were arraigned after publishing a report alleging the government's complicity in a case of drugs-trafficking involving a Ghanaian diplomat based in Geneva, Switzerland. In March the trial of the three journalists was adjourned indefinitely. The NCP and the PCP merged in February to form a single party, known as the Convention People's Party, which later appeared to have broken up. Six people were killed in the Techiman area during violence in the same month, following a dispute over tribal status and authority. Proposals by the government for widely-ranging constitutional amendments came before parliament in February, provoking intense hostility from opposition parties and from many traditional chiefs. The draft legislation contained proposals for changes regarding a number of issues: the composition of the public services; the chairmanship and future nature of the prison service, the armed forces council and the police council; the participation of chiefs in politics; and dual citizenship. Rawlings reshuffled the council of ministers in March. In late May a violent confrontation between two Muslim factions in Atebubu led to one death and severe damage to property.

Presidential and Parliamentary Elections

In April 1996 presidential and parliamentary elections were scheduled for 10 December, although this was later changed to 7 December to meet constitutional requirements. Nominations of candidates were to take place in September. In May Kwame Pianim, prospective presidential candidate for the NPP, was disqualified from the elections on the grounds of his conviction for treason in 1982. In the same month it was announced that the Popular Party for Democracy and Development (PPDD), a group formed in 1992 by supporters of Nkrumah, was to merge with the PCP. The PPDD also announced its support for unity with the NPP. In June Thomas Appiah resigned for personal reasons as chairman of the NCP and vice-chairman of the PCP. In July the NCP announced that it had removed Kow Nkensen Arkaah as its leader, following his selection as presidential candidate by the PCP. In August the NPP and PCP announced their formation of an electoral coalition, to be known as the Great Alliance; it was subsequently announced that John Kufuor, of the NPP, was to be the Great Alliance's presidential candidate, with Arkaah, of the PCP, as the candidate for the vice-presidency. The NCP stated that it would support the NDC in the forthcoming elections, while the PNC announced its intention to contest the elections alone; Edward Mahama was subsequently selected as the PNC's presidential candidate. In September Rawlings was nominated as the NDC's presidential candidate. By 18 September, the official deadline for the nomination of candidates, only the Progressive Alliance (the NDC, the EGLE party and the Democratic People's Party–DPP), the Great Alliance and the PNC had succeeded in having their nomination papers accepted. In early October the NCP, which, according to the national electoral commission, had not presented the appropriate papers, declared its intention to take legal action against the commission to force it to accept the nomination of the party's candidates. In mid-October the electoral commission denied accusations that it had shown bias against the NCP. The selection of common candidates provoked a lengthy dispute between the NPP and the PCP, with the parties contradicting each other regarding previous agreements on the distribution of seats. In late October at least 20 people were wounded in clashes between NDC and NPP militant supporters in Tamale (in the north) and Kibi (in the north-east). In November a network of domestic election observers, comprising 25 groups (including religious councils, the TUC, and civil servants' and journalists' associations), was created to oversee the December elections. The resignation of the minister of the interior in October was followed, in November, by the resignations of the minister of trade and industry and the presidential aide on cocoa affairs, following corruption allegations against them published in an interim report by the CHRAJ. Reports of a number of violent incidents prior to the elections included a fatal attack on an NDC activist near Kumasi, allegedly carried out by NPP supporters, which prompted a temporary ban on all political activity in the area.

The presidential and parliamentary elections took place, as scheduled, on 7 December 1996. Rawlings was re-elected as president by 57.2% of votes cast, while Kufuor secured 39.8% of the votes. In the parliamentary poll the NDC's representation was reduced to 133 seats, while the NPP won 60 seats, the PCP five and the PNC one seat. Voting was postponed in the constituency of Afigya Sekyere East, in Ashanti, because of a legal dispute concerning the eligibility of candidates. (The seat was subsequently won by the NPP in a by-election held in June 1997). Despite opposition claims of malpractice, international observers declared that the elections had been conducted fairly, and a high electoral turnout of 76.8% was reported. Following the announcement of the election results, about 15 people were injured in clashes between NDC and opposition supporters in Bimbila, south-east of Tamale. Later in December Kofi Annan, the Ghanaian candidate, was elected to serve a five-year term as secretary-general of the UN. At the end of that month the PCP announced that its electoral alliance with the NPP had broken down. On 7 January 1997 Rawlings was sworn in as president.

The lengthy process of appointing a new council of ministers resulted in a protracted dispute between the NDC and the opposition, prompting a series of parliamentary walk-outs by the NPP, which insisted that all ministerial appointees be approved by the parliamentary appointments committee prior to assuming their duties. In late February 1997 opposition parties filed a writ in the supreme court preventing Kwame Peprah, the reappointed minister of finance, from presenting the budget. Owing to the NDC's parliamentary majority, however, procedures were approved to allow those ministers who had been retained from the previous government to avoid the vetting process. The majority of ministerial appointments were made during March and April, although a number of posts were not filled until June. In early June the supreme court ruled that all presidential nominees for ministerial positions had to be approved by parliament, even if they had served in the previous government. Following the ruling, the NPP left the chamber on several occasions when ministers attempted to address parliament. The government subsequently announced that ministers who had participated in the previous administration were prepared to undergo vetting procedures.

FOREIGN POLICY UNDER THE RAWLINGS GOVERNMENTS

In 1984 the PNDC established close links with the government of Capt. Thomas Sankara in the neighbouring state of Burkina Faso. Sankara, who seized power in August 1983, based the working structure of his 'revolution' on that of the PNDC. During 1984 Ghana also revived its involvement with the foreign policy structures of the African community, and in September of that year was elected to the chairmanship of the OAU liberation committee. In August 1986 the governments of Ghana and Burkina Faso agreed to establish a high-level political commission which would be responsible for preparing a 10-year timetable for the political union of the two countries. Agreements were also made to harmonize their currencies and their energy, transport, trade and educational systems, and in September and October a joint military exercise was held. Following a military coup in Burkina Faso in October 1987, relations between the two countries were temporarily strained, but subsequently improved, after meetings between Rawlings and Sankara's successor, Capt. Blaise Compaoré.

In July 1985 relations between Ghana and the USA became strained when a distant relative of Rawlings, Michael Agbotui Soussoudis, was arrested by the US authorities and charged with espionage. He was subsequently convicted, and sentenced to 20 years' imprisonment. Shortly afterwards, four members of the diplomatic missions in Accra and Washington were expelled by the respective governments. In December, however, following secret negotiations between the PNDC and the Reagan administration, Boussoudis was exchanged for a number of identified CIA agents in Ghana. In the same month Joseph H. Mensah, the leader of the exiled Ghana Democratic Movement, was arrested in the USA, with two other Ghanaians, and put on trial for attempting to purchase military equipment for shipment to dissidents in Ghana. (However, charges against Mensah were invalidated by legal technicalities.) Tension between the two countries increased in March 1986, when it was discovered that a Panamanian-registered freighter en route from Buenos Aires, Argentina, to Rio de Janeiro was transporting arms and ammunition, while its 18-member crew comprised a number of known mercenaries and US veterans of the Viet Nam war. The PNDC claimed that the vessel had been destined for subversive operations against Ghana, and had been financed by a Ghanaian dissident with alleged links with the CIA. During their trial in Brazil, eight members of the crew admitted that the charges were substantially true and that the dissident, named as Godfrey Osei, had purchased the weaponry in Argentina by posing as an agent of the Ghanaian government. The eight men were sentenced to terms of imprisonment, but three of them subsequently escaped to the USA, with, according to the Ghanaian government, the assistance of the CIA.

Relations with Togo deteriorated sharply in May 1986, following the arrest in Ghana of eight people on charges of subversion: they had allegedly been operating from a base in Togo. In June seven of the defendants were executed. In September an attempted coup in Togo was blamed, in turn, by the Togolese government on infiltrators from Ghana. The frontiers were closed, and in the following month the PNDC accused the Togolese authorities of maltreating the Ghanaians who had been detained in connection with the coup attempt. Although the borders were reopened in February 1987, relations between the two states remained strained.

Between December 1988 and January 1989 more than 130 Ghanaians were deported from Togo, where they were alleged to be residing illegally. In October 1991 the governments of Ghana and Togo signed an agreement on the free movement of goods and persons between the two countries. In October 1992, however, Ghana denied claims by the Togo government that it was implicated in subversive activity by Togolese dissidents based in Ghana. (By late 1992 more than 100,000 Togolese had taken refuge in Ghana, following the deterioration in the political situation in Togo). In January 1993 Ghana announced that its armed forces were to be mobilized, in reaction to concern at the increasing civil unrest in Togo. In March the Togo government accused Ghana of supporting an armed attack on the military camp at Lomé, where the Togolese president, Gen. Gnassingbe Eyadéma, resided. In January 1994 relations with Togo again became strained, following a further attack on Eyadéma's residence, which was claimed by the Togolese authorities to have been staged by armed dissidents based in Ghana. The Ghanaian chargé d'affaires in Togo was subsequently arrested, while Togolese forces killed 12 Ghanaians and bombarded a customs post at Aflao and several villages near the border between the two countries. Ghana, however, denied the accusations of involvement in the coup attempt, and threatened to retaliate against further acts of aggression. In May allegations by the Togolese government that Ghana had been responsible (owing to lack of border security) for bomb attacks in Togo resulted in further tension between the two nations. Later that year, however, relations between the two countries improved, and in November full diplomatic links were formally restored, with the appointment of a Ghanaian ambassador in Togo. In the following month Togo's border with Ghana, which had been closed in January 1994, was reopened. After discussions between Eyadéma and Rawlings in July 1995, an agreement was reached, providing for the reconstitution of the Ghana-Togo joint commission for economic, social and technical co-operation and the Ghana-Togo border demarcation commission. In August the Togolese governmment denied involvement in the assassination of a political opponent who had taken refuge in Ghana. In February 1996 both parliaments established friendship groups to examine ways of easing tensions. By the end of 1996 some 48,000 Togolese refugees were estimated to have received payment for voluntary repatriation.

In November 1993 attacks in Ghana on Ivorian footballers and their supporters prompted violent reprisals against the Ghanaian community in Côte d'Ivoire, leading to 25 deaths. More than 10,400 Ghanaians resident in Côte d'Ivoire were subsequently repatriated, while Ghana formally protested to the Ivorian authorities. However, relations with Côte d'Ivoire improved, following the establishment of a joint commission to investigate the violence in December.

Ghana has participated in the Monitoring Group (ECOMOG) of the Economic Community of West African States (ECOWAS), which was dispatched to Liberia in August 1990 following the outbreak of conflict between government and rebel forces in that country (see chapter on Liberia). In mid-1994 some 1,000 Ghanaian troops remained in Liberia. In August of that year Rawlings, who replaced the Beninois president as chairman of the conference of heads of state and government of ECOWAS, indicated that Ghana was to consider the withdrawal of troops from Liberia. However, it subsequently appeared that the Ghanaian contingent would remain in ECOMOG until peace was achieved, while Rawlings mediated continuing negotiations between the warring Liberian factions. In May 1996 an ECOWAS meeting, to discuss the situation in Liberia, took place at Rawlings' insistence, following intense fighting in Monrovia, Liberia. Ghana granted temporary asylum to some 2,000 Liberian war refugees, but insisted that no more could be accepted in the future. Financial assistance was received from the government of Canada for the care of the Liberian refugees. In July anxiety was expressed by Rawlings and by the government of Mali that the continuance of conflict in Liberia could impede the economic aims of ECOWAS. By mid-1997, however, some 17,000 Liberian refugees had arrived in Ghana. In late July the Nigerian head of state, Gen. Sani Abacha, succeeded Rawlings as chairman of ECOWAS. In June 1997 the Ghanaian government announced the establishment of a task force to monitor the situation in Sierra Leone, following the staging of a military coup in the previous month (see chapter on Sierra Leone); troops were dispatched to participate in an ECOWAS peace-keeping force deployed in that country.

Economy

LINDA VAN BUREN

Based on an earlier article by RICHARD SYNGE

The Ghanaian economy is based primarily on agriculture, although mining has also traditionally been of significance, especially in foreign trade. The dominant commercial activity is cocoa production, which was established in the country, mainly as an African smallholder crop, in the latter part of the 19th century. In the late 1950s, at the time of its political independence, Ghana was the world's leading exporter of cocoa, and this crop continued to account for between 45%–70% of commodity exports in most years from the early 1970s until the 1990s, when increased mineral revenues led to a decline in cocoa's share of exports, to some 33% in 1996. Ghana's other cash crops for export include coffee, bananas, palm kernels, copra, limes, kola nuts and shea nuts. Agricultural raw materials are also grown for processing by local manufacturing industries. Rubber, cotton, oil palms and kenaf are the most important, though productivity has been badly affected in recent years by the lack of foreign exchange for imported inputs and by poor planning. Food farming is based on the production of maize, sorghum, millet, rice, cassava, taro, yams and plantains. Other major export activities are gold and timber production, which were first established in the 1880s; gold enjoyed a major upturn in the 1990s.

At independence in 1957 Ghana possessed one of the strongest economies in Africa. However, the economy declined sharply in the following 25 years. During that period real per caput income fell, bringing about large reductions in the production of most of the main food crops, as well as the agricultural and mineral exports. The government tax base was diminished by a combination of falling incomes and production, and an increase in smuggling, and this in turn created large deficits, which led to rising inflation and enlarged external debts. It also resulted in lower expenditure on, and a general neglect of, the country's infrastructure, as well as its education and health services.

This process of decline commenced during the Nkrumah years (1957–66), and was characterized by ambitious expenditure, a major nationalization programme, and the alignment of Ghana's trade with Eastern Europe. The military government which displaced Nkrumah inherited serious economic problems, including crippling debts, and initiated austerity campaigns and other economic reforms. The successor civilian government headed by Dr Kofi Busia, which assumed power in 1969, continued these efforts and also attempted to liberalize the trade and other policies, which had been tightly regulated from the early days of the Nkrumah administration. However, the unpopularity of many of Busia's economic measures precipitated a coup in January 1972, which established a lengthy period of military government. Following the establishment of the first Rawlings government, efforts to reduce corruption and restore the basis of economic production and growth culminated in the first Economic Recovery Programme (ERP I), which the second Rawlings government introduced in 1983. This programme, which was developed in close collaboration with the World Bank and the IMF, was essentially designed as the stabilization phase of the economy's recovery. A second programme (ERP II), covering the period 1987–90, was regarded as the structural adjustment and development stage of that recovery. Most of the subsequent policy initiatives of the government were designed under the two ERPs.

With the introduction in 1992 of its new multi-party constitution, followed by elections at the end of the year, Ghana suffered a brief period of economic uncertainty, compounded by difficulties in fiscal management and reduced earnings from cocoa and gold. Government expenditure briefly exceeded stipulated levels, after pay increases were awarded to civil servants, resulting in a suspension of programmed assistance from a number of donor agencies. In the aftermath of the elections, President Rawlings' new constitutional government (little changed from its predecessor) was forced to adopt unpopular measures in its 1993 budget, and imposed sharp increases in the price of fuel, which prompted protests from trade unions and from the political parties that had boycotted the parliamentary elections.

Under the 1992 Rawlings government, the emphasis of economic policy shifted more fully towards the stimulation of the private sector as an essential part of its declared strategy of accelerated growth and poverty alleviation. In 1993 the government announced that the investment code would be further liberalized, and that there would be radical revisions to a number of tax and price control laws. The sale of part of the government's stake in Ashanti Goldfields Corpn on the London and Accra stock markets in April 1994 represented a new stage in the opening up of the economy to foreign portfolio investment, a move which proved timely for investors from South Africa who, following the political changes in that country, seized new investment opportunities in Ghanaian mining. Government shares in a number of other companies were also sold, and in 1994 it was expected that shares in public enterprises would progressively be made available to private investors. The government, however, continued to express its awareness of the need to alleviate poverty and significantly raise standards of living for most Ghanaians, and announced that it intended to maintain expenditure on education and basic health.

The continuing financial support of the international community for Ghana's reform efforts was reinforced by the commitment by donors, undertaken in June 1993, to provide finance of US $2,100m. in 1993 and 1994 to meet Ghana's anticipated balance-of-payments difficulties. Borrowing under an IMF structural adjustment facility came to an end in 1992; in mid-1995, however, the IMF approved a further three-year enhanced structural adjustment facility, totalling the equivalent of SDR 164.4m. (about $258m.), in support of the government's economic programme for 1995–97.

POLICY OBJECTIVES OF THE ERP

Exchange rate and trade policy reforms were given priority in the recovery programmes, resulting in a progressive nominal devaluation of the official cedi rate between early 1983 and early 1986. A weekly foreign exchange auction for specified transactions, but excluding cocoa exports, was introduced in September 1986 and remained in operation until mid-1990 (see below). This two-tier structure was unified in February 1987, thereby ending discrimination against cocoa exports and an unrealistically low cedi exchange rate for certain specified imports, particularly petroleum. In conjunction with these exchange-rate changes the long-established quantitative restrictions on imports, which were still necessary in 1986 because of continued currency over-valuation, were lifted and replaced by a fairly uniform rate of customs tariff on most imports. In late 1986 quantitative restrictions were removed from almost all raw materials, spare parts and capital goods. There were two further main reforms in exchange and trade arrangements. The first was the release of foreign exchange to consumer goods by allowing their participation in the auction. The second was the licensing of a number of foreign exchange bureaux, which were empowered to buy and sell foreign exchange independently. Policies adopted in 1992 included the abolition of the weekly foreign auction, with the aim of making exchange rate determination a function of a freely operating interbank market. The cedi has steadily depreciated in value, however, averaging C649.06 against the US dollar in 1993, C956.71 in 1994 and C1,200.43 in 1995.

In the area of public finance the ERP aimed to raise the revenue base of the government, which had declined sharply by the early 1980s. They placed emphasis on a series of policies to simplify and rationalize the major taxes, particularly the sales and customs taxes, improve tax administration, and achieve prompter adjustment of petroleum and other administered prices to reduce the subsidy burden associated with higher import prices. In the case of direct taxes, a main objective was to amend tax brackets and exemptions in order to reduce the degree of progressivity, which was seen as a main incentive for non-compliance. In the case of indirect taxes, the main objective was the integration of the *ad hoc* excise taxes on a wide range of goods with an expanded sales tax to establish the reformed sales tax as the major source of indirect tax revenues. In 1995 the government introduced value-added tax (VAT) at a rate of 17.5%, but public reaction against the move, in the form of political protests and riots, was so strong that the tax was withdrawn. In February 1997 the minister of finance announced that new VAT legislation was to be brought before parliament, with the VAT to become operational from 1 January 1998. He failed to specify the initial rate at which the new tax would be levied. In addition, measures were taken under the ERP to rationalize the import tariff as the central instrument of trade protection. Finally, and as a by-product of exchange rate policies, the major devaluations of the currency have significantly enhanced tax revenues on cocoa earnings.

In the area of budgetary expenditure, the successive IMF programmes have sought to monitor and limit government expenditure while changing the structure of that expenditure; the number of personnel in the civil service and parastatal sector has also been progressively reduced. Overall, the recovery programmes have achieved some success, both in raising the revenue and expenditure shares of GDP, and in achieving reduced fiscal deficits.

Major changes have been introduced in price and subsidy policies. In the case of cocoa prices, ERP I introduced a series of rises in producer prices as a key element of the attempt to achieve a recovery of production levels. The World Bank structural adjustment credit of 1987 consolidated this process by introducing a scheme to relate Ghanaian producer prices to world prices on a formula basis.

In relation to consumer prices, policies focused on the elimination of the endemic price control, under which by 1970, some 6,000 prices, relating to about 700 separate items, were restricted. This formed part of the dissolution of the implicit social contract on wages and prices, which operated through the 1970s and the early 1980s. The liberalization of prices achieved by the recovery programmes achieved improved availability of many items, although for some groups it led to a widening division between the levels of prices and wages. In conjunction with price reforms, there was also a systematic programme of subsidy removal. Reductions in fertilizer and pesticide subsidies were implemented under the ERP from an early stage, and the fertilizer subsidy ceased entirely in 1989.

A final area of policy reform after the 1983 ERP was that of state ownership. At an early stage a consultant study recommended that 80 of 235 state enterprises either be converted into joint ventures with the private sector, be completely divested, or in a few cases be liquidated. Although progress was initially slow, some 52 enterprises had been divested by mid-1993, of which 33 were sold to foreign investors. In addition, some parastatal companies previously considered to be 'strategic', such as Ghana Airways and the Posts and Telecommunications Corpn (now Ghana Telecommunication Co), were designated for transfer to the private sector. Government shares in mining and banking were transferred to the private sector in 1994 and 1995. By the end of 1995 195 state-owned enterprises had been divested. In early 1996 the government indicated that it intended to accelerate the privatization process; a US $70m. private-sector adjustment credit was provided by the World Bank to fund further privatization.

In late 1989 measures agreed under the terms of the enhanced structural adjustment facility (ESAF) included the unification, in mid-1990, of the auction and foreign bureau exchange rates, an increase in privatization, a further relaxation of trade restrictions, and the liberalization of fuel prices. Ghana's first stock exchange, based in Accra, began functioning in late 1990; three stockbroking firms were initially registered. By February 1996 the number of firms listed had grown to 19 and included companies in manufacturing, mining, banking and insurance.

Ghana's economic programme for 1995–97 aimed to increase real GDP growth to 5.5% by 1997, while reducing inflation to 5% (subsequently revised to 15% on an end-of-period basis) and the external current account deficit to 2.7% of GDP. Private investment was to be promoted through the continuation of fiscal policies consistent with reducing the rate of inflation and maintaining a stable exchange rate. The overall budget balance, excluding divestiture receipts, was projected to achieve a surplus of 1.3% of GDP by 1997, as a result of a reduction in current expenditure and an adjustment in taxes on expenditure-based sources of revenue.

ECONOMIC PERFORMANCE UNDER THE ERP

By 1983 the economy of Ghana was severely flawed, as a consequence of two decades or more of economic mismanagement, falling incomes, lower exports, reduced imports, deteriorating infrastructure, endemic corruption, a grossly overvalued currency and a serious distortion of most incentives. Thus, specific imbalances—excessive inflation and unsustainable fiscal and external deficits—were largely symptomatic of the economic recession in the productive sectors. Against this general background, economic performance since 1983 can be considered very successful, although further progress is necessary to achieve broad-based growth at all levels of the economy.

GDP increased by an annual average of 3.0% in 1980–90, and by 4.3% in 1990–95. The growth rate was 3.8% in 1994, 4.5% in 1995, a provisional 5.2% in 1996 and a projected 5.5% in 1997. The deficit on the current account of the balance of payments, which in 1995 amounted to US $403.7m. before (and to $143.7m. after) official transfers, was above 6% of GDP, twice as high as the target stated in the economic programme for 1995–97. In 1996 the current account deficit rose to $458.4m. before, and to $252.8m. after, official transfers, respectively 13.5% and 75.9% higher than in the previous year. Although there has been success in some areas, there is still concern over the sustainability of the structural adjustment process, particularly over the failure to control the growth of government expenditure, which resulted in an increase in money supply, high inflation and the continued rapid depreciation of the national currency. The government's efforts to reduce inflation were only partially successful, even before the 1995 VAT fiasco. After reaching 122.8% in 1983, partly as a result of the severe drought of that year, the rate declined to 10.4% in 1985, but averaged more than 30% in each of the following five years. The rate declined to 10.3% in 1991. The overall consumer price index was dominated by food prices, which were determined largely by domestic food output. Fuel prices and developments in the exchange rate of the cedi were also important factors. Although the rate of inflation was effectively controlled in 1990 and 1991, it increased sharply following the political transition of 1992, reaching 27.7% in 1993 and 34.2% in 1994. The annual inflation rate on an end-of-period basis doubled in 1995, from 34.2% in December 1994 to 70.8% in December 1995. The main reason was the introduction of VAT, but food shortages in the first quarter of 1995 also contributed. The lack of a sufficiently developed financial sector rendered the imposition of high interest rates largely ineffective in curbing inflation in the face of intense currency speculation. Inflation on an end-of-period basis slowed to 32.7% in 1996, and the projection for 1997 was 15.0%.

Private investment has been deterred by perceptions both of financial instability and of political obstacles placed in the way of businesses owned by known opponents of the government, while anticipated flows of foreign and Ghanaian private capital have not been realized. New investment has been concentrated in relatively few areas, principally in gold mining and, to a lesser extent, in tourism. Much of the economy is based on short-term trading activity.

The services sector, in particular trading activity, demonstrated substantial growth over the reform period, while mining also made an important contribution. However, growth in both the agricultural and manufacturing sectors proved disappointing. Services represented some 77% of the growth in the economy between 1984 and 1991, with mining and industry contributing 19% and agriculture 5%. In 1995, according to estimates, services contributed 34.7% of GDP, while agriculture contributed 44.0% and industry contributed 16.5%, more than half of which came from manufacturing. In 1996 services grew by 6.3%, agriculture by 3.9% (cocoa by 6%) and industry by 4.2% (manufacturing by 3.3%).

The recovery in the output of cocoa that might have been expected to result from the government's reforms was constrained by the collapse of world prices for the commodity. Government efforts to increase progressively the share of international prices received by cocoa farmers were impeded by the necessity of maintaining the flow of revenue, by the high marketing costs and by the decline in world prices. The failure of the domestic private sector to invest in productive activity, which was partially attributable to the high cost of credit and generally low level of savings caused largely by the weakness of the cedi, also proved disappointing. The influx of foreign exchange from aid programmes and a growth in tourism has stimulated trade in imported goods, but manufacturing output has failed to respond to the new conditions.

In relation to the balance of payments, the major success has been the reversal of the chronic reduction in imports which had restricted the economy for several years, and the release of enlarged import volumes for both productive sectors and consumers. Imports increased sharply, from US $499.7m. in 1983 to $1,457m. in 1992, and to $1,823.0m. in 1996; world inflationary trends had an adverse effect in some years. Overall, the current account deficit, excluding official transfers, increased from less than 1% of GDP in 1983 to more than 8% by 1990. Although the rise in gold production increased the value of gold exports to more than $300m., and the total value of exports to $986m. in 1992, the growth of cocoa and other exports remained slow. Merchandise exports amounted to $1,431.2m. in 1995 and to a provisional $1,510.2m. in 1996 (falling short of the $1,543.7m. target). Substantial inflows of external concessionary assistance maintained the overall balance-of-payments surplus at $53.2m. in 1993, followed by $167.4m. in 1994. There was an estimated surplus of $249.1m. in 1995. The $83.1m. surplus forecast for 1996 became an $18.9m. overall deficit, however. An overall balance-of-payments surplus of $100.0m. was projected for 1997. The inflows of official grants and long-term concessionary loans increased from less than 1% of GDP in 1983 to about 10% of GDP by 1990, facilitating the elimination of external payments arrears and of official reserves.

POPULATION

According to the result of the March 1984 census, Ghana's population had increased by 43% since 1970, to reach 12.3m. The heaviest concentrations were in the regions of Ashanti (2.1m.), Eastern (1.7m.), Greater Accra (1.4m.), and Volta (1.2m.). The least populous regions were Upper East and Upper West. About 50% of the population are under 15 years of age, and 40% live in and around the principal metropolitan areas. Ghana's population is becoming increasingly urbanized, with an estimated 5.5% rise in the average annual growth rate of the urban population in 1980–85, compared with an average annual growth rate of 3.4% for the whole country over the same period. During 1990–95, according to World Bank estimates, the population increased by an annual average of 2.8%. In August 1996 the minister of finance announced that a population census would be carried out in 1998, at a cost of C2,000m.

At the 1984 census the Ghanaian labour force was about 5.6m., of whom an estimated 41% were in the agricultural sector, and 23% were engaged in service industries. Unemployment in 1983 was officially estimated at 12%–15% of the work-force, although the real level was believed to be considerably higher, owing to the slump in economic activity, the operation of a three-day week in certain sectors and the large influx of returnees from Nigeria. Despite opposition from trade unions, the recognition of chronic over-employment in the public sector resulted in attempts to reduce the public-sector work-force, while raising the wages of remaining employees, by redeployment of labour to the agricultural sector, by voluntary redundancies and by temporary lay-offs. In order to help those affected by its economic retrenchment policies, the government launched the Programme of Action to Mitigate the Social Costs of Adjustment (PAMSCAD) in 1988 and obtained pledges of US $140m. from donors to finance it. The first part of the PAMSCAD comprised a series of schemes to generate employment for those (about 45,000) affected by the job losses in the public sector during 1988–90. The second part aimed to strengthen community social programmes, including self-help groups. The final part was intended to provide the most vulnerable groups in society with basic needs, such as water and sanitation, health care, nutrition and housing. In 1995 redundant staff of the Ghana Cocoa Board (COCOBOD) were to be retrained under a C890m. national programme, funded by the EU and the government. In the following year a C4,000m. Entrepreneurial Scheme, partly funded by the African Development Bank (ADB), was introduced by the government to encourage former civil servants to find employment in the agricultural sector. A further round of public-sector wage and price revisions was implemented in January 1997.

AGRICULTURE

In 1995 the agricultural sector accounted for an estimated 44% of GDP and employed 56% of the working population. Cocoa is traditionally Ghana's most important cash crop, occupying more than one-half of all the country's cultivated land. Output, however, declined steadily during the 1970s, owing to a combination of factors, which included a lack of financial incentives for farmers, caused by fluctuating world cocoa prices, an overvalued cedi, unreliable payment procedures and low producer prices; ageing and diseased trees; shortages of fertilizers and vital pesticides; and poor transport and distribution services. The decline continued into the 1980s, exacerbated by drought, bush fires and smuggling (the latter activity, mainly into Côte d'Ivoire, Togo and Burkina Faso, led to losses of about 50,000 tons of cocoa per year).

In October 1983 the government launched a US $130m. campaign under ERP I to revitalize the cocoa sector, based on an earlier programme for reform and rehabilitation, drafted in 1979. The Cocoa Marketing Board (CMB) was reorganized to implement the campaign more efficiently. Cash incentives were offered to farmers to replant crops, and producer prices were increased by 67%. Essential inputs, such as insecticides, building materials and sprayers, were made available, and improvements were made to transport and distribution services. Financial assistance was provided by the World Bank. Attention was also focused on estate rehabilitation and disease control in the major growing areas in the Ashanti and Western Regions (although the areas worst affected by disease were the Eastern and Central Regions). Progress was slow, owing to shortages of labour, resistance by farmers to the uprooting of old trees in order to prevent the spread of disease to new pods, and continued doubts about the adequacy of price incentives. Although more than 3m. hybrid cocoa pods were distributed to private farms for planting in mid-1985, many farmers chose to plant food crops rather than cocoa. Later in the year the CMB was reorganized as COCOBOD, and in July 1986 a new agreement, proposed by the World Bank, fixed the level of producer prices. In Ghana 320,000 ha of cocoa farming land were designated as special zones for rehabilitation and spraying to prevent black pod disease. Under ERP II, the government aimed to increase cocoa production to more than 350,000 tons per year. However, this target proved to be over-optimistic, and output remained below 300,000 tons per year, totalling only 243,000 tons in 1991/92, 240,000 tons in 1993 and 270,000 tons in 1994. With world prices continuing to decline, the government's measures to increase producer prices proved unsuccessful. Subsidies on fertilizers were abolished and high rates of interest discouraged farmers from seeking credit from the commercial banks. In early 1993 Rawlings promised to maintain appropriate prices for cocoa farmers. In July COCOBOD was deprived of its monopoly, and three trading companies were licensed to purchase cocoa direct from farmers. In 1995 cocoa achieved the highest growth level of any agricultural subsector, at 11.1%, and the harvest reached 325,000 tons. Cocoa production improved further in 1996, when 400,000 tons were harvested, setting a 20-year record. Export earnings reached $508.6m. in that year, exceeding the $425.3m. target by almost 20%. In June 1997 the government announced a 50% increase in the producer price of cocoa, from C1.2m. to C1.8m. per ton, which amounted to 54% of the estimated f.o.b. export price for the 1997 season, nearing the government's target of 60% by the year 2000. The increase meant that, for the first time, more than one-half of the proceeds from cocoa exports accrued to those who grew the commodity. However, the government continued to resist pressure from the IMF and the World Bank to liberalize the external marketing of cocoa. As regards the internal marketing of cocoa, in 1997 the government proposed that the Produce Buying Co be split into two smaller entities, both of which were to be floated on the Ghana Stock Exchange.

Droughts in 1976, 1977 and 1982 necessitated huge imports of staple foodstuffs and increased Ghana's dependence on international food aid. Adverse weather conditions, bush fires and the return of some 1m. Ghanaian migrants from Nigeria led to acute food shortages in 1983, but the return of favourable weather conditions in 1984, combined with new price incentives, helped to increase crop yields considerably. The rise in food production was not, however, sufficient to meet local demand, and 257,000 tons of food aid (of which a considerable proportion came from Eastern Europe) was needed to compensate for the food deficit in 1984. Even the excellent maize harvest in 1984 was substantially below consumption requirements of 1.1m. metric tons. Increased production of maize in Ghana's main producing areas, around the Ashanti and Brong-Ahafo Regions, created added problems for the government. The state-owned Food Distribution Corpn had limited storage facilities, and lacked the resources to purchase and distribute excess stocks. With maize prices declining sharply, consumers were virtually forced to buy maize in the new 'people's shops'. This development, in turn, further depressed prices and led to the accumulation of large unsold stocks. By 1988, however, staple food production had increased to 6.8m. tons. Despite severe floods, crop surpluses were reported in 1989. In 1994 ethnic conflict in the north of the country (a principal agricultural region) necessitated emergency food aid, and it was feared that the harvest in the following year would be adversely affected. In 1995, however, according to the FAO, maize production increased to 1,042,000 tons, compared with 574,000 tons in 1985. In that year production of paddy rice reached 202,000 tons, while output of cassava also increased significantly. Ghana recorded a sorghum harvest of 390,000 tons, and a millet crop of 201,000 tons, in that year. The 1996 cereal crop was 3% down on the volume harvested in 1995, but the output of roots and tubers increased by 8%.

To maintain the continuity of food supplies throughout the year, the government established a national food security and buffer stock system. A price-support structure, to combat fluctuating producer prices, was introduced in 1985, and moves were under way to sell state farms back to the private sector. The ministry of agriculture also set up a national resource allocation committee, which aimed to rationalize the distribution of inputs and equipment. The ministry drew up a pilot scheme for intensive food crop production in the Accra plains, on previously unused land. The area under oil palms was also to be increased to 2,500 ha, and the IDA granted US $25m. towards the second stage of a large palm oil project. Production of palm oil rose to an estimated 51,000 tons in 1987, compared with 13,000 tons in 1982, and by 1994 output had reached 108,000 tons. According to FAO estimates, Ghana produced 176,000 tons of groundnuts (in shell), 34,000 tons of palm kernels and 9,000 tons of copra in 1995. Output of vegetable oils in 1994 reached 25,016 tons of groundnut oil, 9,750 tons of palm kernel oil, 5,568 tons of coconut oil and 4,000 tons of margarine. The plantain harvest in 1995 was 1.64m. tons. The horticultural sector produced 182,000 tons of tomatoes, 169,000 tons of green peppers and chillies, and 6,400 tons of 'garden eggs' (aubergines). Citrus products and other fruits also did well; the 1995 harvests were 50,000 tons of oranges, 30,000 tons of lemons and limes, 12,000 tons of pineapples and 4,000 tons of mangoes. In 1996 export promotion villages were set up to produce high-value export crops such as cashew nuts and black peppercorns.

In 1987 the government introduced a four-year agricultural programme, which included proposals to 'privatize' certain services provided by the secretariat for agriculture and to reorganize its planning and research unit. In 1991 the government implemented a Medium Term Agricultural Development Programme (1991–2000), which aimed to achieve complete self-sufficiency in food by the year 2000. The programme included proposals to diversify staple crops and improve livestock production; farmers were to receive subsidized loans from local banks to purchase high yield seed and fertilizers. In 1997 the government announced that the outgrower scheme in the cultivation of oil palms and other cash crops had been so successful that it was to be used as the basis for similar schemes in other food and cash crops, particularly cereals and tubers. The yield of yams was to be improved by the use of cultivation techniques.

Cattle farming is restricted to the Northern region and the Accra plains. Production of meat is insufficient to meet local annual demand of about 200,000 tons. Imports of livestock from adjacent countries have been considerable, though declining in recent years, owing to shortages of foreign exchange. To revitalize the livestock sector, the government undertook to rehabilitate and restock the six cattle stations at Pong-Tamale, Ejura, Babile, Kintampo, Amrahia and Nungua. Domestic fisheries (marine and Volta Lake) supply only about one-half of the country's total annual demand of 600,000 tons. The total catch in 1995 was 344,460 tons.

Ghana has extensive forests, mostly in the south-west, and developed a substantial timber export industry during the 1960s. The establishment of a Timber Marketing Board (TMB), with powers to fix minimum contract prices, marked the beginning of a decline in this sector, and in 1985 the TMB was replaced by the Forest Products Inspection Bureau and the Timber Export Development Board. Efforts are proceeding to promote timber exports, which are projected eventually to reach 700,000 cu m per year. However, exports declined from 614,000 cu m in 1994 to 364,768 cu m in 1996. The government aims to phase out exports of raw logs and to encourage local processing of timber products, following the introduction in late 1993 of duty incentives for imports of sawmilling and other equipment. Forest replanting, which was being carried out at an annual rate of 11,000 ha in the early 1970s, had declined to 4,000 ha per year by the late 1980s. Ghana, however, possesses enough timber to meet its foreseeable domestic and export requirements until the year 2030. In early 1989 a forest management programme was initiated, financed by $30.6m. from the IDA. The World Bank also made $39.4m. available for forest protection. In early 1996 the government decided to prevent mineral exploration in areas classified as forest reserve. Export earnings from timber increased to $230m. in 1994 (compared with $88m. in 1989), becoming Ghana's third most important export, before falling back to $141.3m. in 1996, 33% short of the $212.4m. target. In 1995 the forestry sector accounted for an estimated 4.2% of GDP and 9.4% of total export earnings in 1996, according to provisional figures. In 1995 more than 800,000 teak trees were planted on a 250-ha site at Somanya, in the Eastern Region, by Bonsuvonberg Farms Ltd. The joint Ghanaian-Dutch company planned to bring a further 450 ha under teak during 1996 and to cover some 10,000 ha with teak in the Ashanti Region by the year 2000.

MANUFACTURING

Apart from traditional industries such as food processing, Ghana has a number of long-established large and medium-sized enterprises, including a petroleum refinery and plants producing textiles, vehicles, cement, paper, chemicals and footwear, and some export-based industries, such as cocoa processing and timber plants.

The manufacturing industries have traditionally been underused, high-cost and strongly dependent on imported equipment and materials. Expansion has been deterred by low levels of investment, by transport congestion and by persistent shortages of imported materials and spares. Moreover, the consistent overvaluation of the cedi and the irregularity of supply increased the attractiveness of imports relative to home-produced goods.

Manufacturing output stagnated in the 1970s and then declined sharply in the early 1980s, and the sector's contribution to Ghana's total GDP fell from 22% in 1973 to under 5% before the start of ERP I in 1983. There was an increase to 8% in 1986, and to nearly 10% of GDP in 1990. This recovery has been assisted by freer access to imports, following the liberalization measures implemented under the adjustment programme. Almost all industries have continued to be affected by shortages of raw materials, spare parts and other imported machinery, irregular electricity supplies, and inflation. These factors, together with poor planning, lack of co-ordination, and duplication, especially in the soap, textile and beverage industries, reduced average capacity utilization to as low as 20% in 1985. However, manufacturing output recovered somewhat in 1986, as more capital equipment was purchased by producers, using the new foreign exchange 'auctions'. In 1988 the rate of capacity utilization reached 62%. Manufacturing GDP increased by an annual average of 3.6% in 1985–95, and by 3.3% in 1996. The contribution of the industrial sector to total GDP increased from less than 12% in 1983 to an estimated 16.5% in 1995. Industrial GDP increased by an annual average of 5.4% in 1985–95, and by 4.2% in 1996.

According to an IMF study in 1991, the response of the private sector to the improved macro-economic environment remained unsatisfactory, reflecting the time needed to restore confidence in a sector undermined by earlier policy mistakes. The process of reform itself has also forced the closure of many industries that had previously been sheltered from foreign and domestic competition. New policy measures implemented after 1990, which were designed to promote private investment in manufacturing, included reductions in tax rates, and an extension of the capital allowances provided under the Investment Code to all manufacturing enterprises.

Among the largest capital-intensive industries in Ghana is an aluminium smelter at Tema, operated by the Volta Aluminium Co (VALCO), which is owned by the multinational Kaiser Aluminium and Chemical Corpn (90%) and the Reynolds Metals Co (10%). Although the Tema plant has a potential output capacity of 200,000 metric tons of primary aluminium per year, production was running at less than 50,000 tons annually in the mid-1980s, owing to lower world demand and reduced energy supplies from the drought-stricken Akosombo hydroelectricity plant. Other developments in the manufacturing sector during the 1980s included the reopening of a glass factory at Aboso, with a capacity of 25,000 tons per year; a US $36m. project to increase palm oil production, including the opening of a new $15m. palm oil mill in 1987, with a capacity of 25,000 tons per year; a new cement factory using local raw materials; the rehabilitation of Ghana Sugar Estates to produce alcohol; Chinese funding for three rice mills; and the construction of a citronella distillation plant at Bonso. Privatization of the manufacturing sector accelerated in 1993, and the Divestiture Implementation Committee undertook to sell the government's shares in a number of enterprises, including the Tema oil refinery, the Tema food complex, the Ghana Industrial Holding Co's pharmaceutical subsidiary, the Bonsa Tyre Co (including its rubber estate) and cocoa processing factories in Tema and Takoradi. The divestiture programme was expanded in 1994 and 1995 to include some important state-owned enterprises. In 1996 a number of enterprises, including Coca-Cola Ltd, experienced higher production, employment and export levels following privatization.

Evidence of increasing foreign investor confidence is apparent in the repurchase by multinationals, such as Unilever and Guinness, of shares in their Ghanaian operations that had been held by government. In an attempt to encourage new investments by US corporations, the government has repealed some restrictive legislation, and in early 1993 prepared a new investment bill for presentation to parliament. The bill sharply reduced the minimum capital requirements for new foreign investment and reserved very few activities exclusively for Ghanaians. Dividends, profits and the original investment capital could be repatriated freely in convertible currency, and tax incentives and benefits were improved. In 1995 the government launched a proposal for free ports and export-processing zones (EPZs). A variety of incentives were outlined to attract investment to the zones, including exemption from tax for the first 10 years. By May 1997 16 companies had received government approval to set up in the EPZs, and some 50 others were awaiting rulings on their applications.

MINING

Gold is Ghana's principal mineral export and has accounted for an increasing proportion of total export earnings in recent years, replacing cocoa as the leading export commodity in 1992. Ghana's export earnings from gold, totalling about US $92m. per year in 1985 and 1986, increased to $300m. in 1991, and to $647m. in 1995, before declining to $612.4m. in 1996, 9.7% below the target of $678.4m. The principal mine is situated at Obuasi and is the ninth-largest in the world. It is operated by the Ashanti Goldfields Corpn, which is 34% owned by Lonrho PLC, a British-based multinational company. The high value of Ashanti Goldfields was demonstrated by the successful flotation of 26% of its shares on the London and Accra stock exchanges in April 1994. With the shares selling at more than $20 per unit, the government received more than $300m. and the company more than $50m. The government retained a 31% share in the company. In August 1995 Ashanti placed 3m. new shares without the participation of the government or Lonrho, whose shareholdings consequently fell to 28.8% and 41.4% respectively. In 1996, amid speculation regarding a possible takeover by South Africa's Anglo American Corpn, Ashanti acquired the UK's Cluff Resources, International Gold Resources of Toronto and GLAMCO, and concluded a merger with Australia's Golden Shamrock Mines. The company also became listed on the New York and Toronto stock exchanges. The government reduced its shareholding to 19%, with Lonrho owning 34%.

In 1992 substantial new investment was under way in the gold mining sector, with Ashanti Goldfields (which accounted for two-thirds of Ghana's official production in 1996) implementing a number of measures to expand its output. The company has initiated a programme, at an estimated cost of US $250m., to increase production capacity from underground sources to 600,000 oz per year, established a new open-pit sulphide operation, and developed a new surface operation, with an estimated output of 38,000 oz per year. Output at the main Obuasi mine reached 940,000 oz in 1995 and exceeded 1m. oz in 1996. Nevertheless, pre-tax profits at Ashanti Goldfields declined by 46% in 1996, to $60.1m., owing to increased operating costs at Obuasi. Corrective action, proposed in 1997, included the renegotiation of large supply contracts, the rationalization of the labour force and the elimination of high-cost contractors. The other major investments in gold were largely from private sources, while the activities of the government-owned State Gold Mining Corporation (SGMC) continued to be hindered by technical difficulties. Following the political changes in South Africa, investors from that country bought Tarkwa Goldfields from the SGMC in the mid-1990s, and almost immediately the inflow of new investment became evident as new facilities were constructed, virtually transforming the Tarkwa site (where gold reserves are measured at 13m. oz). In 1997 plans to develop the northern reef at Tarkwa were strongly opposed by villagers who were dissatisfied with the resettlement package they had been offered.

Following exploration and development by private investors from 1985, several medium-scale producers, mainly using open-pit methods, commenced a stage of production in 1991/92. These included the following companies: Teberebie Goldfields, Billiton Bogusu, Ghana Australian Goldfields, Goldenrae Mining Co (which subsequently ceased operations in 1993) and Bonte. Some have received financial support and equity contributions from development finance companies, particularly the International Finance Corporation (IFC) and European bilateral institutions. Gold mining investment in the period 1987–91 totalled some $600m., and the further investment of $500m. was predicted. By the end of 1996 123 local prospecting companies and 74 foreign companies had been granted exploratory rights.

The highest-producing companies after Ashanti in 1993–95 were Teberebie Goldfields, controlled by Pioneer Group of the USA (235,470 oz in 1995), Ghana Australian Goldfields at Iduapriem (124,279 oz in 1995) and Billiton Bogusu, owned by Gencor of South Africa (107,677 oz in 1995). In 1992 Rawlings announced that the government intended to initiate consultations and discussions with the mining companies in order to draft legislation to regulate the conduct of the companies, following a report on the impact of gold mining on the environment.

Diamonds, which are mainly industrial stones, are mined both by Ghana Consolidated Diamonds (formerly Consolidated Africa Selection Trust) at Akwatia and by local diggers. Total recorded production dwindled from 3.2m. carats in 1960 to 442,000 carats in 1987, and to only 300,000 carats in 1988. Diamond output recovered as a result of efforts to regularize small-scale mining after 1990, and reached about 500,000 carats in 1992, advancing to about 700,000 carats in 1993. Diamond output totalled 739,967 carats in 1994 but declined to 631,337 carats in 1995.

Ghana became a petroleum producer in 1978, when a US company, Agri-Petco International, began extracting petroleum from the continental shelf near Saltpond. Reserves at the

Saltpond oilfield were estimated at 7m. barrels, but average output during the early 1980s was only 1,250 barrels per day (b/d). In 1986 another US company, Primary Fuel (which had acquired Agri-Petco International), halted production at Saltpond, owing to a decline in profits. In 1983 the government established the Ghana National Petroleum Corpn (GNPC) to develop offshore areas under production-sharing contracts. In 1984 foreign oil companies were invited to bid for exploration and production licences in 70% of its offshore blocks. Exploration and production rights were set out under the 1984 Petroleum Law, which allowed the government to take an initial 10% share in any venture, with the option of buying 50% of production and holding a 50% royalty on output. As of 1993, however, following some exploratory drilling, no commercial quantities of oil had been identified, although various gas projects for power generation were in the process of being developed. In June 1997 a US company, Santa Fe Energy Resources (SFR), announced a production-sharing contract with the ministry of mines and energy and the GNPC which entitled SFR to carry out exploratory oil and gas activities in the 10,500 sq km Keta Block, located at the delta of the Volta. Some 80% of the concession is offshore. Ghana's proven reserves of petroleum were estimated at about 16m. barrels in December 1995. In that year the decision was taken to re-appraise a natural gas deposit at Cape Three Points, discovered initially in 1974, and in 1997 the GNPC signed agreements with two foreign consortia for offshore exploration and production in the area. In September 1995 Ghana joined Nigeria, Togo and Benin in signing an agreement to proceed with the construction of a US $270m. pipeline from Nigeria's oilfields to the three recipient countries.

The country's sole refinery is operated by the Ghanaian–Italian Petroleum Co and is located at Tema. Capacity at the refinery, in which the government holds a 50% share, was 1.25m. metric tons in 1997. Nigeria is the principal supplier of crude petroleum to Ghana. Other suppliers include Iran, Libya and Algeria.

Ghana possesses substantial reserves of bauxite, although only a small proportion, at Awaso in the Western Region, is currently mined. Exploitation of these deposits is carried out by the Ghana Bauxite Co (GBC), in which the government holds a 55% interest. Bauxite output, which is all exported, fell from more than 300,000 metric tons per year during the 1950s to less than 30,000 tons by the mid-1980s, owing to the rapid deterioration of the railway line linking Awaso with port facilities at Takoradi. Following the virtual closure of the line in 1984, the GBC temporarily ceased operations, although output recovered to 170,000 tons in 1985, as repairs to the rail link progressed. By 1994 production had increased further to 451,800 tons and reached 530,440 tons in 1995. Plans to utilize the large bauxite deposits at Kibi for the VALCO aluminium smelter at Tema have failed to materialize because of funding difficulties and opposition from Kaiser Aluminium, which currently imports bauxite from Jamaica for use at the Tema plant.

Manganese ore is mined at Nsuta, in the Western Region, by Ghana National Manganese Corpn, which was to be taken over by Elkem International of Norway in late 1995, and managed by Ghana Manganese Co. Despite obsolete equipment and limited transport facilities at Takoradi Port and the main railway, ore production of 230,000–260,000 tons annually was achieved in the second half of the 1980s, increasing to 319,000 tons in 1991, but declining to 238,430 tons in 1994 and 179,360 tons in 1995. Albeit that these figures represent about one-half of the output levels in the 1960s, Ghana ranks as the world's eighth largest producer of manganese.

In 1986 the government introduced a new mineral code, whereby new mining projects were required to be self-financing in foreign exchange and were granted external account status. The new code made Ghana highly attractive to foreign investors, but almost all of their interest has been focused on gold, with remaining finance being directed to the diamond industry.

ELECTRICITY

Until the Akosombo hydroelectricity plant was opened on the Volta Lake in 1966, electricity production came solely from diesel generators that were operated by the Electricity Corpn of Ghana (ECG) or by the mines. In 1986 the Akosombo plant, with an installed generating capacity of 912 MW, and later the 160-MW Kpong plant together provided virtually all of Ghana's electricity needs, and allowed electricity to be exported to Togo and Benin. In the early 1980s the Volta River Authority (VRA), which operates electricity supply from the Volta Lake, was forced to restrict output, owing to a reduction of water levels after two years of drought. Sporadic interruptions in the electricity supply ensued, and major commercial consumers, such as the Volta Aluminium Co (VALCO—which takes, on average, more than 60% of the power supply from Akosombo), were forced to reduce production levels. An improvement in rainfall from 1984 allowed a return to full output. A project to extend the electricity supply to the Northern, Upper West and Upper East Regions from Brong Ahafo, in order to save reliance on diesel generators in the north, is being financed by bilateral and multilateral credits. In May 1994, however, following poor rainfall, the VRA was again obliged to restrict output, with VALCO agreeing to a reduction of 22% in its energy allocation.

The expansion of the Kpong hydroelectricity plant and the linking of the power systems of Ghana and Côte d'Ivoire are expected to facilitate a growth in electricity exports. However, plans to build a 450-MW hydroelectricity plant at Bui, on the Black Volta, to provide electricity for export and to supply northern Ghana, have been delayed, owing to funding difficulties. The construction of the country's first thermal power generation plant (at a projected cost of US $400m.) at Aboadze, near Takoradi, was expected to be completed in 1997 and to add 300 MW to the national grid. An oil/gas depot was also to be built at Aboadze. The construction of a nuclear reactor at Kwabenya, near Accra, which commenced in 1964 (but was suspended during 1966–74) was completed in January 1995. Eleven more district capitals were connected to the national electricity grid in 1995, and the last 25 district capitals were to be linked up in 1996–98, using $165m. of donor funding. By 1996 the ECG owed the VRA more than C50,000m., and the debt was increasing by some C1,500m. per month. In February 1997 the government announced that it was to convert the ECG into a limited-liability company.

PUBLIC FINANCE

Ghana's fiscal base is extremely narrow. Traditionally, the country's high levels of development spending have been funded by revenues from excises (mainly on cocoa—C277,700m. in 1996) and sales taxes, but, to an increasing extent, these funds proved to be inadequate, in relation to expenditure. The loss of cocoa revenues, as a result of smuggling and a downturn in export volumes, added to the already rapid decline in revenues from other trade transactions, caused by the overvaluation of the cedi and persistent shortages of foreign exchange. However, this decline was to some extent reversed, following the introduction of reform programmes in the 1980s.

Since 1983 fiscal policies have been designed to reduce the imbalances in government finances and to foster economic growth. Capital spending, and the proportion of both revenue and expenditure to GDP, have increased significantly. From 1987 increasing emphasis has been laid on improving economic incentives and tax administration, with the result that, in 1992, corporate tax rates were considerably lower than before the reform process. Receipts from import duties expanded during 1987–90, increasing from 16% to 25% of total revenue. In 1995 import taxes brought in C342,751m., exceeding the target of C335,400m., and included C157,200m. from cocoa duties. In 1996 import taxes brought in C424,600m., falling short of the target of C450,300m. Another important source of revenue was petroleum taxes, which earned C282,800m. in 1996. Export duties, recently levied exclusively on cocoa, have declined as a percentage of total revenue, from 35% in 1983 to 5% in 1993, but increased to 9% in 1995. The generally declining contribution of receipts from the cocoa tax to total revenue reflected the reduction in world cocoa prices, as well as substantial real increases in producer prices paid to farmers.

Government expenditure has been realigned, with the aim of increasing both civil service wages and capital expenditure on infrastructure, agriculture, education and health. The rationalization of the civil service involved the redeployment of some 50,000 civil servants in the period 1987–90. Nevertheless, the public-sector wage bill grew from C431,000m. in 1994 to C560,300m. in 1995. Defence expenditure has remained low, representing 7.5% of total expenditure in 1985, according to official statistics, and declining to 3.1% of total expenditure by 1994.

The budget deficit (including foreign grants) remained fairly stable between 1983–90, fluctuating between 2.1% and 3.3% as a percentage of GDP. Excluding grants, the deficit increased to 5.5% in 1990, partly as a result of the declining share of grants in project-related aid. After considerable financing of the deficit (which reached C118,175m. in 1993) the budget for 1994 achieved a surplus of C111,700m., despite substantial interest payments of C114,200m. on domestic debts and C61,300m. on foreign debts. The 1996 budget proposals envisaged total revenue of C2,328,339m. and total expenditure of C2,169,588m., projecting a budgetary surplus of C158,751m. In the event, however, total revenue was lower, at C2,268,524m., and total expenditure was higher, at C2,410,476m., turning the projected surplus into a deficit of C141,952m. The 1997 budget forecast revenue of C2,944,309m. and expenditure of C2,753,120m., to give a budgetary surplus of C191,189m.

Ghana's heavy use of IMF facilities has contributed significantly to the country's foreign debts, which totalled US $4,351m. at 31 December 1991, of which obligations to the IMF accounted for $834m. Most of the country's other borrowings are long-term and at concessionary rates, but the debt-servicing burden remains substantial; the ratio of debt service to exports of goods and services in 1994 was 26.2%. At 31 December 1995 Ghana's total foreign debt totalled $5,874m. The debt-service ratio was 23.1% in that year. Interest due on external debt was forecast to rise from C95,800m. in 1995 to C126,100m. in 1996, according to projections from the ministry of finance. However, debt-servicing payments on Ghana's foreign debt amounted to C144,800m. in 1996, or about 5% of merchandise exports. Moreover, the cost of servicing the government's domestic debt was three times as high as that of servicing its overseas debts, at C434,500m. The government has blamed this sharp increase in domestic borrowing on the need to absorb excess liquidity and to help reduce inflation. Yet during the same year the government increased the money supply by 34%, adding C452,000m., to bring the total to C1,785,000m. The government has, nevertheless, given priority to its debt-servicing obligations, resulting in an improvement in the country's credit rating. Private banks have proved increasingly willing to extend short-term credit to Ghana for a variety of financial operations, including the purchase of the cocoa crop for the 1993/94 season.

DOMESTIC COMMERCE AND FINANCE

A small number of large and long-established foreign companies continue to be important in the import trade, though they have now largely withdrawn from retail transactions, except for department stores in the major towns and for certain 'technical' goods. Since 1962 the publicly-owned Ghana National Trading Corpn (GNTC), created by purchase of A. G. Leventis and Co, has existed alongside the expatriate companies. At the retail level, independent Ghanaian and other African traders compete with the GNTC and with Lebanese and a few Indian businesses. The complex and highly fragmented trade in locally produced foodstuffs is almost wholly in African ownership.

In 1968 the government announced that small-scale retail and wholesale trade and the representation of overseas manufacturers (together with taxi services and small-scale manufacturing) would henceforth be reserved for Ghanaian enterprise. Most of these restrictions came into force in August 1970. Under an investment policy decree of April 1975, Ghanaian participation of 40%–55% was required by December 1976 in the equities of larger foreign businesses in a range of activities including distribution, banking and some manufacturing processes. Insurance was later brought into these arrangements. In 1986 the government introduced a new investment code, offering a range of fiscal and trade incentives and inducements. The priority sectors, designated for special treatment under the new code, were agriculture, import substitution industries, construction and tourism. The government continues to stress the importance of private investment and has reduced public-sector investment in the development of basic key industries. Public-sector investment accounted for only 28% of total proposed investment under ERP I. Shares were floated on the Ghana Stock Exchange in such groups as Paterson Zochonis Ghana Ltd, UTC Estates, CFAO (Ghana) Ltd and Unilever Ghana Ltd.

The banking sector has expanded and undergone substantial reform since the mid-1980s. In 1992 there were five commercial banks as well as three development banks, three merchant banks and a number of rural banks. The Bank of Ghana has strengthened its supervisory role and in June 1992 assumed control of the assets of the Ghana Co-operative Bank. Home Finance Co Ltd, Standard Chartered Bank Ghana Ltd and the Social Security Bank were listed on the stock exchange in 1996. Two new banks for workers were launched in 1995: Metropolitan and Allied Bank and First Atlantic Bank.

TRANSPORT

The country's two major ports are both artificial: Takoradi, built in the 1920s, and Tema, which was opened in 1961 to replace the Accra roadstead, and which became an industrial centre. The rehabilitation of the two ports, at an estimated cost of US $100m., was completed in 1990. An additional programme to rehabilitate Takoradi commenced in mid-1995. Facilities are to be upgraded further in a $365m. project, scheduled to begin in 1998, which also aims to give greater operational autonomy to both ports. The Ghana Ports and Harbours Authority was to oversee the dredging of the ports in 1996. The Ghana merchant shipping fleet had a total displacement of 225,000 gross registered tons in 1982, but its size was subsequently reduced, as the national Black Star Line disposed of some of its ships, owing to recurrent labour disputes and an increasing debt burden. Total displacement stood at 134,686 grt in 1996.

There are 947 km of railway, forming a triangle between Takoradi, Kumasi and Accra-Tema. Exports traditionally accounted for the greater part of railway freight tonnage, but cocoa and timber were diverted to the roads as rail facilities deteriorated, and the railways have required a regular government subsidy since 1976. In 1988 the IDA and the ADB provided a credit of US $42m. towards a project to rehabilitate the Western Line railway from Kumasi to Takoradi. Equipment worth $12.8m. was also provided by the IDA to help to repair faulty track. In 1996 the government committed US $150m. towards further upgrading the Western Line to link the mining areas with Takoradi port. In 1995 Ghana Railway Corpn took delivery of three new locomotives and 60 goods wagons, funded by Germany's Kreditanstalt für Wiederaufbau (KFW) and Japan's Overseas Economic Co-operation Fund (OECF).

In 1995 there were an estimated 37,561 km of classified roads, of which 24.9% were paved. The road system is good by tropical African standards, but its maintenance has been a constant problem since the early 1960s. Vehicle spare parts were also scarce, and the internal distributive system deteriorated physically. In 1991 the government initiated a major five-year programme of road development and rehabilitation, at an estimated cost of US $142.3m. Work was due to begin in 1996 on eight new roads with a combined length of 466 km and a combined cost of C326,500m. The overwhelming focus of construction in the transport sector in both 1996 and 1997 was on roads, with work being completed on four new roads in 1996. In addition, 87 km of roads were gravelled in that year and a further 213 km were resurfaced, including two roads in the Obuasi area. Spending on road construction in 1997 was expected to total C445,400m., C159,800m. of which was to come from budgetary resources, with C285,600m. coming from foreign sources.

The creation of the Volta Lake, stretching some 400 km inland from the Akosombo dam, opened up new possibilities for internal transportation, but lake transport is still relatively modest. In the late 1980s the Federal Republic of Germany financed a project to construct new ports on the lake, and to establish a new cargo and passenger service.

There is an international airport at Kotoka, near Accra, and other airports at Kumasi, Sunyani, Takoradi, Tamale and Wa serving inland traffic. The national airline is Ghana Airways.

FOREIGN TRADE AND AID

Ghana is essentially an exporter of primary products, mainly gold, cocoa and timber, and an importer of capital goods, foodstuffs and mineral fuels. The propensity to import is high, among both consumers and producers, although trade flows fluctuate in response to variations in the cocoa harvest and world commodity prices.

The continued decline in earnings of convertible currency, a growing food deficit and rising world prices for petroleum increased the pressure on import costs and on Ghana's reserves of foreign exchange. The country's terms of trade seriously deteriorated, and 'visible' trade surpluses in 1979 (US $262.6m.) and 1980 ($195.3m.) were followed by a deficit of $243.6m. in 1981, a small surplus in 1982, and a further deficit of $60.6m. in 1983. The trade balance again moved into surplus in 1984; from 1987, however, deficits were recorded, reaching $470.3m. in 1992, $664.3m. in 1993 and $353.1m. in 1994. Substantial deficits on 'invisible' trade (services and transfers), accentuated by increased payments to service the external debt, caused the current account to follow the 'visibles' into deficit in 1981. Following surpluses on the current account of the balance of payments in 1979 ($122m.) and 1980 ($29.2m.), the current account has remained in deficit in each year since 1981. The deficit on the current account amounted to $375.3m. in 1992, $557.9m. in 1993 and $263.8m. in 1994.

In the early 1990s Western industrial nations comprised Ghana's major trading partners, although useful links have been maintained with countries of the former Eastern bloc, with which Ghana developed trade relations in the early 1980s (in 1984 the USSR accounted for one-quarter of Ghanaian exports). In 1989 the principal export destinations were Germany (representing 21.7% of the total), the United Kingdom (13%), the USA (11.4%) and Japan (6%). The major sources of imports in 1989 were Nigeria (22.3%), which provided most of Ghana's petroleum imports, the United Kingdom (16.7%), the USA (10%) and Germany (8%).

Since the mid-1970s the Ghanaian economy has become increasingly reliant upon external finance. Bilateral aid and loans from traditional trading partners, such as the UK, Germany and the USA, have fluctuated with political changes in the country, and in recent years these sources of funds have been replaced by increasing financial support from World Bank affiliates and the IMF.

Although the level of donor pledges has risen dramatically since 1980, the disbursement of funds has been slow, owing to the complexity of donor agreements, and the lack of local expertise in administering aid. The repayment of the short-maturity credits from the IMF, which has contracted since 1983, has increased the pressure on the capital account of the balance of payments. In addition, Ghana's total external debt increased dramatically, to reach US $5,874m. at 31 December 1995; long-term debt amounted to $4,595m., of which $1,159m. was owed to bilateral institutions, and $2,984m. to multilateral institutions. In 1994 ethnic conflict in the north of the country (see Recent History) necessitated additional assistance from the international community to compensate for the increase in budgetary expenditure. In 1997 the government continued to face both domestic and international pressure. Within Ghana, resistance to the second attempt to introduce VAT persisted, and in the international arena the World Bank and the IMF continued to counsel restraint in foreign and domestic borrowing, further openness in the accounting of state-owned enterprises such as the ECG, and a liberalization of the external marketing of cocoa.

Statistical Survey

Source (except where otherwise stated): Central Bureau of Statistics, POB 1098, Accra; tel. (21) 66512.

Area and Population

AREA, POPULATION AND DENSITY

Area (sq km)	238,537*
Population (census results)	
1 March 1970	8,559,313
11 March 1984	
Males	6,063,848
Females	6,232,233
Total	12,296,081
Population (official estimate at mid-year)	
1991	15,400,000
Density (per sq km) at mid-1991	64.6

* 92,100 sq miles.

POPULATION BY REGION (1984 census)

Western	1,157,807
Central	1,142,335
Greater Accra	1,431,099
Eastern	1,680,890
Volta	1,211,907
Ashanti	2,090,100
Brong-Ahafo	1,206,608
Northern	1,164,583
Upper East	772,744
Upper West	438,008
Total	12,296,081

Principal Ethnic Groups (1991 estimates, percentage of total population): Akan 52.4, Mossi 15.8, Ewe 11.9, Ga-Adangme 7.8, Guan 11.9, Gurma 3.3%, Yoruba 1.3%.

PRINCIPAL TOWNS (population at 1984 census)

Accra (capital)	867,459	Takoradi	61,484
Kumasi	376,249	Cape Coast	57,224
Tamale	135,952	Sekondi	31,916
Tema	131,528		

BIRTHS AND DEATHS (UN estimates, annual averages)

	1980–85	1985–90	1990–95
Birth rate (per 1,000)	45.2	44.3	41.7
Death rate (per 1,000)	14.3	13.1	11.7

Expectation of life (UN estimates, years at birth, 1990–95): 56.0 (males 54.2; females 57.8).

Source: UN, *World Population Prospects: The 1994 Revision.*

ECONOMICALLY ACTIVE POPULATION (1984 census)

	Males	Females	Total
Agriculture, hunting, forestry and fishing	1,750,024	1,560,943	3,310,967
Mining and quarrying	24,906	1,922	26,828
Manufacturing	198,430	389,988	588,418
Electricity, gas and water	14,033	1,404	15,437
Construction	60,692	3,994	64,686
Trade, restaurants and hotels	111,540	680,607	792,147
Transport, storage and communications	117,806	5,000	122,806
Financing, insurance, real estate and business services	19,933	7,542	27,475
Community, social and personal services	339,665	134,051	473,716
Total employed	2,637,029	2,785,451	5,422,480
Unemployed	87,452	70,172	157,624
Total labour force	2,724,481	2,855,623	5,580,104

Source: ILO, *Yearbook of Labour Statistics.*

Mid-1995 (estimates in '000): Agriculture, etc. 4,575; Total 8,164 (Source: FAO, *Production Yearbook*).

Agriculture

PRINCIPAL CROPS ('000 metric tons)

	1993	1994	1995
Maize	961	940	1,042
Millet	198	168	201
Sorghum	328	324	390
Rice (paddy)	157	162	202
Sugar cane*	110	110	110
Cassava (Manioc)	4,500*	6,025	6,899
Yams	1,500*	1,700	2,234
Taro (Coco yam)	1,236	1,148	1,360
Onions	28*	24	24*
Tomatoes	107*	182	182*
Green chillies and peppers*	169	169	169
Eggplants (Aubergines)*	6	6	6
Pulses*	20	20	20
Oranges*	50	50	50
Lemons and limes*	30	30	30
Mangoes*	4	4	4
Bananas*	4	4	4
Plantains	1,322	1,475	1,642
Pineapples*	18	21	12
Palm kernels*	34	264	34
Groundnuts (in shell)	100*	176	176*
Coconuts	220*	264	264*
Copra*	9	9	9
Coffee (green)	4‡	3‡	3*
Cocoa beans‡	240	270	325
Tobacco (leaves)*	2	2	2

* FAO estimate(s). ‡ Unofficial figure(s).

Source: FAO, *Production Yearbook*.

LIVESTOCK ('000 head, year ending September)

	1993	1994	1995
Horses*	2	2	2
Asses*	13	13	13
Cattle	1,392‡	1,680‡	1,680*
Pigs	496‡	595‡	595*
Sheep	2,920‡	3,288‡	3,288*
Goats	2,969‡	3,337‡	3,337*

Poultry (million*): 12 in 1993; 12 in 1994; 12 in 1995.

* FAO estimate(s). ‡ Unofficial figure.

Source: FAO, *Production Yearbook*.

LIVESTOCK PRODUCTS (FAO estimates, '000 metric tons)

	1993	1994	1995
Beef and veal	24	29	29
Mutton and lamb	8	9	9
Goat meat	7	8	8
Pig meat	11	13	13
Poultry meat	14	14	14
Other meat	91	91	91
Cows' milk	23	23	23
Hen eggs	14.3	14.3	14.3
Cattle hides	3.0	3.7	3.7

Source: FAO, *Production Yearbook*.

Forestry

ROUNDWOOD REMOVALS ('000 cubic metres, excl. bark)

	1992	1993	1994
Sawlogs, veneer logs and logs for sleepers	1,170	1,682	1,800
Other industrial wood	130	150	150*
Fuel wood	19,512*	22,612	25,190
Total	20,812	24,444	27,140

* FAO estimate.

Source: FAO, *Yearbook of Forest Products*.

SAWNWOOD PRODUCTION ('000 cubic metres, incl. railway sleepers)

	1992	1993	1994
Coniferous (softwood)	—	29	54
Broadleaved (hardwood)	410	475	582
Total	410	504	636

Source: FAO, *Yearbook of Forest Products*.

Fishing

('000 metric tons, live weight)

	1993	1994	1995
Freshwater fishes	52.5	55.2	50.6
Bigeye grunt	11.9	18.2	14.8
Red pandora	7.9	5.6	4.5
Jack and horse mackerels	1.9	2.7	9.5
Sardinellas	111.1	89.9	95.1
European anchovy	81.4	60.5	65.5
Skipjack tuna	26.1	23.5	25.4
Yellowfin tuna	9.2	8.5	5.5
Chub mackerel	4.3	9.8	12.5
Other marine fishes (incl. unspecified)	66.1	58.0	55.5
Total catch (incl. others)	375.7	337.0	344.5
Inland waters	52.5	55.2	50.6
Atlantic Ocean	323.2	281.8	293.9

Source: FAO, *Yearbook of Fishery Statistics*.

Mining

('000 metric tons, unless otherwise indicated)

	1992	1993	1994
Gold (kilograms)*†	31,000	39,200	44,500
Manganese ore*†	106	115	108
Bauxite‡	338	424	426

* Figures refer to the metal content of ores.

† Data from the US Bureau of Mines.

‡ Data from *World Metal Statistics* (London).

Source: UN, *Industrial Commodity Statistics Yearbook*.

Diamonds ('000 carats): 584.5 (1992); 222.0 (1993) 371.1 (1994 estimate).

Source: IMF, *Ghana—Selected Issues and Statistical Annex*.

Industry

SELECTED PRODUCTS ('000 metric tons, unless otherwise indicated)

	1988	1989	1990
Wheat flour	95.2	88.1	108.4
Beer ('000 hectolitres)	614	639	628
Soft drinks ('000 crates)	1,377	1,553	8,147
Cigarettes (millions)	1,831	1,616	1,805
Motor spirit (petrol)	142.4	252.0	203.6
Kerosene	110.0	136.5	117.8
Diesel and gas oil	290.2	262.2	204.7
Cement	412.1	560.7	678.6
Aluminium (unwrought)*	161	169	174
Electric energy (million kWh)	4,863	5,279	5,816

* Primary metal only.

1992 ('000 metric tons, unless otherwise indicated): Cigarettes (million)* 2,100; Motor spirit (petrol)* 212; Kerosene* 123; Gas-diesel oil* 212; Cement† 1,020; Aluminium (unwrought)‡ 179.9; Electric energy (million kWh)* 6,152.

1993 ('000 metric tons, unless otherwise indicated): Motor spirit (petrol)* 215; Kerosene* 125; Gas-diesel oil* 214; Cement† 1,200; Aluminium (unwrought)‡ 175.4; Electric energy (million kWh)* 6,154.

1994: ('000 metric tons, unless otherwise indicated): Motor spirit (petrol)* 217; Kerosene* 126; Gas-diesel oil* 215; Cement† 1,350; Aluminium (unwrought)‡ 140.7; Electric energy (million kWh)* 6,167.

* Provisional or estimated figures.
† Data from US Bureau of Mines.
‡ Data from *World Metal Statistics* (London).

Source: UN, *Industrial Commodity Statistics Yearbook.*

Groundnut oil (metric tons): 13,032 in 1992; 13,535 in 1993; 25,016 in 1994.
Coconut oil (metric tons): 5,472 in 1992; 5,568 in 1993; 5,568 in 1994.
Palm oil (metric tons): 100,000 in 1992; 108,000 in 1993; 108,000 in 1994.
Palm kernel oil (metric tons): 10,080 in 1992; 10,050 in 1993; 9,750 in 1994.

Source: FAO, *Quarterly Bulletin of Statistics.*

Finance

CURRENCY AND EXCHANGE RATES

Monetary Units

100 pesewas = 1 new cedi.

Sterling and Dollar Equivalents (31 March 1997)

£1 sterling = 3,107.73 cedis;
US $1 = 1,892.65 cedis;
10,000 cedis = £3.218 = $5.284.

Average Exchange Rate (cedis per US $)

1994 956.71
1995 1,200.43
1996 1,637.23

GENERAL BUDGET (million cedis)

Revenue*	1993	1994	1995†
Tax revenue	509,152	841,123	1,138,514
Taxes on income, profits and capital gains	110,299	170,497	275,000
Individual	44,317	62,330	80,783
Corporate	54,330	89,491	157,181
Other unallocated taxes on income	11,652	18,676	37,036
Domestic taxes on goods and services	222,868	309,008	363,550
General sales, turnover or value-added tax	31,248	49,761	69,579
Excises (excl. petroleum)	39,727	57,547	69,947
Petroleum revenue	151,893	201,700	224,024
Taxes on international trade and transactions	175,985	361,618	499,964
Import duties	140,237	215,461	342,751
Export duties	35,748	146,157	157,213
Non-tax revenue	148,429	389,949	552,277
Receipts from divestiture of state-owned enterprises	85,750	261,778	111,787
Total	657,581	1,231,072	1,690,791

Expenditure‡	1992	1993	1994
General public services	58,450	83,918	145,432
Defence	23,242	39,481	33,853
Public order and safety	21,479	30,838	73,544
Education	118,363	179,234	255,792
Health	39,450	56,639	79,551
Social security and welfare	34,630	57,752	40,776
Housing and community amenities	8,639	12,403	8,707
Other community and social services	7,026	10,087	20,558
Economic affairs and services	82,691	129,721	110,059
Agriculture, forestry, fishing and hunting	19,815	28,449	26,752
Mining, manufacturing and construction	7,682	11,029	8,344
Transport and communications	47,693	79,474	60,893
Road transport	42,639	72,218	17,667
Other purposes	77,738	162,648	316,232
Interest payments	61,004	134,778	230,485
Sub-total	471,708	762,721	1,084,504
Special efficiency payments§	27,106	50,805	63,999
Total	498,813	813,526	1,148,503
Current	400,364	694,272	960,850
Capital	98,449	119,254	187,653

* Excluding grants received (million cedis): 66,629 in 1993; 49,483 in 1994; 93,785 (provisional) in 1995.
† Provisional.
‡ Excluding lending minus repayments (million cedis): 11,877 in 1992; 8,029 in 1993; 8,259 in 1994.

§ Including provision for redeployment, retraining and relocation of public-sector employees.

1995 (provisional million cedis): Total expenditure 1,697,893 (current 1,321,375, Capital 376,518), excluding net lending (15,804).

Source: IMF, *Ghana—Selected Issues and Statistical Annex.*

INTERNATIONAL RESERVES (US $ million at 31 December)

	1994	1995	1996
Gold*	77.2	77.4	77.2
IMF special drawing rights	4.2	2.4	2.2
Reserve position in IMF	25.4	25.8	25.0
Foreign exchange	554.3	669.2	801.5
Total	661.1	774.9	905.9

* National valuation.

Source: IMF, *International Financial Statistics.*

MONEY SUPPLY ('000 million new cedis at 31 December)

	1994	1995	1996
Currency outside banks	368.80	546.34	723.99
Deposits of non-financial public enterprises	3.49	6.31	7.87
Demand deposits at deposit money banks	320.86	371.07	482.14
Total money (incl. others)	693.55	925.29	1,215.14

Source: IMF, *International Financial Statistics.*

COST OF LIVING (Consumer Price Index for Accra; base: 1990 = 100)

	1992	1993	1994
Food (incl. beverages)	120.3	150.3	189.2
Clothing and footwear	125.6	147.7	187.0
Rent, fuel and light	174.0	228.0	266.7
All items (incl. others)	129.9	163.0	202.7

1995: Food 306.9; All items 323.2.

Source: ILO, *Yearbook of Labour Statistics.*

NATIONAL ACCOUNTS (million new cedis at current prices)

National Income and Product

	1993	1994	1995*
GDP in purchasers' values	3,949,023	4,950,379	7,557,167
Net factor income from abroad	−72,871	−106,087	−155,734
Gross national product	3,876,152	4,844,292	7,421,433
Less Consumption of fixed capital	−230,291	−259,287	−335,958
National income in market prices	3,645,859	4,585,005	7,085,475

* Estimates.

Source: IMF, *Ghana—Selected Issues and Statistical Annex.*

Expenditure on the Gross Domestic Product

	1993	1994	1995*
Government final consumption expenditure	559,494	553,469	781,408
Private final consumption expenditure	3,438,932	4,208,440	6,029,019
Increase in stocks	3,431	3,431	3,431
Gross fixed capital formation	581,025	783,679	1,405,922
Total domestic expenditure	4,582,882	5,549,019	8,219,780
Exports of goods and services	775,985	1,314,560	1,897,844
Less Imports of goods and services	−1,409,844	−1,913,200	−2,540,457
Statistical discrepancy	−3,949	—	—
GDP in purchasers' values	3,949,023	4,950,379	7,557,167
GDP at constant 1975 prices	7,871	8,172	8,539

* Estimates.

Source: IMF, *Ghana—Selected Issues and Statistical Annex.*

Gross Domestic Product by Economic Activity

	1993	1994	1995*
Agriculture and livestock	1,674,386	1,942,650	2,906,613
Forestry and logging	161,910	207,420	316,239
Fishing	51,337	67,410	103,060
Mining and quarrying	75,031	103,710	131,809
Manufacturing	359,361	466,716	712,467
Electricity, gas and water	71,082	98,528	146,288
Construction	126,369	171,129	255,422
Trade, restaurant and hotels	750,314	995,660	1,152,750
Transport, storage and communications	169,808	228,172	474,803
Finance, insurance, real estate and business services	150,063	197,057	292,073
Other services	339,616	451,157	705,312
Sub-total	3,929,278	4,929,609	7,556,836
Import duties	75,031	93,370	131,023
Less Imputed bank service charge	55,286	72,600	110,692
GDP in purchasers' values	3,949,023	4,950,379	7,557,167

* Estimates.

Source: IMF, *Ghana—Selected Issues and Statistical Annex.*

BALANCE OF PAYMENTS (US $ million)

	1992	1993	1994
Exports of goods f.o.b.	986.4	1,063.7	1,226.8
Imports of goods f.o.b.	−1,456.7	−1,728.0	−1,579.9
Trade balance	−470.3	−664.3	−353.1
Exports of services	110.3	136.6	139.4
Imports of services	−372.2	−428.2	−400.7
Balance on goods and services	−732.2	−955.9	−614.4
Other income received	18.6	19.7	19.9
Other income paid	−132.9	−140.1	−142.1
Balance on goods, services and income	−846.5	−1,076.3	−736.6
Current transfers received	484.8	532.0	487.3
Current transfers paid	−13.6	−13.6	−14.5
Current balance	−375.3	−557.9	−263.8
Capital account (net)	−1.0	−1.0	−1.0
Direct investment from abroad	22.5	125.0	233.0
Other investment assets	−3.5	11.3	−90.1
Other investment liabilities	302.6	511.8	368.3
Net errors and omissions	−52.6	−36.0	−79.0
Overall balance	−107.3	53.2	167.4

Source: IMF, *International Financial Statistics.*

External Trade

PRINCIPAL COMMODITIES

Imports (million cedis)	1991	1992
Food and live animals	8,396	97,337
Rice	1,237	32,062
Crude materials (inedible) except fuels	12,748	41,447
Mineral fuels, lubricants, etc.	16,662	163,622
Crude petroleum	14,913	130,570
Petroleum products	608	21,750
Chemicals	8,211	104,369
Basic manufactures	16,830	130,124
Cement	2,448	33,800
Machinery and transport equipment	118,373	315,506
Passenger cars (excl. buses)	2,386	35,756
Lorries and trucks	4,145	44,421
Miscellaneous manufactured articles	6,257	75,788
Total (incl. others)	188,136	937,733

Source: UN Economic Commission for Africa, *African Statistical Yearbook.*

Exports (US $ million)	1993	1994	1995
Cocoa beans	250.5	295.0	361.1
Cocoa products	35.4	25.2	28.4
Timber and timber products	147.4	165.4	190.6
Gold	434.0	548.6	647.2
Electricity	69.1	56.4	53.0
Total (incl. others)	1,063.6	1,226.8	1,431.2

Source: IMF, *Ghana—Selected Issues and Statistical Annex.*

PRINCIPAL TRADING PARTNERS ('000 cedis)

Imports	1985	1986*	1987*
Canada	384,680	1,540,593	2,020,834
China, People's Repub.	445,812	811,612	1,545,731
France	1,036,690	2,669,607	6,222,440
Germany, Fed. Repub.	5,394,777	10,738,609	19,049,744
Italy	1,561,173	2,836,425	3,047,137
Japan	2,845,424	3,714,632	7,188,215
Libya	7,433	34,489	233,279
Netherlands	1,216,629	3,517,359	5,598,598
Nigeria	10,601,454	11,495,206	21,806,475
Norway	201,533	354,515	535,642
United Kingdom	11,843,832	16,361,776	68,495,538
USA	2,725,773	9,065,604	18,310,717
Total (incl. others)	43,142,515	86,366,800	165,463,210

Exports	1985	1986*	1987*
Germany, Fed. Repub.	2,035,879	4,512,882	8,625,993
Japan	3,249,391	5,361,443	9,377,516
Netherlands	3,400,444	8,554,502	14,005,545
USSR	2,156,475	7,453,808	9,515,974
United Kingdom	6,806,297	10,547,658	27,934,600
USA	2,743,024	12,283,339	19,243,017
Yugoslavia	328,770	690,310	2,061,718
Total (incl. others)	24,733,619	70,021,623	103,679,585

* Provisional figures.

Transport

RAILWAYS (traffic)

	1988	1989	1990
Passengers carried ('000)	3,259.4	2,890.4	1,896.8
Freight carried ('000 metric tons)	774.0	751.4	724.1
Passenger-km (million)	389.3	330.5	277.5
Net ton-km (million)	125.5	130.8	126.9

ROAD TRAFFIC ('000 motor vehicles in use at 31 December)*

	1993	1994	1995
Passenger cars	80.1	86.2	89.0
Lorries and vans	96.9	130.0	133.0

* Estimates.

Source: International Road Federation, *World Road Statistics.*.

SHIPPING

Merchant Fleet (registered at 31 December)

	1994	1995	1996
Number of vessels	164	172	195
Total displacement ('000 grt)	105.9	113.5	134.7

Source: Lloyd's Register of Shipping.

International Sea-borne Freight Traffic
(estimates, '000 metric tons)

	1991	1992	1993
Goods loaded	2,083	2,279	2,424
Goods unloaded	2,866	2,876	2,904

Source: UN Economic Commission for Africa, *African Statistical Yearbook.*

CIVIL AVIATION (traffic on scheduled services)

	1992	1993	1994
Kilometres flown (million)	5	4	5
Passengers carried ('000)	206	152	182
Passenger-km (million)	352	387	478
Total ton-km (million)	62	61	72

Source: UN, *Statistical Yearbook.*

Tourism

	1992	1993	1994
Tourist arrivals ('000)	213	257	248
Receipts from tourism (US $ million)	167	206	218

Source: UN, *Statistical Yearbook.*

Communications Media

	1992	1993	1994
Radio receivers ('000 in use)	4,285	4,420	3,880
Television receivers ('000 in use)	250	265	1,500
Telephones ('000 main lines in use)	48	49	50
Daily newspapers			
Number	4	n.a.	4
Average circulation ('000 copies)	280	n.a.	310*

* Provisional or estimated figure.

Sources: UNESCO, *Statistical Yearbook*; UN, *Statistical Yearbook.*

Education

(1989/90, unless otherwise indicated)

	Institutions	Teachers	Students
Pre-primary	4,735	15,152	323,406
Primary[1]	11,064	72,925[2]	2,011,602
Secondary			
General (public only)	n.a.	39,903[3]	841,722[1]
Teacher training	38[4]	1,001	15,723
Vocational (public only)	20[5]	1,247	22,578[1]
University	3[5]	700[6]	9,609[3]

[1] 1991/92 figure(s).
[2] Provisional figure.
[3] 1990/91 figure.
[4] 1988 figure.
[5] 1988/89 figure.
[6] Excluding the University of Ghana.

Source: mainly UNESCO, *Statistical Yearbook.*

1992: *Primary* 10,623 institutions, 1,800,000 students (estimate); *Junior secondary* 5,136 institutions, 569,000 students (estimate); *Senior secondary* 404 institutions, 147,000 students (estimate); *Higher* 52,000 students.

Source: African Development Bank.

Directory

The Constitution

Under the terms of the Constitution of the Fourth Republic, which was approved by national referendum on 28 April 1992, Ghana has a multi-party political system. Executive power is vested in the President, who is Head of State and Commander-in-Chief of the Armed Forces. The President is elected by universal adult suffrage for a term of four years, and appoints a Vice-President. The duration of the President's tenure of office is limited to two four-year terms. It is also stipulated that, in the event that no presidential candidate receives more than 50% of votes cast, a new election between the two candidates with the highest number of votes is to take place within 21 days. Legislative power is vested in a 200-member unicameral Parliament, which is elected by direct adult suffrage for a four-year term. The Council of Ministers is appointed by the President, subject to approval by the Parliament. The Constitution also provides for a 25-member Council of State, principally comprising presidential nominees and regional representatives, and a 20-member National Security Council (chaired by the Vice-President), both of which act as advisory bodies to the President.

The Government

HEAD OF STATE

President and Commander-in-Chief of the Armed Forces: Flt-Lt (retd) JERRY JOHN RAWLINGS (assumed power as Chairman of Provisional National Defence Council 31 December 1981; elected President 3 November 1992; re-elected 7 December 1996).

Vice-President: Prof. JOHN EVANS ATTA MILLS.

COUNCIL OF MINISTERS
(August 1997)

Minister of Defence: Alhaji MAHAMA IDDRISU.

Minister of State: KOFI TOTOBI-QUAKYI.

Minister of Finance: RICHARD KWAME PEPRAH.

Minister of Parliamentary Affairs: J. H. OWUSU-ACHEAMPONG.

Minister of Foreign Affairs: KWAMENA AHWOI (acting).

Attorney-General and Minister of Justice: Dr OBED ASAMOAH.

Minister of Local Government: KWAMENA AHWOI.

Minister of Education: Dr CHRISTINE AMOAKO-NUAMAH.

Minister of the Interior: NII OKAIDJA ADAMAFIO.

Minister of Food and Agriculture: KWABENA ADJEI.

Minister of Health: Dr EUNICE BROOKMAN-AMISSAH.

Minister of Roads and Transport: EDWARD SALIA.

Minister of Tourism: VIDA YEBOAH.

Minister of Trade and Industry: JOHN FRANK ABU.

Minister of Youth and Sports: E. T. MENSAH.

Minister of Lands and Forestry: CLETUS AVOKA.

Minister of Works and Housing: ISAAC ADJEI-MENSAH.

Minister of Communications: EKOW SPIO-GARBRAH.

Minister of Employment and Social Welfare: Alhaji MOHAMMED MUMUNI.

Minister of the Environment, Science and Technology: J. E. AFFUL.

Minister of Mines and Energy: FRED OHENE-KENA.

There are also five Ministers of State.

REGIONAL MINISTERS
(August 1997)

Ashanti: DANIEL OHENE AGYEKUM.

Brong Ahafo: DAVID OSEI-WUSU.

Central: KOJO YANKAH.

Eastern: PATIENCE ADDO.

Greater Accra: JOSHUA ALABI.

Northern: GILBERT IDDI.

Upper East: DONALD ADABRE.

Upper West: AMIDU SULEMANA.

Volta: Lt Col CHARLES K. AGBENAZA.

Western: ESTHER LILY NKANSAH.

MINISTRIES

Office of the President: POB 1627, Osu, Accra.

Ministry of Communications: Accra.

Ministry of Defence: Burma Camp, Accra; tel. (21) 777611; telex 2077.

Ministry of Education: POB M45, Accra; tel. (21) 665421.

Ministry of Employment and Social Welfare: Accra.

Ministry of the Environment, Science and Technology: Accra.

Ministry of Finance: POB M40, Accra; tel. (21) 665421; telex 2132.

Ministry of Food and Agriculture: POB M37, Accra; tel. (21) 665421.

Ministry of Foreign Affairs: POB M53, Accra; tel. (21) 665421; telex 2001.

Ministry of Health: POB M44, Accra; tel. (21) 665421.

Ministry of the Interior: POB M42, Accra; tel. (21) 665421.

Ministry of Justice: Accra.

Ministry of Lands and Forestry: POB M212, Accra; tel. (21) 665421.

Ministry of Local Government: POB M50, Accra; tel. (21) 665421.

Ministry of Mines and Energy: POB M212, Accra; tel. (21) 665421.

Ministry of Parliamentary Affairs: Accra.

Ministry of Roads and Transport: POB M38, Accra; tel. (21) 665421.

Ministry of Tourism: POB 4386, Accra; tel. (21) 666701; fax (21) 666182.

Ministry of Trade and Industry: POB M85, Accra; tel. (21) 665421; telex 2105.

Ministry of Works and Housing: Accra.

Ministry of Youth and Sports: Accra.

President and Legislature

PRESIDENT

Presidential Election, 7 December 1996

Candidates	% of votes
Flt-Lt (retd) JERRY RAWLINGS (NDC)	57.2
JOHN KUFUOR (Great Alliance*)	39.8
EDWARD MAHAMA (PNC)	3.0
Total	100

* An electoral coalition comprising the New Patriotic Party (NPP) and the People's Convention Party (PCP).

PARLIAMENT

Speaker: Justice DANIEL F. ANNAN.

Legislative Election, 7 December 1996

	Seats
National Democratic Congress (NDC)	133
New Patriotic Party (NPP)	60
People's Convention Party (PCP)	5
People's National Convention (PNC)	1
Total*	200

* Voting in one constituency was postponed. At a by-election in June 1997 the seat was won by the NPP.

COUNCIL OF STATE

Chairman: Alhaji MUMUNI BAWUMIA.

Political Organizations

Democratic People's Party (DPP): Accra; f. 1992; Chair. T. N. WARD-BREW.

EGLE (Every Ghanaian Living Everywhere) Party: Accra; pro-Govt alliance; Co-Chair. OWORAKU AMOFA, Capt. NII OKAI.

Ghana Democratic Republican Party (GDRP): Accra; f. 1992; Leader Dr KOFI AMOAH.

Great Consolidated People's Party (GCPP): Leader DAN LARTEY; Chair. E. B. MENSAH.

National Convention Party (NCP): Accra; f. 1992; pro-Govt; Leader EBO TAIWAH.

National Democratic Congress (NDC): Tamale; f. 1992; pro-Govt alliance; Leader Flt-Lt (retd) JERRY JOHN RAWLINGS; Chair. Alhaji ISSIFU ALI; Sec.-Gen. Alhaji HUUDU YAHAYA.

New Generation Alliance (NGA): Accra; f. 1992.

New Patriotic Party (NPP): Accra; f. 1992 by supporters of the fmr Prime Minister, Dr Kofi Busia; Chair PETER ALA ADJETEY; Sec.-Gen. AGYENIM BOATENG.

People's Convention Party (PCP): Accra; f. Dec. 1993 by the National Independence Party, the People's Heritage Party and a faction of the People's National Convention; merged with Popular Party for Democracy and Development in 1996; Chair. Alhaji ASUMAH BANDA; Sec.-Gen. SETH ABLOSO.

People's National Convention (PNC): Accra; f. 1992 by supporters of the fmr Pres., Dr Kwame Nkrumah; Leader Dr HILLA LIMANN.

The opposition movements listed below, some of which continue to operate mainly from outside Ghana, were in existence prior to the restoration of a plural political system in May 1992:

Campaign for Democracy in Ghana (CDG): based in London, England.

Co-ordinating Committee of Democratic Forces of Ghana (CCDFG): f. 1991; an alliance of 11 opposition movements and other orgs; Chair. Maj. (retd) KOJO BOAKYE GYAN.

Democratic Alliance of Ghana (DAG): based in London, England; Chair. BRIGHT ODURO KWARTENG.

Free Democrats' Union (FDU): Leader Maj. (retd) KOJO BOAKYE DJAN.

Ghana Democratic Movement (GDM): based in London, England; f. 1983.

Ghana Democratic Union: Nigeria; Leader Dr EDUKU QUARFO.

Kwame Nkrumah Revolutionary Guards (KNRG): Accra; African socialist; Chair. SONNIE PROVENCAL.

Movement for Freedom and Justice (MFJ): Accra; f. 1990 to campaign for the restoration of a civilian-led democratic system; Sec.-Gen. JOHN NDEBUGRE.

New Democratic Movement (NDM): Accra; socialist; Chair. KWAME KARIKARI.

United Ghana Movement (UGM): f. 1996; Leader Dr CHARLES WEREKO-BROBBY.

United Party (UP): centre-right; Leader J. H. MENSAH.

United Revolutionary Front (URF): based in London, England; coalition of Marxist-Leninist groups.

Diplomatic Representation

EMBASSIES AND HIGH COMMISSIONS IN GHANA

Algeria: 82 Josif Broz Tito Ave, POB 2747, Accra; tel. (21) 776719; Ambassador: HAMID BOURKI.

Benin: 19 Volta St, Second Close, Airport Residential Area, POB 7871, Accra; tel. (21) 774860; Chargé d'affaires a.i.: L. TONOUKOUIN.

Brazil: 5 Volta St, Airport Residential Area, POB 2918, Accra; tel. (21) 774921; telex 2081; Ambassador: HELDER MARTINS DE MORAES.

Bulgaria: 3 Kakramadu Rd, East Cantonments, POB 3193, Accra; tel. (21) 772404; telex 2709; fax (21) 774231; Chargé d'affaires: GEORGE MITEV.

Burkina Faso: 772/3, Asylum Down, off Farrar Ave, POB 651, Accra; tel. (21) 221988; telex 2108; Ambassador: EMILE GOUBA.

Canada: No. 46, Independence Ave, POB 1639, Accra; tel. (21) 228555; telex 2024; fax (21) 773792; High Commissioner: J. R. SCHRAM.

China, People's Republic: No. 7, Agostinho Neto Rd, Airport Residential Area, POB 3356, Accra; tel. (21) 774527; Ambassador: ZHANG DEZHENG.

Côte d'Ivoire: 9 18th Lane, off Cantonments Rd, POB 3445, Christiansborg, Accra; tel. (21) 774611; telex 2131; Ambassador: KONAN NDA.

Cuba: 20 Amilcar Cabral Rd, Airport Residential Area, POB 9163 Airport, Accra; tel. (21) 775868; telex 2234; Ambassador: JUAN CARRETERO.

Czech Republic: C260/5, Kanda High Rd No. 2, POB 5226, Accra-North; tel. (21) 223540; fax (21) 225337; Ambassador: VLADIMIR KLIMA.

Denmark: 67 Dr Isert Rd, 8th Ave Extension, North Ridge, POB C596, Accra; tel. (21) 226972; telex 2746; fax (21) 228061; e-mail danemb@ighmail.com; Ambassador: BIRGIT STORGAARD MADSEN.

Egypt: 27 Fetreke St, Roman Ridge, Ambassadorial Estate, POB 2508, Accra; tel. (21) 776925; telex 2691; fax (21) 776795; Ambassador: MOHAMED EL-ZAYAT.

Ethiopia: 6 Adiembra Rd, East Cantonments, POB 1646, Accra; tel. (21) 775928; fax (21) 776807; Ambassador: Dr KUWANG TUTILAM.

France: 12th Rd, off Liberation Ave, POB 187, Accra; tel. (21) 774480; telex 2733; fax (21) 778321; Ambassador: DIDIER FERRAND.

Germany: Valdemosa Lodge, Plot No. 18, North Ridge Residential Area, 7th Ave Extension, POB 1757, Accra; tel. (21) 221311; telex 2025; fax (21) 221347; Ambassador: HANS-JOACHIM HELDT.

Guinea: 11 Osu Badu St, Dzorwulu, POB 5497, Accra-North; tel. (21) 777921; Ambassador: DORE DIALE DRUS.

Holy See: 8 Drake Ave, Airport Residential Area, POB 9675, Accra; tel. (21) 777759; fax (21) 774019; Apostolic Nuncio: Most Rev. ANDRÉ DUPUY, Titular Archbishop of Selsea.

Hungary: 14 West Cantonments, off Switchback Rd, POB 3072, Accra; tel. (21) 777234; telex 2543; Chargé d'affaires a.i.: IMRE SOSOVICSKA.

India: 12 Mankata Ave, Airport Residential Area, POB 3040, Accra; tel. (21) 777566; telex 2154; fax (21) 772176; High Commissioner: DILJIT SINGH PANNUN.

Iran: 12 Sir Arku Korsah St, Roman Ridge, POB 12673, Accra North; tel. (21) 777043; telex 2117; Ambassador: SHAMEDDIN KHAREGHANI.

Italy: Jawaharlal Nehru Rd, POB 140, Accra; tel. (21) 775621; telex 2039; Ambassador: MARIO FUGAZZOLA.

Japan: 8 Josif Broz Tito Ave, off Jawaharlal Nehru Ave, POB 1637, Accra; tel. (21) 775616; fax (21) 775951; Ambassador: AKIHISA TANAKA.

Korea, Democratic People's Republic: 139 Nortei Ababio Loop, Ambassadorial Estate, POB 13874, Accra; tel. (21) 777825; Ambassador: RI JAE SONG.

Korea, Republic: 3 Abokobi Rd, East Cantonments, POB 13700, Accra North; tel. (21) 776157; Ambassador: HWANG PU-HONG.

Lebanon: 864/1 Cantonments Rd, OSU, POB 562, Accra; tel. (21) 776727; telex 2118; Ambassador: Dr MOUNIR KHREICH.

Liberia: 10 West Cantonments, off Jawaharlal Nehru Rd, POB 895, Accra; tel. (21) 775641; telex 2071; Ambassador: T. BOYE NELSON.

Libya: 14 Sixth St, Airport Residential Area, POB 9665, Accra; tel. (21) 774820; telex 2179; Secretary of People's Bureau: Dr FATIMA MAGAME.

Mali: Agostino Neto Rd, Airport Residential Area, POB 1121, Accra; tel. (21) 666423; telex 2061; Ambassador: MUPHTAH AG HAIRY.

Netherlands: 89 Liberation Rd, Thomas Sankara Circle, POB 3248, Accra; tel. (21) 773644; telex 2128; fax (21) 773655; Ambassador: HELN C. R. M. PRINCEN.

Niger: 104/3 Independence Ave, POB 2685, Accra; tel. (21) 224962; Ambassador: OUMAROU YOUSSOUFOU.

Nigeria: Josif Broz Tito Ave, POB 1548, Accra; tel. (21) 776158; telex 2051; High Commissioner: T. A. OLU-OTUNLA.

Pakistan: 11 Ring Rd East, Danquah Circle, POB 1114, Accra; tel. (21) 776059; telex 2426; High Commissioner: Dr ABDUL KABIR.

Poland: 2 Akosombo St, Airport Residential Area, POB 2552, Accra; tel. (21) 775972; telex 2558; fax (21) 776108; Chargé d'affaires a.i.: KAZIMIERZ MAURER.

Romania: North Labone, Ward F, Block 6, House 262, POB 3735, Accra; tel. (21) 774076; telex 2027; Chargé d'affaires a.i.: GHEORGHE V. ILIE.

Russia: F856/1, Ring Rd East, POB 1634, Accra; tel. (21) 775611; Ambassador: (vacant).

Saudi Arabia: 10 Noi Fetreke St, Roman Ridge, Airport Residential Area, POB 670, Accra; tel. (21) 774311; telex 2407; Chargé d'affaires a.i.: ANWAR ABDUL FATTAH ABDRABBUH.

South Africa: Room 305, Golden Tulip Hotel, Liberation Road, POB 16033, Kia, Accra; tel. (21) 775360; fax (21) 775361; High Commissioner: JOSIAH MOTSOPE.

Spain: Airport Residential Area, Lamptey Ave Extension, POB 1218, Accra; tel. (21) 774004; telex 2680; fax (21) 776217; Ambassador: DIEGO MARÍA SÁNCHEZ BUSTAMANTE.

Switzerland: 9 Water Rd S.I., North Ridge Area, POB 359, Accra; tel. (21) 228125; telex 2197; fax (21) 223583; Ambassador: PIERRE MONOD.

Togo: Togo House, near Cantonments Circle, POB C120, Accra; tel. (21) 777950; telex 2166; fax (21) 777961; Ambassador: ASSIONGBOR FOLIVI.

United Kingdom: Osu Link, off Gamel Abdul Nasser Ave, POB 296, Accra; tel. (21) 221665; telex 2323; fax (21) 664652; High Commissioner: IAN W. MACKLEY.

USA: Ring Road East, POB 194, Accra; tel. (21) 775347; fax (21) 776008; Ambassador: EDWARD BAYNN.

Yugoslavia: 47 Senchi St, Airport Residential Area, POB 1629, Accra; tel. (21) 775761; Ambassador: LAZAR COVIĆ.

Judicial System

The civil law in force in Ghana is based on the Common Law, doctrines of equity and general statutes which were in force in England in 1874, as modified by subsequent Ordinances. Ghanaian customary law is, however, the basis of most personal, domestic and contractual relationships. Criminal Law is based on the Criminal Procedure Code, 1960, derived from English Criminal Law, and since amended. The Superior Court of Judicature comprises a Supreme Court, a Court of Appeal and a High Court of Justice; Inferior Courts include Circuit Courts, District Courts and such other Courts as may be designated by law.

Supreme Court: Consists of the Chief Justice and not fewer than four other Justices. It is the final court of appeal in Ghana and has jurisdiction in matters relating to the enforcement or interpretation of the Constitution.

Chief Justice: ISAAC KOBINA ABBAN.

Court of Appeal: Consists of the Chief Justice and not fewer than five Judges of the Court of Appeal. It has jurisdiction to hear and determine appeals from any judgment, decree or order of the High Court.

High Court: Comprises the Chief Justice and not fewer than 12 Justices of the High Court. It exercises original jurisdiction in all matters, civil and criminal, other than those for offences involving treason. Trial by jury is practised in criminal cases in Ghana and the Criminal Procedure Code, 1960, provides that all trials on indictment shall be by a jury or with the aid of Assessors.

Circuit Courts: Exercise original jurisdiction in civil matters where the amount involved does not exceed C100,000. They also have jurisdiction with regard to the guardianship and custody of infants, and original jurisdiction in all criminal cases, except offences where the maximum punishment is death or the offence of treason. They have appellate jurisdiction from decisions of any District Court situated within their respective circuits.

District Courts: To each magisterial district is assigned at least one District Magistrate who has original jurisdiction to try civil suits in which the amount involved does not exceed C50,000. District Magistrates also have jurisdiction to deal with all criminal cases, except first-degree felonies, and commit cases of a more serious nature to either the Circuit Court or the High Court. A Grade I District Court can impose a fine not exceeding C1,000 and sentences of imprisonment of up to two years and a Grade II District Court may impose a fine not exceeding C500 and a sentence of imprisonment of up to 12 months. A District Court has no appellate jurisdiction, except in rent matters under the Rent Act.

Juvenile Courts: Jurisdiction in cases involving persons under 17 years of age, except where the juvenile is charged jointly with an adult. The Courts comprise a Chairman, who must be either the District Magistrate or a lawyer, and not fewer than two other members appointed by the Chief Justice in consultation with the Judicial Council. The Juvenile Courts can make orders as to the protection and supervision of a neglected child and can negotiate with parents to secure the good behaviour of a child.

National Public Tribunal: Considers appeals from the Regional Public Tribunals. Its decisions are final and are not subject to any further appeal. The Tribunal consists of at least three members and not more than five, one of whom acts as Chairman.

Regional Public Tribunals: Hears criminal cases relating to prices, rent or exchange control, theft, fraud, forgery, corruption or any offence which may be referred to them by the Provisional National Defence Council.

Special Military Tribunal: Hears criminal cases involving members of the armed forces. It consists of between five and seven members.

Religion

At the 1960 census the distribution of religious groups was: Christians 42.8%, traditional religions 38.2%, Muslims 12.0%, unclassified 7.0%. Since August 1989 religious bodies have been required to register with the Religious Affairs Committee of the National Commission for Culture.

CHRISTIANITY

Christian Council of Ghana: POB 919, Accra; tel. (21) 776725; f. 1929; advisory body comprising 14 Protestant churches; Chair. (vacant); Gen. Sec. Rev. DAVID A. DARTEY.

The Anglican Communion

Anglicans in Ghana are adherents of the Church of the Province of West Africa, comprising 12 dioceses, of which seven are in Ghana. In early 1997 it was announced that the dioceses of Sunyani and Tamale had been separated.

Archbishop of the Province of West Africa and Bishop of Koforidua: Most Rev. ROBERT OKINE, POB 980, Koforidua; tel. (81) 2329.

Bishop of Accra: Rt Rev. JUSTICE O. AKROFI (designate), Bishopscourt, POB 8, Accra; tel. (21) 662292.

Bishop of Cape Coast: Rt Rev. KOBINA ADDUAH QUASHIE, Bishopscourt, POB 233, Cape Coast; tel. (42) 2502.

Bishop of Kumasi: Rt Rev. EDMUND YEBOAH, Bishop's House, POB 144, Kumasi; tel. (51) 4117.

Bishop of Sekondi: Rt Rev. THEOPHILUS ANNOBIL, POB 85, Sekondi; tel. (31) 6048.

Bishop of Sunyani and Tamale: Rt Rev. JOSEPH KOBINA DADSON, Bishop's House, POB 110, Tamale; tel. (71) 2018.

The Roman Catholic Church

Ghana comprises three archdioceses and 12 dioceses. At 31 December 1995 there were 2,109,240 adherents in the country, equivalent to 12.3% of the total population.

Ghana Bishops' Conference: National Catholic Secretariat, POB 9712, Airport, Accra; tel. (21) 500491; telex 2471; fax (21) 500493; f. 1960; Pres. Rt Rev. FRANCIS A. K. LODONU, Bishop of Ho.

Archbishop of Accra: Most Rev. DOMINIC ANDOH, Chancery Office, POB 247, Accra; tel. (21) 222728; fax (21) 231619.

Archbishop of Cape Coast: Most Rev. PETER K. APPIAH-TURKSON, Archbishop's House, POB 112, Cape Coast; tel. (42) 32593.

Archbishop of Tamale: Most Rev. GREGORY EEBO KPIEBAYA, Gumbehini Rd, POB 42, Tamale; tel. (71) 2924; fax (71) 2425.

Other Christian Churches

African Methodist Episcopal Zion Church: Sekondi; Pres. Rev. Dr ZORMELO.

Christian Methodist Episcopal Church: POB 3906, Accra; Pres. Rev. YENN BATA.

Evangelical-Lutheran Church of Ghana: POB 197, Kaneshie; tel. (21) 223487; telex 2134; fax (21) 223353; Pres. Rt Rev. Dr PAUL KOFI FYNN; 21,700 mems.

Evangelical-Presbyterian Church: POB 18, Ho; tel. (91) 755; f. 1847; Moderator Rt Rev. D. A. KORANTENG; 295,000 mems.

Ghana Baptist Convention: POB 1979, Kumasi; tel. (51) 5215; f. 1963; Pres. Rev. FRED DEEGBE; Sec. Rev. FRANK ADAMS.

Mennonite Church: POB 5485, Accra; fax (21) 220589; f. 1957; Moderator Rev. Dr TEI-KWABLA; Sec. ISAAC K. QUARTEY; 4,800 mems.

Methodist Church of Ghana: Liberia Rd, POB 403, Accra; tel. (21) 228120; fax (21) 227008; Pres. Rt Rev. Prof. KWESI A. DICKSON; Sec. Rev. MACLEAN AGYIRI KUMI; 341,000 mems.

Presbyterian Church of Ghana: POB 1800, Accra; tel. (21) 662511; telex 2525; fax (21) 665594; f. 1828; Moderator Rt Rev. ANTHONY ANTWI BEEKO; Sec. Rev. Dr D. N. A. KPOBI; 422,500 mems.

Seventh-day Adventists: POB 1016, Accra; tel. (21) 223720; telex 2119; f. 1943; Pres. P. K. ASAREH; Sec. SETH A. LARYEA.

The African Methodist Episcopal Church, the F'Eden Church and the Society of Friends (Quakers) are also active in Ghana.

In June 1989 the activities of the Church of Jesus Christ of Latter-day Saints (Mormons) and the Jehovah's Witnesses were banned. These groups were deemed to have conducted themselves in a manner not conducive to public order.

ISLAM

There is a substantial Muslim population in the Northern Region. The majority are Malikees.

Chief Imam: Alhaji MUKITAR ABASS.

The Press

In 1992 a commission was established to regulate the media.

DAILY NEWSPAPERS

Daily Graphic: Graphic Rd, POB 742, Accra; tel. (21) 228911; fax (21) 669886; f. 1950; state-owned; Editor ELVIS ARYEH; circ. 100,000.

The Ghanaian Times: New Times Corpn, Ring Rd West, POB 2638, Accra; tel. (21) 228282; fax (21) 229398; f. 1958; state-owned; Editor CHRISTIAN AGGREY; circ. 40,000.

PERIODICALS

Weekly

Bombshell: Crossfire Publications , POB 376, Sakumono, Accra; tel. (21) 234750; fax (21) 233172; Editor BEN ASAMOAH.

Catholic Standard: Accra.

Champion: POB 6828, Accra-North; tel. (21) 229079; Man. Dir MARK D. N. ADDY; Editor FRANK CAXTON WILLIAMS; circ. 300,000.

Christian Chronicle: Accra; English; Editor GEORGE NAYKENE.

The Democrat: Democrat Publications, POB 13605, Accra; tel. (21) 76804; Editor L. K. NYAHO.

Echo: POB 5288, Accra; f. 1968; Sun.; Man. Editor M. K. FRIMPONG; circ. 40,000.

Entertaining Eye: Kad Publications, POB 125, Darkuman-Accra; Editor NANA KWAKYE YIADOM; circ. 40,000.

Evening Digest: News Media Ltd, POB 7082, Accra; tel. (21) 221071; Editor P. K. ANANTITETTEH.

Evening News: POB 7505, Accra; tel. (21) 229416; Man. Editor OSEI POKU; circ. 30,000.

Experience: POB 5084, Accra-North; Editor ALFRED YAW POKU; circ. 50,000.

Free Press: Tommy Thompson Books Ltd, POB 6492, Accra; tel. (21) 225994; independent; English; Editor EBEN QUARCOO.

Ghana Life: Ghana Life Publications, POB 11337, Accra; tel. (21) 229835; Editor NIKKI BOA-AMPONSEM.

Ghana Palaver: Palaver Publications, POB 15744, Accra-North; tel. (21) 232495; Editor BRUCE QUANSAH.

Ghanaian Chronicle: General Portfolio Ltd, Private mail bag, Accra-North; tel. (21) 227789; fax (21) 775895; Editor EBO QUANSAH; circ. 60,000.

Ghanaian Dawn: Dawn Publications, POB 721, Mamprobi, Accra; Editor MABEL LINDSAY.

The Ghanaian Voice: Newstop Publications, POB 514, Mamprobi, Accra; Editor DAN K. ANSAH; circ. 100,000.

The Gossip: Gossip Publications, POB 5355, Accra-North; Editor C. A. ACHEAMPONG.

Graphic Sports: Graphic Rd, POB 742, Accra; tel. (21) 228911; state-owned; Editor JOE AGGREY; circ. 60,000.

The Guide: Western Publications Ltd, POB 8253, Accra-North; tel. (21) 232760; Editor KWEKU BAAKO Jnr.

The Independent: Accra.

The Mirror: Graphic Rd, POB 742, Accra; tel. (21) 228911; telex 2475; fax (21) 669886; f. 1953; state-owned; Sat.; Editor E. N. V. PROVENCAL; circ. 90,000.

The New Ghanaian: Tudu Publishing House, POB 751, Tamale; tel. (71) 22579; Editor RAZAK EL-ALAWA.

New Nation: POB 6828, Accra-North; Editor S. N. SASRAKU; circ. 300,000.

The Pioneer: Abura Printing Works Ltd, POB 325, Kumasi; tel. (51) 2204; f. 1939; Editor JOHNSON GYAMPOH; circ. 100,000.

Private Eye: Kad Life Books Channels, POB 125, Accra; tel. (21) 230684; Editor AWUKU AGYEMANG-DUAH.

Public Agenda: P. A. Communications, POB 5564, Accra-North; tel. (21) 231688; fax (21) 231687; Editor YAO GRAHAM.

Sporting News: POB 5481, Accra-North; f. 1967; Man. Editor J. OPPONG-AGYARE.

The Standard: Standard Newspaper Magazines Ltd, POB 247, Accra; tel. (21) 228410; Editor BENEDICT ASSOROW; circ. 50,000.

Statesman: Kinesic Communications, Accra; tel. (21) 661092; official publ. of the New Patriotic Party; Editor HARUNA ATTAH.

Voice: Accra.

The Weekend: Newstop Publications, POB 514, Mamprobi, Accra; tel. and fax (21) 226943; Editor EMMANUEL YARTEY; circ. 40,000.

Weekly Events: Clear Type Image Ltd, 29 Olympic Street (Enterprise House), Kokomlemle, POB 7634, Accra-North; tel. (21) 223085; Editor JORIS JORDAN DODOO.

Weekly Insight: Militant Publications Ltd, POB K272, Accra New Town, Accra; tel. (21) 660148; f. 1993; independent; English; Editor KWESI PRATT Jnr.

Weekly Spectator: New Times Corpn, Ring Road West, POB 2638, Accra; tel. (21) 228282; fax (21) 229398; state-owned; f. 1963; Sun.; Editor WILLIE DONKOR; circ. 165,000.

Other

Africa Flamingo: Airport Emporium Ltd, POB 9194, Accra; monthly; Editor FELIX AMANFU; circ. 50,000.

African Observer: POB 1171, Kaneshie, Accra; tel. (012) 231459; bi-monthly; Editor STEVE MALLORY.

African Woman: Ring Rd West, POB 1496, Accra; monthly.

Akwansosem: Ghana Information Services, POB 745, Accra; tel. (21) 228011; telex 2201; quarterly; in Akuapim Twi, Asanti Twi and Fante; Editor KATHLEEN OFOSU-APPIAH.

Armed Forces News: General Headquarters, Directorate of Public Relations, Burma Camp, Accra; tel. (21) 776111; f. 1966; quarterly; Editor ADOTEY ANKRAH-HOFFMAN; circ. 4,000.

Boxing and Football Illustrated: POB 8392, Accra; f. 1976; monthly; Editor NANA O. AMPOMAH; circ. 10,000.

Business and Financial Concord: Sammy Tech Consult Enterprise, POB 5677, Accra-North; tel. (21) 232446; fortnightly; Editor KWABENA RICHARDSON.

Business and Financial Times: POB 2157, Accra; fortnightly; Editor JOHN HANSEN.

Chit Chat: POB 7043, Accra; monthly; Editor ROSEMOND ADU.

Christian Messenger: Presbyterian Book Depot Bldg, POB 3075, Accra; tel. and fax (21) 662415; telex 2525; f. 1883; English; also **The Presbyterian** (in Twi and Ga); quarterly; Editor G. B. K. OWUSU; circ. 40,000.

Drum: POB 1197, Accra; monthly; general interest.

Ghana Enterprise: c/o Ghana National Chamber of Commerce, POB 2325, Accra; tel. (21) 662427; telex 2687; fax (21) 662210; f. 1961; quarterly; Editor J. B. K. AMANFU.

Ghana Journal of Science: Ghana Science Assen, POB 7, Legon; monthly; Editor Dr A. K. AHAFIA.

Ghana Manufacturer: c/o Assen of Ghana Industries, POB 8624, Accra-North; tel. (21) 777283; f. 1974; quarterly; Editor (vacant); circ. 1,500.

Ghana Official News Bulletin: Information Services Dept, POB 745, Accra; English; political, economic, investment and cultural affairs.

Ideal Woman (Obaa Sima): POB 5737, Accra; tel. (21) 221399; f. 1971; fortnightly; Editor KATE ABBAM.

Independent: Trans Afrika News Ltd, POB 4031, Accra; tel. (21) 661091; bi-weekly; Editor KABRAL BLAY-AMIHERE.

Insight and Opinion: POB 5446, Accra; quarterly; Editorial Sec. W. B. OHENE.

Legon Observer: POB 11, Legon; telex 2556; fax (21) 774338; f. 1966; publ. by Legon Society on National Affairs; fortnightly; Chair. J. A. DADSON; Editor EBOW DANIEL.

Police News: Police HQ, Accra; monthly; Editor S. S. APPIAH; circ. 20,000.

The Post: Ghana Information Services, POB 745, Accra; tel. (21) 228011; telex 2201; f. 1980; monthly; current affairs and analysis; circ. 25,000.

Radio and TV Times: Ghana Broadcasting Corpn, Broadcasting House, POB 1633, Accra; tel. (21) 221161; telex 2114; f. 1960; quarterly; Editor ERNEST ASAMOAH; circ. 5,000.

The Scope: POB 8162, Tema; monthly; Editor EMMANUEL DOE ZIORKLUI; circ. 10,000.

Students World: POB M18, Accra; tel. (21) 774248; telex 2171; f. 1974; monthly; educational; Man. Editor ERIC OFEI; circ. 10,000.

The Teacher: Ghana National Assen of Teachers, POB 209, Accra; tel. (21) 221515; fax (21) 226286; f. 1931; quarterly; circ. 30,000.

Truth and Life: Gift Publications, POB 11337, Accra-North; monthly; Editor Pastor KOBENA CHARM.

The Watchman: Watchman Gospel Ministry, POB 4521, Accra; tel. (21) 220892; bi-monthly; Editor DIVINE KUMAH.

NEWS AGENCIES

Ghana News Agency: POB 2118, Accra; tel. (21) 665135; telex 2400; fax 669840; f. 1957; Gen. Man. SAM B. QUAICOE; 10 regional offices and 110 district offices.

Foreign Bureaux

Associated Press (AP) (USA): POB 6172, Accra; Bureau Chief P. K. COBBINAH-ESSEM.

Xinhua (New China) News Agency (People's Republic of China): 2 Seventh St, Airport Residential Area, POB 3897, Accra; tel. (21) 772042; telex 2314.

Deutsche Presse-Agentur (Germany) and Reuters (UK) are also represented.

Publishers

Advent Press: POB 0102, Osu, Accra; tel. (21) 777861; telex 2119; f. 1937; Gen. Man. EMMANUEL C. TETTEH.

Adwinsa Publications (Ghana) Ltd: Advance Press Bldg, 3rd Floor, School Rd, POB 92, Legoh Accra; tel. (21) 221654; f. 1977; general, educational; Man. Dir KWABENA AMPONSAH.

Afram Publications: 9 Ring Rd East, POB M18, Accra; tel. (21) 774248; telex 2171; f. 1974; textbooks and general; Man. Dir ERIC OFEI.

Africa Christian Press: POB 30, Achimota; tel. (21) 220271; fax (21) 668115; f. 1964; religious, biography, children's; Gen. Man. RICHARD A. B. CRABBE.

Asempa Publishers: POB 919, Accra; tel. (21) 233084; fax (21) 233130; e-mail asempa@ncs.com.gh; f. 1970; religion, social issues, African music, fiction, children's; Gen. Man. Rev. EMMANUEL B. BORTEY.

Baafour and Co: POB K189, Accra New Town; f. 1978; general; Man. B. KESE-AMANKWAA.

Benibengor Book Agency: POB 40, Aboso; fiction, biography, children's and paperbacks; Man. Dir J. BENIBENGOR BLAY.

Black Mask Ltd: POB 7894, Accra North; tel. (21) 229968; f. 1979; textbooks, plays, novels, handicrafts; Man. Dir YAW OWUSU ASANTE.

Editorial and Publishing Services: POB 5743, Accra; general, reference; Man. Dir M. DANQUAH.

Educational Press and Manufacturers Ltd: POB 9184, Airport-Accra; tel. (21) 220395; f. 1975; textbooks, children's; Man. G. K. KODUA.

Encyclopaedia Africana Project: POB 2797, Accra; tel. (21) 776939; f. 1962; reference; Dir J. O. VANDERPUYE.

Frank Publishing Ltd: POB M414, Accra; f. 1976; secondary school textbooks; Man. Dir FRANCIS K. DZOKOTO.

Ghana Publishing Corpn: PMB Tema; tel. (221) 2921; f. 1965; textbooks and general fiction and non-fiction; Man. Dir F. K. NYARKO.

Ghana Universities Press: POB 4219, Accra; tel. (21) 761051; f. 1962; scholarly and academic; Dir K. M. GANU.

Goodbooks Publishing Co: POB 10416, Accra North; tel. (21) 665629; f. 1968; children's; Man. A. ASIRIFI.

Miracle Bookhouse: POB 7487, Accra North; tel. (21) 226684; f. 1977; general; Man. J. APPIAH-BERKO.

Moxon Paperbacks: POB M160, Accra; tel. (21) 665397; fax (21) 774358; f. 1967; travel and guide books, fiction and poetry, Africana; quarterly catalogue of Ghanaian books and periodicals in print; Man. Dir JAMES MOXON.

Sedco Publishing Ltd: Sedco House, Tabon St, North Ridge, POB 2051, Accra; tel. (21) 221332; telex 2456; fax (21) 220107; f. 1975; educational; Man. Dir COURAGE K. SEGBAWU.

Sheffield Publishing Co: Accra; tel. (21) 667480; fax (21) 665960; f. 1970; religion, politics, economics, science, fiction; Publr RONALD MENSAH.

Unimax Publishers Ltd: 42 Ring Rd South Industrial Area, POB 10722, Accra-North; tel. (21) 227443; telex 2515; fax (21) 225215; atlases, educational and children's; Dir EDWARD ADDO.

Waterville Publishing House: POB 195, Accra; tel. (21) 663124; f. 1963; general fiction and non-fiction, textbooks, paperbacks, Africana; Man. Dir H. W. O. OKAI.

Woeli Publishing Services: POB K601, Accra New Town; tel. and fax (21) 229294; f. 1984; children's, fiction, academic; Dir W. A. DEKUTSEY.

PUBLISHERS' ASSOCIATIONS

Ghana Book Development Council: POB M430, Accra; tel. (21) 229178; f. 1975; govt-financed agency; promotes and co-ordinates writing, production and distribution of books; Exec. Dir D. A. NIMAKO.

Ghana Book Publishers' Association: c/o Africa Christian Press, POB 430, Achimota; Sec. E. B. BORTEY.

Private Newspaper Publishers' Association of Ghana (PRINPAG): POB 125, Darkuman, Accra; Gen. Sec. K. AGYEMANG DUAH.

Radio and Television

In 1994 there were an estimated 3,880,000 radio receivers and 1,500,000 television receivers in use.

There are internal radio broadcasts in English, Akan, Dagbani, Ewe, Ga, Hausa and Nzema, and an external service in English and French. There are three sound transmitting stations, with a number of relay stations. Television transmissions began in 1965; there is a total of eight main colour transmitters. In 1995 36 private companies were granted authorization to operate radio and television networks. The Ghana Frequency Registration and Control Board gave approval for 10 new community radio stations in 1996.

Ghana Broadcasting Corporation: Broadcasting House, POB 1633, Accra; tel. (21) 221161; telex 2114; fax (21) 221153; f. 1935; Dir-Gen. Dr KOFI FRIMPONG; Dir of TV Prof. MARK DUODU; Dir of Radio B. A. APENTENG.

Finance

(cap. = capital; res = reserves; dep. = deposits; m. = million; brs = branches; amounts in cedis)

BANKING

Central Bank

Bank of Ghana: Thorpe Rd, POB 2674, Accra; tel. (21) 666902; telex 2052; fax (21) 662996; f. 1957; bank of issue; cap. and res 118,351m., dep. 405,977m. (Dec. 1995); Chair. and Gov. Dr GODFRIED K. AGAMA.

State Banks

Agricultural Development Bank: Cedi House, Liberia Rd, POB 4191, Accra; tel. (21) 662758; telex 2295; fax (21) 662846; f. 1965; 65% state-owned; credit facilities for farmers and commercial banking; cap. and res 53,804m., dep. 109,074.8m. (Dec. 1996); Chair. NATHAN QUAO; Man. Dir P. A. KURANCHIE; 32 brs.

Bank for Housing and Construction (BHC): Okofoh House, 24 Kwame Nkrumah Ave, POB M1, Adabraka, Accra; tel. (21) 220033; telex 2559; fax (21) 229631; f. 1983; 50% state-owned; cap. 1,000m. (Dec. 1995); Chair. K. TWUM BOAFO; Man. Dir J. E. ABABIO.

Ghana Commercial Bank: POB 134, Accra; tel. (21) 664914; telex 2034; fax (21) 662168; f. 1953; 58% state-owned; cap. and res 67,830m., dep. 359,253m. (Dec. 1995); Chair. S. K. APPEA; Man. Dir HELEN K. LOKKO; 145 brs.

Ghana Co-operative Bank Ltd: Kwame Nkrumah Ave, POB 5292, Accra-North; tel. (21) 663131; telex 2446; fax (21) 662359; f. 1970; 81% state-owned; cap. 2,913.7m. (Dec. 1994); Chair. GEORGE K. HAGAN; Man. Dir K. K. MENSAH; 21 brs.

National Investment Bank Ltd (NIB): 37 Kwame Nkrumah Ave, POB 3726, Accra; tel. (21) 669301; telex 2161; fax (21) 669307; f. 1963; 86.3% state-owned; provides long-term investment capital, jt venture promotion, consortium finance man. and commercial banking services; cap. 3,242.0m., dep. 51,798.3m. (Dec. 1995); Chair. JOHN K. RICHARDSON; Man. Dir STEVE DADZIE; 10 brs.

National Trust Holding Co: Dyson House, Kwame Nkrumah Ave, POB 9563, Airport, Accra; tel. (21) 229664; fax (21) 229975; e-mail nthc@ncs.com.gh; f. 1976 to finance Ghanaian acquisitions of indigenous cos; also assists in their development and expansion, and carries out stockbroking, portfolio man., underwriting, trusteeship business, corporate advisory services and real estate development; cap. 500m. (1996); Chair. JOANA FELICITY DICKSON; Man. Dir CHARLES PADDY SAWYERR.

Social Security Bank (SSB): POB 13119, Accra; tel. (21) 221726; telex 2209; fax (21) 668651; f. 1976; cap. 6,734.5m., dep. 277,309.1m. (Dec. 1996); Chair. HENRY DEI; Man. Dir PRYCE K. THOMPSON.

Trust Bank Ghana Ltd: 68 Kwame Nkrumah Ave, POB 1862, Accra; tel. (21) 665708; telex 2782; fax (21) 665710; f. 1996 to take over assets and liabilities of Meridien BIAO Bank Ghana Ltd; cap. 10.1m. (April 1996); Man. Dir DAVID C. JOHNSON.

Merchant Banks

CAL Merchant Bank Ltd: 45 Independence Ave, POB 14596, Accra; tel. (21) 221056; telex 2675; fax (21) 231913; f. 1990 as Continental Acceptances Ltd; cap. and res 2,754.4m., dep. 28,464.4m. (Dec. 1993); Chair. LOUIS CASELY-HAYFORD; Gen. Man. CLIFTON J. BEST.

Ecobank Ghana (EBG): 19 Seventh Ave, Ridge West, Accra; tel. (21) 231931; telex 2718; fax (21) 231934; f. 1989; 58.9% owned by Ecobank Transnational Inc (operating under the auspices of the Economic Community of West African States); cap. 1,300m., res 8,365m., dep. 80,550m. (Dec. 1995); Chair. JOHN SACKAH ADDO; Man. Dir J. N. AKA.

First Atlantic Merchant Bank Ltd: Atlantic Place, 1 Seventh Ave, Ridge West, POB C1620, Cantonments, Accra; tel. (21) 231433; telex 2915; fax (21) 231399; f. 1995; cap. and res 2,066.6m., dep. 13,130.5m. (Dec. 1996); Chair. B. C. F. LOKKO; Man. Dir JUDE ARTHUR.

Merchant Bank (Ghana) Ltd: Merban House, 44 Kwame Nkrumah Ave, POB 401, Accra; tel. (21) 666331; telex 2191; fax (21) 667305; f. 1972; 30% state-owned; cap. 5,000m., dep. 55,701.5m. (Dec. 1994); Chair. J. RICHARDSON; Man. Dir CHRIS N. NARTEY; 3 brs.

Foreign Banks

Barclays Bank of Ghana Ltd (UK): High St, POB 2949, Accra; tel. (21) 667629; telex 2721; fax (21) 667420; f. 1917; 40% state-owned; cap. and res 21,926.8m., dep. 188,749.4m. (Dec. 1995); Chair. NANA WEREKO AMPEM; Man. Dir M. O. BRISTOW; 28 brs.

Standard Chartered Bank Ghana Ltd (UK): Standard Bank Bldg, High St, POB 768, Accra; tel. (21) 664591; telex 2671; fax (21) 667751; f. 1896; cap. and res 41,056m., dep. 275,311m. (Dec. 1996); Chair. DAVID ANDOH; CEO VISHNU MOHAN; 28 brs.

STOCK EXCHANGE

Ghana Stock Exchange (GSE): Cedi House, 5th Floor, Liberia Rd, POB 1849, Accra; tel. (21) 669908; telex 2722; fax (21) 669913; e-mail stockex@ncs.com.gh; 52 mems; Dir YEBOA AMOA.

INSURANCE

Ghana Union Assurance Co Ltd: POB 1322, Accra; tel. (21) 664421; telex 2008; fax (21) 664988; f. 1973; Man. Dir KWADWO DUKU.

The Great African Insurance Co Ltd: POB 12349, Accra North; tel. (21) 227459; telex 3027; fax (21) 228905; f. 1980; Man. Dir KWASI AKOTO.

The State Insurance Corporation of Ghana: POB 2363, Accra; tel. (21) 666961; telex 2171; fax (21) 662205; f. 1962; state-owned; undertakes all classes of insurance; also engages in real estate and other investment; Man. Dir B. K. QUASHIE.

Social Security and National Insurance Trust: Pension House, POB M149, Accra; tel. (21) 667742; telex 2564; fax (21) 662226; f. 1972; covers over 650,000 contributors; Dir-Gen. HENRY G. DEI.

Vanguard Assurance Co Ltd: Insurance Hall, Derby House, Derby Ave, POB 1868, Accra; tel. (21) 666485; telex 2005; fax (21) 668610; f. 1974; general accident, marine, motor and life insurance; Man. Dir NANA AWUAH-DARKO AMPEM; 7 brs.

Several foreign insurance companies operate in Ghana.

Trade and Industry

STATE PROPERTY AGENCY

Divestiture Implementation Committee: F3515 Ring Road East, North Labone, Cantonments, POB C102, Accra; tel. (21) 772049; fax (21) 773126; e-mail dicgh@ncs.com.gh; f. 1988; Exec. Sec. EMMANUEL AGBODO.

PUBLIC BOARDS AND CORPORATIONS

Atomic Energy Commission: POB 80, Legon/Accra; construction of a nuclear reactor at Kwabenya, near Accra, which was begun in 1964, was completed in Jan. 1995; the reactor was to provide training for West African scientists; Chair. Prof. F. K. A. ALLOTEY.

Bast Fibres Development Board: POB 1992, Kumasi; f. 1970; promotes the commercial cultivation of bast fibres and their processing, handling and grading.

Cocoa Processing Co Ltd: Private Mail Bag, Tema; tel. (22) 202926; telex 2082; fax (22) 206657; f. 1981; subsidiary of the Ghana Cocoa Board; mills and processes cocoa beans into semi-finished products; Man. Dir PAUL AWUA.

Food Production Corporation: POB 1853, Accra; f. 1971; state corpn providing employment for youth in large scale farming enterprises; controls 76,900 ha of land (16,200 ha under cultivation); operates 87 food farms on a co-operative and self-supporting basis, and rears poultry and livestock.

Ghana Cocoa Board (COCOBOD): POB 933, Accra; tel. (21) 221212; telex 2082; fax (21) 667104; f. 1985; monopoly purchaser of cocoa until 1993; responsible for purchase, grading and export of cocoa, coffee and shea nuts; also encourages production and scientific research aimed at improving quality and yield of these crops; controls all exports of cocoa; CEO JOHN NEWMAN.

Ghana Consolidated Diamond Co Ltd: POB M108, Accra; telex 2058; f. 1986; grades, values and processes diamonds, buys all locally won, produced or processed diamonds; engages in purchasing, grading, valuing, export and sale of local diamonds; Chair. KOFI AGYEMAN; Man. Dir JOSEPH ANSAFO-MENSAH.

Ghana Cotton Co Ltd: f. 1986; Govt holds 70% interest, private textile cos 30%; 15 regional offices; Chair. HARRY GANDA; Man. Dir MAURICE ABISSA SEIDOU.

Ghana Food Distribution Corporation: POB 4245, Accra; tel. (21) 228428; f. 1971; buys, stores, preserves, distributes and retails foodstuffs through 10 regional centres; Man. Dir E. H. K. AMANKWA.

Ghana Free Zones Board: POB M47, Accra; tel. (21) 780532; telex 2951; fax (21) 780536; approves establishment of companies in export processing zones; Exec. Sec. GEORGE ABOAGYE.

Ghana Industrial Holding Corporation (GIHOC): POB 2784, Accra; tel. (21) 664998; telex 2109; f. 1967; controls and manages 26 state enterprises, including steel, paper, bricks, paint, pharmaceuticals, electronics, metals, canneries, distilleries and boat-building factories; also has three subsidiary cos and four jt ventures; managed since 1989 by an interim superintending secr.

Ghana Investment Promotion Centre: Central Ministerial Area, POB M193, Accra; tel. (21) 665125; telex 2229; fax (21) 663801; e-mail gipc@ncs.com.gh; f. 1981; negotiates new investments, approves projects, registers foreign capital and decides extent of govt participation.

Ghana National Manganese Corporation: POB M183, Ministry PO, Accra; tel. (21) 666607; telex 2046; fax (21) 666562; f. 1975 following nationalization of manganese mine at Nsuta; Chair. NANA AKUAMOAH BOATENG ABABIO (acting); Man. Dir Col E. T. OKLAH (retd).

Ghana National Petroleum Corporation: Private Mail Bag, Tema, Accra-North; tel. (21) 712930; telex 2703; fax (21) 232055; e-mail gnpc@ncs.com.gh; f. 1983; exploration, development, production and disposal of gas and petroleum; also involved in telecommunications, gold and salt mining and tourism; Chair. TSATSU TSIKATA.

Ghana National Trading Corporation (GNTC): POB 67, Accra; tel. (21) 664871; f. 1961; organizes exports and imports of selected commodities; over 500 retail outlets in 12 admin. dists.

Ghana Standards Board: c/o POB M245, Accra; tel. (21) 500065; telex 2545; fax (21) 500092; f. 1967; establishes and promulgates standards; promotes standardization, industrial efficiency and development and industrial welfare, health and safety; operates certification mark scheme; 403 mems; Dir Rev. Dr E. K. MARFO.

Ghana Telecommunication Co Ltd: Posts and Telecommunications Bldg, Accra-North; tel. (21) 221001; telex 3010; fax (21) 667979; f. 1974 as Posts and Telecommunications Corporation; 30% transferred to the private sector in 1997; provides both internal and external postal and telecommunication services; Dir-Gen. JOSEPH AGGREY-MENSAH; Man. Dir ADNAN ROFIEE.

Ghana Water and Sewerage Corporation: POB M194, Accra; f. 1966 to provide, distribute and conserve water for public, domestic and industrial use, and to establish, operate and control sewerage systems.

Grains and Legumes Development Board: POB 4000, Kumasi; tel. (51) 4231; f. 1970; state-controlled; promotes and develops production of cereals and leguminous vegetables.

Minerals Commission: 10 Sixth St, Airport Residential Area, Accra; tel. (21) 772783; telex 2545; fax (21) 773324; f. 1984; supervises, promotes and co-ordinates the minerals industry.

National Board for Small-scale Industries: Ministry of Trade and Industry, POB M85, Accra; f. 1985; promotes small and medium-scale industrial and commercial enterprises by providing credit, advisory services and training.

State Construction Corporation: Ring Rd West, Industrial Area, Accra; f. 1966; state corpn with a labour force of 7,000; construction plans give priority to enhancing agricultural production; Man. Dir DAVID BOATENG.

State Farms Corporation: Accra; undertakes agricultural projects in all regions but Upper Region; Man. Dir E. N. A. THOMPSON (acting).

State Fishing Corporation: POB 211, Tema; tel. (221) 6177; telex 2043; fax (221) 2336177; f. 1961; govt-sponsored deep-sea fishing, distribution and marketing (incl. exporting) org.; transfer to private-sector ownership proposed in 1991; owns 5 deep-sea fishing trawlers; CEO Dr ISAAC C. N. MORRISON.

State Gold Mining Corporation: POB 109, Tarkwa; Accra Office, POB 3634; tel. 775376; telex 2348; f. 1961; manages four gold mines; CEO F. AWUA-KYEREMATEN.

State Hotels Corporation: POB 7542, Accra-North; tel. (21) 664646; telex 2113; f. 1965; responsible for all state-owned hotels, restaurants, etc. in 10 major centres; Man. Dir S. K. A. OBENG; Gen. Man. EBEN AMOAH.

State Housing Construction Co: POB 2753, Accra; f. 1982 by merger; oversees govt housing programme.

Timber Export Development Board: POB 515, Takoradi; tel. (31) 29216; telex 2189; f. 1985; promotes the sale and export of timber; CEO SAMUEL KWESI APPIAH.

Volta River Authority: POB M77, Accra; tel. (21) 664941; telex 2022; fax (21) 662610; f. 1965; controls the generation and distribution of electricity; CEO ERASMUS KALITSI.

CHAMBER OF COMMERCE

Ghana National Chamber of Commerce: POB 2325, Accra; tel. (21) 662427; telex 2687; fax (21) 662210; f. 1961; promotes and protects industry and commerce, organizes trade fairs; 2,500 individual mems and 8 mem. chambers; Pres. ALEX AWUKU; Exec. Sec. JOHN B. K. AMANFU.

COMMERCIAL AND INDUSTRIAL ORGANIZATIONS

Ghana Export Promotion Council: Republic House, POB M146, Accra; tel. (21) 228813; fax (21) 668263; f. 1974; Chair. and mems appointed by Ministry of Trade and Industry, Asscn of Ghana Industries, Customs, Excise and Preventive Services, Bank of Ghana, Ghana Commercial Bank, GIHOC Distilleries, Export Finance Co Ltd, Information Service Dept, Ghana Trade Fair Authority, Asscn of Ghanaian Exporters and Ministry of the Environment, Science and Technology; Exec. Sec. TAWIA AKYEA.

The Indian Association of Ghana: POB 2891, Accra; tel. (21) 776227; f. 1939; Pres. ATMARAM GOKALDAS.

Institute of Marketing (IMG): POB 102, Accra; tel. (21) 226697; telex 2488; fax (21) 222171; f. 1981; reorg. 1989; seeks to enhance professional standards; Chair. Ishmael Yamson; Pres. Frank Appiah.

EMPLOYERS' ASSOCIATION

Ghana Employers' Association: 122 Kojo Thompson Rd, POB 2616, Accra; tel. (21) 228455; fax (21) 228405; f. 1959; 400 mems; Pres. Ishmael E. Yamson; Vice-Pres. Ato Ampiah.

Affiliated Bodies

Association of Ghana Industries: Trade Fair Centre, POB 8624, Accra-North; tel. (21) 777283; telex 3027; fax (21) 773143; f. 1957; Pres. Dr Justice Atta Addison; Exec. Sec. Eddie Imbeah-Amoakuh.

Ghana Booksellers' Association: POB 10367, Accra-North; tel. (21) 773002; fax (21) 773242; Pres. Sampson Brako; Gen. Sec. Fred J. Reimmer.

The Ghana Chamber of Mines: 2nd Floor, Diamond House, POB 991, Accra; tel. (21) 665355; telex 2036; fax (21) 662926; f. 1928; Pres. Peter Bradford; Exec. Dir George M. Osei (acting).

Ghana Electrical Contractors' Association: POB 1858, Accra.

Ghana National Association of Teachers: POB 209, Accra; tel. (21) 221515; fax (21) 226286; f. 1931; Pres. G. N. Naaso; Gen. Sec. Paul Osei-Mensah.

Ghana National Contractors' Association: c/o J. T. Osei and Co, POB M11, Accra.

Ghana Timber Association (GTA): POB 246, Takoradi; f. 1952; promotes, protects and develops timber industry; Chair. Tetteh Nanor.

CO-OPERATIVES

The co-operative movement in Ghana began in the 1920s through government initiative and supervision to ensure the production of high quality cocoa. This effort culminated in the adoption of the first co-operative law in 1932, which was replaced in 1937 and again in 1968. In 1996 there were 11,208 registered co-operatives, grouped into four sectors: industrial, financial, agricultural and service.

Department of Co-operatives: POB M150, Accra; tel. (21) 666212; f. 1944; govt-supervised body, responsible for registration, auditing and supervision of co-operative socs and provision of advisory and social services; Registrar R. Buachie-Aphram.

Ghana Co-operatives Council Ltd: POB 4034, Accra; f. 1951; co-ordinates activities of all co-operative socs; comprises 15 nat. co-operative asscns and five central socs; Sec.-Gen. Thomas Andoh.

The 15 co-operative associations include the Ghana Co-operative Marketing Asscn Ltd, the Ghana Co-operative Credit Unions Asscn Ltd, the Ghana Co-operative Agricultural Producers and Marketing Asscn Ltd, and The Ghana Co-operative Consumers' Asscn Ltd.

MAJOR INDUSTRIAL COMPANIES

The following are among the largest companies in terms of either capital investment or of employment.

ABC Brewery Ltd: POB 114, Achimota, Accra; tel. (21) 402988; fax (21) 400673; f. 1973, as Tata Brewery; name changed to Achimota Brewery Co Ltd in 1979; beer and soft drinks; Chair. C. Stanley-Pierre; Man. Dir K. X. Y. Ahlijah.

Ashanti Goldfields Co Ltd: Gold House, Patrice Lumumba Rd, Roman Ridge, POB 2665, Accra; tel. (21) 722190; telex 20362; fax (21) 775947; f. 1897, reorg. 1994; gold mining; leases mining and timber concessions from the Govt, which holds a 19% interest; 34% is held by Lonrho PLC and 47% by private investors; Chair. R. K. Peprah; CEO Sam Jonah; 9,500 employees.

BP Ghana Ltd: 95 Kojo Thompson Rd, POB 553, Accra; tel. (21) 221445; telex 2093; fax (21) 221453; f. 1965; shares held by BP Africa Ltd, National Investment Bank, National Trust Holding Co Ltd; distribution of petroleum products, fuelling marine vessels at Tema and Takoradi, and aircraft at Kotoka International Airport, Accra; Man. Dir F. J. Mouchet; 173 employees.

Cocoa Processing Co: PMB, Tema; tel. (22) 202926; telex 2082; fax (22) 206657; f. 1981; controlled by COCOBOD; mfrs of cocoa products.

Ghana Bauxite Co Ltd: POB 1, Awaso; 55% state-owned; fmrly British Aluminium Co Ltd; mining of bauxite at Awaso with loading facilities at Takoradi; Man. Dir T. Cregg.

Ghana Consolidated Diamonds Ltd: c/o 34 Seymour St, London, W1H 5WD, England; tel. (71) 724-9398; telex 262899; fax (71) 723-8384; 20% govt-owned; operates diamond mine at Akwatia.

Lever Bros Division: POB 1648, Accra; mfrs of household and toilet soaps, non-soap detergents, scourers, toothpaste, margarine and other edible fats; Man. Dir A. K. Jesani.

Tema Oil Refinery (TOR) Ltd: POB 599, Tema; tel. (21) 302881; telex 2011; fax (22) 302884; f. 1963; sole oil refinery in Ghana; state-controlled since 1977; Man. Dirs W. S. Parker, A. S. K. Aidoo, L. Prempeh; 360 employees.

Total Ghana Ltd: 3 Yiyiwa St, Abelenkpe, Accra; tel. (21) 772309; telex 2681; fax (21) 773662; f. 1960; subsidiary of Total Paris; distribution of petroleum products, incl. liquefied petroleum gas; Man. Dir Jean-Jacques Cestari.

Unilever Ghana Ltd: POB 64, Kwame Nkrumah Ave, Accra; tel. (21) 664985; telex 2008; fax (21) 664808; f. 1955 as United Africa Co of Ghana Ltd; comprises 6 divisions and assoc. cos; subsidiary of Unilever plc, United Kingdom; agricultural, industrial, specialized merchandising, distributive and service enterprises; Chair. Ishmael Yamson; 1,200 employees.

Volta Aluminium Co Ltd (VALCO): POB 625, Tema; tel. (21) 231004; fax (21) 231423; owned by Kaiser Aluminium and Chemical Corpn (90%) and the Reynolds Metal Co (10%); operates an aluminium smelter at Tema (annual capacity 200,000 tons); Chair. Jed Daniel; Man. Dir Neil Darlington.

West African Mills Co Ltd: Effia Junction Industrial Estate, POB 257 and 218, Takoradi; tel. (31) 22511; fax (31) 23394; f. 1992; formerly Cocoa Processing Co; produces high-grade cocoa products for export; Man. Dir Reinhold F. M. Mueller; 440 employees.

TRADE UNIONS

Ghana Trades Union Congress (GTUC): Hall of Trade Unions, POB 701, Accra; tel. (21) 662568; fax (21) 667161; f. 1945; 17 affiliated unions; all activities of the GTUC were suspended in March 1982; Chair. Interim Man. Cttee E. K. Aboagye; Sec.-Gen. Christian Appiah-Agyei.

Transport

State Transport Corporation: Accra; f. 1965; Man. Dir Lt-Col Akyea-Mensah.

RAILWAYS

Ghana has a railway network of 1,300 km, which connects Accra, Kumasi and Takoradi. A project to rehabilitate the railway network, which was supported by the African Development Bank, was completed in 1989.

Ghana Railway Corporation: POB 251, Takoradi; tel. (31) 2181; telex 2297; f. 1977; responsible for the operation and maintenance of all railways; Man. Dir. M. K. Arthur.

ROADS

In 1995 Ghana had an estimated total road network of 37,561 km, including 5,020 km of main roads, and 9,620 km of secondary roads; some 24.9% of the road network was paved. A five-year Road Sector Expenditure Programme, costing US $259m., was initiated in 1995. In 1992 the Government allocated a projected 26.7% of total expenditure to the rehabilitation of roads.

Ghana Highway Authority: POB 1641, Accra; tel. (21) 666591; telex 2359; fax (21) 665571; f. 1974 to plan, develop, classify and maintain roads and ferries; CEO B. L. T. Sakibu.

SHIPPING

The two main ports are Tema (near Accra) and Takoradi, both of which are linked with Kumasi by rail. The rehabilitation of the two ports, at an estimated cost of US $100m., was completed in 1990. A further stage of the programme to rehabilitate Takoradi commenced in mid-1995. In 1990 goods loaded totalled an estimated 1.8m. metric tons, and goods unloaded an estimated 2.8m. tons.

Ghana Ports and Harbour Authority: holding company for the ports of Tema and Takoradi; Dir Gen. K. T. Dovlo.

Alpha (West Africa) Line Ltd: POB 451, Tema; telex 2184; operates regular cargo services to west Africa, the UK, the USA, the Far East and northern Europe; shipping agents; Man. Dir Ahmed Edgar Collingwood Williams.

Black Star Line Ltd: 4th Lane, Kuku Hill Osu, POB 248, Accra; tel. (21) 2888; telex 2019; fax (21) 2889; f. 1957; state-owned; transfer to private sector pending in 1997; operates passenger and cargo services to Europe, the UK, Canada, the USA, the Mediterranean and west Africa; shipping agents; Chair. Magnus Addico; Man. Dir Capt. V. N. Attuquayefio.

Holland West-Afrika Lijn NV: POB 269, Accra; POB 216, Tema; and POB 18, Takoradi; cargo services to and from North America and the Far East; shipping agents.

Liner Agencies (Ghana) Ltd: POB 66, Accra; tel. (21) 712270; telex 2009; fax (21) 213168; freight services to and from UK, Europe, USA, Canada, Japan and Far East; intermediate services between west African ports; shipping agents; Dir J. Ossei-Yaw.

Remco Shipping Lines Ltd: POB 3898, Accra; tel. (21) 224609.

Scanship (Ghana) Ltd: CFAO Bldg, High St, POB 1705, Accra; tel. (21) 664314; telex 2181; shipping agents.

Association

Ghana Shippers' Council: Enterprise House, 5th Floor, opp. Barclay's Bank, High St, POB 1321, Accra; tel. (21) 666915; fax (21) 668768; e-mail shippers@ncs.com.gh; f. 1974; represents interests of c. 3,000 registered Ghanaian shippers; also provides cargo-handling and allied services; CEO M. T. ADDICO.

CIVIL AVIATION

The main international airport is at Kotoka (Accra). There are also airports at Takoradi, Kumasi, Sunyani, Tamale and Wa. In 1988 Ghana received a loan of US $12m. from France to finance the rehabilitation of Kotoka Airport (at a total cost of $55.5m.), which began in 1991.

Gemini Airlines Ltd: America House, POB 7328, Accra-North; tel. (21) 665785; f. 1974; operates weekly cargo flight between Accra and London; Dir V. OWUSU; Gen. Man. P. F. OKINE.

Ghana Airways Ltd.: Plot 9, Ghana Airways Avenue, Ghana Airways House, POB 1636, Accra; tel. (21) 773321; telex 2489; fax (21) 777078; f. 1958; state-owned; operates regional services and international routes to West African and European destinations, and to the USA and South Africa; Chair. EDWARD SALIA; CEO REX LEZARD.

Tourism

Ghana's attractions include fine beaches, game reserves, traditional festivals, and old trading forts and castles. In 1994 tourist arrivals were estimated at 248,000, and revenue from tourism totalled US $218m. In 1990 a government programme to expand tourism was initiated, with the aim of increasing tourist arrivals to 370,000 per year by 1995. In 1996 a national tourism development plan (1996–2010) was initiated. According to the Ministry of Tourism, 300,000 tourists visited Ghana in 1996, with revenue from tourism totalling $248m.

Ghana Tourist Board: POB 3106, Accra; tel. (21) 222153; telex 2714; fax (21) 231779; f. 1968; Exec. Dir EDMUND Y. OFOSU-YEBOAH.

Ghana Association of Tourist and Travel Agencies: Ramia House, Kojo Thompson Rd, POB 7140, Accra; tel. (21) 228933; Pres. JOSEPH K. ANKUMAH; Sec. JOHNNIE MOREAUX.

Ghana Tourist Development Co Ltd: POB 8710, Accra; tel. (21) 776109; telex 2714; fax (21) 772093; f. 1974; develops tourist infrastructure, including hotels, restaurants and casinos; operates duty-free and diplomatic shops; Man. Dir ALFRED KOMLADZEI.

Defence

In August 1996 Ghana had total armed forces of 7,000 (army 5,000, navy 1,000 and air force 1,000) and a paramilitary force of 5,000. The headquarters of the Defence Commission of the OAU is in Accra.

Defence Expenditure: Budgeted at C33,853m. in 1994.

Commander-in-Chief of the Armed Forces: Flt-Lt (retd) JERRY RAWLINGS.

Chief of Defence Staff: Lt-Gen. B. K. AKAFIA.

Commander of the Navy: Rear-Adm. OSEI OWUSO-ANSAH.

Commander of the Air Force: Air Vice-Marshal J. A. BRUCE.

Commander of the Army: Maj.-Gen. J. H. SMITH.

Education

Education is officially compulsory for nine years, between the ages of six and 16 years. Primary education begins at the age of six and lasts for six years. Secondary education, beginning at the age of 12, lasts for a further six years, comprising two three-year cycles. Following three years of junior secondary education, pupils are examined to determine admission to senior secondary school courses, or to technical and vocational courses. At the junior secondary schools pupils are examined to determine admission to senior secondary school courses, which lead to examinations at the 'ordinary' level of the general certificate of education, and technical and vocational courses. In 1991 primary enrolment was equivalent to 76% of children in the relevant age-group (83% of boys; 70% of girls), while the comparable ratio for secondary enrolment was 37% (45% of boys; 29% of girls). It was estimated that 52,000 students were enrolled in higher education in 1992, with about 10,700 students attending the country's five universities. Tertiary institutions also included 38 teacher-training colleges, seven diploma-awarding colleges, 21 technical colleges and six polytechnics. Expenditure on education by the central government in 1994 was 255,792m. cedis (22.3% of total spending). According to UNESCO estimates, the average rate of adult illiteracy in 1995 was 35.5% (males 24.1%; females 46.5%).

Bibliography

Adjei, M. *Death and Pain: Rawlings Ghana, The Inside Story.* London, Black Line Publishing Ltd, 1994.

Afrifa, A. A. *Ghana Coup d'Etat.* London, Frank Cass, 1967.

Agbodeka, F. *An Economc History of Ghana from the Earliest Times.* Accra, Ghana Universities Press, 1993.

Allman, J. M. *The Quills of the Porcupine: Asante Nationalism in an Emergent Ghana.* Madison, University of Wisconsin Press, 1993.

Anin, T. E. *Essays on the Political Economy of Ghana.* London, Selwyn, 1991.

Armah, K. *Nkrumah's Legacy.* London, Rex Collings, 1974.

Austin, D. *Politics in Ghana 1946–60.* Oxford University Press, 1964.

Awoonor, K. N. *Ghana: A Political History from Pre-European to Modern Times.* Accra, Ghana, Woeli Publishing Services, 1990.

Babatope, E. *The Ghana Revolution from Nkrumah to Jerry Rawlings.* Enugu, Fourth Dimension Publishers, 1984.

Baynham, S. *The Military and Politics in Nkrumah's Ghana.* Boulder, CO, Westview Press, 1988.

Boateng, E. A. *A Geography of Ghana.* 2nd Edn. Cambridge University Press, 1970.

Brown, C. K. (Ed.). *Rural Development in Ghana.* Accra, Ghana University Press, 1986.

Busia, K. A. *Africa in Search of Democracy.* London, Routledge and Kegan Paul, 1967.

Chazan, N. *An Anatomy of Ghanaian Politics: Managing Political Recession 1969–1982.* Boulder, CO, Westview Press, 1983.

Cruise O'Brien, D. B., Dunn, J., and Rathbone, R. (Eds). *West African States.* Cambridge, Cambridge University Press, 1989.

Davidson, B. *Black Star. A View of the Life and Times of Kwame Nkrumah.* London, Panaf Books, 1974.

Dickson, K. B. *A Historical Geography of Ghana.* Cambridge University Press, 1969.

Dumor, E. K. *Ghana, OAU and Southern Africa: An African Response to Apartheid (1957–1972).* Oxford, ABC; Ghana University Press, 1991.

Edgerton, R. B. *The Fall of the Ashante Empire.* New York and London, Free Press, 1995.

Foster, P., and Zolberg, A. R. (Eds). *Ghana and the Ivory Coast: Perspectives and Modernization.* University of Chicago Press, 1972.

Frimpong, J. H. *The Vampire State in Africa: The Political Economy of Decline in Ghana.* London, James Currey, 1991.

Graham, R. *The Aluminium Industry and the Third World: Multinational Corporations and Underdevelopment.* London, Zed Press, 1982.

Greenhalgh, P. *West African Diamonds: An Economic History 1919–83.* Manchester University Press, 1985.

Gyimah-Boardi, E. (Ed.). *Ghana under PNDC Rule.* Dakar, CODESRIA, 1993.

Hansen, E. *Ghana under Rawlings: Early Years.* Oxford, ABC; Malthouse Press, 1991.

Hansen, E., and Ninsen, K. A. (Eds). *State Development and Politics in Ghana.* Dakar, CODESRIA, 1990.

Hayward, M. F. *Elections in Independent Africa.* Boulder, CO, Westview Press, 1987.

Herbst, J. *The Politics of Reform in Ghana, 1982–1991.* Berkeley, University of California Press, 1993.

Huq, M. M. *The Economy of Ghana: The First 25 Years since Independence.* London, Macmillan, 1988.

Jeffries, R. *Class, Power and Ideology in Ghana.* Cambridge University Press, 1978.

Jones, T. *Ghana's First Republic.* London, Methuen, 1976.

Kay, G. (Ed.). *The Political Economy of Colonialism in Ghana: A Collection of Documents and Statistics 1900–60.* Cambridge University Press, 1972.

Killick, A. *Development Economics in Action: A Study of Economic Policies in Ghana.* London, Heinemann, 1978.

Kimble, D. *Political History of Ghana.* London, Oxford University Press, 1963.

Ninsin, K. A., and Drah, F. K. (Eds). *The Search for Democracy in Ghana: A Case Study in Political Instability in Africa.* Accra, Asempa Publishers, 1987.

Ghana's Transition to Constitutional Rule. Accra, Ghana University Press; Oxford, ABC, 1991.

Political Parties and Democracy in Ghana's Fourth Republic. Accra, Woeli Publishing Services, 1993.

Obeng-Fosu, P. *Industrial Relations in Ghana: The Law and Practice.* Oxford, ABC; Ghana University Press, 1991.

Ofori, S. *Regional Policy and Regional Planning in Ghana.* Brookfield, VT, Ashgate Publishing, 1997.

Okeke, B. E. *4 June: A Revolution Betrayed.* Enugu, Ikenga Publishers, 1982.

Oquaye, M. *Politics in Ghana 1972–1979.* Accra, Tornado Publications, 1980.

Owusu-Ansah, D., and McFarland, M. D. *Historical Dictionary of Ghana.* 2nd Edn. Lanham, MD, Scarecrow Press, 1995.

Pinkney, R. *Ghana under Military Rule 1966–1969.* London, Methuen, 1972.

Rimmer, D. *The Economies of West Africa.* London, Weidenfeld and Nicolson, 1984.

Staying Poor: Ghana's Political Economy, 1950–1990. Oxford, Pergamon, 1992.

Roe, Alan, Schneider, H., and Pyatt, G. *Adjustment and Equity in Ghana.* Paris, OECD, 1992.

Sarpong, P. *Ghana in Retrospect.* Oxford, ABC; Ghana Publishing Corporation, 1991.

Sarris, A., and Shams, H. *Ghana under Structural Adjustment: The Impact on Agriculture and the Rural Poor.* New York University Press, 1991. (IFAD Studies in Rural Poverty).

Shillington, K. *Ghana and the Rawlings Factor.* London, Macmillan, 1992.

Ward, W. E. F. *A History of Ghana.* London, Allen and Unwin, 1958.

Yeebo, Z. *Ghana: The Struggle for Popular Power—Rawlings: Saviour or Demagogue?* Accra, New Beacon Books, 1992.

GUINEA

Physical and Social Geography

R. J. HARRISON CHURCH

The Republic of Guinea covers an area of 245,857 sq km (94,926 sq miles), containing exceptionally varied landscapes, peoples and economic conditions. The census of 31 December 1996 recorded a population of 7,164,823 (giving an average density of 29.1 inhabitants per sq km). The population is concentrated in the plateau area of central Guinea: about one-fifth of the population is estimated to be living in Conakry and its environs.

Guinea's coast is part of the extremely wet south-western sector of west Africa, which has a monsoonal climate. Thus Conakry, the capital, has five to six months with almost no rain, while 4,300 mm fall in the remaining months. The coastline has shallow drowned rivers and estuaries with much mangrove growing on alluvium eroded from the nearby Fouta Djallon mountains. Much of the mangrove has been removed, and the land bunded for rice cultivation. Only at two places, Cape Verga and Conakry, do ancient hard rocks reach the sea. At the latter they have facilitated the development of the port, while the weathering of these rocks has produced exploitable deposits of bauxite on the offshore Los Islands.

Behind the swamps a gravelly coastal plain, some 65 km wide, is backed by the steep, often sheer, edges of the Fouta Djallon, which occupies the west-centre of Guinea. Much is over 900 m high, and consists of level Primary sandstones (possibly of Devonian age) which cover Pre-Cambrian rocks to a depth of 750 m. The level plateaux, with many bare lateritic surfaces, are the realm of Fulani herders. Rivers are deeply incised in the sandstone. These more fertile valleys were earlier cultivated with food crops by slaves of the Fulani, and then with bananas, coffee, citrus fruits and pineapples on plantations under the French. Falls and gorges of the incised rivers have great hydro-electric potential. This is significant in view of huge deposits of high-grade bauxite located at Fria and Boké. The climate is still monsoonal but, although the total rainfall is lower—about 1,800 mm annually—it is more evenly distributed than on the coasts as the rainy season is longer. In such a mountainous area there are sharp variations in climatic conditions over a short distance, and from year to year.

On the Liberian border the Guinea highlands rise to 1,752 m at Mt Nimba, where substantial deposits of haematite iron ore are eventually to be developed in co-operation with Liberia. These rounded mountains contrast greatly with the level plateaux and deep narrow valleys of the Fouta Djallon. Rainfall is heavier than in the latter, but is again more evenly distributed, so that only two or three months are without significant rain. Coffee, kola and other crops are grown in the forest of this remote area. Diamonds are mined north of Macenta and west of Beyla, and the exploitation of gold reserves is in progress.

Recent History

PIERRE ENGLEBERT

Revised for this edition by the Editor

THE SEKOU TOURÉ PERIOD, 1958–84

In a referendum held in French Guinea on 28 September 1958, 95% of voters rejected membership of a proposed community of self-governing French overseas territories, to be established under the constitution of the new French republic. French Guinea was the only French colony to reject the proposal. Prominent in the campaign against membership was Ahmed Sekou Touré, the secretary-general of the Parti démocratique de Guinée–Rassemblement démocratique africain (PDG–RDA), which had won 58 of the 60 seats in the territorial assembly in 1957, and which demanded complete independence from France. Thus, on 2 October 1958 the territory became independent as the Republic of Guinea; Sekou Touré became its first president, and the PDG–RDA the sole political party. Punitive economic reprisals were taken by the departing French authorities, and French aid and investment were suspended.

Sekou Touré pursued a policy of socialist revolution, and any opposition was ruthlessly suppressed. There were intermittent purges of groups such as merchants, civil servants and the military, and many thousands of opponents of the government were forced into exile, especially in neighbouring Côte d'Ivoire and Senegal and in France. Sekou Touré's security in office was attributable to his dominance of all central government activities, his reliance on a group of close collaborators, and his ability to balance the authority of the armed forces against that of the PDG–RDA's 'people's militia', which was used to enforce government policies.

Guinea withdrew from the Franc Zone in 1960, in a gesture of economic independence, but consequently the Guinean franc became worthless outside the country, and there was widespread trafficking in foreign currency. In 1964 severe measures were adopted to prevent smuggling and unauthorized currency-dealing, and to increase state control of both internal and external trade. Following independence the government initially obtained assistance from the USSR, but after 1961 (when the Soviet ambassador was expelled for allegedly interfering in Guinea's internal affairs) the USA became a more significant source of aid.

Fearing the influence of his exiled opponents, Sekou Touré made repeated allegations of foreign plots to overthrow him: a reported coup attempt in April 1960, for example, was ascribed to the French government, while senior French officials and President Houphouët-Boigny of Côte d'Ivoire were accused of complicity in an 'assassination plot' in October 1965. Exiles based in Abidjan, Dakar and Paris formed an opposition front in 1965, provoking allegations by Sekou Touré that the three countries were training 'mercenaries' for an invasion of Guinea. An abortive invasion in November 1970 originated in the neighbouring territory of Portuguese Guinea (now Guinea-Bissau), where Sekou Touré's government had been supporting the nationalist Partido Africano da Independência da Guiné e Cabo Verde (PAIGC). A force comprising mainly Guinean exiles led by Portuguese officers landed from the sea off Conakry, and, during two days of sporadic fighting, destroyed the offices of the PAIGC and freed some political prisoners but failed to overthrow Sekou Touré. Severe reprisals followed: many prominent Guineans, including seven former government ministers and the Roman Catholic archbishop of Conakry, were arrested, and about 90 were sentenced to death. In February 1973 the assassination in Conakry of the PAIGC leader, Amílcar Cabral, gave rise to renewed suspicion of plots against the Touré regime.

A new currency, the syli, was introduced in 1972. In 1973 there was a reorganization of local government structures, whereby the Pouvoirs révolutionnaires locaux, introduced in 1968 as executive bodies at village level, were given the additional role of planning the production and marketing of commodities. In 1975 all private trading was forbidden. Transactions were to be conducted through official co-operatives, under the supervision of the 'economic police' of the PDG–RDA. These measures apparently encountered opposition in northern Guinea among the nomadic Fulani, and in 1976 the government announced the discovery of a 'Fulani plot', attributed to Diallo Telli, the minister of justice and a former secretary-general of the OAU. He died in a prison camp in 1977, having 'confessed' his collusion in the plot, which had purportedly been sponsored by the US Central Intelligence Agency. In the same year a UN report revealed maltreatment of political prisoners, and in 1978 a prominent human rights organization, Amnesty International, published details of torture, political executions and imprisonment without trial in Guinea. The Guinean government subsequently asserted that such abuses had ceased.

Widespread opposition to the PDG–RDA's 'economic police', who were suspected of extortion and smuggling, culminated in August 1977 in violent demonstrations and rioting, as a so-called 'women's revolt' in Conakry quickly spread to other towns. In response, Sekou Touré disbanded the 'economic police' and permitted the resumption (from July 1979) of small-scale private trading. In late 1978 it was agreed to increase the membership of the central organs of the PDG–RDA and to merge the functions of the party and the state. In January 1979 the country was renamed the People's Revolutionary Republic of Guinea.

Diplomatic relations with France (which had been effectively severed in 1965) were restored in 1976, and in the following year the two countries reached an agreement on economic co-operation, including an undertaking by the French government to curb the activities of Guinean dissidents in Paris. In 1978 Sekou Touré declared a policy of 'co-operation with capitalist as well as socialist states'. The government sought also to improve relations with Côte d'Ivoire and Senegal, and increased its participation in regional organizations.

CONTÉ AND THE CMRN

Sekou Touré died suddenly in March 1984. Before a successor could be chosen, the army staged a *coup d'état* in April, and a Comité militaire de redressement national (CMRN) seized power. Although the CMRN was composed mainly of middle- and lower-ranking officers, its principal leaders, Col (later Gen.) Lansana Conté and Col Diarra Traoré, who became president and prime minister respectively, had both held senior positions for some years. A semi-civilian government was appointed, and efforts were furthered to improve regional relations and links with potential sources of economic aid (most notably France). In May the country resumed the designation of Republic of Guinea. The PDG–RDA and organs of Sekou Touré's 'party state' were dismantled under this second republic, which was initially greeted with great enthusiasm. State surveillance and control were ended, and many political detainees were freed and their places taken by former associates of Sekou Touré. Corruption involving the former leadership was revealed, and the CMRN denounced Sekou Touré's 'bloody and pitiless dictatorship', promising a new era of freedom. Exiled groups of Guineans were eager to return, but, with an estimated 2m. exiles abroad, Guinea's new rulers were unable (and showed no willingness) to accommodate them all at once.

In the first months of his presidency Conté adopted an open style of government, inviting constructive advice and criticism from all quarters. Given the parlous economic situation and domestic uncertainty confronting the CMRN, however, major political change had to be contained within the bounds of fiscal austerity and social acceptability. A devaluation of the currency was long overdue, and local political opinion and external creditors favoured the liberalization of trading practices (a process already initiated in the later years of the Sekou Touré regime) and fostering of private enterprise. However, institutionalized corruption and tax evasion had apparently resulted in inertia in the administrative system.

Undercurrents of Opposition

In December 1984 Conté abolished the office of prime minister, demoting Traoré to a lesser cabinet post. Noting that some of his colleagues had used power to 'satisfy their personal interests', Conté warned that there might be further changes, with the emphasis placed on competence. In July 1985, while Conté was attending a regional summit meeting in Togo, Traoré attempted a *coup d'état,* supported mainly by members of the police force. Troops loyal to Conté swiftly regained control, and the president returned, to public acclaim, two days later. Traoré and many of his family were arrested, and the armed forces conducted a purge of his suspected sympathizers; in all, more than 200 arrests were made. Among those executed in the immediate aftermath of the coup attempt were Traoré and a half-brother of Sekou Touré. About 60 other military officers were later sentenced to death following secret trials. (Sekou Touré's widow and son were released following an amnesty for 67 political prisoners in January 1988.)

The coup attempt effectively strengthened Conté's position, allowing him to pursue the extensive economic reforms demanded by the World Bank and the IMF as a prerequisite for the disbursement of new funds. The syli was devalued and replaced in January 1986 by a revived Guinean franc. A reform of the cumbersome civil service was initiated, with inevitable redundancies; many state-owned enterprises were dissolved or offered for sale, and the banking system was overhauled. In December 1985 Conté reorganized the council of ministers, introducing a majority of civilians for the first time since he took power and creating resident 'regional' ministries. Opposition to the reform programme was revealed in late 1987 by unrest within the armed forces and the civil service, while high levels of inflation provoked public demonstrations in Conakry in January 1988. Conté reorganized the government in the same month, transferring two high-ranking members to regional ministries. Further reshuffles were implemented in April of that year and in June 1989.

Meanwhile, a process of limited democratization was proceeding. In October 1988, commemorating the 30th anniversary of the country's independence, Conté declared an amnesty for 39 political prisoners, including some of those implicated in the 1985 coup attempt. At the same time he announced the establishment of a committee to draft a new constitution to be submitted for approval in a national referendum. In October 1989 Conté revealed plans whereby a Comité transitoire de redressement national (CTRN) would succeed the CMRN and oversee a five-year transitional period prior to the establishment of a two-party political system under an elected president and legislature. In February 1990 an amnesty was announced for all remaining political detainees and exiled dissidents.

As elsewhere in the region, it was in the education sector that discontent at economic austerity tended most frequently to manifest itself. A teachers' strike in early 1990, in protest at inadequate pay and conditions, forced the government to replace an unpopular education minister. Tensions resurfaced in November, when the authorities briefly closed the University of Conakry in response to a boycott of classes by students, and two students were killed by security forces at a demonstration in the capital. The government ordered the resumption of classes, but two further demonstrators were killed in further disturbances in December.

Conté appealed in November 1990 for the return to Guinea of political exiles. In contrast, three members of an illegal opposition movement, the Rassemblement populaire guinéen (RPG) were imprisoned later in the month. Rejecting widespread demands for an accelerated programme of political reform, the government proceeded with its plan for a gradual transition to a two-party political system. The draft constitution (*loi fondamentale*) was submitted to a national referendum in December, and was declared to have been approved by 98.7% of those who voted (some 97.4% of the registered electorate). The period of transition to civilian rule thus began, and in February 1991 the 36-member CTRN was inaugurated, under the chairmanship of Conté. A prior reorganization of the council of ministers had entailed the removal from the government of three close associates of Conté, who were now appointed to the CTRN (under the new constitution, membership of the CTRN was incompatible with ministerial status). Military officers continued to hold the most sensitive posts in the new government, implying that the president intended to ensure the continued loyalty of the armed forces.

In May 1991, as academic staff again took strike action, the government announced a doubling of civil servants' salaries, together with increases in some social allowances and a halving of the salaries of members of the council of ministers and of the CTRN. However, the trade unions deemed these concessions to be insufficient, and a widely-observed general strike effectively paralysed the capital. In the same month the leader of the RPG, Alpha Condé, returned to Guinea after a long period of exile in France and Senegal. Security forces dispersed a meeting of his supporters, and the government subsequently imposed a ban on unauthorized meetings and demonstrations. In June one person was killed when security forces opened fire on a group of demonstrators who had gathered outside the police headquarters in Conakry, to where Condé had been summoned in connection with the seizure of allegedly subversive materials. As many as 60 arrests were reported, while Condé sought refuge in the Senegalese embassy, where he remained for several weeks before being granted political asylum in Senegal.

Contrary to the earlier scheme for political change, in October 1991 Conté announced that the registration of an unlimited number of political parties would come into effect on 3 April 1992 (the eighth anniversary of the coup that had brought him to power), and that legislative elections would take place before the end of 1992 in the context of a full multi-party political system. In late 1991 the Conté administration denied allegations made by Amnesty International of the persecution, imprisonment and torture of political opponents.

THE THIRD REPUBLIC

The constitution of the third republic was promulgated on 23 December 1991. In January 1992 Conté ceded the presidency of the CTRN (whose membership was reduced to 15), in accordance with constitutional provision for the separation of the powers of the executive and legislature. In the following month most military officers and all *Guinéens de l'extérieur* (former dissidents who had returned from exile after the 1984 coup) were removed from the government: it later became apparent that some of these long-serving ministers had left public office in order to establish a pro-Conté political party. The resident ministries were also abolished in the reshuffle.

The RPG was among the first parties to be legalized in April 1992, and Alpha Condé returned to Guinea in June. Other than the RPG, the most prominent challengers to the pro-Conté Parti de l'unité et du progrès (PUP) were the Parti pour le renouveau et le progrès (PRP), led by a well-known journalist, Siradiou Diallo, and the Union pour la nouvelle République (UNR), led by Mamadou Bâ. However, the opposition was generally fragmented, which undermined attempts to persuade the government to convene a national political conference. It was alleged by the opposition that the PUP was benefiting from state funds, and that the government was coercing civil servants into joining the party; moreover, there was evidence that the government was favouring development projects in areas of potential PUP support. Clashes between pro- and anti-Conté activists (seemingly fuelled by ethnic rivalries) occurred frequently from mid-1992, and in October the government again banned all unauthorized public gatherings. In that month Conté was reported to have escaped an assassination attempt when gunmen opened fire on the vehicle in which he was travelling.

In December 1992 the government announced the indefinite postponement of the legislative elections, which had been scheduled for the end of the month, citing technical and financial difficulties. It was later indicated that the elections would be organized in late 1993, and that (contrary to the preference of most opposition parties) they would be preceded by the presidential election. In May 1993 about 30,000 people demonstrated in the capital to demand that the legislative elections be brought forward; three people were reportedly killed in ensuing violence.

The principal opposition parties failed in their attempts to form an electoral alliance, with the aim of preventing a divided opposition vote from benefiting Conté and the PUP. Thus, there were eight candidates for the presidential election, which was scheduled for 5 December 1993. Conté's main challengers were Condé, Diallo and Bâ. In September the government banned all political gatherings and marches, following violent incidents in Conakry when police opened fire on demonstrators, as a result of which, according to official figures, some 18 people were killed (unofficial reports claimed as many as 63 deaths) and almost 200 injured. In October, at an unprecedented meeting between Conté and representatives of 43 political organizations, it was reportedly agreed to establish an independent electoral commission. However, controversy immediately arose regarding its composition and also the government's decision to place it under the jurisdiction of the powerful ministry of the interior and security. Opposition candidates demanded that the presidential election be postponed, citing technical and procedural irregularities and delays. Objections were also voiced that the PUP was able to hold electoral rallies, while the opposition remained subject to the ban announced in September. In late November the government announced a two-week postponement of the presidential poll, admitting that technical preparations for voting were incomplete.

At least four deaths resulted from outbreaks of violence in Conakry and in the interior prior to the presidential election. A further six people were reported to have been killed as voting proceeded on 19 December 1993. Despite confused reports of opposition appeals for a boycott of the poll (and the absence of voters' lists in some polling centres), the rate of participation was, officially, 78.5% of the registered electorate, with supporters of all candidates voting. The official results were confirmed by the supreme court in early January 1994: Conté was elected at the first round of voting, having secured an absolute majority (51.70%) of the votes cast. Condé, his nearest rival, took 19.55% of the votes; however, the supreme court's invalidation (having found evidence of malpractice) of the results of voting in the Kankan and Siguiri prefectures, in both of which Condé had won more than 90% of the votes, fuelled opposition claims that the poll had been manipulated in favour of Conté. Of the other candidates, Bâ took 13.37% of the votes and Diallo 11.86%.

Conté (who had, in accordance with the constitution, resigned from the army in order to contest the presidency as a civilian) was inaugurated as president on 29 January 1994. His stated priorities—to strengthen national security and unity and to promote economic growth, in particular through the development of the primary sector—were apparently reflected in the composition of an enlarged council of ministers, appointed in August.

In May 1994 Bâ, asserting his lack of confidence in the Guinean opposition movement, expressed the UNR's willingness to recognize Conté as the country's legitimately elected head of state. Relations between the government and opposition otherwise remained generally poor, and the RPG in particular protested of the harassment of its activists by members of the armed forces. The national human rights body, the Association guinéenne des droits de l'homme, meanwhile denounced what it alleged was a recent increase in the maltreatment of prisoners and attempts by the authorities to deprive individuals of basic rights and freedoms. The brief detention, in June, of eight senior armed forces officers, including the deputy chief of staff of the air force, prompted rumours of a coup plot; the government confirmed that certain members of the armed forces had participated in a 'political' meeting, in contravention of their terms of service, but denied the existence of any conspiracy. In September the authorities refuted RPG assertions that attempts had been made to assassinate Condé. Opposition activists protested that a government ban on political demonstrations was unconstitutional; the ban was ended in November, but the government emphasized that rallies should not be confused with street demonstrations. The announcement, shortly afterwards, that there would be no facilities abroad to allow expatriate Guineans to vote in the forthcoming legislative elections (following violent disturbances at polling stations outside Guinea at the 1993 presidential election) provoked criticism by opposition parties and by members of the electoral commission, who stated that the disenfranchisement of Guineans abroad was in contravention of both the constitution and the electoral code. Bâ was among those to condemn the policy, and the UNR withdrew its support for Conté. In February 1995 it was announced that the president was to readopt his military rank.

In December 1994 the government announced new measures aimed at combating organized crime and other serious offences. As well as the creation of a special police unit to counter banditry, the enforcement of the death penalty was envisaged, together with stricter policies governing immigration and asylum for refugees: the Conté administration has frequently attributed the increase in insecurity to the presence of large numbers of refugees (see Foreign and Regional Affairs, below) in Guinea. There were, in addition, increasing indications of the government's desire to curb the influence of Islamic fundamentalism. In January 1996 international human rights organizations expressed concern at the rejection by the supreme court of appeals against six death sentences.

In March 1995 it was announced that elections to the new national assembly would take place on 11 June. Parties of the so-called 'radical' opposition (principally the RPG, the PRP and the UNR) immediately denounced the timing of the election, suggesting that the authorities had chosen a date during the rainy season so as effectively to prevent many voters in rural areas from participating in the poll. Opposition leaders frequently alleged harassment of party activists by the security forces, claiming that efforts were being made to prevent campaigning in areas where support for the opposition was likely to be strong. They also denounced the PUP's use of portraits of Conté on campaign posters and literature, since the head of state was, in principle, constitutionally required to distance himself from party politics.

At the elections a total of 846 candidates, from 21 parties, contested the national assembly's 114 seats. As preliminary results indicated that the PUP had won an overwhelming majority in the legislature, the radical opposition protested that voting had been conducted fraudulently, stating that they would take no further part in the electoral process and that they would boycott the national assembly. According to the full results, which were not published until more than one week after the polls, the PUP won 71 seats—having taken 30 of the country's 38 single-member constituencies and 41 of the 76 seats allocated by a system of national proportional representation. Eight other parties won representation, principal among them the RPG, which took 19 seats, the PRP and the UNR, both of which won nine seats. Some 63% of the electorate were reported to have voted. The results were verified by the supreme court in mid-July 1995, whereupon the new legislature formally superseded the CTRN. At local elections in late June the PUP won control of 20 of the country's 36 municipalities, while the RPG, the PRP and the UNR, which had presented a co-ordinated campaign, took 10.

In July 1995 the three radical opposition parties joined forces with nine other organizations in a new opposition front, the Coordination de l'opposition démocratique (Codem). Disagreement was, however, reported between the RPG, the PRP and the UNR, which continued to advocate a boycott of the national assembly, and other parties that had won parliamentary representation and wished to take their seats. Codem indicated its willingness to enter into a dialogue with the authorities. At a subsequent meeting between a representative of Codem and the minister of the interior, Alsény René Gomez, the latter rejected what Codem had presented as evidence of electoral fraud as not affecting the overall credibility of the results. The inaugural session of the national assembly, on 30 August, was attended by representatives of all the elected parties. Boubacar Biro Diallo, of the PUP, was elected as the new parliament's speaker; the PUP and its allies also took control of all other prominent posts in the legislature, despite previous indications that some would be allocated to parties of the opposition.

Addressing the armed forces in November 1995, Conté warned against civilian interference in, and the politicization of, the military. In early February 1996 elements of the military wishing to overthrow Conté's regime apparently took advantage of protests by soldiers in Conakry who were demanding improved pay and allowances. Disaffected soldiers seized control of the airport and offices of the state broadcasting service, and shelling around the presidential palace caused severe damage. Conté was reportedly seized as he attempted to flee the palace, and was held by rebels for some 15 hours until he made concessions including a doubling of salaries and immunity from prosecution for those involved in the mutiny. He had already agreed to the demand that the minister of defence, Col Abdourahmane Diallo, be dismissed, assuming personal responsibility for defence. About 50 people (some of them civilians) were killed and 100 injured as rebels clashed with forces loyal to the Conté regime. Mutineers looted shops and markets, as well as government property, and the seizure of food stocks by rebels was reported to have resulted in shortages in subsequent weeks. In all, as many as 2,000 soldiers, including members of the presidential guard, were believed to have joined the rebellion. Despite Conté's undertaking that there would be no punitive action, several officers—apparently among them some of those detained in June 1994—were arrested shortly afterwards, and both Conté and Gomez stated that any legal proceedings would be a matter for the judiciary. There were, however, concerns that some armed mutineers remained at large. That there had been a coup attempt was only admitted by Conté almost three weeks after the mutiny. Members of Codem subsequently withdrew from a parliamentary commission that had been established to investigate the circumstances surrounding the rebellion, apparently in protest at Conté's allusions to opposition links with anti-government elements within the military.

The initial recommendations of the parliamentary commission, published at this time, included that there should be a complete depoliticization of the military, accompanied by the demilitarization of political life, and the need to restore discipline within the armed forces was emphasized. For its part, the opposition warned that avoidance of further insurrection could be guaranteed only by full observance of the agreement reached by Conté and the military during the rebellion. In late March 1996, none the less, it was announced that eight members of the military (four of them senior officers) had been charged with undermining state security in connection with the coup attempt. A reinforcement of security measures followed the assassination of the commander (a close associate of Conté) of the Alpha Yaya military barracks, where the February rebellion had begun, apparently in reprisal against the charges. Calm was quickly restored, and Conté left his barracks for the first time since early February to meet President Alpha Oumar Konaré of Mali, who arrived in Conakry to discuss terms for the release into Guinean custody of one of the alleged perpetrators of the coup attempt, who had taken refuge in the Malian embassy. In early April it was reported in Guinea that the Malian authorities had handed over the officer, having received assurances that his rights would be respected; however, Mali subsequently recalled its ambassador from Conakry, protesting that Guinean forces had stormed the embassy to make the arrest. By mid-June some 42 members of the armed forces had reportedly been charged in connection with the coup plot. An international warrant had also been issued for the arrest of Commdr Joseph Gbago Zoumanigui, suspected of being a main conspirator, who was rumoured to have fled the country. In addition, in early April 10 people, some of them civilians, were said to have been detained in connection with the assassination of the army commander in the previous month.

The replacement, in mid-April 1996, of the armed forces chief of staff and the governor of Conakry (also a military officer), both of whom had been regarded as close associates of Conté, was regarded as an indication of the president's commitment to a restructuring of both the civilian and military administration. The need was also emphasized to raise moral standards in public life and within the military. An armed forces conference was convened in early June to consider the reorganization of the military, at which there was consensus regarding several of the parliamentary commission's recommendations for reform. In early July Conté announced (for the first time under the third republic) the appointment of a prime minister. The premiership was assigned to a non-partisan economist, Sidia Touré. A comprehensive reorganization of the government included the departure of Gomez and the division of the ministry of the interior into two separate departments (one responsible for territorial administration and decentralization, the other for security), and the appointment of a new minister of justice; Conté retained the defence portfolio. Touré announced that the new government's priorities were to be economic recovery and the combating of institutionalized corruption, with the aim of securing renewed assistance from the international donor community, and of attracting increased foreign investment; the new prime minister assumed personal responsibility for the economy, finance and planning, and immediate measures were announced to reduce public expenditure by one-third—although the salary increases for the military conceded by Conté in February were to be honoured. The installation of Touré's technocrat-led government was generally well received. However, controversy arose in some quarters, most notably within the PUP, after it emerged that Touré (formerly head of cabinet of Alassane Ouattara—Côte d'Ivoire's prime minister in 1990–93) had been appointed premier in accordance with an Ivorian-brokered arrangement. Touré, who held dual Guinean-Ivorian citizenship, responded to criticism that there was no constitutional provision for the post of prime minister by stating that his appointment was in accordance with the article of the constitution empowering the president of the republic to appoint ministers and to delegate part of his functions.

The removal from office of Gomez was welcomed by opposition groups. However, one of his last actions as minister of the interior, authorizing the establishment of a foundation dedicated to the philosophy of Ahmed Sekou Touré, was particularly criticized by the Union des forces démocratiques de Guinée, which was active in representing the interests of victims of the Sekou Touré regime. The party had also condemned the rehabilitation of Sekou Touré and recent legislation granting full privileges to members of the former president's family as trivializing the crimes of the 'party state'.

In early November 1996 the RPG's headquarters in Conakry was ransacked and damaged by fire, apparently following clashes between supporters of Condé and a group of students. Four prominent members of the RPG were subsequently arrested, and in the following month Codem announced its intention to establish a militia, with the aim of resisting further detentions of opposition activists. In mid-January 1997 the minister of territorial administration and decentralization stated that no political party had the right to establish an armed force, and emphasized that the law would be applied vigorously against those seeking to foster what he termed a spiral of violence in Guinea. The four RDP officials were sentenced to two years' imprisonment in mid-June, having been convicted of violence and causing injury to others.

A new financing arrangement was concluded with the IMF in January 1997. In mid-February Touré relinquished control of the economy portfolio to his two ministers-delegate, Ousmane Kaba and Ibrahima Kassory Fofana, who now became, respectively, minister of planning and co-operation and minister of economic affairs and finance. The issue of the premiership remained controversial, and in May, in response to parliamentary appeals for the establishment of a post of constitutional prime minister, the government stated that for the constitution to vest powers directly in an office of prime minister would result in political instability and confusion.

During early August 1996 40 of those detained in connection with the February mutiny were released from custody; charges remained against three suspects (including Zoumanigui). The announcement, in June 1997, that a state security court was to be established to deal with matters of exceptional jurisdiction, and that its first task would be to try the alleged leaders of the previous year's mutiny, provoked outrage among opposition parties and prompted strong protests by the national lawyers' association. Particular concerns were that there was no constitutional provision for such a court, that its members were to be personally appointed by Conté (the tribunal's president was to be Commdr Sama Pannival Bangoura, the head of the Alpha Yaya barracks), and that the trial of the alleged mutineers would be held in camera. The opposition reiterated its concerns regarding the potential consequences should Conté renege on earlier pledges that there would be no reprisals for those involved in the rebellion. Shortly after the announcement of the trial, moreover, unidentified forces were reported to have raided the home of one of Conté's closest civilian advisers, leaving behind a note warning that the president should not seek re-election in 1998. Meanwhile, rumours circulated with increasing frequency that Guinean dissidents were conspiring with rebels and mercenary groups in Sierra Leone and Liberia to overthrow the Conté regime. The fugitive Zoumanigui, notably, was reported to be attempting to recruit mercenary forces, and the planned invasion was said to have the support of Sekou Touré's son. In mid-April 1997 it was reported that three Belgian nationals had been arrested in Guinea, accused of plotting to overthrow Conté; the Belgian authorities vehemently denied that the detainees were mercenaries, and indicated that they had been arrested following a commercial dispute. Opposition parties asserted that rumours of a destabilization plot were false. The leader of the Union pour le progrès de la Guinée, Jean-Marie Doré, stated in July that the armed forces were in full control of the country's borders, and that the only possible source of dissension might come from members of the military disenchanted at their operating conditions.

FOREIGN AND REGIONAL AFFAIRS

France has assumed an increasingly active role in the Conté regime's strategy for aid and investment. French interests have predominated in taking control of the newly-privatized state companies, and there has been a substantial inflow of French advisers and teachers. In addition, Guinea is dependent on France for the provision of civilian and military intelligence, and France has contributed financial and technical assistance for the holding of multi-party elections. However, official French reaction to the attempted *coup d'état* in February 1996 was considered muted, and it was noted that French instructors responsible for training the Guinean presidential guard did not actively prevent members of the force from joining the rebels. France did, none the less, subsequently offer assistance in restoring security. Libya and the People's Republic of China both pledged material assistance following the mutiny. Guinea, a member of the Organization of the Islamic Conference, has also forged links with other Islamic states, notably signing several co-operation agreements with Iran in the mid-1990s.

Of particular concern to the Guinean authorities during the 1990s has been the instability in neighbouring Liberia and Sierra Leone. In August 1990 Guinean armed forces were deployed along the border with Liberia, following a series of incursions by deserters from the Liberian army. Guinean army units also participated in the ECOMOG monitoring group of the Economic Community of West African States (ECOWAS) that was dispatched to Liberia in that month, and in April 1991 it was annnounced that a Guinean contingent was to be deployed in Sierra Leone to assist that country in repelling violations of its territory by the National Patriotic Front of Liberia (NPFL), led by Charles Taylor. Following the *coup d'état* in Sierra Leone in April 1992, ex-president Momoh of that country was granted asylum in Guinea, although the Conté government expressed its wish to establish 'normal' relations with the new regime led by Capt. Valentine Strasser, and announced that Guinean forces would remain in Sierra Leone.

In October 1992 the Conté government confirmed for the first time that Liberian forces were being trained in Guinea; however, assurances were given that those receiving military instruction were not, as had been widely rumoured, members of the anti-Taylor United Liberation Movement of Liberia for Democracy (ULIMO), but that they were to constitute the first Liberian government forces following the eventual restoration of peace. In March 1993 the NPFL protested to the UN that ULIMO had launched an armed attack on NPFL-held territory from Guinea, and threatened reprisals should further offensives occur. Although Guinea continued to deny support for ULIMO, it was admitted in the same month that, contrary to earlier indications, Liberian forces trained in Guinea (at the request of the Liberian interim government) had already returned to Liberia. Efforts were undertaken from early 1994 to reinforce security along Guinea's borders, following recent incursions by both ULIMO and NPFL fighters.

A resurgence of violence in Liberia in September 1994, following a coup attempt in that country, caused as many as 50,000 refugees to cross into Guinea. Moreover, an intensification of hostilities involving government and rebel forces in Sierra Leone, in January 1995, resulted in a further influx of refugees (numbering 20,000–40,000, according to conflicting reports). The Guinean government warned of food shortages in border areas, and appealed for international assistance for its efforts to meet the refugees' basic needs. The Conté administration also established a special commission to monitor the refugee crisis. In July the government issued a statement reaffirming Guinea's determination to ensure the defence of its territory and security of its population, and indicating that attacks by Liberian factions against border areas, which undermined Guinea's territorial integrity and national sovereignty, would not be tolerated.

In December 1995, following the conclusion (in Abuja, Nigeria, in August) of a new peace accord for Liberia, it was reported that arrangements were being finalized for the repatriation of Liberian refugees, at a rate of 150 per week, from Guinea. Several thousand refugees were also reported to have crossed into Liberia in December, following the reopening of a border point that had been blocked by the NPFL since 1994. A population census conducted in Guinea at the end of 1996 enumerated some 640,000 refugees from Liberia and Sierra Leone.

Like his predecessor, Strasser took refuge in Guinea after he was deposed in January 1996. None the less, close co-operation was developed with the new regime, and President Ahmed Tejan Kabbah made several visits to Guinea both before and after his election to the presidency in March of that year. Kabbah in turn fled to Guinea in May 1997, following the seizure of power in Sierra Leone by forces led by Maj. Johnny Paul Koroma. Military reinforcements were deployed to protect Guinea's border, and 1,500 Guinean troops were dispatched in support of the Nigerian-led force in Sierra Leone. Guinea joined other members of the international community in condemning the subversion of constitutional order in Sierra Leone, and following an *ad hoc* conference of ECOWAS ministers of foreign affairs, which was convened in Conakry in late June, Guinea became a member of the 'committee of four' (with Côte d'Ivoire, Ghana and Nigeria) charged with ensuring the implementation of decisions and recommendations pertaining to the situation in Sierra Leone. A conference communiqué appealed for international assistance for Guinea and other countries of the sub-region affected by the influx of refugees as a result of the coup.

The crisis in Sierra Leone served to exacerbate tensions with regard to Guinea's internal security (see above). In April 1997, the commander of ECOMOG forces, Maj.-Gen. Victor Malu, had stated that he would allow no use of Liberian territory for the purposes of mounting an invasion of a neighbouring state. Reports continued to circulate, none the less, both of the recruitment by Guinean dissidents of mercenary forces in Liberia and Sierra Leone, and of the involvement of refugees from those countries in destabilization activities in Guinea.

Economy

EDITH HODGKINSON

With substantial mineral deposits and excellent agricultural potential, Guinea could be one of the richest countries in west Africa. Yet the economic record since independence has been disappointing overall. The country's gross domestic product (GDP) expanded, in real terms, at an average rate of 3.0% per year in 1970–80, reflecting the rapid development of the bauxite sector during that decade, but declined by 1.4% per year in 1980–85. The causes of Guinea's relatively poor performance during this period were largely political. First, there was the abrupt severance of the country's links with France in 1958. Some of the short-term difficulties arising from the sudden withdrawal of French officials, and the discontinuance of aid, were overcome by support from Eastern bloc countries, while the immediate and substantial flight of capital was stemmed when Guinea created its own currency, the Guinean franc (FG), after withdrawing from the Franc Zone in 1960. However, other consequences—the need to find alternative markets for Guinea's exports and alternative sources of capital and technical assistance, and to build up the country's indigenous skills and supplies—took longer to resolve.

Second, the newly independent Guinea immediately sought to set up a socialist economy, with direct state control of production and consumption in virtually every sector—an objective demanding managerial input that Guinea lacked, and which resulted in great inefficiency and waste. Mining, the one economic sector where state control was diluted, developed as an enclave, with admittedly major benefits for Guinea's export earnings but little linkage and feedback into the rest of the economy, which remained essentially based on agriculture and which suffered from Sekou Touré's system of highly centralized management. The economy consequently became even more dualistic, with the development of a large informal sector in response to the near monopoly of the state over formal economic activity. In an attempt to remove at least the domestic constraints on growth, the Conté administration has introduced a series of policy reforms, agreed with the IMF and the World Bank. These include the transfer to private interests, or elimination, of the parastatal organizations, the liberalization of foreign trade and the abolition of price controls, monetary and banking reforms, and a reduction in the number of civil service personnel. The recovery programme has received substantial international support, in the form of debt-relief and new funds from both bilateral and multilateral sources. Such reforms have enjoyed considerable success, and real GDP growth in 1988–96 averaged 4.0% per year, at a fairly stable pace. None the less, GDP per head, at US $483 in 1995, remained low. A more telling indication of living standards is provided by two demographic statistics: life expectancy at birth was only 45 years in 1993 (well below the average for sub-Saharan Africa of 52 years), and one-quarter of all live-born children die before the age of five.

POPULATION AND EMPLOYMENT

Population growth has been relatively slow, owing to the high level of emigration during the Sekou Touré regime. Therefore, while the population was stated to be 4.5m. (excluding adjustment for underenumeration) at the 1983 census, a further 2m. Guineans (some of whom returned following the 1984 coup) were estimated to be living abroad. The census conducted in December 1996 enumerated a population of 7,164,823, including some 640,000 refugees. The urban population numbered 2.1m.

The active labour force in the early 1990s was estimated at about 3m. The majority are employed in the rural sector, although the share has eased from 78% of the total at the 1983 census to about two-thirds in the mid-1990s, with an increasing proportion now engaged in industrial and service activities. A little more than one-half of salaried employees are concentrated in the public sector, which has rendered more difficult the Conté government's aim of reducing the number of civil service personnel by 50%. By early 1995 the number of employees in the public sector had been reduced to about 48,000, compared with some 90,000 in 1986. However, the real contraction is less significant, as some of the losses resulted from the transfer to private ownership of state-owned interests. Thus, 8,000 employees of the state mining companies were removed from the public payroll in May 1990. The diminution in job opportunities in the public sector, previously guaranteed to all university graduates, has caused a rapid increase in urban unemployment and fuelled student unrest.

AGRICULTURE, FORESTRY AND FISHING

Despite the rapid development and potential of the mining sector, agriculture remains an important economic activity in terms of value of output (an estimated 25% of GDP in 1995) and the most significant in terms of employment (see above). Its slow growth (3% per year in 1970–77, and only around 1% per year during the final years of the Sekou Touré regime) offset the much stronger performance of mining. Agricultural production was depressed by the low official prices paid to producers, government controls on marketing, and the production tax on crops and livestock, which led to large-scale smuggling of produce by peasant farmers. The collective agricultural units, which occupied a dominant role in agriculture, and the Pouvoirs révolutionnaires locaux, which controlled the transport and marketing of agricultural production, were highly inefficient. The government of Lansana Conté immediately abolished collectives, raised producer prices and ended the production tax. Improvements to the infrastructure (notably to the road network) and the easier availability of farm credits are beginning to stimulate an increase in production by small-scale farmers.

Production of foods has thus been recovering in recent years, to about 50% more than the average in 1979–81. In 1995 output of paddy rice (cultivated mainly in the Forest Guinea area) was 532,000 metric tons, while production of cassava was 512,000 tons, sweet potatoes 143,000 tons and maize 89,000 tons. The rise in output has, in the long term, failed to keep pace with population growth, so that Guinea—a net exporter of food in the past—now imports large quantities, representing about double the value of its agricultural exports. The staple crops are supplemented by the substantial livestock herd (raised by traditional methods), estimated by the FAO in 1995 at 1.7m. cattle, 475,000 sheep and 580,000 goats.

The major commercial crops are bananas, coffee, pineapples, oil palm, groundnuts and citrus fruit. The banana plantations, which suffered in the late 1950s from disease and, with independence, from the withdrawal of European planters and the closing of the protected French market, have shown a good recovery, with output averaging some 138,000 tons per year in 1992–94. Officially recorded coffee output fluctuated widely in the Sekou Touré era—in some years net imports were recorded—because of smuggling to neighbouring countries, where higher prices were obtainable. Before independence Guinea exported about 20,000 tons of coffee annually. Higher prices paid to producers in the late 1980s prompted more output to be sold on the official domestic market: production rose strongly, from 6,900 tons in 1985/86 to about 29,000 tons per year in the early 1990s. Pineapple production, having fallen from 25,000 tons per year in the late 1960s to about one-half of this level in 1970, had increased to about 94,000 tons per year by the mid-1990s. An export trade in fruit and vegetables for the European market has been developed, as quality-control and transportation links have improved. Because of the overvaluation of the currency until 1985, exports of bananas, coffee, oil palm and other crops were subsidized out of the proceeds of import taxes. This practice ceased under the Conté regime, and production of cash crops is being stimulated by the more realistic exchange rate. In 1986 a nine-year project was launched to plant 13,000 ha with rubber and oil palm in Forest Guinea, with the aim of re-establishing, in a modified form, the plantation agriculture that was characteristic of the colonial period, and of attracting foreign investment to this sector. Meanwhile, a cotton development scheme, aided by France, was inaugurated in 1985, aiming to produce a total of 43,000–50,000 tons from plantations in Haute Guinée (where it is the largest single development project) and Moyenne Guinée. However, progress has been disappointing, with output of seed cotton reaching its highest level at only 19,670 tons in 1992/93 and then falling to only 10,600 tons in 1995/96. This fall is attributed to the decline in yields because of unfavourable weather and a reduction in the area planted as farmers have gradually transferred to other economic activities, notably gold-mining. The government is attempting to keep the programme in operation by means of increasing producer prices, reducing supply costs and subsidizing agricultural equipment.

There is considerable potential for timber production, with forests covering more than two-thirds of the land area. Timber resources are currently used mainly for fuel, with production of roundwood (by small-scale producers) totalling 4.5m. cu m in 1993. An integrated forestry industry is, however, planned.

The fishing sector remains relatively undeveloped. Only a small proportion of the total catch from Guinean waters—some 120,000 tons in recent years—has been accounted for by indigenous fleets, the rest having been taken by factory ships and industrial trawlers. Since 1983 the Guinean government has concluded a series of fishing accords with the European Community (EC, now European Union—EU). The two-year agreement that took effect in January 1990 allowed European trawlers to land an average of 12,000 tons of fish per year, and it has since been agreed to award foreign licences exclusively to EU fleets, in an effort to preserve the viability of fish stocks on the continental shelf. Inadequate local infrastructure has been a constraint on the development of this sector, but improvements are now being made. The African Development Bank is helping to finance the establishment of onshore facilities and the supply of equipment for small-scale fishermen. In addition, the rehabilitation of the port of Conakry includes the installation of deep-freeze equipment to serve the fishing industry.

MINING AND POWER

Guinea's most dynamic sector and most important source of foreign exchange, providing more than 90% of recorded export revenues for much of the 1980s, is mining, which contributed 22.8% of GDP in 1989. Since that year the sector has suffered great upheavals, as operations have been disrupted by industrial disputes and technical difficulties, and has declined in importance. By 1995 its share of GDP had declined to about 19%. The country possesses between one-quarter and one-third of the world's known bauxite reserves, with a very high-grade ore. Guinea ranks second only to Australia in terms of ore production, and is the world's largest exporter of bauxite. Since the mid-1980s, however, bauxite revenues have been affected by a weakening in world demand for aluminium and the considerable surplus in world production capacity. Annual output averaged 13.5m. tons in the period 1981–86 and increased to a yearly average of 17m. tons in 1987–93. Production declined thereafter, to some 14m. tons in 1995–96. Current expansion and rehabilitation programmes at the country's mines are projected to increase annual output to 20m. tons.

The exploitation of bauxite reserves at Fria, by the Cie internationale pour la production de l'alumine Fria (an international consortium that included Pechiney), began in the 1930s. Processing into alumina began in 1960, at what remains the country's only smelter. Following independence, the government took a 49% share in the company, which was renamed Friguia. The smelter's output has eased from a peak of 692,000 tons (recorded in 1980, and close to the plant's total capacity of 700,000 tons annually) to some 640,000 tons in 1995. A rehabilitation programme is under way to raise output to 1.3m. tons per year.

The country's principal bauxite mine is at Boké, in the north-west, which was commissioned in 1973 by the Cie des bauxites de Guinée, a joint venture between the government and the Halco group (an international consortium of US, Canadian, French, German and Spanish aluminium companies). The government holds 49% of the capital and receives 65% of the mine's net profits. The scheme involved investment of US $400m., including infrastructural development—142 km of railway and a port at Kamsar. Output increased from around 900,000 tons per year to the complex's full capacity (at that time) of 10m. tons in 1981, eased subsequently, and then rose to 11.5m. tons per year in 1990 and 1991. The plant's capacity is to be expanded to 13.5m. tons by 1998, drawing on growing output from the new mine under development at Bidikoum.

A similar agreement to that signed with Halco was concluded in 1969 by Guinea and the USSR for the working of bauxite deposits at Debélé, near Kindia. Production by the Office des bauxites de Kindia began in 1974, with capacity of 2.5m. tons per year, and averaged about 3m. tons per year in the late 1980s. Following the dissolution of the USSR, the company suffered severe financial difficulties: it was reorganized as the Société des bauxites de Kindia in 1992, and is scheduled for privatization. Output, which had fallen to 1.1m. tons in 1992, recovered to 2.4m. tons in 1993, but then regressed to the 1992 level in 1994. The Société des bauxites de Dabola-Tougué, established as a joint venture with Iran, plans to develop reserves at Dabola and Tougué and eventually to operate an alumina-processing plant. The first production from the mine was scheduled for 1997, and in late 1996 Iran announced its intention to build a railway connecting the site to Conakry. A joint Russian-Ukrainian scheme to extract bauxite from deposits at Dian-Dian, for processing in those two countries, was announced in 1996, but funding has yet to be finalized.

Working of the iron-ore deposits on the Kaloum peninsula (near Conakry) was begun in 1953 by an Anglo-French group, and provided a stable output of about 700,000 tons per year in 1960–69, when working at Kaloum was abandoned. An ambitious project for the exploitation of the far superior deposits at Mt Nimba, which has proven reserves of 350 tons of high-grade (66.7%) ore (total reserves have been estimated at as much as 1,000m. tons), has been studied and much discussed for many years. It was originally proposed that a consortium of the government (50%) and companies from Japan, the USA, France, Spain, Romania, Yugoslavia, Nigeria, Algeria and Liberia would undertake the project, which, with associated infrastructure, was to cost an estimated US $900m. However, the original proposals failed to attract sufficient capital, since commitments by potential customers for the ore were far below the planned level of output (an eventual 15m. tons per year), and a scaled-down version of the project was to be undertaken by a joint venture of the governments of Guinea and Liberia (each with a stake of 20%) and the Euronimba consortium of Sumitomo, Gencor, Coframines and Cidem. This envisaged shipment via an 18-km rail spur for processing in Liberia, with export through that country's port of Buchanan. There are plans for the eventual construction of a railway (at an estimated cost of $555m.) to Conakry, where a new deep-water port would be constructed. However, the persistent conflict in Liberia since the beginning of the 1990s, as well as international concern at the potential environmental impact of the project, have prevented any further progress.

Production of diamonds rose in the late 1960s, to reach 80,000 carats per year in the early 1970s: the official figure did not include substantial illicit production, and mining was suspended in the late 1970s to prevent smuggling and theft. In 1980 the government allowed the resumption of diamond mining by private companies, and AREDOR–Guinée was founded in 1981 with Australian, Swiss, British and—for the first time in Guinea—International Finance Corpn participation. The government had a 50% holding and was to take 65% of net profits. AREDOR–Guinée began production in 1984, and output reached a peak of 204,000 carats in 1986. However, mining was suspended following violent incidents in 1991, and in 1992 the government revoked the ban (imposed in 1985) on small-scale prospecting in order to stimulate investment by foreign companies. All output is now by independent miners, who export some 80,000–125,000 carats per year, although only a small proportion of this appears in official figures.

Gold is mined both industrially and by individuals (the latter smuggle much of their output abroad). A joint venture with Belgian interests, the Société Aurifère de Guinée, was established in 1985 to develop gold mining in the Siguiri and Mandiana districts. Alluvial production began in 1988, and reached 2,000 kg in the following year; however extraction ceased in 1992, owing to financial and technical difficulties and conflicts with artisanal miners. Golden Shamrock of Australia took a 70% interest in the project (the International Finance Corpn and the Guinean government each hold 15%). It was in turn taken over by Ghana's Ashanti Goldfields in 1996, and hard-rock extraction was scheduled to resume in 1997. The Société minière de Dinguiraye (a joint venture with Norwegian, Australian and French interests) began production at the Léro site in 1995, with an eventual target of 1,200 kg per year. Several other foreign enterprises are also actively prospecting for gold.

The country possesses a wide range of other minerals, but only granite is exploited on an industrial scale. There are no known resources of fossil fuels, but only one-third of Guinea's territorial area has so far been geologically surveyed.

Reflecting the demands of the alumina sector and the development of hydroelectric power, production of electricity rose five-fold between 1960 and 1976, to 500m. kWh, of which about two-thirds was consumed by Friguia. Net installed capacity is 176 MW, of which one-half is privately operated, notably by the mining companies. Supplies of energy outside the mining and industrial sector are vastly inadequate, with only about 6% of households receiving electricity from the national grid; even Conakry is subject to frequent and prolonged power-cuts during dry periods. None the less, the country has a very large, as yet unexploited, hydroelectric potential, estimated at some 6,000 MW. Several ambitious projects for the development of hydroelectric facilities on the Konkouré river finally came to fruition—in a much reduced form—in 1996, when work began on a 75-MW plant at Garafiri. Feasibility studies have been funded by foreign donors for a 125-MW project at Kaléta, 100 km downstream from Garafiri. The two plants are projected to commence production in 1999 and 2002, respectively, meeting forecast demand at those dates. As part of the economic reform programme, the national power corporation has been restructured, and participation has been secured from Hydro-Québec of Canada, Electricité de France and SAUR of France. It is envisaged that the electricity network be extended to cover the whole country by 2004.

MANUFACTURING

The principal aim of Guinea's small manufacturing sector, which accounts for only 4%–5% of GDP, has been import-substitution, but the experience of the state-run projects that were established under Sekou Touré was disappointing. Lack of foreign exchange for raw materials, of skilled workers and of technical expertise, combined with poor management and low domestic purchasing power, meant that most of the plants were, and are still, operating substantially below capacity. A French evaluation in 1985 estimated that utilization was equivalent to only one-tenth of capacity, and it is probable that the situation will have worsened since. The industrial units include a textile factory (with an annual capacity of 24m. m of fabrics), construction materials plant, food and agricultural processing facilities, and a cement factory. The Conté government has liberalized the investment code, giving equal treatment to foreign capital and individuals, with guarantees against expropriation, and has a more positive attitude to the private sector as a whole than the previous regime. Of 200 state enterprises in existence in 1985, all but 23 had been sold to the private sector or dissolved by the end of 1992. However, the programme attracted criticism on two counts: that the government did not put an accurate value on the assets divested, and that the capacity of the new owners to undertake the necessary rehabilitation was not assured.

TRANSPORT INFRASTRUCTURE

The inadequacy of Guinea's transport infrastructure has been cited by the World Bank as the 'single most severe impediment to output recovery'. None the less, some major improvements have been made in the past decade. The road network is being almost entirely reconstructed, to restore links between Conakry and the country's interior, while road tracks have been built to open up rural areas. In 1995 there were an estimated 30,270 km of roads and tracks, including 4,250 km of main roads and 7,920 km of secondary roads; about 5,000 km of the network was paved. The rail network is better developed because of the demands of the bauxite sector: a 135-km heavy-gauge railway links the Boké bauxite deposits with the deep-water port at Kamsar, which handles around 9m. tons per year and is thus the country's major export outlet in tonnage terms. The 662-km public rail line from Conakry to Kankan is in very poor condition, and can take light traffic only. However, it is now being renovated with French aid; in early 1997 a Slovak company was awarded the contract for the first phase of a two-year programme of upgrading. The port of Conakry, which handled 4.4m. tons of foreign trade in 1994, has been extended and modernized as part of a programme that envisages the construction of naval-repair and deep-water port facilities. A petroleum terminal is also planned for Conakry. There is an international airport at Conakry, and there are several smaller airfields.

FINANCE

Government revenue remains heavily reliant on income from the mining companies, but this contribution has declined sharply from a peak of 60% in 1987 to about 20% in the mid-1990s. Although mining revenue rose strongly in the mid- and late 1970s, reflecting the growth of the bauxite sector, current expenditure exceeded revenue, owing to the government's policy of providing jobs in the public sector to all graduates, combined with the rising losses of the state enterprises and the growing burden of servicing the foreign debt.

By 1981 the deficit of the public sector was equivalent to around one-fifth of GDP, with parastatal enterprises alone accounting for some three-quarters of the deficit. As part of Guinea's programme for economic stabilization, inaugurated in 1986 with support from the IMF, consumer subsidies were reduced or eliminated, while the activities of state enterprises were curtailed and employment in the civil service was to be reduced by more than one-half. This severe fiscal austerity proved difficult to implement, and the government was obliged to rescind some of the price increases resulting from the devaluation of the currency in 1986, while the reduction in civil service personnel was finally achieved only in 1995. None the less, the budget balance improved as the government succeeded in raising its revenue from non-mining activities 10-fold in 1987–95, through changes in the tax system and improvements in collection. This was particularly significant, as mining revenue had been falling in every year since 1989. By 1994 non-mining revenues were more than double those from mining. Expenditure, meanwhile, has benefited from the liquidation or sale of the state's industrial and commercial enterprises. The current budget has thus been in surplus in every year since 1989. The overall budget (i.e. taking into account both grants and capital expenditure) remains in deficit, but as a proportion of GDP this has declined in almost every year, from 6.6% in 1988 to only 2% in 1995. (Excluding grants, the deficit has fallen from 8.4% of GDP in 1989 to 6.7% in 1995.) However, this still represents an addition to already high debt stocks, which in turn increases the burden of interest payment on the current budget. The multilateral institutions, the support of which is essential to secure the external funding needed to make up the budgetary shortfall, have maintained their pressure for rigid spending control. The target for 1996—a before-grants deficit equivalent to 5.5% of GDP—came under severe pressure when the military insurrection early in the year extracted a promise from President Conté of substantial pay increases for the army. The prospect of Guinea's failing to meet the agreed fiscal targets prompted the IMF to suspend the enhanced structural adjustment facility (ESAF). However, the new government under prime minister Sidia Touré, appointed in July, set about a restoration of relations with the Fund. The introduction of value-added tax, together with more rigorous controls on the civil service payroll, kept the budget out-turn for the year, at 5.8%, close to target. This rendered Guinea eligible for a new ESAF in early 1997; under the programme this supports, the budget deficit is projected to narrow from 5.7% of GDP in 1997 to 5.1% in 1999.

At all times, the implementation of the government's capital spending programme has been heavily dependent on external funds. Almost two-thirds of development expenditure in the 1960s was covered by foreign aid, with funding for the first (1960–64) Development Plan originating almost exclusively from the Eastern bloc. However, the second (1965–71) Plan received substantial funding from Western countries, principally from the USA. Since the 1984 *coup d'état*, financial support from multilateral agencies and Western governments has been critical to the economic recovery programme.

An important element of the economic liberalization initiated in the final years of the Sekou Touré regime and pursued with vigour by the Conté administration was the reform of the banking sector, ending the state monopoly by allowing the establishment of private commercial banks and then closing down the six state-controlled institutions. This is gradually drawing in funds that previously flowed to the parallel economy. In a further significant disengagement from the banking sector, in late 1996 the government announced plans to privatize the Banque internationale pour le commerce et l'industrie de la Guinée, in which it holds a 51% stake (foreign interests hold 40%). The bank accounts for 45% of the country's banking resources and for about one-third of credits to the private sector.

FOREIGN TRADE AND PAYMENTS

With the development of bauxite resources from the early 1970s, the country's external trade position greatly improved. Previously, exports had stagnated because the initial rise in earnings from bauxite and alumina, to account for nearly two-thirds of exports in 1969, was offset by the ending of iron ore sales after 1967 and the overall poor performance of export crops. Another factor that held down export growth—at least in the official statistics—was the overvaluation of the country's currency. Exporters were required to surrender their foreign-exchange earnings at a rate that effectively reduced their value by around three-quarters. Smuggling was rife during this period. The sharp rise in bauxite exports resulted in strong growth in export earnings after 1975, and sales of bauxite and alumina contributed more than 90% of recorded earnings in the early 1980s. Export earnings were subsequently bolstered by contributions from sales of diamonds and gold, which accounted for 15% of the total in 1990 (when the share of bauxite and alumina was 78%). The sustained growth in exports throughout this period allowed a similarly strong rise in spending on imports, in large part reflecting capital investment in the mining sector. However, as earnings from bauxite and alumina declined from 1991 onwards, while the cost of imports was little changed, the trade account moved into deficit, averaging some US $65m. per year in 1992–95. The value of illicit exports to neighbouring countries (consisting largely of agricultural products) was, in the past, estimated at some $100m. per year, with the proceeds being used mainly to finance illicit imports. It had been hoped that the devaluation of the currency and increases in agricultural producer prices would attract more trade into legal channels. By the mid-1990s, however, these measures seemed to have had relatively little effect. The shortfall in the officially-recorded trade balance has in most years since 1990 kept the current payments account in relatively high deficit, at an average of $211m. per year in 1991–95.

Guinea has relied heavily on foreign capital (in the form of mining investment) and aid. The country's *rapprochement* with France and adherence to the Lomé Conventions (the aid and trade agreements with the EC), in conjunction with the change of political regime in 1984, resulted in a rapid increase in the flow of official development assistance from non-Eastern bloc countries and agencies. This averaged US $367m. (net) per year in 1988–95. While France remains by far the most significant bilateral source of aid funds, the World Bank (through its concessionary lending agency, the International Development Association) and the European Commission are the largest multilateral lenders, providing a net $205m. and $151m., respectively, in 1993–95.

Reflecting its dependence on foreign sources of capital, Guinea's foreign debt rose very sharply, from US $137m. in 1960 to $1,387m. at the end of 1981—equivalent to 86% of the country's gross national product (GNP) in that year—a level that was broadly maintained in the following four years. Although the burden of servicing the debt was alleviated by concessionary interest rates on most of the borrowing and by the buoyancy of Guinean exports, it remained at a high level throughout this period, fluctuating within the range of 14%–24% of exports of goods and services, and obligations were not discharged in full. Arrears on both repayment and interest had apparently reached $300m. at the time of the 1984 coup. With debt-service payments projected to rise steeply over the next few years, and with foreign exchange reserves nearing depletion, a rescheduling of the foreign debt was a necessity.

In early 1986, following final agreement between the IMF and the Conté administration on the terms of the economic stabilization programme (which included a 93% devaluation of the syli and its replacement by a revived Guinea franc), the country's Western creditors agreed to a rescheduling of debt. Some US $200m. in debt liabilities were rescheduled over 10 years, with five years' grace: this arrangement covered all arrears and debt-servicing due up to early 1987. However, the external debt increased strongly again in the late 1980s, to reach $2,255m. at the end of 1988, when the cost of debt-servicing was equivalent to about one-fifth of export earnings. In early 1989 the 'Paris Club' of official creditors agreed to reschedule a further portion of Guinea's external debt. Three creditor governments—most significantly France ($259m.) but also the Federal Republic of Germany and the USA—cancelled some of Guinea's debt. Further rounds of rescheduling of official debt (in 1990, 1991 and 1992), together with the rising share of concessionary loans, meant that, while total foreign debt remained close to 100% of GNP (at $3,242m. at the end of 1995, it was equivalent to 91% in that year), the debt-service ratio was kept at a manageable 14% in most years. Another round of rescheduling, in January 1995, was under the highly concessionary 'Naples terms', and included the cancellation of one-half of debt-servicing liabilities in 1994 and 1995 to France, Germany, Norway and the USA. However, the ratio almost doubled in 1995, to 25.3%, because of a surge in repayment. This enhanced the country's eligibility for further special measures of debt relief: following a favourable assessment by the IMF, and the award of the new ESAF in January 1997, another round of 'Paris Club' restructuring reduced Guinea's debt by $59m. and rescheduled $66m. over 23 years. A significant concession was that Guinea was permitted to convert up to 20% of its outstanding debt (i.e. double the usual limit) into local-currency equity in the form of investment in development projects.

Such debt-relief and continued inflows of new funds are essential to the Guinean economy, since the country's export base remains narrow, over-dependent on one commodity (bauxite) and thus highly vulnerable to fluctuations in international prices for that commodity. The current account of Guinea's balance of payments is expected to continue in deficit for some time, as the country's dependence on imports—particularly of food and petroleum—will still be high. Meanwhile, budgetary support from external sources is vital to the success of the sometimes unpalatable economic adjustment process, by enabling the Conté administration to respond to domestic pressure for an improvement in living standards.

Statistical Survey

Source (unless otherwise stated): Service de la Statistique Générale, Conakry; tel. 44-21-48.

Area and Population

AREA, POPULATION AND DENSITY

Area (sq km)	245,857*
Population (census results)	
4–17 February 1983	4,533,240†
31 December 1996‡	
Males	3,496,150
Females	3,668,673
Total	7,164,823
Density (per sq km) at census of 1996	29.1

* 94,926 sq miles.

† Excluding adjustment for underenumeration.

‡ Provisional figure, including refugees from Liberia and Sierra Leone (estimated at 640,000).

PRINCIPAL TOWNS (population at December 1972)

Conakry (capital) 525,671 (later admitted to be overstated); Kankan 60,000.

BIRTHS AND DEATHS (UN estimates, annual averages)

	1980–85	1985–90	1990–95
Birth rate (per 1,000)	51.3	51.0	50.6
Death rate (per 1,000)	23.8	22.0	20.3

Expectation of life (UN estimates, years at birth, 1990–95): 44.5 (males 44.0; females 45.0).

Source: UN, *World Population Prospects: The 1994 Revision*.

ECONOMICALLY ACTIVE POPULATION

(persons aged 10 years and over, census of 1983, provisional)

	Males	Females	Total
Agriculture, hunting, forestry and fishing	856,971	566,644	1,423,615
Mining and quarrying	7,351	4,890	12,241
Manufacturing	6,758	4,493	11,251
Electricity, gas and water	1,601	1,604	3,205
Construction	5,475	3,640	9,115
Trade, restaurants and hotels	22,408	14,901	37,309
Transport, storage and communications	17,714	11,782	29,496
Finance, insurance, real estate and business services	2,136	1,420	3,556
Community, social and personal services	82,640	54,960	137,600
Activities not adequately defined*	101,450	54,229	155,679
Total labour force	1,104,504	718,563	1,823,067

* Includes 18,244 unemployed persons (not previously employed), whose distribution by sex is not available.

Source: ILO, *Yearbook of Labour Statistics*.

Mid-1995 (estimates in '000): Agriculture, etc. 2,753; Total labour force 3,231 (Source: FAO, *Production Yearbook*).

Agriculture

PRINCIPAL CROPS ('000 metric tons)

	1993	1994	1995
Maize	88	88	89
Millet	4	5	5*
Sorghum	3	4	14*
Rice (paddy)	531	532	532
Other cereals	82	133	133*
Sweet potatoes	130	143	143*
Cassava (Manioc)	485	512	512*
Yams	73	114	114*
Taro (Coco yam)	39	32*	32*
Pulses*	60	60	60
Coconuts	18*	5	5*
Cottonseed*	11	10	10
Cotton (lint)	8†	8	6*
Vegetables*	420	420	420
Sugar cane*	220	220	220
Citrus fruits*	230	230	230
Bananas	137	151	151*
Plantains*	429	429	429
Mangoes	77	105	80*
Pineapples	58	67	67
Other fruits*	37	36	37
Palm kernels	40*	53	53*
Groundnuts (in shell)	122	128	170
Coffee (green)	29*	30	30*
Cocoa beans	4†	4	4*
Tobacco (leaves)*	2	2	2

* FAO estimate(s). † Unofficial figure.

Source: FAO, *Production Yearbook*.

LIVESTOCK ('000 head, year ending September)

	1993	1994*	1995*
Cattle	1,768	1,780	1,780
Sheep	469	475	475
Goats	570	580	580
Pigs	35	38	38
Horses*	2	2	2
Asses*	1	1	1

Poultry (million)*: 14 in 1993; 14 in 1994; 14 in 1995.

* FAO estimates.

Source: FAO, *Production Yearbook*.

LIVESTOCK PRODUCTS (FAO estimates, '000 metric tons)

	1993	1994	1995
Beef and veal	11	12	12
Poultry meat	18	18	18
Mutton and lamb	1	1	1
Goat meat	1	1	1
Pig meat	1	1	1
Other meat	4	4	4
Cows' milk	46	46	46
Goats' milk	4	4	4
Sheep's milk	1	1	1
Poultry eggs	14.5	14.5	14.5
Cattle hides	1.9	2.1	2.1

Source: FAO, *Production Yearbook*.

Forestry

ROUNDWOOD REMOVALS ('000 cubic metres, excluding bark)

	1992	1993	1994
Sawlogs, veneer logs and logs for sleepers	140	140*	140*
Other industrial wood*	426	440	453
Fuel wood	3,849	4,125	4,296
Total	4,415	4,705	4,889

* FAO estimate(s).

Source: FAO, *Yearbook of Forest Products*.

SAWNWOOD PRODUCTION
('000 cubic metres, including railway sleepers)

	1992	1993	1994
Total	63	65	72

Source: FAO, *Yearbook of Forest Products*.

Fishing

('000 metric tons, live weight)

	1993*	1994*	1995
Freshwater fishes	4.0	4.4	4.0*
Sea catfishes	3.0	3.1	4.4
Bobo croaker	2.5	2.6	3.7
Other croakers and drums	2.8	2.9	4.1
Porgies and seabreams	3.3	3.3	4.7
Mullets	1.2	1.3	1.8
Carangids	3.5	3.6	5.0
Sardinellas	3.7	3.8	5.3
Bonga shad	23.0	25.0	23.6
Other marine fishes (incl. unspecified)	13.0	14.4	12.2
Total catch	60.0	64.4	68.8*

* FAO estimate(s).

Mining

	1990	1991	1992
Bauxite ('000 metric tons)	15,341	14,862	13,625
Diamonds ('000 carats)*	127	97	95

Bauxite ('000 metric tons)*: 14,784 in 1993; 13,761 in 1994.

* Data from the US Bureau of Mines.

Source: UN, *Industrial Commodity Statistics Yearbook*.

Gold (Mineral content of ore, metric tons): 4.2 in 1992; 3.8 in 1993; 4.3 in 1994; 6.5 in 1995; 7.0 in 1996 (Source: Gold Fields Mineral Services Ltd, *Gold 1997*).

Industry

SELECTED PRODUCTS ('000 metric tons, unless otherwise indicated)

	1992	1993	1994
Raw sugar	16*	20	10†
Alumina (calcined equivalent)	661	656	n.a.
Electric energy (million kWh)‡	531	536	530

* Data from the FAO.
† Data from the International Sugar Organization.
‡ Provisional or estimated figure(s).

Source: UN, *Industrial Commodity Statistics Yearbook*.

Palm oil (unrefined): 40 in 1992; 40 (estimate) in 1993; 50 in 1994; 50 (estimate) in 1995 (Source: FAO, *Production Yearbook*).

Finance

CURRENCY AND EXCHANGE RATES

Monetary Units

100 centimes = 1 franc guinéen (FG or Guinean franc).

Sterling and Dollar Equivalents (31March 1997)

£1 sterling = 1,758.2 Guinean francs;
US $1 = 1,070.8 Guinean francs;
10,000 Guinean francs = £5.688 = $9.339.

Average Exchange Rate (Guinean francs per US $)

1994	976.6
1995	991.4
1996	1,004.0

Note: The Guinean franc was reintroduced in January 1986, replacing (at par) the syli. At the same time, the currency was devalued by more than 90%. The syli had been introduced in October 1972, replacing the original Guinean franc (at 10 francs per syli).

BUDGET ('000 million Guinean francs)

Revenue*	1993	1994	1995†
Mining-sector revenue	137.5	98.5	110.7
Profit taxes and dividends	17.6	8.7	1.4
Turnover taxes on Société des Bauxites de Kindia (SBK)	8.1	0.9	7.4
Special tax on mining products	105.8	87.1	100.2
Other revenue	214.1	244.8	290.8
Tax revenue	190.1	220.4	265.6
Taxes on income and profits	24.3	30.1	36.6
Personal	16.5	16.2	20.9
Corporate	3.8	8.7	10.7
Taxes on domestic production and trade	114.5	136.5	171.0
Turnover taxes	36.6	38.5	52.4
Excise surcharge	6.9	10.2	13.8
Petroleum excise tax	52.6	65.1	72.6
Taxes on international trade	51.2	53.8	58.0
Import duties	46.0	50.6	54.8
Total	351.6	343.3	401.5

Expenditure‡	1993	1994	1995†
Current expenditure	293.5	311.7	332.8
Wages and salaries	140.3	145.5	154.9
Other goods and services	80.6	76.5	73.1
Subsidies and transfers	31.1	37.3	52.2
Interest payments	41.5	52.4	52.5
Public investment programme	286.1	268.8	313.9
Domestically financed	45.6	38.8	51.2
Externaly financed	240.5	230.0	262.7
Sub-total	579.6	580.5	646.9
Adjustment for payments arrears §	−0.3	−19.2	52.1
Total (cash basis)	579.3	561.3	699.0

* Excluding grants received ('000 million Guinean francs): 112.7 in 1993; 117.5 in 1994; 146.3† in 1995.
† Estimate(s).
‡ Excluding lending minus repayments ('000 million Guinean francs): 0.2† in 1995.
§ Minus sign indicates an increase in arrears.

Source: IMF, *Guinea—Statistical Annex* (March 1997).

INTERNATIONAL RESERVES (US $ million at 31 December)

	1994	1995	1996
IMF special drawing rights	5.53	7.45	0.77
Reserve position in IMF	0.10	0.10	0.11
Foreign exchange	82.22	79.21	89.85
Total	87.85	86.76	90.73

Source: IMF, *International Financial Statistics*.

MONEY SUPPLY (million Guinean francs at 31 December)

	1993	1994	1995
Currency outside banks	166,609	154,748	167,144
Demand deposits at commercial banks	86,763	94,430	104,060
Total (incl. others)	260,854	252,582	274,125

Source: IMF, *International Financial Statistics*.

COST OF LIVING

(Consumer Price Index for Conakry; base: 1990 = 100)

	1992	1993	1994
Food	134.9	147.5	154.5
Fuel and light	144.9	144.5	148.8
Clothing	118.8	129.6	132.5
Rent	135.9	142.7	143.5
All items (incl. others)	139.5	149.4	155.6

1995: Food 166.8; All items 164.0.

Source: ILO, *Yearbook of Labour Statistics*.

NATIONAL ACCOUNTS

Expenditure on the Gross Domestic Product
('000 million Guinean francs at current prices)

	1993	1994	1995*
Government final consumption expenditure	292.4	289.2	306.5
Private final consumption expenditure	2,411.2	2,728.1	2,966.1
Increase in stocks / Gross fixed capital formation }	491.7	451.8	529.7
Total domestic expenditure	3,195.3	3,467.0	3,802.4
Exports of goods and services	681.1	656.5	791.1
Less Imports of goods and services	840.1	809.9	952.0
GDP in purchasers' values	3,036.3	3,315.6	3,641.5
GDP at constant 1989 prices	1,657.3	1,723.6	1,799.4

* Estimates.

Gross Domestic Product by Economic Activity
('000 million Guinean francs at constant 1989 prices)

	1993	1994	1995*
Agriculture, hunting, forestry and fishing	395.8	415.7	430.2
Mining and quarrying	322.2	328.6	336.8
Manufacturing	75.4	79.6	82.1
Electricity, gas and water	3.6	3.7	3.9
Construction	113.8	119.5	128.1
Trade	423.1	448.5	472.7
Transport	85.0	88.4	94.2
Administration	92.9	91.3	91.3
Other services	105.4	105.7	114.1
GDP at factor cost	1,617.2	1,681.0	1,753.4
Indirect taxes	40.1	42.6	46.0
GDP in purchasers' values	1,657.3	1,723.6	1,799.4

* Estimates.

Source: IMF, *Guinea—Statistical Annex* (March 1997).

BALANCE OF PAYMENTS (US $ million)

	1993	1994	1995
Exports of goods f.o.b.	561.1	515.7	582.8
Imports of goods f.o.b.	-582.7	-685.4	-621.7
Trade balance	-21.6	-169.7	-39.0
Exports of services	186.8	152.9	118.7
Imports of services	-334.8	-366.0	-370.8
Balance on goods and services	-169.6	-382.9	-291.1
Other income received	9.3	6.5	12.9
Other income paid	-92.6	-79.8	-97.5
Balance on goods, services and income	-252.9	-456.1	-375.7
Current transfers received	260.3	280.6	258.3
Current transfers paid	-64.2	-72.5	-79.3
Current balance	-56.8	-248.0	-196.7
Capital account (net)	12.4	—	35.2
Direct investment from abroad	2.7	0.2	0.8
Investment assets	-20.1	-14.5	-73.7
Other investment liabilities	79.9	98.5	193.9
Net errors and omissions	-107.5	39.8	-31.8
Overall balance	-89.3	-124.1	-72.5

Source: IMF, *International Financial Statistics*.

External Trade

PRINCIPAL COMMODITIES (US $ million)

Imports c.i.f.	1993	1994	1995†
Public sector	146.6	138.2	148.2
Food aid	5.6	5.4	0.0
Public investment programme	119.0	109.9	124.4
Central Government and public enterprises	22.0	22.9	23.8
Mining companies	217.9	152.6	185.3
Other private sector*	367.7	397.0	475.6
Petroleum products	33.1	33.8	38.6
Total	732.2	687.9	809.2

Exports f.o.b.	1993	1994	1995†
Bauxite	323.7	271.5	298.5
Alumina	108.9	103.4	110.3
Diamonds	70.0	40.2	57.8
Gold	72.1	83.5	112.2
Coffee	36.6	56.7	72.4
Fish	16.6	19.7	29.3
Total (incl. others)	665.0	625.9	747.5

* Including some public-enterprise imports.
† Estimates.

Source: IMF, *Guinea—Statistical Annex* (March 1997).

PRINCIPAL TRADING PARTNERS (percentage of trade)*

Imports f.o.b.	1993	1994	1995
Austria	0.3	1.5	1.6
Belgium-Luxembourg	6.2	7.4	6.2
Brazil	2.1	6.6	3.1
China, People's Repub.	4.4	3.9	3.5
Côte d'Ivoire	13.8	17.2	18.3
France (incl. Monaco)	19.7	20.1	20.5
Germany	2.7	4.1	3.0
Hong Kong	6.8	6.5	5.8
Italy	4.6	3.4	3.5
Japan	2.8	3.5	2.8
Morocco	0.9	0.9	1.4
Netherlands	4.4	3.9	4.3
Nigeria	2.3	2.6	2.5
Senegal	1.8	1.4	1.5
Singapore	4.2	0.0	0.7
Spain	3.9	3.6	3.2
Switzerland	0.3	1.0	0.9
Taiwan	1.0	1.1	0.9
United Kingdom	2.3	5.1	3.3
USA	8.3	7.3	8.4

Exports f.o.b.	1993	1994	1995
Belgium-Luxembourg	24.2	26.5	15.8
Brazil	4.8	4.7	6.7
Cameroon	4.2	3.9	4.1
Canada	0.9	2.0	1.4
China, People's Repub.	2.9	1.6	0.3
Côte d'Ivoire	1.1	1.3	1.6
France (incl. Monaco)	5.8	4.3	6.1
Germany	5.3	5.5	3.6
India	1.1	0.7	0.0
Ireland	9.8	9.1	10.7
Italy	3.3	3.3	5.0
Japan	0.6	1.1	2.0
Norway	1.2	1.1	1.1
Spain	10.1	9.1	11.2
USA	19.1	14.4	15.6

* Data are compiled on the basis of reporting by Guinea's trading partners. Non-reporting countries include, notably, the former USSR.

Source: IMF, *Guinea—Statistical Annex* (March 1997).

Transport

RAILWAYS (estimated traffic)

	1991	1992	1993
Freight ton-km (million)	660	680	710

Source: UN Economic Commission for Africa, *African Statistical Yearbook*.

ROAD TRAFFIC (estimates, '000 motor vehicles in use)

	1993
Passenger cars	23.1
Commercial vehicles	13.0

Source: UN, *Statistical Yearbook*.

SHIPPING
Merchant Fleet (registered at 31 December)

	1992	1993	1994
Number of vessels	26	27	25
Total displacement ('000 grt)	8.1	6.9	6.7

Source: Lloyd's Register of Shipping, *World Fleet Statistics*.

International Sea-borne Freight Traffic
(estimates, '000 metric tons)

	1991	1992	1993
Goods loaded	13,670	14,920	16,760
Goods unloaded	717	722	734

Source: UN Economic Commission for Africa, *African Statistical Yearbook*.

CIVIL AVIATION (traffic on scheduled services)

	1992	1993	1994
Kilometres flown (million)	1	1	2
Passengers carried ('000)	23	24	45
Passenger-km (million)	33	35	33
Total ton-km (million)	4	4	4

Source: UN, *Statistical Yearbook*.

Communications Media

	1992	1993	1994
Radio receivers ('000 in use)	257	270	280
Television receivers ('000 in use)	43	48	50
Telephones ('000 main lines in use)	11	12	9

Newspapers: 1 daily (average circulation 13,000) in 1988; 1 non-daily (estimated average circulation 1,000) in 1990.

Sources: UNESCO, *Statistical Yearbook*; UN, *Statistical Yearbook*.

Education

(1993/94)

	Institu-tions	Teachers	Students		
			Males	Females	Total
Primary	2,849	9,718	317,654	154,138	471,792
Secondary					
General	252	3,632	82,015	26,444	108,459
Teacher training	8	188	805	763	1,568
Vocational	50	1,302	6,538	2,740	9,278
University	2	659	6,786	296	7,082
Other higher	3	221	833	48	881

Source: the former Ministère de l'Enseignement Pré-Universitaire et de la Formation Professionnelle, Conakry.

Directory

The Constitution

The Constitution (*Loi fondamentale*) of the Third Republic of Guinea was adopted in a national referendum on 23 December 1990 and promulgated on 23 December 1991. An 'organic law' of 3 April 1992, providing for the immediate establishment of an unlimited number of political parties, countermanded the Constitution's provision for the eventual establishment of a two-party political system. There was to be a five-year period of transition, overseen by a Comité transitoire de redressement national (CTRN), to civilian rule, at the end of which executive and legislative authority would be vested in organs of state elected by universal adult suffrage in the context of a multi-party political system.

The Constitution defines the clear separation of the powers of the executive, the legislature and the judiciary. The President of the Republic, who is Head of State, must be elected by an absolute majority of the votes cast, and a second round of voting is held should no candidate obtain such a majority at a first round. The President is Head of Government, and is empowered to appoint ministers and to delegate certain functions. The legislature is the 114-member Assemblée nationale. One-third of the assembly's members are elected as representatives of single-member constituencies, the remainder being appointed from national lists, according to a system of proportional representation.

The CTRN was dissolved following the legislative elections of June 1995.

The Government

HEAD OF STATE

President: Gen. LANSANA CONTÉ (took office 4 April 1984; elected 19 December 1993).

COUNCIL OF MINISTERS
(August 1997)

President of the Republic and Minister of National Defence: Gen. LANSANA CONTÉ.

Prime Minister: SIDIA TOURÉ.

Minister of Foreign Affairs: LAMINE CAMARA.

Minister of Territorial Administration and Decentralization: DORANK ASSIFAT DIASSENY.

Minister of Justice and Keeper of the Seals: MAURICE ZOBELEMOU TOGBA.

Minister of Public Works and the Environment: CELLOU DIALLO.

Minister of Health: KANDJOURA DRAME.

Minister of Energy and Natural Resources: FASSINÉ FOFANA.

Minister of Agriculture, Water and Forests: JEAN-PAUL SARR.

Minister of Industrial Promotion and Trade: MADY KABA.

Minister of Communication and Culture: MICHEL KAMANO.

Minister of Town Planning and Housing: OUSMANE DIALLO.

Minister of National Education and Scientific Research: KOZO ZOUMANIGUI.

Minister of Technical Education and Professional Training: ALMAMY DIABY.

Minister of Employment and the Civil Service: GERMAIN DUALAMU.

Minister of Fishing and Livestock: BOUBACAR BARRY.

Minister of Security: MOUSSA SAMPIL.

Minister of Social Affairs, Women and Children: DARABA SARAN.

Minister of Youth, Sport and Civic Education: KOUMBA DIAKITÉ.

General Secretary to the Presidency: ALMAMY FODE SYLLA.

Minister of Planning and Co-operation: OUSMANE KABA.

Minister of Economic Affairs and Finance: IBRAHIMA KASSORY FOFANA.

MINISTRIES

All ministries are in Conakry.

Office of the President: Conakry; tel. 44-11-47; telex 623.

Ministry of Agriculture, Water and Forests: BP 576, Conakry; tel. 44-19-66.

Ministry of Energy and Natural Resources: BP 295, Conakry; tel. 44-11-86; fax 41-49-13.

Ministry of Foreign Affairs: Conakry; tel. 40-50-55; telex 634.

Ministry of Justice: Conakry; tel. 44-16-04.

Ministry of National Education: BP 2201, Conakry; tel. 41-34-41; telex 22331; fax 41-30-41.

President and Legislature

PRESIDENT

Election, 19 December 1993

Candidate	% of votes
LANSANA CONTÉ (PUP)	51.70
ALPHA CONDÉ (RPG)	19.55
MAMADOU BOYE BÂ (UNR)	13.37
SIRADIOU DIALLO (PRP)	11.86
FACINÉ TOURÉ (UNPG)*	1.40
MOHAMED MANSOUR KABA (Djama) ISMAËL MOHAMED GASSIM GUSHEIN (PDG–RDA) JEAN-MARIE DORÉ (UPG)	2.12
Total	100.00

* Union nationale pour la prospérité de la Guinée. See political organizations, below, for expansion of other acronyms.

ASSEMBLÉE NATIONALE

Speaker: BOUBACAR BIRO DIALLO.

General election, 11 June 1995

Party	Seats
PUP	71
RPG	19
PRP	9
UNR	9
UPG	2
Djama	1
PDG–AST	1
PDG–RDA	1
UNP	1
Total	114

Political Organizations

Following the military coup of April 1984, the country's sole political party, the Parti démocratique de Guinée–Rassemblement démocratique africain (PDG–RDA), was dissolved, and party political activity officially ceased until April 1992, when legislation providing for the existence of an unlimited number of political parties came into effect. The following parties won representation in the legislature at the 1995 elections:

Parti démocratique de Guinée–Ahmed Sekou Touré (PDG–AST): f. 1994, following split from PDG–RDA.

Parti démocratique de Guinée—Rassemblement démocratique africain (PDG–RDA): f. 1946, revived 1992; Leader El Hadj ISMAËL MOHAMED GASSIM GUSHEIN.

Parti Djama: Leader MOHAMED MANSOUR KABA.

Parti pour le renouveau et le progrès (PRP): Sec.-Gen. SIRADIOU DIALLO.

Parti de l'unité et du progrès (PUP): supports Pres. Conté; Sec.-Gen. ABOUBACAR SOMPAORÉ.

Rassemblement populaire guinéen (RPG): Leaders ALPHA CONDÉ, AHMED TIDIANE CISSÉ.

Union pour la nouvelle République (UNR): Sec.-Gen. MAMADOU BOYE BÂ.

Union pour le progrès de Guinée (UPG): Sec.-Gen. JEAN-MARIE DORÉ.

Union nationale pour le progrès (UNP): Leader PAUL LOUIS FABER.

Note: The **Coordination de l'opposition démocratique (Codem)** was established in July 1995, under the leadership of MAMADOU BOYE BÂ, as an alliance of 12 opposition groups. Other than the UNR, leading members include the PRP and the RPG. The UPG withdrew from the alliance in May 1996.

Diplomatic Representation

EMBASSIES IN GUINEA

Algeria: BP 1004, Conakry; tel. 44-15-03; Chargé d'affaires a.i.: BOUCHERIT NACEUR.

Canada: Corniche Sud, BP 99, Coleah, Conakry; tel. 41-23-95; Ambassador: DENIS BRIAND.

China, People's Republic: BP 714, Conakry; Ambassador: KONG MINGHUI.

Congo, Democratic Republic: BP 880, Conakry; telex 632; Ambassador: B. KALUBYE.

Côte d'Ivoire: Conakry; telex 2126; Chargé d'affaires a.i.: ATTA YACOUBA.

Cuba: BP 71, Conakry; Ambassador: LUIS DELGADO PÉREZ.

Czech Republic: BP 2097, Conakry; tel. 46-14-37.

Egypt: BP 389, Conakry; Ambassador: HUSSEIN EL-NAZER.

France: Immeuble Chavanel, Babadi Hadiri, BP 373, Conakry; tel. 44-16-55; telex 600; Ambassador: CHRISTOPHE PHILIBERT.

Germany: BP 540, Conakry; tel. 41-15-06; telex 22479; fax 41-22-18; Ambassador: PIUS FISCHER.

Ghana: Immeuble Ex-Urbaine et la Seine, BP 732, Conakry; tel. 44-15-10; Ambassador: Air Vice-Marshal J. E. A. KOTEI.

Guinea-Bissau: BP 298, Conakry; Ambassador: ARAFAN ANSU CAMARA.

Iraq: Conakry; telex 2162; Chargé d'affaires a.i.: MUNIR CHIHAB AHMAD.

Italy: BP 84, Village Camayenne, Conakry; tel. 46-23-32; telex 636; Ambassador: FAUSTO MARIA PENNACCHIO.

Japan: Mayorai, Corniche Sud, BP 895, Conakry; tel. 41-36-07; telex 22482; fax 41-25-75; Ambassador: KEIICHI KITABAN.

Korea, Democratic People's Republic: BP 723, Conakry; Ambassador: HANG CHANG RYOL.

Liberia: BP 18, Conakry; telex 2105; Chargé d'affaires a.i.: ANTHONY ZEZO.

Libya: BP 1183, Conakry; telex 645; Chargé d'affaires a.i.: MUFTAH MADI.

Mali: Conakry; telex 2154; Ambassador: KIBILI DEMBA DIALLO.

Morocco: BP 193, Conakry; telex 22422; Ambassador: MOHAMED AYOUCH.

Nigeria: BP 54, Conakry; telex 633; Ambassador: PETER N. OYEDELE.

Romania: BP 348, Conakry; tel. 44-15-68; Ambassador: MARCEL MĂMULARU.

Russia: BP 329, Conakry; tel. 46-37-25; fax 41-27-77; Ambassador: IGOR I. STOUDENNIKOV.

Saudi Arabia: BP 611, Conakry; telex 2146; Chargé d'affaires a.i.: WAHEEB SHAIKHON.

Senegal: BP 842, Conakry; tel. and fax 44-44-13; Ambassador: MAKHILY GASSAMA.

Sierra Leone: BP 625, Conakry; Ambassador: Commdr MOHAMED DIABY.

Syria: BP 609, Conakry; tel. 46-13-20; Chargé d'affaires a.i.: BECHARA KHAROUF.

Tanzania: BP 189, Conakry; tel. 46-13-32; telex 2104; Ambassador: NORMAN KIONDO.

USA: angle 2e blvd et 9e ave, BP 603, Conakry; tel. 44-15-20; fax 44-15-22; Ambassador: TIBOR P. NAGY Jr.

Yugoslavia: BP 1154, Conakry; Ambassador: DANILO MILIĆ.

Judicial System

The Constitution of the Third Republic embodies the principle of the independence of the judiciary, and delineates the competences of each component of the judicial system, including the Higher Magistrates' Council, the Supreme Court, the High Court of Justice and the Magistrature. A restructuring of the judicial system is being undertaken, with international financial and technical support, as part of the programme of structural adjustment.

Chief Justice of the Supreme Court: Lamine Sidime.

Director of Public Prosecutions: Antoine Ibrahim Diallo.

Note: A State Security Court was established in June 1997, with exceptional jurisdiction to try, 'in times of peace and war', crimes against the internal and external security of the State. Members of the court are appointed by the President of the Republic. There is no constitutional provision for the existence of such a tribunal.

President of the State Security Court: Commdr Sama Pannival Bangoura.

Religion

It is estimated that 95% of the population are Muslims and 1.5% Christians.

ISLAM

Islamic League: Conakry; Sec.-Gen. El Hadj Ahmed Tidiane Traoré.

CHRISTIANITY

The Anglican Communion

Anglicans in Guinea are adherents of the Church of the Province of West Africa, comprising 11 dioceses. The diocese of Guinea (formerly the Río Pongas), was established in August 1985 as the first French-speaking diocese in the Province.

Bishop of Guinea: (vacant), BP 1187, Conakry.

The Roman Catholic Church

Guinea comprises the archdiocese of Conakry and the dioceses of N'Zérékoré and Kankan. There were some 109,297 Roman Catholics in Guinea at 31 December 1995 (comprising about 1.7% of the total population).

Bishops' Conference: Conférence Episcopale de la Guinée, BP 2016, Conakry; tel. 41-32-70; fax 41-22-28; Pres. Most Rev. Robert Sarah, Archbishop of Conakry.

Archbishop of Conakry: Most Rev. Robert Sarah, Archevêché, BP 2016, Conakry; tel. 41-32-70; fax 41-22-28.

The Press

L'Evénement de Guinée: BP 796, Conakry; monthly; independent; Dir Boubacar Sankarela Diallo.

Fonike: BP 341, Conakry; sport and general; Dir Ibrahima Kalil Diare.

Horoya (Liberty): BP 191, Conakry; weekly; Dir Mohamed Mounir Camara.

Journal Officiel de Guinée: BP 156, Conakry; fortnightly; organ of the Govt.

Le Lynx: Conakry; f. 1992; daily; satirical; Editor Souleyman Diallo.

L'Observateur: Conakry; independent; Dir Sekou Kone.

L'Oeil: Conakry; independent; weekly; Dir of Publishing Ismaël Bangoura.

NEWS AGENCIES

Agence Guinéenne de Presse: BP 1535, Conakry; tel. 46-54-14; telex 640; f. 1960; Man. Dir Mohamed Condé.

Foreign Bureaux

Rossiiskoye Informatsionnoye Agentstvo—Novosti (RIA—Novosti) (Russia): BP 414, Conakry; Dir Vasilii Zubkov.

Xinhua (New China) News Agency (People's Republic of China): BP 455, Conakry; tel. 46-13-47; telex 2128; Correspondent Zhang Zhenyi.

Agence France-Presse and Reuters (UK) are also represented in Guinea.

PRESS ASSOCIATION

Association Guinéenne des Editeurs de la Presse Indépendante (AGEPI): Conakry; f. 1991; an asscn of independent newspaper publ; Chair. Boubacar Sankarela Diallo.

Publisher

Editions du Ministère de l'Education Nationale: Direction nationale de la recherche scientifique, BP 561, Conakry; tel. 44-19-50; telex 22331; f. 1959; general and educational; Dir Prof. Kanté Kabiné.

Radio and Television

In 1994, according to UNESCO, there were an estimated 280,000 radio receivers and 50,000 television receivers in use.

Radiodiffusion-Télévision Guinéenne (RTG): BP 391, Conakry; tel. 44-22-05; telex 22341; radio broadcasts in French, English, Créole-English, Portuguese, Arabic and local languages; television transmissions in French and local languages; Dir-Gen. Justin Morel.

The establishment of a network of rural radio stations is in progress.

Finance

(cap. = capital; res = reserves; m. = million; brs = branches; amounts in Guinean francs).

BANKING

Central Bank

Banque Centrale de la République de Guinée (BCRG): 12 blvd du Commerce, BP 692, Conakry; tel. 41-26-51; telex 22225; fax 41-48-98; f. 1960; bank of issue; Gov. Ibrahima Cherif Bah; Dep. Gov. Fodé Soumah.

Commercial Banks

Banque Internationale pour l'Afrique en Guinée (BIAG): blvd du Commerce, BP 1419, Conakry; tel. 41-42-65; telex 22180; fax 41-22-97; f. 1985; 19% state-owned; cap. and res 15,940m. (Dec. 1995); provides 'offshore' banking services; Pres. El Hadj Abdourahmane Cherif Haidara; Man. Dir Jacky Vasseur; 1 br.

Banque Internationale pour le Commerce et l'Industrie de la Guinée (BICI-GUI): ave de la République, BP 1484, Conakry; tel. 41-45-15; telex 22175; fax 41-39-62; f. 1985; 51% state-owned; cap. and res 12,145m. (Dec. 1995); transfer to private ownership pending; Pres. Ibrahima Soumah; Man. Dir Olivier de Belleville; 11 brs.

Banque Populaire Maroco-Guinéenne (BPMG): Immeuble SCIM, 5e ave Manquepas, Kaloum, BP 4400, Conakry; tel. 41-23-60; telex 22211; fax 41-32-61; f. 1991; 35% owned by Banque Centrale Populaire (Morocco), 20% state-owned, cap. and res 262m. (Dec. 1996); Pres. Ben Yalla Sylla; Man. Dir Amrani Sidi Mohamed; 3 brs.

Société Générale de Banques en Guinée: ave de la République, BP 1514, Conakry 1; tel. 41-17-41; telex 22212; fax 41-25-65; f. 1985; 34% owned by Société Générale (France); cap. and res 6,344m. (Dec. 1995); Pres. Alain Bataille; Man. Dir Jean-Claude Robert.

Union Internationale de Banque en Guinée (UIBG): 5e blvd, angle 6e ave, centre ville, BP 324, Conakry; tel. 41-20-96; telex 23135; fax 41-42-77; f. 1987; 51% owned by Crédit Lyonnais (France); cap. and res 2,049m. (Dec. 1995); Pres. Alpha Amadou Diallo; Man. Dir Maurice Tranchant.

Islamic Bank

Banque Islamique de Guinée: 6 ave de la République, BP 1247, Conakry; tel. 44-21-10; telex 22184; fax 41-50-71; f. 1983; 51% owned by Dar al-Maal al-Islami (DMI Trust); cap. and res 4,565m. (Dec. 1995); Pres. Aderraouf Benessaiah; Man. Dir Benjelloun Abdelmajid.

INSURANCE

Union Guinéenne d'Assurance et de Réassurance (UGAR): BP 179, Conakry; tel. 44-48-41; telex 23211; fax 44-17-11; f. 1989; 60% state-owned, 40% owned by L'Union des Assurances de Paris; cap. 2,000m.; Man. Dir Maurice Giboudot.

Trade and Industry

DEVELOPMENT AGENCIES

Caisse Française de Développement (CFD): Conakry; telex 780; fmrly Caisse Centrale de Coopération Economique, name changed 1992; Dir in Guinea Guy Terracol.

Centre de Promotion et de Développement Minier (CPDM): BP 295, Conakry; tel. 44-11-86; fax 41-49-13; f. 1995; promotes investment in mining sector; Dir Alkany Yansane.

Mission Française de Coopération: Conakry; administers bilateral aid; Dir in Guinea André Bailleul.

CHAMBERS OF COMMERCE

Chambre de Commerce, d'Industrie et d'Agriculture de Guinée: BP 545, Conakry; tel. 44-44-95; telex 609; f. 1985; Chair. Capt. THIANA DIALLO; 70 mems.

Chambre Economique de Guinée: BP 609, Conakry.

TRADE ORGANIZATION

Entreprise Nationale Import-Export (IMPORTEX): BP 152, Conakry; tel. 44-28-13; telex 625; state-owned import and export agency; Dir MAMADOU BOBO DIENG.

MAJOR INDUSTRIAL COMPANIES

The following are among the largest companies in terms either of capital investment or employment.

AREDOR-Guinée: BP 1218, Conakry; tel. 44-31-12; telex 22132; f. 1981 (as Association pour la recherche et l'exploitation de diamants et de l'or); operations suspended 1994, restructured 1996; cap. US $8m.; 85% owned by First City Mining Ltd; diamond mining and gold; 1,200 employees.

BONAGUI: Z.I. Matoto, BP 3009, Conakry; tel. 41-18-92; telex 23358; fax 41-24-91; f. 1986; cap. 2,607m. FG; privately owned; soft-drinks bottling factory. Man. ERIC BOULANGER; 147 employees.

Compagnie des Bauxites de Guinée: BP 523, Conakry; f. 1964; cap. US $2m.; 49% state-owned, 51% owned by Halco (Mining) Inc (a consortium of interests from USA, Canada, France, Germany, and Spain); bauxite mining at Boké; Pres. JOHN L. PERVOLA; Vice-Pres. G. COKER ; 2,796 employees.

Compagnie des Eaux Minérales de Guinée: Conakry; f. 1987; owned by Cie générale des eaux (France); mineral water bottling plant.

Enterprise Nationale d'Electricité de Guinée (ENELGUI): BP 322, Conakry; tel. 41-42-43; fax 41-17-51; production and distribution of electricity; Man. Dir BOKARY SYLLA.

Friguia: BP 334, Conakry; tel. 41-31-13; fax 44-34-63; f. 1957; cap. 13,602m. FG; 49% state-owned, 51% owned by Holding Frialco (a consortium of Canadian, French and Norwegian interests); alumina plant at Fria; Man. Dir ALAIN MORALÈS; 1,500 employees.

Nimba International Mining Co (Nimco): BP 837, Conakry; tel. 41-30-68; fax 41-50-04; f. 1990; cap. US $120m.; 60% owned by Euronimba, 20% by Govt of Guinea/MIFERGUI-NIMBA, 20% by Govt of Liberia/LIMINCO; development of high-grade iron deposit at Mt Nimba (12m. tons annually, to be shipped via Buchanan, Liberia).

Office de Développement de la Pêche artisanale et de l'Aquaculture en Guinée (ODEPAG): 6 ave de la République, BP 1581; Conakry; tel. 44-19-48; telex 22315; development of fisheries and fish-processing.

Société d'Aquaculture de Koba (SAKOBA): BP 4834, Conakry; tel. 44-24-75; telex 22111; fax 41-46-43; f. 1991; 49% state-owned, 51% owned by private Guinean and French interests; prawn-farming venture with a planned annual capacity of 1,300 metric tons of frozen shrimps for export by 1997; 700 employees; Mans SEPIA International (France).

Société Aurifère de Guinée (SAG): BP 1006, Conakry; tel. 41-58-09; telex 23237; fax 41-15-45; f. 1985; cap. US $13m.; 70% owned by Ashanti Goldfields Co Ltd (Ghana); gold prospecting and exploitation at Koron; Dir-Gen. DAVID NETHERWAY.

Société des Bauxites de Dabola-Tougué (SBDT): BP 2859, Conakry; tel. and fax 41-47-21; f. 1992; owned jtly by Govts of Guinea and Iran; bauxite mining at Dabola and Tougué; Dir-Gen. A. SAADATI.

Société des Bauxites de Kindia (SBK): Conakry; telex 2148; f. 1969, as Office des Bauxites de Kindia (a jt-venture with the USSR), production began 1974; named changed 1992; state-controlled; transfer to private ownership pending; bauxite mining at Debélé; Dir MAMADOU SYLLA; 1,700 employees.

Société Guinéenne d'Electricité (SOGEL): Conakry; f. 1994; 49% state-owned, 51% held jtly by Hydro-Québec (Canada), Electricité de France and SAUR (France); intended to oversee production, transport and distribution of electricity.

Société Guinéenne des Hydrocarbures (SGH): BP 892, Conakry; tel. 46-12-56; telex 776; f. 1980; 50% state-owned; research into and exploitation of offshore petroleum reserves.

Société Guinéenne de Pêche (SOGUIPECHE): Conakry; f. 1987; 51% state-owned, 49% owned by Jego-Query (France); fishing and processing of fish products.

Société Guinéo-Arabe d'Alumine: BP 554, Conakry; f. 1975 by Guinean govt and six Arab govts; to open and develop production of aluminium at Ayekoe; estimated production 1m. tons annually.

Société Libyo-Guinéenne pour le Développement Agricole et Agro-industrielle (SALGUIDIA): BP 622, Conakry; 44-31-34; telex 22117; fax 41-13-09; cap. 15m. FG; fmrly Société Industrielle des Fruits Africains; fruit growing (pineapples, grapefruit, oranges and mangoes); fruit canning and juice extracting; marketing.

Société Minière de Dinguiraye: Dinguiraye; 85% owned by Delta Gold Mining—owned jtly by Kenor AS (Norway) and La Source (Australia-France); exploitation of gold deposits at Léro and devt of other areas of Dinguiraye concession; Man. Dir DENIS N'GUYEN.

Société Minière et de Participation Guinée-Alusuisse: Conakry; f. 1971; owned by Guinean govt and Alusuisse (Switzerland); to establish bauxite mine and aluminium smelter at Tougué; estimated production of bauxite 8m. tons annually.

Société Nationale des Eaux de Guinée (SONEG): BP 825, Conakry; tel. and fax 41-43-81; f. 1988; national water co.

Société de Pêche de Kamsar (SOPEKAM): Kamsar Free Zone; f. 1984; 40% state-owned, 40% Universal Marine & Shark Products (USA); fishing and processing of fish products; fleet of 18 fishing vessels.

Total Guinée: BP 306, Conakry; tel. 41-50-35; telex 23291; fax 41-38-05; f. 1988 as Société Guinnéenne des Carburants; storage of petroleum products.

TRADE UNION

Confédération des travailleurs de Guinée (CTG): BP 237, Conakry; f. 1984; Sec.-Gen. Dr MOHAMED SAMBA KÉBÉ.

Transport

RAILWAYS

There are 662 km of 1-m gauge track from Conakry to Kankan in the east of the country, crossing the Niger at Kouroussa. The line is to be upgraded over two years: the contract for the first phase was awarded to a Slovak company in early 1997. Three lines for the transport of bauxite link Sangaredi with the port of Kamsar in the west, via Boké, and Conakry with Kindia and Fria, a total of 383 km. In late 1996 the government of Iran announced its intention to construct a railway linking the Dabola-Tougué bauxite deposits with Conakry: the preliminary contract was secured by Slovak State Railways. Plans exist for the eventual use of a line linking the Nimba iron-ore deposits with the port of Buchanan in Liberia.

Office National des Chemins de Fer de Guinée (ONCFG): BP 589, Conakry; tel. 44-46-13; telex 22349; f. 1905; Man. Dir FOFANA M. KADIO.

Chemin de Fer de Boké: BP 523, Boké; operations commenced 1973.

Chemin de Fer Conakry–Fria: BP 334, Conakry; telex 22251; operations commenced 1960; Gen. Man. A. CAMARA.

Chemin de Fer de la Société des Bauxites de Kindia: BP 613, Conakry; tel. 41-38-28; telex 22148; operations commenced 1974; Gen. Man. K. KEITA.

ROADS

In 1995 there were an estimated 30,270 km of roads, including 4,250 km of main roads and 7,920 km of secondary roads; about 5,000 km of the road network were paved. An 895-km cross-country road links Conakry to Bamako, in Mali, and the main highway connecting Dakar (Senegal) to Abidjan (Côte d'Ivoire) also crosses Guinea. The road linking Conakry to Freetown (Sierra Leone) forms part of the Trans West African Highway, extending from Morocco to Nigeria.

La Guinéenne-Marocaine des Transports (GUIMAT): Conakry; f. 1989; owned jtly by Govt of Guinea and Hakkam (Morocco); operates national and regional transport services.

Société Générale des Transports de Guinée (SOGETRAG): Conakry; f. 1984; 63% state-owned; bus operator.

SHIPPING

Conakry and Kamsar are the international seaports. Conakry handled 4.4m. metric tons of foreign trade in 1994, while some 12m. tons of bauxite were transported to Kamsar for shipment.

Port Autonome de Conakry: BP 715, Conakry; tel. 44-27-37; telex 22276.

Port de Kamsar OFAB: Kamsar.

Société Navale Guinéenne (SNG): BP 522, Conakry; tel. 44-29-55; telex 22234; fax 41-39-70; f. 1968; state-owned; shipping agents; Dir-Gen. NOUNKÉ KEITA.

SOTRAMAR: Kamsar; f. 1971; exports bauxite from mines at Boké through port of Kamsar.

CIVIL AVIATION

There is an international airport at Conakry-Gbessia, and smaller airfields at Labé, Kankan and Faranah. In 1995 France agreed to provide some 27.6m. French francs in support of a project (costing 31m. francs) to improve facilities at Conakry.

Nouvelle Air Guinée: 6 ave de la République, BP 12, Conakry; tel. 44-46-02; telex 22349; f. 1960; transfer pending to one-third private ownership; regional and internal services; Dir-Gen. El Hadj NFA MOUSSA DIANE.

Société de Gestion et d'Exploitation de l'Aéroport de Conakry (SOGEAC): Conakry; f. 1987; manages Conakry-Gbessia international airport; 51% state-owned.

Tourism

A major tourism development project was announced in 1995, with the eventual aim of attracting some 100,000 visitors annually: 186 tourist sites are to be renovated, and access to them improved, and it is planned to increase the number of hotel beds from less than 800 to 25,000 by 1999.

Secrétariat d'Etat au Tourisme et à l'Hôtellerie: square des Martyrs, BP 1304, Conakry; tel. 44-26-06; f. 1989.

Defence

In August 1996 Guinea's active armed forces numbered 9,700, comprising an army of 8,500, a navy of 400 and an air force of 800. Paramilitary forces numbered some 9,600, and included a 7,000-strong people's militia. Military service is by conscription and lasts for two years.

Defence Expenditure: Budgeted at 44,000m. FG in 1997.

Chief of Staff of Armed Forces: Col IBRAHIMA SORY DIALLO.

Education

Education is provided free of charge at every level in state institutions. Primary education, which begins at seven years of age and lasts for six years, is officially compulsory. In 1993, however, enrolment at primary schools was equivalent to only 46% of children in the relevant age-group (males 61%; females 30%). As part of government plans to extend the provision of basic education, it was aimed to increase the rate of primary enrolment to 53% by 2000. Secondary education, from the age of 13, lasts for seven years, comprising a first cycle (collège) of four years and a second (lycée) of three years. Enrolment at secondary schools in 1993 was equivalent to only 12% of children in the appropriate age-group (males 18%; females 6%). There are universities at Conakry and Kankan, and other tertiary institutions at Maneah, Boké and Faranah. In 1993, according to the national literary service, the average rate of adult illiteracy was 72% (males 61%; females 83%). Under a six-year transitional education plan, announced in June 1984, ideological education was eliminated and French was adopted as the language of instruction in schools. Teaching of the eight national languages was suspended, although the reintroduction of classes in certain local languages was under consideration in 1996. A ban on private schools operated in 1961–84. Government expenditure on education in 1993 was equivalent to 26% of total budget spending.

Bibliography

Adamolekun, L. *Sekou Touré's Guinea.* London, Methuen, 1976.

Ameillon, B. *La Guinée, bilan d'une indépendance.* Paris, Maspero, 1964.

Amnesty International. *Guinea.* London, 1978.

Canale, J. S. *La République de Guinée.* Paris, Editions Sociales, 1970.

Dhada, M. *Warriors at Work: How Guinea was Set Free.* Niwot, University Press of Colorado, 1994.

Diallo, A. *Le mort de Diallo Telli.* Paris, Editions Karthala, 1983.

Europe Outremer. *La Guinée d'aujourd'hui.* Paris, 1979.

Hair, P. E. H., Jones, A., and Law, R. *Barbot on Guinea.* London, the Hakluyt Society, 1992.

Kake, I. B. *Sékou Touré, le héros et le tyran.* Paris, Jeune Afrique Livres, 1987.

Lewin, A. *La Guinée.* Paris, Presses Universitaires de France, 1984.

O'Toole, T. E. *Historical Dictionary of Guinea.* Metuchen, NJ, Scarecrow Press, 1988.

Rimmer, D. *The Economies of West Africa.* London, Weidenfeld and Nicolson, 1984.

Rivière, C. *Guinea: The Mobilization of a People* (trans. by Thompson, V., and Adloff, R.). Ithaca, NY, Cornell University Press, 1977.

Soriba Camara, S. *La Guinée sans la France.* Paris, Presse de la Fondation nationale des sciences politiques, 1977.

Touré, S. *L'expérience guinéenne et l'unité africaine.* Paris, Présence africaine, 1959.

L'action politique du parti démocratique en Guinée. Conakry, 1962.

GUINEA-BISSAU

Physical and Social Geography

RENÉ PÉLISSIER

The Republic of Guinea-Bissau, formerly Portuguese Guinea, is bounded on the north by Senegal and on the east and south by the Republic of Guinea. Its territory includes a number of coastal islands, together with the Bissagos or Bijagós archipelago, which comprises 18 main islands. The capital is Bissau.

The country covers an area of 36,125 sq km (13,948 sq miles), including some low-lying ground which is periodically submerged at high tide. Except for some higher terrain (rising to about 300 m above sea-level), close to the Guinea border, the relief consists of a coastal plain deeply indented by *rias*, which facilitate internal communications, and a transition plateau, forming the *planalto* de Bafatá in the centre, and the *planalto* de Gabú, which abuts on the Fouta Djallon.

The country's main physical characteristics are its meandering rivers and wide estuaries, where it is difficult to distinguish mud, mangrove and water from solid land. The main rivers are the Cacheu, also known as Farim on part of its course, the Mansôa, the Geba and Corubal complex, the Rio Grande and, close to the Guinean southern border, the Cacine. Ocean-going vessels of shallow draught can reach most of the main population centres, and there is access by flat-bottomed tugs and barges to nearly all significant outposts except in the north-eastern sector.

The climate is tropical, hot and wet with two seasons. The rainy season lasts from mid-May to November and the dry season from December to April. April and May are the hottest months, with temperatures ranging from 20°C to 38°C, and December and January are the coldest, with temperatures ranging from 15°C to 33°C. Rainfall is abundant (1,000–2,000 mm per year in the north), and excessive on the coast. The interior is savannah or light savannah woodland, while coastal reaches are covered with mangrove swamps, rain forest and tangled forest.

The first official census since independence, conducted in April 1979, recorded a population of 753,313. At the census of December 1991 the National Census and Statistics Institute enumerated the population at 983,367. According to UN estimates, the total was 1,073,000 at mid-1995. The main population centre is Bissau, which had 197,610 inhabitants at the 1991 census. Bafatá, Bolama, Farim, Cantchungo, Mansôa, Gabú, Catió and Bissorã are the other important towns. Prior to the war of independence, the main indigenous groups were the Balante (about 32% of the population), the Fulani or Fula (22%), the Mandyako (14.5%), the Malinké or Mandingo (13%), and the Pepel (7%). The non-Africans were mainly Portuguese civil servants and traders, and Syrian and Lebanese traders. Although Portuguese is the official language, a Guinean *crioulo* is the lingua franca. In 1990–95, according to UN estimates, the average life expectancy at birth was 41.9 years for men and 45.1 years for women.

Recent History

LUISA HANDEM PIETTE

Revised for this edition by the Editor

The campaign for independence in Portuguese Guinea (now Guinea-Bissau) began in the 1950s with the formation of the Partido Africano da Independência da Guiné e Cabo Verde (PAIGC), under the leadership of Amílcar Cabral. Armed resistance began in the early 1960s, and by 1972 the PAIGC was in control of two-thirds of the country. In January 1973 Cabral was assassinated in Conakry, Guinea, by PAIGC dissidents. The subsequent escalation of hostilities prompted the deployment of some 40,000 Portuguese troops. Guinea-Bissau unilaterally declared its independence from Portugal on 24 September 1973 under the presidency of Luiz Cabral, the brother of Amílcar Cabral. The heavy losses sustained by the Portuguese in 1973–74 have been cited as a contributory factor in the military *coup d'état* in Portugal in April 1974. In August Portugal withdrew its forces from Guinea-Bissau and on 10 September it recognized the country's independence. Guinea-Bissau became a single party state governed by the PAIGC. The party introduced measures to lay the foundations for a socialist state. However, the government adopted a non-aligned stance in its foreign relations, receiving military aid from the Eastern bloc and economic assistance from Western countries and Arab states. Friendly relations with Portugal were renewed.

By 1980, however, Guinea-Bissau's economic situation had deteriorated, owing partly to drought, but also to the policies of Cabral. Agricultural production had fallen below pre-independence levels, the state-controlled retail network had proved inadequate, and sparse economic resources were being deployed in projects of questionable utility.

Until 1980, the PAIGC supervised both Cape Verde and Guinea-Bissau, the two constitutions remaining separate, but with a view to eventual unification. These arrangements were abruptly terminated by Cape Verde in November 1980, when Cabral was overthrown by the prime minster, João Bernardo Vieira, and a military-dominated revolutionary council took control of government.

VIEIRA AND THE PAIGC

The period following the 1980 coup was one of considerable political ferment, with major shifts in the leadership, although President Vieira remained the dominant force. The unrest was attended by further economic decline, which was as much an effect of the regime's economic policies as of international economic conditions.

A special PAIGC congress in 1981 reaffirmed the regime's commitment to socialism and rebuked the previous administration for deviation from the policies of Amílcar Cabral. The party hierarchy was changed, and some former opponents of the regime were brought into the government, while Portuguese-trained civil servants returned to the bureaucracy.

These events were followed, in May 1982, by the postponement of promised elections and by a government reshuffle in which Vieira assumed the portfolios of defence and security. Vítor Saúde Maria, vice-chairman of the ruling council of the revolution and former minister of foreign affairs, was appointed prime minister. Vasco Cabral and Mário Cabral were among members of the party's radical left wing who lost their ministerial posts, although they remained influential within the PAIGC. In July, following rumours of plots, several members of the pre-coup leadership were arrested, and later in that year they were put on trial. In August 1983 three ministers were dismissed, on the grounds of embezzlement, and the chief of staff of the armed forces was suspended. These departures were apparently part of a struggle for primacy between Vieira and Saúde Maria. The issue was eventually decided in Vieira's favour, and in 1984 it was proposed that a new constitution would abolish the office of prime minister. In March, having been dismissed from office both for corruption and allegedly plotting a coup, Saúde Maria sought asylum in the Portuguese embassy. Several other party members were subsequently accused of colluding with Saúde Maria and were expelled from the PAIGC.

The new constitutional arrangements took effect in May 1984. Elections had been held in March for eight regional councils (comprising PAIGC-approved candidates only) which, in turn, elected 150 members of a new legislative assembly. This body approved the new constitution and selected a council of state to discharge legislative functions when the assembly was not in session. A government reshuffle ensued, which reduced the number of ministers and brought the return to office both of Vasco Cabral, as secretary of the council of state and minister in the presidency for economic affairs, and of Mário Cabral, as minister of trade and tourism. A number of younger and better-trained officials were also appointed, and Bartolomeu Pereira, perhaps the most prominent of the 'technocratic' group and formerly a secretary of state, became minister of economic co-ordination, planning and international co-operation. The overall effect of these changes was to formalize the position of Vieira as head of state, chief of government, c-in-c of the armed forces and head of the PAIGC, and to assemble a government in which the emphasis was placed on economic competence.

In November 1985 the first vice-president, Col Paulo Correia, and several senior army officers were arrested for allegedly attempting to lead a coup, although the precise background of the plot was never clarified. In July 1986 six people, accused of involvement in the alleged conspiracy, were reported to have died in prison. Later in the same month, 12 of those arrested were condemned to death, and 41 were sentenced to hard labour. Correia and five others were executed, but the remaining six had their death sentences commuted, following international appeals for clemency. In order to discourage the creation of personal power-bases, Vieira replaced a number of multi-functional ministries with smaller administrative portfolios. Three ministries for the provinces were created, and the council of ministers was enlarged from 15 to 19 members. In December 1988 four of those imprisoned following the 1985 attempted coup were released under an amnesty. All the remaining prisoners had been released by January 1990.

The policy of economic liberalization, initiated in 1983 in an attempt to halt economic decline, was accelerated in the late 1980s. In August 1986 the government abolished trading restrictions and allowed private traders to import and export goods. At the fourth PAIGC congress, held in November, Vieira introduced further proposals to reduce state controls over trade and the economy, and to increase foreign investment. These moves were supported by the congress, which re-elected him as secretary-general of the PAIGC for a further four years. In February 1987 Vieira ensured future PAIGC support for economic liberalization by appointing Vasco Cabral as permanent secretary of the central committee of the PAIGC. In a subsequent government reshuffle, a new minister of justice and two new secretaries of state for justice and foreign affairs were appointed. In April the government and the World Bank agreed on a structural adjustment programme which included further liberalization measures for the economy. These were accompanied by a restructuring of the state investment programme and a reduction in levels of public-sector employment, and were followed in May by a 41% devaluation of the Guinea peso. Although Vieira promised that the domestic effects of the latter would be offset by government subsidies on essential commodities, political tension increased, amid rumours that about 20 army officers had been arrested for plotting against the president.

In February 1989 a minor reshuffle of the government took place, and in the same month it was announced that the PAIGC had set up a six-member constitutional revision commission. Regional elections were held in early June, at which all candidates were nominated by the PAIGC. The electoral commission reported a 95.8% turnout of eligible voters, although this figure was disputed by other sources. The 473 councillors convened in mid-June to elect the national assembly, which in turn elected the council of state. Vieira was confirmed as president for a second five-year term. In January 1990 Vieira announced the formation of two commissions to review, respectively, the programme and statutes of the PAIGC and the laws on land ownership, in preparation for the fifth PAIGC congress, due to be held in November. In March an extensive government reshuffle took place, in which Vasco Cabral became second vice-president, in charge of social affairs.

Constitutional Transition

In April 1990, from its base in Lisbon, an emigré opposition group, the Resistência da Guiné-Bissau–Movimento Bafatá (RGB–MB), proposed political negotiations with the PAIGC, with the implied threat that civil war might ensue should its demands for reform not be met. Shortly afterwards, in the wake of mounting international pressure for political democratization, Vieira gave approval in principle to the introduction of a multi-party political system. It was stated that the necessary constitutional amendments would be implemented in late 1990, following a special congress of the PAIGC, and that the next presidential election, due in 1994, could be contested by two or more candidates. In early June 1990 another external opposition movement, the Frente da Luta para a Libertação da Guiné (FLING), demanded an immediate conference of all political parties. In August Vieira informed a meeting of the PAIGC central committee that political pluralism was the only system that could bring democratic freedom to Guinea-Bissau. He also announced that members of the national assembly would in future be elected by universal adult suffrage. A national conference on the transition to democracy was held in October, attended by 350 representatives of the government, the ruling party and private organizations. The conference voted in favour of the holding of a national referendum on the nature of political reforms to be introduced. There was also support for the establishment of a transitional government to oversee the democratization process, and for the abolition of the PAIGC's political monopoly. Criticism of the government at the conference was acknowledged by the minister of justice, Mário Cabral, who admitted that the PAIGC had made mistakes, particularly in regard to economic management.

Rumours of an attempted coup were widespread in November and December 1990, although these were consistently denied by the government. Vieira returned early from a visit to Taiwan at the beginning of November, cancelling a planned trip to Japan; some observers linked his return to the flight of Saúde Maria, the former prime minister, and the former armed forces minister, Umaru Djalo, to Portugal, where they were granted political asylum.

At an extraordinary conference of the PAIGC, which opened in January 1991, Vieira confirmed that the transition to a multi-party system would be completed by 1993, when a presidential election would be held. During the transitional period, the armed forces would become independent of the PAIGC, and the party would cease to be the country's dominant social and political force. Vieira appealed to all Guineans, both at home and abroad, to participate in the democratization process.

Constitutional amendments, formally terminating single-party rule, were approved unanimously by the national assembly in May 1991. The reforms terminated the PAIGC's role as the leading political force and Vieira indicated that legislative elections would be held before 1993. The new arrangements also severed the link between the party and the armed forces, and guaranteed the operation of a freemarket economy. To prevent the formation of regionally-based or separatist organizations, it was stipulated that new parties seeking registration must obtain at least 100 signatures from each of the nine provinces, with a total of 2,000 signatures required for registration; these regulations were revised in August, when the numbers of signatures required were halved to 50 and 1,000 respectively. A number of opposition parties were created following the introduction of the legislation. The Frente Democrática Social (FDS), set up clandestinely in 1990 and led by Rafael

Barbosa, gave rise to two splinter groups in mid-1991: the Frente Democrática (FD), led by Aristides Menezes, and the Partido Unido Social Democrático (PUSD), led by Saúde Maria. In November the FD became the first party to be legalized by the supreme court, formally ending 17 years of one-party politics.

The PAIGC met in December 1991 to discuss its strategy for the first democratic elections. As part of this process, Vieira extensively reshuffled the cabinet in late December. The post of prime minister was revived with the appointment of Carlos Correia, previously minister of state for agriculture and rural development, to the position. Other cabinet changes included the appointment of Samba Lamine Mane as minister of defence, a portfolio formerly held by Vieira himself, and of João Cruz Pinto as minister of justice, replacing Vasco Cabral, who also lost his position as second vice-president. In addition Vieira relinquished the post of minister of the interior to Abubacar Baldé. Filinto de Barros, formerly minister of natural resources and industry, was appointed minister of finance. The reshuffle included the removal of Col Camara, the first vice-president, who had been accused of involvement in smuggling of arms to separatist guerrillas in Senegal's southern Casamance region.

Three further opposition parties were registered in December 1991 and January 1992: the Resistência da Guiné-Bissau–Movimento Bah-Fatah (RGB–MB) (the party changed its name prior to legalization, from Resistência da Guiné-Bissau–Movimento Bafatá, because the constitution prohibits parties with names connoting regional or tribal affiliation), led by Domingos Fernandes Gomes, the FDS, and the PUSD. Three other parties had yet to achieve recognition and another was formed in mid-January, following a further split in the FDS: the Partido para a Renovação Social (PRS), led by former FDS vice-chairman Koumba Yalla. At the FD's first public rally in mid-January, party leader Menezes called on the PAIGC to set up a caretaker government bringing in representatives of the opposition. In late January, four opposition parties: the RGB–MB, FDS, PUSD and the Partido da Convergência Democrática (PCD), led by Vítor Mandinga, agreed to set up a 'democratic forum' for consultations. They demanded that the government dissolve the political police and cease using state facilities for political purposes. They also called for a revision of press law, free access to media, the creation of an electoral commission and the declaration of election dates in consultation with all the opposition parties.

An opposition demonstration, the first to be permitted by the government, was held in Bissau in March 1992, attended by an estimated 30,000 people. Election dates were announced on 9 March. Presidential elections were to be held on 15 November, followed by legislative elections on 13 December, despite demands by the opposition that the elections be held in June, with the legislative elections held first. The national council meeting also elected Saturnino Costa as the new permanent secretary to the party's central committee, replacing Vasco Cabral, who had held the post since 1987. Following a second application for official recognition, the FLING was legalized in May. In that month a dissident group known as the 'Group of 121' broke away from the PAIGC to form a new party, the Partido de Renovação e Desenvolvimento (PRD), led by João da Costa, a former minister of health under Luiz Cabral. The PRD called for the establishment of a transitional government pending democratic elections and for the dissolution of the political police. In mid-May the leader of the RGB–MB, Domingo Fernandes, returned from a six year exile in Portugal. Following his return Fernandes and the leaders of the FD, PCD, FDS and the PUSD met Vieira to discuss the political reform programme. As a result of the talks it was decided that commissions would be set up to oversee and facilitate the organization of the forthcoming elections.

In July 1992 the leader and founder of the FLING, François Kankoila Mendy, returned to Guinea-Bissau after 40 years in exile. In the following month, in response to opposition demands for the establishment of a national conference to oversee the transition to multi-party democracy, Vieira inaugurated the Comissão Multipartidária de Transição (Multi-party Transition Commission), charged with drafting legislation in preparation for democratic elections. All officially recognized parties were to be represented on the commission, although it was boycotted by the recently recognized Partido Democrático do Progresso (PDP), led by Amine Michel Saad, which alleged that the commission's work would be biased in favour of the PAIGC. Several other political parties were given legal status during the second half of 1992; these included the PRD, the Movimento para a Unidade e a Democracia (MUDE), led by former education minister Filinto Vaz Martins, and the PRS.

In October 1992 Vieira again reshuffled the council of ministers. Eight ministers who had served in the cabinet since the country's independence in 1974 were dismissed, including the minister of foreign affairs, Júlio Semedo, the minister of justice, João Cruz Pinto, and the minister of industry and natural resources, Manuel dos Santos. Other changes included the establishment of a new ministry of territorial administration, replacing the three resident ministries for the provinces.

In early November 1992 the government announced that the presidential and legislative elections, scheduled for that month, were to be postponed until March 1993. The delay arose from a disagreement concerning the sequence in which the two sets of elections should be held; contrary to government proposals, the opposition parties insisted that the legislative elections take place prior to the presidential elections.

Legislation preparing for the transition to a pluralist democracy was approved by the national assembly in February 1993, and in the following month a four-member commission was appointed to supervise the forthcoming elections. However, reports in mid-March of a coup attempt against the Vieira government threatened to disrupt the progress of democratic transition. Initial reports indicated that Maj. Robalo de Pina, commander of the Forças de Intervenção Rápida (an élite guard of some 30 soldiers responsible for protecting the president), had been assassinated in what appeared to be an army mutiny, provoked by disaffection at poor standards of pay and living conditions. About 50 people were arrested in connection with the mutiny, including the leader of the PRD, João da Costa. Opposition politicians, however, alleged that the incident had been contrived by the government in an effort to discredit its political opponents and to maintain its hold on power. It was announced that the suspects would be brought to trial in August. Da Costa and nine other members of the PRD in detention were released in mid-June, but banned from political activity. In mid-April public-sector unions organized a three-day general strike in support of demands for wage increases and payment of arrears. In May, following a further split in the FDS, a new political party, the Partido da Convenção Nacional (PCN), was formed, although it was not granted official registration. In July Vieira announced that simultaneous presidential and legislative multi-party elections would be held on 27 March 1994. In early August da Costa was rearrested for allegedly violating the conditions of his parole, prompting renewed accusations by opposition politicians that the government's actions were politically motivated. Following a threatened boycott of the national electoral commission by the opposition, da Costa was released.

In January 1994, when da Costa came to trial, several of his co-defendents retracted statements implicating him in the coup attempt, and it was claimed that accusations against him had been fabricated by the director-general of state security, Col João Monteiro, who had presided over the military commission of inquiry which had investigated the coup attempt. In early February da Costa was acquitted.

Multi-Party Elections

One week before the designated election date, set for 27 March 1994, Vieira announced a further postponement of the elections owing to financial and technical difficulties, including delays in the electoral registration process and inadequacies in the functioning of the regional electoral commissions. Voter registration for the postponed elections was conducted between 11–23 April. On 11 May it was announced that the elections would be held on 3 July, with a 21-day period of electoral campaigning to begin on 11 June. In early May six opposition parties, the FD, FDS, MUDE, PDP, PRD and the Liga para a Proteção da Ecologia (LIPE), formed an electoral coalition, the União para a Mudança (UM). Later in May a further five opposition parties, the FLING, PRS, PUSD, RGB–MB and the Foro Cívico da Guiné (FCG), announced the establishment of an informal alliance under which each party reserved the right to present its own candidates in the elections.

The elections took place on schedule on 3 July, although voting was extended for two days owing to logistical problems. Eight candidates contested the presidency, while 1,136 candidates contested the 100 legislative seats. The PAIGC secured a clear majority in the national people's assembly, winning 62 seats, but the results of the presidential election were inconclusive, with Vieira winning 46.29% of the votes, while his nearest rival, Koumba Yalla of the PRS, secured 21.92% of the votes. As no candidate had obtained an absolute majority, a second round presidential election between the two leading candidates was conducted on 7 August. Despite receiving the combined support of all the opposition parties, Yalla was narrowly defeated, securing 47.97% of the votes to Vieira's 52.03%. Yalla subsequently contested the results of the election, accusing the PAIGC of electoral fraud and claiming that the state security police had sought to intimidate opposition supporters. Yalla's claims were, however, rejected and on 20 August he accepted the results of the election, but announced that the PRS would not participate in the new government. International observers later declared the elections to have been free and fair. Vieira was inaugurated as president on 29 September 1994 and, following considerable delays owing to divisions within the PAIGC, eventually appointed Manuel Saturnino da Costa as prime minister in late October. The council of ministers was appointed in mid-November comprising solely members of the PAIGC.

Post-Election Politics

Strike action, commonplace in recent years due to falling living standards, continued under the new government. In February 1995 the national union of teachers conducted a three-day strike in support of demands for wage increases and payment of salary arrears. In May, following a two-day general strike by the União Nacional dos Trabalhadores da Guiné in the previous month, the government conceded a 100% increase in the country's minimum wage.

In April 1995 the FD, FDS, MUDE, PDP and the PRD reconsolidated themselves within the UM coalition and elected João da Costa as president and Amine Michel Saad as its secretary-general. The LIPE, which had two representatives in the legislature and was a member of the original UM coalition, did not join the new organization, which obtained legal status in November. In August registration was granted to a new party, the Partido Social Democrático, which was formed by dissidents from the RGB–MB.

In October 1995 a demonstration, organized by the PRS, was conducted in protest at the country's deteriorating economy. The protest received widespread support from opposition parties, as well as from the Guinea-Bissau Human Rights League, which was formed in 1992 under the leadership of former justice of the supreme court, Fernando Gomes. A similar protest was organized later that month by the RGB–MB. Also in October, following negotiations with the UNTG, the government granted a further increase, of 50%, in the minimum wage.

In January 1996 da Costa reorganized the council of ministers. In May the national people's assembly rejected a motion of censure, proposed by the RGB–MB, against the government. The vote followed sustained demands by opposition parties for the government's resignation on grounds of incompetence and its inability to resolve the socio-economic problems of the country. In early November government plans to join the Union économique et monétaire ouest-africaine (UEMOA, see p. 121) were rejected by the national people's assembly. A report by the parliamentary economic and financial commission recommended a transition period of two years before joining the francophone regional organization. However, in late November, on receiving a plea from Vieira, the legislature approved a constitutional amendment authorizing the government to seek membership of the UEMOA, which it duly attained in January 1997. Guinea-Bissau subsequently entered the Franc Zone on 2 May, when the national currency was replaced by the franc CFA, and the Banque centrale des états de l'Afrique de l'ouest (BCEAO) assumed the central banking functions of the Banco Central da Guiné-Bissau.

In May 1997, in the light of what Vieira described as a serious political crisis, da Costa was dismissed. In the following month Carlos Correia was appointed prime minister and a new 14-member cabinet was inaugurated.

FOREIGN AFFAIRS

In its foreign relations, the Vieira regime is motivated primarily by the need to solicit aid, and secondly by a sense of vulnerability to the economic interests of its larger and more prosperous francophone neighbours, Senegal and Guinea. As a result, the country has actively promoted co-operation with Portugal, even to the point of proposing an 'escudo zone' (an idea in which other lusophone African countries have shown no interest). Relations with Portugal deteriorated in October 1987, after patrol boats detained six Portuguese vessels for alleged illegal fishing in Guinea-Bissau's territorial waters. Portugal retaliated by suspending non-medical aid, but reversed this decision in early November, after the vessels were released. Shortly afterwards, the head of security at the embassy of Guinea-Bissau in Lisbon sought political asylum, alleging that the diplomatic mission was preparing to organize the assassinations of prominent members of the exiled RGB–MB, which had its headquarters in Lisbon. These allegations were vigorously denied by the government of Guinea-Bissau. During a brief visit to Lisbon in October 1988,Vieira raised the question of the RGB–MB's activities with President Soares of Portugal. As a sign of further commitment to *rapprochement* between the two countries, the Portuguese prime minister, Cavaco Silva, visited Guinea-Bissau in March 1989, when both governments promised increased bilateral co-operation, and agreed to continue to promote relations between African lusophone states. President Soares' visit to Guinea-Bissau in November 1989 included discussions on the issue of extending dual nationality to Guinea-Bissau citizens resident in Portugal. In January 1990 a co-operation agreement between Portugal and Guinea-Bissau allowed a credit facility in conversions of the Guinea peso to the Portuguese escudo at an agreed rate. Links with Portugal were strengthened further by visits during 1990 by the Portuguese prime minister, Cavaco Silva, and by the Portuguese ministers for foreign affairs and the environment. In July 1996 Vieira paid an official visit to Portugal, during which agreement was reached on improved bilateral relations, particularly in the area of defence. In the same month Guinea-Bissau was among the five lusophone African nations which, together with Brazil and Portugal, formally established the Comunidade dos Países de Língua Portuguesa (CPLP), a lusophone commonwealth intended to benefit each member state by means of joint co-operation on technical, cultural and social matters. Diplomatic relations were established with Taiwan in May 1990. In October 1995 da Costa headed a ministerial delegation on a six-day official visit to Taiwan, with the aim of strengthening ties between the two nations. Since mid-1995, Guinea-Bissau has also been promoting closer ties with Argentina. In November 1995 Guinea-Bissau became a non-permanent member of the UN Security Council, for a period of two years. In May 1996 Guinea-Bissau and Morocco signed a co-operation agreement establishing the foundations for improved economic, technical, cultural and scientific co-operation.

Relations with neighbouring countries have been improving in recent years and those between Guinea-Bissau and Cape Verde, which had deteriorated following the coup in 1980, have gradually become closer. The two countries signed a bilateral co-operation agreement in February 1988 and agreed to liquidate certain joint shipping interests which predated the 1980 coup. A boundary dispute with the Republic of Guinea was resolved in Guinea-Bissau's favour by the International Court of Justice (ICJ) in February 1985. In August 1989 a similar dispute arose between Guinea-Bissau and Senegal over the demarcation of maritime borders, which had been based on a 1960 agreement between the former colonial powers, France and Portugal. Guinea-Bissau brought proceedings against Senegal in the ICJ after rejecting an international tribunal's ruling in favour of Senegal. Guinea-Bissau requested direct negotiations with Senegal and invited President Mubarak of Egypt (as president of the OAU) and President Soares of Portugal to act as mediators. In April 1990 Guinea-Bissau accused Senegal of repeated territorial violations, following the seizure of a Soviet vessel operating in Guinea-Bissau territorial waters and several infringements of Guinea-Bissau's air-space. In early May Guinea-Bissau and Senegal appeared close to military conflict after a reconnaissance platoon of the Senegalese army entered Guinea-Bissau territory. However, the detachment was withdrawn, and military confrontation was avoided. Following a meeting between Vieira and President Diouf of Senegal in late May, the two heads of state affirmed their commitment to seeking a peaceful solution to the dispute. A meeting of the two countries' joint commission in July failed to make any significant progress towards determining an agreed maritime boundary. The meeting, the first for nine years, did result in an agreement to establish a commission to monitor security on the common land border (a response to claims by Senegal that Guinea-Bissau had supported separatists in Senegal's Casamance region). Action by the Senegalese armed forces against the separatists led to the flight of several hundred refugees to Guinea-Bissau in late 1990. The Bissau government has been involved in negotiations between the Senegal government and the Casamance separatists which led to the signing in Bissau of a cease-fire agreement in May 1991. However, violence again erupted in Casamance in the second half of 1991.

In November 1991 the ICJ ruled that the agreement concluded between France and Portugal in 1960 regarding the demarcation of maritime borders between Guinea-Bissau and Senegal remained valid. In October 1993 the presidents of Guinea-Bissau and Senegal signed an agreement providing for the joint management and exploitation of the countries' maritime zones (see Economy). The agreement, which was for a renewable 20-year period, was expected to put a definitive end to the countries' dispute over the demarcation of their common maritime borders. In December 1995 the legislature authorized the ratification of the October 1993 accord. In November 1995 the ICJ announced that Guinea-Bissau had abandoned all proceedings regarding the border dispute with Senegal.

Relations with Senegal have, however, continued to be strained by separatist violence in the Casamance region. In December 1992, following an attack by separatists that resulted in the deaths of two Senegalese soldiers, Senegalese aircraft bombarded border villages in Guinea-Bissau, killing two people and injuring three. Vieira protested to the Senegalese authorities and denied Senegalese claims that the government was providing support for the rebels. The Senegalese government apologized and offered assurances that there would be no repetition of the incident. In March 1993, in an apparent attempt to convince Senegal that it did not support the rebels, the government handed over Abbé Augustin Diamacouné Senghor, one of the exiled leaders of the Casamance separatists, to the Senegalese authorities. In late 1994 the number of Senegalese refugees in Guinea-Bissau was estimated to total 13,600. In February 1995 the Senegalese air force bombarded the village of Ponta Rosa in Guinea-Bissau, close to the border with Senegal. Despite an acknowledgement by the Senegalese authorities that the bombing had occurred as the result of an error, the Senegalese military conducted a similar attack later in the same month, when the border village of Ingorezinho came under artillery fire. In March, in an attempt to forge a rapprochement between the two countries, President Diouf visited Guinea-Bissau to provide a personal apology for the two recent incidents and to offer the commitment that Senegal would respect Guinea-Bissau's sovereignty. In September, following a meeting at Gabú, in Guinea-Bissau, between representatives of both governments, agreement was reached to strengthen co-operation and establish regular dialogue concerning security on the countries' joint border. However, a further attack by the Senegalese air force in October, which resulted in injuries to several Guinea-Bissau nationals, prompted the legislature to establish a commission of inquiry to investigate such border incidents. In November da Costa paid a three-day visit to Senegal, aimed at strengthening co-operation between the two countries. In June 1996 a meeting held at Kolda, in Senegal, between ministerial delegations from Guinea-Bissau and Senegal resulted in renewed commitments to improved collaboration on security.

Economy

MILES SMITH-MORRIS

Revised for this edition by the Editor

INTRODUCTION

In terms of average income, Guinea-Bissau is among the 15 poorest countries in the world. In 1995, according to estimates by the World Bank, Guinea-Bissau's gross national product (GNP), measured at average 1993–95 prices, was US $265m., equivalent to only $250 per head. During 1985–95, it was estimated, GNP per head increased, in real terms, at an average rate of 1.8% per year. Over the same period the population increased by an annual average of 1.9%. Guinea-Bissau's gross domestic product (GDP) increased by an estimated 4.2% in 1995.

Following independence in 1974, the government established a centrally-planned economy, and an ambitious investment programme, financed mainly by foreign borrowing, was initiated, with emphasis on the industrial sector. However, the economy, which had been adversely affected by the campaign for independence, continued to deteriorate, partly as a result of the government's policies, and by the late 1970s Guinea-Bissau had an underdeveloped agricultural sector, a growing external debt, dwindling exports and escalating inflation.

In the 1980s the government initiated a policy of economic liberalization, in an attempt to reverse the decline in the economy. In 1983 measures were initiated to liberalize the trading sector, to increase producer prices and to encourage private enterprise. Although the measures of adjustment succeeded in increasing agricultural production and exports in 1984, the momentum behind the reforms slowed in 1985–86. By the end of 1986, export earnings had fallen, and the production of many goods had been halted, as the depletion of the country's reserves of foreign exchange made it difficult to import fuel or spare parts. In response to the deteriorating economic situation, the government adopted a structural adjustment programme (SAP) for 1987–90 (see below), which aimed to strengthen the role of the private sector by removing controls over prices and marketing, and by reforming the public sector. In 1990 the government began the reform of the country's public enterprises and initiated the first phase of its programme of privatization. By mid-1995 the process of removing subsidies from public enterprises, which began in 1991, had been virtually completed.

AGRICULTURE AND FISHING

Agriculture is the principal economic activity. The agricultural sector (including forestry and fishing) engaged an estimated 84.3% of the working population and accounted for an estimated 47.3% of GDP in 1995. Agriculture in Guinea-Bissau is entirely an African activity, since there are no European settlers. The main cash crops are cashew nuts (which, according to the IMF, accounted for 85.8% of total merchandise exports in 1995), palm kernels and cotton. In addition, rice, roots and tubers, millet, sorghum and groundnuts are produced. Livestock and timber production are also important. The fishing industry is developing rapidly; earnings from fishing exports and the sale of fishing licences now represent the country's second largest source of export revenue. Among food crops, rice is the staple food of the population. The southern region of Tombali accounts for about 70% of the country's rice production. Production of swamp rice and upland rice amounted to about 70,000 metric tons per annum in the pre-war period, and some rice was exported in years of good harvests. The FAO figure for the production of paddy rice in 1995 was 133,000 tons. The government is promoting a project aimed at achieving an annual harvest of 30,000 tons of rice from new fields. The droughts of 1977, 1979–80 and 1983 drastically reduced rice production, and in 1986/87 the overall food deficit reached an estimated 17,000 tons. By 1989 it had risen to 165,700 tons, owing to locust depredation and late and insufficient rain for the 1988/

89 crop. In response to this situation the World Food Programme (WFP) was to provide $13.8m. for imports of 21,000 tons of food for the period 1989–91. Agricultural output was maintained in 1990, despite another year of inadequate rains. Estimates by the Comité permanent Inter-états pour la Lutte contre la sécheresse au Sahel (CILSS) assessed production at 160,000 metric tons of rice, 23,000 tons of maize and 64,000 tons of millet and sorghum. Nevertheless, President Vieira appealed in January 1991 for international assistance to compensate for the remaining food deficit of 31,000 tons. Cereal output in 1991 declined by 58.2% compared to the previous year, from 250,400 tons in 1990 to 104,704 tons in 1991, but recovered to an estimated 199,000 tons in 1994 and 1995. Maize, beans, cassava, sorghum and sweet potatoes play an important part at the village level. Rice imports increased sharply in recent years, to some 60,000 tons in 1991, depressing the market for domestic produce.

Traditional exports are groundnuts (18,000 tons produced in 1995, according to FAO estimates), grown in the interior as an extension of the Senegalese cultivation, oil-palm products in the islands and on the coast, and coconuts. In 1977 groundnut exports of 16,335 tons, accounted for 60% of total export earnings. However, in 1992 only about 400 tons, worth US $200,000, were exported, and by 1993, according to the IMF, exports of groundnuts had ceased altogether. Exports of palm kernels amounted to 10,600 tons, worth $1.3m., in 1983, but by 1994 had declined to 800 tons, worth about $100,000. Cashew nuts are a relatively recent crop, with an expanding production, estimated at 6,000 tons in 1987, rising to 46,500 tons in 1994. In that year export earnings from cashew nuts totalled $31m., or 93.4% of total export revenue. Cashew nut exports declined to $20.5m. in 1995, accounting for 85.8% of total export revenue. Most of Guinea-Bissau's cashew nuts are purchased by India.

In the government's development plans, priority has been given to agriculture, with the aim of achieving self-sufficiency in food. A sugar refinery (with an annual capacity of 10,000 tons), capable of satisfying domestic needs, is being built at Gambiel and will be supplied from new irrigated plantations covering an area of 6,000 ha. An agro-industrial complex at Cumeré is capable of processing 50,000 tons of rice and 70,000 tons of groundnuts annually. It is estimated that these schemes, together with the projected construction of a thermoelectric power station, will require an investment of US $200m., mainly from external sources. The government has nationalized most of the land but does grant private concessions to work the land and has maintained the rights of those tilling their fields. The regime also confiscated the property of former pro-Portuguese Guineans and introduced state control over foreign trade and domestic retail trade through 'people's shops', whose inefficiency and corruption led to serious shortages of consumer goods and contributed to the downfall of the Cabral regime in 1980. In 1983/84 the government partially 'privatized' the state-controlled trading companies, and raised producer prices by about 70%, in an attempt to accelerate agricultural output. Despite the introduction of these measures, Guinea-Bissau continues to operate a 'war economy', superimposed upon a rudimentary peasant economy where most products are bought and sold by the state. Since 1987, however, plans have been accelerated for the removal of price controls on most agricultural products, except essential goods, and for the liberalization of internal marketing systems. In 1992 the government disbanded the people's militia, a paramilitary corps charged with monitoring the economic sector inside the country.

The fishing industry has expanded rapidly since the late 1970s, and it has been estimated that the potential annual catch in Guinea-Bissau's waters could total nearly 250,000 tons, although by 1995 less than 10% of this level was actually being realized and revenue from fish exports had declined to less than 1% of total export revenue (US $200,000). If illegal fishing could be effectively prevented, fishing could become Guinea-Bissau's main source of revenue. In 1994 it was estimated that annual losses from illegal fishing by foreign vessels in Guinea-Bissau's waters amounted to $25m. In 1987 the USA financed a programme for patrolling Guinea-Bissau's waters to prevent illegal fishing. Industrial fishing is conducted principally by a joint venture between Guinea-Bissau and Estonia and by Russia, which, in addition to purchasing fishing licences, yielded 15% of its catch to Guinea-Bissau. However, the contract with Russia expired in 1992 and a new contract was of paramount importance for Guinea-Bissau since a considerable amount of its fishing export revenue derives from that source. According to IMF figures, artisanal fishing production increased by an annual average of 8.1% in 1990–95, and the total catch stood at 20,088 tons in 1995. In March 1989 an agreement was signed with Portugal for the creation of a joint fishing company. Portugal also provided a grant of $2.1m. towards a fisheries project, and in December 1990 the African Development Bank (ADB) agreed to lend $15m. for a project to develop fishing for export at Cacine, in the south. A new fishing agreement was signed with the European Community (EC, now the European Union–EU) in 1991, increasing the quotas allowed to EC vessels in Guinea-Bissau's waters. Under a further agreement, signed in mid-1995, the EU was to provide Guinea-Bissau with ECU 10m. over a period of two years in return for fishing rights. In June 1997 a new four-year fishing agreement was signed with the EU, allowing European vessels to catch 12,600 tons of fish per year in Guinea-Bissau's waters in return for annual compensation of ECU 9m. In October 1993 an agreement was signed with Senegal providing for the joint management of the countries' maritime zones, with fishing resources to be divided according to the determination of a joint management agency, formally established in December 1995 (see also below).

Cattle-breeding is a very important activity among Balante and Muslim tribes of the interior. In 1995 there were 475,000 head of cattle, 270,000 goats, 255,000 sheep and 310,000 pigs, according to FAO estimates. Meat consumption is significant, and some hides and skins are exported. Tree-felling was temporarily halted while a full assessment of resources was made, but exports resumed in 1986, reaching US $1m., and production totalled 577,000 cu m in 1994, according to FAO estimates. Exports of rough and processed timber earned $1.5m in 1995. In the 1988–91 Development Plan, forestry was allocated a high priority by the government, and a reafforestation programme was to be implemented.

INDUSTRY, MINING AND TRANSPORT

There is little industrial activity other than food-processing, brewing and cotton-processing. Industry (including mining, manufacturing, construction and power) employed 4.1% of the economically active population in 1994 and provided an estimated 18.2% of GDP in 1995. According to the World Bank, industrial GDP declined, in real terms, by an annual average of 1.3% in 1985–95, but increased by an estimated 3.1% in 1995. A car assembly plant, with a capacity of 500 vehicles per year, was reopened in 1986, following the government's encouragement of the private sector. The factory was opened in 1979, but was forced to close in 1984, owing to lack of components. In 1987 the government attempted to attract foreign investment for the rehabilitation and expansion of a fish-processing plant, and the establishment of a factory to produce plywood and furniture. An agreement between Guinea-Bissau, Portugal and the USA was signed in 1987 for the establishment of an experimental credit fund to encourage private enterprise. In July 1989 an agreement was signed with Portugal, under which a Portuguese company was to reopen a plastics factory which had ceased production in 1984. Electricity consumption totalled 14m. kWh in 1985, according to UN estimates. In 1987 work began on the construction of an 8,000-kW diesel-electric power station, funded by the USSR; its completion, together with the rehabilitation of the Bissau thermal power station and purchase of a new 3.5 MW generating unit, formed part of a project aimed at increasing total generating capacity to 15.4 MW. In 1992 the European Investment Bank (EIB) agreed to provide ECU 7.5m. towards financing the project.

The mining sector has still to be developed, and prospecting for bauxite, petroleum and phosphates is in progress. A large deposit of 200m. tons of bauxite was reported in the Boé area in 1972, but exploitation has not yet become economic. In 1981 a French exploration team announced the discovery of 200m. tons of phosphates in Cacheu and Oio. In 1987 the government negotiated for financial backing to exploit phosphate deposits in the northern region. Petroleum exploration has resumed; an offshore zone, contested with Guinea until 1985, may contain significant deposits. A second maritime zone, on the border with

Senegal, was also the subject of a jurisdictional dispute until October 1993, when an agreement was signed with Senegal providing for the joint management of the countries' maritime zones. The agreement, which was to operate for an initial 20-year period, provided for an 85%–15% division of petroleum resources between Senegal and Guinea-Bissau respectively. Guinea-Bissau formally ratified the agreement in December 1995. In 1984 the government reached agreement with a group of foreign petroleum companies concerning prospecting in an offshore concession covering 4,500 sq km, and in 1985 licences for exploration of some 40 offshore blocks were offered on favourable terms, following the relaxation of Guinea-Bissau's hydrocarbons law. A US petroleum company, Pecten, began exploratory drilling in its offshore permits in 1990. In July of that year the government announced that a new exploration programme was to begin in 1991; a joint commission had been formed with Guinea to facilitate exploration in the two countries' maritime border area. In 1996 a Canadian petroleum company, Petrobank, agreed terms for a joint venture with the state petroleum company of Guinea-Bissau to explore an offshore block covering some 280,000 ha. Petrobank's initial investment was to total US $1m.

For strategic reasons, an impressive network of 3,500 km of roads (540 km tarred) was built from Bissau to the north and north-east in 1972. The EU is interested in an international project to construct a road linking Banjul, in The Gambia, to Bissau. The road system is poor, especially during the rainy season. In 1989 the World Bank approved a loan of US $23.6m. towards a $43m. infrastructural rehabilitation scheme. Other donors included the UN Capital Development Fund, the Kuwait Fund for Arab Development, the ADB and the Islamic Development Bank. In early 1989 grants totalling $31.3m. were provided by the ADB, the Arab Bank for Economic Development in Africa and the EC for road improvements. The road from São Domingos to M'Pack in Senegal, built with aid from the EC and Italy, opened in 1990. Water transport could be much developed, as 85% of the population live within 20 km of a navigable waterway. In 1984 work began on a project, expected to cost $47.4m., to enlarge Bissau harbour and to rehabilitate four river ports. The ADB was to lend $2.5m. in 1991 for the purchase of port equipment. The construction of a new river port at N'Pungda began in 1986, to improve rice distribution to the northern region. There are also plans to expand the international airport at Bissau. In 1991 Guinea-Bissau and Portugal signed an air transport agreement, under which the Portuguese national airline, TAP, would provide equipment and technicians to help Air Bissau to improve internal services, as well as increasing the frequency of Lisbon-Bissau flights from two to three per week. An experimental television service, financed by Portugal was introduced in 1989.

EXTERNAL TRADE, FINANCE AND DEVELOPMENT

Serious external trade imbalances persist. Exports rose from about US $12m. in 1982 to $17.4m. in 1984, but fell to $7.5m. in 1986. In 1987 exports rose dramatically to $15.3m., as a result of the devaluation of the peso in May, and to $15.9m. in 1988. The value of exports continued to rise, to $17.5m. in 1989, $21.5m. in 1990 and $23m. in 1991, in spite of the devaluation of the Guinea peso, which in 1991, when the exchange rate averaged 3,659 pesos = $1, was worth less than one-half of its value of two years earlier. According to IMF figures, the value of exports totalled only $6.5m. in 1992, but increased to $16m. in 1993, and to $33.2m. in 1994 before declining to $23.9m. in 1995. Devaluation of the peso continued, with the average exchange rate reaching 6,934 pesos = $1 in 1992, 10,082 pesos = $1 in 1993, 12,892 pesos = $1 in 1994 and 18,073 pesos = $1 in 1995. Meanwhile, the demand for manufactured goods, machinery, fuel and food has ensured a high level of imports, averaging $60m. per year in the 1980s. However, foreign exchange controls and the closure of some state enterprises caused a large fall in imports of industrial raw materials. Imports totalled $51.2m. in 1986, falling to $48.8m. in 1987 and rising again in 1988 to about $57m., according to IMF figures. Imports continued to rise reaching $78m. in 1989 and $93m. in 1990 before falling slightly to $78m. in 1991. According to IMF figures, the value of imports totalled $83.5m. in 1992, but declined to $53.8m. in 1993, and to $52.4m. in 1994, reflecting tightened fiscal and monetary policies, rising slightly to $59.34m. in 1995. In 1995 the principal source of imports (36.9%) was Portugal; other major suppliers were the Netherlands, the People's Repubic of China, Japan and Spain. In that year India, a major importer of cashew nuts, was the principal market for exports (87.8%); other significant purchasers were Portugal (10.2%), France and Spain.

In 1993 the budgetary deficit was equivalent to 13.1% of GDP and stood at 310,134m. Guinea pesos, falling to 244,172m. pesos in 1994 and to 74,000m. pesos in 1995. Grants from abroad continue to be the major source of revenue, accounting for 56.3% of the total for 1995. The deficit on the current account of the balance of payments reached US $79.04m. in 1991, increasing to $104.18m. in 1992, before decreasing to $65.48m. in 1993, to $50.63m. in 1994 and to $41.45m. in 1995. In 1987–95 the average annual rate of inflation was 50.0%. Consumer prices increased by an average of 15.2% in 1994 and by 45.4% in 1995. The shortfalls in the economy are offset by inflows of foreign aid, which averaged more than $60m. per year in 1981–85, increasing from $72.2m. in 1986 to $106.3m. in 1987. The increase was due principally to a rise in multilateral assistance, especially from the World Bank, the African Development Fund (ADF) and the EC. The level of aid fell slightly in 1988, to $100m. In recent years, the Netherlands and the Scandinavian countries have been important aid-donors. Guinea-Bissau has attended various Franco-African summit conferences and has been a signatory to successive Lomé Conventions.

An extensive re-organization of Guinea-Bissau's banking system has been under way since 1989, involving the replacement of Banco Nacional da Guiné-Bissau by three institutions: a central bank, a commercial bank (Banco Internacional da Guiné-Bissau, which began operations in March 1990), and a national credit bank, established in September 1990, to channel investment. A fourth financial institution, responsible for managing aid receipts, was subsequently created with assistance from the EC, the US Agency for International Development, Sweden and Portugal. In 1991 the government authorized the establishment of privately-operated foreign exchange bureaux.

In November 1987 Guinea-Bissau applied to join the Franc Zone, but withdrew its application in January 1990 following the formulation of an exchange rate agreement with Portugal linking the Guinea peso rate to that of the Portuguese escudo. This accord was considered to form the initial stage in the creation of an 'escudo zone'. However, in August 1993 Guinea-Bissau renewed its application to join the Franc Zone. Guinea-Bissau joined the Union économique et monétaire ouest-africaine in January 1997 and was admitted to the Franc Zone on 2 May. The Guinea peso and the franc CFA co-existed for a period of three months to allow for the gradual replacement, at foreign exchange offices, of the national currency at a rate of 1 franc CFA = 65 Guinea pesos. With the entry of Guinea-Bissau into the Franc Zone, the Banco Central da Guiné-Bissau ceased to operate as the country's central bank and its functions were assumed by the Banque Centrale des états de l'Afrique de l'ouest (BCEAO), which has its headquarters in Dakar, Senegal.

President Vieira's government aimed to downgrade many of the prestigious projects that had been initiated by Cabral's administration, and to emphasize rural development. In order to achieve a coherent policy, a Development Plan for 1983–86 was prepared in 1982. In December 1983 the peso was devalued by 50%, with the new official exchange rate set at 88 pesos = SDR 1, as part of a programme of economic stabilization, which aimed to liberalize trade and to increase activity in the private sector. In 1986 trading restrictions were lifted, allowing private traders to import and export goods, although the two state-owned enterprises retained their monopolies in rice, petroleum products and various other commodities.

After consultations with the World Bank, the IMF and other external donors, Guinea-Bissau initiated an SAP covering the period 1987–90. The programme was to be wholly financed by external aid totalling US $46.4m. The SAP included proposals to liberalize the economy and to reform public administration and enterprises. It aimed to achieve a real GDP growth rate of at least 3.5% per year, a lower annual inflation rate (of about 8%) and a reduction in the current account and budgetary deficits. In May 1987 the peso was devalued by about 60%, with the official rate set at 650 pesos = US $1, and new taxes and higher tariffs were introduced. Civil servants' salaries were increased by 25% in 1987, and by 50% in 1988, although one-third of the 16,623 state employees were to be gradually redeployed in the agricultural sector and in public works projects. At the end of 1990, civil servants were granted an extra month's salary to ameliorate the stringencies imposed by the SAP. In 1988 a reduction of government subsidies on petroleum products increased their average price by 40%.

The Development Plan (1989–92) aimed to consolidate the progress made under the SAP in the reduction of the state's role in the economy, and the growth of private investment. Emphasis was on social development. The agricultural and fishing sectors were to be given priority as a means of achieving self-sufficiency and reducing the balance-of-payments deficit. By the end of 1989, Guinea-Bissau's total external debt was estimated at US $458m., of which $427m. was public and publicly-guaranteed long-term debt. Overall debt-servicing charges for that year totalled $11.6m., or 43% of exports. In October 1989, the 'Paris Club' of Western official creditors, including Belgium, France, Sweden and Switzerland, agreed to reschedule $21m. of principal and interest due from end-October 1989 to December 1990. In September 1989 Belgium agreed to reschedule $2.5m. of Guinea-Bissau's debt. Portugal announced in October 1990 that it would convert Guinea-Bissau's debt of $14.5m. into a Guinea peso fund to be used to support development projects. At the end of the year Portugal released a $6m. credit to the government as part of the financial agreement concluded in January (see above). In January 1989, following the removal of subsidies, fuel prices rose a further 40%, and this was quickly followed by a 33% increase in the price of bread. Further fuel price increases followed in January, July and October 1990 and February 1991, linked to the depreciation of the Guinea peso against the US dollar and in response to the rise in world petroleum prices that accompanied the Gulf crisis.

In January 1989 the government announced the adoption of a US $104.6m. investment programme, to be funded entirely by external donors, which was to supplement development projects already proceeding under the SAP. In an attempt to stimulate foreign trade, restrict 'black market' activity and restrain inflation, customs duties and general taxes on imported goods were reduced in April. In the following month international donor countries pledged allocations of $120m., of which 40% was to assist in financing the balance-of-payments deficit, and the remainder to meet general financing requirements. In accordance with these agreements, the World Bank approved a $23.4m. loan to support the second stage of the SAP, introduced in 1987. Joint financing was expected from, among others, the Netherlands ($4.8m.), the USA ($4.5m.) and the ADF ($17.2m.). Under the second stage of the SAP, the government undertook to extend the aims of its economic liberalization programme, with particular emphasis on the privatization of state-owned enterprises.

In June 1990 President Vieira initiated new measures to attract domestic and foreign private investment. It was stated that most of the 50 public enterprises were to be restructured and made more efficient although some strategic sectors, such as telecommunications, electricity and infrastructure, were expected to remain under state control. A decree on privatization was adopted in March 1991, defining areas of state intervention in the economy and outlining the rules for transferring state holdings in public enterprises to the private sector. Nine enterprises were listed for initial privatization, including the 'people's shops', the national brewery and the fishing enterprise, SEMAPESCA. Of these, seven were sold for a total of US $6m. The second phase of privatizations began in early 1994. The government's failure to meet some of the targets of the adjustment programme led, however, to a suspension of international financing when the IMF declined to renew its structural adjustment facility. Among funding suspended as a result was the third tranche of the World Bank's structural adjustment loan, totalling $6.5m.; negotiations on a resumption of World Bank funding began in July 1992 and, in July 1993, it was announced that credits were finally to be resumed. However, in the following month, the World Bank reversed its decision, owing to the government's delay in making repayments on its external debt. In January 1995 the IMF approved a series of loans totalling $13.6m. under an enhanced structural adjustment facility in support of the government's economic reform programme. The loans were to be disbursed over a three-year period. In April 1992 the International Development Association announced a loan of $7.2m. to help finance an economic management project. The project, which aimed to improve the government's management and monitoring of economic policy, was to cost a total of $8m. Among the measures involved in the project were a modernizing of the budget process and reform of the tax structure. In April 1993 the government initiated a $63m. public investment programme. The programme, which concentrates predominantly on public works, was to be funded by $32.5m. in aid and $29.5m. in loans contracted by the government, which was itself to provide the remaining $1m. By the end of 1995 total external debt had risen to $894.0m., of which $848.6m. was long-term public debt. In that year the cost of debt servicing was equivalent to 33.7% of the total value of exports of goods and services. Efforts to renegotiate the country's external debt were being made with the assistance of the UN Development Programme.

The government's economic objectives for 1996–98 included annual GDP growth of at least 4%, and a reduction in the annual rate of inflation, from 45.4% in 1995 to 7.5% by 1998. The balance-of-payments deficit was to be curbed, from 18.9% of GDP in 1995 to 15.5% by 1998. It was envisaged that considerable reductions in customs exemptions and enhanced efforts to recover taxes and duties would contribute to increasing public revenue.

Statistical Survey

Area and Population

AREA, POPULATION AND DENSITY

Area (sq km)	36,125*
Population (census results)	
16–30 April 1979	753,313
1 December 1991	
Males	476,210
Females	507,157
Total	983,367
Population (UN estimates at mid-year)†	
1993	1,028,000
1994	1,050,000
1995	1,073,000
Density (per sq km) at mid-1995	29.7

* 13,948 sq miles.

† Source: UN, *World Population Prospects: The 1994 Revision.*

POPULATION BY REGION (1991 census)

Bafatá	143,377
Biombo	60,420
Bissau	197,610
Bolama/Bijagos	26,691
Cacheu	146,980
Gabú	134,971
Oio	156,084
Quinara	44,793
Tombali	72,441
Total	983,367

PRINCIPAL TOWNS (population at 1979 census)

Bissau (capital)	109,214	Catió	5,170
Bafatá	13,429	Cantchungo†	4,965
Gabú*	7,803	Farim	4,468
Mansôa	5,390		

* Formerly Nova Lamego. † Formerly Teixeira Pinto.

BIRTHS AND DEATHS (UN estimates, annual averages)

	1980–85	1985–90	1990–95
Birth rate (per 1,000)	43.3	42.9	42.7
Death rate (per 1,000)	24.7	23.0	21.3

Expectation of life (UN estimates, years at birth, 1990–95): 43.5 (males 41.9; females 45.1).

Source: UN, *World Population Prospects: The 1994 Revision.*

ECONOMICALLY ACTIVE POPULATION
('000 persons at mid-1994)

	Males	Females	Total
Agriculture, etc.	195	175	370
Industry	15	5	20
Services	80	14	94
Total	290	194	484

Source: UN, *African Statistical Yearbook.*

Mid-1995 (estimates in '000): Agriculture etc. 430; Total 510 (Source: FAO, *Production Yearbook*).

Agriculture

PRINCIPAL CROPS ('000 metric tons)

	1993	1994	1995
Rice (paddy)	126	131	133
Maize	13	14	15
Millet	26	29	35
Sorghum	14	14	16
Roots and tubers	65	65*	65*
Groundnuts (in shell)	18	18	18*
Cottonseed	2	2	2*
Coconuts*	25	25	25
Copra*	5	5	5
Palm Kernels*	7	8	8
Vegetables and melons*	20	20	20
Plantains*	34	34	34
Other fruits*	32	31	31
Sugar cane*	6	6	6
Cashew nuts*	28.0	35.0	35.0
Cotton (lint)*	1	1	1

* FAO estimate(s).

Source: FAO, *Production Yearbook.*

LIVESTOCK (FAO estimates, '000 head, year ending September)

	1993	1994	1995
Cattle	475	475	475
Pigs	310	310	310
Sheep	255	255	255
Goats	270	270	270

Source: FAO, *Production Yearbook.*

LIVESTOCK PRODUCTS (FAO estimates, '000 metric tons)

	1993	1994	1995
Beef and veal	4	4	4
Pig meat	10	10	10
Cows' milk	12	12	12
Goats' milk	3	3	3

Source: FAO, *Production Yearbook.*

Forestry

ROUNDWOOD REMOVALS
(FAO estimates, '000 cubic metres, excluding bark)

	1992	1993	1994
Sawlogs, veneer logs and logs for sleepers*	40	40	40
Other industrial wood	110	112	115
Fuel wood†	422	422	422
Total	572	574	577

* Assumed to be unchanged since 1971.

† Assumed to be unchanged since 1979.

Source: FAO, *Yearbook of Forest Products.*

SAWNWOOD PRODUCTION
(FAO estimates, '000 cubic metres, including railway sleepers)

	1992	1993	1994
Total*	16	16	16

* Assumed to be unchanged since 1971.

Source: FAO, *Yearbook of Forest Products.*

Fishing

(FAO estimates, '000 metric tons, live weight)

	1993	1994	1995
Inland waters	0.3	0.3	0.3
Atlantic Ocean	5.1	5.3	5.3
Total catch	5.4	5.6	5.6

Source: FAO, *Yearbook of Fishery Statistics*.

Industry

SELECTED PRODUCTS

	1993	1994	1995
Vegetable oils (million litres)	6.2	6.0	5.6
Electric energy (million kWh)	44.0	44.9	46.3

Source: IMF, *Guinea-Bissau—Statistical Appendix* (May 1997).

Finance

CURRENCY AND EXCHANGE RATES

Monetary Units

100 centimes = 1 franc de la Communauté financière africaine (CFA).

French Franc, Sterling and Dollar Equivalents
(31 March 1997)

1 French franc = 100 francs CFA;
£1 sterling = 924.20 francs CFA;
US $1 = 562.85 francs CFA
1,000 francs CFA = £1.082 = $1.777.

Average Exchange Rate (francs CFA per US $)

1994 555.20
1995 499.15
1996 511.55

Note: An exchange rate of 1 French franc = 50 francs CFA, established in 1948, remained in force until January 1994, when the CFA franc was devalued by 50%, with the exchange rate adjusted to 1 French franc = 100 francs CFA. Following Guinea-Bissau's admission in January 1997 to the Union économique et monétaire ouest-africaine, the country entered the Franc Zone on 2 May. As a result, the Guinea peso was replaced by the franc CFA, although the peso remained legal tender until 31 July. The new currency was introduced at an exchange rate of 1 franc CFA = 65 Guinea pesos. At 31 March 1997 the exchange rate in relation to US currency was $1 = 36,793.3 Guinea pesos. The average exchange rate (Guinea pesos per US $) was: 12,892 in 1994; 18,073 in 1995; 26,373 in 1996.

BUDGET (million Guinea pesos)

Revenue*	1993	1994	1995
Tax revenue	121,018	207,370	317,700
Income taxes	18,005	25,190	45,700
Business profits	9,223	11,823	28,000
Individuals	5,395	9,474	12,000
Consumption taxes	23,362	27,659	97,900
On imports	22,209	25,572	95,100
Taxes on international trade and transactions	73,535	134,625	159,000
Import duties	25,150	33,476	60,300
Export duties	17,987	57,463	25,900
Port service charges	30,398	43,685	72,800
Other taxes	6,116	19,897	14,700
Non-tax revenue	132,637	168,408	263,100
Fees and duties	114,643	151,300	228,100
Fishing licences	113,659	150,579	219,100
Privatization receipts	4,404	—	4,000
Total	253,654	375,778	580,800

Expenditure†	1993	1994	1995
Current expenditure	343,327	440,757	703,300
Wages and salaries	77,935	80,815	128,200
Goods and services	90,435	135,571	165,900
Transfers	37,540	60,513	103,300
Scheduled external interest payments	137,416	163,858	305,900
Capital expenditure	587,561	604,693	695,700
Total	930,888	1,045,450	1,399,000

* Excluding grants received ('000 million pesos): 404.1 in 1993; 443.3 in 1994; 747.9 in 1995.

† Excluding net lending ('000 million pesos): 37.0 in 1993; 17.8 in 1994; −3.7 in 1995.

Source: IMF, *Guinea-Bissau—Statistical Appendix* (May 1997).

CENTRAL BANK RESERVES (US $ million at 31 December)

	1993	1994	1995
IMF special drawing rights	0.01	—	0.01
Foreign exchange	14.16	18.43	20.26
Total	14.17	18.43	20.27

Source: IMF, *International Financial Statistics*.

MONEY SUPPLY ('000 million Guinea pesos at 31 December)

	1993	1994	1995
Currency outside banks	132.53	195.97	278.08
Demand deposits at deposit money banks	68.25	120.56	187.18
Total money (incl. others)	201.91	319.27	469.24

Source: IMF, *International Financial Statistics*.

COST OF LIVING (Consumer Price Index; base: 1990 = 100)

	1993	1994	1995
Food, beverages and tobacco	395.8	455.9	662.7

Source: IMF, *International Financial Statistics*.

NATIONAL ACCOUNTS

Expenditure on the Gross Domestic Product*
(million Guinea pesos at current prices)

	1991	1992	1993
Government final consumption expenditure	114,640	163,100	212,970
Private final consumption expenditure	791,310	1,700,380	2,246,520
Gross capital formation	231,500	405,660	540,290
Total domestic expenditure	1,137,450	2,269,140	2,999,780
Exports of goods and services	122,560	125,010	292,630
Less Imports of goods and services	405,030	864,140	926,690
GDP in purchasers' values	854,980	1,530,010	2,365,720
GDP at constant 1990 prices	525,400	540,100	556,300

* Figures are rounded to the nearest 10 million pesos.

Source: IMF, *International Financial Statistics*.

Gross Domestic Product by Economic Activity
('000 million Guinea pesos at current prices)

	1992	1993	1994
Agriculture, hunting, forestry and fishing	751	1,262	1,587
Mining and quarrying; Manufacturing; Electricity, gas and water	163	231	330
Construction	125	150	124
Trade, restaurants and hotels	394	538	748
Transport, storage and communications	41	60	74
Finance, insurance, real estate, etc.; Community, social and personal services (excl. government)	14	19	25
Government services	72	103	116
GDP at factor cost	1,561	2,364	3,004

Source: IMF, *Guinea-Bissau—Statistical Appendix* (May 1997).

BALANCE OF PAYMENTS (US $ million)

	1993	1994	1995
Exports of goods f.o.b.	15.96	33.21	23.90
Imports of goods f.o.b.	-53.82	-53.80	-59.34
Trade balance	-37.86	-20.59	-35.44
Imports of services	-11.38	-24.50	-21.09
Balance on goods and services	-49.24	-45.09	-56.53
Other income paid	-28.98	-26.27	-15.02
Balance on goods, services and income	-78.22	-71.36	-71.55
Current transfers received	14.39	21.79	31.42
Current transfers paid	-1.65	-1.06	-1.32
Current balance	-65.48	-50.63	-41.45
Capital account (net)	36.58	44.42	49.20
Other investment liabilities	-13.55	-26.98	-25.60
Net errors and omissions	-15.98	-21.36	-25.53
Overall balance	-58.43	-54.55	-43.38

Source: IMF, *International Financial Statistics.*

External Trade

PRINCIPAL COMMODITIES (US $ million)

Imports c.i.f.	1993	1994	1995
Food and live animals	25.1	17.3	25.6
Rice	17.2	8.6	18.0
Oil	1.1	1.8	2.0
Dairy products	1.2	0.9	1.1
Beverages and tobacco	3.2	3.7	4.3
Other consumer goods	5.1	6.2	6.6
Clothing and footwear	0.6	1.5	1.1
Durable consumer goods	2.7	2.9	2.3
Non-durable consumer goods	1.8	1.9	3.2
Petroleum and petroleum products	3.2	6.3	8.3
Diesel fuel and gasoline	2.5	4.2	5.8
Construction materials	4.9	6.0	7.3
Transport equipment	8.9	14.5	8.4
Passenger vehicles	3.6	5.7	2.2
Freight vehicles	1.8	6.7	5.2
Vehicle parts	3.5	2.1	1.0
Electrical equipment and machinery	5.3	6.5	7.7
Total (incl. others)	61.5	65.2	71.9

Exports f.o.b.	1993	1994	1995
Cotton	0.7	1.1	1.3
Palm kernels	0.3	0.1	n.a.
Cashew nuts	13.0	31.0	20.5
Fish	0.5	0.1	—
Logs	0.9	0.3	1.2
Total (incl. others)	16.0	33.2	23.9

Source: IMF, *Guinea-Bissau—Statistical Appendix* (May 1997).

PRINCIPAL TRADING PARTNERS

Imports (million pesos)	1984
France	232.7
Germany, Fed. Repub.	213.7
Italy	110.4
Netherlands	215.6
Portugal	924.0
Senegal	362.0
Sweden	70.2
USSR	462.7
USA	192.4
Total (incl. others)	3,230.7

Source: Ministry of Planning, Bissau.

Exports (US $ '000)	1981
China, People's Repub.	1,496
France	1,376
Portugal	2,890
Senegal	1,122
Spain	4,058
Sweden	1,627
Switzerland	1,617
United Kingdom	1,211
Total (incl. others)	15,730

Source: UN, *International Trade Statistics Yearbook.*

Transport

ROAD TRAFFIC (motor vehicles in use, estimates)

	1993	1994	1995
Passenger cars	4,930	5,920	6,300
Commercial vehicles	3,700	4,650	4,900

Source: IRF, *World Road Statistics.*

INTERNATIONAL SEA-BORNE SHIPPING
(UN estimates, freight traffic, '000 metric tons)

	1991	1992	1993
Goods loaded	40	45	46
Goods unloaded	272	277	283

Source: UN Economic Commission for Africa, *African Statistical Yearbook.*

CIVIL AVIATION (traffic on scheduled services)

	1992	1993	1994
Kilometres flown (million)	1	1	1
Passengers carried ('000)	21	21	21
Passenger-km (million)	10	10	10
Total ton-km (million)	1	1	1

Source: UN, *Statistical Yearbook.*

Communications Media

	1992	1993	1994
Radio receivers ('000 in use)	40	41	42
Telephones ('000 main lines in use)*	8	9	n.a.
Daily newspapers:			
Number	1	n.a.	1
Average circulation ('000 copies)	6	n.a.	6

* UN estimates.

Sources: UNESCO, *Statistical Yearbook*; UN, *Statistical Yearbook*.

Education

(1988)

	Insti-tutions	Teachers	Students		
			Males	Females	Total
Pre-primary	5	43	384	370	754
Primary	632*	3,065*	50,744	28,291	79,035
Secondary:					
General	n.a.	617†	3,588	1,917	5,505
Teacher training	n.a.	33	137	39	176
Vocational	n.a.	74	593	56	649
Tertiary	n.a.	n.a.	380	24	404

* 1987 figures. † 1986 figure.

Source: UNESCO, *Statistical Yearbook*.

Directory

The Constitution

A new Constitution for the Republic of Guinea-Bissau was approved by the National People's Assembly on 16 May 1984 and amended in May 1991 and November 1996 (see below). The main provisions of the 1984 Constitution were:

Guinea-Bissau is an anti-colonialist and anti-imperialist Republic and a State of revolutionary national democracy, based on the people's participation in undertaking, controlling and directing public activities. The Partido Africano da Independência da Guiné e Cabo Verde (PAIGC) shall be the leading political force in society and in the State. The PAIGC shall define the general bases for policy in all fields.

The economy of Guinea-Bissau shall be organized on the principles of state direction and planning. The State shall control the country's foreign trade.

The representative bodies in the country are the National People's Assembly and the regional councils. Other state bodies draw their powers from these. The members of the regional councils shall be directly elected. Members of the councils must be more than 18 years of age. The National People's Assembly shall have 150 members, who are to be elected by the regional councils from among their own members. All members of the National People's Assembly must be over 21 years of age.

The National People's Assembly shall elect a 15-member Council of State, to which its powers are delegated between sessions of the Assembly. The Assembly also elects the President of the Council of State, who is also automatically Head of the Government and Commander-in-Chief of the Armed Forces. The Council of State will later elect two Vice-Presidents and a Secretary. The President and Vice-Presidents of the Council of State form part of the Government, as do Ministers, Secretaries of State and the Governor of the National Bank.

The Constitution can be revised at any time by the National People's Assembly on the initiative of the deputies themselves, or of the Council of State or the Government.

Note: Constitutional amendments providing for the operation of a multi-party political system were approved unanimously by the National People's Assembly in May 1991. The amendments stipulated that new parties seeking registration must obtain a minimum of 2,000 signatures, with at least 100 signatures from each of the nine provinces. (These provisions were adjusted in August to 1,000 and 50 signatures, respectively.) In addition, the amendments provided for the National People's Assembly (reduced to 100 members) to be elected by universal adult suffrage, for the termination of official links between the PAIGC and the armed forces, and for the operation of a free market economy. Multi-party elections took place in July 1994.

In November 1996 the legislature approved a constitutional amendment providing for Guinea-Bissau to seek membership of the Union économique et monétaire ouest-africaine and of the Franc Zone.

The Government

HEAD OF STATE

President of the Republic and Commander-in-Chief of the Armed Forces: Commdr João Bernardo Vieira (assumed power 14 November 1980; elected President of the Council of State 16 May 1984, and re-elected 19 June 1989; elected President in multi-party elections 3 July and 7 August 1994).

COUNCIL OF MINISTERS
(August 1997)

Prime Minister: Carlos Correia.

Minister of Defence: Samba Lamine Manè.

Minister of Foreign Affairs and Co-operation: Fernando Delfim da Silva.

Minister in the Presidency with Responsibility for Parliamentary Affairs and Information: Malal Sane.

Minister of Economy and Finance: Issuf Sanha.

Minister of the Interior: Francisca Pereira.

Minister of Territorial Administration: Nicandro Pereira Barreto.

Minister of Rural Development, Natural Resources and the Environment: Avito José da Silva.

Minister of Equipment: João Gomes Cardoso.

Minister of Social Affairs and the Advancement of Women: Nharebat N'Gaia N'Tchaso.

Minister of Public Health: Brandão Gomes Co.

Minister of Justice and Labour: Daniel Ferreira.

Minister of National Education: Odette Semedo.

Minister of Veterans' Affairs: Arafan Manè.

Minister of Fishing: Artur Augustro da Silva.

There are seven Secretaries of State.

MINISTRIES

All ministries are in Bissau.

President and Legislature

PRESIDENT

Presidential Election, First Ballot, 3 July 1994

Candidate	Votes	% of Votes
JOÃO BERNARDO VIEIRA (PAIGC)	142,577	46.29
KOUMBA YALLA (PRS)	67,518	21.92
DOMINGOS FERNANDES GOMES (RGB—MB)	53,277	17.30
CARLOS DOMINGOS GOMES (PCD)	15,575	5.06
FRANÇOIS KANKOILA MENDY (FLING)	8,655	2.81
Alhaje BUBACAR DJALÓ (UM)	8,506	2.76
VÍTOR SAÚDE MARIA (PUSD)	6,388	2.07
ANTONIETA ROSA GOMES (FCG)	5,509	1.79
Total	308,005	100.00

Second Ballot, 7 August 1994

Candidate	Votes	%
JOÃO BERNARDO VIEIRA (PAIGC)	159,993	52.03
KOUMBA YALLA (PRS)	147,518	47.97
Total	307,511	100.00

NATIONAL PEOPLE'S ASSEMBLY

President: MALANG BACAI SANHA.

General Election, 3 July 1994

	% of Votes	Seats
Partido Africano da Independência da Guiné e Cabo Verde (PAIGC)	46.0	62
Resistência da Guiné-Bissau—Movimento Bah-Fatah (RGB—MB)	19.2	19
Partido para a Renovação Social (PRS)	10.3	12
União para a Mudança (UM)	12.8	6
Frente da Luta para a Libertação da Guiné (FLING)	2.5	1
Partido da Convergência Democrática (PCD)	5.3	—
Partido Unido Social Democrático (PUSD)	2.9	—
Foro Cívico da Guiné (FCG)	0.2	—
Total (incl. others)	100.0	100

Political Organizations

Foro Cívico da Guiné (FCG): Bissau; Leader ANTONIETA ROSA GOMES.

Frente da Luta para a Libertação da Guiné (FLING): Bissau; f. 1962; officially registered in May 1992; Leader FRANÇOIS KANKOILA MENDY.

Liga Guineense de Protecção Ecológica (LIPE): Bairro Missirá, CP 448, Bissau; tel. and fax 252309; f. 1991; ecology party; Pres. Alhaje BUBACAR DJALÓ.

Partido Africano da Independência da Guiné e Cabo Verde (PAIGC): CP 106, Bissau; f. 1956; fmrly the ruling party in both Guinea-Bissau and Cape Verde; although Cape Verde withdrew from the PAIGC following the coup in Guinea-Bissau in Nov. 1980, Guinea-Bissau has retained the party name and initials; Pres. Commdr JOÃO BERNARDO VIEIRA; Sec.-Gen. MANUEL SATURNINO DA COSTA.

Partido da Convergência Democrática (PCD): Bissau; Leader VÍTOR MANDINGA.

Partido para a Renovação Social (PRS): Bissau; f. 1992 by breakaway faction of the FDS; officially registered in Oct. 1992; Leader KOUMBA YALLA.

Partido Social Democrático (PSD): Bissau; f. 1995 by breakaway faction of RGB—MB; Leader JOAQUIM BALDÉ; Sec.-Gen. GASPAR FERNANDES.

Partido Unido Social Democrático (PUSD): Bissau; f. 1991; officially registered in Jan. 1992; Leader VÍTOR SAÚDE MARIA.

Resistência da Guiné-Bissau—Movimento Bah-Fatah (RGB—MB): Bissau; f. 1986 in Lisbon, Portugal, as Resistência da Guiné-Bissau—Movimento Bafatá; adopted present name prior to official registration in Dec. 1991; maintains offices in Paris (France), Dakar (Senegal) and Praia (Cape Verde); Chair. DOMINGOS FERNANDES GOMES.

União para a Mudança (UM): Bissau; f. 1994 as coalition to contest presidential and legislative elections, re-formed April 1995; Pres. JOÃO DA COSTA (PRD); Sec.-Gen. AMINE MICHEL SAAD (PDP); comprises following parties:

Frente Democrática (FD): Bissau; f. 1991; officially registered in Nov. 1991; Pres. CANJURA INJAI; Sec.-Gen. MARCELINO BATISTA.

Frente Democrática Social (FDS): Bissau; f. 1991; legalized in Dec. 1991; Leader RAFAEL BARBOSA.

Movimento para a Unidade e a Democracia (MUDE): Bissau; officially registered in Aug. 1992; Leader FILINTO VAZ MARTINS.

Partido Democrático do Progresso (PDP): Bissau; f. 1991; officially registered in Aug. 1992; Pres. of Nat. Council AMINE MICHEL SAAD.

Partido de Renovação e Desenvolvimento (PRD): Bissau; f. 1992 as the 'Group of 121' by PAIGC dissidents; officially registered in Oct. 1992; Leaders MANUEL RAMBOUT BARCELOS, AGNELO REGALA, JOÃO DA COSTA.

Diplomatic Representation

EMBASSIES IN GUINEA-BISSAU

Brazil: Rua São Tomé, Bissau; tel. 201327; telex 245; fax 201317; Ambassador: MARCELO DIDIER.

China (Taiwan): Avda Amílcar Cabral 35, CP 66, Bissau; tel. 201501; fax 201466.

Cuba: Rua Joaquim N'Com 1, Bissau; tel. 213579; Ambassador: DIOSDADO FERNÁNDEZ GONZÁLEZ.

Egypt: Avda Omar Torrijos, Rua 15, CP 72, Bissau; tel. 213642; Ambassador: MOHAMED REDA FARAHAT.

France: Avda 14 de Novembro, Bairro de Penha, Bissau; tel. 251031; fax 253142; Ambassador: FRANÇOIS CHAPPELLET.

Guinea: Rua 14, no. 9, CP 396, Bissau; tel. 212681; Ambassador: MOHAMED LAMINÉ FODÉ.

Libya: Rua 16, CP 362, Bissau; tel. 212006; Representative: DOKALI ALI MUSTAFA.

Portugal: Rua Cidade de Lisboa 6, Apdo 276, Bissau; tel. 201261; telex 248; fax 201269; Ambassador: JOÃO PEDRO SILVEIRA DE CARVALHO.

Russia: Avda 14 de Novembro, Bissau; tel. 251036; fax 251050; Ambassador: VIKTOR M. ZELENOV.

Senegal: Bissau; tel. 212636; Ambassador: AHMED TIJANE KANE.

USA: CP 297, 1067 Bissau; tel. 252273; fax 252282; Ambassador: PEGGY BLACKFORD.

Judicial System

Judges of the Supreme Court are appointed by the Conselho Superior da Magistratura.

President of the Supreme Court: MAMADU SALIU DJALO PIRES.

Religion

About 54% of the population are animists, 38% are Muslims and 8% are Christians, mainly Roman Catholics.

CHRISTIANITY

The Roman Catholic Church

Guinea-Bissau comprises a single diocese, directly responsible to the Holy See. The Bishop participates in the Episcopal Conference of Senegal, Mauritania, Cape Verde and Guinea-Bissau, currently based in Senegal. At 31 December 1995 there were an estimated 125,637 adherents in the country.

Bishop of Bissau: Rt Rev. SETTIMIO ARTURO FERRAZZETTA, CP 20, 1001 Bissau; tel. 251057; fax 251058.

The Press

As part of a new national policy on information, a law defining the status of journalists was approved by the Council of Ministers in December 1989. In 1991 the National Assembly approved laws allowing greater press freedom.

Baguerra: Bissau; owned by the Partido da Convergência Democrática.

Banobero: Bissau; weekly; Dir FERNANDO JORGE PEREIRA.

Nô Pintcha: Bissau; daily; Dir Sra CABRAL; circ. 6,000.

NEWS AGENCY

Agência Noticiosa da Guinea (ANG): CP 248, Bissau; tel. 212151; telex 96900.

Radio and Television

According to UNESCO estimates, there were 42,000 radio receivers in use in 1994. An experimental television service began transmissions in November 1989. Regional radio stations were to be established at Bafatá, Cantchungo and Catió in 1990. In September 1990 Radio Freedom, which broadcast on behalf of the PAIGC during Portuguese rule and had ceased operations in 1974, resumed transmissions.

Radiodifusão Nacional da República da Guiné-Bissau: CP 191, Bissau; govt-owned; broadcasts in Portuguese on short-wave, MW and FM; Dir Francisco Barreto.

Rádio Pidjiguiti: f. 1995; independent.

Finance

(cap. = capital; m. = million; brs = branches; amounts in Guinea pesos)

BANKING

The decentralization of banking activities began in 1989.

Central Bank

Banque Centrale des Etats de l'Afrique de l'Ouest (BCEAO): Avda Amílcar Cabral, CP 38, Bissau; tel. 212434; telex 241; fax 201305; headquarters in Dakar, Senegal; f. 1955; bank of issue and central bank for the member states of the Union économique et monétaire ouest-africaine (UEMOA); cap. and res 657,592m. (Dec. 1995); Gov. Charles Konan Banny.

Other Banks

Banco Internacional da Guiné-Bissau: Avda Amílcar Cabral, CP 74, Bissau; tel. 213662; telex 204; fax 201033; f. 1989; cap. 3,260m. (Dec. 1993); 26% state-owned, 25% by Guinea-Bissau enterprises and private interests, 49% by Portuguese interests; Chair. Alvito José da Silva; Gen. Man. José Aníbal C. Tavares.

Banco Totta e Açores (Portugal): Rua 19 de Setembro 15, CP 618, Bissau; tel. 214794; fax 201591; Gen. Man. Carlos Madeira.

Caixa de Crédito da Guiné: Bissau; govt savings and loan institution.

Caixa Económica Postal: Avda Amílcar Cabral, Bissau; tel. 212999; telex 979; postal savings institution.

STOCK EXCHANGE

Côte d'Ivoire's Bourse des Valeurs d'Abidjan was scheduled to become a regional stock exchange, serving the member states of the UEMOA.

INSURANCE

In 1979 it was announced that a single state-owned insurer was to replace the Portuguese company Ultramarina.

Trade and Industry

The Government has actively pursued a policy of small-scale industrialization to compensate for the almost total lack of manufacturing capacity. Following independence, it adopted a comprehensive programme of state control, and in 1976 acquired 80% of the capital of a Portuguese company, **Ultramarina**, a large firm specializing in a wide range of trading activities, including ship-repairing and agricultural processing. The Government also holds a major interest in the **CICER** brewery and has created a joint-venture company with the Portuguese concern **SACOR** to sell petroleum products. Since 1975 three fishing companies have been formed with foreign participation: **GUIALP** (with Algeria), **Estrela do Mar** (with the former USSR) and **SEMAPESCA** (with France; now bankrupt). In December 1976 **SOCOTRAM**, an enterprise for the sale and processing of timber, was inaugurated. It operates a factory in Bissau for the production of wooden tiles and co-ordinates sawmills and carpentry shops throughout the country. In 1979 the **Empresa de Automóveis da Guiné** opened a car-assembly plant at Bissau, capable of producing 500 vehicles per year. A plan to restructure several public enterprises was proceeding in the mid-1990s, as part of the Government's programme to attract private investment.

Empresa Nacional de Pesquisas e Exploração Petrolíferas e Mineiras (PETROMINAS): Rua Eduardo Mondlane 58, Bissau; tel. 212279; state-owned; regulates all prospecting for hydrocarbons and other minerals; Dir-Gen. António Cardoso.

CHAMBER OF COMMERCE

Associação Comercial, Industrial e Agrícola da Guiné-Bissau: Bissau; f. 1987.

TRADE UNION

União Nacional dos Trabalhadores da Guiné (UNTG): 13 Avda Ovai di Vievra, CP 98, Bissau; tel. 212094; telex 900; Sec.-Gen. Mário Mendes Correa.

Legislation permitting the formation of other trade unions was approved by the National People's Assembly in October 1991.

Transport

RAILWAYS

There are no railways in Guinea-Bissau.

ROADS

In 1995, according to International Road Federation estimates, there were about 4,350 km of roads, of which 444 km were paved. A major road rehabilitation scheme is proceeding, and in 1989 donors provided US $31.3m. for road projects. An international road, linking Guinea-Bissau with The Gambia and Senegal, is planned. In 1989 the Islamic Development Bank granted more than US $2m. towards the construction of a 111-km road linking north and south and a 206-km road between Guinea-Bissau and Guinea. A five-year rehabilitation project, funded by international donors, was due to begin in 1990. The programme included repair work on roads, the management and supply of equipment to transport companies, and town planning.

SHIPPING

Under a major port modernization project, the main port at Bissau was to be renovated and expanded, and four river ports were to be upgraded to enable barges to load and unload at low tide. The total cost of the project was estimated at US $47.4m., and finance was provided by the World Bank and Arab funds. In 1986 work began on a new river port at N'Pungda, which was to be partly funded by the Netherlands.

CIVIL AVIATION

There is an international airport at Bissau, which there are plans to expand, and 10 smaller airports serving the interior.

Transportes Aéreos da Guiné-Bissau (TAGB): Aeroporto Osvaldo Vieira, CP 111, Bissau; tel. 201277; telex 268; fax 251536; f. 1977; domestic services and flights to France, Portugal, the Canary Islands (Spain), Guinea and Senegal; Dir Capt. Eduardo Pinto Lopes.

Tourism

Centro de Informação e Turismo: CP 294, Bissau; state tourism and information service.

Defence

In August 1996 the armed forces totalled 9,250 men: army 6,800, navy 350, air force 100, and the paramilitary gendarmerie 2,000.

Defence Expenditure: Estimated at 130,300m. Guinea pesos in 1995.

Commander-in-Chief of the Armed Forces: Commdr João Bernardo Vieira.

Education

Education is officially compulsory only for the period of primary schooling, which begins at seven years of age and lasts for six years. Secondary education, beginning at the age of 13, lasts for up to five years (a first cycle of three years and a second of two years). In 1988 the total enrolment at primary and secondary schools was equivalent to 38% of the school-age population (males 49%; females 27%). In that year enrolment at primary schools of children in the relevant age-group was equivalent to 60% (males 77%; females 42%). The comparable figures for secondary schools was 7% (males 9%; females 4%). Expenditure on education by the central government in 1989 was 5,051m. pesos (2.7% of total spending). In 1997 the IDA approved a credit of US $14.3m. for a project to expand and upgrade the education system. Mass literacy campaigns have been introduced: according to UNESCO estimates, the average rate of adult illiteracy in 1980 was 60.9% (males 46.6%; females 74.4%), but by 1995 the rate had declined to 45.1% (males 32.0%; females 57.5%). In 1991 plans were announced for the establishment of the country's first university.

Bibliography

Andreini, J.-C., and Lambert, M.-L. *La Guinée-Bissau.* Paris, 1978.

Cabral, A. *Unity and Struggle* (collected writings) (trans. by M. Wolfers). London, Heinemann Educational, 1979.

Cabral, L. *Crónica da Libertação.* Lisbon, O Jornal, 1984.

Chabal, P. *Amílcar Cabral—Revolutionary Leadership and People's War.* Cambridge, Cambridge University Press, 1983.

Chaliand, G. *Lutte armée en Afrique.* Paris, Maspero, 1967. As *Armed Struggle in Africa.* New York and London, Monthly Review Press, 1969.

Davidson, B. *The Liberation of Guiné.* Harmondsworth, Penguin Books, 1969.

No Fist is Big Enough to Hide the Sky: The Liberation of Guinea-Bissau and Cape Verde. 2nd Edn. London, Zed Press, 1984.

Fisas Armengol, V. *Amílcar Cabral y la Independencia de Guinea-Bissau.* Barcelona, Nova Terra, 1974.

Freire, P. *Pedagogy in Progress: Letters to Guinea-Bissau.* London, W. & R. Publ. Co-operative, 1978.

Galli, R., and Jones, D. *Guinea-Bissau: Politics, Economics and Society.* New York and London, Pinter Publishers, 1987.

Lobban, R. A. *Historical Dictionary of the Republics of Guinea-Bissau and Cape Verde.* Folkestone, Kent, Bailey Bros and Swinfen, 1981.

Lobban, R. A., and Mendy, P. K. *Historical Dictionary of Guinea-Bissau.* 3rd Edn. Lanham, MD, Scarecrow Press, 1996.

Lopes, C. *Guinea-Bissau: From Liberation Struggle to Independent Statehood.* Boulder, CO, Westview Press, 1987.

Mettas, J. *La Guinée portugaise au vingtième siècle.* Paris, Académie des Sciences d'Outre-mer, 1984.

da Mota Teixeira, A. *Guiné Portuguesa.* 2 vols. Lisbon, 1964.

Núñez, B. *Dictionary of Portuguese-African Civilization.* Vol. I. London, Hans Zell, 1995.

Paulini, T. *Guinea-Bissau, Nachkoloniale Entwicklung eines Agrarstaates.* Göttingen, 1984.

Pereira, L. T., and Moita, L. *Guiné-Bissau: Três Anos de Indepêndencia.* Lisbon, CIDAC, 1976.

Rimmer, D. *The Economies of West Africa.* London, Weidenfeld and Nicolson, 1984.

Rudebeck, L. *Guinea-Bissau.* Uppsala, 1974.

Problèmes de pouvoir populaire et de développement. Uppsala, Scandinavian Institute of African Studies, Research Report 63.

Urdang, S. *Fighting Two Colonialisms.* London, Monthly Review Press, 1979.

World Bank. *Guinea-Bissau: A Prescription for Comprehensive Adjustment.* Washington DC, 1988.

KENYA

Physical and Social Geography

W. T. W. MORGAN

PHYSICAL FEATURES

The total area of the Republic of Kenya is 580,367 sq km (224,081 sq miles) or 569,137 sq km (219,745 sq miles) excluding inland waters (mostly Lake Turkana and part of Lake Victoria). Kenya is bisected by the Equator and extends from approximately 4°N to 4°S and 34°E to 41°E.

The physical basis of the country is composed of extensive erosional plains, cut across ancient crystalline rocks of Pre-Cambrian age. These are very gently warped—giving an imperceptible rise from sea level towards the highlands of the interior which have their base at about 1,500 m above sea-level. The highlands are dominated by isolated extinct volcanoes, including Mt Kenya (5,200 m) and Mt Elgon (4,321 m), while outpourings of Tertiary lavas have created plateaux at 2,500–3,000 m. The Great Rift Valley bisects the country from north to south and is at its most spectacular in the highlands, where it is some 65 km across and bounded by escarpments 600–900 m high. The trough is dotted with lakes and volcanoes which are inactive but generally associated with steam vents and hot springs. Westwards the plains incline beneath the waters of Lake Victoria, and eastwards they have been down-warped beneath a sediment-filled basin, which is attracting exploration for petroleum.

CLIMATE

Although Kenya is on the Equator, its range of altitude results in temperate conditions in the highlands above 1,500 m, with temperatures which become limiting to cultivation at about 2,750 m, while Mt Kenya supports small glaciers. Average temperatures may be roughly calculated by taking a sea-level mean of 26°C and deducting 1.7°C for each 300 m of altitude. For most of the country, however, rainfall is more critical than temperature. Only 15% of the area of Kenya can be expected to receive a reliable rainfall adequate for cultivation (750 mm in four years out of five). Rainfall is greatest at the coast and in the west of the country, near Lake Victoria and in the highlands, but the extensive plains below 1,200 m are arid or semi-arid. In the region of Lake Victoria and in the highlands west of the Rift Valley, rain falls in one long rainy season. East of the Rift Valley there are two distinct seasons: the long rains (March–May) and the short rains (September–October).

NATURAL RESOURCES

The high rainfall areas tend to be intensively cultivated on a small-scale semi-subsistence basis with varying amounts of cash cropping. Food crops are in great variety, but most important and widespread are maize, sorghum, cassava and bananas. The principal cash crops, which provide the majority of exports, are tea, coffee (*arabica*), pyrethrum and sisal. The first three are particularly suited to the highlands and their introduction was associated with the large-scale farming on the alienated lands of the former 'White Highlands'. The herds of cattle, goats, sheep and camels of the dry plains are as yet of little commercial value and support a low density of mainly subsistence farmers.

Forests are largely restricted to the rainy upper levels of the highlands, where the limited output possible from the natural forests led to the introduction of plantations of conifers and of wattle. Fisheries are of local importance around Lake Victoria and are of great potential at Lake Turkana.

Soda ash is mined at Lake Magadi in the Rift Valley. Deposits of fluorspar, rubies, gold, salt, vermiculite and limestone are also exploited. However, mineral resources make a negligible contribution to Kenya's economy.

POPULATION AND CULTURE

A total population of 10,942,705 was recorded at the census of August 1969. At the August 1979 census the figure had risen to 15,327,061, excluding estimated underenumeration of 5%. The provisional results of the August 1989 census (also believed to be underenumerated) indicated a total population of 21,443,636. At mid-1995 the population was officially estimated at 30,522,000. The resultant overall density of 52.6 inhabitants per sq km is extremely unevenly distributed, with approximately three-quarters of the population contained in only 10% of the area; densities approach 400 per sq km on the small proportion of the land that is cultivable. About 15% of the population reside in urban areas, and most of these are in Nairobi (population provisionally estimated to be 1,346,000 at the 1989 census) and Mombasa (provisionally estimated to be 465,000 at the 1989 census). The towns also contain the majority of the non-African minorities of some 89,185 Asians, 34,560 Europeans and 41,595 Arabs (1989 census, provisional results).

Kenya has been a point of convergence of major population movements in the past, and, on a linguistic and cultural basis, the people have been divided into Bantu, Nilotic, Nilo-Hamitic (Paranilotic) and Cushitic groups. Persian and Arab influence at the coast is reflected in the Islamic culture. Kiswahili is the official language, although English, Kikuyu and Luo are widely understood.

Recent History

ALAN RAKE

COLONIAL RULE TO THE KENYATTA ERA, 1895–1978

Kenya, formerly known as British East Africa, was declared a British protectorate in 1895, primarily to secure a route to Uganda. Subsequent white settlement met with significant African armed resistance by 1914, and by the early 1920s some African political activity had begun to be organized, particularly among the Kikuyu in the capital, Nairobi, and among the Luo. Local native councils were introduced in 1925. By the 1940s the white settler farmers had achieved considerable prosperity, cultivating tea and coffee for export. However, agriculture in the African lands could not sustain the rapidly-increasing population, and many migrated to the towns in search of work.

In 1944 the Kenya African Union (KAU), an African nationalist organization, was formed, demanding African access to white-owned land. The movement comprised the educated élite of several tribes, but attracted little popular support, except among the Kikuyu. In 1947 Jomo Kenyatta (a Kikuyu and previously the KAU's representative in the United Kingdom) became president of the organization. From 1952–56 a campaign of terrorism was conducted by the Mau Mau, a predominantly Kikuyu secret society. A state of emergency was declared by the British authorities in October 1952. In June 1953 Kenyatta was imprisoned for alleged involvement in Mau Mau activities, and the KAU was banned. All political activity was proscribed until 1955; nevertheless, during the period of this ban, two Luo political activists, Tom Mboya and Oginga Odinga, came to prominence. In 1957 African members were elected to the legislative council, on a limited franchise (covering 60% of the adult African population). Mboya was the unofficial leader of these members, who refused to accept government posts and demanded a universal adult franchise.

The state of emergency was rescinded in January 1960. A transitional constitution, drafted in January and February of that year, allowed Africans a large majority in the legislative council, and legalized political parties. African members of the council subsequently formed the Kenya African National Union (KANU). James Gichuru, a former president of the KAU, was elected acting president of KANU, and Mboya and Odinga were also elected to the party's leadership.

At a general election in 1961 KANU candidates won a majority of seats in the legislative council, but refused to form an administration before the release of Kenyatta. A coalition government was formed under Ronald Ngala. Following his release in August 1961, Kenyatta assumed the presidency of KANU. KANU won a decisive victory at the general election of May 1963, and Kenyatta became prime minister in June, when internal self-government began. Kenya became independent on 12 December. The country was declared a republic (with Kenyatta as president) exactly one year later. After independence Kenya remained dependent on the United Kingdom for military assistance and for financial aid to compensate European settlers for their land.

By 1965 there was a clear division within KANU, between the party's 'conservative' wing, led by Mboya, and the 'radicals', led by Odinga, who was the country's vice-president until his resignation in April 1966. In 1966 Odinga formed a new party, the Kenya People's Union (KPU), which accused the government of furthering the interests of a small privileged class. Legislation requiring the 30 KPU members of the house of representatives to contest by-elections was immediately approved: only nine KPU members were re-elected. Security legislation was also enacted, giving the government powers of censorship and the right to hold suspects in detention without trial. In December Kenya's two legislative chambers, the senate and the house of representatives, were amalgamated to form a unicameral national assembly. Daniel arap Moi, the minister of home affairs, became vice-president in January 1967.

In July 1969 Mboya (then minister for economic planning and secretary-general of KANU) was assassinated by a Kikuyu. Luo demonstrations against Kenyatta followed, and in the same week the KPU was banned and Odinga was placed in detention, where he remained for 15 months. At a general election in December, in which only KANU candidates took part, two-thirds of the members of the previous national assembly lost their seats.

During the early 1970s President Kenyatta became increasingly reclusive and autocratic, although he was elected, unopposed, for a third five-year term in September 1974. At a general election in October (in which, once again, only KANU members were presented as candidates), more than one-half of the members of the previous assembly were defeated. President Kenyatta died in August 1978.

THE MOI PRESIDENCY

Programme of Reform

With the support of Charles Njonjo, the attorney-general and an influential associate of the elderly Kenyatta, the presidency passed to Daniel arap Moi, the vice-president, in October 1978. A programme to reform Kenya's corrupt bureaucracy was initiated, and in December all political detainees were released. President Moi, a Kalenjin, emphasized regional representation in the new style of government; nevertheless, Odinga and four other former KPU members were barred from participating in the general election of November 1979. This election, however, marked the end of the president's period of grace: student protest began, with predominantly Luo participation, prompted by the KPU bannings.

In early 1980 Moi succeeded in bringing Odinga and his substantial following back into KANU. Nevertheless, Odinga continued to attack the use of military facilities in Kenya by the USA, and to denounce the government's economic management. In April Njonjo resigned as attorney-general, but subsequently returned to the government as minister of home and constitutional affairs. A 'de-tribalization' campaign was introduced in mid-1980, whereby virtually every Kenyan organization title which had a tribal implication was renamed.

During 1981 disagreements between the president's two close associates, Njonjo and Mwai Kibaki, the vice-president, became unbridgeable; intense factional disputes also developed between their respective supporters. Kibaki eventually won the power struggle, gaining Njonjo's home affairs portfolio at a cabinet reshuffle in February 1982. Meanwhile, Moi appeared to be growing increasingly intolerant of criticism. In May 1982 Odinga and another former MP were expelled from KANU for advocating the formation of a new political party, and in the following month Kenya constitutionally became a one-party state.

Coup Attempt

In August 1982 a section of the Kenya air force attempted to overthrow the government. The revolt was swiftly crushed by the army, although sporadic firefights and looting continued for several days. The official death toll was given as 159, but unofficial sources asserted that the true total was much higher.

The instigators of the revolt (who cited corruption and the restriction of freedom as the causes of the insurrection) escaped to Tanzania, but were subsequently deported to Kenya and sentenced to death. Meanwhile, about 2,000 air force personnel and 1,000 civilians were detained, the air force was disbanded, and Nairobi university (which had been a focus of support for the rebellion) was closed. The commander of the air force, the commissioner of police and the commandant of the General Service Unit, an élite military force, were dismissed and detained. By March 1983 the government had sufficiently recovered from the political paralysis which followed the revolt to suspend the death sentences passed on its perpetrators and to grant an amnesty to most of the remaining detainees. The considerable degree of Luo involvement in the coup attempt also had political repercussions: Odinga was placed under house arrest (from which he was freed in October 1983), and the Luo information minister, Peter Aringo, was dismissed. Conciliatory moves, aimed at some of the sources of political unrest, included a new code of conduct for politicians in office, and an investigation of the civil service.

The 'Njonjo Affair'

The country was distracted from the persistent mood of political uncertainty by the spectacular fall from power of Charles Njonjo. In May 1983 Moi alleged that certain unspecified foreign powers were grooming an unnamed Kenyan politician to take over as president. Moi then announced that a general election would be held in September—a year earlier than constitutionally required—in order to 'cleanse the system' of any corruption. After Njonjo's name was mentioned in the national assembly in connection with the allegation, there followed a storm of accusation and invective against him. Denying all charges, Njonjo was suspended from the cabinet and from KANU, and in June he resigned his seat in the assembly, while the president appointed a judicial commission to inquire into the 'Njonjo affair'. Meanwhile, the September election, which returned Moi unopposed for a second term as president, attracted only 48% of the electorate. A major cabinet reshuffle followed the election. The Njonjo inquiry commission began its work in October 1983 and was eventually closed in August 1984, when Njonjo withdrew from public life. When the commission's report finally appeared, Njonjo was pardoned but not rehabilitated. The immediate aftermath of the inquiry was a purge of figures associated with the Njonjo faction.

Moi's Authority Reasserted

While intensive press coverage of the Njonjo inquiry had been absorbing public attention, there were indications that the coup attempt had persuaded the Moi government of the need to respond more flexibly to opposition. The problem of student opposition was approached on several fronts. A programme of national youth service, originally announced soon after Moi's accession but then indefinitely postponed, was finally introduced in 1984. During that year, a controversial restructuring of the education syllabus was also introduced, placing renewed emphasis on technical and vocational studies. During 1984, after the education minister had advocated 'dialogue' between students and government, there were unprecedented meetings between the president and student leaders at Nairobi university. Nevertheless, intermittent outbreaks of student unrest subsequently continued to occur.

During the progress of the Njonjo inquiry, there were also signs that Moi intended henceforth to control his government within certain firm limits, although against a background of freer public debate than had been possible before the attempted coup. Presidential authority over the parliamentary front bench was reaffirmed when cabinet ministers (over 40% of members of the assembly) were required to endorse a letter from the president, stating that they were not at liberty to criticize, or differ from, the government outside immediate government circles. Some conciliation was offered to the political left wing with a presidential amnesty for fugitives abroad.

After dismissals, in late 1984, of prominent civil servants for abuse of office, rationalizations of major parastatal organizations, and a minor cabinet reshuffle in January 1985 (followed by a reshuffle of appointments in the provincial administration), political life in early 1985 was dominated by a recruitment drive to revitalize the membership of KANU as a prelude to local and national KANU elections, held in June.

The 'Mwakenya Conspiracy'

In March 1986 it was revealed that several Kenyans had been detained under the provisions of the Public Security Act, and that others were to face charges of publishing seditious documents: during the ensuing 12 months, a 'conspiracy' known as Mwakenya (a Swahili acronym for the 'Union of Nationalists to Liberate Kenya') became the focal point of Kenyan politics. Although Moi alleged that Mwakenya comprised the same 'tribalistic élite' that had fostered the 1982 coup attempt, it became apparent that the movement embraced a wide spectrum of opposition to the Moi presidency.

In August 1986 the annual KANU party conference approved a 'queue-voting' system to replace the secret ballot in the preliminary stage of a general election. The new procedure, whereby voters were to queue publicly in support of the candidate of their choice, was opposed by church leaders on the grounds that it would discourage voting by church ministers, civil servants and others whose political impartiality was necessary for their work. In December the national assembly adopted constitutional amendments which increased the power of the president by transferring control of the civil service to the president's office, and reduced the independence of the judiciary by giving the head of state the power to dismiss the attorney-general and the auditor-general without endorsement by a legal tribunal. No votes were cast in opposition to the amendments, but two MPs who had openly questioned the virtue of the changes were briefly detained in January 1987. By early 1987, more than 100 people had been detained in connection with Mwakenya, some of them receiving lengthy terms of imprisonment, and the political climate had become reminiscent of the months preceding the 1982 coup attempt. In April 1987 Odinga, still the most prestigious opponent of the government, made an unprecedented public declaration of opposition to Moi's political management; the government, opting for caution, took no action against Odinga, who repeated his criticism of the Moi regime in July and August. The administration did, however, make allegations of involvement with Mwakenya against several influential church leaders.

Although the government may have over-reacted in its anxieties about Mwakenya, the movement none the less represented genuine undercurrents of discontent. Its followers comprised a broad spectrum of opposition elements, including Kikuyu peasants, urban intellectuals (often, but not exclusively, Luo), and elements of the established political network. Most threatening for the government was the fact that Mwakenya was apparently confined to no particular region.

Political Retrenchment

From early 1987, international criticism of Moi's government was intensified, as further allegations emerged of human rights abuses in Kenya. The government's response to this criticism reflected, for the most part, its continuing hostility both to external pressure and internal opposition. In April, however, Moi ordered the dismissal of members of the police force found to be guilty of corruption, criminal activity or brutality. Two months later the minister of foreign affairs was replaced, reportedly on the grounds that he was failing effectively to defend Kenya's record on human rights. In July Amnesty International published a report which accused the Kenyan authorities of seeking to silence political opposition by detention without trial and by torture.

In October and November 1987 serious rioting broke out among Muslims in Mombasa, following a government ban on an Islamic public meeting. The government's fear of destabilization by foreign powers was reflected in the detention, in November, of seven student leaders, one of whom was imprisoned for allegedly spying on behalf of Libya. These arrests led to mass student demonstrations during December; clashes between students and riot police resulted, to the dismay of the government, in the brief detention and alleged mistreatment of four Western journalists. Nairobi university was temporarily closed, and its student organization banned.

In early 1988 the government made some minor concessions to international criticism of its conduct towards its opponents. In January Justus Ole Tipis, the minister of state for security, was demoted following a controversy over the brief detention of two US human rights activists who were allegedly in possession of 'subversive' documents, and in February the president ordered the release of nine political detainees, several of whom later claimed that they had been tortured while in custody.

A general election to the national assembly, held in March 1988, provided only limited indication of Moi's popularity. Prior to the parliamentary polling, the president was returned unopposed for a third term of office. The open-air 'queue-voting' technique of candidate selection, conducted in February, produced a KANU-approved list to contest 123 of the 188 elective seats (65 candidates, including the president, were returned unopposed). Potential candidates who were unpopular with the Moi administration (such as Odinga) were excluded from seeking election, and seats were largely contested on local and personality issues rather than on national policies. In an extensive government reshuffle following the election, Mwai Kibaki was demoted from the vice-presidency to the post of minister of health (it was widely believed that the president was disquieted by Kibaki's popularity among the Kikuyu), and replaced by Josephat Karanja, a relatively obscure politician with no popular following.

The independence of the judiciary from the executive was effectively removed in July 1988, when the national assembly assented to constitutional amendments which allowed the president to dismiss judges at will, and which increased the period of detention, from 24 hours to 14 days, of people suspected of capital offences. These measures led to an intensification of criticism of the government's record on human rights, especially from church leaders and lawyers. Moi subsequently accused foreigners of acting in concert with Kenyan church leaders against the government. Moi indicated that he was considering the arrests of 'roaming' foreigners and the curtailment of freedom of worship.

Elections to the leadership of KANU were held in September 1988; Moi was confirmed as president of the party, and Kibaki was replaced by Karanja as party vice-president. Allegations of malpractice in the KANU elections were made by Kibaki, among others, and in December Kenneth Matiba, the minister of transport and communications, resigned and was expelled from KANU after criticizing the conduct of the party elections.

Karanja's period of influence was short-lived: in February 1989 he became the subject of a campaign of vilification by fellow MPs, which culminated, in late April, in a unanimous parliamentary vote expressing 'no confidence' in him. He was widely accused of attempting to establish himself as a rival to President Moi and of pursuing tribal interests. In addition, he encountered allegations from some quarters of conspiring with the Ugandan government to destabilize Kenya. At the beginning of May Karanja, who had denied the charges against him, resigned from the posts of Kenyan vice-president and vice-president of KANU. Moi appointed Prof. George Saitoti, the minister of finance, as the country's new vice-president and announced a major cabinet reshuffle. Shortly afterwards, Karanja resigned from the national assembly, and in June he was expelled from KANU.

In June 1989 Moi, who was clearly sensitive to continuing international criticism of his human rights record, released all political prisoners who were being detained without trial, and offered an amnesty to dissidents living in exile. While this action was applauded by Amnesty International, that organization repeated allegations that many convicted Kenyan political prisoners had received unfair trials. In November part of Nairobi university was closed, owing to student unrest.

In February 1990, the minister of foreign affairs and international co-operation, Dr Robert Ouko, died in suspicious circumstances. Accusations that the Moi administration was implicated in Ouko's death led to anti-government riots in Nairobi and the western town of Kisumu. Moi responded by banning all demonstrations from the beginning of March, and requested an investigation by British police into Dr Ouko's death (the results of this were presented to the Kenyan authorities in September, and in October Moi ordered a judicial inquiry into the affair). In April the minister of information and broadcasting, Waruru Kanja, was dismissed, following allegations on his part that Ouko's death was politically motivated. Pressure on the government to terminate KANU's political monopoly increased in May with the formation of a broad alliance of intellectuals, lawyers and church leaders (under the leadership of the former cabinet minister, Kenneth Matiba) which sought to legalize political opposition. In July Moi ordered the arrests of several of the alliance's leaders, including Matiba and Raila Odinga, the son of the former vice-president. Serious rioting ensued in Nairobi and its environs, and sporadic unrest was reported in the hinterland of the Kikuyu-dominated Central province; more than 20 people were killed in the disturbances, and more than 1,000 rioters were reportedly arrested. The KANU leadership responded to international criticism by denouncing the advocates of multi-party political reform as 'tribalists' in the pay of 'foreign masters', seeking to undermine national unity. Moi accused the US government of interfering in the country's internal politics after one of the dissident leaders was granted refuge in the US embassy in Nairobi. In August a prominent Anglican bishop, who had publicly criticized the government, died in a car crash, following threats to his life from members of the cabinet; the most senior of these, Peter Okondo, the minister of labour, subsequently resigned his post. The government ordered a public inquest into the bishop's death. In November Amnesty International reported that several hundreds of people detained at the time of the July riots remained in custody, and accused the Kenyan authorities of torturing some prisoners. During late 1990 seven people were arrested and charged with treason.

In December 1990, having considered the findings of a political review committee that had recently tested public opinion, KANU abolished the system of 'queue-voting' approved by the party in 1986, and resolved to cease expulsions of party members. In January 1991 KANU agreed to readmit to the party a number of people who had previously been expelled. Oginga Odinga founded the National Democratic Party (NDP) in the following month, and was subsequently harrassed by the Kenyan authorities: he was arrested briefly in May, shortly before the court of appeal rejected his application to register the NDP as a political party.

In March 1991 a prominent human rights lawyer and magazine editor was arrested and charged with sedition, having accused the president of promoting the interests of his native Kalenjin tribe, and having published the manifesto of the banned NDP. The charge was withdrawn in May, following widespread exposure of the case in the international media. In that month Moi reiterated his offer of an amnesty for dissident Kenyans in exile abroad. Soon afterwards the government announced the release from imprisonment of Kenneth Matiba, who was reportedly suffering from ill health. In June several religious leaders and lawyers formed a body, known as the Justice and Peace Convention, which aimed to promote freedom of political expression. In the following month four of those arrested during the unrest of July 1990 were found guilty of sedition and each sentenced to seven years' imprisonment. During July 1991 the human rights organization, Africa Watch, published allegations that the government was permitting the torture of detainees and exerting undue influence on the judiciary. At the beginning of August six opposition leaders, including Oginga Odinga, formed a new political movement, the Forum for the Restoration of Democracy (FORD); the government immediately outlawed the grouping, but it continued to operate.

In September 1991 the judicial inquiry into the death of Dr Ouko was presented with evidence that he had been murdered. In mid-November Moi dismissed Nicholas Biwott from the post of minister of industry, in response to widespread suspicion that the latter was implicated in the alleged assassination. Shortly afterwards Moi ordered the dissolution of the judicial inquiry. A suspect was eventually charged with the murder, but was acquitted in July 1994.

In November 1991 several members of FORD were arrested prior to a planned pro-democracy rally in Nairobi; protestors at the rally (which took place despite a government ban) were dispersed by the security forces. The Kenyan authorities were condemned internationally for suppressing the demonstration, and most of the opposition activists who had been detained were subsequently released. In late November bilateral and multilateral creditors suspended aid to Kenya for 1992, pending the acceleration of both economic and political reforms; the donors emphasized, in particular, the desirability of an improvement in Kenya's human rights record.

Political Pluralism and Ethnic Tensions

In early December 1991 a special conference of KANU delegates, chaired by President Moi, acceded to the domestic and international pressure for reform, and resolved to permit the introduction of a multi-party political system. Soon afterwards the national assembly approved appropriate amendments to the constitution. Several new political parties were registered from the beginning of 1992.

In mid-December 1991 Moi dismissed the minister of manpower development and employment, Peter Aringo, who had publicly criticized the government; Aringo subsequently resigned as chairman of KANU. Later in that month Mwai Kibaki, the minister of health and former vice-president, resigned from the government, in protest against alleged electoral malpractice by KANU and against the unsatisfactory outcome of the judicial inquiry into the death of Dr Ouko. Kibaki immediately founded the Democratic Party. Five other ministers and deputy ministers resigned their posts in December 1991 and January 1992.

During the first half of 1992 as many as 2,000 people were reportedly killed and some 20,000 made homeless as a result of tribal clashes in western Kenya. Opposition leaders accused the government of covertly inciting the violence as a means of discrediting the progress towards a multi-party political system, while the government countered that the exacerbation of existing ethnic tensions was an inevitable result of the new political freedoms. In March the government banned all political rallies, purportedly in a bid to suppress the unrest, and restrictions were placed on the activities of the press. A two-day general strike, organized by FORD to demand the release of political prisoners and the removal of the ban on political rallies, was held in early April: the government acceded to the latter demand shortly afterwards.

In mid-May 1992 some 34 members of the opposition were arrested, following the publication in the national media of unsubstantiated allegations that elements within the government were plotting to assassinate opponents of the Moi regime. Later in that month the security forces violently suppressed a pro-Islamic demonstration in Mombasa. In June, during the period of voter-registration for the forthcoming presidential and legislative elections (see below), opposition parties protested that administrative and legal obstacles were effectively disenfranchising some sectors of the electorate. In June KANU published draft legislation stipulating that a successful presidential candidate must receive at least one-quarter of all votes cast in at least five of the country's eight provinces: this measure was intended to encourage political participation along national rather than ethnic lines.

From mid-1992 FORD was weakened by mounting internal divisions; in August the organization split into two opposing factions, and in October these were registered as separate political parties, FORD–Asili and FORD–Kenya, respectively led by Kenneth Matiba and Oginga Odinga.

Presidential and parliamentary elections were held concurrently in late December 1992. At the presidential election Moi was re-elected, winning 36.35% of the votes, ahead of Kenneth Matiba (26.00%), Mwai Kibaki (19.45%) and Oginga Odinga (17.48%). Of the 188 elective seats in the national assembly, KANU won 100 (including 16 uncontested), FORD–Asili and FORD–Kenya secured 31 each, the DP took 23, and the remainder were divided between the Kenya Social Congress, the Kenya National Congress and an independent candidate. (In November 1994 one FORD–Kenya representative and the independent member were found guilty of electoral malpractice and retrospectively disqualified from the elections.) Some 15 former cabinet ministers lost their seats. Votes were cast predominantly in accordance with ethnic affiliations, with the two largest tribes, the Kikuyu and Luo, overwhelmingly rejecting KANU. The leaders of FORD–Asili, FORD–Kenya and the DP initially launched a campaign to have the results declared invalid, alleging that gross electoral irregularities had taken place. In January 1993, however, a Commonwealth monitoring group stated that the outcome of the elections reflected 'the will of the people', despite accusing the government of corruption, intimidation and incompetence.

In early January 1993 Moi was sworn in for a fourth five-year term as president. An extensive reshuffle of cabinet posts was implemented in mid-January. In February the government impounded copies of three opposition publications which allegedly contained seditious material, and in April four opposition members were arrested and charged with participating in an illegal demonstration. During April the World Bank agreed to release foreign aid which had been suspended since November 1991. At the beginning of May 1993 a general strike was called by the Central Organization of Trade Unions (COTU) to demand wage increases and the dismissal of the vice-president and minister of planning and national development, Prof. George Saitoti; the former demand was partially acceded to. However, COTU's secretary-general was arrested and charged with inciting industrial unrest.

In May 1993 Sheikh Khalid Balala, a leader of the banned radical-fundamentalist Islamic Party of Kenya (IPK), threatened to declare a 'jihad' against the government and called for the assassination of cabinet ministers; Balala was subsequently arrested on charges of incitement. In an attempt to counter support for the IPK, KANU sponsored a rival Muslim party, the United Muslims of Africa, whose stated objective was to end 'the domination and oppression of indigenous African tribes by rich Arabs'. Behind the ethnic rivalry, however, lay a serious economic conflict centred on local feelings about the purchase of high-value land in tourist coastal areas by 'outsiders'—namely Asians, whites and certain government ministers.

Tribal clashes which occurred during 1993, described by church organizations as the most serious since independence, were most acute in the Rift Valley and on the borders between land occupied by the Masai, Kikuyu and Kalenjin tribes. Hundreds of Kikuyu families were driven from their farms, which were then allegedly occupied mainly by Kalenjins. Foreign observers who toured the Rift Valley in mid-1993 accused the government of failing to contain the fighting and of pursuing a policy of 'ethnic cleansing'. President Moi sealed off part of the region in September, ostensibly to prevent further hostilities, although the opposition claimed that his real aim was to suppress criticism of the government. Following significant escalation of the violence in October, president Moi accused his opponents of fomenting a civil war and increased the powers of the security forces. Five prominent Kikuyu who were arrested in connection with raids on police stations during October included the human rights activist Koigi wa Wamwere, who had been released earlier in the year following his arrest on charges of treason. In November the international human rights organization Africa Watch reiterated allegations that the ethnic violence had been deliberately exploited by Moi and his associates in order to undermine the move towards political pluralism. The organization estimated that 1,500 people had been killed and 300,000 displaced since the clashes began.

In January 1994 Oginga Odinga died; he was succeeded as the chairman of FORD–Kenya by Michael Kijana Wamalwa, hitherto the party's vice-president. At the time of Odinga's death, the rift between FORD–Kenya and FORD–Asili had widened considerably. During January Dr Richard Leakey, director of the Kenya Wildlife Service (KWS) and a third-generation white Kenyan, resigned after coming under attack from a number of government ministers. Although Leakey was respected internationally for his efforts at ending the poaching of elephants and for obtaining substantial financial support for the protection of Kenya's game reserves (a vital element in the country's tourism industry), it was alleged that he was doing little to protect the farmers on and around the reserves whose crops were being ravaged by the wildlife.

In April 1994, following further outbreaks of violence in part of the Rift Valley between the Kikuyu and the Kalenjin, Moi reimposed a security zone and curfew on the area. Roman Catholic bishops and opposition leaders repeated the long-standing allegations that the government was fully responsible for fomenting the unrest. Allegations of serious fraud involving the misappropriation of government funds abounded during 1994, incriminating opposition figures as well as government associates. This apparent widespread corruption together with the continuing adoption of tactics of repression by the government and the ineffectual state of the divided and poorly-organized opposition, resulted in major popular discontent and alienation; the rates of crime and urban violence increased significantly and ethnic unrest continued to simmer. Meanwhile, university staff and employees of the public health sector organized strike action to protest at the government's refusal to recognize their respective trade unions and to grant improved conditions of employment.

In June 1994 the main opposition groups, excluding FORD–Asili, formed a loose coalition, the United National Democratic Front (UNDA), in an attempt to gain a tactical advantage at future elections; however, UNDA was subsequently divided by disagreements. Disunity was also becoming apparent within individual opposition parties, with vying factions evident within both FORD–Kenya and FORD–Asili. Meanwhile, FORD–Kenya was further damaged by the implication of some of its leading supporters in allegations of corruption (see above). The IPK also suffered a set-back when, in December 1994, the government withdrew the right to Kenyan citizenship from its leading spokesman, Sheikh Balala (also a citizen of Yemen); Balala, who was abroad at the time, was also banned from re-entering Kenya. In May 1995 several opposition activists, including Gitobu Imanyara, a former secretary-general of FORD–Kenya, and Paul Muite, a very influential human rights lawyer and also a former FORD–Kenya supporter, formed a new political grouping, Safina (the Swahili term for 'Noah's Ark'). The new party, whose primary stated aims were to combat corruption and human rights abuses and to introduce an electoral system of proportional representation, was chaired by Mutari Kigano, also a human rights lawyer. The former KWS director, Dr Leakey, was appointed as Safina's secretary-general, thereby attracting beneficial international attention to the enterprise. Moi, apparently regarding the party, and, in particular, Dr Leakey as a significant threat, launched a series of bitter personal attacks against the white Kenyan, accusing him of harbouring 'colonialist' ambitions. Safina's application for official registration was rejected. The party strongly rebuffed accusations by the government that it was illegally funded from abroad.

During the mid-1990s Kenya's apparently deteriorating human rights situation came under increasing domestic and international scrutiny. In April 1995 the country's catholic bishops published a pastoral letter in which they once again strongly condemned the government, accusing it of betraying the nation by eroding the independence of the judiciary and by condoning police brutality and endemic corruption. In mid-1995 leading human rights organizations expressed particular concern over physical assaults on Safina officials (including Dr Leakey) by members of KANU's youth wing, as well as the government's refusal officially to register Safina, and the lengthy trial of the human rights activist Koigi wa Wamwere, who had been charged in 1993 in connection with a raid on a police station (see above). Wamwere was eventually found guilty in October 1995 of attempted robbery and sentenced to a term of imprisonment; Amnesty International and opposition members of the national assembly alleged that the prosecution's evidence had been fabricated. In November the Kenyan authorities revealed that 810 prisoners had died in custody since the beginning of 1995. In December Amnesty International reported that the security forces were systematically torturing criminal suspects and opposition activists. In response to its critics (and in order to ensure continuing inflows of foreign assistance), the Moi administration provisionally withdrew controversial draft legislation in January 1996 that would have severely restricted the freedom of the press and, in July, inaugurated a human rights committee to investigate alleged humanitarian abuses by the Kenyan authorities. During July, however, Moi announced, and subsequently reiterated, that constitutional reforms (strongly advocated by foreign donors) would not be considered prior to the next legislative and presidential elections, which were scheduled to take place in late 1997.

The rising rates of crime and urban violence continued to arouse concern. During the latter part of 1995 several foreign diplomatic missions and personnel were attacked by armed robbers; a British high commission official who was shot in his car subsequently died of his injuries. In December the Kenyan authorities, under pressure to allay the fears of the resident foreign communities and to protect the national tourism industry, organized a rounding-up of illegal aliens, who were alleged to be largely responsible for the crime wave.

Despite the prospect of national elections in 1997, during much of the mid-1990s the opposition remained deeply fractured and disorganized. Although the main opposition organizations (excluding FORD–Asili) formed a new alliance in November 1995, with Leakey as its chief co-ordinator, widening divisions in and between the parties ensured that the co-operation was ineffectual and short-lived. By the end of 1995 some 11 national assembly delegates who had been elected in December 1992 as representatives of opposition groupings had reportedly defected to the ruling KANU; several subsequent defections occurred during 1996–97. FORD–Asili and FORD–Kenya were paralysed by leadership struggles in early 1996; Martin Shikuku claimed to have unseated Matiba as chairman of the former, while in the latter Raila Odinga nominated a rival party executive to that led by Kijana Wamalwa. A FORD–Kenya party congress, held in April, to settle Odinga's challenge ended in disorder. Meanwhile, Safina remained effectively powerless, owing to the government's refusal to grant it registered status. In December Odinga was reportedly expelled from FORD–Kenya; Odinga (who claimed to have resigned from the party) subsequently announced that he was joining the little-known National Development Party, of which he was appointed leader in May 1997. Rivalries also began to emerge within KANU itself, apparently motivated by the desire to gain political advantage in anticipation of Moi's demise or retirement, given his age and that the constitution permitted him to stand for only one further term as president.

At a public rally in September 1996 Moi pardoned two self-confessed guerrillas, who were said to have admitted to belonging to a clandestine group that had plotted to assassinate Moi and other prominent Kenyans; they were also claimed to have revealed a plot to free Wamwere from detention, using weapons smuggled from abroad. However, it was widely considered that the allegations had been fabricated in an attempt to discredit the opposition. In December Wamwere was released on bail in order to seek medical treatment abroad. There was, meanwhile, further criticism of Kenya's human rights record: in October the independent Kenya Human Rights Commission condemned Kenya's prisons as among the worst in the world; in December African Rights claimed that Kenya's judicial system was corrupt, and in January 1997 a report by Amnesty International alleged that the Government had failed to halt widespread torture. In the same month, moreover, the reappointment to the cabinet of Biwott (a principal suspect in the inquiry into the assassination of Robert Ouko in 1990) provoked considerable disquiet. In February 1997 Kenya became a signatory to the UN Convention Against Torture and Other Cruel, Inhuman and Degrading Treatment or Punishment. Shortly afterwards the death of a prominent student activist in suspicious circumstances let to anti-government demonstrations on campuses throughout Kenya.

Concerns continued to be voiced in the mid-1990s over levels of corruption in Kenyan society. In May 1996 the opposition-dominated public accounts committee accused a number of senior members of the government of withholding information vital to its investigation into the collapse of several Kenyan banks, a matter believed to be connected with losses of an estimated US $430m. in public funds on allegedly fraudulent claims for export tax rebates. In June 1997 proceedings were abandoned in the high court against a prominent Asian businessman implicated in the scandal; although the attorney-general announced that a retrial would take place, international donors accused the government of doing little to recover the lost revenue or to bring those responsible to justice. Meanwhile, Matiba began to advocate the expulsion of the Kenyan Asian community, alleging that they were primarily responsible for corruption in Kenya, a policy decried as racist and unfounded by other opposition parties as well as by the government. In March 1997 opposition politicians expressed fears that Moi was in a position to use his control over the distribution of famine relif to gain political advantage in the afflicted regions.

It was widely believed by opposition politicians that, short of considerable constitutional reform, Moi and KANU would inevitably win the presidential and parliamentary elections scheduled for 1997. In particular, it was alleged that constituency boundaries had been gerrymandered and should be altered, and that, while Moi would be extremely likely to gain the highest number of votes in a first presidential ballot, given a second round of voting requiring an overall majority of votes, a single opposition candidate might emerge victorious. Moi, however, having promised a constitutional review, repeatedly refused to contemplate its initiation until after the 1997 elections. In April 1997 the National Convention Assembly (along with its executive council, the NCEC) was established at a conference in Limuru as an inclusive forum involving representatives of non-governmental organizations, religious groups and opposition parties (notably excluding supporters of Matiba and Odinga). On 3 May the NCEC attempted to hold a rally in Nairobi, but security forces prevented supporters from entering the venue and violent confrontations ensued. On 31 May, shortly after Matiba announced that he was resigning as a member of parliament on the grounds that he did not recognize the government's authority, security forces intervened to disperse a rally organized by Matiba and Odinga.

On 19 May 1997 the electoral roll was opened for the registration of voters, eventually closing on 30 June; no date for the forthcoming elections was announced, however. Demands for constitutional reform reached a head on 19 June, when opposition parliamentarians rendered the budget speech inaudible and security forces clashed with demonstrators on the streets of Nairobi. The budget was subsequently approved, despite opposition claims that it could not be properly debated as nobody had been able to hear its contents. In early July Balala was allowed to return to Kenya to resolve the issue of his citizenship.

On 7 July 1997, the anniversary of the pro-democracy demonstrations of 1990, illegal rallies were held across Kenya in support of constitutional reform. International outrage was expressed at the conduct of the security forces, who, as well as using excessive force to disperse demonstrators, attacked worshippers in the Anglican cathedral in Nairobi and were widely reported to have committed unprovoked violence against passers-by. The disturbances continued for several days, and a number of people were killed. In mid-July Moi held meetings with opposition and religious leaders to discuss constitutional reform, and announced that the opposition was free to hold registered public meetings, in anticipation of new, more lenient legislation. In what was widely viewed as an attempt to regain control of the reform process, KANU's executive council recommended the establishment of a constitutional review commission; the NCEC agreed, despite misgivings, to enter into dialogue with the government. However, in late August the government withdrew from the talks, following serious outbreaks of criminal violence in and around Mombasa. While the government blamed the NCEC for the attacks (including one on a police station), the NCEC alleged that KANU was inciting inter-ethnic conflict so as to deprive opposition supporters (among them many Luo) of the opportunity to vote in the forthcoming elections, by forcing them to flee their homes.

Following the IMF's decision to suspend loan disbursements to Kenya in August 1997, the government published the Statute Law Miscellaneous Amendments Bill, which proposed the establishment of an anti-corruption authority.

EXTERNAL RELATIONS

President Moi has resumed presidential direction of foreign affairs: Kenyatta, uniquely in Africa, left the conduct of foreign relations to his ministers of foreign affairs, and never travelled outside the country. Throughout the years of Kenyatta's presidency, Kenya remained unconvinced of the benefits of close integration with its neighbours through the East African Common Services Organization and its successor, the East African Community (EAC). During the early 1970s major political and economic tensions developed between the EAC member states, and by July 1977 the Community had ceased to function. Throughout the period of Idi Amin's regime in Uganda, President Kenyatta maintained an official stance of strict neutrality towards that country, although relations with Tanzania gradually deteriorated to a level of outright hostility by the time of Kenyatta's death in 1978. The collapse in April 1979 of the Amin regime raised hopes of better relations generally in east Africa, but Kenya was deeply suspicious of Tanzania's military role in Uganda. A meeting in January 1980 between President Moi and Presidents Nyerere of Tanzania and Binaisa of Uganda failed to allay these anxieties. The accession of Dr Milton Obote to the presidency of Uganda in December 1980, however, was followed by a sustained improvement in Kenya's relations with both Uganda and Tanzania. In November 1983 the three countries reached agreement on the distribution of the assets and liabilities of the EAC. Shortly afterwards, the border between Kenya and Tanzania (closed in 1977) was reopened, and in December the two countries agreed to establish full diplomatic relations. In 1986 agreement was reached on a trade treaty and on the establishment of a joint co-operation commission.

When the National Resistance Army (NRA) seized power in Uganda in January 1986, Moi offered full co-operation to the new Ugandan president, Yoweri Museveni. However, relations became less cordial as Moi became increasingly distrustful of the radical nature of the new regime in Kampala. Additionally, the Kenyan authorities became anxious that continued unrest in Uganda could provide a source of arms for opposition supporters in Kenya. Tension grew during 1986 over alleged Kenyan interference in freight deliveries to Uganda that were routed through Mombasa, and, in early 1987, an open dispute broke out over alleged ill-treatment of Ugandans resident in Kenya, following the death of a Ugandan national in Kenyan police custody. In May Uganda lodged further complaints over Kenya's alleged closing of the land frontier. The tension eased somewhat in June, when it appeared that the movement of traffic between the two countries was possible.

The détente, however, proved to be short-lived. In September 1987 Uganda claimed that Kenya was harbouring anti-Museveni rebels, and stationed troops at its border with Kenya. These claims were denied, and Moi warned that any infiltration by Ugandan troops in Kenya would encounter fierce retaliation. The influx of some 2,000 Ugandan refugees into Kenya strained relations further. In December Ugandan troops were alleged to have entered Kenya illegally in pursuit of rebels, and for several days the Ugandan and Kenyan armed forces exchanged fire across the border, which was temporarily closed to traffic. The Kenyan government expelled the Ugandan high commissioner and a number of other Ugandan citizens. Later in December, Presidents Moi and Museveni agreed to withdraw troops from either side of the border and to allow the resumption of normal traffic. In January 1988 the two countries signed a joint communiqué which provided for co-operation between them in resolving problems relating to the flow of traffic across the common border. This *rapprochement* was disrupted in July, when the Ugandan government accused Kenya of complicity in smuggling weapons to a rebel group in northern Uganda, and security was tightened along the Kenya–Uganda border to prevent alleged incursions by Ugandan troops. In October Uganda complained that Kenya had been intermittently obstructing the movement of Ugandan traffic across the border. In March 1989 the Ugandan government strongly denied Kenyan allegations that Ugandan troops had been involved in an attack by Ugandan cattle-rustlers on Kenyan security forces earlier in that month, and that a Ugandan military aircraft had been responsible for the bombing of a town in north-western Kenya shortly afterwards. In August 1990 Moi visited Museveni, indicating a renewed *détente* between Kenya and Uganda. In November 1991 the presidents of Kenya, Uganda and Tanzania met in Nairobi, and declared their commitment to developing mutual co-operation. In November 1994 the three leaders met at Arusha, Tanzania, and established a permanent tripartite commission for co-operation, with a view to reviving the defunct EAC; progress was hindered, however, by a renewed deterioration in relations between Kenya and Uganda. During early 1995 the Moi administration protested strongly to the UN, following the granting of refugee status in Uganda to Brig. John Odongo (also known as Stephen Amoke), leader of the February Eighteen Popular Resistance Army, a previously unknown outlawed Kenyan guerrilla movement. The Moi administration lent no credence to subsequent claims by the Ugandan government to have deported Odongo to a third country (reported to be Ghana). Following the intervention of the newly-elected President Benjamin Mkapa of Tanzania, Moi and Museveni were publicly reconciled in January 1996, and undertook to co-operate over the planned relaunch of the EAC. In March Moi, Museveni and Mpaka, meeting in Nairobi, formally inaugurated the Secretariat of the Permanent Tripartite Commission for East African Co-operation. The principal aims of this revived EAC were to enhance regional co-operation in political and economic affairs, and to reduce its members' reliance on foreign aid. In September, however, the Kenyan authorities suggested that the Ugandan Government was supporting attempts to subvert the Moi administation: such allegations were strongly denied by Uganda. None the less, in April 1997 a four-year development strategy was launched for the new EAC.

In December 1980 and May 1981 Lt-Col Mengistu Haile Mariam of Ethiopia made state visits to Kenya; the two countries subsequently signed a treaty of friendship and co-operation, and a mutual defence pact. Relations with the government of Meles Zenawi in Ethiopia came under strain in 1997, following an increased incidence of cross-border cattle-rustling, including an attack in March 1997 in which 16 members of the Kenyan security forces were killed. A number of communiqués were subsequently signed by representatives of the two countries, agreeing to tighten border security, to take measures to prevent arms and drugs-smuggling and to enhance trade. Somalia has traditionally laid claim to part of north-eastern Kenya, where there is a large ethnic Somali population. In mid-1981, however, President Moi held talks with the Somali president, Siad Barre, at which the latter renounced these territorial claims. In July 1984, during a state visit to Somalia by the Kenyan leader, Presidents Moi and Siad Barre pledged to increase bilateral co-operation between their respective countries and discussed arrangements for monitoring the Kenya–Somalia border. In November 1987 ministers from both countries signed a joint communiqué in which they undertook to consolidate existing good relations. In early 1989, however, friction developed between the Kenyan government and ethnic Somalis from both north-eastern Kenya and Somalia, when Somali poachers were alleged to be largely responsible for the rapid depletion of Kenyan elephant numbers in recent years; it was reported that several thousand ethnic Somalis had been ordered to evacuate areas near the game parks. In late 1989 the Kenya government began to scrutinize the status of ethnic Somalis, in order to determine whether they held Somali or Kenyan citizenship. In April 1991, following the overthrow and flight of President Siad Barre in January of that year, the new Somali government accused the Moi regime of providing assistance to Barre and his supporters, who had taken refuge in Kenya. During the early 1990s the Kenyan government mediated between the rival factions in the Somali civil war. In May 1992 the Kenyan authorities negotiated permanent asylum for Barre in Nigeria. Relations between Kenya and Libya deteriorated in April 1987, when five Libyan diplomats were expelled for alleged subversive activities. In the following month a Kenyan newspaper published an unsubstantiated report that Libya was training dissidents from Kenya to overthrow the government. In December the government closed the Libyan diplomatic mission in Nairobi. Relations between Kenya and Sudan deteriorated in June 1988, as they exchanged mutual accusations of aiding rebel factions. In early 1989 Sudan renewed a long-standing dispute with Kenya over the sovereignty of territory on the Kenyan side of the Kenya–Sudan border, known as the 'Elemi triangle', which is believed to contain substantial deposits of petroleum. By May 1994, however, relations between the two countries had improved sufficiently for the Sudanese president, Mohammad Omar el-Bashir, to visit Nairobi in connection with the 30th anniversary of the African Development Bank. In October 1995, despite strong condemnation from foreign governments, the Kenyan authorities refused to permit the UN international criminal tribunal for Rwanda, which was investigating war crimes committed in 1994, access to alleged Rwandan perpetrators of genocide who were now in Kenya. In June 1996 Kenya closed the Rwandan embassy in Nairobi in protest at the Rwandan government's refusal to waive diplomatic immunity for an embassy official who was suspected of plotting a murder in Kenya; the diplomat was deported. In September 1996, however, the first arrest in Kenya was made of a Rwandan Hutu suspected of involvement in genocide. Kenya strongly denied accusations, in November, of supplying arms to Rwandan Hutu rebels operating from within Zaire. Following the *coup d'état* in Burundi in July 1996, Kenya, along with other countries of the region, imposed full economic sanctions on the administration of Maj. Pierre Buyoya; these sanctions were subsequently reduced, in line with other regional countries. In November and December regional summit meetings were held in Nairobi to discuss the crisis in the Great Lakes region. Moi's long-standing support for the government of Marshal Mobutu Sese Seko in Zaire (now the Democratic Republic of the Congo) brought into question the pragmatism of this policy, following the ousting of Mobutu by Laurent-Désiré Kabila in May 1997. However, the relative stability which followed in the Great Lakes region encouraged the re-establishment of good relations with Rwanda; it was reported in June that the Rwandan embassy in Nairobi was to reopen, whilst in July seven further Rwandan Hutus were arrested by the Kenyan security forces to stand trial on charges of genocide at the UN tribunal.

At 31 December 1995, according to a report from UNHCR, Kenya was sheltering an estimated 239,500 refugees, including about 200,000 from Somalia. The Moi government, which claims that the refugees place an intolerable burden on the country's resources, has repeatedly requested the UN to repatriate the total refugee population. In July 1995 UNHCR agreed that 29,000 Sudanese refugees should be returned from Kenya to Sudan.

President Moi has made a number of overseas visits and has taken an active interest in continental affairs. In 1989 he offered his services as mediator between vying forces in Ethiopia and Mozambique, and in 1991 he took the chairmanship in peace talks between warring Somali factions. An important development in foreign affairs under Moi has been Kenya's support of US military commitments in the Indian Ocean. In 1980 Kenya permitted the USA to use port and air base facilities in Kenya, in return for increased US military assistance to Kenya.

In recent years Kenya has received international criticism of its records on human rights, particularly from the USA. Following the violent disruption by Kenyan security forces of a meeting in Kenya between a US congressman and a Kenyan church leader in January 1987 the USA temporarily suspended aid allocations to Kenya. In August the US administration suspended military aid of US $5m., in protest at the Kenyan government's arrest of opposition figures in July of that year; the funds were eventually released in February 1991. In October 1990 Kenya severed diplomatic relations with Norway, following protests by the Norwegian government to Kenya about the arrest on treason charges during that month of a Kenyan dissident who had been exiled in Norway; Norway subsequently suspended aid allocations to Kenya. Diplomatic relations were restored in February 1994 although Norway refused to resume aid to the country. In mid-November 1991, following protests by several overseas governments against arrests by the Kenyan security forces of opposition leaders who had organized a pro-democracy rally (see above), the Kenyan government accused US, German and Swedish diplomats of assisting Kenyan dissidents (allegations which were vigorously denied). In response, Germany withdrew its ambassador for 'consultations'. Later in the same month, following the decision by donor nations and organizations to withhold aid to Kenya (see above), the USA announced that it was suspending assistance worth $28m. Nevertheless, strategic considerations continue to ensure that the informal military alliance between Kenya and the USA will remain intact for the foreseeable future. In May 1994 the USA announced the disbursement of development assistance worth K£23.95m. for agricultural research, rural infrastructure and health care programmes. In July 1995 the United Kingdom withheld financial aid to Kenya, pending an improvement in the Moi administration's human rights record and economic management.

In the mid-1990s reports in the international press suggested that Moi's position as a senior African statesman was being undermined both by his government's human rights record at home, and, abroad, by the demise of many of his political allies and the emergence of younger, more radical African leaders who viewed his style of government as outdated and reactionary.

Economy

LINDA VAN BUREN

INTRODUCTION

The population of Kenya at the census of 24 August 1989 (believed to be underenumerated) was 21,443,636. By mid-1994 the total population was officially estimated at 29,292,000, producing an average population density of 50.5 per sq. km. Much of Kenya's population is concentrated in the south-western highlands, the coastal strip and the lake area. The rate of population increase was 3.4% per annum in 1980–90, but fell to 2.9% per annum in 1990–95, according to World Bank estimates. In 1985 the country's average annual birth rate, at 5.4%, was the highest in the world; by 1995, however, the rate stood at 3.5%, one of the lowest in sub-saharan Africa. The rate of infant mortality was 58 per 1,000 live births in 1995, compared with 102 per 1,000 in 1970.

Agriculture is the main occupation and source of income of the majority of the people, but the service and manufacturing sectors are substantially more important than would normally be expected in a country of Kenya's income level. The disproportionate development of manufacturing, processing and service industries was bound up with the early presence in Kenya of a substantial number of non-African settlers, whose high incomes generated demand.

At independence in 1963, the export-orientated agriculture in Kenya was based upon large-scale commercial agriculture of the settled 'White Highlands' and on European- and Asian-owned plantations. Much of the government's agricultural effort in the early years of independence was devoted to a land reform programme designed to transfer land from the European settlers and to resettle Africans upon it. Later, the government turned its attention to the Kenyanization of commerce, which at that time was dominated by non-African and frequently non-citizen businesses.

Kenya's record in the 15 years or so after independence placed it, in terms of the growth of output, among the most successful of African developing countries. From independence until 1980, the economy progressed at a cumulative annual rate of growth of 6.8% in real terms, with growth in the industrial sector reaching 9.7% per year during the 1970s. This expansion was financed by a substantial inflow of capital as well as by domestic sources.

During the period 1970–78 Kenya's gross domestic product (GDP) expanded at an average rate of more than 5% per annum in real terms. In the early 1980s, indications of weakness in the once-booming economy became increasingly evident. Deteriorating terms of trade led to a growing balance-of-payments deficit and a sharp decline in reserves of foreign exchange; burgeoning government expenditure, which was encouraged by the earlier high prices for Kenya's exports of tea and coffee, resulted in substantial budgetary deficits; and the government's high rate of borrowing on the international market created a debt-service ratio of more than 27% of export earnings by 1984. During 1983, however, some degree of economic recovery was achieved as a result of measures introduced by the government, in accordance with conditions imposed by the IMF, and also by way of an inflow of aid from a variety of multilateral and bilateral donors, as well as from funds from the IMF itself. The improved world outlook, together with buoyant tea prices, led observers to take a more optimistic view of Kenya's economic prospects by the start of 1984. Prospects were ruined, however, by the severe drought of that year (the most severe for 50 years): harvests were drastically reduced, necessitating large cereal imports, and growth in GDP fell to only 0.9%. However, as a result of improved rainfall and favourable coffee prices in 1985 and 1986, real GDP expanded by 4.1% and 5.5%, respectively, in those years. The growth rate eased to 4.8% in 1987, owing to a decline in coffee prices and a rise in petroleum prices; however, favourable weather conditions and higher commodity prices led to an increase, to 5.2%, in the growth rate of GDP in 1988. A reversal of these factors resulted, according to figures from the IMF, in a decline in GDP growth to 4.8% in 1989, 4.3% in 1990 and 1.4% in 1991. GDP declined by 0.8% in 1992, owing to a combination of political and ethnic instability, the suspension of bilateral balance of payments assistance and other exogenous factors. The introduction of a programme of economic reform in 1993, together with greater political stability and the resumption of aid, contributed to GDP growth of 0.4% in 1993, 2.7% in 1994, 4.4% in 1995 and 4.6% in 1996, with growth of 4.0% projected for 1997. The annual inflation rate, according to government estimates, was reduced from 10.7% in 1985 to 5.7% in 1986, and to slightly below that level in 1987, but rose to 11.8% in 1988. It averaged 10.5% in 1989, before rising steadily during the early 1990s, to 15.8% per annum in 1990, 19.8% in 1991, 29.5% in 1992 and 45.8% in 1993. During the first three months of 1993 the annual rate of inflation soared to 60% (and, at times, to more than 100%, according to unofficial sources), owing to the effects of the suspension of international donor aid and the deregulation of prices in 1992 (see below). By the end of 1993 the inflation rate had been contained, and the annual rate for 1994 was 29.0%. Consumer prices in 1995 rose by just 0.8%, and by 8.8% in 1996, according to the IMF. The inflation rate officially rose to an annual level of 12.3% in the first quarter of 1997, owing to drought-induced food price increases. In 1995, according to estimates by the World Bank, Kenya's gross national product (GNP) was US $7,583m. at average 1993–95 prices, while GNP per head was $280. During 1990–95, it was estimated, GNP per head grew by 0.1%.

AGRICULTURE

Agriculture continues to dominate Kenya's economy, although its share of GDP has declined slightly in recent years; in 1995 the agricultural sector (including forestry and fishing) contributed 31% of GDP. The principal cash crops, tea and coffee, ranked second and third respectively, behind tourism, as sources of foreign exchange in 1992–95. About 78% of the working population made their living on the land in 1995, compared with 80% in 1980. More than one-half of total agricultural output is subsistence production.

Agricultural output is greatly dependent upon the weather since there is as yet little irrigated production, although the area under irrigation is being increased. The huge Bura scheme on the Tana river was designed to grow mainly cotton. The project, having been beset by financial and management problems, fell several years behind schedule. The main donors were the World Bank, the United Kingdom, the European Development Fund and the Netherlands. By early 1986 about 2,000 families had been settled.

In the early 1960s, as a result of land reform and increased coffee production on African farms, the share of small farms in marketed output grew rapidly. Since 1976 this share has stood at about one-half. There are around 1.7m. smallholders in the monetary sector and 3,200 large farms, ranches and plantations. There is an acute shortage of arable land, and only 7% of the country is classified as first-class land. The majority of smallholders have plots of less than 2 ha, and successive subdivision of plots among farmers' sons impels large numbers of people to towns in search of employment.

Between 1972–81 annual growth of the agricultural sector lagged far behind the net population growth rate, except in 1976 and 1977, when improved performance was largely the result of unprecedentedly high world prices for coffee. In 1981, agricultural output grew by 6.2%, partly as a result of better weather conditions. Growth rates of 4.4% and 4.5% were recorded for 1982 and 1983 respectively. Disappointing 'short' rains in late 1983, followed by the severe drought of 1984, seriously affected almost all crops and created near-famine conditions in many parts of the country. Fortunately, rain returned at the end of 1984 and, with heavy rainfall in early 1985, the agricultural sector made a strong recovery in 1985/86. The output of the sector increased by 4.8% in 1986, but the rate of expansion declined to 3.8% in 1987, when crops were adversely affected by the premature end of the 'long' rains. Agricultural production increased by 4.4% in 1988, but the growth rate retreated to 3.9% in 1989, owing mainly to low international coffee prices and unfavourable weather conditions. The same factors contributed to growth of only 3.4% in 1990. There was a modest recovery in the growth of agricultural production, to 4.3%, in 1991. However, according to the FAO, output increased by only 0.1% in 1991 and declined by 2.4% in 1992 and by 3.5% in 1993, owing partly to the onset of a severe drought and low world prices for coffee. A recovery in the sector in 1994 and 1995 was reflected in growth of 6.8% and 3.7% respectively.

The principal cash crops are tea, coffee, sugar cane, maize, wheat, sisal, pyrethrum and cotton.

Kenya's leading export crops are coffee, almost all of it high-grade arabica, tea and horticultural produce. Until October 1992 the Coffee Board of Kenya (CBK) controlled coffee production and handled much of its marketing. Since then, however, the marketing of coffee has been liberalized and the role of the CBK has been confined to licensing, regulation and research. In addition, coffee auctions are now conducted in US dollars. Small-holders accounted for 117,677 ha of the total 156,304 ha planted with coffee in 1986, and they produce about 60% of the crop. Until the abandonment of coffee quotas by the International Coffee Organization (ICO) in July 1989, Kenya's production consistently exceeded its quota allocations, with the result that buyers were sought on the open market, mainly in the Middle East. Drought in Brazil caused world prices to soar by the end of 1985, and Kenya was able to take advantage of the price boom, earning K£388.5m. from coffee exports in 1986, compared with K£230.6m. in the previous year. However, prices fell sharply again from late 1986, which, compounded by lower output, resulted in a decline in export earnings, to an estimated K£194.6m., in 1987. Despite low market prices, export earnings rose to almost K£245m. in 1988, when a record marketed output of 124,600 metric tons was achieved. Following the suspension of ICO quota arrangements in 1989, together with a decline in production to 119,000 tons in the 1988/89 crop year, coffee export revenue was reduced to K£255.8m. in 1989. Output was 114,000 tons in the 1989/90 season, with exports earning K£180m. in 1990. Output of coffee declined sharply, to 87,000 metric tons, in 1990/91, owing to unfavourable weather conditions; with export earnings of US $159m. Although Kenya's premium arabica coffee has long commanded a high price, the instability of the coffee market (in April 1992 world coffee prices were, in nominal terms, at a 22-year 'low', and overall 1992 prices were only one-third of their 1980 level) acted as a disincentive to Kenyan producers, many of whom decided to abandon coffee-growing in favour of more profitable crops. In late 1989 a coffee development scheme, aimed at raising productivity and improving farmers' access to credit, was initiated with the support of the Commonwealth Development Corpn and the World Bank. The seven-year scheme, at a projected cost of $107m., also provided for the construction of 65 processing factories and the rehabilitation of a further 275 such installations. With the deregulation of coffee marketing in 1992, official production figures declined even further, to 79,000 tons in that year and to 75,000 tons in 1993. Output recovered to 80,000 tons in 1994, to 90,000 tons in 1995, and, according to the International Coffee Organization, to 109,000 tons in 1996. Coffee exports earned $128m. in 1992, $177m. in 1993, $233m. in 1994 and $282m. in 1995. In October 1993 Kenya began taking part in the stock-withholding arrangements of the Association of Coffee Producing Countries, which gradually generated an improvement in prices. The outlook for coffee production received a temporary boost in April 1994, when world coffee prices reached a five-year high. In 1995 coffee accounted for 15% of Kenya's exports. In February 1995 Kenya, together with four other African coffee producers, agreed to participate in coffee price guarantee contract arrangements sponsored by the Eastern and Southern Africa Trade and Development Bank under the auspices of the Common Market for Eastern and Southern Africa (COMESA). This plan sought to promote producer price guarantees in place of stock retention schemes. The contract guarantee arrangements were to indemnify producers against prices falling below an agreed contract price. None the less, during 1994–97 global coffee prices declined by some 40%, with no sign of an imminent recovery. In March 1997 the Coffee Millers' Forum (subsequently the Coffee Millers' Association) was founded to advocate further liberalization of the coffee marketing sector, which remained dominated by the CBK. Although the CBK was instructed to issue marketing licences to all suitable applicants, a deposit of Ks. 1,000m. was required as security, which, it was argued, few applicants would be able to afford.

The decline in coffee production coincided with a sharp rise in output and sales of tea. High-quality tea has been a rapidly expanding crop since the early 1970s, and in 1994 Kenya ranked as the world's second largest exporter of tea, behind Sri Lanka and ahead of China and India. Kenya has replaced India as the United Kingdom's principal tea supplier, and now provides about 40% of British tea imports. Pakistan is also an important customer. The share of tea in Kenya's export earnings rose from 13.7% in 1982 to over 28% in 1984. However, with the onset of sharply falling prices, the proportion fell to 18% in 1986, recovering to 21.7% in 1987 and again declining, to 20.2%, in 1988. Although the 1987 harvest reached 155,808 tons, the continuing decline in world prices led to a fall in export earnings, to an estimated K£163.4m. Production of tea rose to 164,030 tons in 1988, to 181,000 tons in 1989, to 197,000 tons in 1990 and to a record 203,590 tons in 1991. As a result of drought in all growing areas and the disruption to farming caused by ethnic clashes in western regions, output in 1992 fell to 188,000 tons. However, by 1993 tea production had risen again, to 211,170 tons. Output rose from 209,420 tons in 1994 to an estimated 244,530 tons in 1995. Kenya benefited from a rising trend in tea prices in 1989, when revenue from tea, at K£266.2m., exceeded that from coffee for the first time. In 1989 a total of 84,400 ha in Kenya were planted with tea, of which almost 57,000 ha represented smallholder operations. In 1995 approximately 106,000 ha were under tea. Tea exports earned Kenya an estimated US $292m. in 1990, dropping to $277m. in 1991, before rising to $295m. in 1992, $299m. in 1993 and $301m. in 1994. Export earnings stood at $331m. in 1995, accounting for about 18% of Kenya'a total export receipts. Severe drought early in 1997 led to a drop in tea production of more than 30% in January–May of that year, compared with figures for the same months in 1996.

The share of small farms in total area under tea has expanded rapidly under the high-density settlement schemes of the Kenya Tea Development Authority (KTDA), which has established more than 40 tea factories in 14 districts. In July 1992 the government announced the forthcoming transferral of tea factories to the private sector. About 172,000 smallholders grow tea on 69,620 ha, and production of tea from their land accounts for 59% of total output. Estates, grouped in the Kenya Tea Growers' Association, cover about 31,017 ha. Smallholders' yields (at 1,810 kg per ha) are still lower than those of the large plantations (2,929 kg per ha), but are increasing as their bushes reach maturity.

The Kenya Sugar Authority was established in 1971 to develop the growing and processing of sugar cane. In 1980 there was a surplus of 150,000 metric tons of sugar for export after domestic demand of 275,000 tons had been met. By the late 1980s, domestic consumption had increased, and annual imports of sugar exceeded 120,000 tons in some years. Output of sugar cane was about 4.7m. tons annually in both 1987 and 1988. Production of raw sugar achieved successive record levels in 1989, 1990 and 1991, estimated at 457,000, 467,000 and 532,000 tons respectively. However, output fell back to 464,000 tons in 1992 and to 402,000 tons in 1993; production was estimated at 420,000 tons in 1995, while national demand was approximately 160,000 tons. Cane is sold to the sugar companies by smallholders and co-operatives. There are six parastatal sugar companies, with a seventh to be completed by the year 2000, with investment from the Commonwealth Development Corpn and the British company, Tate & Lyle. During the early 1990s sugar produced in western Kenya was being smuggled into Uganda on a scale large enough to cause shortages on the Kenyan market. In 1996 the government announced plans to privatize two of the three most productive sugar companies, Mumias and Chemelil. In February 1997 the government announced an increase in duty on sugar imports, and their temporary suspension, after the market was flooded with cheap foreign sugar, much of it allegedly illegally imported, with which domestic producers could not compete: it was reported that the production of refined sugar had virtually ceased.

Production of cotton increased steadily in the 1970s, but output of lint slumped from 62,179 bales (each of 480 lb or 218 kg) in 1978/79 to 18,306 bales in 1995. Nevertheless, potential output of lint is estimated at more than 220,000 bales. Imported lint is necessary to satisfy the demand of the domestic textiles industry; in 1991 imports of lint amounted to 8,000 metric tons, costing US $13m. The reasons for the poor performance include low prices, an erratic payments system, inefficient marketing, and drought. The Cotton Board of Kenya was radically reorganized during the early 1990s, and the transfer to private-sector ownership of the country's 15 cotton ginneries commenced in 1995. Output of cottonseed oil, which peaked at 3,575 tons in 1989, plunged to 1,961 tons in 1990; a partial recovery, to 2,183 tons, was recorded in 1991, but in 1994 production slumped to 743 tons, and only 74 tons were produced in 1995. Kenya also produced 288 tons of linseed oil. Output of other oil crops in 1995 included 7,000 tons of copra (yielding 3,205 tons of coconut oil) and 15,000 tons of sunflower seeds (producing 3,331 tons of sunflower seed oil); 11,250 tons of maize oil and 1,631 tons of castor-bean oil were also produced.

Kenya became self-sufficient in tobacco in 1983, with production at about 6,600 metric tons. Production of tobacco rose by 24% in 1987, and included 5,212 tons of flue-cured, 126 tons of burley and 1,658 tons of fire-cured tobacco. In 1991 about 4,000 ha of land was planted with tobacco, yielding a total crop of 9,756 tons (an average of 2,439 kg per ha). Output was estimated at 10,000 tons annually in 1993–95.

Kenya is the world's third largest producer of sisal. However, production of sisal, which reached a peak of 86,526 metric tons in 1974, was only an estimated 45,000 tons in 1990 and has successively fallen, to 39,000 tons in 1991 and to 34,000 tons per annum in 1992–95. Revenue from this crop totalled K£12.9m. in 1990 and averaged an estimated US $11m. per annum in 1992–95. The number of large estates has fallen to 19, from about 60 in 1954. Global sisal prices reached a 12-year low in 1992, but recovered during 1993–96, benefiting Kenyan producers. Kenya exports only sisal fibre, having no processing industry.

Kenya supplies 65%–70% of the world market for pyrethrum. In the early 1990s there were about 30,000 ha under pyrethrum, its output being mainly linked to co-operatives. The Pyrethrum Board of Kenya allocates quotas and attempts to improve production and its quality. In the late 1980s production ranged from 7,500 tons to about 10,000 tons annually. By the early 1990s, however, the increasing use of biological insecticides (particularly in the USA, the mainstay of Kenyan pyrethrum exports), had led to declining levels of demand for this commodity.

Kenya's high elevation favours the cultivation of a variety of fruit and vegetables, and in 1995 horticultural produce became Kenya's fourth most important source of foreign exchange, after tourism, tea and coffee. Fresh flowers, fruit and vegetables are air-freighted to Europe and the Middle East. Production increased from 1.5m. kg in 1968 to 548m. kg in 1993, while earnings rose from US $76m. in 1980 to $139m. in 1990, and to an estimated $157m. in 1991. The vegetables and fruit, other than pineapples, are grown mainly by smallholders; two large companies account for most of the cut flowers. Kenya exports about 60,000 metric tons of canned pineapple products and 11,000 tons of pineapple juice per year, and started exporting fresh pineapples in 1988. Output of fresh pineapples totalled 270,000 metric tons in 1995. The United Kingdom imports 44% of the vegetables and fruit. In 1997 a 10% 'suspended duty' was imposed on imports of certain fruits, in order to protect local growers. Kenya is the world's fourth-largest exporter of cut flowers, which are grown mainly on large-scale farms in the Naivasha region of Central province. Horticultural produce accounted for 10% of total export earnings in 1988, compared with 3% of export earnings in 1983. The sector has great potential and is a highly successful example of export diversification, but lack of air-freight space and inadequate cold-storage facilities at Jomo Kenyatta International Airport has placed a major constraint on further expansion, as did the high cost of aviation fuel during the 1980s. Kenya is also faced with growing competition from other new exporters of horticultural products, and from South Africa. In 1994, according to the Export Promotion Board of Kenya, horticultural produce raised some Ks. 8,300m. in export revenue. It was reported that horticultural produce had accounted for more than Ks. 14,000m. in export earnings in 1995, equivalent to some 12% of total export revenue.

Kenya's principal food crop is maize. Imports were needed in 1980 and 1981 to compensate for serious shortfalls, caused by drought, low producer prices and the fact that maize exports were authorized despite low stocks. There were improved harvests in the following two years, but the drought which started in the latter part of 1983 led to a very serious shortfall in maize, as well as other cereals, in 1984. As a result, large quantities of food aid had to be imported. However, improved rainfall enabled Kenya to dispense with emergency famine relief by mid-1985. In 1985/86 there was a record maize harvest of 2.9m. metric tons, and in 1987 some maize was exported. In 1986/87 the harvest declined to an estimated 1.9m. tons, but the excellent harvests in the two preceding years had resulted in a substantial stockpile. Good rains produced a crop of 2.8m. tons in 1989, increasing maize stocks to 1m. tons, and a record crop of 3m. tons in 1990. However, drought adversely affected output in 1991/92, necessitating the importation of food aid valued at K£425,000m. by June 1992. Maize output soon recovered: after the drought-affected crop of 2.1m. tons in 1993, an estimated 3.1m. tons were produced in 1994. Output of an estimated 2.8m. tons was recorded in 1995, in which year some 1.4m. ha were planted with maize, yielding 1,964 kg per ha. The loss-making National Cereals and Produce Board (NCPB) was to be restructured under an agreement that Kenya signed with the World Bank in 1986 for a US $71.5m. agricultural adjustment programme, and with additional aid from the EC (now the EU). The government liberalized grain marketing in 1993 to allow more private-sector involvement, though it reserved for itself the power to 'make selected targeted interventions where market forces may not be effective'. In 1995 Kenya sold 3m. 90-kg bags of surplus maize to drought-stricken countries in southern Africa; following the sale, the NCPB still held surplus stocks of 4m. bags. Drought substantially reduced the 1996/97 maize crop, necessitating the importation of famine-relief maize.

Kenya has a high consumer demand for wheat and needed for years to import about 30% of its requirements. A major wheat expansion programme increased the area under wheat from 95,000 ha in 1993 to 155,000 ha in 1994. Yields, which were 2,025 kg per ha in 1979–81, had fallen to 1,259 kg per ha by 1992, but recovered to an estimated 2,129 kg per ha in 1995. Output increased from 150,000 tons in 1993 to about 277,000 tons in 1994, and to 330,000 tons in 1995. In 1990 production costs for wheat were reported to have a foreign exchange component of about 80%, compared with 50% for maize production.

Livestock and dairy production are important both for domestic consumption and for export. The country had an estimated 13.8m. cattle in 1990, 13m. in 1991, 12m. in 1992 and 11m. in 1993–95. Some 1.8m. head of cattle were slaughtered in 1995, producing 240,000 tons of beef. The national dairy herd numbered an estimated 4.4m. in 1995 and produced 2.17m. tons of milk in that year. A substantial proportion of dairy cattle are in small herds of up to 10 animals. Kenya has traditionally exported butter, cheese and skimmed milk powder, and maintains strategic stocks of these products. In 1997 it was reported that an epidemic of rinderpest was threatening Kenya's cattle population. The country had 104,000 pigs in 1995. In addition, 4.51m. head of sheep and goats were slaughtered in 1995, producing 51,000 tons of mutton, lamb and goat meat. Output of poultry meat in that year was 48,000 tons.

INDUSTRY

Kenya is the most industrially developed country in east Africa, with a good infrastructure, extensive transport facilities and considerable private-sector activity. Nevertheless, the manufacturing sector contributed only 11% of GDP in 1995. The annual increase in the output of the sector averaged 10.5% in 1965–80, but only 4.7% in 1980–83, eventually recovering from a low of 2.7% in 1982 to 5.9% in 1986. Growth declined slightly in 1987, to 5.7%, but increased to 6% in 1988, retreating to 5.9% in 1989, 4.9% in 1990 and to 3.7% in 1991, as a result of selective price increases and diminished domestic demand. Growth in manufacturing output recovered to 4.9% in 1992, partly owing to the effects of the liberalization of foreign exchange controls in that year (see below). The manufacturing sector employs fewer than 200,000 people. It suffered from stringent import controls during the late 1970s and the 1980s, with 60%–70% of its inputs having to be imported, and was also hindered during that period by delays in the issuing of import licences and by controls on ex-factory prices. In addition the steady devaluation of the shilling in recent years has increased the costs of those manufacturers heavily dependent on imported inputs. Manufacturing is, in practice, based on import-substitution, although the government is now putting great emphasis on developing export-orientated industries. In 1990 imports of goods intended for the manufacture of exports were exempted from import duty and value added tax. Kenyan manufacturers hope to find new markets among the member countries of COMESA (formerly the PTA). Major industries include petroleum refining (using imported crude petroleum), the processing of agricultural products, vehicle assembly, the exploitation of soda-ash reserves, the production of chemicals, publishing and printing and the manufacture of textiles and clothing, cement, electrical equipment, tyres, batteries, paper, ceramics, machinery, metal products, rubber, wood and cork products and leather goods. Petroleum refining provided about 9% of export earnings in 1993. About one-half of the investment in the industrial sector is foreign-owned, and, of this, the United Kingdom owns about one-half. The USA is the second most important foreign investor.

The massive Panafrican Paper Mills' plant at Webuye commenced production in 1975. A major expansion raised annual production capacity from 66,000 metric tons to 90,000 tons. The government owns 40% of the company's shares. A partly Swedish-owned company, Tetra Pak Converters, began production of laminated milk cartons in 1983.

The textile industry performed relatively well following independence, and diversification was encouraged in the clothing and leather industries. By 1993 some 65 textile factories were operating in the country, of which some 40 were engaged in manufacturing under bond for export. The expansion in the sector was mostly induced by Kenya's unrestricted access to the US market, which encouraged manufacturers in Asian countries to use Kenya as a conduit for their goods and thus fraudulently to bypass US-imposed quotas. However, in 1994 the US authorities imposed a quota on Kenyan textile imports, quantities of which had increased suspiciously. The industry swiftly collapsed: in 1997 only a few factories remained in operation, and those at a much reduced rate of production. There are three vehicle assembly plants: Associated Vehicle Assemblers, General Motors Kenya and Leyland Kenya. They produce trucks, commercial vehicles, pickups, minibuses and four-wheel drive vehicles and passenger cars from kits supplied from abroad. General Motors Kenya started assembly of a passenger car, the Uhuru, in 1985. Domestic sales of locally-produced vehicles reached 13,600 in 1987, an increase of more than 30% from 1986. A small proportion of Kenyan-assembled vehicles are exported to Uganda, Sudan and Malawi. About 30% of components are produced locally and this proportion is to be increased. The government has announced plans to reduce its 35% interest in Leyland Kenya and its 51% interest in the other two assembly firms. Tyres are manufactured by Firestone East Africa. The parent company, the US-based Firestone Corpn, reduced its share in the enterprise from 80% to 18% in 1985. An expansion programme for 1989–92, with a projected cost of K£22.5m., sought to increase production capacity from 500,000 tyres per year to 700,000 tyres per year. Steel processing, for the construction industry and for re-export, is a growing industry; in May 1997 14 steel mills were operational, with a further three scheduled to open by the end of the year. Controversy arose in 1996 over revelations that a bullet factory was being built at Eldoret by the Belgian corporation Fabrique Nationale de Herstal. Construction briefly ceased after fears were raised that the ammunition might be used in conflicts in volatile countries in the region, but resumed in March 1997. Cement, produced by the Bamburi Portland Cement Co and East African Portland Cement, was one of the most successful industries during the 1980s. However, this industry has been suffering the effects of irregular supplies of imported inputs, an increasingly competitive export market and the fall in the value of the US dollar (the currency in which cement earnings are denominated). Foreign companies own 74% of the Bamburi plant, the government 16% and local private investors 10%. There are three glassware factories, two owned by the Madhvani Group, and one by Kenya Breweries Ltd. There is a sheet glass factory at Mombasa. Charcoal is produced from coffee husks by Kenya Planters' Co-operative Union at Nairobi and is exported to the Middle East, as well as being used locally to replace some of the wood charcoal. The Bata Shoe Co has a factory at Voi, from which it exports to Tanzania and to markets in central Africa. A machine-tool manufacturing plant is being set up at Nairobi, in a joint venture with an Indian firm, and will include a training centre. Kenya Breweries Ltd, part of the East African Breweries Group, has four brewing plants, and it exports a small percentage of its beer. However, a reduction on liquor service duties introduced in 1995 has had a significant negative effect on the domestic brewing industry. In April 1997 South African Breweries announced that it was to invest in a brewery at Thika, scheduled to become operational in 1998 at a production capacity of 800,000 hl.

The Mombasa petroleum refinery, which is half-owned by the state and half by a group of international oil companies (BP, Caltex, Exxon and Shell), first went into production in 1963 and is capable of handling 4.2m. tons of crude petroleum annually, although only 2.1m. tons were handled in 1987. Refined petroleum products were, until recently, Kenya's largest source of foreign exchange, but the refinery needs a huge injection of funds to modernize it. Plans to extend the Mombasa-to-Nairobi oil pipeline as far as the Ugandan border were pledged financing of $120m. in 1990.

MINERALS

Mining activity in Kenya is so far limited, but prospecting is continuing. Soda ash, Kenya's principal mineral export, is extracted at Lake Magadi, in the Rift Valley; about 181,330 tons were produced in 1992 (compared with 231,900 tons in 1990). An estimated 216,000 and 224,000 tons were produced in 1993 and 1994 respectively. In 1997 the Canadian company, Tiomin Resources, announced the discovery of mineral sands along the coast to the north-east of Mombasa, containing substantial reserves of titanium and zircon. The other principal products are gold, salt, vermiculite and limestone. A fluorspar ore deposit in the Kerio valley in Rift Valley province has been mined since 1975: it produced 80,630 tons in 1992, and has a total capacity of 102,000 metric tons. The extraction of extensive deposits of rubies began in 1974; gems of up to 30 kg have been reported. Deposits of garnet crystals discovered at Tsavo have received high valuations. Other minerals identified in the region include apatite, graphite, kaolin, kyanite, rubies, topazes, green tourmalines and tsavolite. Searches for chromite, nickel, fluorspar and vermiculite in Central province, and for chromite, nickel and copper in the Kerio valley are being undertaken. Prospecting for petroleum and gas has continued intermittently on and off shore, but so far without significant results. Under an Oil Exploration Act, introduced in 1984, exploitation by foreign oil companies would be on a production-sharing basis. Exploration concessions have been taken by Amoco, Compagnie Française des Pétroles (CFP–Total), Marathon Oil Co, Mobil, Fina (of Belgium) and Petro-Canada, operating either independently or in consortia. In 1988 CFP–Total discovered traces of gas and oil in a test well drilled in Isiolo district, in the north-west. It was the 20th well to be drilled in Kenya since exploration began in the 1950s; the others, mostly in coastal areas, had all been dry. Several concessions came due for renewal in 1988, and Total's discovery, and the discovery of a deposit in Turkana district, revived the oil companies' flagging interest, although the commercial value of these finds is not yet known. The first exploration agreement since 1985 was awarded in 1989 to a consortium comprising Total, Amoco, Marathon and Texaco. The four-year agreement related to an area covering 32 sq km of the Wajit and Mandera districts in the north-east of the country. New agreements were finalized in mid-1990 with Amoco and Shell Exploration.

POWER

Electricity, apart from small local stations, is supplied inland by hydroelectric plants in the Tana river basin and by the geothermal station at Olkaria, and at the coast by an oil-fired plant. This is supplemented by a bulk supply of 30 MW from Owen Falls in Uganda under a 50-year agreement signed in 1958. However, the revival of Uganda's economy in the 1990s has led to increased demand for electricity there; an agreement was reached in 1997 that Kenya would pay a higher rate for electricity imported from Uganda. Hydroelectric plants supply about 75% of total generating capacity. There are five major stations on the Tana river: Gitaru, Kamburu, Kindaruma, Masinga and Kiambere. The 140-MW station at Kiambere was commissioned in 1988, increasing Kenya's total generating capacity to 715 MW. Another station, with a capacity of 105 MW, operates at Turkwel Gorge in Turkana district. The Olkaria geothermal scheme in the Rift valley, 90 km from Nairobi, began production in 1981 and now has three 15-MW generators in operation, with plans for a further two 64-MW units, to become operational in 2000 and 2001 respectively. In 1997 it was announced that the Japanese government was funding a hydropower project at Sondu-Miriu with a generating capacity of 60-MW. The drought of 1996–97 necessitated seven months of power rationing, and the urgent need for expansion in the sector became apparent. However, the tendering of contracts to Iberafrica of Spain, to supply a 44-MW diesel-fuelled unit for the Nairobi South power plant, and to Sabah Shipyard of Indonesia, to provide a 43-MW barge-mounted unit at Kipevu, near Mombasa, lacked transparency, according to the IMF: together with the government's failure to rationalize the energy sector, this was presented as a reason for the suspension of IMF aid in August 1997 (see below). A major study of the development of rivers in the Lake Victoria basin, for irrigation and hydropower, was begun in 1983. In 1997 the Kenya Power Co was established, to deal exclusively with the generation of electricity; the Kenya Power and Lighting Co continued to be responsible for electricity transmission and distribution.

COMMUNICATIONS

Kenya's extensive transport system includes road, rail, coastal and inland water and air. Full container-handling facilities have been added at Mombasa, the chief port, to deal with the volume of containers, which expanded from 50,000 20-ft (6-m) equivalent units (TEU) in 1982 to nearly 103,000 TEU in 1985. The modern container-handling terminal was opened in 1983, and the country's first inland clearance depot for containers, at Embakasi on the outskirts of Nairobi, began operating in 1984. In 1993 it was announced that Mombasa's Kilindini port was to be expanded by 1,200 ha. Mombasa provides access to the sea for Uganda, eastern Zaire, Burundi and Rwanda. Although faced with competition from Dar es Salaam, in Tanzania, which was undergoing modernization, Mombasa handled 7,991,822 metric tons in 1992, compared with 7,143,876 tons in 1991. Transit cargo passing through the port to neighbouring states (including northern Tanzania) increased sharply from 527,418 tons in 1991 to 1,209,977 tons in 1992. The government acknowledged in 1997 that the diversion into the Kenyan market of goods nominally in transit had become a serious problem, and promised measures to tighten controls on transit cargo.

Kenya Airways has operated its own international services since the break-up of East African Airways. In April 1989 the airline inaugurated a freighter service to Europe: fresh flowers and vegetables were the main outward cargo. In 1992 Kenya Airways underwent a major reorganization in preparation for privatization, which took place in 1996. African Express Airkenya, a private passenger airline, began operating regular services between Kenya and Europe in 1986. A project to construct the country's third international airport, at Eldoret in central Kenya (President Moi's home town) was completed in 1996, at an estimated cost of US $49m. Critics, including international donors, considered the scheme to be an unnecessary waste of resources. Meanwhile, Jomo Kenyatta International and Moi International Airports were undergoing modernization during the mid-1990s.

A 590-km road between Kitale and Juba, in Southern Sudan, provides an all-weather road link between the two countries. Rebuilding of 175 km of Kenyan roads, with financing by the EU and Germany, began in 1990 as part of the 'northern corridor' scheme to improve access for land-locked countries to Mombasa port. In early 1990 Japan promised to provide almost US $200m. in concessionary finance to help develop road infrastructure and airports. In February 1996 the World Bank approved a $165m. loan to finance the urgent rehabilitation of the important Nairobi–Mombasa road link. Construction of the Ks. 349.3m. trans-Mara highway commenced in 1996, with an expected completion date of December 1997. A $155m. programme to rehabilitate urban road surfaces, with financial assistance from the World Bank, was expected to commence in 1997.

The railway in Kenya runs from the coast at Mombasa, through Nairobi, to western Kenya, and on to points in Tanzania and Uganda. A three-year project to improve Kenya Railways Corporation's operations, at an expected cost of US $45.5m., was started in 1987, and was aimed, in particular, at making the railways more competitive in the freight market. In 1995/96 Kenya Railways Corpn made a loss, and in 1997 the government proposed that locomotives and rolling stock be leased out to private operators.

Under a major telecommunications development project, funded by the World Bank and started in 1983, international subscriber dialling was introduced in 1984, and between 1970 and 1984 the number of exchange lines rose from 70,000 to 106,000. In 1994 Kenya had nine telephones for every 1,000 inhabitants. In August 1992 a K£119m. radio transmitter, in the Ngong hills near Nairobi, was inaugurated, reportedly bringing 95% of the population within range of radio transmissions. There is an earth satellite station at Longonot. In February 1997 government plans were announced to install 300,000 new telephone lines in rural areas and 2.4m. new lines in urban centres over a period of some years; moreover, Kenya Posts and Telecommunications Corpn was to be divided, prior to privatization, into three entities: Telkom Kenya, the Postal Corpn of Kenya and the Communications Commission of Kenya (a regulatory body).

TOURISM

In 1989 tourism became Kenya's largest source of foreign exchange, in terms of gross receipts. Earnings from the sector amounted to US $442m. in 1992. Over the period 1983–90 the number of visitors increased steadily. Arrivals totalled 817,550 in 1991. However, the number of visitors declined to 698,540 in 1992. A number of well-publicized attacks on foreign tourists and reports of political unrest in the country were believed to have contributed to this decline. Tourist arrivals recovered to 826,200 in 1993 and to 863,400 in 1994; in the latter year earnings from the sector totalled about $505m. In 1995 tourism receipts dropped to an estimated $430m., with the number of visitors declining to about 690,000; the sector recovered somewhat in 1996, with receipts rising to approximately $440m. and tourist arrivals estimated at 717,000. Germany and the United Kingdom provide the largest number of tourists.

FOREIGN TRADE, BALANCE OF PAYMENTS AND AID

Kenya typically has a substantial deficit in visible trade with countries outside Africa. Its terms of trade have fluctuated quite widely since the mid-1970s, but, overall, there has been a general decline. In 1977 the trade deficit was less than K£30m., but this rose to K£267m. in 1978, with the end of the coffee boom and soaring import costs. Reduced imports and higher export earnings meant that the 1983 deficit was reduced to K£250.5m., from K£375.2m. in 1982. In 1984 export earnings rose by about 19%, owing to high prices for tea and coffee, to K£777.8m., but imports also rose (to K£1,114.8m.), partly because of liberalization measures but also because of additional food imports, made necessary by drought. In 1985 exports increased further, to K£802.4m., but the import bill rose to K£1,201.5m., so that the trade gap widened to K£399.1m., 18% more than in 1984. Higher coffee earnings helped to increase 1986 export earnings to K£958m. (including re-exports worth about K£29m.), while the import bill rose less steeply, to K£1,338m., producing a smaller deficit than in 1985, at K£380m. In 1987, however, export earnings declined sharply to K£790m. (of which K£36m. derived from re-exports), while imports increased to K£1,431m., producing a deficit of K£641m. Although exports improved to K£1,184m. in 1990, the value of imports soared to K£2,434m., producing a trade deficit of K£1,250m. Merchandise exports of US $1,185.3m. and imports of $1,697.3m. produced a visible trade deficit of $511.9m. in 1991.

Merchandise imports of $1,608.7m. exceeded merchandise exports of $1,108.5m. in 1992, yielding a visible trade deficit in that year of $500.2m. In 1993 imports totalled $1,509.6m., while the value of merchandise exports increased to $1,262.6m., producing a reduced trade deficit of $247.0m. A deficit of $238.4m. was recorded in 1994 (the value of merchandise exports in that year was $1,537.0m., while imports stood at $1,775.3m.). In 1995, however, the value of merchandise imports soared to $2,652.4m.; exports grew more modestly, to $1,914.3m., with the trade deficit more than doubling, to $738.1m. The value of imports in 1996 was expected to exceed $3,000m.

In an attempt to reduce dependence on fluctuating world prices for its main agricultural commodities, the government has made efforts to stimulate nontraditional exports including horticultural produce, canned pineapple products, handicrafts, clothing, leather, cement, soda ash and fluorspar. The stimulation of exports of manufactured goods, including textiles, paper and vehicles, has also been a priority. Manufacturing was hampered by restrictions on imports of raw materials, parts and machinery until 1992, when these restrictions began to be removed gradually. In 1993 manufactured products accounted for 29% of Kenya's total exports. After crude oil and petroleum products, the largest import bill in that year was for industrial machinery and transport equipment. Consumer goods accounted for only about 15% of the total.

Pattern of Trade

The major outlet for Kenya's exports, outside east Africa, continues to be Europe. The United Kingdom is still the most important trading partner, accounting for 14.6% of Kenyan exports and 14.3% of its imports in 1993, and according to the IMF, for 10% of exports and 12.6% of imports in 1995. However, the main source of imports is the United Arab Emirates, Kenya's main supplier of crude oil. Kenya's third main source of imports is Japan. Regional trade is important to Kenya, which has consistently had a favourable trade balance with its neighbours, to which it exports petroleum products, food and basic manufactures in particular. After the re-opening of the Kenya/Tanzania border (closed from 1977–83) trade with Tanzania was limited by that country's lack of foreign exchange; but exports to Tanzania increased rapidly during the 1990s, and in 1995, according to the IMF, accounted for some 13% of total exports. Official trade with Uganda was depressed from the 1970s, but Uganda received 8.6% of Kenya's imports in 1993 and by 1995 was Kenya's largest export market, accounting for 15.7% of total exports, according to IMF figures. A vast amount of goods are smuggled into Uganda from Kenya. It was hoped that the revival of the East African Community would boost trade between Kenya, Tanzania and Uganda.

Balance of Payments

Kenya's formerly strong balance of payments has been weak in most years since the early 1970s.

In September 1981 Kenya obtained a US $115m. eight-year Euroloan as balance-of-payments support. In January 1982 the IMF authorized a stand-by arrangement, worth $175.7m. over 12 months, to support the government's economic stabilization programme. However, the government was unable to fulfil the IMF's conditions, and the arrangement was suspended in mid-year. Following a 15% devaluation of the shilling in December 1982, a new arrangement, for SDR 175.95m. over 18 months, was finally approved in March 1983. This, together with additional balance-of-payments aid from bilateral donors, helped to reduce the deficit on the current account from $304.7m. in 1982 to $48.1m. in 1983. Subsequently the effects of drought and the high cost of debt-servicing combined to increase the current account deficit. A 12-month stand-by facility from the IMF, worth SDR 85.2m., was agreed in January 1985, to support the government's 1985 economic programme. The current account deficit was reduced from $173.8m. in 1985 to $68.5m. in 1986; in 1987, however, there was a sharp deterioration in Kenya's terms of trade, and this, combined with the government's somewhat over-inflationary policies, resulted in an overall balance-of-payments deficit of nearly $100m., compared with a surplus of $116.9m. in 1986. The deficit on the current account widened to $579.6m. in 1989, following a period of import-led growth, but was reduced to $527.1m. in 1990 and to $213.3m. in 1991. The current account deficit narrowed to $180.2m. in 1992, and in 1993 the current account showed a surplus of $71.2m. A further surplus, of $97.9m., was recorded in 1994; in 1995, however, there was a current account deficit of $400.4m. Although there was a surplus of $122m. on the overall balance-of-payments account in 1989, deficits of $92.5m., $43.9m. and $256.9m. were registered in 1990, 1991 and 1992 respectively. In 1993 the overall balance-of-payments showed a surplus of $411.8m.; in 1994 the surplus narrowed to $61.6m., and in 1995 a deficit of $142.0m. was registered. In January 1988 a new IMF arrangement, worth SDR 175.2m., was agreed. Of the total, SDR 85m. was a stand-by facility, to be drawn over 18 months, and SDR 90.2m. was a three-year structural adjustment facility (SAF). In accordance with IMF requirements, the government maintained a flexible exchange rate policy and the value of the shilling was allowed to move steadily downwards in relation to the major international currencies. Kenya received the approval of the IMF for its management of the economy during the late 1980s, particularly for having reduced the rate of increase in money supply. However, the budget deficit remained a problem, as did the losses incurred by the country's parastatal bodies. In April 1989 the government reached agreement with the IMF and the World Bank on the release of funds to support an economic programme for 1989–91: the funds included an enhanced structural adjustment facility (ESAF) worth SDR 240m., which was made available in late May, and replaced the SAF that had been arranged in January 1988. In December 1991 the 'Paris Club' of official creditors suspended aid to Kenya (see below).

Kenya's reserves of foreign exchange stood at US $80m. at the end of 1992, compared with $460m. in 1985, having been deliberately depleted to relieve pressure on the balance of payments. By the end of 1993 reserves had recovered to $437m., and at the end of 1994 they stood at $588m., increasing to $853m. at the end of 1995. In November 1996 the government estimated the country's reserves of foreign exchange to be $1,225m. The government has bowed to pressure from the IMF and the World Bank to liberalize the sale of foreign exchange. It is estimated that overseas holdings by Kenyan residents amount to at least $4,000m.

At the end of 1995 Kenya's total external debt was US $7,381m., of which $6,372m. was long-term public debt. The debt-service ratio (as a percentage of the value of exports of goods and services) has declined from 41.7% in 1987 to 25.7% in 1995. The government's borrowing on the domestic market had ballooned to 20.7% of GDP by 1997, prompting the planned flotation of a Eurobond in 1998, to alleviate repayments. Debt-service charges for 1997/98 were forecast at Ks. 9,112m. on foreign debt and Ks. 21,568m. on domestic debt.

Aid

Since independence, Kenya has received substantial amounts of development aid. In 1982 Kenya asked its main donors to provide additional balance-of-payments support to help to halt the serious economic decline. A series of donors' meetings took place over the next few months and more than US $77m. was subsequently pledged. Early in 1984 the World Bank-sponsored Consultative Group of aid donors to Kenya met in Paris to discuss the government's 1984–88 Development Plan, which required external financing of about $520m. in both 1984 and 1985. At a further meeting, held in April 1986, $900m. was pledged for the following two years. In October 1988 donors' commitments for 1989 totalled $1,100m. The sources of aid have diversified considerably in recent years. The share provided by the United Kingdom has fallen, while multilateral agencies, particularly the World Bank and the European Development Fund, have increased their share. In July 1982 the World Bank approved a $131m. structural adjustment programme, the second that it had made to Kenya. However, disbursement of the second tranche of this loan was suspended in 1983, because Kenya had not yet fulfilled the Bank's conditions on de-controlling maize marketing, and it was not completed until early 1984. Discussions concerning a third structural adjustment loan subsequently collapsed, since agreement had still not been reached on grain marketing, and the World Bank decided to revert to sectoral loans from 1986. Following an improvement in relations with the Bank, donors were encouraged to provide larger amounts.

In early 1989 the Federal Republic of Germany, Kenya's principal bilateral creditor, announced that it would cancel the total debt of US $435m. in return for increased Kenyan investment in projects aimed at protecting the environment. Japan also increased its aid to Kenya, becoming the country's largest official donor. An ESAF agreement, concluded with the IMF in April 1989, resulted in the World Bank's approval for two credits, totalling $89m., in October. Of the total amount, $45m. was the second tranche of a $110m. industrial sector adjustment credit (ISAC), which commenced during the previous year. The remaining $44m. was to supplement a $115.3m. financial sector credit approved in mid-1989. Relations with the international donor community were strained towards the end of 1989, when the government proposed building a 60-storey media complex at a cost of $200m., with 'offshore' commercial financing. At a special January 1990 donors' meeting to discuss levels of external commercial borrowing proposed by the Kenyan government since mid-1989, donors expressed concern that the new loans would raise the debt-service ratio and would slow productive investment. The USA agreed to cancel Kenya's debt on condition that the government agreed to abandon its plans for the media complex, which it subsequently did. In November 1991, however, the 'Paris Club' declared a moratorium on aid to Kenya, pending the implementation of economic and political reforms. Following the holding of multi-party elections in December 1992 (see Recent History), lending resumed in April 1993. Total development aid from all sources amounted to $894m. in 1993. In December 1993 the IMF agreed to a one-year ESAF arrangement totalling $61.97m., of which one half was disbursed immediately. At a 'Paris Club' meeting in January 1994 donors pledged a total of $850m. for 1994; a further $800m. was pledged in December 1994, but much of this remained undisbursed, following 'informal talks' between the government and donors in Paris in July 1995, at which strong reservations were expressed about the Moi regime's economic management and human rights record. In September 1995 the IMF withheld a $216m. ESAF, pending decisive action by the Kenyan authorities to eradicate allegedly endemic corruption. At a meeting in Paris in March 1996 donors announced a $730m. aid package for Kenya; however, as a substantial proportion of the assistance pledged for 1994 had not yet been disbursed, it remained unclear whether or not the 1996 assistance represented wholly new funds. The IMF agreed to release the $216m. ESAF in April 1996; however, the second tranche of $37m., scheduled for release in November, was postponed, owing to concerns over the slow progress of privatization and reform, particularly in the power sector. In July 1997, following the collapse of court proceedings in a corruption scandal (see Recent History), the IMF once again delayed disbursement. In August the IMF suspended disbursement of the second and third tranches of the ESAF, shortly after the government's dismissal of a customs official who was taking measures to prevent corruption in revenue collection.

PUBLIC FINANCE

The main features of the 1982/83 budget were increases in many import duties, a halving of capital gains tax and the withdrawal of the export compensation scheme, which had given exporters rebates of up to 20% of the value of their exported goods. In September 1982 President Moi announced that the scheme was to be reintroduced as part of the programme to stimulate manufactured exports. In the 1983/84 budget import duties on raw materials were reduced and rises in sales tax and the price of beer were introduced. Among the main features of the 1984/85 budget were a reduction of import duties on raw materials and capital equipment, the lowering of the commercial bank lending rate, and a reduction in withholding tax, to encourage foreign investment. The cautiously expansionary 1985/86 budget added 300 items of consumer goods to the import priority schedule (with the aim of making local industry more competitive) and abolished capital gains tax. It reduced tariffs on some imported raw materials and capital goods, and introduced a unified rate of export compensation in the hope of speeding up the payment procedure. Under the 1986/87 budget duty was increased on beer and cigarettes, while sales tax on diesel fuel, cooking fats and soap was reduced. The actual budgetary deficit was K£404m. (equivalent to 7% of GDP).

The 1987/88 budget proposals included measures to boost investment, with some reductions in taxes and duties on imported capital goods and raw materials for the manufacturing sector, and incentives for new industries located outside Nairobi and Mombasa. The actual budget deficit was K£328.6m., equivalent to 6.7% of GDP. The 1988/89 budget aimed to reduce the deficit by 20%, and to encourage foreign investment by allowing investors to deduct foreign exchange losses on their investments. Other new measures in the budget included the simplification of the tariff structure, the doubling of airport taxes, and increases in levies on cigarettes, beer, soft drinks and petrol, and the reduction of import duties on motor vehicles and on television and radio receivers. The actual budgetary deficit for 1988/89 was equivalent to 4.5% of GDP. The 1989/90 budget envisaged recurrent expenditure of K£2,472.8m. (an increase of 21% over actual expenditure in 1988/89) and development expenditure of K£922.1m. (14.4% higher than the out-turn for the previous year). Total revenue was forecast at K£2,493.9m. The actual budgetary deficit was equivalent to 4.2% of GDP. The 1990/91 budget envisaged a rapid expansion of exports, based on fiscal management and incentives to the private sector. The actual budgetary deficit was equivalent to 5.6% of GDP.

The budget proposals for 1991/92 envisaged total expenditure of K£3,538.2m., and included the restructuring of the taxation system. The budgetary deficit fell to 1.4% of GDP. Expenditure under the 1992/93 budget was forecast at K£4,670m., the budgetary deficit in that year was equivalent to 5.3% of GDP. The 1993/94 budget produced a K£1,453m. deficit which was equivalent to more than 7% of GNP, well outside the IMF ceiling of 5%. In 1994/95 expenditure of K£6,751m. and revenue totalling K£6,266m. left a more manageable shortfall of K£485.1m., equivalent to about 2% of GDP. In 1995/96 expenditure of K£7,661m. and revenue amounting to K£7,275m. created a budgetary deficit of K£385.6m. The fiscal year 1996/97 saw a significant overspend, incurred by imports of famine-relief maize, high levels of domestic debt-servicing, salary increases and the registration of voters for the forthcoming elections. In order to pay for these additional expenses, a Supplementary Appropriation Bill was passed by the national assembly, releasing some Ks. 5,750m. Budget proposals for 1997/98 (presented amidst turmoil—see Recent History, above) envisaged expenditure of K£7,994m. and revenue of K£7,971m., predicting a slight deficit of K£23.4m.

DEVELOPMENT PLANNING

Development policy in Kenya emphasizes the role of private enterprise in industry and commerce, and foreign investment is actively encouraged. Direct participation by the state in productive enterprises is limited, and in recent years the government has been withdrawing from unprofitable joint ventures. In 1991 the government announced that all remaining unproductive, 'non-strategic' state-owned companies were to be transferred to private-sector ownership; details of the impending privatization of some 207 such companies had been released by mid-1993. By June 1997 148 of these companies had been either privatized or dissolved. However, concerns were raised in 1997 over the slow pace of the privatization process which had been scheduled for completion by the end of the year; this could in part be attributed to the poor performance of some parastatals, but there were also suspicions that the government was unwilling to divest itself of some lucrative assets.

Kenya's first Development Plan, revised in 1966, covered the period 1964–70. Important objectives of the plan included the Kenyanization of the economy, until then largely in expatriate hands. The second Development Plan (1969/70–1973/74) had as a basic objective the acceleration of rural development and the rectification of the imbalance between rural and urban incomes. Annual growth targets under the third Development Plan (1974–78) were assisted by the rise in world coffee prices during 1976 and 1977. One of the main themes of Kenya's fourth Development Plan (1979–83) was the fight against rural poverty. However, the deteriorating economic situation led the government to revise the Plan in May 1980, lowering the target annual growth rate of GDP from 6.3% to 5.4%.

The fifth Development Plan (1984–88) envisaged an average annual growth rate of 4.9%, showing a much more cautious approach than in the previous Plan. It placed greater reliance on domestic resources for financing development. There was to be continued emphasis on projects for the benefit of the poor and on attaining a better balance between urban and rural areas.

In 1986 the government published details of a programme for economic reform (Sessional Paper No. 1), which aimed to increase productivity, provide incentives and stimulate investment in the private sector, develop and diversify agricultural and industrial exports and to create jobs in rural areas.

A sixth Development Plan, covering the period 1989–93, aimed primarily to increase earnings of foreign exchange and to generate employment through the expansion of the industrial sector. The targeted average annual growth rate for the economy as a whole was 5.4%; an annual increase of 4.5% was projected for the agricultural sector, and growth of 6.4% per year for the manufacturing sector. Some reforms of the health and education sectors, including the introduction of charges to users, were to be introduced in order to reduce the budgetary deficit. The plan also aimed to reduce the rate of population growth, by promoting family planning. In 1990 import duty and value added tax were withdrawn from goods intended for the manufacture of exports, in order to stimulate industrial expansion. During the first half of 1992, however, following the imposition by foreign donors in November 1991 of a moratorium on aid (see above), the government implemented a sweeping programme of economic reforms: these included the liberalization of imports, exports and exchange control, the streamlining of government ministries, price deregulation and a reduction in the bureaucracy surrounding incoming foreign investment. Although the reform measures were briefly suspended in March 1993, having been denounced by President Moi as 'dictatorial and suicidal', they were reintroduced in May, following the announcement by the World Bank in April that it would resume aid allocations to Kenya. In a speech delivered for him in early May 1994, President Moi vowed to continue with the policy of economic liberalization already under way. The Kenyan currency was devalued by 32% between July 1991 and June 1992, by 37% in February 1993, and by 23% in April 1993. According to an assessment made by the IMF in May 1994 Kenya has made 'important headway' in tightening monetary conditions. The Kenya shilling, the IMF pointed out, had 'appreciated' from over KSh. 80=US $1 to about KSh. 60=US $1 during the previous 12 months. In May 1994 the government announced the liberalization of foreign exchange controls which would allow commercial banks to undertake foreign exchange transactions without reference to the Central Bank. The new measures, which took immediate effect, meant that the Kenyan shilling became fully convertible against other world currencies. The shilling exhibited marked stability when exposed to market forces: immediately after flotation, in May 1994, its value stood at KSh. 56.48=US $1, and in 1995 it had strengthened to an annual average rate of KSh. 51.43=US $1.

The eighth Development Plan (1997–2001) differed from previous plans in that it aimed primarily to foster an enabling environment for the private sector, rather than emphasizing the state's role in raising and sustaining growth. The targeted average annual growth rate for the economy was 5.9%, entailing annual investment equivalent to more than 25% of GDP. Stated methods included the curbing of corruption and the enhancement of revenue collection, the rationalization of the tax system, reform in the civil service and in public enterprises and further market liberalization. However, the plan was jeopardized by the suspension of IMF assistance in August 1997.

REGIONAL ARRANGEMENTS AND PROBLEMS

In 1967 Kenya, Tanzania and Uganda founded the East African Community (EAC), which comprised a customs union and a range of public services, including the East African Development Bank, operated on a collectively-managed basis. During the early 1970s, however, major economic and political tensions developed between the EAC's member countries. By the beginning of 1977 the railways had effectively become national enterprises, East African Airways had broken up and Kenya had launched its own Kenya Airways. In February Tanzania closed its border with Kenya, and trade between the two countries virtually ceased. In July 1977, for practical purposes, the EAC ceased to exist. The East African Development Bank, however, has continued to function.

Negotiations concerning the distribution of the EAC's assets and liabilities among the former member states continued intermittently for six years, under the chairmanship of a World Bank-appointed mediator. Agreement was eventually reached in November 1983, and a new era of improved relations between the three countries seemed at least a possibility. Kenya was allocated a 42.5% share of the assets, whose value was put at $898m., while Tanzania received 32.5% and Uganda 25%. Long-term external debts totalled about $220m., and a creditors' meeting was arranged to discuss possible rescheduling. In addition, Uganda was to be paid compensation of US $191m. by the other two partners, because their shares of the assets were calculated as greater than the equity shares which they held in the former community corporations. Kenya started to pay this compensation by transferring some of its railway rolling stock to Uganda. An immediate result of the settlement was the re-opening of the Kenya/Tanzania border, which provided some limited opportunities for Kenyan exporters. The two countries' airlines resumed inter-state flights in 1984 and there have been agreements on overland transport, the cross-border transport of tourists, an expanded air service and co-operation in shipping and port services. In November 1994 the leaders of Kenya, Tanzania and Uganda established a permanent tripartite commission for co-operation. In March 1996 the secretariat of the permanent tripartite commission for East African co-operation was formally inaugurated: its aims were to enhance regional co-operation in political and economic affairs, and to reduce its members' reliance on foreign aid. In April 1997 a four-year development strategy was launched for this revived EAC, along with a regional passport designed to facilitate cross-border trade.

PROBLEMS AND PROSPECTS

Kenya's high rate of population growth has imposed major strains upon the economy, in terms of public expenditure, as well as threatening social stability. However, government initiatives to encourage family planning have had significant success in reducing the rate in recent years. The average fertility rate fell from 7.8 children per adult female in 1980 to 4.9 in 1994, and the population growth rate declined from an annual average of 3.4% in 1980–90 to 2.9% in 1990–95. Another major constraint to growth has been the balance-of-payments problem. The period of rapid growth had ended by 1978. External factors contributing to the sharp slowdown included deteriorating terms of trade, with rising prices for petroleum and other imports and generally low world prices for Kenya's commodities. Internal factors included: lack of incentives to agricultural producers in some sectors; shortages of imported inputs for manufacturers; high government spending; an overvalued currency; low wages, which have declined in real terms, and consequent poor productivity; and too much stress on industries relying heavily on expensive imported materials and equipment.

Pressure from the IMF, the World Bank and bilateral donors helped to persuade the government to take a firm grip on the economy and on public spending by late 1982. In September of that year President Moi stressed the government's commitment to encouraging the private sector and foreign investment, both public and private. In June 1986 a radical departure from Kenya's previously liberal policy on foreign investment was indicated in a speech by President Moi, in which he declared that Kenyans should henceforth hold controlling interests in joint ventures with foreigners. The government attempted, however, to dispel fears that this policy would endanger existing foreign investments. Following the collapse of a number of financial institutions, owing to the malpractice and mismanagement of their directors, the government formed a committee in August to investigate the scandal and to restore public confidence in Kenya's financial system. A further wave of bank collapses led the government to take action again in 1994 to strengthen the sector. However, two more banks collapsed in mid-1996, apparently as a result of bad debts linked to major cases of corruption.

Progress has been made in solving some of Kenya's economic problems. Liberalization has made imported inputs more freely available and has eased currency distortions, and government expenditure has been restrained, although further curtailment is required. In addition, productivity levels have improved, with gross output per employee increasing by 135% in 1980–92, and the privatization of unprofitable state-owned companies is taking place. However, there remain many serious flaws in the economy's basic structure, and pressure on land and the lack of alternative employment for the growing numbers of landless people represent serious long-term difficulties. The sweeping programme of economic reforms implemented by the government in 1992 attempted to address these problems, although the positive effects of the reforms may take some time to permeate through the economy. By early 1993 measures to liberalize agricultural marketing had produced mixed results, but the introduction of foreign exchange retention accounts had clearly facilitated the importation of raw materials by manufacturers. The effects on the economy of widespread corruption became increasingly manifest during 1997; the government, however, appeared unwilling to take decisive action against those responsible. Meanwhile, civic unrest in mid-1997 threatened both the tourism industry and foreign investment. The government was expected to make emergency cuts in budgetary expenditure, following the suspension of IMF loans in August 1997; serious repercussions on the economy were feared.

Statistical Survey

Source (unless otherwise stated): Central Bureau of Statistics, POB 30256, Nairobi; tel (2) 33970.

Area and Population

AREA, POPULATION AND DENSITY

Area (sq km)	580,367*
Population (census results)†	
24 August 1979	15,327,061
24 August 1989	
Males	10,628,368
Females	10,815,268
Total	21,443,636
Population (official estimates at mid-year)	
1993	28,113,000
1994	29,292,000
1995	30,522,000
Density (per sq km) at mid-1995	52.6

* 224,081 sq miles. Total includes 11,230 sq km (4,336 sq miles) of inland water.
† Excluding adjustment for underenumeration.

PRINCIPAL ETHNIC GROUPS (census of August 1989)

African	21,163,076	European	34,560
Arab	41,595	Other*	115,220
Asian	89,185	**Total**	21,443,636

* Includes persons who did not state 'tribe' or 'race'.

PRINCIPAL TOWNS (estimated population at census of August 1989)

Nairobi (capital)	1,346,000	Meru	78,100
Mombasa	465,000	Thika	57,100
Kisumu*	185,100	Kitale	53,000
Nakuru	162,800	Kisii	44,000
Eldoret*	104,900	Kericho	40,000
Nyeri*	88,600	Malindi*	35,200

* Boundaries extended between 1979 and 1989.

BIRTHS AND DEATHS (UN estimates, annual averages)

	1980-85	1985–90	1990–95
Birth rate (per 1,000)	48.7	46.1	44.5
Death rate (per 1,000)	13.2	11.7	11.7

Expectation of life (UN estimates, years at birth, 1990–95): 55.7 (males 54.2; females 57.3).

Source: UN, *World Population Prospects: The 1994 Revision.*

ECONOMICALLY ACTIVE POPULATION
(estimates, '000 persons, 1991)

	Males	Females	Total
Agriculture, etc.	4,587	3,270	7,857
Industry	657	159	816
Services	972	615	1,587
Total	6,216	4,044	10,260

Source: UN Economic Commission for Africa, *African Statistical Yearbook*.

Mid-1995 (estimates in '000): Agriculture, etc. 10,621; Total labour force 13,620 (Source: FAO, *Production Yearbook*).

Agriculture

PRINCIPAL CROPS ('000 metric tons)

	1993	1994	1995
Wheat*	150	277	330
Rice (paddy)†	51	60	60
Barley	63*	65†	60†
Maize	2,089	3,085*	2,750*
Millet	58	59*	60†
Sorghum	115	130†	130†
Potatoes	185	162	205
Sweet potatoes†	630	630	630
Cassava (Manioc)†	810	830	840
Pulses	113	254	270†
Cottonseed*	11	6	8
Cotton lint*	5	3	4
Coconuts†	43	43	43
Vegetables (incl. melons)†	655	655	655
Sugar cane†	4,470	3,780	4,300
Pineapples†	270	270	270
Bananas†	220	220	220
Plantains†	360	360	370
Cashew nuts†	15	15	15
Coffee (green)	75	80	93*
Tea (made)	211	209	245*
Tobacco (leaves)†	10	10	10
Sisal	35	34	34†

* Unofficial figure(s). † FAO estimate(s).

Source: FAO, *Production Yearbook.*

LIVESTOCK (FAO estimates, '000 head, year ending September)

	1993	1994	1995
Cattle	12,500	12,500	13,000
Sheep	5,500	5,500	5,600
Goats	7,300	7,300	7,400
Pigs	100	102	104
Camels	810	810	810

Poultry (FAO estimates, million): 24 in 1993; 25 in 1994; 25 in 1995.

Source: FAO, *Production Yearbook*.

LIVESTOCK PRODUCTS ('000 metric tons)

	1993	1994	1995*
Beef and veal*	230	230	240
Mutton and lamb*	22	22	22
Goats' meat*	29	29	29
Pig meat*	5	5	5
Poultry meat*	47	48	48
Other meat*	30	31	31
Edible offals*	56	56	58
Cows' milk*	2,080	2,080	2,170
Sheep's milk*	24	24	25
Goats' milk*	91	91	93
Butter and ghee	2.4†	2.4†	2.5
Cheese	0.2	0.1	0.1
Poultry eggs*	40.3	42.0	42.0
Honey*	23.0	24.0	25.0
Wool:			
greasy*	1.9	1.9	1.9
clean*	0.9	0.9	1.0
Cattle hides*	36.8	36.8	38.2

* FAO estimates. † Unofficial figure.

Source: FAO, mainly *Production Yearbook*.

Forestry

ROUNDWOOD REMOVALS
(FAO estimates, '000 cubic metres, excluding bark)

	1992	1993	1994
Sawlogs, veneer logs and logs for sleepers	460	460	460
Pulpwood	357	357	357
Other industrial wood	1,001	1,038	1,075
Fuel wood	35,788	37,137	38,480
Total	37,606	38,992	40,372

Source: FAO, *Yearbook of Forest Products*.

SAWNWOOD PRODUCTION (FAO estimates, '000 cubic metres)

	1992	1993	1994
Total*	185	185	185

* Annual output of sawnwood is assumed to be unchanged since 1989.

Source: FAO, *Yearbook of Forest Products*.

Fishing

('000 metric tons, live weight)

	1993	1994	1995
Silver cyprinid	42.5	69.1	56.8
Nile tilapia	12.7	11.8	12.4
Other tilapias	7.9	6.4	7.6
Mouthbrooding cichlids	3.5	4.2	4.8
Nile perch	100.0	104.1	102.5
Other fishes (incl. unspecified)	15.9	7.5	8.3
Other aquatic animals	0.7	0.9	1.4
Total catch	183.2	204.0	193.8
Inland waters	177.5	200.1	188.3
Indian Ocean	5.7	3.9	5.5

Source: FAO, *Yearbook of Fishery Statistics*.

Mining

(metric tons)

	1990	1991	1992
Soda ash	231,900	219,500	181,330
Fluorspar	80,529	77,402	80,630
Salt	70,318	72,441	72,494
Limestone products†	35,733	32,017	30,656

† Excluding limestone used for production of cement.

1993 (metric tons): Soda ash 216,000; Fluorspar 78,700.
1994 (metric tons): Soda ash 224,000; Fluorspar 64,000.

Source (for 1993–94): UN, *Industrial Commodity Statistics Yearbook*.

Industry

SELECTED PRODUCTS ('000 metric tons, unless otherwise indicated)

	1992	1993*	1994*
Wheat flour	222	143	191
Raw sugar	397	375	303
Beer ('000 hectolitres)	3,686	3,589	3,250
Cigarettes (million)	7,031	7,267	7,319
Cement	1,507	1,417	1,452
Motor spirit (petrol)	348	329	329
Kerosene and jet fuel	455	426	421
Distillate fuel oils	580	529	539
Residual fuel oil	670	664	630
Electric energy (million kWh)	3,215	3,396	3,538

* Source: UN, *Industrial Commodity Statistics Yearbook*.

Finance

CURRENCY AND EXCHANGE RATES

Monetary Units
100 cents = 1 Kenya shilling (Ks.);
Ks. 20 = 1 Kenya pound (K£).

Sterling and Dollar Equivalents (31 March 1997)
£1 sterling = Ks. 89.82;
US $1 = Ks. 54.70;
Ks. 1,000 = £11.13 sterling = $18.28.

Average Exchange Rate (Ks. per US $)
1994 56.051
1995 51.430
1996 57.115

Note: The foregoing information refers to the Central Bank's mid-point exchange rate. However, with the introduction of a foreign exchange bearer certificate (FEBC) scheme in October 1991, a dual exchange rate system is in effect. In May 1994 foreign exchange transactions were liberalized and the Kenya shilling became fully convertible against other currencies.

BUDGET (Ks. million, year ending 30 June)

Revenue*	1993/94	1994/95	1995/96
Tax revenue	91,537	108,697	123,008
Taxes on income and profits	36,570	43,287	48,054
Taxes on goods and services	40,276	45,099	52,203
Value-added tax	29,049	24,479	28,404
Excise duties	11,227	19,332	22,612
Taxes on international trade	14,691	18,598	21,176
Import duties	14,691	18,598	21,176
Non-tax revenue	11,286	16,615	22,494
Property income	1,604	3,802	8,401
Administrative fees and charges	2,408	4,471	3,786
Total	102,823	125,312	145,502

Expenditure†	1993/94	1994/95	1995/96
General administration	18,486	18,003	33,621
Defence	5,320	7,367	9,039
Social services	32,260	44,195	39,387
Education	22,575	30,717	29,501
Health	7,076	9,595	8,872
Housing, community amenities and social welfare	2,609	3,883	1,014
Economic services	26,514	32,857	29,643
General administration	2,729	2,637	2,929
Agriculture, forestry and fishing	12,031	10,069	9,454
Mining, manufacturing and construction	2,137	4,858	1,572
Electricity, water, gas and steam	2,153	4,191	2,745
Roads	3,536	6,242	7,571
Other transport and communications	2,473	3,336	4,386
Other economic services	1,455	1,524	986
Interest on public debt	46,652	31,823	37,245
Unallocated	1,718	1,428	3,619
Sub-total	130,950	135,672	152,554
Adjustment to cash basis	933	−658	659
Total	131,883	135,014	153,213

* Excluding grants received (Ks. million): 4,025 in 1993/94; 5,508 in 1994/95; 5,815 in 1995/96.

† Including lending minus repayments (Ks. million): 2,516 in 1993/94; 1,592 in 1994/95; 2,840 in 1995/96.

Source: IMF, *Kenya—Statistical Appendix* (May 1997).

INTERNATIONAL RESERVES (US $ million at 31 December)

	1994	1995	1996
Gold*	15.2	15.4	14.8
IMF special drawing rights	0.7	0.3	0.8
Reserve position in IMF	18.0	18.3	17.7
Foreign exchange	538.9	334.8	728.0
Total	572.8	368.8	761.3

* National valuation of gold reserves (80,000 troy oz in each year).

Source: IMF, *International Financial Statistics*.

MONEY SUPPLY (Ks. million at 31 December)

	1994	1995	1996
Currency outside banks	24,817	28,891	30,394
Demand deposits at commercial banks	39,294	38,994	43,094
Total money (incl. others)	66,792	69,337	78,999

Source: IMF, *International Financial Statistics*.

COST OF LIVING (Consumer Price Index for low-income group in Nairobi; annual averages; base: 1990 = 100)

	1992	1993	1994
Food	166.9	242.4	316.8
Fuel and light	122.6	178.6	193.4
Clothing	134.9	166.0	209.1
Rent	154.5	225.2	290.6
All items (incl. others)	154.5	225.2	290.6

1995: Food 309.8; All items 297.1.

Source: ILO, *Yearbook of Labour Statistics*.

NATIONAL ACCOUNTS (Ks. million at current prices)

Expenditure on the Gross Domestic Product

	1993	1994	1995
Government final consumption expenditure	48,307	60,719	69,140
Private final consumption expenditure	210,342	265,663	335,505
Increase in stocks	2,246	1,683	5,000
Gross fixed capital formation	56,505	75,616	87,634
Total domestic expenditure	317,400	403,681	497,279
Exports of goods and services	129,554	148,282	152,482
Less Imports of goods and services	113,277	137,188	181,909
GDP in purchasers' values	333,677	414,775	467,852
GDP at constant 1982 prices	100,419	103,130	107,705

Source: IMF, *Kenya—Statistical Appendix* (May 1997).

Gross Domestic Product by Economic Activity (at factor cost)

	1993	1994	1995
Agriculture, hunting, forestry and fishing	89,406	112,443	122,697
Mining and quarrying	704	714	724
Manufacturing	28,394	36,155	43,185
Electricity, gas and water	3,665	4,481	5,441
Construction	15,260	16,954	18,353
Trade, restaurants and hotels	38,413	52,020	60,501
Transport, storage and communication	19,838	25,259	30,407
Finance, insurance, real estate and business services	47,930	61,794	72,335
Other services	40,162	37,352	42,514
Total	283,772	347,172	396,157

Source: IMF, *Kenya—Statistical Appendix* (May 1997).

BALANCE OF PAYMENTS (US $ million)

	1993	1994	1995
Exports of goods f.o.b.	1,262.6	1,537.0	1,914.3
Import of goods f.o.b.	−1,509.6	−1,775.3	−2,652.4
Trade balance	−247.0	−238.4	−738.1
Exports of services	1,063.5	1,117.3	1,034.5
Imports of services	−569.4	−686.8	−871.3
Balance on goods and services	247.0	192.2	−574.9
Other income received	3.3	20.9	25.6
Other income paid	−392.2	−385.7	−350.5
Balance on goods, services and income	−141.8	−172.6	−899.8
Current transfers received	276.0	333.7	544.8
Current transfers paid	−63.0	−63.2	−45.5
Current balance	71.2	97.9	−400.4
Capital account	28.1	−0.4	−0.4
Direct investment from abroad	1.6	3.7	32.5
Portfolio investment assets	—	—	6.0
Other investment assets	−31.4	171.1	261.6
Other investment liabilities	85.0	−216.5	−52.5
Net errors and omissions	257.5	5.8	11.4
Overall balance	411.8	61.6	−142.0

Source: IMF, *International Financial Statistics*.

External Trade

PRINCIPAL COMMODITIES (distribution by SITC, US $'000)

Imports c.i.f.	1991	1992	1993
Food and live animals	92,493	204,270	152,575
Cereals and cereal preparations	67,919	123,203	102,131
Wheat and meslin (unmilled)	38,205	23,957	62,050
Crude materials (inedible) except fuels	42,471	49,597	50,806
Mineral fuels, lubricants, etc	319,909	451,362	253,889
Petroleum and petroleum products	309,456	435,416	241,823
Animal and vegetable oils and fats	71,878	98,687	70,737
Chemicals and related products	277,296	272,464	346,571
Medicinal and pharmaceutical products	56,040	63,847	98,230
Fertilizers (manufactured)	45,857	46,950	58,484
Plastic materials, etc.	55,549	51,140	61,973
Basic manufactures	263,701	213,367	269,639
Textile yarn, fabrics, etc	21,107	28,171	37,047
Iron and steel	113,807	81,154	108,573
Machinery and transport equipment	568,626	428,210	454,836
Machinery specialized for particular industries	105,383	101,638	69,421
General industrial machinery, equipment and parts	86,398	79,228	70,711
Telecommunications and sound equipment	120,186	68,452	58,575
Other electrical machinery, apparatus, etc.	70,565	48,225	43,814
Road vehicles and parts	101,101	67,527	127,760
Passenger motor cars (excl. buses)	40,104	34,446	55,255
Motor vehicles for goods transport and special purposes	22,306	9,959	35,145
Miscellaneous manufactured articles	75,716	73,552	86,581
Total (incl. others)	1,714,907	1,793,040	1,695,948

Exports f.o.b.	1991	1992	1993
Food and live animals	558,169	556,186	679,918
Fish and fish preparations	27,515	25,777	30,497
Vegetables and fruit	100,208	96,758	95,293
Coffee (green and roasted)	159,376	126,325	194,814
Tea	278,366	289,721	336,871
Crude materials (inedible) except fuels	101,538	103,474	116,861
Cut flowers and flower buds	22,551	27,146	36,236
Mineral fuels, lubricants, etc	194,930	152,388	129,197
Petroleum and petroleum products	194,509	152,006	128,836
Chemicals and related products	42,150	43,687	58,016
Basic manufactures	103,766	115,588	190,220
Cement	12,411	15,616	31,872
Iron and steel	19,711	30,020	61,085
Miscellaneous manufactured goods	91,308	324,264	137,657
Jewellery	56,402	295,376	83,464
Total (incl. others)	1,170,896	1,361,703	1,391,890

Source: UN, *International Trade Statistics Yearbook.*

PRINCIPAL TRADING PARTNERS (US $'000)

Imports c.i.f.	1991	1992	1993
Argentina	40	9,207	17,639
Belgium-Luxembourg	58,838	45,645	49,102
Canada	15,307	17,485	19,129
China	16,554	26,160	29,080
Denmark	26,913	21,035	22,997
Finland	8,095	20,122	17,194
France (incl. Monaco)	87,594	68,630	74,883
Germany	149,057	111,097	126,264
Hong Kong	9,225	10,966	17,793
India	32,682	50,415	54,433
Italy	55,812	48,968	88,686
Japan	154,340	126,422	142,139
Malaysia	64,786	66,540	38,305
Netherlands	40,228	43,442	48,689
Saudi Arabia	33,470	17,615	28,270
SACU*	10,816	47,644	58,821
Singapore	16,768	30,415	20,592
Switzerland-Liechtenstein	25,758	26,156	21,582
United Kingdom	297,195	195,514	243,077
USA	86,756	68,630	140,031
Total (incl. others)	1,714,907	1,793,040	1,695,948

Exports f.o.b.	1991	1992	1993
Belgium-Luxembourg	26,102	25,239	30,330
Egypt	33,614	40,956	55,202
Ethiopia	10,097	11,364	29,931
France (incl. Monaco)	27,820	28,337	25,724
Germany	88,936	71,567	94,449
Italy	28,446	33,978	23,373
Netherlands	45,496	44,364	51,503
Pakistan	74,913	84,190	97,625
Rwanda	21,183	13,393	24,047
Somalia	12,754	30,097	41,390
Spain	23,329	12,511	16,756
Sudan	20,941	12,627	29,046
Sweden	17,383	13,487	21,885
Tanzania	39,359	48,843	95,457
Uganda	77,847	74,772	118,068
United Arab Emirates	3,561	256,772	89,083
United Kingdom	172,828	177,405	200,657
USA	40,141	39,849	48,478
Total (incl. others)	1,148,198	1,343,306	1,376,776

* Southern African Customs Union, comprising Botswana, Lesotho, Namibia, South Africa and Swaziland.

Source: UN, *International Trade Statistics Yearbook.*

Transport

RAILWAYS (traffic)

	1990	1991	1992*
Passengers carried ('000)	3,109	2,635	2,563
Passenger-km (million)	677	658	557
Freight carried ('000 metric tons)	3,317	3,581	2,821
Freight ton-km (million)	1,865	1,627	1,755

* Provisional.

1993: Passenger-km (million) 464; Freight ton-km (million) 1,312 (Source: UN, *Statistical Yearbook*).

ROAD TRAFFIC (motor vehicles in use at 31 December)

	1990	1991	1992*
Motor cars	156,851	164,234	171,813
Buses and coaches	13,445	14,740	16,323
Goods vehicles	32,183	32,794	35,344
Vans	88,396	92,585	95,967
Tractors, trailers and semi-trailers	37,908	39,264	40,699
Motor cycles and mopeds	23,536	24,895	25,912

* Provisional.

SHIPPING

Merchant Fleet (registered at 31 December)

	1994	1995	1996
Number of vessels	33	35	38
Total displacement ('000 grt)	15.7	18.0	19.8

Source: Lloyd's Register of Shipping, *World Fleet Statistics.*.

International Sea-borne Freight Traffic
(estimates, '000 metric tons)

	1990	1991	1992*
Goods loaded	2,297	1,791	2,083
Goods unloaded	5,192	5,310	5,810

* Provisional.

CIVIL AVIATION (traffic on scheduled services)

	1992	1993	1994
Kilometres flown (million)	14	15	16
Passengers carried ('000)	721	770	754
Passenger-km (million)	1,333	1,459	1,737
Total ton-km (million)	174	191	215

Source: UN, *Statistical Yearbook*.

Tourism

	1992	1993	1994
Tourist arrivals ('000)	782	826	863
Tourist receipts (million US dollars)	442	413	505

Source: UN, *Statistical Yearbook*.

Communications Media

	1992	1993	1994
Radio receivers ('000 in use)	2,200	2,300	2,400
Television receivers ('000 in use)	245	280	295
Telephones ('000 main lines in use)*	207	215	229
Daily newspapers:			
Titles	5	n.a.	5
Average circulation ('000 copies)	354†	n.a.	358†

* Year ending 30 June.

† Estimated figure.

Book production (titles, excl. pamphlets): 239 in 1991.

Sources: UNESCO, *Statistical Yearbook*; UN, *Statistical Yearbook*.

Education

(1995)

	Institutions	Teachers	Pupils
Primary	15,804*	181,975	5,545,000
General secondary	2,878	41,484	632,388
Technical†	36	1,147	11,700
Teacher training	26	808‡	18,992§
Universities‖	4	4,392	35,421

* 1993 figure. † 1988 figures. ‡ 1985 figure.

§ 1992 figure. ‖ 1990 figures.

Sources: Ministry of Education, Nairobi; UNESCO, *Statistical Yearbook*.

Directory

The Constitution

The Constitution was introduced at independence on 12 December 1963. Subsequent amendments, including the adoption of republican status on 12 December 1964, were consolidated in 1969. A further amendment in December 1991 permitted the establishment of a multi-party system. The Constitution can be amended by the affirmative vote on Second and Third Reading of 65% of the membership of the National Assembly (excluding the Speaker and Attorney-General).

The central legislative authority is the unicameral National Assembly, in which there are 188 directly elected Representatives, 12 members nominated by the President and two ex-officio members, the Attorney-General and the Speaker. The maximum term of the National Assembly is five years from its first meeting (except in wartime). It can be dissolved by the President at any time, and the National Assembly may force its own dissolution by a vote of 'no confidence', whereupon Presidential and Assembly elections have to be held within 90 days.

Executive power is vested in the President, Vice-President and Cabinet. Both the Vice-President and the Cabinet are appointed by the President, who must be a member of the Assembly and at least 35 years of age. Election of the President, for a five-year term, is by direct popular vote; the winning candidate at a presidential election must receive no less than 25% of the votes in at least five of Kenya's eight provinces. If a President dies, or a vacancy otherwise occurs during a President's period of office, the Vice-President becomes interim President for up to 90 days while a successor is elected.

The Government

HEAD OF STATE

President: DANIEL ARAP MOI (took office 14 October 1978; elected August 1983, commenced further term of office February 1988, re-elected December 1992).

CABINET
(August 1997)

President and Commander-in-Chief of the Armed Forces: DANIEL ARAP MOI.

Vice-President and Minister of Planning and National Development: Prof. GEORGE SAITOTI.

Minister of Agriculture, Livestock and Marketing: DARIUS MBELA.

Minister of Finance: MUSALIA WYCLIFF MUDAVADI.

Minister of Foreign Affairs and International Co-operation: STEPHEN KALONZO MUSYOKA.

Minister of Education: JOSEPH KAMOTHO.

Minister of Land Reclamation, Regional and Water Development: SIMEON NYACHAE.

Minister of Energy: KIRUGI M'MUKINDIA.

Minister of Environment and Natural Resources: HENRY KOSGEI.

Minister of Transport and Communication: WILSON NDOLO AYAH.

Minister of Commerce and Industry: J. M. ANGATIA.

Minister of Tourism and Wildlife: Dr P. K. MOMANYI.

Minister of Health: JACKSON MULINGE.

Minister of Local Government: FRANCIS LOTODO.

Minister of Home Affairs and National Heritage: WILLIAM OLE NTIMANA.

Minister of Lands and Settlement: NOAH KATANA NGALA.

Minister of Labour and Manpower Development: PHILIP MASINDE.

Minister of Information and Broadcasting: JOHNSTONE MAKAU.

Minister of Culture and Social Services: WINFRED NYIVA MWENDWA.

Minister of Co-operative Development: KAMWITHI MUNYI.

Minister of Public Works and Housing: Prof. JONATHAN NG'ENO.

Minister of Research, Technical Training and Technology: M. MUHAMMED.

Ministers of State in the President's Office: J. K. KOECH, NICHOLAS KIPTYATOR BIWOTT.

Attorney-General: AMOS WAKO.

MINISTRIES

Office of the President: Harambee House, Harambee Ave, POB 30510, Nairobi; tel. (2) 27411.

Office of the Vice-President and Ministry of Planning and National Development: Treasury Bldg, Harambee Ave, POB 30007, Nairobi; tel. (2) 338111; telex 22696.

Ministry of Agriculture, Livestock and Marketing: Kilimo House, Cathedral Rd, POB 30028, Nairobi; tel. (2) 718870; telex 22766; fax (2) 720586.

Ministry of Commerce and Industry: Co-operative House, Haile Selassie Ave, POB 30430, Nairobi; tel. (2) 340010; fax (2) 218845.

Ministry of Co-operative Development: Kencom House, Moi Ave, Nairobi; tel. (2) 340081.

Ministry of Culture and Social Services: Reinsurance Plaza, Taifa Rd, POB 45958, Nairobi; tel. (2) 339650.

Ministry of Education: Jogoo House 'B', Harambee Ave, POB 30040, Nairobi; tel. (2) 28411.

Ministry of Energy: Nyayo House, Kenyatta Ave, POB 30582, Nairobi; tel. (2) 331242; telex 23094.

Ministry of Environment and Natural Resources: Kencom House, POB 30126, Nairobi; tel. (2) 29261.

Ministry of Finance: Treasury Bldg, Harambee Ave, POB 30007, Nairobi; tel. (2) 338111; telex 22696; fax (2) 330426.

Ministry of Foreign Affairs: Harambee House, POB 30551, Nairobi; tel. (2) 334433; telex 22003.

Ministry of Health: Medical HQ, Afya House, Cathedral Rd, POB 30016, Nairobi; tel. (2) 717077; fax (2) 725902.

Ministry of Home Affairs and National Heritage: Nairobi.

Ministry of Information and Broadcasting: Jogoo House, POB 30025, Nairobi; tel. (2) 28411; telex 22244.

Ministry of Labour and Manpower Development: National Social Security House, POB 40326, Nairobi; tel. (2) 729800.

Ministry of Land Reclamation, Regional and Water Development: Maji House, Ngong Rd, POB 30521, Nairobi; tel. (2) 716103; fax (2) 713654.

Ministry of Lands and Settlement: POB 30450, Nairobi; tel. (2) 718050.

Ministry of Local Government: Jogoo House 'A', POB 30004, Nairobi; tel. (2) 28411.

Ministry of Public Works and Housing: POB 30260, Nairobi; tel. (2) 723101.

Ministry of Research, Technical Training and Technology: Utalii House, Uhuru Highway, POB 30623, Nairobi; tel. (2) 336173.

Ministry of Tourism and Wildlife: Utalii House, 5th Floor, Uhuru Highway, POB 54666, Nairobi; tel. (2) 331030; telex 25016.

Ministry of Transport and Communication: Transcom House, Ngong Rd, POB 52692, Nairobi; tel. (2) 729200; telex 22272; fax (2) 726326.

President and Legislature

PRESIDENT

Election, 29 December 1992

Candidates	Votes	%
DANIEL ARAP MOI	1,962,866	36.35
KENNETH MATIBA	1,404,266	26.00
MWAI KIBAKI	1,050,617	19.45
OGINGA ODINGA	944,197	17.48
GEORGE MOSETI ANYONA	14,273	0.26
CHIBULE WA TSUMA	10,221	0.19
JOHN HARUN MWAU	8,118	0.15
MUKARU NG'ANG'A	5,776	0.11
Total	5,400,334	100.00

NATIONAL ASSEMBLY

Speaker: FRANCIS OLE KAPARO.

General Election, 29 December 1992

Party	Seats
KANU	100*
FORD–Asili	31
FORD–Kenya	31†
DP	23
KSC	1
KNC	1
Independent	1†
Total	188‡

* By the end of 1995 11 delegates who had been elected as representatives of opposition parties had reportedly defected to KANU.

† In November 1994 the election to the National Assembly of one FORD–Kenya representative and of the independent member was nullified.

‡ In addition to the 188 directly elected seats, 12 are held by nominees of the President. The Attorney-General and the Speaker are, *ex officio*, members of the National Assembly.

Political Organizations

Kenya was a *de facto* one-party state between 1969 and June 1982, when it became a *de jure* one-party state. In December 1991 the Constitution was amended to legalize a multi-party political system.

Democratic Party (DP): Nairobi; f. 1991; Pres. MWAI KIBAKI; rival faction led by NGENGI MUIGAI.

Forum for the Restoration of Democracy–Asili (FORD–Asili): POB 48647, Nairobi; f. 1992; Chair. KENNETH MATIBA; rival faction led by MARTIN J. SHIKUKU.

Forum for the Restoration of Democracy–Kenya (FORD–Kenya): Nairobi; f. 1992; predominantly Luo support; Chair. MICHAEL KIJANA WAMALWA.

Kenya African National Union (KANU): POB 72394, Nairobi; f. 1960; sole legal party 1982–91; Pres. DANIEL ARAP MOI; Chair. WILSON NDOLO AYAH; Sec.-Gen. JOSEPH KAMOTHO.

Kenya National Congress (KNC): f. 1992.

Kenya National Democratic Alliance Party (KENDA): f. 1991; Chair. MUKARU NG'ANG'A.

Kenya Social Congress (KSC): f. 1992; Chair. GEORGE MOSETI ANYONA; Sec.-Gen. ONESMUS MBALI.

Labour Party Democracy: Chair. MOHAMED IBRAHIM NOOR.

National Development Party (NDP): f. 1994; Chair. RAILA ODINGA; Sec.-Gen. Dr CHARLES MARANGA.

Party for Independent Candidates of Kenya (PICK): Leader: HARUN MWAU.

Patriotic Pastoralist Alliance of Kenya: f. 1997 to address the needs of northern Kenyan pastoralist communities; Leaders KHALIF ABDULLAHI, IBRAHIM WOCHE, JACKSON LAISAGOR.

People's Union of Justice and New Order: Kisumu; Islamic support; Leader WILSON OWILI.

Rural National Democratic Party: f. 1992; promotes agrarian interests; Chair. SEBASTIAN MUNENE.

Safina ('Noah's Ark'): Nairobi; f. 1995; unregistered party which aims to combat corruption and human rights abuses and to introduce proportional representation; Chair. MUTARI KIGANO; Sec.-Gen. Dr RICHARD LEAKEY.

Social Democratic Party: Nairobi; f. 1992; Leader CHARITY NGILU.

United Muslims of Africa (UMA): f. 1993; Leader EMMANUEL MAITHA.

United National Democratic Alliance (UNDA): f. 1994; an informal coalition of major opposition parties (excl. FORD–Asili) formed to present an agreed list of candidates at elections.

United Patriotic Party (UPP): f. 1995.

Youth Associated with the Restoration of Democracy (YARD): Chair. ELIUD AMBANI MULAMA.

The following organizations are banned:

February Eighteen Resistance Army: believed to operate from Uganda; Leader Brig. JOHN ODONGO (also known as STEPHEN AMOKE).

Islamic Party of Kenya (IPK): Mombasa; f. 1992; Islamic fundamentalist; Chair. SHEIKH KHALIFA MUHAMMAD (acting); Sec.-Gen. ABDULRAHMAN WANDATI.

Diplomatic Representation

EMBASSIES AND HIGH COMMISSIONS IN KENYA

Argentina: POB 30283, Nairobi; tel. (2) 335242; telex 22544; Ambassador: JOSÉ MARÍA CANTILO.

Australia: POB 39341, Nairobi; tel. (2) 445034; telex 22203; fax (2) 444617; High Commissioner: J. M. TROTTER.

Austria: City House, Wabera St, POB 30560, Nairobi; tel. (2) 228281; telex 22076; fax (2) 331792; Ambassador: FRANZ HÖRLBERGER.

Bangladesh: POB 41645, Nairobi; tel. (2) 562815; telex 25077; fax (2) 562817; High Commissioner: Dr M. AFSARUL QADER.

Belgium: Limuru Rd, POB 30461, Nairobi; tel. (2) 741564; telex 22269; fax (2) 741568; Ambassador: MÁRIO AGUSTO SANTOS.

Brazil: Jeevan Bharati Bldg, Harambee Ave, POB 30751, Nairobi; tel. (2) 337722; telex 22498; fax (2) 336245; Ambassador: MÁRIO AGUSTO SANTOS.

Burundi: Development House, Moi Ave, POB 44439, Nairobi; tel. (2) 218458; telex 22425; Ambassador: VANANT BAATAKANWA.

Canada: Comcraft House, Haile Selassie Ave, POB 30481, Nairobi; tel. (2) 214804; fax (2) 226987; e-mail Pamela.Isfeld@nrobi01.X400.gc.ca; High Commissioner: BERNARD DUSSAULT.

Chile: International House, Mama Ngina St, POB 45554, Nairobi; tel. (2) 331320; telex 22348; fax (2) 215648; Ambassador: Dr VICENTE SÁNCHEZ.

China, People's Republic: Woodlands Rd, POB 30508, Nairobi; tel. (2) 722559; telex 22235; Ambassador: AN YONGYU.

Colombia: International House, 8th Floor, Mama Ngina St, POB 48494, Nairobi; tel. (2) 246770; fax (2) 246772; Ambassador: Dr GERMÁN GARCÍA-DURÁN.

Congo, Democratic Republic: Electricity House, Harambee Ave, POB 48106, Nairobi; tel. (2) 229771; telex 22057; Ambassador: (vacant).

Costa Rica: POB 76639, Nairobi; tel. and fax (2) 569078.

Cyprus: Eagle House, Kimathi St, POB 30739, Nairobi; tel. (2) 220881; telex 22436; fax (2) 331232; High Commissioner: PAVLOS HADJITOFIS.

Czech Republic: Harambee Ave, POB 48785; tel. (2) 210494; telex 25115; fax (2) 223447.

Denmark: HFCK Bldg, Koinange St, POB 40412, Nairobi; tel. (2) 331088; telex 22216; fax (2) 331492; Ambassador: KLAUS DAHLGAARD.

Djibouti: POB 59528, Nairobi; tel. (2) 229633; Ambassador: SALEH HAJI FARAH.

Egypt: Harambee Plaza, 7th Floor, POB 30285, Nairobi; tel. (2) 225991; telex 22335; Ambassador: MARAWAN ZAKI BADR.

Ethiopia: State House Ave, POB 45198, Nairobi; tel. (2) 723027; telex 22864; fax (2) 723401; Ambassador: TOSHOME TOGA.

Finland: International House, City Hall Way, POB 30379, Nairobi; tel. (2) 334777; telex 22010; fax (2) 335986; Ambassador: GLEN LINDHOLM.

France: Barclays Plaza, 9th Floor, POB 41784, Nairobi; tel. (2) 339783; telex 22279; fax (2) 339421; Ambassador: JACQUES DEPAIGNE.

Germany: Williamson House, 4th Ngong Ave, POB 30180, Nairobi; tel. (2) 712527; telex 22221; fax (2) 714886; Ambassador: (vacant).

Greece: Nation Centre, Kimathi St, POB 30543, Nairobi; tel. (2) 340722; telex 22008; Ambassador: E. KATSAREAS.

Holy See: Apostolic Nunciature, Manyani Rd West, POB 14326, Nairobi; tel. (2) 442975; fax (2) 446789; Apostolic Nuncio: Most Rev. GIOVANNI TONUCCI, Titular Archbishop of Torcello.

Hungary: Agip House, 2nd Floor, POB 30523, Nairobi; tel. (2) 226914; telex 22364; fax (2) 569433; Chargé d'affaires a.i.: ZSIGMOND D. PATAY.

India: Jeevan Bharati Bldg, Harambee Ave, POB 30074, Nairobi; tel. (2) 222361; telex 22079; fax (2) 334167; High Commissioner: T. P. SREENIVASAN.

Indonesia: Utalii House, Uhuru Highway, POB 48868, Nairobi; tel. (2) 215873; telex 23171; Ambassador: DALINDRA AMAN.

Iran: POB 49170, Nairobi; tel. (2) 720343; telex 22563; Ambassador: HAMID MOAYYER.

Iraq: Loresho Ridge, POB 49213, Nairobi; tel. (2) 581143; telex 22176; Chargé d'affaires a.i.: HIKMAT A. SATTAR HUSSEIN.

Israel: POB 30354, Nairobi; tel. (2) 722182; telex 22412; fax (2) 715966; Ambassador: MENASHE ZIPORI.

Italy: International Life House, Mama Ngina St, POB 30107, Nairobi; tel. (2) 337356; telex 22251; fax (2) 337056; Ambassador: Dr ROBERTO DI LEO.

Japan: Kenyatta Ave, POB 60202, Nairobi; tel. (2) 332955; fax (2) 216530; Ambassador: Dr SHINSUKE HORIUCHI.

Korea, Republic: Anniversary Towers, University Way, POB 30455, Nairobi; tel. (2) 333581; telex 22300; Ambassador: PARK MYUNG JOON.

Kuwait: Muthaiga Rd, POB 42353, Nairobi; tel. (2) 767144; telex 22467; Chargé d'affaires a.i.: JABER SALEM HUSSAIN EBRAHEEM.

Lesotho: International House, Mama Ngina St, POB 44096, Nairobi; tel. (2) 337493; telex 22489; High Commissioner: (vacant).

Malawi: Waiyaki Way (between Mvuli and Church Rds), POB 30453, Nairobi; tel. (2) 440569; telex 22749; fax 440568; High Commissioner: M. V. L. PHIRI (acting).

Mexico: POB 14145, Nairobi; tel. (2) 582850; telex 23065; fax (2) 581500; Ambassador: ARTURO GONZÁLEZ.

Morocco: POB 61098, Nairobi; tel. (2) 222264; telex 22531; Chargé d'Affaires a.i.: DRISS KASSIMI.

Netherlands: Uchumi House, Nkrumah Ave, POB 41537, Nairobi; tel. (2) 227111; telex 22285; fax (2) 339155; Ambassador: RUUD J. TREFFERS.

Nigeria: Hurlingham, POB 30516, Nairobi; tel. (2) 564116; telex 22194; fax (2) 562776; High Commissioner: CLARKSON N. UMELO.

Norway: Nairobi; Chargé d'affaires a.i.: OVE DANBOLDT.

Pakistan: St Michel Rd, Westlands, POB 30045, Nairobi; tel. (2) 443911; telex 25907; fax (2) 446507; High Commissioner: AMIR M. KHAN.

Poland: Kabarnet Rd, POB 30086, Nairobi; tel. (2) 566288; telex 22266; fax (2) 562588; Ambassador: ADAM T. KOWALEWSKI.

Portugal: POB 34020, Nairobi; tel. (2) 338990; telex 22634; fax (2) 214711; Ambassador: Dr JOSÉ CAETANO DA COSTA PEREIRA.

Romania: POB 48412, Nairobi; tel. (2) 227515; Chargé d'affaires a.i.: GHEORGHE DRAGOS.

Russia: Lenana Rd, POB 30049, Nairobi; tel. (2) 722559; telex 25261; fax (2) 721888; Ambassador: VLADIMIR S. KITAYEV.

Saudi Arabia: POB 58297, Nairobi; tel. (2) 762781; telex 22990; fax (2) 760939; Ambassador: MOHAMMED H. M. AL-KAHTANY.

Slovakia: Milimani Rd, POB 30204, Nairobi; tel. (2) 721896; fax (2) 721898.

South Africa: Lonhro House, Standard St, POB 42441, Nairobi; tel. (2) 228469; fax (2) 223687; High Commissioner: G. M. MEMELI.

Spain: Bruce House, Standard St, POB 45503, Nairobi; tel. (2) 335711; telex 22157; fax (2) 332858; Ambassador: FERMIN PIETRO-CASTRO ROUMIER.

Sri Lanka: Rose Ave, off Lenana Rd, POB 48145, Nairobi; tel. (2) 227577; telex 25081; fax (2) 225391; High Commissioner: J. D. A. WIJEWARDENA.

Sudan: Minet ICDC House, 7th Floor, POB 48784, Nairobi; tel. (2) 720853; Ambassador: OMER EL-SHEIKH.

Swaziland: Silopark House, POB 41887, Nairobi; tel. (2) 339231; telex 22085; High Commissioner: Prince CHURCHILL B. H. DLAMINI.

Sweden: International House, Mama Ngina St, POB 30600, Nairobi; tel. (2) 229042; telex 22264; fax (2) 218908; Ambassador: LARS-GÖRAN ENGFELDT.

Switzerland: International Life House, Mama Ngina St, POB 30752, Nairobi; tel. (2) 228735; telex 22181; Ambassador: Dr ARMIN KAMER.

Tanzania: Continental House, POB 47790, Nairobi; tel. (2) 331056; High Commissioner: MIRISHO SAM HAGGAI SARAKIKYA.

Thailand: POB 58349, Nairobi; tel. (2) 715800; telex 22836; fax (2) 715801; Ambassador: PONGSAK DISYATAT.

Turkey: Gigiri Rd, off Limuru Rd, POB 30785, Nairobi; tel. (2) 520404; telex 22346; fax (2) 521237; Chargé d'affaires a.i.: CUNEYT YAVUZCAN.

Uganda: POB 60855, Nairobi; tel. (2) 330801; telex 22732; High Commissioner: J. TOMUSANGE.

United Kingdom: Upper Hill Rd, POB 30465, Nairobi; tel. (2) 714699; telex 22219; fax (2) 723446; High Commissioner: JEFFREY JAMES.

USA: cnr Moi and Haile Selassie Aves, POB 30137, Nairobi; tel. (2) 334141; telex 22964; fax (2) 340838; Ambassador: PRUDENCE BUSHNELL.

Venezuela: International House, Mama Ngina St, POB 34477, Nairobi; tel. (2) 341078; telex 22671; fax (2) 337487; Ambassador: ALBERTO LIZARRALDE MARADEY.

Yemen: Ngong Rd, POB 44642, Nairobi; tel. (2) 564379; Ambassador: Dr HUSSEIN AL-GALAL.

Yugoslavia: State House Ave, POB 30504, Nairobi; tel. (2) 720671; telex 22515; Ambassador: LJUBE ZAFIROV.

Zambia: Nyerere Rd, POB 48741, Nairobi; tel. (2) 724850; telex 22193; fax (2) 718494; High Commissioner: ENESS CHISHALA CHIYENGE.

Zimbabwe: Minet ICDC House, Mamlaka Rd, POB 30806, Nairobi; tel. (2) 721071; telex 25033; High Commissioner: LUCAS PANDE TAVAYA.

Judicial System

The Kenya Court of Appeal: POB 30187, Nairobi; the final court of appeal for Kenya in civil and criminal process; sits at Nairobi, Mombasa, Kisumu, Nakuru and Nyeri.

Chief Justice: ABDUL MAJID COCKAR.

Justices of Appeal: MATHEW MULI, J. M. GACHUHI, J. R. O. MASIME, J. E. GICHERU, R. O. KWACH.

The High Court of Kenya: Harambee Ave, POB 40112, Nairobi; tel. (2) 21221; has unlimited criminal and civil jurisdiction at first instance, and sits as a court of appeal from subordinate courts in both criminal and civil cases. The High Court is also a court of admiralty. There are two resident puisne judges at Mombasa and at Nakuru, and one resident puisne judge at Eldoret, Kakamega, Kisumu, Nyeri, Kisii and Meru.

Resident Magistrates' Courts: have country-wide jurisdiction, with powers of punishment by imprisonment up to five years or by fine up to K£500. If presided over by a chief magistrate or senior resident magistrate the court is empowered to pass any sentence authorized by law. For certain offences, a resident magistrate may pass minimum sentences authorized by law.

District Magistrates' Courts: of first, second and third class; have jurisdiction within districts and powers of punishment by imprisonment for up to five years, or by fines of up to K£500.

Kadhi's Courts: have jurisdiction within districts, to determine questions of Islamic law.

Religion

Most of the population hold traditional African beliefs, although there are significant numbers of African Christians. The Arab inhabitants are Muslims, and the Indian population is partly Muslim and partly Hindu. The Europeans and Goans are predominantly Christian. Muslims are found mainly along the coastline; however, the Islamic faith has also established itself among Africans around Nairobi and among some ethnic groups in the northern districts. East Africa is also an important centre for the Bahá'í faith.

CHRISTIANITY

National Council of Churches of Kenya: Church House, Moi Ave, POB 45009, Nairobi; tel. (2) 242278; fax (2) 224463; f. 1943 as Christian Council of Kenya; 35 full mems and eight assoc. mems; Chair. Rev. JOSEPH WAITHONGA; Sec.-Gen. Rev. MUTAVA MUSYIMI.

The Anglican Communion

Anglicans are adherents of the Church of the Province of Kenya, which was established in 1970. It comprises 21 dioceses, and had some 2m. members in 1994.

Archbishop of Kenya and Bishop of Nairobi: (vacant), POB 40502, Nairobi; tel. (2) 714755; fax (2) 718442; Acting Primate: Rt Rev. Dr DAVID M. GITARI (Bishop of Kirinyaga), POB 95, Kutus; fax (161) 30824.

Greek Orthodox Church

Archbishop of East Africa: NICADEMUS of IRINOUPOULIS, Nairobi; jurisdiction covers Kenya, Tanzania and Uganda.

The Roman Catholic Church

Kenya comprises four archdioceses, 16 dioceses and one apostolic vicariate. At 31 December 1995 there were an estimated 6,366,989 adherents in the country.

Kenya Episcopal Conference: Kenya Catholic Secretariat, POB 48062, Nairobi; tel. (2) 443133; fax (2) 442910; f. 1976; Pres. JOHN NJUE, Bishop of Embu.

Archbishop of Kisumu: Most Rev. ZACCHAEUS OKOTH, POB 1728, Kisumu; tel. (35) 43950; fax (35) 42415.

Archbishop of Mombasa: Most Rev. JOHN NJENGA, Catholic Secretariat, Nyerere Ave, POB 83131, Mombasa; tel. (11) 471320; fax (11) 473166.

Archbishop of Nairobi: Most Rev. RAPHAEL NDINGI MWANA'A NZEKI, Archbishop's House, POB 14231, Nairobi; tel. (2) 441919; fax 447027.

Archbishop of Nyeri: Most Rev. NICODEMUS KIRIMA, POB 288, Nyeri; tel. (34) 2366.

Other Christian Churches

Africa Inland Church in Kenya: Pres. Rev. Dr TITUS GITHUMBI.

African Christian Church and Schools: POB 1365, Thika; tel. (151) 47; f. 1948; Moderator Rt Rev. JOHN NJUNGUNA; Gen. Sec. Rev. SAMUEL MWANGI; 50,000 mems.

African Church of the Holy Spirit: POB 183, Kakamega; f. 1927; Exec. Sec. Rev. PETER IHAJI; 20,000 mems.

African Israel Nineveh Church: Nineveh HQ, POB 701, Kisumu; f. 1942; High Priest Rt Rev. JOHN KIVULI, II; Gen. Sec. Rev. JOHN ARAP TONUI; 350,000 mems.

Baptist Convention of Kenya: POB 14907, Nairobi; Pres. Rev. ELIUD MUNGAI.

Church of God in East Africa: Pres. Rev. Dr BAIRAM MAKOKHA.

Evangelical Fellowship of Kenya: Co-ordinator Rt Rev. ISAIAH GITONGA; Sec.-Gen. Dr WASHINGTON NG'ENG'I.

Evangelical Lutheran Church in Kenya: POB 874, Kisii; tel. (381) 20237; Bishop Rev. FRANCIS ONDERI NYAMWARO; 55,000 mems.

Methodist Church in Kenya: POB 47633, Nairobi; tel. (2) 724841; f. 1862 (autonomous since 1967); Presiding Bishop Rev. Dr ZABLON NTHAMBURI; 610,000 mems (1996).

Presbyterian Church of East Africa: POB 48268, Nairobi; tel. (2) 504417; fax (2) 504442; Moderator Rt Rev. Dr JESSE KAMAU; Sec.-Gen. Rev. Dr SAMUEL MWANIKI.

Other denominations active in Kenya include the Africa Gospel Church, the African Brotherhood Church, the African Independent Pentecostal Church, the African Interior Church, the Episcopal Church of Kenya, the Free Pentecostal Fellowship of Kenya, the Full Gospel Churches of Kenya, the Lutheran Church in Kenya, the National Independent Church of Africa, the Pentecostal Assemblies of God, the Pentecostal Evangelistic Fellowship of God and the Reformed Church of East Africa.

BAHÁ'Í FAITH

National Spiritual Assembly: POB 47562, Nairobi; tel. (2) 725447; mems resident in 9,654 localities.

ISLAM

Supreme Council of Kenyan Muslims (SUPKEM): Nat. Chair. ALI H. S. AL-BUSAIDY; Sec.-Gen. AHMED KHALIF.

The Press

PRINCIPAL DAILIES

Daily Nation: POB 49010, Nairobi; tel. (2) 337710; English; f. 1960; banned by govt in June 1989 from reporting parliamentary proceedings; Editor-in-Chief WANGETHI MWANGI; Man. Editor TOM MSHINDI; circ. 170,000.

Kenya Leo: POB 30958, Nairobi; tel. (2) 337798; f. 1983; Kiswahili; KANU party newspaper; Man. Editor JOB MUTUNGI.

Kenya Times: POB 30958, Nairobi; tel. (2) 24251; telex 25008; f. 1983; English; KANU party newspaper; Editor-in-Chief JOHN KHAKHUDU AGUNDA; circ. 52,000.

The Standard: POB 30080, Nairobi; tel. (2) 540280; telex 24032; fax (2) 553939; English; f. 1902; Editor-in-Chief PAUL OKWANY ODONDO; Man. Editor KAMAU KANYANGA; circ. 70,000.

Taifa Leo: POB 49010, Nairobi; tel. (2) 337691; Kiswahili; f. 1960; daily and weekly edns; Editor ROBERT MWANGI; circ. 57,000.

Kenya has a thriving vernacular press, but titles are often short-lived. In 1997 newspapers in African languages included:

Kihooto (The Truth): Kikuyu; satirical.

Mwaria Ma (Honest Speaker): Karatina, Nyeri; f. 1997; Publr Canon JAMLICK M. MIANO.

Mwihoko (Expectation): POB 734, Muranga; f. 1997; Roman Catholic publ.

Nam Dar: newspaper in Luo.

Otit Mach (Firefly): newspaper in Luo.

SELECTED PERIODICALS

Weeklies and Fortnightlies

Coast Week: weekly; Editor ADRIAN GRIMWOOD; circ. 40,000.

Kenrail: POB 30121, Nairobi; tel. (2) 221211; telex 22254; English and Kiswahili; publ. by Kenya Railways Corpn; Editor J. N. LUSENO; circ. 20,000.

Kenya Gazette: POB 30746, Nairobi; tel. (2) 334075; f. 1898; official notices; weekly; circ. 8,000.

The People: POB 48647, Nairobi; tel. (2) 449269; fax (2) 446640; f. 1993; weekly; Editor-in-Chief GEORGE MBUGGUSS; circ. 100,000.

Society: Changamwe Rd, Industrial Area, Nairobi; weekly; Editor-in-Chief PIUS NYAMORA.

The Standard on Sunday: POB 30080, Nairobi; tel. (2) 540280; telex 24032; fax (2) 553939; English; Man. Editor ESTHER KAMWERU; circ. 90,000.

Sunday Nation: POB 49010, Nairobi; f. 1960; English; Man. Editor BERNARD NDERITU; circ. 170,000.

Sunday Times: POB 30958, Nairobi; tel. (2) 337798; telex 25008; ROBERT OTANI.

Taifa Jumapili: POB 49010, Nairobi; f. 1987; Kiswahili; Editor ROBERT K. MWANGI; circ. 56,000.

Taifa Weekly: POB 49010, Nairobi; tel. (2) 337691; f. 1960; Kiswahili; Editor ROBERT K. MWANGI; circ. 68,000.

The Weekly Review: POB 42271, Nairobi; f. 1975; English; Editor AMBOKA ANDERE; circ. 32,000.

What's On: Rehema House, Nairobi; tel. (2) 27651; telex 25092; Editor NANCY KAIRO; circ. 10,000.

Monthlies

East African Medical Journal: POB 41632, Nairobi; tel. (2) 712010; fax (2) 724617; English; f. 1923; Editor-in-Chief Prof. WILLIAM LORE; circ. 4,500.

East African Report on Trade and Industry: POB 30339, Nairobi; journal of Kenya Asscn of Mfrs; Editor GORDON BOY; circ. 3,000.

Executive: POB 47186, Nairobi; tel. (2) 555811; telex 24095; fax (2) 557815; f. 1980; business; Editor ALI ZAIDI; circ. 16,000.

Kenya Export News: POB 30339, Nairobi; tel. (2) 25502; English; publ. for Kenya External Trade Authority, Ministry of Commerce and Industry; Editor Prof. SAMUEL NJOROGE; circ. 5,000.

Kenya Farmer (Journal of the Agricultural Society of Kenya): c/o English Press, POB 30127, Nairobi; tel. (2) 20377; f. 1954; English and Kiswahili; Editor ROBERT IRUNGU; circ. 20,000.

Kenya Yetu: POB 8053, Nairobi; tel. (2) 223201; telex 22244; f. 1965; Kiswahili; publ. by Ministry of Information and Broadcasting; Editor M. NDAVI; circ. 10,000.

Nairobi Handbook: POB 30127, Accra Rd, Nairobi; Editor Mrs R. OUMA; circ. 20,000.

The Nairobi Law Monthly: Tumaini House, 4th Floor, Nkrumah Ave, POB 53234, Nairobi; tel. (2) 330480; f. 1987; English; Editor-in-Chief GITOBU IMANYARA.

News from Kenya: POB 8053, Nairobi; tel. (2) 28411; telex 22244; publ. by Ministry of Information and Broadcasting.

Today in Africa: PO Kijabe; English; Editors MWAURA NJOROGE, NJUGUNA NGUNJIRI; circ. 13,000.

Other Periodicals

African Ecclesial Review: POB 4002, Eldoret; scripture, religion and development; 6 a year; Editor AGATHA RADOLI; circ. 2,500.

Afya: POB 30125, Nairobi; tel. (2) 501301; telex 23254; fax (2) 506112; journal for medical and health workers; quarterly.

Busara: POB 30022, Nairobi; literary; 2 a year; Editor KIMANI GECAU; circ. 3,000.

East African Agricultural and Forestry Journal: POB 30148, Nairobi; f. 1935; English; quarterly; Editor J. O. MUGAH; circ. 1,000.

Eastern African Economic Review: POB 30022, Nairobi; f. 1954; 2 a year; Editor J. K. MAITHA.

Economic Review of Agriculture: POB 30028, Nairobi; tel. (2) 728370; telex 33042; f. 1968; publ. by Ministry of Agriculture, Livestock and Marketing; quarterly; Editor OKIYA OKOITI.

Education in Eastern Africa: Nairobi; f. 1970; 2 a year; Editor JOHN C. B. BIGALA; circ. 2,000.

Finance: Nairobi; monthly; Editor-in-Chief NJEHU GATABAKI.

Inside Kenya Today: POB 8053, Nairobi; tel. (2) 223201; telex 22244; English; publ. by Ministry of Information and Broadcasting; quarterly; Editor M. NDAVI; circ. 10,000.

Journal of the Language Association of Eastern Africa: Nairobi; tel. (2) 28411; telex 22244; publ. by Ministry of Information and Broadcasting; 2 a year; Editor T. P. GORMAN; circ. 2,000.

Kenya Education Journal: Nairobi; f. 1958; English; 3 a year; Editor W. G. BOWMAN; circ. 5,500.

Kenya Statistical Digest: POB 30007, Nairobi; tel. (2) 338111; telex 22696; publ. by Ministry of Finance; quarterly.

Target: POB 72839, Nairobi; f. 1964; English; 6 a year; religious; Editor REBEKA NJAU (acting); circ. 17,000.

NEWS AGENCIES

Kenya News Agency (KNA): Information House, POB 8053, Nairobi; tel. (2) 223201; telex 22244; f. 1963; Dir S. MUSANDU.

Foreign Bureaux

Agence France-Presse (AFP): International Life House, Mama Ngina St, POB 30671, Nairobi; tel. (2) 332043; telex 22243; Bureau Chief DIDIER LAPEYRONIE.

Agenzia Nazionale Stampa Associata (ANSA) (Italy): Agip House, POB 20444, Nairobi; tel. (2) 711338; telex 23251; fax (2) 229383; Rep. ADOLFO D'AMICO.

Associated Press (AP) (USA): Chester House, Koinange St, POB 47590, Nairobi; tel. (2) 340663; telex 25101; fax (2) 221449; Bureau Chief SUSAN LINNÉE.

Deutsche Presse-Agentur (dpa) (Germany): Chester House, 1st Floor, Koinange St, POB 48546, Nairobi; tel. (2) 330274; telex 22330; fax (2) 221902; Bureau Chief Dr HUBERT KAHL.

Informatsionnoye Telegrafnoye Agentstvo Rossii—Telegrafnoye Agentstvo Suverennykh Stran (ITAR—TASS) (Russia): Likoni Lane, POB 49602, Nairobi; tel. (2) 721978; telex 22192; fax (2) 721978; Correspondent GRIGORY N. POTAPOV.

Inter Press Service (IPS) (Italy): Press Centre, Chester House, Koinange St, POB 54386, Nairobi; tel. (2) 335418; Correspondent HORACE AWORI.

Kyodo Tsushin (Japan): Mbaaz Ave, POB 58281, Nairobi; tel. (2) 339504; telex 22915; Bureau Chief JUNJI MIURA.

Reuters (UK): Finance House, 12th Floor, Loita St, Nairobi; Bureau Chief NICK KOTCH.

United Press International (UPI) (USA): POB 76282, Nairobi; tel. (2) 337349; fax (2) 213625; Correspondent JOE KHAMISI.

Xinhua (New China) News Agency (People's Republic of China): Ngong Rd at Rose Ave, POB 30728, Nairobi; tel. and fax (2) 711685; Pres. and Editor-in-Chief Prof. FLAMINGO Q. M. CHEN.

Publishers

Amecea Gaba Publications: Amecea Pastoral Institute, POB 4002, Eldoret; tel. (321) 61218; fax (321) 62570; religious; Dir Sister AGATHA RADOLI.

Camerapix: POB 45048, Nairobi; tel. (2) 223511; telex 22576; fax (2) 217244; f. 1960; architecture and design, travel, topography, natural history; CEO MOHAMED AMIN.

East African Educational Publishers Ltd: cnr Mpaka Rd and Woodvale Grove, Westlands, POB 45314, Nairobi; tel. (2) 444700; fax (2) 448753; f. 1965; academic, educational, creative writing; some books in Kenyan languages; Man. Dir HENRY CHAKAVA.

East African Publishing House Ltd: Nairobi; tel. (2) 557417; f. 1965; educational, academic and general; also publs periodicals; Man. Dir EDWARD N. WAINAINA.

Evangel: POB 28963, Nairobi; tel. (2) 802033; f. 1952; Gen. Man. RICHARD ONDENG.

Foundation Books: Nairobi; tel. (2) 761520; f. 1974; Man. Dir F. O. OKWANYA.

Kenya Literature Bureau: Belle Vewarea, off Mombasa Rd, POB 30022, Nairobi; tel. (2) 506142; f. 1977; parastatal body under Ministry of Education; literary, educational, cultural and scientific books and journals; Chair. JANE KIANO; Man. Dir S. C. LANG'AT.

Jomo Kenyatta Foundation: POB 30533, Nairobi; tel. (2) 557222; f. 1966; primary, secondary, university textbooks; Man. Dir HERBERT CHABALA.

Longhorn Kenya Ltd: Funzi Road, Industrial Area, POB 18033, Nairobi; tel. (2) 532579; fax (2) 540037; f. 1965; textbooks and educational materials; Gen. Man. JANET NJOROGE.

Macmillan Kenya (Publishers) Ltd: POB 30797, Nairobi; tel. (2) 224485; fax (2) 212179; e-mail dmuita@macken.co.ke; Man. Dir DAVID MUITA.

Newspread International: POB 46854, Nairobi; tel. (2) 331402; telex 22143; fax (2) 607252; reference, economic development; Exec. Editor KUL BHUSHAN.

Oxford University Press (Eastern Africa): Waiyaki Way, ABC Place, POB 72532, Nairobi; tel. (2) 440555; fax (2) 443972; f. 1954; educational and general; Regional Man. ABDULLAH ISMAILY.

Paulines Publications-Africa: POB 49026, Nairobi; tel. (2) 442097; fax (2) 442144; religious.

Transafrica Press: Kenwood House, Kimathi St, POB 48239, Nairobi; tel. (2) 331762; f. 1976; general, educational and children's; CEO JOHN NOTTINGHAM.

Government Publishing House

Government Printing Press: POB 30128, Nairobi.

PUBLISHERS' ORGANIZATION

Kenya Publishers' Association: POB 18650, Nairobi; tel. (2) 223262; fax (2) 339875; f. 1971; Chair. GACHECHE WARUINGI.

Radio and Television

In 1994, according to UNESCO, there were an estimated 2.4m. radio receivers and 295,000 television receivers in use.

Kenya Broadcasting Corporation (KBC): Broadcasting House, Harry Thuku Rd, POB 30456, Nairobi; tel. (2) 334567; telex 25361; fax (2) 220675; f. 1989 as a state corpn to succeed Voice of Kenya (f. 1959); responsible for radio and television broadcasting; Chair. Dr JULIUS KIANO; Man. Dir SIMEON ANABWANI.

Radio: three services: National (Kiswahili); General (English); Vernacular (Borana, Burji, Hindustani, Kalenjin, Kikamba, Kikuyu, Kimasai, Kimeru, Kisii, Kuria, Luo, Luhya, Rendile, Somali, Suba, Teso and Turkana).

Television: KBC—TV financed by licence fees and commercial advertisements; services in Kiswahili and English; operates on four channels for approximately 50 hours per week. KBC–II: private subscription service.

Kenya Television Network (KTN—TV): POB 56985, Nairobi; tel. (2) 227122; fax (2) 214467; Chair. MWAKIO SIO.

Finance

(cap. = capital; res = reserves; dep. = deposits; m. = million; brs = branches; amounts in Kenya shillings)

BANKING

Central Bank

Central Bank of Kenya (Banki Kuu Ya Kenya): Haile Selassie Ave, POB 60000, Nairobi; tel. (2) 226431; telex 22324; fax (2) 340192; f. 1966; bank of issue; cap. and res 1,672m., dep. 65,048m. (June 1996); Gov. MICAH CHESEREM; Dep. Gov. Dr T. N. KIBUA.

Commercial Banks

African Banking Corporation Ltd: ICEA Bldg, Kenyatta Ave, Nairobi; tel. (2) 251540; fax (2) 251687; f. 1995; cap. and res 208.1m., dep. 2,528.6m. (Dec. 1995); Exec. Chair. ASHRAF SAVANI; CEO KHALIL ZOBAIRI: 7 brs.

Barclays Bank of Kenya Ltd: Bank House, Moi Ave, POB 30120, Nairobi; tel. (2) 332230; telex 22210; fax (2) 335219; f. 1978; cap. and res 5,726m., dep. 38,526m. (Dec. 1996); Chair. SAMUEL NJOROGE WARUHIU; Man. Dir PETER GEER; 64 brs.

Biashara Bank of Kenya Ltd: Investment House, Muindi Mbingu St, POB 30831, Nairobi; tel. (2) 221064; telex 25161; fax 221679; f. 1984; cap. and res 161.3m., dep. 1,531.4m. (Dec. 1996); Chair. SIMEON NYACHAE; CEO S. C. KOCHAR.

CFC Bank Ltd: KCS House, Kaunda St, POB 72833, Nairobi; tel. (2) 340091; fax (2) 223032; cap. and res 959.6m. (March 1996); Chair. P. K. JANI; Man. Dir N. MAJMUDAR.

Commercial Bank of Africa Ltd: Commercial Bank Bldg, cnr Wabera and Standard Sts, POB 30437, Nairobi; tel. (2) 228881; telex 23205; fax (2) 335827; f. 1967; 100% owned by Kenyan shareholders; cap. and res 989m., dep. 6,448m. (Dec. 1996); Chair. M. H. DA GAMA ROSE; Man. Dir J. A. M. DOCHERTY; 10 brs.

Consolidated Bank of Kenya Ltd: Koinange St, POB 51133, Nairobi; tel. (2) 340920; telex 22482; fax (2) 340213; f. 1989; state-owned; cap. and res 1,230m., dep. 756m. (March 1994); Chair. JAPHETH LIJOODI; Man. Dir E. K. MATHIU.

Kenya Commercial Bank Ltd: Kencom House, Moi Ave, POB 48400, Nairobi; tel. (2) 339441; telex 23085; fax (2) 338006; f. 1970; 60% state-owned; cap. and res 8,440m., dep. 46,036m. (Dec. 1995); Exec. Chair. A. T. KAMINCHIA; Gen. Man. ELIJAH K. ARAP BII; 264 brs and sub-brs.

Middle East Bank Kenya Ltd: Kenyatta Ave, POB 47387, Nairobi; tel. (2) 335168; telex 23132; fax (2) 336182; f. 1981; 75% owned by Kenyan shareholders; cap. and res 287.5m., dep. 2,501.3m. (Dec. 1995); Chair. A. K. ESMAIL; Man. Dir S. S. DINAMANI; 2 brs.

National Bank of Kenya Ltd (Banki ya Taifa La Kenya Ltd): National Bank Bldg, Harambee Ave, POB 72866, Nairobi; tel. (2) 226471; telex 22619; fax (2) 330784; f. 1968; 80% state-owned; cap. and res 3,190.8m., dep. 18,384.3m. (Dec. 1996); Exec. Chair. JOHN SIMBA; Gen. Man. AHMED H. AHMED; 33 brs.

Pan African Bank Ltd: ICEA Bldg, 14th Floor, Kenyatta Ave, POB 45334, Nairobi; tel. (2) 225325; telex 23058; fax (2) 218490; f. 1982; cap. 100m. (Dec. 1990); Chair. and Man. Dir MOHAMMAD ASLAM; 8 brs.

Prime Bank Ltd: Kenindia House, Loita St, POB 43825, Nairobi; tel. (2) 211979; telex 23224; fax (2) 334549; cap. and res 153m. (Sep. 1995); Chair. R. C. KANTARIA; Man. Dir G. H. BHATT.

Stanbic Bank Kenya Ltd: Kenyatta Ave, POB 30550, Nairobi; tel. (2) 335888; telex 22397; fax (2) 330227; 40% state-owned; cap. and res 574m., dep. 3,331.6m. (Dec. 1996); Chair. J. B. WANJUI; Gen. Man. P. LEWIS-JONES; 2 brs.

Standard Chartered Bank Kenya Ltd: Stanbank House, Moi Ave, POB 30003, Nairobi; tel. (2) 330200; telex 22209; fax (2) 330506; owned by Standard Chartered Bank Africa; cap. and res 2,126.6m., dep. 21,536.5m. (Dec. 1995); Chair. JULIUS GECAU; CEO ANTONY GROAG; 43 brs.

Trans-National Bank Ltd: Trans-National Plaza, 2nd Floor, Mama Ngina St, POB 75840, Nairobi; tel. (2) 224234; fax (2) 251504; f. 1985; cap. 624m., dep. 862m. (Dec. 1994); Chair. MWAKAI SIO: 5 brs.

Trust Bank Ltd: Trustforte Bldg, Moi Ave, POB 46342, Nairobi; tel. (2) 226413; telex 25143; fax (2) 334995; f. 1988; cap. and res 796m., dep. 12,775.7m. (Dec. 1996); Chair. AJAY I. SHAH; Gen. Mans. P. D. MALKAN, Y. N. MODI, K. D. SONI; 13 brs.

Victoria Commercial Bank Ltd: Victor House, 2nd Floor, Kimathi St, POB 41114, Nairobi; tel. (2) 228732; telex 22471; fax (2) 220548; f. 1987 as Victoria Finance Co Ltd, name changed 1996; cap. and res 240.2m., dep. 3,280.7m. (Dec. 1996); Chair. SILVANO KOLA; Gen. Man. YOGESH KANJI PATTNI.

Merchant Banks

African Merchantile Banking Co Ltd: POB 30090, Nairobi; tel. (2) 333969; fax (2) 333818; wholly-owned by First Chartered Securities Ltd; cap. and res 245.1m. (Dec. 1995); Chair. DUNCAN NDEGWA; Man. Dir B. ROGERS.

Diamond Trust Bank of Kenya Ltd: Nation Centre, 8th Floor, Kimathi St, POB 61711, Nairobi; tel. (2) 210988; fax (2) 336836; f. 1945; cap. and res 1,010.1m. (Dec. 1995); Chair. ZAHER AHAMED; Man. Dir M. P. MANJI.

Kenya Commercial Finance Co Ltd: Kenyan House, 6th Floor, Moi Ave, POB 21984, Nairobi; tel. (2) 339074; fax (2) 215881; f. 1971; cap. 300m., dep. 3,914m. (1995); Chair. A. T. KAMINCHIA; Chief Man. M. S. FAZAL.

Kenya National Capital Corporation Ltd: POB 73469, Nairobi; tel. (2) 336077; fax (2) 338217; f. 1977; 60% owned by National Bank of Kenya, 40% by Kenya National Assurance Co; cap. 80m., dep. 1,024m. (1996); Chair. J. P. N. SIMBA; Gen. Man. C. M. KIBUNJA.

National Industrial Credit Bank Ltd (NIC): NIC House, Masaba Rd, POB 44599, Nairobi; tel. (2) 718200; fax (2) 718232; publicly quoted; cap. and res 759m. (Dec. 1995); Chair. P. O. NYAKIAMO; Man. Dir P. J. BOLTON.

Pan African Credit and Finance Ltd: ICEA Bldg, 5th Floor, Kenyatta Ave, POB 47529, Nairobi; tel. (2) 25325; telex 23058; fax (2) 722410; owned by Pan African Bank; cap. 40m. (Dec. 1990); Chair. and Man. Dir MOHAMMAD ASLAM.

Standard Chartered Financial Services Ltd: International House, 1st Floor, Mama Ngina St, POB 40310, Nairobi; tel. (2) 336333; telex 22089; fax (2) 334934; owned by Standard Chartered Bank Kenya; cap. and res 161.7m., dep. 1,700m. (Dec. 1992); Chair. A. CLEARY; Man. Dir W. VON ISENBURG.

Foreign Banks

ABN AMRO Bank NV (Netherlands): Nyerere Rd, POB 30262, Nairobi; tel. (2) 710455; telex 22262; fax (2) 713391; Gen. Man. W. A. E. J. LEMSTRA; 2 brs.

Bank of Baroda (India): Bank of Baroda Bldg, cnr Mondlane St and Tom Mboya St, POB 30033, Nairobi; tel. (2) 337611; telex 22250; fax (2) 333089; Exec. Chair. C. K. DAIYA; 6 brs.

Bank of India: Kenyatta Ave, POB 30246, Nairobi; tel. (2) 221414; telex 22725; fax (2) 229462; Chief Man. P. V. PALSOKAR.

Banque Indosuez (France): Reinsurance Plaza, Taifa Rd, POB 69562, Nairobi; tel. (2) 215859; telex 23091; fax (2) 214166; Regional Man. JEAN-MICHEL BROCATO.

Citibank NA (USA): Fedha Towers, 6th Floor, Muindi Mbingu St, POB 30711, Nairobi; tel. (2) 334286; telex 22051; fax (2) 337340; Gen. Man. PAUL FLETCHER.

First American Bank of Kenya Ltd (USA): ICEA Bldg, 6th/7th Floors, Kenyatta Ave, POB 30691, Nairobi; tel. (2) 333960; telex 222398; fax (2) 230969; f. 1987; cap. and res 538.8m., dep. 3,677.6m. (Dec. 1996); Chair. N. N. MERALI; Gen. Man. S. S. HASAN RIZVI; 2 brs.

Habib Bank AG Zurich (Switzerland): National House, Koinange St, POB 30584, Nairobi; tel. (2) 334984; telex 22982; fax (2) 218699; Gen. Man. BAKIRALI NASIR.

MashreqBank PSC (UAE): ICEA Bldg, Kenyatta Ave, POB 11129, Nairobi; tel. (2) 330562; telex 22596; fax (2) 330792; Man. S. A. IMAN.

Co-operative Bank

Co-operative Bank of Kenya Ltd: Co-operative House, Haile Selassie Ave, POB 48231, Nairobi; tel. (2) 228453; telex 22938; fax (2) 227747; f. 1968; cap. and res 2,323.4m., dep. 8,422.9m. (Dec. 1996); Chair. HOSEA KIPLAGAT; Man. Dir ERASTUS K. MUREITHI; 24 brs.

Development Banks

Development Finance Co of Kenya Ltd: POB 30483, Nairobi; tel. (2) 340401; telex 22662; fax (2) 338426; cap. and res 793.2m. (Dec. 1995); Chair. Prof. H. K. MENGECH; Gen. Man. J. V. BOSSE.

East African Development Bank: Bruce House, 4th Floor, Standard St, POB 47685, Nairobi; tel. (2) 340642; telex 22689; fax (2) 216651; Man. J. F. OWITI.

Industrial Development Bank Ltd (IDB): National Bank Bldg, 18th Floor, Harambee Ave, POB 44036, Nairobi; tel. (2) 337079; telex 22339; fax (2) 334594; f. 1973; 49% state-owned; cap. 258m. (June 1996); Chair. R. K. CHESHIRE; Man. Dir L. A. MASAVIRU.

STOCK EXCHANGE

Nairobi Stock Exchange: Nation Centre, Kimathi St, POB 43633, Nairobi; tel. (2) 230692; fax (2) 224200; f. 1954; 56 mems (Dec. 1994); Chair. J. M. MBARU; CEO JOB K. KIHUMBA.

INSURANCE

American Life Insurance Co: American Life House, POB 49460, Nairobi; tel. (2) 721124; telex 22621; fax 723140; general.

Blue Shield Insurance Co Ltd: POB 49610; Nairobi; tel. (2) 227932; fax (2) 337808; f. 1983; life and general.

Cannon Assurance (Kenya) Ltd: Haile Selassie Ave, POB 30216, Nairobi; tel. (2) 335478; telex 25482; f. 1974; life and general; CEO I. J. TALWAR.

Corporate Insurance Co Ltd: Corporate House, Banda St, POB 34172, Nairobi; tel. (2) 225302; telex 25134; f. 1983; life and general; CEO K. C. MATHEW.

Heritage Insurance Co Ltd: Norwich Union Bldg, Mama Ngina St, POB 30390, Nairobi; tel. (2) 725303; telex 22476; fax (2) 722835; f. 1975; general; CEO T. C. GOSS.

Insurance Co of East Africa Ltd (ICEA): ICEA Bldg, Kenyatta Ave, POB 46143, Nairobi; tel. (2) 21652; life and general; CEO J. K. NDUNGU.

Intra Africa Assurance Co Ltd: Williamson House, 4th Ngong Ave, POB 43241, Nairobi; tel. (2) 712607; f. 1977; CEO H. G. MKANGI.

Jubilee Insurance Co Ltd: POB 30376, Nairobi; tel. (2) 340343; telex 22199; fax (2) 216882; f. 1937; life and general; Chair. ABDUL JAFFER.

Kenindia Assurance Co Ltd: Kenindia House, Loita St, POB 44372, Nairobi; tel. (2) 333100; telex 23173; fax (2) 218380; f. 1979; life and general; CEO SAIKAT GUHA.

Kenya Reinsurance Corporation: Reinsurance Plaza, Taifa Rd, POB 30271, Nairobi; tel. (2) 332690; telex 22046; fax (2) 339161; f. 1970; CEO WILLIAM MBOTE.

Lion of Kenya Insurance Co Ltd: POB 30190, Nairobi; tel. (2) 338800; telex 22717; f. 1978; general; CEO I. A. GALLOWAY.

Monarch Insurance Co Ltd: Chester House, 2nd Floor, Koinange St, POB 44003, Nairobi; tel. (2) 330042; f. 1979; general; Gen. Man. J. K. KARIUKI.

Pan Africa Insurance Co Ltd: Pan Africa House, Kenyatta Ave, POB 62551, Nairobi; tel. (2) 339544; telex 22750; fax (2) 217675; f. 1946; life and general; CEO WILLIAM OLOTCH.

Phoenix of East Africa Assurance Co Ltd: Ambank House, University Way, POB 30129, Nairobi; tel. (2) 338784; fax (2) 211848; general; Gen. Man. G. O. NANDY; Exec. Dir MOYEZ ALIBHAI.

Provincial Insurance Co of East Africa Ltd: Old Mutual Bldg, Kimathi St, POB 43013, Nairobi; tel. (2) 330173; telex 22852; f. 1980; general; CEO E. C. BATES.

Prudential Assurance Co of Kenya Ltd: Yaya Centre, Argwings Kodhek Rd, POB 76190, Nairobi; tel. (2) 567374; telex 22280; f. 1979; general; CEO E. THOMAS.

Royal Insurance Co of East Africa Ltd: Mama Ngina St, POB 40001, Nairobi; tel. (2) 330171; telex 23249; fax (2) 727396; f. 1979; general; CEO S. K. KAMAU.

Trade and Industry

Kenya National Trading Corporation Ltd: Uchumi House, Nkrumah Ave, POB 30587, Nairobi; tel. (2) 29141; telex 22298; f. 1965; promotes national control of trade in both locally produced and imported items; exports coffee and sugar; CEO S. W. O. OGESSA.

CHAMBER OF COMMERCE

Kenya National Chamber of Commerce and Industry: Ufanisi House, Haile Selassie Ave, POB 47024, Nairobi; tel. (2) 334413; fax (2) 340664; f. 1965; 53 brs; Nat. Chair. G. KASSIM OWANGO; CEO REM O. OGANA.

TRADE ASSOCIATIONS

East African Tea Trade Association: Tea Trade Centre, Nyerere Ave, POB 85174, Mombasa; tel. (11) 315687; fax (11) 225823; f. 1957; organizes Mombasa weekly tea auctions; CEO MARK RADOLI; 167 mems.

Export Processing Zones Authority: POB 50563, Nairobi; tel. (2) 712800; fax (2) 713704; e-mail epza_hq@users.africa.online.co.ke; established by the govt. to promote investment in Export Processing Zones; CEO SILAS ITA.

Export Promotion Council: POB 43137, Nairobi; tel. (2) 333555; telex 22468; fax (2) 226036; promotes exports; Chair. SAM MUUMBI.

Kenya Association of Manufacturers: POB 30225, Nairobi; tel. (2) 746005; fax (2) 746028; Chair. MANU CHANDARIA; CEO Z. N. KAHURA; 580 mems.

STATUTORY BOARDS

Central Province Marketing Board: POB 189, Nyeri.

Coffee Board of Kenya: POB 30566, Nairobi; tel. (2) 332896; telex 25706; fax (2) 330546; f. 1947; Chair. PITHON MWANGI; Gen. Man. AGGREY MURUNGA.

Kenya Dairy Board: POB 30406, Nairobi.

Kenya Meat Corporation: POB 30414, Nairobi; tel. (2) 340750; telex 22150; f. 1953; purchasing, processing and marketing of beef livestock; Chair. H. P. BARCLAY.

Kenya Sisal Board: Mutual Bldg, Kimathi St, POB 41179, Nairobi; tel. (2) 223457; f. 1946; CEO J. H. WAIRAGU; Man. Dir KENNETH MUKUMA.

Kenya Sugar Authority: POB 51500, Nairobi; tel. (2) 710600; telex 25105; fax (2) 723903; Chair. LUKE R. OBOK; CEO F. M. CHAHONYO.

National Cereals and Produce Board: POB 30586, Nairobi; tel. (2) 555288; telex 24109; fax (2) 542024; f. 1995; stores and manages strategic national food reserves, provides market outlet for cereals, undertakes market stabilization programmes, distributes famine relief, provides drying, weighing, storage and fumigation services to farmers; Chair. JAMES MUTUA; Man. Dir Maj. W. K. KOITABA.

Pyrethrum Board of Kenya: POB 420, Nakuru; tel. (37) 211567; telex 33080; fax (37) 45274; f. 1935; 18 mems; Chair. T. O. OMATO; CEO J. M. G. WAINAINA.

Tea Board of Kenya: POB 20064, Nairobi; tel. (2) 569102; fax (2) 562120; f. 1950; regulates tea industry on all matters of policy, licenses tea planting and processing, combats pests and diseases, controls the export of tea, finances research on tea, promotes Kenyan tea internationally; 17 mems; Chair. JOHNSTONE O. MORONGE; CEO GEORGE M. KIMANI.

DEVELOPMENT ORGANIZATIONS

Agricultural Development Corporation: POB 47101, Nairobi; tel. (2) 338530; telex 22856; fax (2) 336524; f. 1965 to promote agricultural development and reconstruction; CEO Dr WALTER KILELE.

Agricultural Finance Corporation: POB 30367, Nairobi; tel. (2) 333733; telex 22649; a statutory organization providing agricultural loans; Gen. Man. G. K. TOROITICH.

Development Finance Company of Kenya Ltd: Finance House, 16th Floor, Loita St, POB 30483, Nairobi; tel. (2) 340401; telex 22662; fax (2) 338426; f. 1963; private co with govt participation; paid-up cap. Ks. 139m. (1991); Chair. H. N. K. ARAP MENGECH; Gen. Man. J. V. BOSSE.

Horticultural Crops Development Authority: POB 42601, Nairobi; tel. (2) 337381; telex 22687; fax (2) 228386; f. 1968; invests in production, dehydration, processing and freezing of fruit and vegetables; exports of fresh fruit and vegetables; Chair. KASANGA MULWA; Man. Dir M. A. S. MULANDI.

Housing Finance Co of Kenya Ltd: Rehani House, Kenyatta Ave, POB 30088; Nairobi; tel. (2) 333910; f. 1965; cap. Ks 20m., dep. 2,300m. (1989); Man. Dir WALTER MUKURIA.

Industrial and Commercial Development Corporation: Uchumi House, Aga Khan Walk, POB 45519, Nairobi; tel. (2) 229213; telex 22429; fax (2) 333880; f. 1954; govt-financed; assists industrial and commercial development; Chair. REUBEN CHESIRE; Exec. Dir DONALD KIMUTAI.

Investment Promotion Centre: National Bank Bldg, 8th Floor, Harambee Ave, POB 55704, Nairobi; tel. (2) 221401; fax (2) 336663; promotes and facilitates local and foreign investment; Exec. Chair. Dr JOSEPH N. K. ARAP NGOK.

Kenya Fishing Industries Ltd: Nairobi; Man. Dir ABDALLA MBWANA.

Kenya Industrial Estates Ltd: Nairobi Industrial Estate, Likoni Rd, POB 78029, Nairobi; tel. (2) 530551; telex 24191; fax (2) 534625; f. 1967 to finance and develop small-scale industries.

Kenya Industrial Research and Development Institute: POB 30650, Nairobi; tel. (2) 557762; f. 1942, reorg. 1979; restructured 1995; research and development in industrial and allied technologies including engineering, commodity technologies, mining and power resources; Dir Dr H. L. KAANE.

Kenya Planters' Co-operative Union: Nairobi; coffee cultivation and processing; Chair. A. MWANGI; Man. Dir JAMES NYAGA.

Kenya Tea Development Authority: POB 30213, Nairobi; tel. (2) 21441; telex 22645; f. 1964 to develop tea growing, manufacturing and marketing among African smallholders; in 1994/95 it supervised an area of 76,968 ha, cultivated by 289,270 registered growers, and operated 44 factories; Chair. STEPHEN M. IMANYARA; Man. Dir EUSTACE G. KARANJA.

Settlement Fund Trustees: POB 30449, Nairobi; administers a land purchase programme involving over 1.2m. ha for resettlement of African farmers.

EMPLOYERS' ASSOCIATIONS

Federation of Kenya Employers: Waajiri House, Argwings Kodhek Rd, POB 48311, Nairobi; tel. (2) 721929; telex 22642; fax (2) 721990; Chair. J. P. N. SIMBA; Exec. Dir TOM D. OWUOR; the following are affiliates:

Association of Local Government Employers: POB 52, Muranga; Chair. S. K. ITONGU.

Distributive and Allied Industries Employers' Association: POB 30587, Nairobi; Chair. P. J. MWAURA.

Engineering and Allied Industries Employers' Association: POB 48311, Nairobi; tel. (2) 721929; Chair. D. M. NJOROGE.

Kenya Association of Building and Civil Engineering Contractors: POB 43598, Nairobi; Chair. G. S. HIRANI.

Kenya Association of Hotelkeepers and Caterers: POB 46406, Nairobi; tel. (2) 726640; fax (2) 721505; f. 1944; Chair. J. MWENDWA.

Kenya Bankers' (Employers') Association: Nairobi; tel. (2) 330200; Chair. J. A. M. DOCHERTY.

Kenya Sugar Employers' Union: POB 262, Kisumu; Chair. L. OKECH.

Kenya Tea Growers' Association: POB 320, Kericho; tel. (2) 21010; fax (2) 32172; Chair. M. K. A. SANG.

Kenya Vehicle Manufacturers' Association: POB 1436, Thika; Chair. C. PETERSON.

Motor Trade and Allied Industries Employers' Association: POB 48311, Nairobi; tel. (2) 721929; fax (2) 721990; Exec. Sec. G. N. KONDITI.

Sisal Growers' and Employers' Association: POB 47523, Nairobi; tel. (2) 720170; telex 22642; fax (2) 721990; Chair. A. G. COMBOS.

Timber Industries Employers' Association: POB 18070, Nairobi; Chair. H. S. BAMBRAH.

MAJOR INDUSTRIAL COMPANIES

The following are among the largest companies in terms either of capital investment or employment.

BAT (Kenya) Ltd: Likoni Rd, Industrial Area, POB 30000, Nairobi; tel. (2) 533555; telex 24131; fax (2) 531717; f. 1957; subsidiary of British American Tobacco Co Ltd, UK; mfrs of tobacco products; Man. Dir T. P. G. MCDOWELL.

Bata Shoe Co (Kenya) Ltd: POB 23, Limuru; tel. (154) 71620; telex 22386; fax (154) 71145; f. 1943; mfrs of footwear; CEO A. FERNANDEZ.

A. Baumann and Co Ltd: Nairobi Baumann House, Haile Selassie Ave, POB 40538, Nairobi; tel. (2) 140538; fax (2) 210315; f. 1926; active in Kenya, Tanzania and Uganda; steamship agents, warehousemen, clearing and forwarding agents, exporters and importers of electrical, engineering and agricultural products, and mfrs of carbon brushes and soft alloys; also involved in the air-conditioning business in Kenya, paint manufacture in Uganda; also holds substantial investments in numerous local cos and industries; Chair. N. NGANGA; Man. Dir H. RANA.

Consolidated Holdings Ltd: POB 11854, Nairobi; telex 22204; fax (2) 553939; f. 1919; cap. K£2,140,410; holding co with interests in Kenya in newspaper publication and the distribution of foreign newspapers and magazines; Chair. M. W. HARLEY; Man. Dir R. S. HOLT.

East Africa Industries: Enterprise Rd, Industrial Area, POB 30062, Nairobi; tel. (2) 542000; telex 22507; fax (2) 543912; f. 1943; mfrs of toothpaste, body lotions, soaps, detergents, edible oils and soft drinks ; CEO J. B. WANJUI.

East African Portland Cement Co Ltd: Longonot Place, Kijabe St, POB 40101, Nairobi; tel. (2) 226551; telex 22151; fax (2) 211936; f. 1933; cement mfrs; Chair. A. LULU; Man. Dir J. G. MAINA.

Firestone East Africa (1969) Ltd: POB 30429, Nairobi; tel. (2) 559922; telex 24052; fax (2) 544241; f. 1969; tyre and tube mfrs; CEO N. N. MERALI.

General Motors East Africa Ltd: cnr Enterprise and Mombasa Rds, Industrial Area, POB 30527, Nairobi; tel. (2) 556588; telex 24071; fax (2) 544178; f. 1975; motor vehicle assembly; CEO D. D. McCarthy.

Kenya Breweries Ltd: Thika Rd, POB 30161, Nairobi; tel. (2) 802701; telex 22628; fax (2) 802054; f. 1920; mfrs of lager beers and malted barley; Chair. J. G. Kiereini; Man. Dir M. J. Karanja.

Kenya Co-operative Creameries Ltd: Dakar Rd, POB 30131, Nairobi; tel. (2) 532535; telex 24128; fax (2) 544879; f. 1925; processes and markets the bulk of dairy produce; Dir Job Mukule.

Kenya Vehicle Manufacturers Ltd: POB 1436, Thika; motor vehicle mfrs; Man. Dir D. Percival.

Magadi Soda Co Ltd: POB 1, Magadi; tel. (303) 33000; fax (303) 32088; f. 1926; processors of salt and soda ash for export.

Panafrican Paper Mills (East Africa) Ltd: Kenindia House, Loita St, POB 30221, Nairobi; tel. (2) 335489; telex 22083; fax (2) 215692; f. 1970; mfrs of paper, paperboard and pulp; CEO N. K. Mohatta.

TRADE UNIONS

Central Organization of Trade Unions (Kenya) (COTU): Solidarity Bldg, Digo Rd, POB 13000, Nairobi; tel. (2) 761375; fax (2) 762695; f. 1965 as the sole trade union fed.; Chair. Peter G. Muthee; Sec.-Gen. Joseph J. Mugalla; the following unions are affiliates:

Amalgamated Union of Kenya Metalworkers: POB 73651, Nairobi; tel. (2) 211060; Gen. Sec. F. E. Omido.

Bakers', Confectionary Manufacturing and Allied Workers' Union: POB 57751, Nairobi; tel. (2) 229920.

Dockworkers' Union: POB 98207, Mombasa; tel. (11) 491427; f. 1954; Gen. Sec. J. Khamis.

Kenya Airline Pilots' Association: POB 57505, Nairobi; tel. (2) 716986.

Kenya Building, Construction, Civil Engineering and Allied Trades Workers' Union: POB 49628, Nairobi; tel. (2) 336414; Gen. Sec. John Murugu.

Kenya Chemical and Allied Workers' Union: POB 73820, Nairobi; tel. (2) 338815. Gen. Sec. Were Dibi Oguto.

Kenya Electrical Trades Allied Workers' Union: POB 47060, Nairobi; tel. (2) 334655.

Kenya Engineering Workers' Union: POB 73987, Nairobi; tel. (2) 333745; Gen. Sec. Justus Mulei.

Kenya Game Hunting and Safari Workers' Union: Nairobi; tel. (2) 25049; Gen. Sec. J. M. Ndolo.

Kenya Jockey and Betting Workers' Union: POB 55094, Nairobi; tel. (2) 332120.

Kenya Local Government Workers' Union: POB 55827, Nairobi; tel. (2) 217213; Gen. Sec. Wasike Ndombi.

Kenya National Union of Fishermen: POB 83322, Nairobi; tel. (2) 227899.

Kenya Petroleum Oil Workers' Union: POB 48125, Nairobi; tel. (2) 338756; Gen. Sec. Jacob Ochino.

Kenya Plantation and Agricultural Workers' Union: POB 1161, Nakuru; tel. (37) 212310; Gen. Sec. Stanley Muiruri Karanja.

Kenya Quarry and Mine Workers' Union: POB 332120, Nairobi; f. 1961; Gen. Sec. Wafula Wa Musamia.

Kenya Scientific Research, International Technical and Allied Institutions Workers' Union: Ngumba House, Tom Mboya St, POB 55094, Nairobi; tel. (2) 339964; Sec.-Gen. Samson Owen Kubai.

Kenya Shipping, Clearing and Warehouse Workers' Union: POB 84067, Mombasa; tel. (11) 312000.

Kenya Shoe and Leather Workers' Union: POB 49629, Nairobi; tel. (2) 533827; Gen. Sec. James Awich.

Kenya Union of Commercial, Food and Allied Workers: POB 46818, Nairobi; tel. (2) 212545.

Kenya Union of Domestic, Hotel, Educational Institutions, Hospitals and Allied Workers: POB 41763, Nairobi; tel. (2) 336838.

Kenyan Union of Entertainment and Music Industry Employees: Nairobi; tel. (2) 333745.

Kenya Union of Journalists: POB 47035, Nairobi; tel. (2) 3376691; Gen. Sec. George Odiko.

Kenya Union of Printing, Publishing, Paper Manufacturers and Allied Workers: POB 72358, Nairobi; tel. (2) 331387; Gen. Sec. John Bosco.

Kenya Union of Sugar Plantation Workers: POB 36, Kisumu; tel. (35) 22221; Gen. Sec. Onyango Midika.

National Seamen's Union of Kenya: Mombasa; tel. (11) 312106; Gen. Sec. I. S. Abdallah Mwarua.

Railway Workers' Union: POB 72029, Nairobi; tel. (2) 26131.

Tailors' and Textile Workers' Union: POB 72076, Nairobi; tel. (2) 338836.

Transport and Allied Workers' Union: POB 45171, Nairobi; tel. (2) 545317; Gen. Sec. Julias Malii.

Union of Posts and Telecommunications Employees: POB 48155, Nairobi; tel. (2) 27314.

Independent Unions

Kenya Medical Practitioners' and Dentists' Union: not officially recognized; Nat. Chair. Gibbon Ateka.

Kenya National Union of Teachers: POB 30407, Nairobi; f. 1957; Sec.-Gen. A. A. Adongo.

University Academic Staff Union: Nairobi; not officially registered; Interim Chair. Dr Korwa Abar.

Transport

RAILWAYS

In 1993 there were 2,740 km of track open for traffic, including sidings.

Kenya Railways Corporation: POB 30121, Nairobi; tel. (2) 221211; telex 22254; fax (2) 340049; f. 1977; Exec. Chair. Prof. J. K. Musuva; Gen. Man. A. Y. Hariz.

ROADS

At the end of 1995 there were 63,663 km of classified roads, of which 6,403 km were main roads and 19,435 km were secondary roads. Only 13.8% of road surfaces were paved. An all-weather road links Nairobi to Addis Ababa, in Ethiopia, and there is a 590-km road link between Kitale (Kenya) and Juba (Sudan). In February 1996 the World Bank approved a US $165m. loan to finance the urgent rehabilitation of the important internal road link between Nairobi and Mombasa.

Abamba Public Road Services: POB 40322, Nairobi; tel. (2) 556062; fax (2) 559884; operates bus services from Nairobi to all major towns in Kenya and to Kampala in Uganda.

East African Road Services Ltd: Nairobi; tel. (2) 764622; telex 23285; f. 1947; operates bus services from Nairobi to all major towns in Kenya; Chair. S. H. Nathoo; Gen. Man. E. H. Malik.

Nyayo Bus Service Corp.: POB 47174, Nairobi; tel. (2) 803588; f. 1986; operates bus services within and between major towns in Kenya.

Speedways Trans-Africa Freighters: POB 75755, Nairobi; tel. (2) 544267; telex 23000; largest private road haulier in East Africa, with over 200 trucks; CEO Hassan Kanyare.

SHIPPING

Major shipping operations in Kenya are handled at the international seaport of Mombasa, which has 16 deep-water berths with a total length of 3,044 m and facilities for the off-loading of bulk carriers, tankers and container vessels. An inland container depot with a potential full capacity of 120,000 20-ft (6-m) equivalent units was opened in Nairobi in 1984. Two further inland depots were scheduled to begin operating in the mid-1990s at Eldoret and Kisumu.

Kenya Ports Authority: POB 95009, Mombasa; tel. (11) 312211; telex 21243; fax (11) 311867; f. 1977; sole operator of coastal port facilities, and operates three inland container depots; Exec. Chair. Robert Brenneisen; Gen. Man. L. J. Mwangola.

Kenya Cargo Handling Services Ltd: POB 95187, Mombasa; tel. (11) 25955; telex 20047; division of Kenya Ports Authority; Man. Dir Joshua Kegode.

Inchcape Shipping Services Kenya Ltd: POB 90194, Mombasa; tel. (11) 314245; telex 21278; fax (11) 314224.

Kenya Shipping Agency Ltd: Southern House, Moi Ave, POB 84831, Mombasa; tel. (11) 20501; telex 21013; fax (11) 314494; 60% govt-owned via Kenya National Trading Corpn Ltd, 40% owned by Southern Shield Group; dry cargo, container, bulk carrier and tanker agents; Chair. Ray Kester; Man. Dir Jonathan Mturi.

Lykes Lines: POB 30182, Nairobi; tel. (2) 332320; telex 22317; fax (2) 723861; services to USA ports.

Mackenzie Maritime Ltd: Maritime Centre, Archbishop Makarios Close, POB 90120, Mombasa; tel. (11) 221273; telex 21205; fax (11) 316260; agents for P&O/Nedlloyd, Thos and Jas Harrison, Mitsui OSK Lines, Shell (Stasco), Cunard, Princess Cruises, Mobil, Orient Lines.

Marship Ltd: Jubilee Bldg, Moi Ave, POB 80443, Mombasa; tel. (11) 314705; telex 21442; fax (11) 316654; f. 1986; shipbrokers, ship management and chartering agents.

Mitchell Cotts Kenya Ltd: Cotts House, Wabera St, POB 30182, Nairobi; tel. (2) 221273; telex 22317; fax (2) 214228; agents for DOAL, Cie Maritime Belge SA, Nippon Yusen Kaisha.

Southern Line Ltd: POB 90102, Mombasa; tel. (11) 20507; telex 21288; operating dry cargo and tanker vessels between East African ports, Red Sea ports, the Persian (Arabian) Gulf and Indian Ocean islands.

Spanfreight Shipping Ltd: Cannon Towers, Moi Ave, POB 99760, Mombasa; fax (11) 312092.

Star East Africa Co: POB 86725, Mombasa; tel. (11) 314060; telex 21251; fax (11) 312818; shipping agents and brokers.

Wigglesworth and Co Ltd: POB 90501, Mombasa; tel. (11) 25241; telex 21246.

CIVIL AVIATION

Jomo Kenyatta International Airport, at Nairobi, was inaugurated in 1978. Moi International Airport, at Mombasa, also handles international traffic. Wilson Airport in Nairobi services domestic flights as do airports at Malindi and Kisumu. Kenya has about 400 airstrips. During the mid-1990s a US$10.9m. programme to rehabilitate and expand Jomo Kenyatta International and Moi International Airports was under way. Construction of a third international airport, at Eldoret, was completed in 1996.

Kenya Airports Authority: Jomo Kenyatta International Airport, POB 19001, Nairobi; tel. (2) 822950; telex 25552; fax (2) 822078; f. 1991; responsible for the provision, management and operation of aerodromes; also approves and supervises private airstrips; Man. Dir B. S. OMUSE.

Air Kenya Aviation: Wilson Airport, POB 30357, Nairobi; tel. (2) 501601; telex 22939; fax (2) 500845; f. 1985; operates internal scheduled and charter passenger services; Man. Dir JOHN BUCKLEY.

Eagle Aviation (International African Eagle): POB 93926, Mombasa; tel. (11) 434502; fax (11) 434249; f. 1986; scheduled regional and domestic passenger and cargo services; Chair. Capt. GILBERT M. KIBE; Man. Dir CHARLES K. MUTHAMA.

Kenya Airways Ltd: Jomo Kenyatta International Airport, POB 19002, Nairobi; tel. (2) 823000; telex 22771; fax (2) 823488; f. 1977 following the dissolution of East African Airways; transfer to private-sector ownership completed in 1996; passenger services to Africa, Asia, Europe and Middle East; freight services to Europe; internal services from Nairobi to Kisumu, Mombasa and Malindi; also operates a freight subsidiary; Chair. ISAAC OMOLO OKERO; Man. Dir BRIAN DAVIES.

CIVIL AVIATION AUTHORITY

Kenya Directorate of Civil Aviation: Jomo Kenyatta International Airport, POB 30163, Nairobi; tel. (2) 822950; telex 25239; f. 1948; under Kenya govt control since 1977; responsible for the conduct of civil aviation; advises the govt on civil aviation policy; Dir J. P. AYUGA.

Tourism

Kenya's main attractions for visitors are its wildlife, with 25 National Parks and 23 game reserves, the Indian Ocean coast and an equable year-round climate. In 1994, when tourist arrivals numbered an estimated 863,400, earnings from the sector totalled about Ks. 28,000m. In 1995 tourist arrivals declined to an estimated 690,000 and earnings from the sector fell to Ks. 24,000m. The decline in the sector, which abated slightly in 1996, with arrivals numbering some 717,000, was attributed both to competition from other countries of the region, and to perceptions of high rates of crime and shortcomings in security within Kenya.

Kenya Tourism Board: Nairobi; f. 1996; promotes Kenya as a tourist destination, monitors the standard of tourist facilities.

Kenya Tourist Development Corporation: Utalii House, Uhuru Highway, POB 42013, Nairobi; tel. (2) 330820; telex 23009; fax (2) 227815; f. 1965; Chair. PAUL KITOLOLO; Man. Dir ELIAS MUSYOKA.

Defence

In August 1996 Kenya's armed forces numbered 24,200, comprising an army of 20,500, an air force of 2,500 and a navy of 1,200. Military service is voluntary. The paramilitary police general service unit was 5,000 strong in 1996. Defence was allocated Ks. 9,039m. in the budget for the financial year to 30 June 1996 (representing 5.9% of total budgeted expenditure by the central government). Military assistance is received from the United Kingdom, and from the USA, whose Rapid Deployment Force uses port and onshore facilities in Kenya.

Defence Expenditure: Budgeted at Ks. 9,039m. for 1995/96.

Commander-in-Chief of the Armed Forces: DANIEL ARAP MOI.

Chief of Armed Forces General Staff: Lt-Gen. DAUDI TONJE

Education

The government provides, or assists in the provision of, schooling. Primary education, which is compulsory, is provided free of charge. The education system involves eight years of primary education (beginning at six years of age), four years at secondary school and four years of university education. The language of instruction from the secondary stage onwards is English. The total enrolment at primary schools increased from about 900,000 in 1963 to 5,545,000 in 1995, taught by some 181,975 teachers. The number of pupils in secondary schools increased from 31,923 in 1963 to 632,388 in 1995, taught by some 41,484 teachers. In 1993 the total enrolment at primary and secondary schools was equivalent to 72% of the school-age population (boys 73%; girls 71%). However, a survey conducted in 1994 revealed that some 30% of pupils leaving primary schools were without access to secondary education. According to estimates by UNESCO, the adult literacy rate in 1995 was 78.1% (males 86.3%; females 70.0%). Enrolment on the government adult literacy programme stood at 111,997 in 1995. There are four state universities, with total enrolment of 35,421 students in 1990, and three chartered private universities (with plans for a further nine mooted in 1997). The education sector was allocated Ks. 29,501m. in the budget for 1995/96 (representing 19.3% of total budgeted expenditure by the central government).

Bibliography

arap Moi, D. T. *Kenya African Nationalism: Nyayo Philosophy and Principles.* London, Macmillan, 1986.

Arnold, G. *Modern Kenya.* London, Longman, 1981.

Bailey, J. *Kenya: The National Epic.* Nairobi, East African Education Publishers, 1993 (Pictorial history).

Bates, R. H. *Beyond the Miracle of the Market: The Political Economy of Agrarian Development in Kenya.* Cambridge, Cambridge University Press, 1992.

Bennett, G. *Kenya, A Political History: The Colonial Period.* London, Oxford University Press, 1963.

Berman, B., and Lonsdale, J. *Unhappy Valley: Clan, Class and State in Colonial Kenya.* London, James Currey, 1988.

Bourmand, D. *Histoire politique du Kenya.* Paris, Editions Karthala, 1988.

Central Bank of Kenya. *Kenya: Land of Opportunity.* Nairobi, Central Bank of Kenya, 1991.

Cohen, D. W., and Odhiambo, E. S. A. *Burying SM: The Politics of Knowledge and the Sociology of Power in Africa.* London, James Currey, 1992.

Coughlin, P., and Gerrishon, K. I. (Eds). *Kenya's Industrialization Dilemma.* Nairobi, Kenyan Heinemann, 1991. [Contains industrial studies carried out under the Industrial Research Project].

Eshiwani, G. S. *Education in Kenya since Independence.* Nairobi, East African Educational Publishers, 1993.

Fogken, D., and Tellegen, W. *Tied to the Land: Living Conditions of Labourers on Large Farms in Trans Nzoia District, Kenya.* Leiden, African Studies Centre, 1995.

Gerzel, C. *The Politics of Independent Kenya.* London, Heinemann; Nairobi, East African Publishing House, 1970.

(Ed.) *Government and Politics in Kenya.* Nairobi, East African Publishing House, 1969.

Govt of Kenya. *Economic Reforms for 1996–1998: The Policy Framework Paper.* Nairobi, Govt Printing Press, 1996.

Greer, J., and Thorbecke, E. *Food Poverty and Consumption Patterns in Kenya.* Geneva, International Labour Office, 1986.

Haugerud, A. *The Culture of Politics in Modern Kenya.* Cambridge, Cambridge University Press, 1995.

Hayward, M. F. *Elections in Independent Africa.* Boulder, CO, Westview Press, 1987.

Himbara, D. *Kenyan Capitalists, the State and Development.* Boulder, CO, Lynne Rienner Publishers, 1993.

Hoorweg, J., Fogken, D., and Klaver, W. *Seasons and Nutrition at the Kenya Coast.* Brookfield, VT, Ashgate Publishing, 1996.

Kanogo, T. *Squatters and the Roots of Mau Mau, 1905–63.* London, James Currey, 1987.

Kenyatta, J. *Facing Mount Kenya*. London, Heinemann, 1979.

Killick, T. (Ed.). *Papers on the Economy of Kenya: Performance, Problems and Politics.* London, Heinemann Educational, 1983.

Kitching, G. N. *Class and Economic Change in Kenya: The Making of an African Bourgeoisie 1905–1970.* Yale University Press, 1980.

Leys, C. *Underdevelopment in Kenya: The Political Economy of Neo-Colonialism.* London, Heinemann Educational, 1975.

Little, P. D. *The Elusive Granary: Herder, Farmer and State in Northern Kenya.* Cambridge, Cambridge University Press, 1992.

Malobe, W. O. *Mau Mau and Kenya: An Analysis of a Peasant Revolt.* Bloomington, Indiana University Press, 1993.

Mboya, T. *The Challenge of Nationhood.* London, André Deutsch, 1970.

Miller, N., and Yeager, R. *Kenya: The Quest for Prosperity.* Boulder, CO, Westview Press, 1994.

Mungeam, G. H. *British Rule in Kenya, 1898–1912.* London, Clarendon Press, 1966.

Mwau, G., and Handa, J. *Rational Economic Decisions and the Current Account in Kenya.* Aldershot, Avebury, 1995.

Ndegwa, P. *Development and Employment in Kenya: A Strategy for the Transformation of the Economy; Report of the Presidential Committee on Employment.* Southwell, Leishman and Taussig, 1991.

Nowrojee, B. *Divide and Rule: State-Sponsored Ethnic Violence in Kenya.* Washington, DC, Human Rights Watch and Africa Watch, 1993.

Ochieng, W. R., and Maxon, R. M. *An Economic History of Kenya.* Nairobi, East African Educational Publishers, 1992.

Ogot, B. A. (Ed.). *Politics and Nationalism in Colonial Kenya.* Nairobi, East African Publishing House, 1972.

Ogot, B. A., and Ochieng, W. R. (Eds). *Decolonization and Independence in Kenya, 1940–1993.* London, James Currey, 1995.

Ojany, F. F., and Ogendo, R. B. *Kenya: A Study in Physical and Human Geography*. London, Longman, 1973.

Otiende, J. E., Wamahiu, S. P., and Karugu, A. M. *Education and Development in Kenya: An Historical Perspective.* Nairobi, Oxford University Press, 1992.

Ouma, S. J. *Development in Kenya through Co-operatives.* Revised Edn. Nairobi, Shirikon, 1989.

Presley. C. A. *Kikuyu Women and Social Change in Kenya.* Boulder, CO, Westview Press, 1992.

Somjee, S. *Material Culture of Kenya.* Nairobi, East African Educational Publications, 1993.

Swainson, N. *The Development of Corporate Capitalism in Kenya, 1918–1977.* London, Heinemann, 1980.

Thomas-Slayter, B., and Rocheleau, D. *Gender, Environment and Development in Kenya: A Grassroots Perspective.* Boulder, CO, Lynne Rienner, 1995.

Throup, D. W. *Economic and Social Origins of Mau Mau, 1945–53.* London, James Currey, 1987.

Trench, C. C. *Men Who Ruled Kenya: The Kenya Administration 1892–1963.* London, Radcliffe Press, 1993.

wa Wamwere, K. *The People's Representative and the Tyrants: or, Kenya, Independence without Freedom.* Nairobi, New Concept Typesetters, 1993.

Widner, J. A. *The Rise of a Party State in Kenya: From 'Harambee' to 'Nyayo'.* Berkeley, University of California Press, 1992.

Willis, J. *Mombasa, the Swahili and the Making of the Mijikenda.* New York, Oxford University Press, 1993.

World Bank. *Kenya: Re-investing in Stabilization and Growth through Public Sector Adjustment.* Washington, DC, World Bank, 1992. (World Bank Country Study).

LESOTHO

Physical and Social Geography

A. MacGREGOR HUTCHESON

PHYSICAL FEATURES

The Kingdom of Lesotho, a small, land-locked country of 30,355 sq km (11,720 sq miles), is enclosed on all sides by South Africa. It is situated at the highest part of the Drakensberg escarpment on the eastern rim of the South African plateau. About two-thirds of Lesotho is very mountainous. Elevations in the eastern half of the country are generally more than 2,440 m above sea-level, and in the north-east and along the eastern border they exceed 3,350 m. This is a region of very rugged relief, bleak climate and heavy annual rainfall (averaging 1,905 mm), where the headstreams of the Orange river have incised deep valleys. Westwards the land descends through a foothill zone of rolling country, at an altitude of 1,830–2,135 m, to Lesotho's main lowland area. This strip of land along the western border, part of the high veld, averages 40 km in width and lies at an altitude of about 1,525 m. Annual rainfall averages in this region are 650–750 mm, and climatic conditions are generally more pleasant. However, frost may occur throughout the country in winter, and hail is a summer hazard in all regions. The light, sandy soils which have developed on the Karoo sedimentaries of the western lowland compare unfavourably with the fertile black soils of the Stormberg basalt in the uplands. The temperate grasslands of the west also tend to be less fertile than the montane grasslands of the east.

POPULATION AND NATURAL RESOURCES

The population at mid-1992 was estimated to be 1,932,879, (including 126,647 absentee workers in South Africa). The noticeable physical contrasts between east and west of Lesotho are reflected in the distribution and density of the population. While large parts of the mountainous east (except for valleys) are sparsely populated, most of the fertile western strip, which carries some 70% of the population, has densities in excess of 200 inhabitants per sq km (the national average in 1989 was 56.0 per sq km). Such population pressure, further aggravated by steady population growth, has resulted in (i) the permanent settlement being pushed to higher levels (in places to 2,440 m) formerly used for summer grazing, and on to steep slopes, thus adding to the already serious national problem of soil erosion; (ii) an acute shortage of cultivable land and increased soil exhaustion, particularly in the west; (iii) land holdings which are too small to maintain the rural population; and (iv) the country's inability, in its current stage of development, to support all its population, thus necessitating the migration of large numbers of workers to seek paid employment in South Africa. It was estimated in 1995 that more than one-quarter of the adult male labour force were employed in South Africa, mainly in the mines. Lesotho's economy depends heavily on their remitted earnings, and a migratory labour system on this scale has grave social, economic and political implications for the country.

Lesotho's long-term development prospects largely rely upon the achievement of optimum use of its soil and water resources. Less than 13% of the country is cultivable and, since virtually all of this is already cultivated, only more productive use of the land can make Lesotho self-sufficient in food (20% of domestic needs are currently imported from South Africa). The high relief produces natural grasslands, well suited for a viable livestock industry, but this has been hindered through inadequate pasture management, excessive numbers of low-quality animals and disease. Lesotho and South Africa are jointly implementing the Highlands Water Project (see Economy), which will provide employment for thousands of Basotho and greatly improve Lesotho's infrastructure. Reserves of diamonds have been identified in the mountainous north-east, and there are small surface workings at Lemphane, Liquobong and Kao. Uranium deposits have been located near Teyateyaneng in the north-west, but their exploitation must await a sustained improvement in world prices. The search for other minerals is continuing.

Recent History

RICHARD BROWN

Revised for this edition by the Editor

Lesotho, formerly known as Basutoland, became a British protectorate in 1868, at the request of the Basotho people's chief, who feared Boer expansionism. Basutoland was annexed to Cape Colony (now part of South Africa) in 1871 but detached in 1884. It became a separate British colony, and was administered as one of the high commission territories in southern Africa (the others being the protectorates of Bechuanaland, now Botswana, and Swaziland). The British Act of Parliament that established the Union of South Africa in 1910 also provided for the possible inclusion in South Africa of these territories, subject to the consent of the local inhabitants. Until 1960, successive South African governments sought the transfer of the high commission territories, which was consistently opposed by the native chiefs.

Modern party politics began in 1952 with the founding of the Basutoland Congress Party (BCP, renamed the Basotho Congress Party in 1966) by Dr Ntsu Mokhehle. A legislative council was introduced in 1956, and a constitution, granting limited powers of self-government, was adopted in 1959.

The BCP decisively won elections to the legislative council, held in 1960. Basutoland's first general election, held on the basis of universal adult suffrage, took place on 29 April 1965, and full internal self-government was achieved on the following day. Moshoeshoe II, the paramount chief, was recognized as king. The majority of seats in the new legislative assembly were won by the Basutoland National Party (BNP, renamed the Basotho National Party at independence), a conservative group which had the support of the South African government. The BNP's leader, Chief Leabua Jonathan, failed to win a seat, but won a by-election in July, whereupon he became prime minister. Basutoland became independent, as Lesotho, on 4 October 1966.

JONATHAN AND THE BNP, 1966–86

A constitutional crisis arose in December 1966, when Moshoeshoe attempted to extend the royal prerogative. In January 1967, however, the king signed an undertaking, on pain of enforced abdication, to abide by the constitution, which effectively transferred executive power to the prime minister. A general election was held in January 1970, when the opposition BCP appeared to have won a majority of seats in the national assembly. However, Chief Jonathan declared a state of emergency, suspended the constitution and arrested Mokhehle and other leaders of the BCP. The election was annulled, and the assembly prorogued. Some 500 people were reported to have been killed by the police during the ensuing disturbances.

King Moshoeshoe was placed under house arrest and later exiled, although he returned in December 1970, after accepting a government order which prohibited him from taking part in politics. From January 1970 the country was effectively under the prime minister's personal control. In March 1973, as a result of pressure from members of his own party (as well as from political opponents), Jonathan established an interim national assembly, comprising chiefs and nominated members, with the declared aim of drafting a new constitution. The state of emergency was revoked in July. The BCP split into an 'internal' faction, whose members were willing to accept nomination to the interim assembly, and an 'external' faction, whose members demanded a return to normal political life: the latter group was led by Mokhehle and was held responsible for an attempted coup in January 1974. Mokhehle and other leading BCP members fled the country. A number of supporters of the BCP were imprisoned and strict new security laws were introduced.

Despite Lesotho's economic dependence on South Africa, the government's official policy during the 1970s was one of 'dialogue' with its neighbour, Jonathan repeatedly criticized the South African government's policy of apartheid, and declared his support for the prohibited African National Congress of South Africa (ANC). During the late 1970s Jonathan accused the South African government of supporting the Lesotho Liberation Army (LLA), the military wing of the 'external' faction of the BCP, which was conducting a campaign of violence: this was denied by South Africa. In 1982 the LLA was blamed for the murder of a government minister and of the secretary-general of the BCP's 'internal' faction. In December of that year South African commando troops launched a raid on Maseru, the capital of Lesotho, killing some 30 ANC members and about 12 private citizens. The UN Security Council unanimously condemned the action. In August 1983 South Africa delivered an ultimatum to Lesotho, either to expel (or repatriate) 3,000 South African refugees or be subjected to economic sanctions. Two groups of refugees left Lesotho after the ultimatum.

In March 1983 Jonathan announced that elections would be held. It was not, however, until January 1985 that the national assembly was dissolved. In July the government announced that the elections would take place in September; however, the elections were cancelled in August, when no candidates from the five opposition parties were nominated to contest them: the opposition parties maintained that the government refused to publish the electoral roll, thus preventing opposition candidates from securing sufficient signatures to qualify for nomination. It was announced that Jonathan and the BNP candidates in all 60 constituencies had been returned to office unopposed. In addition to arousing considerable domestic political opposition, the government's cancellation of the elections also appeared to have increased the hostility of the LLA, which launched a number of attacks on BNP targets during late 1985.

Lesotho's continued refusal to sign a joint non-aggression pact led South Africa to impound consignments of armaments destined for Lesotho, and to threaten to impose further economic sanctions in August 1984. On 1 January 1986 South Africa imposed a blockade on the border with Lesotho, impeding access to vital supplies of food and fuel. Five leading Lesotho politicians opposed to the government were arrested on their return from talks in Pretoria, South Africa, and there were reports of fighting between factions of the armed forces, some members of which opposed the government's contacts with socialist states and the radical policies of the BNP's influential Youth League.

MILITARY RULE, 1986–93

On 15 January 1986 troops of the Lesotho paramilitary force, led by Maj.-Gen. Justin Lekhanya, surrounded government buildings and the Youth League headquarters. Five casualties were reported in the ensuing fighting, and on 20 January Lekhanya (who had recently returned from 'security consultations' in South Africa), together with Maj.-Gen. S. K. Molapo, the commander of the security forces, and S. R. Matela, the chief of police, deposed the Jonathan government.

The new regime established a military council, headed by Lekhanya and including five other senior officers of the paramilitary force (which was subsequently replaced by the Royal Lesotho Defence Force–RLDF). In late January 1986 a council of ministers was sworn in, comprising three officers and 17 civilians, predominantly civil servants and professional men, and including one former member of Jonathan's cabinet. The national assembly was dissolved, and all executive and legislative powers were vested in the king, acting on the advice of the military council. One week after the coup, about 60 members of the ANC were deported from Lesotho, and on the same day the South African blockade was lifted.

The main opposition groups initially welcomed the military take-over. The exception was Mokhehle's wing of the BCP, which demanded the immediate restoration of the 1966 constitution, the integration of the LLA into Lesotho's armed forces and the holding of free elections within six months. All formal political activity was suspended by the military council in March 1986. In August Jonathan, together with six of his former ministers, was placed under house arrest, but in September the high court declared the initial detention order, and then a second detention order, to be invalid. Chief Jonathan died in April 1987.

In September 1986 the council of ministers was restructured (giving increased responsibility to Lekhanya), and the military council held discussions with the leaders of the five main opposition parties. The suspension of political activity continued, however, and opposition to the military council was discouraged. In April 1988 the five main opposition parties appealed to the Organization of African Unity (OAU), the Commonwealth and the South African government to restore civilian rule. In the following month Mokhehle, after 14 years of exile, was allowed to return to Lesotho for peace talks, together with other members of the BCP. The government agreed to guarantee the personal security of those returning, on certain conditions, the most important of these being that members of the LLA were to be prohibited from joining the RLDF. It was widely believed that the South African government had played a part in promoting this reconciliation. In 1989 the LLA was reported to have been disbanded, and by 1990 the two factions of the BCP had apparently reunited under the leadership of Mokhehle.

In mid-1989 some elements within the government were reported to have sought the removal of Lekhanya from the chairmanship of both the military council and the council of ministers, following reports in the international media that implicated him in the fatal shooting of a civilian at Maseru in December 1988: it was claimed that Lekhanya had falsely attributed responsibility for the incident to a subordinate. In September 1989, at an inquest into the civilian's death (which was reportedly instigated at the request of some members of the military council), Lekhanya admitted the truth of the allegations. Nevertheless, in October a verdict of justifiable homicide was returned.

In early 1990 conflict developed between Lekhanya and King Moshoeshoe. In February Lekhanya dismissed three members of the military council and one member of the council of ministers, reportedly owing to their alleged involvement in a coup plot. Following the king's refusal to approve the changes to the military council, Lekhanya suspended his executive and legislative powers. Shortly afterwards, Lekhanya promised that a return to civilian government would take place in 1992, and, to reassure business interests, a programme for privatizing state enterprises was announced. In early March 1990 the military council assumed the executive and legislative powers which were previously vested in the king, and Moshoeshoe (who remained head of state) went into exile, in England. Later in March one of the dismissed members of the military council, Lt-Col Sekhobe Letsie, was charged with the murder in 1986 of two former government ministers (who had been regarded as leading opponents of Lekhanya) and their wives. In June a national constituent assembly was inaugurated to draft a new constitution acceptable to the majority of Basotho; its members included Lekhanya, together with members of the council of ministers, traditional chiefs, local councillors, businessmen and representatives of banned political parties.

In October 1990 Lekhanya invited King Moshoeshoe to return to Lesotho from exile. However, the king announced that his return would be conditional upon the lifting of military rule and the formation, by representatives of all political parties, of an interim government, pending the restoration of the 1966 constitution and the holding of an internationally-supervised general election. On 6 November 1990 Lekhanya responded by promulgating an order which deposed the king with immediate effect. On 8 November Lesotho's 22 principal chiefs elected Moshoeshoe's eldest son, Prince Bereng Seeisa, as the new king, and on 12 November he succeeded to the throne, as King Letsie III, having undertaken not to involve himself in the political life of the country.

On 30 April 1991 Lekhanya was removed as chairman of the military council in a coup led by Col (later Maj.-Gen.) Elias Phitsoane Ramaema, a member of the military council. Col Ramaema succeeded Lekhanya as chairman of that body, which was immediately reorganized, along with the council of ministers; Ramaema's announcement that there would be no changes in government policy indicated that the coup resulted from a conflict of personalities rather than from a divergence of political aims. In mid-May Ramaema announced the repeal of the law which had banned party political activity in 1986. However, a tense atmosphere prevailed following the coup, and in late May resentment of foreign-owned businesses precipitated riots in Maseru and other major towns, which resulted in some 34 deaths and 425 arrests.

In early June 1991 20 officers were dismissed from the RLDF, following an unsuccessful attempt to overthrow Ramaema and to reinstate Lekhanya; the latter was placed under house arrest during August-September, owing to allegations that a further counter-coup was being plotted. By July the national constituent assembly had drafted a new constitution. In September the council of ministers was restructured.

In April 1992 relatives of ex-king Moshoeshoe announced that he intended to return to Lesotho from exile, in defiance of the wishes of the military council. In early June it was announced that elections would take place in late November. The council of ministers was reshuffled in late June. Following talks in England between Moshoeshoe and Ramaema, under the auspices of the secretary-general of the Commonwealth, the former king returned to Lesotho in July. In August two members of the military council were dismissed, following allegations against them of corruption.

MOKHEHLE IN GOVERNMENT

The transition from military rule to democratic government, which had been scheduled to take place in November 1992, was postponed at short notice; the general election eventually took place in late March 1993. The BCP swept to power, winning all 65 seats in the new national assembly (gaining 54% of the votes, compared with the BNP's 16%). Mokhehle, the leader of the BCP, was sworn in as prime minister at the beginning of April, and, on the same day, King Letsie was reported to have sworn allegiance to the new constitution (which took effect following the election). Although independent local and international observers pronounced the general election to be broadly free and fair, the BNP, which had the support of members of the former military regime, alleged widespread irregularities and refused to accept the results; the BNP also subsequently declined the BCP government's offer of two seats in the newly established senate.

Army Unrest

In late 1993 serious discontent emerged within the armed forces. A mutiny in November by about 50 junior officers in the RLDF, was apparently precipitated by a proposal to place the military under the command of a senior member of the LLA—as part of government efforts to integrate LLA activists (many of whom were still in South Africa) with the RLDF. Tensions increased in the first weeks of 1994, after members of the armed forces demanded that their salaries be doubled: Mokhehle responded that any increase in remuneration for the army would only be considered as part of a wider review of public sector pay that was currently in progress. Skirmishes followed near Maseru on two days in mid-January, involving rebellious troops and forces loyal to the government. Although the rebels' leaders maintained that their actions were linked to the demand for increased pay, it was widely believed that the mutiny reflected broader political differences (principally, it was suggested, between supporters of the new regime and of the BNP) within the military. Mediation efforts involving representatives of Botswana, South Africa, Zimbabwe, the Commonwealth, the OAU and the UN failed to prevent a day of more serious fighting (between about 600 rebels and a 150-strong loyalist contingent) before a truce took effect. At the beginning of February the rival factions surrendered their weapons and returned to barracks, in accordance with a Commonwealth-mediated peace accord that envisaged negotiations between the Mokhehle government and the parties involved in the fighting. In all, at least five soldiers and three civilians were reported to have been killed in the conflict.

There was renewed army unrest in mid-April 1994, when the deputy prime minister, Selometsi Baholo (who also held the finance portfolio), was shot dead during an abduction attempt by disaffected troops, who also briefly detained four other ministers. In May police officers (who, with prison guards, were staging a strike in support of demands for increased pay and allowances) briefly took hostage the minister of information and broadcasting and acting finance minister, Mpho Malie. Agreement was subsequently reached on increased allowances (although the demand for 60% salary increases was not met), and the government announced the formation of an independent commission to review the salary structures of civil servants; the three-week strike ended at the end of the month. Meanwhile, the minister responsible for natural resources, Monyane Moleleki, fled to South Africa and subsequently resigned from the government. A commission to investigate the armed forces unrest of January and April began work in mid-July.

'Royal Coup'

In late July 1994 Mokhehle appointed a commission of inquiry into the circumstances surrounding the dethronement of former King Moshoeshoe II in 1990. In early August 1994, however, King Letsie petitioned the high court to abolish the commission on the grounds of bias on the part of its members. In mid-August supporters of the BNP, led by Lekhanya, staged a demonstration in Maseru to demand the resignation of the Mokhehle government and the restoration of Moshoeshoe II to the throne. On 17 August Letsie made a radio broadcast announcing that he had dissolved parliament, dismissed the Mokhehle government and suspended sections of the Constitution, citing 'popular dissatisfaction' with the BCP administration. (The king also denounced as treason Mokhehle's appeal for external assistance in quelling army unrest earlier in the year.) A provisional body would be established to govern, pending fresh elections, which were to be organized by an independent commission. Following the king's broadcast, several thousand people gathered outside the royal palace in Maseru to demonstrate their support for the deposed government. However, army and police support for Letsie's 'royal coup' was evident, and clashes between demonstrators and the security forces resulted in four deaths (a further death was reported in disturbances two days later). A night-time curfew was imposed on the day of the broadcast. A prominent human rights lawyer, Hae Phoofolo, was appointed chairman of the transitional council of ministers; among the other members of the provisional government was the secretary-general of the BNP, Evaristus Retselisitsoe Sekhonyana, who was appointed minister of foreign affairs. Phoofolo identified as a priority for his administration the amendment of the constitution to facilitate the restoration of Moshoeshoe. In the mean time, King Letsie was to act as executive and legislative head of state. A two-day general strike, co-ordinated by the BCP and the Lesotho Council of Non-governmental Organizations, in support of the ousted government effectively paralysed economic activity in Maseru in late August.

The suspension of constitutional government was widely condemned outside Lesotho. The presidents of Botswana, South Africa and Zimbabwe led diplomatic efforts to restore the elected government, supported by the OAU and the Commonwealth. Several countries threatened economic sanctions against Lesotho, and the USA withdrew financial assistance. King Letsie and Mokhehle attended negotiations in Pretoria in late August, at which Letsie was urged to reinstate all elected institutions. Although there was agreement in principle on the restoration of Moshoeshoe II to the throne, subsequent deadlines for a resolution to the crisis failed to be met, owing to disputes regarding a programme for the return of the Mokhehle government to office. A further two-day strike was widely observed in early September, and South African armed forces conducted manoeuvres near Lesotho territory.

On 14 September 1994 King Letsie and Mokhehle signed an agreement, guaranteed by Botswana, South Africa and Zimbabwe, providing for the restoration of Moshoeshoe as reigning monarch, and for the immediate restitution of the elected organs of government; the commission of inquiry into Moshoeshoe's dethronement was to be abandoned; persons involved in the 'royal coup' were to be immune from prosecution; the political neutrality of the armed forces and public service was to be guaranteed, and consultations were to be undertaken with the expressed aim of broadening the democratic process.

In mid-October 1994 Sekhonyana was ordered to pay a heavy fine (or serve two years' imprisonment) after being convicted of sedition and the incitement to violence earlier in the year of army and police troops against former LLA members.

In mid-November 1994 legislation providing for the reinstatement of Moshoeshoe was presented to the national assembly; the bill was unanimously approved on 2 December, and was subsequently endorsed by the senate. Accordingly, on 25 January 1995 Moshoeshoe II, who undertook not to intervene in politics, was restored to the throne, following the voluntary abdication of Letsie III, who took the title of crown prince (the new legislation provided for Letsie to succeed as monarch upon the death of his father).

Internal Discord

Government changes in early February 1995 included the promotion of the minister of education and training, Pakalitha Mosisili, to the post of deputy prime minister (which had remained vacant since Baholo's assassination). In a further government reshuffle later in the month Malie was appointed minister of foreign affairs.

The director and another senior officer of the national security service (NSS) were held hostage by junior officers (who were demanding improved terms and conditions of service) for three weeks in March 1995, and were released only after intervention by the Commonwealth secretary-general. Monyane Moleleki was briefly detained by security forces in late March, following his return from exile in South Africa. The BNP, meanwhile, alleged that the government was forming a private security force with the participation of former members of the Azanian People's Liberation Army (APLA), the military wing of the Pan-Africanist Congress of South Africa.

In early April 1996 government representatives and military officials from Lesotho, Botswana, South Africa and Zimbabwe met in Maseru to discuss progress in the restoration of constitutional order in Lesotho. The conference examined the recommendations of the commission of inquiry into the army mutiny of 1994; these included a streamlining of existing forces, a clearer definition of their functions, and improved training. In late May, none the less, two people were shot dead in Maseru during rioting which had erupted while police were maintaining an indefinite 'go slow', as part of their continuing salary campaign. In June the BCP complained of persistent harassment of its members by the NSS. In previous weeks several members of the national assembly were reported to have been abducted and interrogated; at least one was questioned in connection with the discovery of arms caches allegedly linked to the APLA. Apparently in an attempt to deter further indiscipline, the government announced 15% salary increases for all sectors of the armed and security forces, thus bringing their pay into line with remuneration for other public-sector employees. A reorganization of the cabinet in mid-July 1995 included Malie's departure from the government.

Earlier concerns that the Mokhehle administration was not honouring its expressed commitment to trade union rights were revived in early August 1995, when a 5,000-strong demonstration was organized in Maseru to protest against proposed legislation that would prevent public servants from joining trade unions. The protesters, claiming that the legislation was unconstitutional, presented petitions to Mokhehle and also, urging parliament not to approve the bill, to the president of the senate and the speaker of the national assembly. They demanded, moreover, that Mokhehle abandon plans to reduce earlier salary increases that were now said to have been granted in error. Also in August the opening of the country's university for the new academic year was postponed, owing to an indefinite strike by members of the university teachers' union. A six-day 'national forum' was convened in September to examine the exercise of democracy in Lesotho and the country's stability and development since 1993. In the same month, however, Amnesty International urged the Mokhehle government to act to eliminate abuses of human rights by the security forces, condemning what it alleged were arbitrary arrests and incommunicado detentions, as well as the ill-treatment and torture of detainees.

King Moshoeshoe was killed in a motor accident in January 1996. The crown prince was formally elected by the college of chiefs to succeed his father, and returned to the throne, resuming the title King Letsie III, in February. Like his father in January 1995, Letsie undertook not to involve the monarchy in any aspect of political life. In mid-March 1996 Mokhehle commissioned British detectives to investigate the circumstances surrounding Moshoeshoe's death: they concluded, in June, that Moshoeshoe's driver (who was also killed) had been under the influence of alcohol.

Following a five-month trial, in early February 1996 three former senior public officials were sentenced to a total of 120 year's imprisonment, having been convicted by the high court of the theft of more than M2m. in state funds from the Central Bank of Lesotho. In late February premises of the national radio service were seized by a small group that broadcast an apparently groundless statement that the government had been overthrown. The alleged perpetrators of the 'false coup', reported as being, Makara Sekautu, the president of the opposition United Party, two former members of the RLDF and a former member of the NSS, were charged in March with high treason; in March 1997 three of the accused, including Sekautu, were given prison sentences.

Political Realignments

Five government ministers were removed from office in early May 1996, among them the minister of justice and human rights, law and constitutional affairs, Molapo Qhobela. The dismissed ministers were unofficially said to have been linked to efforts to bring about the nullification of elections that had taken place in March to the national executive committee (NEC) of the BCP (Qhobela, notably, had been replaced as the party's deputy leader by the deputy prime minister, Bethuel Pakalitha Mosisili). Further government changes followed the resignation, in mid-May, of the ministers of finance and economic planning and of trade and industry. In November, none the less, the results were invalidated by the high court, and the previous committee (elected in 1995) was empowered to organize a new internal party election. Divisions within the BCP were exacerbated in mid-January 1997, when Moleleki, who had returned to the government in November 1996 as minister of information and broadcasting, intimated in an official statement that an attempt was under way to destabilize the government. Although Moleleki did not name the suspected conspirators in this statement, Qhobela, reinstated as deputy leader of the BCP, asserted that the minister had, in fact, directly accused Qhobela and other senior members of the party during an interview with the external service of the British Broadcasting Corpn. The conflicting claims apparently led to insubstantiated rumours of an imminent coup attempt. A new NEC, elected later in January, was dominated by Qhobela and his supporters, but in mid-February these elections were in turn invalidated by the high court. The court ordered that Qhobela's 1995 committee organize yet another election, to be held at the end of February 1997, at the BCP annual conference. However, there was considerable confusion as the prime minister and other party members opposed to the 1995 committee were expelled from the conference. In early March, moreover, Qhobela's NEC announced that it had dismissed Mokhehle as BCP leader in accordance with a decision of the conference, prompting uproar in the national assembly. The government issued a statement insisting that Mokhehle remained leader of the BCP, although this did not dispel divisions within the party. Several BCP members opposed to Mokhehle withdrew in protest from the national assembly on two consecutive days, after a motion of support for the prime minister was introduced. In mid-March Mokhehle announced his intention to retire from politics prior to the 1998 elections, citing ill health and old age. The following month the high court ruled that Mokhehle was to remain interim leader, and that elections for his successor were to be held before the end of July. In early June violent clashes between supporters of the opposing groups in the ruling party led to two deaths in Quacha's Nek, in the south-east of the country. As a result of the intense rivalry within the party, and despite his earlier statement suggesting his imminent retirement, Mokhehle resigned from the BCP and formed a new political party, the Lesotho Congress for Democracy (LCD), to which he transferred executive power. Leaders of several opposition parties denounced the move as a political coup, declaring that Mokhehle should have resigned from his position as prime minister, sought a dissolution of the national assembly and held new elections. Some 38 members of the national assembly joined the LCD, and the following day the BCP, which had become the official opposition party, staged a parliamentary walk-out in protest at the formation of the new ruling party. The LCD denied that Mokhehle had contravened the constitution, as he was supported by a majority in the national assembly, and, at a meeting of the council of state, headed by the king, Mokhehle defended his actions. Meanwhile, a demonstration in support of demands for the prime minister's resignation was widely attended. Later that month Mokhehle announced that the NEC which had been elected by the BCP in March 1996 was to perform the executive duties of the LCD. In early July opposition parties organized a protest march to the royal palace, in defiance of a ban imposed by the government in June, to demand the resignation of Mokhehle and the appointment of an interim government. Qhobela was elected leader of the BCP at the party's annual conference in late July.

There was further confusion in early February 1997, when eight police-officers, who were resisting arrest for alleged involvement in the fatal shooting of three officers in October 1995, seized control of the police headquarters in Maseru, with the support of a small group of colleagues; the rebel officers claimed to have dismissed senior officers and appointed their own police commissioner. A strike by supporters of the mutineers within the force resulted in the closure of police stations. In mid-February 1997, after government efforts failed to persuade the rebels to surrender, the RLDF was mobilized and swiftly regained control of the police headquarters. More than 100 police-officers (some of whom had taken refuge in the royal palace) were arrested, and 10 alleged leaders of the rebellion were subsequently remanded in custody on charges of sedition and contravention of internal security legislation. However, two of the instigators of the mutiny (including one of the officers indicted for murder) evaded arrest and fled to South Africa to seek political asylum, which they were reported to have been granted the following month. Meanwhile, suggestions that 14 South Africans arrested in Maseru while the rebellion was in progress belonged to an élite police unit dispatched from South Africa to restore order in Lesotho were denied by the authorities in both countries. The arrests coincided with a claim by Qhobela that mercenaries had been broght into Lesotho to assassinate members of the BCP.

A strike by state telecommunications workers in late July 1996 caused disruption to Lesotho's international telephone links. The strike had been organized over allegations, initially raised in 1994, of corruption and unfair dismissal. There was more serious labour unrest in mid-September 1996, when clashes between security forces and former employees of the Highlands Water Project, after more than 2,000 workers were dismissed for breach of contract, resulted in at least five deaths. The government subsequently announced the establishment of an independent inquiry into the incident. A one-day general strike, called in early October by the Lesotho Council of Non-governmental Organizations in protest against the killings, was reported to have received little support.

In April 1997 the national assembly approved legislation for the establishment of a three-member independent national electoral commission. The creation of such a body had been a recommendation of the 1995 'national forum'.

FOREIGN RELATIONS

Crucial to Lesotho's external affairs has been its relationship with South Africa, to whose support the Jonathan regime owed some of its initial success. In 1970 Lesotho and Malawi were the only countries to abstain on an OAU resolution calling on Western powers not to supply arms to South Africa. Perhaps aware of the extent to which his pro-South African policies were losing him support among the Basotho population, the majority of whom had first-hand experience of apartheid, Jonathan made a number of increasingly sharp criticisms of the South African government from 1972, and in November 1974 revived Lesotho's claim to 'conquered territory' in South Africa's Orange Free State (OFS). A vigorous anti-South African stance at the UN and OAU in the first half of 1975 increased tensions between the two countries. Lesotho's refusal to recognize South Africa's proclamation of an 'independent' Transkei in October 1976 led the Transkeian authorities to demand visas from visiting Lesotho nationals. In December Lesotho protested to the UN that this action had effectively closed the border with Transkei and was seriously disrupting internal communications because the mountainous terrain between Maseru and the south-west of the country made transport impossible except by air. Tension was exacerbated by a South African decision to terminate subsidies on exports of wheat and maize to Lesotho, and by Chief Jonathan's renewed claim to lands in the OFS. In February 1978 the Transkei authorities imposed stringent border controls, which virtually halted all cross-border traffic. In addition to cutting off Basotho migrant workers from mines in South Africa, these measures posed a threat of serious food shortages in the south-eastern region of Lesotho. Jonathan added to South African ire when he attended the non-aligned conference in Havana, Cuba, in September 1979 and again attacked apartheid. The first meeting of the leaders of Lesotho and South Africa since 1967 took place in August 1980 and produced a preliminary agreement on the Highlands Water Project (HWP, see Economy), an advantageous scheme for Lesotho to supply water to South Africa.

During 1982–83 relations with South Africa deteriorated sharply, following allegations of South African armed raids against ANC sympathizers in Lesotho. In April 1983 Jonathan announced that Lesotho was effectively in a state of war with South Africa. South Africa responded in the following month by applying strict border controls on its main frontier with Lesotho, resulting in food shortages. The border controls were eased in June, after a meeting between both countries in which they agreed to curb cross-border guerrilla infiltration, but were re-imposed in July. Further talks with South Africa followed, and, soon afterwards, Lesotho declared that it had received an ultimatum from the republic, either to expel (or repatriate) some 3,000 refugees or to face the economic consequences. In September two groups of refugees left the country.

Relations with South Africa remained at a low ebb for most of 1984. In March Chief Jonathan alleged that the South African government had encouraged dissident exiles to form a new opposition party, the Basotho Democratic Alliance (BDA), as part of a conspiracy to overthrow the government. In April the BDA was officially registered as a political party, and its chairman reportedly confirmed that South Africa had promised to provide financial support to the BDA for the forthcoming election campaign. Relations between the two countries were further marred during 1984 by South African attempts to coerce Lesotho into signing a joint non-aggression pact, similar to the Nkomati Accord, agreed in March 1984 with Mozambique. Lesotho's continued refusal to sign such a pact led South Africa to impound consignments of armaments destined for Lesotho, and to threaten further economic sanctions in August, including the suspension of the HWP. However, after talks between the two countries in the following month, and an announcement by Lesotho that the ANC had agreed to withdraw completely from its territory, relations improved slightly in October, when South Africa released the arms that it had impounded and resumed talks on the HWP.

Tension was renewed during 1985, as, with unrest spreading in South Africa, Jonathan refused South African requests to expel ANC refugees and to discuss a mutual security pact with South Africa. In October the South African minister of foreign affairs visited Maseru in an unsuccessful attempt to persuade the government to take action against the ANC. Subsequently the South African government threatened to deport Basotho workers in South Africa. In December there was a raid on Maseru, ostensibly carried out by the LLA, for which Jonathan publicly blamed South Africa, and again refused to hand over refugees or to discuss a security treaty. On 1 January 1986 South Africa imposed strict controls at border crossing-points (see above), claiming the need to exclude 'terrorists'.

Following the military coup of January 1986 (in which South Africa denied having any role), the new government proved to be more amenable to South Africa's policy on regional security. It was agreed that neither country would allow its territory to be used for attacks on the other; South African refugees began to be flown out, and South Africa withdrew its special border checks on 25 January. By August more than 200 South African refugees, believed to be ANC members, were reported to have been expelled from Lesotho (although the Lesotho government did not permit their extradition directly to South Africa). Additionally, the new government agreed to create a joint security committee and to proceed with the HWP. Technicians from the Democratic People's Republic of Korea (DPRK) were expelled from Lesotho, and the new regime announced that it would resume relations with the Republic of Korea. In March Lekhanya travelled to Pretoria and met President Botha of South Africa. The two leaders reiterated the principles of mutual respect and non-interference. The DPRK embassy was closed in September. In the following month the treaty for the Highlands Water Project was signed by Lesotho and South Africa. In April 1987 the two countries signed an agreement to establish a joint trade mission. Lesotho and South Africa concluded 'friendly and successful' negotiations on issues relating to their common border in March 1988. In April 1990 Lesotho established diplomatic relations with Taiwan, and those with the People's Republic of China were severed but were resumed in January 1994. Lesotho and South Africa agreed to establish diplomatic relations, at ambassadorial level, in May 1992.

In December 1992 South Africa alleged that terrorist attacks on South African targets were being launched from Lesotho. In April 1993, however, the new Lesotho government declared its intention to co-operate closely with South Africa, which, following the election of an ANC-dominated government in 1994, has continued to exercise a powerful influence on the affairs of Lesotho. On an official visit to Lesotho in July 1995, President Mandela stressed the importance of good relations between the two countries, and their mutual interest in the success of the HWP. Friction continues, however, over the persistent problem of cross-border cattle thefts and the unresolved claim by Lesotho to 'conquered territory' in the OFS. Cross-border raids and livestock rustling incidents in February and June 1996, resulting in a number of deaths, prompted discussions between officials from the two countries.

In July 1996 the South African minister of defence, Joe Modise, visited Maseru, in his role as chairman of the Inter-State Defence and Security Committee, for talks with government ministers on a number of issues including the prevention of military coups in the SADC region; the suppression of cross-border crime; and the participation of the SADC member states in peace-keeping operations. They also underlined the need for the completion of the memorandum of understanding between the two countries on South Africa's assistance to Lesotho on military matters. In late August the 16th annual SADC summit meeting took place in Maseru; matters under discussion included trade, energy, transport and telecommunications and combating drug-trafficking.

Economy

LINDA VAN BUREN

Based on an earlier article by RICHARD BROWN

Lesotho is, economically, one of the world's least developed countries. Its resources have been listed as 'people, water and scenery'. The population was estimated at 1.9m. in mid-1994 and at 2.09m. in mid-1997. Between 1990–96, it was estimated, the population increased at an annual rate of 2.5%. About 78% of the resident population is located in rural areas, and an estimated 60% of the male work-force was employed as migrant workers in South Africa in 1996 (compared with an estimated 45% in 1987). The gross remittances of Basotho migrant workers constituted some 45% of Lesotho's gross national product (GNP) in 1996. This phenomenon reflects a continuing lack of opportunities in the domestic formal sector, despite government attempts to develop manufacturing and services, and severe pressure on agricultural land, which continues to support a high proportion (82.6% in 1996) of the resident labour force. This pressure is reflected in the wide disparity of population density, which reaches 200 per sq km in the west, where virtually all arable land and 70% of the population are concentrated, compared with a national average density of an estimated 66.88 per sq km. at mid-1997. The resulting problems of land shortage, soil erosion and falling productivity have been compounded by recurrent drought.

Lesotho's economic performance has also been adversely affected by the problems of the intimately linked South African economy—particularly in terms of the depreciation in the value of the South African rand, which is at par with the Lesotho currency unit, the loti (plural: maloti). Nevertheless, the country's gross domestic product (GDP) increased, in real terms, by an annual average of 7.0% in 1985–95, and is estimated to have increased by 12.6% in 1995. In 1995, according to estimates by the World Bank, Lesotho's GNP, measured at average 1993–95 prices, was US $1,519m., equivalent to $770 per head. During 1985–95, it was estimated, GNP increased, in real terms, at an average annual rate of 1.5%.

The country's internal tensions (see Recent History) probably underlie the record budget of $436m. presented in May 1994. The 1995/96 budget envisaged further increases of revenue (13%) and expenditure (18%). Capital spending was to increase by 17%. Spending on education was the principal item (21%), with health (7%) and defence (6%) the next largest allocations. Buoyant customs revenues, largely due to the construction of the Highland Water Project (see below), underpin the increases, but will diminish in the next few years as the main construction work is completed. In the budget for 1996/97 total revenue and grants were estimated at M2,019m.; M1,006m. of this was from the customs revenue pool of the Southern African Customs Union (SACU, see below). Total expenditure and net lending was budgeted at M1,964.5m., with 20% of public expenditure allocated to education and manpower training; over 6% to health and social welfare; more than 8% to public works; and around 7% to the Lesotho Highlands Development Authority.

AGRICULTURE

Although only about 11% of the total land area of 30,355 sq km is suitable for arable cultivation, a further 66% is usable for pasture, and agriculture is the primary occupation for the great majority of Basotho (82.6% of the internal labour force in 1996). It accounts for about one-fifth of export earnings. The sector's contribution to GDP fluctuates with changes in yields caused by soil erosion, the prevalence of poor agricultural practices, and the impact of drought (most recently during 1982–85 and from 1990). Agriculture accounted for 47% of GDP in 1970 and an estimated 15.1% in 1996. Apart from increases in the use of fertilizers and tractors since 1970, the sector remains largely unmodernized. Most crops continue to be produced, using traditional methods, by peasant farmers who have little security of tenure under existing laws.

Maize is the staple crop, accounting for 60% of the total planted area, followed by sorghum with 30%. The land area devoted to sorghum fell from 50,000 ha in 1994 to 24,000 ha in 1996, while at the same time sorghum yields dropped from 1,207 kg per ha to 740 kg per ha. Beans, dry peas, oats and sunflower oil are also cultivated. Lesotho's harvest of 2,000 metric tons of dry peas in 1995 was half the annual output in

1979–81. The oat crop, although only about 1.5 metric tons, enjoys one of the highest yields in Africa, at 1,410 kg per ha. Summer wheat is so far the only crop to have been exported in significant quantities, with most exports sold to South Africa. Food imports have been required in recent years. In 1991/92 only 20% of basic needs were met from domestic production, owing to exceptionally severe drought conditions. A maize shortfall of 242,000 tons was forecast in the 1992/93 season. Adequate rains in 1993/94 helped to restore output, but the drought emergency programme continued in 1994/95, when widespread drought returned, causing an acute shortage of locally produced maize. In June 1996 it was reported that Lesotho faced an estimated 235,000-ton cereal shortage for that year. However the 1996 maize harvest was believed to have been favourable. Compared with its potential, the livestock sector has been little exploited, although cattle exports have traditionally accounted for about one-third of agricultural exports, with wool and mohair providing a further 30% each. Other agricultural exports in 1996 included wheat, peas and beans. In 1996 the national herd was estimated at 600,000 cattle, 1.8m. sheep and 1.0m. goats, having suffered severe depletion during the early 1980s as a result of the drought. The Livestock Products Marketing Service was established in 1973 as a state monopoly for marketing and improving production. One of its major projects, construction of an export-orientated abattoir in Maseru, was completed in 1983. This facility, and associated fattening pens, aimed initially to satisfy domestic demand, and eventually to extend into exports to regional and European Community (EC, now European Union—EU) markets. Milk production is also being promoted.

The government is implementing a programme for food security, based on the development of small-scale irrigated agricultural schemes and the general improvement of rural water supplies. The Lesotho Agricultural Development Bank (LADB), established in 1980 and the sole source of farmers' credit, plays an important part in the self-sufficiency programme. The slow pace of agricultural improvement led the government, in September 1987, to threaten to expropriate land from inefficient farmers. Traditional chiefs in village councils were ordered to monitor land-use and to set annual production targets and producer prices. In 1988 the World Bank also agreed to provide a US $16m. credit to finance a project to support reform in land management and conservation, while agriculture and rural development were to receive the bulk of the ECU 41m. that was allocated to Lesotho by the EC under the provisions of the third Lomé Convention.

MANUFACTURING, MINING AND TOURISM

Confronted by the chronic problems of agriculture, and by the need to create jobs for a rapidly expanding population, Lesotho has promoted development in other sectors, with varying degrees of success. Its main assets are proximity and duty-free access to the South African market, and abundant labour. Lesotho enjoys one of the lowest average rates of adult illiteracy in Africa (26.6% in 1996, according to UNESCO estimates), and emigrant Basotho workers command an excellent reputation in South Africa. Until recently, South Africa actively discouraged the development of competing industries in Lesotho.

The Lesotho National Development Corpn (LNDC), founded in 1967, and the Basotho Enterprises Development Corpn (BEDCO), which provides finance to local entrepreneurs, have been the main bodies stimulating manufacturing development, promoting a wide variety of small industries, including tyre retreading, tapestry weaving, electric lamp assembly, diamond cutting and polishing, and the production of clothing, candles, ceramics, explosives, furniture, fertilizers and jewellery. Inducements to foreign companies have included generous allowances and tax 'holidays', duty-free access to the EU and SACU markets, the provision of industrial infrastructure and the construction of industrial estates in Maseru and Maputsoe (with further estates planned elsewhere in the country). During the late 1980s, when economic sanctions were imposed against South Africa by the international community, the government intensified its efforts to encourage the involvement of South African firms in Lesotho. In 1996 the government again announced incentives for South African companies relocating to Lesotho. Industrial developments during the 1980s which were supported by the LNDC included a project designed to double the capacity of the Basotho Fruit and Vegetable Cannery at Mazenod, and the establishment of the Maseru Tyre Co, a concern manufacturing parachutes for sporting and military purposes, a brewery and soft drinks plant in Maseru and two new steel plants and a wire products factory near the capital. By 1989 the LNDC was promoting 51 companies which employed more than 10,000 workers. In 1991 a Chinese company opened a television assembly plant. For its part, BEDCO has had some success in encouraging small-scale enterprises, with strong financial support from Canada. Up to 3,000 new jobs are estimated to have been created between 1975 and 1995. As a result of these efforts, the industrial sector grew by an annual average of 13.8% in 1985–95, and manufacturing's contribution to GDP increased from about 6% in 1986 to an estimated 16.4% in 1995. In 1991 the UN provided up to M1.5m. in assistance for a project to develop small industries.

There has also been significant development of tourism, which is now both a major source of employment and the second largest source of 'invisible' earnings, after workers' remittances. Tourist arrivals, mostly from South Africa, increased from 4,000 in 1968 to 171,000 in 1990. They increased dramatically to 417,000 in 1992 before falling back to 343,000 in 1993, 253,000 in 1994 and 212,000 in 1995.

Diamond mining was limited to small diamond diggings, exploited by primitive methods, until 1977, when a small modern mine at Letseng-la Terai, developed and administered by De Beers Consolidated Mines of South Africa, began full production. Most of the diamonds that the mine produced were of industrial quality, although a few unusually large gemstones were also found. Recovery rates, at only 2.8 carats per 100 metric tons, proved to be the lowest of any mine in the De Beers group, and operations ceased in 1982, depriving Lesotho of some 50% of its visible export earnings. However, plans to reopen the Letseng-la Terai mine were being considered in 1996. Co-operatives using labour-intensive methods still recover a small quantity of low-grade diamonds.

POWER

Lesotho's major undeveloped resource is water. After much uncertainty over economic and technical feasibility, the final details of the controversial Highlands Water Project (HWP) were agreed with South Africa in March 1988 (see below). A massive undertaking for any country (particularly for one as small as Lesotho), with costs originally estimated at $3,770m., the HWP proposed the diversion of water from Lesotho's rivers for export to South Africa, with self-sufficiency in hydro-generated electricity as the major by-product. The prospective throughput of water was projected at 77 cu m per second by the time the scheme is completed in the year 2017, although at the end of the first phase, planned for 1997, the rate was to be about 18 cu m per second. The HWP was expected to have a generating capacity of 200 MW by the year 2003. The first phase of the scheme was expected to cost $2,415m. Approximately three-quarters of this sum was raised in southern Africa (including some 57% from banks), with diversified external sources providing the balance. The commercial segment of the debt was to be met from royalty payments received on water sales to South Africa. Excavation began in 1991, and the first stage, which included the Katse dam, was completed in 1997. However, in mid-1997, as the first delivery of water to South Africa and the first M110m. annual royalty payment to Lesotho were about to be made, rumours became widespread that the troubled scheme was far too ambitious and was about to be downsized. The World Bank had observed that the scheme had been under poor management, and there were even suggestions that it might not fund the remaining four phases. The World Bank was to announce its decision in October 1997 as to the funding of the second stage of Phase I, which would involve the construction of the Mohale dam. The first stage had been beset by dismissals, strikes and opposition from environmental, trade-union and other groups. In September 1996, as a result of a labour dispute which led to the dismissal of more than 2,000 workers, at least five workers were shot dead and some 30 others were injured in clashes between the security forces and former employees. The contractors eventually agreed to take back 1,700 workers. A further problem was that many of the 1,750 families who had been displaced by the first stage of

Phase I had received little or none of the compensation they had been promised. The World Bank acknowledged that the scheme's 'social targets' had not been achieved, suggesting a reluctance to proceed with the displacement of upwards of 8,000 more families to allow the construction of a further five dams.

The water treaty negotiated with South Africa covered the legal framework of the project and the pricing and volume of water to be sold. One of the most contentious aspects of the treaty was the control of water delivery. There were strong fears, both in Lesotho and among its neighbours, that, unless Maseru controlled the 'tap', the country would be even more dependent on South Africa as the republic could delay the transfer of water payments as a form of leverage. The treaty addresses part of the problem, with South Africa due to pay monthly royalties in cash, regardless of water delivered, plus a unit cost component based on each cu ft of water delivered.

TRANSPORT AND COMMUNICATIONS

Owing to its mountainous terrain, much of Lesotho was, until recently, virtually inaccessible except by horse or light aircraft. However, a substantial network of tracks, passable by four-wheel drive vehicles, has now been built up, largely by 'food for work' teams in the mountain areas, and by 1995 some 892 km of tarred roads had been constructed. The road between Leribe, in the north, and Tsoaing, beyond Maseru, has been bituminized. In 1983 the first section of the southern perimeter road from Tsoloane to Mohale's Hoek was completed with aid from the Arab Bank for Economic Development in Africa (BADEA), and in 1984 the EC agreed to finance the next stage, to the Mekaling river. Finance from the EC was also made available in 1984 for the third stage, from Mekaling to Quthing. Several other road-building and rehabilitation projects have received funding: these include the construction of a new road linking Mohale's Hoek to Quthing. Construction of 300 km of new roads under the HWP commenced in 1987. In 1996 the International Development Association (IDA) granted US $40m. towards the government's rolling five-year road programme. In 1990 a bilateral agreement was reached with South Africa for the joint construction of a bridge over the Caledon river, for the transportation of equipment to the HWP. In June 1996 the Lesotho Highlands Development Authority invited prequalification submissions for the contract to build Mohale tunnel. Lesotho's economic development has relied heavily on South African road and rail outlets, a dependence which was graphically illustrated in 1983, 1984 and early 1986, when the South African government instituted road blocks and checks, as a form of economic sanctions, which had severely debilitating effects on the Lesotho economy. A greater degree of independence in international communications was reached after the Maseru international airport became operational in mid-1986. The national carrier, Lesotho Airways, operates internal flights as well as international services via South Africa and Swaziland.

EMPLOYMENT, WAGES AND MIGRANT LABOUR

Lesotho's dependence on South Africa is also reflected in the extent of migrant labour. Of the estimated total labour force of 689,000 in 1996, more than one-quarter worked in South Africa, 87,421 of them as miners. This exodus is caused by land shortage, by the depressed state of agriculture, by the lack of employment opportunities and by low wages in the formal sectors. Unemployment is estimated to exceed 35%, and only the labour demands of the HWP have prevented it from reaching an even higher level. During 1990–91 some 10,000 Basotho were dismissed from South African mines, owing to a decline in international prices for gold and the high unemployment rate in that country.

The Lesotho economy's dependence on receipts from services and transfers, in the form of migrants' remittances, has traditionally been reflected in the fact that the country's GNP is generally more than double GDP. (In most other African states the net outflow of services means that GDP is greater than GNP.) Net private capital flows amounted to US $14m. in 1994, or 7.3% of GNP. Apart from their obvious role in financing the large trade gap, the remittances have been central to the income of up to 60% of families and have also been used by the government to finance development. The Lesotho Deferred Payment Scheme was set up in 1974 at the instigation of the Lesotho government, and as it was compulsory, it has been widely condemned by labour-relations groups. Under the scheme, the South African employer of a Lesotho national was required to deposit 60% of his wage into a special account at Lesotho Bank every month; this proportion was reduced to 30% in 1990. Although the employee was permitted to make two withdrawals during the contract period, of up to a total of 50% of the accumulated balance, the remainder was, of course, available to the Lesotho government. The National Union of Miners has called for the abolition of the scheme, and a commission established in South Africa to investigate migrant labour in that country recommended that the scheme be phased out over a period of five years. In any case, South Africa's policy (announced in late 1995) of granting permanent residency rights to migrant workers could deprive Lesotho of this important source of income. It was decided that migrant workers who had voted in the 1994 South African election, and who were in South Africa before 30 June 1996, would be eligible for 'permanent status'. By March 1996 37,000 applications had been approved, although it was not specified how many of these were from Lesotho nationals.

The decline in the number of migrant workers since 1990 holds potentially serious implications for Lesotho's economy. In 1985 the government invited the International Labour Office to assess alternative employment prospects. The resulting report emphasized the creation of small-scale enterprises, employing up to 50 people each, as the main area of potential job development, although such a policy would require far more active investment efforts from government. In 1996 the government announced incentives for South African manufacturing companies, particularly those in labour-intensive industries, relocating to Lesotho.

SACU AND THE MONETARY AGREEMENTS

Together with Botswana, Namibia, South Africa and Swaziland, Lesotho is a member of the Southern African Customs Union (SACU), which dates formally from 1910, when the Union (now the Republic) of South Africa was established. The most recent SACU agreement, made in 1969, provides for payments to Botswana, Lesotho and Swaziland (the BLS countries) to be made on the basis of their share of goods imported by SACU countries, multiplied by an 'enhancement' factor of 1.42 as a form of compensation for the BLS countries' loss of freedom to conduct a completely independent economic policy, and for the costs that this restriction involves in trade diversion and loss of investment. SACU revenue is paid two years in arrears and earns no interest, but for Lesotho it has formed up to 70% of government recurrent revenues in recent years. Lesotho has resisted attempts by South Africa to renegotiate the terms governing SACU. However, pressure on SACU grew after the Mandela government came to power in South Africa. The role SACU would play in southern Africa's changed environment was unclear, in view of South Africa's application to join the EU's Lomé Convention, and the Southern African Development Community's plan to establish a 12-nation free-trade area by the year 2005, which would include all the members of SACU.

In December 1974 the governments of Lesotho, Swaziland and South Africa concluded the Rand Monetary Agreement (RMA). Under this agreement, Lesotho received interest on rand currency circulating in Lesotho, at a rate of two-thirds of the current yield to redemption of the most recent issues of long-dated South African government stock offered the previous year. In January 1980, however, Lesotho followed Botswana and Swaziland in their moves towards monetary independence by introducing its own currency, the loti (plural: maloti), replacing the South African rand at par. This measure was designed to give Lesotho greater control over factors influencing its development and over cash outflows by Basotho visiting South Africa. In July 1986 the RMA was superseded by a new agreement, establishing the Tripartite Monetary Area (TMA, now the Common Monetary Area–CMA) comprising Lesotho, Swaziland and South Africa (including Namibia, which became independent in 1990). Under the CMA arrangements, Lesotho may determine the exchange rate of its own currency, but to date the loti has remained at par with the rand.

EXTERNAL TRADE AND PAYMENTS

Until the 1980s, Lesotho was largely able to ignore its balance of payments, since, as a *de facto* member of the South African rand monetary area, situations which in other countries would have shown up as a balance-of-payments problem would, in Lesotho, have appeared as a general credit shortage. In fact, this happened only rarely until the 1980s, as Lesotho's chronic trade deficit, resulting from a limited export base and large requirements of food imports, was more than offset by current transfers, migrant remittances and surpluses on the capital account of the balance of payments. As a result of a sharp decline in export earnings from 1980, combined with a reduction in aid receipts and an increase in imports, deficits on the current account of the balance of payments were incurred in some of the subsequent years. A deficit of US $10m. in 1983 was followed in 1984 by a small surplus of $2m., and in 1985 receipts and payments were roughly in balance. Lesotho's external position subsequently deteriorated again, with the current account registering a deficit of $17m. in 1986. However, a current account surplus of $24m. was recorded in 1987. Although exports reached $47m. in 1987, imports also increased substantially, to $397m. As donors became concerned about the government's management of the economy, aid disbursements began to be withheld. A deficit of $25m. on the current account was recorded in 1988. During that year an IMF programme of reforms was implemented. In 1989 the current account registered a surplus of $10.4m., and further surpluses were reported in 1990 and 1991, of $65m. and $63.3m. respectively. In 1993 there was a surplus of $29.3m. In 1994 imports of goods and services, at $874.4m., far exceeded exports of goods and services, at $181.3m., leaving a trade deficit of $693.2m. Net current private transfers were $471.2m., yielding a current account surplus of $108.1m. The combined effects of drought and the decline in the level of workers' remittances are expected to make it difficult to sustain this performance. In 1990 workers' remittances totalled M1,102m., more than 600% of the value of Lesotho's exports and equivalent to 73% of GDP (compared with 105% of GDP in 1984). In 1995 miners' remittances totalled M1,242.4m., equivalent to 33% of GDP.

South Africa is Lesotho's main trading partner. In 1995 South Africa was the main source of Lesotho's imports, supplying 94%, and the destination for 42% of its exports, while 28% of exports went to the EU, and a further 25% to North and South America. The principal imports in that year were maize, building materials, clothing, vehicles, machinery, medicines and petroleum products. Lesotho is associated with the EU under the provisions of the Lomé Convention, according duty-free access to EU markets for all exports except those covered by the EU's Common Agricultural Policy, which will benefit only from a small preference. The short-term effect on Lesotho's exports has been small.

PUBLIC FINANCE

Since the renegotiation of the SACU agreement in 1969, revenue from this source has increased, from R1.9m. in 1968/69 to an estimated M548m. in 1992/93. Successive budget deficits during the 1980s (which were exacerbated by high spending on defence) led to substantial cuts, in real terms, in other sectors.

In July 1988 the IMF approved a loan of SDR 9.6m. under its structural adjustment facility (SAF), to support a three-year economic programme agreed with the World Bank. The programme aimed to achieve an annual increase in GDP to 4%; to reduce the budget deficit from 18.8% of GDP in 1987/88 to 4.1% in 1990/91; to lower the debt-service ratio; and to reduce the rate of inflation. The government undertook to adopt policies which would increase the supply of credit from commercial banks to the private sector, encourage private investment in industry (particularly in industrial enterprises which would produce goods for export or provide substitutes for imports) and increase agricultural productivity. Initial delays in the Lesotho government's negotiations with the IMF were caused by the IDA's approval, in May, of an SDR 15m. (US $20.7m.) credit for urban development and an SDR 11.7m. ($16.2m.) credit for land management, which led to concern about Lesotho's ability to meet the targets set for the SAF. In December 1988 a meeting of donor governments and organizations, convened by the UN Development Programme, agreed to provide $390m. in assistance for Lesotho's three-year programme. In the first year of the programme its targets were not met. The budgetary deficit increased to M181.1m. in 1988/89. However, the deficit was equivalent to only 0.6% of GNP in 1990/91. Preliminary estimates indicate budget surpluses in 1992/93 and 1993/94.

In June 1991 the IMF agreed to provide SDR 18.1m. under its enhanced structural adjustment facility (ESAF) in support of an economic development programme covering the period 1991–94. The programme aimed to diversify manufacturing production and exports, to promote the role of the private sector in the economy and to improve the balance-of-payments position. By early 1993 Lesotho was exceeding the targets set by the ESAF. Lesotho's progress and further needs are under review by the IMF. In 1995 the Mokhehle government unveiled its plans for a five-year privatization programme. A Privatization Unit was set up to decide the fate of 31 public enterprises, including the BEDCO (see above), the Drug Service Organization, the Electricity Corpn, the Housing and Development Corpn, the LADB (see above), Lesotho Airways, Lesotho Flour Mills, Lesotho Pharmaceutical Corpn and the Lesotho Telecommunications Corpn. Critics of the privatization programme, led by trade-union organizations, argued that selling off these enterprises would only make Lesotho more dependent on South Africa. They maintained that Lesotho Flour Mills in particular should not be privatized for reasons of food security.

Between 1980–86 Lesotho's receipts of net development assistance fell by over 40% in real terms. The budget allocation for servicing the national debt increased from M36m. in 1982/83 to M60m. in 1984/85, although in 1985/86 and 1986/87 the upward trend in debt servicing costs appeared to have been stemmed, with a drop in real allocations. Lesotho's disbursed public debt more than doubled between 1980–84 to $134m., or 24.3% of GNP. The total external public debt was $471.6m. at the end of 1992, resulting in a debt-service ratio of 5.6%, as a percentage of exports of goods and services; this was equivalent to 42% of GNP. By the end of 1995 total external debt had risen to $659.0m., equivalent to 43.4% of that year's GNP. The 1995 debt-service ratio as a percentage of exports of goods and services was 6.6%.

The first Five-Year Development Plan (1970/71–1974/75) concentrated on the development of roads and agriculture. The second Five-Year Plan (1975/76–1979/80) exceeded its public investment target of R112m., although investment was still insufficient to stimulate economic growth. Under the third Development Plan, originally scheduled to cover 1980/81–1984/85 but extended to 1985/86, long-term investments were targeted at M700m. The plan was pessimistic about the prospects for job creation but did aim to spread economic growth and to make improvements in social welfare and the conservation of resources. In December 1988 donors pledged $390m. in support of a fourth Plan, covering the period 1988/89–1990/91. Severe drought, however, interfered with the plan's implementation. In 1996 increased development assistance was forthcoming: M700m. from the international donor community, over a five-year period, towards health, agriculture, tourism, population and environmental programmes; M330m. from the EU under the National Indicative Programme, in terms of the Fourth Lomé Convention; and a further M19m. from the EU, as part of the Structural Adjustment Support Programme (SASP), to finance education, health and village water supply projects.

Lesotho continues to face formidable economic problems. The acute shortage of fertile land, the problem of soil erosion, and the backward state of agriculture make it highly unlikely that this sector can absorb the increase in population. Much will depend on the attitudes of the government in South Africa, on the benefits to be derived from the HWP, and on the government's ability to find alternative sources of revenue to the Lesotho Deferred Payment Scheme of emigrant workers' remittances and SACU receipts.

Statistical Survey

Source (unless otherwise stated): Bureau of Statistics, POB 455, Maseru 100; tel. 323852.

Area and Population

AREA, POPULATION AND DENSITY

Area (sq km)	30,355*
Population (census results)†	
12 April 1976	
Males	458,260
Females	605,928
Total	1,064,188
12 April 1986 (provisional)	1,447,000
Population (official estimates at mid-year)‡	
1985	1,528,000
1987	1,619,000
1989	1,700,000
Density (per sq km) at mid-1989	56.0

* 11,720 sq miles.

† Excluding absentee workers in South Africa, numbering 152,627 (males 129,088; females 23,539) in 1976.

‡ Including absentee workers in South Arica. Mid-year estimates for 1986 and 1988 are not available.

1992: Estimated population 1,932,879, including 126,647 absentee workers in South Africa.

DISTRICTS (*de jure* population at 1986 census, provisional)*

District	Population
Berea	194,600
Butha-Buthe	100,600
Leribe	257,900
Mafeteng	195,600
Maseru	311,200
Mohale's Hoek	164,400
Mokhotlong	74,700
Qacha's Nek	64,000
Quthing	110,400
Thaba-Tseka	104,100
Total	1,577,500

* Including absentee workers in South Africa.

Note: Each district has the same name as its chief town.

Capital: Maseru, population 45,000 in 1976.

BIRTHS AND DEATHS (UN estimates, annual averages)

	1980–85	1985–90	1990–95
Birth rate (per 1,000)	42.0	38.7	36.9
Death rate (per 1,000)	12.7	11.4	10.0

Expectation of life (UN estimates, years at birth, 1990–95): 60.5 (males 58.0; females 63.0).

Source: UN, *World Population Prospects: The 1994 Revision.*

ECONOMICALLY ACTIVE POPULATION

Mid-1995 (estimates in '000): Agriculture, etc. 329; Total 834 (Source: FAO, *Production Yearbook*).

In 1992 about 38% of the total adult male labour force were in employment in South Africa.

Agriculture

PRINCIPAL CROPS ('000 metric tons)

	1993	1994	1995
Wheat	8	21	2
Maize	92	175	27
Sorghum	52	60	10*
Roots and tubers*	58	60	62
Pulses	3	4	4*
Vegetables*	20	26	20
Fruit*	18	18	15

* FAO estimate(s).

Source: FAO, *Production Yearbook.*

LIVESTOCK (FAO estimates, '000 head, year ending September)

	1993	1994	1995
Cattle	630	640	640
Sheep	1,280	1,300	1,300
Goats	660	670	670
Pigs	40	45	45
Horses	115	120	120
Asses	150	152	152
Mules	1	1	1

Poultry (FAO estimates, million): 1 in 1993; 1 in 1994; 1 in 1995.

Source: FAO, *Production Yearbook.*

LIVESTOCK PRODUCTS (FAO estimates, '000 metric tons)

	1993	1994	1995
Cows' milk	26	26	26
Beef and veal	14	14	14
Mutton and lamb	4	4	4
Goat meat	2	2	2
Pig meat	2	2	2
Poultry meat	1	1	1
Other meat	3	3	3
Hen eggs	0.8	0.8	0.8
Wool:			
greasy	5.0	5.2	5.2
clean	2.5	2.6	2.6

Source: FAO, *Production Yearbook.*

Forestry

ROUNDWOOD REMOVALS
(FAO estimates, '000 cubic metres, excluding bark)

	1992	1993	1994
Total (all fuel wood)	654	672	690

Source: FAO, *Yearbook of Forest Products.*

Fishing

(FAO estimates, metric tons, live weight)

	1993	1994	1995
Common carp	25	25	24
North African catfish	5	5	4
Rainbow trout	5	5	4
Total catch	35	35	32

Source: FAO, *Yearbook of Fishery Statistics*.

Finance

CURRENCY AND EXCHANGE RATES

Monetary Units

100 lisente (singular: sente) = 1 loti (plural: maloti).

Sterling, Dollar and Rand Equivalents (31 March 1997)

£1 sterling = 7.2585 maloti;
US $1 = 4.4205 maloti;
R1 = 1 loti;
100 maloti = £13.777 = $22.622.

Average Exchange Rate (US $ per loti)

1994 0.28177
1995 0.27574
1996 0.23416

Note: The loti is fixed at par with the South African rand.

BUDGET (million maloti, year ending 31 March)

Revenue*	1993/94	1994/95	1995/96†
Tax revenue	1,102.8	1,268.8	1,413.5
Taxes on net income and profits	169.3	228.2	275.8
Company tax	46.4	65.2	56.1
Individual income tax	110.2	140.1	195.1
Taxes on goods and services	176.6	190.8	220.7
Sales tax	141.5	149.8	174.0
Petrol levy	32.5	39.3	45.6
Taxes on international trade and transactions	747.8	840.9	906.5
Customs duties	746.9	840.9	906.5
Non-tax revenue	163.6	173.3	268.1
Administative fees, charges and non-industrial sales	50.8	53.9	85.0
Total	1,266.4	1,442.1	1,681.6

Expenditure‡	1993/94	1994/95	1995/96†
General public services	265.0	294.7	378.5
Public order, safety and defence	138.5	154.7	191.4
Health, social security and welfare	134.6	165.4	175.2
Education and community services	265.4	354.7	437.5
Economic services	448.6	502.3	646.7
Agriculture and rural development	145.4	143.2	207.9
Commerce, tourism and industry	53.1	45.5	44.8
Water, energy and mining	95.6	127.1	228.2
Roads	124.9	153.6	153.1
Other transport and communications	29.6	32.9	12.7
Unallocable and other purposes	137.1	104.5	98.6
Total	1,250.7	1,421.6	1,736.5
Current	842.1	966.7	1,118.1
Capital‡	408.6	454.9	618.4

* Excluding grants received (million maloti): 137.4 in 1993/94; 143.6 in 1994/95; 163.2 (estimate) in 1995/96.

† Estimates.

‡ Including lending minus repayments (million maloti): 63.4 in 1993/94; 76.3 in 1994/95; 60.6 in 1995/96.

Source: IMF, *Lesotho—Recent Economic Developments* (November 1996).

1996/97 (budget proposals, million maloti): Revenue and grants 2,019; Expenditure and net lending 1,964.5.

INTERNATIONAL RESERVES (US $ million at 31 December)

	1994	1995	1996
IMF special drawing rights	0.47	0.35	1.33
Reserve position in IMF	5.13	5.22	5.05
Foreign exchange	367.02	451.17	454.13
Total	372.62	456.74	460.51

Source: IMF, *International Financial Statistics*.

MONEY SUPPLY (million maloti at 31 December)

	1994	1995	1996
Currency outside banks	52.57	74.76	84.82
Demand deposits at commercial banks	434.02	445.91	548.00
Total money	486.59	520.67	632.82

Source: IMF, *International Financial Statistics*.

COST OF LIVING (Consumer Price Index; base: 1990 = 100)

	1993	1994	1995
All items	156.0	168.9	184.5

Source: IMF, *International Financial Statistics*.

NATIONAL ACCOUNTS (million maloti at current prices)

Expenditure on the Gross Domestic Product (year ending 31 March)

	1992/93	1993/94	1994/95
Government final consumption expenditure	394.0	458.2	537.5
Private final consumption expenditure	2,305.7	2,540.5	2,473.4
Increase in stocks	−7.7	1,791.4	2,310.4
Gross fixed capital formation	1,581.7		
Total domestic expenditure	4,273.7	4,790.2	5,321.3
Exports of goods and services	378.9	512.2	592.7
Less Imports of goods and services	2,712.8	2,986.2	3,150.1
GDP in purchasers' values	1,939.8	2,316.2	2,763.8

Source: IMF, *International Financial Statistics*.

Gross Domestic Product by Economic Activity

	1993	1994	1995
Agriculture, forestry and fishing	304.7	408.3	395.5
Mining and quarrying	2.2	2.4	2.7
Manufacturing	377.7	454.2	556.5
Electricity, gas and water	61.3	73.7	90.3
Construction	473.5	668.2	889.5
Trade, restaurants, and hotels	217.1	270.0	332.9
Transport and communications	78.1	100.1	122.7
Finance, insurance, real estate and business services	309.3	380.5	440.9
Government services	323.2	381.8	467.4
Other services	68.2	79.4	99.2
Sub-total	2,215.2	2,818.6	3,397.6
Less Imputed bank service charge	91.0	132.8	158.2
GDP at factor cost	2,124.2	2,685.9	3,239.5
Indirect taxes, *less* subsidies	440.8	446.8	524.6
GDP in purchasers' values	2,564.9	3,132.6	3,764.1
GDP at constant 1980 prices	499.0	567.0	638.5

Sources: IMF, *Lesotho—Recent Economic Developments* (November 1996).

BALANCE OF PAYMENTS (US $ million)

	1992	1993	1994
Exports of goods f.o.b.	109.2	134.0	143.5
Imports of goods f.o.b.	–932.6	–868.1	–810.2
Trade balance	–823.4	–734.1	–666.7
Exports of services	41.3	37.0	37.8
Imports of services	–82.8	–70.5	–64.2
Balance on goods and services	–864.9	–767.6	–693.2
Other income received	496.3	444.5	369.6
Other income paid	–32.6	–22.8	–39.4
Balance on goods, services and income	–401.1	–345.9	–363.0
Current transfers received	542.1	376.5	472.1
Current transfers paid	–103.3	–1.3	–0.9
Current balance	37.6	29.3	108.1
Direct investment from abroad	2.7	15.0	18.7
Other investment assets	–106.4	8.9	–13.4
Other investment liabilities	36.8	31.3	27.6
Net errors and omissions	79.2	17.8	–20.3
Overall balance	49.9	102.3	120.9

Source: IMF, *International Financial Statistics.*

External Trade

PRINCIPAL COMMODITIES ('000 maloti)

Imports c.i.f.	1979	1980	1981
Food and live animals	68,559	76,918	82,902
Beverages and tobacco	13,725	16,233	21,761
Clothing	31,652	34,452	36,733
Machinery and transport equipment	44,084	58,397	74,647
Petroleum products	22,848	31,633	37,766
Chemicals	16,372	18,853	28,229
Footwear	10,556	12,423	14,338
Total (incl. others)	303,612	360,757	439,375

Total imports (million maloti): 497.8 in 1982; 539.7 in 1983; 634.5 in 1984; 751.0 in 1985; 803.3 in 1986; 954.8 in 1987; 1,327.5 in 1988; 1,552 in 1989; 1,738 in 1990; 2,242 in 1991; 2,564 in 1992; 2,839 in 1993; 3,000 in 1994; 3,576 in 1995 (Source: IMF, *International Financial Statistics*).

Exports f.o.b.	1992	1993	1994
Food and live animals	20,978	25,672	26,018
Crude materials (inedible) except fuels	20,163	22,221	32,202
Wool	15,293	16,853	19,358
Mohair	3,816	5,131	11,935
Basic manufactures	6,401	13,426	10,063
Machinery and transport equipment	29,570	25,540	69,840
Miscellaneous manufactured articles	206,860	348,199	366,127
Total (incl. others)*	287,680	438,942	509,287

* Excluding re-exports ('000 maloti): 3,075 in 1992; 1,783 in 1993.

1995 (million maloti): Total exports 581 (Source: IMF, *International Financial Statistics*).

PRINCIPAL TRADING PARTNERS (million maloti)

Imports*	1992	1993	1994†
Africa	2,497.6	2,722.8	2,881.2
Southern African Customs Union‡	2,494.0	2,716.2	2,866.5
Asia	249.8	354.8	377.2
Hong Kong	93.6	90.0	102.3
Japan	43.8	53.0	46.8
Taiwan	54.4	108.3	150.0
European Union	117.6	85.9	78.7
France	31.8	28.6	13.8
Germany	28.8	20.5	16.7
Italy	30.3	9.1	17.9
North America	17.1	37.0	44.9
USA	16.0	33.5	40.6
Total (incl. others)	2,926.0	3,221.8	3,391.8

Exports	1992	1993	1994†
Africa	154.4	206.0	261.8
SACU‡	152.7	201.3	258.9
European Union	70.5	80.0	51.3
North America	83.3	147.0	192.7
Total (incl. others)	310.9	438.9	509.3

* Valuation exclusive of import duties. Figures also exclude donated food.

† Estimated figures.

‡ Comprising Botswana, Lesotho, Namibia, South Africa and Swaziland.

Source: IMF, *Lesotho—Recent Economic Developments* (November 1996).

Transport

ROAD TRAFFIC (estimates, motor vehicles in use at 31 December)

	1993	1994	1995
Passenger cars	8,320	9,830	11,100
Lorries and vans	17,200	20,600	22,200

Source: IRF, *World Road Statistics.*

CIVIL AVIATION (traffic on scheduled services)

	1992	1993	1994
Kilometres flown (million)	1	1	1
Passengers carried ('000)	26	23	27
Passenger-km (million)	9	9	9
Total ton-km (million)	1	1	1

Source: UN, *Statistical Yearbook.*

Tourism

	1992	1993	1994
Tourist arrivals ('000)	417	343	253
Tourist receipts (US $ million)	19	17	17

Source: mainly Lesotho Tourist Board, Maseru.

Communications Media

	1992	1993	1994
Radio receivers ('000 in use)	60	63	65
Television receivers ('000 in use)	11	13	20
Telephones ('000 main lines in use)	11	12	n.a.
Daily newspapers			
Number	2	n.a.	2
Average circulation ('000 copies)	14	n.a.	14

Sources: UNESCO, *Statistical Yearbook;* UN *Statistical Yearbook.*

Education

(1994)

	Institutions	Teachers	Students
Primary	1,232	7,428	366,569
Secondary			
General	193	2,597	61,615
Technical and vocational	9	102	1,697
University	1	229	1,798
Teachers' training college	1	102	755

Source: Ministry of Education and Manpower Development, Maseru.

Directory

The Constitution

The Constitution of the Kingdom of Lesotho, which took effect at independence in October 1966, was suspended in January 1970. A new Constitution was promulgated following the March 1993 general election. Its main provisions are summarized below:

Lesotho is an hereditary monarchy. The King, who is Head of State, has no executive or legislative powers. Executive authority is vested in the Cabinet, which is headed by the Prime Minister, while legislative power is exercised by the 65-member National Assembly, which is elected, at intervals of no more than five years, by universal adult suffrage in the context of a multi-party political system. There is also a Senate, comprising traditional chiefs and 11 nominated members. The Prime Minister is the official head of the armed forces.

The Government

HEAD OF STATE

HM King LETSIE III (acceded to the throne 7 February 1996).

CABINET
(August 1997)

Prime Minister and Minister of Defence and Public Service: Dr NTSU MOKHEHLE.

Deputy Prime Minister and Minister of Home Affairs and Local Government, Rural and Urban Development: BETHUEL PAKALITHA MOSISILI.

Minister of Justice and Human Rights, Law and Constitutional Affairs: SEPHIRI MOTANYANE.

Minister of Foreign Affairs: KELEBONE ALBERT MAOPE.

Minister of Education: LESAO LEHOHLA.

Minister of Finance and Economic Planning: LEKETEKETE VICTOR KETSO.

Minister of Trade and Industry: LIRA MOTETE.

Minister of Agriculture, Co-operatives, Marketing and Youth Affairs: MOPSHATLA MABITLE.

Minister of Health and Social Welfare: TEFO MABOTE.

Minister of Natural Resources (Water, Lesotho Highlands Water Project, Energy, Mining, Technology and the Environment): SHAKHANE ROBONG MOKHEHLE.

Minister of Transport and Telecommunications: MAMOSHEBI KABI.

Minister of Works: MOHAILA MOHALE.

Minister of Information and Broadcasting: MONYANE MOLELEKI.

Minister of Labour and Employment: NOT'SI VICTOR MOLOPO.

Minister of Tourism, Sports and Culture: PASHO MOCHESANE.

MINISTRIES

Office of the Prime Minister: POB 527, Maseru 100; tel. 311000.

Ministry of Agriculture, Co-operatives, Marketing and Youth Affairs: POB 24, Maseru 100; tel. 322741; telex 4330; fax 310349.

Ministry of Defence and Public Service: Private Bag A166, Maseru 100; tel. 323861; fax 310518.

Ministry of Education: POB 47, Maseru 100; tel. 313628; telex 4330; fax 310126.

Ministry of Finance and Economic Planning: POB 395, Maseru 100; tel. 311101; telex 4330; fax 310157.

Ministry of Foreign Affairs: POB 1387, Maseru 100; tel. 311150; telex 4330; fax 310178.

Ministry of Health and Social Welfare: POB 514, Maseru 100; tel. 322714; telex 433010.

Ministry of Home Affairs and Local Government, Rural and Urban Development: POB 174, Maseru 100; tel. 323771; fax 310319.

Ministry of Information and Broadcasting: POB 36, Maseru 100; tel. 323561; telex 4530; fax 310003.

Ministry of Justice and Human Rights, Law and Constitutional Affairs: POB 402, Maseru 100; tel. 311160; telex 4330; fax 310365.

Ministry of Labour and Employment: Private Bag A116, Maseru 100; tel. 322565.

Ministry of Natural Resources (Water, Lesotho Highlands Water Project, Energy, Mining, Technology and the Environment): POB 436, Maseru 100; tel. 311742; telex 4253.

Ministry of Tourism, Sports and Culture: POB 52, Maseru 100; tel. 313034; fax 310194.

Ministry of Trade and Industry: POB 747, Maseru 100; tel. 322138; telex 4384; fax 310121.

Ministry of Transport and Telecommunications: Maseru.

Ministry of Works: Maseru.

Legislature

NATIONAL ASSEMBLY

Elections to the 65-member National Assembly took place in March 1993. The Basotho Congress Party (BCP) won all of the seats. In June 1997 the Prime Minister, Dr Ntsu Mokhehle, resigned from the BCP to form the Lesotho Congress for Democracy, which subsequently held some 38 seats in the National Assembly.

Speaker: Dr J. G. KOLANE.

Political Organizations

Basotho Congress Party (BCP): POB 111, Maseru; f. 1952; Leader MOLAPO QHOBELA.

Basotho Democratic Alliance (BDA): Maseru; f. 1984; Pres. S. C. NCOJANE.

Basotho National Party (BNP): POB 124, Maseru 100; f. 1958; Sec.-Gen. EVARISTUS RETSELISITSOE SEKHONYANA; 280,000 mems.

Communist Party of Lesotho (CPL): Maseru; f. 1962 (banned 1970–91); supported mainly by migrant workers employed in South Africa; Sec.-Gen. MOKHAFISI JACOB KENA.

Ha Reeng ('Let's Go') Basotho Party: Maseru; Leader KHAUTA KHASU.

Kopanang Basotho Party (KBP): Maseru; f. 1992; campaigns for women's rights; Leader LIMAKATSO NTAKATSANE.

Lesotho Congress for Democracy (LCD); Maseru; f. 1997 as a result of divisions within the BCP; Leader Dr NTSU MOKHEHLE; Sec.-Gen. SHAKHANE MOKHEHLE.

Lesotho Labour Party (LLP): Maseru; f. 1991; Leader MAMOLEFI RANTHIMO.

Marematlou Freedom Party (MFP): POB 0443, Maseru 105; tel. 315804; f. 1962; Leader VINCENT MOEKETSE MALEBO; Deputy Leader THABO LEANYA: 300,000 mems.

National Independence Party (NIP): Maseru; f. 1984; Pres. ANTHONY C. MANYELI.

Popular Front for Democracy (PFD): Maseru; f. 1991.

Progressive National Party (PNP): Maseru; f. 1995 following split in the BNP; Leader Chief PEETE NKOEBE PEETE.

Sefate Democratic Union (SDU): Maseru; Leader BOFIHLA NKUEBE.

United Democratic Party (UDP): POB 776, Maseru 100; f. 1967; Chair. BEN L. SHEA; Leader CHARLES D. MOFELI; Sec.-Gen. MOLOMO NKUEBE; 26,000 mems.

United Party (UP): Maseru; Pres. MAKARA SEKAUTU (imprisoned for high treason March 1997).

Diplomatic Representation

EMBASSIES AND HIGH COMMISSIONS IN LESOTHO

China, People's Republic: POB 380, Maseru 100; tel. 316521; fax 310489; Ambassador: LIN TINGHAI.

Denmark: Site 11, Industrial Area, POB 1259, Maseru 100; tel. 323630; fax 310138; Ambassador: ALF JÖNSSON.

Korea, Democratic People's Republic: Maseru; Ambassador: AN KYONG HYON.

South Africa: 10th Floor, Lesotho Bank Tower, Kingsway, Private Bag A266, Maseru 100; tel. 315758; telex 4381; fax 310128; High Commissioner: (vacant).

United Kingdom: POB 521, Maseru 100; tel. 313961; telex 4343; fax 310120; High Commissioner: PETER JOHN SMITH.

USA: POB 333, Maseru 100; tel. 312666; fax 310116; Ambassador: BISMARCK MYRICK.

Judicial System

HIGH COURT

The High Court is a superior court of record, and in addition to any other jurisdiction conferred by statute it is vested with unlimited original jurisdiction to determine any civil or criminal matter. It also has appellate jurisdiction to hear appeals and reviews from the subordinate courts. Appeals may be made to the court of appeal.

Chief Justice: JOSEPH LEBONA KHEOLA.

Judges: M. L. LEHOHLA, W. C. M. MAQUTU, B. K. MOLAI, T. E. MONAPATHI, K. GUNI, G. MOFOLO, M. RAMOLIBELI.

COURT OF APPEAL

Judges: ISMAIL MAHOMED (President), T. BROWDE, G. P. KOTZE, R. N. LEON, J. N. STEYN.

SUBORDINATE COURTS

Each of the 10 districts possesses subordinate courts, presided over by magistrates.

JUDICIAL COMMISSIONERS' COURTS

These courts hear civil and criminal appeals from central and local courts. Further appeal may be made to the high court and finally to the court of appeal.

CENTRAL AND LOCAL COURTS

There are 71 such courts, of which 58 are local courts and 13 are central courts which also serve as courts of appeal from the local courts. They have limited civil and criminal jurisdiction.

Religion

About 90% of the population profess Christianity.

CHRISTIANITY

African Federal Church Council: POB 70, Peka 340; f.1927; co-ordinating org. for 48 African independent churches; Co-ordinator Rev. S. MOHONO.

Christian Council of Lesotho: POB 457, Maseru 100; tel. 323639; telex 4512; fax 310310; f. 1973; six mem. and four assoc. mem. churches; Chair. Rev. LEBOHANG KHEEKHE; Sec. R. M. TAOLE.

The Anglican Communion

Anglicans in Lesotho are adherents of the Church of the Province of Southern Africa. The Metropolitan of the Province is the Archbishop of Cape Town, South Africa. Lesotho forms a single diocese, with an estimated 100,000 members.

Bishop of Lesotho: Rt Rev. PHILIP STANLEY MOKUKU, Bishop's House, POB 87, Maseru 100; tel. 311974; fax 31016.

The Roman Catholic Church

Lesotho comprises one archdiocese and three dioceses. At 31 December 1995 there were an estimated 726,330 adherents in the country.

Lesotho Catholic Bishops' Conference: Catholic Secretariat, POB 200, Maseru 100; tel. 312525; telex 4540; fax 310294; f. 1972; Pres. Rt Rev. EVARISTUS THATHO BITSOANE, Bishop of Qacha's Nek.

Archbishop of Maseru: Most Rev. BERNARD MOHLALISI, Archbishop's House, 19 Orpen Rd, POB 267, Maseru 100; tel. 312565; fax 310425.

Other Christian Churches

African Methodist Episcopal Church: POB 223, Maseru 100; tel. 322616; f. 1903; 11,295 mems.

Dutch Reformed Church in Africa: POB 454, Maseru 100; tel. 314669; f. 1957; 7,396 mems (1991).

Lesotho Evangelical Church: POB 260, Maseru 100; tel. 323942; f. 1833; independent since 1964; Moderator Rev. G. L. SIBOLLA; Exec. Sec. Rev. A. M. THEBE; 211,000 mems (1990).

Methodist Church of Southern Africa: POB 81, Maseru 100; tel. 322412; f. 1927; Supt Rev. D. SENKHANE; c. 10,000 mems and adherents (1989).

Other denominations active in Lesotho include the Apostolic Faith Mission, the Assemblies of God, the Full Gospel Church of God and the Seventh-day Adventists. In addition, there are numerous African independent churches.

BAHÁ'Í FAITH

National Spiritual Assembly: POB 508, Maseru 100; tel. 312346; fax 310092; mems resident in 420 localities.

The Press

Lentsoe la Basotho: POB 353, Maseru 100; tel. 323561; telex 4450; fax 310003; f. 1974; weekly; Sesotho; publ. by Ministry of Information and Broadcasting; Editor K. LESENYA; circ. 10,000.

Leselinyana la Lesotho (Light of Lesotho): POB 7, Maseru 100; tel. 360244; f. 1866; fortnightly; Sesotho, with occasional articles in English; publ. by Lesotho Evangelical Church; Editor A. B. THOALANE; circ. 15,000.

Makatolle: POB 111, Maseru 100; f. 1963; weekly; Sesotho; Editor MOHAILA MOHALE; circ. 2,000.

The Mirror: POB 903, Maseru 100; tel. 315602; telex 4416; fax 310015; f. 1988; weekly; English; Editor T. MLUNGWANE; circ. 4,000.

Moeletsi oa Basotho: Mazenod Institute, POB 18, Mazenod 160; tel. 350254; telex 4271; f. 1933; weekly; Roman Catholic; Sesotho; Editor Rev. M. KHUTLANG; circ. 20,000.

Molepe: Maseru; bi-monthly; magazine for Lesotho Airways; circ. 5,000.

Mphatlatsane: Maseru; daily; independent.

Shoeshoe: POB 36, Maseru 100; tel. 323561; telex 4340; fax 310003; quarterly; women's interest; publ. by Ministry of Information and Broadcasting.

NEWS AGENCIES

Lesotho News Agency (LENA): POB 36, Maseru 100; tel. 315317; telex 4598; fax 310003; f. 1986; Dir LEBOHANG LEJAKANE; Editor KHOELI PHOLOSI.

Foreign Bureau

Inter Press Service (IPS) (Italy): c/o Lesotho News Agency, POB 36, Maseru 100; Correspondent LEBOHANG LEJAKANE.

Publishers

Macmillan Boleswa Publishers Lesotho (Pty) Ltd: POB 7545, Maseru 100; tel. 317340; fax 310047.

Mazenod Institute: POB MZ 18, Mazenod 160; tel. 62224; telex 4271; f. 1931; Roman Catholic; Man. Fr B. MOHLALISI.

Morija Sesuto Book Depot: POB 4, Morija 190; fax 360204; f. 1861; owned by the Lesotho Evangelical Church; religious, educational and Sesotho language and literature.

St Michael's Mission: The Social Centre, POB 25, Roma; f. 1968; religious and educational; Man. Dir Fr M. Ferrange.

Government Publishing House

Government Printer: Maseru.

Radio and Television

In 1994, according to UNESCO, there were an estimated 65,000 radio receivers and 20,000 television receivers in use.

Lesotho National Broadcasting Service: POB 552, Maseru 100; tel. 323561; telex 4340; fax 310003; programmes in Sesotho and English; radio transmissions began in 1964 and television transmissions in 1988; CEO F. N. Letele; Dir of Broadcasting T. Ntsane.

Finance

(cap. = capital; res = reserves; dep. = deposits; m. = million; brs = branches; amounts in maloti)

BANKING

Central Bank

Central Bank of Lesotho: POB 1184, Maseru 100; tel. 314281; telex 4367; fax 310051; f. 1980; bank of issue; cap. and res 161.2m., dep. 1,572.3m. (Dec. 1995); Gov. and Chair. Dr Anthony M. Maruping.

Commercial Banks

Lesotho Bank: Central Services, Lesotho Bank Centre, Kingsway, POB 1053, Maseru 100; tel. 315737; telex 4206; fax 310268; f. 1972; state-owned; commercial bank, also carries out development banking functions; cap. and res 32.3m., dep. 604m. (Dec. 1993); Chair. Dr 'Musi Mokete; Gen. Man. Nkopane Monyane; 15 brs.

Standard Chartered Bank Lesotho Ltd: Standard Bank Bldg, 1st Floor, Kingsway, POB 1001, Maseru 100; tel. 312696; telex 4332; fax 310025; Man. Dir R. C. Dewar; 3 brs and 7 agencies.

Stanbic Bank Lesotho Ltd: Bank Building, 1st Floor, Kingsway, POB 115, Maseru 100; tel. 312423; fax 310235; f. 1957 as Barclays Bank DCO; owned by Standard Bank Investment Corpn Ltd; cap. and res 14.2m., dep. 196.3m. (Dec. 1995); Chair. G. C. Bell; Man. Dir M. Wooler.

Development Banks

Lesotho Agricultural Development Bank (LADB): 58 Kingsway Rd, POB 845, Maseru 100; tel. 313277; telex 4269; fax 310139; f. 1980; state-owned; cap. 13m. (Dec. 1995); Chair. L. B. Mokotoane; Man. Dir C. S. Molelle; 7 brs and 12 agencies.

Lesotho Building Finance Corporation (LBFC): Private Bag A59, Maseru 100; tel. 313514; telex 4326; state-owned; Man. Dir N. Monyane; 3 brs.

INSURANCE

Lesotho National Insurance Co (Pty) Ltd: Private Bag A65, Lesotho Insurance House, Kingsway, Maseru; tel. 323032; telex 4220.

Minet Kingsway (Pty) Ltd: POB 993, Maseru 100; tel. 313540; fax 310033.

Trade and Industry

DEVELOPMENT ORGANIZATIONS

Lesotho Highlands Development Authority: POB 7332, Maseru 100; tel. 311280; telex 4523; fax 310060; f. 1986 to supervise the Highlands Water Project, being undertaken jtly with South Africa; CEO Makase Marumo.

Lesotho National Development Corporation (LNDC): Development House, 1st Floor, Kingsway Rd, Private Bag A96, Maseru 100; tel. 312012; telex 4341; fax 310038; e-mail lndc@pixie.co.za; f. 1967; 90% govt-owned; interests include candle, carpet, tyre-retreading, explosives, fertilizer, clothing, jewellery and furniture factories, potteries, two diamond prospecting operations, an abattoir, a diamond-cutting and polishing works, a housing co, a brewery, an international hotel with a gambling casino and Lesotho Airways Corpn; Man. Dir M. Senaoana.

Basotho Enterprises Development Corporation (BEDCO): POB 1216, Maseru 100; tel. 312094; telex 4370; f. 1980; promotes and assists in the establishment and development of small-scale Basotho-owned enterprises; Man. Dir S. K. Phafane.

Lesotho Co-operatives Handicrafts: Maseru; f. 1978; marketing and distribution of handicrafts; Gen. Man. Khotso Matla.

Trade Promotion Unit: c/o Ministry of Trade and Industry, POB 747, Maseru 100; tel. 322138; telex 4384; fax 310121.

CHAMBER OF COMMERCE

Lesotho Chamber of Commerce and Industry: POB 79, Maseru 100; tel. 323482.

MARKETING ORGANIZATIONS

Livestock Marketing Corporation: POB 800, Maseru 100; tel. 322444; telex 4344; f. 1973; fmrly Livestock Products Marketing Service; sole organization for marketing livestock and livestock products; liaises closely with marketing boards in South Africa; projects include an abattoir, tannery, poultry and wool and mohair scouring plants; Gen. Man. S. R. Matlanyane.

Produce Marketing Corporation: Maseru; telex 4365; f. 1974; Gen. Man. M. Phoofolo.

EMPLOYERS' ORGANIZATION

Association of Lesotho Employers: POB 1509, Maseru 100; tel. 315736; telex 4368; f. 1961; represents mems in industrial relations and on govt bodies, and advises the Govt about employers' concerns; Pres. S. J. Kao; Exec. Dir T. Makeka.

MAJOR INDUSTRIAL COMPANIES

Lesotho Brewing Co Pty Ltd: POB 764, Maseru; tel. 311111; fax 310020; beer and non-alcoholic beverages.

Lesotho Milling Co Pty Ltd: POB 39, Maputsoe; tel. 430062; maize, groats and meal.

Lesotho Pharmaceutical Corporation: POB 256, Mafeteng 900; tel. 700326; telex 4305; fax 700002; pharmaceutical products.

Lesotho Sandstone Co Pty Ltd (LESACO): Private Bag A241, Maseru; tel. 322443; fax 310081; mining and quarrying.

Lesotho Textiles Pty: POB 7432, Maseru 100; tel. 314647; fax 310004; clothing mfrs.

TRADE UNIONS

Construction and Allied Workers Union of Lesotho (CAWULE): Maseru.

Lesotho General Workers' Union: POB 322, Maseru 100; f. 1954; Chair. J. M. Ramarothole; Sec. T. Motlohi.

Lesotho Transport and Telecommunication Workers' Union: Maseru 100; f. 1959; Pres. M. Bereng; Sec. P. Motramai.

Lesotho University Teachers' and Researchers' Union (LUTARU): Maseru.

National Union of Construction and Allied Workers: Maseru; f. 1967; Pres. L. Putsoane; Sec. T. Tlale.

National Union of Printing, Bookbinding and Allied Workers: PO Mazenod 160; f. 1963; Pres. G. Motebang; Gen. Sec. Clement Ratsiu.

Union of Shop Distributive and Allied Workers: Maseru 100; f. 1966; Pres. P. Bereng; Sec. J. Molapo.

CO-OPERATIVE SOCIETIES

Co-op Lesotho Pty Ltd: Ministry of Agriculture, Co-operatives, Marketing and Youth Affairs, POB 24, Maseru 100; tel. 322741; telex 4330.

Registry of Co-operatives: POB 89, Maseru 100; Registrar P. Moeketsi.

Transport

RAILWAYS

Lesotho is linked with the South African railway system by a short line (2.6 km in length) from Maseru to Marseilles, on the Bloemfontein/Natal main line.

ROADS

In 1995 Lesotho's road network totalled 4,955 km, of which 884 km were main roads and 1,285 km were secondary roads. About 18% of roads were paved. Construction of 300 km of new roads, under the Highlands Water Project, began in 1987. In the 1993/94 budget M80m. (5.7% of total expenditure) was allocated for the improvement of the road network. In 1996 the International Development Association granted US $40m. towards the government's rolling five-year road programme. From 1996/67 an extra-budgetary Road Fund was to finance the maintenance of Lesotho's road network.

CIVIL AVIATION

King Moshoeshoe I International Airport, operational since 1986, is at Thota-Moli, some 20 km from Maseru. There are 40 airstrips in Lesotho, of which 14 receive commercial air services.

Lesotho Airways Corporation: Mejametalana Airport, POB 861, Maseru 100; tel. 312453; telex 4347; fax 310126; f. 1970; govt-owned; transfer to private sector pending in 1997; internal and regional flights and scheduled international services via South Africa and Swaziland; Chair. M. MAKHAKHE; Man. Dir LETSABA RATOKI.

Tourism

Spectacular mountain scenery is the principal tourist attraction. In 1994 there were 253,310 tourist arrivals, of whom 241,940 came from South Africa. Receipts from tourism in that year totalled about US $17m. During 1992–94 Lesotho's tourist industry declined by 47%, partly as a result of internal political unrest.

Lesotho Tourist Board (Boto Ea Tsa Boeti Lesotho): POB 1378, Maseru 100; tel. 312896; fax 323638; f. 1983; Man. Dir Mrs K. TLEBERE.

Defence

Military service is voluntary. The Royal Lesotho Defence Force comprised 2,000 men in August 1996.

Defence Expenditure: Budgeted at M191.4m. (11% of total estimated expenditure) for 1995/96, including public order and safety.

Commander of the Royal Lesotho Defence Force: Maj.-Gen. S. K. MOLAPO.

Education

All primary education is available free of charge, and is provided mainly by the three main Christian missions (Lesotho Evangelical, Roman Catholic and Anglican), under the direction of the Ministry of Education and Training, Sports, Culture and Youth Affairs. Lesotho has one of the highest levels of literacy among African countries: according to the population census of 1986, the average rate of adult illiteracy was 30% for males and 11% for females. According to estimates by UNESCO, the rate in 1995 averaged 28.7% (males 18.9%; females 37.7%). Education at primary schools is officially compulsory for seven years between six and 13 years of age. Secondary education, beginning at the age of 13, lasts for up to five years, comprising a first cycle of three years and a second of two years. Of children in the relevant age-group in 1994 an estimated 60% of males and 71% of females were enrolled at primary schools, while the equivalent of 23% of males and 34% of females were enrolled at secondary schools. The National University of Lesotho had 1,612 students in 1992. Of projected expenditure by the central government in the 1995/96 financial year, M437.5m. (25.2%) was allocated to education and community services.

Bibliography

Ambrose, D. *Maseru: An Illustrated History.* Morija, Morija Museum and Archives, 1993.

Ambrose, D. P., and Perry, J. W. B. *Atlas for Lesotho.* Cape Town, Longman Southern Africa, 1974.

Bardill, J. E., and Cobbe, J. *Lesotho: Dilemmas of Dependence in Southern Africa.* Boulder, CO, Westview Press, 1985.

Bardill, J. E., and Cobbe, J. *Lesotho: Profiles.* Boulder, CO, Westview Press, 1985.

Burman, S. *Chiefdom, Politics and Alien Law: Basutoland under Cape Rule, 1871–1884.* London, Macmillan in association with St Antony's College, Oxford, 1981.

Cervenka, Z., et al. *Botswana, Lesotho, Swaziland.* Bonn, Deutsche Afrika-Gesellschaft, 1974.

Duncan, T., et al. *Support Against Apartheid: An Evaluation of 28 Years of Development Assistance to Lesotho: Final Report.* Stockholm, Swedish International Development Authority, 1994.

Eldredge, E. A. *A South African Kingdom: The Pursuit of Security in Nineteenth-Century Lesotho.* Cambridge, Cambridge University Press, 1993.

Ferguson, J. (Ed.). *The Anti-Politics Machine: Development, Depoliticization and Bureaucratic State Power in Lesotho.* Cambridge, Cambridge University Press; Cape Town, David Philip, 1990.

Franklin, A. S. *Land Law in Lesotho: The Politics of the 1979 Land Act.* Aldershot, Avebury; Brookfield, VT, Ashgate Publishing, 1995.

Gay, J., et al (Ed.). *Lesotho's Long Journey: Hard Choices at the Crossroads: A Comprehensive Overview of Lesotho's Historical, Social, Economic and Political Development With a View to the Future.* Maseru, Sechaba Consultants, 1995. (Commissioned and funded by Irish Aid).

Gill, S. J. *A Short History of Lesotho, From the Late Stone Age Until the 1993 Elections.* Morija, Morija Museum and Archives, 1993.

Haliburton, G. *Historical Dictionary of Lesotho.* Metuchen, NJ, Scarecrow Press, 1977.

Konczacki, Z. A., et al. *Studies in the Economic History of Southern Africa.* Vol. II. London, Cass, 1991.

Kowet, D. K. *Land, Labour Migration and Politics in Southern Africa: Botswana, Lesotho and Swaziland.* New York, Africana Publishing, 1979.

Lundahl, M., and Petersson, L. *The Dependent Economy: Lesotho and the Southern Africa Customs Union.* Boulder, CO, Westview Press, 1991.

Machobane, L. B. B. J. *Government and Change in Lesotho, 1800–1966: A Study of Political Institutions.* Maseru, Macmillan Lesotho, 1990.

Mapetla, E. R. M., and Rembe, S.W. *Decentralisation and Development in Lesotho.* Roma, National University of Lesotho, 1989.

Maqutu, W. C. M. *Contemporary Constitutional History of Lesotho.* Mazenod, Mazenod Institute, 1990.

Milazi, D. *The Politics and Economics of Labour Migration in Southern Africa. What are the Key Issues?* Maseru, Lesotho Printing and Publishing Co, 1984.

Mochebelele, M.T., et al. *Agricultural Marketing in Lesotho.* Ottawa, International Development Research Centre, 1992.

Murray, C. *Families Divided: The Impact of Migrant Labour in Lesotho.* Cambridge, Cambridge University Press; Johannesburg, Ravan Press, 1981.

Orpen, J. M. *History of the Basutos of South Africa.* Mazenod, Mazenod Institute, 1988.

Rwelamira, M. *Refugees in a Chess Game: Reflections on Botswana, Lesotho and Swaziland Refugee Policies.* Trenton, NJ, Red Sea Press, 1990.

Southall, R., and Petlane, T. (Eds). *Democratisation and Demilitarisation in Lesotho: The General Election of 1993 and its Aftermath.* Pretoria, Africa Institution of South Africa, 1996.

Van der Wiel, A. C. A. *Migratory Wage Labour: Its Role in the Economy of Lesotho.* Maseru, Mazenod Book Centre, 1977.

Van Rensburg, P. *Another Development for Lesotho: Alternative Development Strategies for the Mountain Kingdom.* Gaborone, Foundation for Education with Production, 1989.

Winai-Strom, G. *Development and Dependence in Lesotho, the Enclave of South Africa.* Uppsala, Scandinavian Institute of African Studies, 1979.

Migration and Development: Dependence on South Africa: A Study of Lesotho. Revised Edn. Uppsala, Scandinavian Institute of African Studies; Trenton, NJ, Red Sea Press, 1986.

Witzsch, G. *Lesotho Environment and Environmental Law.* Roma, National University of Lesotho, 1992.

LIBERIA

Physical and Social Geography

CHRISTOPHER CLAPHAM

The Republic of Liberia was founded in 1847 by freed black slaves from the USA who were resettled from 1821 onwards along the western Guinea coast between Cape Mount (11° 20′ W) and Cape Palmas (7° 40′ W). Liberia extends from 4° 20′ N to 8° 30′ N with a maximum breadth of 280 km between Buchanan and Nimba. The country occupies an area of 97,754 sq km (37,743 sq miles) between Sierra Leone to the west, the Republic of Guinea to the north, and Côte d'Ivoire to the east.

PHYSICAL FEATURES AND POPULATION

An even coastline of 570 km, characterized by powerful surf, rocky cliffs and lagoons, makes access from the Atlantic Ocean difficult, except at the modern ports. The flat coastal plain, which is 15–55 km wide, consists of forest and savannah. The interior hills and mountain ranges, with altitudes of 180–360 m, form part of an extended peneplain, covered by evergreen (in the south) or semi-deciduous (in the north) rain forests. The northern highlands contain Liberia's greatest elevations, which include the Nimba mountains, reaching 1,752 m above sea-level, and the Wologisi range, reaching 1,381 m. The descent from the higher to the lower belts of the highlands is characterized by rapids and waterfalls.

Liberia has two rainy seasons near Harper, in the south, and one rainy season (from May to October) in the rest of the country. From Monrovia, on the coast in north-west Liberia, with an average of 4,650 mm per year, rainfall decreases towards the south-east and the hinterland, reaching 2,240 mm per year at Ganta. Average temperatures are more extreme in the interior than at the coast. Monrovia has an annual average of 26°C, with absolute limits at 33°C and 14°C respectively. At Tappita temperatures may rise to 44°C in March and fall to 9°C during cool harmattan nights in December or January. Mean water temperature on the coast is 27°C.

The drainage system consists of 15 principal river basins, of which those of the Cavalla river, with an area of 30,225 sq km (including 13,730 sq km in Liberia), and of the St Paul river, with an area of 21,910 sq km (11,325 sq km in Liberia), are the largest. The water flow varies considerably and may reach over 100,000 cubic feet per second (cfs) at the Mt Coffee gauge of the St Paul river in August or decrease to 2,000 cfs during the dry season in March.

The first Liberian census enumerated a population of 1,016,443 in April 1962. According to the second census, in February 1974, an increase of 47.9%, to 1,503,368, had taken place, indicating an average annual growth rate of 3.36%, one of the highest in Africa. A third census, held in February 1984, enumerated a total population of 2,101,628. According to official estimates, the population had increased to 2,760,000 at mid-1995, with an average density of 28.2 inhabitants per sq km.

The main groups comprising the Liberian population at the 1974 census were the 16 indigenous African tribes (totalling 1,402,950), 42,834 non-tribal Liberians (mainly descendants of the settlers), 47,654 non-Liberian Africans (including 26,337 Guineans, 8,068 Fanti from Ghana, and 6,440 Sierra Leoneans), 3,430 Lebanese, 2,399 US citizens, and 4,101 Europeans. The major ethnic group is the Kpelle (numbering 298,500 in 1974), who occupy the central section of the country, particularly Bong County. The Bassa in the Buchanan region (214,150) and the Gio in Nimba County (130,300) are the second and third largest groups. Other well-known groups are the seafaring Kru (121,400) and the Vai.

Prior to 1990 the demographic pattern of Liberia was characterized by a number of features typical of developing countries: a high proportion of children under 15 years of age (47% in 1984); a low average population density; a high growth rate in the capital (the population of Monrovia, including Congotown, increased from 80,992 in 1962 to 208,629 in 1978, and to 421,058 in 1984), and in coastal districts; a high rate of migration towards urban centres, and the resulting social problems of slum formation, increasing crime and unemployment. Considerable social and demographic disruption has attended the civil disorder that has dominated Liberian affairs since December 1989. In November 1993 some 400,000– 500,000 people (about 20% of the total population) had taken refuge in the Monrovia area. By May 1995 the population of Monrovia was estimated to have increased to about 700,000, with further concentrations in Buchanan and other 'safe zones'. It was estimated that about 80% of the total population had fled to other West African countries or become internally displaced, while about 10% of the population had been killed since December 1989. Following the installation of new transitional authorities in September 1995, a number of refugees returned to Liberia, but renewed fighting in 1996 led to a further exodus of civilians. In early 1997, according to estimates by the UNHCR, almost 759,000 Liberians were residing in neighbouring countries, including 400,000 in Guinea and 220,000 in Côte d'Ivoire.

Recent History

GILL TUDOR

Based on an earlier article by CHRISTOPHER CLAPHAM

Liberia was founded by liberated black slaves from the USA. During 1822–92 some 16,400 former slaves were resettled along the 'Malagueta' or 'Grain Coast' of west Africa, under the auspices of US philanthropic organizations. They were joined by some 5,700 Africans who had been freed from slaving vessels by the British and US navies. Conditions on the coast were harsh, and many of the settlers died, moved elsewhere or returned to the USA. Liberia was never officially a US colony, and it became an independent republic on 26 July 1847, with a constitution based on that of the USA. For most of the 19th century the republic controlled only scattered coastal settlements with their immediate hinterland. Control was extended inland from the 1890s onwards, in response to encroachment by British and French colonialism, although the people of the interior were not fully subdued until the 1920s. In 1926, however, European influence was reduced when the US-owned

Firestone Plantations Co began operations in Liberia, establishing massive rubber estates, and becoming the country's principal private-sector employer.

TUBMAN AND TOLBERT

For more than 130 years after independence Liberian politics was dominated by descendants of the original settlers, known as Americo-Liberians; the True Whig Party (TWP) maintained uninterrupted rule during 1871-1980. In contrast to his predecessors, President William Tubman, who was inaugurated in 1944, advocated the development of the economy through the encouragement of foreign investment, and a policy of assimilating Liberia's different ethnic groups. Following his death in 1971, Tubman was succeeded as president by the vice-president, William Tolbert, who was re-elected in 1975. During the Tolbert era the Mano River Union, which provided for increased economic co-operation with Sierra Leone, was formed, and Liberia became a member of the Economic Community of West African States (ECOWAS). Although the economy continued to expand, Liberia was adversely affected during the late 1970s by declining world demand for its principal exports, iron ore and rubber, and by a sharp increase in the prices of its imports.

In July 1979 a demonstration in protest at a proposed increase in the price of rice, which was organized by the Progressive Alliance of Liberia (PAL), an opposition group formed in the previous year, resulted in riots and looting. Tolbert assumed emergency powers, but shortly afterwards, introduced price subsidies for rice. In December the PAL was permitted to register as an official opposition party, under the name of the Progressive People's Party (PPP). Support for the PPP increased rapidly, and, in March 1980 its chairman, Gabriel Baccus Matthews, advocated a general strike; he and some 70 supporters were subsequently arrested.

THE PEOPLE'S REDEMPTION COUNCIL

In April 1980 Tolbert was assassinated in a military coup, led by Master Sgt (later Gen.) Samuel Doe. A People's Redemption Council (PRC), which comprised military personnel, with Doe as chairman, was established; the constitution was suspended and political parties were banned. The PRC assumed the government of the country, in conjunction with a 17-member council of ministers, five of whom were soldiers, while the remainder were members of the three movements that had been politically active before the coup: the TWP, the PPP and the radical Movement for Justice in Africa (MOJA). The new regime publicly executed 13 leading officials of the previous administration. Although popular within Liberia, the executions were condemned internationally: the Liberian delegation was excluded from a summit meeting of the Organization of African Unity (OAU) in Lagos, Nigeria later in the same month, and Doe's claim to Tolbert's chairmanship of the OAU was rejected. Doe promised that no further executions would take place, however, and Liberia's international standing was gradually restored. The PRC retained Liberia's close links with Western countries, and US aid was substantially increased.

In April 1981 a commission was established to draft a new constitution. During 1981–82 there were frequent resignations and dismissals from the PRC and the council of ministers, as Doe demonstrated his avowed intention to eradicate official corruption (while also gradually removing those with a different ideological outlook). In August 1981 five members of the PRC, including the vice-chairman, Thomas Weh Syen, were executed for conspiring against the government, and, shortly afterwards, the principal representative of MOJA in the council of ministers, Togba-Nah Tipoteh, resigned as minister of economics. The minister of justice, Chea Cheapoo, was dismissed in September for alleged dishonesty, and Matthews was removed as minister of foreign affairs in November. In 1982 several other ministers and heads of public companies were dismissed, following allegations of malpractice. In October 1983 the army commander, Brig.-Gen. Thomas Quiwonkpa (who had been accused of plotting against the government), was dismissed from the PRC, and fled the country. A number of other members of the PRC, however, continued to attract public criticism, and the government's increasingly conservative orientation proved to be unpopular.

CIVILIAN RULE

A draft constitution was approved by the PRC in March 1983, and subsequently adopted by 78.3% of registered voters in a referendum, which took place in July 1984. The new constitution again provided for a bicameral legislature and the separation of executive and legislative powers, and abolished property qualifications for voters. Doe dissolved the PRC and replaced it with an interim national assembly, under his chairmanship, which comprised the members of the former PRC, together with 36 appointed civilians, mainly former supporters of the TWP. In the same month the ban on political organizations was lifted, in anticipation of presidential and legislative elections, which were due to take place in 1985.

In August 1984 Doe formed the National Democratic Party of Liberia (NDPL) and formally announced his intention to contest the presidential elections. Other newly-established parties included the Liberian People's Party (LPP), the successor to MOJA; the United People's Party (UPP), a reconstituted PPP; the Unity Party (UP), the Liberian Action Party (LAP); and the Liberian Unification Party (LUP). However, the registration of political associations was impeded by considerable legal difficulties (including a prohibitive financial qualification). Opposition leaders were briefly detained, following an attempt to assassinate Doe in April 1985. Only three parties besides the NDPL—the LAP, the LUP and the UP—were eventually registered to contest the elections, which took place in October. There were allegations of electoral malpractice, and the chairman of the government-appointed electoral commission declared that extensive irregularities had taken place. It was later announced that Doe had been elected to the presidency, with 50.9% of the votes cast. (Neutral observers, however, believed the leader of the LAP, Jackson Doe, to have been the actual winner.) At concurrent elections to the bicameral national assembly, the NDPL secured 22 of the 26 seats in the senate and 51 of the 64 seats in the house of representatives. The LAP rejected the results, and refused to occupy the seats assigned to them.

In November 1985 an attempted military coup, led by Brig.-Gen. Quiwonkpa, was suppressed by troops loyal to the government. Quiwonkpa and a number of his supporters were killed, and subsequent fighting between rebels and government forces resulted in at least 600 deaths. Opposition leaders were detained, and meetings of students and others likely to be critical of the government were banned.

The formal installation of a civilian government in January 1986 failed to achieve internal stability and international acceptance. Although Doe appealed for national reconciliation, only a few members of the opposition parties agreed to accept posts in his government. In March the LAP, LUP and UP formed an alliance, known as the Liberia Grand Coalition. In March 1988 Gabriel Kpolleh, the leader of the LUP, was arrested on charges of conspiring to overthrow the government; in October he and nine others were sentenced to 10 years' imprisonment. In July 1988 Doe announced that a former PRC vice-chairman, Nicholas Podier, had been killed while allegedly preparing to stage a coup attempt from bases in Côte d'Ivoire. In the same month the constitution was amended to allow the presidential tenure to be extended for more than two terms. The government's suppression of political opponents and the press was restrained only by US threats to withdraw economic aid. Following allegations of economic mismanagement and diversion of aid funds, a team of US experts arrived in Liberia in late 1987 to supervise government finances, but left the country in December 1988. Liberia's relations with neighbouring countries became strained, during Doe's leadership, although links were established with Nigeria.

CIVIL CONFLICT AND ECOMOG INTERVENTION

In late December 1989 an armed insurrection by rebel forces began in the north-eastern border region of Nimba County. The rebels claimed to represent a previously unknown opposition movement, the National Patriotic Front of Liberia (NPFL), led by Charles Taylor, a former government official who was being sought for trial on charges of corruption. In early 1990 several hundred deaths ensued in the course of fighting between the Liberian army (the Armed Forces of Liberia–AFL) and the rebels, which swiftly developed into a conflict between President Doe's ethnic group, the Krahn, and the local Gio and Mano tribes. Both the Krahn-dominated army and the rebel forces were responsible for numerous atrocities against civilians; a large proportion of the local population took refuge in neighbouring Côte d'Ivoire and Guinea. By April the NPFL had overcome government resistance in Nimba County, and in May it extended its control to the remainder of the country, apart from the capital, Monrovia. The NPFL military offensive on Monrovia began in early July, and Taylor repeatedly demanded Doe's resignation as a precondition for a cease-fire. Taylor's authority as self-proclaimed head of a national patriotic reconstruction assembly (NPRA) was, however, challenged by a breakaway faction, known as the Independent National Patriotic Front of Liberia (INPFL), led by Prince Yormie Johnson, whose troops, estimated to number less than 500, rapidly gained control of parts of Monrovia. During August many foreign nationals and diplomatic staff were evacuated by a US naval force. Repeated efforts by ECOWAS to negotiate a cease-fire proved unsuccessful, and in late August it dispatched a seaborne force, comprising some 4,000 troops, provided by Ghana, Nigeria, Sierra Leone, The Gambia and Guinea, to enforce peace in the region. Doe and Johnson agreed to accept the ECOWAS monitoring group (ECOMOG), but its initial occupation of the port area of Monrovia (which had been under Johnson's control), encountered armed opposition by Taylor's forces.

On 30 August 1990 ECOWAS convened a national conference in the Gambian capital, Banjul, although the NPFL refused to attend. Exiled representatives of Liberia's principal political parties, churches and other groups elected Dr Amos Sawyer, the leader of the LPP, as president of an interim government of national unity (IGNU), with a representative of the Liberian Council of Churches, Bishop Ronald Diggs, as vice-president. In late August it was reported that the AFL, which supported Doe, and Johnson's INPFL, had formed an alliance against the NPFL. In September, however, discussions between the AFL and INPFL, held under ECOMOG supervision, led to armed clashes, during which Doe was captured and subsequently killed by the INPFL.

In October 1990 ECOMOG launched an armed offensive, with the aim of establishing a neutral zone in Monrovia to separate the three warring factions, and subsequently gained control of central Monrovia. Thus, Liberia became effectively divided between two administrations: Monrovia was placed under the jurisdiction of the IGNU, which was maintained in power by ECOMOG, while most of the remainder of the country was controlled by the NPFL. Taylor continued to assert his claim to the presidency, and, later that month, established a rival administration, the NPRA, based at Gbarnga, in Bong County (in central Liberia). On 22 November Sawyer was formally installed as interim president in Monrovia. Numerous attempts were made to negotiate a cease-fire and the restoration of a single elected government for the whole country. An initial cease-fire, signed at Bamako, Mali, in late November, effectively recognized the division of the country into two parts.

Following further negotiations, under the auspices of ECOWAS, a peace agreement was signed in Yamoussoukro, Côte d'Ivoire, in October 1991, whereby all Liberian warring factions were to be encamped and disarmed, and national elections were to be conducted under ECOWAS supervision. Although the cease-fire was maintained, efforts to re-establish a national government failed, largely as a result of Taylor's refusal to disarm NPFL forces and to submit to the authority of ECOMOG, which he believed to be prejudiced in favour of Sawyer. Taylor also cited the increasing military threat presented by ULIMO (see below) as a reason not to disarm.

Progress towards a settlement was also inhibited by the rival sources of external support for ECOMOG and the NPFL. ECOMOG, although formally representing all members of ECOWAS, largely comprised forces of its anglophone members, dominated by Nigeria. However, Guinea also supported ECOMOG, and Senegalese troops (financed by the USA) participated in the force from September 1991 until early 1993. The NPFL received supplies and consignments of armaments from neighbouring Côte d'Ivoire, and from Burkina Faso, although support from both countries was periodically restrained as a result of diplomatic pressure. ECOMOG and the IGNU were backed by the USA, which provided both military and financial assistance, while the NPFL appeared to receive at least tacit support from French interests in Côte d'Ivoire.

The INPFL initially co-operated with the IGNU, and participated in a 28-member interim national assembly, which was established in January 1991. In August, however, the INPFL withdrew from the interim government, following criticism by Sawyer of the execution (reportedly at Prince Johnson's instigation) of four INPFL members accused of criminal activities. The INPFL subsequently attempted to re-establish links with Taylor's NPFL, but its role in the conflict declined. Meanwhile, it was reported that the AFL (which comprised the remaining troops of the late President Doe) continued to perpetrate acts of brutality against civilians. Nominally, at least, both the INPFL and the AFL were disarmed and confined to barracks, under the terms of the Yamoussoukro agreement. (The INPFL was subsequently dissolved in September 1992.)

A new opposition group, the United Liberation Movement of Liberia for Democracy (ULIMO), led by Raleigh Seekie, was formed in Sierra Leone in June 1991 by former supporters of Doe. ULIMO declared its opposition to the NPFL, and denounced the Yamoussoukro accord. Its forces entered north-western Liberia in September 1991, and, from November, were also involved in clashes with the NPFL in the Mano River Bridge area, in the south-west of the country. The Sierra Leone government denied allegations by Taylor that its troops had participated in ULIMO offensives in retaliation for NPFL incursions into Sierra Leone and support for the Sierra Leonean insurgent group, the Revolutionary United Front (RUF).

In early 1992 there appeared to be some prospect of a peaceful settlement. Roads linking Monrovia and territory under the control of the NPFL were opened, and, in April, ECOMOG began to deploy troops in NPFL-controlled areas, with the aim of disarming all factions and creating conditions that would allow elections to take place. In May, however, following the execution of six Senegalese soldiers by NPFL forces, ECOMOG withdrew its troops to Monrovia. This incident further exacerbated relations between ECOMOG and NPFL, and, in late July, ECOWAS announced that it would impose economic sanctions on the NPFL if Taylor did not fully comply with the conditions of the Yamoussoukro agreement within 30 days. In August ULIMO attacked the NPFL from Sierra Leone, with considerable success, gaining control of large areas of Lofa and Cape Mount Counties in western Liberia.

In September 1992, following the expiry of the stipulated date for the implementation of the Yamoussoukro agreement, ECOMOG threatened to enforce the terms of the accord. In mid-October the NPFL launched a major offensive against ECOMOG positions in the outskirts of Monrovia, and captured a number of strategic areas, effectively besieging the capital and resulting in the temporary closure of Spriggs Payne airport, the city's principal link with the international community. The NPFL recruited boys, some as young as eight, and executed large numbers of civilians who refused to join its forces; mass graves were subsequently discovered in the suburbs of Monrovia, which had been occupied by NPFL forces, and at the Firestone plantations. The murder of five American nuns by the NPFL in late October attracted particular international condemnation.

Following the NPFL offensive, ECOMOG abandoned its previous peace-keeping stance for a directly combatant role; Nigerian aircraft under ECOMOG command bombed NPFL positions. Aerial attacks on the border with Côte d'Ivoire, designed to impede NPFL supply routes, prompted protests from the Ivorian government. In late November 1992 the UN security council imposed a mandatory arms embargo on all factions in the conflict (excluding ECOMOG), and authorized the UN secretary-general to send a special envoy to Liberia. The former president of Zimbabwe, Canaan Banana, was appointed as OAU representative, but the combined efforts of the two representatives had little effect. In early January 1993, following a new offensive, ECOMOG forces (which had been reinforced by additional Nigerian and Ghanaian troops) regained control of the outskirts of Monrovia, and advanced along the coast, capturing the airport at Robertsfield (which was severely damaged and closed to civilian traffic) later that month, the Firestone rubber plantation at Harbel in mid-February, and the principal port of Buchanan in early April.

In early 1993 ULIMO intensified its attacks in western Liberia, gaining control of Cape Mount and Bomi Counties and the greater part of Lofa County. In March ULIMO accepted an invitation to join the IGNU, although its relations with the government and ECOMOG remained uneasy, and, in early April, ECOMOG disarmed ULIMO forces in Monrovia, in the interests of public safety. (ULIMO had split into two factions, of which one, led by Raleigh Seekie and subsequently by Maj.-Gen. Roosevelt Johnson, principally comprised Krahn and operated from Sierra Leone. The other faction, led by Alhaji G. V. Kromah, was predominantly Islamic and Mandingo, and operated from Guinea.) In April the UN security council adopted a further resolution, declaring that the UN was prepared to take further measures against any faction unwilling to implement the Yamoussoukro accord. In June more than 600 refugees were killed by troops (alleged to be members of the NPFL) at the Harbel rubber plantation. Following initial investigations, the IGNU accused Taylor and his associates of involvement in the massacre, and stated that they were to be charged accordingly. In September 1993, however, a UN investigation concluded that AFL troops were responsible, and a number of AFL units were withdrawn to Monrovia and disarmed (although the IGNU continued to dispute the results of the inquiry.)

In July 1993 a peace conference, attended by all factions involved in the hostilities, was convened, under the auspices of the UN and ECOWAS, in Geneva, Switzerland. After several days of negotiations, the IGNU, the NPFL and ULIMO agreed to a cease-fire (which was to take effect at the end of that month and was to be monitored by UN observers and a reconstituted peace-keeping force), and to the formation of a transitional government. The peace accord was formally signed on 25 July at an ECOWAS summit meeting, held in Cotonou, Benin. The agreement provided for the IGNU to be replaced by a Liberian national transitional government (LNTG), which was to include a five-member council of state, and the existing legislature by a 35-member transitional parliament (comprising 13 representatives of the IGNU, 13 of the NPFL, and nine of ULIMO), pending presidential and legislative elections, which were to take place in February 1994. In response to demands by Taylor, the dominance of the Nigerian contingent in ECOMOG was to be considerably reduced; the new peace-keeping force, which was to be reconstituted as the ECOWAS cease-fire monitoring group, was to be supplemented with additional troops from other West African states.

At the end of July 1993 the cease-fire was successfully implemented; in early August, however, ECOMOG claimed that the NPFL had violated the peace agreement by repeatedly entering territory under the control of the peace-keeping force. In mid-August the IGNU, the NPFL and ULIMO each appointed one representative to the transitional council of state, while the remaining two members (representatives of the IGNU and ULIMO respectively) were elected by a list of candidates who had been nominated by the three factions. However, the inauguration of the council of state (originally scheduled for 24 August) was to be postponed, pending the disarmament of all warring factions in accordance with the peace agreement. Subsequent delays in the deployment of UN observers and additional peace-keeping troops resulted in a protracted impasse: Taylor refused to permit the disarmament of NPFL forces prior to the arrival of the additional troops (owing to his scepticism regarding ECOMOG's neutrality) while the IGNU continued to insist that the installation of the transitional authorities take place in conjunction with the disarmament process.

In September 1993 the UN security council approved the establishment of the UN Observer Mission in Liberia (UNOMIL), which was to co-operate with ECOMOG and the OAU in supervising the transitional process. In early October a transitional legislative assembly was established, in accordance with the peace agreement (although its installation was also delayed, pending the implementation of the disarmament process). Later in October it was announced that the governments of Tanzania and Uganda were to contribute troops to ECOMOG. Attempts to establish a council of ministers, as part of the LNTG, were delayed, however, owing to the failure of the IGNU, the NPFL and ULIMO to agree on the allocation of ministerial portfolios. Agreement was finally reached in early November on a number of portfolios in the LNTG.

Meanwhile, it was feared that renewed hostilities in several areas of the country would jeopardize the peace accord. An armed faction, known as the Liberia Peace Council (LPC), comprising members of the Krahn ethnic group from Grand Gedeh County, together with a number of disaffected AFL troops, emerged in September 1993, and subsequently entered into conflict with the NPFL in south-eastern Liberia. A large number of civilians fled to Buchanan from Rivercess and Grand Bassa Counties, in response to fighting in the region. The LPC, which was led by Dr George Boley (a prominent member of ULIMO), claimed to be a non-partisan movement established in response to what it claimed to be continued atrocities perpetrated by the NPFL. In December fighting between ULIMO and a newly-formed movement, the Lofa Defence Force (LDF), was also reported in Lofa County, apparently in retaliation against alleged acts of violence committed by ULIMO forces in the region.

In late December 1993 the contingents of additional ECOMOG troops from Tanzania and Uganda began to arrive. In February 1994 further negotiations took place between the IGNU, the NPFL and ULIMO, with the aim of resolving outstanding differences regarding the implementation of the peace accord. At the end of February the council of state elected David Kpomakpor, a representative of the IGNU, as its chairman. In early March units belonging to UNOMIL and the new ECOMOG force were deployed, and the disarmament of all factions commenced. On 7 March the council of state was inaugurated; it was envisaged that the presidential and legislative elections (which were originally scheduled for February) would take place in September. However, the disarmament process was subsequently impeded by an increase in rebel activity; in addition to continuing hostilities involving the LPC and the NPFL (despite a cease-fire agreement, which was mediated by ECOMOG in March), more than 200 people were killed in clashes between members of the two ULIMO factions, particularly in the region of Tubmanburg, north of Monrovia (where the organization was based). The hostilities (which followed the dispute earlier that month between Kromah, a Mandingo, and Johnson, a Krahn) were prompted by resentment within the Krahn at the predominance of the Mandingo among ULIMO representatives in the transitional institutions; the factions henceforth became known as ULIMO–K (led by Kromah) and ULIMO–J (led by Johnson).

By early April 1994 only 1,447 of the estimated 60,000 troops in Liberia had disarmed, of whom the majority were members of the AFL. In May, following continued disputes over its composition a 19-member cabinet was installed, comprising seven members of the NPFL (which held the disputed portfolios of justice and foreign affairs), seven of ULIMO and five of the IGNU. In the same month the USA condemned the widespread violations of human rights perpetrated by a number of factions, particularly by the LPC (which was accused of the massacre of civilians, believed to be NPFL supporters, in south-eastern Liberia).

In early August 1994, following secret negotiations, representatives of the six factions involved in civil conflict (the AFL, the LDF, the LPC, ULIMO–K, ULIMO–J and the NPFL) signed an agreement providing for the cessation of hostilities, and pledged to co-operate in the process of disarmament; it was further agreed that the LPC and the LDF (which had not been party to the Cotonou accord) be allowed to participate in the LNTG.

In early September 1994 (when the original mandate of the LNTG was due to expire), a meeting of the NPFL, the AFL and ULIMO–K was convened, under the aegis of the Ghanaian president, Jerry Rawlings, at Akosombo, Ghana. Meanwhile, following clashes between dissident members of the NPFL and troops loyal to Taylor in the region of Gbarnga, the minister of labour, Thomas Woewiyu, claimed that Taylor had been removed as leader of the NPFL. On 12 September, however, Taylor, Kromah and the chief of staff of the AFL, Lt-Gen. Hezekiah Bowen, signed a peace accord, which provided for an immediate cessation of hostilities and the establishment later that month of a reconstituted council of state, in which four of the members were to be nominated by the three warring factions, while the remaining member was to be selected by a national conference of prominent civilians; presidential and general elections were rescheduled for October 1995, and the new government was subsequently to be installed in January 1996. However, the proposed installation of a predominantly military council of state prompted widespread criticism.

Meanwhile, the NPFL dissidents' Central Revolutionary Council (CRC) reiterated that Taylor had been deposed and replaced by Woewiyu, who rejected the Akosombo agreement. In mid-September 1994 disaffected members of the AFL, led by a former officer who had served in the Doe administration, Gen. Charles Julu, seized the presidential residence in Monrovia, but were subsequently overpowered by ECOMOG forces. Some 78 members of the AFL, including Julu, were later arrested, and a further 2,000 troops were disarmed by ECOMOG. (In July 1995 Julu and a further six senior officers received custodial sentences of seven years—they were pardoned by the government in July 1996.) Later that month the NPFL dissidents (known as the NPFL–CRC), apparently in alliance with elements of the AFL, ULIMO, the LPC and the LDF, took control of Gbarnga; forces loyal to Taylor retreated to the town of Palala, to the east of Gbarnga, while Taylor was said to have taken refuge in Côte d'Ivoire. During September about 75,000 civilians fled to Côte d'Ivoire and Guinea, following the increase in factional hostilities.

In early October 1994 the council of state removed Bowen from the post of AFL chief of staff, on the grounds that he had failed to respond effectively to Julu's coup attempt in September; Bowen, however, refused to relinquish office. In the same month ECOMOG announced a reduction in its peace-keeping forces deployed in Liberia, citing a lack of financial resources, in conjunction with the failure of the international community to assist in the peace process; the UN security council extended the mandate of UNOMIL until January 1995, but also announced a reduction in personnel (which then numbered 368), in view of the lack of progress achieved. In early November 1994 Ghana reiterated its warning that it would withdraw from ECOMOG if the warring factions failed to reach a peace settlement, while the Nigerian government withdrew military equipment from the peace-keeping force. Later that month a conference, attended by Bowen, Taylor, Woewiyu, Boley and the leader of the LDF, François Massaquoi, together with representatives of the LNC and the LNTG, was convened in the Ghanaian capital, Accra, to discuss preparations for the installation of a reconstituted council of state, in accordance with the Akosombo agreement. However, a subsequent decision, endorsed by ECOWAS, that the AFL nominate a representative in conjunction with the 'Coalition Forces' (an informal alliance comprising the NPFL–CRC, the LPC, the LDF and elements of ULIMO–K) resulted in contention, with both Bowen and Boley claiming a seat in the proposed council of state. Negotiations were adjourned at the end of November, after the participants failed to agree on the composition of the new transitional administration.

In early December 1994 it was reported that the NPFL had regained control of much of the territory, including Gbarnga, that the NPFL–CRC had captured in September. On 22 December, after the peace conference was reconvened in Accra, the participants reached agreement on a cease-fire, which was to enter into force later that month. Additional accords reaffirmed the terms of the Akosombo agreement, including provisions for the establishment of demilitarized zones throughout Liberia and for the installation of a reconstituted council of state (which was to comprise a single representative of each of the NPFL, ULIMO, the AFL in conjunction with the 'Coalition Forces', and the LNC, with a fifth member elected jointly by the NPFL and ULIMO from traditional rulers); new institutions were to be installed on 1 January 1996, following multi-party elections, which were to take place by 14 November 1995. Later in December 1994 the UN security council extended the mandate of UNOMIL (now comprising 90 observers) until April 1995, while the Nigerian government reduced its ECOMOG contingent to 6,000 (from about 10,000), in accordance with its stated aim gradually to withdraw from Liberia. The cease-fire, which entered into force on 28 December 1994, was widely observed, despite reports of skirmishes between supporters of ULIMO–J, the AFL and the NPFL around Monrovia.

In January 1995, following continuing disagreement between the AFL and the 'Coalition Forces' regarding their joint representative in the council of state, ECOWAS heads of state submitted a proposal, which was accepted in principle by the armed factions, that the council of state be expanded from five to six members (to include both Bowen and Woewiyu). However, subsequent negotiations were impeded by Taylor's persistent demands that he be granted the chairmanship of the council of state, which was opposed by the other factional leaders. In early February a compromise arrangement was negotiated, whereby Chief Tamba Taylor, the traditional ruler who had been nominated by ULIMO and the NPFL, would assume the office of chairman, while Charles Taylor and Kromah would become joint vice-chairmen; the three remaining seats in the council of state were to be allocated to Bowen, Woewiyu and the representative of the LNC, Oscar Quiah. In the same month reports of renewed hostilities between the NPFL and the LPC in south-eastern Liberia prompted concern that any agreement reached by the armed factions would be undermined; ECOMOG also claimed that elements of the NPFL had infiltrated the outskirts of Monrovia in preparation for an attack on the capital. In early March the Tanzania government announced that its ECOMOG contingent (which numbered 800) was to be withdrawn from Liberia by the end of that month. Later in March Kpomakpor and Tamba Taylor met Ghanaian officials in Accra to discuss the continuing political impasse (which was apparently caused by Charles Taylor's reluctance to assume his seat in the new council of state, in protest at Woewiyu's inclusion as a representative).

In April 1995 about 62 civilians were massacred by unidentified armed groups in the town of Yosi, near Buchanan, after hostilities between the NPFL and the LPC resumed in the region; renewed fighting in other parts of Liberia was also reported. Later that month a meeting between Charles Taylor and an adviser to Rawlings took place in the Libyan capital, Tripoli, with mediation by the Libyan head of state, Col Qaddafi. At the end of April the withdrawal of the Tanzanian contingent of ECOMOG commenced. In May an ECOWAS summit meeting was convened in Abuja, Nigeria, to discuss the Liberian conflict; however, Charles Taylor failed to attend the meeting, and a number of issues regarding the composition of the council of state remained unresolved. It was subsequently announced that the installation of the council of state was to be postponed until the constituent factions demonstrated commitment to the observance of the cease-fire and to the disarmament process.

In June 1995 the NPFL agreed to allow ECOMOG troops to be deployed in the region of the Bong iron mines, and to co-operate with ULIMO–J forces in operations to remove land-mines along a principal road linking Kakata with Gbarnga. In mid-June clashes took place at the border with Côte d'Ivoire, apparently between LPC and NPFL forces; it was reported that about 10 Ivorian citizens had been killed, prompting resentment against Liberian refugees resident in Côte d'Ivoire. In July the Guinean government attributed border incursions, in which several people were killed, to NPFL forces. At the end of that month peace negotiations resumed in Monrovia, which, however, Charles Taylor again failed to attend; it was reported that he continued to demand the position of first vice-president in the new council of state, despite the recommendations of the summit meeting in May that the five members representing the warring factions be granted equal status as joint vice-chairmen. Meanwhile, the UN special representative in Liberia indicated that UNOMIL's mandate (which had again been renewed) would be allowed to expire in mid-September unless sufficient progress was achieved in the peace process.

TRANSITIONAL COUNCIL OF STATE

On 19 August 1995, following a further ECOWAS summit meeting (convened at Abuja, Nigeria), the warring factions signed a peace accord providing for the installation of a reconstituted council of state, which was to remain in power for a period of one year, pending elections: an academic with no factional affiliations, Prof. Wilton Sankawulo, was to assume the office of chairman, while the other seats were to be allocated respectively to Charles Taylor, Kromah, Boley, Quiah and Tamba Taylor. Later that month a cease-fire entered into force, in accordance with the terms of the peace agreement. The new transitional council of state was formally installed on 1 September; at the inauguration ceremony the UN special representative announced that the elections were to take place on 20 August 1996. (Charles Taylor had already indicated that he intended to contest the presidential election, although, under the terms of the peace agreement, members of the council of state were obliged to resign from office prior to participating in the elections.) A new transitional council of ministers, comprising members of the seven factions that had signed the peace agreement, was subsequently formed. Later in September the UN Security Council extended UNOMIL's mandate until the end of January 1996. Reports emerged, however, that clashes between the ULIMO factions had resumed in Lofa County, while the armed factions had failed to commence disarmament in compliance with the peace accord. At the end of September about 65 civilians were killed by NPFL forces in Nimba County.

In October 1995, at an emergency meeting of ECOWAS, the governments of Nigeria, Ghana, Côte d'Ivoire, Burkina Faso and Togo pledged to contribute additional forces to ECOMOG (which then numbered 7,269), to ensure the effective implementation of the peace process. Meanwhile, clashes between NPFL and ULIMO–K forces erupted; Kromah denied claims by Charles Taylor that ULIMO–K had initiated attacks against NPFL troops at Gbarnga. In November, however, the two leaders reaffirmed their commitment to the peace process, and signed a 'memorandum of understanding', which included undertakings to co-operate with humanitarian organizations operating in territory under their control; under the terms of the agreement, a demilitarized zone was subsequently established between NPFL and ULIMO–K forces in the region of St Paul River (between Bong and Lofa Counties). At a UN conference, which was convened at the end of October, donor nations, notably the USA, pledged further humanitarian and military assistance to support the peace process. External aid for ECOMOG was, however, affected by international action against Nigeria, following the execution of the political activist, Ken Saro-Wiwa, in November.

In mid-December 1995 the deployment of ECOMOG forces commenced, in accordance with the Abuja peace agreement. Following continued clashes between the ULIMO factions, however, ULIMO–J attacked ECOMOG troops in the region of Tubmanburg. ECOMOG was obliged to suspend deployment of its forces, and launched a counter-offensive in an attempt to restore order; several members of the peace-keeping force were reportedly killed in subsequent fighting. ULIMO–J forces seized and held hostage 130 Nigerian members of ECOMOG in the region of the Bong mines (who were, however, released in mid-January 1996). Hostilities continued in early 1996, with large numbers of civilians killed or displaced. ECOMOG rejected an offer by Charles Taylor, Kromah and elements of the AFL to assist the peace-keeping force in its efforts to suppress the ULIMO–J uprising. At the end of January unidentified forces attacked members of UNOMIL in the region of Tubmanburg; the UN special representative and the US special envoy in Liberia both subsequently expressed doubts regarding the commitment of the armed factions to the peace process. In February, following a resumption of clashes between the LPC and the NPFL in south-eastern Liberia, eight members of non-governmental organizations were temporarily held hostage by the LPC. Later that month military and executive officials within ULIMO–J issued a resolution to the effect that Johnson had been replaced as leader of the movement in the interests of the peace process. In March the council of state announced the removal of Johnson (who had hitherto held the rural development portfolio) from the cabinet. Following the division within ULIMO–J, clashes erupted between the two factions, in which forces loyal to Johnson allegedly killed a supporter of the new leadership. The council of state subsequently ordered that Johnson be arrested on charges of murder. Johnson, however, refused to surrender to the authorities and became effectively besieged in his private residence in central Monrovia, while a number of ULIMO–J forces remained loyal to him.

In early April 1996 government forces, led by Charles Taylor, engaged in hostilities with Johnson's supporters, in an effort to force him to surrender, with the effective result that the principal factions represented in the transitional authorities became involved in the conflict; members of the LPC and AFL (which were predominantly Krahn) supported Johnson's forces, while the NPFL and ULIMO–K opposed them. Fighting rapidly intensified in central Monrovia, resulting in the displacement of large numbers of civilians, who fled the capital or took refuge in embassy compounds. ECOMOG (which had refrained from military intervention) deployed its forces in the region of Monrovia, with the aim of negotiating between the warring factions; following a lull in the fighting, however, a number of Johnson's supporters staged attacks in the residential area of Mamba Point (where embassies and offices of humanitarian organizations were situated) and seized a number of civilians, including 40 Lebanese nationals and 25 Nigerian members of ECOMOG, as hostages. The US government began to effect the evacuation of US citizens and other foreign nationals from the US embassy (where some 20,000 civilians had taken shelter). Johnson's supporters, together with their hostages and several thousand civilians, took refuge in former army barracks, known as the Barclay Training Centre, in Monrovia; NPFL and ULIMO–K forces subsequently surrounded the barracks. President Rawlings of Ghana (in his capacity as chairman of ECOWAS) urged Johnson to surrender in exchange for pledges of safe conduct, and appealed to the council of state to suspend military action against him. Following negotiations, with mediation by ECOMOG, the warring factions agreed to a cease-fire; Johnson was to surrender to ECOMOG, pending further negotiations, while the hostages held by his supporters were to be released. Johnson's forces subsequently released 27 Lebanese hostages.

The cease-fire agreement proved unsuccessful, however, and NPFL and ULIMO–K forces launched renewed attacks against the Barclay Training Centre. Further discussions took place between an ECOMOG delegation and Johnson's supporters, who, it was reported, demanded guarantees of protection for members of the Krahn ethnic group as a precondition for surrender. The evacuation of foreign nationals continued, while the US government dispatched warships to the region, with the stated aim of ensuring the protection of US diplomatic staff in Monrovia. Later in April 1996 a further cease-fire agreement was reached under the aegis of the US government, the UN and ECOWAS; under the terms of the accord, ECOMOG troops were subsequently deployed throughout Monrovia, while the majority of the remaining hostages, including the foreign nationals, were released by Johnson's supporters.

In early May 1996 an emergency summit meeting was abandoned, after the heads of state of the majority of member countries failed to attend. Rawlings subsequently warned that continued failure of the armed factions to resolve the conflict would oblige ECOWAS to withdraw the peace-keeping force from Liberia. Meanwhile, during the absence of Johnson (who had left the country under US protection, to attend the planned summit meeting), the NPFL launched a further attack against the Barclay Training Centre. The resumption of intense fighting prompted further large numbers of civilians to flee to Monrovia Free Port in an attempt to leave the country, attracting international concern. A Nigerian freighter transporting some 4,000 Liberians was refused entry by other West African coastal nations until, following considerable international pressure, the Ghanaian government agreed to accept the refugees. At the end of May the UN Security Council renewed the mandate of UNOMIL for a further three months, but warned the armed factions that international support would be withdrawn if fighting continued; UNOMIL was henceforth to comprise only the five military and 20 civilian personnel remaining in the country following the evacuation of a further 93 observers in April. In early June Johnson's supporters agreed to disarm and to leave the Barclay Training Centre, while an ECOWAS arbitration mission commenced discussions with the faction leaders in an effort to restore the peace process. ECOMOG troops gained control of the Barclay Training Centre, although a number of Johnson's supporters subsequently refused to leave Monrovia, in contravention of the agreement. Also in June clashes between ULIMO–K and ULIMO–J forces in Grand Cape Mount County resumed. It was reported moreover, that a newly-emerged Americo-Liberian faction, the Congo Defence Force, had clashed with ULIMO–J members in the region of Tubmanburg.

In August 1996, at an ECOWAS conference in Abuja, the principal faction leaders (apart from Johnson, who remained abroad) signed a further peace agreement, whereby a reconstituted council of state was to be installed by the end of that month, with a former Liberian senator, Ruth Perry, replacing Sankawulo as chairman; Taylor and Boley were to remain members of the new administration. Under a revised timetable, elections were to take place at the end of May 1997, and power was to be transferred to an elected government by mid-June, while the armed factions were to be dissolved by the end of January of that year. In order to implement the new timetable, ECOMOG (which then numbered 8,500) was to be reinforced. Faction leaders who failed to comply with the new agreement would be subject to sanctions, including travel restrictions, the 'freezing' of business assets and exclusion from the elections, while the establishment of a war crimes tribunal was recommended. The mandate of UNOMIL was extended for a further three months to the end of November, and the mission was to be expanded to 34 personnel; the announcement was accompanied by further warnings that the international community would withdraw its representatives from the country if the armed factions failed to demonstrate their commitment to the peace process. In early September Perry was inaugurated as chairman of the council of state.

The implementation of the peace process gained impetus, following the new Abuja accord. Taylor, Boley and Kromah ordered their followers to withdraw from territory under their control, and by late August the removal of some roadblocks had commenced. The cease-fire was generally observed, although skirmishes were reported in various areas, notably between the NPFL and the LPC in south-eastern Liberia and between the two ULIMO factions in the west. Under the terms of the peace agreement, Johnson was reinstated to a reorganized cabinet at the end of September 1996, becoming minister of transport. The reopening of roads allowed humanitarian organizations to resume operations in regions that had previously been inaccessible, and reports of severe famine in Tubmanburg, in western Liberia, attracted international attention; however, activity by faction members continued to prevent free movement in much of the country. The delivery of UN relief supplies to Sinje, in Grand Cape Mount County, inadvertently caused a massacre, with members of one of the two ULIMO factions killing a number of civilians in a raid to steal the food supplies. In early October ECOMOG demanded that ULIMO–J remove its roadblocks from the main highways in western Liberia. ECOMOG troops subsequently encountered no armed resistance when they took control of the region; by the end of the month they had also gained control of the southern port of Greenville. In early November it was announced that ECOMOG was to be reinforced by about 2,300 personnel from several West African states, including Nigeria, Ghana and Mali; Niger and Burkina Faso had pledged contingents for the first time, while Côte d'Ivoire was to dispatch medical personnel. UNOMIL's mandate was extended until the end of March 1997.

On 31 October 1996 the peace process suffered another serious threat, with an apparent assassination attempt against Charles Taylor by unidentified assailants when he arrived at the offices of the council of state. Taylor was unharmed but at least three of his aides were killed. Taylor accused Boley and Johnson of instigating the attack, although they both denied involvement. There was speculation that NPFL dissidents might have been responsible for the incident, or that Taylor had staged the attack himself in order to discredit his rivals. ECOMOG arrested about 20 people, mainly members of the LPC. Taylor refused to attend subsequent meetings of the council of state, on security grounds, but the incident remained largely inconclusive and did not prove an impediment to the peace process.

The process of disarmament officially recommenced in late November 1996, with ECOMOG deploying troops throughout much of the country, and establishing demilitarized zones to separate the warring factions. Progress was very slow, however; by the end of December the UN reported that about 6,000 of an estimated total of 60,000 rebel forces had been disarmed at the 11 official demobilization points. In January 1997 the national disarmament and demobilization commission revised the estimated number of combatants, to a total of only 23,416. ECOMOG agreed that the estimate of 60,000 (based on claims by faction leaders) was exaggerated and announced that a more realistic number would be 30,000–35,000. Shortly before the end of January (the stipulated date for the completion of disarmament under the terms of the Abuja accord), the number of combatants demobilizing suddenly increased; by the end of that month ECOMOG announced that about 23,000 had been disarmed. The deadline was extended by a further week to allow the process to be completed, and ECOMOG declared that 91% of forces had been disarmed at the end of that period, although final figures were inconsistent. The faction leaders all declared that their movements had been officially dissolved in accordance with the Abuja agreement, and Taylor and Kromah announced the reconstruction of their military organizations into the civilian National Patriotic Party (NPP) and All Liberian Coalition Party respectively.

THE 1997 ELECTIONS

In mid-February 1997 ECOWAS confirmed that voting by proportional representation would take place on 30 May to elect a president and a bicameral parliament, comprising a 64-seat house of representatives and a 26-seat senate. At the end of February, Taylor, Kromah and Boley resigned from the council of state in order to contest the presidential election; they were replaced by nominees from their respective organizations. The office of the UN high commissioner for refugees (UNHCR) drafted a programme for a mass repatriation of refugees, which was to commence in May and continue for 18 months, at a cost of US $60m. The UNHCR estimated the total number of Liberian refugees residing in neighbouring countries at 758,500, including 400,000 in Guinea and 327,500 in Côte d'Ivoire (but subsequently revised the number in Côte d'Ivoire to 220,000, following a refugee census in that country in March). The mandate of UNOMIL was again extended, to the end of June.

During the course of a nationwide search for illicit armaments in March and April 1997, ECOMOG discovered two large arms caches at Kromah's residences in Monrovia and Voinjama, as well as two major caches in the NPFL stronghold of Nimba County and smaller quantities of armaments at the residences of Taylor and Boley. Kromah was placed under house arrest and threatened with prosecution and exclusion from the elections but was subsequently released without charge, after issuing a public apology. ECOMOG was progressively reinforced during the first half of 1997; in February the USA, supported by the United Kingdom, provided a military airlift for some 500 Ghanaian troops and 637 Malian troops, and 90 Ivorian medical personnel. The arrival in April of an additional 500 troops from Niger, 320 from Burkina Faso and 250 from Benin increased the force to a total strength of about 13,000 by mid-May

Several political parties which had become inactive during the civil conflict re-emerged and a number of civilian candidates presented their candidacy for the presidency, including the former ministers, Gabriel Baccus Matthews and Togba-Nah Tipoteh. An attempt in late March 1997 by an alliance of seven of the long-standing parties (the LPP, UPP, LAP, TWP, NDPL, LUP and UP) to agree on a single presidential candidate failed when some of the parties rejected a poll which had been won by Cletus Wotorson of the LAP. The selection of a new seven-member independent electoral commission was impeded by disagreements, with Taylor contesting the appointment of the chairman. The body was finally inaugurated in early April, but the delay affected the electoral timetable. By early May it was evident that preparations for the poll were not adequately advanced, and all the parties, apart from Taylor's NPP, demanded a postponement; Taylor, however, warned that he would not accept a delay in the elections. ECOWAS acted decisively in the dispute, announcing later that month that the first round of voting would be rescheduled for 19 July, with a second round taking place on 2 August if no presidential candidate won more than 50% of votes cast. A total of 13 candidates were to contest the presidential election, including Ellen Johnson-Sirleaf, a political exile under the Doe government and hitherto a director of the UN development programme. Taylor was generally viewed as the most popular candidate, with a well-organized campaign, financed by profits accrued from unofficial exports and supported by his private radio station (the only one broadcasting nationwide), Kiss FM. Johnson-Sirleaf, who contested the election on behalf of the UP, quickly emerged as his closest rival. A 10-day voter registration census commenced in late June, but was extended by a few days in some areas, owing to adverse weather conditions.

The electoral campaign was conducted peacefully, apart from a few clashes between rival supporters and allegations of a further conspiracy to assassinate Taylor. Voting, which took place on 19 July 1997, was also without serious incident, apart from some logistical difficulties, often caused by poor voter education. More than 500 international observers, who monitored the electoral process, declared that no serious irregularities had occurred (although both Johnson-Sirleaf and Kromah complained of malpractice). According to the final results, Taylor secured an outright victory, with 75.3% of the votes cast, while Johnson-Sirleaf obtained 9.6% of the votes; in the legislative elections, the NPP won 49 seats in the house of representatives and 21 seats in the senate. Taylor was duly inaugurated as president on 2 August. He subsequently appointed a cabinet (which retained some members of the transitional administration), subject to the approval of the senate. A nine-member national security council was established to ensure the maintenance of civil order.

Economy

GILL TUDOR

Based on an earlier article by CHRISTOPHER CLAPHAM

The Liberian economy had been in decline for at least a decade before the outbreak of the civil war, which has destroyed most of the country's productive resources. During 1985–89, according to UN estimates, Liberia's gross domestic product (GDP) increased by an annual average of 1.5% in real terms, compared with an annual average decline of 1.5% in 1980–85. In 1990–92 GDP declined by an annual average of 12.3%. According to government figures, GDP was estimated at US $1,182.8m in 1989. As a result of the conflict, credible data have become extremely scarce; in 1997 the World Bank could provide only the broad estimate that annual GDP per head was in the 'low-income' category of $765 or less.

Following the outbreak of civil war in December 1989, considerable damage was done to Liberia's economic infrastructure, most foreign nationals left the country, and about 80% of the Liberian population became refugees or were internally displaced. GDP was estimated to have declined, in real terms, by 9% in 1990, and by 10% in 1991. In early 1992, some economic activity resumed under the aegis of the National Patriotic Reconstruction Assembly (NPRA), an alternative administration formed by Charles Taylor, whose forces, the National Patriotic Front of Liberia (NPFL), controlled the greater part of Liberian territory; the NPRA, rather than the interim government based in Monrovia, received taxes and export duties from timber, rubber and mining operations. Following the peace agreement that was signed in July 1993 and the subsequent installation of the Liberian National Transitional Government (LNTG, see Recent History), Liberia benefited from the resumption of official exports of rubber and timber to increase foreign exchange revenue. Continuing factional violence proved an impediment to economic reconstruction, however, and most of the remaining economic infrastructure in the capital was destroyed, following the resumption of fighting in April 1996.

AGRICULTURE, FORESTRY AND FISHING

Agriculture (including forestry and fishing) contributed 36.7% of the country's GDP in 1989, with rubber, coffee and cocoa constituting the main cash crops. The principal food crops are rice and cassava (manioc); with palm oil and some fish or meat, these form the basis of the national diet. Other crops, such as yams, eddoes, sweet potatoes, okra and groundnuts, and fruit such as plantains, oranges, mangoes, avocados or grapefruits are of secondary or local importance. However, the civil conflict particularly affected rural areas, prompting much of the population traditionally employed in the sector to take refuge in neighbouring states. Agricultural production, according to the FAO, increased by an annual average of 1.4% in 1985–89, but declined in 1989–95, by an annual average of 9.6%. About 70.1% of the official labour force were employed in the sector in 1995.

In 1988 imports of rice amounted to US $27.9m. (equivalent to 10.2% of the total cost of imports). Following the outbreak of war, production of paddy rice was estimated to have declined from 290,000 tons in 1989 to 50,000 tons in 1994, and much of the population became dependent on relief grain. Nimba County and Lofa County were particularly badly affected, and distribution of relief was impeded by looting by members of the armed factions. Food shortages were also reported in Monrovia, where the population had increased considerably, owing to the influx of refugees from country areas. The installation of new transitional authorities in September 1995 allowed relief agencies to open feeding centres. Relief operations were, however, severely disrupted by the resumption of fighting in April 1996, prompting foreign non-governmental organizations to make an unprecedented joint declaration that they would provide only minimum relief services until faction leaders showed greater commitment to security and freedom of movement. Nevertheless, the FAO estimated that rice production increased to some 94,450 tons in 1996, owing, in part, to improved security in major rice-growing areas such as Nimba and Bong Counties. The FAO said cassava production also rose in 1996, to an estimated 213,260 tons, although this still represented only about half of pre-war output.

In 1983 the Firestone Plantations Co, formerly Liberia's largest private-sector employer, closed the smaller of its two rubber plantations, at Cavalla in Maryland County. It continued to operate the huge Harbel plantation of more than 30,000 ha until 1988, when it sold its Liberian interests to the Japanese tyre company, Bridgestone, although Firestone continued to be responsible for local management. With continued weakness in the world rubber market, all of the Liberian companies found it difficult to compete with South-East Asian producers, and the level of production stagnated. Output in 1985, which earned US $77m. and accounted for 18% of Liberia's exports, represented only 2% of world production. All of the major rubber companies incurred financial losses on their Liberian operations in the 1980s, while many of the small Liberian-owned farms were forced out of production. The war resulted in a severe disruption of exports, and rubber production was estimated to have declined from 106,000 metric tons in 1989 to 14,000 tons in 1996 (according to the International Rubber Study Group). Firestone resumed operations at Harbel in February 1992 (following an agreement with the NPRA), but these were interrupted by the capture of Harbel and Buchanan by ECOMOG forces in early 1993 (see Recent History). Later that year Buchanan was officially reopened to shipping, and exports of rubber subsequently resumed under the aegis of the LNTG. Between June 1994 and January 1995 the government received an estimated $1m. in taxes from rubber plantation owners. In May 1995 a ban on rubber exports was imposed (supposedly in order to determine the legal ownership of the rubber), but was lifted later that year.

Coffee production is centred in northern Liberia, between Voinjama and Kolahun, where mainly *Coffea robusta* is cultivated. Prior to the outbreak of civil conflict, production remained fairly stable, totalling 8,000–10,000 metric tons per year, of which about one-half was consumed locally. The total had fallen to 3,000 tons by 1995, according to FAO estimates. Cocoa has been introduced into Maryland County from Equatorial Guinea, but an attempt to develop a cocoa plantation near Ganta ended in failure. Production during the civil conflict has declined to negligible levels.

Experiments with tobacco in Nimba County were initially promising. However, owing to increasing difficulties, they were practically discontinued and the big tobacco-drying sheds were dismantled. Problems also arose with the Liberia Sugar Corpn plantation at Barrake in Maryland County. By 1980 an area of 600 ha had been cultivated with sugar cane, but the original Taiwanese management withdrew after Liberia recognized the People's Republic of China. In January 1983 Chinese advisers arrived to assist in the management and rehabilitation of the plantation. By 1987, however, the plantation was in need of further rehabilitation, and Cuba agreed to provide the necessary assistance.

Liberia possesses substantial forest reserves; a national forest inventory made from 1960 to 1967 indicated that there was an average timber potential of 10,000–15,000 cu metres per sq km on a closed forest area of 2.5m. ha, and that 1 sq km contained an average number of 15,000–20,000 trees. From the mid-1960s there was a great increase in timber production, and in 1980 about 450,000 cu m of logs, with a value of US $72.5m., were exported. Reafforestation in Liberia began in 1971 and was centralized later on at the independent Forestry Development Authority (FDA), created in 1974 to provide for more effective forest management and improved training and conservation practices. In the mid-1970s a large sawmill and a plywood mill near Greenville began production. Exports declined in the early 1980s, owing to the exhaustion of accessible timber, but recovered to reach 787,000 cu. m in 1988. Further depletion took place after 1990, as a result of the export of timber to support NPFL operations. It was estimated that timber exports from areas under the control of the warring factions averaged $53m. per year in 1990–94.

Another important forest product is palm nuts, from which, according to FAO estimates, some 38,000 metric tons of palm oil were produced in 1995. In addition to some 1,620 ha of smaller plantations (mainly in the Kakata area), there is a large estate at New Cess, near Buchanan in Grand Bassa County, with some 2,940 ha planted; before the war it was operated by the Liberia Industrial Corpn (LIBINC). Another large estate of some 1,860 ha at Wangakor, near Robertsport in Grand Cape Mount County, belonging to the Liberian-owned West African Agricultural Corpn (WAAC) started production in 1972. In south-eastern Liberia the Liberian Palm Products Corpn (LPPC), a subsidiary of the Liberian Produce Marketing Co (LPMC), had been developing two larger programmes at Buto, near Juarzon in Sinoe County (3,040 ha), and at Dube in Grand Gedeh County (4,050 ha), with technical assistance from SODEPALM of Côte d'Ivoire. An agreement to establish a palm oil factory for the Buto project, financed by the Belgian government and a vegetable oil processing firm, was signed in March 1984, and aid of US $3.36m. for various palm oil projects was granted by the European Development Fund in 1985. A palm kernel oil mill was constructed by the LPMC, and in 1987 a French company, Finex International, agreed to construct Liberia's first palm oil refinery and to assume the management of the National Palm Oil Corpn for five years, in an attempt to reorganize and rehabilitate the sector.

FAO estimates indicate that in 1995 there were some 210,000 sheep, 220,000 goats, 120,000 pigs and 36,000 head of cattle. In the same year, the FAO estimated that Liberia produced some 17,000 tons of meat.

Fish production increased from 1,180 metric tons in 1960 to 18,731 tons in 1987, but by 1995, according to FAO estimates, it had fallen to 7,700 tons (including a catch of 4,000 tons in inland waters).

MINING

Since the opening of the Bomi Hills iron ore mine by the Liberia Mining Co (LMC) in 1951, the mining sector has become increasingly important to the Liberian economy, although by 1980 it employed only 5.1% of the labour force. In 1989 mining contributed 10.9% of GDP. Discoveries of diamonds in the lower Lofa river area in 1957 resulted in an influx of thousands of plantation workers to Weasua and other places in the Gola forest. The value of diamond exports achieved a record US $49.4m. in 1973, when 812,000 carats were exported. By the mid-1980s, however, exports were averaging about 200,000 carats annually; much of this volume has been attributed to stones smuggled from adjoining countries and attracted to Liberia by its currency link with the US dollar. In 1988 diamonds accounted for only $8.8m. (2.2%) of total exports. In 1992, according to data from the US Bureau of Mines, production of industrial diamonds totalled 90,000 carats, while production of gem diamonds amounted to 60,000 carats.

Gold-mining is focused on the Tchien area, where 50 of the 67 mining licences were granted in 1976. An extensive gold mining concession was awarded to the Liberia Gold and Diamond Corpn. Gold production increased from 359 kg in 1982, to 700 kg in 1989, but declined slightly, to 600 kg, in 1991.

The diamond and gold deposits provided a significant source of income for the various armed factions which fought for control of the principal areas of production. Diamond exports were estimated to average US $300m. per year in 1990–94, and gold exports $1m. per year.

There have been several other mineral discoveries, notably of bauxite, copper, columbite-tantalite, corundum, lead, manganese, tin and zinc. Of economic significance are the deposits of barite in the Gibi range near Kakata, and kyanite reserves. The discovery of deposits of uranium in Bong and Lofa Counties was announced in July 1981. In 1981, Kantana Resources of Canada signed a production-sharing agreement with the Liberian government for petroleum exploration in the coastal area between Robertsfield and Grand Bassa County. Further exploration agreements were signed with Amoco in 1983, and with the Henry Resources Corpn in 1985. As a result of the civil conflict, however, all exploration has been suspended.

Iron ore mining has been the principal extraction industry of Liberia since 1961, when, in terms of value, iron ore replaced rubber as the leading export commodity. Liberia soon became one of the world's main exporters of iron ore. In the 1980s, however, the reduction in international demand for iron ore severely depressed production and export earnings; in 1989 it accounted for 51% of total export earnings, compared with 62.1% in 1981. The National Iron Ore Co (NIOC) mine, which is 85% Liberian-owned, was opened on the Mano river in Grand Cape Mount County, in 1961. Liberia's largest deposits of iron ore in Nimba County—probably more than 1,000m. metric tons, including at least 235m. tons of high-grade ore of 65%–70% iron content—were exploited by the Liberian-American-Swedish Minerals Co (LAMCO) from 1963. With investments of more than US $300m., covering the construction of Africa's first pelletizing plant at Buchanan (opened in 1968), a new port and a 274-km railway, the Nimba project comprised one of the largest private enterprises in Africa (see Economy of Guinea). Its main shareholders were the Grängesberg Co of Sweden, together with five other Swedish companies, and the US Bethlehem Steel Corpn (25%). Owing to the world recession, LAMCO's production declined sharply in the 1980s, from over 10m. tons in 1981 to 2m. tons in 1989. LAMCO ceased production in July 1989, and in September was transferred to a government-owned holding company, Liberian Mining Co (LIMINCO), which reached agreement with the British-based African Mining Consortium (AMC) to assume control of operations at Yekepa. The civil conflict in the area started two months later, and mining operations were suspended. The fourth of Liberia's open-cast mines, in the Bong range north of Kakata, was opened in 1965 by the Bong Mining Co (70% Federal German, 25% Italian) on behalf of the German-Liberian Mining Co (DELIMCO), of which the Liberian government held a 50% interest. Operations were suspended in June 1990, and the site has been devastated by fighting and looting. According to UN estimates, production of iron ore fell dramatically from 12.9m tons in 1988 to 1.7m. tons in 1992, as a result of the civil conflict. The country's total iron ore earnings were estimated to average $41m. per year in 1990–93.

In early 1997 the transitional government granted the South African Company, Amalia Gold, exclusive rights to explore and develop Liberia's mineral resources through its 67%-owned Holistic Resources. At this time the country was estimated to have about 2,600m. tons of proven iron ore reserves, with probable resources of an additional 2,000m. tons. Southern Liberia, where rebel activity prevented recent exploration, was expected to yield significant reserves of gold and diamonds.

INDUSTRY

Companies such as Firestone and LAMCO assisted in the development of Liberia's technical and social infrastructure by constructing roads, ports, airfields, schools and hospitals. Their contribution to economic development in general was nevertheless limited, as few secondary industries based on iron ore or rubber were established. Small enterprises predominate in the manufacturing sector, mainly construction firms, saw mills, repair shops, and tailors' shops; over 80% have less than 10 employees. Many enterprises were seriously affected by the depressed state of the economy in the 1980s. The few larger plants with over 50 employees included the rubber factories at the concession sites and the beverage industry, represented by a Coca-Cola and other bottling plants and by a brewery. Most manufacturing enterprises suspended activity during the civil conflict, especially those on the outskirts of Monrovia.

The principal Liberian-owned company was the Mesurado Group, which, in addition to its fishing interests, manufactures detergents, soap, industrial gases and animal foods. In 1964 the Industrial Park near Paynesville was created by the Liberian Development Co on behalf of the Liberian government, initially comprising a shoe factory and a metallo-plastics firm. A cement factory was constructed in 1968 in Monrovia by the Lebanese-owned Liberian Cement Corpn (LCC), and in the same year a petroleum refinery with an annual capacity of 650,000 tons was constructed by the Liberian Petroleum Refining Corpn (LPRC). The refinery had, however, ceased operations by 1982, and, although the LPRC leased storage facilities to other corporations, by 1995 it lacked the credit capacity to import on its own account. A steel rolling mill, using scrap metal from ships broken in Liberia, was constructed by Hong Kong shipping interests and began operations in 1988. Other small industrial enterprises include oilseed and rice mills, a sugar factory, a rum distillery, and factories producing umbrellas, aluminium parts, batteries, foam rubber, hand tools, candles, detergents, biscuits and confectionery. The import substitution effect, however, remained small because over 95% of the raw materials were imported; only cement, matches and batteries were eliminated from the Liberian import list before the civil conflict. In January 1991 the cost of rehabilitating the LPRC's facilities after war damage was projected at US $7m. The looting which accompanied the renewed fighting of mid-1996 extensively damaged most of Liberia's remaining manufacturing infrastructure.

Prior to the outbreak of civil conflict, the main impediments to industrialization were the restricted interest in investments, the small number of Liberian entrepreneurs, the concentration of industry in the Monrovia region, and the limited size of the domestic market. In an attempt to overcome the domestic market handicap, the government established an industrial free zone area as an expansion of the Monrovia 'free port', with the assistance of the UN Industrial Development Organization, althouth the civil conflict subsequently prevented its development. It was hoped that the industrial free zone would accommodate 50 factories with direct contacts in the world market and create 10,000 new jobs. The restricted significance of the manufacturing sector in the Liberian economy was indicated by its contribution of 7.3% to the country's GDP in 1989, and by the size of its work-force, which represented about 1.2% of the working population in 1980.

TRANSPORT, POWER AND TELECOMMUNICATIONS

Liberia's road network is inadequate and mostly in very poor repair. In 1995 the road network totalled an estimated 10,300 km, of which about 628 km were paved. Agreements to reconstruct the Gbarnga–Voinjama and Ganta–Harper highways were announced in 1988, but the war has prevented the work from proceeding. A main road between Monrovia and Freetown, completed in 1988, reduced the distance between the two capitals from 1,014 to 544 km. Another major road links Monrovia to Ganta in Nimba County. The principal roads in Liberia were closed for most of the civil conflict (apart from a partial reopening in 1992), and free movement was prevented by roadblocks installed by the various armed factions. In early 1997, however, most of the principal roads were reopened under the disarmament process.

The railways from Monrovia to Mano River via Bomi Hills (145 track-km), from Monrovia to the Bong Mine (78 track-km) and from Buchanan to Nimba (267 track-km) were constructed for the transport of iron ore. The latter railway, owned by LAMCO, was also utilized for the transport of logs and rubber and for the Guinea transit trade. A passenger line linked Buchanan to Yekepa prior to the civil conflict.

In January 1996 the Liberian-registered merchant fleet comprised 1,584 vessels, with a total displacement of about 59.3m. gross registered tons (grt). Although it remained the second largest national fleet in the world in terms of tonnage, it had decreased from 81.5m. grt in 1982, reflecting the decline in the number of oil tankers, competition from other 'open registry' states, and growing international opposition to 'open registry' shipping. Liberia's principal ports are Monrovia Free Port, Buchanan, Greenville and Harper. The EC (European Community, now the European Union—EU) has contributed aid for the development of Harper port. In 1992 the resumption of armed conflict in the region of Monrovia resulted in the suspension of most shipping activity. It subsequently resumed, but activities at all the ports remained dependent on developments in the fighting. Monrovia Free Port was again closed to commercial shipping during the renewed conflict in April–May 1996. The Danish shipping company, Maersk, resumed direct services to Monrovia in late 1996, followed by the British-based OT Africa Lines.

Liberia's principal airports before the civil war were Roberts Field International Airport, at Harbel, 56 km east of Monrovia, and the smaller James Spriggs Payne Airport, at Monrovia. International air traffic reached 52,954 passengers arriving and 55,541 departing in 1985, as compared with 24,724 arriving and 28,281 departing in 1970. During the same period the quantities of cargo loaded and unloaded increased from 242 to 1,247 tons and from 1,142 to 1,624 tons respectively. In 1990 the civil conflict in Monrovia resulted in severe damage to Roberts Field International Airport, which has not reopened to civilian traffic, but was partly rehabilitated, prior to an airlift of ECOMOG reinforcements in February 1997. Air services to James Spriggs Payne Airport were maintained by a variety of airlines, although most were suspended during the fighting in Monrovia in 1992. The airport was damaged, but was reopened in June 1996.

Public power production rose from 328.8m. kWh in 1972 to 904m. kWh in 1985, but dependence on hydroelectric power, especially from the Mt Coffee plant, resulted in shortages of electricity during the dry season. Power production declined to 565m. kWh in 1990, and to 450m. kWh in 1991; in December 1990 the Mt Coffee dam was reported to have been completely destroyed. Mains electricity supplies have been erratic or non-existent during the civil conflict.

PUBLIC FINANCE

A substantial rate of growth in government revenues between 1945–81 failed to keep pace with increased levels of government spending, which, especially with the decline in the growth rate of revenue during the recession of the late 1970s, led to heavy budgetary deficits. Following the 1980 coup, the Doe government inherited a foreign debt of US $800m. and a budgetary deficit of $71m. Increased domestic expectations after the coup of April 1980, together with a decline in foreign business confidence and the weakness of the international iron ore market, placed further strains on the economy. In addition, private-sector liquidity fell sharply, as both local and foreign investors moved their convertible assets abroad. Such disinvestment has continued. Government spending on public order and defence increased from $21m. to $52m. between 1979 and 1981, and civil service salaries were also raised. The reliability of the budgets was in doubt, with extra-budgetary spending reportedly being about 25% of the level of total budget expenditure in 1984 and 1985. Drastic attempts to reduce government spending culminated in a reduction of 25% in the wages of all government employees (except the armed forces) from December 1985. In 1988 the fiscal year was changed to correspond to the calendar year. An overall budgetary deficit of L $91.9m. (equivalent to 7.8% of GDP) was recorded in 1988. In 1991–93 the national budget related only to the small part of the national territory controlled by the Interim Government of National Unity (IGNU), while the NPRA in the interior imposed levies on the local population and on companies exporting through the port of Buchanan and through Côte d'Ivoire. The IGNU budget for 1992 envisaged expenditure of $167m. and income of $129m. arising largely from 'currency gain', or printing money. The 1993 budget of $274m., which was approved in April of that year, was to be funded by taxes of $79m., of which 44% was to be derived from the merchant shipping registry, and 'currency gain' of $171m. The first LNTG finance minister, Wilson Tarpeh, aimed to improve fiscal restraint. It was announced that actual revenue had increased from L $176m. in 1993 to L $225m. in 1994, while total expenditure had declined from L $331m. to L $285m. Government finances were, however, disrupted by the wholesale looting in April–May 1996, and the National Bank of Liberia remained closed for several months.

Since 1940 the Liberian dollar has been nominally maintained at par with the US dollar, and US banknotes are used in Liberia alongside Liberian coins. Following the military coup in 1980, the value of US dollar notes in circulation declined from $10.5m. in that year to $4.2m. in 1984, while Liberian coins in circulation rose from $11.6m. to $31.3m. over the same period, and to $46.6m. by the end of 1985. This resulted in the creation of a two-tier currency, with a substantial premium for US notes, and rapid inflation in local currency terms. By April 1993 the 'black' market exchange rate was reported to be US $1 = L $20. Liberian coins had begun to be officially withdrawn from circulation in July 1989, being replaced by local bank notes which further emphasized the effective separation of Liberian and US currencies. In early 1992 the government introduced new banknotes, in an attempt to demonetize currency held by the NPRA, and a fluctuating exchange rate emerged between new and old notes, depending on local political control. In October 1995 an attempt by the transitional authorities to impose an exchange rate of US $1=L $25, proved unsuccessful. Exchange rates have also fluctuated widely according to developments in the civil conflict, increasing from about US $1=L $50 in early April 1996 to US $1=L $72 in late May, before stabilizing again, at about US $1=L $55 by early June.

The willingness of the USA to increase its aid, from some US $10m. in 1979 to $64m. in 1985, undoubtedly encouraged the Doe government to maintain Liberia's traditional alignment with Western countries. However, US aid was sharply reduced to $43m. in 1986. In February 1987 a US federal agency reported that $12m. of aid had been diverted to unauthorized use, with a further $16.5m. unaccounted for. The release of further US aid was subsequently made conditional upon Liberian acceptance of 17 US-appointed operational experts to supervise revenue collection and government expenditure. The experts arrived in Liberia in late 1987 but left after only one year of a projected two-year stay, owing to their failure to control unauthorized presidential allocations, or the revenues of public corporations. In 1988 US aid was further reduced, to $31m. From 1990, however, the USA provided emergency assistance to counteract the effects of the civil conflict; in 1990–95 economic aid from the USA amounted to $112m. Net foreign aid to Liberia in 1995 totalled £12.3m., of which $92m. was from multilateral institutions, principally UN agencies and the European Union.

Other major aid donors have been the EC, under the Lomé agreements, and the World Bank. In addition, Liberia received successive stand-by credits from the IMF: for SDR 82.7m. in October 1982, for SDR 55m. in September 1983, and for SDR 42.8m. in November 1984, the last of these being suspended within a week, owing to repayment arrears on a previous loan. Successive debt-rescheduling timetables were agreed in December 1981, December 1983 and December 1984. In January 1986 Liberia was declared ineligible for further drawings on the IMF, and in February 1988 the Fund closed its mission in Monrovia, claiming that the government had not seriously attempted to reform the economy. The World Bank suspended disbursements in February 1986. In March 1990 the IMF declared Liberia a 'non-co-operating' country, and threatened expulsion, owing to the government's failure to pay outstanding arrears; Liberia owed an estimated US $396m. to the IMF and $65m. to the African Development Bank (ADB). An appeal for $13.8m. in emergency aid received virtually no response, although emergency donations totalling $127m. were made between December 1989 and May 1991 by individual governments and private charities. In August 1994 the transitional government resumed negotiations with the IMF after paying arrears of L $1m.; however, the continuing conflict and political confusion prevented further discussions. In October 1995 donors at a UN-backed conference in New York pledged a total of $145.7m. to support the peace process, although the disbursement of funds was delayed and incomplete. Total external debt increased from $437m. in 1978 to $1,439m. in 1986 and to $2,127m. in 1995, with interest payment arrears on long-term public debt rising from $27m. in 1984 to $545m. in 1994; since there were scarcely any new disbursements after 1989, accumulated arrears were virtually the sole source of increasing indebtedness.

ECONOMIC PROSPECTS

Liberia's economic growth since the Second World War was reflected in the increase in overseas trade turnover (imports plus exports) from US $32.2m. in 1950 to $151.8m. in 1960, and to $1,130.5m. in 1980. However, following the recession and the 1980 coup, the economy declined. The value of imports fell from $411.6m. in 1983 to $286.3m. in 1985, reflecting a dramatic decline in local purchasing power. Liberia's economic growth was achieved principally by the export of primary products to the industrial economies, and involved a high level of dependence, firstly on rubber (which accounted for 88.1% of total export value in 1951) and then on iron ore (64% of total export value in 1985). In both cases, prices varied considerably. Exports to neighbouring West African countries remained negligible.

In 1987 Liberia recorded a visible trade surplus of US $63m., although there was a deficit of $118m. on the current account of the balance of payments. In 1988 the principal source of imports (21.2%) was the USA, while the principal market for exports (27.3%) was the Federal Republic of Germany. In 1992, according to World Bank estimates, a trade surplus of $110m. was recorded, moving to a deficit of $50m. in 1993. As a result of the civil conflict official figures have become largely meaningless, since many raw materials and looted goods have been smuggled out of the country. Statistics on Liberia's trading patterns are also distorted by the recording of shipping registrations as imports. Thus, IMF figures indicated that Japan and the Republic of Korea were the principal sources of Liberian imports in 1995, accounting for more than 50% of the total. The principal market for exports in that year was Belgium (as a result of exports of diamonds arriving at the Belgian port, Antwerp, mainly from territory under the control of various armed factions).

The civil war has resulted in considerable destruction, looting and deterioration in the modern sector of the country's economy. The hinterland area from which all the export crops and minerals were extracted remained under the control of the various armed factions, which looted and exported resources, including diamonds, iron ore, timber and rubber. Charitable agencies imported food and medical supplies through Buchanan and other ports, including Monrovia, although the commercial import-export and distribution network had broken down. The subsistence economy was maintained, despite political collapse, while local crops such as cassava to some extent compensated for the shortfall in imported rice. Some limited economic recovery took place from 1992, reinforced in Monrovia by the spending capacity of UN and ECOMOG contingents stationed there, but the renewed fighting and accompanying looting in Monrovia in April–May 1996 extensively damaged much of the capital and again halted most formal economic activity. Future prospects for genuine economic reconstruction, involving the long process of rehabilitating the infrastructure and restoring business confidence, were dependent on the maintenance of civil order in the country following the elections in July 1997.

Statistical Survey

Sources (unless otherwise stated): the former Ministry of Planning and Economic Affairs, POB 9016, Broad Street, Monrovia; tel. 222622.

Area and Population

AREA, POPULATION AND DENSITY

Area (sq km)	97,754*
Population (census results)	
1 February 1974	
Males	759,109
Females	744,259
Total	1,503,368
1–14 February 1984	2,101,628
Population (official estimates at mid-year)	
1993	2,640,062
1994	2,699,888
1995	2,760,000
Density (per sq km) at mid-1995	28.2

* 37,743 sq miles.

ADMINISTRATIVE DIVISIONS (population at 1984 census)

Counties:		Nimba	313,050
Bomi	66,420	Rivercess	37,849
Bong	255,813	Sinoe	64,147
Grand Bassa	159,648	Territories:	
Grand Cape Mount	79,322	Gibi	66,802
Grand Gedeh	102,810	Kru Coast	35,267
Lofa	247,641	Marshall	31,190
Maryland	85,267	Sasstown	11,524
Montserrado	544,878	**Total**	2,101,628

PRINCIPAL TOWN

Monrovia (capital), population 421,058 at 1984 census.

BIRTHS AND DEATHS (UN estimates, annual averages)

	1980–85	1985–90	1990–95
Birth rate (per 1,000)	47.2	47.3	47.3
Death rate (per 1,000)	16.7	15.8	14.2

Expectation of life (UN estimates, years at birth, 1990–95): 55.4 (males 54.0; females 57.0).

Source: UN, *World Population Prospects: The 1994 Revision*.

ECONOMICALLY ACTIVE POPULATION

	1978	1979	1980
Agriculture, forestry, hunting and fishing	355,467	366,834	392,926
Mining	25,374	26,184	28,047
Manufacturing	6,427	6,631	7,102
Construction	4,701	4,852	5,198
Electricity, gas and water	245	246	263
Commerce	18,668	19,266	20,636
Transport and communications	7,314	7,549	8,086
Services	49,567	51,154	54,783
Others	28,555	29,477	31,571
Total	496,318	512,193	548,615

Mid-1995 (estimates in '000): Agriculture, etc. 845; Total 1,206 (Source: FAO, *Production Yearbook*).

Agriculture

PRINCIPAL CROPS ('000 metric tons)

	1993	1994	1995
Rice (paddy)	65*	50*	50†
Sweet potatoes†	21	23	23
Cassava (Manioc)†	425	450	450
Yams†	25	30	30
Taro (Coco yam)†	18	20	20
Coconuts†	7	7	7
Palm kernels†	8	9	9
Vegetables and melons†	71	76	76
Sugar cane†	234	234	234
Oranges†	7	7	7
Pineapples†	7	7	7
Bananas†	81	82	82
Plantains†	40	45	45
Natural rubber (dry weight)†	45	31	31

* Unofficial figure. † FAO estimate(s).

Source: FAO, *Production Yearbook*.

LIVESTOCK (FAO estimates, '000 head, year ending September)

	1993	1994	1995
Cattle	36	36	36
Pigs	120	120	120
Sheep	210	210	210
Goats	220	220	220

Poultry (FAO estimates, million): 4 in 1993; 4 in 1994; 4 in 1995.

Source: FAO, *Production Yearbook*.

LIVESTOCK PRODUCTS (FAO estimates, metric tons)

	1993	1994	1995
Pig meat	4,000	4,000	4,000
Poultry meat	5,000	5,000	5,000
Other meat	8,000	8,000	8,000
Cows' milk	1,000	1,000	1,000
Hen eggs	3,600	3,600	3,600

Source; FAO, *Production Yearbook*.

Forestry

ROUNDWOOD REMOVALS ('000 cubic metres, excluding bark)

	1992	1993	1994†
Sawlogs, veneer logs and logs for sleepers	890	800*	800
Other industrial wood†	169	175	181
Fuel wood†	5,040	5,118	5,202
Total	6,099	6,093	6,183

* Unofficial figure.
† FAO estimates.

Source: FAO, *Yearbook of Forest Products*.

SAWNWOOD PRODUCTION
('000 cubic metres, including railway sleepers)

	1992	1993	1994
Total	125*	90*	90†

* Unofficial figure.
Source: FAO, *Yearbook of Forest Products*.

Fishing

('000 metric tons, live weight)

	1993	1994	1995*
Inland waters	4.0	4.0	4.0
Atlantic Ocean	3.8	3.7	3.7
Total catch	7.8	7.7	7.7

* FAO estimates.
Source: FAO, *Yearbook of Fishery Statistics*.

Mining

	1990	1991	1992
Iron ore ('000 metric tons)*	2,490	804	1,142
Industrial diamonds ('000 carats)	60	60	90
Gem diamonds ('000 carats)†	40	40	60
Gold (kilograms)*†	600	600	700

* Figures refer to the metal content of ores.
† Data from the US Bureau of Mines.
Source: UN, *Industrial Commodity Statistics Yearbook*.

Industry

SELECTED PRODUCTS
('000 metric tons, unless otherwise indicated)

	1988	1989	1990
Palm oil*	35	35	30
Beer ('000 hectolitres)	158	n.a.	n.a.
Soft drinks ('000 hectolitres)	171	n.a.	n.a.
Cigarettes (million)†	22	22	22
Cement	130	85‡	50
Electric energy (million kWh)	834	818	565

* FAO estimates.
† Data from the US Department of Agriculture.
‡ Provisional or estimated figure.

Cigarettes (million): 22 in 1991; 22 in 1992.

Electric energy (million kWh): 460 in 1992; 480 in 1993; 485 in 1994.

Source: mainly UN, *Industrial Commodity Statistics Yearbook*.

Palm Oil (FAO estimates, '000 metric tons): 30 in 1993; 38 in 1994; 38 in 1995 (Source: FAO, *Production Yearbook*).

Finance

CURRENCY AND EXCHANGE RATES

Monetary Units
100 cents = 1 Liberian dollar (L $).

Sterling and Dollar Equivalents (31 March 1997)
£1 sterling = L $1.642;
US $1 = L $1.000;
L $100 = £60.90 = US $100.00.

Exchange Rate
Since 1940 the Liberian dollar has been officially at par with the US dollar.

BUDGET (public sector accounts, L $ million, year ending 30 June)

Revenue*	1985/86	1986/87	1988†
Tax revenue	172.7	172.4	203.8
Taxes on income and profits	71.7	61.5	72.1
Taxes on property	1.1	2.3	2.6
Taxes on domestic transactions	44.9	57.7	53.3
Taxes on foreign trade	51.6	48.6	73.6
Other taxes	3.4	2.3	2.2
Other current revenue	7.7	8.0	8.9
Capital revenue	0.3	0.2	0.1
Total	180.7	180.6	212.8

Expenditure‡	1985/86	1986/87	1988†
General public services	51.3	51.3	67.8
Defence	21.0	23.5	26.5
Education	38.8	42.8	31.3
Health	15.6	18.7	14.5
Social security and welfare	2.3	2.5	2.9
Housing and community amenities	2.7	2.6	2.1
Recreational, cultural and religious affairs and services	7.2	6.4	4.2
Economic affairs and services	94.4	72.8	79.8
Fuel and energy	7.3	4.5	17.4
Agriculture, forestry, fishing and hunting	21.0	23.6	14.1
Mining, manufacturing and construction	13.1	6.4	2.1
Transport and communications	19.8	18.2	15.0
Other purposes	40.6	42.9	54.3
Total	273.9	263.5	283.4
Current§	205.3	226.1	244.7
Capital	68.6	37.4	38.7

* Excluding grants received from abroad (L $ million): 25.0 (current 17.0, capital 8.0) in 1985/86; 18.0 (current 12.2, capital 5.8) in 1986/87.
† Beginning in 1988, the fiscal year was changed to coincide with the calendar year.
‡ Excluding net lending (L $ million): 22.7 in 1985/86; 19.0 in 1986/87; 21.3 in 1988.
§ Including interest payments (L $ million): 40.6 in 1985/86; 42.9 in 1986/87; 41.2 in 1988.
Source: IMF, *Government Finance Statistics Yearbook*.

INTERNATIONAL RESERVES (US $ million at 31 December)

	1992	1993	1994
Reserve position in IMF	0.04	0.04	0.04
Foreign exchange	0.94	2.33	5.03
Total	0.98	2.37	5.07

Source: IMF, *International Financial Statistics*.

MONEY SUPPLY (L $ million at 31 December)

	1992	1993	1994
Currency outside banks*	154.94	274.11	302.95
Demand deposits at commercial banks	111.12	149.95	154.32

* Figures refer only to amounts of Liberian coin in circulation. US notes and coin also circulate, but the amount of these in private holdings is unknown. The amount of Liberian coin in circulation is small in comparison to US currency.
Source: IMF, *International Financial Statistics*.

COST OF LIVING
(Consumer Price Index for Monrovia; base: 1980 = 100)

	1986	1987	1988
Food	107.8	108.0	128.8
Fuel and light	127.2	127.4	128.1
Clothing	124.9	144.8	157.5
Rent	103.8	104.1	105.1
All items (incl. others)	123.2	129.4	141.8

1989: Food 141.2 (average for January–October); All items 150.2.
1990 (January–June): Food 160.7; All items 162.4.

Source: ILO, *Yearbook of Labour Statistics*.

NATIONAL ACCOUNTS (L $ million at current prices)

Expenditure on the Gross Domestic Product

	1987	1988	1989
Government final consumption expenditure	143.9	136.3	141.6
Private final consumption expenditure	713.9	733.3	656.8
Increase in stocks*	7.0	3.5	4.0
Gross fixed capital formation	120.4	115.3	96.8
Statistical discrepancy	22.9	39.1	48.2
Total domestic expenditure	1,008.1	1,027.5	947.4
Exports of goods and services	438.2	452.3	521.4
Less Imports of goods and services	356.8	321.5	275.2
GDP in purchasers' values	1,089.5	1,158.3	1,193.6
GDP at constant 1981 prices	1,015.0	1,043.7	1,072.8

* Figures refer only to stocks of iron ore and rubber.

Gross Domestic Product by Economic Activity

	1987	1988	1989
Agriculture, hunting, forestry and fishing	381.8	412.0	410.7
Mining and quarrying	105.0	115.0	122.3
Manufacturing	73.1	80.4	81.6
Electricity, gas and water	19.0	18.8	19.0
Construction	32.7	28.8	26.3
Trade, restaurants and hotels	60.1	64.2	63.3
Transport, storage and communications	75.3	79.1	79.1
Finance, insurance, real estate and business services	119.2	136.1	141.8
Government services	108.5	109.7	139.4
Other community, social and personal services	34.4	35.5	35.5
Sub-total	1,009.1	1,079.6	1,119.0
Less Imputed bank service charge	18.3	27.1	36.5
GDP at factor cost	990.8	1,052.5	1,082.5
Indirect taxes, *less* subsidies	99.0	105.8	111.3
GDP in purchasers' values	1,089.5	1,158.3	1,193.6

Source: UN, *National Accounts Statistics*.

BALANCE OF PAYMENTS (US $ million)

	1985	1986	1987
Exports of goods f.o.b.	430.4	407.9	374.9
Imports of goods f.o.b.	–263.8	–258.8	–311.7
Trade balance	166.6	149.1	63.2
Exports of services	34.6	56.9	52.5
Imports of services	–80.2	–80.5	–74.2
Balance on goods and services	121.0	125.5	41.5
Other income received	3.7	2.1	5.2
Other income paid	–131.8	–183.3	–188.3
Balance on goods, services and income	–7.1	–55.7	–141.6
Current transfers received	130.0	97.9	50.0
Current transfers paid	–67.6	–59.9	–53.5
Current balance	55.3	–17.7	–145.1
Direct investment from abroad	–16.2	–16.5	38.5
Portfolio investment assets	4.4	5.6	—
Other investment assets	–9.3	–7.1	4.3
Other investment liabilities	–128.9	–199.1	–228.1
Net errors and omissions	–108.7	–73.4	30.3
Overall balance	–203.4	–294.0	–300.1

Source: IMF, *International Financial Statistics*.

External Trade

PRINCIPAL COMMODITIES (US $ million)

Imports c.i.f.	1986	1987	1988
Food and live animals	53.6	58.7	47.3
Rice	12.1	17.7	27.9
Mineral fuels, lubricants, etc.	52.9	69.8	55.3
Refined petroleum products	52.5	67.1	n.a.
Motor spirit and other light fuels	12.1	14.2	n.a.
Chemicals and related products	26.3	22.1	15.3
Basic manufactures	36.0	55.3	48.0
Machinery and transport equipment	59.1	73.5	82.3
Miscellaneous manufactured articles	18.1	14.2	15.4
Total (incl. others)	259.0	307.6	272.3

Exports f.o.b.	1986	1987	1988
Coffee and substitutes	16.3	9.0	5.6
Cocoa	9.0	5.9	6.3
Natural rubber and gums	70.9	89.4	110.2
Wood in the rough or roughly squared	33.1	35.5	32.0
Iron ore and concentrates	248.4	218.0	219.7
Diamonds	6.6	11.0	8.8
Total (incl. others)	408.4	382.2	396.3

Source: UN, *International Trade Statistics Yearbook*.

1989 (L $ million): Total exports f.o.b. 461.16 (iron ore 235.05, rubber 119.93, logs 91.98). Source: National Bank of Liberia, *Quarterly Statistical Bulletin*.

PRINCIPAL TRADING PARTNERS (US $ million)*

Imports c.i.f.	1986	1987	1988
Belgium/Luxembourg	8.5	11.2	15.0
China, People's Repub.	7.1	14.7	4.8
Denmark	10.6	7.6	5.9
France (incl. Monaco)	6.5	6.4	4.7
Germany, Fed. Repub.	32.7	52.3	39.5
Italy	2.5	2.2	7.3
Japan	20.1	15.0	12.0
Netherlands	20.6	26.8	14.4
Spain	2.5	6.6	3.1
Sweden	2.4	0.6	4.6
United Kingdom	24.2	18.4	12.7
USA	42.5	58.0	57.7
Total (incl. others)	259.0	307.6	272.3

Exports f.o.b.	1986	1987	1988
Belgium/Luxembourg	29.2	23.2	28.2
France (incl. Monaco)	33.1	33.2	33.2
Germany, Fed. Repub.	114.5	109.2	108.1
Italy	70.3	63.4	63.2
Japan	4.9	1.0	4.8
Netherlands	14.4	11.5	10.5
Spain	16.4	17.8	13.4
United Kingdom	7.2	8.8	6.3
USA	93.2	73.9	74.6
Total (incl. others)	408.4	382.2	396.3

* Imports by country of origin; exports by country of last consignment.

Source: UN, *International Trade Statistics Yearbook.*

Transport

RAILWAYS (estimated traffic)

	1991	1992	1993
Passenger-km (million)	406	417	421
Freight ton-km (million)	200	200	200

Source: UN Economic Commission for Africa, *African Statistical Yearbook.*

ROAD TRAFFIC (estimates, vehicles in use at 31 December)

	1993	1994	1995
Passenger cars	13,400	13,600	10,300
Goods vehicles	22,000	25,900	28,300
Total	35,400	39,500	38,600

Source: International Road Federation, *World Road Statistics.*

SHIPPING

Merchant Fleet (registered at 31 December)

	1994	1995	1996
Number of vessels	1,621	1,666	1,684
Displacement ('000 gross registered tons)	57,647.7	59,800.7	59,988.9

Source: Lloyd's Register of Shipping.

International Sea-borne Freight Traffic (estimates, '000 metric tons)

	1991	1992	1993
Goods loaded	16,706	17,338	21,653
Goods unloaded	1,570	1,597	1,608

Source: UN Economic Commission for Africa, *African Statistical Yearbook.*

CIVIL AVIATION (traffic on scheduled services)

	1990	1991	1992
Passengers carried ('000)	32	32	32
Passenger-km (million)	7	7	7
Total ton-km (million)	1	1	1

Source: UN, *Statistical Yearbook.*

Communications Media

	1992	1993	1994
Radio receivers ('000 in use)	622	645	670
Television receivers ('000 in use)	51	54	55
Telephones ('000 main lines in use)	5	5	n.a.
Daily newspapers			
Number	8	n.a.	8
Average circulation ('000 copies, estimates)	35	n.a.	35

Sources: UNESCO, *Statistical Yearbook*; UN, *Statistical Yearbook.*

Education

	1983	1984	1985
Schools	1,284	1,830	1,691
Teachers	7,202	9,817	9,856
Students	245,673	275,243	260,560

1986: Students 250,322.

Source: Ministry of Education, Monrovia.

Primary school pupils (1986): 80,048.

University (1987): 444 teachers; 4,855 students (males 3,698; females 1,157).

Other higher (1987): 28 teachers; 240 students (males 220; females 20).

Source: UNESCO, *Statistical Yearbook.*

Directory

The Constitution

The Constitution, promulgated on 6 January 1986 (and amended in July 1988), provides for the division of state authority into three independent branches: the executive, the legislature and the judiciary. Executive powers are vested in the President, who is Head of State, Head of Government and Commander-in-Chief of the Liberian armed forces, and who is elected by universal adult suffrage for a six-year term (renewable more than once). Legislative power is vested in the bicameral National Assembly, comprising the 26-member Senate and the 64-member House of Representatives. Members of both houses are directly elected by popular vote. The Constitution provides for a multi-party system of government, and incorporates powers to prevent the declaration of a one-party state, the dissolution of the legislature or the suspension of the judiciary. The Constitution may be amended by a two-thirds majority of both houses of the National Assembly.

An Interim President was inaugurated in November 1990, and an Interim Government of National Unity (IGNU) was appointed in Monrovia in January 1991. Under the terms of a peace agreement that was signed in July 1993, the IGNU was replaced by a Council of State, and the existing legislature by a Transitional Legislative Assembly, pending presidential and general elections. Following a further peace agreement (reached in August 1996), presidential and legislative elections took place on 19 July 1997. The elected President was inaugurated on 2 August, and subsequently appointed a new Cabinet.

The Government

HEAD OF STATE

President: CHARLES GHANKAY TAYLOR (took office 2 August 1997).

Vice-President: ENOCH DOGOLEA.

CABINET
(August 1997)

Minister of Agriculture: Dr ROLAND C. MASSAQUOI.

Minister of Commerce and Industry: BANKALE FOFANA.

Minister of Defence: DANIEL CHEA.

Minister of Education: EVELYNE KANDAKAI.

Minister of Finance: ELIAS SALEEBY.

Minister of Foreign Affairs: MONI CAPTAN.

Minister of Health and Social Welfare: FINEBOY DARKINAH.

Minister of Information, Culture and Tourism: JOE MULBAH.

Minister of Internal Affairs: EDWARD SACKOR.

Minister of Justice: PETER BONA JALLAH .

Minister of Labour: THOMAS J. WOEWIYU.

Minister of Lands, Mines and Energy: JENKINS DUNBAR.

Minister of Posts and Telecommunications: MAXWELL KABA.

Minister of Public Works: JOHN RICHARDSON.

Minister of Transport: (vacant).

Minister of Youth and Sports: FRANÇOIS MASSAQUOI.

Minister of State for Presidential Affairs: T. ERNEST EASTMAN.

MINISTRIES

Ministry of Agriculture: Tubman Blvd, POB 9010, Monrovia.

Ministry of Commerce and Industry: Ashmun St, POB 9014, Monrovia.

Ministry of Defence: Benson St, POB 9007, Monrovia.

Ministry of Education: Broad St, POB 1545, Monrovia.

Ministry of Finance: Broad St, POB 9013, Monrovia.

Ministry of Foreign Affairs: Mamba Point, Monrovia.

Ministry of Health and Social Welfare: POB 9004, Sinkor, Monrovia.

Ministry of Information, Culture and Tourism: 110 United Nations Drive, POB 9021, Monrovia.

Ministry of Internal Affairs: cnr Warren and Benson Sts, POB 9008, Monrovia.

Ministry of Justice: Ashmun St, POB 9006, Monrovia.

Ministry of Labour: Mechlin St, POB 9040, Monrovia.

Ministry of Lands, Mines and Energy: Capitol Hill, POB 9024, Monrovia.

Ministry of Planning and Economic Affairs: Broad St, POB 9016, Monrovia.

Ministry of Posts and Telecommunications: Carey St, Monrovia.

Ministry of Presidential Affairs: Executive Mansion, Capitol Hill, Monrovia.

Ministry of Public Works: Lynch St, POB 9011, Monrovia.

Ministry of Transport: Monrovia.

Ministry of Youth and Sports: POB 9040, Sinkor, Monrovia.

President and Legislature

PRESIDENT

A presidential election, which was contested by 13 candidates, took place on 19 July 1997; CHARLES GHANKAY TAYLOR was elected to the presidency, with 75.3% of votes cast.

LEGISLATURE
Senate

General Election, 19 July 1997

	Seats
National Patriotic Party	21
Unity Party	3
All Liberian Coalition Party	2
Total	26

House of Representatives

General Election, 19 July 1997

	Seats
National Patriotic Party	49
Unity Party	7
All Liberian Coalition Party	3
Alliance of Political Parties*	2
United People's Party	2
Liberian People's Party	1
Total	64

* Coalition of the Liberian Action Party and the Liberian Unification Party.

Political Organizations

At the end of January 1997 the armed factions in Liberia officially ceased to exist as military organizations; a number of them were reconstituted as political parties, while long-standing political organizations re-emerged, prior to elections in July of that year.

All Liberian Coalition Party (ALCOP): f. 1997 from elements of the fmr armed faction, the United Liberation Movement of Liberia for Democracy; Leader Alhaji G. V. KROMAH.

Free Democratic Party: Leader FAYAH GBOLLIE.

Liberian Action Party (LAP): f. 1984; Leader CLETUS WOTORSON.

Liberian National Union (LINU): Leader HENRY MONIBA.

Liberian People's Party (LPP): f. 1984 by fmr members of the Movement for Justice in Africa; Leader TOGBA-NAH TIPOTEH.

Liberian Unification Party (LUP): f. 1984; Leader LAVELI SUPUWOOD.

National Democratic Party of Liberia (NDPL): f. 1997 from the fmr armed faction, the Liberia Peace Council; Leader Dr GEORGE E. SAIGBE BOLEY.

National Patriotic Party (NPP): f. 1997 from the fmr armed faction, the National Patriotic Front of Liberia; won the majority of seats in legislative elections in July; Leader CHARLES GHANKAY TAYLOR; Sec.-Gen. CHRISTIAN HERBERT.

National Reformation Party (NRP): Leader MARTIN SHERIF.

People's Progressive Party (PPP): Leader CHEA CHEAPOO.

Reformation Alliance Party (RAP): Leader HENRY BOIMAH FAHNBULLEH.

True Whig Party (TWP): f. 1868; ruling party prior to April 1980 coup; Leader RUDOLPH SHERMAN.

United People's Party (UPP): f. 1984 by fmr mems of the Progressive People's Party, which led opposition prior to April 1980 coup; Leader GABRIEL BACCUS MATTHEWS.

Unity Party (UP): f. 1984.

Diplomatic Representation

EMBASSIES IN LIBERIA

Algeria: Capitol By-Pass, POB 2032, Monrovia; tel. 224311; telex 44475; Chargé d'affaires a.i.: MUHAMMAD AZZEDINE AZZOUZ.

Cameroon: 18th St and Payne Ave, Sinkor, POB 414, Monrovia; tel. 261374; telex 44240; Ambassador: VICTOR E. NDIBA.

Congo, Democratic Republic: Spriggs Payne Airport, Sinkor, POB 1038, Monrovia; tel. 261326; Ambassador: (vacant).

Côte d'Ivoire: Tubman Blvd, Sinkor, POB 126, Monrovia; tel. 261123; telex 44273; Ambassador: CLÉMENT KAUL MELEDJE.

Cuba: 17 Kennedy Ave, Congotown, POB 3579, Monrovia; tel. 262600; Ambassador: M. GAUNEANO CARDOSO TOLEDO.

Egypt: POB 462, Monrovia; tel. 261953; telex 44308; Ambassador: MUHAMMAD SALEH EL-DIN EL-DAOUR.

Germany: Oldest Congotown, POB 34, Monrovia; tel. 261460; telex 44230; Ambassador: Dr JÜRGEN GEHL.

Ghana: cnr 11th St and Gardiner Ave, Sinkor, POB 471, Monrovia; tel. 261477; Ambassador: G. R. NIPAH.

Guinea: Tubman Blvd, Sinkor, POB 461, Monrovia; tel. 261182; Ambassador: (vacant).

Israel: Gardiner Ave, between 11th and 12th Sts, Sinkor, Monrovia; tel. 262861; telex 44415; Ambassador: MOSHE ITAN.

Italy: Mamba Point, POB 255, Monrovia; tel. 224580; telex 44438; Ambassador: Dr. ENRIC'ANGIOLO FERRONI-CARLI.

Korea, Republic: 10th St and Payne Ave, Sinkor, POB 2769, Monrovia; tel. 261532; telex 44241; Ambassador: KIM YONG-JIP.

Lebanon: 12th St, Monrovia; tel. 262537; telex 44208; Ambassador: MANSUR AL-ABDULLAH.

Libya: Monrovia.

Morocco: Tubman Blvd, Congotown, Monrovia; tel. 262767; telex 44540; Chargé d'affaires a.i.: Dr MOULAY ABBES AL-KADIRI.

Nigeria: Tubman Blvd, Sinkor, POB 366, Monrovia; tel. 261093; telex 44278; Ambassador: JOSHUA IROHA.

Poland: cnr 10th St and Gardiner Ave, Sinkor, POB 860, Monrovia; tel. 261113; Chargé d'affaires a.i.: ZBIGNIEW REJMAN.

Romania: 81 Sekou Touré Ave, Sinkor, POB 2598, Monrovia; tel. 261508; Chargé d'affaires a.i.: SILVESTRA ZUGRAV.

Russia: Payne Ave, Sinkor, POB 2010, Monrovia; tel. 261304; Ambassador: VASILI STEPANOVICH BEBKO.

Senegal: Monrovia; Ambassador: MOCTAR TRAORÉ.

Sierra Leone: Tubman Blvd, POB 575, Monrovia; tel. 261301; Ambassador: WILFRED KANU.

Spain: Capitol Hill, POB 275, Monrovia; tel. 221299; telex 44538; Ambassador: MANUEL DE LUNA.

Sweden: POB 335, Monrovia; tel. 261646; telex 44255; Chargé d'affaires a.i.: OVE SVENSSON.

Switzerland: Old Congo Rd, POB 283, Monrovia; tel. 261065; telex 44559; Chargé d'affaires a.i.: CHARLES HALLER.

United Kingdom: Mamba Point, POB 120, Monrovia; tel. 221491; telex 44287.

USA: 111 United Nations Drive, Mamba Point, POB 98, Monrovia; tel. 222994; Chargé d'affaires a.i.: JOHN BOMAN.

Judicial System

In February 1982 the People's Supreme Tribunal (which had been established following the April 1980 coup) was renamed the People's Supreme Court, and its chairman and members became the Chief Justice and Associate Justices of the People's Supreme Court. The judicial system also comprised People's Circuit and Magistrate Courts. The five-member Supreme Court (composed of representatives of the interim Government and of the NPFL) was established in January 1992 to adjudicate in electoral disputes.

Chief Justice of People's Supreme Court: GLORIA SCOTT.

Religion

Liberia is officially a Christian state, although complete religious freedom is guaranteed. Christianity and Islam are the two main religions. There are numerous religious sects, and many Liberians hold traditional beliefs.

CHRISTIANITY

Liberian Council of Churches: 182 Tubman Blvd, POB 2191, Monrovia; tel. 262820; f. 1982; six mems and two assoc. mems; Pres. Bishop ARTHUR F. KULAH; Gen. Sec. IMOGENE M. COLLINS.

The Anglican Communion

The diocese of Liberia forms part of the Church of the Province of West Africa, incorporating the local Protestant Episcopal Church. Anglicanism was established in Liberia in 1836, and the diocese of Liberia was admitted into full membership of the Province in 1982. In 1985 the Church had 125 congregations, 39 clergy, 26 schools and about 20,000 adherents in the country. The Metropolitan of the Province is the Bishop of Koforidua, Ghana.

Bishop of Liberia: Rt Rev. EDWARD NEUFVILLE, POB 10-0277, 1000 Monrovia 10; tel. and fax 224760.

The Roman Catholic Church

Liberia comprises the archdiocese of Monrovia and the dioceses of Cape Palmas and Gbarnga. At 31 December 1995 there were an estimated 96,864 adherents in the country, equivalent to 5.7% of the total population. The Bishops participate in the Interterritorial Catholic Bishops' Conference of the Gambia, Liberia and Sierra Leone (based in Freetown, Sierra Leone).

Archbishop of Monrovia: Most Rev. MICHAEL KPAKALA FRANCIS, Catholic Mission, POB 2078, Monrovia; tel. 221389; telex 44529; fax 226287.

Other Christian Churches

Assemblies of God in Liberia: POB 1297, Monrovia; f. 1908; 14,578 adherents, 287 churches; Gen. Supt JIMMIE K. DUGBE, Sr.

Lutheran Church in Liberia: POB 1046, Monrovia; 25,600 adherents; Pres. Bishop RONALD J. DIGGS.

Providence Baptist Church: cnr Broad and Center Sts, Monrovia; f. 1821; 2,500 adherents, 300 congregations, 6 ministers, 8 schools; Pastor Rev. A. MOMOLUE DIGGS; associated with:

The Liberia Baptist Missionary and Educational Convention, Inc: POB 390, Monrovia; tel. 222661; f. 1880; Pres. Rev. J. K. LEVEE MOULTON; Nat. Vice-Pres. Rev. J. GBANA HALL; Gen. Sec. CHARLES W. BLAKE.

United Methodist Church in Liberia: cnr 12th St and Tubman Blvd, POB 1010, 1000 Monrovia 10; tel. 223343; f. 1833; c. 70,000 adherents, 487 congregations, 450 ministers, 300 lay pastors, 38 schools; Resident Bishop Rev. ARTHUR F. KULAH; Sec. Rev. JULIUS SARWOLO NELSON.

Other active denominations include the National Baptist Mission, the Pentecostal Church, the Presbyterian Church in Liberia, the Prayer Band and the Church of the Lord Aladura.

ISLAM

The total community numbers about 670,000.

National Muslim Council of Liberia: Monrovia; Leader Shaykh KAFUMBA KONNAH.

The Press

NEWSPAPERS

Daily Observer: 117 Broad St, Crown Hill, POB 1858, Monrovia; tel. 223545; f. 1981; independent; 5 a week; Editor-in-Chief STANTON B. PEABODY; circ. 30,000.

Herald: Monrovia; f. 1987; Catholic weekly; Editor RUFUS DARPOH.

The Inquirer: Monrovia; Man. Editor GABRIEL WILLIAMS.

New Times: Monrovia; Man. Editor RUFUS DARPOH; Editor JEFF MUTADA.

Sunday Express: Mamba Point, POB 3029, Monrovia; weekly; Editor JOHN F. SCOTLAND; circ. 5,000.

Sunday People: POB 3366, Monrovia; 2 a week; Editor D. G. PYNE-DRAPER.

PERIODICALS

Daily Listener: POB 35, Monrovia; monthly; Man. CHARLES C. DENNIS; circ. 3,500.

The Eye: POB 4692, Monrovia; daily; Editor H. B. KINBAH.

Journal of Commerce, Industry & Transportation: POB 9041, Monrovia; tel. 222141; telex 44331.

The Kpelle Messenger: Kpelle Literacy Center, Lutheran Church, POB 1046, Monrovia; Kpelle-English; monthly; Editor Rev. JOHN J. MANAWU.

Liberian Star: POB 691, Monrovia; f. 1954; monthly; Editor HENRY B. COLE; circ. 3,500.

Palm: Johnson and Carey Sts, POB 1110, Monrovia; 6 a year; Editor JAMES C. DENNIS.

The People Magazine: Bank of Liberia Bldg, Suite 214, Carey and Warren Sts, POB 3501, Monrovia; tel. 222743; f. 1985; monthly; Editor and Publr CHARLES A. SNETTER.

Plain Talk: POB 2108, Monrovia; daily; Editor-in-Chief N. MACAULAY PAYKUE.

X-Ray Magazine: c/o Liss Inc, POB 4196, Monrovia; tel. 221674; f. 1985; monthly; health; Man. Editor NMAH BROPLEH.

PRESS ORGANIZATION

Press Union of Liberia: Monrovia; f. 1985; Pres. LAMINI A. WARITAY.

NEWS AGENCIES

Liberian News Agency (LINA): POB 9021, Capitol Hill, Monrovia; tel. 222229; telex 44249; Dir-Gen. ERNEST KIAZOLY (acting).

Foreign Bureaux

Agence France-Presse (AFP): Monrovia; telex 44211; Rep. JAMES DORBOR.

United Press International (UPI) (USA): Monrovia; Correspondent T. K. SANNAH.

Xinhua (New China) News Agency (People's Republic of China): Adams St, Old Rd, Congotown, POB 3001, Monrovia; tel. 262821; telex 44547; Correspondent SUN BAOYU.

Reuters (UK) is also represented in Liberia.

Publisher

Government Publishing House

Government Printer: Government Printing Office, POB 9002, Monrovia; tel. 221029; telex 44224.

Radio and Television

In 1994, according to UNESCO estimates, there were 670,000 radio receivers and 55,000 television receivers in use.

RADIO

ELBC—The Voice of Peace, Harmony and Reconcilation: Liberian Broadcasting System, POB 594, Monrovia; tel. 224984; f. 1960; reorg. 1990, under the aegis of the interim Govt; broadcasts in English, French and Liberian vernaculars; Asst Dir-Gen. (Radio) NOAH A. BORDOLO.

Kiss FM: Privately owned by Charles Ghankay Taylor; nationwide broadcasts.

LAMCO Broadcasting Station (ELNR): LAMCO Information and Broadcasting Service, Nimba; Liberian news, music, cultural, political and educational programmes in English; carries national news and all nation-wide broadcasts from ELBC, and local news in English and African languages (Mano, Gio, Bassa, Vai, Lorma, Kru, Krahn, Grebo and Kpelle); also relays BBC World Service and African Service news programmes; Dir T. NELSON WILLIAMS.

Liberia Rural Communications Network: POB 10-02176, 1000 Monrovia 10; tel. 271368; f. 1981; govt-operated; rural development and entertainment programmes; following outbreak of civil conflict, maintained minimum staffing levels in Monrovia; Dir J. RUFUS KAINE (acting).

Radio ELWA: POB 192, Monrovia; tel. 271669; f. 1954; operated by the Sudan Interior Mission; closed July 1990, owing to civil conflict; resumed religious broadcasts in English in Aug. 1993; Broadcasting Dir LEE J. SONIUS.

Radio Liberia International: international short-wave service; owned by Liberia Communications Network; Deputy Man. JAMES KASSOYEN.

Voice of America: Monrovia; telex 44365; broadcasts in English, French, Swahili, Hausa and Portuguese.

TELEVISION

ELTV: Liberian Broadcasting System, POB 594, Monrovia; tel. 224984; telex 44249; f. 1964; commercial station, partly govt-supported; broadcasts 5½ hours daily Mon.–Fri., 9½ hours daily Sat. and Sun..

Finance

(cap. = capital; res = reserves; dep. = deposits; m. = million; br. = branch; amounts in Liberian dollars)

BANKING

Most banking operations in Liberia were suspended in 1990, as a result of the disruption caused by the civil conflict, although several commercial banks began to resume operations in mid-1996.

Central Bank

National Bank of Liberia: Broad St, POB 2048, Monrovia; tel. 222497; telex 44215; f. 1974; bank of issue; cap. and res 17.1m., dep. 70.7m. (1986); Gov. QUAYE.

Other Banks

Agricultural and Co-operative Development Bank: Carey and Warren Sts, POB 10-3585, Monrovia; tel. 224385; telex 44535; fax 221500; f. 1977; 65% govt-owned; cap. 6.6m. (Dec. 1989), res. 6.7m., dep. 30.6m. (Dec. 1987); Pres. and CEO JEROME M. HODGE; Gen. Man. ETHEL DAVIS; 6 brs.

Citibank (Liberia): Ashmun St, POB 280, Monrovia; tel. 224991; telex 44274; f. 1935; cap. 0.5m.; Gen. Man. THIERRY BUNGINER; 1 br.

Eurobank Liberia Ltd: Broad and Warren Sts, POB 2021, 1000 Monrovia; tel. 224873; telex 44455; fax 225921; cap. 1m. (Dec. 1992); Chair. GEORGES PHILIPPE; Pres. DONALD S. REYNOLDS.

First Commercial and Investment Bank: cnr Ashmun and Mechlin Sts, POB 1442, Monrovia; tel. 222498; telex 44431; fax 222351; cap. 3.6m. (Dec. 1991); Chair. and Pres. EDWIN J. COOPER.

International Trust Co of Liberia: 80 Broad St, POB 10-292, Monrovia; tel. 221600; telex 44588; fax 226092; f. 1948; cap. 2m., dep. 30m. (Dec. 1989); Pres. A. N. STEWART; Gen. Man. Gen. CHARLES H. BAUMANN ; 1 br.

Liberia Finance and Trust Corporation: Broad St, POB 3155, Monrovia; tel. 221020; telex 44386; cap. 0.8m. (Dec. 1984); Chair. G. ALVIN JONES; Pres. C. T. O. KING, III.

Liberian Bank for Development and Investment (LBDI): Ashmun and Randall Sts, POB 547, Monrovia; tel. 223998; telex 44345; fax 226359; f. 1961; cap. 5.2m. (Dec. 1995), dep. 34.1m. (Dec. 1993); Chair. THOMAS D. VOER HANSON; Gen. Man. FRANCIS A. DENNIS.

Liberian Trading and Development Bank Ltd (TRADEVCO): 57 Ashmun St, POB 10-293, Monrovia; tel. 221800; telex 44270; fax 225035; f. 1955; wholly-owned subsidiary of Mediobanca SpA (Italy); cap. and res 3.2m., dep. 64.7m. (June 1995); Chair. and Pres. GIORGIO PICOTTI.

Banking Association

Liberia Bankers' Association: POB 292, Monrovia; an asscn of commercial and development banks; Pres. LEN MAESTRE.

INSURANCE

American International Underwriters, Inc: Carter Bldg, 39 Broad St, POB 180, Monrovia; tel. 224921; telex 44389; general; Gen. Man. S. B. MENSAH.

American Life Insurance Co: Carter Bldg, 39 Broad St, POB 60, Monrovia; f. 1969; life and general; Vice-Pres. ALLEN BROWN.

Insurance Co of Africa: 80 Broad St, POB 292, Monrovia; f. 1969; life and general; Pres. GIZAW H. MARIAM.

Lone Star Insurances Inc: 51 Broad St, POB 1142, Monrovia; tel. 222257; telex 44394; property and casualty.

Minet James Liberia Inc: POB 541, Monrovia; Man. Dir EDWARD MILNE.

National Insurance Corporation of Liberia (NICOL): LBDI Bldg Complex, POB 1528, Sinkor, Monrovia; tel. 262429; telex 44228; f. 1984; state-owned; sole insurer for govt and parastatal bodies; also provides insurance for the Liberian-registered merchant shipping fleet; Man. Dir MIATTA EDITH SHERMAN.

Royal Exchange Assurance: Ashmun and Randall Sts, POB 666, Monrovia; all types of insurance; Man. RONALD WOODS.

United Security Insurance Agencies Inc: Randall St, POB 2071, Monrovia; telex 44568; life, personal accident and medical; Dir EPHRAIM O. OKORO.

Trade and Industry

CHAMBER OF COMMERCE

Liberia Chamber of Commerce: POB 92, Monrovia; tel. 223738; telex 44211; f. 1951; Pres. DAVID A. B. JALLAH; Sec.-Gen. LUESETTE S. HOWELL.

DEVELOPMENT ORGANIZATIONS

Forestry Development Authority: POB 3010, 1000 Monrovia; tel. 224940; responsible for forest management and conservation; Man. Dir BENSON S. GWYAN.

Liberia Industrial Free Zone Authority: Bushrod Island, POB 9047, Monrovia; f. 1975; 98 mems; Man. Dir GBAI M. GBALA.

National Investment Commission (NIC): Former Executive Mansion Bldg, POB 9043, Monrovia; tel. 225163; telex 44560; f. 1979; autonomous body negotiating investment incentives agreements on behalf of Govt; promotes agro-based and industrial development; Chair. G. E. SAIGBE BOLEY; Exec. Dir P. SEBASTIAN SMITH.

MARKETING ORGANIZATION

Liberian Produce Marketing Corporation: POB 662, Monrovia; tel. 222447; telex 44590; f. 1961; govt-owned; exports Liberian produce, provides industrial facilities for processing of agricultural products and participates in agricultural development programmes; Man. Dir ALETHA JOHNSON-FRANCIS.

EMPLOYERS' ASSOCIATION

National Enterprises Corporation: POB 518, Monrovia; tel. 261370; importer, wholesaler and distributor of foodstuffs, and wire and metal products for local industries; Pres. EMMANUEL SHAW, Sr.

MAJOR INDUSTRIAL COMPANIES

The following are among the largest companies in terms either of capital investment or employment. In 1990 the majority of industrial companies were forced to suspend activity, owing to the disruption caused by the civil war. A number of companies resumed operations in 1992.

Bong Mining Co Ltd: POB 538, Monrovia; tel. 225222; telex 44269; fax 225770; f. 1958; cap. $26.5m.; engages in iron ore mining, upgrading of crude ore and transportation of concentrate and pellets to Monrovia Free Port for shipment abroad; capacity: 4.5m. tons of concentrate and 3m. tons of pellets annually; Pres. HANSJOERG RIETZSCH; Gen. Man. HANS-GEORG SCHNEIDER; 2,200 employees.

Firestone Plantations Co: POB 140, Harbel; telex 44499; f. 1926; operated the world's largest natural rubber plantation until 1988, when these interests were acquired by the Japanese co, Bridgestone; resumed operations in 1992; Man. Dir CLYDE TABOR; c. 2,300 employees.

Liberia Cement Corporation (CEMENCO): POB 150, Monrovia; tel. 222650; telex 44558; mfrs of Portland cement.

The Liberia Co: POB 45, Broad St, Monrovia; f. 1947; cap. $1m; shipping agents Delta Steamship Lines; owns COCOPA rubber plantations; Pres. J. T. TRIPPE (New York); Vice-Pres. J. M. LIJNKAMP (Monrovia); 850 employees.

Liberian International American Corporation (LIAC): mining of iron ore.

Liberian Iron and Steel Corporation (LISCO): POB 876, Monrovia; f. 1967; mining of iron ore.

Liberian Mining Co (LIMINCO): Monrovia; govt-owned; mining of iron ore; assumed control of LAMCO JV Operating Co in 1989; operations suspended 1990–92.

Liberia Petroleum Refining Corporation (LPRC): POB 90, Monrovia; sole producer of domestically produced fuels, with designed capacity of 15,000 b/d; products include diesel fuel, fuel oils, liquid petroleum gas; supplies domestic market and has limited export facilities for surplus products.

Mesurado Industrial Complex: POB 142, Monrovia; Liberian-owned cos; products include detergents, soap, industrial gases, windows and animal feeds; Pres. P. BONNER JALLAH.

National Iron Ore Co Ltd: POB 548, Monrovia; f. 1958; 85% govt-owned co mining iron ore at Mano river; Gen. Man. S. K. DATTA RAY.

Shell Liberia Ltd: Bushrod Island, POB 360, Monrovia; f. 1920; inc in Canada; distributors of petroleum products; Man. M. Y. KUENYEDZI; 15 employees.

Texaco Exploration Belize Inc: ULRC Bldg, Randall St and United Nations, Monrovia; oil and gas exploration; Pres. C. R. BLACK.

United States Trading Co: POB 140, Monrovia; f. 1949; distribution of Firestone products; Ford USA and UK vehicle sales and service, wholesalers and retailers of foodstuffs and beverages.

TRADE UNIONS

Congress of Industrial Organizations: 29 Ashmun St, POB 415, Monrovia; Pres. Gen. J. T. PRATT; Sec.-Gen. AMOS N. GRAY; 5 affiliated unions.

Labor Congress of Liberia: 71 Gurley St, Monrovia; Sec.-Gen. P. C. T. SONPON; 8 affiliated unions.

Liberian Federation of Labor Unions: J. B. McGill Labor Center, Gardnersville Freeway, POB 415, Monrovia; f. 1980 by merger; Sec.-Gen. AMOS GRAY; 10,000 mems (1983).

Transport

RAILWAYS

Railway operations were suspended in 1990, owing to the disruption caused by the civil conflict.

Bong Mining Co Ltd: POB 538, Monrovia; tel. 225222; telex 44269; fax 225770; f. 1965; operates 78 km of standard track, transporting iron ore concentrates and pellets from Bong Town mine to Monrovia; Gen. Man. H.-G. SCHNEIDER.

Liberian Mining Co: Monrovia; tel. 221190; telex 44260; govt-owned; assumed control of LAMCO JV Operating Co in 1989; operates 267 track-km between Buchanan and the iron ore mine at Nimba; also operates a passenger railway between Buchanan and Yekepa.

National Iron Ore Co Ltd: POB 548, Monrovia; f. 1951; 145 km of track; transports iron ore from Mano River to Monrovia; Gen. Man. S. K. DATTA RAY.

ROADS

In 1995 the road network in Liberia totalled an estimated 10,300 km, of which about 628 km were paved. The main trunk road is the Monrovia–Sanniquellie motor road, extending north-east from the capital to the border with Guinea, near Ganta, and eastward through the hinterland to the border with Côte d'Ivoire. Trunk roads run through Tapita, in Nimba County, to Grand Gedeh County and from Monrovia to Buchanan. A bridge over the Mano river connects with the Sierra Leone road network, while a main road links Monrovia and Freetown (Sierra Leone). The use of the road network was subject to considerable disruption from 1990, as a result of the armed conflict in Liberia. Following a peace agreement in August 1996, most of the principal roads were reopened to commercial traffic in early 1997.

SHIPPING

In January 1996 Liberia's open-registry fleet (1,584 vessels), the second largest in the world (after Panama) in terms of gross tonnage, had a total displacement of 59.3m. grt. Commercial port activity in Liberia was frequently suspended from 1990, as a result of the armed conflict, but resumed in late 1996.

Liberia National Shipping Line (LNSL): Monrovia; f. 1987; jt venture by the Liberian Govt and private German interests; routes to Europe, incl. the UK and Scandinavia.

National Port Authority: POB 1849, Monrovia; tel. 221454; telex 44275; f. 1967; administers Monrovia Free Port and the ports of Buchanan, Greenville and Harper; Man. Dir ELSIE DOGSIE BADIO.

CIVIL AVIATION

Liberia's principal airports are Roberts Field International Airport, at Harbel, 56 km east of Monrovia, and James Spriggs Payne Airport, at Monrovia. There are more than 100 other airfields and airstrips. As a result of the armed conflict in Liberia, normal air services were suspended in 1990. In late 1996 the ECOWAS Ceasefire Monitoring Group, deployed in Liberia, announced that Roberts Field International Airport (which had been severely damaged during the civil conflict) was to be reopened, with assistance from the European Union. James Spriggs Payne Airport was reopened in mid-1996.

ADC Liberia Inc: Monrovia; f. 1993; services to the United Kingdom, the USA and destinations in West Africa.

Air Liberia: POB 2076, Monrovia; telex 44298; f. 1974 by merger; state-owned; scheduled passenger and cargo services; Man. Dir JAMES K. KOFA.

Defence

In early 1997 troops of the ECOWAS Ceasefire Monitoring Group (ECOMOG) were increased to number about 13,000, prior to elections in July of that year. The UN Observer Mission in Liberia, comprising 34 personnel, was also present. Following the elections, the new government indicated that ECOMOG was to remain in the country until permanent order was restored.

Defence Expenditure: Projected at US $38.1m. (12.9% of total expenditure) for 1993.

Chief of Staff of the Armed Forces: Lt-Gen. ABRAHAM COMAH.

Education

Primary and secondary education are available free of charge, except for an annual registration fee of about L $10. Education is officially compulsory for nine years, between seven and 16 years of age. Primary education begins at seven years of age and lasts for six years. Secondary education, beginning at 13 years of age, lasts for a further six years, divided into two cycles of three years each. In 1986 the total enrolment at primary schools was equivalent to only 35% of children in the relevant age-group; in 1984 the comparable ratio for secondary schools was 17%. In late 1995 total enrolment of school-age children was estimated at only 25%. A total of 5,056 students were enrolled at the University of Monrovia in 1994. Other higher education institutes include the Cuttington University College (controlled by the Protestant Episcopal Church), a college of technology and a computer science institute. Expenditure on education by the central government in 1988 was L $31.3m., representing 11.0% of total spending. UNESCO estimated that 61.7% of the adult population (males 46.1%; females 77.6%) remained illiterate in 1995.

Bibliography

Clapham, C. *Liberia and Sierra Leone: An Essay in Comparative Politics*. Cambridge University Press, 1976.

Corder, S. H. *Liberia under Military Rule*. Monrovia, 1980.

Cruise O'Brien, D. B., Dunn, J., and Rathbone, R. (Eds). *Contemporary West African States*. Cambridge, Cambridge University Press, 1989.

Dunn, D. E. *The Foreign Policy of Liberia During the Tubman Era 1944–71*. Hutchinson Benham, 1979.

Dunn, D. E., and Holsoe, S. E. *Historical Dictionary of Liberia*. Metuchen, NJ, Scarecrow Press, 1986.

Dunn, D. E., and Tarr, S. B. *Liberia: A National Polity in Transition*. Metuchen, NJ, Scarecrow Press, 1988.

Fahnbulleh, H. B., Jr. *The Diplomacy of Prejudice: Liberia in International Politics 1945–1970*. Vantage Press, 1986.

Gifford, P. *Christianity and Politics in Doe's Liberia*. New York, Cambridge University Press, 1993.

Givens, W. *Liberia: The Road to Democracy under the Leadership of Samuel Kanyon Doe*. London, Kensal Press, 1986.

Horton A. P. *Liberia's Underdevelopment*. Lanham, MD, University Press of America, 1994.

Huberich, C. H. *The Political and Legislative History of Liberia*. 2 vols. New York, 1947.

Kappel, R., Korte, W., and Mascher, R. F. *Liberia, Underdevelopment and Political Rule in a Peripheral Society*. Hamburg, Institut für Afrika-Kunde, 1986.

Keih, G. K. Jr. *Dependency and the Foreign Policy of a Small Power*. Lewiston, NY, Edwin Mellen Press, 1992.

Liebenow, J. G. *Liberia: The Quest for Democracy*. Bloomington, Indiana University Press, 1987.

Rimmer, D. *The Economies of West Africa*. London, Weidenfeld and Nicolson, 1984.

Schulze, W. *A New Geography of Liberia*. London, Longman, 1973.

Sisay, H. B. *Big Powers and Small Nations*. Lanham, MD, University Press of America, 1985.

US Library of Congress. *Liberia during the Tolbert Era: A Guide*. Washington, DC, 1984.

van Mourik, D. *Land in Western Liberia. A Reconnaissance. Agricultural Land Evaluation of the Mano River Union Project Area in Liberia*. Freetown, Mano River Secretariat, 1979.

Vogt, M. A. (Ed.). *Liberian Crisis and ECOMOG: A Bold Attempt at Regional Peace-keeping*. Lagos, Gabumo Publishing Co, 1992.

Wonkeryor, E. L. *Liberia's Military Dictatorship: A 'Fiasco' Revolution*. Chicago, Smugglers' Press, 1985.

MADAGASCAR

Physical and Social Geography

VIRGINIA THOMPSON

PHYSICAL FEATURES

The Democratic Republic of Madagascar comprises the island of Madagascar, the fourth largest island in the world, and several much smaller offshore islands. Madagascar lies 390 km from the east African mainland across the Mozambique channel. It extends 1,600 km from north to south and up to 570 km wide. The whole territory covers an area of 587,041 sq km (226,658 sq miles). Geologically, the main island is composed basically of crystalline rock, which forms the central highlands that rise abruptly from the narrow eastern coastal strip but descend gradually to the wide plains of the west coast.

Topographically, Madagascar can be divided into six fairly distinct regions. Antsiranana province, in the north, is virtually isolated by the island's highest peak, Mt Tsaratanana, rising to 2,800 m above sea level. Tropical crops can be grown in its fertile valleys, and the natural harbour of Antsiranana is an important naval base. Another rich agricultural region lies in the north-west, where a series of valleys converge on the port of Mahajanga. To the south-west along the coastal plains lies a well-watered region where there are large animal herds and crops of rice, cotton, tobacco, and manioc. The southernmost province, Toliary (Tuléar), contains most of Madagascar's known mineral deposits, as well as extensive cattle herds, despite the almost total lack of rainfall. In contrast, the hot and humid climate of the east coast favours the cultivation of the island's most valuable tropical crops—coffee, vanilla, cloves, and sugar-cane. Although this coast lacks sheltered anchorages, it is the site of Madagascar's most important commercial port, Toamasina. Behind its coral beaches a continuous chain of lagoons, some of which are connected by the Pangalanes Canal, provides a partially navigable internal waterway. The island's mountainous hinterland is a densely populated region of extensive rice culture and stock raising. Despite its relative inaccessibility, this region is Madagascar's administrative and cultural centre, the focal point being the capital city of Antananarivo.

Climatic conditions vary from tropical conditions on the east and north-west coasts to the hotness and dryness of the west coast, the extreme aridity of the south and the temperate zone in the central highlands. Forests have survived only in some areas of abundant rainfall, and elsewhere the land has been eroded by over-grazing and slash-and-burn farming methods. Most of the island is savannah-steppe, and much of the interior is covered with laterite. Except in the drought-ridden south, rivers are numerous and flow generally westward, but many are interspersed by rapids and waterfalls, and few are navigable except for short distances.

POPULATION AND CULTURE

Geography and history account for the diversity and distribution of the population, which was enumerated at 12,092,157 at the census of August 1993. The island's 18 principal ethnic groups are the descendants of successive waves of immigrants from such diverse areas as south-east Asia, continental Africa and Arab countries. The dominant ethnic groups, the Merina (estimated at 1,993,000 in 1974) and the Betsileo (920,600), who inhabit the most densely populated central provinces of Antananarivo and Fianarantsoa, are of Asian-Pacific origin. In the peripheral areas live the tribes collectively known as *côtiers*, of whom the most numerous are the Betsimisaraka (1,134,000) on the east coast, the Tsimihety (558,100) in the north, and the Antandroy (412,500) in the south. Population density ranges from 30 inhabitants per sq km on the central plateaux to 2 per sq km along much of the west coast. At the 1993 census the average density was 20.6 inhabitants per sq km. Although continuous migrations, improved means of communication, and a marked cultural unity have, to some extent, broken down geographical and tribal barriers, traditional ethnic antagonisms—notably between the Merina and the *côtiers*—remain close to the surface.

Increasing at an average annual rate of 3.1% during 1985–95, the Malagasy are fast exceeding the island's capacity to feed and employ them. Estimates from the 1974–75 census indicated that more than half the population was under 20 years of age, that the large foreign element was rapidly declining, and that the urban component was steadily growing. French nationals, who numbered some 50,000 before 1972, dwindled to fewer than 15,000 by 1986. In 1981 there were some 5,000 Indians holding French nationality and an equal number of creoles. The Comorans, who were formerly the second largest non-indigenous population group and were concentrated in the Mahajanga area (60,000 in 1976), have become an almost negligible element there, owing to the repatriation of about 16,000 after the clashes between them and the Malagasy in December 1976. Also inhabiting the west coast are the 10,000 or so Indian nationals, who are also unpopular with the Malagasys because of their social clannishness and their wealth, acquired through control of the textile and jewellery trades and of urban real estate. Administratively, the Asians are organized into *congrégations*, each headed by a representative chosen by them but appointed by and responsible to the government. A Chinese community, numbering about 10,000, is dispersed throughout the east-coast region, where they are principally employed as grocers, small-scale bankers, and traders in agricultural produce.

More than 82% of the Malagasy still live in rural areas, but the towns are attracting an increasing percentage of the fast-growing youthful population, thus aggravating urban socio-economic problems. Antananarivo, the capital, is by far the largest city (estimated population: 662,585 in 1985) and continues to expand, as do all the six provincial capitals.

Recent History

MERVYN BROWN

FRENCH RULE

Madagascar was annexed by France in 1896. The imposition of colonial rule did not, however, resolve the basic ethnic conflict between the dominant Merina tribe, based on the central plateau, and the coastal peoples (*côtiers*), most of whom had been forcibly incorporated into the Merina kingdom in the early 19th century.

By 1904 the French had completed their conquest of the island and integrated it with France's economy. Nationalist feeling among the educated Merina was subsequently demonstrated by increasing demands for French citizenship. However, the slow pace of the official policy of assimilation caused their leaders to aim instead for independence. Nationalist hopes were encouraged by the introduction in 1946 of a more liberal system of government, whereby Madagascar elected deputies to the French parliament. A predominantly Merina party in favour of independence, the Mouvement démocratique pour la rénovation malgache (MDRM), won all three Malagasy seats in the French national assembly in that year. However, fears of a resumption of Merina domination resulted in the formation by *côtiers* of the Parti des déshérités de Madagascar (PADESM), which was opposed to early independence. The subsequent rapid growth of PADESM was one of the factors that provoked a violent revolt in 1947, organized by extremist factions of the MDRM, in which about 80,000 people were killed. The MDRM was suppressed and all political activity suspended.

INDEPENDENCE

In 1956 the French *loi cadre* instituted universal suffrage and transferred a significant share in executive power to the Malagasy. The predominantly *côtier*-supported Parti social démocrate (PSD), formed from progressive elements of PADESM, and led by a schoolteacher, Philibert Tsiranana, emerged as the principal party. In October 1958 Madagascar became, as the Malagasy Republic, an autonomous state within the French Community. In 1959 Tsiranana was elected president. Full independence followed on 26 June 1960.

Opposition to the PSD

Following Tsiranana's accession to power, the PSD, which practised a moderate, pragmatic socialism, was joined by nearly all of its early rivals. The only significant opposition was the left-wing Parti du congrès de l'indépendance de Madagascar (AKFM), led by Richard Andriamanjato, a Merina Protestant pastor and mayor of Antananarivo. The rivalry between the two parties reinforced the antagonisms between Merina and *côtiers*; however, the PSD's political dominance was maintained throughout the decade following independence.

In the late 1960s, however, the economy deteriorated, and there was increasing opposition to the government's authoritarianism and subservience to French interests. In April 1971 peasants in the region of Toliary, in the south-west, provoked by excessive taxation and abuses committed by local officials, attacked a number of police posts. Tsiranana attributed this revolt, and the first overt student unrest, a medical students' strike in March, to a 'Maoist plot'. Following the suppression of the uprising, a regional left-wing group, the Mouvement national pour l'indépendance de Madagascar (MONIMA), led by Monja Jaona, became a significant opposition movement, attracting support from students and urban radicals.

Tsiranana, increasingly intolerant of opposition, persisted in strengthening relations with South Africa and maintained economic and cultural links with France. As the sole candidate in the presidential election of January 1972, Tsiranana was re-elected with 99.9% of the votes cast, but this result bore little relation to the true state of political opinion. In response to increasing dissatisfaction with government policies, particularly with the continuing French domination of education, students staged a series of strikes, which were joined later by other groups. In May, after 34 people were killed in a violent confrontation between security forces and members of a coalition of students, teachers, workers and urban unemployed, Tsiranana relinquished powers to Gen. Gabriel Ramanantsoa, the Merina chief of staff of Madagascar's armed forces.

MILITARY GOVERNMENT

Under Ramantsoa's leadership, order was quickly restored in the country. At a referendum, which was conducted in October 1972 to determine the future form of Madagascar's government, Ramanantsoa received a mandate from 96% of the voters to govern for a transitional period of five years, pending the establishment of new institutions and a new constitution.

The promotion of Malagasy as the official language and the 'Malagasization' of education was welcomed by student and nationalist opinion, but led to riots and strikes in coastal areas, owing to revived fears of Merina domination. Nationalists and radicals, including the extreme left-wing Mouvement pour le pouvoir prolétarien (MFM), led by Manandafy Rakotonirina, supported the major changes in foreign policy: the establishment of diplomatic relations with the People's Republic of China, the Soviet bloc countries and Arab nations; the withdrawal from the Franc Zone and the Organisation commune africaine et mauricienne (OCAM); and, in particular, the renegotiation of the co-operation agreements with France, which resulted in the evacuation of French air and naval bases.

However, Ramanantsoa's authority was undermined by the country's worsening trade and financial position, disunity in the armed forces and the government, and continuing discord between *côtiers* and Merina. The cabinet was divided between moderates, led by Col Roland Rabetafika, and radicals, led by Col Richard Ratsimandrava, the minister of the interior. The principal cause of contention was the latter's plans for radical administrative and political reform, based on a revival of the traditional communities, known as *fokonolona*.

Ratsimandrava and Ratsiraka

On 31 December 1974 the mobile police, a mainly *côtier* force, staged an attempted coup in protest at Merina domination of the armed forces. A prolonged crisis followed. In February 1975 Ramanantsoa transferred power to Col Richard Ratsimandrava, who was, however, assassinated six days later. Gen. Gilles Andriamahazo immediately assumed power, and formed an 18-member directorate. Martial law and press censorship were imposed, and political parties suspended.

In June 1975 some 300 men who had been charged with involvement in Ratsimandrava's assassination were acquitted, except for three men discovered at the scene of the murder. Later that month Andriamahazo was succeeded as head of state by Lt-Commdr Didier Ratsiraka, a *côtier* and a former minister of foreign affairs. Ratsiraka established a supreme revolutionary council (CSR), originally entirely military, to supervise a government that principally comprised civilians. Martial law was lifted, but press censorship was retained. Banks, insurance and shipping companies, the petroleum refinery and mineral resources were nationalized, as was the leading foreign-owned trading company, the Société Marseillaise. In September Ratsiraka published details of his policy, entitled *boky mena* (Little Red Book) or 'Charter of the Malagasy Socialist Revolution', in which he undertook to carry out administrative and agrarian reforms based on the *fokonolona*, reorganize the armed forces as an 'army of development' and pursue a non-aligned foreign policy. At a referendum, which took place in December, 94.66% of voters approved a new constitution, which incorporated the tenets of the Charter, and the appointment of Ratsiraka as president for a term of seven years. The country was renamed the Democratic Republic of Madagascar, and the 'Second Republic' was proclaimed.

THE SECOND REPUBLIC

The new 'revolutionary' institutions were the presidency, the CSR (which soon became predominantly civilian), the military committee for development (CMD) with purely advisory functions, a constitutional high court, a national people's assembly, and a cabinet of ministers appointed by the president. In March Ratsiraka formed the Avant-garde de la révolution malgache (AREMA) as the nucleus of the Front national pour la défense de la révolution socialiste malgache (FNDR), the only political organization permitted by the constitution. Several existing parties subsequently joined the FNDR, including the AKFM, MONIMA, the MFM and the Elan populaire pour l'unité nationale, (known as the Vonjy), which comprised left-wing elements of the former PSD.

With the help of its administrative network and the traditional support given to the government party in the rural areas, AREMA won the majority of seats in local government elections, which took place between March and June 1977, resulting in division within the FNDR. MONIMA withdrew from the FNDR, and was subsequently proscribed. At legislative elections held in June, AREMA won 112 of the 137 seats in the national assembly. However, a number of disparate right-wing and left-wing factions had meanwhile emerged within AREMA. The main conservative elements comprised the Merina bourgeoisie, based in Antananarivo, and the Christian Council of Churches in Madagascar (FFKM), representing both Protestants and Roman Catholics. Neither group differed openly with Ratsiraka's version of socialism but, for different reasons, criticized its application. Religious leaders complained of widespread corruption, while Merina businessmen, albeit pleased with the nationalization of the economy, felt that the government had unduly favoured the *côtiers* in the distribution of the profits and had been incompetent in economic management. In August the membership of the CSR was extended to include leaders of the former political parties, and more *côtiers,* in an effort to restore political equilibrium.

During 1978–79 sporadic violence occurred in the rural provinces, which suffered from extreme drought. The unrest increased in late 1980, after Monja Jaona called for a general strike and was arrested, prompting demonstrations by university students, who clashed violently with security forces in early February 1981. Ratsiraka, however, released Jaona from detention; MONIMA subsequently rejoined the FNDR, and Jaona was appointed to the CSR. Ratsiraka, meanwhile, attempted to establish himself in the international community as a spokesman for the developing countries and as the leading advocate of the demilitarization of the Indian Ocean. His 'non-aligned' foreign policy manifested itself chiefly in hostility to what he perceived as 'Western imperialism', in conjunction with close relations with the USSR and other Eastern bloc countries. A particularly close link was established with the Democratic People's Republic of Korea, which provided soldiers for Ratsiraka's personal bodyguard.

Political and Economic Challenges

In January 1982 Ratsiraka announced his candidature for a second term as president. Later that month a conspiracy to overthrow the government was discovered. Following a severe deterioration in the economy, Ratsiraka was obliged to adopt austerity measures imposed by the International Monetary Fund (IMF). Consequently, with his prestige impaired and the island's economy weakened, Ratsiraka appeared vulnerable to the challenge raised by Monja Jaona's declaration of his candidacy for election to the presidency. At the presidential election, which took place in November, however, Ratsiraka was re-elected by 80% of the vote, while Jaona won only 20% of the votes cast. Jaona refused to accept the result, attributing it to electoral fraud. In December Jaona called for a general strike in support of demands that the results of the election be annulled, and a new poll conducted. Following rioting in mid-December, Jaona was arrested and expelled from the CSR.

In August 1983 elections to the 137-member national assembly took place. Political apathy, rather than active opposition to the FNDR leadership, accounted for a low turnout of voters; AREMA won nearly 65% of the votes cast, and secured 117 seats in the legislature. However, MONIMA attracted considerable support in the capital. A new government (which closely resembled the previous cabinet) was subsequently appointed.

Social Unrest

Urban violence increased dramatically in the 1970s and early 1980s, with groups of unemployed citizens harassing and extorting money from people in the capital, especially those opposed to the government. To counter their activities, students and other youths, mainly of bourgeois families, organized vigilante societies which practised the oriental martial art of kung-fu. Clashes between the two groups resulted in a ban on the practice of kung-fu in September 1984, which provoked further rioting from kung-fu adherents and resulted in 50 deaths during further disturbances in December. A reorganization of the council of ministers, carried out in February 1985, was intended to confirm the regime's socialist direction in the face of 'deviationist' tendencies and increased liberalism in the economic sector. In August security forces attacked the headquarters of the kung-fu societies, which the government accused of planning a coup attempt; some 50 people were killed and over 200 arrested. (At the trial of 245 kung-fu adherents in March 1988, the majority of the defendants were acquitted.)

In November 1986 Ratsiraka provoked renewed opposition through proposals for a number of reforms of higher education. Following a series of protests and boycotts by students and university authorities, the government decided to postpone the introduction of the reforms for a further academic year. Nevertheless, unrest continued through the early months of 1987, in reaction to the government's refusal to release students arrested during the disturbances, and to withdraw security forces from the university campus and abandon the entire reform programme. Order was restored only after the government agreed to abandon the proposed reforms.

In the rural south of Madagascar there were further disorders in 1986–87, following severe famine in the region. In November 1986 violent demonstrations, resulting in a number of deaths, occurred at Toamasina, the principal Malagasy port, in protest at food shortages and the introduction of measures to rationalize the port. Violence erupted again in early 1987, when Indian and Pakistani traders in southern towns were attacked, and their property burnt and looted. During the disturbances there were about 14 deaths, and Indian families, many holding French nationality, took refuge at the French consulate or fled to Réunion. The Asian community had long been unpopular with the Malagasys, who resented its control of the retail sector and relative prosperity. In June 56 people who had taken part in the riots were imprisoned.

In 1987 opposition within the FNDR to Ratsiraka appeared to be increasing, partly as a result of disagreement with the government's reaction to the student strikes and other disturbances. The MSM and the Vonjy, joined later by the Parti socialiste monima (VSM), began to co-operate openly with MONIMA in opposing government policies and, from May 1987, in demands for the resignation of the government and the holding of new elections. MSM, Vonjy and MONIMA also decided to contest the presidential elections, which were due to take place in 1989. Ratsiraka subsequently announced that legislative and local government elections, scheduled for 1988, would be postponed respectively until May and September 1989. In February 1988 the prime minister, Gen. Désiré Rakotoarijaona, resigned, ostensibly on grounds of ill-health, and was succeeded by the minister of public works, Lt-Col Victor Ramahatra. In January 1989 the constitution was amended to allow Ratsiraka to bring forward the presidential election from November to March. In February the MFM, Vonjy and VSM announced the formation of an opposition alliance, the Alliance démocratique de Madagascar (ADM), but retained separate presidential candidates. In the same month restrictions on the freedom of the press were relaxed, and in the abolition of press censorship was announced.

At the presidential election, which took place in March 1989, Ratsiraka was elected to a third term of office, receiving 62% of the total votes cast (compared with 80% at the previous election). Manandafy Rakotonirina, the candidate of the MFM, (which had now moved from the extreme left to a market-orientated liberalism) obtained 20% of the poll, while the Vonjy candidate, Dr Jérôme Marojama Razanabahiny, secured 15% and Monja

Jaona of MONIMA only 3%. Later in March a new political movement, the AKFM/Fanavaozana, was formed by Richard Andriamanjato, in response to the refusal of the AKFM to support his presidential candidature. Allegations by the ADM of electoral fraud led to subsequent rioting. The membership of the cabinet remained unchanged following Ratsiraka's inauguration, but six members of the CSR, including Manandafy and Andriamanjato, were dismissed for opposing his re-election. At the end of April the ADM declared its intention to boycott the forthcoming legislative elections, but this threat was withdrawn when Ratsiraka promised to allow representatives of the opposition parties to observe polling procedures. At the legislative elections in May, AREMA increased its previously substantial parliamentary majority by a further three seats, winning 120 of the 137 parliamentary seats. The MFM, which obtained seven seats, rejected the results, alleging fraud. The Vonjy secured four seats, the AKFM/Fanavaozana three seats, the original AKFM two seats and MONIMA only one. The abstention rate was high, averaging 25% of registered voters and reaching almost 35% in some urban constituencies.

Political Reform

Despite AREMA's electoral success, widespread discontent with the government continued among the intellectual and urban classes. In August 1989 Ratsiraka reorganized both the CSR and the government, removing members of doubtful loyalty to himself and replacing them with strong supporters. The fragile opposition alliance was divided by the reappointment of Monja Jaona to the CSR, together with the vice-president of the Vonjy and some minor opposition figures, while several economic and technical specialists were appointed to the government. Shortly before the government reshuffle, Ratsiraka convened a meeting of the FNDR, (the first to be held since 1982), at which the constituent parties were invited to submit proposals for the future of the FNDR and a possible revision of the 1975 constitution. He also consulted privately with leaders of the churches and other opinion groups. However, demands by the Council of Malagasy Churches for the abolition of the FNDR's monopoly on political activity, as well as the elimination of socialist references in the constitution, received wide support.

In the first round of local government elections (to the *fokontany*) in September 1989, AREMA again gained the majority of votes, except in Antananarivo, but the average abstention rate was 30%. AREMA's electoral strength and the divisions among his opponents enabled Ratsiraka to limit constitutional changes. The amendments adopted by parliament in December abolished the requirement for political parties to be members of the FNDR, thus effectively dissolving the FNDR itself. However, the privileged status of socialism in the constitution was retained. Nevertheless, provisions were made for a multi-party system, backed by the economic liberalism imposed by the IMF and the new freedom of the press, which opposition newspapers were using increasingly to criticize the government. In the early months of 1990 a number of new parties were formed. Two former PSD ministers established a centre-right party, the Mouvement des démocrates chrétiens malgaches (MDCM), while the Vonjy was seriously weakened by the departure of André Resampa and nine other leading members to relaunch the PSD, with Resampa as secretary-general.

In March 1990 the government formally assented to the resumption of multi-party politics. Numerous organizations subsequently emerged, some of them small left-wing parties supporting the president which joined with AREMA, the old AKFM and elements of Vonjy and MONIMA, to form a new coalition, the Mouvement militant pour le socialisme malagasy (MMSM). Other new parties, notably the Union nationale pour le développement et la démocratie (UNDD), led by a medical professor, Albert Zafy, joined the MFM, AKFM/Fanavaozana and the newly-formed MDC and PSD in opposition to the government. The MFM now changed its name from Mouvement pour le pouvoir prolétarien to Mouvement pour le progrès de Madagascar, while retaining the same Malagasy initials, MFM.

On 13 May 1990 a group of armed rebels seized control of the radio station at Antananarivo and broadcast an announcement that Ratsiraka's regime had been overthrown; and a crowd gathered outside the station to demonstrate its support. Six people were killed and 50 injured in the subsequent suppression of the revolt by security forces. Of the 11 rebels arrested and brought to trial in December, several were acquitted and the others received short prison sentences.

Meanwhile, the withdrawal of Soviet support following the collapse of communism in the USSR compelled Ratsiraka to look to the Western countries, particularly France, for economic aid. These improved relations were demonstrated by a state visit by President Mitterrand in June 1990, during which it was announced that Madagascar's US $750m. debt to France had been cancelled and that France would be permitted to resume use of the facilities at the naval base at Antsiranana.

In mid-1990 the FFKM invited all political associations to attend conferences, which were to take place in August and December, to discuss a programme of reform. However, Ratsiraka criticized the FFKM's intervention, and parties belonging to the MMSM refused to participate in the discussions. At the conference, held in December, 16 opposition factions, together with trade unions and other groups, established an informal alliance, under the name Forces vives (FV), to co-ordinate proposals for constitutional reform. The leading figures of FV were Zafy (UNDD), Manandafy (MFM) and Andriamanjato (AKFM/Fanavaozana). In the same month the national people's assembly adopted legislation that abolished press censorship, ended the state monopoly of radio and television and permitted the establishment of private broadcasting stations in partnership with the government. In January 1991 Ratsiraka announced that further constitutional amendments would be adopted by the assembly at its next meeting in May. It was later indicated that the main change would be the replacement of the supreme revolutionary council by an elected senate.

Confrontation and General Strike

At the session of the national people's assembly in May 1991, FV supporters forced their way into the chamber to submit their alliance's proposals for amending the constitution; these included the elimination of references to socialism, a reduction in the powers of the president and a limit on the number of terms he could serve. However, the only amendments considered were those presented by the government, which, although numerous, did not meet the FV's basic demands. In early June the FV leadership demanded that a constitutional conference be convened. When the government failed to respond, the FV called a general strike from 10 June, and began a series of peaceful demonstrations, in support of demands for the resignation of the president and the appointment of a new 'provisional government', which would include opposition leaders. The army and police did not intervene in the demonstrations, and similar gatherings took place in the provincial capitals.

The strike was widely supported in the civil service, banks, major firms and transport and, together with the daily demonstrations, resulted in the suspension of economic activity in the capital. In July 1991 various negotiations between the FV and the MMSM, with the mediation of the FFKM or the French embassy, failed, owing to the FV's insistence on the resignation of the president. Ratsiraka refused to resign, on the grounds that he had been democratically elected. In response, the FV maintained that the 1989 elections were not democratic (since only political parties adhering to the FNDR were allowed to operate), and denounced abuses of human rights and widespread corruption in the government and in the president's family. In mid-July the FV appointed its own 'provisional government', with a retired general, Jean Rakotoharison, as president and Zafy as prime minister. 'Ministers' of the 'provisional government' then began to occupy various ministry buildings, with the assistance of civil servants observing the strike. Later in July Ratsiraka announced a state of emergency, reimposed censorship, and prohibited mass meetings. This had little effect, however, as the army and police took no action to enforce it. In the next few days Zafy and three other FV 'ministers' were abducted and held in various army camps. There were also murders of several FV leaders in Toamasina and Antsiranana.

On 28 July 1991 Ratsiraka dissolved his government and pledged to organize a referendum on a new constitution by the end of the year. At a demonstration on the folllowing day, however, the FV insisted on the president's resignation, the lifting of the state of emergency and the release of their 'ministers'. (They were released unharmed on the following day.) On

8 August Ratsiraka nominated a new prime minister, Guy Razanamasy, hitherto the mayor of Antananarivo, who invited the FV to join the government. The offer was rejected, and on 10 August the FV organized a large but peaceful protest march on the president's residence to demand his resignation. The president's bodyguard fired into the crowd, killing 100 and wounding many more. On the same day a further 20 people were killed in the suppression of a similar demonstration in Mahajanga. The French government subsequently suspended military aid and advised Ratsiraka to resign, offering him asylum in France. The Roman Catholic archbishop of Antananarivo joined those calling for the president's resignation, and the FFKM announced that it was abandoning its role as mediator and would henceforth support the FV. Later that month Ratsiraka declared Madagascar to be a federation of six states, under his presidency, and claimed to command the support of five provinces, where AREMA held the majority of seats in regional councils. On 26 August Razanamasy formed a government, which contained some defectors from the FV, including Resampa. The state of emergency was modified, but Razanamasy warned that civil servants would be dismissed unless they returned to work by 4 September. On that day, however, the FV, which had denounced the new government as 'puppets' of Ratsiraka, organized a massive demonstration, which halted all economic activity in Antananarivo.

During September and October 1991 the FV continued to organize frequent demonstrations and maintain the general strike at an effective level, ensuring the closure of all ports except for Toamasina. Ratsiraka was sustained by support from the provinces and was able to exploit divisions within the opposition, notably between Manandafy's MFM, which favoured a constitutional settlement, and the majority of radicals led by Zafy. Meanwhile, the army and the aid donors increased their pressure on all parties to reach a settlement including a consensus government.

Interim Settlement

Following an ultimatum from the army, an interim agreement was signed on 31 October 1991 by Razanamasy and representatives of the FV, MMSM and FFKM, providing for the suspension of the constitution and the creation of a transitional government, which was to remain in office for a maximum period of 18 months, pending the adoption of a new constitution and the holding of elections. Under the agreement, Ratsiraka remained as president with the ceremonial duties of head of state and titular head of the armed forces, but relinquished all executive powers. A 31-member Haute autorité de l'état (HAE), under Zafy, and a 130-member advisory Conseil de redressement économique et social (CRES), headed jointly by Andriamanjato and Manandafy, replaced the CSR and the national people's assembly, while Razanamasy's government was to be expanded to include members of the FV.

In February 1992 the interim authorities suspended the elected bodies (nearly all controlled by AREMA and supporting Ratsiraka) at the various levels of local government and replaced them with special delegations. In the same month proposals for a new constitution and electoral code were compiled at a series of regional forums, and delegates were elected to attend a national forum, which was convened in Antananarivo in late March. After attacks against the conference hall and an attempt to assassinate Zafy, the forum was moved to a military camp. At the end of March security forces fired at supporters of Ratsiraka, led by Monja Jaona, who had marched on the camp; eight people, including a former minister, were killed.

Ratsiraka reasserted his intention to stand for re-election, and called for a federalist draft constitution to be submitted to a referendum as an alternative to the unitary draft being considered by the forum. After much debate, a clause was included in the electoral code excluding the candidature of anyone who had been elected president twice under the second republic. The constitution adopted by the forum, subject to approval by the transitional authorities and at a national referendum, was of a parliamentary type, with a constitutional president, a senate and a national assembly elected by proportional representation, and executive power vested in a prime minister elected by the assembly. The referendum on the constitution was scheduled for 21 June 1992, and was to be followed by presidential elections in August and legislative elections in October. However, continuing lack of agreement within the government and the HAE regarding the exclusion of Ratsiraka from the presidential elections and the extent of the future president's powers delayed the publication of the draft constitution and therefore caused the referendum to be postponed. Despite attempts by federalist supporters of Ratsiraka to disrupt the referendum, the new constitution was approved on 19 August by 73% of votes cast.

The federalists subsequently intensified pressure for Ratsiraka's right to stand for re-election. After a number of violent incidents involving federalists, including the temporary seizure of the airport at Antsiranana and the bombing of the railway track linking Toamasina and the capital, the transitional authorities agreed to allow Ratsiraka to contest the election. A further seven candidates, including Zafy and Manandafy, were also to participate in the elections. In the first round of the presidential election, which was conducted peacefully under international supervision on 25 November 1992, Zafy secured 45% of votes cast, while Ratsiraka obtained 29% and Manandafy 10% of the vote. The second round, which was contested by the two leading candidates, took place on 10 February 1993. Most of the other candidates transferred their support to Zafy, who obtained a substantial majority of 67% of the vote, against 33% for Ratsiraka. Zafy was formally invested as president in late March, amid violent clashes between security forces and federalists in northern Madagascar. However, the transitional authorities continued to function, pending the formation of a new government after the legislative elections (which were rescheduled for 16 June). In accordance with a constitutional stipulation, Zafy resigned as president of the UNDD in May.

In early June 1993 two people were killed and a further 40, including Monja Jaona, arrested, after security forces attacked federalists who had seized the prefecture building in Toliary. On 16 June the elections to the national assembly (which had been reduced from 184 to 138 seats) were contested under a system of proportional representation by 121 political parties and some 4,000 candidates. Several elements of the FV coalition presented separate lists of candidates; however, the remaining parties in the alliance, known as the Cartel HVR, proved the most successful group, securing 45 seats; Manandafy's MFM obtained 16 seats, while a new pro-Ratsiraka movement, FAMIMA, won only 11 seats. Intensive inter-party negotiations prior to the first meeting of the assembly resulted in some shifting in party support for the various candidates contesting the post of prime minister. In the election on 9 August, Manandafy obtained 32 votes and Roger Ralison (the candidate of the Cartel) 45 votes. The winner, with 55 votes, was Francisque Ravony, who was the favoured candidate both of Zafy and the business community. Ravony, a respected lawyer and a son-in-law of former president Tsiranana, had served as deputy prime minister in the transitional government. The leader of the AKFM/Fanavaozana, Richard Andriamanjato, was elected speaker of the national assembly.

THE THIRD REPUBLIC

At the end of August 1993 Ravony formed a new council of ministers, which was endorsed by 72% of deputies in the national assembly, together with his programme, which emphasized economic recovery based on free-market policies, and measures to eradicate corruption. The latter resulted in the arrest in September of 12 senior civil servants, who were accused of misappropriating World Bank credits equivalent to US $10m. Effective action regarding economic recovery subsequently proved difficult, however, owing, in part, to the fragmented nature of the national assembly, which comprised some 25 separate parties; these became grouped into two informal coalitions of equal size (and a small number of independent deputies), known respectively as the HVR group (which included supporters of Zafy and Andriamanjato) and G6. However, neither was specifically a government or opposition organization, and ministers were appointed from both alliances and also from the independent members. Despite the immediate necessity for substantial assistance from the World Bank and IMF to sustain the economy, a number of deputies opposed the acceptance of structural adjustment measures, required by the World Bank and IMF as a precondition to the approval of financial credit, owing to the additional widespread hardship that would ensue. A strike by civil servants in January 1994 demonstrated the difficulty in accepting IMF demands for substantial retrenchment in the civil service and a 'freeze' of public sector salaries. In early 1994 a number of severe cyclones further damaged the economy, and weakened the government's ability to resist the demands of the World Bank and IMF. In May agreement was reached with the World Bank and IMF on a framework agreement for 1995–96, including further structural adjustment reforms. In June, however, the reform programme was rejected by a majority in the national assembly.

Ravony's position was undermined by public opposition from Zafy and Andriamanjato, who rejected the IMF and World Bank demands as an affront to national sovereignty and favoured financial arrangements with private enterprises (known as 'parallel financing'). In July 1994 31 deputies belonging to the G6 coalition proposed a motion of censure against Ravony for failing to conclude an agreement with the Bretton Woods institutions, which was, however, defeated with the assistance of the HVR group. In August Ravony reorganized the council of ministers to reflect the HVR's support; the president of the Leader party, Herizo Razafimahaleo, subsequently resigned, after his portfolio was divided.

Andriamanjato, with the support of Zafy and the governor of the central bank, continued to pursue 'parallel financing' arrangements, notably one with Prince Constantin of Liechtenstein, whose company established a subsidiary, Flamco Madagascar. In October 1994 Flamco's directors, who included two of Andriamanjato's sons, were accused of misappropriating funds advanced by the government and other irregularities. The continuing decline of the economy and the inflationary effects of the floatation of the currency and increase in fuel prices in May prompted demands from the main G6 parties for the resignation of the president, the prime minister and the speaker, while the HVR group urged the resignation of the prime minister and the minister of finance.

In January 1995, at the insistence of the Bretton Woods institutions, Ravony dismissed the governor of the central bank. In a balancing move to appease the HVR group, the minister of finance also resigned, with Ravony assuming the portfolio himself. The government subsequently pledged to undertake further austerity measures, while the IMF and World Bank approved the doubling of the minimum wage and additional expenditure on health and education to counteract the effect of the structural adjustment reforms.

In March 1995 two leaders of a minor opposition group were arrested, after announcing the establishment of a 'parallel government', while members of the HVR group staged a demonstration urging the resignation of the prime minister. In June members of the G6 group staged a demonstration urging the impeachment of Zafy, on the grounds that he had exceeded his constitutional powers and supported Andriamanjato's demands for 'parallel financing'. At the same time Ravony strengthened his parliamentary position by recruiting additional deputies to his (hitherto single-member) party, Committee for the Support of Democracy and Development in Madagascar (CSDDM). The CSDDM then joined the G6, which became the G7, constituting a clear majority in the assembly. In July Zafy publicly criticized Ravony, and, at his instigation, the HVR group in the national assembly proposed a motion of censure against the prime minister, which was, however, rejected by a large majority.

Zafy subsequently announced that he could not co-operate with Ravony and called a referendum for 17 September 1995 to endorse a constitutional amendment, whereby the president, rather than the national assembly, would select the prime minister. Ravony, who had reorganized the cabinet to reflect changes in the composition of his support in the national assembly, announced that he would resign when the result of the referendum was formally announced in October. He also declined to campaign against the referendum, and many of his supporters decided to express their disapproval by abstaining from voting. In the referendum, notable for a high degree of abstention, the constitutional amendment was approved by 63.5% of the valid votes.

Ravony and his government duly resigned and President Zafy appointed the leader of his own party, the UNDD, Emmanuel Rakotovahiny, as prime minister. The new government contained no members of the G7 majority group and was heavily weighted in favour of the UNDD at the expense of other groups from the former HVF. Six parties formerly supporting the president immediately demanded a change of government and a new prime minister, and accused Zafy of seeking to create a UNDD one-party state.

The government, with very little support in the assembly, was further weakened by public disagreement between the prime minister and the finance minister over the 1996 budget, and could make no progress in negotiations with the IMF and the World Bank. In February 1996 a new radical extra-parliamentary group, SFFF (led by prominent figures from the Ratsiraka regime), held demonstrations in support of demands for the departure of the president, a provisional government of national recovery and yet another new constitution. Public discontent was expressed by strikes of university students and railway workers and an unprecedented strike by officials of the finance ministry, joined by customs officials at the ports, calling for the resignation of their minister who, it was later revealed, had been convicted of corruption in 1982. Under increasing pressure to change the government, Zafy offered a reshuffle but insisted on retaining Rakotovahiny as prime minister. In April most of the parties which previously supported Zafy joined in a new group, the Rassemblement pour la Troisième République (RP3R), to oppose him. At the same time, the FFKM returned to the public stage to appeal for a new government, an agreement with the IMF and World Bank and the elimination of corruption in the government. The managing director of the IMF, Michel Camdessus, made it clear during a visit to Madagascar that the IMF could negotiate only with a cohesive government united in favour of agreements with the Bretton Woods institutions.

When Zafy failed to carry out even the government reshuffle that he had promised, the G7 and RP3R joined on 16 May 1996 in a motion of censure against the government, which, requiring a two-thirds' majority, was carried by 109 votes to 15. Rakotovahiny resigned and Zafy appointed a non-political prime minister, Norbert Ratsirahonana, hitherto the president of the constitutional high court and a leading member of the Protestant Reformed Church. Ratsirahonana's programme, emphasizing economic reform in the context of agreements with the IMF and World Bank and action on poverty, corruption and crime, won general approval. He proposed a government including a number of members of the G7 majority group and only one UNDD member. However, Zafy vetoed all but one G7 minister and insisted on the retention of five UNDD members and other ministers from the previous government. Most G7 and RP3R deputies therefore walked out when Ratsirahonana presented his government and programme to the assembly on 10 June. However, in July Ratsirahonana obtained a vote of confidence by linking it with legislation necessary for the agreements with the IMF and World Bank. There were further strikes, by transport drivers protesting against an increase in the fuel tax, and by civil servants protesting against the politicization of civil service appointments.

On 26 July 1996 the assembly voted the impeachment of the president, for various violations of the constitution, by 99 votes to 34. After giving Zafy a month to contest the charges, the constitutional high court endorsed the impeachment and removed him from office; on the same day Zafy resigned. The court appointed the prime minister, Ratsirahonana, to act as interim president pending the outcome of a new presidential election, to be held within two months. He formed a new government, excluding those ministers whom Zafy had forced him to accept. Despite the impeachment, Zafy immediately declared himself a candidate for the presidential election, and was joined by ex-president Ratsiraka, acting president Ratsirahonana and 12 other candidates, including most of the leaders of the main political parties.

The Return of Ratsiraka

In the first round of the presidential election on 3 November 1996, marked by a high abstention rate, Ratsiraka came first with 37% of the valid votes, followed by Zafy with 23%. In the runoff on 29 December Ratsiraka won narrowly with 51% of the valid votes to Zafy's 49%, but, with even more abstentions and spoilt votes adding up to 52% of the electorate, less than 25% of the electorate voted for the winning candidate. In February

1997 Ratsiraka appointed as prime minister Pascal Rakotomavo, who formed a government consisting largely of technocrats.

During the election campaign Ratsirahonana had successfully completed negotiations with the IMF, leading in due course to a resumption of international aid and debt-relief arrangements. Ratsiraka's first act was to visit Washington and New York (USA), Paris (France) and Brussels (Belgium) to reassure the donor community of his intention to adhere to the reform programme approved by the IMF. He announced his intention to fulfil an electoral promise to submit to a national referendum two alternative new constitutions, but, owing to practical and constitutional problems, it seemed likely that the referendum would be limited to approving amendments to the existing constitution. The legislative elections due in August 1997 were postponed for 10 months so that they could be held under whatever new constitutional arrangements emerged from the referendum. The opposition, led by Zafy, condemned the delay (which was officially to allow time for the distribution of newly compulsory identity cards for voters), and declared it to be a violation of the constitution; in early August Zafy demanded the resignation of the government, the national assembly and the constitutional high court.

Local government elections, originally scheduled for October 1993, were repeatedly postponed, owing to disagreement over proposals to restructure and decentralize government by the creation of more local authorities. In response to pressure from the World Bank and IMF to reduce administrative expenditure, the government proposed a two-tiered structure of 28 regions (replacing six provinces) and 1,278 communes. Elections to the communes were held in November 1995, but those to the regions, scheduled for August 1996, were postponed because of the crisis over the impeachment of the president. Meanwhile, the establishment of the senate continued to be delayed, owing to the constitutional provision whereby two-thirds of the senators are to be selected by an electoral college comprising all elected local government representatives. Similarly, no progress was made with the establishment of the independent judicial power prescribed by the 1992 constitution.

In complete reversal of Ratsiraka's foreign policies, in the early 1990s Ravony's government established relations with Israel, South Africa, the Republic of Korea and (for trade and economic purposes only) Taiwan. These arrangements were not altered after Ratsiraka's return as president in 1997. The new minister of foreign affairs, Herizo Razafimahaleo, made the promotion of the economy the main focus of foreign policy and moved to strengthen relations with the newly industrialized countries of South-East Asia and the Far East. France remained the principal trading partner and supplier of bilateral aid. Political relations with France also remained close, despite long-standing disputes over compensation for nationalized French assets, and sovereignty of the Iles Glorieuses to the north of Madagascar and three other uninhabited islets in the Mozambique Channel, which are claimed by France.

Economy

GILL TUDOR

Revised for this edition by the Editor

In 1995, according to estimates by the World Bank, Madagascar's gross national product (GNP), measured at average 1993–95 prices, was US $3,178m., equivalent to $230 per head. On the basis of GNP per head, Madagascar was among the world's 18 poorest countries in that year. According to World Bank estimates, Madagascar's gross domestic product (GDP), measured at current prices, was $3,198m. in 1995. In 1985–95, it was estimated, GNP per head declined, in real terms, by an annual average of 2.0%, while the population increased by an annual average of 3.1%. Madagascar's GDP increased, in real terms, by an average of 1.1% annually in 1985–95; the economy registered real GDP growth of 1.8% in 1995, and an estimated 2% in 1996. In the mid-1980s it was estimated that 65% of the population were in the subsistence sector. However, the urban population represented more than 23% of this total in 1990.

THE RURAL SECTOR

The rural economy accounts for 80% of Madagascar's export revenues and supplies most of the raw materials needed for industry. In 1995 the agricultural sector (including forestry and fishing) accounted for an estimated 33.6% of GDP and engaged an estimated 76.3% of the country's labour force. The production of both food and export crops, except cotton, either stagnated or declined after President Ratsiraka took power in 1975, mainly as a result of the imposition of doctrinaire socialist principles and natural disasters. The island's agricultural sector also suffered from adverse climatic conditions, a lack of insecticides, spare parts and fertilizers, and the poor maintenance of rural roads. The imposition of co-operative societies and state farms on a reluctant peasantry also contributed to the agricultural sector's poor performance. Agricultural GDP increased by an annual average of 2.3% in 1985–95, according to the World Bank; in 1994 it shrank by 0.5% but in 1995 it was estimated to have recovered by 2.7%. The introduction of higher producer prices during the 1980s aimed to increase output of food crops, in particular, and eventually to achieve self-sufficiency in food. However, in view of the problems of quotas, low world prices and international competition, a major policy objective is to improve the quality of export crops, while limiting the expansion in output. The diversification of both food and export crops is also a priority. The forestry sector has been badly neglected, and 85% of domestic fuel needs are supplied by wood and charcoal. In 1992, according to FAO estimates, about 27% of the land area was covered by forests. A US $66m. aid arrangement was agreed at a donors' meeting in Paris in February 1990 to support the first stage of a long-term environmental action plan. In August 1989 a 'debt-for-nature' exchange, the first for Africa, was arranged: the USA gave the Worldwide Fund For Nature (WWF) $1m. to buy $2.1m. of government commercial debts at a 55% discount from a consortium of international banks, and to use the money for environmental projects. The experiment proved successful, and further debt-conversion agreements, involving international organizations, were subsequently negotiated. By late 1995 WWF was reported to have purchased about $5m. of Malagasy debt, for $2.3m.

Paddy rice is the main crop grown by 70% of the population, whose basic food is rice (the average annual per caput consumption is about 135 kg, the highest of any country in the world), and it occupies about 1.18m. ha, or approximately one-half the area under cultivation. Output of paddy remained constant at an average annual level of about 2m. metric tons for some years but the cyclones of January 1982 caused flooding which damaged the paddy crop and necessitated imports of about 356,000 tons of rice, at great cost, during that year. In early 1984 a further four cyclones destroyed some 40,000 ha of rice fields, and in March 1986 a cyclone destroyed rice fields and damaged Toamasina, the major port. A further cyclone in January 1990 destroyed rice fields and coffee plantations, especially in the south-east. The area planted to rice was subsequently reduced, while output of potatoes and maize was increased. In 1986 the government abolished virtually all controls on the rice trade, except for a minimum purchasing price of 90 Malagasy francs per kg and the maintenance of buffer stocks by the state. The estimated harvest in 1986 was 2.1m. tons, and in 1987 2.2m. tons. Imports of about 162,000 tons were necessary in both years but these were reduced to 75,000 tons in 1989, and to 50,000 tons in 1990 (with production reaching an estimated 2.4m. tons in that year). Severe drought in 1991–92 necessitated some 60,000 tons of imports. Rice production totalled an estimated 2.3m. tons in 1991, but increased to 2.5m. tons in 1992, and to 2.6m. tons in 1993. It fell back to 2.4m. tons in 1994 as a result of cyclone damage, leading to imports of 179,000 tons in that year, but rebounded to 2.6m. tons in 1995, when imports totalled 71,911 tons. Fresh cyclone damage in January 1996 in the major rice-growing area of Ambatondrazaka was estimated to have destroyed as much as 5% of that year's crop. However, rice imports declined to 34,684 tons in that year. The country suffered extensive crop damage again in early 1997, when cyclones struck both the south-east and the north-east. Heavy rains, brought by the cyclones, led to an increase in the number of locusts, which destroyed rice fields and maize plantations in the south and covered 2m. ha by March 1997. There is a need for improved husbandry and for the introduction of higher-yielding varieties, as well as an improved distribution system. Other important staple crops are maize, cassava, bananas and sweet potatoes.

Madagascar's main cash crops are coffee, vanilla and cloves. The most important is coffee (97% of it robusta, although arabica production is encouraged), which, in the 1980s, accounted for about 24% of total export earnings and engaged 25% of the working population. Output in the 1980s was generally about 80,000–84,000 metric tons per year, almost double the export quota allocated by the International Coffee Organization (ICO). Madagascar thus had considerable quantities for disposal on the non-quota market. Domestic consumption has risen steadily in recent years, to about 15,000 tons per year. There was a dramatic decline in world coffee prices after the ICO agreement collapsed in July 1989, leading to a loss in export revenue of over US $20m. that year; coffee export earnings came to $76.8m. Despite a recovery in prices, export earnings from coffee declined further in 1990, to $38.8m., owing partly to cyclone damage and lower crop quality. Coffee earnings stagnated until 1994, when a surge in world prices raised Madagascar's coffee exports to $79m., equivalent to 24% of total exports. Prices declined dramatically between 1994 and 1996, when coffee exports accounted for 19% of the value of total exports.

Madagascar was the world's largest exporter of vanilla until 1989, since then it has been beaten into second place in most years by Indonesia. Vanilla accounted for 9% of Madagascar's total export revenue in 1995, and only 4% in 1996. The USA and France are the main purchasers. Output has fluctuated widely, between 600 metric tons and 1,800 tons a year. Owing to competition from cheap synthetic substitutes, the value of Madagascar's high-quality natural vanilla is determined by its scarcity, and the government has therefore followed a policy of limiting exports. The country has operated a quota and price cartel system with Réunion and the Comoros, although by late 1994 this was starting to crumble; a huge build-up of stocks led the government to destroy vanilla amounting to more than the total volume of annual world consumption. Madagascar exported only 543 tons in 1993, but exports more than doubled to 1,182 tons in 1994 (yielding earnings of $56m.), before falling back to 602 tons in 1995, and to 640 tons in 1996. Reform of the vanilla sector has been a key prerequisite for further funding from the Bretton Woods institutions (see below), and in 1994 the government implemented a number of changes, including abolition of the guaranteed producer price. Free-market prices for farmers have since plunged, discouraging production. In May 1997, however, the government's decision to abolish export tax (levied at 25%) was welcomed. The government also replaced the state vanilla marketing board by a supervisory parastatal, the Madagascar Vanilla Institute (IVAMA), which had been due to be converted in late 1996 into a company in which the state would be a minority shareholder. In early 1997, however, it was reported that the government had decided to abolish IVAMA, in response to pressure from the World Bank.

Production of cloves in the early 1980s was at a level of 10,000–12,000 metric tons per year and accounted for about a quarter of export earnings, but in 1983 the main buyer, Indonesia, suspended purchases and Madagascar was left with large quantities of unsold stocks. New markets were found in Sri Lanka and the Far East, and exports recovered by 1985 to 11,600 tons. In 1987 there was a collapse in world prices, following the emergence of Indonesia as a clove exporter, while liberalization of marketing in Madagascar caused an excess of cloves on the market, depressing prices further. Production subsequently rose as farmers responded to liberalization. Official figures show a leap in output from 12,500 tons in 1993 to 23,000 tons in 1994. Exports totalled 17,128 tons in 1995, but declined considerably to 7,268 tons in 1996, with revenue falling by more than 50% in the latter year, to 22,814m. Malagasy francs.

Litchis and small quantities of pepper and ylang-ylang (an essence used in the perfume industry) are also exported. Production of seed cotton declined steadily, from 42,900 metric tons in 1984/85 to 27,000 tons in 1987/88. However, 41,000 tons were harvested in 1988/89 and exports resumed, after a period of several years. Production fell back to between 20,000 tons and 27,000 tons a year in the first half of the 1990s. Sisal is a minor export crop, adversely affected for a number of years by synthetic substitutes. World prices have improved, but drought in the south in 1988 caused the closure of three major sisal estates. Annual production is between 10,000 and 20,000 tons. There are five sugar factories, of which four have been rehabilitated with French aid, increasing their output from 80,000 tons a year to an average of some 120,000 tons in the late 1980s. The fifth factory, near Morondava on the west coast, was built with Chinese assistance and began operating in 1987, with an annual capacity of 22,000 tons. All factories are managed by the state-owned Société Siramamy Malagasy. Nevertheless, the sugar estates have suffered from under-investment and several have threatened closure because of debts. Production of sugar cane has averaged about 2m. tons a year in the early 1990s. Imports of sugar are necessary to meet domestic requirements; in 1992 11,092 tons were imported from Mauritius and Réunion. Groundnuts, pineapples, coconuts, butterbeans and tobacco are also grown.

Sea fishing by coastal fishermen is being industrialized, with assistance from Japan and France. Shrimp fishing has expanded considerably, and represents the second largest source of export revenue (after coffee); the shrimp catch reached 8,786 metric tons in 1995. Small quantities of lobster are also exported. In 1995 the total catch amounted to 120,140 tons. Vessels from EC (European Community, now European Union—EU) countries, Japan and Russia fish by agreement for tuna and prawns in Madagascar's exclusive maritime zone, extending to 370 km (200 nautical miles) off the coast. A US $18m. tuna-canning complex has been established as a joint venture with a French company at Antsiranana, financed predominantly by France and the European Investment Bank (EIB). The EIB, the International Finance Corpn (IFC) and France are providing funds for Pêcheries de Nossy Bé to replace three trawlers and to modernize the shrimp-processing plant at Hellville in the north-west.

Madagascar has about 10.3m. head of cattle; however, cattle are generally regarded as an indication of wealth rather than as sources of income, and the development of a commercial beef sector is difficult. Nevertheless, there is some ranching and 144,000 metric tons of beef and veal were produced commercially in 1995, according to FAO estimates. Some beef is exported, but volumes have declined in recent years, to about 800 tons a year, despite an EC quota of 11,000 tons. There is an urgent need to revive veterinary sevices, improve marketing and rehabilitate abattoirs, partly to meet EC import standards. Live animals and some canned corned beef are exported to African countries, the Gulf states and Indian Ocean islands. There are scarcely any dairy cattle and the three milk processing plants use imported milk powder. There were some 1.6m. pigs in 1995, according to FAO estimates, but pigmeat is a luxury item and only about 50,000 tons were produced commercially in that year. According to FAO estimates, there were some 1.3m. goats in 1995. Poultry are raised on a small-scale, non-commercial basis.

INDUSTRY

Industry accounted for an estimated 13.6% of Madagascar's GDP in 1995; the sector employs only about 3% of the working population. The island's major industrial centres, other than mines, are located in the High Plateaux or near Toamasina port. Food processing accounts for about one-half of all industrial value added. Textiles was formerly the second largest sector but has now been superseded by brewing, paper and soap. There are cement plants at Mahajanga and Toamasina. However, in the late 1980s average annual production of cement was only about 40,000 metric tons, necessitating imports of about 250,000 tons per year; by 1993 production had declined to 36,397 tons and in 1994 it plunged to only 8,524 tons before recovering to a provisional 45,009 tons in 1995. A fertilizer plant at Toamasina, which began operations in 1985, produces 90,000 tons per year of urea- and ammonia-based fertilizers. Other industries include the manufacture of wood products and furniture, tobacco, agricultural machinery and the processing of agricultural products. Industrial GDP increased by an annual average of 0.6% in 1985–95, according to the World Bank; growth was estimated at 1.6% in 1995.

In June 1986 the government introduced a new investment code, which provided incentives for domestic and foreign private investment in activities outside the public sector, particularly in manufacturing for the export market. All military and strategic industries, including those in the energy sector, dockyards and ship repair yards, remained in the control of the Office militaire national pour les industries stratégiques (OMNIS), renamed the Office des mines nationales et des industries stratégiques under President Zafy (see Recent History). The country's fifth investment code, which took effect in January 1990, introduced incentives to attract foreign private investors, in particular. This enactment was strongly opposed by many politicians and also by local business people. Rules regarding foreign exchange and the number of expatriate employees have been relaxed and private investors are granted tax incentives. In the case of small and medium-sized enterprises, profits are exempt from corporation tax for the first five years, after which there is tax relief for a further five years. A number of export processing zones (EPZ) have been established, and have attracted foreign investors' interest, particularly from South-East Asia, Mauritius and France. A preliminary agreement has been signed with a consortium of Hong Kong interests, involving projected investment totalling US $650m. over 15 years. At the end of 1993 the EPZ regime covered 370 businesses with a total capital of 452,000m. Malagasy francs. Labour is cheaper and corporation tax lower in the Malagasy EPZ than in those in Mauritius, but there are much higher risks for companies producing for export. A new investment code was approved in mid-1996 to simplify procedures for potential investors.

In March 1990 the International Development Association (IDA) approved a credit of US $48m. to finance the government's project to develop private enterprises. The funds were to be directed towards private businesses, or allocated to the development of training and extension services, to the restructuring of the chamber of commerce and to the establishment of an investment promotion agency. In mid-1994 the IFC approved an equity investment amounting to about $1.1m. in the Madagascar Capital Development Fund (an investment fund established by a French bank), which was to assist export-orientated companies.

MINING

Madagascar has sizeable deposits of a wide range of minerals, but in many cases they are in remote areas, making commercial exploitation difficult and expensive. However, chromite, graphite and mica are all exported, as are small quantities of semi-precious stones, such as topaz, garnet and amethyst. Chromite output (chromium ores and concentrates) before 1976 was approximately 200,000 metric tons per year, although in the early 1980s production had declined to very low levels. In 1993 output increased to 144,311 tons, compared with 64,200 tons in 1988, but declined to 75,000 tons in 1994 and a provisional 74,000 tons in 1995 (despite a maximum annual capacity of 160,000 tons). The main deposits of chromium ore are at Andriamena, but it is also mined at Befandriana Nord. Graphite output was also very low in the early 1980s; after increasing to 18,500 tons in 1990, production again declined, to 14,600 tons in 1994 and a provisional 13,900 tons in 1995. Production of mica reached 1,800 tons in 1986, declining to 693 tons in 1988; it recovered to 1,800 tons in 1990 but fell again, amounting to 563 tons in 1994 and a provisional 387 tons in 1995. The government is inviting private mining companies to exploit the country's gold deposits, which were nationalized in 1975. Official production has been only a few kilograms a year, but it has been estimated that 2–3 tons annually is mined unofficially by small prospectors. In 1994 the government established an agency to purchase the output of these prospectors. A proposed major project to revive the mining of ilmenite (titanium ore), which ceased in 1977, has aroused considerable controversy on environmental grounds; the deposits, whose exploitation could earn an estimated US $550m. over a 30-year period, are located in an area of primeval rain forest and sand-dunes in the south-east of the island. The project would also necessitate the construction of a new port. Other potential mineral projects include the eventual exploitation of an estimated 100m. tons of bauxite at Manantenina in the south-east of the country, and of coal deposits, also estimated at 100m. tons. In mid-1997 plans to exploit nickel and cobalt deposits were awaiting final approval.

ENERGY

Madagascar's prospects for reducing fuel imports have been improved by the development of hydroelectric power and by a reduction in the cost of imported petroleum (which, nevertheless, still absorbed 15% of the country's total export earnings in 1996, compared with 16% in 1989). The Andekaleka hydroelectric scheme, which began operations in 1982, supplies Antananarivo and Antsirabe areas, as well as the Andriamena chromite mine. A second stage to extend this grid to Toamasina is planned, but finance has yet to be secured. There are seven hydroelectric stations, providing just under half of total generating capacity while the remainder is from thermal installations. However, oil imports in 1995 totalled 400,000 tons, whereas hydroelectricity output represented the energy equivalent of only about 90,000 tons of oil. Fuel wood and charcoal is estimated to provide 85% of the country's total energy needs. Many mines and factories have their own small diesel- or steam-powered generators. In April 1994 the government announced plans for the construction of a solar-energy electricity power plant, at a projected cost of US $3,400m. In April 1996 the IDA financed a $46m. project comprising various energy programmes including the promotion of energy efficiency and the rehabilitation and development of equipment, facilities and feasibility studies.

In 1980 the government announced that deposits of petroleum had been located and that the Petroleum Code would be revised. In the following decade several foreign companies signed concession agreements with the government to prospect in a number of areas, particularly in the Morandava basin, in western Madagascar. In 1990 BHP Australia signed an agreement to explore the Mahajanga area in the north west. As a result of the war in the Persian Gulf in late 1990 and early 1991, interest among Western petroleum companies in locating deposits of petroleum outside the Gulf region increased and, in Madagascar, Shell began drilling at three onshore sites in mid-1991. In 1993, however, it completed its exploratory programme and in 1994 announced that it was terminating its activities. So far, only non-commercial deposits of oil and gas have been found. Studies are continuing on deposits of heavy petroleum at Tsimororo.

For some years the USSR provided about two-thirds of Madagascar's imports of petroleum, some on a concessionary financing basis. However, in 1988 the USSR suspended deliveries of petroleum to Madagascar, owing to unpaid bills totalling some US $240m. Madagascar was subsequently obliged to buy Iranian crude petroleum at market prices. Petroleum is also supplied by Libya and Gabon. The Toamasina refinery has the capacity to produce about 747,000 tons annually, but exports fell from 128,912 tons in 1995 to 57,247 tons in 1996. The World Bank has been urging the privatization of the refinery. In late 1995, also under World Bank pressure, the government relinquished the state monopoly on retail sales of petroleum products.

TRANSPORT

Madagascar's mountainous topography has hindered the development of adequate communications and the infrastructure is also prone to cyclone damage. Even major routes may be impassable in bad weather. In 1995 there were 49,837 km of classified roads, of which 8,528 km were main roads and 17,310 km were secondary roads; only 5,731 km of the road network were paved. In 1987 there were 39,500 km of unclassified roads, used only in favourable weather. In 1988 a programme to rehabilitate 4,781 km of roads (of which 1,500 km tarred) by 1993 was initiated. The US $144m. project was to be financed by the IDA, the EC, Switzerland and Norway. In June 1989 the European Development Fund (EDF) granted $10m.

for road rehabilitation in the north and west of the country and in 1992 the Arab Bank for Economic Development in Africa lent a further US $7m. to improve roads in tourist areas.

In 1993 there were 1,095 km of railway. Three lines in the north of the country primarily served the capital, while the fourth (in the south) linked Fianarantsoa to Manakara port. In 1986 the World Bank agreed to lend US $12m. to finance the rehabilitation of the northern railway network, and the 40-km extension of one line. A 72-km extension to a line on the northern system was opened in 1986. In 1994 'Cyclone Geralda' damaged the line from Antananarivo to Toamasina so extensively that the World Bank recommended its replacement by a road link.

Domestic air services are important to Madagascar, on account of its size, difficult terrain and poor quality of road and rail networks. There are 211 airfields, two-thirds of which are privately owned. The main international airport is at Antananarivo. In 1996 the government invited bids for a rehabilitation project including nine of Madagascar's airports. The national airline, Air Madagascar, is 90% owned by the government. Under the government's new liberalization measures, Air Madagascar lost its monopoly on domestic services, although few competitors have emerged. On international routes, Air Madagascar effectively operates a duopoly with Air France. The French charter airline, Air Outre-Mer (AOM), began flights to Antananarivo in 1995, but was banned from landing in Madagascar soon afterwoods. The South African company, Inter Air, began charter flights to Madagascar in 1995 and was joined by a French company, Corsair, in late 1996.

Toamasina and Mahajanga, the principal seaports, suffer from lack of storage space and equipment. Toamasina port handles about 70% of Madagascar's foreign trade and was in the process of being enlarged and modernized, until 80% of the port was destroyed by a cyclone in March 1986. (It suffered further serious damage from 'Cyclone Geralda' in 1994.) In January 1987 the IDA agreed to provide a US $16m. credit for a $34.8m. project to rehabilitate 10 ports. France, Germany and the UK are also financing the project. Toamasina is independently managed but the other ports are operated by the Malagasy Ports Authority. The parastatal Société Malgache de Transports Maritimes operates four ocean-going vessels. Coastal shipping is conducted mainly by private companies. The country's 18 ports handled a total of 1,434,349 tons of freight in 1993 (819,093 tons inward and 615,256 tons outward). In 1984 the government initiated a development project to restore more than 200 km of the Pangalanes canal, which runs for 600 km near the east coast from Toamasina to Farafangana. In early 1990 432 km of the canal between Toamasina and Mananjary were navigable.

TOURISM

In 1989 the government introduced a tourism investment programme, which aimed to achieve 100,000 tourist arrivals by 1995. The government planned to exploit specialist markets represented by the growing number of visitors who are attracted by Madagascar's unusual varieties of wildlife. A number of state-owned hotels were transferred to private-sector ownership, and a French adviser was appointed to prepare a new tourism plan. The French group Savana and its parent company, Pullman–International Hotels, were to implement the tourism project at a total cost of US $234m., of which $30m. was provided by the government, mainly for infrastructural costs. An hotel group, partly owned by Mauritian interests, began the construction of a 200-room luxury hotel in the capital. In 1989 net tourism receipts were estimated at $22m. There were 4,208 hotel rooms and 52,923 tourist arrivals in 1990, when tourist receipts increased to $37m.; in 1991, however, the number of tourist arrivals declined by 34%, to 34,891, in reaction to the country's internal unrest. In 1994 65,839 tourists visited Madagascar, and revenue from tourism was estimated at $46m. The government estimated that arrivals reached 78,800 in 1995, considerably less than the original target number. Revenue from tourism in that year was forecast at $57.6m. The government has declared its aim to attract 230,000 tourist arrivals annually by 2000.

EXTERNAL TRADE AND BALANCE OF PAYMENTS

During the period 1977 to 1987 Madagascar's unfavourable trade balance steadily worsened. Despite a brief rise in the value of exports in 1980, imports increased even faster than before, owing to the official policy of industrialization and overriding emphasis on investment.

As the balance-of-payments problems became increasingly severe, the government was obliged to yield to pressure from the IMF, the World Bank and Western aid donors and creditors to liberalize trade and to adjust the Malagasy franc exchange rate. The reforms succeeded in reducing the external current account deficit from 14.6% of GDP in 1980 to 8.7% in 1986, when it was US $136m. The deficit declined from $149m. in 1988, to $84m. in 1989, as a result of improved export earnings in that year. Following a sharp increase in imports, the deficit on the current account rose to $265m. in 1990; it subsequently recovered slightly, amounting to $198m. in 1992, but increased again to reach $276m. in 1995. The government has aimed to reduce import restrictions and to introduce comprehensive tariff reforms. In February 1988 simplified import procedures were introduced, and the government also announced the removal of export duties from all goods except those, such as coffee, handled by state marketing boards. The trade deficit was converted to a surplus of $1m. in 1989; in 1990, however, a deficit of $249m. was recorded. In 1995 the trade deficit stood at $122m. The principal exports in 1996 were coffee, shrimps, and chromium ores. The principal imports in that year included chemical products, minerals (chiefly crude petroleum), transport equipment, machinery, and electrical manufactures.

The principal source of imports in 1996 was France (31.0%); other major suppliers were Iran, the Southern African Customs Union (SACU) countries, Japan and the USA. France was also the principal market for exports (accounting for 31.7% of exports in that year); other important purchasers were Japan, Germany and Réunion.

ECONOMIC POLICY, PLANNING AND AID

Ratsiraka's initial 'strategy for development', embodied in a Plan covering three stages over the period 1978–2000, proved unsuccessful after only two years, principally as a result of the government's failure to take into consideration Madagascar's inadequate supply of the raw materials which were needed to operate some of the projected (or even existing) factories, the growing rice deficit, and the lack of spare parts and consumer-goods inducements. By mid-1980 the external debt had risen to US $680m.; Ratsiraka appealed successfully to the IMF for an $85m. loan, and later requested that France cancel Madagascar's debt. By 1981 many of Madagascar's traditional suppliers refused to grant credit to its government.

In return for a further stand-by loan of about US $80m. in May 1982, the IMF required the government to devalue the Malagasy franc by 15%; to channel state investments into the agricultural sector, to increase payments to farmers for paddy rice and cotton; and to restrict any increase in the minimum wage to 4.5%. Fulfilment of these and other drastic demands was immediately visible in the 1983 budget allocations, and was also reflected by a revision of national policies under which the state would either retain its monopoly or hold a majority share in certain vital sectors such as mining and hydrocarbons, but in most other areas would allow private entrepreneurs to invest in, and initiate, new projects. Although there was an improvement in the supply of provisions to urban consumers, as a result of the increase in payments to farmers and the liberalization of the rice trade in 1983–84, there was a noticeable rise in the cost of living, while successive devaluations of the Malagasy franc, together with the failure to make any appreciable increase in the wages of non-agricultural workers, placed the cost of basic necessities beyond the means of the average Malagasy. Even with the overall improvements in Madagascar's economic condition, the declining level of production, especially in export crops, caused an increasing dependence on costly imports (particularly fuel and rice) and on foreign aid.

In April 1985 the IMF approved a stand-by arrangement of SDR 29.5m. to support Madagascar's economic and financial programme during 1985–86. At a World Bank-sponsored Consultative Group meeting in April 1986, donors made commitments of about US $600m. for 1986–87. In May the IMF agreed to grant Madagascar two facilities, totalling SDR 32.7m., to offset the effects of the cyclone in March and the shortfalls in export earnings during the previous year. A devaluation of the

Malagasy franc in August (see below), and further liberalization of trade and distribution, encouraged the IMF to provide a three-year stand-by arrangement of SDR 30m. in September. In October the 'Paris Club' of official creditors agreed to reschedule SDR 73.8m. of debts for 1986 and SDR 99.2m. for 1987.

In June 1986 a new investment code was introduced, providing incentives for domestic and foreign investment, particularly in manufacturing for the export market. Also in 1986 the government abolished most state controls on the internal rice trade. In 1987 further measures were introduced to encourage exports by allowing exporters to fix prices directly with foreign purchasers, and imposing a duty, equal to 10% of the import licence, on importers. The Malagasy franc was devalued by 20% in August 1986. There were several subsequent adjustments, and in June 1987 the currency was devalued by a further 41%. The government's reform measures resulted in the approval of a US $100m. structural adjustment loan arrangement from the World Bank and several bilateral donors. In August 1987 the IMF agreed to provide a new stand-by facility of SDR 42.2m. over three years, which included a structural adjustment facility (SAF). In the same month the 'London Club' of commercial creditors agreed to reschedule $59.4m. of debt.

At a meeting in Paris in January 1988, the World Bank-sponsored Consultative Group agreed to provide Madagascar with US $700m. in quick-disbursing aid, conditional upon the rescheduling of debts due to the 'Paris Club' later in the year. The donors strongly commended the Malagasy government's structural adjustment programme. The budget deficit had been reduced to the equivalent of 4% of GDP in 1986 (compared with 18.4% in 1980), and price controls had been lifted from most products and fixed profit margins had been virtually abolished by the end of 1987. In early 1988 the government stated its commitment to rationalize the public sector by closing loss-making nationalized enterprises and selling off many others. At the end of 1988 the IMF approved a 10-month stand-by facility of SDR 13.3m. to replace a credit of SDR 30m. which had expired in March 1988, without being fully drawn. Conditions of the new arrangement included further trade liberalization, stricter controls on government spending, the return of state banks to private-sector ownership, the opening up of financial markets to foreign competition, and improved credit access for producers. This was in addition to the three-year SAF due to expire in August 1990. The IDA released $125m. in July 1988 to support the government's plan to reform the public sector, and made available a credit of $22m. for social programmes.

The new IMF agreement opened the way for further pledges from donors attending a meeting in October 1988 of the 'Paris Club', which agreed to reschedule US $212m. of debt and to cancel $37m. of principal. The Federal Republic of Germany cancelled $116m. of debt in 1988, and in 1989 France decided to write off one-third of the debt owed to it, or about $471.4m. Debt-servicing costs were reduced from $271m. in 1987 to $221m. in 1988. The latest debt relief measures decreased further costs, but in 1988 debt servicing still represented 53.7% of export earnings. In May 1989 the IMF gave approval for a three-year enhanced structural adjustment facility (ESAF), to replace the 10-month stand-by agreement. The credit of SDR 76.9m. was to give support to the programme covering the period 1989–1991 which aims to promote growth of per caput income in real terms and to stabilize the financial sector. As part of the liberalization programme the government removed all price subsidies in March 1989.

Total external debt was estimated at US $3,449m. at the end of 1989, although this represented a decline in US dollar terms compared with 1987, as a result of the devaluation in June of that year. However, total external debt increased to $4,134m. by the end of 1994. Despite the 'Paris Club' rescheduling of debt-service arrangements in 1988, debt-service payments still represented 33.1% of the value of exports of goods and services in 1991; this ratio had declined to 7.6% by 1994, but this was largely because much of the debt service due went unpaid, leading to a steep build-up in arrears. External debt at the end of 1995 totalled $4,302m., of which $3,691m. was long-term public debt; the cost of debt-servicing in that year was estimated to be equivalent to 9.2% of the value of exports of goods and services. Madagascar received a net total of $289m. in official development assistance from members of the OECD's development assistance committee in 1994, of which $273m. was in grant form. The main bilateral donors were France and Japan, while the World Bank's IDA and the EU were the principal multilateral donors. In 1988 the rate of inflation (which had declined to an average of 9.9% in 1984) increased to an average of 27%, owing to the abolition of price controls and the devaluation of the currency, which resulted in higher prices for imported goods. The rate fell back to an average of just over 11% per year in 1990–93, but consumer prices escalated again in 1994 and 1995 (by 39% and 49.1% respectively) as a result of further devaluation, less disciplined monetary policy and the effects of the boom in world coffee prices. The rate of inflation slowed to 19.8% in 1996, giving an average of 22.6% per year in 1990–96.

Liberalization of the banking sector has attracted foreign private banks to Madagascar. Banque Nationale de Paris is the main shareholder owning 55% of Banque Malgache de l'Océan Indien (BMOI), which was officially opened in January 1990. Belgian and German banks own 20% of BMOI, and about 300 Malagasy shareholders own 25%. Privatization of the two remaining state banks, Bankin'ny Tantsaha Mpamokatra (BTM) and Banky Fampandrosoana ny Varotra (BVF), is a key condition of structural adjustment lending, but progress has been slow.

In 1991 a public investment programme (1991–93), financed by the World Bank, IMF and other international donors, was initiated. The programme, which cost an estimated US $1,000m., again emphasized the liberalization of trade and the financial sector, the encouragement of foreign and domestic investment, a reduction in the role of parastatal bodies, and increased producer prices. Following a prolonged general strike in the second half of 1991, however, the programme was deferred, pending the fulfilment of certain conditions, which included the transfer of a number of parastatal organizations to the private sector and a reduction in public expenditure.

The general strike in 1991 severely affected the financial sector: despite a substantial decline in capital expenditure, the ensuing fall in tax revenue, in conjunction with increased expenditure on personnel, prompted a rise in the budgetary deficit in 1991, to 272,400m. Malagasy francs (equivalent to 5.5% of GDP). Reserves of foreign exchange, which totalled US $223.7m. at the end of 1988 (excluding gold), declined to $89m. Economic conditions failed to improve in 1992, owing to the continued lack of political stability. In 1993 the new government initiated negotiations with the Bretton Woods institutions to obtain funding for a further economic reform programme. Following a report by a joint mission by the World Bank and IMF in early 1994, however, the organizations insisted that a number of economic reforms be implemented as a precondition to the disbursement of funds to support a new structural adjustment programme. Severe cyclones in early 1994 resulted in a further deterioration in economic conditions, increasing the necessity for substantial external assistance, while the French government indicated that continuing aid for reforms was conditional on an agreement between Madagascar and the Bretton Woods institutions. In May the government accepted the conditions imposed by the World Bank and IMF, notably the 'floating' of the Malagasy franc (which resulted in an immediate devaluation), the removal of price controls, further 'privatization' (93 state-owned enterprises had been either liquidated or transferred to the private sector in 1988–92), and measures to reduce budgetary expenditure, including substantial retrenchment in the civil service. A 'framework agreement', signed by the government and the Bretton Woods institutions in June, provided for the introduction of further reforms (including the removal of price controls and measures to reduce budgetary expenditure), prior to the adoption of a structural adjustment programme later that year. However, parliamentary opposition to the implementation of the economic austerity measures impeded subsequent progress (see Recent History). In October, in compliance with demands by the IMF and World Bank, the prime minister undertook to suspend arrangements with private enterprises whereby the government obtained financial assistance independently from the Bretton Woods institutions, and the dismissal, in early 1995, of the governor of the central bank fulfilled a further precondition to the resumption of credit from the World Bank and IMF. In February the government accepted a number of economic reforms (similar to those agreed in June

1994), including the imposition of a new tax on petroleum products and restrictions on loans by the central bank to private enterprises; subject to the successful implementation of these measures, the IMF was to reschedule Madagascar's external debt arrears and resume financial disbursements later in 1995. In September of that year, however, a World Bank mission reported delays in the implementation of a number of prescribed economic reforms.

Political paralysis in early 1996, including a bitter feud between the prime minister, Emmanuel Rakotovahiny, and the finance minister, Jean-Claude Raherimanjato, continued to stall reforms deemed necessary for agreement on new structural adjustment financing. The managing director of the IMF, Michel Camdessus, visited Antananarivo at the end of April and subsequently said that no new deal with the Fund would be possible without a cabinet reshuffle. The appointment of Norbert Ratsirahonana as prime minister in May 1996, followed by a government vote of confidence in reforms regarded as conditions for further IMF support, raised hopes of a breakthrough. IMF officials arrived in Madagascar in August for more talks; they agreed the government's economic policy framework document (1996–99) setting out the measures needed to satisfy the aid donors. The document was primarily concerned with controlling inflation, promoting growth and investment, and improving the working of the foreign exchange market. Specific provisions included the ending of monopolies (public or private), a major improvement in tax collection and a concentration of government expenditure on education, security and road improvement. In November the IMF approved a three-year loan (equivalent to US $118m.) in support of the economic reform programme for 1996–99. Following his re-election in December 1996, President Didier Ratsiraka affirmed his commitment to the implementation of the structural adjustment programme. Subsequent negotiations with the 'Paris Club' of creditor governments resulted in the restructuring of Madagascar's debt, with an agreement to reduce its value by 67%. In March 1997 the World Bank approved a structural adjustment loan of $70m., and further aid was forthcoming from the EU and the African Development Bank. In June the government released a list of the 45 companies that it intended to privatize. Economic indicators at the end of 1996 were favourable, with a reduction in the rate of inflation; it was hoped that continued economic liberalization would increase export revenue, and consequently reduce the widespread poverty in the country. However, future concessions by donor and creditor nations were to be conditional on the IMF's assessment of Madagascar's sustained performance under the economic reform programme, which was largely dependent on continued political stability.

Statistical Survey

Source (unless otherwise stated): Banque des Données de l'Etat, BP 485, Antananarivo; tel. 21613.

Area and Population

AREA, POPULATION AND DENSITY

Area (sq km)	587,041*
Population (census results)	
1974–75†	7,603,790
1–19 August 1993	
Males	5,991,171
Females	6,100,986
Total	12,092,157
Population (official estimates at mid-year)	
1990	11,197,000
1991	11,493,000
Density (per sq km) at August 1993	20.6

* 226,658 sq miles.

† The census took place in three stages: in provincial capitals on 1 December 1974; in Antananarivo and remaining urban areas on 17 February 1975; and in rural areas on 1 June 1975.

PRINCIPAL ETHNIC GROUPS (estimated population, 1974)

Merina (Hova)	1,993,000	Sakalava	470,156*
Betsimisaraka	1,134,000	Antandroy	412,500
Betsileo	920,600	Antaisaka	406,468*
Tsimihety	558,100		

* 1972 figure.

PRINCIPAL TOWNS (population at 1974–75 census)

Antananarivo (capital)	406,366	Mahajanga (Majunga)	65,864
Antsirabé	78,941	Toliary (Tuléar)	45,676
Toamasina (Tamatave)	77,395	Antsiranana (Diégo-Suarez)	40,443
Fianarantsoa	68,054		

The population of Antananarivo was estimated to be 662,585 in 1985.

BIRTHS AND DEATHS (UN estimates, annual averages)

	1980–85	1985–90	1990–95
Birth rate (per 1,000)	47.3	47.2	43.9
Death rate (per 1,000)	15.4	13.7	11.8

Expectation of life (UN estimates, years at birth, 1990–95): 56.5 (males 55.0; females 58.0).

Source: UN, *World Population Prospects: The 1994 Revision*.

ECONOMICALLY ACTIVE POPULATION
(ILO estimates, '000 persons at mid-1980)

	Males	Females	Total
Agriculture etc.	1,731	1,583	3,314
Industry	216	28	244
Services	457	82	539
Total labour force	2,405	1,693	4,098

Source: ILO, *Economically Active Population Estimates and Projections, 1950–2025*.

Mid-1985 (official estimates, '000 persons): Total labour force 3,929 (males 2,194; females 1,735) (Source: ILO, *Yearbook of Labour Statistics*).

Mid-1995 (estimates in '000): Agriculture, forestry and fishing 5,357; Total labour force 7,020 (Source: FAO, *Production Yearbook*).

Agriculture

PRINCIPAL CROPS ('000 metric tons)

	1993	1994	1995
Maize	175	155	169*
Rice (paddy)	2,550	2,360	2,596*
Sugar cane	1,960	1,980	1,980†
Potatoes	280	270	270†
Sweet potatoes	500	560	560†
Cassava (Manioc)	2,350	2,413*	2,420†
Taro (Coco yam)†	125	125	125
Dry beans	52	50	50†
Vegetables and melons	343	333	333†
Oranges†	86	80	80
Bananas†	230	210	210
Avocados†	22	20	20
Mangoes†	205	200	200
Pineapples†	50	48	48
Other fruits†	220	202	202
Groundnuts (in shell)	32	28	28†
Cottonseed	16	15*	20*
Cotton (lint)*	11	12	13
Coconuts†	86	80	80
Copra†	10	10	10
Coffee (green)	78	79	79*
Cocoa beans	4	4*	4*
Tobacco (leaves)	2	2†	2†
Sisal	18	17	17†

* Unofficial figure(s). † FAO estimate(s).

Source: FAO, *Production Yearbook*.

LIVESTOCK ('000 head, year ending September)

	1993	1994	1995
Cattle	10,287	10,288*	10,309*
Pigs*	1,525	1,558	1,592
Sheep†	735	740	740
Goats†	1,270	1,300	1,300

* Unofficial figure(s). † FAO estimates.

Chickens (FAO estimates, million): 22 in 1993; 23 in 1994; 23 in 1995.
Ducks (FAO estimates, million): 5 in 1993; 5 in 1994; 5 in 1995.
Turkeys (FAO estimates, million): 3 in 1993; 4 in 1994; 4 in 1995.

Source: FAO, *Production Yearbook*.

LIVESTOCK PRODUCTS (FAO estimates, '000 metric tons)

	1993	1994	1995
Cows' milk	479	481	483
Beef and veal	143	143	144
Pig meat	49	50	52
Poultry meat	78	81	81
Hen eggs	17.4	18.2	18.2
Honey	3.8	3.8	3.8
Cattle hides	20.2	20.2	20.3

Source: FAO, *Production Yearbook*.

Forestry

ROUNDWOOD REMOVALS
('000 cubic metres, excluding bark)

	1992	1993	1994
Sawlogs, veneer logs and logs for sleepers*	468	278	127
Other industrial wood*†	339	339	339
Fuel wood	8,148*	9,211	10,179
Total	8,955*	9,828	10,645

* FAO estimate(s).
† Assumed to be unchanged since 1977.

Source: FAO, *Yearbook of Forest Products*.

SAWNWOOD PRODUCTION
('000 cubic metres, including railway sleepers)

	1992*	1993	1994
Coniferous (softwood)*	5	2	2
Broadleaved (hardwood)	233	139	64
Total	238	141	66

* FAO estimates.

Source: FAO, *Yearbook of Forest Products*.

Fishing

('000 metric tons, live weight)

	1993	1994	1995
Inland waters:			
Freshwater fishes	30.0	32.9	33.2
Indian Ocean:			
Marine fishes	72.9	71.0	72.8
Marine crabs	1.1	1.3	1.3
Tropical spiny lobsters	0.4	0.4	0.4
Shrimps and prawns	9.7	12.1	10.3
Molluscs	0.6	0.6	0.7
Other aquatic animals	0.5	1.8	1.5
Total catch	115.0	120.0	120.1

Source: FAO, *Yearbook of Fishery Statistics*.

Mining

(metric tons)

	1993	1994	1995*
Chromite†	144,311	75,000	74,000
Salt	63,399	75,783	80,000
Graphite (natural)	188	14,600	13,900
Mica	850	563	387

* Provisional figures.
† Figures refer to gross weight. The estimated chromium content is 27%.

Source: IMF, *Madagascar—Selected Issues and Statistical Annex* (June 1996).

Industry

SELECTED PRODUCTS (metric tons, unless otherwise indicated)

	1993	1994	1995*
Raw sugar	71,222	79,280	89,474
Beer ('000 hectolitres)	227.7	219.0	318.8
Cigarettes	2,304	2,000	1,736
Woven cotton fabrics (million metres)	35.1	38.7	25.0
Leather footwear ('000 pairs)	176	180	181
Plastic footwear ('000 pairs)	804	535	517
Paints	2,775	2,600	2,550
Soap	19,276	16,837	15,000
Motor spirit—petrol ('000 cu metres)	81.5	56.8	87.9
Kerosene ('000 cu metres)	74.8	23.4	110.8
Gas-diesel (distillate fuel) oil ('000 cu metres)	101.1	35.4	129.2
Residual fuel oils ('000 cu metres)	183.4	61.0	177.3
Cement	36,397	8,524	45,009
Electric energy (million kWh)†	532	540	552

* Provisional figures.
† Production by the state-owned utility only, excluding electricity generated by industries for their own use.

Source: IMF, *Madagascar—Selected Issues and Statistical Annex* (June 1996).

Finance

CURRENCY AND EXCHANGE RATES

Monetary Units

100 centimes = 1 franc malgache (franc MG—Malagasy franc).

Sterling and Dollar Equivalents (31 January 1997)

£1 sterling = 7,635.0 francs MG;
US $1 = 4,764.4 francs MG;
10,000 francs MG = £1.310 = $2.099.

Average Exchange Rate (Malagasy francs per US $)

1994 3,067.3
1995 4,265.6
1996 4,061.3

BUDGET ('000 million francs MG)

Revenue*	1993	1994	1995
Tax revenue	526.5	702.2	1,120.8
Taxes on income, profits and capital gains	103.6	150.7	167.8
Corporate	66.1	68.5	83.2
Individual	25.9	40.6	58.6
Domestic taxes on goods and services	143.0	201.4	298.5
General sales, turnover or value-added tax	80.0	177.5	242.3
Excises	26.3	5.9	0.8
Taxes on international trade and transactions	269.5	335.6	633.8
Import duties	255.6	320.0	589.8
Export duties	13.9	15.6	43.9
Other current revenue	96.6	55.0	28.0
Entrepreneurial and property income	12.8	18.2	10.6
Capital revenue	10.5	4.8	0.8
Total	633.6	762.0	1,149.6

Expenditure†	1993	1994	1995
General public services (incl. public order)	217.5	181.9	174.6
Defence	80.5	84.6	118.6
Education	181.3	187.0	264.6
Health	47.0	83.3	136.6
Social security and welfare	14.6	32.9	61.6
Housing and community amenities	0.6	49.4	67.0
Recreational, cultural and religious affairs and services	2.9	1.0	13.1
Economic affairs and services	341.2	432.8	658.9
Agriculture, forestry, fishing and hunting	46.7	109.1	143.1
Mining and mineral resources, manufacturing and construction	7.3	58.4	71.1
Transportation and communication	161.0	105.6	121.1
Other purposes	382.0	681.4	849.2
Interest payments	258.4	491.8	687.9
Total	1,267.6	1,734.3	2,344.2
Current	782.2	1,165.5	1,535.4
Capital	485.4	568.8	808.8

* Excluding grants received ('000 million francs MG): 225.4 in 1993; 274.0 in 1994; 392.1 in 1995.

† Excluding lending minus repayments ('000 million francs MG): 55.2 in 1993; 44.3 in 1994; 29.7 in 1995.

Source: IMF, *Government Finance Statistics Yearbook.*

INTERNATIONAL RESERVES (US $ million at 31 December)

	1994	1995	1996
IMF special drawing rights	—	—	0.1
Foreign exchange	71.6	108.9	240.8
Total	71.6	109.0	240.9

Source: IMF, *International Financial Statistics.*

MONEY SUPPLY ('000 million francs MG at 31 December)

	1994	1995	1996
Currency outside banks	614.5	758.7	829.4
Demand deposits at deposit money banks	989.0	1,089.3	1,338.3
Total money	1,603.5	1,848.0	2,167.7

Source: IMF, *International Financial Statistics.*

COST OF LIVING (Consumer Price Index for Madagascans in Antananarivo; base: 1990 = 100)

	1994	1995	1996
Food	193.0	290.7	346.0
All items*	190.1	283.3	339.3

* Excluding rent.

Source: UN, *Monthly Bulletin of Statistics.*

NATIONAL ACCOUNTS ('000 million francs MG at current prices)

Expenditure on the Gross Domestic Product

	1993	1994	1995
Government final consumption expenditure	506.5	628.8	904.2
Private final consumption expenditure	5,805.7	8,215.7	12,361.5
Increase in stocks } Gross fixed capital formation }	738.5	995.6	1,474.9
Total domestic expenditure	7,050.7	9,840.1	14,740.6
Exports of goods and services	988.1	2,011.8	3,182.0
Less Imports of goods and services	1,587.9	2,720.9	4,282.7
GDP in purchasers' values	6,450.9	9,131.1	13,639.9
GDP at constant 1990 prices	4,456.3	4,454.2	4,533.7

Source: IMF, *International Financial Statistics.*

Gross Domestic Product by Economic Activity

	1989	1990	1991
Agriculture, hunting, forestry and fishing	1,181.7	1,334.3	1,488.4
Mining and quarrying	16.1	14.9	14.8
Manufacturing	471.6	492.6	530.6
Electricity, gas and water	42.7	78.7	87.0
Construction	48.7	61.7	52.6
Trade, restaurants and hotels	351.6	426.2	498.0
Transport, storage and communications	623.9	721.6	747.9
Finance, insurance, real estate and business services	58.7	64.6	70.0
Public administration and defence	190.9	240.7	284.4
Other services	658.7	756.9	791.9
GDP at factor cost	3,644.6	4,192.0	4,565.5
Indirect taxes, *less* subsidies	360.7	409.6	340.9
GDP in purchasers' values	4,005.3	4,601.6	4,906.4

Source: UN Economic Commission for Africa, *African Statistical Yearbook.*

BALANCE OF PAYMENTS (US $ million)

	1993	1994	1995
Exports of goods f.o.b.	335	450	507
Imports of goods f.o.b.	–514	–546	–628
Trade balance	–180	–96	–122
Exports of services	187	206	242
Imports of services	–302	–328	–359
Balance on goods and services	–295	–218	–238
Other income received	3	2	7
Other income paid	–154	–158	–174
Balance on goods, services and income	–446	–374	–405
Current transfers received	202	114	141
Current transfers paid	–14	–17	–12
Current balance	–258	–277	–276
Capital account (net)	78	62	45
Direct investment from abroad	15	6	10
Other investment assets	–47	19	–62
Other investment liabilities	–126	–147	–145
Net errors and omissions	4	61	98
Overall balance	–334	–276	–330

Source: IMF, *International Financial Statistics*.

External Trade

PRINCIPAL COMMODITIES
(million francs MG)

Imports c.i.f.	1995	1996
Animal products	58,154	41,489
Vegetable products	178,442	123,160
Wheat and meslin	52,927	58,202
Rice	71,911	34,684
Animal or vegetable fats, oils and waxes	81,526	65,520
Food oils	40,626	40,623
Prepared foodstuffs	60,289	37,167
Mineral products	351,294	295,782
Crude petroleum	257,969	178,453
Chemical products	319,571	305,971
Pharmaceutical products	64,064	61,669
Plastic materials	83,827	56,947
Rubber manufactures	53,942	67,439
Rubber tyres	35,018	49,576
Paper, paperboard, etc.	107,723	79,716
Base metals and articles thereof	263,571	162,796
Iron and steel	176,383	75,202
Machinery and mechanical appliances (non-electric)	227,276	210,186
Electrical machinery and appliances	122,691	193,262
Radio and television equipment	26,852	104,791
Transport equipment	238,830	214,846
Passenger cars and buses	75,020	73,180
Lorries	80,739	80,749
Total (incl. others)	2,300,143	2,056,108

Exports f.o.b.	1995	1996
Animal products	281,100	233,919
Meat and meat preparations	36,932	16,540
Shrimps and prawns	200,695	178,627
Vegetable products	725,980	471,104
Coffee (green)	346,300	232,242
Vanilla	142,383	47,988
Cloves	47,155	22,814
Litchis	29,180	25,052
Prepared foodstuffs	47,817	30,730
Sugar	38,059	21,053
Mineral products	161,474	227,557
Graphite	40,474	33,061
Chromium ores	52,207	151,610
Petroleum products	60,561	39,414
Chemical products	32,227	24,920
Wood, cork and articles thereof	28,437	25,277
Textiles and textile articles	121,328	117,400
Cotton fabrics	48,737	43,612
Total (incl. others)	1,505,875	1,215,702

Source: Ministère du commerce et de la consommation.

PRINCIPAL TRADING PARTNERS (million francs MG)

Imports	1994	1995	1996
Belgium-Luxembourg	16,447	54,136	35,539
China, People's Republic	36,011	75,847	94,410
France	420,039	682,144	638,339
Germany	79,564	18,180	12,193
India	8,602	23,190	35,339
Iran	47,645	231,441	187,198
Italy	27,144	53,041	40,578
Japan	136,088	137,094	118,265
Malaysia	18,644	35,761	33,632
Netherlands	16,447	29,362	23,261
Pakistan	26,685	32,823	2,432
Romania	14,920	5,891	17,440
Saudi Arabia	22,552	30,018	3,529
Singapore	20,066	37,517	47,497
Southern African Customs Union*	114,783	144,261	169,140
Spain	16,037	16,844	14,433
Switzerland	14,182	30,418	14,607
United Kingdom	40,539	54,342	47,459
USA	61,494	86,993	102,889
Viet Nam	14,259	96	3,455
Total (incl. others)	1,380,003	2,300,143	2,056,108

* Comprising Botswana, Lesotho, Namibia, South Africa and Swaziland.

Exports	1994	1995	1996
Belgium-Luxembourg	29,572	73,751	53,179
Canada	11,297	1,061	3,056
France	363,028	427,598	385,865
Germany	120,591	125,176	77,513
Italy	48,990	79,037	53,896
Japan	85,693	33,300	192,659
Mauritius	20,615	58,411	47,691
Netherlands	29,572	31,291	19,333
Poland	15,556	9,024	—
Portugal	7,453	17,651	16,570
Réunion	67,517	89,521	69,184
Singapore	23,105	35,115	19,124
Spain	26,716	52,306	27,563
Switzerland	3,491	24,138	2,511
Tunisia	13,358	5,726	290
United Kingdom	52,428	56,945	36,956
USA	84,343	98,980	50,797
Total (incl. others)	1,060,462	1,505,875	1,215,702

Source: Ministère du commerce et de la consommation.

Transport

RAILWAYS (traffic)

	1985	1986	1987
Passengers carried ('000)	2,564	3,161	2,974
Passenger-km (millions)	178	208	209
Freight carried ('000 metric tons)	808	735	693
Ton-km (millions)	208.5	188	174

Passenger-km (million): 242 in 1988; 204 in 1989; 198 in 1990. Ton-km (million): 174 in 1988; 207 in 1989; 209 in 1990 (Source: UN, *Statistical Yearbook*).

ROAD TRAFFIC (estimates, vehicles in use at 31 December)

	1993	1994	1995
Passenger cars	50,900	54,900	58,100
Buses and coaches	3,530	3,800	4,340
Lorries and vans	9,790	10,600	11,000
Road tractors	430	475	520

Source: International Road Federation, *World Road Statistics*.

SHIPPING

Merchant Fleet (registered at 31 December)

	1994	1995	1996
Number of vessels	94	96	99
Displacement ('000 gross registered tons)	36.1	38.1	39.3

Source: Lloyd's Register of Shipping, *World Fleet Statistics*.

International Sea-borne Freight Traffic ('000 metric tons)

	1987	1988	1989
Goods loaded:			
Mahajanga	17	18	29.4
Toamasina	252	350	360.6
Other ports	79	100	137.4
Total	348	468	527.4
Goods unloaded:			
Mahajanga	37	32	30.8
Toamasina	748	778	708.9
Other ports	48	53	52.0
Total	833	863	791.7

1990 ('000 metric tons): Goods loaded 540; Goods unloaded 984 (Source: UN, *Monthly Bulletin of Statistics*).

CIVIL AVIATION (traffic on scheduled services)

	1992	1993	1994
Kilometres flown (million)	6	7	7
Passengers carried ('000)	344	419	451
Passenger-km (million)	432	499	567
Total ton-km (million)	66	72	74

Source: UN, *Statistical Yearbook*.

Tourism

	1993	1994	1995*
Tourist arrivals	55,355	65,839	78,800
Tourist receipts (US $ million)	39.7	46.1	57.6

* Preliminary figures.

Source: IMF, *Madagascar—Selected Issues and Statistical Annex* (June 1996).

Communications Media

	1992	1993	1994
Radio receivers ('000 in use)	2,565	2,655	2,740
Television receivers ('000 in use)	260	272	280
Telephones ('000 main lines in use)	37	35	34
Book production†:			
Titles	85	143	114
Copies ('000)	402*	537	287
Daily newspapers:			
Number	7	n.a.	7
Circulation ('000 copies)	48	n.a.	60
Non-daily newspapers:			
Number	37	n.a.	31
Circulation	168	n.a.	90*

* Estimate.

† Including pamphlets (39 titles and 219,000 copies in 1992; 57 titles and 359,000 copies in 1993; 42 titles and 106,000 copies in 1994).

Sources: UNESCO, *Statistical Yearbook*; UN, *Statistical Yearbook*.

Education

(1993/94, unless otherwise indicated)

	Institutions	Teachers	Pupils		
			Males	Females	Total
Primary	13,624	37,676	767,027	737,641	1,504,668
Secondary:					
General	n.a.	15,118	148,341	149,900	298,241
Teacher training	n.a.	58	199	142	341
Vocational*	n.a.	1,091	5,348	2,705	8,053
University level*	n.a.	819	18,466	14,909	33,375

* 1992/93 figures.

Source: UNESCO, *Statistical Yearbook*.

Directory

The Constitution

The Constitution of the Third Republic of Madagascar, which was endorsed by national referendum on 19 August 1992, enshrines a unitary state, and provides for a bicameral legislature, comprising a Senate and a National Assembly. Two-thirds of the members of the Senate are selected by an electoral college (which is elected at regional and departmental level) for a term of four years, and the remaining one-third of the members are appointed by the President. The 138-member National Assembly is elected by universal adult suffrage, under a system of proportional representation, for a four-year term of office. The constitutional Head of State is the President, who is elected for a term of five years. If no candidate obtains an overall majority in the presidential election, a second round of voting is to take place a maximum of 30 days after the publication of the results of the first ballot. Executive power is vested in a Prime Minister, who, under an amendment to the Constitution (approved in a referendum of September 1995), is appointed by the President from candidates nominated by the political parties represented in the National Assembly. The Prime Minister appoints the Council of Ministers, subject to the approval of the President.

The Government

HEAD OF STATE

President: Adm. (retd) DIDIER RATSIRAKA (took office 9 February 1997).

COUNCIL OF MINISTERS
(August 1997)

Prime Minister: PASCAL RAKOTOMAVO.

Deputy Prime Minister in charge of Foreign Affairs: HERIZO RAZAFIMAHALEO.

Deputy Prime Minister in charge of Finance and the Economy: TANTELY ANDRIANARIVO.

Deputy Prime Minister in charge of Decentralization and the Budget: PIERROT RAJAONARIVELO.

Minister of Industrialization and Craftsmanship: MANASSÉ ESOAVELOMANDROSO.

Minister of the Private Sector and Privatization: CONSTANT HORACE.

Minister of Trade and Consumption: AUGUSTE PARAINA.

Minister of Energy and Mining: CHARLES RASOZA.

Minister of Tourism: JULIETTE RAHARISOA.

Minister of Secondary and Basic Education: JACQUIT SIMON.

Minister of Higher Education: Prof. ANGE ANDRIANARISOA.

Minister of Technical Education and Vocational Training: BONIFACE LEVELO.

Minister of Youth and Sports: LINA ANDRIAMIFIDIMANANA.

Minister of Information, Culture and Communication: FREDO BETSIMIFIRA.

Minister of Population and Solidarity: ERNEST NJARA.

Minister of Health: HENRIETTE RAHANTALALAO.

Minister of the Civil Service, Labour and Social Legislation: ABEL JEAN DÉSIRÉ RATOVONELINJAFY.

Minister of Public Works: Col JEAN EMILE TSARANAZY.

Minister of Regional and Town Planning: HERIVELONA RAMANANTSOA.

Minister of Posts and Telecommunications: NY HASINA ANDRIAMANJATO.

Minister of Transport and Meteorology: NAIVO RAMAMONJISOA.

Minister of Agriculture: M. RANJAKASON.

Minister of Fishing and Fish Stocks: ABDALLAH HOUSSEN.

Minister of the Environment: COLETTE VAOHITA.

Minister of Water and Forests: RIJA RAJOHNSON.

Minister of Livestock: Lt-Commdr NDRIANASOLO.

Minister of the Armed Forces: Brig. MARCEL RANJEVA.

Minister of the Interior: Col JEAN JACQUES RASOLONDRAIBE.

Minister of Justice and Keeper of the Seals: ANACLET IMBIKI.

Minister of Scientific Research: LILA RATSIFANDRIAMANANA.

Secretary of State for Public Security: BEN MAROUF AZALY.

Secretary of State for the Gendarmerie: Brig. JEAN PAUL BORY.

MINISTRIES

Office of the Prime Minister: BP 248, Mahazoarivo, 101 Antananarivo; tel. (2) 25258; telex 22339; fax (2) 35258.

Ministry of Agriculture: BP 500, Anosy, 101 Antananarivo; tel. (2) 24710; telex 22508; fax (2) 26561.

Ministry of the Armed Forces: BP 08, Ampahibe, 101 Antananarivo; tel. (2) 22211; fax (2) 35420.

Ministry of the Civil Service, Labour and Social Legislation: Tsaralalana, 101 Antananarivo; tel. (2) 24816.

Ministry of Decentralization and the Budget: BP 268, Antaninarenina, Antananarivo; tel. (2) 22636.

Ministry of Energy and Mining: BP 527, Antaninarenina, Antananarivo; tel. (2) 25515; telex 22540; fax (2) 32554.

Ministry of the Environment: Ampandrianomby, 101 Antananarivo; tel. (2) 40908.

Ministry of Finance and the Economy: BP 61, Antaninarenina, 101 Antananarivo; tel. (2) 35422; telex 22489; fax (2) 34530.

Ministry of Fishing and Fish Stocks: BP 1699, Ampandrianomby, 101 Antananarivo; tel. (2) 40650; fax (2) 41655.

Ministry of Foreign Affairs: Anosy, 101 Antananarivo; tel. (2) 21198; telex 22236; fax (2) 34484.

Ministry of Health: Ambohidahy, 101 Antananarivo; tel. (2) 23697.

Ministry of Higher Education: BP 4163, Tsimbazaza, 101 Antananarivo; tel. (2) 27185; fax (2) 23897.

Ministry of Industrialization and Craftsmanship: Antaninarenina, 101 Antananarivo; tel. (2) 25515; fax (2) 27790.

Ministry of Information, Culture and Communications: BP 305, 101 Antananarivo; tel. (2) 27092; fax (2) 29448.

Ministry of the Interior: BP 23, Anosy, 101 Antananarivo; tel. (2) 23084; fax (2) 35579.

Ministry of Justice: BP 231, Faravohitra, 101 Antananarivo; tel. (2) 24030; fax (2) 62376.

Ministry of Livestock: BP 484, Antsahavola, Antananarivo; tel. (2) 24026.

Ministry of Population and Solidarity: Ambohijatovo, 101 Antananarivo; tel. (2) 23075; fax (2) 27394.

Ministry of Posts and Telecommunications: Antaninarenina, 101 Antananarivo; tel. (2) 26121; telex 22250.

Ministry of the Private Sector and Privatization: BP 674, Anosy, 101 Antananarivo; tel. (2) 20647; fax (2) 28505.

Ministry of Public Works: Anosy, 101 Antananarivo; tel. (2) 24224; telex 22343.

Ministry of Regional and Town Planning: BP 3378, Anosy, 101 Antananarivo; tel. (2) 35617; fax (2) 35613.

Ministry of Scientific Research: 21 rue Fernand Kasanga, BP 6224, Andoharano-Tsimbazaza, 101 Antananarivo; tel. (2) 33288; telex 22539; fax (2) 24075; e-mail cidst@bow.dts.mg.

Ministry of Secondary and Basic Education: BP 267, Anosy, 101 Antananarivo; tel. (2) 21325; fax (2) 24765.

Ministry of Technical Education and Vocational Training: Complexe scolaire, Ampefiloha, BP 793, 101 Antananarivo; tel. (2) 26014; fax (2) 25176.

Ministry of Tourism: BP 610, 101 Antananarivo; tel. (2) 26298; fax (2) 26710.

Ministry of Trade and Consumption: Ambohidahy, Antananarivo; tel. (2) 27409.

Ministry of Transport and Meteorology: Anosy, 101 Antananarivo; tel. (2) 24604; telex 22301; fax (2) 24001.

Ministry of Water and Forests: BP 243, Nanisana, Antananarivo; tel. (2) 40610; fax (2) 40230.

Ministry of Youth and Sports: Ambohijatovo, Place Goulette, 101 Antananarivo; tel. (2) 23075.

President and Legislature

PRESIDENT

Presidential Election, First Ballot, 3 November 1996

Candidate	% of votes
Adm. (retd) DIDIER RATSIRAKA	36.6
Prof. ALBERT ZAFY	23.4
HERIZO RAZAFIMAHALEO	15.1
NORBERT RATSIRAHONANA	10.1
Pastor RICHARD ANDRIAMANJATO	4.9
Others	9.9
Total	100.0

Second Ballot, 29 December 1996

Candidate	% of votes
Adm. (retd) DIDIER RATSIRAKA	50.71
Prof. ALBERT ZAFY	49.29
Total	100.00

LEGISLATURE

The August 1992 Constitution provides for a bicameral legislature, comprising a Senate and a National Assembly.

National Assembly

President: Pastor RICHARD ANDRIAMANJATO.

General Election, 16 June 1993

Party	Seats
HVR	46
MFM	15
Leader Fanilo	13
FAMIMA	11
Fihaonana	8
RPSD	8
AKFM–Fanavaozana	5
UNDD–HVR	5
UNDD	2
CSDDM	2
Farimbona	2
Accord	2
Fivoarana	2
Teachers and Educators–HVR	1
GRAD ILOAFO	1
Vatomizana	1
Others	14
Total	138

Political Organizations

Following the restoration of multi-party politics in March 1990, more than 120 political associations emerged, of which 25 secured representation in the National Assembly in 1993. After various changes and shifting alliances, by mid-1997 the parties in the National Assembly had reorganized into three main groups:

Presidential Group: parties supporting Pres. Ratsiraka, consisting mainly of:

Association pour la renaissance de Madagascar (AREMA): party of Pres. DIDIER RATSIRAKA; f. 1975 as Avant-garde de la révolution malgache; adopted present name 1997.

Leader Fanilo: f. 1993 as a party of 'non-politicians'; Leader HERIZO RAZAFIMAHALEO.

AKFM–Fanavaozana (AKFM–Renouveau): f. 1989 as a breakaway group from the Marxist Parti du congrès de l'indépendance de Madagascar (AKFM); supports liberal policies; Leader Pastor RICHARD ANDRIAMANJATO.

Vonjy iray tsy mivaky (VITM–Elan populaire pour l'unité nationale): f. 1973; centrist; Leader Dr JÉRÔME MAROJAMA RAZANABAHINY.

Opposition: sometimes referred to as the extremist opposition; led by fmr Pres. Zafy and consisting mainly of:

Union nationale pour la défense de la démocratie (UNDD): f. 1991 by Prof. Albert Zafy as Union nationale pour le développement et la démocratie; named changed 1996.

GRAD ILOAFO: f. 1992 by its Leader TOVONANAHARY RABETSITONTA.

Panorama Group: a 'third force' led by fmr prime ministers Ravony and Ratsirahonana; named after hotel where party leaders met in June 1997 to form an alliance to provide constructive opposition to the govt:

Committee for the support of democracy and development in Madagascar (CSDDM): f. 1993; Leader FRANCISQUE RAVONY.

Ny asa vita no ifampitsara (AVI)–('People are judged by the work they do'): f. 1997 to promote human rights, hard work and development; Leader NORBERT RATSIRAHONANA.

Parti sociale démocrate (PSD): f. 1957; party of fmr Pres. Tsiranana; ruling party 1958–72; relaunched 1990; Leader Mme RUFFINE TSIRANANA.

Rassemblement pour le socialisme et la démocratie (RPSD): f. 1993 as a breakaway group from PSD; Leader EVARISTE MARSON.

MASTERS: f. 1997 by ALAIN RAMAROSON after he was dismissed as Pres. of political dept of the Hery Velona Rasalama (HVR, now disbanded); Leader ALAIN RAMAROSON.

Outside these groups are some 'independent' deputies and several other parties, notably:

Mouvement pour le progrès de Madagascar (Mpitolona ho amin'ny Fandrosoan'ny Madagasikara–MFM): 101 Antananarivo; f. 1972 as Mouvement pour le pouvoir prolétarien (MFM), adopted present name in 1990; advocates liberal and market-orientated policies; Leader MANANDAFY RAKOTONIRINA; Sec.-Gen. GERMAIN RAKOTONIRAINY.

Fihaonana: f. 1990; Leader GUY RAZANAMASY.

Diplomatic Representation

EMBASSIES IN MADAGASCAR

China, People's Republic: Ancien Hôtel Panorama, BP 1658, 101 Antananarivo; Ambassador: ZHAO BAOZHEN.

Egypt: 47 ave Lénine, BP 4082, Ankadifotsy, 101 Antananarivo; tel. (2) 25233; telex 22364; fax (2) 27959; Ambassador: ALY ELKARAKSY.

France: 3 rue Jean Jaurès, BP 204, 101 Antananarivo; tel. (2) 23700; telex 22201; Ambassador: CAMILLE ROHOU.

Germany: 101 rue du Pasteur Rabeony Hans, BP 516, Ambodirotra; tel. 23802; telex 22203; fax (2) 26627; Ambassador: Dr HUBERT BEEMELMANS.

Holy See: Amboniloha Ivandry, BP 650, 101 Antananarivo; tel. (2) 42376; telex 22432; fax (2) 42384; Apostolic Nuncio: Most Rev. ADRIANO BERNARDINI, Titular Archbishop of Faleri.

India: 4 làlana Emile Rajaonson, BP 1787, 101 Antananarivo; tel. (2) 23334; telex 22484; Ambassador: Dr JOSHI.

Indonesia: 15 rue Radama I Tsaralalana, 101 Antananarivo; tel. (2) 24915; telex 22387; Chargé d'affaires a.i.: SLAMET SUYATA SASTRAMIHARDZA.

Iran: route Circulaire, Lot II L43 ter, 101 Antananarivo; tel. (2) 28639; telex 22510; fax (2) 22298; Ambassador: ALI AMOUI.

Italy: 22 rue Pasteur Rabary, BP 16, Ankadivato; tel. 21217; telex 22293; Ambassador: ROSARIO GUIDO NICOSIA.

Japan: 8 rue du Dr Villette, BP 3863, Isoraka, 101 Antananarivo; tel. (2) 26102; telex 22308; fax (2) 21769; Ambassador: TOSHIO WATANABE.

Korea, Democratic People's Republic: Ambohibao; tel. 44442; telex 22494; Ambassador: RI HYONG YON.

Libya: Lot IIB, 37A route Circulaire Ampandrana-Ouest, 101 Antananarivo; tel. (2) 21892; Chargé d'affaires: MANSUR MILAD AL-KADUSHI.

Mauritius: Anjaharay, route Circulaire, BP 6040, Ambanidia 101, Antananarivo; tel. (2) 21864; fax (2) 21939; Ambassador: GHISLANE HENRY.

Russia: BP 4006, Ivandry-Ambohijatovo, 101 Antananarivo; tel. (2) 42827; fax (2) 42642; Ambassador: YOURI N. MERZLIAKOV.

Switzerland: BP 118, 101 Antananarivo; tel. (2) 62997; fax (2) 28940; Chargé d'affaires: ROSMARIE SCHELLING.

United Kingdom: Immeuble 'Ny Havana', Cité de 67 Ha, BP 167, 101 Antananarivo; tel. (2) 27749; telex 22459; fax (2) 26690; Ambassador: ROBERT SCOTT DEWAR.

USA: 14–16 rue Rainitovo, Antsahavola, BP 620, 101 Antananarivo; tel. (2) 21257; telex 22202; fax (2) 34539; Ambassador: (vacant).

Judicial System

CONSTITUTIONAL HIGH COURT

Haute Cour Constitutionnelle: 101 Antananarivo; interprets the constitution and rules on constitutional issues; seven mems; Pres. VICTOR BOTO.

SUPREME COURT

Cour Suprême: Palais de Justice, Anosy, 101 Antananarivo; Pres. ALICE RAJAONAH (acting); Attorney-General COLOMBE RAMANANTSOA (acting); Chamber Pres. YOLANDE RAMANGASOAVINA, FRANÇOIS RAMANANDRAIBE.

COURT OF APPEAL

Cour d'Appel: Palais de Justice, Anosy, 101 Antananarivo; Pres. AIMÉE RAKOTONIRINA; Chamber Pres CHARLES RABETOKOTANY, PÉTRONILLE ANDRIAMIHAJA, BAKOLALAO RANAIVOHARIVONY, BERTHOLIER RAVELONTSALAMA, LUCIEN RABARIJHON, NELLY RAKOTOBE, ARLETTE RAMAROSON, CLÉMENTINE RAVANDISON, GISÈLE RABOTOVAO, JEAN-JACQUES RAJAONA.

OTHER COURTS

Tribunaux de Première Instance: at Antananarivo, Toamasina, Antsiranana, Mahajanga, Fianarantsoa, Toliary, Antsirabé, Ambatondrazaka, Antalaha, Farafangana, Maintirano; for civil, commercial and social matters, and for registration.

Cours Criminelles Ordinaires: tries crimes of common law; attached to the Cour d'Appel in Antananarivo but may sit in any other large town. There are also 31 Cours Criminelles Spéciales dealing with cases concerning cattle.

Tribunaux Spéciaux Economiques: at Antananarivo, Toamasina, Mahajanga, Fianarantsoa, Antsiranana and Toliary; tries crimes specifically relating to economic matters.

Tribunaux Criminels Spéciaux: judges cases of looting and banditry; 31 courts.

Religion

It is estimated that more than 50% of the population follow traditional animist beliefs, some 43% are Christians (about one-half of whom are Roman Catholics) and the remainder are Muslims.

CHRISTIANITY

Fiombonan'ny Fiangonana Kristiana eto Madagasikara (FFKM)/Conseil Chrétien des Eglises de Madagascar/Christian Council of Churches in Madagascar: Vohipiraisama, Ambohijatovo-Atsimo, BP 798, 101 Antananarivo; tel. (2) 29052; f. 1980; four mems and one assoc. mem.; Pres. Pastor EDMOND RAZAFIMAHALEO; Gen. Sec. Rev. LALA ANDRIAMIHARISOA.

Fiombonan'ny Fiangonana Protestanta eto Madagasikara (FFPM)/Fédération des Eglises Protestantes à Madagascar/ Federation of the Protestant Churches in Madagascar: VK 3 Vohipiraisana, Ambohijatovo-Atsimo, BP 4226, 101 Antananarivo; tel. (2) 20144; f. 1958; two mems; Pres. Pastor EDMOND RAZAFIMAHEFA; Gen. Sec. Rev. Dr ROGER ANDRIATSIRATAHINA.

The Anglican Communion

Anglicans are adherents of the Church of the Province of the Indian Ocean, comprising six dioceses (four in Madagascar, one in Mauritius and one in Seychelles). The Archbishop of the Province is the Bishop of Antananarivo. The Church has about 160,000 adherents in Madagascar, including the membership of the Eklesia Episkopaly Malagasy (Malagasy Episcopal Church), founded in 1874.

Bishop of Antananarivo (also Archbishop of the Province of the Indian Ocean): Most Rev. RÉMI JOSEPH RABENIRINA, Evêché Anglican, Ambohimanoro, 101 Antananarivo; tel. (2) 20827; fax (2) 33749.

Bishop of Antsiranana: Rt Rev. KEITH BENZIES, Evêché Anglican, BP 278, Antsiranana; tel. (8) 22650.

Bishop of Mahajanga: Rt Rev. JEAN-CLAUDE ANDRIANJAFIMANANA, BP 169, 401 Mahajanga.

Bishop of Toamasina: Rt Rev. DONALD SMITH, Evêché Anglican, rue de la Fraternité, BP 531, 501 Toamasina; tel. (5) 32163.

The Roman Catholic Church

Madagascar comprises three archdioceses and 15 dioceses. At 31 December 1995 the number of adherents in the country represented about 21.1% of the total population.

Bishops' Conference: Conférence Episcopale de Madagascar, 102 bis ave Maréchal Joffre, Antanimena, BP 667, 101 Antananarivo; tel. (2) 20478; fax (2) 24854; f. 1969; Pres. Cardinal ARMAND RAZAFINDRATANDRA, Archbishop of Antananarivo.

Archbishop of Antananarivo: Cardinal ARMAND RAZAFINDRATANDRA, Archevêché, Andohalo, 101 Antananarivo; tel. (2) 20726.

Archbishop of Antsiranana: Most Rev. ALBERT JOSEPH TSIAHOANA, Archevêché, BP 415, 201 Antsiranana; tel. (8) 21605.

Archbishop of Fianarantsoa: Most Rev. PHILIBERT RANDRIAMBOLOLONA, Archevêché, place Mgr Givelet, BP 1440, Ambozontany, 301 Fianarantsoa; tel. (7) 50672; fax (7) 24854.

Other Christian Churches

Fiangonan' i Jesoa Kristy eto Madagasikara/Eglise de Jésus-Christ à Madagascar: Lot 11 B18, Tohatohabato Ranavalona 1, Trano 'Ifanomezantsoa', BP 623, 101 Antananarivo; tel. (2) 26845; telex 22467; fax (2) 26372; f. 1968; Pres. Rev. EDMOND RAZAFIMAHEFA; Gen. Sec. Rev. LALA RASENDRAHASINA; 2m. mems.

Fiangonana Loterana Malagasy (Malagasy Lutheran Church): BP 1741, 101 Antananarivo; tel. (2) 22347; telex 22544; Pres. Rev. RABENOROLAHY; 600,000 mems.

The Press

In December 1990 the National People's Assembly adopted legislation guaranteeing the freedom of the press and the right of newspapers to be established without prior authorization.

PRINCIPAL DAILIES

Bulletin de l'Agence Nationale d'Information 'Taratra' (ANTA): 3 rue du R. P. Callet, Behoririka, BP 386, 101 Antananarivo; tel. (2) 21171; telex 22506; f. 1977; French; Man. Dir JEANNOT FENO.

L'Express de Madagascar: BP 3893, 101 Antananarivo; tel. (2) 21934; telex 22287; fax (2) 62894; f. 1995; French and Malagasy; Editor SYLVAIN RANDRIANAHINORO; circ. 10,000.

Imongo Vaovao: 11K 4 bis Andravoahangy, BP 7014, 101 Antananarivo; tel. (2) 21053; f. 1955; Malagasy; Dir CLÉMENT RAMAMONJISOA; circ. 10,000.

Madagascar Tribune: Immeuble SME, rue Ravoninahitriniarivo, BP 659, Ankorondrano, 101 Antananarivo; tel. (2) 22635; telex 22340; fax (2) 22254; f. 1988; independent; French and Malagasy; Editor RAHAGA RAMAHOLIMIHASO; circ. 12,000.

Maresaka: 12 làlana Ratsimba John, Isotry, 101 Antananarivo; tel. (2) 23568; f. 1953; independent; Malagasy; Editor M. RALAIARIJAONA; circ. 5,000.

Midi Madagasikara: làlana Ravoninahitriniarivo, BP 1414, Ankorondrano, 101 Antananarivo; tel. (2) 62122; telex 22543; fax (2) 27351; f. 1983; French; Dir MAMY RAKOTOARIVELO; circ. 25,500.

PRINCIPAL PERIODICALS

Afaka: BP 1475, 101 Antananarivo; Malagasy and French; Dir MAX RATSIMANDISA; circ. 5,000.

Basy Vava: Lot III E 96, Mahamasina Atsimo, 101 Antananarivo; tel. (2) 20448; f. 1959; Malagasy; Dir GABRIEL RAMANANJATO; circ. 3,000.

Bulletin de la Société du Corps Médical Malgache: Imprimerie Volamahitsy, 101 Antananarivo; Malagasy; monthly; Dir Dr RAKOTOMALALA.

Dans les Media, Demain: Immeuble Jeune Afrique, 58 rue Tsiombikibo, BP 1734, Ambatovinaky, 101 Antananarivo; tel. (2) 27788; telex 22225; fax (2) 30629; f. 1986; independent; weekly; Dir HONORÉ RAZAFINTSALAMA; circ. 2,500.

Feon'ny Mpiasa: Lot M8, Isotry, 101 Antananarivo; trade union affairs; Malagasy; monthly; Dir M. RAZAKANAIVO; circ. 2,000.

Fiaraha-Miasa: BP 1216, 101 Antananarivo; Malagasy; weekly; Dir SOLO NORBERT ANDRIAMORASATA; circ. 5,000.

Gazetinao: Lot IPA 37, BP 1758, Anosimasina, 101 Antananarivo; tel. 40560; French and Malagasy; monthly; Dir ETIENNE M. RAKOTOMAHANINA; circ. 3,000.

La Gazette d'Antsirabé: Lot 12 C-190, Antsenakely, 110 Antsirabé; f. 1989; Dir VOLOLOHARIMANANA RAZAFIMANDIMBY; circ. 7,000.

Gazety Medikaly: Lot 12B, Ampahibe, 101 Antananarivo; tel. (2) 27898; f. 1965; medical; monthly; Dir PAUL RATSIMISETA; circ. 2,000.

Isika Mianakavy: Ambatomena, 301 Fianarantsoa; f. 1958; Roman Catholic; Malagasy; monthly; Dir J. RANAIVOMANANA; circ. 21,000.

Journal Officiel de la République de Madagascar: BP 248, 101 Antananarivo; tel. (2) 25258; f. 1883; official announcements; Malagasy and French; weekly; Dir SAMÜEL RAMAROSON.

Journal Scientifique de Madagascar: Antananarivo; f. 1985; Dir Prof. MANAMBELONA; circ. 3,000.

Jureco: Immeuble SOMAGI, 120 rue Rainandriamampandry, 101 Antananarivo; tel. (2) 24145; fax (2) 20397; law and economics; monthly; Dir MBOARA ANDRIANARIMANANA.

Lakroan'i Madagasikara: Maison Jean XXIII, Mahamasina Sud, 101 Antananarivo; tel. (2) 21158; f. 1927; Roman Catholic; French and Malagasy; weekly; Dir LOUIS RASOLO; circ. 25,000.

Mada—Économie: 15 rue Ratsimilaho, BP 3464, 101 Antananarivo; tel. (2) 25634; f. 1977; reports events in south-east Africa; monthly; Editor RICHARD-CLAUDE RATOVONARIVO; circ. 5,000.

Mpanolotsaina: BP 623, 101 Antananarivo; tel. (2) 26845; religious, educational; Malagasy; quarterly; Dir PAUL SOLOHERY.

Ny Mpamangy-FLM: 9 rue Grandidier Isoraka, BP 538, Antsahamanitra, 101 Antananarivo; tel. (2) 32446; telex 22544; f. 1882; monthly; Dir Pastor JEAN RABENANDRASANA; circ. 3,000.

Ny Sakaizan'ny Tanora: BP 538, Antsahaminitra, 101 Antananarivo; tel. (2) 32446; telex 22544; f. 1878; monthly; Editor-in-Chief DANIEL PROSPER ANDRIAMANJAKA; circ. 5,000.

PME Madagascar: rue Hugues Rabesahala, BP 953, Antsakaviro, 101 Antananarivo; tel. (2) 22536; telex 22261; fax (2) 34534; f. 1989; French; monthly; economic review; Dir ROMAIN ANDRIANARISOA; circ. 3,500.

Recherche et Culture: BP 907, 101 Antananarivo; tel. (2) 26600; f. 1985; publ. by French dept of the University of Antananarivo; 2 a year; Dir GINETTE RAMAROSON; circ. 1,000.

Revue Ita: BP 681, 101 Antananarivo; tel. (2) 30507; f. 1985; controlled by the Ministry of Population; monthly; Dir FILS RAMALANJAONA; circ. 1,000.

Revue de l'Océan Indien: Communication et Médias Océan Indien, rue H. Rabesahala, BP 46, Antsakaviro, 101 Antananarivo; tel. (2) 22536; telex 22261; fax (2) 34534; f. 1980; quarterly; Man. Dir GEORGES RANAIVOSOA; Sec.-Gen. HERY M. A. RANAIVOSOA; circ. 5,000.

Sahy: Lot VD 42, Ambanidia, 101 Antananarivo; tel. (2) 22715; f. 1957; political; Malagasy; weekly; Editor ALINE RAKOTO; circ. 9,000.

Sosialisma Mpiasa: BP 1128, 101 Antananarivo; tel. (2) 21989; f. 1979; trade union affairs; Malagasy; monthly; Dir PAUL RABEMANANJARA; circ. 5,000.

Valeurs—L'Hebdomadaire de Madagascar: Antananarivo; f. 1995; weekly; Dir RIJA RASENDRATSIROFO.

Vaovao: BP 271, 101 Antananarivo; tel. (2) 21193; f. 1985; French and Malagasy; weekly; Dir MARC RAKOTONOELY; circ. 5,000.

NEWS AGENCIES

Agence Nationale d'Information 'Taratra' (ANTA): 3 rue du R. P. Callet, Behoririka, BP 386, 101 Antananarivo; tel. (2) 21171; telex 22395; f 1977; Man. Dir JEANNOT FENO.

Foreign Bureaux

Associated Press (AP) (USA): BP 73, 101 Antananarivo; tel. (3) 80971; Correspondent CHRISTIAN CHADEFAUX.

Korean Central News Agency (KCNA) (Democratic People's Republic of Korea): BP 4276, 101 Antananarivo; tel. (2) 44795; Dir KIM YEUNG KYEUN.

Xinhua (New China) News Agency (People's Republic of China): BP 1656, 101 Antananarivo; tel. (2) 29927; telex 22360; Chief of Bureau WU HAIYUN.

Reuters (UK) is also represented in Madagascar.

Publishers

Editions Ambozontany: BP 40, 301 Fianarantsoa; tel. (7) 50603; f. 1962; religious and school textbooks; Dir R. F. GIAMBRONE.

Foibe Filankevitry Ny Mpampianatra (FOFIPA): BP 202, 101 Antananarivo; tel. (2) 27500; f. 1971; textbooks; Dir Frère RAZAFINDRAKOTO.

Madagascar Print and Press Co (MADPRINT): rue Rabesahala, Antsakaviro, BP 953, 101 Antananarivo; tel. (2) 22536; telex 22226; fax (2) 34534; f. 1969; literary, technical and historical; Dir GEORGES RANAIVOSOA.

Maison d'Edition Protestante Antso (Librairie-Imprimerie): 19 rue Venance Manifatra, Imarivolanitra, BP 660, 101 Antananarivo; tel. (2) 20886; f. 1962; religious, school, social, political and general; Dir HANS ANDRIAMAMPIANINA.

Imprimerie Nouvelle: PK 2, Andranomahery, route de Majunga, 101 Antananarivo; tel. (2) 23330; Dir EUGÈNE RAHARIFIDY.

Nouvelle Société de Presse et d'Edition (NSPE): Immeuble Jeune Afrique, 58 rue Tsiombikibo, BP 1734, Ambatorinaky, 101 Antananarivo; tel. (2) 27788; telex 22225; fax (2) 30629.

Office du Livre Malgache: Lot 111 H29, Andrefan' Ambohijanahary, BP 617, 101 Antananarivo; tel. (2) 24449; f. 1970; children's and general; Sec.-Gen. JULIETTE RATSIMANDRAVA.

Edisiona Salohy: BP 7124, 101 Antananarivo; Dir JEAN RABENALISOA RAVALITERA.

Société de Presse et d'Edition de Madagascar: Antananarivo; non-fiction, reference, science, university textbooks; Man. Dir RAJAOFERA ANDRIAMBELO.

Société Malgache d'Edition (SME): BP 659, Ankorondrano, 101 Antananarivo; tel. (2) 22635; telex 22340; fax (2) 22254; f. 1943; general fiction, university and secondary textbooks; Man. Dir RAHAGA RAMAHOLIMIHASO.

Société Nouvelle de l'Imprimerie Centrale (SNIC): làlana Ravoninahitriniarivo, BP 1414, 101 Antananarivo; tel. (2) 21118; f. 1959; science, school textbooks; Man. Dir MARTHE ANDRIAMBELO.

Imprimerie Takariva: 4 rue Radley, BP 1029, Antanimena, 101 Antananarivo; tel. (2) 22128; f. 1933; fiction, languages, school textbooks; Man. Dir PAUL RAPATSALAHY.

Trano Printy Fiangonana Loterana Malagasy (TPFLM): BP 538, 9 ave Grandidier, Antsahamanitra, 101 Antananarivo; tel. (2) 23340; f. 1875; religious, educational and fiction; Man. RAYMOND RANDRIANATOANDRO.

Government Publishing House

Imprimerie Nationale: BP 38, 101 Antananarivo; tel. (2) 23675; all official publs; Dir JEAN DENIS RANDRIANIRINA.

Radio and Television

In December 1990 the state monopoly of broadcasting was abolished, and legislation was adopted authorizing the establishment of private broadcasting stations 'in partnership with the Government or its agencies'; by early 1995 six independent radio stations were operating in Madagascar. According to UNESCO, there were an estimated 2,740,000 radio receivers and 280,000 television receivers in use in 1994.

RADIO

Radio Nationale Malagasy: BP 442, 101 Antananarivo; tel. (2) 35261; telex 22559; fax (2) 31719; state-controlled; broadcasts in French, Malagasy and English; Dir SIMON SEVA MBOINY.

Le Messager Radio Evangélique: BP 1374, 101 Antananarivo; tel. (2) 34495; broadcasts in French, English and Malagasy; Dir JOCELYN RANJARISON.

Radio Antsiva: Lot VA, 21 Ambohitantely, 101 Antananarivo; tel. (2) 34330; broadcasts in French, English and Malagasy; Dir JEAN VICTOR RALIARISON.

Radio Feon'ny Vahoaka (RFV): 103 Immeuble Ramaroson, 8e étage, 101 Antananarivo; tel. (2) 33820; broadcasts in French and Malagasy; Dir ALAIN RAMAROSON.

Radio Korail: BP 6325, 101 Antananarivo; tel. and fax (2) 24494; f. 1993; broadcasts in French and Malagasy; Dir ALAIN RAJAONA.

Radio Lazan'iarivo (RLI): Lot V A49, Andafiavaratra, 101 Antananarivo; tel. (2) 29016; broadcasts in French, English and Malagasy; Dir IRÈNE RAVALISON.

Radio Tsioka Vao (RTV): Lot V T15/16, Ambohimitsimbona, Ankaditapaka; tel. 21749; broadcasts in French, English and Malagasy; Dir THOMAS BARNABE BETKOU DIEUDONNÉ.

TELEVISION

Télévision Nasionaly Malagasy: BP 1202, 101 Antananarivo; tel. (2) 22381; telex 22506; state-controlled; broadcasts in French and Malagasy; one transmitter; Dir-Gen. SIMON ANDRIAMIALISON.

Finance

(cap. = capital; res = reserves; dep. = deposits; m. = million; brs = branches; amounts in Malagasy francs)

BANKING

Central Bank

Banque Centrale de Madagascar: ave de la Révolution Socialiste Malgache, BP 550, 101 Antananarivo; tel. (2) 21751; telex 22329; fax (2) 34532; f. 1973; bank of issue; cap. 1,000m.; Gov. GASTON RAVELOJAONA.

Other Banks

Bankin'ny Tantsaha Mpamokatra (BTM): place de l'Indépendance, BP 183, 101 Antananarivo; tel. (2) 23641; telex 22208; fax (2) 21398; f. 1976 by merger; specializes in rural development; state-owned; cap. and res 49,865.8m., dep. 400,373.4m. (Dec. 1992); Pres. EVARISTE MARSON; 44 brs.

Banky Fampandrosoana ny Varotra (BFV): 14 làlana Jeneraly Rabehevitra, BP 196, 101 Antananarivo; tel. (2) 20691; telex 22257; fax (2) 34535; 73.7% state-owned; f. 1977 by merger; cap. and res 15,681.1m., dep. 569,046.3m. (1995); Chair. TANTELY ANDRIANARIVO; Administrator BERNARD LECOQ; 25 brs.

Banque Malgache de l'Océan Indien (BMOI) (Indian Ocean Malagasy Bank): place de l'Indépendance, BP 25, Antananarivo 101; tel. (2) 34609; telex 22381; fax (2) 34610; f. 1990; 37.5% owned by Banque Nationale de Paris; cap. 10,000m. (Dec. 1996); Pres. GASTON RAMENASON; Dir-Gen. MICHEL LAFONT; 7 brs.

BNI–Crédit Lyonnais Madagascar: 74 rue du 26 Juin 1960, BP 174, 101 Antananarivo; tel. (2) 23951; telex 22205; fax (2) 33749; 33% state-owned; f. 1976 as Bankin'ny Indostria; cap. and res 61,331.7m., dep. 649,642.5m. (Dec. 1995); Dir-Gen. BERNARD FOURNIER; 27 brs.

Union Commercial Bank (UCB): 77 làlana Solombavambahoaka, BP 197, 101 Antananarivo; tel. (2) 27262; telex 22528; fax (2) 28740; f. 1992; cap. and res 5,543m., dep. 80,449m. (Dec. 1995); Pres. RAYMOND HEIN; Dir-Gen. JACQUES GRENOUILLAUD.

INSURANCE

ARO (Assurances Réassurances Omnibranches): Antsahavola, BP 42, 101 Antananarivo; tel. (2) 20154; telex 22265; fax (2) 34464; Pres. DÉSIRÉ RAJOBSON; Dir-Gen. HENRI RAJERISON.

Assurance France-Madagascar: 7 rue Rainitovo, BP 710, 101 Antananarivo; tel. (2) 23024; telex 22321; fax (2) 23024; f. 1951; Dir SAMUELSON RAOILY.

Compagnie Malgache d'Assurances et de Réassurances: Immeuble 'Ny Havana', Zone des 67 Ha, BP 3881, 101 Antananarivo; tel. (2) 26760; telex 22377; fax (2) 24303; f. 1968; cap. 16,050m. (1996); Administrator TOMBO RAMANDIMBISOA.

Mutuelle d'Assurances Malagasy (MAMA): 1F, 12 bis, rue Rainibetsimisaraka, Ambalavao-Isotry, BP 185, 101 Antananarivo; tel. (2) 22508; Pres. RAKOTOARIVONY ANDRIAMAROMANANA.

Société Malgache d'Assurances, Faugère, Jutheau et Cie: 13 rue Patrice Lumumba, BP 673, 101 Antananarivo; f. 1952; tel. (2) 23162; telex 22247; Dir ANDRIANJAKA RAVELONAHIANA.

Trade and Industry

CHAMBER OF COMMERCE

Fédération des Chambres de Commerce, d'Industrie et d'Agriculture de Madagascar: 20 rue Paul Dussac, BP 166,

101 Antananarivo; tel. (2) 21567; 12 mem. chambers; Pres. JEAN RAMAROMISA; Chair. HENRI RAZANATSEHENO; Sec.-Gen. HUBERT RATSIANDAVANA.

TRADE ORGANIZATION

Société d'Intérêt National des Produits Agricoles (SINPA): BP 754, rue Fernand-Kasanga, Tsimbazaza, Antananarivo; tel. (2) 20558; telex 22309; fax (2) 20665; f. 1973; monopoly purchaser and distributor of agricultural produce; Chair. GUALBERT RAZANAJATOVO; Gen. Man. JEAN CLOVIS RALIJESY.

DEVELOPMENT ORGANIZATIONS

Office des mines nationales et des industries stratégiques (OMNIS): 21 làlana Razanakombana, BP 1 bis, 101 Antananarivo; tel. (2) 24439; telex 22370; fax (2) 22985; f. 1976; oversees the management of major industrial orgs and exploitation of mining resources; Dir-Gen. ACKRAM MOHAJY ANDRIAMANDAMINY.

Société d'Etude et de Réalisation pour le Développement Industriel (SERDI): 78 bis, ave Lénine Ankaditapaka, BP 3180, 101 Antananarivo; tel. (2) 21335; telex 22453; fax (2) 29669; f. 1966; Dir-Gen. RAOILISON RAJAONARY.

PRINCIPAL EMPLOYERS' ORGANIZATIONS

Groupement des Entreprises de Madagascar (GEM): Kianja MDRM sy Tia Tanindrazana, BP 1338, 101 Antananarivo; f. 1973; eight nat. syndicates and four regional syndicates comprising 444 cos and 44 directly affiliated cos; Pres. GASTON RAMENASON: Sec.-Gen. ZINAH RASAMUEL RAVALOSON.

Syndicat des Importateurs et Exportateurs de Madagascar: 2 rue Georges Mandel, BP 188, 101 Antananarivo; Pres. M. FONTANA.

Syndicat Indépendant des Exportateurs de Vanille de Madagascar: Antalaha; 18 mems; Pres. MICHEL GERMAIN MING.

Syndicat des Industries de Madagascar: Immeuble Kobana Soanierana; BP 1695, 101 Antananarivo; tel. (2) 23608; fax (2) 33043; f. 1958; Chair. PATRICK RAJAONARY.

Syndicat des Planteurs de Café: 37 làlana Razafimahandry, BP 173, 101 Antananarivo.

Syndicat Professionnel des Agents Généraux d'Assurances: Antananarivo; f. 1949; Pres. SOLO RATSIMBAZAFY; Sec. IHANTA RANDRIAMANDRANTO.

MAJOR INDUSTRIAL COMPANIES

The following are some of the largest companies in terms either of capital investment or employment.

Brasseries STAR Madagascar: BP 3806, Antananarivo; tel. (2) 27711; telex 22315; fax (2) 34682; f. 1953; cap. 10,090.9m. FMG; mfrs of beer and carbonated drinks. Pres. H. FRAISE; Gen. Man. YVAN COUDERC.

Compagnie des Ciments Malgaches: BP 302, Mahajanga; cap. 625m. FMG; cement works; Pres. JULES PLAQUET; Dir J. SCHNEEBERGER.

Compagnie Salinière de Madagascar: rue Béniowsky, BP 29, 201 Antsiranana; tel. (8) 21373; fax (8) 29394; f. 1895; cap. 1,312m. FMG; exploitation of salt marshes; Dir-Gen. JEAN-YVES MORVAN.

La Cotonnière d'Antsirabé (COTONA): route d'Ambositra, BP 45, Antsirabé; tel. (4) 49422; telex 44800; fax (4) 49222; f. 1952; cap. 46,528m. FMG; spinning, weaving, printing and dyeing of textiles; Dirs-Gen. SALIM ISMAIL, AZIZ HASSAM ISMAIL.

Ets Gallois: BP 159, Antananarivo; cap. 220m. FMG; production of graphite and sisal; Pres. and Dir-Gen. HENRY GALLOIS.

Jiro sy Rano Malagasy (JIRAMA): BP 200, 149 rue Rainandriamampandry, Antananarivo; tel. (2) 20031; telex 22235; fax (2) 33806; f. 1975; state-owned; controls production and distribution of electricity and water; Dir-Gen. CALEB RAKOTOARIVELO.

Kraomita Malagasy (KRAOMA): BP 936, Antananarivo; tel. (2) 24304; telex 22234; fax (2) 24654; f. 1966 as Cie Minière d'Andriamena (COMINA); cap. 1,540m. FMG; 100% state-owned; chrome mining and concentration; Dir-Gen. WILLY RANJATOELINA.

Laboratoires Pharmaceutiques Malgaches (FARMAD): BP 828, Antananarivo 101; tel. (2) 46622; pharmaceutical mfrs.

Nouveaux Ateliers de Construction Métallique: 352 route Circulaire, BP 1073, Antananarivo 101; tel. (2) 23136; mfrs of cutlery, tools, implements and metal parts.

Omnium Industriel de Madagascar: BP 207, Antananarivo; tel. (2) 22373; telex 22303; fax (2) 28064; f. 1929; cap. 1,300m. FMG; mfrs of shoes and luggage; operates a tannery; Pres. and Dir-Gen. H. J. BARDAY.

Papeteries de Madagascar (PAPMAD): BP 1756, Ambohimanambola, 101 Antananarivo; tel. (2) 20635; telex 22229; fax (2) 24394; f. 1963; cap. 1,308m. FMG; paper-making; Pres. and Dir-Gen. P. RAJAONARY.

Société Agricole du Domaine de Pechpeyrou: BP 71, Tolagnaro; f. 1947; cap. 192m. FMG; sisal growing.

Société Américaine, Grecque et Malgache 'Industrie de la Viande': Antananarivo; cap. 300m. FMG; abattoir, meat-canning, mfrs of meat products; Pres. and Dir-Gen. G. S. REPAS; Dir T. C. BACOPOLOUS.

Société Commerciale Laitière (SOCOLAIT): BP 4126; Antananarivo; tel. (2) 22282; telex 22279; cap. 2,800m. FMG; dairy products; Pres. SOCOTALY KARMALY.

Société des Cigarettes Melia de Madagascar: route d'Ambositra 110, BP 128, Antsirabé; tel. (2) 48241; telex 44803; f. 1956; cap. 881m. FMG; mfrs of cigarettes; Pres. and Dir-Gen. PHILIPPE DE VESINNE LARUE; Dir GUY RAVELOMANANTSOA.

Société d'Etudes de Constructions et Réparations Navales (SECREN): BP 135, Antsiranana; tel. (8) 29321; telex 93103; fax (8) 29326; f. 1975; transfer to the private sector announced in 1997; cap. 2,600m. FMG; ship-building and repairs; Gen. Man. CHRISTOPHE J. NOSY HARINONY; 1,069 employees.

Société de Fabrication de l'Océan Indien: Tanjombato, BP 132, Antananarivo 101; tel. (2)46776; plastics.

Société de Filature et de Tissage de Madagascar (FITIM): BP 127, Mahajanga; f. 1930; cap. 1,444m. FMG; spinning and weaving of jute; Pres. C. A. WILLIAM RAVONINJATOVO; Dir-Gen. HATIM HASSANALY.

Société Malgache de Collecte et de Distribution: BP 188, 101 Antananarivo; tel. (2) 24871; telex 22207; fax (2) 25024; f. 1972; Chair. HENRI RASAMOELINA; Gen. Man. NORBERT RAZANAKOTO.

Société Malgache de Cosmetiques et de Parfumerie: Tanjombato, BP 852, Antananarivo 101; tel. (2) 46537; fax (2) 46029; perfumery, cosmetics and toothpaste.

Société Malgache d'Exploitations Minières: BP 266, Antananarivo; f. 1926; cap. 130m. FMG; mining of graphite and mica; Pres. JEAN SCHNEIDER; Dir-Gen. LUCIEN DUMAS.

Société Malgache de Pêcherie (SOMAPECHE): BP 324, Mahanga; cap. 200m. FMG; sea fishing; Pres. J. RABEMANANJARA; Dir-Gen. J. BRUNOT.

Société Malgache de Raffinage: BP 433, Toamasina; tel. (5) 32773; telex 55607; fax (5) 33705; f. 1964; cap. 2.5m. FMG; state-owned; refinery for petroleum imported from the Middle East, principally Iran; Dir-Gen. JACQUES GLANTENET.

Société Siramamy Malagasy (SIRAMA): BP 1633, Antananarivo; f. 1949; state-owned; transfer to the private sector announced in 1997; cap. 2,500m. FMG; sugar refinery at St Louis; Pres. GABRIEL DAHER; Dir-Gen. Y. GROUITCH.

Société Textile de Majunga (SOTEMA): BP 375, Mahajanga; tel. (2) 27568; telex 62704; fax (2) 34533; f. 1967; cap. 3,510m. FMG; spinning, weaving, printing and finishing textiles, finished garments; Pres. LÉON RAJAOBELINA; 2,800 employees.

Société Verrerie Malagasy (SOVEMA): BP 84, Toamasina; f. 1970; cap. 235.6m. FMG; bottles and glass articles; Pres. and Dir-Gen. A. SIBILLE.

Solitany Malagasy (SOLIMA): 2 ave Grandidier; BP 140, Antananarivo; tel. (2) 20633; telex 22222; fax (2) 26693; f. 1976; transfer to the private sector pending in 1997; cap. 2,505m. FMG; imports, transports and refines crude petroleum; produces and exports petroleum products; Chair. ALBERT ANDRIANTSOA RASOMANAMA; Dir-Gen. LOUIS CHRISTIAN NTSAY.

TRADE UNIONS

Cartel National des Organisations Syndicales de Madagascar (CARNOSYAMA): BP 1035, 101 Antananarivo.

Confédération des Travailleurs Malgaches (Fivomdronamben'ny Mpiasa Malagasy–FMM): 3 ave Lénine, Ambatomitsanga, 101 Antananarivo; tel. (2) 24565; f. 1957; Sec.-Gen. JEAN RASOLONDRAIBE; 30,000 mems.

Fédération des Syndicats des Travailleurs de Madagascar (Firaisan'ny Sendika eran'i Madagaskara–FISEMA): Lot III, rue Pasteur Isotry, 101 Antananarivo; f. 1956; Pres. DESIRÉ RALAMBOTAHINA; Sec.-Gen. M. RAZAKANAIVO; 8 affiliated unions representing 60,000 mems.

Fédération des Travailleurs Malagasy Révolutionnaires (FISEMARE): Lot IV N 77, Ankadifots, BP 1128, Antananarivo-Befelatanana; tel. (2) 21989; f. 1985; Pres. PAUL RABEMANANJARA.

Sendika Kristianina Malagasy–SEKRIMA (Christian Confederation of Malagasy Trade Unions): Soarano, route de Mahajanga, BP 1035, 101 Antananarivo; tel. (2) 23174; f. 1937; Pres. MARIE RAKOTOANOSY; Gen. Sec. RAYMOND RAKOTOARISAONA; 158 affiliated unions representing 40,000 mems.

Sendika Revolisakionera Malagasy (SEREMA): 101 Antananarivo.

Union des Syndicats Autonomes de Madagascar (USAM): Ampasadratsarahoby, Lot 11 H67, Faravohitra, BP 1038, 101

Antananarivo; Pres. NORBERT RAKOTOMANANA; Sec.-Gen. VICTOR RAHAGA; 46 affiliated unions representing 30,000 mems.

Transport

RAILWAYS

In 1993 there were 1,095 km of railway, all 1-m gauge track. The northern system, which comprised 729 km of track, links Toamasina, on the east coast, with Antsirabé, in the interior, via Brikaville, Moramanga and Antananarivo, with a branch line from Moramanga to Vohidiala which divides to Lake Alaotra and Morarano to collect chromium ore. The southern system, which comprised 170 km of track, links Manakara, on the south-east coast, and Fianarantsoa.

Réseau National des Chemins de Fer Malagasy: 1 ave de l'Indépendance, BP 259, Soarano, 101 Antananarivo; tel. (2) 20521; telex 22233; fax (2) 22288; f. 1909; transfer to private sector pending in 1997; Dir-Gen. RANAIVOHARITAFIKA ANDRIANTSOAVINA.

ROADS

In 1995 there were 49,837 km of classified roads, of which 8,528 km were main roads and 17,310 km were secondary roads; 5,731 km of the road network were paved. In 1987 there were 39,500 km of unclassified roads, used only in favourable weather.

INLAND WATERWAYS

The Pangalanes Canal runs for 600 km near the east coast from Toamasina to Farafangana. In 1984 the Government initiated a project to rehabilitate more than 200 km of the canal by 1988, at a cost of 18.5m. Malagasy francs. In early 1990 432 km of the canal between Toamasina and Mananjary were navigable.

SHIPPING

There are 18 ports, the largest being at Toamasina, which handles about 70% of total traffic, and Mahajanga. In 1987 Madagascar received foreign loans totalling US $34.8m., including a credit of $16m. from the World Bank, to finance a project to rehabilitate 10 ports.

Compagnie Générale Maritime (CGM): BP 69, 501 Toamasina; tel. (5) 32312; telex 55612; f. 1976 by merger; Rep. J. P. BERGEROT.

Compagnie Malgache de Navigation (CMN): rue Toto Radona, BP 1621, 101 Antananarivo; tel. (2) 25516; telex 22263; f. 1960; coasters; 13,784 grt; transfer pending to private-sector ownership; Pres. Mme ELINAH BAKOLY RAJAONSON; Dir-Gen. ARISTIDE EMMANUEL.

Navale et Commerciale Havraise Peninsulaire (NCHP): rue Rabearivelo Antsahavola, BP 1021, 101 Antananarivo; tel. (2) 22502; telex 22273; Rep. JEAN PIERRE NOCKIN.

Société Nationale Malgache des Transports Maritimes (SMTM): 6 rue Indira Gandhi, BP 4077, 101 Antananarivo; tel. (2) 27342; telex 22277; fax (2) 33327; f. 1963; 51% state-owned; transfer to private sector pending in 1997; services to Europe; Chair. ALEXIS RAZAFINDRATSIRA; Dir-Gen. ANDRIONORO RAMANANTSOA.

CIVIL AVIATION

The international airport is at Antananarivo, while the airports at Mahajanga, Toamasina and Nossi-Bé can also accommodate large jet aircraft. There are more than 200 airfields, of which 57 are open to public air traffic. In 1996 the Government invited tenders for a rehabilitation project, which was to include nine of the major airports. Later that year the Government authorized private French airlines to operate scheduled and charter flights between Madagascar and Western Europe.

Société Nationale Malgache des Transports Aériens (Air Madagascar): 31 ave de l'Indépendance, BP 437, 101 Antananarivo; tel. (2) 22222; telex 22332; fax (2) 33760; f. 1962; 89.58% state-owned; transfer to the private sector pending in 1997; extensive internal routes connecting all the principal towns; external services to France, Germany, Italy, the Comoros, Mauritius, Réunion and South Africa; Chair. NIRINA ANDRIAMANANSOA; Dir-Gen. B. R. RAZAFIMAHARO.

Direction des Transports Aériens: BP 921, Anosy, 101 Antananarivo; tel. (2) 24604; telex 22301; fax (2) 24001.

Transports et Travaux Aériens de Madagascar: BP 876; tel. 27036; fax 30540; Dir-Gen. SOLONAIVO RAKOTOMALALA.

Tourism

Madagascar's attractions include unspoiled scenery, many unusual varieties of flora and fauna, and the rich cultural diversity of Malagasy life. The tourism sector is undergoing expansion; the Government has declared a target of 230,000 tourist arrivals annually by 2000. In 1995, according to preliminary figures, a total of 78,800 tourists visited Madagascar. Revenue from tourism in that year was forecast at US $57.6m.

Direction du Tourisme de Madagascar: Ministry of Tourism, Tsimbazaza, BP 610, 101 Antananarivo; tel. (2) 26298; fax (2) 26710.

Maison du Tourisme: place de l'Indépendance, 101 Antananarivo; tel. (2) 31007.

Defence

In August 1996 total armed forces numbered 21,000 men: army 20,000, navy 500 and air force 500. There is a paramilitary gendarmerie of 7,500.

Defence Expenditure: Budgeted at 118,600m. Malagasy francs in 1995.

Chief of Armed Forces General Staff: Gen. ISMAIL MOUNIBOU.

Education

Education is officially compulsory between six and 11 years of age. Madagascar has both public and private schools, although legislation that was enacted in 1978 envisaged the progressive elimination of private education. Primary education generally begins at the age of six and lasts for five years. Secondary education, beginning at 11 years of age, lasts for a further seven years, comprising a first cycle of four years and a second of three years. In 1993 primary enrolment was equivalent to 73% of children in the relevant age-group (males 75%; females 72%), while the comparable ratio for secondary education was 14% (males 14%; females 14%). Enrolment in tertiary education in that year was equivalent to 3.9% of the relevant age-group (males 4.4%; females 3.4%). According to UNESCO estimates, 54.3% of the adult population (males 40.2%; females 68.0%) remained illiterate in 1995. In 1995 expenditure on education by the central government was 264,600m. Malagasy francs (11.3% of total expenditure).

Bibliography

Allen, P. M. *Madagascar: Conflicts of Authority in the Great Island.* Boulder, CO, Westview Press, 1995.

Archer, R. *Madagascar depuis 1972, la marche d'une révolution.* Paris, Editions l'Harmattan, 1976.

Bastian, G. *Madagascar, étude géographique et économique.* Nathan, 1967.

Bradt, H., and Brown, M. *Madagascar.* Oxford, Clio Press, 1993.

Brown, Sir M. *Madagascar Rediscovered.* London, Damien Tunnacliffe, 1978.

A History of Madagascar. London, Damien Tunnacliffe, 1995.

Cadoux, C. *La République malgache.* Paris, Berger-Levrault, 1970.

Chaigneau, P. *Rivalités politiques et Socialisme à Madagascar.* Paris, Centre des Hautes Etudes sur l'Afrique et l'Asie Modernes, 1985.

Covell, M. *Madagascar. Politics, Economics and Society.* London, Frances Pinter, 1987.

Historical Dictionary of Madagascar. Lanham, MD, Scarecrow Press, 1995.

Deleris, F. *Ratsiraka: Socialisme et Misère à Madagascar.* Paris, L'Harmattan, 1986.

Deschamps, H. *Histoire de Madagascar.* 4th Edn. Paris, Berger-Levrault, 1972.

Drysdale, H. *Dancing with the Dead: A Journey through Zanzibar and Madagascar.* London, Hamish Hamilton, 1991.

Duruflé, G. *L'Ajustement structurel en Afrique (Sénégal, Côte d'Ivoire, Madagascar).* Paris, Editions Karthala, 1987.

Feeley-Harnick, G. *A Green Estate: Restoring Independence in Madagascar.* Washington, DC, Smithsonian Institution Press, 1991.

de Gaudusson, J. *L'Administration malgache.* Paris, Berger-Levrault, 1976.

Heseltine, N. *Madagascar.* London, Pall Mall, 1971.

Hugon, P. *Economie et enseignement à Madagascar.* Paris, Institut International de Planification de l'Education, 1976.

Litalien, R. *Madagascar 1956–1960, Etape vers la décolonisation.* Paris, Ecole Pratique des Hautes Etudes, 1975.

Massiot, M. *L'organisation politique, administrative, financière et judiciaire de la République malgache.* Antananarivo, Librairie de Madagascar, 1970.

Mutibwa, P. *The Malagasy and the Europeans: Madagascar's Foreign Relations 1861–95.* London, Longman, 1974.

Pascal, R. *La République malgache: Pacifique indépendance.* Paris, Berger-Levrault, 1965.

Pryor, F. L. *Malawi and Madagascar: The Political Economy of Poverty, Equity and Growth.* New York, Oxford University Press, 1991.

Rabemananjara, J. *Nationalisme et problèmes malgaches.* Paris, 1958.

Rabenoro, C. *Les relations extérieures de Madagascar, de 1960 à 1972.* Paris, Editions l'Harmattan, 1986.

Raison-Jourde, F. *Les souverains de Madagascar.* Paris, Editions Karthala, 1983.

Rajémis-Raolison, R. *Dictionnaire historique et géographique de Madagascar.* Fianarantsoa, Librairie Ambozontany, 1966.

Rajoelina, P. *Quarante années de la vie politique de Madagascar, 1947–1987.* Paris, L'Harmattan, 1988.

Rajoelina, P., and Ramelet, A. *Madagascar, la grande île.* Paris, L'Harmattan, 1989.

Ralaimihoatra, E. *Histoire de Madagascar.* 2 vols. Antananarivo, Société Malgache d'Editions, 1966–67.

Ramahatra, O. *Madagascar: Une économie en phase d'ajustement.* Paris, Editions l'Harmattan, 1989.

Sharp, L. A. *The Possessed and the Dispossessed.* Berkeley, University of California Press, 1993.

Spacensky, A. *Madagascar: Cinquante ans de vie politique (de Ralaimongo à Tsiranana).* Paris, Nouvelles Editions Latines, 1970.

Thompson, V., and Adloff, R. *The Malagasy Republic.* Stanford, CA, Stanford University Press, 1965.

Tronchon, J. *L'insurrection malgache de 1947.* Paris, Editions Karthala, 1986.

Vérin, P. *Madagascar.* Paris, Editions Karthala, 1990.

Vindard, G. R., and Battistini, R. *Bio-geography and Ecology of Madagascar.* The Hague, 1972.

Wilson, J. *Lemurs of the Lost World.* 2nd Edn. London, Impact Books, 1995.

MALAWI

Physical and Social Geography

A. MACGREGOR HUTCHESON

The land-locked Republic of Malawi extends some 840 km from north to south, varying in width from 80 to 160 km. It has a total area of 118,484 sq km (45,747 sq miles), including 24,208 sq km (9,347 sq miles) of inland water, and is aligned along the southern continuation of the east African rift valley system. There are land borders with Tanzania to the north, with Zambia to the west, and with Mozambique to the south and east. Frontiers with Mozambique and Tanzania continue to the east, along the shores of Lake Malawi.

Malawi occupies a plateau of varying height, bordering the deep rift valley trench which averages 80 km in width. The northern two-thirds of the rift valley floor are almost entirely occupied by Lake Malawi, which is 568 km in length and varies in width from 16 km to 80 km. The lake covers an area of 23,310 sq km, and has a mean surface of 472 m above sea-level. The southern third of the rift valley is traversed by the River Shire, draining Lake Malawi, via the shallow Lake Malombe, to the River Zambezi. The plateau surfaces on either side of the rift valley lie mainly at 760–1,370 m, but very much higher elevations are attained; above the highlands west of Lake Malawi are the Nyika and Viphya plateaux and the Dedza mountains and Kirk Range, which rise to between 1,524 and 2,440 m in places. South of Lake Malawi are the Shire highlands and the Zomba and Mulanje mountain ranges; the Zomba plateau rises to 2,100 m, and Mt Mulanje, the highest mountain in central Africa, to 3,050 m above sea-level.

The great variations in altitude and latitudinal extent are responsible for a wide range of climatic, soil and vegetational conditions within Malawi. There are three climatic seasons. During the cool season, from May to August, there is very little cloud, and mean temperatures in the plateau areas are 15.5°C–18°C, and in the rift valley 20°C–24.5°C. The coldest month is July, when the maximum temperature is 22.2°C and the minimum 11.7°C. In September and October, before the rains, a short hot season occurs when humidity increases: mean temperatures range from 27°C–30°C in the rift valley, and from 22°C–24.5°C on the plateaux at this time. During October/November temperatures exceeding 37°C may be registered in the low-lying areas. The rainy season lasts from November to April, and over 90% of the total annual rainfall occurs during this period. Most of Malawi receives an annual rainfall of 760–1,015 mm, but some areas in the higher plateaux experience over 1,525 mm.

Malawi possesses some of the most fertile soils in south-central Africa. Of particular importance are those in the lake-shore plains, the Lake Chilwa-Palombe plain and the upper and lower Shire valley. Good plateau soils occur in the Lilongwe-Kasungu high plains and in the tea-producing areas of Thyolo, Mulanje and Nkhata Bay districts. Although just over half the land area of Malawi is considered suitable for cultivation, rather less than 50% of this area is cultivated at present; this is an indication of the agricultural potential yet to be realized. The lakes and rivers have been exploited for their considerable hydroelectric and irrigation potential.

Malawi is one of the more densely populated countries of Africa, with 7,988,507 inhabitants (an average density of 67.4 per sq km) at the 1987 census. There were an estimated 10,032,600 inhabitants at mid-1994, giving a population density of 84.7 per sq km. According to UN projections, Malawi's population will increase to 11.4m. by the middle of the year 2000. However, population patterns are expected to be affected by the high rate of incidence of AIDS, which is particularly prevalent in urban areas. Labour has been a Malawian resource for many years, and thousands of migratory workers seek employment in neighbouring countries, particularly in South Africa.

As a result of physical, historical and economic factors, Malawi's population is very unevenly distributed. The Southern Region, the most developed of the three regions, contains more than half the population, while the Northern Region has only about 12%. New investment in the Northern and Central Regions and the movement of the capital from Zomba to a new site at Lilongwe in the early 1970s have made some progress towards redressing these regional imbalances.

Recent History

RICHARD BROWN

Revised for this edition by the Editor

THE COLONIAL PERIOD

In 1891 the British government declared a protectorate over the area that came to be known as Nyasaland. An agricultural economy was established by white settlers, while many Africans were given unprotected tenancies, with few legal rights to the land they cultivated. Grievances against the injustices of the colonial system led to an unsuccessful uprising by Africans in early 1915. In 1944 the Nyasaland African Congress (NAC) was formed, linking, on a non-ethnic basis, native associations, independent churches and other groups of educated Africans. In 1951 the British government gave its assent to proposals by white settlers for a federation with the territories of Northern and Southern Rhodesia. Despite the opposition of Africans, who feared that the plan would prevent the achievement of independence, the Federation of Rhodesia and Nyasaland (FRN) was formally established in October 1953.

By 1955 the influence of a radical element within the NAC, led by Henry Chipembere and Kanyama Chiume, had become evident. In 1958 Dr Hastings Kamuzu Banda, a physician who had retained close links with the NAC despite being resident abroad for nearly 40 years, returned to assume the leadership of the party. His vigorous denunciations of the federation, combined with the forceful campaigning of his followers, provoked an outbreak of civil disorder in March 1959: a state of emergency was declared, the NAC was banned and its leaders were detained. After the emergence in September of the new Malawi Congress Party (MCP), led by the imprisoned Dr Banda, the British authorities were obliged to choose between maintaining control through the continued use of armed force, or leaving Malawi completely: they chose the latter alternative. Dr Banda was released in April 1960. Elections held in August 1961 gave the MCP a decisive victory. Full self-government followed in

January 1963; Dr Banda became prime minister in February, and the FRN was dissolved in December. On 6 July 1964 Nyasaland became the independent state of Malawi.

Banda's reluctance to promote the 'Africanization' of the economy or to pursue stronger anti-colonial policies was opposed by a significant proportion of educated Malawians; Banda reacted by giving greater responsibilities to white expatriates and by eliciting popular support from the less educated sections of the population. Opposition to Dr Banda's increasingly authoritarian style of government led, in February 1965, to an open revolt, and subsequently to the flight into exile of its leader, Henry Chipembere.

THE BANDA REGIME

On 6 July 1966 Malawi officially became a republic and a one-party state, with Banda as president: he was voted president-for-life in 1971. In the ensuing years no political opposition was tolerated, and the various exiled opposition groups, of which the most prominent were the Socialist League of Malawi (LESOMA) and the Malawi Freedom Movement (MAFREMO), remained ineffectual, although they claimed to command strong support. In March 1979 Banda admitted that a letter-bomb which had injured the leader of LESOMA, Dr Attati Mpakati, had been sent in accordance with his instructions; the Malawi government, however, denied any responsibility for the murder of Mpakati in March 1983, while he was on a private visit to Zimbabwe. In May 1983 the leader of MAFREMO, Orton Chirwa, and his wife Vera were sentenced to death for treason (having, it was alleged, been kidnapped in Zambia and brought to Malawi by force). Following appeals for clemency by international organizations and heads of state, Banda commuted the sentence to one of life imprisonment. (Orton Chirwa died in prison in October 1992 and Vera Chirwa was released in January 1993.) In November 1989 the government rejected allegations by Amnesty International that several Malawian political detainees had been subjected to torture, and in October 1990 another international human rights organization accused the Malawi government of using detention without trial, torture and assassination to suppress political opposition. In February 1991 a new opposition movement, the Malawi Socialist Labour Party, was formed by Malawians living in exile in Tanzania.

Within Malawi no political figure was permitted to emerge as an obvious successor to the ageing president. In 1983 a dispute was reported to have developed between Dick Matenje, the secretary-general of the MCP and a minister without portfolio, and John Tembo, the governor of the Reserve Bank of Malawi, concerning the eventual succession to the presidency. Matenje and three other senior politicians died in May, apparently in a road accident, but exiled opposition members claimed that they had been murdered while trying to leave the country (see below). The post of MCP secretary-general was left vacant, and the dissolution and reorganization of the government became virtually an annual occurrence, apparently to prevent ministers from establishing secure power bases.

In March 1992 the government was exposed to unprecedented criticism from the influential Roman Catholic church in Malawi, with the publication by its bishops of an open letter criticizing the state's alleged abuses of human rights. Pressure on the government intensified later in that month, when about 80 Malawian political exiles gathered in Lusaka to devise a strategy to precipitate political reforms. In early April Chakufwa Chihana, a prominent trade union leader who had demanded multi-party elections, returned to Malawi from exile and was immediately arrested. The Banda regime was seriously threatened from within the country in early May, when industrial unrest in the southern city of Blantyre escalated into violent anti-government riots; these spread to Lilongwe, and reportedly resulted in at least 40 deaths. Shortly afterwards international donors suspended all non-humanitarian aid to Malawi, pending an improvement in the government's observance of human rights. In early June several hundred people were arrested and charged with circulating seditious material.

Elections to an enlarged legislature took place in June 1992, at which 675 MCP candidates contested 141 elective seats in the national assembly: 45 candidates were returned unopposed, five seats remained vacant, owing to the disqualification of some candidates, and 62 former members of the national assembly lost their seats. Opposition groups challenged the government's claim of a turnout of about 80% of the electorate. Chihana was released from detention in July, but was re-arrested soon afterwards and charged with sedition. (In December Chihana was found guilty and sentenced to two years' hard labour; the sentence was, however, subsequently reduced on appeal to nine months.)

In September 1992 a group of opposition politicians formed the Alliance for Democracy (AFORD), a pressure group operating within Malawi under the chairmanship of Chihana, which aimed to campaign for democratic political reform. Another opposition organization, the United Democratic Front (UDF), was formed in the same month. In October Banda reluctantly conceded to demands for a national referendum by secret ballot on the introduction of multi-party democracy. In early January 1993 more than 100,000 anti-government demonstrators attended a rally in Blantyre. During that month LESOMA and another party, the Malawi Democratic Union, merged to form the United Front for Multi-party Democracy, based in Zambia. In March MAFREMO dissolved itself and its membership joined AFORD.

TRANSITION TO DEMOCRACY

The referendum on the introduction of democratic reform took place in mid-June 1993. Although the government had disrupted the activities of opposition groups prior to the referendum, the latter secured a decisive victory, with 63.2% of voters supporting the reintroduction of multi-party politics. A turnout of 67% of the electorate was recorded. The opposition received especially strong support in the north and south of the country, while voters in the central region mainly remained loyal to the MCP. Following the referendum, Banda rejected opposition demands for the immediate installation of a government of national unity. He agreed, however, to establish a national executive council, to oversee the transition to a multi-party system, and a national consultative council to draft a new constitution. Both councils were to comprise members of the government and the opposition. Banda announced a general amnesty for thousands of political exiles, and stated that a general election would be held, on a multi-party basis, within a year. (Chihana had been released from prison a few days before the referendum, having served six months of his sentence.) In late June the constitution was amended to allow the registration of political parties other than the MCP: by mid-August five organizations, including AFORD and the UDF, had been accorded legal status. A UN-sponsored forum on the transition to democracy was held in Malawi in July; it was agreed that the UN would continue to play a supporting role in the country during the transitional period.

In September 1993 Banda carried out an extensive cabinet reshuffle, including the appointment of Hetherwick Ntaba as minister of external affairs, a post held by Banda himself since 1964. In early October 1993 Banda became seriously ill and underwent neurological surgery in South Africa. Having rejected opposition demands for the election of an apolitical interim head of state, in mid-October the office of the president announced the formation of a three-member presidential council, which was to assume executive power in Banda's absence. As required by the constitution, the council was placed under the chairmanship of the new secretary-general of the MCP, Gwanda Chakuamba. (Chakuamba, a former government minister, had been sentenced to 22 years' imprisonment in 1981, after having been convicted of sedition; he was released in July 1993.) The two other members were also senior MCP officials, John Tembo and Robson Chirwa, the minister of transport and communications. In early November the presidential council reshuffled the cabinet, as a result of which Banda was without ministerial responsibilities for the first time since 1964. In mid-November 1993 the national assembly passed the constitutional amendment bill, which included the repeal of the institution of life presidency, the reduction of the qualifying age for a presidential candidate from 40 to 35 years, the repeal of the requirement that election candidates be members of the MCP, the repeal of the right of the president to nominate members of the legislature exclusively from the MCP, and the lowering of the minimum voting age from 21 to 18 years. The national assembly also amended the public security act, repealing all provisions permitting detention without trial.

Having made a rapid and unexpected recovery, Banda resumed full presidential powers on 7 December 1993 and the presidential council was dissolved. Shortly afterwards, in response to increasing pressure from the opposition, the government amended the constitution to provide for the appointment of an acting president in the event of the incumbent's being incapacitated. In February 1994 the MCP announced that Banda was to be the party's presidential candidate in the forthcoming general election, which was scheduled to take place on 17 May; Chakuamba was selected as the MCP's candidate for the vice-presidency. In the same month the national assembly approved an increase in the number of elected legislative members in the approaching general election from 141 to 177.

Meanwhile, the MCP announced in September 1993 that the Malawi Young Pioneers (MYP), a widely-feared paramilitary section of the ruling party, were to be gradually disarmed. In early December, following the murder of three soldiers by MYP members, members of the regular army undertook a peremptory campaign to close MYP offices and camps. In the ensuing violence, which was believed to have been exacerbated by long-standing tensions between the army and the MYP, 32 people were reported to have been killed. Following his recovery from surgery, Banda appointed a minister of defence (having previously himself retained the defence portfolio) to oversee the MYP disarmament process and investigate army grievances. By early January 1994 it was reported that the disarmament of the MYP had been satisfactorily completed; it was also reported, however, that several thousand MYP members had crossed the border into Mozambique to take refuge in rebel bases. In late January 1994 the governments of Malawi and Mozambique agreed to a programme for the repatriation of the MYP forces from Mozambican territory; however, in May (three months after the MYP was officially disbanded) it was reported that at least 2,000 armed MYP members remained in Mozambique. In June 1996 it was further reported that former MYP members had formed a terrorist group, known as the Movement for the Restoration of Democracy in Malawi (MRDM), in Mozambique.

On 16 May 1994 a provisional constitution was adopted by the national assembly. The new document provided for the appointment of a constitutional committee and of a human rights commission, and abolished the system of 'traditional' courts. Banda's domination of the country finally ended with the multi-party elections held on the following day. In the four-candidate presidential contest, Bakili Muluzi, leader of the UDF, obtained 47.3% of the votes; Banda himself won 33.6%, and Chakufwa Chihana (of AFORD) 18.6%. The UDF won 84 of the 177 parliamentary seats, the MCP 55 seats and AFORD 36 seats. (The results of voting in two constituencies were invalidated.) In the absence of strong ideological differences between the parties, regional and ethnic allegiances predominated: AFORD won all 33 of the Northern Region's seats; the MCP was strongly supported in the Central Region; and the UDF won most of the seats in the Southern Region. The expected UDF–AFORD coalition did not materialize, however, and one month after the elections AFORD agreed instead to work with the MCP, thus compelling the UDF to form a government without a parliamentary majority.

THE MULUZI GOVERNMENT

President Muluzi and his vice-president, Justin Malewezi, were inaugurated later in May 1994. The principal aims of the new administration were defined as being to alleviate poverty and ensure food security, and to combat corruption and the mismanagement of resources. The closure was announced of three prisons where abuses of human rights were known to have taken place; an amnesty was granted to the country's remaining political prisoners, and all death sentences were commuted to terms of life imprisonment. The new government was dominated by the UDF, but also included members of the Malawi National Democratic Party and the United Front for Multi-party Democracy. Attempts to recruit members of AFORD into a coalition administration initially failed, owing to disagreements regarding the allocation of senior portfolios, and in June AFORD and the MCP signed what was termed a 'memorandum of understanding' whereby they would function as an opposition front. The Muluzi government was thus deprived of a majority in the national assembly, which was inaugurated at the end of June. In late August it was announced that Banda, while remaining honorary life president of the MCP, was to retire from active involvement in politics. Chakuamba, as vice-president of the MCP, effectively succeeded to the party leadership.

Government changes in late September 1994 included the appointment of Chihana to the post of second vice-president and minister of irrigation and water development: AFORD members were also allocated responsibility for agriculture, transport, research and the environment. None the less, the AFORD–MCP 'memorandum of understanding' remained in force until January 1995, when AFORD, acknowledging that the new government had made significant progress in the restoration of political stability and the establishment of democracy, announced an end to its co-operation with the MCP. The creation of the post of second vice-president necessitated a constitutional amendment, and provoked severe criticism from the MCP. Moreover, the national constitutional conference, which met in February to consider refinements to the document prior to its official promulgation, recommended that the post be abolished. In late March, however, the national assembly (in the absence of MCP deputies, who boycotted the vote) approved the retention of the second vice-presidency; the assembly also approved the establishment—although not before May 1999—of a second chamber of parliament, the senate, as well as a constitutional clause requiring that senior state officials declare all personal assets within two months of assuming their post. A further reorganization of the cabinet took place in August 1995.

In June 1994 Muluzi announced the establishment of an independent commission of inquiry to investigate the deaths of Matenje and his associates in May 1983. In early January 1995, in accordance with the findings of the commission, Banda was placed under house arrest; Tembo and two former police officers were arrested and detained, and the four were charged with murder and conspiracy to murder. A former inspector-general of the police, who was alleged, *inter alia*, to have destroyed evidence relating to the deaths, was charged later in the month. Cecilia Kadzamira, Tembo's niece and the former president's 'official hostess', was charged in early April with conspiracy to murder. The trial opened in late April, but was immediately adjourned, owing to Banda's absence from court (his defence counsel asserted that he was too ill to stand trial), and to the failure of the state prosecution to submit, as required, certain evidence to the defence. Banda failed to appear at a resumed hearing in early May, and was stated by medical consultants to be unable to attend the trial. Banda remained under house arrest, while proceedings against Tembo, Kadzamira and other defendants resumed in July. In mid-September Tembo and the two former police officers were granted bail, and most restrictions on Banda's movements were ended. The case against Kadzamira was abandoned in mid-December, owing to lack of evidence, and later in the month Banda, Tembo and the other defendants were acquitted of conspiracy to murder and to defeat justice. The director of public prosecutions subsequently appealed against the verdict, complaining that the presiding judge had effectively instructed the jury to acquit the defendants. In early January 1996 an MCP-owned newspaper printed a statement by Banda in which he admitted that he might unknowingly have been responsible for brutalities perpetrated under his regime, and apologized to Malawians for 'pain and suffering' inflicted during his presidency. In early July 1995 Tembo and four other members of the Banda regime were charged with conspiring to murder the Roman Catholic bishops who had published criticisms of the former administration in 1992.

In July 1995 lawyers acting for Banda demanded that Muluzi explain the apparent payment of a substantial sum to a witness in the trial of Banda and his associates. Meanwhile, there were further allegations that the Muluzi administration had been involved in questionable financial transactions. It emerged in mid-1995 that the president had authorized the payment of some K6.2m. from the state poverty alleviation account to UDF members of parliament (to enable the payment of loans to their constituents); there was also evidence of the involvement of government ministers in the smuggling of maize to neighbouring countries. Moreover, few ministers had complied with the constitutional requirement regarding the declaration of assets. An investigation of Banda's financial interests was initiated in

September. Muluzi announced in February 1996 that an independent anti-corruption bureau was to be established to investigate allegations of corruption.

The cabinet was reorganized in July 1995. Later in that month the UDF and AFORD signed a formal co-operation agreement. Many government offices were closed for a week in August, as civil servants undertook industrial action in support of their demands for increases in salary. The government declared the strike illegal, but withdrew threatened sanctions after the industrial action was cancelled; negotiations regarding pay increases ensued. In late October the president and vice-president of the Malawi Democratic Party (MDP) were acquitted on charges of intimidating the head of state: in late July MDP leaders had demanded Muluzi's resignation, stating that the population had lost confidence in his administration.

In December 1995 Chihana warned that AFORD might withdraw from the coalition government, alleging that the UDF was using public funds to secure political influence, and complaining of a lack of openness in the Muluzi administration. Chihana resigned from the government in May 1996, expressing his intention to devote himself more fully to the work of his party. The post of second vice-president remained vacant following a reorganization of the cabinet shortly afterwards. In late May Bitwell Kawonga, another AFORD minister, resigned. In early June AFORD withdrew from its coalition with the UDF (which meant the loss of a parliamentary working majority for the government) and declared that AFORD ministers still in the cabinet should resign; Dr Mponda Mkandawire, the minister of natural resources, subsequently stepped down and the party appointed a new 'shadow cabinet', which included Kawonga and Mkandawire. Five members were dismissed from AFORD's national executive, having refused to relinquish their ministerial posts. A reorganization of the cabinet in July included the reappointment of Mkandawire. International donors were displeased by the creation of another ministerial post in an already large cabinet. Meanwhile, AFORD and the MCP insisted that AFORD ministers who had disobeyed instructions to resign should be regarded as members of the UDF, as they were effectively maintaining that party's parliamentary majority. The rejection of this demand resulted in a parliamentary boycott by both opposition parties. In September a UDF member of the national assembly (a former government minister) resigned from the party, and a further eight members were reportedly threatening to resign, in response to Muluzi's controversial appointment of a new UDF regional governor for the south. At the beginning of December the AFORD ministers remaining in the cabinet asserted, in a letter to the speaker of the national assembly, that they were independent and had not joined the UDF. In early March 1997 AFORD stated that the party would continue its boycott until the ministers resigned both their government posts and parliamentary seats. Meanwhile, the high court dismissed a case, brought by the opposition parties, that the previous sitting of parliament be declared illegal and unconstitutional. In early April the MCP ended its parliamentary boycott, following a meeting between Muluzi and Chakuamba, at which Muluzi had allegedly promised to amend the constitution to prevent parliamentary delegates from changing their political affiliation without standing for re-election. Government changes were made in May; in July the cabinet was again reorganized, and a number of ministries were merged or eliminated altogether.

Tembo and Kadzamira were again arrested in September 1996, and were charged, along with several others, with conspiracy to murder and attempted murder. Although they had been arrested in connection with the recent shooting of a Lebanese trader, the charges were reported to relate to a plot to kill three government ministers in 1995. In January 1997 it was announced that Banda was to be charged with embezzling state funds for the establishment of a private school; however, in May he was discharged as unfit to attend court. In July the supreme court dismissed an appeal against the acquittal of Banda and Tembo on murder charges, shortly after Muluzi reportedly requested that all criminal cases against Banda be discontinued. In the same month Banda announced his intention to resign as president of the MCP.

Strike action by civil servants during April–May 1997 caused considerable disruption, notably to health services and air traffic. A government-appointed commission had recently recommended salary increases of as much as 300% for public-sector employees; however, the government insisted that immediately to grant increases of this order would necessitate unacceptable measures of retrenchment in other areas of public expenditure. In early May, following a number of arrests, it was reported that the majority of striking personnel had returned to work.

REGIONAL RELATIONS

President Banda's establishment of diplomatic relations with South Africa in 1967 alienated him for a time from most other African leaders, as did his promotion of friendly relations with Portugal under the pre-1974 right-wing regime. Following independence, Malawi's relations with its neighbours, Tanzania and Zambia, were strained by disputes over territorial boundaries: during the late 1960s Malawi claimed that its natural boundaries included the whole of the northern half of Lake Malawi, and extended at least 160 km north of Tanzania's Songwo river, as well as east and west into Mozambique and Zambia. Full diplomatic relations with Zambia were established in 1971, but it was not until 1985 that diplomatic relations were established with Tanzania. However, Malawi did become a member of the Southern African Development Co-ordination Conference (SADCC) in 1980, and in 1993 was a founder member of its successor, the Southern African Development Community (SADC—see p. 130). Following talks in April 1994, the presidents of Tanzania and Malawi agreed that social and economic relations between the two countries should be improved, and that the joint commission on co-operation (which had last met in 1983) should be re-established. An agreement formalizing cross-border trade was signed in August 1996.

Dr Banda gave support neither to the Frente de Libertação de Moçambique (Frelimo) nor to the Patriotic Front (PF), during their respective independence struggles in Mozambique and Zimbabwe, and in 1982 the Mozambique government alleged that its opponents, members of the Resistência Nacional Moçambicana (Renamo, also known as the MNR), were operating from bases in Malawi. In October 1984 Malawi and Mozambique signed a general co-operation agreement, establishing a joint commission to regulate their relations. In July 1986, however, the chief of staff of Mozambique's armed forces alleged that Malawi was actively assisting the guerrillas of Renamo. Despite Banda's denial of these allegations, President Machel of Mozambique warned that, if Malawi continued to assist Renamo, he would close the border between the two countries, thereby denying Malawi its most direct access to the sea. In October 1986 President Machel was killed in an aeroplane crash in South Africa. The South African government claimed that documents which had been discovered in the crash wreckage revealed a plot by Mozambique and Zimbabwe to overthrow the Malawi government. Angry protests from the Malawi government to Mozambique and Zimbabwe were met by denials of the accusations. In December Malawi and Mozambique signed a further agreement on defence and security matters, which was believed to include co-operation in eliminating Renamo operations. In April 1987 it was confirmed that Malawi troops had been stationed in Mozambique to protect the strategic railway line linking Malawi to the Mozambican port of Nacala. In July 1988 relations between the two countries were consolidated when President Chissano of Mozambique made a state visit to Malawi, during which he stated that he did not believe Malawi to be supporting Renamo. In December Malawi, Mozambique and the UN High Commissioner for Refugees (UNHCR) signed an agreement to promote the voluntary repatriation of an estimated 650,000 Mozambican refugees who had fled into Malawi over the previous two years, as a result of the continuing unrest in Mozambique, and who were placing a considerable burden on the country's resources; the number of refugees continued to rise, however, reaching about 1m. by mid-1992. Following the signing of a general peace agreement for Mozambique in October 1992, all Malawian troops had been withdrawn from Mozambique by June 1993. However, in mid-1994 an estimated 600,000 Mozambican refugees still remained in Malawi. By early 1996 the majority of the refugees had been repatriated in an operation organized by UNHCR. In March 1995 President Chissano visited Malawi, and the two countries agreed to review their joint defence and security arrangements to reflect problems such as drugs-trafficking and arms-smuggling. Following a meeting of the joint defence and security commission in mid-1996, a sub-committee to regulate border issues, and joint committees on security and police matters at national, regional, district and local levels, were to be established.

Malawi's relations with Zimbabwe improved during the 1980s, despite the Banda regime's hostility to the PF prior to Zimbabwe's independence, and absence from the independence celebrations in 1980. Diplomatic relations were subsequently established, and in 1986 a joint permanent commission was formed. In April 1990 Banda was a guest of honour at celebrations for Zimbabwe's 10th anniversary of independence.

The Muluzi government has undertaken a more active role in foreign affairs, offering troops for the UN peace-keeping operation in Rwanda and undertaking joint military exercises with US troops within Malawi. During 1995, as chairman of the Common Market for Eastern and Southern Africa (COMESA), Muluzi acted as mediator in a long-standing frontier dispute between Sudan and Uganda.

Economy

LINDA VAN BUREN

INTRODUCTION

In terms of average income, Malawi is still among the world's 12 poorest countries. The country has, however, achieved some development successes since independence in 1964, despite problems of subsistence agriculture, low educational levels, shortage of skilled personnel, lack of mineral resources, inadequate infrastructure and import-dependent industries, compounded by the limitations of a land-locked position and a small domestic market. In 1994, according to estimates by the World Bank, Malawi's gross domestic product (GDP) was US $1,302m., and the gross national product (GNP) per head was $170. During 1985–95, it was estimated, GNP per head declined, in real terms, by an annual average of 0.7%. Over the same period the population increased by an annual average of 3.1%. Malawi's GDP also declined, in real terms, by an annual average of 0.7% in 1990–94. Real GDP fell by 10.2% in 1994, but increased, according to provisional figures, by 9.5% in 1995 and, according to the IMF, by about 11% in 1996.

ECONOMIC BACKGROUND

During the 1970s Malawi benefited from a sharp rise in investment, supported by favourable government policies and an influx of foreign aid and capital. The concurrent expansion of commercial output led to a doubling of production of export crops, and also placed Malawi among the few countries of sub-Saharan Africa where food production kept pace with population growth. In the social services sector there were extensive donor-supported programmes to improve the provision of education, health services, water supply and sanitation. Rapid growth in the domestic economy was, however, paralleled by a poor performance of the economy externally.

Malawi was beset by drought during 1979–81. The resulting decline in agricultural output adversely affected export earnings and necessitated the import of food, while associated industries began to experience severe reductions in revenue. With virtually no sector of the economy unaffected, GDP growth, in real terms, declined to 3.1% per year during the period 1980–91. In 1981, in an effort to restore growth, the government, supported by the IMF and the World Bank, initiated a programme of reform.

The economy responded rapidly, helped by the return of favourable rains in 1982 and a resurgence of agricultural output. Restraint in the level of imports and an increase in inflows of aid helped to reduce Malawi's current account deficit while also enabling levels of external borrowing to decline. However, Malawi's terms of trade continued to worsen during the period, and the complete closure in 1984 of the country's regular maritime access routes through war-torn Mozambique raised export freight costs. A further reform programme began in 1986. Although a number of the anticipated measures were implemented during the year (including a reduction in subsidies and the reorganization of some major parastatal bodies) the economy began to falter again, with GDP growth falling to 2.8%, compared with the target of 4.2%, and with the budget deficit amounting to 11% of GDP, compared with a target of 3.5%. As a result of the economy's disappointing performance, the government cancelled its three-year extended facility with the IMF in August 1986, shortly before it was due to expire in October, pending a reassessment of the reform programme. In March 1988 agreement was reached on a 14-month stand-by facility, the government having agreed in August 1987, under pressure from the IMF, to reschedule its debt repayments. In July 1988 the government obtained a four-year enhanced structural adjustment facility (ESAF) from the IMF.

Economic performance in 1992 was adversely affected by severe drought conditions, an unprecedented level of industrial unrest and the decision by international donors in May to link all future non-humanitarian aid to progress in upholding human rights. According to government figures, GDP declined, in real terms, by 7.3% in 1992, while (following two devaluations of the national currency) the annual rate of inflation averaged 23.2% (compared with 8.2% in 1991). More than one-half of the population experienced food shortages in that year. Favourable weather conditions in 1992–93 restored the situation, and official figures estimated real GDP growth at 9.7% in 1993. Serious droughts in both the 1993–94 and 1994–95 seasons undermined agricultural production and necessitated extensive maize imports. GDP decreased by 10.2% in 1994, but rose by an estimated 9.5% in 1995. In addition, the new government inherited an unstable fiscal and monetary situation.

AGRICULTURE

Agriculture is the most important sector of the economy, and (with forestry and fishing) it accounted for 30.9% of GDP (at constant 1978 factor cost) in 1994, and an estimated 35.9% in 1995. During 1980–90 agricultural GDP increased by an annual average of 2.0%, but in 1990–94 it declined by 0.6% per annum. An estimated 86.3% of the working population were engaged in agriculture in 1995. The vast majority of these work in the smallholder sector, which accounts for nearly 80% of the cultivated area and of agricultural output, which is mostly on a subsistence basis. The principal cash crops are tobacco (which accounted for an estimated 67.3% of domestic export earnings in 1996), tea and sugar cane. Maize is the principal food crop, and is grown almost entirely by smallholders; output was 1.66m. metric tons in 1995, up from 1.04m. tons in 1994. The sorghum harvest increased from 17,000 tons in 1994 to some 45,000 tons in 1995. There have been some exports of maize, although imports of cereals have been required in years when unfavourable weather conditions have adversely affected output. Cassava, potatoes, plantains, groundnuts and pulses are also important food crops. Malawi produced about 31,000 metric tons of groundnuts (in shell) in 1994 and a similar amount in 1995. From this was obtained an output of 3,600 tons of groundnut oil per year. The sunflower seed crop of about 9,000 tons in 1994 yielded 1,981 tons of sunflower-seed oil; sunflower seed production stood at 10,000 tons in 1995. The output of cottonseed oil was 3,020 tons in 1994. The output of green coffee beans was about 5,000 metric tons per annum in 1994–96. The leading export crop, tobacco, was grown on an estimated 130,000 ha, with yields of some 1,015 kg per ha, in 1995. Output of tobacco leaves was an estimated 99,000 metric tons in 1994 and 132,000 metric tons in 1995. Malawi's principal agricultural exports are tobacco, tea and sugar. Large, hand-shelled, confectionary-grade groundnuts, coffee, cassava, rice, medium staple cotton and sunflower seed are also exported. Smallholder crops are marketed for export by the Agricultural Development and Marketing Corpn (ADMARC) and, since the mid-1990s, by private traders. Since the implementation, after 1981, of more favourable pricing arrangements, together with the introduction of new hybrid varieties, efforts have been made to diversify the range of commercial smallholder crops, to improve the productivity of food and export crops and to raise rural incomes. Assistance has been obtained from several donors, led by the International Development Association (IDA). The IDA has also helped to finance, in association with the International Fund for Agricultural Development (IFAD), a scheme, instigated in 1988, to improve the availability of credit to small-scale farmers. This scheme formed part of government plans to double the coverage of seasonal credit to about 30% of smallholders by 1995. Efforts to expand commercial production of crops, especially for export, and to raise rural incomes took two forms—the expansion of commercial smallholding schemes and the National Rural Development Programe (NRDP). Among the wide range of donor-supported smallholder schemes was a project sponsored by the European Union (EU) to develop the cultivation of tobacco and coffee in the north, and a tobacco scheme, financed by the Commonwealth Development Corpn (CDC) of the United Kingdom, near Mt Kasungu on the central plateau. The latter, started in 1970, involved more than 1,500 growers, cultivating 1,200 ha of flue-cured tobacco and an equivalent area of maize. The 20-year NRDP, introduced in 1977, centred on eight agricultural development regions, covering one-fifth of the country; by 1985 more than 80% of Malawi's smallholders were involved in the programme. The scheme was aimed at increasing crop yields by encouraging simple improvements in farming techniques, with greater use of fertilizers, pest control and irrigation. This was intended to stimulate farmers with very small plots (40% of all smallholders) to achieve self-sufficiency in food production, and to enable larger smallholders to produce a surplus for market. However, growth in smallholder output lost momentum during the late 1980s, and the programme was suspended in 1988 (growth in smallholder output was only 2.6% in that year, compared with growth of 7% in the estate sector). This decline in the rate of growth resulted from the limited access of the majority of peasants to improved credit facilities and crop varieties; a government decision to phase out fertilizer subsidies from 1986; rising transport costs; and, most significantly, the small size of most plots of land. In 1994 the government launched a programme to redistribute land acquired from commercial farms as part of its policy of poverty alleviation. The liberalization of agricultural marketing and production arrangements undertaken by the Muluzi government in the mid-1990s contributed, together with favourable weather conditions, to substantial increases in smallholder production, estimated by the IMF to amount to 34% in 1995 and 40% in 1996.

Livestock improvements have made the country self-sufficient in meat and liquid milk. Cattle numbered an estimated 980,000 in 1995, sheep and goats 1,086,000 and pigs 247,000. Almost all livestock is kept by smallholders. Fish provide about 70% of animal protein consumption, but the annual catch decreased during 1990–95 by 9.3% per annum, to 45,427 metric tons in 1995. Much of the commercial fishing activity centres on Nkhotakota, on the western shore of Lake Malawi. The lake has more than 500 species of fish.

Timber and pulpwood plantations have been developed since the early 1970s, with the area under state plantations totalling 20,800 ha in 1985. In addition, 54,000 ha of pine and eucalyptus have been planted on the Viphya plateau, in the north, to supply a pulp and paper project. The project focuses on development of part of the Viphya plantation, and the construction of processing facilities. The scheme aimed eventually to provide employment for several thousand people, not only in forestry but also in infrastructural development, which includes the construction of a port on the lake at Chinteche and a new town. The total area under forests in 1990 was 35,000 sq km. Acacia, conifers and baobab trees grow in the highlands.

Major Exports

Malawi is the second largest producer of tobacco in Africa, after Zimbabwe. The crop sustains some 6,500 estates and provides a cash income for about 66,000 tenant smallholders. It is by far the most important export, accounting for an estimated 67.3% of domestic export earnings in 1996, a less than optimal year, as the quality of the crop was reduced, owing to excessive rainfall. Malawi is the only significant African producer of burley, which is the most important of the six types of tobacco cultivated in Malawi. Output of this variety has achieved record levels in each year since 1991, the first year in which its cultivation on smallholdings was permitted (the production of burley had previously been confined to estates). Quotas on burley production at smallholdings were to be eliminated by 1997. The importance of burley has increased greatly since the early 1980s, when strong world demand encouraged a major expansion in output. Output of flue-cured tobacco, which is only grown on estates, and of the four types of tobacco traditionally cultivated by smallholders (Northern and Southern fire-cured, sun/air cured and oriental) is declining. The government is trying to improve smallholder production and output of flue-cured tobacco through a combination of improved prices and instructional and training programmes aimed at improving yields.

Malawi is, after Kenya, Africa's second largest producer and exporter of tea. In 1995 Malawi had about 20,000 ha planted with tea: 88% of the land under cultivation was controlled by large estates, and the remainder by 5,200 smallholders. Output of tea reached 39,500 metric tons in 1993, declining, however, to 35,100 tons in 1994 and further, to an estimated 34,500 tons, in 1995. In 1994 exports of tea by Malawi accounted for almost 14% of all African tea exports. Tea provided 7.5% of total export earnings in 1994. The United Kingdom is by far the most important foreign purchaser. During January 1994–July 1995 world tea prices fell by some 28%. In 1996 renewed demand, coupled with a reduced global supply of quality produce, contributed to a strengthening in the price of Malawian tea; in that year output recovered to 37,200 tons. However, the tea sector was confronted in 1997 by the imposition of an 8% levy on all tea exports (reduced to 4% in the 1997/98 budget), together with a significant fall in world demand for the Indochinese variety of tea predominant in Malawi. Efforts by the government to persuade the country's tea growers to transfer to a more popular hybrid met with strong resistance, despite the establishment by the EU of a US $8m. fund, intended to provide an income for growers until newly-planted bushes became productive.

Much of Malawi's sugar is consumed locally. The principal foreign customer is the EU, followed by the USA. Production is centered on the Dwangwa sugar project, covering some 5,250 ha of the Central Region, which started operations in 1979. Export earnings from sugar were adversely affected in the mid-1980s by low world prices and transport problems. They improved, however, from 1987, owing to a recovery in world prices. In 1994 export earnings from sugar provided 7.4% of total export receipts. A sugar expansion project to meet increasing local demand was announced by the British based trading group Lonrho in 1992. Production of raw sugar increased by 72%, to 197,000 metric tons, in 1994, following the completion of the expansion programme at Nchalo. In 1997 plans were announced for the imminent privatization of the Sugar Corpn of Malawi and Dwangwa Sugar.

INDUSTRY

Development of Malawi's extremely limited industrial base was accorded high priority at independence, and subsequent rapid expansion increased manufacturing output by an average of 11% per year in the 1970s. During the early 1980s growth slowed to less than 3% per year, owing to a combination of factors, including the impact of drought on domestic demand and the scarcity of foreign exchange for imports (the sector is heavily dependent on imports). Manufacturing entered a recession after 1985, but by 1988 the sector recovered slightly, benefiting from the effects of the trade and industrial policy adjustment programme, and from the associated influx of donor funds. Output subsequently contracted, in part due to the aid ban. Industry (including manufacturing, construction and power) contributed 20.7% of GDP (at constant 1978 factor cost) in 1994 and an estimated 19.8% of GDP in 1995, with manufacturing providing 13.6% and about 13.1% respectively. Industrial GDP declined, in real terms, at an average rate of 0.4% per annum in 1990–94, but increased by an estimated 5.5% in 1995.

Government encouragement of private enterprise led initially to the attraction of foreign private direct investment and management expertise, especially in collaboration with the government-owned Malawi Development Corpn (MDC), established in 1964. In common with other major parastatal bodies, however, the MDC became subject to major reorganization and management restructuring in 1985. Small-scale industrial development has been promoted by the Small Enterprise Development Organisation of Malawi (SEDOM). The single largest industrial sector concern during the period when Dr Hastings Banda held power was Press Corpn. Nominally a private company but indirectly controlled by Banda, Press has interests throughout the modern sector of the economy. Often in joint-venture arrangements with foreign companies, these interests included tobacco and sugar estates, cattle ranching, ethanol production, civil engineering, transport, retail and wholesale trade, property development and banking and insurance. The listing of Press Corpn on the stock exchange, which was established in December 1994, continued to be delayed, however, owing mainly to a dispute over ownership between the government and the Malawi Congress Party (MCP), led by Banda. In 1997 it was announced that the Malawi Iron and Steel Corpn and Plastic Products Corpn were to be privatized.

Malawi has provided an attractive range of incentives for potential investors, including low-cost estate sites, tariff protection, exclusive licensing where justified, generous investment allowances and unrestricted repatriation of capital, profits and dividends. However, the rate of new investment has been inhibited partly by the small size of the local market and the limited possibilities for exports. Although new investment has not created as many new jobs as the government had hoped, owing to the capital-intensive nature of some operations, employment in industry more than doubled between 1980 and 1992.

Mining

Deposits of a number of minerals, including bauxite, asbestos, coal, phosphates, gemstones, uranium, vermiculite, graphite and several types of construction stone, have been discovered, but only a few industrial minerals have so far been exploited to any extent, notably limestone by the Portland Cement Co (Malawi). During the 1980s the company's clinker and cement works were rehabilitated and its quarry at Changalame was expanded, with the aim of producing a small surplus of limestone for export. (Cement output stood at approximately 120,000 metric tons in 1996.) There has been small-scale exploitation of Malawi's coal reserves; production at the Kaziwiziwi mine near Livingstonia, in northern Malawi, was terminated in 1984, after less than a year's operation, because it was deemed to be uneconomic. The state-owned Mining Investment and Development Corpn (MIDCOR), however, reopened the mine. Following the depletion of the mine at Kaziwiziwi, coal production transferred in 1992 to the Mchenga mine, which was estimated to contain some 2.8m. metric tons of bituminous coal. Production averaged 7,500 tons a month during January–June 1996, for use in domestic and regional industries. There are further coal deposits, of poorer quality, at Ngana and Mwabvi. In 1989 large high-quality phosphate reserves were discovered, which could be utilized for local fertilizer production.

Reserves of vermiculite exist at Fereme, and in 1997 a feasibility study was being conducted on export of this mineral to Zimbabwe. Semi-precious stones are mined, mostly on an artisanal basis; in 1997 Minex, a joint venture between MIDCOR and a South African company, was involved in the rehabilitation of facilities at Chimwadzulu for the extraction of corundum (including some sapphires and rubies). In 1997 the Geological Survey Department reported that deposits of gold had been found at Mwanza and in the outskirts of Lilongwe and that there were indications of diamond reserves at Livingstonia.

Cost factors have prevented the exploitation of Malawi's most important mineral discovery so far, the bauxite reserves in the Mulanje area, which have been assessed at almost 29m. metric tons of ore, containing an average of 43.9% alumina. Their development would involve heavy transport costs, owing to the remote location of the area, supplemented by transport costs to the coast, making their exploitation uneconomic in present world market conditions. The feasibility of the project could improve if development of Malawi's hydroelectric capacity results in sufficient low cost power to meet the substantial requirements of alumina smelting. Indeed, a major restraint on the sector's expansion is that current levels of electricity generation are insufficient for most heavy industrial mining.

Power

The Electricity Supply Commission of Malawi (ESCOM) operates both thermal and hydroelectric power stations in its grid, although the latter supply 85% of the central grid's generating capacity of 190 MW. Three plants on the Middle Shire river account for 76% of hydro capacity: Tedzani (40 MW); Nkula A (24 MW), which was completed in 1985; and Nkula B (80 MW). Outside the grid, ESCOM operates four small diesel sets in remote areas in the north, and there are 30 MW of privately-owned capacity, of which about 50% is operated by the sugar estates. Although the central grid is currently operating at below capacity (with sales of 620m. kWh in 1994), ESCOM is planning major investments in new capacity, in an attempt to satisfy projected demand in the 1990s, as well as in reinforcing the existing grid. Lack of foreign exchange for spare parts resulted in interruptions to the electric power supply in the mid-1990s. Even with the expansion of electricity output, the majority of Malawi's energy requirements are supplied by fuel wood, which has accounted for some 90% of energy needs (compared with 3% for hydro-power, 4% for petroleum products and 1% for coal) in recent years. The Muluzi government has, however, announced that it intends to reduce dependence on this source. Petroleum and diesel fuel constitute Malawi's principal imports; in 1992 fuels comprised 11% of the value of total imports; in 1996 fuel imports totalled approximately 220m. litres. In 1982 a factory to produce ethyl alcohol (ethanol) from molasses went into production, and in its first five years of operation it produced 6.8m. litres of ethanol annually, for 20% blending with petrol, equivalent to 10% of Malawi's petrol needs. Full design capacity of 8.5m. litres per year was reached in 1988. The government intended to increase ethanol production to 20m. litres per year in the 1990s, subject to its commercial value. Just over 16,000 tons of coal were imported in 1988 (compared with 70,000 tons in 1982). Serious shortfalls in the supply of petroleum products occurred in the mid-1990s, prompting research (funded by the World Bank) which was to produce contingency plans, and to evaluate a minimum level below which rationing of petroleum products should automatically take effect.

Transport and Tourism

Malawi Railways has an internal rail network covering 789 km, extending to Mehinji on the Zambian border. It also operates 465 km of the 830-km single-line rail link from Salima, on the central lake-shore, to the Mozambique port of Beira, Malawi's traditional trade outlet on the Indian Ocean. Another rail link provides access to the port of Nacala, north of Beira. However, increased guerrilla activity in Mozambique after 1981 caused a major disruption in these routes, with freight traffic declining from 745,000 metric tons in 1980 to 274,000 tons in 1983, and to zero from 1984, when the routes were closed. The enforced re-routing of trade through South Africa, a journey of 3,000 km, had a severe impact on the economy. Additional transport costs surged from US $50m. annually between 1984–86, to $75m. in 1987 and to $100m. in 1988. This was partly due to increased import volumes.

The first moves to provide Malawi with a cheaper alternative outlet began in 1983, when the United Kingdom agreed to upgrade the 65-km unpaved road linking Karonga, near the northern end of Lake Malawi, to Mbeya, in southern Tanzania, so providing Malawi with access to the Tanzania–Zambia railway as far as the port of Dar es Salaam. Work on the Karonga–Mbeya road was completed in 1984. In 1985 a new priority 'northern corridor' scheme was proposed, involving a 750-km section of the Tazara railway line between Dar es Salaam and Mbeya, a 250-km road link from Mbeya to Chilumba port, at the northern end of Lake Malawi, and a 400-km journey along the lake to Chipoka port, to link with the southern transport network. The project (costing an estimated US $110m. and co-ordinated by the IDA) was completed in 1992, and was expected to carry up to 30% of Malawi's external trade.

Malawi was also to benefit from the US $600m. Beira 'corridor' scheme, supported by a group of international donors under the guidance of the Southern African Development Community.

Regional political developments have led to recent improvements at the port of Beira and an upgraded road network in the area. Work on the Beira railway line began in late 1985. At the same time rehabilitation of Malawi's rail link to Nacala was being undertaken. An escalation in Mozambican rebel attacks on the line led to the suspension of rehabilitation work for one year from early 1988. In August 1989 a cease-fire was agreed along the line, and in October the Nacala link was reopened. Traffic resumed slowly, owing to the disrepair of the line and to the uncertain security situation.

Malawi's road network, totalling 13,647 km (17% tarred) in 1990, is being steadily upgraded, in particular the lakeshore Kamuzu Highway, which provides the main land link between the remote Northern Region and the Central and Southern Regions. Feeder and crop-extraction roads are also being extended. Road transport grew steadily during the period when Malawi's rail outlets were closed.

Malawi has one main international airport at Lilongwe, three domestic airports and the former main international airport at Blantyre, which still serves some regional airlines. Lilongwe is regularly served by a number of international and regional airlines, as well as by the national carrier Air Malawi.

The government is currently aiming to expand the tourism sector, which has grown substantially since Malawi began seriously to develop its considerable tourist potential in the mid-1970s. The sector was, however, adversely affected in the 1980s by recession in South Africa, which accounts for the majority of visitors to Malawi, but recovered in the early 1990s. Tourism earnings in 1994 were US $15m. The number of visitors reached 154,000 in 1994. In 1997 tourist arrivals reportedly fell, owing to concerns over an alleged outbreak of bilharzia.

EXTERNAL TRADE AND PAYMENTS

Malawi's prospects for sustained development depend upon the achievement of improved export performance, especially in the industrial sector. The primary producer's dependence on international commodity trade is heightened in Malawi's case by a lack, so far, of exportable minerals. Agricultural products still account for about 90% of domestic export receipts, with tobacco providing more than two-thirds of total foreign exchange earnings. Exports of manufactured goods, mainly clothing, footwear and cattle cake, increased during the 1980s, but still provided only 4% of all export earnings in 1994. However, according to the IMF, non-traditional exports increased by more than 150% per annum during 1995–96 in terms of volume, albeit from a restricted base. The principal imports in the 1990s were diesel fuel and petroleum (by far the largest item, accounting for 11% of all imports in 1992), machinery and transport equipment, piece goods and medical and pharmaceutical goods.

Malawi's major trading partners have not changed over the years, although the volume of trade with the United Kingdom has declined. In 1994 the main export destinations were the USA, South Africa, Germany and Japan, while the principal suppliers of Malawi's imports were South Africa, Zimbabwe, the United Kingdom and Japan.

Malawi has sustained a deficit on the current account of its balance of payments in every year since 1966, with a particularly sharp deterioration in 1979 and 1980, when it increased from an average of 8% of GDP to 23.5%. However, following the introduction of the economic stabilization programme in 1981 and an improvement in the trade balance, there was some recovery over the next two years. None the less, the current account deficit increased sharply from US $48.9m. in 1984 to $124.7m. in 1985. There was subsequently an improvement in the level of the deficit, to $89.9m. in 1986 and to $53.1m. by 1988.

As a result of increases in debt-service costs and a reduction in concessionary assistance from 1980, Malawi operated a substantial overall balance-of-payments deficit in most years until 1987, when there was a surplus of K85m., reflecting the marked improvement in the merchandise trade surplus and the impact of the government's decision to suspend debt-service payments pending the conclusion of negotiations on new reschedulings with both the Paris and London 'Clubs' of government and private creditors. The signing of the rescheduling agreements in April and May 1988 (see below) contributed significantly to the K247m. overall balance-of-payments surplus recorded in that year. The surplus also reflected the impact of increased concessionary assistance: the capital account surplus increased by 67%, to K363.7m. in 1988. In 1994 merchandise imports of US $491m. exceeded merchandise exports of $325m., leaving a visible trade deficit of $166m. Imports of goods and services in 1994 reached $639m., dwarfing exports of goods and services at $390m. and yielding a deficit on the goods and services account of $249m. The current-account balance in that year showed a shortfall of $230m. However, the government reported exports of K6,600m. in 1995, double the figure of K3,300m. reported in 1994. In mid-1996 the Eastern and Southern Africa Trade and Development Bank announced the funding of a $50m. stuctured preshipment financing facility to support the growth of exports from Malawi.

PUBLIC FINANCE AND BANKING

In the three years after 1978/79 there was a rapid deterioration in the budgetary position, reflecting the worsening balance-of-payments situation and the decline in domestic growth. In 1980/81 the overall budget deficit reached 16.5% of GDP. With the introduction of the first economic adjustment programme in 1981, the overall deficit began to improve, and by 1985/86 it had fallen to 6.6% of GDP. However, this was largely attributable to a sharp fall in development expenditure, which declined by an annual average of 2% in real terms. Owing to a rise in the costs of debt-servicing and transport, and to an increase in losses by parastatal enterprises, recurrent expenditure expanded, in real terms, by 10% per year, resulting in a deficit that had to be financed by domestic and foreign borrowing. In 1985/86 total borrowing reached K242m.

The overall deficit deteriorated again in 1986/87, when, because revenues were lower than anticipated (owing to economic recession), it reached 11% of GDP. To arrest this trend, the 1987/88 budget proposals were particularly stringent, and it was hoped to reduce the overall deficit to K172.6m., or 6.5% of GDP. However, although an actual deficit of K171.5m. was recorded in that year, recession in the domestic economy (caused by drought and the impact on manufacturing of reduced imports) resulted in the deficit being equivalent to 8.2% of GDP. The budget for 1988/89 was also stringent, with the overall deficit falling to 3.1% of GDP. In 1989/90 the overall deficit rose again, to an estimated 4.9% of GDP. In that financial year the government undertook to keep development expenditure in line with availability of foreign funding, in order to prevent a major increase in future debt-service repayments. In 1990/91 the budget deficit represented 5.6% of GDP and rose to 9.1% in 1992/93. The 1994/95 budget, presented in March 1994, was widely seen as an attempt to influence the election by its emphasis on social expenditure and the reduction in the number of income-tax payers. The government's pre-election spending contributed to a deficit of about K500m. in May 1994, 2.5 times the figure agreed with the IMF. A supplementary budget in October helped to stabilize the downward-floating kwacha, but did not prevent inflation reaching 37% by the end of the year. The regular budget of March 1995 attempted to reduce the deficit by controlling expenditure, enhancing revenue collection and stimulating agricultural exports (which were favoured by the low kwacha). Even so, the budgetary deficit (before grants) was equivalent to 15.1% of GDP in 1994/95, but decreased to 5.7% of GDP in 1995/96.

The network of banking services includes a central bank, two commercial banks, the Post Office Savings Bank and a development bank. The First Merchant Bank of Kenya commenced banking operations in Malawi in July 1995. Foreign exchange bureaux were also licensed. The Reserve Bank of Malawi began issuing its own notes in 1965, the basic currency unit then being the Malawi pound, which stood at par with sterling. In February 1971 a decimal currency was introduced, with the kwacha (divided into 100 tambala) as the unit of exchange. The exchange rate of the kwacha was originally linked to that of sterling, but an active exchange rate policy was introduced in 1974. From 1984 the kwacha exchange rate was related to a 'basket' of the currencies of Malawi's seven principal trading partners. As part of the Reserve Bank's management of the exchange rate, the kwacha was subject to regular trade-related devaluations between 1982 and 1994. In February 1994 the kwacha was 'floated', with the result that it depreciated by 25% in three months, relative to the US dollar. This depreciation contributed to an inflation level of more than 100% in 1994; by March 1997 the annual rate of inflation had been reduced, according to official figures, to 6.7%. A formal inter-bank exchange market was opened in September 1996. A stock exchange was established in late 1994; however, at the end of 1996 only one company was listed.

FOREIGN AID, GOVERNMENT DEBT AND DEVELOPMENT PLANNING

Malawi began to undertake significant commercial borrowing in the mid-1970s, initially to finance development programmes. International organizations have replaced bilateral donors as the main source of foreign funding, granting 78.8% of foreign aid given in 1994, with the IDA as the leading multilateral creditor. As a proportion of outstanding debt, commercial borrowing increased from less than 2% in 1976 to more than 24% in 1980. After 1979, non-concessionary borrowing rose sharply, as the government resorted to the banks to help to finance the budget deficit. This led to a substantial increase in total public debt-service payments. The 1982 and 1983 debt reschedulings, arranged with the 'Paris Club', resulted in a substantial fall in payments. By 1984 the effects of this relief were coming to an end, and in 1984/85 service payments increased sharply. In 1986/87 they were equivalent to 41% of total export earnings.

As a result of the high level of the debt-service ratio in 1987, the government came under pressure from the IMF to undertake a new rescheduling. With the scarcity of foreign exchange acting as an increasing constraint on recovery, the government finally acquiesced in mid-1987, and rescheduling agreements were eventually finalized in April 1988, when the 'Paris Club' agreed to reschedule debt originally due for repayment in 1988, over 20 years, including 10 years' grace. No details of the amount rescheduled were disclosed, but the World Bank estimated that publicly guaranteed debt scheduled for repayment in 1988 was US $88m., of which $59m. was principal owed to official and private creditors. The 'London Club' agreed to an eight-year rescheduling arrangement, including four years' grace. As a result of the reschedulings, service payments were reduced to 31% of export earnings in 1988, falling to an average of 25.9% over the following five years. World Bank figures for 1994 indicate that the Muluzi government inherited a total external debt of $2,009m., equivalent to 161.5% of Malawi's GNP in that year. Debt-service payments were equivalent to 18.3% of export earnings. In 1995 debt-service payments were equivalent to 25.3% of export earnings, and international reserves had increased to $115m.; by January 1997 foreign reserves were sufficient to cover three months' worth of imports.

The United Kingdom was Malawi's major aid donor in the years after independence, and has remained an important source of funding. Similarly, South Africa has been a significant source of donor aid, particularly in providing finance for the new capital of Lilongwe, where construction of government buildings began in 1968. Other major donors are the EU (currently the main donor overall), France, Canada, the USA, Germany, Denmark, Japan, the African Development Bank, the IDA and the World Bank. In real terms, foreign grants and concessionary loans fell sharply between 1980 and 1987, with overall external support in the latter year totalling just US $170m. In June 1988 the consultative group on Malawi approved $555m. in external support for Malawi's economic recovery programme, of which $265m. was to be released in 1988 and $290m. in 1989. The funding arrangements (which also included the April debt reschedulings, the IMF's March stand-by facility and its planned extended facility) represented an increase of almost 60% in external assistance. In May 1990 the consultative group on Malawi approved $508m. for 1990/91 in support of the economic recovery programme. In May 1992, however, the consultative group suspended all non-humanitarian aid, linking future assistance to an improvement in Malawi's human rights record. Following the multi-party elections in 1994 (see Recent History), Germany, the USA and the United Kingdom all indicated that they would provide increased future levels of aid.

In 1981 a five-year programme (for 1981/82–1985/86) was introduced, with an initial target of growth in real GDP of 5% per year. This was subsequently reduced to 3.4%. Under a three-year economic development programme, covering 1985/86–1987/88, transport was the priority, taking 32% of projected investment, with the 'northern corridor' constituting the main project. Agriculture was scheduled to receive 19%, education 9.6%, and industry and commerce 6.4%. A further statement of development policies was published in March 1988, covering the period 1987–96. It projected a limited range of objectives, outlining policies aimed at maintaining a realistic pace of growth in real GDP until the early 1990s, when the major constraints on foreign exchange and economic recovery (debt payments and transport costs) were expected to ease; however, in late 1991, following three years of good performance, the Malawian economy suffered a series of exogenous shocks, including severe drought, worsening terms of trade and the suspension of non-humanitarian aid. After a brief recovery in 1993, inflation increased dramatically in 1994, owing to heavy public borrowing (to finance the forthcoming elections), to drought-induced pressures on food prices and to a major exchange rate adjustment. In November 1994 the World Bank approved a US $40m. supplementary financing arrangement under the Entrepreneurship Development and Drought Recovery Credit. Following an unsuccessful adjustment programme, supported by an eight-month IMF stand-by arrangement, the government adopted a comprehensive economic reform package in 1995. With assistance from the IMF (which in October 1995 approved an ESAF in support of the government's financial programme for 1995/96–1997/98) and other donors, it was aimed to achieve GDP growth of 9.9% in 1995 and of 7% annually during 1996–98, to contain the external current account deficit and to bring about significant reductions in both the rate of inflation and the budget deficit. A wide-ranging programme of economic liberalization was to include the privatization of many state concerns and the ending of most agricultural monopolies and subsidies, and measures were instituted to promote foreign investment in all sectors. Public expenditure was to be restricted through the implementation of a cash budget system, the restructuring of parastatals and reductions in the public payroll, while government revenue would be enhanced by fiscal reforms, including improved efficiency in the collection of import duties, the planned introduction of a value-added tax and the establishment of an independent National Revenue Authority. The privatization process started in early 1996, and in 1996/97 some 26 public enterprises were scheduled to be ready for divestiture, with total net assets amounting to 15% of government holdings (including shares in private companies). A further 20 parastatals were to reach point of sale in 1997/98. A civil service census was conducted in October 1995, and some 20,000 employees were discharged, while restraints were placed on further public recruitment. According to official figures, real GDP increased by some 9.5% in 1996 and inflation stood at 6.7% in the year to April 1997. Donors expressed satisfaction at the progress of the reforms, and the IMF began to release the $22m. second tranche of the ESAF in December 1996. However, the economic and infrastructural problems that the Muluzi government inherited in 1994, coupled with the agricultural sector's vulnerability to climatic conditions, render heavy dependence on foreign aid a continuing necessity.

Statistical Survey

Sources (unless otherwise indicated): Ministry of Information and Tourism, POB 494, Blantyre; Reserve Bank of Malawi, POB 30063, Capital City, Lilongwe 3; tel. 780600; telex 44788; fax 782752.

Area and Population

AREA, POPULATION AND DENSITY

Area (sq km)	118,484*
Population (census results)	
20 September 1977	5,547,460
1–21 September 1987	
Males	3,867,136
Females	4,121,371
Total	7,988,507
Population (official estimates at mid-year)	
1992	9,344,600
1993	9,700,500
1994	10,032,600
Density (per sq km) at mid-1994	84.7

* 45,747 sq miles. The area includes 24,208 sq km (9,347 sq miles) of inland water.

Ethnic groups (1977 census): Africans 5,532,298; Europeans 6,377; Asians 5,682; others 3,103.

REGIONS (mid-1994)

Region	Area (sq km)*	Estimated population	Density (per sq km)	Regional capital
Southern	31,753	4,980,500	156.9	Blantyre
Central	35,592	3,907,000	109.8	Lilongwe
Northern	26,931	1,145,100	42.5	Mzuzu
Total	94,276	10,032,600	106.4	

* Excluding inland waters, totalling 24,208 sq km.

PRINCIPAL TOWNS (estimated population at mid-1994)

Blantyre	446,800	Mzuzu	62,700
Lilongwe (capital)	395,500*	Zomba	62,700

* Including Limbe.

BIRTHS AND DEATHS (UN estimates, annual averages)

	1980–85	1985–90	1990–95
Birth rate (per 1,000)	53.5	52.0	50.5
Death rate (per 1,000)	21.5	20.2	20.0

Expectation of life (UN estimates, years at birth, 1990–95): 45.6 (males 45.0; females 46.2).

Source: UN, *World Population Prospects: The 1994 Revision*.

ECONOMICALLY ACTIVE POPULATION*
(persons aged 10 to 64 years, 1987 census)

	Males	Females	Total
Agriculture, hunting, forestry and fishing	1,293,606	1,674,327	2,967,933
Mining and quarrying	6,977	187	7,164
Manufacturing	79,293	18,483	97,776
Electricity, gas and water	8,306	527	8,833
Construction	45,006	1,869	46,875
Trade, restaurants and hotels	75,491	18,954	94,445
Transport, storage and communications	23,323	1,540	24,863
Financing, insurance, real estate and business services	4,418	1,172	5,590
Community, social and personal services	113,763	33,276	147,039
Activities not adequately defined	9,120	2,765	11,885
Total employed	1,659,303	1,753,100	3,412,403
Unemployed	36,549	8,801	45,350
Total labour force	1,695,852	1,761,901	3,457,753

* Excluding armed forces.

Mid-1995 (estimates in '000): Agriculture, etc. 4,682; Total 5,424 (Source: FAO, *Production Yearbook*).

Agriculture

PRINCIPAL CROPS ('000 metric tons)

	1993	1994	1995
Rice (paddy)	65	42*	52
Maize	2,034	1,040	1,661
Millet	15	10	18
Sorghum	22	17	45
Potatoes	370†	350†	376
Cassava (Manioc)	216	200†	200†
Dry beans†	80	81	82
Chick-peas†	37	38	39
Lentils†	1	1	1
Other pulses†	147	149	151
Groundnuts (in shell)	55	31	32
Sunflower seed	9	9†	10
Cottonseed	18*	20†	45†
Cotton (lint)	7*	8†	18†
Cabbages	33	36	27
Tomatoes	37	37	34
Onions (dry)	20†	20†	20
Other vegetables	170†	171†	171
Mangoes	31†	32†	33
Bananas†	90	91	91
Plantains†	195	200	200
Citrus fruits	2	2†	2†
Other fruit†	181	183	183
Sugar cane†	1,100	2,000	2,200
Coffee (green)*	4	5	5
Tea (made)	39	35	34*
Tobacco (leaves)	130	99*	132†

* Unofficial figure(s). † FAO estimate(s).

Source: FAO, *Production Yearbook*.

LIVESTOCK ('000 head, year ending September)

	1993*	1994*	1995
Cattle	970	980	980*
Pigs	240	245	247
Sheep	195	196	196*
Goats	888	890	890*

* FAO estimate(s).

Poultry (FAO estimates, million, year ending September): 9 in 1993; 9 in 1994; 9 in 1995.

Source: FAO, *Production Yearbook*.

LIVESTOCK PRODUCTS (FAO estimates, '000 metric tons)

	1993	1994	1995
Beef and veal	17	18	18
Goat meat	3	3	3
Pig meat	10	10	10
Poultry meat	9	10	10
Cows' milk	41	42	42
Hen eggs	11.4	11.5	11.5

Source: FAO, *Production Yearbook*.

Forestry

ROUNDWOOD REMOVALS ('000 cubic metres, excluding bark)

	1992	1993	1994*
Sawlogs, veneer logs and logs for sleepers	125	130	130
Pulpwood	7	7	7
Other industrial wood*	372	386	397
Fuel wood*	9,075	9,391	9,678
Total	9,579	9,914	10,212

* FAO estimates.

Source: FAO, *Yearbook of Forest Products*.

SAWNWOOD PRODUCTION
('000 cubic metres, including railway sleepers)

	1992*	1993	1994*
Coniferous (softwood)	28	30	30
Broadleaved (hardwood)†	15	15*	15
Total	43	45	45

* FAO estimate(s).
† Assumed to be unchanged since 1989.

Source: FAO, *Yearbook of Forest Products*.

Fishing

('000 metric tons, live weight)

	1993	1994	1995
Carps, barbels, etc.	6.8	7.3	0.6
Tilapias	10.3	6.7	3.9
Other freshwater fishes	51.1	44.9	41.0
Total catch	68.2	58.8	45.4

Source: FAO, *Yearbook of Fishery Statistics*.

Mining

('000 metric tons, unless otherwise indicated)

	1992	1993	1994
Limestone	183.0	177.4	173.8
Coal	41.9	54.9	n.a.
Lime	2.1	2.4	n.a.
Quarry stone ('000 cubic metres)	135.2	554.5	74.5
Gemstones (kilograms)	833.9	114.9	n.a.

Source: Department of Mines, Lilongwe.

Industry

SELECTED PRODUCTS ('000 metric tons, unless otherwise indicated)

	1992	1993	1994
Raw sugar	200	114	185
Beer ('000 hectolitres)	774	763	811
Cigarettes (million)	1,000	1,020	1,127
Blankets ('000)	1,300	894	895
Cement	108	117	122
Electric energy (million kWh)*	792	795	802

* Provisional or estimated figure(s).

Source: UN, *Industrial Commodity Statistics Yearbook*.

Finance

CURRENCY AND EXCHANGE RATES

Monetary Units

100 tambala = 1 Malawi kwacha (K).

Sterling and Dollar Equivalents (31 March 1997)

£1 sterling = 25.235 kwacha;
US $1 = 15.368 kwacha;
1,000 Malawi kwacha = £39.63 = $65.07.

Average Exchange Rate (kwacha per US $)

1994 8.7364
1995 15.2837
1996 15.3085

BUDGET (K million, year ending 31 March)

Revenue*	1992/93	1993/94	1994/95
Tax revenue	1,126.4	1,407.7	2,031.5
Taxes on income and profits	424.8	509.1	747.8
Companies	207.0	251.8	328.8
Individuals	217.8	257.3	419.0
Taxes on goods and services	422.9	619.4	816.6
Surtax	372.0	548.1	700.4
On imports	191.1	304.2	400.2
On domestic manufactures	180.9	243.9	300.2
Excise duties	38 4	59.6	104.9
Taxes on international trade	256.2	270.0	458.6
Import duties	255.5	267.9	457.0
Non-tax revenue	205.0	220.9	199.5
Departmental receipts	143.1	153.7	n.a.
Total	1,331.4	1,628.6	2,231.0

Expenditure	1992/93	1993/94	1994/95
Current expenditure†	1,713.1	1,900.9	4,522.3
General administration	439.2	475.3	896.4
Defence	99.1	90.4	159.4
Justice and public order	77.2	91.9	180.2
Social services	328.9	408.2	628.2
Education	190.3	251.0	351.8
Health	94.6	113.2	244.9
Economic services	237.1	390.5	1,225.5
Natural resources	141.1	184.7	725.9
Transportation	40.6	60.2	54.5
Unallocable	498.7	444.6	1,432.6
Interest on public debt	218.5	300.5	716.7
Pensions and gratuities	55.0	90.6	123.8
Development expenditure	469.4	464.4	1,066.3
Unidentified expenditure	196.9	62.7	193.6
Total	2,379.4	2,428.0	5,782.2

* Excluding grants received (K million): 174 in 1992/93; 284 in 1993/94; 1,470 in 1994/95.

† Including drought-related expenditure (K million): 450.0 in 1992/93; 124.7 in 1993/94; 920.5 in 1994/95.

1995/96 (estimates, K million): Total revenue 4,436, excluding grants (1,982); Total expenditure 7,738.

Source: IMF, *Malawi—Recent Economic Developments* (August 1996).

INTERNATIONAL RESERVES (US $ million at 31 December)

	1994	1995	1996
Gold*	0.54	0.55	0.54
IMF special drawing rights	6.20	0.88	1.36
Reserve position in IMF	3.25	3.31	3.20
Foreign exchange	33.35	105.82	221.17
Total	43.34	110.55	226.27

* National valuation.

Source: IMF, *International Financial Statistics*.

MONEY SUPPLY (K million at 31 December)

	1993	1994	1995
Currency outside banks	414.17	624.74	987.52
Official entities' deposits with monetary authorities	45.58	14.75	5.55
Demand deposits at commercial banks	560.15	895.94	1,218.14
Total money	1,019.90	1,535.43	2,211.21

Source: IMF, *International Financial Statistics*.

COST OF LIVING (National Consumer Price Index; base: 1990 = 100)

	1993	1994	1995
Food	175.6	242.9	468.6
Clothing	126.2	149.3	n.a.
All items (incl. others)	163.8	220.5	404.2

NATIONAL ACCOUNTS

Expenditure on the Gross Domestic Product
(K million at current prices)

	1993	1994	1995
Government final consumption expenditure	1,529.0	2,565.3	4,181.5
Private final consumption expenditure	7,708.4	7,678.8	15,734.6
Increase in stocks	200.0	240.0	550.0
Gross fixed capital formation	890.0	1,243.0	2,860.0
Total domestic expenditure	10,327.4	11,727.0	23,726.0*
Exports of goods and services	1,470.7	3,394.3	6,733.0
Less Imports of goods and services	2,855.9	3,912.0	7,987.0
GDP in purchasers' values	8,942.2	11,209.3	22,472.0

* Including adjustment.

Source: IMF, *International Financial Statistics*.

Gross Domestic Product by Economic Activity
(K million at constant 1978 prices)

	1993	1994	1995*
Agriculture, forestry and fishing	421.0	297.6	381.8
Manufacturing	126.8	130.8	139.1
Electricity and water	27.2	29.3	30.2
Construction	41.2	39.8	41.5
Trade, restaurants and hotels	118.4	112.6	114.7
Transport and communications	56.7	51.8	53.2
Finance, insurance and business services	67.3	62.3	66.5
Ownership of dwellings	44.9	45.9	47.0
Private social services	45.1	46.4	47.4
Government services	154.2	147.3	142.0
Sub-total	1,102.8	963.6	1,063.2
Less Imputed bank service charges	25.9	11.5	25.4
GDP at factor cost	1,076.9	952.1	1,037.7
Indirect taxes, *less* subsidies	76.4	83.1	96.2
GDP in purchasers' values	1,153.3	1,035.2	1,133.9

* Figures are provisional.

Source: mainly IMF, *Malawi—Recent Economic Developments* (August 1996).

BALANCE OF PAYMENTS (US $ million)

	1992	1993	1994
Exports of goods f.o.b.	399.9	317.5	362.6
Imports of goods f.o.b.	–415.0	–340.2	–639.0
Trade balance	–15.0	–22.8	–276.4
Exports of services	28.5	30.0	22.2
Imports of services	–338.8	–260.1	–233.7
Balance on goods and services	–325.4	–252.9	–488.0
Other income received	6.3	2.2	1.9
Other income paid	–83.4	–70.9	–87.8
Balance on goods, services and income	–402.5	–321.6	–573.9
Current transfers received	155.2	167.9	139.7
Current transfers paid	–37.7	–11.9	–15.4
Current balance	–284.9	–165.6	–449.6
Investment assets	11.9	–11.8	—
Investment liabilities	81.7	200.6	122.0
Net errors and omissions	144.8	0.7	292.6
Overall balance	–46.5	24.0	–35.1

Source: IMF, *International Financial Statistics*.

External Trade

PRINCIPAL COMMODITIES

Imports c.i.f. (US $ '000)	1988	1989	1991*
Food and live animals	31,016	44,934	42,534
Cereals and cereal preparations	23,436	33,903	26,693
Maize (unmilled)	19,330	20,736	5,019
Crude materials (inedible) except fuels	9,115	10,488	9,708
Mineral fuels, lubricants, etc.	49,941	55,154	70,355
Petroleum, petroleum products, etc.	48,826	53,991	69,006
Refined petroleum products	47,118	52,600	65,924
Motor spirit (gasoline) and other light oils	19,502	23,137	n.a.
Motor spirit (incl. aviation spirit)	15,964	19,061	n.a.
Gas oils (distillate fuel oils)	22,610	24,596	n.a.
Chemicals and related products	86,536	103,466	129,638
Medicinal and pharmaceutical products	9,174	9,745	12,264
Manufactured fertilizers	38,902	51,848	65,673
Nitrogenous fertilizers (mineral or chemical)	19,993	37,799	31,349
Calcium nitrate (maximum 16% nitrogen)	8,484	14,355	n.a.
Urea	9,591	20,381	13,116
Phosphatic fertilizers (mineral or chemical)	14,839	10,210	9,266
Superphosphates	13,362	8,928	1,229
Artificial resins, plastic materials, etc.	12,397	14,380	15,594
Products of polymerization, etc.	4,738	8,060	13,873
Basic manufactures	84,546	102,583	125,934
Rubber manufactures	9,948	11,140	12,635
Paper, paperboard, etc.	14,899	19,636	23,907
Paper and paperboard (not cut to size or shape)	10,404	14,030	19,641
Textile yarn, fabrics, etc.	15,791	21,497	26,267
Iron and steel	18,200	16,522	27,436
Universals, plates and sheets	9,633	7,433	13,040
Machinery and transport equipment	121,448	155,968	214,476
Power-generating machinery and equipment	6,477	9,100	15,602
Machinery specialized for particular industries	20,344	34,129	30,269
Tractors not for road use	4,159	12,652	1,647
General industrial machinery, equipment and parts	14,949	19,138	32,305
Telecommunications and sound equipment	23,641	17,736	11,586
Electrical line telephonic and telegraphic apparatus	5,099	14,317	4,292
Other electrical machinery, apparatus, etc.	18,228	20,204	30,700
Road vehicles and parts†	32,333	49,143	77,262
Passenger motor cars (excl. buses)	7,924	18,543	15,684
Motor vehicles for goods transport, etc.	7,693	5,018	30,501
Goods vehicles (lorries and trucks)	1,439	1,068	29,411
Parts and accessories for cars, buses, lorries, etc.†	10,918	17,432	12,150
Miscellaneous manufactured articles	17,924	22,563	39,323
Total (incl. others)	408,805	508,325	647,397

* Detailed figures are not available for 1990. In that year the value of total imports (in US $ '000) was 578,894.
† Excluding tyres, engines and electrical parts.

Source: UN, *International Trade Statistics Yearbook*.

Total imports (K million): 2,653.8 in 1992; 2,404.9 in 1993; 4,264.0 in 1994 (Source: IMF, *International Financial Statistics*).

Exports f.o.b. (US $ million)*	1993	1994	1995†
Tobacco	213.0	256.5	260.2
Sugar	15.6	26.2	30.9
Tea	35.6	29.9	27.5
Coffee	7.9	14.6	16.8
Pulses	1.4	1.5	8.1
Total (incl. others)	308.0	364.6	409.2

* Figures exclude re-exports. Total exports (in US $ million) were: 317.2 in 1993; 372.4 in 1994; 421.2† in 1995.
† Estimate(s).

Source: IMF, *Malawi—Recent Economic Developments* (August 1996).

PRINCIPAL TRADING PARTNERS (US $ million)*

Imports c.i.f.	1993	1994	1995†
Botswana	6.5	7.6	8.7
France	8.0	6.5	12.8
Germany	23.9	17.6	24.1
Japan	25.7	31.8	14.5
Netherlands	15.5	6.2	5.0
South Africa	199.6	192.7	237.0
United Kingdom	29.9	32.9	23.0
USA	17.4	20.8	20.4
Zambia	5.1	3.5	4.3
Zimbabwe	47.1	56.0	68.9
Total (incl. others)	452.1	477.0	533.8

Exports f.o.b.	1993	1994	1995†
Botswana	5.3	6.3	7.8
France	7.7	17.8	10.7
Germany	36.1	50.1	57.9
Japan	47.7	45.4	44.0
Mozambique	20.7	24.6	30.3
Netherlands	19.9	22.2	24.0
South Africa	48.8	52.2	64.2
United Kingdom	29.6	35.8	25.4
USA	60.5	57.0	43.3
Zambia	1.9	3.8	4.6
Zimbabwe	1.9	2.3	2.8
Total (incl. others)	353.6	388.6	397.5

* Data are compiled on the basis of reporting by Malawi's trading partners.
† Estimates.

Source: IMF, *Direction of Trade Statistics*.

Transport

RAILWAYS (traffic)

	1992	1993	1994
Passengers carried ('000)	892	692	446
Passenger-kilometres ('000)	68,186	45,547	18,995
Freight ('000 ton-km, net)	54,477	43,303	56,778

Source: Malawi Railways, Limbe.

ROAD TRAFFIC (estimates, motor vehicles in use at 31 December)

	1993	1994	1995
Passenger cars	22,400	23,400	25,400
Lorries and vans	26,500	25,900	28,900

Source: International Road Federation, *World Road Statistics*.

SHIPPING

Inland waterways (lake transport)

	1992	1993	1994
Freight ('000 ton-km, net)	5,933	3,682	707
Passenger-kilometres ('000)	20,378	10,332	11,995

Source: Malawi Railways, Limbe.

CIVIL AVIATION (traffic on scheduled services)

	1992	1993	1994
Kilometres flown (million)	2	2	3
Passengers carried ('000)	121	132	142
Passenger-kilometres (million)	79	266	289
Total ton-kilometres (million)	9	15	28

Source: UN, *Statistical Yearbook*.

Tourism

	1992	1993	1994
Number of departing visitors ('000)	150	153	154
Tourist receipts (US $ million)	83	7	5

Source: UN, *Statistical Yearbook*.

Communications Media

	1992	1993	1994
Radio receivers ('000 in use)	2,285	2,375	2,450
Telephones ('000 main lines in use)	31	33	33
Book production: titles*	189	206	243
Daily newspapers:			
Titles	1	n.a.	1
Average circulation ('000 copies)	25	n.a.	25

* Including pamphlets (84 in 1993; 106 in 1994).

Non-daily newspapers (1992): 4 titles (average circulation 133,000 copies).

Other periodicals (1986): 14 titles (average circulation 124,000 copies).

Sources: UNESCO, *Statistical Yearbook*; UN, *Statistical Yearbook*.

Education

(1994/95)

	Institutions	Teachers	Students: Males	Students: Females	Students: Total
Primary	3,424	45,775	1,515,508	1,345,311	2,860,819
Secondary:					
Government	76	2,713	20,854	12,033	32,887
Private	31	167	8,577	6,896	15,473
Distance education	192	1,216	38,357	19,124	57,481
Higher:					
Universities	6	400	2,713	888	3,601
Primary teacher training	6	217	1,859	1,126	3,085
Technical and vocational	n.a.	81	n.a.	n.a.	1,080

Source: Ministry of Education, *Basic Education Statistics* (December 1995).

Directory

The Constitution

A new Constitution, replacing the (amended) 1966 Constitution, was approved by the National Assembly on 16 May 1994, and took provisional effect for one year from 18 May. During this time the Constitution was to be subject to review, and the final document was promulgated on 18 May 1995.

THE PRESIDENT

The President is both Head of State and Head of Government. The President is elected for five years, by universal adult suffrage, in the context of a multi-party political system. There are two Vice-Presidents.

PARLIAMENT

Parliament comprises the President, the two Vice-Presidents and the National Assembly. The National Assembly has 177 elective seats, elections being by universal adult suffrage, in the context of a multi-party system. Cabinet ministers who are not elected members of parliament also sit in the National Assembly. The Speaker is appointed from among the ordinary members of the Assembly. The parliamentary term is normally five years. The President has power to prorogue or dissolve Parliament.

In 1995 the National Assembly approved proposals for the establishment of a second chamber, the Senate, to be implemented in 1999.

EXECUTIVE POWER

Executive power is exercised by the President, who appoints members of the Cabinet.

The Government

HEAD OF STATE

President: Dr (Elson) Bakili Muluzi (took office 21 May 1994).

Vice-President: Justin Malewezi.

CABINET

(August 1997)

President and Head of Government: Dr Bakili Muluzi.

Vice-President and Minister of Finance: Justin Malewezi.

Minister of Agriculture and Irrigation: Aleke Banda.

Minister of Health and Population: Harry Thomson.

Minister of Water Development: Edward Bwanali.

Minister of Education: Brown Mpinganjira.

Minister of Lands, Housing, Physical Planning and Surveys: Peter Fatchi.

Attorney-General and Minister of Justice: Cassim Chilumpha.

Minister of Tourism, Parks and Wildlife: Patrick Mbewe.

Minister of Foreign Affairs: Dr Mapopa Chipeta.

Minister of Information: Sam Mpasu.

Minister of State: Edda Chitalo.

Minister of Commerce and Industry: Matembo Nzunda.

Minister of Transport: Kamangadazi K. Chambalo.

Minister of Energy and Mining: Rev. Dumbo Lemani.

Minister of National Heritage: Richard Sembereka.

Minister of Labour and Vocational Training: Kaliyoma Phumisa.

Minister of Local Government and Sports: Chakakala Chaziya.

Minister of Women, Youth and Community Services: Lilian Patel.

Minister of Home Affairs: MELVIN MOYO.

Minister of Works and Supplies: ABDUL PILANI.

Minister of Defence: JOSEPH KUBWALO.

Minister of Forestry, Fisheries and Environmental Affairs: F. V. MAYINGA MKANDAWIRE.

Ministers of State, President's Office: ROBSON J. MAKUWIRA, BUNDAUNDA PHIRI.

MINISTRIES

Office of the President: Private Bag 301, Capital City, Lilongwe 3; tel. 782655; telex 44389; fax 782095.

Ministry of Agriculture and Irrigation: POB 30134, Capital City, Lilongwe 3; tel. 784299; telex 44648; fax 784656.

Ministry of Commerce and Industry: POB 30366, Capital City, Lilongwe 3; tel. 732711; telex 44873; fax 780680.

Ministry of Defence: Private Bag 43, Lilongwe 3; fax 784176.

Ministry of Education: Private Bag 328, Capital City, Lilongwe 3; tel. 784800; telex 44636; fax 782873.

Ministry of Energy and Mining: Private Bag 309, Capital City, Lilongwe 3.

Ministry of Finance: POB 30049, Capital City, Lilongwe 3; tel. 782199; telex 44407; fax 781679.

Ministry of Foreign Affairs: POB 30315, Capital City, Lilongwe 3; tel. 782211; telex 44113; fax 782434.

Ministry of Forestry, Fisheries and Environmental Affairs: Lilongwe 3; fax 635095.

Ministry of Health and Population: POB 30377, Capital City, Lilongwe 3; tel. 783044; telex 44558; fax 783109.

Ministry of Home Affairs: Private Bag 305, Lilongwe 3; tel. 744704; fax 784067.

Ministry of Information: Private Bag 310, Lilongwe 3; tel. 783233; fax 784568.

Ministry of Justice and Constitutional Affairs: Private Bag 333, Capital City, Lilongwe 3; tel. 782411; fax 782176.

Ministry of Labour and Vocational Training: Private Bag 344, Capital City, Lilongwe 3; tel. 783277.

Ministry of Lands, Housing, Physical Planning and Surveys: POB 30548, Lilongwe 3; tel. 780755; fax 732639.

Ministry of Local Government and Sports: POB 30312, Capital City, Lilongwe 3; tel. 780555; fax 780242.

Ministry of National Heritage: Lilongwe 3.

Ministry of Tourism, Parks and Wildlife: Private Bag 326, Lilongwe 3; tel. 782702; fax 781073.

Ministry of Transport: Private Bag 322, Capital City, Lilongwe 3; tel. 730122.

Ministry of Water Development: Private Bag 350, Capital City, Lilongwe 3; tel. 782600; telex 44465; fax 780260.

Ministry of Women, Youth and Community Services: Private Bag 330, Capital City, Lilongwe 3; tel. 780411; telex 44361; fax 732796.

Ministry of Works and Supplies: Private Bag 316, Capital City, Lilongwe 3: tel. 784200; telex 44285; fax 783328.

President and Legislature

PRESIDENT

Presidential Election, 17 May 1994

Candidate	Votes	% of votes
BAKILI MULUZI (UDF)	1,404,754	47.30
Dr HASTINGS KAMUZU BANDA (MCP)	996,363	33.55
CHAKUFWA CHIHANA (AFORD)	552,862	18.62
KAMPELO KALUA (MDP)	15,624	0.53
Total	2,969,603	100.00

NATIONAL ASSEMBLY

Speaker: RODWELL T. C. MNYENYEMBE.

General Election, 17 May 1994

Party	Seats
UDF	84
MCP	55
AFORD	36
Total*	175

* Elections were repeated in two constituencies where irregularities had been found: as a result, the UDF and MCP each won an additional seat, bringing the total number of elective seats in the Assembly to 177.

Political Organizations

Alliance for Democracy (AFORD): Private Bag 28, Lilongwe; f. 1992; in March 1993 absorbed membership of fmr Malawi Freedom Movement; Pres. CHAKUFWA CHIHANA.

Congress for the Second Republic (CSR): Leader KANYAMA CHIUME.

Malawi Congress Party (MCP): Private Bag 388, Lilongwe 3; tel. 730388; f. 1959; sole legal party 1966–93; Pres. (vacant); Vice-Pres. GWANDAGULUWE CHAKUAMBA-PHIRI; Sec.-Gen. LOVEMORE MUNLO.

Malawi Democratic Party (MDP): Pres. KAMPELO KALUA.

Malawi Democratic Union (MDU): Pres. JAMES TABUNA DISENTI-KUBA.

Malawi National Democratic Party (MNDP): Leader TIMOTHY MANGWAZU.

Movement for the Restoration of Democracy in Malawi: f. 1996; terrorist organization based in Mozambique consisting of fmr Malawi Young Pioneers.

People's Democratic Party (PDP).

United Democratic Front (UDF): POB 5446, Limbe; f. 1992; Pres. BAKILI MULUZI; Vice-Pres. JUSTIN MALEWEZI; Sec.-Gen. SAM MPASU.

United Front for Multi-party Democracy (UFMD): f. 1992 by three exiled political groups: the Socialist League of Malawi, the Malawi Freedom Party and the Malawi Democratic Union; Pres. EDMOND JIKA.

Diplomatic Representation

EMBASSIES AND HIGH COMMISSIONS IN MALAWI

China (Taiwan): Area 40, Plot No. 9, POB 30221, Capital City, Lilongwe 3; tel. 783611; telex 44317; Ambassador: ROBERT C. J. SHIH.

Denmark: Plot No. 43/2/180, Private Bag 396, Lilongwe 3; tel. 730463; telex 44218; fax 784961; Ambassador: B. JENSEN.

Egypt: POB 30451, Lilongwe 3; tel. 730300; telex 44538; Ambassador: F. M. Y. ELKHADI.

Germany: POB 30046, Lilongwe 3; tel. 782555; telex 44124; fax 780250; Ambassador: Dr JÜRGEN HELLNER.

Korea, Republic: POB 30583, Lilongwe 3; telex 44834; Ambassador: SON MYONG-SON.

Mozambique: POB 30579, Lilongwe 3; tel. 784100; telex 44793; fax 781342; High Commissioner: DANIEL MBANZE.

South Africa: British High Commission Bldg, Capital Hill, POB 30043, Lilongwe 3; tel. 783722; telex 44255; fax 782571; High Commissioner: LLEWELLYN CREWE-BROWN.

United Kingdom: British High Commission Bldg, Capital Hill, POB 30042, Lilongwe 3; tel. 782400; telex 44727; fax 782657; High Commissioner: JOHN F. R. MARTIN.

USA: Area 40, Plot 18, POB 30016, Lilongwe 3; tel. 783166; telex 44627; fax 740471; Ambassador: AMELIA SKIPPY (designate).

Zambia: POB 30138, Lilongwe 3; tel. 782590; telex 44181; fax 784349; High Commissioner: Col (retd) LAWRENCE M. H. HAAMAUNDU.

Zimbabwe: POB 30187, Lilongwe 3; tel. 733988; High Commissioner: Dr TENDAI MUTUNHU.

Judicial System

The courts administering justice are the Supreme Court of Appeal, High Court and Magistrates' Courts.

The High Court, which has unlimited jurisdiction in civil and criminal matters, consists of the Chief Justice and five puisne judges. Traditional Courts were abolished under the 1994 Constitution. Appeals from the High Court are heard by the Supreme Court of Appeal in Blantyre.

High Court of Malawi: POB 30244, Chichiri, Blantyre 3; tel. 670255; fax 670213; Registrar E. B. TWEA.

Chief Justice: RICHARD A. BANDA.

Justices of Appeal: L. A. UNYOLO, H. M. MTEGHA, J. B. KALAILE, L. A. CHATSIKA, J. B. VILLIERA.

High Court Judges: M. P. MKANDAWIRE, D. G. TAMBALA, I. J. MTAMBO, A. S. E. MSOSA, D. F. MWAUNGULU, A. K. C. NYIRENDA, A. K. TEMBO, D. S. L. KUMANGE, G. M. CHIMASULA PHIRI, E. B. Z. KUMITSONYO, CHIUDZA BANDA, L. B. T. NDOVI, W. M. HANJA HANJA.

Religion

About 75% of the population profess Christianity. The Asian community includes Muslims and Hindus, and there is a small number of African Muslims. Traditional beliefs are followed by about 10% of the population.

CHRISTIANITY

Christian Council of Malawi: POB 30068, Capital City, Lilongwe 3; tel. 783499; fax 783106; f. 1939; 18 mems and nine associates; Chair. Rev. Dr. O. P. Mazunda; Gen. Sec. A. W. Kishindo.

The Anglican Communion

Anglicans are adherents of the Church of the Province of Central Africa, covering Botswana, Malawi, Zambia and Zimbabwe. The Church comprises 12 dioceses, including three in Malawi. The Archbishop of the Province is the Bishop of Botswana. There are about 80,000 adherents in Malawi.

Bishop of Lake Malawi: Rt Rev. Peter Nathaniel Nyanja, POB 30349, Capital City, Lilongwe 3; fax 731966.

Bishop of North Malawi: Rt Rev. Jackson Biggers, POB 120, Mzuzu.

Bishop of Southern Malawi: Rt Rev. Nathaniel Benson Aipa, PO Chilema, Zomba; fax 531243.

Protestant Churches

The Baptist Convention in Malawi: POB 51083, Limbe; tel. 643224; Chair. Rev. S. L. Malabwanya; Gen. Sec. Rev. M. T. Kachaso Gama.

Church of Central Africa (Presbyterian): comprises three synods in Malawi (Blantyre, Livingstonia and Nkhoma); Blantyre Synod: POB 413, Blantyre; tel. and fax 633942; Gen. Sec. Rev. Misanjo E. Kansilanga; 92,000 adherents in Malawi.

Evangelical Fellowship of Malawi: POB 2120, Blantyre; tel. 633543; Chair. K. M. Luwani; Sec. W. C. Musopole.

The Lutheran Church of Central Africa: POB 748, Blantyre; tel. 630821; fax 630821; f. 1963; evangelical and medical work; Co-ordinator J. M. Janosek; 35,000 mems. in Malawi.

Seventh-day Adventists: POB 951, Blantyre; tel. 620264; telex 4216; fax 620528; Pres. W. L. Masoka; Exec. Sec. R. R. Mzumara.

The African Methodist Episcopal Church, the Churches of Christ, the Free Methodist Church, the Pentecostal Assemblies of God and the United Evangelical Church in Malawi are also active.

The Roman Catholic Church

Malawi comprises one archdiocese and six dioceses. At 31 December 1995 some 19% of the total population were adherents of the Roman Catholic Church.

Episcopal Conference of Malawi: Catholic Secretariat of Malawi, Chimutu Rd, POB 30384, Capital City, Lilongwe 3; tel. 782066; fax 782019; f. 1969; Pres. Most Rev. Felix Eugenio Mkhori, Bishop of Chikwawa.

Archbishop of Blantyre: Most Rev. James Chiona, Archbishop's House, POB 385, Blantyre; tel. 633905; fax 636107.

BAHÁ'Í FAITH

National Spiritual Assembly: POB 5849, Limbe; tel. 640996; fax 640910; f. 1970; mems resident in nearly 1,500 localities.

The Press

ABA Today: POB 5861, Limbe; f. 1982; monthly; publ. by African Businessmen's Association of Malawi.

Boma Lathu: POB 494, Blantyre; tel. 620266; telex 44471; fax 620039; f. 1973; monthly; Chichewa; publ. by the Ministry of Information and Tourism; circ. 100,000.

Business and Development News: Blantyre; f. 1973; monthly.

The Daily Times: Private Bag 39, Ginnery Corner, Blantyre; tel. 671566; telex 44112; fax 671114; f. 1895; Mon.–Fri.; English; Editor-in-Chief Poulton Mtenje; circ. 22,000.

Financial Post: Blantyre; f.1992; weekly; English; independent; Editor Alaudin Osman.

The Independent: POB 2094, Blantyre; tel. and fax 624915; f.1993; weekly; English and Chichewa; independent; Editor Janet Karim; circ. 10,000.

Kuunika: PO Nkhoma, Lilongwe; f. 1909; monthly; Chichewa; Presbyterian; Editor Rev. M. C. Nkhalambayausi; circ. 6,000.

Malawi Life: Private Bag 39, Ginnery Corner, Blantyre; tel. 671566; f. 1991; monthly magazine; English.

Malawi Government Gazette: Government Printer, POB 37, Zomba; tel. 523155; f. 1894; weekly.

Malawi News: Private Bag 39, Ginnery Corner, Blantyre; tel. 671566; telex 44112; fax 671114; f. 1959; weekly; English, Chichewa; circ. 30,000.

Moni: POB 5592, Limbe; tel. 651139; telex 44814; f. 1964; monthly; Chichewa and English; circ. 40,000.

Moyo: Health Education Unit, POB 30377, Lilongwe 3; bi-monthly; English; publ. by Ministry of Health; Editor-in-Chief W. G. Bomba.

Nation: Blantyre; f.1993; weekly; English; independent; Editor Ken Lipanga.

New Express: Blantyre; f.1993; weekly; English; independent; Editors Willie Zingani, Felix Mponda.

Odini: POB 133, Lilongwe; tel. 721388; fax 721141; f. 1950; fortnightly; Chichewa and English; Roman Catholic; Dir S. P. Kalilombe; circ. 12,000.

This is Malawi: POB 494, Blantyre; tel. 620266; telex 44471; fax 620807; f. 1964; monthly; English and Chichewa edns; publ. by the Dept of Information; circ. 5,000.

Woman Now: POB 2094, Blantyre; tel. and fax 624915; f. 1989; quarterly; Editor Janet Karim; circ. 3,000.

NEWS AGENCY

Malawi News Agency (MANA): Mzuza; tel. 636122; telex 44234; f. 1966.

Publishers

Christian Literature Association in Malawi: POB 503, Blantyre; tel. 620839; f. 1968; general and religious publs in Chichewa and English; Gen. Man. Willie Zingani.

Likuni Press and Publishing House: POB 133, Lilongwe; tel. 721388; fax 721141; f. 1949; publs in English and Chichewa; Gen. Man. (vacant).

Mzuzu Publishing Co: POB 225, Nkhata Bay; tel. 352353; Exec. Chair. M. W. Kanyama Chiume.

Popular Publications: POB 5592, Limbe; tel. 651139; telex 44814; fax 651171; f. 1961; general and religious.

Government Publishing House

Government Printer: POB 37, Zomba; tel. 523155.

Radio and Television

There were an estimated 2,450,000 radio receivers in use (according to UNESCO) in 1994. In May 1994 the Government announced plans for the reintroduction of the Tumbuka language on national radio. In the same year the existing ban on television broadcasting was ended. A television service was to begin in late 1996.

Malawi Broadcasting Corporation: POB 30133, Chichiri, Blantyre 3; tel. 671222; telex 44425; fax 671257; f. 1964; statutory body; semi-commercial, partly state-financed; domestic service in English, Chichewa, Chitumbuka, Lomwe and Yao; Dir Gen. Sam Gunde; Dir of News and Current Affairs Molland Nkhata.

Finance

(cap. = capital; res = reserves; dep. = deposits; m. = million; brs = branches; amounts in kwacha)

BANKING

Central Bank

Reserve Bank of Malawi: POB 30063, Capital City, Lilongwe 3; tel. 780600; telex 44788; fax 731145; f. 1965; bank of issue; cap. and res 336.5m., dep. 1890.1m. (Dec. 1995); Gov. Mathews Chikaonda; Gen. Mans. G. G. Lengu, I. C. Bonongwe, B. J. A. Khoriyo; br. in Blantyre.

Commercial Banks

Commercial Bank of Malawi Ltd: POB 1111, Blantyre; tel. 620144; telex 44340; fax 620360; f. 1970; cap. and res 324.9m., dep. 2,148.8m. (Dec. 1996); Chair. K. Hassan; CEO Dennis G. Lawrence; 13 brs.

National Bank of Malawi: Victoria Ave, POB 945, Blantyre; tel. 620622; telex 44142; fax 620606; f. 1971; cap. and res 396.2m., dep. 3,028.9m. (Dec. 1996); Chair. J. H. M. Carter; CEO T. J. O. Barnes; 14 brs; agencies throughout Malawi.

Development Bank

Investment and Development Bank of Malawi Ltd (INDEBANK): Indebank House, Haushong Rd, Top Mandala, POB 358, Blantyre; tel. 620055; telex 45201; fax 623353; f. 1972; cap. and res 40.1m. (Dec. 1995); provides loans to statutory corpns and to private enterprises in the agricultural, industrial, tourism, transport and commercial sectors; Chair. Christopher Barrow; Gen. Man. Chadwick L. Mphande.

Merchant Banks

Leasing and Finance Co of Malawi Ltd: Indebank House, 1st Floor, Top Mandala, POB 1963, Blantyre; tel. 620233; telex 44179; fax 620275; f. 1986; cap. and res 21.4m. (Aug. 1995); Chair. C. L. Mphande; Gen. Man. H. M. Ndhlovu.

National Finance Credit Ltd: Plantation House, POB 821, Blantyre; tel. 623670; fax 620549; f. 1958; cap. 13.2m. (Dec. 1996); Chair. T. J. O. Barnes; Gen. Man. M. T. Bamford.

Savings Bank

Malawi Savings Bank: POB 521, Blantyre; tel. 620944; telex 44437; fax 621929; state-owned; Chair. Dr Ngalande Banda; Gen. Man. R. Tucker.

STOCK EXCHANGE

Malawi Stock Exchange: f. 1994; CEO Rob Stangroom.

INSURANCE

National Insurance Co Ltd: NICO House, Private Bag 30421, Capital City, Lilongwe 3; tel. 783311; telex 44622; f. 1971; cap. and res 38.3m. (1994); offices at Blantyre, Lilongwe and Mzuzu, agencies country-wide; Gen. Man. F. L. Mlusu.

Premier Life Office: POB 393, Blantyre; tel. 620677; telex 44690.

Trade and Industry

CHAMBER OF COMMERCE

Malawi Chamber of Commerce and Industry: Chichiri Trade Fair Grounds, POB 258, Blantyre; tel. 671988; telex 43992; fax 671147; f. 1892; 400 mems; Chair. F. P. Kalilombe.

STATUTORY ORGANIZATIONS

Agricultural Development and Marketing Corporation (ADMARC): POB 5052, Limbe; tel. 640044; telex 44121; fax 640486; statutory trading org. that markets agricultural crops produced by smallholder farmers; exporter of confectionery-grade groundnut kernels, maize, cassava and sunflower seed; primary marketing of tobacco, wheat and a wide variety of beans, peas and other seeds; co-operates with commercial cos in the cultivation and processing of agricultural produce; Gen. Man. Eunice Kazembe.

Malawi Posts and Telecommunications Corporation (MPTC): Blantyre; f. 1995 to succeed the Dept of Posts and Telecommunications.

INDUSTRIAL AND COMMERCIAL ORGANIZATIONS

Smallholder Coffee Authority: POB 230, Mzuzu; tel. 332899; fax 332902; producers of arabica coffee.

Smallholder Sugar Authority: Blantyre; telex 44647.

Smallholder Tea Authority: POB 80, Thyolo.

Tea Association of Malawi Ltd: POB 930, Blantyre; tel. 671182; telex 44320; fax 671427; f. 1936; 20 mems.

Tobacco Association of Malawi: POB 31360, Lilongwe 3; tel. 783099; telex 44598; fax 783493; f. 1929; 49,000 mems; Pres. Dr A. B. Mzumacharo.

Tobacco Exporters' Association of Malawi: Private Bag 403, Kanengo, Lilongwe 4; tel. 765663; telex 44360; fax 765668; f. 1930; 10 mems; Chair. S. W. Wallace; Exec. Sec. H. M. Mbale.

DEVELOPMENT CORPORATIONS

Malawi Development Corporation (MDC): MDC House, Glyn Jones Rd, POB 566, Blantyre; tel. 620100; telex 44146; fax 620584; f. 1964; state-owned; provides finance and management advice to commerce and industry; 23 subsidiary and assoc. cos; Chair. Dr J. A. A. Jana; Gen. Man. E. B. Kadzako.

Malawi Export Promotion Council: Delamere House, POB 1299, Blantyre; tel. 620499; telex 44589; fax 635429; f. 1974; Gen. Man. J. B. L. Malange.

Malawi Investment Promotion Agency (MIPA): Private Bag 302, Capital City, Lilongwe 3; tel. 780800; fax 781781; e-mail mipa@eo.wn.apc.org; f. 1993; one-stop government agency; promotion and facilitation of local and foreign investments; Gen. Man. M. J. M. Phiri.

Mining Investment and Development Corporation Ltd (MIDCOR): POB 565, Lilongwe; f. 1985; state-owned; operates coal mines at Kaziwiziwi and Mchenga and explores for other mineral deposits; Gen. Man. Stanley Kalyati.

Small Enterprise Development Organization of Malawi (SEDOM): POB 525, Blantyre; tel. 622555; telex 44666; fax 622781; f. 1982; tech. and management advice to indigenous small-scale businesses.

EMPLOYERS' ASSOCIATIONS

Employers' Consultative Association of Malawi (ECAM): POB 2134, Blantyre; tel. 671337; f. 1963; 500 mems; Chair. D. Kambauwa; Exec. Dir W. L. Dambuleni.

Master Builders', Civil Engineering Contractors' and Allied Trades' Association: POB 311, Blantyre; tel. 622966; f. 1955; 70 mems (1994); Chair. B. Clow.

Master Printers' Association of Malawi: POB 2460, Blantyre; f. 1962; 21 mems; Chair. Paul Frederick.

National Automotive Franchise Holders' Association of Malawi: POB 311, Blantyre; tel. 624754; fax 622966; f. 1954; 42 mems (1989); Chair. D. H. Draude.

MAJOR INDUSTRIAL COMPANIES

The following are among the largest companies in terms of capital investment or employment.

BATA Shoe Company (Malawi) Ltd: POB 936, Blantyre; tel. 670511; telex 44252; mfrs of shoes; Man. Dir H. Strohmayer.

B.A.T. (Malawi) Ltd: POB 428, Blantyre; tel. 670033; telex 44114; fax 670808; mfrs of cigarettes; Man. Dir A. E. Phillip.

Blantyre Netting Co: POB 30575, Blantyre; tel. 636735; fax 635708; polypropylene woven sacks, ropes, bristles, strapping tapes, nylon twines, nets; Man. Dir H. Anadkat.

Brown and Clapperton: POB 1582, Limbe; tel. 634677; telex 44243; fax 635198; mfrs of engineering products.

Carlsberg Malawi Brewery Ltd: POB 1050, Heavy Industrial Area, Blantyre; tel. 670133; telex 44405; fax 671903; mfrs of beer; CEO P. B. Jorgensen.

Chemical Manufacturers Ltd: POB 30242, Chichiri, Blantyre 3; tel. 671536; fax 675956; f. 1981; mfrs and distributers of industrial chemical products.

Chillington Agrimal (Malawi) Ltd: POB 143, Blantyre; tel. 670933; telex 44750; fax 670651; mfrs of agricultural hand tools, hoes and implements; Gen. Man. C. J. Peverelle.

CTM (Malawi) Ltd: POB 5350, Limbe; telex 44183; mfrs of textiles; Man. Dir Christopher George Geasley.

Grain and Milling Co Ltd: POB 5847, Limbe; tel. 645055; telex 44868; fax 643342; grain millers.

Import and Export Co of Malawi (1984) Ltd: POB 1106, Blantyre; tel. 670999; telex 44214; fax 671160; mfrs and wholesalers of brushes.

International Timbers Ltd: POB 5050, Limbe; tel. 640399; telex 4248; fax 640959; f. 1907; cap. K6.6m.; foresters and sawmillers of home-grown eucalyptus timber; mfrs of tobacco packing material, structural laminated timber, woodblock flooring, pallets and wooden packaging material, commercial plywood, blockboard, tea chests and flush panel doors; Man. Dir Edward J. Goreham.

Lever Brothers (Malawi) Ltd: POB 5151, Tsiranana Rd, Limbe; tel. 641100; telex 44253; fax 645720; f. 1963; mfrs of soaps, detergents, cooking oils, foods, beverages and chemicals; Chair. C. Foy.

Lonrho (Malawi) Ltd: POB 5498, Churchill Rd, Limbe; tel. 640000; telex 441127; fax 640427; f. 1963; cap. K5m.; total issued cap. of Lonrho group cos in Malawi: c. K70m.; Chair. G. A. Jaffu; operates the following subsidiaries:

- **The Central Africa Co Ltd:** Tobacco and special crops.
- **Chibuku Products Ltd:** Brewing.
- **Farming and Engineering Services Ltd:** Agricultural equipment.
- **Lonrho Motors (Malawi) Ltd:** Motor trading.
- **Lonrho Properties Ltd:** Construction and property management.
- **Toyota Malawi Ltd:** Motor trading.

Malawi Distilleries Ltd: POB 924, MacLeod Rd, Heavy Industrial Site, Blantyre; tel. 670722; telex 44820; fax 670813; f. 1967; cap. K0.45m.; sole producer of potable spirits for local consumption and export; Man. Dir. N. T. Watson.

Malawi Iron and Steel Corporation: POB 143, Blantyre; tel. 674307; telex 44750; fax 670651; foundry operators.

National Oil Industries Ltd: POB 143; Macleod Rd, Blantyre; tel. 670155; telex 44334; mfrs of cooking oils, cotton-seed cake and millers of rice; Gen. Man. F. A. Jumbe.

Packaging Industries (Malawi) Ltd: POB 30533, Chichiri, Blantyre 3; tel. 670533; telex 44601; fax 671283.

PEW Ltd: POB 30038, Chichiri, Blantyre 3; tel. 671155; telex 44836; fax 671437; fmrly Plumbing and Engineering Works; mfrs of coachworks, bus bodies, road and farm trailers, truck bodies, tankers and GRP products; Man. Dir George French.

Plastic Products Ltd: POB 907, Blantyre.

The Portland Cement Co (1974) Ltd: POB 523, Heavy Industrial Area, Blantyre; tel. 671933; telex 44841; fax 671026; f. 1974; cap. K21.6m. (Dec. 1996); mfrs and distributors of cement; projected annual capacity: 140,000 metric tons; CEO ROGER MORTON.

Press and Shine Clothing Ltd: POB 306, Lilongwe; tel. 720566; fax 720597, mfrs of garments; Gen. Man. R. ZIEGENHARDT.

Press Steel Industries Ltd: POB 30116, Lilongwe 3; tel. 765088; telex 44859; fax 765848; metal rollers.

PROMAT Ltd: POB 30041, Lilongwe 3; tel. 765388; telex 44871; fax 733172; mfrs of polyvinylchloride (PVC)-U pipes, high-density polyethylene pipes, PVC hosepipes.

Southern Bottlers Ltd: POB 406, Blantyre; tel. 670022; telex 44229; mfrs of soft drinks.

Universal Industries Ltd: POB 507, Blantyre; tel. 670055; telex 44402; mfrs of confectionery; Man. Dir D.K. AMIN.

Viply: Private Bag 1, Chikangawa Mzimba; tel. 335377; telex 44097; fax 335126; mfrs of plywood, blockboard and timber.

TRADE UNIONS

Trades Union Congress of Malawi (TUCM): POB 5094, Limbe; f. 1964; 6,500 mems; Chair. KEN WILLIAM MHANGO; Gen. Sec. EATON V. LAITA; the following are among the principal affiliated unions:

Building Construction, Civil Engineering and Allied Workers' Union: Limbe; tel. 650598; f. 1961; 6,000 mems; Chair. W. I. SOKO; Gen. Sec. G. SITIMA.

Railway Workers' Union of Malawi: POB 5393, Limbe; tel. 640844; f. 1954; 3,000 mems; Chair. W. C. CHIMPHANGA; Gen. Sec. F. L. MATTENJE.

Other unions affiliated to the TUCM are the Commercial and Allied Workers' Union, the Civil Servants' Trade Union, the Hotels, Food and Catering Workers' Union, the Local Government Employees' Union, the Plantation and Agricultural Workers' Union, the Teachers' Union of Malawi , the Textile, Garment, Guards and Leather Workers' Union, the Transport and General Workers' Union and the Sugar Plantation and Allied Workers' Union. The TUCM and its affiliated unions had a total membership of 450,000 in 1995.

Transport

RAILWAYS

Malawi Railways and the Central African Railway Co, its wholly-owned subsidiary, operate between Nsanje (near the southern border with Mozambique) and Mchinji (near the border with Zambia) via Blantyre, Salima and Lilongwe, and between Nkaya and Nayuchi on the eastern border with Mozambique, covering a total of about 789 km. Malawi Railways and Mozambique State Railways connect Malawi with the Mozambican ports of Beira and Nacala. These links, which traditionally form Malawi's principal trade routes, were effectively closed during 1983–85, owing to insurgent activity in Mozambique. The rehabilitation of the rail link to Nacala was completed in October 1989. There is a rail/lake interchange station at Chipoka on Lake Malawi, from where Malawi Railways vessels operate services to other lake ports in Malawi. In 1995 the International Development Association approved a credit of US $17.5m., to support the restructuring of the railway system in preparation for the eventual privatization of Malawi Railways and its routes.

Malawi Railways Ltd: POB 5144, Limbe; tel. 640844; telex 44810; fax 640683; f. 1994; Chair. D. LUNGU; Gen Man. E. R. LIMBE.

ROADS

In 1995 Malawi had a total road network of an estimated 27,880 km, including 3,290 km of main roads and 2,790 km of secondary roads; about 5,130 km of the road network was paved. All main roads, and most secondary roads, are all-weather roads. Major routes link Lilongwe and Blantyre with Harare (Zimbabwe) Lusaka (Zambia) and Mbeya and Dar es Salaam (Tanzania). The 480-km highway along the western shore of Lake Malawi, linking the remote Northern Region with the Central and Southern Regions, is currently being upgraded. A project to create a new trade route, or 'Northern Corridor', through Tanzania, involving road construction and improvements in Malawi, was completed in 1992. In early 1996 Germany granted approximately K150m. for the maintenance of bituminous roads and bridges.

Road Transport Operators Association: Makata Industrial Site, POB 30740, Chichiri, Blantyre 3; tel. 670422; fax 671423; f. 1956; 254 mems (1995); Chair. F. D. GHAMBI.

CIVIL AVIATION

Kamuzu International Airport (at Lilongwe) was opened in 1982. There is another main airport, at Blantyre, which serves a number of regional airlines, and three domestic airports.

Air Malawi Ltd: Robins Rd, POB 84, Blantyre; tel. 620811; telex 44245; fax 620042; f. 1967; scheduled domestic and regional services, scheduled services to the Middle East and charter flights; Chair. V. T. LIKAKU; CEO Capt. A. WISDOM B. MCHUNGULA.

Tourism

Fine scenery, beaches on Lake Malawi, big game and an excellent climate form the basis of the country's tourist potential. The number of departures by foreign visitors was 154,000 in 1994; receipts from tourism in that year totalled US $5m.

Department of Tourism: POB 402, Blantyre; tel. 620300; telex 44645; fax 620947; f. 1969; responsible for tourist policy; administers govt rest-houses, sponsors training of hotel staff and publs tourist literature; Chief Tourism Officer M. M. MATOLA.

Tourism Development and Investment Co (TDIC): Blantyre; f. 1988 by Malawi Development Corpn to operate hotels and tours.

Defence

Malawi's defence forces in August 1996 comprised a land army of 9,500, a marine force of 200 and an air force of 80; all form part of the army. There was also a paramilitary police force of 1,000.

Defence Expenditure: Budgeted at an estimated K360m. in 1996.

Commander-in-Chief of the Armed Forces: Gen. O. B. BINAULI.

Education

Primary education, which is officially compulsory, begins at six years of age and lasts for up to eight years. Secondary education, which begins at 14 years of age, lasts for four years, comprising two cycles of two years. In 1994 the total enrolment at primary and secondary schools was equivalent to 87% of the school-age population (males 92%; females 83%). In that year primary school enrolment included 92% of children in the relevant age-group (males 91%; females 93%), but secondary enrolment included only 2% of children in the appropriate age-group for both sexes. The new government is undertaking a programme to expand education at all levels; however, the introduction of free primary education in September 1994 was reported to have resulted in severe overcrowding in schools; primary school enrolment in 1992 had been equivalent to only 52% of the relevant age-group. In January 1996 the IDA granted US $22.5m. for the training of 20,000 new teachers, appointed in response to the influx. The University of Malawi had 3,601 students in 1994/95. Some students attend institutions in the United Kingdom and the USA. Education was allocated 10.3% of total government expenditure in the 1995/96 budget. In 1987, according to census results, the average rate of adult illiteracy was 51.5% (males 34.7%; females 66.5%). A five-year adult literacy programme was launched in 1986, and in 1987 two teacher-training colleges were opened. However, in 1995, according to UNESCO estimates, the average rate of adult illiteracy was 43.6% (males 28.1%; females 58.2%).

Bibliography

Bafael, B. R. *A Short History of Malawi*. Limbe, Popular Publishers, 1980.

Baker, C. *The Evolution of Local Government in Malawi*. Ife, University of Ife, 1975.

Seeds of Trouble: Government Policy and Land Rights in Nyasaland, 1946–1964. London, British Academic Press, 1993.

Catholic Institute for International Relations. *Malawi: Moment of Truth*. London, CIIR, 1993.

Crosby, C. A. *Historical Dictionary of Malawi*. 2nd Edn. Metuchen, NJ, Scarecrow Press, 1993.

Cullen, T. *Malawi: A Turning Point*. Edinburgh, Pentland Press, 1994.

Economist Intelligence Unit. *Country Report: Zimbabwe, Malawi*. No. 2, 1986, London, EIU, 1986.

Jere, N., and Mkandawire, D. S. *An Outline of Our Government*. Blantyre, Christian Literature Association of Malawi, 1982.

Kibble, S. *Dependencey and Choice: Malawi's Links with South Africa.* Leeds, African Studies Unit, University of Leeds, 1988.

Lamport-Stokes, B. *Blantyre: Glimpses of the Early Days.* Blantyre, Society of Malawi, 1989.

Lienau, C. *Malawi.* Darmstadt, Wissenschaftliche Buchgesellschaft, 1981.

Lwanda, J. L. *Kamazu Banda of Malawi: A Study in Promise, Power and Paralysis: Malawi under Dr Banda, 1961 to 1993.* Glasgow, Dudu Nsomba Publishers, 1993.

Macdonald, R. J. (Ed.). *From Nyasaland to Malawi: Studies in Colonial History.* Nairobi, East African Publishing House, 1976.

Martin, C. G. C. *Maps and Surveys of Malawi: A History of Cartography and the Land Survey Profession.* Cape Town, Balkema, 1980.

Meinhardt, H. *Die Rolle des Parlaments in Autoritaeren Malawi.* Hamburg, Institut für Afrika-Kunde, 1993.

Mhone, G. C. Z. (Ed.). *Malawi at the Crossroads: The Post-Colonial Political Economy.* Harare, SAPES Books, 1992.

Milazi, D. *The Politics and Economics of Labour Migration in Southern Africa: What are the Key Issues?* Maseru, Lesotho Publishing Co, 1986.

Mtewa, M. *Malawi: Democratic Theory and Public Policy.* Cambridge, MA, Schenkmann, 1984.

Mwhakasunguru, A. K. *The Rural Economy of Malawi: A Critical Analysis.* Bergen, CMI, 1986.

Nzunda, M. S., and Ross, K. R. (Eds). *Church, Law and Political Transition in Malawi 1992–1994.* Gweru, Mambo, 1995.

Pachai, B. *The Early History of Malawi.* London: Longman, 1972.

Malawi: The History of a Nation. New York, Longman, 1973.

Land and Politics in Malawi 1875–1975. Kingston, Ontario, Limestone Press, 1978.

Phiri, D. D. *From Nguni to Ngoni.* Limbe, Popular Publishers, 1982.

Spring, A. *Agricultural Development and Gender Issues in Malawi.* Lanham, MD, University Press of America, 1995.

Vaughan, M. *The Story of an African Famine: Gender and Famine in Twentieth-Century Malawi.* Cambridge, Cambridge University Press, 1987.

Wells, A. J. *An Introduction to the History of Central Africa: Zambia, Malawi and Zimbabwe.* Oxford, Oxford Univeristy Press, 1985.

White, L. *Magomero: Portrait of an African Village.* Cambridge, Cambridge University Press, 1987.

Williams, T. D. *Malawi: The Politics of Despair.* Ithaca, NY, Cornell University Press, 1978.

World Bank. *Malawi: Human Resources and Poverty: Profile and Priorities for Action.* Washington, DC, World Bank, 1996.

Young, A., and Young, D. *A Geography of Malawi.* 2nd Edn. London, Evans, 1987.

MALI

Physical and Social Geography

R. J. HARRISON CHURCH

With an area of 1.24m. sq km (478,767 sq miles), the Republic of Mali is only slightly smaller than Niger, west Africa's largest state. Like Niger and Burkina Faso, Mali is land-locked. It extends about 1,600 km from north to south, and roughly the same distance from east to west, with a narrowing at the centre. The population was 7,696,348 at the census of April 1987, and was officially estimated at 8,156,000 in mid-1990 (giving an average density of 6.6 inhabitants per sq km). The UN estimated a population of 10.8m. at mid-1995.

The ancient Basement Complex rocks of Africa have been uplifted in the mountainous Adrar des Iforas of the north-east, whose dry valleys bear witness to formerly wetter conditions. Otherwise the Pre-Cambrian rocks are often covered by Primary sandstones, which have bold erosion escarpments at, for example, Bamako and east of Bandiagara. At the base of the latter live the Dogon people, made famous by Marcel Griaule's study. Where the River Niger crosses a sandstone outcrop below Bamako, rapids obstruct river navigation, giving an upper navigable reach above Bamako, and another one below it from Koulikoro to Ansongo, near the border with Niger.

Loose sands cover most of the rest of the country and, as in Senegal and Niger, are a relic of drier climatic conditions. They are very extensive on the long border with Mauritania and Algeria.

Across the heart of the country flows the River Niger, a vital waterway and source of fish. As the seasonal floods retreat, they leave pasture for thousands of livestock desperate for food and water after a dry season of at least eight months. The retreating floods also leave damp areas for man, equally desperate for cultivable land in an arid environment. Flood water is sometimes retained for swamp rice cultivation, and has been made available for irrigation, particularly in the 'dead' south-western section of the inland Niger delta.

The delta is the remnant of an inland lake, in which the upper Niger once terminated. In a more rainy era this overflowed to join the then mighty Tilemsi river, once the drainage focus of the now arid Adrar des Iforas. The middle and lower courses of the Tilemsi now comprise the Niger below Bourem, at the eastern end of the consquential elbow turn of the Niger. The eastern part of the delta, which was formed in the earlier lake, is intersected by 'live' flood-water branches of the river, while the relic channels of the very slightly higher western part of the delta are never occupied naturally by flood water and so are 'dead'. However, these are used in part for irrigation water retained by the Sansanding barrage, which has raised the level of the Niger by an average of 4.3 m.

Mali is mainly dry throughout, with a rainy season of four to five months and a total rainfall of 1,120 mm at Bamako, and of only seven weeks and an average fall of 236 mm at Gao. North of this there is no rain-fed cultivation, but only semi-desert or true desert, which occupies nearly one-half of Mali. The mining of gold reserves, most of which are located near the borders with Senegal and Guinea, is becoming an increasingly important activity. The extraction of diamonds has recently been revived near the border with Senegal.

Distances to the nearest foreign port from most places in Mali are at least 1,300 km, and, not surprisingly, there is much seasonal and permanent emigration.

Recent History

PIERRE ENGLEBERT

Revised for this edition by the Editor

The former French colony of Soudan merged with Senegal in April 1959 to form the Federation of Mali, which became independent on 20 June 1960. Senegal seceded two months later, and the Republic of Mali was proclaimed on 22 September. President Modibo Keita declared the country a one-party state, under his Union soudanaise–Rassemblement démocratique africain (US–RDA). Keita's Marxist regime severed links with France, developing close relations with the Eastern bloc. Mali's withdrawal from the Franc Zone in 1962 severely undermined the economy, despite government efforts to regulate commerce. In 1967 agreement was reached with France for an eventual return to the Franc Zone. This was strongly opposed by radical elements within the US–RDA, and such internal disputes impelled Keita to take decisive action: he dissolved the party's political bureau in 1967 and the national assembly in 1968, replacing them with new bodies. The emergence of a militant youth movement, which undertook purges within the party, administration and military, caused disquiet in the army, and a group of young officers staged a successful *coup d'état* in November 1968. The constitution was abrogated, and all party political activity was banned. A Comité militaire pour la libération nationale (CMLN) was formed, with Lt (later Gen.) Moussa Traoré as president and Capt. Yoro Diakité as head of government.

THE TRAORÉ PERIOD, 1968–91

The new regime promised a return to civilian rule when Mali's economic problems (now exacerbated by drought in the Sahel region) had been overcome. Relations with France improved, and French budgetary aid ensued. In September 1969, following the discovery of a military plot to reinstate Keita, Diakité was demoted to a lesser government post. (He was arrested in 1971, and died in detention in 1973.) There was opposition to Traoré, now also head of government, among civil servants, state employees and students loyal to the former regime, but political dissent was overshadowed by the ravages of the 1968–74 drought.

In 1974 a new constitution was approved by referendum, providing for the establishment, after a five-year transition period, of a one-party state. The future ruling party was to be the Union démocratique du peuple malien (UDPM), the formation of which was announced in 1976. Such changes encountered persistent opposition both from supporters of the old regime and from proponents of multi-party democracy, and hostile demonstrations followed Keita's death in detention in 1977. In 1978 a number of senior officers were tried and imprisoned on charges of threatening state security.

Presidential and legislative elections were held in June 1979. Traoré, as sole candidate for the presidency, won a reported

99% of the votes cast, while a single list of UDPM candidates was elected to the legislature. Unrest among students and teachers in 1980–81 was prompted by the dissolution of the students' union (which had refused to affiliate to the UDPM) and the subsequent death in custody of a student leader. In December 1980 an alleged coup plot led to death sentences for three gendarmes. A constitutional amendment adopted in September 1981 increased the presidential term from five to six years, and reduced that of the national assembly from four years to three. Legislative elections followed in June 1982, again with a single list of UDPM candidates.

From 1981 the Traoré regime undertook a programme of economic liberalization, in co-operation with the World Bank and other Western donors. The reforms were pursued in spite of severe drought in 1983–84. Traoré was re-elected president in June 1985 (obtaining, as sole candidate, 98% of the votes). In June 1986 the president's personal physician, Dr Mamadou Dembélé (hitherto the minister of public health and social affairs), was appointed to the restored post of prime minister. Traoré also ceded the defence portfolio to a close associate, Gen. Sékou Ly. However, the post of prime minister was again abolished in June 1988; Dembélé returned to his former position in the council of ministers, and Traoré also reassumed the defence portfolio. (Dembélé was dismissed from the government one year later, following allegations of his involvement in gold-smuggling.)

The government's decision, in 1987, to curtail elements of its unpopular economic austerity programme resulted in the suspension by the IMF of financing negotiations. However, capital inflows resumed in August 1988, following the introduction of new economic measures. An anti-corruption commission was established in April 1987, and in December nine people were sentenced to death, convicted of embezzling public funds; four others received death sentences in mid-1989. Meanwhile, in August 1987 the minister of finance and trade, Soumana Sacko, was apparently forced to resign as a result of the unpopularity in official circles of his efforts to eliminate corruption: he was rehabilitated in 1988, when he was appointed auditor-general, but subsequently left Mali to work for the UN Development Programme.

At elections to the national assembly in June 1988, provision was made for up to three UDPM-nominated candidates to contest each of the 82 seats. Forty new members were thus elected to the assembly. In September Traoré ordered the closure of the detention facilities at the Taoudenni salt mines, in northern Mali, and reduced the sentences of (or released) its 78 prisoners, among them several of those implicated in the 1978 coup attempt.

Doubtless influenced by political events elsewhere in the region, in March 1990 Traoré initiated a nation-wide series of conferences to consider the exercise of democracy within and by the UDPM. Many political activists at the Bamako conference spoke in favour of reform, although Traoré stated that diverse political opinions must be expressed within the framework of the UDPM. Mali's first cohesive opposition movements began to emerge in the second half of the year: among the most prominent were the Comité national d'initiative démocratique (CNID) and the Alliance pour la démocratie au Mali (ADEMA), which organized mass pro-democracy demonstrations in December.

In January 1991 Traoré relinquished the defence portfolio to Brig.-Gen. Mamadou Coulibaly, the air force chief of staff. Gen. Ly, now minister of the interior and basic development, issued warnings to the nascent opposition groups that their political activities must cease. Rallies were organized to denounce the restrictions, and protests intensified following the arrest of the leader of an unofficial students' organization. Two demonstrators were killed, and 35 injured, when security forces intervened to suppress violent protests in Bamako led by students, school pupils and lawyers. Schools and colleges throughout Mali were closed by the authorities for several weeks, as unrest spread, and armoured vehicles were deployed in the capital.

ARMY INTERVENTION AND POLITICAL REFORM

Violent pro-democracy demonstrations in March 1991 were harshly repressed by the security forces: official figures later revealed that 106 people were killed, and 708 injured, during three days of unrest. Traoré promised political reforms, but refused to accede to demands for his resignation. On 26 March it was announced that Traoré had been arrested. A military Conseil de réconciliation nationale (CRN), led by Lt-Col (later Lt-Gen.) Amadou Toumani Touré, assumed power, and the constitution, government, legislature and the UDPM were dissolved. Following negotiations with ADEMA, the CNID and other reformist political groups, the CRN was swiftly succeeded by a 25-member Comité de transition pour le salut du peuple (CTSP), chaired by Touré, whose function was to be to oversee a transition to a democratic, civilian political system. It was announced that municipal, legislative and presidential elections would be organized by the end of the year, and that the armed forces would withdraw from political life in January 1992. In April 1991 Soumana Sacko accepted an invitation to return to Mali at the head of a transitional, civilian-dominated council of ministers.

The CTSP, while affirming its commitment to the policies of economic adjustment that had been adopted by the Traoré administration, undertook the reform of Malian political life, and sought to remove from positions of influence all those considered to have been implicated in the corrupt practices of the previous regime. Efforts were initiated to recover funds allegedly embezzled by Traoré and his associates, rumoured to total some US $2,000m. (roughly equivalent to the country's foreign debt), which were said to have been deposited in bank accounts overseas. Senior officials including Sékou Ly, Mamadou Coulibaly and Ousmane Coulibaly, the chief of staff of the army, were arrested in connection with the brutal repression of the unrest that had preceded Traoré's overthrow, while other prominent figures were accused of 'economic crimes'. The council of ministers and the CTSP were reorganized following the discovery, in July 1991, of a coup plot, allegedly involving several members of the new regime. Salary increases were announced for military personnel and civil servants, and an amnesty was proclaimed for most political prisoners detained under Traoré.

Meanwhile, provision was made for the registration of political parties. The CNID was legalized as the Congrès national d'initiative démocratique (led by a prominent lawyer, Mountaga Tall), while ADEMA (chaired by Alpha Oumar Konaré, an historian, archaeologist and founder of an influential cultural co-operative, who had briefly been a government minister in the late 1970s) adopted the additional title of Parti africain pour la solidarité et la justice. Modibo Keita was posthumously rehabilitated in May 1991, and his US–RDA was revived.

A national conference was convened in Bamako on 29 July–12 August 1991. Its 1,800 delegates prepared a draft constitution for what was to be designated the third republic of Mali, together with an electoral code and a charter governing political parties. Later in August seven government ministers and about one-half of the members of the CTSP were replaced, following allegations of their implication in the repression prior to the coup.

In November 1991 it was announced that the period of transition to civilian rule was to be extended until 26 March 1992. The delay was attributed principally to the CTSP's desire first to secure an agreement with Tuareg groups in the north (see below), but it was also admitted that the foreign assistance hitherto granted was insufficient to finance the elections. The constitutional referendum, originally scheduled for 1 December 1991, thus took place on 12 January 1992, when the document was approved by 99.76% of those who voted (only about 43% of the electorate). Municipal elections, which followed on 19 January, were contested by 23 of the country's 48 authorized parties. ADEMA enjoyed the greatest success, winning 214 of the 751 municipal seats, while the US–RDA took 130 seats and the CNID 96. The rate of abstention by voters was, however, almost 70%. Legislative elections eventually took place on 23 February and 8 March, amid allegations that the electoral system was unduly favourable to ADEMA. Of the 21 parties contesting the elections, 10 secured seats in the 129-member national assembly: ADEMA won 76 seats (with 48.4% of the votes cast), the CNID nine (with 5.5%) and the US–RDA eight (with 17.6%). Overall, only about one-fifth of the electorate was said to have voted.

Nine candidates contested the delayed first round of the presidential election, on 12 April 1992 (the date for the transition to civilian rule having again been postponed). The largest share of the votes (44.95%) was won by Konaré. A second round of voting, contested by the ADEMA leader and his nearest rival, Tiéoulé Mamadou Konaté of the US–RDA, followed two weeks later, at which Konaré won 69.01% of the votes cast. Again, participation by voters was little more than 20%.

THE KONARÉ PRESIDENCY

Alpha Oumar Konaré was sworn in as president of the third republic on 8 June 1992. (Previously he had resigned as chairman of ADEMA, in accordance with the provisions of the constitution). Younoussi Touré, hitherto the national director of the Banque centrale des états de l'Afrique de l'ouest, was immediately designated prime minister. While most strategic posts in Touré's government were allocated to members of ADEMA, the US–RDA and the Parti pour la démocratie et le progrès (PDP) were also represented. In July (in the absence of opposition deputies, who boycotted the vote in protest against their lack of influence in a political system that they perceived to be excessively dominated by ADEMA) Aly Nouhoun Diallo, ADEMA's political secretary, was elected president of the national assembly.

In February 1993 ex-president Moussa Traoré, Sékou Ly, Mamadou Coulibaly and Ousmane Coulibaly were sentenced to death, after having been convicted of 'premeditated murder, battery and voluntary manslaughter' at the time of the March 1991 disturbances; 29 other defendants were acquitted. Appeals against the death sentences were rejected by the supreme court in May. However, no execution was known to have been carried out since 1980, and, as had been widely expected, Konaré eventually commuted all four sentences. (In early 1996 Konaré asserted that no death penalty would be exacted during his presidency.) Charges relating to 'economic crimes' remained against Traoré, his wife and other members of the discredited regime.

In March 1993 students and school pupils, protesting at the adverse impact on the education sector of the government's economic austerity measures, attacked public buildings and vehicles in Bamako. There were further clashes in April (as a result of which at least one person was killed), when students, angered by government attempts to impose a new leader on their union, set fire to buildings including the seat of the national assembly, the official residence of the minister of state for national education and the headquarters of ADEMA. Younoussi Touré resigned shortly afterwards, and was replaced by Abdoulaye Sekou Sow. The new prime minister, who, while not affiliated to any political party, was known to be sympathetic to Konaré's policies, implemented an extensive government reorganization: his council of ministers remained dominated by ADEMA and its supporters, but also included opposition representatives—with, most notably, three ministries (among them the justice portfolio) being allocated to the CNID. There was evidence, none the less, of increasing tensions among the parties in government. Members of ADEMA, the CNID and the US–RDA expressed dissatisfaction at their exclusion from the decision-making process, which they believed to be excessively dominated by Konaré and the council of ministers. A reorganization of the government in November was prompted by the resignation of ADEMA's vice-president, Mohamed Lamine Traoré, from his ministerial post. Sow's 'streamlined' council of ministers included new ministers responsible for finance (a controversial programme of austerity measures, announced in September, had failed to prevent the suspension of assistance by the IMF and the World Bank) and for foreign affairs. ADEMA remained the majority party in the government, which also included representatives of the CNID, the PDP and the Rassemblement pour la démocratie et le progrès (RDP). Two of the US–RDA's three ministers left the government at the time of the reshuffle, and the party withdrew from the coalition shortly afterwards. In December it was revealed that a plot to assassinate Konaré, Sow and Aly Nouhoun Diallo, orchestrated by Traoré's former aide-de-camp (who had been detained since July, accused of the misappropriation of state funds), had been thwarted. Five junior military officers were arrested for their part in the conspiracy.

Political and social tensions were exacerbated by the 50% devaluation, in January 1994, of the CFA franc. Sow, who had been experiencing increasing difficulty in securing support for his policies from ADEMA, resigned in February, and was replaced as prime minister by Ibrahim Boubacar Keita—since November 1993 the minister of foreign affairs, Malians abroad and African integration, who was said to be both a member of ADEMA's radical tendency and a close associate of Konaré. The CNID and the RDP withdrew from the goverment coalition, protesting that they had not been consulted about the changes; a new, ADEMA-dominated government was appointed, from which the PDP in turn withdrew (although its representative in the council of ministers resigned from the party, in order to retain his portfolio).

Sow's resignation came at a time of renewed unrest in the education sector, as students and school pupils protested against the currency's depreciation and demanded compensatory grant increases. Violent demonstrations in Bamako in February 1994 prompted the closure of schools and colleges, and the detention in March of the students' union leader provoked further violent disturbances. A day of 'inaction', organized by opposition groups in late March, was deemed by the authorities to have been poorly supported, although the opposition claimed that much of the economic life of the capital had been disrupted. Salaries in the state sector were increased by 10% with effect from April, and by a further 5% in October. However, junior army officers staged a brief strike in August, demanding the 'necessary means' to fulfil their duties. In November cadets who had been dismissed from the gendarmerie following a strike prompted by the delayed payment of arrears seized weapons and erected barricades in Bamako: one person was killed, and about 300 cadets were arrested.

Persistent rumours of divisions within ADEMA were apparently confirmed in September 1994, when the election of Keita to the party presidency precipitated the resignation of prominent figures, including Mohamed Lamine Traoré and the secretary-general, Mouhamedou Dicko, from the governing party. Former members of ADEMA formed the Mouvement pour l'indépendance, la renaissance et l'intégration africaines in December. In January 1995 an application for legalization by the UDPM was rejected by the supreme court (an earlier application had been disallowed in 1993). However, the Mouvement patriotique pour le renouveau (MPR), established by several of those who had sought to revive the UDPM, was granted official status later in the month. A split was reported in the CNID in March 1995, when several members of the party's executive, alleging excessive dominance by Tall, formed a 'breakaway' movement; this was registered in September as the Parti pour le renouveau national (PARENA), led by Yoro Diakité and Tiébilé Dramé. ADEMA and PARENA established a political alliance in February 1996, and Diakité and Dramé were appointed to the government in July.

There was renewed disruption in the education sector from November 1995. In early December 25 people, including two police-officers, were injured in clashes in Bamako between security forces and students (who had begun strike action to demand improved conditions of study and the payment of grants). The arrest, in early January 1996, of the students' union secretary-general and other activists provoked a further boycott, which ended in mid-January following an appeal by the union's deputy leader for the resumption of classes. The crisis prompted the CNID to table Mali's first ever parliamentary motion of 'no confidence' in the government, although this was overwhelmingly defeated.

The government adopted a new electoral code in mid-August 1996, introducing a system of proportional representation for municipal elections and a semi-proportional basis for elections to the national assembly. Independent candidates were to be disallowed at parliamentary elections. It was also decided that the Commission électorale nationale indépendante (CENI), to be responsible for overseeing the 1997 presidential, legislative and municipal elections, should include among its 30 members five representatives of the majority party and five members to represent the political opposition. The draft code was condemned by the opposition as being unduly favourable to ADEMA's interests. The code was adopted by the national assembly in late September 1996, in a vote boycotted by opposition deputies.

However, certain clauses were subsequently deemed by the constitutional court to be incompatible with the constitution. Following consultations with opposition groups, the government adopted a revised code at the beginning of December, and this was approved by the legislature in early January 1997. Deputies grouped in the opposition Rassemblement des forces patriotiques (RFP) participated in the parliamentary debate, but did not vote on the amended code. The code restored the two-round system of majority voting for the legislative elections (as employed in 1992) and also allowed independent candidacies. The composition of the CENI was altered to comprise 14 representatives of political parties (seven for the majority party and seven for the opposition parties combined), together with eight representatives of the government and eight of what was termed the civic society. Deputies also approved an increase in the number of parliamentary seats from 129 to 147.

Meanwhile, in late October 1996 it was announced that a prominent member of the MPR and former minister under Traoré, Mady Diallo, had been arrested, together with several armed forces officers, following the discovery of a plot to assassinate Konaré, Keita and other government ministers. Diallo was later released, but was rearrested in early April 1997 upon his return from France, where he had been receiving medical treatment. (Another MPR official was arrested in late March 1997, in connection with his alleged involvement in a land speculation scandal while mayor of a Bamako district.)

Dates for the forthcoming elections were announced in mid-January 1997: the first round of legislative voting was to take place on 9 March (with a second round two weeks later), presidential voting was scheduled for 4 May (with a second round, should no candidate secure an overall majority, on 18 May), and municipal elections for 1 June. In mid-February, however, the CENI announced that it would be unable to organize the parliamentary elections according to this timetable, owing to legal, technical and financial difficulties. In late February the RFP tabled a parliamentary motion of 'no confidence' in the government, citing its failure to hold elections in accordance with legal deadlines: this was easily defeated. (The authorities, meanwhile, emphasized that all elections would have been completed by 8 June—the fifth anniversary of the inauguration of the organs of the third republic.)

The first round of the legislative election was subsequently reset for 13 April 1997, and, despite opposition demands for further postponement, voting proceeded accordingly. More than 1,500 candidates, mainly representing 36 of the country's 63 political parties, sought election to the enlarged national assembly. Considerable confusion was evident at polling stations, with a shortage of electoral materials compounded by anomalies and omissions in voting lists. As early results showed a clear victory for ADEMA, the main opposition parties condemned the results as fraudulent, and announced their intention to withdraw from the second round. A protest march was held in Bamako (in defiance of a government ban) to denounce the conduct of the elections and to demand the resignation of the government and disbandment of the CENI; 20 people (among them an opposition candidate for the presidency) were reported to have been injured as security forces intervened to disperse the protesters. The chairman of the CENI, Kassoum Tapo, admitted that there had been obvious organizational difficulties at the first round, but stated that the poll had been in no way fraudulent and appealed to the opposition to participate in the second round. Konaré and the government similarly acknowledged the problems, and urged that the electoral process continue. (Independent national and international monitors, for their part, recognized that the conduct of the poll had been flawed but not fraudulent.) However, the opposition parties confirmed that they would boycott the second round, and also withdraw their candidates from the presidential election and refuse to participate in the municipal elections. The results of voting, which indicated that ADEMA was the only party to have won any seats at the first round, were subject to confirmation by the constitutional court. On 25 April, following the expiry of the deadline for the submission of appeals, the court annulled the first round of voting. While welcoming the cancellation, the opposition none the less expressed its dissatisfaction that the results had been invalidated on the grounds of irregularities, rather than fraud.

Shortly after the invalidation of the results of legislative voting, the first round of the presidential election was postponed, by one week, until 11 May 1997. Launching his official re-election campaign at the end of April, Konaré emphasized that he had no wish to be the sole candidate. In early May Mamadou Maribatrou Diaby, the leader of the Parti pour l'unité, la démocratie et le progrès, announced that he was prepared to contest the presidency. However, the so-called radical opposition collective adhered to its demands for the cancellation of the ongoing electoral process, for the complete revision of the voters' register, and, in the mean time, for the resignation of the government and the appointment of a transitional administration. The constitutional court rejected a petition filed by the opposition candidates seeking the cancellation of the presidential poll, and voting proceeded on 11 May. A curfew had been imposed in the CNID stronghold of Ségou following disturbances there on the eve of the poll, but voting was reported to have taken place generally in an atmosphere of calm. The results of voting, published by the CENI five days after the poll, confirmed an overwhelming victory for the incumbent Konaré, with 84.36% of the votes, while Diaby took 3.57%. These results included votes cast for the eight boycotting opposition candidates, whose names were posted at polling centres, by order of the constitutional court, since they had not given formal notification of their withdrawal from the contest; the final results, as issued by the constitutional court on 24 May, excluded the votes for boycotting candidates, and thus allocated 95.90% of the valid votes cast to Konaré and 4.10% to Diaby. The radical opposition expressed satisfaction at the success of its campaign for a boycott of the election, stating that the low rate of participation by voters, at 28.4% of the registered electorate, effectively invalidated Konaré's victory. (The turnout was, none the less, higher than that recorded at the 1992 election.) International observers, meanwhile, expressed satisfaction at the fair conduct of the poll.

The political climate deteriorated further following the presidential election, as the radical opposition, refusing to recognize the legitimacy of Konaré's second mandate, resisted the president's attempts at reconciliation. At the end of May 1997 the municipal elections, which the opposition had been intending to boycott, were postponed indefinitely. On 8 June, the day of Konaré's investiture, there were violent disturbances in Bamako, and Tall, Almany Sylla (the RDP chairman and leader of the opposition collective) and Sogal Maïga (the MPR secretary-general) were among five opposition leaders arrested and charged with 'non-recognition of the results of the presidential election' and with opposition to state authority, as well as with arson and incitement to violence. Shortly afterwards several opposition activists were sentenced to three months' imprisonment for their part in recent disturbances. The opposition collective condemned the detentions, denying any involvement in acts of violence or vandalism and stating that the arrests, which were in violation of constitutional guarantees of the right to demonstrate and to hold public gatherings, were intended by the authorities to distract attention from the issue of the holding of free and fair elections. The opposition leaders were released on bail in mid-June, shortly after the first round of the legislative elections, due on 6 July, had been postponed by two weeks. A small number of opposition parties had recently announced their intention to present candidates for the national assembly. However, 18 opposition parties, whose collective embraced the broadest political spectrum, linking the late president Keita's US–RDA with the MPR (the effective successor to Moussa Traoré's UDPM) and the CNID (which had, together with ADEMA, led the opposition to Traoré's one-party state), reiterated their refusal to re-enter the electoral process unless their demands were met in full.

Two people were reported to have been killed in violence in San on the eve of legislative voting, and there were violent disturbances in Bamako and elsewhere, as a result of which, according to opposition claims, some 40 people were injured and 50 arrests were made. Voting proceeded on 20 July 1997: a total of 17 parties (including five 'moderate' opposition parties), as well as small number of independent candidates, contested seats in the national assembly. As at the presidential election, the radical opposition claimed that its appeal to the electorate to boycott the poll had been successful, and that the low rate of participation by voters would render the assembly illegitimate.

The results of voting were released by the CENI four days after the poll and validated by the constitutional court at the end of the month, confirming an overwhelming victory for ADEMA. A second round of voting was held for eight seats on 3 August. The final results allocated 130 seats to ADEMA (including one seat won in alliance with the Convention patriotique pour le progrès), eight to PARENA, four to the Convention démocratique et sociale, three to the Union pour la démocratie et le développement and two to the PDP. Both rounds of legislative voting were stated by international monitors to have been conducted fairly. Later in August several prominent opposition figures were arrested (and subsequently transferred to detention centres far from the capital), following the lynching of a police-officer at an opposition rally; three of the detainees were receiving medical treatment by the end of the month, having undertaken a hunger strike. It was reported at this time that Konaré was prepared to concede the allocation of public funds to opposition parties, acknowledging that ADEMA was disproportionately advantaged by the prevailing system, while the ruling party strong disapproved of the president's relatively conciliatory approach towards the radical opposition. Neither Konaré nor ADEMA, meanwhile, appeared willing to compromise on the issue of the legitimacy of the recently-elected institutions, a key element of the collective's demands. A new government was appointed under Keita in mid-September, including several members of the 'moderate' opposition.

ETHNIC TENSIONS

Ethnic violence emerged in the north in mid-1990, as large numbers of light-skinned Tuaregs, who had migrated to Algeria and Libya during periods of drought, began to return to Mali and Niger (q.v.). In July of that year the Traoré government, which claimed that Tuareg rebels were attempting to establish a secessionist state, imposed a state of emergency in the Gao and Tombouctou regions, and the armed forces began a repressive campaign against the nomads. An effort to restore calm was made in September, when the heads of state of Algeria, Libya, Mali and Niger agreed measures governing border controls and facilitating the return of refugees to their region of origin. In the same month the Malian government announced that a new administrative region was to be established in the north-eastern Kidal area. In January 1991 representatives of the Traoré government and of two Tuareg groups, the Mouvement populaire de l'Azaouad (MPA) and the Front islamique-arabe de l'Azaouad (FIAA), meeting in Tamanrasset, Algeria, signed a peace accord: there was to be an immediate cease-fire, and the state of emergency was revoked. Tuareg military prisoners were released in March.

Following the overthrow of the Traoré regime, the transitional administration affirmed its commitment to the Tamanrasset accord, and representatives of the Tuaregs were included in the CTSP. However, unrest continued in the north, and in June 1991 a prominent human rights organization, Amnesty International, reported incidences of the harsh repression of Tuaregs by the armed forces. Thousands of Tuaregs, Moors and Bella (the descendants of the Tuaregs' black slaves, some of whom remained with the nomads), had fled to neighbouring countries to escape retaliatory attacks by the armed forces and the sedentary black population, while there had been many casualties in the Malian armed forces.

During the second half of 1991 the MPA was reported to have lost the support of more militant members, and a further group, the Front populaire de libération de l'Azaouad (FPLA), emerged to claim responsibility for several attacks. In December a 'special conference on the north' was convened in Mopti. With Algerian mediation, representatives of the transitional government and of four Tuareg groups—the MPA, the FIAA, the FPLA and the Armée révolutionnaire de libération de l'Azaouad (ARLA)—agreed in principle to a peace settlement. Negotiations resumed in the Algerian capital in January 1992, at which the Malian authorities and the MPA, the FIAA and the ARLA (now negotiating together as the Mouvements et fronts unifiés de l'Azaouad—MFUA) formally agreed to implement the Mopti accord; the FPLA was reported not to have attended the Algiers sessions. A truce entered into force in February, and a commission of inquiry was inaugurated in Gao shortly afterwards to examine acts of violence perpetrated and losses suffered in areas affected by the conflict. Further talks in Algiers culminated, in March, in the drafting of a 'national pact', which was signed in Bamako by the Malian authorities and the MFUA on 11 April. In addition to the provisions of the Mopti accord, the pact envisaged special administrative structures for the country's three northern regions, the incorporation of Tuareg fighters into the Malian armed forces, the demilitarization of the north and the instigation of efforts more fully to integrate Tuaregs in the economic and political fields.

Sporadic attacks, particularly against members of the northern majority Songhai, continued. None the less, the implementation of the 'national pact' was pursued, and in October 1992 representatives of the government and the national assembly attended an MFUA congress at Taouardeï. Joint patrols were established, and Konaré visited the north in November to inaugurate the new administrative structures. In February 1993 the Malian government and the MFUA signed an accord facilitating the integration of an initial 600 Tuaregs into the national army. In May the FPLA's secretary-general, Rhissa Ag Sidi Mohamed, declared the rebellion at an end and returned to Mali (from his base in Burkina Faso), urging FPLA fighters to participate in the pact. During the second half of 1993, however, Tuareg leaders expressed concern that difficulties in repatriating refugees and in the implementation of the 'national pact' were the cause of renewed attacks in the north. Indications of a breakdown in security were apparently confirmed in February 1994 by the assassination, allegedly by members of the ARLA, of the MPLA's military leader (a principal architect of the peace process, who had joined the Malian army under the 'national pact'). Clashes between the MPA and the ARLA continued for several weeks before the two groups were reconciled.

In May 1994, at a meeting in Algiers, agreement was reached by the Malian government and the MFUA regarding the integration of 1,500 former rebels into the regular army and of a further 4,860 Tuaregs into civilian sectors; the MFUA undertook to dismantle its military bases in the north, while the government reaffirmed its commitment to the pursuit of development projects in northern areas. The agreement was, however, undermined by an intensification of clashes and acts of banditry in the north, and tensions between the 'integrated' Tuareg fighters and regular members of the Malian armed forces periodically escalated into violence. Meanwhile, a Songhai-dominated resistance movement, the Mouvement patriotique malien Ghanda Koy ('Masters of the Land'), emerged in the north, and there were rumours of official complicity in its actions against the Tuaregs.Violence continued, despite the stated commitment of the Malian government and the MFUA to the 'national pact': the adherence of the FIAA, in particular, was called into question after the death of one of its leaders, in June, as a result of a clash with members of the armed forces. Meeting in Tamanrasset later in the month, the Malian authorities and the MFUA agreed on the need for the reinforcement (initiated in previous weeks) of the army presence in areas affected by the violence, and for the more effective integration of Tuareg fighters. None the less, there was an escalation of violence in July, and in August a grenade attack took place on the home of a prominent Tuareg official in Bamako.

In August 1994 agreement was reached by Mali, Algeria, representatives of the UN High Commissioner for Refugees (UNHCR) and the International Fund for Agricultural Development regarding the voluntary repatriation from Algeria of Malian refugees. The accord, whereby the Malian authorities undertook to protect the fundamental rights and dignity of the Tuaregs, and which guaranteed international protection for Tuareg refugees, was welcomed by the Tuaregs: at a meeting in Tamanrasset, the MFUA pledged the reconciliation of the Tuareg movements and reiterated its commitment to the 'national pact'; however, the talks were not attended by representatives of the 'dissident' Tuaregs, and unrest continued. In September Amnesty International published a report expressing concern at the deaths of increasing numbers of civilians as a result of the conflict, and denouncing what it termed a cycle of violence as a result of which attacks by armed Tuareg and Moorish groups were followed by retaliatory attacks by the Malian armed forces on light-skinned civilians. Hostilities intensified, and in October, following an attack (for which the FIAA claimed responsibility) on Gao and retaliatory action, as a result of which, according to official figures, 66 people were killed, both the government and the MFUA appealed for an end to the violence.

Following the appointment of a new minister of the armed forces and veterans, shortly after the Gao attack, the authorities were widely regarded as having adopted a less conciliatory approach towards the Tuareg rebels, and in subsequent weeks the army announced the capture of several rebel bases. The FIAA appeared increasingly marginalized in the peace process: the Algerian-based FIAA leader, Zahabi Ould Sidi Mohamed (held by the Malian government to be personally responsible for endangering the 'national pact') protested in late 1994 that the Algerian authorities were co-operating with Mali in preventing him from travelling to Belgium to attend a debate at the European parliament on the Tuareg issue. (The session was attended by representatives of the MFUA and by a Malian parliamentary delegation.)

In January 1995 representatives of the FPLA and Ghanda Koy, meeting in Bourem, issued a joint statement appealing for an end to hostilities in the north, and for the implementation of the 'national pact'. Shortly afterwards Zahabi Ould Sidi Mohamed asserted that the FIAA was willing to co-operate with the government and with other Tuareg groups in the restoration of peace. Further discussions involving Tuareg groups, Ghanda Koy and representatives of local communities took place in the north in subsequent weeks, and, following a meeting in Aghlal, in the Mopti region, in April, an agreement was signed providing for joint co-operation in resolving hitherto contentious issues. In May the Malian authorities began a month-long programme aimed at promoting reconciliation and awareness of the peace process, whereby three ministerial delegations, including representatives of the organs of state, the MFUA and Ghanda Koy, toured firstly the northern regions and then refugee areas in Algeria, Burkina and Mauritania. Konaré also visited those countries, and made direct appeals to refugees to return to participate in the process of reconstruction in the north. In June the FIAA unilaterally announced an end to its armed struggle, and expressed its willingness to join national reconciliation efforts.

As part of the programme of 'normalization' in the north, initiatives were undertaken in mid-1995 to restore civilian local government to areas affected by the conflict, as well as education and health-care facilities and basic utilities. In July representatives of the government and of Mali's creditors met at Tombouctou, where they agreed medium- and long-term development strategies for the northern regions; the MFUA and Ghanda Koy issued a joint statement in support of the decisions taken at the conference. Later in the month an official ceremony was held in Bamako to mark the restoration of local government in the north.

By mid-February 1996 some 3,000 MFUA fighters and Ghanda Koy militiamen had registered and surrendered their weapons at designated centres in the north, under an encampment programme initiated in November 1995 in preparation for the eventual integration of former rebels into the regular army or civilian structures. A ceremonial burning of the surrendered weapons, symbolizing the definitive end to the conflict in northern Mali, took place in Tombouctou on 27 March 1996, in the presence of Konaré and President Jerry Rawlings of Ghana; the ceremony was also attended by representatives of the former rebels and by Mali's political, civic and religious dignitaries, members of the diplomatic community and representatives of international organizations. Prior to the ceremony the MFUA and Ghanda Koy had issued a joint statement affirming their adherence to Mali's constitution, national unity and territorial integrity, and advocating the full implementation of the 'national pact' and associated accords. They proclaimed, moreover, the 'irreversible dissolution' of their respective movements.

The persistence of insecurity in the north after 1992 had undermined attempts to repatriate refugees, as envisaged in the 'national pact' and provided for in agreements with neighbouring countries where refugees were sheltering: the escalation of violence in 1994 was reported to have prompted as many as 160,000 people, many of whom had returned to Mali following the signing of the pact, once again to cross into neighbouring countries. During 1995–96, however, significant numbers of refugees were reported to be returning voluntarily to Mali. From mid-1995 such returns were accompanied by repatriations of smaller numbers under UNHCR supervision from Algeria (where there was a total of some 35,000 refugees in October 1995) and Mauritania (although food shortages in refugee camps there in early 1996 were reportedly jeopardizing programmes for the organized return of some 34,000 people). Refugees in Burkina (numbering some 50,000 in mid-1995) were also preparing to return. Konaré toured these countries again in March 1996, urging refugees to return. In November of that year Mali, Niger and UNHCR signed an agreement for the repatriation of 25,000 Malian Tuaregs from Niger; the agreement defined the obligations and responsibilities of its signatories with regard to the voluntary return 'with dignity' of the refugees.

EXTERNAL RELATIONS

In September 1983 the governments of Mali and Upper Volta (now Burkina Faso) agreed to refer their long-standing boundary dispute over the the reputedly mineral-rich Agacher strip to the International Court of Justice (ICJ) for adjudication. In addition, Upper Volta withdrew its opposition to the re-admission of Mali to the Franc Zone and the Union monétaire ouest-africaine, which was finally achieved in 1984. (The CFA franc was reintroduced as Mali's unit of currency in that year.) On 25 December 1985, however, the dispute between Mali and Burkina, compounded by ideological differences, suddenly escalated into armed conflict, resulting in the six-day 'Christmas war'. During this brief conflict, Malian forces demonstrated their military superiority, but both sides were willing to submit to a cease-fire, agreed on 31 December (see the Recent History of Burkina Faso). Throughout 1986 there was a gradual reconciliation with Burkina: prisoners were exchanged in February, and full diplomatic relations, which had been broken off in 1974, were restored in June. A ruling by the ICJ in December awarded Mali sovereignty over the western part of the Agacher strip, comprising about one-half of the disputed area. Both countries expressed satisfaction with this adjudication.

In recent years the presence in neighbouring countries of large numbers of refugees from the conflict in northern Mali, and the attendant issue of border security, has dominated Mali's regional relations. In addition to the refugees in Algeria, Burkina, Mauritania and Niger, some 10,000 Tuaregs were, according to some reports, members of the Libyan armed forces in the mid-1990s. (Zahabi Ould Sidi Mohamed attributed the FIAA's decision to observe a truce, from June 1995, not only to the success of reconciliation efforts already undertaken by the Malian authorities but also to intervention by the Libyan leader, Col Qaddafi.)

The government of France, which had notably extended no military support to the Traoré regime as the influence of the Malian opposition movement increased, granted financial support for the recovery efforts that were necessary after March 1991, and promised continued aid for Mali's programme of economic adjustment. French financial assistance was also forthcoming for the implementation of the national pact between the Malian government and Tuareg leaders. None the less, the Konaré regime has sought to develop what it considers a more equal relationship with its former colonial ruler. In July 1995 Konaré refused to travel to Senegal for informal discussions with Chirac, asserting that Chirac's itinerary, which involved visits to Côte d'Ivoire, Gabon and Senegal (to where regional heads of state were invited to attend a series of talks), indicated that a hierarchy existed in France's relations with its former colonies. From mid-1996, moreover, a series of much-publicized expulsions from France of illegal immigrants, among them many Malians, was generally criticized in Mali, with the process of repatriation by chartered aircraft being condemned by the Konaré administration as a violation of basic dignity. The issue of the expulsions and the resettlement of those migrants returned to Mali was the main focus of bilateral contacts during the second half of 1996. A regional forum was held in Kayes, in western Mali, in January 1997. (The Kayes region, from where most migrants originate, is one of the country's poorest regions.) Some 500 delegates, representing Mali's central and regional administrations, local civic groups, external official donors and non-governmental organizations, as well as migrants' organizations, adopted a programme to develop the region and alleviate its isolation from the rest of the country; France and the European Union were to be principal contributors to its projects.

During his first term in office President Konaré regarded the development of a wider international role for Mali as a priority in foreign policy. Mali has, notably, contributed actively to UN peace-keeping forces, and in October 1996 (following a visit to Mali by the US secretary of state, Warren Christopher) responded positively to US proposals for the establishment of an African military crisis-response force. In the following month Mali expressed willingness to contribute to an African intervention force for the Great Lakes region, and Konaré denounced what he termed the indifference of other African countries with regard to the crisis in eastern Zaire. In late 1996 and early 1997, moreover, Amadou Toumani Touré, who had recently been active in a number of conflict-resolution initiatives undertaken by the US-based Carter Center, led a regional mediation effort to resolve the crisis in the Central African Republic (CAR), and in February 1997 a Malian military contingent was dispatched to the CAR as part of a regional surveillance mission. Mali was also to contribute troops to an enlarged ECOMOG peace-keeping force of the Economic Community of West African States.

Economy

EDITH HODGKINSON

Revised for this edition by ANDREW MANLEY

Mali, the second largest country in francophone west Africa, is sparsely populated (with a density of about 9 inhabitants per sq km at mid-1995) and land-locked, and most parts are desert or semi-desert, with the economically viable area confined to the Sahelian-Sudanese regions irrigated by the River Niger, which comprise about one-fifth of the total land area. The rate of economic growth in recent decades has been affected by drought, changes in the terms of international trade, as well as political upheaval. There have thus been wide fluctuations in trends in gross domestic product (GDP) from year to year, although overall GDP increased at an average rate of 4.9% per year in the 1970s and 2.5% in 1980–91. Progress was particularly erratic in the early 1990s: GDP stagnated in 1991, as political upheaval and difficulties in the agricultural sector depressed the economy. There was renewed growth, of 8.4%, in 1992, with the reflation of the economy assisted by strong expansion in cotton output. GDP declined in 1993, largely owing to the economic paralysis prior to the devaluation of the CFA franc and to pressure from the IMF for fiscal restraint. The stimulus to the agricultural sector as a result of the 50% devaluation of the currency in January 1994 coincided with a strong rise in world commodity prices in that year. Growth of 2.3% in 1994 progressed to 6.4% in 1995, as the agricultural sector prospered, investment in infrastructure stimulated the services sector, and fiscal pressures began to ease. The recovery continued in 1996, with growth again forecast at 6%. With the prospect of futher expansion in exports of cotton (which have recently accounted for about one-half of total export earnings) and gold (as new capacity comes into production), the economy could show steady growth over the rest of the decade. None the less, Mali remains among the world's poorest countries, with gross national product (GNP) per head equivalent to only some US $250m. in 1995, and it remains both highly vulnerable to external shocks and highly dependent on external funds.

Mali's population, which was 7,696,348 at the census of April 1987, is (according to official figures) increasing at a rate of about 2% per year (relatively low because of emigration), and was officially estimated to be some 9m. in 1994. Estimates vary, however: the World Bank estimates a total of 9.8m. in 1995, while the UN mid-year estimate for 1995 was 10.8m. About 5% of the population are nomadic, and 25% urban, with the only significant agglomerations at the capital, Bamako, and the regional capitals. Persistent drought conditions throughout the Sahelian region during the 1970s and early 1980s drew a significant part of the nomadic population to the settled areas, with the result that parts of the Gao and Tombouctou (Timbuktu) regions are now deserted. The conflict between government and Tuareg forces in the first half of the 1990s reinforced this trend, with many thousands seeking refuge in neighbouring countries, although the restoration of peace has resulted in the return of large numbers of refugees.

In the absence of strong economic growth or structural change, employment patterns have changed little since independence. In 1995 more than 80% of the total labour force were estimated to be engaged in agriculture, largely at subsistence level, compared with 90% in 1965. Among these, there is significant seasonal migration (during the agricultural off-season) to Côte d'Ivoire and Senegal, and a total of some 3m. Malians are thought to work abroad, with France also an important host country. Wage employment is very low, and is concentrated in the state sector and in formal-sector businesses in Bamako.

AGRICULTURE

Agricultural production has been affected by periods of severe drought, institutional failings and low prices for producers. The sector accounted for an estimated 44% of GDP in 1995 (compared with about two-thirds in the early 1960s). It is an artisanal activity, with minimal mechanization. Millet and sorghum—two basic food crops—are essentially produced at subsistence level. Output of cereals was badly affected by the droughts of the early 1970s and early 1980s: production of millet, sorghum and maize, which had been 1.3m. metric tons in 1976/77, declined to less than one-half of this level in 1984/85, while that of rice, at 103,400 tons in that year, continued to be substantially below earlier levels. The cereals deficit consequently reached 481,000 tons in 1985, about one-half of which was covered by food aid. Since then there has been an upturn, largely the consequence of the return of adequate rainfall in the late 1980s, and exportable surpluses were recorded in both 1989/90 and in 1994/95. In the latter year output of millet, sorghum and maize together reached a record 1,966,300 tons, and that of rice an unprecedented 469,100 tons. Estimates for 1995/96 were slightly lower, with output of millet, sorghum and maize at 1,699,300 tons, and rice at 458,400 tons. An important factor in the improvement in rice production has been the reform of the parastatal Office du Niger. This agency was originally established by the French colonial authorities to irrigate the Niger delta, mainly for the cultivation of cotton. For many years the agency operated at a substantial financial loss, with about one-third of its irrigated area remaining uncultivated. In 1986 a rehabilitation programme was initiated which aimed to rationalize the organization's management and to increase the total cultivable area to more than 100,000 ha, of which 46,730 ha were to be planted with rice. The restructuring of the Office was largely completed by 1994. In 1988 a programme was inaugurated to improve the irrigation network for the cultivation of rice both on the Office du Niger land and in the inland delta of the Niger in the Ségou region. Yields of rice remained low until the mid-1990s (largely owing to poor levels of rainfall), although yields exceeded 5 tons/ha in 1996.

By far the most important cash crop is cotton, and this dominates the agricultural sector. Mali is easily the leading producer in the Franc Zone and ranks second only to Egypt on the African continent. Production is in the southern region, by means of village co-operatives co-ordinated by the parastatal Cie Malienne pour le développement des textiles (CMDT). After suffering from the droughts of the 1970s and early 1980s output increased very strongly, to reach 367,000 tons (320,000 tons marketed) in 1992/93. It then eased back somewhat, to average some 270,000 tons per year in 1993/94 and 1994/95, before the 47% rise in the producer price following the 1994 devaluation of the CFA franc, in conjunction with strong international prices, and the connected expansion of the area cultivated, boosted output to 406,000 tons in 1995/96. A further sharp expansion was recorded in 1996/97, to a provisional 468,000 tons, aided by increased growth in the west of the country.

Groundnut production, which had reached a high point of 205,000 tons in 1975/76, saw a steep decline in the early 1980s, but recovered over the following decade, attaining a new record of 215,160 tons in 1994/95. However, many growers switched to cotton production in the following season, resulting in a decline in the groundnut harvest in 1995/96, to 147,000 tons. Production is mainly for domestic consumption.

Livestock-raising accounts for about one-half of the agricultural sector's contribution to GDP, and is the principal economic activity in the north. After cotton, livestock currently represents Mali's second highest recorded export (although gold will soon vie for this position), and large numbers of live animals are smuggled across the country's borders. Livestock numbers fell during the droughts of the 1970s and early 1980s (the last is thought to have caused the deaths of 40%–80% of the national herd). None the less, at an estimated 5.5m. cattle and 12.55m. sheep and goats in 1995, Mali's herd remains by far the largest in francophone west Africa. The drought also tended to move livestock-rearing from the north to the south, where it is geared towards export to Côte d'Ivoire and Ghana. This trade has received a strong stimulus from the currency's devaluation.

Fishing on the Niger produces an annual catch of about 65,000 tons (although this was doubled in 1995); however, the sector is very vulnerable to drought, to the effects of large-scale dam building on the upper reaches of the river, and to pollution from urban centres.

MINING AND POWER

Deposits of bauxite, copper, iron ore, manganese and uranium have been located but not yet exploited, largely because of the country's land-locked position and lack of infrastructure. Marble is mined at Bafoulabé, and phosphate rock at Gao, but by far the most important mineral currently being exploited is gold, while there are high hopes for the development of diamond reserves. After considerable delay, production at the Kalana gold deposit began in 1985, supported by credits from the USSR. Planned capacity was 2,000 kg per year, but official output averaged only 400 kg per year in 1985–90. Exploitation of the reserves was suspended in 1992, amid rumours that much of the production had bypassed official channels under the Traoré regime. Syama, in the south—the first post-Traoré mining venture—was established by a consortium led by BHP-Utah (which took 65% of the shares). Although gold production reached 6,200 kg in 1995, BHP sold its interest to Randgold of South Africa in mid-1996, citing operational difficulties and Syama's incompatibility with BHP's global corporate strategy. Randgold has since increased its stake to 75%. Mali's largest gold-mining project, Sadiola Hill, is a joint venture between the Canadian operator Iamgold and South Africa's De Beers offshoot, Anglo American. The deposit is expected to produce 10,000 kg annually from 1997 (the first year of commercial output) to 2005, with some of the lowest operating costs in the world despite the lack of mining infrastructure in the Kayes region. Kalana was acquired in 1996 by a consortium including Ghana's Ashanti Goldfields, although industry sentiment is divided as to whether this was a worthwhile purchase. Other Australian, South African and (especially) Canadian companies are active in exploration. A joint venture between Canada's Mink Minerals and Ashton Pty of Australia is investigating kimberlite pipes in the Kéniéba area of the south-west, in the hope of lucrative diamond finds.

About 80% of the 310m. kWh of electricity generated in 1995 were hydroelectric in origin, provided by the Selingué facility on the Sankarani river. The proportion is scheduled to rise as a second dam is constructed on the river, at Koruba, and as the Manantali project on the Senegal river begins production. The operation of the last is to be supervised by the Organisation pour la mise en valeur du fleuve Sénégal, in which both Mauritania and Senegal participate. Mali is to receive 52% of the annual output of the hydroelectric plant (projected at 800m. kWh). Construction of the dam was completed in 1988, but the installation of generating equipment was delayed by disagreements over supply routes, as well as the deterioration in relations between Mauritania and Senegal in 1989–90, with the effect that the dam was not formally inaugurated until 1992. After further problems with funding and cross-border arrangements, Manantali is now expected to come into operation in 2000, when Mali's network is to be linked to the Ivorian national grid, via a line from the north of Côte d'Ivoire to the Syama gold-mine and thence to Selingué. In the mean time, much of the country's energy demand is met by fuel wood and charcoal, which has resulted in considerable deforestation.

MANUFACTURING

Manufacturing activity, largely directed to meet local demand, is concentrated in Bamako, mainly taking the form of agricultural processing and the manufacture of consumer goods. Manufacturing contributed some 6% of GDP in 1995. The incomplete statistics available suggest general stagnation in industry throughout the 1970s and much of the 1980s, with several agricultural processing plants (particularly oilseed-crushing mills) operating well below capacity owing to a lack of supply. Smuggling of cheaper goods from Nigeria (while the CFA franc remained overvalued) and competition from the more developed manufacturing companies in Côte d'Ivoire also depressed the sector. During the mid-1980s more than 75% of industrial turnover was accounted for by state companies, which operated nine of the 12 major food sector plants—a legacy of the Keita era. The 40 parastatal bodies generally proved to be inefficient and unprofitable. Following the failure of successive governments to improve its performance, the sector is now being reorganized, under pressure from the IMF and other foreign creditors, with full or part-ownership in 30 of the companies to be sold. The remainder are being either liquidated or tendered to foreign management.

TRANSPORT

The first years of the 1960s saw very substantial investment (one-fifth of total planned investment spending) in road-building, after the dissolution of the short-lived federation with Senegal in 1960, followed by Mali's withdrawal from the Franc Zone in 1962, disrupted traditional trading outlets. However, road communications remain poor: of some 15,000 km of classified roads, only about one-third are all-weather roads. Mali's main access to the sea is via the Bamako–Abidjan (Côte d'Ivoire) road. The 575-km all-weather road between Sévaré and Gao, which was opened in 1987, forms part of the Trans-Sahara Highway connecting Algeria with Nigeria. A major programme for the modernization of the transport infrastructure, in progress in the mid-1990s, aims to restore 3,000 km of roads (including the vital link between Mabako and Sévaré) and also part of the very dilapidated 1,286-km rail link from Bamako to Dakar (Senegal). The state-owned Régie du chemin de fer du Mali is seeking private capital. Owing to the inadequacy of the road and rail facilities, the country's inland waterways are of great importance to the transport infrastructure. The River Niger is used for bulk transport during the rainy season, while traffic on the Senegal is expected to improve as a result of the completion of the Manantali hydro-project, which should stabilize the water level and facilitate uninterrupted access to the sea. There are, however, serious environmental concerns regarding this project.

FINANCE

Mali adopted a very ambitious capital spending programme at independence, and state companies were established to operate the main sectors of the economy (including foreign trade, transport and mineral exploration). In the event, the bureaucratic superstructure became highly developed—administrative spending rose by an average 11%–12% per year in 1959–68, while the economy grew by a small fraction of this rate. Most state enterprises were operating at a loss. The simultaneous, and related, deterioration in the payments situation led Mali in 1967 to seek to rejoin the Franc Zone and the Union monétaire ouest-africaine (UMOA), from which it had withdrawn in 1962.

The conditions of the agreement providing for such a reintegration included a reduction in the activities of state enterprises and a 'freeze' on wages, to reduce the budget deficit. These measures undoubtedly contributed to the downfall of the Keita regime in 1968. (The final stage in the return to financial integration with other francophone countries of the region came in 1984, when Mali rejoined UMOA and readopted the CFA franc as its currency.) The recovery programme to cover the period 1970–73, drawn up with French advice, provided for a reduction in infrastructure and social investment, the dismantling of co-operatives, the abandonment of mineral exploration, and the winding up of some state industries. The budget deficit in fact continued, and French subsidies were substantially in excess of the agreed upper limit, as any serious reduction in spending would have alienated the large and influential bureaucracy.

The military government that came to power in November 1968 initially pursued Modibo Keita's economic policies. Beginning in 1981, however, the Traoré government, under pressure from the IMF, the World Bank and bilateral donors, undertook a programme of economic reform. Adjustment measures included the ending of state monopolies, the restructuring or transfer to private ownership of parastatal organizations, the liberalization of the marketing of agricultural products and the easing of price controls. One objective of these measures was to curtail budgetary expenditure. However, the budget deficit remained at a high level, with revenues depressed by the weak foreign trade performance (in 1985) and the sharp decline in world cotton prices (in 1986). The deficit was reduced in 1987, as Mali failed to fulfil its debt-servicing obligations, but increased again in 1988 and 1989, as some debt arrears were paid off in order to secure the resumption of IMF funding: the shortfall thus reached a record 62,100m. francs CFA (after grants) in 1989 (equivalent to 9.5% of GDP). The budget deficit was then brought down to less than one-half of this level by 1991, higher tax revenue in conjunction with a decline in current expenditure (as employment in the civil service was rationalized and the functions of the state agricultural produce boards were scaled down). Compliance with the adjustment programme agreed with the IMF and the World Bank was essential if Mali was to secure the external funds, mostly in the form of grants, needed for the budget. In 1991, for example, grants constituted one-third of total budgetary revenue. However, the unpopularity of the austerity programme, particularly as it affected employment among graduates, contributed to the downfall of President Traoré in March 1991. The new administration recognized none the less that there was no feasible alternative to complete acceptance of IMF-prescribed policies, and the deficit was held at a level similar to the 1990–91 average in 1992 and 1993 essentially by means of cuts in expenditure. However, there was little improvement in the tax regime, and overall fiscal performance was therefore deemed inadequate by the IMF and the World Bank, which suspended all assistance to Mali in October 1993.

Negotiations with the Bretton Woods institutions resumed following the 50% devaluation, in January 1994, of the CFA franc. The World Bank and the IMF agreed, respectively, to provide 157,000m. and 50,000m. francs CFA in budgetary support for 1994–96, thereby allowing the government to establish a special fund to assist those social groups most severely affected by the devaluation, to increase public-sector salaries and to raise the official minimum wage. Reflecting the increase in spending obligations, the 1994 budget recorded a much higher deficit, at 73,100m. francs CFA (after grants). Allowing for currency depreciation, this represented a real increase of about one-sixth. If external grants are excluded, the deficit was 141,200m. francs CFA, equivalent to 13.7% of GDP. In 1995 this ratio declined to 10.5% (129,000m. francs CFA), through a moderate fall in spending and a slight improvement in tax receipts. After grants, the deficit was 50,700m. francs CFA, equivalent to 4.1% of GDP. The programme agreed with the IMF in early 1996, to secure its continued financial support under the enhanced structural adjustment facility (ESAF) for the following three years, provided for further progress along these lines, with the fiscal deficit to narrow gradually to 7.7% of GDP by 1998. In early 1997 the IMF declared itself satisfied with budgetary performance (with a fiscal deficit estimated at 7.9% of GDP) in the previous year. The budget for 1997 envisaged a deficit of 8.8% of GDP, in some part due to the cost of that year's elections. This figure exemplifies Mali's continuing reliance on foreign grants to compensate for its budgetary shortfall.

FOREIGN TRADE AND PAYMENTS

Mali's trade balance is in chronic deficit, although there has been an overall improvement since the early 1970s, when exports typically represented only one-half of the value of imports. However, Mali's trade deficit remained high, as the two rounds of increases in international petroleum prices (in 1973–74 and 1979–80) and the impact of drought on cereals production necessitated increased spending on imports. By 1985 the trade deficit (a record US $152m.) was equivalent to 86.5% of the value of merchandise exports. Significantly lower deficits, averaging some $96m., were recorded annually in 1986–91, as rising sales of gold and an increase in the volume of cotton exports helped to offset weaknesses in international prices for these commodities while imports showed only modest growth. The balance deteriorated once again in 1992, to a deficit of $149m., as exports declined and imports rose, although the situation was somewhat better in 1993 (when the deficit was $105m.). Devaluation had a beneficial impact on the trade balance, lowering the deficit to $102m. in 1994 and probably to some $80m. (according to the Franc Zone secretariat of the Banque de France) in 1995. Export earnings have been boosted by the sharp increase in cotton production (in response to much higher local prices), by higher demand from Côte d'Ivoire for Malian livestock, and by enhanced gold production. Import spending, meanwhile, has been contained as a result of higher prices and improved domestic food supply.

There are two important offsets to the trade deficit, namely aid inflows and emigrants' remittances. The latter averaged about US $85m. annually in 1992–95, according to Franc Zone secretariat figures. Aid inflows are substantially higher, averaging some $450m. per year in 1991–95, equivalent to about one-fifth of GNP. France, in particular, has maintained a high level of support for the structural adjustment programme, in the form of budgetary grants as well as loans for specific projects and programmes. Because of the high grant element in the development assistance that Mali receives, its debt-servicing payments had, until the mid-1980s, remained low—8.3% of total foreign earnings in 1983. However, the drought of 1983–85 necessitated a rapid increase in external borrowing, from $879m. at the end of 1982 (equivalent to less than 75% of GNP) to $1,468m. by the end of 1985 (120% of GNP in that year). Despite the cancellation of significant amounts of bilateral debt during this period, and the increasingly concessional nature of inflows, the burden of servicing the debt rose substantially, owing to the decline in international prices for cotton. In the absence, after 1986, of a formal agreement with the IMF, there were no formal debt-relief concessions. Thus, as the external debt continued to accumulate (reaching $2,040m. by the end of 1988), so did arrears on the servicing of the debt. In October 1988, however, following agreement with the IMF on a programme of economic adjustment, Mali became the first debtor country to benefit from a system of exceptional debt-relief that had been agreed in principle at that year's summit meeting of industrialized nations, held in Toronto, Canada, which made provision for preferential debt-relief for countries with persistent debt-servicing difficulties. In addition, Mali was one of the world's 35 poorest countries whose official debt to France was cancelled at the beginning of 1990 (when Mali's debt of $240m. to that country was forgiven). None the less, the external debt, which had risen again, to $2,618m. by the end of 1991, continued to represent a substantial burden on this poor economy. The debt-service ratio in that year was reduced to a tolerable level—5.4%, from 11.5% in 1990—only because of the non-payment of some obligations. Thus there remained a continuing need for both debt relief and new funding, and the 'Paris Club' of Western official creditors agreed in November 1992 to a further round of rescheduling, on enhanced 'Toronto terms'. However, with debt at the end of 1993 equivalent to 100% of GNP, at $2,656m., Mali was a prime candidate for the special measures of debt-relief that followed the devaluation of the CFA franc in January 1994 (which had doubled the external debt in local currency terms). Major bilateral aid sources, led by France, thus cancelled a proportion of debt and rescheduled repayments. While cancellations meant that the foreign debt increased only modestly in 1994, to $2,796m., this was, owing to devaluation, equivalent to 153% of GNP, while the debt-service ratio increased almost fourfold, to 26.2%. None the less, Mali was now meeting its debt-servicing obligations in full, and it has continued to do so since. Total external debt stood at $3,066m. (of which as much as $500m. was owed to Russia) at the end of 1995, while the debt-service burden was alleviated to 12.2%. With Mali's economic performance continuing to be to the satisfaction of the IMF and the World Bank, and the securing of another three-year access to the ESAF in March 1996, further debt-relief was granted by the country's external creditors in May of that year, under the highly concessionary 'Naples terms', whereby two-thirds of eligible debt was cancelled. The strict guide-lines for the 'Naples terms', however, meant that relatively little debt fell into this category, and the net benefit to Mali is estimated to have been only $50m. Mali thus remains very much dependent on inflows of aid to underpin the government's budget and meet the funding requirement on the current account.

Statistical Survey

Source (unless otherwise stated): Direction de la Statistique et de l'Informatique, Ministère des Finances, BP 234, Koulouba, Bamako; tel. 22-56-87; telex 2559; fax 22-88-53.

Area and Population

AREA, POPULATION AND DENSITY

Area (sq km)	1,240,192*
Population (census results)†	
16 December 1976	6,394,918
1–30 April 1987	
Males	3,760,711
Females	3,935,637
Total	7,696,348
Population (UN estimates at mid-year)‡	
1993	10,135,000
1994	10,462,000
1995	10,795,000
Density (per sq km) at mid-1995	8.7

*478,841 sq miles.

† Figures refer to the *de jure* population.

‡ Source: UN, *World Population Prospects: The 1994 Revision.*

PRINCIPAL ETHNIC GROUPS (estimates, 1963)

Bambara	1,000,000	Malinke	200,000
Fulani	450,000	Tuareg	240,000
Marka	280,000	Sénoufo	375,000
Songhai	230,000	Dogon	130,000

ADMINISTRATIVE DIVISIONS (*de jure* population at 1987 census)

District			
Bamako	658,275		
Regions*			
Ségou	1,339,631	Kayes	1,067,007
Sikasso	1,310,810	Tombouctou	459,318
Mopti	1,282,617	Gao	380,722
Koulikoro	1,197,968		

* A new region, Kidal, was formally established in May 1991.

PRINCIPAL TOWNS (population at 1976 census)

Bamako (capital)	404,000	Sikasso	47,000
Ségou	65,000	Kayes	45,000
Mopti	54,000		

(population at 1987 census)

Bamako	658,275

BIRTHS AND DEATHS (UN estimates, annual averages)

	1980–85	1985–90	1990–95
Birth rate (per 1,000)	50.8	51.0	50.8
Death rate (per 1,000)	22.3	20.7	19.1

Expectation of life (UN estimates, years at birth, 1990–95): 46.0 (males 44.4; females 47.6).

Source: UN, *World Population Prospects: The 1994 Revision.*

ECONOMICALLY ACTIVE POPULATION

Mid-1995 (estimates in '000): Agriculture, etc. 4,496; Total 5,345.

Source: FAO, *Production Yearbook.*

Agriculture

PRINCIPAL CROPS ('000 metric tons)

	1993	1994	1995*
Millet, sorghum and fonio	1,402	1,604	1,604
Rice (paddy)	428	469	469
Maize	283	322	322
Other cereals	25	38	38
Sugar cane	284	262	262
Sweet potatoes*	13	10	10
Cassava (Manioc)	1	2*	2
Other roots and tubers*	23	16	17
Vegetables*	267	267	267
Fruit*	16	16	16
Pulses*	64	65	65
Groundnuts (in shell)	131	215	215
Cottonseed	178*	150	150
Cotton (lint)	100	110†	110

* FAO estimate(s). † Unofficial figure.

Source: FAO, *Production Yearbook.*

LIVESTOCK ('000 head, year ending September)

	1993	1994	1995*
Cattle	5,380	5,542	5,542
Sheep	4,926	5,173	5,173
Goats	7,029	7,380	7,380
Pigs	62	63	63
Horses	92	101	101
Asses	600	611	611
Camels	232	260	260

Poultry (million): 23† in 1993; 23† in 1994; 23* in 1995.

* FAO estimate(s). † Unofficial figure.

Source: FAO, *Production Yearbook.*

LIVESTOCK PRODUCTS (FAO estimates, '000 metric tons)

	1993	1994	1995
Cows' milk	136	136	136
Sheep's milk	80	80	80
Goats' milk	161	161	161
Beef and veal	81	83	83
Mutton and lamb	24	24	24
Goat meat	27	27	27
Poultry meat	25	25	25
Other meat	24	26	26
Poultry eggs	11.9	11.9	11.9
Cattle hides	12.4	12.8	12.8
Sheepskins	5.5	5.7	5.7
Goatskins	3.8	3.8	3.8

Source: FAO, *Production Yearbook.*

Forestry

ROUNDWOOD REMOVALS
(FAO estimates, '000 cubic metres, excluding bark)

	1992	1993	1994
Sawlogs, veneer logs and logs for sleepers*	13	13	13
Other industrial wood	367	379	391
Fuel wood	5,572	5,752	5,936
Total	5,952	6,144	6,340

* Estimated to be unchanged since 1988.

Source: FAO, *Yearbook of Forest Products.*

Fishing

('000 metric tons, live weight)

	1993	1994	1995
Total catch (freshwater fishes)	64.4	63.0	133.0

Source: FAO, *Yearbook of Fishery Statistics.*

Mining

(metal content of ore, metric tons)

	1994	1995	1996
Gold	6.3	7.8	6.1

Source: Gold Fields Mineral Services Ltd, *Gold 1997.*

Salt ('000 metric tons, provisional or estimated figures): 5 in 1993; 5 in 1994 (Source: US Bureau of Mines in UN, *Industrial Commodity Statistics Yearbook*).

Industry

SELECTED PRODUCTS ('000 metric tons, unless otherwise indicated)

	1992	1993	1994
Salted, dried or smoked fish	11.3	11.3	n.a.
Raw sugar	31	26	25*
Cement	16	14	n.a.
Electric energy (million kWh)†	265	282	289

* Data from the International Sugar Organization.

† Provisional or estimated figures.

Source: UN, *Industrial Commodity Statistics Yearbook.*

Finance

CURRENCY AND EXCHANGE RATES

Monetary Units

100 centimes = 1 franc de la Communauté financière africaine (CFA).

French Franc, Sterling and Dollar Equivalents (31 March 1997)

1 French franc = 100 francs CFA;
£1 sterling = 924.20 francs CFA;
US $1 = 562.85 francs CFA;
1,000 francs CFA = £1.082 = $1.777.

Average Exchange Rate (francs CFA per US $)

1994 555.20
1995 499.15
1996 511.55

Note: An exchange rate of 1 French franc = 50 francs CFA, established in 1948, remained in force until January 1994, when the CFA franc was devalued by 50%, with the exchange rate adjusted to 1 French franc = 100 francs CFA.

BUDGET ('000 million francs CFA)*

Revenue†	1993	1994	1995
Budgetary revenue	94.0	126.0	160.7
Tax revenue	83.7	103.2	131.5
Taxes on net income and profits	11.6	16.2	26.6
Payroll tax	2.1	2.6	2.5
Property taxes	3.1	2.6	3.4
Domestic taxes on goods and services	12.4	15.0	17.0
Value-added tax	9.2	11.8	13.8
Taxes on international trade	47.4	55.1	73.0
Value-added tax on imports	11.5	13.3	20.8
Petroleum import duties	14.5	19.2	17.3
Other tax revenue	7.1	11.8	9.0
Stamp duties	2.1	3.6	4.8
Payment of tax arrears	3.4	6.5	2.8
Other current revenue	10.3	20.0	21.9
Capital revenue	n.a.	2.7	7.3
Special funds and annexed budgets	10.7	12.9	16.6
Social security fund	9.7	11.8	15.0
Total	104.7	138.9	177.3

Expenditure	1993	1994	1995
Budgetary expenditure	161.2	268.4	291.9
Current expenditure	88.1	132.1	134.7
Personnel	40.9	44.5	48.0
Supplies	8.8	14.2	18.6
Scholarships	4.8	4.2	3.9
Interest payments (scheduled)	12.2	23.9	17.6
Development expenditure	67.5	128.7	152.1
Externally financed	58.5	115.0	133.5
Public enterprise sector adjustment programme	2.8	5.1	2.3
Special funds and annexed budgets	10.5	11.7	14.5
Social security fund	9.5	10.6	12.9
Extrabudgetary expenditure	5.6	—	—
Total	177.3	280.1	306.4

* Figures represent a consolidation of the central government budget, special funds and annexed budgets. In addition, the data include extra-budgetary expenditure in 1993.

† Excluding grants received ('000 million francs CFA): 42.0 in 1993; 97.8 in 1994; 92.4 in 1995.

Source: IMF, *Mali—Selected Issues and Statistical Annex* (December 1996).

1996 (Draft budget, '000 million francs CFA): Revenue and grants 333.9; Expenditure 380.3.

1997 (Draft budget, '000 million francs CFA): Revenue and grants 379.6; Expenditure 400.3.

INTERNATIONAL RESERVES (US $ million at 31 December)

	1994	1995	1996
Gold*	7.0	7.3	7.1
IMF special drawing rights	0.2	0.5	0.3
Reserve position in IMF	12.7	13.0	12.6
Foreign exchange	208.5	309.5	418.6
Total	228.4	330.3	438.6

* Valued at market-related prices.

Source: IMF, *International Financial Statistics.*

MONEY SUPPLY ('000 million francs CFA at 31 December)

	1993	1994	1995
Currency outside banks	65.07	91.15	107.54
Demand deposits.	52.72	82.99	90.49
Total money (incl. others)	117.79	174.17	198.20

Source: IMF, *International Financial Statistics.*

COST OF LIVING (Consumer Price Index; base: 1990 = 100)

	1992	1993	1994
Food	93.5	92.9	115.7
Clothing.	91.8	89.5	n.a.
Rent*	102.5	104.8	n.a.
All items (incl. others)	95.5	94.9	117.1

* Including fuel and light.

Source: ILO, *Yearbook of Labour Statistics.*

NATIONAL ACCOUNTS ('000 million francs CFA at current prices)

Expenditure on the Gross Domestic Product

	1993	1994	1995
Government final consumption expenditure	113.5	122.8	131.6
Private final consumption expenditure	607.4	840.2	953.5
Increase in stocks	—	5	–2
Gross fixed capital formation	135.8	239.4	286.6
Total domestic expenditure	856.6	1,207.5	1,370.2*
Exports of goods and services	118.5	212.9	274.0
Less Imports of goods and services	267.7	456.6	475.7
GDP in purchasers' values	707.4	963.8	1,168.5

* Including adjustment.

Source: IMF, *International Financial Statistics.*

Gross Domestic Product by Economic Activity

	1990	1991	1992
Agriculture, livestock-rearing, forestry and fishing	286.1	295.8	312.6
Mining	9.5	11.1	12.5
Manufacturing	48.2	49.5	48.6
Electricity and water.	8.6	9.5	10.3
Construction and public works	27.9	33.9	33.4
Transport and telecommunications	29.4	33.2	32.8
Trade	115.7	103.9	113.1
Other marketable services	45.6	46.1	46.7
Public administration	62.3	69.5	70.2
Sub-total	633.3	652.5	680.2
Customs duties	37.8	38.0	38.0
Less Imputed bank service charge	–4.9	–5.0	–4.9
GDP in purchasers' values	666.2	685.5	713.3

Source: Banque centrale des états de l'Afrique de l'ouest.

BALANCE OF PAYMENTS (US $ million)

	1992	1993	1994
Exports of goods f.o.b.	335.9	341.1	319.7
Imports of goods f.o.b.	–484.5	–446.5	–421.6
Trade balance	–148.6	–105.3	–101.9
Exports of services	75.0	75.4	66.8
Imports of services	–406.5	–388.6	–324.0
Balance on goods and services	–480.2	–418.6	–359.1
Other income received	12.8	25.1	5.4
Other income paid	–43.1	–38.1	–41.2
Balance on goods, services and income	–510.4	–431.7	–395.0
Current transfers received	344.9	300.2	275.8
Current transfers paid	–87.6	–81.9	–45.2
Current balance	–253.1	–213.4	–164.4
Capital account (net).	143.6	111.9	111.7
Direct investment from abroad	–7.6	–20.1	45.0
Other investment assets	17.5	11.9	–100.3
Other investment liabilities	–7.0	–17.6	49.4
Net errors and omissions	–31.0	30.1	–5.1
Overall balance	–137.6	–97.2	–63.7

Source: IMF, *International Financial Statistics.*

External Trade

PRINCIPAL COMMODITIES ('000 million francs CFA)

Imports c.i.f.	1993	1994	1995*
Foodstuffs	27.4	47.8	51.7
Cereals	7.2	7.2	10.5
Sugar.	4.2	15.2	16.0
Milk	7.0	10.1	9.8
Machines and vehicles	51.7	107.0	128.0
Petroleum products	21.0	32.0	32.9
Construction materials	18.6	33.7	39.6
Chemical products	20.0	33.9	35.4
Textiles and leather	14.3	22.5	20.8
Total (incl. others)	191.9	349.3	386.4

Exports f.o.b.	1993	1994	1995*
Cotton	41.7	83.2	130.3
Cotton fibre	39.4	79.7	126.9
Cotton yarn and fabrics	1.4	2.2	2.2
Livestock	27.0	51.8	46.5
Hides and leathers	2.1	2.9	2.6
Fish.	1.1	1.7	1.8
Shea-nuts (Karité nuts)	2.0	3.0	3.3
Gold	15.2	27.8	34.6
Total (incl. others)	98.9	185.0	234.7

* Preliminary figures.

Source: IMF, *Mali—Selected Issues and Statistical Annex* (December 1996).

PRINCIPAL TRADING PARTNERS (US $ million)*

Imports	1993	1994	1995
Belgium-Luxembourg	23.97	26.37	35.20
China, People's Repub.	12.71	11.89	27.61
Côte d'Ivoire.	200.52	228.56	293.48
France (incl. Monaco)	131.22	105.14	191.52
Germany	24.20	15.94	17.00
Spain	10.50	6.09	12.43
United Kingdom	15.62	18.27	41.71
Total (incl. others)	911.20	1,261.09	1,105.36

Exports	1993	1994	1995
Belgium-Luxembourg	36.00	20.96	20.65
China, People's Repub.	n.a.	8.27	30.04
Côte d'Ivoire	3.36	3.83	4.92
France (incl. Monaco)	8.43	7.38	6.91
Germany	5.94	3.84	3.73
Spain	2.74	4.48	7.75
Total (incl. others)	224.70	358.53	238.40

* Data are compiled on the basis of reporting by Mali's trading partners.

Source: IMF, *Direction of Trade Statistics*.

Transport

RAILWAYS (traffic)

	1986	1987	1988
Passenger-km (million)	176.9	772.8	731.9
Freight ton-km (million)	225.1	429.3	432.2

1993: Passenger-km (million) 845.9; Freight ton-km (million) 460.9.

Source: Banque centrale des états de l'Afrique de l'ouest.

ROAD TRAFFIC (estimates, '000 motor vehicles in use)

	1991	1992	1993
Passenger cars	24	25	26
Commercial vehicles	14	14	14

Source: UN Economic Commission for Africa, *African Statistical Yearbook*.

CIVIL AVIATION (traffic on scheduled services)*

	1992	1993	1994
Kilometres flown (million)	2	2	2
Passengers carried ('000)	66	68	69
Passenger-km (million)	201	207	215
Total ton-km (million)	34	33	34

* Including an apportionment of the traffic of Air Afrique.

Source: UN, *Statistical Yearbook*.

Communications Media

	1992	1993	1994
Radio receivers ('000 in use)	430	450	465
Television receivers ('000 in use)	11	13	14
Telephones ('000 main lines in use)	13	14	n.a.
Daily newspapers			
Number	2	n.a.	2
Estimated average circulation ('000 copies)	41	n.a.	40

Book production (textbooks, government publications and university theses, including pamphlets): 160 titles (92,000 copies) in 1984.

Sources: UNESCO, *Statistical Yearbook*; UN, *Statistical Yearbook*.

Tourism

	1992	1993	1994
Tourist arrivals ('000)	38	31	28
Tourist receipts (US $ million)	11	13	18

Source: UN, *Statistical Yearbook*.

Education

(1993/94, unless otherwise indicated)

	Institu- tions	Teach- ers	Students		
			Males	Females	Total
Pre-primary	151	503	8,298	7,610	15,908
Primary	1,728	8,363	305,662	192,207	497,869
Secondary					
General	n.a.	4,854*	65,353	34,026	99,379
Teacher training	n.a.	75	257	56	313
Vocational	n.a.	762†	7,827	4,049	11,876
University level†	n.a.	701	5,798	905	6,703

* 1991/92 figure. † 1990/91 figure(s).

1994/95: *Pre-primary:* Teachers 531; Students 17,165 (males 8,954; females 8,211). *Primary:* Institutions 1,732; Teachers 8,274; Students 542,891 (males 330,058; females 212,833).

Source: UNESCO, *Statistical Yearbook*.

Directory

The Constitution

The Constitution of the Third Republic of Mali was approved in a national referendum on 12 January 1992. The document upholds the principles of national sovereignty and the rule of law in a secular, multi-party state, and provides for the separation of the powers of the executive, legislative and judicial organs of state.

Executive power is vested in the President of the Republic, who is Head of State and is elected for five years by universal adult suffrage. The President appoints the Prime Minister, who, in turn, appoints other members of the Council of Ministers.

Legislative authority is exercised by the unicameral Assemblée nationale, which is elected for five years by universal adult suffrage.

The Constitution guarantees the independence of the judiciary. Final jurisdiction in constitutional matters is vested in a Constitutional Court.

The rights, freedoms and obligations of Malian citizens are enshrined in the Constitution. Freedom of the press and of association are guaranteed.

Note: A constitutional bill was adopted by the Assemblée nationale in January 1997, providing for an increase, with effect from that year's legislative elections, in the number of deputies from 129 to 147.

The Government

HEAD OF STATE

President: Alpha Oumar Konaré (took office 8 June 1992; re-elected 11 May 1997).

COUNCIL OF MINISTERS
(September 1997)

Prime Minister: IBRAHIM BOUBACAR KEITA.

Minister of Mines and Energy: YORO DIAKITÉ.

Minister of the Environment: MOHAMED AG ERLAF.

Minister of Foreign Affairs and Malians Abroad: Maj. MODIBO SIDIBÉ.

Minister of Industry, Trade and Handicrafts: FATOU HAIDARA.

Minister of Youth Promotion: BOUBACAR KARAMOKO COULIBALY.

Minister of Finance: SOUMEYLA CISSÉ.

Minister of Territorial Administration and Security: Col SADA SAMAKÉ.

Minister of Urban Development and Housing: SY KADIATOU SOW.

Minister of Rural Development and Water Resources: MODIBO TRAORÉ.

Minister of Secondary and Higher Education and Scientific Research: YOUNOUSS HAMAYE DICKO.

Minister of Justice and Keeper of the Seals: AMADOU DIABATÉ.

Minister of Employment, the Civil Service and Labour: OUSMANE OUMAROU SIDIBÉ.

Minister of Economic Affairs, Planning and Integration: AHMED EL MADANI DIALLO.

Minister of Basic Education and Spokesperson for the Government: ADAMA SAMASSEKOU.

Minister of Health, the Elderly and Solidarity: DIAKITÉ FATOUMATA NDIAYE.

Minister of Culture and Tourism: AMINATA DRAMÉ TRAORÉ.

Minister of the Armed Forces and Veterans: MOHAMED SALIA SOKONA.

Minister of Women's Promotion, Children and Family Affairs: DIARRA HAFSATOU THIERRO.

Minister of Public Works and Transport: IBRAHIMA SIBY.

Minister responsible for Relations with the Institutions and Political Parties: HASSAN BARRY.

Minister of Communications: ASCOFARE OULEYMATOU TAMBOURA.

Minister of Sports: ADAMA KONÉ.

MINISTRIES

All ministries are in Bamako.

Office of the President: BP 1463, Bamako; tel. 22-24-61; telex 2521.

Office of the Prime Minister: BP 97, Bamako.

Ministry of the Armed Forces and Veterans: BP 215, Bamako; tel. 22-26-17.

Ministry of Employment, the Civil Service and Labour: BP 80, Bamako; tel. 22-59-51.

Ministry of Finance: BP 234, Koulouba, Bamako; tel. 22-56-87; telex 2559; fax 22-88-53.

Ministry of Foreign Affairs, Malians Abroad and African Integration: Koulouba, Bamako; tel. 22-54-89; telex 2560.

Ministry of Health, the Elderly and Solidarity: Koulouba, Bamako; tel. 22-53-01.

Ministry of Industry, Trade and Handicrafts: BP 1759, Bamako; tel. 22-80-58; fax 23-02-61.

Ministry of Justice: BP 97, Bamako; tel. 22-24-36.

Ministry of Mines and Energy: BP 238, Bamako; tel. 22-35-47.

Ministry of National Education: BP 71, Bamako; tel. 22-24-50.

Ministry of Public Works and Transport: c/o World Bank Resident Mission, BP 1864, Bamako; tel. 22-66-82.

Ministry of Rural Development and Water Resources: BP 1676, Bamako; tel. and fax 23-19-39.

Ministry of Territorial Administration and Security: BP 78, Bamako; tel. 22-39-37.

President and Legislature

PRESIDENT

Presidential Election, 11 May 1997

Candidate	Votes	% of votes
ALPHA OUMAR KONARÉ	1,056,819	95.90
MAMADOU MARIBATROU DIABY	45,160	4.10
Total	1,101,979	100.0

ASSEMBLÉE NATIONALE

General Election, 20 July and 3 August 1997

Party	Seats
ADEMA	130*
PARENA	8
CDS	4
UDD	3
PDP	2
Total	147

* Including one seat won in alliance with the Convention patriotique pour le progrès.

Advisory Councils

Conseil Economique et Social: Bamako; f. 1987.

Cour Constitutionnelle: BP 213, Bamako; tel. 22-56-32; fax 23-42-41; f. 1994; Pres. ABDOULAYE DICKO; Sec.-Gen. BOUBACAR TAHOUATI.

Political Organizations

Following the dissolution in March 1991 of the Union démocratique du peuple malien (UDPM), which had been the sole legal party since 1979, provision was made for the registration of an unlimited number of political parties. There were 63 registered political parties at the time of the 1997 legislative elections, 17 of which presented candidates for the Assemblée nationale. The collective of 18 'radical' opposition parties, including the CNID, the CPP, the MPR, the RDP and the US–RDA, boycotted the elections. Among the most active parties in mid-1997 were:

Alliance pour la démocratie au Mali–Parti africain pour la solidarité et la justice (ADEMA): BP 1791, Bamako; tel. 22-03-68; f. 1990 as Alliance pour la démocratie au Mali; Chair. IBRAHIM BOUBACAR KEITA; Sec.-Gen. IBA NDIAYE.

Bloc pour la démocratie et l'intégration africaines—Faso Djigui (BDIA–Faso Djigui): Bamako; f. by split in US–RDA.

Congrès national d'initiative démocratique (CNID): BP 2572, Bamako; tel. 22-42-75; fax 22-83-21; f. 1990; Chair. Me MOUNTAGA TALL; Sec.-Gen. N'DIAYE BA.

Convention démocratique et sociale (CDS): Bamako; f. 1996; Chair. MAMADOU BAKARY SANGARÉ.

Convention parti du peuple (CPP): Bamako.

Convention patriotique pour le progrès: Bamako; Leader MAMADOU GACKOU.

Mouvement pour l'indépendance, la renaissance et l'intégration africaines (MIRIA): Bamako; f. 1994, following split in ADEMA; Leaders MOHAMED LAMINE TRAORÉ, MOUHAMEDOU DICKO.

Mouvement patriotique pour le renouveau (MPR): Bamako; f. 1995; linked to fmr UDPM; Sec. Gen. SOGAL MAÏGA.

Parti pour la démocratie et le progrès (PDP): BP 1823, Bamako; tel. and fax 22-64-52; f. 1991; Leader: Me IDRISSA TRAORÉ.

Parti pour le renouveau national (PARENA): Bamako; f. 1995, following split in CNID; Chair. YORO DIAKITÉ; Sec.-Gen. TIÉBILÉ DRAMÉ.

Parti pour l'unité, la démocratie et le progrès (PUDP): Bamako; Chair. MAMADOU MARIBATROU DIABY.

Rassemblement pour la démocratie et le progrès (RDP): BP 2110, Bamako; tel. 22-30-92; fax 22-67-95; f. 1990; Chair. ALMAMY SYLLA.

Rassemblement pour la démocratie et le travail (RDT): Bamako; Leader ALI GNANGADO.

Rassemblement nationale pour la démocratie (RND): Bamako; f. 1997 by 'moderate' breakaway group from RDP; Chair. ABDOULAYE GAFA KAPO.

Union pour la démocratie et le développement (UDD): Bamako; f. 1991 by fmr supporters of ex-President Traoré; Leader MOUSSA BALLA COULIBALY.

Union des forces démocratiques pour le progrès (UFDP): Bamako; f. 1991; Sec.-Gen. Col. YOUSSOUF TRAORÉ.

Union soudanaise–Rassemblement démocratique africain (US–RDA): Bamako; f. 1946, sole legal party 1960–68, revived 1991; Sec.-Gen. MAMADOU BAMOU TOURÉ.

Diplomatic Representation

EMBASSIES IN MALI

Algeria: route de Daoudabougou; tel. 22-51-76; telex 2414; fax 22-93-74; Ambassador: AHMED FERHAT ZERHOUNI.

Burkina Faso: BP 9022, Bamako; Ambassador: HAMADOU KONÉ.

Canada: route de Koulikoro, BP 198, Bamako; telex 2530; Chargé d'affaires a.i.: GUY GAGNON.

China, People's Republic: BP 112, Bamako; telex 2455; Ambassador: LI YONEQIAN.

Egypt: BP 44, Badalabougou; tel. 22-35-03; fax 22-08-91; Ambassador: ABDELSALAM YEHIA EL-TAWIL.

France: square Patrice Lumumba, BP 17, Bamako; tel. 22-29-51; telex 2569; fax 22-31-36; Ambassador: GABRIEL DE REGNAULD DE BELLESCIZE.

Germany: Badalabougou-Est, Lotissement A6, BP 100, Bamako; tel. 22-32-99; telex 2529; fax 22-96-50; Ambassador: HARRO ADT.

Guinea: BP 118, Bamako; tel. 22-29-75; telex 2576; Ambassador: MAMADOU MASS DIALLO.

Iran: quartier de l'Hippodrome, BP 2136, Bamako; Ambassador: MOJTABA SHAFII.

Iraq: BP 2512, Bamako-Badalabougou; tel. 22-38-06; telex 2416; Chargé d'affaires a.i.: JASSIM N. MSAWIL.

Libya: quartier de l'Hippodrome, Bamako; telex 2420; Chargé d'affaires a.i.: ABDEL MANSUR.

Malaysia: Badalabougou-Ouest, BP 98, Bamako; tel. 22-27-83; telex 2423; fax 22-32-32; Ambassador: CHOO SIEW-KIOH.

Mauritania: BP 135, Bamako; telex 2415; Ambassador: BILAL OULD WERZEG.

Morocco: BP 2013, Bamako; tel. 22-21-23; telex 22430; fax 22-77-87; Ambassador: LARBI ROUDIÉS.

Nigeria: BP 57, Badalabougou; tel. 22-57-71; Chargé d'affaires: M. O. KUFORIJI.

Russia: BP 300, Bamako; tel. 22-55-92; fax 22-99-26; Ambassador: PAVEL PETROVSKII.

Saudi Arabia: BP 81, Badalabougou; telex 2408; Chargé d'affaires: MUHAMMAD RAJAMIRI.

Senegal: ave Kassé Keïta, BP 42, Bamako; tel. 22-82-74; fax 23-17-80; Ambassador: MAMADOU LAITY NDIAYE.

USA: angle rue Rochester NY et rue Mohamed V, BP 34, Bamako; tel. 22-54-70; telex 2248; fax 22-37-12; Ambassador: DAVID P. RAWSON.

Judicial System

The 1992 Constitution guarantees the independence of the judiciary.

Supreme Court: BP 7, Bamako; tel. 22-24-06; f. 1969; 25 mems; judicial section comprises two civil chambers, one commercial chamber, one social chamber and one criminal chamber; in addition, there are administrative and financial regulatory sections; Pres. LOUIS BASTIDE; Sec.-Gen. HENRIETTE BOUNSLY.

Court of Appeal: Bamako.

President of the Bar: Me MAGATTÉ SÈYE.

There are two Tribunaux de première instance (Magistrates' Courts) and also courts for labour disputes.

Religion

It is estimated that about 80% of the population are Muslims, while 18% follow traditional animist beliefs and 1.2% are Christians.

ISLAM

Chief Mosque: Bagadadji, place de la République, Bamako.

CHRISTIANITY

The Roman Catholic Church

Mali comprises one archdiocese and five dioceses. At 31 December 1995 there were an estimated 110,003 adherents in the country (1.1% of the total population).

Bishops' Conference: Conférence Episcopale du Mali, BP 298, Bamako; tel. 22-67-84; fax 22-67-00; f. 1973; Pres. Rt Rev. JEAN-GABRIEL DIARRA, Bishop of San.

Archbishop of Bamako: Most Rev. LUC AUGUSTE SANGARÉ, Archevêché, BP 298, Bamako; tel. 22-54-99; fax 22-52-14.

Other Christian Churches

There are several Protestant mission centres, mainly administered by US societies.

The Press

Restrictions on press freedom were formally ended under a new statute that entered force during December 1992 and January 1993.

DAILY NEWSPAPER

L'Essor—La Voix du Peuple: BP 141, Bamako; tel. 22-47-97; f. 1949; pro-Government newspaper; Editor SOULEYMANE DRABO; circ. 3,500.

PERIODICALS

L'Afro-Arabe Revue: rue Mohamed V, BP 2044, Bamako; quarterly; Editor MOHAMED BEN BABA AHMED; circ. 1,000.

L'Aurore: BP 2043, Bamako; f. 1990; fortnightly; independent; Editor CHOUAHIBOU TRAORÉ.

Barakela: Bamako; monthly; publ. by the Union nationale des travailleurs du Mali.

Citoyen: Bamako; f. 1992; fortnightly; independent.

Danbe: Bamako; f. 1990; organ of the CNID.

Les Echos: BP 2043, Bamako; f. 1989; fortnightly; publ. by Jamana cultural co-operative; circ. 25,000; Man. TIÉGOUNÉ MAÏGA.

Jamana—Revue Culturelle Malienne: BP 2043, Bamako; f. 1983; quarterly; organ of Jamana cultural co-operative.

Kabaaru: Mopti; monthly; Fulbé language; rural interest; Editor BADAMA DOUCOURÉ; circ. 5,000.

Kibaru: BP 1463, Bamako; monthly; Bambara and three other languages; rural interest; Editor AMADOU GAGNY KANTÉ; circ. 5,000.

Journal Officiel de la République du Mali: BP 1463, Bamako; official announcements.

Mali Muso (Women of Mali): Bamako; quarterly; publ. by the Union des femmes du Mali; circ. 5,000.

Podium: BP 141, Bamako; weekly; culture and sports.

Nouvel Horizon: BP 942, Bamako; weekly; independent; Editor SEMBI TOURÉ.

Le Républicain: BP 1484, Bamako; f. 1992; weekly; independent; Dir TIÉBILÉ DRAMÉ; Editor EBRAHIM TRAORÉ.

La Roue: Quinzambougou, BP 2043, Bamako; pre-independence journal, revived 1990; independent.

Sunjata: BP 141, Bamako; monthly; social, economic and political affairs; Editor SOUMEYLOU MAÏGA; circ. 3,000.

Yiriwa: BP 2043, Bamako; f. 1990; independent.

NEWS AGENCIES

Agence Malienne de Presse et Publicité (AMAPP): BP 116, Bamako; tel. 22-26-47; telex 2421; f. 1977; Dir GAOUSSOU DRABO.

Foreign Bureaux

Agence France-Presse (AFP): BP 778, Bamako; telex 2480; Correspondent CHOUAÏBOU BONKANE.

Rossiiskoye Informatsionnoye Agentstvo—Novosti (RIA—Novosti) (Russia): BP 193, Bamako; tel. 22-45-25; telex 2528; Correspondent BORIS TARASOV.

Xinhua (New China) News Agency (People's Republic of China): c/o Ambassade de la République Populaire de Chine, BP 112, Bamako; telex 2455; Correspondent NI MANHE.

IPS (Italy) and Reuters (UK) are also represented in Mali.

Publisher

EDIM SA: ave Kassé Keïta, BP 21, Bamako; tel. 22-40-41; f. 1972 as Editions Imprimeries du Mali, reorg. 1987; general fiction and non-fiction, textbooks; Chair. and Man. Dir IBRAHIMA BERTHE.

Radio and Television

In 1994, according to UNESCO, there were an estimated 465,000 radio receivers and 14,000 television receivers in use. Legislation authorizing the establishment of private radio and television stations was promulgated in 1992.

Office de Radiodiffusion-Télévision Malienne (ORTM): BP 171, Bamako; tel. 22-24-74; fax 22-42-05; f. 1957; state-owned; radio programmes in French, Bambara, Peulh, Sarakolé, Tamachek, Sonrai, Moorish, Wolof, English; about 37 hours weekly of television broadcasts; Man. Dir ABDOULAYE SIDIBE; Dir of Television CHEICK HAMALLA TOURÉ.

Chaîne 2: Bamako; f. 1993; radio broadcasts to Bamako.

By the mid-1990s there were some 15 private radio stations, including:

Fréquence 3: Bamako; f. 1992; commercial.

Radio-Bamakan: Marché de Médine, BP E-100, Bamako; tel. 22-27-60; fax 22-53-66; f. 1991; 100 hours of FM broadcasts weekly; Man. MODIBO DIALLO.

Radio Kayira: Bamako; f. 1992; supports the CNID.

Radio Kledu: Bamako; f. 1992; commercial; Propr MAMADOU COULIBALY.

Radio Liberté: Nouveau Marché de Médine, BP 5015, Bamako; tel. 22-05-81; f. 1991; commercial station broadcasting 24 hours daily.

Radio Balanzan: Ségou.

Sahel FM: Kayes.

Radio Tabalé: BP 697, Bamako; tel. and fax 22-78-70; f. 1992; independent public-service station broadcasting 57 hours weekly; Dir TIÉMOKO KONÉ.

Radio France International and the Gabonese-based Africa No. 1 began FM broadcasts in Mali in 1993; broadcasts by Voice of America and the World Service of the British Broadcasting Corpn are also transmitted via private radio stations.

Finance

(cap. = capital; res = reserves; m. = million; brs = branches; amounts in francs CFA)

BANKING

Central Bank

Banque Centrale des Etats de l'Afrique de l'Ouest (BCEAO): square Lumumba, BP 206, Bamako; tel. 22-37-56; telex 2574; fax 22-47-86; f. 1962; headquarters in Dakar, Senegal; bank of issue and central bank for the member states of Union économique et monétaire ouest-africaine (UEMOA); cap. and res 657,592m. (Dec. 1995); Gov. CHARLES KONAN BANNY; Dir in Mali IDRISSA TRAORÉ (acting); br. at Mopti.

Commercial Banks

Bank of Africa–Mali (BOA): ave Kassé Keïta, BP 2249, Bamako; tel. 22-46-72; telex 2581; fax 22-46-53; f. 1982; cap. and res 1,452m. (Dec. 1995); Chair. BOUREIMA SYLLA; Man. Dir RENÉ BACH; 5 brs.

Banque Commerciale du Sahel SA (BCS–SA): ave Kassé Keïta, BP 2372, Bamako; tel. 22-55-20; telex 2580; fax 22-55-43; f. 1982; fmrly Banque Arabe Libyo-Malienne pour le Commerce Extérieur et le Développement; 50% owned by Fore Bank (Libya), 49.5% state-owned; cap. and res 1,278m. (Dec. 1995); Chair. FANGATIGUI DOUMBIA; Man. Dir MOHAMED OMAR JABALLAH.

Banque Internationale pour le Mali (BIM–SA): Immeuble de Bolibana, blvd de l'Indépendance, BP 15, Bamako; tel. 22-51-08; telex 2501; fax 22-45-66; f. 1981; fmrly BIAO–Mali, present name since 1995; cap. and res 2,066m. (Dec. 1995); Chair. MAHAMAR OUMAR MAÏGA; Man. Dir ASSANA SY.

Banque Malienne de Crédit et de Dépôts SA (BMCD): ave Modibo Keita, BP 45, Bamako; tel. 22-53-36; telex 2572; fax 22-79-50; f. 1961; state-owned; partial sale of state holding pending; cap. and res 1,629m. (Dec. 1995); Chair. and Man. Dir AMIDOU OUMAR SY; 5 brs.

Development Banks

Banque de Développement du Mali SA (BDM): ave du Fleuve, BP 94, Bamako; tel. 22-20-50; telex 2522; fax 22-50-85; f. 1968; 20% state-owned, 20% owned by BCEAO, 20% by Banque ouest-africaine de développement; cap. and res 4,884m. (Dec. 1995); Chair. Minister of Finance and Trade; Man. Dir ABDOULAYE DAFFE; 11 brs.

Banque Nationale de Développement Agricole (BNDA): Immeuble Ex-Caisse Autonome d'Amortissement, quartier du Fleuve, BP 2424, Bamako; tel. 22-64-64; telex 2638; fax 22-29-61; f. 1981; 39.5% state-owned; cap. and res 4,625m. (Dec. 1995); Chair. and Man. Dir BAKARY TRAORÉ; 20 brs, etc.

Financial Institution

Direction Générale de la Dette Publique: Immeuble Ex-Caisse Autonome d'Amortissement, Quartier du Fleuve, BP 1617, Bamako; tel. 22-29-35; telex 2676; fax 22-07-93; management of the public debt; Dir NAMALA KONE.

STOCK EXCHANGE

Côte d'Ivoire's Bourse des Valeurs d'Abidjan was scheduled to become a regional stock exchange, serving the member states of the UEMOA.

INSURANCE

Caisse Nationale d'Assurance et de Réassurance (CNAR): Immeuble CNAR, square Patrice Lumumba, BP 568, Bamako; tel. 22-64-54; telex 2549; fax 22-23-29; state-owned; cap. 50m.; Man. Dir FOUNEKE KEITA; 10 brs.

La Soutra: BP 52, Bamako; telex 2469; fax 22-55-23; f. 1979; cap. 150m.; Chair. AMADOU NIONO.

Trade and Industry

DEVELOPMENT ORGANIZATIONS

Caisse Française de Développement (CFD): BP 32, Bamako; tel. 22-28-42; telex 2502; fmrly Caisse Centrale de Coopération Economique, name changed 1992; Dir ROBERT CHAHINIAN.

Compagnie Malienne pour le Développement des Textiles (CMDT): BP 487, Bamako; tel. 22-24-62; telex 2554; fax 22-81-41; f. 1975; cap. 1,500m. francs CFA; 60% state-owned, 40% owned by Cie Française pour le Développement des Fibres Textiles; cotton cultivation, ginning and marketing; Chair. and Man. Dir DRISSA KEITA.

Direction Nationale des Travaux Publics (DNTP): ave de la Liberté, BP 1758, Bamako; tel. and fax 22-29-02; telex 2557; administers public works.

Mission Française de Coopération et d'Action Culturelle: BP 84, Bamako; tel. 22-83-38; fax 22-83-39; administers bilateral aid from France; Dir PIERRE A. RICHEZ.

Office de Développement Intégré du Mali-Ouest (ODIMO): square Patrice Lumumba, BP 72, Bamako; tel. 22-57-59; f. 1991 to succeed Office de Développement Intégré des Productions Arachidières et Céréalières; development of diversified forms of agricultural production; Man. Dir ZANA SANOGO.

Office du Niger: BP 106, Ségou; tel. 32-00-93; fax 32-01-43; f. 1932; taken over from the French authorities in 1958; restructured in mid-1990s; cap. 7,139m. francs CFA; principally involved in cultivation of food crops; Pres. and Man. Dir Dr FERNAND TRAORÉ.

Office des Produits Agricoles du Mali (OPAM): BP 132, Bamako; tel. 22-37-55; telex 2509; fax 22-04-06; f. 1965; cap. 5,800m. francs CFA; state-owned; manages National (Cereals) Security Stock, administers food aid, responsible for sales of cereals and distribution to deficit areas; Man. Dir ABDOULAYE KOITA.

Société Nationale de Recherches et d'Exploitation des Ressources Minières du Mali (SONAREM): BP 2, Kati; tel. 27-20-42; state-owned; Man. Dir MAKAN KAYENTAO.

CHAMBER OF COMMERCE

Chambre de Commerce et d'Industrie du Mali: place de la Liberté, BP 46, Bamako; tel. 22-50-36; telex 2435; fax 22-21-20; f. 1906; Pres. DRAHAMANE HAMIDOU TOURÉ; Sec.-Gen. DABA TRAORÉ.

EMPLOYERS' ASSOCIATIONS

Association Malienne des Exportateurs de Légumes (AMELEF): BP 1996, Bamako; f. 1984; Pres. BADARA FAGANDA TRAORÉ; Sec.-Gen. BIRAMA TRAORÉ.

Association Malienne des Exportateurs de Ressources Animales (AMERA): Centre Malien de Commerce Extérieur, BP 1996, Bamako; tel. 22-56-83; f. 1985; Pres. AMBARKÉ YERMANGORE; Admin. Sec. ALI HACKO.

MAJOR INDUSTRIAL COMPANIES

The following are among the major private and state-owned companies in terms of capital investment or employment.

Abattoir Frigorifique de Bamako: Zone Industrielle, BP 356, Bamako; tel. 22-24-67; telex 2992; f. 1965; cap. 339m. francs CFA; state-owned; transfer to 80% private ownership, as Société des Abattoirs Frigorifiques de Bamako, announced in 1996; Man. Dir El Hadj YOUSSOUF CAMARA.

Béton Mali: BP 2410, Bamako; cap. 350m. francs CFA; mfrs and distributors of construction materials; Chair. and Man. Dir MAMADOU DIATIGUI DIARRA.

Compagnie Malienne des Textiles (COMATEX): route de Markala, BP 52, Ségou; tel. 32-01-83; telex 2584; f. 1968; cap. 4,250m. francs CFA; production of unbleached fibre and textiles; Pres. M. KEITA; 2,027 employees.

Energie du Mali (EDM): square Patrice Lumumba, BP 69, Bamako; tel. 22-30-20; telex 2587; fax 22-84-30; f. 1961, restructuring in progress from 1994; cap. 2,500m. francs CFA; state-owned, managed by consortium of Franco-Canadian interests; planning, construction and operation of all power-sector facilities; Pres. MOCTAR TOURÉ; Man. Dir HAMIDOU DIALLO; 1,350 employees.

Ets Peyrissac–Mali: ave de la République, BP 168, Bamako; tel. 22-20-62; telex 2561; f. 1963; cap. 300m. francs CFA; distributors of motor vehicles; Dir FRANÇOIS GRULOIS.

Grands Moulins du Mali (GMM): BP 324, Bamako; tel. 22-36-64; telex 2513; f. 1979; cap. 600m. francs CFA; mfrs of flour and animal feed; Chair. and Man. Dir GÉRARD ACHCAR.

Huilerie Cotonnière du Mali (HUICOMA): c/o CMDT, BP 487, Bamako; tel. 22-24-62; telex 2554; fax 22-81-41; f. 1979; cap. 1,500m. francs CFA; 50% owned by CMDT, 40% state-owned; processing of oilseeds; Dir of Operations ABEL KEITA.

Mobil Oil Mali: quartier TSF, Zone Industrielle, BP 145, Bamako; tel. 22-25-98; telex 2562; f. 1974; cap. 321m. francs CFA; distribution of petroleum products; Chair. and Man. Dir J. L. VILLALBA.

Pharmacie Populaire du Mali (PPM): ave Houssa Travele, BP 277, Bamako; tel. 22-46-25; telex 2523; f. 1960; cap. 400m. francs CFA; majority state-owned; import and marketing of medicines and pharmaceutical products; Man. Dir Dr ABDOULAYE DIALLO.

Société des Brasseries du Mali (BRAMALI): BP 442, Bamako; f. 1981; cap. 500m. francs CFA; mfrs of beer and soft drinks; Chair. and Man. Dir SEYDOU DJIM SYLLA.

Société d'Exploitation des Mines d'Or de Sadiola SA (SEMOS): Bamako; f. 1994; 38% owned by Anglo American Corpn (South Africa), 38% by Iamgold (Canada); devt of gold deposits at Sadiola Hill.

Société Industrielle de Karité (SIKAMALI): Bamako; telex 2476; f. 1980; cap. 938m. francs CFA; processors of shea-nuts (karité nuts); Dir DRISSA SANGARÉ.

Société Karamoko Traoré et Frères (SOKATRAF): BP 88, Mopti; telex 2428; f. 1975; cap. 318m. francs CFA; import/export; Chair. and Man. Dir DRAMANE TRAORÉ.

Société Malienne d'Etudes et de Construction de Matériel Agricole (SMECMA): BP 1707, Bamako; tel. 22-40-71; f. 1974; cap. 251.4m. francs CFA; mfrs of agricultural equipment; Chair. AHMED AG HAMANI; Man. Dir BOUBACAR NANTÉGUÉ MALLE.

Société Malienne de Piles Electriques (SOMAPIL): route de Sotuba, Zone Industrielle, BP 1546, Bamako; tel. 22-46-87; telex 2401; fax 22-29-80; f. 1975; cap. 500m. francs CFA; mfrs of batteries; Chair. KOUMAN DOUMBIA; Man. Dir GÉRARD HELIX.

Société Malienne de Produits Chimiques (SMPC): BP 1560, Bamako; f. 1987; cap. 250m. francs CFA; sale of part of state holding (c. 20%) authorized in 1996; mfrs and distributors of insecticides; Chair. and Man. Dir ISSA KONDA.

Société Malienne de Profilage et de Transformation des Métaux (TOLMALI): quartier TSF, Zone Industrielle, Bamako; tel. 22-33-35; telex 2547; fax 22-53-77; f. 1978; cap. 250m. francs CFA; mfrs of iron and steel construction materials and aluminium utensils.

Société Malienne de Sacherie (SOMASAC): BP 74, Bamako; tel. 22-49-41; telex 2564; f. 1971; cap. 462.5m. francs CFA; production of sacking from dah and kenaf fibre and manufacture of sacks; Chair. DOSSOLO TRAORÉ; Man. Dir ERNEST RICHARD.

Société des Mines de Loulo (SOMILO): Loulo; fax 22-81-87; f. 1987; cap. 2,133m. francs CFA; 51% owned by Randgold Resources (South Africa); exploration and development of gold deposits at Loulo; Chair. MAMADOU TOURÉ; Man. Dir ROBERT KRUH.

Société Minière de Syama (SOMISY): Syama; f. 1990; 75% owned by Randgold Resources (South Africa), 20% state-owned; exploitation of gold reserves at Syama; Gen. Man. JOHN STEELE.

Société Nationale des Tabacs et Allumettes du Mali (SONATAM): route de Sotuba, Zone Industrielle, BP 59, Bamako; tel. 22-49-65; telex 2537; fax 22-23-72; f. 1968; cap. 2,177m. francs CFA; state-owned: transfer to private ownership pending; production of cigarettes and matches; Chair. MOUSSA BABA DIARRA; Man. Dir BOUBACAR DEMBÉLÉ; 820 employees.

Tanneries Maliennes (TAMALI): route de Sotuba, BP 188, Bamako; tel. 22-28-26; telex 2616; f. 1970; cap. 254m. francs CFA; processing of skins and hides; Man. Dir DU MONG YING.

TRADE UNION FEDERATION

Union nationale des travailleurs du Mali (UNTM): Bourse du Travail, blvd de l'Indépendance, BP 169, Bamako; tel. 22-20-31; f. 1963; Sec.-Gen. ISSÉ DOUCOURÉ.

There are, in addition, several non-affiliated trade unions.

Transport

RAILWAYS

Mali's only railway runs from Koulikoro, via Bamako, to the Senegal border (642 track-km). The line continues to Dakar, a total distance of 1,286 km. In 1995 the Governments of Mali and Senegal agreed to establish, with a view to privatization, a joint company to operate the Bamako–Dakar line. Some 500,000 tons of freight were handled on the Malian railway in 1991. Plans exist for the construction of a new rail line linking Bamako with Kouroussa and Kankan, in Guinea.

Régie du Chemin de Fer du Mali (RCFM): rue Baba Diarra, BP 260, Bamako; tel. 22-29-68; telex 2586; fax 22-83-88; f. 1960; Pres. DIAKARIDIA SIDIBÉ; Man. Dir CISSÉ OUMOU.

ROADS

The Malian road network in 1995 comprised 14,776 km, of which about 5,705 km were main roads and 5,595 km were secondary roads. About 1,770 km of the network were paved. A bituminized road between Bamako and Abidjan (Côte d'Ivoire) provides Mali's main economic link to the coast; construction of a road linking Bamako and Dakar (Senegal) is to be financed by the European Development Fund. In 1995 the OPEC Fund for International Development agreed to provide US $10m. towards the cost of rehabilitating roads and bridges in the north-west, near the border with Mauritania.

Compagnie Malienne de Transports Routiers (CMTR): BP 208, Bamako; tel. 22-33-64; telex 2539; f. 1970; state-owned; Man. Dir MAMADOU TOURÉ.

INLAND WATERWAYS

The River Niger is navigable in parts of its course through Mali (1,693 km) during the rainy season from July to late December. The River Senegal was, until the early 1990s, navigable from Kayes to Saint-Louis (Senegal) only between August and November, but its navigability was expected to improve following the inauguration, in 1992, of the Manantali dam, and the completion of works to deepen the river-bed.

Compagnie Malienne de Navigation (CMN): BP 10, Koulikoro; tel. 26-20-94; fax 26-20-09; f. 1968; state-owned; river transport and shipbuilding; Pres. and Man. Dir LASSINÉ MARIKO (KONÉ).

Société Navale Malienne (SONAM): Bamako; f. 1981; transferred to private ownership in 1986; Chair. ALIOUNE KEÏTA.

CIVIL AVIATION

The principal airport is at Bamako-Senou. The other major airports are at Bourem, Gao, Goundam, Kayes, Kita, Mopti, Nioro, Ségou, Tessalit and Tombouctou. There are about 40 small airfields. Mali's airports are being modernized with external financial assistance.

Air Afrique: BP 2651, Bamako; tel. 22-76-86; fax 22-61-36; see under Côte d'Ivoire; Dir in Mali B. DJIBO.

Mali Tombouctou Air Service (MALITAS): Bamako; f. 1988 to succeed Air Mali; partial sale of state holding (20%) authorized in 1996; domestic services; Chair. AMADOU OUSMANE SIMAGA.

Société des Transports Aériens (STA): BP 1809, Bamako; f. 1984; privately-owned; local services; Man. Dir MELHEM ELIE SABBAGUE.

Tourism

Mali's rich cultural heritage is promoted as a tourist attraction. Some 28,000 tourists visited Mali in 1994; receipts from tourism in that year totalled US $18m. Although unrest in the north after 1990 adversely affected the sector, a marked recovery was evident with the restoration of peace from 1995.

Office Malien du Tourisme et de l'Hôtellerie (OMATHO): porte 71, rue Mohamed V, BP 191, Bamako; tel. 22-56-73; fax 22-55-41; f. 1995; Dir AGUIBOU GUISSÉ.

Defence

In August 1996 the active Malian army numbered some 7,350 men: land army 6,900, naval force about 50 (with three patrol boats on the River Niger), air force 400. Paramilitary forces (gendarmerie, republican guard, militia and national police) numbered 7,800 men. Military service is by selective conscription and lasts for two years.

Defence Expenditure: Budgeted at 25,000m. francs CFA in 1996.

Chief of Staff of the Armed Forces: Col TOUMANI CISSOKO.

Chief of Staff of the Army: Lt SILIMA KEITA.

Education

Education is provided free of charge and is officially compulsory for nine years between seven and 16 years of age. Primary education usually begins at the age of seven and lasts for six years. Secondary education, from 13 years of age, lasts for a further six years, generally comprising two cycles of three years each. The rate of school-enrolment in Mali is among the lowest in the world: in 1993 total enrolment at primary and secondary schools was equivalent to 20% of children in the relevant age-group (males 26%; females 15%). Primary enrolment in 1994 was equivalent to 32% of the appropriate age-group (males 39%; females 25%). Secondary enrolment in 1993 was equivalent to only 8% (males 11%; females 6%). The Government aims to increase the rate of primary enrolment to 35% by 1999; to this end, an additional 2,600 teachers were to be recruited in 1996–2001. Tertiary education facilities include the national university, developed in the mid-1990s. Hitherto, many students have received higher education abroad, mainly in France and Senegal. In 1988, according to official figures, illiteracy among persons aged six years and over averaged 81.2% (males 73.6%; females 88.6%). UNESCO estimated the average rate of adult illiteracy in 1995 at 69.0% (males 60.6%; females 76.9%). Expenditure by the Ministry of National Education in 1993 was 15,369m. francs CFA (equivalent to 13.2% of total government spending).

Bibliography

de Benoist, J.-R. *Eglise et pouvoir colonial au Soudan français.* Paris, Editions Karthala, 1987.

Brasseur, P. *Bibliographie générale du Mali (Anciens Soudan Français et Haut-Sénégal-Niger).* Dakar, Institut français d'Afrique noire, 1964.

Cissé, Y. T., and Kamissoko, W. *La grande geste du Mali, des origines à la fondation de l'empire.* Paris, Editions Karthala, 1988.

Cola Cissé, M., et al. *Le Mali: Le Paysan et L'Etat.* Paris, L'Harmattan, 1981.

Davies, S. *Adaptable Livelihoods: Coping with Food Insecurity in the Malian Sahel.* New York, St. Martin's Press, 1996.

Decraene, P. *Le Mali.* Paris, Presses universitaires de France, 1980.

Diarrah, Cheikh O. *Le Mali de Modibo Keita.* Paris, L'Harmattan, 1986.

Diop, M. *Histoire des classes sociales dans l'Afrique de l'Ouest. Tome 1: Le Mali.* Paris, L'Harmattan.

Dumont, R. *Afrique noire: développement agricole, reconversion de l'économie agricole: Guinée, Côte d'Ivoire, Mali.* Paris, Presses universitaires de France, 1962.

Foltz, W. J. *From French West Africa to Mali Federation.* Yale University Press, 1965.

Gaudio, A. *Le Mali.* Paris, Editions Karthala, 1988.

Gibbal, J. M. *Genii of the River Niger.* Chicago, University of Chicago Press, 1994.

Harrison Church, R. J. *West Africa.* 8th Edn. London, Longman, 1979.

Imperato, P. J. *Historical Dictionary of Mali.* Metuchen, NJ, Scarecrow Press, 1987.

Mali: A Search for Direction. Boulder, CO, Westview Press, 1989.

Maharaux, A. *L'Industrie au Mali.* Paris, L'Harmattan, 1986.

Mariko, K. *Les Touaregs Ouelleminden.* Paris, Editions Karthala, 1984.

Raimbault, M., and Sanogo, K. (Eds). *Recherches archaéologiques au Mali.* Paris, Editions Karthala, 1991.

Rimmer, D. *The Economies of West Africa.* London, Weidenfeld and Nicolson, 1984.

Snyder, F. G. *One-Party Government in Mali: Transition towards Control.* New Haven and London, Yale University Press, 1965.

Sy, M. S. *Recherches sur l'exercice du pouvoir politique en Afrique noire (Côte d'Ivoire, Guinée, Mali).* Paris, 1965.

MAURITANIA

Physical and Social Geography

DAVID HILLING

Covering an area of 1,030,700 sq km (397,950 sq miles), the Islamic Republic of Mauritania forms a geographical link between the Arab Maghreb and Black West Africa. Moors, heterogeneous groups of Arab/Berber stock, form about two-thirds of the population, which totalled 1,864,236 at the April 1988 census. According to official estimates, the population totalled 2,284,000 at mid-1995 (giving an average population density of 2.2 persons per sq km).

The Moors are divided on social and descent criteria, rather than skin colour, into a dominant group, the Bidan or 'white' Moors, and a group, probably of servile origin, known as the Harratin or 'black' Moors. All were traditionally nomadic pastoralists. The country's black African inhabitants traditionally form about one-third of the total population, the principal groups being the Fulani (20%) and the Wolof (12%). They are mainly sedentary cultivators and are concentrated in a relatively narrow zone in the south of the country.

During the drought of the 1970s and early 1980s, there was mass migration to the towns, and the urban population increased from 18% of the total in 1972 to as much as 35% in 1984. The population of Nouakchott was 134,986 at the time of the 1977 census, but this was estimated to have risen to 550,369 by 1994. Towns such as Nouadhibou (population 22,365 in 1977), Kaédi (20,356), Zouérate (17,947) and Rosso (15,888) have since grown considerably. There has been a general exodus from rural areas and an associated growth of informal peri-urban encampments. In 1963 about 83% of the population was nomadic, and 17% sedentary, but by 1988 only 12% remained nomadic, while 88% were settled, mainly in the larger towns.

Two-thirds of the country may be classed as 'Saharan', with rainfall absent or negligible in most years and always less than 100 mm. In parts vegetation is inadequate to graze even the camel, which is the main support of the nomadic peoples of the northern and central area. Traditionally this harsh area has produced some salt, and dates and millet are cultivated at oases such as Atar. Southwards, in the 'Sahelian' zone, the rainfall increases to about 600 mm per year; in good years vegetation will support sheep, goats and cattle, and adequate crops of millet and sorghum can be grown. There is evidence that the 250 mm precipitation line has moved 200 km further south since the early 1960s, as Saharan conditions encroach on Sahelian areas. In 1983 rainfall over the whole country reached an average of only 27% of that for the period 1941–70, and was only 13% in the pasturelands of the Hodh Oriental region. Average annual rainfall in the early 1990s was reported to be only 100 mm. The Senegal river has been at record low levels, and riverine cultivation in the seasonally inundated *chemama* lands has been greatly reduced. Larger areas of more systematic irrigation could be made possible by dams which have been constructed for the control of the river.

Geologically, Mauritania is a part of the vast western Saharan 'shield' of crystalline rocks, but these are overlain in parts with sedimentary rocks, and some 40% of the country has a superficial cover of unconsolidated sand. Relief has a general north-east/south-west trend, and a series of westward-facing scarps separate monotonous plateaux, which only in western Adrar rise above 500 m. Locally these plateaux have been eroded, so that only isolated peaks remain, the larger of these being known as *kedia* and the smaller as *guelb*. These are often minerally enriched; however, reserves of high-grade iron ore in the *djbel le-hadid* ('iron mountains') of the Kédia d'Idjil were nearing exhaustion in the late 1980s, and production ceased in 1992. Mining at a neighbouring *guelb*, El Rhein (some 40 km to the north), began in 1984, while the exploitation of the important M'Haoudat deposit (55 km to the north of Zouérate) began in 1994. Gypsum is currently mined on a small scale, and reserves of gold, phosphates, sulphur and rock salt have been identified.

In 1991 Arabic was declared to be the official language. The principal vernacular languages, Poular, Wolof and Solinke were, with Arabic, recognized as 'national languages'. French is still widely used, particularly in the commercial sector.

Recent History

PIERRE ENGLEBERT

Revised for this edition by the Editor

Mauritania achieved independence from France on 28 November 1960, with Moktar Ould Daddah, whose Parti du regroupement mauritanien (PRM) had won all the seats in the previous year's general election, as head of state. After independence all parties merged with the PRM to form the Parti du peuple mauritanien (PPM), and Mauritania was declared a one-party state in 1964. The 1961 constitution provided for an executive presidency, to which Ould Daddah was duly elected. A highly centralized and tightly controlled political system was imposed on a diverse political spectrum. Some elements among the Moorish population favoured union with Morocco, and, although every government included a small minority of black Mauritanians, the southern population feared Arab domination. In the early years of independence the majority of Arab states refused to recognize Mauritania, which Morocco claimed as part of its own territory. Mauritania relied heavily on the diplomatic support of France, while forming other international alliances, concentrating initially on black African countries. Morocco officially recognized Mauritania in 1969.

OULD DADDAH AND THE PPM

In the early 1970s the Ould Daddah government undertook a series of measures to strengthen Mauritania's political and economic independence. Economic and cultural agreements signed with France at independence were renegotiated, and Mauritania announced its intention to withdraw from the Franc Zone and introduce its own currency, the ouguiya. In 1974 the foreign-controlled operator of the iron-ore mines which provided 80% of national exports was nationalized. The period of reform culminated in a PPM congress in 1975, which adopted a charter for an Islamic, national, central and socialist democracy.

For the next four years Mauritanian political life was dominated by the question of the Spanish-controlled territory of the Western Sahara, sovereignty of which was claimed by both Morocco and Mauritania. In November 1975, despite a ruling made in the previous month by the International Court of Justice that the territory's people were entitled to self-determination, Spain, Morocco and Mauritania concluded the Madrid Agreement, whereby Spain agreed to cede the territory in February 1976 for division between its northern and southern neighbours. However, the occupation of the territory by Mauritania and Morocco met with fierce resistance from guerrillas of the Frente Popular para la Liberación de Saguia el-Hamra y Río de Oro, known as the Frente Polisario (Polisario Front), which had, with Algerian support, proclaimed a 'Sahrawi Arab Democratic Republic' (SADR). With the assistance of Moroccan troops, Mauritania occupied Tiris el Gharbia, the province it had been allocated under the Madrid Agreement, but resistance by Polisario forces continued. Guerrilla attacks were mounted both in the new province and inside Mauritania's 1960 frontiers (most notably on the economically vital railway linking the iron-ore deposits near Zouérate with the port of Nouadhibou).

Despite a rapid expansion of its army, Mauritania became increasingly dependent on support from Moroccan troops and on financial assistance from France and conservative Arab states. Within Mauritania the war was popular only with the pro-Moroccan tendency: large sections of the Moorish population had ties of kinship with the Sahrawi insurgents and felt no commitment to the conflict. Mauritania was unable to defend itself militarily, and its economy was in ruins.

SALEK AND HAIDALLA

In July 1978 Ould Daddah was overthrown and detained in a bloodless military coup. Power was assumed by a self-styled military committee for national recovery (CMRN), headed by the chief of staff, Lt-Col (later Col) Moustapha Ould Mohamed Salek, which suspended the constitution and dissolved the national assembly and PPM. Two days after the coup Polisario announced a cease-fire with Mauritania; this was accepted by the new government but proved difficult to maintain with Moroccan troops still on Mauritanian territory. With an outbreak of racial tensions between blacks and Moors in early 1979 adding to political instability, Salek assumed absolute power in March, dissolving the CMRN in the following month and replacing it with a military committee for national salvation (CMSN). Salek continued to head the CMSN, but relinquished the post of prime minister to Lt-Col Ahmed Ould Bouceif. The new premier was, however, killed in an air crash in May, and the CMSN appointed Lt-Col Mohamed Khouna Ould Haidalla, the minister of defence since April, in his place. In the following month Salek resigned, and the CMSN appointed Lt-Col Mohamed Mahmoud Ould Ahmed Louly as his successor. In July Polisario announced an end to the cease-fire; later in the month the Organization of African Unity (OAU) appealed for a referendum to be held in Western Sahara. These events provided the impetus for Mauritania's withdrawal from the war: Haidalla declared that Mauritania had no territorial claims in Western Sahara, a decision that was formalized in the Algiers Agreement, signed with Polisario in August. King Hassan of Morocco then announced that his country had taken over Tiris el Gharbia 'in response to local wishes'.

Haidalla displaced Louly as president in January 1980, and dismissed several members of the CMSN who were allegedly 'impeding national recovery'. Some of those dismissed were to form the nucleus of exiled opposition movements, including the Paris-based Alliance pour une Mauritanie démocratique, led by Ould Daddah, who had been released from prison in 1979. Following growing tensions within the CMSN, Haidalla formed a civilian government in December 1980, with Sid Ahmed Ould Bneijara as prime minister, and published a draft constitution with provision for a multi-party system. In March 1981 Haidalla's forces defeated an attempted coup led by former members of the CMSN. Allegations of Moroccan involvement led to the suspension of diplomatic relations. In April Ould Bneijara was replaced as prime minister by the army chief of staff, Lt-Col (later Col) Maawiya Ould Sid'Ahmed Taya, who also took the defence portfolio; a new military government was formed and the draft constitution abandoned. A further alleged coup attempt was foiled in February 1982, as a result of which Salek and Ould Bneijara were imprisoned.

Mauritania, which had recognized the legitimacy of Polisario but not that of the SADR, found it increasingly difficult to maintain neutrality in the Western Sahara conflict, especially after October 1981, when Morocco bombed Sahrawi bases in northern Mauritania and threatened reprisals against Mauritania itself. In 1982 Mauritania supported the admission of the SADR to the OAU, although it was not until February 1984 that Mauritania itself formally recognized the SADR—a move which had little impact on Morocco but provoked unrest, notably among students, inside Mauritania. The country was simultaneously affected by the effects of severe drought.

THE TAYA PRESIDENCY

Popular discontent with Haidalla's rule led to a bloodless *coup d'état* in December 1984, when Col Taya, who had returned to his previous post as chief of staff of the armed forces, deposed Haidalla (who was temporarily absent from the country, but nevertheless returned home to face detention). Taya instituted major economic reforms, which attracted support from foreign donors, and, in what was seen as an attempt to achieve a reconciliation with supporters of Ould Daddah, three members of the former president's government were appointed to ministerial posts in 1985. Ould Daddah was himself officially pardoned and invited to return home, but chose to remain in exile. In April diplomatic relations with Morocco were resumed.

Ethnic Unrest

The second half of the 1980s witnessed growing unrest among the black Mauritanian population—resentful at what they perceived as the increasing Arabicization of the country by the Moorish community. The distribution of an 'Oppressed Black African Manifesto' in April 1986 provoked the arrest, in September, on charges of 'undermining national unity', of a number of prominent black Mauritanians. Civil disturbances involving the black community led to further arrests. The government responded by stressing the Islamic, rather than Arab, character of Mauritanian culture and by accelerating the introduction of *Shari'a* (Islamic) law. At municipal council elections in December 1986, provision was made for up to four lists of candidates in each municipality, although formal political organizations remained illegal. The Taya regime pledged to continue the process of democratization, with the eventual introduction of direct legislative and presidential elections.

Racial tensions were again highlighted by the arrest, in October 1987, of 51 members of the black Toucouleur ethnic group, following the discovery of a coup plot. Three military officers were sentenced to death, and 41 others were imprisoned. In January 1988 it was claimed that more than 500 black NCOs had been dismissed from the army, gendarmerie and national guard, as a result of disturbances that had followed the executions of the three Toucouleur officers.

In mid-1988 it was reported that about 600 people, including members of the armed forces, were arrested, as part of a short-lived purge of light-skinned Bidan supporters of the Baath Arab Socialist organization, a movement sympathetic to the governments of Iraq and Morocco which had hitherto been influential in the CMSN. In September 13 opponents of the government, all alleged to have Baathist links, were convicted of undermining state security and of recruiting military personnel on behalf of an unnamed country. This estrangement of the pro-Moroccan faction was viewed in some quarters as a shift in the government's position to that which had been advocated by Haidalla (who was released from detention in December), and raised questions concerning Mauritania's professed neutrality in the Western Sahara question.

Friction with Senegal

The persistence of ethnic divisions within Mauritania was exemplified by the country's three-year border dispute with Senegal. The deaths, in April 1989, of two Senegalese, following a disagreement over grazing rights with Mauritanian livestock-breeders, provoked a crisis that was exacerbated by long-standing ethnic and economic rivalries. In the aftermath of the border incident Mauritanian nationals residing in Senegal were attacked, and their businesses ransacked (the retail trade in

Senegal had hitherto been dominated by some 300,000 mainly light-skinned Mauritanians resident in that country). Senegalese nationals in Mauritania (an estimated 30,000, many of whom were employed in the manufacturing sector),together with black Mauritanians, suffered similar attacks. Estimates of the number of casualties varied, but it was believed that by early May several hundred people, mainly Senegalese, had been killed. Operations to repatriate nationals of both countries commenced, with international assistance. Meanwhile, Mauritania was alleged to be exploiting the crisis to expel members of its black indigenous population, while light-skinned Senegalese were being allowed to remain in their host country. Many others fled, or were expelled, from Mauritania to Mali. In July the human rights organization Amnesty International expressed concern that violations of human rights had occurred in Mauritania at the time of the expulsions, and in November it recommended that the Taya government conduct an inquiry into allegations of the torture and murder of black Mauritanians.

Despite international mediation attempts, and both countries' expressed commitment to the principle of a negotiated settlement to the dispute, Senegal's insistence on the inviolability of the border, as defined at the time of French colonial rule, and Mauritania's demand that its traders returning from Senegal receive compensation from the government of that country remained the greatest impediments to a solution. The two countries suspended diplomatic relations in August 1989. There were further outbreaks of violence at the end of the year, when black Mauritanians sheltering in Senegal crossed the frontier (with, the Taya government asserted, the complicity of the Senegalese armed forces) with the intention of reclaiming their property. In early 1990 attempts at mediation by the OAU were thwarted by military engagements in the border region, resulting in several deaths. Subsequent initiatives were equally unsuccessful, and in July telephone connections between the two countries were severed. (All transport links between Mauritania and Senegal had been suspended during 1989.)

Hopes of a *rapprochement* were further undermined in late 1990, when the Mauritanian authorities accused Senegal of complicity in an alleged attempt to overthrow President Taya. In December several sources reported the arrests of large numbers of black Halpulaars in Mauritania. The government confirmed that many arrests (of both military personnel and civilians) had taken place in connection with an alleged coup conspiracy, but denied suggestions that detainees had been tortured. Although the Senegalese government denied any involvement in the alleged plot, relations between the two countries further deteriorated, and in January and February 1991 incidents were reported in which Mauritanian naval vessels had opened fire on Senegalese fishing boats, apparently in Senegal's territorial waters. In March several deaths were reported to have resulted from a confrontation on Senegalese territory, following an incursion by Senegalese troops into Mauritania.

In March 1991 60 of those who had been detained following the alleged coup plot were released. This was followed by a general amnesty, as a result of which the government stated that almost all the country's political prisoners had been freed; however, other sources maintained that several hundred of those who had been arrested in late 1990 remained in detention.

Constitutional Reform

In April 1991 Taya announced that proposals for a new constitution, which would permit the establishment of a multi-party political system, were to be submitted for approval in a national referendum. This unexpected announcement coincided with an upsurge in overt political opposition. In May and June there were demonstrations in Nouakchott by women demanding to know the fate of their relatives who had 'disappeared' following the alleged coup plot in November 1990; also in June there were anti-government protests in Nouadhibou. Tracts and open letters, condemning the Taya government and demanding that a national conference be convened to deliberate the country's political future, began to circulate. The draft constitution was submitted to a national referendum on 12 July 1991. According to official figures, 97.9% of those who voted (85.3% of the registered electorate) endorsed the proposals. However, opposition movements claimed that the turn-out had been as low as 8% of registered voters. The new constitution accorded extensive powers to the president of the republic, who was to be elected, by universal suffrage, for a period of six years, with no limitation placed on further terms of office. Provision was made for a bicameral legislature (comprising a national assembly, to be elected by universal suffrage every five years, and a senate, to be appointed by municipal leaders with a six-year mandate), as well as for a constitutional council, an economic and social council and a supreme Islamic council. The CMSN would remain in power pending the inauguration of the new organs of state. Under the constitution, Arabic was designated as the sole official language.

Shortly after the adoption of the constitution, legislation permitting registration of political parties took effect. Among the first parties to be accorded official status was the pro-government Democratic and Social Republican Party (DSRP), which was criticized by the opposition for its privileged access to the state apparatus; also influential in the first months of political pluralism were the Mauritanian Party for Renewal (which included ex-president Haidalla among its members) and the Union of Democratic Forces (UDF).

A general amnesty for all those accused or convicted of undermining state security was announced in July 1991, prompting the Dakar-based opposition group, the Forces de libération africaine de Mauritanie (FLAM), which had maintained a sporadic campaign of attacks on official targets, to suspend its military operations. However, the limitations of the democratization process became evident in August, when a further women's demonstration was violently dispersed by the security forces. Later in the month Amnesty International published a list of 339 people (mostly Halpulaars), who were alleged to have died in detention following the disclosure of the November 1990 coup plot.

Four candidates, including Taya, Ahmed Ould Daddah (the half-brother of the country's first president), who, while not at the time affiliated to any party, was supported by the UDF, and former CMRN chairman Salek, participated in the presidential election, which took place on 17 January 1992. According to official results, Taya obtained 62.7% of the poll (51.7% of the registered electorate voted); his nearest rival, Ahmed Ould Daddah, received 32.8% of the votes cast. The defeated candidates denounced Taya's victory as fraudulent, and appealed unsuccessfully to the supreme court to declare the election invalid. (Independent observers stated that some 'administrative' errors had undoubtedly occurred, but otherwise agreed that the election had been fairly conducted.) Unrest following the election led to at least two deaths and more than 160 arrests, and prompted the government to impose a temporary dusk-to-dawn curfew in Nouakchott and Nouadhibou. By early February all those who had been detained in the post-election violence had been released. Shortly before the presidential election FLAM had announced that it was to resume military operations.

'Democratized' Government

By late February 1992 six opposition parties that had initially intended to contest elections to the national assembly had withdrawn their candidates, claiming that the electoral process favoured the DSRP. At the elections, which took place on 6 and 13 March, the DSRP won 67 of the chamber's 79 seats, with all but two of the remaining seats being secured by independent candidates. The rate of participation by voters was reported to have been low. It was stated that each of the country's ethnic groups was represented in the assembly. Other than the DSRP, only one party presented candidates for the senate (elections to which followed on 3 and 10 April). The DSRP emerged with a majority in the upper house, with 36 senators; 17 independent candidates were elected, the remaining three seats being reserved for representatives of Mauritanians resident abroad.

At his inauguration, on 18 April 1992, President Taya designated Sidi Mohamed Ould Boubacar, previously the minister of finance, as prime minister. The only military officer in the new government was Col Ahmed Ould Minnih, as minister of defence. Included in the new government were three black ministers and one opposition representative. Ould Boubacar, a French-trained technocrat, was known to have extensive experience of financial management and had previously been involved in the country's negotiations with the IMF. However, his relative lack of experience in other areas of government suggested that Taya intended to retain a dominant role in the political process. The new government announced plans to restructure the judicial system and to reform the civil service. The two legislative chambers were inaugurated later in April. The national assembly elected Cheikh Sid'Ahmed Ould Baba, a Harratin (black Moors who had formerly been slaves) as its president, and Dieng Boubou Farba, a Toucouleur, became president of the senate. Ahmed Ould Daddah and his supporters formally joined the principal opposition to Taya's administration, the UDF (which was renamed the UDF–New Era), in June.

The devaluation of the ouguiya, in early October 1992, precipitated violent protests in the capital, as traders immediately imposed sharp increases in the prices of basic household commodities. The government gave assurances that measures would be taken to offset the adverse social consequences of the currency's depreciation, and compensatory salary increases were introduced in all sectors in January 1993.

Although the government placed particular emphasis on the multi-ethnic character of its administration, tensions remained. In late May 1993 parliament approved legislation pardoning all those (specifically including members of the army and security forces) convicted of crimes committed in connection with 'armed operations and acts of violence and terrorism' during the three years preceding Taya's inauguration as elected president. Security forces forcibly dispersed a demonstration in Nouakchott organized by opponents of the measure, who protested that the period covered by the amnesty had been one of severe repression by the armed forces of black dissidents.

Several long-serving ministers were removed from the government in January 1993, and in June Mouhamedou Ould Michel left the ministry of planning and development to become governor of the central bank. Government changes in November included the departure from the post of minister of foreign affairs and co-operation of Mohamed Abdrahmane Ould Moine, regarded as a principal architect of Mauritania's recent *rapprochement* with Kuwait and its regional allies in the Gulf conflict (see below). His successor, Mohamed Salem Ould Lekhel, was a former member of the CMSN and minister of the economy and finance under Taya's military regime.

Mauritania's first multi-party municipal elections took place in January and February 1994, at which the DSRP won control of 172 of the country's 208 administrative districts. The UDF–New Era won control of 17 districts, the remainder being taken by independent candidates. Opposition groups, including the UDF–New Era, protested that the elections had been fraudulently conducted, to the benefit of the DSRP. (Prior to the elections several people, reported to be activists of both the DSRP and opposition parties, had been arrested in connection with alleged electoral malpractice, while several parties, anticipating fraud, boycotted the polls.) The DSRP's control of the political process was confirmed at elections to renew one-third of the senate's membership in April and May.

Shortly before the first round of municipal voting the president of the unauthorized Mauritanian Human Rights Association (MHRA), Cheikh Sadibou Camara (who was also a member of the prominent opposition party, the Union for Democracy and Progress –UDP) was detained for several days, reportedly on charges of incitement to agitation. Camara had apparently reported to a visiting delegation of international human rights organizations that children of Harratin had been abducted and sold into slavery. (Mauritanian law regards any reference to slavery, which was formally abolished in 1980, as injurious to national unity.) International human rights monitors protested that the government's assertion that Camara belonged to an unauthorized organization was invalid, since the MHRA had on several occasions applied for and been denied legal status, despite constitutional guarantees of the right of free association. Earlier in January 1994 Mauritania's first independent trade union confederation had been legalized, following a protracted dispute between its leaders and the authorities.

Internal Tensions

Meanwhile, there was renewed concern regarding Mauritania's observance of civil rights. In September 1994 seven independent journals suspended publication, in protest at alleged increased censorship measures (including the temporary suspension of two independent journals earlier in the year). None the less, the authorities continued to enforce strict press controls, suspending journals deemed critical of the Taya administration.

From the final months of 1993 there was increasing evidence of the government's desire to counter activities by fundamentalist Islamic organizations. More than 90 alleged members of illicit fundamentalist organizations were arrested in September 1994, among them a former government minister, 10 religious leaders and several foreign nationals. In the following month an amnesty was granted to the detainees after several of their number had made broadcast 'confessions' regarding their membership of extremist groups. Among those who admitted to belonging to an Islamic Movement in Mauritania (Hasim) were prominent members of the UDF–New Era, whose leadership had condemned, and questioned the justification for, the arrests. The Taya government, which accused foreign Islamist groups of promoting extremism in Mauritania, subsequently prohibited the delivery of political speeches in places of worship and outlawed certain Islamic organizations. In February 1995 Mauritania, Morocco, Tunisia, Egypt and Israel participated in discussions with the North Atlantic Treaty Organization (NATO) regarding the future co-ordination of efforts to counter the rise of Islamic fundamentalism and weapons proliferation in the Middle East and North Africa.

An increase of some 25% in the price of bread in January 1995 (following the imposition of value-added tax on food products and industrial supplies) led to riots in Nouakchott. Several prominent opposition figures, including Ahmed Ould Daddah and the UDP leader, Hamdi Ould Mouknass, were arrested and placed under house arrest, accused of organizing the disturbances; a night-time curfew was imposed in the capital, and public gatherings were temporarily banned. The curfew was revoked in late January, and the opposition leaders were released in February. The government subsequently adopted measures aimed at controlling the prices of essential consumer goods.

Government changes in February 1995 included the appointment of new ministers of finance and of defence. In March the Movement of Independent Democrats, which until 1994 had been a member of the UDF–New Era, announced that it was to join the DSRP, claiming that the alliance would afford it greater influence in government and enable it to monitor respect for human rights. Internal tensions within the UDF–New Era threatened to undermine the influence of the party, as dissident groups complained of excessive centralization around Ahmed Ould Daddah's leadership. In July several members of the UDF–New Era were reported to have defected to the UDP. In mid-1995, none the less, six opposition parties, including the UDF–New Era and the UDP, announced they had agreed a series of joint demands regarding future elections: these included the compilation of an accurate voters' register, the formulation of what they termed a 'consensual' electoral code, and guarantees of judicial independence and impartiality on the part of the administration. In August the government granted legal status to two new political parties, Action for Change (AC) and the United Social Democratic Party. In October Taya announced further changes to the council of ministers.

In late October 1995 the Taya administration declared the Iraqi ambassador *persona non grata*, and demanded his departure from Mauritania within 72 hours. The expulsion coincided with reports of a foiled coup in Mauritania, allegedly sponsored by the Iraqi government, which, it was claimed, had funded 'secret organizations' in Mauritania with the intention of securing confidential information concerning the country's strategic installations. A series of arrests ensued, primarily within the ranks of alleged pro-Iraqi Baathist activists. Among those arrested were several journalists, two parliamentarians (one from the DSRP, the other from the UDP), the secretary-general of the national assembly (Mohamed Yehdih Ould Breideleil—a former minister of information), officers in the armed forces and a police commissioner. In December 52 defendants stood trial on charges of forming a secret illegal organization: eight of the accused were sentenced to one year's imprisonment, 11 (including Breideleil and Memel Ould Ahmed, until October a presidential adviser) received short suspended sentences, and 33 were acquitted. In January 1996, however, all 52 were discharged on appeal.

In early January 1996 Taya appointed Cheikh Afia Ould Mohamed Khouna (hitherto minister of fisheries and marine economy) to replace Boubacar as prime minister. (Boubacar was subsequently elected secretary-general of the DSRP.) A new council of ministers was formed, comprising most members of the previous administration and incorporating six new members. Additional changes in February and March included the appointment of Lemrabott Sidi Mahmoud Ould Cheikh Ahmed (hitherto minister of national education) as minister of foreign affairs and co-operation—replacing Mohamed Salem Ould Lekhel, who had been credited with the 'normalization' of relations with Israel and the improvement of relations with Gulf states after the 1990–91 crisis in the region of the Persian (Arabian) Gulf. Also in February 1996 it was announced that the general election (originally scheduled to be held in early 1997) would be brought forward to October 1996, thus enabling the incoming national assembly to vote on the budget for 1997 at the new session. In late March the UDP announced its intention to boycott elections to renew one-third of the senate (scheduled to be held in mid-April), in protest at the government's failure to address the opposition's electoral demands. The results of the elections confirmed the dominance in the senate of the DSRP, which won 17 of the 18 seats contested; the remaining seat was taken by an independent candidate. In May Taya announced further government changes. Despite their initial reluctance, by mid-1996 most political parties, including the UDF–New Era, had agreed to participate in the forthcoming legislative elections. Meanwhile, in June the UDP expelled four of its senior members for their alleged involvement in a defamation campaign against the party, after it had been proposed that the UDP secretary-general be dismissed.

At the legislative elections, held on 11 and 18 October 1996, the DSRP reaffirmed its authority, winning 71 of the 79 seats in the national assembly. The Rally for Democracy and National Unity, closely allied with the administration, also secured a seat. The AC was the only opposition party to win a seat in the assembly, the remainder being secured by independent candidates. Several opposition parties disputed the validity of the results, and denounced censorship measures imposed in the period preceding the elections. Moreover, the UDP, which had participated in the first round of the elections, withdrew from the second round in protest at what it alleged were unfair electoral procedures. Later in October, following the formal resignation of the government, the prime minister named a new council of ministers. Further government changes were announced in January, February, May and June 1997.

In January 1997 several opposition leaders, including the AC chairman, Messaoud Ould Boulkheir, and Mohamed Hassaoud Ould Ismael, the secretary-general of the People's Progressive Party (PPP), were arrested and accused of maintaining 'suspicious relations' with Libya. Boulkheir and several others were released at the end of the month, and Ismael was freed in early February, although five others (all PPP members) were sentenced to short terms of imprisonment for conspiring to break the law. In April four of the five convicted were acquitted by the court of appeal.

In late February 1997 five prominent opposition parties, including the AC and the UDF—New Era, announced the formation of a coalition Opposition Parties' Front. In April the coalition staged a demonstration in the capital to protest at price increases, corruption, and restrictions placed on political parties and trade unions. During a further demonstration in late June, Ahmed Ould Daddah announced that the coalition would boycott the presidential election (scheduled to take place in December) as it anticipated widespread electoral fraud. In July President Taya confirmed his candidature at the election.

In May 1997 as many as 200 undergraduates and 16 lecturers were arrested, following a series of protests in Nouakchott to demand, *inter alia,* an increase in student grants and an improvement in conditions at the university; the detainees were released in June. Secondary school teachers also staged a strike in April, demanding salary rises.

External Issues

Renewed diplomatic initiatives resulted in a meeting, held in July 1991 in Guinea-Bissau, of the foreign ministers of Mauritania and Senegal, at which it was agreed in principle to reopen the Mauritania–Senegal border and to resume diplomatic relations. (However, the issues of the demarcation of the border and the fate of Mauritanian refugees in Senegal were not discussed.) Bilateral contacts continued during the second half of the year, and in November Presidents Taya and Diouf met while attending the francophone summit meeting in France. Full diplomatic links were restored in April 1992, and the process of reopening the border began in May. None the less major issues still remained unresolved. In June representatives of the refugees published an open letter in which they appealed for international assistance for repatriation efforts, together with the return of property confiscated by the Mauritanian authorities and payment compensation for the 'humiliation' suffered as a result of their earlier expulsion. Moreover, Mauritanian refugees in Senegal insisted that, as long as their national identity (*mauritanité*) were not recognized by the Taya government, they would not return to Mauritania. Further tensions were reported in September 1993, when the Mauritanian authorities announced that Senegalese nationals would henceforth be required to fulfil certain criteria, including currency-exchange requirements, before being allowed to remain in (or enter) Mauritania. Concern was expressed that such conditions might be used to prevent black Mauritanians who had fled to Senegal in 1989 from returning to Mauritania. However, in late 1994 the governments of Mauritania and Senegal agreed new measures to facilitate the free movement of goods and people between the two countries, and in early 1995 it was reported that diplomatic initiatives with a view to the repatriation of black Mauritanians from Senegal were in progress. A census conducted by the office of the UN High Commissioner for Refugees (UNHCR) in mid-1995 indicated that there were some 66,000 Mauritanian refugees in Senegal.

In January 1996 several hundred Mauritanian refugees staged demonstrations in northern Senegal in protest at the Mauritanian government's proposed repatriation programme. The demonstrators insisted that their earlier demands be met and that the repatriation process be organized by UNHCR in co-operation with the two governments. A repatriation programme, scheduled to begin in June 1996, was postponed because of logistical problems. Meanwhile, concern was expressed at the plight of the refugees as UNHCR had ceased providing them with food aid at the beginning of the year.

The issue of refugees was also the subject of a series of senior-level negotiations with Mali (including meetings between the presidents of the two countries) in 1992–96. The problem of Mauritanian refugees in Mali was compounded by the presence in Mauritania of light-skinned Malian Tuaregs and Moors and also Bella (for further details, see Recent History of Mali), who, the Malian authorities asserted, were launching raids on Malian territory from bases in Mauritania. Following reports that Malian troops had, in turn, crossed into Mauritania in pursuit of rebels, the two countries agreed in early 1993 to begin work on a precise demarcation of their joint border, which was concluded in September 1993 (at which time there were some 13,000 black Mauritanian refugees in Mali). In April 1994 Mauritania, Mali and UNHCR representatives signed an agreement for the eventual voluntary repatriation of Malian refugees (estimated to number more than 40,000) from Mauritania. An escalation of unrest in northern Mali in July prompted the Mauritanian authorities, fearing a renewed influx of refugees, to dispatch military reinforcements to the border region. Food shortages in refugee camps in Mauritania in early 1996 were reportedly jeopardizing programmes for the organized return of some 34,000 people.

Meanwhile, in April 1994 the governments of Mauritania, Mali and Senegal agreed to strengthen military co-operation, with the aim of improving joint border security. In January 1995 the governments of the three countries undertook to co-operate in resolving joint border issues and in combating extremism, arms-smuggling and drugs-trafficking. In June 1996, at the conclusion of a meeting in Nouakchott of ministers responsible for the interior, the three established joint security measures on their common borders. (An investigation into drugs-trafficking in Mauritania resulted in July in the imprisonment of seven senior police officers and four magistrates.) In July 1997 the respective countries' chiefs of general staff held a meeting in Mali to discuss measures to combat banditry in the region.

Although France has remained an important source of aid and technical assistance, the Taya regime has sought increasingly to enhance links with the other countries of the Maghreb and with the wider Arab world. In February 1989 Mauritania became a founder member, with Algeria, Libya, Morocco and Tunisia, of a new regional economic organization, the Union of the Arab Maghreb (UMA). The member states subsequently formulated 15 regional co-operation conventions. In February 1993, however, it was announced that, given the differing economic orientations of each signatory, no convention had actually been implemented, and the organization's activities were to be 'frozen'. None the less, meetings of UMA leaders continued to be convened annually. Taya made an official visit to Algeria in mid-1995, which culminated in a joint statement reaffirming both countries' commitment to consolidating bilateral relations and to combating 'all manifestations of terrorism'. Relations were strengthened further when Algeria's prime minister and president visited Mauritania in April and July 1996 respectively.

Mauritania has generally enjoyed cordial relations with Iraq (exemplified by the prominent role of the Baathist movement in Mauritanian public life). In April and May 1990 the government denied persistent rumours that it was allowing Iraq to test long-range missiles on Mauritanian territory. Following Iraq's invasion of Kuwait, in August of that year, Mauritania condemned the deployment of troops in the region of the Persian (Arabian) Gulf by those countries that opposed the Iraqi action. Individual Mauritanians volunteered to support Iraq's armed forces, and demonstrations in protest against what was regarded as a US-led offensive took place in Nouakchott. Mauritanian support for Iraq during the 1990–91 crisis resulted in the loss of financial assistance from other countries of the Gulf region. During 1993, however, Mauritania sought to improve its relations with Kuwait and its allies, and there was a perceived loss of influence for Iraqi sympathizers. In April 1994 Kuwait's first deputy prime minister and minister of foreign affairs visited Mauritania, and the two countries issued a joint communiqué in which the Taya government emphasized its recognition of Kuwait's borders, as defined by the UN in 1993.

Mauritania's relations with France improved significantly in the early 1990s, following the introduction of political reforms. Taya made an official visit to France in December 1993, during which he held discussions, described as 'fruitful' with President François Mitterrand and the prime minister, Edouard Balladur. The Mauritanian authorities expressed the hope that bilateral co-operation would be improved as a result of such contacts. Conversely, in mid-1993 the USA suspended Mauritania's benefits under its generalized system of preferences—a programme whereby developing nations enjoy privileged access to US markets—on account of the Taya administration's poor record on workers' rights.

In late November 1995, during a European-Mediterranean conference in Barcelona, Spain, Mauritania signed an agreement to recognize and establish relations with Israel. The Libyan government denounced the *rapprochement*, closed its embassy in Mauritania and severed all economic assistance to the country. The Mauritanian government responded by closing the Libyan cultural centre in Nouakchott. Diplomatic relations between the two countries were, however, restored in March 1997.

Economy

EDITH HODGKINSON

Revised for this edition by THEO THOMAS

Mauritania has few natural resources other than minerals, and its economy was almost entirely traditional and rural, based on livestock and agriculture, until the rapid development of the mining industry, in the 1960s and 1970s, enormously increased export earnings and government revenues. The country's gross domestic product (GDP) rose, in real terms, at an average rate of 8% per year during the 1960s. The growth rate fluctuated in the 1970s as a result of drought, trends in demand for iron ore, and disturbances in output, owing to the activities of the Polisario Front (see Recent History).

During the early 1980s the economy contracted (by an annual average of 1.0% in 1981–84) in the wake of a world recession in demand for iron ore and the burden of servicing a high level of foreign debt, much of it arising from ill-considered investments that Mauritania had made during the more prosperous years of the mid-1970s. Persistent drought was also a factor. The sole offsetting element was the dynamic growth of the fishing sector. The further expansion of this sector, together with the recovery in agricultural production when the drought ended, resulted in a recovery in GDP growth in 1985–88, to an average of 3.2% annually (slightly below the target of real GDP growth of 4% per year that had been envisaged in the programme for economic and financial recovery for that period). The rate of growth accelerated to 5.5% in 1989; however, decline in revenue from the fishing sector, together with disruption caused by the dispute with Senegal and the withdrawal of funding from Middle Eastern sources—as a consequence of Mauritania's support for Iraq at the time of the crisis in the region of the Persian (Arabian) Gulf—resulted in a decline, of 1.8%, in GDP in 1990. The following year saw growth of 2.6%, despite lower output in both the fishing and mining sectors. There was modest growth, estimated at 1.7%, in 1992, while a growth rate of 5.5% in 1993 was attributed to successes achieved under the government's programme of economic adjustment. GDP growth has since remained solid at 4.6% in 1994 and 1995 with an estimated 4.7% in 1996. In 1995, according to estimates by the World Bank, Mauritania's gross national product (GNP) was US $1,014m., equivalent to $460 per head. This level of GNP per head places Mauritania in the category of low-income developing countries (in earlier years, Mauritania had been classified as a lower middle-income developing country).

The Taya regime formulated a one-year economic recovery programme, in agreement with the IMF, when it came to power at the end of 1984. This was incorporated in the 1985–88 programme, which aimed to reduce budget and balance-of-payments deficits by means of more stringent criteria for selecting public investment projects. Emphasis was given to immediately productive schemes in fishing and agriculture, and to the rehabilitation of existing capacity and infrastructure in mining and transport. The achievements of the programme were to be consolidated under the terms of the 1989–91 economic support and revival programme, supported by an enhanced structural adjustment facility from the IMF (that was awarded in May 1989). The programme aimed to achieve real average GDP growth of 3.5% per year during 1989–91 by fostering private enterprise while restructuring and rehabilitating the banking system. As indicated above, economic growth averaged only 2.1% over the period, below the estimated annual population growth rate of 2.6%. Nevertheless, the broad terms of the programme, and its GDP growth targets, were maintained for the subsequent IMF-supported reforms in 1992–95, while real annual growth targets were revised to 4.4% for the 1995–97 programme.

The total population of Mauritania was 1,864,236 at the census of April 1988, implying an average population growth of about 2.6% per year during the preceding decade. Official estimates for mid-1996 indicate a population of 2.35m, although some uncertainty has been caused by population movements arising from the dispute with Senegal. Mauritania's average population density (about 2 per sq km) is the lowest in west Africa. The severe drought of the early 1970s, with its destruction of livestock, and the growth of the modern sector caused a significant diminution in numbers of those living a nomadic or semi-nomadic way of life. In 1965 these were estimated to total

83% of the population, but by 1988 the proportion had declined to 12%. A trend towards settlement in urban areas has been apparent, with the average annual growth rate of the urban population of 6.8% between 1980–95. About 54% of the population was urban in 1995, compared with 14% in 1970; of these, more than 80% live in the capital, Nouakchott.

AGRICULTURE

As mining has developed, the contribution of agriculture and livestock-rearing to GDP has declined—from about 44% in 1960 to 25.5% in 1994 (although 62.6% of the labour force were employed in the sector in the latter year). Less than 1% of the land receives sufficient rainfall to sustain crop cultivation, which is largely confined to the riverine area in the extreme south.

The serious drought of the early 1970s destroyed a large part of the livestock herds (cattle numbered 2m. in 1970), while the harvest of millet and sorghum fell to below its normal level. The return of drought in subsequent years resulted in a further decline in production and livestock numbers, and the grain crop was estimated at 35,000 metric tons in 1979/80. In 1980/81 and 1981/82 there was a good recovery in output of cereals, but the severe drought of 1982–84 caused production to decline sharply, to only one-tenth of domestic requirements in 1983/84. Improved rainfall brought a very strong recovery in subsequent years, while the introduction of paddy rice cultivation proved highly successful, contributing to a total cereal crop of 183,600 tons in 1989/90. However, inadequate rains reduced the crop out-turn to an average of just over 100,000 tons in the following three years. The area planted with cereals increased dramatically in 1993/94 and 1994/95, by nearly 30% and 90% respectively, which, combined with good rains, produced a bumper harvest of 200,400 tons in 1994/95. Even in non-drought years imports are needed to satisfy domestic demand (which has increased as a result of urbanization). In the drought years 1982–84 commercial grain imports were as high as 300,000 tons, supplemented by more than 100,000 tons of food aid. However, by 1994 the import requirement had fallen to 81,000 tons, supplemented by 25,000 tons of food aid. Herding (which is the main occupation of the rural population, and whose contribution to GDP is more than three times that of crop cultivation) was even more adversely affected by the droughts: in 1984 cattle numbers had fallen to about 1m., and sheep and goats to 5.7m. They subsequently recovered to near pre-drought levels, but then fell again in the early 1990s; in 1995, according to FAO estimates, the number of cattle had decreased again to 1.1m., although sheep and goats numbered 8.8m.

The military regime committed itself to a comprehensive rural development programme, concentrating on rebuilding livestock herds and providing reliable water supplies. The 1985–88 economic and financial recovery programme gave priority to the rural sector, which was allocated 35% of total investment, compared with only 10% in the previous (1981–85) plan. The major project in the 1980s was the Gorgol valley irrigation scheme, representing investment of US $100m., with the World Bank, the European Community (EC, now European Union—EU), Saudi Arabia, Libya and France providing more than 85% of the funds. The scheme has provided irrigation for 3,600 ha of rice, sugar, wheat and maize since the inauguration of the dam in 1985. Two similar projects are in progress: one at Boghé, on the Senegal river, and the other based on a number of small dams in the centre and west of the country. In total, the three schemes are projected to bring some 30,000 ha into cultivation. The construction of dams at Djama, in Senegal (completed in 1985), and at Manantali in Mali (completed in 1988), under the auspices of the Organization for the Development of the Senegal River (OMVS), was expected to provide a further 16,000 ha of irrigated land, but its contribution has been limited by technical and political problems.

An Oasis Development Project, financed by the International Fund for Agricultural Development, was under way in 1994–95. The project, estimated to cost US $17.2m., aimed to improve incomes and living conditions of 9,500 poor and rural families in 120 oases and 20 villages in five of the country's regions through the development of water resources and conveyance systems. In 1996 Mauritania won funding of some $76.5m. from various donors for a major five-year irrigation project along the Senegal river.

FISHING

The fishing sector provides an important contribution to both local food supply and exports, and was the most dynamic sector of the economy in the 1980s. The potential annual catch in Mauritanian waters had until recently been estimated at as much as 600,000 tons, but declining catches and concern about over-exploitation of fish stocks have led to a less optimistic reassessment. The rapid extension of foreign participation in the industry during the 1970s, which exceeded the growth of the fish-processing sector at Nouadhibou, obliged the government to reformulate its fishing policy in 1980. Thus, it abrogated existing agreements permitting foreign-based vessels to fish Mauritanian waters, and required foreign companies or governments fishing therein to form joint ventures with Mauritanian interests, with the latter holding a majority of the equity capital. Since 1983 all catches made in Mauritanian waters have had to be landed in the country for processing and export, and from mid-1984 until the monopoly was ended in 1992 all sales had to be directed through the state fishing company. Agreements have been reached with fishing companies from the EC, Japan, Russia, Ukraine and the People's Republic of China, among others.

After protracted negotiations, a fishing agreement with the EC was signed in 1987. Covering a three-year period, the agreement granted fishing rights to vessels of EC countries in return for US $23.7m. in compensation, but excluded some categories of fish and vessels. The subsequent three-year accord, concluded in 1990, maintained broadly the same terms, but made provision for the protection of fish stocks and for monetary compensation of $64m. A further arrangement with the EC was negotiated in 1993, and in 1996 a five-year accord was signed with the EU. The new accord increases substantially Mauritania's annual compensation entitlement (including licence fees), from around $10.7m. in the previous three-year treaty, to $75.4m. The annual catch quota was raised from 76,050 tons to 183,392 tons. For the first time EU vessels will be allowed to trawl the deep-water (pelagic) species which were previously exploited by Mauritanian joint-venture companies (many of which had become inoperative). As part of the overall package, the EU agreed to increase local employment in the industry from around 400 to 1,000 and observe an annual two-month rest period (September and October) to protect species during their peak reproductive season.

The requirement that foreign enterprises land and process their catch in Mauritania has boosted fish exports and earnings, which in 1983 reached 312,100 tons (from only 14,600 in 1979) and UM 8,773m., causing fish to become, for the first time, a more important source of export earnings than iron ore—a position that was maintained in 1984, despite a recovery in sales of iron ore in that year, and in 1985. In 1986 the value of exports of fish reached a record UM 20,330m. and their volume a record 388,400 tons. In that year the fishing sector (including processing) accounted for about one-tenth of GDP, and the 1985–88 recovery programme allocated almost 9% of total new project investment (UM 3,520m.) to further fisheries development, with around one-half destined for a ship-repair yard in Nouadhibou, which was inaugurated in late 1989. However, the volume and value of catches declined in the late 1980s, as some international operators moved their operations elsewhere and because of the depletion of stocks earlier in the decade. By 1991 the sector's contribution to GDP had declined to 6%, with fish exports (of 205,200 tons) valued at UM 18,926m. Earnings improved by almost 45% in 1993, when exports of fish and fish products accounted for some 56% of the value of total exports, and the contribution of fishing to GDP had recovered to 7%. Export volumes plunged by 38% in 1994, however, to a total of 196,100 tons, reducing the contribution of the fishing sector to 5% of GDP. (In terms of foreign exchange earnings, the decline was partly offset by higher prices.) This provoked the government to rethink its fishing policy; in particular, it addressed serious concerns about over-fishing by imposing a one-month suspension of all fishing operations in late 1995, in an attempt to allow marine stocks (particularly octopus and squid) to recover. It also revised its system of allocating fishing licences, replaced deep-sea export licences with access fees and introduced production-sharing agreements. In spite of the temporary fishing ban, fish exports recovered sharply in 1995, to 287,000 tons before declining to 250,000 in 1996, according to official estimates. Over-fishing will remain a concern, however, while the sector's future is also compromised by the poor state of the Mauritanian fleet, only 60% of which is now considered operational. External assistance (such as a loan of $14.2m., granted by the African Development Fund in late 1993, and a substantial loan from the International Development Association in mid-1995) has been made available for the reform of the fishing sector. Many aid-funded projects have targeted artisanal fishing.

MINING AND POWER

While the vast majority of the population still depends on agriculture and livestock for its livelihood, the country's economic growth prospects were transformed during the 1960s by the discovery and exploitation of reserves of iron ore and copper, which made Mauritania one of west Africa's wealthier countries in terms of per caput income. The Guelbs region has workable reserves of iron ore estimated at 5,000m.–6,000m. tons. These are being developed by the former Société anonyme des mines de fer de Mauritanie (MIFERMA), established in 1959 by the French government. Mauritania nationalized these holdings in 1974, and they became part of the state mining corporation, the Société nationale industrielle et minière (SNIM). Between 1960–72 about 70,800m. francs CFA was invested in the development of the Kédia d'Idjil mines, including the construction of a 670-km railway and a mineral port. Production of ore, which began in 1963, reached 11.7m. tons (gross weight) in 1974, but by 1978 had fallen to 7.3m. tons, owing in part to attacks on the supply line by guerrillas of the Polisario Front. Following the cease-fire of 1978, production began to recover. However, the mines' fortunes were subsequently eclipsed by a fall in foreign demand, because of economic recession. By the late 1980s the Kédia d'Idjil mines were nearing exhaustion, and production ceased in 1992. Meanwhile, SNIM began exploitation of the lower-grade (36%, compared with a metal content of as much as 60% at Kédia d'Idjil) iron ore deposits some 40 km north of the Kédia d'Idjil mines. Production under the first stage of the project, at El Rhein, began in 1984, increasing total national output to 11.5m. tons in 1990. However, production declined to 10.3m. tons in 1991 and to only 8.3m. tons in 1992, as technical problems (notably the cost of ore processing in this isolated region) at El Rhein meant that the deposit yielded little more than 2m. tons per year, far less than the 'break-even' level of 3m. tons annually. The second stage of the project, a new mine at Oum Arwagen, was thus allowed to lapse. The company's main interest has now been transferred to the deposits at M'Haoudat, near Zouérate (estimated to contain recoverable reserves of 100m. tons), which revealed potential for annual production of about 5.6m. tons of high-grade (60%–65%) ore. Financing for the project, estimated to total US $172m., was supplied by the African Development Bank (ADB), the European Investment Bank, France and SNIM. Work on the scheme began in December 1991, and the mine was inaugurated in April 1994. As part of the project the mineral port at Point-Central, 10 km south of Nouadhibou, has been modernized and expanded, with new plant to mix different concentrate types. With the entry into production of the M'Haoudat scheme, the government hoped to sustain overall output averaging 12m. tons of ore annually, over at least 25 years. Total production reached 11.4m. tons in 1994 and 11.3m. tons in 1995, while exports rose from 8.0m. tons in 1992 to 11.5m. tons in 1995. In April 1997 SNIM began construction of its $200m. iron pelletization project, which will increase domestic value-added by reducing impurities in the iron-bearing ore, and provide an estimated 5,000 additional jobs in Nouadhibou. The government hopes to raise output to 15.5m. tons of ore per year.

In 1967 the Société minière de Mauritanie (SOMIMA), of which the government took full control in 1975, was formed to exploit the copper reserves at Akjoujt, then estimated at 32m. tons. Production began in 1970, with 3,000 tons of copper concentrate. Output rose to a peak of 28,982 tons in 1973, but ceased altogether in 1978, owing to the low grades of the deposit. A new company, the Société arabe des mines d'Inchiri, was formed in 1981 by the government and Arab interests in order to reopen the mine, at a projected annual production of 105,000 tons, exploiting more extensive reserves than earlier estimated, at a cost of US $100m. Projected annual output has since been lowered to 65,000 tons, and investment reduced to $40m. In early 1991 SOMIMA established a joint-venture company, Mines d'or d'Akjoujt (MORAK), with Australian interests and the International Finance Corpn, to extract gold from Akjoujt. Operations began in April 1992 and ended in early 1996, when the deposit was depleted, but the partners in MORAK were expected to start a new venture to mine an estimated 25m. tons of deeper copper reserves at the site. In June 1995 the government granted an Australian exploration company, General Gold Resources, exclusive rights to explore and exploit minerals in the south of the country. In November 1996 General Gold Resources applied for a new mining permit covering a region close to the northern border with Western Sahara. In June 1995 France awarded a substantial grant for gold prospecting in the Inchiri region. Mauritania's total gypsum reserves are estimated at 4,000m. tons, among the largest in the world. Production rose substantially with the reopening in 1984 of the N'Drahamcha quarry, north of Nouakchott, by the Société arabe des industries métallurgiques mauritano-koweïtienne (SAMIA). Owing to technical and transport problems, total output declined from a peak of 19,400 tons in 1987 to less than 3,000 tons a year, both in 1991 and 1992.

As part of the reduction in the government's role in the economy, SNIM was opened to private participation in 1978, and Arab governments and institutions now hold 29% of the renamed concern. SNIM is involved in prospecting for tungsten (wolfram), iron, petroleum, phosphates and uranium (the latter, in the north of the country, was temporarily interrupted by the guerrilla war). Phosphate reserves of 95m.–150m. tons have been located at Bofal, near the Senegal river. A consortium was established in 1990 to develop the deposit, although initial attempts to secure external financial support failed, and it is planned to construct a fertilizer plant to process eventual output.

Exploratory drilling for petroleum began at the offshore Autruche field in 1989, although no significant reserves have been discovered. Reserves of gold, sulphur and peat are also being considered for exploitation.

Reflecting the needs of mineral development, electricity generation has expanded rapidly since the late 1960s, from 38.4m. kWh in 1967 to 148m. kWh in 1994. About one-half of the electricity is now generated by hydroelectric installations built on the Senegal river under the OMVS scheme (see above). SNIM generates electrical power for its production centres from two diesel-powered plants at Zouérate, and from the Point-Central plant in Nouadhibou. A power line that will enable Mauritania to utilize electricity generated at the Manantali installation (which was inaugurated in October 1992) is to be constructed; Mauritania would receive 15% of the target of generation of 800m. kWh.

A butane gas depot, with a capacity of 2,500 cu m, was inaugurated in mid-1995 at Kiffa, in southern Mauritania. Consumption of butane gas in the country was reported to have increased from 5,000 tons in 1988 to 13,000 tons in 1994.

MANUFACTURING

There is, as yet, no significant industrial development outside the mining sector, but the manufacturing sector has expanded because of the development of the fish-processing industry. Initially, development had concentrated on import substitution. However, as income from iron mining rose during the early 1970s, the government promoted the development of large-scale, capital-intensive manufacturing projects, in which it participated directly. These included the petroleum refinery at Nouadhibou, which entered production in 1978, with an annual capacity of 1m. tons. In the event, this wholly government-financed project was closed by the new regime. After reopening in 1982 (with Algerian assistance), the refinery closed again after only six months. However, an agreement on rehabilitation was reached with Algeria in 1985, and operations resumed in mid-1987. More than three-quarters of its total annual output of 1.5m. tons are exported. A sugar refinery was completed in 1977, but it was closed after less than one year's operation because its dependence on imported sugar made it uneconomic. The plant was reactivated in 1982, with assistance from Algeria, as a sugar-packaging operation, but finally closed in 1990. The government also planned to establish plants to produce 500,000 tons of steel and 30,000 tons of copper by 1979/80. SAMIA (see above) was formed in 1974, with Kuwaiti participation, to build the plants, and operations at the steel mill, which has product capacity of 36,000 tons and uses both scrap and imported billets, began in 1981. The mill failed to reach capacity production, and closed in 1984, but reopened in 1987 as a joint venture with Jordanian and Kuwaiti participation. In total, however, these projects proved to be unprofitable and a major burden on state finances. Although government enterprises remain of major importance, the Taya administration is no longer placing emphasis on large-scale capital-intensive projects, but is, instead, encouraging development by the private sector and the establishment of small- and medium-scale operations, aimed at low-level import substitution. Long-term tax concessions are offered for private investors, especially for those aiming to create local employment, increase exports or establish projects outside the two main cities. Meanwhile, the development of fish-processing units at Nouadhibou, as a result of the government's fisheries policy, made this sub-sector into the single most important manufacturing activity, accounting for as much as 4% of annual GDP. However, several plants have since closed, mainly because of high utility costs, a lack of skilled labour and inadequate port facilities. In April 1996 poor hygiene standards prompted the EU to impose a three-month ban on imports of fish landed in Mauritania. In 1994 the manufacturing sector (excluding construction) contributed 10.9% of GDP.

A major strand in current policy is the rationalization of the public sector. In mid-1990 the World Bank, in co-operation with Arab donors, Spain and the Federal Republic of Germany, agreed to provide US $40m. in support of a programme to reduce, or eliminate, state monopolies, to transfer some state enterprises to private ownership, and to restructure some strategic enterprises (such as SNIM, the fish-export monopoly and the power utility). It was envisaged that one-half of Mauritania's 80 parastatal organizations would have been thus 'privatized' or liquidated by mid-1991. Although this target was not attained, there has been solid progress. The reform of the banking system, under the 1989–91 programme, had already entailed the streamlining of government banking institutions. Five textile and fishing companies were liquidated, the petroleum-products sector was fully liberalized, and the monopolies in fish-marketing, insurance and tea-importing have been ended. By mid-1996 only seven companies remained wholly under state ownership, with a further 50 majority- or part-owned by the government.

TRANSPORT INFRASTRUCTURE

Transport infrastructure related to mineral development is of a high standard. The iron ore port of Point-Central, 10 km to the south of Nouadhibou, can accommodate 150,000-ton bulk carriers (a 670-km rail line links the port with the iron-ore deposits at Zouérate and has been extended by 40 km to the El Rhein deposit and by 30 km to M'Haoudat), while Nouakchott's capacity was expanded to 950,000 tons with the completion, in 1986, of a 500,000-ton deep-water facility, financed and constructed by the People's Republic of China. This development reduced the country's dependence on transportation through Senegal, and the excess capacity that the port currently represents could be used for gypsum and copper exports, and for traffic to Mali. Outside the mineral shipment network, communications are at present still poor: in 1996 there were some 7,600 km of roads and tracks, of which less than 1,800 km were tarred. The 1,100-km Trans-Mauritania highway, linking Nouakchott with the south-eastern part of the country, was completed in 1985. Its construction was aided by foreign, principally Arab, funds. In late 1994 the European Development Fund granted ECU 7.4m. to help finance the country's second road programme. In 1996 the ADB granted a US $12.8m. loan towards upgrading the road between Akjoujt and Atar. The work is part of the $26m. 'route transmaghrébine', designed to improve access to the north-eastern part of the country and eventually to improve transport links between Mauritania and its north-eastern neighbours. The Senegal river is navigable for 210 km throughout the year (navigability should eventually be extended, with the completion of the Manantali dam), and there are three major river ports, at Rosso, Kaédi and Gouraye. There are international airports at Nouakchott and Nouadhibou.

FINANCE

Mauritania's budget situation was transformed by mineral development. The MIFERMA contract allowed the temporary liquidation of the chronic budget deficit and commitment of funds to capital development. Spending increased as a result of the guerrilla war and the administrative costs associated with the annexed territory of Western Sahara (abandoned in 1979). Consequently, ordinary expenditure rose by 11% in 1977 and was predicted to rise by 18% in 1978. The cease-fire allowed a much slower rise in current spending in 1978 (only 7%) and a projected fall of 9% in 1980, to UM 9,948m. However, the budget continued in deficit, reaching UM 5,423m. on current spending and UM 8,095m. on total spending in 1979. In return for IMF stand-by credits, successive Mauritanian governments have since 1980 attempted to restrain the level of budgetary spending and to raise current revenue. The overall deficit fell sharply, to around UM 1,800m. per year in both 1982 and 1983, but rose to an estimated UM 4,000m. in 1984, owing to the rising cost of servicing the foreign debt and to the impact of the drought. The 1985–88 recovery programme aimed to balance the current budget in 1986 and to generate a surplus by 1988. In its first year, however, the overall deficit reached an unprecedented UM 9,341m., as debt arrears were discharged. None the less, the current budget did achieve the intended balance, and the overall deficit eased to about UM 900m. in 1986, before widening to UM 2,000m. in 1987. The deficit increased again in the following two years, to reach UM 6,300m. in 1989. Improvements in revenue from taxes, in conjunction with strict controls on expenditure, reduced the deficit to an average of UM 5,940m. per year in 1990–92. The deficit widened sharply in 1993 to UM 12,580m. (equivalent to 11% of GDP), largely reflecting the costs of restructuring the banking sector and of servicing the external debt (see below), together with increased social costs. A slight fall in debt-service payments and better revenue collection reduced the deficit to UM 5,740m. in 1994. On 1 January 1995 the government imposed value-added tax of 5% on food products and of 14% on industrial supplies in an attempt to raise current revenue. The tax proved unpopular and riots erupted in Nouakchott when the price of bread increased by some 25%, but the budget deficit fell to UM 1,160m. in that year. The government subsequently announced the introduction of measures to check monopoly and speculation and the expansion of the remit of SONIMEX, the state's essential goods distribution company, to encompass all essentials including rice, milk, vegetable oil and bread. In line with the 1995–97 reform programme, the government has continued to restrain current expenditure while broadening the tax base by reducing exemptions granted to externally financed government projects, and strengthening collection procedures, particularly for imports. According to official estimates, a budget surplus was recorded in 1996 and it was anticipated that in 1997 the budget target surplus of 1.6% of GDP (excluding unbudgeted fishing royalties equivalent to about 2.5% of GDP) would be surpassed, owing to an increase in revenue. The government decided not to incorporate all fishing revenue in the budget: of the UM 11,000m. annual receipts, only UM 4,000m. was included in the current budget; the remainder will be placed in accounts abroad, reflecting concerns both about the economy's growing dependence on a single depletable resource and the short-term capacity of the economy to absorb productively the large influx of resources.

FOREIGN TRADE AND PAYMENTS

Foreign trade has been transformed by the development, firstly, of the mineral sector and, secondly, of fishing. The value of Mauritania's exports increased from 3,200m. francs CFA (mainly cattle)—equivalent to UM 650m.—in 1959 to UM 8,013m. in 1976, of which 6,919m. came from iron ore. Despite the heavy import requirements of mining development, imports rose less rapidly—from 7,000m. francs CFA (UM 1,400m.) in 1959 to UM 8,072m. in 1976. International reserves, which were only US $3m. at the end of 1970, reached $143m. in early 1975. However, the trade account deteriorated in subsequent years, recording a deficit of UM 5,137m. in 1979, on exports of UM 6,733m. (of which iron ore accounted for UM 6,074m.). The major reasons were a weakening in the demand for iron ore, and increased spending on imports of petroleum. Tighter control on the growth in imports of capital equipment and consumer goods, the recovery in iron-ore prices and the sevenfold increase in earnings from fish exports (to UM 4,428m. in 1981) resulted in a narrowing in the trade gap in subsequent years, to only UM 294m. in 1981. After a sharp rise in the deficit in 1982, as a result of the decline in earnings from iron ore and the increase in petroleum imports with the opening of the refinery, foreign trade moved into surplus in 1983. Import spending was curbed by the government's austerity programme and by a decrease in the import of petroleum products, while export revenue benefitted from the near-doubling in earnings from fish, to UM 8,773m. The trade surplus almost doubled in 1984, and again in 1985, as export totals were enlarged by the rise in iron ore shipments and imports eased further, with an increase in food aid (reducing the need for commercial purchases) and the completion of the first stage of investment at the *guelbs* mine project. The devaluation of the ouguiya in 1985 reinforced these trends. The surplus was maintained in 1986, and increased in 1987–89, as expenditure on imports was contained, while higher earnings from sales of iron ore and the further devaluation of the ouguiya in relation to the US dollar effectively doubled ouguiya-denominated export receipts during 1984–89. The balance of trade remained positive in 1990 and 1991 before a sharp fall in earnings from iron ore (resulting from both lower volumes and international prices) and a large increase in capital imports caused a substantial regression into deficit, of some UM 4,743m. (on a balance-of-payments basis), in 1992. Following a small surplus in 1993, a continuing decline in the volume of imports produced a trade surplus of UM 5,857m. in 1994 and UM 23,851m. in 1995. (It must be borne in mind that significant cross-border trade is not recorded in these statistics.) Such fluctuations in the trade balance were largely responsible for changes in the deficit (before official transfers) on the current account of the balance of payments, although this remained substantial throughout the late 1980s and into the 1990s. Net of official transfers, the current-account deficit averaged $146m. per year in 1986–88. The current account continued in deficit, averaging $80m. per year in the period 1990–94. In 1995, however, the current account was estimated to have registered a modest surplus of $22.1m., owing mainly to the large trade surplus of $183.8m.

The substantial trade surpluses that occurred every year between 1965 and 1974 enabled Mauritania to service its extensive foreign borrowing, while reaching a payments surplus in 1971–74. This allowed Mauritania to leave the West African Monetary Union in 1973 and establish its own currency, the ouguiya, not linked to the franc. In the less favourable payments situation in subsequent years, Mauritania's reserves were sustained by continuing capital borrowing. The country's external public debt reached US $632.2m. (disbursed) at the end of 1976, and its service payments in that year reached 33% of total foreign earnings, compared with only 3.8% in 1974. The foreign debt declined in the following years, reaching $590m. at the end of 1979, but the burden of repayment and interest remained at the same level because of the country's substantial borrowing of commercial funds. Despite a rescheduling of debt obtained by the regime that came to power in 1978, indebtedness continued to rise, totalling $1,342m. at the end of 1984, which was almost double the level of GNP in that year. In addition, arrears of more than $100m., not agreed with lenders, had accrued by the end of 1984, and the debt burden was forecast to rise again in subsequent years. Against the background of the economic stabilization programme agreed with the IMF, the Taya government secured reschedulings of its debt to official creditors in 1985, 1986 and 1987, on the latter occasion obtaining a 15-year rescheduling (including five years' grace) on repayment. Moreover, Mauritania continued to receive substantial aid, of which more than one-half was in grant form, from non-communist countries and multilateral agencies: such funding averaged $242m. per year in 1985–88. However, the debt rose inexorably, to $2,054m. at the end of 1987 (equivalent to 247% of annual GNP), and arrears on interest payments had doubled by 1988, to $52m. The debt-service ratio neared 25% of foreign earnings during most of this period. Mauritania was one of the African countries classified by the World Bank as 'debt-distressed' (i.e., without rescheduling, its debt-service ratio would exceed more than 30% of external earnings in 1988–90) and was thus eligible for the system of exceptional debt-relief that was agreed in principle at the summit meeting of industrialized nations, held in Toronto, Canada, in June 1988. Accordingly, in June 1989 the 'Paris Club' of Western official creditors agreed to reschedule $52m. of the country's external debt. Some bilateral donors agreed to relief: in both 1988 and 1989 the Federal Republic of Germany cancelled official trade obligations, and in mid-1990 France cancelled official loans, totalling $60m., contracted before the end of 1988. In all, debts totalling $180m. were cancelled in 1989. While the foreign debt continued to rise, to $2,233m. by the end of 1991, debt-rescheduling agreements meant that the debt-service ratio was reduced to 20.4% of the value of exports of goods and services in that year—although this continued to represent a considerable burden on the Mauritanian economy. Moreover, interest arrears continued to accumulate, totalling $121m. by the end of 1992 (although the total debt fell slightly, to $2,134m.). Mauritania's failure to pay off debt arrears or to achieve the fiscal targets agreed with the IMF for 1989–91 meant that no further debt relief was accorded until early 1993, when, following the IMF's agreement to extend an enhanced structural adjustment facility for the period to September 1995, the 'Paris Club' agreed to cancel one-half of the interest due on non-concessional debt and to reschedule the remainder over 23 years, with payment due to begin only after 10 years. This round of debt relief represented savings for Mauritania amounting to more than $200m. and was followed by debt restructuring packages of $91m. and $67m. in subsequent years. Nevertheless, although arrears were reduced, the total debt continued to rise to $2,174m. at the end of 1993 and to $2,467m. at the end of 1995. The debt-service ratio increased to 30.1% of the value of exported goods and services in 1993, and was 21.5% in 1995. In early 1995 the IMF approved a $63m. loan, extending an enhanced structural adjustment facility to support the government's financial and economic reform programme for 1995–97. Towards the end of 1996 almost the entire stock of foreign privately contracted commercial debt (of $92m.) was retired through a discounted buy-back operation funded by the World Bank and other donors. Nevertheless, Mauritania's debt sustainability position will remain precarious without further relief for which, paradoxically, it may not be eligible, given its improving macroeconomic outlook.

Statistical Survey

Figures exclude Mauritania's section of Western Sahara, annexed in 1976 and relinquished in 1979.

Source (unless otherwise stated): Office National de la Statistique, BP 240, Nouakchott; tel. 530-70; fax 551-70.

Area and Population

AREA, POPULATION AND DENSITY

Area (sq km)	1,030,700*
Population (census results)†	
1 January 1977	1,338,830
5–20 April 1988	
Males	923,175
Females	941,061
Total	1,864,236
Population (official estimates at mid-year)	
1993‡	2,147,778
1994	2,211,000
1995	2,284,000
Density (per sq km) at mid-1995	2.2

* 397,950 sq miles.

† Figures include estimates for Mauritania's nomad population (444,020 in 1977; 224,095 in 1988).

‡ At 24 April.

REGIONS

Region	Chief town	Area ('000 sq km)	Population (1988 census)*
Hodh el Chargui	Néma	183	212,203
Hodh el Gharbi	Aïoun el Atrous	53	159,296
Assaba	Kiffa	37	167,123
Gorgol	Kaédi	14	184,359
Brakna	Aleg	33	192,157
Trarza	Rosso	68	202,596
Adrar	Atar	215	61,043
Dakhlet-Nouadhibou	Nouadhibou	22	63,030
Tagant	Tidjikja	95	64,908
Guidimaka	Sélibaby	10	116,436
Tiris Zemmour	F'Derik	253	33,147
Inchiri	Akjoujt	47	14,613
Nouakchott	Nouakchott	1	393,325
Total		1,030	1,864,236

* Source: UN, *Demographic Yearbook*.

PRINCIPAL TOWNS (population at census of January 1977)

Nouakchott (capital)*	134,986	Zouérate	17,947
Nouadhibou (Port-Etienne)	22,365	Atar	16,394
Kaédi	20,356	Rosso	15,888

* Estimated at 350,000 in 1984.

BIRTHS AND DEATHS (UN estimates, annual averages)

	1980–85	1985–90	1990–95
Birth rate (per 1,000)	42.3	41.0	39.8
Death rate (per 1,000)	18.5	15.9	14.4

Expectation of life (UN estimates, years at birth, 1990–95): 51.5 (males 49.9; females 53.1).

Source: UN, *World Population Prospects: The 1994 Revision*.

ECONOMICALLY ACTIVE POPULATION
(estimates, '000 persons, 1994)

	Males	Females	Total
Agriculture, etc.	332	98	430
Industry	69	11	80
Services	155	22	177
Total	556	131	687

Source: UN Economic Commission for Africa, *African Statistical Yearbook*.

Agriculture

PRINCIPAL CROPS ('000 metric tons)

	1993	1994	1995
Millet and sorghum	96	154	165
Rice (paddy)	65	53	79
Maize	7	6	1
Potatoes	n.a.	1*	1*
Sweet potatoes*	2	2	2
Yams*	2	3	3
Pulses*	15	17	17
Dates	16*	22	25
Watermelons*	5	6	6
Groundnuts (in shell)*	2	2	2

* FAO estimate(s).

Source: FAO, *Production Yearbook*.

LIVESTOCK ('000 head, year ending September)

	1993	1994	1995
Cattle	1,200	1,100	1,125
Goats*	3,520	3,520	3,526
Sheep*	5,280	5,280	5,288
Asses†	155	155	155
Horses†	18	18	18
Camels	1,070	1,080	1,087

Poultry (million)*: 4 in 1993; 4 in 1994; 4 in 1995.

* Unofficial figures. † FAO estimates.

Source: FAO, *Production Yearbook*.

LIVESTOCK PRODUCTS ('000 metric tons)

	1993	1994	1995
Beef and veal	9	9	10
Mutton and lamb*	12	13	13
Goat meat*	8	8	8
Poultry meat*	4	4	4
Other meat	17	20	20
Cows' milk*	113	104	106
Sheep's milk*	70	72	74
Goats' milk*	80	82	83
Poultry eggs*	4.4	4.6	4.6
Cattle hides*	1.4	1.4	1.4
Sheepskins*	1.6	1.7	1.7
Goatskins*	1.0	1.0	1.0

* FAO estimates.

Source: FAO, *Production Yearbook*.

Forestry

ROUNDWOOD REMOVALS
(FAO estimates, '000 cubic metres, excluding bark)

	1992	1993	1994
Sawlogs, veneer logs and logs for sleepers*	1	1	1
Other industrial wood†	4	4	4
Fuel wood	8	8	8
Total	13	13	13

* Assumed by the FAO to be unchanged since 1977.
† Assumed by the FAO to be unchanged since 1987.
Source: FAO, *Yearbook of Forest Products*.

Fishing

('000 metric tons, live weight)

	1993	1994	1995
Freshwater fishes*	5.0	5.0	5.0
Flatfishes*	1.7	1.8	1.8
Groupers and seabasses*	5.8	6.1	6.4
Meagre*	4.8	5.1	5.4
Porgies, seabreams, etc.*	5.7	6.0	6.3
Sardinellas*	2.4	2.6	2.7
Other marine fishes (incl. unspecified)*	19.1	20.0	21.2
Total fish*	44.5	46.5	49.3
Marine crustaceans	0.5	0.5*	0.5*
Cuttlefishes and bobtail squids	6.9	6.1	6.4*
Octopuses	46.1	30.0	31.7*
Other cephalopods	2.4	1.9	2.0*
Total catch*	100.4	85.0	90.0

*FAO estimate(s).
Source: FAO, *Yearbook of Fishery Statistics*.

Mining

('000 metric tons)

	1990	1991	1992
Iron ore: gross weight	11,520	10,264	8,262
metal content*	6,800	6,500	5,330
Gypsum (crude)*	8	3	3

1993: Iron ore ('000 metric tons): gross weight 9,196; metal content* 5,900.
1994: Iron ore: metal content* ('000 metric tons) 5,400.

* Data from the US Bureau of Mines.
Source: mainly UN, *Industrial Commodity Statistics Yearbook*.

Industry

SELECTED PRODUCTS ('000 metric tons, unless otherwise indicated)

	1990	1991	1992
Frozen and chilled fish*	25.0	13.3	8.3
Salted, dried and smoked fish*	1.2	0.8	0.8
Electric energy (million kWh)	140	143†	146†

1993: Frozen and chilled fish* ('000 metric tons) 8.3; Electric energy† (million kWh) 146.
1994: Electric energy† (million kWh) 148.

* Data from the FAO.
† Estimate.
Source: UN, *Industrial Commodity Statistics Yearbook*.

Finance

CURRENCY AND EXCHANGE RATES

Monetary Units
5 khoums = 1 ouguiya (UM).

Sterling and Dollar Equivalents (31 March 1997)
£1 sterling = 237.42 ouguiyas;
US $1 = 144.59 ouguiyas;
1,000 ouguiyas = £4.212 = $6.916.

Average Exchange Rate (ouguiyas per US $)
1994 123.575
1995 129.768
1996 137.222

BUDGET ('000 million ouguiyas)

Revenue*	1993	1994	1995
Budgetary revenue	27.87	28.98	32.79
Tax revenue	21.71	22.72	23.57
Taxes on income and profits	7.39	7.38	8.16
Taxes on goods and services	3.46	4.72	7.52
Value-added tax	—	—	4.50
Turnover taxes	1.16	1.09	0.30
Tax on petroleum products	1.30	2.59	1.54
Other excises	0.88	0.86	0.95
Taxes on international trade	10.44	10.13	7.47
Import taxes	7.15	7.83	4.73
Export tax on fish	3.15	2.31	2.74
Other current revenue	5.41	5.10	7.99
Fishing royalties and penalties	1.82	1.89	3.46
Revenue from public enterprises	1.17	0.40	0.53
Capital revenue	0.75	1.16	1.24
Special accounts	0.61	0.47	0.42
Total	28.48	29.46	33.21

Expenditure	1993	1994	1995
Current expenditure	24.59	23.62	24.89
Wages and salaries	6.44	6.70	6.97
Goods and services	6.02	6.21	6.93
Transfers and subsidies	2.11	2.20	2.30
Military expenditure	3.64	3.64	3.64
Interest on public debt	4.67	3.65	4.48
Other (incl. unclassified)	1.71	1.22	0.57
Capital expenditure and net lending	17.31	11.58	9.49
Fixed capital formation	6.53	7.33	7.03
Restructuring and net lending†	10.78	4.25	2.46
Total	41.90	35.20	34.37

* Excluding grants received. Also excluded is an adjustment for uncashed cheques.
† Relating to the restructuring of public enterprises and commercial banks.
Source: IMF, *Mauritania—Statistical Appendix* (June 1996).
1996 (estimates, million ouguiyas): Budget balanced at 43,188.

INTERNATIONAL RESERVES (US $ million at 31 December)

	1994	1995	1996
Gold*	4.3	4.4	4.2
IMF special drawing rights	—	0.1	1.4
Foreign exchange	39.7	85.4	139.8
Total	44.0	89.9	145.4

* Valued at market-related prices.
Source: IMF, *International Financial Statistics*.

MONEY SUPPLY (million ouguiyas at 31 December)

	1993	1994	1995
Currency outside banks	9,097	8,598	7,383
Demand deposits at deposit money banks	11,508	11,145	10,674
Total money (incl. others)	20,938	19,816	18,202

Source: IMF, *International Financial Statistics*.

COST OF LIVING (Consumer Price Index for Mauritanian households in Nouakchott; base: 1985 = 100)

	1993	1994	1995
Food	185.0	191.4	206.7
Clothing	160.2	169.4	183.4
Housing	193.6	204.0	213.3
All items (incl. others)	180.2	187.6	199.8

Source: IMF, *Mauritania—Statistical Appendix* (June 1996).

NATIONAL ACCOUNTS

Expenditure on the Gross Domestic Product
('000 million ouguiyas at current prices)

	1992	1993	1994
Government final consumption expenditure	10.8	12.5	12.9
Private final consumption expenditure*	85.3	90.5	104.8
Increase in stocks Gross fixed capital formation	21.2	26.8	20.5
Total domestic expenditure	117.3	129.7	138.1
Exports of goods and services	40.2	52.3	53.4
Less Imports of goods and services	53.9	68.0	64.6
GDP in purchasers' values	103.6	114.0	126.9
GDP at constant 1985 prices	62.0	65.4	68.4

* Including public enterprises. Figures are obtained as a residual.

Source: IMF, *Mauritania—Statistical Appendix* (June 1996).

Gross Domestic Product by Economic Activity
('000 million ouguiyas at current prices)

	1992	1993	1994
Agriculture, hunting, forestry and fishing	24,661	27,146	28,746
Mining and quarrying	8,109	10,405	12,860
Manufacturing	10,514	12,617	12,311
Electricity, gas and water Construction	7,052	7,468	10,346
Trade, restaurants and hotels	15,411	15,877	18,045
Transport, storage and communications	7,116	7,392	8,058
Public administration	13,002	13,115	14,203
Other services	7,359	7,508	8,306
GDP at factor cost	93,224	101,527	112,875
Indirect taxes, *less* subsidies	10,393	12,472	14,006
GDP in purchasers' values	103,617	113,999	126,881

Source: IMF, *Mauritania—Statistical Appendix* (June 1996).

BALANCE OF PAYMENTS (US $ million)

	1993	1994	1995
Export of goods f.o.b.	403.0	399.7	476.4
Imports of goods f.o.b.	–400.4	–352.3	–292.6
Trade balance	2.6	47.4	183.8
Exports of services	21.4	26.0	27.9
Imports of services	–184.9	–181.1	–217.0
Balance on goods and services	–160.9	–107.7	–5.3
Other income received	0.8	1.1	1.3
Other income paid	–97.6	–47.7	–49.5
Balance on goods, services and income	–257.8	–154.3	–53.5
Current transfers received	110.3	113.3	94.7
Current transfers paid	–26.5	–28.9	–19.2
Current balance	–174.0	–69.9	22.1
Direct investment from abroad	16.1	2.1	7.0
Portfolio investment liabilities	–0.1	–0.2	–0.5
Other investment assets	170.5	169.3	211.5
Other investment liabilities	–321.3	–182.6	–228.2
Net errors and omissions	26.7	–23.5	–18.1
Overall balance	–282.1	–104.7	–6.2

Source: IMF, *International Financial Statistics*.

External Trade

PRINCIPAL COMMODITIES

Imports c.i.f. (million ouguiyas)	1992	1993	1994
Dairy products	1,969	1,992	2,030
Tea	1,538	617	325
Rice	1,442	1,926	1,214
Sugar	1,937	3,108	2,346
Cement	705	948	1,082
Hydrocarbons	3,974	912	1,367
Total (incl. others)	35,362	53,749	44,694

Total imports (SDR million): 241 (estimate) in 1995 (Source: IMF, *Mauritania—Statistical Appendix* (June 1996)).

Exports f.o.b. (SDR million)	1993	1994	1995
Iron ore	114.0	114.1	129.7
Fish, crustaceans and molluscs	158.0	144.6	184.5
Gold	11.1	14.3	9.2
Total (incl. others)	286.4	275.0	324.8

Source: IMF, *Mauritania—Statistical Appendix* (June 1996).

PRINCIPAL TRADING PARTNERS (million ouguiyas)

Imports c.i.f.	1992	1993	1994
Algeria	2,330	3,698	2,578
Belgium	1,755	1,713	2,091
Canada	n.a.	1,269	n.a.
China, People's Repub.	1,816	1,470	n.a.
France	12,430	18,074	14,665
Germany	2,291	4,749	2,906
Italy	n.a.	n.a.	1,410
Japan	1,051	2,189	1,629
Netherlands	863	2,573	891
Spain	3,010	3,122	2,980
Thailand	1,208	n.a.	1,047
USA	1,810	5,940	4,291
Total (incl. others)	35,362	53,749	44,694

Exports f.o.b.	1992	1993	1994
Belgium	3,023	2,759	3,388
Côte d'Ivoire	1,666	2,283	1,712
France	2,988	5,972	7,141
Germany	n.a.	n.a.	1,441
Italy	4,365	7,001	7,094
Japan	9,981	11,192	14,511
Nigeria	802	1,497	n.a.
Spain	3,768	5,572	5,225
Switzerland	n.a.	1,932	2,643
USSR (former)	2,737	3,320	1,362
United Kingdom	1,606	2,358	1,603
USA	905	n.a.	n.a.
Total (incl. others)	37,019	51,109	50,710

Transport

RAILWAYS

1984: Passengers carried 19,353; Passenger-km 7m.; Freight carried 9.1m. metric tons; Freight ton-km 6,142m.

Freight ton-km (million): 6,365 in 1985; 6,411 in 1986; 6,473 in 1987; 6,535 in 1988; 6,610 in 1989; 6,690 in 1990; 6,720 in 1991; 6,810 in 1992; 6,890 in 1993 (figures for 1988–93 are estimates) (Source: UN Economic Commission for Africa, *African Statistical Yearbook*).

ROAD TRAFFIC (estimates, '000 motor vehicles in use)

	1993	1994	1995
Passenger cars	15.0	16.8	17.3
Commercial vehicles	7.3	9.0	9.2

Source: IRF, *World Road Statistics*.

SHIPPING

Merchant Fleet (registered at 31 December)

	1994	1995	1996
Number of vessels	129	119	131
Total displacement (grt)	42,172	39,448	42,679

Source: Lloyd's Register of Shipping, *World Fleet Statistics*.

International Sea-borne Freight Traffic
(estimates, '000 metric tons)

	1991	1992	1993
Goods loaded	10,100	10,300	10,400
Goods unloaded	690	715	724

Source: UN Economic Commission for Africa, *African Statistical Yearbook*.

CIVIL AVIATION (traffic on scheduled services)*

	1992	1993	1994
Kilometres flown (million)	3	4	3
Passengers carried ('000)	213	215	216
Passenger-km (million)	275	281	289
Total ton-km (million)	41	40	41

* Including an apportionment of the traffic of Air Afrique.

Source: UN, *Statistical Yearbook*.

Tourism

Tourist Arrivals (estimates, '000): 12 in 1984; 13 in 1985; 13 in 1986.

Receipts from Tourism (US $ million): 7 in 1984; 5 in 1985; 8 in 1986; 14 in 1987; 12 in 1988; 13 in 1989; 15 in 1990; 15 in 1991; 15 in 1992; 15 in 1993.

Sources: UN Economic Commission for Africa, *African Statistical Yearbook*; UN, *Statistical Yearbook*.

Communications Media

	1992	1993	1994
Radio receivers ('000 in use)	309	318	327
Television receivers ('000 in use)	50	50	55
Telephones ('000 main lines in use)	7	8	8
Daily newspapers			
Number	1	n.a.	1
Average circulation ('000 copies)	1*	n.a.	0.5*

* Estimate.

Sources: UNESCO, *Statistical Yearbook*; UN, *Statistical Yearbook*.

Education

(1993/94, unless otherwise indicated)

	Institutions	Teachers	Students		
			Males	Females	Total
Pre-primary*	36	108	n.a.	n.a.	800
Primary	1,635	4,686	136,990	111,058	248,048
Secondary					
General	n.a.	1,776	28,194	15,667	43,861
Teacher training	2†	57	544	276	820
Vocational	3†	105	868	261	1,129
University level	4 (combined)	248*	6,452	1,195	7,647
Other higher	4 (combined)	18*	544	276	820

* 1992/93 figure(s).

† 1991/92 figure.

1994/95: Primary: 5,181 teachers; 268,216 pupils (147,712 boys; 120,504 girls).

Source: mainly UNESCO, *Statistical Yearbook*.

Directory

While no longer an official language under the terms of the 1991 Constitution (see below), French is still widely used in Mauritania, especially in the commercial sector. Many organizations are therefore listed under their French names, by which they are generally known.

The Constitution

The Constitution of the Arab and African Islamic Republic of Mauritania was approved in a national referendum on 12 July 1991.

The Constitution provides for the establishment of a multi-party political system. The President of the Republic is elected, by universal adult suffrage (the minimum age for voters being 18 years), for a period of six years: no limitations regarding the renewal of the presidential mandate are stipulated. Legislative power is vested in a National Assembly (elected by universal suffrage for a period of five years) and in a Senate (elected by municipal leaders with a six-year mandate—part of its membership being elected every two years). The President of the Republic is empowered to appoint a head of government. Provision is also made for the establishment of a Constitutional Council and a Supreme Islamic Council (both of which were inaugurated in 1992), as well as an Economic and Social Council.

The Constitution states that the official language is Arabic, and that the national languages are Arabic, Poular, Wolof and Solinke.

The Government

HEAD OF STATE

President: Col MAAWIYA OULD SID'AHMED TAYA (took office 12 December 1984; elected President 17 January 1992).

COUNCIL OF MINISTERS
(August 1997)

Prime Minister: CHEIKH AFIA OULD MOHAMED KHOUNA.

Minister of Foreign Affairs and Co-operation: SOW ABOU DEMBA.

Minister of Defence: MOHAMED YESLEM OULD EL-VILL.

Minister of Justice: MOHAMED LEMINE SALEM OULD DAH.

Minister of the Interior, Posts and Telecommunications: KABA OULD ELEWA.

Minister of Finance: KAMARA ALY GUELADIO.

Minister of Fisheries and Marine Economy: BOIDIEL OULD HOUMEID.

Minister of Planning and Employment: MOHAMED OULD AMAR.

Minister of Trade, Handicrafts and Tourism: Dr ABDELLAHI OULD NEM.

Minister of Industry and Mines: N'GUE DAH LEMINE KAYOU.

Minister of Equipment and Transport: SOW MOHAMED DEYNA.

Minister of National Education: SGHEYET OULD M'BARE.

Minister of Culture and Islamic Affairs: KHATTRY OULD JIDDOU.

Minister of the Civil Service, Labour, Youth and Sports: BAB OULD SIDI.

Minister of Water and Energy: AHMED KELLY OULD CHEIKH SIDYA.

Minister of Rural Development and the Environment: AHMED SALEM OULD SALEK.

Minister of Health and Social Affairs: MOHAMED OULD DAHMANE.

Minister in charge of Relations with Parliament: RACHID OULD SALEH.

Minister, Secretary-General of the Presidency: BA SILEYE.

Secretary of State for the Union of the Arab Maghreb Affairs: CHEIKH OULD ALI.

Secretary of State, in charge of Civil Status: LEVDAHL OULD ABEL WEDOUD.

Secretary of State for Literacy and Basic Education: MOHAMED LEMINE OULD MOHAMED VALL.

Secretary of State, in charge of Women's Issues: SINIYA MINT SIDI HAIBA.

MINISTRIES

Office of the President: Présidence de la République, BP 184, Nouakchott; tel. 523-17; telex 5580.

Ministry of the Civil Service, Labour, Youth and Sports: Nouakchott.

Ministry of Culture and Islamic Affairs: BP 223, Nouakchott; tel. 511-30; telex 5585.

Ministry of Defence: BP 184, Nouakchott; tel. 520-20; telex 5566.

Ministry of Finance: BP 181, Nouakchott; tel. 520-20; telex 5572.

Ministry of Equipment and Transport: BP 237, Nouakchott; tel. 533-37; telex 5585.

Ministry of Fisheries and Marine Economy: BP 137, Nouakchott; tel. 524-76; telex 5595; fax 531-46.

Ministry of Foreign Affairs and Co-operation: BP 230, Nouakchott; tel. 526-82; telex 5585; fax 528-60.

Ministry of Health and Social Affairs: BP 177, Nouakchott; tel. 520-52; telex 5583; fax 522-68.

Ministry of Industry and Mines: BP 387, Nouakchott; tel. 533-37; telex 5508; fax 535-82.

Ministry of the Interior, Posts and Telecommunications: BP 195, Nouakchott; tel. 520-20; telex 5844.

Ministry of Justice: BP 350, Nouakchott; tel. 510-83.

Ministry of National Education: BP 387, Nouakchott; tel. 512-37; fax 512-22.

Ministry of Planning and Employment: BP 238, Nouakchott; tel. 516-12; telex 5540; fax 551-10.

Ministry of Rural Development and the Environment: BP 366, Nouakchott; tel. 515-00; telex 5813; fax 574-75.

Ministry of Trade, Handicrafts and Tourism: BP 182, Nouakchott; tel. 535-72; fax 576-71.

Ministry of Water and Energy: Nouakchott; tel. 526-88; telex 5815; fax 526-99.

Office of the Secretary-General of the Government: BP 184, Nouakchott.

President and Legislature

PRESIDENT

Election, 17 January 1992

	Votes	% of total
MAAWIYA OULD SID'AHMED TAYA	345,583	62.65
AHMED OULD DADDAH	180,658	32.75
MOUSTAPHA OULD MOHAMED SALEK	15,735	2.85
MOHAMED MAHMOUD OULD MAH	7,506	1.36
Total*	551,575	100.00

* Included in the total number of valid votes are 2,093 'neutral votes'.

SENATE

President: DIENG BOUBOU FARBA.

Elections to the 56-member Senate took place on 3 and 10 April 1992. It was reported that 36 candidates of the Democratic and Social Republican Party (DSRP) were elected; 17 seats were won by independent candidates, and a further three senators were to represent the interests of Mauritanians resident abroad. Part of the Senate is subject to re-election every two years: accordingly, elections for 17 senators took place on 15 and 22 April 1994, while elections for the three representatives of Mauritanians abroad were conducted by the Senate on 14 May. The DSRP retained its majority in the upper house following these elections and those held on 12 and 19 April 1996 for 18 senatorial seats.

NATIONAL ASSEMBLY

President: Commdt (retd) CHEIKH SID'AHMED OULD BABA.

General Election, 11 and 18 October 1996

	Seats
Democratic and Social Republican Party	71
Action for Change	1
Rally for Democracy and National Unity	1
Independent	6
Total	79

Advisory Councils

Constitutional Council: f. 1992; includes six mems, three nominated by the Head of State and three designated by the Presidents of the Senate and National Assembly; Pres. DIDI OULD BOUNAAMA; Sec.-Gen. MOHAMED OULD M'REIZIG.

Supreme Islamic Council (al-Majlis al-Islamiya al-A'la'): f. 1992; Chair. MOHAMED MOKTAR OULD M'BALAH.

There is provision in the 1991 Constitution for the establishment of an Economic and Social Council.

Political Organizations

The 1991 Constitution provided for the operation of a plural political system. By mid-1997 some 21 parties had been officially registered. Among the most influential of these were:

Action for Change (AC): f. 1995 to represent the interests of Harratin (black moors who had formerly been slaves); Leader MESSAOUD OULD BOULKHEIR; Sec.-Gen. IBRAHIM ASSAR.

Democratic Centre Party (DCP): Leader MOULAYE MOHAMED.

Democratic and Social Republican Party (DSRP): f. 1991; absorbed Movement of Independent Democrats in 1995; Leader Col MAAWIYA OULD SID'AHMED TAYA; Sec.-Gen. SIDI MOHAMED OULD BOUBACAR.

Mauritanian Party for Renewal (MPR): f. 1991; Leader MOULAYE EL HASSAN OULD JEYID.

People's Progressive Party (PPP): f. 1991; Leader TALEB OULD JIDDOU; Sec.-Gen. MOHAMED HASSAOUD OULD ISMAEL.

Rally for Democracy and National Unity (RDNU): f. 1991; Chair. AHMED OULD SIDI BABA.

Socialist and Democratic People's Union (SDPU): f. 1991; Leader MOHAMED MAHMOUD OULD MAH.

Union for Democracy and Progress (UDP): f. 1993; Pres. HAMDI OULD MOUKNASS; Sec.-Gen. SIDI OULD AHMED DEYA.

Union of Democratic Forces–New Era (UDF–NE): f. 1991 as Union of Democratic Forces; restructured (following internal divisions) 1994; Sec.-Gen. AHMED OULD DADDAH.

United Social Democratic Party (USDP): f. 1995; Leader MOHAMED LEMIND OULD MOHAMED BABOU.

Unauthorized but influential is the Islamic **Ummah Party** (the Constitution prohibits the authorization of religious political organizations), founded in 1991 and led by Imam SIDI YAHYA. The clandestine **Forces de libération africaine de Mauritanie (FLAM)** was formed in 1983 to represent black Africans in Mauritania.

Diplomatic Representation

EMBASSIES IN MAURITANIA

Algeria: BP 625, Nouakchott; tel. 540-07; telex 871; Ambassador: ABDELKRIM BEN HOCINE.

China, People's Republic: BP 196, Nouakchott; Ambassador: ZHANE JUNQI.

Congo, Democratic Republic: BP 487, Nouakchott; tel. 528-36; telex 812; Ambassador: MALU MALU DIANGA.

Egypt: BP 176, Nouakchott; telex 520; Ambassador: MOHAMED WAGI EL JIBALY.

France: BP 231, rue Ahmed Ould M'Hamed, Nouakchott; tel. 517-40; telex 582; Ambassador: JEAN-PAUL TAIX.

Gabon: BP 38, Nouakchott; tel. 529-19; telex 593; Ambassador: JACQUES BONAVENTURE ESSONGHE.

Germany: BP 372, Nouakchott; tel. 517-29; telex 5555; fax 517-22; Ambassador: Dr JOHANNES E. WESTERHOFF.

Korea, Republic: BP 324, Nouakchott; tel. 537-86; fax 544-43; Chargé d'affaires a.i.: WON CHOL-KIM.

Morocco: BP 621, Nouakchott; tel. 514-11; telex 550; Ambassador: BRAHIM MOUSSA.

Nigeria: BP 367, Nouakchott; telex 869; Chargé d'affaires a.i.: Mr SENOUSSI.

Romania: 1 BP 5226, Nouakchott; tel. and fax 525-70; telex 5823; Ambassador: RATALOU DIMITRY.

Russia: BP 251, Nouakchott; tel. 519-73; Ambassador: (vacant).

Saudi Arabia: BP 498, Nouakchott; tel. 526-33; telex 813; Ambassador: MOHAMED AL FADH EL ISSA.

Senegal: BP 611, Nouakchott; Ambassador: M'BODJ SAMBA.

Spain: BP 232, Nouakchott; tel. 520-80; telex 5563; fax 540-88; Ambassador: JUAN MARÍA LÓPEZ-AGUILAR.

Tunisia: BP 681, Nouakchott; tel. 528-71; telex 857; Ambassador: ABDEL WEHAB JEMAL.

USA: BP 222, Nouakchott; tel. 526-60; telex 558; fax 525-89; Ambassador: Ms TIMBERLAKE FOSTER (designate).

Judicial System

The Code of Law was promulgated in 1961 and subsequently modified to integrate modern law with Islamic institutions and practices. The main courts comprise three courts of appeal, 10 regional tribunals, two labour tribunals and 53 departmental civil courts. A revenue court is competent in financial matters.

Shari'a (Islamic) law was introduced in February 1980. A special Islamic court was established in March of that year, presided over by a magistrate of Islamic law, assisted by two counsellors and two *ulemas* (Muslim jurists and interpreters of the Koran).

Supreme Court: Palais de Justice, Nouakchott; tel. 521-63; f. 1961; intended to ensure the independence of the judiciary; the court is competent in juridical, administrative and electoral matters; Pres. MAHFODH OULD LEMRABOTT.

Religion

ISLAM

Islam is the official religion, and the population are almost entirely Muslims of the Malekite rite. The major religious groups are the Tijaniya and the Qadiriya. Chinguetti, in the region of Adrar, is the seventh Holy Place in Islam.

CHRISTIANITY

Roman Catholic Church

Mauritania comprises the single diocese of Nouakchott, directly responsible to the Holy See. The Bishop participates in the Bishops' Conference of Senegal, Mauritania, Cape Verde and Guinea-Bissau, based in Dakar, Senegal. At 31 December 1995 there were an estimated 4,386 adherents, mainly non-nationals, in the country.

Bishop of Nouakchott: Rt Rev. MARTIN ALBERT HAPPE, Evêché, BP 5377, Nouakchott; tel. 504-27; fax 537-51.

The Press

Ach-Chaab: BP 371, Nouakchott; tel. 535-23; telex 583; daily; French and Arabic; publ. by Agence Mauritanienne de l'Information; Dir-Gen. HADEMINE OULD SADY.

Le Calame: Nouakchott; weekly; French and Arabic; independent.

Eveil-Hebdo: BP 587, Nouakchott; weekly; independent.

Journal Officiel: Ministry of Justice, BP 350, Nouakchott; fortnightly.

Mauritanie Demain: Nouakchott; monthly; independent; Editor MUBARAK OULD BEIROUK.

Mauritanie Nouvelles: BP 3901, Nouakchott; tel. 567-78; fax 568-28; f. 1991; weekly; French and Arabic; independent; Editor-in-chief BAH OULD SALECK.

La Tribune: BP 6227, Nouakchott; tel. 544-92; fax 502-09.

NEWS AGENCIES

Agence Mauritanienne de l'Information (AMI): BP 371, Nouakchott; tel. 529-70; telex 525; fmrly Agence Mauritanienne de Presse; state-controlled; Dir MOHAMED OULD HAMADY.

Foreign Bureau

Xinhua (New China) News Agency (People's Republic of China): Nouakchott; telex 541; Correspondent WANG TIANRUI.

Agence France-Presse and Reuters (UK) are also represented in Mauritania.

Publishers

Imprimerie Commerciale et Administrative de Mauritanie: BP 164, Nouakchott; textbooks, educational.

Imprimerie Nationale: BP 371, Nouakchott; tel. 535-23; fax 544-37; f. 1978; state-owned; Pres. MOHAMED ABDERRAHMANE OULD ABEID; Dir ISSELMOU OULD MAHJOUB.

Government Publishing House

Société Nationale d'Impression: BP 618, Nouakchott; Pres. MOUSTAPHA SALECK OULD AHMED BRIHIM.

Radio and Television

In 1994, according to estimates by UNESCO, there were 327,000 radio receivers and 55,000 television receivers in use.

Radio de Mauritanie (RM): BP 200, Nouakchott; tel. and fax 521-64; telex 515; f. 1958; state-owned; five transmitters; radio broadcasts in Arabic, French, Sarakolé, Toucouleur and Wolof; Dir SID BRAHIM OULD HAMDINOU.

Télévision de Mauritanie (TVM): BP 5522, Nouakchott; tel. 540-67; fax 540-69; Dir YESLEM OULD EBNOU ABDEN.

Finance

(cap. = capital; res = reserves; dep. = deposits; m. = million; br. = branch; amounts in UM)

BANKING

Central Bank

Banque Centrale de Mauritanie (BCM): ave de l'Indépendance, BP 623, Nouakchott; tel. 522-06; telex 5532; fax 527-59; f. 1973; bank of issue; cap. 200m.; Gov. MOHAMED OULD MICHEL; 4 brs.

Commercial Banks

Banque al-Baraka Mauritanienne Islamique (BAMIS): ave du Roi Fayçal, BP 650, Nouakchott; tel. 514-24; telex 5535; fax 516-21; f. 1985; 50% owned by al-Baraka Group (Saudi Arabia); cap. 3,700m. (Dec. 1995); Chair. Dr HASSAN ABDALLAH KAMEL; Man. Dir MOHAMED ABDELLAHI OULD MOHAMED LEMINE.

Banque Mauritanienne pour le Commerce International (BMCI): Immeuble Afarco, ave Gamal-Abdel-Nasser, BP 622,

Nouakchott; tel. 524-69; telex 5543; fax 520-45; f. 1974; privately-owned; cap. 1,000m., res 106.0m., dep. 8,807.0m. (Dec. 1995); Chair. and Man. Dir SIDI MOHAMED ABASS; 4 brs.

Banque Nationale de Mauritanie (BNM): ave Gamal-Abdel-Nasser, BP 614, Nouakchott; tel. 526-02; telex 5567; fax 533-97; f. 1988 by merger; privately-owned; cap. 1,500m., res –226m., dep. 9,051m. (Dec. 1995); Pres. ISMAIL OULD ABEIDNA; Man. Dir MOHAMED O. A. O. NOUEIGUED.

Chinguitty Bank: ave Gamal-Abdel-Nasser, BP 626, Nouakchott; tel. 521-42; telex 5562; fax 533-82; f. 1972 as Banque Arabe Libyenne-Mauritanienne pour le Commerce Extérieur et le Développement; name changed 1993; 50% state-owned, 50% owned by Libyan Arab Foreign Bank; cap. 2,000m. (Dec. 1995); Chair. HASSEN OULD SALEH; Man. Dir ABDALLAH TAHER ABDEL AZIZ; br. at Nouadhibou.

Générale de Banque de Mauritanie pour l'Investissement et le Commerce (GBM): ave de l'Indépendance, BP 5558, Nouakchott; tel. 536-36; telex 5751; fax 546-47; f. 1996; privately-owned; Pres. and Gen. Man. MOHAMED HAMYEN BOUAMATOU.

INSURANCE

NASR: 12 ave Gamal-Abdel-Nasser, BP 163, Nouakchott; tel. 526-50; telex 527; fax 518-18; Pres. ABDELLAHI OULD MOCTAR: Dir-Gen. ABDERRAHMANE OULD BOUBOU.

Trade and Industry

CHAMBER OF COMMERCE

Chambre de Commerce, d'Agriculture, d'Elevage, d'Industrie et des Mines de Mauritanie: BP 215, Nouakchott; tel. 522-14; telex 581; f. 1954; Chair. KANE YAYA.

DEVELOPMENT ORGANIZATIONS

Caisse Française de Développement (CFD): quartier des Ambassades, BP 211, Nouakchott; fmrly Caisse Centrale de Coopération Economique; name changed 1992; tel. 523-09; telex 516; Dir (vacant).

Mission Française de Coopération: BP 203, Nouakchott; tel. 521-21; telex 582; administers bilateral aid from France; Dir ROBERT SORBI.

Société Arabe Mauritano-Libyenne de Développement Agricole (SAMALIDA): BP 658, Nouakchott; tel. 537-15; f. 1980; cap. UM 350m.; 51% state-owned, 49% owned by Govt of Libya; Dir-Gen. O. TURKI.

Société Nationale de Développement Rural (SONADER): BP 321, Nouakchott; tel. 521-61; telex 807; Dir-Gen. MOHAMED OULD BABETTA.

TRADE ORGANIZATIONS

NAFTEC, SA: BP 679, Nouakchott; tel. 526-51; telex 849; fax 525-42; f. 1980; cap. UM 120m.; govt is a minority shareholder; import and distribution of petroleum products; fmrly Société Mauritanienne de Commercialisation des Produits Pétroliers; Dir-Gen. BRAHIM NOUH.

Société Mauritanienne de Commercialisation du Poisson (SMCP): BP 259, Nouadhibou; tel. 452-81; telex 420; f. 1984; cap. UM 500m.; govt is a minority shareholder; until 1992 monopoly exporter of demersal fish and crustaceans; Pres. MOHAMED SALEM OULD LEKHAL; Dir-Gen. DAH OULD ABDEL JELIL.

Société Nationale d'Importation et d'Exportation (SONIMEX): BP 290, Nouakchott; tel. 514-72; telex 561; f. 1966; cap. UM 914m.; 74% state-owned; import of foodstuffs and textiles, distribution of essential consumer goods, export of gum-arabic; Pres. MOHAMED KHATTRY OULD SEGANE; Dir-Gen. MOUSSA FALL.

EMPLOYERS' ORGANIZATIONS

Confédération Générale des Employeurs de Mauritanie (CGEM): BP 383, Nouakchott; telex 859; f. 1974; professional assn for all employers active in Mauritania; Sec.-Gen. MOHAMED ALI OULD SIDI MOHAMED.

MAJOR INDUSTRIAL COMPANIES

The following are some of the largest companies in terms of either capital investment or employment:

Compagnie Mauritano-Coréenne de Pêche (COMACOP): BP 527, Nouakchott; tel. 537-47; telex 592; f. 1977; cap. UM 230m.; fishing and freezer complex; Chair. and Man. Dir ABDOU OULD AL HACHEME.

Complexe Minier du Nord (COMINOR): BP 1260, Nouadhibou; tel. 451-74; telex 426; fmrly MIFERMA, nationalized 1974; cap. UM 2,660m.; 100m. tons of iron ore are available for exploitation, yielding 66% pure iron; Operations Man. (at Zouérate) M. MILLIOTTE.

Mines d'Or d'Akjoujt (MORAK): BP 9, Akjoujt; f. 1991; cap. UM 459m.; 45% owned by SAMIN, 42.5% by General Gold Resources (Australia), 12.5% by International Finance Corpn; exploitation of gold deposits and exploration of copper reserves at Akjoujt; Chair. CHEIKH SID'EL MOKTAR OULD CHEIKH ABDELLAHI.

NAFTAL, SA: BP 73, Nouadhibou; tel. 452-40; telex 439; f. 1981 as Société Mauritanienne des Industries de Raffinage (SOMIR); cap. UM 4,600m.; operates a petroleum refinery and negotiates overseas transactions; Chair. MOUSTAFA KANE; Man. Dir MOUSSA FALL.

Société Algéro-Mauritanienne des Pêches (ALMAP): BP 321, Nouadhibou; tel. 451-48; telex 424; f. 1974; cap. UM 180m.; 51% state-owned, 49% owned by govt of Algeria; fishing, processing of fishery products; Dir BRAHIM OULD BOIDAHA; 500 employees.

Société Arabe du Fer et de l'Acier (SAFA): BP 114, Nouadhibou; tel. 453-89; telex 444; f. 1984; cap. UM 450m.; 33% owned by SNIM; steel rolling mill; Chair. MOHAMED SALECK OULD HEYINE; Man. Dir AHMEDOU OULD JIDDOU.

Société Arabe des Industries Métallurgiques Mauritano-Koweïtienne (SAMIA): BP 1248, Nouakchott; tel. 544-55; telex 508; f. 1974; cap. UM 762m.; 50% state-owned, 50% owned by Kuwait Foreign Trade, Contracting and Investment Co; copper refining; Chair. and Man. Dir ALI MOHAMED AL-MUHEIMID; Man. Dir MOHAMED SALEM OULD CHEIKH.

Société Arabe Libyenne-Mauritanienne des Ressources Maritimes (SALIMAUREM): BP 75, Nouadhibou; tel. 452-41; telex 452; f. 1978; cap. UM 2,300m.; 50% state-owned, 50% owned by Libyan-Arab Finance Co; fishing and fish processing; freezer factory; Chair. AHMED OULD GHNAHALLA; Dir-Gen. SALA MOHAMED ARIBI.

Société Arabe des Mines d'Inchiri (SAMIN): BP 9, Akjoujt; tel. 671-04; telex 715; f. 1981; cap. UM 3,276m.; 37.5% state-owned, 62.5% owned by Arab interests; Chair. TAHER TABET; Man. Dir ABDERRAHMANE TAYEB.

Société de Construction et de Gestion Immobilière de Mauritanie (SOCOGIM): BP 28, Nouakchott; tel. 517-75; f. 1974; cap. UM 583m.; 89% state-owned; Chair. ABDALLAH OULD MOHAMEDEN; Man. Dir AHMED OULD MOHAMED KHAIROU.

Société Mauritanienne d'Alumettes: BP 44, Nouakchott; tel. 524-81; telex 539; f. 1971; matches; Chair. ABDALLAHI OULD NOUEIGUED.

Société Mauritanienne des Gaz (SOMAGAZ): BP 39, Nouadhibou; chemical compounds; Man. D. BENDER.

Société Nationale d'Eau et d'Electricité (SONELEC): ave de l'Indépendance, BP 355, Nouakchott; tel. 523-08; telex 587; fax 539-95; f. 1968; cap. UM 400m.; state-owned; production and distribution of electricity and water; Man. Dir Capt. MOHAMED OULD BOUEÏDA.

Société Nationale Industrielle et Minière (SNIM): BP 42, Nouadhibou; tel. 451-90; telex 426; f. 1972; cap. UM 9,059.5m.; 71% state-owned; opened to foreign investment in 1978; research, exploitation, processing and marketing of minerals; Chair. CHEIKH SID'EL MOKTAR OULD CHEIKH ABDALLAHI; Man. Dir MOHAMED SALECK OULD HEYINE; 4,400 employees.

TRADE UNIONS

Confédération Générale des Travailleurs de Mauritanie: Nouakchott; f. 1992; obtained official recognition in 1994.

Confédération Libre des Travailleurs de Mauritanie: Nouakchott; f. 1995; Sec.-Gen. SAMORI OULD BEYI.

Union des Travailleurs de Mauritanie (UTM): Bourse du Travail, BP 630, Nouakchott; f. 1961; Sec.-Gen. MOHAMED BRAHIM (acting); 45,000 mems.

Transport

RAILWAYS

A 670-km railway connects the iron-ore deposits at Zouérate with Nouadhibou; a 40-km extension services the reserves at El Rhein, and a 30-km extension those at M'Haoudat. Motive power is diesel-electric. The Société Nationale Industrielle et Minière (SNIM) operates one of the longest (2.4 km) and heaviest (22,000 metric tons) trains in the world.

SNIM—Direction du Chemin de Fer et du Port: BP 42, Nouadhibou; tel. 451-74; telex 426; fax 453-96; f. 1963; Gen. Man. MOHAMED SALECK OULD HEYINE; Dir KHALIA OULD BEYAH.

ROADS

In 1995 there were about 7,600 km of roads and tracks, of which main roads comprised some 2,750 km, and 11.2% of the road network was paved. The 1,100-km TransMauritania highway, completed in 1985, links Nouakchott with Néma in the east of the country. Plans exist for the construction of a 7,400-km highway, linking Nouakchott with the Libyan port of Tubruq (Tobruk).

Société Mauritanienne des Transports (SOMATRA): Nouakchott; tel. 529-53; f. 1975; Pres. CHEIKH MALAININE ROBERT; Dir-Gen. MAMADOU SOULEYMANE KANE.

INLAND WATERWAYS

The River Senegal is navigable in the wet season by small coastal vessels as far as Kayes (Mali) and by river vessels as far as Kaédi; in the dry season as far as Rosso and Boghé, respectively. The major river ports are at Rosso, Kaédi and Gouraye.

SHIPPING

The principal port, at Point-Central, 10 km south of Nouadhibou, is almost wholly occupied with mineral exports. There is a commercial and fishing port at Nouadhibou, which handled 393,716 metric tons in 1983. The deep-water Port de l'Amitié at Nouakchott, built and maintained with assistance from the People's Republic of China, was inaugurated in 1986. The port, which has a total capacity of 1m. tons annually, handled 636,842 tons in 1991 (compared with 479,791 tons in 1990); the port cleared 281 vessels in 1991 (compared with 244 in 1990).

Port de l'Amitié de Nouakchott: BP 267, Nouakchott; tel. 514-53; telex 538; f. 1986; deep-water port; Dir-Gen. MOHAMED MAHMOUD OULD DEH.

Port Autonome de Nouadhibou: BP 236, Nouadhibou; tel. 451-34; telex 441; f. 1973; state-owned; Pres. HABIB ELY; Dir-Gen. HAMADA OULD DERWICH.

Shipping Companies

Compagnie Mauritanienne de Navigation Maritime (COMAUNAM): 119 ave Gamal-Abdel-Nasser, BP 799, Nouakchott; tel. 536-34; telex 5862; fax 525-04; f. 1973; 51% state-owned, 49% owned by govt of Algeria; nat. shipping co; forwarding agent, stevedoring; Chair. MOHAND TIGHILT; Dir-Gen. KAMIL ABDELKADER.

Société d'Acconage et de Manutention en Mauritanie (SAMMA): BP 258, Nouadhibou; tel. 452-63; telex 4433; fax 452-37; f. 1960; freight and handling, shipping agent, forwarding agent, stevedoring; Dir.-Gen. DIDI O. BIHA; Dept Chief SADEGH O. BABA.

Société Générale de Consignation et d'Entreprises Maritimes (SOGECO): BP 351, Nouakchott; tel. 522-02; telex 5502; fax 539-03; f. 1973; Chair. and Man. Dir ISMAIL OULD ABEIDNA.

CIVIL AVIATION

There are international airports at Nouakchott and Nouadhibou, an airport at Néma, and 23 smaller airstrips. Facilities at Nouakchott were expanded considerably in the late 1980s and early 1990s.

Air Afrique: BP 51, Nouakchott; tel. 525-45; fax 549-44; see under Côte d'Ivoire.

Air Mauritanie (Société d'Economie Mixte Air Mauritanie): BP 41, Nouakchott; tel. 522-11; telex 573; fax 538-15; f. 1974; 60% state-owned, 20% owned by Air Afrique; domestic and regional passenger and cargo services; Dir-Gen. MOHAMED YEHDHIH OULD B'REIDLEIL.

Tourism

Mauritania's principal tourist attractions are its historical sites, several of which have been listed by UNESCO under its World Heritage Programme, and its game reserves and national parks. Some 13,000 tourists visited Mauritania in 1986. Receipts from tourism in 1993 totalled an estimated US $15m.

Direction du Tourisme: BP 246, Nouakchott; tel. 535-72; f. 1988; Dir KANE ISMAILA.

Société Mauritanienne de Tourisme et d'Hôtellerie (SMTH): BP 552, Nouakchott; tel. 533-51; f. 1969; promotes tourism, manages hotels and organizes tours; Man. Dir OULD CHEIKH ABDALLAHI.

Defence

In August 1996 the total armed forces numbered 15,650 men: army 15,000, navy about 500, air force 150. Full-time membership of paramilitary forces totalled about 5,000. Military service is by authorized conscription, and lasts for two years.

Defence Expenditure: Budgeted at UM 4,400m. in 1996.

Chief of Staff of the Armed Forces: Col. MOULAYE OULD BOULKHREIS.

Chief of Staff of the National Gendarmerie: Lt-Col DE OULD NE.

Education

Formal education is not compulsory in Mauritania. At the time of the 1988 census the average rate of adult illiteracy was 64.9% (males 53.9%; females 75.4%). According to UNESCO estimates, adult illiteracy averaged 62.3% (males 50.4%; females 73.7%) in 1995. Primary education begins at six years of age and lasts for six years. In 1994 total enrolment at primary schools was equivalent to only 74% of children in the relevant age group (81% of boys; 66% of girls). It is aimed to increase primary enrolment to 90% of all children in Mauritania by 2000. Secondary education begins at 12 years of age and lasts for six years, comprising two cycles of three years each. The total enrolment at secondary schools in 1993 was equivalent to only 15% of children in the appropriate age-group (19% of boys; 11% of girls). A plan to make Arabic the compulsory first language in all schools (which had been postponed in 1979, following protests from the French-speaking south) was reintroduced in April 1988. In 1993/94 a total of 8,495 students were enrolled at Mauritania's four higher education institutions (including the University of Nouakchott, opened in 1983). Expenditure on education in 1988 was UM 3,188m. (22% of current expenditure in that year). Some UM 1,050m. was to be invested in education in 1993. In April 1995 the World Bank approved a US $35m. loan to improve the country's educational system.

Bibliography

Bader, C., and Lefort, F. *Mauritanie, la vie réconciliée.* Paris, Fayard, 1990.

Balta, P. and Rulleau, C. *Le Grand Maghreb, des indépendances à l'an 2000.* Paris, Editions La Découverte, 1990.

Belvaude, C. *La Mauritanie.* Paris, Editions Karthala, 1989.

Clausen, U. *Demokratisierung in Mauritanien: Einfuehrung und Dokumente.* Hamburg, Deutsches Orient-Institut, 1993.

de Chassey, C. *Mauritania 1900–1975.* Paris, Harmattan, 1984.

Garnier, C., and Ermont, P. *Désert fertile: un nouvel état, la Mauritanie.* Paris, Hachette, 1960.

Gerteiny, A. G. *Mauritania.* London, Pall Mall; New York, Praeger, 1967.

Hudson, S. *Travels in Mauritania.* London, Virgin Books, 1990.

Human Rights Watch, Africa. *Mauritania's Campaign of Terror: State-Sponsored Repression of Black Africans.* New York, 1994.

Ould-May, M. *Global Restructuring and Peripheral States: The Carrot and the Stick in Mauritania.* Lanham, MD, Littlefield Adams, 1996.

Pazzanika, A. G. *Historical Dictionary of Mauritania.* Lanham, MD, Scarecrow Press, 1996.

Rimmer, D. *The Economies of West Africa.* London, Weidenfeld and Nicolson, 1984.

Toupet, C., and Pitte, J.-R. *La Mauritanie.* Paris, PUF, 1977.

Westebbe, R. M. *The Economy of Mauritania.* New York and London, Praeger, 1971.

MAURITIUS

Physical and Social Geography

The Republic of Mauritius, comprising the islands of Mauritius and Rodrigues, together with the Agalega Islands and the Cargados Carajos Shoals, lies in the Indian Ocean 800 km east of Madagascar. The island of Mauritius covers 1,865 sq km (720 sq miles) in area. It is a volcanic island, consisting of a plain rising from the north-east to the highest point on the island, Piton de la Rivière Noire (827 m above sea-level) in the south-west, interspersed by abrupt volcanic peaks and gorges, and is almost completely surrounded by a coral reef. Including Rodrigues and its other islands, the republic occupies a land area of 2,040 sq km (788 sq miles).

The climate is sub-tropical maritime, but with two distinct seasons; additionally, the warm dry coastal areas contrast with the cool rainy interior. Mauritius and Rodrigues are vulnerable to cyclones, particularly between September and May.

Rodrigues, a volcanic island of 104 sq km (40 sq miles) surrounded by a coral reef, lies 585 km east of the island of Mauritius (19°S, 63°E). Its population was enumerated at 34,204 in the 1990 census. Mauritius has two dependencies (together covering 71 sq km and having 167 inhabitants at the 1990 census): Agalega, two islands 935 km north of Mauritius (10°S, 56°E); and the Cargados Carajos Shoals (or St Brandon Islands), 22 islets without permanent inhabitants but used as a fishing station, 370 km north-north-east of Mauritius (16°S, 59°E).

Mauritius claims sovereignty over Tromelin, a small island without permanent inhabitants, 556 km to the north-west. This claim is disputed by Madagascar and France. Mauritius also seeks the return of Diego Garcia, a coral atoll in the Chagos Archipelago, about 1,900 km to the north-east. The archipelago was formerly administered by Mauritius but in 1965 became part (and in 1976 all) of the British Indian Ocean Territory (see p. 710).

The population of Mauritius was enumerated at 1,058,775 at the July 1990 census, and was officially estimated at 1,133,551 in mid-1996, giving a density of 575.7 inhabitants per sq km. During 1985–95 the population increased by an annual average of only 1.0%, owing, in part, to higher emigration and a decline in the birth rate. The population is of mixed origin, including people of European, African, Indian and Chinese descent. Almost 42% of the population reside in the urban area extending from Port Louis (the capital and business centre) on the north-west coast, to Curepipe in the island's centre.

Recent History

Revised by the Editor

Following unsuccessful attempts at colonization by the Dutch in the 17th century, the uninhabited islands of Mauritius and Rodrigues were occupied during the subsequent century by French settlers from the neighbouring island of Réunion, who established sugar plantations. Mauritius passed into British control in 1810. Subsequent settlement came mainly from east Africa and India, and the European population has remained largely French-speaking.

EMERGENCE OF PARTY POLITICS

The Indian community in Mauritius took little part in politics until 1947, when the franchise was extended to adults over the age of 21 years who could establish simple literacy in any language. This expansion of the electorate deprived the Franco-Mauritian and Creole communities of their political dominance, and between 1948–59 the Mauritius Labour Party (MLP), led by Dr (later Sir) Seewoosagur Ramgoolam, consolidated the new political role of the Indian community. Following intense political debate between the MLP and the Ralliement Mauricien, the party representing the traditional Franco-Mauritian and Creole interests (which later became the Parti Mauricien Social Démocrate—PMSD), a new constitution, providing for universal adult suffrage, was introduced in 1959; elections, which took place in March of that year, were won by the MLP. Ramgoolam became chief minister in September 1961, and was restyled premier in March 1964. In November 1965 the United Kingdom transferred the Chagos Archipelago (including the atoll of Diego Garcia), a Mauritian dependency about 2,000 km (1,250 miles) north-east of the main island, to the newly-created British Indian Ocean Territory (see p. 710).

Between 1960–65, with impetus from the MLP, Mauritius progressed steadily towards independence. The PMSD, led by Gaëtan (later Sir Gaëtan) Duval, sought unsuccessfully to rally support for a form of 'association' with the United Kingdom instead of full independence, which the Franco-Mauritian and Creole communities feared would lead to Hindu domination. At elections in August 1967, however, a newly-formed alliance of the MLP and the Comité d'Action Musulman (CAM), known as the Independence Party (IP), led by Ramgoolam, secured a majority of seats in the legislature, and a new constitution, providing for internal self-government, was introduced. On 12 March 1968 Mauritius became independent, within the Commonwealth, with Ramgoolam as prime minister. Ramgoolam subsequently formed an extended coalition government, with PMSD participation.

From 1970, the strongest opposition to the Ramgoolam government came from a newly-formed left-wing group, the Mouvement Militant Mauricien (MMM), led by Paul Bérenger. The MMM demanded a more equitable distribution of wealth, and attracted most support from the young unemployed, student groups and trade unions. In response to a period of intense labour unrest in the early 1970s, the government declared a state of emergency and detained leading members of the MMM. The party continued nevertheless to attract popular support, and at the general election held in December 1976 the MMM emerged as the largest single party in the legislative assembly, although with insufficient seats to form a government. Ramgoolam subsequently formed a new coalition with the PMSD. Despite renewed outbreaks of unrest and public disorder, and further arrests of MMM activists, the coalition retained power for the full term of the legislative assembly.

THE JUGNAUTH COALITIONS, 1982–95

At elections to the legislative assembly in June 1982, an alliance of the MMM and Parti Socialiste Mauricien (PSM) won all 60 elective seats on the main island (42 to the MMM and 18 to the PSM). Anerood (later Sir Anerood) Jugnauth became prime minister and appointed Bérenger as minister of finance. In March 1983, however, following opposition within the cabinet to Bérenger's stringent economic policies and his attempts to make Creole (Kreol) the national language (despite the Indian descent of the majority of the population), 12 ministers, including Bérenger, resigned. Jugnauth subsequently formed a new government, and in early April formed a new party, the Mouvement Socialiste Militant, which, in May, amalgamated with the PSM, led by Harish Boodhoo, and was renamed the Mouvement Socialiste Mauricien (MSM). However, the new government lacked a majority in the legislative assembly, and Jugnauth was obliged to dissolve the assembly in June. At a general election in August, an alliance comprising the MSM, the MLP and the PMSD, led by Sir Gaëtan Duval, won 41 of the 62 elective seats, while the MMM won only 19 seats. Jugnauth remained as prime minister, with Duval as deputy prime minister.

In December 1983 draft legislation that would allow Mauritius to become a republic failed to gain sufficient support in the legislative assembly, owing, in part, to disagreement between the government and the opposition over the nature of the powers to be granted to the president of the proposed republic. In the same month Sir Seewoosagur Ramgoolam was appointed governor-general. Satcam (later Sir Satcam) Boolell subsequently became leader of the MLP, but was dismissed from the cabinet in February 1984. In response, the MLP withdrew from the coalition; however, 11 MLP deputies continued to support the government and formed a faction within the MLP, the Rassemblement des Travaillistes Mauriciens.

In March 1984 proposed restrictions on the press prompted considerable public protest. The government eventually agreed to establish a joint commission, with representatives of the press, to examine the proposed legislation. On the commission's recommendation, the government withdrew the legislation. In April 1985, however, the government introduced similar legislation, which banned the publication of material that was judged to be damaging to the administration.

In December 1985 the MMM won 118 of the 126 contested seats in municipal elections, demonstrating the increasing public dissatisfaction with the Jugnauth government. In the same month four members of the legislative assembly were arrested in the Netherlands on charges of drug smuggling. In January 1986, following Jugnauth's refusal to comment on allegations that other deputies were involved in the affair, four cabinet ministers tendered their resignations. Shortly afterwards, Jugnauth formed a new government, which retained the political balance of his previous administration. In the same month Sir Veerasamy Ringadoo, a supporter of Jugnauth, was appointed governor-general, following the death of Ramgoolam. In March five MSM deputies, including three who had resigned as ministers in January, withdrew their support from the coalition.

In June 1986, in response to pressure from within the MSM, Jugnauth announced the creation of a commission of inquiry to investigate the drugs scandal. In the following month, however, three ministers resigned, citing lack of confidence in Jugnauth's leadership. The government retaliated by expelling 11 MSM dissidents from the party. In November, following a report by the commission of inquiry into the drugs affair, four MSM deputies resigned from the legislative assembly, thus reducing the MSM/PMSD coalition's strength in the legislature to only 30 of the 62 elective seats. In the subsequent political realignment, the MMM regained the support of several deputies who had previously left the coalition. In January 1987 Jugnauth announced that a general election would take place later that year.

In March 1987 the commission of inquiry issued a further report alleging that six deputies of the MSM/PMSD alliance had been involved in drug-trafficking. In the same month further allegations associated Sir Gaëtan Duval, a deputy prime minister, with the affair. However, Duval's subsequent offer of resignation was rejected by Jugnauth. In May Diwakar Bundhun, the minister of industry, was dismissed, after openly criticizing Jugnauth. Having lost majority support in the legislative assembly, Jugnauth announced that a general election was to take place in August.

At the general election on 30 August 1987 an electoral alliance comprising the MSM, the PMSD and the MLP won 39 of the 60 elective seats on the main island, although it received only 49.8% of total votes cast. The MMM, which campaigned within an opposition coalition, the 'Union', with two smaller parties (the Mouvement des Travaillistes Démocrates and the Front des Travailleurs Socialistes), won 21 seats, obtaining 48.1% of votes cast. Dr Paramhansa (Prem) Nababsingh subsequently became the leader of the MMM and of the opposition in the assembly, replacing Bérenger, who had failed to secure a seat. In September Jugnauth appointed a new council of ministers. Later that month the new government announced plans to make Mauritius a republic within the Commonwealth.

In August 1988, following a disagreement over employment policies, Sir Gaëtan Duval, the leader of the PMSD, left the government, together with his brother, Hervé Duval, the minister of industry. The opposition demanded Jugnauth's resignation in February 1989, following his expression of support for Soo Soobiah, the former high commissioner to the United Kingdom, who had been arrested on drug-smuggling charges. Two attempts on Jugnauth's life (in November 1988 and March 1989) were attributed by him to criminals involved in drug-trafficking. In June Sir Gaëtan Duval was temporarily detained on suspicion of involvement in a political assassination in 1971.

In July 1990 the MMM and MSM agreed to form an alliance to contest the next general election, and to proceed with constitutional measures, which would allow Mauritius to become a republic. Under the proposed new constitution, Bérenger would assume the presidency, while Jugnauth would remain as executive prime minister, with Nababsingh as deputy prime minister. However, the draft amendments, which were submitted to the legislative assembly in mid-August, were opposed by members of the MLP (in alliance with the PMSD), and Jugnauth failed to secure the necessary parliamentary majority. He subsequently dismissed Boolell, as well as two ministers belonging to the MSM, who had refused to support the proposed amendments. A further three ministers representing the MLP also resigned, leaving only one MLP member in the government. Boolell subsequently relinquished the leadership of the MLP to Dr Navin Ramgoolam (the son of Sir Seewoosagur). In September Jugnauth announced the formation of a new coalition government, in which the six vacant ministerial posts were allocated to members of the MMM, while Nababsingh was appointed as one of the three deputy prime ministers.

In August 1991 Jugnauth dissolved the legislative assembly; the ensuing general election took place on 15 September. An alliance of the MSM, the MMM and the Mouvement des Travaillistes Démocrates (MTD) won 57 of the 62 elective seats, while the alliance of the MLP and the PMSD secured only three seats. Members of the Organisation du Peuple Rodriguais (OPR) were returned to the remaining two seats. However, members of the opposition, including Dr Ramgoolam and Sir Gaëtan Duval, alleged electoral malpractice, and refused to attend the inaugural session of the legislative assembly. Jugnauth subsequently formed a new government, to which nine representatives of the MMM (including Bérenger, who became minister of external affairs) and one representative of the MTD were appointed. Later in September Sir Gaëtan Duval resigned from the legislative assembly. In the following month the MLP/PMSD alliance boycotted municipal elections, in which the MSM/MMM/MTD alliance won 125 of the 126 contested seats.

In October 1991 Jugnauth announced that, subject to the approval of constitutional amendments by a majority of 75% of members of the legislative assembly, Mauritius would become a republic within the Commonwealth on 12 March 1992. However, Duval asserted that the creation of a republic would allow Jugnauth to assume absolute power, and demanded that the proposed amendments be submitted to a national referendum. In December 1991 the constitutional changes were approved by 59 of the 66 deputies in the legislative assembly. (The seven members of the MLP/PMSD alliance in the assembly refused to vote, on the grounds that the amendments provided for an increase in executive power, to the detriment of the legislature.) Under the terms of the revised constitution, the governor-general, Sir Veerasamy Ringadoo, who had been nominated by Jugnauth, was to assume the presidency for an interim period, pending the election of a president and vice-president, for a five-year term, by a simple majority of the legislative assembly (which would be renamed the national assembly). However, the MLP/PMSD alliance criticized these provisions, and demanded that the president be elected by universal suffrage. The constitution vested executive power in the prime minister, who would be appointed by the president, and would be the deputy best able to command a majority in the national assembly. On 12 March 1992 Ringadoo officially became interim president, replacing the British monarch, Queen Elizabeth II, as head of state. Later that month the government announced that Cassam Uteem, the minister of industry and industrial technology and a member of the MMM, was to be nominated to the presidency after a period of three months. (Under the terms of the alliance between the MSM and the MMM, members of the MMM were to be appointed to the presidency and vice-presidency, while Jugnauth was to remain as prime minister.)

In April 1992 opposition members demanded the resignation of Jugnauth, following the issue of a new bank note depicting his wife; it was reported that the ensuing criticism of Jugnauth had weakened the MSM/MMM alliance. In June, following the resignation of Ringadoo, officially on grounds of ill health, Uteem was elected to the presidency by the national assembly. Sir Rabindrah Ghurburrun, a member of the MMM, was nominated to the vice-presidency. A minor reshuffle of the council of ministers also took place.

In October 1992 Ramgoolam announced that he was to return to the United Kingdom to complete legal studies, despite a constitutional stipulation suspending the mandate of a parliamentary deputy who was absent from sessions of the national assembly for a period of more than three months. Plans by Ramgoolam to return to Mauritius in time to comply with this condition were thwarted by the curtailment of a parliamentary session in December and the convening of a further session, in January 1993, without prior notice. In June, however, an attempt by the government to unseat Ramgoolam was rejected by the supreme court, which criticized the 'unreasonable' timing of the parliamentary session in January.

Following a number of disagreements between the MMM and MSM, the government coalition was further weakened in August 1993, when candidates of the PMSD secured the three vacant seats in a municipal by-election (in a constituency where the MMM traditionally attracted most support). Later in August, following an unexpected success by the PMSD in municipal elections in a constituency that traditionally favoured the MMM, a meeting between Bérenger and Ramgoolam prompted speculation that an alliance between the MMM and MLP was contemplated. Shortly afterwards, Jugnauth dismissed Bérenger from the council of ministers, on the grounds that he had repeatedly criticized government policy.

The removal of Bérenger precipitated a serious crisis within the MMM, whose political bureau decided that the other nine members of the party who held ministerial portfolios should remain in the coalition government. Led by Nababsingh, the deputy prime minister, and the minister of industry and industrial technology, Jean-Claude de l'Estrac, supporters of the pro-coalition faction announced in October 1993 that Bérenger had been suspended as secretary-general of the MMM. Bérenger and his supporters responded by expelling 11 MMM officials from the party, and subsequently obtaining a legal ban on Nababsingh and de l'Estrac from using the party name. The split in the MMM led in November to a government reshuffle, in which the remaining two MMM ministers supporting Bérenger were replaced by members of the party's pro-coalition faction.

In April 1994 the MLP and the MMM announced that they had agreed terms for an alliance to contest the next general elections. Under its provisions, Ramgoolam was to be prime minister and Bérenger deputy prime minister, with cabinet portfolios allocated on the basis of 12 ministries to the MLP and nine to the MMM. In the same month, three MPs from the MSM withdrew their support from the government.

Nababsingh and the dissident faction of the MMM, having lost Bérenger's legal challenge for the use of the party name, formed a new party, the Renouveau Militant Mauricien (RMM), which formally commenced political activity in June 1994. In the same month, Jugnauth declared that the government would remain in office to the conclusion of its mandate in September 1996. In August 1994 a number of cabinet posts were reallocated.

In November 1994, during the course of a parliamentary debate on electoral issues, Bérenger and de l'Estrac accepted a mutual challenge to resign their seats in the national assembly and to contest by-elections. In the following month the MSM indicated that it would not oppose RMM candidates in the two polls. In January 1995, however, Jugnauth unsuccessfully sought to undermine the MLP/MMM alliance by offering electoral support to the MLP. The by-elections, held in February, were both won by MLP/MMM candidates, and Bérenger was returned to the national assembly. Following these results, Jugnauth opened political negotiations with the PMSD, whose leader, Luc Xavier Duval (the son of Sir Gaëtan Duval), agreed to enter the coalition as minister of industry and industrial technology and minister of tourism. The cabinet post of attorney-general and minister of justice, previously held by Jugnauth, was also allocated to the PMSD, and Sir Gaëtan Duval accepted an appointment as an economic adviser to the prime minister. As a result, however, of widespread opposition within the PMSD to participation in the coalition, Luc Xavier Duval left the government in October, and Sir Gaëtan Duval subsequently resumed the leadership of the party. The minister for Rodrigues, representing the OPR, also resigned from the cabinet in October.

MLP/MMM COALITION

In November 1995 the government was defeated in a parliamentary vote, requiring a two-thirds' majority to introduce a constitutional requirement for instruction in oriental languages to be provided in primary schools. Jugnauth dissolved the national assembly, and at the subsequent general election in December the MLP/MMM alliance won a decisive victory: of the 62 elected seats, the MLP secured 35 seats, the MMM obtained 25 seats and the OPR two seats. Under constitutional arrangements providing representation for unsuccessful candidates attracting the largest number of votes, Sir Gaëtan Duval re-entered the national assembly, together with two members of the Mouvement Rodriguais and a representative of Hizbullah, an Islamic fundamentalist group. Ramgoolam became prime minister of the new MLP/MMM coalition, with Bérenger as deputy prime minister with responsibility for foreign and regional relations. The more equitable distribution of the country's recent prosperity was identified as a primary aim of the new government. Sir Gaëtan Duval died in May 1996 and was succeeded in the national assembly and as leader of the PMSD by his brother, Hervé Duval, although Luc Xavier Duval continued to command a significant personal following within the party.

Evidence of strains within the MLP/MMM coalition began to emerge in June 1996, when austerity proposals, put forward by Rundheersing Bheenick, the minister of finance, in the 1995/96 budget, aroused considerable opposition from the MMM. Bheenick subsequently resigned, and the finance portfolio was taken over by Ramgoolam until November, when an extensive reallocation of ministerial responsibilities was carried out.

GOVERNMENT BY THE MLP

More serious divisions within the coalition government became apparent in late 1996, when differences were reported between Ramgoolam and Bérenger over the allocation of ministerial responsibilities, and the perception by the MMM of delays in the implementation of social and economic reforms. In January 1997 rumours had begun to circulate of a possible political alliance between the MMM and the MSM, and in March it was reported that Ramgoolam intended to seek support from certain members of the PMSD should the MMM decide to withdraw from the government. Bérenger's criticism of the coalition's performance intensified in the following months, and culminated in late June in his dismissal from the government and the consequent withdrawal of the MMM from the coalition. Following unsuccessful efforts by Ramgoolam to draw the PMSD into a new administration, an MLP cabinet was formed by Ramgoolam, who additionally asumed Bérenger's former responsibilities for foreign affairs. Bheenick returned to the government as minister of economic development and regional co-operation. Ahmed Rashid Beebeejaun, minister of land transport, shipping and public safety in the former coalition, left the MMM and retained his former portfolio as an independent. Ramgoolam emphasized his determination to remain in office for the full legislative term to December 2000. In late June 1997 the national assembly re-elected Cassam Uteem to a second five-year term as president. A prominent supporter of the MLP, Angidi Verriah Chettiar, was elected vice-president.

Economy*

DONALD L. SPARKS

With revisions by the Editor

Mauritius* is a relatively small island (less than 800 sq miles, with a population of 1.1m.). Unlike most other members of the Organization of African Unity (OAU), Mauritius is classified by the World Bank as an 'upper middle income' economy. Unlike most other countries in the sub-Saharan region, Mauritius has enjoyed good rates of economic growth during the past two decades. Mauritius' gross domestic product (GDP) increased, in real terms, by an annual average of 6.2% in 1985–95; GDP increased by an estimated 4.1% in 1994, by 3.9% in 1995 and by an estimated 5.4% in 1996. Mauritius was traditionally dependent on sugar production, and economic growth was therefore vulnerable to adverse climatic conditions and changes in international prices for sugar. However, the dominance of sugar in the economy has been eclipsed by the steadily expanding manufactured exports and financial services sectors and by tourism; the contribution of revenue from sugar to GDP declined from 13% in 1979 to less than 6% in 1996, when it was estimated to account for about 26% of total export earnings. In 1995, according to estimates by the World Bank, Mauritius' gross national product (GNP), measured at average 1993–95 prices, was US $3,815m., equivalent to $3,380 per head. During 1985–95, it was estimated, GNP per head increased, in real terms, by 5.4% per year. Over the same period, the population rose by an annual average of 1.0%. The inflation rate averaged 7.3% in 1994, declining to 6.0% in 1995, but stood at 7.2% in the year ending November 1996. Unemployment remained at less than 2.0% in the early 1990s.

SUGAR

Until recently, with the increasing importance of tourism and light industry (including textiles), agriculture formed the backbone of Mauritius' economy, and sugar dominated the sector. Sugar cane is grown on a total of 84,400 ha (almost one-half of the entire surface area of the island and 87% of arable land). There are 17 large estates, covering 48,000 ha, all but one privately owned and each with a factory for processing the estate sugar and the cane grown by planters in the surrounding areas. The other land under sugar cane, producing over 40% of the total crop, is owned by 452 'big' planters and 35,000 'small' planters. Legislation pending in 1997 was expected to reduce the number of sugar mills to 10, in accordance with aims to increase efficiency and improve unit costs. Many of the 'small' sugar planters, who are mostly Indo-Mauritian and who cultivate about one-quarter of the total land under cane, have grouped themselves into co-operatives to facilitate the consignment of cane to the factories on the estates. Some 37,000 workers (15% of the labour force in 1994) are employed in the sugar industry, and represent about one-half of the agricultural labour force. A bulk sugar terminal, opened in 1980 with an annual capacity of 350,000 metric tons, is the third largest in the world. The Mauritius Sugar Syndicate markets all manufactured sugar, while the main estates are grouped into the Mauritius Sugar Producers' Association.

In 1986, when the output of raw sugar totalled 707,000 metric tons, yields achieved an all-time record average of 9 tons of raw sugar per ha, reaching 12 tons per ha on some estates. Such yields exceeded those of European sugar beet producers, and were comparable with those of many Asian sugar-growing countries. Cyclones in January and April 1989 caused very severe damage to the crop. However, sugar production totalled 643,168 tons in 1992 (an increase of 5.2% compared with 1991). Further cyclone damage, in February 1994, was expected to reduce the year's sugar output to about 500,000 tons, from 565,000 tons in 1993, which was itself the lowest level of output since 1980. The recurrence of adverse weather conditions prevented any recovery in 1995, when sugar production was estimated at about 525,000 tons. Output recovered to almost 588,500 tons in 1996, partly as a result of better weather conditions, and also through an increase of about 3.2% in the area under sugar cultivation (see below).

Most of the island's sugar was formerly sold to the UK at a guaranteed price, under the Commonwealth Sugar Agreement, but in 1975 this arrangement was replaced by a protocol of the first Lomé Convention, which was signed in that year by the European Community (EC, now the European Union–EU) and 46 developing countries, including Mauritius. Under this protocol and its successors, Mauritius receives an annual quota of 585,000 metric tons of raw cane sugar, and is the principal exporter of sugar to European countries. Other important customers are the USA, Canada and New Zealand. Local consumption is about 37,000 tons per year. Mauritius has benefited from the EC quota arrangement in that, for these exports, the guaranteed price has been much higher than the 'spot' price on the world market. However, since 1982 the EC price has remained almost static, despite annual rounds of protracted and often acrimonious negotiations. In 1989 the price was reduced by 2%. Sugar import quotas operated since 1982 by the USA have been extremely detrimental to Mauritius. The disappointing sugar crop in 1995 (see above) fell short of the 585,000 tons required to meet the EU threshold quota level, and posed the risk that Mauritius could lose its preferential treatment under the EU Sugar Protocol. To meet its full quota allocations (inclusive of an additional EU sugar quota of 85,000 tons annually under the special preferential sugar agreement), Mauritius requires an annual output of approximately 625,000 tons. Average annual production since the early 1980s, however, has remained at about 608,000 tons. In an effort to stimulate production, the government transferred about 1,000 ha from tea to sugar cultivation during 1995–96. It was the government's intention to complete its land realloction programme by June 1997, one year ahead of schedule.

Apart from poor weather in some years, problems affecting the industry in recent years have included low world prices, ageing machinery in the factories, and the high level of the sugar export levy, which was introduced in 1980. Following the report of a commission set up to examine the sugar sector's problems, the government drew up a plan for restructuring the industry, and in 1984, as an initial step, it created the Mauritius Sugar Authority to co-ordinate the plan and to monitor its effects. The resulting Sugar Action Plan (SAP) covered the period 1985–90, and one of its main features was the easing of the levy. Five factories were to be closed during that period, and the area planted with sugar was to be reduced by 1% per year, to encourage the growing of more food crops. Under the SAP, the island has been divided into five sugar regions, each supervised by a public company in which small planters were encouraged to buy shares. The SAP also covered the modernization of sugar factories and the development of power stations fired by bagasse (the fibrous remnants of sugar cane after milling). A Sugar Industry Efficiency Act, which provided for a programme of incentives and other measures, has been in operation since 1989.

Progress has been made in improving yields through the introduction of irrigation and new strains of sugar cane. The large-scale Northern Plains irrigation scheme is expected to increase yields per acre from 25 metric tons of cane to 42 tons. However, there is little value in increasing overall output unless world markets can be found. Molasses and rum are important sugar by-products, and are also exported by Mauritius. A five-year agricultural development plan, launched in 1989–90, aimed to increase the significance of the agricultural sector. About

* Although Rodrigues is an integral part of the Republic of Mauritius, most economic data refer to the island of Mauritius only. The figures in this section therefore refer to the main island only, unless otherwise stated.

one-half of the programme's new funds (Rs 7,300m.) was to be allocated to the sugar industry, with much of it specifically going to bagasse energy production. In 1992 the government initiated a new agricultural plan, and in the following year introduced legislation that provided additional agricultural incentives, and reduced the sugar export duty rate.

AGRICULTURE AND FISHING

Following a significant decline in sugar production, agriculture's contribution to GDP was estimated to have fallen to 9.3% in 1996 (compared with 20% in 1970). Agricultural activity currently faces a number of difficulties unrelated to adverse weather conditions. Labour costs have been rising sharply, as have the prices of agricultural inputs and land. Producer prices have not kept pace with these factors, and the government has not allocated sufficient resources to agricultural extension and other services. In 1996 agricultural employment represented 13.4% of the active labour force, compared with 18.3% in 1990.

Tea production, once a significant component of the island's economy, has been adversely affected since the late 1980s by rising production costs and the low level of prices on world markets. Export revenue from this source fell by 67%, between 1985–88, when the volume of tea exported declined from 7,000 tons to 5,400 tons annually. Exports of tea in 1994 were below 4,100 tons, declining to 2,900 tons in 1995 and to only 1,390 tons in 1996. In that year tea output totalled only 2,500 tons. Most tea-growing is carried out by about 1,500 smallholders, grouped into co-operatives. The supervision of the sector is carried out by the Mauritius Tea Factories Co (TeaFac), owned jointly by several state bodies and by tea producer co-operatives. TeaFac currently operates four factories, which account for about 75% of tea exports, and is responsible for export sales.The tea industry receives support from state subsidies.

Tobacco is the other main cash crop, after sugar and tea. Production has been expanded to the point where locally manufactured cigarettes are composed entirely of local tobacco apart from certain luxury grades. Output, which was 422 tons in 1970, was subsequently expanded to about 1,000 tons per year. Practically all tobacco is grown and processed by British-American Tobacco (BAT–Mauritius).

Subsistence farming is conducted on a small scale, although the cultivation of food crops is becoming more widespread in view of the need to diversify the economy and reduce food imports. Food accounted for 12.1% of the total cost of imports in 1992. The expansion of vegetable cultivation and experiments in intercropping with sugar have resulted in self-sufficiency in potatoes and nearly all other vegetables. Other crops now being experimentally intercropped with sugar are maize, rice, vanilla and groundnuts. A tree-planting programme began in 1982, with the aim of providing one-half of the country's timber needs by the mid-1990s.

Mauritius produces only 10% of its total beef requirements, and about 20% of its total consumption of dairy products, the remainder having to be imported mainly from New Zealand, Australia and South Africa. Mauritius is, however, self-sufficient in pork, eggs and poultry. A National Dairy Board was established in 1985, and several projects were initiated, including a cattle improvement scheme and a study on the potential of deer farming. Most cattle fodder has to be imported, in particular maize from South Africa, at considerable cost. Studies have been conducted on the possible production of high-protein feeding-stuffs, as by-products of sugar cane.

The fishing industry is being regenerated, with assistance from Japan and Australia in particular, and commercial fishing is gradually expanding. Vessels from Japan, Taiwan and the Republic of Korea fish in offshore waters and tranship between 15,000-16,000 tons of fish, mostly tuna, every year. Since the mid-1970s, there has been a noticeable increase in illegal fishing by foreign companies in Mauritian waters. A joint-venture tuna-canning factory, owned 49% by Japanese interests, was set up in 1972 and exports to EU countries. A second tuna-canning plant, with an initial capacity of 10,000 tons per year, was opened in 1988. A new fishing port at Trou Fanfaron, built with Japanese grant aid, was opened in 1985, with a handling capacity of about 6,000 tons of fish per year. The experimental farming of prawns has been a success, and there are hopes for export potential in this field.

INDUSTRY

Until the 1970s, the industrial sector was effectively limited to the import substitution of basic consumer products, such as food, beverages, tobacco, footwear, clothing, metal products, paints and board for furniture, made from bagasse. There is a fertilizer plant producing up to 100,000 tons per year, which also exports small quantities of the product, and a refinery to produce ethyl alcohol (ethanol) from molasses is under construction.

However, in view of the limited domestic market, the high level of unemployment and the emphasis on reducing dependence on the sugar sector, the government adopted a policy of export promotion by developing the Export Processing Zone (EPZ), concentrating on labour-intensive processing of imported goods for the export market. Within the EPZ, the government offers both local and foreign investors attractive incentives, including tax 'holidays', exemption from import duties on most raw materials and capital goods, free repatriation of capital, profits and dividends, low-price electricity, etc. About 60% of invested capital is locally-held, a further 25% is owned by Hong Kong entrepreneurs, and the remainder is supplied mainly by Pakistani, Indian, French, German and British interests. By September 1988 there were 586 enterprises in the EPZ, employing about 90,700 workers. However, the growth of employment subsequently slowed, and in 1993, when there were 554 enterprises (down from 556 in 1992), EPZ employment declined to 83,500, its lowest level since 1987. The decline both in new enterprises and employment continued in 1994 and into 1995, when a total of 494 businesses were employing 82,220 workers. New investment also declined, to Rs 800m. in 1994, a fall of 11% on the 1993 total.

The fastest-growing EPZ sectors have been textiles and clothing, which now account for 80% of total EPZ exports, more than 68% of EPZ enterprises, and 91% of EPZ labour. Mauritius is the world's third largest exporter of new woollen goods. Other rapidly growing sectors include electronics components and diamond processing, and emphasis has been put on the development of precision engineering (electronics, watch and instrument making, etc.) and skilled crafts (diamond cutting and polishing, furniture, quality goods, etc.). Other products include toys, razor blades, nails, industrial chemicals, detergents, rattan furniture, plastic goods, tyres and assembly of recording cassettes. During the 1990s, the government has sought to diversify EPZ activities, with particular emphasis on the textile sector.

In 1986 total exports from the EPZ accounted for 55.5% of total export earnings and replaced sugar as the main source of export receipts. The import content, however, represents about 70%–75% of EPZ export earnings, and the high cost of imported materials and components has been reflected in net foreign exchange revenue. EPZ exports increased by 11.2% in 1992 to Rs 13,500m., by 14.8% in 1993 to Rs 15,500m. and by 6.7% to Rs 16,533m. in 1994, when EPZ exports accounted for 67.4% of the value of all of Mauritius' exports. Increased productivity in the clothing and textile sectors led to a rise of 10.5% in EPZ exports in 1995, to Rs 18,267m. In 1996 EPZ exports were estimated to have advanced by 15%, to Rs 21,001m. The EU is the principal market for these exports, representing about 70% of the total. According to the World Bank, however, poor training and lack of modernization restrict the zone's productivity. Most firms operating in the EPZ have been modernizing their operations in recent years, and their productivity rose by 31.7% between 1990–94.

As a result of increasing labour costs, many firms in the EPZ are using more capital-intensive technologies; this will affect employment in the next few years. The demand for skilled personnel in various business sectors, including marketing, management, accounting and computing, also exceeded the number of suitable candidates. Emphasis on the potential of the textiles sector has prompted the creation of a Rs 200m. fund to modernize textile equipment, and a centre of textile technology has also been established by the University of Mauritius. Following changes in the GATT and the subsequent implementation of the world-wide Multi-fibre Arrangement under the World Trading Organization (WTO), Mauritius' EPZ will be faced by considerable challenges, particularly in relation to increased international competition in its principal export sectors. Additionally, exports by lower-cost producers in China,

India and East Africa could diminish Mauritius' EPZ's comparative advantage.

Mauritius has a large, and growing, informal sector. Women comprise almost one-third of the economically active population, although they represent up to 65% of the work-force in the EPZ. Unemployment has declined sharply in recent years, and was estimated at only 1.6% of the labour force in 1994. In 1995 agriculture employed 61,600 workers (representing 13.4% of the work-force), manufacturing 134,700 (29.3%) and government 111,900 (24.3%). The total work-force, including the informal sector, was 460,500 in 1995.

TOURISM

Mauritius is an attractive destination for European visitors, and tourism is now the third most important source of foreign exchange, after sugar and textiles. Arrivals of foreign tourists increased from 27,650 in 1970 to 422,500 in 1995, when receipts were estimated at Rs 6,600m. In that year the greatest number of visitors were from France (27.6%), Réunion (18.6%), South Africa (10.1%) and Germany (9.9%). In 1996, when an estimated 487,000 tourists visited Mauritius, generating revenue of Rs 9,400m., there were an estimated 13,300 hotel beds. Although there are plans to expand the number of visitors to 500,000 annually by 2000, the government is implementing measures to curtail and, where possible, reverse environmental damage which has been caused by the uncontrolled expansion of tourism in the recent past. In an effort to harmonize environmental considerations with higher rates of hotel room occupancy, the government has, since 1990, largely ceased issuing permits to build new hotels. Although small private hotels are exempt from the ban, their room occupancy rates have remained at around 50%, and government measures have been promised to assist this sector. Tourism provided employment, directly and indirectly, for almost 65,000 people in 1995. This sector, however, also contributes to the rise in costly imports, especially foodstuffs.

COMMUNICATIONS

There are approximately 1,877 km of classified roads, of which 29 km are motorways, 920 km are are other main roads and 577 km are secondary roads. The road network is good, considering the mountainous terrain, and about 93% of the roads are paved. There are a number of road projects planned or under way, including the motorway between Port Louis and the Plaisance international airport, and a new road from Pamplemousse to Grande Baie, and the reconstruction of the Nouvelle France–Mahébourg road. Port Louis, the major commercial port, was being modernized and expanded during the 1990s, with loan finance from the World Bank.

The international airport at Plaisance is served by 15 airlines. In 1994 the airport handled about 32,000 tons of freight and more than 1m. passengers. Plans for its expansion, announced in 1995 and expected to cost about Rs 800m., reflect a 50% increase in the number of international arrivals since the late 1980s. Air Mauritius, which is 51% government-owned, generates about one-half of total passenger traffic.

POWER AND WATER

Mauritius relies on imports for most of its energy needs. However, owing to the normally abundant rainfall and precipitous water courses, about 25% of electricity is generated from hydro sources. Most of the supply, however, is provided by diesel-powered thermal stations. The sugar estates generate electricity from bagasse. The 30-MW Champagne hydroelectric scheme started operating in late 1984. A 20-MW gas-powered generating plant in the north, built with French aid, came on stream in 1988. Energy demand is increasing at about 12% per year. It is estimated that Mauritius could produce up to 350m. kWh of electricity per year by using bagasse as a fuel, compared with current annual production of about 34m. kWh. There is a 21.7-MW bagasse-fuelled station attached to the Flacq United Estates sugar factory, and a French-financed bagasse pelletization pilot plant, Bagapel, operates at the nearby Deep River–Beau Champ sugar estate. The object is to establish bagasse as a year-round fuel; currently it is available only in the harvesting season. Two 15-MW bagasse-fired power stations are planned. Studies on wave power and wind power are also being carried out. Water supply and distribution are well developed, with only 0.75% of the population without piped provision. Subterranean reserves are tapped to supply industry, the principal consumer. Imports of petroleum products comprised about 6.9% of the value of merchandise imports in 1996.

BALANCE OF PAYMENTS, FINANCE AND AID

Following the dramatic increase in world sugar prices in the mid-1970s, Mauritius was able to close its trade gap for the first time in 1974. The trade balance returned to deficit between 1975–86, when a surplus of Rs 214m. reflected the latter year's high sugar output, the advance in EPZ export volume and also the decline in international petroleum prices and in the value of the US dollar. In 1987, however, a sharp increase in imports led to a deficit of Rs 1,000m., and in 1990 and 1991 trade deficits of Rs 5,700m. and Rs 5,300m. respectively were recorded, increasing to Rs 5,800m. in 1992. The visible trade deficits have been caused by increases in EPZ imports for manufacturing inputs, and in imported fuel costs, disappointing sugar harvests and a price freeze on sugar exports to the EC. In 1993 the trade deficit totalled Rs 6,800m., and in 1994 the shortfall advanced to Rs 9,800m. As a result of the decline in exports from the EPZ, export volume rose by only 5%, to Rs 24,700m., in 1994. Imports, however, advanced by 13.7% to a record Rs 34,500m. Exports rose by an estimated 10% in 1995, reflecting growth in both the EPZ and non-EPZ export sectors. In that year agricultural production increased and sugar exports rose in value by about 8%. Tropical flowers, which have become an increasingly important component of agricultural exports attracted revenues exceeding Rs 88m. in 1995. Growth in the chemicals sector has also been impressive in recent years. Mauritius' intake of imports rose by about 7% in 1995, compared with an increase of 13.4% in 1994. This deceleration in import growth was, however, in large part attributable to the cessation of substantial purchases of aircraft and ships, which have affected import totals in recent years. In 1995 Mauritius recorded a visible trade deficit of Rs 7,100m.

The principal domestic exports are sugar, textiles and clothing, tea and molasses, and the principal imports are textile yarn and fabrics, petroleum products and food. In 1996 the principal source of imports was South Africa (12%); other major suppliers were France (11.1%), India and the United Kingdom. The principal market for exports (taking 34.4% of exports in that year) was the United Kingdom; other significant purchasers were France (19.5%), the USA and Germany. The importance of South Africa in Mauritius' trade with Southern Africa is expected to increase significantly as the newly-created Common Market for Eastern and Southern Africa (COMESA) becomes fully operational. Mauritius has also been actively promoting economic initiatives to advance the trading interests of countries on the Indian Ocean rim.

The overall balance of payments remained in surplus from 1985/86 until 1990, when a deficit of US $119.3m. on the current account of the balance of payments was recorded. This declined to $18.2m. in 1991 and to only $100,000 in 1992. In 1993 the deficit on the current account of the balance of payments rose to $92m., advancing to $232.1m. in 1994 but declining to $21.9m. in 1995. Mauritius' external debt totalled $1,801m. at the end of 1995, of which $1,182m. was long-term public debt; in that year the cost of debt-servicing was equivalent to 9% of the value of exports of goods and services. Mauritius has an excellent international credit rating.

Mauritius' economic advances of the mid-1980s, precipitated by the growth of the EPZ sector, enabled the government to introduce far-reaching measures to encourage economic expansion. The 1986/87 budget was generally welcomed by commercial interests and by the general public, owing to its proposals to maintain taxes at their existing level, to extend welfare benefits (particularly to workers in the EPZ sector) and to reduce customs duties on many items. The budget for 1987/88 included proposals to liberalize banking regulations and to provide tax incentives, in order to stimulate international trading interest in the newly established stock exchange and to develop offshore banking activities (see below). To lessen a forecast budgetary shortfall in 1989/90, the government introduced increased excise taxes, although subsidies were maintained on food staples such as rice and flour. Proposals were announced to introduce a harmonized system of customs tariffs and to develop re-export and transhipment activities by establishing a duty-free processing zone for bulk imports. In 1990/91 there was an estimated budgetary deficit of Rs 877m. (equivalent to 1.9% of GDP), which the government financed by increased borrowing on the domestic market. In 1991/92 however, the budgetary deficit declined to Rs 67.2m., and in 1992/93 there was a modest budgeting surplus of Rs 221.4m. A return to deficit spending followed in 1993/94, with a budgetary shortfall of Rs 195.4m. Successive deficits, of Rs 1,065.2m. and Rs 2,449m. were estimated for 1994/95 and 1995/96 respectively.

In 1981 the government obtained a structural adjustment loan (SAL) of US $15m. from the World Bank, to finance the three-year economic programme introduced in 1979. Later in 1981 a second one-year stand-by credit of about $30m. was approved by the IMF, but was suspended in May 1982, as a result of the government's failure to meet IMF conditions. Agreement was reached with the IMF in 1983 for a further facility of SDR 49.8m., and the World Bank subsequently approved a new SAL of $45m. Meanwhile, Mauritius' other main aid donors showed their confidence in the government's austerity programme when, in June 1983, at a meeting of the World Bank-sponsored consultative group, they pledged some $53m. in balance-of-payments support. In early 1984 disagreement arose between Mauritius and the IMF over the release of the remaining half of the stand-by facility. Disbursement of the remainder of the World Bank's second SAL was also delayed until 1985, when the sugar restructuring plan was finally introduced. Sectoral loans of about $25m. for the sugar sector and $25m. for the industrial sector were agreed with the World Bank, following lengthy negotiations during late 1985 and throughout 1986. Agreement was reached with the IMF for an SDR 49m. stand-by facility, over 18 months, and SDR 7.5m. in compensatory financing for the shortfall in export earnings. Owing to the delay in negotiating the new arrangement, the government turned to European money markets for balance-of-payments support to enable the country to meet its immediate external debt-servicing obligations. In 1984 the government signed a $40m. Euroloan agreement with a consortium of banks. When the IMF arrangement expired in 1986, the government decided to defer negotiations on a new facility, owing to the country's strong economic performance. At a special donors' meeting organized by the World Bank, held in Paris in 1989, $90m. was made available to finance a five-year environment protection programme, which laid emphasis on improvements to water and sewage treatment.

A new three-year Development Plan was introduced in 1993, with the aim of further modernizing and diversifying of the economy. The plan envisaged an increased pace of privatization of public enterprises, and provided for the creation of new incentives and institutions to assist the private sector.

As part of a long-term strategy to establish Mauritius as an international financial centre, controls on the movement of foreign exchange were relaxed in 1986. From July 1988 commercial banks were allowed to settle all import payments without having to refer to the central bank. In 1989 the government also announced further measures to liberalize foreign exchange controls. An offshore banking facility was established in that year, under legislation adopted in 1988. By 1997 a total of seven offshore banks were in operation. The government has also implemented a series of incentives to encourage companies to incorporate locally and to offer a minimum of 25% of their shares on the stock exchange, which opened in Port Louis in 1989. Investors in these companies were to be exempt from tax on 35% of all dividend payments, and annual profits of up to Rs 100,000 from the sale of these securities were also to be exempt. Mauritius has strengthened trade and investment relations with South Africa since the early 1990s. China and Mauritius signed a technical co-operation and economic agreement in 1990, which provided Mauritius with an interest-free loan of US $5.3m. for infrastructure projects. The Mauritius financial services sector is actively seeking to attract capital from Hong Kong, following that territory's return to Chinese sovereignty in 1997.

ECONOMIC PROSPECTS

Despite its relatively favourable economic performance in recent years. Mauritius faces a number of problems and uncertainties. Prominent among these is the rate of population growth, which projects a population of more than 1.5m. people by the year 2010, exclusive of the numbers of *émigré* Mauritians, estimated at about 50,000, who are expected to return to the island following retirement. This demographic trend is expected to pose the economy with considerable challenges.

The EPZ sector, which has led the island's industrial expansion in recent years, is expected to show growth of less than 8% annually in the late 1990s. As the base of export diversification is unlikely to be widened in the short term, a sharper decline in this sector can be expected. The government is proceeding with proposals to diversify the EPZ's industrial base and to improve vocational, technical and professional training for the industrial sector. Inflation, which has so far been held within manageable levels, totalled 6.6% in 1996. The expansion of tourism, an economic mainstay of recent years, is challenged by the prospect of overcrowding and environmental damage.

Mauritius' infrastructure is beginning to show need of heavy investment in projects such as roads, telecommunications and public utilities. A World Bank report, published in 1989, stressed the need for economic diversification to minimize the country's vulnerability to fluctuations in the international economy. Mauritius is faced by increased competition in the international textile market, and any future alteration in its privileged access to the EU markets would necessitate the industry's becoming more competitive, with the use of newer, costly technology. Foreign direct investment into Mauritius increased during the 1980s, owing primarily to the expansion in the EPZ. By 1991, however, this investment fell sharply, following a slow-down in EPZ growth. This decreased investment led in turn to a further decline in the EPZ, which continued in the mid-1990s. The new coalition government remains committed to a free market economy, while recognizing the need to raise the living standards of the less prosperous strata of Mauritian society. In 1996 the government reintroduced the cycle of five-year plans into national development strategies, with emphasis on education, housing and health. Given the general diversification, stability and diversity of its economy, Mauritius can reasonably expect to achieve its government's target of GDP growth of between 5.5%-6.5% annually by the start of the 21st century.

Statistical Survey

Source (unless otherwise stated): Central Statistical Office, LIC Centre, President John F. Kennedy St, Port Louis; tel. 212-2316.

Area and Population

AREA, POPULATION AND DENSITY

Area (sq km)	2,040*
Population (census results)	
2 July 1983†	
Males	499,360
Females	502,818
Total	1,002,178
1 July 1990‡	1,058,942
Population (official estimates at mid-year)§	
1994	1,112,607
1995	1,122,118
1996	1,133,551
Density (per sq km) at mid-1996§	575.7

* 788 sq miles.
† Including an adjustment of 1,746 for underenumeration.
‡ Including an adjustment of 2,115 for underenumeration on the island of Mauritius (enumerated total 1,022,456, comprising 510,676 males and 511,780 females). The population of the island of Rodrigues was 34,204 (males 17,084; females 17,120).
§ Islands of Mauritius and Rodrigues only (area 1,969 sq km, population 1,058,775 at 1990 census).

ISLANDS

	Area (sq km)	Population 2 July 1983 Census*	Population 1 July 1990 Census†
Mauritius	1,865	968,609‡	1,024,571‡
Rodrigues	104	33,082	34,204
Other islands	71	487	167

* Figures relate to the *de facto* population.
† Figures relate to the *de jure* population.
‡ Including adjustment for underenumeration.

ETHNIC GROUPS

Island of Mauritius, mid-1982: 664,480 Indo-Mauritians (507,985 Hindus, 156,495 Muslims), 264,537 general population (incl. Creole and Franco-Mauritian communities), 20,669 Chinese.

LANGUAGE GROUPS (census of 1 July 1990)*

Arabic	1,686
Bhojpuri	343,832
Chinese	17,652
Creole	379,288
English	888
French	22,367
Hindi	38,181
Marathi	17,732
Tamil	47,953
Telegu	21,033
Urdu	45,311
Other languages	120,737
Total	1,056,660

* Figures refer to the languages usually spoken at home by the population on the islands of Mauritius and Rodrigues only. The data exclude an adjustment for underenumeration. The adjusted total was 1,058,775.

PRINCIPAL TOWNS (estimated population at mid-1996)

Port Louis (capital)	145,797	Curepipe	77,898
Beau Bassin/Rose Hill	98,232	Quatre Bornes	74,860
Vacoas-Phoenix	96,012		

BIRTHS, MARRIAGES AND DEATHS*

	Registered live births Number	Registered live births Rate (per 1,000)	Registered marriages Number	Registered marriages Rate (per 1,000)	Registered deaths Number	Registered deaths Rate (per 1,000)
1993	22,329	20.3	11,576	10.5	7,433	6.8
1994	21,795	19.6	11,414	10.3	7,402	6.7
1995	20,549	18.3	10,624	9.5	7,465	6.7
1996	20,763	18.3	10,697	9.4	7,670	6.8

* Figures refer to the islands of Mauritius and Rodrigues only. The data are tabulated by year of registration, rather than by year of occurrence.

EMPLOYMENT (persons aged 12 years and over)

	1993	1994	1995
Agriculture, hunting, forestry and fishing	62,400	62,300	61,600
Mining and quarrying	1,300	1,400	1,600
Manufacturing	133,700	134,000	134,700
Electricity, gas and water	3,600	3,500	3,500
Construction	36,800	38,200	36,800
Trade, restaurants and hotels	57,400	61,200	64,900
Transport, storage and communications	27,600	27,800	28,400
Financing, insurance, real estate and business services	13,000	13,600	14,100
Community, social and personal services	107,200	109,700	111,900
Activities not adequately defined	2,900	3,100	3,000
Total employed	445,900	454,800	460,500
Males	307,700	311,800	314,200
Females	138,200	143,000	146,300

Agriculture

PRINCIPAL CROPS ('000 metric tons)

	1994	1995	1996
Maize	1	n.a.	n.a.
Potatoes	18	15	11
Coconuts	2	2	2
Tomatoes	9	13	11
Sugar cane	4,813	5,159	5,260
Bananas	7	9	9
Tobacco (leaves)	1	1	1
Groundnuts (in shell)	1	1	1

Tea (made) ('000 metric tons): 5.1 in 1994; 3.8 in 1995; 2.5 in 1996 (Source: International Tea Committee).

LIVESTOCK ('000 head, year ending September)

	1993	1994	1995
Cattle*	34	34	34
Pigs	15	17*	17*
Sheep*	7	7	7
Goats*	95	95	98

* FAO estimate(s).

Poultry (FAO estimates, million): 3 in 1993; 3 in 1994; 3 in 1995.

Source: FAO, *Production Yearbook*.

LIVESTOCK PRODUCTS ('000 metric tons)

	1993	1994	1995
Meat	21	23	24
Cows' milk	9	8	7
Hen eggs	6.7	7.5	8.4

Forestry

ROUNDWOOD REMOVALS ('000 cubic metres, excluding bark)

	1993	1994	1995
Sawlogs, veneer logs and logs for sleepers	7	8	7
Other industrial wood	3	5	3
Fuel wood	9	11	12
Total	19	24	22

SAWNWOOD PRODUCTION
('000 cubic metres, including railway sleepers)

	1992	1993	1994
Total	4	5	4

Fishing

('000 metric tons, live weight)

	1993	1994	1995
Emperors (Scavengers)	6.3	6.3	6.1
Skipjack tuna	6.9	5.3	3.8
Yellowfin tuna	2.5	2.0	1.7
Other fishes (incl. unspecified)	0.4	0.5	4.9
Crustaceans and molluscs	0.4	0.5	0.5
Total catch	21.1	19.0	17.0

Industry

SELECTED PRODUCTS (metric tons, unless otherwise indicated)

	1993	1994	1995
Raw sugar	565,026	500,209	539,521
Molasses	162,000	144,510	150,400
Rum (hectolitres)	61,000	53,415	99,392
Beer and stout (hectolitres)	291,640	282,578	308,788
Electric energy (million kWh)	869	945	1,047

Finance

CURRENCY AND EXCHANGE RATES

Monetary Units

100 cents = 1 Mauritian rupee.

Sterling and Dollar Equivalents (31 March 1997)

£1 sterling = 32.28 rupees;
US $1 = 19.66 rupees;
1,000 Mauritian rupees = £30.98 = $50.86.

Average Exchange Rate (Mauritian rupees per US $)

1994 17.960
1995 17.386
1996 17.948

BUDGET (million rupees, year ending 30 June)*

Revenue†	1993/94	1994/95	1995/96‡
Taxation	12,254.1	12,024.7	12,295.3
Taxes on income, profits and capital gains	1,497.0	1,804.2	1,955.0
Individual taxes	682.7	863.3	970.0
Corporate taxes	814.3	940.9	985.0
Social security contributions	728.8	844.6	900.0
Taxes on property	776.5	809.3	851.0
Taxes on financial and capital transactions	765.3	784.9	838.0
Domestic taxes on goods and services	3,398.4	3,499.4	3,810.3
General sales, turnover or value-added taxes	1,251.9	1,299.4	1,420.0
Excises	1,126.0	1,100.5	1,155.0
Alcoholic beverages	641.8	614.9	625.0
Taxes on specific services	724.0	773.0	899.3
Taxes on international trade and transactions	5,763.7	4,978.6	4,685.0
Import duties	5,363.3	4,978.5	4,685.0
Customs duties	3,662.9	4,968.3	4,685.0
Other import charges	1,700.4	10.2	—
Export duties	400.3	—	—
Other current revenue	1,821.9	2,428.3	2,499.3
Entrepreneurial and property income	1,324.7	1,820.6	1,919.1
From non-financial public enterprises and public financial institutions	1,240.0	1,684.6	1,756.4
Administrative fees and charges, non-industrial and incidental sales	389.8	477.0	406.6
Total	14,076.0	14,453.0	14,794.6

Expenditure§	1993/94	1994/95	1995/96‡
General public services	1,514.9	1,773.9	1,919.3
Defence	200.3	221.0	238.3
Public order and safety	1,276.1	1,424.2	1,535.1
Education	2,309.9	2,682.1	2,864.2
Health	1,306.1	1,292.8	1,400.5
Social security and welfare	2,368.8	2,671.7	3,094.8
Housing and community amenities	999.4	870.4	943.5
Recreational, cultural and religious affairs and services	231.3	280.6	320.9
Economic affairs and services	2,121.0	2,106.2	2,289.2
Agriculture, forestry, fishing and hunting	821.2	901.6	970.0
Mining, manufacturing and construction	67.8	100.6	124.6
Transport and communications	944.7	813.6	634.2
Other purposes	1,943.6	2,195.3	2,637.8
Public debt interest	1,324.9	1,652.5	1,962.1
Transfers to local government	509.4	525.3	630.7
Other	109.3	17.5	45.0
Total	14,271.4	15,518.2	17,243.6
Current	11,549.7	12,876.4	14,539.1
Capital	2,721.7	2,641.8	2,704.5

* Figures represent a consolidation of the General Budget, the National Pensions Fund and the operations of 22 extra-budgetary units of the central Government. The accounts of local government councils are excluded.

† Excluding grants received from abroad (million rupees): 130.2 in 1993/94; 261.6 in 1994/95; 220.5 in 1995/96.

‡ Provisional.

§ Excluding lending minus repayments (million rupees): 101.8 in 1993/94; –30.5 in 1994/95; 493.1 in 1995/96.

INTERNATIONAL RESERVES (US $ million at 31 December)

	1994	1995	1996
Gold*	4.0	4.1	4.0
IMF special drawing rights	31.2	32.2	31.9
Reserve position in IMF	10.7	10.9	10.6
Foreign exchange	705.7	820.2	853.7
Total	751.6	867.4	900.2

* Valued at market-related prices.

Source: IMF, *International Financial Statistics*.

MONEY SUPPLY (million rupees at 31 December)

	1994	1995	1996
Currency outside banks	4,412.2	4,847.2	5,050.7
Demand deposits at deposit money banks	4,443.3	4,685.4	4,774.0
Total money (incl. others)	8,864.0	9,572.8	9,829.8

Source: IMF, *International Financial Statistics.*

COST OF LIVING (Consumer Price Index, average of monthly figures. Base: June 1992 = 100)

	1994	1995	1996
Food	127.3	135.0	142.2
Fuel and light	107.5	111.3	111.0
Rent	111.1	113.5	116.5
All items (incl. others)	122.7	130.1	138.7

NATIONAL ACCOUNTS (million rupees in current prices)

Components of the Gross National Product

	1994	1995	1996*
Compensation of employees	26,260	28,339	31,920
Operating surplus Consumption of fixed capital	28,289	32,031	35,987
Gross domestic product (GDP) at factor cost	54,549	60,370	67,907
Indirect taxes	8,763	8,688	9,700
Less Subsidies	206	330	600
GDP in purchasers' values	63,106	68,728	77,007
Factor income received from abroad *Less* Factor income paid abroad	−443	−332	−719
Gross national product (GNP) at market prices	62,663	68,396	76,288

Expenditure on the Gross Domestic Product

	1994	1995	1996*
Government final consumption expenditure	7,862	8,370	9,400
Private final consumption expenditure	40,361	44,592	49,313
Increase in stocks	1,112	827	195
Gross fixed capital formation	19,350	16,750	19,320
Total domestic expenditure	68,685	70,539	78,228
Exports of goods and services	36,094	40,847	48,320
Less Imports of goods and services	41,673	42,658	49,541
GDP in purchasers' values	63,106	68,728	77,007
GDP at constant 1992 prices	54,460	56,986	60,088

Gross Domestic Product by Economic Activity (at factor cost)

	1994	1995	1996*
Agriculture, forestry, hunting and fishing	4,960	5,707	6,349
Mining and quarrying	90	100	110
Manufacturing	12,686	14,298	16,373
Electricity, gas and water	1,297	1,514	1,628
Construction	4,019	4,060	4,390
Trade, restaurants and hotels	9,251	10,252	11,917
Transport, storage and communications	6,265	6,899	7,568
Financing, insurance, real estate and business services	8,545	9,733	10,927
Government services	6,023	6,433	7,235
Other services	3,286	3,620	4,027
Less Imputed bank service charges	1,873	2,246	2,617
Total	54,549	60,370	67,907

* Figures are provisional.

BALANCE OF PAYMENTS (US $ million)

	1993	1994	1995
Exports of goods f.o.b.	1,334.4	1,376.9	1,571.7
Imports of goods f.o.b.	−1,576.0	−1,773.9	−1,812.2
Trade balance	−241.6	−397.0	−240.5
Exports of services	566.2	632.7	777.7
Imports of services	−521.7	−546.4	−641.3
Balance on goods and services	−197.1	−310.6	−104.2
Other income received	70.0	31.7	52.2
Other income paid	−66.5	−56.4	−71.3
Balance on goods, services and income	−193.6	−335.3	−123.3
Current transfers received	115.9	129.6	146.8
Current transfers paid	−14.4	−26.3	−45.4
Current balance	−92.0	−232.1	−21.9
Capital account (net)	−1.5	−1.3	−1.1
Direct investment abroad	−33.2	−1.1	−3.6
Direct investment from abroad	14.7	20.0	18.7
Portfolio investment assets	−2.2	−0.3	—
Portfolio investment liabilities	—	2.1	175.9
Other investment assets	−26.7	−64.6	−136.4
Other investment liabilities	66.6	85.2	−29.5
Net errors and omissions	81.2	148.5	106.7
Overall balance	7.0	−43.5	108.8

Source: IMF, *International Financial Statistics.*

External Trade

PRINCIPAL COMMODITIES (million rupees)

Imports c.i.f.*	1994	1995*	1996*
Food and live animals	4,241	n.a.	n.a.
Dairy products	766	849	947
Crude materials (inedible) except fuels	1,004	n.a.	n.a.
Mineral fuels, lubricants, etc.	2,133	n.a.	n.a.
Petroleum products	1,779	2,019	2,821
Chemicals	2,442	n.a.	n.a.
Basic manufactures	11,828	n.a.	n.a.
Textile yarn and thread	2,306	2,653	3,637
Textile fabrics	4,887	4,630	4,461
Cement	653	687	754
Iron and steel	914	887	1,255
Machinery and transport equipment	8,887	n.a.	n.a.
Machinery specialized for particular industries	1,467	1,275	1,548
General industrial machinery	997	933	1,148
Road motor vehicles	1,545	1,487	1,711
Miscellaneous manufactured articles	3,101	n.a.	n.a.
Total (incl. others)	34,548	34,379	40,892

Exports f.o.b. (EPZ)†	1992	1993	1994
Fish and fish preparations	295	384	514
Clothing	10,476	12,719	12,876
Other textiles	468	574	702
Watches and clocks	630	612	512
Total (incl. others)	13,081	15,821	16,545

1995 (million rupees): Total EPZ exports 18,267.

1996 (million rupees): Total EPZ exports 21,001.

Exports f.o.b. (non-EPZ)‡	1994	1995*	1996*
Sugar (raw)	5,742	6,326	8,024
Total (incl. others)	6,651	7,519	9,474

* Figures are provisional.

† Exports from the Export Processing Zone (EPZ) only.

‡ Figures refer to domestic exports, excluding exports from the Export Processing Zone (EPZ). Also excluded are re-exports, totalling (in million rupees): 901 in 1994.

PRINCIPAL TRADING PARTNERS (million rupees)

Imports c.i.f.	1994	1995*	1996*
Australia	1,024	1,110	1,811
Bahrain	64	76	219
Belgium	533	536	686
China, People's Repub.	1,240	1,005	1,740
France	6,380	4,427	4,554
Germany	1,590	1,554	1,903
Hong Kong	1,772	1,641	1,474
India	2,294	2,900	3,629
Indonesia	295	293	447
Italy	989	1,109	1,392
Japan	1,750	1,642	1,795
Korea, Repub.	475	437	493
Malaysia	807	1,121	964
New Zealand	345	430	444
Pakistan	497	365	644
Singapore	991	910	867
South Africa	4,106	3,825	4,893
Switzerland	697	811	878
Taiwan	1,209	1,083	1,120
United Kingdom	2,308	2,288	2,648
USA	788	891	1,022
Total (incl. others)	34,548	34,363	40,892

Exports f.o.b.	1994	1995*	1996*
Belgium	511	511	732
France	4,844	5,662	6,109
Germany	1,423	1,561	1,748
Italy	1,002	1,098	1,269
Netherlands	508	579	769
Réunion	485	490	524
United Kingdom	7,696	9,173	10,799
USA	4,360	3,965	4,092
Total (incl. others)	24,097	26,757	31,391

* Figures are provisional.

Transport

ROAD TRAFFIC (vehicles in use)

	1994	1995	1996
Private vehicles			
Cars	55,336	59,123	63,390
Motorcycles and mopeds	92,370	97,228	101,140
Commercial vehicles			
Buses	2,270	2,362	2,348
Taxis	4,311	4,439	4,673
Goods vehicles	21,049	22,019	22,924
Government vehicles	4,584	4,685	4,813

Source: Ministry of Works, Port Louis.

SHIPPING

Merchant Fleet (registered at 31 December)

	1994	1995	1996
Number of vessels	58	48	50
Total displacement ('000 grt)	206.2	238.3	243.6

Source: Lloyd's Register of Shipping, *World Fleet Statistics*.

Sea-borne Freight Traffic ('000 metric tons)

	1994	1995	1996
Goods unloaded	2,419	2,463	2,753
Goods loaded	834	799	966

Source: Ministry of Works, Port Louis.

CIVIL AVIATION (traffic)

	1994	1995	1996
Aircraft landings	5,717	5,830	6,265
Passenger arrivals	528,565	549,448	630,240
Freight unloaded (metric tons)	12,690	14,367	16,856
Freight loaded (metric tons)	14,855	16,111	18,815

Source: Ministry of Works, Port Louis.

Tourism

FOREIGN TOURIST ARRIVALS

Country of Residence	1994	1995	1996
France	106,268	116,701	130,292
Germany	41,824	41,637	45,221
Italy	18,149	17,384	21,848
Madagascar	6,849	6,885	11,401
Réunion	77,035	78,431	82,272
South Africa	39,762	42,653	50,361
Switzerland	11,453	13,815	15,692
United Kingdom	33,295	31,324	35,271
Total (incl. others)	400,526	422,463	486,867

Communications Media

	1991	1992	1993
Radio receivers ('000 in use)	390	395	399
Television receivers ('000 in use)	236	239	242
Telephones ('000 main lines in use)	64	79	107
Book production*			
Titles	56	80	96
Copies ('000)	157	99	135
Daily newspapers			
Number	n.a.	6	n.a.
Average circulation ('000 copies)	n.a.	80	n.a.
Non-daily newspapers			
Number	n.a.	25	n.a.
Average circulation ('000 copies)	n.a.	n.a.	n.a.
Other periodicals			
Number	n.a.	62	n.a.

* Including pamphlets (20 titles and 92,000 copies in 1991; 24 titles and 14,000 copies in 1992; 21 titles and 29,000 copies in 1993).

Sources: UNESCO, *Statistical Yearbook*; UN, *Statistical Yearbook*.

Education

(1996)

	Institutions	Students
Primary	281	124,589
Secondary	130	93,037
University	1	2,496
Institute of Education	1	3,092
Lycée Polytechnique	1	584

Teachers (1996): Primary 5,215; General Secondary 4,564.

Directory

The Constitution

The Mauritius Independence Order, which established a self-governing state, came into force on 12 March 1968, and was subsequently amended. Constitutional amendments providing for the adoption of republican status were approved by the Legislative Assembly (henceforth known as the National Assembly) on 10 December 1991, and came into effect on 12 March 1992. The main provisions of the revised Constitution are listed below:

HEAD OF STATE

The Head of State is the President of the Republic, who is elected by a simple majority of the National Assembly for a five-year term of office. The President appoints the Prime Minister (in whom executive power is vested) and, on the latter's recommendation, other ministers.

COUNCIL OF MINISTERS

The Council of Ministers, which is headed by the Prime Minister, is appointed by the President and is responsible to the National Assembly.

THE NATIONAL ASSEMBLY

The National Assembly, which has a term of five years, comprises the Speaker, 62 members elected by universal adult suffrage, a maximum of eight additional members and the Attorney-General (if not an elected member). The island of Mauritius is divided into 20 three-member constituencies for legislative elections. Rodrigues returns two members to the National Assembly. The official language of the National Assembly is English, but any member may address the Speaker in French.

The Government

HEAD OF STATE

President: CASSAM UTEEM (took office 30 June 1992; re-elected 28 June 1997).

Vice-President: ANGIDI VERRIAH CHETTIAR.

COUNCIL OF MINISTERS*
(July 1997)

Prime Minister, Minister of Defence and Home Affairs, Minister of External Communications and the Outer Islands, Minister for Civil Service Affairs and Minister of Urban and Rural Development: Dr NAVINCHANDRA RAMGOOLAM.

Deputy Prime Minister, Minister of Foreign Affairs and International Trade: RAJKESWUR PURRYAG.

Minister of Housing and Land Development: CLARIEL DÉSIRÉ MALHERBE.

Attorney-General and Minister of Justice, Minister of Human Rights and Corporate Affairs and Minister of Labour and Industrial Relations: ABDOOL RAZACK MOHAMED AMEEN PEEROO.

Minister of Land Transport, Shipping and Public Safety: Dr AHMED RASHID BEEBEEJAUN.

Minister of Finance: Dr VASANT KUMAR BUNWAREE.

Minister of Local Government and Environment: Dr JAMES BURTY DAVID.

Minister of Education and Human Resource Development: RAMSAMY CHEDUMBARUM PILLAY.

Minister of Agriculture, Fisheries and Co-operatives: Dr ARVIN BOOLELL.

Minister of Social Security and National Solidarity: DHURMA GLAN NATH.

Minister of Arts and Culture: TSANG FAN HIN TSANG MAN KIN.

Minister of Public Infrastructure: Dr MOHUMMUD SIDDICK CHADY.

Minister of Public Utilities: DEVANAND VIRAHSAWMY.

Minister of Women, Family Welfare and Child Development: Mrs INDIRA SAVITREE THACOOR-SIDAYA.

Minister of Youth and Sports: SACHINDEV MAHESS KUMAR SOONARANE.

Minister of Tourism and Leisure: MARIE-JOSEPH JACQUES CHASTEAU DE BALYON.

Minister of Health and Quality of LIfe: NANKESWARSINGH SUNASSEE.

Minister of Industry and Commerce: SATHIAMOORTHY SUNASSEE.

Minister of Telecommunications and Information Technology: SARAT DUTT LALLAH.

Minister for Rodrigues: J. BÉNOIT JOLICOEUR.

* See Late Information.

MINISTRIES

Prime Minister's Office: Government Centre, Port Louis; tel. 201-1001; telex 4249; fax 208-8619.

Ministry of Agriculture and Natural Resources: NPF Bldg, 8th Floor, Port Louis; tel. 212-7946; fax 212-4427.

Ministry of Arts and Culture: NPF Bldg, cnr Jules Koenig and Maillard Sts, Port Louis; tel. 212-2675.

Ministry of Civil Service Affairs: Government Centre, Port Louis; tel. 201-1035; fax 212-9528.

Ministry of Co-operatives: Life Insurance Corpn of India Bldg, 3rd Floor, President John F. Kennedy St, Port Louis; tel. 208-4812; fax 208-9263.

Ministry of Economic Planning and Development: Emmanuel Anquetil Bldg, Sir Seewoosagur Ramgoolam St, Port Louis; tel. 201-1576; fax 212-4124.

Ministry of Education, Science and Technology: Government Centre, Port Louis; tel. 201-3039; fax 212-3783.

Ministry of Employment, Manpower Resources and Technical Training: NPF Bldg, 6th Floor, cnr Jules Koenig and Maillard Sts, Port Louis; tel. 242-1462.

Ministry of Energy and Water Resources: Government Centre, Port Louis; tel. 201-1087; fax 208-6497.

Ministry of the Environment and Quality of Life: Barracks St, Port Louis; tel. 212-8332; fax 212-9407.

Ministry of Finance: Government Centre, Port Louis; tel. 201-1145; fax 208-8622.

Ministry of Fisheries and Marine Resources: Life Insurance Corpn of India Bldg, President John F. Kennedy St, Port Louis; tel. 211-2470.

Ministry of Foreign Affairs, International and Regional Co-operation: Level 5, New Government Centre, Port Louis; tel. 201-1416; fax 212-6764.

Ministry of Health: Emmanuel Anquetil Bldg, Sir Seewoosagur Ramgoolam St, Port Louis; tel. 201-1910; fax 208-0376.

Ministry of Housing, Lands and Town and Country Planning: Moorgate House, Port Louis; tel. 212-6022; fax 212-7482.

Ministry of Industrial Relations: Ming Court, cnr Eugène Laurent and GMD Atchia Sts, Port Louis; tel. 212-3049; fax 212-3070.

Ministry of Industry, Industrial Technology, Scientific Research and Handicraft: Government Centre, Port Louis; tel. 201-1221; fax 212-8201.

Ministry of Information and Telecommunications: Government Centre, Port Louis; tel. 201-1278; fax 208-8243.

Ministry of Justice: Jules Koenig St, Port Louis; tel. 208-5321.

Ministry of Local Government: Emmanuel Anquetil Bldg, Sir Seewoosagur Ramgoolam St, Port Louis; tel. 201-1215.

Ministry of Public Utilities: Treasury Bldg, Port Louis; tel. 208-0281; fax 212-8373.

Ministry for Rodrigues: Fon Sing Bldg, Edith Cavell St, Port Louis; tel. 208-8472; fax 212-6329.

Ministry of Social Security and National Solidarity: NPF Bldg, cnr Pope Hennessy and Maillard Sts, Port Louis; tel. 212-3006.

Ministry of Tourism and Leisure: Emmanuel Anquetil Bldg, Sir Seewoosagur Ramgoolam St, Port Louis; tel. 201-2286; fax 208-6776.

Ministry of Trade and Shipping: Government Centre, Port Louis; tel. 201-1067; fax 212-6368.

Ministry of Women, Child Development and Family Welfare: Rainbow House, cnr Edith Cavell and Brown Sequard Sts, Port Louis; tel. 208-2061; fax 208-8250.

Ministry of Youth and Sports: Emmanuel Anquetil Bldg, Sir Seewoosagur Ramgoolam St, Port Louis; tel. 201-1242; fax 212-2986.

Legislature

NATIONAL ASSEMBLY

Speaker: RAMESH JEEWOOLALL.

General Election, 20 December 1995

Party	Seats*
Mauritius Labour Party	35
Mouvement Militant Mauricien	25
Organisation du Peuple Rodriguais	2

* Four additional members were appointed, two from the Mouvement Rodriguais, one from the Parti Mauricien Social Démocrate and one from Hizbullah, as unsuccessful candidates who attracted the largest number of votes.

Political Organizations

Comité d'Action Musulman (CAM): POB 882, Port Louis; f. 1958; Muslim support; Pres. YOUSSUF MOHAMMED.

Hizbullah: Port Louis; Islamic fundamentalist.

Mauritius Labour Party (MLP): 7 Guy Rozemont Sq., Port Louis; tel. 212-6691; f. 1936; Leader Dr NAVINCHANDRA RAMGOOLAM; Sec.-Gen. JOSEPH TSANG MAN KIN.

Mouvement Militant Mauricien (MMM): Port Louis; f. 1969; socialist; Chair. AHMAD JEEWAH; Leader PAUL BÉRENGER.

Mouvement Rodriguais: Port Mathurin, Rodrigues; represents the interests of Rodrigues; Leader NICHOLAS VON MALLY.

Mouvement Socialiste Militant (MSM): Sun Trust Bldg, 31 Edith Cavell St, Port Louis; tel. 212-8787; fax 208-9517; f. 1983 as the Movement Socialiste Mauricien by fmr mems of the MMM; dominant party in subsequent coalition govts until Dec. 1995; Leader Sir ANEROOD JUGNAUTH; Sec.-Gen. VISHWANATH SAJADAH.

Organisation du Peuple Rodriguais (OPR): Port Mathurin, Rodrigues; represents the interests of Rodrigues; Leader LOUIS SERGE CLAIR.

Parti Mauricien Social Démocrate (PMSD): place Foch-Galende, Rémy Ollier, POB 599, Port Louis; centre-right; Pres. ALAN DRIVER; Leader HERVÉ DUVAL; Sec.-Gen. CLIFFORD EMPEIGNE.

Renouveau Militant Mauricien (RMM): Port Louis; f. 1994 by fmr mems of the Mouvement Militant Mauricien; Chair. DHARMANAND FOKEER; Leader Dr PARAMHANSA (PREM) NABABSINGH; Gen. Sec. J. BOULLÉ.

Minor parties include the **Mouvement des Travaillistes Démocrates,** the **Parti Socialiste Mauricien,** the **Union Démocratique Mauricienne** and the **Movement des Démocrates Libéraux.**

Diplomatic Representation

EMBASSIES AND HIGH COMMISSIONS IN MAURITIUS

Australia: Port Louis; tel. 208-1700; telex 4414; fax 208-8878; High Commissioner: CHRIS MARCHANT.

China, People's Republic: Royal Rd, Belle Rose, Quatre Bornes, Port Louis; tel. 454-9111; Ambassador: ZHENG AQUAN.

Egypt: King George V Ave, Floreal, Port Louis; tel. 696-5012; telex 4332; fax 686-5575. Ambassador: SAMIRA EKDAWI.

France: 14 St George's St, Port Louis; tel. 208-3755; telex 4233; fax 208-8145; Ambassador: RENÉ FORCEVILLE.

India: Life Insurance Corpn of India Bldg, President John F. Kennedy St, Port Louis; tel. 208-3775; telex 4523; fax 208-6859; High Commissioner: SHYAM SARAN.

Madagascar: Guiot St, Pasceau, Floreal, Port Louis; tel. 686-5015; telex 4340; fax 686-7040; Ambassador: BERTRAND RAZAFINTSALAMA.

Pakistan: Anglo-Mauritius House, Intendance St, Port Louis; tel. 212-6547; telex 4609; fax 212-6548; High Commissioner: IKRAM KARIM FAZLI.

Russia: Queen Mary Ave, Floreal, POB 509, Port Louis; tel. 696-1545; telex 4826; Ambassador: N. K. ASSATOUR AGARON.

South Africa: British-American Insurance Bldg, 4th Floor, Pope Hennessy St, POB 908, Port Louis; tel. 212-6925; fax 212-6936; High Commissioner: ANDRÉ BOSMAN.

United Kingdom: Edith Cavell St, POB 1063, Port Louis; tel. 211-1361; fax 211-1369; High Commissioner: JAMES DALY.

USA: Rogers House, President John F. Kennedy St, Port Louis; tel. 208-2347; fax 208-9534; Ambassador: HAROLD W. GEISEL.

Judicial System

The laws of Mauritius are derived both from the old French Codes, suitably amended, and from English Law. The Judicial Department consists of the Supreme Court, presided over by the Chief Justice and eight other Judges who are also Judges of the Court of Criminal Appeal and the Court of Civil Appeal, the Intermediate Court, the Industrial Court and 10 District Courts. There is a right of appeal in certain cases to the Judicial Committee of the Privy Council in the United Kingdom.

Chief Justice: ARIRANGA PILLAY.

Senior Puisne Judge: B. SIK YUEN.

Puisne Judges: V. BOOLELL, K. P. MATADEEN, Mrs R. N. NARAYEN, E. BALANCY, P. LAM SHANG LEEN.

Religion

At the 1972 census, Hindus comprised 51.0% of the population on the island of Mauritius, with Christians accounting for 31.3%, Muslims 16.6% and Buddhists 0.6%.

CHRISTIANITY

The Anglican Communion

Anglicans in Mauritius are within the Church of the Province of the Indian Ocean, comprising six dioceses (four in Madagascar, one in Mauritius and one in Seychelles). The Archbishop of the Province is the Bishop of Antananarivo, Madagascar. In 1983 the Church had 5,438 members in Mauritius.

Bishop of Mauritius: Rt Rev. REX DONAT, Bishop's House,Phoenix; tel. 686-5158; fax 697-1096.

Presbyterian Church of Mauritius

Minister: Pasteur ANDRÉ DE RÉLAND, 11 Poudrière St, Port Louis; tel. 208-2386; f. 1814.

The Roman Catholic Church

Mauritius comprises a single diocese, directly responsible to the Holy See. At 31 December 1995 there were an estimated 287,853 adherents in the country, representing about 25.7·% of the total population.

Bishop of Port Louis: Rt Rev. MAURICE PIAT, Evêché, 13 Mgr Gonin St, Port Louis; tel. 208-3068; fax 208-6607.

BAHÁ'Í FAITH

National Spiritual Assembly: POB 538, Port Louis; tel. 212-2179; mems resident in 190 localities.

ISLAM

Mauritius Islamic Mission: Noor-e-Islam Mosque, Port Louis; Imam S. M. BEEHARRY.

The Press

DAILIES

China Times: 24 Emmanuel Anquetil St, POB 325, Port Louis; tel. 240-3067; f. 1953; Chinese; Editor-in-Chief LONG SIONG AH KENG; circ. 3,000.

Chinese Daily News: 32 Rémy Ollier St, POB 316, Port Louis; tel. 240-0472; f. 1932; Chinese; Editor-in-Chief WONG YUEN MOY; circ. 5,000.

L'Express: 3 Brown Sequard St, POB 247, Port Louis; tel. 212-4365; telex 4384; fax 208-8174; f. 1963; English and French; Editor-in-Chief JEAN-CLAUDE DE L' ESTRAC; circ. 42,000.

Maurice Soir: Port Louis; f. 1996; Editor SYDNEY SELVON; circ. 2,000.

Le Mauricien: 8 St George St, POB 7, Port Louis; tel. 208-3251; fax 208-7059; f. 1908; English and French; Editor-in-Chief GAËTAN SENEQUE (acting); circ. 30,000.

Le Quotidien: Port Louis; f. 1996; Dirs JACQUES DAVID, PATRICK MICHEL.

Le Socialiste: Manilall Bldg, 3rd Floor, Brabant St, Port Louis; tel. 208-8003; English and French; Editor-in-Chief Dr MONAF KHEDARUN; circ. 6,000.

The Sun: 31 Edith Cavell St, Port Louis; tel. 212-4820; fax 208-9517; English and French; Editor-in-Chief SUBASH GOBIN; circ. 22,000.

WEEKLIES AND FORTNIGHTLIES

5-Plus Dimanche: Résidence des Palmiers, 198 Royal Rd, Beau Bassin; tel. 454-3353; fax 454-3420; f. 1994; English and French; Editor-in-Chief FINLAY SALESSE; circ. 30,000.

5-Plus Magazine: Résidence des Palmiers, 198 Royal Rd, Beau Bassin; tel. 454-3353; fax 454-3420; f. 1988; English and French; Editor-in-Chief PIERRE BENOÎT; circ. 10,000.

Business Magazine: TN Tower, 1st Floor, 13 St George St, Port Louis; tel. 211-1925; fax 211-1926; f. 1993; English and French; Editor-in-Chief LYNDSAY RIVIÈRE; circ. 6,000.

Le Croissant: cnr Velore and Noor Essan Mosque Sts, Port Louis; tel. 240-7105; English and French; Editor-in-Chief B. A. OOZEER.

Le Dimanche: 5 Jemmapes St, Port Louis; tel. 212-1177; f. 1961; English and French; Editor RAYMOND RICHARD NAUVEL; circ. 25,000.

Impact News: 6 Grandcourt, Port Louis; tel. 240-8567; English and French; Editor-in-Chief CADER SAIB.

Lalit de Klas: 153B Royal Rd, G.R.N.W., Port Louis; tel. 208-2132; English, French and Creole; Editor ASHOK SUBRON.

Le Lotus: 73 Prince of Wales St, Rose Hill; tel. 208-4068; English and French; Editor-in-Chief MOGANADEN PILLAY.

Le Mag: Industrial Zone, Tombeay Bay; tel. 247-1005; fax 247-1061; f. 1993; English and French; Editor-in-Chief ALAN GORDON-GENTIL; circ. 8,000.

Mauritius Times: 23 Bourbon St, POB 202, Port Louis; tel. and fax 212-1313; telex 4409; f. 1954; English and French; Editor-in-Chief BICKRAMSINGH RAMLALLAH; circ. 15,000.

Le Militant Magazine: 7 Lord Kitchener St, Port Louis; tel. 212-6050; fax 208-2291; f. 1989; English and French; Editor-in-Chief MITRADEV PEERTHUM; circ. 2,000.

Mirror: 39 Emmanuel Anquetil St, Port Louis; tel. 240-3298; Chinese; Editor-in-Chief NG KEE SIONG; circ. 4,000.

Le Nouveau Militant: 21 Poudrière St, Port Louis; tel. 212-6553; fax 208-2291; f. 1979; publ. by the Mouvement Militant Mauricien; English and French; Editor-in-Chief J. RAUMIAH.

Le Rodriguais; Saint Gabriel, Rodrigues; tel. 831-1613; fax 831-1484; f. 1989; Creole, English and French; Editor JACQUES EDOUARD; circ. 2,000.

Star: 14 Orléans St, Port Louis; tel. 212-2736; English and French; Editor-in-Chief Dr HASSAM RUHOMALLY.

Sunday: 31 Edith Cavell St, Port Louis; tel. 208-9516; fax 208-7059; f. 1966; English and French; Editor-in-Chief SUBASH GOBIN.

Sunday Mirror: 6 Saint Denis St, Port Louis; tel. 211-5137; f. 1996; English; Editor-in-Chief VEDAN B. CHOOLUN; circ. 10,000.

La Vie Catholique: 28 Nicolay Rd, Port Louis; tel. 242-0975; fax 242-3114; f. 1930; English and French; Editor-in-Chief MONIQUE DINAN; circ. 15,000.

Week-End: 8 St George St, Port Louis; tel. 208-3252; fax 208-7059; f. 1966; French and English; Editor-in-Chief GÉRARD CATEAU; circ. 35,000.

Week-End Scope: 8 St George St, Port Louis; tel. 208-3251; fax 208-7059; English and French; Editor-in-Chief AHMAD SALARBUX.

OTHER SELECTED PERIODICALS

CCI–INFO: 3 Royal St, Port Louis; tel. 208-3301; telex 4277; fax 208-0076; English and French; f. 1995; publ. of the Mauritius Chamber of Commerce and Industry.

Ciné Star Magazine: 64 Sir Seewoosagur Ramgoolam St, Port Louis; tel. 240-1447; English and French; Editor-in-Chief ABDOOL RAWOOF SOOBRATTY.

Education News: Edith Cavell St, Port Louis; tel. 212-1303; English and French; monthly; Editor-in-Chief GIAN AUBEELUCK.

Le Message de L'Ahmadiyyat: c/o Ahmadiyya Muslim Asscn, POB 6, Rose Hill; tel. 464-1747; fax 454-2223; e-mail jamaatmu@-bow.intnet.mu; French; monthly; Editor-in-Chief ZAFRULLAH DOMUN; circ. 3,000.

Le Progrès Islamique: 51 Solferino St, Rose Hill; f. 1948; English and French; monthly; Editor N. SOOKIA.

PROSI: Plantation House, Port Louis; tel. 212-3302; telex 4214; fax 212-8710; f. 1969; sugar industry journal; monthly; Dir JACQUES DINAN; circ. 2,750.

La Voix d'Islam: Parisot Rd, Mesnil, Phoenix; f. 1951; English and French; monthly.

Publishers

Best Graphics Ltd: Le Mauricien Bldg, 2nd Floor, 8 St George St, Port Louis; tel. 208-6283; fax 212-6285; English and French; Gen. Man. CLIFFORD LILYMAN.

Bukié Banané: 5 Edwin Ythier St, Rose Hill; tel. 454-2327; f. 1979; Creole literature, poetry and drama; Man. Dir DEV VIRAHSAWMY.

Business Publications Ltd: TN Tower, 1st Floor, St George St, Port Louis; tel. 211-1925; fax 211-1926; f. 1993; English and French; Dir LYNDSAY RIVIÈRE.

Editions du Dattier: 6 Bois Chéri Rd, Moka; tel. and fax 433-0875; English and French; Man. Dir VÉRONIQUE LAGESSE.

Editions de l'Océan Indien Ltée: Stanley, Rose Hill; tel. 464-3959; telex 4739; fax 464-3445; f. 1977; textbooks, literature; English and French; Chair. S. BISSOONDOYAL.

Editions Le Printemps: 4 Club Rd, Vacoas; tel. 696-1017; fax 686-7302; Man. Dir A. I. SULLIMAN.

Précigraph Ltd: St Vincent de Paul Ave, Les Pailles; tel. 208-5049; fax 208-5050; English and French; Man. Dir FRANCE DE LABAUVED'ARIFAT.

Radio and Television

In 1993, according to UNESCO estimates, there were 399,000 radio receivers and 242,000 television receivers in use.

Mauritius Broadcasting Corporation: Broadcasting House, Louis Pasteur St, Forest Side; tel. 675-5001; telex 4230; fax 676-7332; f. 1964; independent corpn operating the national radio and television services; Chair. (vacant); Dir-Gen. TRILOCK DWARKA.

Finance

(cap. = capital; res = reserves; dep. = deposits; m. = million; br. = branch; amounts in Mauritian rupees, unless otherwise stated)

BANKING

Central Bank

Bank of Mauritius: Sir William Newton St, POB 29, Port Louis; tel. 208-4164; telex 4253; fax 208-9204; f. 1967; bank of issue; cap. and res 33m. (June 1994), dep. 2,507m. (Dec. 1996); Gov. DAN MARAYE; Man. Dir BUDHESWAR GUJADHUR.

Commercial Banks

Bank of Baroda: Sir William Newton St, POB 553, Port Louis; tel. 208-1504; telex 4237; fax 208-3892; Pres. R. A. ALMEIDA; 5 brs.

Banque Nationale de Paris Intercontinentale: 1 Sir William Newton St, POB 494, Port Louis; tel. 208-4147; telex 4231; fax 208-8143; Pres. MICHEL PÉBEREAU; Man. Dir YANN OZANNE; 2 brs.

Barclays Bank PLC, Mauritius: Sir William Newton St, POB 80, Port Louis; tel. 208-3724; telex 4572; fax 208-2720; Gen. Man. PATRICK H. NOBLE; 21 brs.

Delphis Bank Ltd: 16 Sir William Newton St, POB 485, Port Louis; tel. 208-5061; telex 4294; fax 208-5388; Man. Dir VIJAY KUMAR RAMPHUL.

Hongkong and Shanghai Banking Corporation Ltd: Place d'Armes, POB 50, Port Louis; tel. 208-1801; telex 4235; fax 208-8449; CEO PAUL LEECH.

Indian Ocean International Bank Ltd: 34 Sir William Newton St, POB 863, Port Louis; tel. 208-0121; telex 4390; fax 208-0127; f. 1978; cap. and res 102.2m., dep. 1,008.1m. (June 1995); Chair. and Man. Dir S. M. CUNDEN; Gen. Man. H. BHASKAR KEDLAYA.

Mauritius Commercial Bank Ltd: 9–15 Sir William Newton St, POB 52, Port Louis; tel. 208-2801; telex 4218; fax 208-7054; f. 1838; cap. and res 3,231.8m., dep. 31,908.5m. (June 1996); Pres. J. RAYMOND HAREL; Gen. Man. PIERRE GUY NOEL; 40 brs.

South East Asian Bank Ltd: 26 Bourbon St, POB 13, Port Louis; tel. 208-8825; fax 211-4900; f. 1989; cap. and res 93.7m., dep. 617m. (Dec. 1996); Chair. Tan Sri Dato' Dr ABDUL KHALID SAHAN; CEO VINCENT LEE; 4 brs.

State Bank of Mauritius Ltd: State Bank Tower, 1 Queen Elizabeth II Ave, POB 152, Port Louis; tel. 202-1111; fax 202-1234; f. 1973; 51% state-owned; cap. and res 979.8m., dep. 15,733m. (June 1996); Chair. D. D. MANRAJ; CEO MUNI KRISHNA T. REDDY; 51 brs.

Union International Bank Ltd: 22 Sir William Newton St, POB 1076, Port Louis; tel. 208-8080; telex 4894; fax 208-8085; f. 1987; cap. and res 55.2m., dep. 645m. (Dec. 1994); Chair. VIVEK CHADHA; Man. Dir and CEO K. P. C. HEGDE.

Development Bank

Development Bank of Mauritius Ltd: La Chaussée St, POB 157, Port Louis; tel. 208-0241; telex 4248; fax 208-8498; f. 1964; 65% govt-owned; cap. and res 1,294m., dep. 1,432m. (June 1996); Chair. K. SACCARAM; Exec. Dir RADHA KRISHNA LUXMUN PRABHU.

'Offshore' Banks

'Offshore' banking operations commenced in 1989.

Banque Internationale des Mascareignes: Moorgate House, 4th Floor, Sir William Newton St, POB 489, Port Louis; tel. 212-4978; telex 4701; fax. 212-4983; f. 1991; cap. US $6m. (1993); jt venture between Crédit Lyonnais de France and Mauritius Commercial Bank Ltd; Chair. MICHEL VALIDIRE; Gen. Man. HIMMAT KALSIA.

Banque Privée Edmond de Rothschild (Océan Indien) Ltée: Anglo-Mauritius House, 2nd Floor, 10 Intendance St, Port Louis; tel. 212-2784; telex 4547; fax 208-4561; Man. Dir LUDOVIC VERBIST.

State Bank International Ltd: SICOM Bldg, 10th Floor, Sir Célicourt Antelme St, Port Louis; tel. 212-2054; fax 212-2050; jt venture between the State Bank of Mauritius and the State Bank of India; Man. Dir M. MADHUKAR.

Bank of Baroda, Banque Nationale de Paris Intercontinentale, Barclays Bank PLC and Hong Kong and Shanghai Banking Corporation also operate 'offshore' banking units.

STOCK EXCHANGE

Stock Exchange Commission: SICOM Bldg, Sir Célicourt Antelme St, Port Louis; tel. 208-8735; telex 5291; fax 208-8676; f. 1993; supervisory authority; Chair. DHIREN DABEE (acting); CEO Ms SHARDA DINDOYAL.

Stock Exchange of Mauritius: Cascades Bldg, 6th Floor, Edith Cavell St, Port Louis; tel. 212-9541; fax 208-8409; f. 1989; 11 mems; Chair. MICHAEL LIM TIT CHONG; CEO RICHARD MORIN.

INSURANCE

Albatross Insurance Co Ltd: 22 St George St, POB 116, Port Louis; tel. 212-9007; telex 4299; fax 208-4800; f. 1975; Chair. DEREK TAYLOR; Man. Dir JEAN DE LA HOGUE.

Anglo-Mauritius Assurance Society Ltd: Swan Group Centre, 10 Intendance St, Port Louis; tel. 211-2312; fax 208-8956; inc. 1951; Chair. J. M. ANTOINE; CEO JEAN DE FONDAUMIÈRE.

British American Insurance Co (Mauritius) Ltd: BAI Bldg, 25 Pope Hennessy St, POB 331, Port Louis; tel. 208-3637; fax 208-3713; Chair. DAWOOD RAWAT; Man. Dir ALAIN C. Y. CHEONG.

Indian Ocean General Assurance Ltd: cnr Rémy Ollier and Corderie Sts, Port Louis; tel. 212-4125; fax 212-5850; f. 1970; Chair. SAM CUNDEN; Man. Dir Mrs D. A. CUNDEN.

Island Insurance Co Ltd: 27 St Louis St, Port Louis; tel. 212-4860; fax 208-8762; Chair. CARRIM A. CURRIMJEE; Man. OLIVIER LAGESSE

Jubilee Insurance Co Ltd: 9 Corderie St, Port Louis; tel. 212-3113; fax 240-7643; Man. Dir HAMID PATEL.

Lamco International Insurance Ltd: 12 Barracks St, Port Louis; tel. 212-0233; fax 208-0630; f. 1978; Chair. S. M. LATIFF; Gen. Man. A. S. KARKHANIS.

Life Insurance Corporation of India: LIC Centre, President John F. Kennedy St, Port Louis; tel. 212-5316; telex 4726; fax 208-6392; Chief Man. Mr ATIMBAH.

Mauritian Eagle Insurance Co Ltd: 10 Dr Ferrière St, POB 854, Port Louis; tel. 212-4877; telex 4867; fax 208-8608; f. 1973; Chair. CHRISTIAN DALAIS; Exec. Dir GUY LEROUX.

Mauritius Union Assurance Co Ltd: 4 Léoville l'Homme St, POB 233, Port Louis; tel. 208-4185; telex 4310; fax 212-2962; f. 1948; Chair. Sir MAURICE LATOUR-ADRIEN; Man. Dir GERVAIS SALAÜN.

The New India Assurance Co Ltd: Bank of Baroda Bldg, 3rd Floor, 32 Sir William Newton St, POB 398, Port Louis; tel. 208-1442; telex 4834; fax 208-2160; Man. Dir P. K. KATHURIA.

La Prudence Mauricienne Assurances Ltée: Fon Sing Bldg, 1st Floor, 12 Edith Cavell St, POB 882, Port Louis; tel. 208-8935; fax 208-8936; Chair. ROBERT DE FROBERVILLE; Man. Dir FELIX MAUREL.

Rainbow Insurance Co Ltd: 23 Edith Cavell St, POB 389, Port Louis; tel. 212-5767; telex 4356; fax 208-8750; f. 1976; Chair. B. GOKULSING; Gen. Man. LATIF KUMAR RAMBURN.

Seagull Insurance Ltd: Blendax House, 3rd Floor, Dumas St, Port Louis; tel. 212-0867; telex 4593; fax 208-2417; Chair. Y. V. LAI FAT FUR; Man. Dir O. GUNGABISSOON.

SICOM Ltd: SICOM Bldg, Sir Célicourt Antelme St, Port Louis; tel. 208-5406; telex 4396; fax 208-7662; f. 1975; Chair. R. SUNT; Man. Dir Mrs K. BHOOJEDHUR-OBEEGADOO.

Stella Insurance Co Ltd: 17 Sir Seewoosagur Ramgoolam St, POB 852, Port Louis; tel. 208-6051; telex 4719; fax 208-1639; f. 1977; Chair. and Man. Dir R. KRESHAN JHOBOO.

Sun Insurance Co Ltd: 2 St George St, Port Louis; tel. 212-2522; telex 4452; fax 208-2052; f. 1981; Chair. Sir KAILASH RAMDANEE; Man. Dir Lady (URSULA) RAMDANEE.

Swan Insurance Co Ltd: Swan Group Centre, 10 Intendance St, POB 364, Port Louis; tel. 211-2001; telex 4393; fax 208-6898; incorp. 1955; Chair. J. M. ANTOINE HAREL; CEO JEAN DE FONDAUMIÈRE.

L. and H. Vigier de Latour Ltd: Les Jamalacs Bldg, Old Council St, Port Louis; tel. 212-2034; telex 4386; fax 212-6056; Chair. and Man. Dir L. J. D. HENRI VIGIER DE LATOUR.

Trade and Industry

CHAMBER OF COMMERCE

Mauritius Chamber of Commerce and Industry: 3 Royal St, Port Louis; tel. 208-3301; telex 4277; fax 208-0076; f. 1850; 408 mems; Pres. CADER SAYED-HOSSEN; Sec.-Gen. JEAN-NOËL HUMBERT (designate).

TRADING ORGANIZATIONS

Chinese Chamber of Commerce: 35 Dr Joseph Rivière St, Port Louis; tel. 208-0946; fax 242-1193; Pres. JEAN KOK SHUN.

Indian Traders' Association: POB 231, Port Louis; tel. 212-2934; fax 208-3339.

Mauritius Chamber of Merchants: Louis Pasteur St, Port Louis; tel. 212-1477; telex 4619; fax 208-7088; Pres. AHMED ABDULLA AHMED.

Mauritius Sugar Syndicate (MSS): Port Louis; sugar marketing monopoly.

State Trading Corpn: Fon Sing Bldg, 12 Edith Cavell St, Port Louis; tel. 208-5440; telex 4537; fax 208-8359; f. 1982 to manage import and distribution of rice, wheat, flour, petroleum products and cement; 99% state-owned; Pres. (vacant); Gen. Man. BEEJAYE GOORAH.

DEVELOPMENT ORGANIZATIONS

Mauritius Export Development and Investment Authority (MEDIA): BAI Bldg, 2nd Floor, 25 Pope Hennessy St, POB 1184, Port Louis; tel. 208-7750; fax 208-5965; f. 1985 to promote exports of goods and services and to encourage export-orientated investment; Chair. MARDAY VENKETASAMY; CEO CHAND BHADAIN.

Mauritius Freeport Authority: Deramann Tower, 3rd Floor, 30 Sir William Newton St, Port Louis; tel. 212-9627; fax 212-9626; f. 1990 to promote freeport activities; Chair. Prof. EDOUARD LIM FAT; Dir-Gen. GÉRARD SANSPEUR.

Mauritius Offshore Business Activities Authority (MOBAA): Deramann Tower, 1st Floor, 30 Sir William Newton St, Port Louis; tel. 211-0143; fax 212-9459; e-mail mobaa@bow.intnet.mu; f.1992; regulates and supervises 'offshore' commercial activities; Dir SATYADEV DEONARAIN BIKOO.

State Investment Corporation Ltd (SIC): Fon Sing Bldg, 2nd Floor, 12 Edith Cavell St, Port Louis; tel. 212-2978; telex 4635; fax 208-8948; provides support for new investment and transfer of technology, in agriculture, industry and tourism; Chair. DEV MANRAJ; Man. Dir (vacant).

EMPLOYERS' ASSOCIATIONS

Mauritius Employers' Federation: Cerné House, Chaussée St, Port Louis; tel. 212-1599; fax 212-6725; f. 1962; Pres. AJIT K. GUJADHUR; Dir Dr AZAD JEETUN.

Mauritius Sugar Producers' Association: Plantation House, Duke of Edinburgh Ave, Port Louis; tel. 212-0295; fax 212-5727; Dir P. DE L'. D' ARIFAT.

MAJOR INDUSTRIAL COMPANIES

Compagnie Sucrière de St Antoine Ltée: Cerné House, La Chaussée, Port Louis; tel. 283-9545; fax 283-9551; mfrs of sugar products.

International Distillers (Mauritius) Ltd: POB 661, Plaine Lauzun; tel. 212-6896; telex 42521; fax 208-6076; mfrs and wholesalers of beverages, spirits and vinegar.

Les Moulins de la Concorde Ltée: Cargo Peninsula, Quay D, Port Louis; tel. 240-8180; telex 4405; fax 240-8171; millers; Chair. ARMAND MAUDAVE.

Mauritius Chemical and Fertilizer Industry Ltd: Chaussée Tromelin, POB 344, Port Louis; tel. 242-5077; telex 4250; fax 240-9969; mfrs of agricultural chemicals and fertilizers.

Mauritius Tuna Fishing and Canning Enterprises Ltd: Caudan, Port Louis; tel. 212-3746; telex 4375; fax 212-5876; processors of tuna fish.

TRADE UNIONS

Federations

Federation of Civil Service Unions (FCSU): 33 Corderie St, Port Louis; tel. 242-6621; f. 1975; 52 affiliated unions with 16,500 mems (1992); Pres. D. BHURUTH; Gen.-Sec. RASHID IMRITH.

General Workers' Federation: 19B Poudrière St, Port Louis; tel. 212-3338; Pres. BEEDIANAND JHURRY; Sec.-Gen. FAROOK AUCHOYBUR.

Mauritius Federation of Trade Unions: Arc Bldg, 3rd Floor, cnr Sir William Newton and Sir Seewoosagur Ramgoolam Sts, Port Louis; tel. 208-9426; f. 1958; four affiliated unions; Pres. FAROOK HOSSENBUX; Sec.-Gen. R. MAREEMOOTOO.

Mauritius Labour Congress: 8 Louis Victor de la Faye St, Port Louis; tel. 212-4343; telex 4611; fax 208-8945; f. 1963; 55 affiliated unions with 70,000 mems (1992); Pres. NURDEO LUCHMUN ROY; Gen. Sec. JUGDISH LOLLBEEHARRY.

Principal Unions

Government Servants' Association: 107A Royal Rd, Beau Bassin; tel. 464-4242; f. 1945; Pres. A. H. MALLECK-AMODE; Sec.-Gen. S. P. TORUL; 14,000 mems (1984).

Government Teachers' Union: 3 Mgr Gonin St, POB 1111, Port Louis; tel. 208-0047; fax 208-4943; f. 1945; Pres. JUGDISH LOLLBEEHARRY; Sec. SHIVCOOMAR BAICHOO; 4,468 mems (1995).

Nursing Association: Royal Rd, Beau Bassin; tel. 464-5850; f. 1955; Pres. CASSAM KUREEMAN; Sec.-Gen. FRANCIS SUPPARAYEN; 2,040 mems (1980).

Organization of Artisans' Unity: 42 Sir William Newton St, Port Louis; tel. 212-4557; f. 1973; Pres. AUGUSTE FOLLET; Sec. ROY RAMCHURN; 2,874 mems (1994).

Plantation Workers' Union: 8 Louis Victor de la Faye St, Port Louis; tel. 212-1735; f. 1955; Pres. C. BHAGIRUTTY; Sec. N. L. ROY; 13,726 mems (1990).

Port Louis Harbour and Docks Workers' Union: 19B Poudrière St, Port Louis; tel. 208-2276; Pres. M. VEERABADREN; Sec.-Gen. GERARD BERTRAND; 2,198 mems (1980).

Sugar Industry Staff Employees' Association: 1 Rémy Ollier St, Port Louis; tel. 212-1947; f. 1947; Chair. T. BELLEROSE; Sec.-Gen. G. CHUNG KWAN FANG; 1,450 mems (1997).

Textile, Clothes and Other Manufactures Workers' Union: Thomy d'Arifat St, Curepipe; tel. 676-5280; Pres. PADMATEE TEELUCK; Sec.-Gen. DÉSIRÉ GUILDAREE.

Union of Bus Industry Workers: 19B Poudrière St, Port Louis; tel. 212-3338; Pres. BABOOA; Sec.-Gen. F. AUCHOYBUR; 1,783 mems (1980).

Union of Employees of the Ministry of Agriculture and other Ministries: Royal Rd, Curepipe; tel. 686-1847; f. 1989; 2,131 mems (1988); Sec. P. JAGARNATH.

Union of Labourers of the Sugar and Tea Industry: Royal Rd, Curepipe; f. 1969; Sec. P. RAMCHURN; 2,150 mems (1980).

CO-OPERATIVE SOCIETIES

Mauritius Co-operative Agricultural Federation Ltd: Co-operation House, 3 Dumas St, Port Louis; tel. 212-1360; fax 211-2261; f. 1950; supplies agricultural materials; Chair. KHEMRAJ BHURUTH; Sec. R. HEMOO; 209 mem. socs.

Mauritius Co-operative Union Ltd: Co-operation House, 3 Dumas St, Port Louis; tel. 212-2922; telex 4348; f. 1952; educational and promotional activities; Pres. TOOVAN RAMPHUL; Sec.-Gen. DHARAMJEET BUCKTOWER; 303 mem. socs (1983).

Transport

RAILWAYS

There are no railways in Mauritius.

ROADS

In 1995 there were 1,877 km of classified roads, of which 29km were motorways, 920km were other main roads, and 577 km were secondary roads. About 93% of the road network is paved. The construction of an urban highway, linking the motorways approaching Port Louis, and the extension of one of the motorways to Plaisance airport were completed in 1988.

SHIPPING

Mauritius is served by numerous foreign shipping lines. In 1990 Port Louis was established as a free port to expedite the development of Mauritius as an entrepôt centre. In 1995 the World Bank approved a loan of US $30.5m. for a programme to develop the port. At 31 December 1996 Mauritius had a merchant fleet of 50 vessels, with a combined displacement of 243,635 grt.

Mauritius Marine Authority: Port Administration Bldg, POB 379, Mer Rouge, Port Louis; tel. 240-0415; telex 4238; fax 240-0856; f. 1976; port and maritime authority; Dir-Gen. R. MAUNTHRODA.

Islands Services Ltd: Rogers House, 5 President John Kennedy St, POB 60, Port Louis; tel. 208-6801; telex 4312; fax 208-5045; services to Indian Ocean islands; Chair. Sir RENÉ MAINGARD; Exec. Dir Capt. RENÉ SANSON.

Mauritius Shipping Corporation Ltd: Nova Bldg, 1 Military Rd, Port Louis; tel. 242-5255; telex 4874; fax 242-5245; Pres. KRIS PONNUSAMY; Dir SUREN RAMPHUL.

Société Mauricienne de Navigation Ltée: 1 rue de la Reine, POB 53, Port Louis; tel. 208-3241; telex 4213; fax 208-8931; Dir YVES BELLEPEAU.

CIVIL AVIATION

Sir Seewoosagur Ramgoolam international airport is at Plaisance, 4 km from Mahébourg. In 1994 the airport handled more than 1m. passengers. Plans were announced in 1995 for the construction of additional runway and air traffic control facilities, at an estimated cost of Rs 800m.

Air Mauritius: Air Mauritius Centre, 2 President John F. Kennedy St, POB 441, Port Louis; tel. 208-7700; telex 4415; fax 208-8331; f. 1967; 51% state-owned; services to 28 destinations in Europe, Asia, Australia and Africa; Chair. and Man. Dir NASHIR MALLAM-HASSAM.

Tourism

Tourists are attracted to Mauritius by its scenery and beaches, the pleasant climate and the blend of cultures. Accommodation capacity totalled 13,300 beds in 1996. The number of visitors increased from 300,670 in 1990 to an estimated 422,463 in 1995, when receipts from tourism were estimated at Rs 6,600m. In 1995 the greatest numbers of visitors were from France (27.6%), Réunion (18.6%), South Africa (10.1%) and Germany (9.9%). An estimated 487,000 visitors travelled to Mauritius in 1996.

Mauritius Tourism Promotion Authority: Emmanuel Anquetil Bldg, Sir Seewoosagur Ramgoolam St, Port Louis; tel. 201-1703; telex 4249; fax 212-5142; Chair. ARMAND MAUDAVE.

Defence

The country has no standing defence forces, although there is a special 1,300-strong police mobile unit to ensure internal security and a coastguard numbering 500.

Defence Expenditure: Budgeted at Rs 238.3m. in 1995/96.

Education

In 1995, according to UNESCO estimates, the average rate of adult illiteracy was 17.1% (males 12.9%; females 21.2%), one of the lowest rates in sub-Saharan Africa. Education is officially compulsory for seven years between the ages of five and 12. Primary education begins at five years of age and lasts for six years. Secondary education, beginning at the age of 11, lasts for up to seven years, comprising a first cycle of three years and a second of four years. Primary and secondary education are available free of charge. In 1993 enrolment at primary schools included 94% of both males and females in the relevant age-group. In the same year the number of children attending secondary schools was equivalent to 59% of the appropriate age-group (males 58%; females 60%). Control of the large private sector in secondary education was indirectly assumed by the government in 1977. The University of Mauritius, founded in 1965, had 2,496 students in 1996, and a large number of students receive further education abroad. Of total expenditure by the central government in 1995/96, Rs 2,864.2m. (16.6%) was budgeted for education.

Bibliography

Addison, J., and Hazareesingh, K. *A New History of Mauritius*. Oxford, ABC; Rosehill, Editions de l'Océan Indien,1991.

Alladin, I. *Economic Miracle in the Indian Ocean: Can Mauritius Show the Way?* Port Louis, Editions de l'Océan Indien, 1993.

Baker, P. *Kreol: A Description of Mauritian Creole*. London, Hurst, 1972.

Benedict, B. *Indians in a Plural Society: A Report on Mauritius*. London, HMSO, 1961.

Mauritius, A Plural Society. London, 1965.

Bissoonoyal, B. *A Concise History of Mauritius*. Bombay, Bharatiya Vidya, 1963.

Bowman, L. W. *Mauritius: Democracy and Development in the Indian Ocean*. Boulder, CO, Westview Press, 1991.

Cohen, R. *African Islands and Enclaves*. London, Sage Publications, 1983.

Dukhira, C. D. *Mauritius and Local Government Management*. Oxford, ABC; Port Louis, Editions de l'Océan Indien; Bombay, LSG Press, 1992.

Favoreu, L. *L'île Maurice*. Paris, Berger-Levrault, 1970.

Ingrams, W. H. *A Short History of Mauritius*. London, Macmillan, 1931.

International Monetary Fund. *Mauritius: Recent Economic Developments*. Washington, DC, 1984.

Jones, P., and Andrews, B. *A Taste of Mauritius*. London, Macmillan, 1982.

Lehembre, B. *L'île Maurice*. Paris, Editions Karthala, 1984.

Mahadeo, T. *Mauritian Cultural Heritage*. Port Louis, Editions de l'Océan Indien, 1995.

Mathur, H. *Parliament in Mauritius*. Oxford, ABC; Rosehill, Editions de l'Océan Indien, 1991.

Ramgoolam, Sir S. *Our Struggle: 20th Century Mauritius*. New Delhi, Vision Books, 1982.

Selvon, S. *Historical Dictionary of Mauritius*. 2nd Edn. Metuchen, NJ, Scarecrow Press, 1991.

Simmons, A. S. *Modern Mauritius: The Politics of Decolonization*. Bloomington, IN, Indiana University Press, 1982.

Titmuss, R. M., and Abel-Smith, B. *Social Policies and Population Growth in Mauritius*. Sessional Paper No. 6 of 1960, London, Methuen, reprinted by Frank Cass, 1968.

Toussaint, A. *Port Louis, deux siècles d'histoire (1735–1935)*. Port Louis, 1946.

Bibliography of Mauritius 1501–1954. Port Louis, 1956.

Histoire des îles Mascareignes. Paris, Berger-Levrault, 1972.

World Bank. *Mauritius: Economic Memorandum: Recent Developments and Prospects*. Washington, DC, 1983.

Mauritius: Managing Success. Washington DC, 1989.

Mauritius: Expanding Horizons. Washington, DC, 1992.

Wright, C. *Mauritius*. Newton Abbot, David and Charles, 1974.

OTHER ISLANDS

Rodrigues

The island of Rodrigues covers an area of 104 sq km and contained a population of 34,204 at the 1990 census. Formerly also known as Diego Ruys, Rodrigues is located 585 km east of the island of Mauritius, and is administered by a resident commissioner. Rodrigues is represented in the national assembly by two members. Fishing and farming are the principal activities, while the main exports are cattle, salt fish, sheep, goats, pigs and onions. The island is linked to Mauritius by thrice-weekly air and monthly boat services.

The Lesser Dependencies

The Lesser Dependencies (area 71 sq km, population 167 at the 1990 census) are the Agalega Islands, two islands about 935 km north of Mauritius, and the Cargados Carajos Shoals (St Brandon Islands), 22 islets without permanent inhabitants, lying 370 km north-north-east. Mauritius also claims sovereignty over Tromelin Island, 556 km to the north-west. This claim is disputed by Madagascar, and also by France, which maintains an airstrip and weather station on the island.

THE BRITISH INDIAN OCEAN TERRITORY (BIOT)

The British Indian Ocean Territory (BIOT) was formed in November 1965, through the amalgamation of the former Seychelles islands of Aldabra, Desroches and Farquhar with the Chagos Archipelago, a group of islands 1,930 km north-east of Mauritius, and previously administered by the Governor of Mauritius. Aldabra, Desroches and Farquhar were ceded to Seychelles when that country was granted independence in June 1976. Since then BIOT has comprised only the Chagos Archipelago, including the coral atoll Diego Garcia, with a total land area of 60 sq km (23 sq miles), together with a surrounding area of some 54,400 sq km (21,000 sq miles) of ocean.

BIOT was established to meet British and US defence requirements in the Indian Ocean. Previously, the principal economic functions of the islands were fishing and the production of copra: the islands, together with the coconut plantations, were owned by a private company. The copra industry, however, went into decline after the Second World War, and, following the purchase of the islands by the British crown in 1967, the plantations ceased to operate and the population were offered the choice of resettlement in Mauritius or in Seychelles. The majority (which numbered about 1,200) went to Mauritius, the resettlement taking place during 1969–73, prior to the construction of the military facility. Mauritius subsequently campaigned for the immediate return of the Territory, and received support from the Organization of African Unity and from India. The election victory of the Mouvement Militant Mauricien in 1982 led to an intensification of these demands. Mauritius supported the former island population in a protracted dispute with the United Kingdom over compensation for those displaced, which ended in 1982 when the British government agreed to an *ex gratia* payment of £4m. In early 1984, however, it was reported that people who had been displaced from Diego Garcia were seeking US $6m. from the US government to finance their resettlement in Mauritius. The US administration declined to accept any financial responsibility for the population.

A 1966 agreement between the United Kingdom and the USA provides for BIOT to be used by both countries over an initial period of 50 years, with the option of extending this for a further 20 years. The United Kingdom undertook to cede the Chagos Archipelago to Mauritius when it was no longer required for defence purposes. All US activities in BIOT are conducted in consultation with the British government. Originally the US military presence was limited to a communications centre on Diego Garcia. In 1972, however, construction of a naval support facility was begun, apparently in response to the expansion of the Soviet maritime presence in the Indian Ocean. This plan was expanded in 1974, the agreement being formalized by an 'exchange of notes' in 1976, and again following Soviet military intervention in Afghanistan in December 1979. Facilities on Diego Garcia include a communications centre, a runway with a length of 3,650 m, anchorage, refuelling and various ancillary services. During the 1980s the US government undertook a programme of expansion and improvement of the naval support facility which was to include a space-tracking station. In August 1987 the US navy began to use Diego Garcia as a facility for minesweeping helicopters taking part in operations in the Persian (Arabian) Gulf. Following Iraq's invasion of Kuwait in August 1990, Diego Garcia was used as a base for US B-52 aircraft, which were deployed in the Gulf region. Runway facilities on Diego Garcia were again used in September 1996 as a base for US support aircraft during US missile attacks on Iraq.

In January 1988 Mauritius renewed its campaign to regain sovereignty over the Chagos Archipelago, and reiterated its support for a 'zone of peace' in the Indian Ocean. In November 1989, following an incident in which a military aircraft belonging to the US air force accidentally bombed a US naval vessel near Diego Garcia, a demonstration was held outside the US embassy in Mauritius, demanding the withdrawal of foreign military forces from the area. The Mauritius government announced that it would draw the attention of the UN Security Council to the dangers that it perceived in the execution of US military air exercises. However, the US assistant secretary of state for African affairs reiterated during an official visit to Mauritius, in the same month, that the USA would maintain its military presence in the Indian Ocean.

In January 1994 arrangements were agreed for the establishment of a joint British-Mauritius fisheries commission to promote and co-ordinate conservation and scientific research within the territorial waters of Mauritius and BIOT. In May the Mauritius government ministers of foreign affairs and fisheries paid a two-day official visit to the Chagos Archipelago.

The civil administration of BIOT is the responsibility of a non-resident Commissioner in the Foreign and Commonwealth Office in London, represented on Diego Garcia by a Royal Naval commander and a small British naval presence. A chief justice, a senior magistrate and a principal legal adviser (who performs the functions of an attorney-general) are resident in the United Kingdom.

Land Area: about 60 sq km.

Population: There are no permanent inhabitants. In 1996 there were about 930 US and British military personnel stationed in the Territory.

Currency: The US dollar is used.

Commissioner: Bruce Dinwiddy, Head of African Dept (Southern), Foreign and Commonwealth Office, King Charles St, London, SW1A 2AH, England; tel. (171) 270-3000.

Administrator: Louise Savill, African Dept (Southern), Foreign and Commonwealth Office, King Charles St, London, SW1A 2AH, England; tel. (171) 270-3000.

Commissioner's Representative: Commdr Simon Jackson, RN, Diego Garcia, c/o BFPO Ships; telex 938 6903.

MOZAMBIQUE

Physical and Social Geography

RENÉ PÉLISSIER

The Republic of Mozambique covers a total area of 799,380 sq km (308,641 sq miles). This includes 13,000 sq km of inland water, mainly comprising Lake Niassa, the Mozambican section of Lake Malawi. Mozambique is bounded to the north by Tanzania, to the west by Malawi, Zambia and Zimbabwe, and to the south by South Africa and Swaziland.

With some exceptions towards the Zambia, Malawi and Zimbabwe borders, it is generally a low-lying plateau of moderate height, descending through a sub-plateau zone to the Indian Ocean. The main reliefs are Monte Binga (2,436 m above sea-level), the highest point of Mozambique, on the Zimbabwe border in Manica province, Monte Namúli (2,419 m) in the Zambézia province, the Serra Zuira (2,227 m) in the Manica province, and several massifs which are a continuation into northern Mozambique of the Shire highlands of Malawi. The coastal lowland is narrower in the north but widens considerably towards the south, so that terrain less than 1,000 m high comprises about 45% of the total Mozambican area. The shore-line is 2,470 km long and generally sandy and bordered by lagoons, shoals and strings of coastal islets in the north.

Mozambique is divided by at least 25 main rivers, all of which flow to the Indian Ocean. The largest and most historically significant is the Zambezi, whose 820-km Mozambican section is navigable for 460 km. Flowing from eastern Angola, the Zambezi provides access to the interior of Africa from the eastern coast.

Two main seasons, wet and dry, divide the climatic year. The wet season has monthly averages of 26.7°–29.4°C, with cooler temperatures in the interior uplands. The dry season has June and July temperatures of 18.3°–20.0°C at Maputo. Mozambique is vulnerable to drought and attendant famine, which severely affected much of the country during the 1980s, particularly during the period 1982–84 and again during 1986–87. In late 1992 it was estimated that 3.2m. people were threatened with food shortages as a result of drought.

The census taken by the Portuguese authorities in December 1970 recorded a total population of 8,168,933, and the population increased to 11,673,725, excluding underenumeration (estimated at 3.8%), by the census of 1 August 1980. The population was officially estimated to be 17,423,000 at mid-1995. The population density was 21.8 inhabitants per sq km. Mozambique's population increased by an annual average of 1.8% between 1985–95.

North of the Zambezi, the main ethnic groupings among the African population, which belongs to the cultural division of Central Bantu, are the Makua-Lomwe groups, who form the principal ethno-linguistic subdivision of Mozambique and are believed to comprise about 40% of the population. South of the Zambezi, the main group is the Thonga, who feature prominently as Mozambican mine labourers in South Africa. North of the Thonga area lies the Shona group, numbering more than 1m. Southern ethnic groups have tended to enjoy greater educational opportunities than those of other regions. The government has sought to balance the ethnic composition of its leadership, but the executive is still largely of southern and central origin.

Mozambique is divided into 11 administrative provinces, one of which comprises the capital, Maputo, a modern seaport whose population was estimated to be 882,601 at 1 August 1986. The second seaport of the country is Beira. Other towns of importance include Nampula, on the railway line to Niassa province and Malawi, and Quelimane.

Recent History

JOÃO GOMES CRAVINHO

EMERGENCE OF FRELIMO

Following the military coup in Portugal in April 1974, the Frente de Libertação de Moçambique (Frelimo) demanded full independence for Mozambique and plenary powers for itself. Although it controlled only a small proportion of the territory, Frelimo, formed in 1962, maintained a sizeable armed force, by guerrilla standards, and had an effective and politically astute leadership. It faced no challenge from the Portuguese settlers, who were as alienated politically as the Mozambicans by the colonial administration. A transitional government, Joaquim Chissano as prime minister, was formed in September 1974 and led the country to independence on 25 June 1975, under the presidency of the Frelimo leader, Samora Machel.

There was considerable internal disorder in 1974–75, as the Portuguese, who had controlled the administration and the economy, fled the country. The exclusion of Africans by the colonial regime from almost all administrative positions created a dearth of middle-level managers and others who could fill the vacuum left by the exodus of the Portuguese. Frelimo faced formidable problems in restructuring its internal organization, in establishing new state structures and in maintaining a minimal level of economic activity. In addition, Frelimo's strong support for exiled Rhodesian nationalists exposed it to increasingly damaging attacks from Rhodesian forces. The government's decision in March 1976 to close the border with Rhodesia and apply economic sanctions put an end to the transit traffic that had been a mainstay of the economy.

In 1977 Frelimo transformed itself from a relatively broad political grouping into a 'Marxist-Leninist vanguard party' and declared its long-term goal to be a socialist Mozambique. The armed forces were brought under party control, and mass organizations of women, workers and young people were formed. A system of indirectly elected bodies was created, by which lower assemblies in turn elected higher tiers, with the people's assembly as, nominally at least, the fount of political power.

From 1980 onwards, national life was increasingly dominated by the effects of severe drought and political turbulence in the region. For Mozambique this took the form of direct South African aggression and indirect attacks by that country through its support for the Resistência Nacional Moçambicana (Renamo), a guerrilla force promoted by Rhodesia during its confrontation with Mozambique in 1976–79.

INTERNAL CONFRONTATION

By 1981, the emergence of an independent Zimbabwe and internal dissension within Renamo had reduced it to little more than a gang of armed brigands. However, assistance from South Africa rapidly transformed it into an agent of economic devastation. By late 1981 Renamo had resumed its activities in northern Manica and Sofala provinces and northern Inhambane and had begun attacks on the Beira railway. From 1982 onwards, Zimbabwean troops were deployed along the oil pipeline from Mutare to Beira to prevent sabotage attempts by Renamo.

The Frelimo leadership exercised considerable diplomatic skill in pursuit of Mozambique's national interests, balancing relations with the Soviet bloc with contacts made with Western powers in the interests of bringing pressure to bear on South Africa to desist from the constant destabilization of its neighbours. In 1984 Mozambique joined the World Bank and the IMF, while the government announced a new and liberal foreign investment code.

Frelimo's achievements at this time in the fields of social welfare and education were considerable. Progress was made in expanding school enrolment and in reducing adult illiteracy; there were substantial increases in spending on health care. In 1983 the party's central committee was expanded from 57 to 130 members, with the bulk of the new recruits coming from the provinces, or from outside the state apparatus. Further administrative reforms followed in 1986 when President Machel appointed four leading members of the Frelimo politburo to oversee the activities of government ministries. In July Mário da Graça Machungo was appointed prime minister, taking responsibility for day-to-day administration and freeing the president to concentrate on military operations against Renamo.

Elections to the people's assembly, due in 1982, were finally begun in August 1986 but interrupted by the intensity of the internal conflict and the sudden death, in October, of President Machel (see below). In November, Frelimo's central committee appointed Joaquim Chissano, the former minister of foreign affairs, as president. The elections were completed by December 1986, with 299 Frelimo nominees standing for the 250 seats; all government and political leaders were re-elected.

Fundamental changes in Frelimo's political and economic philosophy began to emerge at the fifth party congress in July 1989, when the party renounced its Marxist-Leninist orientation and agreed to extend the right of membership to religious believers and property owners. In January 1990 draft proposals for a new constitution were published, providing for the direct election of the president and people's assembly by universal suffrage. The eligibility of Renamo to contest the elections was recognized, provided that it abandoned violence and acknowledged the legitimacy of the state. The draft constitution, which was submitted to public debate during 1990, provided for the separation of Frelimo and the state, the independence of the judiciary and the right to strike.

These political developments represented attempts to create a framework for a diplomatic solution to the civil war, by reducing the disparity between the aims of the government and those of Renamo. The process of political change was further advanced in August 1990, when Frelimo announced that multi-party legislative elections were to take place in 1991, and that the country's name was to be changed from the People's Republic of Mozambique to the Republic of Mozambique.

The new constitution was formally approved by the people's assembly at the beginning of November 1990 and took effect at the end of the month. Provisions outlawing censorship and enshrining freedom of expression had been added to the earlier draft after representations by local journalists; the constitution also abolished the death penalty. The new constitution was welcomed by Western aid donors but rejected by Renamo as the product of an unrepresentative, unelected assembly.

Political Liberalization

The renamed assembly of the republic met for the first time in December 1990. One of its first acts was to pass legislation allowing the formation of new political parties, which took effect in February 1991. In March President Chissano announced that general elections would be held in 1992, although no specific date was given. A number of political parties announced their intention to apply for legal status under the new legislation. Prominent among these were the Partido Liberal e Democrático de Moçambique (Palmo), which described itself as 'anti-socialist' and whose manifesto expressed views critical of white, mixed race and Asian Mozambicans; the União Nacional Moçambicana (Unamo), described as 'social democratic' and composed of disaffected guerrillas who had left Renamo, and the Social Democratic Mozambique National Movement (Monamo), based in Portugal. A fourth party, the Congresso Independente de Moçambique (Coimo), founded in Kenya in 1985, was led by Victor Marcos Saene, son of an exiled Frelimo dissident.

Evidence of opposition to the change-over to multi-party democracy emerged in late June 1991 when a conspiracy against the government was discovered, leading to the arrests of a number of serving and retired army officers, as well as civilians. Among those detained was a former chief of staff of the armed forces, Col-Gen. Sebastião Mabote. In August, the minister of the interior, Col Manuel José António, was questioned in connection with the alleged coup conspiracy, although the case against him was dropped in February 1992, on the grounds that he had been instrumental in bringing the coup attempt to the attention of the authorities, and he returned to his duties in April. Mabote was acquitted of all charges by the supreme court in September, and 13 others were released under a general amnesty in October.

Frelimo held its sixth congress in August 1991, re-electing Chissano as party chairman and electing its central committee by secret ballot for the first time. Feliciano Gundana, the minister of the presidency, was appointed to the new post of party secretary-general. New legislation on trade union activity was passed by parliament in December, allowing workers to form trade unions of their choice, to join and resign from unions at will and establishing unions as self-regulating and autonomous organizations, free from outside interference.

New political parties continued to organize during late 1991 and early 1992 in preparation for the forthcoming elections, with several of the newly-registered parties, including Renamo, holding conventions, one of the conditions for registration. The formal end to one-party politics came in March with the announcement that Unamo had fulfilled the conditions for registration as the first legal opposition party. Earlier, a long-standing opponent of Frelimo, Domingos Arouca, in exile in Portugal since 1975, returned to launch the local organization of his Frente Unido de Moçambique (Fumo), formed in exile in 1976. Arouca declared his intention to form a 'third force', between Frelimo and Renamo on the political spectrum, and invited the co-operation of other opposition parties. In late June 1992 the leader of Palmo, Martins Bilal, announced that eight parties, including Palmo, had agreed to work together to present a 'third force' in opposition to Frelimo and Renamo.

Following the signing, in October 1992, of the general peace agreement between the government and Renamo (see below), political activity intensified in preparation for the presidential and legislative elections, initially scheduled for October 1993. The government published a draft electoral law in March 1993 proposing the establishment of a 21-member national electoral commission, chaired by a member of the supreme court, to organize and supervise the elections. A multi-party conference, convened in late April to discuss the law, collapsed when 12 opposition parties announced that they would boycott the conference until their demands for accommodation and logistical support were met. Following the collapse of the discussions, the 12 opposition parties called for the establishment of a transitional coalition administration pending the elections. The demand was rejected by the government. The conference met again in late July, after the opposition parties agreed to end their boycott in return for promises of state funding in 1994, but was again disrupted by the withdrawal of Renamo, which alleged that the draft electoral law contravened the peace agreement.

'DÉTENTE' WITH SOUTH AFRICA

The need to devote increased resources to the struggle against South African intervention eventually forced Mozambique to enter into discussions with the South African government in late 1983 and early 1984. Negotiations in February and March 1984 culminated in the Nkomati Accord, a non-aggression treaty in which both sides bound themselves not to give material aid to opposition movements in each other's countries, and to establish a joint security commission. Effectively, this meant that Mozambique would prevent the African National Congress of South Africa (ANC) from conducting military operations from its territory, while South Africa would cease to support Renamo. It was hoped that, under the accord, Mozambique would be in a position to begin the reconstruction of its shattered economy. The government immediately took steps to limit the activities of the ANC, restricting the organization's presence to a diplomatic mission in Maputo. By late 1984 there had been a noticeable reduction in ANC guerrilla activity in South Africa. For its part, however, the South African government effectively ignored the accord. The disruption resulting from continuing Renamo operations in Mozambique was considerable, and by August 1984, despite major government offensives against the rebels between March and July, Renamo forces were active in all 10 of Mozambique's provinces and the capital came increasingly under threat. While refraining from accusing South Africa directly of contravening the Nkomati Accord, the Mozambique leadership nevertheless made increasingly forthright statements demanding that the accord be implemented. For its part, the South African government repeatedly denied any involvement in the continuing Renamo activity.

The escalating internal conflict led the Frelimo government, none the less, to warn South Africa in August 1984 that both the accord and associated plans for economic co-operation were under threat unless Renamo activity was halted. In a bid to resolve the situation, South Africa responded by convening a number of separate but parallel talks with Renamo and Frelimo government representatives during August and September, which culminated in the so-called 'Pretoria Declaration' of early October, in which a cease-fire was agreed in principle between the Frelimo government and the rebels, and a tripartite commission, comprising Frelimo, Renamo and South African representatives, was established to implement the truce. In November, however, Renamo withdrew from the peace negotiations, citing the Frelimo government's continued refusal to recognize Renamo's legitimacy. The rebel movement also announced the launching of a major country-wide offensive. In December President Machel reportedly accused South Africa of abrogating the Nkomati Accord by continuing to support Renamo. The South African government denied this, and made further, unsuccessful attempts in early 1985 to persuade Renamo to negotiate with the Frelimo government.

Meanwhile, the joint security commission, established between South Africa and Mozambique under the provisions of the accord, continued to meet to review the situation, but Renamo activity in Mozambique continued. In March 1985 the two countries reiterated their continued commitment to the accord, and South Africa announced that a restricted air space, partly aimed at preventing support from reaching Renamo guerrillas from South African territory, would be established in the border area with Mozambique. This was followed in April by an announcement that a joint operational centre, to be used by both countries to deal with security and other matters relating to the Nkomati Accord, would be established on the border between Mozambique and South Africa. However, in the same month, Renamo guerrilla activity effectively severed rail links between the two countries.

The worsening security situation precipitated a meeting in June 1985 in Harare, Zimbabwe, between President Machel, Robert Mugabe (the prime minister of Zimbabwe) and President Nyerere of Tanzania, at which it was agreed that Tanzania and Zimbabwe would support Mozambique, and, in particular, that Zimbabwe would augment its military presence in Mozambique. This arrangement resulted in the capture, in August, of the largest Renamo base, the so-called 'Casa Banana' in Sofala province, and of other major rebel bases in the area. Not only were large quantities of weapons captured, but also incriminating documentation concerning South African support for Renamo since the signing of the Nkomati Accord. Some of these documents were published, compelling the South African government to confirm the allegations, although claiming that its continued contacts with Renamo were designed to promote peace negotiations between the guerrillas and the Frelimo government. In mid-October Mozambique unilaterally suspended the joint security commission.

In early 1986 the Mozambique government's military situation deteriorated sharply. This was most graphically illustrated by the recapture in February of the 'Casa Banana' base by Renamo forces, who encountered no serious opposition from fleeing government troops. This military reverse dismayed the Zimbabweans, who had been instrumental in capturing the base; it was eventually recaptured by them in April.

The second half of 1986 was dominated both by a deterioration in the military situation and by the sudden death of President Samora Machel: in October a Soviet civilian aircraft carrying the president, on his return from a meeting in Zambia of leaders of the 'front-line' states, crashed just inside South African territory, killing the president, together with two of his aides and the minister of transport, Luís Santos. Controversy has continued to surround the causes of the crash, especially over the strong possibility of South African involvement. Following the disaster, Mozambican demonstrators attacked the South African trade mission in Maputo, in protest against South Africa's suspected involvement in the incident. In October the South African government announced that it was to ban recruitment of Mozambican miners, and was to repatriate some 60,000 Mozambicans already employed in South African mines, in retaliation for an alleged increase in activity by ANC guerrillas in the Mozambique border region. (In January 1987 this decision was relaxed in respect of about 30,000 of the Mozambican mineworkers.) In January 1987 a joint report, compiled by Mozambican, Soviet and South African experts, was presented to an international board of inquiry, established to investigate the crash. The board concluded that pilot error, and not sabotage, had caused the accident, although some observers suggested that the examination of the course of events was not sufficiently thorough.

Following the death of Machel in October 1986, Mozambique applied intense pressure on Malawi, including threats of military action, to induce its neighbour to cease accommodating Renamo, and in December a joint security agreement was signed between the two states. In April 1987 Chissano confirmed the presence of some 300 Malawian troops guarding part of the railway line from the Malawi frontier to Nacala, in northern Mozambique. Malawi's willingness to co-operate with Mozambique was endangered in November 1987, when it was reported that Mozambique government forces had shot down a Malawian civilian aircraft (which they claimed to have been violating Mozambican airspace), killing 10 people. The Mozambique government expressed its regret, and a joint investigation by the two countries into the incident led to the drafting of new regulations on air safety. By mid-1988 the number of Malawian troops in Mozambique had increased to 600, and in July, during a state visit to Malawi, Chissano praised the country for its support of his government. In December 1988 Mozambique, Malawi, and the United Nations High Commissioner for Refugees (UNHCR) signed an agreement to promote the voluntary repatriation of Mozambican refugees in Malawi.

The Mozambican army was so ill-equipped and malnourished that it was often unable to hold even well-defended positions. However, government troops became more successful at repulsing rebel attacks during 1987, although Renamo continued to cause widespread disruption. In February Zimbabwean and Mozambican troops recaptured five towns in northern Mozambique which Renamo had seized in late 1986. This signified a general shift in the balance of power, with Renamo increasing its operations in the south, while government troops registered important successes in the north and along the coastline. In March 1987 the government carried out a major reorganization of the armed forces, which included the establishment of highly-trained commandos and the arrival of reinforcements from Zimbabwe and Tanzania. The apparent cessation of covert aid by Malawi to Renamo may also have been significant.

An open raid in late May 1987 by South African security forces on alleged ANC bases in metropolitan Maputo effectively signalled the demise of the Nkomati Accord. Renewed accusations of South African support for Renamo were made in July, when the rebels were allegedly responsible for the massacre of 424 civilians in the southern Mozambican town of Homoine. South Africa denied any involvement in the incident, however, and offered to investigate its circumstances jointly with Mozambique. International opinion was further outraged by successive attacks attributed to Renamo, including the ambush, in October, of a convoy travelling from Maputo on the main north–south road, in which more than 270 people were killed. The rebels were also reported to have conducted a series of cross-border raids into Zambia and, especially, Zimbabwe; between June and

December some 80 Zimbabwean civilians were allegedly killed by Renamo guerrillas.

In December 1987 President Chissano announced a 'law of pardon', whereby convicted prisoners who showed repentance were to be released on parole or served with lenient sentences, and an amnesty for members of Renamo who surrendered their arms. By December 1988 it was claimed by the Mozambican authorities that more than 3,000 rebels had defected; these included two prominent members of the European branch of Renamo, both of whom accused South Africa of continuing complicity in the affairs of the organization. The amnesty was initially to have expired in December 1988, but was extended for a further 12 months. Meanwhile, government troops made important advances against Renamo.

The defection of some Renamo members appeared to have been prompted by bitter divisions within the organization. The main disagreement was between the proponents and opponents, such as Afonso Dhlakama (the leader of Renamo), of a peaceful resolution of the armed conflict by means of negotiation with the Frelimo government and by a reduction of links with South Africa.

In late 1987 and early 1988 the governments of Mozambique and South Africa held discussions aimed at reviving the Nkomati Accord. A bomb attack in Maputo in April 1988, in which an exiled South African anti-apartheid activist was severely injured, threatened to undermine the progress made in negotiations. However, following initiatives from President Chissano to resume discussions, Mozambique and South Africa agreed in May to re-establish, 'as soon as possible', a joint security commission, and thereby effectively to revive the Nkomati Accord. In addition, a series of discussions between Mozambique, South Africa and Portugal led to an agreement by these countries, signed in November 1987, to restore the Cahora Bassa dam in Mozambique (see Economy). In September 1988 President Chissano met the South African president, P. W. Botha, in Mozambique. As a result of this meeting, Mozambique and South Africa established a joint commission for co-operation and development, and South Africa agreed to provide non-lethal military aid for the protection of the Cahora Bassa power lines. In addition, South Africa agreed to give assistance for improvements to Maputo harbour and to the road and rail links between Mozambique and South Africa, and in November restrictions on the recruitment of Mozambican mineworkers in South Africa were withdrawn. In February 1989 South Africa proposed a peace initiative for Mozambique, whereby the USA was to mediate a settlement between the Mozambican government and Renamo; however, the two parties in the conflict rejected this offer. In the following month a senior US government official claimed that supplies were still reaching Renamo from South Africa. Nevertheless, during a visit to Mozambique in July by the then leader of the South African National Party, F. W. de Klerk, Chissano stated that he accepted that the South African government no longer supported the rebel organization.

PEACE INITIATIVES

In June 1989 the government launched a peace initiative containing 12 principles, which demanded the cessation of acts of terrorism, guaranteed the right of political participation to all 'individuals' who renounced violence, recognized the principle that no group should impose its will on another by force and demanded that all parties should respect the legitimacy of the state and of the constitution. In mid-1989 Presidents Moi of Kenya and Mugabe of Zimbabwe agreed to mediate between Renamo and the Mozambique government, and in August officials from the Mozambique Christian Council met representatives from Renamo in Nairobi to discuss the 12 principles. However, Renamo rejected the plan, demanding its recognition as a political entity, the introduction of multi-party elections and the withdrawal of Zimbabwean troops from Mozambique. Nevertheless, there was indirect contact between Renamo and the government during late 1989. In mid-November Presidents Moi and Mugabe invited both parties to hold direct negotiations. Although the government subsequently agreed to this offer in principle, it continued to deny formal recognition to Renamo. The role of Presidents Mugabe and Moi as mediators came to an end after Renamo refused to attend a meeting between the protagonists that had been arranged to take place in Malawi in June 1990. However, the first direct talks between the two sides were held the following month in Rome, Italy, and further talks were held in August.

A third round of talks, due to start in September 1990, was postponed after Renamo alleged that the government had begun a new military offensive. The two sides met again in Rome in November when Renamo presented a list of demands as conditions for a cease-fire, including the withdrawal of all foreign troops from the country and the abandonment of the new constitution. Three weeks of talks culminated in the signing on 1 December of a partial cease-fire agreement. This provided for the withdrawal of Zimbabwean forces to within 3 km of the Beira and Limpopo transport 'corridors'. In exchange, Renamo agreed to cease hostilities and refrain from attacking the 'corridors'. The cease-fire was to be monitored by a joint verification commission (JVC) comprising representatives from 10 countries. The withdrawal of Zimbabwean troops to the 'corridors' was completed by the end of December but a number of violations of the cease-fire, mostly attributed to Renamo, were reported in January 1991.

A brief round of the peace talks was held in mid-December 1990, but proved inconclusive; the fifth round, in late January and early February 1991, collapsed after Renamo rejected a JVC report accusing it of breaching the cease-fire provisions. Later in February, Renamo announced that it would resume attacks. However, in March Renamo was reported to be ready to resume negotiations and declared a unilateral cease-fire over the Easter period. Attacks by Renamo during the early months of 1991 included the first, for more than a year, on the transport 'corridor' from Nacala port in northern Mozambique to Malawi. This had not been covered by the partial cease-fire agreement because of the lack of rebel activity in the area at the time.

Following a meeting between Renamo and members of the JVC in mid-April 1991 to discuss alleged violations of the cease-fire, direct talks resumed in Rome, Italy, on 6 May. The talks, which ended on 10 June, were reported to have agreed on a timetable for the discussion of outstanding issues, including setting a date for the cessation of hostilities and for the calling of general elections.

The seventh round of peace talks began in Rome in August 1991 and was suspended on 9 August, to give Renamo time to consider proposals made by the mediators which would allow it to begin political activities in Mozambique as soon as a cease-fire had been agreed, but requiring it to recognize the existing constitution. Renamo was, however, reported to have made a new demand: that the UN should take control of the administration during the period between a cease-fire and the elections. This demand was abandoned at the next round of talks, in October, which ended with clear signs of progress, including the signing by the two sides of a protocol said to represent a recognition by Renamo of the government's legitimacy and its agreement to begin operating as an opposition political party. In return, the government was reported to have undertaken not to enact legislation before the elections on any of the issues under discussion at the talks. The establishment of a commission to oversee the eventual cease-fire was also agreed. In the following month, it was agreed that Renamo would function as a political party immediately after a cease-fire.

Relations with Malawi deteriorated sharply at the end of December 1991, when Mozambique protested about Malawi's sudden closure of the border crossing at Milange, one of the major entry points to Mozambique. The closure halted international relief consignments to Zambézia province. No official explanation was given for the closure, although observers speculated that it was linked to political conflicts within Malawi. The border crossing was eventually re-opened in mid-January 1992.

The role of President Mugabe of Zimbabwe as a mediator resumed following talks with Chissano in December 1991. In mid-January 1992, Mugabe and President Banda of Malawi held direct discussions with Renamo leader Afonso Dhlakama, in Malawi, in an effort to expedite the peace talks, although it was reported that one of Renamo's main demands—the withdrawal of the 7,000 Zimbabwean troops from Mozambique—was not discussed. The ninth round of peace talks began in Rome on 21 January but were deadlocked for several weeks because of demands by Renamo that the government commit itself to a revision of the constitution. In mid-March, however, a third protocol was signed, establishing the principles for the country's future electoral system. The protocol provided for a system of proportional representation for the legislature, with legislative and presidential elections to take place simultaneously within one year of the signing of a cease-fire. A national electoral commission was to be set up to oversee the elections, with one-third of its members appointed by Renamo. The protocol also guaranteed freedom of the press and media and of association, expression and movement.

Rebel activity within Mozambique, with attacks on the fringes of major cities, including Maputo, Beira and Chimoio, continued during March 1992. Convoys carrying relief supplies were also attacked and in April the Red Cross sought guarantees from Renamo that it would not attack relief shipments. Following appeals by Chissano and the Italian minister of foreign affairs for other countries, including the USA, Portugal, France and Britain, to participate in the peace talks as observers, US assistant secretary of state Herman Cohen met Dhlakama in Malawi in late April, when he was understood to have persuaded the rebel leader to concentrate on discussing proposals for a cease-fire, rather than political issues, at the next round of talks. There was speculation that the increasingly severe drought in Mozambique (see below) was having an impact on Renamo's forces, and increasing the chances for a peaceful settlement. However, when, after a series of delays, the peace talks reopened in Rome in mid-June, Renamo's negotiators immediately departed from the agreed agenda to revive the constitutional issue, resulting in a further deadlock. An offer by Dhlakama of an immediate cease-fire, made after talks held in Botswana with President Mugabe and President Masire of Botswana on 5 July, was greeted with scepticism by the government, which pointed out that the rebel leader's condition for a cease-fire—guarantees of political freedom for Renamo supporters—had already been met in the October 1991 protocol. After meetings in mid-July with the presidents of South Africa and Zimbabwe, Chissano announced on 19 July that he was prepared to meet Dhlakama. On 7 August, following three days of discussions in Rome (in the presence of President Mugabe, Lonrho chief executive Tiny Rowland, and representatives of the Italian government and of the Roman Catholic Church), Chissano and Dhlakama signed a joint declaration committing the two sides to a total cease-fire by 1 October 1992, as part of a general peace agreement which would provide for presidential and legislative elections within one year. Dhlakama rejected Chissano's offer of an immediate armistice, on the grounds that the mechanisms necessary to guarantee such a truce had first to be implemented. The two leaders did agree, however, to guarantee the political rights and freedoms and personal security of all Mozambican citizens and political parties, and to accept the role of the international community, particularly the UN, in monitoring and guaranteeing the peace agreement.

In mid-September 1992 Chissano and Dhlakama met in Gaborone, Botswana, to attempt to resolve the military and security issues which had remained deadlocked since the first substantive talks on the subjects in early July. At the talks Chissano offered to establish an independent commission to monitor and guarantee the impartiality of the Serviço de Informação e Segurança do Estado (SISE, State Information and Security Service), a body which Renamo claimed to be merely a successor to the disbanded political police. It was also agreed that the joint national defence force would number 30,000 troops. As the talks continued, aid agencies warned that up to 3.2m. people in Mozambique were threatened with food shortages due to the drought. In mid-September Renamo agreed to open two transport corridors to allow food aid to reach some of those in need in areas under its control in central Mozambique, although it insisted that most areas could be supplied by air.

The General Peace Agreement

Following a brief delay (during which Dhlakama raised further questions regarding the commission monitoring the SISE and the administration of Renamo-occupied territory pending elections), the general peace agreement was eventually signed on 4 October 1992. It provided that a general cease-fire was to come into force immediately after ratification of the treaty by the assembly of the republic. Both the Renamo and the government forces were to withdraw to assembly points within seven days of ratification. A new 30,000-strong national defence force, the Forças Armadas de Defesa de Moçambique (FADM), would then be created, drawing on equal numbers from each side, with the remaining troops surrendering their weapons to a UN peacekeeping force within six months. A cease-fire commission, incorporating representatives from the government, Renamo and the UN, would be established to assume responsibility for supervising the implementation of the truce regulations. In overall political control of the peace process would be the Comissão de Supervisão e Controle (CSC, Supervision and Control Commission), comprising representatives of the government, Renamo and the UN, with responsibilities including the supervision of the cease-fire commission and other commissions charged with establishing the joint armed forces and reintegrating demobilized soldiers into society, as well as verifying the withdrawal of foreign troops from Mozambique. In addition, Chissano was to appoint a national commission with the task of supervising the SISE. Presidential and legislative elections were to take place, under UN supervision, one year after the signing of the general peace agreement, provided that it had been fully implemented and the demobilization process completed.

The general peace agreement was duly ratified by the assembly of the republic, and came into force on 15 October 1992. However, in the week that followed, the government accused Renamo of systematically violating the accord. The rebels had reportedly occupied four strategically-positioned towns in central and northern Mozambique. Dhlakama subsequently claimed that Renamo's actions had been defensive manoeuvres, and, in turn, accused government forces of violating the accord by advancing into Renamo territory. However, there was speculation as to the extent to which the Renamo leader was able to control his forces. The UN Security Council, meanwhile, agreed to appoint a special representative for Mozambique, former Italian parliamentarian and UN development programme official Aldo Ajello, and dispatch 25 military observers, the first of whom arrived in Maputo on 15 October.

In early November 1992, following delays in the formation of the various peace commissions that were envisaged in the general peace agreement, the timetable for the cease-fire operations was redrafted. In mid-December the UN Security Council approved a plan for the establishment of the UN Operation in Mozambique (ONUMOZ), providing for the deployment of some 7,500 troops, police and civilian observers to oversee the process of demobilization and formation of the new national armed forces, and to supervise the forthcoming elections. A meeting of aid donors in Rome on 15 December agreed to commit most of the estimated US $330m. cost of the operation.

ONUMOZ Intervention

The commander of the UN military force, Maj.-Gen. Lélio Gonçalves Rodrigues da Silva, assumed his post in February 1993. There were continued delays in the deployment of the peacekeeping force, with the UN experiencing difficulty in persuading member nations to commit troops. Renamo, in turn, refused to begin demobilizing its forces until the UN force was in place. The location of the 49 assembly points was not agreed until late February. Renamo withdrew from the CSC and the cease-fire commission in mid-March, protesting that its officials had not been provided with necessary accommodation, transport and food. In early April Dhlakama announced that his forces would begin to report to assembly points only when Renamo received US $15m. to support its political activities. The first UN troops, an Italian battalion, became operational in the Beira corridor on 1 April, and in mid-April the Zimbabwean troops guarding the Beira and Limpopo corridors finally withdrew, six months behind schedule, following their replacement by UN forces. Problems in financing the UN operation were also reported, with only $140m. of the $330m. budget having been approved. On 14 April the UN Security Council unanimously adopted Resolution 818, expressing serious concern at the delays, calling for the timetable for implementation of the peace treaty to be finalized and for both sides to guarantee freedom of movement for ONUMOZ. On 25 April Ajello confirmed that, due to the delays, the elections were unlikely to be held before mid-1994.

By early May 1993 the ONUMOZ force was approaching full strength, with units contributed by 19 countries totalling 4,721 armed and 150 unarmed personnel. Renamo, meanwhile, continued to use its demands for finance to delay the demobilization process, claiming, in late May, that it needed US $100m. from the international community to transform itself into a political party. In early June a meeting in Maputo of the CSC announced a formal postponement of the election date to October 1994 (one year behind the original schedule), and called for immediate action on establishing assembly points and commencing the formation of the new national armed forces. A new timetable published by ONUMOZ envisaged assembly points opening in July–August 1993, with demobilization of the two forces beginning in September. Training of the new armed forces would take place from September 1993 to February 1994. Electoral registers would be prepared between 1 April and 30 June 1994, with the election campaign conducted between 1 September and 14 October, followed by the elections in mid-October. The CSC meeting was followed by a meeting of aid donors which revealed growing impatience among the international community with the repeated delays in implementing the peace agreement and with Renamo's escalating demands for funds. The meeting produced additional promises of support for the peace process, bringing the total pledged by donors to US $520m., including support for the repatriation of 1.5m. refugees from neighbouring countries, the resettlement of 4m.–5m. displaced people and the reintegration of some 80,000 former combatants into civilian life, as well as for emergency relief and reconstruction. The UN also agreed to establish a trust fund of $10m. to finance Renamo's transformation into a political party, with use of the funds requiring approval by both Renamo and the UN. A second trust fund, accessible to all political parties, was to be established once the national electoral commission had been formed, following the eventual approval of a new electoral law.

In July 1993 Renamo announced new conditions to the advancement of the peace process, initially insisting on the recognition of its own administration, to operate parallel to that of the government. This demand was later revised, with Renamo seeking appointments to five of the country's 11 provincial governorships. However, in early September, following direct talks between Chissano and Dhlakama which began in Maputo in late August, an agreement was signed resolving the question of the control of provincial administrations. Under the terms of the agreement, Renamo was to appoint three advisers to each of the incumbent provincial governors to advise on all issues relating to the reintegration of areas under Renamo control into a single state administration. It was also agreed that the UN be requested to provide a police corps to supervise the activities of the national police and ensure neutrality in areas under Renamo control.

In late October 1993 the CSC approved a new timetable covering all aspects of the peace process, including the elections in October 1994. The timetable stipulated the approval of the new electoral law by the end of November 1993. Troops were to be confined to assembly points between November and December, with demobilization beginning in January 1994 and completed by May. Training of the FADM was also to begin in January 1994 and it was to be fully operational by September. However, at the time of announcement of the new timetable only 36 of the 49 designated assembly points had been approved, and only 23 were ready to receive troops.

In early November 1993 the UN Security Council adopted a resolution renewing the mandate of ONUMOZ for a further six months. In addition, it responded to the joint request by the government and Renamo for a UN police corps by authorizing the deployment of 128 police observers. In mid-November consensus was finally reached on the text of the electoral law following agreement that Mozambicans living abroad would be permitted to vote wherever the national electoral commission considered suitable conditions to exist. The new law was promulgated on 29 December.

At a meeting of the CSC in mid-November 1993 an agreement was signed providing for the confinement of troops to begin on 30 November. The process was to have concluded by the end of December. However, by that date less than 15% of the total number of troops for confinement had entered assembly points. In January 1994 the UN expressed concern at the slow pace at which government troops were assembling. In mid-January 540 military instructors (comprising government and Renamo troops who had been trained by British instructors in Zimbabwe) arrived in Mozambique to begin training the FADM. However, owing to logistical problems, the formal date for the initial cycle of training to begin was repeatedly postponed. In late February the definitive date was finally set for 21 March, some two months later than envisaged in the revised timetable for the peace process agreed in October 1993.

The national electoral commission was inaugurated in early February 1994. The composition of the commission, which had finally been agreed (after protracted dispute) in October 1993, included 10 members from the government, seven from Renamo, three from the other opposition parties and an independent chairman. On 23 February the UN Security Council announced that, in response to demands made by Dhlakama for a reinforcement of the UN police corps monitoring the confinement areas, it would be increasing their number from 128 to 1,144 (with simultaneous reductions in the number of UN military personnel to avoid extrabudgetary expenditure). In addition, the UN Security Council urged the government and Renamo to set a specific date for the October general election and appealed for a rapid conclusion to the demobilization process. By the end of February only 50% of troops had entered assembly points and none had officially been demobilized. In early March, in an effort to expedite the confinement process (which, to an extent, had been hampered by the inadequate capacity of assembly points), the government announced its decision to begin the unilateral demobilization of its troops. Renamo responded by beginning the demobilization of its troops on 18 March. In early April Lt-Gen. Lagos Lidimo, the nominee of the government, and former Renamo guerrilla commander Lt-Gen. Mateus Ngonhamo were inaugurated as the high command of the FADM.

On 11 April 1994 Chissano issued a decree establishing the date of the general election as 27–28 October. On 5 May the UN Security Council adopted a resolution renewing the mandate of ONUMOZ for the final period, ending on 15 November, subject to review in July and September. Voter registration for the elections began on 1 June and was due to continue until 15 August, with the total potential electorate estimated at some 7.89m. people. In late July the national electoral commission announced that as a consensus could not be reached on the issue of the enfranchisement of Mozambicans living abroad, emigrants would not be granted the right to vote in the forthcoming general election.

The confinement and demobilization processes continued to make slow progress and consequently the deadline for troop confinement was extended, beyond the beginning of the electoral process, to 8 July 1994, with demobilization to be completed by 15 August. On that date, according to figures issued by ONUMOZ, a total of 64,277 government troops had registered at confinement points, of which 48,237 had been demobilized. The total number of Renamo troops registered was 22,790, of which 14,925 had been demobilized, thus making it impossible for Renamo to supply its quota of 15,000 troops to the FADM. At that point only 7,375 troops from both sides had enlisted in the FADM (4,134 government troops; 3,241 Renamo troops). The deadline for registration at confinement points was subsequently extended to 31 August, after which date it was to continue at three centres in the north, centre and south of the country. On 16 August, in accordance with the provisions of the general peace agreement, the government Forças Armadas de Moçambique were formally dissolved and its functions transferred to the FADM, which was duly inaugurated as the country's official armed forces on the same day. During July and August a series of mutinies and demonstrations occurred involving troops from both sides stationed in confinement areas. The soldiers were protesting at poor conditions and the slow pace of demobilization. In August Renamo formally registered as a political party. In the same month the Partido Nacional Democrático, the Partido Nacional de Moçambique and Palmo formed an electoral coalition, the União Democrático (UD).

Presidential and legislative elections were held on 27–29 October 1994. The extension of the voting to a third day had become necessary following the withdrawal of Renamo from the elections only hours before the beginning of the poll, claiming that conditions were not in place to ensure free and fair elections. However, following concerted international pressure, Renamo abandoned its boycott in the early hours of 28 October.

The official election results were issued by the national electoral commission on 19 November 1994. In the presidential election Chissano secured an outright majority (53.30%) of the votes, thus avoiding the need for a second round of voting. His closest rival was Dhlakama, who received 33.73% of the votes. In the legislative election Frelimo also secured an overall majority, winning 129 of the 250 seats, while Renamo obtained 112 and the UD the remaining nine seats. Renamo received considerable support in central and northern Mozambique, and won a majority of the votes in five of the country's 11 provinces (including the most economically important in the country). The level of participation by the electorate was considerable, with some 80% of the total 6.1m. registered voters exercising their right to vote. Dhlakama subsequently accepted the results of the elections, although he maintained that there had been irregularities. The UN recognized the occurrence of irregularities, but asserted that these were insufficient to have affected the overall credibility of the poll, which it declared to have been free and fair. (This view was endorsed by international observers at the elections, who numbered some 2,300). According to the UN Development Programme the total cost of Mozambique's first multi-party elections was US $63.53m., of which the vast majority (some $59m.) was funded by international donors. In mid-November the UN Security Council adopted a resolution extending the mandate of ONUMOZ until the inauguration of the new government: the withdrawal of ONUMOZ troops and police was to be completed by 31 January 1995. In December 1994 the cease-fire commission issued its final report, according to which ONUMOZ had registered a combined total of 91,691 government and Renamo troops during the confinement process, of whom 11,579 had enlisted in the FADM (compared with the 30,000 envisaged in the general peace accord). In practice, demobilization had continued until 15 September, with special cases still being processed the day before the elections.

POST-ELECTION POLITICS

Chissano was inaugurated as president on 9 December 1994, and the new government was sworn in on 23 December. All the portfolios were assigned to members of Frelimo. Demands by Renamo that it be assigned the governorships of the five provinces where it won a majority of the votes in the legislative elections were rejected by Chissano: three new provincial governors appointed in January 1995 were all members of Frelimo. At the first session of the new legislature, the assembléia da república, which began on 8 December 1994, a dispute concerning the voting procedure employed to elect the assembly's chairman resulted in the withdrawal of the Renamo and UD deputies, who had unsuccessfully demanded a secret ballot; both parties had abandoned the legislative boycott by the end of December, although not before the conclusion of the first session.

In March 1995 the minister of national defence announced that, once legislation had been enacted allowing for the re-introduction of compulsory military service, a further 4,500 troops would be drafted into the FADM in that year. The total strength of the FADM would be defined by government policy, and the figure of 30,000 envisaged in the general peace accord would not necessarily be observed. During that and subsequent months there were several incidents of insurrection involving members of the FADM who were demanding salary increases and improved conditions. By the end of March all ONUMOZ troops and police had withdrawn from Mozambique, two months later than originally envisaged, and only a small unit of ONUMOZ officials remained in the country.

In April 1995 Chissano announced the official appointment of Gen. Lagos Lidimo and Gen. Mateus Ngonhamo—who had been appointed as the joint high command of the FADM in April 1994 (see above)—as chief and deputy chief of the general staff of the FADM, respectively. The swearing-in ceremony was conducted in the following month. At the second national conference of opposition parties, held in May in Inhambane province, an extra-parliamentary forum was established through which parties without representation in the legislature intended to convey their concerns to the executive and legislative bodies. In October there was an outbreak of rioting in Maputo when hundreds of demonstrators looted shops and blockaded roads in protest at the acute increase in the price of basic commodities. In November Mozambique was admitted as a full member of the Commonwealth (see p. 107), in which it had held observer status since 1987.

During 1995 the activities, principally in the border province of Manica, of a group of Zimbabwean dissidents, known as 'Chimwenjes', came under increasing scrutiny. The group, which was alleged to have associations with Renamo, was believed to be preparing for military incursions into neighbouring Zimbabwe, where it sought the overthrow of President Mugabe. In January 1996, following a series of armed confrontations between the 'Chimwenjes' and the Mozambican security forces, the Chissano government announced its intention to expel the dissidents from Mozambique. In June, following a series of armed attacks on both sides of the Mozambique-Zimbabwe border believed to have been perpetrated by 'Chimwenjes', bilateral discussions held between the governments of Mozambique and Zimbabwe resulted in an agreement to combine and intensify efforts to combat the activities of the dissidents.

In February 1996 the government proposed that municipal elections, which the Constitution stipulated must be conducted no later than October 1996, be held in 1997. Delays in the election process had resulted from a dispute between the government and the parliamentary opposition regarding the scope of the elections: the government sought to hold elections only in those areas that had attained municipal status (which would include only some 42% of the population — it was estimated that the process of establishing functioning municipal administrations throughout the country would not be completed before 2003), while the opposition demanded simultaneous local elections throughout Mozambique. In October 1996 parliament approved a constitutional amendment providing for a revision of the municipalities law. The amendment defined two units of local government: municipalities (including 23 cities and 116 other district capitals) and administrative posts (numbering 394). Each of these units would have its own elected council and mayor. In June 1997 the government announced that the municipal elections would be conducted, in 23 cities and 10 towns, on 27 December 1997. However, it was widely assumed that the logistics of the electoral process would require that the elections be delayed for several months. Also in June Renamo and 10 other opposition parties established a co-ordinating council of the opposition, with a view to presenting a concerted political alternative to the ruling party at the forthcoming municipal elections.

In May 1996 the government signed an agreement with South Africa under the terms of which some 200,000 ha of farmland in northern Mozambique were to be leased to South African farmers. The agreement, which was estimated to be worth some US $800m. to Mozambique, was criticized by opposition parties. In May 1997 the governments of Mozambique and South Africa signed an agreement establishing the Mosagrius Development Society to manage the development of this farmland in the Lugenda valley, in Niassa province. Initial capital of US $1m. was provided in equal shares by the Mozambican state and the South African Chamber for Agricultural Development in Africa, and was to benefit both South African and Mozambican farmers in the area. Some 300 South African farmers had committed themselves to the project by mid-1997.

Debate was continuing in mid-1997 concerning the revision of the law on land tenure. Existing legislation placed all land in the hands of the state. Various levels of state authority had the capacity to offer land concessions, giving rise to multiple claims for the same area of land. Moreover, the law did not adequately address matters relating to disputes over land use, particularly when one claim resulted from an official concession and another from customary but unwritten law. Donors had strongly urged the introduction of new land legislation, which was due to be enacted before the end of 1997.

In May 1997 a wave of anti-government demonstrations began in the central city of Beira, spreading gradually to Quelimane, Nampula, Chimoio and Inhambane. The initial demonstration was organized by Renamo in order to protest at the exclusion of a number of towns from the municipal elections. Clashes between the demonstrators and police resulted in some 25 arrests, including those of two local Renamo leaders. Subsequently, demonstrations took place to demand the release of those arrested. With the escalation of the demonstrations, the protests broadened to express opposition to police brutality, the high cost of living, and the disparities in development between southern Mozambique and the rest of the country.

In late May 1997 Frelimo held its seventh party congress, the first such congress since the introduction of the multi-party system. Chissano was re-elected unopposed as the leader of the party.

THE REFUGEE PROBLEM

In January 1993 the office of the United Nations High Commissioner for Refugees (UNHCR) estimated that there were 1.7m. Mozambican refugees in neighbouring countries. As a consequence of the signing of the General Peace Agreement in October 1992, an estimated 800,000 refugees were expected to return to the country in 1993. In June 1993 UNHCR began its official voluntary repatriation programme with the return of a small group from an estimated total of 140,000 refugees in Zimbabwe. In August Mozambique, UNHCR and Swaziland signed a tripartite agreement providing for the return of 24,000 refugees from Swaziland, and in mid-October the first contingent arrived in Mozambique (the programme was completed in June 1994). The first 300 of an estimated 25,000 refugees in Zambia also returned in October. In the same month a tripartite agreement was signed with South Africa, providing for the voluntary repatriation of some 350,000 Mozambican refugees. However, in January 1994 it was reported that South Africa had expressed its intention to begin expelling refugees from April. In February UNHCR reported that some 600,000 refugees had returned from neighbouring countries in 1993, although the majority had done so spontaneously (with the largest number of these coming from Malawi). By January 1994 only 20,167 refugees were reported to have returned through UNHCR repatriation schemes. In 1994 a further 600,000–700,000 refugees were expected to return. The complete repatriation programme was expected to last a total of three years and to cost US $203m. In March 1995 UNHCR reportedly announced that it would cease repatriating Mozambican refugees from South Africa at the end of that month because the process had become too expensive. According to a report by the International Organization of Migration, issued in November 1994, there were still 684,000 'internally displaced' people in Mozambique at that time. However, an estimated 3m. had been successfully resettled since the signing of the general peace agreement. In May 1995 UNHCR reported that a total of 1.7m. refugees had returned to Mozambique from six southern African countries (although only 363,000 had done so through its voluntary repatriation programme), and that only Malawi was still in the process of repatriating an estimated total of 39,000 remaining refugees. Expenditure on the repatriation process then totalled some $152m. In November the process was reported to have been completed, some seven months ahead of schedule.

Economy

JOÃO GOMES CRAVINHO

INTRODUCTION

Mozambique's post-independence economy has suffered the damaging effects of a guerrilla war, drought, floods, famine, the displacement of population, and a severe scarcity of skilled workers and foreign exchange. These difficulties are compounded by a large visible trade deficit, with export earnings covering only about 15-20% of import costs, and high levels of debt repayments, equivalent to about 120% of the value of Mozambique's exports of goods and services in 1994, although substantial debt relief had reduced this figure to a more sustainable 23%. As a result, Mozambique is heavily reliant on foreign credits. Following the signing of the Nkomati Accord with South Africa in March 1984, the US government announced that its ban on direct bilateral aid to Mozambique had been lifted. In the same year Mozambique acceded to the third Lomé Convention, thus becoming eligible for assistance from the European Community (EC, now the European Union–EU), and became a member of the IMF and the World Bank.

In 1995, according to estimates by the World Bank, Mozambique's gross national product (GNP), measured at average 1993–95 prices, was US $1,353m., equivalent to only about $80 per head. Between 1985–95, it was estimated, GNP per head increased, in real terms, at an average rate of 3.6% per year. Signs of economic recovery began to emerge at the end of the 1980s with real growth in gross domestic product (GDP) averaging 5.4% in 1987–89. Economic growth declined during 1990–92, owing to drought, the effects of the war on production and reduced foreign support; GDP growth averaged only 0.8% during this period, according to the World Bank. With an end to the drought and prospects for sustained peace, GDP increased by 19.3% in 1993, by 5.0% in 1994, by 1.5% in 1995, and by 6.4% in 1996. The annual average rate of inflation was 54.6% in 1985–95. With the impact of economic reforms, the rate of inflation fell from 160% in 1987 to 35.2% in 1991, before increasing to 45.2% in 1992 and to 76.2% in 1993, owing to an acute devaluation of the currency. The inflation rate for 1994 was 70%, declining to 54.4% in 1995, and fell sharply to 16.6% in 1996. Under the government's economic programme for 1996-98 it was intended to reduce inflation to 10% by the end of 1998, and by mid-1997 this objective seemed to be well within reach.

In January 1987 the government initiated an economic recovery programme (ERP) for 1987–90, which was supported by the IMF, and which aimed to increase economic efficiency and to reduce internal and external deficits, by a 'liberalization' of the economy (see below). In June the IMF approved an allocation of SDR 38.74m. in support of the ERP. As a consequence, other donors, both bilateral and multilateral, increased aid to US $700m. for 1987.

Meanwhile, the implementation of the ERP began with two substantial devaluations of the metical, from US $1 = 40 meticais to US $1 = 200 meticais in January 1987, and to US $1 = 400 meticais in June 1987. Subsequent devaluations, by 12.5% in January 1988, 22.4% in July 1988, 6.9% in October 1988, and through subsequent monthly adjustments brought the official exchange rate to US $1 = 12,100 meticais by August 1996. Other major components of the ERP included fiscal measures, with a planned reduction of the budget deficit from 50% of expenditure in 1986 to 25% in 1987, an increase in income taxes, and a reduction in government wage costs and government subsidies, and monetary measures, including the maintenance of stringent control on the rate of credit growth and the increased linkage of wages to productivity. Other measures under the programme included a deregulation of some prices previously controlled by the government, the stimulation of the private sector in industry and agriculture, the focusing of resources on activities of import-substitution or those yielding a high level of value added, the stimulation of exports, and a review of procedures for the allocation of foreign exchange. Price rises were duly introduced in April 1988, during the second phase of the ERP, when basic commodity prices were increased. In urban centres the price of maize rose by nearly 300%, that of rice by nearly 600%, and that of sugar by 400%. In an effort to offset the impact of these rises, the government announced an increase in minimum wages. However, enterprises were expected to limit overall increases in wage costs to 45%. The prices of petroleum, electricity and meat were increased in early 1989. In February 1990 further increases in food prices were announced.

In June 1990 the IMF approved an enhanced structural adjustment facility (ESAF) of SDR 85.40m. to support a further programme of economic reforms (1990–92), which aimed to increase the role of the private sector, to promote foreign investment and to improve access to imports and supplies of industrial inputs. The programme was intended to raise the annual growth rate of GDP to 6.0%, and to limit the current account deficit on the balance of payments to 30% of GDP (compared to an estimated 74.4% in 1989). In June 1994 the IMF announced a further loan of SDR 29.4m. under the ESAF to support economic reforms in 1994/5. A meeting of the consultative group of aid donors in Paris in December 1990 resulted in pledges of nearly US $1,200m. for 1991: $400m. for debt relief (including the writing off of $19m. of debt), and $761m. in food and project aid (of which $200m. would be used in the rehabilitation of the Nacala railway). A number of reforms linked to the ERP were introduced in late 1990 and early 1991, including the establishment of a secondary foreign exchange market and the introduction of new incentives for foreign investors. Pledges totalling $1,125m. (48% in grant form) were made at the December 1991 consultative group meeting, although 80% of this consisted of debt relief, rather than new finance. In March 1992 the government unveiled a three-year plan for sharp cuts in public expenditure. The plan, prepared in consultation with the IMF, provided for reductions in investment in agriculture, mining and manufacturing, accompanied by a programme of privatizations in these areas, with the emphasis shifting to rehabilitation of infrastructure. Plans to sell off a number of major state-owned enterprises were announced in early 1992, including cashew nut processor Cajú de Moçambique, engineering company Cometal and forestry project Ifloma. By mid-1993 some 180 state enterprises had been transferred to private ownership, 80% of which were sold to Mozambican investors. A new investment code was approved by the legislature in June 1993, providing identical fiscal and customs benefits to both local and foreign investors. By the end of 1995 some 1,000 state-owned enterprises had been privatized. Further divestments were envisaged in the government's economic programme for 1996–98.

During 1993 the government introduced a national reconstruction plan to account for post-war reconstruction needs. A World Bank report, prepared for the December 1993 consultative group meeting of donors in Paris, estimated that Mozambique would require external funding totalling US $1,494m. in 1994, including $405m. in debt relief. The same document estimated that the cost of the peace process (including demobilization, demining, assistance for returning refugees and displaced people and the conduct of elections) would reach $400m. A further consultative group meeting was held in March 1995 in Paris at which pledges were made for $784m. of the estimated total of $1,105m. needed for 1995. Three of the major donors—the USA, Britain and Germany—stipulated that their funding was conditional on continued democratization and good governance in Mozambique. In June 1995 the minister of planning and finance revealed that delays in the disbursement of funds pledged by donor countries were forcing the state to borrow more heavily than anticipated from banks. As a result restrictions on credit for business were tightened considerably in order to maintain total credit within the limits imposed by the IMF. A meeting of the consultative group of aid donors in Paris in April 1996 resulted in pledges of $567.5m., excluding debt relief, while the government agreed to continue and intensify its programme of privatization and liberalization of the economy. Important steps in this regard are the divestment of two state banks; the controlling share in the Banco Comercial de Moçambique was purchased by the Portuguese bank Banco Mello in August 1996, while divestment of up to 49% of the Banco Popular de Desenvolvimento was pending in mid-1997, although the low level of interest from potential buyers indicated that further restructuring of the bank needed to be undertaken in order to achieve this objective. In June 1996 the IMF approved a three-year loan of $110m., under its enhanced structural adjustment facility, to support the government's economic reform programme for 1996–98. The objectives of the programme included a reduction in the annual inflation rate to 10% by 1998, and average annual GDP growth, excluding energy production, of 5% for the three-year period.

At the May 1997 consultative group meeting of donors in Paris, Mozambique received praise for its success in the implementation of economic reforms, as reflected in its positive economic indicators for 1996. Consequently, the government's funding requirements for 1997 were met with little discussion; pledges amounted to US $641.5m., with an additional $193.5m. for debt reduction. In June 1997 the IMF approved a $35m. loan for Mozambique. The prospect of reducing Mozambique's debt burden improved following the decision by the 'Paris Club' of official creditors to admit Russia as a member. Since Mozambique owed substantial debts to Russia (which inherited them from the Soviet Union) it was possible that Russian membership of the 'Paris Club' would clear the way for Mozambique to benefit from the 'Paris Club's' Highly Indebted Poor Countries (HIPC) debt-reduction initiative.

AGRICULTURE

In periods of stability, 80%–90% of the total working population have been engaged in agriculture, and about 80% of exports in the late 1960s were of agricultural origin. Although only 5% of arable lands are cultivated, agriculture accounts for as much as 65% of Mozambique's GDP. The major cash crops are cotton (accounting for 11.7% of export earnings in 1995), cashew nuts (5.6%), sugar cane (4.3%) and copra. Maize, bananas, rice, tea, sisal and coconuts are also grown, and the main subsistence crop is cassava. Good weather conditions led, in 1996, to an increase in cassava production of 31% on the previous year. Large-scale modern agriculture before independence was mainly under Portuguese control. About 3,000 farms and plantations were known to exist, employing more than 130,000 people on more than 1.6m. ha, while African plots covered some 2.8m. ha. Since independence, agricultural production has been adversely affected by several factors: the internal conflict which prevented nearly 3m. Mozambicans from farming the land; the scarcity of skilled labour, following the post-independence exodus by the Portuguese; low crop yields from some state farms; the collapse of rural transport and marketing systems, owing to general insecurity and disorganization; drought, flooding, cyclones and insect pests which have combined to destroy food crops in large areas of the country (notably in the south and the Zambézia region). Agricultural GDP increased by an estimated annual average of 1.6% during 1980–90 and 2.4% during 1990–94.

During 1996 and 1997 a major programme for the promotion of Mozambican agriculture, entitled Proagri, was drawn up. The five-year programme, which was to receive the support of all major donors, was to cost some US $200m., and aimed to increase state capacity and co-ordination in all areas of agricultural production.

The development of the cultivation of cashew nuts is a relatively recent occurrence. Production of cashew nuts was 204,000 metric tons in 1974. Output decreased by 44% between 1973 and 1976 and continued to decline until 1984, owing to inefficient marketing practices by state enterprises, lack of transportation and the effects of drought. Unofficial estimates assessed the production of cashew nuts at only 20,300 metric tons in 1984. In an attempt to increase production levels, the government doubled producer prices for the crop. Output of cashews was estimated at 25,000 tons in 1985 and, according to official figures, totalled 40,200 tons in the 1986/87 crop year. Output was estimated at 47,000 tons in 1987/88, and at 50,000 tons in 1988/89 but fell to 22,000 tons in 1989/90 due to poor weather conditions and security problems. The expansion in production resulted largely from a French-financed rehabilitation programme. Production recovered to 31,000 tons in 1990/91 and to 54,000 tons in 1991/92, before falling to 24,000 in 1992/93 due to a shortage of rainfall. In the two subsequent seasons marketed cashew production was stable at around 35,000 tons per year, but in 1995/96 a 15-year record high was reached with 60,000 tons. In late 1991 the government authorized the export of cashews in unprocessed form, for the first time since 1976, because of the inability of processing plants to cope with increased output. The processing plant in Nacala was due to be renovated in 1992–93, with Portuguese assistance. In April 1993 the African Development Bank granted US $20m. for a five-year programme to rehabilitate the industry. A proposal by the World Bank that restrictions on the export of unprocessed cashews should not be reintroduced was vociferously opposed by producers and by the government. However, a compromise was subsequently reached whereby the government agreed to impose an export tax of 20% for unprocessed cashew nuts during 1995-6 which would then gradually be phased out by 2000. In 1996 cashew nuts were the third most important export after prawns and cotton, earning $9.5m. for processed cashews and a further $5.6m. for unprocessed cashews. However, by mid-1997 the debate concerning the liberalization of unprocessed cashew exports had resumed as several Mozambican processing plants reduced staff numbers as a result of the increasing proportion of unprocessed exports.

Cotton has traditionally been the main cash crop of northern Mozambique, with more than 500,000 African growers in the Cabo Delgado, Niassa, Nampula and Zambézia provinces. Production of seed (unginned) cotton was 144,000 metric tons in 1973, but by 1984 had fallen to less than 20,000 tons, and in 1985 marketed production reached only 5,700 tons. A programme for rehabilitating the cotton sector is under way, with help from foreign companies. Nearly all cotton is cultivated by peasant producers working in concession areas where large companies have sole right of purchase. The 1995 and 1996 cotton harvests were both excellent, with 51,000 tons and 50,000 tons marketed respectively. Cotton exports earned $20m. in 1996.

Sugar was produced by large cane-growing companies, such as the Sena Sugar Estates Ltd, on a tributary of the Zambezi, the Companhia Colonial do Buzi, south of Beira, and the Sociedade Agrícola do Incomati, north of Maputo. This formerly monopolistic system produced 227,823 metric tons of sugar in 1975, but export earnings fell from 575m. escudos in 1975 to 260m. escudos in 1977. All the companies were nationalized and entrusted to Cuban experts, who sought unsuccessfully to restore pre-independence levels of production. Climatic conditions, combined with production difficulties, reduced raw sugar production to 126,000 tons in 1982, and to a record 'low' of 17,000 tons in 1986. However, output increased to about 55,000 tons in 1987. Sugar production has increased dramatically since the peace agreement. In 1994 some 234,000 tons were produced, increasing to 313,000 tons in 1995 and 434,000 tons in 1996. However, exports declined with the result that revenue from sugar exports was reduced from US $11m. in 1994 to $7.3m. in 1995. As part of government plans to rehabilitate the industry, the African Development Fund provided $55m. for the rehabilitation of the Mafambisse sugar complex in Sofala province. Plans to rehabilitate the Marromeu and Luabo plantations and factories were announced in early 1990 by the Commonwealth Development Corpn. The Maragra sugar company, situated near Maputo, has a production capacity of 60,000 tons but requires some $30m. in investment to fund its rehabilitation. In November 1996 Illoro Sugar Ltd of South Africa announced that it would invest $18m. in the rehabilitation of the Maragra sugar company.

In 1986 Mozambique ranked eighth, after Kenya, Malawi, Tanzania, Zimbabwe, Rwanda, South Africa and Mauritius, among African producers of tea. The Zambézia hills and mountains, close to the Malawi border, are the main producing area. The country produced 18,795 metric tons of made tea in 1973 but output fell to 13,143 tons in 1975. It rose to 22,190 tons in 1981 but declined again, to an estimated 11,000 tons in 1984, and to an estimated 3,000 tons in 1987 and 1,500 tons in 1988. The destruction by Renamo, in February 1987, of equipment at five tea-processing factories, which had been rehabilitated at a cost of about US $30m., led to a further decline in output. An increase in production in 1990 and 1991 was reversed by drought and in 1996 production stood at only 1,500 tons. The principal markets for Mozambican tea are the United Kingdom and the USA, and exports earned 1,212m. meticais in 1981, when shipments totalled 18,000 tons. Following the sharp fall in production since 1981, the value of tea exports declined, to 460m. meticais in 1984 and to only 51m. meticais in 1986, according to government figures. Exports of tea reached a peak of $800,000 in 1991 and have since declined considerably. In 1991 the Arab Bank for Economic Development in Africa (BADEA) agreed to lend $6.4m. towards an $8m. project to rehabilitate tea production.

Copra is produced mainly on immense coconut plantations on the coastal belt of the Zambézia and Nampula provinces. It is also a popular crop among Africans who use the oil and other copra products in daily life. In 1972 copra exports totalled 43,938 metric tons. Production levels have fluctuated in recent years, reaching an estimated 60,000 tons in 1980, but declining to 5,200 tons in 1989, due largely to a fall in prices. Since then output has increased, reaching 34,200 tons in 1996, when exports earned US $6.1m. As in Angola, sisal was introduced by German planters. It is a typical plantation crop, concentrated on about 20 estates west of the ports of Moçambique, Nacala and Pemba. Annual production has been consistent during the 1990s at around 24,000 tons.

Since independence the normal maize crop has been far below the level needed to meet domestic requirements. However, with the advent of peace and successive years of favourable climatic conditions in 1994–96, the shortfall in this staple crop may be eliminated before the end of the decade. A problem remains, nevertheless, in that surpluses from the north and centre of the country reach the areas in deficit in the south (particularly the large urban markets around Maputo) at greatly inflated prices due to high transport costs, making it cheaper to import maize from South Africa. Rehabilitation of the commercial networks that link the areas with surplus maize to neighbouring countries and to the ports of Nacala and Beira is needed to eliminate this problem in the medium term. According to the FAO, the harvest totalled 453,000 tons in 1990, falling to 133,00 tons in 1992 and then increasing to an estimated 734,000 tons in 1995. Early projections for 1996 indicated production of about 947,000 tons, drastically reducing the shortfall. In 1986 only 21,500 tons were available on the market, compared with 59,000 tons in 1985. Marketed production rose to 27,000 tons in 1987, 60,400 tons in 1988 and 93,800 tons in 1989. Between 1987–92 the cereal shortage averaged 900,000 tons per year, rising to 1,209,000 tons in 1993 as a result of the drought which affected much of the country. About 120,000 tons of rice were produced in the irrigated lowlands in 1974 falling to an estimated 66,000 tons in 1993. Estimates for 1995 and 1996 indicate production of 113,000 tons and 139,000 tons, respectively. The government estimated marketed production of rice at about 43,500 tons in 1986 and 1987, falling to 41,300 tons in 1988. Oil seeds, such as sesame and sunflower seeds and, above all, groundnuts (estimated at 102,000 tons in 1995 and 117,000 tons in 1996), allow for some exports to Portugal. Processing of vegetable oils produces more than 25,000 tons annually. Bananas (production estimated at 85,000 tons in 1996) and citrus fruits (37,000 tons produced in 1996, of which 5,500 tons exported) are exported, as well as potatoes (production estimated at 72,000 tons in 1995), tobacco and kenaf (a jute-like fibre).

Livestock is still of secondary importance, owing partly to the prevalence of the tsetse fly over about two-thirds of the country. Most of the cattle are raised south of the Save river, particularly in the Gaza province which has about 500,000 head. In 1996 estimated figures were: 1.29m. cattle; 122,000 sheep; 386,000 goats and 175,000 pigs. During colonial times the Limpopo *colonato* and the area surrounding Maputo had European cattle ranches to provide the capital with meat and dairy products. Mozambique has to import fresh and prepared meat.

In the early years after independence the government sought to establish communal agriculture at the village level. From 1976 onwards, more than 1,500 communal villages were formed, and agricultural co-operatives and state farms established, in an effort to 'socialize' the rural sector. Between 1975–85 the state sector accounted for 40%–50% of marketed production, while the co-operative sector averaged only 1%. However, several state farms proved to be uneconomic, and since 1983 the government has given increased priority to improving production from small farms in the family sector. From 1984 onwards, several state farms were divided into individual peasant holdings. In 1985 the government prepared a basic programme for agricultural rehabilitation, including the involvement of foreign enterprises in joint ventures. Further reforms have taken place as part of the 1987–90 ERP: subsidies have been reduced, and the prices of some agricultural products have been deregulated. Private producers and traders were encouraged with higher producer prices. In October 1987 a fund for agricultural and rural development was established by the Banco Popular de Desenvolvimento, with the aim of assisting peasant farmers and co-operatives to improve their output. However, various difficulties have rendered this programme almost inoperational and rural credit remains inaccessible for the vast majority of peasant producers. Between 1987–90 the number of state farms was reduced from 150 to 109. In April 1988 and February 1990 the consumer prices of many basic commodities were sharply increased.

During 1981–84 a severe drought prevailed in eight out of the 10 provinces and 4m. people were seriously affected. Further problems were caused by floods and cyclones in 1984, and in both 1983 and 1984 there was a steady deterioration in the overall situation in the agricultural sector. In 1983 an estimated 1m. tons of cassava, equivalent to about one-third of the total annual crop, were lost because of drought. In the six southern provinces, agricultural production had declined by about 70%–80%, and some 550,000 tons of cereals were required to offset crop losses in 1983/84. In 1984 it was estimated that 600,000–900,000 tons of maize imports would be required for 1984/85, and the total cereal import requirement for that period (including commercial imports) was estimated at 620,000 tons. Mozambique received considerable international assistance during the drought. However, distribution of food supplies was persistently hampered by security and transport problems, owing to Renamo guerrilla activity. Because of the ravaged state of agriculture, FAO experts believed that a long-term modernization programme of agricultural methods was needed to reduce the national food production deficit.

In 1986 a combination of drought conditions and the escalation of rebel activity in the latter part of the year resulted in a famine: some 4m. people were threatened with starvation. In February 1987 the UN launched an appeal for US $247m. in humanitarian aid to ease the problem; it was estimated that 800,000 tons of food aid would be required in 1987/88. As a result of a meeting of UN member-states held in March 1987, international donors increased their pledges of aid: of increased shipments of cereals pledged, the USA was to send 194,000 tons, and the EC 105,000 tons, in 1987. The outlook was equally bleak in the following year. Agricultural production was further hampered by the inadequate level of rainfall over much of the country in late 1987, and by floods in early 1988. Locusts were reported to have destroyed 80% of the cereal crop in Inhambane province in May 1988. In March of that year the UN launched an appeal, on behalf of the government, for $380m. in emergency aid; it was estimated that 710,000 tons of cereals were needed for 1988/89. In February 1989 the government appealed, through the UN, for $383m. in emergency funding for 1989/90. It was estimated that 916,000 tons of food aid were required to meet the needs of some 7.7m. people who were facing severe food shortages. The government requested a further $136m. in emergency aid for 1990/91. The food supply situation continued to deteriorate during 1990. In December the World Bank warned that half the population faced starvation or serious deprivation. In April 1991 the overall food deficit was put at 1.1m. tons.

With much of southern Africa suffering from severe drought, the food supply situation in Mozambique deteriorated further in 1992, with that year's harvests expected to yield only 30% of normal levels. Total cereal production was estimated at 236,000 tons, compared to 724,000 tons in 1990, the last year of normal rainfall. Almost complete harvest failure was reported from the south and centre of the country. A report prepared by the government and UN agencies to support an appeal for international assistance in May put the number of people threatened with famine at 3.15m., with a further 6m. in need of additional food supplies. The report estimated Mozambique's total food aid needs for the next 12 months at more than 1.3m. tons valued at US $270.7m.; the government appealed for total emergency assistance of $457.5m. to cover food aid and logistical needs. The first deaths from starvation were reported in late May. Conditions among Mozambican refugees in Malawi were also reported to be deteriorating as their numbers continued to grow, reaching 985,000 by June, with the number increasing by 8,000 a month. With the return of normal rains and the establishment of a cease-fire, the food supply improved in 1993, although the UN estimated that 1m. people, excluding refugees, would still require direct food aid in 1993/94. By the end of 1993, however, with hostilities at an end, there were indications that Mozambique was recovering its capacity to support itself. Although noting that it would be premature to declare an end to the emergency, a report prepared with UN assistance put the country's emergency needs for 1994/95 at $211m., less than half the figure for 1993/94, with an estimated 119,340 tons of food aid needed for 500,000–800,000 people. These predictions proved to be correct despite a setback in March 1994 when a cyclone hit the fertile northern province of Nampula.

Forestry has developed chiefly along the Beira railway and in the wetter Zambézia province. Some eucalyptus plantations have been established in the south of the country to produce wood for paper, but the long-term ecological effects of these plantations are a matter of concern. Most of the exports are sawn timber, construction timber, etc., with a ready market in South Africa. In 1990 a South African company formed a joint venture with the Banco Popular de Desenvolvimento to produce timber products in Beira. The forestry sector is affected by widespread coruption, with numerous small companies felling hardwood trees indiscriminately, particularly in the central provinces of Zambézia, Manica and Sofala. Much of the wood is then exported illegally at greatly reduced prices.

Fishing is a relatively recent development on this extensive coast. An estimated 32,000 tons of fish and shrimps were landed in 1980, and a promising future seems likely for industrial fishing. Shrimps and prawns provided 29% of export earnings in 1984, valued at 1,199.1m. meticais. In 1993 exports of prawns accounted for 52% of total export revenue of $131.9m. Exports of shrimps, prawns and lobsters declined from $72.0m. in 1993 to $66.4m. in 1994, owing partly to a cyclone that affected the principal shrimp-production region. In 1995 shrimp exports recovered to $73m. In that year fish catches, including shrimps, totalled 26,900 tons. Although Mozambique is still not self-sufficient in fish, domestic catches cover about 34% of consumption at present, compared with 6% in 1979. The potential annual catch is estimated at 500,000 tons of fish and 14,000 tons of shrimps. In 1984 South Africa and Mozambique signed a three-year fisheries agreement, under which South Africa provided a credit worth R2m. for the development of the fishing sector. In May 1988 it was announced that the EC and Italy were to provide US $40.7m. to finance a fisheries development project in Nampula, Sofala and Inhambane provinces. In April 1991 Japan announced a loan of $5m. for an experimental fishing project.

MINERALS

Mozambique has considerable mineral resources, although exploitation has been limited by internal unrest. The value of mineral exports was US $1.1m. in 1987, $2.4m. in 1988 and $1m. in 1989. During 1991–93 mining contributed a constant 0.2% of GDP. In 1994 output increased to an estimated $19.8m. There are confirmed coal reserves of some 6,000m. tons, but so far output has remained relatively low. The Moatize coal mine, near Tete has an annual production capacity of 600,000 tons, although output was only 84,500 tons in 1989 (compared with 574,800 tons in 1975), owing to a lack of facilities for transporting the coal to Beira port, and to rebel attacks against the railway to Beira. Exports of coal from Moatize declined from pre-independence levels of some 100,000 tons per year to only 9,000 tons in 1986. Coal exports declined from 19,000 tons in 1990 to 400 tons in 1993 owing to flooding in the Moatize mines. However, there are plans to revive the industry, with a new coal-handling terminal at Beira increasing annual capacity from 400,000 tons to 1.2m. tons. Renovation work on the railway to the port, having been repeatedly delayed as a result of the security situation, resumed in July 1990. The EC was providing funding of $72m. for the project. The government signed bilateral agreements which envisaged an increase in annual coal production levels to about 3m. tons by 1995, although the plan was later postponed for several years. The rehabilitation project envisaged foreign investment in mining projects of more than $600m., and in railway and port infrastructural work of almost $500m. The loans were to be repaid in coal. An agreement worth $700m. over seven years for coal prospecting and mining rights at Mucanha Vuzi was concluded with Brazilian companies in 1982.

Mozambique has significant reserves of tantalite, but only small quantities are exported. There are deposits of ilmenite in the area north of the mouth of the Zambezi river. In 1989 the Irish-based Kenmare Resources Co joined the government in a joint venture to exploit graphite deposits at Ancuabe, in Cabo Delgado province. Mining commenced in 1994, and was expected to produce about 5,000 tons annually, at 98% carbon. Investigations have also been proceeding along the coast to confirm deposits of ilmenite, zircon and titano-magnetite, and smaller reserves of rutile and monazite. Preliminary assessments estimated the heavy mineral content at 2.2m.–5m. tons, depending upon the method of extraction, with possible revenues of US $44m. a year. The mining of iron ore began in the mid-1950s and production of ore averaged about 6m. tons (60%–65% iron) annually in the early 1970s. Production was disrupted by the civil war and ceased altogether between 1975 and 1984. At present, output is stockpiled and the resumption of exports of iron ore depends upon the eventual rehabilitation of the rail link between the mines at Cassinga and the coast. A major deposit of 360m. tons estimated reserves exists near Namapa in Nampula province. In 1997 JCI Ltd of South Africa was conducting a feasibility study on the establishment of a US $1,000m. iron ore project in Mozambique and Zimbabwe. The plans involved the use of natural gas from Mozambique to fuel an iron ore reduction plant which would be built on the border of Mozambique and Zimbabwe, in Manica province. Bauxite is mined in the Manica area; in the early 1990s several thousand tons annually were exported direct by licence to Zimbabwe. Further deposits near Tete were reported to be awaiting the completion of the Cahora Bassa power complex to be processed in Vila Fontes on the Zambezi. New deposits of manganese, graphite, fluorite, platinum, nickel, radioactive minerals (e.g. uranium), asbestos, iron, diamonds and natural gas (of which there are confirmed reserves of about 60,000m. cu m) have been found. An Israeli company is mining emeralds and garnets in Zambézia province.

In 1985 a protocol was signed with the multinational company, Lonrho, regarding the possible development of gold mines in Manica province. In October 1987 Lonrho signed a 25-year agreement for rights in five blocks on a seam in Manica; in 1990 the company announced the formation of a joint venture with the Mineral Resources Ministry, Aluviões de Manica, with plans to produce 20 kilos of gold per month from alluvial deposits in the Revuè and Chua river basins. Reserves in the province are estimated at 50 metric tons. Official sources estimated that some 13 tons of gold had been illegally extracted between 1990–95 from the Lupiliche region in Niassa province. In 1996 total official extraction of gold was just 50.3 kg. In June 1993 Italy agreed to provide US $19m. to rehabilitate the Montepuez marble quarry in Cabo Delgado province and to build a processing factory in Pemba. Annual production from the quarry was projected at 8,100 cubic metres, with Portugal and South Africa identified as potential export markets.

Mozambique imports all its petroleum supplies. The Maputo refinery has an annual capacity of 800,000 tons of crude oil; production was 683,000 tons in 1981, compared with 518,716 tons in 1974. Petroleum prospecting was actively pursued by US, French, Federal German and South African companies, both offshore near the Rovuma river basin and Beira and on the mainland, but so far only gas has been found. Extraction of gas from the Pande field in southern Inhambane province was to begin with the assistance of a US $30m. loan from the World Bank agreed in April 1994. The field's reserves are estimated at 55,000m. cubic metres. Sales of the gas to South Africa, which was expected to be the principal consumer, were to begin in 1998, following the construction of a 900-km pipeline. The state-owned Empresa Nacional de Hidrocarbonetos de Moçambique controls concessions for petroleum production and exploration, although many foreign petroleum companies have been deterred from exploring for petroleum in Mozambique by the country's security situation and the fall in the world price of petroleum. Petroleum prospecting resumed in late 1994, following a three-year hiatus, with initial exploration focusing on the Rovuma basin and the southern coast. In recent years a critical shortage of foreign exchange has drastically reduced Mozambique's imports of crude petroleum, and severe shortages of fuel have ensued. The government has aimed to encourage foreign investment in the minerals sector, and during the period 1986–89 foreign mining investment in Mozambique increased from $5m. to $50m.

POWER

Electricity production, totalling 658m. kWh in 1975, increased to 4,940m. kWh in 1977, of which 4,490m. was hydroelectric. Total production reached 14,000m. kWh in 1980, but by 1994 had dwindled to 339.9 kWh. Eventually, however, the Cahora Bassa dam should provide great benefits for Mozambique's economy. (The dam, which has always operated at a loss, is owned and administered by the Portuguese government but by the end of the century, when the capital is reimbursed, ownership of the plant will have reverted to Mozambique.) By 1982 Cahora Bassa had a generating capacity of 2,075 MW. The supply of power to South Africa started belatedly in mid-1977, and by 1983 South Africa was receiving about 98% of Cahora Bassa's output. In March–April 1984 tripartite talks between Mozambique, Portugal and South Africa resulted in an agreement whereby Mozambique was to receive a share of the revenues, which had previously been paid exclusively to Portugal. Under the new agreement, Mozambique was to receive 5m.–10m. rand per year from South African electricity purchases. However, frequent sabotage of power lines by Renamo subsequently halted supplies from the dam to the South African grid. By March 1987 Cahora Bassa was reported to be operating at only 0.5% of its potential capacity. However, following six months of negotiations, Mozambique, Portugal and South Africa signed an agreement in June 1988 to restore operations at the dam. Under the agreement, 1,400 km of power lines (of which 900 km traversed areas under Renamo control) were to undergo rehabilitation (financed in part by the South African government), and an armed force was to be established to protect the lines, following the completion of the repair work. In September 1988 it was announced that South Africa would provide military aid to Mozambique for the protection of the lines. However, rehabilitation was continually delayed as a result of the security situation. A programme to rehabilitate the lines, at an estimated cost of US $125m., began in July 1995, with funding from South Africa ($50m.), Portugal ($25m.) and the remainder from the EU, the European Investment Bank and the Caisse Française. Completion of the rehabilitation work, which was expected to take two years, would make Cahora Bassa the country's greatest source of export earnings, with an estimated $56m. a year. An agreement for Zimbabwe, which faces power shortages, to buy electricity from Cahora Bassa was signed in April 1992. The project would involve constructing a 350-km transmission line to Harare and was expected to take three years to complete. In November 1994 an agreement was signed with Norway securing $24.5m. to finance the project. The new line would allow Zimbabwe to draw 500 MW from Cahora Bassa—about 25% of the dam's installed capacity. Plans for the construction of further lines to supply Malawi and Swaziland were also being pursued following the signing of agreements between Mozambique and those countries in 1994.

The 240-km lake that has been created with the dam reaches the Zambian border, and grandiose plans have been made to irrigate 1.5m. ha in this otherwise economically backward salient of Mozambique. Tete could be developed as an iron and steel industrial centre, and the Zambezi made navigable from Tete to the sea. A second phase of the Cahora Bassa project opened in 1981, including installation of additional generating capacity of 1,750 MW directed to domestic needs.

Other main hydroelectric plants are on the Revuè river, west of Beira at Chicamba Real and Mavúzi. Further south, on the Limpopo, is the dam which helps to irrigate the *colonato*. Another dam at Massingir was expected to increase the irrigation potential of the Limpopo. However, the Massingir dam has been empty since soon after its completion in 1977, owing to the discovery of defects. In January 1988 a French company was contracted to undertake preventive maintenance on the dam and its rehabilitation is planned. A dam at Corumana, costing US $250m., was inaugurated in July 1989; the dam's 15-MW power station, financed by Sweden and Norway at a cost of $20m., opened in September 1990. In 1977 a new state company was given the monopoly of production, transport and distribution of electric energy. Mozambique is connected to the South African grid, and by early 1988, in the absence of regular power supplies from Cahora Bassa, was importing an estimated 1,500m. kWh annually from South Africa, costing R15m. per year and absorbing almost 10% of Mozambique's annual export earnings. Since then imports have fallen to around 500m. kWh. In February 1991 an agreement was signed with South Africa and Swaziland to build three dams for power generation and irrigation in the joint Komati river basin. In July 1996 the state electricity company announced that it was to invest $60m. over a period of three years in the rehabilitation and expansion of the country's electricity grid. The majority of the financing was to be provided by Scandinavian countries. Plans were under review in 1997 for the construction of the Mepandua Ncua hydroelectric power station at a site in the Zambezi valley, some 70 km downstream of Cahora Bassa. The plant, which was expected to have a generating capacity of between 2,000-2,500 MW, was projected to cost some US $1,500m., with a further $500m. for the construction of transmission lines linking it to the South African grid. It was envisaged that the station would be completed by 2007.

There is also a coal-fired power station in Maputo with a capacity of 60 MW, which is supplied by imports of coal from South Africa. A new turbine, donated by France, was installed at the Maputo station in 1991. It is estimated that 400,000 tons of timber are used annually as fuel wood in Mozambique. In 1989 the government instigated a project which aimed to protect the environment by promoting the domestic use of gas, paraffin and coal in place of fuel wood.

INDUSTRY

Industries are mainly devoted to the processing of primary materials, and Mozambique remains dependent on South African industrial products. About 47% of Mozambican manufacturers are located in and around Maputo, although the government is encouraging decentralization towards Beira and northern Mozambique. Under the colonial administration, investments from Portugal, South Africa, Italy and the UK established export-oriented industries. Food processing formed the traditional basis of this sector, with sugar refining, cashew- and wheat-processing predominating. However, textile production and brewing gained in importance during the 1980s. Other industries include the manufacture of cement, fertilizers and agricultural implements. Cotton spinning and weaving are undertaken at Chimoio, Maputo, and in Nampula province. In mid-1987 the Companhia Agro-Industrial Lonrho Moçambique, a joint venture that had been formed in 1985, received a loan of ECU 3m. (US $3.5m.) from the European Investment Bank towards a project for the rehabilitation of its cotton ginnery at Chokwe and its vegetable-processing plant at Chilembene (which supplies Maputo).

The cement industry is operating at a reduced level, producing 62,300 metric tons in 1994, compared with 611,000 tons in 1973. Cement exports reached 192,000 tons in 1978 but dropped dramatically, to 70,000 tons, in 1982, and to a negligible level in 1986. A programme to rehabilitate the cement plant at Matola, enabling it to produce 400,000 tons a year, was expected to be completed by the end of 1993, with finance provided by the World Bank, European Development Bank, France, Norway, Sweden and Denmark. Construction of a small cement factory in Tete City, with a capacity of 2,500 tons per year, was under way during the late 1980s. This is for local use, and is funded by Germany. In 1994 the Portuguese company CIMPOR purchased a 51% share of Cimentos de Moçambique for US $20m. The construction sector expanded by 25% between 1977–81, by a further 4.4% in 1982 (when most other sectors were in decline), by 5% in 1987, and by 7% in 1993. A fertilizer plant is in production at Matola. In late 1995 plans were announced for the construction of a US $4m. ammonia plant in Sofala province. The plant, which was to be operational by the end of 1997, was to be a joint venture between the Empresa Nacional de Hidrocarbonetos (Mozambique), Scimitar Production Limited (Canada) and Zarara Petroleum Resources (UAE). In May 1997 the brewery Fábrica de Cervejas Reunidas was purchased by the Portuguese company Empresa de Cerveja da Madeira for $4.5m. The new owners plan to invest some $10m. in the brewery over the first two years. Following the contraction of the industrial sector by an annual average of 8.4% during 1980–86, official sources estimated that industrial output increased by 6% in 1987, owing partly to restructuring of the sector under the ERP and partly to increased imports of raw materials. In 1988 industrial output increased by 5.1%, according to the government. Under the ERP, resources were to be focused on industries with high domestic added value, and on import-substitution products. Government control of prices was relaxed in several industrial sectors in 1987. During 1990–94 industrial GDP declined by an estimated annual average of 2.4%.

Other secondary industries produce glass, ceramics, paper, tyres and railway carriages. Industrial output may have fallen to less than 50% of its pre-independence level, owing to the exodus of skilled workers, shortages of imported raw materials and spare parts, and the disruption to transport systems. The 1983–85 State Plan aimed to encourage small-scale industries, placing emphasis on the production of basic consumer goods and of import substitutes, using local materials. In 1990 the International Development Association (IDA) provided US $38m. for the rehabilitation and promotion of small- and medium-scale enterprises.

In mid-1997 a South African mining conglomerate, Gencor, approved a project to construct an aluminium smelter in the district of Boane, near Maputo in southern Mozambique. Investment in the project was to total US $1,125m. Construction of the smelter, which (it was envisaged) would produce 245,000 tons of aluminium per year, was projected to begin in mid-1998.

TRANSPORT

Before independence Mozambique derived much of its income from charges on goods carried between Zimbabwe, Zambia, Malawi, Swaziland and South Africa and its ports. Railways play a dominant part in this middle-man economy. In 1987 Mozambique had 3,131 km of track, excluding the Sena Sugar Estates railway (90 km), which serves only the company's properties. The end of the war precipitated a rapid increase in rail traffic. Passenger traffic escalated from 26m. passenger-km in 1992 to 312m. passenger-km in 1995. Freight traffic also increased, to a lesser extent, from 616m. ton-km in 1992 to 893m. ton-km in 1995. Main lines are: from Maputo, the Maputo–Ressano Garcia line to the South African border, the Maputo – Goba line to the Swaziland border, and the Maputo – Chicualacuala line to the Zimbabwe border (the Limpopo rail link) in the south; from Beira, the Beira–Mutare line to the Zimbabwe border, the Trans-Zambézia line to the Malawi border, and the Tete line. In the north the main route is the Nacala–Malawi line, with a branch-line to Lichinga. All these lines are intended primarily to export the products of land-locked countries, and secondarily to transport Mozambican goods. During the war the whole of Mozambique's rail network was subject to frequent disruption by Renamo guerrilla sabotage. Repairs to the Dona Ana railway bridge, spanning the Zambezi river at Sena, which was sabotaged in 1986, were completed in early 1996 at a cost of US $19m.

Most of the international lines are controlled by international conventions, since their effective functioning is vital to Mozambique's neighbours. The operation of the Beira and Maputo lines was highly profitable to the Mozambican treasury. In February 1979 Mozambique concluded an agreement with South Africa that was to raise South African exports through Mozambique from the 1978 level of 15,000 tons per day, to 30,000–35,000 tons per day by 1981. Revenue from South African use of Mozambican railways and harbours amounted to US $93m. in 1977. By the late 1980s South African rail traffic through Mozambique had declined. In 1980 the Harare–Beira line was reopened but, owing to lack of maintenance, the port of Beira could no longer accommodate ships of over 5,000 tons.

In 1983 Mozambique secured several grants for making improvements to the railway network, including the rehabilitation of the vital 450-km rail link between the Moatize coalfields and Beira port.

In October 1986 a short-term programme to reinstate the 'Beira Corridor', linking Zimbabwe to the Beira harbour, was initiated, at a cost of more than US $300m., financed mainly by the Netherlands, Scandinavia and the USA. A major project to rebuild the transport network in the corridor was announced in May 1987, under which Western European countries were to provide most of the $589m. cost. The project was expected to span an eight-year period. In 1987 there was an increase of 25% in traffic through the 'Beira Corridor', although the turnover in the transport sector overall declined by 8%, owing to continued disruption by Renamo and a decline in South African traffic. In March 1988 the volume of traffic through the corridor was 42% greater than in the corresponding period of the previous year. The rehabilitation of the Limpopo railway, which began in 1986, was completed in early 1993, at a cost of some $200m.

In December 1992 the government announced the proposed restructuring of the administration of the Beira, Maputo and Nacala transport corridors, with a view to encouraging private-sector involvement in investment and management. In June

1997 the government invited contractors to tender for private concessions to operate Maputo port and the three railways linking it with South Africa, Swaziland and Zimbabwe. The state ports and railway company, Empresa Nacional dos Portos e Caminhos de Ferro de Moçambique (CFM), were to retain a 33% stake in the companies. The operators were to have a 51% stake, while the remaining 16% was to be open to other investors. It was envisaged that the new operators would take over in early 1998. Similar divestments involving the Beira and Nacala transport corridors were expected to be completed by the end of 1998.

This railway-dominated country lacks good roads. In 1994 there were only 29,195 km of roads and tracks. Unfortunately, the main roads are penetration lines toward the border and are grossly insufficient for Mozambique's purposes. Attempts are being made to construct a paved road from the Tanzanian border to the south. Most of the northern provinces are lacking in roads. There is a bridge across the Zambezi river at Tete, on the Zimbabwe–Malawi route, which was completed in 1972, and a tarred road links Malawi to Maputo via Tete. Prior to the end of hostilities in 1992 the poor security situation all but halted normal road transport to and from most cities, and it was necessary to organize military guards for convoys. Between 1977–82 about 550 km of paved roads were built, as well as 450 km of tracks and 50 bridges, and a major programme, supervised by the Southern African Development Co-ordination Conference (SADCC, now the Southern African Development Community–SADC), was under way in 1989 to improve the road links between Mozambique and neighbouring countries. UN agencies are helping to fund a programme to rehabilitate roads within the country. In April 1994 the IDA announced a credit of US $188m. towards an $814.6m. programme to rehabilitate the country's roads. The five-year programme, covering 3,450 km of main roads, 11,700 km of unasphalted roads and 3,200 Bailey bridges, was also to receive finance from the African Development Bank, EU, USA, France, Germany and Kuwait.

The main ports are Maputo (the second largest port in Africa, with its annexe at Matola), Beira, Nacala and Quelimane. Maputo and Beira ports exist chiefly as outlets for South Africa, Swaziland, Zimbabwe, Zambia, Malawi and Zaire. However, because of the security situation, most of their potential traffic has been re-routed to the South African ports of Durban, East London and Port Elizabeth. The total freight traffic handled by Mozambique's ports was only 4.2m. tons in 1986, but increased to 9m. tons in 1988. In 1994 some 6.2m. tons of cargo were handled, increasing to 7.1m. tons in 1995. Maputo has an excellent, multi-purpose harbour and rehabilitation of its facilities, which aimed to increase the port's annual handling capacity from 7m. tons to 12m. tons, was completed in 1989. The coal terminal at Maputo port, which has a handling capacity of 6m. tons per year, has been rented for a period of 15 years to the South African company CMR Engineers and Project Managers. The sugar terminal reopened in June 1995 following four years of inactivity. In mid-1997 the government was pursuing plans for the privatization of the management of Maputo port (see above). The first phase of the rehabilitation of Beira port, which included a joint terminal for petroleum and 'roll on, roll off' traffic and an increase in the capacity of the coal terminal, was completed in 1987, increasing its overall capacity by one-third, to 3.2m. tons per year. The second phase of the rehabilitation, which included the deepening of the entrance channel, was expected to raise capacity to 5m. tons per year on completion. Goods traffic handled at Beira in 1991 totalled 2.4m. tons, compared with 1.8m. tons in 1987. Repairs to the port of Nacala, damaged by a cyclone in early 1994, were to cost an estimated US $14m. Foreign assistance was being sought to fund the repairs.

In May 1996 the governments of Mozambique and South Africa convened an investors' conference in Maputo in an attempt to secure funding for the development of transport links between Maputo and Johannesburg. The project included the rehabilitation of the Maputo-Ressano Garcia railway line, the construction of a toll road between Maputo and Witbank, in South Africa, and improvements to Maputo harbour.

International air transport is operated by the state-owned LAM, and domestic routes by TTA. There are 16 airports, of which three are international. In August 1990 LAM agreed to buy one Boeing 767 and one 737 and to lease a further 767 and two 737 aircraft. All three of the leased aircraft were returned in early 1995. Despite opposition from within the ruling party, sustained pressure from the World Bank led the government to agree to privatize both LAM and TTA. The latter was privatized in May 1997. In mid-1997 five consortia had qualified for the restricted tender for the privatization of LAM, including one led by the Portuguese airline TAP and another led by the South African airline SAA. In 1996 LAM incurred operating losses of US $1.1m., an improvement over the previous year's losses of $6.7m. A project to provide equipment to seven airstrips, which was supported by the Danish International Development Agency (Danida), was carried out in 1983–85; Danida agreed in March 1988 to expand the project and provide maintenance services for the original work. A $4.7m. rehabilitation programme was planned for Maputo airport. The project included the rebuilding of the terminal to increase handling capacity to 1m. passengers a year. Between 1983 and 1993 most provincial capitals were accessible from Maputo only by air, when fuel was available. With the advent of peace and with large investments in road rehabilitation, air transport is no longer the only option.

The improvement of Mozambique's ports and railways is a priority of the SADC, which aimed to reduce the dependence of southern African states on South Africa.

TOURISM

Formerly a highly profitable activity, tourism relied on the influx of Rhodesians and South Africans to Beira and the southern beaches. Gorongosa Park, half-way between Zimbabwe and Beira, was also a great attraction. In 1972 Mozambique had 282 hotels, motels and boarding houses, containing 5,195 rooms, and received 291,574 visitors. In 1978 it was reported that all organized tourist travel had ceased, but in early 1984 Frelimo received a South African delegation for talks on a resumption of tourism, and in that year a joint-venture tourism company was established with South Africa in order to develop tourism on Inhaca island. Meanwhile, efforts have been made to attract tourists from Zimbabwe again. An estimated 1,000 tourists visited the country in 1981. However, the hopes of an actual resumption of South African tourism in 1984 proved to be premature, and, except on coastal islands and in the immediate vicinity of Maputo, the security situation hampered any improvement in this highly volatile sector. During the late 1980s some hotels were rehabilitated. Since the 1992 peace agreement South African tourism has increased rapidly and a number of South African operated camping sites have been established on beaches in the south of the country, although not all are properly licensed.

The government hopes that nature and game reserves will develop into a major tourist attraction. A controversial game reserve is being developed in Maputo province by an entrepreneur from the USA, with a 9.7% stake belonging to the Mozambican state. Gongorosa game reserve is being rehabilitated, and there are plans for the extension of South Africa's Kruger National Park into Mozambique. In 1996 private investment in the tourism sector totalled US $60m. In that year, according to figures released by the Empresa Nacional de Turismo, 550,000 tourists visited Mozambique.

TRADE AND GOVERNMENT FINANCE

Mozambique's severe balance-of-payments problem (the current deficit was US $344.6m. in 1995) has been accentuated by high defence spending (which was projected to account for 35% of budget expenditure in 1994), much of it in already scarce foreign exchange, and by the drastic decline in tourism. Mozambique has also suffered from adverse movements in the terms of trade. Exports cover only a small proportion of the country's imports: 14.7% in 1994, rising to 21.6% in 1995. In 1994 the total value of exports was US $149.5m., with imports valued at $1,018.5m. In 1995 the respective totals were $168.9m. and $783.6m. Mozambique has a diversified set of trading partners. In 1996 the principal sources of imports were South Africa (33.1%), Portugal (5.9%), France (5%) and India (5%). In that year the principal markets for exports were South Africa (21.2%), Spain (15.4%), the USA (13.4%), India (13%), Zimbabwe (8.2%) and Portugal (8%). The employment of Mozambicans in South African mines also declined from a pre-independence peak of 118,000 to about 60,000 in 1986, creating a major unemployment problem. In October 1986 the South African government ordered the repatriation of Mozambican miners, thereby exacerbating the level of unemployment and reducing earnings of foreign exchange by about one-third. However, in January 1987 South Africa announced that about 30,000 of the miners would be permitted to remain, and in November 1988 restrictions on the recruitment of Mozambican mine-workers in South Africa were withdrawn.

Agreements on the rescheduling of Mozambique's debts, covering more than US $400m. of repayments and arrears repayable in the period up to December 1988, were signed in May and June 1987 with Western official and commercial creditors, in order to reduce repayments on the country's external debt. Despite the 1987 reschedulings, the cost of debt-servicing in 1989 exceeded 200% of the value of Mozambique's exports of goods and services. In June 1990 Western official and commercial creditors agreed a further rescheduling of the country's debts. In March 1993 a restructuring of bilateral debt resulted in $180m. of the $440m. Mozambique was due to pay its official creditors over the next two years being written off. In November 1996 the 'Paris Club' of official creditors agreed to cancel or reschedule debt-servicing obligations of some $600m. Mozambique's total external public debt was estimated by the World Bank at $5,781m. at the end of 1995, of which $5,251m. was long-term public debt. In that year the cost of debt-servicing was equivalent to 35.7% of the total value of exports of goods and services.

Government finances for 1995 represent a considerable improvement over previous years. In relation to 1994, government revenue increased by 58%, while current expenditure increased by 11% and investment expenditure increased by 35%. Defence and security accounted for about 24% of current expenditure, although this figure includes considerable expenditure on demobilization. Early results from 1996 indicate a considerable decline in defence and security expenditure. Around 79% of investment expenditure was derived from foreign grants and loans. One of the major barriers to increasing customs revenue was the endemic corruption within the customs services. Upon donor insistence, management of customs was privatized in 1997 and is now the responsibility of a British company, Crown Agents.

Statistical Survey

Source (unless otherwise stated): Direcção Nacional de Estatística, Comissão Nacional do Plano, Avda Ahmed Sekou Touré 21, CP 493, Maputo; tel. (1) 743117.

Area and Population

AREA, POPULATION AND DENSITY

Area (sq km)	799,380*
Population (census results)	
15 December 1970	8,168,933†
1 August 1980‡	
Males	5,670,484
Females	6,003,241
Total	11,673,725
Population (official estimates at mid-year)	
1993	15,583,000
1994	16,614,000
1995	17,423,000
Density (per sq km) at mid-1995	21.8

* 308,641 sq miles. The area includes 13,000 sq km (5,019 sq miles) of inland water.

† Covering only those areas under Portuguese control.

‡ Excluding an adjustment for underenumeration, estimated at 3.8%. The adjusted total is 12,130,000 (males 5,908,500; females 6,221,500).

PROVINCES (at 1 January 1987)

Province	Area (sq km)	Population (provisional)	Density (per sq km)
Cabo Delgado	82,625	1,109,921	13.4
Gaza	75,709	1,138,724	15.0
Inhambane	68,615	1,167,022	17.0
Manica	61,661	756,886	12.3
City of Maputo	602	1,006,765	1,672.4
Maputo province	25,756	544,692	21.1
Nampula	81,606	2,837,856	34.8
Niassa	129,056	607,670	4.7
Sofala	68,018	1,257,710	18.5
Tete	100,724	981,319	9.7
Zambézia	105,008	2,952,251	28.1
Total	799,380	14,360,816	18.0

PRINCIPAL TOWNS (estimated population at 1 August 1986)

Maputo (capital)	882,601	Nampula	182,505
Beira	264,202		

Source: UN, *Demographic Yearbook*.

BIRTHS AND DEATHS (UN estimates, annual averages)

	1980–85	1985–90	1990–95
Birth rate (per 1,000)	45.7	45.0	45.2
Death rate (per 1,000)	20.0	18.8	18.5

Expectation of life (UN estimates, years at birth, 1990–95): 46.4 (males 44.9; females 48.0).

Source: UN, *World Population Prospects: The 1994 Revision*.

ECONOMICALLY ACTIVE POPULATION
(persons aged 12 years and over, 1980 census)

	Males	Females	Total
Agriculture, forestry, hunting and fishing	1,887,779	2,867,052	4,754,831
Mining and quarrying; Manufacturing	323,730	23,064	346,794
Construction	41,611	510	42,121
Commerce	90,654	21,590	112,244
Transport, storage and communications	74,817	2,208	77,025
Other services*	203,629	39,820	243,449
Total employed	2,622,220	2,954,244	5,576,464
Unemployed	75,505	19,321	94,826
Total labour force	2,697,725	2,973,565	5,671,290

* Including electricity, gas and water.

Source: ILO, *Yearbook of Labour Statistics*.

1991 (estimates, '000 persons): Agriculture 6,870; Industry 766; Services 798; Total labour force 8,434 (Source: UN Economic Commission for Africa, *African Statistical Yearbook*).

Mid-1995 (estimates in '000): Agriculture, etc. 6,831; Total 8,404 (Source: FAO, *Production Yearbook*).

Agriculture

PRINCIPAL CROPS ('000 metric tons)

	1993	1994	1995
Rice (paddy)	65	98	113†
Maize	533†	526	734†
Sorghum	143	164	243†
Potatoes*	72	74	72
Sweet potatoes*	55	60	55
Cassava (Manioc)	3,511†	3,294	4,178†
Pulses†	79†	95	134†
Groundnuts (in shell)	84	74	102
Sunflower seed*	12	13	14
Cottonseed†	31	34	32
Cotton (lint)†	16	17	16
Coconuts*	435	438	438
Copra†	73	74	74
Vegetables and melons*	125	125	126
Sugar cane	185	230*	300*
Oranges*	12	14	15
Mangoes*	30	32	34
Bananas*	80	82	84
Papayas*	40	42	44
Other fruits*	170	183	135
Cashew nuts	24	23†	30*
Tea (made)	2	2*	3*
Tobacco (leaves)*	3	3	3
Jute and jute-like fibres*	4	4	4
Sisal	1†	1*	1*

* FAO estimate(s). † Unofficial figure(s).

Source: FAO, *Production Yearbook.*

LIVESTOCK (FAO estimates, '000 head, year ending September)

	1993	1994	1995
Asses	20	20	20
Cattle	1,260	1,270	1,280
Pigs	170	172	175
Sheep	119	120	121
Goats	382	384	385

Chickens (FAO estimates, million): 22 in 1993; 23 in 1994; 23 in 1995.

Source: FAO, *Production Yearbook.*

LIVESTOCK PRODUCTS (FAO estimates, '000 metric tons)

	1993	1994	1995
Beef and veal	38	38	38
Goat meat	2	2	3
Pig meat	12	12	13
Poultry meat	28	28	29
Cows' milk	58	58	59
Goats' milk	10	10	10
Hen eggs	11.4	11.7	12.0
Cattle hides	5.0	5.1	5.1

Source: FAO, *Production Yearbook.*

Forestry

ROUNDWOOD REMOVALS ('000 cubic metres)

	1992	1993*	1994*
Sawlogs, veneer logs and logs for sleepers	22	60	60
Other industrial wood*	910	933	959
Fuel wood*	15,022	15,022	15,022
Total	15,954	16,015	16,041

* FAO estimates (the annual figure for fuel wood is assumed to be unchanged since 1987).

Source: FAO, *Yearbook of Forest Products.*

SAWNWOOD PRODUCTION (FAO estimates, '000 cubic metres, incl. railway sleepers)

	1992	1993	1994
Coniferous (softwood)	6	13	11
Broadleaved (hardwood)	10	17	15
Total	16	30	26

Source: FAO, *Yearbook of Forest Products.*

Fishing

('000 metric tons, live weight)

	1993	1994	1995
Inland waters:			
Freshwater fishes	4.0	4.1	2.0
Dagaas	0.7	0.9	3.1
Indian Ocean:			
Marine fishes	13.1	11.4	10.0
Shrimps	11.0	10.1	10.7
Other crustaceans	1.2	0.9	0.8
Molluscs	0.2	0.1	0.2
Total catch	30.2	27.6	26.9

Source: FAO, *Yearbook of Fishery Statistics.*

Mining

('000 metric tons)

	1990	1991	1992
Coal	122.2	112.0	27.0
Bauxite	6.6	7.9	9.3
Salt (unrefined)	46.9	45.3	22.8

Source: Ministry of Mineral Resources.

Bauxite ('000 metric tons): 6 in 1993; 10 in 1994 (Source: UN, *Industrial Commodity Statistics Yearbook*).

Industry

SELECTED PRODUCTS ('000 metric tons, unless otherwise indicated)

	1992	1993	1994
Margarine	0.5	0.4	0.5
Wheat flour	51	28	40
Raw sugar	30*	20*	20†
Beer ('000 hl)	211	204	118
Cigarettes (million)	124	377	343
Footwear ('000 pairs)	148	302.6‡	280.5‡
Cement	73	60	62
Electric energy (million kWh)§	490	490	490

* FAO estimates.
† Figure from International Sugar Organization.
‡ Source: Direcção Nacional de Estatística, Maputo.
§ Estimates.

Source: UN, *Industrial Commodity Statistics Yearbook.*

Finance

CURRENCY AND EXCHANGE RATES

Monetary Units

100 centavos = 1 metical (plural: meticais).

Sterling and Dollar Equivalents (31 March 1997)

£1 sterling = 18,871.5 meticais;
US $1 = 11,493.0 meticais;
100,000 meticais = £5.299 = $8.701.

Average Exchange Rate (meticais per US $)

1994 6,038.6
1995 9,024.3
1996 11,293.8

BUDGET ('000 million meticais)

Revenue	1993	1994	1995‡
Taxation	995.0	1,397.2	2,201.0
Taxes on income	156.6	273.3	400.0
Domestic taxes on goods and services	534.6	738.6	1,152.0
Customs duties	278.7	343.2	579.0
Import duties	172.9	241.3	416.0
Other taxes	25.2	42.0	70.0
Non-tax revenue	97.6	128.5	211.0
Total	1,092.6	1,525.7	2,412.0

Expenditure	1993	1994	1995‡
Current expenditure*	1,167.1	1,978.0	2,194.0
Defence and security	416.8	762.0	522.0
Civil service salaries	238.8	329.7	553.0
Other goods and services	230.0	601.8	595.0
Interest on public debt	198.0	150.5	341.0
Other purposes	89.5	159.0	267.0
Investment expenditure†	1,097.0	2,118.5	2,863.0
Liquidation of debt of enterprises	40.0	—	106.0
Total	2,304.1	4,096.5	5,162.0

* Including adjustments relating to preceding or following periods ('000 million meticais): -6.0 in 1993; -25 in 1994.

† Including adjustments relating to preceding or following periods ('000 million meticais): -127.5 in 1993; -289.6 in 1994.

‡ Source: IMF, *Republic of Mozambique—Recent Economic Developments* (December 1996).

Source: the former Ministry of Finance, Maputo.

INTERNATIONAL RESERVES (US $ million at 31 December)

	1994	1995	1996
IMF special drawing rights	0.05	0.05	0.05
Reserve position in IMF	0.01	0.01	0.01
Foreign exchange	173.20	228.80	391.00
Total	173.26	228.86	391.06

Source: IMF, *International Financial Statistics.*

MONEY SUPPLY ('000 million meticais at 31 December)

	1989	1990	1991
Currency outside banks	94.1	147.1	189.6
Demand deposits at commercial banks	129.3	178.2	224.1

Source: IMF, *International Financial Statistics.*

COST OF LIVING

(Consumer Price Index for Maputo; base: 1990=100)

	1993	1994	1995
All items	275.0	448.8	693.1

Source: IMF, *International Financial Statistics.*

NATIONAL ACCOUNTS

National Income and Product ('000 million meticais at current prices)

	1984	1985	1986
Domestic factor incomes*	95.7	137.2	146.3
Consumption of fixed capital	4.0	4.0	4.0
Gross domestic product (GDP) at factor cost	99.7	141.2	150.3
Indirect taxes	9.8	6.9	8.7
Less Subsidies	0.4	0.5	0.5
GDP in purchasers' values	109.1	147.6	158.4
Net factor income from abroad	0.3	0.2	0.6
Gross national product	109.4	147.8	159.0
Less Consumption of fixed capital	4.0	4.0	4.0
National income in market prices	105.4	143.8	155.0

* Compensation of employees and the operating surplus of enterprises.

Source: UN, *National Accounts Statistics.*

Expenditure on the Gross Domestic Product
('000 million meticais at current prices)

	1993	1994	1995
Government final consumption expenditure	915	1,740	1,688
Private final consumption expenditure	3,839	5,718	8,874
Gross capital formation	3,579	6,015	8,290
Total domestic expenditure	8,332	13,471	18,853
Exports of goods and services	1,162	2,016	3,291
Less Imports of goods and services	4,031	6,835	8,614
GDP in purchasers' values	5,463	8,652	13,530
GDP at constant 1990 prices	1,571	1,660	n.a.

Source: IMF, *International Financial Statistics.*

Gross Domestic Product by Economic Activity
(estimates, million meticais at current prices)

	1989	1990	1991
Agriculture, hunting, forestry and fishing	555,480	668,150	801,780
Mining and quarrying	2,610	3,600	4,320
Manufacturing	305,240	420,700	504,840
Electricity, gas and water	54,360	74,920	89,910
Construction	86,030	225,000	270,000
Trade, restaurants and hotels	60,920	83,970	100,760
Transport and communications	124,350	162,400	194,880
Finance, insurance, real estate, etc.	4,460	6,140	7,370
Public administration and defence	37,730	52,000	62,410
Other services	7,120	9,810	11,770
GDP at factor cost	1,238,300	1,706,700	2,048,040
Indirect taxes, *less* subsidies	106,570	146,540	175,840
GDP in purchasers' values	1,344,870	1,853,240	2,223,880

Source: UN Economic Commission for Africa, *African Statistical Yearbook.*

BALANCE OF PAYMENTS (US $ million)

	1990	1991	1992
Exports of goods f.o.b.	126.4	162.3	139.3
Imports of goods f.o.b.	−789.7	−808.8	−798.5
Trade balance	−663.3	−646.5	−659.2
Exports of services	103.0	147.2	164.6
Imports of services	−206.0	−236.8	−246.4
Balance on goods and services	−766.3	−736.1	−741.0
Other income received	70.4	55.6	58.0
Other income paid	−167.8	−165.5	−197.7
Balance on goods, services and income	−863.7	−846.0	−880.7
Current transfers received	448.4	501.7	499.4
Current balance	−415.3	−344.3	−381.3
Direct investment from abroad	9.2	22.5	25.3
Other investment liabilities	−92.7	−210.0	−148.2
Net errors and omissions	66.3	−3.9	32.5
Overall balance	−432.5	−535.7	−471.7

Source: IMF, *International Financial Statistics*.

External Trade

PRINCIPAL COMMODITIES (US $'000)

Imports c.i.f.	1988	1989	1990
Consumer goods:			
Foodstuffs	176,298	173,629	253,924
Other	104,597	155,927	83,888
Primary materials:			
Chemicals	48,547	52,185	31,953
Metals	35,465	42,472	29,808
Crude petroleum and petroleum products	61,104	71,523	95,860
Other	70,893	81,693	97,723
Machinery and spare parts	101,183	87,509	83,628
Capital goods	137,513	142,736	200,736
Total	735,600	807,674	877,520

Total imports (US $ million): 899 in 1991; 855 in 1992; 955 in 1993; 1,019 in 1994 (Source: UN, *Monthly Bulletin of Statistics*).

Exports f.o.b.	1993	1994	1995
Cashew nuts	8,151	3,295	9,500
Shrimps, prawns, etc.	68,793	62,810	73,100
Raw cotton	11,055	18,943	19,800
Sugar	—	10,977	7,300
Copra	2,500	3,423	6,100
Lobsters	3,188	3,550	n.a.
Total (incl. others)	131,899	155,444	168,900

PRINCIPAL TRADING PARTNERS (US $'000)

Imports c.i.f.	1987	1988	1989
Belgium-Luxembourg	4,824	9,668	8,148
Canada	4,917	24,027	11,504
France	35,558	29,200	32,789
German Democratic Repub.	8,677	17,093	29,140
Germany, Fed. Repub.	31,547	31,831	30,594
Italy	85,023	68,092	48,355
Japan	34,581	24,011	45,309
Portugal	31,049	42,627	55,130
Netherlands	27,398	29,313	16,475
South Africa	85,809	110,179	187,652
Sweden	27,653	28,875	24,406
Switzerland	9,685	5,024	4,590
USSR	54,896	73,228	78,842
United Kingdom	29,228	39,750	38,533
USA	62,888	56,222	57,279
Zimbabwe	15,366	31,337	22,858
Total (incl. others)	642,000	735,600	807,676

Exports f.o.b.	1992	1993	1994
India	—	—	16,788
Japan	13,163	20,708	19,430
Portugal	18,221	16,751	14,612
South Africa	23,033	20,049	23,627
Spain	41,028	36,932	34,041
USA	18,610	4,748	13,990
Zimbabwe	8,270	3,957	5,441
Total (incl. others)	139,305	131,899	155,444

Transport

RAILWAYS (traffic)

	1984	1985	1986
Freight carried ('000 metric tons)	3,698.6	2,899.5	2,949.3
Freight ton-km (million)	536.3	289.6	303.3
Passengers carried ('000)	5,296.0	6,723.0	6,619.0
Passenger-km (million)	284.1	225.4	263.6

1987: Passenger-km 105m.; Freight ton-km 353m.
1988: Passenger-km 75m.; Freight ton-km 306m.

Source: UN, *Statistical Yearbook*.

1989: Passenger-km 73.5m.; Freight ton-km 402.2m.
1990: Passenger-km 78.9m.; Freight ton-km 421.4m.
1991: Passenger-km 61.0m.; Freight ton-km 306.7m.
1992: Passenger-km 26.0m.; Freight ton-km 616.0m.
1993: Passenger-km 71.3m.; Freight ton-km 648.9m.
1994: Passenger-km 127.0m.; Freight ton-km 654.0m.
1995: Passenger-km 312.0m.; Freight ton-km 893.0m.

(Source: IMF, *Republic of Mozambique—Recent Economic Developments*, (December 1996)).

ROAD TRAFFIC (motor vehicles in use at 31 December, estimates)

	1993	1994	1995
Passenger cars	59,500	59,500	67,600
Lorries and vans	20,400	19,300	21,200

Source: International Road Federation, *World Road Statistics*.

SHIPPING

Merchant Fleet (registered at 31 December)

	1994	1995	1996
Number of vessels	101	95	96
Total displacement ('000 grt)	35.6	38.3	44.8

Source: Lloyd's Register of Shipping, *World Fleet Statistics.*

International Sea-borne Freight Traffic ('000 metric tons)

	1989	1990	1991*
Goods loaded	2,430	2,578	2,800
Goods unloaded	3,254	3,379	3,400

* Estimates.

Sources: UN, *Monthly Bulletin of Statistics*; UN Economic Commission for Africa, *African Statistical Yearbook.*

Total Freight Handled ('000 metric tons): 6,224 in 1992; 6,053 in 1993; 6,167 in 1994; 7,056 in 1995 (Source: IMF, *Republic of Mozambique—Recent Economic Developments* (December 1996)).

CIVIL AVIATION (traffic on scheduled services)

	1992	1993	1994
Kilometres flown (million)	4	4	5
Passengers carried ('000)	225	206	221
Passenger-km (million)	382	411	443
Total ton-km (million)	44	47	52

Source: UN, *Statistical Yearbook.*

1995: Passenger-km 384.0m.; Freight ton-km 9.0m. (Source: IMF, *Republic of Mozambique—Recent Economic Developments* (December 1996)).

Communications Media

	1992	1993	1994
Radio receivers ('000 in use)	n.a.	n.a.	580
Television receivers ('000 in use)	44	54	55
Telephones ('000 main lines in use)	56	62	57
Daily newspapers:			
Number	2	n.a.	2
Average circulation ('000)	81	n.a.	81

Non-daily newspapers (1988): 2 (estimated average circulation 85,000).

Periodicals (1988): 5 (average circulation 2,263,000).

Book Production (1984): 66 titles (including 37 pamphlets); 3,490,000 copies (including 360,000 pamphlets).

Source: mainly UNESCO, *Statistical Yearbook.*

Education

(1995, unless otherwise indicated)

	Institutions	Teachers	Students: Males	Students: Females	Students: Total
Pre-primary*†	n.a.	n.a.	24,278	20,822	45,100
Primary†	4,149	24,575	823,295	592,133	1,415,428
Secondary:					
General	239‡	3,889‡	99,319†	66,549†	165,868†
Technical‡	31	826	n.a.	n.a.	13,816
Higher	3‡	877†§	3,893†§	1,357†§	5,250†§

* 1986 figures; data refer to initiation classes.

† Source: UNESCO, *Statistical Yearbook.*

‡ 1994 figure(s).

§ 1993 figure.

Directory

The Constitution

The Constitution came into force on 30 November 1990, replacing the previous version, introduced at independence on 25 June 1975 and revised in 1978. Its main provisions, as amended in 1996, are summarized below.

GENERAL PRINCIPLES

The Republic of Mozambique is an independent, sovereign, unitary and democratic state of social justice. Sovereignty resides in the people, who exercise it according to the forms laid down in the Constitution. The fundamental objectives of the Republic include:

The defence of independence and sovereignty;

the defence and promotion of human rights and of the equality of citizens before the law; and

the strengthening of democracy, of freedom and of social and individual stability.

POLITICAL PARTICIPATION

The people exercise power through universal, direct, equal, secret, personal and periodic suffrage to elect their representatives, by referenda and through permanent democratic participation. Political parties are prohibited from advocating or resorting to violence.

FUNDAMENTAL RIGHTS AND DUTIES OF CITIZENS

All citizens enjoy the same rights and are subject to the same duties, irrespective of colour, race, sex, ethnic origin, place of birth, religion, level of education, social position or occupation. In realizing the objectives of the Constitution, all citizens enjoy freedom of opinion, assembly and association. All citizens over 18 years of age are entitled to vote and be elected. Active participation in the defence of the country is the duty of every citizen. Individual freedoms are guaranteed by the State, including freedom of expression, of the press, of assembly, of association and of religion. The State guarantees accused persons the right to a legal defence. No Court or Tribunal has the power to impose a sentence of death upon any person.

STATE ORGANS

Public elective officers are chosen by elections through universal, direct, secret, personal and periodic vote. Legally-recognized political parties may participate in elections.

THE PRESIDENT

The President is the Head of State and of the Government, and Commander-in-Chief of the armed forces. The President is elected by direct, equal, secret and personal universal suffrage on a majority vote, and must be proposed by at least 10,000 voters, of whom at least 200 must reside in each province. The term of office is five years. A candidate may be re-elected on only two consecutive occasions, or again after an interval of five years between terms.

THE ASSEMBLY OF THE REPUBLIC

Legislative power is vested in the Assembly of the Republic. The Assembly is elected by universal direct adult suffrage on a secret ballot, and is composed of 250 Deputies. The Assembly is elected for a maximum term of five years, but may be dissolved by the President before the expiry of its term. The Assembly holds two ordinary sessions each year.

THE COUNCIL OF MINISTERS

The Council of Ministers is the Government of the Republic. The Prime Minister assists and advises the President in the leadership of the Government and presents the Government's programme, budget and policies to the Assembly, assisted by other ministers.

LOCAL STATE ORGANS

The Republic is administered in provinces, municipalities and administrative posts. The highest state organ in a province is the provincial government, presided over by a governor, who is answerable to the central Government. There shall be assemblies at each administrative level.

THE JUDICIARY

Judicial functions shall be exercised through the Supreme Court and other courts provided for in the law on the judiciary, which also subordinates them to the Assembly of the Republic. Courts must safeguard the principles of the Constitution and defend the rights and legitimate interests of citizens. Judges are independent, subject only to the law.

The Government

HEAD OF STATE

President of the Republic and Commander-in-Chief of the Armed Forces: JOAQUIM ALBERTO CHISSANO (took office 6 November 1986; elected President 27–29 October 1994).

COUNCIL OF MINISTERS
(August 1997)

Prime Minister: Dr PASCOAL MANUEL MOCUMBI.

Minister for Foreign Affairs and Co-operation: Dr LEONARD SANTOS SIMÃO.

Minister of National Defence: AGUIAR JONASSANE REGINALDO REAL MAZULA.

Minister of the Interior and Minister in the President's Office, with responsibility for Defence and Security Affairs: ALMERINDO DA CRUZ MARCOS MANHEJE.

Minister of State Administration: ALFREDO GAMITO.

Minister of Economic and Social Affairs: Dr ENEAS DA CONCEIÇÃO COMICHE.

Minister of Justice: JOSÉ IBRAIMO ABUDO.

Minister of Planning and Finance: TOMÁS AUGUSTO SALOMÃO.

Minister of Education: ARNALDO VALENTE NHAVOTO.

Minister of Parliamentary Affairs: FRANCISCO CAETANO J. MADEIRA.

Minister of Health: AURELIO ARMANDO ZILHÃO.

Minister of Mineral Resources and Energy: JOHN WILLIAM KACHAMILA.

Minister of Public Works and Housing: ROBERTO COSTLEY WHITE.

Minister of Environmental Co-ordination: BERNARDO PEDRO FERRAZ.

Minister of Culture, Youth and Sports: JOSÉ MATEUS MUARIA KATUPHA.

Minister of Labour: GUILHERME LUÍS MAVILA.

Minister of Agriculture and Fisheries: CARLOS AGOSTINHO DO ROSÁRIO.

Minister of Industry, Commerce and Tourism: OLDEMIRO J. BALOI.

Minister of Transport and Communications: PAULO MUXANGA.

Minister of Social Action Co-ordination: FILIPE MANDLATE (acting).

MINISTRIES

Office of the President: Avda Julius Nyerere, Maputo; tel. (1) 491121; telex 6243.

Ministry of Agriculture and Fisheries: Praça dos Heróis Moçambicanos, CP 1406, Maputo; tel. (1) 460010; telex 6195; fax (1) 460145.

Ministry of Culture, Youth and Sports: Avda Patrice Lumumba 1217, CP 1742, Maputo; tel. (1) 420068; telex 6621.

Ministry of Economic and Social Affairs: Maputo.

Ministry of Education: Avda 24 de Julho 167, Maputo; tel. (1) 492006; telex 6148; fax (1) 492196.

Ministry of Environmental Co-ordination: Maputo.

Ministry of Foreign Affairs and Co-operation: Avda Julius Nyerere 4, Maputo; tel. (1) 490218; telex 6418.

Ministry of Health: Avdas Eduardo Mondlane e Salvador Allende, CP 264, Maputo; tel. (1) 430814; telex 6239.

Ministry of Industry, Commerce and Tourism: Avda 25 de Setembro 1218, Maputo; tel. (1) 431029; telex 6235.

Ministry of Information: Avda Francisco Orlando Magumbwe 780, Maputo; tel. (1) 491087; telex 6487.

Ministry of the Interior: Avda Olof Palme 46/48, Maputo; tel. (1) 420130; telex 6487.

Ministry of Justice: Avda Julius Nyerere 33, Maputo; tel. (1) 490940; telex 6594; fax (1) 494264.

Ministry of Labour: Avda 24 de Julho 2351-2365, CP 281, Maputo; tel. (1) 427051; telex 6392.

Ministry of Mineral Resources and Energy: Avda Fernão de Magalhães 34, Maputo; tel. (1) 429615.

Ministry of National Defence: Avda Mártires de Mueda, Maputo; tel. (1) 492081; telex 6331.

Ministry of Parliamentary Affairs: Maputo.

Ministry of Planning and Finance: Praça da Marinha Popular, CP 272, Maputo; tel. (1) 425071; telex 6569.

Ministry of Public Works and Housing: Maputo.

Ministry of Social Action Co-ordination: Maputo.

Ministry of State Administration: Maputo.

Ministry of Transport and Communications: Avda Mártires de Inhaminga 306, Maputo; tel. (1) 430151; telex 6466.

PROVINCIAL GOVERNORS

Cabo Delgado Province: JORGE MUANAHUMO.

Gaza Province: EUGÉNIO NUMAIO.

Inhambane Province: FRANCISCO JOÃO PATEGUANA.

Manica Province: ARTUR USSENE CANANA.

Maputo Province: RAIMUNDO MANUEL BILA.

Nampula Province: ROSÁRIO MUALEIA.

Niassa Province: AIRES BONIFACIO.

Sofala Province: FELISBERTO PAULINO TOMÁS.

Tete Province: VIRGILIO FERRÃO.

Zambézia Province: ORLANDO CANDUA.

City of Maputo: JOÃO BAPTISTA COSMÉ.

President and Legislature

PRESIDENT

Presidential Election, 27–29 October 1994

	Votes	% of votes
JOAQUIM ALBERTO CHISSANO (Frelimo)	2,633,740	53.30
AFONSO MACACHO MARCETA DHLAKAMA (Renamo)	1,666,965	33.73
WEHIA MONAKACHO RIPUA (Pademo)	141,905	2.87
CARLOS ALEXANDRE DOS REIS (Unamo)	120,708	2.44
Dr MÁXIMO DIOGO JOSÉ DIAS (Monamo—PMSD)	115,442	2.34
VASCO CAMPIRA MAMBOYA ALFAZEMA (Pacode)	58,848	1.19
YAQUB NEVES SALOMÃO SIBINDY (Pimo)	51,070	1.03
Dr DOMINGOS ANTÓNIO MASCARENHAS AROUCA (Fumo—PCD)	37,767	0.76
CARLOS JOSÉ MARIA JEQUE (Independent)	34,588	0.70
CASIMIRO MIGUEL NHAMITHAMBO (Sol)	32,036	0.65
MARIO CARLOS MACHEL (Independent)	24,238	0.49
Dr PADIMBE MAHOSE KAMATI ANDREA (PPPM)	24,208	0.49
Total*	4,941,515	100.00

* Excluding 312,143 blank votes and 147,282 spoilt votes.

ASSEMBLÉIA DA REPÚBLICA

Chairman: EDUARDO MULEMBUE.

General Election, 27–29 October 1994

	Votes	% of votes	Seats
Frente de Libertação de Moçambique (Frelimo)	2,115,793	44.33	129
Resistência Nacional Moçambicana (Renamo)	1,803,506	37.78	112
União Democrática (UD)	245,793	5.15	9
Aliança Patriótica (AP)	93,051	1.95	—
Partido Social, Liberal e Democrático (Sol)	79,622	1.67	—
Frente Unida de Moçambique—Partido de Convergência Democrática (Fumo—PCD)	66,527	1.39	—
Partido de Convenção Nacional (PCN)	60,635	1.27	—
Partido Independente de Moçambique (Pimo)	58,590	1.23	—
Partido de Congresso Democrático (Pacode)	52,446	1.10	—
Partido de Progresso Popular de Moçambique (PPPM)	50,793	1.06	—
Partido de Renovação Democrático (PRD)	48,030	1.01	—
Partido Democrático de Moçambique (Pademo)	36,689	0.77	—
União Nacional Moçambicana (Unamo)	34,809	0.73	—
Partido do Trabalho (PT)	26,961	0.56	—
Total*	4,773,245	100.00	250

* Excluding 457,382 blank votes and 173,592 spoilt votes.

Political Organizations

Aliança Democrática de Moçambique (ADM): f. 1994; Co-ordinator JOSÉ PEREIRA BRANQUINHO.

Aliança Patriótica (AP): f. 1994; electoral alliance comprising:

Movimento Nacionalista Moçambicana—Partido Moçambicano da Social Democracia (Monamo—PMSD): Sec.-Gen. Dr MÁXIMO DIOGO JOSÉ DIAS.

Frente de Ação Patriótica (FAP): f. 1991; Pres. JOSÉ CARLOS PALAÇO; Sec.-Gen. RAUL DA CONCEIÇÃO.

Confederação Democrática de Moçambique (Codemo): f. 1991; Leader DOMINGOS CARDOSO.

Congresso Independente de Moçambique (Coinmo): Pres. VÍTOR MARCOS SAENE; Sec.-Gen. HILDA RABECA TSININE.

Frente de Libertação de Moçambique (Frelimo): Rua Pereiro do Lago, Maputo; f. 1962 by merger of three nationalist parties; reorg. 1977 as a 'Marxist-Leninist vanguard party'; in July 1989 abandoned its exclusive Marxist-Leninist orientation; Chair. JOAQUIM ALBERTO CHISSANO; Sec.-Gen. MANUEL TOMÉ.

Frente Unida de Moçambique—Partido de Convergência Democrática (Fumo—PCD): Pres. Dr DOMINGOS ANTÓNIO MASCARENHAS AROUCA.

Frente Unida de Salvação (FUS): f. 1994; alliance comprising:

Partido do Congresso Democrático (Pacode): Leader VASCO CAMPIRA MAMBOYA ALFAZEMA.

Partido Independente de Moçambique (Pimo): f. 1993; Sec.-Gen. MAGALHÃES BRAMUGY.

Partido de Progresso do Povo Moçambicano (PPPM): f. 1991; obtained legal status 1992; Pres. Dr PADIMBE MAHOSE KAMATI ANDREA; Sec.-Gen. CHE ABDALA.

Partido Renovador Democrático (PRD): obtained legal status 1994; Pres. MANECA DANIEL.

Partido do Trabalho (PT): f. 1993; breakaway faction of PPPM; Pres. MIGUEL MABOTE; Sec.-Gen. LUÍS MUCHANGA.

Partido Social, Liberal e Democrático (Sol): breakaway faction of Palmo; Leader CASIMIRO MIGUEL NHAMITHAMBO.

União Nacional Moçambicana (Unamo): f. 1987; breakaway faction of Renamo; social democratic; obtained legal status 1992; Pres. CARLOS ALEXANDRE DOS REIS; Sec.-Gen. FLORENCIA JOÃO DA SILVA.

Partido Agrário de Moçambique (PAM): f. 1991.

Partido Comunista de Moçambique (Pacomo): f. 1995.

Partido de Convenção Nacional (PCN): obtained legal status Dec. 1992; Chair. LUTERO CHIMBIRIMBIRI SIMANGO; Sec.-Gen. Dr GABRIEL MABUNDA.

Partido Democrático de Libertação de Moçambique (Padelimo): based in Kenya; Pres. JOAQUIM JOSÉ NIOTA.

Partido Democrático de Moçambique (Pademo): f. 1991; obtained legal status 1993; Co-ordinator WEHIA MONAKACHO RIPUA; Gen. Sec. GIMO GUINDILA.

Partido Internacionalista Democrático de Moçambique (Pidemo): f. 1993; Leader JOÃO KAMACHO.

Partido Patriótico Independente de Moçambique: f. 1995; breakaway faction of Pimo.

Partido Progressivo e Liberal Federalista das Comunidades Religiosas de Moçambique (PPLFCRM): f. 1992; Pres. NEVES SERRANO.

Partido Revolucionário do Povo Socialista Unido de Moçambique (Prepsumo): f. 1992.

Partido Social Democrático (PSD): Leader CARLOS MACHEL.

Partido de Todos os Nativos Moçambicanos (Partonamo): f. 1996; Leader MUSSAGY ABDUL REMANE.

Regedores e Camponeses de Moçambique (Recamo): f. by ARONE SIJAMO.

Resistência Nacional Moçambicana (Renamo): also known as Movimento Nacional da Resistência de Moçambique (MNR); f. 1976; fmr guerrilla group, in conflict with the Govt between 1976 and Oct. 1992; registered as a political party Aug. 1994; Pres. AFONSO MACACHO MARCETA DHLAKAMA; Sec.-Gen. FRANCISCO XAVIER MARCELINO.

União Democrática (UD): f. 1994; Gen. Sec. ANTÓNIO PALANGE; coalition comprising:

Partido Liberal e Democrático de Moçambique (Palmo): obtained legal status 1993; Chair. MARTINS BILAL; Pres. ANTÓNIO PALANGE.

Partido Nacional Democrático (Panade): obtained legal status 1993; Leader JOSÉ CHICUARRA MASSINGA.

Partido Nacional de Moçambique (Panamo): Pres. MARCOS JUMA.

União Democrática de Moçambique (Udemo): f. 1987 as the mil. wing of Unamo, from which it broke away in 1991; adopted present name in April 1992; Leader GIMO PHIRI.

The following armed separatist group was operating in Zambézia province in 1994:

Rombézia: aims to establish separate state in northern Mozambique between Rovuma and Zambezi rivers; reported to receive support from Portuguese residents in Malawi; Leader MANUEL ROCHA.

Diplomatic Representation

EMBASSIES AND HIGH COMMISSIONS IN MOZAMBIQUE

Algeria: CP 1709, Maputo; tel. (1) 492070; telex 6554; fax (1) 490582; Ambassador: ABDELHAMID BOUBAZINE.

Angola: Maputo; Ambassador: PAULO CONDENÇA DE CARVALHO.

Belgium: CP 1500, Maputo; tel. (1) 490077; telex 6511; Ambassador: MICHEL VANTROYEN.

Brazil: Avda Kenneth Kaunda 296, CP 1167, Maputo; tel. (1) 492388; fax (1) 490986; Ambassador: LUCIANO OZORIO ROSA.

Bulgaria: CP 4689, Maputo; tel. (1) 491471; telex 6324; Ambassador: IVAN MARINOV SOKOLARSKI.

China, People's Republic: CP 4668, Maputo; tel. (1) 491560; Ambassador: MI SHIHENG.

Congo, Democratic Republic: CP 2407, Maputo; tel. (1) 492170; telex 6316; fax: 492170; Ambassador: W'EBER M.-B. ANGELO.

Congo, Republic: Avda Kenneth Kaunda 783, CP 4743, Maputo; tel. (1) 490142; telex 6207; Ambassador: EMILIENNE BOTOKA.

Cuba: CP 387, Maputo; tel. (1) 491905; telex 6359; Ambassador: JOSÉ ESPINOSA.

Czech Republic: CP 1463, Maputo; tel. (1) 491484; telex 6216.

Denmark: Avda 24 de Julho 1500, CP 4588, Maputo; tel. (1) 420172; telex 6164; fax (1) 420557; Ambassador: OLE BLICHER-OLSEN.

Egypt: CP 4662, Maputo; tel. (1) 491118; telex 6417; Ambassador: MOHAMED HINDAM.

France: Avda Julius Nyerere 2361, CP 4781, Maputo; tel. (1) 490444; telex 6307; Ambassador: DIDIER DESTREMEAU.

Germany: Rua de Mapulangwene 506, CP 1595; Maputo; tel. (1) 492714; telex 6489; fax (1) 494888; Ambassador: HELMUT RAU.

Holy See: Avda Julius Nyerere 882, CP 2738, Maputo; tel. (1) 491144; fax (1) 492217; Apostolic Nuncio: Most Rev. PETER STEPHAN ZURBRIGGEN, Titular Archbishop of Glastonia (Glastonbury).

India: Avda Kenneth Kaunda 167, Maputo; tel. (1) 490584; telex 6452; fax (1) 492364; High Commissioner: SURENDRA KUMAR.

Iran: Avda Mártires da Machava 1630, Maputo; tel. (1) 490700; telex 6159; fax (1) 492005; Ambassador: ABDOLALI TAVAKKOLI.

Italy: Avda Kenneth Kaunda 387, CP 976, Maputo; tel. (1) 491605; telex 6442; Ambassador: UGO G. DE MOHR.

Libya: CP 4434, Maputo; tel. (1) 490662; telex 6475; Ambassador: MUHAMMAD AHMAD AL-AMARY.

Malawi: CP 4148, Maputo; tel. (1) 491468; telex 6300; High Commissioner: Rev. E. CHINKWITA-PHIRI.

Netherlands: CP 1163, Maputo; tel. (1) 490031; telex 6178; fax (1) 490429; Ambassador: R. A. VORNIS.

Nicaragua: Maputo; tel. (1) 490810; telex 6245; Ambassador: CARLOS JOSÉ GARCÍA CASTILLO.

Nigeria: CP 4693, Maputo; tel. (1) 490105; telex 6414; High Commissioner: ISAIAH UDOYEN.

Norway: CP 828, Maputo; tel. (1) 429411; telex 6556; fax (1) 429410; Ambassador: SIGURD ENDRESEN.

Poland: Rua D. João IV 22, Maputo; tel. (1) 490284; Ambassador: MIROSŁAW DACKIEWICZ.

Portugal: Avda Julius Nyerere 730, CP 4696, Maputo; tel. (1) 490431; telex 1172; fax (1) 491127; Ambassador: RUI GONÇALO CHAVES DE BRITO E CUNHA.

Romania: CP 4648, Maputo; tel. (1) 492999; telex 6397; Chargé d'affaires a.i.: VALERIU NICOLAE.

Russia: Avda Agostinho Neto 1103, CP 4666, Maputo; tel. (1) 420091; telex 6635; Ambassador: VALERII GAMAIOUN.

South Africa: Avda Julius Nyerere 745, CP 1120, Maputo; tel. (1) 493030; telex 6376; fax (1) 493029; High Commissioner: MANGISI C. ZITHA.

Spain: Rua Damião de Gois 347, CP 1331, Maputo; tel. (1) 492025; telex 6579; fax (1) 492055; Ambassador: JOSÉ EUGENIO SALARICH.

Swaziland: CP 4711, Maputo; tel. (1) 492117; telex 6353; High Commissioner: Mr MABUZA.

Sweden: Avda Julius Nyerere 1128, CP 338, Maputo; tel. (1) 490091; telex 6272; fax (1) 490056; Ambassador: HELENA ÖDMARK.

Switzerland: CP 135, Maputo; tel. (1) 492432; telex 6233; Chargé d'affaires a.i.: JEAN PIERRE BALLAMAR.

United Kingdom: Avda Vladimir I. Lénine 310, CP 55, Maputo; tel. (1) 420111; telex 6265; fax (1) 421666; High Commissioner: BERNARD EVERETT.

USA: Avda Kenneth Kaunda 193, CP 783, Maputo; tel. (1) 492797; Ambassador: BRIAN DEAN CURRAN (designate).

Zambia: CP 4655, Maputo; tel. (1) 492452; telex 6415; fax (1) 491893; High Commissioner: Brig.-Gen. B. B. CHISUTA.

Zimbabwe: CP 743, Maputo; tel. (1) 490404; telex 6542; High Commissioner: JOHN MAYOWE.

Judicial System

The Constitution of November 1990 provides for a Supreme Court and other judicial courts, an Administrative Court, courts-martial, customs courts, maritime courts and labour courts. The Supreme Court consists of professional judges, appointed by the President of the Republic, and judges elected by the Assembly of the Republic. It acts in sections, as a trial court of primary and appellate jurisdiction, and in plenary session, as a court of final appeal. The Administrative Court controls the legality of administrative acts and supervises public expenditure.

President of the Supreme Court: MÁRIO MANGAZE.

Attorney-General: SINAI NHATITIMA.

Religion

There are an estimated 5m. Christians and 4m. Muslims, as well as a small Hindu community. Many inhabitants follow traditional beliefs.

CHRISTIANITY

In 1975 educational and medical facilities that had hitherto been administered by churches were acquired by the State. In June 1988 the Government announced that these facilities were to be returned.

Conselho Cristão de Moçambique (Christian Council of Mozambique): Avda Ahmed Sekou Touré 1822, Maputo; tel. (1) 425102; telex 6119; fax (1) 421968; f. 1948; 22 mems; Pres. Rt Rev. BERNARDINO MANDLATE; Gen. Sec. Rev. LUCAS AMOSSE.

The Roman Catholic Church

Mozambique comprises three archdioceses and nine dioceses. At 31 December 1995 adherents represented some 16.7% of the total population.

Bishops' Conference: Conferência Episcopal de Moçambique, Secretariado Geral, Avda Armando Tivene 1701, CP 286, Maputo; tel. (1) 492174; telex 6101; fax (1) 490766; f. 1982; Pres. Rt Rev. FRANCISCO JOÃO SILOTA, Bishop of Chimoio.

Archbishop of Beira: Most Rev. JAIME PEDRO GONÇALVES, Cúria Arquiepiscopal, CP 544, Beira; tel. (3) 322313; fax (3) 327639.

Archbishop of Maputo: Cardinal ALEXANDRE JOSÉ MARIA DOS SANTOS, Paço Arquiepiscopal, Avda Eduardo Mondlane 1448, CP 258, Maputo; tel. (1) 426240; fax (1) 421873.

Archbishop of Nampula: Most Rev. MANUEL VIEIRA PINTO, Paço Arquiepiscopal, CP 84, Nampula; tel. (6) 213025; fax (6) 214194.

The Anglican Communion

Anglicans in Mozambique are adherents of the Church of the Province of Southern Africa. There are two dioceses in Mozambique. The Metropolitan of the Province is the Archbishop of Cape Town, South Africa.

Bishop of Lebombo: Rt Rev. DINIS SALOMÃO SENGULANE, CP 120, Maputo; tel. (1) 734364; telex 6119; fax (1) 401093.

Bishop of Niassa: Rt Rev. PAULINO TOMÁS MANHIQUE, Missão Anglicana de Messumba, Metangula, CP 264, Lichinga, Niassa.

Other Churches

Baptist Convention of Mozambique: Avda Maguiguane 386, CP 852, Maputo; tel. (1) 26852; Pres. Rev. BENTO BARTOLOMEU MATUSSE.

Free Methodist Church: Pres. Rev. LUÍS WANELA.

Presbyterian Church of Mozambique: Avda Ahmed Sekou Touré 1822, CP 21, Maputo; tel. (1) 422950; telex 421968; fax (1) 428066; 80,000 adherents; Pres. of Synodal Council Rev. SIMÃO CHAMANGO.

Other denominations active in Mozambique include the Church of Christ, the Church of the Nazarene, the Reformed Church in Mozambique, the United Congregational Church of Mozambique, the United Methodist Church of Mozambique, and the Wesleyan Methodist Church.

ISLAM

Islamic Congress of Mozambique: represents Sunni Muslims; Chair. HASSANE MAKDÁ.

Islamic Council of Mozambique: Leader Sheikh ABOOBACAR ISMAEL MANGIRÁ.

The Press

DAILIES

Diário de Moçambique: Rua D. João de Mascarenhas, CP 81, Beira; tel. (3) 322501; telex 7347; f. 1981; under state management since Sept. 1991; Dir EZEQUIEL AMBROSIO; Editor FARUCO SADIQUE; circ. 16,000.

Imparcial Fax: CP 2517, Maputo; tel. (1) 428548; fax (1) 428547; news-sheet by subscription only, distribution by fax; sympathetic to Renamo; Editor MIGUIS LOPES, Jr.

Mediafax: Avda Mártires da Machava 1002, Maputo; tel. (1) 490906; telex 6233; fax (1) 490063; f. by co-operative of independent journalists Mediacoop; news-sheet by subscription only, distribution by fax.

Metical: Maputo; f. 1997; news-sheet, distribution by fax; Editor CARLOS CARDOSO.

Notícias: Rua Joaquim Lapa 55, CP 327, Maputo; tel. (1) 420119; telex 6453; fax (1) 420575; f. 1926; morning; under state management since Sept. 1991; Dir BERNARDO MAVANGA; Editor HILARIO COSSA; circ. 33,000.

WEEKLIES

Demos: Avda Ho Chi Min 1436, CP 2011, Maputo; Dir NOE DIMANDE; Editor ELIAS COSSA.

Desafio: Rua Joaquim Lapa 55, Maputo.

Domingo: Rua Joaquim Lapa 55, CP 327, Maputo; tel. (1) 431026; telex 6453; fax (1) 431027; f. 1981; Sun.; Dir JORGE MATINE; Editor MOISES MABUNDA; circ. 25,000.

Savana: c/o Mediacoop, Avda Amílcar Cabral 1049, CP 73, Maputo; tel. (1) 430106; fax (1) 430721; f. 1994; Dir KOK NAM; Editor SALOMÃO MOYOANA.

Tempo: Avda Ahmed Sekou Touré 1078, CP 2917, Maputo; tel. (1) 26191; telex 6486; f. 1970; magazine; under state management since Sept. 1991; Dir ROBERTO UAENE; Editor ARLINDO LANGA; circ. 40,000.

PERIODICALS

Agricultura: Instituto Nacional de Investigação Agronómica, CP 3658, Maputo; tel. (1) 30091; f. 1982; quarterly; publ. by Centro de Documentação de Agricultura, Silvicultura, Pecuária e Pescas.

Aro: Avda 24 de Julho 1420, CP 4187, Maputo; f. 1995; monthly; Dir Policarto Tamele; Editor Bruno Macame, Jr.

Arquivo Histórico: CP 2033, Maputo; tel. (1) 421177; fax (1) 423428; f. 1987; Editor João Paulo Borges Coelho.

Boletim da República: Avda Vladimir I. Lénine, CP 275, Maputo; govt and official notices; publ. by Imprensa Nacional da Moçambique.

Moçambique–Informação Estatística: Comissão Nacional do Plano, CP 2051, Maputo; f. 1982; publ. by Centro de Documentação Económica.

Moçambique–Novos Tempos: Avda Ahmed Sekou Touré 657, Maputo; tel. (1) 493564; fax (1) 493590; f. 1992; Dir J. Mascarenhas.

Mozambiquefile: c/o AIM, Rua da Radio Moçambique, CP 896, Maputo; tel. (1) 430795; telex 6430; fax (1) 421906; e-mail AIM@AIMMPTO.VEM.MZ; monthly; Editor-in-Chief Ricardo Malate.

Mozambique Inview: c/o Mediacoop, Avda Amílcar Cabral 1049, CP 73, Maputo; tel. (1) 430106; fax (1) 430721; f. 1994; two a month; Editor Gil Lauriciano.

Novos Tempos: monthly; Renamo-owned.

Portos e Caminhos de Ferro: CP 276, Maputo; English and Portuguese; ports and railways; quarterly.

Revista Médica de Moçambique: Instituto Nacional de Saúde, Ministério da Saúde e Faculdade de Medicina, Universidade Eduardo Mondlane, CP 264, Maputo; tel. (1) 420368; telex 6239; fax (1) 423726; f. 1982; 4 a year; medical journal; Editor Rui Gama Vaz.

NEWS AGENCIES

Agência de Informação de Moçambique (AIM): Rua da Rádio Moçambique, CP 896, Maputo; tel. (1) 430795; telex 6430; fax (1) 421906; e-mail AIM@AIMMPTO.VEM.MZ; f. 1975; daily reports in Portuguese and English; Dir Ricardo Malate.

Foreign Bureaux

Agence France-Presse (AFP): CP 4650, Maputo; tel. (1) 422940; fax (1) 422940; Correspondent Rachel Waterhouse.

Agência Lusa de Informação (Portugal): Avda Ho Chi Min 111, Maputo; tel. (1) 427591; fax (1) 421690; Bureau Chief Carlos Lobato.

Agenzia Nazionale Stampa Associata (ANSA) (Italy): Maputo; tel. (1) 430723; telex 6252; fax (1) 421906; Correspondent Paul Fauvet.

Reuters (UK) is also represented in Mozambique.

Publishers

Arquivo Histórico: CP 2033, Maputo; tel. (1) 421177; fax (1) 423428; Dir Inês Nogueira da Costa.

Editora Minerva Central: Rua Consiglieri Pedroso 84, CP 212, Maputo; telex 6561; f. 1908; stationers and printers, educational, technical and medical textbooks; Man. Dir J. F. Carvalho.

Empresa Moderna Lda: Avda 25 de Setembro, CP 473, Maputo; tel. (1) 424594; f. 1937; fiction, history, textbooks; Gen. Dir Fernando Henrique dos Santos António.

Instituto Nacional do Livro e do Disco: Avda 24 de Julho 1921, CP 4030, Maputo; tel. (1) 34870; telex 6288; govt publishing and purchasing agency; Dir Arménio Correia.

Government Publishing House

Imprensa Nacional de Moçambique: CP 275, Maputo.

Radio and Television

According to UNESCO, there were an estimated 580,000 radio receivers and 55,000 television receivers in use in 1994.

RADIO

Rádio Moçambique: CP 2000, Maputo; tel. (1) 421814; telex 6712; fax (1) 421816; f. 1975; programmes in Portuguese, English and vernacular languages; Chair. Manuel Fernando Veterano.

By January 1995 the Government had issued licences to 13 private radio stations. Of those, only three were broadcasting at that time.

Voz da Renamo: owned by former rebel movement Renamo; transmitters in Maputo and Gorongosa, Sofala province.

Rádio Miramar: owned by Brazilian religious sect, the Universal Church of the Kingdom of God.

TELEVISION

Radio Televisão Klint (RTK): Avda Agostinho Neto 946, Maputo; tel. (1) 422956; fax (1) 493306; Dir Carlos Klint.

Televisão de Moçambique (TVM): Avda Julius Nyerere 942, CP 2675, Maputo; tel. (1) 493452; fax (1) 492756; f. 1981; Pres. António Júlio Botelho Moniz; Dir Júlio Bicá.

Finance

(cap. = capital; res = reserves; dep. = deposits; m. = million; brs = branches; amounts in meticais)

BANKING

Central Bank

Banco de Moçambique: Avda 25 de Setembro 1695, CP 423, Maputo; tel. (1) 428151; telex 6240; fax (1) 421912; f. 1975; bank of issue; cap. 50,000m. (1994); Gov. Adriano Afonso Maleiane.

Commercial Banks

Banco Comercial e de Investimento (BCI): Avda 25 de Setembro 1230, Maputo; 60% owned by Caixa Geral de Depósitos (Portugal); Chair. and Man. Dir Abdul Magide Ousmane; 2 brs.

Banco Comercial de Moçambique: Avda 25 de Setembro 1800, CP 865, Maputo; tel. (1) 428408; telex 6358; fax (1) 425292; f. 1992 to take over commercial banking activities of Central Bank; 51% transferred to private ownership in 1996, 49% state-owned; cap. 30,000m., dep. 1,054,445m. (1993); Pres. Dr José Lopes Palma; Gen. Man. Natalino Bruno de Morais; 47 brs and agencies.

Banco Internacional de Moçambique (BIM): Avda Samora Machel 247, CP 2657, Maputo; tel. (1) 422095; fax (1) 423208; f. 1995; 50% owned by Banco Comercial Português SA, 45% state-owned, 5% owned by Community Development Foundation; Chair. Dr Mário Fernandes da Graça Machungo; Man. Dir Dr José Alberto de Lima Félix.

Banco Popular de Desenvolvimento: Avda 25 de Setembro 1184, CP 757, Maputo; tel. (1) 428125; telex 6250; fax (1) 423470; f. 1977; partial privatization pending in 1997, state to retain 51%; cap. and res 18,765m., dep. 441,203m. (1993); Chair. Boaventura Celestino Cossa; 193 brs and agencies.

Banco Standard Totta de Moçambique, SARL: Praça 25 de Junho 1, CP 2086, Maputo; tel. (1) 424597; telex 6223; fax (1) 426967; f. 1966; 55% owned by Banco Totta e Açores, SA, 41% owned by Standard Chartered Bank; cap. and res 51,363m., dep. 1,025,500m. (1996); Man. Dir Dr António José Martins Galamba; 24 brs.

Creditcoop—Cooperativa de Crédito e Investimento, SARL: Avda Kenneth Kaunda 682, CP 2930, Maputo; tel. (1) 423349; f. 1994; cap. 1,000m. (1994); Chair. Jacinto Veloso.

Foreign Banks

Banco de Fomento e Exterior SA (Portugal): Avda Vladimir Lenine 624, CP 4233, Maputo; tel. (1) 423915; telex 6947; fax (1) 423981; Gen. Man. Carlos Mendes Alves.

Banco Português do Atlântico (Portugal): Avda 24 de Julho 2096, CP 1717, Maputo; tel. (1) 430954; telex 6957; fax (1) 430241; Gen. Man. Alfredo Primavera.

DEVELOPMENT FUND

Fundo de Desenvolvimento Agrícola e Rural: CP 1406, Maputo; tel. (1) 460349; fax (1) 460157; f. 1987 to provide credit for small farmers and rural co-operatives; promotes agricultural and rural development; Sec. Eduardo Oliveira.

INSURANCE

In December 1991 the Assembléia da República approved legislation terminating the state monopoly of insurance and reinsurance activities.

Empresa Moçambicana de Seguros, EE (EMOSE): Avda 25 de Setembro 1383, CP 1165, Maputo; tel. (1) 422095; telex 6280; f. 1977 as state insurance monopoly; took over business of 24 fmr cos; privatization pending in 1997; cap. 150m.; Gen. Dir Venancio Mondlane.

Seguradora Internacional de Moçambique: Maputo; tel. (1) 422095; fax (1) 423208; Pres. Mário Fernandes da Graça Machungo.

Trade and Industry

CHAMBER OF COMMERCE

Câmara de Comércio de Moçambique: Rua Mateus Sansão Mutemba 452, CP 1836, Maputo; tel. (1) 491970; telex 6498; fax (1) 492211; Pres. Carlos Klint.

INVESTMENT ORGANIZATION

Centro de Promoção de Investimentos (CPI): POB 4635, Maputo; tel. (1) 422456; telex 6876; fax (1) 422459; encourages foreign investment and jt ventures with foreign firms; evaluates and negotiates investment proposals; Dir FERNANDO SUMBANA.

STATE FOREIGN-TRADING ENTERPRISES

Citrinos de Manica, EE: Avda 25 de Setembro, Chimoio, CP 15, Manica; tel. (51) 42316; exports citrus and tropical fruit; Dir OSIAS M. MANJATE.

Citrinos de Maputo, EE: Avda 25 de Setembro 1509, 6° andar, CP 1659, Maputo; tel. (1) 421857; telex 6538; exports citrus fruits; Dir Gen. MAURÍCIO MOTY CARIMO.

Companhia de Desenvolvimento Mineiro (CDM): Avda 24 de Julho 1895, 1°–2° andares, CP 1152, Maputo; tel. (1) 429170; telex 6413; fax (1) 428921; exports marble, tantalite, asbestos anthophylite, beryl, bentonite, agates, precious and semi-precious stones; Dir LUÍS JOSSENE.

Companhia Industrial de Cordoarias de Moçambique (CICOMO), SARL: Avda Zedequias Manganhela 520, 4° andar, CP 4113, Maputo; tel. (1) 427272; telex 6347; sisal; Dir CARLOS CORDEIRO.

Distribuidora de Materiais de Construção (DIMAC): Avda Zedequias Manganhela 520, 11° andar, CP 222, Maputo; tel. (1) 423308; telex 6343; fax (1) 422805; f. 1979; building materials; transfer pending to private ownership; Dir RUI FERNANDES.

Empresa de Comércio Externo de Equipamentos Industriais (INTERMÁQUINA): Rua Consiglieri Pedroso 165, CP 808, Maputo; tel. (1) 424056; telex 6543; industrial equipment and accessories; Dir KONG LAM.

Empresa Distribuidora de Equipamento Eléctrico e Electrónico e Componentes (INTERELECTRA): Avda Samora Machel 162, CP 1159, Maputo; tel. (1) 427091; telex 6203; fax (1) 420723; electrical equipment and components; Dir FRANCISCO PAULO CUCHE.

Empresa Distribuidora e Importadora de Metais (INTERMETAL): Rua Com. Baeta Neves 53, CP 1162, Maputo; tel. (1) 422770; telex 6372; metals and metal products; Man. Dir JORGE SILVESTRE LUÍS GUINDA.

Empresa Estatal de Hidráulica (HIDROMOC): Avda do Trabalho 1501, CP 193, Maputo; tel. (1) 400181; telex 6234; fax (1) 400043; irrigation equipment and chemicals for water treatment; transfer to private ownership pending; Dir EDUARDO J. NHACULE.

Empresa Estatal de Importação e Exportação de Medicamentos (MEDIMOC): Avda Julius Nyerere 500, 1° andar, CP 600, Maputo; tel. (1) 491211; telex 6260; fax (1) 490168; pharmaceuticals, medical equipment and supplies; Gen. Dir RENATO RONDA.

Empresa Moçambicana de Apetrechamento da Indústria Pesqueira (EQUIPESCA): Avda Zedequias Manganhela 520, CP 2342, Maputo; tel. (1) 27630; telex 6284; fishing equipment; transfer to private ownership pending; Dir JOAQUIM MARTINS DA CRUZ.

Empresa Moçambicana de Importação e Exportação de Produtos Pesqueiros (PESCOM Internacional): Rua Consiglieri Pedroso 343, 4° andar, CP 1570, Maputo; tel. (1) 421734; telex 6409; fax (1) 24961; f. 1978; imports and exports fish products; transfer to private ownership pending; Dir FELISBERTO MANUEL.

Empresa Moçambicana de Importação e Exportação de Produtos Químicos e Plásticos (INTERQUIMICA): Rua de Bagamoyo 333, CP 2268, Maputo; tel. (1) 423168; telex 6274; fax (1) 21229; chemicals, fertilizers, pesticides, plastics, paper; Dir AURÉLIO RICARDO CHIZIANE.

Empresa Nacional de Carvão de Moçambique (CARBOMOC): Rua Joaquim Lapa 108, CP 1773, Maputo; tel. (1) 427625; telex 6413; fax (1) 424714; f. 1948; mineral extraction and export; transfer to private ownership pending; Dir JAIME RIBEIRO.

Empresa Nacional de Importação e Exportação de Veículos Motorizadas (INTERMECANO): Rua Consiglieri Pedroso 165, CP 1280, Maputo; tel. (1) 430221; telex 6505; motor cycles, cars, trucks, buses, construction plant, agricultural machinery, spare parts; Dir RODRIGO DE OLIVEIRA.

Empresa Nacional Petróleos de Moçambique (PETROMOC): Praça dos Trabalhadores 9, CP 417, Maputo; tel. (1) 427191; telex 6382; fax (1) 430181; f. 1977 to take over the Sonarep oil refinery and its associated distribution co; state directorate for liquid fuels within Mozambique, incl. petroleum products passing through Mozambique to inland countries; Dir MANUEL PATRÍCIO DA CRUZ VIOLA.

ENACOMO, SARL (Empresa Nacional de Comércio): Avda Samora Machel 285, 1° andar, CP 698, Maputo; tel. (1) 430172; telex 6387; fax (1) 427754; f. 1976; imports, exports, procurement, investment; Man. Dir CARLOS PACHECO FARIA.

Importadora de Bens de Consumo (IMBEC): Rua da Mesquita 33, CP 4229, Maputo; tel. (1) 421455; telex 6350; fax (1) 423650; f. 1982; import of consumer goods; transfer pending to private ownership; Man. Dir CARLOS COSSA.

Lojas Francas de Moçambique (INTERFRANCA): Rua Timor Leste 106, CP 1206, Maputo; tel. (1) 425199; telex 6403; fax (1) 431044; music equipment, motor cars, handicrafts, furniture; Gen. Dir CARLOS E. N. RIBEIRO.

Riopele Têxteis de Moçambique, SARL: Rua Joaquim Lapa 21, CP 1658, Maputo; tel. (1) 31331; telex 6371; fax (1) 422902; textiles; Dir CARLOS RIBEIRO.

OTHER MAJOR STATE ENTERPRISES

Comércio Grossista de Produtos Alimentares (COGROPA): Avda 25 de Setembro 874–896, CP 308, Maputo; tel. (1) 428655; telex 6370; food supplies; transfer pending to private ownership; Dir ANTÓNIO BAPTISTA DO AMARAL.

Companhia da Zambézia, SARL: Avda Samora Machel 245, 4° andar, CP 617, Maputo; tel. (1) 420639; telex 6380; fax (1) 421507; f. 1892; agriculture; Dirs JOSÉ BENTO VEDOR, JOÃO FORTE, CARLOS DE MATOS.

Companhia Siderurgica de Moçambique (CSM), SARL: Avda Nuno Alvares 566, CP 441, Maputo; tel. (1) 401281; telex 6262; fax (1) 400400; steel; Technical Man. HERLANDER PEDROSO.

Companhia Industrial do Monapo, SARL: Avda do Trabalho 2106, CP 1248, Maputo; tel. (1) 400290; telex 6249; fax (1) 401164; animal and vegetable oils and soap; CEO CARMEN RAMOS.

Electricidade de Moçambique: Avda Agostinho Neto 70, CP 2447, Maputo; tel. (1) 492011; telex 6407; production and distribution of electric energy; Dir FERNANDO RAMOS JULIÃO.

Empresa de Construções Metálicas (ECOME): Avda das Industrias-Machava, CP 1358, Maputo; tel. (1) 752282; agricultural equipment; Dir JUSTINO LUCAS.

Empresa de Gestão e Assistência Técnica ao Equipamento Agrícola (MECANAGRO): Avda das FPLM 184, CP 2727, Maputo; tel. (1) 460016; telex 6344; agricultural machinery; Dir RAGENDRA DE SOUSA.

Empresa Metalúrgica de Moçambique, SARL: Avda de Moçambique 1500, CP 1316, Maputo; tel. (1) 475189; telex 6499; fax (1) 475149; f. 1951; metallurgical products; Dir JOÃO GARROCHINHO.

Empresa Moçambicana de Malhas (EMMA), SARL: Avda Zedequias Manganhela 488, CP 2663, Maputo; tel. (1) 423112; telex 6813; textiles; Admin. AMADE OSSUMANE.

Empresa Moçambicana de Chá (EMOCHÁ): Avda Zedequias Manganhela 250, Maputo; tel. (1) 424779; telex 6519; tea production; transfer pending to private ownership; Dir MARCOS BASTOS.

Empresa Nacional de Calçado e Têxteis (ENCATEX): Avda 24 de Julho 2969, CP 67, Maputo; tel. (1) 731258; telex 6421; footwear and textiles; Dir SOVERANO BELCHIOR.

Empresa Nacional de Hidrocarbonetos de Moçambique (ENHM): Avda Fernão de Magalhães 34, CP 2904, Maputo; tel. (1) 460083; telex 6478; controls concessions for petroleum exploration and production; Dir MÁRIO MARQUES.

Empresa Provincial (AVICOLA) EE: Avda 25 de Setembro 1676, CP 4202, Maputo; tel. (1) 34738; Dir MÁRIO BERNARDO.

Fábricas Associadas de Óleos (FASOL), SARL: Avda de Namaacha, CP 1128, Maputo; tel. (1) 723186; telex 6070; oils; transfer pending to private ownership; Dir CARLOS COSTA.

Forjadora, SARL—Fábrica Moçambicana de Equipamentos Industriais: Avda de Angola 2850, CP 3078, Maputo; tel. (1) 465537; telex 6107; fax (1) 465211; metal structures; Man. Dir. JORGE MORGADO.

Indústria Moçambicana de Aço (IMA), SARL: Avda 24 de Julho 2373, 12° andar, CP 2566, Maputo; tel. (1) 421141; telex 6323; fax (1) 423446; steel; Dir MANUEL JOSÉ SEREJO.

Moçambique-Industrial, SARL: Rua Aruangua 39, 1° andar, CP 432, Beira; tel. (3) 322123; telex 7352; fax (3) 325347; vegetable oils and soap; Dir JOSÉ BARROS CARDOSO.

Química-Geral, SARL: Língamo-Matola, CP 15, Maputo; tel. (1) 424713; telex 6448; fertilizers; Dir ALFREDO BADURU.

Sena Sugar Estate Lda: Avda 25 de Setembro 2801, CP 361, Maputo; tel. (1) 427610; telex 6422; fax (1) 426753; fmrly British-owned; govt-administered since 1978; plantations and mills in Sofala and Zambézia provinces; Dir HERMINIO MACHADO.

Texlom, SARL: Avda Filipe Samuel Magaia 514, CP 194, Maputo; telex 6289; textiles; Dir JOSÉ AUGUSTO TOMO PSICO.

TRADE UNIONS

Freedom to form trade unions, and the right to strike, are guaranteed under the 1990 Constitution.

Organização dos Trabalhadores de Moçambique—Central Sindical (OTM—CS) (Mozambique Workers' Organization—Trade Union Headquarters): Rua Manuel António de Sousa 36, Maputo; tel. (1) 426477; telex 6116; fax (1) 421671; f. 1983 as trade union fed. to replace fmr production councils; officially recognized in 1990; 200,000 mems (1993); Pres. JOAQUIM FANHEIRO; Secs-Gen. AUGUSTO MACAMO, SOARES BUNHAZA NHACA.

Sindicato Nacional dos Trabalhadores Agro-Pecuários e Florestais (SINTAF): Avda 25 de Setembro 1676, 1° andar, Maputo; tel. (1) 431182; Sec.-Gen. EUSÉBIO LUÍS CHIVULELE.

Sindicato Nacional dos Trabalhadores da Aviação Civil, Correios e Comunicações (SINTAC): Avda 25 de Setembro 1509, 2° andar, No 5, Maputo; tel. (1) 30996; Sec.-Gen. MANUEL SANTOS DOS REIS.

Sindicato Nacional dos Trabalhadores do Comércio, Banca e Seguros (SINTCOBASE): Avda Ho Chi Min 365, 1° andar, CP 2142, Maputo; tel. (1) 426271; Sec.-Gen. AMÓS JÚNIOR MATSINHE.

Sindicato Nacional dos Trabalhadores da Indústria do Açúcar (SINTIA): Avda das FPLM 1912, Maputo; tel. (1) 460108; f. 1989; Sec.-Gen. ALEXANDRE CÂNDIDO MUNGUAMBE.

Sindicato Nacional dos Trabalhadores da Indústria Alimentar e Bebidas (SINTIAB): Avda Eduardo Mondlane 1267, CP 394, Maputo; tel. (1) 424709; Sec.-Gen. SAMUEL FENIAS MATSINHE.

Sindicato Nacional dos Trabalhadores da Indústria de Cajú (SINTIC): Rua do Jardim 574, 1° andar, Maputo; tel. (1) 475300; Sec.-Gen. BOAVENTURA MONDLANE.

Sindicato Nacional dos Trabalhadores da Indústria de Construção Civil, Madeira e Minas (SINTICIM): Avda 24 de Julho 2341, 5° andar dt°, Maputo; tel. (1) 421159; Sec.-Gen. JOSÉ ALBINO.

Sindicato Nacional dos Trabalhadores da Indústria Hoteleira, Turismo e Similares (SINTHOTS): Avda Eduardo Mondlane 1267, CP 394, Maputo; tel. (1) 420409; Sec.-Gen. ALBERTO MANUEL NHAPOSSE.

Sindicato Nacional dos Trabalhadores da Indústria Metalúrgica, Metalomecânica e Energia (SINTIME): Avda Samora Machel 30, 6° andar, No 6, CP 1868, Maputo; tel. (1) 428588; fax (1) 421671; Sec.-Gen. RUI BENJAMIM COSTA.

Sindicato Nacional dos Trabalhadores da Indústria Química, Borracha, Papel e Gráfica (SINTIQUIGRA): Avda Karl Marx 414, 1° andar, CP 4433, Maputo; tel. (1) 421553; Sec.-Gen. JOAQUIM M. FANHEIRO.

Sindicato Nacional dos Trabalhadores da Indústria Têxtil Vestuário, Couro e Calçado (SINTEVEC): Avda do Trabalho 1276, 1° andar, CP 2613, Maputo; tel. (1) 426753; fax (1) 421671; Sec.-Gen. PEDRO JOAQUIM MANDJAZE.

Sindicato Nacional dos Trabalhadores da Marinha Mercante e Pesca (SINTMAP): Rua Joaquim Lapa 4, 22-5° andares, No 6, Maputo; tel. (1) 421148; Sec.-Gen. DANIEL MANUEL NGOQUE.

Sindicato Nacional dos Trabalhadores dos Portos e Caminhos de Ferro (SINPOCAF): Avda Guerra Popular, CP 2158, Maputo; tel. (1) 420531; Sec.-Gen. DINIS EFRAIME FRANCISCO NHANGUMBE.

Sindicato Nacional dos Trabalhadores dos Transportes Rodoviários e Assistência Técnica (SINTRAT): Avda Paulo Samuel Kankhomba 1568, 1° andar, 14, Maputo; tel. (1) 402390; Sec.-Gen. ALCANO HORÁCIO MULA.

Sindicato Nacional de Jornalistas (SNJ): Avda 24 de Julho, 231, Maputo; tel. (1) 492500; fax (1) 492031; f. 1978; Sec.-Gen. HILÁRIO M. E. MATUSSE.

Sindicatos Livres e Independentes de Moçambique (SLIM): Sec.-Gen. JEREMIAS TIMANE.

Transport

The 'Beira Corridor', where rail and road links and a petroleum pipeline run from Manica, on the Zimbabwean border, to the Mozambican port of Beira, forms a vital outlet for the land-locked southern African countries, particularly Zimbabwe. The development of this route is a major priority of the Southern African Development Community (SADC). Following the General Peace Agreement in 1992, rehabilitation of the transport network, which had been continually disrupted by guerrilla attacks and sabotage, began, funded principally by the SADC. By 1994 the 'Beira Corridor' was fully operational.

RAILWAYS

In 1987 the total length of track was 3,131 km, excluding the Sena Sugar Estates Railway (90 km), which serves only the company's properties. The railways are all state-owned. There are both internal routes and rail links between Mozambican ports and South Africa, Zimbabwe and Malawi. During the hostilities many lines and services were disrupted by Renamo guerrilla operations. Improvement work on most of the principal railway lines began in the early 1980s. The rehabilitation of the 534-km Limpopo railway, linking Chicualacuala, at the Zimbabwe border, with the port of Maputo, was completed in March 1993. In September 1993 it was announced that the implementation of plans, initiated in 1990 but later disrupted, to rehabilitate the railway linking the port of Beira with the coal-mining centre of Moatize had resumed. However, in early 1997 the Government indicated that the rehabilitation of the line, which would cost in excess of US $300m., was dependent on attracting foreign investors to the coal mines of Moatize who would meet the cost of repairs. In November 1993, following the rehabilitation of some 533 km of the 610-km railway linking the port of Nacala with Blantyre, in Malawi, the completed section, which runs from Nacala to Cuamba in Niassa province, was reopened. In June 1996 the rehabilitation of the remaining 77-km section, linking Cuamba with Entre-Lagos on the Malawian border, was completed and plans were announced to repair the 200-km branch line from Cuamba to Lichinga. In early 1996 rehabilitation of the Goba railway, linking Mozambique and Swaziland, which began in 1993, was nearing completion.

Direcção Nacional dos Portos e Caminhos de Ferro de Moçambique (CFM): Avda Mártires de Inhaminga 336, CP 2158, Maputo; tel. (1) 427173; telex 6438; fax (1) 424228; f. 1929; 3,131 km open; there are five separate systems linking Mozambican ports with the country's hinterland, and with other southern African countries, including Malawi, Zimbabwe and South Africa. These systems are administered from Nampula, Beira, Maputo, Inhambane and Quelimane respectively; Dir (vacant).

Empresa Nacional dos Portos e Caminhos de Ferro de Moçambique (CFM), SARL: Praça dos Trabalhadores, CP 2158, Maputo; tel. (1) 427173; telex 6208; Dir-Gen. (vacant).

ROADS

In 1995 there were an estimated 29,810 km of roads in Mozambique, of which 5,545 km were paved. In 1991 a major programme, supervised by the SADCC (now SADC), was in progress to improve the road links between Mozambique and neighbouring countries. In 1994 the Government announced a five-year road rehabilitation programme to reopen 11,000 km of roads closed during the hostilities, and to upgrade 3,000 km of paved roads and 13,000 km of secondary and tertiary roads. The programme, which was to cost an estimated US $24,000m., was to be financed mainly by international donors and the World Bank.

SHIPPING

The main ports are Maputo, Beira, Nacala and Quelimane. Some 7.1m. tons of cargo were handled in 1995. The modernization and expansion of the port of Beira, which began in 1991, was completed in 1994. The construction of a new petroleum terminal doubled the port's capacity, thus facilitating the transportation of petroleum products along the 'Beira Corridor' to Zimbabwe. Rehabilitation of the port of Maputo was completed in 1989, as part of the SADCC (now SADC) transport programme. Repairs to the port of Nacala, damaged by a cyclone in early 1994, were to cost an estimated US $14m. In late 1994 the port was reported to be operating at only 25%–30% of its capacity. Foreign assistance was still being sought in early 1997 to finance the repairs.

Agência Nacional de Frete e Navegação (ANFRENA): Rua Consiglieri Pedroso 396, CP 492, Maputo; tel. (1) 428111; telex 6258; fax (1) 427822; Dir FERDINAND WILSON.

Companhia Nacional de Navegação: CP 2064, Maputo; telex 6237.

Companhia Portuguesa de Transportes Marítimos: Avda Samora Machel 239, CP 2, Maputo; tel. (1) 426912.

Empresa Moçambicana de Cargas (MOCARGO): Rua Consiglieri Pedroso 430, 1°–4° andares, CP 888, Maputo; tel. (1) 431022; telex 6581; fax (1) 421438; f. 1984; shipping, chartering and road transport; Man. Dir MANUEL DE SOUSA AMARAL.

Manica Freight Services, SARL: Praça dos Trabalhadores 51, CP 557, Maputo; tel. (1) 425048; telex 6221; fax (1) 431084; international shipping agents; Dir W. A. VERPLOEGH.

Navique EE (Empresa Moçambicana de Navegação): Rua de Bagamoyo 366, CP 145, Maputo; tel. (1) 425316; telex 6424; fax (1) 426310; Chair. DANIEL C. LAMPIAO; Man. Dir JORGE DE SOUSA COELHO.

CIVIL AVIATION

There are 16 airports, of which three are international airports.

Aerocondor Moçambique: Beira.

Empresa Nacional de Transporte e Trabalho Aéreo, EE (TTA): Aeroporto Internacional de Maputo, CP 2054, Maputo; tel. (1) 465292; telex 6539; fax (1) 465484; scheduled services to 35 domestic points; also operates air taxi services, agricultural and special aviation services; privatized in 1997; Dir ESTEVÃO ALBERTO JUNIOR.

Linhas Aéreas de Moçambique (LAM): Aeroporto Internacional de Maputo, CP 2060, Maputo; tel. (1) 465137; telex 6386; fax (1) 735601; f. 1980; operates domestic services and international services within Africa and to Europe; privatization of 51% share pending in 1997; Chair. and Dir-Gen. José Ricardo Zuzarte Viegas.

Tourism

Tourism, formerly a significant source of foreign exchange, ceased completely following independence, and was resumed on a limited scale in 1980. There were 1,000 visitors in 1981 (compared with 292,000 in 1972 and 69,000 in 1974). In 1984 a joint-venture company was established with South Africa in order to develop tourism on Inhaca island. With the successful conduct of multi-party elections in 1994 and the prospect of continued peace, there is considerable scope for development of this sector.

Empresa Nacional de Turismo (ENT): Avda 25 de Setembro 1203, CP 2446, Maputo; tel. (1) 421794; telex 6303; fax (1) 421795; f. 1985; hotels and tourism; Dir Armindo Langa.

Defence

In June 1990 the National Defence Force (Forças Armandas de Moçambique–FAM) totalled an estimated 72,000, with 60,000 in the army, 1,000 in the navy and 6,000 in the air force, and a paramilitary force of 5,000; there were also provincial and people's militias in villages. In December 1991 the government announced plans to reduce the FAM by 45,000, in anticipation of the signing of a cease-fire agreement, whereupon, it was proposed, a single body of armed forces, incorporating Renamo guerrillas, would be created. Under the provisions of the General Peace Agreement (GPA) of October 1992, the joint armed forces (Forças Armadas de Defesa de Moçambique–FADM), were to number 30,000, comprising equal numbers of government and Renamo troops. All troops from both sides were to register at assembly points throughout the country; those not enlisting in the FADM were to be demobilized. In accordance with the provisions of the GPA, all Zimbabwean and Malawian troops stationed in Mozambique to guard the 'transport corridors' linking the land-locked southern African states with the Indian Ocean were withdrawn—in April 1993 and July 1993, respectively—prior to the holding of presidential and legislative elections in October 1994. On 16 August the FAM were formally dissolved and the FADM inaugurated as the country's official armed forces. According to the final report, issued in December 1994, of the cease-fire commission (established under the GPA to supervise the implementation of truce regulations), a combined total of only 11,579 government and Renamo troops (from a total of 91,691 troops registered at assembly points) had enlisted in the FADM. In mid-1997 the government was seeking to introduce legislation providing for the reintroduction of compulsory military service, which had been suspended under the GPA, in order to increase the strength of the FADM, which stood at less than 11,000 in late 1996. It was envisaged that, once enabling legislation had been introduced, the strength of the FADM would be increased to 15,000. The total strength of the FADM was to be defined by government policy, and the figure of 30,000 envisaged in the GPA would not necessarily be observed. By the end of March 1995 all troops and police belonging to the UN Operation in Mozambique (ONUMOZ), stationed in the country to facilitate the pacification and electoral processes, had withdrawn. After that date only a small unit of ONUMOZ officials remained in the country.

Defence Expenditure: Budgeted at 830,000m. meticais in 1997.

Commander-in-Chief of the Armed Forces: Pres. Joaquim Alberto Chissano.

Chief of General Staff: Gen. Lagos Lidimo.

Deputy Chief of General Staff: Gen. Mateus Ngonhamo.

Education

At independence, between 85%–95% of the adult population were illiterate. In the early 1980s there was a major emphasis on campaigns for adult literacy and other adult education. By 1995, according to estimates by UNESCO, 59.9% of the adult population were illiterate (males 42.3%; females 76.7%). Education is officially compulsory for seven years from the age of seven. Primary schooling begins at six years of age and lasts for five years. Secondary schooling, which begins at twelve years of age, lasts for seven years and comprises a first cycle of two years and a further cycle of five years. The number of children receiving primary education increased from 634,000 in 1973 to 1,495,000 in 1979; the total declined to 1,199,476 in 1992, owing to the security situation, but recovered to 1,415,428 in 1995. As a proportion of the school-age population, the total enrolment at primary and secondary schools increased from 30% in 1972 to 52% in 1979, but declined to the equivalent of 35% in 1995 (males 41%; females 29%). In that year enrolment at primary schools was equivalent to 65% of children in the relevant age-group (males 75%; females 54%), while secondary enrolment was equivalent to 8% of children in the relevant age-group (males 10%; females 6%). There were 5,250 students at the university in 1993. Expenditure on education by all levels of government in 1990, including foreign aid received for the purpose, was 72,264m. meticais (12.0% of total government expenditure). In early 1991 the government introduced a programme to improve primary education and strengthen the overall management of the education sector, at a cost of US $67.9m. (to be provided mainly by the World Bank).

Bibliography

Abrahamsson, H., and Nilsson, A. *Mozambique: The Troubled Transition from Socialist Construction to Free Market Capitalism.* London, Zed Books, 1995.

Azevedo, M. *Historical Dictionary of Mozambique.* Metuchen, NJ, Scarecrow Press, 1991.

Bhagavan, M. R. *Some Aspects of International Development in Mozambique.* Stockholm, Swedish International Development Authority, 1977.

Chingono, M. F. *Conspicuous Destruction: War, Famine and the Reform Process in Mozambique.* New York, Human Rights Watch, 1992.

The State, Violence and Development: The Political Economy of War in Mozambique, 1975–1992. Aldershot, Avebury, 1996.

Davies, R. *South African Strategy Towards Mozambique in the Post-Nkomati Period: A Critical Analysis of Effects and Implications.* Uppsala, Scandinavian Institute for African Studies, 1985.

Egero, B. *Mozambique: A Dream Undone. The Political Economy of Democracy, 1975–1984.* Uppsala, Scandinavian Institute for African Studies, 1987.

Finnegan, W. A. *A Complicated War: The Harrowing of Mozambique.* Berkeley, University of California Press, 1992.

First, R. *Black Gold: The Mozambican Miner, Proletariat and Peasant.* Brighton, Harvester Press; New York, St Martin's Press, 1983.

Hanlon, J. *Apartheid's Second Front: South Africa's War Against its Neighbours.* Harmondsworth, Penguin, 1986.

Harris, P. *Work, Culture and Identity: Migrant Labourers in Mozambique and South Africa, c.1860–1910.* Johannesburg, University of the Witwatersrand Press; London, James Currey, 1994.

Henriksen, T. H. *Mozambique: A History.* London, Rex Collings; Cape Town, David Philips, 1978.

Hermele, K. *Land Struggles and Social Differentiation in Southern Mozambique: A Case Study of Hokwe, Limpopo 1950–1987.* Uppsala, Scandinavian Institute for African Studies, 1988.

Hoile, D. *Mozambique: A Nation in Crisis.* London, Claridge Press, 1989.

Mozambique: Propaganda, Myth and Reality. London, Mozambique Institute, 1991.

Mozambique: Resistance and Freedom: A Case for Reassessment. London, Mozambique Institute, 1994.

Hoile, D. (Ed.). *Mozambique 1962–1993: A Political Chronology.* London, Mozambique Institute, 1994.

Hume, C. *Ending Mozambique's War: The Role of Mediation and Good Offices.* Washington, DC: United States Institute of Peace Press, 1994.

Ishemo, S. L. *Lower Zambezi Basin in Mozambique: A Study in Economy and Society, 1920–1950.* Brookfield, VT, Ashgate Publishing, 1995.

Katzenellenbogen, S. E. *South Africa and Southern Mozambique: Labour, Railways and Trade in the Making of a Relationship.* Manchester, Manchester University Press, 1982.

Marshall, J. *War, Debt and Structural Adjustment in Mozambique: The Social Impact.* Ottawa, North-South Institute, 1992.

Miech-Chatenay, M. *Mozambique: The Key Sectors of the Economy.* Paris, BIDOI, 1986.

Mozambique 1991: The New Phase. Montréal, CIDMAA, 1991.

Newitt, M. *A History of Mozambique.* Bloomington, Indiana University Press; London, Hurst, 1993.

Newitt, M. D. D. *Portugal in Africa: The Last Hundred Years.* London, Hurst, 1981.

Pelissier, R. *Naissance du Mozambique.* 2 vols. France, Editions Pelissier, 1984.

Penvenne, J. M. *African Workers and Colonial Racism: Mozambican Strategies and Struggles in Lourenço Marques, 1877–1962.* London, James Currey, 1995.

Quarterly Economic Review of Tanzania and Mozambique. London, Economist Intelligence Unit, 1978–.

Rotberg, R. I., et al (Eds). *South Africa and its Neighbours: Regional Security and Self-Interest.* Lexington, Lexington Books, 1985.

Saul, J. (Ed.). *A Difficult Road: The Transition to Socialism in Mozambique.* New York, Monthly Review Press, 1985.

Seiler, J. (Ed.). *Southern Africa Under the Portuguese Coup.* Boulder, CO, Westview, 1980.

Sogge, D. *Hammer and Hoe: Local Industries under State Socialism in Mozambique.* The Hague, Institute of Social Studies, 1985.

Torp, J. E. *Mozambique: Politics, Economics, Society.* London, Pinter, 1989.

Verdier, I. (Ed.). *Mozambique: 100 Men in Power.* Paris, Indigo Publication Group, 1996.

Vieira, S. *Southern Africa, Mozambique: From Rivalries to Global Convergence.* Maputo, Centro Estudos Africanos, 1988.

Vines, A. *No Democracy Without Money: The Road to Peace in Mozambique (1981–1992).* London, Catholic Institute for Int. Relations, 1994.

Renamo: Terrorism in Mozambique. Bloomington, Indiana University Press, 1991.

Renamo Mozambique. London, James Currey; Bloomington, Indiana University Press, 1994.

Renamo: From Terrorism to Democracy in Mozambique. USA and Canada, World Press, 1995.

Wuyts, M. E. *Peasants and Rural Economy in Mozambique.* Maputo, Centro Estudos Africanos, 1978.

Money and Planning for Socialist Transition: The Mozambican Experience. Aldershot, Gower, 1989.

NAMIBIA

Physical and Social Geography

A. MacGREGOR HUTCHESON

The Republic of Namibia, lying across the Tropic of Capricorn, covers an area of 824,292 sq km (318,261 sq miles). It is bordered by South Africa on the south and south-east, by Botswana on the east and Angola on the north, while the narrow Caprivi Strip, between the two latter countries, extends Namibia's boundaries to the Zambezi river and a short border with Zambia.

The Namib Desert, a narrow plain 65–160 km wide and extending 1,600 km along the entire Atlantic seaboard, has a mean annual rainfall of less than 100 mm; long lines of huge sand dunes are common and it is almost devoid of vegetation. Behind the coastal plain the Great Escarpment rises to the plateau which forms the rest of the country. Part of the Southern African plateau, it has an average elevation of 1,100 m above sea-level but towards the centre of the country there is a rise to altitudes of 1,525–2,440 m. A number of mountain masses rise above the general surface throughout the plateau. Eastwards the surface slopes to the Kalahari Basin and northwards to the Etosha Pan. Much of Namibia's drainage is interior to the Kalahari. There are no perennial rivers apart from the Okavango and the Cuando, which cross the Caprivi Strip, and the Orange, Kunene and Zambezi, which form parts of the southern and northern borders.

Temperatures of the coastal areas are modified by the cool Benguela Current, while altitude modifies plateau temperatures (cf. Walvis Bay: January 19°C, July 14.5°C; and Windhoek (1,707 m): January 24°C, July 14°C). Mean annual rainfall varies from some 50 mm on the coast to 550 mm in the north. Most rain falls during the summer, but is unreliable and there are years of drought. Grasslands cover most of the plateau; they are richer in the wetter north but merge into poor scrub in the south and east.

Most of the population (enumerated at 1,409,920 at the census of October 1991 and estimated at 1,594,000 at mid-1995) reside on the plateau. Figures for the density of population (1.9 inhabitants per sq km at mid-1995) are misleading, as the better-watered northern one-third of the plateau contains more than one-half of the total population and about two-thirds of the African population, including the Ovambo (the largest single ethnic group), Kavango, East Caprivians and Kaokovelders. Almost the entire European population (80,000 in 1988, including the European population of Walvis Bay, an exclave of South Africa which was ceded to Namibia in March 1994) are concentrated in the southern two-thirds of the plateau, chiefly in the central highlands around Windhoek, the capital, together with the other main ethnic groups, the Damara, Herero, Nama, Rehoboth and Coloured. Excluding ports and mining centres in the Namib and small numbers of Bushmen in the Kalahari, these regions are largely uninhabited.

Namibia possesses scattered deposits of valuable minerals, and its economy is dominated by the mining sector. Of particular importance are the rich deposits of alluvial diamonds, which are exploited by surface mining, notably in the area between Oranjemund and Lüderitz. Operations at the Oranjemund mine are not, however, expected to remain economic after the year 2000, and the development of 'offshore' diamond fields is rapidly proceeding. Uranium ore (although of a low grade) is mined open-cast at Rössing, 39 km north-east of Swakopmund, which is the world's largest open-pit uranium oxide complex. There is another, smaller uranium deposit about 80 km south of Rössing, which is thought to be of a higher grade. Tin, copper, rock salt, lead and zinc are also mined, and Namibia is believed to have significant reserves of coal, iron ore and platinum, although these have yet to be assessed. Other minerals currently produced or awaiting exploitation include vanadium, manganese, gold, silver, tungsten (wolfram), cadmium and limestone. The existence of considerable reserves of offshore natural gas could be of great benefit to Namibia's future economic development.

Despite the limitations imposed by frequent drought, agriculture is a significant economic activity. With the help of water from boreholes, large areas are given over to extensive ranching. Rivers, notably the Orange, Kunene and Okavango, are potential water resources for irrigation and hydroelectric power, while swamps, such as those situated in the Caprivi Strip, could be drained to enhance arable output.

Namibia possesses potentially the richest inshore and deep-water fishing zones in tropical Africa as a consequence of the rich feeding provided by the Benguela Current. Measures are being taken to counter the effects of decades of over-fishing by both domestic and foreign fleets.

Recent History

CHRISTOPHER SAUNDERS

HISTORICAL BACKGROUND

South West Africa (SWA), declared a German protectorate in 1884, was occupied by South Africa following the outbreak of the First World War. Following the war, the League of Nations entrusted South Africa with a mandate to administer the territory. In 1925 the South African government granted limited self-government to the territory's white inhabitants. No trusteeship agreement was concluded after the Second World War, and the refusal of the United Nations (UN) in 1946 to agree to South Africa's request to annex SWA marked the beginning of a protracted dispute. In 1949 South Africa granted the territory's white voters representation in the South African parliament. In 1950 the International Court of Justice (ICJ) ruled that South Africa was not competent to place the territory under the UN trusteeship system, nor able to alter the legal status of the territory unilaterally. In 1966 the UN General Assembly voted to terminate South Africa's mandate and to assume responsibility for the territory; a 'Council for South West Africa' was appointed in 1967, and in the following year the UN resolved that the territory should be renamed Namibia. The South African government, however, refused to allow the UN to take control of the territory's administration.

Political resistance was, meanwhile, taking hold within the territory. In 1957 the Ovamboland People's Congress was formed. It was subsequently renamed the Ovamboland People's Organisation, and in 1960 the South West Africa People's Organisation (SWAPO). Its leaders included Sam Nujoma and Herman (later Andimba) Toivo ja Toivo. From 1963 onwards, SWAPO meetings were effectively banned, although it remained technically a legal organization. In 1966 SWAPO's military wing, the

People's Liberation Army of Namibia (PLAN), began an armed insurgency. In 1968 SWAPO restyled itself as the South West Africa People's Organisation of Namibia.

In 1971 the ICJ ruled that South Africa's presence in Namibia was illegal and that it should withdraw immediately. The South African government's rejection of the ruling provoked a massive strike in the territory in December, to which the administration responded with arrests and the imposition of a partial state of emergency. In early 1973 South Africa set up a short-lived multiracial council for the territory. In December, after the failure of a UN attempt to establish negotiations with South Africa, the UN General Assembly voted to recognize SWAPO as the 'authentic representative of the people of Namibia', and appointed the first UN commissioner for Namibia to undertake 'executive and administrative tasks'.

South Africa's unsuccessful intervention in Angola in the second half of 1975 set the scene for the escalation of the Namibian armed struggle, and, by illegally using Namibia as a military base, South Africa made its position at the UN more vulnerable. With the accession to power in neighbouring Angola of the pro-SWAPO Movimento Popular de Libertação de Angola, PLAN was able to establish bases close to the borders of Namibia. South Africa reacted to this threat by greatly expanding counter-insurgency forces in the territory.

At this time South Africa began to take initiatives on the political front. In September 1975 the South African prime minister, B. J. Vorster, convened a constitutional conference to discuss the territory's future. The Turnhalle conference, as it became known, designated 31 December 1978 as the target date for Namibian independence and, in March 1977, it produced a draft constitution for a pre-independence interim government. This constitution, providing for 11 ethnic administrations, was denounced by the UN and SWAPO, which issued its own constitutional proposals based on a parliamentary system with universal adult suffrage.

THE UN 'CONTACT GROUP'

In order to persuade South Africa to reject the Turnhalle scheme and to adopt instead a plan which would be acceptable to the UN, a 'contact group' comprising the five western members of the UN Security Council was established. The 'contact group' held talks with both the South African government and SWAPO beginning in April 1977. In September of that year South Africa appointed an administrator-general for Namibia, and the territory's representation in the South African parliament was terminated. By April 1978 the 'contact group' was able to present proposals for a settlement providing for UN-supervised elections, a reduction in the numbers of South African troops from Namibia and the release of political prisoners. These proposals were accepted by South Africa in late April and by SWAPO in July, after a delay caused in part by a South African raid on a SWAPO refugee centre at Cassinga in Angola, during which a large number of civilians were killed. The proposals were then incorporated into UN Security Council Resolution 435 of 28 September 1978. South Africa insisted on holding its own election for a Namibian constituent assembly in the territory in December; this was rejected by the international community, which, however, declined to impose sanctions in protest at the action. With SWAPO boycotting the election, 41 of the 50 seats were won by the Democratic Turnhalle Alliance (DTA), a conservative coalition of the ethnic groups involved in the conference. Its leader, Dirk Mudge, became chairman of a ministerial council which was granted limited executive powers. A separate South West African Territory Force (SWATF) was established in 1980, although control of defence and security matters and external affairs remained in the hands of the South African government.

In January 1981 the UN convened a conference at Geneva which was attended by SWAPO, South Africa, the DTA and other internal parties. The UN 'contact group' and the 'front-line' states (Angola, Botswana, Mozambique, Tanzania, Zambia and Zimbabwe) were present as observers. South Africa and the internal parties could not agree on a cease-fire date and the implementation of the UN plan. It was apparent that the South African prime minister, P. W. Botha, believed that SWAPO was communist-controlled and that it therefore could not be allowed to come to power. The DTA for its part needed more time to establish itself as a credible alternative to SWAPO; the South African government, meanwhile, hoped that the newly-elected Reagan administration in the USA would be sympathetic to South African policy.

Under US leadership, the 'contact group' resumed consultations with South Africa and SWAPO during 1981. In July 1982 constitutional guidelines were agreed to by the two parties, which provided that the post-independence constitution should include a bill of rights and be approved by two-thirds of the members of a constituent assembly. Although South Africa and SWAPO were unable to agree on whether the election should be conducted wholly on the basis of proportional representation, the UN secretary-general was able to report that all other points at issue had been resolved. By then, however, a more formidable obstacle to the implementation of the UN plan had arisen. South Africa now insisted that the Cuban troops withdraw from Angola. This concept, known as 'linkage', was initiated in 1981 by the US government, which viewed the war in Namibia and southern Angola as a buffer against Soviet expansionism. This view was not shared by the other members of the 'contact group', particularly France, which eventually left the group in December 1983. The USA then continued the negotiations alone.

Within the territory, the DTA was seriously weakened in February 1982 by the resignation of Peter Kalangula, the leader of the only significant movement supported by the Ovambo (the largest ethnic group in Namibia) other than SWAPO. After several months of dispute with the South African government over the future role of the DTA, Mudge resigned as chairman of the ministerial council in January 1983, and the council itself was automatically dissolved. The administrator-general, in turn, dissolved the national assembly, and assumed direct rule of Namibia on behalf of the South African government.

Even more disturbing to the internal settlement plans, perhaps, was the contempt with which the ethnic administrations came to be regarded. The attempt to enhance support by channelling state funds through these administrations proved counter-productive. In 1983 South Africa appointed a commission of inquiry to investigate allegations of inefficiency and corruption: this revealed major irregularities, and in 1984 the administrator-general assumed powers to allow the central department of finance to control the spending of the ethnic authorities where necessary.

ARMED CONFLICT

During the early 1980s, South African troops and police, based in the north of the territory, were augmented by units from the locally-recruited SWATF, including mercenary and covert police detachments. The result was a severe deterioration in respect for human rights, initially in Ovamboland, but spreading in 1982–83 into the Kavango and Caprivi regions. Internal church reports of torture and killings were supported by a number of international church delegations visiting Namibia during the period 1981–84. Such criticism, however, failed to influence the security policies operated by the territorial administration.

South Africa conducted extensive raids across the frontier into southern Angola from 1981, parts of which were effectively occupied by South African troops which advanced 200 km inside Angolan territory. In February 1984 a cease-fire agreement was concluded in Lusaka, Zambia, following talks between South African and US government officials. Under the terms of the agreement, a joint commission was established to monitor the withdrawal of South African troops from Angola, and Angola undertook to permit neither SWAPO nor Cuban forces to move into the areas vacated by South African troops. SWAPO declared that it would abide by the agreement, but made it clear that it would continue PLAN operations until a cease-fire was established in Namibia as the first stage in the implementation of Resolution 435. US negotiators continued, meanwhile, to aim at achieving a regional accord, in which a settlement in Namibia along the lines of Resolution 435 would be counter-balanced by a removal of the Cuban troops from Angola. In November 1984, in response to US proposals, President dos Santos of Angola suggested a timetable for the withdrawal of Cuban troops from the south of Angola. South African withdrawal from Angola was completed in April 1985, but soon afterwards South Africa established an interim internal government in Namibia.

TRANSITIONAL GOVERNMENT AND POPULAR RESISTANCE

After the dissolution of the DTA ministers' council in January 1983, there was a political hiatus until an informally-constituted Multi-Party Conference (MPC) began to meet in November of that year. At that time, its membership extended beyond the DTA to include the Damara Council, the Rehoboth Liberation Front, the SWAPO–Democrats (SWAPO–D, a breakaway faction of SWAPO), the right-wing National Party of South West Africa (SWANP) and the Herero-dominated South West African National Union (SWANU). SWAPO, however, refused to join, and denounced the MPC as 'another South African puppet show'. In October 1984 the MPC called for an all-party meeting by 31 December of that year, failing which it would negotiate unilaterally with Pretoria for independence.

The credibility of the MPC was not high, owing to the past history of the DTA, the corruption and mismanagement of ethnic authorities under the control of MPC member parties, its failure to attract any Ovambo party, and its readiness to deal with South Africa. Aware of the lack of support for the MPC, the South African government sought to involve at least part of SWAPO in an internal settlement. In March 1984 it released Toivo ja Toivo, who had been imprisoned in South Africa since 1968. A number of SWAPO activists who had been detained since 1978 were also freed. In May 1984 formal talks were held in Lusaka between the administrator-general, SWAPO and the internal parties, under the joint chairmanship of President Kaunda of Zambia and the administrator-general. SWAPO, however, insisted on the implementation of Resolution 435 and the talks ended in failure. The members of the MPC then proceeded with their own plans.

On 17 June 1985 the South African government installed a 'Transitional Government of National Unity' (TGNU) in Windhoek, pending independence, although the arrangement was condemned in advance by the contact group governments and was declared 'null and void' by the UN secretary-general. This interim government consisted of a cabinet and a national assembly. Neither was elected and appointments were made from among the constituent parties of the MPC. A 'bill of rights', drawn up by the MPC, prohibited racial discrimination, and a constitutional council was established, under a South African judge, to prepare a constitution for an independent Namibia. South Africa retained responsibility for foreign affairs, defence and internal security. The administrator-general used his power of legislative veto on several occasions. From 1985, SWAPO and its youth league held a series of rallies, which were disrupted by the police. In July 1986, however, the courts ruled that SWAPO was entitled to hold public meetings, because the violent overthrow of the state was not an integral part of its progamme.

MOVES TOWARDS INDEPENDENCE

In early 1987 Angola secured US agreement to the participation of Cuba in discussions, nominally as part of the Angolan delegation and in January 1988 Angola and Cuba accepted, in principle, the US demand for a complete withdrawal of Cuban troops from Angola, this being conditional on the implementation of the UN independence plan for Namibia. In March proposals for the withdrawal of all Cuban troops were rejected by South Africa as 'insufficiently detailed'. However, South Africa agreed to participate in tripartite negotiations with Angola and Cuba, with the USA acting as mediator.

At these negotiations, which began in London in early May 1988, South Africa agreed to implement Resolution 435, providing that a timetable for the withdrawal of Cuban troops could be agreed. By mid-July the participants in the negotiations had accepted a document containing 14 'essential principles' for a peaceful settlement, and in early August it was agreed that the implementation of Resolution 435 would begin on 1 November. South African troops were withdrawn from Angola by the end of August. The November deadline was not met, however, owing to disagreement on an exact schedule for the evacuation of Cuban troops. In mid-November these arrangements were agreed in principle, although their formal ratification was delayed until mid-December, owing to South African dissatisfaction with verification procedures.

On 22 December 1988 South Africa, Angola and Cuba signed a formal treaty designating 1 April 1989 as the implementation date for Resolution 435. Another treaty was signed by Angola and Cuba, requiring the evacuation of all Cuban troops from Angola by July 1991. Under a further agreement, a joint commission was established to monitor the implementation of the trilateral treaty. Under the terms of Resolution 435, South African forces in Namibia were to be confined to their bases, and their numbers reduced to 1,500 by 1 July 1989; all South African troops were to have been withdrawn from Namibia one week after the election. A multinational UN observer force, the UN Transition Assistance Group (UNTAG), was to monitor the South African withdrawal, and supervise the election.

IMPLEMENTATION OF THE UN INDEPENDENCE PLAN

According to the original proposals regarding Resolution 435, UNTAG was to be composed of 7,500 troops; in February 1989, following disagreement within the UN Security Council over the cost of the operation, it was announced that the number was to be 4,650, with a further 500 police and about 1,000 civilian observers. The UNTAG force began to arrive during February 1989. At the end of that month the TGNU was formally disbanded, and on 1 March the national assembly voted to dissolve itself: from then until independence the territory was governed by the administrator-general, Louis Pienaar, in consultation, from 1 April, with the special representative of the UN secretary-general, Martti Ahtisaari.

The scheduled implementation of the UN Security Council's Resolution 435 was disrupted by large-scale movements, beginning on 1 April 1989, of PLAN troops into Ovamboland. The South African government obtained Ahtisaari's agreement to the release from base of its forces, and more than 300 PLAN troops were reportedly killed in the subsequent fighting. The origins of the sudden and unanticipated conflict apparently lay in differing interpretations of the terms of the UN peace plan; SWAPO, excluded from the 1988 negotiations, relied on provisions under Resolution 435 for the confinement to base of PLAN combatants located within the territory on 1 April, and it was widely claimed that the insurgents had intended to report to UNTAG officials. On 9 April the joint commission produced conditions for an evacuation of the PLAN forces; meanwhile, Sam Nujoma, president of SWAPO, ordered a withdrawal of PLAN forces to Angola. At a meeting of the joint commission on 19 May, the cease-fire was certified to be in force.

In June 1989 most racially discriminatory legislation was repealed and an amnesty was granted to Namibian refugees and exiles: by late September nearly 42,000 refugees, including Nujoma, had returned to Namibia. Meanwhile, South Africa completed its troop reduction ahead of schedule.

The pre-independence election was conducted peacefully in the second week of November 1989; more than 95% of the electorate voted. The 72 seats in the constituent assembly were contested by candidates from 10 political parties and alliances: representatives of seven parties and fronts were elected. SWAPO received 57.3% of all votes cast and won 41 seats, thus obtaining a majority of the seats in the assembly but failing to achieve the two-thirds majority which would have allowed SWAPO to draft the constitution without recourse to wider consultation. It was widely believed that SWAPO would have fared better had evidence not emerged during the election campaign of the torture and death in its camps in Angola of numerous people whom SWAPO had detained—as alleged by South Africa during the war. The DTA, with 28.6% of the votes, won 21 seats. The election was pronounced 'free and fair' by the special representative of the UN secretary-general. Following the election, the remaining South African troops left Namibia, and SWAPO bases in Angola were disbanded.

SWAPO IN GOVERNMENT

In early February 1990 the constituent assembly adopted unanimously a draft constitution, which provided for a multi-party political system, based on universal adult suffrage, with an independent judiciary and a 'bill of rights'. Executive power was to be vested in a president who was permitted to serve a maximum of two five-year terms, while a 72-member national assembly was to have legislative power. In mid-February the constituent assembly elected Nujoma as Namibia's first president. On 21 March 1990 Namibia became independent: the constituent assembly became the national assembly, and the president and his cabinet took office.

Following independence, Namibia became a member of the UN, the Organization of African Unity and the Commonwealth. Full diplomatic relations were established with many states, and partial diplomatic relations with South Africa. In May 1990 Angola and Namibia agreed to form a joint commission to monitor their common border. However, relations became strained in February 1991 when Angolan aircraft bombed a northern Namibian village; the Angolan government claimed that it had attacked covert destabilization bases sponsored by South Africa, and promised to pay compensation to the Namibian government. With the resumption of the civil war in Angola in late 1992, the Namibian government remained concerned over the security of its northern border. Instability in South Africa also threatened to affect Namibia; the government was, therefore, much relieved when South Africa's first democratic election took place peacefully in April 1994.

In March 1990 Namibia became a full member of the Southern African Customs Union (having previously been a *de facto* member of that organization) and a member of the South African Development Co-ordination Conference (SADCC), which sought to reduce the dependence of southern African states on South Africa. In August 1992 Namibia joined the other SADCC members in recreating the organization as the Southern African Development Community (SADC).

In April 1990 a team of British military advisers arrived in Namibia to assist in training the new Namibian Defence Force, comprising former members of both PLAN and the SWATF. In September several ex-members of the national police force and of the disbanded pre-independence paramilitary force, Koevoet, were charged with high treason, following the discovery of a cache of arms in July. The appointment, in October, of the former SWAPO head of security, Maj.-Gen. Solomon Hawala, as commander of the army caused protest among opposition groups, owing to allegations that he had been implicated in the torture and detention of dissidents prior to Namibia's independence. Although the opposition in the assembly continued to raise the matter from time to time, the government refused to agree to an investigation of events which took place during the struggle for independence. Allegations of past violations of human rights by SWAPO have remained a sensitive political issue.

The disclosure by the South African government in July 1991 that it had provided some R100m. in funding to the DTA and other anti-SWAPO political parties during the 1989 election campaign added to the DTA's post-independence problems. In late November 1991 the DTA, formerly a coalition of ethnically-based interests, reorganized itself as a single party, but its support continued to dwindle. In late November and early December 1992 the first elections were held for the country's 13 regional councils and 48 local authorities. SWAPO won nine regional councils while the DTA won only three (in the remaining council there was no clear majority). SWAPO thus secured control of the newly-established second house of parliament, the national council, which comprised two members from each regional council; it began work in May 1993. In June Dirk Mudge, the leading figure in the DTA, resigned from the national assembly and subsequently retired from public life. The DTA repeatedly publicized examples of alleged maladministration and financial extravagance (the most controversial example being the purchase of a presidential aircraft during a period of severe drought) but these efforts failed to revitalize popular support for the DTA.

Walvis Bay, the 1,124-sq km enclave that contains the region's only deep-water port facilities, had remained under South African jurisdiction after Namibian independence. Negotiations between the South African and Namibian governments led to the announcement in August 1992 that a Walvis Bay Joint Administration Authority (JAA) would be established, comprising an equal number of representatives from each country. The JAA began operating in November that year. In August 1993, following pressure from the African National Congress of South Africa, South Africa's multi-party negotiating forum resolved to transfer sovereignty of Walvis Bay to Namibia. Some white residents of the enclave resorted unsuccessfully to legal action in an attempt to block the transfer. The work of the JAA was completed in February 1994, and from the beginning of March the enclave was formally incorporated into Namibia.

Namibia's first post-independence presidential and legislative elections took place on 7–8 December 1994, and resulted in overwhelming victories for Nujoma and SWAPO. Nujoma was elected for a second term as president, securing 76.3% of the votes cast; his only challenger was Mudge's successor as president of the DTA, Mishake Muyongo. SWAPO secured 53 of the elective seats in the national assembly, obtaining 73.9% of the valid votes cast. The DTA retained 15 seats (with 20.8% of the votes), and the coalition United Democratic Front two. The remaining two seats were won by the Democratic Coalition of Namibia (DCN—an alliance of the National Patriotic Front and the German Union) and the Monitor Action Group. SWANU, which had been a founder member of the DCN in August, but subsequently withdrew to contest the elections in its own right, failed to secure representation in the legislature. Although SWAPO thus had a two-thirds' majority in the national assembly, Nujoma gave assurances that no amendments would be made to the constitution without prior approval by national referendum. The election results were released despite evidence of irregularities in four constituencies (three results were the subject of high court adjudication in early 1995), and opposition claims of 'gross irregularities' in electoral procedures—international observers had, however, expressed satisfaction with the conduct of voting. The success of Nujoma and SWAPO was, in part, attributed to the popularity of land reform legislation recently approved by the national assembly.

Nujoma was sworn in for his second presidential term on 21 March 1995. The previous day, as part of a major reorganization of cabinet portfolios, he assumed personal responsibility for home affairs and the police, in what was interpreted as an attempt to curb an increase in crime and discontent within the police force. Geingob remained as prime minister, with Hendrik Witbooi, previously minister of labour, public services and manpower development, as his deputy. Helmut Angula (hitherto minister of fisheries and marine resources) became minister of finance. SWAPO's secretary-general, Moses Garoëb, was appointed minister of labour and human resources development.

At the end of March 1996 the publication of *Namibia: The Wall of Silence*, a book by German Pastor Siegfried Groth, a former SWAPO supporter, describing the detention and torture of people by the organization during the 1980s, was released in Namibia. Nujoma publicly denounced the book as an attempt to discredit SWAPO, and accused its promoters of endangering national reconciliation. Nujoma and his party were, in turn, accused of failing to admit to, and apologize for, the alleged human rights' violations in the SWAPO camps in Angola. Prior to the publication of Groth's book, the Council of Churches in Namibia announced that it was to convene a national conference on the issue of detainees in Angola; following the subsequent controversy regarding the book, however, the planned conference was postponed. SWAPO subsequently published a book, entitled *Their Blood Waters Our Freedom,* listing about 8,000 SWAPO supporters who had died during the war. However, a 'breaking the wall of silence' committee continued to accuse the party of failing to acknowledge the alleged atrocities in its camps. When the South African truth and reconciliation commission (see chapter on South Africa) requested permission to conduct hearings in Namibia in 1997, it was refused, on the grounds that the public discussions might hinder Namibia's own search for reconciliation.

In late May 1997 SWAPO held its second party congress since independence. The most intensive debate was on land reform, with the congress urging the government to expedite measures in that area. An important resolution endorsing the proposal that Nujoma should seek re-election for a third term as president was justified on the grounds that Nujoma had initially been chosen by the constituent assembly, and had only once been elected president on a popular mandate. (SWAPO had the requisite parliamentary majority to adopt a constitutional amendment allowing Nujoma to serve a third term in office.) Witbooi, who had been vice-president of the party since 1983, was re-elected to the post, defeating a challenge by Geingob.

The minister of fisheries and marine resources, Hifikepunye Pohamba, replaced Garoëb as secretary-general of the party.

Critics continued to accuse SWAPO of autocratic practices and various abuses of power. Investigations into allegations of corruption were protracted, and the government often failed to punish those involved. The proposed purchase of a new presidential airplane (to replace one bought in 1992 which was claimed to be too small) prompted much criticism in 1997, which, however, the government was able to disregard. Both the press and the judiciary were attacked by SWAPO supporters who opposed their independence, while efforts to establish new anti-SWAPO parties have attracted little popular support. The dominant trend was to increase the concentration of power in the SWAPO élite.

REGIONAL RELATIONS

In March 1993 the Angolan insurgent movement União Nacional para a Independência Total de Angola (UNITA) alleged that members of the Namibian Defence Force had crossed the border into southern Angola to assist Angolan government forces in offensives against UNITA. The Namibian authorities denied any involvement in the Angolan civil conflict, but a section of the border with Angola was closed from September 1994, following an attack, attributed by the Namibian authorities to UNITA, in which Namibian nationals were killed. In 1996 it was announced that some 1,000 members of a special field force of the Namibia police, created in 1995 to provide employment for former PLAN troops, were to be deployed along the Okavango river on the Angolan border to deter possible UNITA attacks. In August of that year Namibian and Angolan officials agreed on further measures to increase border security. In 1997, however, it was alleged that some of the Namibian forces deployed at the border had been responsible for the disappearance of about 1,700 Angolans since 1994.

Good relations with Botswana were maintained in many fields, but in early 1996 the two countries referred their dispute over the demarcation of their joint border on the Chobe river (specifically, the issue of the sovereignty of the sparsely inhabited island of Kasikili-Sududu) for adjudication by the ICJ. However, in light of speculation concerning a build-up of armaments in Botswana, Namibia substantially increased its defence budget in that year. Additionally, reports in early 1996 of troop movements by Botswana in the area near the island prompted concern, until it was learned that the deployment was intended to assist in the containment of a cattle disease.

Following the change of government in South Africa, President Mandela visited Namibia in August 1994 and indicated the possible cancellation of Namibia's pre-independence debt to South Africa (estimated at N$ 826.6m. in 1990), which Namibia was to have repaid with interest in annual instalments during 1995–2012. Shortly before Namibia's elections in December 1994, Nujoma again met Mandela in South Africa, and the South African president announced that the entire debt would be cancelled. However, when technical experts from the two countries met to discuss the practicalities, they were unable to agree. The issue was given priority during Nujoma's first state visit to South Africa in May 1996, and by August of that year it was reported that the difficulties had been resolved. Legislation providing for the cancellation of the debt was subsequently adopted by the South African parliament. When he addressed the South African parliament on his state visit to Cape Town, Nujoma appealed for South African investment in Namibia; however, relatively few such funds have been forthcoming.

Economy

DONALD L. SPARKS

INTRODUCTION

With a gross domestic product (GDP) per caput of US $2,000 in 1996, Namibia is relatively prosperous in the African context. Namibia's relative wealth reflects a large and fairly diversified mining sector, producing diamonds, uranium and base metals. Despite frequent drought, large ranches generally provide significant exports of beef and karakul sheepskins. Yet the economy is highly extractive and poorly integrated. About 90% of the goods that Namibia produces are exported, and about 90% of the goods that are used in the country, including about one-half of the food, are imported. Furthermore, the figure for GDP per caput disguises an extreme inequality in income distribution—the average income for the white minority is significantly higher than that for the mass of the black population.

The reason for this imbalance lies in the economic structure that was imposed by colonial history. The ranches were established as settlers displaced Africans on two-thirds of the viable farmland. From the African 'reserves' came a stream of migrant workers, on whose low wages the development of the early mines and ranches depended. In the diamond and uranium mines, where profits have been high and the wage bill a small proportion of costs, the situation has changed, and these enterprises now pay the highest wages in the country. Elsewhere, particularly on the ranches, wages remain extremely low.

During the early 1980s Namibia experienced a deep economic recession, intensified by war, severe drought and low world prices for the country's mineral products and for karakul pelts. In real terms, output per head declined by more than 20% over the period 1977–84, representing a fall of about one-third in real purchasing power. The impact of the recession was partly masked by a rapid expansion in state expenditure in the early 1980s, as South Africa tried to buy support for the Democratic Turnhalle Alliance (DTA) and an internal settlement. There were some benefits from this spending. For example, a high-quality road network was built in the north, albeit for military purposes. From the mid-1980s, however, there was a modest economic recovery. GDP increased by 3% in 1986, compared with a decline of 0.8% in 1985, and there were further increases in 1987 and 1988. GDP declined by 0.6% in 1989. This sluggish rate of growth was due to a number of factors, including depressed international prices for Namibia's mineral exports, a corresponding decline in mining production, and the poor performance of the South African economy (in the period prior to and since independence the Namibian and South African economies have remained closely linked). GDP increased by 5.1% in 1991, and by 3.5% in 1992, owing primarily to higher diamond output and increases in the output of the fishing and construction sectors. GDP grew by 6.2% in 1994, after a decline of 1.6% in 1993. The mining sector led the recovery, with diamond production increasing by 13%. GDP increased by 5.2% in 1995 and by 2.6% in 1996 (when it amounted to N $13,804m.), and was projected to grow by 4% in 1997. During 1990–95 average annual GDP per caput increased by 0.6%; however, GDP per head declined, in real terms, by 0.3% in 1996.

FINANCE

During the 1980s South Africa was an important source of public finance for Namibia, its annual contribution rising from R40m. (12% of total revenue) in 1981 to R469.2m. (30% of total revenue) in 1987. South Africa contributed R308m. in 1988 and 1989, and made its final contribution, of R83m., in 1990. The South African government ceased acting as guarantor of Namibian loans in 1990. Following independence Namibia began to receive financial assistance from the international donor community. Official development assistance declined from R125m. in 1991 to R90m. in 1992. However, total aid disbursements increased by nearly 50% (from N$ 282m. to N$ 421m.) from 1990 to 1992. Official development assistance accounts for about 75% of aid. In July 1990 international donors pledged assistance of US $696m. for the period 1990–93; Germany was the largest bilateral donor, agreeing to provide $186m. The USA and Scandinavian countries are the other major bilateral donors. Namibia is not permitted to borrow on concessionary terms from the International Development Association, owing to the country's high level of income per head (the fact that this is unevenly distributed throughout the population, see above, has been emphasized strongly by President Nujoma).

Namibia's budget account was characterized by a succession of deficits during the 1980s. Following independence, the government aimed to increase expenditure on health and education. The first post-independence budget, for the financial year 1990/91, produced a surplus of R200m. The 1991/92 budget represented a 21% increase in spending over the previous year, with capital expenditure doubling. The 1997/98 budget was received with approval by Namibia's business community owing to its resistance of major expenditure increases and provision for firm commitments on greater transparency in government fiscal operations. The 1997/98 expenditure of N$ 5,800m. (US $1,300m.) was only about 6% higher than the revised estimate for the previous year. The projected N$ 555m. deficit amounted to 3.7% of GDP, compared with 4.9% in the previous year. This reflected a 9% rise in estimated revenue (to N$ 5,200m.) for 1997/98, mainly as a result of increases in projected tax receipts. These increased revenues were to depend largely on higher economic growth which should, in turn, increase corporate profitability, since no rises in tax rates were announced for 1997/98. Although the government was considering the replacement of the current indirect taxes by a value-added tax (VAT), it pledged that VAT would not be introduced until 1999 at the earliest. Capital spending was projected at a record level of just under N$ 1,000m., which represented an increase of 17% compared with 1996/97. There was little change in the direction of spending, with basic education and culture continuing to take the largest share of total expenditure, at N$ 1,300m. (representing a slight decrease on the revised estimates of 1996/97), while the shares of health and transport, at N$ 800m. and N$ 700m. respectively, were virtually unchanged. Defence spending increased by 10% to N$ 400m., principally in order to cover higher salary costs. A public-sector salary increase, due at the beginning of April, was postponed until progress was made in reducing the size of the civil service. The salary freeze was sharply criticized by public sector unions, which were likely to resist more determined efforts by the government to reduce the present 67,000 staffing complement. The government acknowledged that it had not achieved the 2% annual reduction in personnel costs from 1996 recommended by the wages and salaries commission; personnel expenditure was to rise by 14% (for the second year in succession) to N$ 2,600m., representing 45% of the total budget. Financing the projected budget deficit was not to involve a significant expansion in government borrowing commitments. Domestic borrowing was to be slightly less than in 1996/97, with the remaining gap covered by a further drawing on cash reserves.

Namibia was expected to follw the example of South Africa and relax most foreign exchange controls. The central bank reaffirmed that Namibia's policy was to move towards full exchange control liberalization in conjunction with the South African Reserve Bank. Since 1 July South African nationals and residents have been entitled to hold foreign-currency accounts in South Africa or to transfer limited funds overseas. Namibia applied for IMF Article VIII status, thus providing for eventual full current-account convertibility. The South African parliament finally approved its debt-cancellation agreement with Namibia, more than two years after South Africa's president announced that Namibia's pre-independence bilateral debt would be cancelled; the writing-off liabilities totalled N$ 1,200m. The conclusion of the debt-cancellation agreement reduced Namibia's outstanding external public debt by 85%, to some N$ 200m., which represented less than 2% of Namibia's GDP. However, Namibia's external debt situation may not be as favourable as official figures indicate. The government has undertaken increased foreign borrowing in recent years, with non-Rand-denominated loans rising from only N$ 16m. in 1991 to N$ 132m. in 1993. These were mainly on highly concessionary terms, but, after the expiry of the initial grace period, repayments of debt principal were to start falling due within the following years.

The new Namibian Stock Exchange (NSE) continued to expand. The market value of shares traded on the exchange increased by nearly 80% in local-currency terms to N$ 150,000m. since the beginning of 1996, due to several large new listings. This confirmed the NSE to be sub-Saharan Africa's second largest stock exchange in capital value, although 98% of it was provided by dual-listed shares in South African firms, and trading volumes, while on the increase, remained relatively modest.

The annual rate of inflation averaged 12.9% in 1988, 15.1% in 1989 and 12.0% in 1990. The rate declined in 1992, from 20.5% in the year to June to 10.8% at the end of the year, and fell further to 8.7% in the year to March 1993 and to 7.0% by October 1993. The annual rate of inflation was 9.9% in 1995, compared with 10.8% in 1994. The rate declined further, to 8.0%, in 1996. The Consumer Price Index (CPI) recorded only changes in prices in the capital, Windhoek; however, a new measurement, which was to come into force in 1996, was to cover prices throughout the economy. The South African central bank's sustained policy of monetary restraint effectively curbs inflation in Namibia (as Namibia's fiscal policies are virtually controlled by South Africa). For example, the 1995 lending rate reached a high of 19%, with a consequent restraining influence on inflation. The nation's money supply increased by 33% in 1995, to N$ 6,500m. Declines in food prices have played a major role in the generally lower overall price level. Some 38% of the labour force were unemployed in early 1995.

MINERALS AND MINING

Namibia is mineral-rich. It is the world's leading producer of gem-quality diamonds, accounting for some 30% of total world output. In addition, Namibia has the world's largest uranium mine, and significant reserves of tin, lithium and cadmium. Namibia is Africa's second largest producer of zinc, its third largest producer of lead and fourth largest source of copper. Other important minerals include hydrocarbons, tungsten, vanadium, silver, gold, columbite/tantalite, germanium and beryl. Under the Minerals (Prospecting and Mining) Act, which came into operation in early 1994, the government has taken action to diversify the mining sector. A new geological survey of Namibia is being undertaken, with technical and financial assistance from the European Union (EU).

In 1980 mining accounted for about one-half of Namibia's GDP, but had declined to about 15% in 1994. The total value of mineral exports peaked at R1,645m. in 1986 and totalled R1,543m. in 1988, accounting for 73% of total export earnings. The real value of mining production declined by 9.8% in 1991. Minerals accounted for 51% of total exports in 1995. Employment in the sector declined from 21,000 in 1977 to 12,265 in 1992, and to 11,441 in 1993.

Diamonds form a key component of Namibia's economy. Measured at constant 1990 prices, diamond-mining contributed 69.2% of the sector's GDP in 1995. Diamonds are the principal mineral export, accounting for an estimated 32.5% of export revenue in 1994. The ownership of Namibia's most important diamond mine, centred on Oranjemund, underwent a significant reorganization in late 1994, when a new operating company, the Namdeb Diamond Corpn (owned in equal shares by the government and De Beers Centenary AG), acquired the diamond assets of Consolidated Diamond Mines (CDM), the De Beers subsidiary that had previously held sole exploitation rights to Namibian alluvial diamond deposits. About 98% of the diamonds recovered in Namibia are of gem quality, and under the new arrangements these stones continue to be marketed by De Beers through the Central Selling Organisation (CSO). Operations at Oranjemund, however, are not expected to remain economic after the year 2000, and the exploitation of an offshore diamond field, extending 300 m from the coast, is proceeding. In 1993 offshore recoveries of gem-quality stones accounted for more than 27.5% of Namibia's diamond output. In 1993 marine exploration concessions were granted to a new privately-financed venture, the Namibian Minerals Corpn (NAMCO). Concession rights held by NAMCO cover three offshore areas totalling almost 2,000 sq km, containing an estimated 80m. carats of gem-quality diamonds. Commercial recoveries began in late 1995. In that year, offshore recoveries of gem-quality stones accounted for 37% of Namibia's diamond output. Operations at a new onshore diamond mine at Auchas commenced in 1990, and a second mine, at Elizabeth Bay, entered production in 1991. Total diamond output, which totalled 1.6m. carats in 1992, fell to 1.1m. carats in 1993. Production recovered to 1.3m.

carats in 1994 and remained at approximately that level in 1995. Production increased to 1.4m. carats in 1996, owing to an increase in both onshore and offshore recoveries by Namdeb Diamond Corpn (Namdeb) and De Beers Marine (Debmar) respectively. Namdeb was expanding operations inland at Auchas, and was expected to commence mining the similar upstream Daberas prospect by 1998. Offshore recoveries accounted for 34% of Namdeb's output, although the production increase was only one-quarter of that recorded in 1995, since one of its four vessels was used for exploratory mining off the South African coast. Output from Namibian waters was expected to increase by about 50% during 1999, since a Debmar ship had been re-equipped, and one-fifth, using a new crawler-mounted mining system, was to be deployed in 1998. Most additional production was to be generated from an expansion in offshore operations by Debmar and from the start of commercial mining by NAMCO off Lüderitz in September, which was expected to increase offshore recoveries by a combined 140,000 carats, to some 610,000 carats. Despite the uncertainties surrounding the conclusion of a draft marketing agreement with Russia, De Beers was confident that demand on the international market would remain firm and was aiming to increase its onshore output, with several deposits inland along the Orange river to be brought on stream.

The huge, although low-grade, Rössing uranium mine, which is the world's largest single producer of uranium, came into production in 1976. After an initial period of profitability for its owner, the Rio Tinto-Zinc group, the mine suffered from the depression in the uranium market. The Rössing mine's uranium is sold by means of long-term contracts to EU countries, Japan and Taiwan, but the persistently weak 'spot' price of uranium has forced renegotiations of the contract prices. In 1986 it was reported that uranium from Rössing was contributing about 16% of Namibia's GDP at current prices. As a result of the continuing decline in world uranium prices, Rössing reduced its output to 2,500 tons in 1991. Production continued to decline, owing to a reduction in world-wide demand, with output of 1,973 tons in 1992, the lowest output since the mine began operations. Rössing began to deliver uranium to Electricité de France under a long-term contract calling for 5,000 tons of uranium oxide annually until 2000. This contract should put Rössing back into producing at capacity, ensuring profits in 1995. Rössing's output totalled 1,665 tons in 1993. As a result of higher international demand, the 'spot' price of uranium has increased since 1995; this upward trend was expected to continue into 1997. Namibia produced 1,901 tons of uranium in 1994 and 2,007 tons in 1995, of which virtually all emanated from Rössing. The company planned to expand its output of uranium oxide production by 12% in 1996. Uranium output rose by one-third in the first quarter of 1997, when production was being increased in conjunction with higher sales commitments. By the end of that year the Rössing mine could be operating at close to full capacity for the first time since 1991.

Tsumeb Corpn Ltd (TCL), a subsidiary of Gold Fields Namibia, is the country's principal metal producer, operating four base-metal mines and a major copper smelter and lead refinery. Operations at the copper, lead and silver mines at Tsumeb were to cease in 1996, since, after about 100 years, the ore quality had declined to such an extent that it was no longer economically viable to mine it. Gold Field Namibia (GFN) was to lose about 600 employees, under an agreement concluded with the Mineworkers' Union of Namibia (MUN). The copper smelter was to continue to remain in operation, while GFN was developing a higher-grade ore mine at Khusib Springs. In 1997 the MUN, which represented most workers in the industry, launched a campaign to force mining firms to eliminate job discrimination and to ensure equal employment opportunities for indigenous Namibians. At its annual congress MUN's acting president announced that the union would press the government not only to change laws permitting foreigners to obtain permanent residence but also to curtail temporary work permits. There were fears that the Tsumeb base metal operations of Gold Fields Namibia (GFN), which had only just begun to recover from strike action in 1996, would be affected by dissent between the union and GFN management. Another strike would seriously undermine GFN's recovery strategy, which aimed to bring up to full efficiency the new Tsumeb tailings retreatment plant and Ausmelt lead furnace. Australia's Great Fitzroy Mines confirmed that the Haib copper mine and on-site refinery would commence production in 1999. With projected output of 115,000 tons of copper cathode, this was to be Namibia's biggest mining development since the Rössing mine in the mid-1970s. The biggest operating cost component was to be power, and Haib's 200-MW projected annual requirement was to make it Namibia's single largest electricity consumer. Supplies initially would be derived from South Africa's power grid, but Haib's development strengthened the case for the planned expansion in domestic generating capacity. A further significant mining operation is Imcor Zinc (Pty) Ltd, a subsidiary of South Africa's state-controlled Iron and Steel Corpn (ISCOR), which owns the Uis tin mine and the Rosh Pinah lead/zinc mine. It is one of the very few companies to have undertaken significant prospecting for base metals in recent years, and has expanded Uis's capacity by 30% and Rosh Pinah's by 25%. The mine was put into provisional bankruptcy in late 1993, and its assets were re-acquired by ISCOR in mid-1995.

A variety of other minerals are already mined on a small scale. The most significant of these is salt, of which 346,800 metric tons were produced in 1994. Namibia is the primary source of industrial salt for the whole of southern Africa. TCL is investigating small gold prospects, and the Navacheb gold mine in central Namibia, a joint Anglo American and CDM venture, began production in 1990, with total revenue reaching R60m. in 1992. Namibia has considerable offshore reserves of natural gas, in an area near Lüderitz known as the Kudo field. A recent World Bank study suggests a proven 14-year reserve at the Kudu fields, which would allow a daily production of 28m. cu m of natural gas. Exploration rights for the offshore Kudu gas fields were awarded to a consortium of Shell and Engen in mid-1993. This was the fifth permit to be allocated under Namibia's current oil leasing negotiations. Exploration for onshore and offshore reserves of petroleum is proceeding.

In early 1993 the European Community (EC, now European Union–EU) approved a grant of ECU 40m., under its Sysmin facility, to help to finance a number of mining projects in Namibia. Most of these funds will be lent at concessionary rates to private firms. About 10% of the funds will go toward a high-resolution aeromagnetic survey of 130,000 sq km of north-central Namibia. Other projects include financing the Namibian Institute of Mining Technology, a drilling project at the Navachab gold mine and other smaller feasibility studies.

AGRICULTURE AND FISHING

War, drought, overgrazing and unscientific farming methods have had an adverse effect on the agricultural sector. The contribution of agriculture and fisheries to GDP, however, increased from 7.3% in 1986 to 9.5% in 1996. Agricultural production increased by an average of 1.9% in 1982–92, and agricultural GDP increased by an average of 5.0% per year in 1988–95. In 1995 the sector employed an estimated 45.1% of Namibia's labour force.

Namibia has a fragile ecology, and most of the land can support only livestock. The major agricultural activities are the processing of meat and other livestock products, and more than 90% of commercial agricultural output comprises livestock production. The most important agricultural product is beef (beef production represents some 87% of Namibia's gross non-fishing agricultural income). Ostrich farming was an expanding sector in the early 1990s. The only large-scale commercial arable farming is in the *karstveld* around Tsumeb, and on the Hardap irrigation scheme in the south. In the southern half of Namibia, farming is based on karakul sheep, but international fashion markets for karakul pelts slumped in the 1980s: in 1990 the value of exports of karakul pelts was equivalent to only one-half of their value in 1980. Subsistence crops include beans, potatoes and maize. Although output of maize was high in 1991, the severe drought conditions of 1991/92 devastated output. In May 1992 President Nujoma appealed to the international donor community for drought relief aid. The total maize crop for 1992/93 was 32,000 tons, a considerable increase on the previous year (when the yield reached only 13,000 tons), but still below normal levels of about 35,000 tons. The agricultural sector in Namibia remains precarious, despite higher than usual amounts of rainfall in the northern part of the country during early 1995.

Output was even lower than in 1994 because commercial and communal farmers planted less cereals. Rainfall in 1997 was higher than average (most dams received substantial inflows), and the situation regarding both crops and livestock was more favourable than at the start of 1996; a coarse grain harvest of 154,400 tons was forecast for 1996/97, almost double the drought-affected production of the previous year. The estimated millet crop of 107,700 tons was to be higher than in any year since independence. Commercial livestock activities were expected to take longer to fully recover and, due to restocking, it was possible that cattle-marketing may remain below 1996 levels.

Colonial history bequeathed Namibia three different agricultural sectors: about 4,000 large commercial ranches, almost all white-owned; 20,000 African stock-raising households, compressed into central and southern reserves; and 120,000 black families practising mixed farming on just 5% of the viable farmland in the far north. At the time of Namibia's independence about 50% of the country's commercial farms were owned by absentee landlords, and the possible re-distribution of such land was an important political issue. In mid-1991 a national land reform conference rejected calls for radical land expropriations and the abolition of freehold ownership. Nevertheless, the conference did make recommendations for reform, including bans on foreign ownership of agricultural land and on purchases of large tracts of land. In 1992 the government proposed the redistribution of 7.3m. ha of farmland owned by absentee landowners or otherwise underutilized, representing almost one-quarter of the 32m. ha owned by commercial (mostly white) farmers at independence. The Namibian government, through the Agricultural Bank of Namibia, began to grant low-interest loans to farmers in 1994. The government announced a draft national agricultural policy in early 1995 but while the policy stresses small-scale agricultural assistance, it does not tackle the controversial problem of communal land tenure. The minister of lands and resettlement was to submit the final version of a communal land reform bill in 1996. Notably, the legislation was to create leasehold titles to existing communal lands. The minister was also to have the responsibility of implementing the commercial land reform act of 1994. By 1997, however, very little farm land had been purchased by the government for redistribution, primarily because the allocated budget, totalling N$ 20m. had proved inadequate.

In 1990, following independence, Namibia signed the Lomé convention, agreeing to supply an EC quota of 10,500 tons of beef in 1991 and 1992, rising to 13,000 tons in 1993. Some 84% of commercial beef production had previously been exported to South Africa. Slaughtering and processing facilities were due to be expanded during the 1990s.

Because of the cold Benguela current, Namibia has potentially one of the richest fisheries in the world. Prior to independence, however, Namibia received no tax or licence fees from fishing because the illegal occupation of the territory deprived it of an internationally recognized fishing zone within the usual limit of 200 nautical miles (370 km). There are, in fact, two separate fisheries off Namibia—inshore and offshore. The inshore fishery, for pilchard, anchovy and rock lobster, is controlled by Namibian and South African companies, based at Lüderitz and Walvis Bay. During the mid-1980s, however, persistent over-fishing left stocks severely depleted, and in March 1990 the new Namibian government requested foreign fleets to cease fishing Namibia's coastal waters, pending an assessment of fish stocks. Following independence the Namibian authorities enforced an exclusive 370-km offshore zone, thereby achieving considerable success in restocking its waters. Under licensing arrangements implemented in 1992, 25 deep-sea trawlers were authorized to fish within Namibian coastal waters. Revenue from exports of fish and fish products provided 22.5% of total export earnings in 1993, and government revenue from sales of fishing concessions was projected at N$ 100m. in the financial year ending 31 March 1997. Fish stocks have recovered substantially since independence, and many foreign commercial companies are pressing the government to increase the annual 30,000-ton interim catch limit. The total commercial fish catch was 639,000 tons in 1994, a decrease of 19% from the previous year's record catch, but export earnings increased by 23% to N$ 1,300m. as a result of higher hake prices and higher production of canned pilchards. Namibia's freezer-trawler hake fleet has increased to some 70 vessels, three times the number in 1991, while the number of foreign-owned ships licensed to fish in Namibian waters has fallen to about a dozen. The fishing industry has declined since 1993 and shows no indications of strong recovery, although the low oxygen levels in the ocean improved in the first half of 1996, and some increase in stocks was expected in 1996–97. The total fish catch declined from 789,000 tons in 1993 to 560,000 tons in 1995. Onshore fish processing has increased the sector's value added; consequently, exports amounted to about N$ 1,300m. in 1995, almost equivalent to the level of the previous year. In 1997 scientific surveys indicated a recovery in the pilchard stock, and the government approved a small catch quota for that year's season. The 25,000-ton total allowable catch, announced by the minister of fisheries and marine resources, was 5,000 tons more than that of 1996 (which was mainly uncaught). The government also approved a 20% increase in the inshore mackerel quota, to 100,000 tons, since the initial 1997 quota had been fully caught by the end of March, with above-average oil yields. The midwater mackerel quota was also increased by almost half, to 250,000 tons. However, while the adverse oceanic conditions affecting Namibian fishing yields during the previous two years had finally receded, a new threat emerged at the end of April, with a massive increase in harmful algae along the central coast; the phenomenon had already severely affected crayfish stocks off Cape Town. However, Namibian fishery ministry officials were hopeful that its impact will be temporary and localized. Several companies reported losses for 1995; Namibian Fishing Industries, one of the largest pelagic operators, incurred a loss of N$ 10.5m. and a planned merger with its associated company, Namibian Sea Products was consequently postponed. A 1997 financial aid package for the industry was to cost the government some N$ 50m. (US $11m.) in revenue during 1997/98, but was expected to reduce the chances of industry bankrupties.

The fishing industry is an important source of employment, and there is considerable scope for job creation in the sector, particularly in fish-processing. Indeed, since independence the number of workers in this industry has increased from 6,000 to 9,000, and the fishing industry could soon replace mining as the largest source of private-sector employment. A fish-processing plant is under construction at Lüderitz. The factory, which will cost R18m. to construct, will provide 250 new jobs. The Kuwait government is to finance a N$ 6m. feasibility study for the construction of a new harbour at Mowe Bay, some 440 km north of Walvis Bay, for the expansion of the fishing industry. A N$ 150m. investment in rehabilitating the fishing fleet and building a fish-processing plant has been planned for Walvis Bay.

OTHER SECTORS

Namibia's manufacturing sector is extremely small. It provided an estimated 10.2% of GDP in 1996, and consists mainly of processing fish, minerals and meat for export, and production of basic consumer products, such as beer and bread: food products account for about 70% of all goods produced in Namibia. In 1991 manufacturing output increased by 5%; during 1986–93 manufacturing GDP increased, in real terms, by an estimated annual average of 6.6%. Manufacturing output was severely affected by lower fish-processing levels in 1996, but its contribution to GDP was expected to be raised in 1997, with a partial recovery in fish production and the initiation of additional plants in the export processing zone (EPZ). There is very little integration with Namibia's mining industry: in 1981 only 0.5% of Rössing's inputs were manufactured in the territory. The development of the sector has been limited by fluctuations in the supply of cattle and fish, by the small domestic market, by the high cost of energy and transport, and by the lack of an educated entrepreneurial class. Namibia has traditionally been dependent on South Africa for most manufactured goods; this has resulted in the underdevelopment of the sector. There are more than 300 manufacturing firms, which are located in or near the main urban centres. A cement plant, with a capacity of 200,000 tons, came into operation in 1991. In 1997 the European Commission granted N$ 32m. (US $7.2m.) to develop the EPZ project and to strengthen Namibia's capacity to attract investment and expand foreign trade. Funding was reserved for

EPZ infrastructure and services, investment promotion and the establishment of a Namibian Exporters' Association. In the Walvis Bay EPZ, the N$ 30m. German-owned Namibia Press and Tools vehicle-components plant, which opened in 1996, was to be expanded. However, several of the approximately 20 EPZ projects approved had been scaled down or abandoned. Construction contributed only 1.8% of GDP in 1991. Construction also recorded negative growth in 1995, with a decline following the 1993–94 expansion in commercial and residential property developments.

By contrast, the electricity and water sectors (which represented 2.0% of GDP in 1991) are somewhat more integrated and extensive than might be expected. The principal mines and towns are linked in a national grid, which can be fed by the 120-MW Van Eck power station outside Windhoek, the hydroelectric station at Ruacana (which has a generating capacity of up to 320 MW) on the Kunene river, and the 45-MW Paratus scheme at Walvis Bay. There is a link to the system that is operated by South Africa's Electricity Supply Commission (ESCOM), and the Zambia Electricity Supply Corpn provides electricity to the Caprivi region. The NDB diamond mine, however, draws its supply directly from ESCOM, and is not connected to the Namibian grid. In 1991 Namibia and Angola signed an agreement on the further development of the Kunene river as a source of energy. The Epupa hydroelectric scheme on the Kunene river continues to attract controversy. Fears have been expressed that the dam will disrupt the area's ecology and displace the Himba people. A 30-month study, costing N$ 4.8m. began in mid-1995. Electricity sales to domestic consumers decreased by 0.5% in 1993, despite an increase of 17% in the number of customers. In that year, municipalities consumed more electricity than the mines for the first time. Drought led to a 49m. kWh reduction in hydroelectric power exports, to 204m. kWh in 1993. Owing to low water levels in the Kunene river, only one of the three turbines at the Ruacana hydroelectric station was operating in 1996. For this reason, the Namibia Power Corpn increased electricity rates by 8.5% for large users, and by 3.5% for smaller users.

Mines and towns in Namibia's white-inhabited areas are also the main places which are served by the long-distance water supply. Windhoek and its surrounding mines are supplied from a number of dams, which came under severe pressure in the recent drought. Rössing, Walvis Bay and Swakopmund draw their water from boreholes in a series of dry river-beds. Both the Tsumeb and coastal underground reserves are under strain, and the long-term plan is to connect the two systems together, and to draw water from the Okavango river in the extreme north of the country. In November 1987 the former interim government and South Africa signed an agreement on the use of water from the Orange river, which forms the border between Namibia and South Africa.

Tourism is playing an increasingly important role in the economy. According to a government study, 282,000 tourists visited Namibia in 1991, contributing R32m. to the economy. The study estimates that the level may rise to 635,000 per year by 1997. In 1995 a new N$ 60m. hotel and entertainment complex was built in Swakopmund, housing Namibia's first casino and employing 700 people in the hospitality sector. Owing to increasing pressure from church leaders, the government has announced the establishment of a new special commission to determine the effects of the casinos and gambling houses act. The minister of environment and tourism was concerned that the government had insufficient resources to monitor the numerous legal (not to mention illegal) gambling establishments, which rapidly came into existence following their legalization in 1995. In 1997 TransNamib was to commence a new twice-weekly "desert express" rail service linking Windhoek and Swakopmund. The ministry of wildlife, conservation and tourism has also recommended the development of 'eco-tourism' in Namibia. The Namibian government appears to intend to introduce a liberalized air policy, with the minister of transport deciding not to object to a proposal by Kalahari Express Airlines that services operate between Windhoek, Cape Town and Johannesburg, despite strong criticism from Air Namibia, the state airline. In 1997 Kalahari Express Airlines was granted a five-year scheduled air-service licence. Air Namibia's international services to Frankfurt and London were under review, although airline officials discounted any prospect that it would cease to operate the routes. However, the airline encountered increased competition on Europe–Southern African routes and was conducting exploratory talks with Lufthansa regarding a possible partnership for the Windhoek–Frankfurt route. Air Namibia was also considering strategic alliances with other airlines in order to maintain its market competitiveness.

FOREIGN TRADE

Namibia's principal trade partners have included the United Kingdom, South Africa, Switzerland, Germany, Japan and the USA. Namibia's exports and imports have continued to grow since 1993. Exports amounted to US $1,279m. in that year, US $1,337m. in 1994, US $1,431m. in 1995 and an estimated US $1,500m. in 1996. Imports have increased from US $1,212m. in 1993, US $1,279m. in 1994, US $1,467m. in 1995 and an estimated US $1,550m. in 1996. In 1994 Namibia sold 37% of its exports (mostly diamonds) to the United Kingdom, 25% to South Africa, 10% to Spain and 8% to Japan. Principal exports in 1995 were diamonds (US $486m.), processed fish (US $320m.), other minerals (US $247m.), live cattle, sheep and goats (US $113m.), meat and meat products (US $115m.), and unprocessed fish (US $57m.). Diamond exports were estimated to have exceeded US $800m. in 1996 for the first time and earnings were expected to rise by some US $50m. in 1997 and by a further US $80m. in 1998. Owing, in addition, to higher uranium earnings, and, from 1998, increased exports of fish, overall export earnings might reach US $1,800m. in 1998. Namibia's principal imports in 1994 were food and beverages (23.9% of total imports), vehicles and transport equipment (17.3%), mineral fuels (12.2%), machinery and electrical goods (11.6%) and chemicals (8.7%). Its main suppliers were South Africa (which accounted for 85% of all imports), Côte d'Ivoire, Japan and Germany. The current account surplus was US $121m. in 1993, increasing to US $169m. in 1994, but declining to US $112m. in 1995 and to US $70m. in 1996.

ECONOMIC PROSPECTS

Namibia will continue to be economically dominated by neighbouring South Africa for the near future. Namibia is part of the Common Monetary Area (CMA), with Lesotho, South Africa and Swaziland, and a member (with Botswana, Lesotho, South Africa and Swaziland) of the Southern African Customs Union. At independence, Namibia used the South African rand as its currency, as it still does. However, in 1993 Namibia created its own central bank and issued its own currency, the Namibian dollar, at par with the rand. In 1995 the exchange rate was US$ 1=3.80 rand/N$. Namibia has no plans of withdrawing from the CMA in the foreseeable future. South Africa is the source of 90% of Namibia's imports; in addition, South Africa has significant control over Namibia's transport infrastructure, as Namibia's only external rail links are with South Africa. In February 1993 Namibia and South Africa agreed to establish joint customs control over Walvis Bay—which handles about 90% of Namibia's sea-borne trade. Although the enclave of Walvis Bay was transferred to Namibia in March 1994, the port facilities (owned by a South African parastatal, Portnet) were not ceded. In late 1995, however, the harbour assets at Walvis Bay were formally transferred to Namibia, after the government paid N$ 30m. for the facilities (considerably below the N$ 66m. asked by Portnet). The Export Processing Zone Act was passed in February 1995, establishing an EPZ in Walvis Bay and allowing others to follow. The Namibian EPZ is based on the successful Mauritian model, with substantial fiscal incentives. Seven companies were approved for EPZ status in 1995. The largest company, Purity Manganese, announced plans to construct a N$ 30m. industrial pipe-manufacturing facility. Although the National Assembly has banned strikes in the EPZ, all other labour legislation was in force there (as of 1996). The majority of EPZ firms were situated at Walvis Bay, although other areas of the country can also be designated as locations. The German Development Bank has financed a N$ 12m. strategic development plan for Walvis Bay and Lüderitz harbour, which was completed in 1995.

At independence Namibia became a member of the Southern African Development Co-ordination Conference (SADCC), which in 1992 was reorganized as the Southern African Development

Community (SADC) with the aim of minimizing the region's economic dependence on South Africa.

The SWAPO government has professed commitment to a mixed economy. Its first Five-Year Development Plan (NDP1), for 1995–2000, envisages increased diversification and growth. In September 1990 Namibia joined the IMF. In December of that year liberal legislation on foreign investment was introduced, and in early 1991 some 140 potential foreign investors attended a conference in Windhoek. The government has adopted a number of investment incentives, including the establishment of an export processing zone (as discussed above), which was the first in mainland Africa, and was expected to generate significant employment and foreign exchange opportunities. In early 1996 the minister of finance announced that the government aimed to increase the nation's annual economic growth to 5% during the NDP1 period. However, in view of the growth in GDP of only 2% in 1995, it appeared unlikely that the target of 5% growth for 1996 would be achieved. Since as much as half of Namibia's population lived below the official poverty level, the new budget also laid emphasis on the reduction of poverty. The budget was to include a new programme to restrain population growth, then estimated at about 3% annually. The government announced that it intended to adopt a more active role in the economy, especially in the medium- and large-scale projects. Some N$ 13m. has been allocated for the establishment of 'enterprise development units' and national industrial parks, while the Nordic Development Bank, the French State Development Bank and the European Investment Bank were to finance a loan programme for small business projects.

Namibia's abundant mineral reserves and rich fisheries are expected to form the basis of the nation's future economic prosperity. Diamond and uranium output was expected to continue to improve and to be the main factor supporting stronger GDP growth in 1998, which was projected to reach 5%. It will be necessary to expand the severely underdeveloped manufacturing sector; at independence most of the country's essential requirements were imported. The development of the impoverished northern region of the country remains a priority. In April 1993 President Nujoma announced a programme of incentives for private-sector investment in manufacturing. The incentives include tax relief, cash grants and low-interest loans for export promotion. Namibia's economic growth rate continues to advance, but this has been accomplished primarily by the extractive industries and has not yet filtered through to the wider economy in terms of increased employment, more equitable income distribution or higher per caput incomes. None the less, Namibia has moved from colonial rule to independence with relatively little social or economic upheaval, and, indeed, with public economic policies and a physical infrastructure which should lead to long-term development and growth.

Statistical Survey

Source (unless otherwise stated): Strategy Network International Ltd, The Namibia Office, Clutha House, 10 Storey's Gate, London, SW1P 3AY, England (no longer in operation).

Area and Population

AREA, POPULATION AND DENSITY*

Area (sq km)	824,292†
Population (census results)	
May 1981	1,033,196
21 October 1991	
Males	686,327
Females	723,593
Total	1,409,920
Population (official estimates at mid-year)	
1993	1,499,000
1994	1,546,000
1995	1,594,000
Density (per sq km) at mid-1995	1.9

* Including data for Walvis Bay, sovereignty over which was transferred from South Africa to Namibia with effect from March 1994. Walvis Bay has an area of 1,124 sq km (434 sq miles) and had a population of 20,800 in 1981.

† 318,261 sq miles.

ETHNIC GROUPS (population, 1988 estimate)

Ovambo	623,000	Caprivian	47,000
Kavango	117,000	Bushmen	36,000
Damara	94,000	Baster	31,000
Herero	94,000	Tswana	7,000
White	80,000	Others	12,000
Nama	60,000	**Total**	1,252,000
Coloured	51,000		

PRINCIPAL TOWN

Windhoek (capital), estimated population 114,500 in December 1988.

BIRTHS AND DEATHS (UN estimates, annual averages)

	1980–85	1985–90	1990–95
Birth rate (per 1,000)	40.3	39.0	37.0
Death rate (per 1,000)	13.5	12.0	10.5

Expectation of life (UN estimates, years at birth, 1990–95): 58.8 (males 57.5; females 60.0).

Source: UN, *World Population Prospects: The 1994 Revision*.

ECONOMICALLY ACTIVE POPULATION
(persons aged 10 years and over, 1991 census)

	Males	Females	Total
Agriculture, hunting, forestry and fishing	99,987	89,942	189,929
Mining and quarrying	13,837	849	14,686
Manufacturing	10,773	12,111	22,884
Electricity, gas and water	2,826	148	2,974
Construction	18,137	501	18,638
Trade, restaurants and hotels	19,678	18,142	37,820
Transport, storage and communications	8,003	1,319	9,322
Financing, insurance, real estate and business services	5,180	3,367	8,547
Community, social and personal services	3,664	2,163	5,827
Activities not adequately defined	39,224	44,490	83,714
Total employed	221,309	173,032	394,341
Unemployed	57,263	41,976	99,239
Total labour force	278,572	215,008	493,580

Source: ILO, *Yearbook of Labour Statistics*.

Agriculture

PRINCIPAL CROPS ('000 metric tons)

	1993	1994	1995
Wheat	6	6	3
Maize	26	44	15
Millet	37	59	35
Sorghum	7	10	6
Roots and tubers*	200	190	190
Pulses*	7	7	6
Vegetables*	8	8	7
Fruit*	10	10	8

* FAO estimates.

Source: FAO, *Production Yearbook*.

LIVESTOCK ('000 head, year ending September)

	1993	1994	1995
Horses	57	59	59*
Mules*	7	7	7
Asses*	71	71	71
Cattle	2,074	2,036	1,890†
Pigs	20	18	18*
Sheep	2,652	2,620	2,620*
Goats	1,580	1,639	1,640*

* FAO estimate(s). † Unofficial figure.

Poultry (FAO estimates, million): 2 in 1993; 2 in 1994; 2 in 1995.

Source: FAO, *Production Yearbook*.

LIVESTOCK PRODUCTS ('000 metric tons)

	1993	1994	1995
Beef and veal*	48	52	44
Mutton and lamb*	13	14	14
Goat meat*	4	4	4
Pig meat*	2	2	2
Poultry meat*	2	2	2
Other meat*	5	5	4
Cows' milk*	70	70	70
Hen eggs*	1.5	1.5	1.5
Wool:			
greasy	1.5*	1.9	1.9*
scoured*	0.9	1.2	1.2
Cattle hides (fresh)*	5.5	5.7	5.0
Sheepskins (fresh)*	1.6	1.7	1.7

* FAO estimate(s).

Source: FAO, *Production Yearbook*.

Forestry

Separate figures are not yet available. Data for Namibia are included in those for South Africa.

Fishing*

('000 metric tons, live weight)

	1993	1994	1995
Cape hakes (Stokvisse)	64.9	104.2	121.7
Cape monk	9.2	11.9	9.9
Cape horse mackerel (Maasbanker)	73.5	34.1	52.2
Southern African pilchard	114.8	116.4	42.8
Southern African anchovy	63.1	25.1	48.0
Other fishes (incl. unspecified)	4.2	8.8	10.9
Total fish	329.8	300.6	285.4
Crustaceans and molluscs	0.2	0.3	0.5
Total catch	330.0	300.9	286.0
Inland waters	1.2	1.0	1.2
Atlantic Ocean	328.8	299.9	284.8

* Figures include quantities caught by licensed foreign vessels in Namibian waters and processed in Lüderitz and Walvis Bay. The data exclude aquatic mammals (whales, seals, etc.). The number of South African fur seals caught was: 35,730 in 1993; 37,853 in 1994; 20,450 in 1995. Also excluded are aquatic plants ('000 metric tons): 0.2 in 1993; 0.2 in 1994; 0.8 in 1995.

Source: FAO, *Yearbook of Fishery Statistics*.

Mining

('000 metric tons, unless otherwise indicated)

	1993	1994	1995
Copper concentrates*	29.3	27.4	22.5
Lead concentrates*	11.4	13.9	16.1
Zinc concentrates*	18.0	33.4	30.2
Silver ore (metric tons)*	72	64	66
Uranium ore (metric tons)*	1,980	2,236	2,007
Gold ore (kilograms)*	1,953	2,394	2,098
Marble	13.4	12.1	16.9
Fluorspar†	43.5	52.2	37.1
Arsenic trioxide (metric tons)‡	2,290	2,775	1,661
Salt (unrefined):			
Sea salt	126.5	349.6	423.5
Rock salt	4.1	4.6	4.0
Diamonds ('000 carats)	1,141.1	1,312.3	1,381.7
Amethyst (metric tons)	100	338	5.3

* Figures refer to the metal content of ores and concentrates.

† 98% calcium fluoride.

‡ 75% arsenic.

Source: Ministry of Mines and Energy.

Industry

SELECTED PRODUCTS (metric tons)

	1993	1994*	1995*
Unrefined copper (unwrought)	34,411	29,781	29,799
Refined lead (unwrought)*	31,236	23,800	26,800
Refined cadmium (unwrought)	13	19	20

* Figures are provisional.

Sources: Ministry of Mines and Energy; Ministry of Trade and Industry.

Finance

CURRENCY AND EXCHANGE RATES

Monetary Units

100 cents = 1 Namibian dollar (N $).

Sterling and US Dollar Equivalents (31 March 1997)

£1 sterling = N $7.2585;
US $1 = N $4.4205;
N $100 = £13.777 = US $22.622.

Average Exchange Rate (N $ per US $)

1994 3.55080
1995 3.62709
1996 4.29935

Note: The Namibian dollar was introduced in September 1993, replacing (at par) the South African rand. The rand remained legal tender in Namibia.

CENTRAL GOVERNMENT BUDGET

(N $ million, year ending 31 March)

Revenue*	1994/95	1995/96†	1996/97‡
Taxation	3,136.1	3,521.7	3,987.5
Taxes on income, profits and capital gains	1,030.6	1,090.4	1,192.5
Individual taxes	605.7	659.8	734.5
Corporate taxes	424.9	430.6	458.0
Mining companies	163.5	139.4	140.0
Non-mining companies	261.4	291.2	318.0
Domestic taxes on goods and services	1,132.4	1,204.2	1,360.0
General sales tax	529.2	551.6	620.0
Additional sales duties	230.3	238.4	295.0
Fuel levies	261.4	299.7	304.0
Fishing quota levies	91.7	91.5	100.0
Taxes on international trade and transactions	905.5	1,155.6	1,348.0
Other current revenue	428.6	422.5	468.4
Entrepreneurial and property income	233.8	182.4	285.8
Royalties on diamond exports	142.4	114.5	160.0
Administrative fees and charges, non-industrial and incidental sales	184.1	232.6	171.1
Capital revenue	3.7	3.5	3.5
Total	3,568.4	3,947.7	4,459.4

Expenditure§	1994/95	1995/96†	1996/97‡
General public services	515.5	724.2	1,043.8
Defence	198.0	232.1	293.8
Public order and safety	267.1	297.8	327.3
Education	952.2	1,049.9	1,176.3
Health	410.0	480.6	524.2
Social security and welfare	249.7	248.3	275.8
Housing and community amenities	343.7	402.8	330.7
Recreational, cultural and religious affairs and services	90.8	111.3	129.1
Economic affairs and services	535.8	671.9	821.6
Agriculture, forestry, fishing and hunting	208.0	271.8	365.4
Transport and communications	226.2	270.8	307.7
Other purposes	131.8	121.0	150.0
Total	3,689.6	4,339.9	5,072.6

* Excluding grants received from abroad (N $ million): 38.4 in 1994/95; 48.6 (estimate) in 1995/96; 35.0 (forecast) in 1996/97.

† Revised estimates.

‡ Budget forecasts.

§ Figures are based on an unadjusted definition of expenditure. The adjusted totals (in N $ million) are: 3,797.4 in 1994/95; 4,392.7 (estimate) in 1995/96; 4,935.1 (forecast) in 1996/97. These amounts exclude lending minus repayments (N $ million): 31.9 in 1994/95; 38.0 (estimate) in 1995/96; 109.1 (forecast) in 1996/97.

Source: Bank of Namibia, Windhoek.

INTERNATIONAL RESERVES (US $ million at 31 December)*

	1994	1995	1996
IMF special drawing rights	0.02	0.02	0.02
Reserve position in IMF	0.01	0.03	0.04
Foreign exchange	202.59	220.94	193.81
Total	202.62	220.98	193.87

* Excluding gold, of which there were no official reserves in 1993–95.

Source: IMF, *International Financial Statistics*.

MONEY SUPPLY (N $ million at 31 December)

	1994	1995	1996
Demand deposits at deposit money banks	1,465.3	1,581.9	2,516.7
Total money (incl. others)	1,682.8	1,822.2	2,799.5

Source: IMF, *International Financial Statistics*.

COST OF LIVING

(Consumer Price Index for Windhoek; base: December 1992 = 100)

	1993	1994	1995
Food	102.42	115.78	129.20
Housing, fuel and power	104.83	118.77	134.06
Clothing and footwear	108.69	117.37	127.57
All items (incl. others)	104.99	116.29	127.93

Source: Bank of Namibia, Windhoek.

NATIONAL ACCOUNTS (N $ million at current prices)

National Income and Product

	1993	1994	1995
Compensation of employees	3,807.8	4,253.8	4,703.1
Operating surplus	1,961.1	3,046.8	3,035.7
Domestic factor incomes	5,768.9	7,300.6	7,738.8
Consumption of fixed capital	1,246.8	1,461.1	1,680.9
Gross domestic product (GDP) at factor cost	7,015.8	8,761.7	9,419.7
Indirect taxes	1,440.7	1,733.9	1,977.3
Less Subsidies	103.5	101.8	129.4
GDP in purchasers' values	8,353.0	10,393.8	11,267.6
Factor income received from abroad	737.1	829.3	848.7
Less Factor income paid abroad	484.0	462.4	543.5
Gross national product	8,606.0	10,760.8	11,572.7
Less Consumption of fixed capital	1,246.8	1,461.1	1,680.9
National income in market prices	7,359.2	9,299.7	9,891.8
Other current transfers from abroad	1,230.4	1,257.4	1,442.5
Less Other current transfers paid abroad	456.3	531.0	600.1
National disposable income	8,133.3	10,026.1	10,734.2

Source: Bank of Namibia, Windhoek.

Expenditure on the Gross Domestic Product

	1993	1994	1995
Government final consumption expenditure	2,997.5	3,274.0	3,702.0
Private final consumption expenditure	4,534.8	5,113.3	6,177.9
Increase in stocks	−430.7	269.6	−208.2
Gross fixed capital formation	1,886.9	2,243.8	2,565.6
Total domestic expenditure	8,988.5	10,900.8	12,237.2
Exports of goods and services	4,951.2	5,651.3	6,045.0
Less Imports of goods and services	5,586.8	6,158.3	7,014.6
GDP in purchasers' values	8,353.0	10,393.8	11,267.6
GDP at constant 1990 prices	6,695.3	7,131.7	7,318.4

Source: Bank of Namibia, Windhoek.

Gross Domestic Product by Economic Activity

	1993	1994	1995*
Agriculture, hunting, forestry and fishing	811.4	1,319.4	1,446.6
Mining and quarrying	862.0	1,282.0	1,096.7
Manufacturing	856.2	846.5	721.7
Electricity, gas and water	97.3	148.7	187.2
Construction	243.6	291.6	346.9
Trade, restaurants and hotels	769.4	902.9	1,042.8
Transport, storage and communications	398.1	490.2	566.2
Finance, insurance, real estate and business services†	1,095.9	1,142.4	1,354.1
Government services	2,170.7	2,375.5	2,700.8
Other community, social and personal services	99.5	111.5	135.3
Other services	209.7	237.8	266.7
Sub-total	7,413.8	9,148.5	9,865.0
Less Imputed bank service charge	299.8	250.2	316.7
GDP at basic prices	7,114.0	8,898.3	9,548.3
Import duties	356.3	408.2	478.1
Other taxes on products	882.6	1,087.2	1,241.0
GDP in purchasers' values	8,352.9	10,393.7	11,267.4

* Figures are provisional.

† Including imputed rents of owner-occupied dwellings (N $ million): 453.2 in 1993; 514.6 in 1994; 580.1 in 1995.

Source: IMF, *Namibia—Statistical Annex* (August 1996).

BALANCE OF PAYMENTS (US $ million)

	1993	1994	1995
Exports of goods f.o.b.	1,279.4	1,336.7	1,369.1
Imports of goods f.o.b.	−1,212.2	−1,279.0	−1,467.1
Trade balance	67.3	57.8	−98.1
Exports of services	235.7	254.8	297.4
Imports of services	−497.6	−455.4	−466.8
Balance on goods and services	−194.6	−142.9	−267.5
Other income received	223.9	235.8	232.9
Other income paid	−147.1	−129.0	−148.5
Balance on goods, services and income	−117.9	−36.0	−183.1
Current transfers received	371.1	346.6	390.0
Current transfers paid	−132.3	−141.3	−156.9
Current balance	120.9	169.2	50.0
Capital account (net)	27.3	43.3	43.6
Direct investment abroad	−10.6	−3.5	−6.1
Direct investment from abroad	38.6	51.5	47.1
Portfolio investment assets	15.5	−19.4	−2.6
Portfolio investment liabilities	60.1	55.8	107.6
Other investment assets	−193.5	−301.8	−280.4
Other investment liabilities	29.7	48.1	55.4
Net errors and omissions	3.3	32.0	14.5
Overall balance	91.3	75.0	29.1

Source: IMF, *International Financial Statistics.*

External Trade

PRINCIPAL COMMODITIES (N $ million)

Imports c.i.f.	1992	1993	1994
Food and live animals Beverages and tobacco	867	940	998
Mineral fuels and lubricants	366	497	510
Chemicals and related products	307	330	361
Wood, paper and paper products (incl. furniture)	209	214	234
Textiles, clothing and footwear	216	233	255
Machinery (incl. electrical)	501	384	488
Transport equipment	626	680	722
Total (incl. others)	3,659	3,883	4,248

Exports f.o.b.	1992	1993	1994
Food and live animals	1,127	1,115	1,461
Live animals chiefly for food	270	279	405
Cattle	110	140	210
Sheep and goats	146	129	173
Meat and meat preparations	293	294	380
Beef and veal	256	238	307
Fish, crustaceans and molluscs	534	512	646
Mineral products	2,091	2,366	2,289
Diamonds	1,334	1,501	1,472
Copper	222	188	188
Zinc	60	44	60
Manufactured products	556*	683*	n.a.
Canned fish, fish meal and fish oil	311*	403*	n.a.
Total (incl. others)	3,826	4,214	4,524

* Provisional.

Source: Bank of Namibia, Windhoek.

Exports f.o.b. (provisional figures, US $ million, 1995): Food and live animals 496.9 (live animals 139.4); Meat and meat preparations 115.3 (Beef and veal 93.0); Fish, lobsters and crabs 233.8 (Hake 145.2); Mineral products 733.3 (Diamonds 485.8); Manufactured products 117.8 (Processed fish 78.1); Total (incl. others) 1,369.3. Source: IMF, *Namibia—Statistical Annex* (August 1996).

PRINCIPAL TRADING PARTNERS (N $ million)

Imports c.i.f.	1993
Côte d'Ivoire	129
France	40
Germany	100
South Africa	3,383
USA	46
Total (incl. others)	3,883

Exports f.o.b.	1993
Belgium	232
Côte d'Ivoire	70
France	87
Germany	140
Japan	411
South Africa	1,153
Spain	258
Switzerland	74
United Kingdom	1,450
USA	51
Total (incl. others)	4,213

Source: Bank of Namibia, Windhoek.

Transport

RAILWAYS

	1994/95	1995/96
Freight (million net ton-km)	1,077	1,082
Passengers carried ('000)	110	124

Source: TransNamib Ltd., Windhoek.

ROAD TRAFFIC (motor vehicles in use at 31 December)

	1993	1994	1995*
Passenger cars	60,100	61,269	62,500
Buses and coaches	5,000	5,098	5,200
Lorries and vans	58,900	60,041	61,300
Motorcycles and mopeds	6,340	6,457	6,590

* Estimates.

Source: International Road Federation, *World Road Statistics*.

SHIPPING

Merchant Fleet (at 31 December)

	1994	1995	1996
Number of vessels	95	99	114
Displacement (gross registered tons)	44,271	51,791	58,591

Source: Lloyd's Register of Shipping, *World Fleet Statistics*.

Sea-borne Freight Traffic (at Walvis Bay, '000 metric tons)

	1995/96
Goods loaded	1,132
Goods unloaded	644

Source: Namibian Ports Authority, Walvis Bay.

CIVIL AVIATION (traffic on scheduled services)

	1994/95	1995/96
Kilometres flown (million)	6.6	7.2
Passengers carried ('000)	209	227
Passenger-km (million)	718	756
Freight ton-km (million)	26	23

Source: TransNamib Ltd., Windhoek.

Tourism

FOREIGN TOURIST ARRIVALS*

Country of origin	1993
Angola	12,719
Botswana	11,889
Germany	29,730
South Africa	155,050
United Kingdom	5,987
Zambia	8,798
Total (incl. others)	254,978

* Excluding same-day visitors, totalling 33,465 in 1993.

Source: Ministry of Environment and Tourism, Windhoek.

Communications Media

	1997
Radio receivers ('000 in use)	208*
Television receivers ('000 in use)	50
Daily newspapers	
Number	4
Average circulation ('000 copies)	9.5
Non-daily newspapers	
Number	5
Average circulation ('000 copies)	9.1

* 1994 figure (Source: UNESCO, *Statistical Yearbook*).

Source: Ministry of Information and Broadcasting, Windhoek.

Telephones ('000 main lines in use, year ending 31 March): 76.4 in 1994/95; 80.9 in 1995/96; 85.0 in 1996/97 (Source: Telecom Namibia, Windhoek).

Education

(1994, unless otherwise indicated)

	Institutions	Teachers	Students: Males	Students: Females	Students: Total
Pre-primary	12*	217†	2,273	2,306	4,579
Primary	974‡	10,912†	186,500‡	185,756‡	372,256‡
Secondary	116‡	3,999†	48,270‡	56,210‡	104,480‡
General	n.a.	3,943†	46,300	55,538	101,838
Vocational	n.a.	56†	83	53	136
Higher education	7*	331§	4,440	6,904	11,344

* 1993. † 1992. ‡ 1996. § 1991.

Sources: UNESCO, *Statistical Yearbook*; Ministry of Information and Broadcasting, Windhoek.

Directory

The Constitution

The Constitution of the Republic of Namibia took effect at independence on 21 March 1990. Its principal provisions are summarized below:

THE REPUBLIC

The Republic of Namibia is a sovereign, secular, democratic and unitary State and the Constitution is the supreme law.

FUNDAMENTAL HUMAN RIGHTS AND FREEDOMS

The fundamental rights and freedoms of the individual are guaranteed regardless of sex, race, colour, ethnic origin, religion, creed or social or economic status. All citizens shall have the right to form and join political parties. The practice of racial discrimination shall be prohibited.

THE PRESIDENT

Executive power shall be vested in the President and the Cabinet. The President shall be the Head of State and of the Government and the Commander-in-Chief of the Defence Force. The President shall be directly elected by universal and equal adult suffrage, and must receive more than 50% of the votes cast. The term of office shall be five years; one person may not hold the office of President for more than two terms.

THE CABINET

The Cabinet shall consist of the President, the Prime Minister and such other ministers as the President may appoint from members of the National Assembly. The President may also appoint a Deputy Prime Minister. The functions of the members of the Cabinet shall include directing the activities of ministries and government departments, initiating bills for submission to the National Assembly, formulating, explaining and assessing for the National Assembly the budget of the State and its economic development plans, formulating, explaining and analysing for the National Assembly Namibia's foreign policy and foreign trade policy and advising the President on the state of national defence.

THE NATIONAL ASSEMBLY

Legislative power shall be vested in the National Assembly, which shall be composed of 72 members elected by general, direct and secret ballots and not more than six non-voting members appointed by the President by virtue of their special expertise, status, skill or experience. Every National Assembly shall continue for a maximum period of five years, but it may be dissolved by the President before the expiry of its term.

THE NATIONAL COUNCIL

The National Council shall consist of two members from each region (elected by Regional Councils from among their members) and shall have a life of six years. The functions of the National Council shall include considering all bills passed by the National Assembly, investigating any subordinate legislation referred to it by the National Assembly for advice, and recommending legislation to the National Assembly on matters of regional concern.

OTHER PROVISIONS

Other provisions relate to the administration of justice (see under Judicial System), regional and local government, the public service commission, the security commission, the police, defence forces and prison service, finance, and the central bank and national planning commission. The repeal of, or amendments to, the Constitution require the approval of two-thirds of the members of the National Assembly and two-thirds of the members of the National Council; if the proposed repeal or amendment secures a majority of two-thirds of the members of the National Assembly, but not a majority of two-thirds of the members of the National Council, the President may make the proposals the subject of a national referendum, in which a two-thirds majority is needed for approval of the legislation.

The Government

HEAD OF STATE

President and Commander-in-Chief of the Defence Force: Dr SAMUEL DANIEL NUJOMA (took office 21 March 1990; elected by direct suffrage 7–8 December 1994).

CABINET
(August 1997)

President: Dr SAMUEL DANIEL NUJOMA.

Prime Minister: HAGE GEINGOB.

Deputy Prime Minister: Rev. HENDRIK WITBOOI.

Minister of Home Affairs: JERRY EKANDJO.

Minister of Foreign Affairs: THEO-BEN GURIRAB.

Minister of Basic Education and Culture: JOHN MUTORWA.

Minister of Higher Education, Vocational Training, Science and Technology: NAHAS ANGULA.

Minister of Information and Broadcasting: BEN AMADHILA.

Minister of Mines and Energy: ANDIMA TOIVO YA TOIVO.

Minister of Justice: Dr NGARIJUTUKE TJIRIANGE.

Minister of Trade and Industry: HIDIPO HAMUTENYA.

Minister of Agriculture, Water and Rural Development: HELMUT ANGULA.

Minister of Defence: PHILEMON MWALIMA.

Minister of Finance: NANGOLD MBUMBA.

Minister of Health and Social Services: Dr LIBERTINE AMATHILA.

Minister of Labour: MOSES GAROËB.

Minister of Regional and Local Government and Housing: NICKEY IYAMBO.

Minister of Environment and Tourism: GERT HANEKOM.

Minister of Works, Transport and Communications: HAMPIE PLICHTA.

Minister of Lands, Resettlement and Rehabilitation: PENDUKENI ITHANA.

Minister of Fisheries and Marine Resources: HIFIKEPUNYE POHAMBA.

Minister of Youth and Sports: RICHARD KAPELWA-KABAJANI.

Minister of Prisons and Correctional Services: MARCO HAUSIKU.

Director of Women's Affairs at the Office of the President: NETUMBO NDAITWAH.

MINISTRIES

Office of the President: State House, Robert Mugabe Ave, PMB 13339, Windhoek; tel. (61) 220010; telex 3222; fax (61) 221780.

Office of the Prime Minister: Robert Mugabe Ave, PMB 13338, Windhoek; tel. (61) 2879111; fax (61) 226189.

Ministry of Agriculture, Water and Rural Development: cnr Robert Mugabe Ave and Peter Muller St, PMB 13184, Windhoek; tel. (61) 2029111; telex 3109; fax (61) 221733.

Ministry of Basic Education and Culture: Troskie House, Uhland St, PMB 13186, Windhoek; tel. (61) 2939311 fax (61) 224277.

Ministry of Defence: Private Bag 13307, Windhoek; tel. (61) 221920; fax (61) 224277.

Ministry of Environment and Tourism: Swabou Bldg, Post St Mall, PMB 13346, Windhoek; tel. (61) 2849111; fax (61) 229936.

Ministry of Finance: Fiscus Bldg, John Meinert St, PMB 13295, Windhoek; tel. (61) 2099111; telex 3369; fax (61) 236454.

Ministry of Fisheries and Marine Resources: Brenden Simbwaye Bldg, Goethe St, PMB 13355, Windhoek; tel. (61) 2053911; fax (61) 233286.

Ministry of Foreign Affairs: Govt Bldgs, East Wing, 4th Floor, Robert Mugabe Ave, PMB 13347, Windhoek; tel. (61) 2829111; telex 655; fax (61) 223937.

Ministry of Health and Social Services: Old State Hospital, Harvey St, PMB 13198, Windhoek; tel. (61) 2032800; telex 3366; fax (61) 227607.

Ministry of Higher Education, Vocational Training, Science and Technology: Winco Bldg, Stuebel St, PMB 13391, Windhoek; tel. (61) 253670; fax (61) 253671.

Ministry of Home Affairs: Cohen Bldg, Kasino St, PMB 13200, Windhoek; tel.(61) 2929111; telex 403; fax (61) 223817.

Ministry of Information and Broadcasting: Govt Bldgs, 2nd Floor, PMB 13344, Windhoek; tel. (61) 2839111; telex 2123; fax (61) 222343.

Ministry of Justice: Justitia Bldg, Independence Ave, PMB 13248, Windhoek; tel. (61) 239280; telex 635; fax (61) 221233.

Ministry of Labour: 32 Mercedes St, Khomasdal, PMB 23115, Windhoek; tel. (61) 2066111; telex 496; fax (61) 212323.

Ministry of Lands, Resettlement and Rehabilitation: Brendan Simbwaye Bldg, Goethe St, PMB 13343, Windhoek; tel. (61) 2852111; telex 826; fax (61) 228240.

Ministry of Mines and Energy: Trust Bank Bldg, cnr J. Meinert and Independence Ave, PMB 13297, Windhoek; tel. (61) 2848111; telex 487; fax (61) 238643.

Ministry of Prisons and Correctional Services: Brendan Simbwaye Bldg, Goethe St, PMB 13323; tel. (61) 233836; fax (61) 233879.

Ministry of Regional and Local Government and Housing: PMB 13289, Windhoek; tel. (61) 2972911; telex 603; fax (61) 226049.

Ministry of Trade and Industry: Govt Bldgs, Private Bag 13340, Windhoek; tel. (61) 2849111; telex 808; fax (61) 220227.

Ministry of Works, Transport and Communications: Private Bag 13341, Windhoek; tel. (61) 2089111; telex 709; fax (61) 228560.

Ministry of Youth and Sports: Educom Bldg, 6th Floor, Independence Ave, PMB 13359, Windhoek; tel. (61) 220066; fax (61) 221304.

President and Legislature

PRESIDENT

Presidential Election, 7–8 December 1994

Candidate	Votes	% of votes
SAMUEL NUJOMA (SWAPO)	370,452	76.34
MISHAKE MUYONGO (DTA)	114,843	23.66
Total	485,295	100.00

NATIONAL ASSEMBLY

Speaker: Dr MOSES TJITENDERO.

General Election, 7–8 December 1994

Party	Votes	% of votes	Seats*
South West Africa People's Organisation of Namibia	361,800	73.89	53
Democratic Turnhalle Alliance of Namibia	101,748	20.78	15
United Democratic Front	13,309	2.72	2
Democratic Coalition of Namibia	4,058	0.83	1
Monitor Action Group	4,005	0.82	1
South West African National Union	2,598	0.53	—
Federal Convention of Namibia	1,166	0.24	—
Workers' Revolutionary Party	952	0.19	—
Total	489,636	100.00	72

* In addition to the 72 directly-elected members, six non-voting members were nominated by the President.

NATIONAL COUNCIL

Chairman: KANDINDIMA NEHOVA.

The second chamber of parliament is the advisory National Council, comprising two representatives from each of the country's 13 Regional Councils, elected for a period of six years.

Political Organizations

Christian Democratic Action for Social Justice (CDA): Ondwangwa; telex 3143; f. 1982; supported by Ovambos and supporters of fmr National Democratic Party; Leader Rev. PETER KALANGULA.

Democratic Coalition of Namibia (DCN): Windhoek; f. 1994 as coalition of the National Patriotic Front, the South West African National Union (withdrew from coalition in Nov. 1994) and the German Union; Leader MOSES KATJIUONGUA.

Democratic Turnhalle Alliance of Namibia (DTA): POB 173, Windhoek; telex 3217; f. 1977 as a coalition of ethnically-based political groupings; reorg. as a single party in 1991; Pres. MISHAKE MUYONGO; Chair. PIET JUNIUS.

Federal Convention of Namibia (FCN): Windhoek; f. 1988; Leader JOHANNES DIERGAARDT; federalist; opposes unitary form of govt for Namibia; an alliance of ethnically-based parties, including:

NUDO–Progressive Party Jo'Horongo: f. 1987; Pres. MBURUMBA KERINA.

Rehoboth Bevryde Demokratiese Party (Rehoboth Free Democratic Party or **Liberation Front) (RBDP):** Leader JOHANNES DIERGAARDT; coalition of the **Rehoboth Bevrydingsparty** (Leader JOHANNES DIERGAARDT) and the **Rehoboth Democratic Party** (Leader K. G. FREIGANG).

Monitor Action Group (MAG): Windhoek; f. 1991; fmrly National Party of South West Africa; Leader KOSIE PRETORIUS.

Namibia Movement for Independent Candidate: Windhoek; f. 1997; Leader JUSTICE KAWADENGE.

Namibia National Democratic Party: Windhoek; Leader PAUL HELMUTH.

Namibia National Front: Windhoek; Leader VEKUII RUKORO.

National Democratic Party for Justice (NDPFJ): f. May 1995 as SWAPO for Justice by breakaway mems of SWAPO; reconstituted as a political party in Nov. 1996, when it claimed to have 3,000 mems; Pres. NGHIWETE NDJOBA.

South West Africa People's Organisation of Namibia (SWAPO): Windhoek; f. 1957 as the Ovamboland People's Congress; renamed South West Africa People's Organisation in 1960; adopted present name in 1968; Pres. Dr SAMUEL DANIEL NUJOMA; Vice-Pres. Rev. HENDRIK WITBOOI; Sec.-Gen. HIFIKEPUNYE POHAMBA.

South West African National Union (SWANU): Windhoek; f. 1959; Leader HITJEVI VEII.

United Democratic Front (UDF): POB 20037, Windhoek; tel. (61) 230683; fax (61) 237175; f. 1989 as a centrist coalition of eight parties; Nat. Chair. ERIC BIWA; Pres. JUSTUS GAROEB.

Workers' Revolutionary Party: Windhoek; f. 1989; Trotskyist; Leaders WERNER MAMUGWE, HEWAT BEUKES.

Diplomatic Representation

EMBASSIES AND HIGH COMMISSIONS IN NAMIBIA

Algeria: 95 John Meinert St, Windhoek; tel. (61) 229896; Chargé d'affaires a.i.: A. I. BENGUEUEDDA.

Angola: Angola House, 3 Ausspann St, Private Bag 12020, Windhoek; tel. (61) 227535; telex 897; fax (61) 221498; Ambassador: Dr ALBERTO D. C. B. RIBEIRO.

Bangladesh: Windhoek; tel. (61) 32301; telex 650; High Commissioner: A. Y. B. I. SIDDIQI (acting).

Botswana: 101 Nelson Mandela Ave, POB 20359, Windhoek; tel. (61) 221942; telex 894; fax (61) 36034; High Commissioner: TUELENYANA ROSEMARY DITLHABI-OLIPHANT.

Brazil: 52 Bismarck St, POB 24166, Windhoek; tel. (61) 237368; telex 498; fax (61) 233389; Chargé d'affaires a.i.: JOSÉ FERREIRA-LOPES.

Canada: Windhoek; tel. (61) 222941; telex 402; fax (61) 224204; High Commissioner: WAYNE HAMMOND.

China, People's Republic: 39 Beethoven St, POB 22777, Windhoek; tel. (61) 222089; telex 675; fax (61) 225544; Ambassador: AN YONGYU.

Congo, Republic: 9 Corner St, POB 22970, Windhoek; tel. (61) 226958; telex 405; fax (61) 228642; Ambassador: A. KONDHO.

Cuba: 31 Omuramba Rd, Eros, POB 23866, Windhoek; tel. (61) 227072; telex 406; fax (61) 231584; Ambassador: ESTHER ARMENTEROS.

Denmark: Sanlam Centre, 154 Independence Ave, POB 20126, Windhoek; tel. (61) 224923; telex 461; fax (61) 35807; Ambassador: ALF JÖNSSON.

Egypt: 10 Berg St, POB 11853, Windhoek; tel. (61) 221501; telex 421; fax (61) 228856; Ambassador: HUSSEIN A. M. WAHBY.

Finland: POB 3649, Windhoek; tel. (61) 221355; telex 671; fax (61) 221349; Ambassador: KIRSTI LINTONEN.

France: 1 Goethe St, POB 20484, Windhoek; tel. (61) 229021; telex 715; fax (61) 231436; Ambassador: FRÉDÉRIC BALEINE DU LAURENS.

Germany: POB 231, Windhoek; tel. (61) 229217; telex 482; fax (61) 222981; Ambassador: Dr HANNS SCHUMACHER.

Ghana: 5 Nelson Mandela Ave, POB 24165, Windhoek; tel. (61) 221341; fax (61) 221343; High Commissioner: H. MILLS-LUTTERODT.

India: 97 Nelson Mandela Ave, POB 1209, Windhoek; tel. (61) 226037; telex 832; fax (61) 237320; High Commissioner: KANWAR SINGH JASROTIA.

Iran: 81 Nelson Mandela Ave, Windhoek; tel. (61) 229974; telex 637; fax (61) 220016; Chargé d'affaires a.i.: ALAMALHODA.

Italy: POB 24065, Windhoek; tel. (61) 228602; telex 620; fax (61) 229860; Ambassador: PIERO DE MASI.

Kenya: Kenya House, 134 Robert Mugabe Ave, POB 2889, Windhoek; tel. (61) 226836; telex 823; fax (61) 221409; High Commissioner: JOSEPH SEFU.

Libya: 69 Burg St, Luxury Hill, POB 124, Windhoek; tel. (61) 221139; telex 868; fax (61) 34471; Chargé d'affaires a.i.: H. O. ALSHAOSHI.

Malawi: 56 Bismarck St, POB 23384, Windhoek; tel. (61) 221291; telex 469; fax (61) 221392; High Commissioner: JAMES KALILANGWE (acting).

Nigeria: 4 Omuramba Rd, Eros Park, POB 23547, Windhoek; tel. (61) 232103; fax (61) 221639; High Commissioner: AKIN OYATERU.

Norway: POB 9936, Windhoek; tel. (61) 227812; telex 432; fax (61) 222226; Ambassador: OLAF MYKLEBUST.

Portugal: 28 Garten St, POB 443, Windhoek; tel. (61) 228736; telex 409; Chargé d'affaires a.i.: JOÃO JOSÉ GOMES.

Romania: 3 Hamerkop St, Hochland Park, POB 6827, Windhoek; tel. (61) 224630; telex 435; fax (61) 221564; Ambassador: P. VLASCEANU.

Russia: 4 Christian St, POB 3826, Windhoek; tel. (61) 228671; telex 865; fax (61) 229061; Ambassador: BAKHTIER M. KHAKIMOV.

South Africa: RSA House, cnr Jan Jonker and Nelson Mandela Aves, POB 23100, Windhoek; tel. (61) 229765; fax (61) 236093; High Commissioner: S. MABIZELA.

Spain: 58 Bismarck St, POB 21811, Windhoek; tel. (61) 223066; fax (61) 223046; Ambassador: GERMÁN ZURITA Y SÁENZ DE NAVARRETE.

Sudan: Windhoek; tel. (61) 228544; Ambassador: ABD ELMONIEM MUSTAFA ELAMIN.

Sweden: POB 23087, Windhoek; tel. (61) 222905; telex 463; fax (61) 222774; Ambassador: ULLA STRÖM.

United Kingdom: 116 Robert Mugabe Ave, POB 22202, Windhoek; tel. (61) 223022; telex 2343; fax (61) 228895; High Commissioner: GLYN DAVIES.

USA: 14 Lossen St, Private Bag 12029, Windhoek; tel. (61) 221601; fax (61) 229792; Ambassador: GEORGE F. WARD.

Venezuela: Southern Life Tower, 3rd Floor, Post Street Mall, Private Bag 13353, Windhoek; tel. (61) 227905; fax (61) 227804; e-mail: Embaven@iwwn.com.na; Chargé d'affaires: ALBERTO VALERO.

Yugoslavia: 10 Chateau St, POB 3705, Windhoek; tel. (61) 36900; telex 3174; fax (61) 222260; Chargé d'affaires: PETKO DELIĆ.

Zambia: 22 Sam Nujoma Drive, POB 22882, Windhoek; tel. (61) 37610; telex 980; fax (61) 228162; High Commissioner: CHANDA SOSALA.

Zimbabwe: cnr Independence Ave and Grimm St, POB 23056, Windhoek; tel. (61) 228134; telex 866; fax (61) 228659; High Commissioner: MARY SIBUSISIWE MUBI.

Judicial System

Judicial power is exercised by the Supreme Court, the High Court and a number of Magistrate and Lower Courts. The Constitution provides for the appointment of an Ombudsman.

Chief Justice: ISMAIL MAHOMED.

Attorney-General: REINHOLD RUKORO.

Religion

It is estimated that about 90% of the population are Christians.

CHRISTIANITY

Council of Churches in Namibia: 8 Mont Blanc St, POB 41, Windhoek; tel. (61) 217621; telex 834; fax (61) 62786; f. 1978; eight mem. churches; Pres. Bishop HENDRIK FREDERIK; Gen. Sec. Dr ABISAI SHEJAVALI.

The Anglican Communion

Namibia comprises a single diocese in the Church of the Province of Southern Africa. The Metropolitan of the Province is the Archbishop of Cape Town, South Africa.

Bishop of Namibia: Rt Rev. JAMES HAMUPANDA KAULUMA, POB 57, Windhoek; tel. (61) 38920; fax (61) 225903.

Dutch Reformed Church

Dutch Reformed Church of South West Africa/Namibia: POB 389, Windhoek; tel. (61) 41144; Moderator Rev. A. J. DE KLERK.

Evangelical Lutheran

Evangelical Lutheran Church in Namibia (ELCIN): Bishop Dr KLEOPAS DUMENI, Private Bag 2018, Ondangwa; tel. (6756) 40241; fax (6756) 40472.

Evangelical Lutheran Church (Rhenish Mission Church): POB 5069, Windhoek; tel. (61) 224531; telex 3107; f. 1967; Pres. Bishop HENDRIK FREDERIK.

German Evangelical-Lutheran Church in Namibia: POB 233, Windhoek; tel. (61) 224294; fax (61) 221470; 8,200 mems; Pres. Rev. Landespropst REINHARD KEDING.

Methodist

African Methodist Episcopal Church: Rev. B. G. KARUAERA, Windhoek; tel. (61) 62757.

Methodist Church of Southern Africa: POB 143, Windhoek; tel. (61) 228921.

The Roman Catholic Church

Namibia comprises one archdiocese, one diocese and one apostolic vicariate. At 31 December 1995 adherents of the Roman Catholic Church in Namibia comprised some 14.2% of the total population.

Archbishop of Windhoek: Most Rev. BONIFATIUS HAUSHIKU, POB 272, Windhoek; tel. (61) 227595; fax (61) 229836.

Other Christian Churches

Among other denominations active in Namibia are the Evangelical Reformed Church in Africa, the Presbyterian Church of Southern Africa and the United Congregational Church of Southern Africa.

JUDAISM

Windhoek Hebrew Congregation: POB 140, Windhoek; tel. (61) 221990; fax (61) 226444.

BAHÁ'Í FAITH

National Spiritual Assembly: POB 20372, Windhoek; tel. and fax (61) 239634; mems resident in 208 localities.

The Press

Abacus: POB 22791, Windhoek; tel. (61) 235596; fax (61) 236467; weekly; English; educational; Editor HEIDI VON EGIDY; circ. 31,000.

AgriForum: 114 Robert Mugabe Ave, PMB 13255, Windhoek; tel. (61) 237838; fax (61) 220193; monthly; Afrikaans, English; Editor PEDRO STEENKAMP; circ. 5,000.

Allgemeine Zeitung: 49 Stuebel St, POB 56, Windhoek; tel. (61) 230331; fax (61) 220225; e-mail aznews@iafrica.com.na; f. 1915; daily; German; Editor-in-Chief EBERHARD HOFFMAN; circ. 4,500 (Mon.-Wed.), 5,900 (Thur.-Fri.).

Aloe: POB 59, Windhoek; tel. (61) 2092911; fax (61) 2902006; monthly; English; edited by the Windhoek Municipality; Editor SIMON HOEBEB; circ. 45,000.

Investor: PMB 13340, Windhoek; tel. (61) 2837111; fax (61) 220278; circ. 5,000.

Monitor: 4 Kepler St, POB 2196, Windhoek; tel. (61) 234141; fax (61) 229242; f. 1945; monthly; Afrikaans, English; Editor JACOBUS WILLEM FRANÇOIS; circ. 3,000.

Namib Times: Seventh St., POB 706, Walvis Bay; tel. (64) 205854; telex 844; fax (64) 204813; 2 a week; Afrikaans, English, German and Portuguese; Editor PAUL VINCENT; circ. 4,300.

Namibia Brief: Independence Ave, POB 2123, Windhoek; tel. and fax (61) 251044; quarterly; English; Editor CATHY BLATT; circ. 7,500.

Namibia Business Journal: POB 9355, Windhoek; tel. (61) 228809; fax (61) 228009; Editor MILTON LOUW; circ. 4,000.

Namibia Focus: Windhoek; tel. (61) 227182; fax (61) 220226; monthly; English; business; Editor JOHAN ENGELBRECHT; circ. 30,000.

Namibia Review: Turnhalle Bldg, Bahnhof St, PMB 13344, Windhoek; tel. (61) 222246; fax (61) 224937; govt-owned monthly; Editor ALEX KAURE; circ. 5,000.

Namibia Today: POB 24669, Windhoek; tel. (61) 229150; fax (61) 229150; 2 a week; Afrikaans, English, Oshiherero, Oshiwambo; publ. by SWAPO; Editor KAOMO-VIJINDA TJOMBE; circ. 5,000.

The Namibian: John Meinert St, POB 20783, Windhoek; tel. (61) 236970; telex 3032; fax (61) 233980; e-mail graham@namibian.com.na; daily; English; Editor GWEN LISTER; circ. 11,000.

The Namibian Worker: POB 50034, Bachbrecht, Windhoek; tel. (61) 215037; fax (61) 215589; Afrikaans, English, Oshiwambo; publ. by National Union of Namibian Workers; Editor-in-Chief C. R. HAIKALI; circ. 1,000.

New Era: PMB 13364, Windhoek; tel. (61) 234924; fax (61) 235419; govt-owned: 2 a week; English; Editor RAJAH MUNAMAVA; circ. 10,000.

Die Republikein: 49 Stuebel St, POB 3436, Windhoek; tel. (61) 230331; telex 3201; fax (61) 223721; e-mail republkn@iwwn.com.na; f. 1977; daily; Afrikaans, English and German; organ of DTA of Namibia; Editor CHRISTO RETIEF (acting); circ. 12,000 (Mon.-Wed.), 15,000 (Thur.-Fri.).

Tempo: 49 Stuebel St, POB 1794, Windhoek; tel. (61) 225822; fax (61) 223110; f. 1992; weekly; English and German; Editor DES ERASMUS; circ. 11,000.

Visitor: POB 23000, Windhoek; tel. (61) 227182; fax (61) 220226; monthly; English; tourist information; Editor JOHAN ENGELBRECHT; circ. 10,000.

The Windhoek Advertiser: 49 Stuebel St, POB 3436, Windhoek; tel. (61) 230331; fax (61) 225863; e-mail advertsr@iwwn.com.na; f. 1919; daily; English; Editor DEON SCHLECHTER; circ. 5,000 (Mon.-Wed.), 7,000 (Thur.-Fri.).

Windhoek Observer: 49 Stuebel St, POB 2255, Windhoek; tel. (61) 221737; fax (61) 226098; f. 1978; weekly; English; Editor HANNES SMITH; circ. 14,000.

NEWS AGENCIES

Namibia Press Agency (Nampa): POB 61354, Windhoek; tel. (61) 221711; fax (61) 221713; Editor-in-Chief MOCKS SHIVUTE.

Foreign Bureaux

Associated Press (AP) (USA): POB 5750, Windhoek; tel. (61) 235573; fax (61) 232476; Correspondent SEAN KELLY.

Informatsionnoye Telegrafnoye Agentstvo Rossii–Telegrafnoye Agentstvo Suverennykh Stran (ITAR–TASS) (Russia): POB 24821, Windhoek; tel. and fax (61) 232909; telex 713; Correspondent KORCHOUNOV.

Inter Press Service (IPS) (Italy): POB 20783, Windhoek; tel. (61) 226645; telex 3032; Correspondent MARK VERBAAN.

South African Press Association (SAPA): POB 2032, Windhoek; tel. (61) 231565; fax (61) 220783; Representative CARMEN HONEY.

Xinhua (New China) News Agency (People's Republic of China): POB 22130, Windhoek; tel. (61) 226484; fax (61) 226484; Bureau Chief TENG WENVI.

Reuters (UK) is also represented in Namibia.

PRESS ASSOCIATIONS

Journalist Association of Namibia (JAN): Windhoek; tel. (61) 232975; fax (61) 248016; f. 1992; Chair. DAVID LUSH.

Press Club Windhoek: POB 2032, Windhoek; tel. (61) 231565; fax (61) 220783; Chair. CARMEN HONEY.

Publishers

BAUM Publishers: POB 3436, Windhoek; tel. (61) 225411; fax (61) 224843; Publr NIC KRUGER.

Clarian Publishers: POB 5861, Windhoek; tel. (61) 251044; fax (61) 237251; Publr CATHY BLATT.

ELOC Printing Press: PMB 2013, Oniipa, Ondangwa; tel. and fax (6756) 40211; f. 1901; Rev. Dr KLEOPAS DUMENI.

Gamsberg McMillan Publishers (Pty) Ltd: POB 22830, Windhoek; tel. (61) 232165; fax (61) 233538; Man. Dir HERMAN VAN WYK.

Longman Namibia: POB 9251, Eros, Windhoek; tel. (61) 231124; fax (61) 224019; Publr LINDA BREDENKAMP.

National Archives of Namibia: 4 Lüderitz St, PMB 13250, Windhoek; tel. (61) 2934308; fax (61) 239042; Editor (vacant).

New Namibia Books (Pty) Ltd: POB 21601, Windhoek; tel. (61) 221134; fax (61) 235279; Publr JANE KATJAVIVI.

Out of Africa Publishers: POB 21841, Windhoek; tel. (61) 221494; fax (61) 221720; Man. VIDA LOCHNER.

Verba Corporate Publishers Ltd: POB 24007, Windhoek; tel. (61) 229778; fax (61) 228085; Man. Dirs JOHN C. STOKES, ALTA F. FOLSCHER.

PUBLISHERS' ASSOCIATION

Association of Namibian Publishers: POB 21601, Windhoek; tel. (61) 235796; fax (61) 235279; f. 1991; Sec. PETER REINER.

Radio and Television

In 1994, according to UNESCO, there were an estimated 208,000 radio receivers in use. There were some 50,000 television receivers in use in 1997.

Namibian Broadcasting Corporation (NBC): POB 321, Windhoek; tel. (61) 291311; telex 622; fax (61) 216209; f. 1990; broadcasts on eight radio channels in 11 languages; television programmes are broadcast in English; Dir-Gen. DANIEL TJONGARERO.

Channel 7: POB 20500, Windhoek; tel. (61) 218969; fax (61) 215572; Man. NEAL VAN DEN BERGH.

Katutura Community Radio: POB 22355, Windhoek; tel. (61) 263768; fax (61) 262786; Dir FREDERICK GOWASEB.

Multi Choice Namibia: POB 1752, Windhoek; tel. (61) 222222; fax (61) 227605; commercial television channels; Gen. Man. HARRY AUCAMP.

Radio Antenna (Radio 99): POB 11849, Windhoek; tel. (61) 223634; fax (61) 230964; private radio service; Man. Dir ROLF LANGE.

Radio Energy (Radio 100): POB 11849, Windhoek; tel. (61) 224947; fax (61) 230964; Man. Dir MARIO AITA.

Finance

(cap. = capital; res = reserves; dep. = deposits; m. = million; brs = branches; amounts in Namibian dollars)

BANKING

Central Bank

Bank of Namibia: 10 Casino St, POB 2882, Windhoek; tel. (61) 226401; telex 710; fax (61) 227649; f. 1990; cap. and res. 74.3m., dep. 493.2m. (Jan. 1997); Gov. T. K. ALWEENDO; Deputy Gov. L. IPANGELWA.

Commercial Banks

Bank Windhoek Ltd: 262 Independence Ave, POB 15, Windhoek; tel. (61) 2991122; telex 660; fax (61) 2991285; f. 1982; cap. and res 60.0m., dep. 953.4m. (March 1996); Chair. J. C. BRANDT; Man. Dir J. L. J. VAN VUUREN; 15 brs.

City Savings and Investment Bank (CSIB): Post St Mall, Windhoek; tel. (61) 221262; fax (61) 221555; f. 1994; CEO ABD AZIZ BIDIN.

Commercial Bank of Namibia Ltd: 12–20 Bülow St, POB 1, Windhoek; tel. (61) 2959111; telex 898; fax (61) 2952079; f. 1973; controlled by Namibian Banking Corpn; cap. and res 69.9m., dep. 1,053.3m. (1996); Chair. V. BURGHAGEN; Man. Dir UDO REINHOLD; 7 brs.

First National Bank of Namibia Ltd: 209/211 Independence Ave, POB 195, Windhoek; tel. (61) 2992341; telex 479; fax (61) 220979; f. 1986; cap. and res 224.6m., dep. 2,065.6m. (Sept. 1996); Chair. H. D. VOIGTS; Man. Dir S. H. MOIR; 27 brs and 22 agencies.

Namibian Banking Corporation: Carl List Haus, Independence Ave, POB 370, Windhoek; tel. (61) 225946; telex 629; fax (61) 223741; Chair. J. C. WESTRAAT; Man. Dir P. P. NIEHAUS; 3 brs.

Standard Bank Namibia Ltd: Mutual Platz, Post St Mall, POB 3327, Windhoek; tel. (61) 2949111; telex 8679; fax (61) 2942369; f. 1915; controlled by the Standard Bank Investment Corpn; cap. and res 86.6m., dep. 1,734.0m. (Dec. 1995); Chair. C. V. KAURAISA; Man. Dir V. B. MOLL; 33 brs.

STOCK EXCHANGE

Namibian Stock Exchange: Shop 11, Kaiserkrone Centre, Post St Mall, POB 2401, Windhoek; tel. (61) 227647; fax (61) 248531; f. 1992; Chair. Exec. Cttee NICO C. TROMP; Gen. Man. TOM MINNEY.

INSURANCE

W. Biederlack & Co: Mettje-Behnsen Bldg, 2nd Floor, Independence Ave, POB 365, Windhoek; tel. (61) 233177; fax (61) 233178; f. 1990.

Commercial Union Insurance Ltd: Bülow St, POB 1599, Windhoek; tel. (61) 37137; telex 3096.

Incorporated General Insurance Ltd: 10 Bülow St, POB 2516, Windhoek; tel. (61) 37453; telex 415; fax (61) 35647.

Lifegro Assurance Ltd: Independence Ave, POB 23055, Windhoek; tel. (61) 33068.

Metropolitan Life Ltd: Goethe St, POB 3785, Windhoek; tel. (61) 37840.

Mutual and Federal Insurance Co Ltd: Mutual and Federal Centre, 227 Independence Ave, POB 151, Windhoek; tel. (61) 237730; telex 3084; fax (61) 235716; Gen. Man. J. STEELE.

Namibia National Insurance Co Ltd: Bülow St, POB 23053, Windhoek; tel. (61) 224539; fax (61) 238737; fmrly Federated Insurance Co Ltd.

Protea Assurance Co Ltd: Windhoek; tel. (61) 225891; telex 414.

SA Mutual Life Assurance Soc.: Independence Ave, POB 165, Windhoek; tel. (61) 36620; fax (61) 34874.

Sanlam Life Assurance Ltd: Bülow St, POB 317, Windhoek; tel. (61) 36680.

Santam Insurance Ltd: Independence Ave, POB 204, Windhoek; tel. (61) 38214.

Southern Life Assurance Ltd: Southern Tower, Post Street Mall, POB 637, Windhoek; tel. (61) 34056; fax (61) 31574.

Trade and Industry

CHAMBERS OF COMMERCE

Namibia National Chamber of Commerce and Industry: POB 9355, Windhoek; tel. (61) 228809; fax (61) 228009; f. 1990.

Windhoek Chamber of Commerce and Industries: SWA Building Society Bldg, 3rd Floor, POB 191, Windhoek; tel. (61) 222000; fax (61) 233690; e-mail: whkchamber@lianam.lia.net; f. 1920; Pres. VIC MOLL; Gen. Man. T. D. PARKHOUSE; 230 mems.

DEVELOPMENT ORGANIZATIONS

Investment Centre: Ministry of Trade and Industry, Govt Bldgs, Private Bag 13340, Windhoek; tel. (61) 2892431; telex 870; fax (61) 220227.

Namibia Development Corporation: 11 Goethe St, Private Bag 13252, Windhoek; tel. (61) 206911; telex 800; fax (61) 2062229; f. 1993; promotes foreign investment and provides concessionary loans and equity to new enterprises; manages agricultural projects; undertakes feasibility studies; Chair. P. T. DAMASEB; Man. Dir A. J. BOTES.

National Building and Investment Corporation: POB 20192, Windhoek; tel. (61) 37224; fax (61) 222301.

National Housing Enterprise: POB 20192, Windhoek; tel. (61) 2927111; fax (61) 222301; f. 1983; provides low-cost housing; Chair. N. SCHOOMBE; CEO A. M. TSOWASELO.

PUBLIC BOARDS AND CORPORATIONS

Meat Board of Namibia: POB 38, Windhoek; tel. (61) 33180; telex 679; fax (61) 228310; f. 1935; Gen. Man. H. W. KREFT.

Meat Corporation of Namibia (MEATCO NAMIBIA): POB 3881, Windhoek; tel. (61) 216810; fax (61) 217045.

Namibian Agronomic Board: POB 5096, Windhoek; tel. (61) 224741; fax (61) 225371; Man. JAH HOFFMANN.

Namibian Karakul Board: Private Bag 13300, Windhoek; tel. (61) 37750; fax (61) 36122.

National Petroleum Corporation of Namibia (NAMCOR): Windhoek; Man. Dir SKERF POTTAS.

Namibia Power Corporation Ltd (NamPower): NamPower Centre, 147 Robert Mugabe St, POB 2864, Windhoek; tel. (61) 2054111; fax (61) 232805; Chair. H. PUPKEWITZ; Man. Dir LEAKE S. HANGALA.

EMPLOYERS' ORGANIZATIONS

Chamber of Mines of Namibia (CMIN): POB 2895, Windhoek; tel. (61) 237925; fax (61) 222638; f. 1979; 33 mems (1995); Pres. ANDREW HOPE; Gen. Man. JOHN ROGERS.

Construction Industries Federation of Namibia: 7 Joule St, Southern Industrial Area, POB 1479, Windhoek; tel. (61) 230028; fax (61) 224534; Pres. STEPHEN PELL.

Electrical Contractors' Association: POB 3163, Windhoek; tel. (61) 37920; Pres. F. PFAFFENTHALER.

Motor Industries Federation of Namibia: POB 1503, Windhoek; tel. (61) 37970; fax (61) 33690.

Namibia Agricultural Union (NAU): Private Bag 13255, Windhoek; tel. (61) 37838; fax (61) 220193; Pres. PAUL SMIT.

Namibia Chamber of Printing: POB 363, Windhoek; tel. (61) 237905; fax (61) 222927; Sec. S. G. TIMM.

MAJOR INDUSTRIAL COMPANIES

Berg Aukas Ltd: POB 2, Grootfontein 9000; tel. (6731) 2047; telex 775; subsidiary of Gold Fields Namibia Ltd; mines lead, zinc and vanadium at Berg Aukas; Chair. P. R. JANISCH.

Imcor Zinc (Pty) Ltd: Private Bag, Rosh Pinah; tel. (63342) 2; telex 443; fax 145; subsidiary of South Africa Iron and Steel Corpn (ISCOR); mines zinc and lead at Rosh Pinah.

Namdeb Diamond Corporation Ltd: POB 1906, Windhoek; tel. (61) 35061 (Windhoek) and (6332) 9111 (Oranjemund); telex 658 (Windhoek) and 440 (Oranjemund); f. 1994; owned 50% by Govt, 50% by De Beers Centenary AG; operates alluvial diamond mine at Oranjemund; also recovers marine diamonds; Chair. J. OGILVIE THOMPSON.

Namibian Copper Joint Venture (Pty) Ltd: POB 11978, Windhoek; tel. (61) 238628; fax (61) 226978; development of cathode copper project at Haib.

Namibian Minerals Corporation (NAMCO): Walvis Bay; f. 1993; operates three marine diamond concessions covering c.2,000 sq km, containing an estimated 80m. carats of gem diamonds; Chair. and CEO ALASTAIR HOLBERTON.

Rössing Uranium Ltd: POB 22391, Windhoek; tel. (61) 236760; telex 3104; fax 233637; f. 1970; operates an open-cast uranium mine in the Namib desert; began production in 1976 and is the world's largest open-pit uranium mine; Chair. C. V. KAURAISA; Man. Dir A. J. HOPE.

Tsumeb Corporation Ltd: POB 40, Tsumeb 9000; tel. (671) 21115; telex 680; fax (671) 21710; produces and sells blister copper, silver, refined lead, refined arsenic trioxide, refined cadmium, refined sodium antimonate and other metals; operates copper smelter at Tsumeb and conducts exploration for base metals; Man. A. R. DE BEER.

TRADE UNIONS

There are several union federations, and a number of independent unions.

Trade Union Federations

Confederation of Labour: POB 22060, Windhoek.

National Allied Unions (NANAU): Windhoek; f. 1987; an alliance of trade unions, representing c. 7,600 mems, incl. Namibia Wholesale and Retail Workers' Union (f. 1986; Gen. Sec. T. NGAUJAKE; 6,000 mems), and Namibia Women Support Cttee; Pres. HENOCH HANDURA.

Namibia Trade Union (NTU): Windhoek; f. 1985; represents 6,700 domestic, farm and metal workers; Pres. ALPHA KANGUEEHI; Sec.-Gen. BEAU TJISESETA.

Namibia Trade Union Council (NTUC): Windhoek; f. 1981; affiliates include Northern Builders' Asscn.

National Union of Namibian Workers (NUNW): POB 50034, Windhoek; tel. (61) 215037; fax (61) 215589; f. 1972; Sec.-Gen. RANGA HAIKAILI; 87,000 mems; affiliates include:

Mineworkers' Union of Namibia (MUN): f. 1986; Chair. ASSER KAPERE; Pres. JACOB NGHIFINDAKA (acting); Gen. Sec. PETER NAHOLO (acting); 12,500 mems.

Namibia Food and Allied Workers' Union: f. 1986; Chair. MATHEUS LIBEREKI; Chair. ELIFAS NANGOLO; Gen. Sec. MAGDALENA IPINGE (acting); 12,000 mems.

Namibia Metal and Allied Workers' Union: f. 1987; Chair. ANDRIES TEMBA; Gen. Sec. MOSES SHIKWA (acting); 5,500 mems.

Namibia Public Workers' Union: f. 1987; Chair. STEVEN IMMANUEL; Gen. Sec. PETER ILONGA; 11,000 mems.

Namibia Transport and Allied Workers' Union: f. 1988; Chair. TYLVES GIDEON; Gen. Sec. IMMANUEL KAVAA; 7,500 mems.

Other Unions

Association for Government Service Officials: Windhoek; f. 1981; Chair. ALLAN HATTLE; 9,000 mems.

Namibia Building Workers' Association: Windhoek; Sec. H. BOCK.

Public Service Union of Namibia: POB 21662, Windhoek; tel. (61) 213083; fax (61) 213047; f. 1981; Sec.-Gen. CORNELIUS PONTAC.

Transport

RAILWAYS

The main line runs from Nakop, at the border with South Africa, via Keetmanshoop to Windhoek, Kranzberg, Grootfontein, Tsumeb, Swakopmund and Walvis Bay. There are three branch lines, from Windhoek to Gobabis, Otjiwarongo to Outjo and Keetmanshoop to Lüderitz. The total rail network covers 2,382 route-km.

TransNamib Ltd: TransNamib Bldg, cnr Independence Ave and Bahnhof St, Private Bag 13204, Windhoek; tel. (61) 2982109; telex 465; fax (61) 2982386; state-owned; Chair. WILLIE KLEIN.

ROADS

In 1994 the road network comprised 42,594 km of roads, including 5,010 km of tarred roads, 26,646 km of gravel roads, 235 km of salt gypsum roads and 10,682 km of natural roads. A major road link from Walvis Bay to Jwaneng, northern Botswana, the Trans-Kalahari Highway, and the Trans-Caprivi highway, linking Namibia with northern Botswana, Zambia and Zimbabwe, are both scheduled for completion in the late 1990s. The Government is also upgrading and expanding the road network in northern Namibia.

SHIPPING

Walvis Bay and Lüderitz are the only ports, although the development of other harbours (notably a fishing port at Moewe Bay, some 440 km. north of Walvis Bay) is planned. Walvis Bay, the region's only deep-water port, is linked to the main overseas shipping routes and handles almost one-half of Namibia's external trade. There are plans to deepen the harbour of Walvis Bay in order to accommodate larger vessels; a new bulk terminal was opened at the port in 1995.

Namibian Ports Authority (NAMPORT): CEO MIKE VAN DER MEER (acting).

Walvis Bay Port Authority: Dir JOHANNES VON DER FECHT.

CIVIL AVIATION

The international airport, located 47 km from Windhoek, registered 308,690 passenger arrivals and departures in 1993. There are a number of other airports throughout Namibia, as well as numerous landing strips.

Air Namibia: TransNamib Bldg, cnr Independence Ave and Bahnhof St, POB 731, Windhoek; tel. and fax (61) 221910; telex 657; f. 1959 as Namib Air; state-owned; domestic flights and services to Southern Africa and Western Europe; Chair. W. A. P. KLEIN; Gen. Man. (vacant).

Kalahari Express Airlines (KEA): Windhoek; f. 1995; domestic and regional flights.

Tourism

In the mid-1990s tourism was one of the fastest growing sectors of the Namibian economy. Nambia's principal tourist attractions are its game parks and nature reserves, and the development of 'eco-tourism' is being promoted. Government investment in expanding the tourism sector was expected to total N$ 547m. during 1993–98. A total of 254,978 tourist arrivals was recorded in Namibia in 1993, excluding 33,465 excursionists. Most were from South Africa (60.8%) and Germany (11.7%). In 1993 receipts from tourism totalled US $95m.

Namibia Tourism: Private Bag 13346, Windhoek; tel. (61) 2849111; fax (61) 221930.

Defence

In August 1996 the Namibian Defence Force numbered 8,100 (army 8,000; coastguard an estimated 100).

Defence Expenditure: Budgeted at N$ 293.8m. in 1996/97 (representing 5.8% of total projected budgetary expenditure for that year).

Commander-in-Chief of the Defence Force: Pres. SAMUEL (SAM) DANIEL NUJOMA.

Commander of the Army: Maj.-Gen. SOLOMON HAWALA.

Education

Education is officially compulsory for nine years between the ages of six and 16 years, or until primary education has been completed (whichever is the sooner). Pre-primary education was abolished in the state sector in 1995. Primary education consists of seven grades, and secondary education of five. In 1992 enrolment at primary schools included 89% of the relevant age-group (males 86%; females 93%). Enrolment at secondary schools in 1994 was equivalent to 63% of the secondary school-age population (males 57%; females 69%). Higher education is provided by the University of Namibia, the Technicon of Namibia, a vocational college and four teacher-training colleges. In 1994 11,344 students were enrolled in tertiary education. Various schemes for informal adult education are also in operation in an effort to combat illiteracy; since 1992 some 42,000 Namibians have followed such programmes. At the 1991 census the average rate of adult illiteracy, excluding unemployed persons, was 24.2% (males 22.2%; females 26%). Budget forecasts for 1996/97 allocated N$ 1,176.3m. (23.2% of total government expenditure) to education.

Bibliography

Afro-Asian Peoples' Solidarity Organization. *Namibia: Road to Independence.* Cairo, 1990.

Allison, C., and Green, R. H. *Political Economy and Structural Change: Namibia at Independence.* Brighton, University of Sussex, Institute of Development Studies, 1989.

Amukugo, E. M. *Education and Politics in Namibia: Past Trends and Future Prospects.* Windhoek, Gamsberg Macmillan, 1995.

Arcadi de Saint-Paul, M. *Namibie: Une Siècle d'Histoire.* Paris, Albatron, 1984.

Catholic Institute for International Relations. *Land Reform in Namibia.* London, 1995.

Cooper, A. D. (Ed.). *Allies in Apartheid: Western Capitalism in Occupied Namibia.* New York, St Martin's Press; Basingstoke, Macmillan, 1988.

Cros, G. *Chroniques Namibiennes: La Dernière Colonie.* Paris, Présence Africaine, 1983.

La Namibie. Paris, Presses Universitaires de France, 1983.

Dale, R. *The UN and the Independence of Namibia: The Longest Decolonization, 1946–1990.* 1994.

Diescho, J. *The Namibian Constitution in Perspective.* Windhoek, Macmillan Gamsberg, 1994.

Du Pisani, A. *SWA/Namibia: The Politics of Continuity and Change.* Johannesburg, Jonathan Ball, 1986.

Duggal, N. K. (Ed.). *Namibia: Perspectives for National Reconstruction and Development.* Lusaka, United Nations Institute for Namibia, 1986.

First National Development Corporation. *Namibia: Development and Investment.* Windhoek, The Corporation, 1989.

Frayne, B. *Urbanisation in Post-Independence Windhoek: (With Special Emphasis on Katutura).* Windhoek, University of Namibia, 1992.

Green, R. H. *From Sudwesafrika to Namibia: The Political Economy of Transition.* Uppsala, Scandinavian Institute for African Studies, 1981.

Groth, S. *Namibia: the Wall of Silence.* Wiepperthal, Germany, Peter Hammer Verlag, 1995.

Grotpeter, J. J. *Historical Dictionary of Namibia.* Metuchen, NJ, Scarecrow Press, 1994.

Harvey, C., and Isaksen, J. (Eds). *Monetary Independence for Namibia.* Windhoek, NEPRU, 1990.

Heribert, W., and Matthew, B. (Eds). *The Namibian Peace Process: Implications and Lessons for the Future.* Freiburg, Arnold-Bergstraesser-Institut, 1994.

Hishongwa, N. *The Contract Labour System and its Effects on Social and Family Life in Namibia.* Windhoek, Gamsberg Macmillan, 1992.

Jezkova, P. *Namibia: New Avenue of Industrial Development.* Vienna, UNIDO, 1994.

Karase, C., and Gutto, S. (Eds). *Namibia: The Conspiracy of Silence.* Harare, Nehanda, 1989.

LeBeau, D. *Namibia: Ethnic Stereotyping in a Post-Apartheid State.* Windhoek, University of Namibia, 1991.

Leys, C., and Saul, J. S. *Namibia's Liberation Struggle: The Two-Edged Sword.* London, James Currey Publishers, 1995.

Lister, S. (Ed.). *Aid, Donors and Development Management.* Windhoek, NEPRU, 1991.

Lush, D. *Last Steps to Uhuru: An Eye-Witness Account of Namibia's Transition to Independence (1988–1992).* Ibadan, Spectrum Books, 1993.

Mbuende, K. *Namibia: The Broken Shield: Anatomy of Imperialism and Revolution.* Uppsala, Scandinavian Institute for African Studies, 1986.

Nangoloh, P. Y. *Namibia: Human Rights Report, 1995.* Windhoek, National Society for Human Rights, 1986.

Omar, G., et al. *Introduction to Namibia's Political Economy.* Cape Town, Southern Africa Labour and Development Research Unit, 1990.

Peltola, P. *The Lost May Day: Namibian Workers' Struggle for Independence.* Uppsala, Finnish Anthropological Society and Nordiske Afrikainstitutet, 1995.

Saunders, C. (Ed.). *Perspectives on Namibia: Past and Present.* Cape Town, Centre for African Studies, 1983.

Singham, A. W. *Namibian Independence: A Global Responsibility.* Westport, Hill, 1985.

Soggot, D. *Namibia: The Violent Heritage.* London, Collings, 1986.

Soiri, I. *Radical Motherhood: Namibian Women's Independence Struggle.* Uppsala, Nordiske Afrikainstitutet, 1996.

Sparks, D. L., and Green, D. *Namibia: The Nation after Independence.* Boulder, CO, Westview Press, 1992.

Totemeyer, G., et al. (Eds). *Namibia in Perspective.* Windhoek, Council of Churches in Namibia, 1987.

Totemeyer, G. *The Reconstruction of the Namibian National, Regional and Local State.* Windhoek, University of Namibia, 1992.

Wilmsen, E. N. *Land Filled with Flies: A Political Economy of the Kalahari.* Chicago, University of Chicago Press, 1989.

NIGER

Physical and Social Geography

R. J. HARRISON CHURCH

The land-locked Republic of Niger is the largest state in west Africa. With an area of 1,267,000 sq km (489,191 sq miles), it is larger than Nigeria, its immensely richer southern neighbour, which is Africa's most populous country. The relatively small size of Niger's population, 7,248,100 in September 1988 (according to provisional census results), rising to an officially-estimated 8,361,000 at mid-1993, is largely explained by the country's aridity and remoteness. Population density in 1993 averaged 6.6 persons per sq km. Two-thirds of Niger consists of desert, and most of the north-eastern region is uninhabitable. Hausa tribespeople are the most numerous (some 53% of the population in 1988), followed by the Djerma Songhai (22%), Tuaregs (10%) and Peulhs (10%).

In the north-centre is the partly volcanic Aïr massif, with many dry watercourses remaining from earlier wetter conditions. Agadez, in Aïr, receives an average annual rainfall of no more than about 180 mm. Yet the Tuaregs keep considerable numbers of livestock by moving them seasonally to areas further south, where underground well-water is usually available. South again, along the Niger–Nigerian border, are sandy areas where annual rainfall is just sufficient for the cultivation of groundnuts and millet by Hausa farmers. Cotton is also grown in small, seasonally flooded valleys and depressions.

In the south-west is the far larger, seasonally flooded Niger valley, the pastures of which nourish livestock that have to contend with nine months of drought for the rest of the year. Rice and other crops are grown by the Djerma and Songhai peoples as the Niger flood declines.

Niger thus has three very disparate physical and cultural focuses. Unity has been encouraged by French aid and by economic advance, but the attraction of the more prosperous neighbouring state of Nigeria is considerable. Distances to the nearest ports (Cotonou, in Benin, and Lagos, in Nigeria) are at least 1,370 km, both routes requiring breaks of bulk.

Recent History

PIERRE ENGLEBERT

Revised for this edition by the Editor

Formerly a part of French West Africa, Niger became a self-governing republic within the French Community in December 1958, and proceeded to full independence on 3 August 1960. Control of government passed to the Parti progressiste nigérien (PPN), whose leader, Hamani Diori, favoured the maintenance of traditional social structures and the retention of close economic links with France. Organized opposition, principally by the left-wing nationalist Union nigérienne démocratique (UND, or Sawaba party), had been suppressed since 1959 and the UND leader, Djibo Bakary, was forced into exile. The Diori regime dealt firmly with periodic manifestations of nationalism, although the president himself gained considerable prestige as a spokesman for francophone Africa.

Niger's valuable reserves of uranium began to be exploited in 1971, but the period 1968–74 was overshadowed by the Sahelian drought. Exports of groundnuts, which formerly accounted for 70% of Niger's export revenue, were badly affected, and the loss of pasture land in the north of the country led to serious food shortages. Widespread civil disorder followed allegations that some government ministers were misappropriating stocks of food aid, and in April 1974 Diori was overthrown by the armed forces chief of staff, Lt-Col (later Maj.-Gen.) Seyni Kountché. A Conseil militaire suprême (CMS) was established to rule the country, with a mandate to distribute food aid fairly and to restore morality to public life. Although political parties were outlawed, Bakary and other opposition activists were permitted to return to the country.

THE KOUNTCHÉ REGIME

The military government's major preoccupation was planning an economic recovery. In the interest of national independence, it obtained the withdrawal of French troops and reduced French influence over the exploitation of Niger's uranium deposits, while none the less maintaining generally amicable relations with the former colonial power. New links were formed with Arab states. Domestically, there was a renewal of political activism following Bakary's return from exile, while personal and policy differences developed within the CMS. Plots to remove Kountché were uncovered in 1975 (resulting in the imprisonment of Bakary and the vice-president of the CMS) and again in 1976 (when nine conspirators received death sentences). From 1978, however, the government released a number of political detainees, including (in 1980) Diori and Bakary—although Diori remained under house arrest until 1984.

Kountché began in 1981 gradually to increase civilian representation in the CMS, and in 1982 preparations were undertaken for a constitutional form of government. In the following year an indirectly-elected Conseil national de développement (CND) began to function as a constituent assembly. A civilian prime minister, Oumarou Mamane, took office in January 1983; he became president of the CND in August, and was replaced as prime minister by Hamid Algabid in November. In January 1984 Kountché established a commission to draft a pre-constitutional document, termed a 'national charter'.

Economic adjustment efforts during this period were impeded by the recurrence of drought in 1984–85 and by the closure of the land border with Nigeria in 1984–86, with the result that Niger's dependence on external financial assistance was increased. Relations with the USA (by now the principal donor of food aid to Niger) assumed considerable importance at this time. Meanwhile, a period of renewed tension between Niger and Libya had fuelled Libyan accusations of the persecution of the light-skinned, nomadic Tuareg population by the Kountché regime. In May 1985, following an armed incident near the Niger–Libya border, all non-Nigerien Tuaregs were expelled. The resultant insecurity apparently prompted the rearrest of Diori; the former president took up residence in Morocco following his release in 1984, where he died in 1989.

The draft 'national charter' was overwhelmingly approved (by some 99.6% of voters) at a national referendum—Niger's first since independence—in June 1987. The charter provided for the establishment of non-elective, consultative institutions at both national and local levels.

SAÏBOU AND THE SECOND REPUBLIC

Kountché died in November 1987, after a year of ill health. The chief of staff of the armed forces, Col (later Brig.) Ali Saïbou, who had assumed the role of acting head of state during Kountché's illness, was formally confirmed in the positions of chairman of the CMS and head of state on 14 November. The new leader promised a continuity of Kountché's ideals and objectives, although he displayed a less austere approach to government. Both Diori and Bakary were received by Saïbou, an appeal was made to exiled Nigeriens to return, and an amnesty was announced for political prisoners. Although the military continued to play a prominent role in government, Oumarou Mamane was reinstated as prime minister in July 1988, and in November a civilian was appointed minister of finance.

A constitutional document (which the CND had been commissioned to draft in mid-1988), which provided for the continued role of the armed forces in what was to be designated the second republic, was endorsed by 99.3% of voters in a national referendum in September 1989. Meanwhile, in August 1988 Saïbou had announced an end to the 14-year ban on all political organizations, with the formation of a new ruling party, the Mouvement national pour une société de développement (MNSD). Saïbou made clear his opposition to the establishment of a multi-party system, but stated that the existence of a single party was not incompatible with the concept of political pluralism. In May 1989 the constituent congress of the MNSD elected a Conseil supérieur d'orientation nationale (CSON) to replace the CMS. As president of the CSN, Saïbou was the sole candidate at a presidential election in December, when he was confirmed as head of state, for a seven-year term, by 99.6% of voters. At the same time a single list of 93 CSON-approved deputies to a new legislative assembly (to succeed the CND) was endorsed by a similar margin. It was subsequently announced that Niger's two remaining political detainees were to be released, to commemorate Saïbou's inauguration as president of the second republic. The post of prime minister was abolished later in December, as part of an extensive reorganization of the council of ministers.

In February 1990 intervention by security forces at a demonstration by university students in Niamey, who had been boycotting classes in protest against proposed education reforms and a reduction in the level of graduate recruitment into the civil service, resulted in three deaths. Saïbou (who had been abroad at the time of the incident) expressed regret at the police action, and announced the appointment of a commission to examine the students' grievances. The ministers of the interior and higher education were dismissed in March, and a prominent industrialist, Aliou Mahamidou, was appointed to the restored post of prime minister; the outgoing minister of the interior was, moreover, among senior figures dismissed from the CSON. There was, none the less, further student action in April and again in June.

The prospect of political reform, following the announcement in June 1990 that the constitution was to be amended to allow for a pluralist system, failed to end a period of industrial unrest, as the trade union federation, the Union des syndicats des travailleurs du Niger (USTN) demanded the cancellation of unpopular austerity measures. In November a five-day general strike effectively halted production of uranium, closed public buildings and disrupted regional and international air links. Later in the month Saïbou announced that, on the basis of the findings of a constitutional review commission, a multi-party political system would be established. He also announced that less stringent austerity measures would be adopted, in consultation with Niger's external creditors. Interim provision was made for the registration of political parties (the constitution was amended to this effect in April 1991), and it was announced that a national conference would be convened during 1991 to determine the country's political evolution. In January 1991 the USTN announced that it was to end its affiliation with the MNSD.

THE TRANSITION PERIOD

In March 1991 it was announced that the armed forces were to withdraw from political life, and serving military officers were, accordingly, removed from the council of ministers. In July Saïbou resigned as chairman of the MNSD–Nassara (as the ruling party had been restyled), in order to distance himself from party politics in preparation for the national conference. He was succeeded as party leader by Col (retd) Tandja Mamadou.

The national conference, convened on 29 July 1991, was initially attended by about 1,200 delegates (representing, among others, the organs of state and some 24 political organizations, together with professional, women's and students' groups). Declaring the conference sovereign, delegates voted to suspend the constitution and to dissolve its organs of state: Saïbou was to remain in office as interim head of state, but his powers were reduced to largely ceremonial functions. The government was deprived of its authority to make financial transactions, and links with external creditors were effectively severed when, in October, the conference voted to suspend adherence to the country's IMF- and World Bank-sponsored programme of economic adjustment. The conference had meanwhile assumed control of the armed forces and the police, appointing in September a new armed forces chief of staff and deputy chief of staff. The government was dissolved, and in October the conference appointed Amadou Cheiffou (a regional official of the International Civil Aviation Organization) to head a transitional government pending the installation (scheduled for early 1993) of elected democratic institutions. The conference ended in early November 1991; its chairman, André Salifou (a dean of the University of Niamey), was designated chairman of a 15-member Haut conseil de la République (HCR). This was to function as an interim legislature, and was intended to ensure the transitional government's implementation of conference resolutions, supervise the activities of the head of state, and oversee the drafting of a new constitution.

An atmosphere of national consensus prevailed in the immediate aftermath of the national conference. New austerity measures, and consequent delays in the payment of public-sector salaries, were initially accepted with few signs of discontent. In February 1992, however, junior-ranking members of the armed forces staged a mutiny, demanding not only the payment of salary arrears but also the release of an army captain found responsible by the national conference for the violent suppression of a Tuareg attack on Tchin Tabaraden in May 1990 (see below), as well as the dismissal of senior armed forces officers (including the deputy chief of staff installed by the national conference). The mutineers detained Salifou and the minister of the interior, Mohamed Moussa (himself of Tuareg extraction), and took control of the offices of the state broadcasting media in Niamey. They briefly returned to barracks when Cheiffou (who had assumed personal responsibility for defence in the interim government) promised to consider their material demands, but troops again seized the broadcasting media in March. A large public demonstration took place in Niamey to condemn the rebellion, and the USTN and several political parties organized a widely-observed general strike to protest against the military's actions. Order was restored when the government agreed to consider all the mutineers' demands. Weakened by the lack of discipline within the military, the country's precarious financial situation and the continuing Tuareg rebellion in the north, Cheiffou admitted that the transitional government had achieved little in its attempts to address the country's problems. The council of ministers was reorganized later in March, with four ministers dismissed and Moussa transferred to a lesser government post. In mid-1992, seemingly motivated by the need to secure external financial assistance (most urgently to fund the payment of salary arrears), the government announced the restoration of diplomatic relations with Taiwan (which had been severed in 1974, upon Niger's recognition of the People's Republic of China). The resumption of links proceeded despite objections from members of the HCR, most notably Salifou, who asserted that the transitional administration had no authority to effect such a reorientation of foreign policy. Diplomatic relations with the People's Republic of China were accordingly severed, and Niger received its first financial assistance from Taiwan shortly afterwards.

Numerous technical difficulties were encountered in the transition process. A constitutional referendum finally took place on 26 December 1992, when the new document was approved by 89.8% of those who voted (56.6% of the electorate: an appeal by Islamic leaders for a boycott of the vote, in view of the secular basis of the constitution, had only limited success). Elections to the new national assembly took place, again after considerable delay, on 14 February 1993, and were contested by 12 of the country's 18 registered political parties. The MNSD–Nassara was the party winning the greatest number of seats (29) in the 83-member assembly, but was prevented from resuming power by the rapid formation, in the aftermath of the election, of an alliance of parties that was able to form a parliamentary majority. This Alliance des forces de changement (AFC) grouped six parliamentary parties with a total of 50 seats (and was also supported by three parties not represented in the legislature), its principal members being the Convention démocratique et sociale–Rahama (CDS–Rahama), which held 22 seats in the assembly, the Parti nigérien pour la démocratie et le socialisme–Tarayya (PNDS–Tarayya), with 13 seats, and the Alliance nigérienne pour la démocratie et le progrès social–Zaman Lahiya (ANDPS–Zaman Lahiya), with 11 seats. The rate of participation by voters was reported to be somewhat higher than at the time of the constitutional referendum.

The MNSD–Nassara, which denounced opposition tactics in the legislative elections, was similarly frustrated at the presidential election. At the first round, on 27 February 1993, Tandja Mamadou won the greatest proportion of the votes cast (34.2%). He and his nearest rival, Mahamane Ousmane (the leader of the CDS–Rahama, who took 26.6% of the first-round votes), proceeded to a second round on 27 March. Ousmane was then elected president by 55.4% of those who voted (just over 35% of the electorate): four of the six other candidates at the first round were members of the AFC, and had urged their supporters to transfer allegiance to Ousmane.

OUSMANE AND THE THIRD REPUBLIC

Mahamane Ousmane, a devout Muslim and the country's first Hausa head of state (his predecessors having been members of the Djerma community), who had consistently expressed his commitment to the principle of a secular state, was inaugurated as president of the third republic on 16 April 1993. Shortly beforehand AFC deputies had elected Moumouni Amadou Djermakoye (the leader of the ANDPS–Zaman Lahiya and a first-round candidate for the presidency) as the speaker of the new national assembly. The vote had been boycotted by the MNSD–Nassara and its allies, protesting that Djermakoye's appointment—in accordance with an agreement made within the AFC prior to the second round of the presidential election—was unconstitutional, and was annulled by the supreme court. Ousmane none the less proceeded to appoint another first-round presidential candidate, Mahamadou Issoufou of the PNDS–Tarayya, to the post of prime minister (again in accordance with a prior AFC arrangement), and in May, in the absence of opposition deputies, Djermakoye was voted in as national assembly speaker.

The incoming president and prime minister were anxious to resume a dialogue with the international financial community, with the aim of securing new credits and debt-relief, and the stated task of Issoufou's first council of ministers was to address the country's economic and social crisis. In the absence of significant external assistance, arrears had accumulated in the public and education sectors under the transitional authorities. A period of violent disruption in the education sector prompted the government, in May 1993, to declare the 1992/93 academic year invalid in state secondary schools. Furthermore, despite pledges of emergency financial assistance from France, allowing the payment of public-sector wages outstanding since April, the announcement that arrears accumulated under the transitional authorities could not be paid provoked renewed unrest. A 48-hour strike by USTN members in July was swiftly followed by unrest in the army, as soldiers at Zinder, Tahoua, Agadez and Maradi took local officials hostage and demanded the payment of three months' salary arrears. The USTN organized a 72-hour strike in September, in protest at the government's austerity budget, which included a 24% reduction in wages in the public sector, the imposition of new taxes and an indefinite suspension of the payment of salary arrears. Further strikes were averted when the authorities agreed to suspend implementation of a new law restricting the right to strike, and in October the government and unions reached an agreement whereby public-sector employees would forgo three months' salary arrears in return for lesser wage reductions.

Social tensions were exacerbated following the 50% devaluation, in January 1994, of the CFA franc. In March students who had been campaigning for the payment of grant arrears blocked roads in Niamey and occupied university buildings. The death of a student in clashes with police precipitated a boycott of classes, as students demanded that those responsible for the death be brought to justice. A government undertaking to pay three months' arrears and to establish a commission to investigate the police actions failed to prevent further violent protests; many police-officers refused to intervene, in support of colleagues implicated in the student's death, thus necessitating the deployment of paramilitary forces. Later in the month Niamey was effectively paralysed by a 24-hour general strike, organized by the USTN to protest against the recent imposition of the controversial 'right to strike' legislation, and also to demand 30%–50% salary increases to compensate for currency devaluation. A three-day strike followed in April, and the announcement of pay increases of 5%–12% for public-sector employees failed to avert a further 72-hour strike in May. An indefinite strike began in June, but at the end of July the USTN agreed to halt industrial action, pending efforts to achieve a negotiated settlement with the government.

Meanwhile, the MNSD–Nassara was leading an opposition campaign of civil disobedience, demanding representation in the government proportionate to the percentage of votes won by Tandja Mamadou at the second round of presidential voting in 1993. The arrest of Mamadou and two other opposition leaders in April 1994, after a violent protest resulted in the death of an activist, prompted further demonstrations; numerous arrests ensued (although the three party leaders were released); 25 opposition members were brought to trial in May, on charges of involvement in an unauthorized demonstration and of causing damage to public and private property: three were sentenced to two or three years' imprisonment, and banned from residence in Niamey for a further year, while 10 received suspended sentences. Later in May, following a meeting between Ousmane and representatives of the MNSD–Nassara, the opposition agreed to end its boycott of the national assembly.

In September 1994 the PNDS–Tarayya withdrew from the AFC, and Issoufou resigned as prime minister, in protest against what was perceived as the transfer of some of the prime minister's powers to the president of the republic. Souley Abdoulaye, a member of the CDS–Rahama, who had hitherto been minister of trade, transport and tourism, was appointed to the premiership. However, his new government did not command a majority in the national assembly, and in October a parliamentary motion of 'no confidence' in the Abdoulaye administration (proposed by the MNSD–Nassara and the PNDS–Tarayya) was approved by 46 votes to 36. Ousmane dissolved the national assembly, confirming the Abdoulaye government in office pending new elections, which were scheduled for December. Ousmane's decision to dissolve the national assembly, rather than designate a prime minister from the new parliamentary majority, provoked criticism from the labour movement, which claimed that the cost of organizing an early general election would be too great, given the country's economic difficulties. From November the USTN co-ordinated weekly 48-hour strikes in support of its demands for pay increases and the payment of salary arrears, for the cancellation of the 'right to strike' ordinance, and to protest against government privatization plans (which would result in the loss of many jobs). The strikes were widely observed throughout the state sector, and action by schoolteachers prevented the commencement of the academic year in Niamey and several other towns.

Financial, technical and logistical difficulties meant that the legislative elections did not take place until 12 January 1995. The results indicated that the MNSD–Nassara, combining its 29 seats with those of its allies, would be able to form a 43-strong majority group in the national assembly. While Ousmane's CDS–Rahama increased its representation to 24 seats, the AFC (having lost the support of the PNDS–Tarayya and also that of the Parti progressiste nigérien–Rassemblement démocratique africain) held 40 seats. Abdoulaye resigned as prime minister in early February, but Ousmane declined to accept the new majority's nominee, Hama Amadou (the secretary-general of the MNSD–Nassara); he appointed instead another member of that party, Amadou Aboubacar Cissé, stating that the latter, as a former official of the World Bank, would be ideally suited to the essential task of negotiating new funding arrangements with external creditors. Cissé was expelled from the MNSD–Nassara, and the party and its allies announced that they would neither participate in, nor co-operate with, his administration. His position was further undermined by continuing strike action, and by the election of Issoufou to the post of speaker of the national assembly. A parliamentary motion of censure against Cissé was approved by 43 votes to 40, and Ousmane was obliged to accept the majority's nomination of Amadou as prime minister. The new government, appointed in late February, included one member of the AFC: Alitor Mano, of the mainly-Tuareg Union pour la démocratie et le progrès social–Amana (UDPS–Amana), was designated minister of agriculture and livestock.

Political and Institutional Conflict

The new government swiftly ended several months of labour unrest, agreeing to cancel the 'right to strike' legislation and to pay two months' salary arrears. Relations between the government and the presidency were, however, less conciliatory, and frequent procedural disputes concerning the prerogatives and competences of the two branches of the executive resulted in much political disruption. Difficulties of 'cohabitation' precipitated an institutional crisis from July 1995, when Ousmane apparently refused to chair a session of the council of ministers at which Amadou's nominations for new senior executives of state-owned organizations (effectively replacing those installed by Ousmane and the AFC government) were to have been adopted. Both Ousmane and Amadou claimed to be acting in accordance with procedures decreed by the supreme court for the organization of sessions of the council of ministers, and each accused the other of impeding the functioning of the organs of state. The government ordered the deployment of security forces at the premises of state enterprises, thereby preventing the incumbent executives from performing their duties. Despite mediation efforts by regional envoys, and the expressed commitment of both Ousmane and Amadou to the principle of defining the respective prerogatives of the president, as elected head of state, and prime minister, as leader of the elected majority, the crisis deepened in subsequent weeks, with the contentious issue of the appointment of state company executives compounded by uncertainty as to Amadou's competence to sign an amnesty decree (for all those involved in the Tuareg conflict—see below). In October a parliamentary motion expressing 'no confidence' in the Amadou government was defeated in the absence of its proponents, who boycotted the vote to protest at the absence from the debate of the speaker (Issoufou was attending a conference in Romania). Security forces were reported to have intervened after fighting broke out at the parliament building between supporters of Ousmane and Amadou.

The USTN (which had in August threatened to force the removal from office of both Ousmane and Amadou, should the institutional conflict not be resolved) renewed strike action in October 1995, with two 48-hour stoppages in support of demands for the payment of salary arrears to civil servants and the restitution of sums deducted from wages in reprisal for earlier strikes. The government's draft legislation for the sale of some 30 state and parastatal enterprises was not only a source of concern for the unions, but also exacerbated institutional frictions, as Ousmane expressed concern at what he regarded as the surrender of national institutions; the president also sought guarantees that proceeds from privatization would be used for public investment, rather than to finance the shortfall in current spending requirements. The unresolved issue of salary arrears prompted further industrial action by teachers and civil servants, and in mid-December there were violent demonstrations in Niamey, involving some 2,000 university students who were demanding the payment of one year's grant arrears. Ousmane appealed for the restoration of national cohesion. However, his rejection, in early January 1996, of the government's draft budget (the president expressed concern that a proposed standardized rate of income tax would exacerbate disparities in living standards) precipitated a severe decline in institutional relations. The ensuing political impasse, together with further strike action by public employees and mineworkers opposed to the new tax, and a campaign of civil disobedience by university students in Niamey, raised fears that approval by the IMF of essential new funding might be withheld.

MILITARY TAKEOVER

On 27 January 1996 the elected organs of state were overthrown by the military, under the command of Col (later Brig.-Gen.) Ibrahim Baré Maïnassara (a former aide-de-camp to the late president Kountché, who had been appointed chief of staff of the armed forces in March 1995). The coup leaders, who formed a 12-member Conseil de salut national (CSN), chaired by Maïnassara, asserted that their seizure of power had been necessitated by Niger's descent into political chaos: it was claimed that the president had been about to dissolve the national assembly, while his opponents within parliament had petitioned the supreme court to declare Ousmane's incapacity as head of state. The CSN suspended the constitution, dissolving the national assembly and other institutions; political parties were suspended, and a state of emergency was imposed. Ousmane, Amadou and Issoufou were placed under house arrest: they were reportedly released at the end of the month, although some restrictions on their movements remained. Clashes between Maïnassara's forces and members of the presidential guard reportedly resulted in several deaths, but order was swiftly restored.

The CSN asserted that it had no wish to 'cling to power'. The military immediately pledged its commitment to the pursuit of policies of economic restructuring, with a view to concluding funding arrangements with the IMF and the World Bank, and undertook to consolidate efforts towards the restoration of peace in the north of the country. A national forum was to be convened to consider the revision of the constitution and the electoral code, with the aim of preventing a recurrence of the paralysis of recent months; the forum would also determine a timetable for a swift return to government by democratically elected authorities. The coup was, none the less, generally condemned internationally; Western donors withdrew all non-humanitarian assistance, and negotiations with the IMF were stalled. However, a delegation of the regional Conseil de l'entente was received by Maïnassara for discussions that were described as cordial, and in February representatives of the new regime, led by ex-president Saïbou, undertook a regional mission to explain and secure support for the military's actions. Strong links with Nigeria, Algeria and Libya were apparent.

In late January 1996 the CSN appointed Boukary Adji, the deputy governor of the Banque centrale des états de l'Afrique de l'ouest (and a former finance minister under Kountché) to the post of prime minister. Adji's transitional government was composed entirely of civilians. Among its members was Salifou (the former chairman of the transitional HCR), who was named minister of state, in charge of higher education and research. The government's stated priorities were economic and financial restructuring and the provision of guarantees of health care, education, food and national security. The CSN, meanwhile, pursued a wide range of contacts; Maïnassara held separate discussions with Ousmane, Amadou and Issoufou at the beginning of February, following which each (although condemning the coup) expressed willingness to co-operate with the new regime in securing a restoration of civilian rule. The USTN (which had denounced the coup and had organized a two-day general strike at the end of January) received assurances regarding the payment of salaries. The appointment, in early February, of military officers to the governorships of Niger's administrative regions was attributed by the CSN to the need to ensure neutrality in the organization of the elections that would precede a return to constitutional government.

In mid-February 1996 the deposed president, prime minister and speaker of the national asembly signed a joint text, in Maïnassara's presence, that effectively endorsed the legitimacy of the CSN and recognized that the assumption of power by the military had been necessitated by the difficulties that were being experienced in the functioning of the organs of state. A preliminary timetable for a return to civilian rule was subsequently released, culminating in a constitutional referendum in September and the installation of new elected authorities by the end of the year. The programme was revised almost immediately (apparently to coincide with a summit meeting of francophone states in Bordeaux, France), rescheduling the referendum for June and the completion of the election programme by September. At a rally in Niamey, Maïnassara appealed for financial donations, as well as foodstuffs and medical supplies, to assist in the funding of the election programme and in alleviating poverty and disease. It was announced that government ministers, members of the armed forces and all other public employees would be required to contribute as much as 40% of their salary to a national solidarity fund. Diplomatic efforts were, moreover, to be intensified to persuade the IMF and other donors to release funds. France, notably, had restored full co-operation by early March.

Two independent consultative bodies were established in late February 1996. It was emphasized that both the advisory Conseil des sages (which elected Saïbou as its chairman) and the co-ordinating committee of the national forum, one of the functions of which was to submit proposals for constitutional changes to the forthcoming forum, would function free from military influence. Each body included former state officials, traditional chiefs, religious leaders and members of the judiciary. The 'national forum for democratic renewal' was convened in Niamey at the beginning of April. Other than the members of the co-ordinating committee and the Conseil des sages, its 700 members included representatives of the dissolved parliament and of workers' and employers' organizations. During its week-long session the forum adopted revisions to the constitution that aimed to guarantee greater institutional stability, essentially by conferring executive power solely on the president of the republic and requiring the prime minister to implement a programme stipulated by the head of state. With the aim of achieving the depoliticization of public administration and of averting the hindrance of the functioning of the elected institutions by political parties' actions, amendments were also made to the electoral code and to the charter governing the activities of political organizations. In mid-April a decree was issued bringing forward the date of the constitutional referendum to 12 May: this would enable the presidential poll to take place in July, prior to the commencement of the rainy season. Later in April it was announced that restrictions on the movements of Ousmane, Amadou and Issoufou had been ended, and all three accompanied Maïnassara to northern Niger to celebrate 'national concord day', on the first anniversary of the signing of the peace agreement with the Tuareg movement (see below). Meanwhile, the USTN cancelled plans for a two-day strike, to demand the payment of salary arrears, after the authorities agreed to abandon proposals for levies on civil servants' salaries.

Although, upon seizing power, Maïnassara had given assurances that he and his associates in the CSN had no personal political ambitions, by the beginning of May 1996 he had confirmed reports of his intention to seek election to the presidency as a non-partisan candidate. Adji's transitional government was reshuffled shortly afterwards. The minister of foreign affairs, Mohamed Bazoum, notably left the government, and his responsibilities were transferred to Salifou. The constitutional referendum took place, as scheduled, on 12 May. According to the official results, which were confirmed by the supreme court one week later, the revised document was approved by 92.3% of voters; an abstention rate of some 65% was, however, recorded. The ban on activities by political organizations was revoked shortly afterwards, and this was followed by the ending of the state of emergency imposed in the aftermath of the *coup d'état*. Ousmane, Issoufou, Mamadou and Djermakoye (Issoufou's predecessor as national assembly speaker) swiftly announced their intention to contest the presidential election. All four candidatures, together with that of Maïnassara, were confirmed by the supreme court in mid-June. Meanwhile, there was criticism among opposition groups of the appointment by the Conseil des sages of a new high court of justice, which was to be solely responsible for trying cases of high treason and other offences committed by public figures (including past officials) in the exercise of their state duties. This end to the political consensus of recent months was compounded by tensions between the authorities and the Commission électorale nationale indépendante (CENI), as the government disregarded the latter's recommendations that the presidential election be postponed, owing to delays in the finalization of voters' lists and in the distribution of election materials. The announcement that difficulties in compiling accurate lists meant that it would be impossible to arrange for Nigeriens abroad to vote was, furthermore, condemned by the CENI as a violation both of citizens' rights and of the prerogatives and autonomy of the commission. A new funding arrangement was, in the mean time, concluded with the IMF.

Voting in the presidential election commenced, as scheduled, on 7 July 1996, but was quickly halted in Niamey and in several other areas where preparations were incomplete: polling took place in these areas the following day. Controversy arose when, shortly before the end of voting, the authorities announced the dissolution of the CENI, in response to what they termed its 'obvious and deliberate' obstruction of the electoral process. A new commission, largely comprising senior civil servants, was appointed to collate the election results. The democratic credentials of the CSN were further brought into doubt after Maïnassara's four rivals for the presidency were placed under house arrest. The provisional results of voting, announced by the new commission on 9 July, showed an outright victory for Maïnassara, with some 52.2% of the votes cast; ex-president Ousmane had won 19.8%, and Mamadou 15.7%. Security measures in the capital were reinforced in response to opposition unrest, the closure was ordered of the headquarters of the main opposition parties, and a curfew was imposed in Zinder (Ousmane's birthplace) following violent clashes between police and demonstrators: the ministry of the interior and territorial administration subsequently confirmed that 86 arrests had been made in the post-election period. Meanwhile, the USTN, which asserted that Nigeriens would not tolerate a further *coup d'état*, called a general strike, although this was stated by the authorities to have been poorly observed. The supreme court validated the election results on 21 July, and the release from house arrest of the defeated presidential candidates was announced the following day. All those detained in the aftermath of the election were reported to have been released by the end of the month, and the curfew was ended in Zinder; however, it transpired that Issoufou remained under surveillance. The USTN abandoned attempts at a general strike in late July.

THE FOURTH REPUBLIC

Maïnassara was installed as president of the fourth republic on 7 August 1996. In his inaugural address, he appealed for national unity as a basis for the forging of lasting economic and social stability, and pledged a continuance of the campaign against corruption, injustice and irresponsibility in public affairs. Issoufou was released from house arrest in mid-August, as was Bazoum (who had also recently been placed under surveillance). A new government, under Boukary Adji, was named later in August: incoming members included former prime minister Souley Abdoulaye, as minister of transport, and Amadou Cissé, who returned from a World Bank posting in Chad to become minister of state for the economy, finance and planning. Members of the CDS–Rahama, the MNSD–Nassara and the PNDS–Tarayya who accepted government posts were subsequently expelled from their parties.

At the end of August 1996 the legislative elections, which had been scheduled to take place in late September, were postponed until 10 November, in order that they might take place in what were termed 'suitable' conditions. In early September a group of eight opposition parties (including the CDS–Rahama, the MNSD–Nassara and the PNDS–Tarayya) stipulated several preconditions for their participation in the elections, foremost among them the annulment of the presidential election and the restitution of the CENI. The subsequent formation by these parties of an opposition Front pour la restauration et la défense de la démocratie (FRDD) was followed by the establishment of the Front pour la démocratie et le progrès (FDP), which brought together several small political organizations that supported President Maïnassara. Later in September the Conseil des sages recommended the further postponement of the legislative elections, pending the resolution of difficulties (including the threatened boycott by the FRDD). Maïnassara subsequently asked the government to pursue inter-party negotiations, with mediation by the Conseil des sages, to bring about a reconciliation. In the ensuing talks it emerged that the government was prepared to concede opposition access to the state media and an end to the ban (in force since the presidential election) on public meetings and demonstrations. In early October, moreover, the government announced the postponement of the legislative election, to 23 November, and the restoration of the CENI, with the same composition as that which had overseen the 1995 election. The commission's prerogatives were, however, amended, and the FRDD reiterated that it would not participate in the forthcoming poll unless the CENI was reinstated with its original powers and the presidential election was annulled.

In mid-October 1996 a prominent human rights organization, Amnesty International, issued a report alleging that Niger's human rights situation had worsened since the coup; the deterioration had been particularly marked since the presidential election. The organization denounced, in particular, arrests, deportations to the north, degrading treatment and intimidation of opposition activists, the denial of press freedom and the harassment of journalists. Maïnassara rejected the allegations, asserting that there were no political prisoners in Niger, that the press was totally free, and that political organizations enjoyed freedom of association and movement.

The Conseil des sages, meanwhile, continued its efforts to broker a compromise between the government and the FRDD. Despite a brief extension of the deadline for the registration of candidates, the main opposition parties refused to modify their preconditions for participation, and in early November 1996 the supreme court formally ruled on the FRDD members' exclusion from the legislative elections. Voting, on 23 November, was contested by 11 parties and movements, as well as by independent candidates. The FRDD claimed that its appeal to supporters to boycott the vote had been successful: turnout was low in all areas other than Dosso (Maïnassara's home province) and Agadez, with polling stations in Niamey almost deserted. However, official figures showed a level of participation similar to that at previous elections. The authorities denied foreign radio reports that Ousmane had been placed under house arrest, stating that security around his home had been increased in order to prevent a scheduled opposition meeting there, following the discovery of a plan to disturb public order. According to official results published by the election commission three days after the poll, the pro-Maïnassara Union nationale des indépendants pour le renouveau démocratique (UNIRD) took 52 of the national assembly's 83 seats. International observers pronounced themselves satisfied with the organization and conduct of the election. (The supreme court later upheld complaints of fraud in three constituencies won by the UNIRD, annulling the results there.)

Following the completion of the constitutional referendum and the presidential and legislative elections, the CSN was formally dissolved on 12 December 1996. A new government was appointed in the following week, with Amadou Cissé as prime minister. André Salifou became minister of state, responsible for relations with parliament. The FRDD leaders had rejected an invitation by Maïnassara to join the government, and the deputy leader of the CDS–Rahama, Jackou Senoussi, was expelled from the party after accepting a ministerial post. The final session of the Conseil des sages took place on 26 December, and the national assembly was inaugurated the following day. Moutari Moussa was elected president of the legislature at the end of the month, despite some controversy regarding the procedure for his appointment. Deputies within the assembly organized themselves into three groups: the ANDPS–Zaman Lahiya/UDPS–Amana, the FDP and UNIRD.

As the first anniversary of the *coup d'état* approached, the government warned that opposition parties were planning 'a genuine campaign of permanent destabilization'. In mid-January 1997 an unauthorized demonstration in Niamey to mark what the opposition termed a 'day of democratic initiative' degenerated into clashes with security forces. Some 62 people were arrested, among them Ousmane, Mamadou and Issoufou (who were initially placed under house arrest but subsequently taken into custody). It was announced that they would be tried by the state security court, which had been restored in the aftermath of the demonstration. Considerable controversy ensued regarding the validity of the court's revival. Neither the constitution nor the penal code made provision for the court, which had been in existence under the Kountché regime; however, the government invoked constitutional provisions whereby, unless specifically repealed, laws in force at the time of the promulgation of the constitution remained valid. Meanwhile, national and international human rights bodies, as well as the governments of France and the USA, expressed concern at the arrests. Violent clashes in Zinder were followed, one week after the 'day of democratic initiative', by a second protest in Niamey to demand the release of the opposition leaders. All were released two days later, reportedly on Maïnassara's direct order, and the president appealed to the Cissé administration and the FRDD to co-operate in forming a government of national unity. However, little progress was made in reconciling the government and opposition. Foremost among the FRDD's preconditions for participation in government was the dissolution of the national assembly and the holding of free and fair elections. Its other demands included guarantees of opposition access to the media, of press freedom and freedom of association; the FRDD also required an end to the privatization programme, to which the government was expressly committed. For its part, the government stated its willingness to negotiate on all issues other than the institutions of the fourth republic, thus precluding fresh elections. A demonstration in Niamey in mid-February proceeded peacefully: participants demanded the dissolution of the state security court, as well as opposition access to the state media. (It was noted at this time that opposition actions were being increasingly covered by the official broadcasting and press services, as were statements by the national human rights association.) A further demonstration took place in the following week. Meanwhile, the FRDD leaders embarked on a tour of Conseil de l'entente countries, in an apparent attempt to secure support for the opposition cause; Maïnassara, similarly, had recently held consultations with regional leaders. Speaking in Benin, Ousmane reiterated that the opposition would be unable to participate in government unless further legislative elections were held. In early March police used tear gas to prevent an unauthorized opposition rally from proceeding near the parliament building.

Tensions were, meanwhile, exacerbated by labour unrest in February–March 1997. Strikes involved most notably schoolteachers, demanding improved pay and conditions, and employees at the state electricity company, protesting against the proposed privatization of the company. The power workers' dispute, which had necessitated the deployment of security forces in order to ensure electricity supplies, was declared illegal by the government, which stated that constitutional guarantees of the right to strike did not extend to some strategic sectors. Following stoppages by customs workers in March, their union was dissolved, since strike action was similarly outlawed in paramilitary sectors. The USTN undertook a 72-hour strike in early April, demanding the payment of salary arrears and the release of power workers detained for acts of sabotage. The strike was reported to have been fully observed in educational establishments, and to have had partial support in other sectors. In mid-April four members of the power workers' union were sentenced to prison sentences of up to two years, having been convicted of sabotage. A further 19 trade unionists, among them the deputy secretary-general of the USTN, were acquitted, but remained in detention pending an appeal by the state.

Addressing the diplomatic corps at the beginning of April 1997, the minister of foreign affairs warned against interference in Niger's internal affairs. Allegations that members of certain diplomatic missions had taken part in demonstrations and issued statements incompatible with diplomatic ethics were widely assumed to be directed at staff at the US, Canadian and German embassies. Speaking in Tchin Tabaraden to commemorate 'national concord day', later in April, Maïnassara appealed to the opposition to engage in dialogue and reconciliation. In early May, none the less, a three-day general strike by civil servants resulted in the closure of schools and colleges and disruption to hospitals and health centres. The strike took place while representatives of the IMF and World Bank were visiting Niger to assess progress in the implementation of the programme agreed in mid-1996. Meanwhile, the government and authorities resumed a dialogue; as before, however, little was achieved, with the opposition continuing to demand the dissolution of the national assembly and the authorities reiterating that there was no constitutional provision for the holding of fresh elections before 2001 (the date of the expiry of the national assembly's mandate). The national assembly, for its part, issued a statement in May 1997 welcoming the resumption of dialogue, but denouncing the opposition for demanding strict observance of the constitution while seeking the dissolution of the document's institutions. Amnesty International issued a further report in May, urging the Nigerien government to put an end to human rights violations carried out by the security forces 'with impunity' since the 1996 coup, and condemning the arbitrary arrests, systematic intimidation and unfair trials of opposition members in recent months.

A reorganization of the government in mid-June 1997 included the appointment of Ahmadou Maiyaki as minister of the economy and finance (a new post) and the addition of responsibility for higher education to Senoussi's portfolio. The reshuffle was followed by a number of other state appointments. Within the military, Col Moussa Moumouni Djermakoye, hitherto prefect-mayor of Niamey, was designated chief of staff of the armed forces, while Lt-Col Issa Kalagbo was named deputy chief of staff. New military prefects were also appointed to Niger's departments. Earlier in June there had been unrest at military garrisons in northern and eastern Niger, involving soldiers who were demanding the payment of arrears in allowances, and the military commander and prefect of Maradi had been taken hostage by mutineers. However, a government statement on the unrest countered reports that the then deputy chief of staff of the armed forces, who was a member of a delegation dispatched to examine the soldiers' grievances, had been among the hostages. Earlier in June the national assembly had appointed members to the high court of justice; the court's president was to be Moumouni Amadou Djermakoye. At the end of the month the legislature approved new measures governing the media, which stipulated stringent penalties for those found to have published or distributed libellous or offensive material. The adoption of the new press code followed a period during which the Maïnassara administration had denounced the use of the communications media by groups wishing to undermine the state.

As the first anniversary of Maïnassara's election to the presidency approached, the government announced a nation-wide ban on demonstrations planned for 7–8 July 1997, stating that it could not tolerate actions that aimed 'continuously to disturb public order'. The authorities denied that the ban was in violation of constitutional guarantees of the right to demonstrate. Security forces were mobilized as demonstrations proceeded in several towns on 8 July, with violent clashes reported in Maradi, Zinder and Tahoua, while in Niamey police surrounded the headquarters of the CDS–Rahama, PNDS–Tarayya and MNSD–Nassara, where opposition leaders had taken refuge.

ETHNIC CONFLICT

As in neighbouring Mali, ethnic unrest was precipitated by the return to Niger, beginning in the late 1980s, of large numbers of Tuareg nomads, who had migrated to Libya and Algeria earlier in the decade to escape the drought. In May 1990 Tuaregs launched a violent attack on the prison and gendarmerie at Tchin Tabaraden, in north-eastern Niger. Reports suggested that the incident reflected Tuareg dissatisfaction that promises, made by Saïbou following his accession to power, regarding assistance for the rehabilitation of returnees to Niger had not been fulfilled (it appeared that funds designated for this purpose had been misappropriated). The alleged brutality of the armed forces in quelling the raid was to provoke considerable disquiet, both within Niger and internationally. In February 1991 an attack on an anti-desertification centre in northern Niger, at the time of a visit to the country by representatives of Amnesty International, was attributed to Tuareg activists. In April 44 Tuaregs were acquitted of involvement in the attack on Tchin Tabaraden.

Although the Tuareg issue was a major concern of the 1991 national conference, rebels mounted a renewed offensive in October. During the months that followed numerous violent attacks were directed at official targets in the north, and clashes took place between Tuareg rebels and the security forces. Many arrests were reported, while Tuareg groups were known to have kidnapped several armed forces members. In January 1992 the transitional government intensified security measures in northern Niger. Shortly afterwards the government formally recognized, for the first time, that there was a rebellion in the north (incidents had hitherto been dismissed as isolated acts of banditry), and acknowledged the existence of a Tuareg movement, the Front de libération de l'Aïr et l'Azaouad (FLAA)—although official reports of the strength of the FLAA appeared to be understated. In the following month the leader of the FLAA, Rissa Ag Boula, stated that the Tuareg rebels were not seeking to achieve independence, but rather the establishment of a federal system, in which each ethnic group would have its own administrative entity.

A two-week truce, agreed in May 1992 by the government and FLAA, in preparation for peace negotiations, failed. Tuareg attacks resumed in subsequent months, and in August the armed forces launched a major offensive against the Tuareg rebellion in the north. According to official figures, 186 Tuaregs were arrested in late August and early September, both in the north and in Niamey. Among those detained were Mohamed Moussa (who, as minister of the interior, had initiated contacts with Tuareg leaders) and the prefect of Agadez. The issue of the Tuaregs held by the security forces, as well as the 44 members of the Nigerien military who had been captured by militant Tuaregs, was to be a major obstacle to the resumption of a dialogue in subsequent months. Military authority was intensified, following renewed Tuareg attacks, by the appointment, in October, of senior members of the security forces to northern administrative posts. In November a commission appointed by the transitional government to consider the Tuareg issue recommended a far-reaching programme of decentralization, according legal status and financial autonomy to local communities. In December the government announced the release from custody of 57 Tuaregs.

In January 1993 five people were killed in a Tuareg attack on an MNSD–Nassara meeting in the northern town of Abala. Although he escaped injury, the principal target of the attack was said to have been Tandja Mamadou, who had been minister of the interior at the time of the suppression of the Tchin Tabaraden raid. Although Tuareg attacks and acts of sabotage persisted, later in January a further 81 Tuaregs, including Mohamed Moussa, were released from detention. In February 30 people were reported to have been killed in raids by Tuaregs (for which the FLAA denied responsibility) around Tchin Tabaraden. In March, following Algerian mediation, Rissa Ag Boula (who was based in Algeria, despite attempts by the Nigerien authorities to secure his extradition) announced a unilateral truce for the duration of the campaign for the second round of the presidential election. Shortly afterwards Tuareg representatives in Niamey signed a similar truce agreement (brokered by France). The election of the new organs of state appeared to offer new prospects for dialogue, and in early April the transitional government and the FLAA reached an agreement for an extension of the truce. About 30 Tuareg prisoners were released shortly afterwards, and in mid-April the Tuaregs released their hostages.

President Ousmane and prime minister Issoufou identified the resolution of the Tuareg issue as a major priority, and, although sporadic resistance was reported, the truce accord was largely respected. In June 1993 it was revealed that representatives of the Nigerien government and the Tuaregs had for some time been negotiating in France, and on 10 June a formal, three-month truce agreement was signed in Paris. The accord provided for the demilitarization of the north, and envisaged the instigation of negotiations on the Tuaregs' political demands. Financial assistance was promised to facilitate the return of Tuareg refugees from Algeria, and development funds were pledged for northern areas. A committee was to be established to oversee the implementation of the agreement. However, the Paris accord encountered some opposition within the Tuareg community: a new group, the Armée révolutionnaire de libération du nord-Niger (ARLN), emerged to denounce the accord, and by July a further split was evident between supporters of the truce (led by Mano Dayak, the Tuareg signatory to the agreement), who broke away from the FLAA to form the Front de libération de Tamoust (FLT), and its opponents (led by Rissa Ag Boula), who stated that they could not support any agreement that contained no specific commitment to discussion of the federalist issue.

In September 1993 the FLT and the Nigerien government agreed to extend the truce for a further three months. The FLAA and the ARLN refused to sign the accord, but in the following month they joined the FLT in a Coordination de la résistance armée (CRA), with the aim of presenting a cohesive programme in future dealings with the Nigerien authorities. It was indicated that the FLAA and the ARLN would henceforth be more willing to compromise in their demands, and efforts were initiated to arrange new talks. However, frustrated by subsequent delays, the French government announced its withdrawal from mediation efforts. Attacks on travellers between Agadez and Zinder, in December, were attributed to Tuaregs (the first time for several months that the authorities had blamed disturbances on Tuaregs), and shortly afterwards government forces were reported to have attacked a Tuareg encampment, killing four people, although the government denied any such offensive.

Unrest continued in January 1994, although discreet mediation efforts continued. In the same month the establishment was reported of a further Tuareg movement, the Front patriotique de libération du Sahara (FPLS). In February the CRA, including the FPLS, announced its willingness to attend preliminary talks in Ouagadougou, Burkina Faso, although it declined to sign a new truce agreement with the Nigerien government. France agreed to rejoin the negotiations, and, meeting in Burkina in February, the CRA (which presented a list of the Tuaregs' demands for consideration by the Nigerien authorities) and the government of Niger agreed to full negotiations in Paris in March, with French, Algerian and Burkinabè mediation. None the less, reports of a Tuareg attack on a uranium installation at Arlit, and of the harassment of travellers in the north and east, undermined peace efforts in subsequent weeks. Moreover, the CRA's demands for regional autonomy, and for the establishment of quotas for Tuaregs in government, parliament and in the armed forces, received little support in Niamey, where the authorities and parliamentary opposition were prepared to concede the rehabilitation of the north and greater political decentralization. The proposed Paris negotiations did not take place in March, and a further round of consultations was postponed indefinitely in April. There was an escalation of violence during May, including clashes some 200 km to the north of Agadez between the Nigerien armed forces and a rebel unit of the FPLS, as a result of which as many as 40 deaths were recorded. Negotiations reopened in Paris in June. Tentative agreement was reached on the creation of 'homogenous' autonomous regions for Niger's ethnic groups, each of which would have its own locally-elected assembly and governor to function in parallel with the central government. There was, however, no agreement regarding the integration of Tuareg fighters into Niger's armed forces and political and administrative structures.

There was renewed unrest in August and September 1994, including three reported attempts by Tuaregs to disrupt power supplies to uranium mines; a grenade attack on a meeting in Agadez of the UDPS–Amana resulted in six deaths (Tuareg groups accused government forces of responsibility for the assault). At a meeting in Ouagadougou in late September, none the less, the CRA presented Nigerien government negotiators with what it termed a 'comprehensive and final' plan for a restoration of peace. The plan was referred to Ousmane, and formal negotiations resumed in Ouagadongou in early October, with mediation by the Burkinabè president, Blaise Compaoré, as well as representatives of France and Algeria. A new peace accord was signed on 9 October, which, while emphasizing that Niger was 'unitary and indivisible', recognized the right of the people to manage their own affairs. Territorial communities were to have their own elected assemblies or councils, to which would be delegated responsibility for the implementation of economic, social and cultural policies at a regional or local level. The Nigerien government was to take immediate measures to ensure the rehabilitation and development of areas affected by the conflict, and to ensure the elimination of insecurity in the north. Provisions were also to be made to facilitate the return and resettlement of refugees. A renewable three-month truce was to take immediate effect, to be monitored by French and Burkinabè military units. By the time of the conclusion of the Ouagadougou agreement the number of deaths since the escalation of the Tuareg rebellion in late 1991 was officially put at 150.

In January 1995 a commission was established to consider the administrative reorganization of the country. Shortly afterwards representatives of the Nigerien government, the CRA, Algeria, Burkina and France met in Agadez, where they agreed to a three-month renewal of the truce. Despite occasional reports of incidents apparently involving renegade Tuareg units, observers confirmed general adherence to the truce, and a further round of negotiations was scheduled to take place in Ouagadougou in late March. The opening of these talks was, however, briefly delayed by a split in the Tuareg movement. Rissa Ag Boula, who in January had withdrawn from the CRA (having repeatedly criticized Dayak's negotiating stance) and refused to participate in the decentralization committee, emerged as the leader of the Tuareg delegation (now renamed the Organisation de la résistance armée–ORA) in Ouagadougou: Dayak and the FLT initially remained within the ORA, which claimed to accord increased autonomy to each of the six movements now reportedly in existence. In mid-April it was announced that a lasting peace agreement had been reached. The accord, which essentially confirmed the provisions of the October 1994 agreement, provided for the establishment of a special peace committee, to be overseen by representatives of the three mediating countries, whose task would be to ensure the practical implementation of the accord, including the disarming of combatants. Demobilized rebels were to be integrated into the Nigerien military and public sector, and special military units were to be accorded responsibility for the security of the northern regions; particular emphasis was to be placed on the economic, social and cultural development of the north, and the government undertook to support the decentralization process. There was to be a general amnesty for all parties involved in the Tuareg rebellion and its suppression, and a day of national reconciliation was to be instituted in memory of the victims of the conflict. The peace agreement, which envisaged the implementation of its provisions within a period of six months, was formally signed by the Nigerien government negotiator, Mai Maigana, and Rissa Ag Boula in Niamey on 24 April 1995. A cease-fire took effect the following day.

Meanwhile, there was increasing evidence in late 1994 and early 1995 of ethnic unrest in southern and eastern Niger, especially in the Lake Chad region. Clashes (frequently over grazing rights) between settled Toubous and nomadic Peulhs resulted in numerous deaths, many of which were attributed to the Front démocratique du renouveau (FDR)—an organization which emerged in October 1994 to demand increased autonomy for south-eastern regions. In November, in compliance with a request by the UN, Niger established a committee whose stated aim was to disarm militias and to combat arms-trafficking: the Agadez and Lake Chad regions were said to be major centres for weapons-trading, with insecurity near the border with Chad being attributed to the presence in Niger, since the overthrow of President Hissène Habré in late 1990, of several thousand (mainly Toubou) Chadian refugees. It was from this region that one of the greatest potential obstacles to national reconciliation seemed to emerge in subsequent months.

Although the ORA expressed concern at the slow implementation of the April 1995 peace agreement, its provisions were gradually enacted: the Comité spécial de la paix (CSP) was inaugurated in May, under the chairmanship of Maigana, and a military observer group, comprising representatives of Burkina and France, was deployed in the north in July. The issue of the amnesty proved more controversial, since the inclusion of Arab militias, which had been established by the transitional authorities in 1992 to act as civilian self-defence units in the north, was opposed by many Tuareg groups. The amnesty decree was, none the less, signed by Hama Amadou in mid-July, and all Tuareg prisoners were reported to have been released shortly afterwards. The peace process was undermined following a clash in the north between Tuaregs and an Arab militia unit, as a result of which a Tuareg leader and at least 12 others were killed. Moreover, there was evidence that Dayak and other Tuareg groups in a revived CRA were making common cause with the FDR in demanding autonomy for their regions. In July at least four deaths were reported following an armed attack, responsibility for which was claimed by the FDR, on a military garrison in the south-east, and in August the FDR accused the armed forces of killing 29 civilians in the Lake Chad region. Despite a threat by Rissa Ag Boula that the ORA would once again take up arms if the implementation of the peace agreement was not accelerated, efforts at reconciliation were evident, and Amadou stated that the FDR would not be excluded from agreements currently under negotiation. However, talks between representatives of the Tuareg movements and the FDR, which took place in northern Niger in September–October, failed either to reunite the CRA and the ORA, or to establish the principle of the FDR's adherence to the April peace accord. In October clashes in the north-east involving rebel Tuaregs and the armed forces (reportedly the first hostilities since April) were attributed to elements of the CRA. Dayak subsequently stated that the fragmentation of the Tuareg movement represented a major obstacle to a lasting peace, but stipulated that the CRA would not join the peace process until the authorities and the ORA recognized all groups (reportedly six) within the CRA. Meeting in Tahoua in late October, bilateral and international donors pledged some 18,700m. francs CFA in support of a two-year emergency programme for the development of the north. A programme for the repatriation of an estimated 25,000 refugees from Algeria, Burkina and Libya was also discussed. In November a clash in the Tchin Tabaraden region between government forces and a security unit of the ORA provoked tensions between the signatories to the peace agreement. However, an extraordinary session of the CSP, convened in December, resulted in agreement on preventing further such incidents. In mid-December Dayak was killed, together with two other leading CRA members, when the aircraft in which they were (according to later reports) travelling to Niamey, for talks on rejoining the peace process, crashed in northern Niger. In early January 1996 the new leader of the FLT (and acting leader of the CRA), Mohamed Akotai, indicated that his movement favoured inter-Tuareg reconciliation and a dialogue with government.

Following the military *coup d'état* of January 1996, Niger's new leadership quickly expressed its commitment to the April 1995 agreement. Maïnassara had previously been involved in the work of the CSP, and the government, the ORA and the CRA all expressed the view that direct contacts between the military and the Tuareg movements would expedite the peace process. The FDR also expressed its willingness to co-operate with the new authorities; in early February, none the less, an armed assault on Dirkou by members of that movement, and an army counter-attack, resulted in the deaths of 11 members of the FDR and of one member of the military. The appointment, later in the month, of an ORA spokesman, Mohamed Aoutchéki, as a special adviser to Maïnassara was said to be indicative of the CSN's wish to accelerate the peace process. In early March agreements were signed by the Nigerien authorities, the office of the UN High Commissioner for Refugees (UNHCR) and the governments of Algeria and Burkina, regarding the repatriation of refugees. Shortly afterwards the CRA, including the FDR, affirmed its recognition of the April 1995 agreement, and announced that it would observe a unilateral truce for one month, pending the outcome of negotiations with the authorities. The ORA pledged its support for the involvement of the CRA in the peace process, and in early April 1996 the government and the CRA signed an agreement formalizing the latter's adherence to the 1995 accord. In late May 1996 the ORA and the CRA agreed to establish a joint committee to co-ordinate their activities and represent the interests of the resistance movements in negotiations with the authorities on the implementation of the peace accord. There was considerable support for the CSN regime in Tuareg areas, and Maïnassara's victory in the presidential election was largely welcomed in the north. (Maïnassara had, in mid-June, held his first electoral rally in Agadez.)

In mid-July 1996, following a month of discussions, the CSP and the resistance movements recommended measures aimed at curbing what was termed 'residual banditry' in northern areas. Preliminary agreement was also reached regarding the integration of demobilized fighters into regular military and civilian sectors, although Tuareg leaders expressed some disappointment that the number of fighters to be integrated into the army and paramilitary forces (1,400) was not greater. Discussions continued in August regarding the demobilization and disarmament of the rebel movement, and in mid-September joint peace-keeping patrols of the Nigerien armed forces and former rebels were inaugurated in the north. At the end of September, however, Rissa Ag Boula, denouncing the inadequacy of arrangements for the reintegration of demobilized fighters, announced that the ORA was no longer bound by the peace treaty. The authorities asserted that this abandonment of the 1995 accord was linked less to concerns regarding the implementation of its provisions than to the arrest of ORA members in connection with the diversion, some months previously, of a large consignment of cigarettes bound for the north. In an apparent gesture of reconciliation, however, the detainees were released at the end of October 1996 and the ORA surrendered the consignment to the authorities. In November it was reported that a new group had emerged, combining movements from both the ORA and the CRA; led by Mohamed Anako, the Union des forces de la résistance armée (UFRA) affirmed its commitment to the peace accord. A meeting between the high commissioner for the restoration of peace and 10 of the reported 12 resistance groups was followed in mid-December by the signing of a protocol for the encampment of some 5,900 former fighters, prior to their disarmament and reintegration into regular armed forces and civilian structures. The ORA, however, remained excluded from this process.

Concerns for the peace process were heightened at the end of 1996 by reports of renewed insecurity, including clashes between renegade fighters and joint patrols. Following a meeting in Niamey between Maïnassara and Rissa Ag Boula in early January 1997, at which mutual co-operation pledges were made, the ORA leader condemned, especially, recent attacks on tourists in the Aïr region. Having received assurances regarding the implementation of provisions of the 1995 accord, the ORA declared its renewed support; it was announced, moreover, that the FLAA and FLT would establish a joint patrol aimed at combating insecurity and banditry. In early February 1997 the UFRA joined members of the regular armed forces, the CRA and the Comité de vigilance de Tassara (CVT) in a peace-keeping patrol in Agadez.

At the end of January 1997 Cissé chaired a donors' consultative meeting on the financing of the peace process. The cost of encampment and reintegration of former fighters and refugees was put at some 18,000m. francs CFA. In April Maïnassara signed a decree establishing a commission, under his direct jurisdiction, charged with overseeing the process. Chaired by the minister of national defence, the commission was to include representatives of other ministries, the military and paramilitary, the high commissioner for the restoration of peace, all signatories to the 1995 accord, and the CVT.

Some insecurity persisted, none the less, particularly in the east. Violent clashes were reported in late March 1997, involving several hundred soldiers and Toubou rebels: the FDR protested that the operation, which was attributed by the authorities to the need to eliminate isolated groups of armed bandits, was endangering the peace accord. In early June it was announced that Toubous and Arabs of the Forces armées révolutionnaires du Sahara (FARS) had, following negotiations in Chad, agreed to join the peace process. The FARS had reportedly been responsible for the recent kidnapping of three civil servants and a Canadian aid worker (who had been released, after 12 weeks, in mid-May), and had suffered heavy losses as a result of the recent army operations. It subsequently appeared that large numbers of armed Toubous had fled to north-eastern Nigeria following the defeat of the FARS; Niger's minister of national defence subsequently proposed the establishment of joint patrols, to involve the armed forces of Niger, Nigeria, Chad and Cameroon, to ensure security in the Lake Chad region. At the beginning of June, meanwhile, the authorities denied reports that, following a military rebellion at the Agadez military barracks, former rebel Tuaregs were besieging the town.

A three-day meeting took place in mid-July 1997 to assess encampment procedures. It was reported that the demobilization and billeting of former fighters, as envisaged in the December 1996 accord, had been completed, and that the incorporation of demobilized groups into the regular armed and paramilitary forces and the civil service was proceeding. Appeals were renewed for funds to expedite the full application of the peace accord: France had agreed to provide finance for the reinforcement of security in northern and eastern areas, but assistance pledged by the European Union (EU) for the development of areas affected by ethnic conflict had not yet been released. It was stated that some 11,000 refugees would return from Burkina and Algeria, with UNHCR assistance, by the end of 1997. Shortly after the meeting, however, the FDR announced its withdrawal from the peace process, stating that Nigerien and Chadian military units had attacked one of its bases in the Lake Chad region; the FDR reported that 17 members of the armed forces had been killed in clashes with its fighters. The Nigerien authorities strenuously denied that any engagement had taken place, denouncing the FDR's submission of such reports to Agence France-Presse, which had broadcast details of the clashes, as an 'act of manipulation'. In subsequent weeks the government expressed optimism that the FDR would rejoin the peace process.

In November 1996, meanwhile, Niger, Mali and UNHCR signed an agreement for the repatriation of 25,000 Malian Tuaregs from Niger; the agreement defined the obligations and responsibilities of its signatories with regard to the voluntary return 'with dignity' of the refugees.

FOREIGN RELATIONS UNDER THE FOURTH REPUBLIC

There was a notable deterioration in relations with the USA in the immediate aftermath of the 1996 presidential election. The US authorities expressed concern that the Maïnassara administration was seeking to manipulate the results of voting, and in late July again announced the suspension of its programme of economic and military assistance, in reaction to what it termed the 'very visible abandonment of democracy' in Niger. France, however, appeared more circumspect, expressing satisfaction that the promised elections had taken place, and, in a message to the new president, Chirac wished Maïnassara success in leading Niger towards stability and development. The French government minister responsible for co-operation, Jacques Godfrain, attended Maïnassara's investiture in early August, and it was implied that France, which stressed its tradition of non-interference in the internal affairs of its former colonies, would intercede on behalf of Niger within Europe, and EU funds were subsequently pledged for the development of northern and eastern Niger.

The Maïnassara administration continued its campaign of regional dialogue, frequently dispatching high-level delegations to neigbouring countries to explain and secure support for its actions. There was a significant reversal of foreign policy in late August 1996, when relations were resumed with the People's Republic of China. Salifou (who had led opposition to the restoration of links with Taiwan in 1992) signed documents to this effect while visiting China in his capacity as minister of state for foreign affairs. Disappointment was expressed at the level and nature of co-operation by Taiwan, which severed links shortly afterwards. Maïnassara made an official visit to the People's Republic of China in May 1997.

Economy

EDITH HODGKINSON

During the 1980s and into the mid-1990s Niger's economy lost much of its earlier momentum towards growth and modernization which had resulted from the development of the uranium-mining industry in the 1970s. After a long-term decline in international demand and prices for uranium, the formal economy has contracted, both in size and diversity. However, the traditional rural economy has remained intact, and growth has been noted in informal trade and in small-scale artisanal manufacturing and repair activities. The country is greatly influenced by its economic relations with its southern neighbour, Nigeria. While Niger's official exports and imports have declined sharply since the beginning of the 1990s, substantial unrecorded trade has continued to flourish across the 2,000-km border with Nigeria: fuel smuggled from Nigeria already accounts for at least one-third of Niger's national consumption, according to official estimates. The informal, or 'grey', economy is thus unusually large in Niger, and the World Bank estimates that it represents about 70% of all economic activity.

In 1994, according to estimates by the World Bank, Niger's gross national product (GNP) was equivalent to only US $220 per head, making it one of the world's poorest countries. The UN's human development index, which takes into account life expectancy and conditions in health and education, ranked Niger last among 174 countries in 1995 and again in 1996. This follows more than two decades of decline in GNP per head, as the economy performed very erratically during the 1970s and then contracted in almost every year of the 1980s, owing to a combination of weakening earnings from uranium, drought and economic turmoil in neighbouring Nigeria. There appears to be little prospect of securing strong and sustained economic growth, even after the 50% devaluation of the CFA franc in January 1994, which has benefited some other Franc Zone countries, since world prices for uranium, Niger's dominant export, remain depressed and the country otherwise has a very limited range of exportable goods. However, it was hoped that the enhanced flows of aid and measures of debt-relief that followed immediately after the devaluation would help achieve the objectives of the development programme for 1994–96. This aimed at economic growth of 4% in 1994 and of more than 5% thereafter. In the event, these targets were not met, with growth in gross domestic product (GDP) just 2.6% in both 1994 and 1995, while 1996 is unlikely to have registered much improvement, owing to the severing of much aid after the military coup in January and a very poor cereals harvest. However, the potentially very damaging boycott by aid donors came to an end relatively rapidly: the signing of an enhanced structural adjustment facility (ESAF) agreement with the IMF in June 1996 was followed by pledges of funding from the World Bank, the African Development Bank, the European Union, France and Japan. President Ibrahim Baré Maïnassara declared his intention to promote a market economy, with the privatization programme 'irreversibly' in progress. Along with enhancing competitivenes, the new administration undertook to reduce poverty, distributing the benefits of still-modest growth (the programme supported by the ESAF aims to achieve annual GDP growth of 4.5% in 1997–98) more widely across the population.

THE TRADITIONAL ECONOMY

Although only a small proportion of Niger's land is capable of supporting settled farming, agriculture and livestock contribute some 35%–40% of GDP, and account for more than 80% of the working population. Principal staple products are millet, maize, sorghum, cow-peas and cassava, all grown mainly for household consumption. Rice is also produced, on the small area that is under modern irrigation, while cotton and groundnuts are the principal cash crops. With the exception of drought periods, expansion in the production of food crops has kept pace with population growth, and Niger became self-sufficient in food grains after the mid-1980s, although distribution problems continued to cause local shortages. At times of drought, however, the situation can become serious. This was the case when, after a relatively poor crop in 1995/96, an inadequate wet season in 1996 and infestation by parasites were expected to result in a harvest in 1996/97 of only 1,197,000 metric tons, compared with a national requirement of some 2,230,000 tons. While the government sought international food aid, large numbers of the population were already moving from rural areas to the towns and also into neighbouring countries.

As food production generally increased, output of groundnuts declined sharply from a peak of 191,307 metric tons (unshelled) in 1967 to an average of only some 25,000 tons per year in the late 1980s. It has since recovered strongly, to 67,400 tons in 1994/95 and an estimated 108,600 tons in 1995/96. Cotton production has not fared so well, after a strong start—9,597 tons (unginned) in 1973/74, 50% up on the level of four years earlier—mainly as a result of investment in irrigated cultivation. Output reached a peak of 11,133 tons in 1975/76 but declined rapidly thereafter. Marketed production averaged less than 4,400 tons per year in 1988/89–1990/91. There has been greater success in the production of cow-peas, with output averaging 200,000 tons per year by the end of the 1980s and reaching about 450,000 tons annually in the early 1990s. The devaluation has made the crop a profitable export to the Nigerian market. However, the single most important activity in this sector is livestock-rearing, which accounted for about 15% of GDP in 1994. Cattle are the second most significant export, in terms of foreign exchange earnings, after uranium, with a significant—if largely unrecorded—trade across the border with Nigeria. As in the rest of the region, extensive stock-rearing made appreciable progress in the years following independence, stimulated by demand from the highly populated coastal region and Nigeria. The droughts of the 1970s and early 1980s, however, caused a sharp fall in numbers, either because of death or because of the removal of livestock to neighbouring countries, and the size of the cattle herd declined by two-thirds between 1972 and 1975, and by one-half in the crisis year of 1984. Although the return of better rains has allowed the partial restoration of the herd, livestock numbers remain significantly below pre-drought levels, at some 2m. cattle and 9.5m. sheep and goats in 1995. The government has been unable to promote either intensive commercial livestock operations or dairy farming, owing to Niger's ecological and demographic conditions. However, the sector did benefit from the strong rise in foreign demand after the 1994 currency devaluation.

The anti-desertification campaign is a priority for the Nigerien government (desertification affected an average of 60,000 ha of land per year in 1980–85), and an effective programme of afforestation and environmental protection is proceeding.

MINING AND POWER

The mining and export of uranium plays a very significant role in Niger's economy, representing an important source of budgetary revenue and providing most of the country's foreign exchange earnings (80% in 1992, but declining to 62% in 1995). However, as demand and prices have weakened, the government has made efforts to encourage the development of the country's other mineral resources, which include cassiterite, coal, phosphates, iron ore, gold and petroleum, although few of these have yet been considered commercially viable.

Proven reserves of uranium are estimated at 280,000 tons. A processing plant at the Arlit uranium mine, in the desolate Aïr mountains, began production in 1971, with 410 tons of metal; output rose to 1,982 tons in 1980. The mining company, Société des mines de l'Aïr (SOMAÏR), is under French control; the majority interest is with the Compagnie générale des matières nucleaires (COGEMA—a subsidiary of the French government's Commissariat à l'énergie atomique) and French private interests, with the Nigerien government's Office nationale des ressources minières du Niger (ONAREM) holding a 33% share. Operating costs at the mine are high, owing to the remoteness of the site, and its output is transported by aircraft or overland to Cotonou, Benin. Production at the country's second uranium mine, at Akouta, was begun in 1978 by a consortium—the Compagnie minière d'Akouta (COMINAK)—of the government, COGEMA, the Japanese Overseas Uranium Resources Development and the Spanish Empresa Nacional del Uranio. Output from the mine reached 2,200 tons in 1980, and total uranium production by Niger reached its peak in 1981 at 4,366 tons. Production subsequently slowed, as world prices plummeted, to a recorded average in the region of 2,900 tons per year in 1987–95 (although this is thought to be an understatement). Most output is sold to equity partners in the mining operations, with France, the principal purchaser, paying a substantial (but still reduced) premium over the world price since the early 1990s. Niger's earnings from sales of uranium were thus only 50,300m. francs CFA in 1992, less than two-thirds of the level (88,415m. francs CFA) recorded in 1986, on volumes that were only one-sixth lower. In 1992 only about 8% of the national budget was financed by sales of uranium, compared with 40% in 1979. While uranium demand is forecast by the industry to recover over the next 10–15 years, Niger will suffer from its high costs in relation to other producers, as well as probable competition from recycled uranium. Plans to increase capacity by, for example, developing the large deposits at Imourarem, 80 km south of Arlit, have therefore been postponed indefinitely.

There is increasing foreign interest in the potential for the industrial-scale mining of Niger's gold reserves, most of which are located in the south-west, near the border with Burkina Faso, and which have been exploited on a small scale since the early 1980s. Surveys of sites at Sirba, Téra and Gourouol, conducted by ONAREM, in co-operation with foreign donors, have yielded encouraging results, and in August 1995 a joint venture with Etruscan (of Canada) was reported to have made a large discovery at Koma-Bangou, in the Liptako region bordering Burkina. The company has invested US $7m. in further exploration, while a Kuwaiti company, Berlant, plans to invest $3.5m. in exploring an area at Kossa (also in Liptako), probably in partnership with Canadian interests.

Other mineral resources include cassiterite, a tin-bearing ore mined in the Aïr region (with an estimated output, in terms of mineral content, of 70 tons in 1991 but of only 20 tons per year in 1992–94), iron ore at Say (deposits, as yet unexploited, of some 650m. tons), calcium phosphates (some 2,000 tons per year were produced from open-cast mines at Tahoua until 1984, and there exists the prospect of much greater output from a 207m.-ton deposit at Tapoa) and gypsum. Coal deposits, estimated at 6m. tons, have been located at Anou-Anaren, to the north-west of Agadez. Production began in 1981, for use in power generation, and now averages some 170,000 tons annually. Deposits of petroleum, located in the south-west, have not hitherto been deemed commercially exploitable. The government introduced legislation in 1991 to attract foreign participation in exploration for petroleum. Elf Aquitaine, of France, and the US Exxon Corpn began seismic work in 1992 in the previously unexplored Agadem region north of Lake Chad. Reserves there have been estimated at 1m. tons, and Elf and Exxon renewed their licence in November 1995, with plans to invest 30,000m. francs CFA over five years.

Electricity consumption has risen rapidly, almost doubling in the 1980s, to reach 356m. kWh in 1991, with the major consumers being the uranium companies. Domestic generation, which is almost entirely thermal, covers about one-half of demand, and the remainder is met by hydroelectric supplies from Nigeria. There is a massive power development programme, stimulated by the unreliability of the Nigerian supply, with a 125-MW hydroelectric plant under construction at Kandadji, on the Niger river.

MANUFACTURING

As in most other west African countries, manufacturing takes the form of the processing of agricultural commodities and import substitution. The sector's contribution to GDP was about 7% in 1994. There is a groundnut oil extraction plant, as well as cotton ginneries, rice mills, flour mills and tanneries. Import substitution has been stimulated by the very high cost of transport. A textile mill (capacity 1,600 tons per year) and a cement works (annual capacity 35,000 tons) are in operation, and there are light industries serving the very limited local market. The European Investment Bank and the French government are lending funds for the modernization of the textile plant. However, activity in the sector remains predominantly small-scale and artisanal (the modern sector is estimated to account for less than one-sixth), and, in that it draws on local inputs, will have been stimulated by the currency devaluation, which has made foreign manufactures correspondingly expensive. The modern sector, which is more dependent on imports, was severely affected by devaluation: several businesses closed down in 1994, with the loss of about 3,000 jobs.

TRANSPORT INFRASTRUCTURE

The transport system is still inadequate, despite considerable road development—funded by the World Bank, the European Development Fund and Saudi Arabia—including the 902-km all-weather road between Niamey and Zinder, opened in 1980, and a 651-km 'uranium road' from Arlit to Tahoua, which opened in 1981. In 1995 there were an estimated 9,863 km of classified roads, of which only a small proportion (less than 8%) was paved. There is, at present, no railway: plans to extend the Cotonou–Parakou line from Benin elicited no interest from aid donors, and the scheme was postponed in 1989. Most foreign trade is shipped through Cotonou, via the Organisation commune Bénin-Niger des chemins de fer et des transports. The emphasis in transport development is on diversifying and improving access to seaports: a road is being built to Lomé, Togo, via Burkina Faso, and the Agadez–Zinder section (428 km) of the Trans-Sahara Highway is being upgraded. There are international airports at Niamey and Agadez, and four major domestic airports.

FINANCE

As in other countries of francophone west Africa, some foreign aid in the years immediately after independence took the form of subsidies to make up the chronic deficit on the budget. In the late 1970s, however, the current budget registered a substantial surplus because of the rapid rise in government revenues from uranium. These financed about one-third of the current budget, as well as nearly all capital investment. The decline in uranium revenues (reflecting lower prices and output) during the early 1980s transformed the current budget balance from a surplus of 15,200m. francs CFA in 1980/81 to a deficit of 51,880m. francs CFA in 1982/83. With the doubling of Niger's debt-servicing burden over the same period (see below), stringent austerity measures were needed in subsequent years to limit the budget deficit. Current spending was first reduced, in 1983/84, and then held steady, partly as a result of cut-backs in public-sector employment and of the sale to private ownership of some parastatal enterprises, which tended to be a drain on government funds. Some modest growth in both current and capital expenditure was envisaged in the budgets for 1986/87–1988/89, which were drafted with the co-operation of the IMF and the World Bank. Government finances were to be aided by the restructuring of 10 state-owned companies and the transfer to private ownership or participation of a further 18 companies. Under the terms of the ESAF granted by the IMF in 1989, fiscal austerity was to be maintained. Although funding agreements with the IMF and the World Bank were suspended following the 1991 national conference, prime minister Amadou Cheiffou's transitional government introduced further austerity measures in late 1991. These included a levy on salaries in the civil service. The budget none the less continued in substantial deficit, and public finances deteriorated to such an extent during 1993 that the government was unable to pay civil servants for three months. In common with previous budgets, that for 1993 depended very heavily on foreign sources for its funding: 40% of government income was in the form of external grants.

With France assisting the Ousmane administration in the preparation of a major restructuring programme, both the IMF and World Bank were quick to respond with financial assistance following the currency devaluation. The IMF approved a US $26m. stand-by credit in March 1994, in support of a programme that aimed to reduce the budget deficit (after grants) to 2% of GDP by 1996, by means of revenue enhancement and limiting the increase in expenditure on salaries. In accordance with the latter policy, when budget spending for 1994 was revised upwards to take account of the halving in value of the CFA franc, the current expenditure component—which includes salaries—was increased by only 27%. France pledged budgetary support of 85,000m. francs CFA for that year (representing a little more than one-half of total expenditure). The fiscal situation remained very poor during 1995, despite some success achieved by the new prime minister, Hama Amadou, in increasing customs revenue and reducing the monthly wage bill by one-seventh. However, this progress proved short-lived, as trade union resistance to austerity effectively paralysed public administration for much of the second half of the year. While the fundamental problem in Nigerien public finances is the gross inadequacy of tax revenue (which has been equivalent to only 6%–7% of GDP in recent years), as governments have failed to bring most of the economy into the tax 'net', the army-backed regime installed in early 1996 brought with it the prospect of tax increases and enforced cuts in public-sector salaries. Although the new regime was unable to implement its planned 40% reduction in civil-service pay, it did manage to put into place a number of new taxes proposed earlier, including a business-licence tax (to bring the informal sector into the tax system) and a property levy on owner-occupied housing. The programme for 1996–98, supported by the ESAF agreed in mid-1996, aims to increase tax receipts to 8% of GDP in 1996 and to more than 10% in 1997. This is intended to narrow the budget deficit (excluding grants) to an average of 7.3% of GDP in 1996–98, from 8.6% in 1995 and 12.5% in 1994. This relatively modest improvement in the fiscal balance reflects the need to increase expenditure on education, health care and sanitation, and on the general programme of poverty alleviation. The aim is to accommodate these higher outlays by means of restrictions on the public-sector payroll. An important contribution to fiscal stability will come from the planned privatization of public utilities (in tandem with the liberalization of prices) and divestment of some other government corporate assets. Thus it is intended to sell off 12 public enterprises, including the electricity utility, the petroleum import company and the post office, before the end of 1997.

FOREIGN TRADE AND PAYMENTS

Exports are only partly recorded, but there was evidently a rise—if erratic—in the 1960s, followed by more sustained growth in later years, as the downturn or stagnation of traditional exports (groundnuts and livestock) was more than offset by the impact of the beginning of uranium production. In 1973 uranium became the major export, and within two years it was accounting for around two-thirds of all export earnings. Uranium earnings were responsible for the rapid rise in export receipts in the late 1970s, and reached a peak of 100,804m. francs CFA in 1980—three times the level of 1977. Imports have, none the less, almost always exceeded exports, although by a less substantial margin than in some countries of francophone west Africa. The rise in uranium earnings was matched by the rise in import spending, reflecting higher petroleum prices and investment in capital equipment for the mining industry. Since 1980 the trade balance has fluctuated widely, and deficits have almost always been very much higher than the levels recorded in the late 1970s (3,000m.–9,000m. francs CFA), owing to the persistent depression in the uranium market and the severe grain shortfall in the drought years. The devaluation of the CFA franc did, however, serve to bring Niger's external trade close to balance in 1995, owing to the increased level of sales to Nigeria of livestock and agricultural goods, while demand within Niger for imports was restricted by higher prices.

With merchandise trade normally in deficit, compounded by high transportation costs (reflecting the country's landlocked position), the deficit on the current account of the balance of payments has been contained only by external aid. Grants from members of the Organisation for Economic Co-operation and Development and of the Organization of the Petroleum Exporting Countries averaged US $332m. per year in 1991–95. External borrowing to compensate the current payments' deficit has resulted in a sharp escalation in the foreign debt, from $863m. at the end of 1980 to $1,614m. in 1993. Meanwhile, export earnings declined, with the result that as early as 1982 Niger's debt-service ratio was equivalent to more than one-half of the country's foreign earnings. With the continuing depression in the world uranium market, Niger's major official creditors agreed in 1983 to reschedule the country's external debt over a nine-year period, with payment to begin after four-and-a-half years. Their action followed the approval of stand-by credits by the IMF and the introduction of austerity budgets for every year since 1982/83. As a result of this accord and subsequent restructuring agreements with both official and commercial creditors, the debt-service ratio was contained below its 1982 peak, despite the continued sharp rise in the foreign debt. However, with a debt-service ratio of 41% in 1988, Niger was classified as 'debt-distressed' by the World Bank, and hence at the December rescheduling of debt by the 'Paris Club' of official creditors, the highly concessional 'Toronto terms' for debt-relief were applied. In 1990 France agreed to cancel debts totalling 80,000m. francs CFA, thereby reducing Niger's external debt by about 18%. This was followed by a further rescheduling of debt by the 'Paris Club', again in accordance with the 'Toronto terms', while Niger secured World Bank funding to buy back commercial debt from Western banks, and a total of $108m. was retired in 1991–92. Debt-servicing obligations were thus reduced to a low point of 16% in 1992, although they were still at 25%–30% in most years. Moreover, as the devaluation of the CFA franc in January 1994 doubled the cost in local currency terms of repayment of and interest on debt, exceptional measures of debt-relief were required. A new agreement with the 'Paris Club' in March 1994, in accordance with the more concessional 'Trinidad terms', rescheduled 85,000m. francs CFA in debt, France cancelled one-half of Niger's liabilities, and the World Bank pledged $60m. in budgetary assistance for that year. However, although Niger's outstanding debt declined in 1994, as a result of relief accorded by bilateral donors, to $1,566m., this remained very high as a proportion of GNP (104%) because of the depreciation of the CFA franc against the US dollar. At $67m. debt-servicing was lower than in 1993 (when it mounted to $91m.), but still represented a heavy burden as a ratio of total foreign earnings—at 24.9%—and accounted for a large share of the government's meagre income from taxation. The external debt increased once again in 1995, to $1,633m., and debt-servicing would have been even higher than in 1994 had Niger not accumulated an additional $30m. in arrears on its long-term debt. However, in the aftermath of the ESAF accorded in 1996, Niger was able to attain a rescheduling of eligible debt to bilateral creditors on 'Naples terms' (effectively allowing two-thirds of debt to be written off). However, with just over one-half of external debt owed to multilateral institutions, which cannot reschedule liabilities, there is limited scope for further restructuring to alleviate the burden. Given that prospects for increasing revenue from exports or from domestic taxation are very modest, while the investment needed to raise basic living conditions to a satisfactory level is substantial, the country will remain highly dependent on external support for the foreseeable future.

Statistical Survey

Source (unless otherwise stated): Direction de la Statistique et de l'Informatique, Ministère de l'Economie et des Finances, BP 720, Niamey; tel. 72-23-74; telex 5463; fax 73-33-71.

Area and Population

AREA, POPULATION AND DENSITY

Area (sq km)	1,267,000*
Population (census results)	
20 November 1977	5,098,427
20 May 1988	
Males	3,590,070
Females	3,658,030
Total	7,248,100
Population (official estimate at mid-year)	
1993	8,361,000
Density (per sq km) at mid-1993	6.6

* 489,191 sq miles.

ETHNIC GROUPS (estimated population at 1 July 1972)*

Hausa	2,279,000	Tuareg, etc	127,000
Djerma-Songhai	1,001,000	Beriberi-Manga	386,000
Fulani (Peulh)	450,000	**Total**	4,243,000

* Provisional figures. Revised total is 4,239,000.

PRINCIPAL TOWNS (population in 1977)

Niamey (capital)	225,314	Tahoua	31,265
Zinder	58,436	Agadez	20,475
Maradi	45,852	Birni N'Konni	15,227

1981 (estimates): Niamey 360,000; Zinder 75,000.

BIRTHS AND DEATHS (UN estimates, annual averages)

	1980–85	1985–90	1990–95
Birth rate (per 1,000)	59.4	56.1	52.5
Death rate (per 1,000)	22.1	20.4	18.9

Expectation of life (UN estimates, years at birth, 1990–95): 46.5 (males 44.9; females 48.1).

Source: UN, *World Population Prospects: The 1994 Revision.*

ECONOMICALLY ACTIVE POPULATION
(1988 census, provisional)

	Males	Females	Total
Agriculture, hunting, forestry and fishing	1,549,600	243,950	1,793,550
Mining and quarrying	4,790	960	5,750
Manufacturing	28,060	35,630	63,690
Electricity, gas and water	2,330	60	2,390
Construction	14,040	390	14,430
Trade, restaurants and hotels	95,670	112,700	208,370
Transport, storage and communications	14,400	470	14,870
Financing, insurance, real estate and business servcies	1,400	450	1,850
Community, social and personal services	100,620	29,110	129,730
Activities not adequately defined	21,250	50,270	71,520
Total employed	1,832,160	473,990	2,306,150

Source: UN, *Demographic Yearbook.*

Mid-1995 (estimates in '000): Agriculture, etc. 3,906; Total 4,372 (Source: FAO, *Production Yearbook*).

Agriculture

PRINCIPAL CROPS ('000 metric tons)

	1993	1994	1995*
Maize	1	1*	1
Millet	1,658	1,725*	1,725
Sorghum	421	420*	420
Rice (paddy)*	70	70	70
Sugar cane*	140	142	142
Sweet potatoes*	35	35	35
Cassava (Manioc)*	220	225	225
Onions (dry)*	175	178	178
Tomatoes*	45	47	47
Other vegetables*	37	39	39
Pulses	433	433*	433
Dates*	7	8	8
Other fruit*	39	39	39
Groundnuts (in shell)*	60	65	65
Cottonseed	2†	2†	2
Cotton (lint)	1†	1†	1
Tobacco (leaves)*	1	1	1

* FAO estimate(s). † Unofficial figure.

Source: FAO, *Production Yearbook.*

LIVESTOCK ('000 head, year ending September)

	1993	1994	1995
Horses*	82	82	82
Asses*	450	450	450
Cattle	1,872	1,968	2,008
Camels	370†	374*	380
Pigs*	39	39	39
Sheep	3,465	3,678	3,789
Goats	5,420	5,566	5,716

Poultry (million)*: 20 in 1993; 20 in 1994; 20 in 1995.

* FAO estimate(s). † Unofficial figure.

Source: FAO, *Production Yearbook*.

LIVESTOCK PRODUCTS (FAO estimates, '000 metric tons)

	1993	1994	1995
Beef and veal	33	33	34
Mutton and lamb	12	13	13
Goat meat	21	21	21
Pig meat	1	1	1
Poultry meat	23	23	23
Other meat	20	21	21
Cows' milk	157	160	164
Sheep's milk	13	14	14
Goats' milk	90	92	98
Cheese	12.5	12.8	13.5
Butter	4.3	4.4	4.5
Poultry eggs	9.0	9.2	9.2
Cattle hides	5.6	5.7	5.9
Sheepskins	1.5	1.6	1.6
Goatskins	3.5	3.6	3.7

Source: FAO, *Production Yearbook*.

Forestry

ROUNDWOOD REMOVALS
(FAO estimates, '000 cubic metres, excluding bark)

	1992	1993	1994
Industrial wood	327	338	350
Fuel wood	4,970	5,142	5,321
Total	5,297	5,480	5,671

Source: FAO, *Yearbook of Forest Products*.

Fishing

('000 metric tons, live weight)

	1993	1994	1995
Total catch	2.2	2.5	3.6

Source: FAO, *Yearbook of Fishery Statistics*.

Mining

('000 metric tons, unless otherwise indicated)

	1992	1993	1994
Salt*†	3	3	3
Gypsum	1*	n.a.	n.a.
Hard coal	170	172†	172†
Tin (metric tons)*†‡	20	20	20

* Data from the US Bureau of Mines.
† Provisional or estimated figure(s).
‡ Data refer to the metal content of ore.

Source: UN, *Industrial Commodity Statistics Yearbook*.

Uranium (metal content of ore, metric tons): 2,966 in 1992; 2,921 in 1993; 2,956 in 1994; 2,974 in 1995 (Source: Banque centrale des états de l'Afrique de l'ouest).

Gold (metal content of ore, metric tons): 0.5 per year in 1992–96 (Source: Gold Fields Mineral Services Ltd, *Gold 1997*).

Industry

SELECTED PRODUCTS ('000 metric tons, unless otherwise indicated)

	1992	1993	1994
Salted, dried or smoked fish	1.0*	n.a.	n.a.
Cement†	29	29‡	29‡
Electric energy (million kWh)‡	171	173	178

* Data from the FAO.
† Data from the US Bureau of Mines.
‡ Provisional or estimated figure(s).

Source: UN, *Industrial Commodity Statistics Yearbook*.

Finance

CURRENCY AND EXCHANGE RATES

Monetary Units

100 centimes = 1 franc de la Communauté financière africaine (CFA).

French Franc, Sterling and Dollar Equivalents (31 March 1997)

1 French franc = 100 francs CFA;
£1 sterling = 924.20 francs CFA;
US $1 = 562.85 francs CFA;
1,000 francs CFA = £1.082 = $1.777.

Average Exchange Rate (francs CFA per US $)

1994 555.20
1995 499.15
1996 511.55

Note: An exchange rate of 1 French franc = 50 francs CFA, established in 1948, remained in force until January 1994, when the CFA franc was devalued by 50%, with the exchange rate adjusted to 1 French franc = 100 francs CFA.

BUDGET ('000 million francs CFA)

Revenue*	1993	1994†	1995‡
General budget	44.0	49.8	68.6
Tax revenue	41.4	46.6	63.9
Taxes on income, profits, payroll and work force	12.9	12.9	19.8
Taxes on goods and services	6.8	9.2	12.4
Taxes on international trade and transactions	19.0	21.7	29.4
Import Duties	14.0	16.9	n.a.
Export duties	4.7	4.4	n.a.
Other taxes	2.6	2.8	2.4
Taxes on property	2.0	1.9	—
Non-tax revenue	2.7	3.3	4.6
Annexed budgets and special accounts	2.0	2.4	1.7
Total	46.0	52.2	70.3

Expenditure§	1993	1994†	1995‡
General budget	107.5	158.5	146.8
Current expenditure	80.7	108.4	102.7
Wages and salaries	40.3	47.4	49.8
Materials and supplies	14.7	28.8	23.7
Subsidies and transfers	13.6	10.8	6.0
Interest payments	10.7	19.8	22.9
Capital expenditure	26.8	50.1	44.1
Annexed budgets and special accounts	2.0	3.8	2.8
Sub-total	109.5	162.3	149.6
Changes in areas‖	−24.6	47.6	−11.4
Adjustment	—	—	5.4
Total	84.9	209.9	143.6

* Excluding grants received ('000 million francs CFA): 35.2 in 1993; 50.3 (provisional) in 1994; 45.4 (estimate) in 1995.
† Provisional figures.
‡ Estimates.
‖ A minus sign indicates an increase in arrears.
Source: IMF, *Niger—Background Paper* (August 1996).

INTERNATIONAL RESERVES (US $ million at 31 December)

	1994	1995	1996
Gold*	4.1	4.3	4.2
IMF special drawing rights	0.4	0.3	1.9
Reserve position in IMF	12.5	12.7	12.3
Foreign exchange	97.3	81.7	64.3
Total	114.4	99.0	82.7

* Valued at market-related prices.
Source: IMF, *International Financial Statistics.*

MONEY SUPPLY ('000 million francs CFA at 31 December)

	1993	1994	1995
Currency outside banks	48.34	48.67	59.64
Demand deposits at deposit money banks*	28.83	40.25	38.42
Checking deposits at post office	1.92	2.10	1.82
Total money (incl. others)*	79.52	91.78	100.24

* Excluding the deposits of public enterprises of an administrative or social nature.
Source: IMF, *International Financial Statistics.*

COST OF LIVING
(Consumer Price Index for Africans in Niamey; base: 1990 = 100)

	1994	1995	1996
All items (incl. others)	118.4	130.9	137.8

Source: IMF, *International Financial Statistics.*

NATIONAL ACCOUNTS ('000 million francs CFA at current prices)
Expenditure on the Gross Domestic Product

	1993	1994	1995*
Government final consumption expenditure	99.3	138.6	130.2
Private final consumption expenditure	523.0	714.4	792.1
Increase in stocks	−2.3	13.0	3.0
Gross fixed capital formation	38.3	77.2	67.2
Total domestic expenditure	658.2	943.1	992.5
Exports of goods and services	84.3	142.7	143.0
Less Imports of goods and services	113.8	218.0	193.4
GDP in purchasers' values	628.7	867.8	942.1
GDP at constant 1987 prices	694.7	722.4	n.a.

* Estimates.

Gross Domestic Product by Economic Activity

	1992	1993*	1994*
Agriculture, hunting, forestry and fishing	230.3	233.3	372.2
Mining and quarrying	34.6	35.1	34.7
Manufacturing	42.3	43.4	56.9
Electricity, gas and water	14.5	14.7	18.4
Construction	11.7	11.9	16.1
Trade, restaurants and hotels	114.7	116.1	130.0
Transport, storage and communications	26.7	27.0	47.2
Other marketable services	64.6	65.5	87.4
Government services	69.0	69.3	94.7
Sub-total	608.4	616.3	857.5
Import duties	12.2	12.4	10.3
GDP in purchasers' values	620.6	628.7	867.8

* Estimates.
Source: IMF, *Niger—Background Paper* (August 1996).

BALANCE OF PAYMENTS (US $ million)

	1992	1993	1994
Exports of goods f.o.b.	347.3	300.4	226.8
Imports of goods f.o.b.	−396.5	−312.1	−271.3
Trade balance	−49.2	−11.7	−44.5
Exports of services	57.7	36.5	30.4
Imports of services	−201.0	−185.6	−149.1
Balance on goods and services	−192.6	−160.9	−163.2
Other income received	19.7	19.3	15.6
Other income paid	−54.1	−30.2	−45.2
Balance on goods, services and income	−227.0	−171.7	−192.8
Current transfers received	133.6	139.5	115.1
Current transfers paid	−65.7	−65.0	−48.5
Current balance	−159.2	−97.2	−126.1
Capital account (net)	109.0	109.3	88.2
Direct investment abroad	−40.7	−5.8	1.8
Direct investment from abroad	56.4	−34.4	−11.3
Other investment assets	10.4	11.2	22.3
Other investment liabilities	24.8	−94.4	17.1
Net errors and omissions	−95.5	87.2	−67.8
Overall balance	−94.9	−23.9	−75.8

Source: IMF, *International Financial Statistics.*

External Trade

PRINCIPAL COMMODITIES ('000 million francs CFA)

Imports f.o.b.	1993	1994	1995*
Consumer goods	50.7	98.0	65.7
Cereals	6.2	14.7	12.0
Petroleum products	6.5	10.4	9.7
Intermediate and capital goods	22.6	37.6	55.0
Total (incl. others)	73.3	135.6	121.7

Exports f.o.b.	1993	1994	1995*
Uranium	45.7	78.4	72.2
Live animals	12.3	20.4	21.7
Hides and skins	2.0	3.7	4.0
Cow-peas	2.5	4.5	5.2
Total (incl. others)	71.1	124.6	123.3

* Estimates.
Source: IMF, *Niger—Background Paper* (August 1996).

PRINCIPAL TRADING PARTNERS (US $ million)*

Imports	1992	1993	1994†
Côte d'Ivoire	37.2	44.2	50.0
France	102.5	110.6	94.0
Germany	20.1	19.0	11.0
Italy	13.3	13.4	8.0
Japan	11.1	9.7	8.0
Nigeria	7.2	n.a.	n.a.
Total (incl. others)	453.3	508.2	460.0

Exports	1992	1993	1994†
Côte d'Ivoire	7.3	8.5	10.0
France	149.1	130.3	78.0
Nigeria	17.5	n.a.	n.a.
Total (incl. others)	202.0	235.5	117.0

* Data are compiled on the basis of reporting by Niger's trading partners.
† Estimates.

Source: IMF, *Direction of Trade Statistics*.

Transport

ROAD TRAFFIC (vehicles in use at 31 December)

	1989	1990
Cars	31,342	31,427
Buses and coaches	2,559	2,695
Goods vehicles	5,968	6,073
Trailers and semi-trailers	2,144	2,217

Source: International Road Federation, *World Road Statistics*.

CIVIL AVIATION (traffic on scheduled services)*

	1992	1993	1994
Kilometres flown (million)	2	2	2
Passengers carried ('000)	66	68	69
Passenger-km (million)	201	207	215
Total ton-km (million)	34	33	34

* Including an apportionment of the traffic of Air Afrique.

Source: UN, *Statistical Yearbook*.

Tourism

	1992	1993	1994
Tourist arrivals ('000)	13	11	11
Tourist receipts (US $ million)	17	16	16

Source: UN, *Statistical Yearbook*.

Communications Media

	1992	1993	1994
Radio receivers ('000 in use)	500	520	540
Television receivers ('000 in use)	38	42	44
Telephones ('000 main lines in use)	10	11	n.a.
Daily newspapers			
Number	1	n.a.	4
Average circulation ('000 copies)	5	n.a.	11

Books published (first editions, 1991): Titles 5; Copies ('000) 11.

Sources: UNESCO, *Statistical Yearbook*; UN, *Statistical Yearbook*.

Education

(1992/93, unless otherwise indicated)

	Institutions	Teachers	Students		
			Males	Females	Total
Pre-primary	88	367	6,234	6,366	12,600
Primary	2,422	10,027	237,311	142,401	379,712
Secondary					
General	n.a.	2,219	52,385	25,514	77,899
Teacher training	n.a.	76	933	389	1,322
Vocational	n.a.	99	688	100	788
University level*	n.a.	232	n.a.	n.a.	4,513

* 1991/92 figures.

1993/94: *Primary:* Institutions 2,656; Teachers 12,216; Students 394,063 (males 246,565, females 147,498). *General Secondary:* Students 88,810.
1994/95: *Primary:* Students 440,460. *General Secondary:* Students 89,773 (males 60,299; females 29,474).

Source: UNESCO, *Statistical Yearbook*.

Directory

The Constitution

Following the *coup d'état* of 27 January 1996, the military Conseil de salut national suspended the Constitution of the Third Republic (promulgated in January 1993), dissolving the institutions provided for therein. A National Forum for Democratic Renewal met in April 1996 to consider amendments to the Constitution, and the revised document was approved in a national referendum on 12 May.

The Constitution of the Fourth Republic, which was promulgated on 22 May 1996, abolishes the principle of a 'dual executive', as enshrined in the previous document. Executive authority is vested solely in the President of the Republic, who decides, implements and directs national policy in conjunction with the legislature. The function of the Prime Minister is defined as to implement a programme decreed by the Head of State. Legislative authority is vested in the 83-member Assemblée nationale. All elections are by universal adult suffrage, in the context of a multi-party political system.

The Constitution states that all laws in force at the time of the promulgation of the Constitution, unless specifically abrogated, remain valid.

The Government

HEAD OF STATE

President: Brig.-Gen. IBRAHIM BARÉ MAÏNASSARA (took office 27 January 1996; elected President 7–8 July 1996).

COUNCIL OF MINISTERS

(August 1997)

Prime Minister: AMADOU ABOUBACAR CISSÉ.

Minister of State, responsible for Relations with Parliament: ANDRÉ SALIFOU.

Minister of State, responsible for Higher Education, Research, Technology and African Integration: JACKOU SENOUSSI.

Minister of State, responsible for National Education: MOUMOUNI AISSATA.

Minister of Transport: SOULEY ABDOULAYE.

Minister of National Defence: OUSMANE ISSOUFOU OUBANDAWAKI.

Minister, Permanent Under-secretary at the Office of the President: MAHAMANE SANI BAKO.

Minister of Justice and Human Rights, Keeper of the Seals: BOUBE OUMAROU.

Minister of Foreign Affairs and Co-operation: IBRAHIM GADJI MAIYAKI.

Minister of Water and the Environment: BRAH MAMANE.

Minister of the Economy and Finance: AHMADOU MAIYAKI.

Minister of Youth, Sports and National Solidarity: Lt-Col ABOURAHMANE SEYDOU.

Minister of Communications and Culture, Spokesperson for the Government: BAYARD MARIAMA GAMATIE.

Minister of Mines and Energy: BOUKAR MAI MANGA.

Minister of the Interior and Territorial Development: IDI ANGO OMAR.

Minister of the Civil Service, Labour and Employment: SEINI ALI GADO.

Minister of Equipment and Infrastructure: CHERIF CHAKO.

Minister of Social Development, Population, and Women's and Children's Promotion: MARIAMA SAMBO ABDOULAYE.

Minister of Public Health and Social Welfare: HAMIDOU HAROUNA SIDICOU.

Minister of Tourism and Crafts: AISSA ABDOULAYE DIALLO.

Minister of Trade and Industry: IBRAHIM KOUSSOU.

Minister of Agriculture and Livestock: AKOLI DAOUEL.

Minister of Planning and Privatization: YACOUBA NABASSOUA.

Secretary of State for Agriculture: MOUSSA DOURAHMANE.

MINISTRIES

All ministries are in Niamey.

Office of the President: Niamey.

Office of the Prime Minister: Niamey.

Ministry of Agriculture and Livestock: BP 10427, Niamey; tel. 73-31-55.

Ministry of the Civil Service, Labour and Employment: Niamey; tel. 72-25-01; telex 5283.

Ministry of Communications and Culture: Niamey; tel. 72-24-89; telex 5214.

Ministry of the Economy and Finance: BP 720, Niamey; tel. 72-23-74; telex 5463; fax 73-33-71.

Ministry of Equipment and Infrastructure: Niamey; tel. 72-25-01; telex 5283.

Ministry of Foreign Affairs and Co-operation: BP 396, Niamey; tel. 72-29-07; telex 5200; fax 73-52-31.

Ministry of the Interior and Territorial Development: Niamey; tel. 72-21-76; telex 5214.

Ministry of Justice and Human Rights: Niamey; tel. 72-20-94; telex 5214.

Ministry of Mines and Energy: BP 11700, Niamey; tel. 73-45-82; telex 5214.

Ministry of National Defence: BP 626, Niamey; tel. 72-20-76; telex 5291.

Ministry of National Education: Quartier Yantala Haut, BP 11897, Niamey; tel. 72-25-26.

Ministry of Public Health and Social Welfare: BP 623, Niamey; tel. 72-27-82; telex 5533.

President and Legislature

PRESIDENT

Presidential Election, 7–8 July 1996

Candidate	% of votes
IBRAHIM BARÉ MAÏNASSARA	52.22
MAHAMANE OUSMANE	19.75
TANDJA MAMADOU	15.65
MAHAMADOU ISSOUFOU	7.60
MOUMOUNI AMADOU DJERMAKOYE	4.77
Total	100.00

ASSEMBLÉE NATIONALE

President: MOUTARI MOUSSA.

General Election, 23 November 1996

	Seats
UNIRD	49
ANDPS–Zaman Lahiya	31
UDPS–Amana	
FDP	
Total	80*

* Results of voting in three constituencies (won by the UNIRD) were subsequently annulled by the Supreme Court.

Political Organizations

Some 20 political organizations held legal status in mid-1997. The following were among the most prominent:

Alliance nigérienne pour la démocratie et le progrès social–Zaman Lahiya (ANDPS–Zaman Lahiya): Leader MOUMOUNI AMADOU DJERMAKOYE.

Convention démocratique et social–Rahama (CDS–Rahama): Chair. MAHAMANE OUSMANE.

Front démocratique nigérien–Mountounchi (FDN–Mountounchi): f. 1995 by fmr mems of PPN–RDA; Chair. OUMAROU YOUSSOUFOU EARBA: Sec.-Gen. MOHAMED MUDUR.

Mouvement national pour une société de développement–Nassara (MNSD–Nassara): f. 1988 as MNSD, name changed in 1991; sole party 1988–90; Chair. Col (retd) TANDJA MAMADOU; Sec.-Gen. HAMA AMADOU.

Parti nigérien pour l'autogestion (PNA): f. 1997; Leader JACKOU SENOUSSI.

Parti nigérien pour la démocratie et le socialisme–Tarayya (PNDS–Tarayya): Sec.-Gen. MAHAMADOU ISSOUFOU.

Parti progressiste nigérien–Rassemblement démocratique africain (PPN–RDA): associated with the late President Diori; Chair. DANDIKO DANKOULODO; Sec.-Gen. IDE OUMAROU.

Parti républicain pour les libertés et le progrès au Niger–Nakowa (PRLPN–Nakowa): Chair. ALKA ALAMOU.

Parti social-démocrate nigérien–Alheri (PSDN–Alheri): Leader KAZELMA OUMAR TAYA.

Parti pour l'unite nationale et le développement–Salama PUND–Salama): Leader PASCAL MAMADOU.

Union pour la démocratie et le progrès–Amici (UDP–Amici): Leader BELLO TIOUSSO GARBA.

Union pour la démocratie et le progrès social–Amana (UDPS–Amana): Chair. MOHAMED ABDULLAHI.

Union des forces populaires pour la démocratie et le progrès–Sawaba (UFPDP–Sawaba): Chair. DJIBO BAKARY.

Union nationale des indépendants pour le renouveau démocratique (UNIRD): f. 1996; supports Pres. IBRAHIM BARÉ MAÏNASSARA.

Union des patriotes démocratiques et progressistes–Shamuwa (UPDP–Shamuwa): Chair. Prof. ANDRÉ SALIFOU.

Note: The **Front pour la restauration et la défense de la démocratie (FRDD)** was established in September 1996 as an alliance of eight opposition parties, including the CDS–Rahama, the MNSD–Nassara and the PNDS–Tarayya. The FRDD boycotted the legislative elections in November of that year. The **Front pour la démocratie et le progrès** (FDP) was established in the same month by supporters of President Maïnassara.

Diplomatic Representation

EMBASSIES IN NIGER

Algeria: route des Ambassades-Goudel; BP 142, Niamey; tel. 72-35-83; telex 5262; fax 72-35-93; Ambassador: MADJID BOUGUERRA.

Belgium: BP 10192, Niamey; tel. 73-34-47; telex 5329; fax 73-37-56; Ambassador: FRANK RECKER.

Benin: BP 11544, Niamey; tel. 72-39-19; Ambassador: KOLAWOLÉ IDJI.

Canada: Niamey.

China, People's Republic: Niamey; Ambassador JI JINGYI.

Egypt: Nouveau Plateau, Niamey; tel. 73-33-55; telex 5245; Ambassador: Dr SOBHY MOHAMED NAFEH.

France: BP 10660, Niamey; tel. 72-24-31; telex 5220; fax 72-25-18; Ambassador: ALBERT PAVEC.

Germany: 71 ave du Général de Gaulle, BP 629, Niamey; tel. 72-25-34; telex 5223; fax 72-39-85; Ambassador: ANGELIKA VÖLKEL.

Iran: ave de la Présidence, Niamey; tel. 72-21-98; Chargé d'affaires: FAGHIH ALI ABADI MEHDI.

Libya: Rond-point du Grand Hôtel, POB 683, Niamey; tel. 73-47-92; telex 5429; Sec. of People's Cttee: MUHAMMAD HUSAYN AL-KUNI.

Mauritania: Yantala, BP 12519, Niamey; tel. 72-38-93; Ambassador: MOHAMED EL HOUSSEIN OULD HABIBOU ALLAH.

Morocco: ave du Président Lubke, BP 12403, Niamey; tel. 73-40-84; telex 5205; fax 74-14-27; Ambassador: TAHAR NEJJAR.

Nigeria: ave du Général Ibrahim Babangida, Goudel, BP 11130, Niamey; tel. 73-24-10; telex 5259; fax 73-35-00; Chargé d'affaires a.i.: ABBA ABDUL KADIR.

Pakistan: BP 10426, Niamey; tel. 72-35-84; telex 5268; Chargé d'affaires: IRFAN-UR-REHMAN RAJA.

Russia: BP 10153, Niamey; tel. 73-27-40; telex 5539; Ambassador: VITALII Y. LITVINE.

Saudi Arabia: Yantala, BP 339, Niamey; tel. 72-32-15; telex 5279; Ambassador: GHASSAN SAID SADEK RACHACH.

Tunisia: ave du Général de Gaulle, BP 742, Niamey; tel. 72-26-03; telex 5379; Ambassador: RHIDA TNANI.

USA: Yantala, BP 11201, Niamey; tel. 72-26-61; telex 5444; Ambassador: JOHN (JACK) S. DAVISON.

Judicial System

Attorney-General: SULI ABDOURAHMANE.

Supreme Court: Niamey; Pres. ALI BANDIARE.

High Court of Justice: Niamey; competent to indict the President of the Republic and all other state officials (past and present) in relation to all matters of state, including high treason; comprises seven perm. mems and three rotating mems; Pres. MOUMOUNI AMADOU DJERMAKOYE.

Court of State Security: Niamey; competent to try cases not within the jurisdiction of the High Court of Justice; incorporates a martial court.

Court of Appeal: Niamey; court of appeal for judgements of **Criminal** and **Assize Courts** (the latter at Niamey, Maradi, Tahoua and Zinder).

Courts of First Instance: located at Niamey (with sub-divisions at Dosso and Tillabéry), Maradi, Tahoua (sub-divisions at Agadez, Arlit and Birni N'Konni) and Diffa (sub-division at Diffa).

Labour Courts: function at each Court of the First Instance and sub-division thereof.

Religion

It is estimated that some 95% of the population are Muslims, 0.5% are Christians and the remainder follow traditional beliefs.

ISLAM

The most influential Islamic groups are the Tijaniyya, the Senoussi and the Hamallists.

CHRISTIANITY

Various Protestant missions maintain 13 centres, with a personnel of 90.

The Roman Catholic Church

Niger comprises a single diocese, directly responsible to the Holy See. The diocese participates in the Bishops' Conference of Burkina Faso and Niger (based in Ouagadougou, Burkina Faso). In Niger the Roman Catholic Church has about 19,000 adherents (31 December 1995).

Bishop of Niamey: (vacant); Apostolic Admin. Mgr GUY ROMANO, Titular Bishop of Caput Cilla, Evêché, BP 10270, Niamey; tel. 73-30-79; fax 74-10-13.

The Press

L'Alternative: Niamey; Editor-in-Chief FUMAZOU KEITA.

Amfani: rue du Danagaram, BP 2096, Niamey; tel. 74-08-80; fax 74-00-52; f. 1992; independent; weekly; circ. 3,000.

Angam: Niamey; f. 1992; monthly; independent; Dir GRÉMAH BOUKAR.

Al-Habari: Niamey; independent.

Haske: BP 297, Niamey; tel. 74-18-44; fax 73-20-06; f. 1990; weekly; independent; Dir IBRAHIM CHEIKH DIOP.

Haske Magazine: BP 297; tel. 74-18-44; fax 73-20-06; f. 1990; quarterly; independent; Dir IBRAHIM CHEIKH DIOP; circ. 3,000.

Horizon 2001: Niamey; f. 1991; monthly; independent; Dir INOUSSA OUSSEÏNI.

Journal Officiel de la République du Niger: BP 116, Niamey; tel. 72-39-30; fax 72-39-43; f. 1960; fortnightly; Man. Editor BONKOULA AMINATOU MAYAKI; circ. 800.

Kakaki: Niamey; f. 1991; monthly; independent; Dir SIRAJI KANÉ.

La Marche: Niamey; f. 1989; monthly; independent; Dir ABDOULAYE MOUSSA MASSALATCHI.

Nigerama: Niamey; quarterly; publ. by the Agence Nigérienne de Presse.

Le Pont Africain: Niamey; independent; satirical.

Le Républicain: Niamey; f. 1991; weekly; independent; pro-Tuareg; Dir MAMANE ABOU.

Le Sahel: BP 13182, Niamey; f. 1960; publ. by Office National d'Edition et de Presse; daily; Dir ALI OUSSEÏNI; circ. 5,000.

Le Sahel Dimanche: BP 13182, Niamey; publ. by Office National d'Edition et de Presse; weekly; Dir ALI OUSSEÏNI; circ. 3,000.

Le Soleil: Niamey; independent; Dir MOULAYE ABDOULAYE.

La Tribune du Peuple: Niamey; independent; Man. Editor IBRAHIM HAMIDOU.

NEWS AGENCIES

Agence Nigérienne de Presse (ANP): BP 11158, Niamey; tel. 740809; telex 5497; f. 1987; state-owned; Dir ABDOURAHMANE ALILOU.

Office National d'Edition et de Presse (ONEP): Niamey; f. 1989; Dir ALI OUSSEÏNI.

Publisher

Government Publishing House

L'Imprimerie Nationale du Niger (INN): BP 61, Niamey; tel. 73-47-98; telex 5312; f. 1962; Dir E. WOHLRAB.

Radio and Television

In 1994, according to UNESCO estimates, there were 540,000 radio receivers and 44,000 television receivers in use.

Office de Radiodiffusion-Télévision du Niger (ORTN): BP 309, Niamey; tel. 72-31-63; telex 5229; state broadcasting authority; Dir-Gen. MAHAMANE ADAMOU; Tech. Dir (Radio and Television) ZOUDI ISSOUF.

La Voix du Sahel: BP 361, Niamey; tel. 72-32-72; fax 72-35-48; f. 1958; govt-controlled radio service; programmes in French, Hausa (Haoussa), Djerma (Zarma), Kanuri, Fulfuldé, Tamajak, Toubou, Gourmantché and Arabic; Dir OMAR TIELLO.

Télé-Sahel: BP 309, Niamey; tel. 72-31-53; telex 5229; fax 72-35-48; govt-controlled television service; broadcasts daily; Dir MAMANE MAMADOU.

Radio Amfani (Dir GREMAH BOUCAR) is among several private radio stations in operation.

Finance

(cap. = capital; res = reserves; m. = million; brs = branches; amounts in francs CFA)

BANKING

Central Bank

Banque Centrale des Etats de l'Afrique de l'Ouest (BCEAO): rond-point de la Poste, BP 487, Niamey; tel. 72-24-91; telex 5218; fax 73-47-43; headquarters in Dakar, Senegal; f. 1962; bank of issue for the member states of the Union économique et monétaire ouest-africaine (UEMOA); cap. and res 657,592m. (Dec. 1995); Gov. CHARLES KONAN BANNY; Dir in Niger MAMADOU DIOP; brs at Maradi and Zinder.

Commercial Banks

Bank of Africa–Niger: Immeuble Sonara II, BP 10973, Niamey; tel. 73-36-20; telex 5321; fax 73-38-18; f. 1994 to acquire assets of Nigeria International Bank Niamey; 42% owned by African Financial Holding; cap. and res 1,473m. (Dec. 1995); Chair. PAUL DERREMAUX (acting).

Banque Commerciale du Niger (BCN): rond-point Maourey, BP 11363/881, Niamey; tel. 73-33-31; telex 5292; fax 73-21-63; f. 1978; fmrly Banque Arabe Libyenne-Nigérienne pour le Commerce Extérieur et le Développement; owned by private Nigerien (50%) and Libyan (50%) interests; cap. and res 950m. (Sept. 1993); Chair. and Man. Dir CHEICK MOHAMED METRI.

Banque Internationale pour l'Afrique au Niger (BIA–Niger): ave de la Mairie, BP 10350, Niamey; tel. 73-31-01; telex 5215; fax 73-35-95; f. 1980; fmrly Banque Meridien BIAO Niger; 35% owned by Groupe Belgolaise SA (Belgium); cap. and res 2,636m. (Dec. 1995); Chair. AMADOU HIMA SOULEY; Man. Dir JEAN-PIERRE CARPENTIER; 5 brs.

Banque Islamique du Niger: ave de la Mairie, BP 12754, Niamey; tel. 73-27-30; telex 5440; fax 73-48-25; f. 1983; fmrly Banque Masraf Faisal Islami, restructured 1994–96; 33% owned by Dar al-Maal al-Islami (DMI Trust), 33% by Islamic Development Bank; cap. and res 1,810m. (Dec. 1995); Chair. ABDERRAOUF BENESSAÏAH; Man. Dir JUNAID IQBAL.

Société Nigérienne de Banque (SONIBANQUE): ave de la Mairie, BP 891, Niamey; tel. 73-47-40; telex 5480; fax 73-46-93; f. 1990; 25% owned by Société Tunisienne de Banque; cap. and res 2,587m. (Sept. 1993); Chair. ALMA OUMAROU; Dir-Gen. CHAKIB SIALA.

Development Banks

Caisse de Prêt aux Collectivités Territoriales (CPCT): route de Torodi, BP 730, Niamey, tel. 72-34-12; f. 1970; 94% state-owned (collectivités territoriales); part-privatization pending; cap. and res 1,146m. (Dec. 1995); Chair. BRIGI RAFINI; Man. Dir IBRAHIM KOMMA.

Crédit du Niger: blvd de la République, BP 213, Niger; tel. 72-27-01; telex 5210; fax 72-23-90; f. 1958; 54% state-owned, 20% owned by Caisse Nationale de Sécurité Sociale; cap. and res 2,610m. (Sept. 1992); Chair. SANI MAHAMANE; Man. Dir ABOU KANÉ.

Fonds d'Intervention en Faveur des Petites et Moyennes Entreprises Nigériennes (FIPMEN): Immeuble Sonara II, BP 252, Niamey; tel. 73-20-98; telex 5569; f. 1990; state-owned; cap. and res 124m. (Dec. 1991); Chair. AMADOU SALLA HASSANE; Man. Dir IBRAHIM BEIDARI.

Savings Bank

Caisse Nationale d'Epargne (CNE): BP 11778, Niamey; tel. 73-24-98; total assets 2,437m. (Sept. 1993); Chair. IDI GADO; Man. Dir BACHIR MALLAM MATO.

STOCK EXCHANGE

Côte d'Ivoire's Bourse des Valeurs d'Abidjan was scheduled to become a regional stock exchange, serving the member states of the UEMOA.

INSURANCE

Agence Nigérienne d'Assurances (ANA): place de la Mairie, BP 423, Niamey; tel. 72-20-71; telex 5277; f. 1959; cap. 1.5m.; owned by L'Union des Assurances de Paris; Dir JEAN LASCAUD.

Société Civile Immobilière des Assureurs de Niamey: BP 423, Niamey; tel. 73-40-71; telex 5277; fax 73-41-85; f. 1962; cap. 14m.; Dir MAMADOU TALATA DOULLA.

Société Nigérienne d'Assurances et de Réassurances 'Leyma' (SNAR—LEYMA): ave du Général de Gaulle, BP 426, Niamey; tel. 73-55-26; telex 5202; f. 1973; cap. 345m.; Pres. AMADOU OUSMANE; Dir-Gen. MAMADOU MALAM AOUAMI.

Union Générale des Assurances du Niger (UGAN): rue de Kalley, BP 11935, Niamey; tel. 73-54-06; telex 5277; fax 73-41-85; f. 1985; cap. 500m.; Pres. PATHÉ DIONE; Dir-Gen. MAMADOU TALATA; 7 brs.

Trade and Industry

DEVELOPMENT ORGANIZATIONS

Caisse de Stabilisation des Prix des Produits du Niger (CSPPN): BP 480, Niamey; telex 5286; price control agency for Nigerien goods; Dir IBRAHIM KOUSSOU.

Mission Française de Coopération: BP 494, Niamey; tel. 72-20-66; telex 5220; administers bilateral aid from France; Dir JEAN BOULOGNE.

Office des Eaux du Sous-Sol (OFEDES): BP 734, Niamey; tel. 73-23-44; telex 5313; govt agency for the maintenance and development of wells and boreholes; Dir ADOU ADAM.

Office du Lait du Niger (OLANI): BP 404, Niamey; tel. 73-23-69; telex 5555; f. 1971; govt agency for development and marketing of milk products; Pres. Dr ABDOUA KABO; Dir MAHAMADOU HAROUNA.

Office National de l'Energie Solaire (ONERSOL): BP 621, Niamey; tel. 73-45-05; govt agency for research and development, commercial production and exploitation of solar devices; Dir ALBERT WRIGHT.

Office National des Ressources Minières du Niger (ONAREM): BP 12716, Niamey; tel. 73-59-26; telex 5300; f. 1976; govt agency for exploration, exploitation and marketing of all minerals; Dir-Gen. OUSMANE GAOURI.

Office des Produits Vivriers du Niger (OPVN): BP 474, Niamey; telex 5323; govt agency for developing agricultural and food production; Dir ADAMOU SOUNA.

Riz du Niger (RINI): BP 476, Tillabéry, Niamey; tel. 71-13-29; f. 1967; cap. 825m. francs CFA; 27% state-owned; development and marketing of rice; Pres. YAYA MADOUGOU; Dir-Gen. OUSMANE DJIKA.

Société Nigérienne de Produits Pétroliers (SONIDEP): BP 11702, Niamey; tel. 73-33-34; telex 5343; f. 1977; govt agency for the distribution and marketing of petroleum products; cap. 1,000m. francs CFA; Man. Dir ADAMOU NAMATA.

TRADE ORGANIZATIONS

Centre Nigérien du Commerce Extérieur (CNCE): place de la Concertation, BP 12480, Niamey; tel. 73-22-88; telex 5434; fax 73-46-68; f. 1984; promotes and co-ordinates all aspects of foreign trade; Dir AÏSSA DIALLO.

Société Nationale de Commerce et de Production du Niger (COPRO-Niger): BP 615, Niamey; tel. 73-28-41; telex 5222; fax 73-57-71; f. 1962; monopoly importer of foodstuffs; cap. 1,000m. francs CFA; 47% state-owned; Man. Dir DJIBRILLA HIMA.

CHAMBERS OF COMMERCE

Chambre de Commerce, d'Agriculture, d'Industrie et d'Artisanat du Niger: place de la Concertation, BP 209, Niamey; tel. 73-22-10; telex 5242; f. 1954; comprises 80 full mems and 40 dep. mems; Pres. AHMADOU MAYAKI; Gen. Sec. SAMA OUMAROU IBRAHIM.

Chambre de Commerce, d'Agriculture, d'Industrie et d'Artisanat du Niger, Antenne d'Agadez: BP 201, Agadez; tel. 44-01-61.

Chambre de Commerce, d'Agriculture, d'Industrie et d'Artisanat du Niger, Antenne de Diffa: BP 91, Diffa; tel. 54-03-92; f. 1988.

Chambre de Commerce, d'Agriculture, d'Industrie et d'Artisanat du Niger, Antenne de Maradi: BP 79, Maradi; tel. 41-03-66.

Chambre de Commerce, d'Agriculture, d'Industrie et d'Artisanat du Niger, Antenne de Tahoua: BP 172, Tahoua; tel. 61-03-84; f. 1984; Sec. ILYESS HABIB.

Chambre de Commerce, d'Agriculture, d'Industrie et d'Artisanat du Niger, Antenne de Zinder: BP 83, Zinder; tel. 51-00-78.

EMPLOYERS' ORGANIZATIONS

Syndicat des Commerçants Importateurs et Exportateurs du Niger (SCIMPEXNI): Niamey; tel. 73-34-66; Pres. ANDRÉ BEAUMONT; Sec.-Gen. C. SALEZ.

Syndicat National des Petites et Moyennes Entreprises et Industries Nigériennes (SYNAPEMEIN): Niamey; Pres. El Hadj ALI SOUMANA; Sec.-Gen. BOUBACAR ZEZI.

Syndicat Patronal des Entreprises et Industries du Niger (SPEIN): BP 415, Niamey; tel. 73-24-01; telex 5370; fax 73-45-26; f. 1945; Pres. AMADOU OUSMANE.

MAJOR INDUSTRIAL COMPANIES

The following are among the largest companies in terms of either capital investment or employment.

Compagnie Minière d'Akouta (COMINAK): BP 10545, Niamey; tel. 73-34-25; telex 5269; fax 73-28-55; f. 1974; cap. 3,500m. francs CFA; 34% owned by Cie générale des matières nucléaires (COGEMA) (France), 31% by ONAREM (Niger govt), 25% by Overseas Uranium Resources Development (Japan), 10% by Empresa Nacional del Uranio (Spain); mining and processing of uranium at Akouta; Chair. BOUKAR MAÏ MANGA; Dir HENRI PELLO.

Office National des Produits Pharmaceutiques et Chimiques (ONPPC): BP 11585, Niamey; tel. 73-27-81; telex 5231; fax 73-23-74; f. 1962; cap. 440m. francs CFA; state-owned; Dir Dr MAIDANA SAIDOU DJERMAKOYE.

Société des Brasseries et Boissons Gazeuses du Niger (BRANIGER): BP 11245, Niamey; tel. 72-20-88; telex 5280; f. 1967; cap. 1,428m. francs CFA; mfrs of ice and soft drinks at Niamey and Maradi; Chair. ALPHONSE DENIS; Dir M. TRAVERSA; 300 employees.

Société d'Exploitation des Produits d'Arachides du Niger (SEPANI): BP 8, Magaria; telex 8216; f. 1970; cap. 405m. francs CFA; 33% state-owned; production of groundnut oil at Magaria; Dir MAURICE CHAINE.

Société des Mines de l'Aïr (SOMAÏR): BP 12910, Niamey; tel. 72-35-31; telex 5494; fax 72-29-33; f. 1968; cap. 4,349m. francs CFA; 49.3% owned by COGEMA (France), 33% by ONAREM; uranium mining at Arlit; Man. Dir FRANÇOIS MEIA; Dir at Arlit DOUDOU ALHASSANE.

Société Minière du Niger (SMDN): Niamey; tel. 73-45-82; telex 5300; f. 1941; cap. 36m. francs CFA; 71% state-owned, 10% owned by Benin govt; cassiterite mining at El Mecki and Tarrouadji; Chair. AMANI ISSAKA; Man. Dir MAMADOU SAADOU.

Société Minière de Tassa N'Taghalgué (SMTT): BP 10376, Niamey; tel. 73-36-66; telex 5393; f. 1979; cap. 10,500m. francs CFA; 33% owned by ONAREM, 33% by COGEMA (France), 33% by Kuwait Foreign Trading, Contracting and Investment Co; owns uranium-mining rights at Taza (leased to SOMAÏR in 1986); Chair. Minister of Mines and Energy; Man. Dir MICHEL HAREL.

Société Nigérienne du Charbon d'Anou Araren (SONICHAR): BP 78, Tchirozérine, Agadez; tel. 44-02-48; fax 44-03-49; f. 1975; cap. 19,730m. francs CFA; 61% state-owned, 10% owned by the Islamic Development Bank, 24% by COMINAK, SMTT and SOMAÏR; exploitation of coal reserves at Anou Araren and generation of electricity; Chair. AKOLI DAOUEL; Man. Dir DIOFFO AMADOU; 375 employees.

Société Nigérienne de Cimenterie (SNC): BP 03, Malbaza; tel. 01-02; telex 8216; f. 1963; cap. 900m. francs CFA; 59% state-owned; production and marketing of cement at Malbaza; Chair. SAIDOU MAMANE; Man. Dir ABOUBACAR KADA LABO.

Société Nigérienne d'Electricité (NIGELEC): BP 11202, Niamey; tel. 72-26-92; fax 72-32-88; f. 1968; cap. 3,357m. francs CFA; 95% state-owned; partial transfer to private ownership pending; production and distribution of electricity; Man. Dir AMADOU MAYAKI.

Société Nigérienne d'Exploitation des Ressources Animales (SONERAN): Niamey; tel. 73-23-75; telex 5537; f. 1968; cap. 270m. francs CFA; 99.9% state-owned; production and export of fresh and processed meat; ranch of 110,000 ha; Man. Dir MOUCTARI MAHAMANE FALALOU.

Société Nouvelle Nigérienne des Textiles (SONITEXTIL): route de Kolo, BP 10735, Niamey; tel. 73-25-11; telex 5241; f. 1978; cap. 1,000m. francs CFA; textile complex at Niamey; 27% state-owned; Chair. SAIDOU MAMANE; Man. Dir ROGER HUBER; 830 employees.

Unimo-Industrie et Chimie: BP 71, Maradi; tel. 41-00-56; telex 8201; f. 1978; cap. 710m. francs CFA; mfrs of foam rubber; Dir ASSAD GHASSAN.

TRADE UNION FEDERATIONS

Confédération des Syndicats Libres des Travailleurs du Niger (CSLTN): Niamey; f. 1993; 4 affiliates.

Union des Syndicats des Travailleurs du Niger (USTN): Bourse du Travail, BP 388, Niamey; tel. and fax 73-52-56; f. 1960; Sec.-Gen. IBRAHIM MAYAKI; 28,000 mems in 37 affiliated unions.

Transport

ROADS

Niger is crossed by highways running from east to west and from north to south, giving access to neighbouring countries. Work on the upgrading of the 428-km Zinder–Agadez road, scheduled to form part of the Trans-Sahara highway, began in 1985.

In 1995 there were an estimated 9,863 km of classified roads, including 3,586 km of main roads and 3,205 km of secondary roads. Only 7.9% of the total network was paved.

Société Nationale des Transports Nigériens (SNTN): BP 135, Niamey; tel. 72-24-55; telex 5370; fax 73-47-07; f. 1961; operates passenger and freight road-transport services; 49% state-owned; Dir AHMADOU MAYAKI.

RAILWAYS

Organisation Commune Bénin-Niger des Chemins de Fer et des Transports (OCBN): BP 38, Niamey; tel. 73-27-90; telex 5253; f. 1959; 50% owned by Govt of Niger, 50% by Govt of Benin; manages the Benin-Niger railway project (begun in 1978). There are as yet no railways in Niger.

INLAND WATERWAYS

The River Niger is navigable for 300 km within the country. Access to the sea is available by a river route from Gaya, in south-western Niger, to the coast at Port Harcourt, Nigeria, between September and March. Port facilities at Lomé, Togo, are used as a commercial outlet for land-locked Niger, and an agreement providing import facilities at the port of Tema was signed with Ghana in November 1986.

Niger-Transit (NITRA): Zone Industrielle, BP 560, Niamey; tel. 73-22-53; telex 5212; fax 73-26-38; f. 1974; 48% owned by SNTN; customs agent, freight-handling, warehousing, etc.; manages Nigerien port facilities at Lomé; Pres. SALEY CHAIBOU; Man. Dir SADE FATIMATA.

Société Nigérienne des Transports Fluviaux et Maritimes (SNTFM): Niamey; tel. 73-39-69; telex 5265; river and sea transport; cap. 64.6m. francs CFA; 99% state-owned; Man. Dir BERTRAND DEJEAN.

CIVIL AVIATION

There are international airports at Niamey and Agadez, and major domestic airports at Arlit, Diffa, Tahoua and Zinder.

Air Afrique: BP 11090, Niamey; tel. 73-30-10; telex 5284; see under Côte d'Ivoire; Dir in Niamey MALLÉ SALL.

Nigeravia SA: BP 10454, Niamey; tel. 73-30-64; fax 74-18-42; f. 1989 as Trans-Niger Aviation; operates domestic and regional services; Man. Dir JEAN SYLVESTRE.

Société Nigérienne des Transports Aériens (SONITA): Niamey; f. 1991; cap. 50m. francs CFA; owned by private Nigerien (81%) and Cypriot (19%) interests; operates domestic and regional services; Man. Dir ABDOULAYE MAIGA GOUDOUBABA.

Tourism

The Aïr and Ténéré Nature Reserve, covering an area of 77,000 sq km, was established in 1988. Tourism has been hampered by insecurity in the north and east during the 1990s. Some 11,000 tourists visited Niger in 1993, compared with 21,000 in 1990. Receipts from tourism in 1993 amounted to US $16m.

Direction du Tourisme et de l'Hôtellerie: BP 12130, Niamey; tel. 73-23-85; telex 5249; Dir ALZOUMA MAÏGA.

Office National du Tourisme (ONT): ave du Président H. Luebke, BP 612, Niamey; tel. 73-24-47; telex 5467; f. 1977.

Société Nigérienne d'Hôtellerie (SONHOTEL): BP 11040, Niamey; tel. 73-23-87; telex 5239; f. 1977; state-owned hotel corpn; Dir-Gen. HABI ABDOU.

Defence

In August 1996 Niger's armed forces totalled 5,300 men (army 5,200; air force about 100). Paramilitary forces numbered 5,400 men, comprising the gendarmerie, the republican guard and the national police force. Conscription is selective and lasts for two years.

Defence Expenditure: Budgeted at 10,800m. francs CFA in 1995.

Chief of Staff of the Armed Forces: Col MOUSSA MOUMOUNI DJERMAKOYE.

Education

Education is available free of charge, and is officially compulsory for eight years from seven to 15 years of age. Primary education begins at the age of seven and lasts for six years. Secondary education begins at the age of 13 years and comprises a four-year cycle followed by a further three-year cycle. Primary enrolment in 1993 was equivalent to only 28% of children in the appropriate age-group (boys 35%; girls 21%). Enrolment was equivalent to 30% in 1994: it is aimed to increase the rate of primary enrolment to 35% by 1999. Secondary enrolment in 1994 was equivalent to only 7% of the relevant age-group (boys 9%; girls 5%). The Abdou Moumouni Diop University, at Niamey, was inaugurated in 1973, and the Islamic University of West Africa, at Say, was opened in January 1987. Expenditure on education by the central Government in the 15 months to the end of December 1990 was projected at 24,409m. francs CFA, representing 10.3% of total spending. Adult illiteracy at the time of the 1988 census averaged 89.1% (makes 83.1%; females 94.6%). In 1995, according to UNESCO estimates, the adult illiteracy rate averaged 86.4% (males 79.1%; females 93.4%).

Bibliography

Asiwaju, A. I. et al., and Barkindo, B. M. *The Nigerian-Niger Transborder Co-operation.* Lagos, Malthouse Press, 1993.

Beckwith, C., and Van Offelen, M. *Nomads of Niger.* London, Collins, 1984.

Bernus, E. *Touaregs, un peuple du désert.* Paris, Editions Robert Laffont, 1996.

Charlick, R. B. *Niger: Personal Rule and Survival in the Sahel.* Boulder, CO, Westview Press, 1991.

Clair, A. *Le Niger indépendant.* Paris, ATEOS, 1966.

Decalo, S. *Historical Dictionary of Niger.* 3rd Edn. Metuchen, NJ, Scarecrow Press, 1996.

La Documentation Française. *Bibliographie sommaire de la République du Niger.* Paris, 1969.

La République du Niger. Paris, 1973.

Donaint, P., and Lancrenon, F. *Le Niger.* Paris, Presses universitaires de France, 1972.

Grégoire, E. *Les Alhazi de Maradi.* Paris, Editions Ostrom, 1986.

Harrison Church, R. J. *West Africa.* 8th Edn, London, Longman, 1979.

Keenan, J. *The Tuareg.* London, Allen Lane, 1978.

Klotchkoff, J.-C. *Le Niger aujourd'hui.* Paris, Editions Jeune Afrique, 1982.

Ramir, S. *Les Pistes de l'oubli: Touaregs au Niger.* Paris, Editions du Félin, 1991.

Raynault, G. (Ed.). *Projet de développement rural de Maradi. Le développement rural de la région au village.* Bordeaux, Groupe de recherche interdisciplinaire pour le développement, 1988.

Rimmer, D. *The Economies of West Africa.* London, Weidenfeld and Nicolson, 1984.

Séré de Rivières, E. *Histoire du Niger.* Paris, Berger-Levrault, 1966.

NIGERIA

Physical and Social Geography

AKIN L. MABOGUNJE

The Federal Republic of Nigeria covers an area of 923,768 sq km (356,669 sq miles) on the shores of the Gulf of Guinea, with Benin to the west, Niger to the north, Chad to the north-east, and Cameroon to the east and south-east. The population was enumerated at 88,514,501 at the census of November 1991, increasing to an estimated 97,223,521 at mid-1995. Population density in 1995 averaged 105.2 persons per sq km.

Nigeria became independent on 1 October 1960, and in 1968 adopted a new federal structure comprising 12 states. A federal capital territory was created in 1979. The number of states was increased to 19 in 1976, to 21 in 1987, to 30 in 1991, and to 36 in 1996.

PHYSICAL FEATURES

The physical features of Nigeria are of moderate dimensions. The highest lands are along the eastern border of the country and rise to a maximum of 2,040 m above sea-level at Vogel Peak, south of the Benue river. The Jos plateau, which is located close to the centre of the country, rises to 1,780 m at Shere Hill and 1,698 m at Wadi Hill. The plateau is also a watershed, from which streams flow to Lake Chad and to the rivers Niger and Benue. The land declines steadily northward from the plateau; this area, known as the High Plains of Hausaland, is characterized by a broad expanse of level sandy plains, interspersed by rocky dome outcrops. To the south-west, across the Niger river, similar relief is represented in the Yoruba highlands, where the rocky outcrops are surrounded by forests or tall grass and form the major watershed for rivers flowing northwards to the Niger and southwards to the sea. Elsewhere in the country, lowlands of less than 300 m stretch inland from the coast for over 250 km and continue in the trough-like basins of the Niger and Benue rivers. Lowland areas also exist in the Rima and Chad basins at the extreme north-west and north-east of the country respectively. These lowlands are dissected by innumerable streams and rivers flowing in broad sandy valleys.

The main river of Nigeria is the Niger, the third longest river of Africa. Originating in the Fouta Djallon mountains of north-east Sierra Leone, it enters Nigeria for the last one-third of its 4,200 km course. It flows first south-easterly, then due south and again south-easterly to Lokoja, where it converges with its principal tributary, the Benue. From here the river flows due south until Aboh, where it merges with the numerous interlacing distributaries of its delta. The Benue rises in Cameroon, flows in a south-westerly direction into the Niger, and receives on its course the waters of the Katsina Ala and Gongola rivers. The other main tributaries of the Niger within Nigeria are the Sokoto, Kaduna and Anambra rivers. Other important rivers in the country include the Ogun, the Oshun, the Imo and the Cross, many of which flow into the sea through a system of lagoons. The Nigerian coastline is relatively straight, with few natural indentations.

CLIMATE

Nigeria has a climate which is characterized by relatively high temperatures throughout the year. The average annual maximum varies from 35°C in the north to 31°C in the south; the average annual minimum from 23°C in the south to 18°C in the north. On the Jos plateau and the eastern highlands altitude moderates the temperatures, with the maximum no more than 28°C and the minimum sometimes as low as 14°C.

The annual rainfall total decreases from over 3,800 mm at Forcados on the coast to under 650 mm at Maiduguri in the north-east of the country. The length of the rainy season ranges from almost 12 months in the south to under five months in the north. Rain starts in January in the south and moves gradually across country. June, July, August and September are the rainiest months country-wide. In many parts of the south, however, there is a slight break in the rains for some two to three weeks in late July and early August. No such break occurs in the northern part of the country, and the rainy season continues uninterrupted for three to six months.

SOILS AND VEGETATION

The broad pattern of soil distribution in the country reflects both the climatic conditions and the geological structure; heavily leached, reddish-brown, sandy soils are found in the south, and light or moderately leached, yellowish-brown, sandy soils in the north. The difference in colour relates to the extent of leaching the soil has undergone.

The nutrient content of the soil is linked to the geological structure. Over a large part of the northern and south-western areas of the country the geological structure is that of old crystalline Basement complex rocks. These are highly mineralized and give rise to soils of high nutrient status, although variable from place to place. On the sedimentary rocks found in the south-east, north-east and north-west of the country the soils are sandy and less variable but are deficient in plant nutrient. They are highly susceptible to erosion.

The vegetation displays clear east-west zonation. In general, mangrove and rain forests are found in the south, occupying about 20% of the area of the country, while grassland of various types occupies the rest. Four belts of grassland can be identified. Close to the forest zone is a derived savannah belt, which is evidently the result of frequent fires in previously forested areas. This belt is succeeded by the Guinea, the Sudan and the Sahel savannah northwards in that order. The height of grass and density of wood vegetation decrease with each succeeding savannah belt.

RESOURCES

Although nearly 180,000 sq km of Nigeria is in the forest belt, only 23,000 sq km account for most of its timber resources. These forests are mainly in Ondo, Bendel and Cross River States. Nigeria exports a wide variety of tropical hardwoods, and internal consumption has been growing rapidly.

Cattle, goats and, to a lesser extent, sheep constitute important animal resources. Most of the cattle are found in the Sudan grassland belt in the far north. Poultry and pigs are increasing in importance.

Coastal waters are becoming important fishing grounds. Traditionally, however, major sources of fish have been Lake Chad in the extreme north-east, the lagoons along the coast, the creeks and distributaries of the Niger delta and the various rivers in the country.

Mineral resources are varied, although considerable exploration remains to be carried out. Tin and columbite are found in alluvial deposits on the Jos Plateau. Nigeria was, until 1968, Africa's main producer of tin, but output has since declined. Extensive reserves of medium-grade iron ore exist, and iron and steel production is being developed.

Fuel resources include deposits of lignite and sub-bituminous coal, exploited at Enugu since 1915; however, total reserves are small. More significant are the petroleum reserves, estimates of which alter with each new discovery in the offshore area. The oil produced, being of low sulphur content and high quality, is much in demand on the European and US markets. Since Libya restricted production in 1973, Nigeria has been Africa's leading producer of petroleum. Natural gas is also found in abundance, and has been undergoing development since the mid-1980s.

POPULATION

The Nigerian population is extremely diverse. There are more than 500 spoken languages, and well over 250 ethnic groups, some numbering fewer than 10,000 people. Ten groups, notably Hausa-Fulani, Yoruba, Ibo, Kanuri, Tiv, Edo, Nupe, Ibibio and Ijaw, account for nearly 80% of the total population. Much of the population is concentrated in the southern part of the country, as well as in the area of dense settlement around Kano in the north. Between these two areas is the sparsely populated Middle Belt.

Urban life has a long history in Nigeria, with centres of population such as Kano (mid-1975 estimate 399,000), Zaria (224,000), Ife (176,000) and Benin (136,000) dating from the Middle Ages. Recent economic development, however, has stimulated considerable rural-urban migration and led to the phenomenal growth of such cities as Lagos, Ibadan, Kaduna and Port Harcourt. In December 1991 the federal capital was formally transferred to Abuja; however, a number of government departments and non-government institutions have remained in the former capital, Lagos.

Recent History

T. C. McCASKIE

Revised for this edition by the Editor

The territory of present-day Nigeria, except for the section of former German-controlled Kamerun (see below), was conquered by the United Kingdom, in several stages, during the second half of the 19th century and the first decade of the 20th century. The British dependencies of Northern and Southern Nigeria were merged into a single territory in 1914, and a legislative council, initially with limited African representation, was created in 1922. However, much of the administration remained under the control of traditional rulers, supervised by the colonial authorities. In 1947 the United Kingdom introduced a new Nigerian constitution, establishing a federal system of government, based on three regions: Eastern, Western and Northern. The federal arrangement sought to reconcile regional and religious tensions, and to accommodate the interests of Nigeria's diverse ethnic groups: mainly the Ibo (in the east), the Yoruba (in the west) and the Hausa and Fulani (in the north). The Northern Region, whose inhabitants were mainly Muslims, contained about one-half of Nigeria's total population.

Nationalists continued to demand the extension of the franchise and the holding of direct elections, and in 1949 the constitution of 1947 was abrogated. Ministerial government was introduced in 1951. During the 1950s a series of constitutional conferences took place, in an attempt to achieve a balance of power between regions and ethnic groups, and political parties coalesced on the basis of regional affiliations. The Eastern Region was dominated by the National Council for Nigeria and the Cameroons (NCNC), led by Dr Nnamdi Azikiwe and the veteran nationalist Herbert Macaulay. The NCNC had emerged from a broadly-based organization that had opposed the 1947 constitution, and it attracted mainly Ibo support. The leading political entity in the Western Region was the Action Group (AG), which was derived from the nationalist Nigerian Youth Movement. The AG was led by the premier of the Western Region, Obafemi Awolowo, and Ijebu Yoruba, and was dominated by educated Yoruba. The largest region in the country, the Northern Region, was dominated by the Northern People's Congress (NPC). The NPC was based on the traditional and mercantile Hausa-Fulani élite; its nominal leader was the premier of the Northern Region, the sardauna of Sokoto, Ahmadu (later Sir Ahmadu) Bello. The NPC's political (later parliamentary) spokesman was Abubakar (later Sir Abubakar) Tafawa Balewa, a former schoolteacher (who was appointed the first federal prime minister in 1957).

In 1954 the federation became self-governing, with the Regions allowed considerable powers of autonomy. Lagos, the capital, was constituted as a federal territory, separate from the Western Region. In 1958 a constitutional conference agreed that Nigeria should become independent in 1960, and, in preparation for this, elections for an enlarged federal legislature took place in December 1959. None of the three major parties achieved an overall majority, but, owing to the greater size of the Northern Region, the NPC commanded the largest representation, and Tafawa Balewa continued in office as federal prime minister, leading a coalition of the NPC and the NCNC. A bicameral federal parliament was formed in January 1960.

CIVILIAN RULE, 1960–66

On 1 October 1960, as scheduled, the Federation of Nigeria achieved independence, initially as a constitutional monarchy. Tafawa Balewa continued as federal prime minister and also became minister of foreign affairs. In November the pre-independence governor-general (representing the British monarch as head of state) was succeeded by Dr Nnamdi Azikiwe of the NCNC, who had been president of the senate and was a former premier of the Eastern Region. In June 1961 the northern section of the neighbouring UN Trust Territory of British Cameroons, formerly part of the German protectorate of Kamerun, was incorporated into Nigeria's Northern Region as the province of Sardauna.

After the 1959 election, the AG was excluded from power at the federal level, and, in addition, was affected by a resurgence of Yoruba factionalism. Awolowo began to quarrel openly with the prime minister of the Western Region, Chief Samuel Akintola, and in early 1962 the AG executive decided to replace Akintola with a protégé of Awolowo, provoking disorder in the Western regional assembly. The federal government declared a state of emergency and took over the regional administration. After the expiry of the six-month period of emergency, Akintola's new United People's Party (UPP) controlled the government of the Western Region, in alliance with the NCNC, which had strong support in the non-Yoruba areas of the region. In 1963 a referendum was held in the Western Region, approving the formation of a separate region for the non-Yoruba areas; following legislative approval in August, the new Mid-Western Region was detached from the Western Region, and the NCNC won the ensuing elections to the Mid-Western regional legislature.

In September 1962 Awolowo and some 30 supporters were arrested and charged with plotting to overthrow the federal government. The trial, which was widely perceived as an attempt to discredit Awolowo, made public the level of corruption prevalent in Nigerian politics. Awolowo revealed that he had attempted to form an alliance with elements of the NCNC in 1961, in order to take over the federal government, and was sentenced to a term of imprisonment.

In October 1963 the country adopted a revised constitution and was renamed the Federal Republic of Nigeria, while remaining a member of the Commonwealth. Dr Azikiwe took office as Nigeria's first president (then a non-executive post). The first national election since independence, to the federal house of representatives, took place in December 1964. It was preceded by a split in the coalition between the NPC and the NCNC (renamed the National Convention of Nigerian Citizens), and by the formation of two new national coalitions. The Nigerian National Alliance (NNA) comprised the NPC and Akintola's breakaway Yoruba party, now renamed the Nigerian National Democratic Party (NNDP). The United Progressive

Grand Alliance (UPGA), led by Dr Michael Okpara, the prime minister of the Eastern Region, was composed of the NCNC, the remainder of the AG (whose leaders were still in prison) and the minority, populist Northern Elements Progressive Union (NEPU). The election campaign was characterized by violence and corruption, and, in protest against alleged irregularities, the UPGA organized a boycott of the poll, which was widely observed in the Eastern Region. The NNA won by default, and Azikiwe reluctantly asked Tafawa Balewa to form a new government. A supplementary election was held in the Eastern Region in March 1965 (at which the UPGA won every seat), followed by a fresh election in the Western Region in November, owing to widespread irregularities. Both the NNDP and the AG subsequently claimed the right to form a government in the Western Region, and the situation deteriorated into anarchy: some 2,000 people were killed during, and immediately following, the election.

MILITARY INTERVENTION AND CIVIL WAR, 1966–70

National rivalries were reflected in the Nigerian armed forces; most of the quota of personnel recruited from the North came from the Middle Belt of the Northern Region and were opposed to the NPC and to Hausa-Fulani dominance. Ibo from the Eastern Region formed the majority of the officer corps, and this provoked intense distrust from other ethnic groups. In January 1966 Tafawa Balewa's government was overthrown by junior (mainly Ibo) army officers; Tafawa Balewa was killed, together with Sir Ahmadu Bello, prime minister of the Northern Region, Chief Akintola, prime minister of the Western Region, and Chief Festus Okotie-Eboh, the federal minister of finance. On the following day the surviving federal ministers requested Maj.-Gen. Johnson Aguiyi-Ironsi, the c-in-c of the army and an Ibo, to take control of the government. He formed a supreme military council (SMC), suspended the constitution, and imposed a state of emergency. The coup was followed by anti-Ibo riots, and in late May many people were killed when violence erupted in most of the major cities of the north, involving Hausa urban dwellers: disturbances indicated the level of Hausa dissatisfaction with Ibo dominance at the federal level, with the increasing centralization of government, and with what was seen as the exclusion of northerners from federal office. On 29 July Aguiyi-Ironsi was killed in a counter-coup by northern troops, and easterners were massacred in barracks throughout the country. Power was transferred to the chief-of-staff of the army, Lt-Col (later Gen.) Yakubu Gowon, a Christian northerner from the Middle Belt. Gowon restored some degree of discipline to the armed forces, and attempted to revive the federal system, appointing a military governor for each region.

Ibo still living in the North began to return to the Eastern Region after the counter-coup of July 1966, and in late September and early October those who remained in the North were massacred by northern army elements. The military governor of the Eastern Region, Lt-Col Chukwuemeka Odumegwu-Ojukwu, was subsequently urged by senior Ibo civil servants, who had fled from Lagos, to declare an independent Ibo state. In early 1967 there was a dispute between the federal government and that of the Eastern Region concerning the distribution of revenues from the Eastern petroleum industry. In May Gen. Gowon announced a proposal to abolish Nigeria's regions and replace them by 12 states. On 30 May Ojukwu announced the secession of the Eastern Region, and proclaimed its independence as the 'Republic of Biafra'. In July 'Biafran' troops crossed into the Western Region in an attempt to surround Lagos: federal troops then attacked 'Biafra' from the north and west, and a naval blockade was imposed. The Ibo achieved a series of initial successes, but by late 1967 the war had degenerated into a violent campaign of attrition. During 1968 most major towns in 'Biafra' were captured by federal forces, and in January 1970 'Biafran' forces surrendered, after Ojukwu's departure into exile. During the civil war military casualties reached an estimated 100,000, but between 500,000 and 2m. 'Biafran' civilians died, mainly from starvation as a result of the federal blockade.

MILITARY RULE, 1970–76

The 12-state structure proposed by Gen. Gowon entered into effect in April 1968, and after the cease-fire in January 1970 East Central State (the heartland of the former 'Biafra') was reintegrated into Nigeria. The SMC implemented various reconciliatory measures, reinstating a number of 'Biafran' military personnel and establishing infrastructural projects. However the government's strategy of reconciliation was seriously impeded by the failure of the national population census, conducted in 1973, to produce credible results; the census purported to show a near-doubling of the population in the three northern states (Kano, North-Eastern and North-Western), while that of the Yoruba heartland of Western State was reported to have declined. In October 1974 Gowon announced that the return to civilian rule, scheduled for 1976, had been indefinitely postponed, on the grounds that a government plan for socio-economic reconstruction had not been fulfilled. Instead, the SMC announced an ambitious new National Development Plan for 1975–80, and promised a new constitution and the creation of new states; by mid-1975, however, none of these expressed intentions had been fulfilled.

In May 1975 Gen. Gowon presided over the signing of the final agreements establishing the Economic Community of West African States (ECOWAS), a Nigerian-funded initiative that aimed to combine the economic potential of the region's states. On 29 July, while Gowon was attending a summit meeting of the Organization of African Unity (OAU) in Uganda, his government was overthrown in a bloodless coup by other senior officers. Gowon was forcibly 'retired' and allowed to go into exile, while his place as head of government was assumed by Brig. (later Gen.) Murtala Ramat Muhammed, hitherto the federal commissioner for communications. Muhammed immediately dismissed the 12 state governors, and undertook a radical and extremely popular purge of the public services. In October he announced that the country would be returned to civilian government by October 1979, following the adoption of a new constitution and the holding of local, state and federal elections.

OBASANJO AND THE RETURN TO CIVILIAN RULE, 1976–79

Despite a substantial popular following, Gen. Muhammed was assassinated in February 1976 by a disaffected army officer, Lt-Col Bukar Dimka, and a number of associates, who demanded the reinstatement of Gen. Gowon. Power was transferred to Muhammed's deputy, Lt-Gen. Olusegun Obasanjo, the chief-of-staff of the armed forces. As head of state, Obasanjo pledged to fulfil his predecessor's programme for the return to civilian rule. In 1976 new legislation attempted to reform the structure of local government (hitherto based on British 'indirect rule' and a series of subsequent partial reforms): local government authorities were henceforth to be administered by councils with a majority of elected members. In 1975 the government established a constitutional drafting committee, comprising two representatives from each state, advised by experts. The committee's recommendations, announced in September 1976, included: the creation of a federal system of government with an executive presidency (similar to that of the USA); a moratorium on the creation of further states (the number of which had been increased by seven to 19 in March of that year); the creation of genuinely national political parties; the holding of open, free and fair elections; and the transfer of the federal capital from Lagos to a 'neutral' site at Abuja, in the geographical centre of Nigeria. A constituent assembly (CA) was created in August 1977 to draft the new constitution. The new local government councils (elected at the end of 1976) were constituted as electoral colleges for the CA, with the regional percentage of membership being determined by population estimates; of the 230 members (including 20 nominated directly by the SMC), many were nationally-known politicians from the 1960–66 period.

The new constitution was produced in 1978 and promulgated by the SMC in September. It envisaged an executive presidency, and a separation of powers between executive, legislative and judicial branches of government. To win the presidential election, a candidate would need to obtain an outright majority of the national vote, and also to win at least 25% of the votes in at least 12 states. Executive governors were to be appointed to each state. The respective powers of federal and state governments were carefully demarcated.

THE SECOND REPUBLIC, 1979–83

The ending of the state of emergency in September 1978 was accompanied by the lifting of the ban on formal activity by political parties. By November more than 50 political groupings had emerged. In its electoral decree of 1977, the SMC had imposed stipulations that aspirant political parties were obliged to fulfil in order to contest the 1979 elections. The monitoring body, the Federal Electoral Commission (FEDECO), was instructed by the SMC to recognize only those parties that possessed a nationwide organization and base; divisive regionalism was to be avoided, and the emphasis was to be on national unity and dedication to the federal concept. In the event, of the 19 associations that applied for registration, only five received approval by FEDECO.

The best prepared of the five parties was the Unity Party of Nigeria (UPN), led by Chief Obafemi Awolowo, formerly vice-chairman of the SMC under Gowon and leader of the Yoruba-dominated AG in the 1950s. The UPN was a Yoruba-based party, which drew support from the western part of the country, and most notably from Oyo, Ondo, Ogun and Lagos States; its programme was viewed as populist. The National Party of Nigeria (NPN) was formed by such veteran politicians as Alhaji Shehu Shagari (later selected as its presidential candidate) and Makaman Bida, both of whom had taken prominent roles in the northern-based NPC. The NPN, which was based in Kaduna, in the north, advocated the enforcement of law and order, respect for tradition, and the operation of a capitalist, free-market economy. The People's Redemption Party (PRP), the northern-based opposition to the NPN, was formed in Kaduna in October 1978, under the leadership of a former member of the NPN, Alhaji Aminu Kano. The PRP was populist in outlook, stressing the issue of multi-national corporations, and advocating a 'social revolution' in the distribution of income. The fourth party, the Nigerian People's Party (NPP), was initially led by Alhaji Waziri Ibrahim, a businessman and contractor from the north-eastern Borno State. At its nominating convention in November, Chief Ogunsanya, a senior member of the party, broke away from Ibrahim, assumed leadership of the NPP and appointed Dr Azikiwe as presidential candidate. Ibrahim immediately formed another party, the Greater Nigeria People's Party (GNPP), in order to advance his presidential aspirations.

Thus, the UPN, the NPN, the PRP, the NPP and the GNPP contested elections to the new bicameral national assembly, and for state assemblies and state governors, which took place in July 1979. The rate of abstention was high; in the presidential election itself, only 35% of the registered electorate voted. (The SMC's decree that the result of each election had to be made known before its successor was held undoubtedly benefited the party that dominated the election series.) The NPN received the most widespread support, securing 37% of the seats in the house of representatives, 36% in the state assemblies, and 38% in the senate, and winning seven of the 19 state governorships. In the presidential election, which took place in August, Shagari received 5.7m. votes, while Awolowo secured 4.9m., Azikiwe 2.8m., Kano 1.7m., and Ibrahim 1.6m.; thus, Shagari obtained the mandatory 25% of the vote in 12, rather than 13, of the 19 States. Following legal debate on this point, the supreme court upheld the election of Shagari. On 1 October military rule ended, the new constitution came into force, and Shagari was sworn in as president of the Second Republic.

Despite the evident volatility of world petroleum prices, the Shagari government introduced an ambitious programme of investment, which, it was hoped, would be financed by a continuing high level of revenue from the petroleum industry. In 1982, however, a decline in international petroleum prices produced a foreign exchange crisis and widespread financial panic. During 1982–83 export revenue from petroleum continued to fall, and drastic measures by the government to curb imports and to control the export of foreign exchange, resulted in widespread corruption and fiscal malpractice. In 1983 Nigeria agreed to a restrictive economic programme, in return for support from the IMF. The population suffered increasing hardship, and this, in turn, generated resentment.

Meanwhile, a series of violent events occurred in the north during 1980-82. In December 1980 the populist preachings of Alhaji Muhammad Marwa (known as Maitatsine) provoked serious rioting in Kano. Maitatsine himself was killed, and the disorder was violently suppressed. In October 1982 police in Maiduguri arrested 16 of Maitatsine's followers, and serious rioting ensued, spreading to Kano and Kaduna. The military suppressed the outbreak, killing hundreds of dissidents. In November the sect was officially banned. The NPN claimed that the events were a product of religious extremism, refusing to acknowledge the underlying cause of economic deprivation.

Decline of the NPN

By the early 1980s it was widely believed in Nigeria that the federal democracy was a façade, which allowed NPN politicians, dominated by a powerful political community in Kaduna, to distribute contracts and rewards in order to ensure their own continuation in power. In order to reinforce its power on the federal legislature, the NPN formed an alliance with Azikiwe's NPP, which, however, was dissolved in July 1981. The NPP then established a coalition, known as the Progressive Parties' Alliance (PPA), with the UPN, the major opposition party, thereby engendering further realignments in the parties that had fought the 1979 elections. The PRP and the GNPP split, with some of their members joining the PPA, while others aligned themselves with the government. In 1982, amid increasing political animosity towards the NPN, an abortive coup attempt was staged, ostensibly led by disaffected army officers. It emerged that the coup attempt had been instigated by Alhaji Zana Bukar Mandara, a businessman, whose main grievance was that he had received fewer public contracts from the NPN than the SMC. He was found guilty of treasonable felony, and sentenced to 50 years in prison.

In 1982, in preparation for the elections of the following year, FEDECO was reconstituted and given extensive powers. Two new parties subsequently applied for registration; FEDECO approved the National Advance Party (NAP), led by the radical Lagos lawyer Tunji Braithwaite, but the 'Rimi faction' of the Progressive People's Party was refused recognition. FEDECO decreed also that the unrecognized splinter factions of the PRP and the GNPP would have to campaign in support of the political programmes of the NPN or the UPN. As campaigning began, the NPN used its entrenched position and financial influence to ensure its return to office. In May the government granted a pardon to Odumegwu-Ojukwu, the former 'Biafran' leader, who returned to Nigeria after more than 12 years of exile, and later aligned himself with the NPN. Later that year the PPA became divided over the issue of choosing a presidential candidate; eventually, Awolowo was selected as the UPN candidate, and Azikiwe as the NPP candidate.

The elections, which were contested by the six political parties, took place in August–September 1983. In the presidential poll, Shagari was returned for a second term, receiving more than 12m. votes, or 47% of the total votes cast. The NPN attained a decisive majority in the elections to the senate (60 seats out of 96) and the house of representatives (264 seats out of 450), and won 13 of the 19 state governorships, with voting for the state assemblies and local governments largely following the same pattern. However, allegations of widespread electoral malpractice on the part of the NPN resulted in litigation and a reinforcement of the belief that the elections had been won by means of misconduct on a vast scale. On 1 October Shagari was sworn in for a second term as president, but he now presided over a country that was more bitterly divided than it had been at the inception of the Second Republic.

THE RETURN OF MILITARY RULE

Buhari and the SMC, 1983–85

On 31 December 1983 Shagari was deposed in a bloodless military coup, led by Maj.-Gen. Muhammadu Buhari, a former military governor of Borno and federal commissioner for petroleum during 1976–78. All political parties were banned, FEDECO was dissolved, and all bank accounts were temporarily 'frozen'. Several high-ranking military personnel were replaced, and prominent NPN members and politicians (including Shagari) were arrested. The new military regime, which was identified with the government of Gen. Muhammed, received widespread popular support. The structure of the new regime, similar to that of the military governments of 1975–79, comprised a reconstituted SMC, headed by Buhari. A national council of states, with a federal executive council, and state executive councils, presided over by military governors, were subsequently established.

In February 1984 the SMC issued a decree which empowered the government to enact laws that could not be challenged in the courts. Further legislation effectively prohibited the publication of information unfavourable to the government. In April it was announced that special tribunals were to be established to try those under arrest, and, *in absentia,* those who had fled the country; it became evident that the special tribunals were designed to recover assets which had been misappropriated by the civilian administration. By July a number of former governors had been sentenced for corruption and fiscal irregularities. However, there were widespread complaints that few of those who had been convicted by the tribunals were members of the NPN. Despite the SMC's denials of partiality, it was evident that former members of the NPN commanded considerable influence within the government.

In July 1984 a diplomatic crisis arose between Nigeria and the United Kingdom as a result of the attempted kidnapping, in London, of Umaru Dikko, a political exile and a former minister in the Shagari administration, who was being sought for trial in Nigeria on charges of corruption. The alleged involvement of Nigerian diplomats in the affair resulted in the mutual withdrawal of the two countries' high commissioners. (Full diplomatic relations were restored in February 1986, although annual bilateral talks at ministerial level remained suspended until 1988.)

Public resentment concerning the delay in the trials of a large number of detainees from the Shagari era increased, following the acquittal, on corruption charges, of two former governors in March 1985. (In January Buhari had announced that the government was to retain the powers of detention without trial, for three months, of citizens who were considered to constitute a threat to the state.) In July Maj.-Gen. Tunde Idiagbon, the chief of staff at supreme military headquarters, urged further economic retrenchment, stated that there was no schedule for a return to civilian rule, and prohibited all debate on the political future of Nigeria. Several journalists were subsequently detained. Following Idiagbon's proclamation, there were widespread rumours of a coup attempt by junior officers and reports of open dissension within the SMC.

Babangida and the AFRC, 1985–93

In August 1985 Buhari's regime was deposed in a peaceful military coup, led by Maj.-Gen. (later Gen.) Ibrahim Babangida, the army chief-of-staff, who was named as the new head of state. The SMC was replaced by a 28-member armed forces ruling council (AFRC) which, unlike the SMC, was composed solely of military personnel. The post of chief-of-staff at supreme military headquarters, upon which Idiagbon had based his power, was replaced by that of chief of the general staff within the AFRC, a position that carried no responsibility for actual control of the armed forces. A national council of ministers was formed, together with a reconstituted national council of state. There was a redistribution of all state governorships, and Buhari's ministers were removed. Following the abolition of the decree on press censorship, a number of journalists were released, together with detainees from the Shagari government. In September Babangida, with the support of Maj.-Gen. Sani Abacha, the chief of the army staff, removed some 40 senior officers, including Buhari and Idiagbon, who were placed in detention.

In October 1985 Babangida declared a state of national economic emergency and assumed extensive interventionist powers over the economy. In December Babangida suspended negotiations with the IMF, a move that received widespread popular support, but caused dissension among certain members of the AFRC, and within the army command. On 20 December the AFRC suppressed a coup attempt by disaffected army officers. In February 1986 13 of the 14 named conspirators were convicted and executed.

In January 1986 Babangida announced that the armed forces would transfer power to a civilian government on 1 October 1990. The government appointed a 17-member political bureau, composed mainly of university academics, to formulate procedures for such a transition, but, at the same time, it insisted that no overt political activity was yet permissible. In May, amid protests from the Nigerian Bar Association, the AFRC extended the period of detention without trial from three to six months. In June sanctions were introduced against public officials convicted of corruption, which included the withdrawal of their passports for five years and the 'freezing' or confiscation of their assets. In July Shagari and former vice-president Ekwueme were released from detention, although they were subsequently banned for life from political activity. In the same month an extensive reshuffle of state governorships took place. In October the chief of general staff, Cdre Ebitu Ukiwe, was dismissed from the AFRC, and four new members were appointed.

In February 1986 Babangida announced that Nigeria's application for full membership of the Organization of the Islamic Conference (OIC) had been accepted; ensuing unrest among the non-Muslim sector of the population reflected alarm at increasing 'Islamization' in the country. In May about 15 people, mostly students, were shot dead by police during demonstrations at the Ahmadu Bello University, in Zaria, and a ban was imposed on further demonstrations. Babangida subsequently established a national commission to examine the advisability of Nigeria's membership of the OIC.

In March 1987 violent clashes broke out between Muslim and Christian youths at Kafanchan, in southern Kaduna State, which were reported to have resulted in some 30 deaths. A curfew was imposed, and an estimated 1,000 people were arrested. In April the AFRC formed an advisory council on religious affairs (ACRA), comprising Muslim and Christian leaders, to investigate the causes of the violence, and the authorities issued decrees banning religious organizations in schools and universities. However, sporadic outbreaks of student unrest continued in late 1987 and early 1988.

In July 1987, after receiving recommendations from the political bureau, the AFRC announced that power was to be transferred to a civilian government in 1992, two years later than envisaged, although a transitional programme would begin later in 1987 with the formation of an electoral commission and a directorate of social mobilization and political education. Political parties would remain banned during the transitional period, although elections for local government authorities were to be contested on a non-party basis by the end of 1987. A constituent assembly, which was to draft a new constitution, was to be established in 1988, and, following the promulgation of the constitution, further local and state elections were to be held in 1990, at which time two political parties were to be permitted. Elections for a bicameral federal legislature and for the presidency were to follow in 1992.

In August 1987 the AFRC established a programme to promote political education, in preparation for the transition to civilian rule. In September the number of states was increased from 19 to 21, in an attempt to resolve the problem, experienced under the Second Republic, of determining what constituted a two-thirds majority of the states in an election. In the same month the AFRC proscribed all categories of former politicians and its own membership from contesting elections in 1992. In addition, the AFRC inaugurated a constitutional review committee to examine proposals for a new constitution, and a national electoral commission (NEC) to supervise future elections. On 12 December local government elections were contested by some 15,000 non-party candidates in 301 electoral areas. However, inadequate preparations for the elections by the NEC resulted in confusion, violence and allegations of electoral fraud and corruption. The NEC annulled the results in 312 local government wards, where further elections took place on 26 March 1988. Babangida subsequently announced that the new constitution would be promulgated in 1989, and proposed that an enlarged constituent assembly should debate the terms of the constitution. Accordingly, in April 1988 local government councillors elected 450 members to the constituent assembly. The AFRC later nominated a further 117 members, to represent various interest groups. Abuja, the future federal capital, was designated as the seat of the new assembly.

At the first session of the constituent assembly in June 1988, it was announced that the new constitution, which was to be modelled on that of 1979, would contain provisions prohibiting groups or individuals from usurping the government by force, and would ensure that all political change was effected by democratic means. Additionally, the constituent assembly was to draft and ratify the new constitution by the end of the year, rather than by May 1989, as originally envisaged. However, debate over the new draft constitution threatened to founder on the issue of religion. Muslims demanded the inclusion of Shari'a courts in the constitution, but in November 1988 further debate on this topic was banned by Babangida, as the progress of the assembly's work was being severely impeded. The AFRC postponed the date of submission of the draft constitution from January to March 1989, and threatened to dissolve the assembly unless it completed its task by the revised date. In January 1989 the assembly ratified the decision that, under the new constitution, a civilian president was to be elected for a six-year term, and was to declare all personal assets and liabilities before taking office.

In February 1989 Babangida reduced membership of the AFRC from 29 to 19, reportedly in order to reduce the power of the armed forces during the transitional period leading to civilian rule. In March a minor reshuffle of the council of ministers took place, and a new NEC was formed. In the same month, electoral legislation was amended to allow the AFRC to decide which of the political groupings recommended by the NEC were to be registered as the two legally permitted political parties when legislation prohibiting political activity was revoked later that year. The constituent assembly presented its report and draft constitution in early April. The assembly refused to include provisions for the transitional period, as this would legitimize a degree of military rule.

In early May 1989 the ban on political parties was lifted, and the constitution was promulgated. The constitution was to enter into force on 1 October 1992, when a civilian government would be installed. Elections for the government of the Third Republic were to be contested by only two registered political parties, which were to be selected by the AFRC from the register compiled by the NEC. To be eligible for registration, a political party was to be founded on national policy-making (and not be allied to any ethnic or religious grouping), and be democratically organized. Six political parties subsequently emerged, and by the beginning of July this number had risen to approximately 40. However, only 13 parties succeeded in fulfilling the registration requirements by the stipulated date of 15 July. In the same month all local government councils were dissolved, pending the election of new councillors in late 1989.

In October 1989, following the recommendation by the NEC of six of the 13 associations to the AFRC, Babangida announced that the AFRC had decided to dissolve all 13 of the political associations, on the grounds that they lacked distinctive ideologies, and were allied to discredited civilian politicians. In their place the AFRC created two new political parties, the Social Democratic Party (SDP) and the National Republic Convention (NRC). The announcement provoked widespread criticism. Local elections, scheduled for December, were immediately postponed until early 1990, and the NEC announced that delays might be expected in the planned transition to civilian rule. In December the NEC published the draft constitutions and manifestos of the SDP and the NRC. In the same month Babangida carried out a major cabinet reshuffle, in which he assumed the defence portfolio, while his closest associate, Lt-Gen. Sani Abacha, the chief of the army staff, was appointed chairman of the joint chiefs of staff. In March 1990 registration began for membership of the SDP and NRC. In the same month legislation which had permitted the detention of criminal suspects for up to six months without charge was amended, and a review panel was created to investigate individual cases.

In April 1990 junior army officers seized the headquarters of the Federal Radio Corpn and attacked the presidential residence. The leader of the attempted coup, Maj. Gideon Orkar, claimed to be acting on behalf of Nigerians in the centre and south of the country, who, he alleged, were under-represented in the government. Orkar declared that the Babangida regime had been overthrown; he also announced that the predominantly Muslim states of Sokoto, Borno, Katsina, Kano and Bauchi were to be 'excised' from Nigeria, owing to the disputed installation, earlier in 1989, of Alhaji Ibrahim Dasuki as the 18th sultan of Sokoto. The coup attempt was suppressed within 24 hours, and Orkar was arrested, together with about 300 other military personnel, and more than 30 civilians. A number of journalists perceived as critical of the government were also detained. In July Orkar and a number of other prisoners were convicted by a military tribunal, on charges of conspiracy to commit treason; later that month 42 prisoners, including Orkar, were executed. Nine other defendants were imprisoned, and the AFRC ordered the retrial by military tribunal of a further 31 of the accused. In September there were a further 27 executions in connection with the attempted coup.

The election of officials from the SDP and NRC to local government councils was held in May 1990. In July more than 44,000 delegates, representing the two political parties, elected party executives for each state. The administration of the SDP and NRC was transferred from government-appointed administrative secretaries to elected party officials in early August. In the same month Chief Tom Ikimi, a southerner, was elected chairman of the NRC, while Baba Kingibe, a northerner, was installed as chairman of the SDP. (It was widely believed that the NRC received most support from the north of the country, and the SDP from the south.) Internal disputes were reported in both parties, concerning the regional affiliation of potential candidates for the presidency of the civilian government. It was also alleged that former politicians who were banned from party membership were involved in both the SDP and NRC.

Later in August 1990 Babangida extensively reshuffled the government, replacing nine ministers and abolishing the position of chief of general staff, whose incumbent, Vice-Adm. Augustus Aikhomu, was subsequently appointed to the newly-created post of vice-president. Babangida also announced that the presidency would be restructured in order to prepare for the transition to civilian rule, and that the size of the armed forces would be substantially reduced. In early September, in an attempt to restrict military influence in the government, three ministers were obliged to retire from the armed forces, leaving the minister of defence, Lt-Gen. Sani Abacha, as the only serving military officer in the council of ministers. 12 military state governors were replaced, and 21 civilian deputy governors were appointed to each state, pending gubernatorial elections, scheduled for 1991.

Legislation was introduced in November 1990 providing for an 'open ballot' system, which was designed to minimize electoral malpractice in the forthcoming elections. In December local government elections took place in some 440 areas, although only an estimated 20% of registered voters participated. 2,934 candidates representing the SDP were elected as councillors, with a further 232 elected to chair local councils, while 2,588 NRC candidates were elected as councillors, with 208 elected as chairmen. In January 1991 the government announced that state subsidies being provided to the NRC and SDP would end in September. Primary elections, which were to be preceded by a three-stage registration process for candidates, were scheduled for 24 August. Later in February a minor government reshuffle was carried out, in which three ministers were replaced. In April the election of 38 chairmen and a number of councillors was annulled, after a tribunal ruled that the candidates concerned failed to fulfil electoral requirements.

At this time the government was also confronted by manifestations of ethnic discontent and religious conflict. In October 1990 the Movement for the Survival of the Ogoni People (MOSOP) was formed to co-ordinate opposition to the exploitation of petroleum reserves in the territory of the Ogoni ethnic group (Ogoniland), in the south-central Rivers State, by the Shell Petroleum Development Co of Nigeria. Following demonstrations, organized by MOSOP, in protest at alleged environmental damage caused by petroleum production, some 80 Ogonis were killed by security forces. In April 1991 a number of demonstrations by Muslims in the northern state of Katsina, in protest against the publication of an article considered to be blasphemous, culminated in violence. In the same month some 130 people, mainly Christians, were killed in riots in Bauchi and other predominantly Muslim states, where Christians proposed to slaughter pigs in a local abattoir that was also used by Muslims. It was later reported that some 120 Muslims had been killed by government troops, which had been sent to the region to suppress the riots. In October demonstrations by Muslims took place at Kano, in the north, in protest against a tour of the state by a Christian preacher (following a decision by the authorities to refuse a Muslim leader permission to visit the area). More than 300 people were reported to have been killed in subsequent clashes between Muslims and Christians, which were suppressed by the army.

In late 1991 violence erupted in Taruba, in the east, as a result of a long-standing land dispute between the Tiv and Jukun ethnic groups. The conflict continued in subsequent months, and by March 1992 up to 5,000 people were reported to have been killed. In January demonstrations in Katsina by Muslim fundamentalists demanding the imposition of Shari'a law were forcibly suppressed. In February some 30 people were killed in the northern state of Kaduna in clashes between the Hausa ethnic group (which was predominantly Muslim) and the Kataf (mainly Christian).

In June 1991 the NRC and SDP selected some 144,950 delegates to stand in the primary elections, which were to take place in August, for the gubernatorial and state assembly elections. By mid-1991 some 45 prospective presidential candidates had declared themselves; the government expressed concern that candidate rivalries within both the NRC and the SDP might undermine the programme for transition to civilian rule. In early September the government created nine new states, increasing the size of the federation to 30 states, in an attempt to ease ethnic tensions prior to the elections. However, violent demonstrations took place in several states where the government had failed to comply with demands to create a new state in the region, or where there was discontent at the relocation of the state capital. As a result of these protests, the government announced that the primary elections (which had already been postponed to September) would take place on 19 October, and would be followed by state assembly and gubernatorial elections on 14 December. It was confirmed, however, that the transition to civilian rule would be completed on 1 October 1992, as scheduled. Military administrators were subsequently appointed for the nine newly-created states, pending the gubernatorial elections.

On 19 October 1991 primary elections took place to select candidates for the forthcoming gubernatorial and state assembly elections. In November, however, following allegations of widespread electoral fraud on the part of both the NRC and the SDP, results were annulled in nine states, and 12 candidates were disqualified; new elections were held in these states in early December. Controversy over the election results led to increased divisions within both parties, especially within the SDP.

In December 1991 the seat of federal government was formally transferred from Lagos to Abuja, which was to be administered by a municipal council. In the gubernatorial and state assembly elections, which took place on 14 December, the SDP gained a majority in 16 state assemblies, while the NRC won control of 14; however, NRC candidates were elected as governors in 16 of the 30 states, many of which were situated in the south-east of Nigeria, where the SDP had previously received more support. Both the SDP and the NRC subsequently disputed the election results in a number of states, on the grounds of voting irregularities. In the same month 11 former ministers, who had contravened the disqualification of former office-holders from contesting elections, were arrested. They were, however, released later in December, and the ban was lifted. (Only Babangida and officials convicted of criminal offences were henceforth prohibited from taking part in elections.) In early January 1992 the new state governors were inaugurated.

In mid-January 1992 Babangida formed a new 20-member national council of ministers, in which a number of portfolios were reallocated. In the same month the government announced that elections for a bicameral national assembly, comprising a 593-member house of representatives and a 91-member senate, would take place on 7 November, and would be followed by a presidential election on 5 December. Primary elections for presidential candidates were to take place between 2 May and 20 June, while the selection of candidates to contest the legislative elections was scheduled for 4 July. The formal installation of a civilian government and the promulgation of the new constitution were to take place on 2 January 1993, rather than on 1 October 1992, as previously planned. Later in January 1992 Babangida rejected demands by former politicians for the establishment of a government of national consensus.

In February 1992 disputed election results in the states of Edo, Jigawa and Abia were annulled, and the state governors removed from office. However, the validity of the elections of the governors of Edo and Jigawa was later upheld on appeal. Later in February the government promulgated legislation empowering state governors to appoint commissioners (local ministers) without the approval of the state assemblies. In March, following discussions between the NEC, the NRC and the SDP, legislative elections were scheduled for 4 July, earlier than envisaged. The selection of candidates for the legislature was to commence on 23 May, while primary elections for presidential candidates were to take place between 1 August and 15 September. (The presidential election was to take place on 5 December, as originally scheduled.) Later in March legislation that allowed the NEC to disqualify electoral candidates deemed to be unfit to hold office was introduced. In April a committee, comprising officials from several government ministries, was established to co-ordinate the transition to civilian rule. Later that month Babangida denied rumours of a coup attempt by senior army officers.

In early May 1992 widespread rioting in protest at sharp increases in transport fares (resulting from a severe fuel shortage) culminated in a number of demonstrations demanding the resignation of the government, which were violently suppressed by the security forces; several people were reported to have been killed. An alliance of 25 organizations opposed to the government, known as the Campaign for Democracy (CD), which had been formed six months earlier, attributed the unrest to widespread discontent at increasing economic hardship. Later in May further rioting broke out in Lagos, following the arrest of the chairman of the CD, Dr Beko Ransome-Kuti, who had accused the government of provoking the violence in order to delay the transition to civilian rule. In the same month some 300 people were reported to have been killed in renewed violence between the Hausa and the Kataf in Kaduna; a curfew was briefly imposed in that state, and some 250 people were arrested. The government subsequently banned all associations with a religious or ethnic base; a security force, to be known as the national guard, was also to be established in order to reduce the role of the army in riot control.

Extensive government changes were carried out in early June 1992, in which the influential minister of finance and economic planning, Alhaji Abubakar Alhaji, was replaced. Later in June a number of human rights activists, including Ransome-Kuti, were released, pending their trial later that year, on charges of conspiring to incite the riots in May. In the same month the NEC disqualified (without explanation) 32 candidates who had been selected to contest the legislative elections.

In elections to the national assembly, which took place on 4 July 1992 the SDP gained a majority in both chambers, securing 52 seats in the senate and 314 seats in the house of representatives, while the NRC won 37 seats in the senate and 275 seats in the house of representatives. However, the formal inauguration of the national assembly, scheduled for 27 July, was subsequently postponed until 2 January 1993, owing to the AFRC's insistence that it retain supreme legislative power until the installation of a civilian government. Primary elections to select an NRC and an SDP presidential candidate commenced on 1 August 1992, but were suspended, owing to widespread electoral irregularities; results in states where elections had taken place were annulled. Further polls to select presidential candidates took place on 12, 19 and 26 September. By the end of the second round of voting, four leading candidates had emerged: Gen. (retd) Shehu Musa Yar'Adua and Chief Olu Falae (SDP), and Alhaji Umaru Shinkafi and Malam Adamu Ciroma (NRC). However, 10 of the original 23 aspirants (including Falae) withdrew from the third and final stage of polling, alleging fraudulent practices. Reports of irregularities were widely believed, and the participation rate in the poll was significantly low. Nevertheless, Yar'Adua claimed to have won the SDP nomination, while Shinkafi and Ciroma were to contest a final poll for the NRC candidacy on 10 October.

On 6 October 1992, however, the AFRC summarily suspended the results of all three stages of the presidential primaries, pending an investigation by the NEC into the alleged incidents of voting irregularities. Despite the AFRC's reaffirmation of its pledge to transfer power to a civilian president by 3 January 1993, widespread suspicion that it intended to extend military rule subsequently increased. Later in October 1992 Babangida cancelled the presidential primaries, following a report by the NEC confirming that malpractice had occurred. The AFRC further decreed that, owing to bribery during the September polls, the finances of both the SDP and NRC were to be audited, after which both parties would be allowed to proceed with internal restructuring. The NEC was subsequently commissioned to suggest new options for the selection of presidential candidates. The local, state and national committees of both the NRC and SDP were dissolved, and replaced by caretaker committees.

In November 1992 Babangida announced that the presidential election (scheduled for 5 December) was to be postponed until 12 June 1993, and the transition to civilian rule until 27 August. All 23 aspirants who had contested the discredited primaries in September 1992 were disqualified as presidential candidates. Under the new arrangements, the AFRC was to be replaced on 2 January 1993 by a national defence and security council (NDSC), and the council of ministers by a civilian transitional council. However, the national assembly was to be inaugurated on 5 December, as scheduled. Babangida also announced a new programme for the installation of an elected civilian president: the restructured parties were each to nominate a new presidential candidate at a series of congresses, conducted at ward, local government, state and national level; the results of the rescheduled presidential election were to be announced during June.

In December 1992 the bicameral national assembly was formally convened in the new federal capital of Abuja. Although it had been planned as a legislature for the postponed civilian administration, the national assembly was obliged to submit legislation for approval by the AFRC. On 2 January 1993 the NDSC and transitional council were duly installed. The 14-member NDSC was chaired by Babangida, and included the vice-president, the chief of defence staff, the service chiefs, and the inspector-general of police. The transitional council, which comprised 29 members, was to be responsible for federal administration, but was accountable to the NDSC. Its chairman, Chief Ernest Shonekan (a prominent businessman), was officially designated as head of government.

Following the registration of party voters in January 1993, some 300 aspirants to the presidency emerged, including Gowon and Ojukwu (the principal protagonists in the 'Biafran' civil war). The NEC subsequently reviewed candidates in view of the NDSC's criteria. Following party congresses at ward level on 6 February, at local government level on 20 February, and at state level on 6 March, the number of candidates was reduced to 62. (Gowon was defeated at the local government congress on 20 February, while Ojukwu was disqualified by the NEC.)

National party congresses took place, as scheduled, during 27–29 March 1993: the NRC selected Alhaji Bashir Othman Tofa, an economist and businessman, to contest the presidential election, while Chief Moshood Kashimawo Olawale Abiola, a wealthy publisher, emerged as the SDP presidential candidate. In April Abiola chose Baba Kingibe (a former chairman of the SDP) as his vice-presidential candidate, and Tofa selected Dr Sylvester Ugoh, who had served in the Shagari administration. Later that month both Tofa and Abiola began to campaign throughout the country. Meanwhile, a number of informal organizations with diverse agendas emerged; the Association for a Better Nigeria (ABN) demanded the extension of military rule for a further four years, on the grounds of political instability.

In early June 1993 the ABN leadership obtained an interim injunction in the Abuja high court prohibiting the presidential election from taking place, pending the results of its appeal for the extension of military rule until 1997. However, the NEC rejected the injunction as invalid and stated that the election would take place, as scheduled. The rate of participation in the presidential election on 12 June was relatively low, owing, in part, to the confusion occasioned by the Abuja court action, but international monitors throughout Nigeria reported that it had been conducted relatively peacefully. Two days later, initial results, released by the NEC, indicated that of the 6.6m. votes cast in 14 of the 30 states the SDP had secured 4.3m. and the NRC 2.3m. In 11 of the 14 states (including Tofa's home state of Kano), Abiola had obtained the majority of votes. Shortly afterwards, however, the NEC announced that the remaining results would not be released until further notice, following a further injunction, secured by the ABN, that prohibited the promulgation of the results; several other applications were presented in a number of courts, in an attempt to delay or suspend the electoral process. Widespread confusion followed, and protests were voiced that the NDSC (principally through the ABN, which was believed to have connections with Babangida) had deliberately sabotaged the elections. Later in June the CD promulgated election results, which indicated that Abiola had won the majority of votes in 19 states, and Tofa in 11 states. Significantly, Tofa did not challenge these results. The NDSC subsequently attracted increasing domestic and international criticism.

Finally, on 23 June 1993, the NDSC declared the results of the election to be invalid, halted all court proceedings pertaining to the election, suspended the NEC, and repealed all decrees relating to the transition to civilian rule. New electoral regulations were introduced that effectively precluded Abiola and Tofa from contesting a further presidential poll. Babangida subsequently announced that the election had been marred by corruption and other irregularities, but insisted that he remained committed to the transition on 27 August; in order to meet this schedule, a reconstituted NEC was to supervise the selection of two new presidential candidates by the SDP and NRC. Abiola, however, continued to claim, with much popular agreement, that he had been legitimately elected to the presidency. The United Kingdom subsequently announced that it was to review its bilateral relations with Nigeria, and imposed a number of military sanctions, while the USA immediately suspended all assistance to the government.

In early July 1993 a demonstration, organized by the CD, led to rioting, prompted by resentment at political developments, in conjunction with long-standing economic hardship. Order was subsequently restored, after security forces violently suppressed protests; however, sporadic unrest was reported throughout the country. The NDSC provisionally announced that a new presidential election was to take place on 14 August in order to fulfil the pledge to transfer power on 27 August, prompting general disbelief. The SDP declared that it intended to boycott an electoral process that superseded its victory on 12 June. Later in July the NDSC proscribed five national publishing groups, including Concord Press, which was owned by Abiola, and detained a number of supporters of democracy.

'Interim National Government'

At the end of July 1993 Babangida announced that an interim national government (ING) was to be established, on the grounds that there was insufficient time to permit the scheduled transition to civilian rule on 27 August. A committee, comprising officials of the two parties and senior military officers, headed by Aikhomu, was subsequently established to determine the composition of the ING. Abiola immediately declared his opposition to the proposed administration, and stated his intention of forming a 'parallel government'. (He subsequently fled abroad, following alleged death threats, and attempted to solicit international support for his claim to the presidency.) In August the CD continued its campaign of civil disobedience in protest at the annulment of the election, appealing for a three-day general strike (which was widely observed in the south-west of the country, where Abiola received most popular support). Several prominent members of the CD were arrested, in an attempt to prevent further protests, while additional restrictions were imposed on the press. Later in August Babangida announced his resignation, reportedly as a result of pressure from prominent members of the NDSC, notably the secretary of defence, Gen. Sani Abacha. On 27 August a 32-member interim federal executive council, headed by Shonekan, was installed; the new administration, which included several members of the former transitional council, was to supervise the organization of local government elections later that year and a presidential election in early 1994, while the transitional period for the return to civilian rule was extended to 31 March 1994. (Shonekan was later designated as head of state and commander-in-chief of the armed forces.) Supporters of democracy criticized the inclusion in the ING of several members of the former NDSC (which had been dissolved), including Abacha, who was appointed to the new post of vice-president, and the proposed establishment of two predominantly military councils as advisory bodies to the president.

At the end of August 1993 the CD staged a further three-day strike, while the Nigerian Labour Congress (NLC) and the National Union of Petroleum and Natural Gas Workers (NUPENG) also announced industrial action in support of the installation of a civilian administration, headed by Abiola. The combined strike action resulted in a severe fuel shortage and widespread economic disruption. Following the establishment of the ING, Shonekan pledged his commitment to the democratic process, and, in an effort to restore order, initiated negotiations with the NLC and effected the release of several journalists and prominent members of the CD, including Ransome-Kuti, who had been arrested in July. In early September the NLC and NUPENG provisionally suspended strike action, after the ING agreed to consider their demands.

In September 1993 a series of military appointments, which included the nomination of Lt-Gen. Oladipo Diya to the office of chief of defence staff, effectively removed supporters of Babangida from positions of influence within the armed forces, thereby strengthening Abacha's position. Diya, who had reportedly opposed the annulment of the presidential election, subsequently declared that military involvement in politics would cease. In the same month Abiola returned to Lagos, amid popular acclaim. Later in September the NRC and SDP agreed to a new timetable, whereby local government elections and a presidential election would take place concurrently in February 1994. The CD subsequently announced the resumption of strike action in support of demands for the installation of Abiola as president; an ensuing demonstration by supporters of the CD in Lagos was violently dispersed by security forces, and Ransome-Kuti, together with other prominent members of the CD, was arrested. In October the SDP (which had previously demonstrated limited support for Abiola, as a result of dissension within the party) demanded that he be inaugurated as president, and refused to participate in the new elections. In the same month Shonekan established a committee to investigate the circumstances that had resulted in the annulment of the presidential election.

In late October 1993 members of a hitherto unknown organization, the Movement for the Advancement of Democracy (MAD), hijacked a Nigerian aircraft and issued a number of demands, principally that the ING transfer power to Abiola; passengers on the aircraft, who were taken hostage, reportedly included high-ranking Nigerian officials. Abiola disowned the hijackers, and appealed to them to surrender to the authorities. Shortly afterwards the hijackers (who had diverted the aircraft to the Nigerien capital, Niamey) were overpowered by members of the Nigerien security forces, reportedly with the assistance of French troops. Other members of the MAD were later arrested in Lagos.

In early November 1993 the president of the senate, a strong supporter of Abiola, was removed. Shortly afterwards the high court in Lagos State ruled in favour of an application by Abiola, declaring the establishment of the ING to be invalid under the terms of the 1979 constitution (whereby the president of the senate was to act as interim head of state). In the same month the ING dissolved the government councils, prior to local elections, and withdrew state subsidies on petroleum products. The resultant dramatic increase in the price of fuel prompted widespread anti-government demonstrations, and the NLC announced the resumption of strike action. Meanwhile, the proposed revision of the electoral register was undermined by the refusal of supporters of the SDP to participate, and it became clear that the new schedule for the transition to civilian rule could not be met.

Abacha and the PRC

On 17 November 1993, following a meeting with senior military officials, Shonekan announced his resignation as head of state, and immediately transferred power to Abacha (confirming widespread speculation that Abacha had effectively assumed control of the government following Babangida's resignation). On the following day Abacha dissolved all organs of state and bodies that had been established under the transitional process, replaced the state governors with military administrators, prohibited political activity (thereby proscribing the NRC and the SDP), and announced the formation of a provisional ruling council (PRC), which was to comprise senior military officials and the principal members of a new federal executive council (FEC). He insisted, however, that he intended to relinquish power to a civilian government, and pledged to convene a conference with a mandate to determine the constitutional future of the country. Restrictions on the media were suspended, and the ban that had been imposed on certain publishing groups in July was revoked. Ensuing demonstrations by supporters of democracy were suppressed by security forces (although protests were generally limited). On 21 November Abacha introduced legislation that formally restored the 1979 constitution and provided for the establishment of the new government organs. In an apparent attempt to counter domestic and international criticism, several prominent supporters of Abiola, including Kingibe, and four former members of the ING were appointed to the PRC and FEC, which were installed on 24 November. Abacha subsequently removed 17 senior military officers, who were believed to be loyal to Babangida. In the same month discussions between Abacha and Abiola took place, while the NLC agreed to abandon strike action after the government acted to limit the increase in the price of petroleum products.

In December 1993 controversy arose over the mandate of the proposed constitutional conference, which, Abacha stated, was not to include the issue of devolution of federal government powers. The CD dismissed the conference plan as an attempt to legitimize the new administration. In the same month the United Kingdom announced that member countries of the European Union (EU) were to impose further sanctions against Nigeria, including restrictions on the export of armaments.

In April 1994 the government announced its proposals for the establishment of the national constitutional conference (NCC): some 273 delegates were to be elected in May, while 96 delegates were to be nominated by the government from a list of eligible citizens submitted by each state. The national constitutional conference was to be convened at the end of June, and was to submit recommendations, including a new draft constitution, to the PRC in late October. A further stage in the transitional programme was to commence in mid-January 1995, when the ban on political activity was to end. In May 1994, however, a new pro-democracy organization, comprising former politicians, retired military officers and human rights activists, the National Democratic Coalition (NADECO), demanded that Abacha relinquish power by the end of that month and urged a boycott of the NCC. Later in May, however, elections duly took place at ward, and subsequently at local government, level to select the 273 conference delegates; the boycott was widely observed in the south-west of the country, and a low level of voter participation was reported. In the same month Ken Saro-Wiwa, the leader of MOSOP, was arrested in connection with the deaths of four Ogoni electoral candidates. At the end of May Abiola announced his intention of forming a government of national unity by 12 June (the anniversary of the presidential election). Violent anti-government protests followed the expiry of the date stipulated by NADECO for the resignation of the military administration.

In early June 1994 members of the former senate (including its president) were detained on charges of treason, after the senators reconvened and declared the government to be illegal. A number of prominent opposition members, including Ransome-Kuti, were also arrested, after the CD urged a campaign of civil disobedience, which received the support of NADECO. (Ransome-Kuti was subsequently charged with treason.) Following a symbolic ceremony, in which Abiola was publicly inaugurated as president and head of a parallel government, a warrant was issued for his arrest on charges of treason; the authorities alleged that he intended to organize an uprising to remove the military administration from power. Later in June security forces arrested Abiola (who had emerged from hiding to attend a rally in Lagos), prompting protests from pro-democracy organizations and criticism from the governments of the United Kingdom and the USA. Further demonstrations in support of demands for an immediate suspension of military rule and the installation of Abiola as president ensued, while NUPENG threatened to initiate strike action unless the government agreed to release Abiola.

At the initial session of the NCC, which was convened on schedule at the end of June 1994, Abacha pledged to relinquish power on a date that would be determined by the conference. (The conference subsequently established committees to consider a number of contentious issues, including that of the annulment of the presidential election in 1993.) In early July the minister of justice was charged with contempt of court, after the government failed to comply with two orders from the high court in Abuja to justify the continued imprisonment of Abiola, who had challenged the legality of his detention. Shortly afterwards, a special high court that had been appointed by the government formally indicted Abiola for 'treasonable felony.'

In early July 1994 NUPENG initiated strike action in support of dual demands for Abiola's release and installation as president, and an increase in government investment in the petroleum industry; the strike was subsequently joined by the senior petroleum workers' union, the Petroleum and Natural Gas Senior Staff Association (PENGASSAN). Government troops distributed fuel in an attempt to ease the resultant national shortage, while it was reported that senior officials of NUPENG and PENGASSAN had been arrested. By mid-July members of affiliate unions in a number of sectors had joined the strike action, resulting in an effective suspension of economic activity in Lagos and other commercially significant regions in the south-west of the country. However, the national impact of the strike was constrained by ethnic and regional divisions; it was reported that unions in northern and eastern regions had failed to join strike action. In addition, petroleum exports were initially unaffected, largely owing to expatriate workers who failed to observe the strike. Later in July union officials suspended negotiations with the government, on the grounds that the authorities had failed to release the secretary-general of NUPENG from detention. At the end of July it was reported that some 20 people had been killed, when security forces violently supressed anti-government demonstrations. Meanwhile, the US special envoy in Nigeria, Rev. Jesse Jackson, announced that the USA was considering the imposition of further sanctions. In early August the NLC initiated an indefinite general strike in support of NUPENG; following the suppression of further anti-government protests, in which about five demonstrators were killed, however, the NLC suspended strike action after two days to allow negotiations with the government to proceed.

In early August 1994 Abiola's trial was adjourned, pending a ruling regarding a defence appeal that the high court in Abuja had no jurisdiction in the case of an offence that had allegedly been committed in Lagos. Abiola (who was reported to be in poor health) refused to accept bail, since the stipulated conditions required him to refrain from political activity. The court finally decided that it had the necessary jurisdiction, although the presiding judge withdrew from the trial. In the same month the authorities banned the national newspaper, *The Guardian*, following the publication of a report suggesting that divisions existed within the government as to whether to proceed with the charges against Abiola. Later in August Abacha replaced the senior officials of NUPENG and PENGASSAN, and ordered petroleum workers to end strike action. Although a number of union members failed to comply, the effects of the strike soon began to recede: in early September the union officials who had been dismissed suspended the strike action, on the grounds of the widespread hardship that would result from its effects on the economy. In the same month Abacha promulgated legislation that extended the period of detention without trial to three months and prohibited legal action challenging government decisions. The minister of justice was subsequently dismissed, after protesting that he had not been consulted regarding the new legislation. In mid-September the state military administrators were reshuffled. Later that month Abacha reconstituted the PRC, which was enlarged from 11 to 25 members, all of whom were senior military officials.

In late September 1994 Wole Soyinka, a prominent critic of the government (who had received the Nobel Prize for Literature in 1986), legally challenged the legitimacy of the Abacha regime at the federal high court. In the following month the court ruled that Abiola's detention was illegal and awarded him substantial financial compensation. Nevertheless, Abiola remained in detention pending the outcome of other legal action before the federal court of appeal in Kaduna.

In October 1994 the NCC adopted constitutional proposals providing for a 'rotational presidency', whereby the office would be held alternately by northerners and southerners; other elective posts, including state governorships, were to be held successively, for a transitional period, by representatives of the territorial districts. In addition, the NCC envisaged a power-sharing arrangement, whereby any political party that secured a minimum of 10% of the seats in the legislature would be guaranteed representation in the government. Under a proposed transitional timetable, a new constitution was to be adopted by March 1995, the ban on political activity was to be rescinded, and multi-party elections were to take place at local and national level in 1996, prior to the installation of a new government in January 1997. In October 1994 Abacha replaced the minister of finance, who had supported the programme of economic liberalization that had been abandoned by the government in January. In November the NCC adopted further constitutional recommendations, providing for the creation of three vice-presidents and the establishment of a federal council of traditional rulers, which would function in an advisory capacity.

In early November 1994 the federal court of appeal in Kaduna granted Abiola unconditional bail; however, the government refused to release Abiola, on the grounds that he was charged with a capital offence. In the same month the human rights organization, Amnesty International, accused the Abacha regime of imprisoning or executing large numbers of opposition members, and particularly condemned violations of human rights that had allegedly been perpetrated against members of the Ogoni ethnic group in an effort to suppress protests at environmental damage caused by petroleum production in Rivers State. In early December the federal court of appeal in Kaduna rescinded its previous ruling granting Abiola bail, and directed that Abiola remain in custody in the interests of national security.

In December 1994 the NCC accepted a proposal that the government relinquish power on 1 January 1996, on the grounds that a prolonged transitional period would result in a further deterioration of the economy; it was agreed that the PRC would draft a new transitional timetable in accordance with the decisions of the conference. In January 1995 Abacha announced the adoption of a new programme of economic reforms, which was designed to secure the approval of the International Monetary Fund (see Economy). In the same month the NCC, which had been scheduled to complete preparations for a draft constitution in October 1994, adjourned until March 1995, prompting increasing impatience that its protracted deliberations were serving to prolong the tenure of the military administration. The trial of Saro-Wiwa and a further 14 MOSOP activists, on charges of complicity in the murder of the four Ogoni traditional leaders, commenced in mid-January 1995; the defendants were to challenge the legitimacy of the special military tribunal, which had been appointed by the government. In February the federal court of appeal dismissed Abiola's legal action challenging the jurisdiction of the high court in Abuja.

In February 1995 Abacha dissolved the FEC, after a number of ministers announced their intention of engaging in political activity in the forthcoming transitional period. In March some 150 military officials were arrested, apparently in response to widespread disaffection within the armed forces. The authorities subsequently confirmed reports (which had initially been denied) of a coup conspiracy. (However, opponents of the Abacha regime claimed that it had fabricated a coup attempt, with the aim of suppressing dissent within the armed forces.) Reports that about 80 members of the armed forces had been summarily executed were officially denied. However, the arrest of the former head of state, Olusegun Obasanjo and his former deputy, Maj.-Gen. Yar'Adua, together with other prominent critics of the government, prompted international protests. In mid-March Abacha reconstituted the FEC, whose 36 members included a number of civilians who were believed to favour an extended period of military rule.

In April 1995 the NCC endorsed the constitutional proposals that had been approved in late 1994. At the end of that month, however, the conference adopted a motion reversing its previous decision that a civilian government be installed on 1 January 1996, on the grounds that the requisite timetable was untenable. The NCC subsequently undertook the incorporation of the necessary amendments to the constitutional recommendations, which were to be submitted for approval by the government. The trial of Saro-Wiwa (which had been suspended while he received medical treatment) resumed in late May. At the end of that month a curfew was imposed in Kano, following ethnic clashes in which five people were killed. In early June it was reported that a number of pro-democracy campaigners had been arrested, following a bomb attack at an official function in Kwara State, in which three people were killed. In the same month about 40 people, including several civilians, were arraigned before a special military tribunal in connection with the alleged coup attempt in March; it was reported that Obasanjo and Yar'Adua had also been secretly charged with conspiring to overthrow the government. Further arrests of pro-democracy activists took place later in June, in an effort by the government to pre-empt protests on the anniversary of the annulled presidential election; nevertheless, a one-day general strike, supported by the CD, was widely observed.

In June 1995 the NCC formally presented proposals for a draft constitution to Abacha, who rescinded the ban on political activity. The PRC was to approve the constitutional recommendations within a period of three months, whereupon Abacha was to announce, on 1 October, a programme for transition to civilian rule. (A number of political organizations subsequently emerged.) At the end of June reports emerged that the military tribunal had sentenced Obasanjo to 25 years' imprisonment for his alleged involvement in the coup attempt, while Yar'Adua and a further 13 military officers had received the death penalty. Numerous international protests and appeals for clemency ensued. Despite indications that the Nigerian government would yield to these pressures, at the end of July a military council ratified the death sentences, which were subject to confirmation by the PRC. Eventually, in early October the PRC commuted the death sentences and reduced the terms of imprisonment. The capital charges against Abiola were not withdrawn. Concurrently, Abacha announced a three-year programme for transition to civilian rule, whereby a new president was to be inaugurated on 1 October 1998, following elections at local, state and national level; the duration of the transitional period was received with international disapproval. New constitutional provisions, which generally accorded with the recommendations of the NCC and were to be formally adopted later in 1995, included the restoration of a multi-party system (whereby any party attaining 10 seats or more in the national assembly would be proportionately represented in the FEC), the division of the country into six regions (and the allocation, in rotation, of the presidency and other principal executive and legislative offices to these regions for a period of 30 years), and the establishment of a national judicial council and constitutional court.

At the end of October 1995 Saro-Wiwa and a further eight Ogoni activists were sentenced to death by the special military tribunal; six other defendants, including the deputy president of MOSOP, were acquitted. Although the defendants were not implicated directly in the incident, the nine convictions were based on the premise that the MOSOP activists had effectively incited the killings. An international campaign (led by Saro-Wiwa's son) against the convictions, and numerous appeals for clemency, ensued (although the Nigerian opposition criticized a number of foreign governments, notably that of South Africa, for favouring a diplomatic approach rather than the imposition of sanctions against Nigeria). However, on 10 November (the same day as a Commonwealth summit meeting, which was to discuss, *inter alia*, events in Nigeria, was convened in Auckland, New Zealand) the nine convicted Ogonis were executed, prompting immediate condemnation by the international community. Nigeria was suspended from the Commonwealth, and threatened with expulsion if the government failed to restore democracy within a period of two years; only The Gambia voted against the suspension. Later that month the EU reaffirmed its commitment to existing sanctions that had been imposed in 1993 (notably an embargo on the export of armaments and military equipment to Nigeria), and extended visa restrictions to civilian members of the administration; the EU also announced the suspension of development co-operation with Nigeria. The governments of the USA, South Africa and the EU member nations recalled their diplomatic representatives from Nigeria in protest at the executions. However, both the United Kingdom and the USA (which suspended military exports to Nigeria) failed to support demands now made by the South African president, Nelson Mandela, for the imposition of an embargo on petroleum imports from Nigeria, seemingly owing to domestic economic considerations. The Shell Petroleum Development Co of Nigeria (which had suspended operations in Ogoniland in 1993, following attacks on its installations) confirmed that it intended to proceed with a natural gas project at Bonny Island, in Rivers State, despite having attracted international criticism for its alleged complicity with the Nigerian regime in suppressing Ogoni activism and for its failure to prevent the executions. The Nigerian government condemned the imposition of sanctions as an international conspiracy to overthrow the administration, and, in turn, withdrew its diplomatic representatives from the USA, South Africa and the EU member countries. Additional security forces were dispatched to Ogoniland to deter any protests against the executions while a further 19 Ogonis were charged with complicity in the May 1994 murders. (However, their trial was subsequently postponed, pending an appeal to the effect that the special military tribunal at Port Harcourt was unconstitutional.) In late November the government established a committee of traditional rulers to advise the FEC in view of Nigeria's increasing isolation within the international community, and initiated a public relations campaign to counter the country's reputation for corruption. Opponents of the government alleged that it had financed advertisements in defence of the executions, placed in foreign newspapers by relatives of the four murdered Ogoni leaders.

In early December 1995 Abacha approved the establishment of a number of committees, including the national electoral commission of Nigeria (NECON), to implement the transitional programme. NECON subsequently divided the country into seven regions (rather than six, as originally envisaged), prior to local government elections in early 1996. In the same month an *ad hoc* meeting of the Southern African Development Community, which was convened in Pretoria, South Africa, at Mandela's instigation, was attended by only five of the 12 member heads of state; the secretary-general of the Organization of African Unity (OAU) also failed to support Mandela's demands for sanctions. Later in December a Commonwealth 'action group', comprising eight member countries' ministers with responsibility for foreign affairs, which had been established at the summit meeting in November, met to discuss further measures to be taken if the Nigerian government failed to restore democratic government, and announced that five of the ministers were to visit Nigeria to initiate negotiations with the military regime. (The diplomatic representatives who had been withdrawn following the executions in November subsequently returned to Lagos, in order to facilitate the Commonwealth mission.) The UN general assembly adopted a resolution condemning the executions (although countries that abstained from voting included two members of the Commonwealth 'action group', Ghana and Malaysia). At the end of December the minister of youth and sports announced that Nigeria was to withdraw from the African group of nations football tournaments in 1998 and in 2000, apparently as a political reprisal against South Africa.

In January 1996 the government announced that the Commonwealth ministerial delegation would only be granted permission to visit Nigeria if the organization undertook to investigate alleged violations of human rights perpetrated in other countries, and demanded that the decision to suspend Nigeria be reviewed. In the same month two minor bomb attacks were reported in northern Nigeria, at Kano and Kaduna. A government minister subsequently accused Wole Soyinka of complicity in the incidents, on the grounds that the instigator of one of the bombings had apparently been in possession of one of Soyinka's works. At the end of January the government announced that the new constitution would be formally adopted in 1998, upon the completion of the transitional period (rather than in late 1995, as proposed in Abacha's original statement).

In February 1996 the 19 Ogonis who remained in detention pending their trial appealed to the Commonwealth for assistance in securing their release. In the same month the South African administration denied accusations by Nigeria that it had assisted exiled opponents of the government. In March a UN mission was dispatched to Nigeria (at the latter's request) to investigate the trial and execution of the nine Ogoni activists in 1995. (However, the government continued to refuse to receive the Commonwealth ministerial delegation.) Also in March 1996 local government elections, which were contested on a non-party basis, took place as part of the transitional programme; although opposition leaders had urged a boycott, NECON claimed that a high level of voter participation had been recorded. In April the UN investigative mission visited Ogoniland, where sizeable anti-government demonstrations had taken place; it was reported that Ogoni activists and other opposition representatives were prevented from meeting the delegation. Later that month, following the government's continued refusal to enter into negotiations with the ministerial group regarding human rights issues and the restoration of democracy, the Commonwealth proposed to adopt a number of sanctions against Nigeria. In May the PRC was reorganized, following the removal of a number of senior military officials.

In early June 1996 Abiola's wife, Kudirat, who had been a prominent critic of the administration, was killed by unidentified assailants. Although the authorities conducted an investigation of the crime, widespread speculation that the government had ordered the killing increased general hostility towards the regime. The university at Ibadan was temporarily closed, following a demonstration, led by students, in protest at the alleged assassination. Abiola's son and a number of his other immediate relatives were subsequently arrested, apparently on suspicion of complicity in the murder. Four members of NADECO were also detained in connection with the incident. Later in June Nigerian officials met the Commonwealth 'action group' in an attempt to avert the threatened imposition of sanctions against Nigeria; shortly before the discussions took place, the government released a number of political prisoners, and promulgated legislation regarding the registration of political parties, in an apparent effort to conciliate critics. The Nigerian delegation demanded that Nigeria be readmitted to the Commonwealth in exchange for the government's adoption of the programme for transition to civilian rule by October 1998. The Commonwealth rejected the programme as unsatisfactory, but remained divided regarding the adoption of consequent measures. It was finally agreed that the Commonwealth would suspend the adoption of sanctions, but that the situation would be reviewed at a further meeting of the 'action group', which was scheduled for September. Canada, however, announced its opposition to this decision and unilaterally imposed a number of sanctions (similar to those already adopted by the EU), including the suspension of military co-operation, the introduction of visa restrictions for members of the administration and their relatives and the cessation of sporting connections.

The legislation that had been promulgated in June 1996 governing the formation of political parties was generally considered to be extremely restrictive, and included a prohibition on associations holding assets abroad. Only 15 of a large number of newly-emerged organizations had applied for registration by the stipulated date in late July; NECON was to begin to confirm the legalization of these parties in September. In August new state military administrators were appointed. In the same month the government, which had agreed to receive the Commonwealth ministerial delegation, imposed a number of restrictions on its visit, claiming that it had already co-operated with the UN mission.

In September 1996 a large demonstration by Muslims in Kaduna, staged in protest at the arrest of their local leader (who had allegedly made broadcasts likely to incite rioting), was violently dispersed by government troops; it was reported that about 50 people had been killed. At the end of that month five of the 15 political organizations that had applied for registration were granted legal status. NADECO condemned the disqualification of the remaining 10 parties, which were subsequently dissolved by decree; it was widely believed that the associations that had been granted registration were largely sympathetic towards the military administration. In early October Abacha announced the creation of a further six states, increasing the total size of the federation to 36 states. At the same time he announced the establishment of a committee of economic representatives, chaired by the former head of state, Chief Ernest Shonekan, which was to draft the government's future policy for economic development (see Economy).

At the end of September 1996 the ministerial 'action group' agreed that the Commonwealth delegation would visit Nigeria, despite the continued insistence of the military authorities that it would not be permitted access to opposition activists or political prisoners. The Canadian minister of foreign affairs accused other members of the 'action group' of adopting a conciliatory stance towards the Nigerian administration. The Canadian representative subsequently withdrew from the delegation, which visited Nigeria in November, after two Canadian security officials were refused entry visas. Later in November the EU renewed its sanctions against Nigeria for a further six months. In December the Nigerian government rejected a UN resolution criticizing its alleged violations of human rights. In February 1997 a planned mission to Nigeria by the UN Human Rights Commission was abandoned, after the government refused to allow it access to political detainees. In the same month a meeting of the Commonwealth ministerial 'action group' failed to reach a decision regarding sanctions; Nigerian opposition movements were invited to submit evidence of human rights' violations to the group. The ministerial group was subsequently to prepare recommendations for submission to a Commonwealth summit meeting in October.

A bomb attack in Lagos in December 1996 was widely interpreted as an attempt to assassinate the state administrator, who was a close associate of Abacha. In February 1997 Abacha attributed delays in the holding of local government elections (which had been rescheduled for March) to a further series of bomb attacks in Lagos, in which, it was reported, about six people had been killed and 40 injured; he also indicated that he intended to contest the presidential election in 1998. International observers, including a US monitoring group, declared that the local government elections, which took place accordingly in mid-March, had been conducted peacefully; it was reported that the United Nigerian Congress Party had secured the highest number of seats in the municipal councils. In the same month, after repeatedly accusing NADECO of responsibility for the bomb attacks, the government charged Soyinka and a further 15 pro-democracy activists, including several NADECO leaders, of treason in connection with the incidents. (Soyinka and a further three of the accused were charged *in absentia*.) In March 1997 the Canadian government suspended its diplomatic representation in Nigeria.

In early 1997 escalating tension between the Ijaw and Itsekiri ethnic groups in the town of Warri, south-west of Nigeria, severely disrupted Shell's petroleum-mining operations in the region. In March a demonstration by members of the Ijaw ethnic group in Warri, in protest at the relocation of local government headquarters from Ijaw to Itsekiri territory, precipitated violent clashes. Protesters seized Shell installations and took about 100 employees of the enterprise hostage, in an attempt to force the government to accede to their demands. A curfew was subsequently imposed in the region in an attempt to restore order. By mid-April it was reported that about 90 people had been killed in the disturbances, while the disruption in petroleum production had contributed to a national fuel shortage, effectively suspending the transportation system in much of the country. The government dispatched armed forces to the region in an attempt to quell the unrest. In early May it appeared that a peace settlement had been reached, following a meeting between leaders of the Ijaw and Itsekiri communities. However, the abduction and killing of two Ijaw in Warri precipitated a resumption in hostilities, and further attacks on Shell installations ensued. Later in May the authorities established a commission of inquiry, which was to investigate the cause of the clashes and submit recommendations for restoring order in the region.

In April 1997 Abacha issued a decree empowering himself to replace the mayors who had been elected in March and to dissolve local municipal councils if he considered that they were acting contrary to national interests. In the same month the UN Human Rights Commission voted in favour of appointing a special investigator for Nigeria, in view of continued violations of human rights by the authorities. In May some 22 pro-democracy and human rights organizations, including MOSOP and the CD, formed a loose alliance, the United Action for Democracy (UAD), with the aim of campaigning for the restoration of democracy in Nigeria. UAD announced that the organization would participate in the forthcoming elections providing that

Abacha did not seek re-election to the presidency, and adopted a programme of demands, which included the release of political detainees, the formation of a government of national unity and the convening of a sovereign national conference. It was reported that UAD planned to organize a nationwide campaign of civil disobedience, with one-day general strikes, to force Abacha to relinquish power. Also in May a total of four people were killed in a further series of bomb attacks, which took place in Lagos, Ibadan and Onitsha (in Anambra State). NADECO denied reiterated claims by the authorities that the organization was responsible for the attacks.

In June 1997 the minister of petroleum resources, Dan Etete, dismissed the directors of the Nigerian Liquefied National Gas Co (NLNG), prompting concern regarding the implementation of the national gas project at Bonny Island by a consortium of the Nigerian National Petroleum Corpn and foreign enterprises, including Shell (see Economy); it was reported that Etete had objected to contractual terms entitling Shell to nominate the NLNG's managing director. In July the authorities announced a new electoral timetable: elections to the state assemblies were to take place on 6 December, followed by elections to the national assembly on 25 April 1998, and presidential and gubernatorial elections on 1 August of that year (despite previous indications that the gubernatorial elections were to be held in late 1997). Although it was confirmed that the new elected organs of government would be installed by 1 October 1998, the rescheduling of the gubernatorial elections was criticized by opposition groups, which voiced concern that the transfer to democratic rule would not be completed on the stipulated date. Also in July 1997 the government of the United Kingdom indicated that it would not accept the re-election of Abacha to the presidency unless reforms to the electoral process, particularly regarding the registration of political parties, were adopted. At the end of that month four prominent opposition members in exile, including Soyinka, were sought by the authorities for alleged involvement in terrorist activities.

REGIONAL RELATIONS

Nigeria has taken a leading role in African affairs and is a prominent member of the Economic Community of West African States (ECOWAS) and other regional organizations. The Nigerian government contributed a significant number of troops to the ECOWAS Monitoring Group (ECOMOG), which was deployed in Liberia from August 1990 in response to the conflict between government forces and rebels in that country (see chapter on Liberia). By mid-1996, the Nigerian contingent deployed in Liberia had been reduced to number about 6,000. However, Nigeria, together with a number of other West African states, dispatched additional troops to Liberia to support the holding of elections in July 1997 (see Recent History of Liberia). In 1993 Nigerian troops were dispatched to Sierra Leone, in response to a formal request by the Sierra Leonean government for military assistance to repulse attacks by rebels in that country. Following a military coup in Sierra Leone in May 1997, the Nigerian government demanded that the newly-installed junta relinquish power, and increased its military strength in the Sierra Leonean capital, Freetown, to about 4,000 troops. In early June Nigerian forces initiated a naval bombardment of Freetown in an unsuccessful attempt to force the reinstatement of the ousted government; some 300 troops were captured by supporters of the coup leaders (assisted by members of the rebel Revolutionary United Front—RUF), but were later released. Meanwhile, the leader of the RUF, Corporal Foday Sankoh, remained in detention in Nigeria (after being arrested there in March).

In mid-1997 the Developing Eight (D8) group, comprising Nigeria, Turkey, Indonesia, Egypt, Pakistan, Malaysia, Bangladesh and Iran, was inaugurated in Istanbul, Turkey; D8 was formed to promote economic co-operation between the eight Islamic nations. In mid-1993 the United Kingdom, together with other European nations and the USA, imposed military sanctions against Nigeria, in response to the suspension of the scheduled transition to civilian rule. Further sanctions were adopted in late 1995 (see above). In May 1997 the Nigerian government imposed an indefinite ban on flights from the United Kingdom, after Nigerian-registered aircraft were banned from British airports on the grounds that they failed to meet safety standards.

In 1991 the Nigerian government claimed that Cameroonian security forces had annexed several Nigerian fishing settlements in Cross River State (in south-eastern Nigeria), following a long-standing border dispute, based on a 1913 agreement between Germany and the United Kingdom that ceded the Bakassi peninsula in the Gulf of Guinea (a region of strategic significance) to the German protectorate of Kamerun; Cameroon's claim to the region was upheld by an unratified agreement in 1975. Subsequent negotiations between Nigerian and Cameroonian officials in an effort to resolve the dispute achieved little progress. In December 1993 some 500 Nigerian troops were dispatched to the region, in response to a number of incidents in which Nigerian nationals had been killed by Cameroonian security forces. Later that month the two nations agreed to establish a joint patrol at the disputed area, and to investigate the cause of the incidents. In February 1994, however, the Nigerian government increased the number of troops deployed in the region. Later in February Cameroon announced that it was to submit the dispute for adjudication by the UN, the OAU, and the International Court of Justice (ICJ), and requested military assistance from France. Subsequent reports of clashes between Cameroonian and Nigerian forces in the region prompted fears of a full-scale conflict between the two nations. In March Cameroon agreed to enter into bilateral negotiations with Nigeria (without the involvement of international mediators) to resolve the issue. Later that month, however, a proposal by the Nigerian government that a referendum be conducted in the disputed region was rejected by Cameroon. Also in March the OAU urged the withdrawal of troops from the region; both governments indicated dissatisfaction with the resolution. In May two members of the Nigerian armed forces were killed in further clashes in the region. Later that month negotiations between the two nations, which were mediated by Togo, resumed in the Cameroonian capital, Yaoundé. In June the heads of state of the two nations met at an OAU summit meeting in Tunis, Tunisia, and agreed to establish a joint committee to achieve a resolution to the dispute. However, a meeting to discuss the issue, which was scheduled to take place in July, was postponed, owing to the unrest in Nigeria. In September 10 members of the Cameroonian armed forces were killed in further confrontations.

In February 1996 renewed hostilities between Nigerian and Cameroonian forces in the Bakassi region resulted in several casualties. Later that month, however, Nigeria and Cameroon agreed to refrain from further military action, and delegations from the two countries resumed discussions, with mediation by the Togolese president, in an attempt to resolve the dispute. In March the ICJ ruled that Cameroon had failed to provide sufficient evidence to support its contention that Nigeria had provoked the border conflict, and ordered both nations to cease military operations, to withdraw troops to former positions, and to co-operate with a UN investigative mission that was to be dispatched to the region. In April, however, clashes continued, with each government accusing the other of initiating the attacks. Although tension in the region remained high, diplomatic efforts to avoid further conflict increased in May; in that month a Cameroonian delegation visited Nigeria, while Abacha accepted an invitation to attend an OAU summit meeting, which was convened in Yaoundé in July. The UN investigative mission visited the Bakassi region in September. In December, however, the Nigerian authorities claimed that Cameroonian troops had resumed attacks in the region. In May 1997 the Cameroonian government denied further allegations by Nigeria that it had initiated hostilities; it was reported that the UN had requested that the Togolese president continue mediation efforts.

Economy

LINDA VAN BUREN

Despite considerable agricultural and mineral resources, Nigeria is ranked by the World Bank as a low-income country. In 1996, according to government estimates, Nigeria's gross national product (GNP), measured at constant 1994 prices, was US $31,651m., equivalent to $279 per head. During 1985–95, it was estimated, GNP per head increased, in real terms, at an average annual rate of 1.2%, while the population increased by an annual average of 2.9%. Nigeria's gross domestic product (GDP) increased, in real terms, by an annual average of 4.1% during 1985–95. The IMF estimated real GDP growth at 2.2% in 1995.

Statistical assessments of the Nigerian economy are subject to wide margins of error, as a result of the lack of reliable data. The census of November 1991 recorded a total of 88,514,501 inhabitants, while the population was officially estimated at 97,223,521 inhabitants at mid-1995. In 1985–95 the population increased by an annual average of 2.9%. According to figures (excluding the contribution of unofficial trade) from the Federal Office of Statistics, the leading economic activities are agriculture, livestock, forestry and fishing, which accounted for 35.5% of GDP in 1996, followed by crude petroleum and gas (34.5%), and wholesale and retail trade (15.3%).

The development of the petroleum industry in the late 1960s and 1970s radically transformed Nigeria from an agriculturally-based economy to a major oil exporter. Increased earnings from petroleum exports generated high levels of real economic growth, and by the mid-1970s Nigeria ranked as the dominant economy in sub-Saharan Africa and as the continent's major exporter of petroleum. Following the decline in world petroleum prices after 1981, however, the government became increasingly over-extended financially, with insufficient revenue from petroleum to pay the rising cost of imports or to finance major development projects. The decline in Nigeria's earnings of foreign exchange led to an accumulation of arrears in trade debts and of import shortages, which, in turn, resulted in a sharp fall in economic activity, with most of Nigerian industry struggling to operate without essential imported raw materials and spare parts. A series of poor harvests, an overvalued currency and a widening budget deficit compounded the problem. The Buhari government responded to the crisis by implementing a range of severe austerity measures, including further cuts in public expenditure, and rigid restrictions on credit and the availability of foreign exchange.

The Babangida military government, which took power in August 1985, continued its predecessor's policies of austerity and monetary control. Babangida declared a state of economic emergency, under which the import of rice and maize was banned, and a national recovery fund was created. However, the dramatic fall in international prices for petroleum in 1986, together with reduced output in all sectors (except agriculture), kept the economy in the depths of recession. In July 1986 the Babangida government announced a two-year structural adjustment programme (SAP), which aimed at expanding non-oil exports, reducing the import of goods which could be manufactured locally, achieving self-sufficiency in food and increasing the role of the private sector. The SAP included the abolition of import licences and a reduction in import duties. One of its principal features, however, was the creation, in September, of two rates for foreign exchange transactions; a first 'tier', which the government used for foreign debt-servicing and other specified outgoings, and a second-tier foreign exchange market (SFEM) for commercial transactions. SFEM rates were determined by means of auctions of available foreign exchange, conducted by the Central Bank. In July 1987 the two-tier exchange mechanism was replaced by fortnightly auctions at a unitary foreign exchange market (FEM). In January 1991 the auction system was replaced; the Central Bank of Nigeria (CBN) was henceforth to fix the rate in consultation with leading commercial banks. The government also permitted the establishment of bureaux de change, which were to sell as much as $30,000 of foreign exchange at market rates that represented a variable premium over the official CBN rate.

In early 1988 the government issued a list of 110 state enterprises to be 'privatized' or partially commercialized. A special technical committee was established to implement the programme, which was to involve the Nigerian Railway Corpn, the National Electric Power Authority, and the telecommunications conglomerate, NITEL. By the end of 1992 90 of the 120 enterprises scheduled for 'privatization', including 12 commercial banks in which the government had a shareholding, had been sold, while the transfer to private ownership of Nigeria Airways and the Nigerian National Shipping Line was also envisaged.

Measures undertaken under the SAP with the aim of attracting private capital from abroad proved largely unsuccessful; investors were deterred by the country's reputation for corruption, and by the government's failure to control expenditure. The budget deficit began to expand rapidly, reaching the equivalent of 11.4% of GDP in 1988 and increasing to more than 12% of GDP in subsequent years. Economic instability was also reflected in a persistently high rate of inflation, which increased from an annual average of 24.0% in 1986–91, to 44.6% in 1992, to 57.2% in 1993, and to 72.8% in 1995. However, official figures indicated that inflation had declined to 28% in 1996. It was reported that in the year to the end of March 1996 the prices of important commodities, such as *garri* (cassava flour), rice and beans, had increased by 100%. The SAP was abandoned in 1994, following a severe deterioration in political and economic conditions in the early 1990s.

In 1994 the Abacha government introduced a fixed exchange rate of ₦22.00 = US $1, and selective import controls, but these policies proved unsuccessful and were replaced in 1995 with a return to earlier adjustment policies, allowing the naira to float more freely, and new measures that favoured foreign investment. However, the government's actions were often contrary to official policy, reflecting a desire to impose administrative and sectional control of both the petroleum industry and the banking system.

The political instability since the early 1990s has severely impeded the ability of successive governments to implement economic policies and has also adversely affected international confidence in the economy. The international community has taken punitive measures against Nigeria (see Recent History), with detrimental effects on the economy.

AGRICULTURE

Until Nigeria attained independence in 1960, agriculture was the most important sector of the economy, accounting for more than one-half of GDP and for more than three-quarters of export earnings. However, with the rapid expansion of the petroleum industry, agricultural development was neglected, and the sector entered a relative decline. Between the mid-1960s and the mid-1980s, Nigeria moved from a position of self-sufficiency in basic foodstuffs to one of heavy dependence on imports. Under-investment, a steady drift away from the land to urban centres, increased consumer preference for imported foodstuffs (particularly rice and wheat) and outdated farming techniques continued to keep the level of food production well behind the rate of population growth. After experiencing growth rates of 8%–10% per annum during the early 1970s, the increase in agricultural production declined to around 4% per annum towards the end of the decade. The slow growth continued into the 1980s, with output rising by only 3.4% in 1981 and by 2.7% in 1982. The effects of drought and the government's austerity programme resulted in a severe 9.4% fall in agricultural output in 1983. However, a succession of good harvests, higher producer prices, reductions in cereal imports and a resurgence of public and private investment in crop production resulted in a sharp recovery in production. Food output showed the strongest growth, rising by 7% in 1984 and by an estimated 10% in 1985, when total agricultural output increased by 3.8%. Agriculture was the only sector to show any significant expansion in 1986, when, owing to further record harvests of rice and maize, overall agricultural production increased by 2.1%. Agriculture (including hunting, forestry and fishing) contributed 35.5% of GDP in 1996, when the sector increased by 3.8%. An estimated 70% of the labour force were employed in the sector in that year.

Traditional smallholder farmers, who use simple techniques of production and the bush-fallow system of cultivation, account for around two-thirds of Nigeria's total agricultural production. The number of state farms is relatively small, and of decreasing importance. Since 1986 many of the loss-making parastatal bodies have been closed down or sold to the private sector. Subsistence food crops (mainly sorghum, maize, taro, yams, cassava, rice and millet) are grown in the central and western areas of Nigeria, and are traded largely outside the cash economy. Cash crops (mainly palm kernels, coffee, cotton, cocoa, rubber and groundnuts) are grown in the mid-west and north of the country. In June 1986 six federal commodity marketing boards ceased trading (they were formally abolished in 1987); the abolition of agricultural marketing monopolies, combined with a devalued naira, contributed to an increase in producer prices and output. Owing to these measures, production of cash crops increased considerably in 1988.

Among the agricultural crops, only cocoa makes any significant contribution to exports, but Nigeria's share of the world cocoa market has been substantially reduced in recent years, owing to ageing trees, low producer prices, black pod disease, smuggling and labour shortages. Moreover, the abolition of the Cocoa Marketing Board in 1986 led to poor quality control and fraudulent trading practices, which adversely affected the market reputation of Nigerian cocoa. The government subsequently reintroduced licences for marketers of cocoa and improved inspection procedures. Recent emphasis has been placed on encouraging domestic cocoa-processing to provide higher-value products for export. According to the International Cocoa Organization, cocoa production in Nigeria fell from 165,000 tons to 110,000 tons in the period 1988/89–1991/92, recovering to 145,000 tons in 1992/93. Output was 135,000 tons in 1993/94, 142,700 tons in 1994/95 and 148,123 tons in 1995/96. Nigeria's exports of cocoa in 1994/95 accounted for about 7.8% of total exports.

The production and export of oil palm products has declined dramatically. The world's leading exporter of palm oil until overtaken by Malaysia in 1971, Nigeria is now heavily dependent on imports in order to satisfy domestic needs. As in other cash-crop sectors, output of palm products has suffered from labour shortages, inefficient traditional harvesting methods, lack of vital inputs and low levels of capital investment. A sharp reduction in imports and large-scale replanting in eastern Rivers State did, however, result in a substantial increase in production during the mid-1980s. Trade liberalization and the exchange rate policy also contributed to the improvement in palm oil production after 1987. Most of the surplus output has been used for import substitution, with some increase in exports of palm products. According to FAO estimates, palm kernel production increased from 350,000 tons in 1986 to 392,000 tons in 1993, followed by 380,000 tons in 1994, 400,000 tons in 1995 and 405,000 tons in 1996. There have been substantial investments in oil-milling facilities to produce vegetable oil for domestic use. Palm oil production was 857,000 tons in 1989, increasing to 965,000 tons in 1993. Output declined to 837,000 tons in 1994, but recovered slightly, to 852,000 tons in 1995, and to 853,000 tons in 1996.

In 1990 Nigeria overtook Liberia as the largest rubber producer in Africa. Production rose from 55,000 tons in 1986 to 152,000 tons in 1990 and 155,000 tons in 1991. Output in 1992 was 129,000 tons. Benefits from a replanting programme in the eastern states have yet to materialize, and local demand from the tyre and footwear industries continues to outstrip domestic supply. A programme to increase output of palm kernels and rubber, with financial assistance from the World Bank, is being implemented.

Production of raw cotton increased to 276,000 tons in 1990 (compared with 187,000 tons in 1989), but declined to 270,000 tons in 1991, despite considerable public and private investment in the sector. Incentives for local textile companies and higher tariffs on imported cotton have stimulated local production, although the textile manufacturers prefer the higher quality of legally or illegally imported cotton from neighbouring countries. Nigeria produced 233,000 tons of cottonseed and 19,800 tons of cottonseed oil in 1995. In 1996 the government agreed to purchase 400,000 bales of excess cotton from farmers. The 1995 crop of 1.5m. tons of groundnuts in shells yielded 311,572 tons of groundnut oil, while copra output of 22,000 tons yielded 14,076 tons of coconut oil. Production of other cash crops included 2,160 tons of soyabean oil, 10,000 tons of tobacco leaves and 3,000 tons of green coffee. Assessments of the amounts of staple food crops produced in Nigeria have varied widely; according to the FAO, Nigeria produced 13.7m. tons of cereals in 1996, including 4.2m. tons of sorghum, 3.7m. tons of millet and 3.5m. tons of paddy rice. Production of other food crops in 1995 amounted to 1.9m. tons of pulses, 1.7m. tons of plantains, 950,000 tons of green peppers and chillies, 500,000 tons of papayas, 400,000 tons of tomatoes and 175,000 tons of carrots.

According to the FAO, output of beef and veal reached 267,000 metric tons in 1995, while the output of goat meat was estimated at 130,000 tons. In 1996, according to FAO estimates, Nigeria's national herd comprised 25.4m. goats, 16.8m. cattle, 14.4m. sheep and 6.9m. pigs; in that year 15.3m. sheep and goats, 5.9m. pigs and 2.8m. cattle were slaughtered, producing 183,000 tons of sheep and goat meat, 258,000 tons of pork and 221,000 tons of beef. Output of poultry meat was estimated at 168,000 tons in 1995. Nigeria's annual fish catch declined from 538,350 tons in 1983 to 241,634 tons in 1985, owing to shortages of trawlers and nets, and the cancellation of industrial fishing licences, but increased in 1986 to 268,500 tons. According to the FAO, the fish catch totalled 282,100 tons in 1994, increasing to 366,100 tons in 1995.

Some 20% of the land area is forested, but exports of timber (mostly obeche, abura and mahogany) are relatively small. Nigeria's annual output of timber declined by 8% in the period 1982–84, and deforestation, particularly in the Niger delta area, remains a considerable problem. Following the removal of a ban on specific timber exports, timber production increased to 99m. cubic metres in 1988, and then to 100.1m. in 1989. About 12% of the country's total land area is threatened by the encroaching Sahara desert in the north, and a National Committee on Arid Zone Afforestation has been established as part of the anti-desertification programme. In June 1989 it was announced that the government was to share the cost of a $135m. afforestation project with the World Bank. Fuelwood is still the main source of domestic energy, and accounts for more than 60% of commercial primary energy consumption.

As with the Buhari government, the military regime of Gen. Babangida made agricultural development and food self-sufficiency key components of its overall economic strategy. Agriculture, arguably the most successful element of the structural adjustment programme, exhibited sharp increases in food crop production and a rise in commodity exports. The increase in agricultural production was attributed to three policy initiatives: the devaluation of the naira, which promoted commodity exports and discouraged cheap food imports; the abolition of the state-controlled commodity boards and removal of restrictions on agricultural pricing; and the imposition of an import ban on wheat, maize and barley. Attention was focused on the smallholder farmer, who produces some 90% of food consumed in Nigeria. In 1997 the government pledged to grant further concessions to smallholder farmers.

Apart from maize, most of the corporate investment in agriculture since 1986 has centred on oil palm and cotton, reflecting the relative success of the vegetable oil and textile industries in the use of local raw materials. The Land Use Decree, introduced in 1978, stipulated that land be vested in the state governors, who would hold it in trust for all Nigerians. The government agreed to amend the Decree, in response to protests from smallholder farmers, who claimed that the Decree discriminated against them. In addition to the problem of land availability, the other key issues facing the agricultural sector are environmental degradation, inadequate storage facilities and transport, leading to massive post-harvest losses (assessed at 40% of total production in 1996), lack of research and training facilities for the transfer of new technologies, and the absence of credit facilities for smallholder farmers. Nigeria's resources are not fully exploited, and many parts of the country remain very poorly developed. Inadequate provision of economic infrastructure such as power, water supply, roads and telecommunications, especially in the rural areas, has proved an impediment to both agricultural and industrial investment. The 1997 budget included a ₦4,300m. allocation to the Family Economic Advancement Programme (FEAP), which aimed to allocate resources to enterprises in rural areas. The initiative envisaged the establishment of viable rural small-scale industries, which would be provided with locally-produced machinery and equipment to produce garri, palm-kernel oil, palm oil, other vegetable oils, pottery and garments.

PETROLEUM

The first commercial discoveries of petroleum were made in 1956 in the Niger River delta region. Exports began in 1958, and production advanced rapidly, until output was disrupted by the outbreak of the 'Biafra' civil war in 1967. By the early 1970s, the petroleum industry had become the dominant sector of the Nigerian economy and the major determinant of the country's economic growth. In 1986 the petroleum sector accounted for around 18% of GDP, more than 97% of total export earnings and over 70% of all government revenues. In 1992 revenue from petroleum represented about 95% of the country's foreign exchange earnings. Petroleum earnings were projected to contribute 60% of total budgetary revenue in 1997. Nigeria's proven reserves were estimated at 20,827m. barrels in December 1995. A five-year investment programme, initiated in 1991, aimed to increase petroleum output capacity to 2.5m. barrels per day (b/d). Output was estimated at 2.01m. b/d at December 1996. The 1997 federal budget was based on an output of 1.79m. b/d earning an average US $17 per barrel. (The actual average price of petroleum was $19.6 per barrel in 1996, but was forecast to decline to $18 per barrel or lower.) A member of the Organization of Petroleum Exporting Countries (OPEC), Nigeria accounted for 7.7% of the organization's petroleum production in that year. Since Libya restricted output in 1973, Nigeria has been Africa's leading petroleum-producing country. Being of low sulphur content and high quality, its petroleum is much in demand on the European market.

Revenues from exports of petroleum, which are shared in decreasing proportions between federal, state and local governments, have largely determined the pace of Nigeria's economic development. Successive governments based their five-year plans on predicted earnings from petroleum, and, more recently, foreign exchange revenue from sales of petroleum has been virtually the sole means of meeting the country's import needs and debt-servicing commitments. The level of revenues from petroleum has fluctuated in line with OPEC's pricing policy and changes in world demand. With the depreciation of the dollar and with free-market prices in the range US $10–$12 per barrel in mid-1986, Nigeria's export earnings from oil declined sharply. Total export earnings from oil in 1986 were 47% lower than in the previous year, at an estimated $6,400m. In 1987 the value of petroleum exports was estimated to have risen slightly, to $6,700m., with the return to a comparatively stable price for petroleum offsetting a fall in the volume of exports, and reached $7,100m. in 1988. According to IMF estimates, earnings rose to $8,500m. in 1989, and to $10,600m. in 1990, declining slightly to $10,200m. in 1991, and to an estimated $10,000m. in 1992. By 1995 these earnings had fallen to $7,001m., but they recovered to $9,727m. in 1996 and were projected to reach $11,045m. in 1997.

Production costs for Nigerian petroleum are up to seven times as high as those in the Middle East, but the Nigerian product's low sulphur content places it at the upper end of OPEC's price scale. The Niger delta remains Nigeria's main petroleum-producing region, containing 78 oilfields, the largest of which is Forcados Yorki. The USA is the major market for Nigeria's petroleum, taking, on average, around one-half of all exports. Spain, Germany, France, Portugal and the United Kingdom are also important customers.

In 1971 the state-owned Nigerian National Oil Corpn (NNOC) was formed to be a participant in the operations of the foreign oil companies. In 1977 the NNOC was merged with the ministry of petroleum resources to form the Nigerian National Petroleum Corpn (NNPC), which gradually increased its equity stake in all operating companies, except Ashland. In 1979 the NNPC nationalized BP's interests in Nigeria, in retaliation for BP's participation in an oil-swapping agreement which led indirectly to the shipment of Nigerian petroleum to South Africa. (In 1992 the government sold the nationalized BP interests to Shell, Elf-Aquitaine and other private enterprises.) Agreements governing the petroleum producing companies' terms of operation were not officially signed until 1984, after being effective for more than 10 years. The NNPC had a 60% interest in the operations of Agip-Phillips, Elf-Aquitaine, Gulf, Mobil, Texaco and Pan Ocean, and has an 80% share in Shell (which accounts for one-half of total production). In November 1984 the rules governing the operation of the equity contracts, under which foreign companies extract Nigerian petroleum, were revised in an attempt to increase production and exploration. Companies in partnership with the NNPC were permitted to extract more than their contracted amount of petroleum on the basis of a government-determined 'allowable' production rate. Additionally, companies could also buy, on equity terms, any of the petroleum that the NNPC was unable to sell, while reimbursing the NNPC for production costs. New 'incentive' agreements were signed with international oil companies in 1986, guaranteeing producers a profit margin of around US $2 per barrel. In July 1991 a new memorandum of understanding (MOU) between the NNPC and its foreign production partners was signed, which guaranteed minimum profit margins to foreign joint-venture operators, depending on their level of capital investment and cost efficiency. The MOU detailed a new five-year plan for exploration and production, with incentives for capital investment in the sector, and guaranteed a profit margin of $2.3 per barrel, on the condition that technical operating costs did not exceed $2.5 per barrel. The minimum guaranteed margin was to increase to $2.5 a barrel if capital investment exceeded $1.5 per barrel, with total operating costs at less than $3.5 per barrel. The MOU also provided bonuses for companies that increased their reserves by more than their annual production in any given year, thereby adding to net reserves. In the same year the NNPC and the foreign oil companies signed joint venture agreements for the new oil fields allocated by the government; these agreements defined procedures for making capital spending decisions, stipulated the foreign companies' obligations to train Nigerian nationals, and allowed the NNPC to become the operator of fields when it chose. In 1993 all major enterprises operating in Nigeria—Shell, Mobil, Chevron, Agip, Texaco and Elf Aquitaine—initiated new development programmes, while BP and Statoil, the Norwegian state-owned oil company, signed a new agreement with the government. The petroleum industry suffered a decline in 1994, as a direct consequence of Nigeria's increasing political and economic instability. After government mismanagement of the NNPC's accounts, the company could no longer meet its financial obligations to the oil companies, and the majority of new drilling work was suspended. This did not at first affect ongoing production facilities, and petroleum output remained at almost 2m. b/d in the first half of 1994, but production began to decline after petroleum workers commenced long-term strike action in July. At the end of that month Shell reported that its production had declined by about one-third (the company's previous output level had been approximately 1m. b/d), while petroleum prices increased to more than $18 per barrel. Following the end of strike action in September, production quickly recovered to close to former levels, although the petroleum producing companies remained dissatisfied with the large amounts of money owed to them by the NNPC for past running costs and developmental work. Unrest continued in early 1997, when protesters occupied flow stations belonging to Shell Petroleum Development Company and held 127 Shell employees hostage. Operations at several stations were suspended, but were subsequently resumed. Increased output from the new offshore Ngo field and from Qua Ibo enabled Nigeria to increase its output level to 2.27m. b/d in late 1996. Official sources indicated that prices continued to increase, however, and the average price for Brent Blend was $20.7 per barrel in December 1996, reaching $24 in January 1997. By April 1997, the price had fallen below $19 per barrel. In mid-1995 the government indicated that continuing criticism from the British administration (see Recent History) would endanger Shell and BP interests in Nigeria. In 1996 the Nigerian government claimed that 150,000 barrels of petroleum were unaccounted for each day, and introduced a new inspection scheme, in addition to existing measures, which would be financed by a 1% levy on non-petroleum commodities and a 0.15% levy on petroleum exports. The principal petroleum enterprises immediately demanded that the levy be abolished. Nigeria would easily be capable of maintaining output at a level of 2.5m. b/d. Elf Aquitaine's offshore Ofon field was due to enter into production on 1 January 1998, with the Amenam field scheduled to commence production in the year 2001.

In March 1988 the government announced that the NNPC was to be restructured by division into three sections, responsible for operations, for corporate services and for national petroleum investment management services. Eleven subsidiaries of the NNPC were to be established, each concentrating on a particular area, such as refining, development, engineering and petrochemicals. The marketing of petroleum was also reorganized in order to eliminate intermediate marketers. Under the new scheme, only the NNPC and local and foreign oil companies involved in production or exploration would be permitted to market petroleum. Investment in maintenance, capital equipment and exploration had fallen in recent years, owing to difficulties in funding. By virtue of its equity ownership in the various oil companies, the government has been responsible for around 75% of total investment in the industry. In early 1993 the IMF increased pressure on the government to reduce subsidies on domestic fuel, which were estimated to cost ₦63,000m. in 1992, and maintained the official petrol price at ₦0.7 per litre—one of the cheapest in the world. In August, despite initial reluctance (owing to concern that the measure would prompt renewed unrest), the government partially removed subsidies on domestic fuel, with the introduction of a new grade of petrol, at a cost of ₦7.50 per litre. Shortages of refined fuel were widespread in 1994, obliging the Nigerian government to import petrol products. It was reported that imports of refined fuel cost $800m. in 1995 and $451m. in January-June 1996. Nevertheless, as a result of the unrest, a new fuel crisis occurred in April 1997, when shortages of refined petroleum products were widespread. The NNPC in March 1996 claimed that the two refineries at Port Harcourt and at Roduna were fully operational. A further refinery, at Warri, was under repair and expected to return to full production by mid-April. In October 1996 it was announced that the government was to divest a major part of its average 57% share in the joint-venture oil partnerships with Shell, Chevron, Mobil, Texaco, Elf Aquitaine and Agip, and to enter into production-sharing arrangements instead. However, subsequent diplomatic disagreements with the USA in particular, prompted criticism over the prospect of foreign nationals owning Nigerian oil. In February 1997 the government announced that a committee would be set up to advise on the matter.

With increased participation from the private sector, greater emphasis is being placed on gas—both liquefied petroleum gas (LPG) and liquefied natural gas (LNG)—and on increasing the capacity of the country's petroleum refineries to enable the export of higher-value petroleum products. Until the completion of the 60,000 b/d petroleum refinery at Port Harcourt in 1965, Nigeria exported its entire output of crude petroleum. A second refinery, with a capacity of 100,000 b/d (later expanded to 125,000 b/d), was constructed in 1978 at Warri, in Bendel State, and a third inland refinery, at Kaduna, was partly operational by 1981. The Kaduna refinery has a capacity of 100,000 b/d, and is divided into two units: one uses the light Nigerian crude, while the second unit, which was not finally commissioned until 1983, uses heavier imported crudes. The NNPC owns the Warri and Kaduna refineries, and has an 80% share in the original refinery at Port Harcourt. Technical problems and the lack of proper maintenance reduced the combined operating capacity of the three refineries to 155,000 b/d in 1985. Because of the under-utilization of refinery capacity, Nigeria has to process up to 80,000 b/d abroad in order to meet domestic requirements. It was announced in June 1989 that the World Bank was to make a US $27.7m. loan to improve efficiency at Warri and Kaduna by supporting the repair and maintenance programmes and by improving investment planning. A fourth refinery was completed in March 1989 at Alesa Eleme (near Port Harcourt), thereby increasing Nigeria's refining capacity to 157,680 b/d. Severe operational problems and delayed maintenance work adversely affected local refining capacity in the first half of 1993, while increased illicit trade in fuel contributed to critical shortages throughout the country, prompting the government to ban exports of petroleum products. In 1993 and 1994 strikes in the petroleum sector resulted in a severe disruption in the refining and distribution of fuel, while disruption also occurred in 1997 (see above).

Development of an integrated petrochemicals industry has been a main priority of successive governments. Construction of a number of processing units at the refineries in Warri and Kaduna was completed in 1987. The units use feedstock from the refineries to produce benzene, carbon black and polypropylene. The construction of a larger petrochemicals complex at Alesa-Eleme, at a projected cost of US $1,000m. was completed in 1996.

NATURAL GAS

Besides its petroleum resources, Nigeria possesses the largest deposits of natural gas in Africa. Proven reserves are assessed at more than 2,800,000m. cu m, most of which is located with petroleum deposits in and around the Niger delta. Probable gas reserves were estimated at a further 1,800,000m. cu m. Production in 1990 was estimated at 27,600m. cu m, of which 77% was flared. Of the gas that was consumed, some 75% was bought by the National Electric Power Authority (NEPA). In a bid to curtail the wasteful flaring of gas, the government issued a decree penalizing oil companies for this practice. Although the decree, which came into force in January 1985, affected only 69 of the 155 oil-producing fields, many of the large operators began to install gas re-injection facilities. Some 18,000m. cu m of gas was flared each year, at a market cost of over US $4,000m., according to oil companies; domestic consumption was estimated at just 3,000m. cu m per year. Utilization of gas increased substantially when the Warri associated gas project, under which 17m. cu m per day was piped from the Niger Delta to Igbin power station, near Lagos, came into operation in 1990. Nevertheless, the flaring of gas was a major source of contention between the Ogoni ethnic group and Shell (see Recent History). In 1996 the Shell Petroleum Development Company of Nigeria Limited awarded a £320m. contract for a new gas-processing plant at Soku in Rivers State. The plant was to enable Shell to flare less gas in the Niger Delta and was to supply the LNG plant, which was under construction at Bonny Island (see below). The plant at Soku, when completed, was to be capable of delivering 12.7m. cu m of gas per day.

Nigeria's most ambitious scheme to utilize flared gas was to construct a gas liquefaction plant, with a daily capacity of at least 45m. cu m, on the River Bonny. To implement the plan to produce LNG, the Bonny LNG consortium, comprising the NNPC (which held a 69% share), Phillips, Shell, BP, Agip and Elf Aquitaine, was formed in 1978. The project received an early boost in 1980, when a consortium of European gas distributors signed a 20-year agreement to buy 23m. cu m per day, starting in 1984. However, the viability of the project hinged on the sale of a further 23m. cu m per day to four US distributors. Negotiations with the US government over access broke down in 1980. Market uncertainties continued to surround the project, and, when the outline of the government's 1981–85 Development Plan deferred investment in the scheme until the late 1980s, the Bonny LNG consortium was dissolved. A scaled-down version of the flared gas project was revived by the military government. In 1988 the government considered a new US $2,000m. scheme to construct a pipeline from gas fields in eastern Nigeria to the LNG plant at Bonny. In May 1989 a joint-venture agreement was signed to implement the scheme. The majority shareholder was the NNPC (49%), followed by Shell, Agip and Elf. After a series of difficulties, however, the initiation of the project was delayed. In 1996 the government predicted that production would commence in 1999, with an estimated annual output of 7,000m. cu m. The project is expected to generate $37,000m. over a period of 30 years, averaging $1,233m. per year from the year 2007. (However, in June 1997 the dismissal of the directors of the consortium's Nigerian Liquefied National Gas Company by the minister of petroleum resources was viewed with concern by the other shareholders.)The NNPC in 1996 acquired a new route for the gas-distribution pipeline linking with the aluminium smelter plant in Akwa Ibom State. Chevron, which owns the Gulf Oil Company of Nigeria (GOCON), announced plans in 1991 to construct a plant to recover 300m. cu ft of associated gas per day; with an estimated cost of $500m., the plant would produce condensates, propane and butane gas for export. There were also plans by the NNPC to use some of this gas to fuel an export-orientated $400m. methanol plant, with a daily output of 2,000–2,500 tons. Discussions were held between the NNPC, Penspen, a UK company, and Mannesman, a German company, on a joint venture agreement for the project.

Other schemes which are aimed at utilizing the country's gas reserves include the National Fertilizer Company gas-fed fertilizer plant (commissioned in April 1987) at Onne, the Warri refinery extension and the Delta steel plant at Aladja. Gas is also planned to be used as a feedstock for the second phase of the NNPC chemicals complex near Port Harcourt. The NNPC agreed to a price rise of 269% (from ₦1.52 to ₦5.24 per thousand cubic feet) in April 1989. A new comprehensive gas development policy, offering incentives for companies investing in gas production, distribution and consumption, was released by the NNPC in 1990. The policy provisions also supported the commercialization of LNG production for export and for domestic consumption, the establishment of gas companies distributing to domestic and industrial consumers, and viable projects, aimed at substituting gas for existing fuels.

COAL AND OTHER MINERALS

Nigeria possesses substantial deposits of lignite and sub-bituminous coal, but the country has yet to exploit their full potential. Coal is mined by the Nigerian Coal Corpn (NCC), and is used mainly by the railway, by traditional metal industries and for the generation of electricity. Coal production declined from a peak of 940,000 tons in 1958 to 144,000 tons in 1986, and to 86,700 tons in 1992. The 1996 budget allocated ₦211m. to the NCC for the completion of a rehabilitation programme. There are long-term plans to exploit the Lafia/Obi coal deposits for use at the Ajaokuta steel complex. Reserves are estimated at more than 270m. tons.

Nigeria's output of tin concentrates has been in decline since the late 1960s, and these exports have reflected the depressed conditions in world tin prices since the late 1980s. Production totalled about 186 tons annually in 1992 and 1993. The country has two tin smelters, with a combined capacity well in excess of total ore production. Columbite is mined near Jos, but output has fallen steadily since the mid-1970s, to 47 tons in 1989. The Nigerian Mining Corpn was allocated ₦211.5m. in the 1996 budget to co-operate with the private sector in the development of Nigeria's deposits of bentonite, gypsum (in Bauchi State), kaolin, rock salt, byrates, phosphates, talc, manganese, copper, gold and tin.

Extensive deposits of iron ore have been discovered in Itakpe, Ajabanoko and Shokoshoko—all in Kwara State. Mining operations at Itakpe started in 1984, with the long-term aim of supplying most of the requirements of the Ajaokuta and Delta steel complexes. More than 180,000 tons of iron ore had been mined by early 1986. The construction of a US $250m. beneficiation plant at Itakpe began in December 1992; the plant was projected to process 5m. tons of iron ore into a concentrated form for the Ajaokuta steel complex. In 1995 work was completed on the establishment of a river port at Ajaokuta, which was to enable the transportation of iron ore for the steel complex. An aluminium smelter at Ikot Abasi has an output capacity of 90,000 tons per year and is run by the Aluminium Smelter Co of Nigeria. Uranium deposits have been discovered at Gombe, but have yet to be exploited, although drilling and sample analysis have taken place.

MANUFACTURING AND CONSTRUCTION

Measured in constant prices, the contribution of the manufacturing sector to GDP increased from 4% in 1977 to 13% in 1982, after which it declined to an estimated 8.2% in 1995. According to the World Bank, manufacturing GDP increased by an annual average of 3.1% in 1985–95.

Industrial development has mainly taken the form of import substitution of consumer goods, although, during the 1970s, greater emphasis was placed on the production of capital goods and on assembly industries. In 1983 textiles, beverages, cigarettes, soaps and detergents together accounted for 60% of total manufacturing output. Investment in manufacturing has come mostly from the government and from foreign multinational companies. Private-sector investment in manufacturing is small, and is centred on industries which are shielded from competition by import barriers.

Manufacturing is heavily reliant on imported raw materials and components. According to the Manufacturers' Asscn of Nigeria (MAN), up to 60% of all the raw materials that local industry used in 1985 were imported. Manufacturing is thus extremely vulnerable to disruption if imports are restricted, as they have been since 1980. Imports of raw materials declined, on average, by 10% per year over the period 1982–85. The combination of import restrictions, over-pricing and industrial disputes favoured cheaper foreign goods and encouraged smuggling and black-marketeering. Import licensing was abolished in September 1986, in tandem with the introduction of the SFEM, and tariffs were reduced. However, the resultant sharp devaluation of the naira increased import costs and hence production costs. A new tariff structure, introduced in 1988, aimed to protect local industries from external competition, while encouraging domestic competition to stimulate efficiency.

Total production from the manufacturing sector declined by more than one-third between 1982 and 1985, while the level of capital expenditure fell by over 50%. In 1986 manufacturing output declined by a further 6%. The most severely affected branches of the sector were: commercial vehicles, chemicals, metals, textiles, sugar, plastics and paper. A further 30% reduction in imports in 1985 and a similar reduction in 1986, coupled with the government's plans to reduce the level of state investment in manufacturing, did not help the sector to revive. Manufacturers asserted that inadequate development funds and the government's stringent fiscal policy had constrained the sector, which was estimated to be operating at only 25% of its capacity in 1987. Manufacturing output increased, in real terms, by 7.6% in 1990, and by 6.1% in 1991. Many manufacturers placed their hopes on the success of the government-backed local sourcing programme, under which all existing industries were actively encouraged to utilize more local raw materials. Various tax and investment incentives were introduced, and a National Raw Materials Development Council and a Raw Materials Data Bank were established. A new tariff structure, to benefit manufacturing based on local resources, was drawn up, although its viability was seriously constrained by the poor state of the country's infrastructure and by the high cost of local materials and parts. In 1996 growth of manufacturing output was estimated at 0.7%, and the average rate of industrial capacity utilization was 32.5% (compared with 29.3% in 1995). Despite successive governments' efforts to encourage industrial dispersal, most manufacturing plants are still based in Lagos State. The Agbara industrial estate, in Ogun State, has attracted some industries away from Lagos, although most of the heavily import-based companies are reluctant to move, owing to the fact that around 70% of all industrial materials are still handled at ports in Lagos State.

The creation of an integrated iron and steel industry has been a high priority of successive development plans. In January 1982 the Delta steel complex at Aladja, in Bendel State, was formally opened. The complex, which has a capacity of 1m. tons per year and operates the direct reduction system, supplies billets and wire rods to three steel-rolling mills at Oshogbo, Katsina and Jos. Each of the three mills has an initial annual capacity of 210,000 tons of steel products. The Ajaokuta Steel Company opened the first light section mill in 1983, and the rolling mill for the production of steel wire rods in 1984, but output was sporadic, owing to shortages of imported billets and to difficulties in obtaining supplies from the Delta complex. In 1996, Nigeria's steel companies were reported to be operating at just 10% of their installed capacity, owing to mismanagement and lack of foreign exchange. Nigeria's annual steel requirements reached 6m. metric tons by 1990, and there were plans at least to double the capacity of the first stage of the Ajaokuta complex. Construction costs, originally estimated at US $1,400m., exceeded $3,000m. at the end of 1989, and had increased to $8,000m. by 1997. A 20-year contract with a Russian firm, Tyazhpromexport, for the plant equipment and technology, which had been criticized by the World Bank, was terminated in December 1996. However, the 1997 federal budget allocated ₦6,600m. for the completion of the project, confirming the government's intention to continue with the Ajaokuta project. In early 1992 a second stage of the project was initiated. The Iwopin Paper Mill and the rehabilitation of damaged sections of Jebba Paper Mill were completed in 1995, but, as of February 1996, a number of projects remained unfinished, as a result of financial difficulties.

Manufacturers using raw materials from local sources were at a strong advantage after the economic reforms of 1986. By 1990 locally sourced operations achieved relatively high levels of capacity utilization: tyres (64%), leather products (63%), beer and stout (59%), textiles (54%) and industrial chemicals (49%). One of the most successful industrial sub-sector projects was the nitrogenous fertilizer plant at Onne, owned by the National Fertilizer Corpn of Nigeria (NAFCON), which was established in 1987; at full capacity it produced 400,000 tons per year of urea and 300,000 tons per year of compound fertilizer. Overall capacity utilization increased from an estimated 33% in 1989 to more than 60% in 1992. The NAFCON plant was temporarily closed in March 1996 to allow major maintenance work, and it was reported that the plant was deteriorating, not only from age but also as a result of the pressure to produce quantities beyond its design capacity.

The assembly of motor vehicles in Nigeria is dominated by Peugeot in passenger cars, and by Mercedes in commercial vehicles. Local demand remains well above supply, but the cost of components and the difficulties in obtaining import licences have reduced output. Government plans to transfer Nigeria's vehicle-assembly plants to private ownership were suspended in early 1993, since it was believed that the prevailing economic recession would reduce their value.

Various government programmes that were aimed at national self-sufficiency in food allowed for the steady growth of agro-business during the 1970s. Sugar refining, textiles, brewing, rubber, fertilizers, footwear, paper, cigarettes and general food-processing industries were among the most significant. However, the expansion and modernization of plants was cut short by the onset of economic recession in 1982. The large brewing industry has continued to flourish, although in 1987 it suffered from a ban on imports of malted barley, imposed with the aim of stimulating local barley production. Funding was arranged in 1995 to increase the working capital of the Nigeria Sugar Corpn and a number of other enterprises. In 1988 Firestone opened a new tyre-manufacturing plant in Bendel State, bringing the number of tyre manufacturers in Nigeria to three. With enlarged capacity at Dunlop Nigeria's plant in Lagos, it was estimated that local manufacturers would be able to meet about 60% of domestic demand.

Activity in the construction sector has declined in recent years. Output fell by 50% in value from 1981 to 1985, and by a further 5% in 1986. The construction sector suffered from serious constraints on growth, following the introduction of the structural adjustment programme in 1986 and further reductions in public sector projects. The construction of a federal capital at Abuja was formally completed in 1991. (However, the expansion of the private sector at Abuja subsequently proved to be slow.) The creation of nine new states in 1991 necessitated several new infrastructure projects, and ongoing investment in the energy sector of some $1,000m. a year has also benefited the sector. However, road construction, and the rehabilitation of railways, airports and seaports virtually ceased in the late 1980s. In February 1996 the rehabilitation of eight roads and bridges was at various stages of completion.

In March 1988 changes were made to regulations concerning foreign investment in Nigeria. The 1972 Nigerian Enterprises Promotion Decree, which was strengthened and extended in 1977, involved three categories of business. The first (Schedule I) had to be 100% Nigerian-owned and covered more than 50 enterprises, including printing, rice-milling, advertising, road haulage, bus services, taxis and tyre retreading. The second category (Schedule II) had to be 60%-owned by Nigerian interests and included breweries, department stores and supermarkets, wholesale distribution, banking, insurance, construction and furniture manufacture. All other enterprises, including food-processing (Schedule III), had to be 40% Nigerian-held. In 1985 the decree was being selectively relaxed in order to encourage foreign private investment in neglected areas, such as large-scale agro-business and manufacturing based on local resources. From March 1988 foreign investors were allowed to increase their holdings in Schedule I enterprises to 20%, and in Schedule III enterprises to 80%. Schedule II enterprises were to be allowed to enter joint ventures with foreign companies. Under a new decree, promulgated in December 1989, foreign companies are permitted to own 100% of any new venture, except for enterprises in banking, oil prospecting, insurance and mining. The government in February 1996 stated its intention of encouraging private-sector competition in sectors, such as power and telecommunications, previously monopolized by NEPA and NITEL, and pledged that, 'apart from exceptional circumstances', it would not fund these enterprises after December 1996. The largest government agency in industrial development is the Nigerian Industrial Development Bank, which, in recent years, has centred its activities on directing multilateral funding into private-sector projects in intermediate and capital goods manufacturing, food processing and other agro-related industries. In August 1995 the Nigerian government promulgated legislation, aimed at stimulating foreign investment, which guaranteed the unconditional transferability of funds through an authorized dealer in freely convertible currency for debt-service payments, dividends and proceeds of sales of assets, although new investments were still required to be processed through the Nigeria Stock Exchange and new companies still had to receive the approval of the Investment Promotion Commission. A new Export Processing Zone (EPZ) at Calabar in Cross River State was reported in February 1996 to be 85% complete. The EPZ was aimed at investors in 14 sectors, including electrical products, electronics, textiles, wood, food-processing, pharmaceuticals, cosmetics, rubber and plastics. By mid-1997, ₦2,500m. had been spent on the EPZ at Calabar, including the construction of an airport and improvements to the port. In 1997 the government announced that henceforth all contracts entered into in Nigeria were to be denominated in naira alone, whereas previously some contracts had been denominated both in foreign currency for the offshore portions and in naira for the onshore components.

POWER

The principal supplier of electricity in Nigeria is the state-owned NEPA, which was formed in 1973 by the merger of the Niger Dams Authority and the Electricity Corpn of Nigeria. In addition to the 1,320-MW power station at Igbin, other major plants include: the Kainji hydroelectric plant (capacity 760 MW); the gas and oil-fired plants in Afam (742 MW); Sapele (696 MW); Lagos (60 MW); and the coal-fired plant on the Oji river (150 MW). The Igbin plant is fired with natural gas piped from fields at Escravos.

Demand for power regularly exceeds capacity, and power cuts have become a regular feature of daily life. Only about 30% of the population have access to mains electricity. Peak demand was estimated to be 2,542 MW in 1997. Improvement of existing facilities has been given preference to the expansion of capacity, although plans are under consideration for the construction of new plants at Onitsha, Kaduna, Makurdi, Oron, Katsina and Mambilla. The Makurdi and Mambilla plants, in addition to three new thermal power stations at Zungeru, Abuja and Kaduna, were due to come on stream in the last quarter of 1997, adding 2,450 MW to the national grid. China agreed in January 1996 to construct two new power stations, one at Abuja and one at Geregu, near Ajaokuta, in Koji State. Under the agreement, China was also to rehabilitate three thermal stations, at Egbin in Lagos State, at Afain in Rivers State and at Sapela in Delta State. Total electricity generated in the late 1980s was about 10,000m. kWh per year, of which about 50% was supplied by hydroelectric plants.

TRANSPORT

In comparison with other west African states, Nigeria has a well-developed transport system. However, congestion, lack of maintenance, and poor planning have resulted in services that are unreliable and often dangerous. The rehabilitation of the transport infrastructure formed a major element of the three-year rolling Investment Plan, announced in January 1990.

Approximately 95% of all traffic in goods and passengers travel by road, most of it to and from the major ports. In 1991 the road network totalled some 112,140 km, of which about 30,900 km were principal roads and 19,550 km were secondary roads; some 31,500 km were tarred. In the 1980s the government's main concern was to repair existing roads, rather than to build new ones. Road safety standards in Nigeria are virtually non-existent, and driving licences are distributed indiscriminately. On average, around 30,000 accidents are reported each year, with the loss of over 8,000 lives.

The railway network covers 3,505 km. The two main narrow-gauge lines run from Lagos to Nguru and from Port Harcourt to Kaura Namoda, with extensions from Kafanchan, through Jos, to Maiduguri, and from Minna to Baro. A new 52-km railway line for iron ore traffic has been constructed between the Ajaokuta steel complex and Itakpe. Despite medium-term expansion plans, the Nigerian Railway Corpn (NRC) reduced services and jobs in 1989; this led to a series of strikes and further operating difficulties. In 1991 the number of passengers carried totalled 3.9m. (compared with 6.3m. in 1990), while the volume of freight declined to 282m. tons (compared with 374m. tons in 1990). A programme to rehabilitate the railway network, at a projected cost of ₦17,000m., was announced in 1993. In 1997 the China Civil Engineering Co-operative Corporation was under contract to rehabilitate Nigeria's railway system, with the provision of technology, locomotives and 70 passenger carriages, which were to be built by China's Sifang Rolling Stock Plant.

There are two international airports, at Ikeja (Lagos) and Kano, and 11 domestic airports. Construction commenced on a new airport at Abuja, with the first stage due for completion in June 1997. It was to have 10 terminals, three of which were to handle international traffic, while the other seven were to serve the domestic market. Under the civilian regime, the parastatal Nigeria Airways' domestic monopoly was ended, and several private charter airlines have since begun operations. International traffic is dominated by foreign airlines. Meanwhile, the military government has put increasing pressure on Nigeria Airways to improve its standard of service and to reduce its costs. However, Nigeria Airways has incurred a series of substantial financial losses. Owing to Nigeria Airways' difficulties, it was announced that private airlines would be allowed to offer international services if they satisfied safety requirements. In early 1993 Nigeria Airways entered negotiations to sell some 40% of ownership to a foreign airline; control of international services was to be transferred to the private sector, while domestic services were to remain state-owned. The number of passengers on domestic flights declined to 556,000 in 1991 (compared with 621,000 in 1990), while the number of passengers on international routes increased to 187,000 (compared with 160,000 in 1990). In April 1996 only 28 of the 85 aircraft intended for use on domestic routes in the country were operative. Sanctions forced Nigeria Airways to cease operating its New York-Lagos route in 1993, and in 1997 the carrier closed its New York office. In March 1997, the government announced a 4.0% increase in domestic air fares.

Nigeria's principal seaports for general cargo are Apapa, Tin Can Island (both of which serve Lagos), Port Harcourt, Warri, Sepele and Calabar. The main ports for petroleum shipments are Bonny and Burutu. After steadily declining since 1982, port utilization was expected to increase in 1990 and 1991 as a result of the rise in import and export volumes. In 1992 a report released by the West African Shipowners Operations Committee indicated that Nigeria's ports charged disproportionately high rates to shipping lines (some 230% above the average rate for west Africa), and that their turnaround times were longer, owing to poor maintenance of equipment. The state-owned Nigerian National Shipping Line handled only 3.3% of non-oil shipments (totalling 10.2m. tons) in 1991 and went into liquidation. Its fixed assets and its seven general cargo vessels were to be sold in 1996 to settle its debts and those of a newly-acquired 6,800-ton vessel. A new national shipping line, the Nigeria Unity Line (NUL), was created, to operate services between Europe and Nigeria. Its initial destination in Europe was Antwerp, in Belgium, but Tilbury, in London, and one French port were to be added by the end of 1996, as well as West African ports, such as Abidjan and Dakar. A ₦329.9m. dredging of the Rivers Niger and Benue was due for completion in 1997.

TRADE

With a sharp fall in export earnings from petroleum and with a continued rise in imports, Nigeria's visible trade balance moved into deficit in 1981, after registering a healthy surplus of US $11,106m. in 1980. The trade deficit widened further in 1982, to $2,714m., as a 33% drop in export earnings exceeded the decline in imports, which fell to $14,801m. A further 15% decline in export earnings in 1983 was offset by a steeper fall in imports, and the trade deficit was reduced to $1,084m. However, the current account remained heavily in deficit, and Nigeria began to accumulate an increasing volume of unpaid trade debts. Considerable improvement was achieved in 1984, with the trade surplus rising to $2,984m. and the current account registering a small surplus of $114m. Export earnings fell sharply, to $6,599m., in 1986, owing to the collapse of petroleum prices on the world market, although efforts to reduce the volume of imports maintained the visible trade account in surplus. In the same year there was a current account surplus of $365m. Exports increased to $7,702m. in 1987, while imports totalled $4,178m., resulting in a trade surplus of $3,524m. The trade balance declined slightly to $2,419m. in 1988 but increased to $4,178m. in 1989. According to IMF figures, exports increased sharply, to $13,585m., in 1990, while imports totalled $4,932m., resulting in a trade surplus of $8,653m.; in that year a surplus of $4,988m. on the current account of the balance of payments was recorded. In 1991 the trade surplus declined to $4,441m. (owing, in part, to the sharp increase in the volume of imports, to $7,813m.), and the current account surplus to $1,203m. In 1992 Nigeria recorded a trade surplus of $4,611m., and there was a surplus of $2,268m. on the current account of the balance of payments. In 1994 imports of goods and services of $12,504m. exceeded imports of goods and services of $9,879m. by $2,625m., and the deficit on the current account of the balance of payments before official transfers was $2,079m. Gross international reserves amounted to $1,649m. in January 1995, increasing to $4,086m. by February 1997.

Following the introduction, in September 1986, of the SFEM, foreign exchange for trade was made available by the central bank at weekly auctions. This initially resulted in an effective 60% devaluation of the naira. However, as the auction mechanism of the SFEM removed the need for import controls, the licensing of imports was abolished. At the same time, the government introduced further measures, which abolished the 30% import levy, reduced import duties, reformed the tariff structure and reduced the list of prohibited imports. The devaluation of the naira, through the currency auction system introduced in 1986, was accompanied by a series of trade liberalization measures, designed to expand the export base. In July 1987 the military government terminated the SFEM, merging the first- and second-tier exchange rates but retaining the auction mechanism, whereby a unitary rate would be determined by fortnightly auctions of available foreign exchange, conducted by the central bank. Under the new arrangement, the naira initially fell by 6.3% against the US dollar, to ₦3.95 = US $1, and reached ₦4.61 = US $1 in May 1988. It was expected that the rate would continue to weaken in the short term, unless the government substantially increased its official funding of the market. In January 1989 the Interbank Foreign Exchange Market (IFEM) was established, in accordance with IMF recommendations, to provide a unified exchange rate for the naira, to be fixed on a daily basis. Exchange rate policy in 1992 and 1993 vacillated between a return to the auction mechanism (which had previously been suspended) and a more managed system. In January 1994 the Abacha government abandoned the auction system, replacing it with occasional allocations of foreign exchange to banks at a fixed rate of ₦22.0 = US $1. The autonomous market for foreign exchange, which had stimulated exports of non-petroleum commodities, was abolished and all foreign exchange entering the country was to be surrendered to the CBN. These policies were again reversed in 1995, with the introduction of the Autonomous Foreign Exchange Market (AFEM). In June 1996 a dual exchange rate was in operation, with the official rate established by the government at a fixed ₦22.0 = US$1 and the market rate allowed to fluctuate and amounting to ₦85.0 = US $1. Although the government acknowledged the long-term aim of unifying the two rates, it was emphasized in February 1997 that it would continue to maintain a dual exchange-rate system. During 1996 the official exchange rate continued to be fixed at ₦22.0 = US $1, while the market rate remained stable at about ₦80.0 = US $1.

Revenue from petroleum accounted for 97.9% of total export earnings in 1992. Non-petroleum exports, mainly cocoa beans and rubber, have remained low, totalling US $500m. in 1992, despite the availability of various incentives for export-based industries. A significant proportion of non-recorded exports of manufactured goods, processed foods and agricultural produce is smuggled through Nigeria's borders.

In 1993 Nigeria's principal source of imports was Germany (16.2%); other major suppliers were the United Kingdom, the USA and France. The principal market for exports (45.3%) in that year was the USA; other significant purchasers were Spain, the Netherlands and Italy.

DEBT

Following the sharp rise in government revenues from petroleum and the launching of several large-scale capital-intensive projects during the late 1970s, external borrowing increased dramatically. Although state borrowing was severely restricted during the 1980s and the level of federal government borrowing was reduced, the external debt rose to ₦12,000m. by late 1983. More than one-half of the outstanding debt consisted of medium-term loans from the international capital market at 'floating' interest rates, most of which were incurred during the late 1970s. The net result was a heavy concentration of maturity dates at a time when real interest rates were high and when Nigeria's earnings of foreign currency were declining. Despite the successful refinancing of some US$2,000m. of the trade debt and of $6,000m. of the short-term debt during the course of 1984, Nigeria's total external loan commitments in October 1985 amounted to ₦21,000m., of which ₦3,146m. was in the form of 'open-account' uninsured trade debts. In 1986 debt-servicing alone was expected to cost $3,400m. With the decline in earnings of foreign exchange from petroleum exports, the debt service ratio would have risen to about 47% of total exports, well above the 30% level that the government had set as its target.

From April 1986, Nigeria obtained successive 90-day moratoria on repayments of debt principal to commercial creditors, but it became clear that a rescheduling would be needed. However, the government declared that it would not seek a loan from the IMF, which was a precondition of rescheduling by the Paris and London 'Clubs' (Western governments and commercial bank creditors respectively). A further problem arose when Nigeria defaulted on the first repayments of debt principal totalling US $1,500m., resulting from promissory notes issued for pre-1984 short-term trade debts. However, a compromise with the IMF was reached, as part of the government's structural adjustment plan, whereby Nigeria agreed to accept 'enhanced surveillance' by the IMF. In November 1986 Nigeria reached agreement with its commercial bank creditors on the rescheduling of $1,500m. of medium-term debts and $2,000m. of arrears on letters of credit, and on the provision of a new commercial loan of $320m. In December the 'Paris Club' of creditor governments agreed to a 10-year rescheduling of medium- and long-term debts, accumulated before the end of 1983, and to a four-year rescheduling of short-term debts accumulated since that date; the amount rescheduled was reported to total $7,500m.

In November 1987, following protracted negotiations, Nigeria reached an agreement with its commercial bank creditors on the rescheduling of US $1,550m. of medium-term debts falling due in 1986–87, and $2,350m. of arrears on letters of credit. A new commercial loan of $320m., to be disbursed in instalments from February 1988, was also agreed but was not implemented, owing to the government's failure to secure a renewal of the IMF endorsement of its economic strategy in January 1988. In January 1988 foreign exporters agreed to reschedule (over 22 years) repayments on $4,000m. of promissory notes representing a portion of the trade debts incurred since 1984 (estimated by creditors to total $9,800m.). In 1988 Nigeria's total debt was estimated at $29,000m. In September another agreement was reached with the creditor banks, to reschedule $5,200m. of debt falling due between January 1988 and December 1991. Repayment of $2,700m. of medium-term debt was to be extended over 20 years, and repayment of $2,500m. in letters of credit over 12 years, with repayment to begin after a three-year period of grace. Both this agreement and the disbursement of loans by various bilateral donors and the World Bank were dependent on Nigeria's gaining approval for its recovery programme from the IMF. This took place in January 1989, and the rescheduling agreement was signed in London in March. During 1986 the World Bank increased its lending to Nigeria to more than $800m., including a major loan of $452m., approved in October. Support from the IMF and World Bank for the reform programme continued in 1987, but was suspended in 1988, following differences of opinion over policy and performance. New adjustment credits were approved by the World Bank in 1989 and 1990, but ceased entirely in 1991, after it emerged that Nigeria could not account for petroleum revenue amounting to about $2,500m. that should have been earned during the Gulf War. The World Bank and the IMF were also discouraged by the government's continuing failure to control budgetary spending and its reluctance to raise domestic fuel prices to cover the costs of refining and distribution.

The size of Nigeria's external debt continued to increase in the late 1980s; in 1990 total foreign debt was US $34,089m. and debt service ratio projected at 34%. According to government estimates, debt service was expected to average $4,200m. a year—about one-third of projected export revenue—until 1997, which implies a financing gap of some $2,500m. over that period. These projections, and the limitations on economic growth and investment that they imply, formed the basis of the Nigerian claim for a 30-year rescheduling of its commercial debt. At the end of 1991 Nigeria's total foreign debt was $34,497m., compared with $2,060m. at the end of 1984. The external debt declined to $32,531m. by the end of 1993, of which $28,237m. was long-term public debt. In that year the cost of debt-servicing was equivalent to 29.4% of the value of exports of goods and services. Total external debt amounted to $33,485m. at the end of 1994, with a debt-servicing ratio of 18.5% of the value of exports of goods and services. At the end of 1995 Nigeria's total debt was estimated at $32,585m., of which 66.5% was owed to the 'Paris Club', 13.5% to other multilateral donors, 9.7% on promissory notes and 6.3% to the 'London Club'. Debt-servicing arrears for 1995 amounted to US $1,124m. The Nigerian government allocated $2,000m. for external debt-servicing payments in the 1997 budget (the same level of debt-servicing that it had paid in each of the preceding six years). In February 1997 the government declared that it had succeeded in reducing external debt to $28,060m. at the end of 1996 without further debt rescheduling. The reduction was achieved primarily through the Debt Conversion Programme, in which Nigeria repurchased some of its debt stock from third parties. Nevertheless, debt-servicing payments due in 1997 were $4,980m., and, with accumulated arrears from 1996 and earlier included, Nigeria's total debt-servicing bill in 1997 was estimated at $16,104m. The Federal Government in April 1997 denied claims by external creditors that Nigeria's debt totalled $48,000m., rather than $28,060m.

Nigerian proposals to convert commercial debt into 30-year bonds, serviced at a 3% interest rate, were discussed at a series of meetings between creditor bank representatives and Nigerian finance officials in 1990. Negotiations, led by the minister of finance, Olu Falae, were suspended in August 1990, when Falae was replaced by Alhaji Abubakar Alhaji. A new accord was reached with the IMF in January 1991, which facilitated the conclusion of negotiations to reschedule the commercial and official debt. The rescheduling of Nigeria's $5,800m. bank debt allowed the government to repurchase as much as 60% of the debt, while the banks were given the option of exchanging the remainder for 30-year bonds at a

6.25% interest rate. The 'Paris Club' agreed to reschedule all development and aid loans that were due before March 1992 for a period of 20 years with a 10-years' grace, and also guaranteed commercial debts for a period of 15 years with an eight-year period of grace. Although Nigeria is defined by the World Bank as a low-income country, it was not accorded the debt concessions for which it applied. In 1992 Nigeria's finance ministry officials initiated a series of negotiations for the renewal of Nigeria's stand-by facility with the IMF (the previous facility had expired in April) and a series of development credits with the World Bank, in an effort to reschedule and to reduce the 'Paris Club' debt, which was the principal burden on the government finance. In May 1993 efforts by the transitional council to obtain a new arrangement with the IMF (which was a precondition to the rescheduling of Nigeria's external debt on concessionary terms) ended in failure, owing to lack of agreement over the exchange rate policy and the proposed removal of subsidies on domestic fuel. In 1994, following the government's abandonment of market reforms, the IMF deferred agreement on the rescheduling of accumulating debt arrears until the administration achieved its stated objectives of controlling expenditure, inflation and the foreign exchange rate. In January 1995 the government announced a number of economic reforms under the projected budget for that year, which included the liberalization of foreign exchange controls. In April the Bretton Woods institutions declared the implementation of the 1995 budget in the first quarter of the year to be satisfactory, and agreed to engage in negotiations with the government regarding a medium-term programme; however, the conclusion of a debt-rescheduling arrangement on concessionary terms remained dependent on sustained economic progress. Negotiations on further loans from the IMF and World Bank continued in 1996 and 1997. The liberalization of the financial sector in the 1980s resulted in a proliferation of banks, from 51 in 1986 to 119 in 1992. By the mid-1990s, however, it was evident that some of these banks were financially instable. The Nigeria Deposit Insurance Company revealed evidence that violations of banking regulations had taken place in a number of institutions. Several banks failed, and other seemed on the point of doing so. In September 1995, the government initiated measures to rescue several banks. By February 1977 eight banks had been offered for privatization; two of these, the National Bank and the African Continental Bank, attracted investor interest, but purchasers were still being sought for the remaining six.

PUBLIC FINANCE

Since the early 1970s, the channelling of earnings from petroleum exports, import and excise duties and other forms of revenue from taxation through the federal, state and local governments has been the main impetus of economic activity in Nigeria. After a period in the late 1970s and early 1980s of inflationary domestic policies (characterized by high levels of public spending, recurrent budget deficit financing and ambitious development planning), the government was faced with serious internal financial difficulties. The sharp reduction in revenues from petroleum, which account for around 70% of total federal revenue, meant that the Shagari government could not meet the public spending targets that it had proposed in the fourth National Development Plan (1981–85) except by borrowing from overseas. By 1983 much of the government's capital programme had been temporarily abandoned in the face of a massive ₦6,200m. budget deficit and heavy debt-servicing commitments. In May 1984 the new military government abandoned the fourth Plan and introduced an austerity budget that was aimed at reducing public expenditure, imports and inflation. A series of deflationary measures followed, including a virtual embargo on new projects, a 'freeze' on wages, the imposition of heavier import duties, higher interest rates, limits on federal and state spending and reductions in state subsidies, the pruning of parastatal companies and a clamp-down on corruption and tax evasion. Aided by a rise in revenues from petroleum and by the introduction of new state taxes and import duties, federally-collected revenue was increased during 1984 by 14%, to ₦11,300m. Moreover, despite an increase in recurrent expenditure (owing largely to debt servicing), a sharp cut in the level of capital expenditure was sufficient to reduce the overall budget deficit for 1984 by 47%, to ₦3,300m. The government announced a new planning strategy in January 1990, consisting of a three-year rolling Investment Plan, costed at ₦144,200m., and a 15-year perspective Plan, incorporating a series of rolling investment plans. The 1997–1999 National Rolling Plan placed emphasis on controlling inflation, commercializing unprofitable government industries, raising industrial capacity-utilization levels, and introducing measures to resolve unemployment. In order to improve performance on plan implementation, a co-ordinated planning review procedure was to be established, to which all ministries and government departments would submit data to allow more effective monitoring. The introduction of the structural adjustment programme in 1986 resulted in a major change in public finance policy; the reforms involved extensive austerity measures in public-sector expenditure, reductions in subsidies and public-sector payrolls, with the aim of balancing the budget, and a lowering of the public-sector borrowing requirement.

The 1992 budget proposals envisaged a surplus of ₦2,000m., or 0.6% of projected GDP, as a result of a further increase in revenue from petroleum, and a sharp rise in federally-collected revenue; however, estimates indicated an actual budgetary deficit of ₦43,800m. (equivalent to about 9.8% of GDP). According to official figures, actual federal revenue in that year totalled ₦101,201m. (of which ₦79,156m. was from petroleum). The 1993 budget proposals forecast federally-collected revenue at ₦148,400m., and an overall deficit of ₦28,600m. However, the actual budgetary deficit in that year totalled ₦101,000m. (equivalent to about 12.3% of GDP). The 1994 budget, which was announced by Abacha in January, projected a federally-collected revenue of ₦231,400m. (of which the federal government planned to retain ₦110,200m.), with a reduced overall deficit of ₦39,000m. (equivalent to 6% of GDP). However, these projections were not realized, and the total deficit in 1994 was ₦81,000m. (equivalent to 8.1% of GDP). Total revenue for 1995 was projected at ₦350,660m., and expenditure at ₦351,160m, it was reported that the government had indeed maintained a budgetary surplus of ₦1,000m. (equivalent to 0.6% of GDP). Value-added tax, introduced in January 1994, increased revenue by ₦8,600m. in 1994 and by ₦21,000m. in 1995. The government pledged to pay US $2,000m. of the external debt-servicing costs of $4,400m. which fell due in 1995, and to end the system of dedicated accounts, into which at least $12,000m. of revenue was directed between 1988 and 1994. The 1996 budget required total expenditure of ₦124,222m., of which ₦76,745m. was recurrent and ₦47,477m. capital, and envisaged a budgetary surplus of ₦19,000m. (equivalent to 1.2% of GDP). Revenue projections were based on an oil price of US $16 per barrel and an official exchange rate of ₦22.0 = US $1. The 1997 budget, announced on 18 January 1997, required ₦99,000m. in recurrent expenditure and ₦88,693m. in capital expenditure.

In November 1996 Gen. Abacha established the Vision 2010 Committee, chaired by a former head of state, Chief Ernest Shonekan; the committee of 172 members (later increased to 194) included the Minister of Finance, a further nine ministers, members of the armed forces and representatives from a number of civilian fields. The Vision 2010 Committee was to devise strategies to achieve sustained annual GDP growth of 6-10%, to keep inflation down to not more than 3-5% per annum by the year 2010, and to attain a high level of employment and was to submit its report in September 1997. Meanwhile, with diplomatic relations with a number of foreign states remaining strained, and with the IMF and the World Bank continuing to insist on reforms, the government failed to address the matter of Nigeria's debt payments; consequently, the problem of arrears, acknowledged to be unsustainable, remained unresolved.

Statistical Survey

Source (unless otherwise stated): Federal Office of Statistics, 7 Okotie-Eboh St, SW Ikoyi, Lagos; tel. (1) 2682935.

Area and Population

AREA, POPULATION AND DENSITY

Area (sq km)	923,768*
Population (census results, 28–30 November 1991)	
Males	44,544,531
Females	43,969,970
Total	88,514,501
Population (official estimates at mid-year)	
1993	93,265,251
1994	95,223,821
1995	97,223,521
Density (per sq km) at mid-1995	105.2

* 356,669 sq miles.

STATES (census of November 1991)*

	Population	Capital
Abia	2,297,978	Umuahia
Adamawa	2,124,049	Yola
Akwa Ibom	2,359,736	Uyo
Anambra	2,767,903	Awka
Bauchi	4,294,413	Bauchi
Benue	2,780,398	Makurdi
Borno	2,596,589	Maiduguri
Cross River	1,865,604	Calabar
Delta	2,570,181	Asaba
Edo	2,159,848	Benin City
Enugu	3,161,295	Enugu
Imo	2,485,499	Owerri
Jigawa	2,829,929	Dutse
Kaduna	3,969,252	Kaduna
Kano	5,632,040	Kano
Katsina	3,878,344	Katsina
Kebbi	2,062,226	Birnin Kebbi
Kogi	2,099,046	Lokoja
Kwara	1,566,469	Ilorin
Lagos	5,685,781	Ikeja
Niger	2,482,367	Minna
Ogun	2,338,570	Abeokuta
Ondo	3,884,485	Akure
Osun	2,203,016	Oshogbo
Oyo	3,488,789	Ibadan
Plateau	3,283,704	Jos
Rivers	3,983,857	Port Harcourt
Sokoto	4,392,391	Sokoto
Taraba	1,480,590	Jalingo
Yobe	1,411,481	Damaturu
Federal Capital Territory	378,671	Abuja
Total	88,514,501	

* In October 1996 the Government announced the creation of six new states.

PRINCIPAL TOWNS (estimated population at 1 July 1975)

Lagos (federal capital)*	1,060,848	Ado-Ekiti	213,000
Ibadan	847,000	Kaduna	202,000
Ogbomosho	432,000	Mushin	197,000
Kano	399,000	Maiduguri	189,000
Oshogbo	282,000	Enugu	187,000
Ilorin	282,000	Ede	182,000
Abeokuta	253,000	Aba	177,000
Port Harcourt	242,000	Ife	176,000
Zaria	224,000	Ila	155,000
Ilesha	224,000	Oyo	152,000
Onitsha	220,000	Ikere-Ekiti	145,000
Iwo	214,000	Benin City	136,000

* Federal capital moved to Abuja in December 1991.

BIRTHS AND DEATHS (UN estimates, annual averages)

	1980–85	1985–90	1990–95
Birth rate (per 1,000)	46.7	46.1	45.4
Death rate (per 1,000)	18.2	16.9	15.4

Expectation of life (UN estimates, years at birth, 1990–95): 50.4 (males 48.8; females 52.0).

Source: UN, *World Population Prospects: The 1994 Revision.*

ECONOMICALLY ACTIVE POPULATION
(sample survey, '000 persons aged 14 years and over, September 1986)

	Males	Females	Total
Agriculture, hunting, forestry and fishing	9,800.6	3,458.4	13,259.0
Mining and quarrying	6.8	—	6.8
Manufacturing	806.4	457.3	1,263.7
Electricity, gas and water	127.0	3.4	130.4
Construction	545.6	—	545.6
Trade, restaurants and hotels	2,676.6	4,740.8	7,417.4
Transport, storage and communications	1,094.7	17.2	1,111.9
Financing, insurance, real estate and business services	109.8	10.3	120.1
Community, social and personal services	3,939.5	962.6	4,902.1
Activities not adequately defined	597.1	147.8	744.9
Total employed	19,704.1	9,797.8	29,501.9
Unemployed	809.8	453.8	1,263.6
Total labour force	20,513.9	10,251.6	30,765.5

Note: Figures are based on a total estimated population of 98,936,800, which may be an overestimate.

Source: ILO, *Yearbook of Labour Statistics.*

Agriculture

PRINCIPAL CROPS ('000 metric tons)

	1993	1994	1995
Wheat	30*	40*	36
Rice (paddy)	2,305*	2,427	2,548
Maize	6,291*	6,902	7,240
Millet	4,602*	4,757	4,900
Sorghum	6,051*	6,197	6,184
Potatoes	80*	90*	94
Sweet potatoes†	40	40	40
Cassava	29,900	31,005	31,404
Yams	24,121	23,153	23,264
Taro (Coco yam)	1,066*	1,204*	1,204†
Pulses	1,626	1,721	1,850†
Soybeans	163	178	185
Groundnuts (in shell)	1,323	1,453	1,502
Sesame seed	52*	56	50
Cottonseed	225†	218	233
Cotton (lint)†	110	105	115
Coconuts	140	148	150
Palm kernels*	390	380	400
Palm oil	825	837	871
Tomatoes†	400	400	400
Green peppers†	900	920	950
Carrots†	175	175	175
Sugar cane	905	633	240
Citrus fruits†	2,200	2,200	2,200
Mangoes†	500	500	500
Pineapples	800	800	800
Plantains	1,629*	1,694*	1,694†
Papayas†	500	500	500
Other fruit (excluding melons)	1,400	1,400	1,400
Cashew nuts†	25	25	25
Cocoa beans	135*	130*	130†
Tobacco (leaves)†	10	10	10
Natural rubber (dry weight)	130*	105*	105†

* Unofficial figure(s). † FAO estimate(s).

Source: FAO, *Production Yearbook*.

LIVESTOCK ('000 head, year ending September)

	1993	1994	1995
Horses*	204	204	204
Asses*	1,000	1,000	1,000
Cattle	16,316	16,316*	17,791
Camels*	18	18	18
Pigs	6,660	6,926	6,926*
Sheep*	14,000	14,000	14,000
Goats*	24,500	24,500	24,500

Poultry (million)*: 120 in 1993; 122 in 1994; 124 in 1995.

* FAO estimate(s).

Source: FAO, *Production Yearbook*.

LIVESTOCK PRODUCTS ('000 metric tons)

	1993	1994	1995
Beef and veal	219*	219*	267
Mutton and lamb*	51	51	51
Goat meat*	127	130	130
Pig meat*	249	259	259
Poultry meat*	165	168	168
Other meat	100*	99*	99
Edible offals*	107	108	119
Cows' milk*	380	380	380
Butter and ghee*	8.6	8.6	8.6
Cheese*	6.9	6.9	6.9
Poultry eggs†	397.0	418.0	320.0
Cattle hides*	53.4	53.4	62.0
Sheepskins*	9.2	9.2	9.2
Goatskins*	20.0	20.4	20.4

* FAO estimate(s). † Unofficial figures.

Source: FAO, mainly *Production Yearbook*.

Forestry

ROUNDWOOD REMOVALS
(FAO estimates, '000 cubic metres, excluding bark)

	1992	1993	1994
Sawlogs, veneer logs and logs for sleepers*	5,984	5,984	5,984
Other industrial wood†	2,279	2,279	2,279
Fuel wood	93,964	96,852	99,796
Total	102,227	105,115	108,059

* Assumed to be unchanged since 1990.
† Assumed to be unchanged since 1980.

Source: FAO, *Yearbook of Forest Products*.

SAWNWOOD PRODUCTION
('000 cubic metres, including railway sleepers)

	1989	1990	1991
Coniferous (softwood)	6	6	—
Broadleaved (hardwood)	2,706*	2,723†	2,723*
Total	2,712	2,729	2,723*

* FAO estimate. † Unofficial figure.

1992–94: Annual production as in 1991 (FAO estimate).

Source: FAO, *Yearbook of Forest Products*.

Fishing

('000 metric tons, live weight)

	1993	1994	1995
Inland waters	111.8	117.7	133.4
Tilapias	15.5	13.4	15.1
Upsidedown catfishes	3.9	11.1	9.8
Characins	4.3	7.2	8.9
Naked catfishes	8.9	5.9	6.6
Torpedo-shaped catfishes	14.8	15.1	21.3
Other freshwater fishes (incl. unspecified)	55.4	58.9	66.7
Nile perch	9.1	6.1	5.0
Atlantic Ocean	143.7	164.4	232.7
West African croakers	8.1	12.0	9.3
Mullets	1.8	3.6	3.7
Threadfins and tasselfishes	4.0	5.2	5.9
Carangids	13.1	7.9	5.8
Sardinellas	26.3	25.8	76.6
Bonga shad	24.5	25.6	15.1
Sharks, rays, skates, etc.	5.8	9.1	6.5
Other marine fishes (incl. unspecified)	42.5	62.6	89.1
Southern pink shrimp	13.8	8.6	14.7
Other marine crustaceans	3.8	4.0	6.0
Total catch	255.5	282.1	366.1

Source: FAO, *Yearbook of Fishery Statistics*.

Mining

('000 metric tons, unless otherwise indicated)

	1992	1993	1994
Hard coal	87	41	50*
Crude petroleum	97,850	95,260	91,045
Natural gas (petajoules)	173	197	382
Tin concentrates (metric tons, metal content)	100†	178	208

* Provisional or estimated figure.
† Data from *World Metal Statistics* (London).

Source: UN, *Industrial Commodity Statistics Yearbook*.

Industry

SELECTED PRODUCTS ('000 metric tons, unless otherwise indicated)

	1992	1993	1994
Raw sugar	45[1]	50[1]	55[2]
Cigarettes (metric tons)	8,608	9,384	9,228
Plywood (cubic metres)	72,000	72,000[3]	72,000[3]
Paper and paperboard[3]	45	43	43
Nitrogenous fertilizers (a)[4]	271.0	267[5]	n.a.
Phosphatic fertilizers (b)[4]	76.0	44.0	n.a.
Jet fuels[5]	40	40	30
Motor spirit—petrol	3,233	3,178	1,675
Kerosene	1,636	1,603	799
Distillate fuel oils	2,761	2,933	1,413
Residual fuel oils	2,569	2,480	1,257
Liquefied petroleum gas[5]	60	60	60
Cement	3,367	3,247	3,086
Crude steel[6]	140	140	140
Tin metal—unwrought (metric tons)	300	300	316
Electric energy (million kWh)	14,834	14,790[5]	14,790[5]

[1] Data from the FAO.
[2] Data from the US Department of Agriculture.
[3] FAO estimate(s).
[4] Production in terms of (a) nitrogen or (b) phosphoric acid (Source: FAO, *Quarterly Bulletin of Statistics*).
[5] Provisional or estimated figure(s).
[6] Data from the US Bureau of Mines.

Source: UN, *Industrial Commodity Statistics Yearbook*.

Finance

CURRENCY AND EXCHANGE RATES

Monetary Units

100 kobo = 1 naira (₦).

Sterling and Dollar Equivalents (31 March 1997)

£1 sterling = 35.94 naira;
US $1 = 21.89 naira;
1,000 naira = £27.83 = $45.69.

Average Exchange Rate (naira per US $)

1994 21.996
1995 21.895
1996 21.884

FEDERAL BUDGET (₦ million)

Revenue*	1993	1994	1995†
Federation Account revenue	51,798	53,661	73,524
Other petroleum revenue	34,681‡	37,607	61,954
Independent revenue	8,121	2,106	19,121
Federation Stabilization Account	11,832	2,453	—
Value-added tax (VAT)	—	1,720	7,443
Total	106,433	97,547	162,042

Expenditure§	1993	1994	1995†
Recurrent expenditure	169,457	112,448	158,234
General administration	10,409	11,934	16,903
Defence	4,645	4,205	6,598
Internal security	3,313	4,396	5,257
Agriculture	1,084	1,183	1,510
Construction	1,396	1,144	1,699
Transport and communications	1,218	446	1,081
Other economic services	959	1,137	1,628
Education	5,336	7,383	9,746
Health	2,326	2,094	3,321
Other social and community services	1,145	609	754
Interest payments due	80,251	71,874	73,909
Other transfers‖	57,376	6,044	35,828
Capital expenditure	16,635	33,355	67,706
General administration	5,807	5,219	9,271
Defence	1,737	2,403	2,763
Internal security	538	1,164	1,304
Agriculture and water resources	1,824	2,179	2,414
Manufacturing, mining and quarrying	2,224	3,321	4,164
Transport and communications	803	1,070	2,511
Special projects	—	—	26,000
Other economic services	124	707	8,060
Education	995	2,052	2,426
Health	242	749	1,312
Housing	1,980	1,836	4,818
Other social and community services	359	357	659
Transfers	3	12,299	2,004
Total	186,092	145,803	225,940

* Figures refer to federally retained revenue. This includes 48.5% of total distributed revenue of the Federation Account, consisting almost entirely of proceeds from the operations of the Nigerian National Petroleum Corporation (NNPC) and foreign oil companies. The remainder of Federation Account revenue is allocated to state governments (24%), local governments (20%) and five special funds (7.5%). The Federal Government retains 20% of federally collected VAT.

† Estimates.

‡ Excluding revenue 'dedicated' to the NNPC to help the company to finance its capital budget.

§ Figures exclude the operations of extrabudgetary accounts, except for recurrent expenditure in 1993 and 1994. Including net lending, supplementary and extrabudgetary outlays, total expenditure (in ₦ million) was: 232,469 in 1993; 178,645 in 1994; 216,952 (estimate) in 1995.

‖ Including pensions, gratuities, grants, subventions and losses from transactions in foreign exchanges.

Source: IMF, *Nigeria—Statistical Appendix* (March 1997).

INTERNATIONAL RESERVES (US $ million at 31 December)

	1993	1994	1995
Gold*	1	1	1
IMF special drawing rights	—	—	1
Foreign exchange	1,372	1,386	1,443
Total	1,373	1,387	1,444

* National valuation of gold reserves (687,000 troy ounces in each year).

Source: IMF, *International Financial Statistics*.

MONEY SUPPLY (₦ million at 31 December)

	1993	1994	1995
Currency outside banks	56,168	90,315	106,411
Demand deposits at commercial banks	55,592	74,398	85,564
Total money (incl. others)	116,276	171,303	200,325

Source: IMF, *International Financial Statistics*.

COST OF LIVING
(Consumer Price Index for rural and urban areas; base: 1990 = 100)

	1993	1994	1995
Food	258.8	379.9	653.7
Clothing	236.7	362.5	n.a.
Rent, fuel and light	230.5	513.0	n.a.
All items (incl. others)	256.8	403.2	687.9

Source: ILO, *Yearbook of Labour Statistics*.

NATIONAL ACCOUNTS (₦ million at current prices)

National Income and Product

	1991	1992	1993*
Compensation of employees	46,869	59,099	74,546
Operating surplus	258,111	468,880	599,822
Domestic factor incomes	304,980	527,979	674,368
Consumption of fixed capital	15,267	16,351	17,240
Gross domestic product (GDP) at factor cost	320,247	544,330	691,608
Indirect taxes	4,271	5,762	5,689
Less Subsidies	508	284	202
GDP in purchasers' values	324,010	549,808	697,095
Factor income received from abroad	2,126	} -64,405	-73,211
Less Factor income paid abroad	26,600		
Gross national product (GNP)	299,536	485,403	623,884
Less Consumption of fixed capital	15,267	16,351	17,240
National income in market prices	284,269	469,052	606,644
Other current transfers from abroad (net)	7,292	12,680	17,925
National disposable income	291,561	481,732	624,569

* Figures are provisional.

Expenditure on the Gross Domestic Product

	1992	1993	1994
Government final consumption expenditure	20,432	27,583	31,720
Private final consumption expenditure	404,182	537,473	750,241
Increase in stocks }	58,940	81,398	85,314
Gross fixed capital formation }			
Total domestic expenditure	483,554	646,447*	867,275
Exports of goods and services	196,904	228,687	217,245
Less Imports of goods and services	130,650	173,661	170,187
GDP in purchasers' values	549,808	701,473	914,334
GDP at constant 1990 prices	281,089	287,488	291,333

* Including adjustments.

Source: IMF, *International Financial Statistics*.

Gross Domestic Product by Economic Activity (at factor cost)

	1993	1994	1995*
Agriculture, hunting, forestry and fishing	231,833	349,245	608,970
Mining and quarrying	251,168	227,729	248,750
Manufacturing	38,431	60,347	116,820
Electricity, gas and water	1,601	1,743	1,840
Construction	8,019	10,325	13,780
Trade, restaurants and hotels	102,066	160,384	284,600
Transport, storage and communications	15,297	31,770	57,280
Finance, insurance, real estate and business services	26,247	40,888	66,940
Government services	19,130	20,614	20,840
Other community, social and personal services	2,194	5,435	10,760
Total	695,986	908,476	1,430,580

Source: IMF, *Nigeria—Statistical Appendix* (March 1997).

BALANCE OF PAYMENTS (US $ million)

	1992	1993	1994
Exports of goods f.o.b.	11,791	9,910	9,459
Imports of goods f.o.b.	-7,181	-6,662	-6,511
Trade balance	4,611	3,248	2,948
Exports of services	1,053	1,163	371
Imports of services	-1,810	-2,726	-3,007
Balance on goods and services	3,853	1,685	312
Other income received	156	58	49
Other income paid	-2,494	-3,335	-2,986
Balance on goods, services and income	1,515	-1,593	-2,626
Current transfers received	817	857	550
Current transfers paid	-64	-44	-52
Current balance	2,268	-780	-2,128
Direct investment from abroad	897	1,345	1,959
Portfolio investment liabilities	1,884	-18	-27
Other investment assets	-5,840	-1,345	-1,286
Other investment liabilities	-4,725	-1,026	-317
Net errors and omissions	-122	-88	-139
Overall balance	-5,638	-1,911	-1,938

Source: IMF, *International Financial Statistics*.

External Trade

PRINCIPAL COMMODITIES
(₦ million)

Imports c.i.f.	1993	1994	1995*
Food and live animals	13,912.9	16,585.8	76,819.1
Crude materials (inedible) except fuels	4,306.4	5,636.0	27,576.1
Chemicals	28,322.6	40,578.8	172,678.8
Basic manufactures	39,751.1	35,909.0	152,324.9
Machinery and transport equipment	70,226.9	50,240.4	180,557.6
Miscellaneous manufactured articles	6,293.9	7,246.2	27,094.8
Total (incl. others)	165,629.4	161,027.0	656,572.2

Exports f.o.b.	1993	1994	1995*
Mineral products	213,803.7	200,826.9	728,648.3
Crude petroleum	213,778.8	200,710.2	728,265.3
Total (incl. others)	218,801.1	206,059.2	748,368.1

* Figures are provisional. A unitary exchange rate of ₦70.3632=US $1 was used as a conversion factor in 1995.

Sources: Central Bank of Nigeria, Lagos, and Federal Office of Statistics.

PRINCIPAL TRADING PARTNERS (US $ '000)*

Imports c.i.f.	1989	1990	1991
Belgium-Luxembourg	122,006	143,671	160,020
Brazil	106,404	175,801	179,085
China, People's Republic	86,591	128,230	189,776
France	271,611	394,209	440,375
Germany	591,509	644,589	881,035
Hong Kong	52,447	96,415	126,287
India	45,141	67,082	85,003
Italy	185,040	193,827	297,904
Japan	231,902	257,434	401,280
Korea, Republic	39,543	53,977	80,463
Netherlands	132,990	207,208	298,537
Spain	44,609	59,463	55,258
Switzerland	79,522	115,829	142,016
United Kingdom	556,105	739,417	2,324,956
USA	420,123	373,963	563,039
Total (incl. others)	3,419,079	4,317,921	7,114,360

Exports f.o.b.	1989	1990	1991
Brazil	82,307	9,423	125,754
Canada	16,275	117,584	150,988
Côte d'Ivoire	192,737	224,270	298,050
France	349,424	292,856	497,179
Germany	335,879	591,369	918,662
Ghana	171,746	224,694	189,966
Italy	340,367	298,146	935,714
Netherlands	651,942	933,627	878,331
Portugal	244,797	282,531	134,992
Spain	862,201	939,451	2,070,045
United Kingdom	142,533	298,914	148,715
USA	4,343,233	5,551,527	6,011,690
Total (incl. others)	8,145,435	10,241,646	12,827,941

* Imports by country of production; exports by country of last consignment.

Source: UN, *International Trade Statistics Yearbook*.

Transport

RAILWAYS (estimated traffic)

	1991	1992	1993
Passenger-km (million)	n.a.	434	555
Freight ton-km (million)	1,930	2,060	2,185

Sources: UN Economic Commission for Africa, *African Statistical Yearbook*; UN, *Statistical Yearbook*.

Freight ton-km (million): 141 in 1994; 108 in 1995 (Source: Central Bank of Nigeria).

ROAD TRAFFIC (estimates, '000 motor vehicles in use)

	1993	1994	1995
Passenger cars	571	617	663
Lorries and vans	65.3	66.8	68.3

Source: IRF, *World Road Statistics*.

SHIPPING

Merchant Fleet (registered at 31 December)

	1994	1995	1996
Number of vessels	279	291	288
Displacement ('000 grt)	473	479	447

Source: Lloyd's Register of Shipping.

International Sea-borne Freight Traffic
(estimates, '000 metric tons)

	1991	1992	1993
Goods loaded	82,768	84,797	86,993
Goods unloaded	10,960	11,143	11,346

Source: UN Economic Commission for Africa, *African Statistical Yearbook*.

CIVIL AVIATION (traffic on scheduled services)

	1992	1993	1994
Kilometres flown ('000)	12,000	11,000	12,000
Passengers carried ('000)	647	608	650
Passenger-km (million)	990	913	985
Total ton-km (million)	103	96	100

Source: UN, *Statistical Yearbook*.

Tourism

	1992	1993	1994
Tourist arrivals ('000)	237	192	193
Tourist receipts (US $ million)	29	31	34

Source: UN, *Statistical Yearbook*.

Communications Media

	1992	1993	1994
Radio receivers ('000 in use)	20,000	20,650	21,300
Television receivers ('000 in use)	3,800	4,000	4,150
Telephones ('000 main lines in use)	321	342	369
Book production (titles)†	1,562	n.a.	n.a.
Daily newspapers			
Number	26	n.a.	27
Average circulation ('000 copies)*	1,850	n.a.	1,950

* Estimates.

† Including pamphlets (540 in 1992), but excluding university theses.

Sources: UNESCO, *Statistical Yearbook*; UN, *Statistical Yearbook*.

Education

(1994)

	Institu-tions	Teachers	Students		
			Males	Females	Total
Primary	38,649	435,210	9,056,367	7,134,580	16,190,947
Secondary	6,162*	152,596	2,419,782	2,031,547	4,451,329
Teacher training†	135	4,531	n.a.	n.a.	108,751
Technical and vocational†	240	5,115	n.a.	n.a.	89,536
Higher education	133*	19,601‡	n.a.	n.a.	383,488*

* 1993 figure.

† 1987 figures.

‡ 1989 figure.

Sources: Federal Ministry of Education, Lagos; UNESCO, *Statistical Yearbook*.

Directory

The Constitution

On 18 November 1993, following the assumption of power of a new military Head of State, all existing organs of state and bodies that had been established under the former process of transition to civilian rule were dissolved, the elected State Governors were replaced with military administrators, and political activity was prohibited. Supreme executive and legislative power was subsequently vested in a Provisional Ruling Council (PRC), comprising senior military officials and principal members of the new cabinet, the Federal Executive Council (FEC). The Head of State, who was Commander-in-Chief of the Armed Forces, chaired the PRC and the FEC. On 21 November the Constitution of 1979 (which provided for an executive President, elected for a term of four years, a bicameral National Assembly and elected local government councils) was formally restored. On 27 June 1995 a National Constitutional Conference (NCC) submitted proposals for a draft constitution for approval by the Government, which rescinded the ban on political activity. In early October the Government announced a three-year programme for transition to civilian rule, whereby a new President was to be inaugurated on 1 October 1998, following elections at local, state and national level. New constitutional provisions (which were largely in accordance with the recommendations of the NCC) included the adoption of a multi-party system whereby any party with a minimum of 10 seats in the National Assembly would be proportionately represented in the FEC, the division of the country into a number of regions, and the rotation of principal executive and legislative offices between these regions for a period of 30 years, and the establishment of a National Judicial Council and a Constitutional Court. The new Constitution was to be formally adopted in 1998, at the end of the transitional period.

The Judiciary comprises the Supreme Court, the Court of Appeal and the Federal High Court at federal level, and High Courts in each state. Judicial appointments below the Supreme Court are made by the Federal Government on the advice of the Advisory Judicial Committee, with the Chief Justice of the Federation as Chairman. Certain states also have a Shari'a Court of Appeal, and others a Customary Court of Appeal, to consider civil cases in Islamic or customary law respectively.

Federal Government

HEAD OF STATE

Head of Government and Commander-in-Chief of the Armed Forces: Gen. SANI ABACHA (assumed power 17 November 1993).

PROVISIONAL RULING COUNCIL

(August 1997)

Gen. SANI ABACHA (Chairman)
Lt-Gen. OLADIPO DIYA (Vice-Chairman)
Maj.-Gen. ABDULSALAM ABUBAKAR
Maj.-Gen. ISHAYA BAMAIYI
Cdre MIKE AKHIGBE
Air Vice-Marshal NSIKAK EDUOK
Alhaji IBRAHIM A. COOMASIE
Air Vice-Marshal A. DAGGASH
Maj.-Gen. CHRIS GARBA
Maj.-Gen. JOHN INIENGER
Brig.-Gen. ABDULLAHI MUKTAR
Brig.-Gen. BASHIR MAGASHI
Brig.-Gen. PETER GYANG SHA
Brig.-Gen. FELIX MUJAKPERUO
Brig.-Gen. PATRICK AZIZA
Rear-Adm. RUFUS EYITAYO
Cdre VICTOR OMBU
Air Cdre EMMANUEL EDEM
Air Vice-Marshal GY KONTAGORA
Lt-Gen. JEREMIAH T. USENI
Lt-Gen. MOHAMMED B. HALADU
Brig.-Gen. TIMOTHY SHELPIDI
Air Cdre IBRAHIM MUSA
Maj.-Gen. MUFU BALOGUN
Capt. ANTHONY OGUGUO
Air Cdre CANNIS UWENWALIRI
Cdre TAYIWO ODENINA

FEDERAL EXECUTIVE COUNCIL

(August 1997)

Minister of Justice: Chief MICHAEL AGBAMUCHE.

Minister of Agriculture: Alhaji GAMBO JIMETA.

Minister of Aviation: Air Cdre UDOH IME.

Minister of Commerce and Tourism: Rear-Adm. JUBRILA AYINLA.

Minister of Communications: Maj.-Gen. ADENIYI T. OLANREWAJU.

Minister of Education: Dr MOHAMMED LIMAN.

Minister of Finance: Chief ANTHONY ANI.

Minister of Federal Capital Territory: Lt-Gen. JEREMIAH T. USENI.

Minister of Foreign Affairs: Chief TOM IKIMI.

Minister of Health: Dr IHECHUKWU MADUBUIKE.

Minister of Industry: Lt-Gen. MOHAMMED B. HALADU.

Minister of Information: Dr WALTER OFONAGORO.

Minister of Internal Affairs: Alhaji BABAGANA KINGIBE.

Minister of Labour: Alhaji UBA AHMED.

Minister of National Planning: Chief AYO OGUNLADE.

Minister of Petroleum Resources: Chief DAN L. ETETE.

Minister of Power and Steel: Alhaji BASHIR DALHATU.

Minister of Science and Technology: Brig.-Gen. SAM I. MOMAH.

Minister of Solid Minerals Development: Alhaji KALOMA ALI.

Minister of Transport: Maj.-Gen. IBRAHIM D. GUMEL.

Minister of Water Resources: Alhaji ALIYU J. YELWA.

Minister of Women's and Social Affairs: JUDITH ATTA.

Minister of Works and Housing: Maj.-Gen. ABDULKARIM ADISA.

Minister of Youth and Sports: Chief JIM NWOBODO.

Minister of State for Agriculture: (vacant).

Minister of State for Education: IYABO ANISULOWO.

Minister of State for Finance: Alhaji ABU GIDADO.

Minister of State for Federal Capital Territory: MARIAM CLARK.

Minister of State for Foreign Affairs: Alhaji ALHASSAN IDRISSA KPAKI.

Minister of State for Health: DAVID SADAUKI.

Minister of State for Petroleum Resources: Dr KABIRU CHAFE.

Minister of State for Power and Steel: Prof. IYORWUESE HAGHER.

Minister of State for Works and Housing: Alhaji ABDULLAHI ADAMU.

Ministers of State with Special Duties: Alhaji WADA NAS, Dr LAZARUS UNAOGU, WOLE OYELESE.

MINISTRIES

Office of the Head of State: Abuja.

Ministry of Agriculture: Gwagwalada Area, PMB 24, Abuja; tel. (9) 8821080.

Ministry of Aviation: Abuja.

Ministry of Commerce and Tourism: Federal Secretariat, PMB 88, Garki, Abuja.

Ministry of Communications: Headquarters, Lafiaji, Lagos; tel. (1) 2633747.

Ministry of Education: PMB 12573, Ahmadu Bello Way, Victoria Island, Lagos; tel. (1) 2616843.

Ministry of Federal Capital Territory: Federal Secretariat, Abuja; tel. (9) 2431250.

Ministry of Finance: New Secretariat Area II, Garki, Abuja; tel. (9) 2341109.

Ministry of Foreign Affairs: Maputo St, PMB 130, Abuja; tel. (9) 5230520.

Ministry of Health: New Federal Secretariat Phase II, Ikoyi Rd, Obalende, Lagos; tel. (1) 2684405.

Ministry of Industry: Gwagwalada Area, PMB 24, Abuja; tel. (9) 2431250.

Ministry of Information: 15 Awolowo Rd, Ikoyi, Lagos; tel. (1) 2610836; telex 22649.

Ministry of Internal Affairs: Old Secretariat, Garki, Abuja.

Ministry of Justice: New Federal Secretariat, Ikoyi, Lagos; tel. (1) 2684414.

Ministry of Labour: Abuja.

Ministry of National Planning: Federal Secretariat Phase I, Ikoyi Rd, Ikoyi, Lagos.

Ministry of Petroleum Resources: Federal Secretariat, Ikoyi Rd, Ikoyi, Lagos.

Ministry of Power and Steel: Federal Secretariat Phase I, Ikoyi Rd, Ikoyi, Lagos.

Ministry of Science and Technology: New Federal Secretariat, Ikoyi Rd, Ikoyi, Lagos; tel. (1) 2614250.

Ministry of Solid Minerals Development: Abuja.

Ministry of Transport: Joseph St, PMB 21038, Ikoyi, Lagos; tel. (1) 2652120; telex 21535.

Ministry of Water Resources: Gwagwalada Area, PMB 24, Abuja; tel. (9) 8821080.

Ministry of Women's and Social Affairs: Abuja.

Ministry of Works and Housing: Tafawa Balewa Sq., Lagos; tel. (1) 2653120.

Ministry of Youth and Sports: Abuja.

Legislature

NATIONAL ASSEMBLY

The National Assembly, which comprised a 91-member Senate and a 593-member House of Representatives, was dissolved on 18 November 1993.

Political Organizations

On 18 November 1993, following the assumption of power by a new military Government, political activity was prohibited. On 27 June 1995 this ban was rescinded, prior to the adoption of a programme for transition to democratic rule. Five political organizations were subsequently granted registration:

Committee of National Consensus (CNC): Chair. Dr ABEL UBEKU.

Democratic Party of Nigeria (DPN): Chair. (vacant).

Grassroots Democratic Movement (GDM): Chair. Alhaji GAMBO LAWAN.

National Centre Party of Nigeria (NCPN): Chair. Alhaji MUGAJI ABDULAHI.

United Nigerian Congress Party (UNCP): Chair. Alhaji ISA MOHAMED ARGUNGU.

The following political pressure groups were active in 1997:

Campaign for Democracy (CD): f. Nov. 1991; alliance of 25 human rights orgs opposed to the Govt; Chair. FREDERICK FASEHUN (acting); Sec.-Gen. JOE OKEI.

Movement for the Survival of the Ogoni People (MOSOP): f. 1990 to organize opposition to petroleum production in Ogoni territory; subsequently demanded that the Ogoni ethnic group be granted compensation for environmental damage to the region and rights to petroleum revenue; Deputy Pres. LEDUM MITEE.

National Democratic Coalition (NADECO): grouping of human rights activists, and fmr politicians and mil. officers; demands the installation of Chief Moshood Abiola as Pres.; Chair. ABRAHAM ADESANYA (acting); Sec.-Gen. OYO OPADOKUN.

United Action for Democracy (UAD): f. May 1997; alliance of 22 opposition groups; seeks the resignation of Gen. Abacha and the restoration of democratic rule.

Diplomatic Representation

EMBASSIES AND HIGH COMMISSIONS IN NIGERIA

Algeria: Plot 203, Etim Inyang Crescent, POB 7288, Lagos; tel. (1) 612092; telex 21676; fax (1) 2624017; Ambassador: EL-MIHOUB MIHOUBI.

Angola: 5 Kasumu Ekomode St, Victoria Island, POB 50437, Lagos; tel. (1) 2611135; Ambassador: B. A. SOZINHO.

Argentina: 93 Awolowo Rd, SW Ikoyi, POB 51940, Lagos; tel. (1) 2682797; telex 21403; Ambassador: NICAROHICIO BOSSO.

Australia: 2 Ozumba Mbadiwe Ave, Victoria Island, POB 2427, Lagos; tel. (1) 2618875; telex 21219; fax (1) 2618703; High Commissioner: H. BROWN.

Austria: Fabac Centre, 3B Ligali Ayorinde Ave, POB 1914, Lagos; tel. (1) 2616081; telex 21463; fax (1) 2617639; Ambassador: Dr WILFRIED ALMOSLECHNER.

Belgium: 1A Murtala Muhammed Dr., Ikoyi, POB 149, Lagos; tel. (1) 2691507; telex 21118; fax (1) 2691444; Ambassador: CHRISTIAAN VAN DRIESSCHE.

Benin: 4 Abudu Smith St, Victoria Island, POB 5705, Lagos; tel. (1) 2614411; telex 21583; Ambassador: PATRICE HOUNGAVOU.

Brazil: 257 Kofo Abayomi St, Victoria Island, POB 1931, Lagos; tel. (1) 2610135; telex 23428; fax (1) 2613394; Ambassador: (vacant).

Bulgaria: 3 Eleke Crescent, Victoria Island, PMB 4441, Lagos; tel. (1) 2611931; telex 21567; fax (1) 2619879; Ambassador: (vacant).

Burkina Faso: 15 Norman Williams St, Ikoyi, Lagos; tel. (1) 2681001; Chargé d'affaires a.i.: ADOLPHE T. BENON.

Cameroon: 5 Elsie Femi Pearse St, Victoria Island, PMB 2476, Lagos; tel. (1) 2612226; telex 21343; Chargé d'affaires a.i.: PROSPER FOMBA NGOM.

Canada: 4 Idowu Taylor St, Victoria Island, POB 54506, Ikoyi Station, Lagos; tel. (1) 2692195; telex 21275; fax (1) 2692919; (High Commission temporarily closed in March 1997); High Commissioner: HANSPETER STRAUCH.

Central African Republic: Plot 137, Ajao Estate, New Airport, Oshodi, Lagos; Ambassador: JEAN-PAUL MOKODOPO.

Chad: 2 Goriola St, Victoria Island, PMB 70662, Lagos; tel. (1) 2622590; telex 28882; fax (1) 2618314; Ambassador: Dr ISSA HASSAN KHAYAR.

China, People's Republic: 19A Taslim Elias Close, Victoria Island, POB 5653, Lagos; tel. (1) 2612586; Ambassador: LU FENGDING.

Colombia: 43 Raymond Njoku Rd, POB 2352, Ikoyi, Lagos; Chargé d'affaires: Dr BERNARDO ECHEVERRI.

Côte d'Ivoire: 3 Abudu Smith St, Victoria Island, POB 7780, Lagos; tel. (1) 2610936; telex 21120; Ambassador: DÉSIRÉ AMON TANOE.

Cuba: Plot 935, Idejo St, Victoria Island, POB 328, Victoria Island, Lagos; tel. (1) 2614836; Ambassador: GIRALDO MAZOLA.

Czech Republic: 2 Alhaji Masha Close, Ikoyi, POB 1009, Lagos; tel. (1) 2683207; fax (1) 2683175; Ambassador: EVZEN VACEK.

Denmark: 4 Eleke Crescent, Victoria Island, POB 2390, Lagos; tel. (1) 2611503; telex 21349; fax (1) 2610841; Ambassador: LARS BLINKENBERG.

Egypt: 81 Awolowo Rd, Ikoyi, POB 538, Lagos; tel. (1) 2612922; Ambassador: FUAD YUSUF.

Equatorial Guinea: 7 Bank Rd, Ikoyi, POB 4162, Lagos; tel. (1) 2683717; Ambassador: A. S. DOUGAN MALABO.

Ethiopia: Plot 97, Ahmadu Bello Rd, Victoria Island, PMB 2488, Lagos; tel. (1) 2613198; telex 21694; fax (1) 2615055; Chargé d'affaires a.i.: NEGGA BEYENNE.

Finland: 13 Eleke Crescent, Victoria Island, POB 4433, Lagos; tel. (1) 2610916; telex 21796; fax (1) 2613158; Ambassador: HEIKKI LATVANEN.

France: 1 Lady Oyinkan Abayomi Drive, POB 51223, Lagos; tel. (1) 2693427; fax (1) 2693430; Ambassador: PHILIPPE PELTIER.

Gabon: 8 Norman Williams St, POB 5989, Lagos; tel. (1) 2684673; telex 21736; Ambassador: E. AGUEMINYA.

Gambia: 162 Awolowo Rd, SW Ikoyi, POB 8037, Lagos; tel. (1) 2681018; High Commissioner: OMAR SECKA.

Germany: 15 Eleke Crescent, Victoria Island, POB 728, Lagos; tel. (1) 2611011; telex 21229; Ambassador: (vacant).

Ghana: 21–25 King George V Rd, POB 889, Lagos; tel. (1) 2630015; fax (1) 2630338; High Commissioner: JOHN K. TETTEGAH.

Greece: Plot 1397, 9B Tiamiyu Savage St, Victoria Island, POB 1199, Lagos; tel. (1) 2614852; telex 21747; fax (1) 2611412; Ambassador: HARIS KARABARBOUNIS.

Guinea: 8 Abudu Smith St, Victoria Island, POB 2826, Lagos; tel. (1) 2616961; Ambassador: KOMO BEAVOGUI.

Holy See: 9 Anifowoshe St, Victoria Island, POB 2470, Lagos; tel. (1) 2614441; telex 22455; fax (1) 2618635; Apostolic Pro-Nuncio: Most Rev. CARLO MARIA VIGANÒ, Titular Archbishop of Ulpiana.

Hungary: 9 Louis Solomon Close, Victoria Island, POB 3168, Lagos; tel. (1) 2613551; fax (1) 2613717; Ambassador: JÁNOS BALASSA.

India: 107 Awolowo Rd, SW Ikoyi, POB 2322, Lagos; tel. (1) 2681297; High Commissioner: SATINDER KUMBER UPPAL.

Indonesia: 5 Anifowoshe St, Victoria Island, POB 3473, Lagos; tel. (1) 2614601; Ambassador: JOHANNES SUTANTIO.

Iran: 1 Alexander Ave, Ikoyi, Lagos; tel. (1) 2681601; telex 22625; Chargé d'affaires a.i. SABRE ANUSLA.

Iraq: Plot 708A, Adeola Hopewell St, Victoria Island, POB 2859, Lagos; tel. (1) 610389; fax (1) 618633; Ambassador TAHA SHUKER MAHMOUD.

Ireland: 34 Kofo Abayomi St, Victoria Island, Lagos; tel. (1) 2615224; telex 21478; Ambassador: DERMOT A. GALLAGHER.

Israel: Abuja; Ambassador: GADI GOLAN.

Italy: 12 Eleke Crescent, Victoria Island, POB 2161, Lagos; tel. (1) 2621046; telex 21202; fax (1) 2619881; Ambassador: UMBERTO PLAJA.

Jamaica: Plot 77, Samuel Adedoyin Ave, Victoria Island, POB 75368, Lagos; tel. (1) 2611085; fax (1) 2610047; High Commissioner: ROBERT MILLER (acting).

Japan: 24–25 Apese St, Victoria Island, PMB 2111, Lagos; tel. (1) 2614929; telex 21364; fax (1) 2614035; Ambassador: TAKANORI KAZUHARA.

Kenya: 53 Queen's Drive, Ikoyi, POB 6464, Lagos; tel. (1) 2682768; telex 21124; High Commissioner: Dr I. E. MALUKI.

Korea, Democratic People's Republic: 31 Akin Adesola St, Victoria Island, Lagos; tel. (1) 2610108; Ambassador: CHOE SANG BOM.

Korea, Republic: Plot 934, Idejo St, Victoria Island, POB 4668, Lagos; tel. (1) 2615353; telex 21953; Ambassador: CHAI KI-OH.

Lebanon: Plot 18, Eleke Crescent, Victoria Island, POB 651, Lagos; tel. (1) 2614511; Ambassador: M. SALAME.

Liberia: 3 Idejo St, Plot 162, off Adeola Odeku St, Victoria Island, POB 70841, Lagos; tel. (1) 2618899; telex 23361; Ambassador: Prof. JAMES TAPEH.

Libya: 46 Raymond Njoku Rd, SW Ikoyi, Lagos; tel. (1) 2680880; Chargé d'affaires a.i.: IBRAHIM AL-BASHAR.

Malaysia: 1 Anifowoshe St, Victoria Island, POB 3729, Lagos; tel. (1) 2619415; High Commissioner: ALFRED KUMARASERI.

Mauritania: 1A Karimu Giwa Close, SW Ikoyi, Lagos; tel. (1) 2682971; Ambassador: MOHAMED M. O. WEDDADY.

Morocco: Plot 1318, 27 Karimu Katun St, Victoria Island, Lagos; tel. (1) 2611682; telex 21835; Ambassador: SAAD EDDINE TAIEB.

Namibia: Victoria Island, PMB 8000, Lagos.

Netherlands: 24 Ozumba Mbadiwe Ave, Victoria Island, POB 2426, Lagos; tel. (1) 2613005; telex 22055; fax (1) 617605; Ambassador: L. P. J. MAZAIRAC.

Niger: 15 Adeola Odeku St, Victoria Island, PMB 2736, Lagos; tel. (1) 2612300; telex 21434; Ambassador: Alhaji MAHAMANG DADO MANSOUR.

Norway: 3 Anifowoshe St, Victoria Island, PMB 2431, Lagos; tel. (1) 2618467; telex 21429; fax (1) 2618469; Ambassador: FRED H. NOMME.

Pakistan: Plot 859, Bishop Aboyade Cole St, Victoria Island, POB 2450, Lagos; tel. (1) 2614129; telex 22758; fax (1) 2614822; High Commissioner: SHAHID M. AMIN.

Philippines: Plot 152, No 302, off 3rd Ave, Victoria Island, Lagos; tel. (1) 2614048; telex 23344; Ambassador: MUKHTAR M. MUALLAM.

Poland: 10 Idejo St, Victoria Island, POB 410, Lagos; tel. (1) 2614634; telex 21729; Ambassador: KAZIMIERZ GUTKOWSKI.

Portugal: Plot 1677, Olukunle Bakare Close, Victoria Island, Lagos; tel. (1) 2619037; telex 22424; fax (1) 2616071; Ambassador: FILIPE ORLANDO DE ALBUQUERQUE

Romania: Plot 1192, off Olugbosi Close, Victoria Island, POB 72928, Lagos; tel. (1) 2617806; telex 28828; fax (1) 2618249; Chargé d'affaires a.i.: EMIL RAPCEA.

Russia: 5 Eleke Crescent, Victoria Island, POB 2723, Lagos; tel. (1) 2613359; telex 22905; fax (1) 2615022; Ambassador: LEV PARSHIN.

Saudi Arabia: Plot 1412, Victoria Island, POB 2836, Lagos; (1) 2603420; Ambassador: SHEHU GALADANCHI.

Senegal: 14 Kofo Abayomi Rd, Victoria Island, PMB 2197, Lagos; tel. (1) 2611722; telex 21398; Ambassador: CHERIF Y. DIAITE.

Sierra Leone: 31 Waziri Ibrahim St, Victoria Island, POB 2821, Lagos; tel. (1) 2614666; telex; 21495; High Commissioner: JOSEPH BLELL.

Slovakia: POB 1290, Lagos; tel. (1) 2694229; telex 28685; fax (1) 2690423; Ambassador: ANTON HAJDUK.

Somalia: Plot 1270, off Adeola Odeka St, POB 6355, Lagos; tel. (1) 2611283; Ambassador: M. S. HASSAN.

South Africa: 4 Maduike St, Ikoyi, Lagos; tel. (1) 685810; High Commissioner: CAROL ALEX (acting).

Spain: 21C Kofo Abayomi Rd, Victoria Island, POB 2738, Lagos; tel. (1) 2615215; telex 28944; fax (1) 2618225; Ambassador MANUEL POMBO BRAVO.

Sudan: 2B Kofo Abayomi St, Victoria Island, POB 2428, Lagos; tel. (1) 2615889; telex 23500; Ambassador: AHMED ALTIGANI SALEH.

Switzerland: 7 Anifowoshe St, Victoria Island, POB 536, Lagos; tel. (1) 2613918; telex 21597; Ambassador: ANTON GREBER.

Syria: 25 Kofo Abayomi St, Victoria Island, Lagos; tel. (1) 2615860; Chargé d'affaires a.i.: MUSTAFA HAJ-ALI.

Tanzania: 45 Ademola St, Ikoyi, POB 6417, Lagos; tel. (1) 2613594; High Commissioner: Maj.-Gen. MIRISHO SAM HAGAI SARAKIKYA.

Thailand: 1 Ruxton Rd, Old Ikoyi, POB 3095, Lagos; tel. (1) 2681337; Ambassador: N. SATHAPORN.

Togo: 96 Awolowo Rd, SW Ikoyi, POB 1435, Lagos; tel. (1) 2617449; telex 21506; Ambassador: FOLI-AGBENOZAN TETTEKPOE.

Trinidad and Tobago: 3A Tiamiyu Savage St, Victoria Island, POB 6392, Marina, Lagos; tel. (1) 2612087; telex 21041; fax (1) 612732; High Commissioner: (vacant).

Turkey: 3 Okunola Martins Close, Ikoyi, POB 56252, Lagos; tel. (1) 2691140; fax (1) 2693040; Ambassador: NUMAN HAZAR.

United Kingdom: 11 Eleke Crescent, Victoria Island, PMB 12136, Lagos; tel. (1) 2619531; telex 21247; fax (1) 2614021; High Commissioner: GRAHAM BURTON.

USA: 2 Eleke Crescent, Victoria Island, Lagos; tel. (1) 2610097; telex 23616; fax (1) 2610257; Ambassador: WALTER CARRINGTON.

Venezuela: 35B Adetokunbo Ademola St, Victoria Island, POB 3727, Lagos; tel. (1) 2611590; telex 28590; fax (1) 2617350; Ambassador: ALFREDO ENRIQUE VARGAS.

Yugoslavia: 7 Maitama Sule St, SW Ikoyi, PMB 978, Lagos; tel. (1) 2680238; Chargé d'affaires a.i.: DORBEJOG KAHANSKI.

Zambia: 11 Keffi St, SW Ikoyi, PMB 6119, Lagos; High Commissioner: B. N. NKUNIKA (acting).

Zimbabwe: 10A Tiamiyu Savage St, POB 50247, Victoria Island, Lagos; tel. (1) 2619328; telex 22650; High Commissioner: GIFT PUNUNGUE (acting).

Judicial System

Supreme Court: Tafawa Balewa Sq., Lagos; consists of a Chief Justice and up to 15 Justices, appointed by the Armed Forces Ruling Council. It has original jurisdiction in any dispute between the Federation and a State, or between States, and hears appeals from the Federal Court of Appeal.

Chief Justice: MUHAMMADU LAWAL UWAIS.

Federal Court of Appeal: consists of a President and at least 35 Justices, of whom three must be experts in Islamic *(Shari'a)* law and three experts in Customary law.

Federal High Court: consists of a Chief Judge and a number of other judges.

Each State has a **High Court,** consisting of a Chief Judge and a number of judges, appointed by the Federal Government. If required, a state may have a **Shari'a Court of Appeal** (dealing with Islamic civil law) and a **Customary Court of Appeal. Special Military Tribunals** have been established to try offenders accused of crimes such as corruption, drug-trafficking and armed robbery; appeals against rulings of the Special Military Tribunals are referred to a **Special Appeals Tribunal**, which comprises retired judges.

Religion

ISLAM

According to the 1963 census, there were more than 26m. Muslims (47.2% of the total population) in Nigeria.

Spiritual Head: Alhaji MOHAMED MACCIDO, the Sultan of Sokoto.

CHRISTIANITY

The 1963 census enumerated more than 19m. Christians (34.5% of the total population).

Christian Council of Nigeria: 139 Ogunlana Drive, Marina, POB 2838, Lagos; tel. (1) 836019; f. 1929; 12 full mems and six assoc. mems; Pres. Rt Rev. C. C. ANYAWU (Anglican Bishop of Mbaise); Gen. Sec. C. O. WILLIAMS.

The Anglican Communion

Anglicans are adherents of the Church of the Province of Nigeria, comprising 48 dioceses. Nigeria, formerly part of the Province of West Africa, became a separate Province in 1979. The Church had an estimated 10m. members in 1990.

Archbishop of Nigeria and Bishop of Lagos: Most Rev. JOSEPH ADETILOYE, Bishopscourt, 29 Marina, POB 13, Lagos; tel. (1) 2635681; fax (1) 2631264.

Provincial Secretary: Ven. SAMUEL B. AKINOLA, 29 Marina, POB 78, Lagos; tel. (1) 2635681; fax (1) 2631264.

The Roman Catholic Church

Nigeria comprises nine archdioceses, 31 dioceses and two Catholic Missions, at Bomadi and at Kano. At 31 December 1994 the total number of adherents represented an estimated 2.8% of the population.

Catholic Bishops' Conference of Nigeria: 6 Force Rd, POB 951, Lagos; tel. (1) 2635849; telex 28636; (1) fax 2636680; f. 1976; Pres. Most Rev. Dr ALBERT KANENE OBIEFUNA, Archbishop of Onitsha.

Catholic Secretariat of Nigeria: 6 Force Rd, POB 951, Lagos; tel. (1) 2635849; telex 28636; fax (1) 2636680; Sec.-Gen. Rev. Fr MATTHEW HASSAN KUKAH.

Archbishop of Abuja: Most Rev. JOHN O. ONAIYEKAN, Archdiocesan Secretariat, Block 64, Area 2, Section II, POB 286, Garki, Abuja; tel. and fax (9) 2340661.

Archbishop of Benin City: Most Rev. PATRICK E. EKPU, Archdiocesan Secretariat, POB 35, Benin City, Edo; tel. (52) 254787; fax (52) 255763.

Archbishop of Calabar: Most Rev. BRIAN D. USANGA, Archdiocesan Secretariat, PMB 1044, Calabar, Cross River; tel. (87) 221666; fax (87) 221407.

Archbishop of Ibadan: Most Rev. FELIX ALABA JOB, Archdiocesan Secretariat, 8 Latosa Rd, PMB 5057, Ibadan, Oyo; tel. (22) 414996; fax (22) 414855.

Archbishop of Jos: Most Rev. GABRIEL G. GANAKA, Archdiocesan Secretariat, 20 Joseph Gomwalk Rd, POB 494, Jos, Plateau; tel. (73) 52878; fax (73) 56880.

Archbishop of Kaduna: Most Rev. PETER YARIYOK JATAU, Archbishop's House, Tafawa Balewa Way, POB 248, Kaduna; tel. (62) 236076.

Archbishop of Lagos: Most Rev. ANTHONY OLUBUNMI OKOGIE, Archdiocesan Secretariat, 19 Catholic Mission St, POB 8, Lagos; tel. and fax (1) 2633841.

Archbishop of Onitsha: Most Rev. ALBERT KANENE OBIEFUNA, Archdiocesan Secretariat, POB 411, Onitsha, Anambra; tel. (46) 210444; fax (46) 214537.

Archbishop of Owerri: Most Rev. ANTHONY J. V. OBINNA, Archdiocesan Secretariat, POB 85, Owerri, Imo; tel. (83) 230115; fax (83) 230760.

Other Christian Churches

Brethren Church of Nigeria: c/o Kulp Bible School, POB 1, Mubi, Gongola; f. 1923; 80,000 mems; Gen. Sec. JOHN BOAZ Y. MAINA.

Church of the Lord (Aladura): Anthony Village, Ikorodu Rd, POB 308, Ikeja, Lagos; tel. (1) 4964749; f. 1930; 1.1m. mems; Primate Dr E. O. A. ADEJOBI.

Lutheran Church of Christ in Nigeria: POB 21, Numan, Adamawa; 575,000 mems; Pres. Rt Rev. Dr DAVID L. WINDIBIZIRI.

Lutheran Church of Nigeria: Obot Idim Ibesikpo, Uyo, Akwa Ibom; tel. and fax (85) 201848; f. 1936; 370,000 mems; Pres. Rev. S. J. UDOFIA.

Methodist Church Nigeria: Wesley House, 21–22 Marina, POB 2011, Lagos; tel. (1) 2631853; 483,500 mems; Patriarch Rev. SUNDAY COFFIE MBANG.

Nigerian Baptist Convention: Baptist Bldg, PMB 5113, Ibadan; tel. (2) 412146; 500,000 mems; Pres. Rev. DAVID H. KARO; Gen. Sec. Dr SAMUEL T. OLA AKANDE.

Presbyterian Church of Nigeria: 26–29 Ehere Rd, Ogbor Hill, POB 2635, Aba, Imo; tel. (82) 222551; f. 1846; 130,000 mems; Moderator Rt Rev. Dr A. A. OTU; Synod Clerk Rev. UBON B. USUNG.

The Salvation Army and the Qua Iboe Church are also active.

AFRICAN RELIGIONS

The beliefs, rites and practices of the people of Nigeria are very diverse, varying between ethnic groups and between families in the same group. In 1963 about 10m. persons (18% of the total population) were followers of traditional beliefs.

The Press

DAILIES

Abuja Times: Daily Times of Nigeria Ltd, New Isheri Rd, Agidingbi, PMB 21340, Ikeja, Lagos; tel. (1) 4900850; telex 21333; f. 1992.

Amana: Concord House, 42 Concord Way, POB 4483, Ikeja, Lagos; Hausa.

Daily Champion: Isolo Industrial Estate, Oshodi-Apapa, Lagos; Editor EMEKA OMEIHE.

Daily Express: Commercial Amalgamated Printers, 30 Glover St, Lagos; f. 1938; Editor Alhaji AHMED ALAO (acting); circ. 20,000.

Daily Sketch: Sketch Publishing Ltd, Oba Adebimpe Rd, PMB 5067, Ibadan; tel. (2) 414851; telex 31591; f. 1964; govt-owned; Chair. RONKE OKUSANYA; Editor ADEMOLA IDOWU; circ. 64,000.

Daily Star: 9 Works Rd, PMB 1139, Enugu; tel. (42) 253561; Editor JOSEF BEL-MOLOKWU.

Daily Times: Daily Times of Nigeria Ltd, New Isheri Rd, Agidingbi, PMB 21340, Ikeja, Lagos; tel. (1) 4900850; telex 21333; f. 1925; 60% govt-owned; Admin. INNOCENT OKPARADIKE; circ. 400,000.

The Democrat: 9 Ahmed Talib Ave, POB 4457, Kaduna South, tel. (62) 231907; f. 1983; Editor ABDULHAMID BABATUNDE; circ. 100,000.

Evening Times: Daily Times of Nigeria Ltd, New Isheri Rd, Agidingbi, PMB 21340, Ikeja, Lagos; tel. (1) 4900850; telex 21333; Editor CLEMENT ILOBA; circ. 20,000.

The Guardian: Rutam House, Isolo Expressway, Isolo, PMB 1217, Oshodi, Lagos; tel. (1) 524111; telex 23283; f. 1983; Publr ALEX IBRU; Editor EMEKA IZEZE; circ. 80,000.

Isokan: Concord House, 42 Concord Way, POB 4483, Ikeja, Lagos; Yoruba.

National Concord: Concord House, 42 Concord Way, POB 4483, Ikeja, Lagos; telex 26681; f. 1980; Editor NSIKAK ESSIEN; circ. 200,000.

New Nigerian: Ahmadu Bello Way, POB 254, Kaduna; tel. (62) 201420; telex 71120; f. 1965; govt-owned; Chair. Prof. TEKENA TAMUNO; Editor (vacant); circ. 80,000.

Nigerian Chronicle: Cross River State Newspaper Corpn, 17-19 Barracks Rd, POB 1074, Calabar; tel. (87) 224976; telex 65104; fax (87) 224979; f. 1970; Editor UNIMKE NAWA; circ. 50,000.

Nigerian Herald: Kwara State Printing and Publishing Corpn, Offa Rd, PMB 1369, Ilorin; tel. and fax (31) 220506; telex 33108; f. 1973; sponsored by Kwara State Govt; Editor RAZAK EL-ALAWA; circ. 25,000.

Nigerian Observer: The Bendel Newspaper Corpn, 18 Airport Rd, POB 1143, Benin City; tel. (52) 240050; telex 41104; f. 1968; Editor TONY IKEAKANAM; circ. 150,000.

Nigerian Standard: 5 Joseph Gomwalk Rd, POB 2112, Jos; telex 33131; f. 1972; govt-owned; Editor SALE ILIYA; circ. 100,000.

Nigerian Statesman: Imo Newspapers Ltd, Owerri-Egbu Rd, POB 1095, Owerri; tel. (83) 230099; telex 53207; f. 1978; sponsored by Imo State Govt; Editor EDUBE WADIBIA.

Nigerian Tide: Rivers State Newspaper Corpn, 4 Ikwerre Rd, POB 5072, Port Harcourt; telex 61144; f. 1971; Editor AUGUSTINE NJOAGWUANI; circ. 30,000.

Nigerian Tribune: African Newspapers of Nigeria Ltd, Imalefalafi St, Oke-Ado, POB 78, Ibadan; tel. (2) 2313410; telex 31186; fax (2) 2317573; f. 1949; Editor FOLU OLAMITI; circ. 109,000.

The Punch: Skyway Press, Kudeti St, PMB 21204, Onipetsi, Ikeja; tel. (1) 4963580; f. 1976; Editor BOLA BOLAWOLE; circ. 150,000.

Vanguard: Kirikiri Canal, PMB 1007, Apapa; f. 1984; Editor FRANK AIGBOGUN.

SUNDAY NEWSPAPERS

Sunday Chronicle: Cross River State Newspaper Corpn, PMB 1074, Calabar; f. 1977; Editor-in-Chief ETIM ANIM; circ. 163,000.

Sunday Concord: Concord House, 42 Concord Way, POB 4483, Ikeja, Lagos; telex 26681; f. 1980; Editor DELE ALAKE.

Sunday Herald: Kwara State Printing and Publishing Corpn, PMB 1369, Ilorin; tel. (31) 220976; telex 33108; f. 1981; Editor CHARLES OSAGIE (acting).

Sunday New Nigerian: Ahmadu Bello Way, POB 254, Kaduna; tel. (62) 201420; telex 71120; Editor (vacant).

Sunday Observer: PMB 1334, Bendel Newspapers Corpn, 18 Airport Rd, Benin City; f. 1968; Editor T. O. BORHA; circ. 60,000.

Sunday Punch: Kudeti St, PMB 21204, Ikeja; tel. (1) 4964691; telex 91470; fax (1) 4960715; f. 1973; Editor DAYO WRIGHT; circ. 150,000.

Sunday Sketch: Sketch Publishing Co Ltd, PMB 5067, Ibadan; tel. (2) 414851; f. 1964; govt-owned; Editor OBAFEMI OREDEIN; circ. 125,000.

Sunday Standard: Plateau Publishing Co Ltd, 5 Joseph Gornwalic Rd, PMB 2112, Jos; f. 1972; govt-owned; Editor SALE ILIYA.

Sunday Statesman: Imo Newspapers Ltd, Owerri-Egbu Rd, PMB 1095, Owerri; tel. (83) 230099; telex 53207; f. 1978; sponsored by Imo State Govt; Editor EDUBE WADIBIA.

Sunday Sun: PMB 1025, Okoro House, Factory Lane, off Upper Mission Rd, New Benin.

Sunday Tide: 4 Ikwerre Rd, POB 5072, Port Harcourt; telex 61144; f. 1971; Editor AUGUSTINE NJOAGWUANI.

Sunday Times: Daily Times of Nigeria Ltd, New Isheri Rd, Agidingbi, PMB 21340, Ikeja, Lagos; tel. (1) 4900850; telex 21333; f. 1953; 60% govt-owned; Editor DUPE AJAYI; circ. 100,000.

Sunday Tribune: POB 78, Oke-Ado, Ibadan; tel. (2) 310886; Editor WALE OJO.

Sunday Vanguard: PMB 1007, Apapa; Editor DUPE AJAYI.

WEEKLIES

Albishir: Triumph Publishing Co Ltd, Gidan Sa'adu Zungur, PMB 3155, Kano; tel. (64) 260273; telex 77357; f. 1981; Hausa; Editor ADAMU A. KIYAWA; circ. 15,000.

Business Times: Daily Times of Nigeria Ltd, New Isheri Rd, Agidingbi, PMB 21340, Ikeja, Lagos; tel. (1) 4900850; telex 21333; f. 1925; 60% govt-owned; Editor GODFREY BAMAWO; circ. 22,000.

Gboungboun: Sketch Publishing Co Ltd, New Court Rd, PMB 5067, Ibadan; tel. (2) 414851; govt-owned; Yoruba; Editor A. O. ADEBANJO; circ. 80,000.

The Independent: Bodija Rd, PMB 5109, Ibadan; f. 1960; English; Roman Catholic; Editor Rev. F. B. CRONIN-COLTSMAN; circ. 13,000.

Irohin Imole: 15 Bamgbose St, POB 1495, Lagos; f. 1957; Yoruba; Editor TUNJI ADEOSUN.

Irohin Yoruba: 212 Broad St, PMB 2416, Lagos; tel. (1) 410886; f. 1945; Yoruba; Editor S. A. AJIBADE; circ. 85,000.

Lagos Life: Guardian Newspapers Ltd, Rutam House, Isolo Expressway, Isolo, PMB 1217, Oshodi, Lagos; f. 1985; Editor BISI OGUNBADEJO; circ. 100,000.

Lagos Weekend: Daily Times of Nigeria Ltd, New Isheri Rd, Agidingbi, PMB 21340, Ikeja, Lagos; tel. (1) 4900850; telex 21333; f. 1965; 60% govt-owned; news and pictures; Editor SAM OGWA; circ. 85,000.

Mid-West This Week: Arin Associates, 50B New Lagos Rd, Benin City; Editors TONY OKODUWA, PRINCE A. R. NWOKO.

The News: Lagos; independent; Editor-in-Chief ODAPO OLORUNYOMI.

Newswatch: 3 Billingsway Rd, Oregun, Lagos; tel. (1) 4960950; telex 27874; fax (1) 4962887; f. 1985; English; Editor-in-Chief DAN AGBESE.

Nigerian Radio/TV Times: Nigerian Broadcasting Corpn, POB 12504, Ikoyi.

Sporting Records: Daily Times of Nigeria Ltd, New Isheri Rd, Agidingbi, PMB 21340, Ikeja, Lagos; tel. (1) 4900850; telex 21333; f. 1961; 60% govt-owned; Editor CYRIL KAPPO; circ. 10,000.

Tell: Lagos; independent; news; Editor-in-Chief NOSO IGIEBOR.

Times International: Daily Times of Nigeria Ltd, 3–7 Kakawa St, POB 139, Lagos; f. 1974; Editor Dr HEZY IDOWU; circ. 50,000.

Truth (The Muslim Weekly): 45 Idumagbo Ave, POB 418, Lagos; tel. (1) 2668455; telex 21356; f. 1951; Editor S. O. LAWAL.

ENGLISH LANGUAGE PERIODICALS

Afriscope: 29 Salami Saibu St, PMB 1119, Yaba; monthly; African current affairs.

The Ambassador: PMB 2011, 1 peru-Remo, Ogun; tel. (39) 620115; quarterly; Roman Catholic; circ. 20,000.

Benin Review: Ethiope Publishing Corpn, PMB 1332, Benin City; f. 1974; African art and culture; 2 a year; circ. 50,000.

Headlines: Daily Times of Nigeria Ltd, New Isheri Rd, Agindingbi, PMB 21340, Ikeja, Lagos; f. 1973; monthly; Editor ADAMS ALIU; circ. 500,000.

Home Studies: Daily Times Publications, 3–7 Kakawa St, Lagos; f. 1964; two a month; Editor Dr ELIZABETH E. IKEM; circ. 40,000.

Insight: 3 Kakawa St, POB 139, Lagos; quarterly; contemporary issues; Editor SAM AMUKA; circ. 5,000.

Journal of the Nigerian Medical Association: 3–7 Kakawa St, POB 139, Apapa; quarterly; Editor Prof. A. O. ADESOLA.

Lagos Education Review: Faculty of Education, University of Lagos Akoka, Lagos; tel. (1) 820448; telex 26983; fax (1) 822644; f. 1978; 2 a year; African education; Editor Prof. M. N. OKENIMKPE.

The Leader: PMB 1017, Owerri; tel. (83) 230932; fortnightly; Roman Catholic; Editor Rev. KEVIN C. AKAGHA.

Management in Nigeria: Plot 22, Idowu Taylor St, Victoria Island, POB 2557, Lagos; tel. (1) 615105; quarterly; journal of Nigerian Inst. of Management; Editor DELE OSUNDAHUNS; circ. 25,000.

Marketing in Nigeria: Alpha Publications, Surulere, POB 1163, Lagos; f. 1977; monthly; Editor B. O. K. NWELIH; circ. 30,000.

Modern Woman: 47–49 Salami Saibu St, Marina, POB 2583, Lagos; f. 1964; monthly; Man. Editor TOUN ONABANJO.

Monthly Life: West African Book Publishers, POB 3445, Lagos; tel. (1) 4900760; telex 26144; f. 1984; monthly; Editor WOLE OLAOYE; circ. 40,000.

The New Nation: 52 Iwaya Rd, Onike, Yaba, Surulere, POB 896, Lagos; tel. (1) 5863629; telex 26517; monthly; news magazine.

Nigeria Magazine: Federal Dept of Culture, PMB 12524, Lagos; tel. (1) 5802060; f. 1927; quarterly; travel, cultural, historical and general; Editor B. D. LEMCHI; circ. 5,000.

Nigerian Businessman's Magazine: 39 Mabo St, Surulere, Lagos; monthly; Nigerian and overseas commerce.

Nigerian Journal of Economic and Social Studies: Nigerian Economic Society, c/o Dept of Economics, University of Ibadan; f. 1959; 3 a year; Editor Prof. S. TOMORI.

Nigerian Journal of Science: University of Ibadan, POB 4039, Ibadan; publ. of the Science Asscn of Nigeria; f. 1966; 2 a year; Editor Prof. L. B. KOLAWOLE; circ. 1,000.

Nigerian Medical Journal: 3 Kakawa St, POB 139, Lagos; monthly.

Nigerian Radio/TV Times: Broadcasting House, POB 12504, Lagos; monthly.

Nigerian Teacher: 3 Kakawa St, POB 139, Lagos; quarterly.

Nigerian Worker: United Labour Congress, 97 Herbert Macaulay St, Lagos; Editor LAWRENCE BORHA.

The President: New Breed Organization Ltd, Plot 14 Western Ave, 1 Rafiu Shitty St, Alaka Estate, Surulere, POB 385, Lagos; tel. (1) 5802690; fax (1) 5831175; fortnightly; management; Chief Editor CHRIS OKOLIE.

Quality: Ultimate Publications Ltd, Oregun Rd, Lagos; f. 1987; monthly; Editor BALA DAN MUSA.

Radio-Vision Times: Western Nigerian Radio-Vision Service, Television House, POB 1460, Ibadan; monthly; Editor ALTON A. ADEDEJI.

Savanna: Ahmadu Bello University Press Ltd, PMB 1094, Zaria; tel. (69) 50054; telex 75241; f. 1972; 2 a year; Editor AUDEE T. GIWA; circ. 1,000.

Spear: Daily Times of Nigeria Ltd, New Isheri Rd, Agidingbi, PMB 21340, Ikeja, Lagos; tel. (1) 4900850; f. 1962; monthly; family magazine; Editor COKER ONITA; circ. 10,000.

Technical and Commercial Message: Surulere, POB 1163, Lagos; f. 1980; 6 a year; Editor B. O. K. NWELIH; circ. 12,500.

Today's Challenge: PMB 2010, Jos; tel. (73) 52230; f. 1951; 6 a year; religious and educational; Editor JACOB SHAIBY TSADO; circ. 15,000.

Woman's World: Daily Times of Nigeria Ltd, New Isheri Rd, Agidingbi, PMB 21340, Ikeja, Lagos; monthly; Editor TOYIN JOHNSON; circ. 12,000.

VERNACULAR PERIODICALS

Abokiyar Hira: Albah International Publishers, POB 6177, Bompai, Kano; f. 1987; monthly; Hausa; cultural; Editor BASHARI F. FOUKBAH; circ. 35,000.

Gaskiya ta fi Kwabo: Ahmadu Bello Way, POB 254, Kaduna; tel. (62) 201420; telex 71120; f. 1939; 3 a week; Hausa; Editor ABDUL-HASSAN IBRAHIM.

NEWS AGENCIES

News Agency of Nigeria (NAN): c/o National Theatre, Iganmu, PMB 12756, Lagos; tel. (1) 801290; telex 22648; fax (1) 832832; f. 1978; Man. Dir Mallam WADA ABDULLAHI MAIDA; Editor-in-Chief DAVE IGIEWE.

Foreign Bureaux

Agence France-Presse (AFP): 26B Keffi St, SW Ikoyi, PMB 2448, Lagos; tel. (1) 2683550; telex 21363; fax (1) 2682752; Bureau Chief GÉRARD VANDENBERGHE.

Informatsionnoye Telegrafnoye Agentstvo Rossii—Telegrafnoye Agentstvo Suverennykh Stran (ITAR—TASS) (Russia): 401 St, POB 6465, Victoria Island, Lagos; tel. (1) 617119; Correspondent BORIS VASILIEVICH PILNIKOV.

Inter Press Service (IPS) (Italy): c/o News Agency of Nigeria, PMB 12756, Lagos; tel. (1) 5801290; Correspondent REMI OYO.

Pan-African News Agency (PANA): c/o News Agency of Nigeria, National Arts Theatre, POB 8715, Marina, Lagos; tel. (1) 5801290; telex 26571; f. 1979.

Xinhua (New China) News Agency (People's Republic of China): 161A Adeola Odeku St, Victoria Island, POB 70278, Lagos; tel. (1) 2612464; telex 21541; Bureau Chief ZHAI JINGSHENG.

Publishers

Africana-FEP Publishers Ltd: Book House Trust, 1 Africana-FEP Drive, PMB 1639, Onitsha; tel. (46) 210669; f. 1973; study guides, general science, textbooks; Man. Dir PATRICK C. OMABU.

Ahmadu Bello University Press: PMB 1094, Zaria; tel. (69) 50054; telex 75291; f. 1974; history, Africana, social sciences, education, literature and arts; Man. Dir Alhaji SAIBU A. AFEGBUA.

Albah International Publishers: 100 Kurawa, Bompai-Kano, POB 6177, Kano City; f. 1978; Africana, Islamic, educational and general, in Hausa; Chair. BASHARI F. ROUKBAH.

Alliance West African Publishers: Orindingbin Estate, New Aketan Layout, PMB 1039, Oyo; tel. (85) 230798; f. 1971; educational and general; Man. Dir Chief M. O. OGUNMOLA.

Aromolaran Publishing Co Ltd: POB 1800, Ibadan; tel. (2) 715980; telex 34315; f. 1968; educational and general; Man. Dir Dr ADEKUNLE AROMOLARAN.

Daystar Press: Daystar House, POB 1261, Ibadan; tel. (2) 8102670; f. 1962; religious and educational; Man. PHILLIP ADELAKUN LADOKUN.

ECWA Productions Ltd: PMB 2010, Jos; tel. (73) 52230; telex 81120; f. 1973; religious and educational; Gen. Man. Rev. J. K. BOLARIN.

Ethiope Publishing Corpn: Ring Rd, PMB 1332, Benin City; tel. (52) 243036; telex 41110; f. 1970; general fiction and non-fiction, textbooks, reference, science, arts and history; Man. Dir SUNDAY N. OLAYE.

Evans Brothers (Nigeria Publishers) Ltd: Jericho Rd, PMB 5164, Ibadan; tel. (2) 2414394; telex 31104; fax (2) 2410757; f. 1966; general and educational; Chair. Dr A. O. OJORA; Man. Dir B. O. BOLODEOKU.

Fourth Dimension Publishing Co Ltd: Plot 64A, City Layout, PMB 01164, Enugu; tel. (42) 339969; telex 51319; f. 1977; periodicals, fiction, verse, educational and children's; Chair. ARTHUR NWANKWO; Man. Dir V. U. NWANKWO.

Gbabeks Publishers Ltd: POB 37252, Ibadan; tel. (62) 217976; f. 1982; educational and technical; Man. Dir TAYO OGUNBEKUN.

Heinemann Educational Books (Nigeria) Ltd: 1 Ighodaro Rd, Jericho, PMB 5205, Ibadan; tel. (2) 2412268; telex 31113; fax (2) 2411089; f. 1962; educational, law, medical and general; Chair. AIGBOJE HIGO.

Heritage Books: 2–8 Calcutta Crescent, Gate 1, POB 610, Apapa, Lagos; tel. (1) 871333; f. 1971; general; Chair. NAIWU OSAHON.

Ibadan University Press: Publishing House, University of Ibadan, PMB 16, IU Post Office, Ibadan; tel. (2) 400550; telex 31128; f. 1951; scholarly, science, law, general and educational; Dir F. A. ADESANOYE.

Ilesanmi Press Ltd: Akure Rd, POB 204, Ilesha; tel. 2062; f. 1955; general and educational; Man. Dir G. E. ILESANMI.

John West Publications Ltd: Plot 2, Block A, Acme Rd, Ogba Industrial Estate, PMB 21001, Ikeja, Lagos; tel. (1) 4925459; telex 26446; f. 1964 general; Man. Dir Alhaji L. K. JAKAUDE.

Kolasanya Publishing Enterprise: 2 Epe Rd, Oke-Owa, PMB 2099, Ijebu-Ode; general and educational; Man. Dir Chief K. OSUNSANYA.

Literamed Publications Ltd (Lantern Books): Plot 45, Alausa Bus-stop, Oregun Industrial Estate, Ikeja, PMB 21068, Lagos; tel. (1) 4962512; telex 21068; fax (1) 4972217; general; Man. Dir O. M. LAWAL-SOLARIN.

Longman Nigeria Ltd: 52 Oba Akran Ave, PMB 21036, Ikeja, Lagos; tel. (1) 4978925; fax (1) 4964370; f. 1961; general and educational; Man. Dir J. A. OLOWONIYI.

Macmillan Nigeria Publishers Ltd: Ilupeju Industrial Estate, 4 Industrial Ave, POB 264, Yaba, Lagos; tel. (1) 4962185; f. 1965; educational and general; Exec. Chair. J. O. EMMANUEL; Man. Dir Dr A. I. ADELEKAN.

Nelson Publishers Ltd: 8 Ilupeju By-Pass, Ikeja, PMB 21303, Lagos; tel. (1) 4961452; general and educational; Chair. Prof. C. O. TAIWO; Man. Dir R. O. OGUNBO.

Northern Nigerian Publishing Co Ltd: Gaskiya Bldg, POB 412, Zaria; tel. (69) 32087; telex 75243; f. 1966; general, educational and vernacular texts; Man. Dir H. HAYAT.

NPS Educational Publishers Ltd: Trusthouse, Ring Rd, off Akinyemi Way, POB 62, Ibadan; tel. (2) 316006; telex 31478; f. 1969; academic, scholarly and educational; CEO T. D. OTESANYA.

Nwamife Publishers: 10 Ibiam St, Uwani, POB 430, Enugu; tel. (42) 338254; f. 1971; general and educational; Chair. FELIX C. ADI.

Obafemi Awolowo University Press Ltd: Obafemi Awolowo University, Ile-Ife; tel. (36) 230284; f. 1968; educational, scholarly and periodicals; Man. Dir AKIN FATOKUN.

Obobo Books: 2–8 Calcutta Crescent, Gate 1, POB 610, Apapa, Lagos; tel. (1) 5871333; f. 1981; children's books; Editorial Dir BAKIN KUNAMA.

Ogunsanya Press Publishers and Bookstores Ltd: SW9/1133 Orita Challenge, Idiroko, POB 95, Ibadan; tel. (2) 310924; f. 1970; educational; Man. Dir Chief LUCAS JUSTUS POPO-OLA OGUNSANYA.

Onibonoje Press and Book Industries (Nigeria) Ltd: Felele Layout, Challenge, POB 3109, Ibadan; tel. (2) 313956; telex 31657; f. 1958; educational and general; Chair. G. ONIBONOJE; Man. Dir J. O. ONIBONOJE.

Pilgrim Books Ltd: New Oluyole Industrial Estate, Ibadan/Lagos Expressway, PMB 5617, Ibadan; tel. (2) 317218; telex 20311; educational and general; Man. Dir JOHN E. LEIGH.

Spectrum Books Ltd: Sunshine House, 1 Emmanuel Alayande St, Oluyole Estate, PMB 5612, Ibadan; tel. (2) 2310058; telex 31588; fax (2) 2318502; f. 1978; educational and fiction; Man. Dir JOOP BERKHOUT.

University of Lagos Press: University of Lagos, PO 132, Akoka, Yaba, Lagos; tel. (1) 825048; telex 21210; university textbooks, monographs, lectures and journals; Man. Dir S. BODUNDE BANKOLE.

University Press Ltd: Three Crowns Bldg, Eleyele Rd, Jericho, PMB 5095, Ibadan; tel. (2) 411356; telex 31121; fax (2) 412056; f. 1978; associated with Oxford University Press; educational; Man. Dir WAHEED O. OLAJIDE.

University Publishing Co: 11 Central School Rd, POB 386, Onitsha; tel. (46) 210013; f. 1959; primary, secondary and university textbooks; Chair. E. O. UGWUEGBULEM.

Vista Books Ltd: 59 Awolowo Rd, POB 282, Yaba, Lagos; tel. (1) 2681656; fax (1) 2685679; f. 1991; general fiction and non-fiction, arts, children's and educational; Man. Dir Dr T. C. NWOSU.

West African Book Publishers Ltd: Ilupeju Industrial Estate, POB 3445, Lagos; tel. (1) 4900760; telex 26144; f. 1967; textbooks, children's, periodicals and general; Dir Mrs A. O. OBADAGBONYI.

Government Publishing House

Government Press: PMB 2020, Kaduna; tel. 213812.

PUBLISHERS' ASSOCIATION

Nigerian Publishers Association: The Ori-Detu, 1st Floor, Shell Close, Onireke, GPO Box 2541, Ibadan; tel. (2) 411557; telex 31113; f. 1965; Pres. V. NWANKWO.

Radio and Television

According to UNESCO estimates, there were 21.3m. radio receivers and 4.2m. television receivers in use in 1994.

RADIO

Federal Radio Corporation of Nigeria (FRCN): Broadcasting House, Ikoyi, PMB 12504, Lagos; tel. (1) 2690301; telex 21484; fax (1) 2690073; f. 1978; controlled by the Fed. Govt and divided into five zones: Lagos (English); Enugu (English, Igbo, Izon, Efik and Tiv); Ibadan (English, Yoruba, Edo, Urhobo and Igala); Kaduna (English, Hausa, Kanuri, Fulfulde and Nupe); Abuja (English, Hausa, Igbo and Yoruba); Dir-Gen. Alhaji ABDURRAHMAN MICIKA.

Voice of Nigeria (VON): Broadcasting House, Ikoyi, PMB 40003, Lagos; tel. (1) 2693075; fax (1) 2691944; f. 1990; controlled by the Fed. Govt; external services in English, French, Arabic, Ki-Swahili, Hausa and Fulfulde; Dir-Gen. Mallam YAYA ABUBAKAR.

Menage Holding's Broadcasting System Ltd: Umuahia, Imo; commenced broadcasting Jan. 1996; commercial.

Radio Kudirat: opposition radio station; broadcasts in several Nigerian languages.

Ray Power 100 Drive: Abeokuta Express Way, Ilapo, Alagbado, Lagos; tel. (1) 2644814; fax (1) 2644817; commenced broadcasting Sept. 1994; commercial; Chair. Chief RAYMOND DOKPESI.

TELEVISION

Nigerian Television Authority (NTA): Television House, Ahmadu Bello Way, Victoria Island, PMB 12036, Lagos; tel. (1) 2615949; telex 21245; f. 1976; controlled by the Fed. Govt; responsible for all aspects of television broadcasting; Chair. IFEANYINWA NZEAKOR; Dir-Gen. Alhaji MOHAMMED IBRAHIM.

NTA Aba/Owerri: Channel 6, PMB 7126, Aba, Abia; tel. (83) 220922; Gen. Man. GODWIN DURU.

NTA Abeokuta: Channel 12, PMB 2190, Abeokuta, Ogun; tel. (39) 242971; f. 1979; broadcasts in English and local languages; Gen-Man. VICTOR FOLIVI.

NTA Abuja: Abuja.

NTA Akure: PMB 794, Akure; tel. (34) 230351; Gen. Man. JIBOLA DEDENUOLA.

NTA Bauchi: PMB 0146, Bauchi; tel. (77) 42748; telex 83270; f. 1976; Man. MUHAMMAD AL-AMIN.

NTA Benin City: West Circular Rd, PMB 1117, Benin City; telex 44308; Gen. Man. J. O. N. EZEKOKA.

NTA Calabar: 105 Marion Rd, Calabar; telex 65110; Man. E. ETUK.

NTA Enugu: Independence Layout, PMB 01530, Enugu, Anambra; tel. (42) 335120; telex 51147; f. 1960; Gen. Man. G. C. MEFO.

NTA Ibadan: POB 1460, Ibadan; tel. (2) 713320; telex 31156; Gen. Man. JIBOLA DEDENUOLA.

NTA Ikeja: Tejuosho Ave, Surulere.

NTA Ilorin: PMB 1478, Ilorin; tel. (31) 220973; fax (31) 224196; Gen. Man. VICKY OLUMUDI

NTA Jos: PMB 2134, Jos; telex 81149; Gen. Man. M. J. BEWELL.

NTA Kaduna: POB 1347, Kaduna; tel. (62) 216375; telex 71164; f. 1977; Gen. Man. SAIDU ABUBAKAR.

NTA Kano: PMB 3343, Kano; tel. (64) 640072; Gen. Man. BELLO ABUBAKAR.

NTA Lagos: Victoria Island, PMB 12005, Lagos; telex 21245; Gen. Man. O. OKUNRINBOYE.

NTA Maiduguri: PMB 1487, Maiduguri; telex 82132; Gen. Man. M. M. MAILAFIYA.

NTA Makurdi: PMB 2044, Makurdi.

NTA Minna: TV House, PMB 79, Minna; tel. (66) 222941; Gen. Man. M. C. DAYLOP.

NTA Port Harcourt: PMB 5797, Port Harcourt; Gen. Man. E. T. HALLIDAY.

NTA Sokoto: PMB 2351, Sokoto; tel. (60) 232670; telex 73116; f. 1975; Gen. Man. M. B. TUNAU.

NTA Yola: PMB 2197, Yola; Gen. Man. M. M. SAIDU.

In July 1993 14 companies were granted licences to operate private television stations.

Finance

(cap. = capital; p.u. = paid up; res = reserves; dep. = deposits; m. = million; brs = branches; amounts in naira unless otherwise stated)

BANKING

In early 1995 there were 120 licensed banks (commercial and merchant banks) operating in Nigeria; however, the Government approved only 68 of these for foreign exchange transactions. In addition, Nigeria had 1,355 licensed community banks at 31 December 1995.

Central Bank

Central Bank of Nigeria: Tinubu Sq., PMB 12194, Lagos; tel. (1) 2660100; telex 21350; f. 1958; bank of issue; cap. and res 6,908.8m., dep. 168,187.0m. (1995); Gov. PAUL AGBAI OGWUMA; 18 brs.

Commercial Banks

Afribank Nigeria Ltd: 94 Broad St, PMB 12021, Lagos; tel. (1) 2663608; telex 28448; fax (1) 2666327; f. 1969 as International Bank for West Africa Ltd; cap. and res 871.7m., dep. 12.0m. (Feb. 1996); Man. Dir JOHN EDOZIEN; 130 brs.

African Continental Bank Ltd: 148 Broad St, PMB 2466, Lagos; tel. (1) 2664833; f. 1947; cap. and res 24.5m., dep. 1,845.1m. (1989); transferred to the private sector in 1997; Chair. Chief J. O. IRUKWU; Man. Dir E. A. EZEKWE; 919 brs.

African International Bank Ltd: 42–44 Warehouse Rd, PMB 1040, Apapa, Lagos; tel. (1) 5870389; telex 22377; fax (1) 5877174; f. 1979; cap. and res 190.5m., dep. 1,397.4m. (1990); acquired assets of Bank of Credit and Commerce International (Nigeria) Ltd; Chair. Alhaji MAMMAN DAURA; Man. Dir Alhaji ABDULLAHI MAHMOUD; 47 brs.

Allied Bank of Nigeria Ltd: Allied House, 214 Broad St, PMB 12785, Lagos; tel. (1) 2669623; telex 21512; fax (1) 2663960; f. 1962 as Bank of India; cap. and res 191.5m., dep. 3,437.7m. (1993); Chair. Dr SIMI JOHNSON; Man. Dir Alhaji SHEHU MOHAMMED; 68 brs.

Bank of the North Ltd: Ahmadu Bello House, 2 Zaria Rd, POB 211, Kano; tel. (64) 660290; telex 77233; f. 1959; cap. and res 400m., dep. 5,259.3m. (1995); Chair. Alhaji MUHAMMAD LUGGA; Man. Dir Alhaji MOHAMMED BULAMA; 97 brs.

Chartered Bank Ltd: Plot 1619, Danmole St, POB 73069, Victoria Island, Lagos; tel. (1) 2620380; telex 21155; fax (1) 2615094; cap. and res 516.2m., dep. 3,704.7m. (Dec. 1995); Chair. Lt-Gen. (retd) M. I. WUSHISHI; Man. Dir O. OLAGUNDOYE.

Citizens International Bank Ltd: Ahmadu Bello Way, Plot 130, Victoria Island, Lagos; tel. (1) 26010390; telex 22952; fax (1) 2615138; f. 1990; cap. and res 284.1m., dep. 2,440.6m. (1994); Chair. Chief D. U. IFEGWU.

Commercial Bank (Crédit Lyonnais Nigeria) Ltd: Elephant House, 214 Broad St, PMB 12829, Lagos; tel. (1) 2665594; telex 23157; fax (1) 2665308; f. 1983; cap. p.u. 120m.(1995), dep. 1,700m. (1993); Chair. ALLISON A. AYIDA; Man. Dir R. CESSAC; 21 brs.

Crown Merchant Bank Ltd: 8 Idowu Taylor St, Victoria Island, Lagos; tel. (1) 2613728; telex 22831; fax (1) 2615545; cap. and res 43.6m., dep. 275.8m. (1991); Man. Dir ORE S. A. ONAKOYA.

Ecobank Nigeria Ltd: 2 Ajose Adeogun St, Victoria Island, POB 72688, Lagos; tel. (1) 2612953; telex 21157; fax (1) 2616568; cap. p.u. 89m. (Sept. 1995); Chair. OTUNBA A. OJORA; Man. Dir OLADISUN HOLLOWAY.

Eko International Bank: cnr Nnamdi Azikiwe and Alli Balogun Sts, PMB 12864, Lagos; tel. (1) 2600350; telex 28657; fax (1) 2665176; cap. and res 123.4m., dep. 1,335.4m. (1994); Chair. J. O. EMANUEL; Man. Dir OLATUNDE FASINA; 9 brs.

Federal Savings Bank: 23 Awolowo Rd, Ikoyi, PMB 12512, Lagos; tel. (1) 2686071; telex 23671; fax (1) 2690397; f. 1974; cap. and res 215.7m., dep. 1,590.8m. (March 1995); Gen. Man. I. T.UDO.

First Bank of Nigeria Plc: Samuel Asabia House, 35 Marina, POB 5216, Lagos; tel. (1) 2665900; telex 21231; fax (1) 2669073; f. 1894 as Bank of British West Africa; cap. and res 6,393.9m., dep. 55,497.6m. (1996); Chair. MAHMOUD IBRAHIM ATTA; CEO and Man. Dir JOSEPH OLADELE SANUSI; 291 brs.

Habib Nigeria Bank Ltd: 1 Keffi St, POB 54648, Falomo, Ikoyi, Lagos; tel. (1) 2663121; cap p.u. 52.5m. (Dec. 1992), dep. 364.6m. (1989); Chair. Maj.-Gen. (retd) SHEHU MUSA YAR'ADUA; Man. Dir Alhaji FALALU; 65 brs.

Investment Banking and Trust Co Ltd (IBTC): Wesley House, 21–22 Marina, PMB 12557, Lagos; tel. (1) 2600200; telex 28747; fax (1) 2634146; cap. and res 1,075.7m., dep. 300.8m. (1995); Chair. DAVID DANKARO; Man. Dir ATEDO A. PETERSIDE.

Lion Bank of Nigeria: 34 Ahmadu Bello Way, PMB 2126, Jos, Plateau; tel. (73) 52223; telex 81165; fax (73) 54602; f. 1987; cap. and res 86.9m., dep. 868.0m. (1993); Man. Dir S. P. Y. GANG.

Magnum Trust Bank: 67 Marina, PMB 12933, Lagos; tel. (1) 2640060; telex 28322; fax (1) 2640069; f. 1991; cap. and res 64.4m., dep. 225.5m. (June 1995); Chair. Dr P.N.C. OKIGBO; Man. Dir JEAN-GEO PASTOURET.

Nigeria International Bank Ltd (NIB): Commerce House, 1 Idowu Taylor St, Victoria Island, POB 6391, Lagos; tel. (1) 2622000; telex 23424; fax (1) 2618916; f. 1984; cap. and res 1,078m., dep. 6,130m. (1995); Chair. Chief CHARLES S. SANKEY; Man. Dir MICHEL ACCAD; 12 brs.

Nigeria Universal Bank Ltd: Yakubu Gowon Way, POB 1066, Kaduna; tel. (62) 233928; telex 71156; fax (62) 235024; f. 1974; owned by Katsina and Kaduna State Govts; cap. 50m. (1994), dep. 447m. (1992); Chair. Alhaji MUHAMMADU HAYATUDDINI; Man. Dir Alhaji USMAN ABUBAKAR; 27 brs.

Owena Bank (Nigeria) Ltd: Engineering Close, PMB 1122, Victoria Island, Lagos; tel. (1) 877901; telex 28692; 30% owned by Ondo State Govt; cap. p.u. 60m. (Dec. 1992); Chair. PETER AJAYI; Man. Dir SEGUN AGBETUYI.

Pan African Bank Ltd: 31 Azikiwe Rd, PMB 5239, Port Harcourt; tel. (84) 2667045; telex 61157; fax (84) 330616; f. 1971; cap. and res 140.3m., dep. 514.7m. (1991); transfer to the private sector pending in 1997; Chair. W. T. DAMBO; Man. Dir B. A. KONYA; 10 brs.

People's Bank of Nigeria: 33 Balogun St, PMB 12914, Lagos; tel. (1) 2664241; fax (1) 2664631; f. 1989; state-owned; cap. p.u. 230m. (Dec. 1991); Chair. Chief E. A. O. OYEYIPO; Man. Dir HAMRA IMAM.

Progress Bank of Nigeria Ltd: Plot 91, Ikenegbu Layout, POB 1577, Owerri; tel. (83) 23476; telex 53203; f. 1982; controlled by Imo State Govt; cap. and res 48.8m., dep. 873.5m. (1990); transfer to the private sector pending in 1997; Chair. Chief R. E. ODINKEMELU; Man. Dir I. K. UCHE (acting)

Savannah Bank of Nigeria Ltd: 62–66 Broad St, POB 2317, Lagos; tel. (1) 2600470; telex 21876; f. 1976; cap. 52.4m., dep. 4,338.7m. (March 1993); Chair. (vacant); Man. Dir Alhaji M. SHARIFF; 70 brs.

Société Générale Bank (Nigeria) Ltd: Sarah House, 13 Martins St, PMB 12741, Lagos; tel. (1) 2661834; telex 28681; fax (1) 2663731; f. 1977; cap. and res 128.3m., dep. 1,599.3m. (Dec. 1994); Chair. Dr EBENEZER A. IKOMI; Man. Dir G. A. OYENOLA; 35 brs.

Tropical Commerical Bank Ltd: 72B Murtala Mohammed Way, POB 4636, Kano; tel. (64) 640050; telex 77299; fax (64) 644506; 15% state-owned; cap. p.u. 184.8m. (Feb. 1997), res 764.7m., dep. 37,151m. (Dec. 1996); CEO LAWAN ZAKARIA GANA.

Union Bank of Nigeria Ltd: 40 Marina, PMB 2027, Lagos; tel. (1) 2665439; telex 21222; fax (1) 669873; f. 1969 as Barclays Bank of Nigeria Ltd; cap. and res 397m., dep. 55,141m. (Sept. 1996); Chair. KALU U. KALU; Man. Dir Alhaji MOHAMMAD IMAM YAHAYA; 255 brs.

United Bank for Africa (Nigeria) Ltd: UBA House, 57 Marina, POB 2406, Lagos; tel. (1) 2644651; telex 28493; fax (1) 2644722; f. 1961; cap. and res 4,373.8m., dep. 37,019.2m. (March 1997); Chair. HAKEEM BELO-OSAGIE; Man. Dir and CEO Mallam ABBA KYARI; 204 brs.

Universal Trust Bank of Nigeria Ltd: 4/6 Ajose Adeogun St, Victoria Island, POB 52160, Lagos; tel. (1) 2637849; telex 28481; fax (1) 615874; f. 1985; cap. and res 226.4m., dep. 3.3m. (1994); Chair. Lt-Gen. T. Y. DANJUMA; Man. Dir Alhaji I. O. SULAIMON; 31 brs.

Wema Bank Ltd: Wema Towers, 54 Marina, Lagos; tel. (1) 2668105; telex 22515; fax (1) 2669411; f. 1945; cap. and res 898.5m., dep. 7,785.3m. (March 1996); Chair. Prof. T. I. RAJI; Man. Dir Chief S. I. ADEGBITE; 75 brs.

Merchant Banks

Abacus Merchant Bank Ltd: Williams House, 8th Floor, 95 Broad St, POB 7908, Lagos; tel. (1) 2660212; telex 21243; cap. and res 24.6m., dep. 312.0m. (1990); Chair. and Man. Dir JULIUS OLAWOLE ADEWUNMI.

African Banking Consortium (ABC) Merchant Bank (Nigeria) Ltd: 13 Olosa St, Victoria Island, POB 70647, Lagos; tel. (1) 2616069; telex 23152; fax (1) 2611117; f. 1982; cap. p.u. 40m. (March 1993), dep. 246.4m. (1992); Chair. Chief E. C. IWUANYANWU; Man. Dir C. N. ABARA; 3 brs.

Century Merchant Bank Ltd: 11 Burma Rd, PMB 1307, Apapa, Lagos; tel. (1) 2803160; telex 22039; fax (1) 2871603; cap. and res 33.9m., dep. 608.7m. (1991); Chair. Alhaji BASHIR OTHMAN TOFA; Man. Dir CHRIS ENUENWOSU.

Continental Merchant Bank Nigeria Ltd: 1 Kingsway Rd, Ikoyi, POB 12035, Lagos; tel. (1) 2690501; telex 21585; fax (1) 2690900; f. 1986; cap. p.u. 43.6m. (Dec. 1992); Chair. Alhaji MOHAMMED SHEKARAU OMAR; Man. Dir Dr CHICHI ASHWE; 3 brs.

Fidelity Union Merchant Bank Ltd: Savannah House, 62-66 Broad St, Lagos; tel. (1) 2601960; telex 22845; fax (1) 2636868; f. 1988; cap. and res 201.5m., dep. 745.5m. (June 1995); Chair. Chief ONWUKA KALU; CEO NEBOLISHA O. ARAH.

First City Merchant Bank Ltd: Primrose Tower, 17A Tinubu St, POB 9117, Lagos; tel. (1) 2665944; telex 22913; fax (1) 2665126; f. 1983; cap. and res 326.8m., dep. 1,058.6m. (1994); Chair. and CEO OTUNBA M. O. BALOGUN; Dr JONATHAN A. D. LONG.

First Interstate Merchant Bank (Nigeria) Ltd: Unity House, 37 Marina, Victoria Island, POB 72295, Lagos; tel. (1) 2667183; telex 23881; fax (1) 2668273; cap. p.u. 40.0m. (March 1992), dep. 801.2m. (1991); Man. Dir O. ODEJIMI (acting).

ICON Ltd: ICON House, Plot 999F, cnr Idejo and Danmole Sts, Victoria Island, Lagos; tel. (1) 2660434; f. 1974; cap. p.u. 50.4m. (1991), dep. 1,545.4m. (1990); Chair. Alhaji SAIDU KASSIM; Man. Dir A. A. FEESE; 6 brs.

Industrial Bank Ltd (Merchant Bankers): Plot 1637, Adetokunbo Ademola St, Victoria Island, PMB 12637, Lagos; tel. (1) 2622454; telex 28735; fax (1) 2619024; cap. p.u. 60.1m. (Dec. 1993); Chair. Dr SAMUEL ADEDOYIN; Man. Dir Chief E. AYO AWODEYI (acting).

International Merchant Bank (Nigeria) Ltd: IMB Plaza, 1 Akin Adesola St, Victoria Island, PMB 12028, Lagos; tel. (1) 2612204; telex 28511; fax (1) 2616792; f. 1974; cap. and res 432.7m., dep. 1,365.5m. (June 1995); Chair. Maj.-Gen. MOHAMMED SHUWA (retd); Man. Dir EDWIN CHINYE; 5 brs.

Merchant Banking Corpn (Nigeria) Ltd: 16 Keffi St, S W Ikoyi, POB 53289, Lagos; tel. (1) 2690261; telex 28945; fax (1) 2690767; f. 1982; cap. and res 260.8m., dep. 1,068.6m. (March 1996); Chair. Dr M. A. MAJEKODUNMI; Man. Dir FUNKE OSIBODU.

NAL Merchant Bank: NAL Towers, 20 Marina, PMB 12735, Lagos; tel. (1) 2600420; telex 28588; fax (1) 2633294; f. 1960; cap. and res 444.5m., dep. 3,423.7m. (March 1996); Chair. Alhaji E. Y. ABDULLAHI; Man. Dir Dr SHAMSUDDEEN USMAN; 6 brs.

New Africa Merchant Bank Ltd: 4 Waff Rd, PMB 2340, Kaduna; tel. (62) 235276; telex 71684; fax (62) 237311; cap. and res 118.7m., dep. 253.1m. (Dec. 1995); Chair. Alhaji SAMAILA MAMMAN; Man. Dir Mallam UMAR YAHAYA.

Nigbel Merchant Bank (Nigeria) Ltd: 77 Awolowo Rd, Ikoyi, POB 52463, Lagos; tel. (1) 2690380; telex 28472; fax (1) 2693256; f. 1987; cap. p.u. 60m. (Dec. 1995), dep. 367.7m. (1991); Chair. Chief N. O. IDOWU; CEO GUY SAUVANET.

Nigerian-American Merchant Bank Ltd: Boston House, 10–12 Macarthy St, PMB 12759, Lagos; tel. (1) 2600360; telex 28412; fax (1) 2631712; f. 1979; affiliate of First National Bank of Boston (USA); cap. and res 433.7m., dep. 763.4m. (1996); Chair. Alhaji IBRAHIM DAMCIDA; Man. Dir OSARO ISOKPAN; 3 brs.

Nigeria-Arab Bank Ltd: 96–102 Broad St, POB 12807, Lagos; tel. (1) 2661955; telex 28939; f. 1969; cap. and res 38.8m., dep. 1,313.3m.

(1991); Chair. Alhaji ABIDU YAZIB; Man. Dir MUJTABA ABUBAKAR GUMI; 41 brs.

Nigeria Intercontinental Merchant Bank Ltd: Plot 999C, Intercontinental Plaza, Danmole St, Victoria Island, POB 80150, Lagos; tel. (1) 2622940; telex 28342; fax (1) 2623010; cap. p.u. 202.3m. (Dec. 1995); Chair. RAYMOND C. OBIERI; Man. Dir ERASTUS B. O. AKINGBOLA.

Rims Merchant Bank Ltd: Kingsway Bldg, Second Floor, 51–52 Merina, POB 73029, Lagos; tel. (1) 2662105; telex 28815; fax (1) 2669947; f. 1988; cap. and res 69.3m., dep. 617.8m. (1992); Chair. Alhaji A. IBRAHIM OFR'SAN; CEO EMMANUEL OCHOLI.

Stanbic Merchant Bank Nigeria Ltd: 188 Awolowo Rd, Ikoyi, POB 54746, Lagos; tel. (1) 2690402; telex 28963; fax (1) 2692469; f. 1983 as Grindlays Merchant Bank of Nigeria; cap. p.u. 100m. (Dec. 1996); Chair. Alhaji ISIYAKU RABIU; Man. Dir ANDREW H. S. MACLEOD.

Development Banks

Federal Mortgage Bank of Nigeria: Mamman Kontagora House, 23 Marina St, POB 2078, Lagos; tel. (1) 2647371; telex 21840; f. 1977; loans to individuals and mortgage institutions; cap. p.u. 150m. (1992), dep. 463.8m. (1991); Chair. Alhaji H. B. KOLO; Man. Dir Alhaji KASSIM MUSA BICHI; 61 brs.

Nigerian Agricultural and Co-operative Bank Ltd (NACB): Hospital Rd, PMB 2155, Kaduna; tel. (62) 201000; telex 71115; fax (62) 210611; f. 1973; for funds to farmers and co-operatives to improve production techniques; cap. p.u. 500m., dep. 4,455.4m. (1992); Chair. Alhaji SULE LAMIDO; Man. Dir Prof. M. B. AJAKAIYE; 38 brs.

Nigerian Bank for Commerce and Industry (NBCI): Bankers' House, Plot 19C Adeola Hopewell, Victoria Island, POB 4424, Lagos; tel. (1) 2616194; telex 21917; fax (1) 2614202; f. 1973; govt bank to aid indigenization and development of small and medium-sized enterprises; cap. p.u. 200m. (1990); Admin. UBADIGBO OKONKWO; 19 brs.

Nigerian Industrial Development Bank Ltd: NIDB House, 63–71 Broad St, POB 2357, Lagos; tel. (1) 2663495; telex 21701; fax (1) 2667074; f. 1964 to provide medium and long-term finance to industry, manufacturing, non-petroleum mining and tourism; encourages foreign investment in partnership with Nigerians; cap. p.u. 106m. (Dec. 1995); Man. Dir Alhaji SAIDU YAYA KASIMU; 6 brs.

Bankers' Association

Chartered Institute of Bankers of Nigeria: 19 Adeola Hopewell St, POB 72273, Victoria Island, Lagos; tel. (1) 2615642; telex 22838; fax (1) 2611306; Chair. JOHNSON O. EKUNDAYO; CEO A. A. ADENUBI.

STOCK EXCHANGE

Securities and Exchange Commission (SEC): Mandilas House, 96–102 Broad St, PMB 12638, Lagos; f. 1979 as govt agency to regulate and develop capital market; responsible for supervision of stock exchange operations; Dir-Gen. GEORGE A. AKAMIOKHOR.

Nigerian Stock Exchange: Stock Exchange House, 2–4 Customs St, POB 2457, Lagos; tel. (1) 2660287; telex 23567; fax (1) 2668724; f. 1960; Pres. PASCAL DOZIE; Dir-Gen. HAYFORD ALILE; 6 brs.

INSURANCE

In December 1994 there were some 134 insurance companies operating in Nigeria. Since 1978 they have been required to reinsure 20% of the sum insured with the Nigeria Reinsurance Corporation.

Insurance Companies

African Alliance Insurance Co Ltd: 112 Broad St, POB 2276, Lagos; tel. (1) 2664300; telex 23461; fax (1) 2660943; f. 1960; life assurance and pensions; Man. Dir OPE OREDUGBA; 30 brs.

African Insurance Co Ltd: 134 Nnamdi Azikiwe St, Idumota, POB 274, Lagos; tel. (1) 2661720; f. 1950; all classes except life; Area Man. N. E. NSA; 4 brs.

American International Insurance (AIICO): AIICO Plaza, Plot PC 12, Afribank St, Victoria Island, POB 2577, Lagos; tel. (1) 2610651; fax (1) 2617433; CEO M. E. HANSEN.

Continental Reinsurance Co Ltd: Reinsurance House, 11th Floor, 46 Marina, POB 2401, Lagos; tel. (1) 2665350; telex 28426; fax (1) 2665370; CEO ADEYEMO ADEJUMO.

Great Nigeria Insurance Co Ltd: 47–57 Martins St, POB 2314, Lagos; tel. (1) 2662590; telex 22272; f. 1960; all classes; Man. Dir R. O. ORIMOLOYE.

Guinea Insurance Co Ltd: Akuro House, 3rd Floor, 24 Campbell St, POB 1136, Lagos; tel. (1) 2665201; telex 21680; f. 1958; all classes; CEO Alhaji M. A. MUSTAPHA.

Industrial and General Insurance Co Ltd: Plot 741, Adeola Hopewell St, POB 52592, Falomo, Lagos; tel. (1) 2613534; fax (1) 614922; CEO REMI OLOWUDE.

Kapital Insurance Co Ltd: 116 Hadeja Rd, POB 2044, Kano; tel. (64) 645666; telex 71108; fax (64) 636962; CEO Alhaji M. G. UMAR.

Law Union and Rock Insurance Co of Nigeria Ltd: 88–92 Broad St, POB 944, Lagos; tel. (1) 2663526; telex 28427; fax (1) 2664659; fire, accident and marine; 6 brs; ; CEO S. O. AKINYEMI.

Leadway Assurance Co Ltd: NN 28–29 Constitution Rd, POB 458, Kaduna; tel. (62) 200660; telex 71101; fax (62) 236838; f. 1970; all classes; Man. Dir OYEKANMI ABIODUN HASSAN-ODUKALE.

Lion of Africa Insurance Co Ltd: St Peter's House, 3 Ajele St, POB 2055, Lagos; tel. (1) 2600950; telex 23536; fax (1) 2636111; f. 1952; all classes; Man. Dir G. A. ALEGIEUNO.

Mercury Assurance Co Ltd: 17 Martins St, POB 2003, Lagos; tel. (1) 2660216; telex 21952; general; Man. Dir S. N. C. OKONKWO.

National Insurance Corpn of Nigeria (NICON): 5 Customs St, POB 1100, Lagos; tel. (1) 2640230; telex 28780; fax (1) 2666556; f. 1969; transferred to private ownership in 1990; all classes; cap. 200m.; Man. Dir Alhaji MOHAMMED U. A. KARI; 28 brs.

N.E.M. Insurance Co (Nigeria) Ltd: 22A Borno Way, Ebute, POB 654, Lagos; tel. (1) 5861920; telex 23287; all classes; Chair. T. J. ONOMIGBO OKPOKO; Man. Dir J. E. UMUKORO.

Niger Insurance Co Ltd: 47 Marina, POB 2718, Lagos; tel. (1) 2664452; fax (1) 2662196; all classes; CEO A. K. ONIWINDE; 6 brs.

Nigeria Reinsurance Corpn: 46 Marina, PMB 12766, Lagos; tel. (1) 2667049; telex 21092; fax (1) 2668041; all classes of reinsurance; Man. Dir O. OSOKA.

Nigerian General Insurance Co Ltd: 1 Nnamdi Azikiwe St, Tirubu Square, POB 2210, Lagos; tel. (1) 2662552; f. 1951; all classes; Chair. Prince SOLAGBADE D. ARAOYE; Man. Dir A. F. KILADEJO; 15 brs.

Phoenix of Nigeria Assurance Co Ltd: Mandilas House, 96–102 Broad St, POB 2893, Lagos; tel. (1) 2661160; fax (1) 2665069; f. 1964; all classes; cap. 10m.; Chair. Chief O. FALEYE; Man. Dir A. A. AKINTUNDE; 5 brs.

Prestige Assurance Co (Nigeria) Ltd: 54 Marina, POB 650, Lagos; tel. (1) 2661213; telex 28516; fax (1) 2664110; all classes except life; Chair. Alhaji S. M. ARGUNGU; Man. Dir K. C. MATHEW.

Royal Exchange Assurance (Nigeria) Group: New Africa House, 31 Marina, POB 112, Lagos; tel. (1) 2663120; telex 27406; fax (1) 2664431; all classes; Chair. Alhaji MUHTAR BELLO YOLA; Man. Dir JONAH U. IKHIDERO; 6 brs.

Summit Insurance Co Ltd: Summit Centre, 9 Bishop Aboyade Cole, Victoria Island, POB 52462, Falomlo, Ikoyi, Lagos; tel. (1) 687476; telex 22652; fax (1) 615850; Man. Dir O. O. LADIPO-AJAYI.

Sun Insurance Office (Nigeria) Ltd: Unity House, 37 Marina, POB 2694, Lagos; tel. (1) 2661318; telex 21994; all classes except life; Man. Dir A. T. ADENIJI; 6 brs.

United Nigeria Insurance Co (UNIC) Ltd: 53 Marina, POB 588, Lagos; tel. (1) 2663201; telex 22186; fax (1) 2664282; f. 1965; all classes except life; CEO E. O. A. ADETUNJI; 17 brs.

Unity Life and Fire Insurance Co Ltd: 25 Nnamdi Azikiwe St, POB 3681, Lagos; tel. (1) 2662517; telex 21657; fax (1) 2662599; all classes; Man. Dir R. A. ODINIGWE.

Veritas: NIGUS House, Plot 1412, Victoria Island, Lagos; tel. (1) 2610485; telex 21826; fax (1) 2633688; all classes; Man. Dir SAIDU USMAN.

West African Provincial Insurance Co: 27–29 King George V Rd, POB 2103, Lagos; tel. (1) 2636433; telex 21613; fax (1) 2633688; all classes except life; Man. Dir C. O. IDOWU SILVA.

Insurance Association

Nigerian Insurance Association: Nicon House, 1st Floor, 5 Customs St, POB 9551, Lagos; tel. (1) 2640825; f. 1971; Chair. J. U.IKHIDERO.

Trade and Industry

CHAMBERS OF COMMERCE

Nigerian Association of Chambers of Commerce, Industry, Mines and Agriculture: 15A Ikorodu Rd, Maryland, PMB 12816, Lagos; tel. and fax (1) 4964737; telex 21368; Pres. Chief M. O. ORIGBO; Dir-Gen. L. O. ADEKUNLE.

Aba Chamber of Commerce and Industry: UBA Bldg, Ikot Expene Rd/Georges St, POB 1596, Aba; tel. (82) 225148; Pres. Dr S. C. OKOLO.

Abeokuta Chamber of Commerce and Industry: 29 Kuto Rd, Ishabo, POB 937, Abeokuta; tel. (39) 241230; Pres. Chief S. O. AKINREMI.

Abuja Chamber of Commerce and Industry: Wuse, PMB 86, Garki, Abuja; tel. (9) 52341887; Pres. Alhaji ABDULLAHI ADAMU.

Adamawa Chamber of Commerce and Industry: c/o Palace Hotel, POB 8, Jimeta, Yola; tel. (75) 255136; Pres. Alhaji ISA HAMMAN-YERO.

Akure Chamber of Commerce and Industry: 57 Oyemekun Rd, Akure; tel. (34) 231051; Pres. GABRIEL AKINJO.

Awka Chamber of Commerce and Industry: 220 Enugu Rd, POB 780, Awka; tel. (45) 550105; Pres. Lt-Col (retd) D. ORUGBU.

Bauchi Chamber of Commerce and Industry: 96 Maiduguri Rd, POB 911, Bauchi; tel. (77) 42620; telex 83261; f. 1976; Pres. Alhaji MAGAJI MU'AZU.

Benin Chamber of Commerce, Industry, Mines and Agriculture: 10 Murtala Muhammed Way, POB 2087, Benin City; tel. (52) 255761; Pres. C. O. EWEKA.

Benue Chamber of Commerce, Industry, Mines and Agriculture: 71 Ankpa Qr Rd, PMB 102344, Makurdi; tel. (44) 32573; Chair. Col (retd) R. V. I. ASAM.

Borno Chamber of Commerce and Industry: 3 Jos Rd, PMB 1636, Maiduguri; tel. (76) 232942; telex 82112; Pres. Alhaji A. ALI KOTOKO.

Calabar Chamber of Commerce and Industry: Desan House Bldg, 38 Ndidem Iso Rd, POB 76, Calabar, Cross River; tel. (87) 221558; 92 mems; Pres. Chief TAM OFORIOKUMA.

Enugu Chamber of Commerce, Industry and Mines: International Trade Fair Complex, Abakaliki Rd, POB 734, Enugu; tel. (42) 330575; f. 1963; Dir S. C. NWAEKEKE.

Franco-Nigerian Chamber of Commerce: Plot 24, Adeola Odeku St, POB 70001, Victoria Island, Lagos; tel. (1) 2621423; telex 21047; fax (1) 2621422; f. 1985; Chair. M. Y. A. OYOLEKE; Pres. J. J. ENGELS.

Gongola Chamber of Commerce and Industry: Palace Hotel, POB 8, Jimeta-Yola; tel. (75) 255136; Pres. Alhaji ALIYU IBRAHIM.

Ibadan Chamber of Commerce and Industry: Commerce House, Ring Rd, Challenge, PMB 5168, Ibadan; tel. (2) 317223; telex 20311; Pres. JIDE ABIMBOLA.

Ijebu Chamber of Commerce and Industry: 51 Ibadan Rd, POB 604, Ijebu Ode; tel. (37) 432880; Pres. DOYIN DEGUN.

Ikot Ekpene Chamber of Commerce and Industry: 47 Aba Rd, POB 50, Ikot Ekpene; tel. (85) 400153; Pres. G. U. EKANEM.

Kaduna Chamber of Commerce, Industry and Agriculture: 24 Waff Rd, POB 728, Kaduna; tel. (62) 211216; telex 71325; fax (62) 214149; Pres. Alhaji MOHAMMED SANI AMINU.

Kano Chamber of Commerce, Industry, Mines and Agriculture: Zoo Rd, POB 10, Kano City, Kano; tel. (64) 667138; Pres. Alhaji AUWALU ILU.

Katsina Chamber of Commerce and Industry: 1 Nagogo Rd, POB 92, Katsina; tel. (65) 31014; Pres. ABBA ALI.

Kwara Chamber of Commerce, Industry, Mines and Agriculture: 208 Ibrahim Taiwo Rd, POB 1634, Ilorin; tel. (31) 221069; Pres. W. O. ODUDU.

Lagos Chamber of Commerce and Industry: Commerce House, 1 Idowu Taylor St, Victoria Island, POB 109, Lagos; tel. (1) 2613898; telex 21368; fax (1) 2610573; f. 1885; 900 mems; Pres. OLUDAYO SONUGA.

Niger Chamber of Commerce and Industry: Trade Fair Site, POB 370, Minna; tel. (66) 223153; Pres. Alhaji U. S. NDANUSA.

Nnewi Chamber of Commerce and Industry: 31A Nnobi Rd, POB 1471, Nnewi; f. 1987; Pres. Chief C. M. IBETO.

Osogbo Chamber of Commerce and Industry: Obafemi Awolowo Way, Ajegunle, POB 870, Osogbo, Osun; tel. (35) 231098; Pres. Prince VICTOR ADEMLE.

Owerri Chamber of Commerce and Industry: OCCIMA Secretariat, 123 Okigwe Rd, POB 1640, Owerri; tel. (83) 234849; Pres. Chief BONIFACE N. AMAECHI.

Oyo Chamber of Commerce and Industry: POB 67, Oyo; Pres. Chief C. A. OGUNNIYI.

Plateau State Chambers of Commerce, Industry, Mines and Agriculture: Shama House, 32 Rwang Pam St, POB 2092, Jos; tel. (73) 53918; telex 81348; f. 1976; Pres. Chief M. E. JACDOMI.

Port Harcourt Chamber of Commerce, Industry, Mines and Agriculture: 169 Aba Rd, POB 71, Port Harcourt; tel. (84) 330394; telex 61110; f. 1952; Pres. Chief S. I. ALETE.

Remo Chamber of Commerce and Industry: 7 Sho Manager Way, POB 1172, Shagamu; tel. (37) 640962; Pres. Chief S. O. ADEKOYA.

Sapele Chamber of Commerce and Industry: 144 New Ogorode Rd, POB 154, Sapele; tel. (54) 42323; Pres. P. O. FUFUYIN.

Sokoto Chamber of Commerce and Industry: 12 Racecourse Rd, POB 2234, Sokoto; tel. (60) 231805; Pres. Alhaji ALIYU WAZIRI BODINGA.

Umahia Chamber of Commerce: 65 Uwalaka St, POB 86, Umahia; tel. (88) 220055; Pres. Chief S. B. A. ATULOMAH.

Uyo Chamber of Commerce and Industry: 141 Abak Rd, POB 2960, Uyo, Akwa Ibom; Pres. Chief DANIEL ITA-EKPOTT.

Warri Chamber of Commerce and Industry: Block 1, Edewor Shopping Centre, Warri/Sapele Rd, POB 302, Warri; tel. (53) 233731; Pres. MOSES F. OROGUN.

TRADE ASSOCIATIONS

Abeokuta Importers' and Exporters' Association: c/o Akeweje Bros, Lafenwa, Abeokuta.

Ijebu Importers' and Exporters' Association: 16 Ishado St, Ijebu-Ode.

Nigerian Association of Native Cloth Dealers and Exporters: 45 Koesch St, Lagos.

Nigerian Association of Stockfish Importers: 10 Egerton Rd, Lagos.

Union of Importers and Exporters: POB 115, Ibadan; f. 1949; Chair. E. A. SANDA.

PROFESSIONAL AND EMPLOYERS' ORGANIZATIONS

Association of Master Bakers, Confectioners and Caterers of Nigeria: 13–15 Custom St, POB 4, Lagos; f. 1951; 250 mems; Pres. J. ADE TUYO (acting).

Federation of Building and Civil Engineering Contractors in Nigeria: Construction House, Plot 6, Adeyemo Alakija St, Professional Centre, Victoria Island, POB 282, Lagos; tel. (1) 2616564; f. 1954; Exec. Sec. T. A. ADEKANMBI.

Institute of Chartered Accountants of Nigeria: Plot 16, Professional Layout Centre, Idowu Taylor St, Victoria Island, POB 1580, Lagos; tel. (1) 2622394; fax (1) 610304; f. 1965; CEO and Registrar P. O. OMOREGIE.

Manufacturers' Association of Nigeria: Unity House, 12th Floor, 37 Marina, POB 3835, Lagos; tel. (1) 2660755; f. 1971; Pres. HASSAN ADAMU.

Nigerian Chamber of Mines: POB 454, Jos; tel. (73) 55003; f. 1950; Pres. A. A. KEHINDE.

Nigeria Employers' Consultative Association: Commercial House, 1–11 Commercial Ave, POB 2231, Yaba, Lagos; tel. (1) 800360; fax (1) 860309; f. 1957; Pres. Chief R. F. GIWA.

Nigerian Institute of Architects: 2 Idowu Taylor St, Victoria Island, POB 178, Lagos; tel. (1) 2617940; fax (1) 2617947; f. 1960; Pres. Chief O. C. MAJOROH.

Nigerian Institute of Building: 1B Market St, Oyingbo, Ebute-Metta, POB 3191, Marina, Lagos; f. 1970; Pres. S. T. OYEFEKO.

Nigerian Institution of Estate Surveyors and Valuers: Flat 2B, Dolphin Scheme, Ikoyi, POB 2325, Lagos; tel. (1) 2685981; Pres. W. O. ODUDU.

Nigerian Livestock Dealers' Association: POB 115, Sapele.

Nigerian Recording Association: 9 Breadfruit St, POB 950, Lagos.

Nigerian Society of Engineers: National Engineering Centre, 1 Engineering Close, POB 72667, Victoria Island, Lagos; tel. and fax (1) 2617315; Pres. Dr O. AJAYI.

Pharmaceutical Society of Nigeria: 4 Tinubu Sq., POB 546, Lagos.

DEVELOPMENT ORGANIZATIONS

Anambra State Agricultural Development Corporation: Garden Ave, PMB 1024, Enugu.

Anambra-Imo Basin Development Authority: Chair. SAMUEL C. ELUWA; Gen. Man. WITLY OKONKWO.

Benin–Owena River Basin Development Authority: 24 Benin-Sapele Rd, PMB 1381, Obayantor, Benin City; tel. (52) 254415; f. 1976 to conduct irrigation; Gen. Man. Dr G. E. OTEZE.

Chad Basin Development Authority: Dikwa Rd, PMB 1130, Maiduguri; tel. (76) 232015; f. 1973; irrigation and agriculture-allied industries; Chair. MOHAMMED ABALI; Gen. Man. Alhaji BUNU S. MUSA.

Cross River Basin Development Authority: 32 Target Rd, PMB 1249, Calabar; tel. (87) 223163; f. 1977; Gen. Man. SIXTUS ABETIANBE.

Cross River State Agricultural Development Corporation: PMB 1024, Calabar.

Federal Capital Development Authority: Abuja; govt agency for design, construction and management of Abuja; Perm. Sec. Alhaji ABUBAKAR KOKO.

Federal Housing Authority: Gen. Man. S. P. O. FORTUNE EBIE.

Federal Institute of Industrial Research, Oshodi (FIIRO): Murtala Muhammed Airport, Bilnd Centre St, Oshodi, Ikeja, PMB 21023, Lagos; tel. (1) 523260; telex 26006; fax (1) 4525880; f. 1956; plans and directs industrial research and provides tech. assistance and information to industry; specializes in foods, minerals, textiles, natural products and industrial intermediates; Dir. Prof. S. A. ODUNFA.

Gongola State Housing Corpn: Yola; Chair. DOMINIC M. MAPEO; Gen. Man. DAVID A. GARNVWA.

Hadejia Jama'are Basin Development Authority: Bauchi; f. 1976; began building four dams for irrigation and hydroelectric power in 1980; Gen. Man. Alhaji AHMADU RUFAI.

Imo State Housing Corpn: Uratta Rd, PMB 1224, Owerri, Imo; tel. (83) 230733; f. 1976; develops housing and industrial estates, grants finance for house purchase and operates a savings scheme; Gen. Man. O. A. KALU.

Industrial Training Fund: Federal Secretariat, 8th Floor, PMB 2199, Jos; tel. (73) 55297; telex 81154; f. 1971 to promote and encourage skilled workers in trade and industry; Dir-Gen. Alhaji LAWAL TUDUNWADA.

Kaduna Industrial and Finance Co Ltd: Investment House, 27 Ali Akilu Rd, PMB 2230, Kaduna; tel. (62) 240751; telex 20711; fax (62) 241764; f. 1989; provides development finance; Chair. ISAIAH C. BALAT; Man. Dir Alhaji DAHIRU MOHAMMED.

Kwara State Investment Corpn: 109–112 Fate Rd, PMB 1344, Ilorin, Kwara; tel. (31) 220510.

Lagos State Development and Property Corpn: Ilupeju Industrial Estate, Ikorodu Rd, PMB 21050, Ikeja; POB 907, Lagos; f. 1972; planning and development of Lagos; Gen. Man. O.R. ASHAFA.

New Nigerian Development Co Ltd: 18/19 Ahmadu Bello Way, Ahmed Talib House, PMB 2120, Kaduna; tel. (62) 236250; telex 71108; fax (62) 235482; f. 1968; owned by the Govts of 16 northern States; investment finance; 7 subsidiaries, 36 assoc. cos; Chair. Alhaji ABDULLAHI IBRAHIM.

New Nigeria Development Co (Properties) Ltd: 18–19 Ahmadu Bello Way, PMB 2040, Kaduna; housing devt agency.

Niger Delta Basin and Rural Development Authority: 21 Azikiwe Rd, PMB 5676, Port Harcourt; f. 1976.

Niger River Basin Development Authority: f. 1976; Chair. Alhaji HALIRU DANTORO.

Nigerian Enterprises Promotion Board: 72 Campbell St, PMB 12553, Lagos; f. 1972 to promote indigenization; Chair. MINSO GADZAMA.

Nigerian Export Promotion Council: Kumba St, PMB 133, Garki, Abuja; tel. (9) 5230930; telex 91510; fax (9) 5230931; f. 1976; promotes development and diversification of exports; Dir M. A. ADESINA.

Nigerian Livestock and Meat Authority: POB 479, Kaduna; telex 71307.

Northern Nigeria Investments Ltd: 4 Waff Rd, POB 138, Kaduna; tel. (62) 239654; telex 71110; fax (62) 230770; f. 1959 to identify and invest in industrial and agricultural projects in 16 northern States; cap. p.u. 20m.; Chair. Alhaji ABUBAKAR G. ADAMU; Man. Dir GIMBA H. IBRAHIM.

Odu'a Investment Co Ltd: Cocoa House, PMB 5435, Ibadan; tel. (2) 417710; telex 31225; fax (2) 413000; f. 1976; jtly owned by Ogun, Ondo and Oyo States; Man. Dir Alhaji R. S. ARUNA.

Ogun-Oshun River Basin Development Authority: f. 1976; Chair. Mrs D. B. A. KUFORIJI; Gen. Man. Dr LEKAN ARE.

Ogun State Agricultural Credit Corpn: PMB 2029, Abeokuta; f. 1976.

Ogun State Housing Corpn: PMB 2077, Abeokuta; f. 1976 to develop housing and industrial estates and to grant finance for house purchase; also operates a savings plan; Gen. Man. F. O. ABIODUN.

Ondo State Housing Corpn: PMB 693, Akure; f. 1976 to develop housing and industrial estates and to grant finance for house purchase; also operates a savings plan.

Ondo State Investment Corpn: PMB 700, Akure; f. 1976 to investigate and promote both agricultural and industrial projects on a commercial basis in the State.

Oyo State Property Development Corpn: f. 1976 to develop housing, commercial property and industrial estates and to grant finance for house purchase; also operates a savings plan.

Plateau State Housing Corpn: Jos; plans to build 1,000 housing units a year in addition to another 1,000 units built in the State by the Fed. Govt.

Plateau State Water Resources Development Board: Jos; incorporates the fmr Plateau River Basin Devt Authority and Plateau State Water Resources Devt Board.

Price Intelligence Agency: c/o Productivity, Prices and Income Board, Lagos; f. 1980; monitors prices.

Projects Development Institute: 3 Independence Layout, POB 609, Enugu; tel. (42) 451593; fax (42) 457691; f. 1974; promotes the establishment of new industries and develops industrial projects utilizing local raw materials; Dir L. K. NWOSU (acting).

Rivers State Development Corpn: Port Harcourt; f. 1970.

Rivers State Housing Corpn: 15/17 Emekuku St, PMB 5044, Port Harcourt.

Rubber Research Institute of Nigeria: PMB 1049, Benin City; telex 41190; f. 1961; conducts research into the production of rubber and other latex products; Dir Dr E. K. OKAISABOR.

Sokoto-Rima Basin Development Authority: f. 1976; Chair. Alhaji MU'AZU LAMIDO.

Trans Investments Co Ltd: Bale Oyewole Rd, PMB 5085, Ibadan; tel. (2) 416000; telex 31122; f. 1986; initiates and finances industrial and agricultural schemes; Gen. Man. M. A. ADESIYUN.

Upper Benue Basin Development Authority: Chair. Alhaji MOHAMMADU MAI.

PUBLIC CORPORATIONS

In early 1995 the Government announced plans to lease a number of state-owned enterprises to private operators.

Ajaokuta Steel Co Ltd: PMB 1000, Ajaokuta, Kwara; tel. (31) 400450; telex 36390; CEO M. M. INUWA.

Delta Steel Co Ltd: Ovwian-Aladja, POB 1220, Warri; tel. (53) 621001; telex 43456; fax (53) 621012; f. 1979; state-owned; operates direct-reduction steel complex; Chair. Chief TUNJI AROSANYIN; Man. Dir TIM C. EFOBI.

Gaskiya Corpn Ltd: Tadun Wada, Zaria; tel. (69) 32201; f. 1938; owned by Kaduna State Govt, New Nigerian Development Co and Jama'atu Nasril Islam; printers; CEO ABDULLAHI HASSAN.

National Electric Power Authority (NEPA): 24–25 Marina, PMB 12030, Lagos; tel. (1) 2600640; telex 21212; f. 1972 by merger of the Electricity Corpn of Nigeria and the Niger Dams Authority; Man. Dir (vacant).

Nigerian Cement Co Ltd (NIGERCEM): Nkalugu, POB 331, Enugu; tel. and fax (42) 253829; telex 51113; f. 1954; Chair. Chief S. N. ANYANWU; Man. Dir Dr OZO NWEKE OZO.

Nigerian Coal Corpn: PMB 01053, Enugu; tel. (42) 335314; telex 51115; f. 1909; operates four mines; Gen. Man. F. N. UGWU.

Nigerian Engineering and Construction Co Ltd (NECCO): Km 14, Badagry Expressway (opp. International Trade Fair Complex), PMB 12684, Lagos; tel. (1) 5880591; telex 21836; building, civil, mechanical and electrical engineers, furniture makers and steel fabricators; Chair. EHIOZE EDIAE.

Nigerian Liquefied Natural Gas Co: Lagos; Chair. (vacant); Man. Dir (vacant).

Nigerian Mining Corpn: Federal Secretariat, 7th Floor, PMB 2154, Jos; tel. (73) 55245; telex 81139; f. 1972; exploration, production, processing and marketing of minerals; nine subsidiaries and eight assoc. cos; CEO YOHANNA B. KWA.

Nigerian National Petroleum Corpn (NNPC): Plot 639, Usuma St, Maitama, Abuja; tel. (9) 5234761; fax (9) 5234760; f. 1977; reorg. 1988; holding corpn for fed. govt interests in petroleum cos; 11 operating subsidiaries; Man. Dir DALHATU BAYERO.

Nigerian National Supply Co Ltd: 29 Burma Rd, PMB 12662, Apapa, Lagos; state-owned import org.; Chair. Brig. J. I. ONOJA; Gen. Man. Maj. A. DAHIRU.

Port Harcourt Refining Co Ltd: POB 585, Port Harcourt Rivers State; tel. (84) 300420; telex 61166; f. 1965; Man. Dir MANSUR AHMED.

CO-OPERATIVES

There are more than 25,000 co-operative societies in Nigeria.

Co-operative Federation of Nigeria: PMB 5533, Ibadan; tel. (2) 711276; telex 31224; fax (2) 711276; Pres. REMI OBISESAN.

Anambra State Co-operative Federation Ltd: 213 Agbani Rd, PMB 1488, Enugu; tel. (42) 331157; Pres. C. G. O. NWABUGWU.

Association of Nigerian Co-operative Exporters Ltd: New Court Rd, POB 477, Ibadan; f. 1945; producers/exporters of cocoa and other cash crops.

Co-operative Supply Association Ltd: Ance Bldg, Jericho, Ibadan; importers and dealers in agricultural chemicals and equipment, fertilizers, building materials, general hardware, grocery and provisions.

Co-operative Union of Western Nigeria Ltd: PMB 5101, Jericho Rd, Ibadan.

Kabba Co-operative Credit and Marketing Union Ltd: POB 25, Kabba; f. 1953; producers of food and cash crops and retailers of consumer goods; Pres. Alhaji S. O. ONUNDI; Man. H. A. ORISAFUNMI.

Kano State Co-operative Federation Ltd: 1 Zaria Rd, PMB 3030, Kano; tel. (64) 622182; Pres. G. B. YAKO.

Kwara State Co-operative Federation Ltd: PMB 1412, Ilorin; operates transport and marketing services in Kwara State; Gen. Man. J. OBARO.

Lagos State Co-operative Federation Ltd: 13 Isaacstan Close, Wemco Rd, POB 8632, Ikeja, Lagos; co-operative education and publicity.

Oyo State Co-operative Federation Ltd: 3 Olubadan Estate, New Ife Rd, PMB 5101, Ibadan; tel. (2) 710985; Pres. J. A. Aderibigbe.

MAJOR INDUSTRIAL COMPANIES

The following are some of the largest companies in terms either of capital investment or employment.

African Petroleum Ltd: AP House, 54–56 Broad St, POB 512, Lagos; tel. (1) 635290; telex 21242; cap. ₦72m.; fmrly BP Nigeria Ltd; markets lubricants, fuel oil, automotive gas oil, motor spirits, liquefied petroleum gas and kerosene; CEO Gana Abba.

African Timber and Plywood (AT & P): PMB 4001, Sapele; f. 1935; a division of UAC of Nigeria Ltd and an assoc. co of UAC International Ltd, London; loggers and mfrs of plywood, particleboard, flushdoors, lumber and machined wood products; Gen. Man. L. Hodgson.

Blackwood Hodge: Asogun Rd, Km 15, Badagry Expressway, POB 109, Apapa, Lagos; tel. (1) 880507; telex 21870; cap. p.u. ₦8.1m.; earthmoving, construction, irrigation, mining and agricultural equipment; Chair. Dr I. B. Jose; Man. Dir M. A. Pigou; 153 employees.

Chemical and Allied Products Co Ltd: POB 1004, 24 Commercial Rd, Apapa, Lagos; tel. (1) 803220; telex 21446; mfrs of paints, pesticides and pharmaceuticals, distributors of chemicals, dyestuffs, explosives, plastic raw materials and associated products.

Guinness (Nigeria) Ltd: Oba Akran Ave, Ikeja, PMB 1071, Lagos State: f. 1950; cap. p.u. ₦25m.; brewers; breweries in Ikeja (700,000 hl), Ogba (700,000 hl) and Benin (900,000 hl); Man. Dir M. F. Oteri.

Gulf Oil Co (Nigeria) Ltd: 19 Tinubu Sq., PMB 2469, Lagos; onshore and offshore petroleum exploration and production; Man. Dir Carroll Cox.

Henry Stephens Group: Head Office: 90 Awolowo Rd, SW Ikoyi, POB 2480, Lagos; tel. (1) 603460; telex 21752; subsidiary cos include:

Gilco (Nigeria) Ltd: 292 Apapa Rd, Apapa; import and export.

Henry Stephens Engineering Co Ltd: 2 Ilepeju By-Pass, Ikeja, PMB 21386, Lagos; tel. (1) 901460; telex 21752; fax (1) 2690758; for construction machinery, motors and agricultural equipment.

Nigerian Maritime Services: 13–15 Sapele Rd, Apapa, PMB 1013, Lagos; tel. (1) 873018; telex 21286; f. 1964; Chair. Prof. Ayo Ogunsheye; Gen. Man. W. P. D. Davson.

IBRU: 33 Creek Rd, PMB 1155, Apapa, Lagos; tel. (1) 876634; telex 21086; agricultural equipment, machinery and service; fishing and frozen fish distribution, civil and agricultural engineering.

A. G. Leventis Group: Iddo House, Iddo, POB 159, Lagos; tel. (1) 800220; telex 26030; fax (1) 860574; activities include wholesale and retail distribution, vehicle assembly, food production and farming, manufacture of glass, plastics, beer, technical and electrical equipment, property investment and management.

Lever Brothers (Nigeria) Ltd: 15 Dockyard Rd, POB 15, Apapa, Lagos; tel. (1) 803300; telex 21520; fax (1) 617873; f. 1923; cap. ₦112.0m.; mfrs of detergents, edible fats and toilet preparations; Chair. and CEO R. F. Giwa.

Leyland Nigeria: POB 5024, Lagos; f. 1976; 35% govt-owned; commercial vehicle assemblers and mfrs of components; Chair. Chief Olu Akinkugbe; Man. Dir P. Quick.

Mandilas Group Ltd: 96–102 Broad St, POB 35, Lagos; telex 21383; subsidiaries include Mandilas Enterprises Ltd, Mandilas Travel Ltd, Norman Industries Ltd, Electrolux-Mandilas Ltd, Phoenix of Nigeria Assurance Co Ltd, Sulzer Nigeria Ltd, Mandilas Ventures Ltd, Original Box Co Ltd.

Mobil Producing Nigeria: PMB 12054, 50 Broad St, Lagos; tel. (1) 600560; telex 21228; offshore petroleum production; Chair. Alfred K. Koch.

National Oil and Chemical Marketing Co Ltd: 38–39 Marina, PMB 2052, Lagos; tel. (1) 2665880; telex 21591; fax (1) 2662802; f. 1975 (fmrly Shell Nigeria Ltd); 40% state-owned; Man. Dir S. I. C. Okoli; 685 employees.

Nigerian Breweries Ltd: 1 Abebe Village Rd, Iganmu, POB 545, Lagos; tel. (1) 5801340; telex 263070; fax (1) 2646624; f. 1946; also facilities at Aba, Kaduna, Ibadan and Enugu; Chair. and Man. Dir Felix Ohiwerei; 3,000 employees.

Nigerian Metal Fabricating Ltd: POB 23, Kano; tel. (64) 632427; telex 77244; fax (64) 634677; part of Cedar Group; mfrs of aluminium household utensils, brassware and silverware; also light engineers.

Nigerian Oil Mills Ltd: POB 342, Kano; tel. (64) 632427; telex 77244; fax (64) 634677; import and production of vegetable oil products.

Nigerian Paper Mill Ltd: POB 1648, Lagos; also at Jebba; Chair. Brig. Usman Abubakar.

Nigerian Sugar Co Ltd: PMB 65, Bacita Estate, Jebba; tel. 641035; f. 1961; cap. ₦79.4m.; growers of sugar cane and mfrs of cane sugar and allied products; Chair. Alhaji Ibrahim Ahmed; Man. Dir Suleiman Abdullahi; 5,600 employees.

Nigerian Textile Mills Ltd: Oba Akran Ave, Industrial Estate, PMB 21051, Ikeja; tel. (1) 962012; telex 26206; fax (1) 962011; f. 1960; cap. ₦40m.; spinners, weavers and finishers; Chair. Prof. S. O. Biobaku; Dir Fernand Picciotto; 2,700 employees.

Nigerian Tin Mining Co Ltd: PMB 2036, Jos; tel. (73) 80634; f. 1986 by merger of Amalgamated Tin Mines of Nigeria Ltd and five other mining cos operating on the Jos plateau; owned by Nigerian Mining Corpn and fmr non-national shareholders in the above five cos; cap. p.u. ₦9.5m.; production of tin concentrate from alluvial tin ore and separation of columbite, zircon and monazite; Chair. E. A. Ifaturoti; Gen. Man. Alhaji M. Adamu.

Nigerian Tobacco Co Ltd: POB 137, Lagos; tel. (1) 2690471; telex 21561; fax (1) 2690470; f. 1951; cap. ₦200m.; mfrs of tobacco products; Chair. Oludolapo Ibukun Akinkugbe; Man. Dir B. Selby; 773 employees.

Phillips Oil Co (Nigeria) Ltd: Plot 853, 19 Bishop Aboyade-Cole St, Victoria Island, PMB 12612, Lagos; tel. (1) 2615656; telex 28460; fax (1) 2615663; petroleum exploration and production; Man. Dir M. O. Taiga.

PZ Industries Ltd: Planning Office Way, Ilupeju Industrial Estate, Ikeja, PMB 21132, Lagos; tel. (1) 901110; fax (1) 962076; fmrly Paterson Zochonis Nigeria Ltd; soaps, detergents, toiletries, pharmaceuticals and confectionery; factories at Ikorodu, Aba and Ilupeju.

SCOA Nigeria Ltd: 67 Marina, POB 2318, Lagos; tel. (1) 663095; telex 21017; cap. ₦44.8m.; vehicle assembly and maintenance, distribution and maintenance of heavyweight engines, industrial air-conditioning and refrigeration, home and office equipment, textiles, tanning, general consumer goods, mechanized farming.

Shell Petroleum Development Co of Nigeria Ltd: Freeman House, 21–22 Marina, PMB 2418, Lagos; tel. (1) 601600; telex 21235; the largest petroleum operation in Nigeria; carries out onshore and offshore exploration and production; 60% govt-owned; Chair. and Man. Dir Ron Burr.

Tate & Lyle (Nigeria) Ltd: 47–48 Eric Moore Rd, Iganmu Industrial Estate, POB 1240, Lagos; tel. (1) 801930; telex 26990; sugar, invert syrup, PVC pipes, plastic goods, stationery.

Texaco Nigeria Ltd: 241 Igbosere Rd, POB 166, Lagos; f. 1913; petroleum marketing; Chair. H. C. Minor; Man. Dir G. E. Smith.

Texaco Overseas (Nigeria) Petroleum Co: 36 Gerrard Rd, Ikoyi, POB 1986, Lagos; tel. (1) 680070; telex 21293; fax (1) 682520; offshore petroleum mining; Man. Dir R. Bucaram.

Triana Ltd: 18–20 Commercial Rd, PMB 1064, Apapa, Lagos; tel. (1) 5803040; telex 2122; fax (1) 5876161; f. 1970; shipping, clearing and forwarding, warehousing, air-freighting; Man. Dir M. P. Aguba.

UAC of Nigeria Ltd: Niger House, 1-5 Odunlami St, POB 9, Lagos; tel. (1) 2663010; telex 21233; fax (1) 2662628; fmrly United Africa Co; divisions include brewing, foods, electrical materials, packaging, business equipment, plant hire, timber; Man. Dir Bassey U. Ndiokho.

The West African Portland Cement Co Ltd: Elephant House, 237–239 Ikorodu Rd, POB 1001, Lagos; tel. (1) 901060; telex 26695; f. 1959; production and sale of cement and decorative materials; cap. p.u. ₦60.3m.; Chair. Prof. M. A. Adeyemo.

TRADE UNIONS

Federation

Nigerian Labour Congress (NLC): 29 Olajuwon St, off Ojuelegba Rd, Yaba, POB 620, Lagos; tel. (1) 5835582; f. 1978; comprised 42 affiliated industrial unions representing 3.5m. mems in 1985; reorg. under workers' control in 1988; Admin. Alhaji Ahmed Gusau.

Principal Unions

In 1990 a technical committee was created to restructure the 42 industrial unions, and to reduce their number. In early 1996 the Nigerian Labour Congress announced that the existing 19 unions were to be reorganized to form seven unions:

Amalgamated Union of Public Corporations, Civil Service, and Technical and Reparational Services Employees: 9 Aje St, PMB 1064, Yaba, Lagos; tel. (1) 5863722.

Maritime Workers' Union of Nigeria.

National Union of Chemical, Footwear, Rubber, Leather and Non-Metallic Workers.

National Union of Printing, Publishing and Paper Products Workers.

Nigerian Union of Civil Engineering, Construction, Furniture and Woodworkers: 51 Kano St, Ebute Metta, PMB 1064, Lagos; tel. (1) 5800263.

Nigerian Union of Mine Workers: 95 Enugu St, POB 763, Jos; tel. (73) 52401.

Steel and Engineering Workers' Union of Nigeria.

Transport

RAILWAYS

There are about 3,505 km of mainly narrow-gauge railways. The two principal lines connect Lagos with Nguru and Port Harcourt with Maiduguri.

Nigerian Railway Corporation: Ebute-Metta, Lagos; tel. (1) 5834302; telex 26584; f. 1955; restructured in 1993 into three separate units: Nigerian Railway Track Authority; Nigerian Railways; and Nigerian Railway Engineering Ltd; Admin. GREG IHIKUE.

ROADS

In 1995 the Nigerian road network totalled an estimated 32,810 km, of which about 13,300 km were principal roads and 16,400 km secondary roads; some 27,100 km were tarred.

Nigerian Road Federation: Ministry of Transport and Aviation, Joseph St, PMB 21038, Ikoyi, Lagos; tel. (1) 2652120; telex 21535.

INLAND WATERWAYS

Inland Waterways Department: Ministry of Transport, Joseph St, PMB 21038, Ikoyi, Lagos; tel. (1) 2652120; telex 21535; responsible for all navigable waterways.

SHIPPING

The principal ports are the Delta Port complex (including Warri, Koko, Burutu and Sapele ports), Port Harcourt and Calabar; other significant ports are situated at Apapa and Tin Can Island, near Lagos. The main petroleum ports are Bonny and Burutu.

National Maritime Authority: Lagos; f. 1987; Chair. Alhaji MOHAMMED MUNIR JA'AFARU.

Nigerian Ports Authority: 26–28 Marina, PMB 12588, Lagos; tel. (1) 2655020; telex 21500; f. 1955; Gen. Man. (vacant).

Nigerian Green Lines Ltd: Unity House, 15th Floor, 37 Marina, POB 2288, Lagos; tel. (1) 2663303; telex 21308; 2 vessels totalling 30,751 grt; Chair. Alhaji W. L. FOLAWIYO.

Nigerian Unity Line: Development House, 21 Wharf Rd, POB 326, Apapa, Lagos; tel. (1) 5804240; telex 21253; fax (1) 5870260; f. 1995, following the dissolution of the Nigerian National Shipping Line; govt-owned.

Association

Nigeria Shipping Federation: NPA Commercial Offices, Block 'A', Wharf Rd, POB 107, Apapa, Lagos; f. 1960; Chair. (vacant); Gen. Man. D. B. ADEKOYA.

CIVIL AVIATION

The principal international airports are at Lagos (Murtala Muhammed Airport), Kano, Port Harcourt, Calabar and Abuja. There are also 14 airports for domestic flights. In early 1997 a two-year programme to develop the airports at Lagos, Abuja, Port Harcourt and Kano was announced.

Federal Airport Authority of Nigeria: Murtala Muhammed Airport, PMB 21607, Ikeja, Lagos; tel. (1) 4900800; telex 26626; Man. Dir PETER IGBINEDION.

Principal Airlines

General and Aviation Services (Gas) Air Nigeria: Plot 5A, Old Domestic Airport, Ikeja, Lagos; tel. (1) 4933510; fax (1) 4962841; domestic and international cargo services; Pres. S. K. S. OLUBADEWO.

Kabo Air: 6775 Ashton Rd, POB 3439, Kano; tel. (64) 639591; telex 77277; fax (64) 645172; f. 1981; domestic services and international charters; Dir SHITU ADAMU.

Nigeria Airways: Airways House, Ikeja, PMB 136, Lagos; tel. (1) 4900470; telex 26127; fax (1) 2777675; f. 1958; scheduled domestic and services to Europe, the USA, West Africa and Saudi Arabia; Man. Dir Alhaji JANI IBRAHIM.

Okada Air: 17B Sapele Rd, Benin City; tel. (19) 241054; f. 1983; domestic and international charter passenger services, domestic scheduled services; Chair. Chief GABRIEL O. IGBINEDION.

Tourism

Potential attractions for tourists include fine coastal scenery, dense forests, and the rich diversity of Nigeria's arts. An estimated 193,000 tourists visited Nigeria in 1994, when receipts from tourism amounted to US $34m.

Nigerian Tourism Development Corporation: Zone 4, PMB 167, Abuja; tel. (9) 5230418; fax (9) 5230962; Chair. S. A. ALAMATU; Dir Alhaji S. M. JEGA.

Defence

In August 1996 the total strength of the armed forces was 77,100 men: the army totalled 62,000 men, the navy 5,600 and the air force 9,500. Military service is voluntary.

Defence Expenditure: Budgeted at ₦7,023m. in 1995.

Commander-in-Chief of the Armed Forces: Gen. SANI ABACHA.

Chief of Defence Staff: Maj.-Gen. ABDULSALAM ABUBAKAR.

Chief of Army Staff: Maj.-Gen. ISHAYA BAMAIYI.

Chief of Naval Staff: Cdre MIKE AKHIGBE.

Chief of Air Staff: Air Vice-Marshal NSIKAK EDUOK.

Education

Education is partly the responsibility of the state governments, although the federal government has played an increasingly important role since 1970. Primary education begins at six years of age and lasts for six years. Secondary education begins at 12 years of age and lasts for a further six years, comprising two three-year cycles. Education to junior secondary level (from six to 15 years of age) is free and compulsory. In 1994 total enrolment at primary schools was equivalent to 89% of children in the relevant age-group (100% of boys; 79% of girls), while the comparable ratio for secondary enrolment was only 30% (33% of boys; 28% of girls). In 1993 383,488 students were enrolled in 133 higher education institutions. Estimated expenditure on education in 1995 was ₦12,172m., equivalent to 5.4% of total expenditure in the federal budget. According to UNESCO estimates, the rate of adult illiteracy in 1995 averaged 42.9% (males 32.7%; females 52.7%).

Bibliography

Adamokekun, L. *The Fall of the Second Republic.* Ibadan, Spectrum Books, 1985.

Adejumobi, S., and Momah, A. (Eds). *The Political Economy of Nigeria under Military Rule, 1984–1993.* Nigeria, Southern Africa Printing and Publishing House, 1995.

Adejumobi S., and Momoh, A. (Eds). *The Enigma of Military Rule in Africa.* Harare, SAPES Books, 1995.

Ajayi, J. F. Ade., Ikoku, S. G., and Ikara, B. (Eds). *Evolution of Political Culture in Nigeria.* Kaduna State Council for Arts and Culture, and the University Press, 1985.

Ake, C. (Ed.). *Political Economy of Nigeria.* London and Lagos, Longman, 1985.

Akindele, R. A., and Ate, B. E. (Eds). *Nigeria's Economic Relations with the Major Developed Market-Economy Countries, 1960–1985.* Ikeja, Nelson, 1988.

Akpan, N. U. *The Struggle for Secession 1966–1970.* London, Frank Cass, 1972.

Aniagolu, A. N. *The Making of the 1989 Constitution of Nigeria.* Ibadan, Spectrum Books, 1993.

Anyanwu, U. D., and Aguwa, J. C. U. (Eds). *The Igbo and the Tradition of Politics.* Enugu, Fourth Dimension, 1993.

Asiegbu, J. U. J. *Nigeria and its British Invaders 1851–1920.* Lagos, Nok Publishers International, 1984.

Ate, B. E., and Akinterinwa, B.A. (Eds). *Nigeria and its Immediate Neighbours: Constraints and Prospects of Sub-Regional Security in the 1990s.* Lagos, Nigerian Institute of International Affairs, 1992.

Ayeni, V., and Soremekun, K. (Eds). *Nigeria's Second Republic.* Lagos, Daily Times Publications, 1988.

Babatope, E. *Murtala Muhammed: A Leader Betrayed.* Enugu, Roy and Ezete Publishing Co, 1986.

The Abacha Regime and the 12 June Crisis. London, Beacons Books, 1995.

Bach, D. C. *Nigéria, un pouvoir en puissance.* Paris, Editions Karthala, 1989.

Bach, D. C., Egg, J., and Philippe, J. *Nigéria, un pouvoir en puissance.* Paris, Karthala, 1988.

Bangura, Y. *Intellectuals, Economic Reform and Social Change: Constraints and Opportunities in the Formation of a Nigerian Technocracy.* Dakar, CODESRIA, 1994.

Clarke, P. B. *West Africans at War 1914–18, 1939–45: Colonial Propaganda and its Cultural Aftermath.* London, Ethnographica, 1986.

Cohen, R. *Labour and Politics in Nigeria.* London, Heinemann Educational, 1982.

Crowder, M. *The Story of Nigeria.* 4th Edn. London, 1978.

Cruise O'Brien, D. B., Dunn, J., and Rathbone, R. (Eds). *Contemporary West African States.* Cambridge University Press, 1989.

Ekundare, R. O. *An Economic History of Nigeria 1860–1960.* London, Methuen, 1973.

Ekwe-Ekwe, H. *Conflict and Intervention in Africa: Nigeria, Angola and Zaire.* London, Macmillan, 1990.

Enwerem, I. M. *Dangerous Awakening: The Politicization of Religion in Nigeria.* Ibadan, FRA, 1996.

Essien, E. *Nigeria Under Structural Adjustment.* Fountain Publications (Nigeria) Ltd, 1990.

Forrest, T. *Politics and Economic Development in Nigeria.* Boulder, CO, Westview Press, 1993.

The Advance of African Capital: The Growth of Nigerian Private Enterprise. Charlottesville, VA, University Press of Virginia, 1994.

Graf, W. D. *The Nigerian State: Political Economy, State, Class and Political System in the Post-Colonial Era.* London, James Currey, 1988.

Hayward, M. F. *Elections in Independent Africa.* Boulder, CO, Westview Press, 1987.

Ihonvbere, J. O. *Nigeria: The Politics of Adjustment and Democracy.* New Brunswick, NJ, Transaction, 1993.

Ikoku, S. G. *Nigeria's Fourth Coup d'Etat.* Enugu, Fourth Dimension, 1985.

Ikpuk, J. S. *Militarism of Politics and Neo-colonialism: The Nigerian Experience 1966–1990.* London, Janus Publishing Co, 1995.

Iweriebor, E. E. G. *Radical Politics in Nigeria, 1945–1950: The Significance of the Zikist Movement.* Zaria, Ahmadu Bello University Press, 1996.

James, D. *Nigeria to 2000: After the Generals?* London, Economist Intelligence Unit, 1993.

Kastfelt, N. *Religion and Politics in Nigeria: A Study in Middle Belt Christianity.* London, British Academic Press, 1994.

Khan, S. A. *Nigeria: The Political Economy of Oil.* New York, Oxford University Press, 1994.

King, M. C. *Basic Currents of Nigerian Foreign Policy.* Baltimore, Harvard University Press, 1996.

Kirk-Greene, A. H. M., and Rimmer, D. *Nigeria Since 1970: A Political and Economic Outline.* London, Hodder and Stoughton, 1981.

Kukah, M. H. *Religion, Politics and Power in Northern Nigeria.* Ibadan, Spectrum Books, 1993.

Mbadiwe, K. O. *Rebirth of a Nation.* Oxford ABC, Enugu, Fourth Dimension Publishing, 1991.

Momah, S., and Momah, A. (Eds). *Political Economy of Nigeria under Military Rule, 1894–1993.* Harare, SAPES Books, 1995.

Muhammadu, T. *The Nigerian Constitution, 1979: Framework for Democracy.* Enugu, Fourth Dimension, 1982.

Nnoli, O. *Ethnicity and Development in Nigeria.* Aldershot, Avebury, 1995.

(Ed.). *Dead-End to Nigerian Development: An Analysis of the Political Economy of Nigeria 1979–1989.* Dakar, CODESRIA, 1993.

Nwabueze, B. O. *Military Rule and Constitutionalism in Nigeria.* Ibadan, Spectrum Books, 1992.

Nwabueze, B. O., and Akinola, A. (Eds). *Military Rule and Social Justice in Nigeria.* Ibadan, Spectrum Books, 1993.

Nwankwo, A. A. *The Nationalities Question in Nigeria: The Class Foundation of Conflicts.* Enugu, Fourth Dimension, 1990.

Nigeria: The Political Transition and the Future of Democracy. Enugu, Fourth Dimension, 1993.

Obasanjo, O. *My Command: An Account of the Nigerian Civil War 1967–1970.* London, Heinemann, 1981.

Obichere, B. (Ed.). *Studies in Southern Nigerian History.* London, Frank Cass, 1980.

Obiozor, G. A. *The Politics of Precarious Balancing: An Analysis of Contending Issues in Nigerian Domestic and Foreign Policy.* Nigerian Institute of International Affairs, 1994.

Odole, Chief M. A. F. *Ife: The Genesis of the Yoruba Race.* Ijeka, John West, 1986.

Ogbondah, C. W. *Military Regimes and the Press in Nigeria, 1968–1993; Human Rights and National Development.* Lanham, MD, University Press of America, 1993.

Ogwu, U. J., and Olaniyan, R. O. (Eds), *Nigeria's International Economic Relations: Dimensions of Dependence and Change.* Lagos, Nigerian Institute of International Affairs, 1990.

Ohiorthenuan, J. F. E. *Capital and the State in Nigeria.* Westport, CT, Greenwood Press, 1989.

Okadigbo, C. *Power and Leadership in Nigeria.* Enugu, Fourth Dimension, 1988.

Okigbo, P. N. C. *National Development Planning in Nigeria, 1900–1992.* Portsmouth, NH, Heinemann, 1989.

Olanrewaju, S. A., and Falola, T. (Eds). *Rural Development Problems in Nigeria.* Aldershot, Avebury, 1992.

Olashore, O. *Challenges of Nigeria's Economic Reforms.* Fountain Publications (Nigeria) Ltd, 1991.

Olowu, D. *Constitutionalism and Development in Nigeria: Lagos State Governance, Society and Economy.* Lagos, Malthouse Press, 1990.

Olowu, D., and Soremekun, K. *Governance and Democratisation in Nigeria.* Ibadan, Spectrum Books, 1995.

Olowu, D., Ayo, S. B., and Akande, B. *Local Institutions and National Development in Nigeria.* Ile-Ife, Obafemi Awolowo University Press, 1991.

Olukoshi, A. O. (Ed.). *The Politics of Structural Adjustment in Nigeria.* London, James Currey, 1993.

Olupona, J. (Ed.) *Religion and Peace in Multi-Faith Nigeria.* Ile-Ife, Obafemi Awolowo University Press, 1992.

Olurode, L. *A Political Economy of Nigeria's 1983 Elections.* Lagos, John West, 1991.

Olusanya, G. O., Ate, B. E., and Olukoshi, A. (Eds). *Economic Development and Foreign Policy in Nigeria.* Lagos, NIIA Press, 1990.

Onyemelukwe, J. O. C., and Filani, M. O. *Economic Geography of West Africa.* London, Lagos, New York, Longman, 1983.

Otobo, D. *The Trade Union Movement in Nigeria.* Lagos, Malthouse Press, 1995.

Oyediran, O. *Essays on Local Government and Administration in Nigeria.* Surulere, Projects Publications, 1988.

Oyeleye, O. (Ed.). *Nigerian Government and Politics under Military Rule.* Lagos, Friends Foundation Publishers, 1988.

Peel, J. D. Y. *Ijeshas and Nigerians: The Incorporation of a Yoruba Kingdom.* Cambridge University Press, 1983.

Post, K. W. J., and Vickers, M. *Structure and Conflict in Nigeria 1960–65.* London, Heinemann, 1973.

Rimmer, D. *The Economies of West Africa.* London, Weidenfeld and Nicolson, 1984.

Sklar, R. L. *Nigerian Political Parties: Power in an Emergent African Nation.* New York and Lagos, Nok Publishers, 1983 (reissue).

Smith, R. S. *Kingdoms of the Yoruba.* 3rd Edn. London, James Currey, 1988.

Stevens, C. A. *The Political Economy of Nigeria.* London, Economist Books, 1984.

Synge, R. *Nigeria, the Way Forward.* London, Euromoney Books, 1993.

Uchendu, P. K. *Politics and Education in Nigeria.* Enugu, Fourth Dimension Publishing, 1995.

Udoma, U. *History and the Law of the Constitution of Nigeria.* Lagos, Malthouse Press, 1994.

Vogt, M. A., and Ekoko, A. E. (Eds). *Nigeria in International Peace Keeping, 1960–1992.* Lagos, Malthouse Press, 1993.

Zwingini, J. S. *Capitalist Development in an African Economy: The Case of Nigeria.* Ibadan, UP PLC, 1992.

RÉUNION

Physical and Social Geography

Réunion is a volcanic island in the Indian Ocean lying at the southern extremity of the Mascarene Plateau. Mauritius lies some 190 km to the north-east and Madagascar about 650 km to the west. The island is roughly oval in shape, being about 65 km long and up to 50 km wide; the total area is 2,507 sq km (968 sq miles). Volcanoes have developed along a north-west to south-east angled fault; Piton de la Fournaise (2,624 m) most recently erupted in 1992. The others are now extinct, although their cones rise to 3,000 m and dominate the island. The heights and the frequent summer cyclones help to create abundant rainfall, which averages 4,714 mm annually in the uplands, and 686 mm at sea-level. Temperatures vary greatly according to altitude, being tropical at sea-level, averaging between 20°C (68°F) and 28°C (82°F), but much cooler in the uplands, with average temperatures between 8°C (46°F) and 19°C (66°F), owing to frequent winter frosts.

The population of Réunion has more than doubled since the 1940s, reaching 597,828 at the March 1990 census. During 1985–95 the population increased at an average rate of 1.6% per year. According to official estimates, the population was 664,200 at 1 January 1996, giving a population density of 265 inhabitants per sq km. During 1982–90 the proportion of Réunion's population under 20 years of age declined from 47% to 40%; in the same period the proportion aged between 20 and 59 years increased from 45% to 51%. The capital is Saint-Denis, with 121,999 inhabitants at the March 1990 census. Other major towns include Saint-Paul, with 71,669 inhabitants, and Saint-Pierre and Le Tampon, with 58,846 and 47,593 inhabitants, respectively, in 1990. The population is of mixed origin, including people of European, African, Indian and Chinese descent.

Recent History

Revised for this edition by the Editor

Réunion (formerly known as Bourbon) was first occupied in 1642 by French settlers expelled from Madagascar, and was governed as a colony until 1946, when it received full departmental status. In 1974 it became an overseas department with the status of a region. Réunion administers the small and uninhabited Indian Ocean islands of Bassas da India, Juan de Nova, Europa and the Iles Glorieuses, which are also claimed by Madagascar, and Tromelin, which is also claimed by both Madagascar and Mauritius. In 1997 Réunion became the administrative centre for the French Southern and Antarctic Territories. Since 1973 Réunion has been the headquarters of French military forces in the Indian Ocean.

In 1978 the liberation committee of the Organization of African Unity (OAU) adopted a report recommending measures to hasten the independence of the island, and condemned its occupation by a 'colonial power'. However, this view seemed to have little popular support in Réunion. Although the left-wing political parties on the island advocated increased autonomy (amounting to virtual self-government), few people were in favour of complete independence.

In 1982 the French government proposed a decentralization scheme, envisaging the dissolution of the general and regional councils in the overseas departments and the creation in each department of a single assembly, to be elected on the basis of proportional representation. However, this proposal received considerable opposition in Réunion and the other overseas departments, and the plan was eventually abandoned. Revised legislation on decentralization in the overseas departments was approved by the French national assembly in December.

In the elections to the French national assembly, which took place in March 1986 under a system of proportional representation, the number of deputies from Réunion was increased from three to five. The Parti Communiste Réunionnais (PCR) won two seats, while the Union pour la Démocratie Française (UDF), the Rassemblement pour la République (RPR) and a newly-formed right-wing party, France-Réunion-Avenir (FRA), each secured one seat. In the concurrent elections to the regional council, the centre-right RPR–UDF alliance and FRA together received 54.1% of the votes cast, winning 18 and eight of the 45 seats respectively, while the PCR won 13 seats.

In September 1986 the French government's plan to introduce a programme of economic reforms provoked criticism from the left-wing parties, which claimed that the proposals should grant the overseas departments social parity with metropolitan France through the introduction of similar levels of taxation and benefits. In October Paul Vergès, the PCR secretary-general and a deputy to the French national assembly, accused France of instituting 'social apartheid' in the overseas departments, and appealed to the European parliament in Strasbourg. In October 1987 Vergès and the other PCR deputy, Elie Hoarau, resigned from the national assembly, in protest against the government's proposals, and Laurent Vergès, Paul Vergès's son, and Claude Hoarau, the PCR mayor of Saint-Louis, assumed the vacated seats.

In the second round of the French presidential election, which took place on 8 May 1988, François Mitterrand, the incumbent president and a candidate of the Parti Socialiste (PS), received 60.3% of the votes cast in Réunion. At the ensuing general election for the French national assembly in June, the system of single-member constituencies was reintroduced. As in the previous general election, the PCR won two of the Réunion seats, while the UDF, the RPR (these two parties allying to form the Union du Rassemblement du Centre–URC) and the FRA each won one seat. In July the PCR criticized the socialist government for continuing to allocate lower levels of benefits and revenue to the overseas departments, despite Mitterrand's pledge, made during his visit to Réunion in February, to operate a uniform policy for the overseas departments and metropolitan France.

In the elections for the newly-enlarged 44-member general council in September and October 1988, the PCR and the PS won nine and four seats respectively, while other left-wing candidates won two seats. The UDF secured six seats and other right-wing candidates 19, but the RPR, which had previously held 11 seats, won only four. Later in October, Eric Boyer, a right-wing independent, was elected to succeed Legros as president of the general council. In the same month, the PCR deputy, Laurent Vergès, was killed in a road accident, and his seat was taken by Alexis Pota, also of the PCR.

The results of the municipal elections in March 1989 represented a slight decline in support for the left-wing parties. Nevertheless, for the first time since the 1940s, a PS candidate, Gilbert Annette, became mayor of Saint-Denis, replacing Legros. At Saint-Pierre the incumbent mayor and PCR deputy to the

French national assembly, Elie Hoarau, unilaterally declared himself the winner, discounting 1,500 votes which had been secured by two minor lists. The result was therefore declared invalid by the administrative tribunal. This incident led to a rift between the PS and the PCR, and, when a fresh election in that municipality was held in September, Elie Hoarau was unable to form an alliance. Hoarau was, however, re-elected mayor, securing just over 50% of the votes cast.

In September 1990, following the restructuring of the RPR under the new local leadership of Alain Defaud, a number of right-wing movements, including the UDF and the RPR, announced the creation of an informal alliance, known as Union pour la France (UPF), to contest the regional elections in 1992. During a visit to Réunion in November the French minister for overseas departments and territories announced a series of proposed economic and social measures, in accordance with pledges made by Mitterrand in 1988 regarding the promotion of economic development and social equality between the overseas departments and metropolitan France. However, these measures were criticized as insufficient by right-wing groups and by the PCR. Following representations by Réunion, a 'solidarity pact' of 60 proposed social and economic changes was agreed in April 1991 (see Economy).

In March 1990 violent protests took place in support of a popular, but unlicensed, island television service, Télé Free-DOM, following a decision by the French national broadcasting commission, the Conseil supérieur de l'audiovisuel (CSA), to award a broadcasting permit to a rival company. In February 1991 the seizure by the CSA of Télé Free-DOM's broadcasting transmitters prompted further violent demonstrations in Saint-Denis. Some 11 people were killed in ensuing riots, and the French government dispatched police reinforcements to restore order. The violence was officially ascribed to widespread discontent with the island's social and economic conditions, and a parliamentary commission was established to ascertain the background to the riots.

A visit to Réunion in March 1991 by the French prime minister, Michel Rocard, precipitated further rioting. In the same month the commission of enquiry attributed the riots in February to the inflammatory nature of television programmes, which had been broadcast by Télé Free-DOM in the weeks preceding the disturbances, and blamed the station's director, Dr Camille Sudre, who was also a deputy mayor of Saint-Denis. However, the commission refuted allegations by right-wing and centrist politicians that the PCR had orchestrated the violence. Later in March President Mitterrand expressed concern over the outcome of the enquiry, and appealed to the CSA to reconsider its policy towards Télé Free-DOM. In April, however, the CSA indicated its continued opposition to Télé Free-DOM. In October Sudre claimed that the continuing sequestration of the broadcasting transmitters would jeopardize Télé Free-DOM's opportunity to obtain a franchise, and announced that he would contest the decision.

In March 1992 the mayor of Saint-Denis, Gilbert Annette, expelled Sudre, who was one of the deputy mayors, from the majority coalition in the municipal council, after Sudre presented a list of independent candidates to contest regional elections later that month. In the elections to the regional council, which took place on 22 March, Sudre's list of candidates secured 17 seats, while the UPF obtained 14 seats, the PCR nine seats and the PS five seats. In concurrent elections to the general council (which was enlarged to 47 seats), right-wing candidates secured 29 seats, maintaining a substantial majority, although the number of PCR deputies increased to 12, and the number of PS deputies to six; Boyer retained the presidency of the council. Shortly after the elections, Sudre's independent candidates (known as Free-DOM) formed an alliance with the PCR, whereby members of the two groups held a majority of 26 of the 45 seats in the regional council. Under the terms of the agreement, Sudre was to assume the presidency of the regional council, and Paul Vergès the first vice-presidency. On 27 March, with the support of the PCR, Sudre was elected as president of the regional council by a majority of 27 votes. The UPF and the PS rejected Sudre's subsequent offer to join the Free-DOM–PCR coalition. The PS subsequently appealed against the results of the regional elections, on the grounds that, in contravention of regulations, Sudre's privately-owned radio station, Radio Free-DOM, had campaigned on his behalf prior to the elections.

Following his election as president of the regional council, Sudre announced that Télé Free-DOM was shortly to resume broadcasting. However, the CSA maintained that if transmissions were resumed Télé Free-DOM would be considered to be illegal, and would be subject to judicial proceedings. Jean-Paul Virapouillé, a deputy to the French national assembly, subsequently proposed the adoption of legislation which would legalize Télé Free-DOM and would provide for the establishment of an independent media sector outside the jurisdiction of the CSA. In April 1992 Télé Free-DOM transmitters were returned, and at the end of May broadcasting was resumed (without the permission of the CSA).

In June 1992 Sudre, Vergès and the former president of the regional council, Pierre Lagourgue, met President Mitterrand to submit proposals for economic reforms, which would establish greater parity between the island and metropolitan France. In early July, however, the French government announced increases in supplementary income, which were substantially less than had been expected, prompting widespread discontent on the island.

In September 1992 the French government agreed to an economic programme that had been formulated by the regional council. In the same month the PCR advocated a boycott of the French referendum on the ratification of the Treaty on European Union, which was to be conducted later that month, in protest at the alleged failure of the French government to recognize the needs of the overseas departments. At the referendum only 26.25% of the registered electorate voted, of whom 74.3% approved the ratification of the treaty. Later that month Boyer and Lagourgue were elected as representatives to the French senate. (The RPR candidate, Paul Moreau, retained his seat.) In October an investigation into allegations that leading politicians had misappropriated funds and obtained contracts by fraudulent means was initiated. In December increasing discontent with living standards and economic conditions on the island led to renewed rioting at Saint-Denis and at the town of Le Port.

In March 1993 Sudre announced that he was to contest Virapouillé's seat on behalf of the Free-DOM–PCR alliance in the forthcoming elections to the French national assembly. (However, a number of members of the PCR objected to the arrangement for a joint candidacy.) At the elections, which took place in late March, Sudre was defeated by Virapouillé in the second round of voting, while another incumbent right-wing deputy, André Thien Ah Koon, who contested the elections on behalf of the UPF, also retained his seat. The number of PCR deputies in the assembly was reduced from two to one (Vergès), while the PS and RPR each secured one of the remaining seats.

In May 1993 the results of the regional elections in March 1992 were annulled, and Sudre was prohibited from engaging in political activity for one year, on the grounds that programmes broadcast by Radio Free-DOM prior to the elections constituted political propaganda. Sudre subsequently selected his wife, Margie, to assume his candidacy in fresh elections to the regional council. In the elections, which took place on 20 June, the Free-DOM list of candidates, headed by Margie Sudre, secured 12 seats, while the UDF obtained 10, the RPR eight, the PCR nine and the PS six seats. Margie Sudre was subsequently elected as president of the regional council, with the support of the nine PCR deputies and three dissident members of the PS, by a majority of 24 votes.

In April 1993 several prominent businessmen were arrested in connection with the acquisition of contracts by fraudulent means, while a number of members of the principal political organizations, including Boyer and Pierre Vergès, the mayor of Le Port and a member of the PCR, were also implicated in malpractice. Both Boyer and Vergès subsequently fled, following investigations into their activities, and warrants were issued for their arrest. In August Boyer, who had surrendered to the security forces, was placed in detention, pending his trial on charges of corruption. (Joseph Sinimalé, a member of the RPR, temporarily assumed the office of president of the general council). In the same month the mayor of Saint-Paul and vice-president of the general council, Cassam Moussa, was also arrested and charged with corruption.

In January 1994 Jules Raux, a deputy mayor of Saint-Denis who was also the local treasurer of the PS, was arrested on charges of financial corruption , and in February two municipal councillors from Saint-Denis were arrested on suspicion of involvement in the affair. In the same month a French citizen (who was believed to have connections with members of the Djibouti government) was arrested on Réunion and charged with having transferred the funds that were alleged to have been illegally obtained to Djibouti. In March Annette, who was implicated in the affair, resigned as mayor of Saint-Denis, and was subsequently charged with corruption. Boyer was tried and sentenced to four years' imprisonment, while Moussa received a term of two years. In the same month Pierre Vergès (who remained in hiding) resigned as mayor of Le Port.

At elections to the general council, which took place in late March 1994, the PCR retained 12 seats, while the number of PS deputies increased to 12 (despite adverse publicity attached to associates of Annette within the PS). The number of seats held by the RPR and UDF declined to five and 11 respectively (compared with six and 14 in the incumbent council). The RPR and UDF subsequently attempted to negotiate an alliance with the PCR; despite long-standing inter-party dissension, however, the PCR and PS established a coalition within the general council, thereby securing a majority of 24 of the 47 seats. On 4 April a member of the PS, Christophe Payet was elected president of the general council by a majority of 26 votes, defeating Sinimalé; the right-wing parties (which had held the presidency of the council for more than 40 years) boycotted the poll. The PS and PCR signed an agreement, whereby they were to control the administration of the general council jointly, and indicated that centrist deputies might be allowed to enter the alliance. In July Boyer's prison sentence was reduced on appeal to a term of one year.

In November 1994 an official visit to Réunion by Edouard Balladur, the French prime minister (and declared candidate for the presidential election in 1995), provoked strike action in protest at his opposition to the establishment of social equality between the overseas departments and metropolitan France. Jacques Chirac, the official presidential candidate of the RPR, visited the island in December 1994, when he was endorsed by the organ of the PCR, *Témoignages*, after declaring his commitment to the issue of social equality. In the second round of the presidential election, which took place in early May 1995, the socialist candidate, Lionel Jospin, secured 56% of votes cast on Réunion, while Chirac won 44% of the votes (although Chirac obtained the highest number of votes in total); the PCR and Free-DOM had advised their supporters not to vote for Balladur, because of his opposition to the principle of social equality. Following Chirac's election to the French presidency, Margie Sudre was nominated minister of French language and culture, prompting concern among right-wing elements on Réunion. In municipal elections, which took place in June, the joint candidate of the PCR and the PS, Guy Etheve, was elected mayor of Saint-Louis, although the candidate of the RPR–UDF alliance, Marc-André Hoarau, submitted an official appeal against the results of the ballot; Elie Hoarau was re-elected mayor of Saint-Pierre. In August Pierre Vergès was sentenced *in absentia* to 18 months' imprisonment; an appeal was rejected in July 1996. In September 1995 the mayor of Salazie, who was a member of the RPR, was also charged with corruption. Following a period of enforced exile in Réunion following a coup attempt in September 1995, the Comoran president, Saïd Mohamed Djohar, returned to the Comoros in January 1996, agreeing to retain only symbolic presidential powers. In November 1995 Boyer lost an appeal against his 1994 conviction and was expelled from the French senate.

In February 1996 Alain Juppé, the French prime minister, invited more than 300 representatives from the overseas departments to Paris to participate in discussions on social equality and development; participants came from political parties, trade unions and other associations. The main issue uniting all the political representatives from Réunion was the need to align the salaries of civil servants on the island with those in metropolitan France. Several trade unionists declared themselves willing to enter into negotiations, on the condition that only new recruits would be affected. The French government remained undecided. President Chirac's visit to Réunion in March coincided with the 50th anniversary of France's establishment of overseas departments. The main issues that the president addressed during his visit were unemployment, the reinforcement of social policy, and equality with metropolitan France. Paul Vergès, joint candidate of the PCR and the PS, was elected to the French senate on 14 April 1996, securing 51.9% of the votes cast. Fred K/Bidy won 40.0% of the votes, failing to retain Eric Boyer's seat for the RPR. In the by-election to replace Paul Vergès, which took place in September, Claude Hoarau, the PCR candidate, was elected with 55.98% of the votes cast, while Margie Sudre obtained 44.01%. A new majority alliance between Free-DOM, the RPR and the UDF was subsequently formed in the regional council, with the re-election of its 19-member permanent commission in October. In November Jean-Paul Virapoullé was re-elected mayor of Saint-André, following the annulment of the results of the election of June 1995 (which he had also won), although Claude Hoarau, the PCR candidate, questioned the legitimacy of electoral proceedings. Wilfried Bertile, the candidate for the PS, secured the highest number of votes in both the municipal and district elections of Saint-Philippe.

In October 1996 the trial of a number of politicians and business executives, who had been arrested in 1993–94 on charges of corruption, took place, after three years of investigations. Gilbert Annette and Jules Raux were convicted and, in December, received custodial sentences. Jacques de Châteauvieux, the chairman of Groupe Sucreries de Bourbon (principally concerned with the production and exportation of sugar), was found guilty of bribing members of the commission responsible for issuing permits for the construction of supermarkets on the island, and also received a custodial term. Senior executives from the French enterprise, Compagnie Générale des Eaux and its subsidiaries, were given suspended sentences. Pierre Vergès surrendered to the authorities in December and appeared before a magistrate in Saint-Pierre, where he was subsequently detained; in February 1997 he was released by the court of appeal. Also in December 1996 voting on the regional budget for 1997 was postponed three times, as a result of the abstention of eight Free-DOM councillors, led by the first vice-president of the regional council, Jasmin Moutoussamy, who demanded the dismissal of Gilbert Payet, a sub-prefect and special adviser to Sudre, and greater delegation of power to the vice-presidents. They also objected to Sudre's alliance with the RPR-UDF majority. In late March 1997 the regional budget was eventually adopted, although Sudre and many right-wing councillors abstained from voting because of the opposition's insistence on a number of amendments, most significantly to the composition of the council's permanent commission, in which it had no representation. Following the vote, Sudre suspended the session to allow for discussion between the political organizations. Also in March Joseph Sinimalé of the RPR was re-elected mayor of Saint-Paul, defeating Paul Vergès.

Meanwhile, civil servants and students protested violently against a French government proposal, made earlier in March 1997, to undertake reform of the civil service, including a reduction in the incomes of new recruits to bring them closer to those in metropolitan France. Senator Pierre Lagourgue was designated to mediate between the French government and the civil servants' trade unions, but strike action and demonstrations continued into April, leading to violent clashes with the security forces.

Four left-wing candidates were successful in elections to the French national assembly held in late May and early June 1997. Claude Hoarau (PCR) retained his seat and was joined by Huguette Bello and Elie Hoarau, also both from the PCR, and Michel Tamaya (PS), while André Thien Ah Koon, representing the RPR–UDF coalition, was re-elected.

In January 1986 France was admitted to the Indian Ocean Commission (IOC), owing to its sovereignty over Réunion. Réunion was given the right to host ministerial meetings of the IOC, but is not eligible to occupy the presidency, owing to its status as a non-sovereign state.

Economy

Revised for this edition by the Editor

As a result of its connection with France, Réunion's economy is relatively developed, especially in comparison with its sub-Saharan African neighbours. Réunion's gross national product (GNP) per head in 1991 was estimated at 40,000 French francs. During 1989–90, it was estimated, GNP increased at an average annual rate of 4%. In 1985–95, according to World Bank estimates, Réunion's population increased at an average rate of 1.6% per year. The population density remained very high, averaging 264.9 inhabitants per sq km at 1 January 1996. In 1994 Réunion's gross domestic product (GDP) per caput was estimated at 54,431 French francs. In 1988–94 GDP increased, in real terms, at an average rate of 3.4% per year.

The economy has traditionally been based on agriculture, which engaged an estimated 4.8% of the employed labour force in 1995, and contributed 3.7% of GDP in 1989, although by 1990 about 73% of the employed population worked in the service sector. Agricultural production increased by 0.9% during 1988–94, declining by 10.1% in 1993, but increasing by 3.4% in 1994. Sugar cane is the principal crop and has formed the basis of the economy for over a century. In 1995 sugar accounted for 63% of export earnings. Only 24% of the land area can be cultivated because of the volcanic nature of the soil, but some 50% of the arable land is used for sugar plantations. The cane is grown on nearly all the good cultivable land up to 800 m above sea-level on the leeward side of the island, except in the relatively dry north-west, and up to 500 m on the windward side. Although the volcanic soil is fertile, the quality and yield are not as high as in Mauritius, and the modernization of agricultural practices is hindered in part by archaic restrictions on land tenure. Sugar cane harvests entered a decline in the early 1970s, owing to drought, ageing plants, rising production costs and inefficient harvesting techniques and transport systems. In 1974 a modernization plan was put into effect, and by 1976 production had begun to reflect both higher yields and an increase in the land used for sugar cultivation. By 1981, when the plan ended, average annual production of raw sugar had risen to 247,000 tons, despite several tropical storms. Annual production fluctuated in the range 224,000–258,000 tons annually until 1987, when output fell to less than 226,000 tons, owing to severe damage to the cane crop, resulting from a cyclone in February 1987. In 1986 state aid of 45 French francs per ton of sugar was given directly to farmers for the first time, and in 1987 this subsidy was increased to 48 French francs per ton. In 1989 sugar production declined to 170,965 tons, compared with 252,230 tons in 1988 (as a result of damage caused by a further cyclone), but increased to 192,000 tons in 1990, to 214,500 tons in 1991, and to 226,700 tons in 1992. In subsequent years, however, the sugar industry was adversely affected by increasing urbanization, which resulted in a decline in the area of agricultural land. In 1995 sugar production was 205,000 tons. The French-owned sugar producer, Quartier, announced the closure of one of its refineries in that year, owing to unprofitability; only two refineries (Gol, owned by Quartier, and Bois Rouge, owned by the local producer, Groupe Sucreries de Bourbon) remained on Réunion. In mid-1996 the sugar harvest was delayed, as planters refused to sign an agreement regarding payment terms for sugar cane for the period 1996–2001.

Geraniums, vetiver and ylang-ylang are grown for the production of aromatic essences. Exporters of oil of geranium and vetiver have experienced difficulty in competing with new producers whose prices are much lower. In 1985 measures were introduced to increase the output of oil of geranium; output had increased to 25.4 tons by 1991, but declined to 14.7 tons in 1992. Output of vetiver totalled 12.1 tons in 1987, but subsequently declined to 1.9 tons in 1992, and is expected to become insignificant as an export crop. Vanilla is produced for export in the south-east; production totalled 132.8 tons in 1987, but declined to 54.4 tons in 1988, and to 31.2 tons in 1990; however, output increased to 70.4 tons in 1991, and to 116.5 tons in 1992. An agreement between Réunion, Madagascar and the Comoros concerning price and export quotas on vanilla ended in 1992; in early 1995, however, negotiations regarding a new agreement between Réunion and the Comoros commenced. Tobacco cultivation (introduced at the beginning of the century) produced a crop of 192.8 tons in 1988. Unfavourable climatic conditions intervened in the 1989/90 crop year, however, and the sector was further adversely affected by cyclone damage, which destroyed 115 of the island's 400 tobacco drying sheds; production declined sharply, to 107.8 tons in 1990, to 73.3 tons in 1991, and to 22 tons in 1992. A variety of vegetables and fruits is grown, and the island is self-sufficient in cattle and pigs. Overall, however, substantial food imports are necessary to supply the dense population.

Although fish are not abundant off Réunion's coast, the commercial fishing industry is an important source of income and employment, especially in the deep-sea sector. The largest fishing vessels make voyages lasting several months, to catch spiny lobsters (langoustes) that breed in the cold waters near Antarctica. Other commercial fishing activities have increased in recent years, although total landings declined from 2,787 tons in 1982 to 1,554 tons in 1987. A recovery, to 1,931 tons (including 348 tons of crustaceans), was achieved in 1988. In an attempt to preserve resources of langoustes, the fishing quota for 1989 was reduced, and the total catch declined to 1,725 tons, increasing slightly to 1,731 tons in 1990. The total catch increased substantially thereafter reaching 2,772 tons in 1993, 4,487 tons in 1994, and 4,821 tons in 1995.

Industry (including mining, manufacturing, construction and power) contributed 19.0% of GDP in 1989, and employed an estimated 13.7% of the working population in 1993. The principal branch of manufacturing is food-processing, particularly the production of sugar and rum. Other significant sectors include the fabrication of construction materials, mechanics, printing, metalwork, textiles and garments, and electronics. In January 1989 there were a total of 958 industrial enterprises in Réunion, 89.6% of which employed fewer than 20 salaried staff; by January 1996 the number of industrial enterprises had increased to 2,328. In early 1997 operations commenced at a steel pipe mill (Ecopipe) at Le Port. The plant, largely financed by private South African investment, was expected to employ up to 80 people, and to reach capacity production of 15,000 metric tons per year by 1998. It was hoped that this would encourage further growth in the industrial sector.

No mineral resources have been identified on Réunion. Imports of petroleum products accounted for 4.7% of the value of total imports in 1995. Energy is derived principally from thermal and hydroelectric power, which constituted 53.7% and 46.3%, respectively, of total electricity production (1,298.4m. kWh) in that year. Bagasse (a by-product of sugar cane) is used to fuel thermal power installations.

In 1995 the principal source of imports was France (66.3%), which was also the principal market for exports (71.4%). Other major trading partners included Bahrain, Japan, Italy, Germany and the Comoros. In 1994 the main imports were foodstuffs (especially cereals, meat and dairy produce), motor vehicles, chemicals, petroleum products and metal products. Principal exports included sugar, fish and shellfish, machinery and transport equipment, and rum. There is a substantial trade deficit, which is partly financed by aid from France and receipts from expatriates; exports in the 1980s covered, on average, only about 10% of the cost of imports. In 1993 Réunion recorded a trade deficit of 10,772.8m. French francs, which increased to 12,116.5m. French francs in 1994, and to 12,458.1m. French francs in 1995. The contribution of exports to GDP declined from 12% at the beginning of the 1970s to 2% in 1992, owing partly to a decline in world sugar prices, and stood at an estimated 2.9% in 1994. In 1995 the volume of goods passing through the ports and the airport increased, principally as a result of a rise in imports. At the ports the tonnage of goods handled increased by 5% on average between 1990 and 1995. Imports of kerosene and other fuels were boosted by the growing number of motor vehicles and a greater number of direct flights from Réunion.

The development of tourism is actively promoted, and it is hoped that increased investment in this sector will lead to higher receipts and will help to reduce the trade deficit, as well as providing new jobs. In 1988 Réunion received aid from the European Community (EC, now the European Union–EU) to stimulate the sector. Tourist arrivals subsequently increased considerably, rising by an annual average of 8.7% in 1990–95. In 1995 304,000 tourists visited Réunion (an increase of 15.8% compared with 1994), and revenue from tourism increased to 1,116m. French francs. Of the total number of visitors in that year, 82% were from France, 9% from Mauritius, and 3% from Madagascar. The tourism sector contributed only 3%-4% of GDP in 1993.

The close connection with France protects the island from the dangers inherent in the narrowness of its economic base. Nevertheless, unemployment and inflation, compounded after 1974 by a number of bankruptcies among small sugar planters, have been the cause of major social and economic problems. The rise in the cost of imported fertilizers and of labour has exceeded the rise in the price of sugar. The annual rate of inflation averaged 6.8% in 1980–88 and 2.6% in 1990–95. Consumer prices increased by 3.8% in 1993, but the inflation rate declined to 1.9% in 1994 and to 1.7% in 1995. The rate was 1.9% in 1996. The 1982 census recorded 54,338 people, or 31.4% of the labour force, as unemployed. In 1995 an estimated 34.3% of the labour force were unemployed, compared with 31.7% at December 1994. By 1996 it was estimated that more than 37% of the labour force were unemployed. Since 1980 the government has invested significant sums in a series of public works projects in an effort to create jobs and to alleviate the high level of seasonal unemployment following the sugar cane harvest. However, large numbers of workers emigrate in search of employment each year, principally to France. In 1986 Réunion benefited from French legislation reducing employers' payments to young persons' social security contributions, which encouraged youth employment. In 1995 the budgetary deficit was estimated at 9,244.5m. French francs.

The French government has increased its infrastructural spending in Réunion, particularly on improvements to health services, housing, electricity supply and communication facilities for low-income families. In 1979 an estimated 75% of the population received welfare payments from France, and direct subsidies averaged 25% higher per recipient in Réunion than in metropolitan France. In October 1986 the French government introduced a programme of reforms to enhance the island's economic status by 1991. The programme included the abolition of tax liability on investments in all sectors for an initial period of 10 years. Under the Integrated Development Operation (OID) for the French overseas departments, initiated in 1979, Réunion was allocated 400m. French francs, over a five-year period to 1991, from various sources, including the French government and the EC, and from revenue generated by the implementation of the 1986 economic reform programme. During 1989–93 the EC also provided aid to assist Réunion to adapt to the requirements of the single European Market.

In December 1988 the French government announced that it would instigate a regional development programme in the overseas departments in 1989, to be financed partly by EC aid. In January 1989 legislation which established a guaranteed minimum income was introduced. In January 1990 a French government commission, appointed in 1989 to examine the economic condition of the overseas departments, published a report containing 58 proposals for the rectification of social and economic shortcomings, and recommended an improvements programme to be phased over two three-year stages. In November 1990 the French government announced measures aimed at establishing parity of the four overseas departments with metropolitan France in social and economic programmes. The reforms included the standardization by 1993 of family allowances, while from January 1992 minimum wage levels in Réunion were to be equalized with those operating in the other three overseas departments. It was envisaged that minimum wages in the overseas departments would be equal with those in metropolitan France by 1995, although this was to be achieved by way of trade union negotiations with employers rather than by government wage guarantees. In August 1996 a committee, established to compare incomes and prices in Réunion with those in metropolitan France, reported that the gross disposable income per inhabitant in Réunion was only 57% of the average income per inhabitant in metropolitan France. The average net salary for state employees was, however, found to be 51% higher on the island, as a result of various benefits, some dating back to colonial times. The disparity between prices for many consumer goods was emphasized, with minimum prices in Réunion being as much as three times the French level. The island's political organizations were united in their insistence that civil servants' salaries and benefits should be reduced, thereby releasing funds that could be used to create more employment. Reactions from trade unions were mixed, and the French government, although willing to hold discussions, delayed making any decision on this politically sensitive issue. In March 1997, however, civil servants and their trade unions were angered by the French government's proposal to reduce the incomes of new recruits to the civil service (see Recent History), despite a promise to create 2,500 jobs in education over a period of five years.

A 'solidarity pact', which was formalized in April 1991, comprised 60 proposals, including the establishment of a fund for local youth initiatives and of a professional training body to stimulate the recruitment of teachers from within the island. In the same month, representatives of the four overseas departments in the French national assembly and senate formed an interparliamentary group to safeguard and promote the agricultural economies of these territories. In July 1992, however, the French government announced an increase in minimum income of 3.3%, and in family allowance of 20%, (far less than required to establish parity with metropolitan France). In September the regional council adopted an economic development programme, known as the emergency plan, which provided for the creation of an export free zone (EFZ). Under the emergency plan, the French government would subsidize wages and some employer's contributions of companies operating within the EFZ. By 1993 levels of family allowance in the overseas departments had reached parity with those in force in metropolitan France, as envisaged. In early 1994, however, the French government indicated that it intended to give priority to the reduction of unemployment rather than the standardization of minimum wage levels, and announced a programme of economic and social development for the overseas departments, whereby approximately one-third of the unemployed population were to be involved in community projects, enterprises were to receive incentives to engage the unemployed, and a number of economic sectors that had been disadvantaged by international competition were to be exempted from certain taxes. In June the regional council drafted a five-year development plan, at a projected cost of 10,000m. French francs, of which 4,900m. French francs were to be financed by the EU: these funds were principally designated to support export initiatives and to improve infrastructure and the environment; allocations were also made to the tourism sector. Part of the Chaudron district of Saint-Denis was designated as a 'special urban zone' in May 1996, with fiscal incentives on offer to companies establishing themselves in the area. In early 1995 the minimum wage level in Réunion was about 14% below that in metropolitan France. However, by 1 January 1996 the minimum wage on Réunion was equal to that in metropolitan France, having increased on average by 23% since the end of 1993. Satisfactory economic progress was reported in 1995 (although the rate of unemployment remained the highest of the overseas departments).

Statistical Survey

Source (unless otherwise indicated): Institut National de la Statistique et des Etudes Economiques, Service Régional de la Réunion, 15 rue de l'Ecole, 97490 Sainte-Clotilde; tel. 29-51-57; fax 29-76-85.

AREA AND POPULATION

Area: 2,507 sq km (968 sq miles).

Population: 515,798 (males 252,997, females 262,801) at census of 9 March 1982; 597,828 (males 294,256, females 303,572) at census of 15 March 1990; 664,200 (official estimate) at 1 January 1996.

Density (1 January 1996): 264.9 per sq km.

Principal Towns (population at census of 15 March 1990): Saint-Denis (capital) 121,999; Saint-Paul 71,669; Saint-Pierre 58,846; Le Tampon 47,593.

Births and Deaths (1995, provisional figures): Registered live births 13,077 (birth rate 19.8 per 1,000); Registered deaths 3,499 (death rate 5.3 per 1,000).

Economically Active Population (persons aged 15 years and over, 1990 census): Agriculture. hunting, forestry and fishing 11,141; Mining, manufacturing, electricity, gas and water 11,295; Construction 16,563; Wholesale and retail trade 17,902; Transport, storage and communications 7,250; Financing, insurance, real estate and business services 3,005; Other services (incl. activities not adequately defined) 79,097; Total employed 146,253 (males 90,526, females 55,727); Unemployed 86,108 (males 45,889, females 40,219); Total labour force 232,361 (males 136,415, females 95,946). Figures exclude persons on compulsory military service. Source: International Labour Office, *Yearbook of Labour Statistics*.

Mid-1995 (estimates in '000): Agriculture, etc. 13; Total labour force 261. Source: FAO, *Production Yearbook*.

AGRICULTURE, ETC.

Principal Crops (FAO estimates, '000 metric tons, 1995): Sugar cane 1,817; Raw sugar 205 (unofficial figure); Maize 17; Vegetables 58; Fruit 35. Source: FAO, *Production Yearbook*.

Livestock (agricultural census, year ending August 1989): Cattle 18,601; Pigs 70,921; Goats 31,318; Chickens 1,348,000. *1995* (FAO estimates, '000 head, year ending September): Cattle 26; Pigs 83; Goats 32; Chickens 8,000. Source: FAO, *Production Yearbook*.

Forestry (FAO estimates, '000 cubic metres): Roundwood removals: 36 in 1992; 36 in 1993; 36 in 1994. Source: FAO, *Yearbook of Forest Products*.

Fishing (metric tons, live weight): Total catch 2,772 in 1993; 4,487 in 1994; 4,821 in 1995.

INDUSTRY

Production (metric tons, 1992): Oil of geranium 14.7; Oil of vetiver root 1.9; Tobacco 22.0; Vanilla 116.5; Ginger 95.0; Pimento 405.6; Rum (hectolitres) 52,534.

FINANCE

Currency and Exchange Rates: 100 centimes = 1 French franc. *Sterling and Dollar Equivalents* (31 March 1997): £1 sterling = 9.2420 francs; US $1 = 5.6285 francs; 1,000 French francs = £108.20 = $177.67. *Average Exchange Rate* (French francs per US dollar): 5.5520 in 1994; 4.9915 in 1995; 5.1155 in 1996.

Budget (million francs, 1995): *State Budget:* Revenue 6,009.0, Expenditure 13,426.5; *Regional Budget:* Revenue 2,165, Expenditure 2,162; *Departmental Budget:* Revenue 4,520, Expenditure 3,992.

Money Supply (million francs at 31 December 1994): Currency outside banks 4,977; Demand deposits at banks 6,649; Total money 11,626.

Cost of Living (Consumer Price Index for urban areas, average of monthly figures; base: 1990 = 100): 113.5 in 1994; 115.5 in 1995; 117.7 in 1996. Source: UN, *Monthly Bulletin of Statistics*.

Expenditure on the Gross Domestic Product (provisional figures, million francs at current prices, 1994): Government final consumption expenditure 10,188; Private final consumption expenditure 27,514; Increase in stocks 38; Gross fixed capital formation 9,925; *Total domestic expenditure* 47,665; Exports of goods and services 1,015; *Less* Imports of goods and services 13,414; *GDP in purchasers' values* 35,266.

Gross Domestic Product by Economic Activity (million francs at current prices, 1989): Agriculture, hunting, forestry and fishing 918; Mining and manufacturing 2,089; Electricity, gas and water 1,156; Construction 1,479; Trade, restaurants and hotels 4,921; Transport, storage and communications 1,233; Government services, 6,906; Other services 6,174; *Sub-total* 24,836; Import duties 1,036; Value-added tax 933; *Less* Imputed bank service charge 1,192; *Total* 25,613. Source: UN, *National Accounts Statistics*.

EXTERNAL TRADE

Principal Commodities (distribution by SITC, US $ million, 1994): *Imports c.i.f.:* Food and live animals 381.2 (Meat and meat preparations 79.5, Dairy products and birds' eggs 53.2, Cereals and cereal preparations 89.2, Vegetables and fruit 51.8); Beverages and tobacco 61.4; Mineral fuels, lubricants, etc. 116.8 (Petroleum, petroleum products, etc. 100.4); Chemicals and related products 240.3 (Medicinal and pharmaceutical products 116.4, Essential oils, perfume materials and cleansing preparations 49.3); Basic manufactures 347.6 (Paper, paperboard and manufactures 60.6, Non-metallic mineral manufactures 67.7, Iron and steel 49.1); Machinery and transport equipment 742.3 (Power-generating machinery and equipment 47.8, Machinery specialized for particular industries 48.5, General industrial machinery, equipment and parts 85.5, Office machines and automatic data-processing equipment 48.2, Telecommunications and sound equipment 58.8, Other electrical machinery, apparatus, etc. 103.1, Road vehicles and parts 292.4, Other transport equipment and parts 53.2); Miscellaneous manufactured articles 368.9 (Furniture and parts 59.5, Clothing and accessories, excl. footwear 92.5); Total (incl. others) 2,358.4. *Exports f.o.b.:* Food and live animals 124.7 (Fish, crustaceans and molluscs 13.4, Vegetables and fruit 4.3, Raw sugar 102.6); Beverages and tobacco 6.7 (Alcoholic beverages 6.3); Basic manufactures 6.0; Machinery and transport equipment 21.4 (Road vehicles and parts 8.1); Miscellaneous manufactured articles 8.1; Total (incl. others) 171.0. Source: UN, *International Trade Statistics Yearbook*. **1995** (million francs): *Imports* 13,494.2; *Exports* 1,036.2 (Sugar 653.0).

Principal Trading Partners (US $ million, 1994): *Imports c.i.f.:* Bahrain 82.9; Belgium-Luxembourg 51.1; France (incl. Monaco) 1,575.5; Germany 64.6; Italy 75.1; Japan 42.5; Madagascar 24.0; Mauritius 26.1; Netherlands 24.6; Southern African Customs Union 57.0; Thailand 24.0; United Kingdom 31.6; USA 45.0; Total (incl. others) 2,358.3. *Exports f.o.b.:* Comoros 7.6; France (incl. Monaco) 127.1; Germany 2.0; Japan 10.6; Madagascar 5.7; Mauritius 3.4; Netherlands 2.7; United Kingdom 3.2; Total (incl. others) 171.0. Source: UN, *International Trade Statistics Yearbook*.

TRANSPORT

Road Traffic (1 Jan. 1996): Motor vehicles in use 196,800.

Shipping: *Merchant Fleet* (total displacement at 31 December 1992): 21,000 grt (Source: UN, *Statistical Yearbook*); *Traffic* (1995): Vessels entered 585; Freight unloaded 2,290,700 metric tons; Freight loaded 424,700 metric tons; Passenger arrivals 6,302; Passenger departures 6,960.

Civil Aviation (1995): Passenger arrivals 566,668; Passenger departures 562,605; Freight unloaded 13,531 metric tons; Freight loaded 4,598 metric tons.

TOURISM

Tourist Arrivals (by country of residence, 1995): France 249,100, Mauritius 27,700, Madagascar 10,300, EU countries (excl. France) 5,600; Total (incl. others) 304,000.

Tourist Receipts (million francs): 855 in 1993; 907 in 1994; 1,116 in 1995.

COMMUNICATIONS MEDIA

Radio Receivers (1994): 158,000 in use. Source: UNESCO, *Statistical Yearbook*.

Television Receivers (1 Jan. 1993): 116,181 in use.

Telephones (main lines at 31 Dec. 1995): 218,723.

Book Production (1992): 69 titles (50 books; 19 pamphlets). Source: UNESCO, *Statistical Yearbook*.

Daily Newspapers (1994): 3 (estimated average circulation 55,000 copies). Source: UNESCO, *Statistical Yearbook*.

Non-daily Newspapers (1988, estimates): 4 (average circulation 20,000 copies). Source: UNESCO, *Statistical Yearbook*.

EDUCATION

Pre-primary (1994/95): Schools 175; teachers 1,336 (1986); pupils 44,312.

Primary (1994/95): Schools 343; teachers 3,917 (1986); pupils 73,250.

Secondary (1994/95): Schools 102; teachers 6,402; pupils 93,968 (1995/96).

University: (1993/94): Teaching staff 206; students 6,671. There is also a teacher training college, a technical institute and an agricultural college.

Directory

The Government

(August 1997)

Prefect: ROBERT POMMIÈS.

President of the General Council: CHRISTOPHE PAYET.

President of the Economic and Social Committee: TONY MANGLOU.

Deputies to the French National Assembly: HUGUETTE BELLO (PCR), CLAUDE HOARAU (PCR), ELIE HOARAU (PCR), MICHEL TAMAYA (PS), ANDRÉ THIEN AH KOON (UPF).

Representatives to the French Senate: EDMOND LAURET (RPR), PIERRE LAGOURGUE, PAUL VERGÈS (PCR).

REGIONAL COUNCIL

Hôtel de la Région, ave René Cassin, Moufia BP 7190, 97719 Saint-Denis; tel. 48-70-00; fax 48-70-71.

President: MARGIE SUDRE (Independent).

Election, 25 June 1993

Party	Seats
Free-DOM*	12
UDF	10
RPR	8
PCR	9
PS	6
Total	45

* List of independent candidates affiliated to Margie Sudre.

Political Organizations

Front National (FN): Saint-Denis; f. 1972; extreme right-wing; Leader ALIX MOREL.

Mouvement des Radicaux de Gauche (MRG): Saint-Denis; f. 1977; advocates full independence and an economy separate from, but assisted by, France; Pres. JEAN-MARIE FINCK.

Mouvement pour l'Egalité, la Démocratie, le Développement et la Nature: affiliated to the PCR; advocates political unity; Leader RENÉ PAYET.

Mouvement pour l'Indépendance de la Réunion (MIR): f. 1981 to succeed the fmr Mouvement pour la Libération de la Réunion; grouping of parties favouring autonomy.

Parti Communiste Réunionnais (PCR): 21 bis rue d l'Est, 97400 Saint-Denis; f. 1959; Pres. PAUL VERGÈS; Sec.-Gen. ELIE HOARAU.

Parti Socialiste (PS)–Fédération de la Réunion: Saint-Denis; tel. 21-77-95; telex 916445; left-wing; Sec.-Gen. JEAN-CLAUDE FRUTEAU.

Rassemblement des Démocrates pour l'Avenir de la Réunion (RADAR): Saint-Denis; f. 1981; centrist.

Rassemblement des Socialistes et des Démocrates (RSD): Saint-Denis; Sec.-Gen. DANIEL CADET.

***Rassemblement pour la République (RPR):** 6 bis blvd Vauban, BP 11, 97400 Saint-Denis; tel. 20-21-18; telex 916080; Gaullist; Pres. ANDRÉ MAURICE PIHOUÉE; Sec.-Gen. TONY MANGLOU.

***Union pour la Démocratie Française (UDF):** Saint-Denis; f. 1978; centrist; Sec.-Gen. GILBERT GÉRARD.

* The RPR and the UDF jointly contested the 1992 regional elections as the Union pour la France (UPF).

Judicial System

Cour d'Appel: Palais de Justice, 166 rue Juliette Dodu, 97488 Saint-Denis; tel. 40-58-58; telex 916149; fax 21-95-32; Pres. JEAN CLAUDE CARRIÉ.

There are two **Tribunaux de Grande Instance**, one **Cour d'Assises,** four **Tribunaux d'Instance**, two **Tribunaux pour Enfants** and two **Conseils de Prud'hommes**.

Religion

A substantial majority of the population are adherents of the Roman Catholic Church. There is a small Muslim community.

CHRISTIANITY

The Roman Catholic Church

Réunion comprises a single diocese, directly responsible to the Holy See. At 31 December 1995 there were an estimated 574,000 adherents, equivalent to almost 90% of the population.

Bishop of Saint-Denis-de-La Réunion: Mgr GILBERT AUBRY, Evêché, 36 rue de Paris, BP 55, 97462 Saint-Denis; tel. 21-28-49; fax 41-77-15.

The Press

DAILIES

Journal de l'Ile de la Réunion: 42 rue Alexis de Villeneuve, BP 98, 97463 Saint-Denis Cédex; tel. 21-32-64; telex 916453; fax 41-09-77; f. 1956; Dir PHILIPPE BALOUKJY; circ. 26,000.

Quotidien de la Réunion: BP 303, 97712 Saint-Denis Messag Cédex 9; tel. 92-15-15; fax 28-43-60; f. 1976; Dir MAXIMIN CKANE KI CKUNE; circ. 30,000.

PERIODICALS

Al-Islam: Centre Islamique de la Réunion, BP 437, 97459 Saint-Pierre; tel. 25-45-43; fax 35-58-23; f. 1975; 4 a year; Dir SAÏD INGAR.

Cahiers de la Réunion et de l'Océan Indien: 24 blvd des Cocotiers, 97434 Saint-Gilles-les-Bains; monthly; Man. Dir CLAUDETTE SAINT-MARC.

L'Economie de la Réunion: c/o INSEE, 15 rue de l'Ecole, BP 13 Le Chaudron, 97408 Saint-Denis; tel. 48-89-00; fax 48-89-89; 6 a year; Dir RENÉ JEAN; Editor-in-Chief COLETTE PAVAGEAU.

L'Eglise à la Réunion: 18 rue Montreuil, 97469 Saint-Denis; tel. 41-56-90; Dir P. FRANÇOIS GLÉNAC.

L'Enjeu: Saint-Denis; tel. 21-75-76; fax 41-60-62; Dir BLANDINE ETRAYEN; Editor-in-Chief JEAN-CLAUDE VALLÉE; circ. 4,000.

Le Journal de la Nature: 97489 Saint-Denis; tel. 29-45-45; fax 29-00-90; Dir J. Y. CONAN.

Le Memento Industriel et Commercial Réunionnais: 80 rue Pasteur, 97400 Saint-Denis; tel. 21-94-12; fax 41-10-85; Dir CATHERINE LOUAPRE POTTIER; circ. 10,000.

974 Ouest: Montgaillard, 97400 Saint-Denis; monthly; Dir DENISE ELMA.

La Réunion Agricole: Chambre d'Agriculture, 24 rue de la Source, BP 134, 97463 Saint-Denis Cédex; tel. 21-25-88; fax 41-17-84; f. 1967; monthly; Dir JEAN-YVES MINATCHY; Chief Editor HERVÉ CAILLEAUX; circ. 8,000.

Télé 7 Jours Réunion: 6 rue Montyon, BP 405, 93200 Saint-Denis; weekly; Dir MICHEL MEKDOUD; circ. 25,000.

Témoignage Chrétien de la Réunion: 21 bis rue de l'Est, 97465 Saint-Denis; weekly; Dir RENÉ PAYET; circ. 2,000.

Témoignages: 21 bis rue de l'Est, BP 192, 97465 Saint-Denis; tel. 21-13-07; f. 1944; publ. of the PCR; weekly; Dir ELIE HOARAU; circ. 6,000.

Visu: 97712 Saint-Denis Cédex 9; tel. 90-20-60; fax 90-20-61; weekly; Editor-in-Chief J. J. AYAN; circ. 53,000.

Radio and Television

There were an estimated 158,000 radio receivers in use in 1994 and 116,181 television receivers in use at 1 January 1993.

Antenne Réunion: 33 rue des Vavangues, 97490 Sainte-Clotilde; tel. 48-28-28; fax 48-28-29; f. 1991; broadcasts 12 hours daily; Dir THIERRY NICHAUT.

Canal Réunion: 2D ave de Lattre de Tassigny, 97490 Sainte-Clotilde; tel. 21-16-17; fax 21-46-61; subscription television channel; broadcasts a minimum of 12 hours daily; Chair. DOMINIQUE FAGOT; Dir JEAN-BERNARD MOURIER.

Radio Free-DOM: BP 666, 97473 Saint-Denis Cédex; tel. 41-51-51; telex 916174; fax 21-68-64; privately-owned radio station; Dir Dr CAMILLE SUDRE.

Société Nationale de Radio-Télévision Française d'Outre-Mer (RFO): 1 rue Jean Chatel, 97716 Saint-Denis Cédex; tel. 40-67-67; fax 21-64-84; home radio and television relay services in French; operates two television channels; Chair. JEAN-MARIE CAVADA; Dir ALBERT-MAX BRIAND.

Télé Free-DOM: BP 666, 97474 Saint-Denis Cédex; tel. 41-51-51; telex 916174; fax 21-68-64; f. 1986; privately-owned TV service, not licensed by the French nat. broadcasting comm.; transmitters confiscated in Feb. 1991; resumed broadcasting in May 1992; Dir Dr CAMILLE SUDRE.

TV-4: 8 chemin Fontbrune, 97400 Saint-Denis; tel. 52-73-73.

TV Sud: 10 rue Aristide Briand, 97430 Le Tampon; tel. 57-42-42; commenced broadcasting in Oct. 1993.

Other privately-owned television services include TVB, TVE, RTV, Télé-Réunion and TV-Run.

Finance

(cap. = capital; res = reserves; dep. = deposits; m. = million; brs = branches; amounts in French francs)

BANKING

Central Bank

Institut d'Emission des Départements d'Outre-Mer: 1 cité du Retiro, 75008 Paris, France; Office in Réunion: 4 rue de la Compagnie, 97487 Saint-Denis Cédex; tel. 21-18-96; telex 916176; fax 21-41-32; Dir YVES ESQUILAT.

Commercial Banks

Banque Française Commerciale Océan Indien (BFCOI): 60 rue Alexis de Villeneuve, BP 323, 97468 Saint-Denis Cédex; tel. 40-55-55; telex 916162; fax 40-54-55; Chair. PHILIPPE BRAULT; Dir PHILIPPE LAVIT D'HAUTEFORT; 8 brs.

Banque Nationale de Paris Intercontinentale: 67 rue Juliette Dodu, BP 113, 97463 Saint-Denis; tel. 40-30-30; telex 916133; fax 41-39-09; Chair. RENÉ THOMAS; Man. Dir JEAN-CLAUDE LALLEMANT; 11 brs.

Banque de la Réunion, SA: 27 rue Jean-Chatel, 97711 Saint-Denis Cédex; tel. 40-01-23; telex 916134; fax 40-00-61; f. 1849; affiliate of Crédit Lyonnais; cap. and res 465.3m., dep. 4,519.0m. (Dec. 1995); Pres. JACQUES BARILLET; Gen. Man. CLAUDE NOMBLOT; 12 brs.

Caisse Régionale de Crédit Agricole Mutuel de la Réunion: parc Jean de Cambiaire, cité des Lauriers, BP 84, 97462 Saint-Denis Cédex; tel. 40-81-81; telex 916139; fax 40-81-40; f. 1949; affiliate of Caisse Nationale de Crédit Agricole; Chair. CHRISTIAN DE LA GIRODAY; Dir ERIC PRADEL.

Development Bank

Banque Populaire Fédérale de Développement: 33 rue Victor MacAuliffe, 97400 Saint-Denis; tel. 21-18-11; telex 916582; Dir OLIVIER DEVISME; 3 brs.

INSURANCE

More than 20 major European insurance companies are represented in Saint-Denis.

Trade and Industry

CHAMBER OF COMMERCE AND INDUSTRY

Chambre de Commerce et d'Industrie de la Réunion: 5 bis rue de Paris, BP 120, 97463 Saint-Denis Cédex; tel. 21-53-66; telex 916278; fax 41-80-34; f. 1830; Pres. ROGER ROLAND; Man. Dir LAURENT BARRAUD.

PRINCIPAL DEVELOPMENT AGENCIES

Association pour le Développement Industriel de la Réunion: 18 rue Milius, BP 327, 97466 Saint-Denis Cédex; tel. 21-42-69; telex 916666; fax 20-37-57; f. 1975; 190 mems; Pres. PAUL MARTINEL.

Chambre d'Agriculture: 24 rue de la Source, BP 134, 97463 Saint-Denis Cédex; tel. 21-25-88; telex 916843; Pres. JEAN-YVES MINATCHY; Dir FATMA BADAT.

Direction de l'Action Economique: Secrétariat Général pour les Affaires Economiques, ave de la Victoire, 97405 Saint-Denis; tel. 21-86-10; telex 916111.

Jeune Chambre Economique de Saint-Denis de la Réunion: 25 rue de Paris, BP 1151, 97483 Saint-Denis; f. 1963; 30 mems; Chair. JEAN-CHRISTOPHE DUVAL.

Société de Développement Economique de la Réunion—SODERE: 26 rue Labourdonnais, 97469 Saint-Denis; tel. 20-01-68; telex 916471; fax 20-05-07; f. 1964; Chair. RAYMOND VIVET; Man. Dir ALBERT TRIMAILLE.

PRINCIPAL INDUSTRIAL ORGANIZATIONS

Syndicat des Exportateurs d'Huiles Essentielles, Plantes Aromatiques et Medicinales de Bourbon: Saint-Denis; tel. 20-10-23; exports oil of geranium, vetiver and vanilla; Pres. RICO PLOENIÈRES.

Syndicat des Fabricants de Sucre de la Réunion: BP 57, 97462 Saint-Denis; tel. 90-45-00; fax 41-24-13; Chair. XAVIER THIEBLIN.

Syndicat des Producteurs de Rhum de la Réunion: BP 57, 97462 Saint-Denis; tel. 90-45-00; fax 41-24-13; Chair. XAVIER THIEBLIN.

Syndicat Patronal du Bâtiment de la Réunion: BP 108, 97463 Saint-Denis; tel. 21-03-81; fax 21-55-07; Pres. P. PAVARD; Sec.-Gen. C. OZOUX.

MAJOR COMPANIES

Coopérative d'Achats des Détaillants Réunionnais (CADRE): Zone Industrielle Port Sud, rue de Bordeaux, 97420 Le Port; tel. 42-09-08; telex 916046; fax 42-17-15; Chair. GEORGES CHEUNG-LUNG.

Établissements Jules Caille: 31 rue Jean Chatel, BP 23, 97400 Saint-Denis; tel. 21-12-30; telex 916591; fax 21-63-77; f. 1919; agent for Peugeot motors; Chair. JACQUES CAILLE; Dir GASTON CAILLE.

Établissements Ravate: 131 rue Maréchal Leclerc, 97400 Saint-Denis; tel. 21-06-63; telex 916155; fax 41-26-63; trades in construction materials, wood, hardware; Chair. ISSOP RAVATE; Dir ADAM RAVATE.

Groupe Sucreries de Bourbon (SB): 2 chemin Bois Rouge, BP 2, 97438 Sainte-Marie; tel. 53-46-02; fax 53-06-33; holding co for nine subsidiaries; producing, refining and exporting sugar; also interests in shipping, fishing and food retailing; Chair. JACQUES DE CHÂTEAUVIEUX.

Renault Réunion: 11 blvd du Chaudron, 97490 Sainte-Clotilde; tel. 29-54-62; retails motor vehicles and parts; Chair. REGIS PICOT; Man. M. COSTANTINI.

Société Réunionnaise de Produits Petroliers (SRPP): BP 2015, 97824 Le Port Cedex; tel. 42-07-11; telex 916156; fax 42-11-34; storage and retail of petroleum; Chair. ROBERT LAUROUA; Dir XAVIER CALLOT.

TRADE UNIONS

Confédération Générale du Travail de la Réunion (CGTR): 144 rue du Général de Gaulle, BP 1132, 97482 Saint-Denis Cédex; Sec.-Gen. GEORGES MARIE LEPINAY.

Réunion also has its own sections of the major French trade union confederations, **Confédération Française Démocratique du Travail (CFDT), Force Ouvrière (FO), Confédération Française de l'Encadrement** and **Confédération Française des Travailleurs Chrétiens (CFTC).**

Transport

ROADS

A route nationale circles the island, generally following the coast and linking the main towns. Another route nationale crosses the island from south-west to north-east linking Saint-Pierre and Saint-Benoît. In 1994 there were 370 km of routes nationales, 754 km of departmental roads and 1,630 km of other roads; 1,300 km of the roads were bituminized.

SHIPPING

In 1986 work was completed on the expansion of the Port de la Pointe des Galets, which was divided into the former port in the west and a new port in the east (the port Ouest and the port Est). In 1995 more than 2.7m. tons of freight were loaded and discharged at the two ports.

Compagnie Générale Maritime (CGM): 2 rue de l'Est, BP 2007, 97822 Le Port Cédex; tel. 42-00-88; telex 916106; fax 43-23-04; agents for Mitsui OSK Lines, Safmarine and Unisaf; Dir RENAUD SAUVAGET.

Maritime Delmais-Vieljeux: BP 2006, 97822 Le Port Cédex; tel. 42-03-46; telex 916151; fax 43-72-06; Dir ARMAND BARUCH.

Réunion Maritime: f. 1991; consortium of 15 import cos; freight only.

Shipping Mediterranean Co: Le Port.

Société de Manutention et de Consignation Maritime (SOMACOM): BP 7, Le Port; agents for Scandinavian East Africa Line, Bank Line, Clan Line, Union Castle Mail Steamship Co and States Marine Lines.

Société Réunionnaise de Services Maritimes: 81 rue de St Paul, BP 2006, 97822 Le Port Cédex; tel. 42-03-46; telex 916170; fax 43-34-79; freight only; Man. DENIS LAURE.

CIVIL AVIATION

There is an international airport at Saint-Denis Gillot. A programme to develop the airport was completed in 1994. A project to develop the Pierrefonds airfield, near Saint-Pierre, as an international airport, at an estimated cost of nearly 50m. French francs, was due for completion by the end of 1997.

Air Austral: BP 611, 97473 Saint-Denis; tel. 28-27-27; telex 916236; fax 29-28-95; f. 1975; subsidiary of Air France; scheduled services to Madagascar, South Africa, Mauritius and the Comoros; Chair G. ETHEVE; Gen. Man. Mme B. POPINEAU.

Air Outre-Mer: Saint-Denis; f. 1990; scheduled services to Paris; Chair. RENÉ MICAUD.

Tourism

Tourism is being extensively promoted. Réunion's attractions include spectacular scenery and a pleasant climate. In 1995 the island had 44 hotels with a total of 1,878 rooms. In that year a total of 304,000 tourists visited Réunion, and revenue from tourism totalled about 1,116m. French francs.

Comité du Tourisme de la Réunion: BP 615, 97472 Saint-Denis Cédex; tel. 41-84-41; telex 916068; fax 20-25-93; Pres. JASMIN MOUTOUSSAMY.

Délégation Régionale au Commerce, à l'Artisanat et au Tourisme: Préfecture de la Réunion, 97400 Saint-Denis; tel. 40-77-58; telex 916111; fax 40-77-01; Dir JEAN-FRANÇOIS DESROCHES.

Office du Tourisme: 48 rue Sainte-Marie, 97400 Saint-Denis; tel. 41-83-00; fax 21-37-76; Vice-Pres. YASMINA HATIA.

Defence

Réunion is the headquarters of French military forces in the Indian Ocean. In August 1996 there were 4,000 troops stationed on Réunion and Mayotte, the French Overseas Collectivité Territoriale in the Comoros archipelago.

Education

Education is modelled on the French system, and is compulsory for 10 years between the ages of six and 16 years. Primary education begins at six years of age and lasts for five years. Secondary education, which begins at 11 years of age, lasts for up to seven years, comprising a first cycle of four years and a second of three years. For the academic year 1994/95 there were 44,312 pupils enrolled at 175 pre-primary schools, 73,250 at 343 primary schools and 92,281 at 102 secondary schools (comprising 64 collèges and 38 lycées). There is a university, with several faculties, a teacher-training college, a technical institute and an agricultural college. In 1982 the illiteracy rate among the population over 15 years of age averaged 21.4% (males 23.5%; females 19.5%).

Bibliography

Bunge, F. M. (Ed.). *Indian Ocean: Five Island Countries.* Washington, DC, American University, 1983.

Cornu, H. *Paris et Bourbon, La politique française dans l'Océan indien.* Paris, Académie des Sciences d'Outre-mer, 1984.

Defos du Rau, J. *L'Ile de la Réunion. Étude de géographie humaine.* Institut de Géographie, Bordeaux, 1960.

Lavaux, C. *La Réunion: du battant des lames au sommet des montagnes.* Montligeon, 1975.

Leguen, M. *Histoire de l'Ile de la Réunion.* Paris, Editions l'Harmattan, 1979.

Leymarie, P. *Océan indien, nouveau coeur du monde.* Paris, Editions Karthala, 1983.

Prudhomme, C. *Histoire religieuse de la Réunion.* Paris, Editions Karthala, 1984.

Scherer, A. *La Réunion.* Paris, Presses Universitaires de France, 1980.

Service Régional de la Réunion. *Panorama de l'économie de la Réunion 1983.* Saint-Denis, Institut National de la Statistique et des Etudes Economiques, 1984.

Références bibliographiques dans les domaines démographique, économique et social sur la Réunion. Saint-Denis, Institut National de la Statistique et des Etudes Economiques, 1984.

Liste d'addresses des établissements commerciaux, industriels et artisanaux. Saint-Denis, Institut National de la Statistique et des Etudes Economiques, 1984.

Toussaint, A. *Histoire des Iles Mascareignes.* Paris, Berger-Levrault, 1972.

RWANDA

Physical and Social Geography

PIERRE GOUROU

The Rwandan Republic, like the neighbouring Republic of Burundi, is distinctive both for the small size of its territory and for the density of its population. Covering an area of 26,338 sq km (10,169 sq miles), Rwanda had an enumerated population of 7,142,755 at the census of 15 August 1991, with a density of 271 inhabitants per sq km. However, political and ethnic violence during 1994 was estimated to have resulted in the death or external displacement of 35%–40% of the total population. Prior to these events, the population had been composed of Hutu (about 85%), Tutsi (about 14%) and Twa (1%). The official languages are French, English (which is widely spoken by the Tutsi minority) and Kinyarwanda, a Bantu language with close similarities to Kirundi, the main vernacular language of Burundi.

It seems, at first sight, strange that Rwanda has not been absorbed into a wider political entity. Admittedly, the Rwandan nation has long been united by language and custom and was part of a state that won the respect of the east African slave-traders. However, other ethnic groups, such as the Kongo, Luba, Luo and Zande, which were well established in small territorial areas, have not been able to develop into national states. That Rwanda has been able to achieve this is partly the result of developments during the colonial period. While part of German East Africa, Rwanda (then known, with Burundi, as Ruanda-Urundi) was regarded as a peripheral colonial territory of little economic interest. After the First World War it was entrusted to Belgium under a mandate from the League of Nations. The territory was administered jointly with the Belgian Congo, but was not absorbed into the larger state. The historic separateness and national traditions of both Rwanda and Burundi have prevented their amalgamation, although both countries participate, with the Democratic Republic of the Congo, in the Economic Community of the Great Lakes Countries.

Although the land supports a high population density, physical conditions are not very favourable. Rwanda's land mass is very rugged and fragmented. Basically it is part of a Pre-Cambrian shelf from which, through erosion, the harder rocks have obtruded, leaving the softer ones submerged. Thus very ancient folds have been raised and a relief surface carved out with steep gradients covered with a soil poor in quality because of its fineness and fragility. Rwanda's physiognomy therefore consists of a series of sharply defined hills, with steep slopes and flat ridges, which are intersected by deep valleys, the bottoms of which are often formed by marshy plains. The north is dominated by the lofty and powerful chain of volcanoes, the Virunga, whose highest peak is Karisimbi (4,519 m) and whose lava, having scarcely cooled down, has not yet produced cultivable soil.

The climate is tropical, although tempered by altitude, with a daily temperature range of as much as 14°C. Kigali, the capital (117,749 inhabitants in 1978), has an average temperature of 19°C and 1,000 mm of rain. Altitude is a factor which modifies the temperature (and prevents sleeping sickness above about 900 m), but such a factor is of debatable value for agriculture. Average annual rainfall (785 mm) is only barely sufficient for agricultural purposes, but two wet and two relatively dry seasons are experienced, making two harvests possible.

Recent History

FILIP REYNTJENS

Revised for this edition by THOMAS OFCANSKY

HUTU ASCENDANCY

Unlike most African states, Rwanda and its southern neighbour Burundi were not an artificial creation of colonial rule. When they were absorbed by German East Africa in 1899, they had been established kingdoms for several centuries. In 1916, during the First World War, the area was occupied by Belgian forces. From 1920, Rwanda formed part of Ruanda-Urundi, administered by Belgium under a League of Nations mandate and later as a UN Trust Territory. Dissensions between the majority Hutu (traditionally comprising about 85% of the population) and their former overlords, the Tutsi (14%) led, in 1959, to a rebellion. In September 1961 it was decided by referendum to replace the monarchy with a republic. Internal autonomy was granted in 1961 and full independence followed on 1 July 1962. Serious tribal strife erupted in December 1963, with large-scale massacres of the Tutsi by the Hutu. During 1964–65 large numbers of displaced Rwandans were resettled in neighbouring countries. In 1969 Grégoire Kayibanda, the country's first president, was re-elected, and all seats in the legislative assembly were retained by the ruling party, the Mouvement démocratique républicain (MDR), also known as the Parti de l'émancipation du peuple Hutu (Parmehutu).

Tension between Hutu and Tutsi was renewed in late 1972 and early 1973. In July the minister of defence and head of the national guard, Maj.-Gen. Juvénal Habyarimana, led a bloodless coup against president Kayibanda, proclaimed a second republic and established a military administration under his presidency. The normal legislative processes were suspended, and all political activity was banned until July 1975, when a new ruling party, the Mouvement révolutionnaire national pour le développement (MRND), was formed. Its establishment was preceded by an extensive government reshuffle in which a number of civilian ministers joined the administration.

A referendum in December 1978 approved a new constitution, aimed at returning the country to normal government in accordance with an undertaking by Habyarimana in 1973, to end the military regime within five years. An unsuccessful coup attempt took place in April 1980, and elections to the legislature, the Conseil national du développement (CND), were held in December 1981 and in December 1983; in the same month Habyarimana was re-elected president.

From 1982, cross-border refugee problems began to affect Rwanda's relations with Uganda, which in 1980 had joined Rwanda, Burundi and Tanzania in a major regional plan to develop the water, power and mineral resources of the Kagera river basin. In October 1982 Rwanda closed its border with Uganda after an influx of 45,000 refugees, most of whom were Rwandan exiles fleeing Ugandan persecution. A further 32,000 refugees collected in camps on the Ugandan side of the border. In March 1983 Rwanda agreed to resettle more than 30,000 refugees, but Ugandan persecution of ethnic Rwandans continued, and in December thousands crossed into Tanzania. In November 1985 it was reported that 30,000 ethnic Rwandan refugees had been repatriated to Uganda. In 1986 the UN High Commissioner for Refugees (UNHCR) reported that there were about 110,000 registered Rwandan refugees living in Uganda, while an even greater number of refugees were believed to have settled in Uganda without registering with UNHCR. In July the central committee of the MRND issued a declaration that Rwanda would not allow the return of large numbers of refugees, since the country's economy was incapable of sustaining such an influx. In the same year President Museveni of Uganda announced that Rwandans who had been resident in Uganda for more than 10 years would automatically be entitled to Ugandan citizenship. In January 1987 a Ugandan government minister visited Rwanda for discussions concerning the problem of border security, and in February 1988 Habyarimana visited Uganda for talks with President Museveni. A subsequent joint communiqué confirmed that relations between the two countries had improved. A resurgence of ethnic tensions in Burundi led to the flight, in August 1988, of an estimated 80,000 refugees, mainly Hutu, into Rwanda. With assistance from the international community, the Rwandan authorities were able to cater for their needs. By June 1989 all but approximately 1,000 of the refugees had been repatriated to Burundi.

At a presidential election held in December 1988, Habyarimana, as sole candidate, secured 99.98% of the votes cast. Elections for the CND were held in the same month, and the government was reshuffled in January 1989. During 1989 economic conditions deteriorated sharply, as the combined effects of soil degradation, population pressure and crop disease affected harvests and led to several hundred deaths from starvation. In addition, the collapse in world coffee prices, combined with a low output of poor-quality beans, led to serious balance-of-payments and budgetary problems. The introduction of an economic austerity programme in December added to public discontent.

In May 1990, the first report of a commission established in 1989 to examine the situation of Rwandan refugees urged the adoption of a more liberal approach on the part of the government, while indicating that *émigré* demands were unlikely to be satisfied. The subject was subsequently discussed at the third meeting of a joint Rwandan-Ugandan ministerial commission. In early July 1990, Habyarimana conceded that political reform was needed and announced that a national commission would be appointed. The Commission nationale de synthèse (CNS) was duly established in September with a mandate to make recommendations for political renewal. However, these measures did little to alleviate the acute sense of political crisis.

REBEL INVASION AND POLITICAL UPHEAVAL

On 1 October 1990 an estimated force of 10,000 guerrillas, representing the exiled, Tutsi-dominated Front patriotique rwandais (FPR, or Inkotanyi), crossed the border from Uganda into north-eastern Rwanda, where they swiftly occupied several towns. Numerically, the troops were dominated by Tutsi refugees, but also included significant numbers of disaffected elements of Uganda's ruling National Resistance Army (NRA). The invasion force was reported to have been led by Maj.-Gen. Fred Rwigyema, a former Ugandan deputy minister of defence. In response to a request for assistance by Habyarimana, Belgian and French paratroopers were dispatched to Kigali to protect foreign nationals and to secure evacuation routes, but in the event did not engage in combat. However, a contingent of troops sent by Zaire (now the Democratic Republic of the Congo—DRC) assisted the small Rwandan army in turning back the FPR some 70 km from Kigali. During the first week of hostilities, an estimated 8,000 people throughout Rwanda were arrested and imprisoned, of whom the vast majority were Tutsi. However, in only a few cases was there any evidence of complicity with the invaders and almost all were released in April 1991, while those convicted were subsequently released under an amnesty introduced in November.

Internationally, the FPR successfully presented itself as a democratic and multi-ethnic movement seeking to depose a corrupt and incompetent regime, with the result that the Belgian government encountered increasing pressure to terminate military aid to Habyarimana. Visits were paid to the region by the Belgian prime minister and other senior ministers with the aim of securing a cease-fire, to be followed by a regional conference on the Rwandan refugee problem. In October 1990 a summit meeting at Mwanza, Tanzania, was attended by the presidents of Rwanda, Uganda and Tanzania, who agreed in principle to the holding of a regional conference. Although numerous other bilateral contacts took place, there was no direct dialogue between the Rwandan government and the FPR. Despite the obvious frailty of the agreements, Belgium decided to extricate itself from the crisis and by 1 November had withdrawn its troops from Rwanda. Their departure coincided with a statement by the Rwandan government that victory had been achieved and that the invaders had fled to Uganda. The FPR, however, now began to attack border areas in the north and north-west from bases within Uganda, raising accusations, strongly denied by Uganda, that the country was actively aiding the FPR.

The conflict continued throughout 1991 and into 1992, as the FPR made frequent guerrilla forays into Rwanda. Thousands of casualties were reported on both sides while many civilians resident in the border region were killed and as many as 100,000 were displaced. Increasing racial tension, exacerbated by the war, resulted in a series of unprovoked attacks upon Tutsis, and prompted accusations of government involvement, particularly in the Bugesera region. In late July 1992 it was reported that a cease-fire had been negotiated, providing for the establishment of a 'neutral area'. The cease-fire arrangements were to be overseen by a 50-member African military monitoring team.

Regional refugee problems came once again to the fore in early 1992, when the presidents of Rwanda, Burundi and Zaire met in an attempt to resolve border difficulties arising from the flight of Hutu refugees from Burundi into Rwanda and Zaire. The three presidents agreed to intensify border controls and to work together to facilitate the voluntary return of refugees to their country of origin. Further bilateral talks between Rwanda and Burundi sought to consolidate this agreement.

The political reform process, initiated before the conflict, was accelerated by the FPR invasion. The CNS published its report and a draft constitution in March 1991, following widespread public discussion of proposals put forward by the commission in December 1990. In June 1991 the new constitution, providing for the legalization of political parties, entered into force. Full freedom of the press was declared, leading to the establishment of a number of magazines and newspapers critical of government policy. In April 1992, following a series of unsuccessful attempts to negotiate a transitional government, the composition of a broadly-based coalition government, incorporating four opposition parties (the revived MDR, the Parti social-démocrate–PSD, the Parti libéral–PL and the Parti démocratique chrétien–PDC), together with the Mouvement républicain national pour la démocratie et le développement–MRNDD (the new party name adopted by the MRND in April 1991), was announced. The cabinet was to be headed by Dismas Nsengiyaremye of the MDR as prime minister, a post established by the new constitution. It was also announced that multi-party elections for municipalities, the legislature and for the presidency would take place before April 1993. In late April 1992, to comply with the new constitutional prohibition of participation in the political process by the armed forces, Habyarimana relinquished his military title and functions.

Renewed dialogue was initiated between the new transitional government and FPR representatives in May 1992, and formal discussions were conducted in Paris during June. Further negotiations, in Arusha, Tanzania, in July, resulted in an agreement on the implementation of a new cease-fire, to take effect from the end of July, and the creation of an OAU-sponsored military observer group (GOM), to comprise representatives from both sides, together with officers drawn from the armed forces of Nigeria, Senegal, Zimbabwe and Mali. However, subsequent negotiations in Tanzania, during August, September and

October, failed to resolve outstanding problems concerning the creation of a 'neutral zone' between the Rwandan armed forces and the FPR (to be enforced by the GOM), the incorporation of the FPR in a future combined Rwandan national force, the repatriation of refugees, and the demands of the FPR for full participation in a transitional government and legislature.

A resurgence in violence followed the breakdown of negotiations in early February 1993, resulting in the deaths of hundreds on both sides. An estimated 1m. civilians fled southwards and to neighbouring Uganda and Tanzania, in order to escape the fighting, as the FPR advanced as far as Ruhengeri and seemed, for a time, poised to occupy Kigali. The actions of the FPR were denounced by Belgium, France and the USA. French reinforcements were dispatched to join a small French military contingent, stationed in Kigali since October 1990 in order to protect French nationals. Meanwhile, the commander of the GOM declared that the group had inadequate manpower and resources to contain the FPR front line, and requested the deployment of an additional 400 troops from the OAU.

In late February 1993 the government accepted FPR terms for a cease-fire in return for an end to attacks against FPR positions and on Tutsi communities, and the withdrawal of foreign troops. Although fighting continued with varying intensity, new peace negotiations were convened in March, in Arusha. In late March the French government began to withdraw its troops.

Negotiations conducted during April 1993 failed to produce a solution to the crucial issue of the structure of future unitary Rwandan armed forces. In the same month, the five participating parties in the ruling coalition agreed to a three-month extension of the government's mandate, in order to facilitate the achievement of a peace accord. Significant progress was made during fresh talks between the government and the FPR in the northern town of Kinihira, during May, when a timetable for the demobilization of 19,000-strong security forces was agreed. Later in the month further consensus was reached on the creation of a 'neutral zone'. In June agreement was concluded on a protocol for the repatriation of all Rwandan refugees resident in Uganda, Tanzania and Zaire, including recommendations that compensation should be made available to those forced into exile more than 12 years ago. In late June the UN Security Council approved the creation of UN Observer Mission Uganda-Rwanda (UNOMUR), to be deployed on the Ugandan side of the border for an initial period of six months, in order to ensure that no military supply lines would be maintained for the FPR.

In July 1993, with improved prospects for a prompt resolution of the conflict, Habyarimana met representatives of the five political parties represented in the government and sought a further extension to the mandate of the coalition government. However, the prime minister's insistence that the FPR should be represented in any newly-mandated government exacerbated existing divisions within the MDR, prompting Habyarimana to conclude the agreement with a conciliatory group of MDR dissidents, including the education minister, Agathe Uwilingiyimana, who was elected to the premiership. The council of ministers was reshuffled to replace the disaffected MDR members. The outgoing prime minister, Dismas Nsengiyaremye, accused Habyarimana of having deliberately jeopardized the peace accord with the FPR, and of having acted irregularly in the selection of Uwilingiyimana as his successor.

On 4 August 1993 a peace accord was formally signed by Habyarimana and Col Alex Kanyarengwe of the FPR, in Arusha. A new transitional government, to be headed by a mutually-approved prime minister (later named as the MDR moderate faction leader, Faustin Twagiramungu), would be installed by 10 September. Multi-party general elections were to take place after a 22-month period, during which the FPR would join the political mainstream and participate in a transitional government and national assembly. In mid-August the curfew in Kigali was lifted, and military road-blocks were removed from all but three northern prefectures. By the end of the month, however, the prime minister was forced to make a national appeal for calm, following reports of renewed outbreaks of violence in Kigali and Butare. The failure to establish a transitional government and legislature by 10 September was attributed by the government and the FPR to the increasingly fragile security situation, and both sides urged the prompt dispatch of a neutral UN force to facilitate the implementation of the accord. Meanwhile, relations between the government and the FPR deteriorated, following the rebels' assertion that the government had infringed the terms of the accord by attempting to dismantle and reorganize those government departments assigned to the FPR under the terms of the agreement.

UN INTERVENTION

On 5 October 1993 the UN Security Council adopted Resolution 872, endorsing the recommendation of the UN secretary-general for the creation of UN Assistance Mission to Rwanda (UNAMIR), to be deployed in Rwanda for an initial period of six months, with a mandate to monitor observance of the cease-fire, to contribute to the security of the capital and to facilitate the repatriation of refugees. UNAMIR, which was to incorporate UNOMUR and GOM, was formally inaugurated on 1 November, and was to comprise some 2,500 personnel when fully operational. (Resolution 928, approved by the Security Council in June 1994, provided for the termination of UNOMUR on 21 September 1994.) In early December 1993, in compliance with the stipulations of the Arusha accord, the French government announced the withdrawal of its military contingent in Kigali, and in mid-December the UN secretary-general's special representative in Rwanda, Jacques-Roger Booh-Booh, declared that the UN was satisfied that conditions had been sufficiently fulfilled to allow for the introduction of the transitional institutions by the end of the month.

In late December 1993 a 600-strong FPR battalion was escorted to the capital by UNAMIR officials (as detailed in the Arusha accord), in order to ensure the safety of FPR representatives selected to participate in the transitional government and legislature. However, dissension within a number of political parties had obstructed the satisfactory nomination of representatives to the transitional institutions, forcing a further postponement of their inauguration. On 5 January 1994 Juvénal Habyarimana was invested as president of a transitional government, for a 22-month period, under the terms of the Arusha accord. (Habyarimana's previous term of office, in accordance with the constitution, had expired on 19 December 1993.) The inauguration of the transitional government and legislature, scheduled for the same day, was again postponed when several major participants, notably representatives of the FPR, the MDR, the PSD and the PDC, and the president of the constitutional court, failed to attend. While government spokesmen identified the need to resolve internal differences within the MDR and the PL as the crucial expedient for the implementation of the new government and legislature, a joint statement, issued by the PSD, the PDC and factions of the MDR and the PL, accused the president of having abused the terms of the Arusha accord by interfering in the selection of prospective ministers and deputies. This charge was reiterated by the FPR in late February, when it rejected a list of proposed future gubernatorial and legislative representatives (tentatively agreed following several days of discussions between the president, the prime minister and the five participating parties of the current administration) as having been compiled as the result of a campaign of intimidation and manipulation by the president in order to secure the participation of his own supporters, and thereby prolong his political influence. The FPR insisted that a definitive list of each party's representatives in the future transitional institutions had been approved by the constitutional court in January. In March the prime minister-designate, Faustin Twagiramungu, declared that he had fulfilled his consultative role as set out in the Arusha accord, and announced the composition of a transitional government, in an attempt to accelerate the installation of the transitional bodies. However, political opposition to the proposed council of ministers persisted, and Habyarimana insisted that the list of proposed legislative deputies, newly presented by Agathe Uwilingiyimana, should be modified to include representatives of additional political parties, including the reactionary Coalition pour la défense de la république–CDR (whose participation was strongly opposed by the FPR, owing to its alleged failure to accept the code of ethics for the behaviour of political parties which proscribed policies advocating tribal discrimination), prompting a further postponement of the formation of a transitional administration.

Meanwhile political frustration had erupted into violence in late February 1994, with the murder of the minister of public works and energy, Félicien Gatabazi of the PSD, who had actively supported the Arusha agreement and the transitional administration. Hours later, the CDR leader, Martin Bucyana, was killed, in apparent retaliation, by an angry mob of PSD supporters, provoking a series of violent confrontations resulting in some 30–40 deaths.

In April 1994 the UN Security Council (which in February had warned that the UN presence in Rwanda might be withdrawn in the absence of swift progress in the implementation of the Arusha accord) agreed to extend UNAMIR's mandate for four months, pending a review of progress made in implementing the accord, to be conducted after six weeks.

COLLAPSE OF CIVIL ORDER

On 6 April 1994 the presidential aircraft, returning from a regional summit meeting in Dar es Salaam, Tanzania, was fired upon, above Kigali airport, and exploded on landing, killing all 10 passengers, including Habyarimana. The president of Burundi, Cyprien Ntaryamira, two Burundian cabinet ministers, the chief of staff of the Rwandan armed forces, and a senior diplomat were among the other victims. In Kigali the presidential guard immediately initiated a brutal campaign of retributive violence against political opponents of the late president, although it remained unclear who had been responsible for the attack on the aircraft, and UNAMIR officials attempting to investigate the site of the crash were obstructed by the presidential guard. As politicians and civilians fled the capital, the brutality of the political assassinations was compounded by attacks on the clergy, UNAMIR personnel and members of the Tutsi tribe. Hutu civilians were forced, under pain of death, to murder their Tutsi neighbours, and the mobilization of the Interahamwe, or unofficial militias (allegedly affiliated to the MRNDD and the CDR), apparently committed to the massacre of government opponents and Tutsi civilians, was encouraged by the presidential guard (with support from some factions of the armed forces) and by inflammatory broadcasts from Radio-Télévision Libre des Mille Collines in Kigali. The prime minister, Agathe Uwilingiyimana, the president of the constitutional court, the ministers of labour and social affairs and of information, and the chairman of the PSD were among the prominent politicians murdered, or declared missing and presumed dead, within hours of the death of Habyarimana.

On 8 April 1994 the speaker of the CND, Dr Théodore Sindikubwabo, announced that he had assumed the office of interim president of the republic, in accordance with the provisions of the 1991 constitution. The five remaining participating political parties and factions of the government selected a new prime minister, Jean Kambanda, and a new council of ministers (drawn largely from the MRNDD) from among their ranks. The legality of the new administration was immediately challenged by the FPR, which claimed that the constitutional right of succession to the presidency of the speaker of the CND had been superseded by Habyarimana's inauguration, in January, as president under the terms of the Arusha agreement. (However, Félicien Ngango, who had been nominated to lead the transitional national assembly, and therefore became next in line to the presidency, had been murdered by the presidential guard.) The legitimacy of the new government (which had fled to the town of Gitarama to escape escalating violence in the capital) was subsequently rejected by factions of the PL and MDR (led by Faustin Twagiramungu), and by the PDC and the PSD (which in May announced that they had allied themselves as the Democratic Forces for Change).

FPR Offensives and the Refugee Crisis

In mid-April 1994 the FPR resumed military operations from its northern stronghold, with the stated intention of relieving its beleaguered battalion in Kigali, restoring order to the capital and halting the massacre of civilians. Grenade attacks and mortar fire intensified in the capital, prompting the UN to mediate a fragile 60-hour cease-fire, during which small evacuation forces from several countries escorted foreign nationals out of Rwanda. Belgium's UNAMIR contingent of more than 400 troops was also withdrawn, having encountered increasing hostility as a result of persistent rumours of Belgian complicity in the attack on Habyarimana's aircraft, and of providing logistical support to the FPR (accusations which were formally levelled by the Rwandan ambassador to Zaire later in the month), which were emphatically denied by the Belgian government.

In late April 1994 the government embarked upon a diplomatic offensive throughout Europe and Africa, seeking to enhance the credibility of the government through international recognition of its legitimacy. However, these efforts achieved only limited success (notably in France, Egypt and Togo), and the FPR's continued refusal to enter into dialogue with the 'illegal' administration proved a major obstacle to attempts, undertaken by the UN and the presidents of Tanzania and Zaire, to sponsor a new cease-fire agreement in late April and early May.

As the violent political crusade unleashed by the presidential guard and the Interahamwe (described by Amnesty International as a well-trained militia numbering some 30,000) gathered momentum, the militia's identification of all members of the Tutsi tribe as political opponents of the state promoted tribal polarization, resulting in an effective pogrom. Reports of mass Tutsi graves and unprovoked attacks on fleeing Tutsi refugees, and on those seeking refuge in schools, hospitals and churches, provoked unqualified international condemnation and outrage, and promises of financial and logistical aid for an estimated 2m. displaced Rwandans (some 250,000 had fled across the border to Tanzania in a 24-hour period in late April 1994) who were threatened by famine and disease in makeshift camps. By late May attempts to assess the full scale of the humanitarian catastrophe in Rwanda were complicated by unverified reports that the FPR (which claimed to control more than one-half of the country) was carrying out retaliatory atrocities against Hutu civilians. However, unofficial estimates indicated that between 200,000–500,000 Rwandans had been killed since early April.

On 21 April 1994, in the context of intensifying violence in Kigali, and the refusal of the Rwandan armed forces to agree to the neutral policing of the capital's airport (subsequently secured by the FPR), the UN Security Council resolved to reduce significantly its representation in Rwanda to 270 personnel, a move which attracted criticism from the government, the FPR, international relief organizations and the international community in general. However, on 16 May, following intense international pressure and the disclosure of the vast scale of the humanitarian crisis in the region, the UN Security Council approved Resolution 917, providing for the eventual deployment of some 5,500 UN troops with a revised mandate, including the policing of Kigali's airport and the protection of refugees in designated 'safe areas'. In late May the UN secretary-general criticized the failure of the UN member nations to respond to his invitation to participate in the enlarged force (only Ghana, Ethiopia and Senegal had agreed to provide small contingents). Further UN-sponsored attempts to negotiate a cease-fire failed in late May and early June, and the FPR made significant territorial gains in southern Rwanda, forcing the government to flee Gitarama and seek refuge in the western town of Kibuye.

In early June 1994 the UN Security Council adopted Resolution 925, whereby the mandate of the revised UN mission in Rwanda (UNAMIR II) was extended until December 1994. However, the UN secretary-general continued to encounter considerable difficulty in securing equipment and armaments requested by those African countries which had agreed to participate. By mid-June the emergence of confirmed reports of retributive murders committed by FPR members (including the massacres, in two separate incidents in early June, of 22 clergymen, among them the Roman Catholic archbishop of Kigali) and the collapse of a fragile truce (negotiated at a summit meeting of the OAU in Tunis, Tunisia) prompted the French government to announce its willingness to lead an armed police action, endorsed by the UN, in Rwanda. Although the French government insisted that the French military presence (expected to total 2,000 troops) would maintain strict political neutrality, and operate, from the border regions, in a purely humanitarian capacity pending the arrival of a multinational UN force, the FPR was vehemently opposed to its deployment, citing the French administration's maintenance of high-level contacts with representatives of the self-proclaimed Rwandan government as an indication of political bias. While the UN secretary-general welcomed the French initiative, and tacit endorsement of the project was contained in Resolution 929, approved by the Security Council in late June, the OAU expressed serious reservations regarding the appropriateness of the action. On 23 June a first contingent of 150 French marine commandos launched 'Operation Turquoise', entering the western town of Cyangugu, in preparation for a large-scale operation to protect refugees in the area. By mid-July the French had successfully relieved several beleaguered Tutsi communities, and had established a temporary 'safe haven' for the displaced population in the south-west, through which a massive exodus of Hutu refugees began to flow, encouraged by reports (disseminated by supporters of the defeated interim government) that the advancing FPR forces were seeking violent retribution against the Hutu. An estimated 1m. Rwandans sought refuge in the Zairean border town of Goma, while a similar number attempted to cross the border elsewhere in the south-west. The FPR had swiftly secured all major cities and strategic territorial positions, but had halted its advance several kilometres from the boundaries of the French-controlled neutral zone, requesting the apprehension and return for trial of those responsible for the recent atrocities. (At the end of June the first report of the UN's special rapporteur on human rights in Rwanda — appointed in May — confirmed that as many as 500,000 Rwandans had been killed since April, and urged the establishment of an international tribunal to investigate allegations of genocide; in early July the UN announced the creation of a commission of enquiry for this purpose.)

The FPR Takes Power

On 19 July 1994 Pasteur Bizimungu, a Hutu, was inaugurated as president for a five-year term. On the same day the FPR announced the composition of a new government of national unity, to be headed by Faustin Twagiramungu as prime minister. The majority of cabinet posts were assigned to FPR members (including the FPR military chief Maj.-Gen. Paul Kagame, who became minister of defence and also assumed the newly-created post of vice-president), while the remainder were divided among the MDR, the PL, the PSD and the PDC. The new administration urged all refugees to return to Rwanda and issued assurances that civilian Hutus could return safely to their homes. The prime minister identified the immediate aims of the administration as the restoration of peace and democracy, the reactivation of the economy and the repatriation of refugees. Identity cards bearing details of ethnic origin were to be abolished forthwith. The new government declared its intention to honour the terms of the Arusha accord within the context of an extended period of transition. However, the MRNDD and the CDR were to be excluded from participation in government.

The FPR victory and the new administration were promptly recognized by the French government, which urged the new Rwandan government to assume responsibility for relief operations. In return, Twagiramungu was reported to have expressed his appreciation for the humanitarian and stabilizing nature of the French operation. The French government announced its intention to begin a reduction in personnel by the end of July 1994, with a view to complete withdrawal by the end of August. In mid-July France began to equip a force of 500 troops drawn from Senegal, the (Republic of) Congo, Chad, Niger and Guinea-Bissau, to assist the French contingent and facilitate the eventual transfer of responsibility to a UN force. The claims of the former government were seriously undermined by the recognition by the European Union (EU) of the new Rwandan government of national unity in mid-September 1994.

Meanwhile, conditions in refugee camps in Zaire had continued to deteriorate, as hunger and cholera became more widespread. By the end of July 1994, despite an intensification of international relief efforts in the region, at least 2,000 refugees were dying each day, adding to a refugee camp death toll already in excess of 20,000. Non-government relief agencies were highly critical of the inadequate and overdue nature of the international response to the crisis. In late July Bizimungu met the presidents of Zaire and Tanzania, and concluded agreements on the disarmament and gradual repatriation of refugees.

Amid persistent rumours that the Rwandan armed forces were attempting to regroup and rearm in Zaire in preparation for a counter-offensive strike against the FPR, on 20 August 1994 the UN began to deploy some 2,500 UNAMIR II forces, largely drawn from Ghana and Ethiopia, in the security zone (which was redesignated 'zone four'). On the following day French troops began to withdraw from the area (the final contingent departed on 20 September), prompting hundreds of thousands of internally displaced Hutu refugees within the zone to move to Zairean border areas. An estimated 500,000 refugees remained at camps in the former security zone at the end of August, as the first Rwandan government officials were assigned to customs and immigration and army recruitment duties in the region.

In early August 1994 the prime minister, Faustin Twagiramungu, had declared the country technically bankrupt, accusing the former government of having fled to Zaire with Rwanda's exchange reserves. (New banknotes were subsequently printed in order to invalidate the former currency.) Twagiramungu stressed that economic recovery could only be achieved following the return to their farms and workplaces of the country's displaced population. The government suffered a further financial setback in October, when the minister of foreign affairs and co-operation, Jean-Marie Ndagijimana, was reported to have absconded, while abroad, with government funds intended for diplomatic missions. A successor minister, Anastase Gasana, was named in December.

In November 1994 a multi-party protocol of understanding was concluded, providing for a number of amendments to the terms of the August 1993 Arusha accord relating to the establishment of a transitional legislature. The most notable of the new provisions was the exclusion from the legislative process of members of those parties implicated in alleged acts of genocide during 1994. A 70-member national transitional assembly, whose membership included five representatives of the armed forces and one member of the national police force, was installed on 12 December. On 5 May 1995 the new legislature announced its adoption of a new constitution based on selected articles of the 1991 constitution, the terms of the August 1993 Arusha accord, the FPR's victory declaration of July 1994 and the November multi-party protocol of understanding.

Refugee Repatriation Problems

In late 1994 Hutu refugees within Rwanda and in neighbouring countries were continuing to resist the exhortations of the UN and the new Rwandan administration to return to their homes, despite the deteriorating security situation in many camps which had forced the withdrawal of a number of relief agencies. Hutu militia were reported to have assumed control of several camps, notably Katale in Zaire and Benaco in Tanzania, where it was reported that a state of near lawlessness existed. Reports also emerged that Hutu civilians intending to return to their homes were subjected to violent intimidation by the militia. It was further alleged that male Hutu refugees were undergoing enforced military training in preparation for a renewed armed conflict. In early November the UN secretary-general appealed to the international community for contributions to a 12,000-strong force to police the refugee camps. By late January 1995, however, the UN had abandoned attempts to raise the force, having failed to secure a commitment from member countries for the provision of equipment or personnel for such a mission. A compromise agreement was subsequently concluded with Zairean troops for the supervision of camps in Zaire. At the end of November 1994 the UNAMIR II mandate was extended for a further six months, and in June 1995, at the request of the Rwandan government, the strength of the force was reduced from 5,586 to 2,330 personnel (to be further reduced by September), and the six-month mandate was again renewed.

The reluctance of many refugees to return to their homes was also attributed to persistent allegations that the Tutsi-dominated FPR armed forces (the Armée patriotique rwandaise–APR) were conducting a systematic campaign of reprisals against returning Hutu civilians. In an address to the UN General Assembly in early October 1994, President Bizimungu denied these allegations (presented by investigating officers of UNHCR) and insisted that the government should not be held responsible for what a UN inquiry, conducted earlier in the month, had concluded were frequent but individual acts of retaliation. In late August Bizimungu had announced the execution of two FPR members, following their court martial for involvement in violent acts of reprisal. It was reported that some 50–70 FPR members were awaiting trial for similar offences. In February 1995 the UN Security Council adopted Resolution 977, whereby Arusha was designated the venue for the International Criminal Tribunal for Rwanda (ICTR). The six-member tribunal, to be headed by a Senegalese lawyer, Laity Kama, was inaugurated in late June for a four-year term. It was reported that the tribunal intended to investigate allegations made against some 400 individuals (many of them resident outside of Rwanda) of direct involvement in the planning and execution of a series of crimes against humanity perpetrated in Rwanda during 1994. At a national level, preliminary hearings against an estimated 35,000 Rwandan nationals, imprisoned in Kigali on similar charges, began in early 1995, but were immediately suspended owing to lack of funds. In mid-1995 reports emerged of severely overcrowded conditions in Rwandan prisons, where diseases such as malaria, pneumonia and dysentery were resulting in as many as 300 deaths each week. Meanwhile, lack of finance and personnel had resulted in the virtual collapse of Rwanda's judicial system, and it was estimated that the majority of suspects had been imprisoned without formal charge. The prosecutor's office in Kigali also estimated that as many as 20% of prisoners could be innocent individuals denounced by others who intended to acquire their land and property. In October the supreme court was established by the transitional national assembly.

The ICTR began formal proceedings in late November 1995. The tribunal's first indictment, against eight unnamed individuals implicated in massacres committed on four sites in Kibuye between April and June 1994, was published in December. Exhumation of bodies at the sites was begun in January 1996, in order to assist the prosecutions. In the same month the ICTR cited three further suspects (two former mayors and a former cabinet minister) accused of involvement in massacres in Butare. The Belgian government, which had detained the suspects in mid-1995, agreed to co-operate fully in their extradition to face charges. However members of the Rwandan government have expressed frustration with the slow prosecution of individuals. Consequently, in February 1996, the prime minister announced the creation of special courts within the country's existing judicial system. Under these arrangements, Rwanda's chief supreme court prosecutor was to oversee investigations in each of the country's 10 districts, and establish three-member judicial panels in each district to consider cases. The latter were to be drawn from some 250 lay magistrates who were to receive a four-month legal training course. Additionally, 320 judicial police inspectors, all of whom have received a three-month training course, will compile dossiers on those detained on suspicion of having committed genocide. Newly established assessment commissions were to review possible detentions on the basis of available evidence.

International scepticism regarding the government's programme of refugee repatriation increased in early 1995, following a series of uncompromising initiatives to encourage the return of internally displaced Rwandans (including the interruption of food supplies to refugee camps), culminating in the forcible closure of the camps through military intervention. An attempt to dismantle the Kibeho camp in southern Rwanda, in late April, provoked widespread international condemnation after APR troops opened fire on refugees amid confusion arising from the activities of some hostile elements within the camp and a sudden attempt by large numbers of refugees to break through the military cordon. While the government stated that the number of fatalities (many as a result of suffocation) from the ensuing panic was 338, independent witnesses estimated as many as 5,000 deaths. The report of an international enquiry into the incident, published in mid-May, concluded that the massacre had not been premeditated but that the armed forces had employed excessive force in their response to the situation. The commission also estimated the number of fatalities to be far in excess of the official total.

In August 1995, in response to requests made by the Rwandan government, the UN Security Council voted to suspend the arms embargo to Rwanda (imposed against the previous administration in May 1994) for one year, in order to allow the government to safeguard against the threat of a military offensive to be launched by Hutu extremists encamped in neighbouring countries. In April 1996 the UN Security Council had unanimously voted to investigate alleged illegal shipments of weapons to the former Forces armées rwandaises (FAR) in eastern Zaire. Under the August UN directive, weapons could be purchased only for use by the APR and could be imported only through specified entry points. In September the Security Council adopted Resolution 1013, which created a commission of enquiry to examine allegations that ex-FAR personnel were receiving military training to destabilize Rwanda; to investigate reports of illegal arms-trafficking throughout the Great Lakes region; and to recommend ways to end this trade. Despite this action, weapons were reported to be readily available in the region, since a number of nations, such as Bulgaria, the People's Republic of China, South Africa and Zaire (all of which were allegedly involved in the illegal arms trade), refused to co-operate with the UN commission of enquiry. As a result, the commission's final report failed to make any specific accusations regarding the countries involved. However, the commission's findings did implicate Zaire in an illegal arms sale, conducted in June 1994, whereby weapons were shipped from Seychelles to Goma for distribution to the former FAR. The Seychelles government, which co-operated fully with the commission of enquiry, denied any knowledge of the transaction. In March 1996 the Rwandan government urged the UN Security Council to increase its efforts to end regional arms-trafficking and to consider the imposition of diplomatic and other sanctions against governments that failed to co-operate with the commission of enquiry. Consequently, in April 1996, the UN Security Council adopted Resolution 1053, which urged all Central African states to observe the arms embargo against former FAR troops and to ensure that their territories were not used as a base for armed groups to launch cross-border raids into Rwanda. In June President Mobutu of Zaire agreed to authorize the deployment of UN monitors in eastern Zaire to record any violation of the arms embargo against the former FAR. Despite Mobutu's action, many Western observers remained convinced that Zaire would continue to be a major source of weapons for the former FAR.

In December 1995 the UN Security Council unanimously adopted Resolution 1029, which extended the mandate of UNAMIR until 8 March 1996. Under the terms of the mandate the UNAMIR contingent was reduced by one-third, leaving 1,200 troops and 200 military observers and staff to assist in the repatriation of Rwandan refugees from neighbouring countries. This resolution also adjusted UNAMIR's mandate, authorizing it to attempt actively to facilitate national reconciliation and to encourage refugees to repatriate voluntarily. In addition, UNAMIR was mandated henceforth to perform monitoring tasks to help to re-establish stability and to restore confidence in the Rwandan government. On 19 April 1996 the last member of the UN peace-keeping contingent left Rwanda. Many Rwandans remained critical of the UN's performance during and following the 1994 genocide, and welcomed the termination of UNAMIR operations. In April 1996 the Rwandan government accepted the establishment of a UN Office for Rwanda (UNOR), to comprise a special representative to the UN secretary-general, aided by five UN officials and a maximum of 12 local staff. The UNOR is expected to serve as a small co-ordinating, advocacy and advisory office, while the UNOR special representative will continue to co-ordinate UN activities in Rwanda and to facilitate the repatriation of Rwandan refugees.

By mid-August 1995 the security situation in refugee camps along the Zairean border had deteriorated to such an extent that the Zairean government initiated a programme of forcible repatriation. Some 15,000 Rwandans were deported in a number of days, prompting widespread international concern for their welfare. Later in the month in Geneva, at a meeting with UNHCR, the prime minister of Zaire, Kengo Wa Dondo, agreed to entrust the repatriation process to UNHCR officials until the end of 1995, after which time the Zairean government would resume the forcible return of all remaining refugees. In early September a formal agreement was concluded between UNHCR and the Zairean government for a more regulated and bilateral approach to the refugee crisis. An APR attack on the village of Kanama, near the border with Zaire, some days later, resulted in the deaths of more than 100 civilians (including the local mayor) and did little to reassure returning refugees of the safety of such an undertaking. The Rwandan minister of national defence, Maj.-Gen. Paul Kagame, attributed the atrocity to an exaggerated response by frustrated army elements to repeated anti-government activities in the area, perpetrated by armed militias from camps in Zaire. Kagame declared his intention to bring to justice those responsible for the massacre (separate government and military investigations into the incident were inaugurated during September) and later in the month, following a further meeting of representatives of UNHCR, Rwanda and Zaire in Geneva, further commitments were made by both governments to improve security conditions on both sides of the border. Following a subsequent APR attack on a suspected rebel base on the island of Iwawa, in Lake Kivu, in early November, a UN mission verified government claims that there had been no civilian casualties. The UN officials estimated the number of dead at 25, while Rwandan defence ministry sources reported the deaths of more than 100 militiamen, and the discovery of a large weapons cache, allegedly amassed in preparation for an attack on the mainland to be launched from Lake Kivu. (In June Amnesty International claimed that dealers based in the United Kingdom were organizing the illegal supply, to members of the former Rwandan armed forces and the Interahamwe militia based at camps in Zaire, of consignments of armaments purchased in Eastern Europe.) At a conference of the Great Lakes Countries, convened in Cairo, Egypt in late November, and attended by the presidents of Burundi, Rwanda, Uganda and Zaire and by a Tanzanian presidential envoy, the member nations recognized the need to disarm and demilitarize displaced groups within their borders that threatened the security of neighbouring nations. President Mobutu of Zaire also indicated (and in December confirmed) that the forcible return of remaining refugees in early 1996 was no longer a realistic objective. The conference also accepted the Rwandan president's assertion that the participation of UNAMIR forces in peace-keeping operations in Rwanda was no longer necessary, but urged the Rwandan government to accept the extension of a revised, three-month mandate for the forces to provide assistance in the refugee repatriation process.

During 1995 UNHCR assisted in the repatriation of 240,388 Rwandan refugees from neighbouring countries. The Rwandan authorities were reported to have detained a small number of these returnees, on suspicion that they had participated in the 1994 genocide or had committed other related crimes. Despite the large number of returnees, by February 1996 little progress had been made in repatriating displaced Rwandans who still remained in Zaire. A new initiative, endorsed by UNHCR, was launched early in that month. Zairean troops, deployed at the Kibumba camp in eastern Zaire, sought to encourage the return of refugees by dismantling the unofficial commercial zones that had been established in the camp. However, the difficulties of the initiative were further compounded by the publication in a French newspaper, at the end of February, of reports (based on alleged firsthand accounts) detailing violent acts of reprisal committed by the FPR against fleeing and returning refugees, which had claimed the lives of some 100,000 Hutus since April 1994. These allegations were strenuously denied by the Rwandan government, while UNHCR sources were unable to confirm or deny the alleged scale of the slaughter, owing to lack of evidence.

In March 1996 UNHCR estimated that there were 1,684,645 Rwandan refugees scattered throughout several countries in the region, including Zaire (with 1,057,350), Tanzania (531,016), Burundi (92,279) and Uganda (4,000). Concern regarding the security situation in Rwanda was cited as the single most important factor preventing the repatriation and resettlement of these refugees. During the course of 1996 more than 1.3m. refugees were repatriated, and by the end of that year the number of Rwandan refugees in neighbouring countries had fallen to 257,000. In particular, Tanzania, with the support of UNHCR, initiated a policy of forced repatriation of all Rwandan refugees. This provoked criticism from Amnesty International and Human Rights Watch, Africa, as UNHCR's charter states a commitment to voluntary repatriation, and many refugees moved further east into Tanzania as a result. However, these were turned back by the Tanzanian authorities, and by the end of 1996 an estimated 475,000 refugees had returned from that country to Rwanda. Within Rwanda itself, however, there were reported to be about 20,000 refugees from Zaire and Burundi. A programme for the Return of Qualified Rwandan Nationals (RQRN), sponsored by the EU, began in February 1996, with the aim of encouraging skilled Rwandan refugees to return home. As a result of the mass influx of refugees, the Rwandan government, together with the UN World Food Programme (WFP) and other relief agencies, distributed food aid to the returnees in an attempt to avert a humanitarian crisis. In August 1997 the WFP announced the completion of this distribution programme, and stated its intention to help to construct houses for the repatriated refugees. In late 1996, owing to the deterioration of the security situation in eastern Zaire, pressure for UN-sponsored international intervention in the region increased, and Canada agreed to lead an international military force with the dual aim of securing Goma airport and establishing a secure humanitarian corridor between Rwanda and Zaire. However, the subsequently high level of refugee repatriations rendered these arrangements unnecessary.

Political Dissension and Human Rights Issues

A political crisis emerged in August 1995, following an expression of dissatisfaction by Twagiramungu with the government's lack of adherence to the provisions of the Arusha accord regarding power-sharing. The prime minister also criticized the security forces' repeated recourse to violence in their management of the refugee crisis. Twagiramungu and four other ministers were subsequently replaced, and in a cabinet reshuffle in late August, Pierre Célestin Rwigyema of the MDR, the former minister of primary and secondary education, was named as the new prime minister. The new council of ministers contained representatives of both major ethnic groups and four political parties, largely dispelling fears that the government had rejected its former commitment to power-sharing. In Brussels, Belgium, in March 1996, Twagiramungu and Sendashonga announced the formation of a new party in exile, the Forces de résistance pour la démocratie (FRD), which advocates the return of Rwanda to the status of a UN trust territory, pending the resolution of its internal security difficulties.

The minister of justice, Marthe Mukamurenzi, left the government in September 1996, following allegations of financial impropriety. In the following February the speaker of the transitional national assembly, Juvénal Nkusi, was relieved of his duties following a vote of 'no confidence' in his leadership. In March 1997 a new speaker, Joseph Sebarenzi, was elected. A reshuffle of the council of ministers followed later in the month.

In September 1996 a report compiled by international human rights groups accused Hutu extremists of engaging in the systematic abuse of Tutsi women. The report urged the ICTR to investigate the allegations and prosecute those responsible, although by July 1997 only one such case had been brought. Hundreds of Rwandan civilians were killed by the APR, although after the repatriation of refugees from Tanzania and the DRC in late 1996 reports of such killings temporarily diminished. In early 1997 former FAR personnel began a campaign of political assassinations, killing a number of aid workers and UN monitors. This action prompted aid agencies to reduce the size of their operations and to confine their workers to Kigali. The Rwandan government doubled the size of its police force in response to UN demands that their patrols be accompanied. There have also been FAR attacks on schools, missionaries and witnesses to the ICTR. Both Amnesty International and the PHRO claim that the APR's response to this was revenge killing, resulting in the deaths of up to 3,000 civilians in three months. The Rwandan government initially rejected these claims, and later said that the figures given were exaggerations.

Rwanda has progressed slowly in bringing to justice the perpetrators of the 1994 genocide: according to the International Committee of the Red Cross, by mid-1997 73,000 prisoners were being held, many of them in connection with the massacres in 1994. (By early 1997 the ICTR had indicted 21 people, and started only one trial, while the Rwandan courts had tried more than 120 cases, of which more than 40 had resulted in death sentences.) A further report, published in July 1997, acknowledged that improvements had been made in several areas, but that the ICTR still had many problems to overcome, including matters involving the safety of witnesses and arrangements for defence representation. The Rwandan government has expressed determination to utilize its domestic legal system to try those accused of genocide.

REGIONAL RELATIONS

Rwandan–Tanzanian relations have been defined primarily by the presence of large numbers of Rwandan refugees in the north-west Tanzanian districts of Ngara and Kibondo. By August 1995 there were 421,000 refugees in the five camps that comprised the Benaco complex in Ngara District, and another 13,000 refugees in Kanembwa camp in Kibondo District. Despite repeated efforts by the two countries to encourage the repatriation of these refugees, only 13,060 of them returned to their homes in 1995, as the majority feared retributive violence from the FPR.

Rwandan–Kenyan relations have deteriorated since the 1994 genocide. The Kenyan president, Daniel arap Moi (who had been a personal friend of ex-president Habyarimana), had strenuously opposed the actions of the FPR. In addition, Moi was allegedly suspicious of Uganda's attempts to extend its influence in Central Africa by providing military and financial support to the FPR. After the events of April 1994, thousands of Rwandan Hutus, many of whom were accused of complicity in the organization of Tutsi massacres, sought refuge in Kenya. According to claims made by international human rights organizations (including Amnesty International and African Rights), these Rwandans subsequently travelled freely to Europe and to the DRC, and also arranged for illegal arms shipments to be made to the former FAR. Moi initially refused to co-operate with the ICTR, and threatened to arrest any tribunal member who came to Kenya. In October 1995, however, Moi, reacting to mounting international pressure, abandoned this uncompromising policy and urged the ICTR to broaden its mandate to include an investigation of the April 1994 attack on the aircraft which was transporting the Rwandan and Burundian presidents. Days later, Moi announced that Kenya would not shelter Rwandans who participated in the 1994 genocide. Later in the year, Kenyan police arrested dozens of Rwandan refugees in Nairobi, at least some of whom were being sought by the Rwandan authorities in connection with atrocities perpetrated in Rwanda during 1994. These actions, however, did little to improve relations between the two nations. Relations with Nairobi further deteriorated following attacks on Rwandan nationals in Kenya in early 1996. Finally, in June, the Kenyan ministry of foreign affairs ordered the closure of the Rwandan embassy and suspended diplomatic relations. As a result, Kenya became a safe haven for Rwandan refugees. However, diplomatic relations were restored in July 1997, and after this the Kenyan police launched operations in which Rwandan Hutus, suspected of participation in the 1994 genocide, were arrested.

Relations between Rwanda and Uganda have remained cordial, largely because of the good personal relationship between the Ugandan president, Lt-Gen. Yoweri Museveni, and the Rwandan vice-president and minister of national defence, Maj.-Gen. Paul Kagame (the latter had served in the Ugandan armed forces before taking command of the APR). In August 1995 Museveni undertook an official visit to Rwanda, during which he conferred with Kagame and other Rwandan officials, addressed the national transitional assembly, and spoke at public rallies in Gisenyi and Kigali. As a result of the visit, the two countries made commitments to enhance co-operation in the economic, social, cultural and security sectors, and to co-ordinate their positions at international forums, with regard to issues of common interest. Both nations also reaffirmed their commitment to the Organization for the Management and Development of the Kagera River Basin. In the months following Museveni's visit to Rwanda, there were numerous reports that the two nations had significantly increased their military co-operation. Although Uganda has rejected these allegations and asserted that there is no military alliance between the two countries, many observers remained convinced that President Museveni is seeking to impose stability on the Central African region by supporting the Tutsi, not only in Rwanda but also in Burundi. In August 1996 the Rwandan government announced that it would participate in the regional economic blockade of Burundi. Rwanda also took action to prevent Burundian Hutus from fleeing into the south-west of Rwanda.

Relations between Rwanda and the DRC began to deteriorate in early 1996, largely as a result of the threat posed by former FAR troops based in the eastern DRC. In early June 1996 nine central African states signed a non-aggression pact, but Rwanda refused to do so, and threatened to use force to prevent the former FAR from attacking Rwandan refugees in the DRC. It also began to provide support to insurgent forces in the DRC. However, relations between the two countries began to improve following the Rwanda government's formal recognition of the DRC regime in May 1997.

During 1995 and 1996 relations between Rwanda and France have continued to experience difficulty. However, both countries have remained committed to improving relations. In September 1995 President Bizimungu held talks with the French secretary of state for emergency humanitarian affairs, Xavier Emmanuelli, during his fact-finding mission to Rwanda. The two officials announced a commitment to co-operate in restructuring the judicial system. Emmanuelli also pledged aid for the rehabilitation of the health, education and agriculture sectors. In March 1996 the French government announced funding for several programmes, including the rehabilitation of the ministry of justice and the Ruhengeri hospital, the expansion of the electricity network in Kigali, a water purification programme for 20 towns and a food-provision scheme for the country's secondary-school system. In December of that year, an aid package of vital supplies was received from Israel, and in July 1997, two South African companies agreed to assist Rwanda in exploiting substantial reserves of methane in Lake Kivu.

The USA has remained committed to facilitating the process of national reconciliation and reconstruction in Rwanda. To this end, the US government provided an array of assistance to Kigali, during the 1994 and 1995 financial years, amounting to some US $557.6m. in assistance to various UN agencies, non-governmental organizations (NGO) and international bodies administering relief programmes in Rwanda. Two US department of justice prosecutors and four US investigators were also assigned to assist the work of the ICTR in Rwanda.

Economy

FRANÇOIS MISSER

Based on an earlier article by FILIP REYNTJENS

Rwanda has two main physical handicaps to economic development: the extreme population density and the distance from the sea. The population problem, with its concomitant effect on food resources, is aggravated by soil erosion, caused by leaching and other natural factors. The 1977–78 and 1982–86 Development Plans gave priority to population resettlement in unoccupied areas, in an effort to restrict the exodus to the towns from the countryside (where some 90% of the population resided prior to the ethnic violence and associated refugee problems that began in 1994—see Recent History).

In 1995, according to estimates by the World Bank, Rwanda's gross national product (GNP), measured at average 1993–95 prices, was US $1,128m., equivalent to $180 per head. Rwanda's level of GNP per head is one of the lowest in the world. During 1985–95, it was estimated, GNP per head decreased, in real terms, at an average annual rate of 5.0%. Rwanda's gross domestic product (GDP) increased, in real terms, by an annual average of 1.1% in 1980–93. During 1994, it was estimated, Rwanda's GDP contracted by some 57%, from $1,359m to $585m. In 1995 a 25% recovery was recorded in comparison with the catastrophic results of 1994. The government's three-year programme of rehabilitation and reconciliation aims to restore the economy to the level of its achievements for 1990, by 1998. In 1985–93 the average annual rate of inflation was 6.4%, and consumer prices increased by 12.4% in 1993.

AGRICULTURE

The agricultural sector accounted for about 41% of Rwanda's GDP in 1993, and engaged an estimated 91% of the labour force (mainly at subsistence level in 1994). Agriculture's share of GDP was estimated to have increased to 51% in 1994 and then decreased to 37% in 1995. About 95% of the total value of agricultural production is provided by subsistence crops. While these have failed to meet the needs of the population, the annual increase in production of subsistence crops broadly kept pace with the population growth until 1977. Since then, the area of land annually made available for subsistence crops has increased only marginally and, moreover, crop yields are declining in many areas, owing to erosion and the traditional intensive cultivation methods used. (The problem of erosion was exacerbated during 1990–94 by the felling, by displaced Rwandans, of trees for timber and charcoal.) This led, in the late 1980s, to increasing strains on food production and consequently to severe food shortages. Attempts to increase the yield of small farm plots have included a recent initiative to cultivate climbing beans. In late 1989 and early 1990 many parts of the country, in particular the south, were affected by famine, following drought and crop failure. Subsequently, the government had recourse to emergency food aid to avert widespread starvation.

The principal food crops are bananas (the single most important, with production of about 2.6m. tons in 1995), sweet potatoes, cassava, potatoes, beans, sorghum, rice, maize and peas, in descending order of importance. The major cash crop is coffee, exports of which provided 7,209.8m. Rwanda francs (60.2% of total export earnings) in 1991, compared with 12,569m. Rwanda francs (82% of total export earnings) in 1986. In dollar terms, revenues decreased from US $85m. in 1988 to $42m. in 1993 and to $17m. in 1994. However, a rise in world coffee prices and an increase in production contributed to receipts of $48m. (78% of total export earnings) in 1995. Revenue from coffee fluctuates considerably, and in the late 1980s declined sharply because of the combined effects of a low level of production, falling international prices and the weakness of the US dollar in relation to the currencies of Rwanda's other major trading partners. Even before the catastrophic political events of 1994, it had seemed unlikely that Rwanda would benefit from the resurgence in world coffee prices at the end of 1993. The volume of production had been dwindling for several years, partly owing to price instability. Reduced revenues had also forced farmers to abandon the purchase and introduction of pesticides and fertilizers. In addition, during 1993 the Seventh-day Adventist church had urged adherents to destroy coffee plants, having denounced the plant as a 'drug'. The impact of the political and humanitarian crisis was considerable and production declined from 28,135 metric tons in 1992–93 to 1,994 tons in 1993–94. Output for 1994–95 was 21,041 tons, equivalent to some 50%–60% of annual production in the late 1980s. Unfavourable climatic conditions and a shortage of manpower led to a further decrease, to 15,667 tons, in 1995–96. According to government forecasts, annual output is unlikely to exceed 22,500 tons by 1998. Indeed, the government has prioritized agricultural diversification in its three-year rehabilitation and reconciliation programme. In 1995, however, the price payable to growers for parchment coffee was increased, reflecting the government's continuing commitment to provide incentives for producers.

Prior to 1994, the government had attempted to diversify the crops grown for export through the Office des cultures industrielles du Rwanda (OCIR), established in 1964. This concentrated its efforts on tobacco, cotton, pyrethrum, quinquina, forestry and, pre-eminently, tea. Rwanda's output of made tea has increased steadily in recent years, rising from 2,522 metric tons in 1972 to 8,669 tons in 1984, and to 13,546 tons in 1991. Exports of tea earned 2,796.6m. Rwanda francs, or 23.4% of total export earnings, in 1991, and the proportion increased to 32.3% in 1992. However, production declined to 10,493 tons in 1993, and export earnings decreased to US $16m. (equivalent to 23.5% of the value of total exports), following the occupation of the lucrative Mulindi plantations by forces of the Front patriotique rwandais (FPR). In 1993–94 production collapsed to just 4,902 tons, largely owing to the adverse effects of the war and to the former government's removal to Zaire of the Cyangugu tea factory. Production in 1994–95 increased to 5,346 tons, still considerably below the government's target for 1998 of 13,500 tons (1991 production levels). In November 1994 the European Union (EU) allocated ECU 20m. to Rwanda for the rehabilitation of the coffee and tea sectors. The four tea plantations of Mulindi, Shagasha, Kitabi and Mata (which together account for 80% of national production) were expected to be among the first beneficiaries of these funds. The African Development Bank (ADB) also pledged $2.2m. for the rehabilitation of export agriculture. By November 1995, however, the EU had disbursed only $6.4m. of the allocated funds. An agricultural diversification programme was aided by the EU. In addition, the European Development Fund (EDF), together with the Food and Agriculture Organization of the United Nations (FAO) and the World Bank, is involved in aiding the creation of local farming communes (*paysannats*). In late 1993 the International Development Association (IDA), an affiliate of the World Bank, approved a $15m. loan to help finance agricultural research projects and the transformation of existing research institutes in Rwanda. Prior to the political events of 1994, it was envisaged that the full implementation of the research development programme would generate an annual increase in the sector's growth of some 4%. Rwanda's agriculture was expected to benefit from the nitrogenous fertilizers which can be processed from the country's resources of methane gas. In 1987 Socigaz, a joint venture between Rwanda and Zaire (now the Democratic Republic of the Congo—DRC), was established to exploit this commodity. The success of a proposal to diversify agricultural exports through the sale of 'karamasenge' bananas to Europe was likely to be dependent on the success of a marketing campaign to promote the superior quality of the fruit over more competitively priced and more accessible central American fruits.

By July 1994 the sector was in extreme crisis and the majority of the country's livestock had disappeared (although some cattle were introduced by refugees returning from Uganda). Limited livestock-vaccination programmes were undertaken by the FAO and smaller agencies in the north-east, but the main problem remains the overstocking of cattle (and the consequent environmental strain) in this region, while livestock numbers are hopelessly insufficient elsewhere in the country. Food crops were also decimated. An FAO-World Food Programme report estimated that food production in 1994 amounted to just 45% of the 1993 yield. It was also estimated that hundreds of hectares of natural forests had been damaged by displaced persons and that support systems for agriculture were almost completely destroyed. Food aid requirements (mainly grains and pulses) were estimated at more than 150,000 metric tons in 1994 and 116,000 tons in 1995. During the two seasons following the war, 10,000 tons of bean, maize, vegetable and other seeds, together with 700,000 hoes, were distributed to some 690,000 households. It was estimated that 62% of farmers received seeds, while tools were distributed to some 72%. A conference of potential donors, sponsored by the United Nations Development Programme (UNDP), was convened in Geneva during January 1995, at which pledges of financial assistance totalling US $587m. were made, including a substantial share for agriculture recovery programmes. By the end of 1995 pledges amounted to $1,260m., of which $189.5m. was to be allocated to the agriculture sector. At the same time, however, disbursements amounted to just $28.6m., slowed, in part, by the suspension of aid channelled through the government in the months following the April 1995 massacre of displaced persons by security forces at the Kibeho refugee camp. Disputes involving land tenure were still common in mid-1997, and discouraged farmers from making long-term investments. However, by the end of 1996, part of the $500m. pledged to facilitate the return of refugees had been allocated to basic rural and agricultural infrastructures. A programme of reform was also announced at this time. The government intends to encourage a system of population regroupment known as *Imidugu* (grouped habitat), which is believed to reduce social and economic costs by enabling shared use of expensive items and the maximization of water supplies.

INDUSTRY AND MINING

The industrial sector follows the usual pattern for the less developed African states, and food-based industries, such as the processing of coffee and tea, a sugar factory, a brewery, a cigarette factory, etc., predominate. In 1992 the Netherlands brewer Heineken invested 1,000m. Rwanda francs in its Rwandan subsidiary BRALIRWA–SOBOLIRWA, which markets soft drinks in Rwanda and quadrupled its turnover between 1988–92. In late 1992 the Régie Sucrière de Kibuye sugar plant acquired new equipment which it hoped would help to treble its output for 1990. Otherwise, before April 1994, there were two small textile concerns, small-scale chemical and engineering works, cement and match factories, a plant producing pyrethrum extract and various other enterprises based on transistors, sandals and plastics, agricultural tools, stoneware and printing. The OVIBAR factory produced banana wine and liquors. In 1993 manufacturing accounted for an estimated 14% of GDP while in the same year industry accounted for 21% of GDP.

By July 1994 the country's political turmoil had brought the sector to a standstill. Factories and plants which had been virtually paralysed by power shortages earlier in the year were looted, destroyed or abandoned. By early October 1994, the BRALIRWA plant had resumed production. In 1994 manufacturing accounted for an estimated 3% of GDP, while industry provided 9% of GDP in the same year. In 1995, although only 40% of enterprises had resumed production, manufacturing was estimated to have recovered sufficiently to provide 12.5% of GDP, with industry accounting for 16.3%. Government officials claimed that the slow disbursement of some US $72.9m. in international donor aid, allocated to the trade and industry sectors (only $5.4m. had been activated by the end of 1995), together with competition from tax-free imports of goods such as soap and plastics, had seriously hindered the recovery of the sector.

Cassiterite (a tin-bearing ore) is Rwanda's principal mineral resource (exports of tin ores and concentrates were worth 320m. Rwanda francs in 1991), followed by wolframite (a tungsten-bearing ore) and there are small, known quantities of beryl, colombo-tantalite, and gold. While tin concentrates (about 1,500 tons) were the third-largest export earner in 1985, high transport costs and the sharp decline in world tin prices left the sector virtually inactive in the late 1980s. At the end of 1985 Géomines, the Belgian company with a 51% shareholding in the Rwandan mining company SOMIRWA, went into liquidation; SOMIRWA itself was declared insolvent a few months later. A tin-processing plant built at a cost of 1,000m. Rwanda francs in Karuruma near Kigali had never operated at more than 20% of capacity, and the profitability of SOMIRWA's other operations had also been poor. Plans for other foundries were consequently suspended. Despite the insolvent state of the company, the government's annual maintenance costs for SOMIRWA installations have continued to exceed 70m. Rwanda francs. In 1992 the Régie Minière mining concern was established, with state involvement, and began to exploit the SOMIRWA mines in an artisanal capacity. However, the company was reported to be operating on an annual deficit of some 50m. Rwanda francs, and in 1996 the government announced its plans to privatize it. From 1992 the SOMIRWA smelter resumed activity for six months of the year, processing cassiterite supplied by the ALICOM gold concern. Some efforts were made with EU support to stimulate the artisanal tin sector, and the UNDP provided some funds towards an increase in gold production. Mining activities were resumed at a modest level in 1988 by artisans regrouped in COOPIMAR, an independent co-operative offering managerial and commercial support. In 1992 a new company, Saphirs du Rwanda, began exploration for sapphires.

Another important mineral to be exploited is natural gas, which was discovered beneath Lake Kivu on the border with the DRC. Reserves of an estimated 57,000m. cu m (about one-half of which are in the DRC) are thought to be among the largest in the world. Two pilot plants, funded by the EU, produce gas, but here again the small size of the potential market casts doubt on the likely profitability of large-scale processing. However, in 1993 the national electricity and gas company, Electrogaz, was hoping to receive Belgian funding for a programme to increase its daily output of gas from 5,000 cu m to 25,000 cu m. Government plans to privatize Electrogaz have attracted interest from Franco-Canadian and Franco-Belgian consortia.

POWER AND COMMUNICATIONS

Rwanda's electricity needs are supplied almost entirely from hydroelectric sources, as the land relief is ideal for power generation. According to studies undertaken by the Rwanda-Burundi-DRC tripartite organization, Energie des Pays des Grands Lacs (EGL), the Ruzizi river alone offers a total 500 MW potential, of which only a fraction is being used currently. Rwanda imported only 4% of its electricity in 1977 but, with the connection of the national supply to the Mururu station on the Ruzizi river in Zaire in 1978, and after the closure in 1979 of all but one of seven thermal plants, Zaire provided more than one-half of Rwanda's electricity in 1979. This proportion increased until the opening of the Mukungwa station (with a capacity of 12 MW) in 1981. By 1980 about one-tenth of the country's estimated hydroelectric potential of 200 MW had been harnessed. In 1977 Rwanda, Burundi and Tanzania formed an organization to develop the water, power and mineral resources of the Kagera river basin, with financial support from the UNDP, and in 1982 Rwanda and Tanzania decided to construct a hydroelectric power station (60 MW) at the Rusumo falls on the Kagera river. Work has begun on the Mukungwa-II hydroelectric power station, supported by a $24m. loan from Japan, while work on the Ruzizi-II plant (a joint venture with the DRC and Burundi, with a maximum generating capacity of 42 MW) is nearing completion. In the meantime Rwanda continues to import more than half (54% in 1990) of its total electricity requirements. In early 1994 the European Investment Bank, together with French and German credit institutions, pledged more than $1m. to help rehabilitate the Ntaruka power station, which had been damaged by FPR guerrillas, and the work, to be carried out by a French company, had begun in 1997. By October 1994, as a result of the catastrophic sequence of political events, the Mukungwa power station alone was supplying Kigali, Ruhengeri and Gisenyi with insufficient amounts of electricity. By early 1995, however, following the EU's allocation of ECU 5m.

for the rehabilitation of the power sector, the situation had improved vastly and Butare, Gitarama and all areas of Kigali were receiving adequate power supplies. Further reconstruction enabled the Gihira and Gisenyi power stations and also the Gatsata thermal plant to resume production. A new 15-MW diesel power station, supplied by Canada, was installed by January 1996, but one-third of the country's energy requirements were still not being met. In April 1997, it was announced that a feasibility study would be conducted into the possibility of linking the power grids in Rwanda and Uganda in order to lessen Rwanda's deficit. Canada had offered some financial support and the World Bank was seeking other donors. Also in early 1996 the government announced partial privatization plans for the national electricity company, ELECTROGAZ, which was to entrust management of network exploitation to private interests. Similar divestment was envisaged for the national water company. Reserves of peat are being assessed as an additional source of energy, mainly for homes and small factories in rural areas. Since the mid-1980s the Rwandan government has also expressed its commitment to the development of biogas in the rural areas.

Internal communications in Rwanda are operated almost exclusively along the relatively well-developed road system (13,173 km in 1990), as there are no railways nor navigable waterways (except Lake Kivu). Asphalted highways link Rwanda with Burundi, Uganda, the DRC and Tanzania. They also connect the principal towns (Kibuye remaining the only district capital without direct access to the asphalted road system). Tarmac roads extend to just over 1,000 km, which, given the small size of the country, is one of the highest densities in Africa. EU funding for the surfacing of the 91-km Gitarama–Kibuye road, secured before April 1994, was subsequently delayed for either political or logistical reasons. Rwanda's external trade is heavily dependent on the ports of Mombasa, Dar es Salaam and Matadi, and about 80% of Rwandan exports and imports pass through Uganda and Kenya. Insecurity caused by the war in the north of Rwanda led to the closure of the northern transport 'corridor' through Uganda. With the Gatuna and Kagitumba roads unavailable, most traffic had to be diverted to the difficult and unreliable route through Tanzania. In 1992 several projects had been approved by the EU and the World Bank to improve road links between eastern Zaire and western Uganda, hoping to facilitate the passage of Rwandan trade across the Zairean border, and thereby bypass the troubled border with Uganda. Following the FPR victory in July 1994, however, the northern transport 'corridor' was immediately reopened. In January 1997 the EU approved funding to upgrade the main roads in and around Kigali. Feasibility studies have been discussed for a railway network to link Uganda, Rwanda, Burundi and Tanzania. Prior to the escalation of hostilities in April 1994, a number of international airlines, most prominently Sabena and Air France, operated services to Kigali, while the small national carrier, Air Rwanda (scheduled for privatization), operated domestic passenger and cargo services and international cargo flights to Burundi, Kenya, Tanzania, Uganda, the DRC and destinations in Europe. Only Sabena has resumed flights to Kigali since the FPR took power in July 1994, although the airport is to be upgraded to meet international standards with the aid of the EU.

DEVELOPMENT PLANNING

The DRC, Burundi and Rwanda, the members of the Economic Community of the Great Lakes Countries (CEPGL), agreed to form a joint development bank in 1978 and to co-operate on the development of a transport system and the construction of a hydroelectric power station (the Ruzizi-II project) on the Rwanda-DRC border, the exploitation of methane gas deposits beneath Lake Kivu and the promotion of a fishing industry. The bank was formally established in 1980, with its headquarters at Goma, in the DRC. Since the change of regime in the DRC, all the CEPGL states have expressed their desire for continuing regional co-operation.

A severe drought in 1984 resulted in poor harvests, which, in conjunction with transport disruptions in Uganda, greatly increased the cost of Rwandan imports and penalized exports. This prompted President Habyarimana, in April 1984, to initiate a programme of 'rigour and austerity', which led to the suspension of many non-essential projects. This policy was maintained and intensified dramatically at the end of 1989, following successive years of rapidly declining export revenue and poor harvests.

In 1986 a major project was launched to improve rural water supplies in the Lava district. It was to cost an estimated US $47m., and was to be financed mainly by the World Bank, the European Community (EC, now the EU) and the Arab Bank for Economic Development in Africa (BADEA). The water was required for an area rich in agricultural potential, where the existing supply systems had fallen into disrepair. A second project, involving the construction of new transmission mains in order to rehabilitate and extend existing supply systems, was under way in 1987, and was expected to take some four years to reach completion. This project, which was to cost more than $70m., was to receive initial funding from the ADB, the IDA, the BADEA and the Rwandan government. Further loans were expected to be forthcoming from the French government's Caisse centrale de coopération économique, the Swiss and Austrian governments and the UNDP. By the end of 1988 more than 70% of the population had access to safe water.

In 1986 a new international airport was opened at Kigali. Built at a cost of 3,500m. Rwanda francs, the new airport has an expanded capacity to serve up to 500,000 passengers per year. In August of the same year a scheme to modernize the country's telecommunications system was initiated, with financial assistance to be provided by a number of international organizations. The total cost was estimated at US $45m., and work was expected to continue until the year 2000. A satellite ground station began operation in 1987, providing direct automatic telephone and telex links with the rest of the world.

Road-building programmes have been accelerated, in order to solve the problems of transport through Kenya and Uganda. New roadways to Tanzania have been constructed, and the major roads leading to Kenya have been upgraded. The main roads to Uganda (Kayonza–Kagitumba and Kigali–Gatuna) were upgraded between 1988–90.

Improvement in the performance of the public sector has been a more recent concern. A three-year project for its restructuring and the enhancement of its planning capacity has been funded by a 'soft' loan of US$7.4m. from the IDA and a grant of $2.5m. from the UNDP. In 1991 the IDA committed substantial credits towards the reform of the primary school sector ($23m.) and family planning ($15.6m.).

The government has sought, unsuccessfully, to limit the overall budget deficit, which reached 19.2% of GDP in 1993, compared with 9% in 1989, despite an 11% increase in tax revenue and a 25% decline in capital expenditure until 1992 (project implementation slowed owing to escalating hostilities), and notwithstanding the government's failure to finance adequately the social contingency fund agreed under the terms of its adjustment programme. Budget expenditure increased in order to finance the war and internal security, and to support producer prices for coffee. The situation deteriorated further in 1993, with revenues declining by an estimated 6% while expenditure increased by an estimated 5%. As a consequence domestic and external arrears accumulated and the cost of debt-servicing increased from 13.3% of the value of exports and services in 1988 to an estimated 20.2% for 1992. In 1992 the deficit on the current account of the balance of payments was estimated at 21% of GDP. By the end of 1993 Rwanda's total external debt was US $910.1m., of which $835.8m. was long-term public debt. The debt outstanding and disbursed in that year was equivalent to almost 60% of GDP, compared with 16.3% in 1980 and 32.1% in 1990. By the end of October 1993 foreign reserves were estimated to be insufficient to sustain imports for one week.

The overall budget deficit amounted to 16% of annual GDP by the end of 1994, and to 12.5% by the end of 1995. Furthermore, the high level of military expenditure (33% of the total) in the national budget was a matter of concern for donors, particularly when compared with the share allocated to social sectors, which declined from 38% to 18% between 1985 and 1995. At the end of 1994 Rwanda's total external debt was US $954m., of which $905m. was long-term public debt. One year later, the country's total external debt exceeded $1,000m. (including $73m. in arrears), equivalent to 91% of the country's annual GDP. Scheduled debt-service obligations were equivalent to 46% of the value of exports of goods and non-factor services by late 1995.

Rwanda's heavy dependence on foreign assistance (equivalent to as much as 90% of public investment in recent years) has made the economy vulnerable to civil and political instability. By the end of 1995 external assistance was equivalent to 172.5% of imports, or US $56 per capita. Of the $587m. pledged by donors at the UNDP-sponsored conference convened in Geneva in January 1995, only $69m. had been disbursed by June, largely as a result of the Kibeho refugee camp massacre and the government's failure to embrace a broader political and ethnic base. In that month, however, the EU and other donors began resuming aid disbursements, and subsequent pledges brought the total amount to US $1,260m., of which $404m. (32%) had been spent by the end of 1995. With such transfers, by the end of 1995, foreign reserves increased sufficiently to sustain 3.7 months of imports, compared with 1.3 months in 1994. Delays to aid disbursements were not only prompted by security issues, but also by disagreements between the World Bank and the government over the assignment of a procurement of commodities and technical assistance under the World Bank Emergency Recovery Credit. Other delaying factors were the government's limited capacity to absorb aid, due to its own limited technical and administrative staff and its unwillingness to accept foreign technical assistance. In June 1996, at a second donors' conference held in Geneva, additional funds of $617m. were pledged, although effectively, according to some participants at the meeting, the new money made available amounted to just $240m. Indeed, the EU attached very stringent conditions for the disbursement of its funds, which were unlikely to be fulfilled by the government in the short term. Such conditions included appropriate measures for the repatriation of the refugees in Zaire and in Tanzania, and the improvement of the judicial system. In late 1996 accusations were raised that external aid had been used by the Habyarimana government to purchase weapons. It was also alleged that bank transfers, again used to purchase weapons, had been allowed, even during the genocide.

In 1995, mainly as a result of external assistance funds, a surplus on the current account of the balance of payments of US $65m. was registered. However, government sources anticipate an annual deficit of $197m. by 1998.

FOREIGN TRADE

In April 1976 Rwanda's economy came almost to a standstill as the result of a blockade imposed by President Amin of Uganda in a dispute with neighbouring Kenya. Amin's ban on heavy vehicles from neighbouring countries from using Uganda's roads in 1977, added to rising petrol prices, led to further hardship and strengthened the government's determination to find alternative outlets. An air cargo service, used in 1977 and 1978 to move stocks of coffee, was found to be scarcely more expensive than land transport and appreciably more reliable. The complete closure of the border from February to May 1979, caused by the fighting in Uganda, again severely disrupted trade and, as a result, stockpiles of coffee and tea rose to unprecedented levels, while serious shortages of petroleum and cement were experienced. Road transport on routes through Uganda was further disrupted by civil disorder during 1984 and 1985, and in 1986 a series of major initiatives was taken in order to assure Rwanda's vital trade links through Uganda. The October 1990 guerrilla invasion again demonstrated the extreme vulnerability of Rwanda's geographical position. Both trade and road communications with Uganda and Kenya virtually ceased as a result of the hostilities. The FPR victory in July 1994 improved this situation considerably and the Ugandan border, with ready access to the port of Mombasa, was reopened immediately.

Rwanda has long been experiencing a trade deficit, which stood at US $69m. in 1986 and deteriorated in 1987 to the extent that it exceeded the total of export earnings, which covered only 36% of imports (17.6% in 1993). This imbalance appears unlikely to be rectified in the foreseeable future (despite an increase in world coffee prices), owing to war damage inflicted on the economic infrastructure, the death and displacement of a vast number of the working population. In 1994 coffee production amounted to just 7% of the 1993 total whereas the production of tea represented only 43% of the previous year's crop. In 1995 the situation improved considerably, with output of coffee and tea at 75% and 50% of 1993 production levels, respectively. However, the trade deficit for 1995 was estimated at $173m. (or $250m., taking imports and exports of non-factor services into account). Export earnings covered 26% of imports, compared with 6.9% in 1994 and 43% in 1985. However, hopes have been expressed that the restoration of peace might facilitate the implementation of a free-trade zone for Burundi and Rwanda (as envisaged by Presidents Ndadaye and Habyarimana in October 1993) to encourage the bilateral exchange of goods and services and to enhance the sales of Rwandan cement and Burundian glass in the respective neighbouring country. As well as increased investment in cash crops, the government's three-year rehabilitation programme also envisages the creation of free export zones to promote trade by 1998. Liberalization of the coffee sector and the foreign exchange regime are also planned during 1996–98.

According to statistics presented by the Belgian office of foreign trade, Rwanda also exported 538m. Belgian francs (some US $18m.) of precious stones and minerals in 1992, an amount which decreased to 523m. Belgian francs in 1993 and 133m. in 1994. Mining experts have suggested that these revenues, which do not feature in official Rwandan statistics, are derived from the re-export of (possibly smuggled) Zairean gold.

STRUCTURAL ADJUSTMENT

Following negotiations that lasted for over a year, an agreement on structural adjustment between the Rwandan government and the IMF was announced in November 1990. Clearly, continued insecurity resulting from the war and its resultant economic set-backs were expected to hinder the initial implementation of the agreement, whose provisions included a devaluation of 40%, the introduction of a more liberal system of import licensing, the increase of import taxes, other tax changes (including the increase of sales tax), the suppression, except for monopolies, of profit-margin control, a suspension of the advantageous clauses of the Investment Code, and new credit and interest rate policies. Contrary to many other agreements of this kind, it imposes no significant cut-backs in public sector employment, and health and education spending are left virtually untouched. However, purchasing power was severely diminished as the result of increased consumer prices. In 1991 substantial international financial aid for the programme was pledged, amounting to more than US $170m., including $46m. from the EU, $41m. from the IMF, $25m. from the USA and $17m. from Belgium.

One area of concern for the government is the low level of fiscal revenue, which amounted to just 7% of GDP in 1995, compared with 12% in 1990, and which was equivalent to only 36% of total expenditure. In the 1996–98 three-year programme the government aims to curtail public expenditure. One of the challenges for the new administration will be the application of stricter budgetary control and greater discipline in this area. The former prime minister, Faustin Twagiramungu, and the former minister of the interior, Seth Sendashonga, who left the government in August 1995, claimed that, since the FPR victory, the ministry of defence has withdrawn as much as US $3m. from the public treasury without providing the ministry of finance with a detailed explanation of the money's intended use. Other problems facing the present government include the rationalization of the fiscal administration, the prioritization of long-term development expenditures and the restructuring, and in some cases privatization, of state-owned companies. By mid-1996 the administration had announced its intention to reform the taxation system by abolishing tax exemptions previously extended to new companies, and by increasing measures to suppress practices such as under-invoicing of import bills and smuggling, although a new tax on turnover provoked much criticism, including a strike, as companies wanted the government to return to the previous tax on profits. It was hoped that annual state receipts would increase from 22,500m. to 40,800m. Rwanda francs by 1998.

Statistical Survey

Source (unless otherwise stated): Office rwandais d'information, BP 83, Kigali; tel. 75724.

Area and Population

AREA, POPULATION AND DENSITY

Area (sq km)	26,338*
Population (census results)	
15–16 August 1978	4,830,984
15 August 1991†	
Males	3,487,189
Females	3,677,805
Total	7,164,994
Density (per sq km) at 1991 census	272.0†

* 10,169 sq miles.

† Provisional results. The revised total is 7,142,755 (density 271.2 per sq km).

PREFECTURES (1991 census)

	Area (sq km)	Population*	Density (per sq km)
Butare	1,830	765,910	418.5
Byumba	4,897	779,365	159.2
Cyangugu	2,226	517,550	232.5
Gikongoro	2,192	462,635	211.1
Gisenyi	2,395	728,365	304.1
Gitarama	2,241	849,285	379.0
Kibungo	4,134	647,175	156.5
Kibuye	1,320	472,525	358.0
Kigali	3,251	921,050	355.2
Kigali-Ville		233,640	
Ruhengeri	1,762	765,255	434.3
Total	26,338	7,142,755	271.2

* Source: UN, *Demographic Yearbook*.

PRINCIPAL TOWNS (population at 1978 census)

Kigali (capital)	117,749	Ruhengeri	16,025
Butare	21,691	Gisenyi	12,436

BIRTHS AND DEATHS (UN estimates, annual averages)

	1980–85	1985–90	1990–95
Birth rate (per 1,000)	50.4	45.1	44.1
Death rate (per 1,000)	18.6	16.6	16.7

Source: UN, *World Population Prospects: The 1994 Revision*.

Expectation of life (census results, years at birth, 1978): males 45.1; females 47.7.

ECONOMICALLY ACTIVE POPULATION
(persons aged 14 years and over, official estimates at January 1989)

	Males	Females	Total
Agriculture, hunting, forestry and fishing	1,219,586	1,612,972	2,832,558
Mining and quarrying	4,652	40	4,692
Manufacturing	32,605	12,483	45,088
Electricity, gas and water	2,445	116	2,561
Construction	37,674	563	38,237
Trade, restaurants and hotels	61,169	18,857	80,026
Transport, storage and communications	6,796	536	7,332
Financing, insurance, real estate and business services	2,202	926	3,128
Community, social and personal services	89,484	30,537	120,021
Activities not adequately defined	5,392	4,021	9,413
Total employed	1,462,005	1,681,051	3,143,056

Source: ILO, *Yearbook of Labour Statistics*.

Mid-1995 (estimates, '000 persons): Agriculture, etc. 3,853; Total labour force 4,219 (Source: FAO, *Production Yearbook*).

Agriculture

PRINCIPAL CROPS ('000 metric tons)

	1993	1994	1995
Maize	74	60	71
Sorghum	109	85*	72
Potatoes	204	149	150*
Sweet potatoes*	1,150	800	1,100
Cassava (Manioc)*	300	150	250
Yams*	8	4	4
Taro (Coco yam)*	62	20	30
Dry beans	130*	120*	118
Dry peas*	18	12	12
Groundnuts (in shell)	12	8	8
Plantains*	2,900	2,600	2,600
Coffee (green)†	29	2	22
Tea (made)	10†	5†	5*

* FAO estimate(s). † Unofficial figure(s).

Source: FAO, *Production Yearbook*.

LIVESTOCK ('000 head)

	1993	1994	1995
Cattle	300*	454	465
Pigs*	100	90	80
Sheep*	300	280	250
Goats*	980	950	920

* FAO estimate(s).

Source: FAO, *Production Yearbook*.

LIVESTOCK PRODUCTS (FAO estimates, '000 metric tons)

	1993	1994	1995
Beef and veal	12	10	10
Goat meat	3	3	3
Pig meat	2	2	2
Other meat	11	11	10
Cows' milk	85	80	80
Goats' milk	14	14	14
Poultry eggs	2.0	2.0	2.0
Cattle hides	1.7	1.5	1.5

Source: FAO, *Production Yearbook*.

Forestry

ROUNDWOOD REMOVALS ('000 cubic metres, excluding bark)

	1990	1991	1992
Sawlogs, veneer logs and logs for sleepers	20	20	60
Other industrial wood*	208	208	208
Fuel wood	5,353	5,392	5,392*
Total	5,581	5,620	5,660

* FAO estimate(s).

1993–94: Figures assumed to be unchanged since 1992.

Source: FAO, *Yearbook of Forest Products*.

SAWNWOOD PRODUCTION
('000 cubic metres, including railway sleepers)

	1990	1991	1992
Total	8	8	36

1993–94: Figure assumed to be unchanged since 1992.
Source: FAO, *Yearbook of Forest Products*.

Fishing

(FAO estimates, '000 metric tons, live weight)

	1993	1994	1995
Total catch (freshwater fishes)	3.6	3.5	3.3

Source: FAO, *Yearbook of Fishery Statistics*.

Mining*

(metric tons, unless otherwise indicated)

	1992	1993	1994
Tin concentrates	500†‡	500§	200§
Tungsten concentrates‖	175†	175	30

* Figures refer to the metal content of ores and concentrates.
† Estimate.
‡ Source: Metallgesellschaft AG (Frankfurt).
§ Source: *World Metal Statistics*.
‖ Source: US Bureau of Mines.
Source: UN, *Industrial Commodity Statistics Yearbook*.
Natural gas: about 1 million cubic metres per year.

Industry

SELECTED PRODUCTS

	1989	1990	1991
Beer ('000 hectolitres)	717	592	915
Soft drinks ('000 hectolitres)	161	130	101
Cigarettes (million)	552	290	331
Footwear ('000 pairs)	32	22	24
Soap ('000 metric tons)	9	10	9
Cement ('000 metric tons)	67	60	57
Radio receivers ('000)	8	6	2
Electric energy (million kWh)	105	78	81

Electric energy (estimates, million kWh): 176 in 1992; 159 in 1993; 166 in 1994. Source: UN, *Industrial Commodity Statistics Yearbook*.

Finance

CURRENCY AND EXCHANGE RATES

Monetary Units

100 centimes = 1 franc rwandais (Rwanda franc).

Sterling and Dollar Equivalents (31 March 1997)

£1 sterling = 505.6 Rwanda francs;
US $1 = 307.9 Rwanda francs;
1,000 Rwanda francs = £1.978 = $3.248.

Average Exchange Rate (Rwanda francs per US $)

1994 n. a.
1995 262.20
1996 306.82

Note: Since September 1983 the currency has been linked to the IMF special drawing right (SDR). Until November 1990 the mid-point exchange rate was SDR 1 = 102.71 Rwanda francs. In November 1990 a new rate of SDR 1 = 171.18 Rwanda francs was established. This remained in effect until June 1992, when the rate was adjusted to SDR 1 = 201.39 Rwanda francs. The latter parity was maintained until February 1994, since when the rate has been frequently adjusted. In March 1995 the Government introduced a market-determined exchange rate system.

BUDGET ('000 million Rwanda francs)

Revenue*	1993	1994	1995
Tax revenue	23.9	6.0	21.7
Taxes on income and profits	5.9	1.5	2.8
Company profits tax	2.5	0.7	0.8
Individual income tax	2.1	0.4	1.6
Domestic taxes on goods and services	10.3	2.3	9.9
Excise taxes	5.9	1.1	5.7
Turnover tax	2.8	1.0	3.0
Road fund	1.6	n.a.	1.2
Taxes on international trade	7.2	2.2	8.9
Import taxes	7.0	1.8	6.9
Export taxes	n.a.	0.1	1.8
Non-tax revenue	2.0	—	1.4
Total	25.9	6.0	23.1

Expenditure†	1993	1994	1995
Current expenditure	43.5	22.2	42.1
General public services	11.1	5.7	6.6
Defence	12.9	5.7	14.7
Social services	10.9	12.6	8.4
Education	8.2	9.2	5.3
Health	2.2	2.1	1.6
Economic services	2.5	2.2	4.1
Energy and public works	1.1	1.1	2.9
Interest on public debt	6.1	7.4	8.3
Capital expenditure	21.6	4.4	27.3
Sub-total	65.2	26.6	69.4
Adjustment for payment arrears‡	−10.0	−15.8	−13.3
Total	55.2	10.8	56.1

* Excluding grants received ('000 million Rwandan francs): 18.1 in 1993; 1.5 in 1994; 38.4 in 1995.
† Excluding lending minus repayments ('000 million Rwanda francs): 2.0 in 1993.
‡ Minus sign indicates increase in arrears.
Source: IMF, *Rwanda — Selected Issues and Statistical Appendix* (December 1996).

INTERNATIONAL BANK RESERVES (US $ million at 31 December)

	1994	1995	1996
IMF special drawing rights	2.55	20.29	18.28
Reserve position in IMF	14.29	—	—
Foreign exchange	15.11	105.50	136.48
Total	31.96	125.80	154.76

Source: IMF, *International Financial Statistics*.

MONEY SUPPLY (million Rwanda francs at 31 December)

	1994	1995	1996
Currency outside banks	11,924	17,257	19,908
Demand deposits at deposit money banks	16,165	22,586	24,979
Total money (incl. others)	28,810	40,658	45,423

Source: IMF, *International Financial Statistics*.

COST OF LIVING
(Consumer Price Index for Kigali; base: 1990 = 100)

	1988	1989	1991
Food	92.5	95.2	113.6
Fuel and light	98.9	97.1	114.2
Clothing	99.7	99.4	120.8
Rent	92.2	92.9	100.0
All items (incl. others)	95.1	96.0	119.6

1992: Food 121.6; All items 131.0.
1993: All items 147.2.
Source: ILO, *Yearbook of Labour Statistics*.

NATIONAL ACCOUNTS
(million Rwanda francs at current prices)
National Income and Product*

	1987	1988	1989
Compensation of employees	42,530	45,050	46,970
Operating surplus	102,920	105,310	116,250
Domestic factor incomes	145,450	150,360	163,220
Consumption of fixed capital	11,080	12,360	14,540
Gross domestic product (GDP) at factor cost	156,530	162,720	177,760
Indirect taxes	14,910	15,460	12,460
Less Subsidies	—	250	
GDP in purchasers' values	171,440	177,930	190,220
Factor income from abroad	800	690	750
Less Factor income paid abroad	3,540	4,260	2,980
Gross national product (GNP)	168,700	174,360	187,990
Less Consumption of fixed capital	11,080	12,360	14,540
National income in market prices	157,620	162,000	173,450
Other current transfers from abroad	6,290	7,120	6,470
Less Other current transfers paid abroad	2,010	1,950	1,810
National disposable income	161,900	167,170	178,110

* Figures are rounded.

Expenditure on the Gross Domestic Product

	1993	1994*	1995*
Government final consumption expenditure†	32,897	13,636	30,954
Private final consumption expenditure	252,704	242,202	328,222
Increase in stocks	–2,523	–4,300	1,556
Gross fixed capital formation	44,896	9,920	42,901
Total domestic expenditure	327,974	261,458	403,632
Exports of goods and services	14,726	9,691	19,820
Less Imports of goods and services	58,334	106,090	95,967
GDP in purchasers' values	284,366	165,059	327,485
GDP at constant 1990 prices	203,382	103,816	129,312

* Estimates.
† Defined as budgetary current expenditure less interest payments and transfers.
Source: IMF, *Rwanda—Selected Issues and Statistical Appendix* (December 1996).

Gross Domestic Product by Economic Activity

	1993	1994*	1995*
Agriculture, hunting, forestry and fishing	93,347	66,043	114,622
Mining and quarrying	196	4	81
Manufacturing	32,667	23,114	46,841
Electricity, gas and water	1,350	858	1,382
Construction	17,947	4,568	5,034
Trade, restaurants and hotels	53,630	33,709	58,251
Transport, storage and communications	16,384	4,796	17,055
Public administration	20,945	9,272	16,508
Other services	29,790	13,875	48,882
Sub-total	266,257	156,239	308,655
Indirect taxes	18,110	8,819	18,831
GDP in purchasers' values	284,366	165,059	327,485

* Estimates.
Source: IMF, *Rwanda—Selected Issues and Statistical Appendix* (December 1996).

BALANCE OF PAYMENTS (US $ million)

	1991	1992	1993
Exports of goods f.o.b.	95.6	68.5	67.7
Imports of goods f.o.b.	–228.1	–240.4	–267.7
Trade balance	–132.5	–171.9	–200.0
Exports of services	43.0	31.4	34.3
Imports of services	–111.6	–114.6	–136.4
Balance on goods and services	–201.1	–255.1	–302.1
Other income received	3.5	4.7	3.0
Other income paid	–17.2	–16.1	–18.2
Balance on goods, services and income	–214.8	–266.5	–317.3
Current transfers received	209.3	213.6	208.5
Current transfers paid	–28.3	–30.4	–20.1
Current balance	–33.8	–83.3	–128.9
Capital account (net)	–0.3	0.1	–1.3
Direct investment from abroad	4.6	2.2	5.8
Portfolio investment assets	–0.1	—	—
Other investment assets	23.8	19.2	—
Other investment liabilities	70.8	41.0	82.7
Net errors and omissions	0.2	16.7	–9.5
Overall balance	65.2	–4.0	–51.2

Source: IMF, *International Financial Statistics*.

External Trade

PRINCIPAL COMMODITIES (million Rwanda francs)

Imports c.i.f.	1989	1990	1991
Consumer goods	7,610.7	n.a.	10,819.7
Food	2,323.8	2,673.0	4,366.9
Clothing	1,143.4	554.0	915.9
Mineral fuels and lubricants	3,850.5	3,689.2	4,913.1
Capital goods	6,909.9	4,826.2	6,725.8
Transport equipment	1,832.5	901.8	1,322.2
Machinery and tools	3,969.5	2,496.0	4,260.6
Semi-manufactures	8,329.3	7,999.0	16,015.9
Construction materials	1,570.0	1,316.1	1,486.5
Total (incl. others)	26,700.4	23,057.4	38,474.5

Exports f.o.b.	1989	1990	1991
Coffee (green)	4,691.0	5,424.5	7,209.8
Tea	1,557.3	1,736.8	2,796.6
Tin ores and concentrates	381.2	294.5	319.7
Pyrethrum	151.4	160.2	279.3
Quinquina	60.6	29.9	24.1
Total (incl. others)	8,376.6	8,478.0	11,971.2

Sources: Banque Nationale du Rwanda; Ministère des Finances et de l'Economie, Kigali.

1993 (estimates, US $ million): *Imports c.i.f.:* Capital goods 72.0, Intermediate goods 91.2; Energy products 35.1; Food 59.3; Total (incl. others) 345.6. *Exports f.o.b.:* Coffee 37.6; Tea 18.6; Cassiterite and tin 1.5; Hides and skins 2.5; Pyrethrum and quinquina 0.6; Total (incl. others) 67.7.

1994 (estimates, US $ million): *Imports c.i.f.:* Capital goods 36.0, Intermediate goods 22.8; Energy products 23.3; Food 218.1; Total (incl. others) 458.4. *Exports f.o.b.:* Coffee 17.4; Tea 5.8; Cassiterite and tin 0.5; Hides and skins 1.2; Pyrethrum and quinquina 0.3; Total (incl. others) 32.2.

1995 (estimates, US $ million): *Imports c.i.f.:* Capital goods 51.3, Intermediate goods 32.4; Energy products 21.4; Food 102.5; Total (incl. others) 291.5. *Exports f.o.b.:* Coffee 38.1; Tea 5.1; Cassiterite and tin 1.0; Hides and skins 2.5; Pyrethrum and quinquina 0.5; Total (incl. others) 51.2. Source: IMF, *Rwanda—Selected Issues and Statistical Appendix* (December 1996).

PRINCIPAL TRADING PARTNERS (million Rwanda francs)

Imports	1989	1990	1991
Belgium-Luxembourg	5,020.0	4,468.7	6,588.9
Burundi	149.2	102.8	259.1
France	1,899.2	1,782.4	2,616.3
Germany, Fed. Repub.	2,189.8	2,540.4	2,324.9
Italy	866.3	584.9	1,088.9
Japan	3,177.3	n.a.	n.a.
Kenya	3,907.1	3,818.4	5,153.0
Netherlands	790.7	837.2	1,043.3
Uganda	145.9	257.0	3.6
United Kingdom	556.2	527.0	808.3
USA	236.5	168.9	402.8
Zaire	303.6	190.8	266.9
Total (incl. others)	26,700.4	23,057.3	38,474.5

Exports	1989	1990	1991
Belgium-Luxembourg	1,610.8	1,158.4	1,412.7
Burundi	15.0	23.7	120.1
France	313.4	54.7	137.7
Germany, Fed. Repub.	1,515.9	1,822.8	2,552.7
Italy	299.8	190.9	199.6
Kenya	20.4	14.3	4.3
Netherlands	945.4	1,083.4	2,246.9
Uganda	133.8	64.2	22.0
United Kingdom	546.4	708.1	767.2
USA	427.9	448.1	689.1
Zaire	45.1	27.7	37.7
Total (incl. others)	8,376.6	8,478.2	11,971.2

Source: Banque Nationale du Rwanda, Kigali.

Transport

ROAD TRAFFIC (motor vehicles in use at 31 December)

	1989	1990	1991
Motor cycles and scooters	8,202	8,054	8,207
Passenger cars	8,135	9,255	10,217
Other vehicles	11,692	9,150	8,670
Total	28,029	26,459	27,094

Source: Banque Nationale du Rwanda, Kigali.

CIVIL AVIATION (traffic on scheduled services)

	1992	1993	1994
Passengers carried ('000)	9	9	9
Passenger-km (million)	2	2	2

Source: UN, *Statistical Yearbook*.

Tourism

	1992	1993	1994
Tourist arrivals ('000)	5	2	1
Tourist receipts (US $ million)	4	2	2

Source: UN, *Statistical Yearbook*.

Communications Media

	1992	1993	1994
Radio receivers ('000 in use)	485	500	520
Telephones ('000 main lines in use)	12	12	15
Daily newspapers (number)	1	n.a.	1

Source: mainly UNESCO, *Statistical Yearbook*.

Education

(1991/92, unless otherwise indicated)

	Institutions	Teachers	Pupils		
			Males	Females	Total
Primary	1,710	18,937	556,731	548,171	1,104,902
Secondary	n.a.	3,413	52,882	41,704	94,586
Tertiary*	n.a.	646	2,750	639	3,389

* Figures are for 1989/90.

Source: UNESCO, *Statistical Yearbook*.

Directory

The Constitution

On 10 June 1991 presidential assent was granted to a series of amendments to the Constitution in force since 19 December 1978. The document, as amended, provided, *inter alia*, for a multi-party political system, the separation of the functions of the executive, judiciary and legislature, the limitation of presidential tenure to no more than two consecutive five-year terms of office, the establishment of the office of Prime Minister, freedom of the press, and the right of workers to withdraw their labour. On 5 May 1995 the Transitional National Assembly announced its adoption of a new Constitution based on selected articles of the 1991 Constitution, the August 1993 Arusha peace accord, the FPR victory declaration of July 1994 and the multi-party protocol of understanding concluded in November 1994 (see Recent History).

The Government

HEAD OF STATE

President: Pasteur Bizimungu (took office 19 July 1994).

Vice-President: Maj.-Gen. Paul Kagame.

COUNCIL OF MINISTERS
(August 1997)

A coalition council of national unity, comprising the Mouvement démocratique républicain (MDR), the Front patriotique rwandais (FPR), the Parti social-démocrate (PSD), the Parti libéral (PL), and the Parti démocratique chrétien (PDC).

Prime Minister: PIERRE CÉLESTIN RWIGYEMA (MDR).

Vice-President and Minister of National Defence: Maj.-Gen. PAUL KAGAME (FPR).

Minister of Internal Affairs, Communal Development and Resettlement: ABDUL KARIM HARERIMANA (FPR).

Minister of Foreign Affairs and Co-operation: ANASTASE GASANA (MDR).

Minister of Finance and Economic Planning: JEAN-BERCHMANS BIRARA (Independent).

Minister of Agriculture, Livestock, Environment and Rural Development: AUGUSTIN IYAMUREMYE (PSD).

Minister of Public Works: LAURIEN NGIRABANZI (MDR).

Minister of Public Service and Labour: JOSEPH NSENGIMANA (PL).

Minister of Health: Dr VINCENT BIRUTA.

Minister of Youth, Sports and Vocational Training: Dr JACQUES BIHOZAGARA (FPR).

Minister of Information: JEAN-NEPOMUCÈNE NAYINZIRA (PDC).

Minister of Justice: FAUSTIN NTEZIRYAYO.

Minister of Education: Dr JOSEPH KAREMERA (FPR).

Minister of Communications: CHARLES NTAKIRUTINKA (PSD).

Minister of Handicrafts, Mining and Tourism: MARC RUGENERA (PSD).

Minister of Commerce, Industry, and Co-operatives: BONAVENTURE NIYIBIZI.

Minister of Women's Affairs, Social Affairs and the Family: ALOYSIA INYUMBA (FPR).

Minister in the President's Office: PATRICK MAZIMPAKA (FPR).

MINISTRIES

Office of the President: BP 15, Kigali; tel. 75432; telex 517.

Ministry of Agriculture, Livestock, Environment and Rural Development: BP 621, Kigali; tel. 75324.

Ministry of Commerce, Industry and Co-operatives: BP 476, Kigali; tel. 73875.

Ministry of Communications: BP 720, Kigali; tel. 72424.

Ministry of Education: BP 624, Kigali; tel. 85422.

Ministry of Finance and Economic Planning: BP 158, Kigali; tel. 75410; telex 502.

Ministry of Foreign Affairs and Co-operation: BP 179, Kigali; tel. 75257.

Ministry of Handicrafts, Mining and Tourism: BP 2378, Kigali; tel. 77415; fax 74834.

Ministry of Health: BP 84, Kigali; tel. 76681.

Ministry of Internal Affairs, Communal Development and Resettlement: BP 446, Kigali; tel. 86708.

Ministry of Justice: BP 160, Kigali; tel. 866626.

Ministry of the Public Service and Labour: BP 403, Kigali; tel. 86578.

Ministry of Public Works: BP 24, Kigali; tel. 86649.

Ministry of Women's Affairs, Social Affairs and the Family: BP 790, Kigali; tel. 73481.

Ministry of Youth, Sports and Vocational Training: BP 1044, Kigali; tel. 75861; telex 22502.

Legislature

In November 1994 a multi-party protocol of understanding provided for a number of amendments to the terms of the August 1993 Arusha accord relating to the establishment of a transitional legislature. The most notable of the new provisions was the exclusion from all legislative processes of members of those parties implicated in alleged acts of genocide during 1994. A 70-member Transitional National Assembly was installed on 12 December 1994.

Speaker of the Transitional National Assembly: JOSEPH SEBARENZI.

Political Organizations

Coalition pour la défense de la République (CDR): Kigali; f. 1992; operates an unofficial Hutu militia known as Impuzamugambi; participation in transitional Govt and legislature proscribed by FPR-led admin. in 1994; Leader (vacant).

Front patriotique rwandais (FPR): f. 1990; also known as Inkotanyi; comprises mainly Tutsi exiles, but claims multi-ethnic support; commenced armed invasion of Rwanda from Uganda in Oct. 1990; took control of Rwanda in July 1994; Chair. Col ALEX KANYARENGWE; Sec.-Gen. Dr THÉOGÈNE RUDASINGWA.

Mouvement démocratique républicain (MDR): Kigali; banned 1973–91; fmrly also known as Parti de l'émancipation du peuple Hutu (Parmehutu), dominant party 1962–73; split into two factions in late 1993 early 1994: pro-MRNDD faction led by FRODUALD KARAMIRA, with mainly Hutu support; anti-MRNDD faction led by FAUSTIN TWAGIRAMUNGU, with multi-ethnic support.

Mouvement républicain national pour la démocratie et le développement (MRNDD): BP 1055, Kigali; f. 1975 as the Mouvement révolutionnaire national pour le développement (MRND); sole legal party until 1991; adopted present name in April 1991; draws support from hard-line Hutu elements; Chair. MATHIEU NGIRUMPATSE; operates unofficial militia known as Interahamwe (Leader ROBERT KADJUGA); banned by FPR in 1994 from participation in transitional Govt and legislature.

Parti démocrate chrétien (PDC): BP 2348, Kigali; tel. 76542; fax 72237; f. 1990; Leader JEAN NEPOMUCÈNE NAYINZIRA.

Parti démocratique islamique (PDI): Kigali; f. 1992.

Parti démocratique rwandais (Pader): Kigali; f. 1992; cen. cttee of four mems; Sec. JEAN NTAGUNGIRA.

Parti écologiste (Peco): Kigali; f. 1992.

Parti libéral (PL): BP 1304, Kigali; tel. 77916; fax 77838; f. 1991; split into two factions in late 1993–early 1994: pro-MRNDD faction led by JUSTIN MUGENZI and AGNÈS NTAMBYARIRO; anti-MRNDD faction led by PROSPER HIGIRO, JOSEPH MUSENGIMANA and ESDRA KAYIRANGA.

Parti progressiste de la jeunesse rwandaise (PPJR): Kigali; f. 1991; Leader ANDRÉ HAKIZIMANA.

Parti républicain rwandais (Parerwa): Kigali; f. 1992; Leader AUGUSTIN MUTAMBA.

Parti social-démocrate (PSD): Kigali; f. 1991 by a breakaway faction of the MRND; Pres. (vacant).

Parti socialiste rwandais (PSR): Kigali; f. 1991; workers' rights.

Rassemblement travailliste pour la démocratie (RTD): BP 1894, Kigali; tel. 75622; fax 76574; f. 1991; Leader EMMANUEL NIZEYIMANA.

Union démocratique du peuple rwandais (UDPR): Kigali; f. 1992; Pres. VINCENT GWABUKWISI; Vice-Pres. SYLVESTRE HUBI.

Other political organizations have been formed by exiled Rwandans and function principally from abroad; these include:

Forces de résistance pour la démocratie (FRD): Brussels, Belgium; f. 1996 by Hutu moderates in exile; advocates return of Rwanda to UN Trust Territory status; Leaders FAUSTIN TWAGIRAMUNGU, SETH SENDASHONGA.

Rassemblement pour le retour des réfugiés et la démocratie au Rwanda (RDR): f. 1995 by fmr supporters of Habyarimana admin.; draws support from refugee camps in the Democratic Repub. of the Congo and Tanzania; Chair. FRANÇOIS NSABAHIMANA.

Union du peuple rwandais (UPR): Brussels, Belgium; f. 1990; Hutu-led; Pres. SILAS MAJYAMBERE; Sec.-Gen. EMMANUEL TWAGILIMANA.

Diplomatic Representation

Note: Many diplomatic missions closed in April 1994, when diplomatic personnel were withdrawn, owing to the escalation of civil disorder.

EMBASSIES IN RWANDA

Algeria: Kigali; tel. 85831; Ambassador: MOHAMED LAALA.

Belgium: rue Nyarugenge, BP 81, Kigali; tel. 75554; fax 73995; Ambassador: FRANK DE CONINCK.

Burundi: rue de Ntaruka, BP 714, Kigali; tel. 75010; telex 536; Ambassador: SALVATOR NTIHABOSE.

Canada: rue Akagera, BP 1177, Kigali; tel. 73210; fax 72719; Ambassador: BERNARD DUSSAULT.

China, People's Republic: ave Député Kayuku, BP 1345, Kigali; tel. 75415; Ambassador: HUANG SHEJIAO.

Congo, Democratic Republic: 504 rue Longue, BP 169, Kigali; tel. 75289; Ambassador: (vacant).

Egypt: BP 1069, Kigali; tel. 82686; telex 22585; fax 82686; Ambassador: SAMEH SAMY DARWISH.

France: 40 ave Député Kamuzinzi, BP 53, Kigali; tel. 75225; telex 522; Ambassador: JACQUES COURBIN.

Germany: 8 rue de Bugarama, BP 355, Kigali; tel. 75222; telex 22520; fax 77267; Ambassador: AUGUST HUMMEL.

Holy See: 49 ave Paul VI, BP 261, Kigali (Apostolic Nunciature); tel. 75293; fax 75181; Apostolic Nuncio: Most Rev. JULIUSZ JANUSZ, Titular Archbishop of Caorle.

Kenya: BP 1215, Kigali; tel. 82774; telex 22598; Ambassador: PETER KIHARA MATHANJUKI.

Korea, Democratic People's Republic: Kigali; Ambassador: LEE GWANG ROK.

Libya: BP 1152, Kigali; tel. 76470; telex 549; Secretary of the People's Bureau: MOUSTAPHA MASAND EL-GHAILUSHI.

Russia: ave de l'Armée, BP 40, Kigali; tel. 75286; telex 22661; Ambassador: (vacant).

Uganda: BP 656, Kigali; tel. 76495; telex 22521; fax 73551; Ambassador: (vacant).

United Kingdom: Parcelle 1071, Kimihururu, Kigali; Ambassador: KAYE OLIVER.

USA: blvd de la Révolution, BP 28, Kigali; tel. 75601; fax 72128; Ambassador: DAVID P. RAWSON.

Judicial System

The judicial system comprises a Council of State with administrative jurisdiction, a Court of Cassation, a Constitutional Court consisting of the Court of Cassation and the Council of State sitting jointly, a Court of Accounts responsible for examining all public accounts, and courts of appeal, courts of first instance and provincial courts.

It was estimated that three-quarters of Rwanda's judges were killed during the violent political events of 1994.

In October 1995 the Transitional National Assembly elected eight magistrates to establish the Rwandan Supreme Court. Together with the President of the Supreme Court, the Presidents of the Council of State, the Court of Cassation, the Constitutional Court and the Court of Accounts are Vice-Presidents of the Supreme Court and constitute its directorate.

SUPREME COURT

Chair of the Supreme Court: JEAN MUTSINI.

Presiding Judge: BALTHAZAR KANOBANA.

Vice-President and President of the Council of State: VINCENT NKEZABAGANWA.

Vice-President and President of the Court of Accounts: PAUL RUYENZI.

Vice-President and President of the Constitutional Court: PAUL RUTAYISIRE.

Vice-President and President of the Court of Cassation: Maj. AUGUSTIN CYIZA.

Religion

AFRICAN RELIGIONS

About one-half of the population hold traditional beliefs.

CHRISTIANITY

The Roman Catholic Church

Rwanda comprises one archdiocese and eight dioceses. At 31 December 1995 there were an estimated 3,361,977 adherents in the country, representing around 48% of the total population.

Bishops' Conference: Conférence Episcopale du Rwanda, BP 357, Kigali; tel. 75439; telex 566; f. 1980; Pres. (vacant).

Archbishop of Kigali: Most Rev. THADDÉE NTIHINYURWA, Archevêché, BP 715, Kigali; tel. 75769; fax 76371.

The Anglican Communion

The Church of the Province of Rwanda, established in 1992, has eight dioceses. The Archbishop of Rwanda and Bishop of Shyira, the Most Rev. Augustin Nshamihigo, is currently in exile.

Dean of the Province and Bishop of Byumba: Rt Rev. ONESPHORE RWAJE, BP 17, Byumba; fax 64242.

Provincial Secretary: Canon ANDREW KAYIZARI, BP 2487, Kigali; tel. 76338; fax 73213.

Other Protestant Churches

Eglise Baptiste: Nyantanga, BP 59, Butare; Pres. Rev. DAVID BAZIGA; Gen. Sec. ELEAZAR ZIHERAMBERE.

There are about 250,000 other Protestants, including a substantial minority of Seventh-day Adventists.

BAHÁ'Í FAITH

National Spiritual Assembly: BP 652, Kigali; tel. 75982.

ISLAM

There is a small Islamic community.

The Press

Bulletin Agricole du Rwanda: OCIR-Café, BP 104, Kigali-Gikondo; telex 13; f. 1968; quarterly; in French; Pres. of Editorial Bd Dr AUGUSTIN NZINDUKIYIMANA; circ. 800.

L'Ere de Liberté: BP 1755, Kigali; fortnightly.

Etudes Rwandaises: Université Nationale du Rwanda, Rectorat, BP 56, Butare; tel. 30302; telex 605; f. 1977; quarterly; pure and applied science, literature, human sciences; in French; Pres. of Editorial Bd CHARLES NTAKIRUTINKA; circ. 1,000.

Hobe: BP 761, Kigali; f. 1955; monthly; for children; in Kinyarwanda; Dir ANDRÉ SIBOMANA; circ. 95,000.

Imboni: BP 694, Kigali; tel. 74520; fortnightly.

Ingoboka: BP 635, Kigali; fortnightly.

Inkingi: BP 969, Kigali; tel. 77626; fax 77543; monthly.

Intaremara: BP 83, Kigali; fortnightly.

Kaberinka: BP 83, Kigali; tel. 76182; fortnightly.

Kinyamateka: 5 blvd de l'OUA, BP 761, Kigali; tel. 76164; f. 1933; fortnightly; economics; Editorial Dir ANDRÉ SIBOMANA; circ. 11,000.

La Lettre du Cladho: BP 3060, Kigali; tel. 74292; monthly.

Libération: BP 398, Kigali; tel 82008; monthly.

The New: BP 635, Kigali; tel. 73409; fax 74166; monthly.

Nouvelles du Rwanda: Université Nationale du Rwanda, BP 117, Butare; every 2 months.

Nyabarongo—Le Canard Déchaîné: BP 1585, Kigali; tel. 76674; monthly.

Le Partisan: BP 1805, Kigali; tel. 73923; fortnightly.

La Patrie—Urwatubyaye: BP 3125, Kigali; tel. 72552; monthly.

La Relève: Office Rwandais d'Information, BP 83, Kigali; tel. 75665; telex 557; f. 1976; monthly; politics, economics, culture; in French; Dir CHRISTOPHE MFIZI; circ. 1,700.

Revue Dialogue: BP 572, Kigali; tel. 74178; f. 1967; monthly; Christian issues; Belgian-owned; circ. 2,500.

Revue Medicale Rwandaise: Ministry of Health, BP 83, Kigali; tel. 76681; f. 1968; quarterly; in French.

Revue Pédagogique: Ministry of Primary and Secondary Education, BP 622, Kigali; tel. 85697; telex 5697; quarterly; in French.

Rwanda Renaître: BP 426, Butare; fortnightly.

Rwanda Rushya: BP 83, Kigali; tel. 72276; fortnightly.

Le Tribun du Peuple: BP 1960, Kigali; tel. 82035; 3 per month.

Ukuri Gacaca: BP 3170, Kigali; tel. 73327; monthly.

Umuhinzi-Mworozi: OCIR–Thé, BP 104, Kigali; f. 1975; monthly; circ. 1,500.

Umusemburo—Le Levain: BP 117, Butare; monthly.

Urunana: Grand Séminaire de Nyakibanda, BP 85, Butare; tel. 30792; f. 1967; 3 a year; religious; Editor-in-Chief THARCISSE GATARE.

NEWS AGENCIES

Agence Rwandaise de Presse (ARP): 27 ave du Commerce, BP 83, Kigali; tel. 75735; telex 557; f. 1975.

Office Rwandais d'Information (Orinfor): Kigali; Dir Maj. WILSON RUTAYISIRE.

Foreign Bureau

Agence France-Presse (AFP): BP 83, Kigali; tel. 72997; telex 557; Correspondent MARIE-GORETTI UWIBAMBE.

Publishers

Implico: BP 721, Kigali; tel. 73771.

Imprimerie de Kabgayi: BP 66, Gitarama; tel. 62252; fax 62345; f. 1932.

Imprimerie de Kigali, SARL: place du 5 juillet, BP 956, Kigali; tel. 85795; fax 84047; f. 1980; Dir THÉONESTE NSENGIMANA.

Imprimerie URWEGO: BP 762, Kigali; tel. 86027; Dir JEAN NSENGIYUNVA.

Pallotti-Presse: BP 863, Kigali; tel. 74084.

Printer Set: BP 184, Kigali; tel. 74116; fax 74121; f. 1984.

Government Publishing Houses

Imprimerie Nationale du Rwanda: BP 351, Kigali; tel. 75350; f. 1967; Dir Juvénal Ndisanze.

Régie de l'Imprimerie Scolaire: BP 1347, Kigali; tel. 85695; fax 85695; f. 1985; Dir Stanislas Sinibagiwe.

Radio and Television

In 1994, according to UNESCO estimates, there were 520,000 radio receivers in use.

Radiodiffusion de la République Rwandaise: BP 83, Kigali; tel. 75665; telex 22557; fax 76185; f. 1961; state-controlled; daily broadcasts in Kinyarwanda, Swahili, French and English; Chief of Programmes Louise Kayibanda; Dir of Information Wilson Rutayisire.

Deutsche Welle Relay Station Africa: Kigali; daily broadcasts in German, English, French, Hausa, Swahili, Portuguese and Amharic.

A privately-controlled station, Radio-Télévision Libre des Mille Collines (RTLM), broadcast pro-MRNDD and pro-CDR transmissions from Kigali (and subsequently from Gisenyi) during 1993 and 1994. Radio Muhabura, the official station of the FPR, broadcast to Rwanda in Kinyarwanda from 1991 until July 1994. A humanitarian station, Radio Amaharo, based in Brussels, Belgium, began broadcasting (in Kinyarwanda) to Rwanda and neighbouring countries where Rwandan refugees were sheltering, from transmitters in Gabon and Ethiopia, in August 1994. Radio Agatashya, operated by UNHCR and the Hirondelle Foundation in Kigali, began broadcasting in Kinyarwanda in August 1995. Broadcasts in Kinyarwanda, French and English on Radio UNAMIR were operated by the UN Assistance Mission to Rwanda and began in February 1995.

Finance

(cap. = capital; res = reserves; dep. = deposits; m. = million; brs = branches; amounts in Rwanda francs)

BANKING

Central Bank

Banque Nationale du Rwanda: BP 531, Kigali; tel. 75249; fax 72551; f. 1964; bank of issue; cap. and res 10,720m. (Dec. 1995); Gov. François Mutemberezi; Vice-Gov. Dr Laurean Rutayisire.

Commercial Banks

Banque Commerciale du Rwanda, SA: BP 354, Kigali; tel. 75591; telex 22505; fax 73395; f. 1963; 44.5% state-owned; cap. 773.1m. (Dec. 1995); Admin. Faustin Musare; 11 brs.

Banque Continentale Africaine (Rwanda), SA (BACAR): 20 blvd de la Révolution, BP 331, Kigali; tel. 74456; telex 22544; fax 73486; f. 1983; 51% owned by Banque Continentale du Luxembourg; cap. 500m. (Dec. 1995); Pres. Valens Kajeguhakwa; Dir-Gen. Eustache Ndayisabye.

Banque de Kigali, SA: 63 ave du Commerce, BP 175, Kigali; tel. 76931; telex 22514; fax 73461; f. 1966; cap. 300m., total assets 27,839.1m. (Dec. 1995); Gen. Man. Edouard Bovy; 10 brs.

Development Banks

Banque Rwandaise de Développement, SA (BRD): BP 1341, Kigali; tel. 75079; telex 22563; fax 73569; f. 1967; 56% state-owned; cap. and res 2,152.1m., total assets 4,202.6m. (Dec. 1995); Pres. Edith Gasana.

Union des Banques Populaires du Rwanda (Banki z'Abaturage mu Rwanda): BP 1348, Kigali; tel. 73559; telex 584; fax 73579; f. 1975; cap. 136.1m., dep. 4,919.9m. (Dec. 1993); Pres. Augustin Bizimana; 145 brs.

Savings Bank

Caisse d'Epargne du Rwanda: BP 146, Kigali; tel. 75928; telex 22553; f. 1963; 100% state-owned; cap. 162m., dep. 2,127m. (Dec. 1992); Chair. Dr Donat Hakizimana; Dir-Gen. Dominique Munyangoga; 16 brs.

INSURANCE

Société Nationale d'Assurances du Rwanda (SONARWA): BP 1035, Kigali; tel. 73350; telex 540; fax 72052; f. 1975; cap. 500m.; Dir-Gen. Hope Murera.

Société Rwandaise d'Assurances, SA (SORAS): BP 924, Kigali; tel. 73716; fax 73362; f. 1984; cap. 201m.; Dir-Gen. (Admin.) Charles Mhoranyi.

Trade and Industry

CHAMBER OF COMMERCE

Chambre de Commerce et d'Industrie du Rwanda: BP 319, Kigali; tel. 83537; telex 22662; fax 83532; f. 1982; co-ordinates commerce and industry at national level; Pres. Boniface Rucagu; Sec.-Gen. Thomas Kigufi.

INDUSTRIAL ASSOCIATION

Association des Industriels du Rwanda: BP 39, Kigali; tel. and fax 75430; Sec. Jean de Dieu Habineza.

DEVELOPMENT ORGANIZATIONS

Cimenterie du Rwanda (CIMERWA): Kigali; f. 1984; mfrs of cement; post-war activities resumed in Aug. 1994; 1995 production estimated at 60% of pre-war capacity.

Coopérative de Promotion de l'Industrie Minière et Artisanale au Rwanda (COOPIMAR): BP 1139, Kigali; tel. 82127; fax 72128; Dir Jean Mburanumwe.

Electrogaz: Kigali; state-owned water, electricity and gas supplier; Dir Alphonse Kalinganvie.

Institut de Recherches Scientifiques et Technologiques (IRST): BP 227, Butare; tel. 30396; fax 30939; Dir-Gen. François Gasengayire.

Institut des Sciences Agronomiques du Rwanda (ISAR): BP 138, Butare; tel. 30642; fax 30644; for the development of subsistence and export agriculture; Dir Munyanganizi Bikoro; 12 centres.

Office des Cultures Industrielles du Rwanda–Café (OCIR–Café): BP 104, Kigali; tel. 75004; telex 22513; fax 73992; f. 1978; development of coffee and other new agronomic industries; operates a coffee stabilization fund; Dir Sylvestre Munyaneza.

Office des Cultures Industrielles du Rwanda–Thé (OCIR–Thé): BP 1344, Kigali; tel. 75956; telex 22582; fax 73943; development and marketing of tea; Dir Michel Bagaragaza.

Office National pour le Développement de la Commercialisation des Produits Vivriers et des Produits Animaux (OPROVIA): BP 953, Kigali; tel. 82946; fax 82945; Dir Innocent Butare.

Office du Pyrèthre du Rwanda (OPYRWA): BP 79, Ruhengeri; tel. 46306; telex 22606; fax 46364; f. 1978; cultivation and processing of pyrethrum; post-war activities resumed in Oct. 1994; 1995 production estimated at 63% pre-war capacity; Dir Joseph Ntamfurayinda.

Office de la Valorisation Industrielle de la Banane du Rwanda (OVIBAR): BP 1002, Kigali; tel. 85857; f. 1978; mfrs of banana wine and juice; post-war activities resumed in Dec. 1994; 1995 production estimated at only 1% of pre-war capacity; Dir Gaspard Nzabamwita.

Régie des Mines du Rwanda (REDEMI): BP 2195, Kigali; tel. 73632; f. 1988; state org. for mining tin, tantalum and tungsten; Man. Dir Jean Bosco M. Bicamumpaka.

Régie Sucrière de Kibuye: Kigali; f. 1969; sugar mfrs and distributors; post-war activities resumed in Dec. 1994; 1995 production estimated at 30% of pre-war capacity.

Riziculture du Rwanda: Kigali; development and cultivation of rice.

MAJOR INDUSTRIAL COMPANIES

BRALIRWA: BP 131, Kigali; tel. 82995; fax 85693; f. 1959; mfrs and bottlers of beer in Gisenyi and soft drinks in Kigali.

MIRONKO Plastic Industries: Kigali; tel. 76231; telex 550; plastic wares.

Murri Frères: BP 110, Chantier de Kigali, Kigali; telex 535; f. 1963; heavy engineering and construction; Propr Pietro Murri; Dir R. Camenzind.

Savonnerie de Kicukiro (SAKIRWA): BP 441, Kigali; tel. 72678; telex 556; fax 75450; soap and washing powders; edible oil refinery.

Société Rwandaise pour la Production et la Commercialisation du Thé (SORWATHE), SARL: Kigali; tel. 75461; telex 548; f. 1978; tea; Dir Cyohoha-Rukeri.

SODEPARAL: Kigali; telex 565; produces leather shoes.

SONATUBE: polyvinyl chloride and metal piping.

Sulfo-Rwanda Industries, SARL: BP 90, Kigali; tel. 75353; telex 22523; fax 74573; f. 1964; soap, cosmetics, plastic products, confectionery; Dir-Gen. Tajdin Hussain Jaffer.

UTEXIRWA: Kigali; production of textiles.

TRADE UNIONS

Centrale d'Education et de Coopération des Travailleurs pour le Développement/Alliance Coopérative au Rwanda

(CECOTRAD/ACORWA): BP 295, Kigali; f. 1984; Pres. ELIE KATABARWA.

Centrale Syndicale des Travailleurs du Rwanda: BP 1645, Kigali; tel. 84012; Sec.-Gen. MELCHIOR KANYAMIRWA.

Transport

RAILWAYS

There are no railways in Rwanda although plans exist for the eventual construction of a line passing through Uganda, Rwanda and Burundi, to connect with the Kigoma–Dar es Salaam line in Tanzania. Rwanda has access by road to the Tanzanian railways system.

ROADS

In 1990 there were 13,173 km of roads, of which 5,200 km were main roads. Around 954 km of roads were paved in 1993 and it was hoped that the total length of paved roads would increase to 1,085 km by 1995. There are international road links with Uganda, Tanzania, Burundi and the Democratic Republic of the Congo. Internal armed conflict during 1994 resulted in considerable damage to the road network, including the destruction of several important bridges.

Office National des Transports en Commun (ONATRACOM): BP 720, Kigali; tel. 75064; Dir (vacant).

INLAND WATERWAYS

There are services on Lake Kivu between Cyangugu, Gisenyi and Kibuye, including two vessels operated by ONATRACOM.

CIVIL AVIATION

The Kanombe international airport at Kigali can process up to 500,000 passengers annually. There is a second international airport at Kamembe, near the border with the Democratic Republic of the Congo. There are airfields at Butare, Gabiro, Ruhengeri and Gisenyi, servicing internal flights.

Rwandair Cargo (Société Nationale des Transports Aériens du Rwanda): BP 808, Kigali; tel. 75492; telex 554; fax 72462; f. 1975 as Air Rwanda, adopted current name in 1994; operates domestic passenger and cargo services and international cargo flights within Africa to Bujumbura (Burundi), Goma (the Democratic Republic of the Congo), Entebbe (Uganda), Tanzania, Kenya and to Ostend in Belgium; Chair. JUVÉNAL UWILINGIYIMANA; Gen. Man. JORAM MUSHIMIYIMANA.

Tourism

Attractions for tourists include the flora and fauna of the national parks, Lake Kivu and fine mountain scenery. In 1994 there were an estimated 1,000 foreign visitors to Rwanda. Total receipts from tourism were estimated at US $2m. in that year. The subsequent fortunes of the tourism sector have been overshadowed by the country's internal conflicts.

Ministry of Environment and Tourism: BP 2378, Kigali; tel. 77415; fax 74834.

Office rwandais du tourisme et des parcs nationaux (ORTPN): BP 905, Kigali; tel. 76514; fax 76512; f. 1973; the status and structure of ORTPN is currently under review.

Defence

All armed services form part of the army. In June 1993 the total strength of the army was 5,200 (including 200 air force personnel), and paramilitary forces totalled 1,200 men. Following the victory of the Front patriotique rwandais (FPR) over the Rwandan armed forces in July 1994, responsibility for national defence was assumed by the FPR's military wing, the Armée patriotique rwandaise (APR). No reliable information regarding troop strength has emerged since the FPR victory. By mid-1996 the headquarters of a new gendarmerie had been established, and seven of 11 proposed police units had been commissioned and were beginning to carry out a number of internal security activities previously undertaken by the armed forces.

Defence Expenditure: Estimated at 14,700m. Rwanda francs in 1995.

Chief of Staff of the Army: Col SAM KAKA.

Education

Primary education, beginning at seven years of age and lasting for seven years, is officially compulsory. Secondary education, which is not compulsory, begins at the age of 15 and lasts for a further six years, comprising two equal cycles of three years. Schools are administered by the state and by Christian missions. In 1991 the enrolment at primary schools included an estimated 71% of children in the relevant age-group, but the comparable ratio for secondary enrolment was only 8%. In 1995, according to estimates by UNESCO, the average rate of adult illiteracy was 39.5% (males 30.2%; females 48.4%). Rwanda has a university, with campuses at Butare and Ruhengeri, and several other institutions of higher education, but some students attend universities abroad, particularly in Belgium, France or Germany. In 1991/92 there were 1,104,902 pupils enrolled at primary schools and 94,586 pupils enrolled at secondary schools, including agricultural and technical vocational schools. In 1989/90 an estimated 3,389 students were receiving higher education. In 1995 an estimated 9.4% of total government expenditure was allocated to education.

Bibliography

Abdulai, N. (Ed.). *Genocide in Rwanda: Background and Current Situation.* London, Africa Research and Information Centre, 1994.

Braekman, C. *Rwanda: Histoire d'un genocide.* Paris, Fayard, 1994.

Brauman, R. *Devant le mal. Rwanda, un génocide en direct.* Paris, Arléa, 1994.

Destexhe, A. *Rwanda and Genocide in the Twentieth Century.* London, Pluto Press, 1994.

Erny, P. 'L'enseignement au Rwanda', in *Tiers Monde,* July–December 1974, XV, 59/60, pp. 707–722.

Guichaoua, A. (Ed.). *Les crises politiques au Burundi et au Rwanda (1993–1994).* Paris, Editions Karthala, 1995.

Harroy, J.-P. *Rwanda: de la Féodalité à la Démocratie: 1955–62.* Paris, Académie des Sciences d'Outre-mer.

d'Hertefelt, M., and de Lame, D. *Société, Culture et Histoire du Rwanda.* Tervuren, 1987.

Kagame, A. *Un abrégé de l'ethno-histoire du Rwanda.* Butare, Editions universitaires du Rwanda, 1972.

Kamukama, D. *Rwanda Conflict: Its Roots and Regional Implications.* Kampala, Fountain Publishers, 1993.

Keane, F. *Season of Blood: A Rwandan Journey.* London, Viking.

McCullum, H. *The Angels Have Left Us: The Rwanda Tragedy and the Churches.* Geneva, World Council of Churches.

Misser, F. *Vers un nouveau Rwanda?—Entretiens avec Paul Kagame.* Brussels, Editions Luc Pire, 1995.

Omaar, R. *Rwanda: Death, Despair and Defiance.* London, African Rights, 1994.

Prunier, G. *The Rwanda Crisis 1959–1964: History of a Genocide.* London, Hurst, 1995.

Reyntjens, F. *Pouvoir et droit au Rwanda: Droit public et évolution politique 1916–1973.* Tervuren, Musée royal de l'Afrique centrale, 1985.

Sirven, P., Gotanegre, J.-F., and Prioul, G. *Géographie du Rwanda.* Brussels, Editions A. de Boeck, 1974.

Sparrow, J. *Under the Volcanoes: Rwanda's Refugee Crisis.* Geneva, Federation of Red Cross and Red Crescent Societies, 1994.

Vanderlinden, J. 'La République rwandaise', in *Encyclopédie politique et constitutionnelle.* Paris, Berger-Levrault, 1970.

Waller, D. *Rwanda: Which Way Now?* Oxford, Oxfam, 1993.

ST HELENA

(WITH ASCENSION AND TRISTAN DA CUNHA)

Physical and Social Geography

St Helena, a rugged and mountainous island of volcanic origin, lies in the South Atlantic Ocean, latitude 16° S, longitude 5° 45′ W, 1,131 km south-east of Ascension and about 1,930 km from the south-west coast of Africa. The island is 16.9 km long and 10.5 km broad, covering an area of 122 sq km (47 sq miles). The highest elevation, Diana's Peak, rises to 823 m above sea-level. The only inland waters are small streams, few of them now perennial, fed by springs in the central hills. These streams and rainwater are sufficient for domestic water supplies and a few small irrigation schemes.

The cool South Atlantic trade winds blow throughout the year. The climate is mild and varies little: the temperature in Jamestown, on the sea-coast, is 21°C–29°C in summer and 18°C–23°C in winter. Inland it is some 5°C cooler.

Figures for annual rainfall over the period 1985–88 show a similar variation between Jamestown, with 208–295 mm, and the eastern district, with 614–810 mm.

The most recent census was held on 22 February 1987, when the total population was enumerated at 5,644. In mid-1993 the population was estimated to have risen to 6,488, giving a density of 53.2 inhabitants per sq km.

Jamestown, the capital, is the only town and had a population of 1,413 at the 1987 census.

The language of the island is English and the majority of the population belong to the Anglican communion.

St Helena has one of the world's most equable climates. Industrial pollution is absent from the atmosphere, and there are no endemic diseases of note. The island is of interest to naturalists for its rare flora and fauna; there are about 40 species of flora which are unique to St Helena.

Recent History

Revised by the Editor

The then uninhabited island of St Helena was discovered on 21 May 1502 by a Portuguese navigator, João da Nova, on his homeward voyage from India. He named it in honour of Saint Helena, mother of the Emperor Constantine the Great, whose festival falls on that day. The existence of the island appears to have remained unknown to other European nations until 1588, when it was visited by Capt. Thomas Cavendish on his return from a voyage round the world. In 1633 the Dutch formally claimed St Helena but made no attempt to occupy it. The British East India Co first established a settlement there in 1659, in order that the island might serve as a distant outpost from which to protect England's trade interests. The island was captured and briefly held by the Dutch in 1673. In that year a charter to occupy and govern St Helena was issued by King Charles II to the East India Co. In this charter the king confirmed the status of the island as a British outpost, and bestowed full rights of British citizenship on all those who settled on the island and on their descendants in perpetuity. During 1815–21 the British government temporarily assumed direct control of the island, owing to the presence there in exile of Napoleon Bonaparte, following his abdication as French emperor. In 1834 control over the island's affairs was transferred on a permanent basis from the British East India Co to the British government. However, St Helena was administered by the foreign and colonial office (and classified as a colony), and not, as might have been expected, given its continuing use as a British outpost, by the war office or the admiralty. Its importance as a port of call on the trade route between Europe and India came to an end after the opening of the Suez canal in 1869.

Temporary revivals in St Helena's importance as an outpost and as a place of exile occurred during the Zulu and Anglo-Boer wars and during the First and Second World Wars. However, further periods of economic depression followed. It has been alleged that efforts to render the island economically self-supporting overlook the fact that the island was originally occupied, not as a colony, but as a strategic base, which, given its isolation and lack of resources, never could be fully independent financially and would require substantial assistance on a permanent basis.

In 1968 a South African concern, the South Atlantic Trading and Investment Co, acquired ownership of Solomon & Co (St Helena) Ltd, the local trading company. However, in view of the latter's dominant role in the island's economy, the British government decided in 1974 to take full control of the enterprise. At the general election held in 1976, all but one of the 12 members elected to the legislative council strongly supported a policy of maintaining close economic links with the United Kingdom. This policy has been advocated by almost all members of the legislative council brought to office at subsequent elections (normally held every four years) up to and including that of July 1997.

In October 1981 the governor announced the appointment of a commission to review the island's constitution. The commission reported in 1983 that it was unable to find any proposal for constitutional change that would command the support of the majority of the islanders. In 1988, however, the government obtained the introduction of a formal constitution to replace the order in council and royal instructions under which St Helena was governed. This constitution entered into force on 1 January 1989.

St Helena's persistently high rate of unemployment (estimated at 18% in 1996) has resulted in widespread reliance on welfare benefit payments and a concurrent decline in living standards for the majority of the population. Underlying social discontent was expressed in two protest marches held in Jamestown during 1996, followed in April 1997 by an incident involving alleged arson attacks on police vehicles and a bus at Longwood. In the same month, the governor (who exercises full executive and legislative authority in St Helena) refused to accept the nomination of a prominent critic of government policy to the post of director of the department of social welfare. Two members of the executive council (which acts in an advisory capacity) resigned in protest at the action of the governor, who announced that elections to the legislative council would be held in July. The governor, meanwhile, left the island for a six-week period of home leave. Following the elections, held on 9 July, the governor agreed to the nomination as chairman of the education committee of the candidate he had previously refused to nominate to the social welfare directorate. The newly elected legislative council became the first in which members were to receive a fixed salary to serve on a full-time basis, relinquishing any other paid employment during their term of office.

Owing to the limited range of economic activity on the island, St Helena is dependent on development and budgetary aid from the United Kingdom. Since 1981, when the United Kingdom adopted the British Nationality Act, which effectively removed the islanders' traditional right of residence in Britain, opportunities for overseas employment have been limited to contract work, principally in Ascension and the Falkland Islands. In 1992 an informal 'commission on citizenship' was established by a number of islanders to examine St Helena's constitutional relationship with the United Kingdom, with special reference to the legal validity of the 1981 legislation as applied to St Helena. In April 1997 the commission obtained a legal opinion from a former acting attorney-general of St Helena to the effect that the application of the Act to the population of St Helena was in contravention of the royal charter establishing British sovereignty in 1673. The commission indicated that it intended to pursue the matter further. In July 1997 private legislation was introduced in the British parliament to extend full British nationality to 'persons having connections with' St Helena. In the following month the British government indicated that it was considering arrangements under which islanders would be granted employment and residence rights in the United Kingdom.

Economy

Revised by the Editor

St Helena's principal crops are potatoes and vegetables. In the past the islanders grew formio (New Zealand flax), used in the manufacture of flax fibre (hemp). However, at the end of 1965 the market price of hemp fell sharply dropped considerably and production ceased in 1966.

Since 1979/80 increased benefits have been made available to private farmers in a major effort to encourage greater local production, local utilization and farming efficiency. Grants, loans (of capital and labour) and free technical assistance have been offered and an increasing number of full-time smallholders are taking advantage of the scheme. Two major irrigation schemes using butyl-lined reservoirs have been completed. Following a notable rise in food production in the early 1980s, more land is being rented or leased from the government for this purpose. The Agricultural Development Authority farmed approximately one-half the arable area and one-third of the grazing areas during 1975–96. Commonage grazing areas are now made available by government to private stock owners on a per caput per mensem basis. Individuals hold land either in fee simple or by lease. Immigrants require a licence to hold land. Crown land may be leased on conditions approved by the governor.

A major reafforestation programme was begun during the mid-1970s, aimed at replacing flax and fostering land reclamation. A sawmill/timber treatment plant, opened in 1977, produces a proportion of the timber needed for construction and fencing requirements, but most timber continues to be imported. No mineral resources have been identified.

Fish of many kinds are plentiful in the waters around St Helena, and a fisheries corporation was formed in 1979 to make the best use of this resource. A freezing/storage unit, built in 1977, is capable of storing 20 metric tons, allowing fish to be frozen for export as well as the local market. A drying and salting plant was built at Rupert's Bay in 1981 to process skipjack for export and a deep-sea fishing/survey vessel was acquired in 1982. Fish exports, which commenced in 1979, comprise tuna, skipjack and dried salted skipjack. In 1989 147 tons of fish were exported, with a value of £125,842; in 1995 fish exports totalled 226 metric tons, and export revenue from this source amounted to £430,070. A small quantity of coffee is the only other commodity exported.

Unemployment is a serious problem, and a large proportion of the labour force (the economically active population numbered 2,416 in April 1991) is forced to seek employment overseas, principally on Ascension and the Falkland Islands. The rate of unemployment in St Helena was estimated at 18% in 1996. In March 1997 750 St Helenians were working on Ascension.

The main imports, by value, are foodstuffs, liquor, timber, motor spirit, fuel oils, animal feed, building materials, motor vehicles and parts, machinery and parts. Total imports for 1990/91 were valued at £5,774,351, of which 60.3% were supplied by the United Kingdom and 38.6% by South Africa.

In 1993/94 St Helena received £7.98m. in British aid. Budget revenue (including budgetary aid of £3.56m.) totalled £10.46m. in 1995/96, and expenditure in that year balanced at £10.46m.

The St Helena Growers' Co-operative Society is the only such association on the island. It is both a consumers' and a marketing organization, and provides consumer goods, such as seeds, implements and feeding stuffs, to its members, and markets their produce, mainly vegetables, locally, to visiting ships and to Ascension Island. The local market is limited and is soon over-supplied, and this, together with the decrease in the number of ships calling over recent years, has inhibited the growth of this enterprise.

The only port in St Helena is Jamestown, which is an open roadstead with a good anchorage for ships of any size.

There is no airport or airstrip on St Helena and no railway. There are 98 km of all-weather roads, and a further 20 km of earth roads, which are used mainly by animal transport and are usable by motor vehicles only in dry weather. All roads have steep gradients and sharp curves.

In 1978, with the establishment of the St Helena Shipping Co, the St Helena government assumed responsibility for the operation and maintenance of a charter vessel, which carries cargo and passengers four times a year between Avonmouth, in the UK, and Cape Town, in South Africa, with calls at the Canary Islands, Ascension Island and St Helena, and to Tristan da Cunha once a year. The vessel currently operating this service entered operation in 1990. The St Helena Shipping Co receives an annual subsidy of more than £1m. from the British government. There is a bulk fuel farm at Rupert's Valley, which is supplied at approximately 3-month intervals with fuel from Europe.

Statistical Survey

AREA AND POPULATION

Area: 122 sq km (47 sq miles).

Population: 5,147 (males 2,514; females 2,633) at census of 31 October 1976; 5,644 (males 2,769; females 2,875) at census of 22 February 1987; 6,488 (males 3,320; females 3,168) at mid-1993 (official estimate).

Density (mid-1993): 53.2 per sq km.

Principal town: Jamestown (capital), population 1,413 (1987 census).

Births and Deaths (1995): Registered live births 72; Registered deaths 30.

Employment: 2,516 (1,607 males, 909 females) at census of 22 February 1987; 2,416 in April 1991.

AGRICULTURE, ETC.

Livestock (1994): Cattle 673; Sheep 1,051; Pigs 622; Goats 1,203; Poultry 8,814.

Fishing (metric tons, live weight, including Ascension and Tristan da Cunha): Total catch 651 in 1992; 726 in 1993; 631 in 1994. Figures include catches of rock lobster from Tristan da Cunha during the 12 months ending 30 April of the year stated. Source: FAO, *Yearbook of Fishery Statistics*.

FINANCE

Currency and Exchange Rate: 100 pence (pennies) = 1 St Helena pound (£). *Sterling and Dollar Equivalents* (31 March 1997): £1 sterling = St Helena £1; US $1 = 60.90 pence; £100 = $164.20. *Average Exchange Rate* (US $ per £): 1.5316 in 1994; 1.5785 in 1995; 1.5617 in 1996. Note: The St Helena pound is at par with the pound sterling.

Budget (1995/96): *Revenue* £10,459,011 (including budgetary aid of £3,560,000); *Expenditure* £10,458,241.

Cost of Living (Consumer Price Index; base: 1990 = 100): 118.1 in 1993; 122.8 in 1994; 128.5 in 1995. Source: UN, *Monthly Bulletin of Statistics*.

EXTERNAL TRADE

Principal Commodities: *Imports* (1990/91): £5,774,351 (including food and drink £1,154,568, tobacco £107,273, motor spirits and fuel oils £423,824, animal feed £123,403, building materials £477,298, motor vehicles and parts £355,562, electrical equipment, other machinery and parts £757,090); *Exports* (1995): fish £430,070; coffee n.a. Trade is mainly with the United Kingdom and South Africa.

TRANSPORT

Road Traffic (1995): 1,663 vehicles in use.

Shipping (1995): Vessels entered 141.

EDUCATION

Primary (1997): 5 schools; 32 teachers; 404 pupils.

Intermediate (1997): 3 schools; 31 teachers; 303 pupils.

Secondary (1997): 1 school; 47 teachers; 446 pupils.

Directory

The Constitution

The St Helena Constitution Order 1988, which entered into force on 1 January 1989, replaced the Order in Council and Royal Instructions of 1 January 1967. Executive and legislative authority is reserved to the British Crown, but is ordinarily exercised by others in accordance with provisions of the Constitution. The Constitution provides for the office of Governor and Commander-in-Chief of St Helena and its dependencies (Ascension Island and Tristan da Cunha). The Legislative Council for St Helena consists of the Speaker, three *ex-officio* members (the Chief Secretary, the Financial Secretary and the Attorney-General) and 12 elected members; the Executive Council is presided over by the Governor and consists of the above *ex-officio* members and five of the elected members of the Legislative Council. The elected members of the legislature choose from among themselves those who will also be members of the Executive Council. Although a member of both the Legislative Council and the Executive Council, the Attorney-General does not vote on either. Members of the legislature provide the Chairmen and a majority of the members of the various Council Committees. Executive and legislative functions for the dependencies are exercised by the Governor.

The Government

(August 1997)

Governor and Commander-in-Chief: David Smallman.

Chief Secretary: J. Perrott.

Financial Secretary: M. Young.

Chairmen of Council Committees:

- **Agriculture and Natural Resources:** Terrence F. Richards.
- **Education:** Robert M. Robertson.
- **Employment and Social Services:** William E. Drabble.
- **Public Health:** Eric W. George.
- **Public Works and Social Services:** Stedson W. George.

GOVERNMENT OFFICES

Office of the Governor: The Castle, Jamestown; tel. 2555; telex 4202; fax 2598.

Office of the Chief Secretary: The Castle, Jamestown; tel. 2470; telex 4202; fax 2598.

Political Organizations

There are no political parties in St Helena. Elections to the Legislative Council, the latest of which took place on 9 July 1997, are conducted on a non-partisan basis.

Judicial System

There are four Courts on St Helena: the Supreme Court, the Magistrate's Court, the Small Debts Court and the Juvenile Court. Provision exists for the St Helena Court of Appeal, which can sit in Jamestown or London.

Chief Justice: B. W. Martin (non-resident).

Attorney-General: Kurt de Freitas (designate).

Sheriff: G. P. Musk.

Magistrates: J. Beadon, D. Bennett, D. Clarke, J. Corker, L. Crowie, J. Flagg, P. Francis, B. George, E. W. George, I. George, C. Lawrence, H. Legg, G. P. Musk, G. Sim, J. Thomas, D. Wade, C. Yon, P. Yon.

Religion

The majority of the population belongs to the Anglican Communion.

CHRISTIANITY

The Anglican Communion

Anglicans are adherents of the Church of the Province of Southern Africa. The Metropolitan of the Province is the Archbishop of Cape Town, South Africa. St Helena forms a single diocese.

Bishop of St Helena: Rt Rev. John Ruston, Bishopsholme, POB 62, St Helena; tel. 4471; fax 4330; diocese f. 1859; has jurisdiction over the islands of St Helena and Ascension.

The Roman Catholic Church

The Church is represented in St Helena, Ascension and Tristan da Cunha by a Mission, established in August 1986.

Superior: Rev. Fr Anton Agreiter (also Prefect Apostolic of the Falkland Islands); normally visits Tristan da Cunha once a year and Ascension Island two or three times a year; Vicar Delegate Rev. Fr Joseph Whelan, Sacred Heart Church, Jamestown; tel. and fax 2535.

Other Christian Churches

Baptists (since 1845) and (more recently) the Salvation Army, Seventh-day Adventists, New Apostolics and Jehovah's Witnesses are active on the island.

BAHÁ'Í FAITH

The Bahá'í faith has a few active members on the island.

The Press

St Helena News: Broadway House, Jamestown; tel. 2612; telex 4202; fax 2802; f. 1986; govt-sponsored; weekly; Editor Nicola Dillon; circ. 1,350.

Radio and Television

There were an estimated 2,500 radio receivers in use in 1990. A satellite television link came into operation in July 1994.

Government Broadcasting Service: Information Office, Broadway House, Jamestown; tel. 4669; telex 2202; fax 4542; 81 hours weekly; Information Officer NICOLA DILLON; Station Man. ANTHONY D. LEO.

Finance

BANK

Government Savings Bank: Jamestown; tel. 2345; telex 4202; total deposits (31 March 1996): £8,782,269.

INSURANCE

Royal and SunAlliance Insurance Group PLC: Agents: Solomon & Co (St Helena) PLC, Jamestown; tel. 2380; telex 4204; fax 2423.

Trade and Industry

CHAMBER OF COMMERCE

St Helena Chamber of Commerce: Jamestown.

CO-OPERATIVE

St Helena Growers' Co-operative Society: Jamestown; fax 2511; vegetable marketing and suppliers of agricultural tools, seeds and animal feeding products; 77 mems (1995); Chair. LIONEL LAWRENCE; Sec. PETER W. THORPE.

Transport

There are no railways or airfields in St Helena. Proposals were pending in 1997 for the construction of a small airfield.

ROADS

In 1995 there were 98 km of bitumen-sealed roads, and a further 20 km of earth roads, which can be used by motor vehicles only in dry weather. All roads have steep gradients and sharp bends.

SHIPPING

St Helena Line Ltd: Jamestown; mailing address: The Shipyard, Porthleven, Helston, Cornwall, TR13 9JA, England; tel. (1326) 563434; telex 46564; fax (1326) 564347; operates services to and from the United Kingdom four times a year, calling at the Canary Islands, Ascension Island and Cape Town, South Africa, and at Tristan da Cunha once a year; commenced operation of a scheduled service with one passenger/cargo ship in 1978; this vessel was replaced by the RMS *St Helena* in 1990; Man. Dir ANDREW BELL.

Education

Education is compulsory and free for all children between the ages of five and 15 years, although power to exempt after the age of 14 can be exercised by the Education Committee. The standard of work at the secondary comprehensive school is orientated towards 'GCSE' and 'Advanced' Level requirements of the United Kingdom. During the second half of the 1980s, the educational structure was reorganized from a two-tier to a three-tier comprehensive system, for which a new upper-school building was constructed. Free part-time further education classes at London University 'GCSE' and 'Advanced' Level certificate standard are available. The adult literacy rate is 97%.

There is a free public library in Jamestown, financed by the government and managed by a committee, and a mobile library service in the country districts.

ASCENSION

The island of Ascension lies in the South Atlantic Ocean (7° 55′ S, 14° 20′ W), 1,131 km north-west of St Helena. It was discovered by a Portuguese expedition on Ascension Day 1501. The island was uninhabited until the arrival of Napoleon, the exiled French emperor, on St Helena in 1815, when a small British naval garrison was placed there. Ascension remained under the supervision of the British admiralty until 1922, when it was made a dependency of St Helena.

Ascension is a barren, rocky peak of purely volcanic origin, which was previously destitute of vegetation except above 450 m on Green Mountain (which rises to 875 m). The mountain supports a small farm producing vegetables and fruit. Since 1983 an alteration has taken place in the pattern of rainfall in Ascension. Total average annual rainfall has increased and the rain falls in heavy showers and is therefore less prone to evaporation. Grass, shrubs and flowers have grown in the valleys. These plants survived the dry periods experienced in 1987 and 1990. Some topsoil has been produced by the decay of previous growth and root systems. The island is famous for green turtles, which land there from December to May to lay their eggs in the sand. It is also a breeding ground of the sooty tern, or wideawake, vast numbers of which settle on the island every 10 months to lay and hatch their eggs. All wildlife except rabbits and cats is protected by law. Shark, barracuda, tuna, bonito and other fish are plentiful in the surrounding ocean.

The population in March 1996 was 1,152 (excluding British military personnel), of whom 750 were St Helenians. The majority of the remainder were expatriate personnel of the British Broadcasting Corpn (BBC), Cable and Wireless PLC and the US military base. The population varies from time to time as it is largely determined by the employment offered by these three stations. The island is an important communications centre, being a relay station for cables between South Africa and Europe, operated by the South Atlantic Cable Co. The BBC operates a relay station on the island, and a local broadcasting station has been established. Ascension does not raise its own finance; the costs of administering the island are borne collectively by the user organizations.

Cable and Wireless PLC provides an international telecommunications service, via satellite and submarine cable, to all parts of the world. Ascension Island Services took over the running of the island's schools, power, water and medical services from Cable and Wireless PLC in 1984.

In 1942 the US government, by arrangement with the British government, established an air base, which it subsequently reoccupied and extended by agreement with the British government in 1956, in connection with the extension of the long-range proving ground for guided missiles, centred in Florida. A further agreement in 1965 allowed the USA to develop tracking facilities on the island in support of the National Aeronautics and Space Administration's 'Apollo' space programme. This operation was terminated in 1990.

Facilities on Ascension underwent rapid development in 1982 to serve as a major staging post for British vessels and aircraft on their way to the Falkland Islands, and the island has continued to provide a key link in British supply lines to the South Atlantic.

Area: 88 sq km (34 sq miles).

Population (excluding British military personnel, March 1997): 1,054 (St Helenians 750, UK nationals 142, US nationals 162).

Budget (estimates for year ending 31 March 1997): Revenue £1,200,000; Expenditure £2,900,000.

Government: The Government of St Helena is represented by an Administrator.

Administrator: ROGER C. HUXLEY, The Residency, Ascension; tel. 6311; telex 3214; fax 6152.

Magistrate: ROGER C. HUXLEY.

Justices of the Peace: A. GEORGE, S. A. YOUDE, G. F. THOMAS, S. N. BOWERS, J. PETERS, C. PARKER.

Religion: Ascension forms part of the Anglican diocese of St Helena, which normally provides a resident chaplain who is also available to minister to members of other denominations.

Transport (1995): *Road vehicles:* 1,092. *Shipping:* ships entered and cleared 129. The St Helena Line Ltd (q.v.) serves the island with a two-monthly passenger/cargo service between Cardiff, in the United Kingdom, and Cape Town, in South Africa. A vessel under charter to the British Ministry of Defence visits the island monthly on its United Kingdom–Falkland Islands service. *Air services:* A twice-weekly Royal Air Force Tristar service between the United Kingdom and the Falkland Islands transits Ascension Island both southbound and northbound. There is a weekly US Air Force military service linking the Patrick Air Force Base in Florida, USA, with Ascension Island, via Antigua.

TRISTAN DA CUNHA

Tristan da Cunha lies in the South Atlantic Ocean, 2,800 km west of Cape Town, South Africa and 2,300 km south-west of St Helena. Also in the group are Inaccessible Island, 37 km west of Tristan; the three Nightingale Islands, 37 km south; and Gough Island (Diego Alvarez), 425 km south. Tristan is volcanic in origin and nearly circular in shape, covering an area of 98 sq km (38 sq miles) and rising in a cone to 2,060 m above sea-level. The climate is typically oceanic and temperate. Rainfall averages 1,675 mm per annum on the coast.

The British navy took possession of the island in 1816 during Napoleon's residence on St Helena, and a small garrison was stationed there. When the garrison was withdrawn, three men, headed by Cpl William Glass, elected to remain and became the founders of the present settlement. Because of its position on a main sailing route the colony thrived until the 1880s, but with the replacement of sail by steam a period of decline set in. No regular shipping called and the islanders suffered at times from a shortage of food. Nevertheless, attempts to move the inhabitants to South Africa were unsuccessful. The islanders were engaged chiefly in fishing and agricultural pursuits.

The United Society for the Propagation of the Gospel has maintained an interest in the island since 1922, and in 1932 one of its missionary teachers was officially recognized as honorary commissioner and magistrate. In 1938 Tristan da Cunha and the neighbouring uninhabited islands of Nightingale, Inaccessible and Gough were made dependencies of St Helena, and in 1950 the office of administrator was created. The administrator is also the magistrate. The island council was established in 1952.

In 1942 a meteorological and wireless station was built on the island by a detachment of the South African defence force and was manned by the Royal Navy for the remainder of the war. The coming of the navy reintroduced the islanders to the outside world, for it was a naval chaplain who recognized the possibilities of a crayfish industry on Tristan da Cunha. In 1948 a Cape Town-based fishing company was granted a concession to fish the Tristan da Cunha waters.

On 10 October 1961 a volcanic cone, thought to have been long extinct, erupted close to the settlement of Edinburgh and it was necessary to evacuate the island. The majority of the islanders returned to Tristan da Cunha in 1963. The administration was fully re-established, and the island council re-formed. The population in December 1996 was 288, including 6 expatriates.

The island is remote, and regular communications are restricted to about six calls each year by vessels from Cape Town (usually crayfish trawlers), an annual visit from a British vessel, the RMS *St Helena*, from Cape Town and the annual call by a South African vessel with supplies for the island and the weather station on Gough Island. There is, however, a wireless station on the island which is in daily contact with Cape Town. A local broadcasting service was introduced in 1966 and a closed-circuit television system operated between 1983–89, when it was replaced by a video lending-library. In 1969 electricity was extended to all of the islanders' homes, and in the same year a radio-telephone service was established. A satellite system which provides direct dialling for telephone and fax facilities was installed in 1992, and radio telex was installed at the island radio station in 1994.

The island's major source of revenue derives from a royalty for the crayfishing concession, supplemented by income from the sale of postage stamps and other philatelic items, and handicrafts. The fishing industry and the administration employ all of the working population. Some 20 power boats operating from the island land their catches to a fish freezing factory built by the Atlantic Islands Development Corpn, whose fishing concession was transferred in January 1997 to a new holder, Premier Fishing (Pty) Ltd, of Cape Town. Premier also operates two large fishing vessels exporting the catch to the USA, France and Japan.

Estimated expenditure for the 1995/96 financial year was £653,772 and revenue was estimated at £847,000. Development aid from the United Kingdom ceased in 1980, leaving the island financially self-sufficient. The United Kingdom, however, has continued to supply the cost of the salaries and passages of the administrator, a doctor and visiting specialists (a dentist every two years and an optician every two years).

Area: Tristan da Cunha 98 sq km (38 sq miles); Inaccessible Island 10 sq km (4 sq miles); Nightingale Island 2 sq km (¾ sq mile); Gough Island 91 sq km (35 sq miles).

Population (December 1996): 288 (including six expatriates) on Tristan; there is a small weather station on Gough Island, staffed, under agreement, by personnel employed by the South African Government.

Fishing (catch, metric tons, year ending 30 April): Tristan da Cunha rock lobster 426 in 1990/91; 361 in 1991/92; 362 in 1992/93. Source: FAO, *Yearbook of Fishery Statistics*.

Budget (estimates for 1995/96): Revenue £847,000; Expenditure £653,772.

Government: The Administrator, representing the British Government, is aided by a council of eight elected members (of whom at least one must be a woman) and three appointed members, which has advisory powers in legislative and executive functions. The Council's advisory functions in executive matters are performed through small committees of the Council dealing with the separate branches of administration. The most recent election was held in November 1994.

Administrator: Brendan G. P. Dalley, The Residency, Tristan da Cunha; tel. (satellite) 874-1445434; fax (satellite) 874-1445435.

Legal System: The Administrator is also the Magistrate and Coroner.

Religion: Adherents of the Anglican church predominate on Tristan da Cunha, which is within the Church of the Province of Southern Africa, and is under the jurisdiction of the Archbishop of Cape Town, South Africa. There is also a small number of Roman Catholics.

Transport: The St Helena Line Ltd (q.v.) and the SA *Agulhas* from Cape Town visit the island once each year, and crayfish trawlers from South Africa call about six times annually.

Bibliography

Blackburn, J. *The Emperor's Last Island: A Journey to St Helena.* London, Secker and Warburg, 1992.

Blakeston, O. *Isle of Helena.* London, Sidgwick and Jackson, 1957.

Booy, D. M. *Rock of Exile: A Narrative of Tristan da Cunha.* London, Dent, 1957.

Castell, R. *St Helena: Island Fortress.* Old Amersham, Bucks, Byron Publicity Group, 1977.

Christopherson, E., et al. *Tristan da Cunha* (trans. R. L. Benham). London, Cassell, 1940.

Christopherson, E. (Ed.) *Results of the Norwegian Scientific Expedition to Tristan da Cunha, 1937–1938,* 16 parts. Oslo University Press, 1940–62.

Cohen, R. (Ed.) *African Islands and Enclaves.* London, Sage Publications, 1983.

Crawford, A. *Tristan da Cunha and the Roaring Forties.* Edinburgh, Charles Skilton, 1982.

Cross, T. *St Helena: with chapters on Ascension and Tristan da Cunha.* Newton Abbot, David and Charles, 1981.

Gosse, P. *St Helena, 1502–1938.* London, Thomas Nelson, 1990 (reissue).

Hart-Davis, D. *Ascension: The Story of a South Atlantic Island.* London, Constable, 1972.

Hughes, C. *Report of an enquiry into conditions on the Island of St Helena . . . (and) observations by the St Helena Government on Mr Hughes' report.* London, 1958.

Martineau, G. *Napoleon's St Helena.* London, John Murray, 1968.

Munch, P. A. *Crisis in Utopia.* New York, Crowell, 1971.

Thompson, J. A. K. *Report on a Visit to Ascension Island.* St Helena Government Printer, 1947.

SÃO TOMÉ AND PRÍNCIPE

Physical and Social Geography

RENÉ PÉLISSIER

The archipelago forming the Democratic Republic of São Tomé and Príncipe is, after the Republic of Seychelles, the smallest independent state in Africa. Both the main islands are in the Gulf of Guinea on a south-west/north-east axis of extinct volcanoes. The boundaries take in the rocky islets of Caroço, Pedras and Tinhosas, off Príncipe, and, south of São Tomé, the Rôlas islet, which is bisected by the line of the Equator. The total area of the archipelago is 1,001 sq km (386.5 sq miles), of which São Tomé occupies an area of 854 sq km.

São Tomé is a plantation island where the eastern slopes and coastal flatlands are covered by huge cocoa estates (*roças*) formerly controlled by Portuguese interests, alongside a large number of local smallholders. These plantations have been carved out of an extremely dense mountainous jungle which dominates this equatorial island. The highest point is the Pico de São Tomé (2,024 m), surrounded by a dozen lesser cones above 1,000 m in height. Craggy and densely forested terrain is intersected by numerous streams. The coast of Príncipe is extremely jagged and indented by numerous bays. The highest elevation is the Pico de Príncipe (948 m). Both islands have a warm and moist climate, with an average yearly temperature of 25°C. Annual rainfall varies from over 5,100 mm on the south-western mountain slopes to under 1,020 mm in the northern lowlands. The dry season, known locally as *gravana*, lasts from June to September.

The total population was 117,504 at the census of 4 August 1991, when São Tomé had 112,033 inhabitants and Príncipe 5,471. The population was officially estimated at 127,076 in mid-1995, giving a density of 126.9 inhabitants per sq km. During 1985–95 the population increased by an annual average of 2.3%. The capital city is São Tomé, with an estimated 45,700 inhabitants in 1994. It is the main export centre of the island. Inland villages on São Tomé are mere clusters of houses of native islanders. Príncipe has only one small town of about 1,000 people, Santo António.

The native-born islanders (*forros*) are the descendants of imported slaves and southern Europeans who settled in the 16th and 17th centuries. Intermarriage was common, but subsequent influxes of Angolan and Mozambican contract workers until about 1950 re-Africanized the *forros*. Descendants of slaves who escaped from the sugar plantations from the 16th century onwards, who formed a formidable maroon enclave in the south of São Tomé and became known as Angolares, are now mainly fishermen.

The widespread exodus of skilled Portuguese plantation administrators, civil servants and traders during the period just prior to independence in July 1975, together with the departure of most of the Angolan and Mozambican workers and the repatriation of more than 10,000 São Tomé exiles from Angola, caused considerable economic dislocation, whose effects have not yet fully receded.

Recent History

GERHARD SEIBERT

São Tomé and Príncipe were colonized by Portugal in the 15th century. A nationalist group, the Comité de Libertação de São Tomé e Príncipe, was formed in 1960 and became the Movimento de Libertação de São Tomé e Príncipe (MLSTP) in 1972, under the leadership of Dr Manuel Pinto da Costa. Following the military coup in Portugal in April 1974, the Portuguese government recognized the right of the islands to independence, although negotiations were delayed until September. In December Portugal appointed a transitional government which included members of the MLSTP, which was recognized as the sole legitimate representative of the people. At elections for a constituent assembly held in July 1975, the MLSTP won all 16 seats. Independence as the Democratic Republic of São Tomé and Príncipe took effect on 12 July, with Pinto da Costa as president and Miguel Trovoada as prime minister. The constitution promulgated in November effectively vested absolute power in the hands of the president and the political bureau of the MLSTP. Radical socialist policies were introduced, and any activity deemed contrary to MLSTP directives was viewed as treason.

MLSTP GOVERNMENT

During 1976–82 serious ideological as well as personal divisions arose within the MLSTP, and a number of prominent members who favoured a more moderate approach to social, economic and agrarian reforms were forced into exile. In March 1978 Angolan soldiers were brought to the islands to provide protection for the president and his associates, following an alleged coup attempt. In March 1979 Dr Carlos da Graça, a former minister of health who had left for Gabon in 1977, was tried *in absentia* and sentenced to 24 years' imprisonment. In April 1979 Trovoada was dismissed as prime minister. In September he was arrested, accused of complicity in the 1978 coup attempt and detained without trial until 1981, when he was permitted to leave the islands. Another alleged coup attempt was forestalled in November 1980. In December 1981 rioting broke out on Príncipe, where food shortages had led to agitation for that island's autonomy. During 1982 Leonel d'Alva, a former prime minister and minister of foreign affairs, fled to exile in Cape Verde, and Daniel Daio, the minister of defence and national security, was removed from office.

In its foreign relations, São Tomé and Príncipe avoided any formal commitment to the Eastern bloc, although close economic ties existed with the People's Republic of China and the German Democratic Republic. Cuba and the USSR provided the regime with military advisers. Gabon, the islands' nearest mainland neighbour, viewed these developments with disquiet, and relations consequently deteriorated. However, the republic extended the range of its international contacts by joining the International Monetary Fund (IMF) in 1977, acceding to the Lomé Convention in 1978 and participating in the foundation of the francophone Communauté économique des états de l'Afrique central (CEEAC) in 1983. The bulk of the country's trade continued to be transacted with western Europe, and relations with Portugal remained generally cordial.

In 1985, confronted by the threat of the complete collapse of the economy, Pinto da Costa began to abandon economic ties with the Eastern bloc in favour of capitalist strategies. Trade agreements with Eastern bloc countries were allowed to lapse, and Pinto da Costa and his ministers made extensive visits to Western Europe and North America to solicit support for measures of economic liberalization. The two main Western nations seeking to exert influence in the country were Portugal and France; however, trade with Portugal was much more substantial than with France, and negotiations concerning São Tomé's admission to the Franc Zone were eventually inconclusive. The USA accredited its first ambassador to São Tomé in 1985, and provided the country with a limited amount of military aid.

Ideological Liberalization

From 1985 a wider range of ideological views was represented in the newly elected national people's assembly, which confirmed Pinto da Costa as president, and in the new central committee of the MLSTP. By the end of 1985 there was an atmosphere of reconciliation in São Tomé politics: Carlos da Graça was pardoned and Miguel Trovoada was invited to return from exile. In October 1987 the central committee of the MLSTP announced a major constitutional reform, which included the election by universal adult suffrage of the president of the republic, and of members of the national people's assembly. The amended constitution also allowed 'independent' candidates to contest elections for the national people's assembly, although the president of the MLSTP, chosen by the MLSTP congress from two candidates proposed by the central committee, would continue to be the sole candidate for the presidency of the republic. In January 1988 the national people's assembly approved a constitutional amendment providing for the re-establishment of the post of prime minister, to which Celestino Rocha da Costa, until then the minister of education, labour and social security, was appointed. Rocha da Costa formed a new government in which Carlos da Graça became minister of foreign affairs.

Da Graça, however, was one of the few political exiles to return, as the majority of the opposition groups abroad regarded these reforms as insufficient. Although Miguel Trovoada, now resident in France, chose not to create any alternative political organization, three overseas opposition movements were already in existence: the Frente de Resistência Nacional de São Tomé e Príncipe (FRNSTP), the Acção Democrática Nacional de São Tomé e Príncipe (ADNSTP) and the União Democrática Independente de São Tomé e Príncipe (UDISTP). The FRNSTP was originally based in Gabon under the leadership of Carlos da Graça, but as relations between Gabon and São Tomé improved, the movement was expelled from Gabon in 1986. Carlos da Graça ceased to be a member and remained in Gabon, before returning to São Tomé as minister of foreign affairs. The major part of the FRNSTP moved to Lisbon, formed a coalition with the UDISTP, and agreed to seek political changes by non-violent means. A small faction of the FRNSTP, led by Afonso dos Santos, refused to give up the armed struggle as a means of overthrowing the São Tomé régime and moved to Cameroon, taking the name of Frente de Resistência Nacional de São Tomé e Príncipe–Renovada (FRNSTP–R). In March 1988 Afonso dos Santos led a sea-borne expedition of 44 men from his headquarters in southern Cameroon, in an attempt to invade São Tomé and seize power. The operation was poorly planned and executed, and the invaders were quickly captured. In September 1989 dos Santos was sentenced to 22 years' imprisonment, and 38 other defendants were also jailed.

Democratic Transition

Somewhat shaken by the failed coup attempt, increasingly alarmed by the domestic economic crisis, encouraged by Western exponents of economic reform, and by a progressive faction within the MLSTP, the regime embarked in late 1989 on a transition to full multi-party democracy, after strenuous debate at a national party conference. In August 1990, in a national referendum, 72% of the electorate voted in favour of the introduction of the constitution proposed by the MLSTP central committee. The new constitution provided for a multi-party political system, together with the abolition of the death penalty, guarantees on human rights, and a maximum of two five-year terms of office for the president.

In April 1990 Afonso dos Santos and his accomplices in the March 1988 coup attempt were granted an amnesty by presidential decree and dos Santos founded the Frente Democrata Cristã (FDC). Further organized opposition came from the Coligação Democrática de Oposição (CODO), a merger of the three opposition groups formerly in exile, under the leadership of Albertino Neto. But the major challenge to the MLSTP came from the local opposition. A coalition of former MLSTP dissidents, independents and young professionals, formed the Partido de Convergência Democrática–Grupo de Reflexão (PCD–GR). Leonel d'Alva, returning from exile in Cape Verde, was elected president of the PCD–GR, while Daniel Daio became secretary-general. The MLSTP party congress, held in October 1990, appointed a new secretary-general, Carlos da Graça (the minister of foreign affairs), in succession to Manuel Pinto da Costa, the party's founding president. In addition, the party's name was amended to the Movimento de Libertação de São Tomé e Príncipe–Partido Social Democrata (MLSTP–PSD).

On 20 January 1991 elections to the new national assembly resulted in defeat for the MLSTP–PSD, which secured only 30.5% of the votes and 21 seats in the 55-member legislature. The PCD–GR obtained 54% of the votes and 33 seats in the assembly. CODO, with 5% of the votes, took the remaining seat.

In February 1991 a transitional government, headed by Daniel Daio, was installed, pending the presidential election, to be held in March. In the same month, President Pinto da Costa confirmed his earlier decision that he would be retiring from politics and would not be contesting the forthcoming election. The MLSTP–PSD did not present an alternative candidate. In late February two of the three remaining presidential candidates, Afonso dos Santos, of the FDC (which had received little support at the January legislative elections), and an independent candidate, Guadalupe de Ceita, withdrew from the election. Miguel Trovoada, who stood as an independent candidate (with the support of the PCD–GR and CODO), remained as sole contender, and in March was elected president, receiving 81% of the votes cast. Trovoada took office in the following month. The new government promised to expedite the process of political and economic liberalization, indicated that the harassment of the Roman Catholic church was at an end, and called for national reconciliation.

THE TROVOADA PRESIDENCY

In early 1992 a political crisis erupted when co-operation between the government and the presidency began to break down. The PCD–GR, which wished to limit the extent of powers granted to the president under the constitution of September 1990, attempted to introduce a constitutional amendment limiting the presidential powers. Meanwhile, widespread popular dissatisfaction followed the imposition in June 1991 of stringent austerity measures that had been imposed by the IMF and the World Bank as preconditions for economic assistance. These measures, which included a 40% devaluation of the currency and a substantial increase in petroleum prices, had contributed to a sharp decline in the islanders' living standards. Following two mass demonstrations held in April 1992 to protest against the austerity programme, Trovoada dismissed the Daio government, citing as his main reason the 'institutional disloyalty' of the prime minister, who had publicly blamed the president for the country's economic plight and attendant political unrest. Trovoada did, however, affirm his support for the economic recovery measures that had been implemented by Daio. The PCD–GR, which initially condemned Trovoada's actions as an 'institutional coup', was invited to designate a new prime minister. In May Norberto Costa Alegre (the minister of economy and finance in the former administration, who had been instrumental in the negotiation of the structural adjustment measures) replaced Daio as prime minister and formed a new administration.

Violent clashes in early August 1992 between the police and members of the armed forces resulted when some 40 soldiers forced entry into a police station in the capital to secure the release of two soldiers who were being detained. The conflict followed mounting tensions between the two forces, which observers attributed to a lack of definition as to their respective roles in the country, and to discontent within the armed forces at its impending reorganization.

On 6 December 1992, in the first local elections to be held since independence, the PCD–GR suffered a considerable reverse, obtaining only 15 of the total of 59 seats and failing to gain outright control of any of the seven districts. Conversely, the MLSTP–PSD won 38 seats and gained control of five districts. The newly formed Acção Democrática Independente (ADI) won the remaining six seats and secured control of one district. However, the government refused to accede to opposition demands that it resign, form a government of national unity or call new legislative elections.

In February 1993 Daio resigned as secretary-general of the ruling PCD–GR, and in April was replaced, in an interim capacity, by the more moderate João do Sacramento Bonfim. Opposition expectation that the appointment of Bonfim would facilitate political dialogue, and perhaps lead to the formation of a government of national unity, proved unfounded; in November four opposition parties issued a joint statement accusing the government of authoritarianism and incompetence, and, in turn, were accused of fomenting instability.

In August 1993 the national assembly appointed a five-member commission of inquiry to investigate allegations of corruption against the minister of justice, labour and public administration, Olegário Pires Tiny, and the minister of commerce, industry, fisheries and tourism, Arzemiro dos Prazeres. However, the commission concluded that the allegations against both ministers were unfounded.

In April 1994 the national assembly adopted legislation, drafted by the MLSTP–PSD, reinforcing the rights of the parliamentary opposition. Under the provisions of the law, all opposition parties represented in the legislature were to be consulted on major political issues, including defence, foreign policy and the budget. In the same month the national assembly began discussion of a draft bill providing local autonomy for the island of Príncipe. Its proposals, which were approved later that year, included provision for the creation of a regional assembly and a five-member regional government. This measure was intended to allay discontent expressed by inhabitants of Príncipe, who felt that the island had been neglected by the central administration.

In early 1994 relations between the government and the presidency began to deteriorate. In April Trovoada publicly dissociated himself from government policy. In June political tension increased when the PCD–GR accused Trovoada of systematic obstruction of the government's programme. The same month opposition parties petitioned the president to dismiss the government and to appoint foreign auditors to investigate the management of public funds under its term of office. On 2 July 1994 Trovoada dismissed the Alegre administration citing 'institutional conflict' as the justification for the decision. Moreover, the president accused the ruling party of ignoring presidential vetoes and of attempting to replace the semi-presidential system with a parliamentary regime without executive powers for the head of state. On 4 July Trovoada appointed Evaristo do Espírito Santo de Carvalho (the minister of defence and security in the outgoing administration) as prime minister. The PCD–GR, which refused to participate in the new government, subsequently expelled Carvalho from the party. An interim administration, comprising eight ministers, took office on 9 July. On the following day, in an attempt to resolove the political crisis, Trovoada dissolved the national assembly and announced that a legislative election would be held on 2 October.

This election resulted in a decisive victory for the MLSTP–PSD, which secured 27 seats, one short of an absolute majority. The PCD–GR and the ADI each obtained 14 seats. The level of voter participation, which was as low as 52%, was believed to reflect public disillusionment at the failure of democracy immediately to realize their expectations of a transformation of the country's social and economic prospects. In late October 1994 da Graça was appointed prime minister and subsequently announced his intention to form a government of national unity with those parties represented in the legislature. However, both the ADI and the PCD–GR rejected the proposal. The council of ministers that took office in late October thus comprised solely members of the MLSTP–PSD.

In mid-October 1994 employees in the banking sector began an indefinite strike, in support of demands that compensation be paid to those made redundant since the rationalization of the sector began in 1992. In December 1994 da Graça removed a number of senior civil servants, including the administrative heads of all public enterprises. Among those dismissed was the governor of the central bank, Adelino Santiago Castelo David, who was accused of misappropriation of funds.

Social and Economic Problems

In early February 1995 the government appealed for international aid to mitigate the economic effects of the imminent return of some 6,000–7,000 Santomeans from Gabon, from where all immigrants who had not by that month legalized their status were to be expelled. In the event some 1,500 migrant workers were forced to return to São Tomé. In April about 50 returnees attempted to occupy the prime minister's office in protest at the alleged disappearance of foreign funds intended to support their reintegration.

In mid-February 1995 the government announced that a general salary increase, of 64%–90%, for public- and private-sector employees would be introduced at the end of the month, in an effort to assuage increasing social tension caused by the constantly rising cost of living. Later that month, with the aim of securing the release of suspended funds from the World Bank, the government announced the introduction of austerity measures, including a 25% increase in fuel prices, the dismissal of some 300 civil servants, and an increase in interest rates.

In March 1995 the first elections to a new seven-member regional assembly and five-member regional government were conducted on Príncipe, which had been granted local autonomy by the national assembly in 1994. The elections resulted in victory for the MLSTP–PSD, which won an absolute majority. The ADI and the PCD–GR did not themselves offer candidates, but instead supported a local opposition group. The new regional government began functioning in April. In March the minister of defence abolished the provisional command of the armed forces, created for a transitional period in 1991, and appointed Capt. António Paquete da Costa, the former chief of the provisional command, as the new chief of the general staff of the armed forces. At the end of March 1995, a privatization agreement with an Angolan commercial enterprise, the Mello Xavier Group, provoked a wave of protest in the country. The agreement provided for Mello Xavier to assume control of the Porto Alegre cocoa estate and gave the Angolan company priority in the privatization of a further four non-agricultural enterprises. In addition, the government was to grant Mello Xavier a concession for offshore banking. Both Trovoada and the opposition parties strongly rejected the agreement, and, in the light of the protest, Mello Xavier did not pursue the original agreement. In early 1996 Mello Xavier finally acquired the management contract for the Porto Alegre estate.

In early June 1995 the police assumed control of the national radio station following several days of strike action by employees of the station in support of salary increases of up to 300%. In the wake of the dispute the government suspended a 350% salary increase awarded earlier to bank employees, and created a commission to review state administration salaries. Social unrest continued in the following months with teachers and doctors striking in support of demands for increased salaries and improved working conditions. In June the minister of planning and finance, Carlos Quaresma Batista da Sousa, was dismissed and assumed fully the position of governor of the central bank, a post which he had held in an acting capacity since December 1994. The finance portfolio was assumed by the minister of economic affairs, Joaquim Rafael Branco.

Coup Attempt

On 15 August 1995 a group of some 30 soldiers, led by five junior officers of the armed forces, seized control of the presidential palace. Trovoada was detained at the headquarters of the armed forces, da Graça was placed under house arrest, the constitution was suspended and a curfew imposed. The insurgents cited widespread corruption and political incompetence as justification for the coup. Saõ Tomé's principal aid donors, including the USA and Portugal, immediately condemned the coup and demanded the reinstatement of constitutional order under penalty of the withdrawal of development assistance. Confronted by both international pressure and the lack of professionals to establish a military regime, the five-member military commission, headed by Lt Manuel Quintas de Almeida, abandoned its initial proposal to establish a junta of national salvation and began negotiations with Trovoada, the government and political parties. Talks were mediated by an Angolan delegation, led by the Angolan minister of foreign affairs, Dr Venâncio da Silva Moura. Six days after the initial coup attempt, the military insurgents and the government signed a 'memorandum of understanding', providing for the reinstatement of Trovoada and the restoration of constitutional order. In return, the government gave an undertaking to restructure the armed forces, and the national assembly granted a general amnesty to all those involved in the coup. Following the coup attempt, Alberto Paulino was replaced as minister of defence by Capt. Carlos Carneiro Paquete da Silva. In early September da Silva's appointment as c-in-c of the army prompted a protest by the officers who had promoted the coup, on the grounds that it contravened the 'memorandum of understanding'. As a consequence, da Silva was replaced in that role by Capt. António do Nascimento. In a national address that month Trovoada expressed his wish to form a government of national unity in order to establish a more stable foundation for government. In addition, he acknowledged the high level of corruption prevalent in São Tomé and the rising incidence of crime.

Consensus Government

At the end of December 1995 Armindo Vaz d'Almeida was appointed prime minister, at the head of the government of national unity. The new administration, which took office in early January 1996, included six members of the MLSTP–PSD, four members of the ADI and one of the PDSTP–CODO. The three parties had formed a political alliance in late December 1995, with the aim of ensuring political stability. The PCD–GR, however, refused to participate in the new government. In February 1996, at the request of the national electoral commission, the forthcoming presidential election, which had been scheduled for early March, was postponed pending the finalization of the electoral rolls. In March the date of the election was set for 30 June, and in early April the national assembly approved the extension of the existing presidential mandate by a further five months. At the congress of the MLSTP–PSD, held in March, Pinto da Costa was selected as the party's official candidate in the forthcoming presidential election, while Francisco Fortunato Pires was appointed secretary-general of the party. In April Trovoada declared his candidacy for the presidential election, in which he was supported by the ADI and the PDSTP–CODO.

At the presidential election of 30 June 1996 no candidate secured an absolute majority. Consequently, a second ballot, between the two leading candidates, was conducted on 21 July, at which Trovoada won 52.74% of the votes, defeating Pinto da Costa, who secured 47.26% of the votes. In late July da Costa, who had initially acknowledged Trovoada's victory, contested the results of the election, claiming that irregularities had occurred in the registration process. In early August the supreme court declared that it was unable to adjudicate on the appeal made by Pinto da Costa, and recommended that the government seek international legal arbitration. However, on 20 August Pinto da Costa withdrew his challenge and Trovoada was confirmed as president. Despite the fact that he did not command majority support in the national assembly, Trovoada dismissed the possibility of new legislative elections, announcing instead his intention to seek a broadly-based government of national consensus. In mid-September the Vaz d'Almeida administration was dissolved, following its defeat in a confidence motion in the national assembly. The motion had been proposed by Vaz d'Almeida's own party, the MLSTP–PSD, which accused the government of inefficiency and corruption, and had received the support of the PCD–GR. Vaz d'Almeida remained as prime minister in a caretaker capacity, pending the appointment of a successor. In late October the MLSTP–PSD and the PCD–GR signed an accord providing for the establishment of a nine-member coalition government. In mid-November, following Trovoada's refusal earlier that month to appoint Fortunato Pires as prime minister, the president appointed Raul Vagner da Conceição Bragança Neto, assistant secretary-general of the MLSTP–PSD, to the position. The new coalition government, which included five members of the MLSTP–PSD, three members of the PCD–GR and one independent, was inaugurated later that month. The ADI had refused to participate in the new administration.

In July 1996 São Tomé and Príncipe was among the five lusophone African countries which, together with Portugal and Brazil, formed the Comunidade dos Países de Língua Portuguesa (CPLP), a Portuguese-speaking commonwealth seeking to achieve collective benefits from co-operation in technical, cultural and social matters.

In mid-August 1996 demonstrators blockaded roads in the capital in protest at the shortage of energy and water supplies. The demonstration had been prompted by reports that the government had spent US $500,000 of state funds, derived from a structural adjustment credit disbursed in January, on luxury cars for cabinet ministers. Several injuries resulted as riot police were deployed to disperse the demonstrators.

In December 1996 the Bragança administration accused the former government of Vaz d'Almeida of corrupt practices, including embezzlement and the illegal diversion of public funds. Earlier that month Vaz d'Almeida had been expelled by the MLSTP–PSD, having declined the party's request that he volunteer his resignation. In mid-December the MLSTP–PSD and the PCD–GR presented the national assembly with a proposal for a revision of the constitution. The proposal, which aimed to redefine the extent of the powers invested in the president, included provision for the establishment of a state council which would have to be consulted before the president could dissolve the legislature. In addition, the president would no longer direct foreign policy. Whilst Trovoada recognised the need for a review of the constitution, he favoured a strengthening of the presidential powers and advocated the replacement of the existing semi-presidential system with a presidential regime.

In April 1997, as part of an initiative to promote national reconciliation and political stability, Trovoada held discussions with former president Pinto da Costa. In order to end the continuous political struggle between the presidency and the government, Trovoada proposed the creation of a unity forum for national reconciliation to debate the country's problems. In July Trovoada announced that there would be a referendum on a far-reaching revision of the constitution.

In April 1997 an increase of some 140% in fuel prices, and a concomitant rise in the prices of transport, food and consumer goods, precipitated violent popular protests in São Tomé city. Hundreds of anti-government demonstrators blockaded roads, and the security forces were deployed to quell rioting. In that month the government announced a 200% salary increase for the public sector. The announcement was criticized by the IMF, which stressed that the increase would hinder efforts to control the budget deficit, and recommended that the government postpone the increase, pending a rationalization of the civil service (which would entail the dismissal of some 1,000 employees).

Following Trovoada's unilateral decision in May 1997 to establish diplomatic relations with Taiwan, in July the People's Republic of China (PRC) suspended diplomatic relations with São Tomé, ceased all development co-operation, and demanded the repayment, within 90 days, of bilateral debts amounting to US $17m. In exchange for diplomatic recognition, Taiwan promised São Tomé $30m. in development aid over a three-year period. Trovoada declared that, in view of the economic condition of São Tomé, the Taiwanese aid could not be rejected. By contrast, the government declared that the aid promised by Taiwan could not compensate for the loss of the long-standing co-operation enjoyed with the PRC. Since 1975 the PRC had granted donations totalling $32.7m., as well as providing interest-free loans totalling $18.7m. Consequently, the government refused to accept $4.3m. in aid offered by Taiwan and prohibited its officials from receiving the four high-ranking diplomats appointed to represent Taiwan in São Tomé.

Economy

GERHARD SEIBERT

The economy of São Tomé and Príncipe, which is based almost exclusively on the export of cocoa, has experienced a long period of decline since independence in 1975. The sudden loss of protected markets in Portugal and the mass exodus of skilled personnel were compounded by the negative effects of systematic nationalizations and the relentless fall in the world price of cocoa after 1979. São Tomé and Príncipe's gross domestic product (GDP) declined in real terms during 1980–86, and grew at an average of only 1.3% per year during 1987–91, according to UN estimates. According to estimates by the World Bank, São Tomé's GDP increased, in real terms, by an annual average of 1.0% in 1985–95. Real GDP growth in 1996 was 1.2%, well below the target of 3.0%. During 1985–95, it was estimated, gross national product (GNP) per head declined, in real terms, at an annual average of 2.1%. Over the same period the population increased by an annual average of 2.3%. In 1995, it was estimated, 26.4% of GDP was derived from the primary sector, 19.8% from the secondary sector, and 53.8% from the tertiary sector, the latter figure mainly reflecting the considerable size of the bureaucracy.

The Marxist economic policies implemented during the decade following independence were a prime factor in the country's economic deterioration. President Pinto da Costa, who had been trained as a Marxist economist, decided at independence to nationalize virtually all enterprises of any size. The government also took a monopoly of foreign trade, and controlled prices and distribution through a network of 'people's shops'. São Tomé became a member of the International Monetary Fund (IMF) and the World Bank in 1977, and introduced a new currency unit, the dobra, to replace the Portuguese escudo at par. The dobra became increasingly overvalued, placing considerable strain on the balance of payments, but the government refused to devalue the currency.

In 1985, confronted by the threat of economic collapse, the president initiated a process of economic liberalization. Foreign companies were invited to bid for management contracts for the state farms, and a cautious process of privatization of the non-agricultural sector was begun. In 1986, the 'people's shops' were leased to private traders, a new investment code was promulgated to attract foreign capital, and a donors' conference was held. Following discussions during 1986 with the World Bank and the IMF, the government widened the scope of its reforms with the introduction in June 1987 of a three-year structural adjustment programme (SAP). This aimed to reduce the large trade and budget deficits, to increase agricultural production, to stimulate exports, and to increase foreign earnings from tourism and fishing. The SAP included measures to restructure the public investment programme and unprofitable public enterprises, to liberalize prices, and to improve incentives for investment by the private sector. The SAP received financial support from the World Bank and the African Development Bank (ADB).

The first step in the SAP was taken in July 1987, when the government devalued the dobra by 54.75%, and increased duties on local and imported consumer goods by between 15%–150%. Price controls were abolished on all goods except rice, sugar, wheat flour, beans, milk and edible oil, and wages were increased by 10%–30% to compensate for the higher prices. Reductions in government spending were announced and taxes were raised. Foreign trade was liberalized with the abolition of the monopoly of the state enterprise, Ecomex, over the import and export of goods. Under the SAP any productive enterprise or registered trader could import or export all but six strategic goods. In July 1988 the dobra was devalued by about 20%, the prices of consumer goods and fuels were raised by 60%–100%, and state subsidies were reduced to less than 20% of import prices, compared with 40% previously. In an attempt to compensate for the steep increase in prices, the wages of workers in the agricultural sector and agro-based industries were raised by 15%. The value of the dobra drifted downwards towards parallel rates, while further adjustments to controlled prices were made to bring these rates closer to market levels. Public sector wages were raised periodically, but did not keep pace with the cost of living. In recognition of these reforms, a donors' meeting in Geneva in March 1989 pledged new loans and a rescheduling of debts, and in June the IMF approved a three-year SDR 2.8m. structural adjustment facility (SAF). The resultant structural adjustment programme, however, began to lose momentum in 1990, as the government subordinated economic concerns to its own survival. The IMF suspended payments under the SAF, and the World Bank threatened to do the same. The budget deficit increased to $4.5m., and inflation reached 47%. Additionally, the gap between official and parallel rates of exchange widened, and foreign exchange reserves were severely depleted.

The priority of the government since 1991 has been a return to fiscal and economic austerity in accordance with the IMF and World Bank guidelines. The currency was repeatedly devalued and by June 1993 the dobra was trading officially at approximately US $1 = 425 dobras, while 'black market' rates stood at about US $1 = 600 dobras. This was outside the 15% margin between official and parallel market rates demanded by the IMF. In 1992 the banking system was reorganized. The Banco Nacional de São Tomé e Príncipe (BNSTP) went into liquidation and its central banking functions were taken over by the new Banco Central de São Tomé e Príncipe. In early 1993 the Banco Internacional de São Tomé e Príncipe was founded to undertake the commercial operations of the former BNSTP. In mid-1993 the government announced that it was studying proposals to transfer responsibility for currency transactions entirely to dealers licenced by the central bank. The inflation rate fell to 22% in the year to December 1992, but still considerably exceeded the 10% guideline established by the IMF. The estimated current deficit on the 1993 budget stood at 2,300m. dobras, and the IMF and World Bank expressed concern over the high levels of funds allocated to the military and the civil service. Electricity and fuel prices were increased sharply, and privatization of the non-agricultural sector was scheduled for completion by the end of 1993. Ecomex was liquidated in 1993 and the government ceased to set prices for imported basic goods, although maximum profit margins on such goods were retained. A new import tariff adopted in January 1993 reduced duties on essential goods and taxes on emigrants' remittances, while increasing duties on non-essential imports. By mid-1992 the IMF indicated that enough progress had been made for payments under the SAF to be resumed. This was a precondition to addressing the problem of the country's high level of external debt, estimated at $215m. at the end of 1991. In 1993 the total external debt stood at $254m., of which $225.8m. was long-term debt. Of the long-term debt, 63.7% was owed to multilateral creditors, while 35.8% was owed to bilateral creditors and another 0.5% to private creditors. In that year total external debt per caput was some $2,100, while GDP per caput, measured at average 1991–93 prices, was only $330. In the 1994 budget 13,000m. dobras, of a projected total expenditure of 18,000m. dobras, were set aside for external debt financing.

In early 1994 the World Bank threatened to suspend structural adjustment credits due to delays in the implementation of agreed economic adjustment measures. Subsequently São Tomé failed to qualify for an IMF enhanced structural adjustment facility (ESAF). However, despite its criticism of the slow pace of the restructuring of public enterprises, a World Bank mission indicated in June that it would recommend the release of US $10m. in structural adjustment credits.

In 1994 the current account of the balance of payments, which had recorded a surplus equivalent to 1.3% of GDP in 1991–93, registered a deficit equivalent to 9.6% of GDP. Inflation increased from 20% in 1993 to 40% in 1994. Expansionary monetary policies also resulted in a widening discrepancy between the official and the parallel exchange rate in 1993–94. By September 1994 none of the public finance targets set by the IMF had been met. Due principally to the shortfall of contributions from state enterprises, only 71% of projected receipts of 4,400m. dobras were realized. Current expenditure (excluding interest payments on debt) totalled 3,700m. dobras, representing 83.1% of total projected expenditure for the nine-month period, while only 5.4% of 2,900m. dobras in programmed interest payments on the external debt had been paid. Instead of a surplus of 1,040m. dobras, as scheduled by the IMF for the 1994 national budget, by September the deficit (excluding interest payments on debt) had already reached 442.4m. dobras. In order to reverse the negative trend, in December 1994 the government increased fuel prices by some 30%. In addition the official and free market exchange rates were unified. Successive devaluations of the currency implemented during 1994 totalled some 50%.

In February 1995, following negotiations with a joint mission of the IMF and the World Bank, the government announced a series of austerity measures aimed at facilitating the disbursement of a third tranche of credit (US $3.2m.) under the SAF. The measures included a further 25% increase in fuel prices and the dismissal of 300 civil servants (civil service salaries represent 4.1% of GDP). In addition, the privatization of state-owned companies was to be expedited, salary increases for the public sector limited to 30% and the interest base rate increased from 35% to 50%. During the negotiations the joint mission had proposed the liquidation of the Caixa Nacional de Poupança e Crédito, which had apparently issued loans exceeding its credit limit. With the implementation of successive increases in fuel prices in March and September 1995, the government succeeded in facilitating the release of the structural adjustment credit of $3.2m., which was disbursed in early 1996. Further increases in fuel prices were imposed in February and May 1996. At July 1996 the official exchange rate was US $1=2,363 dobras, while the parallel rate stood at US $1=2,500 dobras. In mid-1996 the government announced a series of measures aimed at stemming the rapid depreciation of the currency and at reducing the annual rate of inflation from 48% to about 25% by the end of the year. The measures included efforts to prevent widespread tax evasion.

In January 1997 a parliamentary commission of enquiry into the implementation of the 1996 budget revealed several instances of fiscal impropriety. The commission accused the government of Armindo Vaz d'Almeida of exceeding the budget limits defined by fiscal legislation. In September 1996 the government had illegally borrowed 13,500m. dobras from the central bank to finance the budget deficit. Unofficial extra-budgetary expenditure by the treasury totalled 4,274m. dobras.

In February 1997 the World Bank issued an ultimatum to São Tomé, threatening the withdrawal of support if the country should fail to implement the necessary measures to qualify for the Highly Indebted Poor Countries (HIPC) initiative. The ultimatum followed a review of the country's public finances, conducted by a World Bank mission in December 1996, which had observed increasing macro-economic imbalances. By October 1996 the current fiscal balance (excluding donations) had reached a deficit of 7,800m. dobras, compared with a targeted surplus for the year of 4,400m. dobras. The deficit resulted from low revenues, owing to tax evasion, the exemption of import duties on 73% of all imports, and excessive public spending. The World Bank urged the government to take immediate measures to increase fiscal discipline and to combat corruption.

In May 1997 the IMF advised the government to take urgent measures to curb inflation and to stem the rapid devaluation of the currency. It was envisaged that measures aimed at containing the budgetary deficit within 1% of GDP, including restrictions on expenditure and strengthened financial discipline, would reduce the annual rate of inflation from 51.7% in 1996 to 40% in 1997.

AGRICULTURE

Agriculture (including forestry and fishing) contributed an estimated 26.4% of GDP in 1995, and employed 38.1% of the economically active population in 1994. At independence, São Tomé inherited a plantation economy dominated by cocoa and partially protected from international price movements by a guaranteed home market. Most land was farmed by 29 large Portuguese-owned enterprises. In September 1975 the government nationalized all landholdings of over 200 ha and grouped them into 15 state enterprises, two of them on Príncipe. They covered over 80% of the cultivable land area, and ranged in size from 1,500–6,000 ha. The nationalization of the estates led to the exodus of many of the skilled agricultural personnel. Equipment on the plantations ceased to function through poor maintenance and lack of spare parts. Wages fell in real terms, and food for the labourers was in short supply, leading to a fall in employment and productivity. Portuguese consumers turned to cheaper sources of supply, especially as the overvaluation of the dobra raised the prices of São Tomé produce. The state farms incurred substantial deficits and, within a decade, were brought to the point of financial collapse.

In 1985, the government initiated a policy of partial privatization. Ownership of the estates was kept in the hands of the state, but foreign aid was sought to rehabilitate the plantations and foreign companies were invited to tender for management contracts of 15–20 years' duration. Privatization proceeded slowly under this system, and was confined to the prime land in the north-east of São Tomé island. A management contract for the Agua-Izé estate was granted in 1987 to two Portuguese companies, Refinarias de Açúcar Reunidas and Pereira Coutinho. In the same year, the World Bank provided a US $7.9m. concessionary loan for the rehabilitation of the Belavista and Ubabudo estates, with a further $6m. provided by the Arab Bank for Economic Development (BADEA). Management of the Belavista estate was awarded to the Portuguese Francisco Mantero enterprise, which had formerly owned some of the largest plantations in the country. Management of the Ubabudo estate was granted to the Société Française de Réalisation et de Gestion des Projets Café et Cacao (Soca II), part of the Franco-Belgian Socfin-Rivaud plantation group. Another company from the same group, GIE-Sedeci-Terres Rouges, was, in 1989, awarded the management contract for the 2,300 ha Santa Margarida estate, which in 1988 received a rehabilitation grant of 43m. French francs from the Caisse centrale de coopération économique (CCCE). Management of the Monte Café estate, covering 1,800 ha, was transferred in 1990 to the Portuguese Espírito Santo group, with the ADB providing $10.9m. for its rehabilitation. However, in 1997 the government revoked the second stage of the contract with the Espírito Santo group, owing to inadequate management of the estate. In 1990 a Luso-Santomean company, Sociedade de Desenvolvimento Agro-Pecuária (Sodeap), obtained a contract for the Diogo Vaz estate, and in 1992 it secured a rehabilitation grant of $5m. from the World Food Programme and French donors. In 1996 the management contract for the Porto Alegre estate, in the south of São Tomé island, was awarded to the Angolan Mello Xavier group. In June 1997 employees of the Porto Alegre estate declared a strike, in support of demands for improved working and living conditions. The plantation workers protested that, since assuming the management of the estate, the Mello Xavier group had made no major investments and that the payment of salaries was two months in arrears.

By the early 1990s, the strategy of estate management contracts was in crisis. Managers complained that the contracts, which gave the government a right of supervision over major decisions and specified that 80% of all profits went to the state, denied them effective control. Critics pointed out that the state took the risk of major losses, and alleged that the foreigners were merely collecting their management fee from aid money and were doing little to rehabilitate the estates. This latter accusation appears misplaced, as the majority of estates under foreign management show clear signs of improved output and quality, in contrast to those remaining in the public sector (The cocoa yields of estates under private management are as high as 400 kg per ha, whereas the national average is just 190 kg per ha). However, declining cocoa prices soon stifled the optimism of the late 1980s. In July 1991 the two Portuguese companies managing the Agua-Izé estate announced that they were withdrawing. Faced with falling cocoa prices and the aftermath of a two-month strike in late 1990, the Portuguese managements had wished to break up the 5,000-ha estate into smallholdings, retaining only the central processing facilities. When the government refused to allow this, the companies declared that their losses had become excessive and that they were giving up the management contract by mutual agreement. In 1992 the United Nations Development Programme (UNDP) announced that it would provide US $3.5m. to rehabilitate the estate over the period 1993–95. In mid-1993, on the advice of the World Bank, the government began the process of replacing management contracts with long leases. Companies gained managerial autonomy (subject to maintaining the value of the assets entrusted to them by the state), obtained control over the size of their labour force, were no longer able to finance investments with public funds, and had to pay the government rents commensurate with their economic performance. In 1994 long-term leases were granted by the government to the companies managing the Belavista and Ubabudo estates.

The alternative strategy of breaking up the estates into smallholdings has been pursued since 1985. About 10,000 ha of land were distributed to small farmers during 1985–89, although these were usually marginal lands from the fringes of the large estates. The government viewed these areas as suitable only for domestic food production, rather than for cash crops for export. The authorities were unwilling to grant full freehold tenure and in 1989, only one-third of the distributed land was under cultivation. At the instigation of the World Bank, which was providing finance of US $17.2m. for the process of land reform, the government announced that some 20,000 ha of land would be transferred to smallholders between 1993–98. Land distributed to smallholders since 1985 which had not been cultivated would be repossessed and redistributed by the state. Surveying for suitable sites is proceeding, but the rate at which land is being transferred is slow. In 1993 some 1,488 ha of former plantation land were distributed to smallholders, with a further 2,957 ha distributed in 1994 and 1,838 ha in the first half of 1995. In addition some 4,000 ha have been distributed to small enterprises since 1993. In January 1995 the government signed an agreement with the UNDP providing financing of $3.4m. for a five-year project to support smallholder agriculture. In March a six-year national programme for the support and promotion of family agriculture was established with financing of 51.1m. French francs, from the Caisse française de développement and the International Fund for Agricultural Development. In May the International Development Association (IDA) granted a loan of $9.8m. for the development of the smallholder sector.

By mid-1996 the Agua-Izé, Ponta Figo and Milagrosa estates had been liquidated and their land redistributed to former workers and to medium-sized enterprises. A further five estates were to be completely dismantled as part of the redistribution programme. By 1996 the government had invested some US $40m. of donor funds in the rehabilitation of state-owned plantations. Although it was projected that all plantations would become profitable by 1995, only the Bela Vista estate achieved this aim. In view of the relative success of the redistribution programme (average incomes from redistributed land were three times greater than those from non-privatized land), and the failure of all but one of the remaining state plantations to become profitable, the World Bank recommended an increase in the area of land scheduled for redistribution to smallholders.

A parliamentary commission of enquiry, established in November 1996 to investigate the process of land distribution, reported in January 1997 that since late 1994 land distribution to medium-sized enterprises had become increasingly irregular. Land was distributed directly by the government of Carlos da Graça and Armindo Vaz d'Almeida, without consulting the national committee for land distribution or observing the pertinent legislation. According to the enquiry, proceeds derived from the sale of state property at the former estates of Milagrosa, Mesquita, Colonia Açoriana and Agua-Izé were not transferred to the treasury.

By May 1997 some 9,000 ha of former plantation land had been distributed to more than 3,000 smallholders. Two estates, Ribeira Peixe and Santa Catarine, were distributed entirely to former plantation workers. An additional 3,000 ha of plantation land were distributd to medium-sized enterprises in plots of up to 50 ha.

Since independence, cocoa has regularly accounted for well over 90% of exports by value, reaching 94% in 1987. Cocoa covered 61% of the cultivated area on the 15 large estates in 1986. Production fell from some 11,500 tons in 1973 to less than 5,000 tons in 1976, but by 1979 had recovered to more than 7,000 tons in response to high world prices, before falling back once again as market demand receded. Output remained stagnant at around 4,000 tons a year in the 1980s, and export earnings from cocoa fell by 67% between 1979–88. Yields had dwindled to 0.32 tons per ha by 1985, compared with 0.5 tons per ha prior to independence, and with yields of up to 2.0 tons per ha on some modern plantations in other areas of the world. In 1985 the islands' cocoa trees were 30 years old on average, and some were much older. Black pod disease has spread because of a lack of phytosanitary treatment, and soil fertility has declined with the lack of fertilizer application. As cocoa prices fell still further in the early 1990s, production drifted down to a low point of 3,193 tons in 1991. Output then increased slightly to 3,688 tons in 1992 and reached 4,305 tons in 1993. Prices were set to rise gently again in 1993, and the combined production of the three most successful foreign managed estates (Belavista, Ubabudo and Santa Margarida) was forecast to reach some 5,000 tons by 1994. However, in that year production totalled only 3,392 tons. Total cocoa production for 1995 was 4,577 tons.

The islands' principal secondary crops are copra, coffee and palm oil and kernels. In 1986, coconut palms covered 23% of the cultivated area on the 15 state-owned estates, and copra was the country's only export of any significance apart from cocoa. In 1987, less than 2,000 tons of copra were exported, compared to over 5,000 tons in 1973. By 1995 production of copra had fallen to only 501 tons. Oil palms accounted for 10% of the cultivated area on the estates in 1986 and coffee for 3%, but exports of these commodities ceased altogether in the latter half of the 1980s. In the early 1990s hopes for agricultural diversification in the export sector rested principally on pepper and arabica coffee. Coffee output increased from 14 tons in 1992 to 29 tons in 1995. Exports of cocoyam (also known as taro, or matabala), plantain and citrus fruit to Gabon were also targeted for development.

Self-sufficiency in basic food crops has eluded the government since independence, despite the high fertility of the islands' volcanic soils, the long growing season, the variety of microclimates, and abundant rainfall. The apportionment of centrally-fixed planning targets for food production among the nationalized estates proved unsuccessful, and by the mid-1980s the country was estimated to be importing 90% of its food requirements. The emphasis after 1985 was on developing smallholder agriculture on the fringes of the great estates. By 1992 it was estimated that imports of food had fallen to around 45% of consumption. The only surviving large-scale food project is the oil palm plantation at Ribeira Peixe. Since the early 1980s, the European Community (EC, now the European Union–EU) has been providing funds to plant 610 ha of high yielding oil palms and to establish a publicly-owned palm oil factory on the 1,500-ha Ribeira Peixe estate in the south-east of São Tomé island. By 1992 the project was producing about 80,000 litres of oil a month and was able to meet the country's internal requirements. However, although the project had been conceived as an exercise in import substitution, it was announced that export markets would be sought if the oil proved unpopular with domestic consumers. A French-financed market gardening project at Mesquita established in 1981 experimented with seeds, techniques and training, and concluded in 1994. The greatest obstacles to self-sufficiency in food are the virtual absence of a smallholder tradition due to the plantation economy and the impossibility of growing wheat for a population increasingly accustomed to eating bread and other wheat-based products. Average food consumption in the country is 300 tons per month, comprising mainly local food crops including plantain, bread-fruit, matabala (taro), cassava, sweet potatoes and vegetables. Annual plantain production increased from 10,250 tons in 1992 to 13,650 tons in 1994. Annual matabala production increased from 5,000 tons in 1992 to 8,245 tons in 1995.

The livestock sector has been seriously affected by the decline in veterinary services since independence. Pork has traditionally been the main source of animal protein, but all 30,000 pigs in the islands had to be slaughtered in 1979 after an outbreak of African swine fever. With the help of foreign donors production was restored to pre-1979 levels by 1986, but swine fever recurred on São Tomé island in 1992 and pork production decreased from

220 tons in 1992 to 34 tons in 1995. Chicken and egg production were also badly affected by disease in 1993 when chicken production fell to 100 tons, before recovering slightly in 1994 to 126 tons, and declining to 118 tons in 1995. Egg production, however, continued to fall, from 2m. in 1992 to 1.6m. in 1994 and 1995. Goats are widely reared, and are sometimes exported to Gabon. The islands are free of tsetse fly, but cattle have been badly affected by bovine tuberculosis. Beef production increased, however, from 12 tons in 1992 to 24 tons in 1995.

Similar difficulties have beset the fishing sector, a priority area for economic diversification which contributed 6% of GDP in 1984. In the early 1990s fishing was the second largest source of foreign exchange, due principally to revenue from fishing licences, and employed some 10% of the economically active population. A state-owned fishing company, Empesca, was formed at independence. Its two modern trawlers had on-board freezing facilities, and cold store facilities were installed at the port of Neves on São Tomé island. In June 1978, the government established an exclusive economic zone around the islands of 370 km (200 nautical miles), although the trawlers actually spent most of their time fishing in Angolan waters. The industrial catch rose to just over 2,500 tons in 1984, but subsequently lack of maintenance on the trawlers led to a rapid decrease. The industrial catch in 1988 was only one ton. Empesca was then reconstituted as a joint venture, but refitting the trawlers has proved more difficult than originally expected. In the long term, the government is basing its hopes for the fishing industry on the tuna resources of the area, and it is estimated that tuna catches could reach 17,000 tons a year without affecting stocks. In the meantime, fishing licences were granted to EC and USSR-flag vessels. São Tomé refused to renew Soviet licences in 1989, owing to a dispute over the terms of payment but signed a new three-year agreement with the EC in 1993. Since the 1985 reforms, the main emphasis of foreign donors has been on upgrading artisan fishing, which has increased the total catch from 1,138 tons in 1980 to 2,873 tons in 1988. In 1993 there were some 2,500 artisan fishing boats in the country, of which about 600 were motorized. The EC, Japan and Canada have provided funds for this purpose. São Tomé's role in the regional fishing scheme operated by the EC since 1987 has been to build and repair fishing boats in the Neves yards. However, the local market for fish in São Tomé has been sated and exports are impeded by bureaucratic regulations. The total catch by artisan fishermen decreased from 3,572 tons in 1990 to 2,334 tons in 1993. A fish-processing plant, the Sociedade Nacional de Comércio e Pesca (SNCP), financed with US $2m. of private capital, began operations in September 1995 in Ribeira Funda, some 20 km from the capital. The SNCP was expected to employ 600 workers by the end of the year. Production was mainly destined for export. In 1996 São Tomé renewed, for a further three-year period, its fishing agreement with the EU, in return for a grant of ECU 2.1m.

São Tomé and Príncipe's considerable forestry resources have been neglected, although it was estimated in 1984 that two-thirds of the country's energy consumption came from fuelwood and most housing is of wooden construction. Colonial legislation for the protection of forests was replaced by a new law in 1979, but it was not enforced and no barriers were placed to the uncontrolled cutting of trees. A commission was set up in 1988 to study the problems of forest preservation and reafforestation, and it began by drawing up a national forest inventory with foreign assistance. This revealed that 29% of the country was still covered in primary forest (*obó*), mainly in the inaccessible south-western quadrant of both islands. Some 245 sq km on São Tomé island and 45 sq km on Príncipe were identified as needing to be demarcated as 'ecological reserves', in areas where commercial agriculture is uneconomic. In addition, the inventory noted the existence of 30,000 ha of secondary forest, largely on abandoned plantation land and 32,000 ha of 'shade forest', covering commercial crops. The resources exploitable on a sustainable basis outside the 'ecological reserves' were estimated at between 70,000–105,000 cu m of construction wood and between 43,000–65,000 cu m of fuelwood per year. However, it was also estimated that the country needed 20,000 cu m of fuelwood for dry-processing cocoa, copra and other commercial crops, and a further 140,000 cu m for domestic purposes. In 1990, São Tomé was included in a Central African forest conservation project, financed by the EC, which was intended to lead to the demarcation and enforcement of forest reserves. Although a provisional code of forest regulations was issued in 1993, the current programme of land distribution to smallholders has led to increasing deforestation, with the new occupants arbitrarily felling trees. Local observers fear serious ecological consequences. With the assistance of the UN Environment Programme, the government has undertaken to formulate legislation concerning management of the environment in order to address increasing problems of this kind.

MANUFACTURING AND SERVICES

Industry, including construction and public utilities, accounted for an estimated 19.8% of GDP in 1995, and employed 15.5% of the economically active population in 1994. The secondary sector comprises some 50 small- and medium-sized enterprises and several hundred microenterprises. Of the 25 manufacturing companies in existence at independence in 1975, 12 had closed down completely by 1993, eight were functioning well below capacity, and five had been rehabilitated and expanded. Three new enterprises had been created. Apart from a printing workshop, beer, soft drinks, spirits, bread, vegetable oil, soap, sawn wood, furniture, ceramics, bricks and garments are produced. Industry is generally confined to production for the local market, but garments are exported to Angola. Many basic manufactured products are still imported, especially from Portugal. The government aims to develop food processing and the production of construction materials. All industrial companies were originally scheduled for privatization by the end of 1993. By early 1995 ten non-agricultural public enterprises had been privatized, liquidated or placed under foreign management. In mid-1997 the government announced the sale of its minority shares in three enterprises: the brick manufacturer Cerámica de São Tomé (in which it held a 40% share), the clothing manufacturer Confecções Agua Grande Lda (35%), and the construction materials supplier Cunha Gomes S.A. (30%). In addition, the World Bank and the IMF urged the government to privatize the Pousada Boa Vista hotel and to liquidate the pharmaceutical company Empresa Nacional de Medicamentos, the slaughterhouse Empresa de Transformação de Carnes, the insurance company A Compensadora, and the savings bank Caixa Nacional de Poupança e Crédito. Those enterprises to remain under state control were the palm oil manufacturer EMOLVE, the ports administration ENAPORT, the airport administration company ENCO, the telecommunications company CST (49%) and the airline Air São Tomé e Príncipe (35%), all of which were to be transformed into limited-liability companies.

There are no mineral resources on the islands, but offshore prospecting for hydrocarbons since the late 1980s has produced encouraging preliminary findings. In May 1997 the government signed an accord with the US Environmental Remediation Holding Corporation (ERHC) and the South African Procura Financial Consultants (PFC) concerning the exploration and exploitation of petroleum, gas and mineral reserves in São Tomé's territory. The agreement, which was valid for 25 years, provided for an initial payment to the government of US $5m. ERHC and PFC were then to finance the evaluation of the petroleum reserves, and a petroleum company was to be established with the government, from which the state would receive 40% of the revenue. Petroleum products were imported from Angola at concessionary rates after independence, but are now being supplied at commercial prices by Angola and Gabon. In 1989, 53% of electricity generation was derived from thermal sources, and 47% from hydroelectric sources. Donors are proposing to place more emphasis on small hydroelectric schemes, either repairing those installed in colonial times or setting up new ones. In early 1994, following completion of a rehabilitation project financed by Sweden, a hydroelectric plant at Guêguê with a capacity of 350 kw was reopened. However, due to low water levels, the plant was operating below its full potential in 1996. The capital city's recently rehabilitated generators still rely on fuel oil, and power cuts have become increasingly frequent as fuel prices have risen sharply. A project aimed at increasing, by 50%, the fuel storage capacity of the state fuel company, with finance of 20.6m. French francs from the Caisse française de developpement, was concluded in late 1995 and was expected to help curb problems arising from erratic supplies.

In 1991, the public company responsible for electricity and water supplies, EMAE, which had become much criticized for its inefficiency, was handed over to a French company to manage. In 1995, in the light of the French company's failure to improve the energy supply, the government declined to renew the management contract. In 1996, with the installation of a new electricity generator with a capacity of 1,200 kw, EMAE succeeded in reducing the energy deficit by 40%. A comprehensive energy plan was scheduled for the end of 1993, and the entire electricity and water distribution systems were to be replaced from 1994.

The asphalted road network of some 250 km suffered serious deterioration following independence, although a repair programme financed by foreign aid began in 1989, and by 1995 most roads outside of the capital had been repaired. Foreign donors are also upgrading three of the country's ports, although São Tomé city lacks a natural deep-water harbour and has been losing traffic to the better-endowed port of Neves, which handles petroleum imports and industrial fishing. Joint ventures were established in 1989 to replace the inefficient state enterprises for maritime communications and telecommunications. In 1984 the first phase of a long-term plan for modernizing the main airport near São Tomé city was completed at a cost of US $10m., with the new runway allowing some long-haul aircraft to land. The second phase costing $18m. and consisting of a new control tower and passenger terminal was completed in 1992. The joint venture airline established in 1986 under the name Equatorial Airlines of São Tomé and Príncipe went into liquidation in 1992. In late 1993 a new airline, Air São Tomé e Príncipe, began operations. The company is managed by TAP-Air Portugal which also holds a 40% share of the capital. The government of São Tomé holds a 35% share while the French companies Golfe International Air Service and Mistral Voyages hold 24% and 1% respectively. In 1990 a telecommunications company, Companhia Santomense de Telecomunicações, was established as a joint venture between the state (49%) and the Portuguese Rádio Marconi (51%).

The improvement in communications has been of great importance in sustaining efforts to develop tourism, which is currently the sector of the economy attracting the most foreign capital. The islands benefit from spectacular volcanic mountains and craters, unpeopled beaches, unique bird life and flora, and have ample potential for game-fishing. However, the high rainfall during most of the year limits the duration of the tourist season, and the sea is usually dangerous to bathe in because of strong currents. Nevertheless, the first modern tourist hotel, the Miramar, was completed in 1986 with a capacity of 50 beds, and it has attracted a modest current of tourists, mainly European expatriates and wealthy Gabonese. The Bombom luxury tourist complex on Príncipe island, which caters particularly for game-fishing, and the Santana tourist complex south of São Tomé city, also with emphasis on marine activities, were opened in late 1992. Renovation of the colonial Pousada Boa Vista, financed by TAP-Air Portugal, was completed in mid-1993. In 1994 a new hotel, the Marlin Beach Hotel, was opened near the airport. In late 1995 the government leased the Miramar Hotel, for a period of 20 years, to a group of German investors, São Tomé Invest S.A. The hotel, which had been renovated at a cost of US $2.5m., reopened in June 1997. The World Bank and the ADB have expressed an interest in providing US $300m. to promote the growth of the country's tourist industry, and there are plans for several new hotels and tourist facilities.

In May 1992 the government and Voice of America (VOA) signed an agreement providing for the establishment of a radio relay station at Pinheira, on São Tomé island. The agreement is for a duration of 30 years, and, since 1994, has provided São Tomé with an annual revenue of US $210,000. Broadcasts to some 25m. listeners throughout Africa began in 1996. In early 1997 VOA began local transmissions on FM. In 1994 the government and Radio France Internationale signed an agreement allowing for the installation of a relay station. Broadcasting began in June 1995. In the same month Rádio Televisão Portuguesa Internacional began relaying television broadcasts to the archipelago.

In 1996 the government signed a memorandum of understanding with a South African enterprise, the Western African Development Corporation, providing for the creation of a service and distribution orientated free zone at Príncipe island's deep-water Agulhas Bay. Total investment in the 600-ha zone was estimated at US $290m.

FOREIGN TRADE AND PAYMENTS

Because of the overwhelming importance of the cocoa plantations, the islands' economic life is entirely dependent on external markets. Until 1980, the trade balance was usually positive because of the small value of imports. However, since then low world cocoa prices and low cocoa production, combined with the higher cost of food imports, have led to a continuing trade deficit. The deficit reached a record total of US $21.5m. in 1991, and stood at $18.4m. in 1995. Shortages of essential supplies, especially fuel, have become more frequent. Portugal is the country's main supplier of goods, accounting for an estimated 38.2% of total imports in 1995, although there are considerable fluctuations from year to year. Most other imports come from Western Europe and East Asia. Since the mid-1980s, São Tomé has sold its cocoa mainly to Germany and the Netherlands. In 1995 the Netherlands accounted for 70.6% of total exports.

São Tomé is reputed to be one of the largest recipients per caput of international aid. In 1990 net foreign aid was equivalent to US $200 per caput. UNDP, the World Bank, the EU, Portugal, France, Italy, Sweden, Canada, Japan, the People's Republic of China and Arab countries have been especially prominent as donors. However, the institutional weakness of the country and the lack of co-ordination between donors has led to problems in the efficiency with which aid is utilized. The influx of aid has helped to deal with the deficit on the current account, but it has distorted prices. Total external debt stood at US $266.7m. at the end of 1995, of which 63% was owed to multilateral creditors, principally the ADB and the IDA. The major bilateral creditors were Angola ($23.4m.) and Portuguese commercial banks ($28.3m.). According to UN figures, in 1993 São Tomé received official development assistance of $378 per caput, the highest level of any developing country. Total development assistance stood at $57.4m. in 1995, of which technical assistance accounted for $34.3m., investment projects $16.1m., balance-of-payments support $2.4m., and food aid $0.4m.

Statistical Survey

Sources (unless otherwise stated): Banco Central de São Tomé e Príncipe, Praça da Independência, CP 13, São Tomé; tel. 21901; Direcção de Estatística, São Tomé; Ministry of Finance and Planning, Largo Alfândega, CP 168, São Tomé; tel. 21083; fax 22790.

AREA AND POPULATION

Area: 1,001 sq km (386.5 sq miles).

Population: 96,611 (males 48,031; females 48,580) at census of 15 August 1981; 117,504 (males 57,577; females 59,927) at census of 4 August 1991; 127,076 at mid-1995 (official estimate).

Density (mid-1995): 126.9 per sq km.

Births and Deaths (1994): Registered live births 4,077 (birth rate 32.78 per 1,000); Registered deaths 1,015 (death rate 8.16 per 1,000).

Expectation of Life (years at birth, 1995): 64.9.

Economically Active Population (1994): Agriculture 12,106; Fishing 1,916; Industry, electricity, gas and water 2,327; Public works and civil construction 3,365; Trade, restaurants and hotels 5,184; Financing, insurance, real estate and business services 194; Transport, storage and communications 2,829; Public administration 4,023; Other activities 4,845; Total employed 36,789.

AGRICULTURE, ETC.

Principal Crops (metric tons, 1995): Bananas 12,685; Bread-fruit 1,800; Cabbages 700 (1994); Cassava 3,000 (FAO estimate, 1995); Cocoa 4,577; Coconuts 22,000 (FAO estimate, 1995); Copra 501; Maize 4,300; Matabala (Taro) 8,245; Palm kernels 3,000 (FAO estimate, 1995); Tomatoes 4,200 (1994). Source: partly FAO, *Production Yearbook*.

Livestock ('000 head, year ending September 1994): Cattle 0.3; Sheep 2; Goats 30; Pigs 7; Poultry 80. Source: Ministério da Agricultura e Desenvolvimento Rural.

Livestock Products (estimates, metric tons unless otherwise indicated, 1995): Beef 24; Pork 34; Mutton and goat meat 32; Poultry meat 118; Eggs 1.6 (million); Milk 1.5 ('000 litres, 1994); Honey 1.5. Source: mainly Ministério da Agricultura e Desenvolvimento Rural.

Forestry ('000 cubic metres): Roundwood removals 9 in 1989; 1990–94 annual production as in 1989 (FAO estimates). Source: FAO, *Yearbook of Forest Products*.

Fishing ('000 metric tons, live weight): Total catch 2.6 in 1993; 3.0 in 1994 (FAO estimate); 2.8 in 1995 (FAO estimate). Source: FAO, *Yearbook of Fishery Statistics*.

INDUSTRY

Production (estimates, metric tons, unless otherwise indicated, 1995): Bread and biscuits 3,855; Soap 135; Beer (litres) 1,823,000; Soft drinks (litres) 230,000; Palm oil (litres) 717,000; Electric energy (million kWh) 20.6 (1994). Source: IMF, *São Tomé and Príncipe—Selected Issues and Statistical Appendix* (August 1996).

FINANCE

Currency and Exchange Rates: 100 cêntimos = 1 dobra (Db). *Sterling and Dollar Equivalents* (31 March 1997): £1 sterling = 5,557.5 dobras; US $1 = 3,384.6 dobras; 10,000 dobras = £1.799 = $2.955. *Average Exchange Rate* (dobras per US $): 429.9 in 1993; 732.6 in 1994; 1,429.0 in 1995.

Budget (million dobras): 1995: *Revenue:* Taxation 6,329 (Consumption taxes 1,839); Import taxes 1,954; Export taxes 616; Other taxes 1,920); Other current revenue 4,357 (Transfers from enterprises 668); Total 10,686, excl. grants (16,295). *Expenditure:* Current expenditure 15,480 (Personnel costs 2,163; Goods and services 2,322; Interest on external debt 7,782; Transfers 1,015; Defence 717; Other current expenditure 1,276; Redeployment fund 206); Capital 34,363; Total 49,843, excl. net lending (–72). Source: IMF, *São Tomé and Príncipe—Selected Issues and Statistical Appendix* (August 1996). 1996: *Revenue*: Total (incl. donations) 16,074. *Expenditure*: Total 28,708.

Cost of Living (Consumer Price Index; base: 1990 = 100): 268.8 in 1993; 370.2 in 1994; 461.1 in 1995.

Gross Domestic Product by Economic Activity (estimates, million dobras at current prices, 1995): Agriculture, forestry and fishing 17,070; Manufacturing, electricity, gas and water 3,375; Construction 9,431; Trade and transport 12,156; Public administration 13,211; Financial institutions 3,864; Other services 5,507; *Total* 64,613. Source: IMF, *São Tomé and Príncipe—Selected Issues and Statistical Appendix* (August 1996).

Balance of Payments (US $ million, 1995): Exports of goods f.o.b. 5.1; Imports of goods f.o.b. –23.5; *Trade balance* –18.4; Exports of services 4.3; Imports of nonfactor services –22.1; *Balance on goods and services* –36.2; Other income (net) –5.5; *Balance on goods, services and income* –41.7; Private unrequited transfers (net) 0.5; Official unrequited transfers (net) 23.6; *Current balance* –17.6; Direct investment (net) 1.9; Other long-term capital (net) 9.4; Short-term capital (incl. net errors and omissions) –1.1; *Overall balance* –7.4. Source: IMF, *São Tomé and Príncipe—Selected Issues and Statistical Appendix* (August 1996).

EXTERNAL TRADE

Principal Commodities (estimates, US $ million, 1995): *Imports c.i.f.*: Food and live animals 7.4; Petroleum and petroleum products 2.6; Capital goods 12.4; Total (incl. others) 29.3. *Exports f.o.b.:* Cocoa 4.7; Total (incl. others) 5.1. Source: IMF, *São Tomé and Príncipe—Selected Issues and Statistical Appendix* (August 1996).

Principal Trading Partners (estimates, US $ million, 1995): *Imports c.i.f.:* Angola 1.3; Belgium 1.9; France 4.9; Germany 0.6; Italy 2.1; Japan 4.2; Netherlands 0.8; Portugal 11.2; Total (incl. others) 29.3. *Exports f.o.b.:* Netherlands 3.6; Portugal 0.1; Total (incl. others) 5.1. Source: IMF, *São Tomé and Príncipe—Selected Issues and Statistical Appendix* (August 1996).

TRANSPORT

Road Traffic (registered vehicles, 1994): Light vehicles 4,581, Heavy vehicles 561; Motor cycles 815; Tractors 299.

International Sea-borne Shipping (estimated freight traffic, metric tons, 1992): Goods loaded 16,000; Goods unloaded 45,000.

Civil Aviation (traffic on scheduled services, 1994): Passengers carried ('000) 22; Passenger-km (million) 8; Total ton-km (million) 1. Source: UN, *Statistical Yearbook*. (1992) Passengers carried 29,975; Freight 297,422 metric tons.

TOURISM

Tourist arrivals ('000): 3 in 1992; 3 in 1993; 5 in 1994. Source: UN, *Statistical Yearbook*.

Tourist receipts (US $ m): 2 in 1992; 2 in 1993; 2 in 1994. Source: UN, *Statistical Yearbook*.

Hotels (1996): 9.

COMMUNICATIONS MEDIA

Radio receivers (1994): 35,000 in use. Source: UNESCO, *Statistical Yearbook*.

Television receivers (1994): 21,000 in use. Source: UNESCO, *Statistical Yearbook*.

Non-daily newspapers and periodicals (1996): Titles 3; Estimated average circulation 500 copies.

Telephones (1994): 2,457 lines in use.

EDUCATION

Pre-primary (1989): 13 schools; 116 teachers; 3,446 pupils (males 1,702; females 1,744).

Primary (1995): 64 schools; 654 teachers; 21,760 pupils.

General Secondary (1995): 9 schools; 415 teachers; 12,047 pupils.

Teacher Training: 10 teachers (1983); 188 students (males 74; females 114) (1987).

Vocational Secondary (1989): 18 teachers; 101 students (males 68; females 33).

Source: mainly UNESCO, *Statistical Yearbook*.

Directory

The Constitution

The Constitution came into force on 10 September 1990 as the result of a national referendum, in which 72% of the electorate voted in favour of a draft that had been introduced by the Central Committee of the Movimento de Libertação de São Tomé e Príncipe and approved in March 1990 by the Assembléia Popular Nacional. The following is a summary of its main provisions:

The Democratic Republic of São Tomé and Príncipe is a sovereign, independent, unitary and democratic state. There shall be complete separation between Church and State. Sovereignty resides in the people, who exercise it through universal, direct and secret vote, according to the terms of the Constitution.

Legislative power is vested in the Assembléia Nacional, which comprises 55 members elected by universal adult suffrage. The Assembléia Nacional is elected for four years and meets in ordinary session twice a year. It may meet in extraordinary session on the proposal of the President, the Council of Ministers or of two-thirds of its members. The Assembléia Nacional elects its own President. In the period between ordinary sessions of the Assembléia Nacional its functions are assumed by a permanent commission elected from among its members.

Executive power is vested in the President of the Republic, who is elected for a period of five years by universal adult suffrage. The President's tenure of office is limited to two successive terms. He is the Supreme Commander of the Armed Forces and is accountable to the Assembléia Nacional. In the event of the President's death, permanent incapacity or resignation, his functions shall be assumed by the President of the Assembléia Nacional until a new president is elected.

The Government is the executive and administrative organ of State. The Prime Minister is the Head of Government and is appointed by the President. Other ministers are appointed by the President on the proposal of the Prime Minister. The Government is responsible to the President and the Assembléia Nacional.

Judicial power is exercised by the Supreme Court and all other competent tribunals and courts. The Supreme Court is the supreme judicial authority, and is accountable only to the Assembléia Nacional. Its members are appointed by the Assembléia Nacional. The right to a defence is guaranteed.

The Constitution may be revised only by the Assembléia Nacional on the proposal of at least three-quarters of its members. Any amendment must be approved by a two-thirds' majority of the Assembléia Nacional.

Note: In 1994 the Assembléia Nacional granted political and administrative autonomy to the island of Príncipe. Legislation was adopted establishing a seven-member regional assembly and a five-member regional government; both are accountable to the Minister-Delegate for the Region of Príncipe, who is appointed by the President of São Tomé and Príncipe.

The Government

HEAD OF STATE

President and Commander-in-Chief of the Armed Forces: MIGUEL DOS ANJOS DA CUNHA LISBOA TROVOADA (took office 3 April 1991; re-elected 21 July 1996).

COUNCIL OF MINISTERS

(August 1997)

Prime Minister: RAUL VAGNER DA CONCEIÇÃO BRAGANÇA NETO.

Minister of Foreign Affairs and Communities: HOMERO JERÓNIMO SALVATERRA.

Minister of Justice, Labour and Public Administration: AMARO PEREIRA DE COUTO.

Minister of Finance and Planning: ACÁCIO ELBA BONFIM.

Minister of Health: EDUARDO DO CARMO FERREIRA DE MATOS.

Minister of Education, Culture and Sport: ALBERTINO HOMEM DOS SANTOS SEQUEIRA BRAGANÇA.

Minister of Social Facilities and Environment: ARLINDO AFONSO DE CARVALHO.

Minister of Defence and Internal Security: Maj. JOÃO QUARESMA VIEGAS BEXIGAS.

Minister of Agriculture and Fishing: HERMENGILDO DE ASSUNÇÃO SOUSA E SANTOS.

Minister of Industry, Trade and Tourism: COSME BONFIM AFONSO DA TRINDADA RITA.

There is also a Minister-Delegate for the Autonomous Region of Príncipe.

Government of the Autonomous Region of Príncipe

(August 1997)

President: DAMIÃO VAZ D'ALMEIDA.

Secretary for Social Affairs: ZEFERINO VAZ DOS SANTOS DOS PRAZERES.

Secretary for Infrastructure and Environment: OZÓRIO UMBELINA.

Secretary for Economic Affairs: SILVESTRE UMBELINA.

Secretary for Finance: EPIFÁCIO CASSANDRA.

MINISTRIES

Office of the Prime Minister: Praça Yon Gato, CP 302, São Tomé; tel. 22890; fax 21670.

Ministry of Agriculture and Fishing: Avda 12 de Julho, CP 47, São Tomé; tel. 22714; fax 22347.

Ministry of Defence and Internal Security: Avda 12 de Julho, CP 427, São Tomé; tel. 21092.

Ministry of Education, Culture and Sport: Rua Misericórdia, CP 41, São Tomé; tel. 21398; fax 21466.

Ministry of Finance and Planning: Largo Alfândega, CP 168, São Tomé; tel. 21083; fax 22790.

Ministry of Foreign Affairs and Communities: Avda 12 de Julho, CP 111, São Tomé; tel. 22309; telex 211; fax 23237.

Ministry of Health: Avda Patrice Lumumba, CP 23, São Tomé; tel. 22290; fax 21306.

Ministry of Industry, Trade and Tourism: Largo Alfândega, São Tomé; tel. 22372; fax 22182.

Ministry of Justice, Labour and Public Administration: Avda 12 de Julho, CP 4, São Tomé; tel. 23263; fax 22256.

Ministry of Social Facilities and Environment: Avda 12 de Julho, CP 130, São Tomé; tel. 22648; telex 242.

President and Legislature

PRESIDENT

Presidential Election, First Ballot, 30 June 1996

Candidate	Votes	% of Votes
MIGUEL TROVOADA	15,344	41.38
MANUEL PINTO DA COSTA	13,627	37.75
ALDA BANDEIRA	5,970	16.10
CARLOS DA GRAÇA	1,973	5.32
ARMINDO TOMBA	168	0.45
Total	37,082	100.00

Second Ballot, 21 July 1996

Candidate	Votes	% of Votes
MIGUEL TROVOADA	19,885	52.74
MANUEL PINTO DA COSTA	17,818	47.26
Total	37,703	100.00

ASSEMBLÉIA NACIONAL

General Election, 2 October 1994

	Seats
Movimento de Libertação de São Tomé e Príncipe–Partido Social Democrata	27
Acção Democrática Independente	14
Partido de Convergência Democrática–Grupo de Reflexão	14
Total	55

Political Organizations

Acção Democrática Independente (ADI): São Tomé; f. 1992; Leader CARLOS AGOSTINHO DAS NEVES.

Aliança Popular–Partido Trabalhista (AP–PT): São Tomé; f. 1993; Leader ANACLETO ROLIN.

Frente Democrata Cristã–Partido Social da Unidade (FDC–PSU): São Tomé; f. 1990; Leader JOÃO MANUEL.

Movimento de Libertação de São Tomé e Príncipe–Partido Social Democrata (MLSTP–PSD): São Tomé; f. 1972 as MLSTP; adopted present name in 1990; sole legal party 1972–90; Sec.-Gen. FRANCISCO FORTUNATO PIRES.

Partido de Convergência Democrática–Grupo de Reflexão (PCD–GR): São Tomé; f. 1990; Pres. ALDA BANDEIRA.

Partido Democrático de São Tomé e Príncipe–Coligação Democrática da Oposição (PDSTP–CODO): São Tomé; f. 1990; Leader MANUEL GOMES DA SILVA.

Diplomatic Representation

EMBASSIES IN SÃO TOMÉ AND PRÍNCIPE

Angola: Avda Kwame Nkrumah 45, São Tomé; tel. 22206; telex 227; Chargé d'affaires: ADRIANO NUNES TIAGO.

China (Taiwan): Avda Marginal de 12 de Julho, CP 839, São Tomé; tel. 23529; fax 21376; Chargé d'affaires: TEH-YANG JACQUES WU.

Gabon: Rua Damão, São Tomé; tel. 21280; Ambassador: HENRI MBIRA NZE.

Portugal: Avda Marginal de 12 de Julho, CP 173, São Tomé; tel. 22470; telex 261; fax 21190; Ambassador: MÁRIO LINO DA SILVA.

Judicial System

Judicial power is exercised by the Supreme Court of Justice and the Courts of Primary Instance. The Supreme Court is the ultimate judicial authority.

President of the Supreme Court: PASCOAL DAIO.

Religion

More than 90% of the population are Christians, almost all of whom are Roman Catholics.

CHRISTIANITY

The Roman Catholic Church

São Tomé and Príncipe comprises a single diocese, directly responsible to the Holy See. At 31 December 1995 there were an estimated 101,182 adherents in the country, representing about 85% of the population. The bishop participates in the Episcopal Conference of Angola and São Tomé (based in Luanda, Angola).

Bishop of São Tomé e Príncipe: Rt Rev. ABÍLIO RODAS DE SOUSA RIBAS, Centro Diocesano, CP 104, São Tomé; tel. and fax 23455.

The Press

Diário da República: Cooperativa de Artes Gráficas, Rua João Devs, CP 28, São Tomé; tel. 22661; f. 1836; official gazette; Dir OSCAR FERREIRA.

O Independente: São Tomé; tel. 22675; f. 1994; Dir CARLOS BORBOLETA.

Notícias: Avda 12 de Julho, CP 112, São Tomé; tel. 22087; f. 1991; state-owned; Dir. MANUEL BARROS.

O Parvo: CP 535, São Tomé; tel. 21031; f. 1994; Editor ARMINDO CARDOSO.

NEWS AGENCY

STP-Press: c/o Rádio Nacional de São Tomé e Príncipe, Avda Marginal de 12 de Julho, CP 44, São Tomé; tel. 21342; telex 217; f. 1985; operated by the radio station in asscn with the Angolan news agency, ANGOP.

Radio and Television

In 1994, according to UNESCO, there were an estimated 35,000 radio receivers and 21,000 television receivers in use. Portuguese technical and financial assistance in the establishment of a television service was announced in May 1989. Transmissions commenced in 1992, and currently broadcasts seven days per week. The creation of the Companhia Santomense de Telecomunicações (CST), agreed in 1989 between a Portuguese company, Rádio Marconi, and the Government of São Tomé, was to allow increased telecommunications links and television reception via satellite. In 1995 Radio France Internationale and Rádio Televisão Portuguesa Internacional began relaying radio and television broadcasts, respectively, to the archipelago. In 1997 Voice of America, which had been broadcasting throughout Africa since 1993 from a relay station installed on São Tomé, began local transmissions on FM.

Rádio Nacional de São Tomé e Príncipe: Avda Marginal de 12 de Julho, CP 44, São Tomé; tel. 23293; f. 1958; state-controlled; home service in Portuguese and Creole; Dir ADELINO LUCAS DOS SANTOS.

Televisão de São Tomé e Príncipe (TVS): Bairro Quinta de Santo António, São Tomé; tel. 21493; fax 21942; state-controlled; Dir VICTOR CORREIA.

Finance

BANKING

Central Bank

Banco Central de São Tomé e Príncipe (BCSTP): Praça da Independência, CP 13, São Tomé; tel. 22407; telex 264; fax 22501; f. 1992 to succeed fmr Banco Nacional de São Tomé e Príncipe; bank of issue; Gov. CARLOS QUARESMA BATISTA DA SOUSA.

Commercial Banks

Banco Comercial do Equador (BCE): Rua de Moçambique, CP 361, São Tomé; tel. 21898; telex 240; fax 21989; f. 1995; Dir AGOSTINHO RITA.

Banco Internacional de São Tomé e Príncipe (BISTP): Praça da Independência, CP 536, São Tomé; tel. 21445; telex 293; fax 22427; f. 1993; 33% government-owned, 30% owned by Banco Totta e Açores, SA (Portugal), 22% by Banco Nacional Ultramarino (Portugal), 15% by BCSTP; cap. US $415,420 (Dec. 1995); Chair. DIONÍSIO TOMÉ DIAS; CEO CARLOS A. M. M. MORAIS.

Savings Bank

Caixa Nacional de Poupança e Crédito (CNPC): Rua Soldado Paulo Ferreira, CP 390, São Tomé; tel. 21309; fax 21811; f. 1993 to succeed fmr Caixa Popular de São Tomé e Príncipe; savings; loans for housing; Pres. and Exec. Dir ADELINO SANTIAGO CASTELO DAVID.

INSURANCE

Empresa Nacional de Seguros e Resseguros 'A Compensadora': Rua Viriato Cruz, CP 190, São Tomé; tel. 22907; f. 1980; privatization pending in 1997.

Instituto de Segurança Social: Rua Soldado Paulo Ferreira, São Tomé; tel. 21382; f. as Caixa de Previdência dos Funcionários Públicos, renamed as above 1994; insurance fund for civil servants; Pres. of Admin. Bd ALBINO GRAÇA DA FONSECA.

Trade and Industry

CHAMBER OF COMMERCE

Câmara do Comércio da Indústria e Agricultura (CCIA): CP 527, Rua de Moçambique, São Tomé; tel. 22723; Pres. NELSON SILVA.

DEVELOPMENT ORGANIZATION

Instituto para o Desenvolvimento Económico e Social (INDES): Travessa do Pelourinho, CP 408, São Tomé; tel. 22491; fax 21931; f. 1989 as Fundo Social e de Infrastructuras, renamed as above 1994; channels foreign funds to local economy; Dir PAULO JORGE ESPÍRITO SANTO.

TRADE UNIONS

Organizacão Nacional de Trabalhadores de São Tomé e Príncipe (ONTSTP): Rua Cabo Verde, São Tomé; tel. 22431; Sec.-Gen. AVELINO ESPÍRITO SANTO.

União Geral dos Trabalhadores de São Tomé e Príncipe (UGSTP): Avda Kwame Nkrumah, São Tomé; tel. 22443; Sec.-Gen. (vacant).

Transport

RAILWAYS

There are no railways in São Tomé and Príncipe.

ROADS

In 1994 there were 380 km of roads, of which 250 km were asphalted.

SHIPPING

The principal ports are at São Tomé city and at Neves on São Tomé island. In 1997 plans were proceeding to construct a deep-water port at Agulhas Bay on Príncipe island.

CIVIL AVIATION

The international airport is at São Tomé. A US $16m. modernization project, including a runway extension, and a new control tower, was financed mainly by the African Development Bank and completed in 1992.

Air São Tomé e Príncipe: Avda Marginal de 12 de Julho, CP 45, São Tomé; tel. 21976; fax 21375; f. 1993; owned by Govt of São Tomé (35%), TAP-Air Portugal, SA (40%), Golfe International Air Service (France) (24%) and Mistral Voyages (France) (1%); operates domestic service between the islands of São Tomé and Príncipe and international connection to Libreville (Gabon); Pres. RAUL BRAGAÇO; Gen. Man. FRANCISCO SIMUS.

Tourism

The islands benefit from spectacular mountain scenery, unspoilt beaches and unique species of flora and wildlife. Although still largely undeveloped, tourism is currently the sector of the islands' economy attracting the highest level of foreign investment. However, the high level of rainfall during most of the year limits the duration of the tourist season, and the expense of reaching the islands by air is also an inhibiting factor. There were approximately 5,000 tourist arrivals in 1994, when receipts totalled some US $2m. In 1996 there were nine hotels and nine guest houses, with a total of 520 beds.

Defence

In 1995 the armed forces were estimated to number some 600. Military service, which is compulsory, lasts for 30 months. In 1992 a reorganization was initiated of the islands' armed forces and the police into two separate police forces, one for public order and another for criminal investigation. However, in December 1993, following increasing pressure from the military high command, parliament approved the new legal status of the armed forces, maintaining their role as military defenders of the nation. In late 1996 restructuring of the armed forces resumed, with technical assistance from Portugal.

Commander-in-Chief of the Armed Forces: Pres. MIGUEL DOS ANJOS DA CUNHA LISBOA TROVOADA.

Chief of General Staff of the Armed Forces: Lt-Col ANTÓNIO DO NASCIMENTO.

Defence Expenditure: Budgeted at 717m. dobras (excl. capital expenditure) in 1995.

Education

Primary education is officially compulsory for a period of four years between seven and 14 years of age. Secondary education lasts for a further seven years, comprising a first cycle of four years and a second cycle of three years. In 1995 the country had 64 primary schools, with a total enrolment of 21,760 pupils. In that year there were nine secondary schools, with a total enrolment of 12,047 pupils, and one vocational training centre in the country. In 1991 the average rate of adult illiteracy was 75% (males 83%; females 68%). In 1995 21.2% of the public investment programme was spent on education. Two secondary schools, financed by the OPEC Fund for International Development, and a teacher training college were completed in 1997.

Bibliography

Ambrósio, A. *Subsidios para a história de São Tomé e Príncipe*. Lisbon, Livros Horizonte, 1984.

Bredero, J. T., Heemskerk, W., and Toxopeus, H. *Agriculture and Livestock production in São Tomé and Príncipe (West Africa)*. Wageningen, Foundation for Agricultural Plant Breeding, 1977.

da Cruz, C. B. *São Tomé e Príncipe: do colonialismo à independência*. Lisbon, 1975.

Economist Intelligence Unit. *Congo, São Tomé & Príncipe, Guinea-Bissau, Cape Verde, Country Report*. London, quarterly.

Congo, São Tomé & Príncipe, Guinea-Bissau, Cape Verde, Country Profile. London, annual.

Espírito Santo, C. *Contribuição para a história de São Tomé e Príncipe*. Lisbon 1979.

Eyzaguirre, P. 'The Independence of São Tomé e Príncipe and Agrarian Reform', in *Journal of Modern African Studies,* April 1989.

Ferraz, L. I. *The Creole of São Tomé*. Johannesburg, Witwatersrand University Press, 1979.

'São Tomé and Príncipe: Combating Cocoa Colonialism', in *Africa Report,* January 1986.

Garfield, R. *A History of São Tomé Island 1470–1655: The Key to Guinea*. New York, Edwin Mellen Press, 1992.

Hodges, T., and Newitt, M. *São Tomé and Príncipe: From Plantation Colony to Microstate*. Boulder, CO, Westview Press, 1988.

Jones, P. J., Burlison, J. P., and Tye, A. *Conservação dos ecossistemas florestais da República Democrática de São Tomé e Príncipe*. Gland and Cambridge, UICN, 1991.

Jones, P. J., and Tye, A. *A Survey of the Avifauna of São Tomé and Príncipe*. Cambridge, International Council for Bird Preservation, 1988.

das Neves, C. A. *São Tomé e Príncipe na Segunda Metade do Século XVIII*. Região Autónoma da Madeira, 1989.

Núñez, B. *Dictionary of Portuguese–African Civilization*. Vol. I. London, Hans Zell, 1995.

Oliveira, J. E. *A Economia de São Tomé e Príncipe*. Lisbon, Instituto de Investigação Científica Tropical, 1993.

Pélissier, R. *Le Naufrage des Caravelles (1961–75)*. Orgeval, Editions Pélissier, 1979.

Explorar. Voyages en Angola et autres lieux incertains. Orgeval, Editions Pélissier, 1980.

Schümer, M. *São Tomé und Príncipe, Ausbruch aus der Isolation*. Bonn, Forschungsinstitut der Deutschen Gesellschaft für Auswärtige Politik eV, 1987.

Torp, E., Denny, L. M., and Ray, D. I. (Eds). *Mozambique and São Tomé and Príncipe: Politics, Economics and Society*. New York, Pinter, 1989.

de Unzueta y Yuste, A. *Islas del Golfo de Guinea (Elobeyes, Corisco, Annobón, Príncipe y Santo Tomé)*. Madrid, Instituto de Estudios Políticos, 1945.

SENEGAL

Physical and Social Geography

R. J. HARRISON CHURCH

The Republic of Senegal, the most westerly state of Africa, covers an area of 196,722 sq km (75,955 sq miles). The population was 6,896,808 at the census of May 1988, and was estimated at 8,572,000 (43.6 persons per sq km) at mid-1996. The southern border is first with Guinea-Bissau and then with Guinea on the northern edge of the Primary sandstone outcrop of the Fouta Djallon. In the east the border is with Mali, in the only other area of bold relief in Senegal, where there are Pre-Cambrian rocks in the Bambouk mountains. The northern border with Mauritania lies along the Senegal river, navigable for small boats all the year to Podor and for two months to Kayes (Mali). The river has a wide flood plain, annually cultivated as the waters retreat. The delta soils are saline, but dams for power, irrigation and better navigation are being built or proposed. The commissioning in 1985 of the Djama dam has considerably improved navigability at the Senegal river delta. The completion in 1988 of the Manantali scheme will eventually extend the all-year navigability of the river from 220 km to 924 km, as far as Kayes, in Mali.

The Gambia forms a semi-enclave between part of southern Senegal and the sea, along the valley of the navigable Gambia river. This has meant that, since the colonial delimitation of the Gambia–Senegal borders in 1889, the river has played no positive role in Senegal's development and that the Casamance region, in the south, was isolated from the rest of Senegal until the opening of the Trans-Gambian highway in 1958.

The Cap Vert (Cape Verde) peninsula, on which the capital, Dakar, is located, results in part from Tertiary volcanic activity. Cap Vert is formed by one of the two extinct volcanoes known as les Mamelles. Exposure to south-westerly winds is responsible for Cap Vert's verdant appearance, in contrast to the yellow dunes to the north. Basalt underlies much of Dakar, and its harbour was constructed in a sandy area east of (and sheltered by) the basaltic plateau. South of the peninsula, particularly in Casamance, the coast is a drowned one of shallow estuaries.

Apart from the high eastern and south-eastern borderlands most of the country has monotonous plains, which in an earlier period were drained by large rivers in the centre of the country. Relic valleys, now devoid of superficial water, occur in the Ferlo desert, and these built up the Sine Saloum delta north of The Gambia. In a later dry period north-east to south-west trending sand dunes were formed, giving Senegal's plains their undulating and ribbed surfaces. These plains of Cayor, Baol, and Nioro du Rip are inhabited by Wolof and Serer cultivators of groundnuts and millet. The coast between Saint-Louis and Dakar has a broad belt of live dunes. Behind them, near Thiès, calcium phosphates are quarried (aluminium phosphates are also present) and phosphatic fertilizer is produced.

Although Senegal's mineral resources are otherwise relatively sparse, there are potentially valuable reserves of gold, in the south-east (production of which began in mid-1997), as well as deposits of high-grade iron ore, in considerable quantity, in the east. Reserves of natural gas are exploited offshore from Dakar, and there is petroleum off the Casamance coast.

Senegal's climate is widely varied, and the coast is remarkably cool for the latitude (Dakar 14° 38′ N). The Cap Vert peninsula is particularly breezy, because it projects into the path of northerly marine trade winds. Average temperatures are in the range 18°C–31°C, and the rainy season is little more than three months in length. Inland both temperatures and rainfall are higher, and the rainy season in comparable latitudes is somewhat longer. Casamance lies on the northern fringe of the monsoonal climate. Thus Ziguinchor (12° 35′ N) has four to five months' rainy season, with average annual rainfall of 1,626 mm, nearly three times that received by Dakar. The natural vegetation ranges from Sahel savannah north of about 15°N, through Sudan savannah in south-central Senegal, to Guinea savannah in Casamance, where the oil palm is common.

Recent History

PIERRE ENGLEBERT

Revised for this edition by the Editor

At independence in 1960, after 300 years of French rule, Senegal already had a limited experience of democracy. Inhabitants of the principal towns had received a form of French citizenship in the 19th century, and had been represented in the French national assembly. As the administrative centre of French West Africa, Dakar was an active centre for African politics. During the 1950s a variety of political forces emerged, including a strong trade union movement, Islamic sects and exponents of Marxism. The Union progressiste sénégalaise (UPS) was founded in 1958 by Léopold Sédar Senghor, a widely respected poet and academic, who combined the support of foreign and local business interests, Islamic leaders and socialists. The success of the UPS was aided by a ban on the activities of the Marxist Parti africain de l'indépendance (PAI). In November 1958 Senegal became a self-governing member of the French Community. The Mali Federation with Soudan (now Mali) was formed in April 1959 and became independent on 20 June 1960. However, the incompatibility of the two leaderships caused the federation to fail, and Senegal seceded after two months to become a separate independent state. The Republic of Senegal was proclaimed on 5 September, with Senghor as its president. His prime minister was the socialist Mamadou Dia, who attempted, despite French opposition, to introduce comprehensive national planning. Senghor assumed the premiership after Dia was arrested in December 1962 and sentenced to life imprisonment, convicted of plotting a coup. French private investment was encouraged, as was French use of military facilities in Senegal.

A revised constitution, strengthening the powers of the president, was approved in a referendum in March 1963. Later in the year the UPS won a decisive victory in elections to the national assembly. The principal legal opposition movement, Cheikh Anta Diop's Bloc des masses sénégalaises, was banned following a serious rioting in Dakar. Other parties were either outlawed or absorbed into the UPS, which by 1966 was the sole legal party. Unrest in the education sector and in the trade union movement in 1968 prompted the government to promise educational reforms and concessions to workers. Government attempts subsequently to co-opt union leaders into its Confédération nationale des travailleurs sénégalais (CNTS) were resisted by the more militant labour activists.

In 1970 the office of the prime minister was revived and assigned to a young provincial administrator, Abdou Diouf. Elections in January 1973 returned both Senghor and the UPS with huge majorities, but further student unrest ensued. In March 1974 Dia was released from detention, and in July the government permitted the registration of a new political party, the Parti démocratique sénégalais (PDS), led by a lawyer, Abdoulaye Wade. In 1976 Senghor announced the formation of a three-party system, comprising the UPS (which in December was renamed the Parti socialiste—PS), the PDS and a Marxist-Leninist party, to be formed by members of the PAI. Most PAI supporters, however, refused to co-operate in the proposed arrangement. Other prominent politicians who were not included formed unofficial parties: Cheikh Anta Diop established the Rassemblement national démocratique (RND), and in 1978 Dia founded the Coordination de l'opposition sénégalaise unie. At elections in February 1978 the PS won 83 of the 100 seats in the national assembly, while Senghor overwhelmingly defeated Abdoulaye Wade in the presidential election. In December a fourth political grouping, the right-wing Mouvement républicain sénégalais, was officially recognized.

DIOUF'S LEADERSHIP

A period of economic decline and resultant austerity measures, in conjunction with intense pressure for imaginative political reforms, were the background to Senghor's announcement in December 1980 that he would resign at the end of the month. Diouf assumed the presidency in January 1981 (also becoming secretary-general of the PS), and undertook a vigorous reorganization of the political system. Restrictions on political activity were removed in April, and in the following months the RND and numerous smaller parties—many of which had Marxist tendencies—were officially registered. The PDS saw its support steadily eroded and some of its members arrested on suspicion of having received Libyan funds. (Diplomatic links with Libya, believed to have for some time been financing Islamist militants in Senegal, had been severed in July 1980, following outspoken attacks on Senghor by the Qaddafi regime.)

In August 1981, following a *coup d'état* in The Gambia, Diouf agreed to a request by the deposed president, Sir Dawda Jawara, to use Senegalese troops to restore him to power. Senegalese forces were subsequently asked to remain, and Diouf and Jawara swiftly established a confederation of the two states, with co-ordinated policies in defence, foreign affairs and economic and financial matters. An agreement establishing the Senegambian confederation came into effect in February 1982. Diouf was designated permanent president of a joint council of ministers, and a confederal assembly was established. However, The Gambia resisted attempts by Senegal to proceed towards the full political and economic integration of the two countries.

In February 1983 Diouf led the PS to a clear victory in presidential and legislative elections. During 1982 the government had amended the electoral law for the legislature so that one-half of its members would be elected on a basis of proportional representation, with the remainder being chosen by direct contest. The PS had mustered the full support of the *marabout* Islamic leaders, while Diouf had enhanced his own image by a gradual anti-corruption campaign, with the result that Diouf received 83.5% of the votes cast, and the PS candidates for the national assembly secured 111 seats, with 79.9% of the votes. The PDS won eight seats, and the RND only one. Disputing the results, the government's opponents resolved to boycott the assembly, although most had taken their seats by the end of the year. Despite Diouf's overwhelming success at the elections, he was regarded in some quarters as having become unduly involved in party politics, and some of the admiration engendered by his early liberalization of the political system began to dissipate.

In forming a new government in April 1983, Diouf continued his purge of the party 'old guard', while strengthening his own powers with the abolition of the premiership. Habib Thiam, the prime minister since 1981, was transferred to the presidency of the national assembly and named as Diouf's automatic successor. However, the 'old guard' of the PS sought to reassert some of its power in the national assembly, and in April 1984 Thiam was forced to resign as president of the assembly, following a decision to re-elect a new parliamentary leader every 12 months.

Opposition Pressures

Meanwhile, the PS benefited from persistent disunity among the opposition groupings, with a boycott by 12 of the country's 15 registered parties contributing to the success of the PS in municipal and rural elections in November 1984. In September 1985 the government banned an alliance of five opposition parties, on the grounds of unconstitutionality. Wade and the leader of the Ligue démocratique–Mouvement pour le parti du travail (LD–MPT), Abdoulaye Bathily, had been among alliance members detained for several days in August, on charges of 'unauthorized demonstration'. The emergence of a PDS splinter group, the Parti démocratique sénégalais–Rénovation (PDS–R), under the leadership of Serigne Diop, was announced in June 1987, following a period of defections and resignations from Wade's party.

Classes at the University of Dakar were boycotted in early 1987 by students who were protesting against the late payment of grants and poor living conditions. In February the university was renamed in honour of Cheikh Anta Diop (who had died the previous year). The student demonstrations were followed by an unprecedented (and illegal) strike by police forces in April, which led to the dismissal of the minister of the interior and the suspension from duty of more than 6,000 police-officers. By August nearly 5,000 police-officers had been reinstated, with the main antagonists permanently dismissed.

Preliminary results of the February 1988 presidential and legislative elections indicated decisive victories for both Diouf and the PS. The PDS, which had long demanded reform of the electoral code, alleged that fraud had been widespread, and rioting erupted in the Dakar region. A state of emergency was declared, public gatherings were banned and educational establishments closed. Abdoulaye Wade and Amath Dansokho, the leader of the Marxist-Leninist Parti de l'indépendance et du travail (PIT), were arrested, together with other opposition activists. The official results allocated 73.2% of the votes cast in the presidential election to Diouf, and 25.8% to Wade (there were three other candidates). In the legislative election, the PS returned 103 deputies to the national assembly, and the PDS 17. Trials began in April for incitement to violence and attacks on the internal security of the state. Dansokho and five others were acquitted, but in May Wade received a one-year suspended prison sentence, while three other PDS activists received prison terms of between six months and two years. However, Diouf swiftly terminated the state of emergency, and all those who had been convicted of involvement in the post-election violence were included in a presidential amnesty later in the month.

Secondary school pupils (who had been boycotting classes since October 1987) and university students failed to return to classes after the elections. In October 1988 a programme for the rehabilitation of the national education system was announced, and in the following month the government agreed to the students' demands for improved welfare provisions, and gave assurances regarding the independence of Cheikh Anta Diop University. The 1988/89 academic year was, none the less, disrupted by a three-month strike by academic staff in early 1989, and by continuing protests by students concerning academic and welfare issues.

In March 1989 Wade, who had left for France in mid-1988, following the failure of attempts by the government and opposition to establish multi-party commissions to consider Senegal's political, economic and social problems, returned, asserting that Diouf had agreed to his demands that a transitional government of national unity be established (in which the PDS leader was to hold a prominent position) pending new presidential and legislative elections; the president, however, denied that such an agreement existed. In October the national assembly approved a series of electoral reforms, in accordance with the recommendations of a PS committee appointed earlier in the year. Changes to the electoral code were said to ensure a fair system of voter registration; a new system of proportional representation (within administrative departments) was to be introduced for legislative elections, and opposition parties were to be granted access to the state media. Also approved was a 'national democratic charter', governing the activities of political parties, and controversial new labour code. The reforms were approved in the absence of PDS deputies, who were boycotting legislative sessions in protest against what they alleged was partial and selective media coverage of parliamentary debates.

Wade returned to Senegal in February 1990, after a further absence of more than six months. Although the PDS leader stated that he no longer disputed Diouf's victory in the 1988 elections, he demanded that, in view of the deteriorating economic and social conditions in Senegal, the electorate be allowed to choose new leaders. A series of days of action were subsequently organized by the opposition parties. Among the most significant features of an extensive government reshuffle in March 1990 was the dismissal, as minister of state and secretary-general of the presidency of the republic, of Jean Collin, an influential public figure since the colonial period; Collin subsequently relinquished prominent posts within the PS. (He was appointed special adviser to President Gnassingbe Eyadéma of Togo in early 1991, and died in France in October 1993.) Many parties boycotted municipal and rural elections in November 1990 (at which the PS reportedly received the support of 70% of voters), claiming that Senegal's electoral code still permitted widespread malpractice.

Constitutional Concessions

In March 1991 the national assembly approved several constitutional amendments, notably the restoration of the post of prime minister. It was also agreed that opposition parties would, henceforth, be allowed to participate in government. Accordingly, in April Habib Thiam was restored to his former post as premier. His government included four representatives of the PDS, among them Wade, as minister of state, and Ousmane Ngom (the party's parliamentary leader), who became minister of labour and professional training; Amath Dansokho also joined the new administration as minister of housing and town planning. In September the national assembly adopted a series of amendments to the electoral code, in accordance with recommendations that had been made by a national commission established in May. Under the amended code, presidential elections would henceforth take place, in two rounds if necessary (the new regulations stipulated that the president would have to be elected by at least one-quarter of registered voters, and by an absolute majority of the votes cast), every seven years, and the president would be limited to a maximum of two terms of office. Elections to the presidency would no longer coincide with legislative elections, which would continue to take place at five-yearly intervals. The amendments also included the lowering of the age of eligibility to vote from 21 to 18 years of age. A major reform of the organs of the judiciary was, meanwhile, implemented in May, as a result of which the supreme court was abolished and its functions divided between three new bodies: a constitutional council, a council of state and a court of higher appeal.

In October 1992 Wade (who had already declared his intention to contest the 1993 presidential election) and his three PDS colleagues resigned from the council of ministers, stating that they had been excluded from the governmental process. In subsequent months Wade protested that the PS retained privileged access to the state-owned media, and alleged that the government was attempting to hinder the registration of certain categories of voter prior to the presidential and legislative elections.

The presidential election, which took place on 21 February 1993, was contested by eight candidates. Despite some irregularities, voting was reported to be well-ordered in most areas, although there were serious incidents in the Casamance region (see below). The opposition denounced preliminary results, which indicated that, while Wade had enjoyed considerable success in Dakar and in the nearby manufacturing town of Thiès, Diouf had won a majority of the overall votes. Disagreements within the electoral commission (a body comprising a presiding magistrate and representatives of the candidates) delayed the process of determining the official outcome of the election, and eventually prompted the resignation of the president of the constitutional council. It was not until 13 March that the council was able to confirm that Diouf had been re-elected by 58.4% of the votes cast (51.6% of the electorate had voted). Wade secured 32.0% of the votes, with none of the other candidates obtaining more than 2.9%. The declaration of the official results precipitated some unrest in Dakar, but order was quickly restored, and Wade appealed for passive resistance to Diouf's victory. Diouf announced that the electoral code was to be modified, with the immediate aim of avoiding similar delays in announcing the results of the forthcoming legislative elections.

Post-election Unrest

Elections to the national assembly took place on 9 May 1993, and on 14 May the electoral commission (now required to submit the results to the constitutional council within five days) announced that the PS had won 84 of the assembly's 120 seats. The PDS, with considerable support in urban areas, took 27 seats, the remainder being divided between three other parties and one electoral alliance. Participation by voters was only 40.7%. Shortly after the announcement of the results the vice-president of the constitutional council, Babacar Seye, was assassinated. Although an organization styling itself the 'Armée du peuple' claimed responsibility, Wade (who had recently declared that he had no confidence in the supposed impartiality of Seye and the council) and three other PDS leaders were detained for three days in connection with the murder. The PDS protested that its opponents were plotting to discredit the party, and suggested that attempts to implicate Wade in the assassination may have been orchestrated by those who sought to prevent any *rapprochement* of Diouf and the opposition leader. The official results of the legislative elections were confirmed by the constitutional council on 24 May. Meanwhile, four people suspected of involvement in Seye's murder were arrested: among those detained were Samuel Sarr, a close associate of Wade, and a PDS deputy, Mody Sy.

Wade and the PDS were excluded from Habib Thiam's new government, which was formed in June 1993. Dansokho, who had supported Diouf's presidential campaign, retained his position in the council of ministers, while the LD–MPT leader, Abdoulaye Bathily (himself a candidate for the presidency), was appointed minister of the environment and nature conservation. Other new appointments included Serigne Diop of the PDS–R, as minister of employment and professional training, and Papa Ousmane Sakho, hitherto the national director of the Banque centrale des états de l'Afrique de l'ouest, as minister of the economy, finance and planning.

In July 1993 six PDS and LD–MPT deputies were briefly detained after security forces intervened at a violent demonstration in Dakar, organized to demand the release of Mody Sy—who, it was alleged, had been tortured while in custody. A descent into social crisis followed. Citing the need to reduce the budget deficit in order to secure vital economic support from the international financial community, in August the government announced wide-ranging austerity measures. Trade unions and the political opposition denounced, especially, the proposed 15% reduction in salaries in the public sector, and in September, following the failure of attempts to reach a compromise, a 24-hour general strike, organized by the CNTS, was widely observed. Diouf postponed the imposition of the measures, pending further negotiations with the CNTS and other unions. However, the talks again failed, and the salary cuts were imposed in October. Two 72-hour general strikes (denounced as illegal by the government, which threatened to withdraw the right to strike) were organized, with only partial success, by trade unions later in October. In the same month Wade was charged with complicity in the assassination of Seye; Wade's wife and a PDS deputy were also charged with 'complicity in a breach of state security'. None was detained, although Mody Sy, Sarr and three others remained in custody in connection with the murder. A PDS motion expressing 'no confidence' in the government was defeated in the national assembly, and the party announced a boycott of parliamentary sessions, in protest against what it considered to be biased coverage by the state media of the vote. In November 1993 Ousmane Ngom and Landing Savané, the leader of And Jëf–Parti africain pour la démocratie et le socialisme (AJ–PADS), were among those detained following a protest in Dakar to demand the cancellation of the austerity measures. The action coincided with a demonstration, at which further arrests were made, to appeal for the release of Moustapha Sy, the leader of an Islamist youth movement, Dahira Moustarchidine wal Moustarchidate, who had recently been arrested after having criticized the government (and who had also reportedly claimed to know the circumstances and authors of Seye's assassination). Ngom, Savané and more than 80 others were convicted of participating in an unauthorized demonstration, and received six-month suspended prison sentences. In January 1994 Moustapha Sy was sentenced to one year's imprisonment.

Diouf was widely regarded as a principal architect of the 50% devaluation, in January 1994, of the CFA franc, and the opposition accused the president of responsibility for resultant hardships. (Government measures to compensate for the devaluation included the cancellation of the previous year's wage reductions and 10% increase, effective from April, in salaries.) A demonstration in Dakar in February, organized by opposition parties grouped in a Coordination des forces démocratiques (CFD), degenerated into serious rioting throughout the capital, as a result of which eight people (including six police-officers) were killed. Dahira Moustarchidine wal Moustarchidate, identified by the authorities as being implicated in much of the violence, was outlawed, and the government stated that it regarded the CFD (which the authorities stressed was an unauthorized organization) as responsible for the unrest. Wade, Savané and more than 70 others were subsequently detained and charged with attacks on state security. Opposition activists alleged that some of the accused had been tortured while in custody (as a result of which one detainee had died), and Wade and Savané instigated a hunger strike, in support of their demands for access to proper legal procedures (they were not formally charged before a court for several weeks). In May charges against Wade and his associates (including Mody Sy and Samuel Sarr) in connection with the murder of the vice-president of the consitutional council were dismissed on the grounds of insufficient evidence, although Wade and Savané, awaiting trial in connection with the post-devaluation violence, were not released from custody. Sarr and Mody Sy, who also remained in detention pending a state-prosecution appeal, began a hunger strike in June, and were subsequently released on bail. Wade, Savané and four others, also refusing food, were provisionally released in July. Legal proceedings against them and 140 others implicated in the February riots were dismissed later in July, again on the grounds of insufficient evidence. In September 24 alleged members of Dahira Moustarchidine wal Moustarchidate received prison sentences of between six months and two years for their part in the violence. Shortly beforehand Moustapha Sy had been granted a presidential pardon and released from custody. In October three of those accused of Seye's murder were convicted and sentenced to between 18 and 20 years' imprisonment, with hard labour; the fourth defendant was acquitted.

In August 1994 the 1993/94 academic year at Cheikh Anta Diop University was declared invalid, following almost three months of disruption by students who were protesting against proposed reforms of the higher education system.

During the latter part of 1994 both the government and opposition expressed their desire to restore a national consensus. In January 1995 Diouf and Wade held their first private meeting since the PDS leader's departure from the council of ministers in 1992, and in February 1995 Wade was formally invited to rejoin the government. Thiam named a new council of ministers in March: Wade was designated minister of state at the presidency, while four other PDS members, including Ngom (as minister of public health and social action), were also appointed to the new administration. Djibo Ka, a long-serving government member who recently, as minister of the interior, had been associated with the legal proceedings against Wade and other opposition leaders, left the government. In September Dansokho and the minister-delegate responsible for planning, also a member of the PIT, were dismissed from the council of ministers, shortly after their party had issued a statement effectively denouncing the poor governance of Senegal.

In August 1995 the government announced that municipal and local elections, scheduled for November, would, for reasons of economy, be postponed by one year to coincide with regional voting. However, opposition groups attributed the decision to delay the elections to difficulties within the PS itself. There were subsequent reports that the conduct of internal elections for PS officials throughout the country was at times resulting in severe violence. In late March 1996 the 13th congress of the PS overwhelmingly elected Diouf to the new post of party chairman. The post of secretary-general, hitherto held by Diouf, was abolished and a new position of executive secretary created: Ousmane Tanor Dieng, the minister of state responsible for presidential affairs and services, was elected to this post. Critics of the PS leadership denounced a lack of debate prior to the implementation of the changes.

In January 1996 Diouf announced that a senate was to be established as a second chamber of the legislature. Local organs of government would thereby be afforded greater representation within the country's legislative framework, as part of a programme of regionalization for which legislation was approved by the national assembly in February. The abolition of independent candidatures for municipal, rural and regional elections prompted widespread criticism, and in subsequent months opposition activists accused the PS of manipulating voters' lists, alleging that likely opposition voters had been removed from electoral registers while the names of potential PS supporters had appeared on lists after the revision process had formally ended. It was claimed, moreover, that only by the establishment of an independent electoral commission could the credibility of the elections be ensured. Following consultations in the second half of July involving the minister of the interior, Abdourahmane Sow, and representatives of some 20 political parties, it was announced that adjustments would be considered to certain aspects of the electoral code, although the government remained disinclined to consider the opposition's principal demands regarding independent candidatures and an autonomous commission. In mid-September the PDS, AJ–PADS and the LD–MPT announced the formation of an electoral coalition, with a view to presenting joint candidates to challenge the PS at the regional, rural and municipal elections. Within the government there was marked antipathy between the PS and the PDS and LD–MPT, prompting Ousmane Tanor Dieng to issue a formal warning to Wade and Bathily, in early October, that they must either cease their criticism or leave the government. In response to a threat by PS parliamentary members to table motion of 'no confidence' in the government, Wade asserted that he would not be compelled to resign, and intimated that the 'no confidence' issue was directly targeted at Thiam by supporters of Tanor (who was increasingly regarded as having ambitions not only to be prime minister but also to be Diouf's eventual successor). Political tensions were heightened later in October when the PDS accused the ministry of the interior of stockpiling 1m. voting cards (in addition to the 3m. to be issued to eligible voters) that could be used fraudulently: Sow stated that the additional cards had been ordered to cover 'unforseen circumstances'.

Elections for some 44,000 regional, municipal and rural councillors took place on 24 November 1996. Logistical and administrative difficulties were widespread, and necessitated a rerun of voting at about 100 polling stations in Dakar three days later. Opposition parties demanded that all the elections be annulled, alleging official complicity in the chaos that had been especially evident in areas where support for the PS was considered doubtful. The official results confirmed an overwhelming victory for the PS, which won control of the country's 10 regions, of all the main towns (including those in which the PDS had polled well in the 1993 presidential and legislative elections), and in the vast majority of rural communities. The opposition continued to dispute the election results, despite the failure of legal challenges to the outcome in certain areas. None the less, the PDS resolved, at an extraordinary session in early February 1997, to remain in the government, and the party was among 19 opposition groups that joined the PS in a 'cellular commission' to examine the issue of establishing an independent electoral commission (to which the PS had hitherto been strongly opposed). The commission began its deliberations in late March. Tensions were, meanwhile, revived in early March, when the PS issued writs for defamation against representatives of 12 parties (including the PDS and LD–MPT), in respect of allegations that the success of the PS in the local elections was attributable to the complicity of the authorities and to the misappropriation, for the purpose of organizing unfair elections, of foreign assistance. The opposition denounced the defamation suits as an attempt by the government to distract attention from the country's genuine economic, social and political difficulties. After a month of discussions, the 'cellular commission' succeeded in drafting a constitutional bill, to be submitted to Diouf, defining the legal framework for a nine-member electoral body. In early May, however, the opposition withdrew from the commission, alleging that the PS was unwilling entirely to relinquish control of the electoral process. In the following month the PS formally rejected the establishment of an independent electoral commission, although the party reiterated its desire to improve the management of the electoral process prior to the next legislative elections, due in 1998.

Meanwhile, the education sector suffered several months of severe disruption from early 1997, as a strike by teachers, whose principal demands included the withdrawal of recent changes to pension and retirement provisions, was accompanied by protests by secondary school pupils and students at Cheikh Anta Diop University, who feared that the academic year might be declared invalid as a result of their teachers' actions. Classes finally resumed in late June.

SEPARATISM IN CASAMANCE

For many years there has been separatist sentiment among Diola communities in the southern region, which is virtually cut from the rest of Senegal by the enclave of The Gambia, and the emergence from the early 1980s of the Mouvement des forces démocratiques de la Casamance (MFDC) periodically presented the Diouf administration with considerable security difficulties. After demonstrations in the regional capital, Ziguinchor, in December 1982, several leaders of the MFDC were detained without trial. A more serious demonstration in December 1983 was suppressed by force, reportedly resulting in more than 100 deaths. Casamance was divided into two administrative regions, Ziguinchor and Kolda, in 1984. In January 1986 a leading Casamance independence campaigner was sentenced to life imprisonment, while other demonstrators received prison sentences ranging from two to 15 years; further arrests were made in October. However, almost 100 detainees were provisionally released in April 1987, and a further 320 separatists reportedly benefited under the conditions of the May 1988 presidential amnesty. There were renewed clashes between supporters of the MFDC and the Senegalese security forces at the end of 1988.

The MFDC initiated a further offensive in 1990 with a series of attacks, most of which were directed at administrative targets in the Casamance region. Tensions escalated when military reinforcements were dispatched to the region, and in September 1990 a military governor was appointed for Casamance. A prominent human rights organization, Amnesty International, issued several reports expressing concern at events in Casamance, although allegations of the torture and summary executions of suspected separatists were investigated and subsequently refuted by the Senegalese government. By April 1991 at least 100 people were said to have been killed as a result of violence in the region, while more than 300 Casamançais had been transported to Dakar to await trial for sedition. Among those in detention was the presidet of the MFDC, Abbé Augustin Diamacouné Senghor. In that month renewed action by separatists violated a truce that had apparently been negotiated by leaders of the MFDC and the new Thiam government. In May Diouf announced the immediate release of more than 340 detainees (including Diamacouné Senghor) who had been arrested in connection with the unrest in Casamance. This facilitated the conclusion, at talks in Guinea-Bissau, of a cease-fire agreement by representatives of the Senegalese government and the MFDC. In June the military governor was replaced by a civilian (as part of the demilitarization of the region that had been envisaged in the cease-fire accord). An amnesty was ratified by the national assembly later in June, benefiting some 400 Casamançais (including separatists released in the previous month). In December a PS deputy and a local village chief were assassinated near the town of Ziguinchor, although MFDC leaders denied involvement in the killings.

In January 1992 a peace commission (the Comité de gestion de la paix en Casamance), comprising government representatives and members of the MFDC, was established, with mediation by Guinea-Bissau. However, a resurgence of violence during July and August prompted the government to redeploy armed forces in the region: this further exacerbated tensions, and gave rise to MFDC protests that the 'remilitarization' of Casamance was in contravention of the cease-fire agreement. The death of a police-officer, in July, was followed in August by a violent clash near Ziguinchor, in which, according to official figures, 50 separatist rebels and two members of the armed forces were killed. Evidence emerged of a split within the MFDC: the so-called 'Front nord' and the MFDC vice-president, Sidi Badji, appealed to the rebels to lay down their arms, while the 'Front sud', based in areas of dense forest near the border with Guinea-Bissau, and led by Diamacouné Senghor (himself now based in Guinea-Bissau), appeared determined to continue the armed struggle. Negotiations between representatives of the Senegalese government and the MFDC achieved little, and in October 32 people (mostly seasonal fishermen from other regions of Senegal) were killed when separatist rebels attacked a fishing village near the Cap-Skirring tourist resort, causing local residents and tourists to flee the region. A further attack on a fishing village in the same area in November resulted in at least seven fatalities. Following the deaths of two Senegalese soldiers in December, the army instigated a major security operation, launching air attacks on supposed rebel bases along the border with Guinea-Bissau (see below).

Indications in advance of the 1993 presidential and legislative elections that MFDC rebels would seek to prevent voting in Casamance prompted Diouf to begin his electoral campaign in the province. His visit, in January, proceeded amid strict security measures, following the recent deaths of seven aid workers to the south-east of Ziguinchor. About 30 people were reported to have been killed in rebel attacks on voters on the day of the presidential election. Army reinforcements were dispatched to Casamance in March (raising the total number of armed forces personnel in the region to as many as 5,000), following further clashes. In April Diamacouné Senghor (who had returned to Senegal in March, having apparently been expelled from Guinea-Bissau) reportedly expressed a willingness to negotiate with the Senegalese government. Shortly afterwards, however, at least 100 rebels and three members of the armed forces were killed in a clash near the border with Guinea-Bissau. In late April the Senegalese authorities confirmed their willingness to observe a truce, stating that the military would henceforth act only in a defensive capacity, and gave assurances regarding the continuation of negotiations and the resumption of economic initiatives in Casamance. A period of relative calm followed, and in July a cease-fire agreement was signed in Ziguinchor by the Senegalese government and, on behalf of the MFDC, Diamacouné Senghor. The accord envisaged the release of Casamançais prisoners, and made provision for the return of those who had fled the region. Guinea-Bissau was to act as a guarantor of the agreement, and the government of France was to be asked to submit an historical arbitration regarding the Casamance issue: the Senegalese authorities had consistently refuted MFDC assertions that documents from the colonial era indicated that France favoured independence for Casamance. Later in July 256 Casamançais were released from detention. At the time of the conclusion of the new cease-fire, the total number of casualties of the conflict was uncertain, since the Senegalese authorities had not given details of military operations in Casamance for some months; however, it was believed that in the year preceding the Ziguinchor accord between 500 and 1,000 people had been killed and many hundreds injured, while humanitarian organizations estimated that 25,000–30,000 people may have fled to The Gambia and Guinea-Bissau, or to other regions of Senegal.

Although there were sporadic reports of clashes in Casamance during the remainder of 1993, as a result of which at least five deaths were recorded, the cease-fire was generally observed. In December France issued its judgment that Casamance had not existed as an autonomous territory prior to the colonial period, and that independence for the region had been neither demanded nor considered at the time of decolonization.

Casamance was widely regarded as being among the regions of Senegal that benefited most from the devaluation of the CFA franc at the beginning of 1994. Tourists returned to the region, and the fishing sector flourished, while several donor-sponsored development initiatives were undertaken with the aim of enhancing the region's economic potential. From early 1995, however, renewed violence near the border with Guinea-Bissau indicated a re-emergence of divisions between the northern and southern factions of the MFDC. Rebels in the south were reportedly frustrated at the slow progress of the dialogue between the MFDC and the authorities, and accused the Senegalese armed forces, by their operations in the south, of violating the provisions of the Ziguinchor accord. At least 20 soldiers were reported to have been killed in military operations in southern Casamance in January and May 1995, and there were believed to have been heavy casualties among the rebels and among the civilian population of the region. A major military operation was instigated following the disappearance, in April, of four French tourists in the Basse-Casamance region. More than 1,000 élite troops were deployed in southern Casamance, and were assisted in their search by French reconnaissance aircraft. In subsequent weeks the aim of the operation appeared increasingly to be to dislodge MFDC dissidents from the border region. Both the northern and southern factions of the MFDC denied any involvement in the apparent abduction of the tourists, and Diamacouné Senghor accused the Senegalese army of responsibility for the disappearances. The MFDC leader was placed under house arrest in Ziguinchor in late April, and his four fellow-members of the movement's 'political bureau' were transported to Dakar and imprisoned. In June MFDC rebels announced an end to their cease-fire, again accusing the government forces of violating the 1993 accord. Although Diamacouné Senghor appealed to the separatists not to break the truce, by early September 60 deaths had been reported among the rebels, the armed forces and the civilian population in the south-west. In the most serious incident at this time, in late July at least 23 soldiers were killed in an ambush as they advanced on what was stated by the armed forces to be a rebel base near Babanda. The army claimed to have regained control of this area (which the MFDC rebels denied having occupied) by mid-August.

In September 1995 Thiam established a Commission nationale de paix (CNP), headed by a Casamance-born former minister of foreign affairs, Assane Seck. Members of the commission travelled to Ziguinchor in late September, where they reportedly sought a dialogue with Diamacouné Senghor (who remained under house arrest) and the MFDC's four other political leaders (who were returned to Ziguinchor and placed under house arrest there in mid-October). During October, none the less, renewed rebel attacks on government forces were accompanied by a major army offensive in the south-western border region—apparently in an effort to reinforce security prior to the forthcoming tourist season. By the end of the month it was reported that about 100 separatists and nine members of the armed forces had been killed, and that three rebel bases near the border with Guinea-Bissau had been destroyed. In late November military sources disclosed that some 51 rebels and six members of the armed forces had been killed in a clash in the border region. Representatives of the armed forces asserted that an intensification of anti-rebel operations had been prompted by a recent series of armed attacks on civilians.

Meanwhile, the CNP was reported to be seeking to arrange a meeting between those members of the MFDC who wished to secure a peace accord and those whose supporters were in direct conflict with the armed forces. In November 1995 the MFDC's representative in Europe, Mamadou Sane N'Krumah, indicated the organization's willingness to enter negotiations with the government if Diamacouné Senghor and his four associates were released from house arrest. In December, following discussions with representatives of the government and the CNP, Diamacouné Senghor made a televised appeal to the MFDC rebels to lay down their arms. He proposed that preliminary talks between his organization and the CNP take place in early January 1996, to be followed by peace negotiations, in a neutral country, three months later. The members of the MFDC 'political bureau' were released from house arrest at the end of December 1995; it was also reported that the CNP had secured the release of 50 of some 150 suspected separatists detained in recent months. Salif Sadio, reported as the MFDC military leader, confirmed observance of a truce in early January 1996. The preliminary discussions between the MFDC and the CNP took place as scheduled in that month, at which Diamacouné Senghor presented his organization's requirements for the conduct of peace talks.

In mid-February 1996 it was announced that the office of the UN High Commissioner for Refugees (UNHCR) was to supervise the voluntary movement of some 20,000–30,000 refugees from the conflict in Casamance, who were currently encamped at several locations along the border with Guinea-Bissau, to two sites within that country. At the end of February Amnesty International denounced detentions without trial, the use of torture and summary executions in Senegal, with specific reference to the conflict in Casamance. The organization condemned incidents of the abuse of human rights by both the armed forces and the MFDC, and considered that the torture of detainees in Senegal was widespread and 'officially tolerated'. The Diouf government strongly denied the allegations, and also expressed surprise at an announcement by the German government that it would no longer automatically reject applications for political asylum made by Senegalese nationals, since it now regarded Senegal's human rights record as unsatisfactory. (Germany reversed this decision in November.)

While there was considerable optimism regarding the commitment of the government and the MFDC to the peace process, it emerged in early April 1996 that Diamacouné Senghor and his associates were unwilling to attend the formal opening of peace talks in Ziguinchor. The MFDC leaders based their refusal to attend on the grounds that a request that they be issued with passports, to enable them to travel to Europe for discussions with 'exiled' members of the movement, had not been fulfilled, and also that Diamacouné Senghor had stipulated that negotiations be conducted abroad. (For its part, the Senegalese government asserted that it had been willing to allow MFDC representatives to travel for discussions with its membership abroad regarding the composition of the movement's delegation at the planned negotiations, but that the actual intention of the visit was to have been to discuss the independence issue.) The peace talks were postponed indefinitely, and in late April there were reports of renewed tensions in the region. Diouf visited Ziguinchor in May (his first visit to Casamance since the 1993 election campaign): he expressed his commitment to the pursuit of peace, stating that the ongoing process of administrative decentralization would afford greater autonomy to regional structures, but reiterated that it was a 'permanent and historical' fact that Casamance was an integral part of Senegal.

In early July 1996, following the deaths of three soldiers outside Ziguinchor, the armed wing of the MFDC warned all those 'unfamiliar' with the southern Casamance region not to enter the territory. At his inauguration in mid-July, however, the new chief of general staff of the Senegalese armed forces, Maj.-Gen. Lamine Cissé, asserted that the military would be denied access to no part of Senegalese territory. In late August there was renewed optimism regarding the likely resumption of negotiations between a united MFDC and the authorities, following discussions in Ziguinchor between Diamacouné Senghor and Diouf's personal chief of staff. There were few reports of unrest until March 1997, when more than 40 rebels and two members of the armed forces were killed in clashes near the border with Guinea-Bissau. The MFDC denied that it had ended its cease-fire, stating that it would investigate these incidents. In that month four representatives of the MFDC had been permitted to travel to France, where they had spent three weeks meeting with representatives of the movement based in Europe. A delegation of the MFDC, led by the movement's second-in-command, Edmond Brora, made a further visit to France in early July, and members of the external wing made a reciprocal visit to Ziguinchor shortly afterwards: the two wings expressed their desire to establish a harmonized position in preparation for future negotiations with the authorities. Sane Nkrumah did not personally attend the talks in Ziguinchor, despite a specific request by Diamacouné Senghor that he do so, stating that he feared for his safety should he enter Senegal. While both the Senegalese authorities and the MFDC leadership appeared committed to reviving the peace process, several incidents in the Ziguinchor region in July and August were attributed by the Senegalese authorities to separatists, and a clash between members of the armed forces and a rebel group in mid-August reportedly resulted in the deaths of 25 soldiers. In early September it was reported that some 2,000 refugees had fled to The Gambia to escape the recent resurgence of violence in Casamance.

REGIONAL RELATIONS

Beginning in 1989 Senegal's traditional policy of peaceful coexistence with neighbouring countries was severely undermined by a series of regional disputes. The deaths, in April 1989, of two Senegalese farmers, following a disagreement with Mauritanian livestock-breeders regarding grazing rights in the border region between the two countries, precipitated a crisis that was fuelled by long-standing ethnic and economic rivalries. Mauritanian nationals residing in Senegal were attacked, and their businesses ransacked (the retail trade in Senegal had hitherto been dominated by an expatriate community of mainly light-skinned Mauritanians, estimated to number about 300,000), and Senegalese nationals in Mauritania (some 30,000, many of whom worked in the manufacturing sector) suffered similar attacks. By early May it was believed that several hundred people, mostly Senegalese, had been killed. Operations to repatriate nationals of both countries were undertaken with international assistance, and Senegal granted asylum to black Mauritanians who feared official persecution. Mediation attempts were initiated by the OAU, the Arab states, France and the heads of state of several countries in the region. However, despite the expressed commitment of both Senegal and Mauritania to the principle of a negotiated settlement of the dispute, Senegal's insistence on the inviolability of the border as defined at the time of French colonial rule, together with Mauritanian demands that the Senegalese government offer compensation for traders returning to Mauritania, remained among the main impediments to a solution. Diplomatic relations were severed in August. Renewed outbreaks of violence were reported in late 1989, when black Mauritanians sheltering in Senegal crossed into their former homeland (abetted, the government of Mauritania alleged, by the Senegalese armed forces) to recover their property. In early 1990 attempts at mediation were thwarted by military engagements in the border region, as a result of which several deaths were reported. Relations deteriorated further in late 1990, when the Mauritanian authorities accused Senegal of complicity in an alleged attempt to overthrow the Taya government (an accusation denied by the Diouf administration). In January and February 1991 incidents were reported in which Mauritanian naval vessels had opened fire on Senegalese fishing boats, apparently in Senegal's territorial waters, and in March several deaths were reported to have resulted from a military engagement, on Senegalese territory, between members of the two countries' armed forces, following an incursion by Senegalese troops into Mauritania. Further diplomatic initiatives resulted, in July, in a meeting in Guinea-Bissau of the foreign ministers of Senegal and Mauritania, at which they agreed in principle to the reopening of the Mauritania–Senegal border and to a resumption of diplomatic relations. Bilateral contacts continued during the second half of the year, and in November Diouf met with Taya while both were attending a francophone summit meeting in France.

Diplomatic links, at ambassadorial level, were finally restored in April 1992, and the process of reopening the border began in May. None the less, the issues of border demarcation and the status of Mauritanian refugees in Senegal remained to be resolved. Further tensions were reported in September 1993, when the Mauritanian authorities announced that Senegalese nationals would henceforth be required to fulfil certain criteria, including currency exchange formalities, before being allowed to remain in (or enter) Mauritania. In December 1994, however, the governments of Senegal and Mauritania agreed new co-operation measures, including efforts to facilitate the free movement of goods and people between the two countries. In January 1995, moreover, the governments of Senegal, Mauritania and Mali undertook to co-operate in resolving joint border issues and in combating extremism, arms-smuggling and drugs-trafficking. In July UNHCR undertook a census of Mauritanian refugees in Senegal (estimated to number some 66,000), as part of initiatives to achieve their eventual repatriation. In October the Mauritanian minister of the interior, posts and telecommunications, who was visiting Dakar (as part of efforts to achieve the full normalization of relations), gave assurances that nationals of his country were free to return to Mauritania. In January 1996, none the less, several hundred Mauritanian refugees took part in protests in northern Senegal to denounce the Mauritanian authorities' arrangements for their return, and to demand that their repatriation be organized under UNHCR auspices. In late June the repatriation of a group of 4,000 refugees was postponed, owing to what were termed 'logistical' difficulties.

A dispute with Guinea-Bissau regarding the sovereignty of a maritime zone that is believed to contain reserves of petroleum, together with valuable fishing grounds, has caused tensions between the two countries. In July 1989 an international arbitration panel (to which the issue had been referred in 1985) judged the waters to be part of Senegalese territory. However, the government of Guinea-Bissau refused to accept the judgment, and referred the matter to the International Court of Justice (ICJ). Moreover, the Vieira government accused Senegal of repeated violations of both Guinea-Bissau's maritime borders and airspace during April 1990, and in the following month several skirmishes involving Senegalese and Guinea-Bissau troops occurred in the border region. The situation was exacerbated by Senegalese allegations that Guinea-Bissau was allowing members of the MFDC to train on its territory. None the less, meetings between representatives of the two countries culminated, in late May, in the signing of an accord whereby each country undertook to refrain from harbouring organizations hostile to the other, to maintain troops at a 'reasonable distance' from the border and to promote more frequent bilateral contacts. In November 1991 the ICJ ruled that the delimitation of the maritime border, as agreed by the French and Portuguese colonial powers in April 1960, remained valid, thereby confirming Senegal's sovereignty over the disputed zone, and Senegal and Guinea-Bissau signed a treaty recognizing this judgment in February 1993.

Although Guinea-Bissau (together with France) played an important role in the formulation of the 1991 cease-fire agreement between the Senegalese government and the MFDC, relations were again strained in late 1992. In December an offensive by the Senegalese armed forces against MFDC strongholds close to the border with Guinea-Bissau (some reports suggested that MFDC bases within Guinea-Bissau had been targeted) resulted in the deaths of two nationals of that country. The Vieira government formally protested at Senegalese violations of Guinea-Bissau's airspace, and reiterated that, as a guarantor of the 1991 accord, it was not assisting the rebels. Although Senegal apologized for the incident, a further violation was reported in January 1993. None the less, Guinea-Bissau was again active in efforts to bring about a new cease-fire agreement between the Senegalese authorities and the MFDC in mid-1993. In October of that year, moreover, the two countries signed a major 20-year agreement regarding the joint exploitation and management of fishing and petroleum resources in their maritime zones.

Renewed operations by the Senegalese military against MFDC rebels in southern Casamance, from early 1995, again affected relations with Guinea-Bissau. In March Diouf visited Guinea-Bissau to discuss joint security issues and to apologize for two recent attacks perpetrated by the Senegalese armed forces on villages in Guinea-Bissau during February. In April Guinea-Bissau temporarily deployed as many as 500 troops near the border with Senegal, as part of attempts to locate the four missing French tourists: the government of Guinea-Bissau subsequently announced that it was satisfied that the tourists were not on its territory, and reiterated that it was not harbouring separatists (although reports persisted of sightings of the French nationals, apparently with MFDC members, in Guinea-Bissau). In May, following the withdrawal of its troops from the border region, Guinea-Bissau pledged assistance in the establishment of an enduring settlement between the Senegalese authorities and the MFDC. The October 1993 treaty on the joint exploration of maritime wealth was ratified in December 1995: fishing resources were to be shared equally between the two countries, while Senegal was to benefit from a majority share (85%) of petroleum deposits. A joint agency (to be based in Dakar, and headed by Guinea-Bissau's ambassador to Senegal) for the management of mutual resources was formally established during a visit to Guinea-Bissau by Diouf in February 1996. Meanwhile, during bilateral contacts in 1995–96 the two countries pledged co-operation in matters of joint defence and security, while the government of Guinea-Bissau continued to give assurances that it was not assisting MFDC rebels. Through the movement of refugees from the conflict in Casamance to sites within Guinea-Bissau (see above), it was hoped that efforts to restore security in the border region between Senegal and Guinea-Bissau would be expedited. Following a resurgence of unrest in Casamance in mid-1997, Vieira offered to mediate between the Senegalese government and rebels.

In August 1989 the Diouf government announced the withdrawal of 1,400 Senegalese troops from The Gambia, apparently in protest at a request by Jawara that his country be accorded more power within the Senegambian confederal agreement (and also, it seemed, in response to The Gambia's alleged lack of commitment to combating cross-border smuggling, as well as to Senegal's continuing dispute with Mauritania). Later in that month Diouf stated that, in view of The Gambia's reluctance to proceed towards full political and economic integration with Senegal, the functions of the confederation should be suspended, and the two countries should endeavour to formulate more attainable co-operation accords. The confederation was formally dissolved in September. The Jawara government subsequently accused Senegal of imposing customs and travel regulations that were unfavourable to Gambian interests, and of preventing supplies of important commodities from entering The Gambia via Senegal. Relations remained strained during 1990, and in October of that year the Diouf government accused the Gambian authorities of allowing members of the MFDC to operate from Gambian territory. By January 1991, none the less, relations had improved sufficiently to permit the foreign ministers of the two countries to sign a bilateral treaty of friendship and co-operation. In July Diouf visited The Gambia for the first time since the dissolution of the confederation, and in December Jawara attended a summit meeting in Dakar of the Organization of the Islamic Conference. However, Senegal's abrupt, unilateral decision to close the Senegalese–Gambian border in September 1993, apparently to reduce smuggling between the two countries, again strained relations, although negotiations subsequently took place between representatives of Senegal and The Gambia, in an attempt to minimize the adverse effects of the closure on The Gambia's regional trading links. Following the *coup d'état* in The Gambia in July 1994, Jawara was initially granted asylum in Senegal; in subsequent months, however, it was widely believed that Senegal's failure openly to condemn the suspension of constitutional rule by the military regime in The Gambia had influenced the generally muted regional response to Jawara's overthrow. Despite the presence in Senegal of prominent opponents of the Gambian military regime, in January 1996 the two countries signed an agreement aimed at increasing bilateral trade and at minimizing cross-border smuggling. The agreement was signed on behalf of Senegal by Diouf, who was visiting The Gambia for the first time since the coup in that country. A further accord, concluded in April 1997, was to facilitate the trans-border movement of goods destined for re-export.

During the 1990s the Senegalese armed forces have been active in peace-keeping initiatives (many under UN auspices) worldwide. In January 1993, however, it was announced that Senegal was to withdraw its contingent, estimated to number about 1,500 men, from the ECOMOG monitoring group of the Economic Community of West African States (ECOWAS) in Liberia. Senegal had committed troops to Liberia in September 1991, but was rumoured to have been increasingly dissatisfied with the conduct of ECOMOG operations (for further details, see Recent History of Liberia). The decision to withdraw from ECOMOG was said to have been necessitated by domestic security imperatives, given the forthcoming presidential and legislative elections and the escalation of violence in Casamance. None the less, Senegal confirmed that it would continue to co-operate with ECOWAS in initiatives to secure an enduring peace settlement in Liberia. In February 1997 a Senegalese contingent joined the inter-African surveillance mission in the Central African Republic.

Jacques Chirac, reported to be a close associate of Diouf, travelled to Senegal in July 1995, as part of his first visit to sub-Saharan Africa following his election to the French presidency. Presidents Conté of Guinea and Taya of Mauritania also visited Dakar for informal discussions with the new French leader. Visiting Senegal in August 1996, France's minister of defence, Charles Millon, gave assurances that a restructuring of the French armed forces being undertaken by the Chirac administration would not entail any substantial changes in the French military presence in Senegal, and that existing defence arrangements would be respected. This was apparently confirmed by the details of the intended reduction of French forces in Africa, announced by the government of Lionel Jospin in mid-1997, whereby a base was expected to be maintained in Senegal.

In January 1996 it was announced that Senegal was to restore diplomatic relations with Taiwan (which had been severed following Senegal's recognition of the People's Republic of China in December 1971). Senegal, which became the 10th African country to establish links with Taiwan, was subsequently reported to be in receipt of significant financial assistance from that country. In response, the People's Republic of China severed links with Senegal, and ceased all development projects and technical assistance.

Economy

EDITH HODGKINSON

Revised for this edition by THEO THOMAS

Senegal retains some of the economic advantages derived from its leading position in pre-independence French West Africa. In 1995 Senegal's gross national product (GNP) was equivalent to US $580 per head, one of the highest levels in west Africa. However, its economic performance has been disappointing. Growth in the gross domestic product (GDP)—averaging only 2.3% per year in 1970–80, before improving slightly, to 2.8% annually, in 1980–94—has partly kept pace with the rate of population growth (estimated at 2.5% per year in 1980–94). In 1996 the population was officially estimated at 8.57m. The World Bank put total GDP at $5,770m. in 1993. Nominal GDP fell to $3,911m. in 1994, because of the 50% devaluation of the CFA franc in January of that year; however, it increased, in real terms, by 2.0% (having declined by 0.4% in 1993). Real GDP growth accelerated to 4.8% in 1995, and reached 5.6% in 1996 (according to official estimates), suggesting that the devaluation was beginning to yield some economic benefits.

Senegal's economy is vulnerable to competition in almost all areas of productive activity, and remains highly dependent on comparatively large inflows of foreign financial assistance. The agricultural base of the economy has been eroded by periodic droughts and the gradual desertification of large tracts of land. The agricultural sector's contribution to GDP declined from 24% in 1970 to 20% in 1993, although its contribution increased marginally, to 21%, in 1996, according to World Bank figures.

Following a substantial drift of population from rural to urban areas, more than 40% of the country's total population is urban, of whom about one-half live in the overcrowded Dakar region. As the role of the public sector has declined, as part of the economic reform programme, unemployment is growing—an estimated 25% of the active population in Dakar were unemployed in 1992.

Fishing, phosphate-mining and tourism have developed to rival groundnuts and groundnut products as the principal sources of foreign exchange. The importance of these sectors has been further enhanced as a result of the devaluation, of the CFA franc, although many of Senegal's more import-dependent industrial activities have suffered payments' difficulties. Senegal's industrial base, which was comparatively well-developed at independence, is threatened by competing industrial investment in the west African region, particularly in Côte d'Ivoire. Many Senegalese industries have been protected by monopoly rights and tax concessions, and there is much excess capacity. From 1995, however, the government announced plans to end artificial protection of many industries, prompting speculation that some would be forced to close, although others could benefit from a more market-orientated operating environment. Most sectors appeared to show some recovery in 1995 and 1996, although the overall situation remains fragile. The services sector, including government services, trade and transport, is calculated to have contributed 59% of GDP in 1996. With the prevailing difficulties in both agriculture and industry, economic activity has been conducted increasingly outside the formal sectors.

Following the devaluation of currency, Senegal received significant financial support from the IMF, the World Bank, France and other external donors. The government undertook to accelerate its economic reforms, including the elimination of subsidies on some food commodities and the privatization of agricultural marketing, industrial units and some public utilities, such as the supply of drinking water. An ambitious privatization programme was adopted in 1996, with 18 major state-owned companies offered for sale in 1997; among the largest of these are the Société nationale de commercialisation des oléagineaux du Sénégal (SONACOS) in the groundnut sector, the Société nationale d'électricité (SENELEC) and the Société nationale des telecommunications du Sénégal (SONATEL). However, Senegalese state companies are highly unionized, and recent privatization proposals have resulted in serious disruption in some sectors.

AGRICULTURE

The principal food crops are millet, sorghum, rice and maize. Groundnuts are the leading cash crop, but the area under cultivation has declined in recent years. Annual groundnut harvests now average considerably less than 800,000 metric tons, compared with more than 900,000 tons per year in the 1960s. There has been a long-term shift from cash to food crop cultivation, a process that is generally believed to be responsible for a decline in the real income of the rural population.

In an attempt to stimulate marketing through official channels, groundnut purchasing was opened to private traders in 1985/86 and producer prices were increased sharply. Improved weather conditions in the following years resulted in a strong rise in output, to 710,789 tons in 1987/88. Output declined to only 415,210 tons in 1988/89, but recovered strongly, to 844,045 tons, in 1989/90. After late rains, production in 1990/91 contracted to 702,584 tons; output remained at a similar level (728,368 tons) in 1991/92, before declining to 578,498 tons in 1992/93. There has since been some recovery: with output rising to 631,300 tons in 1993/94, to 735,400 tons in 1994/95, and to 790,600 tons in 1995/96. However, poor rainfall resulted in a decline in the groundnut crop in 1996/97, to an estimated 630,000 tons. The government is continuing more closely to link its producer prices to international price trends, and, as part of structural adjustment efforts, has almost abandoned its policy of providing inputs (such as seed and fertilizer) to farmers of groundnuts and other agricultural products. One result has been the reversal of smuggling trends, with a significant portion of the Gambian crop reaching Senegalese markets in the early 1990s.

The government has attempted to reduce dependence on groundnuts by diversifying cash and food crops, in particular by expanding cotton, rice, sugar and market-garden produce. Production of unginned cotton rose very rapidly, from only 698 tons in 1965 to 45,400 tons in 1976/77. Output subsequently fluctuated, with production being particularly influenced by prices for groundnuts, as farmers transfer to cultivation of the latter when prices are more favourable than those for cotton. In 1988/89 marketed production of unginned cotton was 38,730 tons; output declined to 29,303 tons in 1989/90, but had recovered to 51,176 tons by 1992/93. Production regressed to 37,000 tons in 1994/95 and to 28,800 tons in 1995/96, partly reflecting a reduction in the planted area, although there was some improvement, to an estiamted 38,000 tons, in 1996/97, as the producer price (and the area under cultivation) increased. Sugar is produced at the Richard Toll complex in the north, near Saint-Louis. Output, all of which is for domestic consumption, has risen steadily since 1979, and totalled an estimated 96,000 tons in 1994.

Output of rice has fluctuated widely, and, at an annual average of 186,000 tons since the beginning of the 1990s, falls far short of domestic demand (some 500,000 tons annually). The shortfall is met by cheap imports of rice from the Far East; however, this seriously jeopardizes the viability of local produce, which in the past attracted a state subsidy of 50–60 francs CFA per kilo. A number of small- and medium-scale projects, supported by foreign aid, have so far been largely unsuccessful in extending the area under irrigation for rice, although the completion of the Manantali project (see below) is expected to have a great impact on output levels and production costs in the future. Market gardening was begun in 1971, and, following initial difficulties, exports from this sector are viewed as having considerable potential, although Senegal's price competitiveness compared with other African producers is declining. The traditional food sector has suffered sharp set-backs from repeated droughts, but the overall production level has risen. Output of millet and sorghum averaged 650,000 tons per year in the mid-1970s, around 100,000 tons higher than at the beginning of the decade, but fell to 351,800 tons in 1983/84, because of drought. Production has since rebounded, to average 700,000 tons per year in 1988/89–1994/95; the 1995/96 crop was officially estimated at 794,100 tons. Output of maize, which reached a record 146,500 tons in 1985/86, declined to 123,327 tons in 1988/89, recovered slightly, to 133,147 tons in 1990/91, before falling back to 114,561 tons in 1992/93. A good crop of 138,300 tons was produced in 1993/94, but has since fallen, to an estimated 88,600 tons in 1996/97.

In recent drought years concessionary grain supplies have amounted to more than 100,000 tons annually, while apparent consumption levels per head have been declining. The attainment of food self-sufficiency remains a major priority. Of great relevance to this objective is the enormous increase in irrigated land which is due to result from the completion of the Manantali dam in Mali. The combined benefits of the anti-salt barrage at Diama and of the Manantali dam are expected to provide newly-irrigated land totalling 240,000 ha in Senegal over the next 25 years. (However, a World Bank report has criticized the project's immediate impact on traditional farming methods, which rely on annual floods.) In the short term, it is hoped to stabilize rice imports at 340,000 tons a year, while promoting the increased cultivation and consumption of millet and sorghum.

Food crops are supplemented by output from fishing. This sector has considerable potential and, including processing, now accounts for about 4% of GDP. Annual catches averaged 307,000 tons during 1988–92, with output of 417,000 tons in 1993 rising to 439,000 tons in 1995. Small-scale fishing continues to predominate, with about 45,000 fishers providing some 60%–70% of the total national catch and about 45% of fish exports although the political insecurity in the Casamance region (the main fishing area) has at times adversely affected the sector. Industrial fishing is practised both by national and foreign operators. Of 244 fishing licences issued in 1990, 113 were for Senegalese-owned vessels. The fishing sector as a whole provides employment for about 10,000 people, including those engaged in local canning factories. Senegal's contribution to the international fish market remains very small, however, at about 0.3%. Since 1979 regular fishing agreements have been concluded with the European Community (now European Union—EU), for which Senegal receives financial compensation of about ECU 30m. annually, and part of the catch made by EU vessels is landed in Senegal for processing locally. In 1986 fish overtook groundnuts to become Senegal's principal export, and fish and fish products provided about 33% of export earnings (excluding re-exports) in 1996. None the less, the fishing industry is suffering some sectoral problems, while increasing competition from Côte d'Ivoire has eroded Senegal's share of the French market. Moreover, concern has been increasingly expressed that industrial fishing activities by EU vessels are not only depleting Senegal's fish stocks but also undermining the traditional fishing sector.

Livestock is a significant sector of the traditional economy (although less important than in most other countries of this area), and is the base for the dairy and meat-processing industries. In 1995 numbers of cattle were estimated by the FAO at 2.85m., sheep and goats at 8.1m., pigs at 320,000 and horses at 500,000.

MINING AND POWER

The mining sector contributed only an estimated 1.4% of GDP in 1996, but is the country's fourth largest source of export earnings. Mining in Senegal is dominated by the extraction of phosphates: reserves of calcium phosphates are estimated at 100m. tons, while there are reserves of 50m.–70m. tons of aluminium phosphates. Senegal accounts for about 1.5% of world output and 3% of world exports of phosphates. The Cie sénégalaise des phosphates de Taïba (CSPT) and the Société sénégalaise des phosphates de Thiès (SSPT), both 50% state-owned, have been the two companies extracting phosphates, which are then processed by Industries chimiques du Sénégal (ICS), in which the Senegalese government has a 33% stake. The merger of the activities of the CSPT and the ICS was announced in September 1996, and is expected to result in a twofold increase in the production of chemical fertilizers over the next seven years. The new company took the name ICS. The CSPT has been the principal producer of calcium phosphates, although the SSPT has modest reserves of some 2m.–3m. tons of lower-quality chalk phosphates at Lam Lam. In 1981 1.8m. tons of calcium phosphates were produced (compared with 198,000 tons in 1960). Output of calcium phosphates increased from 1.8m. tons in 1985 to 2.3m. tons per year in both 1988 and 1989, then declined to 2.1m. tons in 1990 and 1.7m. tons in 1991. A marked improvement in 1992, when production recovered to 2.3m. tons, preceded a further period of decline, from 1.7m. tons in 1993 to 1.6m. tons in 1994, and to 1.5m. tons and 1.4m. tons, respectively, in 1995 and 1995. Exports to countries of the EU have fallen, partly because of the high cadium content of Senegalese phosphates, although EU funding has been provided to finance plant to remove the chemical. Expansion is planned both at existing facilities and at new ones at Tobène, while a plant for the recovery of phosphates from tailings has been constructed at the ICS fertilizer complex, with World Bank support, which will increase the life of the mine through the utilization of lower-quality deposits. There are also unexploited deposits at Semmé, estimated to contain 60m. tons of calcium phosphates. Plans to exploit further the country's reserves of phosphates were impeded in the late 1980s by low international prices (development of the Semmé deposits would cost an estimated US $110m.). European and south-east Asian markets remained tight in the early 1990s, but from 1994 the ICS benefited from an increase in international prices for phosphoric acid in conjunction with enhanced competitiveness arising from the devaluation of the CFA franc.

Reserves of aluminium phosphates have been exploited by the SSPT. Output fluctuated widely in the 1970s and 1980s, with a peak of 405,000 tons in 1974, a halving of that figure in subsequent years, and a slight recovery, to 366,000 tons, in 1985. Concerns regarding the environmental consequences of the use of aluminium phosphates have since adversely affected the international market for this commodity, and Senegal's aluminium phosphates are no longer sold in their natural state. Most of SSPT's production is now processed locally into clinker, with the production of aluminium phosphates reduced to an estimated 27,200 tons in 1996.

Some 330m. tons of high-grade iron ore have been located at Falémé, in the east, but development would require new sources of electricity (the installation of the hydroelectric plant at the Manantali dam could provide such a source), a new, 740-km rail link to Dakar and new port facilities. The persistent over-supply in the world iron-ore market caused the target initial output to be halved, to 6m. tons per year. A gradual increase is then projected, to reach 12m. tons. At the lower capacity, the project, including transport investment, would require funding of some US $700m., but adequate financial support is still being sought. Gold deposits (estimated in mid-1997 to contain 30 tons of metal) have been discovered at Sabodala, in the south-east, and the Société minière de Sabodala, a joint venture by the Senegalese government and French official interests (with Australian participation from 1993), began production in May 1997. Several other foreign companies, including South Africa's Anglo American Corpn and Randgold, as well as Samax of the United Kingdom and several Canadian interests, have been awarded gold exploration permits in south-eastern Senegal. Exploration for diamonds is also in progress. Commercially-viable reserves of titanium were discovered in 1991: workable ores are estimated at some 10m. tons.

Deposits of petroleum, estimated at 52m.–58m. tons, have been located in the Dôme Flore field, off the Casamance coast, but the development of these reserves (which are overwhelmingly of heavy oil) was long regarded as economically unfeasible. Disagreement with Guinea-Bissau regarding sovereignty of waters in this region was a further obstacle to their development. In mid-1995, none the less, the two countries signed an agreement envisaging joint co-operation in prospecting for petroleum in adjoining territorial waters, and exploration rights were subsequently awarded to US interests, operating in partnership with the Société nationale des pétroles du Sénégal (PETROSEN). A small offshore natural gas deposit, of 50m. cu m, at Diam Niadio, near Rufisque, was developed to fuel the Cap des Biches power station, but output was only some 42,000 cu m per day, and production ceased in late 1992. However, a much larger source has been located nearby, and was supplying the Cap des Biches plant in mid-1993. In early 1997 PETROSEN announced the discovery of a major natural gas deposit, with reserves estimated at 10,000m. cu m, in the Thiés region. The deposit could be exploited for the production of electricity over a 30-year period. The development of peat deposits, in the Niayès area, is being examined with external financial support. It was hoped that these would provide fuel for electricity generation (a 20–30 MW station) and also substitute for firewood as domestic fuel. After a period of inactivity, the project was revived in 1990. In 1988 the government adopted a new mining code, in an attempt to encourage the further exploitation of Senegal's mineral resources. The incentives include automatic 25-year exploration rights if a deposit is located, while there is no requirement for government equity participation.

Electric power is supplied from six thermal stations, with a total installed capacity of 231 MW. The rehabilitation of existing capacity forms part of a project currently being implemented at a cost of US $84m., which also included the construction of the 40-MW power station at Cap des Biches. Work began in 1982 on the Manantali hydroelectric plant, on the Senegal river, in a joint scheme with Mali and Mauritania, under the auspices of the Organisation pour la mise en valeur du fleuve Sénégal (OMVS). Construction was completed in March 1988, but the installation of generators has been delayed by arguments among the three OMVS members regarding the distribution of electricity and the routeing of power lines. Agreement was apparently reached in late 1995, and the plant is now targeted to begin production in 2000. The scheme should eventually provide total generating capacity of 200 MW, of which Senegal will have a 30% share. Under a letter of development policy agreed with the World Bank, an enabling law is due to be submitted to the national assembly with regard to the privatization of the electricity generating company, SENELEC. As with many of the other proposed privatizations, there has been considerable opposition from the trade unions, and in June 1997 the government modified its plan to sell off a majority stake in SENELEC, opting instead to transfer 49% of the company to private investors and to operate the company as a commercial entity with majority state ownership. The partial privatization was to be achieved by means of increasing the company's capital, rather than by the divestment of existing equity.

MANUFACTURING

Senegal has the most developed manufacturing sector in francophone west Africa after Côte d'Ivoire, with production accounting for some 13% of GDP in 1995. The main activity is light industry (most of which is located in or near Dakar), transforming basic local commodities and import substitution to satisfy domestic demand. The agro-industrial sector mainly comprises oil mills, sugar refineries, fish-canning factories, flour mills and drinks, dairy-products and tobacco industries, which together account for 40% of total value added. Extractive industries (mainly the processing of phosphates) constitute the second most important branch of industrial activity. The manufacturing of textiles, leather goods and chemicals are also important, while subsidiary activities include paper and packaging and the manufacture of wood products and building materials. Senegal's textiles industry is well equipped and is potentially the most important in black francophone Africa, but has performed badly hitherto. The immediate, short-term impact of devaluation was, moreover, detrimental, as cotton was sold for higher prices abroad, leaving the domestic industry short of raw materials. The chemicals industry (soap, paints, insecticides, plastics, pharmaceuticals and a petroleum refinery) is aimed at import substitution, as are nearly all the metalworking, engineering and electrical plants (including three shipyards, and truck and bicycle assembly plants).

In line with the emphasis on the processing of raw materials, ICS built plants to produce sulphuric acid (625,000 tons per year), phosphoric acid (475,000 tons), ammonium phosphate (250,000 tons) and triple superphosphate (250,000 tons). Production started in 1984, with 180,000 tons of the fertilizer output to be sold in the Senegalese and Malian markets, and the rest to be exported, mainly to other west African markets, eventually representing earnings of up to 24,000m. francs CFA per year. The total cost of this complex, including related infrastructure, was US $312m., making it the single most important industrial project in Senegal. Funds have been contributed by the African Development Bank (ADB), the European Investment Bank (EIB), the International Finance Corporation, France and Arab agencies, including the Arab Bank for Economic Development in Africa, while the governments of Nigeria, Côte d'Ivoire, Cameroon and India have equity shares in ICS. The annual capacity of the cement plant at Rufisque was expanded from 380,000 to 800,000 tons by the end of 1983, at a cost of 16,000m. francs CFA (with France and the EIB contributing loans), and further expansion is planned. In addition, the petroleum refinery's annual capacity rose to 1.2m. tons at the end of 1983, and has since expanded to 1.4m. tons.

The government introduced a New Industrial Policy in 1986, with the purpose of improving the competitiveness of Senegalese companies and encouraging the development of activities generating high value-added, while reducing the role of the state. There were two strands to this policy: firstly, to reduce and harmonize customs tariffs and to remove quantitative restrictions on imports, and, secondly, to restructure enterprises and to improve the economic and regulatory environment by reducing the cost of key inputs, including labour. However, within three years the programme was effectively abandoned. As cheap imports flooded the market, through formal and informal channels, the government decided in 1989 to restore customs tariffs to their previous high levels. The reduction of costs and enactment of an enabling environment were never implemented, largely because of resistance to labour law reforms from the trade unions.

There has been a decline in output in many industrial subsectors since 1986, although the production of phosphates, water and electricity have shown overall increases, and there has been resilience in output of petroleum products, soap, fertilizers and cement. Most has been achieved in those industries that have not been directly affected by the industrial reforms introduced after 1986. The decline was particularly severe in light manufacturing industries such as textiles and shoes, which were vulnerable to competition from imported goods.

After the devaluation of the currency, new measures were undertaken in an attempt to stimulate private-sector participation in industry. Import licensing was abolished, and the government made further commitments to end the effective monopolies enjoyed by a few large companies, to reduce the rigidity of the statutory labour code, and to privatize several state-owned companies and parastatals—including SONACOS, the main groundnut-oil producer. However, the government's rejection in 1996 of several unacceptably-low offers for state enterprises was endorsed by the World Bank. Performance in the manufacturing sector since the devaluation has been uneven, with some sectors (such as food-processing and electronics) suffering a decline in output. There was no immediate increase in private investment, although some textile and shoe factories were rehabilitated for improved production. Loans for private-sector development and small and medium-sized enterprises were awarded by the International Development Association (the World Bank's concessionary lending agency) and the ADB.

TRANSPORT INFRASTRUCTURE

Industrial development has been stimulated by, and has in turn boosted, the port at Dakar. Container-handling facilities were increased from 29,000 tons to more than 100,000 when a new terminal was inaugurated in 1988, and the extension of container facilities was completed in 1993. The port handles some 6m. tons of freight per year. Improvements to the fishing port at Dakar have also been carried out. There were proposals to construct a naval repair yard, to service bulk oil carriers, but plans were scaled down because of a downturn in the tanker market, and a smaller-scale dock, able to handle vessels up to 60,000 tons, entered service in 1981. In that year more than 400 ships were serviced. Completion of the Manantali project will eventually extend the all-year navigability of the Senegal river, currently just 220 km, to 924 km, as far as Kayes in Mali.

Senegal possesses a good road network. In 1995 there were an estimated 14,580 km of classified roads, of which about 4,200 km were surfaced. In mid-1986, as part of the economic adjustment programme, the government suspended virtually all new road-building projects, concentrating instead on financing the maintenance of existing roads. None the less, a 163-km road between Dialakoto and Kédougou, the construction of which (at a cost of some 23,000m. francs CFA) was financed by regional donor organizations, was inaugurated in March 1996. The rail infrastructure is also well-developed, with 1,225 km of track, although only 70 km of this is two-way and the network would benefit from modernization. The two main lines run from Dakar to Kidira, from the west to the east and across the border with Mali to Bamako, and from Dakar, via Thiès, to Saint-Louis in the north, near the border with Mauritania. In late 1995 the governments of Senegal and Mali agreed to establish, with a view to privatization, a joint company to operate the Dakar–Bamako line. There is an international airport at Dakar, which handles about 700,000 passengers and 24,000 tons of freight annually; in addition there are three other major airports and about 15 smaller airfields. A second airport for the capital is to be constructed at Keur Massar (about 30 km east of Dakar), at an estimated cost of US $200m., with capacity for 2.5m. passengers annually. Meanwhile, facilities at Cap-Skirring and Ziguinchor are being upgraded, with the aim of improving direct access to the Casamance region. In accordance with the government's overall strategy in the transport sector, the national carrier, Air Sénégal, is in the final stages of privatization: the process was scheduled to be completed by the end of 1997.

TOURISM

Tourism has grown in importance since the early 1970s, and it now ranks as one of the country's major sources of foreign earnings. In 1995 gross earnings from tourism reached 55,000m. francs CFA, and visitor arrivals totalled 387,708. Senegal has about 16,000 hotel beds of international tourist standard, and Dakar is of considerable importance as an international conference centre. The sector, which provides 4,500 direct and 15,000 indirect jobs, contributed almost 3% of GDP in 1995. The devaluation of the CFA franc improved the competitiveness of tourism in Senegal, hitherto regarded as a high-cost destination. However, further violence in Casamance and the failure to secure an enduring peace settlement in the region, where much tourist activity is located, could prevent a sustained recovery in the sector.

INVESTMENT AND FINANCE

Despite overall economic difficulties, the level of investment increased steadily in the 1960s, from the rather low figure of 9% of GDP in 1961 to 17% in 1971, although it had fallen back to about 13% by the early 1990s. Public investment has accounted for the majority of total gross investment (69% in 1990), with government borrowing—both internal and external—increasing, as budgetary revenue declined. The fall in groundnut production had an adverse impact on current revenue, but the scope for budget austerity was restricted by the high wage bill (reflecting the size of Senegal's civil service—unusually large even among francophone west African countries), by the deficits of state agencies and by the need to service a rising public debt, as borrowing for the capital programme increased.

While phosphate revenues allowed a balance or even a small fiscal surplus on rising expenditure in the mid-1970s, the downturn in economic activity towards the end of the decade severely depressed revenues, and the government adopted a programme of fiscal restraint, agreed with the IMF in 1980. This resulted in a very modest increase in spending over the period 1979/80 (July/June)–1981/82, by an average of 6% annually, which represented a decline in real terms, while budget revenues were to rise, with increases in both taxation and the prices of goods and services that are supplied by the public sector. The broad objectives of the programme were maintained into 1984/85 and 1985/86, with spending restrained by means of reductions in subsidies to state enterprises.

Considerable progress was made, under the austerity programmes of the early 1980s, in reducing the budget deficit, which declined from 8.2% of annual GDP in 1982/83 to 3.8% of GDP in 1987/88. However, the economic situation was severely undermined in 1988/89 by Senegal's dispute with Mauritania, while the implementation of 'liberalization' policies, such as the reduction in customs tariffs, has also affected the level of government revenue. As a result, the budget deficit nearly doubled in 1988/89, to 30,900m. francs CFA, compared with 16,800m. francs CFA in the previous year. The deficit widened further, to 46,400m. francs CFA in 1989/90. However, estimates for 1990/91 indicated that improvements in revenue collection and restraints on expenditure led to an initial surplus in government finances (on a commitment basis) of 31,200m. francs CFA. However, the overall deficit in that year, on a cash basis, was only 400m. francs CFA, reflecting the implementation of a programme to pay off arrears. In the equivalent period of 1991/92 there was a surplus, on a commitment basis, of 3,700m. francs CFA; this budgetary period was extended to the end of 1992, so that subsequent financial years were to coincide with the calendar year. The increasing overvaluation of the currency had a negative impact on government revenues, resulting in a fiscal deficit of 47,200m. francs CFA in 1993 (equivalent to 3.0% of GDP in that year). Although the subsequent fiscal reforms restrained the budget deficit to about 1.8% of GDP in 1994 (on a commitment basis), the deficit on a cash basis continued to widen, reaching 9.3% of GDP, or 200,000m. francs CFA, in that year. None the less, continued fiscal austerity has continued to improve the budgetary position, and the cash deficit narrowed to 2.7% of GDP in 1995. The estimated deficit for 1996 (on both a cash and commitment basis) was in the region of 6,100m. francs CFA—equivalent to 0.2% of GDP. One of the main aims of the government's policy is to eliminate the budget's reliance on sizeable foreign grants.

Since independence, Senegal has benefited from the consistent support of Western donors, who have been keen to assist the country's relatively stable, conservative governments. Donors have always recognized that Senegal is poorly-endowed with natural resources, and external aid and funding have been forthcoming. Moreover, relations with both the World Bank and the IMF have generally remained good.

In 1987 the consultative group of aid donors pledged funds of US $1,800m. to support the public investment programme and to provide payments support for 1987–90. Throughout the period of the economic reform programme the IMF accorded stand-by and structural adjustment facilities. In November 1988 an enhanced structural adjustment facility (ESAF), of SDR 145m. over three years, was approved. However, attempts in mid-1993 to reduce current expenditure—in accordance with creditors' demands that the problem of the public-sector deficit, of some 180,000m. francs CFA, be addressed—principally by means of reductions in civil servants' salaries prompted considerable domestic disquiet. In March 1994 Senegal was the first Franc Zone member to reach agreement with the IMF on new funding (a stand-by credit of $67m.), following the devaluation of the CFA franc, and a new ESAF, of SDR 138.8m., was approved in August 1994. Almost all the new assistance pledged by multilateral and bilateral donors was conditional upon the government's continued adherence to the programme of reforms. Principal among the donors of new loans were the World Bank, the ADB and France. In July 1995 the consultative group of donors, expressing broad satisfaction at the progress of adjustment measures hitherto, pledged $1,500m. over a two-year period. Senegal has since continued to observe the performance criteria defined under the ESAF programme, and the government is expected to request further support from the multilateral donors upon the expiry, in January 1998, of the current facility.

FOREIGN TRADE AND PAYMENTS

Senegal's foreign trade and current-account balance have consistently been in deficit, with the size of the former varying in response to the groundnut crop. Since the mid-1970s, however, the fluctuations have tended to narrow, as exports have stabilized at higher levels, reflecting the expansion, first, of exports of phosphates (to an average of 22,000m. francs CFA per year during the 1980s) and, later, of fishery products (an average of 18,000m. francs CFA per year in 1978–80, rising to 55,000m. francs CFA in 1990, and to 138,300m. francs CFA in 1994—the year of the currency devaluation). The very strong rise in imports in the early 1980s, as petroleum prices rose, the food deficit widened, and purchasing power was maintained through foreign borrowing, resulted in a trade deficit of 130,000m. francs CFA in 1985. The 1985–92 adjustment programme aimed to increase export earnings by 12.9% annually, with exports of fish and chemical products from the ICS complex rising strongly, while import growth was to be held to an average 9.8% per year. This was still to leave Senegal with a substantial trade deficit; in the event, the value of merchandise exports declined by an annual average of 0.7% during 1985–92, while that of imports declined by an average of 1.7% per year. Exports in 1989–93 averaged 228,000m. francs CFA annually, compared with imports averaging some 316,000m. francs CFA per year. The trade deficit in 1994 was 128,300m. francs CFA. In nominal CFA franc terms the value of both imports and exports increased substantially following the 50% devaluation of the currency in January. Exports increased by 119%, to 439,100m. francs CFA, while the increase in expenditure on imports was limited to 84%, at 567,400m. francs CFA. The value of exports and imports continued to expand in 1995, to 483,400m. francs CFA and 607,500m. francs CFA respectively, resulting in a trade deficit of 124,000m. francs CFA.

The chronic deficit on foreign trade and on imports and exports of services are to a large degree offset on the current account by inward cash transfers, consisting mainly of official development grants. The current-account deficit remained relatively stable during the 1980s and early 1990s: it fell from 122,400m. francs CFA in 1985 to a low point 49,300m. francs CFA in 1990, but regressed somewhat, to 79,000m. francs CFA in 1993. A sharp narrowing of the trade deficit and a surge in official development assistance in 1994 resulted in a small current-account surplus, of 1,800m. francs CFA, in that year. However, the surplus was not sustained, and a current-account deficit of 12,700m. francs CFA was recorded for 1995, while the government estimated a deficit of some 32,400m. francs CFA in 1996; both were largely attributable to the decline in the level of foreign official transfers.

Since the late 1970s, the government has had increasing recourse to external borrowing, and outstanding external long-term debt increased from US $1,114m. in 1980 to $2,071m. in 1985 and to $3,235m. in 1995, more than 60% of which is made up of bilateral and multilateral concessional credits. Debts of only $50m. were outstanding to commercial banks at the end of 1995. The rise in debt-servicing payments, which reached 29% of total foreign earnings in 1980, was restricted by a series of debt-rescheduling agreements by the 'Paris Club' of Western official creditors, linked to the IMF-backed austerity programme. None the less, the debt-service ratio reached a record level of 32.4% in 1987, before easing to 28.6% in 1989, to 20.5% in 1990, and to 8.4% in 1993. Subdued export performance in 1994, in conjunction with the clearing of some servicing arrears and the effects of devaluation (which resulted in the doubling, in local-currency terms, of the external debt), meant that the debt-service ratio was 15.1% in 1994, rising to 17.3% in 1995. Since 1988, reschedulings of debt by the 'Paris Club' have been made in accordance with the exceptional terms formulated at the summit meeting of industrialized nations that had been held in Toronto in 1988. Further substantial debt-relief, including cancellations and reschedulings in accordance with the 'Trinidad terms' (devised in 1990), was approved by the 'Paris Club' in March 1994, while France agreed to cancel one-half of Senegal's bilateral debt. Even more concessional relief, involving some 87,000m. francs CFA of debt, was granted by official creditors in early 1995, in accordance with the new 'Naples terms', which allow the cancellation or rescheduling of as much as 67% of public debt. However, the outstanding debt, at $3,845m., continues to represent a considerable burden, with a total debt-to-export ratio of 224.3% in 1995, and further reschedulings and a commercial debt 'buy-back' scheme are expected in the medium term.

Statistical Survey

Source (unless otherwise stated): Direction de la Statistique, Ministère l'Economie, des Finances et du Plan, rue René Ndiaye, BP 4017, Dakar; tel. 21-06-99; telex 3203; fax 22-41-95.

Area and Population

AREA, POPULATION AND DENSITY

Area (sq km)	196,722*
Population (census results)†	
16 April 1976	5,085,388
27 May 1988	
Males	3,353,599
Females	3,543,209
Total	6,896,808
Population (official estimates at mid-year)	
1994	8,130,000
1995	8,347,000
1996	8,572,000
Density (per sq km) at mid-1996	43.6

* 75,955 sq miles.

† Figures refer to the *de jure* population. The *de facto* population at the 1976 census was 4,907,507, and at the 1988 census was 6,773,417.

POPULATION BY ETHNIC GROUP (at 1988 census)

Ethnic group	Number	%
Wolof	2,890,402	42.67
Serere	1,009,921	14.91
Peul	978,366	14.44
Toucouleur	631,892	9.33
Diola	357,672	5.28
Mandingue	245,651	3.63
Rural-Rurale	113,184	1.67
Bambara	91,071	1.34
Maure	67,726	1.00
Manjaag	66,605	0.98
Others	320,927	4.74
Total	6,773,417	100.00

Source: UN, *Demographic Yearbook*.

REGIONS AND PRINCIPAL TOWNS
(*de jure* population at 1988 census)

	Area (sq km)	Population	Density (per sq km)	Population of capital*
Dakar	550	1,488,941	2,707.2	1,375,067
Diourbel	33,547	619,245	33.1	n.a.
Louga		490,077		n.a.
Fatick	7,935†	509,702	64.2	n.a.
Kaolack	16,000†	811,258	50.7†	150,961
Kolda	21,000†	591,833	28.2†	n.a.
Saint-Louis	44,127	660,282	15.0	113,917
Tambacounda	59,602	385,982	6.5	n.a.
Thiès	6,601	941,151	142.6	175,465
Ziguinchor	7,300†	398,337	54.6†	124,283
Total	196,722	6,896,808	35.1	

* Each region has the same name as its capital.

† Figures are approximate.

Note: The city of Dakar is the national capital.

Principal towns (official estimates at mid-1994): Dakar 1,641,358; Thiès 216,381; Kaolack 193,115; Ziguinchor 161,680; Saint-Louis 132,499.

Source: UN, *Demographic Yearbook*.

BIRTHS AND DEATHS (UN estimates, annual averages)

	1980–85	1985–90	1990–95
Birth rate (per 1,000)	47.2	45.5	43.0
Death rate (per 1,000)	19.4	17.7	16.0

Expectation of life (UN estimates, years at birth, 1990–95): 49.3 (males 48.3; females 50.3).

Source: UN, *World Population Prospects: The 1994 Revision*.

ECONOMICALLY ACTIVE POPULATION

Mid-1995 (estimates in '000): Agriculture, etc. 2,756; Total 3,714 (Source: FAO, *Production Yearbook*).

Agriculture

PRINCIPAL CROPS ('000 metric tons)

	1993	1994	1995
Rice (paddy)	193	162	155
Maize	138	108	107
Millet and sorghum	753	680	794
Potatoes	14*	10	9*
Cassava (Manioc)	43	77	56
Pulses	44	29	42
Groundnuts (in shell)	628	718	791
Cottonseed*	28	24	24
Cotton (lint)	20†	20†	18*
Palm kernels*	6.3	6.3	6.3
Tomatoes	62*	20	45*
Dry onions	32*	45	40*
Other vegetables	49*	50	49*
Mangoes	58*	70	66*
Oranges	24*	31	28*
Bananas	5*	7	6*
Other fruit	19*	20	22*
Coconuts*	5	5	5
Sugar cane	850*	856	883

* FAO estimate(s). † Unofficial figure.

Source: FAO, *Production Yearbook*.

LIVESTOCK ('000 head, year ending September)

	1993	1994	1995*
Cattle*	2,750	2,800	2,850
Sheep	4,400†	4,600†	4,800
Goats	3,118†	3,200†	3,250
Pigs*	320	320	320
Horses	498	500*	500
Asses	364	364*	364
Camels*	6	7	6

Poultry (million): 34 in 1993; 38* in 1994; 40* in 1995.

* FAO estimate(s). † Unofficial figure.

Source: FAO, *Production Yearbook*.

LIVESTOCK PRODUCTS (FAO estimates, '000 metric tons)

	1993	1994	1995
Beef and veal	45	46	46
Mutton and lamb	15	15	15
Goat meat	13	14	14
Pig meat	7	7	7
Horse meat	6	6	6
Poultry meat	52	55	58
Other meat	6	6	7
Cows' milk	103	103	103
Sheep's milk	17	17	17
Goats' milk	14	14	14
Poultry eggs	27.0	30.0	31.5
Cattle hides	9.0	9.1	9.2
Sheepskins	3.1	3.2	3.3
Goatskins	2.8	2.9	3.0

Source: FAO, *Production Yearbook*.

Forestry

ROUNDWOOD REMOVALS ('000 cubic metres, excluding bark)

	1992	1993*	1994*
Sawlogs, veneer logs and logs for sleepers	40	40	40
Other industrial wood*	629	645	661
Fuel wood	4,223	4,312	4,404
Total	4,892	4,997	5,105

* FAO estimates.

Source: FAO, *Yearbook of Forest Products*.

Fishing

('000 metric tons, live weight)

	1993	1994	1995
Freshwater fishes	28.7	30.8	32.4
Flatfishes	7.2	11.9	10.5
Grunts, sweetlips, etc.	6.9	8.4	4.2
Croakers and drums	6.3	7.8	9.3
Dentex, seabreams, etc.	8.9	9.4	10.9
Round sardinellas	142.2	128.1	116.8
Madeiran sardinellas	73.9	51.4	64.7
European anchovy	0.1	8.2	0.1
Bonga shad	12.2	13.5	17.3
Other marine fishes (incl. unspecified)	75.5	55.9	56.7
Total fish	362.0	325.5	323.0
Gastropods	5.2	5.6	7.5
Octopuses	4.8	8.4	4.2
Other crustaceans and molluscs	10.2	11.0	13.6
Total catch	382.2	350.5	348.3

Note: Figures cover the artisanal Senegalese fishery, the industrial Senegalese tuna fishery, the industrial Senegalese and French trawler fishery, and the industrial Senegalese sardine fishery.

Source: FAO, *Yearbook of Fishery Statistics*.

Mining

('000 metric tons)

	1991	1992	1993
Natural phosphates	1,741	2,300	1,863
Fuller's earth (attapulgite)*	129	112	112†
Salt (unrefined)	61	20	22

1994 ('000 metric tons): Fuller's earth (attapulgite)* 112†.

* Data from the US Bureau of Mines.

† Provisional or estimated figure.

Source: UN, *Industrial Commodity Statistics Yearbook*.

Industry

SELECTED PRODUCTS ('000 metric tons, unless otherwise indicated)

	1992	1993	1994
Frozen fish*	59.9	60.4	n.a.
Tinned fish*	15.0	19.0	n.a.
Salted, dried or smoked fish*	31.4	n.a.	n.a.
Groundnut oil—crude	114	57	n.a.
Wheat flour	137	139	n.a.
Raw sugar	90*	86*	95†
Cigarettes (million)‡	3,350	n.a.	n.a.
Footwear—excl. rubber ('000 pairs)	644	508	n.a.
Nitrogenous fertilizers§	26.8	25.0‖	24‖
Phosphate fertilizers§	46.4	33.0‖	38‖
Jet fuel‖	92	92	94
Motor spirit (Petrol)‖	115	117	118
Kerosene‖	15	17	18
Gas-diesel (Distillate fuel) oils‖	292	294	295
Residual fuel oils‖	224	225	227
Lubricating oils‖	3	3	3
Liquefied petroleum gas‖	3	3	3
Cement	602	591	n.a.
Electric energy (million kWh)	762	765	769

* Data from the FAO.

† Data from the International Sugar Organization.

‡ Data from the US Department of Agriculture.

§ Figures for fertilizers are in terms of nitrogen or phosphoric acid, and relate to output during the 12 months ending 30 June of the year stated.

‖ Provisional or estimated figure(s).

Source: mainly UN, *Industrial Commodity Statistics Yearbook*.

Finance

CURRENCY AND EXCHANGE RATE

Monetary Units

100 centimes = 1 franc de la Communauté financière africaine (CFA).

French Franc, Sterling and Dollar Equivalents
(31 March 1997)

1 French franc = 100 francs CFA;
£1 sterling = 924.20 francs CFA;
US $1 = 562.85 francs CFA;
1,000 francs CFA = £1.082 = $1.777.

Average Exchange Rate (francs CFA per US $)

1994 555.20
1995 499.15
1996 511.55

Note: An exchange rate of 1 French franc = 50 francs CFA, established in 1948, remained in force until January 1994, when the CFA franc was devalued by 50%, with the exchange rate adjusted to 1 French franc = 100 francs CFA.

BUDGET ('000 million francs CFA)

Revenue	1991	1993*†	1994†
Current revenue	300.9	306.2	363.3
Tax receipts	241.4	241.1	281.0
Other current revenue	59.5	65.1	82.3
Grants, aid and subsidies	—	50.4	106.3
Borrowing	26.3	71.1	66.4
Total	327.2	427.7	536.0

Expenditure	1991	1993*†	1994†
Administrative expenditure	252.4	279.1	277.6
Investment expenditure	44.5	139.0	151.0
Debt-servicing	—	69.1	206.9
Total	296.9	487.2	635.5

* Figures for 1992 are not available.

† Forecasts.

Source: Banque centrale des états de l'Afrique de l'ouest.

INTERNATIONAL RESERVES (US $ million at 31 December)

	1994	1995	1996
Gold*	10.8	11.2	10.9
IMF special drawing rights	1.1	3.8	1.7
Reserve position in IMF	1.7	1.8	1.8
Foreign exchange	176.9	266.2	284.8
Total	190.4	283.0	299.2

* Valued at market-related prices.

Source: IMF, *International Financial Statistics*.

MONEY SUPPLY ('000 million francs CFA at 31 December)

	1993	1994	1995
Currency outside banks	93.03	145.64	152.05
Demand deposits at deposit money banks	101.43	155.35	160.15
Checking deposits at post office	2.96	3.94	4.33
Total money (incl. others)	197.75	305.34	316.76

Source: IMF, *International Financial Statistics*.

COST OF LIVING (Consumer price index, Dakar. Base: 1990 = 100)

	1994	1995	1996
All items	129.1	139.2	143.1

Source: IMF, *International Financial Statistics*.

NATIONAL ACCOUNTS ('000 million francs CFA at current prices)

Expenditure on the Gross Domestic Product

	1993	1994	1995
Government final consumption expenditure	203.9	260.8	278.5
Private final consumption expenditure	1,277.1	1,683.2	1,873.8
Increase in stocks } Gross fixed capital formation }	218.2	315.8	363.6
Total domestic expenditure	1,699.2	2,259.8	2,515.9
Exports of goods and services	357.1	755.5	809.7
Less Imports of goods and services	-467.7	-867.5	-912.3
GDP in purchasers' values	1,588.6	2,147.8	2,413.3

Source: IMF, *International Financial Statistics*.

Gross Domestic Product by Economic Activity*

	1992	1993	1994
Agriculture, hunting, forestry and fishing	318.8	301.8	431.6
Mining and quarrying } Manufacturing }	198.4	197.7	274.3
Electricity, gas and water	36.3	35.6	47.7
Construction and public works	53.3	53.4	69.0
Trade, restaurants and hotels	387.4	380.1	538.4
Transport, storage and communications	168.7	166.6	207.7
Other marketable services	268.3	273.1	379.8
Government services	155.0	153.3	170.8
Non-profit services to households	26.4	27.0	28.5
GDP in purchasers' values	1,612.6	1,588.6	2,147.8

Source: Banque centrale des états de l'Afrique de l'ouest.

BALANCE OF PAYMENTS (US $ million)

	1992	1993	1994
Exports of goods f.o.b.	860.6	736.8	818.8
Imports of goods f.o.b.	−1,191.8	−1,086.7	−1,022.0
Trade balance	−331.1	−349.9	−203.2
Exports of services	532.8	462.1	439.0
Imports of services	−654.2	−581.3	−492.7
Balance on goods and services	−452.5	−469.1	−256.9
Other income received	45.1	34.6	36.7
Other income paid	−173.0	−162.3	−164.5
Balance on goods, services and income	−580.4	−596.8	−384.7
Current transfers received	489.0	432.9	467.5
Current transfers paid	−127.1	−115.4	−79.6
Current balance	−218.5	−279.2	3.2
Direct investment abroad	−51.3	−0.3	−17.4
Direct investment from abroad	21.4	−0.8	66.9
Portfolio investment assets	—	—	−1.5
Portfolio investment liabilities	0.7	5.8	0.5
Other investment assets	−24.9	4.1	−92.5
Other investment liabilities	167.4	120.7	120.8
Net errors and omissions	−19.6	8.4	−57.2
Overall balance	−124.9	−141.5	22.8

Source: IMF, *International Financial Statistics*.

External Trade

PRINCIPAL COMMODITIES (distribution by SITC, US $ million)

Imports c.i.f.	1991	1992	1993
Food and live animals	257.2	282.6	293.7
Dairy products and birds' eggs	41.7	60.6	70.4
Milk and cream	35.9	54.5	63.3
Milk and cream, preserved, concentrated or sweetened	34.9	53.3	61.9
Fish, crustaceans and molluscs	24.5	21.3	13.4
Fresh, chilled or frozen fish	23.2	16.9	12.7
Cereals and cereal preparations	115.0	112.7	126.1
Wheat and meslin (unmilled)	28.1	29.9	35.2
Rice	71.3	71.9	80.7
Rice, milled, broken	70.9	69.3	80.6
Vegetables and fruit	24.8	23.1	24.4
Coffee, tea, cocoa and spices	16.7	25.0	22.8
Crude materials (inedible) except fuels	28.6	42.4	45.9
Mineral fuels, lubricants, etc.	120.4	103.4	103.9
Petroleum, petroleum products, etc.	120.1	103.0	103.4
Crude petroleum oils, etc.	91.4	79.4	84.1
Refined petroleum products	25.9	21.6	16.9
Animal and vegetable oils, fats and waxes	50.1	52.1	63.9
Fixed vegetable oils and fats	45.8	45.0	62.2
Fixed vegetable oils, 'soft', crude, refined or purified	32.0	27.7	45.8
Rape, colza and mustard oils	30.4	26.8	24.1
Chemicals and related products	155.1	151.0	134.1
Inorganic chemicals	30.6	26.7	11.4
Inorganic chemical elements, oxides and halogen salts	27.1	22.8	7.7
Medicinal and pharmaceutical products	44.4	45.8	45.0
Medicaments (incl. veterinary)	41.3	42.3	41.2
Artificial resins, plastic materials, etc.	26.9	25.8	22.4
Polymerization and copolymerization products	22.1	21.8	18.0
Basic manufactures	168.1	190.3	175.5
Paper, paperboard, etc.	29.2	31.7	29.1
Textile yarn, fabrics, etc.	28.6	34.3	24.3
Iron and steel	39.7	49.2	51.9
Universals, plates and sheets, of iron or steel	20.0	18.7	24.0
Machinery and transport equipment	249.0	271.1	252.4
Machinery specialized for particular industries	46.6	49.9	44.0
Civil engineering and contractors' plant and equipment	25.1	29.7	26.5
Construction and mining machinery	21.7	25.7	21.7
General industrial machinery, equipment and parts	42.3	45.5	44.3
Electrical machinery, apparatus, etc.	52.2	56.5	47.8
Road vehicles and parts (excl. tyres, engines and electrical parts)	66.7	80.9	79.9
Passenger motor cars (excl. buses)	26.6	37.0	37.2
Miscellaneous manufactured articles	53.1	66.3	55.5
Total (incl. others)	1,097.0	1,172.5	1,139.2

Exports f.o.b.	1991	1992	1993
Food and live animals	241.1	215.9	176.3
Fish, crustaceans and molluscs	215.3	186.9	143.6
Fresh, chilled or frozen fish	45.1	50.5	57.0
Fresh, chilled, frozen, salted or dried crustaceans and molluscs	30.2	22.3	15.4
Prepared or preserved fish, crustaceans and molluscs	136.2	108.9	66.9
Fish (incl. caviar)	90.4	82.1	48.3
Crustaceans and molluscs	45.7	26.7	18.5
Feeding stuff for animals (excl. unmilled cereals)	18.8	20.4	13.6
Oil-cake, etc.	17.5	18.9	11.9
Groundnut cake	17.3	17.0	11.4
Crude materials (inedible) except fuels	96.1	126.2	103.4
Textile fibres (excl. wool tops) and wastes	21.1	28.0	27.4
Cotton	20.2	27.4	27.2
Raw cotton (excl. linters)	20.2	27.4	27.2
Crude fertilizers and crude minerals	55.9	82.7	64.9
Crude fertilizers	43.9	66.4	51.2
Natural calcium phosphates, etc.	43.9	66.4	51.2
Minerals fuels, lubricants, etc.	104.4	80.3	87.4
Petroleum, petroleum products, etc.	104.2	79.9	86.9
Refined petroleum products	104.1	79.7	86.4
Motor spirit (gasoline) and other light oils	50.6	38.1	33.6
Spirit-type jet fuel	46.9	33.6	28.5
Gas oils (distillate fuels)	28.0	24.5	28.6
Animal and vegetable oils, fats and waxes	72.3	55.7	34.4
Fixed vegetable oils and fats	72.2	55.6	34.3
Fixed vegetable oils, 'soft', crude, refined or purified	72.2	55.5	34.3
Groundnut (peanut) oil	69.5	55.0	33.7
Chemicals and related products	95.1	127.5	103.8
Inorganic chemicals	64.1	83.0	56.7
Inorganic chemical elements, oxides and halogen salts	64.0	82.8	56.6
Inorganic acids and oxygen compounds of non-metals	63.8	82.3	55.4
Phosphorus pentoxide and phosphoric acids	63.7	82.1	55.3
Manufactured fertilizers	21.9	31.8	26.8
Basic manufactures	23.5	41.3	44.2
Paper paperboard and manufactures	6.0	13.2	14.6
Metal containers for storage and transport	7.9	12.6	12.7
Casks, drums, cans, boxes, etc., of iron, steel or aluminium	7.9	12.5	12.5
Machinery and transport equipment	13.7	21.8	39.3
Machinery specialized for particular industries	2.5	7.1	13.8
Miscellaneous manufactured articles	5.5	12.2	13.5
Total (incl. others)	652.2	683.0	605.1

Source: UN, *International Trade Statistics Yearbook*.

PRINCIPAL TRADING PARTNERS (US $ million)*

Imports c.i.f.	1991	1992	1993
Belgium-Luxembourg	41.0	37.1	30.4
Brazil	15.1	16.5	20.4
Canada	14.0	23.5	10.5
China, People's Repub.	13.7	24.3	23.4
Côte d'Ivoire	61.6	70.8	57.8
France (incl. Monaco)	376.7	389.7	403.1
Gabon	23.7	17.1	19.9
Germany	38.7	42.1	42.4
Italy	57.5	70.1	48.1
Japan	32.4	44.2	40.7
Netherlands	29.0	29.3	38.7
Nigeria	79.5	71.8	71.0
Pakistan	9.5	21.1	7.0
Spain	36.5	42.0	40.1
Thailand	57.0	35.0	46.7
United Kingdom	17.2	22.0	17.0
USA	79.2	71.2	59.2
Viet Nam	0.1	12.1	16.1
Total (incl. others)	1,096.9	1,172.4	1,139.2

Exports f.o.b.	1991	1992	1993
Belgium-Luxembourg	9.1	9.0	7.1
Benin	5.0	6.3	10.2
Cameroon	10.4	7.8	7.3
Côte d'Ivoire	17.8	19.7	13.4
Ethiopia	n.a.	0.0	6.1
France (incl. Monaco)	206.1	185.7	157.3
Gambia	9.5	11.9	12.6
Germany	8.3	9.5	9.6
Guinea	5.4	15.2	11.8
India	76.9	105.2	76.9
Iran	6.7	21.6	13.5
Italy	66.0	39.5	41.4
Japan	12.0	13.7	10.3
Mali	24.2	36.7	31.3
Mauritania	0.0	4.5	12.4
Netherlands	10.2	25.3	7.1
Philippines	10.6	12.3	3.3
Spain	20.3	14.0	9.4
USA	6.8	2.9	12.2
Total (incl. others)	652.2	683.0	605.1

* Imports by country of production; exports by country of last consignment.

Source: UN, *International Trade Statistics Yearbook*.

Transport

RAILWAYS (estimated traffic)

	1991	1992	1993
Passenger-km (million)	174	179	206
Freight ton-km (million)	610	650	695

Source: UN Economic Commission for Africa, *African Statistical Yearbook*.

ROAD TRAFFIC (motor vehicles in use)

	1993	1994	1995*
Passenger cars	73,254	75,515	80,600
Buses and coaches	9,087	9,255	9,810
Lorries and vans	20,241	21,081	22,600
Road tractors	2,089	2,133	2,230
Motor cycles and mopeds	2,950	3,185	3,480

* Estimates.

Source: IRF, *World Road Statistics*.

SHIPPING

Merchant Fleet (vessels registered at 31 December)

	1994	1995	1996
Number of vessels	182	184	189
Total displacement ('000 grt)	50	48	50

Source: Lloyd's Register of Shipping, *World Fleet Statistics*.

International Sea-borne Freight Traffic (at Dakar, '000 metric tons)

	1995
Goods loaded	2,979
Goods unloaded	3,247

Source: Banque centrale des états de l'Afrique de l'ouest.

CIVIL AVIATION (traffic on scheduled services)*

	1992	1993	1994
Km flown (million)	3	3	3
Passengers carried ('000)	138	140	141
Passenger-km (million)	222	216	224
Total ton-km (million)	36	35	36

* Including an apportionment of the traffic of Air Afrique.

Source: UN, *Statistical Yearbook*.

Tourism

FOREIGN TOURIST ARRIVALS

Country of origin	1989	1990	1991
Benelux	7,363	5,908	5,474
Canada	2,809	1,866	1,858
France	155,839	147,524	132,254
Germany, Federal Republic	13,661	13,736	13,106*
Italy	11,322	12,786	16,280
Spain	2,339	2,161	1,762
Switzerland	4,085	4,545	4,315
United Kingdom	3,064	3,457	3,533
USA	9,452	8,736	6,220
Total (incl. others)	259,096	245,881	233,512

* The figure for 1991 is for the united Germany.

1992: Total foreign tourist arrivals 245,581.
1993: Total foreign tourist arrivals 167,770.
1994: Total foreign tourist arrivals 239,629.

Source: Ministère du Tourisme et des Transports aériens, Dakar.

Communications Media

	1992	1993	1994
Radio receivers ('000 in use)	890	920	945
Television receivers ('000 in use)	282	290	297
Daily newspapers			
Number	1	n.a.	3
Average circulation ('000 copies)	50	n.a.	48
Non-daily newspapers			
Number	n.a.	n.a.	87

Source: UNESCO, *Statistical Yearbook*.

Telephones ('000 in use): 55 in 1993 (Source: Société Nationale des Télécommunications du Sénégal, Dakar).

Education

(1992/93, unless otherwise indicated)

	Institu-tions	Teachers	Students		
			Males	Females	Total
Primary	2,454	1,711	424,536	314,020	738,556
Secondary					
General	n.a.	n.a.	117,888	64,252	182,140
Teacher training*	n.a.	n.a.	616	173	789
Vocational	n.a.	n.a.	4,766	2,535	7,301
Tertiary	n.a.	965	n.a.	n.a.	23,001

* 1991/92 figures.

1993/94: *Pre-primary* Institutions 196; Teachers 751; Students 17,305 (males 8,779; females 8,526). *Primary* Institutions 2,559; Teachers 14,436; Students 773,386 (males 444,305; females 329,081).

Source: UNESCO, *Statistical Yearbook*.

Directory

The Constitution

The Constitution of the Republic of Senegal was promulgated on 7 March 1963. It has since been amended, with the most recent amendments being effected in May 1992. The main provisions are summarized below:

PREAMBLE

Affirms the Rights of Man, liberty of the person and religious freedom. National sovereignty belongs to the people who exercise it through their representatives or by means of referendums. There is universal, equal and secret suffrage for adults of 18 years of age and above. French is the official language.

THE PRESIDENT

The President of the Republic is elected by direct universal suffrage for a seven-year term and may seek re-election only once. The President holds executive power and, as Commander of the Armed Forces, is responsible for national defence. The President of the Republic appoints the Prime Minister. He may, after consultation with the President of the Assemblée nationale, with the Prime Minister and with the appropriate organ of the judiciary, submit any draft law to referendum. In circumstances where the security of the State is in grave and immediate danger, he can assume emergency powers and rule by decree. The President of the Republic can be impeached only on a charge of high treason or by a secret ballot of the Assemblée nationale carrying a three-fifths' majority.

THE PRIME MINISTER

The Prime Minister is appointed by the President of the Republic, and, in turn, appoints the Council of Ministers in consultation with the President.

THE LEGISLATURE

Legislative power is vested in the Assemblée nationale, which is elected by universal direct suffrage for a five-year term. The Assembly discusses and votes legislation and submits it to the President of the Republic for promulgation. The President can direct the Assembly to give a second reading to the bill, in which case it may be made law only by a three-fifths' majority. The President of the Republic can also call upon the Constitutional Court to declare whether any draft law is constitutional and acceptable. Legislation may be initiated by either the President of the Republic or the Assemblée nationale. Should the Presidency fall vacant, the President of the legislature is automatic successor to the Head of State. A motion expressing 'no confidence' in the Government can be considered if it has been endorsed by one-tenth of the members of the Assembly.

LOCAL GOVERNMENT

Senegal is divided into 10 regions, each having a governor and an elected local assembly.

POLITICAL PARTIES

There is no limit to the number of political parties.

AMENDMENTS

The President of the Republic and Deputies to the Assemblée nationale may propose amendments to the Constitution. Draft amendments are adopted by a three-fifths majority vote of the Assemblée nationale. Failing this, they are submitted to referendum.

Note: The establishment is envisaged of a second legislative chamber, the Senate.

The Government

HEAD OF STATE

President: Abdou Diouf (took office 1 January 1981; elected President on 27 February 1983, re-elected 28 February 1988 and 21 February 1993).

COUNCIL OF MINISTERS
(September 1997)

A coalition of the Parti socialiste sénégalais (PS); Parti démocratique sénégalais (PDS); Ligue démocratique–Mouvement pour le parti du travail (LD–MPT); Parti démocratique sénégalais–Rénovation (PDS–R).

President of the Republic and Head of Government: Abdou Diouf (PS).

Prime Minister: Habib Thiam (PS).

Minister of State at the Presidency: Me Abdoulaye Wade (PDS).

Minister of State, Minister of Foreign Affairs and Senegalese Abroad: Moustapha Niasse (PS).

Minister of State, Minister of Agriculture: Robert Sagna (PS).

Minister of State, Minister of Presidential Services and Affairs: Ousmane Tanor Dieng (PS).

Minister of the Interior: Abdourahmane Sow (PS).

Minister of Justice and Keeper of the Seals: Jacques Baudin (PS).

Minister of the Armed Forces: Cheikh Amidou Kane (PS).

Minister of the Economy, Finance and Planning: Papa Ousmane Sakho (no party affiliation).

Minister of the Environment and Nature Conservation: ABDOULAYE BATHILY (LD–MPT).

Minister of Public Health and Social Action: OUSMANE NGOM (PDS).

Minister of National Education: ANDRÉ SONKO (PS).

Minister of Energy, Mines and Industry: MAGUED DIOUF (PS).

Minister of Modernization of the State: BABACAR NÉNÉ MBAYE (PS).

Minister of Culture: ABDOULAYE ELIMANE KANE (PS).

Minister of Communications: SERIGNE DIOP (PDS–R).

Minister of Labour and Employment: ASSANE DIOP (PS).

Minister of Women's, Children's and Family Affairs: AMINATA MBENGUE NDIAYE (PS).

Minister of Equipment and Land Transport and acting Minister of Housing and Town Planning: LANDING SANÉ (PS).

Minister of Trade, Crafts and Industrialization: IDRISSA SECK (PDS).

Minister of Youth and Sports: OUSMANE PAYE (PS).

Minister of Fisheries and Maritime Transport: ALASSANE DIALY NDIAYE (PS).

Minister of Tourism and Air Transport: TIJANE SYLLA (PS).

Minister of Water Resources: MAMADOU FAYE (PS).

Minister of Scientific Research and Technology: Dr MARIE-LOUISE CORREA (PS).

Minister of Towns: DAOUR CISSÉ (PS).

There are also nine ministers-delegate.

MINISTRIES

Office of the President: ave Léopold Sédar Senghor, BP 168, Dakar; tel. 23-10-88; telex 258.

Office of the Prime Minister: Dakar.

Ministry of Agriculture and Water Resources: Immeuble Administratif, Dakar; tel. 23-10-88; telex 3151.

Ministry of the Armed Forces: BP 176, Dakar; tel. 23-10-88; telex 482.

Ministry of Communications: 58 blvd de la République, Dakar; tel. 23-10-65; fax 21-41-04.

Ministry of Culture: Immeuble Administratif, Dakar; tel. 23-10-88; telex 482.

Ministry of the Economy, Finance and Planning: rue René Ndiaye, BP 4017, Dakar; tel. 21-06-99; telex 61203; fax 22-41-95.

Ministry of Energy, Mines and Industry and of Trade, Crafts and Industrialization: 122 bis ave André Peytavin, BP 4037, Dakar; tel. 22-99-94; telex 61149; fax 22-55-94.

Ministry of the Environment and Nature Conservation: Dakar.

Ministry of Equipment, of Land and Maritime Transport and Fisheries: Immeuble Communal, blvd du Général de Gaulle, Dakar; tel. 21-42-01; telex 3151.

Ministry of Foreign Affairs and Senegalese Abroad: place de l'Indépendance, Dakar; tel. 21-62-84; telex 482.

Ministry of Housing and Town Planning: ave André Peytavin, BP 4028, Dakar; tel. 23-91-27; fax 22-56-01.

Ministry of the Interior: Rond-point de la République, Dakar; tel. 21-41-51; telex 3351.

Ministry of Justice: BP 784, Dakar; tel. 23-10-88; telex 482.

Ministry of Labour and Employment: BP 403, Dakar; tel. 23-10-88; telex 482.

Ministry of Modernization of the State: Dakar.

Ministry of National Education: rues Calmette et René Ndiaye, BP 4025, Dakar; tel. 22-12-28; fax 21-89-30.

Ministry of Public Health and Social Action: Immeuble Administratif, Dakar; tel. 23-10-88; telex 482.

Ministry of Tourism and Air Transport: 23 rue Calmette, BP 4049, Dakar; tel. 23-65-02; fax 22-94-13.

Ministry of Women's, Children's and Family Affairs: Dakar.

Ministry of Youth and Sports: ave Abdoulaye Fadiga, Dakar.

President and Legislature

PRESIDENT

Presidential Election, 21 February 1993

	Votes	% of votes
ABDOU DIOUF (PS)	757,311	58.40
ABDOULAYE WADE (PDS)	415,295	32.03
LANDING SAVANÉ (AJ–PADS)	37,787	2.91
ABDOULAYE BATHILY (LD–MPT)	31,279	2.41
IBA DER THIAM (CDP)	20,840	1.61
MADIOR DIOUF (RND)	12,635	0.97
MAMADOU LÔ (Independent)	11,058	0.85
BABACAR NIANG (PLP)	10,450	0.81
Total	1,296,655	100.00

ASSEMBLÉE NATIONALE

President: CHEIKH ABDOUL KHADRE CISSOKHO.

General Election, 9 May 1993

Party	Votes	% of votes	Seats
PS	602,171	56.56	84
PDS	321,585	30.21	27
Japoo*	52,189	4.90	3
LD–MPT	43,950	4.13	3
PIT	32,348	3.04	2
UDS–R	12,339	1.16	1
Total	1,064,582	100.00	120

* An electoral alliance of AJ—PADS, the CDP and the RND, as well as independent candidates.

Advisory Council

Conseil Economique et Social: 25 ave Pasteur, BP6100, Dakar; tel. 23-59-35; f. 1964; Pres. BABACAR NDOYE.

Political Organizations

There were 26 authorized political parties in early 1997. Among the most influential of these were:

And Jëf–Parti africain pour la démocratie et le socialisme (AJ–PADS): BP 12025, Dakar; tel. 22-54-63; f. 1991 by merger of And Jëf–Mouvement révolutionnaire pour la démocratie nouvelle, Organisation socialiste des travailleurs and Union pour la démocratie populaire; progressive reformist; Sec.-Gen. LANDING SAVANÉ.

Convention des démocrates et des patriotes (CDP): 96 rue 7, Bopp, Dakar; f. 1992; Sec.-Gen. Prof. IBA DER THIAM.

Ligue démocratique–Mouvement pour le parti du travail (LD–MPT): BP 10172, Dakar Liberté; tel. 25-67-06; regd 1981; social-democrat; Sec.-Gen. ABDOULAYE BATHILY.

Mouvement pour le socialisme et l'unité (MSU): Villa no 54, rue 4, Bopp, Dakar; f. 1981 as Mouvement démocratique populaire; socialist; Sec.-Gen. MAMADOU DIA.

Parti africain des écologistes–Sénégal (PAES): Ecole Normale Germaine Legoff, Dakar; Sec.-Gen. ABOUBACRY DIA.

Parti africain de l'indépendance (PAI): BP 820, Dakar; f. 1957, reorg. 1976; Marxist; Sec.-Gen. MAJHEMOUTH DIOP.

Parti africain pour l'indépendance des masses (Pai–M): 440, Cité Abdou Diouf Guédiawaye, Dakar; tel. 34-75-90; f. 1982; social democratic; Sec.-Gen. ALY NIANE.

Parti démocratique sénégalais (PDS): 5 blvd Dial Diop, Dakar; f. 1974; liberal democratic; Sec.-Gen. Me ABDOULAYE WADE.

Parti démocratique sénégalais–Rénovation (PDS–R): 343 Gibraltar II, Dakar; regd 1987; breakaway group from PDS; Sec.-Gen. SERIGNE DIOP.

Parti de l'indépendance et du travail (PIT): BP 5612, Dakar Fann; regd 1981; Marxist-Leninist; Sec.-Gen. AMATH DANSOKHO.

Parti pour la libération du peuple (PLP): 4025 Sicap Amitié II, Dakar; f. 1983 by RND dissidents; neutralist and anti-imperialist; Sec.-Gen. Me BABACAR NIANG; Asst Sec.-Gen. ABDOULAYE KANE.

Parti populaire sénégalais (PPS): Clinique Khadim Diourbel, Dakar; regd 1981; populist; Sec.-Gen. Dr OUMAR WANE.

Parti socialiste sénégalais (PS): Maison du Parti, ave Cheikh Amadou Bamba, Rocade Fann, Bel Air, BP 12010, Dakar; f. 1958 as Union progressiste sénégalaise, reorg. under present name 1978;

democratic socialist; Chair. ABDOU DIOUF; Exec. Sec. OUSMANE TANOR DIENG.

Rassemblement national démocratique (RND): Villa no 29, Cité des Professeurs, Fann Résidence, Dakar; f. 1976, legalized 1981; progressive; Sec.-Gen. MADIOR DIOUF.

Union démocratique sénégalaise–Rénovation (UDS–R): Villa no 273, Ouagou Niayes, Dakar; f. 1985 by PDS dissidents; progressive nationalist; Sec.-Gen. MAMADOU PURITAIN FALL.

Diplomatic Representation

EMBASSIES IN SENEGAL

Argentina: 34-36 blvd de la République, BP 3343, Dakar; tel. 21-51-71; telex 51457; Ambassador: HÉCTOR TEJERINA.

Austria: 24 blvd Djily Mbaye, BP 3247, Dakar; tel. 22-38-86; telex 51611; fax 21-03-09; Ambassador: Dr PETER LEITENBAUER.

Bangladesh: Immeuble Kébé, Appts 11–12, 7e étage, ave André Peytavin, BP 403, Dakar; tel. 21-68-81; telex 51298; Ambassador: M. D. MANIRUZZAMAN MIAH.

Belgium: route de la Petite Corniche-Est, BP 524, Dakar; tel. 22-47-20; telex 51265; fax 21-63-45; Ambassador: XAVIER VAN MIGEM.

Brazil: Immeuble Fondation Fahd, 4e étage, blvd Djily Mbaye, angle Macodou Ndiaye, BP 136, Dakar; tel. 23-25-92; fax 23-71-81; Ambassador: JORGE SALTARELLI JUNIOR.

Cameroon: 157–9 rue Joseph Gomis, BP 4165, Dakar; tel. 21-33-96; telex 21429; Ambassador: EMMANUEL MBONJO EJANGUE.

Canada: Immeuble Daniel Sorano, 45 blvd de la République, BP 3373, Dakar; tel. 23-92-90; telex 51632; fax 23-87-49; Ambassador: JACQUES BILODEAU.

Cape Verde: Immeuble El Fahd, BP 2319, Dakar; tel. 21-18-73; telex 61128; Ambassador: VÍCTOR AFONSO GONÇALVES FIDALGO.

Congo, Democratic Republic: Fann Résidence, 16 rue Léo Frobénius, BP 2251, Dakar; tel. 25-19-79; telex 21661; Ambassador: KALENGA WA BELABELA.

Congo, Republic: Mermoz Pyrotechnie, BP 5243, Dakar; tel. 24-83-98; Ambassador: CHRISTIAN GILBERT BEMBET.

Côte d'Ivoire: 2 ave Albert Sarraut, BP 359, Dakar; tel. 21-01-63; telex 61170; Ambassador: JULES HIÉ NÉA.

Czech Republic: rue Aimé Césaire, Fann Résidence, BP 3253, Dakar; tel. 24-65-26; fax 24-14-06; Ambassador: LADISLAV SKEŘÍK.

Egypt: Immeuble Daniel Sorano, 45 blvd de la République, BP 474, Dakar; tel. 21-24-75; fax 21-89-93; Ambassador: MOHAMED ABDEL-RAHMAN DIAB.

Ethiopia: 39 rue Jules Ferry, BP 379, Dakar; 21-98-94; fax 21-98-95; Ambassador: MOHAMED HASSEN KAHIN.

France: 1 rue Amadou Assane Ndoye, BP 4035, Dakar; tel. 23-91-81; telex 51597; fax 22-18-05; Ambassador: ANDRÉ LEWIN.

Gabon: Villa no 7606 Mermoz, BP 436, Dakar; tel. 24-09-95; fax 25-98-26; Ambassador: SIMON OMBEGUE.

Gambia: 11 rue de Thiong, BP 3248, Dakar; tel. 21-44-76; telex 51617; Ambassador: Col (retd) ANTOUMAN SAHO.

Germany: 20 ave Pasteur, angle rue Mermoz, BP 2100, Dakar; tel. 23-48-84; telex 21686; fax 22-52-99; Ambassador: Dr ELEONORE LINSMAYER.

Guinea: point E, rue 7, angle B&D, BP 7123, Dakar; tel. 24-86-06; telex 61242; Ambassador: AHMADOU TIDJANE TRAORÉ.

Guinea-Bissau: Point E, rue 6, BP 2319, Dakar; tel. 21-59-22; telex 243; Ambassador: PIO GOMES CORREIA.

Holy See: rue Aimé Césaire, angle Corniche-Ouest, Fann Résidence, BP 5076, Dakar; tel. 24-26-74; fax 24-19-31; Apostolic Nuncio: Most Rev. ANTONIO MARIA VEGLIÒ, Titular Archbishop of Aeclanum.

India: 5 ave Carde, BP 398, Dakar; tel. 22-58-75; telex 51514; fax 22-35-85; Ambassador: VIDYA BHUSHAN SONI.

Indonesia: 126 ave Cheikh Anta Diop, angle ave Bourguiba, BP 5859, Dakar; tel. 25-73-16; telex 21644; Ambassador: UTOJO YAMTOMO.

Italy: rue Alpha Hachamiyou Tall, BP 348, Dakar; tel. 22-00-76; fax 21-75-80; Ambassador: PAOLO GUIDO SPINELLI.

Japan: Immeuble Electra II, rue Malan, BP 3140, Dakar; tel. 23-91-41; telex 51677; fax 23-73-51; Ambassador: TAKESHI NAKAMURA.

Korea, Democratic People's Republic: rue Aimé Césaire, Fann Résidence, BP 3156, Dakar; tel. 23-09-99; Ambassador: RI IN SOK.

Korea, Republic: Immeuble Fayçal, BP 3338, Dakar; tel. 22-58-22; Ambassador: KIM IL-KUN.

Kuwait: blvd Martin Luther King, Dakar; tel. 24-17-23; telex 3327; Ambassador: KHALAF ABBAS KHALAF.

Lebanon: 18 blvd de la République, BP 234, Dakar; tel. 22-09-20; telex 3190; Ambassador: NAJI ABDOU ASSI.

Mali: 46 blvd de la République, BP 478, Dakar; tel. 23-48-93; telex 51429; Ambassador: MOHAMED ALI BATHILY.

Mauritania: Fann Résidence, Corniche Ouest, BP 2019, Dakar; tel. 25-98-07; fax 25-72-64; Ambassador: MALIFOND OULD DADDAH.

Morocco: ave Cheikh Anta Diop, BP 490, Dakar; tel. 24-69-27; telex 51567; fax 25-70-21; Ambassador: DRISS ENNAHDI ELIDRISSI.

Netherlands: 37 rue Kléber, BP 3262, Dakar; tel. 23-94-83; telex 51610; fax 21-70-84; Ambassador: GERARD J. H. C. KRAMER.

Nigeria: Point E, rue 1, angle Fa, BP 3129, Dakar; tel. 21-69-22; telex 51404; fax 25-81-36; Chargé d'affaires a.i.: O. A. D. NWAOBASI.

Pakistan: 10 ave Borgnis Desbordes, BP 2635, Dakar; tel. 21-20-31; Ambassador: RASHEED AHMED.

Poland: Fann Résidence, angle Corniche-Ouest, BP 343, Dakar; tel. 24-23-54; fax 24-95-26; Chargé d'affaires a.i.: JANUSZ MROWIEC.

Portugal: 5 ave Carde, BP 281, Dakar; tel. 23-58-22; telex 61134; fax 23-50-96; Ambassador: FERNANDO PINTO DOS SANTOS.

Romania: Point E, blvd de l'Est, angle rue 4, Dakar; tel. and fax 25-19-13; telex 61115; Chargé d'affaires: IONEL ILIE.

Russia: ave Jean-Jaurès, angle rue Carnot, BP 3180, Dakar; tel. 22-48-21; telex 21432; Ambassador: VALERII N. LIPNYAKOV.

Saudi Arabia: 33 rue Kléber, BP 3109, Dakar; tel. 22-23-67; telex 51294; Ambassador: ABDULLAH A. ALTOBAISHI.

South Africa: 12 ave Albert Sarraut, BP 21010, Dakar; tel. 23-65-81; fax 21-48-78; Ambassador: M. N. N. J. MOSIA.

Spain: 45 blvd de la République, BP 2091, Dakar; tel. 21-30-80; fax 21-68-45; Ambassador: MIGUEL ANGEL GARCÍA MINA ORAA.

Switzerland: rue René Ndiaye, angle rue Seydou Nourou Tall, BP 1772, Dakar; tel. 22-58-48; Ambassador: JEAN-CLAUDE RICHARD.

Syria: Point E, rue 1, angle blvd de l'Est, BP 498, Dakar; tel. 21-62-77; telex 62102; Chargé d'affaires a.i.: HILAL AL-RAHEB.

Thailand: Fann Résidence, 10 rue Léon Gontran Damas, BP 3721, Dakar; tel. 24-30-76; telex 61279; Ambassador: NARONK KHEMAYODHIN.

Tunisia: rue El Hadj Seydou Nourou Tall, BP 3127, Dakar; tel. 23-47-47; telex 54564; fax 23-72-04; Ambassador: ALI HACHANI.

Turkey: ave des Ambassadeurs, Fann Résidence, BP 6060, Etoile, Dakar; tel. 24-58-11; telex 51472; fax 25-69-77; Ambassador: MEHMET GORKAY.

United Kingdom: 20 rue du Dr Guillet, BP 6025, Dakar; tel. 23-73-92; fax 23-27-66; Ambassador: DAVID SNOXELL.

USA: ave Jean XXIII, BP 49, Dakar; tel. 23-42-96; telex 21793; fax 22-29-91; Ambassador: DANE F. SMITH.

Zimbabwe: Fann Résidence, BP 15153, Dakar; tel. 25-03-25; telex 61231; fax 25-89-59; Ambassador: CHIMBIDZAYI EZEKIEL SANYANGARE.

Judicial System

Under the terms of a revision of the judicial system, implemented in May 1992, the principal organs of the judiciary are as follows:

Conseil Constitutionnel: Pres. YOUSSOUPHA NDIAYE.

Conseil d'Etat: Pres. OUSMANE CAMARA; Sec.-Gen. DOUDOU NDIR.

Cour de Cassation: Procurator-Gen. ANDRÉSIA VAZ; Sec.-Gen. MOUSTAPHA TOURÉ.

Cour d'Appel: Procurator-Gen. PAPA BOUGOUMA DIENE.

Religion

At the time of the 1988 census almost 94% of the population were Muslims, while some 4% professed Christianity (the dominant faith being Roman Catholicism); a small number followed traditional beliefs.

ISLAM

There are four main Islamic brotherhoods: the Mourides, the Tidjanes, the Layennes and the Qadiriyas.

Grand Imam: El Hadj MAODO SYLLA.

Association pour la coopération islamique (ACIS): Dakar; f. 1988; Pres. Dr THIERNAO KÂ.

National Association of Imams: Dakar; f. 1984; Pres. El Hadj MAODO SYLLA.

CHRISTIANITY

The Roman Catholic Church

Senegal comprises one archdiocese and five dioceses. At 31 December 1995 adherents of the Roman Catholic Church comprised about 4.6% of the total population.

Bishops' Conference: Conférence des Evêques du Sénégal, de la Mauritanie, du Cap-Vert et de Guinée-Bissau, BP 941, Dakar; f. 1973; Pres. Rt Rev. THÉODORE-ADRIEN SARR, Bishop of Kaolack.

Archbishop of Dakar: Cardinal HYACINTHE THIANDOUM, Archevêché, ave Jean XXIII, BP 1908, Dakar; tel. 23-69-18; fax 23-45-63.

The Anglican Communion

The Anglican diocese of The Gambia, part of the Church of the Province of West Africa, includes Senegal and Cape Verde. The Bishop is resident in Banjul, The Gambia.

Protestant Church

Eglise Protestante du Senegal: 65 rue Wagane Diouf, BP 22390, Dakar; tel. 21-55-64; fax 21-71-32; f. 1862; Pastor ETITI YOMO DJERIWO.

BAHÁ'Í FAITH

National Spiritual Assembly: BP 1662, Dakar; tel. 24-23-59; registered 1975; mems resident in 363 localities.

The Press

NEWSPAPERS

Réveil de l'Afrique Noire: Dakar; f. 1986; daily; Dir MAM LESS DIA.

Le Soleil: Société sénégalaise de presse et de publications, route du Service géographique, BP 92, Dakar; tel. 32-46-92; telex 51431; fax 32-03-81; f. 1970; daily; publ. by PS; Man. Dir ALIOUNE DRAME; circ. 45,000.

Sud au Quotidien: Immeuble Fahd, BP 4130, Dakar; tel. 22-53-93; fax 22-52-90; daily; fmrly Sud Hebdo; Editor ABDOULAYE NDIAGA SYLLA; circ. 30,000.

Wal Fadjiri (The Dawn): Dakar; Islamic daily; circ. 15,000.

PERIODICALS

Afrique Economique: Dakar; f. 1975; monthly; Editor ASSANE SECK; circ. 10,000.

Afrique Médicale: 10 rue Abdou Karim Bourgi, BP 1826, Dakar; tel. 23-48-80; telex 1300; fax 22-56-30; f. 1960; monthly; review of tropical medicine; Editor JOËL DECUPPER; circ. 7,000.

Afrique Nouvelle: 9 rue Paul Holle, BP 283, Dakar; tel. 22-51-22; telex 1403; f. 1947; weekly; development issues; Roman Catholic; Dir RENÉ ODOUN; circ. 15,000.

Amina: BP 2120, Dakar; monthly; women's magazine.

Bingo: 17 rue Huart, BP 176, Dakar; f. 1952; monthly; illustrated; Editor E. SOELLE; circ. 110,750.

Le Cafard Libéré: 10 rue Tolbiac, angle autoroute, 3e étage, Dakar; tel. 22-84-43; f. 1987; weekly; satirical; Editor LAYE BAMBA DIALLO; circ. 10,000.

Combat pour le Socialisme: Dakar; f. 1987; politics; circ. 10,000.

Construire l'Afrique: BP 3770, Dakar; tel. 23-07-90; fax 24-19-61; f. 1985; six a year; African business; Dir and Chief Editor CHEIKH-OUSMANE DIALLO.

Le Démocrate: 10 rue de Thiong, Dakar; f. 1974; monthly; publ. by PDS.

Ethiopiques: BP 2035, Dakar; f. 1974; a year; publ. by PDS.

Fippu: Dakar; f. 1987; quarterly; feminist; Dir FATOUMATA SOW.

Journal Officiel de la République du Sénégal: Rufisque; f. 1856; weekly; govt journal.

Momsareew: BP 820, Dakar; f. 1958; monthly; publ. by PAI; Editor-in-Chief MALAMINE BADJI; circ. 2,000.

L'Observateur Africain: Dakar; Dir ALIOUNE DIOP.

Le Politicien: Dakar; f. 1977; fortnightly; satirical; Editor MAM LESS DIA.

Promotion: Ancienne Maison des Artistes Plasticiens, Colobane, BP 1676, Dakar; tel. 21-70-23; f. 1972; weekly; Dir BOUBACAR DIOP; circ. 5,000.

Le Rénovateur: BP 12172, Dakar; monthly; publ. by PDS–R.

Sénégal d'Aujourd'hui: 58 blvd de la République, BP 4027, Dakar; monthly; publ. by Ministry of Culture; circ. 5,000.

Sopi (Change): Dakar; f. 1988; weekly; publ. by PDS; Dir of Publishing JOSEPH NDONG.

L'Unité Africaine: BP 22010, Dakar; f. 1974; monthly; publ. by PS.

Xareli (Struggle): BP 12136, Dakar; tel. 22-54-63; fortnightly; publ. by AJ–PADS; circ. 7,000.

NEWS AGENCIES

Agence de Presse Sénégalaise: 72 blvd de la République, BP 117, Dakar; tel. 21-14-27; telex 51520; f. 1959; govt-controlled; Dir AMADOU DIENG.

Pan-African News Agency (PANA): BP 4650, Dakar; tel. 24-14-10; fax 24-13-90; f. 1979, services began 1983; restructured 1992–93, further restructuring and partial privatization pending; agency of the OAU providing news service to 47 mem. countries; Co-ordinator-Gen. BABACAR FALL.

Foreign Bureaux

Agence France-Presse (AFP): Immeuble Maginot, 7e étage, BP 363, Dakar; tel. 23-21-92; telex 51564; fax 22-16-07; Dir FRANÇOIS-XAVIER HARISPE.

Agenzia Nazionale Stampa Associata (ANSA) (Italy): Dakar; tel. 22-11-97; telex 61338; Correspondent ALIOUNE TOURÉ DIA.

Xinhua (New China) News Agency (People's Republic of China): Villa 1, 2 route de la Pyrotechnie, Stele Mernoz, BP 426, Dakar; tel. 23-05-38; telex 283; Chief Correspondent ZHOU WEIBO.

IPS (Italy), ITAR—TASS (Russia), Reuters (UK) and UPI (USA) are also represented in Dakar.

Publishers

Africa Editions: BP 1826, Dakar; tel. 23-48-80; telex 1300; fax 22-56-30; f. 1958; general, reference; Man. Dir JOËL DECUPPER.

Agence de Distribution de Presse: km 2.5, blvd du Centenaire de la Commune de Dakar, BP 374, Dakar; tel. 32-02-78; fax 32-49-15; f. 1943; general, reference; Man. Dir LAURENT TONNELLE.

Altervision: BP 3770, Dakar; tel. 23-07-90; fax 24-19-61; f. 1985; business; Dir-Gen. CHEIKH-OUSMANE DIALLO.

Editions Juridiques Africaines (EDJA): 18 rue Raffenel, BP 2875, Dakar; tel. 21-66-89; fax 23-60-72; f. 1986; law.

Editions des Trois Fleuves: blvd de l'Est, angle Cheikh Anta Diop, BP 123, Dakar; tel. 25-79-23; fax 25-59-37; f. 1972; general non-fiction; luxury edns; Dir GÉRARD RAZIMOWSKY; Gen. Man. BERTRAND DE BOISTEL.

Enda (Environmental Development Action in the Third World): 4–5 rue Kléber, BP 3370, Dakar; tel. 22-42-29; fax 22-26-95; f. 1972; third-world environment and development; Dir GIDEON PRINSLER OMOLU.

Grande imprimerie africaine: 9 rue Amadou Assane Ndoye, BP 51, Dakar; tel. 22-14-08; fax 22-39-27; f. 1917; law, administration; Man. Dir CHEIKH ALIMA TOURÉ.

Institut fondamental d'Afrique noire (IFAN): BP 206, Dakar; scientific and humanistic studies of black Africa.

Librairie Clairafrique: 2 rue El Hadji Mbaye Guèye, BP 2005, Dakar; tel. 22-21-69; fax 21-84-09; f. 1951; politics, law, sociology, anthropology, literature, economics, development, religion, school books.

Nouvelles éditions africaines du Sénégal (NEAS): 10 rue Amadou Assane Ndoye, BP 260, Dakar; tel. 22-15-80; fax 22-36-04; f. 1972; general; Man. Dir DOUDOU NDIAYE.

Per Ankh: Dakar; co-operative publishing venture.

Société africaine d'édition: 16 bis rue de Thiong, BP 1877, Dakar; tel. 21-79-77; f. 1961; African politics and economics; Man. Dir PIERRE BIARNES.

Société d'édition 'Afrique Nouvelle': 9 rue Paul Holle, BP 283, Dakar; tel. 22-38-25; telex 1403; f. 1947; information, statistics and analyses of African affairs; Man. Dir ATHANASE NDONG.

Société nationale de Presse, d'édition et de publicité (SONAPRESS): Dakar; f. 1972; Pres. OBEYE DIOP.

Sud-Communication: BP 4100, Dakar; operated by a journalists' co-operative; periodicals.

Government Publishing House

Société sénégalaise de presse et de publications (SSPP): route du Service géographique, BP 92, Dakar; tel. 32-46-92; telex 51431; fax 32-03-81; f. 1970; 62% govt-owned; Pres. and Man. Dir ALIOUNE DRAME.

Radio and Television

In 1996, according to official figures, there were an estimated 2.8m. radio receivers and 660,000 television receivers in use.

Société Nationale de Radiodiffusion Télévision Sénégalaise (RTS): BP 1765, Dakar; tel. 21-78-01; telex 21818; fax 22-34-90; f. 1972; fmrly Office de Radiodiffusion-Télévision du Sénégal; state broadcasting co; Man. Dir GUILA THIAM; Dir (Radio) IBRAHIM SANÉ; Dir (Television) BABACAR DIAGNE.

RADIO

RTS radio broadcasts are made in French, Portuguese, Arabic, English and six vernacular languages from Dakar, Saint-Louis, Ziguinchor, Tambacounda and Kaolack.

FM 94: Dakar; 20 hours of local broadcasts daily.

Commercial Station

Sud FM: Immeuble Fahd, 5e étage, BP 4130, Dakar; tel. 22-27-65; fax 22-52-90; f. 1994; operated by Sud-Communication; Man. Dir CHERIF ELVALIDE SEYE.

Broadcasts by the Gabonese-based Africa No. 1 and by Radio France International are received in Dakar.

TELEVISION

There are 10-kW transmitters at Dakar, Thiès, Ziguinchor, Tambacounda and Louga. Following an agreement with France in 1989, Senegal was to receive direct transmissions from that country.

Canal Horizons Sénégal: 31 ave Albert Sarrant, BP 1390, Dakar; tel. 23-50-50; fax 23-30-30; f. 1990; private coded channel; 18.8% owned by RTS and Société Nationale des Télécommunications du Sénégal, 15% by Canal Horizons (France); Man. Dir JACQUES BARBIER DE CROZES.

SUPERVISORY AUTHORITY

Haut Conseil de la Radio Télévision: Dakar; f. 1991; Pres. BABACAR KEBE.

Finance

(cap. = capital; res = reserves; m. = million; brs = branches; amounts in francs CFA)

BANKING

Central Bank

Banque Centrale des Etats de l'Afrique de l'Ouest (BCEAO): ave Abdoulaye Fadiga, BP 3108, Dakar; tel. 23-16-15; telex 21815; fax 23-93-35; National headquarters: blvd du Géneral de Gaulle, angle Triangle Sud, BP 3159, Dakar; tel. 23-53-84; telex 21839; fax 23-57-57; central bank of issue for mems of the Union économique et monétaire ouest africaine (UEMOA); f. 1962; cap. and res 657,592m. (Dec. 1995); Gov. CHARLES KONAN BANNY; Dir in Senegal SEYNI NDIAYE (acting); domestic brs at Kaolack and Ziguinchor.

Commercial Banks

Banque Internationale pour le Commerce et l'Industrie du Sénégal (BICIS): 2 ave Léopold Sédar Senghor, BP 392, Dakar; tel. 39-03-90; telex 21800; fax 23-37-07; f. 1962; 28% owned by Société Financière pour les Pays d'Outre-Mer, 25% state-owned, 22% owned by Banque Nationale de Paris; cap. and res 4,264m. (Dec. 1995); Pres. SERIGNE LAMINE DIOP; Man. Dir AMADOU KANE; 15 brs.

Compagnie Bancaire de l'Afrique Occidentale (CBAO): 2 place de l'Indépendance, BP 129, Dakar; tel. 23-10-00; telex 21663; fax 23-20-05; f. 1980; fmrly BIAO-Sénégal; 65% owned by Société Africane du Fleuve; cap. and res 7,700m. (Dec. 1995); Pres. JEAN-CLAUDE MIMRAN; Dir-Gen. ABDOUL MBAYE; 10 brs.

Crédit Lyonnais Sénégal (CLS): blvd Djily Mbaye, angle rue Huart, BP 56, Dakar; tel. 23-10-08; telex 21622; fax 23-84-30; f. 1989; 95% owned by Crédit Lyonnais (France); cap. and res 5,575m. (Dec. 1995); Pres. BERNARD NORMAND; Dir-Gen. RENÉ BERARDENGO; 1 br.

Crédit National du Sénégal (CNS): 7 ave Léopold Sédar Senghor, BP 319, Dakar; tel. 23-34-86; telex 61283; fax 23-72-92; f. 1990 by merger, commencement of activities pending approval by BCEAO and UEMOA; 87% state-owned; cap. and res 2,021m. (Dec. 1996); Pres. ABDOU NDIAYE.

Société Générale de Banques au Sénégal SA (SGBS): 19 ave Léopold Sédar Senghor, BP 323, Dakar; tel. 23-13-33; telex 21801; fax 23-90-36; f. 1962; 38% owned by Société Générale (France); cap. and res 7,911m. (Dec. 1995); Chair. IDRISSA SEYDI; Man. Dir BERNARD LABADENS; 3 brs.

Development Banks

Banque de l'Habitat du Sénégal (BHS): blvd du Général de Gaulle, BP 229, Dakar; tel. 23-10-04; telex 61275; fax 23-80-43; f. 1979; cap. and res 3,371m. (Dec. 1995); Pres. MAMADOU NDONG; Man. Dir OUSMANE DIÈNE; 1 br.

Banque Sénégalo-Tunisienne (BST): 57 ave Georges Pompidou, BP 4111, Dakar; tel. 23-62-30; telex 61169; fax 23-82-38; f. 1986; cap. 1,100m. (Sept. 1991); Pres. ABOUBAKRY KANE; Dir-Gen. TAOUFIK BAAZIZ.

Caisse Nationale de Crédit Agricole du Sénégal (CNCAS): 45 ave Albert Sarraut, BP 3890, Dakar; tel. 22-23-90; telex 61345; fax 21-26-06; f. 1984; 28% state-owned; cap. and res 2,320m. (Sept. 1992); Man. Dir SAMCIDINE DIENG; 4 brs.

Islamic Banks

Banque Islamique du Senegal (BIS): BP 3381, Dakar; tel. 23-99-20; telex 51255; fax 22-49-48; f. 1996 and restructured Masraf Faisal al-Islami—Senegal; 45% owned by Dar al-Maal al-Islami, 33% by Islamic Development Bank, 22% stated-owned; cap. and res 1,892m. (Dec. 1996); Pres. ABDERRAOUF BENESSAIAH; Man. Dir ABDELLAH NEZZAGHY.

Banque Mouridoulah: Dakar; f. 1996; cap. 3,000m.; Dir SALIDOU FALL.

Banking Association

Association Professionnelle des Banques et des Etablissements Financiers du Sénégal (APBEF): c/o CBAO, 2 place de l'Indépendance, BP 129, Dakar; Pres. ABDOUL MBAYE.

STOCK EXCHANGE

Côte d'Ivoire's Bourse des Valeurs d'Abidjan was scheduled to become a regional stock exchange, serving the member states of the UEMOA.

INSURANCE

Assurances Générales Sénégalaises (AGS): 43 ave Albert Sarraut, BP 225, Dakar; tel. 23-49-94; telex 51647; fax 23-37-01; f. 1977; cap. 2,990m.; Man. Dir A. SOW.

Compagnie d'Assurances-Vie et de Capitalisation (La Nationale d'Assurances-Vie): 7 blvd de la République, BP 3853, Dakar; tel. 22-11-81; telex 51251; fax 21-28-20; f. 1982; cap. 80m.; Pres. MOUSSA DIOUF; Man. Dir BASSIROU DIOP.

Compagnie Sénégalaise d'Assurances et de Réassurances (CSAR): 5 place de l'Indépendance, BP 182, Dakar; tel. 23-27-76; telex 61125; fax 23-46-72; f. 1972; cap. 945m.; 49.8% state-owned; Pres. MOUSTAPHA CISSÉ; Man. Dir MAMADOU ABBAS BA.

SA Capillon V-Assurances: 5 ave Léopold Sédar Senghor, BP 425, Dakar; tel. 22-90-26; telex 684; f. 1951; cap. 10m.; Pres. and Man. Dir GILLES DE MONTALEMBERT.

Nouvelle Société Inter-Africaine de Courtage de Réassurances (Nouvelle SIACRE): 3 ave Albert Sarraut, BP 3135, Dakar; tel. 21-71-38; telex 61244; fax 23-83-91; f. 1977; cap. 50m.; Dir DEMBA SAMBA DIALLO.

La Sécurité Sénégalaise (ASS): Gare Routière, BP 2623, Dakar; tel. 23-75-95; telex 3207; f. 1984; cap. 100m.; Pres. LOBATT FALL; Man. Dir MBACKE SENE.

Société Africaine d'Assurances: ave Léopold Sédar Senghor, angle Victor Hugo, BP 508, Dakar; tel. 23-64-75; fax 23-44-72; f. 1945; cap. 9m.; Dir CLAUDE GERMAIN.

Société Nationale d'Assurances Mutuelles (SONAM): 6 ave Léopold Sédar Senghor, BP 210, Dakar; tel. 23-10-03; telex 51571; fax 20-70-25; f. 1973; cap. 1,464m.; Pres. ABDOULAYE FOFANA; Man. Dir DIOULDÉ NIANE.

Société Sénégalaise de Courtage et d'Assurances (SOSECODA): 16 ave Léopold Sédar Senghor, BP 9, Dakar; tel. 23-54-81; telex 51436; fax 21-54-62; f. 1963; cap. 10m.; 55% owned by SONAM; Man. Dir A. AZIZ NDAW.

Société Sénégalaise de Réassurances SA (SENRE): 6 ave Léopold Sédar Senghor; angle Carnot, BP 386, Dakar; tel. 22-80-89; telex 61144; fax 21-56-52; cap. 600m.

Insurance Association

Syndicat Professionel des Agents Généraux d'Assurances du Sénégal: 43 ave Albert Sarraut, BP 1766, Dakar; Pres. URBAIN ALEXANDRE DIAGNE; Sec. JEAN-PIERRE CAIRO.

Trade and Industry

DEVELOPMENT AND MARKETING ORGANIZATIONS

Caisse Française de Développement (CFD): 15 ave Mandéla, BP 475, Dakar; tel. 23-11-88; telex 51653; fax 23-40-10; f. 1941 as Caisse Centrale de Coopération Economique, name changed 1992; Dir in Senegal ALAIN CÉLESTE.

Mission Française de Coopération: BP 2014, Dakar; telex 3103; administers bilateral aid from France; Dir FRANÇOIS CHAPPELLET.

Société de Développement Agricole et Industriel (SODAGRI): Immeuble Fondation Fahd, 9e étage, blvd Djily Mbaye, angle Macodou Ndiaye, BP 222, Dakar; tel. 21-04-26; fax 22-54-06; cap. 120m. francs CFA; agricultural and industrial projects; Pres. and Man. Dir AMADOU TIDIANE WANE.

Société de Développement des Fibres Textiles (SODEFITEX): km 4.5, blvd du Centenaire de la Commune de Dakar, BP 3216, Dakar; tel. 32-47-80; telex 280; f. 1974; 70% state-owned, 30% owned by Cie Française pour le Développement des Fibres Textiles; responsible for planning and development of cotton industry; cap. 750m. francs CFA; Dir-Gen. FALILOU MBACKE.

Société de Développement et de Vulgarisation Agricole (SODEVA): 92 rue Moussé Diop, BP 3234, Dakar; tel. 23-16-78; telex 51638; fax 21-01-53; f. 1968; cap. 100m. francs CFA; 55% state-owned; development of intensive farming methods and diversified livestock breeding; Dir-Gen. PAPA OUSMANE DIALLO.

Société d'Exploitation des Ressources Animales du Sénégal (SERAS): km 2.5, blvd du Centenaire de la Commune de Dakar, BP 14, Dakar; tel. 32-31-78; telex 51256; fax 32-06-90; f. 1962; cap. 619.2m. francs CFA; 28.5% state-owned; livestock development; Dir Dr MAMADOU FAYE; Man. Dir MACODOU SEYE.

Société Nationale d'Aménagement et d'Exploitation des Terres du Delta du Fleuve Sénégal et des Vallées du Fleuve Sénégal et de la Falémé (SAED): route de Khor, BP 74, Saint-Louis; tel. 61-15-33; telex 75124; fax 61-14-63; f. 1965; cap. 2,500m. francs CFA; state-owned; controls the agricultural development of 30,000 ha around the Senegal river delta; Pres. and Man. Dir SIDY MOCTAR KEITA.

Société Nationale de Commercialisation des Oléagineux du Sénégal (SONACOS): Immeuble SONACOS, 32–36 rue du Dr Calmette, BP 639, Dakar; tel. 23-10-52; telex 51418; fax 23-88-05; f. 1975; cap. 4,800m. francs CFA; 80% state-owned; transfer to majority private ownership pending; processing of groundnuts and groundnut products; Pres. and Man. Dir ABDOULAYE DIOP.

Société Nationale d'Etudes et de Promotion Industrielle (SONEPI): derrière Résidence Seydou Nourou Tall, ave Bourguiba Prolongée, BP 100, Dakar; tel. 25-21-30; telex 61178; fax 24-65-65; f. 1969; cap. 150m. francs CFA; 28% state-owned; promotion of small and medium-sized enterprises; Chair. and Man. Dir HADY MAMADOU LY.

Société Nationale des Pétroles du Sénégal (PETROSEN): 2 rue Malan, blvd Pinet Laprade, Dakar; f. 1981; 90% state-owned; exploration and exploitation of hydrocarbons; Man. Dir. OUSMANE NDIAYE.

Société Nouvelle des Etudes de Développement en Afrique (SONED–AFRIQUE): Immeuble SONACOS, 32–36 rue Calmette, BP 2084, Dakar; tel. 23-94-57; telex 51464; fax 23-42-31; f. 1974; cap. 98m. francs CFA; 61% state-owned; Pres. El Hadj IBRAHIMA NDAO; Man. Dir RUDOLPH KERN.

CHAMBERS OF COMMERCE

Chambre de Commerce, d'Industrie et d'Agriculture de la Région de Dakar: 1 place de l'Indépendance, BP 118, Dakar; tel. 23-71-89; telex 61112; fax 23-93-63; f. 1888; Pres. MAMADOU LAMINE NIANG; Sec.-Gen. MBAYE NDIAYE.

Chambre de Commerce, d'Industrie et d'Artisanat de la Région de Diourbel: BP 7, Diourbel; tel. 71-12-03; f. 1969; Pres. El Hadj OUMAR FALL; Sec.-Gen. MAMADOU NDIAYE.

Chambre de Commerce de la Région de Fatick: BP 66, Fatick; tel. 49-51-27; Sec.-Gen. SEYDOU NOUROU LY.

Chambre de Commerce et d'Industrie de la Région du Kaolack: BP 203, Kaolack; tel. 41-20-52; telex 7474; Pres. IDRISSA GUÈYE; Sec.-Gen. AROHA TRAORÉ.

Chambre de Commerce d'Industrie et d'Agriculture de la Région de Kolda: BP 23; Kolda; tel. 96-12-30; fax 96-10-68; Sec.-Gen. YAYA CAMARA.

Chambre de Commerce de la Région de Louga: BP 26, Louga; tel. 67-11-14; Pres. El Hadj AMADOU BAMBA SOURANG; Sec.-Gen. SOULEYMANE N'DIAYE.

Chambre de Commerce, d'Industrie et d'Agriculture de la Région de Saint-Louis: rue Bisson Nord, BP 19, Saint-Louis; tel. 61-10-88; f. 1879; Pres. El Hadj MOMAR SOURANG; Sec.-Gen. MASSAMBA DIOP.

Chambre de Commerce, d'Industrie et d'Agriculture de la Région de Tambacounda: BP 127, Tambacounda; tel. 81-10-14; Pres. DJIBY CISSÉ; Sec.-Gen. TENGUELLA BA.

Chambre de Commerce, d'Industrie et d'Agriculture de la Région de Thiès: ave Lamine-Guèye, BP 3020, Thiès; tel. 51-10-02; f. 1883; 38 mems; Pres. El Hadj ALIOUNE PALLA M'BAYE; Sec.-Gen. ABDOUL KHADRE CAMARA.

Chambre de Commerce, d'Industrie et d'Artisanat de la Région de Ziguinchor: BP 26, Ziguinchor; tel. 91-13-10; f. 1908; Pres. YOUSSOUF SEYDI; Sec.-Gen. MAMADI DIATTA.

PRINCIPAL EMPLOYERS' ASSOCIATIONS

Confédération Sénégalaise du Patronat (CSP): Dakar; Pres. MANSOUR CAMA.

Groupement Professionnel de l'Industrie du Pétrole du Sénégal (GPP): rue 6, km 4.5, blvd du Centenaire de la Commune de Dakar, BP 479, Dakar; tel. 32-10-80; telex 21838; fax 32-90-65; Pres. DENIS LENORMAND; Sec.-Gen. JEAN-PIERRE NOËL.

Syndicat des Commerçants Importateurs, Prestataires de Services et Exportateurs de la République du Sénégal (SCIMPEX): 2 rue Parent, angle ave Abdoulaye Fadiga, BP 806, Dakar; tel. and fax 21-36-62; f. 1943; Pres. JACQUES CONTI; Sec.-Gen. MAURICE SARR.

Syndicat Patronal de l'Ouest Africain des Petites et Moyennes Entreprises et des Petites et Moyennes Industries: 41 blvd Djily Mbaye, BP 7015, Dakar; tel. 21-35-10; fax 22-28-42; f. 1937; Pres. BABACAR SEYE; Sec.-Gen. MOCTAR NIANG.

Syndicat Professionnel des Entrepreneurs de Bâtiments et de Travaux Publics du Sénégal: ave Abdoulaye Fadiga, BP 593, Dakar; tel. 23-43-73; telex 3167; f. 1930; 130 mems; Pres. CHRISTIAN VIRMAUD.

Syndicat Professionnel des Industries du Sénégal (SPIDS): ave Abdoulaye Fadiga, angle Thann, BP 593, Dakar; tel. 23-43-73; fax 22-08-84; f. 1944; 110 mems; Pres. DONALD BARON; Sec. Gen. PHILIPPE BARRY.

MAJOR INDUSTRIAL COMPANIES

The following are some of the largest companies in terms of either capital investment or employment.

BP Sénégal SA: rue 6, km 4.5, blvd du Centenaire de la Commune de Dakar, BP 59, Dakar; tel. 23-10-80; telex 21838; fax 32-90-65; f. 1951; cap. 3,000m. francs CFA; 99.99% owned by BP Africa Ltd (UK); import, storage and distribution of petroleum products, mfrs of lubricating oil; Man. Dir FERDINAND DA COSTA.

CarnaudMetalbox Sénégal: route du Service géographique, Hann Village, BP 3850, Dakar; tel. 32-05-59; telex 51292; fax 32-37-25; f. 1959; cap. 900m. francs CFA; 72% owned by CarnaudMetalbox (France); mfrs of metal packaging; Chair. BRIAN APPLEYARD; Man. Dir MAURICE PRANGÈRE.

Compagnie Commerciale Industrielle du Sénégal (CCIS): route du Front de Terre, angle Service géographique, BP 137, Dakar; tel. 32-33-44; telex 21415; fax 32-68-22; f. 1972; cap. 1,969.6m. francs CFA; mfrs of PVC piping and plastic for shoes; Man. Dir NAYEF DERWICHE.

Compagnie Sucrière Sénégalaise (CSS): BP 49, Richard Toll; tel. 63-33-20; telex 75130; fax 63-31-47; f. 1970; cap. 13,586m. francs CFA; growing of sugar cane and refining of cane sugar; Chair. and Man. Dir ROBERT MIMRAN.

Les Grands Moulins de Dakar (GMD): ave Félix Eboué, BP 2068, Dakar; tel. 32-19-35; fax 32-89-47; f. 1946; cap. 1,180m. francs CFA; production of flour and animal food; Chair. ROBERT MIMRAN; Dir JEAN-CLAUDE BEGUINOT; 280 employees.

Industrial Drip Irrigation System (Senegal) (IDIS): BP 2031, Dakar; tel. 32-28-86; telex 75130; fax 32-91-92; f. 1976; cap. 405m. francs CFA; subsidiary of CSS; mfrs of plastic pipes; Chair. JEAN-CLAUDE MIMRAN.

Industries Chimiques du Sénégal (ICS): km 18, blvd du Centenaire de la Commune de Dakar, BP 3835, Dakar; tel. 34-01-22; telex 31434; fax 34-08-14; f. 1976; restructured by merger with Cie Sénégalaise des Phospates de Taïba in 1996; cap. 55,300m. francs CFA; 52% state-owned; mining of high-grade calcium phosphates, production of sulphuric and phosphoric acid, fertilizer factory at M'Bao; Chair. and Man. Dir PIERRE BABAKAR KAMA; 570 employees.

Lesieur Afrique (Dakar): place Amílcar Cabral, BP 236, Dakar; tel. 23-10-66; telex 538; f. 1942; cap. 1,796m. francs CFA; groundnut-shelling plant (capacity 350,000 metric tons per year) and vegetable oil refining plant (capacity 30,000 tons) at Dakar; Man. Dir MAMBAYE DIAW.

Manufacture de Tabacs de l'Ouest Africain (MTOA): km 2.5, blvd du Centenaire de la Commune de Dakar, BP 76, Dakar; tel. 23-68-80; telex 21807; fax 23-89-19; f. 1951; cap. 3,129.6m. francs CFA; mfrs of tobacco products; Chair. PIERRE IMBERT; Man. Dir BRUNO GUÉRIN; 330 employees.

Les Moulins Sentenac SA (MS): 50 ave du Président Lamine Guèye, BP 451, Dakar; tel. 23-94-04; telex 51545; fax 23-80-69; f. 1943; cap. 1,056m. francs CFA; milling, production of flour and other food products and of livestock feed; Chair. and Man. Dir DONALD BARON.

Nestlé Senegal: km 14, blvd du Centenaire de la Commune de Dakar, BP 796, Dakar; tel. 34-05-75; telex 31441; fax 34-17-02; f. 1961; cap. 1,620m. francs CFA; mfrs of sweetened and unsweetened condensed milk and culinary products; Man. Dir JEAN-MARIE MAUDUIT.

La Rochette Dakar (LRD): km 13.7, blvd du Centenaire de la Commune de Dakar, BP 891, Dakar; tel. 34-01-24; telex 31420; fax 34-28-26; f. 1946; cap. 500m. francs CFA; mfrs of paper and cardboard packaging; Chair. and Man. Dir ADEL SALHAB.

Sénégal–Pêche, SA: Môle 10, Nouveau Quai de Pêche, BP 317, Dakar; owned by China Nat. Fisheries Corpn.

Société Africaine de Raffinage (SAR): 15 blvd de la République, BP 203, Dakar; tel. 23-46-84; telex 527; f. 1961; cap. 1,000m. francs CFA; petroleum refinery at M'Bao.

Société des Brasseries de l'Ouest Africain (SOBOA): route des Brasseries, BP 290, Dakar; tel. 32-01-90; telex 51286; fax 32-54-69; f. 1928; cap. 820m. francs CFA; mfrs of beer and soft drinks; Man. Dir PIERRE TRAVERSA.

Société de Conserves Alimentaires du Sénégal (SOCAS): 50 ave du Président Lamine Guèye, BP 451, Dakar; tel. 23-94-04; telex 51545; fax 23-80-69; f. 1963; cap. 726m. francs CFA; cultivation of tomatoes and other food crops, mfrs of tomato concentrate and other preserves at Savoigne; Chair. and Man. Dir DONALD BARON.

Société Industrielle Moderne des Plastiques Africains (SIMPA): 50 ave du Président Lamine Guèye, BP 451, Dakar; tel. 23-43-25; telex 51545; fax 21-80-69; f. 1958; cap. 551m. francs CFA; mfrs of injection-moulded and extruded plastic articles; Chair. and Man. Dir RAYMOND GAVEAU.

Société Industrielle de Papeterie au Sénégal (SIPS): km 11, route de Rufisque, BP 1818, Dakar; tel. 34-09-29; telex 31438; fax 34-23-03; f. 1972; cap. 750m. francs CFA; mfrs of paper goods; Chair. OMAR ABDEL KANDER GHANDOUR; Man. Dir ALI SALIM HOBALLAH.

Société Minière de Sabodala (SMS): 7 rue Jean Mermoz, Dakar; tel. 22-37-36; telex 51274; f. 1982; cap. 2,100m. francs CFA; 41% state-owned; exploration and exploitation of gold mines in Sabodala region; Chair. BARDY DIENE; Man. Dir MOHAMED HANN.

Société Nationale d'Electricité (SENELEC): 28–30 rue Vincens, BP 93, Dakar; tel. 23-72-82; telex 21845; fax 23-82-46; f. 1983; cap. 63,000m. francs CFA; state electricity utility; transfer to 49% private ownership pending; Chair. AZIZ NDAO; Man. Dir ABDOURAHMANE NDIR.

Société Nouvelle des Salins du Sine Saloum (SNSSS): BP 200, Kaolack; tel. 41-10-13; telex 7477; f. 1965; cap. 723m. francs CFA; 49% state-owned; production and marketing of sea-salt; Chair. AMADOU LY; Man. Dir HENRI DUNESME.

Société de Produits Industrielles et Agricoles (SPIA): 56 ave Faidherbe, BP 3806, Dakar; tel. 21-43-78; telex 21433; fax 21-66-37; f. 1980; cap. 640m. francs CFA; mfrs of plant-based medicines at Louga; Chair. DJILLY MBAYE; Man. Dir Cheikh DEMBA NAMARA.

Société Sénégalaise d'Engrais et de Produits Chimiques (SSEPC): km 13, blvd du Centenaire de la Commune de Dakar, BP 656, Dakar; tel. 34-02-79; telex 582; f. 1958; cap. 727m. francs CFA; mfrs of fertilizers, insecticides and livestock feed; Chair. BERNARD PORTAL; Man. Dir PAUL SASPORTES.

Société Sénégalaise des Phosphates de Thiès (SSPT): 39 ave Jean XXIII, BP 241, Dakar; tel. 23-32-83; telex 21683; fax 23-83-84; f. 1948; cap. 1,000m. francs CFA; 50% state-owned, 50% owned by Rhône-Poulenc (France); sale of part of state-owned interest pending; production of phosphates and attapulgite, mfrs of phosphate fertilizers; Chair. MAHENTA BIRIMA FALL; Man. Dir DANIEL DUCRET.

Société de Teinture, Blanchiment, Apprêts et d'Impressions Africaines (SOTIBA-SIMPAFRIC): km 9.5, blvd du Centenaire de la Commune de Dakar, BP 527, Dakar; tel. 34-03-78; telex 31421; fax 34-52-68; f. 1951; cap. 2,600m. francs CFA; owned jtly by UB International (India) and CBAO; bleaching, dyeing and printing of textiles; Chair. and Man. Dir SERIGNÉ NDIAYE BOUNA; 1,100 employees.

Société Textile de Kaolack (SOTEXKA): 57 ave Georges Pompidou, BP 4101, Dakar; tel. 21-89-99; telex 21616; fax 21-23-01; f. 1977; cap 8,628m. francs CFA; 63% state-owned; transfer to private ownership pending; textile and garment-assembling complex; Man. Dir ABDOURAHMANE TOURÉ.

TRADE UNIONS

Collectif National des Pêcheurs Sénégalais (CNPS): Dakar; Sec.-Gen. DAO GAYE; 35,000 mems.

Confédération Nationale des Travailleurs Sénégalais (CNTS): 15 rue Escarfait, BP 937, Dakar; f. 1969; affiliated to PS; Sec.-Gen. MADIA DIOP; 120,000 mems.

Confédération des Syndicats Autonomes (CSA): Dakar.

Union Démocratique des Travailleurs du Sénégal (UDTS): Dakar.

Union Nationale des Commerçants et Industriels du Sénégal (UNACOIS): Dakar.

Union Nationale des Syndicats Autonomes du Sénégal (UNSAS): Dakar; Sec.-Gen. MADEMBA SOCK.

TRADE FAIR

Foire Internationale de Dakar: Centre International du Commerce Extérieur du Senegal, route de l'Aéroport, BP 8166, Dakar-Yoff, Dakar; tel. 20-13-75; fax 20-46-05; f. 1986; Man. Dir AMINATA MBAYE.

Transport

RAILWAYS

There are 1,225 km of main line including 70 km of double track. One line runs from Dakar north to Saint-Louis (262 km), and the main line runs to Bamako (Mali). All the locomotives are diesel-driven. The rehabilitation and expansion of the railway network (which was in a poor state of repair in the mid-1990s) is proceeding, and responsibility for the operation of rolling-stock was transferred to a Canadian company, under a two-year contract, from late 1994. In late 1995 the Governments of Senegal and Mali agreed to establish, with a view to privatization, a joint company to operate the Dakar–Bamako line.

Société Nationale des Chemins de Fer du Sénégal (SNCFS): BP 175, Cité Ballabey, Thiès; tel. 51-10-13; telex 77129; fax 51-13-93; state-owned; Pres. ALIEU DIENE DRAME; Man. Dir MBAYE DIOUF.

ROADS

In 1995 there were an estimated 14,580 km of roads, of which 4,150 km were main roads and 1,330 km were secondary roads. About 4,200 km of the network were paved. A 162.5-km road between Dialakoto and Kédougou, the construction of which (at a cost of some 23,000m. francs CFA) was largely financed by regional donor organizations, was inaugurated in March 1996. The road is to form part of an eventual transcontinental highway linking Cairo (Egypt) with the Atlantic coast, via N'Djamena (Chad), Bamako (Mali) and Dakar.

INLAND WATERWAYS

Senegal has three navigable rivers: the Senegal, navigable for three months of the year as far as Kayes (Mali), for six months as far as Kaédi (Mauritania) and all year as far as Rosso and Podor, and the Saloun and Casamance. Senegal is a member of the Organisation de mise en valeur du fleuve Gambie and of the Organisation pour la mise en valeur du fleuve Sénégal, both based in Dakar. These organizations aim to develop navigational facilities, irrigation and hydroelectric power in the basins of the Gambia and Senegal Rivers respectively.

SHIPPING

The port of Dakar is the second largest in west Africa, after Abidjan (Côte d'Ivoire), and the largest deep sea port in the region, serving Senegal, Mauritania, The Gambia and Mali. It handled more than 6m. metric tons of international freight in 1996. The port's facilities include 10 km of quays, and also 45,900 sq m of warehousing and 65,000 sq m of open stocking areas.

Société nationale de Port Autonome de Dakar (PAD): 21 blvd de la Libération, BP 3195, Dakar; tel. 23-45-45; telex 21404; fax 23-36-06; f. 1865; state-operated port authority; Pres. El Hadj MALICK SY; Man. Dir PATHÉ NDIAYE.

Compagnie Sénégalaise de Navigation Maritime (COSENAM): rue le Dantec, angle Huart, BP 683, Dakar; tel. 21-57-66; telex 61301; fax 21-08-95; f. 1979; 26.1% state-owned, 65.9% owned by private Senegalese interests, 8.0% by private French, German and Belgian interests; river and ocean freight transport; Pres. ABDOURAHIM AGNE; Man. Dir SIMON BOISSY.

SDV: 8–10 allée Robert Delmas, BP 164, Dakar; tel. 23-56-82; telex 21652; fax 21-45-47; f. 1936; fmrly Union Sénégalaise d'Industries Maritimes; shipping agents, warehousing; Pres. GASTON GUILLABERT.

Société pour le Développement de l'Infrastructure de Chantiers Maritimes du Port de Dakar (DAKAR-MARINE): blvd de l'Arsenal, BP 438, Dakar; tel. 23-36-88; telex 61104; fax 23-83-99; f. 1981; privately-controlled; operates facilities for the repair and maintenance of supertankers and other large vessels; Man. YORO KANTE.

SOCOPAO-Sénégal: 47 ave Albert Sarraut, BP 233, Dakar; tel. 23-10-01; telex 21496; fax 23-56-14; f. 1926; warehousing, shipping agents, sea and air freight transport; Man. Dir GILLES CUCHE.

CIVIL AVIATION

The international airport is Dakar-Yoff. There are other major airports at Saint-Louis, Ziguinchor and Tambacounda, in addition to about 15 smaller airfields. Facilities at Ziguinchor and Cap-Skirring were being upgraded during the mid-1990s, with the aim of improving direct access to the Casamance region, while construction is planned of a second international airport for the capital, at Keur Massar.

African West Air: 19 bis rue Robert Brun, Dakar; tel. 22-45-38; fax 22-46-10; f. 1993; services to western Europe and Brazil; Man. Dir J. P. PIEDADE.

Air Afrique: place de l'Indépendance; BP 3132, Dakar; tel. 39-42-00; fax 23-89-37; see under Côte d'Ivoire; Dir at Dakar MAHAMAT BABA ABATCHA.

Air Sénégal—Société Nationale des Transports Aériens du Sénégal: BP 8010, Dakar-Yoff, Dakar; tel. 20-09-13; telex 31513; fax 20-00-33; f. 1971; transfer to majority private ownership pending; domestic and international services; Gen. Man. IBRAHIMA FAYE.

Tourism

Senegal's attractions for tourists include six national parks (one of which, Djoudj, is listed by UNESCO as a World Heritage Site) and its fine beaches. The island of Gorée, near Dakar, is of considerable historic interest as a former centre for the slave-trade. Some 245,581 tourists (of whom 52.4% were from France) visited Senegal in 1992. In that year receipts from tourism totalled about 39,200m. francs CFA. However, the number of foreign tourist arrivals declined to 167,770 in 1993, while income from tourism was expected to have fallen to an estimated 27,000m. francs CFA, owing largely to the suspension of tourist activity in the Casamance region in that year. A strong recovery in the sector in 1994–95 was attributed principally to the devaluation, in January 1994, of the national currency. Visitor arrivals in 1995 totalled 387,708; receipts from tourism in that year were 55,000m. francs CFA.

Ministry of Tourism and Air Transport: 23 rue Calmette, BP 4049, Dakar; tel. 23-65-02; fax 22-94-13.

Defence

In August 1996 Senegal's active armed forces comprised a land army of 12,000 (mostly conscripts), a navy of 700, and an air force of 650. There is also a 4,000-strong paramilitary gendarmerie. Military service is by selective conscription and lasts for two years. France and the USA provide technical and material aid, and in August 1996 there were 1,500 French troops stationed in Senegal.

Defence Expenditure: Budgeted at 38,000m. francs CFA in 1996.

Chief of General Staff of the Armed Forces: Maj.-Gen. LAMINE CISSÉ.

Education

Primary education, which is officially compulsory, usually begins at seven years of age and lasts for six years. In 1993 primary enrolment was equivalent to 60% of children in the relevant age-group (males 68%; females 51%); it is aimed to increase the level of enrolment at primary schools to 65% by 1998. Secondary education usually begins at the age of 13, and comprises a first cycle of four years and a further cycle of three years. In 1992 secondary enrolment was equivalent to only 16% of children in the relevant age-group (males 21%; females 11%). In accordance with the policy of 'negritude', the Université Cheikh Anta Diop, at Dakar, specializes in local studies. The Université Gaston-Berger, at Saint-Louis, was established in 1990. Construction of a pan-African university began at Sebikotane, near Dakar, in 1996. Since 1981 the reading and writing of national languages has been actively promoted. The 1988 census recorded a rate of adult illiteracy of 73.1% (males 63.1%; females 82.1%), while UNESCO estimated an adult illiteracy rate of 66.9% in 1995 (males 57.0%; females 76.8%). Current expenditure on education in 1993 was 67,008m. francs CFA (representing 32.6% of total current government expenditure).

Bibliography

Adam, A. *Le long voyage des gens du fleuve.* Paris, Maspero, 1978.

Barry, B. *Le royaume du Waalo: le Sénégal avant la conquête.* Paris, Karthala, 1985.

Clark, A. F., and Phillips, L. C. *Historical Dictionary of Senegal.* 2nd Edn. Metuchen, NJ, Scarecrow Press, 1994.

Coulon, C. *Le Marabout et Le Prince: Islam et Pouvoir en Sénégal.* Paris, Editions A. Pedone, 1981.

Crowder, M. *Senegal: A Study in French Assimilation Policy.* London, 1967.

Cruise O'Brien, D. B., Dunn, J., and Rathbone, R. (Eds.). *Contemporary West African States.* Cambridge, Cambridge University Press, 1989.

Cruise O'Brien, D. B. 'Sénégal: la démocratie a l'épreuve', in *Politique Africaine,* No. 45. Paris, 1992.

Cruise O'Brien, R. (Ed.). *The Political Economy of Underdevelopment: Dependence in Senegal.* London, Sage Publications, 1979.

Deschamps, H. *Le Sénégal et la Gambie.* Paris, Presses universitaires de France, 1964.

Dia, M. *Mémoires d'un militant du tiers-monde.* Paris, Publisud, 1986.

Diagne, A. *Abdou Diouf, le maître du jeu.* Dakar, Agence Less Com, 1996.

Diarassouba, V. C. *L'Evolution des structures agricoles du Sénégal.* Paris, Editions Cujas, 1968.

Diop, A.-B. *La société Wolof.* Paris, Editions Karthala, 1983 (reissue).

Diop, M. *Histoire des classes sociales dans l'Afrique de l'ouest: Vol. 2: Le Sénégal.* Paris, Editions Maspero, 1972.

Diop, M. C. (Ed.). *Senegal: Essays in Statecraft.* Dakar, CODESA, 1993.

Diouf, M. *Sénégal, les ethnies et la nation.* Paris, UN Research Institute for Social Development, Forum du Tiers-Monde and l'Harmattan, 1994.

Dumont, P. *Le français et les langues africaines du Sénégal.* Paris, Editions Karthala, 1983.

Duruflé, G. *L'ajustement structurel en Afrique (Sénégal, Côte d'Ivoire, Madagascar).* Paris, Editions Karthala, 1987.

Fatton, R. Jr. *The Making of a Liberal Democracy. Senegal's Passive Revolution, 1975–1985.* Boulder, CO, Westview Press, and London, Lynne Rienner Publishers, 1987.

Gagnon, G. *Coopératives ou autogestion: Sénégal, Cuba, Tunisie.* Paris, Presses de l'Université de Montréal, 1976.

Gellar, S. *Senegal: An African Nation between Islam and the West.* London, Gower, 1983.

Gersovitz, M., and Waterbury, J. (Eds). *The Political Economy of Risk and Choice in Senegal.* London, Frank Cass, 1987.

Harrison Church, R. J. *West Africa.* 8th Edn, London, Longman, 1979.

Hayward, M. F. *Elections in Independent Africa.* Boulder, CO, Westview Press, 1987.

Hesseling, G. *Histoire politique du Sénégal.* Paris, Editions Karthala, 1983.

Hymans, J. L. *Léopold Sédar Senghor.* Edinburgh University Press, 1972.

Johnson, G. W. *Naissance du Sénégal contemporain.* Paris, Editions Karthala, 1991.

Ka, S. 'Uneasy Passage: Senegal in 1993', in *CSIS Africa Notes,* No. 149. Washington, DC, Center for Strategic and International Studies, 1993.

Makédonsky, E. *Le Sénégal, La Sénégambie.* Paris, L'Harmattan, 1987.

Milcent, E., and Sordet, M. *Léopold Sédar Senghor et la naissance de l'Afrique moderne.* Paris, Editions Seghers, 1969.

Peterec, R. J. *Dakar and West African Political Development.* New York, Columbia University Press, 1967.

Pfefferman, G. *Industrial Labor in the Republic of Senegal.* New York, Praeger, 1968.

Rémy, M. *Le Sénégal aujourd'hui.* Jeune Afrique, 1974.

Rimmer, D. *The Economies of West Africa.* London, Weidenfeld and Nicolson, 1984.

Rocheteau, G. *Pouvoir financier et indépendance économique en Afrique noire. Le cas du Sénégal.* Paris, Editions Karthala, 1983.

Saint-Martin, Y.-J. *Le Sénégal sous le second empire.* Paris, Editions Karthala, 1989.

Sene, M., and Ricou, M.-J. *Le Sénégal.* Centre d'Information du Sénégal, 1974.

Senghor, L. S. *Liberté I, Négritude et Humanisme; Liberté II, Nation et voie africaine du socialisme.* Editions du Seuil, 1964 and 1971.

Wade, A. *Un destin pour l'Afrique.* Paris, Editions Karthala, 1992.

Zarour, C. *La Coopération arabo-sénégalaise.* Paris, L'Harmattan, 1989.

SEYCHELLES

Physical and Social Geography

The Republic of Seychelles comprises a scattered archipelago of granitic and coralline islands ranging over some 1m. sq km of the western Indian Ocean. The exact number of islands is unknown, but has been estimated at 115, of which 41 are granitic and the remainder coralline. The group also includes numerous rocks and small cays. At independence in June 1976, the Aldabra Islands, the Farquhar group and Desroches (combined area 28.5 sq km, or 11 sq miles), part of the British Indian Ocean Territory since 1965 (see p. 710), were reunited with the Seychelles, thus restoring the land area to 308 sq km (119 sq miles). Including the Aldabra lagoon, the country's area is 454 sq km (175.3 sq miles).

The islands take their name from the Vicomte Moreau de Séchelles, controller-general of finance in the reign of Louis XV of France. The largest of the group is Mahé, which has an area of about 148 sq km (57 sq miles) and is approximately 27 km long from north to south. Mahé lies 1,800 km due east of Mombasa, 3,300 km south-west of Bombay, and 1,100 km north of Madagascar. Victoria, the capital of Seychelles and the only port of the archipelago, is on Mahé. It is the only town in Seychelles of any size and had a population of 24,324 (including suburbs) at the census of August 1987. The islanders have a variety of ethnic origins—African, European, Indian and Chinese. In 1981 Creole, the language spoken by virtually all Seychellois, replaced English and French as the official language. The total population of Seychelles was enumerated at 68,598 at the August 1987 census, and at 75,304 at the census of 1996, giving a density of 166 persons per sq km.

The granitic islands, which are all of great scenic beauty, rise fairly steeply from the sea and Mahé has a long central ridge which at its highest point, Morne Seychellois, reaches 912 m. Praslin, the second largest island in the group, is 43 km from Mahé and the other granitic islands are within a radius of 56 km. The coral islands are reefs in different stages of formation, rising only marginally above sea-level.

For islands so close to the Equator, the climate is surprisingly equable. Maximum shade temperature at sea-level averages 29°C, but during the coolest months the temperature may drop to 24°C. At higher levels temperatures are rather lower. There are two seasons, hot from December to May, and cooler from June to November while the south-east trade winds are blowing. Rainfall varies over the group; the greater part falls in the hot months during the north-west trade winds and the climate then tends to be humid and somewhat enervating. The mean annual rainfall in Victoria is 2,360 mm and the mean average temperature nearly 27°C. All the granitic islands lie outside the cyclone belt.

Recent History

Revised for this edition by the Editor

The archipelago now forming the Republic of Seychelles was discovered by the French in 1741, but remained uninhabited until 1770, when French settlers arrived to exploit the islands' abundant resources of tortoises and timber. Following its capture in 1811 by British naval forces, Seychelles was formally ceded by France to Britain in 1814. The islands were administered as a dependency of Mauritius until 1903, when Seychelles became a crown colony.

During the 1960s political activity was focused on the socialist-orientated Seychelles People's United Party (SPUP), led by Albert René, and the centre-right Seychelles Democratic Party (SDP), led by James (later Sir James) Mancham, who became the islands' chief minister in 1970. The SPUP demanded full independence for the islands, while the SDP favoured a form of economic integration with the United Kingdom. This option was not acceptable to the British government, and in 1974 the SDP adopted a pro-independence policy. The two parties formed a coalition government in 1975, and the independent Republic of Seychelles, with Mancham as president and René as prime minister, was proclaimed on 29 June 1976.

The coalition was abruptly terminated in June 1977, when supporters of the SPUP staged an armed coup while Mancham was absent in Britain, and installed René as president. René claimed that Mancham had intended to postpone the 1979 elections (a charge that Mancham denied), but there is little doubt that the ex-president's extravagant lifestyle and capitalist philosophy had displeased many of the islanders. The SDP had intended to develop Seychelles as a financial and trading centre and placed great emphasis on the tourist industry. The SPUP considered the development of agriculture and fishing to be as important as tourism to the economy, and planned to ensure a more equitable distribution of wealth.

ONE-PARTY GOVERNMENT

A new constitution was promulgated in 1979. The SPUP, now redesignated the Seychelles People's Progressive Front (SPPF), was declared the sole legal party, and legislative and presidential elections were held to legitimize the new political order. The government's socialist programme, however, led to discontent, particularly among the islands' small middle class. Two plots to overthrow René were uncovered in 1978, and a third, and more serious coup attempt, involving South African mercenaries, was thwarted in 1981. In 1982 the government put down both an army mutiny and a further coup plot. In 1983, another attempt to depose René was quelled. This sustained anti-government activism was ascribed by the government to pro-Mancham exile groups, although Mancham denied any involvement in the conspiracies. Dissent within the SPUP itself was evident, however, in the enforced resignations of two cabinet ministers; Dr Maxime Ferrari, the minister of planning and external relations, left the islands in 1984, and two years later the minister of youth and defence, Col Ogilvy Berlouis, was removed from office after the discovery of another alleged conspiracy against the government.

During the mid-1980s there was a series of violent attacks upon, and disappearances of, exiled opponents of the SPPF. Notable among these was the murder in London in 1985 of Gérard Hoarau, a former government official and leader of the Mouvement pour la Résistance. In 1987 an elaborate plan to overthrow the Seychelles government was discovered by police in the UK, with details of a consipiracy to abduct leading members of the African National Congress of South Africa (ANC), who were based in London.

Until the early 1990s, exiled opposition to René remained split among a number of small groups based principally in

London. In July 1991 five of these parties, including the Rassemblement du Peuple Seychellois pour la Démocratie (subsequently renamed the Seychelles Christian Democrat Party–SCDP), founded by Dr Maxime Ferrari, established a coalition, the United Democratic Movement (UDM), under Ferrari's leadership, while ex-president Mancham rallied his supporters in a 'Crusade for Democracy'.

During 1991 the René government came under increasing pressure from France and the United Kingdom, the islands' principal aid-donors, to return Seychelles to a democratic political system. Internally, open opposition to the SPPF was voiced by the newly-formed Parti Seychellois (PS), led by a Protestant clergyman, Wavel Ramkalawan. In August Maxime Ferrari returned from exile to organize support for the UDM, and in November René invited all political dissidents to return to the islands. In December the minister of tourism and transport, Jacques Hodoul, left the government and subsequently formed the Seychelles Movement for Democracy.

RETURN TO MULTI-PARTY POLITICS

In December 1991 the SPPF convened an extraordinary congress, at which it was agreed that, from January 1992, political groups numbering at least 100 members would be granted official registration, and that multi-party elections would take place in July for a constituent assembly, whose proposals for constitutional reform would be submitted to a national referendum, with a view to holding multi-party parliamentary elections in December 1992. In April Mancham returned from exile to lead the New Democratic Party (NDP), and was officially received by President René.

Elections for a 20-seat commission to draft a new constitution took place in July 1992. The SPPF won 58.4% of the votes, while the NDP received 33.7%. The PS, which took 4.4% of the votes, was the only other political party to obtain representation on the commission. The commission, which comprised 11 representatives from the SPPF, eight from the NDP (now renamed the Democratic Party–DP) and one from the PS, completed its deliberations in October. In September, however, the DP withdrew its delegation, on the grounds that the SPPF had allegedly refused to permit a full debate of reform proposals. It also expressed objections that the commission's meetings had been closed to the public and news media. Following publication of the draft constitution, the DP focused its opposition on proposed voting arrangements for a new national assembly, whose members were to be elected on a basis of one-half by direct vote and one-half by proportional representation. The latter formula was to reflect the percentage of votes obtained by the successful candidate in presidential elections,and was intended to ensure that the president's party would secure a legislative majority. Other sections of the proposed constitution, relating to social issues, were strongly opposed by the Roman Catholic Church, to which more than 90% of the islanders belong.

The draft constitution, which required the approval of at least 60% of voters, was endorsed by only 53.7% and opposed by 44.6% at a referendum held in November 1992. A second constitutional commission, whose meetings were opened to the public, began work in January 1993 on proposals for submission to a further referendum, which was to be held later in the year. In April President René reshuffled the cabinet, relinquishing the defence portfolio.

In May 1993 the second commission unanimously agreed on a new draft constitution, in which a compromise plan was reached on the electoral formula for a new national assembly. With the joint endorsement of René and Mancham, the draft constitution was submitted to a national referendum in June, at which voters approved the constitutional plan by 73.9% to 24.0%. Opponents of the new constitutional arrangements comprised the PS, the Seychelles National Movement (SNM) and the National Alliance Party (NAP). At the presidential and legislative elections that followed in July, René received 59.5% of the vote, against 36.7% for Mancham and 3.8% for Philippe Boullé, the United Opposition candidate representing the PS, the SCDP, the SNM and the NAP. In the legislative elections, the SPPF secured 21 of the 22 seats elected by direct vote, and the DP one seat. Of the 11 additional seats allocated on a proportional basis, the SPPF received a further seven seats, the DP three seats and the PS one seat. Immediately following the elections, René, whose decisive victory was widely attributed to his promise of increased expenditure on social programmes, carried out an extensive reshuffle of the cabinet.

Socio-Economic Transition

Following the 1993 elections, the government began to promote a gradual transition from socialism to free-market policies, aimed at maximizing the country's potential as an 'offshore' financial and business centre. State-owned port facilities were transferred to private ownership in 1994, when plans were also announced for the creation of a duty-free international trade zone to provide transhipment facilities. Arrangements were proceeding during 1995 for the privatization of government activities in tourism, agriculture and tuna-processing. The economic liberalization, accompanied by diminished levels of aid and the consequent pressure to reduce budgetary deficits, led the government to announce, in February 1995, that some state-funded welfare services were to be reduced.

In early 1995 tensions developed within the opposition DP, whose only directly elected MP, Christopher Gill, sought to remove Mancham from the party leadership on the grounds that the former president was insufficiently vigorous in opposing the policies of the René government. Gill was suspended from the DP in June, and subsequently formed a breakaway 'New Democratic Party' with the aim of restructuring the DP under new leadership. The official registration of active political organizations, affording them corporate status, led to the formal amalgamation of the PS, the SNM, the SCDP and the NAP as a single party, the United Opposition (UO), under the leadership of Wavel Ramkalawan of the former PS.

In the furtherance of its efforts to promote Seychelles as an international 'offshore' financial centre, the government introduced, in November 1995, an Economic Development Act (EDA), under whose provisions investors of a minimum US $10m. would receive immunity in Seychelles from extradition or seizure of assets. It was feared in international financial circles, however, that the operation of the EDA would make Seychelles a refuge for the proceeds of drugs-trafficking and other crimes. Protest was led by the United Kingdom, France and the USA, and in February 1996 the EDA was described by the Financial Action Task Force, the investigative branch of the 'Group of Seven' leading industrial countries, as a 'serious threat to world financial systems.' Within Seychelles, aspects of the EDA were criticized by Mancham. The government, while refusing to rescind the EDA, established an Economic Development Board under the chairmanship of René, to vet potential EDA investors. In April the government introduced legislation aimed at preventing the use of the EDA for 'laundering' illicit funds. It was disclosed in April 1997 that 243 foreign nationals had obtained Seychelles passports, in return for individual payments of $25,000, under an Economic Citizenship Programme introduced in the previous year to attract foreign investors to the republic. It was claimed, however, by opposition groups that many of the grantees had never visited the islands, and that the names of some of these absentee citizens had been added to electoral lists.

In July 1996 the SPPF introduced a series of constitutional amendments, creating the post of vice-president, to which James Michel, the minister of finance, communications and defence and a long-standing political associate of René, was appointed in August. The constitutional changes also provided for revisions in constituency boundaries, which were generally interpreted as favouring SPPF candidates in future legislative elections. Measures were also implemented whereby the number of directly elected members of the national assembly was to be increased from 22 to 25, and the number of seats allocated on a proportional basis reduced from 11 to a maximum of 10.

EXTERNAL RELATIONS

Seychelles, a member of the Commonwealth, the African Development Bank and the Organization of African Unity, has traditionally pursued a policy of non-alignment in international affairs. Under the René government, the country has strengthened its ties with continental Africa and declared its sympathy with various liberation movements.

In 1983 Seychelles, Madagascar and Mauritius agreed to form an Indian Ocean Commission (IOC) with the aim of increasing regional co-operation. The first such agreement under the IOC was signed by the three countries in January 1984. Comoros joined the IOC in 1985. In early 1986 Seychelles withdrew its objections to the admission to membership of France (as the representative of Réunion) despite its reluctance to recognize permanent French sovereignty over Réunion, and disagreements over the demarcation of regional tuna-fishing rights. Relations with France improved in 1987, despite Seychelles' opposition to the accession of France to the presidency of the IOC. France signed three new economic assistance agreements with Seychelles during that year, and the French minister of co-operation visited the islands and opened an electricity generator that had been supplied by the French government. In June 1990 President Mitterrand of France visited Seychelles as part of an Indian Ocean tour.

In 1988 Seychelles established diplomatic relations with the Comoros and with Mauritius, and an agreement was made with the latter to co-operate in health matters. In 1989 diplomatic relations were established with Morocco, Madagascar and Côte d'Ivoire, and in 1990 with Kenya. During 1992 formal relations were established with Israel and South Africa.

During the 1980s President René actively pursued initiatives for the creation of an Indian Ocean 'peace zone' and the demilitarization of the British Indian Ocean Territory, which includes the atoll of Diego Garcia. Until 1983, Seychelles allowed limited use of its naval facilities to warships of all nations, but only on condition that a guarantee was issued that they were not carrying nuclear weapons. Neither the British nor the US governments would agree to this condition, and their refusal to do so caused their respective naval fleets to be effectively banned from using Seychelles port facilities. It is thought that this embargo lost Seychelles a considerable amount of foreign exchange, and that this may have been one reason for the lifting of the guarantee requirement in September 1983. Seychelles continues, theoretically, to refuse entry to ships carrying nuclear weapons.

In 1986 Seychelles and the USA renegotiated an agreement, originally signed in 1976 and renewed in 1981, which allowed the USA to maintain a satellite tracking station on Mahé. In 1988 the USA increased its annual level of economic support to US $3m., exclusive of the $4.5m. paid annually in rental fees for the satellite tracking facilities. Direct economic aid to Seychelles, however, was reduced by the US government in 1993 to $1m. annually, and in September 1995 the US authorities informed the Seychelles government that the station was to close in October 1996. The US diplomatic mission in Victoria was closed in 1996, also as a cost-saving measure.

Economy

DONALD L. SPARKS

In 1995, according to estimates by the World Bank, Seychelles' gross national product (GNP), measured at average 1993–95 prices was US $487m., equivalent to $6,620 per head. During 1985–95, it was estimated, GNP per caput increased, in real terms, at an average annual rate of 4.2%. Over the same period, the population increased by an annual average of 1.2%. Seychelles' gross domestic product (GDP) increased, in real terms, by an annual average of 5.4% in 1985–95. Real GDP rose by 6.9% in 1992 and by 5.8% in 1993, but declined by 1.6% in 1994 and by an estimated 1.8% in 1995. Following the multi-party elections held in 1993, the government has introduced a number of important reforms in the economy, notably towards encouraging the greater involvement of the private sector in tourism, industry and agriculture.

AGRICULTURE AND FISHERIES

As the area of cultivable land is extremely limited (about 1,000 ha of a total of 14,000 ha on Mahé) and the soil is generally poor, it is unlikely that Seychelles will ever become self-sufficient in agriculture. New lands, however, are being opened up for farming on some of the outlying islands, which are managed by the Islands Development Co, a parastatal body, which is responsible for land on 10 islands. Seychelles is heavily dependent on imported food which, together with drink and tobacco, accounted for 19.1% of the total import bill in 1993, although this proportion is being slowly reduced. The government is seeking to stimulate greater self-sufficiency in vegetables, fruit, meat and milk. There are a number of large farms and about 650 small farms and thousands of smallholdings, about one-half of them run by 'part-time' farmers. In 1993, in accordance with the government strategy for reduced state involvement in the economy, the ministry of agriculture withdrew from the management of its five state owned farms. Their profitability had been overtaken by the increasing cost of subsidies and poor productivity. These farms are being sub-divided into small plots and leased to private individuals, and the ministry of agriculture is now to concentrate on stressing increased extension services to small farmers in its continuing attempts to stimulate food production. The transfer of government-owned agricultural land to smallholder farmers was proceeding in 1996. In addition, the African Development Bank (ADB) has offered SR 40m. to assist an integrated agricultural development project to develop roads and irrigation facilities. Agriculture and fishing was estimated to have contributed 4.3% of GDP in 1995.

The main exports from this sector have traditionally been coconuts (especially for copra), frozen fish and cinnamon (exported as bark). In 1987, the first year of its production, canned tuna became the most significant export commodity; in 1994 canned tuna accounted for 74.6% of total merchandise exports (excluding re-exports). Minor export crops include patchouli, vanilla, tea and limes. Cup copra is processed locally into oil, and the by-product made into animal feed. By the early 1990s, exports of copra, which in the late 1960s were about 6,000 tons per year, had fallen to only 10% of 1968 levels, mainly as a result of competition for land from food crops. The value of copra exports declined by an annual average of 40.7% between 1990–1994, and totalled only SR 202,000 in 1994. In the late 1980s exports of cinnamon bark, traditionally an important export item, fell to about one-third of 1986 totals, and remained depressed in the early 1990s. However, exports subsequently recovered; the value of cinnamon bark exports increased by an annual average of 55.5% between 1990–94, and stood at SR 2.3m. in 1994. Tea is grown for domestic consumption, and there is a small surplus for export. Output ranged from 245–250 tons annually in the early 1990s. The government is seeking to stimulate production of bananas, mangoes and avocados. Seychelles is self-sufficient in eggs and poultry, and there has been a large increase in the number of pigs, although animal feed has to be imported. The islands' first fruit and vegetable canning plant and an integrated poultry unit started operating in 1982, and a dairy plant was opened in 1986.

Seychelles expects to be self-sufficient in timber by the year 2000. A reafforestation scheme, with new plantings of 100 ha per year, has been started to provide timber for the sawmill established in 1979 at Grande Anse by the state-owned Seychelles Timber Co (SEYTIM).

Seychelles' consumption of fish per caput is one of the highest in the world, at 85 kg per year. The local catch, by largely traditional methods (the artisanal catch was 4,256 tons in 1995), satisfied domestic demand, leaving a small surplus for export as frozen fish. Until relatively recently, there was little exploitation of the islands' substantial marine resources. A modern fishing industry, operated by the Fishing Development Co (FIDECO), is concentrating on industrial tuna fishing through joint-venture operations, including the Société Thonière de Seychelles (of which 49% is owned by French interests), which has two freezer ships, and a tuna canning plant at Victoria that began operation in 1987, Conserveries de l'Océan Indien (a joint venture between the governments of Seychelles and France). Output at the cannery, which totalled 1,045 tons in the first year of production, reached 4,531 tons in 1993 and 7,200 tons in 1994. In 1995 the US foods multinational, H. J. Heinz, invested US $8m. to acquire a 60% interest in the tuna-canning factory. The government retained a 40% holding in the company, which was reorganized as Indian Ocean Tuna. In 1997 production at the cannery was averaging 110 tons per day, compared with 40 tons per day in the previous year. In early 1997 Heinz announced plans to invest some $20m. to increase production to 300–400 tons per day by 2000. The annual turnover of the factory was forecast at SR 250m. in 1997, compared with SR 90m. in 1996.

In 1978 Seychelles declared an exclusive economic zone (EEZ), extending 370 km (200 nautical miles) from the coast, to curtail the activities of large foreign fleets, which until then had been freely catching almost 24,000 tons per year of deep-sea tuna. Since 1979, when Seychelles began to enforce its control over the EEZ, agreements have been concluded with several foreign governments. The most important of these is with the European Union (EU, formerly the European Community–EC), which has the right to operate 40 purse-seiners within the EEZ. In 1993 a further three-year agreement was signed with the EC. Additional revenue is earned through the supplying of vessels at Victoria and through leasing the newly expanded port facilities to foreign vessels. Seychelles' industrial fish catch more than doubled between 1984–88, and in 1989 reached 227,000 tons. However, the catch declined to 193,000 tons in 1991, before recovering to an estimated 280,000 tons in 1995. An indigenous fleet of 10 purse-seiners is under construction, the first of which was launched in 1991. Seychelles' first tuna-seiner, with a capacity of 250 tons, began operations in late 1991. Assistance in expanding the fishing industry sector has been forthcoming from Japan, France, the United Kingdom and the ADB. In 1991 Seychelles joined Mauritius and Madagascar to form a Tuna Fishing Association. A study on the potential for prawn fishing estimated that the annual catch could total 8 tons. About 3 tons of prawns a year are currently imported, mainly for the tourist industry. There is also future potential for Seychelles to exploit its rich stock of marine algae, for use in the manufacture of fertilizers, adhesives, beverages and medicines. Exports of canned tuna, fresh and frozen fish contributed 82.2% of the total value of merchandise exports (excluding re-exports) in 1994.

TOURISM

The economy is heavily dependent on tourism, which in 1994 provided about 60% of total earnings from goods and services and generated 18% of GDP, 15% of formal employment and a substantial proportion of secondary employment (tourism directly employed 4,615 people in 1994). However, it has been estimated that more than 60% of gross earnings from tourism leaves the country to pay for imported food and other goods, and to tour operators.

The tourism industry began in 1971 with the opening of Mahé international airport. In that year there were only 3,175 visitors; however, by 1981 the number had risen to 60,425, after, however, approaching 79,000 in 1979. The reasons for the setback included general world recession, high local prices (partly caused by the revaluation of the Seychelles rupee in March 1981), increased air fares and the ban on landings imposed on South African Airways in September 1980. An agreement with Swaziland's national airline allowed the important South African trade to resume, but in November 1981 the entry by this route of a group of mercenaries, seeking to oust the government, had a highly damaging effect on tourism. These factors, combined with the army rebellion in August 1982 (which deterred many potential visitors), led to a further fall in arrivals. However, the final figure for 1982 was 47,280 visitors, partly owing to a strenuous campaign, launched during the year, to revive the sector. The number of tourist arrivals had recovered to 72,542 in 1985 and achieved a total of 103,900 in 1990, when there were some 3,590 hotel beds. The Gulf War caused arrivals to decline to about 90,000 in 1991, although 1992 and 1993 both brought a strong recovery, to more than 116,000 visitors in the latter year. Arrivals of tourists and business visitors totalled 109,901 in 1994: almost 82% of these were from Europe. Arrivals increased to 120,717 in 1995, and to 130,995 in 1996. Foreign exchange receipts from tourism rose from SR 521.8m. in 1989, to SR 607m. in 1993, but were estimated to have declined to SR 510m. in 1994, when there were some 4,240 hotel beds.

Seychelles has developed an extensive network of international air links. Air France flies three times each week from Paris to Seychelles, in conjunction with Air Seychelles. In August 1991 Air Seychelles began weekly scheduled flights to Johannesburg. Air Seychelles also operates international services to London, Paris, Frankfurt, Rome, Singapore and Bombay. A service to Spain was introduced by Air Seychelles in 1993, substantially increasing the number of visitors from that country. Late in 1993, Seychelles and Kenya signed a joint marketing agreement to promote combined tour programmes. Air Seychelles extended its network to Israel, and Ukraine in 1995, and was seeking increased services between Seychelles and Johannesburg. In late 1996 Air Seychelles took possession of a new Boeing 767. However, in early 1997 the airline scaled down its international network, discontinuing its services to Spain and Israel as well as one of its twice-weekly flights to Singapore.

Since the mid-1980s the government has rehabilitated and improved existing tourist facilities, and developed new ones, including a craft village, a national aquarium and historical sites. However, care has been taken to control the development of tourism in order to protect both the natural and the social environments, and the emphasis on promoting tourism on a year-round basis has been aimed at restricting visitor numbers to under 4,000 at any one time. The government has estimated the islands' total tourist capacity at 200,000 visitors annually. A conglomerate based in Dubai, in the United Arab Emirates, has purchased land near Victoria with a view to constructing a marina village, to include yachting facilities, a golf course, a conference centre and a 320-room hotel. Despite concerns that this type of development is inconsistent with Seychelles' ethos of sustainable tourism, the ministry of finance affirmed that it would welcome as many as 15 further hotel developments on a similar scale by 2000. Following the 1993 elections, the government began to lessen its involvement, through parastatal corporations, in the tourism sector, and foreign investment has been actively sought. A series of new taxes on the tourism industry, introduced by the government, includes a hotel licence fee, which is levied according to the number of beds per hotel and is expected to contribute additional revenue of SR 23m. in 1997.

MINERALS

The islands' sole mineral export is guano (of which 6,000 metric tons were exported in 1990). The government is investigating the possibility of processing local coral into lime for a cement factory. In July 1986 an Italian firm signed a contract to study the potential for exporting Seychelles granite, of which small quantities had been exported in 1982. India is collaborating in surveys for polymetallic nodules in the EEZ.

In 1977 the government signed a petroleum exploration agreement, covering an offshore concession area of 16,000 sq km, with a consortium including Amoco of the USA, which later bought out its partners. In 1982 Amoco Seychelles signed a new agreement, covering five more offshore wells in addition to those already drilled. Other concessions are held by Elf-Aquitaine of France and Santa Fe Industries of the USA. An exploration promotion programme was launched by the government in 1985. In 1987 the government signed an agreement with Enterprise Oil Exploration, a British company. Under the agreement, the company gained exclusive rights to explore an offshore area south-east of Mahé and to develop any viable fields. Exploratory drilling by Enterprise Oil commenced in August 1994 but proved unsuccessful and was discontinued in the following year. Other petroleum companies have subsequently expressed interest in conducting exploration operations, and the Seychelles government has received technical assistance and funding from Norway to further offshore exploration activities.

INFRASTRUCTURE AND MANUFACTURING

The network of roads is generally good and an improvement programme is proceeding. In 1994 there were 322 km of roads, of which 219 km were paved. The Pointe Larue International airport has been expanded, its runway has been strengthened to take Boeing 747s, and a new domestic terminal has been built. There are 10 airstrips on the islands. Plans are proceeding for the creation of an air control centre.

Seychelles' major infrastructural project, the Mahé east coast development plan, includes the modernization and expansion of Victoria port and the construction of a new road linking Victoria to the airport. The World Bank agreed in 1985 to lend US $6.2m. for dredging work, quayside paving and rehabilitation of roads on Mahé. The total cost of the scheme is likely to be $40m.–$42m., of which $12m. will be spent on the fisheries development project. As well as the World Bank, the ADB, the Banque Arabe pour le Développement Economique en Afrique (BADEA) and the Kuwait Fund have provided finance for the east coast project. The commercial port can accommodate vessels of up to 214 m in length, but there is only one berth. Additional berthing capacity is planned, with some facilities for containerization, and possibly a repair dock. At present there is a small yard for repairing fishing boats and yachts. In March 1994 the government established a commission to prepare the reorganization of port activities at Victoria. The ship-handling, stevedoring and agency activities of the Union Lighterage Co, have been transferred from state to private-sector ownership.

The Seychelles Electricity Corpn was set up in 1980 as a parastatal organization which is to finance its own recurrent costs. The extension of electricity supply to the islands of Mahé, Praslin and La Digue has been completed. Power supplies are generated entirely from petroleum. In 1993 mineral fuels accounted for 14.2% of the value of total imports. (However, the vast majority of fuel imports are re-exported, mainly as bunker sales to visiting ships and aircraft—exports of refined petroleum products contributed 55.1% of total export earnings in that year.) Studies on the use of windmills, solar and wave power for electricity generation have been conducted.

The recurring problem of water shortages should eventually be eased by the completion of the Baie Lazare water supply scheme, in the south of Mahé, by the Seychelles Water Authority. It is the authority's largest project and will supply 18,000 people in the Victoria area. Work was scheduled to start in early 1987, but encountered delays, resulting from negotiations over finance. A project to extend La Digue's water supply to 80% of the population, from the existing level of 50%, began in 1988. Funds for the scheme, which was estimated to cost SR 8m. were provided by France and the USA.

Several small industries have been established, covering brewing, plastic goods, salt, coconut oil, cinnamon essence distilling, soft drinks, detergents, cigarettes, soap, boat building, furniture, printing and steel products. Others include animal feed, meat and fish processing, dairy products, paints, television assembly, and handicrafts for the tourist industry. The tuna-canning factory (see above) is, to date, the major enterprise in the industrial sector.

TRADE, FINANCE AND PLANNING

Seychelles traditionally sustains a substantial visible trade deficit. Despite the imposition of import controls, the deficit rose from SR 660m. in 1991 to SR 763m. in 1992 and to a record SR 856m. in 1993. The trade balance improved significantly in 1994, when exports totalling SR 236.6m. and imports of SR 630.4m. reduced the deficit to SR 393.8m. This improvement was attributable to a reduced level of imports, as export receipts were slightly below 1993 levels. However, exports totalling SR 267.3m. and increased imports of SR 1,131.2m. produced a deficit of SR 863.9m. in 1995. Seychelles' main suppliers of imports in that year were the People's Republic of China (25.5% of the total), Singapore (18.8%), South Africa (11.3%) and the United Kingdom (10.9%). Seychelles' principal export markets in that year were the People's Republic of China (15% of total exports), the United Kingdom (12.4%), Germany (2.6%) and Japan (1.7%).

Following the election in 1994 of a democratically-based government in South Africa, increased trade with (as well as investment from) South Africa can be expected in the near future. In 1993 Seychelles joined the Preferential Trade Area for Eastern and Southern Africa (PTA, which in 1994 became the Common Market for Eastern and Southern Africa–COMESA) and should benefit from the clearing house function which facilitates the use of member countries' currencies for regional transactions. This will reduce the pressure on foreign exchange resources, particularly from trade with Mauritius, another COMESA member.

Seychelles' visible trade deficit is partly offset by earnings from tourism and by capital inflows in the form of aid and private investment, together with rental income from the US satellite tracking station (see Recent History). According to the IMF, in 1992 the current account deficit stood at a manageable US $6.9m., rising to $38.82m. in 1993 before declining to $14.72m. in 1994, and then increasing to $33.13m. in 1995. Seychelles' total external debt was US $164.4m. at the end of 1995, of which $151.1m. was long-term public debt. In that year the cost of debt-servicing was equivalent to 7.1% of the value of exports of goods and services. Reserves of foreign exchange, which declined steadily during the late 1980s, totalled $16.5m. at the end of 1990. These reserves increased to $30.1m. in 1992 and to $34.5m. in 1993, but declined to $29.0m. in 1994, to $25.9m. in 1995 and to $20.6m. in 1996.

In 1996 legislation came into effect under which it was compulsory to remit all foreign currency earnings to local banks. In January 1997 the existing foreign exchange allocation system was abandoned and commercial banks assumed control of the allocation of foreign currency. Recipients of foreign exchange can claim up to 20% of their earnings in foreign exchange, but the amount allocated is decided on a discretionary basis by the commercial bank concerned.

Government spending increased dramatically following independence in 1976, as the new administration expanded its provision of social services and raised its levels of defence spending. British grant support ended in 1979. Revenue deficits expanded steadily between 1984–86. In 1987 the government introduced an austerity budget, restricting public spending, and reduced the deficit to 3.8% of GDP. The deficit rose to nearly 10% of GDP in 1989, but fell to 1.0% in 1994 before rising to 2.8% of GDP in 1995. It was estimated that the deficit could be as great as 6.5% of GDP in 1996, owing to declining revenue (with the postponement of the divestment of several state assets, revenue declined by 19% from the previous year). The government introduced a 'transitional' budget in 1993, reflecting the political uncertainty of the new constitution. This budget included the relaxation of import controls, which had been introduced in 1992, and included proposals for a three-year public-sector investment programme. This awarded priority during the period 1995–97 to projects in education, public utilities, transport and tourism. The 1997 budget estimates predicted a reversal of the decline in revenue recorded in 1996. Improved control of foreign exchange earnings was forecast to generate additional revenue of SR 25m.–30m., while it was envisaged that a further SR 246m. would be raised by a range of increases in tax rates and fees, contributing to a forecast rise in total revenue of 24.5% in 1997. The 1997 budget allowed for a 7.2% increase in overall government expenditure. Recurrent expenditure, however, remained largely unchanged, with a total allocation of SR 1,100m. Most of the increase was allocated to the police and to health and education.

Until recently, most aid came from the UK, but now Seychelles attracts aid from a wide variety of sources, including the World Bank, the EU and other Western European countries (particularly France), the ADB, BADEA, the USA, India, Canada, Arab countries and funds and the People's Republic of China. In 1993 Australia pledged SR 2.8m. for projects in Seychelles' plan for human resources development, and in the same year India provided loan finance of SR 8.5m. for the purchase of Indian-made buses and transport equipment.

The Seychelles rupee, previously tied to sterling, was linked to the IMF Special Drawing Right (SDR) in November 1979. In March 1981 the mid-point exchange rate was set at SDR 1 = 7.2345 Seychelles rupees. This remained in effect until February 1997, when the fixed link with the SDR was ended.

The government has been generally successful in controlling inflation. The annual rate of inflation averaged 1.8% in 1985–95; consumer prices increased by 1.3% in 1993 and 1.9% in 1994, but declined by 0.5% in 1995 and by 0.9% in 1996.

Trade between Seychelles and other members of the Indian Ocean Commission (IOC, see Recent History) accounts for only 2%–3% of the country's total official trade, owing principally to Seychelles' high import duties. Seychelles has applied for membership of the Indian Ocean Rim Initiative (IORI), the World Trade Organization (WTO) and the Southern African Development Community (SADC).

ECONOMIC PROSPECTS

Although the government has taken over a majority shareholding in certain key sectors, through the Seychelles National Investment Corpn set up in 1979, it never promoted a policy of full nationalization. The Seychelles government is now actively encouraging foreign investment, both public and private, particularly in tourism, farming, fisheries and small-scale manufacturing, although joint ventures are preferred where foreign investors are concerned. Taxed profits can be freely repatriated. Certain aspects of the Economic Development Act (EDA), introduced in 1995 to assist in establishing Seychelles as a centre for international 'offshore' financial services, attracted intense criticism, on the grounds that they could provide a shelter for illegally obtained funds (see Recent History). The government has, however, established procedures for vetting investors bringing more than US $10m. to Seychelles under EDA provisions. Seychelles' desire to become an international business centre is gaining momentum. By 1996 nearly 1,200 international companies and five international trusts had been incorporated in the country. Legislation introduced in early 1997 aimed to increase the appeal of the 'offshore' sector by facilitating taxation agreements with other countries. The legislation is specifically intended to further Seychelles' aim to become a major centre serving the Far East.

After more than a decade of conservative economic public policies, the government began to introduce more liberal programmes in 1990. In July 1993 President René created the National Economic Consultative Committee, with a membership including business leaders as well as members of the political opposition. In 1994, with the implementation of the Investment Promotion Act, the government offered a range of incentives to stimulate increased private sector investment in tourism, agriculture, manufacturing and services. As many of the highly skilled Seychellois professional people (many of whom left the islands during the period of single-party rule) return to Seychelles, and as political openness translates into genuine economic reform, the republic may well be within reach of further rises in per caput incomes and an extended period of sustained economic growth and development.

Statistical Survey

Source (unless otherwise stated): Department of Information and Telecommunications, Union Vale, POB 321, Victoria; tel. 224220; telex 2320.

AREA AND POPULATION

Area: 454 sq km (175.3 sq miles), incl. Aldabra lagoon (145 sq km).

Population: 68,598 (males 34,125, females 34,473) at census of 17 August 1987; 75,304 at 1996 census.

Density (1996 census): 165.9 per sq km.

Principal Town: Victoria (capital), population 24,324 (incl. suburbs) at the 1987 census.

Births and Deaths (registered in 1995): Live births 1,582 (birth rate 21.0 per 1,000); Deaths 525 (death rate 7.0 per 1,000). Source: UN, *Population and Vital Statistics Report*.

Expectation of Life (years at birth, 1981–85): Males 65.26; Females 74.05. Source: UN, *Demographic Yearbook*.

Economically Active Population: 1981–82 (persons aged 12 years and over): Employed 18,835 (males 12,228, females 6,607); Unemployed 9,527 (males 2,097, females 7,430); Total labour force 28,362. June 1989 (persons aged 15 years and over): Total labour force 29,494 (males 16,964, females 12,530).

Employment (1989): Agriculture, hunting, forestry and fishing 2,212; Manufacturing, electricity and water 2,537; Construction, mining and quarrying 1,651; Trade, restaurants and hotels 4,419; Transport, storage and communications 3,141; Financing, insurance, real estate and business services 705; Public administration (incl. activities not adequately defined) 3,106; Other community, social and personal services 4,567; Total 22,338. Figures exclude self-employed persons, unpaid family workers and employees in private domestic services. Source: ILO, *Yearbook of Labour Statistics*.

AGRICULTURE, ETC.

Principal Crops (metric tons, 1995): Coconuts 3,000*; Vegetables 2,000*; Bananas 2,000*; Tea (green leaf) 246†; Cinnamon bark (exports) 435†. (*FAO estimate. †1993 figure.) Source: mainly FAO, *Production Yearbook*.

Livestock (FAO estimates, '000 head, year ending September 1995): Cattle 2; Pigs 19; Goats 5. Source: FAO, *Production Yearbook*.

Livestock Products (FAO estimates, metric tons, 1994): Pig meat 1,000; Poultry meat 1,000; Hen eggs 2,400; Other poultry eggs 12. Source: FAO, *Production Yearbook*.

Fishing (metric tons, live weight): Total catch 5,278 in 1993; 4,633 in 1994; 4,177 in 1995. Source: FAO, *Yearbook of Fishery Statistics*.

MINING AND INDUSTRY

Mining (1990): Guano 6,000 metric tons (exports). Source: UN Economic Commission for Africa, *African Statistical Yearbook*.

Industrial Production (1994): Tinned fish 5,100 metric tons; Beer 58,380 hectolitres; Soft drinks 80,380 hectolitres; Cigarettes 49 million; Electric energy 126 million kWh. Source: mainly UN, *Industrial Commodity Statistics Yearbook*.

FINANCE

Currency and Exchange Rates: 100 cents = 1 Seychelles rupee (SR). *Sterling and Dollar Equivalents* (31 March 1997): £1 sterling = 8.200 rupees; US $1 = 4.994 rupees; 100 Seychelles rupees = £12.195 = $20.025. *Average Exchange Rate* (Seychelles rupees per US $): 5.0559 in 1994; 4.7620 in 1995; 4.9700 in 1996. Note: In November 1979 the value of the Seychelles rupee was linked to the IMF's special drawing right (SDR). In March 1981 the mid-point exchange rate was set at SDR 1 = 7.2345 rupees. This remained in effect until February 1997, when the fixed link with the SDR was ended.

Budget (SR million, 1995): *Revenue:* Taxation 844.7 (Taxes on income, etc. 125.8, Social security contributions 175.9, Domestic taxes on goods and services 46.4, Import duties 487.7); Other current revenue 213.4 (Entrepreneurial and property income 111.2, Administrative fees and charges, non-industrial and incidental sales 97.7); Capital revenue 100.3; Total 1,158.4, excl. grants received (13.8). *Expenditure:* General public services 155.3; Defence 55.2; Public order and safety 45.0; Education 155.7; Health 102.2; Social security and welfare 184.0; Housing and community amenities 3.9; Recreational, cultural and religious affairs and services 12.3; Economic affairs and services 149.0 (Agriculture, forestry, fishing and hunting 25.4, Transport and communications 58.7); Other purposes 413.9 (Interest payments 244.0); Total 1,276.5 (Current 1,125.5, Capital 151.0), excl. lending minus repayments (96.2). Note: Figures represent the consolidated accounts of the central Government, covering the operations of the Recurrent and Capital Budgets and of the Social Security Fund. Source: IMF, *Government Finance Statistics Yearbook*.

International Reserves (US $ million at 31 December 1996): IMF special drawing rights 0.03; Reserve position in IMF 1.16; Foreign exchange 20.57; Total 21.76. Source: IMF, *International Financial Statistics*.

Money Supply (SR million at 31 December 1996): Currency outside banks 165.7; Demand deposits at commercial banks 284.0; Total money (incl. others) 450.4. Source: IMF, *International Financial Statistics*.

Cost of Living (Consumer Price Index; base: 1990 = 100): 108.7 in 1994; 108.2 in 1995; 107.2 in 1996. Source: UN, *Monthly Bulletin of Statistics*.

Expenditure on the Gross Domestic Product (SR million at current prices, 1993): Government final consumption expenditure 714.7; Private final consumption expenditure 1,273.5; Increase in stocks 46.0; Gross fixed capital formation 651.2; *Total domestic expenditure* 2,385.1; Exports of goods and services 1,310.2; *Less* Imports of goods and services 1,576.4; *GDP in purchasers' values* 2,419.2. Source: IMF, *International Financial Statistics*.

Gross Domestic Product by Economic Activity (SR million at current prices, 1993): Agriculture, hunting, forestry and fishing 89.4; Mining and manufacturing 259.5; Electricity, gas and water 13.7; Construction 188.2; Trade, restaurants and hotels 627.1;

Transport, storage and communications 254.0; Finance, insurance, real estate and business services 214.0; Government services 343.3; Other services 51.3; *Sub-total* 2,040.7; Import duties 476.6; *Less* Imputed bank service charge 98.1; *GDP in purchasers' values* 2,419.2. Source: IMF, *Seychelles—Recent Economic Developments* (June 1996).

Balance of Payments (US $ million, 1995): Exports of goods f.o.b. 55.45, Imports of goods f.o.b. –218.29, *Trade balance* –162.83; Exports of services 224.05, Imports of services –86.78, *Balance on goods and services* –25.56; Other income received 6.49, Other income paid –22.4, *Balance on goods, services and income* –41.48; Current transfers received 19.55, Current transfers paid –11.21, *Current balance* –33.13; Direct investment abroad –1.51, Direct investment from abroad 40.31, Portfolio investment assets –2.67, Portfolio investment liabilities –0.18, Other investment assets –4.36, Other investment liabilities –1.44, Net errors and omissions –13.93, *Overall balance* –14.03. Source: IMF, *International Financial Statistics*.

EXTERNAL TRADE

Principal Commodities (US $ '000, 1993): *Imports c.i.f.*: Food and live animals 37,865 (Dairy products and birds' eggs 4,851, Fish and fish preparations 7,060, Cereals and cereal preparations 8,150, Vegetables and fruit 7,164); Beverages and tobacco 8,366 (Beverages 7,451); Mineral fuels, lubricants, etc. 34,361 (Refined petroleum products 33,629); Chemicals and related products 14,373 (Essential oils, perfume materials and cleansing preparations 5,045); Basic manufactures 44,770 (Paper, paperboard, etc. 5,030, Non-metallic mineral manufactures 7,575, Metal containers for storage and transport 6,862); Machinery and transport equipment 60,497 (Machinery specialized for particular industries 6,079, General industrial machinery, equipment and parts 6,090, Telecommunications and sound equipment 9,954, Other electrical machinery, apparatus, etc. 9,139, Road vehicles and parts 16,554); Miscellaneous manufactured articles 35,907 (Professional, scientific and controlling instruments, etc. 13,634); Total (incl. others) 241,580. *Exports f.o.b.*: Food and live animals 15,125 (Fish and fish preparations 14,397); Mineral fuels, lubricants, etc. 28,466 (Refined petroleum products 28,434); Machinery and transport equipment 4,012 (Telecommunications and sound equipment 2,141, Aircraft, associated equipment and parts 1,365); Miscellaneous manufactured articles 3,219 (Professional, scientific and controlling instruments, etc. 2,981); Total (incl. others) 51,641. Source: UN, *International Trade Statistics Yearbook*.

Principal Trading Partners (US $ '000, 1993): *Imports c.i.f.*: France 14,962; Germany 7,780; India 5,081; Italy 6,254; Japan 13,940; Singapore 31,632; Southern African Customs Union* 31,072; Thailand 5,157; United Kingdom 32,196; USA 18,689; Yemen 31,665; Total (incl. others) 241,546. *Exports f.o.b.*: France 2,486; Mauritius 1,828; Réunion 1,454; United Kingdom 10,516; USA 3,529; Yemen 27,980; Total (incl. others) 51,641. * Comprising Botswana, Lesotho, Namibia, South Africa, Swaziland. Source: UN, *International Trade Statistics Yearbook*.

TRANSPORT AND TOURISM

Road Traffic (motor vehicles in use, 1989): Passenger cars 4,072; Commercial vehicles 1,105; Buses 216; Motor cycles 102.

Shipping: *Merchant Fleet* (registered at 31 December 1996): Vessels 7; Total displacement 3,720 grt (Source: Lloyd's Register of Shipping, *World Fleet Statistics*); *Sea-borne Freight Traffic* (1990): Vessels entered 953; Freight ('000 metric tons): Loaded 11.2; Unloaded 347.7.

Civil Aviation (traffic on scheduled services, 1994): Kilometres flown 6 million; Passengers carried 297,000; Passenger-km 685 million; Total ton-km 77 million. Source: UN, *Statistical Yearbook*.

Tourism (1994): Foreign visitor arrivals 109,901, excl. cruise-ship passengers (9,897); Gross receipts SR 510m.

COMMUNICATIONS MEDIA

Radio Receivers (1994): 35,000 in use. Source: UNESCO, *Statistical Yearbook*.

Television Receivers (1994): 6,000 in use. Source: UNESCO, *Statistical Yearbook*.

Telephones (1994/95): 12,000 main lines in use. Source: UN, *Statistical Yearbook*.

Book Production (1980): 33 titles (2 books, 31 pamphlets).

Daily Newspapers (1994): 1 (average circulation 3,000 copies). Source: UNESCO, *Statistical Yearbook*.

Non-daily Newspapers (1988): 4 (estimated average circulation 9,000 copies). Source: UNESCO, *Statistical Yearbook*.

EDUCATION

Pre-Primary (1994): 35 schools; 175 teachers; 3,167 pupils.

Primary (1994): 26 schools; 588 teachers; 9,911 pupils.

Secondary

General (1994): 579 teachers; 7,877 pupils.

Teacher-training (1994): 46 teachers; 347 pupils.

Vocational (1994): 132 teachers; 1,056 pupils.

Special Education (1990): 1 school, 78 pupils.

Source: mainly UNESCO, *Statistical Yearbook*.

Directory

The Constitution

The independence Constitution of 1976 was suspended after the coup in June 1977 but reintroduced in July with important modifications. A successor Constitution, which entered into force in March 1979 was superseded by a new Constitution, approved by national referendum on 18 June 1993.

The President is elected by popular vote simultaneously with elections for the National Assembly. The President fulfils the functions of Head of State and Commander-in-Chief of the armed forces and may hold office for a maximum period of three consecutive five-year terms. The Assembly consists of 33 seats, of which 22 are filled by direct election and 11 are allocated on a proportional basis. Constitutional amendments, introduced in July 1996, provided for an Assembly of 25 directly elective seats and a maximum of 10 proportionally allocated seats. There is provision for an appointed Vice-President. The Council of Ministers is appointed by the President and acts in an advisory capacity to him.

The Government

HEAD OF STATE

President: FRANCE ALBERT RENÉ (assumed power 5 June 1977; elected President 26 June 1979, re-elected 18 June 1984, 12 June 1989 and 23 July 1993).

Vice-President: JAMES MICHEL.

COUNCIL OF MINISTERS
(August 1997)

President: FRANCE ALBERT RENÉ.

Vice-President and Minister of Finance, Communications, Defence and the Environment: JAMES MICHEL.

Minister of Foreign Affairs: JÉRÉMY BONNELAME.

Minister of Administration, Manpower and Planning: JOSEPH BELMONT.

Minister of Industry: RALPH ADAM.

Minister of Local Government, Youth and Sports: SYLVETTE FRICHOT.

Minister of Health: JAQUELIN DUGASSE.

Minister of Tourism and Transport: SIMONE DE COMARMOND.

Minister of Employment and Social Affairs: WILLIAM HERMINIE.

Minister of Education and Culture: PATRICK PILLAY.

Minister of Lands and Community Development: DOLOR ERNESTA.

Minister of Agriculture and Marine Resources: ESMÉ JUMEAU.

MINISTRIES

Office of the President: State House, Victoria; tel. 224391; telex 2217; fax 224200.

Ministry of Administration and Manpower: National House, POB 56, Victoria; tel. 383000; telex 2333; fax 224936.

Ministry of Agriculture and Marine Resources: Independence House, POB 166, Victoria; tel. 224030; telex 2418; fax 225245.

Ministry of Education and Culture: POB 48, Mont Fleuri; tel. 224777; telex 2305; fax 224859.

Ministry of Employment and Social Affairs: Unity House, POB 190, Victoria; tel. 322321; telex 2352; fax 321880.

Ministry of Finance and Communications: Central Bank Bldg, POB 313, Victoria; tel. 225252; telex 2363; fax 225265.

Ministry of Foreign Affairs: POB 656, Mont Fleuri; tel. 224688; telex 2260; fax 224845.

Ministry of Health: POB 52, Victoria; tel. 388000; telex 2302; fax 224792.

Ministry of Industry: Maison du Peuple, Victoria; tel. 224030; fax 225784.

Ministry of Lands and Community Development: Independence House, Independence Ave, POB 199, Victoria; tel. 224030; telex 2312; fax 225187.

Ministry of Local Government, Youth and Sports: POB 731, Victoria; tel. 225477; telex 2240; fax 225262.

Ministry of Tourism and Transport: Independence House, Independence Ave, POB 92, Victoria; tel. 225313; telex 2275; fax 224035.

President and Legislature

PRESIDENT

Election, 23 July 1993

Candidate	Votes	% of total
FRANCE ALBERT RENÉ (SPPF)	25,627	59.5
JAMES MANCHAM (DP)	15,815	36.7
PHILIPPE BOULLÉ (United Opposition*)	1,631	3.8

* An electoral coalition comprising the Parti Seychellois, the Seychelles Christian Democrat Party, the National Alliance Party and the Seychelles National Movement.

NATIONAL ASSEMBLY

Speaker: FRANCIS MACGREGOR.

Election, 23 July 1993

Party	Number of votes	% of votes	Seats*
Seychelles People's Progressive Front	24,642	57.5	28
Democratic Party	14,062	32.8	4
United Opposition	4,163	9.7	1

* The Assembly consists of 33 seats, of which 22 are filled by direct election and 11 are allocated on a proportional basis to parties obtaining at least 9% of total votes cast.

Political Organizations

Democratic Party (DP): POB 169, Mont Fleuri; tel. 224916; fax 224302; f. 1992; successor to the Seychelles Democratic Party (governing party 1970–77); Leader Sir JAMES MANCHAM; Sec.-Gen. DANIEL BELLE.

Mouvement Seychellois pour la Démocratie: Mont Fleuri; tel. 224322; fax 224460; f. 1992; Leader JACQUES HODOUL.

New Democratic Party: Victoria; f. 1995 by a breakaway faction of the Democratic Party; Leader CHRISTOPHER GILL.

Seychelles People's Progressive Front (SPPF): POB 91, Victoria; tel. 224455; telex 2226; fax 225351; fmrly the Seychelles People's United Party; renamed in 1978; sole legal party 1978–91; socialist; Pres. FRANCE ALBERT RENÉ; Sec.-Gen. JAMES MICHEL.

United Opposition (UO): Arpent Vert, Mont Fleuri, POB 81, Victoria; tel. 224124; fax 225151; comprises the fmr mem. parties of the political coalition which contested the 1993 elections; Leader Rev. WAVEL RAMKALAWAN.

Diplomatic Representation

EMBASSIES AND HIGH COMMISSIONS IN SEYCHELLES

China, People's Republic: POB 680, St Louis; tel. 266808; fax 266866; Ambassador: ZHANG DAXUN.

Cuba: Bel Eau, POB 108, Victoria; tel. 224094; telex 2354; Ambassador: (vacant).

France: Immeuble Arpent Vert, POB 478, Victoria; tel. 224523; telex 2238; fax 225248; Ambassador: MARCEL SURBIGUET.

India: Le Chantier, POB 488, Victoria; tel. 224489; telex 2349; fax 224810; High Commissioner: PRANAB MUKHOPADHYAY.

Russia: Le Niol, POB 632, Victoria; tel. 266590; telex 2392; fax 266653; Ambassador: GENNADII I. FEDOSOV.

South Africa: British-American Insurance Bldg, 4th Floor, Pope Hennessy St, POB 908, Victoria; tel. 226925; fax 226936.

United Kingdom: Victoria House, POB 161, Victoria; tel. 225225; telex 2269; fax 225127; High Commissioner: PETER A. B. THOMSON.

Judicial System

There are three Courts, the Court of Appeal, the Supreme Court and the Magistrates' Courts. The Court of Appeal hears appeals from the Supreme Court in both civil and criminal cases. The Supreme Court is also a Court of Appeal from the Magistrates' Courts as well as having jursidiction at first instance. The Constitutional Court, which forms part of the Supreme Court, determines matters of a constitutional nature, and considers cases bearing on civil liberties. The judicial system also includes an industrial court and a rent tribunal.

Chief Justice: V. ALLEEAR.

President of the Court of Appeal: HARRY GOBURDHUN.

Justices of Appeal: ANNEL SILUNGWE, EMMANUEL AYOOLA, LOUIS VENCHARD; MAHOMED ALI ADAM.

Puisne Judges: A. PERERA, C. A. AMERASINGHE, S. J. BWANA.

Religion

Almost all of the inhabitants are Christians, of whom more than 90% are Roman Catholics and about 8% Anglicans.

CHRISTIANITY

The Anglican Communion

The Church of the Province of the Indian Ocean comprises six dioceses: four in Madagascar, one in Mauritius and one in Seychelles. The Archbishop of the Province is the Bishop of Antananarivo.

Bishop of Seychelles: Rt Rev. FRENCH CHANG-HIM, POB 44, Victoria; tel. 224242; fax 224296.

The Roman Catholic Church

Seychelles comprises a single diocese, directly responsible to the Holy See. At 31 December 1995 there were an estimated 69,489 adherents in the country, representing about 90% of the total population.

Bishop of Port Victoria: Rt Rev. XAVIER BARONNET, Bishop's House, Olivier Maradan St, POB 43, Victoria; tel. 322152; fax 324045.

The Press

L'Echo des Iles: POB 138, Victoria; tel. 322620; monthly; French, Creole and English; Roman Catholic; Editor P. SYMPHORIEN; circ. 2,800.

The People: Maison du Peuple, Revolution Ave, Victoria; tel. 224455; monthly; Creole, French and English; publ. by the SPPF; circ. 1,000.

Popsport: Premier Bldgs, POB 485, Victoria; tel. 323158.

Regar: Arpent Vert, Victoria; tel. 224507; fax 224987; opposition political weekly.

Seychelles Nation: Information, Culture and Sports Division, POB 800, Victoria; tel. 225775; telex 2320; fax 221006; govt-owned; Mon. to Sat.; also weekend edn; English, French and Creole; Chief Editor RENÉ MORRELL; circ. 3,500.

Seychelles Review: POB 29, Victoria; tel. 323700; monthly.

Seychellois: POB 32, Victoria; f. 1928; publ. by Seychelles Farmers Assen; quarterly; circ. 1,800.

NEWS AGENCY

Seychelles Agence de Presse (SAP): Victoria Rd, POB 321, Victoria; tel. 224161; telex 2320; fax 226006.

Radio and Television

In 1996 there were about 50,000 radio receivers and 12,000 television receivers in use.

Seychelles Broadcasting Corpn (SBC): Hermitage, POB 321, Victoria; tel. 224161; telex 2315; fax 225641; f. 1983 as Radio-Television Seychelles; reorg. as independent corpn in 1992; programmes in Creole, English and French; Man. Dir IBRAHIM AFIF.

RADIO

FEBA Radio (Far East Broadcasting Association): POB 234, Mahé; tel. 282000; fax 242146; Christian programmes; Dir STEWART PEPPER.

SBC Radio: Union Vale, POB 321, Victoria; tel. 224161; telex 2315; fax 224515; f. 1941; programmes in Creole, English and French; Programme Man. (Radio) MARGUERITE HERMITTE.

TELEVISION

SBC TV: Hermitage, POB 321, Mahé; tel. 224161; telex 2315; fax 225641; f. 1983; programmes in Creole, English and French; Programme Man. (Television) JEAN-CLAUDE MATOMBE.

Finance

(cap. = capital; res = reserves; dep. =deposits; m. = million; brs = branches; amounts in Seychelles rupees)

BANKING

Central Bank

Central Bank of Seychelles (CBS): Independence Ave, POB 701, Victoria; tel. 225200; telex 2301; fax 224958; f. 1983; bank of issue; cap. and res 11m., dep. 619.8m. (Dec. 1996); Chair. NORMAN WEBER.

National Banks

Development Bank of Seychelles: Independence Ave, POB 217, Victoria; tel. 224471; telex 2348; fax 224274; f. 1978; 55% state-owned; cap. and res 70m., total assets 184m. (1995); Chair. ANTONIO LUCAS; Man. Dir R. TOUSSAINT.

Seychelles International Mercantile Banking Corpn Ltd (Nouvobanq): Victoria House, State House Ave, POB 241, Victoria; tel. 225011; telex 2253; fax 224670; f. 1991; 78% state-owned, 22% by Standard Chartered Bank (UK); cap. and res 74.1m., dep. 389.7m. (Dec. 1995); Chair. CONRAD BENOITON; Pres. AHMAD SAEED; 1 br.

Seychelles Savings Bank Ltd: Kingsgate House, POB 531, Victoria; tel. 225251; telex 2416; fax 224713; f. 1902; state-owned; term deposits, savings and current accounts; cap. and res 7.8m. (Dec. 1992); Man. Dir ROGER TOUSSAINT; 4 brs.

Foreign Banks

Bank of Baroda (India): Albert St, POB 124, Victoria; tel. 323038; telex 2241; fax 324057; f. 1978; Man. K. N. SUVARNA.

Banque Française Commerciale–Océan Indien (France): POB 122, Victoria; tel. 323096; telex 2261; fax 322676; f. 1978; Man. HENRI ALLAIN D'OFFAY; 3 brs.

Barclays Bank (United Kingdom): Independence Ave, POB 167, Victoria; tel. 224101; telex 2225; fax 224678; f. 1959; Man. M. P. LANDON; 3 brs and 5 agencies.

Habib Bank Ltd (Pakistan): Frances Rachel St, POB 702, Victoria; tel. 224371; telex 2242; fax 225614; f. 1976; Man. JAVED IQBAL SHEIKH.

INSURANCE

H. Savy Insurance Co Ltd: Maison de la Rosière, 2nd Floor, Victoria; tel. 322272; fax 321666; all classes.

State Assurance Corpn of Seychelles (SACOS): Pirate's Arms Bldg, POB 636, Victoria; tel. 225000; telex 2331; fax 224495; f. 1980; all classes of insurance; Exec. Chair. ANTONIO LUCAS.

STOCK EXCHANGE

Proposals for the establishment of a Stock Exchange in Victoria were pending in 1997.

Trade and Industry

CHAMBER OF COMMERCE

Seychelles Chamber of Commerce and Industry: Premier Bldg, Rm 301, POB 599, Victoria; tel. 323812; fax 321422; Chair. ALBERT PAYET.

EMPLOYERS ASSOCIATION

Federation of Employers' Associations of Seychelles: POB 214, Victoria; tel. 224710.

DEVELOPMENT CORPORATION

Seychelles International Business Authority (SIBA): Central Bank Bldg, Victoria; tel. 225402; fax 225851; e-mail siba@seychelles.net; f. 1995 to supervise registration of companies, transhipment and 'offshore' banking in international free trade zone covering area of 23 ha near Mahé international airport; Man. Dir CONRAD BENOITON.

TRADING ORGANIZATIONS

Seychelles Agricultural Development Co Ltd (SADECO): POB 172, Victoria; tel. 375888; f. 1980; Gen. Man. LESLIE PRÉA (acting).

Seychelles Fishing Authority: POB 449, Fishing Port, Victoria; tel. 224597; fax 224508.

Seychelles Industrial Development Corpn(SIDEC): POB 537, Victoria; tel. 323151; telex 2415; fax 324121; promotes industrial development and manages leased industrial sites; CEO MAXWELL JULIE.

Seychelles Marketing Board (SMB): Latanier Rd, POB 634, Victoria; tel. 224444; telex 2368; fax 224735; f. 1984; state trading org. for food production and processing, fisheries development and toiletries; transfer to private sector of agro-industries subsidiaries announced in 1992; CEO MUKESH VALABHJI.

Seychelles National Oil Co: Maison du Peuple, POB 230, Victoria; tel. 225182; fax 225177; Man. Dir EDDIE BELLE.

Seychelles Timber Co (SEYTIM): Grand Anse, Mahé; tel. 278343; telex 2368; logging, timber sales, joinery and furniture; operates sawmill at Grande Anse.

MAJOR INDUSTRIAL COMPANY

Indian Ocean Tuna Co: POB 676, Victoria; tel. 224600; telex 2223; fax 224628; fmrly Conserveries de l'Océan Indien; reorg. 1995; H. J. Heinz owns 60% and Seychelles govt 40%; tuna-processing.

TRADE UNION

Seychelles Federation of Workers' Unions: Maison du Peuple, Latanier Rd, POB 154, Victoria; tel. 224455; fax 225351; f. 1978 to amalgamate all existing trade unions; affiliated to the Seychelles People's Progressive Front; 25,200 mems; Pres. OLIVIER CHARLES; Gen. Sec. BERNARD ADONIS.

Transport

RAILWAYS

There are no railways in Seychelles.

ROADS

In 1994 there were 322 km of roads, of which 219 km were tarmac roads. Most surfaced roads are on Mahé and Praslin.

SHIPPING

Government inter-island ferry and private licensed schooner services connect Victoria and the islands of Praslin and La Digue.

Port and Marine Services Division, Ministry of Tourism and Transport: POB 47, Victoria; tel. 224701; fax 224004; Dir-Gen. (Port of Victoria) SAM ANDRADE.

Allied Agencies Ltd: POB 345, Victoria; tel. 224441; fax 224226; shipping agents.

Aquarius Shipping Agency Ltd: POB 865, Victoria; tel. 225050; fax 225043.

Hunt, Deltel and Co Ltd: Victoria House, POB 14, Victoria; tel. 225352; telex 2249; fax 225367; e-mail hundel@seychelles.net.

Mahé Shipping Co Ltd: Shipping House, POB 336, Victoria; tel. 322100; telex 2216; fax 322978; agents for Royal Fleet Auxiliary, US Navy, P & O, Nedlloyd Lines and numerous other shipping cos; Chair. Capt. G. C. C. ADAM.

Harry Savy & Co: POB 20, Victoria; tel. 322120; fax 321421; shipping agents.

Seychelles Shipping Line Ltd: POB 977, Providence, Victoria; tel. 373655; fax 373185; f. 1994; 90% owned by private interests, 10% by Seychelles Govt; operates freight services between Seychelles and Durban, South Africa; Chair. SELWYN GENDRON; Man. Dir BARRY HIGHAM.

Union Trading Co Ltd: POB 475, Victoria; tel. 322708.

CIVIL AVIATION

The international airport is at Point Larne, 10 km from Victoria.

Air Seychelles: Victoria House, POB 386, Victoria; tel. 381000; telex 2289; fax 224305; f. 1979; operates scheduled internal flights from Mahé to Praslin and charter services to Bird, Desroches and Denis Islands; international services to Europe, Far East, mainland and South Africa; Chair. NORMAN WEBER; CEO Capt. DAVID SAVY.

Tourism

Seychelles enjoys an equable climate, and is renowned for its fine beaches and attractive scenery. There are more than 500 varieties of flora and many rare species of birds. Most tourist activity is concentrated on Mahé, Praslin and La Digue. It is government policy that the development of tourism should not blight the environment, and strict laws govern the construction of hotels. However, the average number of available beds increased from 3,590 in 1990 to 4,240 in 1994. Receipts from tourism totalled an estimated SR 510m. in 1994, when there were 109,901 tourist and business arrivals; most visitors (81.5% in 1994) are from Europe. Visitor arrivals numbered 130,995 in 1996.

Compagnie Seychelloise de Promotion Hotelière Ltd: POB 683, Victoria; tel. 224694; telex 2407; fax 225291; promotes govt-owned hotels.

Seychelles Tourist Office: Independence House, POB 92, Victoria; tel. 225313; telex 2275; fax 225131; parastatal body; Dir-Gen. MONICA CHETTY.

Defence

In August 1996, the army numbered 300 men. Paramilitary forces comprised a 1,000-strong national guard and a coastguard of about 500.

Defence Expenditure: Budgeted at SR 55.2m. in 1995.

Commander-in-Chief of Seychelles Armed Forces: Col LEOPOLD PAYET.

Education

In 1979 free and compulsory primary education was introduced for children between six and 15 years of age, and in 1980 the government initiated a programme of educational reform, based on the British comprehensive system. In 1991 a two-year National Youth Training Scheme, which catered for the secondary education of most children between 15 and 17 years of age, was to be reduced to 12 months. In the same year the duration of primary education was reduced from nine to six years, while that of general secondary education was increased from two to five years (of which the first three years are compulsory), beginning at 12 years of age. Pre-primary and special education facilities are also available. Seychelles Polytechnic, inaugurated in 1982, had 1,428 students in 1993. Several students study abroad, principally in the United Kingdom. In 1990 the average rate of adult illiteracy was estimated at 15%. Government expenditure on education in 1995 was SR 155.7m., or about 12.2% of total expenditure.

Bibliography

Barclays Bank International. *Seychelles: Economic Survey*. London, William Lea, 1972.

Beamish, A. *Aldabra Alone*. London, 1970.

Belling, L. N. *Seychelles: Islands of Love*. Boulogne, Editions Delroise, 1971.

Benedict, B. *People of the Seychelles*. London, HMSO, 1966.

Benedict, M., and Benedict, B. *Men, Women and Money in Seychelles*. Berkeley, University of California Press, 1982.

Bradley, J. T. *History of Seychelles*. Victoria, Clarion Press, 1940.

Central Bank of Seychelles. *Quarterly Review*. Victoria, Central Bank of Seychelles.

Cohen, R. (Ed.) *African Islands and Enclaves*. London, Sage Publications, 1983.

Franda, M. *Quiet Turbulence in the Seychelles: Tourism and Development*. Hanover, NH, American Field Staff Reports, Asia Series No. 10, 1979.

The Seychelles. Boulder, CO, Westview Press, 1981.

Gabby, R., and Ghosh, R. N. *Seychelles Marketing Board: Economic Development in a Small Island Economy*. Singapore, Academic Press International, 1992.

International Monetary Fund. *Seychelles—Recent Economic Developments*. Washington, DC, IMF, 1996.

Lee, C. *Seychelles: Political Castaways*. London, Hamish Hamilton, 1976.

Leymarie, P. *Océan indien, nouveau coeur du monde*. Paris, Editions Karthala, 1983.

Lionnet, G. *The Seychelles*. Newton Abbot, David and Charles, 1972.

Mancham, Sir J. R. *Paradise Raped: Life, Love and Power in the Seychelles*. London, Methuen, 1983.

Island Splendour. London, Methuen, 1984.

Maubouche, R., and Hadjitarkhani, N. *Seychelles Economic Memorandum*. Washington, DC, World Bank, 1980.

Thomas, A. *Forgotten Eden*. London, Longman, 1968.

Toussaint, A. *History of the Indian Ocean*. London, Routledge and Kegan Paul, 1966.

Waugh, A. *Where the Clock Strikes Twice*. New York, Farrar, Strauss and Young, 1951.

Webb, A. W. T. *Story of Seychelles*. Seychelles, 1964.

World Bank. *Seychelles' Economic Memorandum*. Washington, DC, World Bank, 1980.

SIERRA LEONE

Physical and Social Geography

PETER K. MITCHELL

The Republic of Sierra Leone, which covers an area of 71,740 sq km (27,699 sq miles), rises from the beaches of the south-west to the broad plateaux of the Atlantic/Niger watershed at the north-eastern frontier. Despite the general horizontal aspect of the landscapes, developed over millennia upon largely Pre-Cambrian structures there are a number of abrupt ascents to older uplifted erosion surfaces—most impressively along sections of a major escarpment, 130 km inland, separating a western lowland zone (c. 120 m above sea-level) from the country's more elevated interior half (c. 500 m). Incised valleys, interspersed by minor waterfalls, carry drainage south-westwards; only locally or along a coastal sedimentary strip do rivers flow through open terrain.

A geologically recent submergence of major floodplains, particularly north of Cape St Ann, has brought tide-water into contact with the rocky margins of the ancient shield, barring the way to up-river navigation. Water-borne trade has found compensation in sheltered deep-water anchorages, notably off Freetown, the principal port and capital, where a line of coastal summits rising to almost 900 m above sea-level facilitates an easy landfall.

Intrusive gabbros form the peninsular range; elsewhere, isolated blocks or hill groups consist of rock-bare granites or the metamorphic roots of long-vanished mountain chains, which provide mineral deposits: iron, chromite, gold, rutile and bauxite. Reserves of kimberlite in the southern high plateaux are approaching exhaustion. The pipes and dikes of kimberlite may provide the basis for future deep mining.

Differences in seasonal and regional incidence of humidity and rainfall are important. Prolonged rains (May to October, with heaviest rains from July to September) are bracketed by showery weather with many squally thunderstorms, such spells beginning earlier in the south-east. Consequently, the growing season is longest here (although total rainfall—over 5,000 mm locally—is greater along the coast) and the 'natural' vegetation is tropical evergreen forest; the cultivation of cash crops such as cocoa, coffee, kola and oil-palm is successful in this area, and the more productive timber areas, though limited, are concentrated here. The savannah-woodlands of the north-east have less rain (1,900–2,500 mm), a shorter period for plant growth and a dry season made harsh by harmattan winds, with cattle-rearing, groundnuts and tobacco as potential commercial resources. Semi-deciduous forest occupies most intervening areas, but long peasant occupation has created a mosaic of short-term cropland, fallow regrowth plots and occasional tracts of secondary forest.

Permanent rice-lands have been created from mangrove swamp in the north-west, and much encouragement is being given to the improvement of the many small tracts of inland valley swamp throughout the east. Such innovation contrasts with a widespread bush-fallowing technique, giving low yields of rain-fed staples, normally rice, but cassava (especially on degraded sandy soils) and millet in the north. Sierra Leone's agricultural sector is able to provide most of the country's food requirements.

Sierra Leone's third national census, which was held in December 1985, enumerated 3,515,812 inhabitants, representing a population density of 49 inhabitants per sq km. However, there was believed to have been underenumeration, and the census total was subsequently adjusted to 3.7m. At mid-1995, according to UN estimates, Sierra Leone had 4,509,000 inhabitants and a population density of 62.9 inhabitants per sq km.

Traditional *mores* still dominate, in spite of the Westernizing influences of employment in mining, of education and of growing urbanization. A large proportion of the population follows animist beliefs, although there are significant Islamic and Christian communities. Extended family, exogamous kin-groups and the paramount chieftaincies form a social nexus closely mirrored by a hierarchy of hamlet, village and rural centre: 29,000 non-urban settlements including isolated impermanent homesteads. The towns, however, are expanding. Greater Freetown had almost 470,000 inhabitants at the 1985 census, while Koindu, the centre of the Kono diamond fields, has about 80,000 inhabitants; there are, in total, 10 towns with over 10,000 people. Diamond mining has attracted settlers to many villages in the mining areas.

The official and commercial language of the country is English, while Krio (Creole), Mende, Limba and Temne are also spoken.

Recent History

CHRISTOPHER CLAPHAM

Revised for this edition by the Editor

In 1896 a British protectorate was proclaimed over the hinterland of the coastal colony of Sierra Leone, which had been under British administration since 1787. In 1951 a unitary constitution was introduced, which provided for universal adult suffrage. Elections were won by the Sierra Leone People's Party (SLPP), led by Dr (later Sir) Milton Margai, who became chief minister in 1953 and prime minister in 1958. On 27 April 1961 Sierra Leone became an independent state, within the Commonwealth, with Margai remaining as prime minister. The SLPP retained power in elections in 1962. Sir Milton died in 1964 and was succeeded as prime minister by his half-brother, Dr (later Sir) Albert Margai, previously minister of finance. The main opposition party, the All-People's Congress (APC), led by Dr Siaka Stevens, gained a majority of seats in the house of representatives in the general election of March 1967, but was prevented from taking power by a military coup. Following an army mutiny in April 1968, however, a civilian government was restored, with Dr Stevens as prime minister. A period of political instability followed, culminating in an attempted military coup in March 1971, which was suppressed with the aid of troops from neighbouring Guinea. In April Sierra Leone was declared a republic, with Dr Stevens as executive president.

The 1972 by-elections and May 1973 general elections were not contested by the opposition SLPP, and subsequently no official opposition was represented in parliament. Dr Stevens, the sole candidate, was re-elected to the presidency for a second five-year term of office in March 1976.

The economy deteriorated during the second half of the 1970s, as income from mineral resources, the main source of government revenue, declined. Following further political unrest, a general election was held in May 1977, a year earlier than scheduled, at which the SLPP secured 15 of the 85 elective seats in the legislature. In June 1978, however, a new constitution, which provided for a one-party system, was approved by a referendum, and subsequently adopted by the house of representatives. The APC thus became the sole legal party. Stevens was sworn in on 14 June for a seven-year presidential term. The SLPP members of parliament joined the APC, and several were allocated ministerial posts.

The government encountered increasing opposition in 1981, following a scandal involving government officials and several cabinet ministers in the misappropriation of public funds. In August a state of emergency was declared, in an attempt to suppress a general strike, which had been staged in protest against rising prices and food shortages. President Stevens temporarily assumed the additional post of minister of finance in December, following a second financial scandal implicating senior officials. Amid serious outbreaks of violence, a general election took place in May 1982, under the one-party constitution. A new government was subsequently formed, in which the finance ministry was reorganized and efforts were made to control foreign exchange.

THE MOMOH PRESIDENCY, 1985–92

In April 1985 President Stevens announced that he was to retire upon the expiry of his existing mandate later that year. At a conference of the APC in August, Maj.-Gen. Joseph Saidu Momoh, a cabinet minister and the commander of the armed forces, was nominated as sole candidate for the presidency and for the leadership of the party. In October Momoh received 99% of votes cast in a presidential election, and was inaugurated as president on 28 November. Although retaining his military affiliation, Momoh installed a civilian cabinet, which included several members of the previous administration. Elections to the house of representatives took place in May 1986; 335 candidates (all APC members) contested the 105 elective seats. About half of the incumbent representatives, including four cabinet ministers, were replaced. Momoh subsequently appointed a new cabinet, with five new members. In December 27 political prisoners were released, including 12 who had been implicated in the 1974 coup attempt.

Momoh's initial popularity declined in 1986, owing to his administration's failure to improve the serious economic situation, and to the inflationary effects of IMF-sponsored austerity measures. In March the government announced that it had foiled an attempted coup; more than 60 people were arrested (of whom 18 were later charged). In early April the first vice-president, Francis Minah, was arrested and subsequently charged with treason. In an ensuing government reshuffle, a new minister of finance was appointed, and a ministry concerned with rural development and social services was created. In October Minah and 15 others were sentenced to death for plotting to assassinate Momoh and to overthrow the government. Minah and five others were executed in October 1989; the remaining death sentences were commuted to life imprisonment.

In 1987 Momoh initiated measures to combat financial corruption in the public sector. In July 1987 the minister of agriculture, natural resources and forestry resigned, after allegations of accountancy irregularities in the distribution of domestic sugar supplies, and was later ordered by Momoh to make financial restitution. In August and September a deputy minister and a number of senior officials in the civil service and the Bank of Sierra Leone were charged with financial malpractice. In November, following a series of strikes by workers in the public sector, which resulted from the government's inability to pay their salaries, Momoh declared a state of emergency in the economy, announced measures to prevent hoarding of currency and essential goods, and intensified the campaign against smuggling. Under the new measures, corruption was redefined as a criminal offence, and people accused of any crime could be tried *in absentia*. Severe penalties were introduced for the publication of 'defamatory' articles in newspapers; government censorship was imposed, and private mail became subject to inspection. The deputy minister of development and economic planning resigned in January 1988; he and five other people were later charged with fraud. In November a number of ministers were removed in a cabinet reshuffle, which was apparently prompted by accusations of official corruption. At a conference of the APC in January 1989, during which an official code of conduct for political leaders and public servants was adopted, Momoh was re-elected unopposed as secretary-general of the party.

In August 1989 public servants who wished to participate in forthcoming legislative elections (scheduled to be held in 1991), were required to leave government employment no later than May 1990. In December 1989 a new minister of finance took office, following allegations of corruption in the finance ministry. The registration of voters for provincial elections took place in early 1990, but was suspended in three constituencies, following complaints of alleged irregularities.

During early 1990 there was widespread popular support for the establishment of a multi-party system; this was initially rejected by Momoh, although he emphasized that he would continue to encourage broadly-based participation in the one-party state. In mid-August, however, Momoh conceded the necessity of electoral reforms, and announced an extensive review of the constitution. The central committee of the APC approved a number of proposed amendments to the constitution, and in November Momoh appointed a 30-member national constitutional review commission. In late 1990 a constitutional amendment, which reduced the minimum voting age from 21 to 18 years, was adopted.

In March 1991 the commission submitted a draft constitution, which provided for the restoration of a plural political system. The revised constitution stipulated that the president was to be elected by a majority of votes cast nationally and by at least 25% of the votes cast in more than one-half of the electoral districts. The maximum duration of the president's tenure of office was to be limited to two five-year terms. The president was to appoint the cabinet, which was to include one vice-president, rather than two. Legislative power was to be vested in a bicameral legislature, elected by universal adult suffrage for a term of five years. The government subsequently accepted the majority of the commission's recommendations. The proposed formation of an upper legislative chamber was, however, rejected; instead, the government approved the establishment of a 22-member state advisory council, which was to comprise 12 paramount chiefs (one from each district) and 10 members appointed by the president. In early June the government presented the draft constitution to the house of representatives, and announced that the parliamentary term, which was due to end that month, was to be extended for a further year, owing to the disruption caused by the conflict between government forces and Liberian rebels in the south of the country. In addition, the general elections, which were scheduled for May, were to be postponed for a year to allow time for the transition to a multi-party system.

In mid-July 1991 the minister of social affairs, rural development and youth, Musa Kabia, resigned, following disputes within the APC over the new constitution. Ten members of the house of representatives, including Kabia, were temporarily suspended from the APC for alleged activities contrary to the interests of the party. In August the house of representatives approved the new constitution, subject to endorsement by a national referendum, which was to be conducted at the end of that month. However, political activity by parties other than the APC remained illegal until the new constitution took effect. (Following the publication of the constitution in March, some 10 opposition movements had emerged.) At the national referendum, which was conducted during 23–30 August, the new constitution was approved by 60% of voters, with 75% of the electorate participating. The new constitution was formally adopted in September (although the constitution of 1978 also remained officially in force).

In late September 1991 six newly-created political associations allied themselves as the United Front of Political Movements (UNIFOM) and demanded that the government give way to an interim administration. In the same month the government announced that the minister of national development and economic planning, Sheka Kanu, had been dismissed. Shortly afterwards, the first vice-president, Abubakar Kamara, and the second vice-president, Salia Jusu-Sheriff, resigned from both the APC and the government. On 23 September Momoh announced the formation of a new 18-member cabinet, which retained only seven members of the previous government. In late September legislation was introduced to provide for the registration of political associations; a number of political parties, including the APC, were subsequently granted legal status. In December Momoh and leaders of the registered political parties agreed to co-operate in the establishment of a multi-party system. In March 1992 Hassan Gbassay Kanu, who had resigned from the APC and formed the Democratic People's Party (DPP), declared his support of Momoh's policies and announced that the DPP was to be merged with the APC.

MILITARY RULE, 1992–96

On 29 April 1992 members of the armed forces seized a radio station in Freetown and occupied the presidential offices. Their leader, Capt. Valentine E. M. Strasser, subsequently declared that the government had been replaced by a five-member military junta. Momoh sought assistance from the Guinean government, which dispatched troops to Freetown, and more than 100 people were killed in the ensuing violence. On 30 April Momoh fled to Guinea, and Strasser announced the establishment of a national provisional ruling council (NPRC). Strasser affirmed the NPRC's commitment to the introduction of a multi-party system, pledged to end the conflict in the country and assured the Economic Community of West African States (ECOWAS) of the continued participation of Sierra Leone in the ECOWAS Monitoring Group (ECOMOG), which had been engaged since August 1990 in peace-keeping operations in Liberia (see below). The NPRC suspended both the constitutions of 1991 and 1978, dissolved the house of representatives, imposed a state of emergency and curfew, and temporarily closed the country's air, sea and land borders.

On 1 May 1992 the NRPC (which comprised 18 military officers and four civilians) was formally convened under Strasser's chairmanship. On 3 May the NPRC appointed a 19-member cabinet, which retained two members of the Momoh administration. All political activity was suspended, and it was subsequently reported that some 55 people, including members of the former cabinet, had been arrested. On 6 May Strasser was sworn in as head of state. Later that month the government established a commission of inquiry to investigate the activities of members of the former regime.

In early July 1992 Strasser reorganized the cabinet; three members of the armed forces were replaced by civilians, and it was decreed that civilian cabinet ministers were not to hold membership of the NPRC. Later in the month, however, Strasser introduced extensive measures that were designed to reduce the role of the armed forces in government administration: the NPRC was officially designated the supreme council of state, and the cabinet was to be replaced by a council of secretaries, headed by a chief secretary of state, which was to be responsible for the management of the government, subject to the authority of the NPRC. The chairman and deputy chairman of the NPRC were no longer to be involved in government administration (although Strasser retained his defence portfolio in the council of secretaries). Each secretary of state was to assume responsibility for a ministry (henceforth known as a department). The three members of the NPRC who had been removed from the cabinet earlier that month were appointed as principal liaison officers, who were each allocated a number of departments in which they were to supervise government administration. (However, the NPRC was henceforth principally concerned with the suppression of the civil conflict.) In the same month the government introduced legislation which imposed severe restrictions on the media and authorized state censorship. John Benjamin, hitherto the secretary of state in the office of the chairman, became chief secretary of state.

In August 1992 Strasser announced the establishment of an advisory council, which, among other functions, was to review the provisions of the 1991 constitution. In early September 1992 Capt. Solomon Musa, the deputy chairman of the NPRC, became the acting head of state during Strasser's absence in the United Kingdom to obtain medical treatment for injuries sustained during counter-insurgency operations in the south-east of the country (see below). In November about 30 people, who were alleged to be supporters of Momoh, were arrested and charged with subversion. In early December Strasser reorganized the council of secretaries, replacing the two remaining members of the Momoh administration. In the same month Musa was appointed chief secretary of state. Later in December, in an apparent attempt to regain public support, the government established a 15-member advisory council, which was to formulate a programme for transition to civilian rule.

In late December 1992 the government announced that it had foiled a coup attempt by a group known as the Anti-Corruption Revolutionary Movement (which included former members of the army and security forces). Among those reported to have been killed by security forces was the alleged instigator of the plot, Sgt Lamin Bangura. Shortly afterwards, nine of those accused of involvement in the conspiracy were tried by a military tribunal, and, together with 17 prisoners who had been convicted in November on charges of treason, were summarily executed. In January 1993 the United Kingdom announced the suspension of economic aid to Sierra Leone, in protest at the executions. Later that month, in an apparent attempt to allay further accusations of human rights violations, the military regime released several former members of the Momoh government, who had been detained since May 1992. In mid-January 1993, however, the government imposed further press restrictions: all newspapers were required to reapply for registration, which was subject to the fulfilment of certain criteria regarding finance and personnel.

In February 1993 the commissions of inquiry that had been established in May 1992 published reports containing evidence of corruption on the part of former members of the Momoh administration. In April 1993 Strasser promised that all political prisoners would be released and announced that a programme providing for a return to civilian government by 1996 had been adopted. He also stated that measures were being taken to reduce the powers of the security services. In a government reorganization in July, Musa was replaced as deputy chairman of the NPRC and chief secretary of state by Capt. Julius Maada Bio, ostensibly on the grounds that false allegations against him had proved detrimental to the stability of the administration. Musa (who was widely blamed for the repressive measures undertaken by the government) took refuge in the Nigerian high commission in Freetown, amid widespread speculation regarding his dismissal, and subsequently sought refuge in the United Kingdom. Also in July a number of political prisoners were released. In August, however, the human rights organization, Amnesty International, accused the government of detaining more than 170 civilians, including a number of children, on suspicion of involvement with the alleged coup conspiracy of December 1992. In September 1993 the government expropriated the assets of several former politicians, including Momoh, in accordance with the findings of the commissions of inquiry that had investigated their activities. In October a former minister in the Stevens administration, Dr Abbas Bundu, was appointed secretary of state for foreign affairs and international co-operation.

Transitional Arrangements

In late November 1993 Strasser announced the details of a two-year transitional programme, which provided for the installation of a civilian government by January 1996: the national advisory council was to promulgate constitutional proposals in December 1993, and, in conjunction with a committee of legal experts, was to produce a draft constitution by June 1994, which was to be submitted for approval in a national referendum in May 1995; a national commission for democracy was to be established to instruct the population about the new constitution; district council elections (which were to be contested by candidates without political affiliations) were scheduled for November 1994; the registration of political parties was to take place in June 1995, prior to a presidential election in November and legislative elections in December of that year. In December 1993, in accordance with the transitional programme, a five-member interim national electoral commission (INEC), under the chairmanship of Dr James Jonah (the assistant secretary-general of the UN, in charge of political affairs), was established to organize the registration of voters and the demarcation of constituency boundaries, in preparation for the forthcoming local government elections. In the same month the national advisory council submitted several constitutional proposals (which included a number of similar provisions to the 1991 constitution), stipulating that: executive power was to be vested in the president, who was to be required to consult with the cabinet (except in the event of a national emergency), and was to be restricted to a tenure of two four-year terms of office; only Sierra Leonean nationals of more than 40 years of age were to qualify to contest a presidential election (thereby precluding Strasser and the majority of members of the NPRC, on the grounds of age); the president was to be elected by a minimum of 50% of votes cast nationally, and at least by 25% of the votes cast in each of the four provinces; the legislature was to comprise a house of representatives, which was to be elected by universal adult suffrage for a term of five years, and a 30-member upper chamber, the senate, which was to include a number of regional representatives and five presidential nominees; members of the house of representatives were not to be permitted concurrently to hold ministerial portfolios.

At the end of December 1993 the government ended the state of emergency that had operated since April 1992 (although additional security measures remained in force). In March 1994 the authorities introduced further legislation regulating the registration of newspapers, which effectively prevented a number of independent publications from renewing their licences. In April 13 senior members of the armed forces were dismissed, following criticism of the government's failure to end the civil conflict (see below), and rumours of complicity between military officers and the rebels. In May 20 former members of the Momoh government were arrested, after failing to pay compensation for funds that they had misappropriated during their service. In early August Strasser reorganized the council of secretaries (which subsequently included nine civilians). In a further reshuffle in September, the three regional secretaries of state were replaced. Later that month the attorney-general and secretary of state for judicial affairs, Franklyn Kargbo, resigned in protest at the death sentence imposed on an elderly military official, who had been convicted by military tribunal on charges of collaborating with the rebels; Kargbo fled into exile, and was subsequently granted political asylum in the United Kingdom.

In October 1994 a draft constitution was submitted to the NPRC. In November, in accordance with the transitional programme, a five-member national commission for civil education was established to inform the public regarding the principles of the new constitution. However, an increase in rebel activity (see below) prevented the organization of district council elections, which had been scheduled to take place later that month, and was expected to impede the further implementation of the transitional programme.

In January 1995 Strasser reorganized the council of secretaries. In March Musa was apparently ordered to retire from the armed forces, after Strasser rejected his proposal for the installation of a transitional civilian government. Later that month the council of secretaries was reorganized to allow principal military officials in the government to assume active functions within the armed forces (following the advance of rebel forces towards Freetown); Lt-Col Akim Gibril became chief secretary of state, replacing Maada Bio, who was appointed chief of the defence staff. The government claimed that the higher proportion of civilians within the reconstituted council of secretaries reflected the commitment of the NPRC to the transitional process. In late April, on the third anniversary of the NPRC coup, Strasser announced that the ban on political activity would be lifted and that a national consultative conference was to be convened to discuss the transitional process. He further indicated that elections would take place by the end of the year, with the installation of a civilian president and government in January 1996, in accordance with the provisions of the transitional programme. The ban on political parties was formally rescinded on 21 June. The insurgent Revolutionary United Front (RUF, see below) refused to participate in the political process, however, although about 15 parties were subsequently granted registration. The government subsequently announced that 56 former government officials, including ex-president Momoh, would be banned from holding public office for a period of 10 years, on the grounds of their alleged misuse of public funds while in office. The replacement of the chief of staff of the armed forces and of two ministers (including Bundu) was widely interpreted as indicative of divisions within the NPRC. Bundu was expected to represent a new political grouping, the People's Progressive Party, at the forthcoming elections.

The Fall of Strasser

In October 1995, while Strasser was abroad, a coup attempt was suppressed by government forces; seven military officers were subsequently arrested in connection with the incident. In early December it was announced that the presidential and legislative elections were to take place concurrently on 26 February 1996. In January 1996, however, Strasser was deposed by military officers, led by Bio, in a bloodless coup. Bio, who assumed the office of head of state, announced that the coup had been instigated in response to efforts by Strasser to remain in power. (It was reported that Strasser had indicated that he intended to amend restrictions on the age of prospective candidates to enable himself to contest the elections.) Strasser (who had been expelled to Guinea) claimed, however, that the new military administration planned to delay the transition to civilian government. A reconstituted supreme council of state and council of secretaries were formed, and, following a meeting of the new military leadership, the political parties and INEC, it was announced that the elections would proceed as scheduled. The RUF indicated that it was prepared to enter into negotiations with the new government, and declared a temporary cease-fire to allow voter registration to proceed throughout the country; however, it urged a postponement of the elections, pending a peace settlement that would allow the movement to participate in the democratic process. In early February a number of paramount chiefs also requested that the elections be postponed until a peace agreement with the RUF was negotiated (thereby removing obstacles to the electoral process). However, delegates at the national consultative conference, which was convened by INEC, voted in favour of adherence to the scheduled date.

RETURN OF THE SLPP

On 26 February 1996 presidential and legislative elections, which were contested by 13 political parties and were monitored by international observers, took place as scheduled. However, some 27 people were killed in attacks by armed groups, particularly in Bo and parts of Freetown, which were generally attributed to efforts by the RUF to disrupt the electoral process; voting was consequently extended for a further day. The reconstituted SLPP secured 36.1% of votes cast in the legislative elections, while its presidential candidate, Ahmed Tejan Kabbah, also received most support, with 35.8% of votes. Seven of the political parties, including the National Unity Party (which had supported Bio), demanded that the results be annulled, owing to the disruption of the elections in several regions caused by the civil violence. Since none of the candidates had achieved the requisite majority of 55% of the votes, a second round of the presidential election, which took place on 15 March, was contested by Kabbah and the candidate of the United National People's Party (UNPP), John Karefa-Smart (who had obtained 22.6% of votes cast in the first round): Kabbah was elected president by 59.5% of the votes. Later in March seats in the new 80-member parliament were allocated on a basis of proportional representation, with the SLPP securing 27, the UNPP 17, the People's Democratic Party 12 and the reconstituted APC only five; the 12 provincial districts were represented in the legislature by paramount chiefs. Kabbah was inaugurated on 29 March, when the military government officially relinquished power to the new civilian administration. In April Kabbah appointed a cabinet, which was subsequently approved by parliament. In July the national assembly adopted legislation that formally reinstated the constitution of 1991.

In September 1996 Kabbah ordered the compulsory retirement of some 20 officers, including Strasser and Bio, from the armed forces. Shortly afterwards it was reported that a conspiracy to overthrow the government had been thwarted by senior military officers. Later that month the government announced that a team of specialists from Nigeria was to assist the armed forces in the investigation of the planned coup attempt. About 17 members of the armed forces were arrested, of whom nine were subsequently charged with involvement in the conspiracy. In November Kabbah carried out a government reorganization, in which a number of ministries were amalgamated. Following reports of a further conspiracy to overthrow the government in January 1997, Kabbah announced that the Nigerian investigative mission had concluded that former members of the NPRC administration had instigated the coup attempt of the previous September. In April 1997 disagreement within the UNPP resulted in the expulsion of 14 parliamentary deputies from the party by Karefa-Smart. However, the parliament rescinded the expulsions, and imposed a one-year suspension on Karefa-Smart.

REIMPOSITION OF MILITARY RULE

On 25 May 1997 dissident members of the armed forces, led by Maj. Johnny Paul Koroma, seized power, deposing Kabbah, who fled to Guinea. Koroma claimed that the coup, which prompted international condemnation, was in response to the government's failure to implement a peace agreement with the RUF, reached in November 1996 (see below). (The coup leaders were believed to have connections with members of the former NPRC, many of whom, it was reported, planned to return to Sierra Leone.) The Nigerian government demanded that the junta relinquish power, and increased its military strength in Freetown. The new authorities imposed a curfew in Freetown, following widespread violent looting by armed factions; most foreign nationals were evacuated. In early June Nigerian forces initiated a naval bombardment of Freetown in an effort to force the new military leaders to resign. However, forces loyal to the coup leaders, assisted by RUF members, succeeded in repelling Nigerian attacks; it was reported that about 62 people were killed in the fighting. Some 300 Nigerian troops were taken hostage, but were subsequently released. Koroma announced the establishment of a 20-member armed forces revolutionary council (AFRC), with himself as chairman and the RUF leader, Foday Sankoh, as vice-chairman (*in absentia*); the AFRC (which was not internationally recognized as the legitimate government) included a further three members of the RUF and several civilians. All political activity, the existing constitution and government bodies were suspended, although Koroma pledged that democratic rule would be restored, following new elections. Nigeria reiterated that it intended to reinstate the ousted government with the support of ECOWAS, and a further two Nigerian warships were dispatched to the region; further clashes between Nigerian troops and supporters of the new military leaders occurred at the international airport at Lungi. An AFRC delegation, which visited Accra, Ghana, urged the Ghanaian government to refrain from participating in any military action against the junta.

In mid-June 1997 the AFRC announced that it had suppressed a coup attempt, following the arrest of 15 people, including several senior military officers. In the same month it was reported that troops supporting the junta had repulsed an attack by the traditional fighters known as Kamajors (see below), who remained loyal to Kabbah, at the town of Zimmi, 250 km south-east of Freetown. The junta claimed that the former deputy minister of defence in the Kabbah government had organized an attack by the Kamajors, with the assistance of Nigerian troops, from Liberian territory. More than 50 people were later reported to have been killed in hostilities between government supporters and the Kamajors near Kenema. On 17 June Koroma was formally installed as the self-proclaimed head of state. However, despite appeals from Koroma, civilians continued to observe a campaign of civil disobedience, which had been organized by the labour congress in protest at the coup. In the same month members of the disbanded legislature, who had met in defiance of the ban on political activity, proposed a peace agreement, under which a government of national unity representing all political parties and the RUF would be established, and ECOMOG and UN forces would be deployed throughout the country. At the end of June ECOMOG stated that Nigerian troops operating in Sierra Leone (by then numbering about 4,000) were not part of the peace-keeping force.

By early July 1997 the new military government had become completely isolated by the international community. The Commonwealth ministerial action group which had been established to respond to unlawful activities by member states) suspended Sierra Leone from meetings of the Commonwealth, pending the restoration of constitutional order and the reinstatement of a democratically-elected government. The UN security council also condemned the coup, and expressed support for ECOWAS efforts to resolve the situation. The effective imposition of an ECOWAS embargo against Sierra Leone, enforced through the naval blockade and occupation of Lungi airport by Nigerian troops, resulted in increasing shortages of food, crude petroleum and other essential commodities. Meanwhile, a four-nation committee, comprising representatives of Nigeria, Côte d'Ivoire, Guinea and Ghana, which had been established by ECOWAS to monitor a return to constitutional rule, urged the government to relinquish power during a series of negotiations with an AFRC delegation.

In mid-July 1997, in an apparent effort to consolidate power, Koroma formed a cabinet, known as the council of secretaries, comprising representatives of the RUF and the army, together with a number of civilians. Later that month, following further reports of clashes between Kamajors and government forces in the south of the country, AFRC representatives and the ECOWAS committee, meeting in Abidjan, Côte d'Ivoire, agreed to an immediate cease-fire; negotiations were to continue, with the aim of restoring constitutional order. However, Nigeria subsequently accused the AFRC of violating the cease-fire, while further clashes between the Kamajors and the AFRC forces were reported at Zimmi. Renewed skirmishes between Nigerian and AFRC troops also occurred at Lungi airport, following an attempt by forces loyal to the junta to locate a clandestine radio station, which had allegedly been established by supporters of Kabbah. At the end of July continuing discussions between the ECOWAS committee and AFRC representatives in Abidjan were abandoned, after Koroma insisted that he retain power for a tenure of four years, and refused to restore the constitution and to end the ban on political activity. It was reported that the minister of defence in the AFRC cabinet, who had headed the delegation, had subsequently defected in Abidjan. Later in August former members of the RUF (which had been reconstituted as a government security force, known as the People's Army) clashed with civilians, after suppressing a protest against the coup. At the end of that month, in response to the failure of the negotiations, an ECOWAS conference, which was convened at Abuja, Nigeria, formally agreed to increase sanctions against Sierra Leone, with the aim of obliging the AFRC to relinquish power; however, the conference rejected demands by Kabbah, which were supported by the Nigerian government, for military intervention to reinstate his administation.

CIVIL CONFLICT AND REGIONAL CONCERNS

Following the outbreak of civil conflict in Liberia in December 1989 (see Recent History of Liberia), an estimated 125,000 Liberians took refuge in Sierra Leone. Some 500 Sierra Leonean troops joined ECOMOG, which was dispatched to Liberia in August 1990. In November 1990 Charles Taylor, the leader of the principal Liberian faction, the National Patriotic Front of Liberia (NPFL), threatened to attack the international airport at Lungi, north of Freetown, which was used as a base for ECOMOG offensives against rebel strongholds. In March 1991 repeated border incursions by Liberian rebels, reported to be members of the NPFL, resulted in the deaths of several Sierra Leoneans. The Sierra Leone government subsequently deployed 2,150 troops on the Liberian border, and, in early April, attacked rebel bases in Liberian territory. The government alleged that the rebel offensive had been instigated by Charles Taylor, in an attempt to force Sierra Leone's withdrawal from ECOMOG, and also accused the government of Burkina Faso of assisting the rebels. Although the NPFL denied involvement, it was reported that members of a Sierra Leonean guerrilla movement, known as the Revolutionary United Front (RUF), led by Foday Sankoh, had joined forces with the NPFL in attacks against government army positions. In mid-1991 Sierra Leonean troops, assisted by military units from Nigeria and Guinea, initiated a counter-offensive against the rebels, and succeeded in recapturing several towns in the east and south of the country. Government forces were also assisted by some 1,200 Liberian troops, who had fled to Sierra Leone in September 1990, while a number of other countries, including the United Kingdom and the USA, provided logistical support to Sierra Leone. In September 1991 former supporters of the Liberian president, Samuel Doe, known as the United Liberation Movement of Liberia for Democracy (ULIMO), initiated attacks from Sierra Leone against NPFL forces in north-western Liberia. The Sierra Leone government denied allegations by Taylor that Sierra Leonean troops were involved in the offensive. In October clashes between ULIMO and the NPFL continued in the Mano River Bridge area on the border with Liberia. In December Momoh claimed that, contrary to the terms of a peace agreement, which had been signed between the Liberian interim government and the NPFL at the end of October (see Recent History of Liberia), the NPFL had continued its offensive in Sierra Leone; it was reported that the NPFL had regained control of several villages near the border with Liberia.

In January 1992 discussions took place in the Liberian capital, Monrovia, under the auspices of ECOWAS, between members of the Sierra Leone government and leaders of the Liberian factions, in an attempt to resolve the conflict. In May ECOMOG began to establish units along the border between Sierra Leone and Liberia, in accordance with the terms of the October peace agreement; however, the deployment of troops was impeded by renewed ULIMO forays into Liberia. In the same month the RUF (which was reported to have gained control of territory in the south of the country) rejected appeals by the government to end the civil conflict, and demanded that all foreign troops be withdrawn from Sierra Leone as a precondition to the cessation of hostilities. In June Sankoh rejected Strasser's offer of an amnesty for members of the RUF. In August government forces, with the assistance of Guinean troops, launched an offensive against rebel positions near the border with Liberia and succeeded in recapturing a number of villages; in subsequent months, however, territorial gains on both sides were constantly reversed. In early 1993 the RUF became militarily disadvantaged by the reduction of logistical support from the NPFL, after ULIMO gained control of the greater part of western Liberia (see chapter on Liberia); by April it was reported that only Kailahun District in the extreme east of Sierra Leone, near the border with Liberia, and Pujehun District in the south of the country remained under the control of rebel forces. Later that year government forces advanced within Kailahun District, regaining control of the significant diamond-mining town of Koindu, 250 km east of Freetown, in November. In January 1994 the government claimed that it had regained control of further rebel bases in Pujehun District and the town of Kenema near the border with Liberia. Later that year fighting in the south and east of Sierra Leone intensified, and in April it was reported that the RUF, which had been joined by disaffected members of the armed forces, had initiated attacks in the north of the country. (In addition, it was reported that another rebel movement, the National Front for the Restoration of Democracy, had launched attacks from Guinea.)

In early May 1994 government troops destroyed a major rebel base in the Northern Province. In July Israeli-trained government units assisted in the recapture of two important towns, Mongeri and Matotoka, in eastern Sierra Leone, following a military co-operation agreement between the governments of Sierra Leone and Israel. In the same month Strasser announced that a national war council would be established in which the paramount chiefs would be expected to play a significant role in resolving the civil conflict. During July and August government troops initated offensives against rebel bases in the region of Kenema, following reports that the RUF were exploiting diamond reserves in the area in order to finance their activities.

Later in 1994 reports emerged of an increase in insurgent activity, with widespread looting and killing by unidentified armed groups. In October the government announced that a newly-established organization, the Sierra Leonean Initiative for Peace, had assisted the RUF in military operations against government forces. In early November the RUF seized two British members of a voluntary relief organization, following an attack against the northern town of Kabala. Strasser subsequently renewed his offer of negotiations; however, the RUF rejected the conditions stipulated by the government, which included the declaration of an immediate cease-fire and the release of the two British prisoners. The RUF leadership insisted that the United Kingdom suspend military assistance to the Strasser regime as a precondition to the release of the two hostages, and further demanded that the British authorities recognize the RUF as a political organization and provide it with armaments and medical supplies. The British government denied claims by the RUF that it was supplying armaments to the Strasser regime.

In January 1995 the RUF gained control of the mining installations owned by the Sierra Leone Ore and Metal Co (SIEROMCO) and Sierra Rutile Ltd, and seized a number of employees of the two enterprises, including eight foreign nationals. Later in January seven Roman Catholic nuns (who were Italian and Brazilian nationals), together with a number of Sierra Leonean citizens, were abducted, following an attack by the RUF against the north-western town of Kambia. In the same month the RUF threatened to kill the British hostages if the Sierra Leonean authorities executed an officer, who had been convicted by military tribunal of collaborating with the rebels. In early February Sankoh indicated that the RUF was prepared to negotiate with the government, and invited the International Committee of the Red Cross (ICRC) to mediate in the discussions. Later that month, however, the RUF rejected appeals by the UN and the OAU that peace negotiations be initiated, and demanded that all foreign troops assisting the government be withdrawn as a precondition to discussions. In mid-February government forces (which had succeeded in recapturing the Sierra Rutile mining installations) launched an offensive against a principal rebel base in the Kangari region, east of Freetown. Meanwhile, continued atrocities perpetrated against civilians were increasingly attributed to 'sobels', disaffected members of the armed forces who engaged in acts of looting, banditry and indiscriminate killing. By mid-February some 900,000 civilians had been displaced as a result of the increase in the civil conflict, of which about 185,000 had fled to Guinea, 90,000 to Liberia and some 500,000 had settled around the capital.

In February 1995 the Sierra Leone government (which had ordered the total mobilization of the armed forces to repulse rebel attacks) engaged 58 Gurkha mercenaries, who had previously served in the British army, prompting further concern regarding the safety of the British hostages in Sierra Leone. In March government forces regained control of the mining installations owned by SIEROMCO and the principal town of Moyamba, 100 km south-east of Freetown (which had been captured by the RUF earlier that month). Later that month the rebels released the seven nuns who had been abducted in January. Despite the successful counter-offensives by government forces, by April it was reported that the RUF had advanced towards Freetown and had initiated a series of attacks against towns in the vicinity (including Songo, which was situated only 35 km east of Freetown), apparently prior to besieging the capital. The government of Guinea announced that it was to provide additional troops to assist government operations against the RUF. Later in April the 10 remaining foreign nationals who had been seized by the RUF, together with six Sierra Leoneans, were released to the ICRC. (It was reported, however, that the rebels continued to hold a number of Sierra Leonean civilians as hostages.) At the end of April the RUF rejected an unconditional offer by Strasser to initiate peace negotiations.

In May 1995 government forces initiated a number of counter-attacks, and succeeded in recapturing Songo. The governments of Guinea and Nigeria dispatched additional troops to Sierra Leone, while it was reported that mercenaries recruited from South Africa were assisting the authorities with military training and logistics. Later in May Strasser requested that ECOWAS mediate in negotiations between the RUF and the government; however, the RUF rejected the initiative and reiterated its demands that all foreign troops leave the country as a precondition to negotiations. By the end of June government forces had regained control of diamond-mining areas in the eastern Kono District, and part of Bo District, in a successful counter-offensive which was generally attributed to the assistance of the mercenaries. In early September the RUF requested that civilian groups mediate in discussions between the rebel movement and the government; this proposal was subsequently abandoned, however, and large numbers of civilians were killed in further RUF offensives against towns in Bo District (which were recaptured by government forces in early October). Sankoh indicated that humanitarian organizations would be prevented from operating in territory controlled by the RUF, while increasing reports of massacres and other violations of human rights perpetrated by the rebels against the civilian population emerged. In November the RUF regained control of Kailahun, and a further 10 towns in Moyamba District. In December an OAU mission conducted negotiations with RUF representatives in Abidjan, Côte d'Ivoire.

Following the replacement of Strasser by Bio at the head of a new military administration in January 1996 (see above), the RUF withdrew its earlier preconditions to negotiations. The Ivorian head of state subsequently offered to mediate in discussions, and RUF and government delegations met for the first time in February, in Abidjan. Nevertheless, in response to the refusal of Bio to accede to the RUF's request for a postponement of multi-party elections pending a peace agreement, the rebels abandoned a cease-fire in early February and subsequently launched a series of attacks in various parts of the country, killing large numbers of civilians, in an apparent attempt to undermine the electoral process. After the elections took place, however, the government announced in March that the RUF had agreed to a cease-fire; at a meeting between Sankoh and Bio in Yamoussoukro later that month, the RUF agreed to observe the cease-fire for a period of two months and to continue negotiations with the newly-elected civilian government. Following discussions between Sankoh and the new president, Ahmed Kabbah, which took place in April, the government and RUF reaffirmed their commitment to a permanent cessation of hostilities, and announced the establishment of three joint committees, which would consider issues regarding the demobilization of rebel forces. However, Sankoh continued to refuse to recognize the legitimacy of the new government, and demanded that a transitional administration be installed pending further elections. In the same month the RUF released some 250 civilian hostages. At continuing negotiations in May, agreement was reached on a number of issues, although the RUF demanded that the mercenaries be withdrawn from the country as a precondition to the demobilization of its forces. Despite the official cease-fire, sporadic attacks by the RUF were subsequently reported. Additional clashes occurred later that year between government forces and the Kamajors (traditional fighters reconstituted as an auxiliary defence force), who had proved highly successful in repelling rebel attacks, apparently prompting resentment from members of the armed forces. At further discussions between the government and the rebel leadership in July, Sankoh demanded that members of the RUF be allocated government posts as a precondition to the cessation of hostilities.

In November 1996 Kabbah demanded that the RUF relinquish armaments within a period of two weeks, threatening that government forces would resume military operations. At the end of that month Kabbah and Sankoh signed a peace agreement in Abidjan, whereby RUF forces were to be demobilized and the movement was to be reconstituted as a political organization (although members were not to be granted ministerial portfolios), while all foreign troops were to be withdrawn from the country and replaced with foreign observers. A national commission for the consolidation of peace was subsequently established to monitor the peace settlement. By February 1997 all foreign mercenaries had left Sierra Leone in accordance with the agreement, while the repatriation of Sierra Leonean refugees from Liberia had commenced. However, at the end of that month (when the implementation of the peace agreement was scheduled for completion) it was reported that members of the RUF had repeatedly violated the peace agreement and had failed to report to designated centres for disarmament. In March members of the political wing of the RUF issued a declaration that Sankoh had been removed as leader of the organization, owing to his opposition to the peace process; Sankoh was accused of provoking further unrest and failing to attend scheduled discussions with UN officials and members of the national commission for the consolidation of peace regarding the implementation of the peace accord. Later that month, however, RUF forces loyal to Sankoh kidnapped members of the movement who had supported his replacement, together with the Sierra Leonean ambassador to Guinea; the faction issued demands for the release of Sankoh, who had been detained in Nigeria earlier that month (being reportedly in possession of armaments). In May Sankoh (who remained in Nigeria) announced his support for a military coup which ousted the civilian government (see above). A makeshift alliance between the RUF and the new military authorities was established, and the RUF was subsequently reconstituted as a security force, known as the People's Army.

Economy

LINDA VAN BUREN

Sierra Leone's economy was poorly developed, even prior to the civil conflict of the 1990s. Gross national product (GNP) per caput amounted to only US $140 in 1995, according to estimates by the World Bank. In 1996 the UN Development Programme (UNDP) ranked Sierra Leone as one of the five poorest countries in the world. The lack of progress in infrastructural development has rendered large areas of the country untouched by monetization or by the valorization of formal trade. A majority of the population survive by subsistence agriculture and by informal trading activities, which, however, suffered much disruption owing to the civil conflict. Poor implementation of economic policies has meant that modernization projects have failed, while political instability, the associated activities of rebel groups, and economic isolation after the coup in May 1997 have caused severe disruption as much to the traditional economy as to the few high-value mining operations that provide earnings of foreign exchange. In 1994 the estimated gross domestic product (GDP) was $843m., of which agriculture contributed 47%, services 35% and industry only 18%. For many years the modern economy has been affected by high rates of inflation, which averaged 85.7% annually during 1985–92, and 25.1% per year in 1993–95. During 1985–94, it was estimated, GNP per head declined, in real terms, at an average annual rate of 1.9%. In 1995, according to the IMF, Sierra Leone's GDP declined by an estimated 10%, to about $760m. (following an increase of 0.3% in 1993 and 3.5% in 1994).

The economy became export-orientated early in the colonial period, when emphasis was placed on the production of primary commodities for overseas industrial markets which were also the principal suppliers of the country's import requirements. Favourable terms of trade in the 1950s and an expansion in the diamond industry, resulted in a rapid increase in incomes, allowing imports and government expenditure to rise sharply. Rising government expenditure, together with slow export and revenue growth in the early 1960s, led to a financial crisis, which was exacerbated in the mid-1960s by an overambitious programme of investment in plantations and oil palm mills by the Sierra Leone Produce Marketing Board (SLPMB), the sole exporter of the country's crops.

The increase, in the 1970s, of international petroleum prices, in conjunction with Sierra Leone's total dependence on fuel imports, intensified the country's economic problems. During the 1980s there was a high rate of inflation, an acute shortage of foreign exchange, and heavy external debt, while the country's natural mineral resources remained underutilized. Official revenue from exports (particularly diamonds) was adversely affected by smuggling, which was encouraged by governmental policy on price controls and the exchange rate. In 1986 the government implemented an economic reform programme, based on IMF recommendations, which included the introduction of a 'floating' exchange rate, the elimination of government subsidies on rice and petroleum, the liberalization of trade, and increases in producer prices with the aim of encouraging self-sufficiency in rice and other foods. In 1988, however, the IMF withdrew its support for the programme, declaring Sierra Leone ineligible for assistance until arrears in repayments were received. In early 1989 the government announced a further series of economic measures, which aimed to increase revenue from the mining sector and to reorganize loss-making state-owned companies. In December 1989 the government adopted a three-year structural adjustment programme, which was approved by the IMF. The implementation of the programme was, however, postponed, owing to the IMF's concern at the government's continued failure to reduce expenditure or to control debt arrears.

Conditions of internal unrest since 1991 have impeded government efforts to achieve economic stability, although the regime that assumed power in April 1992 agreed to implement the final stage in the IMF-endorsed economic programme, which aimed to increase monetary controls, to develop a foreign exchange market and to improve the management of the country's natural resources. The government also aimed to continue the implementation of structural reforms, including the reduction of civil service staff and privatization. Under an agreement with the IMF, Sierra Leone was able to accumulate 'rights' through its progress during the economic programme, which would then be used as the first disbursement of debt arrears under a successive IMF-supported structural adjustment programme. In March 1994 Sierra Leone became eligible to receive new credits from the IMF (see below). An extensive privatization programme, involving 19 enterprises (including the Sierra Leone Petroleum Refining Co), was initiated in that month; it was announced that a certain percentage of shares would be reserved for Sierra Leone citizens, while the state would also place shares on the international market. The civil war, which had affected mainly the southern and eastern regions of the country, escalated in early 1995, forcing the closure of the bauxite and rutile mining operations which formed the principal sources of official export earnings. Major long-term foreign investors announced that they were to withdraw from the country. With the disruption of nearly all export activity, Sierra Leone become increasingly dependent on the small amounts of foreign assistance that were available from the International Development Association (IDA) and the European Union (EU), as well as on emergency humanitarian aid. Following the coup on 25 May 1997, the UN World Food Programme commenced the limited distribution of emergency food aid in June.

AGRICULTURE AND FISHING

Sierra Leone's economy is predominantly agricultural; in 1995 this sector accounted for 66.8% of the working population. Some 70 different crops are generally cultivated in the country, but only a few (mainly coffee, cocoa, palm kernels and piassava, a fibre crop) are exported, and these are produced by less than 10% of the country's farmers. Prior to the civil conflict, about three-quarters of farmers were engaged in the cultivation of the staple food crop, rice, but production was insufficient to satisfy domestic demand, and the shortfalls were offset by imports (accounting for about 25% of annual consumption in recent years). The harvest of paddy rice declined from 405,000 metric tons in 1994 to 284,000 tons in 1995. Yields remained fairly constant, however, at 1,233 kg per ha in 1995; the lower output of rice resulted from the disruption caused by the civil war, which reduced the surface area under cultivation from 328,000 ha in 1994 to 230,000 ha in 1995. In 1996 total cereal production was estimated at 38,000 metric tons (of which rice constituted 85%). The government opened the rice import trade to the private sector in 1989, with demand determining selling prices (except for the official subsidy on supply to the security forces). However, the ultimate success of moves towards privatization depended crucially on the response of investors to the new opportunities being provided, as well as the prevailing political and economic environment. Other cereal crops declined less dramatically: output of millet fell from 26,000 tons in 1994 to 24,000 tons in 1995, while that of sorghum fell from 24,000 tons in 1994 to 22,000 tons in 1995. However, the 1995 output of plantains, amounting to 27,860 tons, was about the same as that of the previous year. Groundnut production declined slightly, from 40,000 tons in 1994 to 36,000 tons in 1995, while the coffee crop declined from 28,000 tons of green coffee in 1994 to 25,000 tons in 1995. Output of cocoa beans remained constant at 10,000 tons per year in both 1994 and 1995. Production of palm kernels declined from 32,000 tons in 1994 to 29,000 tons in 1995, while output of palm oil dropped from 50,264 tons to 45,238 tons.

With funds provided by the IDA, Sierra Leone introduced Integrated Agricultural Development Projects (IADP) in 1972. These projects, which were designed to revolutionize agriculture in Sierra Leone, combined the provision of simple social and infrastructural amenities, such as water wells and feeder roads, with output-augmenting strategies, mainly in the form of credit facilities, seed distribution, and technical advice. In the early 1990s, however, the civil insurgency (see Recent History) adversely affected agricultural exports (which accounted for 8% of total export earnings in 1993).

Since 1993, Sierra Leone's fishing sector, particularly marine fisheries, has been seriously affected by the civil war. In 1995 the total catch was 62,313 metric tons. Overfishing by foreign vessels within Sierra Leone's coastal waters (including the continental shelf of some 25,000 sq km) is believed to have depleted the available stocks of sardinellas and other common species. It was estimated that illegal fishing deprived the government of some US $30m. per year in revenue.

MINING

Mining, which began in Sierra Leone in the 1930s, is the second most important commodity-producing sector and main source of foreign exchange. In 1994 the mining sector contributed 16% of GDP and 84% of export earnings. Diamonds, for many years the principal export commodity of Sierra Leone, attract widespread illicit trafficking, despite large expenditures on security. Alluvial diamond mining was carried out by numerous small prospectors, while larger-scale mining operations were conducted by the Sierra Leone Selection Trust (SLST), in which the government-controlled National Diamond Mining Co (NDMC, also known as DIMINCO) held a majority share. This enterprise, however, was beset by management, financial and technical problems and by 1992 its production, at 600,000 carats, made only a negligible contribution to foreign exchange receipts. By 1995, when official diamond output was only 300,000 carats, the NDMC had ceased its operations. The marketing of Sierra Leone diamonds has subsequently been conducted by the Government Gold and Diamond Office (GGDO). Legal exports of diamonds declined from 2m. carats in 1970 to 395,000 carats in 1980, and to 132,000 carats in 1989, recovering to 344,000 carats in 1992, before falling to 200,000 carats in 1993. Official diamond output recovered to 400,000 carats in 1994, before declining once again, to 300,000 carats in 1995 and 200,000 carats in 1996. In 1996 official exports of diamonds amounted to 31,929 carats, with a value of US $3.3m. Following the coup of May 1997, fighting continued in the region of the Kono diamond-mining areas, and parts of Kono district were reported to have been occupied by forces opposed to the new military junta in June. In the same month Rex Diamond Mining Corpn of South Africa announced its withdrawal from the country, pending the restoration of civil order. In 1995 mercenaries were recruited via a private South African concern to recapture the Kono diamond-mining areas held by RUF rebels, and by August the province had been secured. (The mercenaries left the country in February 1997.) The most recent agreement regarding the kimberlite project was reached with a South African-linked company, Branch Energy, which would control 60%, with 30% going to the government and 10% to the public. The project was expected to absorb many former employees of the NDMC. However, a legal dispute occurred in 1995 over the leases for the kimberlite pipes at Koindu, previously held by Sunshine Mining until the government assigned the rights to Branch Mining: Sunshine was reported in 1995 to be taking legal action to recover these rights. Output from the Koindu pipe was projected at 250,000 carats per year, with reserves estimated at 2.4m. carats.

In response to the uncertainties in the organization of production and marketing of Sierra Leone diamonds, operators have increasingly turned to the 'black market'. In early 1994, in an effort to reduce illicit trade, the government offered informants rewards of up to 40% of the value of anything recovered. This offer resulted in the recovery in June of that year of a particularly large (172-carat) diamond, which obtained US $2.8m. for the government from its sale by public auction. In August the government granted a South African enterprise, De Beers Consolidated Mines Ltd, a concession to explore 15,800 sq km off the coast of Sierra Leone. In May 1996 illicit exports of diamonds were estimated to cost $200m. per year.

Sierra Leone's second most important mineral export was formerly iron ore, which was mined by the foreign-owned Sierra Leone Development Co (DELCO). In the early 1970s, when the mine's ore output averaged 2m. metric tons annually, the company experienced serious technical difficulties and a depressed market for iron ore, and operations were suspended during 1975–81. In 1981 the government-owned Marampa Iron Ore Co was formed, with the help of an Austrian loan and with management provided by Austro-Mineral. Exports resumed in 1983, but the new company encountered administrative, technical and financial difficulties, and it suspended its operations in October 1985. An operation to recover scrap metal from the mine began in 1988; efforts were made to attract new investors to reopen the mine, whose ore deposits have an iron content of 69%.

The Sierra Leone Ore and Metal Co (SIEROMCO), a subsidiary of Alusuisse of Switzerland, began mining bauxite at Mokanji in 1964. Exports averaged 631,000 tons per year in 1972–79 but declined to 576,000 tons in 1983. Export levels increased sharply to an annual average of 1.7m. tons in 1984–88 but declined to 1.6m. tons in 1989 and to 1.3m. tons in 1992. The mine site was overrun by RUF forces in January 1995, forcing SIEROMCO to suspend all operations. Government forces regained control in February, but the company did not resume operations. Looters subsequently inflicted damage estimated at US $30m., and in September 1996 the company announced its withdrawal from the country, owing to the cost that the resumption of operations would involve.

Rutile (titanium dioxide), an essential ingredient of paint pigment, was first exported by Sherbo Minerals in 1967 but in 1971 the company became bankrupt and closed its alluvial mine near Bonthe. The mine was taken over the following year by Sierra Rutile, a US-owned company. Production was resumed in 1980, and exports rose from 21,000 tons in that year to 148,000 tons in 1992. In 1992 a major rehabilitation of rutile production facilities was announced, for which external finance exceeding US $13m. was obtained. Prior to the disruption resulting from the civil war, Sierra Leone was, after Australia, the world's second largest producer of rutile. Australia's Consolidated Rutile bought a 50% interest in Sierra Rutile in 1994, and undertook, in partnership with the US Nord Resources Corporation, to continue expansion of the mining activity and to increase production to 190,000 tons per year by 1996, with investment amounting to $72m. In 1993 rutile provided 57% of Sierra Leone's mineral export earnings, which totalled $108m. In the year to June 1994 rutile production was 144,000 tons, but in January 1995 all production was suspended when RUF forces overran the mining operation. After the rebels were driven out in February, the company took renewed steps to secure the property, but was unable to resume production. In September 1996 Sierra Rutile indicated that the IMF and World Bank had pledged $18m. towards the reopening of the mine, which was projected to cost a total of $80m.

There has been no significant investment in the gold industry, although some corporate interest had been shown in this activity prior to the civil conflict. Gold-mining is principally carried out by petty diggers, and most of the current production is believed to be smuggled out of the country.

Mining policy, under the IMF-supported economic reform measures, aimed to encourage reputable companies to participate in mining and exporting minerals, but progress in this direction has been slow, owing to the magnitude of investment involved, bureaucratic restrictions and other official practices deterring potential investors, and the civil war. In the early 1990s the government revised its agreements with SIEROMCO and Sierra Rutile in a renewed effort to raise the companies' contributions to government revenue. A new mining policy, introduced in 1994, involved the imposition of a 2.5% royalty on precious mineral exports and a range of licence fees related to the size of mining operations. There was provision for foreign nationals to form companies, and it was proposed that there would be assistance in the provision of security of tenure for artisanal mining activity.

MANUFACTURING, TRADE AND TRANSPORT

With the introduction in 1960 of the Development Ordinance, Sierra Leone adopted a policy of industrial development, using an import-substitution strategy. Under the Ordinance, the government extended generous tax incentives, which included duty-free importation of equipment and raw materials and tax 'holidays', and established an industrial estate at Wellington, near Freetown, with basic services and an employment exchange. At first the prospects for this sector were good, as the country began to produce alcoholic and non-alcoholic beverages, cigarettes and several other goods which had been principal imports. By the late 1970s, however, the manufacturing sector had suffered as a result of the extensive shortages of foreign exchange, electricity and water supplies, poor telecommunications and rising costs of imported raw materials. The sector now comprises mainly palm oil production and other agro-based industries, textiles and furniture-making, and in 1994 accounted for only 2% of GDP.

High priority has been accorded to road construction, especially after the closure in 1971 of the 292-km, narrow-gauge government railway. The country had 11,674 km of roads in 1995, including 1,390 km of main roads and 1,630 km of secondary roads; however, only about 1,284 km of the network was paved and most of the network is in a poor state of repair. Inland waterways and coastal shipping are important features of internal transport. There are almost 800 km of recognized launch routes, including the coastal routes from Freetown northward to the areas served by the Great and Little Scarcies rivers and southward to the important seaport of Bonthe. The services and facilities of the international airport at Lungi, north of Freetown, were improved, with financial assistance from the UNDP. In 1982 the government formed a national airline, Sierra Leone Airlines (subsequently renamed Sierra National Airlines), but the enterprise proved to be unprofitable, and operations had to be suspended in 1987. Limited services, including a weekly flight from Freetown to Paris, were restored in May 1990. Services have, for financial and other reasons, remained subject to periods of interruption.

EXTERNAL TRADE AND PAYMENTS

Sierra Leone is heavily dependent on foreign trade. In 1994 Sierra Leone recorded a trade deficit of US $72.7m., and there was a deficit of $89.1m. on the current account of the balance of payments. In 1994 the principal source of imports was the USA, providing 42.7% of the total; other major suppliers were the Netherlands and the United Kingdom. The USA was also the principal market for exports (taking 44.8% of the total); other significant purchasers were the United Kingdom and Belgium. The principal exports in 1994 were rutile, diamonds and bauxite; however, the civil conflict severely affected exports, with a complete suspension of rutile and bauxite production in early 1995.

In current prices, recorded exports increased from an annual average of Le 126m. in the 1970s to Le 2,940m. in the 1980s and to an estimated Le 14,878m. in 1990. Rebel activity in the eastern and southern parts of the country, where the bulk of the country's exports are produced, resulted in the collapse of the export sector, with exports in 1994 earning only Le 67,930m. Imports increased from an annual average of Le 183m. in the 1970s to Le 668m. in 1980–86 and approximately Le 7,160m. in 1987–89; imports were Le 87,973m. in 1994. Owing to extensive smuggling of diamonds, the contribution of minerals to total exports declined from 77.2% in 1981 to 69% in 1989, rising to 85% in 1990 (rutile 52%, bauxite 18%, diamonds 9%) and increasing considerably to 93% in 1992 (reflecting the disruption of cocoa and coffee farming, owing to guerrilla activity in producing areas), before falling to 84% in 1994 (rutile 48%, diamonds 22%, bauxite 14%). The contribution of agricultural commodities to exports increased from 21% in 1981 to 28% in 1984 but declined to 21% in 1989, 10% in 1990 (coffee 5%, cocoa 4%), 6%

in 1992 (coffee 2%, cocoa 3%), and to 5% in 1994 (coffee 2%, cocoa 3%).

Imports have traditionally been dominated by manufactured goods. However, Sierra Leone has become more dependent on imports of food (mainly rice), which in 1990–92 accounted for one-third of total imports; in the same period manufactures accounted for 35%, and mineral fuels and lubricants 18%. The residue consisted of semi-processed materials, beverages and chemicals. In 1994 machinery and transport equipment accounted for 58% of total imports, while food and live animals represented 17%, basic manufactures 6%, chemicals 6%, and mineral fuels and lubricants 4%.

Unfavourable terms of trade since the early 1970s, in conjunction with the dramatic increases in crude oil prices in the 1970s, led to rising import costs. As a result, large deficits on the current account of the balance of payments were incurred: Le 45m. in 1979/80 (4.2% of GDP), Le 140m. in 1981/82 (9.1% of GDP), Le 220m. in 1983/84 (7.5% of GDP), and Le 8,400m. in 1990/91 (6% of GDP). Owing to the shortage of foreign exchange, the government, in the early 1990s, mortgaged the future export earnings of the SLPMB, in order to finance the country's essential imports, especially of rice and petroleum, and (before the exchange rate was 'floated' in April 1990) bought foreign currencies at rates in excess of its own official rates. The ratio of scheduled external debt-servicing charges to exports of goods and services was 18% in 1977/78, 26% in 1980/81 and 48% in 1990/91. As a result of its protracted foreign exchange crisis (see below), Sierra Leone has a poor record of servicing its foreign debt and has had little access to loans at concessionary rates. External debt totalled US $1,226m. at the end of 1995, of which $968m. was long-term public debt. In that year the cost of debt-servicing was equivalent to 78.5% of the total value of exports of goods and services.

PUBLIC FINANCE

Recurrent revenue increased from Le 5,500m. (about $11m.) in 1989/90 to Le 57,200m. (officially about US $104m.) in 1992/93, the bulk of which was derived from indirect taxes, accounting for approximately 63% of the total in 1960/61–1988/89 (import duties 37%, excise duties 17%, export duties 5%). During the same period, direct taxes contributed 26% of recurrent revenue (companies 16%, personal 10%), while the remainder was derived from non-tax sources, mainly in the form of licences and fees. The provisional recurrent revenue figure of Le 7,984m. for 1989/90 shows a sharp increase in the contribution of indirect tax to 74%, almost certainly reflecting the expanding informal sector, as well as the weakness of the nationalized diamond-mining and iron-ore operations. The 1994/95 budget projected revenue from tax and non-tax sources at Le 81,800m.

Total expenditure increased from Le 890.6m. in 1985/86 (current 66%; development 29%; unallocable 5%) to Le 32,300m. in 1990/91 (current 53%; development 39%; unallocable 8%). Recurrent expenditure for 1992/93 was expected to total Le 44,300m. In the period 1960/61–1988/89, about 28% of the budget was allocated to general services (administration 9%, law and order 7%, defence 12%), 25% to economic services (agriculture 4%, infrastructure 21%), 27% to social services (education 20%, health and social welfare 7%) and 20% to transfers (debt service 10%, personal 2%, subsidies 8%). The 1994/95 budget envisaged expenditure of Le 110,800m., and placed emphasis on improvements in social sectors, in addition to measures to stimulate agriculture, fisheries and mining.

Successive government budgets have been in almost continuous deficit during the last three decades; the deficit on a commitment basis increased from 2.5% of GDP in 1976/77 to 12.7% in 1979, and to 16.8% in 1986/87. It declined to an estimated 7.8% in 1989/90, but increased again to 18% in 1991/92, when the actual deficit (including grants) was Le 26,000m. as opposed to a planned deficit of Le 14,000m. The deficit for 1992/93 was expected to represent 7.4% of GDP. The projected deficit for 1994/95 of Le 29,000m. was expected to be equivalent to 5.2% of GDP, compared with a deficit of about 6.1% of GDP in 1993/94, but the actual deficit was equivalent to 7.3%. In 1995/96 the overall budget deficit was estimated at Le 55,187m., equivalent to 7.8% of GDP. The ratio of government expenditure to GDP increased from 28.9% in 1978/79 to 31.4% in 1980/81, and to 32% in 1985/86 but declined to an estimated 18% in 1989/90, a decrease which reflects the increasing difficulty of financing the deficit, as well as growing pressure from multilateral creditors for the adoption of more effective expenditure control measures. The ratio of central government revenue to GDP was 16.2% in 1978/79, 17.7% in 1980/81, 5.8% in 1985/86 and 6.9% in 1989/90. It increased sharply to an estimated 12.8% in 1990/91. Development expenditure declined from 39% of the total in 1981/82 to 14% in 1987/88, and to an estimated 4% in 1989/90. Total public debt was equivalent to 69% of GDP in 1980/81, 127% in 1990/91 and 187.3% in 1994/95.

Negotiations between the government and multilateral donors resulted in the adoption, in 1986, of a structural adjustment programme, under which the government agreed, among other things, to float the exchange rate, remove all subsidies on rice and petroleum, liberalize trade, increase producer prices and repay $3m. in arrears to the IMF. The IMF promised financial support of SDR 50.36m., comprising a stand-by arrangement for the following 12 months of SDR 23.16m., and a structural adjustment facility, available over the following three years, totalling SDR 27.2m. Meanwhile, the 'Paris Club' of Western creditor governments agreed, in principle, to reschedule Sierra Leone's immediate debt obligations. The 1986 programme ended prematurely when the IMF withdrew its financial support in 1988, stating that the government had not met the agreed conditions. In the same year, Sierrra Leone was declared ineligible to use IMF resources and was under threat of suspension from membership of the Fund for failing to service its foreign debt and to implement IMF-approved economic reforms.

In December 1989 the government adopted an IMF-approved programme of economic reform measures, leading to a three-year IMF-monitored programme covering the period 1990/91 to 1992/93. In conjunction with these measures, import and export licensing was abolished for all commodities in December 1989; the leone was devalued by 85% in January 1990, from Le 65 = US $1 to Le 120 = US $1; and in April 1990 the currency was 'floated', with the result that it depreciated rapidly. Revenue measures, introduced in December 1989, included sharp increases in excise duties on tobacco, beer, petroleum products and a new tax (in the form of an excise duty) on petroleum products. A 'freeze' was imposed on civil service recruitment (except for essential services) in order to limit expenditure; the exercise of deleting the names of non-existent or 'ghost' workers from the payroll, initiated in July 1988, was pursued more vigorously, while a new retrenchment exercise, designed to reduce civil service employment levels (estimated at some 75,000) by about 30% before the end of 1992/93, was introduced in early 1991. All official subsidies were terminated, except those on rice for the security forces (which were considerably reduced in January 1997). In the financial sector, interest rates on treasury bills and on commercial bank loans were raised substantially in an attempt to attract savers. However, the high rate of inflation only continued to deter saving, with the price of 50kg of rice increasing from Le 8,000 in June 1994 to Le 15,000 in October 1995 (in Freetown). Although the government implemented most of the measures foreseen in this programme of economic reforms, the introduction of the proposed 1992/93 programme was delayed until mid-April 1992 by the IMF's concern at the government's continued inability to control expenditure or address the problem of overdue arrears on its foreign debt.

In May 1992 the IMF reiterated its willingness to implement the 1992/93 programme in co-operation with the new military government, which declared its intention of strengthening fiscal discipline in the public sector, as well as imposing tighter open-market monetary controls and maximising revenue collection. At the outset of the IMF-supervised programme, Sierra Leone's outstanding financial obligations to the Fund totalled the equivalent of SDR 87.8m. (about US $120m.), compared with its existing quota of SDR 57.9m. ($79m.). The 1992/93 Rights Accumulation Programme (RAP) permitted Sierra Leone to accumulate IMF repayment 'credits' up to a maximum of its IMF liabilities during the period to end-February 1994. Under this programme, Sierra Leone paid outstanding arrears to the IMF, with the assistance of loans from France, Norway and the USA. In April 1996 the Paris Club of official creditors agreed to a rescheduling of the country's foreign debt repayments under concessionary terms; debt relief amounted to 67%.

At the end of March 1994 the IMF announced the resumption of credit to Sierra Leone, and approved loans totalling SDR 116m. (equivalent to about US $163m.), following the payment of the country's outstanding debt arrears, which was facilitated by loans from France, Norway and the USA. Of the total credit, SDR 88.8m. was to be provided under a three-year enhanced structural adjustment facility, and a further SDR 27m. under a one-year structural adjustment facility, which was to support the government's economic and financial reform programme for 1994/96. Contrary to the recommendations of a joint delegation of the World Bank and the IMF, however, the budget for 1994/95 awarded a salary increase of 20% to public sector workers. Performance during the 1994/95 fiscal year again fell short of expectations, with the budget deficit increasing to 7.3% of GDP. The minister of finance blamed the civil war for the loss of export revenue and damage to agricultural production. The minister announced a short-term budget for the remainder of 1995 in which income and expenditure were to be balanced at Le 75,300m. The fiscal year was henceforth to coincide with the calendar year. The only other foreign assistance credits to be announced in 1994/95 were a facility of $36m. from the IDA for the rehabilitation of the water supply and sewerage networks in Freetown and another facility of $27.5m. from the EU towards the rehabilitation of the road network in the capital. A donors' conference, which was convened in Geneva, Switzerland, in September 1996, pledged $212m. towards the first part of a $1,000m. programme of recovery measures; Canada, France, Germany, Italy, India and Japan pledged loans.

ECONOMIC PROSPECTS

The protracted civil conflict throughout the 1990s resulted in the cumulative deterioration of the economy. Agricultural activity, both in food and cash crops, was severely reduced, leaving the mining sector to generate essential foreign exchange. In 1995 the two most lucrative mining operations were also suspended; the Sierra Leone Ore and Metal Co ceased bauxite production permanently, while rutile-mining was halted, pending an improvement in the security situation. Only diamond-mining continued, but, although several major deposits were discovered (indicating that Sierra Leone's diamond resources might be of international distinction), the sector was adversely affected by smuggling, rebel attacks and the controversy over South African mercenaries brought in to maintain security in the region. After the mercenaries were forced to leave and the elected government was overthrown, armed conflict to gain control of the diamond fields continued, and international condemnation of the May 1997 coup led to the imposition of an ECOWAS blockade (see Recent History). Even the distribution of emergency food aid to civilians was disrupted by the activities of armed groups, and by lack of co-operation from the ruling junta, which, in July, ordered the Red Cross to halt all operations in Sierra Leone.

Statistical Survey

Source (unless otherwise stated): Central Statistics Office, Tower Hill, Freetown.

Area and Population

AREA, POPULATION AND DENSITY

Area (sq km)	71,740*
Population (census results)†	
8 December 1974	2,735,159
14 December 1985	
Males	1,746,055
Females	1,769,757
Total	3,515,812
Population (UN estimates at mid-year)‡	
1993	4,297,000
1994	4,402,000
1995	4,509,000
Density (per sq km) at mid-1995	62.9

* 27,699 sq miles.

† Excluding adjustment for underenumeration, estimated to have been 10% in 1974. The adjusted total for 1974 (based on a provisional total of 2,729,479 enumerated) is 3,002,426, and that for 1985 is 3,700,000 (estimate).

‡ Source: UN, *World Population Prospects: The 1994 Revision*.

PRINCIPAL TOWNS (population at 1985 census)

Freetown (capital)	384,499	Kenema	52,473
Koindu	82,474	Makeni	49,474
Bo	59,768		

BIRTHS AND DEATHS (UN estimates, annual averages)

	1980–85	1985-90	1990–95
Birth rate (per 1,000)	48.9	49.1	49.1
Death rate (per 1,000)	28.6	27.1	25.2

Expectation of life (UN estimates, years at birth, 1990–95): 39.0 (males 37.5; females 40.6).

Source: UN, *World Population Prospects: The 1994 Revision*.

ECONOMICALLY ACTIVE POPULATION
(sample survey, '000 persons, 1988/89)

	Males	Females	Total
Agriculture, etc.	551.2	673.3	1,224.5
Industry	235.9	98.9	334.8
Services	198.4	223.0	421.4
Total	985.5	995.2	1,980.7

Mid-1995 (estimates in '000): Agriculture, etc. 1,123; Total 1,680 (Source: FAO, *Production Yearbook*).

Agriculture

PRINCIPAL CROPS ('000 metric tons)

	1993	1994	1995
Maize	10	9	8
Millet	21	26	24
Sorghum	21	24	22
Rice (paddy)	486	405	284
Sweet potatoes	14	44	40
Cassava (Manioc)	106	244	219
Taro (Coco yam)	3	3*	3*
Tomatoes*	21*	28	32
Dry broad beans	1	1*	1*
Citrus fruit*	75	75	75
Mangoes	5	5*	5*
Palm kernels	32.9	32.4	29.2
Palm oil	47.0	50.3	45.2
Groundnuts (in shell)	20	40	36
Coconuts	3	3*	3*
Coffee (green)	25	28	25
Cocoa beans	5	12	10*

* FAO estimate(s).

Source: FAO, *Production Yearbook*.

LIVESTOCK ('000 head, year ending September)

	1993	1994*	1995*
Cattle	360	360	360
Pigs*	50	50	50
Sheep	302	302	302
Goats	166	166	166

Poultry (million)*: 6 in 1993; 6 in 1994; 6 in 1995.

* FAO estimates.

Source: FAO, *Production Yearbook*.

LIVESTOCK PRODUCTS (FAO estimates, '000 metric tons)

	1993	1994	1995
Beef and veal	5	5	5
Poultry meat	9	9	9
Other meat	5	6	6
Cows' milk	17	17	17
Poultry eggs	6.9	6.9	6.9

Source: FAO, *Production Yearbook*.

Forestry

ROUNDWOOD REMOVALS ('000 cubic metres, excl. bark)

	1992	1993	1994
Sawlogs, veneer logs and logs for sleepers	—	4	4*
Other industrial wood*†	120	120	120
Fuel wood*	2,978	3,050	3,123
Total	3,098*	3,174	3,247*

* FAO estimate(s).

† Annual output assumed to be unchanged since 1980.

Source: FAO, *Yearbook of Forest Products*.

SAWNWOOD PRODUCTION
('000 cubic metres, incl. railway sleepers)

	1992	1993	1994
Total	9*	5	5*

* FAO estimate.

Source: FAO, *Yearbook of Forest Products*.

Fishing

('000 metric tons, live weight)

	1993	1994	1995
Freshwater fishes	14.0	15.0	15.0
Sardinellas	7.7	7.7	7.7
Bonga shad	22.8	21.8	21.7
Other marine fishes (incl. unspecified)	17.2	17.2	17.4
Crustaceans and molluscs	0.3	0.3	0.3
Total catch	61.0	61.9	62.3

Source: FAO, *Yearbook of Fishery Statistics*.

Mining

('000 metric tons, unless otherwise indicated)

	1992	1993	1994
Bauxite	1,257	1,165	729
Ilmenite	60	64	54
Rutile concentrates	149	150	144
Diamonds ('000 metric carats)	312	157	197*
Salt ('000 bags)	155	360	166

* Shipments.

Industry

SELECTED PRODUCTS
(estimates, '000 metric tons, unless otherwise indicated)

	1992	1993	1994
Beer ('000 hectolitres)	36	n.a.	n.a.
Cigarettes (million)	1,200	n.a.	n.a.
Jet fuels	14	16	16
Motor spirit (petrol)	26	28	28
Kerosene	6	7	7
Distillate fuel oils	65	67	67
Residual fuel oils	51	50	50
Electric energy (million kWh)	230	233	237

Source: mainly UN, *Industrial Commodity Statistics Yearbook*.

Finance

CURRENCY AND EXCHANGE RATES

Monetary Units
100 cents = 1 leone (Le).

Sterling and Dollar Equivalents (31 March 1997)
£1 sterling = 1,345.9 leones;
US $1 = 819.7 leones;
10,000 leones = £7.430 = $12.200.

Average Exchange Rate (leones per US $)
1994 586.74
1995 755.22
1996 920.73

BUDGET (Le million, year ending 30 June)

Revenue*	1993	1994	1995
Tax revenue	51,633	64,907	59,462
Taxes on income, profits and capital gains	13,030	14,900	10,092
Individual taxes	4,108	4,914	4,686
Taxes on corporate income	8,482	9,233	4,842
Taxes on payroll and workforce	116	211	109
Domestic taxes on goods and services	19,646	23,186	23,166
Sales tax	2,285	2,657	2,824
Excise duties	12,463	16,275	15,479
Taxes on international trade and transactions	18,792	26,608	26,083
Import duties	18,792	26,608	25,715
Other taxes	49	2	12
Other current revenue	2,661	2,507	2,281
Entrepreneurial and property income	1,893	655	100
Administrative fees and charges, non-industrial and incidental sales	768	878	881
Total	54,294	67,414	61,743

Expenditure	1993	1994	1995
Current expenditure	63,994	75,538	82,534
Expenditure on goods and services	28,023	35,988	39,426
Wages and salaries	15,145	19,723	22,150
Interest payments	19,652	15,538	12,582
Subsidies and other current transfers	16,319	24,012	30,526
Capital expenditure	25,434	33,465	25,481
Sub-total	89,428	109,003	108,015
Adjustment	–10,733	–4,349	–703
Total	78,695	104,654	107,312

* Excluding grants received (Le million): 7,302 in 1993; 11,117 in 1994; 5,734 in 1995.

CENTRAL BANK RESERVES (US $ million at 31 December)

	1994	1995	1996
IMF special drawing rights	9.0	17.1	7.6
Foreign exchange	31.6	17.5	18.9
Total	40.6	34.6	26.6

Source: IMF, *International Financial Statistics*.

MONEY SUPPLY (Le million at 31 December)

	1994	1995	1996
Currency outside banks	23,604	30,023	36,185
Private sector deposits at central bank	219	417	n.a.
Demand deposits at commercial banks	14,719	19,462	15,616
Total money	38,542	49,902	53,215

Source: IMF, *International Financial Statistics*.

COST OF LIVING
(Consumer Price Index for Freetown; base: 1990 = 100)

	1994	1995	1996
All items	509.2	641.5	790.4

Source: IMF, *International Financial Statistics*.

NATIONAL ACCOUNTS
(Le million at current prices, year ending 30 June)

National Income and Product

	1992/93	1993/94	1994/95*
Compensation of employees	86,503.1	107,650.3	138,658.6
Operating surplus	313,873.8	352,605.6	467,380.1
Domestic factor incomes	400,376.9	460,255.8	606,038.7
Consumption of fixed capital	30,097.2	35,104.2	41,907.3
Gross domestic product (GDP) at factor cost	430,474.1	495,360.0	647,946.1
Indirect taxes, *less* subsidies	36,713.4	48,351.0	62,443.2
GDP in purchasers' values	467,187.5	543,711.0	710,389.3
Factor income received from abroad *Less* Factor income paid abroad	–66,914.8	–70,237.5	–84,216.0
Gross national product (GNP)	400,272.7	473,473.5	626,173.3
Less Consumption of fixed capital	30,097.2	35,104.2	41,907.3
National income in market prices	370,175.5	438,369.3	584,265.9
Other current transfers received from abroad *Less* Other current transfers paid abroad	11,483.0	12,438.6	15,067.8
National disposable income	381,658.5	450,807.9	599,333.7

* Provisional figures.

Expenditure on the Gross Domestic Product

	1992/93	1993/94	1994/95*
Government final consumption expenditure	47,119.0	58,384.0	62,837.0
Private final consumption expenditure	341,641.3	382,913.6	538,422.4
Increase in stocks	–3,947.4	2,548.2	–987.9
Gross fixed capital formation	26,943.0	42,066.4	40,969.6
Total domestic expenditure	411,755.9	485,912.2	641,241.1
Exports of goods and services	154,685.6	167,651.6	203,126.4
Less Imports of goods and services	99,254.0	109,852.7	133,978.2
GDP in purchasers' values	467,187.5	543,711.0	710,389.3

* Provisional figures.

Gross Domestic Product by Economic Activity

	1992/93	1993/94	1994/95*
Agriculture, hunting, forestry and fishing	162,194.6	188,884.1	275,327.5
Mining and quarrying	98,615.8	96,748.8	119,229.2
Manufacturing	39,567.0	47,816.7	61,475.3
Electricity, gas and water	469.8	757.3	2,816.8
Construction	4,655.4	12,544.4	15,788.2
Trade, restaurants and hotels	69,139.9	77,251.0	98,270.1
Transport, storage and communications	37,056.5	50,047.1	61,267.5
Finance, insurance, real estate and business services	15,947.0	17,988.0	14,732.2
Government services	14,500.0	17,884.0	19,844.9
Other community, social and personal services	8,998.3	9,769.0	12,308.9
Sub-total	451,144.3	519,690.4	681,060.6
Import duties	18,994.0	27,410.0	32,942.0
Less Imputed bank service charge	2,950.8	3,389.8	3,612.3
GDP in purchasers' values	467,187.5	543,711.0	710,389.3

* Provisional figures.

BALANCE OF PAYMENTS (US $ million)

	1992	1993	1994
Exports of goods f.o.b.	150.4	118.3	116.0
Imports of goods f.o.b.	–139.0	–187.1	–188.7
Trade balance	11.4	–68.8	–72.7
Exports of services	47.0	58.5	100.2
Imports of services	–62.9	–61.5	–107.6
Balance on goods and services	–4.5	–71.9	–80.1
Other income received	6.8	2.3	1.5
Other income paid	–15.1	–5.6	–57.0
Balance on goods, services and income	–12.8	–75.2	–135.7
Current transfers received	8.2	19.1	47.5
Current transfers paid	–0.8	–1.7	–0.9
Current balance	–5.5	–57.8	–89.1
Capital account (net)	0.1	0.1	0.1
Direct investment from abroad	–5.6	–7.5	–4.2
Other investment assets	–31.2	–14.6	–0.8
Other investment liabilities	18.6	71.2	–21.8
Net errors and omissions	39.8	16.1	56.4
Overall balance	16.2	7.5	–59.5

Source: IMF, *International Financial Statistics*.

External Trade

PRINCIPAL COMMODITIES (Le million)

Imports	1992	1993	1994
Food and live animals	30,347	75,286	31,855
Beverages and tobacco	664	5,169	2,419
Crude materials (inedible) except fuels	1,735	4,356	3,010
Mineral fuels, lubricants, etc.	10,407	6,529	6,776
Animal and vegetable oils and fats	1,898	3,008	1,424
Chemicals	5,328	18,235	10,459
Basic manufactures	21,650	20.003	11,146
Machinery and transport equipment	24,366	63,151	106,395
Miscellaneous manufactured articles	4,722	26,223	8,922
Total (incl. others)	101,672	222,697	183,550

Exports	1992	1993	1994
Coffee	1,351.0	1,301.3	1,549
Cocoa beans	1,053.1	2,115.9	1,704
Palm kernels	6.9	—	—
Bauxite	19,408.3	13,764.5	9,687
Piassava	50.1	49.9	51
Diamonds	15,360.0	11,089.3	15,075
Rutile	32,878.6	32,461.7	32,454
Other items	4,764.4	6,048.3	6,185
Re-exports	161.9	246.2	1,224
Total	75,034.3	67,077.3	67,930

PRINCIPAL TRADING PARTNERS (Le million)

Imports	1992	1993	1994
Belgium	5,828	5,889	4,377
China, People's Repub.	4,986	8,160	4,794
Côte d'Ivoire	1,315	1,762	4,026
France	2,440	14,639	2,525
Germany	8,750	19,564	5,578
Hong Kong	325	7,465	5,536
Indonesia	261	4,377	6,838
Italy	8,896	4,618	2,019
Japan	6,256	6,521	3,715
Netherlands	6,015	40,506	26,050
Pakistan	2,678	1,719	1,626
Switzerland	881	9,647	855
United Kingdom	6,809	43,680	10,453
USA	23,295	19,960	78,288
Total (incl. others)	101,672	222,697	183,550

Exports	1992	1993	1994
Belgium	25,770	54	11,412
Germany	1,060	2,486	1,328
Guinea	1,315	817	1,331
Netherlands	5,307	1,201	2,815
Switzerland	7,546	486	215
United Kingdom	5,567	5,988	11,767
USA	13,832	17,564	30,431
Total (incl. others)	75,034	67,077	67,930

Transport

ROAD TRAFFIC (motor vehicles in use at 31 December)

	1993	1994	1995
Passenger cars	32,415	34,288	20,860
Buses and coaches	1,092	1,103	933
Goods vehicles	10,810	11,201	10,081
Motorcycles	10,198	10,977	9,879

Source: International Road Federation, *World Road Statistics*.

SHIPPING

Merchant Fleet (registered at 31 December)

	1994	1995	1996
Number of vessels	62	57	56
Displacement (gross registered tons)	23,979	23,178	19,361

Source: Lloyd's Register of Shipping, *World Fleet Statistics*.

International Sea-borne Freight Traffic
(estimates, '000 metric tons)

	1991	1992	1993
Goods loaded	1,930	2,190	2,310
Goods unloaded	562	579	589

Source: UN Economic Commission for Africa, *African Statistical Yearbook*.

CIVIL AVIATION (traffic on scheduled services)

	1992	1993
Freight loaded (metric tons)	25.2	18.7
Freight unloaded (metric tons)	375.7	120.5
Passenger arrivals ('000)	45	39
Passenger departures ('000)	50	41

Sources: Bank of Sierra Leone and Sierra Leone Port Authority, Freetown.

Tourism

	1992	1993	1994
Tourist arrivals ('000)	89	91	72
Tourist receipts (US $ million)	17	18	10

Source: UN, *Statistical Yearbook*.

Communications Media

	1992	1993	1994
Radio receivers ('000 in use)	980	1,000	1,025
Television receivers ('000 in use)	45	47	48
Telephones ('000 main lines in use)	14	14	16
Daily newspapers	1	2	1
Average circulation ('000 copies)	10	n.a.	10

Sources: UNESCO, *Statistical Yearbook*, and UN, *Statistical Yearbook*.

Non-daily newspapers: 6 (average circulation 65,000 copies) in 1988 (Source: UNESCO, *Statistical Yearbook*).

Education

(1992/93)

	Institu-tions	Teachers	Pupils		
			Males	Females	Total
Primary	1,643	10,595	157,781	109,644	267,425
Secondary:					
General	167	4,313	41,831	29,069	70,900
Vocational	38	459	3,237	2,249	5,486
Teacher training	6	250	1,339	931	2,270
Higher	1	1,130	2,005	566	2,571

Source: Central Statistics Office and the former Department of Education, Freetown.

Directory

The Constitution

Following the transfer of power to a democratically-elected civilian administration on 29 March 1996, the Constitution of 1991 (which had been suspended since April 1992) was formally reinstated. The Constitution provided for the establishment of a multi-party system, and vested executive power in the President, who was to be elected by the majority of votes cast nationally and by at least 25% of the votes cast in each of the four provinces. The maximum duration of the President's tenure of office was limited to two five-year terms. Legislative power was vested in a unicameral 80-member Parliament, elected by universal adult suffrage for a five-year term. The President was to appoint and head the Cabinet. The parties that had secured a minimum of 5% of votes in the legislative elections were allocated seats on a system of proportional representation while 12 Paramount Chiefs also represented the provincial districts in the legislature. Members of the Parliament were not permitted concurrently to hold office in the Cabinet. Following a military coup on 25 May 1997, the Constitution was suspended. A 22-member governing body, the Armed Forces Revolutionary Council, was subsequently installed, and a new Cabinet, known as the Council of Secretaries, formed.

The Government

HEAD OF STATE

President and Commander-in-Chief of the Armed Forces: Maj. Johnny Paul Koroma (assumed power 17 June 1997)

ARMED FORCES REVOLUTIONARY COUNCIL
(August 1997)

Maj. Johnny Paul Koroma (Chairman)
Cpl Foday Sankoh (Vice-Chairman)
Brig. (retd) M. N. Laimon
Brig. H. K. Conteh
Brig. S. F. Y. Koroma
Col Mark Kangah
Capt. A. B. Sesay
Col K. I. S. Kamara
Col A. K. Sesay
Col S. O. Williams
Squadron Leader V. L. Keith
Col Sam Bakary
Col Denis Mingle
Lt Eldred Collins
Insp.-Gen. Teddy Williams
Kermo Lumumba Fofana
Sgt Abu Sankoh
Sgt Alex Braimah
Sgt Mazi Kamara
S. A. T. Baya
Charles Magai
M. A. Shawa

COUNCIL OF SECRETARIES
(August 1997)

Chief Secretary of State, responsible for Mineral Resources: Capt. Solomon Musa.

Secretary of State in the Chairman's Office: Maj. Victor King.

Secretary of State for Foreign Affairs: Paulo Bangura.

Secretary of State for Internal Affairs: Brig. (retd) Leslie Lymon.

Secretary of State for Finance: Joe Amara Bangali.

Secretary of State for Justice: Manley Spaine.

Secretary of State for Development: Victor Brandon.

Secretary of State for Transport and Communications: Osho Williams.

Secretary of State for Health: Col K. I. S. Kamara.

Secretary of State for Women's Affairs: Maj. Kula Samba.

Secretary of State for Sports: Umaru Deen Sesay.

MINISTRIES

All ministries are in Freetown.

Ministry of Agriculture: Youyi Bldg, Freetown; telex 3418.

Ministry of Development: Freetown.

Ministry of Education: New England, Freetown; tel. (22) 240846.

Ministry of Finance: Secretariat Bldg, George St, Freetown; tel. (22) 226911; telex 3363.

Ministry of Foreign Affairs: Gloucester St, Freetown; tel. (22) 224778; telex 3218.

Ministry of Health: Youyi Bldg, 4th Floor, Brookfields, Freetown; tel. (22) 241500.

Ministry of Information: Youyi Bldg, 8th Floor, Brookfields, Freetown; tel. (22) 240034; telex 3218.

Ministry of Justice: Guma Bldg, Lamina Sankoh St, Freetown; tel. (22) 226733.

Ministry of Marine Resources: Youyi Bldg, Brookfields, Freetown.

Ministry of Mineral Resources: Youyi Bldg, 5th Floor, Brookfields, Freetown; tel. (22) 241500.

Ministry of Trade, Industry and State Enterprises: Ministerial Bldg, George St, Freetown; tel. (22) 225211; telex 3218.

Ministry of Transport and Communications: Ministerial Bldg, 5th Floor, George St, Freetown; tel. (22) 225211.

Ministry of Works, Energy and Power: New England, Freetown; tel. (22) 240101.

President and Legislature

PRESIDENT*

Presidential Election, First Ballot, 26–27 February 1996

Candidate	Votes	% of votes
Ahmed Tejan Kabbah (SLPP)	266,893	35.8
John Karefa-Smart (UNPP)	168,666	22.6
Thaimu Bangura (PDP)	119,782	16.1
Dr John Karimu (NUP)	39,617	5.3
Edward Mohammed Turay (APC)	38,316	5.1
Adu Aiah Koroma (DCP)	36,779	4.9
Abass Chernor Bundu (PPP)	21,557	2.9
Amadu M.B. Jalloh (NDA)	17,335	2.3
Edward John Kargbo (PNC)	15,798	2.1
Desmond Luke (NUM)	7,918	1.1
Andrew Victor Lungay (SDP)	5,202	0.7
Andrew Turay (NPP)	3,925	0.5
Mohamed Yahya Sillah (NADP)	3,723	0.5
Total	745,511	100.0

Second Ballot, 15 March 1996

Candidate	Votes	% of votes
Ahmed Tejan Kabbah (SLPP)	608,419	59.5
John Karefa-Smart (UNPP)	414,335	40.5
Total	1,022,754	100.0

* In accordance with the election results, Ahmed Tejan Kabbah took office as President on 29 March 1996. However, he was deposed by a military coup on 25 May 1997.

PARLIAMENT*

Speaker: Sheku Mohamed Kutubu.

General Election, 26–27 February 1996

Party	Votes	% of votes	Seats
SLPP	269,486	36.1	27
UNPP	161,618	21.6	17
PDP	114,409	15.3	12
APC	42,443	5.7	5
NUP	39,280	5.3	4
DCP	35,624	4.8	3
PPP	21,354	2.9	0
NDA	20,105	2.7	0
PNC	19,019	2.5	0
NUM	8,884	1.2	0
SDP	5,900	0.8	0
NADP	4,653	0.6	0
NPP	3,989	0.5	0
Total	746,764	100.0	68†

* Following the military coup of 25 May 1997, Parliament was dissolved.

† A further 12 seats were allocated to Paramount Chiefs, who represented the 12 provincial districts.

Political Organizations

Under the provisions of a transitional programme, which was initiated in 1993, a ban on political activity was officially rescinded in June 1995; some 15 political parties were subsequently granted registration. Following a military coup on 25 May 1997, all political activity was suspended.

All-People's Congress (APC): 39 Siaka Stevens St, Freetown; f. 1960; sole authorized political party 1978–91; merged with the Democratic People's Party in 1992; reconstituted in 1995; Leader EDWARD TURAY.

Coalition for Progress Party (CPP): Leader GEREDINE SARHO.

Democratic Centre Party (DCP): Leader ADU AIAH KOROMA.

National Alliance Democratic Party (NADP): Leader MOHAMED YAHYA SILLAH.

National Democratic Alliance (NDA). Leader AMADU M.B. JALLOH.

National People's Party (NPP): Leader ANDREW TURAY.

National Republican Party (NRP).

National Unity Movement (NUM): Leader DESMOND LUKE.

National Unity Party (NUP): Leader Dr JOHN KARIMU.

People's Democratic Party (PDP): Leader THAIMU BANGURA.

People's National Convention (PNC): Leader EDWARD JOHN KARGBO.

People's Progressive Party (PPP): Leader ABASS CHERNOR BUNDU.

Sierra Leone People's Party (SLPP): official opposition party 1968–78; emerged as the largest party in Parliament, following elections in Feb. 1996; party of Pres. Kabbah.

Social Democratic Party (SDP): Leader ANDREW VICTOR LUNGAY.

United National People's Party (UNPP): Leader JOHN KAREFA-SMART.

Diplomatic Representation

EMBASSIES AND HIGH COMMISSIONS IN SIERRA LEONE

China, People's Republic: 29 Wilberforce Loop, Freetown; tel. (22) 231797; Ambassador: QU WEMING.

Côte d'Ivoire: 1 Wesley St, Freetown; tel. (22) 223983; Chargé d'affaires a.i.: EDO VAN AS.

Egypt: 174C Wilkinson Rd, POB 652, Freetown; tel. (22) 231499; telex 3300; Ambassador: MOHAMED ABDEL SALAM MOUSSA.

Gambia: 6 Wilberforce St, Freetown; tel. (22) 225191; High Commissioner: (vacant).

Germany: Santanno House, 10 Howe St, POB 728, Freetown; tel. (22) 222511; telex 3248; fax (22) 226213; Chargé d'affaires a.i.: ASTRID ILPER.

Guinea: 4 Liverpool St, Freetown; tel. (22) 223080; Ambassador: CHARLES EMMANUEL DE STEFAN.

Holy See: 23 Jomo Kenyatta Rd, PMB 526, Freetown; tel. (22) 242131; fax (22) 240509; Apostolic Delegate: Most Rev. LUIGI TRAVAGLINO, Titular Archbishop of Lettere.

Italy: 32A Wilkinson Rd, POB 749, Freetown; tel. (22) 230995; telex 3456; Ambassador: RANIERI FORNARI.

Korea, Republic: 22 Wilberforce St, POB 1383, Freetown; tel. (22) 224269; telex 3313; Ambassador: KIM CHANG-SOK.

Lebanon: 22 Wilberforce St, POB 727, Freetown; tel. (22) 223513; Ambassador: Dr FAWAZ FAWAD.

Liberia: 30 Brookfields Rd, POB 276, Freetown; tel. (22) 240322; telex 3229; Chargé d'affaires a.i.: SAMUEL B. PETERS.

Nigeria: 37 Siaka Stevens St, Freetown; tel. (22) 224202; telex 3258; fax (22) 224219; High Commissioner: MUHAMMED CHADI ABUBAKAR.

United Kingdom: Spur Rd, Wilberforce, Freetown; tel. (22) 232563; fax (22) 228169; High Commissioner: IAN MCCLUNEY.

USA: Walpole and Siaka Stevens Sts, Freetown; tel. (22) 226481; telex 3509; fax (22) 225471; Ambassador: LAURALEE PETERS.

Judicial System

The Supreme Court: The ultimate court of appeal in both civil and criminal cases. In addition to its appellate jurisdiction, the Court has supervisory jurisdiction over all other courts and over any adjudicating authority in Sierra Leone, and also original jurisdiction in constitutional issues.

Chief Justice: S. BECCLES-DAVIES (acting).

Supreme Court Justices: C. A. HARDING, AGNES AWUNOR-RENNER.

The Court of Appeal: The Court of Appeal has jurisdiction to hear and determine appeals from decisions of the High Court in both criminal and civil matters, and also from certain statutory tribunals. Appeals against its decisions may be made to the Supreme Court.

Justices of Appeal: S. C. E. WARNE, C. S. DAVIES, S. T. NAVO, M. S. TURAY, E. C. THOMPSON-DAVIS, M. O. TAJU-DEEN, M. O. ADOPHY, GEORGE GELAGA KING, Dr A. B. Y. TIMBO, VIRGINIA A. WRIGHT.

High Court: The High Court has unlimited original jurisdiction in all criminal and civil matters. It also has appellate jurisdiction against decisions of Magistrates' Courts.

Judges: FRANCIS C. GBOW, EBUN THOMAS, D. E. M. WILLIAMS, LAURA MARCUS-JONES, L. B. O. NYLANDER, A. M. B. TARAWALLIE, O. H. ALGHALLI, W. A. O. JOHNSON, N. D. ALHADI, R. J. BANKOLE THOMPSON, M. E. T. THOMPSON, C. J. W. ATERE-ROBERTS (acting).

Magistrates' Courts: In criminal cases the jurisdiction of the Magistrates' Courts is limited to summary cases and to preliminary investigations to determine whether a person charged with an offence should be committed for trial.

Local Courts have jurisdiction, according to native law and custom, in matters which are outside the jurisdiction of other courts.

Religion

A large proportion of the population holds animist beliefs, although there are significant numbers of Islamic and Christian adherents.

ISLAM

In 1990 Islamic adherents represented an estimated 30% of the total population.

Ahmadiyya Muslim Mission: 15 Bath St, Brookfields, POB 353, Freetown; Emir and Chief Missionary KHALIL A. MOBASHIR.

Kankaylay (Sierra Leone Muslim Men and Women's Association): 15 Blackhall Rd, Kissy, POB 1168, Freetown; tel. (22) 250931; f. 1972; 500,000 mems; Pres. Alhaji IBRAHIM BEMBA TURAY; Lady Pres. Haja ISATA KEBE; Vice-Pres. Haja SERAY SILLAH.

Sierra Leone Muslim Congress: POB 875, Freetown; Pres. Alhaji MUHAMMAD SANUSI MUSTAPHA.

CHRISTIANITY

Council of Churches in Sierra Leone: 4A Kingharman Rd, Brookfields, POB 404, Freetown; tel. (22) 240568; telex 3210; f. 1924; 17 mem. churches; Pres. Rev. HENRY A. E. JENKINS; Gen. Sec. Rev. AMADU F. KAMARA.

The Anglican Communion

Anglicans in Sierra Leone are adherents of the Church of the Province of West Africa, comprising 11 dioceses, of which two are in Sierra Leone. The Archbishop of the Province is the Bishop of Koforidua, Ghana.

Bishop of Bo: Rt Rev. SAMUEL SAO GBONDA, MacRobert St, POB 21, Bo, Southern Province.

Bishop of Freetown and Makeni: Rt Rev. JULIUS O. PRINCE LYNCH, Bishopscourt, Fourah Bay Rd, POB 128, Freetown.

Baptist Churches

Sierra Leone Baptist Convention: POB 64, Lunsar; Pres. Rev. JOSEPH S. MANS; Sec. Rev. N. T. DIXON.

The Nigerian Baptist Convention is also active.

Methodist Churches

Methodist Church Sierra Leone: Wesley House, George St, POB 64, Freetown; tel. (22) 222216; autonomous since 1967; Pres. of Conf. Rev. GERSHON F. H. ANDERSON; Sec. Rev. CHRISTIAN V. A. PEACOCK; 26,421 mems.

United Methodist Church: Freetown; Presiding Bishop T. S. BANGURA; 36,857 mems.

Other active Methodist bodies include the African Methodist Episcopal Church, the Wesleyan Church of Sierra Leone, the Countess of Huntingdon's Connexion and the West African Methodist Church.

The Roman Catholic Church

Sierra Leone comprises one archdiocese and two dioceses. At 31 December 1995 there were an estimated 134,958 adherents in the country, representing about 3.0% of the total population.

Inter-territorial Catholic Bishops' Conference of The Gambia, Liberia and Sierra Leone: Santanno House, POB 893, Freetown; tel. (22) 228240; telex 3311; fax (22) 228252; f. 1971; Pres. Rt Rev. BENEDICT DOTU SEKEY, Bishop of Gbarnga (Liberia).

Archbishop of Freetown and Bo: Most Rev. JOSEPH HENRY GANDA, Santanno House, POB 893, Freetown; tel. (22) 224590; fax (22) 224075.

Other Christian Churches

The following are represented: the Christ Apostolic Church, the Church of the Lord (Aladura), the Evangelical Church, the Missionary Church of Africa, the Sierra Leone Church and the United Brethren in Christ.

AFRICAN RELIGIONS

There is a diverse range of beliefs, rites and practices, varying between ethnic and kinship groups.

The Press

DAILY

Daily Mail: 29–31 Rawdon St, POB 53, Freetown; tel. (22) 223191; f. 1931; govt-owned; Editor Aiah Martin Mondeh; circ. 10,000.

PERIODICALS

African Crescent: 15 Bath St, POB 353, Brookfields, Freetown; Editor Maulana-Khalil A. Mobashir.

The Catalyst: Christian Literature Crusade Bookshop, 35 Circular Rd, POB 1465, Freetown; tel. (22) 224382; Editor Dr Leopold Foullah.

Concord Times: 139 Pademba Rd, Freetown; 3 a week; Editor Kingsley Lington.

Leonean Sun: 49 Main Rd, Wellington, Freetown; tel. (22) 223363; f. 1974; monthly; Editor Rowland Martyn.

Liberty Voice: 139 Pademba Rd, Freetown; tel. (22) 242100; Editor A. Mahdieu Savage.

New Breed: Freetown; weekly; independent; Man. Editor (vacant).

New Citizen: 5 Hanna Benka-Coker St, Freetown; tel. (22) 241795; Editor I. Ben Kargbo.

The New Globe: 49 Bathurst St, Freetown; tel. (22) 228245; weekly; Man. Editor Sam Tumoe; circ. 4,000.

The New Shaft: 60 Old Railway Line, Brookfields, Freetown; tel. (22) 241093; 2 a week; independent; Editor Franklin Bunting-Davies; circ. 10,000.

Progress: 1 Short St, Freetown; tel. (22) 223588; weekly; independent; Editor Fode Kandeh; circ. 7,000.

Sierra Leone Chamber of Commerce Journal: Sierra Leone Chamber of Commerce, Industry and Agriculture, Guma Bldg, 5th Floor, Lamina Sankoh St, POB 502, Freetown; tel. (22) 226305; telex 3712; fax (22) 228005; monthly.

Unity Now: 82 Pademba Rd, Freetown; tel. (22) 227466; Editor Frank Kposowa.

The Vision: 60 Old Railway Line, Brookfields; tel. (22) 241273; Editor Siaka Massaquoi.

Weekend Spark: 7 Lamina Sankoh St, Freetown; tel. (22) 223397; f. 1983; weekly; independent; Editor Rowland Martyn; circ. 20,000.

NEWS AGENCY

Sierra Leone News Agency (SLENA): 15 Wallace Johnson St, PMB 445, Freetown; tel. (22) 224921; telex 3603; fax (22) 224439; f. 1980; Dir and Editor-in-Chief Rod Mac-Johnson.

Publishers

Njala University Publishing Centre: Njala University College, PMB, Freetown; science and technology, university textbooks.

Sierra Leone University Press: Fourah Bay College, POB 87, Freetown; tel. (22) 22491; telex 3210; fax (22) 224439; f. 1965; biography, history, Africana, religion, social science, university textbooks; Chair. Prof. Ernest H. Wright.

United Christian Council Literature Bureau: Bunumbu Press, POB 28, Bo; tel. (32) 462; books in Mende, Temne, Susu; Man. Dir Robert Sam-Kpakra.

Government Publishing House

Government Printer: New England, Freetown; tel. (22) 241146.

Radio and Television

In 1994 there were an estimated 1,025,000 radio receivers and 48,000 television receivers in use.

Sierra Leone Broadcasting Service: New England, Freetown; tel. (22) 240403; telex 3334; f. 1934; state-controlled; programmes mainly in English and the four main Sierra Leonean vernaculars, Mende, Limba, Temne and Krio; weekly broadcast in French; television service established 1963; colour transmissions since 1978; Dir-Gen. Babatunde Roland-May.

Finance

(cap. = capital; res = reserves; dep. = deposits; m. = million; brs = branches; amounts in leone)

BANKING

Central Bank

Bank of Sierra Leone: Siaka Stevens St, POB 30, Freetown; tel. (22) 226501; telex 3232; fax (22) 224764; f. 1964; cap. and res 24,426.6m., dep. 83,116.6m. (Dec. 1995); Gov. Steve Swaray (acting); Dep. Gov. Yvonne Gibril; 1 br.

Other Banks

Barclays Bank of Sierra Leone Ltd: 25–27 Siaka Stevens St, POB 12, Freetown; tel. (22) 222501; telex 3220; fax (22) 222563; f. 1971; cap. and res 2,319.1m., dep. 19,093.0m. (Dec. 1995); Chair. Augustus D. A. M'Cormack; Man. Dir Emyr Lloyd-Davies; 9 brs and agencies.

National Development Bank Ltd: Leone House, 6th Floor, 21–23 Siaka Stevens St, Freetown; tel. (22) 226791; telex 3589; fax (22) 224468; f. 1968; 99% state-owned; provides medium- and long-term finance and tech. assistance to devt-orientated enterprises; cap. and res 1,568.2m., dep. 1,229.6m. (Dec. 1994); Man. Dir Mohamed M. Turay; 3 brs.

Sierra Leone Commercial Bank Ltd: 29–31 Siaka Stevens St, Freetown; tel. (22) 225264; telex 3275; fax (22) 225292; f. 1973; state-owned; cap. and res 3,378.2m., dep. 7,626.1m. (Dec. 1995); Chair. I. I. May-Parker; Man. Dir S. B. Kanu; 7 brs.

Standard Chartered Bank Sierra Leone Ltd: 9 and 11 Lightfoot-Boston St, POB 1155, Freetown; tel. (22) 226220; telex 3523; fax (22) 225760; f. 1971; cap. and res 2,964.9m., dep. 17,011.7m. (Dec. 1996); Chair. Lloyd A. During; Man. Dir John A. H. Janes; 12 brs.

Union Trust Bank Ltd: Lightfoot Boston St, PMB 1237, Freetown; tel. (22) 226954; telex 3233; fax (22) 226214; fmrly Meridien BIAO Bank Sierra Leone Ltd; commenced operations under present name in July 1995; Chair. S. B. Nicol-Cole: Man. Dir James Sanpha Koroma.

INSURANCE

Aureol Insurance Co Ltd: Kissy House, 54 Siaka Stevens St, POB 647, Freetown; tel. (22) 223435; telex 3222; fax (22) 229336; f. 1987; Chair. Lloyd A. During; Man. Dir S. G. Benjamin.

National Insurance Co Ltd: 18–20 Walpole St, PMB 84, Freetown; tel. (22) 223892; telex 3344; fax (22) 226097; f. 1972; state-owned; Chair. J. T. Sarjah-Wright; CEO A. N. Yaskey.

New India Assurance Co Ltd: 18 Wilberforce St, POB 340, Freetown; tel. (22) 226453; telex 3510; fax (22) 222494; Man. Dir V. Krishnan.

Reliance Insurance Trust Corp. Ltd: 24 Siaka Stevens St, Freetown; tel. (22) 225115; telex 3664; fax (22) 228051; f. 1985; Chair. S. S. Deen; Man. Dir E. B. Koroma.

Sierra Leone Insurance Co Ltd: 31 Lightfoot Boston St, POB 836, Freetown.

Trade and Industry

CHAMBER OF COMMERCE

Sierra Leone Chamber of Commerce, Industry and Agriculture: Guma Bldg, 5th Floor, Lamina Sankoh St, POB 502, Freetown; tel. (22) 226305; telex 3712; fax (22) 228005; f. 1961; 215 mems; Pres. Alhaji Mohamed Musa King.

GOVERNMENT ORGANIZATION

Government Gold and Diamond Office (GGDO): c/o Bank of Sierra Leone, Siaka Stevens St, Freetown; tel. (22) 222600; telex 3566; fax (22) 229064; f. 1985; govt regulatory agency for diamonds and gold; combats illicit trade; Chair. Alhaji M. S. Deen.

EMPLOYERS' ASSOCIATIONS

Sierra Leone Employers' Federation: POB 562, Freetown; Chair. Donald C. Smythe-Macaulay; Exec. Officer A. E. Benjamin.

Sierra Leone Chamber of Mines: POB 456, Freetown; tel. (22) 226082; f. 1965; mems comprise the prin. mining concerns; Pres. D. J. S. Fraser; Exec. Officer N. H. T. Boston.

MAJOR INDUSTRIAL COMPANIES

Aureol Tobacco Co Ltd: Wellington Industrial Estate, POB 109, Freetown; telex 3361; fax (22) 263138; f. 1959; cigarette mfrs; Chair. Prof. K. Koso-Thomas; Man. Dir A. D. A. M'Cormack; 75 employees.

Bata Shoe Co Sierra Leone Ltd: Wallace Johnson St, POB 111, Freetown; footwear mfrs and distributors. Assoc. Co:

Plastic Manufacturing Sierra Leone Ltd: Wilkinson Rd, POB 96, Freetown; footwear mfrs.

Chanrai Sierra Leone Ltd: Wellington Industrial Estate, POB 57, Freetown; tel. (22) 263292; telex 3267; fax (22) 263305; f. 1893; importers of motor spares, air-conditioners, refrigerators, building materials, textiles and provisions; mfrs of soaps and polyethylene bags; Dir R. K. LAKHANPAL; 115 employees.

Compagnie française de l'Afrique occidentale: Howe St, POB 70, Freetown; tel. (22) 22030; telex 3332.

The Diamond Corporation (West Africa) Ltd: 25–27 Siaka Stevens St, POB 421, Freetown; telex 3221; purchase and export of diamonds; Dir S. L. MATTURI.

Rokel Leaf Tobacco Development Co Ltd: POB 29, Makeni; f. 1974; production of leaf tobacco; Chair. J. T. SHORT.

Sierra Leone Brewery Ltd: POB 721, Freetown; fax (22) 263118; f. 1961; brewing and marketing of Guinness stout and Star lager; Man. Dir O. A. SMITH.

Sierra Leone Diamonds Ltd: Freetown; diamond cutting and polishing.

Sierra Leone National Petroleum Co: NP House, Cotton Tree, POB 277, Freetown; tel. (22) 225040; fax (22) 226892; petroleum products; CEO VINCENT LAMIN KANU.

Sierra Leone Ore and Metal Co (SIEROMCO): POB 725, Freetown; tel. (22) 226777; telex 3380; fax (22) 227276; mining of bauxite; operations suspended since 1995; Chair. K. WOLFENSBERGER; Man. Dir JAMES WESTWOOD.

Sierra Leone Petroleum Refining Co Ltd: PMB, Kissy Dockyard, Freetown; 50% state-owned; operates a refinery.

Sierra Rutile Ltd: PMB, Freetown; tel. and fax (22) 228144; telex 3259; f. 1971; jtly-owned by US and Australian interests; mining of rutile and ilmenite (titanium-bearing ores); CEO BRIAN CALVER; 1,600 employees.

UAC of Sierra Leone Ltd: 6-8 Blackhall Rd, Freetown; fmrly United Africa Co; mfrs agents: construction, mining, marine, agriculture and power plants; Chair. LLOYD A. DURING; Man. Dir VICTOR G. THOMAS.

TRADE UNIONS

Artisans', Ministry of Works Employees' and General Workers' Union: 4 Pultney St, Freetown; f. 1946; 14,500 mems; Pres. IBRAHIM LANGLEY; Gen. Sec. TEJAN A. KASSIM.

Sierra Leone Labour Congress: 35 Wallace Johnson St, POB 1333, Freetown; tel. (22) 226869; f. 1966; c. 51,000 mems in 19 affiliated unions; Pres. H. M. BARRIE; Sec. Gen. KANDEH YILLA.

Principal affiliated unions:

Clerical, Mercantile and General Workers' Union: 35 Wallace Johnson St, Freetown; f. 1945; 3,600 mems; Pres. M. D. BENJAMIN; Gen. Sec. M. B. WILLIAMS.

Sierra Leone Association of Journalists: Freetown; Pres. SIAKA MASSAQUOI.

Sierra Leone Dockworkers' Union: 165 Fourah Bay Rd, Freetown; f. 1962; 2,650 mems; Pres. D. F. KANU; Gen. Sec. A. C. CONTEH.

Sierra Leone Motor Drivers' Union: 10 Charlotte St, Freetown; f. 1960; 1,900 mems; Pres. A. W. HASSAN; Gen. Sec. ALPHA KAMARA.

Sierra Leone Teachers' Union: Regaland House, Lowcost Step—Kissy, POB 477, Freetown; f. 1951; 18,500 mems; Pres. FESTUS E. MINAH; Sec.-Gen. A. O. TIMBO.

Sierra Leone Transport, Agricultural and General Workers' Union: 4 Pultney St, Freetown; f. 1946; 1,600 mems; Pres. S. O. SAWYERR-MANLEY; Gen. Sec. S. D. KARGBO.

United Mineworkers' Union: 35 Wallace Johnson St, Freetown; f. 1944; 6,500 mems; Pres. H. M. BARRIE; Gen. Sec. S. D. GBENDA.

Also affiliated to the Sierra Leone Labour Congress: **General Construction Workers' Union, Municipal and Local Government Employees' Union, Sierra Leone National Seamen's Union.**

Transport

RAILWAYS

There are no passenger railways in Sierra Leone.

Marampa Mineral Railway: Delco House, POB 735, Freetown; tel. (22) 222556; telex 3460; 84 km of track linking iron ore mines at Marampa (inactive since 1985) with Pepel port; Gen. Man. SYL KHANU.

ROADS

In 1995 there were an estimated 11,674 km of classified roads, including 1,390 km of main roads and 1,630 km of secondary roads; about 1,284 km of the total network was paved. In 1993 the Government announced a seven-year road rehabilitation programme, which, at an estimated cost of US $100m., was to be financed by the World Bank.

Sierra Leone Road Transport Corpn: Blackhall Rd, POB 1008, Freetown; tel. (22) 250442; telex 3395; fax (22) 250000; f. 1965; state-owned; operates transport services throughout the country; Gen. Man. DANIEL R. W. FAUX.

INLAND WATERWAYS

Recognized launch routes, including the coastal routes from Freetown northward to the Great and Little Scarcies rivers and southward to Bonthe, total almost 800 km. Although some of the upper reaches of the rivers are navigable only between July and September, there is a considerable volume of river traffic.

SHIPPING

Sierra Leone National Shipping Co Ltd: 45 Cline St, POB 935, Freetown; tel. (22) 250881; telex 3260; fax (22) 223222; f. 1972; state-owned; shipping, clearing and forwarding agency; representatives for foreign lines; Gen. Man. PAUL K. NIELSEN.

Sierra Leone Ports Authority: Queen Elizabeth II Quay, PMB 386, Cline Town, Freetown; tel. (22) 250111; telex 3262; fax (22) 250616; f. 1965; parastatal body, supervised by the Ministry of Transport and Communications; operates the port of Freetown, which has full facilities for ocean-going vessels; Gen. Man. Capt. P. E. M. KEMOKAI.

Sierra Leone Shipping Agencies Ltd: Deep Water Quay, Clinetown, POB 74, Freetown; tel. (22) 250882; telex 3260; fax (22) 250400; f. 1949; Man. Dir I. HEDEMANN.

UMARCO (Freetown) Ltd: POB 417, Freetown; telex 3216; shipping agents; Gen. Man. R. HUGHES.

CIVIL AVIATION

There is an international airport at Lungi.

Directorate of Civil Aviation: Department of Transport and Communications, Ministerial Bldg, 5th Floor, George St, Freetown; tel. (22) 222106; Dir T. T. A. VANDY.

Sierra National Airlines: Leone House, 25 Pultney St, POB 285, Freetown; tel. (22) 222075; telex 3242; fax (22) 222026; f. 1982; state-owned; operates domestic and regional services, and scheduled flights to Paris, France; Pres STANLEY A. PALMER.

Tourism

The main attractions for tourists are the coastline, the mountains and the game reserves. In 1994, when an estimated 72,000 tourists visited Sierra Leone, receipts from tourism totalled US $10m.

National Tourist Board: International Conference Centre, Aberdeen Hill, POB 1435, Freetown; tel. (22) 272520; fax (22) 272197; f. 1990; Gen. Man. CECIL J. WILLIAMS.

Defence

In August 1996 the armed forces comprised an army of approximately 14,000 men and a navy of 200. Following a military coup in May 1997, the Nigerian government (which had signed a defence agreement with the ousted administration) increased its military strength in the country to about 4,000 troops. The Revolutionary United Front, a rebel faction which had been engaged in protracted hostilities with the former administration, established an alliance with the coup leaders, and was reconstituted as a government security force, known as the People's Army. Forces supporting the new military junta clashed with both Nigerian troops and with traditional fighters, known as Kamajors, who were loyal to the ousted president.

Defence Expenditure: Estimated at Le 25,000m. in 1996.

Commander-in-Chief of the Armed Forces: Maj. JOHNNY PAUL KOROMA.

Chief of Staff of the Army: Col S. O. WILLIAMS.

Education

Primary education begins at six years of age and lasts for six years. Secondary education, beginning at the age of 12, also lasts for a further six years, comprising two three-year cycles. In 1987 tuition fees for government-funded primary and secondary schools were abolished. In 1990 primary enrolment was equivalent to 51% of children in the appropriate age-group (boys 60%; girls 42%), while the comparable ratio for secondary enrolment was 17% (boys 22%; girls 12%). There is one university, which comprises six colleges; in

1992/93 2,571 students were enrolled in higher education. Budgetary expenditure on education and social welfare by the central government in the financial year 1990/91 was estimated at Le 2,775.1m. (11.7% of total spending). In 1995, according to UNESCO estimates, adult illiteracy averaged 68.6% (males 54.6%; females 81.8%).

Bibliography

Abraham, A. *Topics in Sierra Leone History*. Freetown, 1977.

Allie, Joe. *A New History of Sierra Leone*. London, Macmillan, 1990.

Cartwright, J. R. *Politics in Sierra Leone 1947–67*. Toronto, 1970.

Political Leadership in Sierra Leone. Toronto, 1978.

Clapham, C. *Liberia and Sierra Leone: An Essay in Comparative Politics*. Cambridge University Press, 1976.

Clarke, J. I. *Sierra Leone in Maps*. London, 1966.

Cruise O'Brien, D. B., Dunn, J., and Rathbone, R. (Eds). *Contemporary West African States*. Cambridge University Press, 1989.

Daramy, S. B. *Constitutional Developments in the Post-Colonial State of Sierra-Leone 1961–1984*. Lewiston, Edwin Mallen, 1993.

Fashole Luke, D. *Labour and Parastatal Politics in Sierra Leone: A Study in African Working-class Ambivalence*. Lanham, MD, University Press of America, 1984.

Funna, S. M. 'Structure and Performance of the Sierra Leone Economy: 1971–81', in *Sierra Leone Studies at Birmingham, 1983*. Birmingham University Press, 1984.

Fyle, C. M. *The History of Sierra Leone: A Concise Introduction*. London, 1981.

(Ed.) *The State and Provision of Social Services in Sierra Leone Since Independence*. Dakar, CODESRIA, 1993.

Greenhalgh, P. *West African Diamonds: An Economic History 1919–83*. Manchester University Press, 1985.

Gwynne-Jones, D. R. G., et al. *A New Geography of Sierra Leone*. Longman, 1978.

Harrell-Bond, B., Howard, A. M., and Skinner, D. E. *Community Leadership and the Transformation of Freetown, 1801–1976*. Leiden, 1978.

Hayward, M. F. *Elections in Independent Africa*. Boulder, CO, Westview Press, 1987.

International Labour Organisation. *Ensuring Equitable Growth: A Strategy for Increasing Employment, Equity and Basic Needs Satisfaction in Sierra Leone*. Addis Ababa, 1981.

Jones, A. *From Slaves to Palm Kernels: A History of the Galinhas Country, 1730–1890*. Wiesbaden, Franz Steiner Verlag, 1983.

Kilson, M. *Political Change in a West African State—A Study of the Modernization Process in Sierra Leone*. Cambridge, MA, 1966.

Koroma, A. K. *Sierra Leone: Agony of a Nation*. Freetown, Afro Media, 1996.

Lee, M. M. *UNICEF in Sierra Leone*. Abidjan, UNIPACI, 1988.

Luke, D. F., and Riley, S. P. *Economic Decline and the New Reform Agenda in Africa: The Case of Sierra Leone*. Manchester, University of Manchester, 1991.

Makannah, T. J. (Ed.). *Handbook of the Population of Sierra Leone*. Freetown, Toma Enterprises, 1996.

Reno, W. *Corruption and State Politics in Sierra Leone*. Cambridge University Press, 1995.

Rimmer, D. *The Economies of West Africa*. London, Weidenfeld and Nicolson, 1984.

Stevens, S. *What Life Has Taught Me*. London, Kensal Press, 1984.

Thomas, A. C. *The Population of Sierra Leone: An Analysis of Population Data*. Freetown, Fourah Bay College, 1983.

Thompson, B. *The Constitutional History and Law of Sierra Leone, 1961–1995*. Lanham, MD, University Press of America, 1997.

Turay, E. D. A., and Abraham, A. *The Sierra Leone Army: A Century of History*. London, Macmillan, 1988.

Weeks, J. *Development Strategy and the Economy of Sierra Leone*. New York, St Martin's Press, 1992.

Wyse, A. *The Krio of Sierra Leone: An Interpretive History*. London, Hurst, 1989.

Zack-Williams, A. *Tributors, Supporters and Merchant Capital: Mining and Underdevelopment in Sierra Leone*. Aldershot, Avebury, 1995.

SOMALIA

Physical and Social Geography

I. M. LEWIS

The Somali Democratic Republic covers an area of 637,657 sq km (246,201 sq miles). It has a long coastline on the Indian Ocean and the Gulf of Aden, forming the 'Horn of Africa'. To the north, Somalia faces the Arabian peninsula, with which it has had centuries of commercial and cultural contact. To the north-west, it is bounded by the Republic of Djibouti, while its western and southern neighbours are Ethiopia and Kenya. The country takes its name from its population, the Somali, a Muslim Cushitic-speaking people who stretch far beyond its present frontiers into these neighbouring states.

Most of the terrain consists of dry savannah plains, with a high mountain escarpment in the north, facing the coast. The climate is hot and dry, with an average annual temperature of 27°C, although temperate at higher altitudes and along the coast during June–September, with an annual rainfall which rarely exceeds 500 mm in the most favourable regions. Only two permanent rivers—the Juba and Shebelle—water this arid land. Both rise in the Ethiopian highlands, but only the Juba regularly flows into the sea. The territory between these two rivers is agriculturally the richest part of Somalia, and constitutes a zone of mixed cultivation and pastoralism. Sorghum, millet and maize are grown here, while along the rivers, on irrigated plantations, bananas (the mainstay of Somalia's exports) and citrus fruits are produced. This potentially prosperous zone contains remnants of Bantu groups—partly of ex-slave origin—and is also the home of the Digil and Rahanwin, who speak a distinctive dialect and are the least nomadic element in the population. Of the other Somali clans—the Dir, Isaaq, Hawiye and Darod, primarily pastoral nomads who occupy the rest of the country—the Hawiye along the Shebelle valley are the most extensively engaged in cultivation. A small subsidiary area of cultivation (involving Dir and Isaaq) also occurs in the north-west highlands.

In this predominantly pastoral country, permanent settlements are small and widely scattered, except in the agricultural regions, and for the most part are tiny trading centres built around wells. There are few large towns. Mogadishu, the capital, which dates from at least the 10th century as an Islamic trading post, had an estimated population of 500,000 in 1981. The other main centres are Kismayu (population 70,000 in 1981) and Berbera (65,000 in 1981), the main southern and northern ports respectively. The northern town of Hargeysa (population 70,000 in 1981) was declared the capital of the secessionist 'Republic of Somaliland' in 1991.

According to the results of a census taken in February 1975, the population of Somalia was 3,253,024 (excluding adjustment for underenumeration). The 1986–87 census estimated the total to have risen to 7,114,431. According to UN estimates, the population at mid-1994 had increased to 9,077,000. Important demographic changes have taken place in recent years, beginning with the serious drought which affected the north of the country in 1974–75 and led to the resettlement of large numbers of people in the south. During 1980–88 successive influxes of refugees from Ethiopia created a serious refugee problem before repatriations began in 1990. Of greatest consequence, however, has been the dislocation of Somalia's population during the civil unrest that began in the late 1980s. In early 1993 it was estimated that three-quarters of the population had been internally displaced by civil conflict; by late 1996 there were an estimated 250,000 internally displaced Somalis, and a further 475,000 refugees outside the country, of whom about 240,000 were resident in Ethiopia and 150,000 in Kenya.

Recent History

PATRICK GILKES

Revised for this edition by THOMAS OFCANSKY

Having drawn up bilateral treaties with the clans of the area, the British declared a protectorate over northern Somalia in 1886, with the objectives of safeguarding the trade links of its colony Aden and excluding other interested powers (especially France). With the latter objective in mind, Italy established a colony in southern regions in the same period, completing its control of coastal and inland areas by 1927. Italian Somaliland became, with Eritrea, a base for the Italian conquest of Ethiopia in 1936. The Italian colony was captured by British forces in 1941 and following the defeat of the Italians in east Africa, both it and British Somaliland (which had been briefly occupied by the Italians in 1940–41) were placed under British military administration. Under the provisions of the peace treaty of February 1947, Italy renounced all rights to Italian Somaliland. In December 1950, however, the former Italian colony became the UN Trust Territory of Somalia, placed under Italian administration for a 10-year transitional period prior to independence. The British protectorate had meanwhile reverted to civilian rule, while most of the Somali areas in Ethiopia had been returned to Ethiopian administration.

The trust territory's first general election on the basis of universal adult suffrage was held in March 1959, when 83 of the 90 seats in the legislative assembly were won by the Somali Youth League (SYL). Britain, meanwhile, prepared its protectorate for self-government. British Somaliland became independent on 26 June 1960, and on 1 July, having secured its own independence, the former Italian Somaliland united with the former British Somaliland as the independent Somali Republic. The president of the southern legislative assembly was proclaimed head of state and the two legislatures merged to form a single assembly in Mogadishu. A coalition government was formed by the SYL and the two leading northern political parties, with Dr Abd ar-Rashid Ali Shirmake, a leading SYL politician and a member of the Darod clan, as the first prime minister. Shirmake's government, constituting a balance of northern and southern members representative of the main clans, set the pattern of Somali political life for the next decade.

The problems of merging the administrative systems of the two former colonies were offset to an extent by the shared Somali culture and by the presence of clans straddling the old colonial boundaries. Internal harmony was further encouraged, at the price of external conflict, by the commitment of all political leaders to a policy of extending the boundaries of the new state to include Somali communities in Ethiopia, French Somaliland (now Djibouti) and northern Kenya. Accordingly, liberation movements were established for these areas. In the 1964 elections the SYL comfortably secured a majority of seats in the assembly. However, a split within the SYL's Darod leadership, leading to the appointment of a new Darod prime minister, Abd ar-Razak Hussein, left the party seriously divided and culminated in the election as president in 1967 of Shirmake, who formed a new government with Mohamed Ibrahim Egal (a northerner from the Isaaq clan) as prime minister. Acknowledging the failure so far of its efforts to promote Somali unification, the government, through the mediation efforts of President Kaunda of Zambia, reached agreement with Ethiopia and Kenya to negotiate a lasting settlement of the frontiers issue.

With external pressure on the republic diminished, the smaller constituent units of the traditional political structure again came to the fore, with an upsurge of divisive tribalism. The March 1969 legislative elections were contested by more than 1,000 candidates, representing 68 political parties and the most important lineages and sub-lineages of the Somali clan system. With the resources of the state at its disposal, and with considerable manipulation of the electoral arrangements, the SYL again secured victory, and Egal was reappointed prime minister. Following the formation of the customary clan-coalition government, all but one of the members of the assembly joined the ruling party. Because of the prevailing political fragmentation, however, the government and the assembly were in reality no longer representative of the public at large. Discontent was aggravated by the increasingly autocratic style of both the president and prime minister, and by the prime minister's efforts to provide political and administrative posts for northerners (who had persistently complained that earlier administrations, dominated by southerners, had failed to serve their interests).

THE SIAD BARRE REGIME, 1969–91

In October 1969 Shirmake was assassinated in the course of factional violence. When it became clear that the assembly would elect a new president supported by Egal, the army seized control in a bloodless *coup d'état*. A supreme revolutionary council (SRC), formed of army and police officers, announced that it had acted to preserve democracy and justice and to eliminate corruption and tribalism (clanism) and that the country had been renamed the Somali Democratic Republic to symbolize these aims. The president of the SRC, the army commander Maj.-Gen. Mohamed Siad Barre, became head of state.

Siad Barre swiftly assumed personal control of the government, introducing a policy of 'scientific socialism'. The Somali Revolutionary Socialist Party (SRSP) was established in 1976 under Soviet influence, although it operated more as a mechanism for control than as an ideological vehicle. Medical services, schools, banks, electricity and transport services were nationalized, and the government took control of exports and imports. In 1975 land was nationalized: farmers received holdings on 50-year renewable leases from the state, but from the outset the system was subject to manipulation and corruption. (Subsequent efforts to recover land became a significant element in inter-clan conflict after 1991.) Prices and salaries were subject to state controls. A mass literacy campaign was launched, building on the adoption of Somali as the official language in 1972, using a modified Roman alphabet.

Somalia suffered from severe drought in the mid-1970s, although a programme of resettlement, accomplished with the help of a massive Soviet airlift, relocated some 140,000 people to farming colonies in the agricultural south and experimental fishing settlements along the coast. This impressive response contributed to a relatively low death toll (about 18,000) but could do little to prevent devastating livestock losses.

During this period, the army's dependence on Soviet equipment and training greatly increased Soviet influence in Somalia. The USSR acquired a variety of military facilities, notably at the northern port of Berbera. Somalia nevertheless emphasized its traditional links by joining the Arab League in 1974, when Siad Barre also acted as chairman of the Organization of African Unity (OAU). Ethiopia's revolutionary transformation to military socialism in September 1974 at first seemed to offer the prospect of an acceptable accommodation for Somali aspirations to self-determination in the Ogaden. These hopes were soon dashed, however, and as internal chaos spread in Ethiopia, Somalia saw an opportunity to reactivate claims to the Ogaden and the Somali-speaking regions of Ethiopia. In 1976 Siad Barre restructured the Western Somali Liberation Front (WSLF) and allowed it to operate inside Ethiopia. The Ogaden, the main clan in the Ogaden region and within the WSLF, represented a crucial element of Barre's clan support.

New urgency was given to Somalia's intentions by preparations for Djibouti's independence in June 1977 (both Somalia and Ethiopia had an interest in the strategic port of Djibouti and its rail link to Addis Ababa via Dire Dawa—passing through Somali inhabited areas), and by Soviet overtures to Ethiopia's Col Mengistu after he took power in February 1977. (Ethiopia expelled US personnel in May.) Despite Soviet attempts to dissuade him, Siad Barre's forces invaded Ethiopia, unofficially, in July 'in support of the WSLF'. Within three months Somali troops had overrun the Ogaden region and reached Harar. The USSR began to supply Ethiopia with weapons; in November Somalia abrogated its treaty of friendship with the Soviet Union and expelled 6,000 Soviet advisers and experts. Somalia obtained some financial assistance from Saudi Arabia, but hopes of Western assistance were largely frustrated, and by March 1978 the Soviet and Cuban-led counter-attack had re-established Ethiopian control in the main centres of the Ogaden and the Somali government announced the withdrawal of its forces.

Defeat in the Ogaden war and the break with the USSR led to a gradual strengthening of links with the USA, stemming from US strategy in the Gulf, following the Soviet intervention in Afghanistan in late 1979. A defence agreement, announced in 1980, permitted the use by US military personnel of the air and naval facilities at Berbera. The USA provided Somalia with substantial amounts of aid during the 1980s, but remained hesitant about providing the military aid often sought by the Somali government as long as Somali forces continued to operate in Ethiopia. The US administration also expressed reservations regarding renewed Somali links with Libya after 1985.

The Ethiopian government's recovery of the Ogaden and its response to continued guerrilla operations as well as Somali army incursions (together with prevailing drought conditions), resulted in the flight, to Somalia, of hundreds of thousands of refugees. Food aid from Western relief agencies became a significant factor in the Somali economy. There was considerable disagreement over refugee numbers, with government estimates of as many as 1.5m., in contrast to a figure of 400,000 quoted by some relief agencies. The failure of rains in 1985 and 1986, and the recurrence of famine in 1987, led to further refugee movements. A compromise refugee figure of 800,000 was accepted for the provision of food relief in the later 1980s.

Military defeat, shifts in alliance and ideology, as well as famine and the influx of refugees, had considerable impact on internal politics. Opposition movements began to appear, notably the Somali Salvation Democratic Front (SSDF), a largely Majerteen-supported movement, and the Somali National Movement (SNM), whose support was primarily drawn from the northern Isaaq clan. The Majerteen are a Darod clan living largely in the north-east. Both movements received Ethiopian support. The SSDF took control of two small central Somali towns near the border in 1981 but virtually collapsed with internal divisions in the mid-1980s. In 1988, after a meeting in which Siad Barre and Mengistu agreed to restore diplomatic relations, withdraw troops from border areas, and end support for each other's dissidents, the SNM were ordered to leave their Ethiopian bases. This precipitated a premature guerrilla offensive. In May the SNM seized Burao and captured most of Hargeysa, in the north. They were promptly ousted by a full-scale armed government response under the command of Gen. Mohamed Siad 'Morgan' (a son-in-law of the president). His uncompromising operations included the systematic bombardment of Hargeysa (by South African mercenary pilots), resulting in an estimated 40,000 deaths and the flight of around 400,000 refugees into Ethiopia. The brutal suppression of the insurgency resulted in far greater support for the SNM within the Isaaq and other northern clans than it had ever managed to achieve by its own efforts. Siad Barre's response to political and economic difficulty was to tighten his own control, although he allowed the introduction of a new constitution with an elected assembly, within the single-party system, in 1979. However, the assembly's lack of power was underlined in November 1984 when it effectively transferred all government powers to the president. Although seriously injured in an automobile accident in May 1986, Siad Barre (as sole candidate) was re-elected president for a further seven-year term. In 1987 Siad Barre reluctantly agreed to the creation of the post of prime minister, which was occupied by Gen. Mohamed Ali Samatar, formerly first vice-president and defence minister.

Siad Barre's temporary incapacitation in 1986 precipitated a struggle for the succession within his own Marehan clan and significantly weakened the government's position. The main claimants were his eldest surviving son, Gen. Maslah, and his cousin, Abd ar-Rahman Jama Barre, a veteran foreign minister; their rivalry divided the clan and also the armed forces. Economic difficulties were also increasing, as remittances from Somalis working in the Persian (Arabian) Gulf region declined in the aftermath of the Iran-Iraq war and then during the 1990–91 conflict in that region; international aid was also being reduced, as a result of concern over the regime's human rights record.

With the collapse of the economy, Siad Barre no longer had the resources to continue the manipulation of clan rivalries, which he had ruthlessly employed to ensure his political survival, and opposition continued to grow. In early 1989 a group of Hawiye notables established the United Somali Congress (USC), in exile, in Rome. The USC included a guerrilla wing, operating from Ethiopia, and commanded by Gen. Mohamed Farah 'Aidid'. (The Hawiye are the dominant group in Mogadishu and are particularly prominent in commercial and intellectual life.) Hawiye opposition was also expressed through the 'Manifesto' movement in Mogadishu which produced a declaration, in June 1990, appealing for the resignation of Siad Barre, the establishment of a transitional government to organize democratic elections, and the immediate abolition of all security structures. Siad Barre's response was to arrest about half of the signatories, including the country's highly respected first president, Aden Abdullah Osman. In turn, the 'Manifesto' group began to nurture a military wing, although it was widely considered to be a part of the USC. The growth of opposition was further demonstrated by the arrest of a number of Muslim religious leaders, accused of supporting various opposition elements, which led to demonstrations in Mogadishu in July 1989. These were ruthlessly suppressed by the security police, with reports of as many as 1,500 dead and injured, including one instance in which 46 people, all northerners, were summarily executed. During 1989 the government also lost the support of the Ogaden clan, which together with the Dolbuhunta, had been the main supporters of Siad Barre's Marehan clan. Following the dismissal and arrest of the Ogadeni minister of defence, Gen. Aden Abdullahi 'Gebiyou', Ogadeni army deserters established the Somali Patriotic Movement (SPM) in the south. This gained considerable support from the Ogaden who had long considered that the Marehan, as the president's clan, had been able to expand their grazing at the expense of the Ogaden in the Juba valley. In response to mounting military and civil opposition, the government made some conciliatory gestures, but they were largely dismissed as superficial exercises.

In August 1989 Siad Barre announced that opposition parties would be allowed to contest elections, scheduled to take place before the end of 1990, and additionally offered to relinquish power. One effect of this was to encourage the creation of political parties within those major clans that had yet to evolve a political identity. In January 1990 the president dismissed his government, castigating the prime minister, Gen. Samatar, for the government's poor performance. However, Siad Barre failed to persuade any opposition figures to join the administration, and was finally forced to reappoint Samatar.

A renewed military offensive in the north in early 1990 was largely successful in its aims, with the government temporarily recapturing a couple of towns from the SNM. Significantly, much of the fighting was carried out by clan militia, armed by the government. In July, following the appearance of the 'Manifesto' group, the government announced a constitutional referendum for October to be followed by elections in February 1991. In September, Samatar was again dismissed, and replaced by Mohamed Hawadle Madar, an Isaaq from the north. A month later it was announced that the multi-party system would take immediate effect, and Siad Barre relinquished the post of secretary-general of the SRSP, in accordance with the provisions of the new constitution, which proscribed the president's maintenance of additional official responsibilities. However, by late 1990 the government retained little authority outside Mogadishu. The army, its administration and command structure in decay owing to the over-promotion of untrained Marehan, had virtually disintegrated. Indeed, its clan support was essentially confined to the Marehan which was itself divided on the wisdom of continued support for Siad Barre, some believing that the fortunes of the president had become too closely allied to those of the clan. In November widespread fighting erupted in Mogadishu when Siad Barre attempted to exploit an inter-clan dispute in order to attack the Hawiye. A full-scale uprising followed indiscriminate shelling of Hawiye areas of the city; USC guerrillas arrived in force and steadily advanced on the government's positions. Desperate efforts to form an acceptable government, headed by Umar Arteh Ghalib, an Isaaq and a former minister of foreign affairs recently released by Siad Barre, and an announcement by Siad Barre that he would relinquish power in exchange for a cease-fire, were ignored. Italian efforts to negotiate a peaceful transfer of power were also unsuccessful. On 27 January 1991, Siad Barre fled with the remnants of his army and the USC announced it had assumed the government of the country.

DESCENT TO CIVIL WAR

On announcing its take-over the USC had also urged all opposition forces to participate in a national reconciliation conference. However, on 29 January 1991, the USC unexpectedly appointed one of the 'Manifesto' group, Ali Mahdi Mohamed, a prominent businessman, and former politician from the pre-1969 period, as interim president. The USC emphasized that it did not intend to form a permanent government, but other political groups saw the move as an attempt to pre-empt their participation, despite the appointment of non-Hawiye to government. On 2 February, Umar Arteh Ghalib was appointed prime minister at the head of a new government; other appointments included Gen. Mohamed Abshir, of the Majerteen clan. Umar Arteh, however, was considered to have compromised his position by his acceptance of the premiership shortly before Siad Barre's overthrow, and was unpopular with the SSDF and the SNM. The majority of government posts were allocated to Hawiye clan members, in particular those from the 'Manifesto' group.

In the north the SNM, which expelled the remnants of Siad Barre's forces in January and February 1991, convened a series of clan elders' meetings which led to the declaration of an independent 'Republic of Somaliland' in May. The SNM chairman, Abd ar-Rahman Ahmed Ali 'Tur', was declared acting president. The secession was denounced by the USC and by the Mogadishu government. In the south, fighting erupted between the USC and elements from the Darod clan as Siad Barre tried to rally support under the banner of a Somali National Front (SNF). The move split one Darod clan, the Ogaden, and its political group, the SPM. One faction co-operated with the SNF and forces raised by Gen. Mohamed Siad 'Morgan', who led several advances of SNF forces towards Mogadishu during 1991. The other section of the SPM, led by Col Ahmed Omar Jess, united with the USC to oppose any attempts by Siad Barre to return. The southern port of Kismayu changed hands several times during the year. Much of the fighting was on a clan basis, between Hawiye (USC) and Darod (SNF or SPM), or between sub-clans of the Ogaden, which supported different factions of the SPM.

In June 1991 President Gouled of Djibouti sponsored the first of two reconciliation conferences. The conference was chaired by ex-president Aden Abdullah Osman, and included delegations from the USC, the Somali Democratic Movement (SDM, a Rahanwin organization), the SSDF (Majerteen), and the SPM (Ogaden). Although the SNM refused to attend a second meeting or participate in a transitional government for all Somalia, two additional groups, the Somali Democratic Alliance (Gadabursi), and the United Somali Front (Issa), took part in the second conference, convened in July. An agreement was negotiated, committing all those attending to resist the forces of Siad Barre, implement a general cease-fire, respect national unity, re-adopt the 1960 constitution, and recognize Ali Mahdi's two-year mandate as interim president. Much discussion was devoted to dividing ministerial portfolios equitably among the clan groups. The Darod groups (the SSDF and the SPM) wanted a Darod prime minister, while others requested a northerner, although not Umar Arteh. Other major difficulties arose concerning Darod demands for the return of property seized after Siad Barre's overthrow. Darod and Isaaq clans were estimated to have owned as much as 60% of land and property in Mogadishu before 1989. Most was looted in 1991 and appropriated by Hawiye, who were reluctant to return it. The issues of property and blood debt for deaths in the fighting have since remained highly contentious, and unresolved, problems.

The Mogadishu government's difficulties were compounded during 1991 by a major split in the USC, between the factions led by Ali Mahdi and by Gen. Mohamed Farah 'Aidid' who had been the main USC guerrilla leader. These factions had different origins, but more importantly, they also represented different sub-clans within the Hawiye—Ali Mahdi being from the Abgal, a prominent group in and around Mogadishu; and Gen. Aidid being from the Habr Gidir, who comprise a significant element of the more rural, pastoral Hawiye, living in the central regions of the country. The Abgal provided much of the support for the 'Manifesto' group while the Habr Gidir comprised most of the Hawiye guerrilla forces. Many Habr Gidir felt that the 'Manifesto' politicians had benefited undeservedly, after coming late to the struggle and doing little fighting. Gen. Aidid made it clear he felt he had a much better right to the presidency than Ali Mahdi. In July, at the third congress of the USC, he was elected USC chairman, affording him a significant power base. When Ali Mahdi failed to award ministerial posts to Gen. Aidid's supporters in the reshuffle that followed the Djibouti conferences, confrontation seemed inevitable.

The first clash occurred in September 1991, when four days of fighting resulted in heavy casualties. More serious hostilities erupted in November and lasted until March 1992, when a cease-fire was eventually negotiated. Both sides were exhausted, with food supplies short and no international body prepared to intervene until hostilities ceased. Stores of ammunition were also depleted. By then at least 30,000 people had died and thousands more had been injured, with Mogadishu in disarray and divided between the two sides. The struggle was complicated by two other Hawiye clan militias in Mogadishu, the Hawadle and the Murasade. The Hawadle, in possession of the airport, originally supported Gen. Aidid, the Murasade, in control of the port, backed Ali Mahdi.

The March 1992 cease-fire had been organized by the United Nations, which had first investigated the possibility of a UN peace-keeping force being sent to Somalia early in the year. On 23 January a resolution was adopted unanimously by the UN Security Council, imposing an arms embargo on Somalia, requesting humanitarian aid and urging the parties to cease hostilities. By the end of the month, hundreds of thousands of people displaced by the conflict were reported by the International Committee of the Red Cross to be in danger of starvation, and thousands of refugees from Somalia were continuing to cross the border into Kenya. Following the March cease-fire a UN technical team arrived to act in a supervisory capacity. In late April the UN Security Council approved the establishment of a 'UN Operation in Somalia' (UNOSOM) and the dispatch of 50 observers to Mogadishu. An Algerian diplomat, Mohammed Sahnoun, was appointed by the UN secretary-general as his representative in Somalia. Sahnoun arrived in Mogadishu on 9 May to establish a UN presence. Deployment of the UN observers was slow, partly because Gen. Aidid temporarily suspended co-operation with the UN, alleging that UN aid flights to Mogadishu had been used to supply arms and funding for supporters of Ali Mahdi. The cease-fire monitors eventually arrived in late July. A further UN Security Council resolution approved an urgent airlift of food aid to Somalia, the dispatch of a technical team and 48 military observers to assess the situation in preparation for deploying 500 UN peace-keeping troops. Agreement was finally reached with Aidid on the presence of UN peace-keeping forces and the first elements of a Pakistani battalion arrived in Mogadishu in mid-September. The UN also approved the dispatch of a further 3,000 troops to Somalia, although this was opposed by Aidid.

The UN's gradual involvement during 1992 failed to interrupt continuing fighting. Although the cease-fire in Mogadishu held, forces loyal to Siad Barre attempted to recapture the capital. In April these forces advanced to within 30 km of Mogadishu, only to be halted by Gen. Aidid's forces in a battle at Afgoi on 18 April. Aidid capitalized upon his victory by repulsing Siad Barre's forces, and Siad Barre himself, initially to Guerbaharre, where Siad Barre had been based since his overthrow, and then on into Kenya. The Kenyan government offered Siad Barre temporary refuge for 'humanitarian reasons'; however, following protests by more than 200 members of the Kenyan legislature, he moved on to Nigeria, where he died in exile in January 1995. Following his victory over Siad Barre's forces, in mid-May 1992 Aidid's troops, in alliance with Col Ahmed Omar Jess of one SPM faction, recaptured the southern port of Kismayu from the forces of Gen. 'Morgan'. 'Morgan' and his supporters also fled into Kenya. Aidid's military successes and his efforts to establish administrative control of the whole of southern Somalia, generated considerable opposition. He himself formed a coalition, the Somali National Alliance (SNA), comprising his own USC, a faction of the SPM, a faction of the SDM, and the Southern Somali National Movement, a political group of non-Darod clans to the south of Mogadishu. In response to this and to Aidid's recent victories, Ali Mahdi strengthened his links with other opponents of Aidid, notably the SSDF, the other SPM faction, and the SNF. After mid-1992, the SNF, although a largely Marehan organization, disassociated itself from Siad Barre, while allying itself with 'Morgan', who became one of its main military commanders. In October 1992, fighting again intensified. Aidid's opponents, led by 'Morgan' and Gen. Ahmed Warsame of the SNF, recaptured Bardera, a strategic southern town and advanced towards Kismayu.

The escalation of fighting in October 1992 underlined the serious nature of food shortages in rural areas, particularly in the areas around Bardera. With the country in a state of anarchy, all aid agencies encountered enormous difficulty in ensuring the security of relief supplies and of their own personnel, and many were forced to hire armed guards from local clans for their protection. There were growing differences of opinion between the UN, which wished to secure a general cease-fire with the aid of peace-keeping forces, in order to protect relief supplies from looting, and the relief agencies which identified an urgent need to maximize food distribution as quickly as possible. By mid-1992 it had become apparent that a major humanitarian crisis had arisen in and around Bardera and Baidoa in the south of the country, largely owing to the destruction of food stocks in the area by the forces of Siad Barre in the months before and after their last attack on Mogadishu in April. The failure of Aidid's efforts to establish control in the area contributed to the severity of the problem. It was subsequently estimated that some 300,000 people may have died from starvation in this period. The UN's slow response to the humanitarian crisis was widely criticized. At a conference in Geneva in October, convened for the launch of the UN's 100-Day Programme for Somalia (a relief programme requesting more food aid, and the provision of basic health services—but including the rehabilitation of civil society), the UN secretary-general's special representative took the opportunity to criticize UN agencies, itemizing them as inert and incompetent; he also questioned the continued lack of operations in Somalia of the World Health Organization. Sahnoun also advocated local reconciliation and a gradual approach to a national reconciliation conference, and was resistant to the idea of any rapid deployment of UN peace-keeping forces. His criticism of senior UN officials, and his disagreement with the UN secretary-general over future policy, forced his resignation later in the month.

INTERNATIONAL INTERVENTION

Deteriorating conditions in Somalia in the latter part of 1992 prompted a response from the US government. In late November President Bush, who had earlier authorized a US airlift to assist in food distribution, offered up to 30,000 US troops to ensure food deliveries to those in need, and to prevent looting. The offer was a cause for concern among many aid workers in

Somalia, who felt that since the death toll had already slowed significantly, and food distribution had improved considerably, intervention on such a scale was unnecessary. The US proposition, however, coincided with the aim of UN secretary-general, Boutros Boutros-Ghali, to increase the UN's capacity to intervene in such crisis situations, and the UN welcomed the offer. It was suggested that an additional motivation for the US offer of intervention might have been the emergence of an Islamic political group in June in Somalia. A number of towns in the north-east of the country had been temporarily seized by the al-Ittihad party. While they were quickly expelled by the SSDF, Islamic groups continued to gain prominence in several other areas of the country, prompting US concern at the possibility of the spread of Iranian influence in Somalia, Kenya and Ethiopia.

Following the (albeit brief) convergence of UN and US interests, the first US troops of the Unified Task Force (UNITAF) landed at Mogadishu on 9 December 1992 as part of 'Operation Restore Hope'. Contingents from 21 countries, including France, Belgium, Saudi Arabia, Zambia, Canada, Morocco and Australia participated. UNITAF forces were deployed throughout the country over the next few weeks, entering Baidoa on 16 December and Kismayu four days later. Under pressure from UNITAF, Gen. Aidid and Ali Mahdi held peace talks, and on 27 December announced that they had signed a 'reconciliation agreement'. The scope and aims of UNITAF's operation, however, were both ill-defined and controversial. The US administration was determined to limit the activity of its forces to protecting the flow of aid. The UNITAF commander, a US officer, made it clear that he would not be prepared to carry out disarmament on a substantive scale. The UN, however, wanted the role of UNITAF to include complete disarmament of the rival factions and the establishment of security in the country, which it argued could not be achieved without full-scale disarmament of the factions and indeed of bandits, whose activities remained a considerable threat to security. UNITAF forces did carry out some seizures of weapons and the US claimed that the military task of restoring security had been completed by early February 1993, allowing the free movement of relief aid throughout Somalia. Nevertheless, violent incidents continued as the US administration negotiated the withdrawal of its forces and the transfer of operations to a multinational peace-keeping force under direct UN command. The strength of UNITAF (some 38,300 men in mid-January 1993) had been reduced to 24,000 by early February, although there was disappointment among US officials at the poor level of UN preparedness for any transfer. One of the main areas of conflict remained Kismayu, where the forces of Gen. 'Morgan' and those of Col Ahmed Omar Jess' faction of the SPM were in conflict at the end of February. Clashes continued into March, prompting the US to dispatch marines in an attempt to restore order and reinforce the existing US and UN troops already deployed there.

Meanwhile, negotiations continued among the factions on proposed peace talks, which were scheduled to be held in Addis Ababa, Ethiopia, in March 1993. The national reconciliation conference was attended by representatives of 15 leading factions; members of the SNM from the self-declared 'Republic of Somaliland' (see below) were present with observer status. The conference nearly collapsed at the outset when Gen. Aidid's supporters were ousted from Kismayu by Gen. 'Morgan' despite the presence of UN forces there. However, on 27 March, the leaders reached a compromise agreement, to form a 74-member transitional national council as the supreme authority in Somalia, with a mandate to hold elections within two years. The council was to have three representatives from each of the 18 administrative regions of Somalia (inclusive of 'Somaliland'), as well as five representatives from Mogadishu and one from each of the 15 signatory factions to the agreement (which was not signed by the SNM). The agreement committed the factions to disarmament within 90 days and required the peace-keeping forces of the UN to administer the cease-fire by taking sanctions against violators. However, concern was expressed that ambiguities contained within the final communiqué would lead to future disagreement over interpretation of the terms of the agreement. On the day preceding the signing of the agreement, the UN Security Council adopted Resolution 813, authorizing the deployment of UNOSOM II to replace UNITAF, and instructing it to use whatever means necessary to uphold peace, disarm combatants and protect relief workers. UNOSOM II, the largest peace-keeping operation to be dispatched under UN auspices, was also the first such operation to engage in peace enforcement without the consent of parties in the relevant country. It was to operate under Chapter VII of the UN Charter, allowing its forces to initiate military action as UNITAF had done. The creation of UNOSOM II followed proposals made by the UN secretary-general in March, that operations in Somalia should be transferred to a multinational force of 28,000 men on 1 May. In March a retired US admiral, Jonathan Howe, was appointed as special representative of the secretary-general in Somalia, with a mandate to oversee the transition from UNITAF to UNOSOM II.

UNOSOM II, under the command of Gen. Çevik Bir of Turkey, formally took control of the peace-keeping operation on 4 May 1993, with more than 30 countries contributing to a force which numbered some 30,000 at full strength. UNOSOM II inherited a series of difficulties from UNITAF and from US policies. The view that 'Somaliland' should be considered part of Somalia complicated UNOSOM's dealings with the north, while failure to disarm the militias and the factions meant that violent confrontation was difficult to prevent. UNITAF's acceptance of politicians and warlords as key negotiators rather than making serious efforts to widen the basis of political consultancy, meant that the existing political structures, responsible for the previous two years of anarchy, were reinforced. This also resulted in the promotion of personal conflicts at the expense of understanding clan hostilities. UNOSOM took this a stage further by taking sides and effectively declaring war on Gen. Aidid, after US advisers had decided that he was the one figure with no future role in negotiations, owing to his independent attitude towards UNITAF and towards the UN's presence in Somalia. A final legacy inherited by UNOSOM II was the independence of the US Rapid Deployment Force which remained under direct US command. It was this unit which was responsible for a series of attacks against Aidid in Mogadishu, during 1993. Conflict began on 5 June in Mogadishu when fighting between Aidid's SNA and UNOSOM left 23 Pakistani soldiers dead and 50 wounded. There were several hundred Somali casualties. The next day the UN Security Council condemned the 'unprovoked attack' on the Pakistani force and demanded the arrest and punishment of those responsible. Adm. Howe made it clear that he believed Aidid was responsible for the attack and, in response, on 12 June UNOSOM forces launched a series of attacks on the SNA. These failed in their main objective of seizing Aidid, and also provoked hostile reactions in Mogadishu. In one attack, on 13 June, Pakistani soldiers fired on a crowd of civilians, killing 20 and injuring 50 others. On 17 June the UN issued a warrant for Aidid's arrest on charges of war crimes. On the same day US helicopters attacked Aidid's home in Mogadishu, destroying ammunition dumps. Increasingly violent operations, which sought to disarm the SNA and arrest Aidid, continued over the next few months. One of the worst incidents occurred on 12 July when US helicopters attacked without warning a building they claimed was used by Aidid as a command centre. The SNA subsequently claimed that the building had been occupied by a meeting of Somali elders seeking an end to the violence and that 73 people had been killed. The Red Cross assessed the number of dead at 52, while UNOSOM claimed that only 20 had died. In the aftermath of the attack, four foreign journalists were killed by enraged Somali crowds. The attack revealed clear divisions within UNOSOM's command structure. Italy, providing the third largest contingent, urged a suspension of military operations to defuse tension and promote dialogue. There were claims that UNOSOM's original humanitarian mission had been sacrificed to US government preoccupations with capturing Aidid. The Italian view was echoed by aid agencies, the OAU and even by the UN's own department of humanitarian affairs. However, the secretary-general insisted that initiatives for disarmament should continue. Italy was asked to withdraw its commander in Somalia amid allegations that he was obeying Italian government orders rather than those of UN commanders, and unilaterally negotiating with Aidid. A compromise agreement was eventually arrived at, whereby Italian troops in Mogadishu were to be redeployed elsewhere in the country.

UNOSOM continued to ignore all criticism of its actions, and in August 1993 the death of four US soldiers in another clash led to the dispatch of an élite US military unit to Mogadishu to reinforce efforts to capture Gen. Aidid. Embarrassingly, four days after the rangers' arrival in Mogadishu in August, they mistakenly raided a UN compound and briefly arrested several UN employees. Subsequent US operations were more successful and some senior members of the SNA were detained though no warrants had been issued, raising questions about the legality of the detentions. UNOSOM claimed preventive detention was permissible under its mandate, and there was no obligation to allow access to lawyers. Human rights organizations strongly criticized UNOSOM's arguments. Criticism was also levelled at UNOSOM's refusal to provide figures for Somalis killed as a result of its operations. In two further clashes, in September, Somali casualties, including many civilians, were estimated at 500 dead and wounded. On 3 October an effort by US soldiers to seize Aidid's supporters in a heavily-populated district led to an all-night battle in which there were 19 UNOSOM fatalities, and at least 200 Somalis were killed and more than 700 injured. The incident provoked renewed scrutiny of UNOSOM operations, which had become increasingly characterized by indiscriminate military action and damage to non-military installations.

The events of 3 October 1993 prompted an immediate change in US policy, encouraged by massive popular support for the withdrawal of their troops. Although President Clinton's response was to dispatch reinforcements to the area, he made it clear that the US would promote a political rather than military solution to the conflict with Aidid. Following the release of the two servicemen captured on 3 October and Aidid's declaration of a unilateral cease-fire in mid-October, UNOSOM abandoned demands for Aidid's arrest. Efforts were subsequently concentrated on a political settlement, although the last of the SNA political detainees held by UNOSOM were only finally released in January 1994 after an independent inquiry into the reasons for their detention.

Another UNOSOM objective during 1993 was the rehabilitation of local government through the establishment of district and regional councils, as detailed in the Addis Ababa conference of March 1993. However, local observers were again critical of the methods employed by UNOSOM, claiming that council members were often imposed or excluded (particularly in the case of SNA members) by UN officials. It was also suggested that the local administration rehabilitation programme had been precipitantly implemented, and had failed to address the problem of refugee resettlement.

Another reconciliation conference was convened in Addis Ababa in December 1993, and was again attended by faction leaders. No agreement was reached between the four factions of Aidid's SNA and the 11 factions comprising Ali Mahdi's Somali Salvation Alliance. However, at an affiliated humanitarian conference convened simultaneously, it was made clear that UNOSOM intended to link further aid and assistance to political stability. This had the effect of encouraging local clan and regional agreements, some of which were concluded under UNOSOM auspices, while others were independently negotiated. The first of several regional conferences had been the Jubaland peace conference which took place in Kismayu between May and August 1993. Discussions included recommendations for a cease-fire and for the forcible encampment of militia forces. Negotiations also covered the creation of district councils, of local police and security forces, the rehabilitation of roads and the return of property (though the question of ownership was left undefined). However, this conference and a subsequent Kismayu meeting, convened in June 1994, failed to produce any binding agreement between the Majerteen-Harti and the Ogaden (both Darod—the major clan in the region), nor for an equitable division of resources with other claimants. Indeed the Ogaden elders did not attend the meeting in June 1994, owing to preoccupation with their own efforts to achieve Ogaden unity. (Other issues that remain to be resolved include the settlement of returning refugees and their role in already created councils, and outstanding claims and counter-claims regarding the ownership of land dating from the 1970s.) UNOSOM's reaction to elders' conferences was inconsistent. While it supported the Jubaland peace conferences, UNOSOM was accused of having attempted to sabotage a successful conference organized by Aidid in May 1993 to settle conflicts between the Hawiye and Majerteen clans in central Somalia. It was also suggested that UNOSOM's negative attitude to the continued independence of 'Somaliland', during meetings with clans from the north-east at Garowe in late 1993, undermined considerable progress in inter-clan co-operation proceeding from discussions which took place in Engavo between August and November, at which UNOSOM was not officially represented.

The decision of the US, and most European contingents, to withdraw from Somalia by March 1994, meant that the UN's mandate had to be revised. Although both India and Pakistan increased their contingents, UNOSOM no longer had sufficient personnel to carry out its larger mission. In February 1994 the UN Security Council revised UNOSOM's mandate, authorizing a progressive reduction of troops to a maximum of 22,000. This meant an end to UNOSOM's programme of disarmament of Somali factions, in favour of the protection of ports, airports and roads. In May the UN Security Council voted to extend UNOSOM's mandate for four months (rather than six, as requested by the secretary-general), and in early November the Security Council extended UNOSOM's mandate to a final date of 31 March 1995, by which time the whole operation was to have been withdrawn. There was growing alarm at the cost of UNOSOM, with daily running costs of US $2.5m., while the cost of the deployment of US troops in Somalia between December 1992 and March 1994 was estimated at $1,200m.

There was also considerable consternation in early 1994 at the failure of Somali faction leaders to make further political progress. Meetings in Nairobi, Kenya, in March had resulted in another agreement between Aidid and Ali Mahdi to establish a government, but by the end of July there had been five postponements, and no meeting, because of disagreements over the timing and location of future meetings. Aidid's return to Mogadishu in May did not improve prospects for peace. Renewed conflict erupted between factions of the Hawiye clan and there were indications that Aidid was encountering dissension within his own clan and political organization. Aidid's Habr Gidir and the Hawadle clan disputed control of the airport, and their conflict extended north to Beled Weyne in late July where the Habr Gidir took control. UNOSOM subsequently evacuated its troops from the region after the entire 168-strong Zimbabwe contingent was disarmed by Aidid's forces.

In September 1994 several clashes betweeen UN troops and Somali militias were reported, in which an unknown number of Somalis were killed. In late October fierce fighting erupted in the Bermuda area of Mogadishu, this time betwen Ali Mahdi's Abgal clan and the Murusade clan, although the two groups had previously been in alliance (there were rumours that Gen. Aidid had engineered the estrangement). Hostilities continued into early November, with more than 40 people killed and many wounded; fighting broke out again between the same clans in early December and continued sporadically into January 1995, resulting in as many as 200 fatalities. In early January a peace agreement was brokered by elders from the Abgal and Murusade communities. As the deadline for UNOSOM's departure approached, the competition for control of installations currently in UN hands, in particular the port and airport, became the focus of factional hostility.

In late November 1994 UN forces began to withdraw from positions outside Mogadishu in the first stages of UNOSOM's departure. In December Harti and Marehan clansmen fought for control of the port of Kismayu in the wake of the UN's withdrawal from that town. 'Operation United Shield', to ensure the safe evacuation of the UN troops and civilian personnel, as well as most of the equipment brought in under UNOSOM, was organized and led by the USA. The USA stationed several thousand marines in warships off the Somali coast in December, and in early 1995 they were joined by a multinational force of naval and air force units comprising some 10,000 armed personnel. The strength of this force was intended to provide sufficient protection to departing UN personnel to avoid any further killings (by early 1995 some 136 members of UNOSOM had been killed since the beginning of the operation). Contingents of UN soldiers began to be airlifted out of the country.

In early February 1995 UN troops left their compound in Mogadishu, which had served as UNOSOM's headquarters, and withdrew to positions in the port and airport. The compound buildings were immediately plundered for remaining equipment and materials by Somali looters. In mid-February thousands of

SNA supporters demonstrated against the return of US forces, although Aidid gave assurances that they would not be attacked. Even though Aidid and Ali Mahdi reached agreement on joint management of the port and airport, as well as a cessation of hostilities, including the removal of weapons from the streets of the capital during the UN withdrawal, in late February fighting was reported around both the port and airport areas. The combatants in the airport area appeared to be rival factions of the Habr Gidir sub-clan, with some supporting Aidid and others his former aide, Osman Hassan Ali 'Ato'. At the end of February 1,800 US and 400 Italian marines landed on Mogadishu's beaches, and command of the remaining 2,400 UN troops and of the whole operation was passed from the UN to the US commander. The marines secured the port and airport, and evacuated the last UN soldiers in an operation the execution of which was designed to minimize casualties, although several Somalis were killed and more injured as they threatened US positions. The departure of the last UN personnel on 2 March was closely followed by that of the US and Italian marines themselves. UNOSOM was thus terminated almost one month earlier than had originally been planned. Somali looters overran the airport, but armoured cars from Aidid's faction, reportedly accompanied by UN-trained police-officers, took control of the area. Ali Mahdi's Abgal clansmen, however, gained control of the eastern section of the airport and skirmishes were reported between the two sides. Nevertheless, Aidid and Ali Mahdi agreed on the reopening of the port and set out detailed terms for the 'technical peace committee' that was to administer the port and airport. In late May both sides met in an attempt to consolidate the port and airport administration agreement, but the terms of the agreement were promptly violated by both sides and fighting for control of the crucial sites was resumed. In early May the heaviest fighting since the UN withdrawal was reported in the Bermuda area of Mogadishu.

RESURGENCE OF MILITIA RIVALRY

Significant divisions within the SNA became more apparent in June 1995, following an attempt, made by a group of disaffected party members, to replace Aidid with Osman Hassan Ali 'Ato' as chairman of the party. SNA members loyal to Aidid, however, immediately broadcast a rejection of the legitimacy of the actions of the Ali 'Ato' faction and announced the expulsion of the faction from the SNA. On 15 June a conference of reconciliation, convened in southern Mogadishu by representatives of 15 pro-Aidid factions, elected Aidid president of the Republic of Somalia for a three-year term. Five vice-presidents, representing the interests of distinct clans, were also elected, and the composition of a comprehensive cabinet was subsequently announced. However, Aidid's presidency and mandate to govern were immediately rejected in a joint statement issued by Ali Mahdi and Ali 'Ato'. In mid-August Aidid announced a weapons collection programme in Mogadishu. However, many militias refused to comply and continued to clash with pro-Aidid factions. In mid-September Aidid's forces, which included some 600 troops and 30 armoured vehicles, occupied the south-western city of Baidoa, reportedly in an attempt to seize food supplies. The capture of Baidoa was widely considered to be the most significant military development since Aidid's forces were ejected from the port of Kismayu in 1993. More than 20 foreign aid workers, captured during the battle for Baidoa, were subsequently released unharmed by Aidid's followers. In October it was reported that Aidid had lost control of the airport at Balidogle (some 90 km south-west of Mogadishu) to Ali 'Ato' forces. In the same month a joint committee representing the interests of supporters of Ali Mahdi and those of Ali 'Ato' was established to consider the future of banana exports (a crucial source of revenue) in the context of Aidid's increasingly effective stranglehold on all operations at the port of Mogadishu. (Some goods were being imported through the neighbouring natural harbour at Ceel Macaan.) The committee announced that it would extend a ban on all banana exports from the port of Mogadishu for as long as all revenues were diverted into Aidid's war efforts. Ships attempting to dock at the port were subsequently shelled by the committee's supporters, while Aidid's gunboats returned fire in an attempt to secure the safe passage of merchant vessels.

In early December 1995 there was renewed fighting in Mogadishu between forces loyal to Aidid and Ali Mahdi, and in January 1996 Ali Mahdi's Abgal clansmen battled with Aidid's Murosade clansmen in the northern part of the city. At least 30 people died and 60 were injured as a result of the fighting. Meanwhile, Aidid's forces captured Hoddur, the third largest town in southern Somalia. In March Aidid's supporters captured Dolow, a commercial centre in the Somali-Ethiopian border region, and the southern port of Merca. In April 120 people were killed and 400 were injured in clashes in Mogadishu and southern Somalia.

Meanwhile, Gen. Aidid attempted to prevent the spread of Islamic fundamentalism in Somalia, which he perceived as a threat to his power. In May 1995 Sheikh Abbas bin Omar, the leader of the Islamic organization Jihad al-Islam, threatened to launch a holy war against Aidid and Ali Mahdi if they failed to reach an accommodation within two months. He also claimed that Jihad al-Islam maintained offices in Kenya, Sudan, Yemen, and Pakistan. Despite the threats, no Muslim uprising was reported. After the departure of the international peace-keepers, 17 men, based in north Mogadishu, formed the Shari'a Implementation Club (SIC) which sought to enforce *Shari'a* (Islamic) law throughout Somalia. In June 1995 SIC spokesman Mohamed Hassan Ahmed announced that more than 200 military volunteers had joined his organization. In February 1996, gunmen loyal to Aidid killed three people and wounded four others at the residence of an Islamic cleric. Later in the month Aidid followers wounded two people at an Islamic tribunal.

Sporadic fighting between Aidid's followers and those of Ali Mahdi and Ali 'Ato' continued between May and August 1996. In July more than 90 people were killed and some 350 were wounded during clashes between rival factions in Mogadishu. Gen. Aidid was wounded during the skirmishes, and on 1 August he died as a result of his injuries. Despite initial hopes that Aidid's demise might precipitate peace negotiations, on 4 August one of Aidid's sons, Hussein Mohamed Aidid (a former US marine and hitherto Aidid's chief of security), was elected interim president by the SNA leadership council. Hussein Aidid (who was subsequently elected chairman of the SNA) pledged to continue his father's struggle, and factional fighting quickly resumed.

The Rahanwin Resistance Army (RRA) captured Hoddur in August 1996, and in the following months the RRA clashed with pro-Aidid forces on several occasions. In addition, there was fighting in the port of Kismayu, when warring factions in the SNF clashed as a result of disagreements over the allocation of fees collected from ships using the port. Hostilities also continued in Mogadishu. In mid-October Ali 'Ato', Hussein Aidid and Ali Mahdi attended negotiations in Nairobi, under the auspices of Kenya's president, Daniel arap Moi. Measures agreed by the leaders included ceasing hostilities, removing all road-blocks, allowing the free movement of people in Mogadishu, halting media propaganda and facilitating the delivery of humanitarian aid. Nevertheless, in late October the cease-fire was broken, reportedly by supporters of Ali 'Ato' who fired at civilians in south Mogadishu. Clashes continued in Mogadishu in late 1996 and early 1997, resulting in the deaths of at least 300 people.

In December 1996 representatives of some 26 Somali factions (notably not including the SNA) held protracted talks in Sodere, Ethiopia, under the auspices of the Ethiopian government and the Intergovernmental Authority on Development (IGAD). The conference culminated, in early January 1997, in the creation of a 41-member national salvation council (NSC). The NSC, which is governed by an 11-member executive committee and a five-member joint chairmanship committee, has nine representatives from each of the major clans (Darod, Hawiye, Rahanwin and Dir) and five from smaller clans. The NSC was charged with drafting a transitional charter and holding a national reconciliation conference, with the eventual aim of establishing a provisional government. However, Hussein Aidid condemmed the establishment of the NSC, insisting that he was the legitimate president of Somalia.

In January 1997 the NSC drew attention to the fact that payments for many shipments of weapons were being made with revenue earned by the country's banana industry, and urged the European Union (EU) to refrain from supporting individuals who had secured illegal banana concessions and their parent companies abroad. The NSC also appealed to the international community to enforce arms sanctions against Somalia. The NSC's second ordinary session ended in Addis

Ababa in mid-July. The council urged the EU to impose a temporary ban on banana imports from Somalia and appealed for international assistance to help finance the national reconciliation conference, scheduled to be held in Boosaaso, northern Somalia, in November.

Meanwhile, Hussein Aidid and Ali Mahdi attended a meeting in mid-January 1997, organized by Giuseppe Cassini, Italy's special representative for Somalia. The two leaders pledged to observe the Nairobi agreement of October 1996. (Cassini also persuaded Aidid to rescind the residency ban on the EU representative to Somalia, Sigurd Illing (based in Kenya).) In May Ali 'Ato' and Aidid reaffirmed their commitment to the Nairobi agreement during a meeting in San'a, under the auspices of the Yemeni government. Later in the month Ali Mahdi and Aidid signed a reconciliation agreement in Cairo; however, Aidid maintained that he would not attend the national reconciliation conference in Boosaaso (in November), as he opposed the Ethiopian-supported peace initiative.

There was a steady deterioration in security after March 1994 with an increase in banditry, abductions of aid workers and attacks on UNOSOM personnel. The World Food Programme suspended operations in Kismayu in April, after persistent threats to its employees. In the same month US $2.6m. of UN personnel salaries were stolen from the organization's compound in Mogadishu. The creation of an 8,000-strong police force by the end of June was one of UNOSOM's more successful initiatives. However, the force was insufficiently equipped to deal effectively with the factions. UNOSOM's problems were compounded by an outbreak of cholera early in the year. By the time it had been contained (mid-year) more than 1,000 people had died and 27,000 had been affected. In late 1993 the UN had established a commission of inquiry to investigate the violent exchanges which had resulted in the deaths of more than 100 peace-keeping troops and several thousand Somalis (the SNA claimed at the beginning of 1994 that 13,000 Somalis had been killed by UNOSOM). The report, which was extensively leaked prior to its publication, attributed responsibility for some atrocities to Aidid's forces, but was also highly critical of UNOSOM methods. Among prominent criticisms were those of inadequate training and equipment, and a lack of co-ordination between military and civilian elements. UNOSOM was also accused of having underestimated Somali military capacity, and political advisers were said to have lacked expertise and to have been insensitive to Somali culture. The US was criticized for its 'premature' withdrawal and for its insistence on retaining command of its own troops. The report suggested that the UN should consider compensation for innocent Somali victims of the conflict. It also concluded that UNOSOM, rather than providing assistance for Somalia, as was intended, 'tried to impose a political solution' inconsistent with the UN mandate. In June 1995 the UN announced that the total cost of the UNOSOM mission had been $1,640m. Of the $70.3m. requested by the organization for emergency relief and short-term rehabilitation projects, only $13.1m. had been contributed by that date.

EXTERNAL RELATIONS

Historically, relations between Somalia and Kenya have been close. After the downfall of the Siad Barre regime the Kenyan government declined to express its support for any particular Somali faction striving for power. However, in July 1995 Kenyan police detained Osman Hassan Ali 'Ato', who had been in Nairobi to participate at a conference. Kenyan President Daniel arap Moi personally expressed regrets at the arrest when Ali 'Ato' was released the following day. Ali 'Ato' returned to Nairobi in August to attend a meeting sponsored by the Organization of the Islamic Conference (OIC), resulting in the release of a communiqué urging Gen. Aidid to renounce violence and to support the national reconciliation process. In June 1996 Kenya hosted a European Commission-financed conference regarding political decentralization for Somalia, which was attended by some 30 Somali intellectuals. In October President Moi hosted negotiations between Hussein Aidid, Ali Mahdi and Ali 'Ato' (see above).

Somali-Ethiopian relations have been defined largely by the Ogaden, a Somali-inhabited region in Ethiopian territory. Since the 1977–78 war between Somalia and Ethiopia regarding the Ogaden, conditions along the common border have been unstable. In January 1996 the Ogaden National Liberation Front (ONLF), which supposedly receives support from Col Ahmed Omar Jess (minister of defence in Aidid's government), clashed with Ethiopian government troops in the Ogaden. According to the ONLF, it killed 139 Ethiopian soldiers while losing 17 of its men. The Ethiopian authorities also became increasingly alarmed about the activities of al-Ittihad al-Islam, an Islamic fundamentalist organization based in Somalia but fighting to create an independent homeland in eastern Ethiopia. Al-Ittihad was suspected of having launched several terrorist operations in Ethiopia, including an attack in August 1996 on a hotel in Addis Ababa. Ethiopia responded by deploying two battalions of soldiers, supported by helicopter gunships, tanks and armoured personnel carriers, into Somalia and quickly occupied several al-Ittihad strongholds. The Ethiopian authorities claimed that 232 fundamentalists had been killed and that three al-Ittihad camps had been destroyed. In January 1997 al-Ittihad announced its intention to become a political party, causing considerable alarm to the Ethiopian authorities. Moreover, the Ethiopian administration maintained that Hussein Aidid was acting as an intermediary between Sudan and al-Ittihad. In December 1996 Ethiopian troops launched a cross-border raid into the Gedo region, establishing a 10-km zone of control on the Somali side of the border. Such raids, which continued during early 1997, were not condemned by Somalia's newly-established NSC, as it was dependent on Ethiopia's support for the successful implementation of the Sodere agreement (see above). The situation was exacerbated in February, when al-Ittihad announced that it had concluded an alliance with the ONLF and a faction of the Islamic Front for the Liberation of Oromia, both of which were active in Ethiopia. In June Ethiopia responded by launching another major attack against al-Ittihad in the Gedo region, occupying al-Ittihad's main base at Luq and a rebel stronghold at Bulohawo. These developments precipitated clashes between al-Ittihad and the SNF in the Gedo region. By mid-1997 fighting between these two groups had claimed more than 60 lives.

Libya was the only country to recognize the interim government of Gen. Aidid. The Libyan authorities allegedly also financed Aidid's plan to extend his control over all of Somalia by providing military aid. Nevertheless, in December 1995 the Libyan government informed the Arab League that it supported a united Somalia and to this end it sought to co-operate with all clan factions.

Somali-Canadian relations focused on human rights violations committed by Canadian troops who participated in UNOSOM operations. A Canadian commission of inquiry was established in August 1995 to investigate allegations of abuses committed by Canadian troops in Somalia. In July 1997 the commission concluded that, in March 1993, Canadian troops had murdered a young Somali; as a result, two Canadian soldiers had been imprisoned. Moreover, the commission accused the army's senior leadership of trying to conceal the incident. Meanwhile, in June 1997 two Belgian soldiers, who had participated in UNOSOM operations, were acquitted by a military tribunal of committing atrocities in Somalia. In Italy, however, photographs published in the press in that month, apparently showing members of the Folgore Paratroop Regiment torturing and sexually abusing Somali civilians, led to the resignations of two Italian generals and the launching of an official inquiry.

Despite withdrawing its peace-keeping forces, the UN continued to monitor events in Somalia. In January 1996 the UN expressed concern about the lack of progress towards a peaceful political settlement. While it encouraged all clan factions to work towards this goal, the UN reaffirmed its weapons embargo against Somalia (the embargo, however, failed to prevent weapons, ammunition, and other equipment from entering Somalia). The UN also indicated that, until peace was achieved, it would not provide any financial or other support to Somalia. In May Gen. Aidid addressed a letter to Italy's incoming prime minister, Romano Prodi, alleging that Sigurd Illing (the EU representative to Somalia), and UN secretary-general Boutros Boutros-Ghali were not only conspiring against him but also funding and arming Somali factions opposed to his government. Additionally, he accused the two officials of encouraging the secession of the 'Republic of Somaliland'. In January 1997 the UN Security Council refused an appeal by the NSC to prevent

Hussein Aidid from receiving an alleged arms and counterfeit currency shipment from Hong Kong. Shortly afterwards Aidid announced his desire to improve relations with the UN in order to facilitate the delivery of relief supplies to drought-stricken areas of Somalia. However, at a meeting in Rome in May, the Italian government and representatives from the EU and the US Agency for International Development rejected a UN plan to assume control over the Somali Aid Co-ordination body (SACB), arguing that the UN should not become further involved in Somalia and that the SACB should take greater responsibility for co-ordinating international humanitarian aid.

THE 'REPUBLIC OF SOMALILAND'

The 'Great Conference of the Northern Peoples', convened in May 1991, entrusted the SNM with the task of forming a government and drafting a constitution for the 'Republic of Somaliland'. From the outset the SNM was divided on the issue of independence. Several SNM leaders had expressed opposition to secession from Somalia. In addition, clan divisions arose over the distribution of ministerial portfolios and the allocation of resources. These divisions rendered the government virtually inoperative. However, the major problem for the government, headed by President Ahmed Ali 'Tur' was a shortage of resources. Without international recognition it proved extremely difficult to attract aid, and this in turn meant the government had no means to settle the claims of ex-guerrilla fighters, nor could it afford to demobilize them. Only assistance from non-governmental organizations enabled the government to begin the work of repairing the war-damaged infrastructure of the region, and some progress was made in the removal of mines (it has been calculated that there are about 2m. such devices to be cleared).

Progress in reconstruction was hampered by clan fighting that broke out in Burao in January 1992, and in Berbera twice during the year. The conflict, between Isaaq sub-clans (the Habr Yunis, the clan of President 'Tur', and the Habr Awal) was exacerbated by the grievances of the guerrillas and by government inactivity. Peace negotiations initiated by clan elders brought the conflict to an end in October, though the key economic port of Berbera remained outside government control. With the SNM leadership divided, political power passed into the hands of the national council of elders, who met at Boroma between February and May 1993 in a national reconciliation conference attended by 150 elders from all 'Somaliland' clans, with support from another 150 advisers and observers. Following the SNM's failure to establish a constitution and an effective government, the meeting formulated a national peace charter and a transitional structure of government. This was to comprise a council of elders (an upper house), an elected constituent assembly and an executive council (council of ministers). On 5 May 1993 Mohamed Ibrahim Egal (a former prime minister of Somalia during the 1960s) from the Habr Awal clan, was elected president, defeating the incumbent president, Ahmed Ali 'Tur', by 97 votes to 24. However, Egal's election failed to resolve clan differences. In June, following the announcement of Egal's cabinet, the Habr Yunis clan claimed that the appointments were calculated to foment clan rivalry and that assembly seats had been unjustly distributed. Habr Yunis opposition has since continued and a clan conference in June 1994 rejected Egal's government. (Ahmed Ali 'Tur' had publicly renounced secession early in the year.)

Somaliland leaders have continued to express concern at their relationship with the UN. They have consistently made clear their opposition to the deployment of UN peace-keeping forces in 'Somaliland'. Demonstrations against the possible deployment in the region of UNOSOM II forces took place in Hargeysa in April 1993. Adm. Howe, as special representative of the UN secretary-general, visited 'Somaliland' after Egal's election and pledged UN support for reconstruction. However, the UN stance at regional and political conferences still indicated that it would continue to consider 'Somaliland' as part of Somalia. By mid-1994 the 'Republic of Somaliland' had made no progress in its attempts to achieve international recognition. In July Egal, following an invitation from President Mubarak to visit Egypt, expressed the hope that international attitudes were changing. However, a few weeks later he intimated that the solution for 'Somaliland' might be to reconsider the 1960 independence agreement and adopt a fresh approach to federation. Meanwhile, influential Western nations have identified the region's lack of political and civil stability as reasons for their refusal to recognize an independent Somaliland, denying the aid and investment necessary to address the region's problems.

In February 1994 Egal announced that a referendum would be organized in the north-western region, in order to ascertain the level of popular support for an independent 'Somaliland'. By mid-1997, however, no such referendum had taken place. In August 1994 Egal expelled UN representatives from 'Somaliland', accusing them of interfering in the country's internal affairs. This was apparently precipitated by talks held between the new UN special representative to Somalia, James Victor Gbeho (appointed in July), and Ahmed Ali 'Tur', who was courted by both the UN and Gen. Aidid following his disavowal of secession for 'Somaliland'. In October and November there were violent confrontations in Hargeysa between military units remaining loyal to Egal and those defecting to support Ahmed Ali 'Tur'. There were reports of many fatal casualties, including a defence minister of Egal's administration. By mid-December it was estimated that three-quarters of the population of Hargeysa had fled, many thousands of them seeking refuge in Ethiopia. The rebel militias continued launching attacks on government positions in Hargeysa during early 1995, although their success was difficult to ascertain. Fighting spread to other parts of 'Somaliland', and in April government forces were in armed conflict with fighters from the Garhadji clan who had recently formed an alliance with Issa militiamen belonging to the anti-secessionist United Somali Front (USF). Fighting between rival factions of the SNM continued south of Hargeysa airport in August. In addition, clashes between 'Somaliland' government forces and Issa militias were reported in August and November near the border with Djibouti. In January 1996 more than 60 people were killed during fighting near Burao between troops loyal to Egal and militias apparently supporting Gen. Aidid's aim to become president of a unified Somalia. Instability within the territory led the EU to postpone new rehabilitation projects. Egal had retaliated by banning all EU activities in 'Somaliland'; however, in June 1995 the two sides reached an accommodation allowing the EU to resume operations.

Despite Egal's obviously weakened position he persevered with the introduction of a new currency for the territory, the 'Somaliland shilling', which was completed by the end of January 1995. In August 1995 four subcommittees were established to draft a new constitution for 'Somaliland'. A provisional document comprising 183 articles was published in March 1996. In late 1996 the third congress of 'Somaliland' communities began deliberations on the adoption of a constitution and the selection of a new president for the 'Republic of Somaliland'. On 16 February 1997 the congress approved the constitution, which would be effective for a three-year interim period, prior to ratification by public referendum. On 23 February Egal was re-elected president of 'Somaliland' for a five-year term, having won 223 votes in the 315-member national communities conference. However, opposition to the Egal regime continued to mar efforts to create a national polity. In March, for example, the anti-Egal United Somali Party and the USF merged into the Northern Somali Alliance (NSA). Notwithstanding, by mid-1997 the NSA had done little to weaken Egal or to present a viable alternative to his government. Meanwhile, in an attempt to defend the republic's national security, Egal supported the acquisition of new equipnment for the 15,000-strong armed forces. During 1996 the military's logistics capabilities were improved by the purchase of numerous vehicles, including tanks. In addition, Egal used diplomacy to facilitate the stabilization process, meeting the Edagale community, an Isaaq sub-clan, in January 1997 to review security issues. The two sides had been at odds since clashes betweeen them erupted in 1994 and 1996. The 120-man Edagale team, led by Sultan Mohamed Abdullahi Galal, pledged to support national reconciliation.

In March 1997 Egal demanded that the UN and its agencies recognize the 'Republic of Somaliland' and appoint a UN resident representative in Hargeysa. He indicated that any agency that refused to meet these demands would have to terminate its activities in the region within three weeks. By mid-1997, however, 'Somaliland' had not received official international recognition and the UN agencies remained in place.

In August 1997 an Eritrean delegation visited Hargeysa, ostensibly to brief the 'Somaliland' leadership about the IGAD summit in Nairobi and the Sodere peace process. Other sources suggested that the delegation wished to determine if there were any Islamic fundamentalist groups based in 'Somaliland'. Relations with Djibouti remain tense, largely because Egal believes that President Gouled has failed to take adequate action against Issa militia units campaigning for part of western 'Somaliland' to be transferred to Djibouti. Additionally, Egal maintains that Djibouti, by supporting a united Somalia, has obstructed his efforts to gain international recognition for 'Somaliland'. Egal opposed the Sodere peace conference in Ethiopia in early 1997, fearing that the establishment of an internationallly recognized provisional government in Somalia would hinder the recognition of 'Somaliland'. He therefore supported the third congress of 'Somaliland' communities when it refused to join the NSC.

Economy

MILES SMITH-MORRIS

Revised for this edition by THOMAS OFCANSKY

AGRICULTURE

Since independence in 1960, Somalia's economic growth has failed to keep pace with the rise in the country's population, which has been expanded by the influx of refugees. Over the period 1985–95 the population increased by an annual average of 1.9%. In 1990, according to estimates by the World Bank, Somalia's gross national product (GNP), measured at average 1988–90 prices, was US $946m., equivalent to $150 per head. During 1980–90, it was estimated, GNP grew, in real terms, at an average annual rate of 1.1%, while real GNP per head declined by 2.3% per year in the period 1985–93. In 1990 agriculture contributed 66% of gross domestic product (GDP) and the sector engaged an estimated 74.1% of the labour force in 1995. During 1980–90 agricultural GDP increased by an annual average of 3.3%; in 1991, however, output declined by 8.8%.

The economy is traditionally based, principally on the herding of camels, sheep, goats and cattle (the latter mainly in the southern regions), which still provide for the subsistence needs of about 75% of the population and furnish a substantial export trade in live animals, skins, clarified butter and canned meat. After independence, exports of these items rose dramatically and, until 1988, outstripped the other main export, bananas, which accounted for 40.3% of the total value of exports in that year. In 1989 livestock products accounted for about 49% of GDP.

Exports of livestock products accounted for about 80% of Somalia's total earnings of foreign exchange in 1982. However, this sector—and, indeed, the entire economy—was severely dislocated by the suspension of imports in 1983 by Saudi Arabia, Somalia's largest customer. A supply agreement with Egypt failed to compensate for this, and earnings from livestock exports fell to 1,122m. Somali shillings in 1983, and to only 514m. Somali shillings in 1984. In 1985, however, earnings recovered to 2,604m. Somali shillings, as exports of sheep and goats to Saudi Arabia resumed. In 1986 and 1987 earnings from livestock exports increased dramatically to 4,420m. and 7,300m. Somali shillings, respectively, but declined to 3,807m. Somali shillings in 1988 (approximately 67% of total export earnings) and about 2,300m. Somali shillings in 1989, owing to the fighting in the northern regions of Somalia, where the majority of the livestock is raised. The livestock sector was also severely affected by drought in the mid-1970s and in 1984/85. In March 1985 the government requested emergency international assistance for a US $51m. programme to construct 120 water reservoirs in the north, but by the middle of the year it was estimated that up to 30% of Somalia's livestock faced death from drought. A six-year programme to control livestock diseases, based in Hargeysa, was launched in 1986 with support from the International Fund for Agricultural Development. In April 1989 Italy's official aid programme financed a $37m. joint venture between the Italian company Giza and the Somali government to operate a 14,000 ha farm, whose livestock will be for export to the Arabian peninsula. In 1990 the African Development Fund approved a $24.4m. loan to help finance cattle-breeding and fishing projects; in November 1990 the Islamic Development Bank (IDB) also expressed willingness to assist Somalia in increasing its livestock exports. A significant loss of livestock, suffered as a result of famine and civil conflict in the early 1990s, was reported to have been largely recovered by mid-1995—when it was reported that large quantities of livestock were being exported to the states of the Persian (Arabian) Gulf region.

Bananas are grown on plantations along the Juba and Shebelle rivers. Output increased by more than 70% in the first five years after independence, but declined steadily from 1972, when production totalled 188,500 metric tons, to 75,000 tons in 1986, but rose to 116,000 tons in 1989. Bananas, which, with livestock, form the backbone of Somalia's exports, earned 2,469m. Somali shillings in 1987 and 3,992m. Somali shillings in 1988 (equivalent to some 40% of total export earnings in that year). A decision in 1983 to sell the majority of shares in the National Banana Board—which controlled exports after 1970—to the private sector led to optimism about a revival in production, as did the October 1985 agreement by Italy, the major importer, to abolish tax on bananas imported from Somalia, and the continuing efforts to improve agricultural technology. By May 1995 exports of bananas had also recovered from the adverse effects of famine and civil war. Reports suggested that exports to the European Union (EU) for 1994 had exceeded the quota recommended by the terms of the Lomé Convention. However, concern has been expressed that the most productive plantations, in the lower Shebelle region, are now controlled by competing Itabr Gidir clansmen who are channelling revenues into their war efforts. Exports of bananas were expected to total 27,000 metric tons in 1995.

Other fruits, as yet chiefly for local consumption, are grown on plantations in the same area. Sugar cane is a significant crop, and a number of rehabilitation schemes are under way with the aim of making the country self-sufficient in sugar, with a small surplus available for export. To this end, a second sugar factory was built as part of the Juba sugar estate development, established in 1977. Production of cotton has more than doubled, with output of seed (unginned) cotton reaching about 7,000 tons per year in the 1980s, but there is still insufficient locally-grown cotton to meet the demands of the textile factory at Balad, and the balance must be imported. Large-scale expansion of this factory made it, by 1979, one of the best-equipped textile mills in Africa, but by late 1984 a major rehabilitation was needed, and by 1985 output had fallen to just 30% of capacity. In 1983, however, Somalia overtook Ethiopia to become the world's leading producer of incense, selling more than 2,000 tons annually.

The area between the rivers, of which at present only some 700,000 ha of an estimated potential of 8.2m. ha are under cultivation, also provides the subsistence maize and sorghum crops of the southern Somali. The full utilization of this fertile belt, envisaged in development plans, could eventually satisfy the grain needs of the domestic market and provide a subsidiary export crop. Experiments in rice cultivation, assisted by the People's Republic of China (PRC), may eventually enable Somalia to dispense with costly imports of this grain. Government agricultural programmes since the early 1980s have promoted 'self-help' programmes in the villages, with the ultimate aim of enabling Somalia to achieve self-sufficiency in basic foodstuffs. In 1985 Somalia became self-sufficient in maize and sorghum, but has not managed to maintain this achievement. A spectacular advance in sorghum production in 1994, from 80,000 tons to 252,000 tons, was largely attributed to increased rainfall and the 'low-value' nature of the crop, which makes it unattractive to looters. The country's potential as a producer of grain has been affected by the imbalance caused by imports of food (of which about one-half was food aid), which increased by an annual average of 8% between 1980–84. Three vast new agricultural settlement schemes in southern Somalia, for the victims of the 1974–75 drought, offered scope for increased production. However, the heavy influx of refugees (from the Ogaden and then from Ethiopia's Hararge Administrative Region), during the late 1980s, together with the civil war, posed serious economic problems, despite aid from the office of the UN High Commissioner for Refugees (UNHCR) and other international organizations. Although crop production in 1996 was reported to have increased by 50% compared with the previous year, output was still some 37% lower than it had been prior to the civil war.

One of the largest agricultural schemes, at Afgoi-Mordile, was reactivated in 1985, after being suspended since the late 1970s. It provides for bananas, grapefruit, papaya and vegetables to be grown by a joint Libyan–Somali company, with rice, maize and sesame seed being produced by smallholders over a total of 2,500 ha. The planned Bardera dam, on the Juba river, is regarded as a vital step towards self-sufficiency in food, and has received priority in development planning. The dam is intended to fulfil three separate functions: flood control, irrigation and power supply. It will irrigate a minimum of 175,000 ha of agricultural land, and, by providing power for Mogadishu, should enable the cost of petroleum imports to be reduced by 20%. Finance was to come from the European Development Fund (EDF), the IDB, Abu Dhabi, France, Italy, Saudi Arabia and Germany. Under the public investment programme announced in 1987, the project was to be allocated US $106m. during the period 1987–90, with the total cost estimated at $317m. and completion scheduled for 1992. By 1990, however, work had yet to start and estimated costs had risen to $780m.

FISHING

Before 1972 fishing along the Somali coast was mainly a small-scale subsistence activity. By 1980 it was coming to be regarded as one of the country's leading priorities. During the 1974–75 drought some 12,000 nomads were settled and organized in fishing co-operatives, which have shown considerable promise. There were 4,000 full-time and 10,000 part-time fishermen in 21 co-operatives in 1981. The annual fish catch doubled between 1975 and 1980, reaching 10,000 tons per year. However, fish is still a negligible part of the Somali diet. Originally organized with Soviet assistance, the industry was hampered in 1977 by the expulsion of Soviet advisers and the withdrawal of their trawlers from the projects. The industry is currently receiving aid from the EU and other Western sources. In 1979 Somalia helped to found a joint Arab fisheries company, created under the auspices of the Arab League. Agreement was reached with Italy, in 1980, on a joint fishing venture in which the Italians were to provide four trawlers as well as training and technology. The Food and Agriculture Organization (FAO) has identified the Hafuna region as one of excellent potential for sardine fishing, and is expanding its training and technical assistance. The World Bank lent US $13.5m. to develop traditional fishing on the north-east coast, while Japan constructed two cold chambers and two fish markets for Mogadishu. In 1986 the PRC provided a further $17m. for fisheries development. Under the 1987–89 public investment programme, the sector was allocated $88m., of which almost one-half was to be spent on upgrading and expanding the fishing fleet. Further assistance was promised in 1987 by the EU, under the aid provisions of the third Lomé Convention. In 1988 Somalia's potential annual catch of fish was assessed at 200,000 metric tons and potential revenue at $26m. per year; however, according to estimates by the FAO, the actual annual catch for that year was only 18,200 tons. It was estimated that the total catch subsequently declined, and was 15,500 tons in 1995. In north-east Somalia fishermen currently export about 600 tons of lobster tails and some $800,000 worth of shark fins annually. Sardines are also exported. Vessels illegally fishing in the Red Sea have been seized periodically by the Somali Salvation Democratic Front. Meanwhile, the increase in piracy has hampered economic activity.

MINERALS AND INDUSTRIAL PRODUCTS

Petroleum exploration has so far proved disappointing. Since the mid-1940s more than 60 exploratory wells have been sunk, but by early 1986 only one-third of the concessions on offer were under contract to European or North American oil companies for exploration. Plans to start oil exploration off Somalia's Indian Ocean coast were announced by Mobil Corpn and Pecten, the US subsidiary of Shell, in 1990, but postponed as the civil war intensified later in that year. The government of the 'Republic of Somaliland' made contacts with a number of international oil companies during 1991 and 1992 and an exploration agreement for a block between Hargeysa and Burao was reported to have been signed with US-based Alliance Resources. However, the company failed to take up its permit, and other companies, while expressing interest, appeared reluctant to commit themselves until 'Somaliland' had obtained international recognition. In April 1979 a petroleum refinery, jointly developed with Iraq, went into operation with a throughput of 10,000 barrels per day. Somalia assumed ownership of the refinery in 1984. Production of petroleum products, which has been hindered by the irregularity of supplies of crude oil and by technical problems, amounted to 227,000 tons in 1983, 143,000 tons in 1984 and 156,000 tons in 1985. However, production declined to 44,000 in 1987, and to just 30,000 in 1988. The construction of a petroleum refinery in Mogadishu, with finance provided by two Saudi Arabian firms and Somali entrepreneurs, has been pending for some time. Petroleum accounted for about one-third of total expenditure on imports in 1988.

Somalia's mineral resources include salt, limestone, gypsum, gold, silver, nickel, copper, zinc, lead, manganese, uranium and iron ore. Iron ore reserves estimated at 170m. tons have been located in the Bur region, and deposits of uranium ore exist to the west of Mogadishu. Work began in 1984 on their development, although currently depressed conditions in world uranium markets suggest that their economic potential lies in the long term. Somalia contains some of the world's largest gypsum deposits, near Berbera. The mining sector contributed only 0.3% of GDP in 1988.

Industry is small in scale and mostly based on agriculture: meat- and fish-processing, textiles and leather goods. Between 1974–77 employment in the industrial sector increased by 20% and gross output by 65%. In 1991 the sector employed an estimated 10.5% of the labour force, and in 1988 contributed 8.6% of GDP. Manufacturing GDP decreased by an average of 1.7% annually between 1980–90. In 1988 the sector contributed almost 5% of GDP. More than 80% of enterprises were formerly state-owned, but the government subsequently gave priority to plans to attract private investment. The country's first pharmaceuticals factory, built mainly with Italian aid, was completed in 1984, but has yet to enter into production. In early 1986 the Italian government proposed renovating the factory, and operating it as a joint venture. France has agreed to finance the inauguration of the Berbera cement works (with a capacity of 200,000 tons per year), which lay idle for more than a year, after its completion in early 1985, because of foreign exchange problems. Opportunities for further development under the 1987–89 public investment programme were limited. Manufacturing was allocated only US $84m., the bulk of which was to go to the Juba sugar estate and factory. In May 1989 a hide and skin processing plant (financed by the Italian government) was completed in Mogadishu.

PUBLIC FINANCE

Despite the rise in exports after independence, imports, and the country's external debt, also increased. Budgetary expenditure has risen sharply since independence, and receipts, which derived principally from indirect taxation (especially customs and excise dues) have failed to cover the shortfall.

From 1969 the government made vigorous attempts to increase the country's self-sufficiency. Since 1971 the national budget has been divided into the ordinary budget, which is financed from internal sources, and the development budget, of which about 65% is financed from abroad. In 1988 Somalia recorded a budget deficit of 10,009.4m. Somali shillings. A provisional budget for 1991 was projected to balance at 268,283.2m. Somali shillings. The country's total external debt was US $2,678m. at the end of 1995, of which $1,961m. was long-term public debt. In 1990 (when the long-term debt totalled $1,926m.) the cost of debt-servicing was equivalent to 11.7% of the value of exports of goods and services.

The current deficit on the balance of payments increased sharply after the Ogaden war and continued to increase until 1980. Despite a stabilization programme adopted in 1980 with the help of a US $14m. stand-by credit from the IMF, loans of $9m. from OPEC and of $47m. from the Arab Monetary Fund were required to offset balance-of-payments deficits. In July 1981 a further stand-by credit of $46.6m. was granted by the IMF in support of a new fiscal policy, involving the introduction of a two-tier exchange rate, with a 'parallel' rate (representing a 50% devaluation of the Somali shilling) for exports. The two-tier exchange rate was abolished after one year and a further IMF stand-by credit was granted. The government sought to liberalize the economy by abolishing the state trading companies and introducing strict measures to control currency.

The economy showed some encouraging signs of revival during 1981–83, but deteriorated badly in 1984. An IMF stand-by credit expired in January 1984, and negotiations for an extension of these arrangements collapsed over Somali reluctance to undertake a further currency devaluation. The Somali economy passed through 1984 without IMF support and with the additional handicap of a huge trade deficit, resulting from the ban on livestock exports to Saudi Arabia. Inflation reached 100%, and the 'black market' thrived. The government eventually agreed to a 32% devaluation of the Somali shilling in September, and to a further 29% devaluation, with the introduction of a two-tier exchange rate, in January 1985. An IMF stand-by credit of US $54.7m. was duly announced, as part of a programme which included a further liberalization of the economy, especially in the import/export sector, and a reduction of price controls. However, disbursements were suspended after just a few weeks, because of a major dispute over Somalia's exchange rate policy.

In December 1985 the Somali shilling was again devalued, by about 50%, and in early 1986 the IMF resumed lending to Somalia, after the central bank agreed to the introduction of a system whereby the currency's value would be determined by means of fortnightly auctions of available foreign exchange. The auctions began in September 1986, assisted by a 'soft' loan of US $50m. from the International Development Association (IDA), and by balance-of-payments support from the USA and Italy. Shortages of funds led to the suspension of the auctions in mid-January 1987, but they were resumed in February, after the USA and Italy agreed to make additional contributions. In June, after the government had acted to clear $29m. of arrears owed to the IMF, loans totalling SDR 53.9m. were approved by the IMF, of which SDR 33.15m. was to be drawn over the next 20 months under a stand-by arrangement, while the remainder was to be available over the next three years under the Fund's Structural Adjustment Facility. In July the 'Paris Club' of Western creditor governments agreed to reschedule $170m. of Somali government debt over a period of 20 years. However, debt principal and interest due to be repaid in 1987 and 1988 ($138m. and $146m. respectively) remained substantially in excess of Somalia's forecast export earnings in those years, while outstanding arrears were estimated at $100m.

In September 1987 it was announced that the system of auctioning foreign currency by the central bank was to be abandoned and that there would be a return to a fixed rate of exchange, set at 100 Somali shillings = US $1. This reversal of financial policy was believed to have been prompted by a 14% depreciation of the Somali shilling which had occurred between August and September, and by protests at rising prices. Since the continuation of the foreign exchange auctions had been one of the principal conditions of Somalia's agreement with the IMF in June, the IMF suspended disbursement of the loans, and the World Bank also suspended the remaining $10m. of a credit of $50m. for agricultural adjustment that had been approved in 1986.

In February 1988 a committee was established by the government to review Somalia's relationship with the IMF and other Western financial institutions; however, talks held with the IMF in March foundered on the government's reluctance to readopt the auction system to determine the value of the Somali shilling. In May the IMF declared Somalia to be ineligible for further borrowing, owing to its overdue financial obligations to the Fund, which totalled SDR 26.8m. In June, in an effort to resume negotiations with the IMF, the government effected a 45% devaluation of the Somali shilling and in July it was reported that Somalia had signed an economic and financial agreement with the IMF, under the terms of which it undertook to repay its debts to the Fund with livestock, fish and other natural resources. A further devaluation of the Somali shilling, of about 20%, took place in August, and in January 1989 the government indicated that the foreign exchange auctions would be resumed on a monthly basis in March. The government also introduced significant reforms in both the agricultural and financial sectors, with the liberalization of the trade in hides and skins and veterinary pharmaceuticals, together with plans to permit the opening of foreign banks and the abolition of the state monopoly of insurance. These measures facilitated the adoption in mid-1989 of an IMF-supported structural adjustment programme. This, however, did little to help the government solve its financial problems. In September a Somali government delegation visited the IMF headquarters in Washington to discuss debt arrears and to seek eligibility for fresh loans. The delegation failed in its mission, however, despite an attempt on the part of the IMF to form a support group to raise resources to pay Somalia's US $100m. arrears. Of the seven largest donor countries, only Italy agreed to provide further lending to clear arrears, although this was made conditional on the participation of other members of the support group in financing the debt. The government's financial position continued to deteriorate during 1990, owing to growing instability and donors' reluctance to provide support because of concern about the government's human rights record. There were hopes, however, that Somalia might benefit from a new initiative by the IMF, the rights accumulation programme, allowing countries in arrears to the Fund to accumulate borrowing rights by implementing an adjustment programme and making regular interest payments. In 1991 the annual rate of inflation was estimated at more than 100%; it was estimated to have averaged 45.7% annually during 1980–88.

Somalia's long history of civil unrest (which intensified following the overthrow of President Siad Barre in January 1991), together with erratic climatic conditions, have undermined the traditional agricultural base of the economy. Agricultural production in 1991–92 was estimated at just 5%-10% that of 1987–88, although an increase in rainfall contributed to more encouraging forecasts for 1992–93. In the absence of government-led initiatives for economic reform, an 'unconventional economy' regulated by clans and sub-clans evolved, fuelled by workers' remittances from abroad (often in the form of foreign exchange and household goods and appliances), unrecorded sales of livestock and the cultivation and sale of qat (a mild stimulant). The response of international relief and assistance organizations to the humanitarian crisis in Somalia has contributed to this economy, with clans competing for revenues proceeding from the provision of equipment and accommodation for foreign personnel, the sale of food supplies looted from aid deliveries, and—prior to the arrival of the Unified Task Force (UNITAF) in December 1992—the exaction of protection money from relief organizations.

FOREIGN AID AND DEVELOPMENT, 1960–91

During 1960–69 Somalia received a substantial amount of foreign aid, chiefly from Italy, the USA and the USSR, but without producing any proportionate return. During 1963–70 a series of plans was launched by the government to improve the resources of the country. Although the plans proved too ambitious, much was accomplished during those years, notably in road-building, the construction of ports at Berbera (with aid from the USSR) and Kismayu (with US aid), the building of schools, and a large hospital at Mogadishu, financed by the European Community (EC, now European Union—EU). Few projects for livestock management and agricultural development had successfully progressed beyond the planning stage by 1969.

Under the Siad Barre regime, many of these projects became operational. The government initially sought to encourage 'self-help' rural development projects (e.g. in school-building or well-digging) which produced good results before 1969. The policy was to develop the Somali economy along socialist lines, although private enterprise on a small scale was encouraged, and to aim for self-sufficiency, particularly in food production.

The 1974–78 Five-Year Plan was delayed, since resources had to be diverted for drought relief in 1974–75. Total economic losses and the relief operations actually cost £218m. In April 1976 the World Bank issued a US $8m. loan to help to repair the effects of the drought.

About one-half of the expenditure of 7,104m. Somali shillings envisaged in the 1979–81 Development Plan was to finance projects carried forward from the previous Five-Year Plan. Of this budget, 35.4% was allocated to agriculture and fisheries, 18% to economic infrastructure and 7.4% to education. There was a new emphasis on the needs of small producers rather than large-scale schemes. The 1982–86 Plan envisaged overall expansion in real GDP of 27% over five years, equivalent to an annual average growth of 4.6%. Between 1980–87, GDP increased by an estimated 2.2%. The 1982–86 Plan attracted declarations of intent totalling US $1,200m. from a donors' meeting in October 1983. However, many projects had to be deferred when the economy was severely dislocated by the problems over livestock exports. Under the 1987–91 Plan, GDP growth was expected to average 5%. The Plan projected expenditure at $1,742.2m., with transport and telecommunications accounting for $401.8m. and agricultural development for $499.3m.

At the consultative group meeting with aid donors in April 1987, pledges, at US $835m., fell short of the $1,025m. which the government had sought for its 1987–89 public investment programme. This agreement covered commodity, project and cash aid, of which $428m. was to be allocated in 1987 and $407m. in 1988. The IDA would provide $24m. for a programme to modernize Kismayu, Mogadishu and Berbera ports, while, under the third Lomé Convention, the EC would provide ECU 5m. for the construction of bridges over the Juba and Shebelle rivers, ECU 3m. for road modernization and ECU 3m. for a project to increase fish production in the Mogadishu area. Total project aid, at $720m. over three years, would cover only 70% of the public investment programme for 1987–89. Donors asserted, however, that the shortfall was attributable to the government's inclusion of projects outside the 'core' investment programme. Following the April consultative meeting, the government agreed to establish a project-monitoring system to ensure the observance of strict expenditure guidelines.

Until 1977 the major source of aid was the USSR, together with the PRC (which has been particularly active in road-building), the EDF, UN specialized agencies, the IDA and the Federal Republic of Germany. Since 1974 Arab states have also been very important contributors, especially Libya, the United Arab Emirates (UAE) and Saudi Arabia, which is reported to have supplied over £250m. for military aid in the war with Ethiopia. However, Arab aid was reduced substantially in 1985, with new commitments falling to US $12.1m., only one-fifth of the amount that Arab states supplied in 1984. In April 1987 bilateral discussions were reported to have taken place with the Arab funds to reschedule Somalia's external debt. After Siad Barre's visits to Abu Dhabi, in early 1989, the UAE reportedly provided substantial financial aid to Somalia. Following the 1980 agreement permitting US forces to use Somalia's military bases, the USA became a major donor. Its support was particularly important for Somalia's transport systems, which were among Africa's poorest.

In 1985 work finished on a US-sponsored US $37.5m. project to double the number of berths at Berbera port and to deepen its harbour, which handles a large volume of cattle exports. Soon afterwards, a $42m. development of Kismayu port began, designed to equip it to handle livestock in addition to bananas. The USA also provided finance for the expansion of the runway at Mogadishu airport. US aid, which was suspended in 1988 because of the Somali government's alleged abuses of human rights and the protracted civil war, was resumed in 1989 following the release of more than 200 political prisoners in January. In May the USA supplied 6,536 tons of edible oil worth $5m. and in June signed a grant agreement worth $15.1m. However, a further $36.3m. of aid for 1988/89 remained blocked because of the continuing conflict in the north. In February 1990 the US suspended all financial aid for 1990/91 in protest at Somalia's 'long pattern of human rights abuses'. During that financial year the USA was to provide only $750,000 for some projects already in progress. A more traditional benefactor is Italy, which in 1985 offered more than $200m. in special assistance from its emergency aid fund for Africa, mostly for the construction of a road linking Garowe to Boosaaso, to provide access to the isolated north-east. In 1989 Italy financed the reconstruction and expansion of Mogadishu airport.

In October 1988 the EDF provided ECU 5m. for a programme to improve Somalia's satellite communications links with Europe and the Gulf states. Somalia received a further ECU 15m. in December for specific imports in the agriculture, industry and transport sectors. A US $83m. project to improve and expand Somalia's telecommunications network, due to be completed in 1991, was financed by Italy, the African Development Bank and Japan. In July 1988 Japan also donated $6.5m. in financial aid, cancelled its Somalia debt and pledged to increase its aid disbursements. In January 1989 the Japanese government provided an additional 350m. yen in food aid and in March promised a further 900m. yen to support Somalia's economic recovery programme. In July the EDF granted $54m. for the construction of a 230-km road between Gelib and Bardera. The road was intended to provide access to the fertile Juba valley, which was to be developed following the completion of the Bardera dam project, originally scheduled for 1992. A further grant, of ECU 16m., to fund the purchase of oil imports, was provided by the EU. The EU also donated ECU 2m. in aid to cattle breeders for the purchase of veterinary drugs.

In March 1989 a three-year agreement was signed with the IMF, under the terms of which US $260,000 were to be allocated by the Fund to development projects in the agriculture, livestock and fisheries sectors during 1989–91. In August the World Bank released the first $20m. of a $70m. loan provided for agricultural development. Of the overall credits disbursed through the IDA over the two-year period, $44.5m. was allocated to finance imports of goods and materials for both the private and public sectors, and $16.5m. for fuel purchases. In early 1990 the IDA agreed to provide $26.1m. towards a seven-year $32.5m. education project; the share of education in the national budget had fallen from 10% in 1980 to only 1.9% in 1988. In October 1990 the IDA also pledged $18.5m. for rehabilitation work on the country's road network and telecommunications infrastructure and Mogadishu's water supply.

FOREIGN TRADE

Somalia's foreign trade deficit (which is almost entirely financed by foreign aid) increased to around US $300m. in 1987, and only an increase in official transfers in that year prevented the current account deficit from rising far above the 1986 level of $88m. Despite a considerable narrowing of the trade deficit in 1988, to $157.6m., the trade gap widened to $278.6m. in the following year, with the deficit on the current account of the balance of payments increasing from $98.5m. to $156.7m. Total external debt amounted to $2,678m. at the end of 1995. In February 1993 the Arab Monetary Fund suspended Somalia's membership because of arrears totalling $113.9m. at the end of 1991.

Control over the port of Mogadishu and the lucrative banana trade was repeatedly contested by Gen. Aidid and Ali Mahdi. In August 1995 Ali Mahdi announced that his government had started to construct a new port, at a cost of US $500,000, some 30 km north of Mogadishu. In October Ali Mahdi and Ali 'Ato' banned the export of bananas from Mogadishu port, in an attempt to prevent Aidid from collecting taxes to finance his war efforts. Clashes between the two sides ensued, and vessels attempting to dock at the port were shelled. Meanwhile, in September, Aidid announced the implementation of a new code of taxation, under which all tradable items would be taxable. Other taxable assets included buildings, vehicles and land.

REHABILITATION, FOOD AID AND DEVELOPMENT

In 1989 and 1990 the economy deteriorated rapidly, largely due to the continuing civil strife in many parts of the country. Severe shortages of food, fuel and medical supplies were reported following the overthrow of the Siad Barre government in January 1991, with many aid agencies reluctant to return to the country. Fighting in agricultural regions in mid-1991 was reported to have severely disrupted production, and, as fighting intensified in late 1991 and early 1992, agriculture, and domestic and foreign trade all virtually halted and large numbers of people were displaced from their homes. By July 1992 the UN estimated that 1.5m. people were in immediate danger of starvation, with a further 4.5m. at risk; cereal import needs were assessed at about 480,000 tons. At that time, almost 1m. Somalis were refugees. By late 1995 it was estimated that there were 240,000 Somali refugees in Ethiopia, 150,000 in Kenya, 45,000 in Yemen, 20,000 in Djibouti and 20,000 elsewhere. There were approximately 250,000 internally displaced Somalis, of whom 100,000 lived in 170 locations in the 'Republic of Somaliland'. As a result of the extended civil conflict, considerable damage was inflicted on the infrastructure, telecommunications and electricity and water supplies of many urban areas, notably the capital. Large-scale reconstruction and the exploitation of Somalia's underdeveloped resources (including large areas of uncultivated arable land between the Juba and Shebelle rivers, and rich fishing grounds along the country's coastline) were expected to be hampered by unwieldy foreign debt, in the unlikely event of the prompt negotiation of a durable peace accord. In 1993–94 the UN became Somalia's largest employer and introduced a significant amount of foreign currency. With the withdrawal of the UN operation in early 1995 hundreds of Somalis lost their employment and the country's largest source of income was removed.

Despite continuing insecurity in Mogadishu and other parts of the country, the UNITAF peace-keeping operation, which arrived in December 1992, was successful in facilitating the distribution of food aid. By late January 1993, relief workers were feeding 1m. people daily at 1,000 centres throughout the country. Nevertheless, pockets of famine persisted in rural areas, particularly in the south. In March the FAO estimated that 1m. people would continue to require food aid throughout 1993; the FAO also estimated that 300,000 people had died of hunger-related causes during 1992, although other sources estimated the total to be as high as 500,000. A UN-sponsored conference of donors in Addis Ababa in March pledged US $130m. towards the reconstruction of Somalia, although this fell short of the UN's target of $166m., already revised downwards from $253m. The programme aimed to restore administrative infrastructure, repatriate refugees, restore livestock herds and restart primary education. Donors warned, however, that Somalis needed to find ways to restore stability and security if aid was to continue. Improving conditions in rural areas and good rains in early 1993 allowed agricultural activity to resume, with good harvests reported and even the resumption of small-scale exports of livestock and fruit.

In March 1995 it was reported that more than 500,000 people in southern Somalia were in imminent danger of dying of starvation and disease, and urgently required food and medical aid. In June the European Community Humanitarian Office (ECHO) announced that it had approved a grant of ECU 350,000 for medical aid and for a survey on food requirements. In July the International Committee of the Red Cross (ICRC) provided emergency food aid, seeds and fishing equipment to more than 9,000 families in southern Somalia. In August ECHO agreed to provide an additional US $441,000 to support ICRC's activities in southern Somalia and in Somali refugee camps in Kenya. In September the EU announced it would provide ECU 505,000 to fund food and medical aid in Mogadishu. A further ECU 1m. was made available in October to relieve the acute food shortages in the Juba valley. Relief agencies funded programmes in disease control, education, farming, water chlorination, and the repair of roads, hospitals and schools. (By November 1995 health facilities in Somalia included 21 hospitals, 470 health centres and 99 out-patient dispensaries.) However, despite the advances made by relief agencies, the UN Co-ordination Team (meeting in Kenya in August 1995) indicated that it was not food supplies that were lacking, but the resources for most people to purchase them.

In July 1996 the EU announced plans to fund a modernization project for the port of Boosaaso, providing trained personnel and adequate equipment to develop the port's capabilities. It was anticipated that the scheme would improve the prospects of the 100,000 local inhabitants. The EU also announced a two-year US $60m. rehabilitation programme for Somalia, encompassing 115 projects to advance humanitarian aid, infrastructure, education and health services. The EU subsequently pledged ECU 600,000 to rehabilitate wells in Nugaal Province and ECU 1.5m. for a measles vaccination programme, food and medical aid for war victims. It also allocated ECU 47m. to improve the social, agricultural, private and public sectors.

During 1996 a combination of continued warfare, drought, floods and internal displacement made approximately 1m. Somalis dependent on emergency food aid. In some areas of southern Somalia malnutrition rates reached 22%, although by November the national malnutrition rate totalled 7%. Ten UN agencies and 32 international non-governmental organizations (NGOs) were active in the country in 1996, but relief operations continued to be hampered by violence, banditry and the lack of law enforcement. Three of Somalia's Red Crescent Society workers died in August as the result of shelling in Mogadishu, and in October relief agencies temporarily suspended non-emergency aid deliveries to Mogadishu to protest at kidnappings of their employees. In late 1996 UN agencies launched an appeal for US $100m. to sustain their humanitarian operations in Somalia. In August 1996 UNHCR appealed for $5m. to cover a funding shortage for the repatriation and rehabilitation of returnees. The UNHCR also continued to provide aid to some 500,000 Somalis who have returned to their homes in recent years, and to work on a variety of returnee projects in southern Somalia, including the improvement of infrastructure, the construction of water wells and programmes to develop health services, sanitation, education, agriculture, livestock and small businesses. In December the UN announced that more than $46m. of donor aid would be required to avoid a crisis similar to that of 1991/92, which claimed at least 300,000 lives. Assistance was needed to finance emergency food shipments, rehabilitation projects, international repatriation programmes and improved security. Meanwhile, civil unrest has contributed to a sharp deterioration in public health.

In January 1997 the US government released a study indicating that a serious food emergency might occur later in the year. The report suggested that some 58,000 metric tons of cereals might be required to avert a catastrophe, especially in the Bay and Bakool regions. In April the EU announced that it would provide ECU 3.7m. in humanitarian aid for victims of conflict in Somalia. The assistance, which was to be managed by ECHO, would allow the ICRC and several NGOs to undertake an eight-month feeding programme and a health care project. In June the UN World Food Programme (WFP) appealed for US $2m. to help pay for food distribution in drought-affected areas of southern Somalia, where a crop failure had left 360,000 Somalis short of food. The WFP subsequently distributed 3,240 tons of food to vulnerable Somalis in 78 locations in the Bay, Bakool, Hiran, Lower Juba, Middle Juba, and Lower Shebelle regions.

In October 1996 a group of Somali businessmen opened the Barakat Bank of Somalia in Mogadishu. With an initial capital of US $2m., the bank intends to specialize in small loans to Somali merchants, foreign currency exchange, and currency exchanges abroad. The bank aimed gradually to establish 90 branches in Somalia. In early 1997 the Somali-Malaysian Commercial Bank opened in Mogadishu, with capital of $4m.

THE 'REPUBLIC OF SOMALILAND'

The relative stability of the self-proclaimed 'Republic of Somaliland', following its secession in 1991, contributed to an improvement in the economy of that territory, with an estimated increase in GNP per head of 20% in 1991–94. The Egal administration introduced tax, banking and customs systems in late 1993, and a new currency, the Somaliland shilling, in late 1994. However, during 1994 the 'Somaliland' government was placed increasingly under threat by rebels from the armed forces, which, together with the refusal of the international community to recognize the territory's independence, jeopardized the future prosperity of 'Somaliland'. Furthermore, during 1995 the annual rate of inflation reached as much as 400% in some parts of the territory, resulting in a five-fold increase in the price of basic foodstuffs. In September Egal announced a comprehensive programme to control inflation and to improve the republic's economy. According to the programme, traders and wholesalers were obliged to maintain a minimum deposit of 10m. Somaliland shillings (US $125,000) in the state bank, where foreign organizations working in the territory were obliged to exchange their currencies. However, the disparity between the official and unofficial exchange rates in 'Somaliland' led some foreign organizations to announce in January 1996 that, as a result of the new regulations, they would be reviewing their activities in the territory. In February Egal banned the use of foreign currencies in 'Somaliland', with the exception of the Ethiopian birr and the Djibouti franc. Penalties for violating the measures included lengthy terms of imprisonment. In addition, Egal sought to reduce inflation by requiring banks to hold auctions of US dollars, and by establishing a ministerial committee to supervise exchange rates. Meanwhile, budgetary expenditure for 1996 was projected at 3,252m. Somaliland shillings.

The pursuit of international aid for projects in 'Somaliland' remained a priority of Egal's government. In February 1996 the EU agreed to finance the reconstruction of Berbera port; under the terms of the project, local contractors would upgrade the port's security, infrastructure and cargo-handling facilities. The improvements were expected to increase livestock exports through the port (some 3m. head in 1995). Activity at Berbera port is central to the economy of the 'Republic of Somaliland', as it provides considerable employment and generates much-needed convertible currency. Notable exports include camels, while there are also plans to increase the trade in frankincense and myrrh. It was estimated that in 1996 'Somaliland' exported 500,000 sheep to Saudi Arabia (its principal petroleum supplier). In January 1997 the Intergovernmental Authority on Development (IGAD) announced a project (estimated to cost US $18m.) to improve communications between Berbera and several other East African ports. Meanwhile, the EU has agreed to fund the reconstruction of several roads, and an Italian relief agency, Cooperazione Internazionale, is to rehabilitate Berbera's water system.

In late 1995 the fishing industry in 'Somaliland' was assisted by the resumption of operations of the Somali Highseas Fishing Co after it concluded an agreement with the tribal chief of the Osman Mahmoud sub-clan of the Majerteen, who allegedly had allowed pirates to operate in the Red Sea. Notwithstanding, reports of piracy continued during 1996.

Statistical Survey

Sources (unless otherwise stated): Economic Research and Statistics Department, Central Bank of Somalia, Mogadishu, and Central Statistical Department, State Planning Commission, POB 1742, Mogadishu; tel. (1) 80385; telex 715.

Area and Population

AREA, POPULATION AND DENSITY

Area (sq km)	637,657*
Population (census results)†	
7 February 1975	3,253,024
1986–87 (provisional)	
Males	3,741,664
Females	3,372,767
Total	7,114,431
Density (per sq km) at 1986–87 census	11.2

* 246,201 sq miles.
† Excluding adjustment for underenumeration.

PRINCIPAL TOWNS (estimated population in 1981)

Mogadishu (capital)	500,000
Hargeysa	70,000
Kismayu	70,000
Berbera	65,000
Merca	60,000

BIRTHS AND DEATHS (UN estimates, annual averages)

	1980–85	1985–90	1990–95
Birth rate (per 1,000)	50.4	50.4	50.2
Death rate (per 1,000)	21.8	20.1	18.5

Expectation of life (UN estimates, years at birth, 1990–95): 47.0 (males 45.4; females 48.6).

Source: UN, *World Population Prospects: The 1994 Revision.*

ECONOMICALLY ACTIVE POPULATION
(estimates, '000 persons, 1991)

	Males	Females	Total
Agriculture, etc.	1,157	1,118	2,275
Industry	290	46	336
Services	466	138	604
Total labour force	1,913	1,302	3,215

Source: UN Economic Commission for Africa, *African Statistical Yearbook.*

Mid-1995 (estimates in '000): Agriculture, etc. 3,001; Total 4,049 (Source: FAO, *Production Yearbook*).

Agriculture

PRINCIPAL CROPS ('000 metric tons)

	1993	1994	1995
Maize	79*	150	146*
Sorghum	80*	252	136*
Rice (paddy)	5†	2	2†
Cassava (Manioc)	40†	35	40†
Pulses	11†	12	13†
Groundnuts	2†	3	3†
Sesame seed	22†	22	25†
Sugar cane†	200	200	200
Grapefruit	17†	18	19†
Bananas	55†	43	45†
Vegetables	63†	72	73†

* Unofficial figure. † FAO estimate(s).

Source: FAO, *Production Yearbook.*

LIVESTOCK ('000 head, year ending September)

	1993	1994	1995
Cattle	4,000*	5,000	5,200*
Sheep	11,000*	13,000	13,500*
Goats	11,000*	12,000	12,500*
Pigs*	6	6	9
Asses*	23	24	24
Mules*	20	21	21
Camels	5,900*	6,000	6,200*

* FAO estimate(s).

Poultry (FAO estimates, million): 3 in 1993; 3 in 1994; 3 in 1995.

Source: FAO, *Production Yearbook*.

LIVESTOCK PRODUCTS ('000 metric tons)

	1993	1994	1995
Cows' milk	450*	550	560*
Goats' milk*	350	400	415
Sheep's milk	340*	420	430*
Beef and veal*	37	44	46
Mutton and lamb*	26	33	34
Goat meat*	31	34	36
Poultry eggs*	2.0	2.4	2.4
Cattle hides*	6.8	8.0	8.4
Sheepskins*	5.0	6.3	6.5
Goatskins*	4.8	5.2	5.5

* FAO estimate(s).

Source: FAO, *Production Yearbook*.

Forestry

ROUNDWOOD REMOVALS
(FAO estimates, '000 cubic metres, excl. bark)

	1992	1993	1994
Sawlogs, veneer logs and logs for sleepers*	28	28	28
Other industrial wood	75	76	77
Fuel wood	8,325	8,413	8,529
Total	8,428	8,517	8,634

* Annual output assumed to be unchanged since 1975.

Source: FAO, *Yearbook of Forest Products*.

Fishing

(FAO estimates, '000 metric tons, live weight)

	1993	1994	1995
Freshwater fishes	0.3	0.3	0.3
Marine fishes	14.0	15.0	14.3
Spiny lobsters	0.4	0.4	0.4
Marine molluscs	0.6	0.6	0.6
Total catch	15.2	16.3	15.5

Source: FAO, *Yearbook of Fishery Statistics*.

Mining

	1992	1993	1994
Salt (estimates, 000 metric tons)*	1	1	1

* Data from the US Bureau of Mines.

Source: UN, *Industrial Commodity Statistics Yearbook*.

Industry

SELECTED PRODUCTS
('000 metric tons, unless otherwise indicated)

	1986	1987	1988
Sugar*	30.0	43.3	41.2
Canned meat (million tins)	1.0	—	—
Canned fish	0.1	—	—
Pasta and flour	15.6	4.3	—
Textiles (million yards)	5.5	3.0	6.3
Boxes and bags	15.0	12.0	5.0
Cigarettes and matches	0.3	0.2	0.1
Petroleum products	128	44	30
Electric energy (million kWh)†	253	255‡	257‡

Sugar (Unofficial estimates, '000 metric tons): 28* in 1992; 15* in 1993; 25§ in 1994.

Electric energy (provisional figures, million kWh)†: 258 in 1992; 258 in 1993; 259 in 1994.

* Data from FAO.

† Source: UN, *Industrial Commodity Statistics Yearbook*.

‡ Provisional figure.

§ Data from International Sugar Organization.

Finance

CURRENCY AND EXCHANGE RATES

Monetary Units

100 cents = 1 Somali shilling (So. sh.).

Sterling and Dollar Equivalents (31 October 1994)

£1 sterling = 7,990 Somali shillings;
US $1 = 4,900 Somali shillings;
10,000 Somali shillings = £1.252 = $2.041.

Average Exchange Rate (Somali shillings per US $)

1987 105.18
1988 170.45
1989 490.68

Note: A separate currency, the 'Somaliland shilling', was introduced in the 'Republic of Somaliland' in January 1995. The exchange rate was set at US $1 = 80 'Somaliland shillings' in July 1995.

CURRENT BUDGET (million Somali shillings)

Revenue	1986	1987	1988
Total tax revenue	8,516.4	8,622.4	12,528.1
Taxes on income and profits	1,014.8	889.7	1,431.0
Income tax	380.5	538.8	914.8
Profit tax	634.3	350.9	516.2
Taxes on production, consumption and domestic transactions	1,410.4	1,274.2	2,336.4
Taxes on international transactions	6,091.2	6,458.5	8,760.6
Import duties	4,633.2	4,835.2	6,712.1
Total non-tax revenue	6,375.2	8,220.4	7,623.4
Fees and service charges	274.1	576.1	828.8
Income from government property	633.4	656.4	2,418.9
Other revenue	5,467.2	6,987.9	4,375.7
Total	14,891.6	16,842.8	20,151.5

Expenditure	1986	1987	1988
Total general services	11,997.7	19,636.7	24,213.6
Defence	2,615.9	3,145.0	8,093.9
Interior and police	605.0	560.7	715.4
Finance and central services	7,588.3	14,017.8	12,515.6
Foreign affairs	633.0	1,413.9	2,153.1
Justice and religious affairs	248.5	290.2	447.0
Presidency and general administration	93.0	148.0	217.4
Planning	189.0	24.9	24.3
National Assembly	25.0	36.2	46.9
Total economic services	1,927.6	554.1	600.3
Transportation	122.2	95.2	94.5
Posts and telecommunications	94.3	76.7	75.6
Public works	153.9	57.5	69.8
Agriculture	547.2	59.4	55.3
Livestock and forestry	459.0	89.5	109.9
Mineral and water resources	318.8	85.2	93.1
Industry and commerce	131.0	45.1	43.9
Fisheries	101.2	45.5	58.2
Total social services	1,050.5	900.1	930.8
Education	501.6	403.0	478.1
Health	213.8	203.5	255.2
Information	111.5	135.0	145.8
Labour, sports and tourism	139.6	49.3	51.7
Other	84.0	109.3	—
Total	14,975.8	21,091.0	25,744.7

1989 (estimates): Budget to balance at 32,429m. Somali shillings.
1990 (estimates): Budget to balance at 86,012.0m. Somali shillings.
1991 (estimates): Budget to balance at 268,283.2m. Somali shillings.

CENTRAL BANK RESERVES (US $ million at 31 December)

	1987	1988	1989
Gold*	8.3	7.0	6.9
Foreign exchange	7.3	15.3	15.4
Total	15.6	22.3	22.3

* Valued at market-related prices.

Source: IMF, *International Financial Statistics.*

MONEY SUPPLY (million Somali shillings at 31 December)

	1987	1988	1989
Currency outside banks	12,327	21,033	70,789
Private-sector deposits at central bank	1,771	1,555	5,067
Demand deposits at commercial banks	15,948	22,848	63,971
Total money	30,046	45,436	139,827

Source: IMF, *International Financial Statistics.*

COST OF LIVING
(Consumer Price Index for Mogadishu; base: 1985 = 100)

	1986	1987	1988
Food	123.6	161.4	319.8
Beverages and tobacco	117.5	155.5	249.3
Clothes	119.2	153.4	271.3
Rent	131.5	169.5	250.6
Water, fuel and power	156.0	203.2	222.8
Transport and petrol	130.2	155.4	260.1
Miscellaneous items	121.5	140.9	253.0
All items	125.8	161.2	292.9

NATIONAL ACCOUNTS

Expenditure on the Gross Domestic Product*
(estimates, million Somali shillings at current prices)

	1988	1989	1990
Government final consumption expenditure	33,220	58,530	104,760
Private final consumption expenditure	240,950	481,680	894,790
Increase in stocks	14,770	n.a.	n.a.
Gross fixed capital formation	44,780	134,150	240,030
Total domestic expenditure	333,720	674,360	1,239,580
Exports of goods and services	7,630	8,890	8,660
Less Imports of goods and services	49,430	57,660	58,460
GDP in purchasers' values	291,920	625,580	1,189,780

* Figures are rounded to the nearest 10m. Somali shillings.

Source: UN Economic Commission for Africa, *African Statistical Yearbook.*

Gross Domestic Product by Economic Activity
(million Somali shillings at constant 1985 prices)

	1986	1987	1988
Agriculture, hunting, forestry and fishing	54,868	59,378	61,613
Mining and quarrying	291	291	291
Manufacturing	4,596	4,821	4,580
Electricity, gas and water	77	62	57
Construction	3,289	3,486	2,963
Trade, restaurants and hotels	8,587	9,929	8,599
Transport, storage and communications	6,020	6,153	5,873
Finance, insurance, real estate and business services	3,743	4,095	3,890
Government services	1,631	1,530	1,404
Other community, social and personal services	2,698	2,779	2,863
Sub-total	85,800	92,524	92,133
Less Imputed bank service charges	737	748	748
GDP at factor cost	85,064	91,776	91,385
Indirect taxes, *less* subsidies	5,301	4,250	3,262
GDP in purchasers' values	90,365	96,026	94,647

GDP at factor cost (estimates, million Somali shillings at current prices): 249,380 in 1988; 500,130 in 1989; 923,970 in 1990 (Source: UN Economic Commission for Africa, *African Statistical Yearbook*).

BALANCE OF PAYMENTS (US $ million)

	1987	1988	1989
Exports of goods f.o.b.	94.0	58.4	67.7
Imports of goods f.o.b.	−358.5	−216.0	−346.3
Trade balance	−264.5	−157.6	−278.6
Imports of services	−127.7	−104.0	−122.0
Balance on goods and services	−392.2	−261.6	−400.6
Other income paid	−52.0	−60.6	−84.4
Balance on goods, services and income	−444.2	−322.2	−485.0
Current transfers received	343.3	223.7	331.2
Current transfers paid	−13.1	—	−2.9
Current balance	−114.0	−98.5	−156.7
Investment liabilities	−22.8	−105.5	−32.6
Net errors and omissions	39.0	22.4	−0.8
Overall balance	−97.9	−181.7	−190.0

Source: IMF, *International Financial Statistics.*

External Trade

PRINCIPAL COMMODITIES (million Somali shillings)

Imports*	1986	1987	1988
Foodstuffs	1,783.3	3,703.6	1,216.1
Beverages and tobacco	298.1	183.6	6.2
Textiles, household goods	156.0	304.1	115.5
Medicinal and chemical products	89.2	133.9	97.9
Manufacturing raw materials	230.0	626.9	661.4
Fertilizers	1.8	238.0	2,411.4
Petroleum	2,051.0	3,604.2	3,815.9
Construction materials	981.4	2,001.9	307.8
Machinery and parts	1,098.3	1,203.6	957.1
Transport equipment	1,133.8	1,027.6	195.2
Agricultural machinery	4.2	62.7	113.4
Total (incl. others)	8,443.4	13,913.7	11,545.5

* Figures cover only imports made against payments of foreign currencies. The total value of imports in 1986 was 20,474 million Somali shillings.

Exports	1986	1987	1988
Livestock	4,420.3	7,300.0	3,806.5
Bananas	1,207.2	2,468.8	3,992.3
Fish	45.2	70.4	291.8
Hides and skins	294.0	705.2	492.0
Myrrh	43.6	229.9	252.8
Total (incl. others)	6,372.5	10,899.9	9,914.1

1992 (estimates, US $ million): Imports 150; Exports 80.

PRINCIPAL TRADING PARTNERS ('000 Somali shillings)

Imports	1980	1981	1982
China, People's Repub.	46,959	40,962	89,772
Ethiopia	43,743	146,853	155,775
Germany, Fed. Repub.	104,117	430,548	214,873
Hong Kong	5,351	13,862	3,972
India	41,467	19,638	4,801
Iraq	2,812	67,746	402
Italy	756,800	662,839	1,221,146
Japan	28,900	54,789	48,371
Kenya	86,515	105,627	198,064
Saudi Arabia	120,208	160,583	82,879
Singapore	18,569	15,592	73,652
Thailand	19,296	40,527	106,474
United Kingdom	172,613	935,900	238,371
USA	201,662	141,823	154,082
Total (incl. others)	2,190,627	3,221,715	3,548,805

Exports	1980	1981	1982
Djibouti	6,640	3,209	2,458
Germany, Fed. Repub.	11,376	1,956	20,086
Italy	107,661	58,975	77,870
Kenya	2,425	6,929	4,211
Saudi Arabia	583,768	803,631	1,852,936
United Kingdom	1,233	—	3,169
USA	1,301	—	6,970
Yemen, People's Dem. Repub.	3,182	—	—
Total (incl. others)	844,012	960,050	2,142,585

Source: the former Ministry of Planning, Mogadishu.

1986: *Imports* (estimates, million Somali shillings) USA 1,816; Japan 836; China, People's Repub. 553; United Kingdom 773; France 341; Germany, Fed. Repub. 1,481; Total (incl. others) 8,443; *Exports* (estimates, million Somali shillings) USA 5; China, People's Repub. 4; United Kingdom 31; France 27; Germany, Fed. Repub. 11; Total (incl. others) 6,373. (Source: UN Economic Commission for Africa, *African Statistical Yearbook*.)

Transport

ROAD TRAFFIC (estimates, '000 motor vehicles in use)

	1993	1994	1995
Passenger cars	3.8	2.7	2.0
Commercial vehicles	8.6	7.4	7.3

Source: International Road Federation, *World Road Statistics*.

SHIPPING

Merchant Fleet (registered at 31 December)

	1994	1995	1996
Number of vessels	25	24	22
Total displacement ('000 grt)	16.8	16.4	13.9

Source: Lloyd's Register of Shipping, *World Fleet Statistics*.

International Sea-borne Freight Traffic ('000 metric tons)

	1989	1990	1991
Goods loaded	325	324	n.a.
Goods unloaded	1,252*	1,118	1,007*

* Estimate.

Source: UN Economic Commission for Africa, *African Statistical Yearbook*.

CIVIL AVIATION (traffic on scheduled services)

	1989	1990	1991
Kilometres flown (million)	3	3	1
Passengers carried ('000)	89	88	46
Passenger-km (million)	248	255	131
Freight ton-km (million)	8	9	5

Source: UN, *Statistical Yearbook*.

Communications Media

	1992	1993	1994
Radio receivers ('000 in use)	350	370	375
Television receivers ('000 in use)	113	118	120
Telephones ('000 main lines in use)	15	15	15
Daily newspapers	1	n.a.	1

Sources: UNESCO, *Statistical Yearbook*; UN, *Statistical Yearbook*.

Education

(1985)

	Institutions	Teachers	Pupils
Pre-primary	16	133	1,558
Primary	1,224	10,338	196,496
Secondary			
General	n.a.	2,149	39,753
Teacher training	n.a.	30*	613*
Vocational	n.a.	637	5,933
Higher	n.a.	817†	15,672†

* Figures refer to 1984. † Figures refer to 1986.

Source: UNESCO, *Statistical Yearbook*.

1990 (UN estimates): 377,000 primary-level pupils; 44,000 secondary-level pupils; 10,400 higher-level pupils.

1991: University teachers 549; University students 4,640.

Directory

The Constitution

The Constitution promulgated in 1979 and amended in 1990 was revoked following the overthrow of President Siad Barre in January 1991. Proposals to reinstate the independence Constitution of 1960 were subsequently abandoned. A preparatory commission for a Transitional National Council, formed in March 1993, presented a draft transitional national charter in November 1993, providing the constitutional framework for the country during a two-year transitional period.

The Government

(August 1997)

In January 1997 a 41-member National Salvation Council, with an 11-member executive committee and a five-member joint chairmanship committee, was established to act as an interim government charged with drafting a transitional charter and holding a national reconciliation conference; however, Hussein Aidid challenged the legitimacy of the new body.

Representatives of the self-proclaimed 'Republic of Somaliland' announced in February 1997 that a three-year interim constitution had been promulgated in 'Somaliland', and that Mohamed Ibrahim Egal had been re-elected (by an electoral college) as the territory's President.

MINISTRIES

Office of the President: People's Palace, Mogadishu; tel. (1) 723.

Ministry of Agriculture: Mogadishu; tel. (1) 80716.

Ministry of Civil Aviation and Transport: Mogadishu; tel. (1) 23025.

Ministry of Commerce: Mogadishu; tel. (1) 33089.

Ministry of Defence: Mogadishu; tel. (1) 710; telex 726.

Ministry of Finance and Economy: Mogadishu; tel. (1) 33090.

Ministry of Foreign Affairs: Mogadishu; tel. (1) 721; telex 639.

Ministry of Health: Mogadishu; tel. (1) 31055; telex 776.

Ministry of Higher Education and Culture: POB 1182, Mogadishu; tel. (1) 35042.

Ministry of Industry: Mogadishu; telex 747.

Ministry of Information and National Guidance: POB 1748, Mogadishu; tel. (1) 20947; telex 621.

Ministry of the Interior: Mogadishu.

Ministry of Justice and Islamic Affairs: Mogadishu; tel. (1) 36062.

Ministry of Labour, Youth and Sports: Mogadishu; tel. (1) 33086.

Ministry of National Planning: POB 1742, Mogadishu; tel. (1) 80384; telex 715.

Ministry of Public Works: Mogadishu; tel. (1) 21051; telex 700.

Ministry of Telecommunications: Mogadishu; tel. (1) 29005; telex 615.

Political Organizations

Islamic Union Party (al-Ittihad al-Islam): operates in northern Somalia; aims to unite ethnic Somalis from Somalia, Ethiopia, Kenya and Djibouti in an Islamic state.

Northern Somali Alliance (NSA): f. 1997 as alliance between the United Somali Front and the United Somali Party.

United Somali Front (USF): f. 1989; represents Issas in the north-west of the country; Chair. ABD AR-RAHMAN DUALEH ALI; Sec.-Gen. MOHAMED OSMAN ALI.

United Somali Party (USP): opposes SNM's declaration of the independent 'Republic of Somaliland'; Leader MOHAMED ABDI HASHI.

Somali Democratic Alliance (SDA): f. 1989; represents Gadabursi ethnic grouping in north-west; opposes Isaaq-dominated SNM and its declaration of an independent 'Republic of Somaliland'; Leader MOHAMED FARAH ABDULLAH.

Somali Democratic Movement (SDM): represents Rahanwin clan; movement split in early 1992, with this faction in alliance with Ali Mahdi Mohamed; Leader ABDULKADIR MOHAMED ADAN.

Somali Eastern and Central Front (SECF): f. 1991; opposes SNM's declaration of the independent 'Republic of Somaliland'; Chair. HIRSI ISMAIL MOHAMED.

Somali National Alliance (SNA): f. 1992 as alliance between the Southern Somali National Movement (which withdrew in 1993) and the factions of the United Somali Congress, Somali Democratic Movement and Somali Patriotic Movement given below; Chair. HUSSEIN MOHAMED AIDID.

Somali Democratic Movement (SDM): represents Rahanwin clan; Chair. ADAM UTHMAN ABDI: Sec.-Gen. Dr YASIN MA'ALIM ABDULLAHI.

Somali Patriotic Movement (SPM): f. 1989; represents Ogadenis (of the southern Darod clan); Chair. GEDI UGAS MADHAR.

United Somali Congress (USC): f. 1989; overthrew Siad Barre in 1991; party split in mid-1991, and again in mid-1995.

Somali National Front (SNF): f. 1991; guerrilla force active in southern Somalia, promoting Darod clan interests and seeking restoration of SRSP Govt; Leader Gen. MOHAMED SIAD HERSI 'MORGAN'.

Somali National Movement (SNM): Hargeysa; f. 1981 in London; conducted guerrilla operations in north and north-west Somalia, with early support from Ethiopia, until 1991; support drawn mainly from nomadic Isaaq clan; in May 1991 declared independent 'Republic of Somaliland' with the capital at Hargeysa; mems hold a majority of ministerial portfolios in 'Govt of Somaliland'; in 1994 Mohamed Ibrahim Egal, the elected President of 'Somaliland', disputed that the SNM was still led by Ahmed Ali 'Tur'; Chair. ABD AR-RAHMAN AHMED ALI 'TUR'; Vice-Chair. HASAN ISA JAMA.

Somali Patriotic Movement (SPM): f. 1989 in southern Somalia; represents Ogadenis (of the Darod clan) in southern Somalia; this faction of the SPM has allied with the SNF in opposing the SNA; Chair. Gen. ADEN ABDULLAHI NOOR ('GABIO').

Somali People's Democratic Union (SPDU): f. 1997; breakaway group from SSDF; Chair. Gen. MOHAMED JIBRIL MUSEH.

Somali Revolutionary Socialist Party (SRSP): f. 1976 as the sole legal party; overthrown in Jan. 1991; conducts guerrilla operations in Gedo region, near border with Kenya; Sec.-Gen. (vacant); Asst Sec.-Gen. AHMED SULEIMAN ABDULLAH.

Somali Salvation Democratic Front (SSDF): f. 1981, as the Democratic Front for the Salvation of Somalia (DFSS), as a coalition of the Somali Salvation Front, the Somali Workers' Party and the Democratic Front for the Liberation of Somalia; operates in central Somalia, although a smaller group has opposed the SNA around Kismayu in alliance with the SNF; Chair. Col ABDULLAHI YUSSUF AHMED.

Southern Somali National Movement (SSNM): based on coast in southern Somalia; Chair. ABDI WARSEMEH ISAR.

United Somali Congress (USC): f. 1989 in central Somalia; overthrew Siad Barre in Jan. 1991; party split in 1991, with this faction dominated by the Abgal sub-clan of the Hawiye clan, Somalia's largest ethnic group; Leader ABDULLAHI MA'ALIN; Sec.-Gen. MUSA NUR AMIN.

United Somali Congress—Somali National Alliance (USC—SNA): f. 1995 by dissident members of the SNA's USC faction; represents Habr Gidir sub-clan of the Hawiye; Leader OSMAN HASSAN ALI 'ATO'.

In November 1993 interim President Ali Mahdi Mohamed was reported to have assumed the leadership of the **Somali Salvation Alliance (SSA),** a new alliance of 12 factions opposed to Gen. Aidid, including the Somali African Muki Organization (SAMO), the Somali National Union (SNU), the USF, the SDA, the SDM, the SPM, the USC (pro-Mahdi faction), the SSDF, the Somali National Democratic Union (SNDU), the SNF and the SSNM. In May 1994 the SNU announced its intention to leave the alliance and join the SNA. The majority of Somalia's political organizations have split into two factions, with one aligned to the SNA and the other to the SSA.

Diplomatic Representation

EMBASSIES IN SOMALIA

Note: Following the overthrow of Siad Barre in January 1991, all foreign embassies in Somalia were closed and all diplomatic personnel left the country. Some embassies were reopened, including those of France, Sudan and the USA, following the arrival of the US-led Unified Task Force (UNITAF) in December 1992; however, nearly all foreign diplomats left Somalia in anticipation of the withdrawal of the UN peace-keeping force, UNOSOM, in early 1995.

Algeria: POB 2850, Mogadishu; tel. (1) 81696.

Bulgaria: Hodan District, Km 5, off Via Afgoi, POB 1736, Mogadishu; tel. (1) 81820.

China, People's Republic: POB 548, Mogadishu; tel. (1) 20805.

Cuba: Mogadishu.

Djibouti: Mogadishu; telex 771.

Egypt: Via Maka al-Mukarama Km 4, POB 76, Mogadishu; tel. (1) 80781.

Ethiopia: POB 368, Mogadishu; telex 3089.

France: Corso Primo Luglio, POB 13, Mogadishu; tel. (1) 21715; telex 625.

Germany: Via Mahamoud Harbi, POB 17, Mogadishu; tel. (1) 20547; telex 3613.

India: Via Jigjiga, Shingani, POB 955, Mogadishu; tel. (1) 21262; telex 716.

Iran: Via Maka al-Mukarama, POB 1166, Mogadishu; tel. (1) 80881; telex 616.

Iraq: Via Maka al-Mukarama, POB 641, Mogadishu; tel. (1) 80821; telex 638.

Italy: Via Alto Giuba, POB 6, Mogadishu; tel. (1) 20544; telex 777.

Kenya: Via Mecca, POB 618, Mogadishu; tel. (1) 80857; telex 610.

Korea, Democratic People's Republic: Via Km 5, Mogadishu; Ambassador: KIM RYONG SU.

Kuwait: First Medina Rd, Km 5, POB 1348, Mogadishu; telex 608.

Libya: Via Medina, POB 125, Mogadishu; Ambassador: MUSTAFA SALIM AL-AMUSH.

Nigeria: Via Km 5, Mogadishu; tel. (1) 81362; telex 637.

Oman: Via Afgoi, POB 2992, Mogadishu; tel. (1) 81658; telex 796.

Pakistan: Via Afgoi, Km 5, POB 339, Mogadishu; tel. (1) 80856.

Qatar: Via Km 4, POB 1744, Mogadishu; tel. (1) 80746; telex 629.

Romania: Via Lido, POB 651, Mogadishu.

Saudi Arabia: Via Benadir, POB 603, Mogadishu; tel. (1) 22087; telex 618.

Sudan: Via Mecca, POB 552, Mogadishu; Chargé d'affaires: ALI HASSAN ALI.

Syria: Via Medina, POB 986, Mogadishu; telex 636.

Turkey: Via Km 6, POB 2833, Mogadishu; tel. (1) 81975; telex 784.

United Arab Emirates: Via Afgoi, Km 5, Mogadishu; tel. (1) 23178; telex 614.

United Kingdom: Hassan Geedi Abtow 7/8, POB 1036, Mogadishu; tel. (1) 20288; telex 3617.

USA: Via Afgoi, Km 5, POB 574, Mogadishu; tel. (1) 39971; telex 789.

Yemen: Via Km 5, POB 493, Mogadishu.

Yugoslavia: Via Mecca, POB 952, Mogadishu; tel. (1) 81729; telex 3778.

Zimbabwe: Mogadishu.

Judicial System

Constitutional arrangements in operation until 1991 provided for the Judiciary to be independent of the executive and legislative powers. Laws and acts having the force of law were required to conform to the provisions of the Constitution and to the general principles of Islam.

The Supreme Court: Mogadishu; the court of final instance in civil, criminal, administrative and auditing matters; Chair. Sheikh AHMAD HASAN.

Military Supreme Court: f. 1970, with jurisdiction over members of the armed forces.

National Security Court: heard cases of treason.

Courts of Appeal: sat at Mogadishu and Hargeysa, with two Divisions: General and Assize.

Regional Courts: There were eight Regional Courts, with two Divisions: General and Assize.

District Courts: There were 84 District Courts, with Civil and Criminal Divisions. The Civil Division had jurisdiction over all controversies where the cause of action had arisen under *Shari'a* (Islamic) Law or Customary Law and any other Civil controversies where the matter in dispute did not involve more than 3,000 shillings. The Criminal Division had jurisdiction with respect to offences punishable with imprisonment not exceeding three years, or fine not exceeding 3,000 shillings, or both.

Qadis: Districts Courts of civil jurisdiction under Islamic Law.

In September 1993, in accordance with Resolution 865 of the UN Security Council, a judiciary re-establishment council, composed of Somalis, was created in Mogadishu to rehabilitate the judicial and penal systems.

Judiciary Re-establishment Council (JRC): Mogadishu; Chair. Dr ABD AL-RAHMAN Haji GA'AL.

Following the withdrawal of the UN peace-keeping force, UNOSOM, in early 1995, most regions outside of Mogadishu reverted to clan-based fiefdoms where *Shari'a* Law (comprising an Islamic Supreme Council and local Islamic high courts) prevailed. In October 1996 Ali Mahdi Mohamed announced the approval of a new Islamic judicial system under which appeals could be lodged on all sentences passed by Islamic courts, and no sentence imposed by the courts could be implemented prior to an appeal court ruling.

Religion

ISLAM

Islam is the state religion. Most Somalis are Sunni Muslims.

Imam: Gen. MOHAMED ABSHIR.

CHRISTIANITY

The Roman Catholic Church

Somalia comprises a single diocese, directly responsible to the Holy See. At 31 December 1995 there were an estimated 200 adherents.

Bishop of Mogadishu: (vacant); POB 273, Ahmed bin Idris, Mogadishu; tel. (1) 20184.

The Anglican Communion

Within the Episcopal Church in Jerusalem and the Middle East, the Bishop in Egypt has jurisdiction over Somalia.

The Press

Al Mujeehid: Hargeysa; weekly.

The Country: POB 1178, Mogadishu; tel. (1) 21206; telex 621; f. 1991; daily.

Dalka: POB 388, Mogadishu; f. 1967; current affairs; weekly.

Heegan (Vigilance): POB 1178, Mogadishu; tel. (1) 21206; telex 621; f. 1978; weekly; English; Editor MOHAMOUD M. AFRAH.

Horseed: POB 1178, Mogadishu; tel. (1) 21206; telex 621; weekly; in Italian and Arabic.

Huuriya (Liberty): Hargeysa; daily.

Jamhuuriya (The Republic): Hargeysa; independent; daily; Editor-in-Chief MAHMOUD ABDI SHIDE; circ. 2,500.

New Era: POB 1178, Mogadishu; tel. (1) 21206; telex 621; quarterly; in English, Somali and Arabic.

Qaran (Nation): Mogadishu; financial information; daily; Editor ABDULAHI AHMED ALI; circ. 2,000.

Somalia in Figures: Ministry of National Planning, POB 1742, Mogadishu; tel. (1) 80384; telex 715; govt publication; statistical information; 3 a year; in English.

Xiddigta Oktobar (October Star): POB 1178, Mogadishu; tel. (1) 21206; telex 621; in Somali; daily.

Other periodicals, published in Mogadishu at irregular intervals, include *Ayaamaha* and *Xog Ogaal*.

NEWS AGENCIES

Horn of Africa News Agency: Mogadishu; f. 1990.

Somali National News Agency (SONNA): POB 1748, Mogadishu; tel. (1) 24058; telex 621; Dir MUHAMMAD HASAN KAHIN.

Foreign Bureaux

Agence France-Presse (AFP) (France): POB 1178, Mogadishu; telex 615; Rep. MOHAMED ROBLE NOOR.

Agenzia Nazionale Stampa Associata (ANSA) (Italy): POB 1399, Mogadishu; tel. (1) 20626; telex 3761; Rep. ABDULKADIR MOHAMOUD WALAYO.

Publishers

Government Printer: POB 1743, Mogadishu.

Somalia d'Oggi: Piazzale della Garesa, POB 315, Mogadishu; law, economics and reference.

Radio and Television

In 1994, according to UNESCO, there were an estimated 375,000 radio receivers and 120,000 television receivers in use. Some radio receivers are used for public address purposes in small towns and villages. A television service, financed by Kuwait and the United Arab Emirates, was inaugurated in 1983. Programmes in Somali and Arabic are broadcast for two hours daily, extended to three hours on Fridays and public holidays. Reception is limited to a 30-km radius of Mogadishu.

Holy Koran Radio: Mogadishu; f. 1996; religious broadcasts in Somali.

Radio Awdal: Boorama, 'Somaliland'; operated by the Gadabursi clan.

Radio Free Somalia: f. 1993; operates from Galacaio in north-eastern Somalia; relays humanitarian and educational programmes.

Radio Hargeysa, the Voice of the 'Republic of Somaliland': POB 14, Hargeysa; tel. 155; serves the northern region ('Somaliland'); broadcasts in Somali, and relays Somali and Amharic transmission from Radio Mogadishu; Dir of Radio IDRIS EGAL NUR.

Radio Mogadishu, Voice of the Masses of the Somali Republic: southern Mogadishu; f. 1993 by supporters of Gen. Aidid after the facilities of the fmr state-controlled radio station, Radio Mogadishu (of which Gen. Aidid's faction took control in 1991), were destroyed by UNOSOM; broadcasts in Somali, Amharic, Arabic, English and Swahili; Chair. FARAH HASAN AYOBOQORE.

Radio Mogadishu, Voice of Somali Pacification: Mogadishu; f. 1995 by supporters of Osman Hassan Ali 'Ato'; broadcasts in Somali, English and Arabic.

Radio Mogadishu, Voice of the Somali Republic: northern Mogadishu; f. 1992 by supporters of Ali Mahdi Mohamed.

Voice of Peace: POB 1631, Addis Ababa, Ethiopia; f. 1993; aims to promote peace and reconstruction in Somalia; receives support from UNICEF and the OAU.

Finance

(cap. = capital; res = reserves; m. = million; brs = branches; amounts in Somali shillings unless otherwise stated)

BANKING

Central Bank

Central Bank of Somalia (Bankiga Dhexe ee Soomaaliya): Corso Somalia 55, POB 11, Mogadishu; tel. (1) 725; telex 604; f. 1960; bank of issue; cap. and res 132.5m. (Sept. 1985); Gov. OMAR AHMED OMAR; Gen. Mans MOHAMED MOHAMED NUR, BASHIR ISSE ALI.

A central bank (with 10 branches) is also in operation in Hargeysa (in the self-proclaimed 'Republic of Somaliland').

Commercial Bank

Commercial Bank of Somalia: Via Primo Luglio, POB 203, Mogadishu; tel. (1) 22861; telex 602609; f. 1990 to succeed the Commercial and Savings Bank of Somalia; state-owned; cap. 1,000m. (May 1990); 33 brs.

Private Banks

Barakat Bank of Somalia: Mogadishu; f. 1996; cap. US $2m.; Chair. AHMED NUR ALI JUMALE.

Somali-Malaysian Commercial Bank: Mogadishu; f. 1997; cap. US $4m.

Development Bank

Somali Development Bank: Via Primo Luglio, POB 1079, Mogadishu; tel. (1) 21800; telex 635; f. 1968; state-owned; cap. and res 2,612.7m. (Dec. 1988); Pres. MAHMUD MOHAMED NUR; 4 brs.

INSURANCE

Cassa per le Assicurazioni Sociali della Somalia: POB 123, Mogadishu; f. 1950; workers' compensation; Dir-Gen. HASSAN MOHAMED JAMA; 9 brs.

State Insurance Co of Somalia: POB 992, Mogadishu; telex 710; f. 1974; Gen. Man. ABDULLAHI GA'AL; brs throughout Somalia.

Trade and Industry

CHAMBER OF COMMERCE

Chamber of Commerce, Industry and Agriculture: Via Asha, POB 27, Mogadishu.

TRADE ORGANIZATION

National Agency of Foreign Trade: POB 602, Mogadishu; major foreign trade agency; state-owned; brs in Berbera and over 150 centres throughout Somalia; Dir-Gen. JAMA AW MUSE.

DEVELOPMENT ORGANIZATIONS

Agricultural Development Corpn: POB 930, Mogadishu; telex 713; f. 1971 by merger of fmr agricultural and machinery agencies and grain marketing board; supplies farmers with equipment and materials and purchases growers' cereal and oil seed crops; Dir-Gen. MOHAMED FARAH ANSHUR.

Livestock Development Agency: POB 1759, Mogadishu; Dir-Gen. HASSAN WELI SCEK HUSSEN; brs throughout Somalia.

Somali Co-operative Movement: Mogadishu; Chair. HASSAN HAWADLE MADAR.

Somali Oil Refinery: POB 1241, Mogadishu; Chair. NUR AHMED DARAWISH.

Water Development Agency: POB 525, Mogadishu; Dir-Gen. KHALIF Haji FARAH.

INDUSTRIAL COMPANY

Industrie Chimique Somale: POB 479, Mogadishu; soap and detergent mfrs; Man. Dir HIREI GASSEM.

TRADE UNION

General Federation of Somali Trade Unions: POB 1179, Mogadishu; Chair. MOHAMED FARAH ISSA GASHAN.

Transport

RAILWAYS

There are no railways in Somalia.

ROADS

In 1995 there were an estimated 23,700 km of roads, of which an estimated 2,806 km of road were paved. A 122-km road between Berbera and Burao, financed by the United Arab Emirates, was inaugurated in 1981, and work on a 257-km road between Goluin and Gelib, completing a link between Mogadishu and Kismayu, was begun in 1977, with financial aid from the EC and the Arab Fund for Economic and Social Development. In September 1988 work began on a 120-km US-funded road between Mogadishu and Cadale. In July 1989 the European Development Fund granted US $54m. for the construction of a 230-km road between Gelib and Bardera, to provide access to the Juba valley.

SHIPPING

Merca, Berbera, Mogadishu and Kismayu are the chief ports.

At 31 December 1996 Somalia's merchant fleet totalled 22 vessels, with a combined displacement of 13,941 grt.

In the context of continuing civil unrest, the dispatch of a UN-sponsored port management team for Mogadishu, for an initial period of six months, was announced in May 1993. An EU-sponsored development project for the port of Berbera (in 'Somaliland') was announced in February 1996.

Linea Messina, Medite Line and Lloyd Triestino provide regular services. Other lines call irregularly.

Somali Ports Authority: POB 935, Mogadishu; tel. (1) 30081; telex 708; Port Dir UGAS KHALIF.

Juba Enterprises Beder & Sons Ltd: POB 549, Mogadishu; privately-owned.

National Shipping Line: POB 588, Mogadishu; tel. (1) 23021; telex 611; state-owned; Gen. Man. Dr ABDULLAHI MOHAMED SALAD.

Shosman Commercial Co Ltd: North-Eastern Pasaso; privately-owned.

Somali Shipping Corpn: POB 2775, Mogadishu; state-owned.

CIVIL AVIATION

Mogadishu has an international airport. There are airports at Hargeysa and Baidoa and six other airfields. It was reported that a daily service had been inaugurated in April 1994 between Hargeysa (in the self-declared 'Republic of Somaliland') and Nairobi, Kenya.

Somali Airlines: Via Medina, POB 726, Mogadishu; tel. (1) 81533; telex 3619; fax (1) 80489; f. 1964 (suspended operations in 1991); state-owned; operates internal passenger and cargo services and international services to destinations in Africa, Europe and the Middle East; Pres. MOHAMOUD MOHAMED GULAID.

In addition, two airlines, Bulisafia and African Air, operate services from Mogadishu international airport.

Defence

Of total armed forces of 64,500 in June 1990, the army numbered 60,000, the navy 2,000 and the air force 2,500. In addition, there were 29,500 members of paramilitary forces, including 20,000 members of the people's militia. Following the overthrow of the Siad Barre regime in January 1991, there were no national armed forces; Somalia was divided into areas controlled by different armed groups, which were based on clan, or sub-clan, membership. In March 1994 the UN announced that 8,000 former Somali police officers had been rehabilitated throughout the country, receiving vehicles and uniforms from the UN. Following the UN withdrawal from Somalia in early 1995, these police officers ceased receiving payment, and their future and their hitherto neutral stance appeared uncertain.

Education

All private schools were nationalized in 1972, and education is now provided free of charge. Despite the introduction of the Somali script in 1972, the level of literacy remains low. According to estimates by UNESCO, the average rate of adult illiteracy declined from 83.1% in 1985 to 75.9% (males 63.9%; females 86.0%) in 1990. Primary education, lasting for eight years, is officially compulsory for children aged six to 14 years. However, the total enrolment at primary schools of children in this age-group declined from 14% (boys 18%; girls 10%) in 1980 to only 8% (boys 11%; girls 6%) in 1985. Secondary education, beginning at the age of 14, lasts for four years but is not compulsory. In 1985 enrolment of children at secondary schools included 3% (boys 4%; girls 2%) of those in the relevant age-group. In 1985 enrolment at primary and secondary schools was equivalent to 10% of the school-age population (boys 13%; girls 7%). Current expenditure on education in the 1988 budget was 478.1m. Somali shillings (equivalent to 1.9% of total current spending). Following the overthrow of Siad Barre's government in January 1991 and the ensuing internal disorder, Somalia's education system has collapsed. In January 1993 a primary school was opened in the building of Somalia's only university, the Somali National University in Mogadishu (which had been closed in early 1991). The only other schools operating in the country were a number under the control of fundamentalist Islamic groups and some that had been reopened in the 'Republic of Somaliland' in mid-1991.

Bibliography

Africa Watch. *A Government at War with its Own People.* New York, Africa Watch, 1990.

Ahmed, A. J. (Ed.). *The Invention of Somalia.* Lawrenceville, KS, Red Sea Press, 1995.

Aidid, M. F., and Ruhela, S. P. (Eds). *The Preferred Future: Development in Somalia.* New Delhi, Vikas Publishing House, 1993.

Beachey, R. *The Warrior Mullah: The Horn Aflame 1892–1920.* London, Bellew Publishing, 1990.

Besteman, C., and Cassanelli, L. V. (Eds). *The Struggle for Land in Southern Somalia: The War Behind the War.* Boulder, CO, and Oxford, Westview Press, 1996.

Bongartz, M. *The Civil War in Somalia: Its Genesis and Dynamics.* Uppsala, Scandinavian Institute for African Studies, 1991.

Cassanelli, L. V. *The Shaping of Somali Society: Reconstructing the History of A Pastoral People, 1600–1900.* Philadelphia, Pennsylvania University Press, 1982.

Castagno, M. *Historical Dictionary of Somalia.* Metuchen, NJ, Scarecrow Press, 1975.

Contini, P. *The Somali Republic: An Experiment in Legal Integration.* 1969.

DeLong, K., and Tuckey, S. *Mogadishu: Heroism and Tragedy.* Westport, CT, and London, Praeger, 1994.

de Waal, R., and de Waal, A. *Somalia: Crimes and Blunders.* London, James Currey Publishers, 1995.

Drysdale, J. *The Somali Dispute.* 1964.

Whatever Happened to Somalia?. London, Haan Associates, 1994.

Dualeh, H.A. *From Barre to Aidid: The Story of Somalia and the Agony of a Nation.* Nairobi, Stellagraphics, 1994.

Ghalib, J.M. *The Cost of Dictatorship. The Somali Experience.* New York and Oxford, Lilian Barber Press, 1995.

Hess, R. L. *Italian Colonialism in Somalia.* 1966.

Hirsch, J.L., and Oakley, R.B. *Somalia and 'Operation Restore Hope': Reflections on Peacemaking and Peacekeeping.* Washington, DC, United States Institute of Peace Press, 1995.

Issa-Salwe, A.M., and Cissa-Salwe, C. *The Collapse of the Somali State.* London, Haan Associates, 1994.

Jardine, D.J. *The Mad Mullah of Somaliland.* New York, Negro Universities Press, 1969.

Karp, M. *The Economics of Trusteeship in Somalia.* 1960.

Laitin, D.D., and Saïd, S.S. *Somalia: Nation in Search of a State.* Boulder, CO, Westview Press, 1987.

Lewis, I. M. *A Modern History of Somalia: Nation and State in the Horn of Africa.* Boulder, CO, Westview Press, 1988.

Blood and Bone: The Call of Kinship in Somali Society. Trenton, NJ, Red Sea Press, 1994.

Lyons, T., and Samatar, A.I. *Somalia: State Collapse, Multilateral Intervention and Strategies for Political Reconstruction.* Washington, DC, Brookings Institution, 1995.

Makinda, S.M. *Seeking Peace from Chaos: Humanitarian Intervention in Somalia.* Boulder, CO, Lynne Rienner Publishers, 1993.

Metz, H.C. (Ed.). *Somalia: A Country Study.* Washington, DC, US Government Printing Office, 1993.

Mubarak, J.A. *From Bad Policy to Chaos in Somalia: How an Economy Fell Apart.* Westport, CT, and London, Praeger, 1996.

Omar, M.O. *Somalia: A Nation Driven to Despair.* New Delhi, Somali Publications, 1996.

Pankhurst, E.S. *Ex-Italian Somaliland.* New York, Philosophical Library, 1951.

Sahnoun, M. *Somalia: The Missed Opportunities.* Washington, DC, United States Institute of Peace Press, 1994.

Salih, M. A. M., and Wohlgemuth, L. (Eds). *Crisis Management and the Politics of Reconciliation in Somalia.* Uppsala, Scandinavian Institute for African Studies, 1994.

Samatar, A.I. *The State and Rural Transformation in Northern Somalia, 1884–1986.* Madison, University of Wisconsin Press, 1989.

(Ed.). *The Somali Challenge: From Catastrophe to Renewal?* Boulder, CO, Lynne Rienner, 1994.

Samatar, S.S. *Somalia: A Nation in Turmoil.* London, Minority Rights Group, 1991.

Sheik-Abi, A. *Divine Madness: Mohammed Abdulle Hassan (1856–1920).* Atlantic Highlands, NJ, Humanities Press, 1992.

Simons, A. *Networks of Dissolution: Somalia Undone.* Boulder, CO; Oxford, Westview Press, 1995.

Stevenson, J. *Losing Mogadishu: Testing US Policy in Somalia.* Annapolis, MD, Naval Institute Press, 1995.

United Nations, Dept of Public Information. *The United Nations and Somalia 1992–1996.* New York, United Nations, 1996.

SOUTH AFRICA

Physical and Social Geography

A. MACGREGOR HUTCHESON

The Republic of South Africa occupies the southern extremity of the African continent and, except for a relatively small area in the northern Transvaal, lies poleward of the Tropic of Capricorn, extending as far as latitude 34° 51′ S. The republic covers a total area of 1,219,080 sq km (470,689 sq miles) and has common borders with Namibia on the north-west, with Botswana on the north, and with Zimbabwe, Mozambique and Swaziland on the north-east. Lesotho is entirely surrounded by South African territory, lying within the eastern part of the republic.

PHYSICAL FEATURES

Most of South Africa consists of a vast plateau with upwarped rims, bounded by an escarpment. Framing the plateau is a narrow coastal belt. The surface of the plateau varies in altitude from 600 m to 2,000 m above sea-level, but is mostly above 900 m. It is highest in the east and south-east and dips fairly gently towards the Kalahari Basin in the north-west. The relief is generally monotonous, consisting of undulating to flat landscapes over wide areas. Variation is provided occasionally by low ridges and *inselberge* (or *kopjes*) made up of rock more resistant to erosion. There are three major sub-regions:

(i) the High Veld between 1,200 m and 1,800 m, forming a triangular area which occupies the southern Transvaal and most of the Free State;

(ii) a swell over 1,500 m high, aligned WNW–ESE, part of which is known as the Witwatersrand, rising gently from the plateau surface to the north of the High Veld and forming a major drainage divide; and

(iii) the Middle Veld, generally between 600 m and 1,200 m, comprising the remaining part of the plateau.

The plateau's edges, upwarped during the Tertiary Period, are almost everywhere above 1,500 m. Maximum elevations of over 3,400 m occur in the south-east in Lesotho. From the crests the surface descends coastwards by means of the Great Escarpment which gives the appearance of a mountain range when viewed from below, and which is known by distinctive names in its different sections. An erosional feature, dissected by seaward-flowing rivers, the nature of the escarpment varies according to the type of rock which forms it. Along its eastern length it is known as the Drakensberg; in the section north of the Olifants river fairly soft granite gives rise to gentle slopes, but south of that river resistant quartzites are responsible for a more striking appearance. Further south again, along the KwaZulu/Natal–Lesotho border, basalts cause the Drakensberg to be at its most striking, rising up a sheer 1,800 m or more in places. Turning westwards the Great Escarpment is known successively as the Stormberg, Bamboes, Suurberg, Sneeuberg, Nieuwveld, and Komsberg, where gentle slopes affording access to the interior alternate with a more wall-like appearance. The Great Escarpment then turns sharply northwards through the Roggeveld mountains, following which it is usually in the form of a simple step until the Kamiesberg are reached; owing to aridity and fewer rivers the dissection of this western part of the escarpment is much less advanced than in the eastern (Drakensberg) section.

The Lowland margin which surrounds the South African plateau may be divided into four zones:

(i) The undulating to flat Transvaal Low Veld, between 150 m and 600 m above sea-level, separated from the Mozambique coastal plain by the Lebombo mountains in the east, and including part of the Limpopo valley in the north;

(ii) The south-eastern coastal belt, a very broken region descending to the coast in a series of steps, into which the rivers have cut deep valleys. In northern KwaZulu/Natal the republic possesses its only true coastal plain, some 65 km at its widest;

(iii) The Cape ranges, consisting of the remnants of mountains folded during the Carboniferous era, and flanking the plateau on the south and south-west. On the south the folds trend E–W and on the south-west they trend N–S, the two trends crossing in the south-western corner of the Cape to produce a rugged knot of mountains and the ranges' highest elevations (over 2,000 m). Otherwise the Cape ranges are comparatively simple in structure, consisting of parallel anticlinal ridges and synclinal valleys. Narrow lowlands separate the mountains from the coast. Between the ridges and partially enclosed by them, e.g. the Little Karoo, is a series of steps rising to the foot of the Great Escarpment. The Great Karoo, the last of these steps, separates the escarpment from the Cape ranges; and

(iv) The western coastal belt is also characterized by a series of steps, but the slope from the foot of the Great Escarpment to the coast is more gentle and more uniform than in the south-eastern zone.

The greater part of the plateau is drained by the Orange river system. Rising in the Drakensberg within a short distance of the escarpment, as do its two main perennial tributaries the Vaal and the Caledon, the Orange flows westward for 1,900 km before entering the Atlantic Ocean. However, the western part of its basin is so dry that it is not unknown for the Orange to fail to reach its mouth during the dry season. The large-scale Orange River Project, a comprehensive scheme for water supply, irrigation and hydroelectric generation, aids water conservation in this western area and is making possible its development. The only other major system is that of the Limpopo, which rises on the northern slopes of the Witwatersrand and drains most of the Northern Province to the Indian Ocean. Apart from some interior drainage to a number of small basins in the north and north-west, the rest of the republic's drainage is peripheral. Relatively short streams rise in the Great Escarpment, although some rise on the plateau itself, having cut through the escarpment, and drain directly to the coast. With the exception of riparian strips along perennial rivers most of the country relies for water supplies on underground sources supplemented by dams. None of the republic's rivers are navigable.

CLIMATE AND NATURAL VEGETATION

Except for a small part of the Northern Province the climate of South Africa is subtropical, although there are important regional variations within this general classification. Altitude and relief forms have an important influence on temperature and on both the amount and distribution of rainfall, and there is a strong correlation between the major physical and the major climatic regions. The altitude of the plateau modifies temperatures and because there is a general rise in elevation towards the Equator there is a corresponding decrease in temperature, resulting in a remarkable uniformity of temperature throughout the republic from south to north (cf. mean annual temperatures: Cape Town, 16.7°C; and Pretoria, 17.2°C). The greatest contrasts in temperature are, in fact, between the east coast, warmed by the Mozambique Current, and the west coast, cooled by the Benguela Current (cf. respectively, mean monthly temperatures: Durban, January 24.4°C, July 17.8°C; and Port

Nolloth, January 15.6°C, July 12.2°C). Daily and annual ranges in temperature increase with distance from the coast, being much greater on the plateau (cf. mean annual temperature range: Cape Town, 8°C; Pretoria, 11°C).

The areas of highest annual rainfall largely coincide with the outstanding relief features, over 650 mm being received only in the eastern third of South Africa and relatively small areas in the southern Cape. Parts of the Drakensberg and the seaward slopes of the Cape ranges experience over 1,500 mm. West of the Drakensberg and to the north of the Cape ranges there is a marked rain-shadow, and annual rainfall decreases progressively westwards (cf. Durban 1,140 mm, Bloemfontein 530 mm, Kimberley 400 mm, Upington 180 mm, Port Nolloth 50 mm). Virtually all the western half of the country, apart from the southern Cape, receives less than 250 mm and the western coastal belt's northern section forms a continuation of the Namib Desert. Most of the rain falls during the summer months (November to April) when evaporation losses are greatest, brought by tropical marine air masses moving in from the Indian Ocean on the east. However, the south-western Cape has a winter maximum of rainfall with dry summers. Only the narrow southern coastal belt between Cape Agulhas and East London has rainfall distributed uniformly throughout the year. Snow may fall occasionally over the higher parts of the plateau and the Cape ranges during winter, but frost occurs on an average for 120 days each year over most of the interior plateau, and for shorter periods in the coastal lowlands, except in KwaZulu/Natal, where it is rare.

Variations in climate and particularly in annual rainfall are reflected in changes of vegetation, sometimes strikingly, as between the south-western Cape's Mediterranean shrub type, designed to withstand summer drought and of which the protea—the national plant—is characteristic, and the drought-resistant low Karoo bush immediately north of the Cape ranges and covering much of the semi-arid western half of the country. The only true areas of forest are found along the wetter south and east coasts—the temperate evergreen forests of the Knysna district and the largely evergreen subtropical bush, including palms and wild bananas, of the eastern Cape and KwaZulu/Natal, respectively. Grassland covers the rest of the republic, merging into thorn veld in the north-western Cape and into bush veld in the Northern Province.

MINERAL RESOURCES

South Africa's mineral resources, outstanding in their variety, quality and quantity, overshadow all the country's other natural resources. They are mainly found in the ancient Pre-Cambrian foundation and associated intrusions and occur in a wide curving zone which stretches from the Northern Province through the Free State and Northern Cape to the west coast. To the south of this mineralized zone, one of the richest in the world, the Pre-Cambrian rocks are covered by Karoo sedimentaries which generally do not contain minerals, with the exception of extensive deposits of bituminous coal, the republic's only indigenous mineral fuel. These deposits occur mainly in the eastern Transvaal High Veld, the northern Free State and northern KwaZulu/Natal, mostly in thick, easily worked seams fairly near to the surface. In the mid-1980s reserves were estimated to exceed 110,000m. tons, of which 58,000m. tons were considered to be economically extractable by current technology. Coal is of particular importance to South Africa because of relatively low production elsewhere in the continent south of the Equator, and South Africa's current dependence on imported petroleum.

The most important mineral regions are the Witwatersrand and the northern Free State, producing gold, silver and uranium; the diamond areas centred on Kimberley, Pretoria, Jagersfontein and Koffiefontein; and the Transvaal bushveld complex containing multiple occurrences of a large number of minerals, including asbestos, chrome, copper, iron, magnesium, nickel, platinum, tin, uranium and vanadium. In the Northern Cape important deposits of manganese, iron ore and asbestos occur in the Postmasburg, Sishen and Kuruman areas, while in the north-western Cape reserves of lead, zinc, silver and copper are being exploited. This list of occurrences and minerals is by no means exhaustive, and prospecting for new mineral resources is continuing. In 1988 exploitable petroleum deposits were discovered near Hondeklip Bay, off the western Cape coast, and a substantial reserve of gas and petroleum was discovered south-west of Mossel Bay, off the south coast of the Cape.

ETHNIC GROUPS AND POPULATION

Five major ethnic groups make up South Africa's multiracial society. The 'Khoisan' peoples—Bushmen, Hottentots and Bergdamara—are survivors of the country's earliest inhabitants. The negroid Bantu-speaking peoples fall into a number of tribal groupings. The major groups are formed by the Nguni, comprising Zulu, Swazi, Ndebele, Pondo, Tembu and Xhosa on the one hand, and by the Sotho and Tswana on the other. The European or 'white' peoples, who once dominated the political and social organization of the republic and continue to exercise considerable economic influence, are descended from the original 17th-century Dutch settlers in the Cape, refugee French Huguenots, British settlers from 1820 onwards, Germans, and more recent immigrants from Europe and ex-colonial African territories. The remainder of the population comprises Coloureds (people of mixed race) and Asians, largely of Indian origin. At mid-1995 the total population was estimated to be 41,244,500. According to the preliminary results of an October 1996 census, however, the total population was 37.9m. A post-censal survey indicated undernumeration of 6.8%. The adjusted population at the previous census, held in March 1991, was 37,944,018. In April 1994 the estimated ethnic composition of the total population was: Africans 76.1%; Europeans 12.8%; Coloureds 8.5%; and Asians 2.6%. The official languages are Afrikaans, English, isiNdebele, Sesotho sa Leboa, Sesotho, siSwati, Xitsonga, Setswana, Tshivenda, isiXhosa and isiZulu.

The overall density of the population was officially estimated to be 33.8 per sq km at mid-1995, but its distribution is extremely uneven. It is generally related to agricultural resources, more than two-thirds living in the wetter eastern third of the republic and in the southern Cape. The heaviest concentrations are found in the Witwatersrand mining area—the Johannesburg Metropolitan Area had 1,916,061 people at the 1991 census—and in and around the major ports of Cape Town, Port Elizabeth and Durban. Europeans have a widespread geographical distribution, but more than 80% reside in towns. Relatively few Africans are resident in the western Cape, and, while an increasing number are moving to the large black townships on the periphery of the major urban centres, more than 60% continue to reside in those rural areas which comprised the former tribal reserves. These extend in a great horseshoe along the south-eastern coast and up to the Northern Province and then south-westwards to the north-eastern Cape. The Coloured population are mainly resident in the Cape, and the Asian population is concentrated largely in KwaZulu/Natal and the Witwatersrand.

Recent History

J. D. OMER-COOPER

Revised for this edition by CHRISTOPHER SAUNDERS

HISTORICAL BACKGROUND

European interest in the area that now comprises the Republic of South Africa dates from 1652, with the establishment by the Dutch East India Co of a provisioning station at the Cape of Good Hope to service its maritime trade route to the Far East. Flourishing agricultural settlements were created by subsequent arrivals of white immigrants, principally from the Netherlands, Germany, Britain and France. The expansion of British influence in the Cape after 1795, and the territory's eventual annexation by Britain in 1806, led to increasing friction with the Dutch (Afrikaner, or Boer) frontier farmers. Following the abolition of slavery in 1834, many Afrikaner farmers, already hard-pressed for land, embarked upon a northward trek to establish an independent polity. In the aftermath of this Great Trek, Britain annexed Natal (KwaZulu), while permitting the creation of two Boer republics, the Orange Free State (OFS) and the South African Republic of Transvaal. Discoveries of diamonds near Kimberley in the 1860s, and subsequently of large deposits of gold in the Transvaal, initiated an economic revolution, which prompted the extension of white authority into remaining areas of African land in order to obtain additional reserves of labour, both for the mines and for the construction of a railway transport infrastructure. Increasing requirements for low-cost labour also led to the importation of Indian workers to Natal. The rapid development of gold-mining in the Transvaal, together with the emergence of the South African Republic as the most powerful state in the region, were perceived by British interests as a threat to their paramountcy; the consequent exertion of pressure on the Transvaal and the OFS provoked the Anglo–Boer War of 1899–1902. At its conclusion, the Boer republics passed under effective British control, and on 31 May 1910 the Union of South Africa was formally declared a dominion under the British crown.

The Union constitution gave the franchise to white males only, except in the Cape, where the existing voting rights were retained and protected. The two Afrikaner parties in the ex-republics amalgamated with the Cape's South Africa Party to form the national South Africa Party (SAP). Led by two Boer generals, Louis Botha and Jan Smuts, the SAP formed the first government of the new Union. The pro-imperial and pro-capitalist attitudes of the two leaders, however, antagonized many poorer rural Afrikaners. In 1912 the SAP split, and Gen. J. B. M. Hertzog founded the National Party (NP). In the same year members of the African élite, under the chairmanship of Pixley Seme, established the African Native National Congress, soon renamed the African National Congress (ANC). In order to coerce African peasants into migrant labour for mine owners and white farmers, the 1913 Land Act denied Africans the right to buy land outside the Native Reserves, or to lease white-owned land.

The outbreak of the First World War in 1914, accompanied by Botha's decision to lead South Africa against Germany, sparked off a minor Afrikaner rebellion, which was quickly suppressed. After the war, the former German colony of South West Africa (Namibia) was entrusted to South African administration as a League of Nations mandated territory. In 1918 a group of young Afrikaner professionals formed the nucleus of the secret Broederbond society, which established cells in many branches of South Africa's professional and public service organizations in its struggle to advance the status of Afrikaners. Its 'front' organization, the Federation of Afrikaner Cultural Organizations (FAK), promoted Afrikaner culture and language.

The war also brought about substantial urbanization of the African population. The resulting squalid living conditions and the death rate in the 1918 influenza pandemic were used as a justification for the passage of the 1923 Natives (Urban Areas) Act, based on the principle that Africans had no rights in the towns except to serve white needs. The segregationist approach was pressed further in response to the interests of white workers, poor whites and Afrikaner farmers. Mine owners could no longer afford to reserve numbers of semi-skilled jobs for highly paid whites, and in 1922 they repudiated the 1918 status quo agreement. White mineworkers launched a prolonged strike, culminating in an uprising led by unskilled Afrikaner workers. Government troops suppressed the rebellion. The white workers' Labour Party then formed an alliance with the Afrikaner farmers' NP won the 1924 parliamentary election. Under the new government's 'civilized labour' policy, blacks were removed from many jobs to be replaced by whites. It also legislated for racial job reservation. It failed, however, to achieve the majority required to alter the entrenched clause protecting African voting rights in the Cape and preventing extension of the 1913 Land Act to the province. Re-elected in 1928, it lost popularity during the period of economic hardship which followed the 1929–30 financial crisis in the USA. The NP, now realigned with the SAP, emerged victorious from parliamentary elections held in 1933, after which the two parties formally merged as the United Party (UP). Hertzog, the prime minister, was then able, with Smuts' assistance, to remove black voters from the Cape electoral roll and, by means of the 1936 Land Act, to extend the 1913 Act to the Cape. Coloured voters' rights in the Cape were, however, retained. The fusion of the NP with the SAP catalysed a split. A small group of extreme Afrikaner nationalist MPs, under Daniel Malan, formed the 'purified' NP, which drew substantial support from the Broederbond.

The outbreak of the Second World War in 1939 split the UP. Smuts won a small majority for participation on the Allied side, while Hertzog and some of his followers went into opposition. The war compelled South Africa to produce many goods for itself, transforming the economy into one based predominantly on manufacturing industry. Labour needs were met by a massive expansion of the urbanized African population and an attendant, but limited relaxation of the industrial colour bar. The ANC, gravely weakened during the pre-war economic depression, quickly revived and demanded the implementation of democratic reforms, including universal suffrage. African trade unionism expanded and a wellorganized (although officially unrecognized) union established itself among African mineworkers on the Rand. Although Smuts rejected the ANC's political proposals and used armed force to suppress a black mineworkers' strike in 1946, the UP began to adopt marginally more liberal attitudes in the immediate post-war period, accepting the need for increasing African urbanization and some liberalization of racial criteria in job reservation.

APARTHEID

According to the doctrine of apartheid, each race and nation was to be kept apart so that each was to develop to the full along its own inherent lines. Inter-racial contacts, above all miscegenation, were to be avoided. The doctrine assumed that cultural attainments were racially determined and races were inherently unequal. Each racial group was to have its own territorial area within which to develop its unique cultural personality. Of the areas envisaged for the African peoples, the overwhelming majority, however, were the poverty-stricken Native Reserves, comprising little more than 13% of the national territory.

As South Africa approached the 1948 election, the elderly Smuts no longer commanded his previous authority, while his liberal deputy, Jan Hofmeyr, lacked popularity. Many Afrikaner farmers, badly affected by the loss of low-cost African labour to the towns, and Afrikaner workers fearful of black competition, found apartheid attractive. The NP secured a narrow parliamentary majority. Daniel Malan formed a government and commenced putting apartheid into practice. In 1954 Malan was replaced by the hard-line J. G. Strydom, who died in 1958 and was succeeded by Hendrik Verwoerd, apartheid's chief architect and leading ideologue.

The period 1948–59 saw the introduction of a series of interrelated laws and measures aimed at restructuring South African society to conform to apartheid doctrine. The Population Registration Act provided for the classification of the entire population on the basis of race. Inter-racial marriages were forbidden and the Immorality Act, banning sexual relations between whites and blacks, was extended to include relations between whites and coloureds. Urban segregation was intensified by the Group Areas Act, which provided for the designation of particular residential areas for specific races. Controls over Africans seeking to move to the towns were tightened. Many of the huge number of blacks thus criminalized were encouraged to work as prison labour on farms in the Transvaal. Existing provisions for the reservation of categories of employment for particular races were strengthened. Race segregation in public places, trains and buses, post-offices, hospitals and even ambulances was introduced wherever it had not been previously practised. Beaches were fenced off into separate bathing areas for the different races. The Separate Amenities Act gave legislative sanction for this and stated that the amenities provided for different races need not be of equal standard. The Bantu Education Act removed black education from the care of the ministry of education to that of native affairs. In 1959 the Extension of University Education Act removed the right of non-white students to attend the previously open universities of Cape Town and the Witwatersrand.

To strengthen its hand against radical opposition the government introduced the Suppression of Communism Act. Apart from banning the South African Communist Party (SACP), it decreed that persons named as communists could be subjected to a wide range of restrictions. The definition of communism was framed to cover almost any fundamental opposition to apartheid. The government did take some steps towards enabling Africans to develop along 'their own lines' in the Reserves. As these 'lines' were envisaged in terms of pre-industrial tribal culture, however, it was to traditional (though government-appointed) chiefs that increased powers were delegated in the Bantu Authorities Act.

A significant government measure, both for doctrinal reasons and in order to reduce the UP vote in the Cape, was the removal of Coloured voters from the Cape voting rolls. The UP made this the main focus of its opposition. Failing to achieve its purpose by constitutionally prescribed procedures the government created a special high court of parliament with overriding powers in constitutional matters. In response, white ex-servicemen formed the 'Torch Commando' to defend the constitution, and tensions within the white community ran high. Support for the 'Torch Commando', however, largely reflected English speakers' fears for the status of their language. Once the appeal court had invalidated the act establishing the high court of parliament and the government had accepted that decision, the 'Torch Commando' soon collapsed. The government was subsequently able to achieve its aims regarding the Cape voting rolls, securing the requisite majority by inflating the senate with its own nominees.

The repressive policies of the NP compelled the ANC to employ the tactics of mass civil disobedience, for which its Youth Wing had been pressing. An alliance was formed between the ANC and the South African Indian Congress (SAIC). In 1952 they launched a campaign of 'Mass Defiance against Unjust Laws'. Throughout the country well-disciplined protesters broke discriminatory regulations and allowed themselves to be arrested. The government disposed of the movement by means of police action and harsh penalties for civil disobedience. This repression was facilitated by the outbreak of race riots in Port Elizabeth, East London and Kimberley. Occurring during the course of the defiance campaign, although unrelated to it, these disturbances served to discredit the movement in the eyes of some of its supporters as well as most whites. The campaign, however, by attracting unprecedented mass support for the ANC, consolidated its position as an authentic vehicle of African aspirations.

In 1955 the ANC, the SAIC, the Coloured People's Organisation and the white Congress of Democrats united in convening a 'Congress of the People', at which about 3,000 representatives of all races formulated a 'Freedom Charter', setting out a non-racial democratic approach and suggesting the nationalization of land, mines and industries. In 1956 the government took drastic action against the movement, putting 156 participants of all races on trial for plotting the violent overthrow of the state. The treason trial, continued until 1961 and ended with the acquittal of all the accused. In the meantime, however, the ANC was deprived of many of its senior leaders. In this atmosphere some of the more Africanist-minded members reacted aginst alliances with other races, and, led by Robert Sobukwe, formed the Pan-Africanist Congress (PAC).

In 1960 Hendrik Verwoerd achieved the long cherished ambition of Afrikaner nationalists when he won a white referendum to make the country a republic. However, this raised the question of South Africa's membership of the British Commonwealth. In response to the strong opposition of African members, South Africa was forced to withdraw.

In 1959 Verwoerd introduced the Promotion of Bantu Self-Government Bill and proclaimed that white South Africans must allow the 'Bantustans' to proceed towards full political independence. The need to improve South Africa's international standing and defuse internal African opposition was made strikingly evident in March 1960, when police in Sharpeville opened fire on a crowd of unarmed blacks who were surrounding the police station in response to a PAC demonstration, leaving 67 dead and many more injured. The Sharpeville massacre aroused international indignation to an unprecedented degree, South Africa sustained a net outflow of foreign investment capital, and appeals for military, economic and sporting boycotts began to be given serious attention. Within South Africa the government reacted by banning both the ANC and the PAC. In 1961 the ANC formed a military wing, Umkhonto we Sizwe (MK—'Spear of the Nation'). Under the leadership of Nelson Mandela, it aimed to force the government to negotiate by attacking white-owned property, while avoiding harm to people. In 1962 the PAC also formed an armed wing, called Poqo. Some leaders of both movements escaped abroad to organize an armed liberation struggle. Mandela was detained in 1962 and sentenced to life imprisonment on charges of sabotage in 1964, but remained a focus for opposition to apartheid.

The government, however, modified its formerly overtly racist doctrine. Territorial segregation was now to be rationalized on the grounds that the Native Reserves constituted the historic 'homelands' of different African nations. These were to be encouraged to develop towards self-government and eventual full independence, a process portrayed as 'decolonization'. Denial of rights to blacks in the economic heartland would be justified on the internationally acceptable grounds of foreign nationality, instead of the impermissable pretext of race. The new approach to the 'homelands' led to increased expenditure on their development. Instead of establishing industries in these areas, however, they were established on their borders. Blacks could work in the white areas, but they would have foreign nationality imposed upon them. 'Bantustan' frontiers were sometimes redrawn to include existing black townships on the outskirts of white towns.

The 'homelands' were to be led to self-government under constitutions giving scope to the elective principle but with the balance of power in the hands of government-appointed chiefs. Transkei was accorded 'self-government' under such a system in 1963. Ciskei, Bophuthatswana, Lebowa, Venda, Gazankulu, Qwaqwa and KwaZulu followed in the early 1970s.

The abandonment of explicit racism opened the way to contacts with the élites of African countries and the Bantustans. South Africa sought diplomatic contacts with black states. The first steps towards this new version of apartheid were taken under the leadership of Verwoerd, but in September 1966 he was assassinated in the house of assembly, and was succeeded by J. B. Vorster. Under Vorster's more pragmatic leadership the new approach to apartheid was taken much further. While African leaders in general rejected South African advances, diplomatic relations were established with Malawi. Domestically, racial job reservation began to be more openly relaxed. The alliance between the Afrikaner élite and white manual workers began to disintegrate and a constituency for policies to the right of the NP began to emerge. The Afrikaner élite, however, was increasingly divided between *verligtes* (the enlightened) and the hard-liner *verkramptes*. Albert Hertzog and a small group of extreme *verkramptes* formed the Herstigte

Nasionale Party (HNP). It was unable, however, to secure the support of the Broederbond. The HNP failed to win a seat in the 1970 or subsequent elections but did effectively function as a restraining influence on the *verligtes* in the NP. A much larger number of *verkramptes* remained in the wing of the party led by Dr Andries Treurnicht.

The replacement of explicit racism by separate nationality as a rationale for the denial of civil rights to blacks gave new urgency to reducing the settled African population in white areas. Stricter controls were imposed to prevent Africans acquiring permanent residence in urban areas. Immigrant workers from the Bantustans were discouraged from bringing their families to town, and single men's hostels were built for them. Wherever possible, jobs performed by settled blacks were transferred to migrant labour. A massive campaign was launched to rid the white areas of 'surplus Bantu' and force them into the overcrowded 'homelands'. During 1960–70 more than 1.5m. people were forcibly resettled.

These measures, more drastic than those of the first phase of apartheid, required more ruthless repression to enforce them. The powers of the security police were massively extended. In 1968 the state security services were centralized under the authority of the Bureau of State Security (BOSS). Reports of the widespread use of torture were given credence by the lengthening lists of those who died in police custody.

REGIONAL CONCERNS

South Africa's control over South West Africa (Namibia) had been a subject of international criticism ever since the territory had been entrusted to South Africa as a League of Nations mandated territory. In 1964, despite the opposition of the UN which had assumed responsibility for the mandate, the South African government developed a scheme for the introduction of formal apartheid in the territory. In 1966 the UN General Assembly resolved to revoke South Africa's mandate and place the territory under direct UN administration. This was confirmed by the Security Council in 1968 and South Africa was ordered to withdraw its forces. South Africa refused to co-operate or to admit UN authorities to the country. The apartheid plan was embodied in the 1968 Development of Self-Government for Native Nations in South West Africa Act.

The collapse of the Central African Federation, and the emergence of Malawi and Zambia posed new problems for South Africa which were much increased by the Unilateral Declaration of Independence (UDI) by Southern Rhodesia (now Zimbabwe) in 1965. South Africa initially confined itself to tacit support. After 1972, as the armed freedom struggle escalated, units of the South African police were sent to assist the illegal regime, while less formal military help was also given to the Portuguese against African freedom movements in Mozambique and Angola. Until 1973, the white regimes seemed able to hold the liberation movements in check.

The strategic situation was transformed by the revolution in Portugal in 1974. The Marxist-inspired Frente de Libertação de Moçambique (Frelimo), led by Samora Machel, consolidated its control of that country. South Africa initially refrained from intervention, but allowed itself to be drawn into the post-independence civil war in Angola. While the USA provided massive aid to the Frente Nacional de Libertação de Angola (FNLA) in the north against the Marxist-inspired government of the Movimento Popular de Libertação de Angola (MPLA) in Luanda, South African troops entered the country from Namibia in support of the União Nacional para a Independência Total de Angola (UNITA), led by Jonas Savimbi. The MPLA, however, was reinforced by Cuban troops. After the US congress prohibited further military expenditure in Angola in 1975 the FNLA rapidly collapsed, UNITA forces were driven back and South African troops withdrew across the border. MPLA co-operation with the South West Africa People's Organisation (SWAPO) and the ANC, however, gave the incentive for repeated military incursions into southern Angola in support of UNITA, which also received renewed US support. With the Frelimo victory in Mozambique, the internationally isolated regime in Rhodesia had become unviable in the opinion of South African policy makers. Overt military support was withdrawn and pressure exerted on the regime to negotiate with African leaders in the hope of creating a moderate African government prepared to coexist with South Africa.

South Africa also sought a political solution in Namibia by modifying its original apartheid plan to a proposal for Namibia to attain independence as a federation of ethnic states. This was rejected by both SWAPO and the UN. In December 1978 South Africa conducted elections in the territory. Their results appeared to demonstrate majority support for the ethnically-based Democratic Turnhalle Alliance (DTA). In 1978 South Africa proposed the establishment of a Constellation of Southern African States (Consa), which it hoped would include Zimbabwe Rhodesia and Malawi, along with Lesotho, Swaziland, and Botswana, and South Africa's 'Bantustans'.

INTERNAL PRESSURES FOR CHANGE

In 1973 African workers launched a wave of strikes which paralysed mines and industries in many parts of South Africa. Technological changes were now making obsolescent South Africa's reliance on low-cost unskilled labour. In addition,a chronic shortage of white recruits was necessitating the re laxation of race restrictions in the employment hierarchy. Ensuing pay rises significantly increased the real wages of black workers, while labour law reforms allowed for the registration of black trade unions. A massive expansion of black trade unions and of industrial action followed. The permanent presence of a black resident population in the urban areas was accepted, and policies aimed at entrenching the system of migrant labour were abandoned. The 'Bantustans' now began to be seen as areas where surplus labour could be housed at minimum cost. Barriers against 'Bantustan' residents settling permanently in the towns were further increased. As the demand for migrant labour declined, the advantages of blacks with urban residence rights over migrant workers increased and the level of poverty in the 'Bantustans' became extremely grave. The new situation increased incentives for the South African regime to confer formal independence on the 'Bantustans'. Transkei accepted this status in 1976, Bophuthatswana in 1977, Venda in 1979 and Ciskei in 1981. All remained dependent on South African financial support and their 'independence' was not internationally recognized. The imposition of 'independence' was resisted by KwaNdebele and, still more determinedly, by KwaZulu under the leadership of Chief Mangosuthu Buthelezi, who used the political immunity conferred by his position to attack the apartheid system. He attempted to transform Inkatha, the Zulu cultural movement that he had founded, into a national political force and to consolidate an alliance with Coloured and Indian political movements. His activities aroused suspicion among supporters of the ANC and other radical political groups, who felt that he had compromised his political integrity by participating in the 'Bantustan' system.

By the end of the 1960s there was an increase in overt black political activity. In 1969 Steve Biko led a secession from the multiracial National Union of South African Students and formed an exclusively black student body, the South African Students Organization. He went on to form a nation-wide Black People's Convention, aiming to unite Africans, Coloureds and Indians against white oppression. A substantial network of associated social and cultural organizations was established. The racial exclusiveness of the movement encouraged an initially tolerant reception from the government.

In June 1976 the agglomeration of segregated African townships to the south-west of Johannesburg known as Soweto (South-West Townships) erupted in the most serious racial violence in South Africa since the establishment of the Union. It began with a protest by school children at being forced to use Afrikaans as the medium of instruction for some of their school subjects. When police opened fire on the demonstrators rioting followed; this spread not only to other black townships around the Rand and Pretoria but to Natal and the Cape, where Coloured and Indian youths joined in. Repeatedly and violently repressed, the disturbances were not brought under control until the end of the year. Thousands of young people were arrested but many others escaped across the borders to join the liberation movements. The ANC proved far more successful than the PAC in attracting this cadre of prospective freedom fighters, thus consolidating its political hold over the loyalties of the majority. In October 1977 18 'black consciousness' organizations were suppressed and 50 of their leaders detained. International opinion was further incensed to learn that Steve Biko had been arrested and died from injuries suffered while in police custody.

The increasing pressures on white manpower in the military as well as the industrial field, and the need for allies to support the white power élite in response to black militancy, led Vorster's government to seek a solution to the problem of the political future of the Coloured and Indian peoples for whom no credible separate 'homelands' could be provided. Vorster proposed the formation of separate houses of parliament for Coloureds and Indians. These would be represented along with members of the white parliament in the national cabinet and participate in the choice of a president, who would exercise wide executive powers. This plan was put to the electorate in elections in 1977. The long moribund UP now dissolved itself. One section joined the small Progressive Party, which, in the person of Helen Suzman as its sole parliamentary member until the 1974 elections, had been the only effective white opposition party in the legislature. Relaunched as the Progressive Federal Party (PFP), it now became the official parliamentary opposition. The government obtained a landslide majority, but *verkramptes* within its ranks led to the suspension of the plan for a tricameral parliament.

In 1978 Vorster announced his intention to resign as prime minister and seek election to the mainly ceremonial post of state president. While manoeuvring for the succession was under way a scandal emerged in connection with the activities of the minister of information, Dr Cornelius Mulder, concerning the use of substantial sums of money in covert operations, initially aimed at gaining control of South Africa's English language press and later re-focused on exerting influence over publications, politicians and other prominent people in the USA and Europe. In September Vorster was succeeded as prime minister by P. W. Botha, hitherto the minister of defence. In November, however, Mulder resigned from the new government. He was also forced out of the NP, and formed the National Conservative Party (NCP). In June 1979 Vorster had to resign in disgrace from his new position as president.

Botha altered the balance of influence within the state security network in favour of the armed forces, as opposed to the police. The BOSS was abolished and replaced by a more modest organization. The state security council became the main decision-making organ, with the roles of the NP and parliament increasingly reduced. The previous c-in-c of the army, Magnus Malan, became the new minister of defence, and his view that South Africa faced an assault from the forces of communism, requiring the adoption of an anti-communist strategy, became the basic postulate of government policy. This involved internal reform as well as measures to ensure the denial of bases to the ANC in neighbouring countries. Racial job restrictions were abolished and trade union rights further extended. Africans were permitted to acquire long-term leases on their houses in the urban townships, and finally to purchase them outright. Africans with urban rights of residence could now move freely from one town to another. Restrictions on multiracial sports were reduced and the laws against interracial marriage and extra-marital sexual relations were repealed. The ineffective senate was abolished and replaced by a president's council made up of nominated Coloureds and Indians along with white nominees. It proposed a modified version of the tri-cameral parliament scheme. The need for some political representation for the black population resident in the towns was recognized, but the intention of including them in the central parliament denied. The reforms precipitated a conflict with the remaining *verkramptes* (hardliners) in the NP. Treurnicht challenged the prime minister but was defeated. In March 1982 he founded the Conservative Party of South Africa (CPSA), which absorbed the NCP. The changes in legislation on job reservation ensured the new party a significant white constituency.

Externally, the government's attention at this period was focused on Namibia, where the implementation of UN Security Council Resolution 435, calling for the evacuation of South African military forces from Namibia and for the election of a constituent assembly under UN supervision, was declared conditional by South Africa on the withdrawal of Cuban forces from Angola. Beginning in August 1981 South African armed forces launched a series of invasions in southern Angola, in support of UNITA. In Namibia counter-insurgency units were developed, notably the Koevoet ('Crowbar') unit. In Mozambique, South African security took over the support of the anti-government terrorist movement the Resistência Nacional Moçambicana (Renamo, also known as the MNR). Its widespread attacks on civilian targets as well as industrial installations and communications reduced the country to economic paralysis and famine. South African security forces also orchestrated armed raids into Zambia, Botswana, Lesotho and Swaziland. In London the ANC offices were bombed. The first phase of this programme of destabilization was concluded in 1984 when Mozambique and South Africa signed the Nkomati Accord, under which Mozambique was to deny military bases to the ANC and South Africa to cease supporting Renamo. It was announced in 1984 that South Africa and Swaziland had secretly signed a non-aggression pact in 1982.

Following the departure of Treurnicht and his followers from the NP, Botha proceeded to implement his constitutional plan. In November 1983 the creation of a tricameral legislature was approved by a referendum restricted to white voters. Elections for the Coloured house of representatives and the Indian house of delegates followed in August 1984, and in September the electoral college chose P. W. Botha as the country's first executive president. Meanwhile, in August 1983, a number of groups opposed to apartheid, many with church affiliations and with multiracial memberships, formed the United Democratic Front (UDF) to promote the rejection of the constitutional plan, on the grounds of its failure to provide representation for the black majority. The UDF won strong support from Coloured voters, only 18% of whom participated in the election. Indian participation was even lower.

The introduction of the new constitution catalysed a rebellion in the black townships which exceeded the scale of the 1976 Soweto upheaval. It was supported by strikes, notably in the economically crucial mining industry. The Congress of South African Trade Unions (COSATU), a federation of black trade unions that were politically aligned with the ANC, was formed in December 1984, and demanded the abolition of pass restrictions, the withdrawal of foreign investment and the release of Nelson Mandela. The township rebellion escalated dramatically when, on 21 March 1985 (the 25th anniversary of the Sharpeville massacre), the police opened fire on an unarmed African procession in Uitenhage, killing 20 and wounding many more. In July the government declared a state of emergency in 36 magisterial districts, but the violence continued to increase. Black policemen, community councillors and suspected informers were killed in growing numbers. The government lost control of some townships for significant periods, while groups of young 'comrades' enforced boycotts and their version of law and order through informal 'people's courts'. Continuing throughout 1985 and much of 1986, the disturbances encouraged conflicts between sections of the black communities, which tended to undermine the will to resistance. Migrant workers and some township-based workers were alienated by the boycotts and high handed behaviour of the 'comrades'. They formed 'vigilante' groups which, often with the tacit support of the police, attacked the 'comrades' and burned down their dwellings. These divisions were especially acute in Natal where members of the mainly rural Zulu-supported Inkatha movement, led by Chief Mangosuthu Buthelezi (chief minister of the KwaZulu 'homeland' since 1976), became involved in escalating hostilities with ANC supporters, who were mainly urban-based Zulu and Xhosa speakers from southern Natal.

On 12 June 1986 the government extended the state of emergency to cover the whole country. As many as 24,000 people, many of them children, were detained without trial. Disturbances in the townships continued into 1987 but, with army units largely replacing the police and with massive injections of funds for house-building and improved services, they gradually subsided. The upheavals aroused international opinion against South Africa still further. European banks suspended new lending and the EC introduced a number of economic sanctions. Even the USA applied some limited sanctions. The value of the currency unit, the rand, fell heavily in foreign exchange markets. At a Commonwealth heads of government meeting held in October 1985 a group of distinguished persons reflecting the racial diversity of the Commonwealth was formed to visit South Africa. The Eminent Persons Group (EPG) was initially well received by the government. It was permitted to consult a wide range of opinion and held talks with Nelson Mandela in prison. Its progress, however, abruptly ceased in May 1986 when the South African defence force launched a series of raids into Botswana, Zimbabwe and Zambia. Following the collapse of the EPG, the EC widened its programme of sanctions and the Commonwealth implemented sanction measures. The US congress also voted to intensify its programme of economic embargoes.

Among Afrikaner intellectuals, professionals and businessmen and within the NP itself, opinion was aleady growing that apartheid would have to be abandoned and an accommodation reached with an effective African leadership. Initially, Chief Buthelezi was viewed as a possible negotiating partner. However, the ANC, which commanded overwhelming support in the townships, was backed by COSATU and had the general support of church leaders and the UDF, came increasingly to be seen as the only credible negotiating partner. While liberal Afrikaner opinion was moving towards this view, a proliferation of movements on the extreme right expressed the growing desperation of the poorer sections of the white community at the erosion of their privileged position. A paramilitary organization, the Afrikaanse Weerstandsbeweging (AWB), founded in 1977 and led by Eugene Terre'Blanche, now attracted a mass following, and actively recruited among the police forces within whose ranks it had many sympathisers.

General elections for the white house of parliament in 1987 resulted in a partial realignment of forces. The NP emerged with a secure majority but a considerably reduced vote. The CPSA obtained more seats than the PFP and became the official opposition. In 1989 the PFP, augmented by two small splinter groups and a number of other individual members who broke away from the National Party, was reconstituted as the Democratic Party (DP).

Botha's reform programme, meanwhile, continued to falter. Bold new initiatives were repeatedly promised but little actually materialized. Some relaxation in the application of the Group Areas Act was permitted. Plans for a form of multiracial regional government were drawn up, although a plan for the governance of Natal prepared by an indaba ('meeting') of businessmen and leaders of all races in Natal under the initiative of Chief Buthelezi had recently been ignored. Reforms which once might have appeared substantive now did nothing to satisfy African opinion, church leaders or the UDF. Calls for the release of Nelson Mandela became increasingly insistent. Numerous groups belonging to the UDF were banned and the entire movement barred from receiving external contributions. It dissolved itself to reappear as the Mass Democratic Movement.

Repression within South Africa was accompanied by an intensification of the destabilization of neighbouring black-ruled countries. In Mozambique covert support for Renamo continued, despite the initial Nkomati Accord and its subsequent renewal in 1988. In Angola, South African military involvement increased. In 1987 South African forces defeated a major offensive by Angolan and Cuban forces; in pursuing their advantage, however, they were themselves halted by the Angolan and Cuban forces. The stalemate occurred in a changed international environment. Following the summit meeting held in October 1986 between Presidents Reagan and Gorbachev, the USSR had relinquished any intention of contesting Western hegemony in Africa. This atmosphere thus favoured the opening of negotiations, which resulted in an agreement on 22 December 1988 that opened the way to the solution of the interlinked problems of Angola and Namibia. Cuban forces were gradually repatriated, and Angola withdrew permission for ANC bases on its territory. (South African troops left Angola prior to the agreement.) South Africa permitted the entry into Namibia of UN forces, in accordance withs the provisions of Security Council Resolution 435. A constituent assembly was elected, a national constitution was drafted, and Namibia became independent on 21 March 1990.

THE ABANDONMENT OF APARTHEID

The resolution of the Namibian issue re-focused attention on political conditions within South Africa. Liberal whites, including influential Afrikaners, initiated direct contact with the ANC, at a meeting held in Dakar, Senegal, in July 1987. In spite of Botha's disapproval, further contacts followed. In January 1989 Botha withdrew from official duties on the grounds of ill health and, in early February, he relinquished the NP leadership to F. W. de Klerk. Before finally retiring from office, Botha had a meeting with Nelson Mandela, thus effectively recognizing the ANC leader's position as the potential alternative head of government. Botha relinquished the presidency, with some unwillingness, in mid-August. Prior to the September parliamentary election, de Klerk, still the acting head of state, gave little indication of any radical intentions. At the election, the CPSA and the liberal DP both made considerable gains. The NP retained a clear majority, however, and de Klerk was confirmed as state president.

During 1989 international and internal pressures on the government increased. The economy, weighed down by expenditure on security, was suffering from the effects of international sanctions. There was no possibility of winning black loyalty by reforms along the lines of the tricameral parliament. The illegal influx to the urban areas of migrants from the poverty-stricken 'Bantustans' was not containable by the security forces. The greater part of the NP, the Broederbond and the Afrikaner intellectual élite was already convinced that apartheid was unsustainable and that the ANC must be accepted as a negotiating partner. The ANC, after losing its facilities in Angola, had no military bases from which to operate. The eclipse of communism in the USSR deprived the ANC of backing for the continuation of its armed struggle and undermined the ideological position of SACP members in its governing bodies. In the USA President Bush initiated a more active approach towards democratic change in South Africa. During 1989 informal meetings were held in Britain of representatives of the ANC, the NP, a number of African states and of the USA and USSR. In September US officials indicated that if no move to release Mandela had taken place in six months President Bush would assent to an extension of economic sanctions.

Addressing the three houses of parliament on 2 February 1990, President de Klerk made the dramatic announcement that Nelson Mandela would be released and that the ban had been lifted on the ANC, the PAC, the SACP and 33 other organizations, including the UDF. It was the government's intention to open negotiations with black leaders, with a view to devising a new constitution based on universal franchise. Equality of all citizens, regardless of race, was to be guaranteed by an independent judiciary, and protection for individual rights entrenched.

On 11 February 1990 Nelson Mandela was released after 27 years in prison. ANC refugees soon began to return from exile. However, the ANC faced major problems in bringing the spontaneous loyalties of the great majority of the black population within a disciplined organizational framework, especially in the case of the young 'comrades' who had played such a role in the township upheavals. There were problems of ideological divisions between dedicated Marxists and others in the ANC leadership, as well as rivalries and misunderstandings between returning exiles and internal supporters. Additionally, the ANC had no direct access to power. The ANC called for the continuation of sanctions until the abandonment of apartheid had become demonstrably irreversible. This attracted significant support but was to become increasingly difficult to sustain as the reform process continued.

By the end of 1990 the remnants of traditional social segregation had largely disappeared and people of all races were making common use of beaches, swimming baths, hospital wards, railway carriages, hotels and restaurants. In October the Separate Amenities Act was formally repealed. A beginning of school desegregation had also been made, as white schools could, with the consent of parents, admit a proportion of children of other races. The CPSA protested bitterly and the AWB held demonstrations threatening a violent struggle against black rule. It was unable, however, to attract crowds large enough to give it much political credibility.

ANC and government members met in May 1990 to discuss conditions for the opening of full constitutional negotiations, and again in August, when the ANC agreed to the formal suspension of its guerrilla activities. The ANC favoured the election by universal franchise of a constituent assembly to draw up the new constitutional order, while the government instead favoured a multi-party conference giving each party an equal voice. In January 1991 the government agreed to a proposal by the ANC that a multi-party conference should determine the procedures for drawing up a new constitution.

Prospects of expeditious constitutional negotiations were threatened by continuing and expanding violence between followers of Inkatha and those of the ANC. In August 1990 these disturbances spread from Natal to the townships around the Rand. The ANC became increasingly convinced that the government itself was implicated in a form of internal destabilization strategy aimed at weakening ANC bargaining power.

On 1 February 1991 de Klerk again took the initiative in an address to parliament by announcing that all the remaining legislative pillars of apartheid, including the Group Areas Act and the Population Registration Act, were to be repealed. By the end of June this legal revolution was complete. The NP even changed its own constitution to open membership to all races, and began to attract significant numbers of Indian and Coloured, as well as smaller numbers of African members. The EC and the USA abandoned most economic sanctions, despite ANC appeals. Contacts between South Africa and black African states multiplied and trade was expanded, although Commonwealth countries voted to maintain sanctions for the present. The ANC supported the abandonment of international boycotts for those sports which accepted genuine non-racial management and participation. In July 1991 the International Olympic Committee agreed to South Africa's readmission.

In a series of meetings culminating in a conference in Harare, Zimbabwe in April 1991, the ANC pursued a *rapprochement* with the PAC. A formal alliance was projected, although this was not subsequently carried through. In the first week of July, at its national congress, the ANC elected a new national executive, successfully fusing new elements with 'old guard' members. Mandela became president, with the mineworkers' leader, Cyril Ramaphosa, as secretary-general. In May the ANC published its preliminary constitutional proposals. These included a bicameral legislature (with the lower house elected by proportional representation) and a bill of rights. The government's suggestions, issued in September, had much in common with these but included provisions for a collegial presidency and a constitutional role for the upper house which appeared to build in a white veto, and were rejected by the ANC. At a secret meeting held in February 1992 the government and ANC agreed on the release of political prisoners, the return of exiles and the formal abandonment by the ANC of armed struggle.

CONSTITUTIONAL NEGOTIATIONS

The main obstacle impeding constitutional negotiations, however, was the continuing violence between Inkatha and ANC supporters and the suspicion that elements of the state security forces were involved. Despite meetings between Mandela and Buthelezi held in January and April 1991, the bloodshed in the townships continued. In early April the ANC threatened to withdraw from negotiations if the government failed to take effective action to stop the violence, and demanded the dismissal of the minister of defence, Magnus Malan, and the minister of law and order, Adriaan Vlok. In July it was admitted that secret payments had been made from government funds to Inkatha during 1989–90, and Malan and Vlok were demoted to minor cabinet posts. Suspicions of official complicity in the violence were not fully dispelled, however, and the ANC insisted on the formation of an interim government in which it would be represented during the finalization of constitutional negotiations.

The multi-party conference on procedures for drawing up the new constitution, the Convention for a Democratic South Africa (CODESA), met on 20 December 1991. The government found itself under pressure to agree to the idea of an interim government and an elected constituent assembly.

The commencement of constitutional discussions intensified the hostility of the extreme right and, after losing a parliamentary by-election to the CPSA, de Klerk called a referendum of white voters for 17 March 1992. Despite demonstrations and campaigning by the far right the government achieved a more than two-thirds majority in support of continuing negotiations towards a democratic constitution. The CODESA talks were resumed, but government insisted on provisions that appeared to give it a veto. The talks became deadlocked and the ANC called for a campaign of non-violent mass action by its supporters to put pressure on the government. Then, on 17 June, a number of residents of the settlement of Boipatong, including women and children, were massacred, apparently by Inkatha supporters who had allegedly been brought to the scene by police trucks. The ANC broke off negotiations with the government, and demanded effective action to stop the violence, including the disbandment of groups involved in covert operations. The ANC was invited to resume constitutional negotiations, but refused to do so unless the government modified its insistence on a veto in the constitution-making procedure. During July 1992 mounting criticism of the activities of the security forces and a public outcry at the rising number of deaths in police custody strengthened the ANC's resolve to continue its campaign of mass action. In mid-July President de Klerk announced the dissolution of a number of police and army units. In late July the UN Security Council, acting upon a request by Nelson Mandela, sent a UN special representative to South Africa on a fact-finding mission. As a result of the visit, the UN recommended the establishment of an independent investigation into the activities of the security forces and, in mid-August, the Security Council authorized the deployment of UN observers in South Africa to monitor political violence.

In early August 1992 the ANC, SACP and COSATU joined forces to organize an unprecedented level of mass action against the government, involving political rallies and a two-day general strike. Shortly afterwards, the PAC met the government to discuss the possibility of introducing an alternative negotiating forum to the suspended CODESA. In mid-August talks between the ANC and the government on the resumption of constitutional negotiations failed, as the government refused to meet the demands articulated in June by the ANC. In late August the government announced a major restructuring of the police force and the authorization of an independent body, the Goldstone Commission (established in October 1991), to investigate alleged police complicity in serious crimes.

In early September 1992 the armed forces of the nominally independent 'homeland' of Ciskei fired on a procession of ANC supporters, killing 28 people and wounding about 200 others. The ANC blamed the South African government for complicity in the massacre, and demanded the removal of the Ciskei 'head of state'. President de Klerk agreed to conduct an enquiry into the incident, and in mid-September it was announced that legislation was to be introduced to reintegrate 'homeland' security forces and educational bodies into the South African system. Measures to reduce the 'independence' of the 'homelands' were also promised.

While formal talks between the ANC and the government were suspended, informal contacts continued, and in mid-September 1992 the ANC announced its agreement to a summit meeting between Mandela and de Klerk. This resulted in a 'record of understanding', which allowed for the resumption of full bilateral negotiations. In November the ANC announced its acceptance of a proposal (originating from the SACP and sponsored by Chris Hani, a leading militant radical in the ANC/SACP leadership) that an interim government of national unity should be formed, which would include the major parties that had won seats in the constituent assembly. The interim government would hold office for a five-year period, during which the constituent assembly would act as the interim legislature, while also finalizing the new constitution. The government welcomed this idea and proposed a number of procedural steps, including the resumption of multi-party talks in order to discuss the formation of a transitional executive committee (which was to have control over key ministries), to set the date for the election of the constituent assembly and to draft an interim constitution under which the proposed interim government of national unity and the constituent assembly would function. The ANC accepted the procedural programme, but rejected the government's suggested timetable, pressing for elections for the constituent assembly to be held before the end of 1993. In response to initial reports of the Goldstone Commission, de Klerk took the strong measure of dismissing several high-ranking officers. Gen. Constand Viljoen, a former head of the army, and a committee of former generals subsequently began to take a major overt role in the leadership of the white extreme right.

With substantial agreement between the two main negotiating partners achieved, multi-party talks in a format known as the multi-party negotiating forum were reconvened in April 1993. Agreement between the government and the ANC and the prospect of a NP–ANC coalition in the interim government of national unity placed great strains on the loyalties of some members of both organizations. Within the National Party divisions between those concerned to entrench regional autonomy and those drawn towards an alliance with the ANC at central government level became more pronounced, and within the ANC the emergence of a revolutionary socialist wing was discernible. The imminence of agreement on a new constitutional order aroused even stronger reactions among the right-wing white groups and black political movements opposed to a political solution on the lines favoured by the two major parties. Chief Buthelezi, who protested vigorously at the bilateral agreements between the government and the ANC, initiated meetings between representatives of Inkatha, a number of 'homeland'-based movements and the CPSA. This led to the formation of the Concerned South Africans Group (COSAG), including Inkatha, Bophuthatswana, Ciskei, KwaZulu and the CPSA, to act as a pressure group at the negotiating forum, in favour of extreme regional autonomy. In early April 1993, on the eve of the talks, Chris Hani (the initial sponsor of the idea of a government of national unity and the man best placed to persuade young black radicals to accept it) was assassinated by a white right-wing extremist; several members of the CPSA were implicated in the affair, and three of them were subsequently charged in connection with the murder which was believed to be part of a right-wing plot to disrupt the constitutional negotiations. At this time a series of random terrorist attacks against whites began, which were alleged to be the work of the Azanian People's Liberation Army (APLA—the military wing of the PAC).

As the negotiating forum approached a final decision on the date for the elections which would bring the old constitutional order formally to an end, the white extreme right openly threatened recourse to arms. Then, as the forum was about to confirm the election date as 27 April 1994, an armed commando of some 2,000 white right-wingers occupied the negotiating centre. The ANC criticized the failure of the security forces to prevent the attack. The intruders eventually withdrew and, a few days later, several arrests were made. As committees of the negotiating forum worked on the details of the future transitional executive committee and the interim constitution, the ANC was obliged to concede to decisions being taken on key issues, such as the level of regional autonomy, which would effectively tie the hands of the subsequent constituent assembly. Even this did not satisfy the members of COSAG, and in July Inkatha and the CPSA withdrew from the negotiating forum in protest at the rejection of demands for full regional autonomy.

In late July the draft interim constitution was presented to the negotiating forum. This document embodied major compromises by both the main negotiating partners. Its regional proposals went a long way towards federalism, but still did not suffice to enable de Klerk to persuade Buthelezi to resume participation in the talks. The CPSA proclaimed the proposals had put an end to all possibility of further negotiations. At this time political violence between supporters of Inkatha and those of the ANC in the Rand and Natal escalated again. At the beginning of August Inkatha supporters from a migrant workers' hostel in a Rand township went on the rampage, killing more than 100 people. A week later, substantial army contingents moved into the East Rand townships in a new attempt to bring the situation under control.

TOWARDS DEMOCRATIC ELECTIONS

In late September 1993 parliament approved legislation authorizing the formation, from late October, of a transitional executive council to oversee procedures. Immediately afterwards, in response to an appeal by Mandela to the UN, the USA and Commonwealth countries withdrew all economic sanctions against South Africa.

During November 1993 the Forum completed details of an interim constitution, which was approved by the tricameral parliament in December. The national territory was re-divided into nine regions: Western Cape, Eastern Cape, Northern Cape, Orange Free State (renamed 'Free State' in June 1995), North-West, KwaZulu/Natal, Eastern Transvaal (subsequently renamed Mpumalanga), Northern Transvaal (renamed 'Northern Province' in June 1995) and P W V (Pretoria, Witwatersrand and Vereeniging—subsequently renamed 'Gauteng'). The former 'Bantustans', including those purported to be 'independent', disappeared as distinct entities and were absorbed into one or more of the new regions. Even the names disappeared from the new political map, except in the case of KwaZulu/Natal, which was retained as a concession to Buthelezi and Inkatha. Each of the new regions was provided with an elected assembly, to be chosen by proportional representation, and a regional government with extensive local authority and autonomy.

The central parliament was to comprise a house of assembly of 400 members, all elected by proportional representation but on a basis of one-half from national and one-half from regional lists. There was to be an upper house of 90 members chosen by the regional assemblies. The executive would be headed by an executive president, to be chosen by parliament, and at least two executive vice-presidents. Under the terms of the agreement on a government of national unity, any party obtaining 20% of the national vote would be entitled to one of the vice-presidential positions. In the event that only one party achieved this total, the second position would go to any grouping with the second largest support. Any party receiving 5% or more of the vote would be entitled to a position in the national cabinet. The national and regional assemblies and governments were to function within the limitations of a justiciable interim bill of rights. The interim parliament was to subsist for a maximum of five years. During this period it is to act as the national legislature. It is also to act as a constituent assembly charged with the responsibility for drafting the definitive new constitution for the country. This is to be done within the first two years. Thereafter it will have the duty of introducing the necessary legislation and other arrangements for elections under this new constitution to take place by the end of the five-year period. The adoption of constitutional clauses by the constituent assembly will require a two-thirds majority. In framing the constitution the constituent assembly is required to preserve the principles of the interim constitution.

The Forum did not succeed in winning the assent of Buthelezi, the Afrikaner Volksfront and the representatives of Bophuthatswana and the Ciskei. They now formed a new alliance—the Freedom Front (FF)—and threatened to boycott the April 1994 elections. The intensity of the violence between Inkatha and supporters of the ANC in Natal and the African townships on the Rand escalated further. After repeated attempts at negotiations, Buthelezi was persuaded to register the Inkatha Freedom Party (IFP) for the election before reverting to demanding postponement and threatening a boycott. Negotiations between Mandela, de Klerk and the Afrikaner Volksfront were somewhat more productive. The Volksfront was offered the possibility of the subsequent creation of an Afrikaner 'boerestaat', given sufficient support and provided that such a state would remain part of South Africa and subject to the provisions of the bill of rights. Viljoen agreed to register the movement for the elections. However, Terre'Blanche and the more militant of his AWB supporters rejected this outright and threatened civil war if the election proceeded.

During March 1994 the killings in Natal and KwaZulu continued; the declaration of a state of emergency in the area and the dispatch of troops failed to bring the violence to an end. Buthelezi's followers mounted repeated armed demonstrations; on 30 March this resulted in a bloody battle around the ANC headquarters in the heart of Johannesburg. The possibility that the IFP and the armed force of the KwaZulu police might attempt to forcibly prevent the holding of the election there and that the army, with many right-wingers in its ranks, might be unwilling to suppress such a rebellion seemed to threaten South Africa with generalized anarchy and civil war.

In mid-March 1994, however, the militant section of the Afrikaner extreme right suffered a serious blow. The Bophuthatswana army and police mutinied against the highly unpopular government of Chief Mangope, who was forced to flee from his 'Bantustan'. Over 2,000 Afrikaner extremists then invaded the Bophuthatswana capital, Mmabatho, with the intention of restoring Mangope and securing all or part of the area for their projected boerestaat. Bophuthatswana armed forces attacked them, however, and they fled in panic. President de Klerk reacted to news of the mutiny by sending in units of the South African army, who swiftly restored order, oversaw the departure of the remaining white militants, established an interim administration and effectively reintegrated the 'homeland' into South Africa. Shortly afterwards, the security forces of the Ciskei put an end to both the regime of Brig. Gqoza and of that 'Bantustan's' separate existence. The Bophuthatswana fiasco had seriously discredited the military and political potential of the extreme right and had demonstrated that the army and police would be loyal to the constitutional government, however unpalatable to their earlier political views it might be.

In spite of the collapse of his 'Bantustan' allies, Buthelezi continued on alone. Even the international mediation which he requested and received failed to placate him. By early April 1994, however, his exposed situation was becoming increasingly evident and he was under great pressure from many of his own supporters who wished to take advantage of the opportunities offered by the election. Buthelezi held on to the very last minute before agreeing that the IFP would participate in the elections in return for the enhancement of the status of the Zulu monarchy by the transfer of extensive state lands to a trust in the name of the Zulu monarch, King Goodwill Zwelithini. For this the tricameral parliament had to be hastily recalled.

These issues were only resolved, and the IFP's participation assured, on 21 April 1994. In the mean time, the election timetable had been amended in the light of practical considerations to cover three days commencing on 26 April. Only five days thus remained before voting was to begin. Inkatha had missed the deadline for the registration of candidates and Inkatha names were not on the ballot papers which had already been printed. Additional stick-on strips had therefore to be provided, to be attached to ballot papers during the voting procedure.

With the IFP's last-minute participation, the long-running bloody conflict in Natal and the Rand townships faded dramatically. In a last desperate attempt to abort the election and prevent the transition to majority rule, members of the white extreme right set off a series of bomb blasts, including one at Johannesburg's international airport. The violence failed, however, in its purpose of disrupting the election, merely serving to illustrate the isolation and impotence to which the movement (30 of whose members were subsequently arrested) had been reduced. By this stage the security forces had decisively aligned themselves in support of constitutional order.

The election itself, involving 19 political parties, was marked by a quite extraordinary atmosphere of goodwill. The logistical difficulties of organizing an election on this scale for the first time, compounded by the complex procedures which were exacerbated by the need to affix the Inkatha strips to voting ballots during the actual proceedings, resulted in much frustration and long delays. (Organizational failures were especially severe in the KwaZulu area, resulting in the extension of the voting period there for an extra day.) Despite this, blacks and whites voted together without conflict.

The various electoral problems resulted in abundant opportunities for errors as well as election fraud and in spite of the presence of UN and Commonwealth observers, the precise results in many areas remain distinctly dubious. The overall outcome of the election was, however, clear beyond doubt. The ANC gained an overwhelming majority at national level, although just short of the two-thirds majority which would have enabled it to rewrite the constitution unilaterally. It also gained control of all but two of the nine regional assemblies. The National Party was the only other grouping to top 20% of the poll. It also gained control of the Western Cape regional assembly. Inkatha trailed well behind the leaders with just over 10% of votes, but was credited with a 51% victory in KwaZulu/Natal. The constitutional wing of the Afrikaner Volksfront achieved significant support, but less than the 5% needed for a place in the cabinet. The PAC, with its radical africanist approach, received less than 2% of the vote.

For all its problems, the election was a resounding political success. It provided a quite extraordinary emotional as well as politically-liberating catharsis for the vast majority of South Africans of all races. As the results became known, jubilant crowds poured out into the streets in previously unimaginable scenes of goodwill. Thus the new South Africa was born in a far more joyous atmosphere than even the most optimistic had dared to imagine.

THE NEW GOVERNMENT

On 9 May 1994 the national assembly elected Mandela as president, and on the following day he was inaugurated as head of state at a ceremony which was attended by a large number of international dignitaries. In accordance with the interim constitution (which had taken effect on 27 April), an interim government of national unity was formed, in which the ANC, the NP and the IFP were represented in proportion to the number of seats that they had won in the election. Mbeki and de Klerk both became deputy presidents, while the former minister of finance, Derek Keys, was re-appointed to that position, and Buthelezi was allocated the portfolio of home affairs. Cyril Ramaphosa, the secretary-general of the ANC, remained outside the cabinet, but was selected to preside over the constitutional assembly, which comprised the national assembly and the senate. In accordance with the interim constitution, all the former 'homelands' were reincorporated into South Africa, which was henceforth divided into nine (replacing the previous four) provinces, each with its own legislature and executive.

Following the installation of a democratic government, South Africa was admitted into the OAU, the Commonwealth and the SADC, and resumed its seat in the general assembly of the UN. The arms embargo that the UN had imposed in 1977 was finally removed. Mandela, who personified the 'miracle' of the peaceful transition from apartheid to democracy, was widely revered. South Africa's standing in the Commonwealth was acknowledged by a visit by the British prime minister, John Major, in September 1994, and subsequently by a royal visit from Queen Elizabeth II in March 1995. In return, Mandela made a state visit to the United Kingdom in July 1996.

The interim government of national unity focused on the maintenance of stability and the promotion of economic growth, with initial emphasis laid on a reconstruction and development programme (RDP), which included an undertaking to construct 1m. homes in a period of five years, and to extend basic educational and health facilities to all. The government planned to finance the RDP through savings on security-related expenses and increased revenue resulting from economic growth, while Japan and other countries provided sizeable contributions to the programme. Implementation of the RDP proved much more difficult than the government had anticipated, however. In early 1996 it was announced that the separate ministry for the RDP was to be abolished, and the programme was transferred to the office of Mbeki. By then, fewer homes had been constructed than in the last decade of the apartheid government, largely owing to bureaucratic difficulties. Joe Slovo, the first minister of housing in the interim government of national unity, died in January 1995. The government's schemes to provide electricity and clean water to those without these services were initially among its most successful, but unemployment remained very high in the townships, and many communities continued to refuse to pay for services and rents, despite the efforts of the government's campaign to persuade them to do so. It was evident that the alleviation of poverty was dependent on economic growth, while economic growth required substantial foreign investment, which was not forthcoming.

In June 1994 Keys announced he was to resign the finance portfolio for personal reasons, prompting a loss in international business confidence. Mandela acted swiftly to reassure the business community by appointing an Afrikaner banker, Christo Liebenberg, in his place. When he, in turn, was replaced in March 1996 by Trevor Manuel, an ANC member (who was hitherto minister of trade and industry), there was an even greater loss of confidence, exacerbated by rumours that Dr Christian Stals, the governor of the South African Reserve Bank, was to resign (which, in the event, proved unfounded).

Following the announcement, in June 1996, of a macro-economic plan, which included the privatization of state assets and the gradual removal of exchange controls, COSATU challenged the government, particularly regarding the effects that the measures would have on employment. When strikes were threatened over wage demands, Mandela appealed for moderate increases to be accepted, in the interests of economic growth and job creation. COSATU's criticism of the government's growth, employment and redistribution programme, and its campaign of industrial action in support of demands for improved working conditions, increased the concern of foreign investors regarding the influence that COSATU continued to exert on the ANC. Despite government plans for privatization, little was achieved, although the sale of a stake in Telkom, the state-owned telecommunications company, was completed. While the government aimed to generate 400,000 new jobs annually by the year 2000, more than 100,000 jobs in the formal economy were lost in 1996, and few new ones created. Some prominent black politicians, most notably Cyril Ramaphosa and Tokyo Sexwale (the premier of Gauteng), abandoned politics for business, but the impact of 'black empowerment' was limited.

The first population census since the transition to democracy was conducted in October 1996; preliminary results, which were released in mid-1997, indicated that the population totalled only about 37.9m., but there was widespread speculation that the true figure was considerably higher, and excluded large numbers of illegal immigrants from African countries to the north of the country. Meanwhile, Cape Town was selected as one of five cities which might host the Olympic Games in the year 2004, despite considerable opposition from its inhabitants. At the same time there were debates as to whether Cape Town should remain the seat of parliament; the issue was to be resolved by the end of 1997.

Mandela remained aware of a possible threat from right-wing extremists and continued efforts to appear reconciliatory towards this element. The FF, which had participated in the election, was allowed to establish a 'volkstaat council', which was to debate the issue of self-determination for right-wing Afrikaners. Various plans were proposed (one concerning Pretoria, another a region principally located in the Northern Cape), but none of these was practicable, and Mandela insisted that he would not consider a new structure based on racial criteria. In mid-August 1995 he visited the small settlement of Orangia, developed as a model segregated community, to meet the widow of Verwoerd. He also met ex-president P.W. Botha, but was unable to persuade him to co-operate with the truth and reconciliation commission (see below). Many Afrikaners opposed the downgrading of Afrikaans from one of two official languages to one of 11, which was reflected, for example, in the great reduction in the use of Afrikaans in television broadcasting. Right-wing groups supported the continuation of Afrikaans as a medium for teaching in schools and universities (although the government insisted that the maintenance of racially-segregated schools would not be permitted). Both Afrikaners and English-speaking whites resented 'affirmative action' (discrimination in favour of Africans) in job appointments. However, there was no significant protest by whites against the new system, and the extreme right-wing threats of armed resistance receded after the election in April 1994.

The integration of the various armed forces into the new South African National Defence Force (SANDF) proceeded without difficulty, after an incident in late 1994 in which some 3,000 former members of the MK protested at what they claimed to be discriminatory treatment. Mandela ordered them to return to barracks, or be dismissed, and some 2,000 were subsequently discharged. In 1996 a senior post in the SANDF was allocated to the wife of the minister of defence, himself a former MK official. (The commander of the former defence forces, Gen. George Meiring, had been reappointed head of the SANDF.)

KwaZulu/Natal (where the IFP commanded a majority) was the first province to draft its own constitution, which was accepted unanimously by the local legislature in March 1996. The Western Cape, which was dominated by the NP, also decided to draft its own constitution. However, the provinces had been granted limited powers under the new system of government, and the constitutional court eventually rejected the KwaZulu/Natal constitution, which provided for a devolution of powers from central to provincial government. In KwaZulu/Natal the conflict between supporters of the IFP and the ANC (in which an estimated 20,000 people had been killed since the mid-1980s) continued sporadically, increasing prior to the adoption of the provincial constitution, and to local elections, but declining again in mid-1996, owing, in part, to mediation by Mbeki. Tension in the province was compounded by Zwelethini's replacement of Buthelezi as traditional prime minister with a senior ANC official. Buthelezi continued to demand devolution for KwaZulu/Natal and to accuse the ANC of failing to fulfil a pledge, made prior to the election in April 1994, to refer the matter of provincial powers to international mediation.

Local elections were held successfully in November 1995, except in Western Cape (as a result of boundary disputes) and in KwaZulu/Natal (owing to the persistent violence). The postponed elections in Western Cape took place in May 1996, with the NP increasing its share of votes cast, compared with the election in April 1994. The election in KwaZulu/Natal took place relatively peacefully in June; the IFP secured 44.5% of votes cast, although support for the ANC increased, especially in the urban areas, compared with the general election.

A number of communities began increasingly to use vigilante methods in response to the police force's apparent inability to combat an increase in violent crime. In Western Cape a vigilante group, known as 'People Against Gangsterism and Drugs', patrolled the streets and openly carried weapons. The government, which had previously tended to deny that crime was a serious problem or had merely attributed it to apartheid, appeared unable to take effective measures to counter criminal activity, although the carrying of weapons in public was prohibited. The increase in crime prompted demands for the restoration of the death penalty, which the constitutional court had, in June 1995, ruled to be unconstitutional. Mandela maintained, however, that the death penalty would not be reintroduced. Continued corruption within the police force and the use of old methods of policing were among the reasons for the government's inability to combat successfully the increase in crime. The process of transforming the police into a force that was regarded by the public as legitimate and credible was hindered by evidence which emerged about the measures that had, during the period of apartheid, been used against opponents of that system. A number of members of the former police force were placed on trial, notably, Col Eugene de Kock, the former head of a clandestine police base near Pretoria. After proceedings lasting 18 months, de Kock was convicted in 1996 on 89 charges of murder and other crimes. In another trial, which came to an end in that year, Gen. Magnus Malan, the former minister of defence, and prominent officials in the former armed forces were acquitted of complicity in a massacre, perpetrated in KwaZulu in 1987 by commandos who had been trained in Namibia. As a result of such trials, and the proceedings of the truth and reconciliation commission, much was revealed of the illicit activities which had been employed during apartheid and the transitional period, although more would have been learned if relevant evidence on these matters had not been deliberately destroyed, including all information on covert operations prior to 1994.

CONSTITUTIONAL AND POLITICAL DEVELOPMENTS

Following intense negotiations within the constitutional assembly, a final draft of the new constitution was submitted shortly before the expiry of the deadline stipulated in the interim constitution. Since none of the parties favoured a constitutional referendum, a number of concessions were made on significant outstanding issues. On 8 May 1996 parliament approved the final version of the constitution, with the NP voting in favour; only the representatives of the small African Christian Democratic Party voted against the draft, while, despite its recognition of the right of communities to self-determination, the FF abstained. (The IFP had withdrawn from the constitutional assembly, owing to the government's failure to fulfil its pre-election pledge of international mediation.) The new constitution was subsequently referred to the constitutional court for confirmation that it accorded with the constitutional principles that had been established in negotiations prior to the 1994 election. In September the court returned sections of the constitution to the constitutional assembly, which was to reconvene to consider the court's objections. The court subsequently ratified the constitution, which was signed by Mandela at Sharpeville on 10 December 1996, and entered into force on 4 February 1997. The new constitution provided for the establishment of a 'commission for the promotion and protection of the rights of cultural, religious and linguistic communities', while a national council of provinces replaced the existing senate, increasing the influence of the provinces on central government policy.

Although members of parliament agreed in 1996 to a code of conduct requiring disclosure of their financial assets, widespread evidence of corruption, particularly within the government, continued to prompt criticism, and concern for future stability. In August Bantu Holomisa, the former ruler of Transkei and a deputy minister, claimed, at a hearing of the truth and reconciliation commission that part of a donation, which a hotel owner, Sol Kerzner, had made in 1989 to the government of Transkei, in order to secure casino rights, had been used by Stella Sigcau, also an ANC minister. Holomisa further alleged that Mbeki had also received funds from Kerzner for personal use. Holomisa was removed from his post and was subsequently expelled from the ANC for indiscipline.

Following the approval of the draft constitution, the NP announced that it was to leave the government of national unity from the end of June 1996, to form a parliamentary opposition. Although Buthelezi continued to assert his differences with the ANC, the IFP remained in the government of national unity. Efforts by Mandela to persuade the PAC to join the government were unsuccessful. After the NP ministers left the cabinet, their portfolios were allocated to ANC members and de Klerk became the official leader of the opposition. The NP had been restyled as a non-racial party, but continued to receive almost all its support from the white and Coloured communities. Roelf Meyer, who had played a significant role in the negotiations of 1992–93 and (as secretary-general of the party) was the designated successor to de Klerk, became increasingly concerned with the NP's inability to attract black voters. Following his suggestion that the NP disband and re-form as part of a realigned opposition, he was obliged to resign from the party. He subsequently formed the New Movement Process, and developed close links with Holomisa (after the latter's expulsion from the ANC). Meyer and Holomisa declared their intention to launch a new political party in September 1997, together with the ex-leader of the former 'homeland' of Bophuthatswana, Chief Lucas Mangope. Meanwhile, de Klerk had been the subject of increasing criticism from Western Cape members of his party, who accused him of having betrayed the Afrikaner community in the constitutional negotiations. In August 1997 he unexpectedly resigned as leader of the NP, on the grounds that he was hampering the party, owing to his associations with past events. A number of senior members of the IFP also resigned at this time, including its most prominent white member, Walter Felgate, who accused Buthelezi of administering the party undemocratically. In September the leadership of the NP passed to its secretary-general, Marthinus van Schalkwyk.

Mandela's announcement that he would resign as ANC leader at the end of 1997, and would not serve a second term as president, was received with concern. The majority of observers believed that Mbeki would be elected president at the ANC's national conference, which was to take place in December 1997, would subsequently assume the presidency of the country after the 1999 elections, and would govern pragmatically. By mid-1997 Mbeki was already effectively in control of the government. Economic growth remained essential, however; unless the majority of the population began to experience real improvements in living standards, the country's long-term prospects for stability and development were uncertain.

THE TRUTH AND RECONCILIATION COMMISSION

In 1995, following protracted disputes regarding its method of operating, parliament approved the establishment of a truth and reconciliation commission, and in December of that year 17 members were appointed to the commission by Mandela. Desmond Tutu (whose term of office as Anglican archbishop of Cape Town ended in 1996) became chairman of the commission. The commission began by conducting public hearings throughout the country, at which former victims of human rights' violations gave evidence. The commission's amnesty committee considered applications by perpetrators of such abuses, and from August 1996 began to grant amnesty to those who had appeared before it and given a full account of their actions. Considerable interest was aroused when Janusz Walus and Clive Derby-Lewis, who had been convicted of the murder of Chris Hani, testified before the commission. After the mandate of the commission had been extended from December 1993 to 10 May 1994, as requested both by the FF and the PAC, large numbers of applications for amnesty were received. Following some 8,000 applications by the stipulated date in May, it was decided that the amnesty committee would continue to function after the commission itself had completed its reports. The commission's reparations committee was to recommend how surviving victims could, within the means of the government, be compensated for their suffering.

From August 1996 the commission heard representations from political parties. Although de Klerk formally apologized for the policy of apartheid, he denied that he or other members of the previous government had ordered or condoned illegal activities. The ANC admitted responsibility for some violations of human rights, committed by its members in the 1980s, asserting that these were justified in the context of the struggle against apartheid. However, Buthelezi refused to co-operate with the commission, claiming that he had already apologized for acts of violence perpetrated by IFP supporters. In May 1997 the NP suspended participation in the commission and threatened legal action against Tutu, after he accused de Klerk of responsibility for human rights' violations.

FOREIGN POLICY

Following Mandela's assumption of office, it became evident that the new government intended to maintain cordial relations with regimes which were regarded with disapproval by the USA and other Western countries, but which had provided substantial support to the ANC during the apartheid era, most notably those of Iran, Cuba and Libya. Nevertheless, South Africa's links with the USA strengthened following the transition to democratic rule. The two nations established a joint commission, chaired by Mbeki and the US vice-president, Albert Gore. South Africa was the location for a number of important international meetings, and Mandela's personal stature, in addition to the success of the country's transition to democracy, enhanced South Africa's prestige internationally.

Following a prolonged debate, the EU in March 1996 agreed on a framework for negotiations with South Africa on the proposed establishment of a joint 'free-trade area'. In March 1997 South Africa was granted partial access to the EU's Lomé Conventions with developing countries. In November 1996 Mandela announced that South Africa would transfer diplomatic recognition from Taiwan to the People's Republic of China, with effect from the end of 1997. Taiwan immediately severed diplomatic relations, announced the suspension of most of its aid projects in South Africa, and banned South African Airways from flying to the Taiwanese capital, Taipeh. The South African decision was influenced by the return of Hong Kong to Chinese rule in 1997, and by its aim to secure a permanent seat on an enlarged UN Security Council.

In November 1995 Mandela attracted international criticism for failing to intervene effectively to prevent the execution in Nigeria of the Ogoni activist, Ken Saro-Wiwa, and eight others. He had rejected the proposed imposition of sanctions, in favour of a more conciliatory approach, as a means of exerting pressure on the Nigerian military regime. Following the executions, Mandela denounced the Nigerian government and supported Nigeria's suspension from the Commonwealth. After becoming chairman of the SADC in September 1996, he pursued a more active foreign policy, frequently intervening personally in an effort to resolve regional problems. In early 1997 Mandela was involved in intensive diplomatic activity which was aimed at ending the civil war in Zaire (now the Democratic Republic of the Congo), meeting both the then Zairean rebel leader, Laurent Kabila, and the Zairean president, Mobutu Seso Seko. Mandela also sought to mediate in the dispute over Indonesia's annexation of East Timor in 1976, and in the ongoing conflict in Southern Sudan. However, South Africa was subject to criticism for continuing to supply armaments to governments accused of human rights' violations, such as those of Rwanda and Indonesia; negotiations on a proposed sale of arms to Syria were suspended in response to criticism from the USA in early 1997.

Economy

LINDA VAN BUREN

NATURAL RESOURCES

South Africa's diverse climate permits the cultivation of a wide range of crops but, largely because of inadequate and erratic rainfall, only 13% of the land surface is suitable for arable farming. Indeed, only 11% of the total land area, or 132,000 sq km, was under major crops in 1993, according to the World Bank. Topographic difficulty is the main factor limiting the extent of irrigation to less than 8,000 sq km. However, the ambitious Orange River Project is expected eventually to increase the total irrigated area by about 300,000 ha, or 40%. In spite of improvements in farming methods and conservation techniques in recent years, South Africa remains a relatively poor crop-raising country. This also imposes limits on animal husbandry, for which South Africa is better suited, although even here, the carrying capacity of the land is fairly low by international standards. Nevertheless, because of a high degree of specialization, experience, advanced methods and considerable capital investment, certain branches of farming, such as the fruit and wool sectors, continue to make a substantial contribution to the economy and to exports in particular.

It is in mineral deposits, though, that South Africa's greatest wealth lies. The discovery of first diamonds and then, more importantly, gold during the latter part of the 19th century was the basis of the country's modern economic development. A huge complex of heavy and light industry, based initially on the gold mining industry, has grown up in the interior, although South Africa's share in the volume of world gold production (excluding the former USSR) declined from 70% in 1980 to 27% in 1993, owing to a fall in the average grade of ore mined and an increase in output in other parts of the world. Nevertheless, South Africa remained the largest gold producer in the world, with output totalling 523 metric tons in 1995. There are also abundant deposits of nearly every other important mineral in the country. The production of minerals other than gold accounted for 50% of the total value of mining production of R53,526.3m. in 1994. There are huge reserves of iron ore and coal (with a pit-head price which is probably the lowest in the world). In 1990 South Africa possessed more than three-quarters of the world's reserves of manganese ore (83%) and more than half of world reserves of platinum-group metals (66%) and chromium, as well as 40% of the world's gold and vermiculite, 37% of its alumino-silicates, 33% of its vanadium and 26% of world zirconium metal reserves. In addition, it is a major producer of copper, lead and zinc.

South Africa's long coastline has few natural harbours, but close to its shores are some of the richest fishing areas in the world. The catch includes Southern African anchovy, Cape hakes, Southern African pilchard, Cape horse mackerel and Whitehead's round herring. In 1995 the total catch amounted to 575,200 metric tons, compared with 521,100 metric tons in 1994.

POPULATION

The chief characteristic of South Africa's population, and the one that dominates its society, is the great racial, linguistic and cultural heterogeneity of its people, with Africans, Asians, Europeans and mixed-race citizens making up the population.

At the March 1985 census the total population (excluding the former 'independent homelands') was enumerated as 23,385,645. The total population at the March 1991 census was 37,944,018; an official estimate in mid-1995 gave the total population as 41,244,500. In April 1994 the estimated ethnic composition was: Africans 30,645,157 (76.1%); whites 5,171,419 (12.8%); Coloureds 3,435,114 (8.5%); Asians 1,032,943 (2.6%). According to the preliminary results of the October 1996 census, which were announced in July 1997, the total population was 37.9m. (10% lower than envisaged).

The occupational distribution of the economically active population in 1995 was as follows: out of a total labour force of 14,356,000, 1,295,000 were engaged in agriculture, forestry and fishing (9.0%), 471,000 in mining and quarrying (3.3%), 1,526,000 in manufacturing (10.6%), 95,000 in electricity, gas and water (0.6%), 483,000 in construction (3.4%), 1,769,000 in commerce, restaurants and hotels (12.3%), 520,000 in transport and communications (3.6%), 654,000 in finance and business services (4.6%), and 3,137,000 in other services (21.9%). The most drastic structural change in the economy has been an apparently sharp decline in the proportion of the population engaged in agriculture (28% at the 1970 census).

NATIONAL INCOME

In the 50 years from 1911/12 to 1961/62, net domestic product, at current prices, grew from R266m. to R5,036m. Allowing for price increases and population growth, real income per head more than doubled in this period, with an average growth of 1.8% per annum. Growth in the 1960s was exceptionally high, rivalling that of Japan. GDP, at current market prices, more than doubled between 1960–70, growing at an average rate of 8.9% per annum. In real terms, the rate of increase was 5.9%, and 2.9% per caput, per annum. This rate fell sharply in the 1970s, however, with real GDP growing at an average of only 3.9% (and about 1% per caput) per annum in the period 1970–80. This was followed by an exceptionally high increase of nearly 8% in real GDP in 1980, brought about largely by the high price of gold in that year. During the 1980s growth in real GDP declined further, averaging only 1.4% per year in 1980–90. Negative real growth rates of GDP were recorded during four of the 10 years (i.e. 1982, 1983, 1985 and 1990). With the population increasing at an annual average rate of 2.6% in that decade, income per head was in decline. In 1995, according to estimates by the World Bank, South Africa's gross national product (GNP), measured at average 1993–95 prices, was US $130,918m., equivalent to $3,160 per head. During 1985–95, it was estimated, GNP per head declined, in real terms, by an annual average of 1.0%, while the population increased by an annual average of 2.3%. GDP increased, in real terms, by an annual average of 1.3% in 1980–90, and by 0.6% in 1990–95; real GDP increased by 2.3% in 1994, by 3.3% in 1995, and by 3.1% in 1996.

Despite an improvement in the racial distribution of personal income in recent years, income remains very unevenly distributed in South Africa. It was estimated in 1988 that the white population received about 54% of total personal income, while Africans received only 36%. In 1988 the differential in earnings per employee between whites and Africans in the manufacturing sector was 3.5:1, rising to 5:1 in mining and quarrying. The greatest differential was to be found between those residing in metropolitan areas (white and black) and the rural former 'homelands' (mainly black), estimated to be 18:1 in 1985. (The October 1996 census indicated that 55% of South Africans resided in urban areas.) In 1992 the average monthly income per head was R1,572 for whites, R523 for Asians, R325 for Coloureds, and R165 for black Africans.

The contribution to national income of the three main productive sectors—manufacturing, mining and agriculture—has changed markedly over the years. Manufacturing steadily increased its relative position, overtaking mining as the leading sector during the Second World War. By 1995 manufacturing contributed 23.4% of GDP at factor cost, mining and quarrying 7.5% and agriculture only 4.2%. The expansion of manufacturing since 1910 is the most important structural change to have taken place in the economy.

INVESTMENT AND SAVING

Since the discovery of diamonds and gold in the 19th century, foreign investment has played a vital role in developing these industries and the economy in general. By 1936 it was estimated that R1,046m. had been invested in South Africa, representing 43% of total foreign investment in Africa. Another large wave of foreign investment, associated with goldfields in the then Orange Free State, took place after the Second World War, but there was a subsequent slowing down, with an actual outflow in the years 1959–64. From 1965–76 (with the exception of 1973), foreign investment was again positive. Following the Soweto riots in mid-1976, however, there was a sharp decline in foreign investment, with negative outflows of both long-term and short-term capital from 1977–80. From 1981–83 foreign investment was again positive, but from 1984 it began to move sharply into a negative direction again. At first this was owing to speculative movements against the currency, brought on by a large balance-of-payments deficit and a weakening rand. However, with a deepening recession and the serious political disturbances that flared up in 1985, accompanied by the refusal of foreign banks to defer repayment of short-term loans, negative short-term capital movements reached record levels. Further deterioration was avoided only by the reintroduction, in September 1985, of the two-tier (financial–commercial) system of exchange rates for foreign investors. In the same month, the government also declared a moratorium on repayments of debt principal on foreign loans until the end of the year (later extended until the end of March 1986), although interest payments were to continue. In October negotiations began with creditor banks on rescheduling short-term debt, and in March 1986 the negotiations resulted in a one-year interim agreement whereby South Africa was to make a series of payments of 5% of debts due before the end of June 1987. In March 1987 it was announced that a further agreement had been reached with creditor banks, allowing a three-year rescheduling of US $13,000m. of foreign debt.

At the end of 1995 South Africa's government debt was R280,042m., of which R10,944m. was foreign debt. With a level of foreign borrowing which has been especially low for a country at South Africa's level of development, it can be expected that this situation may change now that South Africa, following its political transition, has access to institutions such as the World Bank and is more favourably treated by the international financial community. The 1996/97 budget provided for a gross borrowing requirement of R45,100m. in the domestic market and R2,500m. in foreign funding.

Gross domestic investment was R59,984m., equivalent to 15.6% of GDP at market prices in 1993, and to 19% of GDP in 1995. This capital formation was financed by gross domestic savings of R65,917m. (17.2% of GDP), allowing for net capital outflows to the rest of the world of R8,874m., and a decrease in holdings of gold and other reserves of R2,941m. Real gross domestic fixed investment increased by 8.7% in 1994, by an estimated 10% in 1995, and by an estimated 6% in 1996.

MANUFACTURING INDUSTRY

Unlike its counterparts in the rest of Africa, South Africa's manufacturing industry is the largest sector of the national economy, measured in terms of contribution to GDP. In 1993 it contributed R81,167m. to GDP at factor cost, employing 1,438,409 (more than 75% of the work-force being non-white) in 1992. In 1995 the manufacturing sector contributed 23.4% of GDP, and employed about 1,526,000 (10.6% of the labour force).

The mining industry, except for a limited number of industries servicing it, did not, at first, stimulate local manufacturing to any extent. As the mining industry favoured cheap imports, little protection was offered to local manufacturers. It was only in 1925 that an active policy of protecting local industry was first adopted. As a consequence, industry grew significantly in the latter half of the 1920s, particularly in the production of consumer goods. That period also saw the foundation of heavy industry under state auspices, with the establishment of the Iron and Steel Corpn of South Africa (ISCOR) in 1928. By 1939 net industrial output was double the 1929 level, and expansion continued in the post-war period. Industrial progress in the 1960s was particularly rapid. Its contribution to GDP, at factor cost, increased by an average of 10.2% per annum between 1961–70, the physical volume of production by 8.5% per annum and employment by 6.1% per annum, indicating increases in productivity over the same period. Real growth was slower in the 1970s, with the physical volume of production increasing by an average of only 2.9% per annum, while employment grew by 2.6% annually. During 1980–93 industrial GDP declined by an annual average of 0.2%.

Industry is heavily concentrated in four industrial areas—Gauteng, Western Cape, Durban-Pinetown and Port Elizabeth-Uitenhage—accounting for more than 75% of net industrial output and employment. More than 50% of the country's industry is now located in Gauteng alone and the tendency has been for this concentration to increase at the expense of the ports and rural areas. Largely to stem the flow of Africans to 'white' industrial areas, the state attempted, from 1960, to decentralize industrial location to proclaimed border areas near to the former 'homelands'. Financial assistance (in the form of tax concessions, loans, reduced railway rates, exemption from wage regulation, etc.) was granted to industrialists in these areas. Between 1960–80, tax and interest concessions (including rental concessions) amounting to R222.8m. were given and 181,198 jobs (142,061 for Africans) were created in border areas. In 1982 the government introduced a revised Regional Industrial Development Programme (RIDP), which provided substantial relocation incentives to industrialists, including wage subsidies, training grants, transport rebates, housing subsidies and soft loans. Over the period 1982–90 about 450,000 jobs were created in the target areas at an average cost (in 1990 prices) of R18,000 per job—for a huge total cost of R8,100m. It was felt, however, that the policy had failed in its primary purpose of job creation as most of the jobs would have existed somewhere else in the absence of relocation incentives, at no cost to the taxpayer. Uneconomic location decisions were encouraged by this policy, as is confirmed by a study which concluded that 34%–42% of firms would be unprofitable if incentives were withdrawn.

In 1991 a new RIDP was adopted, which shifted the emphasis away from decentralized industrial development in rural areas to broader regional development. Incentives were to be more cost-effective in being performance-linked. In April 1995 RIDP incentives were in the form of an establishment grant for the first two years, a profit-based incentive for the following three years and a relocation incentive for foreign firms. In addition, a Simplified Regional Industrial Development Programme (SRIDP) offered incentives to manufacturers, processors and assemblers whose total investment did not exceed R2.5m.

Metal Products and Engineering

This is the largest sector of industry (including basic metals, metal products, machinery and transport equipment), employing 465,600 workers in 1988. The steel industry is the most important branch of this sector, with production of crude steel valued at R12,593m. in 1992, R13,476m. in 1993 and R14,070m. in 1994. The industry is dominated by ISCOR, the transfer of which from state to private-sector ownership was completed in November 1989. In 1997 ISCOR operated 10 ore mines and four steel mills, while a fifth was under construction at Saldanha Bay, at a projected cost of $1,550m., and was due for completion by 1999. In addition, a $280m. ISCOR stainless-steel plant, which was under construction at Pretoria, was due for completion by 1998. There were six other steel-producing companies in the private sector. Because of favourable costs of location, raw materials and labour, and an efficient scale of production, South African steel is among the cheapest in the world. Three manganese plants were being upgraded in 1997, at Sasolburg, Meyerton and Witbank, and were due for completion in January 1998. Gencor was also rehabilitating its Impala platinum refinery at a cost of $100m.; the project was also scheduled for completion in January 1998. The aluminium enterprise, ALUSAF (of which 45% was owned by Gencor and 20% by the Industrial Development Corporation—IDC) commissed its Hillside aluminium smelter in April 1997, five months earlier than scheduled. The total cost of the project was finally estimated at R6,000m.; it had already achieved full production in June 1996, and its output reached 636,000 tons in its first year. ALUSAF's production cost, at $750 per metric ton, was one of the lowest in the world. An estimated 490,000 tons of its output was to be exported, of which 230,000 tons was to be sold under long-term contracts.

The motor industry is another important branch of the engineering sector. In 1992 the transport equipment industry employed 91,000 workers and produced 206,600 passenger cars and 93,600 commercial vehicles. The volume of production in the motor-vehicle subsector increased by 5.1% in 1993 and by 6.8% in 1994. The vast majority of new cars contain at least 66% local content by weight, thereby qualifying for special tariff rates as 'locally manufactured' models. In common with this industry in other developing countries, vehicle manufacturing faces the problem of rising costs with increasing local content, because of the lack of those economies of scale which are enjoyed in the major producing countries. With its potential market size of almost 40m. people, South Africa would offer better opportunities to achieve economies of scale if incomes were more evenly distributed and a larger proportion of the population could afford to buy basic luxuries such as automobiles.

Food, Beverages and Tobacco

Industries processing local farm produce were among the first to develop in South Africa. While this sector has expanded and contributes importantly to exports, its relative position declined from 32% of the net value of manufacturing output in 1925 to 17% in 1963. Food, beverages and tobacco accounted for 19.3% of the value of manufacturing output in November 1994, down from 20.7% for the whole year in 1993, when combined output in these sub-sectors amounted to R44,367.2m. In 1986 the gross value of output of these industries was R18,193m. (21% of the total for all manufacturing industry), and in 1992 they employed 197,300 workers (13.7% of the manufacturing industry labour force). This subsector experienced difficulties in 1993, when volume output declined by 12.6% in beverages, by 2.7% in food and by 1.0% in tobacco. In 1994, however, both food and beverages recovered, by 4.6% and 3.1% respectively; only tobacco remained in decline, at 3.5%. In 1997 South African Breweries was to construct a new $175m. brewery at East London. In a major example of new inward foreign investment, the US enterprise, Coco-Cola, in 1995 joined South African Bottling Company in a $400m. venture, which was aimed at not only the South African market but also that of other African countries.

Clothing and Textiles

The clothing industry, which was well established before the Second World War, now supplies 90% of local demand, and employed 113,500 workers in 1992. The textile industry (other than clothing) was essentially a post-war development; it now meets 60% of the country's textile needs, and employed 82,600 workers in 1992. In November 1994 textiles, wearing apparel and footwear contributed 7% of the value of manufacturing output, up from 6.7% for the whole of 1993, when combined output from these sub-sectors was R14,411.9m. Output of non-clothing textiles increased by 5.6% in 1994 in terms of volume, while that of clothing grew by 3.0% and that of footwear declined by 1.5%.

Chemicals

This industry had an early beginning, with the manufacture of explosives for the gold mines. The Modderfontein factory, near Johannesburg, is now probably the world's largest privately owned explosives factory. Production of fertilizers is also a significant branch of this industry. However, the most important development in recent years was the establishment by the state-owned South African Coal, Oil and Gas Corpn (SASOL) of its first oil-from-coal plant (SASOL 1), which began production in the northern Free State in 1955. Based on cheap, low-grade coal with a high ash-content, this establishment was, until the commissioning of SASOL 2 and 3, the largest plant of its kind in the world. Besides producing a small but significant percentage of South Africa's petrol requirements, the development of synthetic fuel production led to the establishment of a huge petrochemical complex which manufactures about 110 products, some of which, like coal-tar products, are only by-products of a coal-using process. Because of the absence of local supplies of natural mineral oil, attempts at a petroleum embargo and the huge rise in world petroleum prices in 1973, it was decided in 1974 to build SASOL 2 with 10 times the capacity of SASOL 1. SASOL was privatized in 1979. Production at SASOL 2, which had a capital cost of R2,400m., reached full capacity in 1982. Following the change of government in Iran in 1979 and the consequent loss by South Africa of its main source of supply of crude petroleum, it was decided to build SASOL 3, almost an exact copy of SASOL 2, at a capital cost of R3,200m. This plant began operation in 1983, and reached full production in 1985. The three plants in full production provided about 40% of South Africa's fuel requirements, and a fourth plant was planned. Part of the huge capital cost of these plants was provided by private sector investment. In April 1997 SASOL announced a co-operation agreement with Statoil of Norway, under which the two companies were to convert South African natural gas to synthetic crude oil. In June of that year SASOL also commissioned a new acetic acid plant at Secunda; the R167m. plant had the capacity to produce 16,000 metric tons per year of acetic acid and 7,000 metric tons per year of propionic acid. In 1992 the chemical industry employed 120,800 workers. In November 1994 industrial chemicals and chemical products (excluding petroleum) contributed 11.3% of the value of manufactured output, down from 13.2% for the whole of 1993, when these two sub-sectors' combined output was R28,237.5m. Production of industrial chemicals, in terms of volume, declined by 2.9% in 1993, but increased by 2.3% in 1994, while that of non-industrial chemicals declined by 0.2% in 1993, but increased by 1.8% in 1994.

AGRICULTURE

Reference has already been made to the declining role of agriculture as a source of income in the South African economy. The vagaries of climate and unstable world prices are largely responsible for this. The effect of recurrent drought can be dramatically seen in the fluctuations in production of maize—the staple food of the African population and the most important single item in South African farming. From a record output of 13.6m. tons in the 1981/82 season, production fell to only 3.4m. tons in the 1983/84 drought resulting in maize imports of 2.4m. tons in that year. Again, from a peak of 11.7m. tons in 1989/90 output fell to 2.9m. tons in the disastrous drought of 1992/93, necessitating imports of 4.5m. tons at a cost of R2,570m. Maize production amounted to only 9.7m. tons in 1993, and, although it recovered strongly in 1994 to 13.2m. tons, it declined to 4.8m. tons in 1995. However, the 1996 crop doubled to 10m. tons, and exports of maize were resumed. The oat harvest increased from 37,000 tons in 1994 to 42,000 tons in 1995, while the rye crop remained constant at 3,000 tons in both years. Wheat production grew from 1.8m. tons in 1994 to 2.0m. tons in 1995, and to 2.4m. tons in 1996. However, the total cereal harvest of 7.4m. tons in 1995 was less than half that of 1994, at 15.9m. tons. Wool, although prone to wide fluctuations in price, is one of South Africa's most important exports (along with maize, fruit and cane sugar), earning R590.7m. in 1986. Agricultural products contributed R9,857.6m. to exports in 1994 (10.9% of the total). Following the abandonment of sanctions, the export of wine, and various fruit and vegetables to Europe increased dramatically. The low overall productivity of farming, relative to other sectors, is also reflected in the fact that, although employing about 12.9% of the economically active population in 1991, it contributed only 4.5% of GDP in 1994. This is mainly because large numbers of inefficient African subsistence farmers in the former 'homelands' obtain very low crop yields. However, even commercial farms, which are relatively efficient, obtain comparatively low yields by international standards. In maize farming, for example, yields per hectare are only 38% of those in the USA; according to the Food and Agriculture Organization (FAO), South Africa's average maize yield in 1994 (a year not affected by drought) was 3,308 kg per hectare, compared with the USA's 8,685 kg per hectare.

MINING

Despite having given way to manufacturing as the leading sector, mining is still of great importance in external trade. The sector contributed 7.5% of GDP in 1995. In 1993 total sales of minerals amounted to R50,219.4m., of which 63.5% was exported. In 1994 total exports of minerals amounted to R53,526.3m. (up by 6.6% compared with 1993). Mining and quarrying employed a total work-force of 471,000 in 1995.

South Africa is the world's leading gold producer. Since the Second World War, new gold mines in the Free State, Far West Rand, Klerksdorp and Evander areas not only have replaced output from the worked-out mines on the old Rand but have also greatly increased total production. In the absence of new discoveries, however, gold output is expected to continue the decline that began in the early 1970s after a record 1,000 tons in 1970. This has been largely due to the policy of the industry of lowering the grade of ore mined as the price rises. Unless there is a compensating increase in tonnage milled when the average grade of ore mined is lowered, output falls. Since the late 1980s, however, the industry has come under pressure from falls in both the US dollar and rand price of gold and continued increases in costs, forcing several economically marginal mines to close. Gold production amounted to 613.7 tons, valued at R19,512.6m., in 1992, rising to 619.9 tons, valued at R23,239.3m., in 1993. Net gold exports generated R22,229m. in 1993 and R22,661m. in 1994. Having remained well below $350 per ounce throughout 1992, the price of gold began to rise in 1993, briefly exceeding $400 per ounce in mid-1993. In August 1996 the world gold price stood at US $387 per ounce; by August 1997, however, it had dropped to $320.5 per ounce, prompting concern that seven unprofitable gold mines might be closed. In 1996 South Africa's production of gold fell below 500 tons for the first time since 1956.

The output of other minerals has rapidly gained in importance since the Second World War. Gold accounted for about 80% of South Africa's mineral production in 1946 but the proportion had fallen to only 50% by 1993; all mining exports were valued in that year at R46,872.3m. (including gold) or at R23,632.9m. (excluding gold). There has been a great expansion in the output of uranium, platinum, nickel, copper, coal, antimony, diamonds, vanadium, asbestos, iron ore, fluorspar, chromium, manganese and limestone, to name only the most important. (In 1992 South Africa's output of chromium ore, at 3.36m. metric tons, was a close second, in terms of world production, to Kazakstan's 3.6m. metric tons.) Sales of platinum-group metals generated earnings of R6,600m. in 1995. When it was reported that the Impala platinum refinery had been affected by strike action in 1997, the international price of petroleum increased from US $445 to $460 per ounce. These minerals are prominent in South Africa's exports, earning R10,177m. in 1990. A new underground copper mine at Phalaborwa, which was undertaken by Palabora Mining Co, at a projected cost of R1,500m., was due to enter into production in the year 2002.

Diamonds were traditionally the country's second most important export commodity (after gold), but in recent years they have also been overtaken by coal. South African diamond production had been conducted for some time at five mine locations. A sixth mine, Venetia, discovered in 1980 and opened in 1992, was expected during the 1990s to become South Africa's largest-producing diamond mine. Output in 1993 was 9.8m. carats, compared with 10m. carats in 1992 and 8.2m. carats in 1991. Production in 1994 was 10.2m. carats. In 1995 production declined to 9.1m. carats. In 1996 the Venetia mine accounted for about 41% of South Africa's output of 10.2m. carats. In April 1997 Benguela Concessions and Moonstone Diamonds completed a project to exploit marine diamonds off South Africa's west coast.

The coal-mining industry, which stagnated for many years because of low prices and slow growth, acquired renewed vigour after the petroleum crisis in 1973. Exports have grown rapidly in recent years, helped by the opening of the new rail link and coal terminal at Richards Bay in northern KwaZulu/Natal, which, by 1987, with the completion of Phase III of the export programme, had increased its capacity to 44m. tons per annum. However, the spread of international sanctions and especially a fall in international prices had a particularly adverse effect on this industry. Exports fell from 44.9m. tons, earning R3,127m. in 1986, to 42.6m. tons, valued at R2,294m., in 1987. The decline in exports led to some 3,000 workers, mostly Africans, being laid off. By 1991, with the recovery of international prices for coal and the removal of sanctions by most of the countries which have traditionally been South Africa's major export markets for coal, exports increased significantly, with shipments of 50.1m. tons earning R4,300m. in foreign exchange. In 1993 total production of coal was 183m. tons, valued at R9,674.4m. In 1994 output was 197m. tons, valued at R10,427m., an increase of 7.4% in volume terms. Exports of coal amounted to 60.3m. tons and earned R6,500m. in 1995. In 1996 exports of coal increased to 61.7m. tons, generating income of R8,000m. The industry employed 76,200 workers in 1992. SASOL's new US $90m. coal mine at Bosjesspruit was due to be completed in January 1998.

South Africa is the continent's leading producer of iron ore, and exports, to Japan in particular, have also become important since the late 1980s, despite declining world demand for steel. A railway line from the high-grade deposits of the Sishen area, in the northern Cape, carries iron ore to Saldanha Bay. As a result of falling demand, South Africa's exports of iron ore declined from a peak of 14.7m. tons in 1980 to 8.8m. tons in 1986. Despite persistently depressed market conditions, export volume recovered to 15.5m. tons in 1990. In 1991, when shipments declined to 14.9m. tons, this export earned R772.1m. Production of iron ore amounted to 28.2m. tons, valued at R1,127.6m., in 1992, 29.4m. tons, valued at R1,278.9m., in 1993 and 32.3m. tons, valued at R1,327m., in 1994. In May 1996 the IDC announced that it was conducting a feasibility study into the construction of a R2,500m. iron-ore reduction plant in Northern Province.

Only two major mineral products—petroleum and bauxite—have not been found in economic quantities. However, in February 1985 the Southern Oil Exploration Corpn (SOEKOR), a government-owned company which had been involved since 1965 in an intensive search for petroleum deposits, announced that a recent discovery offshore at Mossel Bay, off the south coast of Cape Province, had yielded a daily output of 2,600 barrels of light crude and 1m. cu ft of natural gas. While the oil potential of this field is thought to be limited, the natural gas reserves are estimated to be substantial: in the region of 30,000m. cu m. In 1987 the government decided to proceed with the establishment of a plant to convert this natural gas into liquid fuel, at a cost of R5,500m. This plant was designed to supply 10% of South Africa's liquid fuel requirements when it came into operation in 1992. SOEKOR announced in May 1997 that Petrol S. A. Ltd and Phillips Petroleum of the USA were to explore an area of the Indian Ocean, off South Africa's east coast. Other participants in the venture, for which Phillips was the operator, with a 40% share, were Pan Canadian Petroleum (Africa) Ltd. of Canada (20%), Energy Africa Bredasdorp (Proprietary) Ltd. of South Africa (20%), and SASOL (20%). Phillips was to spend $8m. in gathering seismic data and was to drill at least one exploratory well over the four-year period of the lease (which could be extended for up to two subsequent periods of three years each).

TRANSPORT AND COMMUNICATIONS

With no navigable rivers, South Africa's transport system is entirely dependent on its rail and road network, with air transport playing a small but increasing role. The state-owned railways covered 21,303 route-km in 1993 (about one-third of all the railway track length in sub-Saharan Africa); some 87% of the rail network is electrified and the system was computerized in 1980. A R300m. project, aimed at upgrading the Majuba line, is due for completion by 1997. In the year ending 31 March 1989 total freight traffic was 174.2m. metric tons and 579.5m. passenger journeys were made. South African harbours handled 122.59m. tons of cargo in 1993, including transhipments of cargo but excluding petroleum products. The Richards Bay Coal Terminal handled 58.7m. tons of coal exports in 1996. Plans, announced in August 1997, to construct a new $146m. dry dock and a R500m. container terminal were aimed at developing Richards Bay into a principal transhipment port. Safmarine and Unicorn, the two largest shipping companies, are both in the private sector. Transnet Ltd, which controls the national railways, harbours, and oil pipelines, is the largest commercial undertaking in South Africa, employing 168,419 people in 1990. On 6 August 1993 the country's nine major airports were placed under the management of The Airports Company Limited, which is 100% owned by the government but is nevertheless operating the airports on a commercial basis. The national carrier is South African Airways (SAA), but the sector was deregulated in 1990, and the airline is now exposed to competition, both on domestic and on international routes, from other private-sector carriers. More than 20 private-sector airlines provided 80 routes to 50 towns in South Africa in 1996. Following the end of apartheid, SAA began to expand services to the rest of Africa.

An extensive road network serves the country, with an estimated 182,580 km of roads in 1995. Road transport has grown rapidly since the Second World War. In 1995 there were an estimated 3,810,000 passenger cars in use, 260,000 buses and coaches, 1,380,000 goods vehicles and 270,000 motor cycles. Private long-distance road haulage is restricted, however, by government legislation, designed to protect the railways.

Telecommunications are fairly extensively developed, with 3.7m. telephone lines in use in March 1994 (about 39% of the total in Africa), of which about 96% are automatic. In 1997 the state telecommunications company, Telkom and Telecom Malaysia revealed plans for the construction of a \$360m. cable under the Indian Ocean, which would link Cape Town to Penang, Malaysia, via Port Louis, Mauritius. Telkom, which had accrued debt totalling R8,000m., was offered for privatization in 1997, in the hope that the sale of part of its equity would generate revenue amounting to about R5,000m. In March of that year the sale of a 30% stake in Telkom was completed. The government's ambitious R16,000m. Vision 2000 scheme proposed to extend the telecommunications network to a far greater proportion of the population by installing 12m. new telephone lines, at a cost of R6,000m., by the year 2000.

POWER AND WATER

Electricity

In 1993 South Africa consumed 174,581m. kWh of electricity, with a per caput consumption equal to that of Western Europe. In South Africa, however, only 15m. people, or 37% of the population, have access to electricity in their homes. The bulk of this supply (97% in 1995) was generated by the state-controlled Electricity Supply Commission (ESKOM) via a national grid system which came into operation in 1973. Coal, owing mainly to its low cost, is the main source of fuel for power generation (78% in 1993). South Africa's electricity is among the cheapest in the world (\$0.079 per kWh in 1990). Nearly one-half of the country's coal production goes to electricity production. A very small amount of peak-load power is now being provided by the hydroelectric stations of the Orange River Project. The first nuclear power station to be constructed in South Africa, Koeberg, was commissioned by ESKOM in 1976. It was built at Duynefontein, between Cape Town and Saldanha Bay, by a French consortium. The plant was damaged in a sabotage attack in December 1982, but began operating in March 1984. The first of its two 920-MW units was connected to the national grid in April, and reached full generating capacity in June. The second unit came into operation in 1985. With both units in full operation, the plant has a generating capacity of 1,842 MW, representing about 10% of South Africa's total capacity. In February 1985, however, the Koeberg plant was temporarily closed, following the discovery of defects. In 1993 nuclear generation supplied the equivalent of only 2.3m. tons of coal, or 1.7% of the total. The construction, at a cost of R17,500m., of five coal-fired power stations, each designed to generate 3,600 MW, was being reviewed in 1986. In June 1988 South Africa finalized an agreement with Mozambique and Portugal to restore electricity supplies from the Cahora Bassa dam, in Mozambique (the supplies had been interrupted since 1983 by the destruction of power lines in Mozambique linking the dam to the South African grid). Reconstruction work on the power lines was scheduled to begin in August 1993, with the aim of achieving a full resumption of electricity supply to South Africa by 1996. In 1995 ESKOM exported electricity to Botswana, Lesotho, Mozambique, Namibia, Swaziland and Zambia, and was engaged in discussions with authorities in a number of other African countries. Exports of electricity by ESKOM earned R8,000m. in 1996 (an increase of 7.7% compared with 1995).

Water

Water supply is increasingly becoming a problem for the future location of industry. The Vaal river, which is the main source of water supply for the large concentration of manufacturing industry and mining in Gauteng and the northern Free State, is nearing the limit of its capacity. Even with planned increases in supply to the Vaal from the Tugela basin in KwaZulu/Natal, it is unlikely that this river will meet future requirements by the end of the century. It is likely, therefore, that KwaZulu/Natal with its much greater water supply will have a higher rate of growth of industry than Gauteng in the future. In March 1988 South Africa and Lesotho signed the final protocols for the Highlands Water Project. Its completion, which is scheduled for the year 2017, would provide South Africa with 2,200m. cu m of water annually. The first stage of the Highlands Water Project was completed in 1997, although creditors, including the World Bank, expressed doubt as to whether the venture would ever reach final completion. In the same year the Rand Water Board planned to construct a second reservoir, at a cost of R100m., which was located at Klipriviersberg, south of Johannesburg, and was to serve Johannesburg and Gauteng.

FOREIGN TRADE

South Africa is highly dependent on international trade. The value of merchandise imports (including arms and petroleum) was R76,251m., equal to about 18.2% of GNP at market prices, in 1994, R98,443m. in 1995, and an estimated R113,800m. in 1996. The value of imports was projected at R130,700m. in 1997. In spite of rapid industrialization, with the encouragement of import-replacement industries by protective tariffs and comprehensive direct import control machinery in operation since 1948, imports as a rule are not a much smaller proportion of national income than their average of 24% in the 1930s; in recent years, however, they have been significantly below average and below the level of exports, including gold, owing to the need to finance capital repayments overseas. The composition of imports, however, has changed considerably over the years. Whereas in 1910 food, drink, clothing and textiles constituted 46% of total imports, these consumer goods are usually only a small fraction today (11.7% in 1994), with intermediate and capital goods making up the bulk of imports. In 1968 about 92% of imports were manufactured, whereas only 38% of exports were in this category, and even here a large proportion of exports classified as manufactured were lightly processed agricultural and mineral products. The country remains heavily dependent, therefore, on agriculture and mining (gold in particular) to pay for imports.

The total value of merchandise exports, including gold, was R87,599m., equal to 20.9% of GNP at market prices, in 1994, R101,144m. in 1995 and an estimated R123,500m. in 1996. Revenue from exports was projected at R148,100m. in 1997. The United Kingdom, traditionally South Africa's main trading partner, slipped down the rankings in the 1990s. In 1994 the United Kingdom's share as a supplier of South Africa's imports (11.3%) was surpassed by Germany (16.4%) and the USA (15.7%); Japan supplied 9.9%. As a market for South African exports, the United Kingdom's share (6.6%) was surpassed by Switzerland (6.7%), an important destination of South African diamonds; the USA took 4.8% of exports, and Japan 4.6%. In 1994, exports to all African countries were nearly R8,632m. (9.6%), while imports were only R2,354m. (3.0%). The chief African markets for exports in 1992 were Zimbabwe (2.3%), Zambia (1.6%) and Mozambique (1.0%). The only substantial supplier of imports to South Africa was Zimbabwe (1.5%). On 29 August 1994 South Africa became a member of the Southern African Development Community (SADC).

With import control machinery set up in the late 1940s and strict exchange control regulations imposed in 1961 (after the massive outflow of foreign capital following the political disturbances of 1960), South Africa was generally able to protect itself against disruptions to the balance of payments on both current and capital accounts. In favourable times these regulations were relaxed, but not abolished. They were again stringently applied after the political disturbances which commenced in the second half of 1984, but, despite massive outflows of foreign capital in 1985–93 (net movement of long- and short-term capital: 1985 –R9,231m.; 1986 –R6,097m.; 1987 –R3,069m.; 1988 –R6,663m.; 1989 –R5,555m.; 1990 –R2,410m.; 1991 –R4,775m.; 1992 –R3,673m.; 1993 –R15,021m., mostly short-term), the balance-of-payments position and reserves remained fairly steady, although South Africa was forced to draw heavily upon its reserves of gold and foreign exchange during 1988 in order to fulfil foreign debt commitments for that year. This was achieved only by large surpluses on the balance of trade, offsetting the outflows of capital. With the widespread abandonment of international sanctions on trade and investment from 1991, a more favourable climate for South Africa's balance of payments was forecast. The year-end figures for 1994 confirmed that the flow of capital could indeed be reversed: South Africa achieved a net inflow of short-term capital of R1,430m. as well as a net inflow of long-term capital of R3,780m., totalling a net capital inflow of R5,210m. The improvement continued in 1995; figures for the first quarter of 1995 show a net inflow of short-term capital of R577m. and a net inflow of long-term capital of R4,800m. This long-term figure is particularly significant; a year earlier, in the run-up to the April 1994 election, the first quarter of 1994 still showed a net outflow of long-term capital of –R1,026m. The current account deficit was R12,656m. in 1995 and an estimated R8,000m. in 1996, with a deficit of R2,000m. projected for 1997. South Africa's external balance remains highly vulnerable to adverse external factors such as falls in the price of gold or other commodities. In addition, because of South Africa's high marginal propensity to import, imports tend to increase rapidly as soon as growth approaches 3%.

FINANCE

The South African currency is the rand, issued by the South African Reserve Bank. Since December 1971 there have been several changes in the external value of the rand in both directions. It was briefly linked to the floating pound in 1972 but from October 1972 only the rand-US dollar rate was fixed. In September 1975 the rand was devalued from R1 = US $1.40 to R1 = US $1.15. In January 1979 the 'commercial' rand's link with the dollar was freed and allowed to float, and non-residents were allowed to buy 'security' rand at a discount for direct investment purposes. In February 1983 the 'security' rand was abolished and merged with the commercial rand for non-residents. Owing to the outbreak of political disturbances in the second half of 1984, the rand depreciated sharply against the US dollar and all other major currencies, falling from R1 = US $0.80 in early 1984 to R1 = US $0.42 in January 1985. In spite of measures taken by the Reserve Bank to curtail speculation against the rand, the escalation of violence generated a lack of confidence in the country, politically, and a further flight of capital led to the value of the rand falling to R1 = US $0.35 by August 1985. Coupled with the unwillingness of foreign banks to reschedule short-term loans, a moratorium on debt repayments was imposed in September 1985, together with the reintroduction of the two-tier system of exchange control on foreign investors. In March 1987, however, an agreement was reached with foreign creditor banks allowing a three year rescheduling of $13,000m. of outstanding debt. In August 1994 the commercial rand stood at R1 = US $0.28 and the financial rand at R1 = £0.18, while the discount on the financial rand was 20.59%, reflecting the continued outflow of foreign capital. By March 1995, however, the outflow had been reversed (see above), and the minister of finance, Christo Liebenberg, announced the abolition of the financial rand and the termination of the dual exchange-rate system. Following speculation regarding government policy and the fact that the exchange rate had become overvalued, the rand depreciated by 17% against a number of trade-weighted currencies and by 18% against the US dollar between mid-February and the end of May 1996. The exchange rate stood at R4.33 = US $1 in July 1996 and at R4.67 = US $1 in August 1997. The rand was considered to be sufficiently stable for the government in the 1997/98 budget to relax exchange controls for South African residents (although not for those who had emigrated and who still had assets blocked in the country).

Although South Africa was a member of the Sterling Area until its disbandment, it had not been the practice of the commercial banks since 1942, and more stringently since 1961, to keep reserves in London. Banking follows the British tradition, with a few large branch banks dominating the scene. In addition to commercial banks, a whole range of financial institutions has developed since the Second World War, including merchant banks, discount houses and a fairly well developed short-term money market. These institutions have, over the years, suffered from the fragility of business confidence, engendered by unrest.

Public finance is conducted along orthodox lines, although there has been a steady trend for public spending to grow as a proportion of GDP in spite of repeated attempts to prevent further increases in real terms. In 1991/92, expenditure was 29.7% of GDP compared with 25.5% in 1977/78. The envisaged expenditure of R86,400m. in 1991/92 exceeded expected revenue of R72,100m. by $14,300m., or 4.8% of GDP. A consequence of government expenditure persistently exceeding revenue in the early 1990s has been a rise in the ratio of public debt to GDP from a post-war low of 27% in 1983 to in excess of 40% in 1992, with the budget deficit before borrowing at a record high, equivalent to more than 8% of GDP. An additional effect was an increase in the level of interest payments on the public debt (about 5.5% of GDP in 1992, compared with only 2.5% in 1981). Recent economies in outlays on defence expenditure have been more than offset by large increases in social expenditure on housing, health and education for the African population, which, together with the weak performance of the economy, led to stagnating revenues and spiralling deficits. The first post-election budget, presented in June 1994, essentially followed the conservative tradition of previous budgets. The planned 6.5% increase in expenditure to R135,100m. was below the current rate of inflation so that the fiscal deficit was forecast to shrink substantially to some 6.6% of GDP. The out-turn of the 1994/95 budget, however, showed total estimated expenditure to have been R140,004.9m., and attributed the larger figure to higher inflation (9% in 1994) than had been forecast a year earlier. Nevertheless, the 1994/95 budget deficit was stated to be R28,500m., or 6.4% of the latest estimate of GDP. The 1995/96 budget proposals, announced on 15 March 1995, projected total expenditure at R123,248.3m. (an increase of 9.5% on actual 1994/95 expenditure) and total revenue and grants at R124,191.0m. (an increase of 11.3% on actual 1994/95 revenue), leaving a projected deficit of R29,057.3m., equivalent to 5.8% of projected GDP. In 1994/95 a special budget of R2,500m. for post-apartheid reconstruction was to be financed by budgetary trimming elsewhere, with small savings being made in such areas as forestry, transport and foreign affairs. Initially the cost of defence, previously a source of economizing, was to rise owing to the absorption of ex-guerrillas into a single force. The total cost of transition—the dismantling of the old state and the creation of a new one—was estimated to be some R4,000m. in 1994 alone (the election itself cost nearly R1,000m.). The short-term costs were to be met by a non-recurring levy of 5% on individuals and companies with an annual taxable income of over R50,000. At the same time, the company tax rate was reduced from 40% to 35%, although the dividends tax rose from 15% to 25% to help make up the difference. The 1996/97 budget projected total expenditure at R173,700m. (an increase of 10.4% compared with the revised estimate of the previous year), and total revenue at R144,900m., leaving a budgetary deficit of R28,800m. (or 5.1% of GDP). The company tax rate remained unchanged, at 35%. The 1997/98 budget, which was announced in March 1997, was described by leading private-sector bankers as 'conservative'; it projected expenditure at R186,700m. and revenue at R161,900m., leaving a deficit of R24,800m. (4% of projected GDP).

The combined fixed investment of public authorities and public corporations was 29% of total gross fixed investment in 1993. Although still officially committed to a basically private enterprise economic system, the state under white rule became increasingly involved, through the IDC, in a whole new range of commercial activities, in addition to traditional infrastructure and public utility enterprises. The post-apartheid government, however, committed itself to a programme of privatization of public enterprises. The 1997/98 budget emphasized the government's commitment to the privatization programme, which was to be accelerated.

ECONOMIC OUTLOOK

South Africa undoubtedly achieved remarkable economic development in the 1960s, with one of the highest growth rates in the world during that decade. The fruits of that development, however, were very unevenly distributed, with the 'homelands' remaining as wretched and over-populated as ever. Growth in the 1970s was much slower, with the economy reaching its full potential only in part of 1974 and again in 1979/80, owing to a boom in world commodity prices and a big increase in the price of gold. In the recession of 1975–77 real GNP remained almost stationary. The main reason, of course, for this relatively poor performance was the instability of the world economy in this period, but mention must also be made of the aggravating effect of the disturbances following the Soweto riots in June 1976 and the unsettled political situations of South Africa's neighbours. These factors had a particularly discouraging effect on foreign investment in South Africa. In 1979, however, the economy grew significantly, at a real rate of 4.2%, and in 1980 a real growth rate of 8% was recorded, as the high price of gold and other export commodities compensated for the lack of foreign capital. Growth in the 1980s was even slower than in the 1970s, averaging only 1.4% per annum in real terms over the decade and, therefore, resulting in a fall in real income per head compared with a small average increase of 1% per annum per caput in the 1970s. Factors that contributed to this poor performance included unfavourable commodity prices in international markets, in particular a weakening of the price of gold; drought in 1983 and 1984; the damaging effect of political instability in causing a net outflow of foreign investment and low overall investment in the economy in the late 1980s and early 1990s; and the effect of sanctions on foreign trade in some markets such as coal exports.

Between the first quarter of 1989 and the first quarter of 1993, real GDP fell by 4%, creating South Africa's longest recession of this century. International recession, as well as severe drought and the volatility of the political climate, all played their part. The most serious manifestation of the recession was the decline in investment, which was equivalent to only 15% of GDP in 1992 and had been well below earlier levels (24% on average during 1982–85) since the late 1980s. A low level of investment undermined the economy's future ability to generate growth and absorb work-seekers. Following the establishment of the ANC administration, a major reversal of the flow of investment took place. In 1994 South Africa achieved a record net inflow of foreign investment of R821m., while in 1995 this figure increased almost fivefold, to R3,900m. Disinvestment, in contrast, was less than R50m. per year in 1994 and 1995.

More than 100,000 jobs were lost in mining, and over 60,000 in manufacturing, in the first half of the 1990s. The Reserve Bank estimated that from the first quarter of 1989 (the beginning of the recession) to the third quarter of 1993, employment in the formal non-agricultural sectors fell by some 410,000. During this period 8% of workers were made redundant. Unemployment figures continued to rise even with recovery in the second half of 1993. The employment situation had, however, been weak for much longer. Whereas in the period 1963–70 numbers employed in the non-agricultural sectors of the economy increased at an average annual rate of 4.2%, well in excess of the rate of population increase, this fell to 2.7% in the period 1970–78, barely equal to the increase in population. During the period 1978–87, African employment grew by only 1.2% per annum, well below the increase in population and reflecting the low overall growth in the economy in that period. No accurate figures were available for African unemployment, as official unemployment statistics covered only a limited number of registered African unemployed. A major structural change in the South African economy since the abolition of all forms of influx control, was a huge migration to the large towns. Disguised unemployment in the rural areas was increasingly registered as overt unemployment in the urban areas. However, there were also positive signs of a big increase in the size of the 'informal' sector, assisted by the removal of most of the petty restrictions that have hampered this sector in the past. According to an official survey, open unemployment amounted to 32% of the labour force (about 4.6m.) at October 1994. Most of the unemployed (4m.) were Africans, among whom unemployment was more than 40%; half of these lived in rural areas. In early 1996 the rate of unemployment was estimated at 33% of the labour force. In 1995 employment increased by only 0.6%, while the labour force grew by 2.5%; unemployment increased by some 280,000 in that year. A significant two-year wage contract between the Chamber of Mines and the National Union of Mineworkers, which was announced in July 1997, established strict linkages between productivity and wage increases; gold production was to increase by 90 tons in 1997, and this higher level was to be sustained in 1998. If this target was reached the lowest-paid, least-skilled workers would receive a 25% rise in wages, which would effectively amount to a minimum wage of R1,000 per month for official work and R1,150 per month for unofficial work.

Following the election in April 1994, the new government acted to address the prevailing negative investor sentiment, with a number of prudent financial and structural policies; these included a programme of progressive fiscal deficit reduction, the constitutional guarantee of the independence of the reserve bank, plans for trade liberalization, measures to begin to redress social imbalances, the reform of labour legislation to reduce tension in industrial relations, and commitment to a progressive elimination of capital controls. The impact of these extensive policies was reflected in the strong increase in investor confidence during 1994 and 1995 and subsequent years. Much was to depend on the government's success in fostering the creation of new jobs and in narrowing the earnings gap between the lowest-paid and the highest-paid workers. If the productivity target agreed in the gold miners productivity-linked wage deal was reached, a major landmark in South Africa's economic development would be achieved.

Statistical Survey

Source (unless otherwise indicated): Central Statistical Service, Steyn's Arcade, 274 Schoeman St, Private Bag X44, Pretoria 0001; tel. (12) 3108911; telex 320450; fax (12) 3108500.

Area and Population

AREA, POPULATION AND DENSITY*

Area (sq km)	1,219,080†
Population (census results)	
7 March 1991‡	
Males	18,430,089
Females	19,513,929
Total	37,944,018
Population (official estimates at mid-year)	
1994	40,436,000
1995	41,244,500
Density (per sq km) at mid-1995	33.8

* Excluding data for Walvis Bay (area 1,124 sq km or 434 sq miles, population 23,641 in 1970), sovereignty over which was transferred from South Africa to Namibia on 1 March 1994.

† 470,689 sq miles.

‡ Including adjustment for underenumeration.

9 October 1996 (provisional census results): Total population 37,900,000 (males 18,200,000; females 19,700,000). A post-censal survey indicated underenumeration of 6.8%.

ETHNIC GROUPS (estimates, 27 April 1994)*

	Number	% of total
Africans (Blacks)	30,645,157	76.07
Europeans (Whites)	5,171,419	12.84
Coloureds	3,435,114	8.53
Asians	1,032,943	2.56
Total	40,284,634	100.00

* Figures have been estimated independently, so the total is not the sum of the components.

POPULATION BY PROVINCE (estimates, mid-1995)

Western Cape	3,721,200
Eastern Cape	6,481,300
Northern Cape	742,000
KwaZulu/Natal	8,713,100
Free State*	2,782,500
North-West	3,351,800
Northern Province†	5,397,200
Mpumalanga‡	3,007,100
Gauteng§	7,048,300
Total	41,244,500

* Formerly the Orange Free State.

† Formerly Northern Transvaal.

‡ Formerly Eastern Transvaal.

§ Formerly Pretoria-Witwatersrand-Vereeniging.

PRINCIPAL TOWNS (population at 1991 census)

	City Proper	Metropolitan Area
Cape Town*	854,616	2,350,157
Durban	715,669	1,137,378
Johannesburg	712,507	1,916,061
Pretoria*	525,583	1,080,187
Port Elizabeth	303,353	853,205
Umlazi	299,275	n.a.
Roodepoort	162,632	870,066
Pietermaritzburg	156,473	228,549
Germiston	134,005	n.a.
Bloemfontein*	126,867	300,150
Boksburg	119,890	n.a.
Benoni	113,501	n.a.
East London	102,325	270,127
Kimberley	80,082	167,060
Springs	72,647	700,906
Vereeniging	71,255	773,594

* Pretoria is the administrative capital, Cape Town the legislative capital and Bloemfontein the judicial capital.

BIRTHS AND DEATHS (official estimates, annual averages)

	1975–80	1980–85	1985–90
Birth rate (per 1,000)	34.3	33.1	32.1
Death rate (per 1,000)	12.1	11.0	9.9

October 1994 (household survey): Birth rate 23.4 per 1,000; Death rate 9.4 per 1,000.

Expectation of life (UN estimates, years at birth, 1990–95): 62.9 (males 60.0; females 66.0) (Source: UN, *World Population Prospects: The 1994 Revision*).

IMMIGRATION AND EMIGRATION

	1994	1995	1996
Immigrants			
Africa	1,628	1,343	1,601
Europe	2,784	2,272	2,315
Asia	1,645	1,063	1,137
Americas	249	281	257
Oceania	80	85	86
Total (incl. unspecified)	6,398	5,064	5,407
Emigrants			
Africa	942	1,180	1,223
Europe	4,198	2,963	3,198
Asia	531	444	402
Americas	1,744	1,612	1,786
Oceania	2,766	2,449	3,035
Total (incl. unspecified)	10,235	8,725	9,708

ECONOMICALLY ACTIVE POPULATION
(household survey, persons aged 15 years and over, 1995)*

	Males	Females	Total
Agriculture, hunting, forestry and fishing	1,030,000	265,000	1,295,000
Mining and quarrying	452,000	19,000	471,000
Manufacturing	1,058,000	468,000	1,526,000
Electricity, gas and water	83,000	12,000	95,000
Construction	452,000	31,000	483,000
Trade, restaurants and hotels	999,000	770,000	1,769,000
Transport, storage and communications	441,000	79,000	520,000
Financing, insurance, real estate and business services	362,000	292,000	654,000
Community, social and personal services	1,274,000	1,863,000	3,137,000
Activities not adequately defined	121,000	80,000	201,000
Total employed	6,272,000	3,879,000	10,152,000
Unemployed	1,824,000	2,380,000	4,204,000
Total labour force	8,096,000	6,259,000	14,356,000

* Figures have been assessed independently, so that totals are not always the sum of the component parts.

Agriculture

PRINCIPAL CROPS ('000 metric tons)

	1994	1995	1996*
Maize	13,275	4,866	10,168
Sorghum	520	291	536
Wheat	1,984	1,977	2,765
Barley	275	300	176
Oats	37	38	33
Dry beans	64	54	60
Cottonseed	48	42	77
Cotton (lint)	28	24	44
Sugar cane	15,683	16,714	20,951
Tobacco (leaves)	19	18	18
Potatoes	1,281	1,424	1,541
Sweet potatoes	66	57	54
Soybeans	68	59	80
Groundnuts (in shell)	117	79	145
Sunflower seed	366	539	784
Cabbages	217	229	207
Tomatoes	386	435	411
Pumpkins, squash and gourds	298	291	312
Onions (dry)	247	293	280
Carrots	86	135	101
Watermelons	53	54	51
Apples	551	512	607
Grapefruit and pomelo	120	120	121
Grapes	1,286	1,373	1,359
Lemons and limes	74	74	75
Oranges	877	769	795
Peaches and nectarines	140	158	109
Pears	214	224	191
Bananas	131	135	163
Mangoes	28	30	26
Avocados	48	45	54
Apricots	47	60	55
Pineapples	79	147	136

* Preliminary estimates.

Sources: Department of Agriculture, Pretoria, and FAO, mainly *Production Yearbook*.

LIVESTOCK ('000 head, year ending September)

	1994	1995	1996*
Cattle	12,584	13,015	13,389
Pigs	1,511	1,628	1,603
Sheep	29,134	28,784	28,934
Goats	6,402	6,457	6,674
Horses	230	230	n.a.
Asses and Mules	224	224	n.a.

* Preliminary estimtes.

Chickens (FAO estimates, million): 41 in 1993; 42 in 1994; 42 in 1995.

Sources: Department of Agriculture, Pretoria, and FAO, mainly *Production Yearbook*.

LIVESTOCK PRODUCTS ('000 metric tons)

	1994	1995	1996*
Beef and veal	557.0	520.0	463.0
Mutton and lamb	104.6	94.6	98.3
Goat meat	10.4	9.4	9.7
Pig meat	115.0	121.0	130.0
Poultry meat	667.0	736.0	804.0
Edible offals	149.4	n.a.	n.a.
Cows' milk	2,468.0	2,688.0	n.a.
Butter	12.0	13.0	n.a.
Cheese	38.0	39.0	n.a.
Hen eggs	235.0	251.0	287.0
Wool:			
greasy	69.7	61.1	n.a.
clean	40.0	35.0	n.a.
Cattle hides (fresh)	36.5	26.6	29.0
Sheepskins (fresh)	28.5	28.2	n.a.

* Preliminary estimates.

Sources: Department of Agriculture, Pretoria, and FAO, mainly *Production Yearbook*.

Forestry

(including Namibia)

ROUNDWOOD REMOVALS ('000 cubic metres, excl. bark)

	1992	1993	1994
Sawlogs, veneer logs and logs for sleepers	4,020	4,155	4,264
Pulpwood	8,777	8,806	10,166
Other industrial wood	2,476	2,193	2,578
Fuel wood*	7,150	7,210	7,210
Total	22,423	22,364	24,218

* FAO estimates.

Source: FAO, *Yearbook of Forest Products*.

SAWNWOOD PRODUCTION
('000 cubic metres, incl. railway sleepers)

	1992	1993	1994
Coniferous (softwood)	1,639	1,251	1,401
Broadleaved (hardwood)	179	132	136
Total	1,818	1,383	1,537

Source: FAO, *Yearbook of Forest Products*.

Fishing

('000 metric tons, live weight)

	1993	1994	1995
Freshwater and diadromous fishes	2.0	2.0	1.6
Cape hakes (Stokvisse)	108.3	136.9	136.5
Cape horse mackerel (Maasbanker)	35.4	20.0	10.3
Southern African pilchard	50.7	93.4	115.2
Whitehead's round herring	56.3	54.1	76.9
Southern African anchovy	235.6	155.6	170.3
Snoek (Barracouta)	15.2	13.2	15.3
Silver scabbardfish	12.2	4.7	4.9
Chub mackerel	4.7	4.5	4.7
Other marine fishes (incl. unspecified)	29.7	24.6	26.1
Total fish	550.2	509.1	561.8
Crustaceans	3.0	2.3	3.1
Cape Hope squid	6.3	5.8	7.0
Other molluscs	3.6	3.9	3.3
Total catch*	563.1	521.1	575.2

* Excluding aquatic plants ('000 metric tons): 8.0 in 1993; 4.4 in 1994; 6.3 in 1995. Also excluded are crocodiles. The number of Nile crocodiles captured was: 18,451 in 1993; 25,416 in 1994; 13,704 in 1995.

Source: FAO, *Yearbook of Fishery Statistics*.

Mining

('000 metric tons, unless otherwise indicated)

	1991	1992	1993
Hard coal	178,196	174,392	182,031
Iron ore[1]	18,119	18,460	18,367
Copper ore[1]	192.9	167.0	166.0
Nickel ore[2,3]	30.0	28.4	n.a.
Lead concentrates[1]	76.3	75.4[4]	98.4*
Zinc ore[1]	66.6	69.8[4]	78.2[4]
Tin concentrates (metric tons)[1,4]	1,600	600	500
Manganese ore[1,3]	1,369.0	1,077.0	n.a.
Chromium ore*[1,3]	1,500	1,000	800
Rutile—Titanium dioxide (metric tons)	75,000	n.a.	n.a.
Vanadium ore (metric tons)[1]	15,477[3]	15,000*	n.a.
Zirconium concentrates (metric tons)[3]	230,000	n.a.	n.a.
Antimony concentrates (metric tons)[1]	4,485[3]	4,000*	3,750[4]
Silver ore (metric tons)[1]	171	176	n.a.
Uranium ore (metric tons)[1]	1,712	1,569	3,385
Gold (metric tons)[1]	599.2	614.1	n.a.
Kaolin	134	132	n.a.
Magnesite—crude	92.6	53.3	n.a.
Natural phosphates[3]	3,050	3,051	n.a.
Fluorspar—Fluorite[5]	270.3*	258.1	n.a.
Salt—unrefined	665	702	n.a.
Diamonds: industrial ('000 metric carats)[3]	4,530	5,750	n.a.
gem ('000 metric carats)[3]	3,900	4,400	n.a.
Gypsum—crude	420	334	n.a.
Asbestos	149	124	n.a.
Mica (metric tons)[3]	1,883	2,088	n.a.

* Provisional or estimated figure(s).

[1] Figures relate to the metal content of ores or concentrates.

[2] Nickel content of matte and refined nickel.

[3] Data from the US Bureau of Mines.

[4] Data from *World Metal Statistics* (London).

[5] Acid, metallurgical and ceramic grade.

Source: UN, *Industrial Commodity Statistics Yearbook*.

1994 (provisional, '000 metric tons): Hard coal 182,500; Copper ore 184; Lead concentrates 93.1.

1995 (provisional, '000 metric tons): Copper ore 200; Lead concentrates 87.7.

Source: UN, *Monthly Bulletin of Statistics*.

Industry

SELECTED PRODUCTS

('000 metric tons, unless otherwise indicated)

	1994	1995	1996
Wheat flour	1,872	n.a.	n.a.
Sugar—refined	1,246	1,303	1,373
Wine ('000 hectolitres)[1]	2,150	n.a.	n.a.
Cotton yarn—incl. mixed	69.8	74.7	70.3
Woven cotton fabrics (million sq metres)	179.1	n.a.	n.a.
Footwear (million pairs)	41.1	43.5	n.a.
Mechanical wood pulp[2]	258	n.a.	n.a.
Chemical wood pulp*[2]	1,210	n.a.	n.a.
Newsprint paper	571	574	653
Other printing and writing paper*	380	n.a.	n.a.
Other paper and paperboard*[2]	937	n.a.	n.a.
Synthetic rubber	51.0	56.5	57.5
Rubber tyres ('000)	8,111	8,947	8,714
Nitrogenous fertilizers	1,259	1,077	1,111
Phosphate fertilizers	530	701	775
Motor spirit—petrol (million litres)[3]	8,720	10,047	9,672
Kerosene (million litres)[3]	980	935	1,055
Jet fuel (million litres)[3]	1,629	1,704	1,762
Distillate fuel oils (million litres)[3]	5,736	6,551	6,371
Residual fuel oils	2,793	3,371	3,464
Lubricating oils (million litres)[3]	219	260	286
Petroleum bitumen—asphalt*	265	n.a.	n.a.
Coke-oven coke*	1,850	n.a.	n.a.
Cement	7,065	7,437	7,664
Pig-iron[4]	6,050	n.a.	n.a.
Crude steel*	8,320	10,150	7,970
Refined copper—unwrought*	129.6	132	124
Colour television receivers ('000)	320	337	n.a.
Passenger motor cars—assembled ('000)	227.0	288.4	281.1
Lorries—assembled ('000)	118.2	147.8	131.2
Electric energy (million kWh)[5]	165,985	171,301	178,938

* Estimates.

[1] Natural and sparkling wines.

[2] Including data for Namibia.

[3] Excluding data for Transkei, Bophuthatswana, Venda and Ciskei.

[4] Data from the US Bureau of Mines.

[5] Electricity available for distribution.

Sources: Central Statistical Service, Pretoria; National Productivity Institute, Pretoria; UN, *Industrial Commodity Statistics Yearbook* and *Monthly Bulletin of Statistics*; FAO, *Yearbook of Forest Products*.

Finance

CURRENCY AND EXCHANGE RATES

Monetary Units

100 cents = 1 rand (R).

Sterling and Dollar Equivalents (31 March 1997)

£1 sterling = 7.2585 rand;
US $1 = 4.4205 rand;
100 rand = £13.777 = $22.622.

Average Exchange Rate (US $ per rand)

1994	0.28177
1995	0.27574
1996	0.23416

BUDGET (million rand, year ending 31 March)*

Revenue	1993/94	1994/95	1995/96
Income taxes:			
Gold mines	500	805	1,485
Other companies	11,283	13,149	15,020
Individuals	38,246	42,160	50,630
Value-added tax	24,858	28,600	32,750
Gold-mining leases	115	128	50
Interest and dividends	195	654	504
Customs duty	3,132	3,885	4,700
Surcharge on imports	1,635	1,200	1,100
Fuel levy	7,738	8,045	8,600
Excise duty	4,856	5,387	5,701
Other revenue	2,012	5,250	3,301
Sub-total	94,570	109,263	123,841
Less Transfers to neighbouring countries	5,675	3,250	3,890
Total	88,895	106,013	119,957

Expenditure	1993/94	1994/95	1995/96
Defence	10,683	12,124	11,027
Other general services	9,805	10,239	9,842
Education	27,762	30,850	33,443
Health	13,920	14,299	15,565
Other social services	16,253	17,945	23,238
Interest on public debt	22,150	24,573	29,492
Other expenditure	30,735	30,067	35,247
Sub-total	131,308	140,097	157,854
Less Own revenues†	12,972	7,750	5,281
Total	118,336	132,347	152,573

* Figures represent revenue and expenditure on State Revenue Fund. Accounts of Transnet and Telkom are not included.

† Revenue from provincial administrations, Bophuthatswana, Ciskei, Transkei, Venda and the other former 'homelands'.

INTERNATIONAL RESERVES (US $ million at 31 December)

	1994	1995	1996
Gold*	1,445	1,481	1,261
IMF special drawing rights	1	5	1
Foreign exchange	1,684	2,815	940
Total	3,130	4,301	2,203

* National valuation, based on market prices.

Source: IMF, *International Financial Statistics*.

MONEY SUPPLY (million rand at 31 December)

	1994	1995	1996
Currency outside banks	12,237	14,332	15,954
Demand deposits at deposit money banks	81,736	97,050	130,858
Total (incl. others)	94,511	111,844	147,664

Source: IMF, *International Financial Statistics*.

COST OF LIVING (Consumer Price Index; base: 1995 = 100)

	1993	1994	1996
Food	80.9	92.0	106.1
Fuel and light	84.6	92.7	107.1
Clothing	92.1	95.5	103.7
All items (incl. others)	84.5	92.0	107.4

NATIONAL ACCOUNTS (million rand at current prices)

Note: Data cover the whole of South Africa (including African 'homelands' that had been declared 'independent').

National Income and Product

	1992	1993*	1994*
Compensation of employees	190,003	210,024	231,467
Operating surplus	68,810	80,772	91,557
Domestic factor incomes	258,813	290,796	323,024
Consumption of fixed capital	50,272	54,121	59,537
Gross domestic product (GDP) at factor cost	309,085	344,917	382,561
Indirect taxes	38,803	46,015	57,736
Less Subsidies	6,925	7,861	7,544
GDP in purchasers' values	340,963	383,071	432,753
Factor income received from abroad	2,606	-9,458	-10,561
Less Factor income paid abroad	11,751		
Gross national product	331,818	373,613	422,192
Less Consumption of fixed capital	50,272	54,121	59,537
National income in market prices	281,546	319,492	362,655
Other current transfers from abroad (net)	300	429	205
National disposable income	281,846	319,921	362,860

* Figures are provisional.

Expenditure on the Gross Domestic Product

	1994	1995	1996
Government final consumption expenditure	91,394	99,883	113,237
Private final consumption expenditure	259,743	295,227	330,476
Increase in stocks	5,880	99,303	5,411
Gross fixed capital formation	69,226	81,926	92,557
Statistical discrepancy	-2,355	-90,817	-2,702
Total domestic expenditure	423,888	485,522	538,979
Exports of goods and services	103,098	120,418	143,682
Less Imports of goods and services	95,275	120,188	139,647
GDP in purchasers' values	431,711	485,752	543,014
GDP at constant 1990 prices	278,143	287,506	296,469

Source: IMF, *International Financial Statistics*.

Gross Domestic Product by Economic Activity (at factor cost)

	1994	1995	1996
Agriculture, forestry and fishing	19,802	18,779	22,550
Mining and quarrying	33,172	33,742	39,122
Manufacturing	90,177	104,600	114,916
Electricity, gas and water	15,506	17,029	18,960
Construction (contractors)	12,281	13,509	14,315
Wholesale and retail trade, catering and accommodation	61,450	70,189	77,752
Transport, storage and communication	29,030	33,321	37,154
Finance, insurance, real estate and business services	63,473	73,214	84,152
Government services	59,233	65,463	73,449
Other community, social and personal services	7,573	8,479	9,436
Other producers (non-profit institutions and domestic servants)	7,954	8,999	9,949
Sub-total	399,651	447,324	501,755
Less Imputed bank service charges	14,559	16,452	18,781
Total	385,092	430,872	482,974

BALANCE OF PAYMENTS (US $ million)*

	1993	1994	1995
Exports of goods f.o.b.	24,138	24,947	28,611
Imports of goods f.o.b.	−18,287	−21,452	−27,001
Trade balance	5,850	3,494	1,610
Exports of services	3,571	3,989	4,459
Imports of services	−5,101	−5,483	−6,430
Balance on goods and services	4,321	2,000	−362
Other income received	872	1,075	1,085
Other income paid	−3,449	−3,444	−3,561
Balance on goods, services and income	1,744	−369	−2,837
Current transfers received	262	246	244
Current transfers paid	−132	−196	−228
Current balance	1,873	−319	−2,820
Capital account (net)	1	−5	16
Direct investment abroad	−27	327	332
Direct investment from abroad	−285	−143	−557
Portfolio investment liabilities	1,097	2,133	2,163
Other investment assets	−284	−243	−327
Other investment liabilities	−2,077	331	4,355
Net errors and omissions	−3,038	−1,172	−584
Overall balance	−2,738	909	2,578

* Including Botswana, Lesotho, Namibia and Swaziland.

Source: IMF, *International Financial Statistics*.

External Trade

Figures refer to the Southern African Customs Union, comprising South Africa, Namibia, Botswana, Lesotho and Swaziland. Trade between the component territories is excluded.

PRINCIPAL COMMODITIES (million rand)

Imports f.o.b.	1992	1993	1994*
Chemical products, etc.	5,789.1	6,598.8	8,291.7
Plastics and plastic articles, rubber and rubber articles	2,249.7	2,638.9	3,255.9
Paper, paperboard, etc.	1,463.1	1,740.1	2,182.6
Textiles and textile articles	2,437.2	2,654.0	3,295.0
Base metals and articles of base metal	2,502.2	2,605.7	3,399.5
Machinery and mechanical appliances, electrical equipment, parts thereof	14,944.0	17,130.9	24,804.5
Transport equipment	6,619.0	8,915.9	11,283.6
Optical and photographic instruments, surgical instruments, etc.	2,241.6	2,716.1	3,299.7
Total (incl. others)	52,514.1	59,017.7	75,601.6

Exports f.o.b.	1992	1993	1994*
Vegetable products	2,290.7	2,436.5	4,197.3
Prepared foodstuffs; beverages, spirits and vinegar; tobacco	1,856.8	1,812.5	2,826.0
Mineral products	7,083.3	8,443.7	7,712.4
Chemical products, etc.	3,220.8	3,377.9	4,756.8
Textiles and textile articles	1,809.0	1,812.1	1,923.4
Pearls, precious and semi-precious stones, precious metals, etc.	7,160.4	10,137.7	10,213.3
Base metals and articles of base metal	9,484.8	9,905.2	11,853.0
Total (incl. others)†	68,996.8	79,214.2	90,328.2

* Preliminary figures.

† Figures include exports of gold. The net value of gold output (in million rand) was: 18,195 in 1992; 22,229 in 1993; 22,661 in 1994.

Source: South African Reserve Bank, Pretoria.

SELECTED TRADING PARTNERS (million rand)

Imports	1992	1993	1994*
Australia	629	693	1,074
Belgium	1,138	1,273	1,739
China, People's Repub.	652	1,003	1,284
France	2,052	2,094	2,717
Germany	8,588	9,281	12,986
Hong Kong	885	1,110	1,464
Italy	1,843	2,085	2,985
Japan	5,563	7,445	7,893
Netherlands	1,248	1,386	1,892
Singapore	645	788	994
Switzerland	1,223	1,310	1,935
Taiwan	1,767	2,039	2,604
United Kingdom	5,381	6,549	8,961
USA	7,142	7,766	8,584
Total (incl. others)	52,514	59,018	75,602

* Preliminary figures.

Source: South African Reserve Bank, Pretoria.

Exports	1991	1992	1993
Belgium	1,644	1,998	2,314
France	950	n.a.	n.a.
Germany	3,392	3,008	3,084
Hong Kong	1,354	1,471	1,750
Israel	n.a.	973	1,680
Italy	1,598	1,656	1,465
Japan	4,074	3,761	4,363
Korea, Repub.	n.a.	993	1,275
Netherlands	2,373	1,928	2,151
Switzerland	5,719	5,382	7,896
Taiwan	n.a.	2,149	2,166
United Kingdom	5,039	4,525	4,740
USA	3,967	4,858	5,454
Zambia	n.a.	1,112	1,307
Zimbabwe	n.a.	1,553	1,748
Total (incl. others)	64,355	68,999	79,214

Source: National Productivity Institute, Pretoria.

Transport

RAILWAYS (traffic, year ending 31 March)*

	1990/91	1991/92	1992/93
Passenger-km (million)	103,781	89,466	71,573
Freight ton-km (million)	85,524	88,586	89,716

* Including Namibia.

Source: UN, *Statistical Yearbook*.

ROAD TRAFFIC (motor vehicles in use at 30 June)

	1993	1994	1995*
Passenger cars	3,522,129	3,814,904	3,810,000
Buses and coaches	245,391	251,202	260,000
Goods vehicles	1,338,737	1,345,610	1,380,000
Motor cycles and mopeds	285,034	273,244	270,000

* Estimates.

Source: IRF, *World Road Statistics*.

SHIPPING

Merchant Fleet (vessels registered at 31 December)

	1994	1995	1996
Total displacement ('000 grt)	331	340	371

Cargo Handled ('000 metric tons, year ending 31 March)

	1995/96
Landed	22,203
Shipped	114,331

Source: Department of Transport, Pretoria.

Vessels Handled (year ending 31 March)

	1995/96
Number	13,422
Displacement ('000 gross tons)	528,567

Sources: Portnet; Department of Transport, Pretoria.

CIVIL AVIATION (traffic on scheduled services)

	1991	1992	1993
Kilometres flown (million)	39.9	83.8	128.3
Passengers carried ('000)	11,736.8	16,433.5	18,763.0
Freight ton-km (million)	228.5	278.5	344.3

Source: Department of Transport, Pretoria.

Tourism

FOREIGN TOURIST ARRIVALS
(number of visitors by region of origin)

	1994	1995	1996
Africa	3,125,958	3,452,164	3,606,757
Europe	463,477	721,878	771,166
Asia	113,724	158,463	157,969
Americas	115,621	160,473	169,579
Oceania	36,658	61,085	73,680
Total (incl. unspecified)	3,896,547	4,684,064	4,944,430

Communications Media

	1993	1994	1995
Radio receivers ('000 in use)	12,450	12,750	n.a.
Television licences ('000)	n.a.	2,149	2,331
Telephones ('000 main lines in use)	3,660	3,805	3,988
Daily newspapers			
Number	17	17	17
Average circulation ('000)*	1,294	1,271	1,201
Book production (titles)	4,751	4,574	n.a.

* Estimates.

Sources: Central Statistical Service, Pretoria; UNESCO, *Statistical Yearbook*; UN, *Statistical Yearbook*.

Education

Primary and Secondary Levels (1993, preliminary figures)

	Africans	Whites	Coloureds	Asians
Teachers				
Primary, Secondary and Special	196,169	75,919	50,520	14,703
Pupils				
Primary, Secondary and Special	6,486,588	1,041,707	897,002	256,579

Tertiary Level (1993, preliminary figures)

	Africans	Whites	Coloureds	Asians
University				
Students	135,482	153,513	17,406	23,491
Teachers	9,521	17,388	3,734	1,404
Teacher Training				
Students	43,368	8,481	6,449	1,640
Teachers	4,777	2,867	940	286
Technical				
Students	28,060	53,575	6,021	5,388
Teachers	2,042	3,407	529	184
Technikons				
Students	42,674	74,887	11,820	7,787
Teachers	1,730	4,580	586	445

Source: Department of Education, Pretoria.

Directory

The Constitution

Following multi-party negotiations (see Recent History), the interim Constitution of the Republic of South Africa was ratified on 22 December 1993, and officially came into effect on 27 April 1994; it was to remain in force pending the adoption of a new constitution. The new Constitution was adopted by the Constitutional Assembly (comprising the National Assembly and the Senate) on 8 May 1996, and entered into force on 4 February 1997. The main provisions of the new Constitution are summarized below:

FOUNDING PROVISIONS

The Republic of South Africa is one sovereign democratic state founded on the following values: human dignity, the achievement of equality and advancement of human rights and freedoms; non-racialism and non-sexism; supremacy of the Constitution and the rule of law; universal adult suffrage, a national common voters' roll, regular elections, and a multi-party system of democratic government, to ensure accountability, responsiveness and openness. There is common South African citizenship, all citizens being equally entitled to the rights, privileges and benefits, and equally subject to the duties and responsibilities of citizenship.

BILL OF RIGHTS

Everyone is equal before the law and has the right to equal protection and benefit of the law. The state may not unfairly discriminate directly or indirectly against anyone on one or more grounds, including race, gender, sex, pregnancy, marital status, ethnic or social origin, colour, sexual orientation, age, disability, religion, conscience, belief, culture, language and birth. The rights that are enshrined include: protection against detention without trial, torture or any inhuman form of treatment or punishment; the right to privacy; freedom of conscience; freedom of expression; freedom of assembly; political freedom; freedom of movement and residence; the right to join or form a trade union or employers' organization; the right to a healthy and sustainable environment; the right to property, except in the case of the Government's programme of land reform and redistribution, and taking into account the claims of people who were dispossessed of property after 19 June 1913; the right to adequate housing; the right to health care, food and water and social security assistance, if needed; the rights of children; the right to education in the official language of one's choice, where this is reasonably practicable; the right to use the language and to participate in the cultural life of one's choice, but not in a manner inconsistent with any provision of this Bill of Rights; access to state information; access to the courts; the rights of people who have been arrested or detained; and the right to a fair trial.

CO-OPERATIVE GOVERNMENT

Government is constituted as national, provincial and local spheres of government, which are distinctive, interdependent and interrelated. All spheres of government and all organs of state within each sphere must preserve the peace, national unity and indivisibility of the Republic; secure the well-being of the people of the Republic; implement effective, transparent, accountable and coherent government for the Republic as a whole; respect the constitutional status, institutions, powers and functions of government in the other spheres; not assume any power or function except those conferred on them in terms of the Constitution.

PARLIAMENT

Legislative power is vested in a bicameral Parliament, comprising a National Assembly and a National Council of Provinces. The National Assembly has between 350 and 400 members and is elected, in general, by proportional representation. National and provincial legislatures are elected separately, under a 'double-ballot' electoral system. Each provincial legislature appoints six permanent delegates and nominates four special delegates to the 90-member National Council of Provinces, which is headed by a Chairperson, who is elected by the Council and has a five-year term of office. Parliamentary decisions are generally reached by a simple majority, although constitutional amendments require a majority of two-thirds.

THE NATIONAL EXECUTIVE

The Head of State is the President, who is elected by the National Assembly from among its members, and exercises executive power in consultation with the other members of the Cabinet. No person may hold office as President for more than two terms. Any party that holds a minimum of 80 seats in the National Assembly (equivalent to 20% of the national vote) is entitled to nominate an Executive Deputy President. If no party, or only one party, secures 80 or more seats, the party holding the largest number of seats and the party holding the second largest number of seats in the National Assembly are each entitled to designate one Executive Deputy President from among the members of the Assembly. The President may be removed by a motion of no-confidence or by impeachment. The Cabinet comprises a maximum of 27 ministers. Each party with a minimum of 20 seats in the National Assembly (equivalent to 5% of the national vote) is entitled to a proportional number of ministerial portfolios. The President allocates cabinet portfolios in consultation with party leaders, who are entitled to request the replacement of ministers. Cabinet decisions are reached by consensus.

JUDICIAL AUTHORITY

The judicial authority of the Republic is vested in the courts, which comprise the Constitutional Court; the Supreme Court of Appeal; the High Courts; the Magistrates' Courts; and any other court established or recognized by an Act of Parliament. (See Judicial System.)

PROVINCIAL GOVERNMENT

There are nine provinces: Eastern Cape, Free State (formerly Orange Free State), Gauteng (formerly Pretoria-Witwatersrand-Vereeniging), KwaZulu/Natal, Mpumalanga (formerly Eastern Transvaal), Northern Cape, Northern Province (formerly Northern Transvaal), North-West and Western Cape. Each province is entitled to determine its legislative and executive structure. Each province has a legislature, comprising between 30 and 80 members (depending on the size of the local electorate), who are elected by proportional representation. Each legislature is entitled to draft a constitution for the province, subject to the principles governing the national Constitution, and elects a Premier, who heads a Cabinet. Parties that hold a minimum of 10% of seats in the legislature are entitled to a proportional number of portfolios in the Cabinet. Provincial legislatures are allowed primary responsibility for a number of areas of government, and joint powers with central government in the principal administrative areas.

LOCAL GOVERNMENT

The local sphere of government consists of municipalities, with executive and legislative authority vested in the Municipal Council. The objectives of local government are to provide democratic and accountable government for local communities; to ensure the provision of services to communities; to promote social and economic development, and a safe and healthy environment; and to encourage the involvement of communities and community organizations in the matters of local government. The National Assembly is to determine the different categories of municipality that may be established, and appropriate fiscal powers and functions for each category. Provincial Governments have the task of establishing municipalities, and of providing for the monitoring and support of local government in each province.

STATE INSTITUTIONS SUPPORTING CONSTITUTIONAL DEMOCRACY

The following state institutions are designed to strengthen constitutional democracy: the Public Protector (whose task is to investigate any conduct in state affairs, or in the public administration in any sphere of government, that is alleged or suspected to be improper); the Human Rights Commission; the Commission for the Protection and Promotion of the Rights of Cultural, Religious and Linguistic Communities; the Commission for Gender Equality; the Auditor-General; and the Electoral Commission.

TRADITIONAL LEADERS

The institution, status and role of traditional leadership, according to customary law, are recognized, subject to the Constitution. A traditional authority that observes a system of customary law may function subject to any applicable legislation and customs. National and provincial legislation may provide for the establishment of local or provincial houses of traditional leaders; the National Assembly may establish a national council of traditional leaders.

The Government

HEAD OF STATE

President: Nelson Rolihlahla Mandela (took office 10 May 1994).
Deputy President: Thabo Mbeki.

CABINET
(August 1997)

The interim Government of National Unity comprises representatives of the African National Congress of South Africa (ANC) and the Inkatha Freedom Party (IFP).

Minister of Foreign Affairs: ALFRED B. NZO (ANC).

Minister of Public Enterprises: STELLA SIGCAU (ANC).

Minister of Justice: ABDULLAH MOHAMMED OMAR (ANC).

Minister of Defence: JOE MODISE (ANC).

Minister of Posts, Telecommunications and Broadcasting: JAY NAIDOO (ANC).

Minister of Correctional Services: Dr SIPHO E. MZIMELA (IFP).

Minister of Education: Prof. SIBUSISO M. E. BENGU (ANC).

Minister of Mineral and Energy Affairs: PENUELL MADUNA (ANC).

Minister of Health: Dr NKOSAZANA C. DHLAMINI-ZUMA (ANC).

Minister of Safety and Security: F. SYDNEY MUFAMADI (ANC).

Minister of Transport: S. R. MAHARAJ (ANC).

Minister of Provincial Affairs and of Constitutional Development: VALLI MOOSA (ANC).

Minister of Labour: TITO T. MBOWENI (ANC).

Minister of Arts, Culture, Science and Technology: LIONEL MTSHALI (IFP).

Minister of Finance: TREVOR A. MANUEL (ANC).

Minister of Welfare and Population Development: GERALDINE FRASER-MOLEKETI (ANC).

Minister of Sport and Recreation: STEVE V. TSHWETE (ANC).

Minister of Housing: SANKIE MTHEMBI-MAHANYELE (ANC).

Minister of Trade and Industry: ALEC ERWIN (ANC).

Minister of Environmental Affairs and Tourism: Dr PALLO JORDAN (ANC).

Minister of Agriculture and Land Affairs: DEREK M. HANEKOM (ANC).

Minister of Home Affairs: Chief MANGOSUTHU GATSHA BUTHELEZI (IFP).

Minister of Public Service and Administration: Dr ZOLA S. T. SKWEYIYA (ANC).

Minister of Public Works: JEFF T. RADEBE (ANC).

Minister of Water Affairs and Forestry: Prof. KADER ASMAL (ANC).

MINISTRIES

Office of the President: Union Bldgs, West Wing, Government Ave, Pretoria 0001; Private Bag X1000, Pretoria 0001; tel. (12) 212222; fax (12) 3262719.

Ministry of Agriculture and Land Affairs: 184 Jacob Mare Bldg, cnr Jacob Mare and Paul Kruger Sts, Pretoria 0002; Private Bag X844, Pretoria 0001; tel. (12) 3235212; fax (12) 3211244.

Ministry of Arts, Culture, Science and Technology: Oranje Nassau Bldg, Schoeman St, Pretoria 0002; Private Bag X727, Pretoria 0001; tel. (12) 3244096; fax (12) 3242687.

Ministry of Correctional Services: Poyntons Bldg, West Block, cnr Church and Schubart Sts, Pretoria 0002; Private Bag X853, Pretoria 0001; tel. (12) 3238198; fax (12) 3234111.

Ministry of Defence: Armscor Bldg, Block 1, Nossob St, Erasmusrand 0181; Private Bag X427, Pretoria 0001; tel. (12) 3556101; fax (12) 3470118.

Ministry of Education: 123 Schoeman St, Magister Bldg, Pretoria 0002; Private Bag X603, Pretoria 0001; tel. (12) 3260126; fax (12) 3235989.

Ministry of Environmental Affairs and Tourism: 240 Vermeulen St, Pretoria 0002, Private Bag X883, Pretoria 0001; tel. (12) 3219587; fax (12) 3235181.

Ministry of Finance: 240 Vermeulen St, Pretoria 0002; Private Bag X115, Pretoria 0001; tel. (12) 3238911; fax (12) 3233262.

Ministry of Foreign Affairs: Union Bldgs, East Wing, Government Ave, Pretoria 0002; Private Bag X152, Pretoria 0001; tel. (12) 3510005; fax (12) 3510253.

Ministry of Health: 2027 Civitas Bldg, cnr Andries and Struben Sts, Pretoria 0002; Private Bag X399, Pretoria 0001; tel. (12) 3284773; fax (12) 3255526.

Ministry of Home Affairs: 1005 Civitas Bldg, cnr Andries and Struben Sts, Pretoria 0002; Private Bag X741, Pretoria 0001; tel. (12) 3268081; fax (12) 216491.

Ministry of Housing: 240 Walker St, Sunnyside, Pretoria 0002; Private Bag X645, Pretoria 0001; tel. (12) 441879; fax (12) 3418513.

Ministry of Justice: Presidia Bldg, 8th Floor, cnr Pretorius and Paul Kruger Sts, Pretoria 0002; Private Bag X276, Pretoria 0001; tel. (12) 3238581; fax (12) 211708.

Ministry of Labour: Laboria Bldg, Schoeman and Paul Kruger Sts, Pretoria 0002; Private Bag X499, Pretoria 0001; tel. (12) 3226523; fax (12) 3201942.

Ministry of Mineral and Energy Affairs: DRC Synod Centre, cnr Andries and Visagie Sts, Pretoria 0002; Private Bag X646, Pretoria 0001; tel. (12) 3228695; fax (12) 3228699.

Ministry of Posts, Telecommunications and Broadcasting: Mutual and Federal Bldg, cnr Vermeulen and Paul Kruger Sts, Pretoria 0002, Private Bag X882, Pretoria 0001; tel. (21) 4621632; fax (21) 4621646.

Ministry of Provincial Affairs and of Constitutional Development: 260 Walker St, Sunnyside, Pretoria 0002; Private Bag X802, Pretoria 0001; tel. (12) 3411380; fax (12) 3411389.

Ministry of Public Enterprises: Infotech Bldg 401, 1090 Arcadia St, Hatfield, Pretoria 0083, Private Bag X15, Hatfield 0028; tel. (12) 3427111; fax (12) 3427224.

Ministry for the Public Service and Administration: Transvaal House, cnr Vermeulen and van der Walts Sts, Pretoria 0002; Private Bag X884, Pretoria 0001; tel. (12) 3230331; fax (12) 3286529.

Ministry of Public Works: Central Government Bldg, cnr Bosman and Vermeulen Sts, Pretoria 0002; Private Bag X890, Pretoria 0001; tel. (12) 3241510; fax (12) 3256380.

Ministry of Safety and Security: Wachthuis, 7th Floor, 231 Pretorius St, Pretoria 0002; Private Bag X463, Pretoria 0001; tel. (12) 3238880; fax (12) 3205065.

Ministry of Sport and Recreation: Frans du Toit Bldg, cnr Schoeman and Paul Kruger Sts, Pretoria 0002; Private Bag X869, Pretoria 0001; tel. (12) 211781; fax (12) 218493.

Ministry of Trade and Industry: House of Trade and Industry, 11th Floor, Prinsloo St, Pretoria 0002; Private Bag X274, Pretoria 0001; tel. (12) 3227677; fax (12) 3233262.

Ministry of Transport: Forum Bldg, cnr Struben and Bosman Sts, Pretoria 0001; Private Bag X193, Pretoria 0001; tel. (12) 3093131; fax (12) 3283194.

Ministry of Water Affairs and Forestry: 120 Plein St, Cape Town 8001; Private Bag X9052, Cape Town 8000; tel. (21) 457246; fax (21) 453362; e-mail zao@dwaf-par.wcape.gov.za.

Ministry of Welfare and Population Development: Hallmark Bldg, Vermeulen St, Pretoria 0002; Private Bag X885, Pretoria 0001; tel. (12) 3284600; fax (12) 3257071.

Legislature

PARLIAMENT

National Council of Provinces

Chairman: PATRICK LEKOTA.

The National Council of Provinces (NCOP), which replaced the Senate under the new Constitution, was inaugurated on 6 February 1997. The NCOP comprises 90 members, with six permanent delegates and four special delegates from each of the nine provinces.

National Assembly

Speaker: Dr FRENE NOSHIR GINWALA.

General Election, 26–29 April 1994

Party	Votes	% of votes	Seats
African National Congress of South Africa	12,237,655	62.65	252
National Party	3,983,690	20.39	82
Inkatha Freedom Party	2,058,294	10.54	43
Freedom Front	424,555	2.17	9
Democratic Party	338,426	1.73	7
Pan-Africanist Congress	243,478	1.25	5
African Christian Democratic Party	88,104	0.45	2
Africa Muslim Party	27,690	0.14	—
African Moderates Congress Party	27,690	0.14	—
Dikwankwetia Party	19,451	0.10	—
Federal Party	17,663	0.09	—
Minority Front	13,433	0.07	—
SOCCER Party	10,575	0.05	—
African Democratic Movement	9,886	0.05	—
Women's Rights Peace Party	6,434	0.03	—
Ximako Progressive Party	6,320	0.03	—
Keep It Straight and Simple Party	5,916	0.03	—
Workers' List Party	4,169	0.02	—
Luso South African Party	3,293	0.02	—
Total*	19,533,498	100.00	400

* Excluding spoilt ballot papers, which numbered 193,081.

Provincial Governments

(August 1997)

EASTERN CAPE

Premier: Rev. ARNOLD STOFILE (ANC).

Speaker of the Legislature: GUGILE NKWINTI (ANC).

FREE STATE

Premier: Dr IVY MATSEPE-CASABURRI (ANC).

Speaker of the Legislature: Rev. MOTLALEPULE CHABAKU (ANC).

GAUTENG

Premier: TOKYO SEXWALE (ANC).

Speaker of the Legislature: TREVOR FOWLER (ANC).

KWAZULU/NATAL

Premier: BEN NGUBANE (IFP).

Speaker of the Legislature: GIDEON H. S. MDLALOSE (IFP).

MPUMALANGA

Premier: MATTHEWS PHOSA (ANC).

Speaker of the Legislature: MBALEKELWA GININDZA (ANC).

NORTHERN CAPE

Premier: M. A. DIPICO (ANC).

Speaker of the Legislature: ETHNE PAPENFUS (DP).

NORTHERN PROVINCE

Premier: NGOAKO RAMATHLODI (ANC).

Speaker of the Legislature: T. G. MASHAMBA (ANC).

NORTH-WEST

Premier: POPO MOLEFE (ANC).

Speaker of the Legislature: JERRY THIBEDI (ANC).

WESTERN CAPE

Premier: HERMANUS KRIEL (NP).

Speaker of the Legislature: WILLEM DOMAN (NP).

Political Organizations

African Christian Democratic Party (ACDP): POB 3578, Cape Town 8000; tel. (21) 246591; fax (21) 241307; f. 1993; Leader Rev. KENNETH MESHOE.

African National Congress of South Africa (ANC): 51 Plein St, Johannesburg 2001; POB 61884, Marshalltown 2107; tel. (11) 3307000; fax (11) 3360302; e-mail info@anc.org.za; f. 1912; in alliance with the South African Communist Party (SACP) and the Congress of South African Trade Unions (COSATU); dominant party in interim Govt of Nat. Unity, following 1994 elections; Pres. NELSON MANDELA; Deputy Pres. THABO MBEKI; Nat. Chair. JACOB ZUMA; Sec.-Gen. CHERYL CAROLUS (acting).

Afrikaner Weerstandsbeweging (AWB) (Afrikaner Resistance Movement): POB 274, Ventersdorp 2710; tel. (18) 2642005; fax (18) 2642032; f. 1973; extreme right-wing paramilitary group; Leader EUGENE TERRE'BLANCHE; Sec.-Gen. PIET 'SKIET RUDOLPH.

Azanian People's Organization (AZAPO): Kopanong Centre 3, cnr Luthuli and Main Rds, Dobsonville; POB 4230, Johannesburg 2000; tel. (11) 9881255; fax (11) 9883925; f. 1978 to seek the establishment of a unitary, democratic, socialist republic; excludes white mems; Pres. M. MANGENA; Sec.-Gen. JAIRUS KGOKONG.

Blanke Bevrydingsbeweging (BBB) (White Protection Movement): f. 1987; extreme right-wing activist group; Leader Prof. JOHAN SCHABORT.

Boerestaat Party (Boer State Party): POB 3456, Randburg 2125; tel. and fax (11) 7081988; f. 1988; seeks the establishment of an Afrikaner state; mil. wing (f. 1990) known as Boere Weerstandsbeweging (BWB); Leader ROBERT VAN TONDER.

Boere Vryheidsbeweging (Boer Freedom Movement): f. 1989 by fmr mems of the Afrikaanse Weerstandsbeweging.

Cape Democrats: f. 1988; white support; liberal.

Conservative Party of South Africa (CP): 203 Soutpansberg Rd, Rietondale, Pretoria; Private Bag X847, Pretoria 0001; tel. (12) 3291220; fax (12) 3291229; f. 1982 by breakaway faction of the National Party; seeks the establishment of a separate Afrikaner state as part of a South African confed.; Leader Dr FERDINAND HARTZENBERG; Dep. Leader Dr WILLIE SNYMAN.

Democratic Party (DP): 123 Louis Botha Ave, Fellside, Johannesburg; POB 46400, Orange Grove 2119; tel. (11) 4832743; fax (21) 4615276; f. 1989 by merger; supports the implementation of a democratic, multiracial society by peaceful means; Leader ANTHONY (TONY) LEON; Exec. Dir JAMES SELFE.

Democratic Reform Party (DRP): f. 1988; Coloured support; Leader CARTER EBRAHIM.

Democratic Workers' Party (DWP): Cape Town; f. 1984 by breakaway faction of the People's Congress Party; mainly Coloured support; Leader DENNIS DE LA CRUZ.

Federal Independent Democratic Alliance (FIDA): POB 10528, Johannesburg 2000; tel. (11) 4034268; fax (11) 4031557; f. 1987; black support; centrist; Leader JOHN GOGOTYA.

Freedom Front (FF/VF): 4 Perseus Park Atrium, 6th Floor, cnr Priory and Camellia Aves, POB 74693, Lynnwood Ridge 0040; tel. (12) 3481168; fax (12) 474387; f. 1994; right-wing electoral alliance; included some mems of the Conservative Party of South Africa; Leader Gen. (retd) CONSTAND VILJOEN; Chief Sec. FLIP BUYS.

Freedom Party: Coloured support; Leader ARTHUR BOOYSEN.

Herstigte Nasionale Party (HNP) (Reconstituted National Party): 1043 Pretorius St, Hatfield, POB 1888, Pretoria 0001; tel. (12) 3423410; fax (12) 3423417; f. 1969 by fmr mems of the National Party; advocates 'Christian Nationalism'; Leader JAAP MARAIS; Chair. WILLEM MARAIS; Gen. Sec. L. J. VAN DER SCHYFF.

Inkatha Freedom Party (IFP): Albany House North, 4th Floor, Albany Grove, POB 4432, Durban 4000; tel. (31) 3074962; fax (31) 3074964; f. as Inkatha Movement, a liberation movement with mainly Zulu support; reorg. in 1990 as a multiracial political party; represented in interim Govt of Nat. Unity, following 1994 elections; Leader Chief MANGOSUTHU GATSHA BUTHELEZI; Nat. Chair. BEN NGUBANE (acting); Sec.-Gen. ZAKHELE KHUMALO.

National Party (NP): F. W. de Klerk Bldg, cnr Leyds and Sibelius Sts, Lukasrand, Pretoria; Private Bag X402, Pretoria 0001; tel. (12) 3446050; fax (12) 3446047; e-mail mcjvs@natweb.co.za; f. 1912; ruling party 1948–94; opened membership to all racial groups in 1990; represented in interim Govt of Nat. Unity, following 1994 elections, withdrew from Govt in June 1996 to form the official opposition; Leader MARTHINUS VAN SCHALKWYK.

National People's Party: Private Bag X54330, Durban 4000; Indian support; Leader AMICHAND RAJBANSI.

New Freedom Party of Southern Africa: 15 Eendrag St, Bellville 7530; Coloured support.

New Solidarity: POB 48687, Qualbert 4078; tel. (11) 3055692; fax 3011077; f. 1989; Indian support; Leader Dr J. N. REDDY.

Die Orangjewerkers: seeks to establish several small, self-governing white states; Leader HENDRIK FRENSCH VERWOERD.

Pan-Africanist Congress (PAC): SA Centre, 4th Floor, 253 Bree St, Johannesburg; POB 25245, Ferreirastown 2048; tel. (11) 8360407; fax (11) 8383705; f. 1959 by breakaway faction of the ANC; advocates the achievement of a democratic society through black and not multiracial orgs; Pres. STANLEY MOGOBA; Sec.-Gen. MICHAEL MUENDANE.

Progressive Independent Party (PIP): Indian support; Leader FAIZ KHAN.

South African Communist Party (SACP): Cosatu House, 3rd Floor, 1 Leyds St, Braamfontein; POB 1027, Johannesburg 2000; tel. (11) 3393621; fax (11) 3396880; e-mail sacp@wn.apc.org; f. 1921 as Communist Party of South Africa; reorg., under present name, 1953; supports interim Govt of Nat. Unity; Chair. (vacant); Gen. Sec. M. NCUNU.

Transvaal Indian Congress: f. 1902, reactivated 1983; Pres. Dr ESSOP JASSAT.

United Christian Conciliation Party: Johannesburg; f. 1986; multiracial; Pres Bishop ISAAC MOKOENA, TAMASANQA LINDA.

United Democratic Reform Party: POB 14048, Reigerpark 1466; f. 1987 by merger; mainly Coloured and Indian support; Leader JAKOBUS (JAC) ALBERT RABIE; Nat. Chair. NASH PARMANAND.

Workers' Organization for Socialist Action (WOSA): Cape Town; f. 1990; Chair. Dr NEVILLE ALEXANDER; Gen. Sec. C. BRECHER.

Other political parties that contested the 1994 elections included the Africa Muslim Party; the African Moderates Congress Party; the Dikwankwetia Party; the Federal Party; the Minority Front; the SOCCER Party; the African Democratic Movement; the Women's Rights Peace Party; the Ximako Progressive Party; the Keep it Straight and Simple (KISS) Party; the Workers' List Party; and the Luso South African Party.

Diplomatic Representation

EMBASSIES AND HIGH COMMISSIONS IN SOUTH AFRICA

Algeria: 950 Arcadia St, POB 57480, Hatfield, Pretoria 0001; tel. (12) 3426479; fax (12) 3426479; Ambassador: SAÏD KETOUNI.

Angola: 1030 Schoeman St, POB 8585, Hatfield, Pretoria 0083; tel. (12) 3420049; fax (12) 461477; Ambassador: M. A. DUARTE RODRIGUES.

Argentina: 200 Standard Plaza, 440 Hilda St, POB 11125, Hatfield, Pretoria 0083; tel. (12) 433527; fax (12) 433521; Ambassador: PEDRO R. HERRERA.

Australia: 292 Orient St, Arcadia, 8442 Pretoria 0083; Private Bag X150, Pretoria 0001; tel. (12) 3423740; fax (12) 3428442; High Commissioner: I. W. PORTER.

Austria: 1109 Duncan St, Brooklyn 0181; POB 95572, Waterkloof 0145; tel. (12) 462483; telex 320541; fax (12) 461151; Ambassador: Dr F. PALLA.

Bangladesh: 410 Farenden St, Sunnyside, Pretoria 0002; tel. (12) 3432105; fax (12) 3435222; High Commissioner: A. T. KARIM.

Belgium: 625 Leyds St, Muckleneuk, Pretoria 0002; tel. (12) 443201; telex 320508; fax (12) 443216; Ambassador: LEO WILLEMS.

Botswana: 24 Amos St, Colbyn, POB 57035, Arcadia 0007; tel. (12) 3424760; fax (12) 3421845; High Commissioner: O. J. TEBAPE.

Brazil: 201 Leyds St, Arcadia 0083; POB 3269, Pretoria 0001; tel. (12) 3411712; fax (12) 3417547; Ambassador: O. AGRIPINO MAIA.

Bulgaria: 1071 Church St, Hatfield 0083; POB 26296, Arcadia 0007; tel. (12) 3423720; fax (12) 3423721; Ambassador: PETKO DRAGANOV.

Burundi: 1315 Church St, POB 12914, Hatfield, Pretoria 0083; tel. (12) 3424881; fax (12) 3424885; Chargé d'affaires a.i.: C. SAMBIRA.

Canada: 1103 Arcadia St, cnr Hilda St, Hatfield, Pretoria 0028; tel. (12) 4223000; fax (12) 4223052; High Commissioner: ARTHUR PERRON.

Chile: Campus Centre 1102, 5th Floor, Burnett St, Hatfield 0083; POB 12672, Pretoria 0028; tel. (12) 3421511; fax (12) 3421658; e-mail chile@iafrica.com; Ambassador: JORGE HEINE.

Colombia: First National Bank Bldg, 3rd Floor, 1105 Park St, Pretoria 0083; tel. (12) 3420211; fax (12) 3420216; Ambassador: Dr. A. F. QUINTERO MARIN.

Congo, Democratic Republic: 423 Kirkness St, Pretoria 0002; POB 28795, Sunnyside 0132; tel. (12) 3441478; fax (12) 3441510; Ambassador: G. L. WA DONDO.

Congo, Republic: 960 Arcadia St, Arcadia, Pretoria; POB 40427, Arcadia 0007; tel. (12) 3425507; fax (12) 3425510. Ambassador: D. M. MAHOUNGU.

Côte d'Ivoire: 795 Government Ave, Arcadia 0083; tel. (12) 3426913; fax (12) 3426713; Ambassador: P. Y. AKOTO.

Croatia: 1160 Church St, Pretoria 0083; POB 11335, Hatfield 0028; tel. (12) 3421206; fax (12) 3421819; Ambassador: T. A. MURSALO.

Cuba: 45 Mackenzie St, Brooklyn 0181; POB 11605, Hatfield 0028; tel. (12) 3462215; fax (12) 3462216: Ambassador: ANGEL DALMAU.

Czech Republic: 936 Pretorius St, Arcadia 0083; POB 3326, Pretoria 0001; tel. (12) 3423477; fax (12) 432033; Ambassador: Dr PAVEL VOŠALÍK.

Denmark: POB 2942, Pretoria 0001; tel. (12) 3220595; telex 323133; fax (12) 3220596; Ambassador: ALF JÖNSSON.

Egypt: 270 Bourke St, Muckleneuk 0002; POB 30025, Sunnyside 0132; tel. (12) 3431590; fax (12) 3431082; Ambassador: M. M. KHATTAB.

Eritrea: 1281 Cobham Rd, POB 11371, Queenswood 0186; tel. (12) 3331302; fax (12) 3332330; Ambassador: TSESSAI TESFAZION.

Estonia: 16 Hofmeyer St, Cape Town 7530; tel. (21) 9133850.

Ethiopia: Southern Life Plaza, 2nd Floor, 1059 Schoeman St, Pretoria 0038; POB 11469, Hatfield 0028; tel. (12) 3426321; fax (12) 3428035; Ambassador: AMAN HASSEN.

Finland: 628 Leyds St, Muckleneuk, Pretoria; POB 443, Pretoria 0001; tel. (12) 3430275; fax (12) 3433095; Ambassador: TAPANI BROTHERUS.

France: 807 George Ave, Arcadia 0083; POB 4619, Pretoria 0001; tel. (12) 435564; fax (12) 433481; Ambassador: J. T. D'ALBI.

Gabon: Southern Life Plaza, cnr Festival and Schoeman Sts, Pretoria 0083; tel. (12) 3424376; fax (12) 3424375; Ambassador: T. SOUAH.

Germany: POB 2023, Pretoria 0001; tel. (12) 3443854; telex 321386; fax (12) 3439401; Ambassador: Dr UWE KAESTNER.

Greece: 1003 Church St, Arcadia, Pretoria 0083; tel. (12) 437351; telex 320520; fax (12) 434313; Ambassador: I. THEOPHANOPOULOS.

Guinea: 336 Orient St, Arcadia 0083; tel. (12) 3428465; fax (12) 3428467; Ambassador Dr O. SYLLA.

Holy See: 800 Pretorius St, Arcadia, Pretoria 0083; tel. (12) 3443815; fax (12) 3443595; Apostolic Nuncio: Most Rev. AMBROSE B. DE PAOLI, Titular Archbishop of Lares.

Hungary: 959 Arcadia St, Arcadia, Pretoria 0083; POB 27077, Sunnyside 0132; tel. (12) 433030; fax (12) 433029; Ambassador: JÁNOS BUDAI.

India: 852 Schoeman St, Arcadia 0083; POB 40216, Arcadia 0007; tel. (12) 3425392; fax (12) 3425310; High Commissioner: GOPAL KRISHNA GANDHI.

Indonesia: 949 Schoeman St, Arcadia 0083; POB 13155, Hatfield 0028; tel. (12) 3423350; fax (12) 3423369; Ambassador: R. ISKANDAR.

Iran: 1002 Schoeman St, Hatfield 0083; POB 12546, Hatfield 0028; tel. (12) 3425880; fax (12) 3421878; Ambassador: M. S. MAHDAVI.

Ireland: First Floor, Delheim Suite, Tulbagh Park, 1234 Church St, Colbyn, Pretoria 0083; tel. (12) 3425062; fax (12) 3424752; Ambassador: EAMON O'TUATHAIL.

Israel: 3rd Floor, 339 Hilda St, Hatfield, Pretoria 0083; POB 3726, Pretoria 0001; tel. (12) 3422693; fax (12) 3421442; Ambassador: (vacant).

Italy: 796 George Ave, Arcadia, Pretoria 0083; tel. (12) 435541; telex 321397; fax (12) 435547; Ambassador: BRUNO CABRAS.

Japan: Sanlam Bldg, 2nd Floor, 353 Festival St, Hatfield 0083; POB 11434, Hatfield 0028; tel. (12) 3422100; fax (12) 433922; Ambassador: Y. KONISHI.

Jordan: 209 Festival St, Hatfield 0083; POB 55755, Arcadia 0007; tel. (12) 3428026; fax (12) 3427847; Ambassador: S. BAK.

Kenya: 302 Brooks St, Menlo Park, Pretoria 0081; tel. (12) 3622249; fax (12) 3622252; High Commissioner: J. A. A. MUDAVADI.

Korea, Republic: Greenpark Estates, Block 3, 27 George Storrar Drive, Groenkloof 0181; POB 939, Groenkloof 0027; tel. (12) 462508; fax (12) 461158; Ambassador: Y. S. KIM.

Kuwait: 890 Arcadia St, Pretoria 0001; Private Bag X920, Arcadia 0007; tel. (12) 3420877; fax (12) 3420875; Ambassador: N. AL-MULLA.

Latvia: Bedford Centre, 17th Floor, cnr Bedford and Smith Sts, Johannesburg 2008; tel. (11) 7825812; fax (11) 8885500.

Lebanon: 7 Sixteenth Ave, Johannesburg 2198; tel. (11) 4831106; fax (11) 4831810; Chargé d'affaires a.i.: CHARBEL STEPHAN.

Lesotho: West Tower Momentum Centre, 6th Floor, 343 Pretoria St, Pretoria 0002; tel. (12) 3226090; fax (12) 3220376; High Commissioner: L. R. MOKOSE.

Libya: 900 Church St, Arcadia, Pretoria 0083; tel. (12) 3423902; fax (12) 3423904; Ambassador: Dr. A. A. AL-ZUBEDI.

Malawi: 770 Government Ave, Arcadia, Pretoria 0083; POB 11172, Hatfield 0028; tel. (12) 3420146; fax (12) 3420146; High Commissioner: W. S. KHOZA.

Malaysia: 950 Pretorius St, Arcadia, Pretoria 0083; POB 11673, Hatfield 0028; tel. (12) 3425990; Fax (12) 437773; High Commissioner: A. K. B. M. DEEN.

Mali: Infotech Bldg, Suite 106, 1090 Arcadia St, Pretoria 0083; tel. (12) 3427464; fax (12) 3420670; Ambassador: (vacant).

Mauritius: 1163 Pretorius St, Hatfield, Pretoria 0083; tel. (12) 3421283; fax (12) 3421286; High Commissioner: MAHEN KUNDASAMY.

Mexico: Southern Life Plaza, 1st Floor, Hatfield, Pretoria 0083; tel. (12) 3425190; Ambassador: CASSIO LUISELLI FERNÁNDEZ.

Mongolia: Pretoria; Ambassador: I. OCHIRBAL.

Morocco: 799 Schoeman St, Arcadia, Pretoria 0083; tel. (12) 3430230; fax (12) 3430613; Ambassador: SAÏD BENRYANE.

Mozambique: 199 Beckett St, Arcadia, Pretoria 0083; POB 57465, Pretoria 0001; tel. (12) 3437840; fax (12) 3436714; High Commissioner: Lt-Gen. ARMANDO A. PANGUENE.

Myanmar: 23 Amos St, Colbyn, Pretoria 0083; tel. (12) 3420706; fax (12) 43432039; Ambassador: U HLA MYINT OO.

Namibia: 702 Church St, Pretoria 0083; tel. (12) 3423520; fax (12) 3423565; High Commissioner: S. N. KAUKUNGUA.

Netherlands: 825 Arcadia St, Pretoria; POB 117, Pretoria 0001; tel. (12) 3443910; telex 321332; fax (12) 3439950; Ambassador: H. R. R. V. FROGER.

New Zealand: Saambou Bldg, 2nd Floor, 424 Hilda St, Hatfield, Pretoria 0083; Private Bag X17, Hatfield 0028; tel. (12) 3428656; fax (12) 3428640; High Commissioner: B. W. P. ABSOLUM.

Nigeria: 138 Beckett St, Arcadia, Pretoria 0083; tel. (12) 3432021; fax (12) 3431668; High Commissioner: A. S. MALAMI OFR.

Norway: Sancardia, 7th Floor, 524 Church St, Arcadia, Pretoria 0084; POB 9843, Pretoria 0001; tel. (12) 3234790; fax (12) 3234789; Ambassador: P. Ø. GRIMSTAD.

Oman: Export House, 3rd Floor, cnr Maude and West Sts, Johannesburg 2196; tel. (11) 8840999; fax (11) 8836569.

Pakistan: 97 Charles St, Brooklyn, Pretoria 0181; tel. (12) 3464605; fax (12) 467824; e-mail pakistan@icon.co.za; High Commissioner: A. AHMED.

Paraguay: POB 95774, Waterkloof, Pretoria 0145; tel. (12) 3471047; fax (12) 3470403; Ambassador: Chargé d'affaires a.i.: VÍCTOR AQUINO FORNERA.

Peru: Infotech Bldg, Suite 202, 1090 Arcadia St, Hatfield, Pretoria 0083; tel. (12) 3422390; fax (12) 3424944; Ambassador: JUAN JOSÉ MEIER.

Philippines: Southern Life Plaza, 1st Floor, cnr Schoeman and Festival Sts, Pretoria 0083; tel. (12) 3426920; fax (12) 3426666 Ambassador: E. R. BELLO, III.

Poland: 14 Amos St, Colbyn, Pretoria 0083; tel. (12) 432631; fax (12) 432608; Ambassador: S. CIENIUCH.

Portugal: Office 201, Barclay Sq., 296 Walker St, Sunnyside, Pretoria 0002; POB 27102, Sunnyside 0132; tel. (12) 3412340; fax (12) 3413975; Ambassador: (vacant).

Romania: 117 Charles St, Brooklyn 0181; POB 11295, Pretoria 0011; tel. (12) 466941; fax (12) 466947; Chargé d'affaires a.i.: DUMITRU NEAGU.

Russia: POB 6743, Pretoria 0001; tel. (12) 3621337; fax (12) 3620116; Ambassador: YEVGENII GUSAROV.

Rwanda: 35 Marais St, Brooklyn, Pretoria 0181; tel. (12) 460709; fax (12) 460708; Ambassador: Dr B. KARENZI.

Saudi Arabia: 711 Duncan St, Pretoria 0083; POB 13930, Hatfield 0028; tel. (12) 3431426; fax (12) 3431439; Chargé d'affaires a.i.: Dr. S. M. ZEDAN.

Singapore: 173 Beckett St, Arcadia, Pretoria 0083; POB 11809, Hatfield 0028; tel. (12) 3434371; fax (12) 3433083; High Commissioner: H. HOCHSTADT.

Slovakia: 930 Arcadia St, Pretoria 0083; POB 12736, Hatfield 0028; tel. (12) 3422051; fax (12) 3423688; Ambassador: LADISLAV VLAŠIČ.

Spain: 169 Pine St, Arcadia, Pretoria 0001; tel. (12) 3443875; telex 320705; fax (12) 3434891; Ambassador: MIGUEL ANGEL CARRIEDO MONPIN.

Sudan: 1187 Pretorius St, Pretoria 0083; POB 25513, Monumentpark 0105; tel. (12) 3424538; fax (12) 3424539; Ambassador: N. A. M. IDRIS.

Swaziland: Infotech Bldg, Suite 105, 1090 Arcadia St, Pretoria 0028; tel. (12) 3425782; fax (12) 3425682; High Commissioner: M. HLOPHE.

Sweden: Old Mutual Centre, 167 Andries St, POB 1664, Pretoria 0001; tel. (12) 3211050; fax (12) 3266677; Ambassador: B. HEINEBÄCK.

Switzerland: 818 George Ave, Arcadia, Pretoria 0083; POB 2289, Pretoria 0001; tel. (12) 436707; telex 322106; fax (12) 436771; Ambassador: R. MAYOR.

Tanzania: 845 Government Ave, Arcadia, Pretoria 0083; POB 56572, Arcadia 0007; tel. (12) 3424393; fax (12) 434383; High Commissioner: AMI MPUNGWE.

Thailand: 840 Church St, Eastwood, Pretoria 0083; POB 12080, Hatfield 0028; tel. (12) 3425470; fax (12) 3424805 Ambassador: B. SOTIPALALIT.

Tunisia: 850 Church St, Arcadia, Pretoria; POB 56535, Arcadia 0007; tel. (12) 3425282; fax (12) 3426284; Ambassador: HATEM ATALLAH.

Turkey: 1067 Church St, Hatfield, Pretoria 0083; POB 56014, Arcadia 0007; tel. (12) 3426053; fax (12) 3426052; Ambassador: K. ÖZGÜVENÇ.

Uganda: Infotech Bldg, Suite 402, 1090 Arcadia St, Pretoria 0083; POB 12442, Hatfield 0083; tel. (12) 3426031; fax (12) 3426206; High Commissioner: Prof. E. RUGUMAYO.

Ukraine: 398 Marais St, Brooklyn, Pretoria 0181; POB 57291, Arcadia 0007; tel. (12) 461946; fax (12) 461044; Ambassador: L. M. GURYANOV.

United Arab Emirates: 980 Park St, Arcadia, Pretoria 0083; POB 57090, Arcadia 0007; tel. (12) 3427736; fax (12) 3427738; Ambassador: ALI T. AL-SUWAIDI.

United Kingdom: 'Greystoke', 255 Hill St, Pretoria 0083; tel. (12) 433121; fax (12) 433207; High Commissioner: MAEVE FORT.

USA: Thibault House, 7th Floor, 877 Pretorius St, Pretoria 0083; POB 9536, Pretoria 0001; tel. (12) 3421048; fax (12) 3422244; Ambassador: JAMES A. JOSEPH.

Uruguay: 301 M.I.B. House, 1119 Burnett St, Hatfield Sq., Pretoria 0083; POB 3247, Pretoria 0001; tel. (12) 432829; fax (12) 432833; Ambassador: J. L. ALDABALDE.

Venezeula: 474 Hatfield Gables South, Hilda St, Pretoria 0083; POB 11821, Hatfield 0028; tel. (12) 3420471; fax (12) 3420480; Ambassador: Dr V. VALLENILLA.

Yemen: Unit 2, Block F, Hatfield Gardens, cnr Hilda and Arcadia Sts, Pretoria 0083; POB 13343, Hatfield 0028; tel. (12) 3428650; fax (12) 3428653; Chargé d'affaires a.i.: ALI MOHAMED AL-THAUR.

Yugoslavia: 163 Marais St, Brooklyn, Pretoria; POB 13026, Hatfield 0028; tel. (12) 465626; fax (12) 4660023; Chargé d'affaires a.i.: D. M. EGIĆ.

Zambia: Sanlam Centre, 353 Festival St, POB 12234, Pretoria 0083; tel. (12) 3421541; fax (12) 3424963; High Commissioner: J. M. KABINGA.

Zimbabwe: 798 Merton St, Arcadia, Pretoria 0083; POB 55140, Arcadia 0007; tel. (12) 3425125; fax (12) 3425126; High Commissioner: N. P. MOYO .

Judicial System

The common law of the Republic of South Africa is the Roman-Dutch law, the uncodified law of Holland as it was at the time of the secession of the Cape of Good Hope in 1806. The law of England is not recognized as authoritative, though the principles of English law have been introduced in relation to civil and criminal procedure, evidence and mercantile matters.

The Constitutional Court consists of a President, Deputy President and nine other judges. Its task is to ensure that the executive, legislative and judicial organs of government adhere to the provisions of the Constitution. It has the power to reverse legislation that has been adopted by Parliament. The Supreme Court of Appeal comprises a Chief Justice, Deputy Chief Justice and a number of judges of appeal, and is the highest court of appeal in all but constitutional matters. There are also High Courts and Magistrates' Courts. A National Director of Public Prosecutions is the head of the prosecuting authority and is appointed by the President of the Republic. A Judicial Service Commission makes recommendations regarding the appointment of judges and advises central and provincial government on all matters relating to the judiciary.

THE SUPREME COURT

Chief Justice: ISMAIL MAHOMED.

THE CONSTITUTIONAL COURT

President: ARTHUR CHASKALSON.

Religion

Some 80% of the population profess the Christian faith. Other religions that are represented are Hinduism, Islam, Judaism and traditional African religions.

CHRISTIANITY

The South African Council of Churches: Khotso House, 62 Marshall St, POB 4921, Johannesburg 2000; tel. (11) 4921380; fax (11) 4921448; f. 1936; 26 mem. churches; Pres. Dr K. MGOJO; Gen. Sec. HLOPHE BAM.

The Anglican Communion

Most Anglicans in South Africa are adherents of the Church of the Province of Southern Africa, comprising 23 dioceses (including Lesotho, Namibia, St Helena, Swaziland and two dioceses in Mozambique). The Church had more than 2m. members in 1988.

Archbishop of Cape Town and Metropolitan of the Province of Southern Africa: Most Rev. NJONGONKULU WINSTON HUGH NDUNGANE, Bishopscourt, Claremont 7700; tel. (21) 7612531; fax (21) 7614193.

The Dutch Reformed Church (Nederduitse Gereformeerde Kerk—NGK)

In 1996 the Dutch Reformed Churches in South Africa consisted of the Dutch Reformed Church with 1,288,837 (mainly white) mems, the Uniting Reformed Church with 1,216,252 (mainly Coloured and black) mems, and the Reformed Church in Africa with 2,386 Indian mems. All congregations were desegregated in 1986.

General Synod: POB 4445, Pretoria 0001; tel. (12) 3227658; fax (12) 3223803; Moderator Rev. FREEK SWANEPOEL; Scribe Dr F. M. GAUM; CEO Dr W. J. BOTHA.

The Lutheran Churches

Lutheran Communion in Southern Africa (LUCSA): POB 7170, Bonaero Park 1622; tel. (11) 9731873; fax (11) 3951615; f. 1991; co-ordinating org. for the Lutheran churches in southern Africa, incl. Angola, Botswana, Malawi, Mozambique, Namibia and Zimbabwe; 1,581,730 mems (1997); Pres. Bishop P. J. ROBINSON; Exec. Dir F. F. GRAZ.

Evangelical Lutheran Church in Southern Africa (ELCSA): POB 7095, 1622 Bonaero Park; tel. (11) 9731851; telex 451751; fax (11) 3951862; f. 1975 by merger of four non-white churches; the largest Lutheran church in southern Africa; Gen. Sec. Rev. T. MBULI; 624,567 mems.

Evangelical Lutheran Church in Southern Africa (Cape): 240 Long St, Cape Town 8001; tel. (21) 244932; fax (21) 249618; Pres. Bishop NILS ROHWER; 4,745 mems.

Evangelical Lutheran Church in Southern Africa (Natal–Transvaal): POB 7095, Bonaero Park 1622; tel. (11) 9731851; fax (11) 3951862; Pres. Bishop D. R. LILJE.

Moravian Church in Southern Africa: POB 24111, Lansdowne 7780; tel. (21) 6962926; fax (21) 6963887; f. 1737; Pres. W. M. MAJIKIJELA; 50,000 mems (1997).

The Roman Catholic Church

South Africa comprises four archdioceses, 21 dioceses and one Apostolic Prefecture. At 31 December 1995 there were an estimated 2,840,304 adherents in the country, representing about 7.5% of the total population.

Southern African Catholic Bishops' Conference (SACBC): Khanya House, 140 Visagie St, Pretoria 0002; POB 941, Pretoria 0001; tel. (12) 3236458; fax (12) 3266218; f. 1951; 34 mems representing South Africa, Botswana, Namibia and Swaziland; Pres. Rt Rev. LOUIS NDLOVU, Bishop of Manzini (Swaziland); Sec.-Gen. Br JUDE PIETERSE.

Archbishop of Bloemfontein: Most Rev. PETER BUTELEZI, Archbishop's House, 7A Whites Rd, Bloemfontein 9300; POB 362, Bloemfontein 9300; tel. and fax (51) 481658.

Archbishop of Cape Town: Most Rev. LAWRENCE HENRY; Cathedral Place, 12 Bouquet St, Cape Town 8001; POB 2910, Cape Town 8001; tel. (21) 4622417; fax (21) 4619330.

Archbishop of Durban: Most Rev. WILFRID NAPIER, Archbishop's House, 154 Gordon Rd, Durban 4001; POB 47489, Greyville 4023; tel. (31) 3031417; fax (31) 231848.

Archbishop of Pretoria: Most Rev. GEORGE DANIEL, Archbishop's House, 125 Main St, Waterkloof 0181; POB 17245, Groenkloof, Pretoria 0027; tel. (12) 462048; fax (12) 462452.

Other Christian Churches

In addition to the following Churches, there are a large number of Pentecostalist groups, and more than 4,000 independent African Churches (with 8,563,000 members in 1994).

African Gospel Church: POB 32312, 4060 Mobeni; tel. (31) 9074377; Moderator Rev. F. D. MKHIZE; Gen. Sec. O. MTOLO; 100,000 mems.

Afrikaanse Protestaante Kerk (Afrikaans Protestant Church): POB 11488, Pretoria 0001; tel. (12) 434461; fax (12) 3243946; f. 1987 by fmr mems of the Dutch Reformed Church (Nederduitse Gereformeerde Kerk) in protest at the desegregation of church congregations; c. 53,000 mems.

Apostolic Faith Mission of South Africa: POB 890197, Lyndhurst 2106; tel. (11) 7868550; fax (11) 8871182; f. 1908; Gen. Sec. Pastor M. G. MAHLABO; 136,000 mems.

Assemblies of God: POB 51065, Musgrave 4062, tel. (31) 231341; fax (31) 231342; f. 1915; Chair. Rev. ISAAC HLETA; Gen. Sec. Rev. C. P. WATT; 300,000 mems.

Baptist Union of Southern Africa: Private Bag X45, Wilropark 1731; tel. (11) 7685980; fax (11) 7685983; f. 1877; Pres. Dr L. MARAIS; Gen. Sec. Rev. T. G. RAE; 45,371 mems.

Black Dutch Reformed Church: POB 137, Bergvlei 2012; Leader Rev. SAM BUTI; c. 1m. mems.

Church of England in South Africa: POB 185, Gillitts 3603; tel. (31) 752876; fax (31) 7655150; 207 churches; Bishops: Rt Rev. J. BELL, Rt Rev. J. NGUBANE, Rt Rev. F. RETIEF, Rt Rev. M. MORRISON.

Evangelical Presbyterian Church in South Africa: POB 31961, Braamfontein 2017; tel. (11) 3391044; Gen. Sec. Rev. S. NGOBE; Gen. Sec. Rev. J. S. NGOBE; Treas. Rev. H. D. MASANGU; 60,000 mems.

The Methodist Church of Southern Africa: Methodist Connexional Office, POB 50216, Musgrave 4062; tel. (31) 224214; fax (31) 217674; f. 1883; Pres. Bishop H. M. DANDALA; Sec. Rev. VIVIAN W. HARRIS; 627,952 mems.

Nederduitsch Hervormde Kerk van Afrika: POB 2368, Pretoria 0001; tel. (12) 3228885; fax (12) 3227909; Chair. Dr D. J. C. VAN WYK; Gen. Sec. Dr S. P. PRETORIUS; 193,561 mems.

Nederduitse Gereformeerde Kerk in Afrika: Portland Place, 37 Jorissen St, 2017 Johannesburg; tel. (11) 4031027; 6 synods (incl. 1 in Swaziland); Moderator Rev. S. P. E. BUTI; Gen. Sec. W. RAATH; 350,370 mems.

Presbyterian Church of Africa: POB 54840, Umlazi 4031; tel. (31) 9072366; f. 1898; 8 presbyteries (incl. 1 in Malawi and 1 in Zimbabwe); Chief Clerk Rev. S. A. KHUMALO; 1,231,000 mems.

Presbyterian Church of Southern Africa: POB 96188, Brixton 2019; tel. (11) 8371258; fax (11) 8371653; f. 1897; Moderator Rt Rev. Dr M. J. MASANGO; Gen. Sec. and Clerk of the Assembly Rev. A. RODGER; 90,000 mems.

Reformed Church in South Africa (Die Gereformeerde Kerke): POB 20004, Noordbrug 2522, Potchefstroom; tel. (148) 2973986; fax (148) 2931042; f. 1859; Prin. Officer H. S. J. VORSTER; 158,973 mems.

Seventh-day Adventist Church: POB 468, Bloemfontein 9300; tel. (51) 4478271; fax (41) 4488059; Pres. Pastor V. S. WAKABA; Sec. Pastor B. H. PARKERSON; 150,000 mems.

United Congregational Church of Southern Africa: POB 61305, Marshalltown 2107; tel. (11) 8366537; fax (11) 8369249; f. 1799; Gen. Sec. Rev. S. M. ARENDS; 234,451 mems.

Zion Christian Church: Zion City, Moria; f. 1910; South Africa's largest black religious group, with c. 4m. mems; Leader Bishop BARNABAS LEKGANYANE.

JUDAISM

There are about 100,000 Jews in South Africa, and about 200 organized Jewish communities.

South African Jewish Board of Deputies: POB 87557, Houghton 2041; tel. (11) 4861434; fax (11) 6464940; f. 1902; the representative institution of South African Jewry; Pres. M. SMITH; Chair. M. BETHLEHEM; Nat. Dir SEYMOUR KOPELOWITZ.

BAHÁ'Í FAITH

National Spiritual Assembly: 10 Acorn Lane, Houghton Estate, Houghton 2198; POB 2142, Houghton 2041; tel. (11) 4872077; fax (11) 4871809; e-mail nsa.sec@pixie.co.za; f. 1956; 11,000 mems resident in 320 localities; Sec. SHOHREH RAWHANI.

The Press

In December 1993 legislation was adopted that provided for the establishment of an Independent Media Commission, which was to ensure the impartiality of the press.

South African Communication Service: Midtown Bldg, cnr Vermeulen and Pretorius Sts, Pretoria; Private Bag X745, Pretoria 0001; tel. (12) 3142911; fax (12) 3233831; govt agency.

South African Media Council: Nedbank Gardens, 8th Floor, 33 Bath Ave, Rosebank 2196; POB 31559, Braamfontein; tel. (11) 4032878; fax (11) 4032879; f. 1983 by the Newspaper Press Union and the Conf. of Editors to promote press freedom; 14 media and 14 public representatives; Chair. Prof. KOBUS VAN ROOYEN.

DAILIES

Eastern Cape

Die Burger (Oos-Kaap): 52 Cawood St, POB 525, Port Elizabeth 6000; tel. (41) 5036111; fax (41) 5036138; f. 1937; morning; Afrikaans; Editor JOHN RELIHAN; circ. 17,000.

Cape Times: Newspaper House, 122 St George's St, POB 56, Cape Town 8000; tel. (21) 4884911; fax (21) 4884717; f. 1876; morning; English; Editor MOEGSIEN WILLIAMS; circ. 53,000.

Daily Dispatch: 33 Caxton St, POB 131, East London 5200; tel. (431) 430010; telex 250678; fax (431) 435159; f. 1872; morning; English; Editor Prof. G. STEWART; circ. 39,000.

Eastern Province Herald: Newspaper House, 19 Baakens St, POB 1117, Port Elizabeth 6000; tel. (41) 5047911; telex 243351; fax (41) 554966; f. 1845; morning; English; Editor RIC WILSON; circ. 30,000 (Mon.–Fri.), 25,000 (Sat.).

Evening Post: Newspaper House, 19 Baakens St, POB 1121, Port Elizabeth 6000; tel. (41) 5047911; telex 243351; fax (41) 554966; f. 1950; evening; English; Editor NEVILLE WOUDBERG; circ. 19,000.

Free State

Die Volksblad: 79 Voortrekker St, POB 267, Bloemfontein 9300; tel. (51) 473351; telex 267612; fax (51) 306949; f. 1904; morning; Afrikaans; Editor PAUL MARAIS; circ. 28,000 (Mon.–Fri.), 23,000 (Sat.).

Gauteng

Beeld: 32 Miller St, POB 5425, Johannesburg 2000; tel. (11) 4064600; fax (11) 4064643; f. 1974; morning; Afrikaans; Editor WILLIE KÜHN; circ. 111,958 (Mon.–Fri.), 81,000 (Sat.).

Business Day: 4 Biermann Ave, Rosebank 2196; tel. (11) 2803000; fax (11) 2805505; f. 1985; morning; English; financial; Editor JIM JONES; circ. 41,000.

The Citizen: POB 7712, Johannesburg 2000; tel. (11) 4022900; telex 424053; fax (11) 4026862; f. 1976; morning; English; Editor M. A. JOHNSON; circ. 14,000 (Mon.–Fri.), 108,000 (Sat.).

The Pretoria News: 216 Vermeulen St, Pretoria 0002; tel. (12) 3255382; fax (12) 3257300; f. 1898; morning; English; Editor A. DUNN; circ. 25,500 (Mon.–Fri.), 14,000 (Sat.).

Sowetan: 61 Commando Rd, Industria West, POB 6663, Johannesburg 2000; tel. (11) 4740128; telex 5425992; fax (11) 4748834; f. 1981; Mon.–Fri.; English; Editor Z. AGGREY KLAASTE; circ. 225,000.

The Star: 47 Sauer St, POB 1014, Johannesburg 2000; tel. (11) 6339111; telex 487083; fax (11) 8368398; f. 1887; English; Editor PETER J. SULLIVAN; circ. 209,000 (Mon.–Fri.), 156,000 (Sat.).

Transvaaler: 28 Height St, Doornfontein, POB 845, Johannesburg 2000; tel. (11) 7769111; fax (11) 4020037; afternoon; Afrikaans; Editor G. JOHNSON; circ. 40,000.

KwaZulu/Natal

The Daily News: 18 Osborne St, Greyville 4001, POB 47549, Greyville 4023; tel. (31) 3082100; fax (31) 3082111; f. 1878; Mon.-Fri., evening; English; Editor P. DAVIS; circ. 85,000.

Natal Mercury: 18 Osborne St, Greyville, POB 950, Durban 4001; tel. (31) 3082300; telex 622301; fax (31) 3082333; f. 1852; morning; English; Editor J. PATTEN; circ. 61,000.

Natal Witness: 244 Longmarket St, POB 362, Pietermaritzburg 3200; tel. (31) 551111; fax (31) 551122; f. 1846; morning; English; Editor J. CONYNGHAM; circ. 28,000.

Northern Cape

Diamond Fields Advertiser: POB 610, Kimberley 8300; tel. (531) 26261; telex 280229; fax (531) 25881; morning; English; Editor Prof. J. G. WILLIAMS; circ. 8,000.

North-West

Rustenburg Herald: 28 Steen St, POB 2043, Rustenburg 0300; tel. (1421) 28329; fax (1421) 28350; f. 1924; English and Afrikaans; Editor C. THERON; circ. 11,000.

Western Cape

The Argus: 122 St George's St, POB 56, Cape Town 8000; tel. (21) 48184911; telex 527383; fax (21) 4884075; f. 1857; English; independent; Editor-in-Chief SHAUN JOHNSON; circ. 85,000.

Die Burger: 40 Heerengracht, POB 692, Cape Town 8000; tel. (21) 4062222; telex 527751; fax (21) 4062913; f. 1915; morning; Afrikaans; Editor E. DOMMISSE; circ. 105,841 (Mon.–Fri.), 97,881 (Sat.).

WEEKLIES AND FORTNIGHTLIES

Eastern Cape

Imvo Zabantsundu (Black Opinion): 35 Edes St, POB 190, King William's Town 5600; tel. (433) 23550; fax (433) 33865; f. 1884; weekly; English and Xhosa; Editor W. MNYIKIZO; Gen.Man. WILL FERREIRA; circ. 31,000.

Weekend Post: POB 1141, Port Elizabeth 6000; tel. (41) 5047911; telex 243047; fax (41) 554966; English; Editor N. M. WOUDBERG; circ. 38,000.

Free State

Vista: POB 1027, Welkom 9460; tel. (57) 3571304; fax (57) 3532427; f. 1971; 2 a week; English and Afrikaans; Editor P. GOUWS; circ. 26,000 (Tues.), 26,000 (Fri.).

Gauteng

African Jewish Newspaper: POB 6169, Johannesburg 2000; tel. (11) 6468292; f. 1931; weekly; Yiddish; Editor LEVI SHALIT.

Die Afrikaner: POB 1888, Pretoria 0001; tel. (12) 3423410; fax (12) 3423417; f. 1970; Wednesday; organ of Herstigte Nasionale Party; Editors Dr J. L. BASSON, J. J. VENTER; circ. 10,000.

Benoni City Times en Oosrandse Nuus: 28 Woburn Ave, POB 494, Benoni 1500; tel. (11) 8451680; telex 748942; fax (11) 4224796; English and Afrikaans; Editor H. LEE; circ. 27,000.

City Press: POB 3413, Johannesburg 2000; tel. (11) 4021632; fax (11) 4026662; f. 1983; weekly; English; Editor KHULU SIBIYA; circ. 160,000.

Finance Week: Private Bag 78816, Sandton 2146; tel. (11) 4440555; fax (11) 4440424; f. 1979; Editor S. MURRAY; circ. 15,000.

Financial Mail: 4 Biermann Ave, Rosebank, Johannesburg 2196; tel. (11) 2803000; fax (11) 2805800; weekly; English; Editor NIGEL BRUCE; circ. 32,000.

The Herald Times: POB 31015, Braamfontein 2017; tel. (11) 8876500; telex 431078; weekly; Jewish interest; Man. Dir R. SHAPIRO; circ. 5,000.

Mail and Guardian: 139 Smit St, Braamfontein, Johannesburg; POB 32362, Braamfontein 2017; tel. (11) 4037111; fax (11) 4031025; f. 1985; English; Editor PHILLIP VAN NIEKERK; circ. 32,510.

Mining Week: Johannesburg; tel. (11) 7892144; telex 422125; f. 1979; fortnightly; Editor VAL PIENAAR; circ. 10,000.

The New Nation: POB 10674, Johannesburg 2000; tel. (11) 3332721; telex 482226; fax (11) 3332733; f. 1986; weekly; English; Editor ZWELAKHE SISULU; circ. 64,000.

Die Noord-Transvaler: POB 220, Ladanna, Pietersburg 0704; tel. (152) 931831; fax (152) 932586; weekly; Afrikaans; Editor A. BUYS; circ. 12,000.

Northern Review: 16 Grobler St, POB 45, Pietersburg 0700; tel. (152) 2959167; fax (152) 2915148; weekly; English and Afrikaans; Editor R. S. DE JAGER; circ. 10,300.

Potchefstroom and Ventersdorp Herald: POB 515, Potchefstroom 2520; tel. (148) 930750; fax (148) 930750; f. 1908; 2 a week; English and Afrikaans; Editor H. STANDER; Man. G. WESSELS; circ. 4,000 (Tues.), 5,000 (Fri.).

Rapport: POB 8422, Johannesburg 2000; tel. (11) 4022620; telex 422027; fax (11) 4026163; f. 1970; weekly; Afrikaans; Editor IZAK DE VILLIERS; circ. 353,000.

South African Industrial Week: Johannesburg; Man. Editor W. MASTINGLE; circ. 19,000.

Springs and Brakpan Advertiser: POB 138, Springs 1560; tel. (11) 8121600; fax (11) 8121908; English and Afrikaans; Editor CATHY STAGG; circ. 12,000.

Sunday Times: POB 1742, Saxonwold 2132; tel. (11) 2803000; fax (11) 2803232; English; Editor B. C. POTTINGER; circ. 458,000.

Vaalweekblad: 27 Ekspa Bldg, D.F. Malan St, POB 351, Vanderbijlpark 1900; tel. (16) 817010; fax (16) 810604; weekly; Afrikaans and English; Editor W. J. BUYS; circ. 16,000.

Vrye Weekblad: 153 Bree St, Newtown, Johannesburg 2001; tel. (11) 8362151; fax (11) 8385901; f. 1988; weekly; Afrikaans; Editor MAX DU PREEZ; circ. 13,000.

KwaZulu/Natal

Farmers' Weekly: POB 32083, Mobeni 4060; tel. (31) 422041; telex 624422; fax (31) 426068; f. 1911; weekly; agriculture and horticulture; Editor M. FISHER; circ. 17,000.

Ilanga: 128 Umgeni Rd, POB 2159, Durban 4000; tel. (31) 3094350; fax (31) 3093489; f. 1903; 2 a week; Zulu; Editor A. MAPHUMULO; circ. 126,000.

Keur: POB 32083, Mobeni 4060; tel. (31) 422041; telex 5624422; fax (31) 426068; f. 1967; Afrikaans; Editor GERHARD BURGER; circ. 61,815.

Ladysmith Gazette: POB 10019, Ladysmith 3370; tel. (361) 26801; fax (361) 22283; f. 1902; weekly; English, Afrikaans and Zulu; Editor BEVIS FAIRBROTHER; circ. 7,000.

Natal On Saturday: 18 Osborne St, Greyville 4001, POB 47549, Greyville 4023; tel. (31) 3082500; fax (31) 3082355; f. 1878; English; Editor G. PARKER; circ. 84,000.

Personality: POB 32083, Mobeni 4060; tel. (31) 422041; telex 624422; fax (31) 426068; weekly; Editor DAVID MULLANY; circ. 65,000.

Post: 18 Osborne St, Greyville 4000, POB 47549, Greyville 4023; tel. (31) 3082400; fax (31) 3082427; f. 1935; weekly; English; general; Editor BRIGLALL RAMGUTHEE; circ. 45,000.

Rooi Rose: POB 2595, Johannesburg 2000; tel. (11) 4831070; fax (11) 4833206; Afrikaans; fortnightly; women's interest; Editor J. KRUGER; circ. 165,000.

Sunday Tribune: 18 Osborne St, POB 47549, Greyville 4023; tel. (31) 3082100; telex 622301; fax (31) 3082715; f. 1937; English; weekly; Editor DAVID WIGHTMAN; circ. 126,000.

Umafrika: POB 11002, Mariannhill 3601; tel. (31) 7002720; fax (31) 7003707; f. 1911; weekly; Zulu and English; Editor CYRIL MADLALA; circ. 60,000.

Northern Cape

Die Gemsbok: POB 60, Upington 8800; tel. 27017; fax 24055; English and Afrikaans; Editor D. JONES; circ. 8,000.

Western Cape

Eikestadnuus: 44 Alexander St, POB 28, Stellenbosch 7600; tel. (2231) 72840; fax (2231) 99538; weekly; English and Afrikaans; Editor R. GERBER; circ. 7,000.

Fair Lady: 40 Heerengracht, POB 1802, Cape Town 8000; tel. (21) 4062044; telex 527751; fax (21) 4062930; fortnightly; English; Editor ROZ WROTTESLEY; circ. 116,769.

Huisgenoot: 40 Heerengracht, POB 1802, Cape Town 8000; tel. (21) 4052115; telex 527751; fax (21) 4062937; f. 1916; weekly; Afrikaans; Editor WILLIE KÜHN; circ. 517,000.

Sarie: POB 1802, Cape Town 8000; tel. (21) 4062203; telex 527751; fax (21) 4062913; fortnightly; Afrikaans; women's interest; Editor A. ROSSOUW; circ. 227,000.

South: 6 Russel St, Castle Mews, Woodstock 7925; POB 13094, Sir Lowry Rd 7900; tel. (21) 4622012; fax (21) 4615407; weekly; black interest; Editor Dr GUY BERGER; circ. 25,000.

The Southern Cross: POB 2372, Cape Town 8000; tel. (21) 455007; fax (21) 453850; f. 1920; weekly; English; Roman Catholic; Editor M. SHACKLETON; circ. 10,000.

Tyger-Burger: 40 Heerengracht, POB 2271, Cape Town 8000; tel. (21) 4062121; telex 527751; fax (21) 4062913; weekly; Afrikaans and English; Editor BAREND VENTER.

Weekend Argus: 122 St George's Mall, POB 56, Cape Town 8000; tel. (21) 4884911; telex 527383; fax (21) 4884075; f. 1857; Sat. and Sun.; English; Editor JONATHAN HOBDAY; circ. 120,000.

You Magazine: 40 Heerengracht, POB 7167, Cape Town 8000; tel. (21) 4062116; telex 527751; fax (21) 4062937; f. 1987; weekly; English; Editor-in-Chief ANDRIES VAN WYK; circ. 316,252.

MONTHLIES

Free State

Wamba: POB 1097, Bloemfontein; educational; publ. in seven vernacular languages; Editor C. P. SENYATSI.

Gauteng

Centre News: Johannesburg; tel. (11) 5591781; English; publ. by R.J.J. Publications; circ. 30,000.

The Mail of Rosebank News: Johannesburg; tel. (11) 3391781; English; publ. by R.J.J. Publications; circ. 40,000.

Nursing News: POB 1280, Pretoria 0001; tel. (12) 3432315; fax (12) 3440750; f. 1978; magazine of the Democratic Nursing Org.; English and Afrikaans; circ. 70,000.

Pace: POB 48985, Roosevelt Park 2129; tel. (11) 8890600; fax (11) 8805942; Man. Editor FORCE KOSHANI; circ. 131,000.

Postal and Telkom Herald: POB 9186, Johannesburg 2000; tel. (11) 7255422; fax (11) 7256540; f. 1903; English and Afrikaans; Staff Asscn (Workers' Union); Editor F. A. GERBER; circ. 13,000.

Technobrief: POB 395, Pretoria 0001; tel (12) 8414078; fax (12) 8413789; f. 1991; publ. by the Council for Scientific and Industrial Research (CSIR); Editor VENE MUSKETT; circ. 16,500.

Telescope: POB 925, Pretoria 0001; tel. (12) 3112495; fax (12) 3114031; f. 1970; English, Afrikaans and vernacular languages; telecom staff journal; Editor WERNA HOUGH; circ. 50,000.

KwaZulu/Natal

Bona: POB 32083, Mobeni 4060; tel. (31) 422041; telex 624422; fax (31) 426068; f. 1956; English, Sotho, Xhosa and Zulu; Editor R. BAKER; circ. 263,000.

Home Front: POB 2549, Durban 4000; tel. (31) 3071574; fax (31) 3054148; f. 1928; ex-servicemen's magazine; Editor REG SWEET; circ. 14,000.

Living and Loving: POB 32083, Mobeni 4060; tel. (31) 422041; telex 624422; fax (31) 426068; English; Editor ANGELA STILL; circ. 113,000.

South African Garden and Home: POB 32083, Mobeni 4060; tel. (31) 422041; telex 624422; fax (31) 426068; f. 1947; Editor MARGARET WASSERFALL; circ. 123,050.

Tempo: POB 16, Pinetown 3600; tel. (31) 7013225; fax (31) 7012166; f. 1984; weekly; Afrikaans; Editor Dr HILDA GROBLER; circ. 7,000.

World Airnews: POB 35082, Northway, Durban 4065; tel. (31) 841319; fax (31) 837115; f. 1973; aviation news; Editor T. CHALMERS; circ. 13,500.

Your Family: POB 32083, Mobeni 4060; tel. (31) 422041; telex 624422; fax (31) 426068; f. 1973; English; cooking, crafts, DIY; Editor ANGELA WALLER-PATON; circ. 216,000.

Western Cape

Boxing World: Unit 17, Park St, POB 164, Steenberg 7945; tel. 7015070; fax 7015863; Editor BERT BLEWETT; circ. 10,000.

Car: POB 180, Howard Place 7450; tel. (21) 5311391; (21) fax 5313333; Editor J. WRIGHT; circ. 130,000.

Drum: POB 784696, Sandton 2146; tel. (11) 7837227; fax (11) 7838822; f. 1951; English; Editor BARNEY COHEN; circ. 135,850 in southern Africa.

Femina: 2 the Avalon, POB 3647, Cape Town 8000; tel. (21) 4623070; telex 522991; fax (21) 4612500; Editor JANE RAPHAELY; circ. 109,000.

Finansies & Tegniek: POB 53171, Troyeville 2139; tel. (11) 4026372; fax (11) 4041701; Afrikaans and English; Publisher G. L. MARAIS; circ. 25,791.

Learning Roots: POB 1161, Cape Town 8000; tel. (21) 6968414; fax (21) 6968346; f. 1980; newsletter for black schools in the Western Cape; circ. 50,000.

Nursing RSA Verpleging: Private Bag XI, Pinelands 7430; tel. (21) 5312691; fax (21) 5314126; f. 1986; professional nursing journal; Editor LILLIAN MEDLIN; circ. 10,000.

Reader's Digest (South African Edition): POB 2677, Cape Town 8000; tel. (21) 254460; telex 520333; fax (21) 4191090; English; Editor-in-Chief W. PANKHURST; circ. 371,000.

South African Medical Journal: Private Bag XI, Pinelands 7430; tel. (21) 5313081; fax (21) 5314126; f. 1926; publ. by the Medical Asscn of South Africa; Editor Dr DANIEL J. NCAYIYANA; circ. 20,000.

Die Unie: POB 196, Cape Town 8000; tel. (21) 4616340; fax (21) 4619238; f. 1905; educational; publ. by the South African Teachers' Union; Editor Prof. C. G. DE VRIES; circ. 7,200.

Die Voorligter: POB 1444, Cape Town 8000; tel. (21) 259233; fax (21) 255522; f. 1937; journal of the Dutch Reformed Church of South Africa; Editor Dr F. M. GAUM; circ. 84,000.

Woman's Value: POB 1802, Cape Town 8000; tel. (21) 4062205; telex 527751; fax (21) 4062929; English; Editor RIETA BURGERS; circ. 146,000.

Wynboer: K. W. V. Van SA Bpk, POB 528, Suider-Paarl 7624; tel. (21) 8073267; fax (21) 8631562; f. 1931; viticulture and the wine and spirit industry; Editor HENRY HOPKINS; circ. 8,750.

QUARTERLIES

Gauteng

The Motorist/Die Motoris: POB 31015, Braamfontein 2017; tel. (11) 8876500; fax (11) 8876551; f. 1966; journal of the Automobile Asscn of SA; Editor MICHAEL WANG; circ. 184,000.

South African Journal of Economics: 4-44 EBW Bldg, University of Pretoria, Pretoria 0002; tel. (12) 4203525; fax (12) 437589; English and Afrikaans; Man. Editor Prof. D. J. J. BOTHA.

Vuka SA: POB 1758, Pretoria 0001; tel. (12) 3226404; fax (12) 3207803; f. 1952; publ. by the Foundation for Education, Science and Tech.; Editor JOHAN VAN ROOYEN; circ. 5,000.

Western Cape

New Era: Cape Town.

South African Law Journal: POB 30, Cape Town 8000; tel. (2721) 7975101; fax (2721) 7627424; f. 1884; Editor ELLISON KAHN; circ. 3,000.

NEWS AGENCIES

South African Press Association: Kine Centre, 1st Floor, Commissioner St, POB 7766, Johannesburg 2000; tel. (11) 3310661; telex 488061; fax (11) 3317473; f. 1938; 40 mems; Chair. J. L. MALHERBE; Man. W. J. H. VAN GILS; Editor MARK A. VAN DER VELDEN.

Foreign Bureaux

Agence France-Presse (AFP): Nixdorf Centre, 6th Floor, 37 Stanley Ave, Milpark; POB 3462, Johannesburg 2000; tel. (11) 4822170; telex 422660; fax (11) 7268756; Bureau Chief MARC HUTTEN.

Agenzia Nazionale Stampa Associata (ANSA) (Italy): POB 32312, Camps Bay, Cape Town 8040; tel. (21) 7903991; telex 522211; fax (21) 7904444; Correspondent LICINIO GERMINI.

Associated Press (AP) (USA): 15 Napier St, Richmond, Johannesburg 2092; tel. (11) 7267022; fax (11) 7267834; Bureau Chief JOHN DANISZEWSKI.

Central News Agency (Taiwan): Kine Centre, 1st Floor, 141 Commissioner St, Johannesburg 2001; tel. (11) 3316654; fax (11) 3319463; Chief CHANG JER SHONG.

Deutsche Presse-Agentur (dpa) (Germany): 96 Jorrisen St, POB 32521, Braamfontein 2017; tel. (11) 4033926; fax (11) 4032849; Chief Dr ARNO MAYER.

Informatsionnoye Telegrafnoye Agentstvo Rossii—Telegrafnoye Agentstvo Suverennykh Stran (ITAR—TASS) (Russia): 1261 Park St, Atfield, Pretoria; tel. (12) 436677; telex 320142; fax (12) 3425017; Bureau Chief YURII K. PICHUGIN.

Inter-Press Service (IPS) (Italy): POB 30764, Braamfontein 2017, Johannesburg; tel. (11) 4034967; fax (11) 4032516; Correspondent GUMISAI MUTUME.

Kyodo News Service (Japan): 3rd Floor, Mentone Center, 1 Park Rd, Richmond, Johannesburg 2000; tel. (11) 4826524; fax (11) 4826534; Rep. NOAHITO ISOYA.

Reuters Ltd (UK): Surrey House, 7th and 8th Floors, 35 Rissik St, Johannesburg; Man. CHRIS INWOOD.

United Press International (UPI) (USA): Nedbank Centre, 2nd Floor, POB 32661, Braamfontein 2017; tel. (11) 4033910; telex 423428; fax (11) 4033914; Bureau Chief PATRICK COLLINS.

Agencia EFE (Spain) is also represented.

PRESS ASSOCIATIONS

Newspaper Press Union of Southern Africa: Nedbank Gardens, 8th Floor, 33 Bath Ave, Rosebank 2196, Johannesburg; POB 47180, Parklands 2121; tel. (11) 4471264; fax (11) 4471289; f. 1882; represents 26 urban daily, weekly and independent nat. newspapers; Pres. J. F. VAN HEERDEN; Gen. Man. P. S. C. POTÉ.

Print Media Association of Southern Africa: POB 47180, Parklands 2121; tel. (11) 4471264; fax (11) 4471289; f. 1995, following the restructuring of the Newspaper Press Union of Southern Africa; represents all aspects of the print media (newspapers and magazines); 502 mems; Pres. J. F. HEERDEN; Gen. Man. P. S. C. POTÉ.

Publishers

Acorn Books: POB 4845, Randburg 2125; tel. (11) 8805768; fax (11) 8805768; f. 1985; Africana, general, natural history.

Albertyn Publishers (Pty) Ltd: Andmar Bldg, Van Ryneveld St, Stellenbosch 7600; tel. (21) 8871202; fax (21) 8871292; f. 1971; encyclopaedias; Editorial Man. S. CARSTENS.

BLAC Publishing House: POB 17, Athlone, Cape Town; f. 1974; general fiction, poetry; Man. Dir JAMES MATTHEWS.

Jonathan Ball Publishers: POB 33977, Jeppestown 2043; tel. (11) 6222900; fax (11) 6223553; fiction, reference, bibles, textbooks, general. Subsidiary:

A. Donker (Pty) Ltd: POB 33977, Jeppestown 2043; tel. (11) 6222900; fax (11) 6223553; Africana, literature, history, academic.

Bible Society of South Africa: POB 6215, Roggebaai 8012; tel. (21) 212040; telex 527964; fax (21) 4194846; f. 1820; Gen. Sec. Dr D. TOLMIE.

Book Promotions (Pty) Ltd: POB 5, Plumstead 7800; tel. (21) 720332; fax (21) 720383; Man. Dir. R. MANSELL.

Book Studio (Pty) Ltd: POB 121, Hout Bay 7872.

Books of Africa (Pty) Ltd: POB 10, Muizenberg 7950; tel. (21) 888316; f. 1947; biography, history, Africana, art; Man. Dir T. V. BULPIN.

Brenthurst Press (Pty) Ltd: POB 87184, Houghton 2041; tel. (11) 6466024; fax (11) 4861651; f. 1974; Southern African history.

Butterworth Publishers (Pty) Ltd: POB 4, Mayville 4058; tel. (31) 2683111; fax (31) 2683100; law, tax, accountancy; Man. Dir WILLIAM J. LAST.

Clever Books: POB 20113, Alkantrant 0005; tel. (12) 3423263; fax (12) 432376; f. 1981; Propr J. STEENHUISEN.

College of Careers/Faircare Books: POB 10207, Caledon Sq., Cape Town 7905; tel. (21) 4614411; f. 1946; general, educational; Man. Dir MICHAEL IRVING.

CUM Books: POB 1599, Vereeniging 1930; tel. (16) 214781; fax (16) 211748.

Da Gama Publishers (Pty) Ltd: MWU Bldg, 6th Floor, 19 Melle St, Braamfontein 2017; tel. (11) 4033763; fax (11) 4031263; travel; Publr DERMOT SWAINE.

Digma Publications: POB 95466, Waterkloof 0145; tel. (11) 3463840; fax (11) 3463845.

Dreyer Printers and Publishers: POB 286, Bloemfontein 9300; tel. (51) 4479001; fax (51) 4471281.

Educum Publishers: POB 3068, Halfway House 1685.

Eksamenhulp: POB 55555, Arcadia 0007.

Fisichem Publishers: POB 6052, Stellenbosch 7600.

Flesch, W. J., & Partners: 4 Gordon St, Gardens, POB 3473, Cape Town 8000; tel. (21) 4617472; fax (21) 4613758; f. 1954; Prin. Officer S. FLESCH.

Fortress Books: POB 189, Rondebosch 7700; tel. and fax (21) 7884927; f. 1973; military history, biographies, financial; Man. Dir I. UYS.

T. W. Griggs & Co: 341 West St, Durban 4001; tel. (31) 3048571; Africana.

F.J.N. Harman Publishers: Menlo Park; tel. (12) 469575; f. 1981; educational; Man. Dir F. J. N. HARMAN.

HAUM: Prima Park 4 and 6, cnr Klosser and King Edward Rds, Porow 7500; tel. (21) 926123; f. 1894; Man. C. J. HAGE. Subsidiaries include:

Kagiso Publishers: POB 629, Pretoria 0001; tel. (12) 3284620; fax (12) 3284705; school textbooks and other materials for schools and tertiary institutions in all 11 official South African languages; Man. Dir L. M. MABANDLA.

University Publishers & Booksellers (Pty) Ltd: POB 29, Stellenbosch 7599; tel. (21) 8870337; fax (21) 8832975; f. 1947; educational; Man. Dir B. B. LIEBENBERG.

Heinemann Publishers (Pty) Ltd: POB 781940, Sandown, Sandton 2146; tel. (11) 7848619; fax (11) 7848360; educational; incl. imprints Lexicon, Isando and Centaur; Man. Dir K. KROEGER.

Home Economics Publishers: POB 7091, Stellenbosch 7600; tel. (21) 8874630.

Human and Rousseau (Pty) Ltd: POB 5050, Cape Town 8000; tel. (21) 251280; fax (21) 4192619; f. 1959; English, Afrikaans, Xhosa and Zulu; general adult and children's trade books; Gen. Man. C. T. BREYTENBACH.

Incipit Publishers: POB 28754, Sunnyside, Pretoria 0132; tel. and fax (12) 463802; f. 1987; music; Man. MARIANNE FEENSTRA.

Juta and Co Ltd: POB 14373, Kenwyn 7790, Cape Town; tel. (11) 7975101; fax (11) 7627424; f. 1853; academic, educational, law, electronic; Man. R. J. H. COOKE.

Klipbok Publishers: POB 170, Durbanville 7550; tel. and fax (21) 962293; f. 1979; prose, poetry, drama.

Knowledge Unlimited (Pty) Ltd: POB 781337; Sandton 2146; tel. (11) 6521800; fax (11) 3142984; children's fiction, educational; Man. Dir MIKE JACKLIN.

Konsensus Publishers: 213 Orion St, Waterkloof 0180.

Lemur Books (Pty) Ltd: POB 1645, Alberton 1450; tel. (11) 9072029; fax (11) 8690890; military, political, history, hunting, general; Man. Dir F. STIFF.

Lovedale Press: Private Bag X1346, Alice; tel. (0404) 31135; fax (0404) 31871; f. 1841; Gen. Man. Rev. B. B. FINCA.

Lux Verbi: POB 1822, Cape Town 8000; tel. (21) 253505; telex 526922; fax (21) 4191865; Exec. Chair. W. J. VAN ZIJL.

Macdonald Purnell (Pty) Ltd: POB 51401, Randburg 2125; tel. (11) 7875830; telex 424985; South African flora, fauna, geography and history; Man. Dir E. ANDERSON.

Marler Publications (Pty) Ltd: POB 27815, Sunnyside, Pretoria 0132; tel. (12) 573770; f. 1987; educational; Man. Dir C. J. MULLER.

Maskew Miller Longman (Pty) Ltd: Howard Drive, Pinelands 7405, POB 396, Cape Town 8000; tel. (21) 5317750; telex 5726053; fax (21) 5314049; f. 1983; educational and general; CEO M. A. PEACOCK.

Methodist Publishing House: POB 708, Cape Town 8000; tel. (21) 4618214; fax (21) 4618249; religion and theology; Gen. Man. D. R. LEVERTON.

Nasionale Boekhandel: POB 122, Parow 7500; tel. (21) 5911131; telex 526951; fiction, general, educational, academic; English, Afrikaans and several African languages; Man. Dir P. J. BOTMA.

Nasou—Via Afrika: POB 5197, Cape Town 8000; tel. (21) 4063313; fax (21) 4062922; educational; Gen. Man. D. H. SCHROEDER.

Orion: POB 3068, Halfway House 1685; tel. (21) 3153647; fax (21) 3152757; f. 1947; Sen. Publr NEELS DU PLOOY.

Oudiovista Productions (Pty) Ltd: Parow; tel. (21) 5911131; telex 527751; Man. Dir P. J. BOTMA.

Oxford University Press: POB 12119, Goodwood 7463; tel. (21) 5954400; f. 1914; Man. Dir KATE MCCALLUM.

Perskor Publishers: POB 3068, Halfway House 1685 tel. (11) 3153647; fax (11) 3152757; f. 1940; general and educational; Sr Gen. Man. W. F. STRUIK.

David Philip Publishers (Pty) Ltd: POB 23408, Claremont 7735; tel. (21) 644136; fax (21) 643358; f. 1971; general, academic, literature, reference, fiction, juvenile; Dirs D. H. PHILIP, M. PHILIP, R. MARTIN, B. IMPEY.

Pretoria Boekhandel: POB 23334, Innesdale, Pretoria 0031; tel. (12) 761531; f. 1971; Prin. Officer L. S. VAN DER WALT.

Random House SA (Pty) Ltd: POB 2263, Parklands 2121; tel. (11) 4843538; fax (11) 4846180; f. 1966; Man. Dir S. JOHNSON.

Ravan Press (Pty) Ltd: POB 145, Randburg 2125; tel. (11) 7897636; fax (11) 7897653; f. 1972; political, sociological, fiction, business studies, gender, history, autobiography, biography, educational; Exec. Chair. G. E. DE VILLIERS.

Saayman and Weber (Pty) Ltd: POB 673, Cape Town 8000; f. 1980.

Sasavona Publishers and Booksellers: Private Bag X8, Braamfontein 2017; tel. (11) 4032502; fax (11) 3397274; Northern Sotho, Tshwa, Tsonga, Tswana, Venda and Zulu; Man. A. E. KALTENRIEDER.

Shuter and Shooter (Pty) Ltd: 199 Pietermaritz St, Pietermaritzburg 3201; POB 109, Pietermaritzburg 3200; tel. (331) 946830; fax (331) 427419; f. 1921; educational, general and African languages; Man. Dir D. F. RYDER.

The Struik Publishing Group (Pty) Ltd: POB 1144, Cape Town 8000; tel. (21) 4624360; fax (21) 4619378; Dirs G. STRUIK, A. D. L. CRUZEN, M. C. H. JAMES, C. M. HANLEY, N. D. PRYKE, J. D. WILKINS, J. L. SCHOEMAN, A. S. VERSCHOYLE.

Study Aids Ltd: 13 Darrock Ave, Albemarle Park, Germiston 1401; study aids.

Hans Strydom Publishers: Private Bag 10, Mellville 2109.

Sunray Publishers: 96 Queen St, Durban 4001; tel. (31) 3052543.

Tafelberg Publishers Ltd: 28 Wale St, POB 879, Cape Town 8000; tel. (21) 241320; fax (21) 242510; f. 1950; juvenile, fiction and non-fiction, arts and crafts; Gen. Man. J. J. LABUSCHAGNE.

Thomson Publications: Johannesburg 2123; tel. (11) 7892144; telex 422125; fax (11) 7893196; f. 1948; trade and technical; Man. Dir JOE M. BRADY.

UCCSA Publications Dept: POB 31083, Braamfontein 2017; tel. (11) 8360065; f. 1946; Gen. Man. W. WESTENBORG.

University of Natal Press: Private Bag X01, Scottsville 3209; tel. (331) 2605802; fax (331) 2605599; Man. Editor Dr J. EDLEY.

Van der Walt and Son, J. P. (Pty) Ltd: POB 123, Pretoria 0001; tel. (12) 3252100; fax (12) 3255498; f. 1947; general; Man. Dir C. J. STEENKAMP.

Chris van Rensburg Publications (Pty) Ltd: POB 29159, Mellville 2109; tel. (31) 7264350; yearbooks, general; Man. Dir. C. C. VAN RENSBURG.

Van Schaik, J. L. Publishers: POB 12681, Hatfield 0083; tel. (11) 3422765; fax (11) 433563; f. 1914; educational, general, religion; English, Afrikaans and vernaculars; Gen. Man. G. Louw.

Waterkant Publishers: POB 4539, Cape Town 8000; tel. (21) 215540; fax (21) 4191865; f. 1980; Exec. Chair. W. J. van Zijl.

Witwatersrand University Press: PO Wits, Johannesburg 2050; tel. (11) 4845910; fax (11) 4845971; f. 1922; academic; Head Franscois McHardy.

PUBLISHERS' ASSOCIATION

Publishers' Association of South Africa: POB 116, St James, Cape Town 7946; tel. (21) 7886470; fax (21) 7886469; e-mail pasa@iafrica.com; f. 1992; Chair. B. van Rooyen; Admin. E. van Greunen.

Radio and Television

In 1992 there were some 2.6m. television licences issued; in 1994 (according to UNESCO) there were 12.8m. radio receivers in use.

In December 1993 legislation providing for the establishment of an Independent Broadcasting Authority was adopted, effectively ending state control of radio and television. All stations were required to reapply for licences.

Independent Broadcasting Authority: 26 Baker St, Rosebank, Private Bag X31, Parklands, Johannesburg 212; tel. (11) 4476180; fax (11) 4476187; e-mail theiba@wn.apc.org; f. 1993; Chair. S. M. Matabane; CEO Harris Gxaweni (suspended May 1997).

South African Broadcasting Corporation (SABC): Broadcast Centre, Henley Rd, Private Bag X1, Auckland Park 2006; tel. (11) 7149000; telex 424116; fax (11) 7143569; e-mail shaikz@sabc.co.za; f. 1936; statutory body; revenue from licences and advertising; operates 22 internal radio services broadcasting in 11 languages, one external radio service broadcasting in seven languages, and three TV channels broadcasting in seven languages; Chair. of Board Prof. P. Zulu; CEO Zwelakhe Sisulu.

RADIO

SABC–Radio: Private Bag X1, Auckland Park 2006; tel. (11) 7149111; telex 424116; fax (11) 7143106; CEO Govan Reddy.

Domestic Services

Radio South Africa; Afrikaans Stereo; Radio 5; Radio 2000; Highveld Stereo; Good Hope Stereo; Radio Kontrei; RPN Stereo; Jacaranda Stereo; Radio Algoa (regional services); Radio Lotus (Indian service in English); Radio Metro (African service in English); Radio Lebowa; Radio Ndebele; Radio Sesotho; Setswana Stereo; Radio Swazi; Radio Tsonga; Radio Xhosa; Radio Zulu.

External Service

Channel Africa Radio: POB 91313, Auckland Park 2006; tel. (11) 7142551; fax (11) 7142546; f. 1966; SABC's external service; broadcasts 217 hours per week in Chichewa, Chinyanja, English, French, Lozi, Portuguese, Shona, Swahili and Tsonga to Africa; Exec. Editor Lebona Mosia.

TELEVISION

SABC–Television: Private Bag X41, Auckland Park 2006; tel. (11) 7149111; telex 424116; fax (11) 7145055; transmissions began in 1976; operates television services in seven languages over three channels; English and Afrikaans programmes on Channel one (TV1); Channel two (CCV-TV) broadcasts in English, Northern and Southern Sotho, Tswana, Xhosa and Zulu; Channel three (NNTV) broadcasts documentaries, educational programmes and sport.

Finance

(cap. = capital; auth. = authorized; res = reserves; dep. = deposits; m. = million; brs = branches; amounts in rand)

BANKING

Central Bank

South African Reserve Bank: 370 Church St, POB 427, Pretoria 0001; tel. (12) 3133911; telex 322411; fax (12) 3133197; e-mail info@gweis.resbank.co.za; f. 1921; cap. and res 1,015.1m., dep. 9,474.1m. (March 1996); Gov. Dr Christian L. Stals; Dep. Govs C. J. de Swardt, T. T. Thahane, J. H. Cross; 7 brs.

Commercial Banks

ABSA Bank Ltd: ABSA Towers, 19th Floor, 160 Main St, Johannesburg 2001; tel. (11) 3303222; telex 489399; fax (11) 3303511; f. 1990; cap. and res 5,473m., dep. 97,988m. (March 1996); Chair. David C. Brink; CEO Dr Danie Cronje; 726 brs.

African Bank Limited: 56 Marshall St, Johannesburg 2001; POB 61352, Marshall 2107; tel. (11) 8362331; telex 483089; fax (11) 8382845; f. 1975; cap. 13.9m., dep. 602.6m. (March 1994); Chair. Dr S. M. Motsuenyane; CEO J. C. D. Theron.

Bank of Transkei Ltd: POB 232, Bank of Transkei Bldg, 60 Sutherland St, Umtata; tel. (471) 311368; fax (471) 22546; f. 1977; cap. and res 34.8m., dep. 392.6m. (March 1996); Chair. E. R. Bosman; Man. Dir. E. G. Kaltenbrünn; 5 brs.

Boland Bank Pks Ltd: 333 Main St, POB 4, Paarl 7622; tel. (21) 8072911; telex 522136; fax (21) 8072811; f. 1900; cap. and res 538.1m., dep. 5,163m. (March 1996); Chair. C. H. Wiese; CEO M. S. du P. le Roux; 98 brs.

First National Bank of Southern Africa Ltd: 1 First Place, 6th Floor, BankCity, Johannesburg 2001; POB 1153, Johannesburg 2000; tel. (11) 3712111; fax (11) 3712402; f. 1971; cap. and res 5,131.3m., dep. 79,878.3m. (Sept. 1996); Chair. T. N. Chapman; Man. Dir V. W. Bartlett; 1,360 brs.

French Bank of Southern Africa Ltd: 4 Ferreira St, Marshalltown, Johannesburg 2001; POB 61523, Marshalltown 2107; tel. (11) 8322433; telex 482896; fax (11) 8360625; f. 1949; subsidiary of Banque Indosuez (France); cap. and res 97.6m., dep. 1,968.8m. (Dec. 1993); Chair. P. Brault; Man. Dir M. Verhille; 3 brs.

Habib Overseas Bank Ltd: 2nd Floor, 78 Fox St, Johannesburg 2001; tel. (11) 8347441; fax (11) 8347446; f. 1990; cap. 11.0m., dep. 74.1m. (Dec. 1996); Chair. Mohammad Hassan Hanafi; Man. Dir Bande Hassan; 4 brs.

Mercantile Bank Ltd: Mercantile Lisbon House, 142 West St, Sandton, Gauteng 2196; tel. (11) 3020300; telex 485076; fax (11) 3020700; f. 1965; cap. 149.8m., dep. 1,563.7m. (Dec. 1995); Chair. H. V. Vorster; Man. Dir D. P. Cohen.

Nedcor Bank: 100 Main St, Johannesburg 2001, POB 1144, Johannesburg 2000; tel. (11) 6307111; telex 482765; fax (11) 6302465; f. 1888; cap. and res 3,361m., dep. 26,170m. (Dec. 1995); Chair. C. L. Liebenberg; CEO R. C. M. Laubscher; 317 brs.

The New Republic Bank Ltd: NRB House, 110 Field St, Durban 4001; tel. (31) 3047544; telex 625354; fax (31) 3053547; f. 1971; cap. 89m., dep. 901m. (1993); Man. Dir M. Mia; 13 brs.

The South African Bank of Athens Ltd: Bank of Athens Bldg, 116 Marshall St, POB 7781, Johannesburg 2001; tel. (11) 8321211; telex 486976; fax (11) 8381001; f. 1947; associated with National Bank of Greece; cap. and res 33.7m., dep. 442.8m. (Dec. 1995); Chair. G. Mirkos; Man. Dir A. Stringos; 13 brs.

The Standard Bank of South Africa Ltd: Standard Bank Centre, 5 Simmonds St, Johannesburg 2001; POB 7725, Johannesburg 2000; tel. (11) 6364718; telex 489707; fax (11) 6364207; f. 1862; cap. and res 4,202.7m., dep. 91,782.8m. (Dec. 1996); Chair. Dr Conrad B. Strauss; CEO Miké H. Vosloo; 1,002 brs.

Merchant Banks

ABSA Merchant Bank Ltd: Johannesburg; tel. (11) 3315741; telex 486965; fax (11) 3311040; f. 1977; cap. and res 96.9m., dep. 699m. (March 1991); Man. Dir J. J. Brown; 1 br.

FirstCorp Merchant Bank Ltd: Bankcity 4, First Place, Johannesburg 2001; POB 9773, Johannesburg 2000; tel. (11) 3718336; telex 487092; fax (11) 3718351; f. 1987; cap. 10m. (Sept. 1996), dep. 3,309.2m. (Sept. 1994); Chair. V. W. Bartlett; CEO A. Roux; 1 br.

Rand Merchant Bank Ltd: 1 Merchant Place, cnr Fredman Drive and Rivonia Rd, Sandton 2199; POB 786273, Sandton 2146; tel. (11) 2828000; telex 427796; fax (11) 2828008; cap. and res 583.3m., dep. 6,441.1m. (June 1996); Chair. Gerrit Ferreira; Man. Dir P. K. Harris; 2 brs.

Standard Corporate and Merchant Bank Ltd: 78 Fox St, 16th Floor, Johannesburg 2001; POB 61344, Marshalltown 2107; tel. (11) 6369115; telex 487629; fax (11) 6362371; f. 1964; cap. and res 234.9m., dep. 3,555.5m. (Dec. 1993); Chair. D. R. Geeringh; Man. Dir J. H. Maree.

UAL Merchant Bank Ltd: UAL Gardens, 1 Newtown Ave, Killarney 2193; POB 582, Johannesburg 2000; tel. (11) 4801000; fax (11) 4801525; f. 1955; cap. 6m. (Sept. 1996), res 245.8m., dep. 3,348m. (Sept. 1994); Chair R. C. M. Laubscher; Dep. Chair. G. F. Richardson.

Savings Banks

British Kaffrarian Savings Bank Society: POB 1432, King William's Town 5600; tel. (433) 21478; telex 5250117; f. 1860; dep. 28.8m.; CEO D. E. Daubermann.

Pretoria Bank Ltd: Woltemade Bldg, 118 Paul Kruger St, POB 310, Pretoria; cap. 601,250; dep. 7.6m.; Chair. M. D. Marais; Gen. Man. I. W. Ferreira.

Staalwerkersspaarbank: 417 Church St, POB 1747, Pretoria; cap. 240,630; dep. 2.5m.; Chair. and Man. Dir L. J. van den Berg.

Investment Bank

Investec Bank Ltd: 55 Fox St, POB 11177, Johannesburg 2000; tel. (11) 4982000; telex 488381; fax (11) 4982100; f. 1974; cap. and res 2,204.9m., dep. 8,719.3m. (March 1996); Chair. H. S. Herman; Man. Dir S. Koseff; 4 brs.

Development Bank

Development Bank of Southern Africa (DBSA): 1 Lever Rd, Midrand, POB 1234, Halfway House 1685; tel. (11) 3133911; telex 425546; fax (11) 3133628; e-mail sandalem@dbsaperiod.org.za; f. 1983; CEO Dr Ian Goldin.

Discount Houses

Discount House Merchant Bank Ltd: 66 Marshall St, Johannesburg 2001; POB 61574, Marshalltown 2107; tel. (11) 8367451; fax (11) 8369636; f. 1957; cap. 18.8m.; Exec. Chair. C. J. H. Dunn; Man. Dir M. R. Thompson.

Interbank Ltd: 108 Fox St, POB 6035, Johannesburg; tel. (11) 8344831; fax (11) 8345357; f. 1971; cap. 15.5m., dep. 564m. (1990); Chair. A. Kelly; Man. Dir M. Swart.

The National Discount House of South Africa Ltd: Loveday House, 1st Floor, 15 Loveday St, Johannesburg; tel. (11) 8323151; telex 485081; f. 1961; auth. cap. 10m., dep. 357.1m. (1987); Chair. M. MacDonald; Man. Dir G. G. Lund.

Bankers' Association

Institute of South African Bankers (COSAB): 17 Harrison St, 10th Floor, POB 61674, Marshalltown 2107; tel. (11) 8384978; fax (11) 8346512; f. 1904; 15,000 mems; CEO C. N. Axton.

STOCK EXCHANGE

Johannesburg Stock Exchange: 17 Diagonal St, POB 1174, Johannesburg 2000; tel. (11) 3772200; fax (11) 8387106; e-mail pr@jse.co.za; f. 1887; in late 1995 legislation was enacted providing for the deregulation of the Stock Exchange; automated trading was to commence in 1996; Exec. Pres. R. M. Laubser.

INSURANCE

ACA Insurers Ltd: 35 Symons Rd, Auckland Park; tel. (11) 7268900; telex 4896262; f. 1948; Man. Dir L. G. Y. Nemorin.

Aegis Insurance Co Ltd: Aegis Insurance House, 91 Commissioner St, Johannesburg; tel. (11) 8367621; telex 487512; fax (11) 8384559; Man. Dir B. H. Seach.

African Mutual Trust & Assurance Co Ltd: 34 Church St, POB 27, Malmesbury; f. 1900; Chief Gen. Man. R. A. L. Cuthbert.

Allianz Insurance Ltd: Allianz House, 13 Fraser St, Johannesburg 2001; POB 62228, Marshalltown 2107; tel. (11) 4970400; telex 487103; fax (11) 8383827; Man. Dir Dr A. Gossner.

Anglo American Life Assurance Co Ltd: Life Centre, 45 Commissioner St, POB 6946, Johannesburg 2000; telex 487780; Exec. Chair. Dr Z. J. de Beer; Man. Dir Dr M. Bernstein.

Commercial Union of South Africa Ltd: Commercial Union House, 26 Loveday St, POB 3555, Johannesburg 2000; tel. (11) 4911911; fax (11) 8382600; f. 1964; Chair. A. M. D. Gnodde; Man. Dir J. A. Kinvig.

Credit Guarantee Insurance Corpn of Africa Ltd: 31 Dover St, POB 125, Randburg 2125; tel. (11) 8897000; telex 420508; fax (11) 8861027; f. 1956; Man. Dir C. T. L. Leisewitz.

Fedlife Assurance Ltd: Fedlife House, 1 de Villiers St, POB 666, Johannesburg 2000; tel. (11) 3326000; fax (11) 4921102; f. 1944; Chair. J. A. Barrow; Man. Dir A. I. Basserabie.

General Accident Insurance Co of South Africa Ltd: POB 32424, Braamfontein 2017; tel. (11) 4086000; telex 9450092; fax (11) 3397732; Man. Dir I. L. Maxwell.

I. G. I. Insurance Co Ltd: 162 Anderson St, POB 8199, Johannesburg 2000; tel. (11) 3351911; telex 485393; fax (11) 290491; f. 1954; Chair. I. M. A. Lewis; Man. Dir P. S. Denniss.

Liberty Life Association of Africa Ltd: Liberty Life Centre, 1 Ameshoff St, Johannesburg 2001; POB 10499, Johannesburg 2000; tel. (11) 4082100; telex 422530; fax (11) 4033171; f. 1958; Chair. Donald Gordon; Man. Dir A. Romanis.

Metropolitan Life Ltd: 7 Coen Steytler Ave, Foreshore, Cape Town; POB 2212, Bellville 7535; tel. (21) 9405911; fax (21) 9405730; Chair. Dr Nthato Motlana; Man. Dir Marius Smith.

Momentum Life Assurers Ltd: Momentum Park, 267B West Ave, Centurion 0157; POB 7400, Centurion 0046; tel. (12) 6718911; fax (12) 6718209; f. 1967; Man. Dir H. P. Meyer.

Mutual & Federal Insurance Co Ltd: Mutual Federal Centre, 28th Floor, 69 President St, Johannesburg 2001; tel. (11) 3749111; telex 487641; f. 1970; Chair. M. J. Levett; Man. Dir K. T. M. Saggers.

Old Mutual (South African Mutual Life Assurance Society): Mutualpark, Jan Smuts Drive, POB 66, Cape Town 8001; tel. (21) 5099111; telex 527201; fax (21) 5094444; f. 1845; Chair. M. J. Levett; Man. Dirs G. Griffin, G. S. van Niekerk.

President Insurance Co Ltd: Rentmeester Park, 74 Watermeyer St, Val de Grace 0184; tel. (12) 868100; telex 323281; Man. Dir J. K. Wasserfall.

Protea Assurance Co Ltd: Protea Assurance Bldg, Greenmarket Sq., POB 646, Cape Town 8000; tel. (21) 4887911; fax (21) 4887110; Man. Dir A. L. Tainton.

The Rand Mutual Assurance Co Ltd: POB 61413, Marshalltown 2107; tel. (11) 4976600; fax (11) 8344150; f. 1894; Chair. M. D. Tombs; Man. Dir A. J. E. Fivaz.

Santam Ltd: Santam Bldg, Burg St, Cape Town 8001, POB 653, Cape Town 8000; tel. (21) 4804111; fax (21) 244572; f. 1918; Chair. M. H. Daling; Man. Dir J. J. Geldenhuys.

South African Eagle Insurance Co Ltd: Eagle House, 70 Fox St, Johannesburg 2001; POB 61489, Marshalltown 2107; tel. (11) 3709111; telex 485370; fax (11) 8365541; CEO P. T. Martin.

South African National Life Assurance Co (SANLAM): Strand Rd, Bellville, POB 1, Sanlamhof 7532; tel. (21) 9479111; fax (21) 9478066; f. 1918; Chair. Marinus Daling; Man. Dir Desmond Smith.

South African Trade Union Assurance Society Ltd: Capital Alliance Life Ltd, 162 Anderson St, Johannesburg 2000; tel. (11) 3301000; fax (11) 3301013; f. 1941; Chair. E. van Tonder; Gen. Man. A. Sumner.

The Southern Life Association Ltd: Great Westerford, Main Rd, Rondebosch, Cape Town 7700; tel. (21) 6580911; telex 527621; fax (21) 6891323; f. 1891; Chair. T. N. Chapman.

Standard General Insurance Co Ltd: Standard General House, 12 Harrison St, POB 4352, Johannesburg 2000; tel. (11) 8362723; telex 487320; fax (11) 8344935; f. 1943; Man. Dir Dr R. Grandi.

Swiss Re Southern Africa Ltd: Swiss Park, 10 Queens Rd, Parktown, POB 7049, Johannesburg 2000; tel. (11) 4895600; telex 427556; fax (11) 6432929; f. 1950; Chair. and Man. Dir L. Keel.

UBS Insurance Co Ltd: United Bldgs, 6th Floor, cnr Fox and Eloff Sts, Johannesburg; Chair. P. W. Sceales; Gen. Man. J. L. S. Hefer.

Westchester Insurance Co (Pty) Ltd: Mobil Court, POB 747, Cape Town 8000; tel. (21) 4034000.

Association

The South African Insurance Asscn: POB 30619, Braamfontein 2017; tel. (11) 4038150; f. 1973; represents short-term insurers; CEO B. Scott.

Trade and Industry

CHAMBER OF COMMERCE

South African Chamber of Business (SACOB): JCC House, 3rd Floor, Empire Rd, Milpark, Johannesburg; POB 91267, Auckland Park 2006; tel. (11) 4822524; fax (11) 7261344; f. 1990 by merger of Asscn of Chambers of Commerce and Industry and South African Federated Chamber of Industries; 85 chambers of commerce and industry are mems; Pres. R. Heinz; Dir-Gen. R. W. K. Parsons.

DEVELOPMENT ORGANIZATIONS

Industrial Development Corporation of South Africa Ltd (IDCSA): 19 Fredman Drive, POB 784055, Sandton 2146; tel. (11) 2693000; fax (11) 2693116; f. 1940; Chair. C. H. Wiese; Man. Dir K. Ngqula.

The Independent Development Trust: 129 Bree St, Cape Town 8001, POB 16114, Vlaeberg 8018; tel. (21) 238030; fax (21) 238401; f. 1990; finances health and rural devt, housing and urban devt, micro-enterprises, education, school and clinic-building projects; Chair. Dr Mamphela Ramphele.

National Productivity Institute: POB 3971, Pretoria 0001; tel. (12) 3411470; fax (12) 441866; e-mail npiinfo@cis.co.za; f. 1968; Exec. Dir Dr J. H. Visser.

CHAMBERS OF INDUSTRIES

Bloemfontein Chamber of Trade and Industry: POB 87, Kellner Heights, Bloemfontein 9300; tel. (51) 473368; fax (51) 475064.

Cape Chamber of Commerce and Industry: Cape Chamber House, 19 Louis Gradner St, Foreshore, Cape Town 8001; tel. (21) 4184300; fax (21) 4181800; f. 1994; Exec. Dir Alan Lighton; 3,800 mems.

Durban Regional Chamber of Business: POB 1506, Durban 4000; tel. (31) 3013692; fax (31) 3045255; Dir G. W. Tyler; 8,500 mems.

Johannesburg Chamber of Commerce and Industry: JCC House, 6th Floor, Empire Road, Milpark; Private Bag 34, Auckland

Park 2006; tel. (11) 7265300; fax (11) 4822000; e-mail jcci@cis.co.za; Pres. M. LEOKA; 5,000 mems.

Northern Transvaal Chamber of Industries: Showground Office, Soutter St, Pretoria 0001; tel. (12) 3271487; telex 320245; fax (12) 3271501; f. 1929; Exec. Dir J. G. TOERIEN; 350 mems (secondary industries).

Pietermaritzburg Chamber of Industries: POB 637, Pietermaritzburg 3200; tel. (331) 452747; fax (331) 944151; f. 1910; Dir R. J. ALLEN; 300 mems.

Port Elizabeth Regional Chamber of Commerce and Industry: Chamber House, 22 Grahamstown Rd, Port Elizabeth 6001, POB 2221, North End 6056; tel. (41) 544430; fax (41) 571851; f. 1995; CEO Chamber Div. K. WAKEFORD; 1,100 mems.

Wesvaal Chamber of Business: POB 7, Klerksdorp 2570; tel. (18) 4627401; fax (18) 4627402; Pres. J. LENNOX.

INDUSTRIAL ORGANIZATIONS

Armaments Corporation of SA Ltd (ARMSCOR): Private Bag X337, Pretoria 0001; tel. (12) 4281911; telex 320217; fax (12) 4285635; Exec. Chair. RON HAYWOOD.

Building Industries Federation South Africa: POB 1619, Halfway House 1685; tel. (11) 3151010; fax (11) 3151644; f. 1904; 5,300 mems.

Chamber of Mines of South Africa: Chamber of Mines Bldg, 5 Hollard St, POB 61809, Marshalltown 2107; tel. (11) 4987100; fax (11) 8341884; e-mail twood@bullion.org.za; f. 1889; Pres. Dr N. S. SEGAL.

Clothing Federation of South Africa: 42 Van der Linde St, Bedfordview 2008, POB 75755, Gardenview 2047; tel. (11) 6228125; fax (11) 6228316; f. 1945; Dir H. W. VAN ZYL.

ESKOM: POB 1091, Johannesburg 2000; tel. (11) 8008111; telex 424481; f. 1923; electricity supply; Chair. Dr JOHN B. MAREE.

FOSKOR Ltd: POB 1, Phalaborwa 1390; tel. (1524) 892911; telex 361012; fax (1524) 5531; Man. Dir D. R. VORSTER.

Grain Milling Federation: Johannesburg; f. 1944; Sec. J. BARENDSE.

Industrial Rubber Manufacturers' Asscn of South Africa: POB 91267, Auckland Park 2006; tel. (11) 4822524; fax (11) 7261344; f. 1978; Chair. Dr D. DUNCAN.

Master Diamond Cutters' Asscn of South Africa: S.A. Diamond Centre, Suite 511, 240 Commissioner St, Johannesburg 2001; tel. (11) 3348890; fax (11) 3341748; f. 1928; 76 mems.

Motor Industries' Federation: POB 2940, Randburg 2125; tel. (11) 7892542; fax (11) 7894525; f. 1910; Dir W. FOURIE; 7,800 mems.

National Asscn of Automobile Manufacturers of South Africa: Nedbank Plaza, 1st Floor, cnr Church and Beatrix Sts, Pretoria 0002; POB 40611, Arcadia 0007; tel. (12) 3232003; fax (12) 3263232; f. 1935; Dir N. M. W. VERMEULEN.

National Chamber of Milling, Inc: Braamfontein; tel. (11) 4033739; f. 1936; Dir Dr J. B. DE SWARDT.

National Textile Manufacturers' Asscn: POB 1506, Durban 4000; tel. (31) 3013692; fax (31) 3045255; f. 1947; Sec. PETER MCGREGOR; 9 mems.

Plastics Federation of South Africa: 18 Gazelle Rd, Corporate Park, Old Pretoria Rd, Midrand, Private Bag X68, Halfway House 1685; tel. (11) 314-4021; fax (11) 314-3764; f. 1979; Exec. Dir W. NAUDÉ; 3 mems.

Printing Industries Federation of South Africa: Printech Ave, Laser Park, POB 1084, Honeydew 2040; tel. (11) 7943810; fax (11) 7943964; f. 1916; CEO C. W. J. SYKES.

SOEKOR (Pty) Ltd: POB 307, Parow 7500; tel. (21) 9383911; fax (21) 9383144; f. 1965; responsible for all offshore petroleum and natural gas prospecting in South Africa; CEO M. J. HEÜSER.

South African Brewing Industry Employers' Asscn: Private Bag 34, Auckland Park 2006; tel. (11) 7265300; telex 425594; f. 1927; Sec. L. I. GOLDSTONE; 2 mems.

South African Cement Producers' Asscn: POB 168, Halfway House 1685; tel. (11) 3150300; fax (11) 3150584.

South African Dairy Foundation: POB 72300, Lynnwood Ridge 0040; tel. (2712) 3485345; fax (2712) 3486284; f. 1980; Sec. S. L. VAN COLLER; 59 mems.

South African Federation of Civil Engineering Contractors: POB 644, Bedfordview 2008; tel. (11) 4551700; fax (11) 4551153; f. 1939; Exec. Dir R. R. VALENTE; 230 mems.

South African Fruit and Vegetable Canners' Asscn (Pty) Ltd: Canning Fruit Board Bldg, 258 Main St, POB 6172, Paarl 7622; tel. (2211) 611308; fax (2211) 25930; f. 1953; Sec. T. R. M. MALONE; 12 mems.

South African Inshore Fishing Industry Asscn (Pty) Ltd: POB 2066, Cape Town 8000; tel. (21) 251500; telex 527259; f. 1953; Chair. W. A. LEWIS; Man. S. J. MALHERBE; 4 mems.

South African Lumber Millers' Asscn: Private Bag 686, Isando 1600; tel. (11) 9741061; fax (11) 9749779; f. 1941; Exec. Dir J. H. MORTIMER; 88 mems.

South African Oil Expressers' Asscn: Cereal Centre, 6th Floor, 11 Leyds St, Braamfontein 2017; tel. (11) 7251280; telex 422526; f. 1937; Sec. Dr R. DU TOIT; 14 mems.

South African Paint Manufacturers' Asscn: 39 Field St, Durban 4001, POB 1506, Durban 4000; tel. (31) 3013692; fax (31) 3045255.

South African Petroleum Industry Asscn (SAPIA): Cape Town; Dir. COLIN MCCLELLAN.

South African Sugar Asscn: 6 Durban Club Place, Durban 4001; POB 507, Durban 4000; tel. (31) 3056161; telex 622215; fax (31) 3044939; Exec. Dir MICHAEL J. A. MATHEWS.

South African Wool Board: POB 2191, Port Elizabeth 6056; tel. (41) 544301; telex 242329; fax (41) 546760; f. 1946; 12 mems: nine appointed by wool-growers and three by the Minister of Agriculture; Chair. H. F. PRINSLOO; CEO Dr J. W. GIESELBACH.

South African Wool Textile Council: POB 2201, North End, Port Elizabeth 6056; tel. (41) 545252; fax (41) 545629; f. 1953; Sec. C. THOMAS.

Steel and Engineering Industries Federation of South Africa (SEIFSA): POB 1338, Johannesburg 2000; tel. (11) 8336033; fax (11) 8381522; f. 1943; Exec. Dir. B. ANGUS; nine affiliated trade asscns representing 2,700 mems.

Sugar Manufacturing and Refining Employers' Asscn: 6 Durban Club Place, 11th Floor, POB 2278, Durban 4001; tel. (31) 3043551; fax (31) 3074241; f. 1947; Chair. L. FULLARTON.

TRADE ORGANIZATION

South African Foreign Trade Organization (SAFTO): POB 782706, Sandton 2146; tel. (11) 8833737; telex 424111; fax (11) 8836569; e-mail safto@apollo.is.co.za; f. 1963; Chair. W. C. VAN DER MERWE; CEO J. J. SCHEEPERS; 1,500 mems.

MAJOR INDUSTRIAL COMPANIES

The following are among the leading companies in South Africa.

AECI Limited: POB 1122, Johannesburg 2000; tel. (11) 8068700; fax (11) 8068701; f. 1924; cap. R4,000m.; mfrs of explosives, industrial and agricultural chemicals, paints, synthetic yarns and plastic raw materials; Chair L. BOYD; Man. Dir M. P. SMITH; 15,600 employees.

Alpha Ltd: 94 Rivonia Rd, POB 781868, Sandton 2146; tel. (11) 7835143; telex 422075; f. 1934; cap. R15,038,000; major producer of cement, stone aggregates, lime, industrial minerals and ready-mixed concrete, with extensive interests in manufacture of paper sacks and fertilizers; Chair. P. BYLAND; Man. Dir J. G. PRETORIUS; 4,079 employees.

Barlow Rand Ltd: POB 782248, Sandton 2146; tel. (11) 8019111; fax (11) 4443643; f. 1902; auth. cap. R22.3m. (1984); South Africa's largest industrial group with about 400 operating cos, employing 151,000 people; these operations are managed through a central group exec. cttee and 11 decentralized autonomous divisions; consolidated group turnover in 1991 was R31,994m., and total assets were R19,050m.; Rand Mines administers group's gold, coal and base minerals interests. Industrial interests include manufacture of cement and lime, electronics and telecommunications, electrical engineering, paint, consumer electrical products, packaging and paper products, sugar, food, animal feeds, pharmaceuticals and textiles; distributors of computers, earthmoving equipment, motor vehicles, building and construction supplies; operates mainly in southern Africa, with trading investments in UK, Europe and USA; Chair. W. A. M. CLEWLOW; Man. Dir D. E. COOPER.

CNA Gallo Ltd: POB 9380, Johannesburg 2000; tel. (11) 4822600; fax (11) 7261374; cap. R930m.; core businesses of the group are the CNA and Literary Group chains of retail stores and manufacture and distribution of gramophone records, music cassettes, compact discs and video cassettes, and music publishing; activities of support subsidiaries and associate cos include manufacture and sale of greeting cards and stationery, general book publishing, freight forwarding and clearing, business training and film production and distribution; Chair. D. D. B. BAND.

Consolidated Textile Mills Ltd (Frame Group): POB 12017, Jacobs 4026, Natal; telex 650070; f. 1930; group of cos in South Africa, Malawi and Zimbabwe producing clothing and textiles; Jt Man. Dirs A. BERMAN, S. LURIE, S. R. PEIMER; over 35,000 employees.

ICS Holdings Ltd: Harrowdene Office Park, Bldg 4, Western Service Rd, Woodmead, POB 783854, Sandton 2152; tel. (11) 8045780; fax (11) 8044173; f. 1902; cap. R11.5m.; processes and distributes red meat, poultry and meat products, milk and milk products, ice cream, fish; Chair. R. A. WILLIAMS; Man. Dir R. V. SMITHER; 16,000 employees.

Irvin and Johnson Ltd: Standard Bank Centre, 20th Floor, POB 1628, Cape Town 8000; tel. (21) 216400; telex 527268; fax (21)

217258; f. 1937; trawler operators; processors, distributors and exporters of frozen fish, vegetables and pastries; Sec. C. SCHOEMAN; 8,000 employees.

LTA Ltd: POB 312, Johannesburg 2000; tel. (11) 9235000; telex 744811; fax (11) 3973422; f. 1889; investment holding co; active in all aspects of the construction industry, inc. building, civil and electrical engineering, steel reinforcing and industrialized building systems; Chair. C. J. M. WOOD; Man. Dir C. V. CAMPBELL; 15,000 employees.

Nampak Ltd: 114 Dennis Rd, Athol Gardens, POB 784324, Sandton 2146; tel. (11) 4447418; telex 424179; fax (11) 4444794; f. 1968; cap. R16.3m.; mfrs of packaging in various forms based on paper, paper board, metal, glass and plastics; there are subsidiaries in the service area and fields allied to packaging; Chair. BRIAN CONNELLAN; Man. Dir TREVOR EVANS; 20,000 employees.

Premier Group Holdings Ltd: POB 1530, Johannesburg 2000; tel. (11) 4469111; telex 430735; f. 1913; cap. R1,777m. (1985); holding co controlling Premier Food Industries Ltd with wheat and maize mills, bakeries, edible oils, fats, margarine and derivatives, animal feed factories, poultry and crop farms, sugar and cotton processing, retail liquor outlet, music companies, bookshops, distribution and wholesaling division, stationery division, and pharmaceutical divisions both manufacturing and wholesale; Chair. (vacant); 31,000 employees.

Pretoria Portland Cement Co Ltd: POB 3811, Johannesburg 2000; tel. (11) 4821300; telex 245033; fax (11) 7263537; f. 1892; cap. R40m.; mfrs and distributors of cement, lime and limestone products, paper sacks and other containers; also mines and markets gypsum; Chair. J. C. HALL; Group Man. Dir J. E. GOMERSALL; 3,490 employees.

Protea Holdings Cape (Pty) Ltd: POB 3839, Cape Town 8000; tel. (21) 512357; telex 577551; f. 1963; Man. Dir A. WOLFAARDT; 100 employees.

SAPPI Ltd: POB 31560, Braamfontein 2017; tel. (11) 4078111; telex 422050; fax (11) 3391846; f. 1936 as South African Pulp and Paper Industries Ltd; eight pulp and paper mfg and processing subsidiaries; turnover: R15,271m. (1996); Exec. Chair. EUGENE VAN AS; 23,000 employees.

C. G. Smith Sugar Ltd: POB 194, Durban 4000; tel. (31) 3051511; telex 620610; f. 1913; cap. R419m.; operation of five sugar mills in Natal and one in Transvaal, accounting for 40% of all South African sugar production, and of three white sugar refineries and ancillary packaging, warehousing and distribution concerns; manufacture of syrup; operation of three chemical factories producing furfural, furfuryl alcohol, ethyl alcohol, hydrogen peroxide and dimethyl ether; Man. Dir G. TAYLOR; 6,020 permanent employees.

The South African Breweries Ltd: 2 Jan Smuts Ave, POB 1099, Johannesburg; tel. (11) 3394711; telex 422482; fax (11) 3391830; f. 1895; cap. R155.7m.; largest non-mining industrial group in sub-Saharan Africa; brewing and marketing of beer; mfrs, wholesalers and retailers of furniture, footwear, domestic appliances, plate glass, textiles, natural fruit juices and soft drinks; discount department, food and fashion chain stores; also owns and operates hotels; Exec. Chair. (vacant); Man. Dir GRAHAM MACKAY; 91,000 employees.

SASOL Ltd: POB 5486, Johannesburg 2000; tel. (11) 4413111; telex 426778; fax (11) 7885092; group of cos operating the world's largest complex of oil-from-coal petrochemical installations; produces c. 130 products; Chair. J. A. STEGMANN; Exec. Dir ANDRÉ DU TOIT; 33,000 employees.

Stewarts and Lloyds Export: POB 1137, Johannesburg 2000; tel. (11) 4933000; telex 487010; fax (11) 4931440; f. 1902; cap. R12m.; export trading co manufacturing and distributing industrial metal products, e.g. steel tubing and fittings, valves, diesel engines and generators, pumps, irrigation equipment. Export Man. P. KEMP; 10,000 employees.

L. Suzman Ltd: 2 Elray St, Raedene POB 2188, Johannesburg 2192; tel. (11) 4851020; telex 422523; fax (11) 6401325; f. 1889; cap. R2.1m.; wholesale distribution of tobacco products and other consumer products; operates 26 brs in South Africa; Chair. P. R. S. THOMAS; Man. Dir C. J. VAN DER WALT; 1,000 employees.

The Tongaat-Hulett Group Ltd: POB 3, Tongaat, Natal 4400; tel. (322) 994000; telex 650171; fax (322) 923333; f. 1892 as Huletts Corpn; cap. R5,500m.; divisions operating in sugar cane growing and processing, food production and processing, textiles manufacture, building materials, aluminium products, speciality starches, property administration; Chair. Dr C. J. SAUNDERS; Man. Dir C. M. L. SAVAGE; 25,000 employees.

USKO Ltd: General Hertzog Rd, POB 48, Vereeniging, Transvaal; telex 743051; f. 1911; cap. R35m.; mfr of copper and aluminium conductor and associated products; Chair. F. P. KOTZEE; 770 employees.

Mining Companies

Anglo American Corporation of South Africa Ltd: POB 61587, Marshalltown 2107; tel. (11) 6389111; telex 487167; fax (11) 6383221; f. 1917; cap. and res exceeded R22,000m. in March 1995; market value of listed investments is R46,000m.; a mining financial house holding interests in mining, financial, industrial, insurance, commerce, banking and property cos. The corpn also makes available tech. and admin. services to, and acts as secretary of, mining and other cos; Chair. JULIAN OGILVIE THOMPSON.

Anglovaal Ltd: POB 1885, Saxonwold 2132; tel. (11) 2830000; fax (11) 2830007; f. 1933; mining, financial and industrial group with divisions operating in precious metal and base mineral mining and beneficiation, fishing, food and rubber production, packaging, construction, engineering, electronics, information technology, textiles; Chair. BASIL E. HERSOV; 80,000 employees.

De Beers Consolidated Mines Ltd: 36 Stockdale St, POB 616, Kimberley 8300; tel. (531) 807111; telex 280654; fax (531) 807210; cap. R24.9m.; group of diamond mining cos and allied interests; reorg. 1990, when foreign interests were transferred to De Beers Centenary AG (Switzerland); Chair. JULIAN OGILVIE THOMPSON (until Dec. 1997), N. OPPENHEIMER (designate); 14,000 employees.

Gencor Ltd: 6 Holland St, Johannesburg 2001; tel. (11) 3769111; telex 85830; fax (11) 8384716; fmrly General Mining Union Corpn; cap. R226m.; diversified group with investments in several cos incl. GENMIN, which administers mines producing gold, coal, platinum, ferro-alloys, and ENGEN, which has interests in petroleum refining and retail petrol sales; Chair. BRIAN GILBERTSON.

Gold Fields of South Africa Ltd: 75 Fox St, Johannesburg 2001, POB 61525, Marshalltown 2107; tel. (11) 6399111; telex 450044; fax (11) 6392101; includes four gold-producing cos, platinum, coal and base metals; Chair. ROBIN PLUMBRIDGE.

JCI Ltd: Consolidated Bldg, cnr Fox and Harrison Sts, Johannesburg 2001, POB 590, Johannesburg 2000; tel. (11) 3739111; telex 483787; fax (11) 8366130; f. 1889; mining house with major investments in gold, ferrochrome, coal and base metals; Man. Dir BILL NAIRN.

Palabora Mining Co Ltd: POB 65, Palaborwa 1390; tel. (1524) 802911; telex 331827; fax (1524) 2448; cap. R28,315,500; 39% held by Rio Tinto-Zinc Corpn; mining of copper, with by-products of magnetite, zirconia metals, uranium oxide, anode slimes, nickel sulphate, sulphuric acid and vermiculite; copper refining; Chair. A. J. LEROY; Man. Dir F. FENWICK.

Rand Mines Ltd: The Corner House, 15th Floor, 63 Fox St, Johannesburg 2001, POB 62370, Marshalltown 2107; tel. (11) 4912911; telex 489671; fax (11) 8345936; cap. and res exceed R718.4m.; 74.4% held by Barlow Rand Ltd; mining of gold, coal, mineral exploration, property development, management and financial services; Chair. and Dir D. T. WATT; 52,212 employees.

TRADE UNIONS

In 1994 the number of registered unions totalled 213, with a membership that represented about 24% of the economically active population. In addition there were an estimated 65 unregistered unions, with a membership of about 510,000.

Trade Union Federations

Congress of South African Trade Unions (COSATU): POB 1019, Johannesburg 2000; tel. (11) 3394911; fax (11) 3394060; f. 1985; 19 trade union affiliates representing about 1.6m. mems; Pres. JOHN GOMOMO; Gen. Sec. SAM SHILOWA.

Principal affiliates include:

Chemical Workers' Industrial Union: POB 18349, Dalbridge 4014; tel. (11) 259510; fax (11) 256680; Pres. D. GUMEDE; Gen. Sec. R. CROMPTON.

Construction and Allied Workers' Union: POB 1962, Johannesburg 2000; tel. (11) 230544; Pres. D. NGCOBO; Gen. Sec. L. MADUMA.

Food and Allied Workers' Union: POB 234, Salt River 7925; tel. (21) 6379040; fax (21) 6383761; Pres. ERNEST THERON; Gen. Sec. M. GXANYANA.

Health and Allied Workers' Union: POB 47011, Greyville 4023; tel. (11) 3063993; Gen. Sec. S. NGCOBO.

National Education, Health and Allied Workers' Union: POB 7549, Johannesburg 2000; tel. (11) 299665; Pres. R. MKHIZE; Gen. Sec. S. NJIKELANA.

National Union of Metalworkers of South Africa (NUMSA): POB 260483, Excom 2023; tel. (11) 8322031; fax (11) 8384092; Pres. M. TOM; Gen. Sec. ENOCH GODONGWANA; 240,000 mems (1994).

National Union of Mineworkers: POB 2424, Johannesburg 2000; tel. (11) 8337012; Pres. JAMES MOTLATSI; Gen. Sec. KGALEMA MOTLANTHE ; 350,000 mems.

Paper, Printing, Wood and Allied Workers' Union: POB 3528, Johannesburg 2000; tel. (11) 8344661; Pres. M. Ndou; Gen. Sec. S. Kubheka.

Post and Telecommunications Workers' Association: POB 260100, Excom 2023; tel. (11) 234351; Pres. K. Mosunkulu; Gen. Sec. V. A. Khumalo.

South African Clothing and Textile Workers' Union: POB 18359, Dolbridge 4014; tel. (11) 3011391; fax (11) 3017050; Pres. A. Ntuli; Gen. Sec. J. Copalyn; 185,000 mems.

South African Railways and Harbours Workers' Union: POB 8059, Johannesburg 2000; tel. (11) 8343251; fax (11) 8344664; Pres. J. Langa; Gen. Sec. M. Sebekoane.

Transport and General Workers' Union: POB 9451, Johannesburg 2000; tel. (11) 3319321; fax (11) 3315418; Pres. A. Ndlovu; Gen. Sec. R. Howard.

National Council of Trade Unions (NACTU): POB 10928, Johannesburg 2000; tel. (11) 3368031; fax (11) 3337625; f. 1986; fed. of 22 African trade unions; Pres. James Mdlalose; Gen. Sec. Cunningham McGukamu.

Principal affiliates include:

Building, Construction and Allied Workers' Union: POB 96, Johannesburg 2000; tel. (11) 236311; Pres. J. Seisa; Gen. Sec. V. Thusi.

Food Beverage Workers' Union of South Africa: POB 4871, Johannesburg 2000; tel. (11) 299527; Pres. M. L. Kwelemtini; Gen. Sec. L. Sikhakhane.

Hotel, Liquor and Catering Trade Employees' Union: POB 1409, Johannesburg 2000; tel. (11) 234039; Pres. E. Nkosi (acting); Gen. Sec. K. Keele (acting).

Metal and Electrical Workers' Union of South Africa: POB 3669, Johannesburg 2000; tel. (11) 3311012; fax (11) 3311117; e-mail mewusa@cis.co.za; f. 1989; Pres. Russell Sabor; Gen. Sec. Zithulele Cindi.

National Union of Farm Workers: POB 10928, Johannesburg 2000; tel. (11) 233054; fax (11) 237625; Pres. E. Musekwa; Gen. Sec. T. Moletsane.

National Union of Public Service Workers: POB 10928, Johannesburg 2000; tel. (11) 232812; Pres. K. Nthute; Gen. Sec. S. Radebe.

South African Chemical Workers' Union: POB 236, Johannesburg 2000; tel. (11) 288907; Pres. W. Thuthani; Gen. Sec. O. H. Ndaba.

Steel, Engineering and Allied Workers' Union of South Africa: POB 4283, Johannesburg 2001; tel. (11) 294867; fax (11) 294869; Pres. G. Mabidikama; Gen. Sec. N. Ramaema.

Transport and Allied Workers' Union of South Africa: POB 4469, Johannesburg 2000; Pres. A. Mahlatjie; Gen. Sec. M. Ramela.

SAAWU Federation of Unions: POB 10419, Marine Parade 4050; tel. (11) 3019127; 19 mems; Pres. M. Maboso; Gen. Sec. S. K. B. Kikine.

South African Confederation of Labour: POB 19299, Pretoria West 0117; tel. (12) 793271; 7 mems; Pres. I. J. Els; Sec. L. N. Celliers.

South African Independent Trade Unions Confederation—SAITUCO: f. 1995 by 14 independent trade unions that opposed the new draft legislation on labour relations; Pres. Piet Skhosana; Gen. Sec. Themba Ncalo.

Unaffiliated Trade Union

United Workers' Union of South Africa: f. 1986; controlled by the Inkatha Freedom Party.

Transport

Most of South Africa's railway network and the harbours and airways are administered by the state-owned Transnet Ltd. There are no navigable rivers. Private bus services are regulated to complement the railways.

Transnet Ltd: 8 Hillside Rd, Parktown, Johannesburg; POB 72501, Parkview 2122; tel. (11) 4887111; fax (11) 4887010; Chair. Prof. L. A. Tager; Man. Dir Dr Anton T. Moolman.

RAILWAYS

With the exception of commuter services, the South African railways system is operated by Spoornet Ltd (the rail division of Transnet). The network comprised 31,400 track-km in 1996, of which 16,946 km was electrified. Extensive rail links connect Spoornet with the rail networks of neighbouring countries.

Spoornet: Paul Kruger Bdg, 30 Wolmarans St, Private Bag X47, Johannesburg 2001; tel. (11) 7735090; telex 424087; fax (11) 7733033; CEO A. S. Le Roux.

ROADS

In 1995 the total road network was estimated at 182,580 km. This total comprised 2,480 km of motorways, 56,100 km of main roads and 124,000 km of secondary roads. Some 32.8% of the network was paved.

South African Roads Board: Dept of Transport, Private Bag X193, Pretoria 0001; tel. (12) 3283084; fax (12) 3283194; responsible for location, planning, design, construction and maintenance of national roads.

SHIPPING

The principal harbours are at Richards Bay, Cape Town, Port Elizabeth, East London, Durban and Saldanha Bay. The deep-water port at Richards Bay has been extended and its facilities upgraded. Both Richards Bay and Saldanha Bay are major bulk-handling ports, while Saldanha Bay also has an important fishing fleet.

More than 30 shipping lines serve South African ports. At the end of 1996 South Africa's merchant fleet had a total displacement of 371,396 grt.

Chief Directorate of Shipping: Dept of Transport, Private Bag X193, Pretoria 0001; tel. (12) 3093707; fax (12) 3237009; advises the Govt on matters connected with sea transport to, from or between South Africa's ports, incl. safety at sea, and prevention of pollution by oil; Chief Dir of Shipping Capt. B. R. Watt.

CIVIL AVIATION

Civil aviation is controlled by the Minister of Transport. The Chief Directorate: Civil Aviation Authority at the Department of Transport is responsible for licensing and control of domestic and international air services. The Airports Company owns and operates South Africa's nine principal airports, of which three (at Johannesburg, Cape Town and Durban) are classified as international airports.

South African Airways (SAA): Airways Towers, cnr Wolmarans and Rissick Sts, Braamfontein, POB 7778, Johannesburg 2000; tel. (11) 3561111; telex 425020; fax (11) 3338132; f. 1934; state-owned; internal passenger services linking all the principal towns; international services to Africa, Europe, N and S America and Asia; CEO Mike Myburgh.

COMAIR (Commercial Airways (Pty) Ltd): POB 7015, Bonaero Park 1622; tel. (11) 9210111; telex 746738; fax (11) 9733913; f. 1946; scheduled domestic, regional and international services; Chair. D. Novick; Man. Dir P. Van Hoven.

Airlink Airline: POB 7529, Bonaero Park 1622; tel. (11) 9732941; fax (11) 9732501; f. 1992; internal scheduled and chartered flights; Man. Dirs Rodger Foster, Barrie Webb.

Safair (Pty) Ltd: POB 938, Kempton Park 1620; tel. 9280000; telex 746043; fax 3951314; f. 1969; subsidiary of Safmarine Aircraft Charters and Leasing; aircraft charters, leasing, engineering and maintenance services; Chair. A. Z. Farr; CEO R. J. Boettger.

Air Cape (Pty) Ltd: POB D.F. Malan Airport, Cape Town 7525; tel. (21) 9340344; telex 520246; fax (21) 9348379; scheduled internal passenger services and charters, engineering services and aerial surveys; Chair. Dr P. van Aswegen; Gen. Man. G. A. Nortje.

Tourism

Tourism is an important part of South Africa's economy. The chief attractions for visitors are the climate, scenery and wildlife reserves. Tourist receipts provided an estimated US $2,100m. in foreign exchange in 1996. In 1994 Satour (see below) announced a five-year tourism development strategy that was aimed at maximizing the industry's contribution to the South African economy. In 1996 4,944,430 tourists visited South Africa.

South African Tourism Board (SATOUR): 442 Rigel Ave South, Erasmusrand 0181, Private Bag X164, Pretoria 0001; tel. (12) 3470600; fax (12) 454889; e-mail gcoetzee@is.co.za; f. 1947; 13 overseas brs; Exec. Dir R. Swart (acting).

Defence

In August 1996 the armed forces totalled 137,900: army an estimated 118,000, navy 5,500, air force 8,400 and a medical corps numbering 6,000. In addition, there was a paramilitary force within the police service numbering 140,000. Following the installation of a new government in May 1994, a new South African National Defence Force (SANDF), which numbered some 91,000, was established over a period of three years. The SANDF comprised members of the former South African armed forces, including an estimated 30,000 personnel from the former military wing of the African National Congress of South Africa, the Pan-Africanist Congress and the former 'homelands'.

Defence Expenditure: R11,027m. in the year ending 31 March 1996.

Chief of the South African National Defence Force: Gen. GEORGE MEIRING.

Education

School attendance is compulsory for children of all population groups between the ages of seven and 16 years. In 1992 total enrolment at primary and secondary schools was equivalent to 94% of the school-age population (91% of boys and 96% of girls). From 1991 state schools were permitted to admit pupils from all races, and in 1995 the government promised the right to free state education for all population groups. In 1993 the total enrolment at primary and secondary schools was equivalent to 98% of the school-age population (96% of boys; 100% of girls). During the 1980s universities, which were formerly racially segregated, began to admit students of all races. In 1996 there were 22 universities and 15 'technikons' (tertiary education institutions offering technical and commercial vocational training). In 1995, according to estimates by UNESCO, the rate of adult illiteracy averaged 18.2% (males 18.1%; females 18.3%). Expenditure on education by the central government in the year ending 31 March 1996 was R33,443m. (21.2% of total expenditure).

Bibliography

Abedian, I., and Standish, P. (Eds). *Economic Growth in South Africa: Selected Policy Issues*. Cape Town, Oxford University Press, 1992.

Abel, R. L. *Politics by Other Means: Law in the Struggle Against Apartheid, 1980–1994*. London, Routledge, 1995.

African National Congress. *The Reconstruction and Development Programme*. Johannesburg, Umanyano Publications, 1994.

Asmal, K., Asmal, L., and Robert, R. S. *Reconciliation Through Truth: A Reckoning of Apartheid's Criminal Governance*. Cape Town, David Philip, 1996.

Barnard, N., and Du Toit, J. *Understanding the South African Macro-Economy*. Pretoria, Van Schaik, 1992.

Bloomberg, C. *Christian Nationalism and the Rise of the Afrikaner Broederbond in South Africa, 1918–1948*. Bloomington, Indiana University Press, 1989.

Bond, P. *Commanding Heights and Community Control: New Economics for a New South Africa*. Johannesburg, Ravan Press, 1991.

Callinicos, L. *People's History of South Africa*. Johannesburg, Ravan Press. 3 vols. 1981–93.

Cameron, T., and Spies, S. B. (Eds). *Illustrated History of South Africa*. 3rd Edn. Gauteng, Halfway House, Southern Book Publishers, 1996.

Central Statistical Services, *South African Statistics*. Pretoria, Government Printer, biennial.

Christopher, A. J. *South Africa*. London, Longman, 1982.

Cloete, J. J. N. *Accountable Government and Administration for the Republic of South Africa*. Pretoria, Van Schaik, 1996.

Cole, K. (Ed.). *Sustainable Development for a Democratic South Africa*. London, Earthscan, 1994.

Davenport, T. R. H. *South Africa: A Modern History*. 4th Edn. London, Macmillan, 1991.

Davies, R., O'Meara, D., and Dlamini, S. *The Struggle for South Africa: A Reference Guide to Movements, Organizations and Institutions*. 2 vols. London, Zed Books, 1984.

De Beer, J., and Lourens, L. *Local Government: The Road to Democracy*. Midrand, Educum Publishers, 1995.

De Ville, J., and Steytler, N. (Eds). *Voting in 1999: Choosing an Electoral System*. Durban, Butterworth Publishers, 1996.

Du Pre, R. H. *Separate but Unequal: The 'Coloured' People of South Africa: A Political History*. Johannesburg, Jonathan Ball, 1994.

Du Toit, P. *State Building and Democracy in Southern Africa: Botswana, Zimbabwe and South Africa*. Washington, DC, US Institute of Peace Press, 1995.

Elphick, R., and Giliomee, H. (Eds). *The Shaping of South African Society, 1652–1820*. Cape Town, Longman, 1979.

Falkena, H. B. *Fundamentals of the South African Financial System*. Gauteng, Halfway House, Southern Book Publishers, 1993.

Falkena, H. B. (Ed.). *South African Financial Institutions*. Gauteng, Halfway House, Southern Book Publishers, 1992.

Faure, M., and Lane, J. E. (Eds). *South Africa: Designing New Political Institutions*. London, Sage Publications, 1996.

Gastrow, S. *Who's Who in South African Politics*. 5th Edn. Johannesburg, Ravan Press, 1995.

Hain, P. *Sing the Beloved Country: The Struggle for the New South Africa*. London, Pluto Press, 1996.

Hall, M. *The Changing Past: Farmers, Kings and Traders in Southern Africa, 1800–1860*. Cape Town, Philip, 1987.

Hammond-Tooke, D. *The Roots of Black South Africa: An Introduction to the Traditional Culture of the Black People of South Africa*. Johannesburg, Jonathan Ball, 1993.

Harber, A., and Ludman, B. *A-Z of South African Politics: The Essential Handbook 1994 / Weekly Mail and Guardian*. London, Penguin, 1995.

Heyns, S. *Parliamentary Pocketbook*. Cape Town, Institute for Democracy in South Africa, 1996.

James, W., et al. (Eds). *Now That We Are Free: Coloured Communities in a Democratic South Africa*. Rondebosch, Institute For a Democratic South Africa, 1996.

Johnson, R. W., and Schlemmer, L. (Eds). *Launching Democracy in South Africa: The First Open Election, April 1994*. New Haven, Yale University Press, 1996.

Konczacki, Z. A., and Konczacki, J. M. (Eds). *An Economic and Social History of South Africa*. London, Frank Cass, 1980.

Konczacki, Z. A., Parpart, J. L., and Shaw, T. M. (Eds). *Studies in the Economic History of Southern Africa*. Vol. II. London, Frank Cass, 1991.

Laband, J. P. C. *Rope of Sand: The Rise and Fall of the Zulu Kingdom in the Nineteenth Century*. Johannesburg, Jonathan Ball, 1995.

Le May, G. H. L. *The Afrikaners: An Historical Interpretation*. Oxford, Blackwell Publishers, 1995.

Lipton, M. *Capitalism and Apartheid: South Africa 1910–1984*. Aldershot, Hampshire, Maurice Temple Smith/Gower, 1985.

Lodge, T. *Black Politics in South Africa Since 1945*. London, Longman, 1983.

Marks, S., and Trapido, S. *The Politics of Race, Class and Nationalism in Twentieth Century South Africa*. London and New York, Longman, 1987.

Mayekiso, M. *Township Politics: Civic Struggles For a New South Africa*. New York, Monthly Review Press, 1996.

Meli, F. *South Africa Belongs To Us: A History of the ANC*. London, James Currey; Cape Town, Philip; Bloomington, Indiana University Press, 1989.

Nattrass, N., and Ardington, E. (Eds). *Political Economy of South Africa*. Cape Town, Oxford University Press, 1990.

Nicholson, J. (Ed.). *User's Guide to the South African Economy*. Durban, Y Press, 1994.

Oden, B., et al. *The South African Tripod: Studies on Economics, Politics and Conflict*. Uppsala, Nordiska Afrikainstitutet, 1994.

O'Meara, D. *Forty Lost Years: The Apartheid State and the Politics of the National Party*. Johannesburg, Ravan Press, 1996.

Omer-Cooper, J. D. *History of Southern Africa*. 2nd Edn. Cape Town, Philip, 1994.

Pakenham, T. *The Boer War*. London, Weidenfeld and Nicolson, 1979; Johannesburg, Jonathan Ball, 1992 (reprint).

Pampallis, J. *Foundations of the New South Africa*. London, Zed Books; Cape Town, Maskew Miller Longman, 1991.

Pollock, N. C., and Agnew, S. *An Historical Geography of South Africa*. London, Longman, 1963.

Preston-Whyte, E., and Rogerson, C. (Eds). *South Africa's Informal Economy*. Cape Town, Oxford University Press, 1991.

Ramphela, M. *The Affirmative Action Book: Towards an Equity Government*. Rondebosch, Institute for a Democratic South Africa, 1995.

Reader's Digest. *Illustrated History of South Africa*. 3rd Edn. Cape Town, 1994.

Reynolds, A. (Ed.). *Election '94 South Africa: The Campaigns, Results and Future Prospects.* Cape Town, David Philip, 1994.

Rogerson, C., and McCarthy, J. (Eds). *Geography in a Changing South Africa: Progress and Prospects.* Cape Town, Oxford University Press, 1992.

Roux, A. *Everyone's Guide to the South African Economy.* 4th Edn. Wynberg, Sandton, Zebra Books, 1996.

Sampson, A. *Black and Gold.* London, Hodder and Stoughton, 1987.

Saunders, C. *Historical Dictionary of South Africa.* Metuchen, NJ, Scarecrow Press, 1983.

Saunders, C. (Ed.). *Illustrated Dictionary of South African History.* Sandton, Ibise, 1994.

Schrire, R. (Ed.). *Wealth or Poverty: Critical Choices for South Africa.* Cape Town, Oxford University Press, 1992.

Simons, H. J., and Simons, R. E. *Class and Colour in South Africa, 1850–1950.* Harmondsworth, Middlesex, Penguin Books, 1969.

Smollan, R. *Black Advancement in the South African Economy.* Johannesburg, Macmillan Boleswa, 1993.

South African Institute of Race Relations. *South African Survey.* Johannesburg, annual.

Sparks, A. *Tomorrow is Another Country: The Inside Story of South Africa's Road to Change.* New York, Hill and Wang, 1995.

Thompson, L. *The Unification of South Africa 1902–1910.* Oxford, Clarendon Press, 1960.

History of South Africa. New Haven, Yale University Press, 1990.

United Nations. *United Nations and Apartheid 1984–1994.* New York and Geneva, United Nations Publications, 1995.

Vosloo, W. B. (Ed.). *Entrepreneurship and Economic Growth.* Pretoria, Human Sciences Research Council, 1994.

Wentzel, J. *The Liberal Slideaway.* Johannesburg, South African Institute of Race Relations, 1995.

Wilson, M., and Thompson, L. (Eds). *The Oxford History of South Africa.* Oxford, Clarendon Press, 1969–71.

History of South Africa to 1870. Cape Town, Philip, 1982. (Revised Edn of Vol. 1 of *The Oxford History of South Africa.*)

SUDAN

Physical and Social Geography

J. A. ALLAN

THE NILE

The River Nile and its tributaries form the basis of much of the economic activity of Sudan, and of most of the future activity that is now envisaged. The river traverses diverse landscapes, from the relatively humid tropical forest in the south to the arid deserts in the north. The Republic of Sudan has a total area of 2,505,813 sq km (967,500 sq miles), and the Nile waters which enter Sudan just south of Juba either evaporate or flow 3,000 km until they reach Lake Nubia on the Egyptian border. Even those which flow down the Blue Nile travel 2,000 km. The distances are vast, and the remoteness of places on the Nile system, not to speak of those in the deserts, savannah and swamps of the rest of the country, explains much of the character of Sudan's land use. The other important factor is climate, which influences vegetation and, more significantly, affects the seasonal flow of the Nile tributaries.

The Blue Nile is the main tributary, both in the volume of water which it carries (four-sevenths of the total average flow of the system) as well as in the area of irrigated land, of which it supports over 40% of the present area and 70% of potential irrigable land. The Blue Nile and other east-bank tributaries are sustained by monsoon rains over the Ethiopian highlands which cause the river to flood at the end of July, reach a peak in August and remain high through September and the first half of October. The Atbara, another seasonal east-bank tributary, provides a further one-seventh of the flow in the system, and the remaining two-sevenths come from the White Nile. The sustained flow of the White Nile arises firstly because its main source is Lake Victoria, which regulates the flow, and secondly because the swamps of the Sudd and Machar act as a reservoir, absorbing the irregular stream flow from the south while discharging a regular flow, much reduced by evaporation, in the north.

The River Nile is an international river system, and Sudan depends on river flows from seven other states. Sudan does not yet use all of the 18,500m. cu m of annual flow agreed with Egypt in 1959 as its share of the total average flow at Aswan of 84,000m. (Egypt receives 55,500m. cu m, while 10,000m. cu m are assumed to evaporate annually from Lake Nasser/Nubia). In anticipation of future additional demand by upstream states such as Ethiopia, and in view of Egypt's rising demand for water, Sudan and Egypt jointly embarked in 1978 on the construction of the Jonglei Canal project, which will eventually conserve some 4,000m. cu m of the 33,000m. cu m of water lost annually through evaporation in the Sudd swamp. The Machar swamps will also yield water at a rate as yet undetermined, but likely to be about 4,000m. cu m per year (3,240m. cu m at Aswan).

PHYSICAL FEATURES AND CLIMATE

Sudan is generally a flat, featureless plain reflecting the proximity to the surface of the ancient Basement rocks of the African continent. The Basement is overlain by the Nubian Sandstone formation in the centre and north-west of the country, and by the Umm Ruwaba formation in the south. These formations hold groundwater bodies which are of agricultural significance. No point in the country is very high above sea-level. Elevations rise to 3,187 m on Mt Kinyeti, near the Uganda border, and to 3,071 m on Jabel Marrah, an extinct volcano, in west central Sudan near the frontier with Chad. Some idea of the level character of the landscape is provided by the small amount of the fall in the Blue Nile, which starts its 2,000-km flow through Sudan at 500 m above sea-level at the Ethiopian border and formerly flowed past Wadi Halfa (now flooded) at an elevation of 156 m. It now flows into Lake Nubia at 180 m above sea-level. The White Nile, as it emerges from Uganda, falls some 600 m between the border and Khartoum, a distance of 1,700 km, but falls only 17 m in the last 700 km from entering the southern clay plains.

Average temperatures and rainfall change steadily from month to month, except where the effect of the Ethiopian highlands disturbs the east-west trend in the climatic belts in the south-east. The north of Sudan is a desert, with negligible rainfall and high average daily temperatures (summer 35°C, winter 20°C). Low temperatures occur only in winter. Rainfall increases steadily south of Khartoum (200 mm per year), reaching over 1,000 mm per year at the southern border. Rainfall varies from year to year, especially in the north, and is seasonal. In the south it falls in the period April–October; the rainy season is progressively shorter towards the north, where it lasts only from July until August. Potential evaporation approaches 3,000 mm per year in the north and is always over 1,400 mm per year, even in the humid south.

VEGETATION AND SOILS

The soil resources of Sudan are rich in agricultural potential. Their exploitation, however, depends on the availability of the limiting factor, water, and only a small proportion of the clay plains of central and east Sudan are currently farmed intensively. Clay soils also occur in the south, being deposits of the White Nile and Sobat streams. Recent alluvium provides a basis for productive agriculture in the narrow Nile valley north of Khartoum. Elsewhere, in the west and north the soils are sandy, with little agricultural potential, except in the dry valleys, which generally contain some soil moisture.

Vegetation is closely related to the climatic zones. From the desert in the north vegetation gradually improves through semi-arid shrub to low woodland savannah characterized by acacia and short grasses. Progressively higher rainfall towards the south promotes trees and shrubs as well as herbs, while the more reliably watered rangeland of the Bahr al-Arab provides an important seasonal resource for the graziers from the poor pastures of Darfur and Kordofan. The flooded areas of the Sudd and Machar and environs support swamp vegetation and grassland. On the uplands of the southern border, rainfall is sufficient to support tropical rain forest.

During 1984–85 and again in the early 1990s large areas of Sudan were affected by drought, and it was estimated that thousands of people faced starvation, particularly in the western provinces of Darfur and Kordofan.

POPULATION

The population of Sudan was enumerated at 24,940,683 at the census held in April 1993, compared with 20,594,197 in February 1983 and 14,113,590 in April 1973. According to official estimates, the population increased at an annual average rate of 3.0% in 1985–94. According to provisional estimates, the population was 28,947,000 at mid-1994. At the 1983 census about 71% of the population resided in rural areas, 18% in urban and semi-urban areas and the remaining 11% were nomadic. The population is concentrated in Khartoum province and the Central Region, where population densities were, respectively, 55 and 28 per sq km in 1973, compared with 3.6–6.8 per sq km elsewhere. Agricultural development in the two most populous regions created employment opportunities and this led to the doubling of these populations between 1956 and 1973, compared with rises of between zero and 50% elsewhere. There are local concentrations of population in the Nuba mountains and higher densities than average in better-farmed parts of the Southern and Darfur Regions.

The ethnic origin of the people of Sudan is mixed, and the country is still subject to significant immigration by groups from Nigeria and Chad, such as the Fulani. In the south the Nuer, the Dinka and the Shilluki are the most important of the Nilotic peoples. The Arab culture and language predominate in the north, which includes the most populous provinces and the capital, Khartoum. The south is predominantly Christian and this cultural difference, added to the ethnic separateness and its extreme remoteness, has been expressed in economic backwardness and a tendency to political distinctness, which have been the main cause of persistent unrest in Southern Sudan.

The capital, Khartoum, had an estimated population of 924,505 at the 1993 census. It is the main administrative, commercial and industrial centre of the country. The neighbouring city of Omdurman had 228,778 inhabitants, thus creating, with Khartoum, a conurbation of some 1.2m. inhabitants. As communications are very poor and since Khartoum is at least 1,000 km away from 80% of the country, the influence which the capital exerts on the rest of the country is small. The relatively advanced character and general success of much of the irrigated farming on the east-central clay plains has led to a predominance of investment there and to the misguided impression that the success of the east-central plains could be transferred to other parts of the country where the resources are unfortunately much less favourable. Much of Sudan is so dry for part of each year that the only possible way to use the land and vegetation resources is by grazing, and tribes such as the Bagara traverse the plains and plateaux of Darfur and Kordofan in response to the availability of fodder.

Recent History

THOMAS OFCANSKY

With revisions by the Editor

The scramble for Africa which dominated the closing decades of the 19th century convinced the British government that it was necessary to bring the Sudan under British control. In order to avoid direct conflict with the French and other European powers in central Africa, it was decided that the conquest should be undertaken in the name of Egypt, as a reaffirmation of control over what was described as Egyptian territory temporarily disrupted by the Mahdist rebellion. The reconquest, begun in 1896 by combined British and Egyptian forces, culminated in the defeat of the Mahdist forces at Omdurman in 1898.

The Anglo-Egyptian agreement of 1899 established a nominally Anglo-Egyptian administration that was, in fact, a British colonial government, headed by a governor-general. Egyptian groups and officials who served as intermediaries between British and Sudanese were withdrawn in 1924, following the assassination in Cairo of Sir Lee Stack, the governor-general of the Sudan and c-in-c of the Egyptian army, and a system of 'Indirect Rule' through tribal chiefs was introduced. This was paralleled in the South by a new 'Southern Policy' aimed at eventually assimilating the three Southern provinces into a British-controlled East African Federation. Both forms of administration were unpopular with the growing nationalist movement, which began to mobilize in the mid-1930s. In response to this pressure for increased Sudanese participation in government in preparation for full independence, changes in the administration were introduced, leading to the establishment of an advisory council for Northern Sudan in 1943 and a legislative assembly for the whole country in 1948. The establishment of these institutions provoked a split in the nationalist ranks, with one group—led by the Umma Party (UP) and supported by the Mahdists—feeling that independence could be best achieved by co-operating with the British in the new institutions. Another group, distrustful of the British, supported co-operation with Egypt. Standing for 'The Unity of the Nile Valley' and supported by the Khatmiyya, the chief rival of the Mahdists among the religious fraternities, this group boycotted both council and assembly. However, the latter group's links with the Egyptian establishment were broken by the Egyptian revolution of 1952, clearing the way for a separate settlement of the Sudan question.

An agreement between Britain and the new Egyptian administration in 1953 set out a programme for self-determination for the Sudan and elections were held, resulting in a victory for the National Unionist Party (NUP), whose leader, Ismail al-Azhari, became the first Sudanese prime minister in January 1954. It soon became clear that Sudanese opinion was overwhelmingly in favour of independence, with Southern members of parliament calling for a federal form of government. On 19 December 1955 parliament unanimously declared the Sudan an independent republic. Britain and Egypt were left with no choice but to recognize the Sudan's independence, which formally took effect on 1 January 1956.

POST-INDEPENDENCE UNREST

Soon after independence, Azhari's government was replaced by an uneasy coalition of the Mahdist-supported UP and the People's Democratic Party (PDP), the political organ of the Khatmiyya, with Abdallah Khalil, the UP secretary, as prime minister. After an inconclusive election in February 1958, the UP president, Sadiq al-Mahdi, sought an alliance with the NUP. This was opposed by Khalil, who sought the involvement of the military.

A military coup was launched in November 1958 by a group of officers led by Gen. Ibrahim Abboud, who won the support of civilian politicians with assurances that the junta aimed merely to restore stability and would relinquish power when this was achieved. The Abboud regime had some success in the economic sphere, but the extent of military involvement in government and allegations of corruption created growing discontent. The government also pursued a military solution to the problem of the South, where its operations against the *Anya Nya* rebels forced thousands of Southerners to flee to neighbouring countries. A campaign for the restoration of democratic government gathered momentum during 1964. This became a revolution when in October police fired on student demonstrators in Khartoum. A general strike brought the country to a standstill and Abboud was forced to surrender power to a civilian committee.

A transitional government was formed with representatives from all parties, including for the first time, the Sudanese Communist Party (SCP) and the Muslim Brotherhood. One of its first acts was to declare a general amnesty in the South. A conference of Northern and Southern parties, opening in Khartoum in March 1965, failed to reach agreement on the country's constitutional future—with Northern parties favouring a regional government for the South and the Southern parties divided between those which favoured federation and those seeking full independence—but did agree on a programme of immediate action, including repatriation of refugees and freedom of religion. Elections held in June led to the formation of a coalition government by the UP and the NUP, with the UP's Muhammad Ahmad Mahgoub as prime minister and Azhari as permanent president of the committee of five that acted as collective head of state.

The new government faced serious rebel activity in the South and large numbers of Southerners were killed in the course of reprisals by government troops. The government itself became increasingly right-wing, and in November 1965 the SCP was banned. A split meanwhile developed within the UP, with the more moderate members rallying around the party president, Sadiq al-Mahdi, in opposition to the prime minister. Defeated on a vote of censure in July 1966, Mahgoub resigned and al-Mahdi was elected prime minister at the head of another UP–NUP coalition.

With the help of stringent controls and loans from the World Bank and the International Monetary Fund (IMF), the economy began to revive. Meanwhile, progress had been made towards the settlement of the Southern problem on the basis of regional government. In April 1967 a 'parties conference' submitted a report recommending a regional solution. By this time the long-awaited supplementary elections in the South had been held, bringing 36 members to the constituent assembly, of whom 10, led by William Deng, represented the Sudan African National Union (SANU), the principal Southern party.

The relative success of al-Mahdi's government, however, led to a split in the coalition with the NUP, and in May 1967 al-Mahdi was defeated in the assembly and Mahgoub again became prime minister. The new government severed diplomatic relations with the USA and Britain following the Arab-Israeli war in June and developed closer relations with the Eastern bloc. Domestic problems, however, were neglected. After a series of defeats for the government in the constituent assembly, the assembly was dissolved in January 1968. At elections held in April, the Democratic Unionist Party (DUP), a new party formed by a merger of the NUP and PDP, won the largest number of seats. A coalition government, comprising the DUP and a faction of the UP, took office in May, again with Mahgoub as prime minister. Faced by worsening violence in the South and growing divisions within the coalition, the government survived only a little over a year, until it was overthrown in a bloodless coup, led by Col Gaafar Muhammad Nimeri, in May 1969.

THE NIMERI REGIME, 1969–85

Nimeri's first two years in power were characterized by the adoption of socialist policies and the forging of an alliance between the new military leadership and the SCP. The new regime claimed to be the true heirs of the October revolution of 1964, which it claimed had been betrayed by the traditional parties. The foundations for a one-party state, based on the Egyptian model, were laid with the formation of the Sudanese Socialist Union (SSU), and the country was renamed the Democratic Republic of the Sudan. Internal opposition was ruthlessly suppressed. The government declared its commitment to regional administrative autonomy for the South and set up a ministry for southern affairs. It developed closer relations with the Eastern bloc and followed a policy of militant support for the Palestinian cause. However, the announcement in November 1970 that presidents Nimeri, Qaddafi and Sadat had decided to unite Sudan, Libya and Egypt as a single federal state proved unacceptable to the communists, who staged a military coup, led by Maj. Hashim al-Ata, which resulted in the temporary overthrow of Nimeri in July 1971. With popular support, Nimeri was restored to power within three days. A purge of communists followed and 14 people were executed.

The attempted coup was followed by a cooling of relations with the Eastern bloc and a surge in the personal popularity of Nimeri, who won the first presidential election in Sudanese history in October 1971, gaining almost 4m. votes, with only 56,000 opposed. A new government was formed and the SSU recognized as the sole legal political party. The Addis Ababa Agreement, signed in March 1972 between the government and the *Anya Nya* rebels, appeared to establish the basis for a settlement by introducing regional autonomy for the three Southern provinces. A regional people's assembly was established in Juba with representatives in the national people's assembly and a higher executive council (HEC) of its own. The government also took a pragmatic line on economic policy, denationalizing companies previously taken over by the state and encouraging foreign investment.

The leaders of the traditional parties and their largely right-wing supporters, excluded from involvement in politics, organized themselves into a National Front (NF) which operated as a largely external opposition to the regime. Supported at different times by Libya, Iraq, Saudi Arabia and Ethiopia, the NF made several attempts to overthrow Nimeri. However, as the ideological differences between the government and the NF diminished, attempts at reconciliation began. In July 1977 Sadiq al-Mahdi, who had been under sentence of death, met Nimeri at Port Sudan. Subsequently large numbers of political detainees were released and many exiled members of the NF, including al-Mahdi, returned to Sudan, some to take up government posts.

Sudan's relations with Egypt, normally close, came under strain at the beginning of the 1980s, partly because of Sudan's desire to preserve close links with the rest of the Arab world at a time when Egypt was increasingly isolated by its signing of the Camp David accord with Israel. The assassination of President Sadat of Egypt in October 1981, and growing fears of Libyan attempts to destabilize the Nimeri regime, reinforced the feeling of need in the two regimes for closer co-operation. In October 1982 this culminated in the signing of a charter of integration between Egypt and Sudan, a 10-year agreement providing for political and economic integration and close co-operation in foreign policy, security and development. The charter created a 120-member Nile Valley parliament, a higher council for integration and a joint fund for financial and administrative independence. The charter was greeted with scepticism by many Sudanese and with opposition by Southern leaders who feared it would lead to a diminution of their role.

Prolonged discussions about decentralization led to the adoption in January 1980 of a plan whereby Sudan was to be divided into five regions (Northern, Eastern, Central, Kordofan and Darfur) in addition to Khartoum and the South, which would continue to enjoy a special status and administrative structure. Elections for a new people's assembly were held in December 1981, with its membership reduced from 366 to 155, as many of its powers had been devolved to the regions.

Meanwhile, relations between the government in Khartoum and the South were again deteriorating. A decision to sub-divide the South into three sub-regions to avoid the domination of one ethnic group (the Dinka), eventually implemented in May 1983, was opposed by many Southerners, who feared it would weaken their collective position *vis-à-vis* the North. Southern resentment was also aroused by the decision that petroleum from the newly-discovered oilfields astride the traditional boundaries of the two regions would not be refined locally but exported via a pipeline to Port Sudan, and by fears that the Jonglei Canal project would benefit Northerners and Egypt but have an adverse effect on the Southern population.

A major factor in the deepening crisis was the adoption by the Nimeri regime, after September 1983, of certain aspects (mainly penalties for criminal offences) of Islamic *Shari'a* law, followed by the introduction, after April 1984, of martial law. Despite the general popularity, in principle, of Islamization among the Northern Muslim majority, and regardless of official assurances that non-Muslims would not be adversely affected, many Southern Sudanese were now alienated to the point of armed insurrection. Commonly known as *Anya Nya II*, the revitalized rebel groups were organized into political and military wings, the Sudanese People's Liberation Movement (SPLM) and Sudanese People's Liberation Army (SPLA) respectively. In the course of 1983–84, the rebels engaged government forces in a series of battles, especially in Upper Nile and Bahr al-Ghazal.

Meanwhile, Nimeri's commitment to Islamization continued to attract some support among the mainly Muslim population of the North. The harsher penalties of the new legal code were enforced regardless of, and even contrary to, the teachings of the *Shari'a* itself. Corruption, which was inconsistent with the principles of the *Shari'a*, continued to proliferate within the ruling élite. No effective action was taken to institutionalize the principle of *shura*, or consultation, in government. On the contrary, proposals to amend the 1973 constitution were formally introduced in the people's assembly in July 1984. Under these proposals, Nimeri was to be created Imam and given even greater powers than he had previously exercised. Prominent among the burgeoning opposition was Sadiq al-Mahdi, who viewed Nimeri's Islamization policies as a gross distortion of Islamic principles. Relations between Nimeri and Hassan at-Turabi's faction of the Muslim Brotherhood deteriorated, both because the Brotherhood was ignored in the formulation of Islamization policies and because it was potentially a formidable contender for political power, although formally allied to the regime since 1977.

As the country sank deeper into economic disarray, Nimeri's dependence on his Western allies (especially the USA), and their influence over him, correspondingly increased. Eventually he was persuaded not only to acquiesce in the wishes of the IMF in the removal of food subsidies and the further devaluation of the currency, but also to consent to participate in the evacuation from Ethiopia to Israel of several thousand Falasha Jews, an action which contravened Sudan's commitments as a member of the Arab League. By the end of February 1985 disillusionment with the regime and its policies, both internal and external, was rapidly crystallizing. At this late juncture, Nimeri moved to deal with the Muslim Brotherhood by putting its leaders on trial for sedition and, by so doing, alienated his last vestiges of popular support. Public sentiment was also being rapidly alienated by the government's failure to deal with the effects of the prolonged drought and the problems created by the continued influx of refugees from Ethiopia, Chad and Uganda. Nimeri reacted to this situation by adopting a conciliatory stance. The state of emergency was lifted, and the operation of the special courts was suspended, while an offer was made to revoke the redivision of the South if a majority of Southerners desired it. Nimeri also reshuffled the council of ministers and presidential council. Among those appointed in March 1985 was Lt-Gen. Abd ar-Rahman Swar ad-Dahab, receiving the posts of minister of defence and c-in-c of the armed forces.

MILITARY COUP

Public discontent with Nimeri's regime reached its culmination in March 1985, exacerbated by substantial increases in the price of food and fuel, and Khartoum was immobilized by a general strike. On 6 April, while Nimeri was visiting the USA, he was deposed in a bloodless military coup, led by Lt-Gen. Swar ad-Dahab. A state of emergency was declared, and a transitional military council (TMC) was appointed. After two weeks of negotiations with the various organizations which had worked for Nimeri's downfall, a 15-member council of ministers, including three non-Muslim Southerners, was announced. Dr Gizuli Dafallah, a trade unionist who had been a prominent organizer of the general strike, was appointed prime minister. The council of ministers was to be responsible to the TMC during a 12-month transitional period prior to the holding of free elections, scheduled for April 1986. Hundreds of Nimeri's officials were arrested, and the SSU was dissolved.

In response to the coup, the SPLM initially declared a cease-fire, but presented the new regime with a series of demands concerning the Southern Region. Swar ad-Dahab offered various concessions to the South, including the cancellation of the redivision and the reinstatement of the Southern HEC in Juba, with Maj.-Gen. James Loro, a member of the TMC, as its interim president. The SPLM rejected these terms, broke off negotiations with the TMC, and resumed hostilities. The civil war in the South continued throughout 1985, with many Southern towns under siege. In an attempt to reach agreement with the SPLM, a conference was held in March 1986 in Addis Ababa, Ethiopia, between the SPLM and the National Alliance for Salvation (NAS), a semi-official alliance of trade unionists and politicians who supported the government. The SPLM insisted that the retention of the *Shari'a* remained a major obstacle to national unity; the NAS agreed to abolish the *Shari'a* and, in response to another of the rebels' demands, to end military links with Libya and Egypt; however, these measures were not implemented by the TMC before the April 1986 election.

Despite these difficulties, Swar ad-Dahab promised a return to civilian rule after a 12-month interim period. A transitional constitution was signed in October 1985; under its provisions, numerous political groupings began to emerge in preparation for the forthcoming general election. In December the name of the country was changed to 'the Republic of Sudan', thus restoring the official designation to its pre-1969 form.

The TMC's foreign policy during its 12-month rule reversed Nimeri's strongly pro-Western stance. While advocating a policy of non-alignment, the TMC sought to improve relations with Ethiopia, Libya and the USSR, to the concern of Sudan's former allies, Egypt and the USA. A military co-operation agreement was signed with Libya in July 1985, and diplomatic relations were quickly restored between Sudan, Libya and Ethiopia. Relations also improved with Iran, which had been one of the main adversaries of Nimeri's government. In November links with Egypt were reaffirmed. Relations with the USA, already viewed with suspicion (owing to the US government's former support for Nimeri), were further strained after an attack on Libya by US aircraft in April 1986.

CIVILIAN COALITIONS AND REGIONAL UNREST

More than 40 political parties participated in the general election held in April 1986. As expected, no single party won an outright majority of seats in the assembly, but Sadiq al-Mahdi's UP won the largest number (99), followed by the DUP, led by Osman al-Mirghani (63 seats), and the National Islamic Front (NIF) of Dr Hassan at-Turabi (with 51 seats). The newly elected assembly was, however, unable to agree on the composition of the new government; following protracted negotiations over the allocation of portfolios, a broadly-based administration was formed in May; the council of ministers comprised of a coalition of the UP and the DUP, with, in addition, four portfolios allocated to Southern parties. Sadiq al-Mahdi became prime minister and minister of defence. He urged the Southern rebels to negotiate a peaceful settlement, and promised that *Shari'a* law would be abolished and the state of emergency lifted. In foreign policy, al-Mahdi undertook to maintain the non-aligned policy of the TMC, which was dissolved in preparation for the return to civilian rule. Swar ad-Dahab relinquished the posts of head of state (being replaced by a six-member supreme council, installed on 6 May) and of military c-in-c.

In an attempt to make the new government acceptable to the Southerners, a special portfolio, the ministry of peace and unity, had been created for a member of the NAS, and Col John Garang, leader of the SPLM, had been offered a post in the council of ministers. However, the SPLM refused either to recognize or take part in the new government. Tensions in the South continued to worsen; in early 1986 the SPLM launched a new offensive, and captured the town of Rumbek. In July 1986, however, al-Mahdi and Garang held direct talks for the first time, in Addis Ababa, but the only result was an agreement to maintain contacts.

In August 1986 further negotiations took place between the NAS and the SPLM, with the aim of convening a constitutional conference as a prelude to resolving the civil conflict. These discussions, however, ended abruptly when the SPLM shot down a Sudan Airways aircraft in the same month, killing 60 civilians on board. The SPLM launched a new offensive, with the aim of recapturing the four strategic Southern towns of Juba, Wau, Malakal and Bentiu.

Al-Mahdi attempted a new peace initiative in April 1987, with a suggestion to the SPLM of a two-week cease-fire, to be followed by a reopening of negotiations. By May, the military situation in the South had become so unstable that it appeared possible that the government might consent to the outright secession of three Southern provinces. In the same month a temporary council for the Southern Sudan (CSS) was established under the leadership of a Southern politician, Matthew Abor Ayang. The formation of this body was intended as a transitional measure, pending the convening of a constitutional conference to decide the final system of government, but the CSS seemed unlikely to have any influence on the two contending *de facto* governments which by now existed in the South: the army and the SPLM. In January 1988, following the signing of the 'transitional charter' by the government and 17 political parties (see below), Ayang resigned as chairman of the CSS, whose administrative functions were transferred to the regional governors of the Southern provinces.

In May 1987 al-Mahdi asked the supreme council to dissolve his coalition government, citing as his reasons alleged incompetence on the part of certain ministers, lack of progress in addressing the country's serious economic problems, and divisions within the council of ministers. These disagreements arose from widening divisions within the DUP, where contending factions of liberals and religious traditionalists had led al-Mahdi during April to enter into secret negotiations with the opposition NIF, with a view to forming a new coalition. In the event, neither the NIF nor the UP were willing to participate in a single administration, and al-Mahdi's reconstructed council of ministers, announced in June, differed little from the outgoing administration. Following the formation of the new council of ministers, al-Mahdi stated that the coalition parties had agreed on mutually acceptable guidelines for the conduct of government policy, with special reference to the abrogation of religiously-based legislation unacceptable to the South. Progress was also to be made on the long-delayed convening of a constitutional conference. On the former point, it was stated that laws based on a 'Sudanese legal heritage' would replace those unacceptable to non-Muslims, who would be exempted from Islamic punishments and the system of *zakat* (alms) taxation. Such a compromise, however, was rejected by the SPLM, which continued to demand the total abrogation of *Shari'a* law as a precondition to peace negotiations, while the fundamentalist NIF restated its demand that the Islamic code be applied to the country as a whole. In late July the government imposed a 12-month state of emergency, aimed at resolving the country's worsening economic crisis. In August the DUP temporarily withdrew from the coalition government, after the party's proposed candidate for a vacancy on the supreme council had been rejected by the UP. However, efforts to replace the coalition with an all-party government of national unity were unsuccessful, and in October the UP and the DUP agreed to form a joint administration once again, the NIF having elected to remain in opposition.

In September 1987 representatives of Southern Sudanese political parties met in Nairobi, Kenya; they issued a joint appeal for all Sudanese political forces to join the peace efforts, and requested that the government should convene a national constitutional conference. However, the conflict in the South continued unabated. In November SPLM forces, allegedly with Ethiopian assistance, captured the town of Kurmuk (near the border with Ethiopia and lying within Sudan's Northern provinces). Although the capture of this town was of little strategic significance, it was nevertheless regarded as damaging to government morale, as the SPLA had previously confined its operations to the South. Kurmuk was recaptured by government forces in December, and in the same month the government entered into secret peace negotiations in London with representatives of the SPLM. Although no agreement was reached, the SPLM was reported to have abandoned its demand for the abrogation of Islamic law as a precondition for talks. In December al-Mahdi announced that a number of provisions of the *Shari'a* had been repealed, and that preparations were being made to replace those remaining in force with a new legal code.

In January 1988 representatives of the government and 17 political parties signed a 'transitional charter' which aimed to define Sudan's political structure pending a proposed constitutional conference. The 'transitional charter' stressed Sudan's commitment to multi-party democracy; stipulated that the government of the South would be in accordance with the 1972 system of autonomous regional government; and requested the government to replace *Shari'a* law with an alternative legal system before the constitutional conference was convened.

In April 1988 al-Mahdi requested the supreme council to dissolve his coalition government, following a vote by the national assembly in favour of the formation of a new 'government of national unity'. In order to expedite its formation, al-Mahdi resigned as prime minister on 16 April. On 27 April he was re-elected to a further two-year term, obtaining 196 of 222 votes cast by the 260-member national assembly. In early April, during negotiations on the formation of a new government, the UP, the DUP and the NIF had agreed to proceed with the implementation of an Islamic legal code within two months of taking office. Following his re-election as prime minister, al-Mahdi declared that, while the precise nature of the relationship between the state and religion should be established at the proposed constitutional conference, the Muslim majority had the right to choose laws that governed Muslims in so far as they did not infringe upon the rights of non-Muslims.

The formation of a new 27-member 'government of national unity', comprising members of the UP, the DUP, the NIF and a number of Southern Sudanese political parties, was completed in May 1988. Al-Mahdi announced that the new government would deal with the critical economic and security problems facing the country. Few observers, however, expected the new administration to be able to resolve the problem of the war in the South, especially since the fundamentalist NIF had joined the coalition on condition that a 'replacement' *Shari'a* code be introduced within 60 days of its formation.

In November 1988 representatives of the SPLM met senior members of the DUP and reached agreement on proposals to end the civil war. A statement issued by the two sides stipulated that, in the period preceding the convening of a national constitutional conference, the Islamic legal code should be suspended, that military agreements between Sudan and other countries should be abandoned, and that the state of emergency should be lifted and a cease-fire implemented in the South. In December, however, a state of emergency was again declared amid reports that a military coup had been attempted (see below). The DUP withdrew its six ministers from the coalition government, following a request by al-Mahdi that the national assembly convene a national constitutional conference, without the agreement between the SPLM and the DUP being incorporated into his proposal. In the same month the government was compelled to revoke substantial increases in the prices of basic commodities, following a national strike and demonstrations in Khartoum in protest at the measure.

In February 1989 Dr Hassan at-Turabi, the leader of the NIF, was appointed deputy prime minister. This appointment, while strengthening the position of the NIF in the government, reduced the likelihood of an early solution to the war in the South. In late February al-Mahdi threatened to resign as prime minister unless senior army officers allowed him leeway to form a new government and to work for peace in the South. However, the army refused to guarantee that it would not intervene if necessary to arrest Sudan's continued perceived drift towards Libya and to expedite negotiations to end the war in the South. In March al-Mahdi agreed to form a new, broadly-based government which would begin negotiations with the SPLM. Thirty political parties and 17 trade unions had previously signed an agreement endorsing the peace agreement drawn up by the DUP and the SPLM in November 1988. However, the NIF refused to endorse the agreement (which called for the suspension of Islamic laws as a prelude to the negotiation of a peace settlement to the civil war), and was excluded from the new government formed on 23 March 1989. Peace negotiations between a government delegation and the SPLM commenced in Ethiopia in April. In early May the SPLM proclaimed a 45-day cease-fire, but by mid-June negotiations had become deadlocked.

In the field of foreign relations, al-Mahdi carried out a number of foreign tours, including visits in 1986 to the USSR, Saudi Arabia, the USA and Italy. Following the legislative elections in April, contacts with Egypt became less cordial, as al-Mahdi sought to introduce a more independent policy for Sudan, and it was reported that all joint institutions with Egypt were to be dissolved. In February 1987, however, al-Mahdi visited Cairo to sign a new agreement on economic and cultural co-operation. Despite the lessening of Libya's military involvement in Chad, some Libyan forces remained in north-western Sudan, in defiance of repeated Sudanese demands for their withdrawal. Al-Mahdi stated in March that the question of their presence had been 'settled', although it was not clear whether or not they had been withdrawn. In April 1988 President Habré of Chad urged the Sudanese government to curb the activities of Libyan-backed forces in Darfur, and to end its diplomatic policy which, he claimed, effectively supported Libya.

During 1988 there were increasing reports of alleged violations of human rights by the government, in particular of atrocities committed against civilians in the war in the South. The SPLM alleged that government forces had allowed, and, in some instances, participated in, the massacre of civilians of the Dinka tribe (from which the SPLM drew most of its support) by pro-government militia from the Islamic North. These allegations were corroborated by Western human rights organizations, which accused the government of pursuing a policy of genocide against the Dinka in its effort to defeat the SPLA.

MILITARY RULE AND CIVIL WAR

By late 1988 there were signs of widespread discontent in military circles at the government's continuing lack of progress in resolving the civil conflict. A coup attempt in December, promoted by supporters of ex-president Nimeri, was quickly suppressed, but subsequent political manoeuvres by al-Mahdi (see above) did little to allay the increasing frustration of senior army officers. On 30 June 1989, a bloodless *coup d'état* led by Brig. (later Lt-Gen.) Omar Hassan Ahmad al-Bashir removed al-Mahdi's government and formed a 15-member Revolutionary Command Council for National Salvation (RCC), which declared its primary aim to be the resolution of the Southern conflict. Al-Bashir rapidly dismantled the civilian ruling apparatus. The constitution, national assembly and all political parties and trade unions were abolished, a state of emergency was declared, and civilian newspapers were closed. About 30 members of the former government were detained, including al-Mahdi, although three of the ex-ministers were included in the new 21-member cabinet which was announced in early July. Its composition included 16 civilians, of whom four were Southerners, as well as several members who were understood to be sympathetic towards Islamic fundamentalism. Internationally, the RCC regime received immediate diplomatic recognition from Chad, Egypt, Libya, the People's Democratic Republic of Yemen and Saudi Arabia, and the new government was generally welcomed as a potentially stabilizing influence in the region.

The SPLA response to the coup was cautious. Al-Bashir declared a one-month unilateral cease-fire on 5 July 1989 and offered an amnesty to those opposing the Khartoum government 'for political reasons'. In an effort to restart negotiations, al-Bashir requested Ethiopia, Egypt and Kenya to act as mediators. At the same time, however, the government's announcement of proposals for a national referendum on *Shari'a* law alienated the SPLA, which demanded its suspension as a precondition for talks. A plan by the RCC to introduce military conscription foreshadowed an escalation in the conflict.

Peace negotiations were, however, renewed in Ethiopia in August 1989. By this time the SPLM's terms for a negotiated settlement to the conflict included the immediate resignation of the RCC prior to the establishment of an interim government, which would represent the SPLM, the banned political parties and other groupings; and the new regime's proximity to the fundamentalist NIF had become apparent. The negotiations immediately collapsed over the issue of Islamic law. Col Garang was invited to attend a government-sponsored peace conference in Khartoum in early September, but declined to do so while the curfew and the state of emergency remained in force. Delegates who did attend the conference were believed to be close to the fundamentalist NIF, and were thought to favour the secession of Southern Sudan if it proved impossible to achieve a negotiated settlement to the conflict. Further peace negotiations, mediated by the former US president, Jimmy Carter, began in Kenya at the beginning of December, but quickly collapsed over the issue of *Shari'a* law. By the end of January 1990 the SPLM, which had been achieving significant military advances after resuming hostilities in October 1989, was preparing a full-scale assault on the important garrison town of Juba. In March President Mobutu of Zaire held talks, separately, with both Lt-Gen. Bashir and Col Garang, in an unsuccessful attempt to reactivate peace negotiations.

In late March 1990 57 people, including both army officers and civilians, were reported to have been arrested after allegedly having attempted to stage a *coup d'état.* A reshuffle of the cabinet on 10 April was believed to have strengthened the influence of Islamic fundamentalists on the government, since two of the new appointees were known to be close to the NIF. It was claimed that a further coup attempt, on 23 April, was followed by the executions of 28 army officers.

In May 1990 a senior official of the US department of state met Col Garang in an attempt to revive the peace talks, while US diplomats in Khartoum reportedly held talks with representatives of the government with the aim of facilitating further peace negotiations. It was claimed, in late September, that another coup attempt had been thwarted. Like those alleged to have taken place earlier in the year, its origins remained conjectural. Reports of a fourth coup attempt, in November, were denied by the government. The reports followed growing internal unrest, including strike action by railway and other workers and student demonstrations in Khartoum; the University of Khartoum had been closed since September after clashes between student factions.

An opposition government-in-exile was formed in January 1991 by Col Garang and a former c-in-c of the army, Lt-Gen. Fatih Ahmed Ali. A cabinet reshuffle followed in late January, in which al-Bashir created three new ministries and redesignated several existing departments. At the beginning of February, al-Bashir signed a decree introducing a new penal code, based, like its predecessor, on *Shari'a* law. (Although the earlier Islamic penal code had remained in force, the punishments it prescribed had not been applied since the overthrow of Nimeri in 1985.) The code, which was to take effect from 22 March, was not to apply, for the present, in the three Southern regions of Equatoria, Upper Nile and Bahr al-Ghazal. This exemption, however, appeared to cover only five of the code's 186 articles (those concerned with specified punishments), and it was stated that the code would be applicable to non-Muslim Sudanese residents in the North, notably the estimated 2m. refugees who had fled to the Khartoum area from the civil war in the South.

A new administrative structure for the provinces was introduced in February 1991. According to the government, the changes would be conducive to greater regional autonomy—an issue in the civil war. The previous 18 administrative regions were replaced with nine states: Khartoum, Central, Kordofan, Darfur, Northern, Eastern, Bahr al-Ghazal, Upper Nile and Equatoria, which were in turn sub-divided into 66 provinces and 281 local government areas. Each of the nine new states was to have its own governor, deputy governor and cabinet of ministers, and was to assume responsibility for local administration and the collection of some taxes. The central government retained control over foreign policy, military affairs, the economy and the other main areas of administration. The SPLA rejected the measures as inadequate.

Renewed indications of dissent within the regime emerged following the execution of 20 army officers in April 1991 for their alleged involvement in a coup attempt. Faisal Abu Salih, the minister of the interior and a member of the RCC, together with another RCC member, Brig.-Gen. Uthman Ahmed Hassan, were subsequently dismissed. At the end of April, al-Bashir announced the immediate release of all the country's political prisoners. Human rights organizations subsequently claimed, however, that at least 60 of the government's opponents remained in detention. Among those released was the former prime minister, Sadiq al-Mahdi, who had been under house arrest, and Muhammad Ibrahim Nugud, secretary of the SCP. A one-month amnesty for all opponents of the government was declared, and was further renewed in June without limit on time. The announcements coincided with the holding, in Khartoum between 29 April– 2 May, of a national conference on Sudan's political future, attended by some 1,600 delegates chosen by the regime. Following this conference, al-Bashir announced, on 29 June, that a political system based on Libyan-style 'people's congresses' was to be introduced.

In May 1991 Col Garang marked the eighth anniversary of the start of the civil war by inviting the government to take part in peace negotiations. The government responded by stating that it was willing at any time to discuss terms for a settlement, but it reiterated its view that the administrative reforms introduced in February already represented a considerable degree of compromise. Rebel forces remained in control of most of Southern Sudan. The overthrow, on 21 May, of the Ethiopian government led by Mengistu Haile Mariam had implications for the SPLA, which had in the past enjoyed Ethiopian support; armed clashes within Ethiopia between SPLA forces and those of the new Ethiopian regime were reported in late May. On 29 May the Sudanese government declared its recognition of, and support for, the new Ethiopian government.

International efforts to achieve a peace settlement within Sudan gained renewed momentum in mid-1991. In mid-June the government announced that it would consider proposals made by the US government, providing for the partial withdrawal of government forces from Southern Sudan, the withdrawal of the SPLA forces from government-held areas and the declaration of Juba, the Southern capital, as an 'open' city. On 14 June the SPLA endorsed the government's suggestion that the president of Nigeria, Ibrahim Babangida, should act as a mediator. However, this diplomatic progress coincided with a new government offensive against the SPLA. At the beginning of July, following further initiatives by the USA, Garang was reported to have agreed to begin unconditional peace negotiations with the government. However, in August 1991, as part of a cabinet reshuffle, which was carried out during the absence abroad of President al-Bashir, a prominent Islamic fundamentalist, Tayib Ibrahim Muhammad Khair, was appointed governor of the Southern Province of Darfur. This appointment was viewed as unlikely to improve the prospects of a definitive peace settlement in the immediate future.

An alleged coup attempt in late August 1991, resulted in the arrest of 10 army officers and a number of civilians and was officially ascribed to unspecified 'foreign powers'. Subsequent official statements alleged that those implicated included members of the National Democratic Alliance (NDA, a grouping formed in 1989 by the SPLA and some of the other former political parties, including the UP and the DUP) and the previously unknown organization, *Ana al-Sudan* ('I am Sudan'). The NDA claimed at the end of September that more than 70 people had been arrested and that the former prime minister, Sadiq al-Mahdi, had been among those interrogated. The subsequent trial by a military court of 15 people accused of involvement in the coup attempt, resulted in death sentences for 10 army officers, commuted in December to life imprisonment.

Reports of a split within the SPLA, circulated from Khartoum at the end of August 1991, were immediately denied by Garang. Three SPLA field commanders—Riek Mashar Teny-Dhurgon, Lam Akol and Carabino Kuany Bol—claimed to have taken over the leadership of the SPLA and accused Garang of dictatorial behaviour. The dissidents, based at Nasir in eastern Sudan, were reported to favour a policy of secession for the South, whereas the aim of Garang and his supporters, based at Kapoeta, remained a united, secular state. The split was also along ethnic lines, with the Dinka supporting Garang and the Nuer the breakaway faction. The SPLA's divisions led to a postponement of the first round of peace talks due to be held under the auspices of the OAU in Abuja, Nigeria, at the end of October. Fierce fighting between the two SPLA factions was reported in November and resulted in the massacre of several thousand civilians in the southern towns of Bor and Kongor before a cease-fire was negotiated in mid-December. At the end of November the government announced a one-month amnesty for rebels who wished to surrender.

Proposals for constitutional reform were announced by al-Bashir on 1 January 1992. A 300-member transitional parliament was to be appointed, with full legislative functions and the power to veto decisions of the RCC. The parliament, which convened for the first time on 24 February, included—as well as all members of the RCC (excluding al-Bashir), state governors and representatives of the army and police—former members of the banned UP and DUP, and former aides to ex-president Nimeri, reflecting the government's desire to broaden its support in the wake of the introduction of an unpopular programme of economic austerity measures (see Economy). There were reports of widespread political unrest in early February, with demonstrations against the new economic policies and the reported arrest of a number of army officers who were alleged to be planning an attack on the military leadership. A further alleged coup attempt was reported to have been foiled in mid-April.

The government, while still declaring its willingness to take part in peace talks, launched a new military offensive against the SPLA in late February 1992. With the SPLA weakened by its internal divisions and the loss of Ethiopian support, the town of Pochala, on the Ethiopian border and held by the SPLA since 1985, was captured in March. During April 1992 the towns of Bor, Kongor, Yirol, Pibor and Mongalla also fell to government forces. In late April Col Garang claimed that the government offensive had been halted and that the towns lost by the SPLA had been in the hands of the dissident faction, which he accused of defecting to the government. However, on 1 May government forces were reported to have captured a larger rebel camp at Bahr al-Ghazal in western Sudan, followed on 12 May by Liria, on the road east from Juba to Garang's Torit headquarters. On 28 May, Kapoeta, near the Kenyan border, also fell to government forces. Strengthened by its military successes and by Kenya's reported agreement to stop supporting the SPLA, the government announced its willingness to participate in peace talks. These discussions were convened in Abuja on 26 May by President Babangida of Nigeria, the current OAU chairman, and were attended by a government delegation and two from the SPLA: one representing Col Garang's faction, the other the dissident group based at Nasir and led by Lam Akol. The talks concluded on 5 June, with an agreement by all parties to continue 'peaceful negotiations' at a future date, under Nigerian mediation, although there was no mention of a cease-fire. The final communiqué referred to Sudan as a 'multi-ethnic, multi-lingual, multi-cultural and multi-religious country' but a demand by the two SPLA factions for a referendum on self-determination for the South was withdrawn at government insistence.

The government's military offensive continued to make progress in Southern Sudan, with the opening, for the first time in seven years, of a river passage to Juba in mid-June 1992 and of the railway to Wau later in the month. On 12 July the government announced the capture of Torit, near the Ugandan border, which had been Col Garang's headquarters and the last major town in rebel hands. Garang himself was reported to have escaped to Kajo Kaji, closer to the Ugandan border, shortly before the fall of Torit and the SPLA quickly mounted a counter-attack on the town. Eager to re-establish its credibility after a series of setbacks, the rebel movement launched a new offensive as the rainy season started, mounting an attack on Juba and attempting to disrupt government supply lines to the newly-recaptured Southern towns. There were indications that the two rebel factions had achieved a measure of reconciliation since the Abuja meeting, enabling them to offer a united response to the government advance. The shelling of Juba led to the suspension of relief flights to the city and by mid-August the city's 300,000 people were reported to be close to starvation. Meanwhile, the SPLA claimed that government troops had massacred 900 civilians in the city. Conflicting reports emerged about fighting around Malakal, the capital of Upper Nile province, with the Nasir faction of the SPLA claiming to have captured the town from government forces in early October.

Attempts by Nigeria to reactivate the peace process that had begun in May continued during the second half of 1992, but were obstructed by the increasingly fragmented nature of the SPLA. A round of talks that was scheduled to be held in Abuja in December was abandoned because of disagreements over which factions should attend.

Evidence of divisions between the RCC leadership and the NIF over the continued military domination of the government emerged in early 1993. In statements that he later retracted, the leader of the NIF, Dr Hassan at-Turabi, declared that he expected the RCC to resign and to transfer power to a transitional assembly. In mid-January a cabinet reshuffle disbanded three ministries nd created two new ones. Brig.-Gen. Dominic Kassiano Bakhit was assigned to the new ministry of labour and administrative reform, and Ali el-Haj Muhammad became the new minister of economic planning and investment. Abd ar-Rahim Muhammad Hussain, a close aide of al-Bashir, was appointed minister of the interior, replacing Brig.-Gen. Zubair Muhammad Salih, who remained vice-chairman of the RCC. The minister of health, Faisal Madani, also lost his ministerial portfolio as well as his seat on the RCC. In February the minister of foreign affairs, Ali Sahloul, was replaced by Hussein Suleiman Abu Salih.

Contacts between the government and the various rebel factions took place in Uganda and Kenya during February 1993, with a view to resuming the peace process. Col Garang announced a unilateral cease-fire on 17 March, in honour of the Muslim holiday of Id al-Fitr, and aimed at providing a favourable atmosphere for the peace talks, a gesture to which the government responded with its own announcement of a cease-fire two days later. Garang also urged the establishment of safety zones to allow the delivery of food supplies to starving people. However, at the end of March fighting was reported at Kongor between Garang's forces and the 'Forces of Unity' faction of the SPLA, led by William Nyuon.

Peace talks between the government and the faction of the SPLA led by Col Garang resumed in Abuja in April 1993. After preliminary discussions on 8 April, at which it was agreed to continue to observe a cease-fire, the two sides met again for substantive talks on 26 April. Meanwhile, in Nairobi, talks were also taking place between a government delegation and SPLA–United, an alliance formed in early April between the Nasir faction, the 'Forces of Unity' and a faction led by Carabino Kuany Bol. The Abuja talks adjourned on 18 May, having made little progress on the main issues dividing the parties. Although the government claimed the talks would resume in June, the SPLA side said they had been a failure and that the cease-fire was at an end. The Nairobi talks, after a break in early May, resumed during 7–26 May and ended with agreement on the concept of a unified federal state and on the rights of state governments to introduce laws supplementary to federal legislation—allowing the implementation of *Shari'a* law in the North, but not in the South. No agreement was reached, however, on the length of the period of transition before the holding of a referendum on future divisions of power.

The collapse of the Abuja negotiations was quickly followed by allegations of cease-fire violations from both the government and rebel factions, and in July 1993 the faction of the SPLA led by Col Garang announced that it had launched a major offensive after attacks by government troops, aided by rival SPLA factions. In August government forces attacked SPLA-held towns near the Ugandan border in an offensive aimed at cutting supply routes to rebel forces in Southern and Western Sudan. They were reported to have gained control of the town of Morobo and to have blocked the road route for relief supplies to Bahr al-Ghazal and Western Equatoria. Also in August, the Nuba people were reported to be threatened by government forces in central Sudan. Independent observers urged the UN to establish 'safe havens' for refugees and to extend its Operation Lifeline Sudan to the Nuba mountains. In early September the SPLA was reported to have checked the advance of the government forces in Southern Sudan.

A reshuffle of the cabinet in July 1993 was regarded as having strengthened the position of the NIF within the government, and as a further step towards the establishment of a civilian administration. On 19 October al-Bashir announced political reforms in preparation for presidential and legislative elections to be held in 1994 and 1995 respectively. The RCC had been dissolved three days previously—after it had appointed al-Bashir as president and as head of a new civilian government. Cabinet ministers were requested to remain in office until elections took place. Al-Bashir appointed a new minister of defence—a portfolio that he had formerly held himself—and a new vice-president. Western observers regarded the dissolution of the RCC as reinforcing the position of the NIF within the government during the transition to civilian rule. At the end of October the cabinet was reshuffled.

In early February 1994, by constitutional decree, Sudan was redivided into 26 states instead of the nine that had formed the basis of administration since 1991. The executive and legislative powers of each state government were to be expanded, and Southern states were expected to be exempted from *Shari'a* law.

At the beginning of 1994 the civil war in Southern Sudan remained in stalemate. The government maintained garrisons in Yei, Juba, Rumbek, Kapoeta, Torit, Bor, Wau, Aweil, Gogrial, and Bentiu. Rebel forces, while largely deployed in the countryside, also controlled many towns and villages, including Tambura, Nzara, Yambio, Maridi, Kaya, Nimule, Mugiri, Amadi, Akobo, Tonga, Nasir, Mundiri, Kajo Kaji, Mugiri, and Kongor. As in previous years, the government's 1993–94 Southern offensive involved the deployment of army and Popular Defence Force (PDF) units from sizeable garrisons in Juba and Wau, largely along main roads, to locations along the borders with Zaire (now the Democratic Republic of the Congo) and Uganda. The objective was to capture border towns such as Tambura and Nimule, which the rebels used as transhipment points to bring troops, weapons and other supplies into the war zone from bases in Zaire and Uganda. Rebel forces, which remained divided into warring factions, suffered from a lack of arms and ammunition. As a result, government troops made some minimal advances. On 11 June 1994, for example, army units recaptured Kajo Kaji, a town about 16 km from the Ugandan border. At about the same time, government forces opened a land route between Renk in Sobat state and the Upper Nile regional capital of Malakal, for the first time in some 10 years.

On 13 July 1994 a restructuring of the cabinet was announced, in which Lt-Col Altayeb Ibrahim Mohommed Khair was appointed minister of the interior. On 29 October, President al-Bashir announced the start of a dual offensive to sever the SPLA's supply lines from Uganda and Zaire before the next government offensive. The president also announced that his goal was to liberate Southern Sudan from the SPLA and, at the same time, to pursue efforts to negotiate with the rebels. The offensive did not proceed as planned, however, and army and PDF units suffered several defeats in the area of Mangall and Terakeka, north of Juba. By mid-December the fighting was taking place primarily around the government-held town of Kapoeta. The government acknowledged that its forces had suffered another military defeat east of Torit, on the supply route to Kapoeta. According to Col Garang, the SPLA had killed more than 1,000 government troops. By January 1995 there were reports that rebel forces had surrounded Kapoeta, and had captured part of the town. On 25 March, in spite of these losses, government forces managed to capture Nasir, a stronghold of the South Sudan Independence Movement (SSIM) near the Ethiopian border. On 31 March, however, the SSIM captured intact an armoured military convoy of government forces at the town of Lafon. This development was significant in that the Sudanese government had previously provided support to the SSIM. With the SSIM now in conflict with the government, a reconciliation between the SSIM commander, Riek Mashar Teny-Dhurgon, and Col Garang became more likely. Indeed, on 27 April the two commanders signed the Lafon Declaration, which provided for a cease-fire and a cessation of hostilities between their forces; reunification; reintegration of military forces; and a general amnesty. In early February the cabinet was reshuffled, the pattern of changes suggesting a reinforcement of the Islamic character of the government.

An unexpected development in the Southern conflict occurred on 27 March 1995, when former US president Jimmy Carter persuaded the Sudanese government to declare a unilateral two-month cease-fire and to offer the rebel groups an amnesty if they surrendered their weapons. Three days later the SPLA also declared a two-month cease-fire and requested the deployment of international observers to monitor the truce. Finally, on 3 April, the SSIM issued a cease-fire declaration. On 27 May the Sudanese government extended its cease-fire for two months. However, it soon became apparent that the army was continuing to conduct military operations. Four days prior to the extension of the government cease-fire, the SSIM claimed that government forces had launched a new offensive in Latjor state, which brought the number of government violations of the Carter-mediated cease-fire to 21. On 4 June army units temporarily entered Pariang in Upper Nile province, which had been under the control of the SPLA for 12 years. It was also reported that the government was preparing another dry season offensive in Southern Sudan.

On 15-23 June 1995 a conference took place in Asmara, Eritrea, of groups and parties opposed to the government. The conference, hosted by the Eritrean People's Front for Democracy and Justice (PFDJ) and organized by the Asmara- (formerly Cairo-) based NDA, was attended, among others, by representatives of the DUP, the UP, the SCP and the SPLA. At its conclusion the conference issued a communiqué in which opposition leaders pledged (once the al-Bashir regime had been ousted) to support the right of self-determination for all Sudanese peoples, based on the results of future referendums; and to establish a decentralized government for a four-year interim period. The communiqué also envisaged the future separation of religion and politics and the abolition of *Shari'a* law. The creation of a government-in-exile was announced and the conference was also reported to have achieved a *rapprochement* between the SPLA and the other opposition groups: The NDA announced details of a forthcoming military campaign to be undertaken by its military wing in alliance with, among others, Col Garang's faction of the SPLA.

On 12 August 1995 a cabinet reshuffle was announced. The DUP claimed that ministers who were dismissed had been involved in planning the attempted assassination of President Mubarak of Egypt in June (see below). Later in August President al-Bashir announced that legislative and presidential elections which had been scheduled to take place in 1994 and 1995, respectively, would now be held in 1996. Political prisoners who were released in a government amnesty on 24-25 August 1995 included the UP leader, Sadiq al-Mahdi, who had been placed under arrest in May for having alleged that state funds were being misused.

In September 1995 the government imposed strict security measures in response to rioting in Khartoum. Some reports suggested that the disturbances had been provoked by the arrest of student demonstrators in the city earlier in the month, but the government blamed the SCP for fomenting the unrest. In the same month the government issued a formal denial of any responsibility for the attempted assassination of Egypt's President Mubarak in June.

In November 1995, having begun a new offensive in late October, the forces of the SPLA faction led by Col Garang were reported to be advancing on the Southern town of Juba. The retreat of government forces which this provoked appeared to be regarded as more serious than other, similar retreats in the past: the government declared a mass mobilization, urging all sectors of the population to defend the country. On 11 November the government claimed that its forces had inflicted a major defeat on the SPLA and on Ugandan and Eritrean forces allied with it. The governments of Uganda and Eritrea denied the involvement of their forces in the fighting. By late 1996 the SPLA claimed to have taken control of all of Western Equatoria, all of the rural regions of Eastern Equatoria and 13 towns in central Equatoria.

The first legislative and presidential elections to be held in Sudan since 1989 took place during 6-17 March 1996. Some 5.5m. of Sudan's 10m. eligible voters were reported to have participated in the election of 275 deputies to a new, 400-seat national assembly. The remaining 125 deputies had been appointed at a national conference in January. Representatives of opposition groups and parties alleged that electoral malpractice had been widespread and that many voters had been intimidated into participating. In the presidential election the incumbent president, Lt-Gen. al-Bashir (opposed by some 40 candidates, none of them representatives of the principal opposition groups and parties) obtained 75.7% of the total votes cast, and formally commenced a five-year term of office on 1 April. On the same day Dr Hassan at-Turabi, the secretary-general of the NIF, was unanimously elected president of the national assembly.

Rumours of an attempted *coup d'état* in late March 1996 prejudiced the newly-constituted regime's claim that the elections signified the beginning of a new period of stability and reconciliation, as did reports of serious unrest in Khartoum in early April and the decision not to appoint a new cabinet until it became clear whether the UN would impose sanctions on Sudan for its failure to comply with the terms of Resolution 1044 (see below). The attempted coup reportedly led to another purge of dissident elements within the armed forces.

A unilateral cease-fire declared by the government throughout Southern Sudan on 3 March 1996 did not lead to a cessation of hostilities there. Rather, Col Garang's faction of the SPLA ignored it, attacking towns close to the Sudanese-Ethiopian border, one of which was only a short distance from the Roseires dam and thus provoked speculation that an attack on this key installation might be imminent. However, another peace agreement concluded by the government and the SSIM in February – initially in order to facilitate the provision of emergency food aid to areas of need in Southern Sudan – appeared, in April, to culminate in a substantial breakthrough in the Southern conflict. On 10 April the government, the SSIM and the SPLA-United signed an agreement — described as a 'political charter for peace' — under which they pledged to preserve Sudan's national unity and to take joint action to develop those areas of the country which had been affected by the civil war. The charter also provided for the holding of a referendum as a 'means of realizing the aspirations of Southern citizens' and affirmed that *Shari'a* law would be the basis of future legislation. Other opposition groups, however, rejected the charter as a publicity stunt. On 17 April Sudan's first vice-president was reported to have invited Col Garang to sign the charter on behalf of the faction of the SPLA under his control, and there was speculation that this was part of an attempt to form a new government of national unity. However, the new cabinet, announced on 21 April, retained the military, Islamic cast of its predecessor.

In June 1996 the NDA issued an ultimatum to the government, urging it to relinquish power without further bloodshed. It predicted that its fall was, in any case, imminent and announced plans for a popular uprising for which it forecast support among the armed forces. In the same month anti-government demonstrations by student supporters of the NDA were reported to have taken place in Khartoum, followed by similar agitation in Omdurman. Further student demonstrations were reported to have taken place in Khartoum in early September.

In late August 1996 opponents of the government based in Cairo, Egypt, claimed that 11 military officers had been executed for having taken part in a conspiracy to occupy government facilities in Port Sudan. In October, however, the government denied that any of the conspirators had been executed. In early October al-Bashir appointed eight deputies to the national assembly to represent constituencies in the south where, owing to the civil war, it had not been possible to hold elections in March. In late 1996, in a newspaper interview, Col. Garang disclosed details of the Sudanese opposition's future military campaign. This would include increased activity in the South and the Nuba mountains, and popular uprisings in Khartoum and other cities. In December Sadiq al-Mahdi fled the country to Eritrea. Al-Mahdi claimed that he had left Sudan in order not to become a government hostage.

In January 1997 the government was reported to be seeking assistance from Egypt, after its forces suffered a series of defeats at the hands of an allianace of various rebel forces. Sudan claimed that Ethiopia was lending active support to the rebels and appealed to the UN Security Council to intervene. In late January rebel forces were reported to be advancing on the southern city of Damazin; and in February government forces were reported to have lost control of all but a few Southern towns to rebel forces.

In early March 1997 reports indicated that the Sudanese People's Armed Forces (SPAF) were rounding up young men in Khartoum for military service, and at the end of May President al-Bashir announced that all male secondary school-leavers would be subject to compulsory military service. Various international human rights organizations maintained that the SPAF were assigning young men to combat units against their will, although the government claimed that in such cases non-combative duties were assigned. On 21 April a peace agreement was concluded between the government and six of the southern factions. In this agreement self-determination is promised for the southern states, as is, after a four-year transitional period, a referendum on independence. The SPLA refused to sign, claiming that the pact was devised in such a way as to divide and weaken the southern opposition. In the same month, the southern rebels came within 40km of Juba, the southern capital, althought they lacked the capabilities to seize the town. In the north-east the situation was less clear, as the NDA was exaggerating its military gains, although it did advance towards its target, the Roseires dam. This exaggeration undermined its credibility and masked its ineffective action, which alienated the SPLA and Eritrea—its principal ally. This led the Eritrean government to advocate the creation of a replacement 'Progressive Alliance', but by mid-1997 no such grouping had been formed.

IGADD Initiatives

In September 1993 the Intergovernmental Authority on Drought and Development (IGADD, now IGAD—see below), under the chairmanship of President Moi of Kenya, sought to mediate an end to the civil war in Southern Sudan. Two months later, the IGADD convened its first meeting with the warring Sudanese parties in Kampala, Uganda. Further meetings followed in January, March, May, July, and September 1994, and January and May 1995. The IGADD mediation committee comprised two sections: a committee of the heads of state of Eritrea, Ethiopia, Kenya, and Uganda; and a standing committee composed of their ministers. The IGADD believed that the civil war in Southern Sudan was a regional rather than a national conflict.

At its May 1994 meeting, the IGADD adopted a Declaration of Principles, which gave priority to national unity, but also acknowledged the right of self-determination for all Sudanese people. The SPLA and the SSIM immediately accepted the Declaration of Principles, but the Sudanese government opposed it. Eventually, the government agreed to discuss the principles in question and to make any objections it had on specific points. The right of self-determination and a proposed separation between religion and the state proved to be the most contentious issues. Neither government nor rebel negotiators could devise a compromise which avoided using the terms 'self-determination' and 'secularism'; however, all parties agreed to attend another IGADD-sponsored meeting.

On 18–29 July 1994 the warring parties met in Nairobi, Kenya, and continued to debate the terms 'self-determination' and 'secularism'. As during the May meeting, the rebel groups were willing to accept the terms. The government's position, however, was that secularism was out of the question; indeed, it wanted Islamic law to apply not only throughout Sudan but also the rest of Africa. The government also rejected the term 'self-determination', which it regarded as a ploy for partitioning the country; and expressed its preference for 'shuttle diplomacy', rather than the face-to-face sessions adopted by the IGADD. Finally, it sought support for its own internal peace process instead of IGADD mediation.

On 7 September 1994 the latest round of IGADD-sponsored peace negotiations collapsed in Nairobi, after President al-Bashir reiterated the aforementioned terms. The government subsequently sought a new mechanism for the talks, which would have involved it in separate meetings with the SPLA and the SSIM. Although the negotiations which it had sponsored were effectively stalled, the IGADD remained engaged in the peace process. After convening another session of talks on 4 January 1995, the IGADD called attention to the need for co-operation between itself, the OAU and the international community, led by the UN. However, this did nothing to relieve the deadlock in the negotiations.

In mid-1995 those countries designated as the Friends of IGADD, at a meeting chaired by the Netherlands minister of co-operation, Jan P. Pronk, and attended by delegates from Canada, the United Kingdom, Italy, the Netherlands, Norway, and the USA, sought to persuade the IGADD to resume its work as mediator in the Sudanese civil war. On 17–18 May 1995 Pronk visited Nairobi and Khartoum in order to persuade the warring parties to extend a previously declared cease-fire, which was due to expire on 28 May 1995. The Kenyan president eventually convinced President al-Bashir, the SPLA, and the SSIM to extend the cease-fire by two months. Despite this achievement, military action continued in Southern Sudan, the army capturing the town of Pariang on 4 June 1995.

Meanwhile, the Friends of IGADD continued to advocate a longer cease-fire, the introduction of joint surveillance patrols assisted by international monitors, and a new round of IGADD-sponsored peace talks. Pronk promised that Western countries would finance the surveillance patrols and supply technical equipment, and that they would help to establish a secretariat in Nairobi for the IGADD peace-talks committee. Although it had reservations about some members of the Friends of IGADD, especially the USA, Canada and the United Kingdom, Sudan subsequently approved the Friends of IGADD peace initiative.

In March 1996 al-Bashir attended an IGADD conference in Nairobi at which the mandate of the IGADD was expanded to include regional economic co-operation and the co-ordination of political and social policies. President Moi of Kenya's chairmanship of the Authority was extended for a further year and it was agreed to change the organization's name to the Intergovernmental Authority on Development (IGAD).

In early July 1997 IGAD announced that the Sudanese government had agreed to accept the 1994 Declaration of Principles (see above) as a framework for peace. However, the government declared that it did not consider the declaration to be binding, but merely a basis for future discussions. The SPLA, on the other hand, felt that it could not resume peace negotiations without such a binding agreement. At the end of August President al-Bashir attended talks convened by President Mandela of South Africa. The presidents of Uganda and Zimbabwe were also present, although Col Garang, the leader of the SPLA, did not attend.

FOREIGN RELATIONS

Owing to the strong influence of the NIF on Sudanese politics after the al-Bashir regime came to power, the status of Sudan's relations with any particular country since 1989 has been determined by the extent to which it opposes or supports Sudan's determination to spread radical Islamic fundamentalism throughout eastern Africa and the Middle East. Sudan's closest allies include Iraq, Iran and, interestingly (because the alliance is not based solely on economic interest), France. Relations with neighbouring countries, such as Uganda, Eritrea, Ethiopia, Kenya and Egypt, are characterized either by acrimony or co-operation, often related to the civil war being waged in Southern Sudan. The People's Republic of China (PRC), South Africa and Russia have all pursued economic opportunities in Sudan.

The USA, meanwhile, has condemned Sudan in the strongest terms for its alleged role in the organization of international terrorism and has actively sought the international isolation of the al-Bashir regime. Sudan's alleged involvement in the attempted assassination of President Mubarak of Egypt in June 1995 provoked international outrage. In January 1996 the UN Security Council accused Sudan of supporting terrorism, condemned the attempt on President Mubarak's life and unanimously approved Resolution 1044, demanding that Sudan immediately extradite three Islamists implicated in the attack. On 28 April the Security Council adopted Resolution 1054, imposing sanctions on Sudan (with effect from 10 May 1996) for its failure to comply with Resolution 1044. Under the sanctions, the number of Sudanese diplomatic personnel serving abroad was to be reduced, and international organizations were requested not to hold conferences in the country. The Security Council stated that the sanctions would remain in force until Sudan complied with Resolution 1044, ceased its support for terrorism and conducted its foreign relations in accordance with the charters of the UN and the OAU. On 16 August, in view of Sudan's continued failure to comply with Resolution 1044, the Security Council adopted a resolution (to take effect three months from that date) which would ban all international flights operated by Sudan Airways. However, by mid-1997 the air embargo had still not been implemented, owing to concerns over its humanitarian implications.

Sudan's support for Iraq's invasion of Kuwait in 1990 was a cause of increasing international isolation for the country from the second half of 1990, alienating foreign aid donors, as well as contributing to internal tensions. As a result of this support Sudan and Iraq now have particularly close relations. In April 1994 President al-Bashir held talks with an Iraqi envoy and restated Sudan's support for the lifting of the UN trade embargo on Iraq. In June Sudan and Iraq signed a technical co-operation agreement and Iraq has also agreed to help Sudan exploit its petroleum reserves and to train Sudanese technicians.

A rift developed between Sudan and Iran because of the former's support of Iraq during the 1990–91 Gulf crisis. Since then, however, relations have gradually improved. In June 1994, the head of the Sudan judiciary, Jallal Ali Lutfi, met the speaker of the Iranian parliament, Ali Akbar Nateq Nouri, and the President of Iran, Hashemi Rafsanjani, and expressions of mutual support were exchanged. In October, a delegation from the Iranian Majlis visited Khartoum in order to explore ways of improving relations between Iran and Sudan. The Sudanese government tried unsuccessfully to persuade Iran to provide it with $340m. to finance the war in Southern Sudan. Sudan and Iran have also concluded an accord under which Iran is permitted to use naval facilities at Port Sudan for military purposes. In exchange, Iran agreed to resume military aid to Sudan; help train Sudanese naval and PDF personnel; establish a joint security organization to exchange intelligence; create eight cultural centres for the dissemination of information about the Iranian revolution; and expand tourism. In November 1995 the secretary-general of the Iran supreme council for national security was reported to have visited Sudan in order to assess the country's military requirements. Iran was later reported to have agreed to supply Sudan with armoured vehicles, heavy artillery and radar equipment. An agreement concluded in May 1996 expanded the scope of Sudanese-Iranian co-operation.

Relations between Sudan and France experienced a dramatic improvement on 14 August 1994, when French security officials left Khartoum on a French military aircraft with the Venezuelan-born terrorist Illich Ramirez Sanchez, better known as 'Carlos the Jackal', in their custody. The Sudanese government claimed that its co-operation in the extradition proved that Sudan did not sponsor terrorism but this assertion failed to impress the USA which kept Sudan on its list of nations accused of sponsoring terrorism. In return for Sudan's co-operation, the French government reportedly financed the purchase of four Airbus planes and interceded on Sudan's behalf with the IMF and the UN. In addition, France provided security assistance to Sudan for use in the war against the SPLA. In October, in order to promote trade between Sudan and France, a Franco-Sudanese council on economic affairs was established in the Franco-Arab chamber of commerce in Paris. There have also been reports of French interest in obtaining additional petroleum exploration concessions in Southern Sudan, and in resuming work on the Jonglei Canal and the international airport at Juba. In late 1995 and early 1996 French companies successfully pursued Sudanese contracts in the fields of mining, telecommunications and power. Nevertheless, France observed the UN diplomatic sanctions imposed on Sudan in April (see above).

The USA has been one of the severest critics of the present Sudanese government. On 1 April 1994, Madeleine Albright, the US ambassador to the UN, visited Khartoum, and warned President al-Bashir that Sudan faced further international isolation unless it took immediate steps to improve its human rights record. She also accused the government of blocking food relief shipments to Southern Sudan, and indicated that Sudan would remain on the US list of state sponsors of terrorism. Sudanese officials denied these accusations, defended the country's human rights record and maintained that the USA had failed to produce any evidence that Sudan harboured international terrorists. In June the US president's envoy, Melissa Wells, visited Sudan, and met with President al-Bashir. Wells delivered a letter from the US president and emphasized the importance of maintaining humanitarian relief shipments to southern Sudan and the need to pursue a negotiated settlement of the Southern conflict. President al-Bashir, for his part, unsuccessfully sought the removal of Sudan from the US list of states which sponsor terrorism.

In January 1996 the USA announced that it was transferring all of its diplomatic personnel from Khartoum to Nairobi, Kenya, owing to its doubts about the Sudanese government's ability to guarantee their security. In April a Sudanese diplomat was expelled from the USA for alleged involvement in terrorist activities and espionage. In May a Sudanese army officer attached to the ministry of foreign affairs announced details of a plan aimed at improving relations with the USA. Under this, Sudan would arrange a permanent cease-fire in the Southern conflict; cease its attacks on the Middle East peace process; deport all known terrorists; increase the freedom of the press; distance itself from Iran and Iraq; rescind emergency laws; and avoid future criticism of US policies. These proposals were apparently formulated independently of the government, which expressed no support for them. In November the USA offered US $20m. in military aid to Uganda, Ethiopia and Eritrea, which, despite denials by the USA, Sudan believed to be intended to assist the Sudenese opposition forces.

Relations between Sudan and Uganda remain poor, largely because of Uganda's support of the SPLA and Sudan's links to Ugandan rebel groups, such as the Lord's Resistance Army (LRA) and the West Nile Bank Front (WNBF). For many years Sudan has tried to dissuade Uganda from giving aid to the SPLA by bombing targets in Northern Uganda. While these have caused little military damage, they have proved a valuable psychological weapon, prompting tens of thousands of Southern Sudanese to flee to refugee camps in northern Uganda and placing a further strain on Uganda's already limited resources. In May 1994 President al-Bashir and President Yoweri Museveni of Uganda met in Vienna, Austria, ostensibly to attempt to improve relations between the two countries. Museveni was reported to have promised to try to persuade Col Garang to participate in peace talks, while al-Bashir pledged to end Sudan's support of the LRA. Despite these mutual assurances, relations between the two countries failed to improve. After Sudanese armed forces attacked targets in Northern Uganda in April 1995 Uganda severed diplomatic relations with Sudan. Shortly thereafter representatives from the two countries met in Tripoli, Libya, to try to resolve their differences. However, the talks collapsed after the Sudanese-supported LRA massacred 250 civilians at Atiak, a town in Northern Uganda. In June Presidents al-Bashir and Museveni met in Blantyre, Malawi, and agreed to restore diplomatic relations 'gradually' and to establish a multilateral border-monitoring group and a permanent joint ministerial team. In spite of this progress Uganda demanded that Sudan dismantle LRA camps at Paloteka and Parajok and a WNBF camp at Morobo—all in Southern Sudan. When Sudan failed to respond to this demand the Blantyre agreement collapsed, although Uganda claimed it was committed to a peaceful resolution of the dispute between the two nations. In July the former US president, Jimmy Carter, who was visiting Sudan, announced that Sudan and Uganda had agreed to cross-border monitoring of each other's activities. Under the terms of the envisaged agreement, Sudan was to deploy an army unit in Northern Uganda to ensure that the SPLA did not engage in the cross-border trafficking of arms. Uganda was to undertake similar action. In October, however, Sudan accused Uganda of providing military support — arms, ammunition and troops — to Col Garang's faction of the SPLA in Southern Sudan. Uganda responded by accusing Sudan of providing similar assistance to the LRA. A further deterioration of relations in December was so serious that it prompted speculation that the two countries were on the brink of open war. President Museveni threatened to take military action against Sudan if it did not eradicate units of the LRA which had allegedly launched cross-border raids on Ugandan territory from Sudan, causing the displacement of some 5,000 Ugandan civilians. Some observers suggested that Uganda's threat of military action signalled an alliance of Sudan's Southern and Eastern neighbours against the al-Bashir regime. The extent of the rift was emphasized by Museveni's expression of support for the secession of Southern Sudan if the North of the country continued to treat the South unjustly. He had previously been a staunch opponent of secession. In April 1996 the Ugandan government alleged that Sudanese armed forces had carried out artillery attacks against targets in Uganda and condemned the aggression; and in July claimed that the Sudanese government was co-ordinating a military campaign waged by Christian fundamentalist rebels with the aim of destabilizing Northern Uganda. In September, however, following mediation by President Rafsanjani of Iran, Sudan and Uganda were reported to have agreed to restore diplomatic relations, such restoration being dependent upon each side undertaking to cease its support for rebel factions operating from the other's territory and to participate in an international committee (also comprising Iran, Libya and Malawi) to monitor the agreement. In November there were reports that a peace agreement had been signed, although Uganda later denied this.

Sudan's relations with Eritrea have also been marred by repeated border incidents, and deteriorated in December 1993, when Eritrean security forces killed 20 members of the Sudanese-supported Eritrean Islamic Jihad (EIJ) after its units had infiltrated into Western Eritrea from bases in eastern Sudan. The EIJ, an Islamic fundamentalist group, reportedly aims to overthrow the Eritrean government. Over the following months, there were numerous other low-level EIJ cross-border raids into Western Eritrea. During 1994 Sudan and Eritrea made at least two diplomatic efforts to resolve their differences. In April an Eritrean delegation arrived in Khartoum, and held discussions with a Sudanese counterpart with the aim of improving relations between the two countries. A joint statement, issued at the end of the talks, committed Sudan and Eritrea to take the steps necessary to stabilize the border region. In August Sudan and Eritrea also signed an agreement under which each undertook not to intervene in the internal affairs of the other; and to ban terrorist activities in their territories. Despite this accord, the EIJ continued to raid locations in Western Eritrea. In December 1994 Eritrea severed diplomatic relations with Sudan, largely because of Sudan's continued support for the EIJ. President Afewerki of Eritrea stated that relations would not be restored until Sudan had severed its ties with the EIJ. The Sudanese government denied that it had provided any aid to the EIJ.

On 27 December 1994 Eritrea sponsored a meeting between various Sudanese opposition groups, which resulted in a 'Declaration of Political Agreement'. The signatories included the SPLA, the UP, the DUP, and the Sudanese Allied Forces (SAF), which had split from the Egyptian-based Legitimate High Command owing to the latter's inability to launch military operations against Sudanese government forces. While stressing national unity, the Declaration acknowledged the possibility of independence for Southern Sudan and expressed support for the IGADD-sponsored peace negotiations (see above). On 31 December negotiations between Sudan and Eritrea, sponsored by Yemen, ended in failure. In January 1995 Sudan demanded that Eritrea withdraw from the IGADD peace committee, which also included Ethiopia, Kenya, and Uganda. A further deterioration in relations occurred after a conference of the Sudanese opposition, organized by the NDA, was held in Asmara in June (see above). In July 1996 Sudanese government forces claimed that attacks had been launched against them from within Eritrea. In October the national assembly endorsed a report by the Sudanese security and national defence committee which recommended — with reference to Eritrea — the strengthening of defence facilities and a firm response to military provocation. On 7–12 October the NDA held a conference in Asmara. Among the conclusions reached at the conference was that the al-Bashir regime was responsible for the sanctions imposed on the country by the UN. Attention was also drawn to the threat which Iranian support for the al-Bashir regime allegedly posed to regional stability. The NDA urged regional instutions and governments to support the Sudanese people's struggle agains the al-Bashir regime.

Until late 1995 Sudan enjoyed relatively harmonious links with Ethiopia. Indeed, during the 1994–95 period, most contact between the two countries was focused on improving co-operation. In May 1994, for example, Sudan and Ethiopia agreed to upgrade their economic ties by establishing trade centres in each others' countries. In January 1995 a Sudanese-Ethiopian meeting took place in Addis Ababa in order to discuss ways of implementing friendship and co-operation agreements which had been concluded in 1991. In April 1995 talks between the two countries on the issues of the Nile waters and environmental protection ended in Khartoum with the signing of a technical co-operation agreement on hydrological studies, the equitable distribution of the Nile waters, the protection of wildlife and forests and the Nile river catchment areas in Ethiopia. In July Ethiopia's minister of foreign affairs, Seyoum Mesfin, urged greater co-operation between Sudan and Ethiopia in order to prevent border clashes and to stop Sudanese farmers from illegally crossing into Ethiopia to establish farms there. In September, however, Ethiopia accused Sudan of harbouring three terrorists implicated in the attempted assassination of President Mubarak of Egypt in June and announced that it would close some Sudanese diplomatic facilities in the country and all non-governmental organizations connected with Sudan. In January 1996 Sudan complained to the UN Security Council about alleged Ethiopian aggression. Ethiopia denied the allegation. In April Sudan claimed that Ethiopian government forces had collaborated with the SPLA in attacks on two towns in South Eastern Sudan in which many civilians had been killed. Again Ethiopia denied the allegation. In June Ethiopia's President Zenawi accused Sudan of attempting to destabilize the region after Sudanese armed forces had allegedly carried out cross-border raids on Ethiopian territory in May. In January 1997 the University of Khartoum closed to allow its students to join the forces fighting Ethiopia.

The Kenyan government has sought to maintain good relations with all of the warring parties in Sudan. The SPLA and most of the other Sudanese rebel factions have maintained a strong presence in Nairobi, which has also served as headquarters for the UN-administered Operation Lifeline Sudan (OLS). The president of Kenya serves as chairman of the IGADD's committee of heads of state and has played a major role in peace negotiations between the Sudanese government and the rebels. A rift developed between Sudan and Kenya in early 1995, when the SPLA claimed that the Islamic Party of Kenya (IPK), an unregistered political party which is active largely in Mombasa, was engaging in subversive activities against the Kenyan government from a base in Sudan. The Sudanese government denied the accusation. On 25 May Presidents al-Bashir and Moi issued a joint communiqué committing their countries to the IGADD peace process. The two presidents met again, in Nairobi, in February 1996, noted the excellent state of relations between their countries and reiterated their commitment to the IGADD-sponsored peace process.

Sudan is opposed to what it regards as Egypt's illegal occupation of the Halaib triangle, a small wedge of territory located along the Sudan-Egypt border. In July 1994 Sudan announced that it had sent memoranda to the UN Security Council, the OAU and the Arab League explaining the nature of the Halaib triangle dispute. According to the memorandum, there had been more than 39 military and administrative incursions into Sudanese territory since Sudan had complained about similar incidents in May 1993. In September Sudan accused Egypt of having attacked Challal port, in the disputed Halaib region. Egypt denied the charge and retaliated by temporarily suspending the ferry service between Aswan and Wadi Halfa. In late October the NIF leader, Hassan at-Turabi, justified the use of force by Egyptian Islamist militants, claiming that such activity was an expression of revolt against a government that did not grant freedom of expression. In response, the Egyptian government alleged that Sudan supported international terrorism. In November Sudan claimed that Egypt's President Mubarak had 'violated Arabism for the benefit of the Jews'. On 30 September Egypt had expelled two Sudanese diplomats on charges of threatening state security. In January 1995 Egypt rejected a Sudanese request to place the Halaib triangle dispute before the 61st ordinary session of the OAU foreign ministers' council being held in Addis Ababa, Ethiopia.

On 26 June 1995 Sudan's relations with Egypt suffered a further setback after an unsuccessful assassination attempt was made on President Mubarak, on his arrival in Addis Ababa to attend the annual OAU conference. The Egyptian government immediately accused Sudan of complicity in the attack and during the following weeks relations deteriorated sharply. Egypt immediately strengthened its control of the Halaib triangle and in July, in contravention of an agreement concluded with Sudan in 1978, imposed visa and permit requirements on Sudanese nationals visiting or resident in Egypt. Relations between the two countries deteriorated further in September, when the OAU accused Sudan of direct involvement in the attempted assassination, and in December when it demanded that Sudan should immediately extradite three individuals wanted in connection with the attack. In February 1996 Sudan introduced permit requirements for Egyptian nationals resident in Sudan. Egypt has opposed the imposition of more stringent, economic sanctions on Sudan by the UN (see above), however, on the grounds that they would harm the Sudanese people more than the government.

Sudan and Libya have traditionally maintained very close relations. In March 1990, for example, they signed a 'declaration of integration' which provided for the merging of the two countries. The declaration of integration was not realized and the increasingly Islamic fundamentalist character of the Sudanese regime after 1989 meant that the two countries could no longer be counted as natural allies. However, the Libyan leader, Col Qaddafi, was reported on various occasions to have attempted to mediate between the al-Bashir regime and its more hostile neighbours, notably Uganda in 1996. Trade links remain strong and the expulsion by Libya, in late 1995, of thousands of Sudanese expatriate workers did not, apparently, detract from the two countries' commitment to eventual integration, reiterated in May 1996.

Sudan has close links with the PRC, not least because the PRC is its principal supplier of arms. In September 1995 an agreement of co-operation in such areas as mining, petroleum and textiles was signed and President al-Bashir expressed his support for the PRC's 'one China' policy. In June 1996 Sudan and the PRC signed an economic and technical agreement under which the PRC granted Sudan some US $3.6m. in order to fund development projects.

In February 1996 Sudan, Chad and the Central African Republic (CAR) announced that they had concluded a so-called 'triangle agreement' in order to improve border security and promote greater co-operation. Among other things, the three countries agreed to reinforce military units stationed along their common borders and to co-ordinate future security operations.

FOOD AID AND REFUGEE PROBLEMS

The population of Sudan has suffered from both natural disasters and the civil war in recent years. In August 1988 it was estimated that up to 2m. people had been displaced by heavy flooding, while estimates by the UN for the whole of 1988 suggested that 250,000 people had died of starvation. In April 1989 the UN initiated an emergency relief operation that was intended to ease the country's plight. In March 1990, a report by the US-based organization, Human Rights Watch (Africa), claimed that as many as 500,000 Sudanese civilians had been killed by war and 'man-made' famine since 1986. In September 1990 Sudan reportedly faced shortages of food as serious as those which had occurred in 1984/85, and it was feared that supplies of emergency food aid would be exhausted by the end of October 1990. The Sudanese government, however, continued to claim that international warnings of an impending famine were exaggerated and formed part of a Western conspiracy to undermine the regime. After claiming for some months that Sudan was suffering merely a 'temporary food gap', in December Sudanese officials conceded that the country faced a shortage of 1m. tons of cereals. UN officials estimated the deficit at 1.8m. tons, and forecast that up to 7.8m. Sudanese were at risk from famine. The government was also widely criticized for hampering the work of foreign relief agencies, apparently on the grounds that some aid workers were sympathetic to the SPLA. A number of aid workers were expelled in late 1990, when the government announced that all aid agencies would be required to re-register with the authorities by the end of the year if they wished to continue operating in Sudan. In December the UN World Food Programme (WFP) was allowed to resume relief flights from Uganda to Juba in the South, which had been suspended in 1989, following threats by Sudan to shoot down any aircraft flying without prior government approval.

In February 1991 the government was strongly criticized by the EC (European Community, now the European Union–EU) for its handling of the famine situation. Al-Bashir responded by telling a rally that foreign relief organizations were 'defaming Sudan by begging on behalf of the Sudanese people', and he added that Sudan would 'free itself from dependence on relief supplies and achieve self-sufficiency in food production in a year or two'. However, after continuing international pressure had eventually forced the government to concede both the need for a large-scale relief operation and its own inability to organize such an effort without outside assistance, UN agencies were, by April, able to resume their activities. The delay in organizing relief shipments led to concern, however, that food would not reach those in need in time. By late April it was estimated that only 6% of essential supplies had been moved from Port Sudan to areas of need. Relief efforts were placed under increasing strain by the return of more than 200,000 Sudanese refugees from Ethiopia following the overthrow of the Ethiopian government in late May. At the end of June, the WFP began an airdrop of food to about 110,000 refugees in the Nasir area of Southern Sudan. Large numbers of Ethiopian soldiers were also crossing the border into Sudan; by late June, about 400,000 refugees were reported to have arrived in Sudan from Ethiopia, most of them Sudanese who had fled the fighting in Southern Sudan in the mid-1980s, but who returned because of increased violence in Ethiopia following the overthrow of the Mengistu regime.

The government's relationship with aid agencies remained a troubled one. At the end of August 1991, the government briefly suspended permission for UN agencies to operate relief flights into rebel-held areas, following statements by UN officials accusing the government of obstructing relief efforts. In November government officials announced that Sudan was self-sufficient in food, as a result of policies to switch plantings on the most productive land from export crops, such as cotton, to cereals. Officials described western claims that millions of Sudanese were threatened with starvation as hostile propaganda. Nevertheless, it remained clear that severe shortages were being experienced in many areas in the war-afflicted South, as well as in the western state of Darfur, where crops failed in 1991/92 after a further year of drought. By early 1992, the UN estimated that, despite good harvests in much of the country, about 7.2m. Sudanese were in need of food aid. Aid agencies had enormous problems, however, maintaining supply lines into Southern Sudan in the face of insecurity and government suspicion of their activities. Relief flights from Kenya to the southern town of Wau were suspended during September 1991–January 1992 after a Red Cross aircraft hit a land mine on the runway. Relief operations were also severely disrupted during the government's offensive against the SPLA in March and April 1992, when the government ordered a six-week suspension of aid flights.

International relief efforts in Southern Sudan in 1993 continued to be hampered by insecurity and by lack of funds. A UN appeal, launched in January, for US $190m. in aid had by May raised only some $40m. In late May the Torit faction of the SPLA and the SPLA–United signed an agreement, mediated by the US ambassador to Sudan, to withdraw their forces from the area around Ayod, Kongor and Waat, known to aid workers as the 'famine triangle', in order to allow the free movement of relief supplies to an estimated 60,000 people on the verge of starvation. In June, as the UN began air-drops of food in the Ayod area, an EC delegation visited Khartoum in an effort to persuade the government to establish aid corridors to people trapped by fighting in the South. By mid-1993, some 1.5m. people were reported to be in need of food aid, with 600,000 having no other source of supply.

In March 1994 the SPLA and the SPLA–United concluded an agreement under which they undertook to deliver food aid to all those in need of it, regardless of their locations; to ensure that humanitarian aid benefited civilians rather than military personnel; and to carry out all humanitarian actions with the full knowledge of all parties. Despite this pledge, both factions continued to obstruct the famine relief process. In early April, for example, the government, the SPLA, and the SPLA–United concluded an agreement under the auspices of the IGADD, which provided for the safe shipment of food to Southern Sudanese war zones. According to the Sudanese government, the agreement collapsed when Col Garang refused to sign the final document. As a result, relief activities came to a halt throughout many parts of Southern Sudan. Nevertheless, the government succeeded in delivering some relief food to areas under its control. By mid-1994 the UN estimated that about 1.3m. Sudanese required emergency food aid. The situation in Southern Sudan subsequently improved, however, and in January 1995, the UN resident co-ordinator in Sudan announced that better security in some areas had allowed people to acquire food on their own rather than rely on humanitarian aid. In September the Sudan Relief and Rehabilitation Association (SRRA) — the humanitarian wing of the SPLA — convened a conference to discuss the operations of the UN-administered OLS. A subsequent meeting in November was attended by representatives of the SPLA, of various UN agencies, human rights organizations and donor countries. In December the UN announced that it would carry out a comprehensive review of the OLS, scheduled for completion in late 1996. In late 1995 the UN also concluded an assessment which indicated that in 1996 at least 4.25m. Sudanese would require some form of relief assistance. Of these, some 3.6m. were located in the South and some 300,000 in camps outside Khartoum.

In January 1996 a meeting of donor nations in Geneva, Switzerland, approved the establishment of the UN Inter-Agency Consolidated Appeal for Sudan in order to assist in the co-ordination of relief activities. In the same month an FAO/WFP assessment team, working in conjunction with the OLS, estimated that at least 2.1m. Sudanese would require some 61,395 metric tons of food aid during 1996. However, the Sudanese minister of agriculture claimed that international food aid was unnecessary as the country produced enough food to feed the population, and rejected the UN's assessment. In February, nevertheless, the UN requested its members to provide US $107.6m. in aid for Southern Sudan, in particular the war-afflicted provinces of Bahr al-Ghazal, Jonglei and Upper Nile. In addition to food shortages, conditions were worsened in 1997 by an outbreak of sleeping sickness in Western Equatona, which by September had infected as many as one in five people.

At the end of 1996 there were about 431,000 Sudanese refugees in seven countries (200,000 in Uganda; 100,000 in Zaire; 70,000 in Ethiopia; 30,000 in Kenya; 30,000 in the CAR; and approximately 1,000 in both Eritrea and Egypt). There were also as many as 4m. internally displaced Sudanese, and large numbers outside Sudan without refugee status. In Sudan, there were some 395,000 refugees (340,000 from Eritrea; 50,000 from Ethiopia; and 5,000 from other countries).

During 1995 the office of the UN High Commissioner for Refugees (UNHCR) repatriated some 15,000 Eritreans, while a further 25,000 were reported to have returned to their homes without assistance. UNHCR claimed that it was providing aid to some 250,000 Eritrean refugees. UNHCR originally aimed to repatriate some 60,000 Ethiopian refugees in 1995. However, lack of funds and increased tension between Sudan and Ethiopia caused this figure to be reduced to about 7,000. In late January 1997 Eritrea refused to sign an agreement designed to facilitate the repatriation of refugees from Sudan to Eritrea on the grounds that its conclusion would have constituted diplomatic recognition of the al-Bashir regime. In December 1995 the Ethiopian government complained to UNHCR that the Sudanese authorities were arresting, torturing and killing Ethiopian refugees. UNHCR subsequently agreed to finance the voluntary repatriation of Ethiopian refugees. In January 1997

UNHCR reported that Sudanese were crossing into Ethiopia at a daily rate of 80 in order to escape violence and famine in Sudan.

HUMAN RIGHTS ISSUES

Many different sources have alleged, and documented, the widespread denial of human rights in Sudan. In addition to atrocities committed in connection with the fighting in the South, these include the denial by the government of civil liberties such as the freedom of association, the freedom of speech and the suppression of opposition political activity. While the most significant reports have concentrated on abuses allegedly committed by the government and the armed forces, many of the rebel factions in conflict with the government in Southern Sudan have been similarly accused.

In October 1994 Gaspar Biró, the UN special rapporteur on human rights for Sudan, presented a report to the UN General Assembly which claimed that the Sudanese government had engaged in indiscriminate aerial bombardment of civilian targets in Southern Sudan; recruited minors for military service; and interfered with the delivery of food relief shipments. It also alleged that all of the warring parties in Sudan had used land mines. In December the UN General Assembly's social, humanitarian and cultural committee adopted a resolution which censured the Sudanese government for these abuses and for arresting individuals who had met UN human rights personnel. The Sudanese government rejected the report's findings as 'outrageous, repetitive, untruthful and politicized'.

On 25 January 1995 Amnesty International launched a six-month campaign against human rights violations in Sudan. According to the UK-based organization, the Sudanese government had purged the civil service, trade unions, the judiciary, and educational institutions of elements opposed to it; and had virtually destroyed all political opposition in the country. Amnesty International also accused the Sudanese rebel movements of widespread human rights' violations, and, in order to stop them, recommended the establishment of an international civilian monitoring group.

Allegations of large-scale human rights' violations in the Nuba mountains have persisted for several years. Confirming such allegations has been difficult because the government restricts access to this region. In mid-1995, however, African Rights, a UK-based humanitarian organization, published a report detailing conditions in the Nuba mountains. It alleged that the army, often supported by units of the PDF, had systematically attacked civilian targets and removed villagers to garrison towns and so-called peace camps in order to isolate them from the SPLA. Government forces were also reported to have destroyed food stocks and animals. Women had allegedly been raped, and suspected opponents of the government robbed, kidnapped, tortured and killed.

In November 1995 the UN special rapporteur on human rights for Sudan reported that there had been a substantial increase in reported abductions, and cases of torture and rape perpetrated, mainly, by the Sudanese security forces. He also expressed his concern at an increase in 'slavery, servitude and forced labour'. After a visit to Sudan in August 1996 he reported that there had been no improvement in the human rights situation there since the presentation of his first official report to the UN General Assembly. In April the UN had published a report which included Sudan in a list of countries allegedly guilty of using physical and psychological torture on prisoners. In May the US-based Human Rights Watch (Africa) accused the government of permitting the enslavement of women and children captured by its forces in the South as spoils of war.

Representatives of Sudan's Roman Catholic community — and of other Christian minorities — have also documented alleged human rights' violations. In April 1996 the Sudan Catholic Information Office (SCIO) claimed that in March government forces had attacked civilians in the villages of Kaunda and Toror, destroying crops and livestock.

The government has denied all of the allegations detailed above. In mid-1996, however, it continued to restrict the freedom of representatives of human rights organizations to investigate allegations of violations; and, in some instances, to deport them.

Economy

THOMAS OFCANSKY

Sudan is primarily an agricultural and pastoral country, with about 68% of the economically active population engaged in the agricultural sector—the majority in essentially subsistence production. Industry is mostly agriculturally-based and accounted for an estimated 17.5% of gross domestic product (GDP) in 1993/94 (compared with 2% in the early 1960s). A major expansion of rain-fed production, which provides most staple foods and some export crops, in the 1970s helped to generate vigorous economic growth. By the early 1980s, however, the progressively deteriorating rainfall in the west and east of Sudan began to reduce production, and the contribution of agriculture to GDP declined sharply. Nevertheless, agriculture has remained the largest single component of GDP, accounting for about one-third; agriculture is also the source of virtually all of Sudan's earnings of foreign exchange.

In 1990, according to estimates by the World Bank, Sudan's gross national product (GNP), measured at average 1988–90 prices, was US $10,107m., equivalent to $400 per head. During 1980–90, it was estimated, GNP increased, in real terms, at an average annual rate of 0.3%, but real GNP per head declined by 2.4% per year. During 1985–94 the population increased by an annual average of 3.0%. According to World Bank estimates, Sudan's GDP, expressed in constant 1986/87 prices, increased by an annual average of 0.6% in 1980–90 and by 6.8% in 1990–95.

Until the early 1970s Sudan's trade deficit was minimal despite a steady growth of imports, thanks to high domestic production and good world prices for cotton (the crop which has dominated Sudan's exports since the late 1920s). After 1971, however, there was a dramatic decline in cotton production, which was only partially compensated for in terms of earnings by a major expansion to rain-fed exports (notably of sorghum). Despite some recovery in cotton production after 1982, total export earnings have continued to decline, owing to drought and poor world prices. In 1996 the value of Sudan's export earnings was estimated at only US $600m., while that of imports amounted to a estimated $1,344m., compared with $556m. and $1,219m. respectively in 1995.

Prospects for the economy remained bleak in the early 1990s, with production of cotton and sorghum (which accounted for over 47% of total exports in 1988) fluctuating. In 1995 the visible trade deficit amounted to US $510.3m. In the same year the deficit on the current account of the balance of payments was $499.9m. The phasing-out of subsidies on many basic commodities and the devaluation of the Sudanese pound in 1991 and 1992 led to a sharp increase in inflation. During 1985–95 the average annual rate of inflation was 83%, but in 1996 the rate of inflation averaged 133%. Consumer prices increased by an average of 101.4% in 1993. In early 1995 the annual rate of increase was reported to be 65%.

The deterioration in Sudan's economic position in the 1970s was a result of the policies pursued by the Nimeri government. Encouraged by the willingness of Western and Arab states to channel vast amounts of concessionary and commercial finance into Sudan, the regime embarked upon a grandiose development programme which emphasized new, capital-intensive projects, such as the Kenana sugar complex and an ambitious road-building programme, at the expense of traditional, irrigated infrastructure and the railways which produced and transported the bulk of Sudan's cotton and other exports. By 1980, such policies, combined with the heavy borrowing involved and growing mismanagement, inefficiency and corruption in the public sector (which controlled some 60% of productive capacity), had brought the economy to the verge of collapse and burdened the country with a level of foreign debt which is now the prime obstacle to economic recovery.

Attempts to resolve Sudan's economic crisis began in 1978 and for the next five years consisted of repeated debt reschedulings and donor aid, underpinned by the IMF, World Bank-sponsored austerity measures and structural adjustment programmes aimed at restoring some balance to the external account by stimulating the production of export crops. After 1981 the new policies, especially towards the irrigated sector, began to have an effect. However, the Islamization, in 1983, of economic policies and the legal code, in an attempt to suppress growing popular opposition to Nimeri's government and to the fall in living standards associated with the austerity programmes, brought this improvement to an abrupt end. This dislocation of the domestic economy alienated foreign donors and creditors, leading to the suspension of several important rehabilitation schemes and the collapse of the vital support programme of debt relief and economic aid. By exacerbating civil unrest in the South, Islamization also created security uncertainties, which led to the suspension of activity, in 1984, on two projects that had been viewed as vital to Sudan's long-term recovery: the Jonglei canal scheme and the exploitation of the country's petroleum reserves.

The situation remained little changed for the first two years following the overthrow of Nimeri in April 1985, with drought compounding the problems of political instability and continuing civil conflict in the South. Various programmes aimed at attracting multilateral and bilateral loans were initiated by the al-Mahdi government, but all eventually lapsed (see below). Following the June 1989 coup, the military regime of Lt-Gen. al-Bashir introduced strict measures in its attempt to ameliorate the economic situation, and government economic policies have since attempted—with little success—to achieve food self-sufficiency, stricter control of the budget and a reduction of the government deficit through the privatization of state enterprises. In mid-1995 the economy remained handicapped by high inflation, a huge external debt (US $17,623m. at the end of 1995), a lack of hard currency and declining foreign aid. In mid-1997 it appeared that Sudan had resolved its dispute with the IMF over the management of its debt to the Fund. However, it appeared increasingly likely that the country would be subjected to economic sanctions by the UN for its alleged involvement in terrorist activities.

AGRICULTURE

Approximately one-third of Sudan's total area of about 2.5m. sq km is considered to be suitable for some form of agriculture. Of this, about 84m. ha is potential arable land and the remainder pastoral. Only about 15%, however, of the available arable area is cropped, reflecting the critical role of water availability in the development of the sector. The vast majority of settled cultivation has, until recently, been limited to the permanent watercourses of the Blue and White Niles and their tributaries in north-central Sudan. It is these areas which, within the framework of Sudan's 2m. ha of irrigation schemes, have been the focus of modern, commercial agriculture—producing the major export crop, cotton, as well as vital import substitutes such as sugar and wheat.

In contrast, some 60% of Sudan's area is occupied by the 11% of the population (enumerated at 25m. in the June 1993 census) who are fully or partly nomadic—combining cultivation of subsistence crops and some cash crops with seasonal migration, with their herds, along well-defined routes, determined by the location of sources of drinking water during the wet and dry seasons.

The rainlands account for virtually all output of the staple grains—sorghum, millet and wheat—as well as of meat, milk and some vegetable products, and output in normal rainfall years has usually been enough for self-sufficiency. Livestock have also been an important export, as have other rain-fed products such as sesame seed, gumarabic and groundnuts. According to FAO estimates, the rate of growth of agricultural production declined in the 1980s, and revived to an average annual growth rate of only 1.7% in the period 1985–95.

In January 1985 Sudan was included on the UN list of 10 most severely drought-affected countries. With Sudan's annual food deficit estimated by the FAO at over 1m. tons, excluding some 900,000 tons of food aid pledged after late 1984, it was feared the country was facing a famine disaster paralleling that afflicting Ethiopia. Nearly all the deficit was subsequently pledged, mainly by the USA, but transport difficulties hampered distribution to the most severely affected areas in Darfur and Kordofan. The establishment, in June and July, of an EC-co-ordinated airlift came too late to prevent the death, from starvation, of thousands of people.

In 1986 famine also became a major problem in the South, where inadequate rains and the disruptions caused by the civil war created major food shortages. The civil war caused relief efforts to be constantly interrupted during 1987 and 1988, and the problem of distribution, both of local surpluses and food aid, has remained acute. In September 1988 it was stated that the levels of malnutrition and the percentage of those dying from starvation among the thousands of refugees from the civil war in the South were the worst hitherto recorded world-wide. In March 1989 the government endorsed a UN-sponsored proposal to call a one-month cease-fire in the war in the South in order to facilitate the supply of 170,000 tons of food and medical supplies to victims of the conflict. 'Operation Lifeline Sudan (OLS)' was launched in April and its first phase ended in October 1989. After a four-month delay, the second phase of 'OLS' got under way in early April 1990 after the government and the insurgent Sudan People's Liberation Army (SPLA) ended their opposition to relief flights. The 1990 programme of 'OLS' aimed to transport 100,000 tons of relief supplies by air, road, river and rail. The World Food Programme maintained airlifts of food under 'OLS' from Uganda to the South in 1990 and 1991.

The consequences of the drought made a significant impact on livestock exports, which had been a major source of overseas earnings in the early 1980s. The national herd was estimated to have fallen by about one-third during the drought years, although by the early 1990s overseas sales of cattle, sheep, goats and camels were estimated by the FAO to have contributed about 18% of the total value of exports, compared with 17% in the mid-1980s. In 1996 the proportion fell to 12.5%.

Almost 12% of Sudan's area is classified as forest land, but a minimal amount is under commercial plantations, largely fuel-wood developments in the central region. Exploitation of the natural forest is also predominantly limited to fuel wood, other than gum arabic, which is by far the most important forest product. Until the 1970s Sudan was the world's largest single producer of edible gum, accounting for some 92% of production, but this was reduced to about 80% with the advent of new producers and artificial substitutes and with it the importance of gum in exports. In 1987 this commodity benefited from a consumer reaction against artificial substitutes, and gum arabic regained its place as Sudan's second most important export after cotton, accounting for 22% of total exports. In 1990 exports of gum arabic amounted to 40,000 tons, worth US $62m. Production amounted to about 30,000 tons in 1991, earning some $50m. in export revenues, but fell to 9,000 tons in the following year, owing to locust infestation. In 1995 the value of exports of gum arabic was estimated at $51.4m., about 9.2% of the total value of exports, although in 1996 earnings from this source fell to $28.2m., about 4.7% of the total value of exports.

Sesame, which is also used locally as a source of vegetable oil, has pursued a similar trend in production and exports. Sesame was the third most important export crop in 1988, when the harvest exceeded 300,000 tons. Output subsequently declined, however, with production totalling only 83,000 tons in 1990 before recovering to an average of about 120,000 tons annually during 1991-93. In 1996 exports of sesame seed represented about 21.7% of the total value of Sudan's exports.

Groundnuts were until recently Sudan's second most important cash crop, and in 1993 the country was the fourth largest producer in Africa, after Nigeria, Senegal and Zaire. Groundnuts are grown both under rain-fed conditions in the far west and in the irrigated areas, and have major local use as a source of food and oil, as well as being a key export crop. Groundnut output has fluctuated considerably, but the trend since the mid-1970s has been downwards as a result of low producer prices, falling world prices, problems related to aflatoxin disease in the west, and drought. In the late 1980s the area under groundnuts totalled 1.2m. feddans (1 feddan = 4,201 sq m). Production, which totalled 218,000 tons in 1989, fell to 123,000 tons in 1990, recovering to 315,000 tons in 1992. Production totalled 714,000 tons in 1994, declining to 630,000 tons in 1995.

Of the 2m. ha of land under irrigation, about 50% is in the Gezira scheme, which is located between the Blue and White Niles. First developed by the British in the 1920s, the Gezira is now the world's largest farming enterprise under one management—the parastatal Sudan Gezira Board. The remaining irrigated land is also predominantly under publicly-administered schemes: the small-scale farmer pump schemes on the Blue, White and main Niles; the New Halfa scheme developed in the 1960s on the Gash river to resettle people displaced by the Aswan high dam flooding; and the Rahad scheme, on the Blue Nile, inaugurated in 1977. Although these schemes account for over 60% of Africa's total irrigated area, they represent less than 50% of Sudan's estimated potential.

Expansion into new areas has been limited by capital costs, and by the terms of agreements with Egypt governing the use of the Nile waters. By the late 1970s Sudan was close to drawing its full quota of 20,500m. cu m per year and began, in joint venture with Egypt, construction of the Jonglei canal in Southern Sudan. This scheme aimed at conserving, by the construction of a 360-km canal, some 4,000m. cu m of the 33,000m. cu m of water lost annually through evaporation in the Sudd swamp. The additional yield was to have been divided equally between the two countries, enabling Sudan to develop an additional 12,600 ha on the west bank of the Nile and reclaim up to 1.5m. ha of potential agricultural land. Work began in 1978 but had to be suspended in 1984, with 250 km completed, following attacks on construction workers by the SPLA. The persistence of civil conflict in the South has effectively delayed any substantial progress towards completing this scheme.

The irrigated sector normally accounts for 40%–70% of export earnings, reflecting the fact that the major irrigated crop is cotton. The main types of cotton grown in Sudan are long-medium staple Shambat B variety (which accounted for about 57% of total plantings in the late 1980s); long-staple Barakat (36%); and medium-staple Akala (less than 8%). A small amount of rain-fed short-staple cotton is also grown.

The share of cotton in Sudan's total exports declined from 65% in 1979 to less than 45% in 1980, partly as a result of government policies which emphasized the development of wheat and other new crops, and the expansion of the mechanized rain-fed sector. A reversal of official policy in mid-1979, under IMF pressure to improve export crop production, brought the start of a large-scale rehabilitation programme for the irrigated sector, which was focused on the Gezira scheme. Gezira currently provides more than one-half of Sudan's cotton output, which totalled 295,000 bales in 1993/94 (compared with around 1.3m. bales in 1970/71). In 1992/93 the total area under cotton was 119,000 ha, compared with 324,000 ha in the early 1980s. In 1996 overseas sales of cotton represented about 22% of the total value of Sudan's exports.

The development of sugar production began in the 1960s to reduce the cost of Sudan's single most expensive import commodity after petroleum. The largest of the parastatal sugar enterprises, the Kenana Scheme, was officially opened in 1981, and played a major role in eliminating Sudan's sugar import costs in 1986. However the development of the sugar sector has been variously impeded by drought, inadequate provision for recurrent expenditure and technical and managerial problems. Shortfalls in sugar production have occurred, as in 1988/89, when output fell short of domestic demand by 200,000 tons. Production amounted to 515,000 tons in 1992/93, 425,000 in 1993/94 and 428,000 in 1994/95.

Wheat, Sudan's other major irrigated crop, is also an import substitute, although attempts to increase irrigated domestic production have had very limited success owing to the unsuitability of the climate south of the Egyptian border area. This causes yields to be very low.

Sudanese economists have forecast that the value of agricultural production will increase to US $611m. in 1996, compared with US $566m. in 1995. It was estimated that production of cotton will amount to 638,110 bales in 1996, an increase of 46% compared with 1995. Opportunities for marketing the cotton crop were also expected to benefit from a decline in world production.

INDUSTRY

The ginning of cotton encouraged the beginning of industry in Sudan in the early 20th century. With the expansion of cotton production, the number of ginning factories has increased, with the Gezira Board alone operating the world's largest single ginning complex. The country is not yet self-sufficient in basic cotton cloth, however, owing to a disparity between spinning and weaving capacity. Cotton seeds are partly decorticated, while exports of cotton-seed oil and oil-cake are increasing. Groundnuts are also partly processed, with oil and cake dominating exports of groundnut products. Minerals (copper, iron, mica, chromite and, most recently, gold), which constitute less than 1% of exports, are exported in the crudest form.

With the exception of enterprises producing cement, soap, soft drinks and vegetable oils, large-scale manufacturing of import substitutes started in Sudan only after 1960. This is reflected in the manufacturing sector's contribution to GDP, which (expressed in constant 1981/82 prices) totalled only an estimated 8.0% in 1996. State involvement expanded dramatically after the 1971 nationalizations. A shift in emphasis towards a more mixed economy followed the overthrow of Nimeri in 1985, but the trend towards 'privatization' gained new momentum in 1988 as part of the medium-term economic recovery programme approved by the IMF and the World Bank. Plans were announced to privatize two agricultural schemes, as well as the four state-owned commercial banks and some new industrial concerns. At the same time, plans were announced to rehabilitate existing public sector concerns, and in March 1989 the government initiated a programme for the rehabilitation and modernization of the cotton-spinning sector.

Average annual industrial growth declined from 3.1% between 1965–80 to 2.9% during the period 1980–90. The amount of idle capacity in the textile and food industries has been of particular concern as Sudan has imported many goods which it could produce itself. At the time of the military coup of June 1989 it was estimated that many factories were operating at only 5% of capacity.

The military government proclaimed an 'open-door' policy to the private sector. It announced in April 1990 that private local and foreign investors would be invited to purchase loss-making state corporations. The National Economic Salvation Programme, unveiled in June, named several parastatal bodies in the agricultural sector and many others in the industrial, hotel and transport and communication sectors which would be sold or reorganized as joint ventures. Further privatization plans were announced by the minister of finance in July 1991.

In March 1992, in an attempt to attract foreign investment, the government announced that it would establish four free-trade zones: at Port Sudan, Juba, Janaynat (in western Sudan) and at Melot (in central Sudan).

MINERALS

Since 1973 a number of international companies have shown an interest in exploring for petroleum. More than 80% of available concessions were allocated by 1983, but to date Chevron, a subsidiary of the US company Standard Oil, is the only exploration company to have made any commercial discoveries. These were identified in south-western Sudan, and were forecast to have an eventual production capacity of 190,000 barrels per day (b/d). In early 1984 attacks by the SPLA on Chevron's oilfield operations compelled the company to suspend all operations, and associated plans to construct an oil-export pipeline were also subsequently abandoned. Chevron had continued until early 1986 to carry out some small-scale exploratory drilling in its concession areas outside the South, but neither the Nimeri regime nor the al-Mahdi government accepted security problems as a justification for Chevron and other foreign concessionaires suspending their exploration operations in the South. However, following representations from the government, Chevron agreed to resume drilling on a limited basis in southern Kordofan, but this programme had to be postponed in April 1988 as the civil war spread into the province. During 1988 a number of companies, including Amoco and Conoco of the USA, were reported to have expressed interest in drilling in a previously unallocated area near the Libyan border. Chevron estimated that its concession area, comprising in mid-1990 about 100 wells in western Sudan, had around 1,000m. barrels of reserves, of which around 270m. barrels were recoverable with present technology. The only other international oil company operating in the country is Sun International, which began exploratory drilling at an oil well in its Nile block in November 1989. According to the Institute of Petroleum, Sudan's total proven reserves of petroleum exceeded 3,000m. barrels at the end of 1994. Reserves of natural gas off the coast of Suakin, 30 km from Port Sudan, have been estimated by Chevron to total 70m. barrels of condensate and 3,000,000m. cu ft of natural gas.

During the early 1990s, the government appeared to be renewing its efforts to develop the petroleum sector without the assistance of western companies. In June 1992 Lt-Gen. al-Bashir announced that Chevron had transferred its concessions in Southern Sudan to a local enterprise, Concorp. In August Concorp announced that the Muglad well had begun production at a rate of 600 b/d of crude petroleum, adding that a refinery capable of processing some 20,000 b/d of crude was to be constructed at Muglad. Sudan has pursued a dispute with Egypt over exploration rights in the Halaib triangle, on the Red Sea coast. In December 1992 Sudan signed an agreement with Iraq to co-operate in petroleum exploration.

As part of its strategy to escape international isolation, Sudan is seeking to become a modest exporter of crude oil. To achieve this goal, the government concluded an agreement with a Canadian entrepreneur, Arakis Energy, which has acquired a number of the petroleum fields in Southern Sudan previously abandoned by Chevron. (Total of France also retains concessions in petroleum.) However the success of any future scheme would require substantial financial investment as well as technical assistance. According to Arakis Energy, investment of US $300m.–$400m. would be required to build a pipeline from Southern Sudan's petroleum fields to Port Sudan; and of a further $100m. for operational expenses (other construction estimates are as high as $1,300m.). Arakis has so far unsuccessfully sought funding from Italy, Japan, the Republic of Korea and Russia, although in 1995 a Saudi Arabian investment group acquired a 43% interest in Arakis. In August 1995 Arakis' shareholders were reported to have concluded a $750m. arrangement with a Saudi Arabian financier to fund the pipeline project, but this collapsed one month later and Arakis was subsequently reported to be seeking financing for the project from French and Asian sources. It appeared likely, however, that any effective development of the scheme would have to await the settlement of the conflict in Southern Sudan. In January 1997 China was granted the right to exploit Sudan's largest oilfield with proven oil reserves at 220m. tons. In March it was awarded a contract to build a refinery in Khartoum with a capacity of 50,000 b/d.

Sudan has pursued other opportunities to develop its petroleum industry. In June 1995 Sudan and the People's Republic of China established a joint venture to explore for petroleum. Sudan was to provide 30% of the finance for the company, while China agreed to provide the remaining 70% and to train Sudanese technicians. China subsequently agreed to make Sudan a grant of US $15m. for the exploitation of its petroleum reserves. In October 1995 the Qatar General Petroleum Corpn agreed to participate in a joint venture with Sudan's Concorp to exploit petroleum reserves in central Sudan, while the French bank Paribas was reported to be involved in discussions with the Sudanese ministry of finance and the Bank of Sudan regarding a $25m. rehabilitation scheme for the oil refinery at Port Sudan. In March 1997 an agreement was signed with four international companies — from Malaysia, Canada, China and Sudan — allowing for shared petroleum production and the construction of a $1,000m. pipeline which will transport petroleum to Port Sudan.

Sudan's other known mineral resources include marble, mica, chromite and gypsum. Gold deposits in the Red Sea hills have been known since Pharaonic times, and there are uranium reserves on the western borders with Chad and the Central African Republic. Until recently, only the chromite deposits in the Ingessana Hills near the Ethiopian border were exploited on a substantial scale by the state-owned Sudan Mining Co, which produces 10,000-15,000 metric tons a year for export. The known reserves exceed 1m. tons of high-quality chromite. In November 1988 it was reported that Northern Quarries and Mines (UK) was planning to develop an iron ore and gypsum mine in the Fodikwan area. These deposits were discovered in 1910 but were not exploited on a large scale until the 1960s. About 83,000 metric tons of ore were exported before political disturbances disrupted work. It is now estimated that there are four or five deposits in the Fodikwan area, with reserves of more than 500m. tons of ore. It was planned to resume the commercial extraction of iron ore in the first half of 1990, after a break of more than 20 years. In recent years Sudan has benefited from a resurgence of interest among foreign companies in reworking gold deposits in the Red Sea hills, which, using new processing technology, have a high recoverable gold content. Gold production at the Hassai mine, which is carried out by a joint Sudanese-French venture, reached an estimated 1.6 tons in 1993 and was expected to advance to 4 tons in 1994. British and Irish mining interests have also become involved in developing the country's gold-mining sector. In late 1996 the Ariab mining company announced that it had mined 3 metric tons of gold to the year ending August 1996. Sudan's offshore sea-bed is known to be rich in precious minerals, as well as copper, zinc and iron, and plans are under consideration for these to be exploited jointly with Saudi Arabia.

FOREIGN TRADE AND BALANCE OF PAYMENTS

More than 90% of Sudan's export earnings are from primary agricultural products. Cotton remains the dominant export, although its share of earnings has declined from 65% in the late 1970s to around 20%, reflecting both a decline in cotton production and world prices and rising output of other agricultural products, such as sorghum and livestock. Petroleum and its products have historically dominated imports, accounting for about one-fifth of the import total in recent years. Other major imports are machinery and transport equipment, which together accounted for more than 27% of imports in 1996, and wheat and other foodstuffs, which accounted for around 16%.

The dominant position of petroleum imports is illustrated by Saudi Arabia's position as Sudan's leading supplier, accounting for an estimated 12.6% of imports in 1996. Saudi Arabia has also emerged as Sudan's single largest export market in recent years, reflecting the increasing importance of sorghum and livestock exports as cotton production has declined. The United Kingdom has steadily lost its former position as Sudan's leading trading partner, but remains its second largest source of imports. Japan and the USA have succeeded the United Kingdom as Sudan's largest OECD export markets as a result of their imports of cotton and, in the case of the USA, groundnuts and gum arabic. Libya, with Saudi Arabia, provided Sudan with substantial amounts of essentially 'free' petroleum in 1985/86, but subsequent attempts to develop barter arrangements (exchanging oil for livestock and other agricultural products) proved less successful. Petroleum shortages were compounded by military requisitions for the war in the South, and by mid-1988 the country faced a major fuel crisis. In January 1989 Sudan agreed to purchase US $150m. worth of Libyan crude petroleum and an arms deal was concluded in March. By 1996, France was Sudan's third lagest supplier, and several contracts, for the supply of goods and services, were concluded in that year.

A trade co-operation protocol with China was signed in February 1989, and technical and military agreements between the two countries were renewed. Imports from China rose from an average of US $26m. per year to a high of $76m. in 1988, while Sudanese exports fell from $57m. in 1983 to less than $1m. in 1985. Commercial protocols, which were signed in April 1990 and July 1991, provided for Sudan to export cotton, gum arabic and other agricultural produce, and import Chinese medicine, food, light industrial goods and construction materials. Official bilateral trade with Egypt was in decline before the overthrow of Nimeri, and subsequently declined still further. In April 1988, however, Sudan and Egypt signed a trade protocol worth $225m., indicating an improvement in trade relations. Unofficial trade, or smuggling, with Egypt (as with Libya and across the Red Sea) continues to flourish nevertheless, with Sudanese camels, sheep and gum arabic securing a premium in exchange for consumer goods. Egypt's initial support for the military coup of June 1989 was expected to lead to a further increase in Sudanese-Egyptian trade, but relations between the two countries have fluctuated. A trade agreement worth $350m. was signed by Sudan and Egypt in January 1991 and ratified by the Sudanese government in June. However, it was with Libya that the military government signed an integration pact in March 1990, during a visit to Tripoli by Lt-Gen. al-Bashir. The agreement provided for the merging of the two countries within four years. A supplementary agreement signed at a joint ministerial meeting in July provided for the removal of border and customs barriers and co-operation in the area of banking, as well as moves to encourage Libyan investors in Sudan. Under an 'implementation programme', signed the following month, Libya agreed to supply large quantities of petroleum to Sudan. Under a trade exchange deal signed in December 1989, Libya agreed to import $27m. worth of livestock, cereals and fodder, and oil seeds, yarn and perfumes, while Sudan was to buy Libyan fuel, chemicals, fertilizer, cement and caustic soda. A further trade agreement, which was worth $57m., was signed by Libya and Sudan in February 1991. Libya's role as Sudan's main supplier of oil came to an end in 1992, however, owing to Sudan's failure to maintain payments. Talks in April 1993 failed to resolve the issue and the government announced that it would continue to purchase its oil requirements on the spot market. However, a lack of foreign exchange subsequently led to severe fuel shortages.

Sudan has had a deficit on the current account of its balance of payments since independence in 1956, but the deficits were relatively insignificant until the mid-1970s, when government policies resulted in escalating deficits on the balance of trade and rising debt-service requirements. Sudan reached its first agreement with the IMF in 1979. This agreement marked the onset of a long series of currency devaluations as well as the beginning of continuing austerity programmes. Further agreements with the IMF were negotiated in 1980, 1981, 1983 and 1984, but none ran its full course. Popular reaction to the economic rigours imposed by Nimeri's attempts to reach accommodation with the IMF ultimately resulted in the coup that overthrew him in April 1985. The military regime that succeeded him continued to face popular hostility to IMF-sponsored reforms. The civilian coalition government that followed in 1986 was riven with internal divisions which prevented, until 1987, the formulation of a reform programme acceptable to the IMF. This programme was endorsed by the IMF in August and was followed, in October, by a devaluation of the Sudanese pound of almost 45%. Efforts were also made to increase the flow of remittances through the introduction of preferential exchange rates. In March 1988 a medium-term recovery programme (approved by both the IMF and the World Bank) was announced. The programme called for a further devaluation of the Sudanese pound, liberalization of exchange controls and trade policy, budget restraint and revenue-generating measures. At the same time further talks were held with commercial bank creditors and donors. In October a dual exchange rate for the Sudanese pound was reintroduced, providing a floating rate in addition to the unaltered official rate of US $1 = £S4.50. The move was regarded as heralding a comprehensive devaluation of the Sudanese pound, one of the IMF's principal conditions for a rescheduling of Sudan's debt. However, the political sensitivity of the IMF conditions was underlined in December when the government was forced to revoke increases in the prices of essential commodities, which had caused a general strike and violent demonstrations in Khartoum.

In October 1989, following the replacement of the civilian government by Lt-Gen. al-Bashir, wide-ranging economic measures were proposed in line with the reforms demanded by the IMF. These included a review of the performance of state concerns and banking institutions, as well as the effect of subsidies on the economy and measures to increase direct and indirect taxes, cuts in spending, and the possible introduction of user fees in the health and education sectors. The price of bread was increased by 15%, to reduce the state subsidy, while bakers were instructed to mix sorghum with wheat to reduce import costs. Wheat and flour were estimated to account for 7.6% of total imports in 1988, representing the principal item in the food import bill; the al-Bashir government has made the achievement of food self-sufficiency one of its main policy goals.

FOREIGN AID

Since 1971 the majority of foreign aid has come from Western sources, with the exception of the People's Republic of China. Arab aid, led by Saudi Arabia and Kuwait, has also been substantial.

Assistance from the USA increased dramatically during the 1970s, in accordance with US assessments of Sudan's strategic importance, and by the mid-1980s the USA was the largest single donor to Sudan, which as a recipient was second only to Egypt in Africa. Owing to the identification in Sudan of the US government as a major supporter of President Nimeri, the USA's relations with the military regime that succeeded him, and subsequently the elected coalition government, were initially strained, particularly as Sudan began to improve its relations with Libya. In March 1986 the US $158m. programme of economic and military assistance for the year was suspended when Sudan fell into arrears on its repayment obligations. The programme was subsequently reactivated, but there was a delay in disbursements until early 1988, when $50m. of funds originally allocated towards the plan to liquidate arrears to the IMF were diverted to support key imports. In May 1989 the USA announced that aid totalling $140m. would be suspended, including $40m. of wheat sales on concessionary terms, which provided half of Sudan's annual requirements. This was attributable to a general re-evaluation of the strategic importance of the Horn of Africa to the USA and the belief that aid has no appreciable effect under the conditions of economic crisis and civil war. With effect from March 1990, the USA banned all new economic and military aid to the country under a law prohibiting all but humanitarian assistance to non-elected governments that have not moved towards democracy within eight months of taking power.

The United Kingdom's US $140m. contribution to the Power III programme had made Sudan the largest recipient of British aid after India. In January 1988 the British government pledged a further £10m. for balance of payments support. In January 1991, however, the United Kingdom suspended all development aid to Sudan following the Sudanese government's decision to release the five Palestinians convicted of killing five Britons and two Sudanese at a hotel in Khartoum in 1988. Substantial infrastructural aid was received from Japan during the early 1990s. Sudan has been high on the list of recipients of aid from the Federal Republic of Germany and Norway, while the EC (European Community, now the European Union—EU) has expanded its aid considerably over the last decade. Allocations to Sudan under the third Lomé Convention, linking the EC with a group of African, Caribbean and Pacific countries, totalled around $150m., compared with some $110m. and $93.5m. under Lomé II and I. The most important of the multilateral agencies has been the World Bank. Its loans, which are granted on generous terms, have included $80m. toward the Gezira rehabilitation programme, together with a $50m. credit for agricultural imputs, and $60m. for the sugar rehabilitation project. In January 1988 the World Bank approved a further loan of $107m. for Sudan's third agricultural rehabilitation programme. However, Sudan's substantial and increasing arrears on repayments meant that not only the USA, but also the United Kingdom, the Federal Republic of Germany and Saudi Arabia, among other bilateral donors, have suspended disbursements on aid programmes at various times since 1984. France and the Netherlands also reduced aid in 1989. In 1986 Saudi Arabia and Kuwait began to disburse their contributions to the programmes for the rehabilitation of the Gezira scheme and sugar projects. Arab aid amounted to $208m. in 1986 and to $228m. in 1987. However, in 1988 it fell to only $127m.—its lowest level since the late 1970s.

The impact of arrears on donors is reflected in figures for gross official development assistance which, after having reached a record US $1,180m. in 1983, fell to $745m. in 1984. A new record level, of $1,223m., was reached in 1985, reflecting external support for the new government, but the figure fell back to $937m. in 1988 and to $760m. in 1989. Sudan's failure to maintain payments was only one aspect of the foreign-exchange crisis which had been growing since the late 1970s, as a result of falling export earnings and rising debt-service obligations.

Efforts to reschedule Sudan's foreign debt and thereby enable the government to maintain Sudan's repayment obligations both to the 'Paris Club' of Western official creditors and the 'London Club' of commercial creditors were unsuccessfully pursued through the 1980s. By March 1989, however, there had been no improvement in Sudan's external financial situation, and the country's total foreign debt had risen to US $13,000m., or $600 per caput, more than double the estimated per caput GDP. Sudan's debt liabilities (including principal and interest) in 1988/89 were estimated at $980m., more than twice the country's projected export earnings. However, the 1988/89 budget provided only $100m. for debt repayment. By early 1990 Sudanese government debt was being traded at just two US cents to the dollar in the inter-bank secondary debt market—the lowest rate applied to any developing country's debt. In April 1991 the Bahrain-based Sudan Development Fund (a group of Islamic financial institutions) proposed a recovery which involved, among other things, making a grant available for Sudan to repurchase some of its commercial bank debts.

The al-Bashir government opened talks with the IMF in mid-May 1990, after being given until July to begin settling debt arrears to the Fund of US $1,150m.—the largest in Africa—or face expulsion. Sudan's total foreign debt exceeded $13,000m. by mid-1990, one-quarter of which was then due for repayment. However, Denmark agreed to cancel out-standing debts of around $23m., and the USA announced it would also cancel debts owed. In March France agreed to cancel debts and interest totalling 378m. French francs. In September 1990, however, the IMF adopted a Declaration of Non-co-operation regarding Sudan, noting that it had remained in arrears in its financial obligations to the Fund since July 1984. It was also pointed out, furthermore, that Sudan had made payments to other creditors while failing to discharge its obligations to the Fund, thus ignoring the preferred creditor status that members are expected to give to the Fund.

After assuming power in July 1989, the al-Bashir government cut bread subsidies, ended sugar imports and reduced wheat imports by half. Following the introduction of strict measures to curtail illegal foreign currency transactions, however, the parallel market rate for the US dollar fell from about £S40 = US $1 to approximately £S30 =1, compared with an official rate of £S4.50 =US $1. A new exchange rate, £S8.30 = US $1, was introduced for cotton exporters, and an incentive rate of £S12.25 = US $1 was made available for remittances sent home by expatriate workers. In May 1991 the government recalled large denomination banknotes and issued new ones in an effort to curb inflation and to control excessive liquidity. This was partly in the hope of gaining the approval of the IMF which sent a technical delegation to Khartoum for discussions with the government. At that meeting al-Bashir stated that Sudan was 'determined to co-operate' with the IMF.

In October 1991 the government announced the reduction of subsidies on a number of basic commodities, including sugar and petrol, which resulted in immediate rises in consumer prices of 65%–75%. To mitigate the effect, a wage rise of £S300 a month was awarded to government employees and grants were made available to low-paid workers. Later in October the Sudanese pound was devalued by 70%, to a rate of £S15 = US $1, with the abolition of the previous two-tier rate. The devaluation was welcomed by the IMF.

An IMF mission visited Khartoum in January 1992 for consultations with the government. In February a rigorous programme of economic reforms and austerity measures was announced by the minister of finance, Abd ar-Rahim Hamdi, who denied, however, that the measures had resulted from pressure from the IMF. The reforms included the floating of the pound, which resulted in an immediate devaluation of 83%. Measures taken to reduce the budget deficit included increases of 30% in import and export duties, and cuts of 10% and 60% respectively in recurrent and capital spending. Further cuts in commodity subsidies were announced, although these were accompanied by increases in allowances to poor families. In his announcement, Hamdi stated that the government was spending £S8,700m. annually on wheat and flour subsidies alone, and that this could not continue. However, the subsidy cuts led to a doubling of the price of petrol, a 50% rise in sugar prices and a halving of the size of a standard loaf of bread and were greeted by demonstrations in Khartoum and Omdurman which were dispersed by police with tear gas. A further doubling of fuel prices was announced in April, in anticipation of UN economic sanctions against Libya, which had been supplying Sudan with 100,000 tons of petroleum a month at a special rate. By late July Sudan was suffering increasing fuel shortages, blamed by the government on difficulties in transporting fuel from Port Sudan, and a rationing system was introduced. With inflation running at an annual rate of around 120%, the government announced that basic consumer goods would be sold through co-operatives at controlled prices.

Sudan's continuing debt arrears to the World Bank, totalling US $1,142m., led it to suspend new lending at the end of 1992 and, in April 1993, to withhold the financing of 15 existing projects, including the Gezira rehabilitation scheme (see above). With Sudan's arrears to the IMF standing at $1,600m., in August 1993 the Fund suspended the country's voting rights—the first time such action had been taken against a member nation.

In February 1994 Sudan's arrears to the Fund were estimated to be the largest ever recorded, at US $1,700m. In the same month the Executive Board of the IMF was reported to have voted to commence proceedings to withdraw Sudan's membership of the Fund. Withdrawal proceedings were suspended in July, however, after the government undertook to reform the economy. In September the IMF postponed withdrawal proceedings until January 1995, allowing the government time to develop debt management policies and economic reforms. In November 1994 Sudan and the IMF conducted a series of successful discussions concerning the status of economic reforms. Sudanese officials claimed that the IMF was impressed with Sudan's foreign exchange policy, which had stabilized the Sudanese pound. The IMF also agreed with the government's forecast of GDP growth of about 7% in fiscal 1994/95 as a result of improved agricultural performance. Sudan had also begun to prepare to implement a structural adjustment programme and had lifted the ban on imports of consumer goods. The government promised to increase taxes by raising petroleum prices, customs duties, airport tax, and sales tax on new vehicles; and to repay some $35m. to the Fund by the end of 1995. In January 1995 the IMF announced that it had decided not to recommend Sudan's expulsion from the Fund, and that it had lifted a ban on technical aid to Sudan. In March IMF representatives arrived in Khartoum to assess the progress of Sudan's economic reform programme. There was to be a further review in mid-1995, when the IMF would decide on whether to initiate a rights accumulation programme (RAP). In April the minister of finance reaffirmed Sudan's commitment to meeting all of the IMF targets, including a reduction of the inflation rate and an increase in export revenue. In June, however, the governor of the Bank of Sudan indicated that a further dispute with the IMF had arisen owing to a request by the Fund to extend its review of Sudan's economy from three to six months, during which time Sudan would remain ineligible for loans. Sudan considered such an extension unnecessary in view of the satisfaction with the economic reform programme which the Fund had expressed in November 1994. In August 1995 the IMF renewed its threat to expel Sudan from the Fund after its executive directors had failed to reach agreement with the Sudanese minister of finance on the monthly amount by which Sudan should reduce its arrears of $1,700m. The IMF was reported to be seeking repayment in monthly instalments of $7m., to which the government responded by offering to repay at a monthly rate of $4m. The dispute over the level of Sudan's monthly repayments appeared to have been resolved in May 1996, when an agreement with the IMF was reported to have been concluded. However, no details of the agreement were published and in July 1996 further negotiations with the IMF were reported to be deadlocked over this and other issues. In March 1997 Sudan avoided expulsion from the IMF by agreeing to a series of economic reforms intended to increase growth and cut inflation. Sudan's progress was to be monitored monthly, and any failure to comply would result in expulsion. Both the Arab Monetary Fund and the Arab Fund for Economic and Social Development decided to freeze Sudan's membership in 1997, as a result of the government's inability to clear its arrears.

PUBLIC FINANCE, PLANNING AND DEVELOPMENT

The Sudanese government, like governments in many other less-developed countries, has historically depended heavily on indirect taxes, especially import duties, for its main source of revenue. Since the late 1970s, however, the share of indirect taxes in total revenue has declined in parallel with the economy, reflecting the cut-backs in imports that have been imposed in continuing attempts to reduce the balance-of-payments deficit.

Government finances began to experience serious disruption in September 1984, when the Nimeri government replaced the 20 direct taxes with Islamic taxation, following the adoption of the Zakat and Taxation Act. One of the first economic moves of the military regime, after it took power in April 1985, was to restore the former tax system. Revenue estimates in the successive budgets of the military government nevertheless proved to be over-optimistic, with more than 50% expected to be provided by taxes on imports and exports, and with the collapse of imports (owing to continuing limitations in the issue of import licences) and of exports (owing to the drought and the impact of disease and weak markets on cotton sales), it was clear by the time the civilian government took office in May 1986 that these projections could not be achieved.

Notwithstanding the deterioration of the revenue base, the new government proved even more optimistic in its projections when it presented its first budget, three months late, in October 1986. Revenue for 1986/87 was estimated at £S2,682.8m., with taxation expected to provide over 60% of the total. Estimated expenditure showed an overall reduction from 1985/86 to £S5,542m., owing mainly to the government's decision to limit debt-service payments to about 25% of export earnings. As a result only £S520m. was allocated to this item. The deficit, at £S2,859.2m., was expected to be financed mainly out of commodity aid grants. The government stated, at the time, that it had delayed presentation of the budget because of preparations for a comprehensive economic recovery programme. However, this had still not materialized by the time the 1987/88 budget was presented at the end of June 1987. This showed a deficit of £S2,884.5m., with expenditure projected to rise by 22% over 1986/87 to £S6,790m., owing largely to a near tripling of the allocation for debt servicing. Estimated revenue, at £S3,905.5m., was 45% higher than 1986/87 projections, with 61% due to be provided by taxation. Actual revenue for the year, however, amounted to only £S2,727m. It thus appeared unlikly that revenue projections for 1988/89 of £S5,885m. would be realized, despite the announcement of substantial rises in the prices of a wide range of goods in January 1989. Expenditure in 1988/89 was set at £S9,767m., including £S2,581m. for the development budget, which would be financed almost entirely by concessionary assistance. In June 1989 it was anticipated that the budget deficit for 1988/89 would reach the record figure of £S8,000m., double the forecast of the previous year. The minister of finance forecast a budget deficit of £S13,200m. in 1989/90, £S5,600m. of which would be financed from foreign aid. Following the coup of June 1989, the military government decreed that all foreign currency was to be traded in by citizens, in an attempt to restore the government's reserves. By early August, US $57m. had been deposited in commercial banks, an amount equal to about 43% of total private unrequited transfers for the whole of 1987. However, the government was compelled to print £S1,500m. to relieve the cash shortage caused by the enforced currency exchange.

The first budget of the al-Bashir government, covering 1990/91, announced price increases on petrol, heating oil, tea and cigarettes, a lowering of maximum tax rates and a reduction of central government allocations for regional governments. An increase in tax revenue was to come from a broadening of the tax base, enhanced collection, and a new sales tax on some non-food commodities. The budget was set at £S15,457m., while recurrent expenditure was projected at £S16,163m., leaving a deficit of £S706m. The allocation for defence was increased to £S4,300m., from £S3,600m. in 1989/90. A separate development budget, based on foreign grants and loans of £S19,000m. and other domestic loans, was set at £S5,200m. Total domestic revenue for 1989/90 was estimated at £S9,200m., against recurrent expenditure of £S14,300m. (or 89% of total projected expenditure) the previous year. Public sector spending was estimated to have taken up more than 65% of total domestic revenue in 1989/90. As a means of alleviating pressure on central government resources, the new budget announced an 'open-door' policy towards the private sector.

The impact of the Gulf crisis, particularly the rise in oil prices and the decline in remittances from Sudanese workers in the Gulf, compelled the government to introduce an emergency supplementary budget in January 1991. Measures included a doubling of the price of bread and diesel fuel and a one-third increase in the price of sugar, resulting in a saving of £S1,600m. in government subsidies. Other spending cuts brought total savings on 1990/91 budgeted expenditure to £S2,200m. A £S1,000m. increase in customs and excise receipts was also projected. In July the minister of finance and economic planning reported that the 1990/91 budget had raised a current account surplus of £S400m. instead of the anticipated deficit of £S705m. The 1991/92 budget, which was approved on 26 May 1991, envisaged an increase in domestic revenue, to £S32,600m., with government expenditure being set at £S42,500m. The overall deficit was expected to be £S1,300m., compared with £S3,800m. in 1990/91. There were to be no increases in taxation on sugar, petrol and bread; however, state employees would receive large pay rises. The 1992/93 budget, presented in May 1992, reflected the impact of the floating of the currency in February, with expenditure projected at £S156,000m. and revenue at £S73,700m., leaving a deficit of £S82,300m. Presenting the budget, the minister of finance stated that revenue expectations had been damaged by a sharp decline in the price of cotton and other export crops. Actual revenue in 1992/93 amounted to £S78,200m., while expenditure reached £S254,940m., resulting in an actual deficit of £S176,740m. Military spending dominated the budget for 1993/94, rising by more than 100% to £S41,070m. The budget also allocated £S150,000m. to debt repayment, and increased subsidies on bread and petroleum prices by 13% and 19% respectively. With inflation rising to an annual rate of 105% in July 1993, further measures to protect consumers were taken in August, including the reintroduction of subsidies on some essential commodities and of price controls on other goods. The minimum monthly wage was increased by 24% to £S3,100. The budget for 1996 (1 January-31 December) projected revenue of £S679,600m., while it was estimated that expenditure would amount to £S2,377,100m. The 1997 budget anticipated revenue of US $704m. and expenditure of $870m., and tax on tobacco was raised to 70% from 50%.

Following the disappointing course of development programmes in the 1970s, there were no further attempts to implement a co-ordinated planning policy until the introduction, in 1987, of an economic recovery programme. This was successfully completed and was succeeded in 1988 by a three-year medium-term recovery programme, the priorities of which were the reform of the exchange rate and trade policy, the reduction of the budget deficit and subsidies, the promotion of exports and a privatization programme. The military government formed in July 1989 by Lt-Gen. al-Bashir presented a three-year National Economic Salvation Programme (NESP) to coincide with the 1990/91 budget. Efforts to reform the economy were to include a reallocation of resources towards agriculture and other productive sectors, and a refinement of the Investment Encouragement Act to create a more conducive investment climate for the local and foreign private sector. Measures to attract investment included the removal of the government monopoly in all areas except oil exploitation, as well as liquidation with full or part privatization of government parastatals. Other measures announced included a review of the banking system, export liberalization and price decontrol, and introduction of a 'social solidarity' system to cushion the effects of economic restructuring for low-income groups. In August 1990 the government announced that it was implementing four measures under the NESP: cuts in government expenditure; increases in tax revenues; a reduction in imports; and wage freezes and widespread job cuts. In May 1991 the government announced that, in order to encourage production, it was lifting restrictions on the price of farm products.

POWER, TRANSPORT AND COMMUNICATIONS

Sudan's publicly operated generating capacity in the mid-1980s was about 1,000 MW, of which about 53% was hydroelectricity and the remainder thermally generated. Some 83% of the total was accounted for by the Blue Nile grid, centred on the Roseires and Sennar hydroelectric schemes. However, because of problems related to shortages of spare parts, siltation at the dams and fluctuations in river levels, actual output was less than 50% of this level. These problems with the public supply led to a major growth in private generation. Estimated at a total 177 MW in 1982, including some 70 MW generated by the sugar schemes (of which some 50 MW comes from Kenana), self-generated capacity is since estimated to have grown by some 50%, with a particularly large growth in the number of private household and company generators in the main urban areas to combat the frequent power cuts.

The growth in private generation also reflects Sudan's highly irregular electricity consumption patterns, with Khartoum and the central region accounting for 87% of total consumption and the south and west only 2%. Sectorally, industry accounts for 39% and residential customers 37%. The completion of new thermal units in 1982, at Dongola, el-Fasher, Shendi and Wau, redressed the balance somewhat, and work is also under way to complete the long-delayed Juba power station and construct new stations at Karima and Nyala. The largest addition to Sudan's generating capacity in recent years came in 1986, with the completion of the Power III eletricity scheme, which almost doubled generating capacity in the Blue Nile grid. A new 60-MW thermal power station at Khartoum North came on stream in May 1985. In 1986 work began to add a 40-MW extension to the adjacent Burri thermal power station, and in 1988 work was due to begin on the first of two 40-60 MW units at Khartoum North. Finance for subsequent projects to enhance Sudan's thermal power capacity has been forthcoming from Germany, Japan, the USA, the Netherlands and Saudi Arabia. In addition, the African Development Bank has promoted a study on power generation and desalination in Port Sudan which would determine the feasibility of a project to supply Port Sudan, Suakin and the surrounding areas with drinking water and electricity. In April 1997 the Islamic Development Bank (IDB) agreed a $22m. loan to raise the height of the Roseires dam on the Blue Nile. This project will increase water storage and power generating capacity. The IDB also agreed a $1.44m. loan for the construction of 13 health centres.

Although Sudan still depends heavily on railways for transport, the road network has played an increasingly important role since 1980. More than 48,000 km of tracks are classed as 'motorable'; there were more than 3,160 km of main roads and 739 km of secondary roads in 1985. The completion in 1980 of a 1,190-km highway between Khartoum and Port Sudan encouraged a rapid increase in the number of road haulage firms and as a result road transport now accounts for over 60% of internal haulage traffic. Only a few of the road projects planned received financing after 1983. By 1997, work had been completed on a 270-km road linking Jaili with Atbara, as part of a project to provide an alternative route from Khartoum to the coast and work on a 510-km road from Omdurman to Dongola began in mid-1992. In the same year Iran agreed to assist in the construction of the road from Kosti to Malakal and Juba. Also in progress in 1992 were studies for a road from Gedaref to Doka and Gullalat, linking eastern Sudan with Ethiopia, and for the rehabilitation of the road from Port Sudan to Gedaref. In January 1997, Lt-Gen. al-Bashir inaugurated the second phase of the Challenge Highway which is expected to link eastern and northern Sudan. He also laid the foundation stone for the third phase of the Atbara-Hayya road.

The total length of railway in operation 1991 was 4,725 route-km. The main line runs from Wadi Halfa, on the Egyptian border, to al-Obeid, via Khartoum. Lines from Atbara and Sinnar connect with Port Sudan. There are lines from Sinnar to Damazine on the Blue Nile (227 km) and from Aradeiba to Nyala in the south-western province of Darfur (689 km), with a 445-km branch line from Babanousa to Wau in Bahr al-Ghazal province. In July 1989, shortly after the military coup, it was estimated that railways and ports were operating at less than 20% of capacity. Shortages of spare parts and the impact of import controls on the rehabilitation requirements of track and rolling stock have considerably hampered the country's railway system.

Although Sudan has about 4,068 km of navigable river, with some 1,723 km open throughout the year, river transport has, until recently, been minimal. The waterway which is most frequently used in the 1,435-km section of the White Nile route betwen Karima and Dongola. Since 1981 the government has been attempting to remedy past neglect, and foreign assistance has been sought to upgrade the rivers through dredging, improving quays and providing navigation aids.

Following the reopening of the Suez Canal in 1975, work began on modernizing and enlarging the facilities at Sudan's principal port, Port Sudan. Work on the project, financed by the World Bank and the United Kingdom, started in 1978. It will increase cargo-handling capacity to 13m. tons per year, and container, 'roll on, roll off' and new deep-water berths are being added. The first phase was completed in 1982, and a revised second phase began in 1983. The port at Suakin has the capacity to handle about 1.5m. tons of cargo annually.

Sudan Airways, the national carrier, operates internal and international services. It connects Khartoum with 20 internal points as well as with Europe, the Middle East and Africa. Plans originally announced in 1983, to transfer the airline to private-sector ownership were deferred following the coup in April 1985, but revived in 1991. Following considerable delays, a US $40m. contract, financed by the Saudi Fund for Development and the IDB, to build an international airport in Port Sudan was finalized in early 1990. A programme has been implemented to restore runways at regional airports which had been damaged by drought, and by the early 1990s most of the work to improve Juba airport had been completed.

Sudan has a fixed telephone network of some 64,000 lines. A mobile telephone network for Khartoum State was inaugurated in February 1997, and it is expected that this will later be expanded to cover other states. In early 1997, three contracts were signed with a French company, Alcatel, concerning the provision of equipment for an ARABSAT ground station, operated by the Arab Satellite Telecommunications Organization (an agency of the Arab League), and the improvement of both the domestic and international exchanges in Khartoum.

Statistical Survey

Source (unless otherwise stated): Department of Statistics, Ministry of Finance and Economic Planning, POB 700, Khartoum; tel. (11) 777003.

Area and Population

AREA, POPULATION AND DENSITY

Area (sq km)	2,505,813*
Population (census results)†	
1 February 1983	20,594,197
15 April 1993‡	
Males	12,518,638
Females	12,422,045
Total	24,940,683
Population (official estimates at mid-year)	
1992	27,323,000
1993	28,129,000
1994	28,947,000
Density (per sq km) at mid-1994	11.6

* 967,500 sq miles.
† Excluding adjustments for underenumeration.
‡ Provisional result.

PROVINCES (1983 census, provisional)*

	Area (sq miles)	Population	Density (per sq mile)
Northern	134,736	433,391	3.2
Nile	49,205	649,633	13.2
Kassala	44,109	1,512,335	34.3
Red Sea	84,977	695,874	8.2
Blue Nile	24,009	1,056,313	44.0
Gezira	13,546	2,023,094	149.3
White Nile	16,161	933,136	57.7
Northern Kordofan	85,744	1,805,769	21.1
Southern Kordofan	61,188	1,287,525	21.0
Northern Darfur	133,754	1,327,947	9.9
Southern Darfur	62,801	1,765,752	28.1
Khartoum	10,883	1,802,299	165.6
Eastern Equatoria	46,073	1,047,125	22.7
Western Equatoria	30,422	359,056	11.8
Bahr al-Ghazal	52,000	1,492,597	28.7
Al-Bohayrat	25,625	772,913	30.2
Sobat	45,266	802,354	17.7
Jonglei	47,003	797,251	17.0
Total	967,500	20,564,364	21.3

* In 1991 a federal system of government was inaugurated, whereby Sudan was divided into nine states, which were sub-divided into 66 provinces and 281 local government areas. A constitutional decree, issued in February 1994, redivided the country into 26 states.

PRINCIPAL TOWNS (population at 1993 census*)

Nyala	1,267,077	Omdurman	228,778
Khartoum (capital)	924,505	El-Obeid	228,096
Sharg en-Nil	879,105	Medani	218,714
Port Sudan	305,385	Gedaref	189,384
Kassala	234,270	Juba	114,980

* Provisional.

BIRTHS AND DEATHS (UN estimates, annual averages)

	1980–85	1985–90	1990–95
Birth rate (per 1,000)	43.5	41.5	39.8
Death rate (per 1,000)	15.8	14.4	13.1

Expectation of life (UN estimates, years at birth, 1990–95): 53.0 (males 51.6; females 54.4).

Source: UN, *World Population Prospects: The 1994 Revision.*

ECONOMICALLY ACTIVE POPULATION*
(persons aged 10 years and over, 1983 census, provisional)

	Males	Females	Total
Agriculture, hunting, forestry and fishing	2,638,294	1,390,411	4,028,705
Mining and quarrying	5,861	673	6,534
Manufacturing	205,247	61,446	266,693
Electricity, gas and water.	42,110	1,618	43,728
Construction.	130,977	8,305	139,282
Trade, restaurants and hotels.	268,382	25,720	294,102
Transport, storage and communications	209,776	5,698	215,474
Financing, insurance, real estate and business services	17,414	3,160	20,574
Community, social and personal services	451,193	99,216	550,409
Activities not adequately defined	142,691	42,030	184,721
Unemployed persons not previously employed	387,615	205,144	592,759
Total	4,499,560	1,843,421	6,342,981

* Excluding nomads, homeless persons and members of institutional households.

Mid-1995 (estimates in '000): Agriculture, etc. 7,071; Total 10,379 (Source: FAO, *Production Yearbook*).

Agriculture

PRINCIPAL CROPS ('000 metric tons)

	1993	1994	1995
Wheat	453†	475	520
Maize	40	48*	50*
Millet	221	970	650
Sorghum (Durra)	2,386	3,648	2,600†
Sugar cane	4,900	5,000*	4,800*
Potatoes*	14	16	15
Sweet potatoes*	6	8	7
Cassava (Manioc)*	7	8	9
Yams*	120	128	125
Onions	80	85*	80*
Dry beans	5	6*	6*
Dry broad beans	18†	45*	40*
Other pulses*	62	64	61
Oranges*	14	15	15
Lemons and limes*	50	58	55
Grapefruit*	60	65	63
Mangoes*	130	140	135
Dates*	130	142	140
Bananas	20	23*	21*
Groundnuts (in shell).	428	714	630*
Cottonseed	99	174	260*
Cotton lint	50*	87†	131†
Sesame seed.	175	170	195*
Castor beans*	6	7	6
Tomatoes*	160	170	165
Pumpkins, etc.*	50	56	55
Aubergines*	70	75	73
Melons*	20	21	20
Water melons*	110	122	120

* FAO estimate(s). † Unofficial figure.

Source: FAO, *Production Yearbook.*

LIVESTOCK ('000 head, year ending September)

	1993	1994	1995
Cattle*	21,650	21,750	22,000
Sheep*	22,700	22,800	23,000
Goats*	16,200	16,400	16,500
Horses*	23	23	24
Asses*	670	675	678
Camels	2,849†	2,886†	2,903*

Poultry (FAO estimates, million): 36 in 1993; 36 in 1994; 37 in 1995.

* FAO estimate(s). † Unofficial figure.

Source: FAO, *Production Yearbook*.

LIVESTOCK PRODUCTS ('000 metric tons)

	1993	1994	1995
Beef and veal*	237	238	241
Mutton and lamb*	75	76	76
Goat meat*	36	37	37
Poultry meat*	24	25	25
Other meat*	66	67	69
Cows' milk*	2,496	2,544	2,592
Sheep's milk	430*	435*	440†
Goats' milk*	566	571	576
Butter and ghee*	13.7	14.0	14.2
Cheese*	70.6	72.5	73.8
Poultry eggs	37.5	38.8*	38.0
Wool:			
greasy*	25.0	28.0	30.0
clean*	12.5	14.0	15.0
Cattle hides*	36.3	36.5	37.0
Sheepskins*	11.3	11.4	11.5
Goatskins*	6.9	7.0	7.1

* FAO estimate(s). † Unofficial figure.

Source: FAO, *Production Yearbook*.

Forestry

ROUNDWOOD REMOVALS (FAO estimates, '000 cubic metres)

	1992	1993	1994
Sawlogs, veneer logs and logs for sleepers	5	5	5
Other industrial wood	2,165	2,224	2,284
Fuel wood	21,287	21,858	22,453
Total	23,457	24,087	24,742

Source: FAO, *Yearbook of Forest Products*.

GUM ARABIC PRODUCTION (metric tons, year ending 30 June)

	1984/85	1985/86	1986/87
Gum kashab	11,313	18,047	37,500
Gum talh	2,775	2,375	2,500
Total	14,066	20,422	40,000

Source: Bank of Sudan.

1990: Total production (metric tons): 40,000.

Fishing

(metric tons, live weight)

	1993	1994	1995*
Inland waters	37,700	40,245	41,000
Indian Ocean	2,500	4,000	4,000
Total catch	40,200	44,245	45,000

* FAO estimates.

Source: FAO, *Yearbook of Fishery Statistics*.

Mining

(estimated production)

	1992	1993	1994
Salt (unrefined) ('000 metric tons)	75	75	75
Chromium ore ('000 metric tons)*	3	3	3
Gold ore (kilograms)*	1,000	1,600	2,500

* Figures refer to the metal content of ores.

Source: UN, *Industrial Commodity Statistics Yearbook*.

Industry

PETROLEUM PRODUCTS (estimates, '000 metric tons)

	1992	1993	1994
Motor spirit (petrol)	95	97	95
Aviation gasoline	5	5	5
Naphtha	22	22	24
Jet fuels	85	88	90
Kerosene	22	24	25
Distillate fuel oils	325	326	327
Residual fuel oils	315	315	316
Liquefied petroleum gas	6	6	6

Source: UN, *Industrial Commodity Statistics Yearbook*.

SELECTED OTHER PRODUCTS (year ending 30 June)

	1992/93	1993/94	1994/95
Flour ('000 metric tons)	530	423	300
Raw sugar ('000 metric tons)	515	425	428
Vegetable oils ('000 metric tons)	180	90	90
Soft drinks (million bottles)	480	336	348
Textiles (million metres)	64	69	27
Footwear (million pairs)	2.4	1.3	5.2
Cigarettes (metric tons)	890	1,935	1,417
Rubber tyres ('000)	300	111	133
Cement ('000 metric tons)	170	186	249

Source: IMF *Sudan—Recent Economic Developments* (March 1997).

Finance

CURRENCY AND EXCHANGE RATES

Monetary Units

1,000 millièmes = 100 piastres = 1 Sudanese pound (£S).

Sterling and Dollar Equivalents (31 March 1997)

£1 sterling = £S2,345.7;
US $1 = £S1,428.6;
£S10,000 = £4.263 sterling = $7.000.

Average Exchange Rate (£S per US $)

1994 289.61
1995 n.a.
1996 1,250.79

CENTRAL GOVERNMENT BUDGET*
(£S '000 million)

Revenue	1994/95	1995	1996†
Tax revenue	212.3	288.7	561.2
Taxes on income and profits	75.1	104.9	173.3
Personal income tax	4.3	7.1	14.3
Business profit tax	64.7	83.6	129.8
Remittances from expatriate Sudanese	5.0	10.2	23.4
Taxes on goods and services	54.1	69.8	120.3
Excise duties	44.1	59.8	113.8
Sales taxes	10.0	10.0	6.5
Taxes on international trade and transactions	74.9	105.9	253.2
Import duties	42.1	60.2	139.0
Export tax	7.2	8.0	36.8
Defence tax	24.2	32.3	61.7
Non-tax revenue	72.9	76.7	118.4
Fees and charges on public services	4.6	45.3	75.0
Public enterprise profits, interest, rent and dividends	5.2	9.3	31.1
Commodity price differentials (petroleum)	37.6	—	—
Commodity price differentials (sugar)	4.7	9.3	—
Receipts from sales of public enterprises	7.8	2.0	3.6
Total	285.2	365.4	679.6

Expenditure	1994/95	1995	1996†
Current expenditure (excl. interest arrears)	278.1	376.0	759.2
Wages and salaries	48.9	60.0	79.5
Goods and services	105.9	155.7	365.5
Ministries	32.8	55.4	78.8
Defence	65.5	80.6	208.2
Social support (incl. medical treatment)	7.6	19.7	78.5
Current transfers	39.1	38.5	122.6
To regions	20.0	16.7	102.0
To institutions	19.1	21.7	20.6
Interest paid	34.0	39.6	107.2
Capital expenditure and net lending	59.5	67.0	97.3
Development expenditure	58.8	67.0	97.3
Foreign expenses	31.0	39.0	41.3
Local expenses	23.5	23.7	56.0
Extrabudgetary expenditure	—	58.0	129.0
Interest arrears on external debt	333.7	501.3	1,391.6
Total	671.3	1,005.0	2,377.1

* Starting in 1996, all official accounting moved from a fiscal year (July–June) to a calendar year basis.
† Estimates.

Source: IMF, *Sudan—Recent Economic Developments* (March 1997).

1997 (estimates): Revenue US $704m.; Expenditure US $870m.

INTERNATIONAL RESERVES (US $ million at 31 December)

	1993	1994	1995
Foreign exchange	37.4	78.1	163.3
Total (incl. others)	37.4	78.2	163.4

Source: IMF, *International Financial Statistics.*

MONEY SUPPLY (£S'000 million at 31 December)

	1993	1994	1995
Currency outside banks	94.54	147.90	248.63
Demand deposits at deposit money banks	62.50	94.87	156.01
Total money	157.04	242.77	404.64

Source: IMF, *International Financial Statistics.*

COST OF LIVING
(Retail Price Index; estimates; base: 1970 = 100)

	1991	1992	1993
Food	27,279.9	40,756.2	60,889.8
Clothing	19,054.6	28,696.2	43,216.5
Rent	21,501.4	31,650.1	46,588.9
Housing	24,778.9	36,895.8	54,937.8
Other goods and services	22,852.3	34,027.1	54,937.8
All items	25,167.5	37,474.4	55.794.4

Source: UN Economic Commission for Africa, *African Statistical Yearbook.*

1993/94 (base: 1992 = 100): All items 753.8.
1994/95 (base: 1992 = 100): All items 859.7.
1995 (base: 1992 = 100): All items 1,287.6.

Source: IMF, *Sudan—Recent Economic Developments* (March 1997).

NATIONAL ACCOUNTS
(£S million in current prices, year ending 30 June)

	1988/89	1989/90	1990/91
Gross domestic product	82,562	110,111	192,660

Source: IMF, *International Financial Statistics.*

Expenditure on the Gross Domestic Product
(estimates, £S million in current prices)

	1990	1991	1992
Government final consumption expenditure	12,138	17,562	28,099
Private final consumption expenditure	90,626	184,859	295,775
Gross fixed capital formation	14,995	25,072	40,116
Total domestic expenditure	117,759	227,493	363,990
Exports of goods and services	7,967	10,719	17,150
Less Imports of goods and services	15,751	40,851	65,362
GDP in purchasers' values	109,975	197,361	315,778
GDP at constant 1980 prices	4,560	4,592	5,070

Source: UN Economic Commission for Africa, *African Statistical Yearbook.*

Gross Domestic Product by Economic Activity
(£S million at constant 1981/82 prices)

	1994/95	1995/96	1996*
Agriculture and forestry	3,178	3,471	3,659
Mining and quarrying	13	90	72
Manufacturing	653	671	698
Electricity, gas and water	193	199	206
Construction	548	538	548
Government services	630	585	571
Other services	2,950	2,965	2,960
GDP at factor cost	8,165	8,518	8,714

* Starting in 1996, all official accounting moved from a fiscal year (July–June) to a calendar year basis.

Source: IMF, *Sudan—Recent Economic Developments* (March 1997).

BALANCE OF PAYMENTS (US $ million)

	1993	1994	1995
Exports of goods f.o.b.	306.3	523.9	555.7
Imports of goods f.o.b.	–532.8	–1,045.4	–1,066.0
Trade balance	–226.5	–521.5	–510.3
Exports of services	69.4	76.2	125.3
Imports of services	–109.8	–223.7	–172.3
Balance on goods and services	–266.9	–669.0	–557.3
Other income received	0.7	1.6	1.9
Other income paid	–20.9	–15.9	–4.9
Balance on goods, services and income	–287.1	–683.3	–560.3
Current transfers received	84.9	120.1	346.2
Current transfers paid	—	–38.5	–285.8
Current balance	–202.2	–601.7	–499.9
Investment liabilities	326.6	276.0	473.7
Net errors and omissions	–82.6	344.8	89.3
Overall balance	41.8	19.1	63.1

Source: IMF, *International Financial Statistics.*

External Trade

PRINCIPAL COMMODITIES (US $ million)

Imports c.i.f.	1994/95*	1995	1996†
Foodstuffs	181.4	214.5	215.5
Wheat flour	40.0	58.9	45.2
Tea	26.9	26.6	32.0
Animal and vegetable oils	25.6	5.8	9.2
Crude materials	196.8	224.8	283.4
Petroleum	178.2	194.2	239.5
Chemicals	116.8	134.0	177.4
Pharmaceuticals	40.4	38.1	27.5
Fertilizers	11.0	15.7	58.6
Insecticides	25.0	31.8	11.5
Basic manufactures	228.6	276.6	261.8
Machinery and equipment	188.5	209.8	238.7
Transport equipment	70.4	112.4	126.4
Automobiles	18.2	38.1	27.5
Trucks	8.9	18.0	51.1
Spare parts for automobiles	21.8	17.8	16.3
Total (incl. others)	1,023.4	1,218.8	1,344.4

Exports f.o.b.	1994/95*	1995	1996†
Cotton	95.5	123.0	133.1
Groundnuts	23.1	21.2	21.4
Sesame seed	60.6	80.6	130.1
Sorghum	21.4	44.0	10.1
Gum arabic	44.7	51.4	28.2
Sugar	15.8	22.0	34.9
Livestock	61.7	84.1	75.1
Sheep and lambs	57.5	71.6	68.4
Hibiscus	11.8	13.1	11.8
Yarn	2.9	7.2	13.8
Watermelon seeds	6.6	8.1	21.2
Hides and skins	15.1	20.5	21.8
Gold	16.8	46.7	48.5
Total (incl. others)	421.7	555.6	600.0

* Year ending 30 June.
† Estimates.

Source: IMF, *Sudan—Recent Economic Developments* (March 1997).

PRINCIPAL TRADING PARTNERS (£S million)

Imports c.i.f.	1986	1987	1990*
Africa	187	215	818
EC	971	919	625
France	87	91	51
Germany, Federal Republic	205	190	150
United Kingdom	283	273	163
Eastern Europe	58	49	40
USSR	2	2	1
USA	186	272	149
Japan	121	194	50
China, People's Republic	68	27	11
Total (incl. others)	2,402	2,613	2,783

* Figures for 1988 and 1989 unavailable.

Exports f.o.b.	1986	1987	1990*
Africa	14	9	158
EC	234	735	443
France	48	60	48
Germany, Federal Republic	47	109	82
United Kingdom	34	123	84
Eastern Europe	96	28	10
USSR	22	4	n.a.
USA	45	70	55
Japan	55	95	118
China, People's Republic	0	0	188
Total (incl. others)	833	1,497	1,683

* Figures for 1988 and 1989 unavailable.

Source: UN Economic Commission for Africa, *African Statistical Yearbook*.

1989: Exports f.o.b. £S3,023.2 million (Source: IMF, *International Financial Statistics*).

Transport

RAILWAY TRAFFIC*

	1991	1992	1993
Freight ton-km (million)	2,030	2,120	2,240
Passenger-km (million)	1,020	1,130	1,183

* Estimates.

Source: UN Economic Commission for Africa, *African Statistical Yearbook*.

ROAD TRAFFIC* (registered motor vehicles, '000)

	1991	1992	1993
Passenger cars	199	201	211
Commercial vehicles	26	26	26

* Estimates.

Source: UN Economic Commission for Africa, *African Statistical Yearbook*.

INTERNATIONAL SEA-BORNE SHIPPING*
(freight traffic, '000 metric tons)

	1991	1992	1993
Goods loaded	1,290	1,387	1,543
Goods unloaded	3,800	4,200	4,300

* Estimates.

Source: UN Economic Commission for Africa, *African Statistical Yearbook*.

CIVIL AVIATION (traffic on scheduled services)

	1992	1993	1994
Kilometres flown (million)	12	12	13
Passengers carried ('000)	480	408	432
Passenger-km (million)	511	580	615
Total ton-km (million)	85	91	96

Source: UN, *Statistical Yearbook*.

Tourism

	1992	1993	1994
Tourist arrivals ('000)	17	15	12
Tourist receipts (US $ million)	5	3	3

Source: UN, *Statistical Yearbook*.

Communications Media

	1992	1993	1994
Radio receivers ('000 in use)	6,670	6,860	7,050
Television receivers ('000 in use)	2,060	2,121	2,180
Telephones ('000 main lines in use)	64	64	64
Daily newspapers:			
Number	5	n.a.	5
Average circulation ('000 copies)	620*	n.a.	620*

* Estimate.

Source: mainly UNESCO, *Statistical Yearbook*.

Education

(1991)

	Institutions	Teachers	Pupils/ Students
Pre-primary	6,525	8,478	350,306
Primary	8,016	64,227	2,168,180
Secondary:			
General	n.a.	29,208	683,982
Teacher training	n.a.	640	5,328
Vocational	n.a.	794	28,988
Universities etc.*	n.a.	2,043	59,824

* Figures refer to 1990.

Source: UNESCO, *Statistical Yearbook*.

Directory

The Constitution

Following the coup of 6 April 1985, the Constitution of April 1973 was suspended, pending the drafting and promulgation of a new Constitution. A transitional Constitution, approved in October 1985, was suspended following the military coup of 30 June 1989.

The Government

HEAD OF STATE

President: Lt-Gen. Omar Hassan Ahmad al-Bashir (took power as Chairman of the Revolutionary Command Council for National Salvation (RCC) on 30 June 1989; appointed President by the RCC on 16 October 1993; elected in March 1996 for a five-year term of office).

First Vice-President: Maj.-Gen. Zubair Muhammad Salih.

Second Vice-President: Maj.-Gen. George Kongor.

CABINET

(August 1997)

Prime Minister: Lt-Gen. Omar Hassan Ahmad al-Bashir.

Deputy Prime Minister: Maj.-Gen. Zubair Muhammad Salih.

Minister at the Presidency: Brig. Abd ar-Rahim Muhammad Hussain.

Minister of Defence: Lt-Gen. Hassan Abd ar-Rahman Ali.

Minister of the Interior and Adviser on Security Affairs: Brig. Bakri Hassan Salih.

Minister of Cabinet Affairs: Brig. (retd) Salih ad-Din Muhammad Ahmad Karrar.

Minister of Foreign Affairs: Ali Uthman Muhammad Taha.

Minister of Finance and National Economy: Dr Abd al-Wahab Osman.

Minister of Higher Education and Scientific Research: Prof. Ibrahim Ahmad Umar.

Minister of Education: Dr Kabosho Kuku.

Minister of the Environment and Tourism: Muhammad Tahir Eilla.

Minister of Energy and Mining: Awad Ahmad al-Jaz.

Minister of Federal Relations: Dr Ali el-Haj Muhammad.

Minister of Social Planning: Muhammad Osman Khalifa.

Minister of Culture and Information: Brig. at-Tayeb Ibrahim Muhammad Khair.

Minister of Agriculture and Forestry: Dr Nafie Ali Nafie.

Minister of Health: Ihsan al-Ghabshawi.

Minister of Irrigation: Dr Yaqub Abu Shura Musa.

Minister of Justice: Abd al-Bassit Sabdarat.

Minister of Trade: Osman el-Hadi Ibrahim.

Minister of Transport: Maj.-Gen. (retd) al-Bino Akol Akol.

Minister of Industry: Badr ed-Din Suleiman.

Minister of Public Services: Angelo Beda.

Minister of Roads and Communications: Maj.-Gen. (retd) al-Hadi Bushra.

Minister of Aviation: Maj.-Gen. (retd) at-Tigania Adam Tahir.

Minister of Animal Resources: Musa al-Muk Kur.

Minister of National Assembly Affairs: Abul Gasim Muhammad Ibrahim.

Minister of State at the Presidency: Dr Qutbi Mahdi.

Ministers of State for Foreign Affairs: Dr Mustafa Osman Ismail, Bishop Gabriel Rorega.

Minister of State for the Interior: Dr Ahmad Muhammad al-As.

Ministers of State for Finance and National Economy: Dr Izz ed-Din Ibrahim, Dr Sabir Muhammad al-Hassan.

Ministers of State for Defence: Omer Abd al-Marouf al-Magzoub, Maj.-Gen. Muhammad ar-Radi Nasr ad-Din, Lt-Gen. Muhammad Abd al-Qadir.

Ministers of State for Federal Relations: Dr Ibrahim Ibn Oaf, Abdullah Safi an-Nur, John Dor.

Ministers of State for Social Planning: Yousif Abd al-Fatah Muhammad, Syda Muhammad Bashar, Maj.-Gen. Hasan Muhammad Dahawi Adam.

Minister of State for Transport: Omer Suleiman.

Minister of State for Roads and Communications: Maj.-Gen. (retd) Sayed al-Hussein Abd al-Karimat.

Minister of State for Public Services: Abd ar-Rahman Nur ed-Din.

Minister of State for Animal Resources: Adam Balouh Muhammad.

Presidential Advisers with ministerial status: Lt-Col Ibrahim Shams ed-Din (Defence), Ahmed Ibrahim at-Tahir (Legal Affairs).

MINISTRIES

Ministry of Agriculture and Natural Resources: Khartoum; tel. (11) 72300.

Ministry of Culture and Information: Khartoum; tel. (11) 79850; telex 22275.

Ministry of Defence: Khartoum; tel. (11) 74910; telex 22411.

Ministry of Education: Khartoum; tel. (11) 78900.

Ministry of Energy and Mining: POB 2087, Khartoum; tel. (11) 75595; telex 22256.

Ministry of Finance and Economic Planning: POB 700, Khartoum; tel. (11) 77003; telex 22324.

Ministry of Foreign Affairs: Khartoum; tel. (11) 73101.

Ministry of Health: Khartoum; tel. (11) 73000.

Ministry of the Interior: Khartoum; tel. (11) 79990; telex 22604.

Ministry of Irrigation and Water Resources: Khartoum; tel. (11) 77533.

Ministry of Transport and Communications: POB 300, Khartoum; tel. (11) 79700.

Legislature

NATIONAL ASSEMBLY

On 6–17 March 1996 legislative elections were held in Sudan for the first time since 1989. The new National Assembly, which replaced the transitional legislature appointed by Lt-Gen. al-Bashir in February 1992, comprised 400 seats, of which 275 were elective. The remaining 125 seats had been filled directly at a national conference in January 1996 by representatives of what were described as Sudan's 'modern forces'. Sixty of the elective seats were occupied by candidates who were unopposed. Elections were not held in 10 of the country's southern constituencies, owing to a lack of security there. All candidates for election to the Assembly campaigned as independent of any party-political allegiance. About 5.5m. of Sudan's 10m. eligible voters were reported to have participated in the legislative elections, and in the presidential election which was held concurrently. In October 1996 deputies were appointed to 8 of the 10 vacant seats representing southern constituencies, where it had not been possible to hold elections in March. The term of the National Assembly is four years.

President: Dr HASSAN AT-TURABI.

Political Organizations

All political organizations were banned following the military coup of 30 June 1989. The more influential parties prior to the coup included:

Baath Party: Khartoum.

Democratic Unionist Party (DUP): Khartoum; Leader OSMAN AL-MIRGHANI.

Muslim Brotherhood: Khartoum; Islamic fundamentalist; Leader Dr HABIR NUR AD-DIN.

National Alliance for Salvation (NAS): Khartoum; f. 1985; grouping of professional asscns, trade unions and political parties.

National Congress Party: Khartoum; f. 1985; aims include nat. unity, decentralization, non-alignment; Leader Dr RIYAD BAYYUMI.

National Islamic Front (NIF): Khartoum; Sec.-Gen. Dr HASSAN AT-TURABI.

Nationalist Unionist Party: Khartoum; Leader UTHMAN AL-MIRGHANI.

Progressive People's Party (PPP): Khartoum.

Southern Sudanese Political Association (SSPA): Juba; largest Southern party; advocates unity of the Southern Region.

Sudan African National Union (SANU): Malakal; Southern party; supports continuation of regional rule.

Sudanese African Congress (SAC): Juba.

Sudanese African People's Congress (SAPCO): Juba.

Sudanese Communist Party: Khartoum; Sec.-Gen. IBRAHIM NUGUD.

Sudanese National Party (SNP): Khartoum; Leader HASAN AL-MAHI; participates in the National Democratic Alliance (see below).

Sudanese People's Federal Party (SPFP): Khartoum.

Umma Party (UP): Khartoum; Mahdist party based on the Koran and Islamic traditions; Leader Dr UMAR NUR AD-DA'IM; member of the National Democratic Alliance (see below).

Opposition movements include the **Sudan People's Liberation Movement (SPLM)** (Leader Dr MANSUR KHALID), its military wing, the **Sudan People's Liberation Army (SPLA)** (Leader Col JOHN GARANG; Sec.-Gen. JAMES WANI IGGA), and the **Liberation Front for Southern Sudan (LFSS)**. A rival faction to the original SPLM, the **Southern Sudan Defence Force (SSDF**; led by RIEK MASHAR TENY-DHURGON), was formed in 1997 from several rebel groups, including the **South Sudan Independence Movement (SSIM)** and the **SPLA-United**. Many of the movements opposed to the Government are grouped together in the Asmara-based **National Democratic Alliance (NDA)** (Chair. OSMAN AL-MIRGHANI). The **Sudan Federal Democratic Alliance (SFDA)** (Chair. AHMED DREIGE) was formed in London in February 1994. It advocates a new federal structure for Sudan, based on decentralization.

Diplomatic Representation

EMBASSIES IN SUDAN

Algeria: St 31, New Extension, POB 80, Khartoum; tel. (11) 741954; Ambassador: SALIH BEN KOBBI.

Bulgaria: St 31, Middle Road, New Extension, POB 1690, Khartoum; tel. (11) 743414; Ambassador: T. F. MITEV.

Chad: 21, St 17, New Extension, POB 1514, Khartoum; tel. (11) 742545; Ambassador: MBAILAOU BERAL MOISE.

China, People's Republic: 93, St 22, POB 1425, Khartoum; tel. (11) 222036; Ambassador: WU DUCHENG.

Congo, Democratic Republic: St 13, Block 12CE, New Extension, 23, POB 4195, Khartoum; tel. (11) 742424; telex 24192; Ambassador: MGBAMA MPWA.

Czech Republic: 39, St 39, POB 1047, Khartoum; tel. (11) 743448.

Egypt: Al-Gamma St, POB 1126, Khartoum; tel. (11) 772836; telex 22545; Ambassador: HASSAN ABD AL-HAK GAD AL-HAK.

Ethiopia: 6, 11A St 3, New Extension, POB 844, Khartoum; Chargé d'affaires a.i.: Dr AWOKE AGONGFER.

France: Plot No. 163, Block 8, Burri, POB 377, Khartoum; tel. (11) 225608; telex 22220; Ambassador: MICHEL RAIMBAUD.

Germany: Baladia St, Block No. 8DE, Plot No. 2, POB 970, Khartoum; tel. (11) 777990; telex 22211; fax (11) 777622; Ambassador: Dr WERNER DAUM.

Greece: Sharia al-Gamhouria, Block 5, No. 30, POB 1182, Khartoum; tel. (11) 773155; Ambassador: VASSILIS COUZOPOULOS.

Holy See: Kafouri Belgravia, POB 623, Khartoum (Apostolic Nunciature); tel. (11) 774692; telex 26032; Apostolic Pro-Nuncio: Most Rev. ERWIN JOSEF ENDER, Titular Archbishop of Germania in Numidia.

India: 61 Africa Rd, POB 707, Khartoum; tel. (11) 740560; telex 22228; Ambassador: VIRENDRA P. SINGH.

Iran: House No. 8, Square 2, Mogran, Khartoum; tel. (11) 748843; Chargé d'affaires a.i.: NIMATALLAH GADIR.

Iraq: Khartoum; tel. (11) 745428; telex 24035; Ambassador: TARIQ MOHAMMED YAHYA.

Italy: St 39, POB 793, Khartoum; tel. (11) 745326; telex 24034; Ambassador: Dr MAURIZIO BATTAGLINI.

Japan: 24, Block AE, St 3, New Extension, POB 1649, Khartoum; tel. (11) 744554; telex 24019; Ambassador: YOSHINORI IMAGAWA.

Jordan: 25, St 7, New Extension, Khartoum; tel. (11) 743264; telex 24047; Ambassador: MOHAMMED JUMA ASANA.

Kenya: POB 8242, Khartoum; tel. (11) 440386; telex 24190; fax (11) 452265; Ambassador: GIDEON NYAMWEYA NYAANGA.

Korea, Republic: House 2, St 1, New Extension, POB 2414, Khartoum; tel. (11) 451136; telex 24029; fax (11) 452822; Ambassador: SAE DON CHANG.

Kuwait: Africa Ave, near the Tennis Club, POB 1457, Khartoum; tel. (11) 781525; telex 24043; Ambassador: (vacant).

Libya: 50 Africa Rd, POB 2091, Khartoum; Secretary of People's Bureau: GUMMA AL-FAZANI.

Morocco: 32, St 19, New Extension, POB 2042, Khartoum; tel. (11) 743223; Ambassador: MOHAMMED KAMLICHI.

Netherlands: St 47, House No. 47, POB 391, Khartoum; tel. (11) 471200; telex 24013; fax 471204; Ambassador: P.R. POST.

Nigeria: St 17, Sharia al-Mek Nimr, POB 1538, Khartoum; tel. (11) 779120; telex 22222; Ambassador: IBRAHIM KARLI.

Oman: St 1, New Extension, POB 2839, Khartoum; tel. (11) 745791; Ambassador: MOSLIM EBIN ZAIDAN AL-BARAMI.

Pakistan: House No. 94, Block 16, ar-Riyadh, POB 1178, Khartoum; tel. (11) 742518; telex 24219; Ambassador: KHALID NIZAMI.

Poland: 73 Africa Rd, POB 902, Khartoum; tel. (11) 744248; Chargé d'affaires a.i.: WALDEMAR POPIOLEK.

Qatar: St 15, New Extension, POB 223, Khartoum; tel. (11) 742208; telex 22223; Chargé d'affaires a.i.: HASSAN AHMED ABDULLAH ABU HINDI.

Romania: Kassala Rd, Plot No. 172–173, Kafouri Area, POB 1494, Khartoum North; tel. (11) 613445; telex 24188; Chargé d'affaires a.i.: GHEORGHE GUSTEA.

Russia: B1, A10 St, New Extension, POB 1161, Khartoum; Ambassador: VALERII Y. SUKHIN.

Saudi Arabia: St 11, New Extension, Khartoum; tel. (11) 741938; Ambassador: SAYED MOHAMMED SIBRI SULIMAN.

Somalia: St 23–25, New Extension, POB 1857, Khartoum; tel. (11) 744800; Ambassador: MUHAMMAD Sheikh AHMED.

Spain: St 3, New Extension, POB 2621, Khartoum; tel. (11) 745072; telex 22476; Ambassador: JUAN ALFONSO ORTIZ RAMOS.

Switzerland: Amarat, Street 15, POB 1707, Khartoum; tel. (11) 451010; telex 24327; fax (11) 452804; Chargé d'affaires a.i.: GIANBATTISTA MONDADA.

Syria: St 3, New Extension, POB 1139, Khartoum; tel. (11) 744663; Ambassador: MOHAMMED AL-MAHAMEED.

Turkey: 31, St 29, New Extension, POB 771, Khartoum; tel. (11) 451197; fax 451197; Ambassador: ERDINÇ ERDÜN.

United Arab Emirates: St 3, New Extension, POB 1225, Khartoum; tel. (11) 744476; telex 24024; Ambassador: MOHAMMED SULTAN AS-SUAIDI.

United Kingdom: St 10, off Baladia St, POB 801, Khartoum; tel. (11) 777105; telex 22189; fax (11) 776457; Ambassador: ALAN F. GOULTY.

Yemen: St 11, New Extension, POB 1010, Khartoum; tel. (11) 743918; Ambassador: ABD AS-SALAM HUSSEIN.

Yugoslavia: St 31, 49A, POB 1180, Khartoum 1; tel. (11) 741252; Ambassador: VLADIMIR PETKOVSKI.

Judicial System

Until September 1983 the judicial system was divided into two sections, civil and Islamic, the latter dealing only with personal and family matters. In September 1983 President Nimeri replaced all existing laws with Islamic (Shari'a) law. Following the coup in April 1985, the Shari'a courts were abolished, and it was announced that the previous system of criminal courts was to be revived. In June 1986 the Prime Minister, Sadiq al-Mahdi, reaffirmed that the Shari'a law was to be abolished. It was announced in June 1987 that a new legal code, based on a 'Sudanese legal heritage', was to be introduced. In July 1989 the military Government established special courts to investigate violations of emergency laws concerning corruption. It was announced in June 1991 that these courts were to be incorporated in the general court administration. Islamic law was reintroduced in March 1991, but was not applied in the southern states of Equatoria, Bahr al-Ghazal and Upper Nile.

Chief Justice: OBIED HAJ ALI.

Religion

The majority of the northern Sudanese population are Muslims, while in the south the population are mostly either animists or Christians.

ISLAM

Islam is the state religion. Sudanese Islam has a strong Sufi element, and is estimated to have more than 15m. adherents.

CHRISTIANITY

Sudan Council of Churches: Inter-Church House, St 35, New Extension, POB 469, Khartoum; tel. (11) 742859; telex 24099; f. 1967; 12 mem. churches; Chair. Most Rev. PAOLINO LUKUDU LORO (Roman Catholic Archbishop of Juba); Gen. Sec. Rev. CLEMENT H. JANDA.

Roman Catholic Church

Latin Rite

Sudan comprises two archdioceses and seven dioceses. At the end of 1995 there were about 2.8m. adherents in the country, representing about 8% of the total population.

Sudan Catholic Bishops' Conference: General Secretariat, POB 6011, Khartoum; tel. (11) 225075; telex 24261; fax (11) 703518; f. 1971; Pres. Most Rev. GABRIEL ZUBEIR WAKO, Archbishop of Khartoum.

Archbishop of Juba: Most Rev. PAOLINO LUKUDU LORO, Catholic Church, POB 32, Juba, Equatoria State; tel. 2930; fax 24261.

Archbishop of Khartoum: Most Rev. GABRIEL ZUBEIR WAKO, Catholic Church, POB 49, Khartoum; tel. (11) 782174; fax (11) 783518.

Maronite Rite

Maronite Church in Sudan: POB 244, Khartoum; Rev. Fr YOUSEPH NEAMA.

Melkite Rite

Patriarchal Vicariate of Egypt and Sudan: Patriarcat Grec-Melkite Catholique, 16 rue Daher, Cairo, Egypt; tel. (2) 5905790 (Vicar Patriarchal: Most Rev. PAUL ANTAKI, Titular Archbishop of Nubia); Vicar in Sudan: Fr GEORGE BANNA, POB 766, Khartoum; tel. (11) 776466.

Orthodox Churches

Coptic Orthodox Church: Bishop of Nubia, Atbara and Omdurman: Rt Rev. BAKHOMIOS; Bishop of Khartoum, Southern Sudan and Uganda: Rt Rev. ANBA YOUANNIS.

Greek Orthodox Church: POB 47, Khartoum; tel. (11) 772973; Metropolitan of Nubia: Archbishop DIONYSSIOS HADZIVASSILIOU.

The Ethiopian Orthodox Church is also active.

The Anglican Communion

Anglicans are adherents of the (Episcopal) Church of the Province of the Sudan. The Province, with four dioceses and about 1m. adherents, was established in 1976.

Archbishop in Sudan and Bishop of Juba: Most Rev. BENJAMIN W. YUGUSUK; POB 110, Juba.

Other Christian Churches

Evangelical Church: POB 57, Khartoum; c. 1,500 mems; administers schools, literature centre and training centre; Chair Rev. RADI ELIAS.

Presbyterian Church: POB 40, Malakal; autonomous since 1956; 67,000 mems (1985); Gen. Sec. Rev. THOMAS MALUIT.

Sudan Interior Mission (SIM): Dir R. WELLING, POB 220, Khartoum; tel. (11) 452790; fax (11) 467213; f. 1937.

The Africa Inland Church and the Sudanese Church of Christ are also active.

The Press

DAILIES

Press censorship was imposed following the coup of 30 June 1989. The only publications permitted were the armed forces' weekly newspaper, *Al-Guwwat al-Musallaha*, and the government-controlled dailies, *Al-Engaz al-Watan* and *As-Sudan al-Hadeeth*. The principal publications in circulation prior to the coup included:

Al-Aban: Khartoum; state-controlled.

Al-Ayyam (The Days): POB 2158, Khartoum; tel. (11) 774321; f. 1953; Arabic; Chair. and Editor-in-Chief HASSAN SATTI; circ. 60,000 (publication suspended since Aug. 1986).

Al-Khartoum: Khartoum; Arabic.

Al-Midan (The Field): Khartoum; Arabic; supports Sudanese Communist Party.

Ar-Rayah (The Banner); Khartoum; Arabic.

Sudan Times: Khartoum; English; Editor BONA MALWAL.

As-Sudani (The Sudanese): Khartoum.

Ath-Thawra (The Revolution): Khartoum; Arabic.

Al-Usbu (The Week): Khartoum; Arabic.

PERIODICALS

Al-Guwwat al-Musallaha (The Armed Forces): Khartoum; f.1969; publs a weekly newspaper and monthly magazine for the armed forces; Editor-in-Chief Maj. MAHMOUD GALANDER; circ. 7,500.

New Horizon: POB 2651, Khartoum; tel. (11) 777913; telex 22418; f. 1976; publ. by the Sudan House for Printing and Publishing; weekly; English; political and economic affairs, development, home and international news; Editor-in-Chief MATTHEW OBUR AYANG; circ. 7,000.

Sudanow: POB 2651, Khartoum; tel. (11) 777913; telex 22956; f. 1976; publ. by the Sudan House for Printing and Publishing; monthly; English; political and economic affairs, arts, social affairs and diversions; Editor-in-Chief AHMED KAMAL ED-DIN; circ. 10,000.

NEWS AGENCIES

Sudan News Agency (SUNA): Sharia al-Gamhouria, POB 1506, Khartoum; tel. (11) 775770; telex 22418; Dir-Gen. TAYYIB HAI ATIYAH.

Sudanese Press Agency: Khartoum; f. 1985; owned by journalists.

Foreign Bureaux

Agence France-Presse (AFP): POB 1911, Khartoum; telex 22418; Rep. MUHAMMAD ALI SAID.

Middle East News Agency (MENA) (Egypt): Dalala Bldg, POB 740, Khartoum.

Xinhua (New China) News Agency (People's Republic of China): No. 100, 12 The Sq., Riad Town, POB 2229, Khartoum; tel. (11) 224174; telex 24205; Correspondent SUN XIAOKE.

The Iraqi News Agency and the Agence Arabe Syrienne d'Information (Syria) also have bureaux in Khartoum.

Publishers

Ahmad Abd ar-Rahman at-Tikeine: POB 299, Port Sudan.

Al-Ayyam Press Co Ltd: POB 363, Aboulela Bldg, United Nations Sq., Khartoum; f. 1953; general fiction and non-fiction, arts, poetry, reference, newspapers, magazines; Man. Dir BESHIR MUHAMMAD SAID.

As-Sahafa Publishing and Printing House: POB 1228, Khartoum; f. 1961; newspapers, pamphlets, fiction and govt publs.

As-Salam Co Ltd: POB 944, Khartoum.

Claudios S. Fellas: POB 641, Khartoum.

Khartoum University Press: POB 321, Khartoum; tel. (11) 776653; telex 22738; f. 1964; academic, general and educational in Arabic and English; Man. Dir KHALID AL-MUBARAK.

Government Publishing House

El-Asma Printing Press: POB 38, Khartoum.

Radio and Television

In 1994, according to UNESCO, there were an estimated 7m. radio receivers and 2.2m. television receivers in use.

RADIO

Sudan National Broadcasting Corpn: POB 1094, Omdurman; tel. (11) 552100; state-controlled service broadcasting daily in Arabic, English, French and Swahili; Dir-Gen. SALAH AD-DIN AL-FADHIL USUD.

TELEVISION

An earth satellite station operated on 36 channels at Umm Haraz has much improved Sudan's telecommunication links. A nationwide satellite network is being established with 14 earth stations in the provinces. A microwave network of television transmission covered 90% of inhabited areas in 1983. There are regional stations at Gezira (Central Region) and Atbara (Northern Region).

Sudan Television: POB 1094, Omdurman; tel. 550022; telex 28002; f. 1962; state-controlled; 60 hours of programmes per week; Head of Directorate HADID AS-SIRA.

Finance

(cap. = capital; res = reserves; dep. = deposits; m. = million; brs = branches; amounts in Sudanese pounds unless otherwise stated)

BANKING

All domestic banks are controlled by the Bank of Sudan. Foreign banks were permitted to resume operations in 1976. In December 1985 the government banned the establishment of any further banks. It was announced in December 1990 that Sudan's banking system was to be reorganized to accord with Islamic principles.

Central Bank

Bank of Sudan: Gamaa Ave, POB 313, Khartoum; tel. (11) 778064; telex 22352; f. 1960; bank of issue; cap. and res 70.1m. (Dec. 1989); Gov. ABDULLAH HASSAN AHMED; 9 brs.

Commercial Banks

Al-Baraka Bank: Al-Baraka Tower, Sharia al-Kasr, POB 3583, Khartoum; tel. (11) 774104; telex 22555; fax (11) 778948; f. 1984; investment and export promotion; cap. 55.3m., total assets 7,159.1m. (Dec. 1993); Pres. Sheikh SALIH ABDALLA KAMIL; 33 brs.

Bank of Khartoum: 8 Gamhouria Ave, POB 1008, Khartoum; tel. (11) 772880; telex 22181; fax (11) 781120; f. 1913; absorbed National Export/Import Bank and Unity Bank in 1993; cap. and res 4,457.7m., total assets 121,308.2m. (1995); Gen. Man. Dr ISMAIL MUHAMMAD GORASHI; 118 brs.

Islamic Bank for Western Sudan: United Nations Sq., POB 3575, Khartoum; tel. (11) 779918; telex 23046; f. 1984; cap. 393m., total assets 8,908m. (Dec. 1994); Chair. IBRAHIM MOUNIEM MANSOUR; Gen. Man. ESH-SHARIEF EL-KHATIM; 28 brs.

National Bank of Sudan: Kronfli Bldg, Al-Qasr Ave, POB 1183, Khartoum; tel. (11) 78154; telex 22058; fax (11) 779497; f. 1982; cap. 39.2m. (Dec. 1991); Chair. HASSAN IBRAHIM MALIK; 16 brs in Sudan, 2 abroad.

Omdurman National lBank: POB 11522, Khartoum; tel. (11) 770400; telex 22873; fax (11) 770392; f. 1993; cap. and res 2,000.4m, dep 10,881.8m., total assets 14,908.3m. (Dec. 1994); Chair. SID AHMED SIRAG; 11 brs.

People's Co-operative Bank: POB 922, Khartoum; tel. (11) 773555; telex 22247; Chair. KARAMALLAH AL-AWAD.

Sudan Commercial Bank: Al-Qasr Ave, POB 1116, Khartoum; tel. (11) 779836; telex 22434; fax (11) 774194; f. 1960; cap. 10m., total assets 10,143.7m. (Dec. 1993); Chair. ET-TAYB ELOBEID BADR; 19 brs.

Sudanese French Bank: Zubair Basha St, POB 2775, Khartoum; tel. (11) 776542; telex 22204; fax (11) 71740; f. 1978 as Sudanese Investment Bank; cap. 555m. (Dec. 1993); Chair. Dr ABBAS MUSTAFA OSMAN; 16 brs.

Tadamun Islamic Bank: Baladia Ave, POB 3154, Khartoum; tel. (11) 771848; telex 22158; fax (11) 773840; f. 1983; cap. 49.7m., dep. 32,965.1m., total assets 44,313.4m. (Dec. 1995); Pres. ET-TIGANI HASSAN HILAL; 28 brs.

Foreign Banks

Blue Nile Bank Ltd: Zubeir Pasha Ave, POB 984, Khartoum; tel. (11) 778925; telex 22905; f. 1983; cap. 31.9m., total assets 197.2m. (Dec. 1991); jtly controlled by the Govts of Sudan and the Repub. of Korea; Chair. CHAN SUP LEE.

Citibank NA (USA): SDC Bldg, St 19, New Extension, POB 8027, Khartoum; tel. (11) 747615; telex 22454; f. 1978; cap. and res 48m., total assets 400m. (Dec. 1989); Gen. Man. ADNAN MOHAMED.

Faisal Islamic Bank (Sudan) (Saudi Arabia): Ali Abdel Latif Ave, POB 10143, Khartoum; tel. (11) 781848; telex 22519; fax (11) 80193; f. 1977; cap. 117.7m., total assets 16,490m. (Dec. 1993); Chair. Prince MUHAMMAD AL-FAISAL AS-SAUD.

Habib Bank (Pakistan): Baladia St, POB 8246, Khartoum; tel. (11) 781497; telex 22490; f. 1982; cap. and res 13.8m., total assets 27.3m. (Dec. 1987); Gen. Man. BAZ MUHAMMAD KHAN.

Mashreq Bank PSC (United Arab Emirates): Baladia St, POB 371, Khartoum; tel. (11) 772969; telex 22124; fax (11) 772743; Man. ZULFIQAR MUHAMMAD.

Middle East Bank Ltd (United Arab Emirates): Kronfli Bldg, Al-Qasr Ave, POB 1950, Khartoum; tel. (11) 773794; telex 22516; fax (11) 773696; f. 1982; cap. and res 9.9m., total assets 8.9m. (Dec. 1987); Chief Man. FAISAL HASSOUN.

National Bank of Abu Dhabi (United Arab Emirates): Atbara St, POB 2465, Khartoum; tel. (11) 774870; telex 22249; f. 1976; cap. and res 16.9m., total assets 12.5m. (Dec. 1987); Man. GAAFAR OSMAN.

Saudi Sudanese Bank: Baladia St, POB 1773, Khartoum; tel. (11) 776700; telex 22899; fax (11) 81836; f. 1986; Saudi Arabian shareholders have a 60% interest, Sudanese shareholders 40%; cap. 25m., res 282.3m., total assets 3,909m.; Chair. Sheikh MAHFOUZ SALIM BIN MAHFOUZ.

Development Banks

Agricultural Bank of Sudan: POB 1363, Khartoum; tel. (11) 77432; telex 22610; fax (11) 778296; f. 1957; cap. p.u. 200m.; provides finance for agricultural projects; Dir-Gen. BADR AD-DIN TAHA; 40 brs.

Arab-African International Bank: POB 2721, Khartoum; tel. 775573; telex 22624; Rep. SHEIKH HASSAN BELAIL.

Islamic Co-operative Development Bank (ICDB): POB 62, Khartoum; tel. (11) 780223; telex 22906; fax (11) 777715; f. 1983; cap. 16.4m. (Dec. 1990); 6 brs.

National Development Bank: Tower No. 1, 8th Floor, Khwaiti Bldg, An-Nil St, POB 655, Khartoum; tel. (11) 779496; telex 22835; f. 1982; finances or co-finances economic and social development projects; cap. 5m. (Dec. 1992); Chair. MUHAMMAD DAOUD ALKHALIFA; 6 brs.

Nilein Industrial Development Bank: United Nations Sq., POB 1722, Khartoum; tel. (11) 780929; telex 22456; fax (11) 80776; f. 1993 by merger; provides tech. and financial assistance for private-sector industrial projects and acquires shares in industrial enterprises; cap. and res 3,005m., total assets 11,821m. (Dec. 1995); Chair. ELSAED OSMAN MAHGOUB; 41 brs.

Sudanese Estates Bank: Baladia St, POB 309, Khartoum; tel. (11) 777917; telex 22439; fax (11) 779465; f. 1967; mortgage bank financing private-sector urban housing development; cap. and res 1,700m. (Dec. 1994); Chair. Eng. MUHAMMAD ALI EL-AMIN; 6 brs.

Sudanese Savings Bank: POB 159, Wad Medani; tel. 3013; telex 50005; f. 1974; cap. 10m., total assets 1,613.4m. (Dec. 1991); Chair. MANSOUR AHMAD ESH-SHEIKH; 22 brs.

STOCK EXCHANGE

Sudanese Stock Exchange: Khartoum; f. 1995; Chair. ABD AR-RAHIM HAMDI; 27 mems.

INSURANCE

African Insurance Co (Sudan) Ltd: Muhammad Hussein Bldg, Al-Baladiya Ave, POB 149, Khartoum; f. 1977; fire, accident, marine and motor; Gen. Man. AN-NOMAN AS-SANUSI.

Blue Nile Insurance Co (Sudan) Ltd: POB 2215, Khartoum; telex 22389; Gen. Man. MUHAMMAD AL-AMIN MIRGHANI.

General Insurance Co (Sudan) Ltd: El-Mek Nimr St, POB 1555, Khartoum; tel. (11) 780616; telex 22303; f. 1961; Gen. Man. Abd al-Fattah Muhammad Siyam.

Islamic Insurance Co Ltd: Al-Faiha Commercial Bldg, POB 2776, Khartoum; tel. (11) 772656; telex 22167; f. 1979; all classes.

Khartoum Insurance Co Ltd: POB 737, Khartoum; tel. (11) 778647; telex 22241; f. 1953; Chair. Mudawi M. Ahmad; Gen. Man. Abd al-Menim al-Hadari.

Middle East Insurance Co Ltd: POB 3070, Khartoum; tel. (11) 772202; telex 22191; f. 1981; fire, marine, motor, general liability; Chair. Ahmad I. Malik; Gen. Man. Ali al-Fadl.

Sudanese Insurance and Reinsurance Co Ltd: Sharia al-Gamhouria, Nasr Sq., POB 2332, Khartoum; tel. (11) 770812; telex 22292; f. 1967; Gen. Man. Izz ad-Din as-Said Muhammad.

United Insurance Co (Sudan) Ltd: Makkawi Bldg, Sharia al-Gamhouria, POB 318, Khartoum; tel. (11) 776630; telex 22390; fax (11) 770783; f. 1968; Dir-Gen. Muhammad Abdeen Babiker.

Trade and Industry

STATE CORPORATIONS

Agricultural Research Corpn: POB 126, Wadi Medani; tel. (51) 2226; telex 50009; fax (51) 3213; f. 1967; Gen. Man. Dr Osman Ageeb.

Alaktan Trading Co: POB 2067, Khartoum; tel. (11) 781588; telex 22272; Gen. Man. Abd ar-Rahman Abd al-Moneim.

Animal Production Public Corpn: POB 624, Khartoum; tel. (11) 740611; telex 24048; Gen. Man. Dr Fouad Ramadan Hamid.

General Petroleum Corpn: POB 2986, Khartoum; tel. (11) 771554; telex 22638; f. 1976; Chair. Dr Osman Abdulwahab; Dir-Gen. Dr Abd er-Rahman Osman Abd er-Rahman.

Gum Arabic Co: POB 857, Khartoum; tel. (11) 777288; telex 22314; f. 1969; Gen. Man. Omer el-Mubarak Abu Zeid.

Industrial Production Corpn: POB 1034, Khartoum; tel. (11) 771278; telex 22236; Dir-Gen. Osman Tammam; Dep. Chair. Abd al-Latif Widatalla; incorporates:

Cement and Building Materials Sector Co-ordination Office: POB 2241, Khartoum; tel. (11) 774269; telex 22079; Dir T. M. Khogali.

Food Industries Corpn: POB 2341, Khartoum; tel. (11) 775463; Dir Muhammad al-Ghali Suliman.

Leather Trading and Manufacturing Co Ltd: POB 1639, Khartoum; tel. (11) 778187; telex 22298; f. 1986; Man. Dir Ibrahim Salih Ali.

Oil Corpn: POB 64, Khartoum North; tel. (11) 332044; telex 22198; Gen. Man. Bukhari Mahmoud Bukhari.

Spinning and Weaving General Co Ltd: POB 765, Khartoum; tel. (11) 774306; telex 22122; f. 1975; Dir Muhammad Salih Muhammad Abdallah.

Sudan Tea Co: POB 1219, Khartoum; tel. (11) 781261; telex 22320.

Sudanese Mining Corpn: POB 1034, Khartoum; tel. (11) 770840; telex 22298; Dir Ibrahim Mudawi Babiker.

Sugar and Distilling Industry Corpn: POB 511, Khartoum; tel. (11) 778417; telex 22665; Man. Mirghani Ahmad Babiker.

Mechanized Farming Corpn: POB 2482, Khartoum; Man. Dir Awad al-Karim al-Yass.

National Cotton and Trade Co Ltd: POB 1552, Khartoum; telex 22267; Gen. Man. Zubair Muhammad al-Bashir.

Port Sudan Cotton Trade Co Ltd: POB 261, Port Sudan; telex 22270; POB 590, Khartoum; Gen. Man. Said Muhammad Adam.

Public Agricultural Production Corpn: POB 538, Khartoum; Chair. and Man. Dir Abdallah Bayoumo; Sec. Saad ad-Din Muhammad Ali.

Public Corpn for Building and Construction: POB 2110, Khartoum; tel. (11) 774544; Dir Naim ad-Din.

Public Corpn for Irrigation and Excavations: POB 619, Khartoum; tel. (11) 780167; Gen. Sec. Osman an-Nur.

Public Corpn for Oil Products and Pipelines: POB 1704, Khartoum; tel. (11) 778290; Gen. Man. Abd ar-Rahman Suliman.

Public Electricity Corpn: POB 1380, Khartoum; Dir-Gen. Issa Abdin.

Rahad Corpn: POB 2523, Khartoum; tel. (11) 775175; financed by the World Bank, Kuwait and the USA; by 1983 300,000 ha had been irrigated and 70,000 people settled in 15,000 tenancies; Man. Dir Hassan Saad Abdalla.

The State Trading Corpn: POB 211, Khartoum; tel. (11) 778555; telex 22355; Chair. E. R. M. Tom.

Automobile Corpn: POB 221, Khartoum; tel. (11) 778555; telex 22230; importer of vehicles and spare parts; Gen. Man. Dafalla Ahmad Siddiq.

Engineering Equipment Corpn: POB 97, Khartoum; tel. (11) 773731; telex 22274; importers and distributors of agricultural, engineering and electronic equipment; Gen. Man. Izz ad-Din Hamid.

Gezira Trade and Services Co: POB 215, Khartoum; tel. (11) 772687; telex 22302; fax (11) 779060; f. 1980; importer of agricultural machinery, spare parts, electrical and office equipment, foodstuffs, clothes and footwear; exporter of oilseeds, grains, hides and skins and livestock; provides shipping insurance and warehousing services; agents for Lloyds and P and I Club.

Khartoum Commercial and Shipping Co: POB 221, Khartoum; tel. (11) 778555; telex 22311; import, export and shipping services, insurance and manufacturing; Gen. Man. Idris M. Salih.

Silos and Storage Corpn: POB 1183, Khartoum; stores and handles agricultural products; Gen. Man. Ahmad at-Taieb Harhoof.

Sudan Cotton Co Ltd: POB 1672, Khartoum; tel. (11) 771567; telex 22245; fax (11) 770703; f. 1970; exports raw cotton; Chair. Abbas Abd al-Bagi Hammad; Dir-Gen. Abdin M. Ali.

Sudan Gezira Board: POB 884, HQ Barakat Wadi Medani, Gezira Province; tel. 2412; telex 50001; Sales Office, POB 884, Khartoum; tel. 740145; responsible for Sudan's main cotton-producing area; the Gezira scheme is a partnership between the Govt, the tenants and the board. The Govt provides the land and is responsible for irrigation. Tenants pay a land and water charge and receive the work proceeds. The Board provides agricultural services at cost, technical supervision and execution of govt agricultural policies relating to the scheme. Tenants pay a percentage of their proceeds to the Social Development Fund. The total potential cultivable area of the Gezira scheme is c. 850,000 ha and the total area under systematic irrigation is c. 730,000 ha. In addition to cotton, groundnuts, sorghum, wheat, rice, pulses and vegetables are grown for the benefit of tenant farmers; Man. Dir Prof. Fathi Muhammad Khalifa.

Sudan Oilseeds Co Ltd: Parliament Ave, POB 167, Khartoum; tel. (11) 780120; telex 22312; f. 1974; 58% state-owned; exporter of oilseeds (groundnuts, sesame seeds and castor beans); importer of foodstuffs and other goods; Chair. Sadiq Karar at-Tayeb; Gen. Man. Kamal Abd al-Halim.

CHAMBER OF COMMERCE

Sudan Chamber of Commerce: POB 81, Khartoum; tel. (11) 772346; f. 1908; Pres. Saad Abou al-Ela; Sec.-Gen. Haroun al-Awad.

INDUSTRIAL ASSOCIATION

Sudanese Industries Association: Africa St, POB 2565, Khartoum; tel. (11) 773151; f. 1974; Chair. Fath ar-Rahman al-Bashir; Exec. Dir A. Izz al-Arab Yousuf.

DEVELOPMENT CORPORATIONS

Sudan Development Corpn (SDC): 21 al-Amarat, POB 710, Khartoum; tel. (11) 472151; telex 24078; fax (11) 472148; f. 1974 to promote and co-finance development projects with special emphasis on projects in the agricultural, agri-business, and industrial sectors; cap. p.u. US $200m.; Man. Dir Dr Muhammad Khier Ahmed el-Zubier; affiliates:

Sudan Rural Development Co Ltd (SRDC): POB 2190, Khartoum; tel. (11) 773855; telex 22813; f. 1980; SRDC has 27% shareholding; cap. p.u. US $2m.; Gen. Man. Omran Muhammad Ali.

Sudan Rural Development Finance Co (SRDFC): POB 2190, Khartoum; tel. (11) 773855; telex 22813; fax (11) 773235; f. 1980; Gen. Man. Omran Muhammad Ali.

MAJOR INDUSTRIAL COMPANIES

The following are among the larger companies, either in terms of capital investment or employment.

Aboulela Cotton Ginning Co Ltd: POB 121, Khartoum; tel. (11) 770020; cotton mills.

AGIP (Sudan) Ltd: POB 1155, Khartoum; tel. (11) 780253; telex 22317; f. 1959; cap. £S15.8m.; distribution of petroleum products; Pres. E. Campoli; Gen. Man. G. Baronio; 187 employees.

Bata (Sudan) Ltd: POB 88, Khartoum; tel. (11) 732240; telex 22327; f. 1950; cap. £S1.7m.; mfrs and distributors of footwear; Man. Dir A. A. Ali; 1,065 employees.

The Blue Nile Brewery: POB 1408, Khartoum; f. 1954; cap. £S734,150; brewing, bottling and distribution of beer; Man. Dirs Ibrahim Elyas, Hussein Muhammad Kemal, Omer az-Zein Sagayroun; 336 employees.

The Central Desert Mining Co Ltd: POB 20, Port Sudan; f. 1946; cap. £S150,000; prospecting for and mining of gold, manganese and iron ore; Dirs Abd al-Hadi Ahmad Bashir, Abou-Bakr Said Bashir; 274 employees.

Cotton Textile Mills Ltd: POB 203, Khartoum; tel. (11) 731414; telex 26002; f. 1976; yarns and fabrics; Man. ABDEL MAROUF ZEIN ELABDEEN.

Kenana Sugar Co Ltd: POB 2632, Khartoum; tel. (11) 744297; telex 24033; f. 1971; financed by Sudan govt and other Arab nations; 18,000 employees; Man. Dir OSMAN ABDULLAH AN-NAZIR.

Maxim Co Ltd: POB 1785, Khartoum; tel. (11) 780904; telex (11) 22360; iron and steel foundries.

Sudan Tobacco Co Ltd: POB 87, Khartoum; mfrs of tobacco products.

TRADE UNIONS

All trade union activity was banned following the coup of 30 June 1989. The following organizations were active prior to that date. Many of their officers are reported to have been imprisoned.

Federations

Sudan Workers Trade Unions Federation (SWTUF): POB 2258, Khartoum; tel. (11) 777463; includes 42 trade unions representing c. 1.75m. public-service and private-sector workers; affiliated to the Int. Confed. of Arab Trade Unions and the Org. of African Trade Union Unity; Pres. MUHAMMAD OSMAN GAMA; Gen. Sec. YOUSUF ABU SHAMA HAMED.

Principal Affiliates

Agricultural Sector Workers' Trade Union: Workers' Club, Khartoum North; Pres. AWAD WIDATALLA; Sec. MUHAMMAD OSMAN SALIM; 30,000 mems.

Gezira Scheme Workers' Trade Union: Barakat; Pres. IBRAHIM MUHAMMAD AHMAD ASH-SHEIKH; Sec. AS-SIR ABDOON; 11,500 mems.

Health Workers' Trade Union: Khartoum Civil Hospital, Khartoum; Pres. Dr HARITH HAMED; Sec. GAAFAR MUHAMMAD SID AHMAD; 25,000 mems.

Local Government Workers' Trade Union: Workers' Union, Khartoum; Pres. ISMAIL MUHAMMAD FADL; Sec. SALEM BEDRI HUMAM; 25,000 mems.

Post, Telegraph and Telephone Workers' Trade Union: Workers' Club, Khartoum; Pres. MANSOUL AL-MANNA; Sec. YASSIN ABD AL-GALIL; 8,463 mems.

Public Service Workers' Trade Union: Al-Baladiya Ave, Khartoum; Pres. MOHI AD-DIN BAKHEIT; Sec. ALI IDRIS AL-HUSSEIN; 19,800 mems.

Railway Workers' Trade Union: Railway Workers' Club, Atbara; Pres. MUHAMMAD AL-HASSAN ABDALLAH; Sec. OSMAN ALI FADL; 32,000 mems.

Sudan Irrigation Workers' Trade Union: Ministry of Education, Wadi Medani; Pres. MUHAMMAD HABIB; Sec. MUHAMMAD AHMAD; 19,150 mems.

Taxi Workers' Trade Union: Workers' Union, Khartoum; Pres. AR-RAYAN YOUSIF; Sec. AT-TAYEB KHALAFALLA; 15,000 mems.

Sudanese Federation of Employees and Professionals Trade Unions: POB 2398, Khartoum; tel. (11) 773818; f. 1975; includes 54 trade unions representing 250,000 mems; Pres. IBRAHIM AWADALLAH; Sec.-Gen. KAMAL AD-DIN MUHAMMAD ABDALLAH.

Principal Affiliates

Bank Officials' Union: Bank of Sudan, Gamaa Ave, POB 313, Khartoum; Pres. MUHAMMAD SALLAM; Sec. ABDALLAH MAHMOUD ABDALLAH.

Gezira Board Officials' Union: Barakat; Pres. GALAL HAMID; Sec. OSMAN ABD AR-RAHIM KHEIRAWY.

Local Government Officials' Union: Dept of Local Government, Khartoum; Pres. SALAH IBRAHIM KHALIL; Sec. MUHAMMAD AWAD GABIR.

Post, Telegraph and Telephone Officials: PO, Khartoum; Pres. ABD AR-RAHMAN AL-KHIDER ALI; Sec. AWAD AL-KARIM OSMAN.

Railway Officials' Union: Sudan Railways Corpn, POB 65, Atbara; Pres. HASSAN HAQ MUSA; Sec. Gen. ABBAS BASHIR AR-RAIEH.

Teachers' Union: Teachers' House, Khartoum; Pres. ABDALLAH ALI ABDALLAH; Sec. HASSAN IBRAHIM MARZOUG.

CO-OPERATIVE SOCIETIES

There are about 600 co-operative societies, of which 570 are officially registered.

Central Co-operative Union: POB 2492, Khartoum; tel. (11) 780624; largest co-operative union operating in 15 provinces.

Transport

RAILWAYS

The total length of railway in operation in 1991 was 4,725 route-km. The main line runs from Wadi Halfa, on the Egyptian border, to al-Obeid, via Khartoum. Lines from Atbara and Sinnar connect with Port Sudan. There are lines from Sinnar to Damazine on the Blue Nile (227 km) and from Aradeiba to Nyala in the south-western province of Darfur (689 km), with a 445-km branch line from Babanousa to Wau in Bahr al-Ghazal province.

Sudan Railways Corpn: POB 43, Atbara; tel. 2000; telex 40002; f. 1875; Chair. and Gen. Man. Dr AL-FATIH MOHAMMAD ALI.

ROADS

Roads in Northern Sudan, other than town roads, are only cleared tracks and often impassable immediately after rain. Motor traffic on roads in the former Upper Nile province is limited to the drier months of January–May. There are several good gravelled roads in Equatoria and Bahr al-Ghazal provinces which are passable all the year, but in these districts some of the minor roads become impassable after rain. Rehabilitation of communications in Southern Sudan is hampered by the continuing hostilities in the area.

Over 48,000 km of tracks are classed as 'motorable'; there were 3,160 km of main roads and 739 km of secondary roads in 1985. A 1,190-km tarmac road linking the capital with Port Sudan was completed during 1980. By 1997 a 270-km road linking Jaili with Atbara had been completed, as part of a scheme to provide an alternative route from Khartoum to the coast.

National Transport Corpn: POB 723, Khartoum; Gen. Man. MOHI AD-DIN HASSAN MUHAMMAD NUR.

Public Corpn for Roads and Bridges: POB 756, Khartoum; tel. (11) 770794; f. 1976; Chair. ABD AR-RAHMAN HABOUD; Dir-Gen. ABDOU MUHAMMAD ABDOU.

INLAND WATERWAYS

The total length of navigable waterways served by passenger and freight services is 4,068 km, of which approximately 1,723 km is open all year. From the Egyptian border to Wadi Halfa and Khartoum navigation is limited by cataracts to short stretches but the White Nile from Khartoum to Juba is almost always navigable.

River Transport Corpn (RTC): POB 284, Khartoum North; operates 2,500 route-km of steamers on the Nile; Chair. ALI AMIR TAHA.

River Navigation Corpn: Khartoum; f. 1970; jtly owned by Govts of Egypt and Sudan; operates services between Aswan and Wadi Halfa.

SHIPPING

Port Sudan, on the Red Sea, 784 km from Khartoum, and Suakin, are the only commercial seaports.

Axis Trading Co Ltd: POB 1574, Khartoum; tel. (11) 775875; telex 22294; Chair. H. A. M. SULIMAN.

Red Sea Shipping Corpn: POB 116, Khartoum; tel. (11) 777688; telex 22306; Gen. Man. OSMAN AMIN.

Sea Ports Corpn: Port Sudan; tel. 2910; telex 70012; f. 1906; Gen. Man. MUHAMMAD TAHIR AILA.

Sudan Shipping Line Ltd: POB 426, Port Sudan; tel. 2655; telex 22518; and POB 1731, Khartoum; tel. (11) 780017; telex 22301; f. 1960; 10 vessels totalling 54,277 dwt operating between the Red Sea and western Mediterranean, northern Europe and United Kingdom; Chair. ISMAIL BAKHEIT; Gen. Man. SALAH AD-DIN OMER AL-AZIZ.

United African Shipping Co: POB 339, Khartoum; tel. (11) 780967; Gen. Man. MUHAMMAD TAHA AL-GINDI.

CIVIL AVIATION

Civil Aviation Authority: Khartoum; tel. (11) 772264; telex 22650; Dir-Gen. Brig. MAHGOUB MUHAMMAD MAHDI.

Sudan Airways Co Ltd: POB 253, SDC Bldg Complex, Amarat St 19, Khartoum; tel. (11) 747953; telex 24212; fax (11) 747987; f. 1947; internal flights and international services to Africa, the Middle East and Europe; Chair. Col SALIH AD-DIN MUHAMMAD AHMAD KARRAR.

Tourism

Public Corpn of Tourism and Hotels: POB 7104, Khartoum; tel. (11) 781764; telex 22436; f. 1977; Dir-Gen. Maj.-Gen. EL-KHATIM MUHAMMAD FADL.

Defence

In August 1996 the armed forces comprised: army 85,000, navy an estimated 1,000, air force 3,000. A paramilitary Popular Defence Force included 15,000 active members and 60,000 reserves. Military service is compulsory for males aged 18–30 years and lasts for up to 36 months.

Defence Expenditure: Budgeted at £S190,000m. (including internal security) for 1996.

Commander-in-Chief of the People's Armed Forces: Lt-Gen. Omar Hassan Ahmad al-Bashir.

Education

The government provides free primary education from the ages of seven to 12 years. Secondary education begins at 13 years of age and lasts for up to six years, divided into two cycles of three years each. The average rate of illiteracy in the population aged 15 years and over was estimated by UNESCO at 53.9% (males 42.3%; females 65.4%) in 1995, compared with 67.6% (males 55.5%; females 79.0%) in 1983. In 1991 the total enrolment at primary and secondary schools was equivalent to 38% of children in the appropriate age-groups (43% of boys; 34% of girls). About 15% of current government expenditure in 1985 was for primary and secondary education. Pupils from secondary schools are accepted at the University of Khartoum, subject to their reaching the necessary standards. (The University of Khartoum was closed in January 1997 to allow students to join the armed forces.) The Khartoum branch of Cairo University was appropriated and renamed Nilayn University by the Sudanese government in April 1993. There are three universities at Omdurman. Omdurman Islamic University; Omdurman Ahlia University; and Ahfad University for Women. New universities were opened at Juba and Wadi Medani (University of Gezira) in 1977. There is also a University of Science and Technology in Khartoum.

Bibliography

Abdel-Rahim, M. *Imperialism and Nationalism in the Sudan: A Study in Constitutional and Political Developments 1899–1956.* Oxford University Press, 1969.

Abdel-Rahim, M., et al. *Sudan since Independence.* London, Gower, 1986.

Africa Watch. *War in South Sudan: The Civilian toll.* New York, Africa Watch, 1993.

African Rights. *Facing Genocide: The Nuba of Sudan.* London, African Rights, 1995.

Albino, O. *The Sudan: A Southern Viewpoint.* London, Oxford University Press, 1970.

Alier, A. *Southern Sudan: Too Many Agreements Dishonoured.* Exeter, Ithaca Press, 1990.

Amnesty International. *The Ravages of War: Political Killings and Humanitarian Disaster.* New York, Amnesty International, 1993.

An-Náim, A.A., and Kok, P.N. *Fundamentalism and Militarism: A Report on the Root Causes of Human Rights Violations in the Sudan.* New York, The Fund for Peace, 1991.

Arkell, A. J. *History of Sudan from Earliest Times to 1821.* 2nd Edn. London, Athlone Press, 1961.

Barbour, K. M. *The Republic of the Sudan: A Regional Geography.* University of London Press, 1961.

Beasley, I., and Starkey, J. (Eds). *Before the Winds Changes: Peoples, Places and Education in the Sudan.* Oxford, Oxford University Press, 1991.

Bechtold, P. K. *Politics in the Sudan.* London, 1978.

Beshir, M. O. *The Southern Sudan: Background to Conflict.* C. Hurst, London, 1968, New York, Praeger, 1968.

Revolution and Nationalism in the Sudan. New York, Barnes and Noble, 1974.

(Ed.) *Sudan: Aid and External Relations, Selected Essays.* University of Khartoum, Graduate College Publications No. 9, 1984.

Brown, R. P. C. *Public Debt and Private Wealth: Debt, Capital Flight and the IMF in Sudan.* Basingstoke, Macmillan (in association with the Institute of Social Studies), 1992.

Burr, J. M., and Collins, R. O. *Requiem for the Sudan: War, Drought and Disaster Relief on the Nile.* Boulder, CO, Westview Press, 1995.

Collins, R. O. *Shadows in the Grass: Britain in the Southern Sudan 1918–1956.* Yale University Press, 1983.

Collins, R. O., and Tignor, R. L. *Egypt and the Sudan.* New York, Prentice, 1967.

Craig, G. M. (Ed.) *Agriculture of the Sudan.* Oxford, Oxford University Press, 1991.

Daly, M. W. *Imperial Sudan.* New York, Cambridge University Press, 1991.

Daly, M. W., and Sikainga, A. A. *Civil War in the Sudan.* London, British Academic Press, 1993.

Deng, F. M. *War of Visions: Conflict of Identities in the Sudan.* Washington, DC, Brookings Institution, 1995.

Deng, W. *The Problem of Southern Sudan.* London, Oxford University Press, 1963.

Doornbos, M., Cliffe, L., Ahmed, A. G. M., and Markakis, J. (Eds). *Beyond Conflict in the Horn: The Prospects of Peace and Development in Ethiopia, Somalia, Eritrea and Sudan.* Lawrenceville, KS, Red Sea Press, 1992.

El-Affendi, A. *Turabi's Revolution: Islam and Power in Sudan.* London, Grey Seal Books, 1991.

El-Nasri, A. R. *A Bibliography of the Sudan 1938–1958.* Oxford University Press, 1962.

Eltigani, E. E. (Ed.). *War and Drought in Sudan: Essays in Population Displacement.* Gainesville, University of Florida Press, 1955.

Eprile, C. L. *Sudan: The Long War.* London, Institute for the Study of Conflict, 1972

War and Peace in the Sudan 1955–1972. Newton Abbot, David and Charles, 1974.

Fluehr-Lobban, C., Fluehr-Lobban, R.A., and Voll, J. *Historical Dictionary of the Sudan.* 2nd Edn. Metuchen, NJ, Scarecrow Press, 1992.

Fruzzetti, L., and Ostor, A. *Culture and Change Along the Blue Nile.* Boulder, CO, Westview Press, 1989.

Fukui, K., and Markakis, J. (Eds). *Ethnicity and Conflict in the Horn of Africa.* London, James Currey, 1994.

Gaitskell, A. *Gezira: A Story of Development in the Sudan.* London, Faber, 1959.

Garang, J. *The Call for Democracy in Sudan* (Ed. Khalid, M.). 2nd Edn. London, Kegan Paul International, 1992.

Grandin, N. *Le Soudan nilotique et l'administration britannique (1898–1956).* Leiden, Brill, 1982.

Gurdon, C. *Sudan at the Crossroads.* London, Menas Press, 1985.

Sudan in Transition. London, Economist Publications, 1986.

(Ed.). *The Horn of Africa.* London, University College London Press, 1994.

Hill, R. *Egypt in the Sudan 1820–1881.* London, Oxford University Press, 1959.

Hill, R., and Hogg, P. *A Black Corps d'Elite.* East Lansing, Michigan State University Press, 1995.

Hodgkin, R. A. *Sudan Geography.* London, 1951.

Holt, P. M., and Daly, M. W. *The History of the Sudan from the Coming of Islam to the Present Day.* 4th Edn. London and New York, Longman, 1988.

Hurst, H. E., and Philips, P. *The Nile Basin.* 7 vols. London, 1932–38.

International Labour Office. *Growth, Employment and Equity: A Comprehensive Strategy for the Sudan.* Geneva, 1976.

International Monetary Fund. IMF Staff Country Report No. 95/12: *Sudan—Recent Economic Developments.* Washington, DC, International Monetary Fund, 1995.

Johnson, D. H. *The Root Causes of Sudan's Civil Wars.* London, James Currey, 1995.

Karrar, A. S. *The Sufi Brotherhoods in the Sudan.* London, Hurst, 1992.

Katsuyoshi, F., and Markakis, J. *Ethnicity and Conflict in the Horn of Africa.* London, James Currey, 1994.

Keen, D. *The Benefits of Famine: A Political Economy of Famine and Relief in Southwestern Sudan, 1983–1989.* Princeton, NJ, Princeton University Press, 1994.

Khalid, M. *Nimeiri and the Revolution of Dis-May.* London, Routledge and Kegan Paul, 1985.

The Government They Deserve: The Role of the Elite in Sudan's Political Evolution. London, Kegan Paul, 1990.

Khalifa, M. E. *Reflections on the Sudanese Political System.* Khartoum, Sudan House, 1995.

Kibreab, G. *People on the Edge: Displacement, Land Use and the Environment in the Gedaref Region, Sudan.* London, James Currey, 1996.

Mackie, I. *Trek into Nuba.* Edinburgh, Pentland Press, 1994.

Malwal, B. *People and Power in the Sudan.* London, Ithaca Press, 1981.

Metz, H. C. (Ed.). *Sudan: A Country Study.* Washington, DC, US Government Printing Office, 1991.

Minority Rights Group. *Sudan: Conflict and Minorities.* London, Minority Rights Group, 1995.

Niblock, T. *Class and Power in Sudan: The Dynamics of Sudanese Politics 1898–1985.* Albany, State University Press of New York, 1987.

O'Ballance, E. *The Secret War in the Sudan 1955–1972.* London, Faber and Faber, 1977.

Oduho, J., and Deng, W. *The Problem of the Southern Sudan.* Oxford University Press, 1963.

Peters, C. *Sudan: A Nation in the Balance.* Oxford, Oxfam, 1996.

Prendergast, J. *Sudanese Rebels at a Crossroads: Opportunities for Building Peace in a Shattered Land.* Washington, DC, Center of Concern, 1994.

Prunier, G. *From Peace to War: The Southern Sudan (1972–1984).* Hull, University of Hull, 1986.

Rone, J., et al. (Eds). *Civilian Devastation: Abuses by the Parties in the War in Southern Sudan.* New York, Human Rights Watch, 1994.

Ruay, D. D. A. *The Politics of Two Sudans: The South and the North, 1921–1969.* Uppsala, Nordiska Afrikainstitutet, 1994.

Santi, P., and Hill, R. (Eds). *The Europeans in the Sudan 1834–1878.* Oxford University Press, 1980.

Sidahmed, A. S. *Politics and Islam in Contemporary Sudan.* Richmond, Curzon Press, 1996.

Sikainga, A. A. *Slaves into Workers: Emancipation and Labor in Colonial Sudan.* Austin, University of Texas Press, 1996.

Simone, T. A. M. *In Whose Image?* Chicago, University of Chicago Press, 1994.

Sylvester, A. *Sudan under Nimeri.* London, Bodley Head, 1977.

Thomas, G. F. *Sudan: Struggle for Survival, 1984–1993.* London, Darf, 1993.

Voll, J. O. (Ed.). *Sudan: State and Society in Crisis.* Bloomington, Indiana State University Press, 1991.

Wai, D. *The African-Arab Conflict in the Sudan.* New York, Africana Publishing Co, 1981.

(Ed.). *The Southern Sudan: The Problem of National Integration.* London, Oxford University Press, 1973.

Woodward, P. *Condominium and Sudanese Nationalism.* London, 1979.

Sudan 1898–1989: The Unstable State. Boulder, CO, Lynne Rienner, 1990.

Zulfo, I. H. *Karari: The Sudanese Account of the Battle of Omdurman.* London, Frederick Warne, 1980.

SWAZILAND

Physical and Social Geography

A. MacGREGOR HUTCHESON

The Kingdom of Swaziland is one of the smallest political entities of continental Africa. Covering an area of only 17,363 sq km (6,704 sq miles), it straddles the broken and dissected edge of the South African plateau, surrounded by South Africa on the north, west and south, and separated from the Indian Ocean on the east by the Mozambique coastal plain.

PHYSICAL FEATURES

From the High Veld on the west, averaging 1,050 to 1,200 m in altitude, there is a step-like descent eastwards through the Middle Veld (450 to 600 m) to the Low Veld (150 to 300 m). To the east of the Low Veld the Lebombo Range, an undulating plateau at 450–825 m, presents an impressive westward-facing scarp and forms the fourth of Swaziland's north–south aligned regions. Drainage is by four main systems flowing eastwards across these regions: the Komati and Umbeluzi rivers in the north, the Great Usutu river in the centre, and the Ngwavuma river in the south. The eastward descent is accompanied by a rise in temperature and by a decrease in mean annual rainfall from a range of 1,150–1,900 mm in the High Veld to one of 500–750 mm in the Low Veld, but increasing again to about 850 mm in the Lebombo range. The higher parts, receiving 1,000 mm, support temperate grassland, while dry woodland savannah is characteristic of the lower areas.

RESOURCES AND POPULATION

Swaziland's potential for economic development in terms of its natural resources is out of proportion to its size. The country's perennial rivers represent a high hydroelectric potential and their exploitation for irrigation in the drier Middle Veld and Low Veld has greatly increased and diversified agricultural production. Sugar, however, is the dominant industry and has traditionally been the principal export commodity. Other major crops include cotton (in terms of the number of producers, this is the most important cash crop), maize, tobacco, rice, vegetables, citrus fruits and pineapples. The well-watered High Veld is particularly suitable for afforestation and over 120,000 ha (more than 100 plantations) have been planted with conifers and eucalyptus since the 1940s, creating the largest man-made forests in Africa.

Swaziland is also rich in mineral wealth. Once a major exporter of iron ore, this industry ceased with the exhaustion of high-grade ores, although considerable quantities of iron ore of inferior grade remain. World demand for Swaziland's exports of chrysolite asbestos has declined in recent years as the result of health problems associated with this mineral. Coal holds the country's most important mineral potential, with reserves estimated at 250m. tons. Coal is currently mined at Mpaka, mostly for export, and further reserves have been identified at Lobuka. The exploitation of anthracite deposits at Maloma began in 1993. Gold and diamond deposits are being exploited in the north-west of the country. Other minerals of note are cassiterite (a tin-bearing ore), kaolin, talc, pyrophyllite and silica.

Nearly one-half of the population live in the Middle Veld, which contains some of the best soils in the country. This is Swaziland's most densely peopled region, with an average of 50 inhabitants per sq km, rising to more than 200 per sq km in some rural and in more developed areas. The total population of Swaziland (excluding absentee workers) was enumerated at 681,059 at the census of August 1986, and was officially estimated to be 908,000 at mid-1995.

A complex system of land ownership, with Swazi and European holdings intricately interwoven throughout the country, is partly responsible for considerable variations in the distribution and density of the population. Only about 40% of the country was under Swazi control at the time of independence in 1968, but this proportion steadily increased in subsequent years, as non-Swazi land and mineral concessions were acquired through negotiation and purchase. The Swazi Nation, to which most of the African population belongs, has now regained all mineral concessions.

Recent History

RICHARD LEVIN

Revised for this edition by the Editor

Swaziland, which emerged as a cohesive nation in the early 19th century, became a British protectorate following the Boer War in 1903 and in 1907 became one of the high commission territories. A preoccupation of King Sobhuza II during his 61-year reign, which began in 1921, was the recovery of lands granted to settlers and speculators in the late 19th century by his predecessor.

Moves towards the restoration of independence in the early 1960s were accompanied by a growth in political activity. The Ngwane National Liberatory Congress (NNLC), an African nationalist party formed in 1962 and led by Dr Ambrose Zwane, advocated independence on the basis of universal adult suffrage and a constitutional monarchy. The increasingly radical stance of the NNLC and growing worker militancy prompted royalist interests to form the Imbokodvo National Movement (INM). The INM won all 24 seats in the new house of assembly in the pre-independence elections of April 1967; the NNLC secured 20% of the votes, owing to strong support in urban areas, but failed to gain any seats because of an electoral system that favoured rural areas. The independence constitution vested legislative authority in a bicameral parliament with a large proportion of its membership nominated by the king. Formal independence followed on 6 September 1968.

The 14-year post-independence rule of Sobhuza was characterized by stability and a significant expansion of the economy as investment flowed in, much of it from South Africa. Growing reliance on South African capital, along with Swaziland's membership of the Southern African Customs Union (SACU), produced an increasing dependence on South Africa and severely restricted the country's economic and political choices. During this period the royal authorities acquired a significant material base in the economy, through their control of the Tibiyo Taka Ngwane and Tisuka Taka Ngwane, royal corporations which managed the investment of mineral royalties. Politically, Sobhuza extended his influence on executive and legislative decisions through his indirect control of the country's traditional 'tinkhundla', local authorities each grouping a small number of chieftaincies. In 1973 Sobhuza decreed a suspension of the constitution and a formal ban on party political activity. By the time of Sobhuza's diamond jubilee in 1981, the authority of the Swazi monarchy was absolute, with royal dominance over political affairs becoming increasingly personal and conservative, appealing to reinterpretations of 'tradition' to find solutions to constitutional problems.

Sobhuza's death in August 1982 precipitated a prolonged power struggle within the royal family. The queen mother, Dzeliwe, assumed the regency and appointed the 15 members of the liqoqo, a traditional advisory body which Sobhuza had sought to establish as the supreme council of state. A confrontation ensued between the prime minister, Prince Mabandla Dlamini, and members of the liqoqo, led by Prince Mfanasibili Dlamini. Dzeliwe, who opposed the liqoqo's dismissal of the prime minster and his replacement with the more conservative Prince Bhekimpi Dlamini, was herself removed from the position of queen regent and replaced by Queen Ntombi Laftwala, mother of the 14-year-old heir apparent, Prince Makhosetive. In November 1983, elections were held and a new cabinet formed, purged of members suspected of supporting Mabandla or Dzeliwe. In December 17 people who had been in detention since August, including four members of the royal family, were charged with plotting to overthrow Ntombi. All the detainees were later released.

In April 1984 Bhekimpi announced that a coup plot against him had been foiled the previous month; the minister of finance, Dr Sishayi Nxumalo, was accused of instigating the alleged conspiracy. In June Nxumalo was dismissed and in November he was arrested, together with several other prominent Swazis. The detentions followed Nxumalo's allegations that several prominent Swazi politicians, including Prince Mfanasibili, had illegally diverted funds owed to the SACU. Despite pressure from South Africa for an investigation of the allegations, a decree was issued in September granting immunity from prosecution to members of the liqoqo. Amid growing opposition to the liqoqo's monopoly of power, Mfanasibili and another influential liqoqo member, Dr George Msibi, were removed from their positions on the liqoqo in October 1985. Subsequently it was announced that the liqoqo had reverted to its former status as an advisory council, with executive power being restored to the prime minister and the cabinet. In February 1986 Mfanasibili was charged with subversion, and in May was sentenced to seven years' imprisonment.

ACCESSION OF MSWATI III

Prince Makhosetive was crowned as King Mswati III on 25 April 1986. The young king moved quickly to assert his authority. The liqoqo was disbanded in May and the cabinet reshuffled. In October Mswati dismissed Bhekimpi and replaced him as prime minister with Sotsha Dlamini, a former assistant commissioner of police. In May 1987 12 prominent public figures (including Bhekimpi and other members of the royal family) were arrested on charges of sedition and treason, in connection with the removal from power of Queen Regent Dzeliwe in 1983. Bhekimpi and nine other detainees were brought to trial in November 1987. All were found guilty of treason in March 1988 and sentenced to terms of imprisonment of up to 15 years. In July, however, Bhekimpi and eight of the other defendants were released after receiving royal pardons. Mfanasibili was included in the amnesty, but returned to prison to serve the remainder of his earlier seven-year sentence.

Despite the high incidence of factionalism and personal intrigue within the royal family, both the king and the new prime minister indicated a determination to eliminate corruption from the administration. In the absence of democratic institutions and public accountability, however, corruption thrived. In September 1987 parliament was dissolved in preparation for elections to be held in November, one year early. In November the electoral college duly appointed 40 members of the house of assembly (none of whom had previously been members). Of the 10 additional members nominated by the king, eight were former MPs, including the former prime minister, Sotsha Dlamini. The new house of assembly and King Mswati each appointed 10 members of the senate. A new cabinet, appointed in late November, included Sotsha Dlamini, as prime minister, and three members of the previous cabinet. The low turn-out at the polls for the election of the electoral college was widely interpreted as an indication of growing dissatisfaction among the Swazi population with the tinkhundla system. The limited impact of Swazi voters on the composition of government was revealed in the fact that it was the king's nominees in both houses who were installed as cabinet ministers. Developments within parliament reflected growing public dissatisfaction with the political system when, in October 1988, a majority of the members of the upper house supported a motion demanding a comprehensive review of the legislative structure. The prime minister strongly opposed the motion on the familiar grounds that it would be 'un-Swazi' to challenge an established traditional institution. King Mswati has voiced the opinion that political stability in the kingdom can best be achieved through the maintenance of the tinkhundla, as vectors of 'unity and democracy' in the kingdom. Opposition to the tinkhundla, perceived as potential challenges to their own authority, has been expressed by some of the chiefs, and in May 1989 about 40 chiefs advocated the introduction of direct elections to parliament. In January 1990 the founder and former leader of the NNLC, Dr Ambrose Zwane, in his first public address since the party's suppression in 1973, also urged the introduction of a system of direct legislative elections.

RE-EMERGENCE OF PUDEMO

In July 1989 the king abruptly dismissed the prime minister, Sotsha Dlamini, for 'disobedience'. He was replaced by Obed Dlamini, a founder member and former secretary-general of the Swaziland Federation of Trade Unions (SFTU). His appointment was expected to calm labour unrest which had prompted recent strikes in the banking and transport systems. The second half of 1989, however, witnessed an escalation in labour disputes, which spread to brewery workers, plantation workers, miners and the public service sector; disaffection was also expressed by students, prompting the king to order the closure of the University of Swaziland for one month from the end of September. These manifestations of discontent, together with a more broadly-based popular opposition of political and civic organizations, began to pose a serious challenge to the continuance of royal hegemony. Until late 1989 active criticism of Mswati's maintenance of autocratic rule had been restricted to sporadic appearances of anti-liqoqo pamphlets linked to the People's United Democratic Movement (PUDEMO), an organization which had been formed during the regency. PUDEMO returned to prominence in 1990 with the distribution of new pamphlets which questioned the legitimacy of the monarchy in its present form, without explicitly demanding a republican constitution. PUDEMO criticized the king for his alleged excesses, condemned corruption and called for democratic reform, thus echoing public criticism of the tinkhundla.

In mid-July 1990 the police began systematically to suppress PUDEMO, arresting about 20 people of whom 11 were variously charged with treason, sedition, or conspiring to form a political party. By the end of October, all the accused had been released. In the following month, however, police and army units violently dispersed a peaceful protest held at the university, injuring up to 300 of those involved in the demonstration. The government promised to appoint a judicial commission of enquiry into the events, although this was not carried out until March 1991. Shortly after the violence, the minister of justice, Reginald Dhladhla, was replaced by Zonkhe Khumalo, a former deputy prime minister who had earlier been implicated in a financial scandal surrounding the royal investment fund, Tisuka Taka Ngwane. Early in 1991 Dhladhla's removal was raised in parliament by Dzingalive Dlamini, who asserted that a 'secret group' within the kingdom's power structure was taking major decisions. In March Dzingalive Dlamini briefly fled the country, stating that he feared arrest and indefinite detention by the authorities. Diplomatic activity by a number of countries, notably the USA, led to Dlamini's return and to the release of Mfanasibili and five PUDEMO detainees.

By mid-1991 there appeared to be widespread public support for the PUDEMO activists and their cause, and in the second half of the year the organization began to establish civic structures in order to advance its objectives through legal organizations. The most prominent of these were the Swaziland Youth Congress (SWAYOCO) and the Human Rights Asscn of Swaziland (HUMARAS). The king finally agreed to review the tinkhundla, and established a commission, which became known as the vusela ('greeting') committee, to conduct a series of public forums throughout the country in order to elicit popular opinion on political reforms. Prince Masitsela, a cabinet minister under King Sobhuza II during the 1970s, was appointed chairman of the vusela. There was widespread criticism of the political system as well as of the composition of the vusela itself. At the tinkhundla review meeting held in Mbabane, speakers demanded the abolition of the system, asserting that it was undemocratic and promoted corruption and nepotism, since it provided no system of accountability. In Manzini the meeting of the vusela planned for early November was cancelled, following a demonstration march by supporters of PUDEMO and SWAYOCO. The non-violent march was dispersed by the police, who arrested 19 people for staging an illegal demonstration.

In the months following this event, SWAYOCO was involved in a number of confrontations with the police over its right to engage in peaceful protest and community welfare activities, as increasingly militant Swazi youth seized the initiative in the campaign for democracy. Divisions began to emerge within the government concerning its response to the activities of SWAYOCO, with royal advisory council members, in particular, advocating that the youth congress be suppressed. These influences were resisted by more moderate forces, led by the prime minister, who asserted that political and social change in Swaziland was inevitable.

PUDEMO's activities, meanwhile, were also intensified. In the second half of 1991 the organization's national executive committee rejected the process of review by the vusela committee, and set out five demands whose fulfilment was deemed necessary to create conditions conducive to democratic transition. These included the establishment of an interim government, the suspension of the effective state of emergency, the holding of a constitutional referendum, and the establishment of a constituent assembly to determine a new and appropriate constitution for Swaziland. These demands were officially ignored, but in February 1992, when the king announced the establishment of a second vusela committee (Vusela 2), he included a member of PUDEMO and a member of HUMARAS among the commissioners.

A further two opposition movements, the Swaziland United Front (SUF) and the Swaziland National Front (SWANAFRO), subsequently re-emerged. In February 1992 PUDEMO declared itself a legal opposition party, in contravention of the prohibition of political associations. Kislon Shongwe was named as president, and, among other members of the party executive, Mandla Hlatshwako was appointed national organizer. In a decree, published at the beginning of April, setting out the terms of reference of Vusela 2, the king appointed Hlatshwako as one of the commissioners. The terms of reference of Vusela 2 included a study of the submissions made by Vusela 1, receiving further submissions in camera from any Swazi, examining shortcomings in the existing system of voting and investigating ways in which customary and modern political institutions could be integrated. Following protracted negotiations with the commission over its function and influence, Hlatshwako withdrew from the committee, on the grounds that the purpose of Vusela 2 appeared to be to sustain the tinkhundla rather than to democratize. HUMARAS also rejected Vusela 2 as a waste of resources. HUMARAS president Sam Mkhombe, also a commissioner, was dismissed as president of the organization, having ignored HUMARAS demands that he should resign from Vusela 2.

PRESSURE FOR REFORM

In October 1992 the king approved a number of proposals, which had been submitted by Vusela 2. Under new amendments to the electoral system, the house of assembly (which was redesignated as the national assembly) was to be expanded to 65 deputies (of whom 55 were to be directly elected by secret ballot from candidates nominated by the tinkhundla, and 10 appointed by the king), and the senate to 30 members (of whom 10 were to be selected by the national assembly and 20 appointed by the king); in addition, detention without trial was to cease, and a new constitution, which incorporated the amendments, enshrining an hereditary monarchy and confirming the fundamental rights of the individual and the independence of the judicial system, was to be drafted. However, opposition groups protested at the committee's failure to recommend the immediate restoration of a multi-party political system; the issue was to be postponed until the forthcoming elections in order to determine the extent of public support.

PUDEMO announced its opposition to the electoral reforms, and demanded that the government organize a national convention to determine the country's constitutional future. King Mswati subsequently dissolved parliament, one month prior to the expiry of its term of office, and announced that he was to rule by decree, with the assistance of the cabinet (which was redesignated as the council of ministers), pending the adoption of the new constitution and the holding of parliamentary elections. A third committee (Vusela 3) was established to inform the population about the forthcoming amendments to the electoral system. Later in October 1992 the king announced that elections to the national assembly were to take place in the first half of 1993. At a series of public meetings, which were convened by Vusela 3 from December 1992, doubts regarding the viability of the reformed electoral system were expressed; in early 1993, in response to public concern, it was announced that legislation preventing the heads of the tinkhundla from exerting undue influence in the nomination of candidates had been introduced.

In December 1992 an informal alliance of organizations that advocated democratic reform (principally comprising HUMARAS, PUDEMO and SWAYOCO), known as the Convention for a Full Democratic Swaziland, was formed. In the same month PUDEMO rejected a proposal by SWAYOCO that a 'Vusela Resistance Movement' be established, to impede the implementation of economic reforms by disrupting essential services. In early 1993, in response to attempts by the opposition to impede the elections, the government moved to suppress political gatherings. In March more than 50 opposition activists, including leaders of PUDEMO and SWAYOCO, were arrested and charged in connection with the organization of illegal political meetings. Although those arrested were subsequently released on bail, legal restrictions prevented them from participating in opposition activity, thereby effectively undermining efforts to co-ordinate a campaign in protest at the elections. Despite the opposition's failure to organize an official electoral boycott, however, a low level of voter registration appeared to reflect public response to the proposed reforms.

The first round of elections to the expanded national assembly, which was contested by 2,094 candidates nominated by the tinkhundla, took place on 25 September 1993. At the end of September the king repealed the legislation providing for detention without trial for a period of 60 days. The second round of parliamentary elections, which took place on 11 October, was contested by the three candidates in each tinkhundla who had obtained the highest number of votes in the first poll; the majority of members of the former cabinet (which had been dissolved in late September), including Obed Dlamini, failed to secure seats in the national assembly. (The king subsequently appointed an acting prime minister, with responsibility for all ministerial portfolios, pending the formation of a new cabinet.) Shortly afterwards, Mfanasibili questioned the loyalty to the king of the elected parliamentary deputies, and claimed that certain elements planned to transfer executive power to the prime minister and redesignate the head of state as a constitutional monarch. Later in October the king nominated a further 10 deputies to the national assembly, which elected 10 of its members to the senate; the king subsequently appointed the remaining 20 senators, who included Obed Dlamini and Bhekimpi. In early November the former minister of works and construction, Prince Jameson Mbilini Dlamini, who was regarded as a traditionalist, was appointed prime minister, and a new cabinet (which included Nxumalo, in the office of deputy prime minister) was formed.

In February 1994, following a report by the US department of state that described the parliamentary elections as 'undemocratic', the government claimed that the majority of the Swazi people were opposed to the establishment of a multi-party political system. It was announced, however, that the king was to appoint a five-member committee, comprising representatives of state organs and non-governmental organizations, to draft a new constitution, and a national policy council, which was to prepare a manifesto of the Swazi people. In March elections to the tinkhundla, which were scheduled to take place later that month in accordance with the reforms, were postponed, owing to lack of preparation. (The heads of the tinkhundla had previously been appointed by the king.)

In early 1995 there were outbreaks of arson and incendiary attacks on the property of government officials, and on the parliament and high court buildings. Although crude in execution, these attacks were the first manifestations for almost 20 years of overt political violence against established authority. Simultaneously, the focus of opposition shifted from unauthorized political organizations to the trade union movement. On 13–14 March the SFTU brought the economy to a standstill with a general strike, staged in protest at the government's failure to respond to a set of 27 demands which had been put forward in January of the previous year. Although the demands of the SFTU focused on labour issues, the strike was clearly part of the wider political context. In July a second general strike was narrowly averted following government threats, including an announcement by the king, that the proposed strike would provoke a violent official response. Allegations of official malfeasance continued, meanwhile, to heighten political discontent. The ministers of information and finance were dismissed from their posts in February, on the grounds of alleged corrupt conduct. In May the new minister of finance, Derrick von Wissel, asked the central bank to take over the state-owned Swaziland Development and Savings Bank after the discovery of possible irregularities in loans to prominent public figures. In August the senate approved a motion supporting a statement, made by the king during a visit to South Africa, to the effect that the Swazi population was not in favour of a multi-party system. In November, however, a conference of political organizations (including PUDEMO and SWAYOCO) and the SFTU urged Mswati to leave the country for a temporary period of exile, pending the establishment of a multi-party democracy.

In January 1996 PUDEMO announced that a campaign of protests and civil disobedience would be initiated, following the government's failure to respond to demands for the installation of a multi-party system and for the adoption of a constitution that would restrict the monarch to a symbolic role in government. Strike action, which was scheduled by the SFTU for later that month, was declared to be illegal by the authorities. However, an attempt by the government to have the industrial action pronounced illegal in the high court was rejected, and the indefinite general strike was staged as planned, despite the arrest of three senior SFTU officials (who were subsequently released, following a further legal ruling). Demonstrations by SFTU members were firmly suppressed by security forces, leading to violent clashes in which three people were reported to have been killed. The SFTU refused to enter into negotiations with the government, demanding that the prohibitions on political activity and restrictions on trade unions be revoked prior to discussions. At the end of January the king accused the SFTU membership of attempting to overthrow the monarchy and demanded that they abandon industrial action, threatening to order his traditional warriors to suppress the strike. The SFTU subsequently suspended its industrial action to allow negotiations with the government to proceed. In February the SFTU threatened to resume strike action, but again agreed to a postponement pending negotiations, after the king announced that the process of drafting a new constitution would begin later that year, and that the legislation prohibiting political activity would also be reviewed. In March PUDEMO recommended that a 'government of national unity' be installed to supervise the transitional process. During early May the king indicated that a 'people's parliament', comprising a series of consultative meetings between citizens and government leaders, had been initiated to solicit public opinion regarding constitutional reform, leading to the formation of a committee to prepare proposals for a draft constitution for submission to a referendum. The European Union (EU) offered to assist in this exercise. At the same time the king removed Mbilini from the office of prime minister, and announced that he would appoint his successor in consultation with the Swaziland national council. (Nxumalo assumed the duties of acting prime minister pending the appointment.)

In late July 1996, following an emergency meeting (attended by Nxumalo and the heads of state of Mozambique, Botswana, Zimbabwe and South Africa) to discuss Swaziland's political situation, King Mswati appointed a constitutional review commission, comprising chiefs, political activists and unionists, to collate submissions from the Swazi people and subsequently draft proposals for a new constitution. At the same time, Dr Barnabas Sibusiso Dlamini, an executive director of the IMF and a former finance minister, was appointed prime minister. In August PUDEMO expressed its dissatisfaction with the composition of the constitutional review commission under the chairmanship of the king's brother, Prince Mangaliso, and appealed for South African and other regional and international support in expediting the constitutional review.

In early November 1996 the council of ministers was reorganized, and four ministers were dismissed. Derrick von Wissel, who as minister of finance had attempted to recover debts owed to the central bank by several senior establishment figures, resigned after he was transferred to the tourism portfolio. (He subsequently became governor of the central bank.) Later that month teachers and civil servants withdrew from pay negotiations with the government.

General Strike

In early December 1996 the prime minister announced that a 'task force', composed of workers, employers and government representatives, had discussed the SFTU's 27 demands of January 1994, and that the implementation of the recommendations outlined in the resulting report was to be overseen by the labour advisory board. In mid-January 1997, however, the SFTU claimed that there had been no response to its demands for democratic reform, and resolved to begin indefinite strike action from early February. Meanwhile, the president of PUDEMO, Mario Masuku, declared that Swaziland's leaders were not committed to change, and withdrew from the constitutional review commission. At the end of January the four main leaders of the SFTU were arrested and were subsequently charged with intimidating bus owners into joining the forthcoming strike; it was believed that the arrests had been made at the behest of the Swaziland national council. The strike, declared illegal by the government, proceeded as planned, however, and was apparently observed by approximately one-half of the labour force, with particular support from workers in agriculture and forestry. Several SFTU and PUDEMO members were arrested at a meeting to assess the first day of the strike, although they were released without charge shortly afterwards. Some days later, PUDEMO reportedly distributed a pamphlet containing threats to attack and assassinate journalists whose coverage of the strike favoured the government. On the ninth day of industrial action six strikers were seriously injured in violent clashes with the security forces. A number of southern African leaders expressed concern at the length of the dispute, and a 10-member international delegation of trade unionists threatened to organize a blockade of the kingdom, following inconclusive talks with the government. The SFTU leaders declined the government's offer to release them on condition that they end the strike; their trial began, but was dismissed in late February, owing to lack of evidence. At the beginning of March commercial activity was disrupted by a one-day blockade of the Swazi border, initiated by the Congress of South African Trade Unions (COSATU), which had asserted its support for the SFTU throughout the strike. The SFTU urged workers to support the blockade, although it decided to suspend the strike shortly afterwards, as the government had agreed to commence negotiations. However, it was resolved to continue industrial action on the first two days of each month until the SFTU's 27 demands, made in 1994, had been met. It was subsequently announced that Mswati was reviewing King Sobhuza's 1973 decree. In early April 1997 the SFTU postponed a further blockade, in order to allow the government adequate time to review the situation. In late May Nxumalo warned that he believed a violent revolution would take place, unless a referendum was held to ascertain whether Swazis wished to retain the present political system or to establish a multi-party democracy. In early June the king appealed to the nation to contribute to the constitutional debate. Shortly afterwards South Africa offered assistance in the preparation of the constitution, in response to a request from the king. In July, however, differences were apparently emerging within the commission, with four members having threatened to resign.

INTERNATIONAL RELATIONS

Despite Swaziland's professed neutrality in international affairs, the country has remained distinctly pro-Western, maintaining no diplomatic relations with socialist and former socialist states of the Eastern bloc. US congressional committees have long viewed Swaziland as a moderating force, committed to peaceful change in southern Africa, and the USA has therefore supported programmes of security assistance in the belief that stability in Swaziland aids regional security. A similar perception by South Africa contributed to a strengthening of relations between the two countries during the 1980s, while geographical location has necessitated amicable relations with neighbouring Mozambique, despite that country's commitment to socialism. These relations have improved considerably since mid-1989, when the Mozambique government renounced its exclusive commitment to Marxism-Leninism. The relocation, from Swaziland to Botswana, of the United States Agency for International Development (USAID) and the withdrawal of the US Peace Corps from the kingdom were announced in July 1996. The outgoing US ambassador stressed the need for Swaziland to become more self-reliant, although he offered US assistance with constitutional reform.

There were two aspects to Swaziland's expanding links with South Africa during the 1980s. One was the proposed transfer of land; the other was Swaziland's increasing embroilment in the vortex of spreading violence in southern Africa, and its alignment with the South African government in the latter's confrontation with the African National Congress of South Africa (ANC).

The land transfer scheme provided for the cession to Swaziland of the KaNgwane 'Bantustan' ('homeland' of the Swazi ethnic group in South Africa) and the Ingwavuma region of KwaZulu, an area which would have afforded Swaziland direct access to the sea. Swaziland has long held territorial claims against South Africa, but it was only in the late 1970s that South Africa indicated its readiness to consider these claims seriously. It is generally believed that the proposed transfer of land was intended as an incentive to Swaziland to enter into a security agreement with South Africa.

The prospect of regaining 'lost lands' and reuniting the Swazi people, a large proportion of whom live in South Africa, persuaded Sobhuza to sign a then secret security agreement with South Africa in February 1982. The result was Swaziland's intensified harassment of the ANC. Within weeks, the organization's veteran representative had been expelled from the country, and his deputy assassinated. Sobhuza's death in August 1982 removed the only obstacle to an all-out offensive on the ANC, and by the end of that year the first of a series of round-ups and 'voluntary deportations' of alleged ANC members had occurred. However, as a result of legal obstacles and strong opposition, both in white and black political circles, in South Africa, the proposals for the land transfer were finally abandoned in 1984. Despite this, Swazi security forces continued to harass the ANC.

In 1984, within days of the signing of the Nkomati Accord between South Africa and Mozambique, the Swazi government revealed the existence of its security agreement with South Africa. The systematic suppression of ANC activities intensified, and open collaboration between the two countries inspired gun battles in Manzini as speculation increased that this policy was being orchestrated by a South African trade mission which was established in Mbabane in 1984. In January 1985 the Swazi prime minister defended his government's close relationship with South Africa and implied that the attacks against the ANC would continue. The ANC responded by creating a sophisticated underground network in Swaziland, as conflict within Swazi territory between itself and South Africa intensified. This war escalated in 1986, and in June, July and August armed raids by South African security personnel resulted in a number of ANC deaths in border areas and in Manzini. Increased public outrage at these activities led the Swazi prime minister publicly to accuse South Africa of responsibility and to condemn the August raid as an 'illegal act of aggression', the first open attack on South African policies by a Swaziland government. Nevertheless South African covert security forces continued to carry out operations within Swaziland, in which ANC activists were abducted or murdered. The era of political reform within South Africa that followed the release of Nelson Mandela in February 1990 has brought a general improvement in relations between the two countries, and in late 1993 formal diplomatic relations were established.

In 1995 South African press criticism of the absolute monarchy in Swaziland, the only country in southern Africa not to have adopted a multi-party democratic system, strained relations between the two neighbours. King Mswati paid a state visit to South Africa in mid-1995 and was honoured by President Mandela, who also recalled Sobhuza's role in the ANC in its early years. These events went some way towards improving relations, but international pressure for constitutional reform continues to mount. During 1996–97 prominent South African organizations, including the ANC and COSATU, expressed support for the SFTU's demands for political reform, prompting the Swazi government to protest at interference in its domestic affairs. The establishment of a constitutional review commission, in July 1996, was welcomed by the governments of the UK, Botswana, Tanzania and South Africa. In April of that year the South African government announced that it had rejected a long-standing claim by Swaziland to a region in Mpumalanga Province (formerly Eastern Transvaal).

During the prolonged period of civil unrest within Mozambique, considerable numbers of Mozambicans crossed into Swaziland in search of food and employment, an influx which was linked by Swazi police to an increase in armed crime, and resulted in several mass arrests in urban areas. A sizeable 'unofficial' population of Mozambicans has gathered in urban areas; these Mozambicans, many of whom are highly skilled workers, are perceived as a threat to the jobs of Swazi urban residents. The presence of Mozambican refugees in rural areas has also caused tension, owing to a shortage of land to accommodate them. The officially-maintained refugee settlement camps are crowded and, in the absence of sufficient co-operative agricultural facilities, are heavily dependent on food rations. In June 1990 the governments of Swaziland and Mozambique signed an extradition agreement providing for the repatriation of alleged criminals and illegal immigrants, which was designed to reduce the incidence of smuggling between the two countries. In 1992, however, tension at the border with Mozambique increased, following reports of raids against Swazi farms by members of the Mozambican armed forces. Following the ratification of a Mozambican peace accord in October 1992, an agreement, which was signed by the governments of Swaziland and Mozambique and the UN high commissioner for refugees in August 1993, provided for the repatriation of some 24,000 Mozambican nationals resident in Swaziland; in October 500 Mozambican refugees returned from Swaziland under the programme. In December the number of Swazi troops deployed at the border with Mozambique was increased, following clashes between Swazi and Mozambican forces in the region. Mozambique subsequently protested at alleged border incursions by members of the Swazi armed forces. In early 1994 discussions took place between Swazi and Mozambican officials to seek mutually satisfactory arrangements for the joint patrol of the border, and in 1995 it was announced that the Mhlumeni border post, closed since the 1970s, would re-open as the second official transit point between the two countries. In June 1996 the Mozambican foreign minister praised the efforts of the border patrol set up by the joint security commission, which had, he noted, been successful in reducing cross-border crime.

Economy

GRAHAM MATTHEWS

Revised for this edition by Donald L. Sparks

Although it is, after The Gambia, the smallest state in mainland Africa, Swaziland has one of the continent's highest per caput income levels. In 1995, according to World Bank estimates, the kingdom's gross national product (GNP), measured at average 1993–95 prices, was US $1,051m., equivalent to $1,170 per caput: enough to rank Swaziland as a 'middle income' economy. The World Bank estimates real GNP per caput to have grown at an average 0.6% per annum in 1985–95, while the population increased by an annual average of 3.1% during the same period. Since independence there has been diversification of the economy away from early dependence upon agriculture and mining. According to national estimates, manufacturing contributed the largest share of gross domestic product (GDP) with 33.1% in 1995/96. Manufacturing also accounted for some 18% of formal employment in 1994. After government services, which contributed 21.4% in 1995/96, the other main sectors' contributions to GDP were agriculture and forestry 11.6%, trade, restaurants and hotels 9.6%, financial and business services 7.6%, transport and communications 6.4%, and construction 4.8%. Despite its relative diversification and wealth, however, Swaziland has not escaped the extremes of income distribution familiar elsewhere in Africa. More than two-thirds of the resident population comprises families earning generally poor incomes from smallholder cashcropping or subsistence agriculture on Swazi Nation Land (SNL), where the average land holding was just 1.35 ha in 1991. Moreover, the condition of the rural poor has been largely unimproved by periods of rapid growth since independence.

The most recent period of accelerated growth began with the record sugar crop of 1986 and continued until the regional drought broke the pattern with its disastrous effects upon rain-fed agriculture in 1992. In 1985–89 the average annual rate of GDP growth was 9.4%, while population growth averaged 3.7% per year for the same period. Swaziland's 'open' economy (exports of goods and services accounted for 81.4% of GDP in 1995/96) was severely affected by the depressed commodity prices and drought in the early 1980s; 'Cyclone Domoina', which battered the kingdom in 1984, also took its toll. Finally, the initial impact of the currency's decline during 1983–85 was additionally damaging and led to a period of rapid inflation, among other problems. During 1990–95, according to the IMF, GDP increased, in real terms, by an annual average of 2.6%. Regional recession and drought cut agricultural value added by 20% in 1992/93, although improved construction and manufacturing figures cushioned the blow and the economy grew marginally by 1.2%. In 1993/94 real GDP expanded by 3.8%, when the beneficial demand-side effects of improved growth in South Africa were offset by the agricultural sector's slow recovery from the drought and a drift back across the border of capital previously relocated from South Africa. Real GDP increased by 2.5% in 1995, and by an estimated 3% in 1996. However, this rate of growth has been barely equal to the pace of population expansion. Real incomes per caput have been stagnant as a result. The ministry of economic planning and development estimated that the strike action of early 1997 would reduce that year's GDP growth by 1%.

Swaziland's development has been dominated by its relation to South Africa, the dominant regional power. South African capital and imports, the Southern African Customs Union (SACU), the South African labour market and the Common Monetary Area (CMA, successor to the Rand Monetary Area) have shaped the economy and restricted the scope for independent economic policy. However, a consistent determination to maintain an investment climate attractive to foreign business and a policy of accepting the dominance of its powerful neighbour has brought Swaziland a rate of post-independence capital formation not achieved in most African states. In the late 1980s the kingdom benefited as foreign and South African companies relocated from the republic. In the early 1990s, however, Swaziland experienced the negative repercussions of political uncertainty and economic recession in South Africa. In the immediate aftermath of the installation of a democratically elected government in South Africa in 1994, there were mixed implications for Swaziland, such as the likelihood of a renegotiation of SACU to the country's disadvantage. Nevertheless, in the longer term, regional reintegration in the post-apartheid era should be of net benefit to the Swazi economy.

In the mid-1990s Swaziland's economy was at a critical juncture. With a rising budgetary deficit and pressure for increased spending, the government needs to prepare itself for the time when SACU trade-based taxation will cease to be a major source of revenue. There are very low levels of new investment, growing unemployment and a poor climate of industrial relations. Tourism has stagnated as a result of the expanding South African tourist industry and Swaziland's failure to become more attractive to tourist visitors, by refusing to extend the opening of the main border with South Africa. In addition, the region is becoming increasingly competitive and the economy must further diversify if the necessary jobs are to be created. In February 1997 the government presented the economic and social reform agenda, prepared in consultation with the IMF and the World Bank, which aimed to accelerate economic growth, reduce the level of unemployment and encourage investment in the private sector. However, long-term prospects for investment in Swaziland could depend on a satisfactory political settlement, in view of strike action which disrupted economic activity in 1996 and early 1997 (see Recent History).

The national currency is the lilangeni (plural: emalangeni) introduced in 1974. The terms of the Trilateral Monetary Agreement, signed with South Africa and Lesotho to form the CMA in 1986, allowed the Swazi authorities the option of determining the lilangeni's exchange rate independently. Under the amended Multilateral Monetary Agreement (signed in early 1992 to formalize Namibia's *de facto* membership) this freedom is maintained but the currency has remained pegged at par to the South African rand. Although they are formally no longer legal tender, rand notes still circulate freely in the kingdom.

As a member of the CMA, Swaziland was affected by South Africa's decision in 1997 to relax further its controls on the availability of foreign exchange. The limits on capital investment by companies in the Southern African Development Community (SADC) region have also been relaxed, and thus Swaziland will have to become more competitive if it is to attract further capital and investment from South Africa. Progress on the renegotiation of the SACU agreement slowed in 1997, as South Africa needed to address a number of additional pressing international economic issues, including accession to the Lomé Convention, the proposed free-trade agreement with the European Union (EU), and the SADC trade protocol revisions.

AGRICULTURE AND FORESTRY

Although the agricultural sector accounts for a declining share of GDP (an estimated 11.6% in 1995/96), it remains the backbone of the economy, employing some 33.6% of the labour force in mid-1995. Agro-industry continues to contribute the majority of manufacturing value added; the sector provided about 25% of formal employment in 1995; and the bulk of the population is still engaged in subsistence agriculture or small-scale cash cropping on SNL. Some 56% of the total land area is SNL, where traditional subsistence farming is conducted on land held by the monarchy, access to which is managed by the Swazi aristocracy and local chiefs. However, more than one-half of all SNL is designated as Rural Development Areas, and cash cropping of rain-watered crops, particularly maize and cotton, contribute significantly to total agricultural production when climatic conditions are favourable. In 1994/95 total SNL crop production represented 2.4% of GDP. Smallholders' rain-fed crops were most severely affected by the drought in 1992 (when this sub-sector's share of GDP fell to just 0.9%). The remainder of the land comprises individual tenure farms, owned by commercial companies, wealthy Swazis and white settlers. The principal agricultural commodities are sugar (of which Swaziland is continental Africa's second largest exporter), maize, citrus fruits, pineapples (for canning) and cotton. Livestock-rearing is an important sub-sector of the economy, particularly on SNL.

Sugar is the dominant agricultural export, providing 15.7% of domestic export earnings in 1995, with a value of US $122m. Following exceptionally good weather conditions, production of raw sugar reached 506,349 metric tons in 1986/87, an increase of 33.8% over the 1985/86 season, raising this commodity's share of export receipts to almost 40% in that year. However, production declined to around 440,000 tons in 1987/88 and 1988/89, before increasing to 475,140 tons in 1989/90. Annual output has subsequently stabilized at around 490,000 tons. In 1995 total sales were 421,000 tons, the largest part of which was sold to the EU (147,170 tons), mostly under the quota terms of the Lomé Convention. Other important customers were the USA and Canada. Meanwhile, since 1987 increased quantities have been sold and refined locally, with the establishment of Coca-Cola's soft drink concentrate plant, Cadbury's confectionery factory and a new refinery. Local sales amounted to an estimated 43% of raw sugar production in 1994/95, as new local refining capacity was added. There are three sugar mills in the country, in which the Swazi Nation has substantial shareholdings. The sugar industry was adversely affected by the industrial action which disrupted economic activity across the country in 1996 and 1997. In February 1997 Ubombo Ranches, Swaziland's only producer of refined white sugar, lost four weeks of factory maintenance work, off-crop sugar refining and preparatory work for the milling season. In terms of production, 12,000 tons of white sugar, worth E24m., were lost.

Swazi and South African government officials continued to negotiate in 1997 in an attempt to resolve the dispute over the penetration of Swazi sugar into the South African market, and to develop a common approach to the SADC trade protocol. South Africa wanted to place sugar on the list of excluded items for SADC free trade, fearing competition from lower-cost producers in Swaziland and Zimbabwe. Swaziland wants to adhere to the SACU agreement, which provides for the free movement of goods, but it is in agreement with South Africa on protecting the SACU market from other SADC competitors.

Rain-fed maize production on SNL, where the bulk of the crop is raised, was severely affected by the drought of the early 1980s, and again in 1992. However, with improved rainfall and increased plantings in response to the import of unpopular yellow maize, this smallholder harvest recovered to 83,800 metric tons in 1983/84, from 29,900 tons the previous year. Thereafter about 100,000 tons were produced annually, with the harvest attaining a record 125,800 tons in 1990/91, until drought returned in 1992. The 1991/92 crop was estimated to have fallen to just 45,600 tons, against annual consumption needs of 116,000 tons. A partial recovery followed over the subsequent two seasons (84,500 tons in 1992/93 and 88,800 tons in 1993/94), but poor rains cut production again in 1994/95, when output fell to 76,000 tons, against annual needs of 123,100 tons. In 1995/96, however, the harvest was an estimated 107,575 tons.

An increase in livestock slaughterings in the early 1980s was the result of increased offtake brought about by drought and did not represent sustainable growth in output. A similar pattern emerged in 1992 with the recurrence of drought. The national cattle herd declined to 614,000 head in 1984, but had recovered to number 740,000 in 1991. Numbers slaughtered rose to 65,606 in 1992, although herd numbers rose to 753,000 head. In the wake of the drought, cattle mortality rose to 11% in 1993 and the herd declined to 607,000. Numbers recovered to 626,000 in 1994 before declining to 597,000 in 1995. Supported by the role of cattle as a store of wealth in customary society, at this level the national herd represents a significant environmental problem in terms of the overgrazing of SNL. Factory slaughterings virtually ceased, following the collapse of the Swaziland Meat Corpn in 1988. They recovered with the operation's relaunch as Swaziland Meat Industries in late 1989 but the company collapsed again in early 1992, although the abattoir at Matsapha was re-opened later that year. Frozen and canned meat is exported to the EU under quota.

In 1984 Swaziland's production of citrus fruit (oranges and grapefruit) declined dramatically to 43,000 metric tons following the devastation wreaked by 'Cyclone Domoina'. In the following year there was a mixed performance, with grapefruit production recovering strongly (a rise of 18%) but a further small decline in the orange harvest due to root-rot problems and trees coming to the end of their productive lives. By 1987, however, the citrus industry had recovered and total production increased to 82,700 tons. Steadier output in the range of 66,000–72,000 tons was achieved annually through the early 1990s. In 1994 the first fruits of recent new plantings combined with favourable weather conditions (there was no repeat of the hail damage of 1993) to produce a bumper harvest of 104,100 tons. In the following year output declined to 80,000 tons, but export earnings were sustained at E56m.

In the main, sturdy low-level pineapple plants were undamaged by the 1984 cyclone. The crop and fruit-canning production were thus unaffected; 43,431 metric tons of pineapple were harvested, almost matching the substantial 1983 crop, and 23,350 tons were canned. Subsequent production levels have fluctuated. In 1991 the total crop declined to 31,567 tons, owing to poor rainfall, while cannery output decreased to 14,600 tons. During 1992/93 adverse weather and world market conditions threatened the survival of the country's sole processing plant, Swazican, as export unit prices fell while costs rose. In 1992 cannery output was 14,709 tons, falling to 11,934 tons in 1993. In 1994 output rose to 13,806 tons, and 1,885 tons of jam were produced in addition. The total crop declined to 13,000 tons in 1995. The company continues to restructure and diversify away from the traditional dependence upon pineapple.

Most of the kingdom's cotton is grown by smallholders on SNL, but the diversification of certain of the sugar estates into raising an irrigated crop and the rapid expansion of the area planted to cotton by SNL farmers combined to raise output from 9,000 metric tons of seed cotton in 1982/83 to a record 32,538 tons in 1988/89. In 1989/90 the crop fell to 26,000 tons owing to adverse weather conditions. A similar quantity was produced in the following year, but production was hindered by drought in 1991/92, when output fell to 5,879 tons. Production has since remained depressed, with 10,000 tons in 1992/93, 7,500 tons in 1993/94 and 6,183 tons in 1994/95.

At December 1993 Swaziland had 98,153 ha of planted forest, representing 6% of the country's total land area. Of the total, more than half was devoted to supplying the kingdom's main forestry industry, the Usutu pulp mill which produces unbleached wood pulp. The mill is Swaziland's second largest source of export earnings (those of the Coca-Cola concentrate plant are probably higher but are not publicly disclosed). Wood pulp production was consistent at 170,000–180,000 metric tons throughout the 1980s until boiler problems reduced the figure to 147,000 tons in 1989 and 142,000 tons in 1990. A recovery to above 158,000 tons was recorded in 1991, and the company has produced at or around 170,000 tons annually since then. In 1994 170,800 tons were produced, when improved world market conditions led the mill owners to approve an E224m. expansion plan which is to raise annual capacity to 220,000 tons. Production of wood pulp in 1995 was 170,857 tons, when strong international prices took export earnings to US $122m., equal to sugar earnings. Wood and wood products earned a further $25m. in export revenue in that year. After South Africa, Far Eastern markets are the principal importers of Swazi wood pulp products. Of the remaining area planted to timber, 27,331 ha was for sawlogs in 1991; a further 12,331 ha (mostly gum) was planted for mine timber. The kingdom has three saw mills supplying a small but diversified timber products industry, and pine shelving of Swazi manufacture is sold in the British market, in 'kit' form.

MINING

Mining and quarrying have represented a declining proportion of GDP overall since independence, although the kingdom is relatively rich in mineral resources. From 10% in the 1960s, the sector's contribution fell to only 1.3% in 1993/94 as a result of the closure of one of the country's three commercial mines. By 1993/94 the opening of a new coal mine raised the sector's contribution to 1.9% of GDP; its share was 2.0% in 1994/95, but declined to 1.4% in 1995/96. Revenue from mining barely increased in 1996, at E86.88m. compared with E86.83m. in 1995. The asbestos mine remained the major contributor to this sector, accounting for E46.5m. The poor performance was due to reduced output at the Maloma colliery (which, at 62,000 tons, was worth only E8.25m.) and to the phasing-out of the diamond mine, which closed at the end of 1996. In addition to the three exported minerals, quarry stone is produced to meet the needs of the local construction industry. Iron ore and (on a smaller scale) gold have been significant export minerals in the past, but neither has been mined for more than a decade. Asbestos was the first mineral product to be exploited in the country on a large scale. The Havelock mine was developed in the 1930s, and it was not until 1962 that it was overtaken by the sugar industry as the territory's leading export earner. Since then, however, the identification of health problems associated with asbestos and the depletion of reserves have resulted in the decline of this sub-sector. A steady 30,000–40,000 metric tons were exported annually for decades, but production declined to 22,804 tons in 1988. In 1989 development of the new Far West orebody returned output to 27,291 tons and this figure rose to 35,938 tons in 1990. Beset with financial and labour problems the mine went into provisional liquidation in early 1991, when output fell to just 13,888 tons, but was subsequently re-opened under new ownership, and output recovered to 33,862 tons in 1993. Production fell to 26,988 tons in 1994, recovering a little to 27,914 tons in 1995. However, weaker world prices depressed earnings in the latter year.

Coal holds the country's most important mineral potential, with reserves estimated at 1,000m. metric tons. Production at Emaswati Coal's Mpaka mine fell from 165,122 metric tons in 1989 to 122,502 tons in 1991, as the result of strikes and a cave-in during the year. Mpaka's potential capacity has been consistently under-utilized, and in 1992 the mine closed, owing to lack of consumer demand (potential local users have failed to adapt existing facilities to burn coal). Output in that year consequently fell to 100,200 tons. A second coal-mine, near Maloma, came on stream in late 1993: its output brought total coal production to 227,700 tons in 1994, declining to 171,666 tons in 1995, as the company prepared to shift from open-cast operations to underground workings. Coal output appeared to be beginning to recover in mid-1997.

Production of mainly industrial-quality diamonds began at the Dokolwako mine in 1984. Output rose steadily to 72,676 carats in 1988, before the open pit operation encountered poorer ground and production fell to 55,264 carats in 1989 and 42,488 carats in 1990. A recovery to 57,420 carats in 1991 coincided with weakening world prices. After a fall to 50,547 carats in 1992, output rose to 61,686 carats in 1993 but declined to an estimated 52,800 carats in 1994, when sales earned E24m. Earnings rose marginally to E25.4m. in 1995. Recovery in the global economy strengthened demand, but the mine's longer-term future is uncertain.

MANUFACTURING

Excluding the processing of agricultural and forestry products, the majority of Swaziland's manufacturing is based at the Matsapha industrial estate. Prior to the new investment in the sector in the latter part of the 1980s, four-fifths of manufacturing's value added derived from agro-industries of various kinds, ranging from sugar, timber and wood-pulp mills to fruit, cotton and meat-processing plants. Manufacturing contributes about 35% of GDP annually. In 1984 the Swaziland Chemical Industries fertilizer factory ceased operations, as a combined result of drought conditions and South Africa's adjustment of SACU tariffs. At the end of 1984 the Finnish-owned Salora Swaziland television factory was closed, following its take-over by a South African firm. As a result, the kingdom lost combined exports of E44m., and real manufacturing value added fell slightly in 1985. As a result of industrial action in early 1997, a shortage of sugar supplies from the country's three mills led to the depletion of stocks in the sugar-based industries, which were obliged to import at a higher price from South Africa. Major agroindustrial companies were estimated to have lost E100m. during the strike.

One of the most serious impediments to the growth of manufacturing in Swaziland was the policy of incentives being offered by the South African government and its 'homelands' administrations in their efforts to attract and decentralize industry. Subsequently, however, conditions for investment in Swaziland were made more attractive, and more competitive when compared with the situation in neighbouring states. In 1985 the government introduced a programme of incentives for investment and also embarked upon a promotion exercise to advertise the benefits of Swaziland to industrialists. In 1996, however, the government put an end to the five-year tax-exempt period offered to investors in Swaziland; studies had apparently shown that this incentive had little effect on potential investors. In 1987 the effective replacement of the National Industrial Development Corpn of Swaziland by the Swaziland Industrial Development Co (SIDC) was also a watershed in the history of manufacturing in the kingdom. The SIDC has since established itself as an effective catalyst of industrial development.

Despite these developments within the kingdom, arguably the single most important factor in the improved fortunes of the manufacturing sector in the late 1980s was renewed unrest in South Africa in 1986 and the imposition of international sanctions against that country in the aftermath of its suppression under a state of emergency. It was against this background that Coca-Cola relocated its regional concentrate plant to Swaziland in 1987. This single decision added some 5% to real value added in manufacturing by 1988. Sanctions against South Africa also brought less welcome 'investment' interest to Swaziland. It was reported that a number of South African products were being exported from the kingdom with false 'Made in Swaziland' labels. Several companies, mainly foreign textile concerns, were formally instructed to cease this practice in 1988, but the problem only began to ease as South African domestic reform brought the progressive removal of sanctions after 1990.

Since the late 1980s there has been encouraging diversification of the manufacturing sector, and Swaziland now ranks among the most industrialized of African economies. The pace of investment has slowed in the 1990s, however, as a combined result of drought, regional recession, labour unrest and a drift back to post-apartheid South Africa of earlier relocations. Natex Swaziland (successor to an earlier national textile company) has been installing the capacity for a vertically-integrated national cotton and textile industry, but once again a South African adjustment of SACU tariffs now threatens an important industry in the kingdom. With its protective tariff shield removed the company has been struggling for survival since 1992. Several smaller factories producing knitwear, footwear, gloves, refrigerators, office equipment, beverages, confectionery, pine furniture, safety glass and bricks were established during the investment boom, creating many new jobs. Formal employment grew strongly over the five years to 1990, when the total in formal employment reached an estimated 92,000. Employment has since stagnated, the total being 91,873 in 1994. In 1997 Swaziland's unemployment rate was officially 22% of the labour force, although many observers estimated the real number to be much higher. In 1996 there were high levels of retrenchment in the manufacturing sector and relatively low levels of new investment. The result was a rate of job creation of less than 1% per year. The problem of unemployment, therefore, is serious and growing, especially among young people: 54% of the jobless are under 25 years of age and a further 29% are aged between 25 and 34.

Unfortunately, the country has not received any major foreign investment in recent years, with industrial action having no doubt left many investors cautious. However, despite persistent press claims that some companies are contemplating leaving Swaziland for more stable conditions, there is no indication that any major company is seriously considering relocation. On the contrary, a number of new enterprises have been established or have announced plans to locate in the country. A bus assembly plant opened in 1997 with South African investment. There is expansion in the confectionery industry, and a E12m. Taiwanese nylon-casting operation is under construction. Swaziland has been consolidating its economic ties with Taiwan, with the prime minister paying a visit there in 1997 to discuss new investment projects. Ironically, South Africa's decision to recognize the People's Republic of China may greatly benefit Swaziland. Taiwan has suspended new investment in South Africa, and is reducing its trade and commercial ties with that country. Much Taiwanese investment, originally intended for South Africa, is now expected to find its way to Swaziland.

POWER, TRANSPORT AND COMMUNICATIONS

The country has a comparatively well-developed and maintained physical infrastructure, but the Swaziland Electricity Board (SEB) still imports from South Africa most of the power it supplies, and the proportion has risen steadily during the recent period of historically low rainfall. In 1995 imports, of 597 GWh, amounted to 85% of total supply of 705 GWh. The 20-MW capacity Luphohlo-Ezulwini hydroelectric station, completed under drought conditions in 1983/84, represents the largest part of domestic installed capacity of 50 MW. The link to the South African grid had a capacity of 96 MW, with new capacity planned. Delays and engineering problems elevated the cost of the Luphohlo scheme far beyond budget, but it was the subsequent slump in the exchange value of the lilangeni which burdened the SEB with unserviceable foreign loans.

'Cyclone Domoina' destroyed large parts of Swaziland's transport and communications infrastructure in 1984, bringing down major bridges and ruining large sections of the road network. The 1995/96 season brought unusually heavy rains once more, but flood damage was modest as compared with that of a decade earlier. Rehabilitation costs in 1984 were estimated at E60m., and substantial provisions of international aid were forthcoming.

The kingdom's first railway line was built during 1962–64 to connect the Ngwenya iron ore mine in the far west of the country, via the then railhead across the eastern border at Goma, to the port of Maputo (then Lourenço Marques) and so to its Japanese customers. Long disused west of the Matsapha industrial estate, the line was finally taken up in 1995. A southern link via Lavumisa and connecting to the South African port of Richards Bay was completed in 1978, while a northern link, crossing the border near Mananga and running to the South African town of Komatipoort, was opened in 1986. These lines established a direct link between the eastern Transvaal and the Natal ports, integrating the Swazi lines into the South African network. In the year to March 1995 the northern link carried 3.3m. tons of transit traffic, which represented 78% of all tonnages hauled by the Swaziland Railway Board.

The kingdom's road network is comparatively well developed. In 1995 there were an estimated 3,825 km of roads. About 28.2% of the road network was paved in 1994. Road projects have dominated the capital expenditure programmes of recent development plans and in 1991 work began on the rebuilding of the kingdom's main road artery connecting the capital, Mbabane, to Manzini, via Matsapha. By late 1995 the work had advanced to the laying of new surface on stretches blasted out of the rocky hills on the climb in to the capital.

Much of Swaziland can now be reached telephonically by dialling directly; a satellite link was inaugurated in 1983 allowing the kingdom's subscribers to bypass South Africa when contacting Europe and North America. At the end of 1994 Swaziland had 18,605 telephone exchange connections. An estimated 95% of the population have access to two radio stations operated by the Swaziland Broadcasting and Information Service. One television channel is run by the Swaziland Television Broadcasting Corpn. There are two national daily newspapers, one of which is privately owned.

TOURISM

Tourism in Swaziland was largely depressed during the early 1980s, owing primarily to the economic recession in South Africa (whence the majority of the tourists come; 63% in 1993), together with strong competition from new hotel complexes in the South African 'homelands'. There were significant improvements after 1985, when the total number of arrivals was stimulated by growth in the number of business visitors as well as by renewed tourist interest. Since 1992 regional recession has depressed the sector once more, although some encouragement has been provided by an increase in arrivals from Mozambique following increased stability in the border region.

Facilities in the central Ezulwini valley (the heart of the Swazi tourism industry) are dominated by the South African Sun International chain. A new hotel complex, owned by the government but managed by Protea of South Africa, was opened in Piggs Peak in 1986. Visitor arrivals rose to 287,796 in 1990, but thereafter stagnated. In 1993 287,023 arrivals at hotels were recorded, when 317,000 bed nights were sold and gross earnings were E93.9m. In 1994 an improvement in the industry's fortunes was reflected in a 17% increase in bed nights sold (reaching 370,900), and the trend continued into 1995, when 404,231 bed nights were sold. The peaceful political transition in South Africa was the principal cause of the recovery.

BALANCE OF PAYMENTS

Swaziland's balance-of-payments position improved considerably after the mid-1980s. From the latter part of 1983 until the end of 1985 the value of the lilangeni fell sharply. In terms of the IMF's 'basket' of major currencies, the special drawing right (SDR), the lilangeni exchange rate was SDR 0.78 = E1 at the end of 1983, but had declined to SDR 0.36 = E1 two years later (the decline against the surging US dollar being even more precipitous). This raised the local currency value of commodity exports sold on world markets, albeit at depressed prices in real terms. However, import prices rose sharply. Most imports are supplied by or via South Africa, and the shared currency devaluation fuelled inflation in both countries; the South African index of the cost of imported goods rose by 24% in 1985. The initial impact of this was a widening of the trade deficit in lilangeni terms, but a narrowing in real terms. Distortions further down the external accounts included a sudden rise in the burden of the service of external debt and substantial real valuation losses on reserves held in South Africa. However, as the currency stabilized and exports rose strongly, following the record sugar crop of 1986, the trade deficit of the balance of payments fell from US $95.9m. in 1985 to $18.6m. As a result, the current account moved into surplus for the first time since 1977, and, with new investment supporting capital inflows, the overall balance-of-payments position was also in surplus, signalling the beginning of a sustained period of rising foreign reserves. This improved performance was reversed after 1992, as wider trade deficits and outflows of short-term capital (related to trade credit and pension-fund investments in South Africa) brought about a decline in external reserves.

In 1996 a trade deficit of an estimated US $131m. was recorded, compared with $100.1m. in 1995. In 1995 Swaziland's principal exports were edible concentrates, sugar, wood pulp, refrigerators and cotton yarn. Principal imports in that year included machinery and transport equipment, basic manufactures, food and live animals, chemicals and chemical products and miscellaneous manufactured articles. The major destination for Swaziland's exports in that year was South Africa, accounting for 58% of the total, followed by the EU (19.8%), Mozambique (5.8%) and the USA (3.1%). South Africa was also the principal source of imports (88%); other suppliers included Japan, the United Kingdom and the USA.

Over 1986–92 the current account recorded consistent surpluses, which peaked at US $66.5m. in 1990. Since 1993, however, deficits have occurred, reaching an estimated $68m. in 1996, compared with $51.1m. in 1995 and $41.4m. in 1994. The balance on trade in services has remained in deficit. Inflated by reinsurance claims following the cyclone damage of 1984, earnings were subsequently supported by increased workers' remittances, resulting from pay increases in the South African mining industry, higher tourism receipts and returns on the increased holdings of foreign financial assets. Service debits have been augmented by the transfer of dividends and profits from foreign-owned businesses. Official unrequited transfers also make a significant contribution. Apart from grant aid from abroad, these flows comprise SACU transfers over and above the reimbursement of the duty raised on Swaziland's own trade and production. SACU receipts are expected to contribute a declining share of balance-of-payments and budgetary income as a result of the ongoing renegotiation of the customs union agreement.

The recovery in capital flows in the mid-1980s was very marked. Supported in the early 1980s by the activities of the official sector (the government borrowing abroad), the capital account recorded, after 1985, strong net private inflows as political and commercial considerations combined to bring about the relocation of manufacturing capacity from South Africa or attracted new investment to Swaziland in preference to the South African 'homelands'. Private inflows peaked at E170m. in 1989. New investment flows have since declined, but increased private-sector drawings on foreign loans and reinvestment of profits have maintained the surplus on long-term capital inflows. Government budget surpluses in the five years to 1991/92 led to net redemptions of foreign debt (meaning public sector outflows), but this trend has since reversed. The overall position strengthened considerably after 1986, and by the end of 1992 official holdings of foreign reserves had increased to E912m. Holdings fell over 1993–94 (the first decrease in seven years) to stand at E845m. at the end of 1994. The total rose again to E995m. in 1995, representing a comfortable 16 weeks' import cover.

PUBLIC FINANCE

Swaziland's public finances are characterized by a heavy dependence upon receipts from South Africa from the SACU revenue pool. Over and above the revenue raised in customs and excise duty on the kingdom's own trade and excisable production, these include cash compensation for the distorting effects of high import tariffs which protect South African producers' dominance of the Swazi market. With the installation of a government in South Africa which no longer needs to buy goodwill in the region, the future of these receipts is uncertain and the customs union agreement is being renegotiated. A sales tax was introduced in 1984 to lessen the dependence upon SACU receipts. Its tighter application increased revenue from this source from the 1986/87 (April–March) fiscal year, but it still represented less than a quarter of the contribution of customs union receipts in 1995/96. Overall receipts stagnated in the early 1990s as a result of the general economic downturn. Compounded by the wasteful growth of current expenditure and improved capital budget implemention, this trend took the government's finances into deficit again in 1992/93. Capital spending previously peaked with the internationally-backed reconstruction effort which followed the cyclone damage of 1984, but the general inability of the authorities to spend their investment budget is a structural problem characteristic of the administrative inefficiencies inherent in the dichotomous nature of Swaziland's governance. Finally, there has been significant net lending to public sector industries, some inefficiently run and others struggling with foreign debt, following the sharp decline in the exchange rate during the mid-1980s. In 1989 a public enterprise unit was formed within the finance ministry, charged with reviewing the performance of the public sector companies and advising on future policy in their regard. As a result, an improved performance has been achieved by this sector, although this too has been compromised by the general downturn in the economy since 1992.

In late 1995 a programme for the reform of public enterprises was introduced, and in 1996 an extensive reform of the tax system was initiated, as part of the government's continuing austerity programme. The government intends to establish a non-discriminatory tax regime in which investors in all sectors are subject to the same rate of tax. In place of the discriminatory incentives, the government proposes to reduce the corporate tax rate from 37.5% to 30% in 1997/98, with the ultimate aim of a 25% rate in the medium term. This would give Swaziland the lowest general corporate tax rate in the region. The sales tax on luxury goods will be increased, and the fuel tax will also rise, although the retail price of fuel will remain below that prevailing in neighbouring countries.

The budgets of the early 1980s were introduced against a background of chronic public finance problems, successive (often large) deficits and growing domestic and external debt. However, the economy's buoyancy in the late 1980s and early 1990s turned the deficits into persistent, large and embarrassing surpluses since the effects of the record sugar crop of 1986 entailed a near doubling of direct taxation receipts in 1987/88. In 1987 the finance minister tabled a budget projecting an E24m. deficit; the 1986/87 deficit of E49m. had represented 4.8% of GDP. In the event, company tax delivered E73m. rather than the budgeted E35m. in 1987/88, while personal taxes also came in well above expectations as formal sector employment grew strongly in the boom conditions. Current expenditure was held almost exactly to budget, while net lending was greater than expected at E14m. and the capital budget was 13% underspent at E66m. The result was a surplus, the first since 1980/81, of E22m.

The pattern was repeated over the next five years. The finance ministry's routine revisions of the budget projections in July and December/January of each fiscal year showed higher than expected revenue, tight control of recurrent outgoings and underspending of the capital budget. In 1988/89 the original projection was of an E9.5m. deficit; the eventual surplus for the year was E59m. (3.8% of GDP). In 1989/90 an E1m. deficit was expected; the result was an E95m. surplus (some 5.0% of GDP). In 1990/91 the surplus was only contained at E1m. by the introduction of an E165m. Capital Investment Facility (CIF) established to save from the surplus and so reduce it. In 1991/92 a budgeted E7m. deficit was, in effect, eventually recorded as a surplus of E21m. (E100m. having been diverted by the CIF). One response to this trend was for the authorities to ease the personal tax burden. The government also embarked upon a programme of accelerated debt redemption.

The 1992/93 financial year was a turning-point in the kingdom's public finances. Growth in revenue slowed to 9% (a decline, in real terms, given inflation of some 13%), while expenditure increased by 17%. This latter increase reflected civil service pay and benefits increases, as well as improvements in capital budget implementation. An overall deficit of E42m. was recorded. The 1993/94 budget projected an E120m. deficit. In the event, an E171m. shortfall was recorded. The first signs that the tide was about to turn once more came in 1994/95, when the final deficit turned out at less than that budgeted, albeit still larger, at E198m. (equivalent to 5.2% of GDP), than in 1993/94. Although the 1995/96 budget showed a surplus of E68m., the country's macroeconomic situation deteriorated and the 1996/97 budget resulted in a forecast deficit of E217m. Revenue was revised downwards as a result of the late implementation of sales tax reforms. Furthermore, estimated recurrent expenditure was higher than originally budgeted because of additional allocations for the Swaziland Development and Savings Bank. The extent to which the government adheres to the adjustment programme adopted in 1996 will determine the size of the deficit. The budget has been based on the expectation that additional revenue will be obtained through improved tax collection and the widening of the tax net; that all expenditure will be financed within the budget reallocation; and that there will be no real growth in capital expenditure. Education absorbs the highest proportion of the budget's recurrent expenditure, at 25%. In the mean time the debt burden remains modest. Total public external debt stood at E778m. at the end of March 1996, and debt-service payments consumed just 2.5% of earnings from exports of goods and services in 1995/96. In 1985–96 the average annual rate of inflation was 12.3%; consumer prices increased by 14.7% in 1995 and by 12.2% in 1996.

Statistical Survey

Source (unless otherwise stated): Central Statistical Office, POB 456, Mbabane.

AREA AND POPULATION

Area: 17,363 sq km (6,704 sq miles).

Population (excluding absentee workers): 494,534 (males 231,861, females 262,673) at census of 25 August 1976; 681,059 (males 321,579, females 359,480) at census of 25 August 1986; 908,000 (official estimate) at mid-1995.

Density (mid-1995): 52.3 per sq km.

Ethnic Groups (census of August 1986): Swazi 661,646; Other Africans 14,468; European 1,825; Asiatic 228; Other non-Africans 412; Mixed 2,403; Unknown 77; Total 681,059.

Principal Towns (population at census of August 1986): Mbabane (capital) 38,290; Manzini 18,084.

Births and Deaths (UN estimates, 1990–95): Average annual birth rate 38.5 per 1,000; average annual death rate 10.7 per 1,000. Source: UN, *World Population Prospects: The 1994 Revision*.

Expectation of Life (UN estimates, years at birth, 1990–95): 57.5 (males 55.2; females 59.8). Source: UN, *World Population Prospects: The 1994 Revision*.

Economically Active Population (persons aged 12 years and over, census of August 1986): Agriculture, hunting, forestry and fishing 30,197; Mining and quarrying 5,245; Manufacturing 14,742; Electricity, gas and water 1,315; Construction 7,661; Trade, restaurants and hotels 12,348; Transport, storage and communications 7,526; Financing, insurance, real estate and business services 1,931; Community, social and personal services 32,309; Activities not adequately defined 3,156; Total employed 116,430 (males 79,528, females 36,902); Unemployed 43,925 (males 25,663, females 18,262); Total labour force 160,355 (males 105,191, females 55,164). Source: UN, *Demographic Yearbook*.

Mid-1995 (estimates in '000): Agriculture, etc. 102; Total labour force 303. Source: FAO, *Production Yearbook*.

AGRICULTURE

Principal Crops ('000 metric tons, 1995): Rice (paddy) 1*; Maize 76; Potatoes 6†; Sweet potatoes 2†; Pulses 6; Cottonseed 4†; Cotton (lint) 2†; Oranges 35; Grapefruit 45; Pineapples 13; Sugar cane 3,798.

* Unofficial figure.

† FAO estimate.

Livestock ('000 head, year ending September 1995): Horses 1*; Asses 12*; Cattle 597; Pigs 30; Sheep 24; Goats 435.

* FAO estimate.

Livestock Products ('000 metric tons, 1995): Beef and veal 15*; Goat meat 3*; Cows' milk 42; Cattle hides 1.8*.

* FAO estimate.

Source: FAO, *Production Yearbook*.

FORESTRY

Roundwood Removals ('000 cubic metres, 1993): Sawlogs, veneer logs and logs for sleepers 319 (FAO estimate); Pulpwood 1,324; Other industrial wood 76 (FAO estimate); Fuel wood 560 (FAO estimate); Total 2,279.

1994: Annual output as in 1993 (FAO estimates).

Sawnwood Production ('000 cubic metres, 1982): 103.

1983–94: Annual output as in 1982 (FAO estimates).

Source: FAO, *Yearbook of Forest Products*.

FISHING

Total catch (FAO estimates, metric tons, live weight): 110 in 1993; 110 in 1994; 115 in 1995. Source: FAO, *Yearbook of Fishery Statistics*.

MINING

Production (estimates, 1994): Coal 227,700 metric tons; Asbestos 27,000 metric tons; Quarrystone 211,500 cubic metres; Diamonds 52,800 carats. Source: partly IMF, *Swaziland—Recent Economic Developments* (April 1997).

INDUSTRY

1994: Electric energy 568m. kWh; Wood pulp 170,800 metric tons; Raw sugar 457,300 metric tons.

FINANCE

Currency and Exchange Rates: 100 cents = 1 lilangeni (plural: emalangeni). *Sterling and Dollar Equivalents* (31 March 1997): £1 sterling = 7.2585 emalangeni; US $1 = 4.4205 emalangeni; 100 emalangeni = £13.777= $22.622. *Average Exchange Rate* (US $ per lilangeni): 0.28177 in 1994; 0.27574 in 1995; 0.23416 in 1996. Note: The lilangeni is at par with the South African rand.

Budget (provisional, million emalangeni, year ending 31 March 1996): *Revenue:* Taxes on net income and profits 393; Taxes on property 3; Taxes on goods, services and international trade 968 (Receipts from Southern African Customs Union 744, Sales tax 173, Road levy and oil tax 36); Other current revenue 39; Total 1,403, excl. grants received (44). *Expenditure:* Current expenditure 1,122 (Wages and salaries 634, Other purchases of goods and services 252, Interest payments 32, Subsidies and other current transfers 204); Capital expenditure 290; Total 1,412, excl. lending minus repayments (60). Source: IMF, *Swaziland—Recent Economic Developments* (April 1997).

1996/97 (forecasts, million emalangeni): Revenue (incl. grants) 1,652; Expenditure (incl. net lending) 1,793. Source: Ministry of Finance.

International Reserves (US $ million at 31 December 1996): IMF special drawing rights 8.52; Reserve position in IMF 4.32; Foreign exchange 241.16; Total 254.00. Source: IMF, *International Financial Statistics*.

Money Supply (million emalangeni at 31 December 1996): Currency outside banks 90.85; Demand deposits at commercial banks 331.99; Total money (incl. others) 423.03. Source: IMF, *International Financial Statistics*.

Cost of Living (Retail Price Index, excluding rent, for low-income wage-earners' families in Mbabane and Manzini; base: 1990 = 100): 160.4 in 1994; 184.0 in 1995; 207.1 in 1996. Source: IMF, *International Financial Statistics*.

Expenditure on the Gross Domestic Product (million emalangeni at current prices, 1995/96): Government final consumption expenditure 951.0; Private final consumption expenditure 2,794.2; Increase in stocks 37.4; Gross fixed capital formation 830.9; *Total domestic expenditure* 4,613.5; Exports of goods and services 3,387.1; *Less* Imports of goods and services 3,839.6; *GDP in purchasers' values* 4,161.0. Source: IMF, *Swaziland—Recent Economic Developments* (April 1997).

Gross Domestic Product by Economic Activity (million emalangeni in current purchasers' values, 1995/96: Agriculture and forestry 383.8; Mining and quarrying 45.2; Manufacturing 1,092.6; Electricity, gas and water 68.1; Construction 157.1; Trade, restaurants and hotels 316.6; Transport and communications 209.8; Finance, insurance, real estate, etc. 250.8; Government services 704.6; Other non-marketable services 67.6; *Sub-total* 3,296.2; *Less* Imputed bank service charge 127.1; *GDP at factor cost* 3,169.1; Indirect taxes, *less* subsidies 991.9; *GDP in purchasers' values* 4,161.0. Source: IMF, *Swaziland—Recent Economic Developments* (April 1997).

Balance of Payments (US $ million, 1995): Exports of goods f.o.b. 798.3; Imports of goods f.o.b. –898.4; *Trade balance* –100.1; Exports of services 102.2; Imports of services –161.0; *Balance on goods and services* –158.8; Other income received 137.9; Other income paid –128.0; *Balance on goods, services and income* –149.0; Current transfers received 201.7; Current transfers paid –103.8; *Current balance* –51.1; Capital account (net) –0.2; Direct investment abroad –17.4; Direct investment from abroad 57.7; Portfolio investment assets –1.8; Portfolio investment liabilities –0.1; Other investment assets –46.5; Other investment liabilities 0.4; Net errors and omissions 88.8; *Overall balance* 29.9. Source: IMF, *International Financial Statistics*.

EXTERNAL TRADE

Principal Commodities (estimates, US $ million, 1995): *Imports c.i.f.*: Food and live animals 149.1; Beverages and tobacco 34.5; Inedible crude materials 85.0; Mineral fuels, lubricants 46.5; Chemicals and chemical products 120.2; Manufactures classified by material 158.9; Machinery and transport equipment 227.6; Miscellaneous manufactured articles 106.3. Total (incl. others) 907.7. *Exports f.o.b.*: Sugar 122; Wood pulp 122; Wood and wood products 25; Canned fruits 16; Edible concentrates 189; Cotton yarn 48; Refrigerators 53; Paper products 18; Total (incl. others) 776. Figures refer to domestic exports, excluding re-exports (22). Source: IMF, *Swaziland—Recent Economic Developments* (April 1997).

Principal Trading Partners ('000 emalangeni): *Imports* (year ending 31 March 1993): France 1,552.2; Netherlands 10,726.9; South Africa 2,428,294.0; Switzerland 7,499.6; United Kingdom 75,117.8; Total (incl. others) 2,587,338.5. *Exports* (excl. re-exports, 1991):

South Africa 804,103.7; United Kingdom 56,561.3; Total (incl. others) 1,711,539.0.

TRANSPORT

Railways (traffic estimates, million, 1995): Passenger-km 1,210 (1988); Freight net ton-km 2,910. Source: UN Economic Commission for Africa, *African Statistical Yearbook*.

Total freight ('000 metric tons, 1993): 4,203.

Road Traffic (estimates, motor vehicles in use, 31 December 1995): Passenger cars 27,300; Buses and coaches 2,440; Lorries and vans 23,900; Road tractors 1,503 (1994); Motor cycles and scooters 2,910. Source: International Road Federation, *World Road Statistics*.

Civil Aviation (traffic on scheduled services, 1994): Passengers carried 65,000; Passenger-km 48 million. Source: UN, *Statistical Yearbook*.

TOURISM

Tourist Arrivals by Nationality (1992): South Africa 137,000; United Kingdom 31,181; Total (incl. others) 268,071. Figures cover only tourists staying in hotels. Including other visitors, the total number of arrivals was 1,568,198. In 1993 a total of 287,023 arrivals at hotels was recorded.

Total Receipts (million emalangeni): 76.4 in 1991; 85.7 in 1992; 93.9 in 1993.

COMMUNICATIONS MEDIA

Radio Receivers (1994): 136,000 in use.

Television Receivers (1994): 17,000 in use.

Source: UNESCO, *Statistical Yearbook*.

Daily Newspapers (1995): 2.

Telephones (1992): 25,888 in use.

EDUCATION

Primary (1994): Institutions 535; Teachers 5,887; Students 192,599.

General Secondary (1994): Institutions 165; Teachers 2,872; Students 52,571.

Teacher Training (1993/94): Institutions 3; Teachers 88; Students 924.

Technical and Vocational Training (1993/94): Institutions 2; Teachers 140; Students 2,034.

University Education (1993/94): Institution 1; Teachers 190; Students 1,730.

Directory

The Constitution

The Constitution of 13 October 1978 vests supreme executive and legislative power in the hereditary King (Ngwenyama—the Lion). Succession is governed by traditional law and custom. In the event of the death of the King, the powers of Head of State are transferred to the constitutional dual monarch, the Queen Mother (Indlovukazi—Great She Elephant), who is authorized to act as Regent until the designated successor attains the age of 21. The Constitution provides for a bicameral legislature (Libandla), comprising a House of Assembly and a Senate. The functions of the Libandla are confined to debating government proposals and advising the King. Executive power is exercised through the Cabinet (later redesignated the Council of Ministers), which is appointed by the King. The Swaziland National Council, which comprises members of the royal family, and is headed by the King and Queen Mother, advises on matters regulated by traditional law and custom. The Constitution affirms the fundamental rights of the individual.

Following a number of amendments to the electoral system, which were approved by the King in October 1992, the House of Assembly (which was redesignated as the National Assembly) was expanded to 65 deputies (of whom 55 are directly elected from candidates nominated by traditional local councils, known as Tinkhundla, and 10 appointed by the King), and the Senate to 30 members (of whom 20 are appointed by the King and 10 elected by the National Assembly). Elections to the National Assembly are conducted by secret ballot, in two rounds of voting; the second round of the elections is contested by the three candidates from each of the Tinkhundla who secure the highest number of votes in the first poll. In July 1996 the King appointed a commission to prepare proposals for a draft constitution, which would subsequently be submitted for approval by the Swazi people.

The Government

HEAD OF STATE

HM King Mswati III (succeeded to the throne 25 April 1986).

COUNCIL OF MINISTERS
(August 1997)

Prime Minister: Dr Barnabas Sibusiso Dlamini.

Deputy Prime Minister: Dr Sishayi S. Nxumalo.

Minister of Justice and Constitutional Development: Chief Maweni Simelane.

Minister of Foreign Affairs and Trade: Arthur R. V. Khoza.

Minister of Finance: Themba Masuku.

Minister of Home Affairs: Prince Guduza.

Minister of Education: Solomon Dlamini.

Minister of Agriculture and Co-operatives: Chief Dambuza Lukhele II.

Minister of Enterprise and Employment: Rev. Absalom Dlamini.

Minister of Economic Planning and Development: Albert H. Shabangu.

Minister of Health and Social Welfare: Phetsile Dlamini.

Minister of Public Service and Information: Muntu Mswane.

Minister of Public Works and Transport: Dumsane Masango.

Minister of Natural Resources and Energy: Majahenkhaba Dlamini.

Minister of Tourism and Communications: Musa Nkambule.

Minister of Housing and Urban Development: John Carmichael.

MINISTRIES

Office of the Prime Minister: POB 395, Mbabane; tel. 42251; fax 43943.

Ministry of Agriculture and Co-operatives: POB 162, Mbabane; tel. 42731; telex 2343; fax 44700.

Ministry of Economic Planning and Development: POB 602, Mbabane; tel. 43765; fax 42157.

Ministry of Education: POB 39, Mbabane; tel. 42491; telex 2293; fax 43880.

Ministry of Enterprise and Employment: POB 170, Mbabane; tel. 43521; fax 45379.

Ministry of Finance: POB 443, Mbabane; tel. 42142; telex 2109; fax 43187.

Ministry of Foreign Affairs and Trade: POB 451, Mbabane; tel. 42661; telex 2036; fax 42669.

Ministry of Health and Social Welfare: POB 5, Mbabane; tel. 42431; fax 42092.

Ministry of Home Affairs: POB 432, Mbabane; tel. 42941; telex 2328; fax 44303.

Ministry of Housing and Urban Development: POB 1832, Mbabane; tel. 46510; fax 44085; e-mail minhouse@realnet.co.sz.

Ministry of Justice and Constitutional Development: POB 924, Mbabane; tel. 43531; fax 44796.

Ministry of Natural Resources and Energy: POB 57, Mbabane; tel. 46244; telex 2301; fax 42436.

Ministry of Public Service and Information: Mbabane.

Ministry of Public Works and Transport: POB 58, Mbabane; tel. 42321; telex 2104; fax 42364.

Ministry of Tourism and Communications: POB 338, Mbabane; tel. 42761; fax 42774.

Legislature

LIBANDLA

The Senate

There are 30 senators, of whom 20 are appointed by the King and 10 elected by the National Assembly.

President: Lawrence Mncina.

National Assembly

There are 65 deputies, of whom 55 are directly elected from candidates nominated by the Tinkhundla and 10 appointed by the King. The latest elections to the National Assembly took place, in two rounds of voting, on 25 September and 11 October 1993.

Speaker: MUSA SIBANDZE.

Political Organizations

Party political activity was banned by royal proclamation in April 1973, and formally prohibited under the 1978 Constitution. Since 1991, following indications that the Constitution was to be revised, a number of political associations have re-emerged.

Imbokodvo National Movement (INM): f. 1964 by King Sobhuza II; traditionalist movement, but also advocates policies of development and the elimination of illiteracy; Leader (vacant).

Ngwane National Liberatory Congress (NNLC): Ilanga Centre, Martin St, Manzini; tel. 53935; f. 1962, by a breakaway faction of the SPP; advocates democratic freedoms and universal suffrage, and seeks abolition of the Tinkhundla electoral system; Pres. Dr AMBROSE ZWANE; Sec.-Gen. DUMISA DLAMINI.

Confederation for Full Democracy in Swaziland: f. 1992 as an alliance of orgs advocating democratic reform; includes:

People's United Democratic Movement (PUDEMO): f. 1983; seeks constitutional reform to limit the powers of the monarchy; affiliated orgs, incl. the Human Rights Asscn of Swaziland and the Swaziland Youth Congress (SWAYOCO); Pres. MARIO MASUKU; Sec.-Gen. DOMINIC MNGOMEZULU.

Swaziland National Front (SWANAFRO): Mbabane; Pres. ELMOND SHONGWE; Sec.-Gen. GLENROSE DLAMINI.

Swaziland Progressive Party (SPP): POB 6, Mbabane; tel. 22648; f. 1929; Pres. J. J. NQUKU.

Swaziland United Front (SUF): POB 14, Kwaluseni; f. 1962 by a breakaway faction of the SPP; Leader MATSAPA SHONGWE.

Diplomatic Representation

EMBASSIES AND HIGH COMMISSIONS IN SWAZILAND

China (Taiwan): Embassy House, Warner St, POB 56, Mbabane; tel. 42379; telex 2167; fax 46688; Ambassador: ENTI LIU.

Israel: Mbabane House, Warner St, POB 146, Mbabane; tel. 42626; telex 2098; fax 45857; Ambassador: (vacant).

Mozambique: Princess Drive, POB 1212, Mbabane; tel. 43700; telex 2248; fax 43692; High Commissioner: LOPES TEMBE NDALANE.

South Africa: The New Mall, 2nd Floor, Plasmall St, POB 2507, Mbabane; tel. 44651; telex 2341; fax 44335; High Commissioner: WALTER LOUW.

United Kingdom: Allister Miller St, Private Bag, Mbabane; tel. 42581; fax 42585; High Commissioner: JOHN DOBLE.

USA: Central Bank Bldg, Warner St, POB 199, Mbabane; tel. 46441; telex 2285; fax 46446; Ambassador: ALAN MCKEE.

Judicial System

The judiciary is headed by the Chief Justice. There is a High Court (which is a Superior Court of Record) with six subordinate courts in all the administrative districts, and there is a Court of Appeal which sits at Mbabane.

There are 17 Swazi Courts, including two Courts of Appeal and a Higher Court of Appeal, which have limited jurisdiction in civil and criminal cases. Their jurisdiction excludes non-Swazi nationals.

Chief Justice: S. SAPIRE (acting).

Religion

About 60% of the adult Swazi population profess Christianity. Most of the remainder hold traditional beliefs. There is also a small Muslim community.

CHRISTIANITY

Council of Swaziland Churches: Mandelenkhosi House, 142 Esser St, Manzini; POB 1095, Manzini; tel. 53931; f. 1976; nine mem. churches; Chair. Rev. G. MASHWAMA; Gen. Sec. MARIA MBELU.

League of African Churches: POB 230, Lobamba; asscn of 48 independent churches; Pres. ISAAC DLAMINI.

Swaziland Conference of Churches: 175 Ngwane St, Manzini; POB 115, Manzini; tel. 55259; f. 1929; Pres. Rt Rev. NICHOLAS NYAWO.

The Anglican Communion

Swaziland comprises a single diocese within the Church of the Province of Southern Africa. The Metropolitan of the Province is the Archbishop of Cape Town, South Africa.

Bishop of Swaziland: Rt Rev. LAWRENCE BEKISISA ZULU, POB 118, Mbabane; tel. 43624; fax 46759.

The Roman Catholic Church

The Roman Catholic Church was established in Swaziland in 1913. For ecclesiastical purposes, Swaziland comprises the single diocese of Manzini, suffragan to the archdiocese of Pretoria, South Africa. At 31 December 1995 there were an estimated 47,800 adherents in Swaziland, equivalent to about 5.0% of the total population. The Bishop participates in the Southern African Catholic Bishops' Conference (based in Pretoria, South Africa).

Bishop of Manzini: Rt Rev. LOUIS NCAMISO NDLOVU, Bishop's House, Sandlane St, POB 19, Manzini; tel. 52348; fax 54876.

Other Christian Churches

Church of the Nazarene: POB 1460, Manzini; tel. 54732; f. 1910; 7,649 adherents (1994).

The Evangelical Lutheran Church in Southern Africa: POB 117, Mbabane; tel. 46453; f. 1902; Bishop R. SCHIELE; 2,800 adherents in Swaziland (1994).

Lutheran Development Service: Lutheran World Federation, POB 388, Mbabane; tel. 42562; fax 43870.

Mennonite Central Committee: POB 329, Mbabane; tel. 42805; fax 44732; f. 1971; Co-ordinators JON RUDY, CAROLYN RUDY.

The Methodist Church in Southern Africa: POB 218, Mbabane; tel. 42658; f. 1880; 2,578 adherents (1992).

United Christian Church of Africa: POB 253, Nhlangano; tel. 22648; f. 1944; Pres. Rt Rev. JEREMIAH NDZINISA; Founder and Gen. Sec. Dr J. J. NQUKU.

The National Baptist Church, the Christian Apostolic Holy Spirit Church in Zion and the Religious Society of Friends (Quakers) are also active.

BAHÁ'Í FAITH

National Spiritual Assembly: POB 298, Mbabane; tel. 52689; f. 1960; mems resident in 153 localities.

ISLAM

Ezulwini Islamic Institute: Al Islam Dawah Movement of Swaziland, POB 133, Ezulwini; c. 3,000 adherents (1994).

The Press

The Swazi News: Sheffield Rd, POB 156, Mbabane; tel. 42520; fax 42438; f. 1983; weekly (Sat.); English; owned by *The Times of Swaziland*; Editor KIMBER FRASER; circ. 18,000.

Swaziland Observer: Swazi Plaza, POB A385, Mbabane; tel. 23383; telex 2322; f. 1981; daily (Mon.–Sat.); English; Man. Editor CYRIL DLAMINI; circ. 11,000.

Swaziview: POB 1532, Mbabane; tel. 42716; monthly magazine; general interest; circ. 3,500.

The Times of Swaziland: Sheffield Rd, POB 156, Mbabane; tel. 42520; fax 42438; f. 1897; English; daily (Mon.–Fri.); also monthly edn; Editor MASHUMI THWALA; circ. 18,000.

Publishers

Apollo Services (Pty) Ltd: POB 35, Mbabane; tel. 42711.

GBS Printing and Publishing (Pty) Ltd: POB 1384, Mbabane; tel. 52779.

Jubilee Printers: POB 1619, Matsaka; tel. 84557; fax 84558.

Longman Swaziland (Pty) Ltd: POB 2207, Manzini; tel. 53891.

Macmillan Boleswa Publishers (Pty) Ltd: POB 1235, Manzini; tel. 84533; telex 2221; fax 85247; Man. Dir L. A. BALARIN.

Swaziland Printing & Publishing Co Ltd: POB 28, Mbabane; tel. 42716.

Whydah Media Publishers Ltd: POB 1532, Mbabane; tel. 42716; f. 1978.

Radio and Television

In 1994, according to UNESCO, there were an estimated 136,000 radio receivers and 17,000 television receivers in use.

RADIO

Swaziland Broadcasting and Information Service: POB 338, Mbabane; tel. 42761; telex 2035; fax 42774; f. 1966; broadcasts in English and siSwati; Dir ABNER TEMBE.

Swaziland Commercial Radio (Pty) Ltd: POB 1586, Alberton 1450, South Africa; tel. (11) 4344333; fax (11) 4344777; privately-owned commercial service; broadcasts to southern Africa in English and Portuguese; music and religious programmes; Man. Dir I. KIRSH.

Trans World Radio: POB 64, Manzini; tel. 52781; fax 55333; f. 1974; religious broadcasts from five transmitters in 28 languages to southern, central and eastern Africa and to the Far East; Pres. THOMAS J. LOWELL.

TELEVISION

Swaziland Television Broadcasting Corporation: POB A146, Swazi Plaza, Mbabane; tel. 43036; telex 2138; fax 42093; f. 1978; state-owned; broadcasts seven hours daily in English; colour transmissions; Gen. Man. DAN S. DLAMINI.

Finance

(cap. = capital; res = reserves; dep. = deposits; m. = million; br. = branch; amounts in emalangeni)

BANKING

Central Bank

Central Bank of Swaziland: POB 546, Mbabane; tel. 43221; telex 2029; fax 45417; f. 1974; bank of issue; cap. and res 7.2m., dep. 333.7m. (March 1996); Gov. Dr DERRICK VON WISSEL; Dep. Gov. M. G. DLAMINI.

Commercial Banks

Barclays Bank of Swaziland Ltd: Allister Miller St, POB 667, Mbabane; tel. 42691; telex 2096; fax 43413; f. 1974; 40% state-owned; cap. and res 28.7m., dep. 460.4m. (Dec. 1995); Chair. DANIEL M. DLAMINI; Man. Dir W. G. PRICE; 13 brs and agencies.

First National Bank of Swaziland Ltd: Meridien BIAO House, cnr West Warner St, POB 261, Eveni, Mbabane; tel. 45401; telex 2380; fax 44735; f. 1988; cap. and res 5.6m., dep. 11.9m. (Sept. 1991); Chair. B. J. SWART; Man. Dir D. W. PARSONS; 4 brs and 1 agency.

Nedbank (Swaziland) Ltd: 21 Allister Miller St, POB 68, Mbabane; tel. 43351; telex 2220; fax 44060; f. 1974; fmrly Standard Chartered Bank Swaziland Ltd; 30% state-owned; cap. and res 19.9m., dep. 242.4m. (Dec. 1995); Chair. A. R. B. SHABANGU; Man. Dir P. R. SOUTHEY; 4 brs and 1 agency.

Development Banks

Stanbic Bank Swaziland Ltd: Stanbic House, 1st Floor, Swazi Plaza, POB A294, Mbabane; tel. 46587; telex 2216; fax 45899; f. 1988; 10% state-owned; cap. and res 28.8m., dep. 213.9m. (Dec. 1995); Chair. G. C. BELL; Man. Dir M. P. LUBBE; 4 brs.

Swaziland Development and Savings Bank: Engungwini, Allister Miller St, POB 336, Mbabane; tel. 42551; telex 2396; fax 41214; f. 1965; state-owned; cap. and res 25.3m., dep. 214.5m. (March 1994); Chair. Chief DAMBUZA II; Man. Dir S. S. KUHLASE; 8 brs.

Financial Institution

Swaziland National Provident Fund: POB 1857, Manzini; tel. 53731; telex 3011; fax 54377; total assets 290m. (June 1996).

STOCK EXCHANGE

Swaziland Stockbrokers Ltd: POB 2818, Mbabane; tel. 46163; fax 44132; f. 1993; CEO A. MCGUIRE.

INSURANCE

Although the state-controlled Swaziland Royal Insurance Corporation (SRIC) operates as the country's sole authorized insurance company, cover in a number of areas not served by SRIC is available from several specialized insurers.

Insurance Companies

Bowring & Minet: Swazi Plaza, POB A32, Mbabane; tel. 42929; telex 2120; fax 45254.

Swaziland Employee Benefit Consultants (Pty) Ltd: POB 222, Mbabane; tel. 44776; telex 2101; fax 46413; specialized medical cover.

Swaziland Insurance Brokers: POB 222, Mbabane; tel. 43226; telex 2101; fax 46412; f. 1970; Man. Dir F. PETTIT.

Swaziland Royal Insurance Corporation (SRIC): Gilfillian St, POB 917, Mbabane; tel. 43231; telex 2043; fax 46414; 51% state-owned; sole auth. insurance co since 1974; Gen. Man. M. MKWANAZI.

Tibiyo Insurance Brokers: Swazi Plaza, POB A166, Mbabane; tel. 42010; telex 2170; fax 45035; Man. Dir C. FAUX.

Insurance Association

Insurance Brokers' Association of Swaziland (IBAS): Swazi Plaza, POB A32, Mbabane; tel. 42929; f. 1983; four mems.

Trade and Industry

DEVELOPMENT CORPORATIONS

National Industrial Development Corporation of Swaziland (NIDCS): POB 866, Mbabane; tel. 43391; telex 2052; fax 45619; f. 1971; state-owned; administered by Swaziland Industrial Development Co since 1987; Admin. Dir P. K. THAMM.

Small Enterprise Development Co (SEDCO): POB A186, Mbabane; tel. 42811; telex 2130; fax 40723; govt development agency; supplies workshop space, training and expertise for 120 local entrepreneurs at seven sites throughout the country.

Swaziland Industrial Development Co (SIDC): Dhlan'Ubeka House, 5th Floor, cnr Tin and Walker Sts, POB 866, Mbabane; tel. 43391; telex 2052; fax 45619; f. 1986; 34.9% state-owned; finances private-sector projects and promotes local and foreign investment; cap. E24.1m.; Chair. A. R. SHABANGU; Gen. Man. P. K. THAMM.

Swaki (Pty) Ltd: Liqhaga Bldg, 4th Floor, Nkoseluhlaza St, POB 1839, Manzini; tel. 52693; telex 2244; fax 52001; jtly owned by SIDC and Kirsh Holdings; comprises a number of cos involved in manufacturing, services and the production and distribution of food (especially maize).

Tibiyo Taka Ngwane (Bowels of the Swazi Nation): POB 181, Kwaluseni; tel. 84390; telex 2116; fax 84399; f. 1968; national development agency, with investment interests in all sectors of the economy; participates in domestic and foreign jt investment ventures; total assets E260m. (1992); Man. Dir A. T. DLAMINI.

STATE AUTHORITIES

National Agricultural Marketing Board: POB 1713, Mbabane; tel. 85211; fax 84088.

National Maize Corporation: POB 158, Manzini; tel. 52261; fax 52265.

Posts and Telecommunications Corporation: POB 125, Mbabane; tel. 42341; fax 43130; f. 1986.

Swaziland Citrus Board: POB 343, Mbabane; tel. 44266; telex 2018; fax 43548; f. 1969.

Swaziland Commercial Board: POB 509, Mbabane; tel. 42930; Man. Dir J. M. D. FAKUDZE.

Swaziland Cotton Board: POB 230, Manzini; tel. 52775; Gen. Man. T. JELE.

Swaziland Dairy Board: POB 1789, Manzini; tel. 84411; fax 85313.

Swaziland Electricity Board: POB 258, Mbabane; tel. 42521; fax 42335.

Swaziland Meat Industries Ltd: POB 446, Manzini; tel. 84165; fax 84418; f. 1965; operates an abattoir and deboning plant at Matsapha to process beef for local and export markets; Gen. Man. J. WILLIAMS.

Swaziland National Housing Board: POB 798, Mbabane; tel. 45610; fax 45224.

Swaziland National Trust Commission: POB 100, Lobamba; tel. 61151; fax 61875.

Swaziland Sugar Association: POB 445, Mbabane; tel. 42646; telex 2031; fax 45005; responsible for all sugar storage, transport and sales; Gen. Man. ANDREW COLIN.

Water Services Corporation: POB 20, Mbabane; tel. 45584; fax 45355.

CHAMBERS OF COMMERCE

Sibakho Chamber of Commerce: POB 2016, Manzini; tel. 54409.

Swaziland Chamber of Commerce and Industry: POB 72, Mbabane; tel. 44408; fax 45442; Sec. HARVEY BIRD.

EMPLOYERS' ASSOCIATIONS

The Building Contractors Association of Swaziland: Mbabane; tel. 45566.

Swaziland Association of Architects, Engineers and Surveyors: Swazi Plaza, POB A387, Mbabane; tel. 42309.

Swaziland Institute of Personnel and Training Managers: c/o UNISWA, Private Bag, Kwaluseni; tel. 84545; fax 85276.

Employers' Federation

Federation of Swaziland Employers: POB 777, Mbabane; tel. 22768; fax 46107; f. 1964; 376 mems; Pres. R. SEAL; Exec. Dir E. HLOPHE.

MAJOR INDUSTRIAL COMPANIES

Beral Swaziland: POB 015, Ngwenya; tel. 42164; fax 46093; mfrs of friction materials for the automotive and transport industries.

Bromor Foods: Matsapha Industrial Estate, POB 1638, Matsapha; tel. 84554; fax 84510; f. 1986; mfrs of soft drink concentrates and confectionery.

Cadbury Swaziland: POB 679, Matsapha; tel. 86168; fax 86173; f. 1989; mfrs of confectionery.

Fridgemaster: POB 1604, Matsapha; tel. 84186; fax 84069; f. 1993; mfrs of domestic refrigerators and freezers; Dirs M. S. Shear, C. H. Palmer.

GMH Manufacturing (Pty) Ltd: POB 503, Matsapha; tel. 85386; f. 1990; manufacture, preparation and packaging of food-related products.

Mantenga Craft: Swazi Plaza, POB A5, Mbabane; tel. 61136; fax 61040; handcrafts.

Natex Swaziland Ltd: Matsapha Industrial Sites, POB 359, Manzini; tel. 86133; fax 86140; f. 1987; textiles.

Neopac Swaziland Ltd: Matsapha Industrial Sites, POB 618, Manzini; tel. 86204; fax 84277; f. 1968; mfrs of corrugated containers for agriculture and industry.

Ngwane Mills (Pty) Ltd: Matsapha Industrial Sites, POB 1169, Manzini; tel. 85011; fax 85112; f. 1992; flour and related products.

Spintex Swaziland (Pty) Ltd: POB 6, Matsapha; tel. 86166; fax 86038; mfrs of cotton and poly-cotton combed yarns, sewing thread, core yarns, lycra core yarns and open-end yarns.

Swazi Paper Mills Ltd: POB 873, Mbabane; tel. 86144; telex 2372; fax 86091; f. 1987; Swaziland's largest privately-owned concern; produces paper and paper products.

Swazi Timber Products Ltd: POB 2313, Manzini; tel. 86335; fax 86312; f. 1987.

Swaziland Brewers Ltd: POB 100, Matsapha; tel. 86033; fax 86309; annual production of 250,000 hl of beer.

Swaziland Laminated Timbers (Pty) Ltd: POB 4, Piggs Peak; tel. 71344; telex 2023; fax 71386; mfrs of pine furniture.

Swaziland Safety Glass: Matsapha Industrial Estate, POB 3058, Manzini; tel. 85366; fax 85361; f. 1990; mfrs of glass for transport industry.

Ubombo Ranches Ltd: Private Bag, Big Bend; tel. 36511; fax 36330; f. 1958; produces raw and refined sugar.

Usutu Pulp Co Ltd: Private Bag, Mbabane; tel. 26010; telex 2003; fax 26025; mfrs of unbleached Kraft pulp.

YKK Zippers (Swaziland) (Pty) Ltd: POB 1425, Mbabane; tel. 84188; telex 2125; fax 84182; f. 1977; mfrs of zip fasteners.

TRADE UNIONS

The following trade unions are recognized by the Ministry of Labour and Public Service:

The Association of Lecturers and Academic Personnel of the University of Swaziland, the Building and Construction Workers Union of Swaziland, Swaziland Agriculture and Plantation Workers' Union, Swaziland Commercial and Allied Workers' Union, Swaziland Conservation Workers' Union, Swaziland Electricity Supply, Maintenance and Allied Workers' Union, Swaziland Engineering, Metal and Allied Workers' Union, Swaziland Hotel, Catering and Allied Workers' Union, Swaziland Manufacturing and Allied Workers' Union, Swaziland Mining, Quarrying and Allied Workers' Union, Swaziland National Association of Civil Servants, Swaziland National Association of Teachers, Swaziland Post and Telecommunications Workers' Union, Swaziland Transport Workers' Union, Swaziland Union of Financial Institutions and Allied Workers, University of Swaziland Workers' Union, Workers Union of Swaziland Security Guards, Workers' Union of Town Councils.

Trade Union Federation

Swaziland Federation of Trade Unions (SFTU): Mbabane; f. 1973; prin. trade union org. since mid-1980s; mems from public and private sectors, incl. agricultural workers; 83,000 mems; Pres. Richard Nxumalo; Sec.-Gen. Jan Sithole.

Staff Associations

Three staff associations exist for employees whose status lies between that of worker and that of management:

The Nyoni Yami Irrigation Scheme Staff Association, the Swazican Staff Association and the Swaziland Electricity Board Staff Association.

CO-OPERATIVE ASSOCIATIONS

Swaziland Central Co-operatives Union: POB 551, Manzini; tel. 52787.

There are more than 123 co-operative associations, of which the most important is:

Swaziland Co-operative Rice Co Ltd: handles rice grown in Mbabane and Manzini areas.

TRADE FAIR

Swaziland International Trade Fair: POB 877, Manzini; tel. 54242; telex 2232; fax 52324; annual 10-day event beginning in late August.

Transport

Buses are the principal means of transport for many Swazis. Bus services are provided by private operators who are required to obtain annual permits for each route from the Road Transportation Board, which also regulates fares.

RAILWAYS

The rail network, which totalled 294.4 km in 1991 provides a major transport link for imports and exports. The railways do not carry passengers. Railway lines connect with the South African ports of Richards Bay and Durban in the south, the South African town of Komatipoort in the north and the Mozambican port of Maputo in the east. Goods traffic is mainly in wood pulp, sugar, molasses, coal, citrus fruit and canned fruit.

Swaziland Railway Board: Swaziland Railway Bldg, POB 475, Johnstone St, Mbabane; tel. 42486; telex 2053; fax 45009; f. 1962; Chair. B. A. G. Fitzpatrick; CEO G. J. Mahlalela.

ROADS

In 1995 there were an estimated 3,825 km of roads, including 1,360 km of main roads and 1,640 km of secondary roads. About 28.2% of the road network was paved in 1994. The rehabilitation of about 700 km of main and 600 km of district gravel-surfaced roads began in 1985, financed by World Bank and US loans totalling some E18m. In 1991 work commenced on the reconstruction of Swaziland's main road artery, connecting Mbabane to Manzini, via Matsapha.

Ministry of Public Works and Transport: POB 58, Mbabane; tel. 42321; telex 2104; fax 42364; Prin. Sec. Evart Madlopha; Sr Roads Engineer A. Manana.

SHIPPING

Royal Swazi National Shipping Corporation Ltd: POB 1915, Manzini; tel. 53788; telex 2065; fax 53820; f. 1980 to succeed Royal Swaziland Maritime Co; owns no ships, acting only as a freight agent; Gen. Man. M. S. Dlamini.

CIVIL AVIATION

Swaziland's only airport is at Matsapa, near Manzini, about 40 km from Mbabane. In mid-1997 a government three-year programme to upgrade the airport was initiated.

African International Airways (AIA): POB 2117, Mbabane; tel. 43875; telex 2283; fax 43876; f. 1985; operates cargo services; Dirs P. J. M. Corbin, T. M. Longmore, L. N. Longmore.

Air Swazi Cargo: Dhlan'Ubeka House, Walker St, POB 2869, Mbabane; tel. 45575; telex 3026; fax 45003; charter services for freight to destinations in Africa and Europe; Man. Brian Parmenter.

Royal Swazi National Airways Corporation: POB 939, Matsapa Airport, Manzini; tel. 86155; telex 2064; fax 84538; f. 1978; 50% state-owned; scheduled passenger and cargo services to destinations in Africa; also operates charter flights; Exec. Chair. Prince Gabheni Dlamini; CEO Prince Matatazela Dlamini.

Tourism

Swaziland's attractions for tourists include game reserves and magnificent mountain scenery. In 1992 268,071 tourist arrivals were registered at hotels; the total number of visitors to Swaziland was 1,568,198. A total of 287,023 arrivals at hotels was recorded in 1993. Revenue from the tourist sector in that year totalled E93.9m.

Hotel and Tourism Association of Swaziland: POB 462, Mbabane; tel. 42218.

Ministry of Tourism and Communications: POB 338, Mbabane; tel. 44556; fax 42774; Tourism Officer Simeone Simelane.

Defence

The Umbutfo Swaziland defence force, created in 1973, totalled 2,657 regular troops in November 1983. There is also a paramilitary police force. Compulsory military service of two years was introduced in 1983.

Defence Expenditure: Budgeted at E94.3m. for 1994/95 (including public safety).

Education

Education is not compulsory in Swaziland. Primary education begins at six years of age and lasts for seven years. Secondary education begins at 13 years of age and lasts for up to five years, comprising a first cycle of three years and a second of two years. In 1994 some 95% of children in the relevant age-group (boys 95%; girls 96%) were enrolled at primary schools, while secondary enrolment included 37% of children in the appropriate age-group (boys 34%; girls 40%). Higher education is provided by the University of Swaziland, with campuses in Luyengo and in Kwaluseni, and a number of other institutions of higher education. At the 1986 census the rate of adult illiteracy averaged 32.7% (males 30.3%; females 34.8%). According to estimates by UNESCO, the rate of adult illiteracy in 1995 averaged 23.3% (males 22.0%; females 24.4%). Government expenditure on education was E306.5m. for 1994/95, representing 22.0% of total budgetary expenditure.

Bibliography

Bischoff, P.-H. *Swaziland's International Relations and Foreign Policy: A Study of a Small African State in International Relations.* Berne, P. Lang, 1990.

Booth, A. R. *Swaziland: Tradition and Change in a Southern African Kingdom.* Boulder, CO, Westview Press, 1983; London, Gower Publishers, 1984.

Crush, J. *The Struggle for Swazi Labour, 1890–1920.* Montréal, McGill and Queen's University Press, 1988.

Daniel, J., and Stephen, M. F. (Eds). *Historical Perspectives on the Political Economy of Swaziland.* Kwaluseni, University of Swaziland, 1986.

Davies, R. H., et al. (Eds). *The Kingdom of Swaziland: A Profile.* London, Zed Press, 1985.

Funnell, D. C. *Under the Shadow of Apartheid: Agrarian Transformation in Swaziland.* Aldershot, Avebury, 1991.

Grotpeter, J. J. *Historical Dictionary of Swaziland.* Metuchen, NJ, Scarecrow Press, 1975.

Konczacki, Z. A., et al. (Eds). *Studies in the Economic History of Southern Africa.* Vol. II. London, Cass, 1991.

Leliveld, A. *Social Security in Developing Countries: Operation and Dynamics of Social Security Mechanisms in Rural Swaziland.* Amsterdam, Thesis Publishers, 1994.

Matsebula, J. S. *A History of Swaziland.* 2nd Edn. Cape Town, Maskew Miller, Longmans, 1988.

Rose, L. L. *The Politics of Harmony: Land Dispute Strategies in Swaziland.* Cambridge, Cambridge University Press, 1992.

Schwager, D. *Swaziland.* Mbabane, Websters, 1984.

Simelane, N. C. (Ed.). *Social Transformation: The Swaziland Case.* Dakar, CODESRIA, 1995.

TANZANIA

Physical and Social Geography

L. BERRY

PHYSICAL FEATURES AND CLIMATE

The 945,087 sq km (364,900 sq miles) of the United Republic of Tanzania (incorporating mainland Tanganyika and a number of offshore islands, including Zanzibar, Pemba, Latham and Mafia) have a wide variety of land forms, climates and peoples. The country includes the highest and lowest points in Africa—the summit of Mt Kilimanjaro (5,895 m above sea-level) and the floor of Lake Tanganyika (358 m below sea-level). The main upland areas occur in a northern belt—the Usambara, Pare, Kilimanjaro and Meru mountains; a central and southern belt—the Southern highlands, the Ugurus and the Ulugurus; and a north–south trending belt, which runs southwards from the Ngorongoro Crater. The highest peaks are volcanic, although block faulting has been responsible for the uplift of the plateau areas. Other fault movements have resulted in the depressed areas of the rift valleys; Lakes Tanganyika, Malawi, Rukwa, Manyara and Eyasi occupy part of the floor of these depressions. Much of the rest of the interior comprises gently sloping plains and plateaux, broken by low hill ranges and scattered isolated hills. The coast includes areas with wide sandy beaches and with developed coral reefs, but these are broken by extensive growth of mangroves, particularly near the mouths of the larger rivers.

With the exception of the high mountain areas, temperatures in Tanzania are not a major limiting factor for crop growth, although the range of altitude produces a corresponding range of temperature regimes from tropical to temperate. Rainfall is variable, both from place to place and time to time, and is generally lower than might be expected for the latitude. About 21% of the country can expect with 90% probability more than 750 mm of rainfall, and only about 3% can expect more than 1,250 mm. The central third of the country is semi-arid (less than 500 mm), with evaporation exceeding rainfall in nine months of the year. For much of the country most rain falls in one rainy season, December–May, though two peaks of rainfall in October–November and April–May are found in some areas. Apart from the problem of the long dry season over most parts of the country, there is also a marked fluctuation in annual rainfall from one year to the next, and this may be reflected in the crop production and livestock figures.

The surplus water from the wetter areas drains into the few large perennial rivers. The largest of these, the Rufiji, drains the Southern highlands and much of southern Tanzania. With an average discharge of 1,133 cu m per second, it is one of the largest rivers in Africa, and has major potential for irrigation and hydroelectric power development. The Ruvu, Wami and Pangani also drain to the Indian Ocean. The Pangani has already been developed for hydroelectric power, which supplies Arusha, Moshi, Tanga, Morogoro and Dar es Salaam. Apart from the Ruvuma, which forms the southern frontier, most other drainage is to the interior basins, or to the Lakes Tanganyika, Victoria and Malawi.

The most fertile soils in Tanzania are the reddish-brown soils derived from the volcanic rocks, although elsewhere *mbuga* and other alluvial soils have good potential. The interior plateaux are covered with tropical loams of moderate fertility. The natural vegetation of the country has been considerably modified by human occupation. In the south and west-central areas there are large tracts of woodland covering about 30% of the country, while on the uplands are small but important areas of tropical rain forest. Clearly marked altitudinal variations in vegetation occur around the upland areas and some distinctive mountain flora is found. Tanzania has set aside about one-third of its land for national parks and game and forest reserves.

POPULATION AND RESOURCES

Tanzania had an estimated mid-1995 population of 28,251,511, of whom almost 27.5m. resided in mainland Tanzania. Most of the country's inhabitants are of African origin, although people of Indian and Pakistani ancestry comprise a significant component of the urban population. Tanzania is one of the least urbanized countries of Africa. According to official estimates, the population of the principal towns at mid-1985 was: Dar es Salaam (1,096,000), Mwanza (252,000), Tabora (214,000), Mbeya (194,000) and Tanga (172,000). There are more than 120 ethnic groups in Tanzania, of which the largest are the Sukuma and the Nyamwezi. None, however, exceeds 10% of the total population.

Traditionally, the main features of the pattern of population distribution have been, firstly, sharp variations in density, with a number of densely populated areas separated from each other by zones of sparse population; secondly, the comparatively low density of population in most of the interior of the country; and, thirdly, the way in which, in most parts of the country, rural settlements have tended to consist of scattered individual homesteads rather than nucleated villages.

The highest population densities, reaching over 250 per sq km, occur on the fertile lower slopes of Mt Kilimanjaro and on the shores of Lake Malawi. Most other upland areas have relatively high densities, as does the area south of Lake Victoria known as Sukumaland. The problem of the traditionally scattered nature of the rural population has been a focus of development effort, and attempts at both capital-intensive villagization and the formation of co-operative nucleated settlements (*ujamaa* or 'familyhood' villages) have been made.

Agriculture, which employs about four-fifths of the economically active population, is geared in large part towards subsistence farming. The principal cash crops are coffee, cotton, cashew nuts, tobacco, sisal, coconuts, sugar, cardamom and groundnuts. Cloves, cultivated mainly on the island of Pemba, are Zanzibar's principal export crop. Tanzania's mineral resources include diamonds, other gemstones, gold, salt, phosphates, coal, gypsum, kaolin and tin, all of which are exploited. There are also reserves of nickel, copper, cobalt, lead, soda ash, iron ore, uranium and natural gas.

Dar es Salaam is the main port, the dominant industrial centre, and the focus of government and commercial activity, although the administrative functions of the capital city are scheduled to be transferred to Dodoma by 2005. Dar es Salaam has been growing at a substantial rate and attempts are being made to decentralize industrial development to other centres. Arusha has also been growing rapidly in recent years, partly because of its importance to tourism.

Considerable variation in the pattern of development occurs within Tanzania. In some areas agriculture is becoming much more orientated towards cash crops. In such a large country distance to market is an important factor, and in successive development plans major attempts have been made to improve the main and subsidiary communication networks. The TanZam road and Tazara railway are an important addition, leaving only the far west and the south-east without good surface links to the rest of the country.

Recent History

GRAHAM MATTHEWS

Revised for this edition by the Editor

The 19th-century history of the area that is now the United Republic of Tanzania was fashioned by the extension of the caravan trade from Zanzibar into the far interior, to the eastern Congo and Buganda. Dominated by Omanis, whose sultan transferred his capital to Zanzibar in 1840, it was this trade which carried the Swahili language from the coast and established it as the commercial lingua franca of the region. By the same agency, Islam was conveyed inland. Tanganyika was declared a German protectorate in 1885 and was later incorporated into German East Africa, which also included present-day Rwanda and Burundi. Resistance to German rule culminated in the Maji Maji rebellion in 1905–06, which engulfed much of the south of the country and was eventually suppressed only with resort to a policy of induced famine, which was variously estimated to have caused between 75,000–300,000 deaths. In 1920 Tanganyika was placed under a League of Nations mandate, with the United Kingdom as the administering power, and in 1946 became a UN trust territory, still under British administration. Opposition to the alienation of land to immigrant white farmers, and to unequal representation of Africans in local government was led by the Tanganyika African Association, founded in 1929 and converted in 1954 by its president, Julius Nyerere, into the Tanganyika African National Union (TANU). TANU won a sweeping victory in Tanganyika's first general election, held in two phases in September 1958 and February 1959; a new council of ministers, including African ministers for the first time, was formed in July. At the next election, in September 1960, TANU won 70 of the 71 seats in the national assembly, and Nyerere became chief minister.

THE NYERERE PERIOD, 1961–85

Tanganyika achieved internal self-government in May 1961, with Nyerere as prime minister. Full independence followed on 9 December. TANU's weaknesses soon became apparent. Democratic local government was ill-developed and the institutional vacuum had to be filled from limited party resources. In addition, it had also become apparent that TANU's two main supports in opposition, the flourishing producers' co-operatives and the trade unions, might now become its chief rivals in government. In January 1962 Nyerere resigned as prime minister; he was succeeded by Rashidi Kawawa. In December Tanganyika became a republic, with Nyerere returning to power as the country's first president, having been elected in the previous month. Kawawa became vice-president.

Zanzibar (together with the neighbouring island of Pemba and several smaller islets), a British protectorate since 1890, became an independent sultanate in December 1963. The sultan was overthrown in an armed uprising in January 1964, following which a republic was declared and the Afro-Shirazi Party (ASP) took power. In April Nyerere signed an act of union with the new government of Zanzibar. The leader of the ASP, Abeid Karume, became the United Republic's first vice-president as well as chairman of the ruling supreme revolutionary council of Zanzibar. The union was named Tanzania in October.

A new constitution, introduced in July 1965, provided for a one-party state (although, until 1977, TANU and the ASP remained the respective official parties of mainland Tanzania and Zanzibar, and co-operated in affairs of state). In September 1965 Nyerere was returned to power in the first one-party election. Nyerere was re-elected president in 1970, 1975 and 1980. Early in 1967, TANU accepted a programme of socialism and self-reliance, known as the Arusha Declaration. Party leaders were required to divest themselves of private sources of income; rural development was to come not through large farms but community (*ujamaa*) villages; the small urban sector was not to exploit the countryside; the education system was to be completely reorganized in order to serve the mass of the population rather than to train a privileged few. Commercial banks and many industries were immediately nationalized, but the rest of the programme was much more difficult to implement, as it ran counter to existing trends of social change.

In Zanzibar, Karume survived two coup plots, in 1967 and 1971, but was assassinated in April 1972. His successor, Aboud Jumbe, reorganized the Zanzibari government in that month by extending the powers of the ASP. Despite its incorporation into Tanzania, Zanzibar retained a separate administration, which ruthlessly suppressed all opposition.

In 1972 Rashidi Kawawa was reappointed to the revived post of prime minister, relieving Nyerere of some of his responsibilities. In June 1975 the national assembly voted to incorporate the fundamental principles of socialism and self-reliance into the constitution and to establish TANU as the national political party. A proposal to unite TANU and the ASP was submitted by Nyerere in September 1975, and in February 1977 the two parties merged to form the Chama Cha Mapinduzi (CCM–Revolutionary Party), of which Nyerere was elected chairman and Jumbe vice-chairman. A government reshuffle followed, in which Kawawa was replaced as prime minister by Edward Sokoine. In April 1977 the national assembly adopted a permanent constitution for Tanzania, providing for the election of 10 Zanzibari representatives to the assembly. In October 1979 the supreme revolutionary council of Zanzibar adopted a separate constitution, governing Zanzibar's internal administration, with provisions for a popularly-elected president and a legislative house of representatives elected by delegates of the CCM.

At presidential and legislative elections in October 1980 Nyerere was re-elected president of the United Republic for a further five-year term, which he announced would be his last. However, about one-half of the members of the national assembly, including several ministers, lost their seats, in what was seen as a protest against Tanzania's parlous economic condition and bureaucratic inefficiency. Constitutional amendments were adopted in October 1984, limiting the president's tenure of office to two five-year terms and strengthening the powers of the national assembly.

Evidence of the existence of dissident opinion, fuelled by the economic crisis, emerged with the hijacking of an Air Tanzania flight in February 1982, as an expression of political protest, and the discovery of a coup plot in January 1983, as a result of which 20 soldiers and nine civilians were detained. Nine people received sentences of life imprisonment in December 1985 for their part in the conspiracy. (All those convicted eventually received a presidential pardon in October 1995.) A political crisis arose in Zanzibar in early 1984 as a result of growing dissatisfaction with the union and calls for greater autonomy for the islands. Jumbe and three of his ministers resigned in January in a climate of growing tension, and in April Ali Hassan Mwinyi, the islands' former minister of natural resources and tourism, was elected president of Zanzibar (thus also becoming vice-president of Tanzania). Mwinyi, a supporter of the union, made sweeping changes to Zanzibar's supreme revolutionary council. A new more liberal constitution for the islands was introduced in January 1985, providing for the house of representatives to be directly elected by universal suffrage and for the introduction of a Commonwealth legal system.

At his retirement in November 1985, Nyerere was succeeded by Mwinyi, his vice-president, who had been elected in the previous month with 96% of the valid votes cast. In this way the union was to be cemented by establishing a pattern of alternate mainland and Zanzibari presidents of the United Republic. Idris Abdul Wakil (formerly speaker of the Zanzibar house of representatives) was elected president of Zanzibar to replace Mwinyi. After taking office in November, Mwinyi appointed Joseph Warioba, previously minister of justice, as prime minister and first vice-president.

THE MWINYI PRESIDENCY, 1985–95

The change of president coincided with a worsening economic crisis (see below) which forced the new administration to alter the direction of its economic policy. Greater encouragement was given to the private sector, and acceptance of proposals from the International Monetary Fund (IMF) on budgeting, agricultural reform and management of the shilling persuaded donors to sponsor the country with large disbursements of aid.

Nyerere, who described Tanzania's new economic policy as 'unplanned retreats from socialism', was re-elected chairman of the CCM for a further five-year term in October 1987. His re-election also represented a victory for Rashidi Kawawa (who was himself re-elected almost unanimously as secretary-general of the party) and for other socialist radicals and militants who looked to Nyerere to strengthen the party and to act as a counter-balance against Mwinyi's controversial economic reforms. Two important 'liberal-modernists' failed to secure re-election to the CCM's central committee: Seif Sharrif Hamad, the chief minister of Zanzibar (who subsequently also lost this office), and Cleopa Msuya, the minister of finance, who was closely concerned in negotiations with the IMF. However, Mwinyi was re-elected vice-chairman of the party, and in December 1987, he recast the balance of power by dismissing three cabinet ministers who were perceived as opponents of his liberalization policies. The cabinet was again reorganized in early 1989; among the new appointees were three ministers of state considered to be sympathetic to Islamic fundamentalism, thus redressing a perceived predominance of Christian influence in the cabinet. In a further reshuffle of the cabinet carried out in September, Mwinyi assumed responsibility for the defence and national service portfolio.

In February 1990 the CCM initiated a campaign against corruption among government officials. In March an extensive reshuffle of the cabinet took place: Mwinyi dismissed seven ministers who had allegedly opposed plans for economic reform and presided over corrupt or irresponsible ministries. The president's position was further consolidated in August when, following the resignation of Nyerere, he was appointed chairman of the CCM. During 1990 the CCM experienced no cohesive internal challenge to its political monopoly, except in Zanzibar (see below). The Tanzania Democratic Forum, calling for the establishment of a multi-party political system, was, however, formed in London in early 1990 under the leadership of Oscar Kambona, a former secretary-general of the CCM. In addition, Moussa Membar, who had led the hijack of a Tanzanian airliner in 1982, organized another opposition party operating from the United Kingdom, the Tanzania Youth Democratic Movement. In September 1990 he entered Tanzania from Kenya, and was promptly arrested and charged with treason. Abruptly released from detention in May 1991, Membar died soon afterwards of uncertain causes.

In October 1990 concurrent parliamentary and presidential elections were held in Zanzibar. Wakil did not stand for re-election as president and chairman of the supreme revolutionary council; the sole presidential candidate, Dr Salmin Amour was elected as Wakil's successor by 97.7% of the votes cast. At the end of October parliamentary and presidential elections took place throughout Tanzania. Mwinyi, the sole candidate in the presidential election, was re-elected for a second term, receiving 95.5% of the votes cast. At the elections to the 216 directly elective seats in the 291-member Tanzanian national assembly, 33 delegates lost their seats. In a government reshuffle following the elections, Mwinyi replaced his prime minister, Joseph Warioba, with John Malecela, a former minister and high commissioner to the United Kingdom.

At the end of February 1991 10 prominent opposition figures gave their support to an independent forum, the Tanzania Legal Education Trust, under the leadership of Abdullah Fundikira (a former minister of justice), to steer national opinion towards a multi-party democratic system. In March Mwinyi established a presidential commission to ascertain public opinion on possible electoral reform; in December the commission published recommendations for the establishment of a plural political system. In February 1992 proposed constitutional amendments to this effect were ratified by a special congress of the CCM, which stipulated, however, that all new political organizations should command support in both Zanzibar and mainland Tanzania, and should be free of tribal, religious and racial bias, in order to protect national unity. In May both the United Republic's constitution and the Zanzibar constitution were duly amended to implement these changes.

Mwinyi reallocated cabinet portfolios in late May 1992, and shortly afterwards membership qualification restrictions were abolished by the CCM in preparation for eventual multi-party elections. Several political organizations were officially registered from mid-1992; however, the government continued to impose restrictions on opposition activities.

At the beginning of 1993 it emerged that the Zanzibar government had unilaterally arranged for the islands to join the Organization of the Islamic Conference (OIC). This action was a double infringement of the 1964 articles of union and the 1977 union constitution, whereby the United Republic was established as a secular state and the Zanzibar administration was denied any separate competence in foreign affairs, which became the exclusive responsibility of the union government. In an atmosphere of worsening inter-religious communalism, predominantly Christian mainlanders demanded the resignation of Mwinyi (a Muslim and a Zanzibari). In February 1993 a parliamentary commission ruled that the action of Zanzibar in relation to OIC membership was unconstitutional. The incident led to a cabinet reshuffle, in which the minister of foreign affairs, Ahmed Hassan Diria (a Zanzibari and presidential confidant), was transferred to a lesser post.

In August 1993 Zanzibar withdrew from membership of the OIC, but significant damage had been done to relations between the mainland and the islands. In the same month, during the budget debate in the national assembly, a group of 55 mainland MPs successfully sponsored a private member's bill (the so-called 'G55 motion') providing for the establishment of a third level of government within the union to administer the mainland separately from Zanzibar. The legislation was passed unanimously, despite the intense opposition of ex-president Nyerere, who denounced both the national assembly and the CCM for abandoning a basic tenet of party policy (a commitment to maintaining and enhancing the union) without obtaining a consensus of the entire CCM membership. As a result of Nyerere's intervention, the G55 motion was referred for approval by the CCM membership, which was prevailed upon to reject it. Parliament eventually reversed its decision in August 1994.

Nyerere continued to exert his influence over the political scene, with the publication, in November 1994, of a controversial short book in which he accused Malecela, the prime minister, and Horace Kolimba, the CCM secretary-general, of 'poor leadership', particularly in connection with the OIC affair and the G55 motion. Later in the month a wider political crisis was precipitated when foreign donors began to suspend aid disbursements in protest at official connivance in widespread tax evasion. In December Mwinyi responded to these pressures by dismissing Malecela, Kolimba and Kighoma Ali Malima, the minister of finance, from their posts. Cleopa Msuya, hitherto the minister of industry and trade and previously prime minister during 1980–83, was appointed to the premiership.

In July 1995 the CCM convened a special national conference in order to choose a candidate to contest the presidential election which was due to take place (concurrently with legislative elections) in October of that year (see below). Once again Nyerere's influence was evident. At his behest the list of candidates was restricted to three: Msuya, Jakaya Kikwete, the minister of finance, and Benjamin Mkapa, the minister of science, technology and higher education. Mkapa, who was widely believed to have been Nyerere's first choice from the outset, was eventually selected.

Opposition and Division

Between July 1992, when the CCM-appointed registrar of political parties, George Liundi, began work, and by mid-1996 more than a dozen opposition movements were officially recognized. However, when the CCM fought its first multi-party by-election in April 1993 the poll was boycotted by all but one of the newly registered parties. The CCM won the contest, in a Zanzibari constituency, by default.

In January 1993 the anti-Asian rhetoric of the leader of the unregistered Democratic Party, Rev. Christopher Mtikila, provoked a number of attacks on Asian residents and their businesses in Dar es Salaam. In early April young Muslim radicals took to the streets in a series of attacks on pork butchers (Islam considers the meat unclean). These outbreaks of violence reflected separate but overlapping divisions that had long been contained within Tanzanian society: that between black African and Asian Tanzanians; and that between Christianity and Islam. Set alongside the crisis in the union itself, these completed a picture of deepening divisions in a state that had once been taken as a model of African nation-building.

In February 1994 the CCM won the third by-election of the multi-party era. In a significant judgement delivered in August, the high court asserted a new-found independence when it upheld the petition of the opposition Chama Cha Demokrasia na Maendeleo (Chadema) that the seat had been won by unfair means. The CCM's authority was further challenged in February 1995, when Augustine Mrema, the minister of home affairs, precipitated his own dismissal from the cabinet and, soon after, joined the opposition National Convention for Construction and Reform (NCCR–Mageuzi). In June, following allegations of personal financial irregularities, the minister of industry and trade (and former minister of finance), Kighoma Ali Malima, was forced to resign from the government. Malima defected to the opposition National Reconstruction Alliance (NRA), briefly leading the party until his sudden death in August.

THE 'THIRD PHASE' GOVERNMENT

In October 1995 multi-party legislative elections were held for the first time, concurrently with presidential elections, both in Zanzibar (see below) and throughout the Tanzanian union. The CCM achieved a convincing majority at the national legislative elections, winning 186 of the 232 elective seats in the national assembly, while the Civic United Front (CUF), a party favouring Zanzibari autonomy (see below), secured 24 seats, NCCR–Mageuzi 16, and both Chadema and the United Democratic Party took three seats. The ballots in seven constituencies in Dar es Salaam were cancelled and restaged in November, owing to apparent administrative inefficiency. Benjamin Mkapa was elected national president, winning 61.8% of the votes cast. President Mkapa was inaugurated in late November; Omar Ali Juma (hitherto the chief minister of Zanzibar) was appointed vice-president. Shortly afterwards Mkapa (whose election campaign had promised a crusade against high-level corruption) announced a new cabinet, with Frederick Sumaye (formerly minister of agriculture) as prime minister; many long-standing ministers were not reappointed to their posts. The opposition refused to participate in the new administration (known as the 'third phase' government) in protest at alleged electoral fraud by the CCM.

In his election campaign Mkapa had promised a crusade against corruption in high public office, and in January 1996 he appointed a special presidential commission, under the chairmanship of the former prime minister, Joseph Warioba, to carry out a full investigation of the matter. At a special congress of the CCM, held in June, Mkapa was elected party chairman, and there were many new appointees to the party's central committee. (In order to secure the support of the Zanzibari wing of the CCM at the party elections, Mkapa refrained from taking a firm line in the dispute over the re-election of Dr Amour as Zanzibari president—see below.) During June the allegedly corrupt Dar es Salaam city council was disbanded. In September a parliamentary select committee investigating bribery allegations against the minister of finance, Simon Mbilinyi (a former diplomat and managing director of the National Development Council, who had been appointed to the government in late 1995), published a report recommending that he be made accountable for having illegally granted tax exemptions. Mbilinyi resigned. He was replaced on an acting basis by Daniel Yona Ndhiwa (hitherto minister of state for planning), who was confirmed as finance minister in February 1997. Meanwhile, in October 1996, Mrema unexpectedly won a parliamentary by-election for NCCR–Mageuzi in a Dar es Salam constituency; although his campaign had focused on financial impropriety in government, Mrema had recently been accused of having presented false evidence to the parliamentary select committee on corruption in order to undermine the government's credibility. In December the Warioba commission issued a report asserting that corruption was widespread in the public sector; Dr Juma Alifa Ngasongwa, minister of natural resources and tourism, subsequently resigned; he was replaced in February 1997 by Zakia Meghji, hitherto minister of health.

In May 1997 elements within NCCR–Mageuzi attempted to oust Mrema from his post as party chairman, reportedly after he ordered an investigation into the disappearance of substantial sums of money belonging to the party. In June an NCCR–Mageuzi special congress was banned from taking place by the high court, purportedly in order to prevent violent confrontation between members of opposing factions within the party. It was alleged that the government was manipulating such political divisions to frustrate attempts to form an effective political opposition. Following allegations that the state security forces were not independet of CCM interests, and that the harassment of the government's political opponents was a regular occurrence, reports emerged in August that certain political groupings had formed their own private militias.

TENSIONS IN ZANZIBAR

Tensions in Zanzibar once again surfaced in early 1988, reflecting both continuing rivalries between the islands, and also the underlying discord between the majority African and ethnic minority populations. In January President Wakil accused unnamed ministers in his government of plotting against him, and alleged that a group of dissidents was conspiring to engage mercenaries to overthrow his government. These allegations clearly signalled a power struggle within the Zanzibar administration, in which the Pembans, who produce most of the cloves that have traditionally been the mainstay of the Zanzibar economy, have regarded themselves as under-represented. Those most vociferous in their complaints were thought to have been supported by Arab exiles, who were seeking means of reasserting their previous influence in the islands. Wakil suspended the supreme revolutionary council and assumed control of the armed forces. The chief minister, Seif Sharrif Hamad (a Pemban), was dismissed, together with five other ministers, who were mostly Pembans favouring policies of economic liberalization. All were subsequently expelled from the CCM, and in May 1989 Hamad was arrested for allegedly being in possession of secret government documents and for attending an 'illegal meeting' in Pemba.

Wakil's reshuffle of the revolutionary council was widely interpreted as a triumph for the supporters of the former Afro-Shirazi Party. Omar Ali Juma, a senior government official, was appointed as the new chief minister. Restrictions were subsequently imposed on the Zanzibari press. In December about 4,000 troops were dispatched to Zanzibar from the mainland, in response to reports that a coup was being plotted.

Although no coup attempt materialized, continuing undercurrents of discontent have persisted on Zanzibar and Pemba. The islands, whose links with the Arab Gulf stretch back to the ninth century, have in recent years looked increasingly to Oman for financial and development aid which has not been forthcoming from the Tanzanian mainland. In addition, certain religious and other groups began to perceive an erosion of traditional cultural values. Since late 1988 the value to Zanzibar of the union has come increasingly under question, and dissident groups such as the Movement for Democratic Alternative (MDA) and the smaller, religiously-based group on Pemba, the Bismillah Party, became active even before multi-party politics were officially sanctioned in 1992.

In the immediate prelude to the multi-party era, opposition in Zanzibar coalesced around the Kamati ya Mageuzi Huru (Kamahuru), led by Shaaban Mloo. In order to comply with the requirement that all political movements should function throughout Tanzania, Kamahuru merged in 1992 with the mainland-based Chama Cha Wananchi to form the CUF.

At the October 1995 multi-party elections to the house of representatives the CCM secured 26 of the 50 elective seats, while the CUF, campaigning for increased Zanzibari autonomy, took 24 seats, including every constituency on Pemba. The Zanzibar electoral commission credited Amour with victory by a narrow margin at the presidential election, attributing 50.2% of the votes to the incumbent president and 49.8% to Seif Sharrif Hamad (the former chief minister), who represented the CUF. Rejecting Nyerere's advice to form a government of national unity with the opposition, Amour appointed a new supreme revolutionary council, with Dr Mohamed Gharib Bilali, formerly a government official, as chief minister. However, the CUF refused to accept the election result, alleging that the ballot had been rigged in Amour's favour, and demanded that the contest be restaged. The newly-elected CUF delegates boycotted the house of representatives, and the party sought to mobilize international support.

In February 1996 the Zanzibari government banned demonstrations by the CUF in southern Pemba; allegations persisted that numerous abuses of human rights were being perpetrated by the authorities against supporters of the CUF. Mkapa's failure to intervene in the islands' affairs was attributed in part to his need for the support of Zanzibari members of the CCM at the party elections in June. During 1996 external donors began to suspend aid disbursements to Zanzibar; in September, accordingly, Zanzibar was allotted a share of aid donated to the Tanzanian government. In December the Zanzibari authorities threatened to take punitive action against civil servants on Pemba who were said to be refusing to obey official instructions. However, there were signs of a *rapprochement* when, in January 1997, representatives of the mainland branch of the CUF reportedly agreed to recognize the legitimacy of the Amour administration, also urging members of the CUF to cease political confrontation with the Zanzibari government.

FOREIGN RELATIONS

Tanzania's relations with neighbouring Burundi deteriorated in 1973, when many thousands of refugees poured into Tanzania, and Tanzanian border villages were raided by Burundi troops. Trouble also arose with Uganda in 1973, when Gen. Amin, of whom President Nyerere had been a persistent critic, accused Tanzania of plotting against his regime; supporters of ex-president Obote had attempted an invasion of Uganda from Tanzanian territory in September 1972.

Following the collapse of the East African Community (EAC) in 1977, Tanzania's strained relations with Uganda worsened in late 1978. Renewed border fighting was reported in October, and in the following month Uganda announced the annexation of Tanzania's bordering Kagera region. Ugandan troops withdrew after pressure from the OAU but border fighting continued. Then, in January 1979, a Tanzania-based invasion force entered Uganda. The force, comprising approximately 20,000 members of the Tanzanian defence forces and 1,200 members of the Uganda National Liberation Front (UNLF), rapidly gained control of Uganda's southern region. Amin's army capitulated and an interim UNLF government was proclaimed in April. Tanzania's intervention, which led to the restoration to the presidency of Milton Obote, was condemned by the OAU as a violation of territorial integrity, despite Nyerere's claim to have acted in response to Ugandan aggression.

In October 1993 a failed coup attempt in Burundi sent a wave of refugees into Tanzania's Kigoma and Kagera regions. Their numbers were subsequently far exceeded by the massive and sudden influx of Rwandans which followed the outbreak of civil war in that country in April 1994 and the renewed offensive by the Uganda-based Front patriotique rwandais (FPR). By March 1995 further influxes of both Rwandan and Burundian refugees, combined with Tanzanian frustration at the international community's perceived preoccupation with the Zairean refugee camps, resulted in the controversial closure by Tanzania of its border with Burundi. In early 1996 ex-president Nyerere mediated in peace talks between the warring parties in Burundi; these failed, however, and in July the democratically elected Hutu government was overthrown in a Tutsi-led military coup. The Mkapa administration subsequently imposed economic sanctions against the new Burundi regime, in co-operation with other regional governments. In April 1997 it was agreed that most of these sanctions should be revoked, when Pierre Buyoya, the Burundian president, agreed to enter into talks with opposition politicians. Relations remained uneasy, however, owing both to the presence of Burundian rebels in northern Tanzania and to the increasing number of Burundians seeking refuge in Tanzania throughout 1996 and early 1997, despite notional controls on their movements. In December 1996 many of the Rwandan refugees remaining in Tanzania returned to their homes, following the threat of forcible repatriation by the Tanzanian government. In March 1997 the Tanzanian government appealed for international assistance in coping both with the remaining refugees (an estimated 200,000 Burundians and 250,000 Zaireans) and with domestic food shortages that were expected, owing to drought. In June 1997, at talks with a delegation from the Democratic Republic of the Congo (DRC, as Zaire had been renamed in the previous month), it was agreed to repatriate some 100,000 refugees to the DRC. In July 1997 the office of the United Nations high commissioner for refugees estimated that the number of Burundian refugees in Tanzania had increased to more than 300,000.

The escalation of the civil war in Rwanda undid a peace agreement signed, under Tanzanian auspices, in Arusha in August 1993. Although it pursued its efforts to settle the Rwandan conflict, the Tanzanian government appeared to be siding with the interim administration installed by the Rwandan army. The eventual victory of the FPR thus represented a foreign policy reversal for the Tanzania government, which blamed President Museveni of Uganda for undermining its efforts at mediation by urging the FPR to seek a decisive military victory. These events further strained historically troubled relations between potential partners in a new initiative to revive the EAC. However, in November 1993 the presidents of Tanzania, Uganda and Kenya signed a protocol on renewed co-operation among their countries. In March 1996 President Mkapa and the presidents of Kenya and Uganda met in Arusha to sign a protocol establishing the East African Co-operation Secretariat, which was to implement a revived EAC. In April 1997 the three presidents met again to inaugurate a four-year development strategy for the region, as well as an East African passport and a regional flag.

Economy

LINDA VAN BUREN

Tanzania is one of the five poorest countries in the world. Between independence in 1961 and the mid-1980s, the main preoccupation of the nation's policy-makers was to lift the majority of the population out of illiteracy, poverty and disease. The Arusha Declaration of 1967 put great emphasis on the elimination of those ills, by means of a programme of socialism and self-reliance. At the time, a large proportion of the population was either nomadic or dispersed in widely scattered homesteads. By 1974, however, the majority of the rural population had been settled into planned and permanent villages (*ujamaa vijijini*). The main objective of villagization was originally to raise output through collectivization and larger scale farming methods; however, from an agronomic viewpoint, the results were largely unsuccessful, with ineffective management and shortages of materials contributing to low levels of crop production. The emphasis was gradually moved from the agricultural to the social benefits, with the *ujamaa* villages envisaged as centres for social and infrastructural services. The government also pursued a policy of nationalizing important economic sectors, particularly major industries and distribution and marketing. However, more than a decade of severe economic decline, from the late 1970s onwards, brought the country to a condition of economic collapse, and, in order to obtain continuing aid from international donors, from the mid-1980s the government adopted a more pragmatic approach to economic planning.

NATIONAL INCOME AND DEVELOPMENT PLANNING

In 1995, according to estimates by the World Bank, the gross domestic product (GDP) of mainland Tanzania was US $3,602m., and the gross national product (GNP) per caput was $120. During 1980–94, it was estimated, GNP per caput, in real terms, remained almost static, with average annual growth of only 0.8%, Results of the national census carried out in 1988 assess the total population at 23.13m., compared with 17.51m. at the 1978 census. This indicates an average annual growth rate of 2.8%, as do figures from the national Planning Commission for 1988–95. The World Bank, however, has based its calculations on an estimated annual average population growth rate of 3.1% during 1980–95. Agriculture's share of GDP in 1995 was 53%, that of industry was 13% (manufacturing 6%) and that of services 34% (in 1965 the proportions were agriculture 46%, industry 14%, manufacturing 8% and services 40%). The annual rate of inflation declined from 42.9% in 1984 to 28.2% in 1985, but increased to 44% in 1986, mainly as a result of measures stipulated by the IMF (see below). Despite further devaluations of the shilling and the continuing relaxation of price controls, the inflation rate was subsequently reduced to 19.7% in 1990, stabilizing at 22.3% in 1991 and 21.8% in 1992. The annual rate rose to 25.3% in 1993 and to 34.1% in 1994, falling back to 25.3% in 1995 and to 17.6% in 1996.

The first Five-Year Development Plan, inaugurated in 1964, was abandoned in 1966, partly because the required amounts of foreign aid did not materialize. With the Arusha Declaration, President Nyerere placed Tanzania's economic and social policies firmly along a line of 'African socialism', rejecting both Western capitalism and the ideology of the extreme left. The second Five-Year Plan (1969–74) achieved an average annual GDP growth rate of 4.8%.

A third Five-Year Plan was introduced in 1977. However, by 1980 the extent of Tanzania's shortage of foreign exchange was severely disrupting economic performance. A fourth Five-Year Development Plan was announced in 1981, but was immediately abandoned and replaced by a National Economic Survival Programme.

The balance-of-payments problem had become so acute by early 1982 that Nyerere suspended all new development projects and launched a three-year structural adjustment programme (SAP), which was prepared jointly by the ministry of planning and economic affairs and advisers from the World Bank. This aimed to stimulate the productive sectors (particularly the main export crops), to curtail government spending, and to relax price controls. Although GDP had continued to decline, in real terms, in 1982 and 1983, adjustments introduced in the June 1984 budget soon began to take effect, and GDP grew by 3.4% during that year. In 1985 the rate of growth fell back to 2.6%, partly because of drought. IMF assistance was withheld until mid-1986, when agreement was finally reached on a package involving US $45m. in a stand-by credit, to be drawn in the first 12 months, and $24m. in a structural adjustment facility.

In the June 1986 budget a new three-year Economic Recovery Programme (ERP) was announced which was closely allied to the IMF agreement, and to the associated new aid arrangements agreed with the World Bank (see below). The ERP provided for some downward adjustment of the shilling's official exchange rate and further producer price rises in the first year. The target of 4.5% average annual growth in GDP was over-ambitious, but there was an improvement in the growth rate, to 3.6% and 3.9% in 1986 and 1987 respectively. This resulted from high coffee prices during 1986, improved weather conditions, better producer incentives and slightly better availability of imported inputs, thanks to the inflow of new aid funds. The rate of growth, in real terms, was 5.1% in 1988, 3.6% in 1989, 3.2% in 1990, 3.7% in 1991, 3.6% in 1992 and 4.1% in 1993, 3.0% in 1994 and an estimated 4.5% in 1995.

The second three-year phase of the recovery programme, the Economic and Social Action Plan (ESAP), was launched in January 1990; it aimed to continue the ERP policies but also to alleviate the social costs of adjustment measures. Five-year plans have now been abandoned, and development planning is undertaken year by year; the priority areas in the early 1990s were transport infrastructure, health and education. In 1997 expenditure was to be focussed on primary and secondary education, community and preventative health care and the provision of water and sanitation services.

AGRICULTURE

The agricultural sector is the mainstay of Tanzania's economy, providing a livelihood for about 83% of the economically active population and accounting for 56% of export earnings in 1995. Subsistence farming accounts for about one-half of total agricultural output. No more than about 8% of the country's land area is cultivated, and only about 3% of the cultivated land is irrigated. The northern and south-western areas are the most fertile, receiving the highest rainfall. The main food crop is maize followed by cassava, sorghum, rice, millet and plantains. The main export crops in 1995 were coffee beans and raw cotton, followed by cashew nuts, tobacco, cloves (from Zanzibar), tea and sisal.

During the 1980s there were successive increases in producer prices for all the major crops, and increased availability of imported agricultural inputs, made possible by new foreign-exchange support from international aid donors, contributed to improved harvests. Agricultural output increased, according to the FAO, at an average annual rate of 2.9% during 1984–89. However, production declined by some 0.8% annually in 1989–94; output increased by 3.3% in 1995. In March 1990 the International Development Association (IDA), an affiliate of the World Bank, approved a credit for about US $200m. to support an agricultural adjustment programme, which aimed to make agricultural marketing more efficient. In 1991 legislation was adopted to end the state monopoly over agricultural marketing, permitting private traders to market crops alongside co-operatives; implementation of the legislation was particularly slow regarding the marketing of cotton. Government agencies continued to dominate the official marketing of agricultural produce in the mid-1990s.

Coffee is grown mainly by smallholders and mostly in the Kilimanjaro region; it accounted for 49% of export earnings in 1986, but this share had fallen to 22% by 1994. A record crop of 67,300 metric tons was produced in 1980/81. Since then, output has fluctuated. Production fell from 57,367 tons in 1992/93 to 34,057 tons in 1993/94, but recovered to 42,044 tons in 1994/95 and further, to 50,068 tons, in 1995/96. Production was estimated at 50,000 tons for 1996/97, and was forecast to decrease substantially in 1997/98, owing to the failure of the short rains. Tanzania's total coffee exports in recent years have been about 860,000 bags (each of 60 kg), including those to countries not included in export quota agreements of the International Coffee Organization (ICO), of which Tanzania is a member. The fall in world prices from 1989, following the collapse of the ICO quota arrangements, affected robustas more severely than arabicas, which make up about 75% of Tanzania's coffee output. During the mid-1990s African and Latin American producers implemented schemes to withhold a proportion of their output from world export markets, resulting in an improvement in global coffee prices and prospects and, consequently, a revival in Tanzania's export revenue from coffee. The value of coffee exports in 1994 was US $115.3m., rising by 23% in 1995 to $142.6m., with a decline of more than 30% forecast for 1996. Buyers expressed concern in the mid-1990s that the declining quality of Tanzanian coffee was leading to a reduction in foreign demand.

Production of cotton lint increased steadily during the late 1980s, from 289,390 bales (each of 480 lb, or 218 kg) in 1987 to 390,450 bales in 1988 and 395,040 bales in 1989. The improved performance of the cotton sector was assisted by a major rehabilitation programme, funded by the Netherlands, which covered ginneries and transport in particular. The United Kingdom and the European Investment Bank (EIB) also funded rehabilitation schemes during the 1980s. Although output fell to an estimated 261,000 bales in 1990/91, a record 510,000 bales were produced in 1991/92. Production declined to 334,862 bales in 1992/93, to 256,880 bales in 1993/94, and to 243,119 bales in 1994/95, but recovered to 386,771 bales in 1995/96, according to the Ministry of Agriculture; the failure of the short rains was expected to reduce the cotton crop to some 300,000 bales in 1996/97. About 400,000 ha was under cotton in 1997, the majority in the Mwanza region. Local textile mills bought nearly 74,000 bales in 1989/90. Earnings from cotton exports in 1988/89 were US $83.5m., but in 1989/90, despite rising world prices, they fell to $47m., mainly because of transport difficulties. The value of cotton exports improved to $78m. in 1993, $105m. in 1994 and $120m. in 1995. In 1992 the African Development Bank pledged sh. 1,800m. for the rehabilitation of Tanzania's cotton treatment factories. Tanzania produced a record 22,510 metric tons of cottonseed oil in 1995.

Production of cashew nuts slumped from 145,000 metric tons in 1973/74 to only about 16,500 tons in 1986/87, as a result of low producer prices and long delays in payments to growers, disease, poor husbandry and lack of imported inputs. Output rose steadily during the 1990s to 81,729 tons in 1995/96 and an estimated 90,000 tons in 1996/97. The total annual processing capacity is 103,000 tons, but in some years the whole crop is exported raw in order to earn foreign exchange quickly. In 1994 the Cashewnut Board of Tanzania (known as the Cashewnut Authority of Tanzania until the reform of the crop-purchasing authorities) exported produce to the value of US $51m., and export earnings were estimated at $64m. in 1995. An IDA credit of about $25m. was approved in 1989 to finance a project designed to double production of both cashew nuts and coconuts within 10 years. Coconut production stagnated during the 1980s, partly because of ageing trees. The project covers research into improved varieties and hybrids, training, and credit for farmers.

There has been a significant increase in tobacco production during the 1990s. Although output declined from 19.1m. kg in 1975/76 to 10.7m. kg in 1988/89, production recovered to 17m. kg in 1991 and 17.1m. kg in 1992 before soaring to successive all-time records of 24m. kg in 1993 and 27m. kg in 1995.

Cloves, cultivated mainly on Pemba, are the main export of Zanzibar, providing about 80% of the islands' foreign exchange earnings. Zanzibar, once the world's largest clove exporter, now ranks fourth internationally. When Indonesia, the world's largest consumer, became self-sufficient in cloves in 1983, Zanzibar had to compete for much smaller markets in India, Thailand, Singapore and the Netherlands. Compared with up to 20,000 tons per year in the mid-1960s, output had fallen to 5,800 tons in 1990 and to only 1,575 tons in 1995. It was reported that much of the 1996 crop (the largest in many years) was likely to remain unpicked, owing to a shortage of workers and insufficient profit incentives; fires in early 1997, the result of prolonged drought, destroyed thousands of clove trees. Together with low producer prices, the industry has suffered the effects of smuggling and tree diseases. The state monopoly on the marketing of cloves, as of Zanzibar's other crops, was terminated in 1989. There is a clove distillery on Pemba which produces clove-stem oil for export. Alternative export crops now being encouraged, and increasingly widely grown on the islands, include tobacco, rubber, cardamom, vanilla and peppermint. In 1995 seaweed became the second-largest source of foreign exchange for Zanzibar, with production at 4,975 tons.

Tea production has become increasingly important in recent years. The output of made tea rose from 8,492 metric tons in 1970 to 23,764 tons in 1994. Production was 23,705 tons in 1995, but declined to 19,768 tons in 1996. Tanzania exported 20,511 tons of tea in 1995; earning some US $23m., but the volume of sales retreated to 18,443 tons in 1996. The Tanzania Tea Authority (TTA) accounts for about one-quarter of tea output, has four tea factories and is building three more. Brooke Bond Liebig Tanzania is the largest producer, accounting for 40% of total output. The UK-based Lonrho group has bought back into the Mufindi and Luponde tea estates, which it owned before nationalization. The TTA retains 25% in both companies. The estates are being rehabilitated, and are already selling organic teas, which command high prices. Lonrho announced in early 1991 that it would invest US $5.6m. in a five-year programme aimed at doubling yields at the Mufindi estates to 3,000 kg per ha and extending the planted area from 730 to 1,000 ha. In 1988 the East Usambara Tea Co was formed, with the UK-based Commonwealth Development Corpn (CDC) taking a 60% interest, and the TTA the remainder. The company acquired two TTA estates in Tanga region. The CDC is planning to establish a 600-ha tea estate at Njombe in Iringa region.

Production of sisal in 1964 was just over 250,000 metric tons, but output fell drastically when more than one-half of the estates were nationalized in 1976; only on the remaining privately-owned estates was production maintained at a fairly steady level. Marketing was undertaken by the Tanzania Sisal Development Board (TSDB). In 1986 the government began to dispose of many of its 37 estates to private interests. By 1989 only about one-third of annual production came from TSDB estates, and in 1992 the government announced its intention to return all its estates to the private sector. World prices for sisal began to recover in the late 1980s from the very low levels of the 1970s, as the product began to compete successfully with synthetic substitutes, particularly in some specialized uses. Output, which declined to 30,000 tons in 1987, recovered to 36,000 tons in 1991, when new plantings reached maturity. However, production fell back to 24,309 tons in 1992, improved to about 31,000 tons in 1993 and then slumped to 17,000 tons in 1994. Annual output recovered to an estimated 30,000 tons in 1995. Output for 1996 was estimated at about 26,000 tons. Renewed world demand is encouraging investment in sisal, and several foreign groups have bought estates or started joint ventures with the TSDB.

Other cash crops include sugar cane, cocoa, copra, palm kernels, soya beans, sunflower seeds, pyrethrum and groundnuts. Tanzania's output of sugar cane was 1,410,000 metric tons in 1995, according to the FAO, producing about 88,000 tons of sugar, while local demand is about 400,000 tons per year. Despite this deficit, Tanzania exports 10,000 tons per year to the EU countries. Cocoa output totalled about 1,000 tons in 1995, while 33,000 tons of copra, 6,500 tons of palm kernels, 2,000 tons of soya beans and 30,000 tons of sunflower seeds were produced in that year. Production of pyrethrum, cultivated mainly in the Southern Highlands, fell from about 6,000 tons per year in the 1960s to 1,232 tons in 1986/87, before recovering gradually to 2,396 tons by 1991/92. However, output fell back to 2,050 tons in 1992/93, before plunging to 466 tons in 1993/94 and 460 tons in 1994/95. Nevertheless, world prices have improved, and the government is making efforts to reorganize the industry; the Tanzania Pyrethrum Board has raised prices in line with higher world prices, and it supplies free seeds to growers. In 1995/96 pyrethrum output was projected to have improved to 2,000 tons. A project is under way to rehabilitate the Arusha processing factory. In 1995 72,000 tons of groundnuts were harvested. Fresh fruit and vegetables and flowers are potentially important export crops, and small quantities are being air-freighted to European markets. This non-traditional trade has been stimulated by the encouragement of private enterprise, but it is still severely constrained by many factors, including the very limited chilled storage facilities at Dar es Salaam international airport. In 1995 Tanzania produced 187,000 tons of mangoes, 73,000 tons of pineapples, 1,302,000 tons of bananas and plantains, 22,000 tons of chick peas, 220,000 tons of beans, 22,000 tons of dry peas, 52,000 tons of dry onions and 1,700 tons of garlic. Exports of flowers earned abut US $5m. in 1996. Honey and beeswax produced by Tabora Beekeepers' Co-operative are being exported in small quantities, after a gap of some years. In 1995 Tanzania produced 22,510 tons of cottonseed oil, 19,320 tons of coconut oil, 18,000 tons of maize oil, 8,206 tons of sesame seed oil, 7,800 tons of sunflower seed oil, 6,415 tons of groundnut oil, 5,810 tons of palm oil, 3,240 tons of palm-kernel oil and 1,632 tons of castor-bean oil. Tanzania is one of Africa's largest cattle producers, with an estimated 13.4m. head in 1995; epidemics of lung disease and rinderpest threatened stocks in the mid-1990s. The country's resources of commercial species of timber, including camphorwood, podo and African mahogany, are exploited. In 1995 the total fish catch was 360,000 tons, including Nile perch and tilapia from inland waters and tuna and sardines from the Indian Ocean. The country's first deep-sea fishing company was licensed in 1997.

During the early 1990s severe food shortages were experienced in some areas, owing to a combination of generally poor rains and, particularly in the south-west, serious flooding, as well as inadequate storage facilities (an estimated 30%–40% of all crops are lost through post-harvest pest infestation and other damage). Maize output fell from 3.13m. metric tons in 1988/89 to 2.11m. tons in 1991/92, and in May 1992 the government announced that it would import 400,000 tons of cereals in order to cover shortfalls. In 1995 Tanzania harvested 2.57m. tons of maize, 723,000 tons of paddy rice, 839,000 tons of sorghum and 411,000 tons of millet. Severe drought in 1996/97 necessitated the distribution of food aid, under the auspices of the UN World Food Programme, at a cost of some US $2.5m. It was projected that harvests of food crops in 1997 could be reduced by as much as 50% from the previous year's levels.

INDUSTRY AND POWER

According to estimates by the World Bank, the average annual growth rate of industrial production was 2.6% in 1970–80 and 3.4% in 1980–90. However, many factories closed down, or suspended operations for long periods during the 1980s. Industries suffered from the rising cost of fuel and other imports and the severe lack of foreign exchange to pay for raw materials, machinery, equipment and spares, as well as from frequent interruptions to the water and electricity supply. There were a few signs of improvement from 1986, mainly as more foreign exchange became available through the IMF and Tanzania's main aid donors. By mid-1990, most factories were operating at 20%–40% of capacity, and a few had reached 70%. During 1990–94 industrial output increased by an annual average of 9.7%.

The industrial sector is based on the processing of local commodities and on import substitution. However, the government is seeking to encourage the production of manufactured goods for export, in order to lessen dependence on agricultural commodities, and some industrial goods—textiles, clothing, footwear, tyres, batteries, transformers, switchgear, electric cookers, bottles, cement and paper—are exported to neighbouring countries. A major success was achieved in 1988, when an electrical firm, NEM, exported wall lamps and fluorescent light fittings to Sweden and the Federal Republic of Germany. Devaluation of the shilling helped to make these goods competitive with those from European or Far Eastern suppliers. According to the IMF, exports of manufactured goods fell from US $105m. in 1989 to $53m. in 1993, before recovering to $77m. and $88m. in 1994 and 1995 respectively. High production costs and reliance on import content remain a barrier to international competitiveness.

The principal industries, after food processing, are textiles, brewing and cigarettes. Others include oil refining, fertilizers, rolling and casting mills, pulp and paper, paperboard, metalworking, cement, vehicle assembly, soft drinks, fruit canning, gunny bags, engineering (spares for industrial machinery and for vehicles), railway wagon assembly, glassware, ceramics, hoes, pharmaceutical products, oxygen, carbon dioxide, bricks and tiles, light bulbs, electrical goods, wood products, machine tools and disposable hypodermic syringes. While target output of textiles for 1990 was 61.1m. sq m of cloth, 47.5m. sq m were produced just in the first six months of the year, compared with 38.9m. sq m in the whole of 1988. The removal of protective barriers in the early 1990s, however, placed at least two textile companies in severe financial difficulty, causing them to seek large investments of capital from the government to modernize their machinery. The National Bicycle Co began producing again in 1990 for the first time since 1982, when it closed down owing to lack of foreign exchange. There are three cement plants, at Mbeya, Wazo Hill, near Dar es Salaam, and Tanga. After several years of severe cement shortage, rehabilitation of the plants, mainly with Danish and Swedish assistance, allowed production to increase in 1989 to 700,000 metric tons, meeting domestic needs of about 580,000 tons and allowing exports of 70,000 tons, with the remainder held as stock; combined capacity in 1997 was about 1m. tons per year. Finnish Valmet tractors, Swedish Scania trucks and Italian Fiat tractors are among the vehicles assembled. Southern Paper Mills' US $260m. pulp- and paper-mill at Mufindi commenced production in 1985. The nearby Sao Hill forest will eventually supply the mill's timber needs but, meanwhile, the plant uses imported chemical pulp. The eventual target output was 66,000 tons per year, in seven grades of paper. Tanzania was importing about 30,000 tons of paper per year in the mid-1980s. In 1996 the Kilwa Ammonia Co. (KILAMCO) announced that it was to build an ammonia-urea fertilizer plant at Kilwa Masoka. East African Agro-Industries was formed in 1990 to trawl for nile perch in Lake Victoria; it is to build a plant near Mwanza airport to process 20–25 tons of fish per day for export. The African Fishing Co was licensed in 1997, with six vessels for deep-sea trawing; it was also planned to construct processing facilities. The Tanzanian Italian Petroleum Refinery (TIPER), in Dar es Salaam, is jointly owned by Italy's AGIP and the Tanzanian Petroleum Development Corpn (TPDC). It underwent rehabilitation, at a cost of $18m., in 1990–93. The refinery has a capacity of 875,000 tons per year. The IDA has extended a loan of $44m. towards a $104m. petroleum distribution improvement project, which is regarded as a key component of overall infrastructure improvement plans. During the mid-1990s the government aimed to sell, restructure or dissolve 368 state-owned companies; by February 1997 only 138 concerns had been disposed of. Several former parastatal organizations acquired foreign joint venture partners. In 1995 Tanzania Breweries Ltd, which had been taken over by South Africa's Indol, paid a dividend for the first time in 20 years.

Tanzania's total electricity generating capacity is 600 MW. A large proportion of the country's electricity is generated by hydro-power. Expansion of the major Kidatu hydroelectric complex on the Great Ruaha river was completed in the late 1980s. An eight-year investment programme for the power sector was initiated in 1991; it includes the development of the 200-MW Kihansi power station (with a projected cost of US $410m.), to be commissioned in 1998, and expansion of the Pangani Falls power station. A 220-kv transmission line from Singida to Arusha is also to be built, at an estimated cost of $107m. The national grid is being extended in a major distribution project, taking electricity from Kidatu to six mainland regions. Growth in demand is expected to be 11%–13% per year, and further expansion of generating capacity and of the distribution network will be needed. In 1997 electricity supply to Zanzibar was scheduled to be transferred to Electrogen Ltd, a South African company, via gas-powered generators to be built on the island. The Tanzania Electric Supply Co raised electricity prices by 27% in March 1993 and by a further 71% in July 1993. In 1994 the country's energy consumption, in oil equivalent, was 975m. kg. Total electricity generation in 1995/96 was 1,979m. kWh, according to the Bank of Tanzania. Power shortages in 1994–95 depressed industrial output considerably.

MINERALS

Tanzania exploits diamonds, gold, salt, various gemstones, phosphates, coal, gypsum, kaolin and tin. Deposits of lead, iron ore, tungsten, pyrochlore, magnesite, nickel, copper, cobalt, soda ash, uranium, natural gas, niobium, titanium and vanadium have also been identified. Output of diamonds fell from a peak of 988,000 carats in 1967 to 150,000 carats in 1987, but then recovered slightly to 190,000 carats in 1988. By 1992 output of diamonds had declined again, to 100,000 carats. A continuing problem is that small-scale diamond prospectors sell their finds outside the Tanzanian buying system. Exports of diamonds in 1989 were worth US $14.4m. The Mwadui diamond pipe, covering an area of 146 ha in the Shinyanga region, is the world's largest. However, production at the Williamson mine, which is 75% owned by the government and 25% by De Beers, began to suffer in the late 1980s from deterioration in diamond grades as well as technical and mine maintenance problems, and output temporarily ceased. These difficulties are being overcome, and in 1996 production totalled 117,000 carats. In 1993 De Beers Centenary, together with Canadian interests, obtained exploration rights and mining leases covering almost 9,000 sq km. Following extensive rehabilitation, operations at Mwadui recommenced in August 1995, and exports were resumed in December. However, resources are almost depleted, and production is continuing primarily in order to repay outstanding debts. TANEX, a joint venture between Anglo-American and De Beers, is continuing exploration work near Mwadui.

Gold production virtually ceased in the 1970s, but the Buckreef mine, in Geita, was reopened in 1982 and is currently operated by Ashanti Goldfields of Ghana. A Canadian company is investing US $86m. in a gold mine at Bulyanhulu in Kahama district, which is expected to be capable of producing 180,000 oz of gold annually over 15 years; in 1997 artisanal miners were resisting eviction from the site and delaying excavation. Tancan Gold, a Tanzanian-Canadian joint venture, is to mine at Matinje in Tabora region. In 1996 15 gold-mining companies were active in Tanzania, with a combined exploration budget of $25m.

Tanzania's gold output totalled 6.5 metric tons in 1994, 5.3 tons in 1995. and 5.5 tons in 1996. Official gold exports earned $35m. in 1990, a 52% increase over 1989, and purchases rose sharply in early 1991, as reforms to the official buying mechanism began to take effect. Official purchases were only 41 kg in 1988, but rose to 1,640 kg in 1990, to 3,770 kg in 1991, to 4,100 kg in 1992 and, by more than 70%, to 7,000 kg in 1993, with a value of $26.25m. in 1990, $44.3m. in 1991 and $55m. in 1992. Foreign exchange earnings declined dramatically in 1995 to $3.2m., from $25.7m. 1994; this was largely the result of financial institutions abandoning a scheme to purchase gold at above the parallel market rate and of a failure to institute proper marketing mechanisms.

The Longido ruby mine is the largest in the world, and the Umba River Valley is yielding rubies and sapphires. Deposits of tanzanite (a blue semi-precious stone that was first discovered in the Arusha region in 1967) have been exploited by unlicensed miners, but the government is now severely restricting this activity and at the same time is reviving the Tanzania Gemstone Industry which buys and processes gemstones. Large soda ash deposits in Lake Natron are to be used for the production of caustic soda. Salt is produced at coastal salt pans, and is a potential export. The feasibility of extracting salt from Lake Eyasi, 200 km west of Arusha, is being investigated. Romex International of Canada has signed an agreement to develop nickel deposits in the western Ngara district. Tanzania has nickel deposits estimated at 31.4m. metric tons. In 1992 Canada's Sutton Resources commenced exploration of 26,400 sq km of the Kagera basin, searching for nickel, cobalt, copper, lead, zinc and platinum. In that year a scheme to exploit deposits of nickel, copper and cobalt, which had already been located in the region, was launched, at a projected cost of US $750m. The Chinese-built Songwe-Kiwira coal mine in the south-west, which came into production in 1988, has an annual capacity of 100,000 tons, but the coal's high ash content rendered it unsuitable for use by the intended major customers, Southern Paper Mills and Mbeya Cement Co. Coal is mined on a smaller scale at Ilima in the Mbeya region. In September 1996 a $2m. rehabilitation of the Kiwira coal mine was announced, which would increase its annual production capacity to 150,000 tons. Iron ore is mined at Chunya. Tin is mined on a small scale near the Congolese border. Graphite deposits at Merelani were being developed in 1997.

Prospecting for petroleum and natural gas has been continuing for many years. In the 1970s there were reports of the discovery of petroleum in the Songo Songo island area, off shore from Kilwa, south of Dar es Salaam; the presence of an estimated 42,890m. cu m of natural gas in the area was later confirmed. The proposed KILAMCO fertilizer plant was to use gas from the field. There is a much larger offshore gas field at Kimbiji, 40 km south-east of Dar es Salaam, where recoverable reserves are estimated at 130,000m. cu m. Results of petroleum exploration so far have been disappointing, but a number of international companies have been active, in both on- and offshore areas (in some cases grouped in consortia), including Shell and Esso, Elf Aquitaine, Petrofina, PetroCanada, AGIP, Amoco, Statoil of Norway, Exxon, BP, Broken Hill (Pty) Co, Texaco, the Oil and Natural Gas Commission of India and the Swiss-based International Energy Development Corpn. Tanzania imports about 700,000 tons of crude oil annually, and fuel accounted for 19% of the import bill in 1991 and 13% in 1992. The value of petroleum imports totalled US $167.2m. in 1993, $148.9m. in 1994 and $182.1m. in 1995.

TOURISM

During the period when the East African Community (EAC) was active, the tourism sector in Tanzania was an adjunct of the Kenyan tourist industry. Most travellers merely visited Tanzania's tourist attractions on one-day excursions, pre-paid in Kenya. The dissolution of the EAC and the closure of the Kenya–Tanzania border in 1977 led to a fall in visitor arrivals; only 60,218 tourists visited Tanzania in 1983, compared with 178,000 in 1974. Hotels, lodges and access roads were allowed to deteriorate badly. From 1986 onwards, however, the tourism sector began to recover, with the growing recognition of Tanzania's very promising potential as a tourist destination (based on the country's unspoiled beaches and superb game parks, covering one-third of its area, as well as its long-term political stability). By 1996 tourist arrivals had reached a record (estimated) 326,000. Gross receipts from tourism totalled some sh. 146,840m. in 1993, rising to sh. 192,100m. in 1994 and to sh. 205,000m. in 1995; receipts in 1996 were estimated at US $322m. Devaluation of the shilling has been a major boost to tourism, because Tanzania was previously an extremely expensive destination. The sector is co-ordinated by the state-owned Tanzania Tourist Board. Investment has been forthcoming from several local and foreign private companies. Zanzibar, which receives about 50,000 visitors annually, is encouraging an expansion in tourist arrivals, in particular through an agreement signed with the Aga Khan Fund for Economic Development to build two new hotels (one of which was opened in March 1997), develop a tourism centre and repair historic buildings in the old capital.

TRANSPORT AND COMMUNICATIONS

The concentration of Tanzania's population on the periphery of the country, leaving the central part relatively sparsely populated, poses considerable problems in transport and communications.

The Tanzania-Zambia Railway Authority (Tazara) rail line and the Tanzania-Zambia highway, designed to provide an alternative sea outlet to land-locked Zambia, have eased the problem of transportation to the rich Kilombero valley as well as the Iringa and Mbeya regions. The Chinese-built, 1,860-km Tazara line initially experienced financial and technical problems, together with lack of equipment and spare parts. Tazara made its first profit in the June quarter of 1983, although it did not consistently achieve profits until 1988. Large rises in fares and freight charges were announced at the beginning of 1991. Following the political changes which took place in South Africa during the early 1990s, Zambia started to make greater use of the much more reliable southern transport routes, creating new problems for the Tazara line. Traffic levels fell from approximately 1m. metric tons of freight in 1990 to an estimated 600,000 tons in 1994/95. In 1990 there were only 36 locomotives and 1,446 wagons in operation on the Tazara line, while 90 and 3,200, respectively, were required. The USA undertook to supply 17 locomotives under a US $46m. grant agreement signed in 1987. China signed a 10-year agreement on engineering, managerial and technological co-operation in 1988. Tanzania's central railway line, and its branches, are operated by Tanzania Railways Corpn (TRC). Canada has provided finance and technical assistance for TRC's development programme. The IDA agreed in 1991 to lend $76m. for the TRC's five-year rehabilitation project, which was expected to cost a total of $279m. There is a rail connection with Kenya, as well as marine services and ferry services across Lake Victoria. The TRC also operates ferry links across Lake Victoria to Uganda, across Lake Tanganyika to the Democratic Republic of the Congo and across Lake Malawi to Malawi.

Air Tanzania Corpn (ATC), which was founded in 1977, operates domestic and regional services. ATC has persistently suffered severe financial difficulties and technical problems. The airline has on several occasions had to suspend international flights because of financial problems. In 1992 the government proposed the partial privatization of ATC. Alliance Air was founded in 1994 as a joint venture between ATC, the Ugandan and South African national airlines and the Tanzanian and Ugandan governments, in order to be able to compete with major international airlines. Zanzibar's airport runway has been extended, with aid from Oman, to enable long-haul aircraft to land. Air Zanzibar started operations in 1990, and aims mainly to cater for the tourist trade. The Tanzania Harbours Authority's US $220m. improvement programme for Dar es Salaam port, including the development of container-handling facilities, has received funding from the World Bank, Finland, Denmark, Italy, the Netherlands, Norway, the United Kingdom and the EIB. The project, which was due for completion during the mid-1990s, would raise the port's annual throughput capacity from 3m. metric tons to 7m. tons. The new container terminal came into service in 1989 and an inland container depot is being developed at Ubungo, 15 km from Dar es Salaam. The number of containers handled in 1990 was 73,000 TEU (20-foot equivalent units) and this was expected to rise to 147,000

TEU per year by 1995. Zambia accounted for over 40% of cargo handled at the port in 1993. In 1996 it was reported that port tariffs were to be substantially reduced, in order to encourage the use of Tanzanian ports by Ugandan traders.

A 10-year $650m. integrated road project, funded by the World Bank and several other multilateral and bilateral donors, commenced in 1991. The programme aims to repair and improve 70% of the country's primary roads and to construct 2,828 km of roads and 205 bridges. In September 1996 it was announced that a feasability study was to be conducted on the construction of a bridge over the Rovuma river, linking Tanzania and Mozambique. A new international telephone service giving direct dialling facilities was inaugurated in 1991. A satellite earth station at Mwenge, built in 1979, has been replaced by a new installation supplied by an Italian company, giving access to Atlantic as well as Indian Ocean satellites. Plans to privatize the Tanzanian Telecommunications Co Ltd (TTCL) were announced in 1996. The telephone network is extremely limited, with fewer than four lines per 1,000 inhabitants in 1996, and often faulty. A new exchange came into operation in Dar es Salaam in 1997. The first cellular network in the capital was inaugurated in 1994.

EXTERNAL TRADE

The leading exports are coffee beans, raw cotton, cashew nuts, tobacco, cloves, tea, beans, diamonds, sisal and pyrethrum. Industrial exports include textiles, hides, wattle bark extract and spray-dried instant coffee. Timber, fish and prawns are also exported in small quantities. Recently introduced non-traditional exports include fresh fruit, vegetables and flowers. Honey exports were resumed in 1989, after a gap of several years. Fluctuating world prices lead to wide variations in coffee's share of Tanzania's total exports. In 1996 manufactures of all types accounted for 18% of total exports, according to the Bank of Tanzania, compared with 23% in 1995 and 7% in 1985.

Tanzania's terms of trade were estimated to have declined by 36% between 1972–80 (or by 21.5% if petroleum imports are excluded). However, they began to level off during the second half of the 1980s, and by 1989 they stood at 108 (1987 = 100). By 1992, however, Tanzania's terms of trade had worsened to 71; they recovered slightly, to 83, in 1993. Official merchandise exports earned, according to the IMF, US $408m. in 1990, $362m. in 1991, $401m. in 1992, $440m. in 1993, $549m. in 1994 and $683m. in 1995. Exports amounting to $720m. were estimated for 1996. An encouraging feature has been the success of small private exporters, who in 1989 earned $62m., demonstrating how quickly many of them have responded to trade liberalization measures. In 1994 the United Nations Development Programme provided $30m. for a project which aimed to assist and expand small-scale enterprises. Imports have improved with the implementation of the economic recovery programme; in 1995 total expenditure was $1,340m., compared with $1,309m. in 1994, $1,289m. in 1993, $1,362m. in 1992, $1,270m. in 1991 and $1,227m. in 1990. Imports were estimated at $1,466m. in 1996; the trade deficit was expected to widen considerably in 1997, owing to the effects of drought on crop output.

An Open General Licensing (OGL) scheme was introduced in 1988, with aid from the IDA and the United Kingdom, to give small importers access to foreign exchange, which was made available through the National Bank of Commerce and could initially only be used for importing items on an approved list. The scheme was subsequently expanded and altered, so that any goods are now eligible for a licence unless they appear on a list of excluded items. The original ceiling of US $1m. worth of goods a year per importer was discontinued; for any order worth more than $1m., however, the importer must obtain at least three quotations from potential suppliers. Unfortunately the OGL scheme has been affected by severe leakage problems. Fiscal audits for 1992 revealed that while the Bank of Tanzania (central bank) remitted to the Treasury the full counterpart value of foreign exchange disbursed, the commercial banks had failed to turn over to the Bank of Tanzania some sh. 17,000m. worth of the counterpart funds. This situation, in addition to a lack of disclosure in the allocation of resources, led to a nearly complete withdrawal of donor support. Banking reforms were therefore announced (see below).

In 1962 about 32% of exports went to the Unitd Kingdom, but by 1989 the proportion had declined to about 8.8%. Germany was the main customer in 1993, with 16% of the total, followed by the United Kingdom, Japan, the Netherlands, Kenya, Hong Kong and the USA. The United Kingdom's share of Tanzanian imports in 1962 was 29%, but by 1993 the proportion was only 11%. Germany was the main source of imports in 1993, followed by the USA, Japan and Italy.

BALANCE OF PAYMENTS AND INTERNATIONAL AID

According to IMF figures, the deficit on the current account of the balance of payments (excluding official transfers) shrank steadily from US $1,310m. in 1992 to $983m. in 1995; in the latter year the current account deficit after official transfers stood at $629m., while there was a surplus of $237m. on the capital account. The total external debt at the end of 1995 was $7,333m., of which $6,086m. was long-term public debt and $1,007m. was short-term debt, mostly related to suppliers' credits. Debt-servicing continues to consumer a significant proportion of government recurrent expenditure. The cost of debt-servicing was equivalent to 17.4% of exports of goods and services in 1995, down from 40.0% in 1991, according to World Bank figures. Debt rescheduling agreements were reached at meetings of the 'Paris Club' of Western official creditors held in September 1986, July 1987, March 1990, July 1992 and December 1996. Under a debt conversion programme inaugurated by the Bank of Tanzania in 1990, foreign private creditors can convert their claims into equity or into cash to invest in certain sectors, on a basis which reduces the local costs involved in starting a business in Tanzania. Reserves of foreign exchange declined to $1.2m. in mid-1981, enough for only two days' imports cover. They subsequently improved, and they represented two months' import cover at the end of 1994 and, at $270m., 1.5 months' cover at the end of 1995.

After years of fruitless negotiations, Tanzania finally reached agreement with the IMF in 1986 for a $77m. stand-by facility over 18 months, and $24m. under the Fund's structural adjustment scheme. The IMF demanded the devaluation of the shilling to sh. 58.9 = US $1 by June 1986. The actual official rate at mid-1986 was sh. 40 = $1. Among other IMF conditions were abolition of the subsidy on the staple maize meal (sembe), a 'freeze' on the level of minimum wages, a reduction in the annual budget deficit to sh. 2,500m., the removal of price controls, and the raising of producer prices by at least 45% in real terms. Prior to the 1986 agreement, the government had already introduced some far-reaching measures, and had proposed graduated moves towards fulfilling the IMF's conditions. It reduced the subsidy on maize meal (at the risk of causing urban unrest), dissolved some parastatal bodies, and reorganized or amalgamated others, cutting back their subsidies in order to force them into greater efficiency.

The negotiations with the IMF were closely linked with parallel talks with the World Bank, which subsequently agreed to lend US $50m. to support the government's Economic Recovery Programme (ERP), with a further $46.2m. from the Special Africa Facility. These agreements cleared the way for a World Bank-sponsored Consultative Group meeting on Tanzania held in Paris in June 1986, the first to take place since 1977. Donors strongly endorsed the recovery programme, which required $1,200m. to finance imports in 1986/87. At the meeting of the Consultative Group held in July 1987, Tanzania's main donors pledged a further $740m. for 1987/88. The IMF had also approved a structural adjustment facility (SAF) totalling nearly SDR 68m. to support the ERP. In February 1988 the World Bank approved a $56m. balance-of-payments support plan, also to back the ERP, with $30m. from the IDA and $26m. from the Bank's Special Africa Facility. The Consultative Group met again in Paris in July 1988. It expressed support for the ERP and about $800m. was pledged for 1988/89. In November 1988 the IMF released the second tranche of the three-year SAF, following agreement with the government on further devaluation of the shilling, restructuring of export crop and food marketing, reform of the tax system and continued reform of public enterprises. This agreement unblocked funds from other donors, and in December two IDA credits were approved, totalling about $143m., mostly for financing general imports and also for helping agricultural research. The EC (now the EU) unblocked about $39m. which had been 'frozen' pending finalization of the IMF agreement, and bilateral donors followed suit. The exchange rate of the shilling had dropped to sh. 110.39 = US $1. The 1989/90 budget devalued the shilling further, to sh. 145 = US $1. Tanzania was hoping to obtain an enhanced structural adjustment facility (ESAF) from the IMF to replace the third tranche of the SAF. However, the 1989/90 budget appeared not to have included sufficiently radical measures to satisfy the Fund, and in general, donors regarded the pace of reforms as too slow. A major devaluation of the shilling in December 1989, to sh. 190 = US $1, followed negotiations with the IMF in November, and released the third and final tranche of the three-year SAF. It also opened the way for a new meeting of the Consultative Group in December, at which donors pledged $865m. towards the country's financing needs of $1,300m. for 1990.

The exchange rate underwent a series of minor adjustments following the December 1989 devaluation, and by June 1992 it had declined to sh. 297.68 = US $1. The parallel rate at this date was about sh. 425 = US $1, suggesting that the shilling was still considerably overvalued. The official rate continued to fall, to sh. 378.6 = US $1 in June 1993, to sh. 516 = US $1 in June 1994 and to sh. 602 = US $1 in June 1997.

New negotiations with the IMF were concluded in July 1991, after an interruption caused by the Gulf War, with agreement on a three-year ESAF to replace the SAF which had expired in October 1990. The outline agreement envisaged that more than US $100m. would be made available in each year, starting in 1991/92. The Consultative Group meeting held in Paris in June 1991 pledged up to $980m. in aid for 1991/92. The donors praised Tanzania's progress to date in implementing economic reforms, but asked for the programme to be accelerated. The Consultative Group pledged a further $990m. in aid for 1992/93 in June 1992 and an additional $1,200m. in aid for 1993/94 in July 1993. Of the 1993/94 aid, $360m. was in the form of balance-of-payments support. In November 1992 the IMF approved a loan of SDR 64.2m. ($89m.), to support the second annual arrangement under the ESAF.

In November 1994 foreign donors began to suspend aid disbursements in protest at alleged high-level government connivance in widespread tax evasion. In response, the government established a new regulatory body, the Tanzania Revenue Authority (TRA), which became operational in July 1996. During that month the Consultative Group on Tanzania met in Paris and pledged some US $1,200m. in assistance for 1996/97. In February 1997 the TRA enforced a harmonization of import tariffs throughout the country, following donor concerns that the lower rate of duty in Zanzibar encouraged smuggling to the mainland. IMF credit was restored in November 1996, with the approval of a three-year ESAF of $234m., following the implementation of measures to improve revenue collection, to reduce expenditure and to contain inflation. In December the 'Paris Club' agreed to a rescheduling of some $1,700m. in debts.

A new investment code was approved by parliament in April 1990; this aimed to encourage both local and foreign investment in the economy. Measures to deregulate the banking sector were introduced during the 1990s. By March 1996 the Bank of Tanzania (in its new role as 'regulator and supervisor' of the banking sector) had licensed eight private commercial banks and four non-bank financial institutions. From April 1991 a number of bureaux de change opened throughout the country, and in 1996 the government announced plans to remove all remaining controls on currency convertibility. It was announced in 1997 that the state-owned National Bank of Commerce (NBC) was to be reorganized into three separate units, dealing with trade, corporate business and micro-finance respectively. The NBC had dominated the banking sector, but had accumulated considerable debts.

PUBLIC FINANCE

The 1988/89 budget continued the government's cautious policies directed at economic recovery; measures included an increase in the minimum wage, salary increases for civil servants, a reduction in income tax, higher tuition fees for secondary education, and increases in taxes on cigarettes, beer, soft drinks and wine. The 1989/90 budget aimed to cut public expenditure and to reduce annual inflation from 28.2% to 20% by the end of the financial year, while placing a 20% ceiling on the growth of bank borrowing. Recurrent spending was to go up by 31% and the development budget was cut in absolute terms by 20%. New taxes were expected to raise sh. 3,000m. through increases in education fees, increases in various licence fees, income from six new road toll stations, increases of the duty on alcohol and cigarettes and a doubling of the airport tax. Minimum wages were raised by 26%. Nevertheless, inflation averaged 25.3% per annum during the period 1980–92, according to the World Bank. The 1990/91 budget aimed to alleviate the country's transport and communications problems. Increased revenue was to be derived from an increase in land rents, some licence fees and airport tax. The budget was not too austere, probably because elections were imminent; however, recurrent spending was to be restrained and the overall budget deficit was forecast at under 1% of GDP, therefore well within the IMF 5% limit. Measures included the lowering of some income tax rates, a reduction in customs duty on some items and the abolition of road tolls. In April 1992 the statutory minimum wage was increased from sh. 2,500 per month to sh. 3,500 per month. Under the 1992/93 budget, the minimum wage was raised to sh. 5,000 per month, while total expenditure of sh. 353,605m. was envisaged, of which sh. 251,543m. was recurrent and sh. 102,062m. was for development. The 1994/95 budget envisaged total expenditure of sh. 514,284m. of which sh. 362,797m. was recurrent and sh. 151,487m. was for development; however, actual recurrent expenditure was sh. 55,000m. in excess of the proposed estimate, while actual development spending was only sh. 138,858m. Measures announced included a broadening of the tax base, an increase in customs tariffs from 40% to 50% and further anti-inflationary controls. In July 1994 it was reported that the government had increased by 100% the salaries of all its employees and of those working for parastatal companies. Civil service reforms under the budget included the elimination of 50,000 jobs and the introduction of a mandatory retirement age of 55 years. The 1995/96 budget envisaged total expenditure of sh. 627,688m., of which sh. 488,830m. was recurrent and sh. 138,858m. development expenditure. The higher than expected cost of funding the October 1995 legislative and presidential elections represented a set-back to the government's public finance planning. The 1996/97 budget forecast a deficit of sh. 68,150m. The 1997/98 budget envisaged total expenditure of sh. 975,639m., of which sh. 666,842m. was recurrent expenditure and sh. 308,776m. development expenditure. Airport and harbour fees were increased, as were fuel prices, while three taxes were eliminated in an attempt to simplify business procedures. Budgetary targets included an annual GDP growth rate of 5.5% and a reduction in the inflation rate to 10% annually by June 1998.

CONCLUSION

There is little doubt that, under the Arusha Declaration policies, much was achieved in education and health, and in other social fields. Nevertheless, these achievements were gained at the expense of the productive sectors, leading the economy into a situation which jeopardized the future of these resources. From about 1979 Nyerere's socialist policies increasingly came under attack from aid donors and foreign investors, and—less overtly—from many Tanzanians as well.

Despite having the basic advantages of a wide range of agricultural commodities, of hydroelectric potential, and of more than three decades of relative political stability, Tanzania's prospects of economic advance remain inhibited by a persistent and severe shortage of foreign exchange. Export crops are subject to violent fluctuations in world prices, and since the late 1980s the government has been striving, successfully, to increase non-traditional exports, both agricultural and industrial.

The succession of Ali Hassan Mwinyi as president of Tanzania in 1985 did not signal any definite alteration in economic policies, but allowed a steady, albeit slow, intensification of the liberalization process which was already in progress. In February 1986 the government announced a 'revised import-export policy' allowing exporters of non-traditional industrial products to retain up to 50% of the foreign exchange that they earned from a wide range of goods, and to use one-half of such earnings for importing any inputs or spare parts, while using the remaining half for importing certain goods for sale in the local market.

A determined campaign against corruption, launched in 1991, achieved some success. Despite the fact that many potential investors remain deterred by administrative delays and bureaucracy, as well as by Tanzania's infrastructural shortcomings, the Investment Promotion Centre set up in July 1990 had approved 58 project proposals with total planned investment of some US $100m., and had received 150 applications altogether, by the end of that year. Among the projects which have attracted investor interest are copper/nickel/cobalt mining, tourism development in Zanzibar, private-sector air services, mainland tourist hotels and shrimp fishing.

Signs that economic decline had been arrested were apparent by mid-1987. Two good harvests and the fall in world petroleum prices lessened the potentially threatening inflationary effects of the devaluation of the currency and of other measures introduced in successive budgets. Shortages of essential goods had become less acute and many services had improved. The government has persevered with the policies formulated in the ERP and approved by the IMF and other donors, albeit less rapidly than the donors would wish.

Since the late 1980s the rise in inflation has been tempered, government recurrent expenditure has been reduced, and non-traditional exports have expanded. Nevertheless, the administration of President Mkapa, elected in 1995, inherited many economic challenges. Among major problems are excessive bureaucracy, continuing corruption, the severe shortage of management and entrepreneurial skills, the lack of access to credit by private businesses, transport congestion and other infrastructural weaknesses and the weak purchasing power of the shilling. At best, economic recovery will be a very slow process, with many obstacles to overcome. However, the reform process was firmly on course in the mid-1990s, and forecasts for Tanzania's economic future were tinged with some optimism.

Statistical Survey

Source (unless otherwise stated): Economic and Research Policy Dept, Bank of Tanzania, POB 2939, Dar es Salaam; tel. (51) 110946.

Area and Population

AREA, POPULATION AND DENSITY

Area (sq km)	945,087*
Population (census results)	
26 August 1978	17,512,611
28 August 1988†	
Males	11,327,511
Females	11,846,825
Total	23,174,336
Population (official estimates at mid-year)	
1993	26,712,910
1994	27,471,441
1995	28,251,511‡
Density (per sq km) at mid-1995	29.9

* 364,900 sq miles. Of this total, Tanzania mainland is 942,626 sq km (363,950 sq miles), and Zanzibar 2,461 sq km (950 sq miles).

† Figures are provisional. The revised total is 23,126,952.

‡ Tanzania mainland 27,472,111; Zanzibar 779,400.

ETHNIC GROUPS

(private households, census of 26 August 1967)

African	11,481,595	Others	839
Asian	75,015	Not stated	159,042
Arabs	29,775	**Total**	11,763,150
European	16,884		

REGIONS (estimated population at mid-1995)

Arusha	1,640,399	Mtwara	1,079,495
Dar es Salaam	1,651,534	Mwanza	2,280,206
Dodoma	1,502,344	Pemba*	322,466
Iringa	1,467,144	Pwani (Coast)	774,297
Kagera (Bukoba)	1,652,991	Rukwa	843,424
Kigoma	1,043,491	Ruvuma	950,649
Kilimanjaro	1,345,523	Shinyanga	2,151,539
Lindi	784,658	Singida	960,947
Mara	1,178,340	Tabora	1,257,650
Mbeya	1,791,522	Tanga	1,590,381
Morogoro	1,525,577	Zanzibar*	456,934

* The island regions of Pemba and Zanzibar comprise the autonomous territory of Zanzibar.

PRINCIPAL TOWNS (estimated population at mid-1985)

Dar es Salaam	1,096,000	Tanga	172,000
Mwanza	252,000	Zanzibar	133,000
Tabora	214,000	Dodoma	85,000
Mbeya	194,000		

Source: UN, *Demographic Yearbook*.

BIRTHS AND DEATHS (UN estimates, annual averages)

	1980–85	1985–90	1990–95
Birth rate (per 1,000)	46.5	45.2	43.1
Death rate (per 1,000)	14.8	13.8	13.6

Expectation of life (UN estimates, years at birth, 1990–95): 52.1 (males 52.4; females 55.1).

Source: UN, *World Population Prospects: The 1994 Revision*.

ECONOMICALLY ACTIVE POPULATION (1967 census)

	Males	Females	Total
Agriculture, forestry, hunting and fishing	2,549,688	2,666,805	5,216,493
Mining and quarrying	4,918	99	5,017
Manufacturing	85,659	13,205	98,864
Construction	32,755	318	33,073
Electricity, gas, water and sanitary services	5,704	158	5,862
Commerce	71,088	7,716	78,804
Transport, storage and communications	46,121	711	46,832
Other services	169,693	38,803	208,496
Other activities (not adequately described)	35,574	18,081	53,655
Total labour force	3,001,200	2,745,896	5,747,096

1978 census: Total labour force 7,845,105 (males 3,809,135; females 4,035,970) aged 5 years and over.

Mid-1980 (ILO estimates, '000 persons): Agriculture etc. 8,140 (males 3,787, females 4,353); Industry 431 (males 353, females 78); Services 938 (males 630, females 308); Total 9,508 (males 4,769, females 4,739) (Source: ILO, *Economically Active Population Estimates and Projections, 1950–2025*).

Mid-1995 (estimates in '000): Agriculture, etc. 12,731; Total labour force 15,299 (Source: FAO, *Production Yearbook*).

Agriculture

PRINCIPAL CROPS ('000 metric tons)

	1993	1994	1995
Wheat	59	59	75
Rice (paddy)	600	614	723
Maize	2,282	2,159	2,567
Millet	210	218	411*
Sorghum	719	478	839*
Potatoes†	220	230	240
Sweet potatoes	260	277	451
Cassava (Manioc)	6,833	7,209	5,969
Yams†	10	10	10
Dry beans†	205	190	230
Dry peas†	20	15	22
Chick-peas†	20	15	22
Other pulses†	92	82	104
Groundnuts (in shell)†	70	72	72
Sunflower seed†	30	30	30
Sesame seed†	24	25	25
Cottonseed*	159	95	88
Coconuts†	360	365	365
Copra†	32	33	33
Palm kernels†	6.4	6.5	6.5
Tomatoes†	19	20	20
Onions (dry)†	51	52	52
Other vegetables†	829	929	929
Sugar cane†	1,470	1,530	1,410
Citrus fruits†	35	36	36
Mangoes†	186	187	187
Pineapples†	72	73	73
Bananas	800	834	651
Plantains	800	834	651
Other fruit	262	264	263
Cashew nuts	42.3	46.5	48.0
Coffee (green)	57	34	40
Tea (made)	21	22	22†
Tobacco (leaves)	24	18	27*
Sisal	31	26	30†
Cotton (lint)	81	48	45

* Unofficial figure(s). † FAO estimate(s).

Source: FAO, *Production Yearbook*.

LIVESTOCK ('000 head, year ending September)

	1993	1994	1995
Asses†	177	178	178
Cattle	13,296*	13,376*	13,376†
Pigs	335*	335*	335†
Sheep	3,828*	3,955*	3,955†
Goats	9,373*	9,682*	9,682†

* Unofficial figure. † FAO estimate(s).

Chickens (FAO estimates, million): 27 in 1993; 24 in 1994; 27 in 1995.
Ducks (FAO estimates, million): 1 in 1993; 1 in 1994; 1 in 1995.

Source: FAO, *Production Yearbook*.

LIVESTOCK PRODUCTS ('000 metric tons)

	1993	1994	1995
Beef and veal*	200	202	202
Mutton and lamb*	11	11	11
Goat meat*	24	24	24
Pig meat*	9	9	9
Poultry meat	35*	31	36
Other meat	12	13	13
Cows' milk	545*	555	590
Goats' milk*	90	93	93
Butter*	4.8	4.8	4.9
Hen eggs*	54.1	48.1	54.1
Other poultry eggs*	1.5	1.5	1.5
Honey*	23.5	24.0	24.5
Cattle hides*	40.8	41.0	41.0
Sheepskins*	2.6	2.7	2.7
Goatskins*	4.9	5.1	5.1

* FAO estimate(s).

Source: FAO, *Production Yearbook*.

Forestry

ROUNDWOOD REMOVALS
('000 cubic metres, excluding bark)

	1992	1993	1994
Sawlogs, veneer logs and logs for sleepers*†	317	317	317
Pulpwood	381	234	153
Other industrial wood*	1,569	1,609	1,650
Fuel wood	31,428	32,386	33,626
Total	33,695	34,546	35,746

* FAO estimates.
† Annual output assumed to be unchanged since 1987.

Source: FAO, *Yearbook of Forest Products*.

SAWNWOOD PRODUCTION
(FAO estimates, '000 cubic metres, including railway sleepers)

	1992	1993	1994
Coniferous (softwood)	26	21	13
Broadleaved (hardwood)	22	18	11
Total	48	39	24

Source: FAO, *Yearbook of Forest Products*.

Fishing

('000 metric tons, live weight)

	1993	1994	1995
Tilapias	20.4	20.8	26.1
Mouth-brooding cichlids	9.1	9.3	12.0
Torpedo-shaped catfishes	4.5	4.6	7.9
Other freshwater fishes (incl. unspecified)	59.7	60.8	65.1
Dagaas	44.6	45.4	50.4
Nile perch	156.4	159.2	155.9
Emperors (Scavengers)	4.3	5.4	6.5
Other marine fishes (incl. unspecified)	29.2	33.5	32.1
Other marine animals	3.2	4.0	4.2
Total catch	331.5	342.9	360.0
Inland waters	294.8	300.0	317.2
Indian Ocean	36.7	42.9	42.8

Source: FAO, *Yearbook of Fishery Statistics*.

Mining

	1993	1994	1995
Diamonds ('000 carats)	40.7	22.7	49.1
Gold (kg)	3,370	2,861	320
Salt ('000 metric tons)	83.4	84.3	66.9

Industry

SELECTED PRODUCTS
('000 metric tons, unless otherwise indicated)

	1993	1994	1995*
Sugar	120.5	97.5	88.0
Cigarettes (million)	3.9	3.4	3.7
Beer (million litres)	57.0	56.8	111.2
Soft drinks (million litres)	80.2	109.3	n.a.
Textiles (million sq metres)	60.3	21.4	12.3
Shoes (million pairs)	0.5	0.9	n.a.
Cement	749.0	686.0	796.3
Iron sheets	25.8	22.9	18.3
Aluminium	3.2	2.7	1.1
Petroleum products	348.0	340.0	63.0
Sisal ropes	24.8	21.3	n.a.
Paint (million litres)	2.1	2.0	2.0
Electric energy (million kWh)†	907	912	n.a.

* Provisional figures.
† Data from the UN.

Source: IMF, *Tanzania—Selected Issues and Statistical Appendix* (December 1996).

Finance

CURRENCY AND EXCHANGE RATES

Monetary Units
100 cents = 1 Tanzanian shilling.

Sterling and Dollar Equivalents (31 March 1997)
£1 sterling = 985.4 Tanzanian shillings;
US $1 = 600.1 Tanzanian shillings;
10,000 Tanzanian shillings = £10.148 = $16.663.

Average Exchange Rate (Tanzanian shillings per US $)
1994 509.63
1995 574.76
1996 579.98

BUDGET (million shillings, year ending 30 June)*

Revenue†	1993/94	1994/95	1995/96
Tax revenue	220,758	299,900	383,744
Taxes on imports	50,229	91,121	121,243
Sales taxes and excises on local goods	70,788	72,771	94,712
Imcome taxes	58,505	86,645	103,871
Other taxes	41,236	49,363	63,918
Non-tax revenue	22,063	31,260	64,629
Total	242,821	331,160	448,373

Expenditure‡	1993/94	1994/95	1995/96
Recurrent expenditure	338,364	407,858	417,274
Wages and salaries	77,884	111,494	156,087
Interest payments	44,025	50,164	59,605
Other goods and services and transfers	216,455	246,200	201,582
Development expenditure‡	74,689	31,692	n.a.
Total	413,053	439,550	n.a.

* Figures refer to the Tanzania Government, excluding the revenue and expenditure of the separate Zanzibar Government.
† Excluding grants received (million shillings): 106,790 in 1993/94; 58,505 in 1994/95; 31,096 in 1995/96.
‡ Including lending minus repayments.

INTERNATIONAL RESERVES
(Tanzania mainland, US $ million at 31 December)

	1994	1995	1996
IMF special drawing rights	—	0.1	0.1
Reserve position in IMF	14.6	14.8	14.3
Foreign exchange	317.5	255.3	425.6
Total	332.1	270.2	440.0

Source: IMF, *International Financial Statistics.*

MONEY SUPPLY
(Tanzania mainland, million shillings at 31 December)

	1994*	1995	1996
Currency outside banks	176,310	244,314	257,663
Demand deposits at commercial banks	153,320	183,971	194,448
Total money	329,630	428,285	452,111

* Figures are rounded to the nearest 10 million shillings (Source: IMF, *International Financial Statistics*).

COST OF LIVING
(Consumer Price Index for Tanzania mainland; base: December 1994 = 100)

	1994	1995	1996
Food	88.8	116.6	138.6
Fuel, light and water	92.0	128.0	166.1
Clothing	95.2	114.9	136.3
Rent	94.3	107.2	137.4
All items (incl. others)	95.6	119.8	140.9

NATIONAL ACCOUNTS
(Tanzania mainland, million shillings at current prices)

National Income and Product (provisional)

	1992	1993	1994
Compensation of employees	88,230	119,119	148,194
Operating surplus	906,923	1,132,774	1,462,193
Domestic factor incomes	995,153	1,251,894	1,610,387
Consumption of fixed capital	35,802	36,697	49,542
Gross domestic product (GDP) at factor cost	1,030,955	1,288,591	1,659,929
Indirect taxes	109,442	183,389	260,039
Less Subsidies	9,801	67,611	97,398
GDP in purchasers' values	1,130,596	1,404,369	1,822,570
Factor income received from abroad	2,563	7,934	8,648
Less Factor income paid abroad	72,969	67,842	78,173
Gross national product (GNP)	1,060,190	1,344,460	1,753,045
Less Consumption of fixed capital	35,802	36,697	49,542
National income in market prices	1,024,387	1,307,763	1,703,504
Other current transfers from abroad (net)	282,813	291,673	308,518
National disposable income	1,307,200	1,599,436	2,084,022

Expenditure on the Gross Domestic Product

	1994	1995	1996
Government final consumption expenditure	393,501	462,315	435,329
Private final consumption expenditure	1,931,976	2,532,842	3,130,072
Increase in stocks	4,841	5,856	6,640
Gross fixed capital formation	561,819	591,936	620,597
Total domestic expenditure*	2,827,878	3,547,061	4,220,009
Exports of goods and services	473,888	727,177	751,161
Less Imports of goods and services	1,002,880	1,253,739	1,203,527
GDP in purchasers' values	2,298,886	3,020,499	3,767,643
GDP at constant 1990 prices	975,642	n.a.	n.a.

* Including adjustment (million shillings): −64,259 in 1994; −45,888 in 1995; 27,371 in 1996.

Source: IMF, *International Financial Statistics.*

Gross Domestic Product by Economic Activity
(at factor cost)

	1994	1995	1996*
Agriculture, hunting, forestry and fishing	947,980	1,209,622	1,589,420
Mining and quarrying	26,842	29,526	40,277
Manufacturing	126,397	142,576	185,670
Electricity, gas and water	37,634	46,365	60,889
Construction	86,482	75,245	140,571
Trade, restaurants and hotels	254,458	315,273	419,350
Transport, storage and communications	125,616	153,690	201,923
Finance, insurance, real estate and business services	163,992	194,972	266,017
Community, social and personal services	83,155	106,355	138,262
Sub-total	1,852,556	2,273,624	3,042,379
Less Imputed bank service charge	121,109	143,071	190,099
Total	1,731,447	2,130,553	2,852,280

* Provisional figures.

BALANCE OF PAYMENTS (US $ million)

	1993	1994	1995
Exports of goods f.o.b.	444.6	519.4	682.9
Imports of goods f.o.b.	−1,288.6	−1,309.3	−1,340.4
Trade balance	−844.0	−790.0	−657.5
Exports of services	312.6	410.5	566.4
Imports of services	−595.8	−538.9	−754.5
Balance on goods and services	−1,127.2	−918.3	−845.5
Other income received	21.6	30.9	3.9
Other income paid	−170.8	−153.4	−141.2
Balance on goods, services and income	−1,276.4	−1,040.8	−982.8
Current transfers received	536.7	385.1	385.9
Current transfers paid	−30.3	−25.0	−32.3
Current balance	−770.0	−680.7	−629.2
Capital account (net)	202.8	262.6	236.7
Direct investment from abroad	20.2	50.0	150.0
Other investment assets	−68.6	−75.6	−162.5
Other investment liabilities	155.3	99.4	166.7
Net errors and omissions	13.4	−5.0	−53.5
Overall balance	−447.0	−349.3	−291.8

Source: IMF, *International Financial Statistics.*

External Trade

PRINCIPAL COMMODITIES (US $ million)

Imports c.i.f.	1993	1994	1995
Capital goods	537.3	656.5	413.3
Transport equipment	335.2	242.3	162.6
Building and construction	47.1	107.5	32.8
Machinery	155.0	306.7	217.8
Intermediate goods	203.5	290.4	473.0
Petroleum and petroleum products	99.4	149.0	134.4
Crude petroleum	n.a.	79.8	83.5
Petroleum products	n.a.	69.2	50.8
Consumer goods	308.9	359.5	330.0
Food and foodstuffs	67.2	127.5	27.9
Unclassified	131.6	199.5	—
Total	1,181.3	1,505.5	1,216.3

Exports f.o.b.	1993	1994	1995*
Coffee	87.63	115.35	142.60
Cotton	65.30	105.12	120.15
Tea	23.11	39.53	23.36
Tobacco	15.91	20.56	27.13
Cashew nuts	22.42	51.16	64.00
Minerals	38.81	29.99	44.88
Total (incl. others)	367.19	519.34	661.18

* Estimates.

Source: IMF, *Tanzania—Selected Issues and Statistical Appendix* (December 1996).

PRINCIPAL TRADING PARTNERS (million shillings)

Imports c.i.f.	1988	1989	1990
Belgium	1,596	4,523	6,408
Canada	1,875	3,232	3,927
China, People's Repub.	1,423	1,854	3,660
Denmark	4,545	4,751	5,621
France (incl. Monaco)	1,084	3,123	8,556
Germany, Fed. Repub.	11,791	14,651	20,059
Hong Kong	670	9,191	1,030
India	1,560	2,757	3,436
Ireland	114	113	5,300
Italy	8,240	13,342	13,391
Japan	8,546	14,244	15,426
Kenya	3,681	4,140	3,533
Netherlands	—	5,905	8,719
Norway	955	1,613	2,485
Singapore	969	2,249	1,764
Sweden	1,893	2,101	6,108
Switzerland	28	2,146	2,249
United Kingdom	1,468	23,912	34,104
USA	1,198	2,141	3,112
Zambia	945	1,197	1,010
Total (incl. others)	87,893	146,705	199,260

Exports	1988	1989	1990
Belgium	1,183	1,481	1,368
France	328	572	613
Germany, Fed. Repub.	4,798	7,422	10,044
Hong Kong	1,302	2,200	2,178
India	2,166	1,298	1,352
Indonesia	235	216	797
Italy	1,637	2,467	2,336
Japan	1,595	2,440	3,140
Kenya	1,102	2,088	2,368
Netherlands	1,974	2,993	4,353
Singapore	869	2,704	2,565
Spain	648	538	968
Switzerland	180	148	1,448
Taiwan	1,409	2,728	3,329
Uganda	341	560	780
United Kingdom	3,432	6,267	8,578
USA	869	1,638	5,495
Zaire	272	802	319
Zambia	393	244	388
Total (incl. others)	27,041	52,777	64,571

Transport

RAILWAYS (estimated traffic)

	1989	1990	1991
Passenger-km (million)	3,630	3,690	3,740
Freight ton-km (million)	1,420	1,470	1,490

Source: UN Economic Commission for Africa, *African Statistical Yearbook.*

ROAD TRAFFIC (estimates, '000 motor vehicles in use)

	1993	1994	1995
Passenger cars	30.2	28.0	25.8
Buses and coaches	71.0	77.8	80.3
Lorries and vans	24.6	27.1	27.7
Road tractors	6.7	6.6	6.6

Source: IRF, *World Road Statistics.*

SHIPPING

Merchant fleet (registered at 31 December)

	1994	1995	1996
Number of vessels	46	54	53
Displacement ('000 grt)	42.5	46.1	45.2

Source: Lloyd's Register of Shipping, *World Fleet Statistics.*

International sea-borne freight traffic (estimates '000 metric tons)

	1988	1989	1990
Goods loaded	1,208	1,197	1,249
Goods unloaded	3,140	3,077	2,721

Source: Government Printer, *Economic Survey 1990.*

CIVIL AVIATION (traffic on scheduled services)

	1992	1993	1994
Kilometres flown (million)	4	3	3
Passengers carried ('000)	216	188	199
Passenger-km (million)	174	157	165
Total ton-km (million)	18	16	17

Source: UN, *Statistical Yearbook.*

Tourism

	1993	1994	1995
Tourist arrivals	230,170	261,600	280,000
Tourist receipts (million shillings)	146,840	192,100	205,000

Communications Media

	1992	1993	1994
Radio receivers ('000 in use)*	640	720	740
Television receivers ('000 in use)*	45	55	60
Telephones ('000 main lines in use)	81	85	88
Daily newspapers:			
Number	3	n.a.	3
Average circulation ('000 copies)*	220	n.a.	220

* Estimates.

Sources: UNESCO, *Statistical Yearbook*; UN, *Statistical Yearbook.*

Education

(1993, unless otherwise indicated)

	Teachers	Pupils
Primary	101,816	3,736,734
General secondary	9,568	180,899
Teacher training colleges	1,171	15,824
Higher*		
Universities	939	3,327
Other institutions	267	1,927

* 1989 figures.

Sources: Ministry of Education and Culture, Dar es Salaam; UNESCO, *Statistical Yearbook.*

Directory

The Constitution

The United Republic of Tanzania was established on 26 April 1964, when Tanganyika and Zanzibar, hitherto separate independent countries, merged. An interim Constitution of 1965 was replaced, on 25 April 1977, by a permanent Constitution for the United Republic. In October 1979 the Revolutionary Council of Zanzibar adopted a separate Constitution, governing Zanzibar's internal administration, with provisions for a popularly-elected President and a legislative House of Representatives elected by delegates of the then ruling party. A new Constitution for Zanzibar, which came into force in January 1985, provided for direct elections to the Zanzibar House of Representatives. The provisions below relate to the 1977 Constitution of the United Republic, as subsequently amended.

GOVERNMENT

Legislative power is exercised by the Parliament of the United Republic, which is vested by the Constitution with complete sovereign power, and of which the present National Assembly is the legislative house. The Assembly also enacts all legislation concerning the mainland. Internal matters in Zanzibar are the exclusive jurisdiction of the Zanzibar executive, the Supreme Revolutionary Council of Zanzibar, and the Zanzibar legislature, the House of Representatives.

National Assembly

The National Assembly comprises both directly-elected members (chosen by universal adult suffrage) and nominated members (including five members elected from the Zanzibar House of Representatives). The number of directly-elected members exceeds the number of nominated members. The Electoral Commission may review and, if necessary, increase the number of electoral constituencies before every general election. The National Assembly has a term of five years.

President

The President is the Head of State, Head of the Government and Commander-in-Chief of the Armed Forces. The President has no power to legislate without recourse to Parliament. The assent of the President is required before any bill passed by the National Assembly becomes law. Should the President withhold his assent and the bill be repassed by the National Assembly by a two-thirds majority, the President is required by law to give his assent within 21 days unless, before that time, he has dissolved the National Assembly, in which case he must stand for re-election.

The President appoints a Vice-President to assist him in carrying out his functions. The President presides over the Cabinet, which comprises a Prime Minister and other ministers who are appointed from among the members of the National Assembly.

JUDICIARY

The independence of the judges is secured by provisions which prevent their removal, except on account of misbehaviour or incapacity when they may be dismissed at the discretion of the President. The Constitution also makes provision for a Permanent Commission of Enquiry which has wide powers to investigate any abuses of authority.

CONSTITUTIONAL AMENDMENTS

The Constitution can be amended by an act of the Parliament of the United Republic, when the proposed amendment is supported by the votes of not fewer than two-thirds of all the members of the Assembly.

The Government

HEAD OF STATE

President: BENJAMIN WILLIAM MKAPA (took office 23 November 1995).

Vice-President: OMAR ALI JUMA.

CABINET
(August 1997)

President and Commander-in-Chief of the Armed Forces: BENJAMIN WILLIAM MKAPA.

Prime Minister: FREDERICK SUMAYE.

Ministers of State in the President's Office: MATEO QUARESI, NASSORO MALOCHO.

Minister of State in the Vice-President's Office: BAKARI MBONDE.

Ministers of State in the Prime Minister's Office: MUSSA NKHANGAA, MOHAMMED SEIF KHATIB, KINGUNGE NGOMBALE MWIRU.

Minister of Foreign Affairs and International Co-operation: Lt-Col JAKAYA MRISHO KIKWETE.

Minister of Home Affairs: ALI AMEIR MUHAMMED.

Minister of Finance: DANIEL YONA NDHIWA.

Minister of Industry and Trade: Dr WILLIAM SHIJA.

Minister of Communications and Transport: WILLIAM JONATHAN KUSILA.

Minister of Agriculture and Co-operatives: PAUL KIMITI.

Minister of Health: Dr AARON CHIDUO.

Minister of Education and Culture: Prof. JUMA ATHUMANI KAPUYA.

Minister of Energy and Mineral Resources: Dr ABDALLAH OMAR KIGODA.

Minister of Water: PIUS NG'WANDU.

Minister of Natural Resources and Tourism: ZAKIA MEGHJI.

Minister of Lands, Housing and Urban Development: GIDEON CHEYO.

Minister of Science, Technology and Higher Education: JACKSON MAKWETA.

Minister of Works: ANNA ABDALLAH.

Minister of Labour and Youth Development: SEBASTIAN KINYONDO.

Minister of Community Development, Women's Affairs and Children: MARY NAGU.

Minister of Justice and Constitutional Affairs: HARITH BAKARI MWAPACHU.

Minister of Defence and National Service: EDGAR MAOKOLA MAJOGO.

MINISTRIES

All Ministries in Dar es Salaam are to be transferred to Dodoma by 2005.

Office of the President: The State House, POB 9120, Dar es Salaam; tel. (51) 116898; telex 41264; fax (51) 113425.

Office of the Vice-President: POB 776, Zanzibar; tel. (54) 20511.

Office of the Prime Minister: POB 980, Dodoma; tel. (61) 20511; telex 53159.

Ministry of Agriculture and Co-operatives: POB 9192, Dar es Salaam; tel. (51) 112323.

Ministry of Community Development, Women's Affairs and Children: Dar es Salaam.

Ministry of Defence: POB 9544, Dar es Salaam; tel. (51) 28291.

Ministry of Education: POB 9121, Dar es Salaam; tel. (51) 27211; telex 41742.

Ministry of Energy and Mineral Resources: POB 9153, Dar es Salaam; tel. (51) 117153.

Ministry of Finance: POB 9111, Dar es Salaam; tel. (51) 111174; telex 41329; fax (51) 38573.

Ministry of Foreign Affairs and Co-operation: POB 9000, Dar es Salaam; tel. (51) 111906; telex 41086.

Ministry of Health: POB 9083, Dar es Salaam; tel. (51) 20261.

Ministry of Home Affairs: POB 9223, Dar es Salaam; tel. (51) 112034; telex 41231.

Ministry of Industry and Trade: POB 9503, Dar es Salaam; tel. (51) 27251.

Ministry of Justice and Constitutional Affairs: Dar es Salaam.

Ministry of Labour and Youth Development: POB 2483, Dar es Salaam; tel. (51) 20781.

Ministry of Lands, Housing and Urban Development: POB 9372, Dar es Salaam; tel. (51) 27271.

Ministry of Natural Resources and Tourism: Dar es Salaam.

Ministry of Science, Technology and Higher Education: Dar es Salaam.

Ministry of Water and Livestock Development: Dar es Salaam.

Ministry of Works, Communications and Transport: POB 9423, Dar es Salaam; tel. (51) 23235; telex 41392.

SUPREME REVOLUTIONARY COUNCIL OF ZANZIBAR
(August 1997)

President and Chairman: Dr SALMIN AMOUR.

Chief Minister: Dr MOHAMED GHARIB BILALI.

Deputy Chief Minister, Minister of Education: OMAR RAMADHAN MAPURI.

Minister of State for Constitutional and Legal Affairs: IDI PANDU HASSAN.

Minister of the Treasury: AMINA SALIM ALI.

Minister in the President's Office: MOHAMED RAMIYA.

Minister of Planning and Investments: ALI JUMA SHAMHUNA.

Minister of Agriculture: Brig.-Gen. ADAM MURAKANJUKI.

Minister of Information, Tourism, Youth and Cultural Affairs: ISA MOHAMED ISA.

Minister of Transport and Communications: AMAN ABEID KARUME.

Minister of Health: SAID BAKARI JECHA.

Minister of Regional Administration: ALI HAJI ALI.

Minister of Women's and Children's Affairs: ASHA BAKARI.

Minister of Water, Works, Land and Energy: KAMALI PANDU.

Minister of Trade, Industry and Marketing: KHAMIS AHMAD.

President and Legislature

PRESIDENT

Election, 29 October 1995

Candidate	Votes	%
BENJAMIN WILLIAM MKAPA	4,026,422	61.8
AUGUSTINE LYATONGA MREMA	1,808,616	27.8
Prof. IBRAHIM HARUNA LIPUMBA	418,973	6.4
JOHN MOMOSE CHEYO	258,734	4.0
Total	6,512,745	100.0

NATIONAL ASSEMBLY

Speaker: PIUS MSEKWA.

Election, 29 October 1995

Party	Seats*
CCM	186
CUF	24
NCCR–Mageuzi	16
CHADEMA	3
UDP	3
Total	232

* In addition to the 232 elective seats, 37 nominated seats are allocated to women, five to members of the Zanzibar House of Representatives, and one to the Attorney-General.

ZANZIBAR PRESIDENT

Election, 22 October 1995

Candidate	Votes	%
Dr SALMIN AMOUR	165,271	50.2
SEIF SHARRIF HAMAD	163,706	49.8
Total	328,977	100.0

ZANZIBAR HOUSE OF REPRESENTATIVES

Speaker: P. A. KILIFICHO.

Election, 22 October 1995

Party	Seats*
CCM	26
CUF	24
Total	50

* In addition to the 50 elective seats, five seats are reserved for regional commissioners, 10 for presidential nominees, and 10 for women.

Political Organizations

Bismillah Party: Pemba; seeks a referendum on the terms of the 1964 union of Zanzibar with mainland Tanzania.

Chama Cha Demokrasia na Maendeleo (CHADEMA–Party for Democracy and Progress): Plot No. 922/7, Block 186005, Kisutu St, POB 5330, Dar es Salaam; supports democracy and social development; Chair. EDWIN I. M. MTEI; Sec.-Gen. BOB NYANGA MAKANI.

Chama Cha Mapinduzi (CCM–Revolutionary Party of Tanzania): Kuu St, POB 50, Dodoma; tel. (61) 2282; telex 53175; f. 1977 by merger of the mainland-based Tanganyika African National Union (TANU) with the Afro-Shirazi Party, which operated on Zanzibar and Pemba; sole legal party 1977–92; socialist orientation; Chair. BENJAMIN WILLIAM MKAPA; Sec.-Gen. PHILIP MANGULA.

Civic United Front (CUF): Mtendeni St, Urban District, POB 3637, Zanzibar; f. 1992 by merger of Zanzibar opposition party Kamahuru and the mainland-based Chama Cha Wananchi; commands substantial support in Zanzibar and Pemba, for which it demands increased autonomy; Leaders SEIF SHARRIF HAMAD, Prof. IBRAHIM HARUNA LIPUMBA.

Democratic Party (DP): Dar es Salaam; Leader Rev. CHRISTOPHER MTIKILA.

Movement for Democratic Alternative (MDA): Zanzibar; seeks to review the terms of the 1964 union of Zanzibar with mainland Tanzania; supports democratic institutions and opposes detention without trial and press censorship.

National Convention for Construction and Reform (NCCR–Mageuzi): Plot No. 48, Mchikichi St, Kariakoo Area, POB 5316, Dar es Salaam; f. 1992; Chair. AUGUSTINE LYATONGA MREMA; Sec.-Gen. MABERE MARANDO.

National League for Democracy (NLD): Sinza D/73, POB 352, Dar es Salaam; Chair. EMMANUEL J. E. MAKAIDI; Sec.-Gen. MICHAEL E. A. MHINA.

National Reconstruction Alliance (NRA): House No. 4, Mvita St, Jangwani Ward, POB 16542, Dar es Salaam; Chair. ULOTU ABUBAKAR ULOTU; Sec.-Gen. SALIM R. MATINGA.

Popular National Party (PONA): Plot 104, Songea St, Ilala, POB 21561, Dar es Salaam; Chair. WILFREM R. MWAKITWANGE; Sec.-Gen. NICOLAUS MCHAINA.

Tanzania Democratic Alliance Party (TADEA): Block 3, Plot No. 37, Buguruni Malapa, POB 63133, Dar es Salaam; Pres. FLORA M. KAMOONA; Sec.-Gen. JOHN D. LIFA-CHIPAKA.

Tanzania People's Party (TPP): Mbezi Juu, Kawe, POB 60847, Dar es Salaam; Chair. ALEC H. CHE-MPONDA; Sec.-Gen. GRAVEL LIMO.

United Democratic Party (UDP): Leader JOHN MOMOSE CHEYO.

United People's Democratic Party (UPDP): Al Aziza Restaurant, Kokoni and Narrow Sts, POB 3903, Zanzibar; Chair. KHALFANI ALI ABDULLAH; Sec.-Gen. AHMED M. RASHID.

Union for Multi-Party Democracy of Tanzania (UMD): 77 Tosheka St, Magomeni Mapiga, POB 41093, Dar es Salaam; Chair. Chief ABDALLA SAID FUNDIKIRA.

Diplomatic Representation

EMBASSIES AND HIGH COMMISSIONS IN TANZANIA

Albania: 93 Msese Rd, POB 1034, Kinondoni, Dar es Salaam; telex 41280; Ambassador: MEHDI SHAQIRI.

Algeria: 34 Upanga Rd, POB 2963, Dar es Salaam; telex 41104; Ambassador: (vacant).

Angola: Plot 78, Lugalo Rd, Upanga, POB 20793, Dar es Salaam; tel. (51) 117674; telex 41251; fax (51) 32349; Ambassador: JOSÉ AGOSTINHO NETO.

Belgium: NIC Investment House, 7th Floor, Samora Machel Ave, POB 9210, Dar es Salaam; tel. (51) 112688; telex 41094; fax (51) 117621; Ambassador: BEATRIX VAN HEMELDONCK.

Brazil: IPS Bldg, 9th Floor, POB 9654, Dar es Salaam; tel. (51) 21780; telex 41228; Ambassador: JOSÉ FERREIRA LOPES.

Burundi: Plot No. 10007, Lugalo Rd, POB 2752, Upanga, Dar es Salaam; tel. (51) 38608; telex 41340; Ambassador: (vacant).

Canada: 38 Mirambo St, POB 1022, Dar es Salaam; tel. (51) 112831; fax (51) 112639; High Commissioner: VERONA EDELSTEIN.

China, People's Republic: 2 Kajificheni Close at Toure Drive, POB 1649, Dar es Salaam; tel. (51) 667212; telex 41036; Ambassador: XIE YOUKUN.

Congo, Democratic Republic: 438 Malik Rd, POB 975, Upanga, Dar es Salaam; tel. (51) 150282; telex 41407; Ambassador: DUBAKO BETEMA.

Cuba: Plot No. 313, Lugalo Rd, POB 9282, Upanga, Dar es Salaam; telex 41245; Ambassador: A. ROLANDO GALLARDO FERNÁNDEZ.

Denmark: Ghana Ave, POB 9171, Dar es Salaam; tel. (51) 113887; telex 41057; fax (51) 116433; Ambassador: FLEMMING BJØRK PEDERSEN.

Egypt: 24 Garden Ave, POB 1668, Dar es Salaam; tel. (51) 117622; telex 41173; Ambassador: BAHER M. EL-SADEK.

Finland: Mirambo St and Garden Ave, POB 2455, Dar es Salaam; tel. (51) 119170; telex 41066; fax (51) 116548; Ambassador: ILARI RANTAKARI.

France: Ali Hassan Mwinyi Rd, POB 2349, Dar es Salaam; tel. (51) 666021; telex 41006; fax (51) 668435; Ambassador: JACQUES MIGOZZI.

Germany: NIC Investment House, Samora Ave, POB 9541, Dar es Salaam; tel. (51) 117409; telex 41003; fax (51) 112944; Ambassador: Dr BURGHART NAGEL.

Guinea: 35 Haile Selassie Rd, POB 2969, Oyster Bay, Dar es Salaam; tel. (51) 68626; Ambassador: M. BANGOURA.

Holy See: Msasani Peninsula, POB 480, Dar es Salaam (Apostolic Nunciature); tel. (51) 68403; fax (51) 40193; Apostolic Nuncio: Most Rev. FRANCISCO-JAVIER LOZANO, Titular Archbishop of Penafiel.

Hungary: Plot 294, Chake Chake Rd, POB 672, Dar es Salaam; tel. (51) 668573; telex 41428; fax (51) 667214; Ambassador: JÁNOS ZEGNAL.

India: 28 Samora Ave, POB 630, Dar es Salaam; tel. (51) 117175; telex 41335; fax (51) 46747; High Commissioner: OM PRAKASH GUPTA.

Indonesia: 229 Upanga Rd, POB 572, Dar es Salaam; telex 41575; Ambassador: R. CHARIS.

Iran: Plot 31, Upanga Rd, POB 5802, Dar es Salaam; tel. (51) 112255; fax (51) 118805; Ambassador: ABDUL ALI TAVAKKOLI.

Iraq: Dar es Salaam; tel. (51) 25728; telex 41193; Ambassador: FAWZ ALI AL-BANDER.

Ireland: Plot 1131, Msasani St, Msasani Peninsular, POB 9612, Dar es Salaam; tel. (51) 667816; fax (51) 667852; Chargé d'affaires a.i.: PAULINE CONWAY.

Italy: Plot 316, Lugalo Rd, POB 2106, Dar es Salaam; tel. (51) 115935; telex 41062; fax (51) 115938; Ambassador: TORQUATO CARDILLI.

Japan: 1018 Upanga Road, POB 2577, Dar es Salaam; tel. (51) 115831; telex 41065; Ambassador: MITSURU EGUCHI.

Kenya: NIC Investment House, Samora Machel Ave, POB 5231, Dar es Salaam; tel. (51) 112955; telex 41700; fax (51) 113098; High Commissioner: DICKSON I. KATHAMBANA.

Korea, Democratic People's Republic: Plot 460B, United Nations Rd, POB 2690, Dar es Salaam; Ambassador: RO MIN SU.

Madagascar: Magoret St, POB 5254, Dar es Salaam; tel. (51) 41761; telex 41291; Chargé d'affaires a.i.: RAHDRAY DESIRÉ.

Malawi: IPS Bldg, POB 23168, Dar es Salaam; tel. (51) 37260; telex 41633; High Commissioner: L. B. MALUNGA.

Mozambique: 25 Garden Ave, Dar es Salaam; tel. (51) 33063; telex 41214; High Commissioner: AMOS ESTÊVÃO MAHANJANE.

Netherlands: New ATC Town Terminal Bldg, cnr Ohio St and Garden Ave, POB 9534, Dar es Salaam; tel. (51) 118566; telex 41050; fax (51) 112828; Ambassador: S. LEENSTRA.

Nigeria: 3 Ali Hassan Mwinyi Rd, POB 9214, Oyster Bay, Dar es Salaam; tel. (51) 666000; telex 41240; fax (51) 112828; High Commissioner: SOLOMON A. YISA.

Norway: Plot 160, Mirambo St, POB 2646, Dar es Salaam; tel. (51) 113623; telex 41221; fax (51) 116564; Ambassador: ARILD EIK.

Pakistan: 149 Malik Rd, Upanga, POB 2925, Dar es Salaam; tel. (51) 117630; fax (51) 113205; High Commissioner: (vacant).

Poland: 63 Alykhan Rd, POB 2188, Dar es Salaam; tel. (51) 115812; telex 41022; fax (51) 115812; Chargé d'affaires: EUGENIUSZ RZEWUSKI.

Romania: Plot 11, Ocean Rd, POB 7795, Dar es Salaam; Chargé d'affaires a.i.: IOAN BUNEA.

Russia: Plot No. 73, Ali Hassan Mwinyi Rd, POB 1905, Dar es Salaam; tel. (51) 666005; telex 41747; fax (51) 666818; Ambassador: Dr KENESH N. KULMATOV.

Rwanda: Plot 32, Upanga Rd, POB 2918, Dar es Salaam; tel. (51) 117631; fax (51) 115888; Ambassador: JOY MUKANYANGE.

South Africa: Plot 1338/1339, Mwanya Rd, Msaski, POB 10723, Dar es Salaam; tel. (51) 600484; fax (51) 600618; High Commissioner: T. LUJABE RANKOE.

Spain: 99B Kinondoni Rd, POB 842, Dar es Salaam; tel. (51) 666936; telex 41589; fax (51) 666938; Ambassador: LUIS GÓMEZ DE ARANDA GUILLÉN.

Sudan: 'Albaraka', 64 Ali Hassan Mwinyi Rd, POB 2266, Dar es Salaam; tel. (51) 117641; telex 41143; fax (51) 115811; Ambassador: CHARLES DE WOL.

Sweden: Mirambo St and Garden Ave, POB 9274, Dar es Salaam; tel. (51) 111235; telex 41013; Ambassador: THOMAS PALME.

Switzerland: 17 Kenyatta Drive, POB 2454, Dar es Salaam; tel. (51) 666008; telex 41322; fax (51) 666736; Ambassador: LISE FAVRE.

Syria: POB 2442, Dar es Salaam; tel. (51) 117655; telex 41339; Chargé d'affaires: KANAAN HADID.

Uganda: Extelcoms Bldg, 7th Floor, Samora Machel Ave, POB 6237, Dar es Salaam; tel. (51) 117646; fax (51) 112974; High Commissioner: S. KATONGOLE.

United Kingdom: Hifadhi House, Samora Machel Ave, POB 9200, Dar es Salaam; tel. (51) 117659; telex 41004; fax (51) 112952; High Commissioner: ALAN E. MONTGOMERY.

USA: 36 Laibon St and Ali Hassan Mwinyi Rd, POB 9123, Dar es Salaam; tel. (51) 666010; telex 41250; fax (51) 666701; Ambassador: BRADY ANDERSON.

Viet Nam: 9 Ocean Rd, Dar es Salaam; Ambassador: TRAN MY.

Yemen: 353 United Nations Rd, POB 349, Dar es Salaam; tel. (51) 21722; fax (51) 66791; Chargé d'affaires: MOHAMED ABDULLA ALMAS.

Yugoslavia: Plot 35/36, Upanga Rd, POB 2838, Dar es Salaam; tel. (51) 115891; fax (51) 115893; Ambassador: (vacant).

Zambia: 5–6 Ohio St/City Drive Junction, POB 2525, Dar es Salaam; tel. (51) 118481; telex 41023; High Commissioner: JOHN KASHONKA CHITAFU.

Zimbabwe: NIC Life Bldg, 6th Floor, POB 20762, Dar es Salaam; tel. (51) 116789; telex 41386; fax (51) 112913; High Commissioner: J. M. SHAVA.

Judicial System

Permanent Commission of Enquiry: POB 2643, Dar es Salaam; tel. (51) 26181; Chair. and Official Ombudsman I. S. A. KAJEMBO; Sec. R. J. D. MLAMA.

Court of Appeal: Consists of the Chief Justice and four Judges of Appeal.

Chief Justice of Tanzania: FRANCIS NYALALI.

Chief Justice of Zanzibar: HAMID MAHMOUD HAMID.

High Court: Its headquarters are at Dar es Salaam but it holds regular sessions in all Regions. It consists of a Jaji Kiongozi and 29 Judges.

Jaji Kiongozi: BARNABAS SAMATTA.

District Courts: These are situated in each district and are presided over by either a Resident Magistrate or District Magistrate. They have limited jurisdiction and there is a right of appeal to the High Court.

Primary Courts: These are established in every district and are presided over by Primary Court Magistrates. They have limited jurisdiction and there is a right of appeal to the District Courts and then to the High Court.

Attorney-General: ANDREW CHENGE.

Director of Public Prosecutions: KULWA MASSABA.

People's Courts were established in Zanzibar in 1970. Magistrates are elected by the people and have two assistants each. Under the Zanzibar Constitution, which came into force in January 1985, defence lawyers and the right of appeal, abolished in 1970, were reintroduced.

Religion

ISLAM

Islam is the religion of about 98% of the population in Zanzibar and of about one-third of the mainland population. A large proportion of the Asian community is Isma'ili.

Ismalia Provincial Church: POB 460, Dar es Salaam.

National Muslim Council of Tanzania: POB 21422, Dar es Salaam; tel. (51) 34934; f. 1969; supervises Islamic affairs on the mainland only; Chair. Sheikh HEMED BIN JUMA BIN HEMED; Exec. Sec. Alhaj MUHAMMAD MTULIA.

Supreme Muslim Council: Zanzibar; f. 1991; supervises Islamic affairs in Zanzibar.

Wakf and Trust Commission: POB 4092, Zanzibar; tel. (54) 30853; f. 1980; Islamic affairs; Exec. Sec. YUSUF ABDULRAHMAN MUHAMMAD.

CHRISTIANITY

In 1993 it was estimated that about one-half of the mainland population professed Christianity.

Jumuiya ya Kikristo Tanzania (Christian Council of Tanzania): Church House, POB 1454, Dodoma; tel. (61) 21204; fax (61) 24445; f. 1934; Chair. (acting) Most Rev. JOHN ACLAND RAMADHANI (Archbishop of the Anglican Church); Gen. Sec. ANGETILE YESAYA MUSOMBA.

The Anglican Communion

Anglicans are adherents of the Church of the Province of Tanzania, comprising 16 dioceses. There were an estimated 647,000 members in 1985.

Archbishop of the Province of Tanzania and Bishop of Zanzibar and Tanga: Most Rev. JOHN ACLAND RAMADHANI, POB 35, Korogwe.

Provincial Secretary: Rev. MKUNGA MTINGELE, POB 899, Dodoma; tel. (61) 21437; fax (61) 24265.

Greek Orthodox

Archbishop of East Africa: NICADEMUS of IRINOUPOULIS (resident in Nairobi, Kenya); jurisdiction covers Kenya, Uganda and Tanzania.

Lutheran

Evangelical Lutheran Church in Tanzania: POB 3033, Arusha; tel. (57) 8855; telex 42054; fax (57) 8858; 1.5m. mems; Presiding Bishop Rt Rev. Dr SAMSON MUSHEMBA (acting); Exec. Sec. AMANI MWENEGOHA.

The Roman Catholic Church

Tanzania comprises four archdioceses and 25 dioceses. There were an estimated 7,354,860 adherents at 31 December 1995.

Tanzania Episcopal Conference: Catholic Secretariat, Mansfield St, POB 2133, Dar es Salaam; tel. (51) 50309; telex 41989; f. 1980; Pres. Rt Rev. JUSTIN TETEMU SAMBA, Bishop of Musoma.

Archbishop of Dar es Salaam: Most Rev. POLYCARP PENGO, Archbishop's House, POB 167, Dar es Salaam; tel. (51) 22031; fax (51) 850941.

Archbishop of Mwanza: Most Rev. ANTHONY MAYALA, Archbishop's House, POB 1421, Mwanza; tel. and fax (68) 41616.

Archbishop of Songea: Most Rev. NORBERT WENDELIN MTEGA, Archbishop's House, POB 152, Songea; tel. (635) 2004; telex 40036; fax (635) 2593.

Archbishop of Tabora: Most Rev. MARIO EPIFANIO ABDALLAH MGULUNDE, Archbishop's House, Private Bag, PO Tabora; tel. (62) 2329; telex 47306; fax (62) 4000.

Other Christian Churches

Baptist Mission of Tanzania: POB 9414, Dar es Salaam; tel. (51) 170130; telex 41014; fax (51) 170127; f. 1956; Admin. FRANK PEVEY.

Christian Missions in Many Lands (Tanzania): German Branch; POB 34, Tunduru, Ruvuma Region; f. 1957; Gen. Sec. KARLGERHARD WARTH.

Moravian Church: POB 377, Mbeya; 113,656 mems; Gen. Sec. Rev. SHADRACK MWAKASEGE.

Pentecostal Church: POB 34, Kahama.

Presbyterian Church: POB 2510, Dar es Salaam; tel. (51) 29075.

BAHÁ'Í FAITH

National Spiritual Assembly: POB 585, Dar es Salaam; tel. (51) 21173; mems resident in 2,301 localities.

OTHER RELIGIONS

Many people follow traditional beliefs. There are also some Hindu communities.

The Press

NEWSPAPERS

Daily

Daily News: POB 9033, Dar es Salaam; tel. (51) 110165; telex 41071; fax (51) 112881; f. 1972; govt-owned; Man. Editor CHARLES RAJABU; circ. 50,000.

Kipanga: POB 199, Zanzibar; Swahili; publ. by Information and Broadcasting Services.

Shaba: Dar es Salaam; independent; Editor YASIN SADIKI.

Uhuru: POB 9221, Dar es Salaam; tel. (51) 865377; telex 41239; fax (51) 862974; f. 1961; official publ. of CCM; Swahili; Man. Editor YAHYA BUZARAGI; circ. 100,000.

Weekly

Business Times: POB 71439, Dar es Salaam; tel. (51) 38901; telex 41996; independent; English; Editor B. PALELA; circ. 15,000.

The Express: POB 20588, Dar es Salaam; tel. (51) 110165; telex 41071; independent; English; Editor PASCAL SHIJA; circ. 20,000.

Gazette of the United Republic: POB 9142, Dar es Salaam; tel. (51) 31817; telex 41419; official announcements; Editor H. HAJI; circ. 6,000.

Government Gazette: POB 261, Zanzibar; f. 1964; official announcements.

Mfanyakazi (The Worker): POB 15359, Dar es Salaam; tel. (51) 26111; telex 41205; Swahili; trade union publ.; Editor HAMIDU NZOWA; circ. 100,000.

Mwananchi: POB 20588, Dar es Salaam; tel. (51) 33013; Swahili; circ. 13,593.

Mzalendo: POB 9221, Dar es Salaam; tel. (51) 865377; telex 41239; fax (51) 862974; f. 1972; publ. by CCM; Swahili; Man. Editor YAHYA BUZARAGI; circ. 115,000.

Sunday News: POB 9033, Dar es Salaam; tel. (51) 116072; telex 41071; f. 1954; govt-owned; Man. Editor CHARLES RAJABU; circ. 60,000.

PERIODICALS

The African Review: POB 35042, Dar es Salaam; tel. (51) 43500; 2 a year; journal of African politics, development and international affairs; publ. by the Dept of Political Science, Univ. of Dar es Salaam; Chief Editor Dr. C. GASARASI; circ. 1,000.

Eastern African Law Review: POB 35093, Dar es Salaam; tel. (51) 43254; f. 1967; 2 a year; Chief Editor Dr N. N. N. NDITI; circ. 1,000.

Elimu Haina Mwisho: POB 1986, Mwanza; monthly; circ. 45,000.

Habari za Washirika: POB 2567, Dar es Salaam; tel. (51) 23346; telex 41809; monthly; publ. by Co-operative Union of Tanzania; Editor H. V. N. CHIBULUNJE; circ. 40,000.

Jenga: POB 2669, Dar es Salaam; tel. (51) 113618; telex 41068; fax (51) 113618; journal of the National Development Corpn; circ. 2,000.

Kiongozi (The Leader): POB 9400, Dar es Salaam; tel. (51) 29505; f. 1950; fortnightly; Swahili; Roman Catholic; Editor ROBERT MFUGALE; circ. 33,500.

Kweupe: POB 222, Zanzibar; weekly; Swahili; publ. by Information and Broadcasting Services.

Mbioni: POB 9193, Dar es Salaam; English; publ. monthly by the political education college, Kivukoni College; circ. 4,000.

Mlezi (The Educator): POB 41, Peramiho; tel. 30; f. 1970; every 2 months; Editor Fr GEROLD RUPPER; circ. 8,000.

Mwenge (Firebrand): POB 1, Peramiho; tel. 30; f. 1937; monthly; Editor JOHN P. MBONDE; circ. 10,000.

Nchi Yetu (Our Country): POB 9142, Dar es Salaam; tel. (51) 110200; telex 41419; f. 1964; govt publ.; monthly; Swahili; circ. 50,000.

Nuru: POB 1893, Zanzibar; tel. (54) 32353; fax (54) 33457; f. 1992; bi-monthly; official publ. of Zanzibar Govt; circ. 8,000.

Safina: POB 21422, Dar es Salaam; tel. (51) 34934; publ. by National Muslim Council of Tanzania; Editor YASSIN SADIK; circ. 10,000.

Sauti Ya Jimbo: POB 899, Dodoma; tel. (61) 21437; fax (61) 24265; quarterly; Swahili; Anglican diocesan, provincial and world church news.

Sikiliza: POB 635, Morogoro; tel. (56) 3338; fax (56) 4374; quarterly; Seventh-day Adventist; Editor MEL H. M. MATINYI; circ. 100,000.

Taamuli: POB 35042, Dar es Salaam; tel. (51) 43500; 2 a year; journal of political science; publ. by the Dept of Political Science, Univ. of Dar es Salaam; circ. 1,000.

Tantravel: POB 2485, Dar es Salaam; tel. (51) 111244; fax (51) 116420; quarterly; publ. by Tanzania Tourist Board; Editor STEPHEN H. FISHER.

Tanzania Education Journal: POB 9121, Dar es Salaam; tel. (51) 27211; telex 41742; f. 1984; 3 a year; publ. by Institute of Education, Ministry of Education and Culture; circ. 8,000.

Tanzania Trade Currents: POB 5402, Dar es Salaam; tel. (51) 117752; telex 41408; fax (51) 115623; bimonthly; publ. by Board of External Trade; circ. 2,000.

Uhuru na Amani: POB 3033, Arusha; tel. (57) 3221; telex 42054; fax (57) 8858; quarterly; Swahili; publ. by Evangelical Lutheran Church in Tanzania; Editor ELIZABETH LOBULU; circ. 15,000.

Ukulima wa Kisasa (Modern Farming): POB 2308, Dar es Salaam; tel. (51) 22335; fax (51) 113260; f. 1955; bimonthly; Swahili; publ. by Ministry of Agriculture and Co-operatives; Editor E. M. K. SABUNI; circ. 15,000.

Wela: POB 180, Dodoma; Swahili.

NEWS AGENCIES

SHIHATA: 304 Nkomo Rd, POB 4755, Dar es Salaam; tel. (51) 29311; telex 41080; f. 1981; Dir ABDULLA NGORORO.

Foreign Bureaux

Inter Press Service (IPS) (Italy): 304 Nkomo Rd, POB 4755, Dar es Salaam; tel. (51) 29311; telex 41080; Chief Correspondent PAUL CHINTOWA.

Rossiyskoye Informatsionnoye Agentstvo—Novosti (RIA—Novosti) (Russia): POB 2271, Dar es Salaam; tel. (51) 23897; telex 41095; Dir ANATOLII TKACHENKO.

Xinhua (New China) News Agency: 72 Upanga Rd, POB 2682, Dar es Salaam; tel. (51) 23967; telex 41563; Correspondent HUAI CHENGBO.

Reuters (UK) is also represented in Tanzania.

Publishers

Central Tanganyika Press: POB 1129, Dodoma; tel. (61) 304180; fax (61) 24565; f. 1954; religious; Man. Canon JAMES LIFA .

Dar es Salaam University Press: POB 35182, Dar es Salaam; tel. (51) 43137; fax (51) 43023; e-mail director@dup.udsm.ac.tz; f. 1981; educational, academic and cultural texts in Swahili and English; Dir N. G. MWITTA.

Eastern Africa Publications Ltd: POB 1002 Arusha; tel. (57) 3176; telex 42121; f. 1978; general and school textbooks; Gen. Man. ABDULLAH SAIWAAD.

Inland Publishers: POB 125, Mwanza; tel. (68) 500398; general non-fiction, religion, in Kiswahili and English; Dir ADDISON TANNER.

Oxford University Press: Maktaba Rd, POB 5299, Dar es Salaam; tel. (51) 29209; f. 1969; Man. LUCIUS M. THONYA.

Tanzania Publishing House: 47 Samora Machel Ave, POB 2138, Dar es Salaam; tel. (51) 32164; telex 41325; f. 1966; educational and general books in Swahili and English.

Government Publishing House

Government Printer: POB 9124, Dar es Salaam; tel. (51) 20291; telex 41631; Dir JONAS OFORO.

Radio and Television

According to estimates by UNESCO, there were 740,000 radio receivers in use in Tanzania and 60,000 television receivers in use in Zanzibar in 1994. There is no television service on the mainland.

RADIO

Radio One: Dar es Salaam; Dir REGINALD MENGI.

Radio Tanzania: POB 9191, Dar es Salaam; tel. (51) 860760; telex 41201; f. 1951; domestic services in Swahili; external services in English; Dir (vacant).

Radio Tumaini (Hope): 1 Bridge St, POB 9916, Dar es Salaam; tel. (51) 117307; fax (51) 112594; e-mail tumaini@maf.org; broadcasts in Swahili within Dar es Salaam; operated by the Roman Catholic Church; broadcasts on religious, social and economic issues; Dir Fr JEAN-FRANÇOIS GALTIER.

Sauti Ya Tanzania Zanzibar (The Voice of Tanzania Zanzibar): POB 1178, Zanzibar; tel. (54) 31088; telex 57207; f. 1951; broadcasts in Swahili on three wavelengths; Dir YUSSEF OMAR SHUNDA.

TELEVISION

Television Zanzibar: POB 314, Zanzibar; tel. (54) 32816; telex 57200; f. 1973; colour service; Dir JUMA SIMBA.

Finance

(cap. = capital; res = reserves; dep. = deposits; m. = million; br. = branch; amounts in Tanzanian shillings)

BANKING

Central Bank

Bank of Tanzania (Benki Kuu Ya Tanzania): 10 Mirambo St, POB 2939, Dar es Salaam; tel. (51) 21291; telex 41024; fax (51) 37485; f. 1966; bank of issue; cap. and res 19,612.2m., dep. 105,806 (June 1992); Gov. and Chair. Dr IDRIS RASHID; Dep. Gov. N. N. KITOMARI.

Principal Banks

Co-operative and Rural Development Bank (CRDB): Azikiwe St, POB 268, Dar es Salaam; tel. (51) 113181; telex 41643; fax (51) 26518; f. 1984; provides commercial banking services and loans for rural development; 51% govt-owned, 30% owned by Co-operative Union of Tanzania Ltd (Washirika), 19% by Bank of Tanzania; transfer pending to private ownership; cap. 1,678m. (June 1993), dep. 1,822m. (June 1987); Chair. PIUS B. NGEZE; 20 regional and 25 dist. offices, 8 brs.

Eurafrican Bank Tanzania Ltd: cnr Kivukoni Front and Ohio St, POB 3054, Dar es Salaam; tel. (51) 111229; telex 81001; fax (51) 113740; f. 1994; 30% owned by Banque Belgolaise SA (Belgium); other shareholders: International Finance Corpn (20%), PROPARCO (10%), Tanzania Development Finance Co (9%), UB Holdings BV (5%), Afrimex (5%), others (21%); cap. 1,444m. (Dec. 1994); Chair. FULGENCE KAZAURA; Man. Dir LOUIS L. VIEILLEDENT.

The National Bank of Commerce (NBC): NBC House, POB 1863, Dar es Salaam; tel. (51) 116528; telex 41581; fax (51) 41581; f. 1967; state-owned; reorg. into three banking units pending in 1997; cap. and res 37,439m. (Sept. 1996), dep. 382,000m. (Dec. 1995); Man. Dir DONALD KAMORI; 145 brs.

People's Bank of Zanzibar Ltd (PBZ): Gizenga St, POB 1173, Forodhani, Zanzibar; tel. (54) 31118; telex 57365; fax (54) 31121; f. 1966; controlled by Zanzibar Govt; cap. 16m. (June 1991); Chair. MOHAMED ABOUD; Gen. Man. N. S. NASSOR.

Stanbic Bank Tanzania Ltd: Sukari House, cnr Ohio St/Sokaine Drive, POB 72647, Dar es Salaam; tel. (51) 112195; telex 41415; fax (51) 113742; f. 1993; wholly owned by Standard Bank Investment Corpn Ltd (South Africa); cap. and res 5,765m. (March 1996), dep. 37,195m. (Dec. 1995); Chair A. D. B. WRIGHT; Man. Dir I. J. MITCHELL.

Standard Chartered Bank Tanzania Ltd: 1st Floor, NIC Life House, cnr Ohio St/Sokoine Drive, Dar es Salaam; tel. (51) 117347; fax (51) 113775; f. 1992; wholly owned by Standard Chartered PLC (United Kingdom); cap. 1,000m. (Dec. 1993); Man. Dir Dr N. MOYO.

Tanzania Development Finance Co Ltd (TDFC): TDFL Bldg, cnr Upanga Rd/Ohio St, POB 2478, Dar es Salaam; tel. (51) 25091; telex 41153; fax (51) 116418; f. 1962; owned by the Tanzania Investment Bank, govt agencies of the Netherlands and Germany, the Commonwealth Development Corpn and the European Investment Bank; cap. and res 3,948m. (Dec. 1995); Chair. F. M. KAZAURA; Gen. Man. H. K. SENKORO.

Tanzania Investment Bank (TIB): Samora Machel Ave, POB 9373, Dar es Salaam; tel. (51) 111708; telex 41259; fax (51) 113438; f. 1970; provides finance, tech. assistance and consultancy for economic devt; 99.5% govt-owned; cap. and res 9,253m., dep. 529m. (June 1994); Chair. JUMA V. MWAPACHU; Man. Dir WILLIAM A. MLAKI.

Tanzania Postal Bank (TPB): Texco House, Pamba Rd, POB 9300, Dar es Salaam; tel. (51) 38212; telex 41663; fax (51) 32818; f. 1991; dep. 15,715.7m. (1994); Gen. Man. R. D. SWAI; 207 brs.

STOCK EXCHANGE

A stock exchange was scheduled to open in Dar es Salaam in 1997.

INSURANCE

National Insurance Corporation of Tanzania Ltd (NIC): POB 9264, Dar es Salaam; tel. (51) 113823; telex 41146; fax (51) 113403; f. 1963; nationalized 1967; all classes of insurance; Chair. Prof. J. L. KANYWANYI; Man. Dir OCTAVIAN W. TEMU; 21 brs.

Trade and Industry

CHAMBERS OF COMMERCE

Dar es Salaam Chamber of Commerce: Kelvin House, Samora Machel Ave, POB 41, Dar es Salaam; tel. (51) 21893; telex 41628; Exec. Officer I. K. MKWAWA.

Tanzania Chamber of Commerce, Industry and Agriculture: POB 9713, Dar es Salaam; tel. (51) 37370; telex 41424; fax (51) 30898; Nat. Chair. DAVID MWAIBULA.

TRADE, MARKETING AND PRODUCER ASSOCIATIONS AND BOARDS

The privatization of various nationalized industries was proceeding in 1997.

Board of External Trade (BET): POB 5402, Dar es Salaam; tel. (51) 117752; telex 41408; fax (51) 115623; f. 1978; trade and export information and promotion, market research, marketing advisory and consultancy services; Dir-Gen. MBARUK K. MWANDORO.

Board of Internal Trade (BIT): POB 883, Dar es Salaam; tel. (51) 28301; telex 41082; f. 1967 as State Trading Corpn, reorg. 1973; state-owned; supervises seven national and 21 regional trading cos; distribution of general merchandise, agricultural and industrial machinery, pharmaceuticals, foodstuffs and textiles; shipping and other transport services; Dir-Gen. J. E. MAKOYE.

Cashewnut Board of Tanzania: POB 533, Mtwara; tel. (59) 333445; telex 56134; fax (59) 333536; govt-owned; regulates the marketing, processing and export of cashews; Chair. GALUS ABEID; Gen. Man. Dr ALI F. MANDALI.

Coffee Marketing Board of Tanzania: POB 732, Moshi; telex 43088; Chair. W. KAPINGA; Gen. Man. A. M. RULEGURA.

National Coconut Development Programme: POB 6226, Dar es Salaam; tel. (51) 74606; fax (51) 75549; e-mail arim@arim.africaonline.co.tz; f. 1979 to revive coconut industry; processing and marketing via research and devt in disease and pest control, agronomy and farming systems, breeding and post-harvest technology; based at Mikocheni Agricultural Research Inst.; Project Co-ordinator PETER N. D. KABONGE.

National Milling Corporation (NMC): 74/1 Mandela/Nyerere Rd, POB 9502, Dar es Salaam; tel. (51) 860260; telex 41343; fax (51) 863817; f. 1968; stores and distributes basic foodstuffs, owns grain milling establishments and imports cereals as required; Chair. T. SIWALE; Gen. Man. VINCENT M. SEMESI.

State Mining Corporation (STAMICO): POB 4958, Dar es Salaam; tel. (51) 150243; fax (51) 150097; f. 1972; provides mineral consultancy and marketing services; engaged in contract drilling and mining; mining interests currently undergoing privatization; Dir-Gen. Augustine Y. Hangi.

State Motor Corporation: POB 1307, Dar es Salaam; telex 41152; f. 1974 to control all activities of the motor trade; sole importer of cars, tractors and lorries; Gen. Man. H. H. Iddi.

Sugar Development Corporation: Dar es Salaam; tel. (51) 112969; telex 41338; fax (51) 30598; Gen. Man. George G. Mbati.

Tanganyika Coffee Growers' Association Ltd: POB 102, Moshi.

Tanzania Cotton Lint and Seed Board: POB 9161, Dar es Salaam; tel. (51) 46139; telex 41287; fax (51) 22564; f. 1984; regulates the marketing and export of cotton lint; Gen. Man. Angelo K. Mpuya.

Tanzania Pyrethrum Board: POB 149, Iringa; f. 1960; Chair. Brig. Luhanga; CEO P. B. G. Hangaya.

Tanzania Tea Authority: POB 2663, Dar es Salaam; tel. (51) 116596; telex 41130; fax (51) 23322; Chair. J. J. Mungai; Gen. Man. M. Francis L. Shirima.

Tanzania Tobacco Board: POB 227, Mazimbu Rd, Morogoro; tel. (56) 4517; telex 55347; fax (56) 4401; Chair. S. Galinoma; CEO Hamisi Hasani Liana.

Tanzania Wood Industry Corporation: POB 9160, Dar es Salaam; Gen. Man. E. M. Mnzava.

Tea Association of Tanzania: POB 2177, Dar es Salaam; tel. (51) 22033; f. 1989; Chair. David A. Harrison; Exec. Dir David E. A. Mgwassa.

Zanzibar State Trading Corporation: POB 26, Zanzibar; tel. (54) 30272; telex 57208; fax (54) 31550; govt-controlled since 1964; sole exporter of cloves, clove stem oil, chillies, copra, copra cake, lime oil and lime juice; Gen. Man. Abdulrahman Rashid.

DEVELOPMENT CORPORATIONS

Capital Development Authority: POB 1, Dodoma; tel. (61) 24053; telex 53177; f. 1973 to develop the new capital city of Dodoma; govt-controlled; Chair. Pius Msekwa; Dir-Gen. Abdallah S. Illonga (acting).

Economic Development Commission: POB 9242, Dar es Salaam; tel. (51) 112681; telex 41641; f. 1962 to plan national economic development; state-controlled.

Investment Promotion Centre: Dar es Salaam; Dir-Gen. Sir George Kahama.

National Development Corporation: POB 2669, Dar es Salaam; tel. (51) 112893; telex 41068; fax (51) 113618; f. 1965; state-owned; cap. 21.4m. sh.; promotes progress and expansion in production and investment.

Small Industries Development Organization (SIDO): POB 2476, Dar es Salaam; tel. (51) 151945; telex 41123; fax (51) 152070; f. 1973; promotes and assists development of small-scale enterprises in public, co-operative and private sectors, aims to increase the involvement of women in small businesses; Chair. E. M. K. Msella; Dir-Gen. E. B. Toroka.

Tanzania Petroleum Development Corporation (TPDC): POB 2774, Dar es Salaam; tel. (51) 180145; fax (51) 180047; f. 1969; state-owned; overseas petroleum exploration and undertakes autonomous exploration, imports crude petroleum and distributes refined products; Man. Dir Yona Killagane.

There is also a development corporation for textiles.

INDUSTRIAL ASSOCIATION

Confederation of Tanzania Industries (CTI): POB 71783, Dar es Salaam; telex 41587; fax (51) 46752; Dir Juma Mwapachu.

MAJOR INDUSTRIAL COMPANIES

The following are some of the largest companies in terms either of capital investment or employment.

Agip (Tanzania) Ltd: cnr Msimbazi Mikunguni St, POB 9540, Dar es Salaam; tel. (51) 180110; telex 41027; fax (51) 181374; f. 1966; cap. 300m. sh.; 50% state-owned; distribution and marketing of petroleum products; Man. Dir Guido Romeo; 431 employees.

Aluminium Africa Ltd: POB 2070, Dar es Salaam; tel. (51) 863306; telex 41265; fax (51) 864690; mfrs of aluminium circles, corrugated and plain sheets, galvanized corrugated iron sheets, furniture tubes, steel billets, galvanized pipes, cold rolled steel sheets and coils, asbestos cement sheets; Chair. M. P. Chandaria.

Friendship Textile Mill Ltd: POB 20842, Dar es Salaam; telex 41387; f. 1966; wholly owned by National Textile Corpn; dyed and printed fabric mfrs; 5,400 employees.

Gapco Tanzania Ltd: Mafuta St, Kurasini, POB 9103, Dar es Salaam; tel. (51) 117225; telex 41044; fax (51) 113265; took over operations of Esso Tanzania Ltd (f. 1990); marketing of petroleum products; Man. Dir Y. G. Kotak; 61 employees.

Mwanza Textiles Ltd: POB 1344, Mwanza; tel. (068) 40466; telex 46118; f. 1966; spinners, weavers, dyers and printers of cotton; 3,901 employees.

Southern Paper Mills Co Ltd: POB 1, Mgololo; tel. (64) 2416; fax (64) 2427; mfrs of industrial and cultural paper.

Tanganyika Instant Coffee Co Ltd: POB 410, Bukoba; tel. (66) 20352; telex 58366; fax (66) 20526; mfrs and exporters of spray-dried instant coffee.

Tanganyika Packers Ltd: POB 60138, Dar es Salaam; tel. (51) 47511; telex 41333; f. 1947; govt-owned; mfrs of corned beef and other food products; 470 employees.

Tanzania Breweries Ltd: POB 9013, Dar es Salaam; tel. (51) 182787; telex 41288; fax (51) 181457; f. 1960; subsidiary of Indol (South Africa); manufacture, bottling and distribution of malt beer; Man. Dir A. B. S. Kilewo; 2,000 employees.

Tanzania Cigarette Co Ltd: POB 40114, Dar es Salaam; tel. (51) 860150; telex 41165; fax (51) 865210; f. 1975; privatized 1995; 49% state-owned; manufacture and marketing of cigarettes; Chair. and CEO Natwa Gotecha; 940 employees.

Tanzania Portland Cement Co Ltd: POB 1950, Dar es Salaam; tel. (51) 37660; telex 41401; fax (51) 116648; e-mail twiga@intafrica.com; f. 1959; jt venture; mfrs of ordinary Portland cement; capacity 520,000 metric tons per annum; Gen. Man. Uwe Jönsson; 885 employees.

Williamson Diamonds Ltd: POB 9470, Dar es Salaam; PO Mwadui, Shinyanga; tel. (68) 762960; telex 48165; fax (68) 762965; f. 1942; State Mining Corpn owns 25% of capital; diamond mining; Man. Dir J. W. B. D. Acland; 900 employees.

TRADE UNIONS

Union of Tanzania Workers (Juwata): POB 15359, Dar es Salaam; tel. (51) 26111; telex 41205; f. 1978; Sec.-Gen. Joseph C. Rwegasira; Dep. Secs-Gen. C. Manyanda (mainland Tanzania), I. M. Issa (Zanzibar); 500,000 mems (1991); comprises eight sections:

Agricultural Workers: Sec. G. P. Nyindo.

Central and Local Government and Medical Workers: Sec. R. Utukulu.

Commerce and Construction: Sec. P. O. Olum.

Communications and Transport Workers: Sec. M. E. Kaluwa.

Domestic, Hotels and General Workers: Sec. E. Kazoka.

Industrial and Mines Workers: Sec. J. V. Mwambuma.

Railway Workers: Sec. C. Sammang' Ombe.

Teachers: Sec. W. Mwenura.

Principal Unaffiliated Unions

Organization of Tanzanian Trade Unions (OTTU): Dar es Salaam; Sec.-Gen. Bruno Mpangal.

Workers' Department of Chama Cha Mapinduzi: POB 389, Vikokotoni, Zanzibar; f. 1965.

CO-OPERATIVES

There are some 1,670 primary marketing societies under the aegis of about 20 regional co-operative unions. The Co-operative Union of Tanzania is the national organization to which all unions belong.

Co-operative Union of Tanzania Ltd (Washirika): POB 2567, Dar es Salaam; tel. (51) 23346; telex 41809; f. 1962; Sec.-Gen. D. Holela; 700,000 mems.

Department of Co-operative Societies: POB 1287, Zanzibar; tel. (54) 30747; telex 57311; f. 1952; promotes formation and development of co-operative societies in Zanzibar.

Principal Societies

Bukoba Co-operative Union Ltd: POB 5, Bukoba; 74 affiliated societies; 75,000 mems.

Kilimanjaro Native Co-operative Union 1984 Ltd: POB 3032, Moshi; tel. (55) 54410; telex 43014; fax (55) 54204; f. 1984; 88 regd co-operative societies.

Nyanza Co-operative Union Ltd: POB 9, Mwanza.

Transport

RAILWAYS

Tanzania Railways Corporation (TRC): POB 468, Dar es Salaam; tel. (51) 26241; telex 41308; f. 1977 after dissolution of East African Railways; operates 2,600 km of lines within Tanzania; also operates vessels on Lakes Victoria, Tanganyika and Malawi; a major restructuring scheme was to be completed during the mid-1990s; Chair. J. V. Mwapachu; Dir-Gen. Linford Mboma.

Tanzania-Zambia Railway Authority (Tazara): POB 2834, Dar es Salaam; tel. (51) 62191; telex 41097; fax (51) 62474; jtly owned and administered by the Tanzanian and Zambian Govts; operates a 1,860-km railway link between Dar es Salaam and New Kapiri Mposhi, Zambia, of which 969 km are within Tanzania; plans to construct an additional line, linking Tanzania with the port of Mpulungu, on the Zambian shore of Lake Tanganyika, were announced in 1990; Chair. RICHARD MARIKI; Gen. Man. AYUB RITTI (acting); Regional Man. (Tanzania) H. M. TEGGISA.

ROADS

In 1995 Tanzania had an estimated 88,100 km of classified roads, of which 10,300 km were primary roads and 17,800 km were secondary roads. A 1,930-km main road links Zambia and Tanzania, and there is a road link with Rwanda. A 10-year Integrated Roads Programme, funded by international donors and co-ordinated by the World Bank, commenced in 1991: its aim was to upgrade 70% of Tanzania's trunk roads and to construct 2,828 km of roads and 205 bridges, at an estimated cost of US $650m.

The island of Zanzibar has 619 km of roads, of which 442 km are bituminized, and Pemba has 363 km, of which 130 km are bituminized.

INLAND WATERWAYS

Steamers connect with Kenya, Uganda, the Democratic Republic of the Congo (formerly Zaire), Burundi, Zambia and Malawi. A joint shipping company was formed with Burundi in 1976 to operate services on Lake Tanganyika. A rail ferry service operates on Lake Victoria between Mwanza and Port Bell.

SHIPPING

Tanzania's major harbours are at Dar es Salaam (eight deep-water berths for general cargo, three berths for container ships, eight anchorages, lighter wharf, one oil jetty for small oil tankers up to 36,000 tons, offshore mooring for oil supertankers up to 100,000 tons, one 30,000-ton automated grain terminal) and Mtwara (two deep-water berths). There are also ports at Tanga (seven anchorages and lighterage quay), Bagamoyo, Zanzibar and Pemba. A dredging of the port of Dar es Salaam to extend its capacity was scheduled to begin in March 1997.

Tanzania Harbours Authority (THA): POB 9184, Dar es Salaam; tel. (51) 110371; telex 41346; fax (51) 32066; Exec. Chair. J. K. CHANDE; Gen. Man. A. S. M. JANGUO; 3 brs.

National Shipping Agencies Co Ltd (NASACO): POB 9082, Dar es Salaam; telex 41235; f. 1973; state-owned shipping co with which all foreign shipping lines are required to deal exclusively.

Sinotaship (Chinese/Tanzanian Joint Shipping Line): POB 696, Dar es Salaam; tel. (51) 113389; telex 41127; fax (51) 113388; f. 1967; services to People's Republic of China, South East Asia, Eastern and Southern Africa, Red Sea and Mediterranean ports.

Tanzania Coastal Shipping Line Ltd: POB 9461, Dar es Salaam; tel. (51) 37034; telex 41124; fax (51) 116436; regular services to Tanzanian coastal ports; occasional special services to Zanzibar and Pemba; also tramp charter services to Kenya, Mozambique, the Persian (Arabian) Gulf, Indian Ocean islands and the Middle East; Gen. Man. RICHARD D. NZOWA.

CIVIL AVIATION

There are 53 airports and landing strips. The major international airport is at Dar es Salaam, 13 km from the city centre, and there are also international airports at Kilimanjaro and Zanzibar.

Air Tanzania Corporation: ATC House, Ohio St/Garden Ave, POB 543, Dar es Salaam; tel. (51) 110245; telex 41077; fax (51) 113114; f. 1977; operates an 18-point domestic network and international services to Africa, the Middle East and Europe; Chair. JOSEPH MUNGAI; CEO JOSEPH S. MARANDUS; Dir-Gen. MELKIZEDECK SANARE.

Air Zanzibar: POB 1784, Zanzibar; tel. (54) 32512; telex 57380; fax (54) 33098; f. 1990; operates scheduled and charter services between Zanzibar and destinations in Tanzania, Kenya and Uganda.

Alliance Air: f. 1994; jtly owned by South African Airways, Air Tanzania Corpn, Uganda Airlines Corpn and the Tanzanian and Ugandan Govts; operates regional services and intercontinental routes to Asia, the Middle East and Europe; Man. Dir CHRISTO ROODT.

New ACS Ltd: Peugeot House, 36 Upanga Rd, POB 21236, Dar es Salaam; fax (51) 37017; operates domestic and regional services; Dir MOHSIN RAHEMTULLAH.

Precisionair: POB 70770, Dar es Salaam; tel. (51) 30800; telex 41928; operates domestic and regional services.

Tanzanair: Sheraton Hotel, Dar es Salaam; tel. (51) 843131; operates domestic charter services.

Tourism

Tanzania has set aside about one-third of its land area as national parks and game and forest reserves. Other attractions for tourists include beaches and coral reefs along the Indian Ocean coast. Visitor arrivals were estimated at a record 326,000 in 1996, compared with 138,000 in 1987. Zanzibar receives about 50,000 tourists annually. Revenue from tourism totalled an estimated US $322m. in 1996.

Tanzania Tourist Board: IPS Bldg, Samora Machel Ave, POB 2485, Dar es Salaam; tel. (51) 111244; telex 41061; fax (51) 116420; e-mail ttb@unindar.gn.apc.org; state-owned; supervises the development and promotion of tourism; Man. Dir CREDO SINYANGWE.

Tanzania Wildlife Corporation: POB 1144, Arusha; tel. (57) 8830; fax (57) 8239; organizes safaris; also exports and deals in live animals, birds and game-skin products; Gen. Man. DAVID S. BABU.

Zanzibar Tourist Corporation: POB 216, Zanzibar; tel. (54) 32344; telex 57144; fax (54) 33430; f. 1985; operates tours and hotel services; Gen. Man. ALPHONCE KATEMA.

Defence

In August 1996 the total armed forces numbered 34,600, of whom an estimated 30,000 were in the army, 1,000 in the navy and 3,600 in the air force. Paramilitary forces comprise a 1,400-strong Police Field Force and an 80,000-strong reservist Citizens' Militia. The total strength of the armed forces was scheduled to be reduced to 25,000 by the end of 1996.

Defence Expenditure: Budgeted at 49,000m. shillings in 1996.

Commander-in-Chief of the Armed Forces: President BENJAMIN WILLIAM MKAPA.

Head of the People's Defence Forces: Lt-Gen. G. F. SAYORE.

Education

Education at primary level is officially compulsory and provided free of charge. In secondary schools a government-stipulated fee is paid: from January 1995 this was 8,000 shillings per year for day pupils at state-owned schools and 50,000–60,000 shillings per year for day pupils at private schools. Villages and districts are encouraged to build their own schools with government assistance. Almost all primary schools are government-owned. Universal primary education was introduced in 1977, and was made compulsory by the 1988 Education Act. Primary education begins at seven years of age and lasts for seven years. Secondary education, beginning at the age of 14, lasts for a further six years, comprising a first cycle of four years and a second of two years. As a proportion of the school-age population, total enrolment at primary and secondary schools rose from 22% in 1970 to 57% in 1980, but was equivalent to only 44% in 1993. Enrolment at primary schools in 1993 included 70% of children in the relevant age-group (males 71%; females 69%). Secondary enrolment in that year was equivalent to only 5% of children in the appropriate age-group (males 6%; females 5%). In 1993 there were 3,736,734 primary pupils and some 180,899 pupils attending secondary schools. There is a university at Dar es Salaam. Tanzania also has an agricultural university at Morogoro, and a number of vocational training centres and technical colleges. In 1995, according to UNESCO estimates, adult illiteracy averaged 32.2% (males 20.6%; females 43.2%), compared with a rate of some 67% in 1967. Education was allocated 4.0% of expenditure by the central government in 1991/92.

Bibliography

Angelsen, A., and Fjeldstad, O.-H. *Land Reforms and Land Degradation in Tanzania: Alternative Economic Approaches.* Bergen, CMI, 1995.

Bagachwa, M.S.D. *Financial Integration and Development in Sub-Saharan Africa: A Study of Informal Finance in Tanzania.* London, Overseas Development Institute, 1995.

(Ed.). *Poverty Alleviation in Tanzania: Recent Research Issues.* Dar es Salaam University Press, 1994.

Bagachwa, M. S. D., and Mbelle, A. V. Y. (Eds). *Economic Policy under a Multiparty System in Tanzania.* Dar es Salaam University Press, 1993.

Bennett, Norman R. *A History of the Arab State of Zanzibar.* London, Methuen, 1978.

Bienen, H. *Tanzania: Party Transformation and Economic Development.* Princeton, NJ, 1967; expanded edn, 1970.

Bryceson, D. F. *Liberalizing Tanzania's Food Trade: Public and Private Faces of Urban Marketing Policy 1939–1988.* Geneva, UN Research Institute for Social Development; Tanzania, Mkuki na Nyota, 1993.

Buchert, L. *Education in the Development of Tanzania, 1919–1990.* London, James Currey Publishers, 1994.

Campbell, H., and Stein, H. *Tanzania and the IMF: The Dynamics of Liberalization.* Boulder, CO, Westview Press, 1990.

Cliffe, L., and Saul, J. *Tanzania Socialism—Politics and Policies: An Interdisciplinary Reader.* 2 vols. Nairobi, East African Publishing House, 1972.

Creighton, C., and Omazi, C. K. (Eds). *Gender, Family and Household in Tanzania.* Brookfield, VT, Ashgate Publishing, 1995.

Drysdale, H. *Dancing with the Dead: A Journey through Zanzibar and Madagascar.* London, Hamish Hamilton, 1991.

Dumont, R., *Tanzanian Agriculture after the Arusha Declaration.* Dar es Salaam, Ministry of Economic Affairs and Development Planning, 1969.

Elgstrom, O. *Foreign Aid Negotiations: The Swedish-Tanzanian Aid Dialogue.* Aldershot, Avebury, 1992.

Feierman, S. *Peasant Intellectuals: Anthropology and History in Tanzania.* Madison, University of Wisconsin Press, 1990.

Forster, P. G., and Maghimbi, S. (Eds). *The Tanzanian Peasantry: Economy in Crisis.* Aldershot, Avebury, 1992.

Forster, P., and Maghimbi, S. *The Tanzanian Peasantry: Further Strides.* Brookfield, VT, Ashgate Publishing, 1995.

Gibbon, P. (Ed.). *Liberalized Development in Tanzania: Studies on Accumulation Processes and Local Institutions.* Uppsala, Nordiska Afrikainstitutet, 1995.

Havenik, K. J. *Tanzania: The Limits to Development From Above.* Uppsala, SIAS, 1993.

Hayward, M. F. *Elections in Independent Africa.* Boulder, CO, Westview Pres, 1987.

Hyden, G. *Beyond Ujamaa in Tanzania: Underdevelopment and an Uncaptured Peasantry.* London, Heinemann Educational, 1980.

Iliffe, J. *Tanganyika under German Rule, 1905–12.* Cambridge University Press, 1969.

A Modern History of Tanganyika. Cambridge University Press, 1979.

Kahama, C. G., Maliyamkono, L. and Wells, S. *The Challenge for Tanzania's Economy.* London, James Currey Publishers, 1986.

Kaniki, M. H. Y. (Ed.). *Tanzania under Colonial Rule.* London, Longman, 1980.

Kim, K. S., Mabele, R. B., and Schultheis, E. R. (Eds). *Papers on the Political Economy of Tanzania.* London, Heinemann Educational, 1979.

Kimambo, I. N. *Penetration and Protest in Tanzania: The Impact of the World Economy on the Pare, 1860–1960.* London, James Currey Publishers, 1991.

Lange, S. *From Nation-Building to Popular Culture: The Modernization of Performance in Tanzania.* Bergen, CMI, 1995.

Legum, C., and Mmari, G. (Eds). *Mwalimu: The Influence of Nyerere.* London, James Currey Publishers, 1995.

Liebenow, J. G. *Colonial Rule and Political Development in Tanzania.* Nairobi, East African Publishing House, 1972.

Lofchie, M. *Zanzibar: Background to Revolution.* Princeton, New Jersey; London, Oxford University Press, 1965.

Maddox, G., Giblin, J. L., and Kimambo, I. N. (Eds). *Custodians of the Land: Environment and Hunger in Tanzanian History.* London, James Currey Publishers, 1995; Athens, OH, Ohio University Press, 1996.

McHenry, D. E. Jr. *Limited Choices: The Political Struggle for Socialism in Tanzania.* Boulder, CO, Lynne Rienner Publishers, 1994.

Martin, D.-C. *Tanzanie, L'invention d'une culture politique.* Paris, Karthala, 1988.

Mmuya, M. (Ed.). *Functional Dimensions of the Democratization Process: Tanzania and Kenya.* Dar es Salaam University Press, 1994.

Mmuya, M., and Chaligha, A. *Political Parties and Democracy in Tanzania.* Dar es Salaam University Press, 1994.

Mukandala, R., and Othman, H. *Liberalization and Politics: The 1990 Election in Tanzania.* Dar es Salaam University Press, 1994.

Nyerere, J. K. *Freedom and Socialism, a selection from writings and speeches, 1965–67.* Dar es Salaam and London, Oxford University Press, 1968; contains the Arusha Declaration and subsequent policy statements.

Ofcansky, T. P., and Yeager, R. *Historical Dictionary of Tanzania.* Lanham, MD, Scarecrow Press, 1997.

Othman, H. I. B., and Okema, M. *Tanzania: Democracy in Transition.* Dar es Salaam University Press, 1990.

Pratt, C. *The Critical Phase in Tanzania: 1945–1968.* Oxford University Press, 1980.

Rosch, P. G. *Der Prozess der Strukturanpassung in Tanzania.* Hamburg, Institut für Afrika-Kunde, 1995.

Sheriff, A. *Slaves, Spices and Ivory in Zanzibar: Integration of an East African Commercial Empire into the World Economy, 1770–1873.* London, James Currey Publishers, 1987.

Shivji, I. G. *Law, State and the Working Class in Tanzania.* London, James Currey Publishers, 1986.

Skarstein, R., and Wangwe, S. M. *Industrial Development in Tanzania.* Stockholm, Scandinavian Institute for African Studies, 1986.

Stephens, H. W. *The Political Transformation of Tanganyika: 1920–67.* New York, Praeger; London, Pall Mall, 1968.

Stoecker, H. (Ed.) *German Imperialism in Africa.* London, Hurst Humanities, 1986.

von Freyhold, M. *Ujamaa Villages in Tanzania.* London, Heinemann Educational, 1979.

World Bank. *Tanzania: the Challenge of Reforms: Growth, Incomes and Welfare.* Washington, DC, World Bank, 1996.

Yeager, R. *Tanzania: An African Experiment.* 2nd Edn. Boulder, CO, Westview Press, 1989.

TOGO

Physical and Social Geography

R. J. HARRISON CHURCH

The Togolese Republic, a small state of western Africa (bordered to the west by Ghana, to the east by Benin and to the north by Burkina Faso), covers an area of 56,785 sq km (21,925 sq miles), and comprises the eastern two-thirds of the former German colony of Togoland. From a coastline of 56 km on the Gulf of Guinea, Togo extends inland for about 540 km. In January 1988 the population was officially estimated to be 3,296,000, giving a density of 58.0 persons per sq km, higher than average for this part of Africa. According to official estimates, the population numbered 3,928,000, giving a density of 69.2 persons per sq km, at mid-1994. Northern Togo is more ethnically diverse than the south, where the Ewe predominate. Among the northern peoples the Kabiye are notable for their terracing of hillsides and intensive agriculture.

The coast, lagoons, blocked estuaries and Terre de Barre regions are identical to those of Benin, but calcium phosphate, the only commercially-exploited mineral resource, is quarried north-east of Lake Togo. Pre-Cambrian rocks with rather siliceous soils occur northward, in the Mono tableland and in the Togo-Atacora mountains. The latter are, however, still well wooded and planted with coffee and cocoa. To the north is the Oti plateau, with infertile Primary sandstones, in which water is rare and deep down. On the northern border are granite areas, remote but densely inhabited, as in neighbouring Ghana and Burkina Faso. Togo's climate is similar to that of Benin, except that Togo's coastal area is even drier: Lomé has an average annual rainfall of 782 mm. Thus Togo, though smaller in area than Benin, is physically, as well as economically, more varied than its eastern neighbour.

Recent History

PIERRE ENGLEBERT

Revised for this edition by the Editor

Togoland, of which the Togolese Republic was formerly a part, was annexed by Germany in 1894, occupied by Anglo-French forces in 1914, and proclaimed a League of Nations mandate in 1919. France became responsible for the larger eastern section, while the United Kingdom administered the west. The partition divided the homeland of the Ewe people, who inhabit the southern part of the territory, and this has been a continuing source of internal friction. Ewe demands for reunification were intensified during the UN trusteeship system which took effect after the Second World War. In May 1956 a UN-supervised plebiscite in British Togoland produced, despite Ewe opposition, majority support for a merger with the neighbouring territory of the Gold Coast, then a British colony. The region accordingly became part of the independent state of Ghana in the following year. In October of that year, in a separate plebiscite, French Togoland voted to become an autonomous republic within the French Community.

Political life in French Togoland was dominated by the Comité de l'unité togolaise, led by Sylvanus Olympio, and the Parti togolais du progrès, led by Nicolas Grunitzky, Olympio's brother-in-law. In 1956 Grunitzky became prime minister in the first autonomous government, but, following a UN-supervised election in 1958, he was succeeded by Olympio, a campaigner for Ewe reunification. Following independence on 27 April 1960, Olympio became president.

EYADÉMA TAKES POWER

In January 1963 the Olympio regime, which had become increasingly authoritarian, was overthrown, and Olympio killed, in a military coup led by Sgt (later Gen.) Etienne (Gnassingbe) Eyadéma, a Kabiye from the north of the country, who invited Grunitzky to return from exile as head of state. Subsequent efforts by Grunitzky to achieve constitutional multi-party government proved unsuccessful, and in January 1967 Eyadéma, by then army chief of staff, assumed power. Political activity remained effectively suspended until the creation in 1969 of the Rassemblement du peuple togolais (RPT), which served as a means of integrating the army into political life. Plots to overthrow Eyadéma were suppressed in 1970 and again in 1977, when the exiled sons of ex-president Olympio were accused of organizing a mercenary invasion. From the mid-1970s, Eyadéma began to implement a campaign for cultural 'authenticity', in which foreign personal and place names were abandoned and the two main national languages, Ewe and Kabiye, were to replace French as the language of education.

The introduction of a new constitution in 1980 made little difference to Eyadéma's style of government, or to the furtherance of the personality cult surrounding the president. Although Olympio's supporters maintained an exiled Mouvement togolais pour la démocratie (MTD), by the mid-1980s Eyadéma's rule had entered a more tranquil phase politically, with the focus of national attention shifting to the country's economic problems. At national elections in March 1985 voters were able to choose between more than one candidate for each seat. A total of 216 candidates, all of whom were members of the RPT, contested the 77 seats in the national assembly. The RPT remained the only legal political party, but in May of that year the constitution was amended to allow deputies to the national assembly to be elected by direct universal suffrage without prior approval by the RPT.

POLITICAL REPRESSION

An unprecedented wave of bomb attacks in Lomé in August 1985 led to the arrest, in September and October, of at least 15 people accused of involvement in the bombings and of distributing subversive literature. When one of the detainees died shortly following his arrest, the exiled MTD claimed that the government had used the pretext of the bomb attacks to unleash a 'wave of repression'. The Togolese government accused the Ghanaian authorities of complicity in the attacks, prompting allegations in the Ghanaian press that the explosions had in fact been perpetrated by members of Eyadéma's entourage. In 1986 attempts by the human rights organization, Amnesty International, to investigate allegations of torture of political prisoners, were blocked by the government. However, a visiting delegation of French jurists concluded that torture was being used, and condemned the conditions under which political prisoners were being detained. Many of those who had been arrested following the August 1985 bombings were released under a presidential amnesty in January 1986.

In September 1986 19 people were detained following an apparent attempt by what was described as a 'terrorist commando unit' to occupy the Lomé military barracks (which was also the president's home), the RPT headquarters and the national radio station. About 13 people, including six civilians, were reported to have been killed during the attack. The government subsequently accused both Ghana and Burkina Faso of involvement in the alleged coup attempt. The border with Ghana was closed agreement, and 250 French paratroopers were sent briefly to Togo (in accordance with a previously unpublished defence). Some 350 Zairean troops were also dispatched to Togo. In December Eyadéma was re-elected as president for a further seven-year term, reportedly winning 99.95% of votes cast. At trials in the same month 13 people were sentenced to death, and 14 to life imprisonment, for complicity in the events in September. Gilchrist Olympio, son of the former president and the alleged instigator of the attack, was one of three people sentenced to death *in absentia*.

In the aftermath of the alleged coup attempt Eyadéma combined measures to increase his personal security with reforms aimed at apparent political democratization. In October 1987 a national human rights commission, the Commission nationale des droits de l'homme (CNDH), was established, while most of the death sentences imposed in the previous December were commuted. Amnesties were also extended to common-law offenders. However, the appointment, in December 1988, of the former joint chief of staff of the security forces, Brig.-Gen. (later Maj.-Gen.) Yao Mawulikplimi Amegi, to the position of minister of the interior and security, was regarded as indicative of Eyadéma's preoccupation with national security.

At elections to the national assembly in March 1990, 230 candidates, all of whom declared their allegiance to the RPT, contested the assembly's 77 seats. Only 18 members of the outgoing legislature were re-elected.

By the end of the 1980s demands for political change were increasingly apparent. In December 1989 two Togolese dissidents, who were allegedly members of an opposition movement, the Convention démocratique des peuples africains du Togo (CDPA–T), were expelled from Côte d'Ivoire, after having reportedly been found in possession of tracts denouncing Eyadéma and advocating political pluralism. In August of that year Eyadéma stated that he would assent to a multi-party system, if that were the will of the people. However, in May 1990 a national congress of the RPT unanimously rejected the possibility of a return to multi-party politics. The congress agreed that more freedom of expression within Togo was needed, and it was also decided that proposals made by Eyadéma for the separation of the functions of the party and state would be examined at a later date. In late July, during an official visit to the USA, Eyadéma indicated that the process of democratization in Togo would inevitably include the development of a two-party system.

The establishment, in August 1990, of the independent Ligue togolaise des droits de l'homme (LTDH) was widely regarded as a direct challenge to the integrity of the official CNDH. In the same month 13 people, allegedly members of the CDPA–T and of an unofficial students' organization, were arrested on suspicion of distributing anti-government tracts. Eleven of the detainees were later released, after they had admitted to having been 'manipulated and used by external organizations hostile to Togo', while two others, Logo Dossouvi and Doglo Agbelenko, remained in detention. An official inquiry was ordered to investigate allegations of the torture of the detainees: the CNDH found that four detainees, including Dossouvi and Agbelenko, had been subjected to torture while in custody. In early October Dossouvi and Agbelenko were convicted of distributing defamatory tracts and inciting the army to revolt, and were sentenced to five years' imprisonment. Violent demonstrations erupted in Lomé during the trial, leading to four deaths. The government claimed that the unrest had been orchestrated by 'international machinations', and many of the 170 people who were arrested in connection with the violence were said to be foreigners. In mid-October Dossouvi and Agbelenko were granted presidential pardons, and clemency was subsequently extended to all those who had been detained during the riots.

THE COLLAPSE OF LEGITIMACY

In October 1990 a commission was established to draft a new constitution, which, it was announced, would be submitted for approval in a national referendum in December 1991. The constitutional commission presented its draft document, which (apparently at Eyadéma's instigation) provided for the establishment of a multi-party political system, at the end of the year. In January 1991 Eyadéma declared an amnesty for all those (including exiles) who had been implicated in political offences other than the September 1986 coup attempt. The sentences of criminal offenders were also reduced, and mandatory contributions to the RPT were abolished. However, such concessions were rejected by Togo's emergent opposition, which demanded that a national conference be convened.

A boycott of classes by university students and secondary school pupils, during the first half of March 1991, provoked violent clashes between striking students and the security forces and supporters of Eyadéma. Meanwhile, several opposition movements formed a co-ordinating organization, the Front des associations pour le renouveau (FAR), to campaign for the immediate introduction of a multi-party political system. Following a meeting between Eyadéma and the leader of the FAR, Yao Agboyibo, an agreement was reached whereby Eyadéma consented to an amnesty for all political dissidents, and agreed to the legalization of political parties and to the organization of a national forum to discuss the country's political evolution.

In early April 1991 further student unrest erupted, prompted by a demonstration in Lomé by pupils at Roman Catholic mission schools in support of their teachers' demands for salary increases. Two deaths were reported following intervention by the security forces. Further deaths resulted from similar action by the security forces in Kévé (to the north-west of Lomé) to disperse a demonstration to demand Eyadéma's resignation. Violent protests broke out in the capital; all educational establishments were closed, and a night-time curfew imposed. The official endorsement, by the national assembly, of legislation regarding the general amnesty and the legalization of political parties was overshadowed by the discovery, in mid-April, of about 26 bodies in a lagoon in Lomé. Opposition allegations that the bodies were those of demonstrators who had been beaten to death by the security forces were denied by the government, which ordered the CNDH to investigate the deaths. Retrieval of the bodies provoked further protests, at which the security forces again intervened. Fearing an ethnic conflict between the Kabiye and Ewe ethnic groups, Eyadéma appealed for national unity, and announced that a new constitution would be introduced within one year, and that multi-party legislative elections would be organized. In May Eyadéma relinquished the defence portfolio to Maj.-Gen. Yao Mawulikplimi Amegi, who was succeeded at the ministry of the interior and security by Yao Komlavi (hitherto minister of the environment and tourism).

The FAR was disbanded in late April 1991, to allow for the establishment of independent political parties. Agboyibo formed his own party, the Comité d'action pour le renouveau (CAR). Numerous other movements obtained official status, and in early May 10 parties (including the CAR) announced the formation of a new political coalition, the Front de l'opposition démocratique (FOD), which was later renamed the Coalition de l'opposition démocratique (COD), to co-ordinate the activities of opposition groups in preparation for the national forum.

Negotiations between the government and the opposition, in preparation for the national forum, took place amid conditions of renewed social and labour unrest. In early June 1991 the FOD organized a widely-observed general strike, in an attempt to force Eyadéma's resignation. Shortly afterwards a rally in the capital that had been organized by the FOD was reportedly disrupted by Kabiye supporters of Eyadéma, while demonstrations in Lomé and Sokodé, in central Togo, were dispersed by the security forces. In mid-June it was announced that the government and the FOD had reached agreement regarding the mandate of what was to be known henceforth as the national conference. (The government's previous insistence that the convention be termed a national forum was widely thought to indicate its desire to limit the competence of the meeting, as sovereign national conferences elsewhere in the region, notably in Benin, had imposed radical political reforms.) The FOD subsequently suspended its industrial action. Shortly afterwards the government announced that ex-presidents Olympio and Grunitzky were to be posthumously rehabilitated. Also rehabilitated was Gilchrist Olympio, who returned to Togo in early July to participate in the national conference.

The national conference was opened, after some delay, on 8 July 1991. It was attended by 700–1,000 delegates (representing, among others, the organs of state and the country's newly legalized political organizations, together with workers', students' and religious leaders). A resolution by the conference, in mid-July, to declare itself sovereign, to suspend the constitution and to dissolve the national assembly prompted the government to boycott the proceedings for one week. Upon their return to the conference, government representatives stated that they did not consider such resolutions binding. In late July the conference resolved to 'freeze' the assets of the RPT and the Confédération nationale des travailleurs du Togo (CNTT—which had been reported in April to have terminated its links with the RPT), and to create a commission to examine the financial affairs of these organizations, together with an authority to control the finances of state and parastatal organizations, with the aim of preventing the transfer of state funds abroad. Exit visa requirements were imposed on foreign travel by government ministers.

Meanwhile, renewed allegations had emerged concerning violations of human rights by the Eyadéma regime. In mid-July 1991 the CNDH concluded that the security forces had been responsible for the deaths of at least 20 of those whose bodies had been discovered in mid-April. In late July the national conference heard allegations that a 'death camp' had been established in northern Togo in 1983, and that among those who had died as a result of maltreatment was Antoine Meatchi (Grunitzky's vice-president following the 1963 coup). At the same time, Komla Alipui, hitherto minister of the economy and finance, deplored such violations of human rights, and also condemned the Eyadéma government's record of economic planning and its conduct of financial affairs.

On 26 August 1991 Eyadéma, deprived by the national conference of most of his powers, abruptly suspended the conference. However, opposition delegates defied the order, and proclaimed a provisional government under the leadership of Joseph Kokou Koffigoh, a prominent lawyer and the head of the LTDH. The conference also voted to dissolve the RPT and to form an interim legislature, the Haut conseil de la république (HCR). Fearing renewed unrest, Eyadéma hastily signed a decree confirming Koffigoh as transitional prime minister; the conference ended on 28 August.

Koffigoh's council of ministers, appointed in early September 1991, was composed mainly of technocrats who had not previously held political office. The prime minister assumed personal responsibility for defence, and it was envisaged that Eyadéma would remain only nominally head of the military. However, the events of subsequent months were to show that the Kabiye-dominated armed forces looked to Eyadéma for their command. On 1 October a group of soldiers, apparently dissatisfied at the failure of the HCR to sanction pay increases for the lower ranks of the armed forces, seized control of the offices of the state broadcasting service in Lomé. The troops claimed to have dissolved the HCR, and demanded the resignations of Koffigoh and his government, but returned to barracks on Eyadéma's orders. Five people were killed, and about 50 injured, during the incident. Later the same day members of the presidential guard, led by Eyadéma's half-brother, were rumoured to have staged a second rebellion. One week later presidential guards attempted unsuccessfully to kidnap Koffigoh. Although Eyadéma condemned the incident, and ordered a return to barracks, the rebels claimed to be supporters of the president. Seven deaths and more than 50 injuries were reported, as demonstrations by civilian supporters of Koffigoh degenerated into looting and violence, which was seemingly exacerbated by ethnic rivalries. Three senior armed forces officers, including the president's half-brother (whose death was subsequently reported on more than one occasion), were arrested in early November, in connection with the disturbances.

CONSTITUTIONAL TRANSITION

Work began in October 1991 on drafting the new constitution. The brief political calm ended on 26 November, when the HCR responded to attempts to convene a congress of the RPT by reaffirming the ban on the former ruling party. Clashes between supporters of Eyadéma and Koffigoh, again aggravated by inter-ethnic differences, resulted in further casualties. The military retook the broadcasting headquarters and surrounded government offices, demanding that the transitional authorities be disbanded and that Eyadéma be empowered to nominate a new prime minister. A night-time curfew was imposed, and the borders and main airport were closed. The troops returned to barracks on 30 November, and conciliation talks began. Two days later, however, the military reoccupied strategic positions in the capital, and on the following day captured the prime minister. Following negotiations between Eyadéma and Koffigoh, it was announced that a broadly-based 'government of national unity' (including, it was implied, the RPT) would be appointed. The provisonal government that was formed in late December included many members of the outgoing council of ministers, although two key portfolios were allocated to close associates of Eyadéma: Yao Komlavi again became responsible for national security, and Aboudou Assouma was appointed minister-delegate for the armed forces. Also in late December the HCR adopted a 'social contract for a peaceful transition', compiled by Koffigoh, which (among other provisions) restored legal status to the RPT. (Despite the armed forces' earlier demands, the HCR continued to function, although its members were subject to frequent harassment by the military.)

Delays in the transition process prompted sporadic outbreaks of unrest in the early part of 1992. However, the fragility of the political situation was exemplified in early May, when a failed assassination attempt on Gilchrist Olympio, in which the involvement of the armed forces was widely alleged, resulted in the death of another political leader. A subsequent investigation by the International Federation of Human Rights apparently substantiated these allegations. As a result of the unrest, Lomé was effectively paralysed by a two-day general strike, organized by independent trade unions, and some 15,000 people demonstrated in the capital to demand the resignations of Eyadéma and Koffigoh. At the end of the month it was revealed that preparations for the election of democratic institutions were incomplete, and the electoral timetable (already delayed) was abandoned. Tensions were further exacerbated by ethnic unrest involving the Kabiye and Kotokoli communities in central Togo.

Proposals for a new electoral schedule were announced later in July 1992, beginning with a constitutional referendum at the end of August. In the same month the government was reorganized (Aboudou Assouma had been dismissed in mid-June, and one minister had subsequently resigned his post). The political climate deteriorated shortly after the reshuffle, when a prominent opposition leader, Tavio Ayao Amorin, was shot and seriously wounded, and later died. Eyadéma denounced the assassination; none the less, a new opposition coalition, the Collectif de l'opposition démocratique (COD–2), comprising some 25 political organizations and trade unions, organized a widely-observed general strike in Lomé, and violent confrontations took place between protesters and the police.

Disarray among the country's political parties (estimated to number about 40 by mid-1992) contributed to the atmosphere of instability. Many opposition parties had withdrawn support for Koffigoh following what was perceived to be his 'capitulation' in late 1991, and political alliances were frequently formed and disbanded. An attempt to resolve the political crisis was made in late July 1992, when representatives of Eyadéma and of the country's eight leading political parties began a series of meetings. The negotiations made faltering progress in subsequent weeks. Confidence was undermined by an armed attack (in which the complicity of the security forces was rumoured) on a centre for the processing of electoral data, and by an assassination attempt on the minister of equipment and mines. None the less, agreement was reached on opposition access to the state-controlled media and on the extension, until 31 December, of the transitional period. In late August the HCR restored a number of important powers to the president, empowering Eyadéma to preside over the council of ministers and to represent the country abroad, and obliging the prime minister to make government appointments in consultation with the head of state. Moreover, in an important concession to Eyadéma and his supporters, the draft constitution was amended to permit members of the armed forces seeking election to the new democratic organs of state to retain their commissions.

The transitional government was dissolved on 1 September 1992, and a new electoral schedule was announced: a referendum on the new constitution was to take place later in September, local and legislative elections in October and November, and presidential elections in December. In mid-September a new transitional government was formed: Koffigoh remained as prime minister, and 10 parties were reportedly represented in the new administration, but the most influential posts (including the national defence, foreign affairs and justice portfolios) were allocated to members of the RPT. On 27 September the new constitution was approved in a referendum by 98.11% of the votes cast (the rate of participation by voters was about 66%). At the end of the month, however, it was announced that the elections were to be rescheduled yet again. In late October members of the armed forces stormed a meeting of the HCR, holding some of its members hostage and demanding that it authorize the reimbursement of contributions made to the RPT, whose assets had remained 'frozen' since 1991. Although Eyadéma stated that disciplinary measures would be taken against the men involved, the COD–2 successfully organized a general strike in protest at the incident. In November Koffigoh dismissed two ministers (both supporters of the RPT) for their conduct during the attack on the HCR, but his decision was overruled by Eyadéma. In the same month another general strike was organized by the COD–2 and the Collectif des syndicats indépendants labour movement, to support their demands for elections, the neutrality of the armed forces, the formation of a non-military 'peace force', and the bringing to justice of those responsible for the attacks on the HCR. The strike was widely observed, except in the north of Togo (where support for Eyadéma was strongest), and continued during the first half of 1993, causing considerable economic disruption.

In mid-January 1993 Eyadéma dissolved the government, but reappointed Koffigoh as prime minister. The president stated that he would appoint a new 'government of national unity', whose task would be to organize elections as soon as possible. His action provoked protests by the opposition parties, who claimed that, according to the constitution, the HCR should appoint a prime minister since the transition period had now expired. Later in the same month representatives of the French and German governments visited Togo to offer mediation in the political crisis. During their visit at least 20 people were killed when police opened fire on anti-government protesters. Thousands of Togolese (including most opposition leaders who were not already in exile) subsequently fled from Lomé, many taking refuge in Benin and Ghana. In early February discussions took place, under French and German auspices, in Colmar, France, attended by representatives of Eyadéma, the RPT, Koffigoh, the HCR and the COD–2, but these failed when the presidential delegation left after one day. The formation of a new 'crisis government' was announced shortly afterwards: eight new ministers were appointed, but supporters of Eyadéma retained the principal posts. The COD–2 declared that they now regarded Koffigoh as an obstacle to democratization, and in March COD–2 member parties, meeting in Benin, nominated a 'parallel' prime minister, Jean-Lucien Savi de Tové (the leader of the Parti des démocrates pour l'unité).

On 25 March 1993 there was an armed attack on the military camp in Lomé where Eyadéma had his residence: more than 20 people, including the deputy chief of staff of the armed forces, Col Kofi Tepe, were killed during the attack, after which about 110 members of the armed forces fled the country. The government identified Tepe as the principal military organizer of the attack, but declared that it had been instigated by Gilchrist Olympio, with assistance from the Ghanaian authorities.

In early April 1993 the government announced a new electoral timetable, beginning with the presidential election in early June. This was rejected by the opposition, which reiterated that legitimate polls could only be organized following the restoration of a national consensus. A revised schedule, formulated one month later (apparently following secret negotiations in Ouagadougou, Burkina Faso, between Togolese government representatives and members of the COD–2), was similarly rejected by the opposition. A series of bomb attacks on both government and opposition targets in the second half of May was said by the authorities to have been plotted outside Togo by persons who wished to sabotage democratization. The election was modified twice during June, and was abandoned in early July, in anticipation of renewed negotiations in Ouagadougou (talks there in mid-June had failed, when the participants failed to reach agreement on procedures for the organization of elections). In mid-July those meeting in Ouagadougou (including Eyadéma and President Compaoré of Burkina Faso, Koffigoh and members of the transitional government, representatives of the COD–2 and French and German diplomats) set 25 August as the date for the presidential poll. Agreement was reached on both the issue of security during the election campaign (the Togolese armed forces would be confined to barracks, under the supervision of a multinational military team), and also the establishment and functions of an independent national electoral commission to oversee the polling. International observers were also to be invited to monitor the elections.

However, divisions within the opposition were evident (the total number of political parties at this time exceeded 60). Gilchrist Olympio denounced the Ouagadougou accord, protesting that the government had been allowed too much control over the election process and that no provision had been made for the return of refugees in advance of the elections (international human rights organizations estimated the number of people who had fled Togo in recent months at 200,000, most of whom were sheltering in Benin and Ghana, while Olympio put the total number at about 350,000). Shortly after the conclusion of the Ouagadougou agreement, Edem Kodjo, the leader of the Union togolaise pour la démocratie (UTD), was chosen as the presidential candidate of the COD–2. Four other opposition candidates, including Yao Agboyibo and Gilchrist Olympio, were selected to contest the election. However, the supreme court disallowed Olympio's candidature, on a legal technicality. Meanwhile, the authorities revealed that a warrant for Olympio's arrest, in connection with the March 1993 attack on Eyadéma's residence, had been issued in May. Olympio challenged the legality of the warrant and refused to return from Ghana in the absence of a guarantee of his security by the Togolese authorities.

As the election campaign gained momentum during August 1993, opposition demands, supported by the national electoral commission, that the election be postponed intensified, and Kodjo (widely regarded as Eyadéma's strongest challenger) and Agboyibo effectively withdrew from the election. The COD–2 and Olympio's Union des forces de changement appealed to their supporters to boycott the poll, and US and German observers withdrew from Togo, alleging irregularities in the compilation of voting lists and in electoral procedures. As voting began, on 25 August, the government announced that a coup attempt, plotted by Togolese dissidents in Ghana, had been detected on the eve of polling. Shortly after the poll, it was revealed that at least 15 opposition supporters, arrested in connection with attacks on polling stations in Lomé, had died while in detention (the authorities alleged that the prisoners had been intentionally poisoned by their associates). According to official election results, published in late August, Eyadéma was re-elected president by 96.49% of voters. Only about 36% of the electorate voted in the election.

THE FOURTH REPUBLIC

In September 1993 the COD–2 announced that it would only participate in the forthcoming legislative election if the electoral register was revised, equitable access to state media granted and international observers present. The government subsequently agreed to revise the electoral registers. Eyadéma was sworn in as first president of the fourth republic on 24 September. In November the government announced that the legislative election would take place in two stages in December and January, but both the national electoral commission and the opposition parties declared these dates to be premature, and, following consultation with the international monitoring committee, the government agreed to postpone the first round of the election to 23 January 1994.

In early January 1994 an armed attack on Eyadéma's official residence was reported. As in March 1993, the government alleged that the attack had been organized by Gilchrist Olympio, with Ghanaian support: this was denied both by Olympio and by the Ghanaian government. A total of 67 people were officially reported to have died in the violence. It was claimed by the human rights organization, Amnesty International, that at least 48 summary executions were carried out by the armed forces. On the day after the disturbances the government announced that the election would now take place on 6 February and 20 February 1994, rejecting requests by the CAR and the UTD for a further postponement.

In the legislative election of February 1994, 347 candidates contested 81 seats in the assemblée nationale. Despite the murder of a newly-elected CAR candidate after the first round, and some incidents of violence at polling stations during the second round, international observers expressed themselves satisfied with the conduct of the election. The final result revealed a narrow victory for the opposition, with the CAR winning 36 seats and the UTD seven; the RPT obtained 35 seats and two smaller pro-Eyadéma parties won three. During March Eyadéma consulted the main opposition parties on the formation of a new government. In late March the CAR and the UTD reached agreement on the terms of their alliance and jointly proposed the candidacy of Agboyibo for prime minister (a stipulation of the agreement was that the candidate for prime minister should be a member of the CAR). In rulings issued in late March and early April the supreme court declared the results of the legislative election invalid in three constituencies (in which the CAR had won two seats and the UTD one) and ordered by-elections. The CAR and the UTD refused to attend the new assemblée nationale, in protest at the annulment. In April Eyadéma nominated Kodjo as prime minister. Kodjo accepted the appointment despite assertions by the CAR that to do so was a violation of the agreement of March 1994 between the two parties on which their parliamentary majority was based. The CAR subsequently announced that it would not participate in an administration formed by Kodjo. On 25 April Kodjo took office, citing his priorities as national reconciliation, the return of refugees, economic recovery, and the integration of the armed forces into democratic life. It was not until late May that he announced the formation of his government, which comprised eight members of the RPT and other pro-Eyadéma parties, three members of the UTD, and eight independents. Kodjo maintained, however, that this was an 'interim' government and that, should the CAR decide to join the government, there would be a reorganization of the cabinet to accommodate it. Shortly beforehand, the CAR had announced (in response to the postponement of the parliamentary by-elections, originally scheduled for May) that it was to end its boycott of the assemblée nationale.

In October 1994 the government announced that an attempted terrorist attack on installations of the Office togolais des phosphates had been thwarted by the security forces. It was alleged that an armed group had infiltrated from Ghana with the intention of destroying a transformer at the phosphate mines in Hahotoé, some 50 km north-east of the capital. The group claimed to have been recruited by Togolese political exiles living in Ghana.

In November 1994 the CAR again withdrew from the assemblée nationale, and indicated that it would return only when agreement had been reached with the government on the conduct of the by-elections, ordered by the supreme court in April and due to be held on 27 November. The CAR's demands included the establishment of a joint electoral commission, the reinforcement of security measures and the entrustment of the electoral process to an independent body, such as the constitutional court. In the light of the dispute, on 25 November the by-elections were postponed. Later that month the CAR informed the speaker of the assemblée nationale that it would resume participation in the legislature only when the government had shown a commitment to reaching a general consensus on the organization of free and fair elections.

In December 1994 the assemblée nationale declared a general amnesty covering all persons who had been charged with political offences committed before 15 December 1994, including those alleged to have participated in attacks on the presidential residence in March 1993 and January 1994. The release of those held in detention for such offences began later in December.

In March 1995 Amnesty International expressed concern at the lack of effective measures for ensuring the observance of human rights in Togo, and criticized the absence of independent legal inquiry into abuses committed during the period of political transition in 1991-94. In the following month the CAR announced that it was to end its boycott of the assemblée nationale, following an agreement between the government and the major opposition parties. The terms of the agreement provided for the government and the legislative opposition to have equal representation on national, district and local electoral commissions. In June, following five weeks of negotiations with employers and trade unions, the government agreed to pay, by the end of 1996, wage arrears owing to civil servants that had been accumulated during the nine-month general strike of 1992-93. The amount of arrears was estimated to total 13,500m. francs CFA. In August 1995 the CAR, whose return to the assemblée nationale had been postponed pending the resolution of issues relating to the electoral process, officially resumed participation in the legislature. The CAR's eventual return had also been prompted by the approval, in early August, of legislation concerning the independence of the judiciary.

In November 1995 Kodjo implemented a major reorganization of the cabinet, increasing the number of portfolios from 21 to 23. The CAR, which was not represented in the new government, expressed concern at the level of representation of supporters of Eyadéma; of the 13 new members, 11 (including the ministers responsible for foreign affairs and defence) were considered to be close allies of the president.

In March 1996 the German government issued a formal protest and demanded prompt clarification from the Togolese government, following an incident in which a member of staff at the German embassy was shot dead by a military unit at a road-block in the capital.

In April 1996 a legislative deputy of the CAR resigned from the party, thus reducing the CAR's representation in the assemblée nationale to 33 seats. In June the by-elections that had been postponed in November 1994 were finally rescheduled for August 1996. The CAR subsequently issued demands, dismissed by the government, that the by-elections be organized on the basis of the Ouagadougou accord of July 1993, specifically that the polls be conducted in the presence of an international monitoring committee. In May 1996 the CAR announced its withdrawal from the by-elections, owing to the government's failure to adhere to the terms of the Ouagadougou accord. In the same month a legislative deputy of the UTD was dismissed from the party, thus reducing the UTD's representation in the assemblée nationale to five seats.

At by-elections to the assemblée nationale held in August 1996, conducted in the presence of 22 international observers, the RPT won an absolute majority in the three constituencies being contested. As a result of the by-elections, the RPT and its political allies were able to command a legislative majority, thus forcing the resignation of the Kodjo administration. On leaving office, Kodjo criticized the lack of support that his administration had received for the establishment of the institutions enshrined in the constitution of the fourth republic, and in particular the failure to establish a constitutional court, as a result of which constitutional issues were still referred to the supreme court. On 20 August Eyadéma appointed Kwassi Klutse as prime minister. Klutse, a technocrat and the minister of planning and territorial development in the outgoing administration, cited the recovery of the national economy as the priority of the new government. Both the CAR and the UTD refused to participate in a proposed government of national union, and consequently the new cabinet, appointed in late August, comprised, almost exclusively, supporters of Eyadéma.

In October 1996 a further CAR deputy left the party, transferring his allegiance to the RPT. In the following month the Union pour la justice et la démocratie, which held two seats in the legislature, announced that it was to merge with the RPT, thus giving the RPT 41 seats and an overall majority. In December the remaining 32 deputies of the CAR boycotted a vote on the law governing the constitutional court. The CAR abandoned the session following the legislature's rejection of its proposal that the constitutional court be empowered to rule on disputes arising from legislative and presidential elections. In the absence of the CAR and the UTD, which also boycotted the vote, the government's legislation was unanimously approved. The seven members of the new constitutional court were installed in February 1997.

In May 1997 the CAR organized a demonstration in the capital to protest against what it alleged to be manoeuvres by the RPT aimed at stifling the political activities of the opposition. The RPT responded by staging a demonstration on the following day which, according to its organizers, was attended by some 100,000 government supporters.

FOREIGN RELATIONS

The issue of Ewe reunification has at times led to difficult relations with Ghana. President Nkrumah assisted Togo in its campaign for independence but with the intention of integrating Togo into Ghana. When this objective failed, Nkrumah subjected Togo to constant harassments, through trade embargoes and border closures. Relations improved after the assassination of Olympio, and Nkrumah was the first to recognize the new government. There have been periodic rises in tension, notably following Ghana's decision in 1969 to expel alien workers without permits; also over the problems of smuggling and subversive activity by exiles of each country resident in the other. Ghana has continued to be suspicious of campaigns for Ewe reunification initiated in Togo, which have been tolerated but not supported by Eyadéma. Relations between the two countries deteriorated as Togo's political crisis of the early 1990s intensified, and the presence of Togolese opposition leaders in Ghana prompted renewed suspicion in Lomé that the Ghanaian authorities were supporting elements that might seek to destabilize the Eyadéma regime. In January 1993 the Ghanaian government criticized Eyadéma and expressed fears of a breakdown in law and order in Togo. In March of that year, and again in January 1994, the Rawlings administration in Ghana refuted allegations made by the Togolese government of Ghanaian complicity in armed attacks on Eyadéma's residence (see above). Relations were also strained by the presence of Togolese refugees (numbering at least 100,000 in mid-1993) in Ghana. By late 1994 relations with Ghana had improved considerably. In November full diplomatic relations, suspended since 1982, were formally resumed with the appointment of a Ghanaian ambassador to Togo. In the following month Togo's border with Ghana, which had been closed since January 1994, was reopened. In July 1995, following talks between Eyadéma and Rawlings (held in Kara, northern Togo), a communiqué was issued reiterating both countries' adherence to a protocol of non-aggression between ECOWAS member states. In addition, agreement was reached providing for the reactivation of the Ghana-Togo joint commission for economic, social and technical co-operation and the Ghana-Togo border demarcation commission.

Relations with Benin have similarly been bedevilled by the problems of smuggling and political activities by exiles, and the border between the two countries has frequently been closed. In March 1993 the Eyadéma regime criticized the government of Benin for allowing Togolese opposition leaders to meet on Beninois territory. Some 100,000 Togolese refugees were believed to be sheltering in Benin in mid-1993. In November 1994, following a visit by the president of Benin in the previous month, the Benin-Togo border demarcation commission, which had been dormant since 1978, resumed its activities. In August 1995 Togo signed an accord with the UN High Commissioner for Refugees, providing for the introduction of a programme of voluntary repatriation of Togolese exiles from Ghana and Benin. By December 1996 some 40,500 Togolese exiles, of an estimated total of 48,000, had reportedly been repatriated from Ghana.

Dependence on France increased under Grunitzky. Co-operation agreements with France were concluded in 1963 and Togo became a member of the Conseil de l'entente (and of the now defunct Organisation commune africaine et malgache) in 1966. Although generally anxious to maintain good relations with France, Eyadéma has tended to avoid too close identification with the French sphere of influence in Africa. While not accepting full membership of the francophone west African Communauté économique de l'Afrique de l'ouest, Togo has observer status and is a full member of the defence pact.

During the latter part of 1991 the transitional government, faced with opposition from the armed forces, appealed to France for military assistance. The initial response was the dispatch, in early November, of 10 military instructors to the French embassy in Lomé, and at the end of the month, as the situation in Togo deteriorated, two army units were deployed in neighbouring Benin. Despite appeals, both within Togo and elsewhere in the region, for direct French action in support of Koffigoh's administration, France restricted its intervention to the transfer into Togo of about 30 French troops, ostensibly to strengthen security around the French embassy. None the less, it was widely believed that the French military presence in Benin had constrained Eyadéma's response to his supporters' actions, and that without the threat of direct intervention by French units the president would have dismissed the civilian government.

With the escalation of the political crisis in Togo in 1992–93, many of Togo's external creditors, including France, Germany, the USA and the EC, attempted (with limited success) to exert political pressure on Eyadéma and Koffigoh by withdrawing all but the most urgent economic assistance. The victory of centre-right parties in the French legislative elections of March 1993 prompted speculation that the new government of Edouard Balladur might display a more conciliatory attitude towards the Eyadéma regime. In June 1994 France announced that it was to resume civil co-operation with Togo. By March 1995 the majority of Togo's external creditors had resumed co-operation.

Economy

EDITH HODGKINSON

Revised for this edition by ANDREW MANLEY

At independence in 1960, Togo's economy, compared with those of most of its neighbours, was relatively advanced. Moreover, the country possessed the potential for sustained economic growth. In recent years, however, the economy has declined to such an extent that Togo is now classified as a least developed country, and is experiencing difficulties in servicing a foreign debt acquired in earlier, more prosperous, times.

EARLY ECONOMIC EXPANSION

German Togoland, like the neighbouring Gold Coast, achieved rapid economic advances by 1914. At the outbreak of the First World War, the proportion of Togoland's gross domestic product (GDP) accounted for by exports was already almost the same as in 1970. Tax revenue represented a relatively large share of GDP, thus making it possible to finance the country's infrastructure without resort to German capital and to achieve the highest level of educational development in Africa. The economic advance was attributable primarily to the rapid development of the plantation economy in the south of the country. There were both German plantations (13,000 ha in 1914) and native-owned holdings, which the colonial power had helped to develop on modern capitalist lines with private ownership of the land. During the First World War the Togolese managers on German plantations appropriated the land, thus pre-empting its seizure by the British and French.

POST-WAR DEVELOPMENT

During the period 1920–40 the economy of Togoland remained virtually stagnant. Indeed, in 1949 the volume of exports was still much the same as it had been during German times; but the post-war period, up to independence, was one of relatively swift development. The volume of exports more than doubled in 1949–54. This was mainly attributable to greatly increased investment in infrastructure. This second phase of Togo's development was characterized by a rise in the population growth rate and by increasing urbanization.

Rates of population growth and urbanization have continued at a high level. The population was estimated at 3,928,000 at mid-1994 (representing a fairly high population density of 69.2 per sq km), with the capital, Lomé, having an estimated 450,000 inhabitants. According to World Bank estimates, annual population growth in 1985–95 averaged 3.0%. In most years there is seasonal migration, of around 100,000 Togolese annually, to neighbouring Ghana. The escalation of the political crisis in late 1992 prompted large numbers of Togolese to flee to Ghana and Benin, and by mid-1993 the population was estimated to have fallen by more than 400,000. Thousands of refugees have since returned.

In 1995, according to estimates by the World Bank, Togo's gross national product (GNP), measured at average 1993–95 prices, was US $1,266m., equivalent to $310 per head. Economic growth, which had eased off in the early 1960s (only just keeping pace with population, compared with 1948–60's average annual growth of 5%), accelerated again, to an average of 4.5% per year in 1965–80, as development programmes took effect. However, the severe economic problems which beset the country during the 1980s (see below) reduced GDP growth to an average of 0.5% per year in 1981–90. Compared with the 6.5% average annual growth target set in the 1981–85 Development Plan, GDP is estimated to have fallen each year in 1981–83 because of drought, the slump in phosphate production, the recession in neighbouring economies, and measures of economic adjustment in response to these adverse trends. The end of the drought in 1984 and the upturn in phosphate production caused GDP to increase by 5.5% in that year and by 3.1% in 1985, but growth rates declined again in the following two years, to 2.2% and 1.5% respectively, as a result of lower international prices for the country's major commodities and the impact of fiscal austerity on development expenditure and on overall demand. However, there was an upturn, to 4.7%, in 1988, reflecting increases in both production of and international prices for phosphates and an easing in the financing constraint following the rescheduling of the public debt (see below). The rate of growth declined to 3.2% in 1989, and GDP fell by 1% in 1990, as a result of the decline in the volume of cash crops and other primary commodities, in conjunction with the decline in world prices for Togo's export commodities. Although the three-year programme of economic reform that was adopted in 1989 (with support from IMF funds) projected average real GDP growth of more than 4% annually, GDP continued to contract: a decline of an estimated 5% in 1991 was followed by falls of 10.5% in 1992 and 13.7% in 1993, as political unrest disrupted agricultural distribution and phosphate production. In January 1994 the franc CFA underwent a devaluation, and in mid-year the government adopted a comprehensive adjustment strategy. The resultant increase in economic activity led to real GDP growth of 12.9% in that year, although this represented little more than economic recovery from the disastrous downturns of 1992–93. Further GDP growth of 7.2% was recorded in 1995, owing largely to improved performances in the mining and manufacturing sectors. According to the IMF, GDP growth was 6% in 1996, and growth of 5.8% was envisaged for 1997.

AGRICULTURE

Agriculture is by far the dominant economic activity, accounting for an estimated 32.0% of GDP and for some 61.9% of the working population in 1995. However, after rising rapidly in the mid-1960s, agricultural output grew slowly in the 1970s, and the drought of 1981–83 resulted in an average annual decline in output of 1% in the following five years. In non-drought years Togo is self-sufficient in basic foodstuffs. According to estimates issued by the Banque centrale des états de l'Afrique, the yam crop totalled 411,100 metric tons in 1995/96, while production of manioc was 466,800 tons, maize 225,100 tons, millet and sorghum 191,100 tons and rice 39,700 tons. Food supplies are supplemented by fishing, but Togo's narrow coastline constrains activity, which is mainly artisanal. None the less, modern vessels are used, although the total catch—13,723 tons in 1995—is insufficient to satisfy domestic demand. The livestock sector contributes to—but does not satisfy—the local meat and dairy market. Livestock numbers in 1995, according to FAO figures, were 1.2m. sheep, 1.9m. goats, 850,000 pigs and 248,000 cattle.

Production in the cash-crop sector has, on the whole, recovered after the decline recorded in the mid-1970s. The most important contribution has come from cotton, which is now the country's principal export crop. After falling to negligible levels in the second half of the 1970s, output of seed cotton rose strongly, reaching 100,247 tons in 1990/91, reflecting increases in the area under cultivation. However, owing to political disruption, output in 1991/92 declined to an estimated 90,000 tons, contracting further to 65,000 tons in 1992/93, before recovering in 1993/94 to 84,500 tons. Favourable growing conditions and strong world prices resulted in expanding production in 1994/95, when output reached 125,700 tons. In 1995/96 production declined to 102,000 tons, amid fears of soil depletion. Coffee output fluctuated widely in the 1980s, reaching a low of 2,701 tons in 1983/84, but recovered strongly in 1989/90, reaching a record 16,100 tons (reflecting the improvement in climatic conditions, the impact of replanting programmes, and higher producer prices). Production then declined, by 40%, to 9,653 tons, in 1990/91 before recovering to an estimated 12,000 tons in 1991/92. In 1995, according to FAO estimates, coffee production totalled 16,000 tons. Groundnut production has also fluctuated markedly, from a peak of 19,561 tons in 1986/87 to about 9,000 tons in 1990/91. In 1995, according to FAO estimates, groundnut production totalled 32,000 tons. Similarly, output of shea-nuts (karité nuts) varies enormously, although the bulk goes to subsistence consumption and therefore is not recorded. From a peak of 28,200 tons in 1971/72, output of cocoa beans has since declined, and by the late 1980s averaged less than 9,000 tons a year. The decline in output, which stood at only 7,278 tons in 1990/91 (and totalled 5,000 tons in 1995, according to FAO estimates), was due largely to the ageing of cocoa bushes, which were consequently producing lower yields. (It must also be borne in mind that production figures are greatly distorted by the smuggling of cocoa from Ghana.)

The government's agricultural development programme has received substantial foreign support, including grants from the European Development Fund (EDF), and France's Fonds d'aide et de coopération (FAC) for the development of coffee, cocoa and cotton production in the south, the most developed area. The World Bank has also provided US $9.5m. for this area, and credits have come from the International Development Association (IDA) for rural development projects, intended to increase the area under cultivation and to introduce cotton, maize, sorghum and groundnut crops. It is also planned to develop irrigated agriculture—rice, sugar cane, fruits and vegetables. The Anié sugar complex, in central Togo, was inaugurated in 1987. The complex has the capacity to refine 60,000 tons of sugar cane annually. Other projects intend to increase self-sufficiency in animal protein by encouraging the rearing of cattle, pigs and poultry.

MINING AND POWER

Traditionally the main stimulus to Togo's exports—and overall economic growth—has come from phosphate mining. Phosphates were discovered in Togo in 1952, and exports began in 1961. Togo's phosphate deposits are the richest in the world, with a mineral content of 81%. Reserves of first-grade ore are estimated at 260m. tons, while there are more than 1,000m. tons of carbon phosphates, which, although of a lower quality, have the advantage of a significantly lower cadmium content (see below). The country now ranks fifth among the world's producers of calcium phosphates, and they currently account for almost half of Togo's export receipts (48.5% in 1991). Exports of phosphates from the reserves at Akoupamé and Hahoté by the Compagnie togolaise des mines du Bénin (CTMB), subsequently merged into the Office togolais des phosphates (OTP), rose from 199,000 tons in 1962 to 2.6m. tons in 1974. In 1974 the government nationalized the company, in which it previously had a 35% holding. When, in the following year, prices slumped, owing to the energy crisis and a fall in world demand, Togolese phosphate rock's high quality made it more difficult to place on the market, and production fell to 1.1m. tons. Demand subsequently recovered, and production was around 2.9m. tons per year in 1977–80. Additional treatment and recovery plant costing 4,000m. francs CFA, financed by Arab and French interests, brought total annual capacity to 3.6m. tons in 1980, but the downturn in demand for Togo's relatively high-priced ore in 1981 caused the extra capacity to be closed in that year, and production declined to only 2.01m. tons in 1982. There was a subsequent recovery in foreign demand, and output reached 3.36m. tons in 1989, stimulated by the strength of international prices for phosphates; however, production declined by 27% in 1990, to just 2.44m. tons. Following a recovery to 2.96m. tons in 1991, output declined once more, to 2.03m. tons in 1992. With the mine out of operation for much of the first half of 1993, owing to the general strike, output was reduced to only 1.79m. tons in that year. Output recovered in 1994 to 2.12m. tons. However, in that year the OTP was reported to have incurred large debts and prospects of recovery were hindered by unfavourable conditions on the international market for phosphates. It is planned to exploit lower-grade phosphate deposits if the phosphoric acid plant proceeds (see below). However, the future development of the phosphate-mining sector may be adversely affected by concerns regarding the high cadmium content of Togolese phosphates. The European Union (EU), which has banned the agricultural use of certain categories of phosphate fertilizers, is to provide the OTP with funds for the research and development of sources of phosphates with a lower cadmium content. After lengthy negotiations with creditors, the government agreed to open the OTP to private ownership, and in 1997 a 38% share in the company's capital was offered for sale.

Togo also possesses extensive limestone reserves (some 200m. tons), utilization of which began in 1981 at a large-scale cement plant run by Ciments de l'Afrique de l'ouest (CIMAO), with an output of 600,000 tons of clinker (one-half of capacity). It was hoped to increase annual output to 1.8m. tons during the 1981–85 Plan period. The governments of Ghana and Côte d'Ivoire, as well as French, British and Canadian interests, participated in the scheme, which cost US $285m. Credits were provided by the World Bank and the European Investment Bank (EIB), but the programme was cut back in 1984 and CIMAO went into liquidation in March 1989. However, the construction industry revived in the following two years, with continued work on the Nangbeto dam (see below) and on offices of the regional central bank and the Economic Community of West African States. Cement production has therefore continued under the Société des ciments du Togo (CIMTOGO), a parastatal organization operated in co-operation with Norwegian interests, with an annual capacity of 780,000 tons. Exploitation of reserves of marble at Gnaoulou and Pagola (estimated at 20m. tons) began in 1970 by the Société togolaise de marbrerie (now restructured and operating, with Norwegian participation, as the Nouvelle société togolaise de marbrerie et de matériaux). Exploration for petroleum and uranium was in progress in the early 1990s. Mining and quarrying accounted for 5.4% of GDP in 1994. The GDP of the mining sector increased by an annual average of 3.4% in 1982–91, but declined by an estimated annual average of 3.2% in 1991–95; the IMF estimated an increase of 17.9% in 1995.

Electricity was, in the past, generated mainly at a thermal plant in Lomé and a small hydroelectric installation at Kpalimé, built with Yugoslav assistance. Togo formerly derived electric power principally from the Akosombo hydroelectric installation in Ghana. Beginning in 1988, however, supplies were enhanced by the 65 MW hydroelectric plant at Nangbeto, on the Mono river, constructed in co-operation with Benin. The project, which cost US $144m., received financial support from multilateral agencies (the IDA, the African Development Bank, the Arab Bank for Economic Development in Africa, and the OPEC Fund for International Development) and from Kuwait, France, the Federal Republic of Germany and Canada. The plant has a maximum capacity of 150m. kWh, and also provides irrigation for 43,000 ha of land. Total electricity generation was 334m. kWh in 1994.

INDUSTRY

The manufacturing sector is small and relatively little developed, accounting for an estimated 9.9% of GDP in 1995, but it has shown some expansion in recent years. Manufacturing was, in the past, centred on the processing of agricultural commodities (palm oil extraction, coffee roasting, cassava flour milling, and cotton ginning) and import substitution of consumer goods—textiles, footwear, beverages, confectionery, salt and tyres. During the 1970s, however, major investments were made in a number of heavy industrial schemes, including the CIMAO cement plant (see above) and a petroleum refinery at Lomé with an annual capacity of 250,000 tons, which closed in 1983. A steel works (Société nationale de sidérurgie) with a capacity of 20,000 tons per year started production in 1979. An integrated textile mill, which cost 10,000m. francs CFA and has a capacity of 24,000 tons per year, began operations at Kara in 1981, and the expansion of domestic cotton production led to the establishment of two further plants, at Notse and Atakpamé. A new cotton-ginning plant was inaugurated at Talo in January 1991, with a total capacity of 50,000 tons of seed cotton per year. Total investment, of 3,000m. francs CFA, was provided by France and the Banque ouest-africaine de développement. New palm oil mills have been installed, including one with EC funds equivalent to ECU 5.4m., to complement the development of plantations. On the whole, however, the industrialization programme of the late 1970s proved to be an expensive failure, and large-scale projects have not featured in subsequent plans. Meanwhile, to improve efficiency in the economy, the government has sold or leased a number of state enterprises to private interests. By the end of 1990 the assets of 30 companies had been transferred to private ownership, and 18 others were intended for privatization. Meanwhile, it was expected that manufacturing aimed at export markets would be stimulated by the establishment of a free-trade zone at Lomé, which was inaugurated in 1990. By the end of 1991 15 companies had invested some 56,000m. francs CFA in the zone; most of these, however, suspended operations during 1992–93, owing to the political upheaval. In 1994 the government resumed the promotion of its free-trade zone project, and by mid-1996 some 30 companies were operating in the zone, with a further 20 companies in the process of being established.

TRANSPORT AND TOURISM

Communications are made difficult by the country's long, narrow shape. However, the road network (7,519 km in 1995, of which 2,376 km were paved) is currently being improved, with aid from the EDF, IDA and FAC. The 1981–85 Plan projected investment of 8,000m. francs CFA in this sector, mainly to improve the north-south highway and to develop the east-west route via Kara. Of the US $310m. scheduled for the improvement of the transport infrastructure in 1988–90, $217m. was to be devoted to the rehabilitation and maintenance of the road network. The railways, with 537 km of track, are generally in need of modernization, and two lines, to Palimé and Aného, have been closed to passenger traffic. The port of Lomé handled about 2m. tons of freight per year in the late 1980s and early 1990s, following an increase in its capacity at the beginning of the 1980s, which afforded new facilities for handling minerals and for fishing. However, hopes of attracting a greater volume of regional transit trade from land-locked west African countries such as Mali, Niger, and Burkina Faso have been disappointed because of the recession in these economies in recent years. During the Sahel drought of the early 1980s Lomé served as a major shipment point for food aid, and work began there in 1986 on the first bulk grain trans-shipping facility in west Africa. The level of freight handled declined to 1.8m. tons in 1992 and to 1.1m. tons in 1993, as the political crisis in Togo resulted in the diversion of a large proportion of transit trade to Benin. The level of freight handled stood at 0.9m. tons in 1994, but recovered to 1.3m. tons in 1995. In that year the Banque ouest-africaine de développement approved a loan of 5,000m. francs CFA to help finance the rehabilitation of the infrastructure at Lomé port. There are international airports at Tokoin, near Lomé, and at Niamtougou, in the north of the country, as well as several smaller airfields.

Tourism, formerly a major source of foreign exchange, suffered from the economic downturn of the 1980s and, above all, from the political crisis of the early 1990s. Visitor numbers, which reached a record 143,000 in 1982, declined to a low of 24,000 in 1993, but recovered to 44,000 in 1994 and were estimated to have reached some 80,000 by 1996. The privatization of most state-owned hotels was initiated in early 1997, following studies into the restructuring of the sector by the government and the World Bank. In addition to recreational tourism, efforts have been made to promote Togo as an international conference centre, for which the country is reasonably well equipped.

DEVELOPMENT AND FINANCE

In the past, Togo's official investment targets have been attained or even exceeded, but in the late 1970s, as the result of a deterioration in the country's economic situation (owing mainly to a decline in international prices for phosphates), development spending had to be reduced as part of the government's austerity programme. The 1976–80 Plan provided for total investment of 250,600m. francs CFA, of which just over one-third was projected to come from foreign official sources. However, expenditure fell considerably short of these projections and averaged around three-quarters of the original target.

The 1981–85 Plan projected investment, under a priority programme, at the same level as in 1976–80, which meant a reduction of about one-third in real terms, with infrastructure receiving 74,100m. francs CFA, industry 73,400m. and rural development 66,600m. A supplementary 'optional' programme provided for an additional 117,500m. francs CFA in development spending. Foreign aid was expected to cover two-thirds of the programme. In view of Togo's payments difficulties (see below), this latter projection was over-optimistic, while the downturn in phosphate production since 1980, and the budget cuts (see below), meant that the development programme was behind schedule. Reflecting the influence of the IMF, the six-year Development Plan for 1985–90 involved relatively modest targets: an average rise in real GNP of 1.9% per year, and an absence of new investment projects in favour of the maintenance and rehabilitation of existing ones. Proposed spending on national projects was 360,800m. francs CFA (with infrastructure allocated 53% of the total, and rural development 35%), while a further 19,200m. francs CFA was allocated to small-scale local projects, and 88,000m. to support the balance of payments and budgetary operations. Total planned spending was 468,000m. francs CFA, almost 90% of which, it was hoped, was to be covered by foreign sources. By the late 1980s, however, funding at this level had not been procured, rendering the investment target unattainable.

One of the major objectives of the Development Plans has been the strengthening of the government's revenue position. Togo was able to finance a rising capital programme in the 1970s because of the strong expansion in budget revenue, largely owing to higher receipts from phosphate mining and indirect taxation. However, the worsening in the payments situation since 1978 (see below) necessitated recourse to IMF capital support, which required, in turn, an economic stabilization programme (begun in 1979), including a reduction in the growth of spending to an average 5% per year in 1979–81, with development spending down sharply in each year. Fiscal austerity continued in 1982–84, with increases in taxation, further constraints on development spending (which remained well below the rate required under the 1981–85 Plan), and a five-year 'freeze' on public-sector salaries. These trends were scheduled to continue throughout the 1985–90 Plan period, with current spending projected to fall in real terms, as the rise in spending on salaries was kept below the rate of inflation at the same time as tax receipts increased. However, with the ending of the public-sector salary 'freeze' in January 1987, and the deterioration in state marketing finances as a result of lower commodity prices and higher producer prices, the budget deficit almost doubled in 1987, to the equivalent of 6.8% of GDP. However, the proportion was more than halved in 1988, to 3.3%, as a result of higher receipts from taxation (mostly additional import duties), strict controls on current expenditure, and a sharp decline in capital spending. The deficit was little changed in 1989 and 1990, with small increases in revenue in both years, and the primary budget (excluding interest payments) was estimated to have been almost in balance in 1991. However, with the onset of political unrest and suspension of financial support by major external creditors—to put pressure on the regime to democratize—total budget receipts declined considerably, by 8% in 1992 and by 47.4% in 1993. The situation in 1993 was exacerbated by the seven-month general strike (beginning in November 1992), which directly affected both generation and collection of revenue. The government revised its budget revenue forecast for 1993 from 90,000m. francs CFA to 50,000m. francs CFA, although the eventual out-turn was as low as 38,220m. francs CFA. Budget expenditure for 1993 was revised to 93,010m. francs CFA, with the shortfall to be met by drawing on foreign reserves. With the return to work, in the second half of 1993, of civil servants, renewed expenditure on wages, which had been reduced by the general strike, had a detrimental effect on the cash flow position. However, a complete collapse of the fiscal and financial system was avoided. By March 1995 the majority of major external creditors had resumed financial co-operation. In June the government agreed to meet civil servants' claims for wage arrears that had accrued during the general strike and were estimated to total 13,500m. francs CFA. Most arrears were paid by the end of 1996. The draft budget for 1995 balanced revenue and expenditure at 149,500m. francs CFA. The increase in revenue reflected the government's intention to improve methods of tax collection. In July the government introduced value added tax on commercial operations, replacing the general business tax, primarily in order to simplify fiscal management. However, reductions in domestic and external debt arrears, undertaken following pressure from creditors, resulted in an overall budget deficit of 123,500m. francs CFA in 1995. The 1996 budget envisaged revenue of 111,908m. francs CFA and expenditure of 134,181m. francs CFA, although the eventual deficit was equivalent to 6.5% of GDP. The 1997 budget envisaged revenue of 126,020m. francs CFA and expenditure of 136,444m. francs CFA.

The government's economic programme for 1997 aimed, with the support of a US $30m. tranche of the enhanced structural adjustment facility approved by the IMF in 1994 (see below), to achieve real economic growth of about 5.8%. Inflation was to be reduced to 3.9%, from 4.6% in 1996, and the current account deficit cut to 6.6% of GDP, from 8.5% in 1996. Reforms of the tax system and tax administration were to be continued, while expenditure was to be channelled towards the health and education sectors and the rehabilitation and maintenance of infrastructure.

FOREIGN TRADE AND PAYMENTS

Togo's chronic deficit on foreign trade worsened after the mid-1970s, as export earnings declined as a proportion of import spending. Despite a continuing rise in phosphate receipts (reflecting the higher volume shipped), export earnings were depressed by adverse fluctuations in cocoa production, while the import bill was rising very rapidly (more than doubling over the period 1976–78). Foreign trade registered a record deficit of US $173.8m. in 1979, with exports financing just under two-thirds of imports. The trade deficit then narrowed substantially (and 1984 even recorded a modest surplus) as earnings from both phosphates and cocoa improved, while the level of imports was restricted by the economic adjustment programme. In 1986, with the renewed decline in international prices for Togo's export commodities, the deficit widened again, to $59.9m. It remained close to this level for the rest of the 1980s, with the impact of generally weak prices for export commodities offset by import restraint resulting from government policies directed at suppressing growth in domestic demand. The situation worsened considerably in 1992, as political disorder resulted in a decrease in exports exceeding the concurrent contraction in imports, producing a deficit of $127.7m., according to the IMF. However, these figures do not take into account smuggling, the importance of which would have increased substantially during the political unrest. According to IMF figures, the deficit declined to $111.3m. in 1993 and to $37.1m. in 1994. In that year the principal source of imports (24.0%) was France; other major suppliers were Germany, Côte d'Ivoire and the USA. The principal market for exports was Canada (which took 17.0% of Togo's exports in that year); other significant purchasers were Bolivia, Indonesia, the Philippines and France.

Since the services side of the current payments account normally shows a deficit, it is usually left to grants and loans to cover the shortfall. Togo's receipts of official development assistance (ODA) from non-communist countries and multilateral agencies have tended to be lower, and slightly less concessionary, than those of other countries in francophone west Africa. In 1986–91 the country received an annual average of US $209.4m. In 1991–95 the average declined to $168m., reflecting the impact on donor confidence of the political crisis of 1992–93. In 1991, in order to exert pressure on the Eyadéma administration to proceed towards democratic reform, France, Germany and the USA (the three leading sources of bilateral aid) suspended development aid, while military assistance from the USA and France was suspended in 1992. This contributed to a sharp deterioration in the balance of payments in 1992 and 1993, with a capital deficit of $55m. contributing to a record overall deficit of $187.5m. in 1993. In 1994 the overall deficit was reduced to $97.1m.

The steep rise in foreign borrowing in the late 1970s, stimulated by the commodity price increases which took place in preceding years, brought Togo's external debt to US $1,045m. at the end of 1980 (95.3% of total GNP in that year), of which $899m. was long-term public debt. Debt-rescheduling was necessary in 1979 and again in 1981 and 1983, as exports and GNP contracted and arrears accumulated. In 1982 Togo's reclassification by its official creditors as a least developed country resulted in the cancellation of one-sixth of its outstanding debt to creditor countries. In 1984 and 1985, however, the increase in the exchange value of the US dollar, in which much of Togo's foreign debt is denominated, kept the debt-service ratio at a high level (an estimated 27.3% of foreign earnings in 1985) despite a continued growth in the value of exports. This necessitated the conclusion of further rescheduling agreements, within the context of the austerity programme negotiated with the IMF and scheduled to be continued until the 1990s. Togo clearly could not service its debt at such rates, and further agreements were reached in 1988, under the terms of which the 'Paris Club' of Western official creditors agreed to reschedule all debts due to the end of that year over 16 years, with eight years' grace and with lower interest spreads. More rescheduling of official debt liabilities over a 12-month period followed, in 1989 (covering $76m.), 1990 ($184m.) and 1992, when relief was accorded on payments due on one-half of Togo's total external debt, with creditors taking the option either of cancelling 50% of payments due and rescheduling the remainder over 23 years, with a six-year grace period, or of reducing the interest rate payable on long-term debt so as to reduce the amount due by one-half. These agreements helped to reduce the debt-service ratio, in relation to the value of exports of goods and services, from 22% in 1989 to only 6.6% in 1992. However, political uncertainty obstructed further rescheduling agreements, while external debt, which stood at $1,352m. at the end of 1992, remained substantial in relation to the size of the economy, being equivalent to 84% of GNP in that year. Moreover, the devaluation of the franc CFA in January 1994 effectively doubled the external debt in local currency terms, and Togo, while it benefited from the French government's cancellation of debt following the devaluation, was unable initially to draw on the special grants and concessionary loans promised by France, the IMF and the World Bank. In September 1994 France resumed financial co-operation with Togo with the release of 26,000m. francs CFA towards economic restructuring and rural development. That month the IMF approved a series of credits, totalling $95m., in support of Togo's 1994-97 economic programme. By March 1995 the majority of donor nations had resumed funding. In February the 'Paris Club' rescheduled some $252m. of Togo's debt-service obligations. In May France agreed to the cancellation of 17,000m. francs CFA of Togolese debt and to the rescheduling of a further 19,000m. francs CFA. Togo's total external debt was $1,486m. at the end of 1995, of which $1,297m. was long-term public debt. In that year the cost of debt-servicing was equivalent to 9.5% of the value of exports of goods and services.

Statistical Survey

Source (except where otherwise indicated): Direction de la Statistique, BP 118, Lomé; tel. 21-22-87.

Area and Population

AREA, POPULATION AND DENSITY

Area (sq km)	56,785*
Population (census results)	
1 March–30 April 1970	1,997,109
22 November 1981	2,703,250
Population (official estimate at mid-year)	
1994	3,928,000
Density (per sq km) at mid-1994	69.2

* 21,925 sq miles.

PRINCIPAL TOWNS
(estimated population at 1 January 1977)

Lomé (capital)	229,400	Tsevie	15,900
Sokodé	33,500	Anécho	13,300
Palimé	25,500	Mango	10,930
Atakpamé	21,800	*Bafilo	10,100
Bassari	17,500	*Tabligbo	5,120

* 1975 figure.

BIRTHS AND DEATHS (UN estimates, annual averages)

	1980–85	1985–90	1990–95
Birth rate (per 1,000)	44.9	44.7	44.5
Death rate (per 1,000)	15.7	14.1	12.8

Expectation of life (UN estimates, years at birth, 1990–95): 55.0 (males 53.2; females 56.8).

Source: UN, *World Population Prospects: The 1994 Revision*.

ECONOMICALLY ACTIVE POPULATION
(census of 22 November 1981)

	Males	Females	Total
Agriculture, hunting, forestry and fishing	324,870	254,491	579,361
Mining and quarrying	2,781	91	2,872
Manufacturing	29,307	25,065	54,372
Electricity, gas and water	2,107	96	2,203
Construction	20,847	301	21,148
Trade, restaurants and hotels	17,427	87,415	104,842
Transport, storage and communications	20,337	529	20,866
Financing, insurance, real estate and business services	1,650	413	2,063
Community, social and personal services	50,750	12,859	63,609
Activities not adequately defined	14,607	6,346	20,953
Total employed	484,683	387,606	872,289
Unemployed	21,666	7,588	29,254
Total labour force	506,349	395,194	901,543

Mid-1995 (estimates in '000): Agriculture, etc. 1,069; Total 1,726 (Source: FAO, *Production Yearbook*).

Agriculture

PRINCIPAL CROPS ('000 metric tons)

	1993	1994	1995
Rice (paddy)	34	39	35
Maize	393	270	296
Millet and sorghum	201	130	130*
Sweet potatoes	27	9	9*
Cassava (Manioc)	389	412	469
Yams	530	375	375
Taro (Coco yam)	20	12	12*
Dry beans	39	22	29
Other pulses	4	4	4
Groundnuts (in shell)	35	30	32
Sesame seed*	2	2	2
Cottonseed*	44	61	44
Coconuts*	14	14	14
Copra*	2	2	2
Palm kernels*	8	8	8
Tomatoes*	9	9	9
Other vegetables*	150	150	150
Oranges*	12	12	12
Bananas*	16	16	16
Other fruit*	20	20	20
Coffee (green)	28	26*	16
Cocoa beans	7	5†	5*
Tobacco (leaves)*	2	2	2
Cotton (lint)	40†	40†	40*

* FAO estimate(s). † Unofficial figure.

Source: FAO, *Production Yearbook*.

LIVESTOCK ('000 head, year ending September)

	1993	1994*	1995*
Cattle	248	248	248
Sheep	1,200	1,200	1,200
Pigs*	850	850	850
Goats	1,900	1,900	1,900
Horses*	2	2	2
Asses*	3	3	3

Poultry (million): 6 in 1993; 6* in 1994; 6* in 1995.

* FAO estimate(s).

Source: FAO, *Production Yearbook*.

LIVESTOCK PRODUCTS (FAO estimates, '000 metric tons)

	1993	1994	1995
Beef and veal	5	5	5
Mutton and lamb	3	3	3
Goat meat	4	4	4
Pig meat	12	12	12
Poultry meat	8	8	8
Cows' milk	10	10	10
Hen eggs	6.3	6.3	6.3

Source: FAO, *Production Yearbook*.

Forestry

ROUNDWOOD REMOVALS ('000 cubic metres, excluding bark)

	1992	1993*	1994*
Sawlogs, veneer logs and logs for sleepers	7	7	7
Other industrial wood*	185	191	197
Fuel wood*	1,072	1,097	1,122
Total	1,264	1,295	1,326

* FAO estimates.

Source: FAO, *Yearbook of Forest Products*.

Fishing

('000 metric tons, live weight)

	1993	1994	1995
Tilapias	5.2	3.7	3.5
Other freshwater fishes	1.0	1.5	3.0
Sardinellas	0.5	0.5	0.4
European anchovy	7.8	4.6	4.8
Other clupeoids	0.5	0.7	0.5
Other marine fishes (incl. unspecified)	2.1	2.3	1.5
Total catch (incl. others)	17.1	13.2	13.7

Source: FAO, *Yearbook of Fishery Statistics*.

Mining

('000 metric tons)

	1992	1993	1994
Natural phosphates (gross weight)	2,030.7	1,794.3	2,121.5

Source: Banque centrale des états de l'Afrique de l'ouest.

Industry

SELECTED PRODUCTS

('000 metric tons, unless otherwise indicated)

	1985	1986	1987
Salted, dried or smoked fish*	3.7	2.7	3.6
Wheat flour	32	42	58
Palm oil*	14	14	14
Beer ('000 hectolitres)	423	464	452
Soft drinks ('000 hectolitres)	83	89	142
Footwear—excl. rubber ('000 pairs)	521†	286	29
Cement	284	348	370
Electric energy (million kWh)	249	260	292

1988 ('000 metric tons, unless otherwise indicated): Salted, dried or smoked fish 3.7*; Palm oil 14*; Footwear—excl. rubber ('000 pairs) 100; Cement 383; Electric energy (million kWh) 302.

1989 ('000 metric tons, unless otherwise indicated): Salted, dried or smoked fish 3.8*; Palm oil 14*; Footwear—excl. rubber ('000 pairs) 100; Cement 389; Electric energy (million kWh) 319.

1990 ('000 metric tons, unless otherwise indicated): Salted, dried or smoked fish 3.6*; Palm oil 14*; Footwear—excl. rubber ('000 pairs) 100; Cement 399; Electric energy (million kWh) 339.

1991 ('000 metric tons, unless otherwise indicated): Salted, dried or smoked fish 2.8*; Footwear—excl. rubber ('000 pairs) 100; Cement 386; Electric energy (million kWh) 350.

1992: Salted, dried or smoked fish ('000 metric tons) 2.8*; Footwear—excl. rubber ('000 pairs) 100; Cement ('000 metric tons) 104.

1993: Cement ('000 metric tons) 147; Electric energy (million kWh) 296.

1994: Cement ('000 metric tons) 298; Electric energy (million kWh) 334.

1995: Cement ('000 metric tons) 484.

* Estimate(s) by the FAO.

† Provisional or estimated figure.

Sources: mainly UN, *Industrial Commodity Statistics Yearbook*, and Banque centrale des états de l'Afrique de l'ouest.

Finance

CURRENCY AND EXCHANGE RATES

Monetary Units

100 centimes = 1 franc de la Communauté financière africaine (CFA).

French Franc, Sterling and Dollar Equivalents (31 March 1997)

1 French franc = 100 francs CFA;
£1 sterling = 924.20 francs CFA;
US $1 = 562.85 francs CFA;
1,000 francs CFA = £1.082 = $1.777.

Average Exchange Rate (francs CFA per US $)

1994	555.20
1995	499.15
1996	511.55

Note: An exchange rate of 1 French franc = 50 francs CFA, established in 1948, remained in force until January 1994, when the CFA franc was devalued by 50%, with the exchange rate adjusted to 1 French franc =100 francs CFA.

BUDGET (estimates, million francs CFA)

Revenue	1993	1994	1995
Fiscal receipts	30,800	60,300	88,800
Taxes on income and profits	11,800	26,700	40,200
Individual taxes	3,400	8,300	9,300
Corporate and business taxes	3,900	15,900	23,300
Other direct taxes	4,600	2,500	7,700
Taxes on goods and services	3,200	5,400	11,000
Sales tax	2,900	4,800	5,500
Taxes on international trade and transactions	13,500	27,200	36,300
Import duties	10,300	21,100	29,700
Other current receipts	7,400	6,300	8,300
Property income	400	700	1,900
Total	38,200	66,600	97,100

Expenditure	1993	1994	1995
Current expenditure of ministries	53,000	63,000	67,300
General administration	3,700	8,500	8,500
Defence	14,200	14,100	15,400
Education	7,300	25,200	23,800
Health	2,200	5,800	5,900
Agriculture	1,400	3,300	2,800
Other	24,200	6,100	10,900
Other current expenditure	18,600	33,700	30,800
Common expenditures	3,000	5,300	5,600
Scholarships and training	2,100	3,400	3,700
Interest on domestic debt	1,500	2,100	2,200
Contribution to state agencies	2,900	1,200	1,500
Subsidies and transfers	4,300	12,300	9,800
Extrabudgetary expenditure	3,400	5,600	5,500
Other	1,400	3,700	2,400
Interest due on external debt	13,300	27,900	20,400
Investment expenditure	8,200	12,400	22,900
Total (incl. others)	93,000	137,000	147,200

Source: IMF, *Togo—Recent Economic Developments* (March 1997).

1996 (estimates, million francs CFA): Revenue 111,908; Expenditure 134,181.

1997 (estimates, million francs CFA): Revenue 126,020; Expenditure 136,444.

INTERNATIONAL RESERVES
(US $ million at 31 December)

	1994	1995	1996
Gold*	4.7	4.8	4.7
IMF special drawing rights	0.1	0.4	0.4
Reserve position	0.4	0.4	0.4
Foreign exchange	94.0	129.6	87.8
Total	99.1	135.2	93.2

* Valued at market-related prices.

Source: IMF, *International Financial Statistics*.

MONEY SUPPLY ('000 million francs CFA at 31 December)

	1993	1994	1995
Currency outside banks	10.32	44.83	73.48
Demand deposits at deposit money banks	35.13	49.35	56.37
Total money (incl. others)	46.57	95.29	131.20

Source: IMF, *International Financial Statistics*.

COST OF LIVING
(Consumer price index, low-income households; base: 1987 = 100)

	1993	1994	1995*
Food	107.3	132.9	157.4
Beverages	95.4	168.8	193.8
Household supplies and maintenance	88.7	115.1	142.9
Clothing	106.8	162.0	183.2
Housing	57.6	118.4	141.4
Services	115.6	151.5	161.6
All items (incl. others)	103.3	139.7	161.8

* Estimates.

Source: IMF, *Togo—Recent Economic Developments* (March 1997).

NATIONAL ACCOUNTS
(million francs CFA at current prices)

Expenditure on the Gross Domestic Product

	1993	1994*	1995*
Government final consumption expenditure	61,300	75,600	85,400
Private final consumption expenditure	290,500	389,800	495,800
Increase in stocks	−20,400	9,400	4,000
Gross fixed capital formation	38,000	58,400	86,500
Total domestic expenditure	369,400	533,300	671,700
Exports of goods and services	85,200	166,700	220,100
Less Imports of goods and services	112,100	186,900	245,100
GDP in purchasers' values	342,600	513,100	646,700
GDP at constant 1978 prices	174,100	200,600	216,700

* Estimates.

Source: IMF, *Togo—Recent Economic Developments* (March 1997).

Gross Domestic Product by Economic Activity

	1993	1994*	1995*
Agriculture, hunting, forestry and fishing	154,200	171,100	207,200
Mining and quarrying	13,400	28,100	32,300
Manufacturing	29,900	49,000	64,000
Electricity, gas and water	6,100	15,900	24,400
Construction	19,600	24,800	30,500
Trade, restaurants and hotels	49,800	104,800	143,200
Transport, storage and communications	14,300	37,300	49,500
Public administration and defence	27,500	36,100	37,300
Other services	27,700	46,000	58,400
GDP in purchasers' values	342,600	513,100	646,700

* Estimates.

Source: IMF, *Togo—Recent Economic Developments* (March 1997).

BALANCE OF PAYMENTS (US $ million)

	1992	1993	1994
Exports of goods f.o.b.	419.7	264.0	328.4
Imports of goods f.o.b.	−547.4	−375.3	−365.5
Trade balance	−127.7	−111.3	−37.1
Exports of services	129.2	71.5	73.5
Imports of services	−203.3	−142.0	−78.3
Balance on goods and services	−201.8	−181.8	−42.0
Other income received	31.4	16.2	5.2
Other income paid	−58.6	−48.7	−50.3
Balance on goods, services and income	−229.0	−214.3	−87.0
Current transfers received	111.1	54.0	35.1
Current transfers paid	−22.7	−13.4	−4.9
Current balance	−140.6	−173.7	−56.8
Investment assets	0.2	24.7	—
Investment liabilities	−24.0	−79.7	−16.0
Net errors and omissions	4.0	41.2	−24.3
Overall balance	−160.3	−187.5	−97.1

Source: IMF, *International Financial Statistics.*

External Trade

PRINCIPAL COMMODITIES (US $ million)

Imports c.i.f.	1989	1990	1991
Food and live animals	88.4	86.1	72.4
Fish, crustaceans and molluscs	14.3	15.3	16.6
Fresh, chilled or frozen fish	10.4	11.5	14.6
Fish, frozen (excl. fillets)	9.6	11.4	14.1
Cereals and cereal preparations	35.4	33.4	21.5
Wheat (incl. spelt) and meslin, unmilled	16.5	19.4	11.3
Durum wheat, unmilled	14.8	17.7	10.3
Rice	10.6	7.8	6.4
Rice, semi-milled, milled	10.4	7.7	6.4
Sugar, sugar preparations and honey	11.3	9.6	7.7
Sugar and honey	10.4	8.7	7.1
Refined sugars, etc	10.2	8.6	2.3
Miscellaneous edible products and preparations	4.3	7.6	11.0
Soups and broths	0.7	3.8	9.1
Beverages and tobacco	25.2	35.5	25.2
Tobacco and tobacco manufactures	17.8	25.1	18.1
Tobacco, manufactured	17.8	24.9	17.9
Cigarettes	17.7	24.7	17.7
Crude material (inedible) except fuels	9.1	10.9	9.0
Mineral fuels, lubricants and related materials	29.0	48.1	43.6
Petroleum, petroleum products and related materials	28.7	47.7	43.3
Petroleum products, refined	28.3	45.9	42.7
Motor spirit (gasoline) and other light oils	11.6	19.3	42.6
Motor spirit (gasoline), including aviation spirit	11.6	19.3	—
Other light petroleum oils	—	—	42.6
Chemicals and related products	42.9	71.9	52.7
Medicinal and pharmaceutical products	15.4	30.0	21.0
Medicaments	14.1	25.4	19.7
Medicaments containing antibiotics	13.3	23.6	16.5
Other chemical materials	5.5	21.6	14.5
Pesticides, disinfectants	4.2	19.8	13.1
Insecticides, for retail sale	2.1	18.9	9.6
Basic manufactures	119.8	146.2	78.5
Textile yarn, fabrics, etc	61.3	61.2	30.0
Woven cotton fabrics (excl. narrow or special fabrics)	53.0	49.3	23.1
Bleached and mercerized fabrics	50.9	48.0	22.5
Bleached cotton fabrics (containing 85% or more by weight of cotton)	49.2	47.0	22.4
Non-metallic mineral manufactures	17.1	30.0	12.8
Lime, cement and fabricated construction materials	12.8	23.9	8.7
Cement	11.5	22.3	7.1
Iron and steel	12.6	16.4	8.6
Other metal manufactures	12.6	16.8	10.2
Machinery and transport equipment	118.8	131.2	125.5
Power-generating machinery and equipment	3.9	4.4	9.3
Machinery specialized for particular industries	20.0	13.0	14.5
General industrial machinery, equipment and parts	16.7	20.2	17.6
Telecommunications and sound equipment	11.4	11.8	16.7
Other electrical machinery, apparatus, etc	17.1	18.0	16.8
Road vehicles and parts	39.8	49.6	41.4
Passenger motor cars (excl. buses)	14.3	19.5	14.5
Miscellaneous manufactured articles	29.5	40.4	28.6
Total (incl. others)	471.9	581.4	443.9

Exports f.o.b.	1989	1990	1991
Food and live animals	47.6	57.3	43.6
Cereals and cereal preparations	8.8	17.3	9.2
Flour of wheat or meslin	7.4	12.3	6.8
Coffee, tea, cocoa, spices, and manufactures thereof	34.6	33.5	20.6
Coffee (not roasted), coffee husks and skins	22.1	17.8	9.1
Cocoa beans, raw, roasted	12.3	15.2	11.0
Crude materials (inedible) except fuels	173.2	178.9	186.6
Textile fibres and waste	39.4	55.7	60.4
Cotton	38.7	55.6	55.4
Raw cotton (excl. linters)	38.6	55.6	55.2
Crude fertilizers and crude minerals	130.6	119.6	124.7
Natural calcium phosphates, etc	130.4	119.1	122.8
Mineral fuels, lubricants and related materials	—	0.1	5.9
Petroleum, petroleum products and related materials	—	—	5.8
Petroleum products, refined	—	—	5.8
Motor spirit (gasoline) and other light oils	—	—	5.8
Other light petroleum oils	—	—	5.8
Basic manufactures	12.0	19.5	7.7
Textile yarn, fabrics, etc	0.7	6.5	1.1
Textile articles	0.1	5.7	0.5
Sacks and bags of textile materials	—	5.7	0.5
Non-metallic mineral manufactures	5.2	7.0	3.0
Lime, cement and fabricated construction materials	5.2	6.9	3.0
Cement	5.1	6.9	3.0
Total (incl. others)	245.1	267.9	253.2

Source: UN, *International Trade Statistics Yearbook*.

Total imports c.i.f. (million francs CFA): 104,461 in 1992; 50,810 in 1993; 123,265 in 1994; 191,812 in 1995.

Total exports f.o.b. (million francs CFA): 72,779 in 1992; 38,512 in 1993; 90,053 in 1994; 104,218 in 1995.

Source: IMF, *International Financial Statistics*.

PRINCIPAL TRADING PARTNERS (US $ million)

Imports c.i.f.	1992	1993	1994
Belgium-Luxembourg	9.5	3.2	6.8
Benin	4.7	5.4	3.3
China, People's Repub.	9.5	6.7	5.9
Côte d'Ivoire	11.9	7.5	13.9
Denmark	2.1	1.1	2.8
France (incl. Monaco)	134.9	50.1	53.3
Germany	23.1	10.6	21.9
Ghana	4.3	1.8	2.0
Greece	4.5	0.7	1.1
Hong Kong	11.0	8.0	7.4
Italy	10.7	5.2	6.6
Japan	20.5	8.0	7.8
Mauritania	5.2	4.1	11.4
Netherlands	23.8	9.4	11.5
Nigeria	9.9	9.9	5.7
Norway	1.3	1.3	3.3
Pakistan	3.2	2.0	2.0
Southern African Customs Union*	3.6	4.8	3.5
Spain	7.9	2.8	5.9
Thailand	4.4	1.9	0.8
United Kingdom	9.1	3.2	7.5
USA	3.5	11.0	12.2
Total (incl. others)	394.7	179.5	222.0

Exports f.o.b.	1992	1993	1994
Australia	1.2	—	3.3
Belgium-Luxembourg	4.2	2.7	3.3
Benin	6.2	4.4	4.3
Bolivia	—	4.2	12.4
Brazil	—	7.0	1.6
British Indian Ocean Territory	14.3	2.6	—
Burkina Faso	4.9	1.4	3.8
Canada	56.2	17.9	27.5
France (incl. Monaco)	14.1	6.7	8.1
Germany	6.2	2.6	2.6
Ghana	4.2	2.3	3.5
Greece	3.5	1.5	2.1
India	15.6	3.7	2.9
Indonesia	1.4	4.0	9.2
Italy	6.4	2.0	2.5
Morocco	3.2	2.4	2.8
Netherlands	10.1	8.9	5.8
Niger	3.5	1.1	0.6
Nigeria	25.6	8.7	6.2
Pacific Islands (fmr Trust Territory)†	2.8	0.7	1.7
Philippines	5.4	9.8	8.8
Poland	15.5	1.8	4.0
Portugal	1.5	1.5	2.9
Southern African Customs Union*	—	—	3.6
Spain	11.8	0.7	1.6
Thailand	12.9	6.6	5.2
Total (incl. others)	275.0	136.0	162.2

* Comprising Botswana, Lesotho, Namibia, South Africa and Swaziland.

† Now Marshall Islands, Federated States of Micronesia, the Northern Mariana Islands and Palau.

Source: UN, *International Trade Statistics Yearbook*.

Transport

RAILWAYS (estimated traffic)

	1991	1992	1993
Passenger-km (million)	27.1	28.3	9.9
Freight (million ton-km)	6.4	7.0	2.1

Source: Banque centrale des états de l'Afrique de l'ouest.

ROAD TRAFFIC (motor vehicles registered at 31 December)

	1993	1994	1995
Passenger cars	64,709	67,936	74,662
Buses and coaches	503	529	547
Goods vehicles	30,581	31,457	32,514
Tractors (road)	1,408	1,466	1,544
Motor cycles and scooters	37,132	39,019	52,902

Source: IRF, *World Road Statistics*.

SHIPPING

Merchant Fleet (registered at 31 December)

	1994	1995	1996
Number of vessels	6	6	6
Total displacement (grt)	1,073	1,073	1,128

Source: Lloyd's Register of Shipping, *World Fleet Statistics*.

International Sea-borne Freight Traffic
('000 metric tons)

Port Lomé	1993	1994	1995
Goods loaded	304.4	147.6	174.4
Goods unloaded	785.1	709.0	1,139.0

Source: Banque centrale des états de l'Afrique de l'ouest.

Port Kpémé	1979	1980	1981
Freight loaded* ('000 metric tons)	2,990	2,895	2,200

* Phosphate from the OTP mines.

Source: *Statistiques douanières du Togo.*

CIVIL AVIATION (traffic on scheduled services)*

	1992	1993	1994
Km flown (million)	2	2	2
Passengers carried ('000)	66	68	69
Passenger-km (million)	201	207	215
Total ton-km (million)	34	33	34

* Including an apportionment of the traffic of Air Afrique.

Source: UN, *Statistical Yearbook.*

Tourism

	1992	1993	1994
Tourist arrivals ('000)	49	24	44
Tourist receipts (US $ million)	39	18	18

Source: UN, *Statistical Yearbook.*

Communications Media

	1992	1993	1994
Radio receivers ('000 in use)	795	820	850
Television receivers ('000 in use)	24	26	30
Telephones ('000 main lines in use)	15	17	21
Daily newspapers			
Number	2	n.a.	1
Circulation ('000 copies)	12*	n.a.	10

* Estimate.

Sources: UNESCO, *Statistical Yearbook*; UN, *Statistical Yearbook.*

Education

(1993, unless otherwise indicated)

	Institutions	Teachers	Students: Males	Students: Females	Students: Total
Pre-primary	241	395	5,291	5,235	10,526
Primary	2,594	12,487	397,874	265,252	663,126
Secondary					
General	n.a.	2,918	93,902	32,433	126,335
Vocational*	n.a.	261	6,231	2,161	8,392
University level	n.a.	276†	9,514‡	1,480‡	10,994‡

* 1990 figures. † 1988 figure. ‡ 1994 figure.

Source: UNESCO, *Statistical Yearbook.*

Directory

The Constitution

The Constitution that was approved in a national referendum on 27 September 1992 defines the rights, freedoms and obligations of Togolese citizens, and defines the separation of powers among the executive, legislative and judicial organs of state.

Executive power is vested in the President of the Republic, who is elected, by direct universal adult suffrage, with a five-year mandate. The legislature, the Assemblée nationale, is similarly elected for a period of five years, its 81 members being directly elected by universal suffrage. The President of the Republic appoints a Prime Minister who is able to command a majority in the legislature, and the Prime Minister, in consultation with the President, appoints other government ministers. A Constitutional Court is designated as the highest court of jurisdiction in constitutional matters.

The Government

HEAD OF STATE

President: Gen. GNASSINGBE EYADÉMA (assumed power 13 January 1967; proclaimed President 14 April 1967; elected 30 December 1979; re-elected 21 December 1986 and 25 August 1993).

COUNCIL OF MINISTERS
(August 1997)

President: Gen. GNASSINGBE EYADÉMA.

Prime Minister and Minister of Planning and Territorial Development: KWASSI KLUTSE.

Minister of State in charge of Economy and Finance: BARRY MOUSSA BARQUE.

Minister of State in charge of Industry and Commerce: ELOM KOUAMI DADZIE.

Minister of National Defence: YAGINIM BITOKOTIPOU.

Minister of Interior and Security: Col. SEYI MEMENE.

Minister of Foreign Affairs and Co-operation: KOFFI PANOU.

Minister of Justice and Human Rights and Keeper of the Seals: EUPHREM DORKENOU.

Minister of State Enterprises and the Development of the Free Trade Zone: FAYADOWA BOUKPESSI.

Minister of Technical Education: BAMOUNI SOLOMOU BABA.

Minister of Professional Training and Cottage Industry: STANISLAS TEMELE.

Minister of Mines, Equipment, Transport and Telecommunications: TCHAMDJA ANDJO.

Minister of Youth, Sports and Culture: KOUAMI AGBOGBOLI IHOU.

Minister of National Education and Research: KODJO EDO MAURILLE AGBOBLI.

Minister of Decentralization, Urban Development and Housing: KOFFIUI VICTOR AYASSOU.

Minister of the Promotion of Labour and the Civil Service: SAMBIANI LIWAB.

Minister of Communication and Civic Education: ESSO SOLITOKI.

Minister of Women's Affairs and Social Welfare: TCHANGAI KISSEM WALLA.

Minister of Agriculture, Animal Breeding and Fisheries: DAKE KOKOU DOGBE.

Minister of Public Health: KOFFI SAMA.

Minister of the Environment and Forest Resources: YAO KOMLAVI.

Minister of Tourism and Leisure: DAFO ELIA.

Minister in charge of Relations with the National Assembly: DOTSE KOMI AMOUDOKPO.

MINISTRIES

Office of the President: Palais Présidentiel, ave de la Marina, Lomé; tel. 21-27-01; telex 5201.

Ministry of Agriculture, Animal Breeding and Fisheries: ave de Sarakawa, Lomé; tel. 21-56-71.

Ministry of Communications and Civic Education: Lomé.

Ministry of Decentralization, Urban Development and Housing: Lomé.

Ministry of the Economy and Finance: Ancien Palais, ave de la Marina, BP 387, Lomé; tel. 21-23-71; telex 5286; fax 21-76-02.

Ministry of the Environment and Forest Resources: Lomé.

Ministry of Foreign Affairs and Co-operation: place du Monument aux Morts, Lomé; tel. 21-29-10; telex 5239.

Ministry of Industry and Commerce: rue de Commerce, Lomé; tel. 21-09-09.

Ministry of the Interior and Security: rue Albert Sarraut, Lomé; tel. 21-23-19.

Ministry of Justice and Human Rights: ave de la Marina, rue Colonel de Roux, Lomé; tel. 21-26-53.

Ministry of Mines, Equipment, Transport and Telecommunications: ave de Sarakawa, Lomé; tel. 21-11-01; telex 5115; fax 21-68-12.

Ministry of National Defence: Lomé; tel. 21-28-91; telex 5321.

Ministry of National Education and Research: rue Colonel de Roux, BP 12175, Lomé; tel. 21-38-01; telex 5322.

Ministry of Planning and Territorial Development: Lomé; tel. 21-27-01; telex 5380.

Ministry of Professional Training and Cottage Industry: Lomé.

Ministry of the Promotion of Labour and the Civil Service: angle ave de la Marina et rue Kpalimé, Lomé; tel. 21-26-53.

Ministry of Public Health: rue Branly, Lomé; tel. 21-29-83.

Ministry of State Enterprises and the Free Trade Zone: BP 2748, Lomé; tel. 21-07-44; telex 5396.

Ministry of Technical Education: Lomé.

Ministry of Tourism and Leisure: Lomé.

Ministry of Women's Affairs and Social Welfare: Lomé.

Ministry of Youth, Sports and Culture: BP 3193, Lomé; tel. 21-23-52; telex 5103.

President and Legislature

PRESIDENT

Presidential Election, 25 August 1993

Candidate	% of votes
Gen. GNASSINGBE EYADÉMA	96.49
KWAMI MENSAH JACQUES AMOUZOU	1.87
ADANI IFÉ ATAKPAMEVI	1.64
Total	100.00

ASSEMBLÉE NATIONALE

Speaker: DAHUKU PERE.

General Election, 6 and 20 February 1994

Party	Seats
Comité d'action pour le renouveau (CAR)	36*
Rassemblement du peuple togolais (RPT)	35
Union togolaise pour la démocratie (UTD)	7*
Union pour la justice et la démocratie (UJD)	2
Coordination nationale des forces nouvelles (CFN)	1
Total	81

* The Supreme Court declared the election result invalid in two constituencies where the seats had been allocated to the CAR, and in one where the seat had been allocated to the UTD. Following the resignation, in April 1996, from the CAR of one of its deputies, the dismissal, in July, by the UTD of one of its legislative representatives, and the victory, in August, of the RPT at all three by-elections, the RPT and its allies gained control of the legislature. In October a further CAR deputy resigned, and allied himself with the RPT. In November the UJD officially merged with the RPT, giving it a legislative majority with 41 seats. In August 1997 the seats were divided as follows: RPT 41; CAR 32; UTD five; independents two, CFN one.

Political Organizations

In mid-1993 there were 63 registered political parties. Of those operating in mid-1997, the following were among the most influential:

Alliance togolaise pour la démocratie (ATD): Leader: ADANI IFÉ ATAKPAMEVI.

Comité d'action pour le renouveau (CAR): Leader YAOVI AGBOYIBO.

Convention démocratique des peuples africains (CDPA): Leader Prof. LÉOPOLD GNININVI.

Coordination nationale des forces nouvelles (CFN): f. 1993; Pres. Me JOSEPH KOKOU KOFFIGOH.

Démocratie sociale togolaise (DST): linked to PDT; Leader ABOU DJOBO BOUKARI.

Mouvement du 5 octobre (MO5): radical; Leader BASSIROU AYEVA.

Mouvement nationaliste de l'unité (MNU): f. 1992; Gen. Sec. KOFFITSE ADZRAKO.

Parti d'action pour la démocratie (PAD): Leader FRANCIS EKOH.

Parti démocratique togolais (PDT): linked to DST; Leader MBA KABASSEMA.

Parti des démocrates pour l'unité (PDU): Leader JEAN-LUCIEN SAVI DE TOVÉ.

Parti pour la démocratie et le renouveau (PDR): Leader ZARIFOU AYIVA.

Parti pan-africain socialiste (PPS): radical; Leader FRANCIS AGBOBLI.

Rassemblement du peuple togolais (RPT): place de l'Indépendance, BP 1208, Lomé; tel. 21-20-18; telex 5207; f. 1969; sole legal party 1969–91; Pres. Gen. GNASSINGBE EYADÉMA; Sec.-Gen. VIGNIKO AMEDEGNATO.

Union pour la démocratie et la solidarité (UDS): Sec.-Gen. ANTOINE FOLY.

Union des forces de changement (UFC): Leader GILCHRIST OLYMPIO.

Union pour la justice at la démocratie (UJD): supports Pres. Eyadéma; Leader LAL TAXPANDJAN.

Union des libéraux indépendants (ULD): f. 1993 to succeed Union des démocrates pour le renouveau; Leader KWAMI MENSAH JACQUES AMOUZOU.

Union togolaise pour la démocratie (UTD): Leader EDEM KODJO; Sec.-Gen. ADAN MESSAN AJAVON.

Union togolaise pour la réconciliation (UTR): Leader BAWA MANKOUBU.

Diplomatic Representation

EMBASSIES IN TOGO

Belgium: 165 rue Pelletier Caventou, BP 7643, Lomé; tel. 21-03-23; telex 5363; Ambassador: PIERRE VAESEN.

Brazil: 119 rue de l'OCAM, BP 1356, Lomé; tel. 21-00-58; telex 5346; Chargé d'affaires a.i.: JOSÉ ROBERTO PROCOPIAK.

China, People's Republic: Tokoin-Ouest, BP 2690, Lomé; tel. 21-31-59; telex 5070; Ambassador: ZHOU XIANJUE.

Congo, Democratic Republic: 325 blvd du 13 janvier, BP 102, Lomé; tel. 21-51-55; telex 5263; Ambassador: LOKOKA IKUKELE BOMOLO.

Egypt: route d'Aného, BP 8, Lomé; tel. 21-24-43; telex 5310; Ambassador: HUSSEIN EL-KHAZINDAR.

France: 51 rue du Golfe, BP 337, Lomé; tel. 21-25-71; telex 5202; Ambassador: RÉGIS KOETSCHET.

Gabon: Tokoin Super-Taco, BP 9118, Lomé; tel. 21-47-76; telex 5307; Ambassador: ALAIN MAURICE MAYOMBO.

Germany: blvd de la République, BP 1175, Lomé; tel. 21-23-38; telex 5204; fax 22-18-88; Ambassador: Dr RAINALD STECK.

Ghana: 8 rue Paulin Eklou, Tokoin-Ouest, BP 92, Lomé; tel. 21-31-94; fax 21-77-36; Ambassador: NELSON KOJO DUMEVI.

Israel: 159 rue de l'OCAM, BP 61187, Lomé; tel. 21-79-58; telex 5424; fax 21-88-94; Ambassador: JACOB TOPAZ.

Korea, Democratic People's Republic: Tokoin-Est, Lomé; tel. 21-46-01; Ambassador: PAK SONG IL.

Libya: blvd du 13 janvier, BP 4872, Lomé; tel. 21-40-63; telex 5288; Chargé d'affaires a.i.: AHMED M. ABDULKAFI.

Nigeria: 311 blvd du 13 janvier, BP 1189, Lomé; tel. 21-34-55; Ambassador: VINCENT OKOBI.

USA: angle rue Pelletier Caventou et rue Vauban, BP 852, Lomé; tel. 21-29-91; fax 21-79-52; Ambassador: JOHNNY YOUNG.

Judicial System

Justice is administered by the Cour Constitutionnelle (Constitutional Court), the Cour Suprême (Supreme Court), two Cours d'Appel (Appeal Courts) and the Tribunaux de première instance, which hear civil, commercial and criminal cases. There is a labour tribunal and a tribunal for children's rights. In addition, there are two exceptional courts, the Cour de sûreté de l'Etat, which judges crimes against internal and external state security, and the Tribunal spécial chargé de la répression des détournements de deniers publics, which deals with cases of misuse of public funds.

Cour Constitutionnelle: Lomé; f. 1997; seven mems; Pres. ATSU-KOFFI AMEGA.

Cour Suprême: BP 906, Lomé; tel. 21-22-58; f. 1961; consists of three chambers; judicial, administrative and auditing; Pres. EMMANUEL MAWULI KOUAMI APEDO; Attorney-Gen. KOUAMI AMADOS-DJOKO.

Religion

It is estimated that about 50% of the population follow traditional animist beliefs, some 35% are Christians (mainly Roman Catholics) and 15% are Muslims.

CHRISTIANITY

The Roman Catholic Church

Togo comprises one archdiocese and six dioceses. At 31 December 1995 there were an estimated 956,205 adherents in the country, representing about 22.7% of the total population.

Bishops' Conference: Conférence Episcopale du Togo, 10 rue Maréchal Foch, BP 348, Lomé; tel. 21-22-72; fax 22-48-08; statutes approved 1979; Pres. Most Rev. PHILIPPE FANOKO KOSSI KPODZRO, Archbishop of Lomé.

Archbishop of Lomé: Most Rev. PHILIPPE FANOKO KOSSI KPODZRO, Archevêché, 10 rue Maréchal Foch, BP 348, Lomé; tel. 21-22-72; fax 22-48-08.

Protestant Churches

There are about 250 mission centres, with a personnel of some 250, affiliated to European and US societies and administered by a Conseil Synodal, presided over by a moderator.

Directorate of Protestant Churches: 1 rue Maréchal Foch, BP 378, Lomé; Moderator Pastor AWUME (acting).

Eglise Evangélique Presbyterienne du Togo: 1 rue Tokmake, BP 2, Lomé; tel. 21-46-69; fax 22-23-63; Moderator Rev. YAWO FATSEME AMIDU.

BAHÁ'Í FAITH

National Spiritual Assembly: BP 1659, Lomé; tel. 21-21-99; mems resident in 640 localities.

The Press

DAILIES

Journal Officiel de la République du Togo: EDITOGO, BP 891, Lomé; tel. 21-37-18; telex 5294; fax 21-31-63.

Togo-Presse: EDITOGO, BP 891, Lomé; tel. 21-37-18; telex 5294; fax 21-31-63; f. 1961; official govt publ.; French, Kabiye and Ewe; political, economic and cultural; circ. 8,000.

PERIODICALS

Bulletin de la Chambre de Commerce: angle ave de la Présidence, BP 360, Lomé; tel. 21-70-65; telex 5023; fax 21-47-30; monthly; directory of commercial, industrial and agricultural activities.

Bulletin d'Information de l'Agence Togolaise de Presse: 35 rue Binger, Lomé; weekly; publ. by govt information service.

Courrier du Golfe: Lomé; f. 1990; independent.

Espoir de la Nation Togolaise: EDITOGO, BP 891, Lomé; tel. 21-37-18; telex 5294; monthly; Dir M. AWESSO; circ. 3,000.

L'Eveil du Travailleur Togolais: BP 163, Lomé; tel. 21-57-39; quarterly; Elrato; publ. by Confédération Nationale des Travailleurs du Togo; Chief Editor M. K. AGBEKA; circ. 5,000.

Forum Hebdo: Lomé; weekly; independent; Dir GABRIEL KOMI AGAH (in exile since 1993).

Game su: 19 ave de la Nouvelle Marche, BP 1247, Lomé; tel. 21-28-44; f. 1972; monthly; Ewe; govt publ. for the newly literate; circ. 6,000.

La Parole: Lomé; weekly; independent; Dir BERTIN KANGHI FOLY.

Kpakpa Désenchanté: Lomé; weekly; independent.

Le Secteur Privé: angle ave de la Présidence, BP 360, Lomé; tel. 21-70-65; telex 5023; fax 21-47-30; monthly; publ. by Chambre de Commerce, d'Agriculture et d'Industrie du Togo.

Tev fema: 19 ave de la Nouvelle Marche, BP 1247, Lomé; tel. 21-28-44; f. 1977; monthly; Kabiye; govt publ.; circ. 3,000.

Togo-Dialogue: EDITOGO, BP 891, Lomé; tel. 21-37-18; telex 5294; monthly; publ. by govt information service; circ. 5,000.

Togo-Images: BP 4869, Lomé; tel. 21-56-80; f. 1962; monthly series of wall posters depicting recent political, economic and cultural events in Togo; publ. by govt information service; Dir AKOBI BEDOU; circ. 5,000.

La Tribune des Démocrates: Lomé; weekly; independent; Editor MARTIN NBENOUGOU (imprisoned May 1994).

NEWS AGENCIES

Agence Togolaise de Presse (ATOP): 35 rue des Media, BP 2327, Lomé; tel. 21-25-07; telex 5320; f. 1975; Dir SESHIE SEYENA BIAVA.

Foreign Bureau

Xinhua (New China) News Agency (People's Republic of China): BP 2984, Lomé; tel. 21-39-20; telex 5273; Correspondent QIN DIANJIE.

Publishers

Centre Togolais de Communication Evangélique (CTCE): 1 rue de Commerce, BP 378, Lomé; tel. 21-45-82; fax 21-29-67; Dir MARC K. ETSE.

Editions Akpagnon: BP 3531, Lomé; tel. 22-02-44; f. 1979; general literature; Man. Dir YVES-EMMANUEL DOGBÉ.

Nouvelles Editions Africaines du Togo (NEA TOGO): 239 blvd du 13 janvier, BP 4862, Lomé; tel. 21-67-61; telex 5393; fax 22-10-03; general fiction and non-fiction; Man. Dir DOVI KAVEGUE.

Société National des Editions du Togo (EDITOGO): BP 891, Lomé; tel. 21-61-06; telex 5294; f. 1961; govt-owned; general and educational; Pres. BIOSSEY KOKOU TOZOUN; Man. Dir WIYAO DADJA POUWI.

Radio and Television

In 1994, according to UNESCO, there were an estimated 850,000 radio receivers and 30,000 television receivers in use.

Radiodiffusion du Togo (Internationale)—Radio Lomé: BP 434, Lomé; tel. 21-24-93; telex 5320; fax 21-36-73; f. 1953; renamed Radiodiffusion-Télévision de la Nouvelle Marche 1979–91; state-controlled; radio programmes in French, English and vernacular languages; Dir BAWA SEMEDO.

Radiodiffusion du Togo (Nationale): BP 21, Kara; tel. 60-60-60; f. 1974 as Radiodiffusion Kara (Togo); state-controlled; radio programmes in French and vernacular languages; Dir M'BA KPENOUGOU.

Radio Kara: BP 21, Kara; tel. 60-60-60; Dir KAO PÉRÉZI.

Radio Liberté: operated by the COD–2 opposition alliance.

Télévision Togolaise: BP 3286, Lomé; tel. 21-53-57; telex 5320; fax 21-57-86; f. 1973; state-controlled; three stations; programmes in French and vernacular languages; Dir MARTIN AHIAVI.

Finance

(cap. = capital; res = reserves; dep. = deposits; m. = million; br. = branch; amounts in francs CFA)

BANKING

Central Bank

Banque Centrale des Etats de l'Afrique de l'Ouest (BCEAO): rue des Nîmes, BP 120, Lomé; tel. 21-53-84; telex 5216; fax 21-76-02; headquarters in Dakar, Senegal; f. 1955; bank of issue and central bank for the member states of the Union économique et monétaire ouest-africaine (UEMOA); cap. and res 657,592m. (Dec. 1995); Gov. CHARLES KONAN BANNY; Dir in Togo YAO MESSAN AHO; br. at Kara.

Commercial Banks

Banque Togolaise pour le Commerce et l'Industrie (BTCI): 169 blvd du 13 janvier, BP 363, Lomé; tel. 21-46-41; telex 5221; fax 21-32-65; f. 1974; 24.8% owned by Société Financière pour les Pays d'Outre-mer, 23.8% by Banque Nationale de Paris, 21.0% by SNI & FA; cap. 1,700m. (Sept. 1994); Pres. BARRY MOUSSA BARQUE; Man. Dir MAX KODJO OSSEYI; 8 brs.

BIA—Togo: 13 rue de Commerce, BP 346, Lomé; tel. 21-32-86; telex 5218; fax 21-10-19; f. 1981; fmrly Meridien BIAO—Togo; cap. and res 1,575m., dep. 31,543m. (Sept. 1993); Pres. KOSSI R. PAASS; Dir-Gen. DANIEL HASSER; 6 brs.

Ecobank—Togo: 20 rue de Commerce, BP 3302, Lomé; tel. 21-72-14; telex 5440; fax 21-42-37; f. 1984, operations commenced 1988; 65% owned by Ecobank Transnational Inc (operating under the auspices of the Economic Community of West African States), 35% by Togolese private interests; cap. and res 1,481m., dep. 23,178m. (Sept. 1994); Pres. YAO PALI TCHALLA; Man. Dir AMIN UDDIN.

Société Interafricaine de Banques (SIAB): route d'Aného, BP 4874, Lomé; tel. 21-28-30; telex 5301; fax 21-58-29; f. 1975; fmrly Banque Arabe Libyenne-Togolaise du Commerce Extérieur; 50% state-owned, 50% owned by Libyan Arab Foreign Bank; cap. 3,100m. (Sept. 1994); Pres. YENTCHABRE YANDJA; Dir-Gen. IDRISSA DERMAN.

Union Togolaise de Banque (UTB): blvd du 13 janvier, BP 359, Lomé; tel. 21-64-11; telex 5215; fax 21-22-06; f. 1964; state-owned; cap. 2,000m. (Sept. 1992); Pres. Minister of the Economy and Finance; Dir-Gen. ALEXIS LAMSEH LOOKY; 9 brs.

Development Banks

Banque Togolaise de Développement (BTD): angle rue des Nîmes et ave N. Grunitzky, BP 65, Lomé; tel. 21-36-41; telex 5282; fax 21-44-56; f. 1966; 44% state-owned, 20% owned by BCEAO, 20% by private Togolese interests; cap. and res 4,171m., dep. 18,056m. (Sept. 1993); Pres. Minister of Industry and Commerce; Man. Dir MENSAVI MENSAH; 8 brs.

Société Nationale d'Investissement et Fonds Annexes (SNI & FA): 11 ave du 24 janvier, BP 2682, Lomé; tel. 21-62-21; telex 5265; fax 21-62-25; f. 1971; state-owned; cap. 500m. (Sept. 1993); Pres. OGAMO BAGNAH; Man. Dir TANKPADJA LALLE.

Bankers' Association

Association Professionnelle des Banques et Etablissements Financiers du Togo: Lomé.

STOCK EXCHANGE

Côte d'Ivoire's Bourse des Valeurs d'Abidjan was scheduled to become a regional stock exchange, serving the member states of the UEMOA.

INSURANCE

CICA—RE/Compagnie Commune de Réassurance des Etats Membres de la CICA: ave du 24 janvier, BP 12410, Lomé; tel. 21-62-69; telex 5066; fax 21-49-64; reinsurance co operating in 12 west and central African states; cap. 600m.; Chair. JACQUELINE OKILI; Gen. Man. DIGBEU KIPRE.

Groupement Togolais d'Assurances (GTA): route d'Atakpamé, BP 3298, Lomé; tel. 25-60-75; telex 5069; fax 25-26-78; f. 1974; 62.9% state-owned; all classes of insurance and reinsurance; Pres. Minister of the Economy and Finance; Man. Dir KOSSI NAMBEA.

Trade and Industry

ECONOMIC AND SOCIAL COUNCIL

Conseil Economique et Social: Lomé; tel. 21-53-01; telex 5237; f. 1967; advisory body of 25 mems, comprising five trade unionists, five reps of industry and commerce, five reps of agriculture, five economists and sociologists, and five technologists; Pres. KOFFI GBODZIDI DJONDO.

DEVELOPMENT AND MARKETING ORGANIZATIONS

Agricultural development is under the supervision of five regional development authorities, the Sociétés régionales d'aménagement et de développement.

Caisse Française de Développement: ave de Sarakawa, BP 33, Lomé; tel. 21-04-98; telex 5313; fax 21-79-32; f. 1992 to succeed the Caisse Centrale de Coopération Economique; Dir M. TYACK.

Mission Française de Coopération: BP 91, Lomé; telex 5413; fax 21-21-28; administers bilateral aid from France; Dir SUZANNE FAUCHEUX.

Office de Développement et d'Exploitation des Forêts (ODEF): 15 rue des Conseillers Municipaux, BP 334, Lomé; tel. 21-51-59; f. 1971; develops and manages forest resources; Man. Dir KOFFI AGOGNO.

Office National des Produits Vivriers (TOGOGRAIN): 141 ave de la Libération, BP 3039, Lomé; tel. 21-59-55; telex 5220; develops and markets staple food crops; Man. Dir M. WALLA.

Office des Produits Agricoles du Togo (OPAT): angle rue Branly et ave no. 3, BP 1334, Lomé; tel. 21-44-71; telex 5220; f. 1964; agricultural development, marketing and exports; Dir-Gen. ABALO KELEM.

Office Togolais des Phosphates (OTP): BP 3200, Lomé; tel. 21-22-28; telex 5287; f. 1974; cap. 15,000m. francs CFA; production and marketing of phosphates; Dir-Gen. EKUE LIKOU.

Société d'Appui a la Filière Café-Cacao-Coton (SAFICC): Lomé; f. 1992; development of coffee, cocoa and cotton production.

Société Nationale de Commerce (SONACOM): 29 blvd Circulaire, BP 3009, Lomé; tel. 21-31-18; telex 5281; f. 1972; cap. 2,000m. francs CFA; importer of staple foods; Dir-Gen. JEAN LADOUX.

Société Togolaise du Coton (SOTOCO): Lomé; f. 1974 to promote cotton cultivation.

CHAMBER OF COMMERCE

Chambre de Commerce, d'Agriculture et d'Industrie du Togo (CCAIT): angle ave de la Présidence et ave Georges Pompidou, BP 360, Lomé; tel. 21-70-65; telex 5023; fax 21-47-30; f. 1921; Pres. ALEXIS LAMSEH LOOKY; Sec.-Gen. MICHEL KWAME MEYISSO.

EMPLOYERS' ORGANIZATIONS

Groupement Interprofessionnel des Entreprises du Togo (GITO): BP 345, Lomé; Pres. CLARENCE OLYMPIO.

Syndicat des Commerçants Industriels Importateurs et Exportateurs du Togo (SCINPEXTO): BP 1166, Lomé; tel. 22-59-86; Pres. C. SITTERLIN.

Syndicat des Entrepreneurs de Travaux Publics, Bâtiments et Mines du Togo: BP 12429, Lomé; tel. 21-19-06; fax 21-08-30; Pres. JOSÈPHE NAKU.

MAJOR INDUSTRIAL COMPANIES

The following are among the country's largest companies in terms of either capital investment or employment:

Brasserie BB Lomé SA: 47 rue du Grand Marché, BP 896, Lomé; tel. 21-50-62; telex 5228; fax 21-38-59; f. 1964 as Brasserie du Bénin SA; cap. 2,500m. francs CFA; 25% state-owned; mfrs of beer and soft drinks at Lomé and Kara; Chair. and Man. Dir JOACHIM HAASE; Dirs ELMAR VAN BOEMMEL, OSCAR BOSSHARD; 523 employees.

CEREKEM Exotic Togo: BP 2082, Lomé; f. 1987; cap. 400m. francs CFA; agro-industrial complex at Adétikopé for cultivation and processing of aromatic plants; Chair. and Man. Dir OLE RASMUSSEN; 400 employees.

Communauté Electrique du Bénin: rue de l'Hôpital, BP 1368, Lomé; tel. 21-61-32; telex 5355; f. 1968 as a jt venture between Togo and Benin to exploit the energy resources in the two countries; Chair. S. B. TIDJANI-DOURODJAYE; Man. Dir BOUKARY ALIDOU.

Compagnie Energie Electrique du Togo (CEET): 10 ave du Golfe, BP 42, Lomé; tel. 21-27-43; telex 5230; fax 21-64-98; f. 1963; state-owned; production, transportation and distribution of electricity; Chair. YAO BANA DAGADZI; Man. Dir ELI YAO KPEGBA.

Industrie Togolaise des Plastiques (ITP): Zone Industrielle, BP 9157, Lomé; tel. 27-49-83; telex 5018; fax 27-15-58; f. 1980; cap. 735m. francs CFA; owned by a consortium of private Togolese, Dutch, German and Danish interests; mfr and marketing of moulded articles, etc.; Man. Dir S. VICTOIRE DOGBE.

Nouvelle Industrie des Oléagineux du Togo (NIOTO): BP 1755, Lomé; f. 1976; cap. 1,000m. francs CFA; 51% owned by Cie Française pour le Développement des Textiles, 49% by private Togolese interests; production and marketing of plant oils; Man. Dir ANANI ERNEST GASSOU.

Nouvelle Société Togolaise de Marbrerie et de Matériaux (Nouvelle SOTOMA): Zone Portuaire, BP 2105, Lomé; tel. 21-29-

22; telex 5229; fax 21-71-32; cap. 500m. francs CFA; exploitation of marble at Gnaoulou and Pagola; Man. Dir K. PEKEMSI.

Régie Nationale des Eaux du Togo (RNET): ave de la Libération, angle rue du Chemin de Fer, BP 1301, Lomé; tel. 21-34-81; telex 5004; fax 21-46-13; f. 1964; cap. 252m. francs CFA; state-owned; production and distribution of drinking water; Chair. ANATO AGBOZOUHOUE; Man. Dir KPANDJA I. BINGUITCHA-FARE.

Sagefi et PS: route de l'Aéroport, BP 4566, Lomé; tel. 21-55-43; telex 50321; fax 21-64-24; f. 1976; mfrs of electronic equipment; Chair. K. HOFFER.

Société Agricole Togolaise-Arabe-Libyenne (SATAL): 329 blvd du 13 janvier, BP 3554, Lomé; tel. 21-69-18; telex 5051; f. 1978; cap. 1,400m. francs CFA; 50% state-owned, 50% owned by govt of Libya; production, processing and marketing of agricultural goods; Chair. KATANGA KOFFI WALLA; Man. Dir ASSAID MOHAMED RAAI.

Société des Ciments du Togo (CIMTOGO): Zone Industrielle Portuaire PK 12, BP 1687, Lomé; tel. 21-08-59; telex 5234; fax 21-71-32; f. 1969; cap. 750m. francs CFA; owned by SCANCEM International (Norway); production and marketing of cement and clinker; turnover in 1991: 9,700m. francs CFA; Pres. Minister of State Enterprises and the Free Trade Zone; Man. Dir H. RASMUSSEN.

Société Générale du Golfe de Guinée-Togo (SGGG-TOGO): 7 rue Koumoré, BP 330, Lomé; tel. 21-23-90; telex 5236; fax 21-51-65; f. 1972; cap. 2,744.9m. francs CFA; import-export agency and transporters; turnover in 1991 13,315m. francs CFA; Chair. and Man. Dir MATÉ KWAME ABBEY; 309 employees.

Sociéte Générale des Moulins du Togo (SGMT): Zone Industrielle Portuaire, BP 9098, Lomé; tel. 21-35-59; telex 5272; f. 1971; cap. 300m. francs CFA; 45% state-owned; flour milling at Lomé; Chair. KOUDJOLOU DOGO; Man. Dir VASKEN BAKALIAN.

Société Nationale pour le Développement de la Palmeraie et des Huileries (SONAPH): BP 1755, Lomé; tel. 21-22-32; telex 5268; f. 1968; cap. 1,320m. francs CFA; state-owned; cultivation of palms and production of palm-oil and palmettoes; Chair. Dr FOLI AMAIZO BUBUTO; Man. Dir ANANI ERNEST GASSOU.

Société Togolaise des Boissons (STB): Zone Industrielle Portuaire, BP 2239, Lomé; tel. 27-58-80; f. 1970; cap. 264m. francs CFA; manufacture, bottling and sale of soft drinks; Chair. PIERRE CASTEL; Dir-Gen. E. VAN BÖMMEL; 88 employees.

Société Togolaise du Coton (SOTOCO): BP 219, Atakpamé; tel. 40-01-53; telex 5179; f. 1974; cap. 200m. francs CFA; state-owned; development of cotton growing; Man. Dir KAMBIA ESSOBEHEYI.

Société Togolaise et Danoise de Savons (SOTODAS): ZoneIndustrielle Portuaire, BP 1669, Lomé; tel. 21-52-03; fax 21-52-04; f. 1987; cap. 205m. francs CFA; 40% owned by Domo Kemi (Denmark) 20% by private Togolese interests; mfrs of detergents and cleansers; Man. Dir S. RAZVI.

Société Togolaise de Sidérurgie (STS): route d'Aného, Zone Portuaire, BP 13472, Lomé; tel. 21-10-16; telex 5385; cap. 700m. francs CFA; steel production; Chair. JOHN MOORE; Man. Dir STANLEY CLEVELAND.

Société Togolaise de Stockage de Lomé (STSL): BP 3283, Lomé; tel. 21-50-64; telex 5210; f. 1976; cap. 4,000m. francs CFA; exploitation and commercialization of hydrocarbons; Dir-Gen. M. BLAZJENVICZ.

Sogotel Co Ltd: Chateau d'Eau Be, BP 497, Lomé; tel. 21-05-43; fax 21-10-71; f. 1973; processors of fish and meat; Pres. CLARENCE ANSAH JOHNSON.

Togotex International: BP 3511, Lomé; tel. 21-33-25; telex 5108; fax 21-60-49; f. 1990; cap. 2,250m. francs CFA; owned by Cha Chi Ming (Hong Kong); operates textile mills; Pres. CHA CHI MING; Man. Dir VICTOR CHA.

TRADE UNIONS

Collectif des Syndicats Indépendants (CSI): Lomé; f. 1992 as co-ordinating org. for three trade union confederations:

Confédération Syndicale des Travailleurs du Togo (CSTT): Lomé.

Groupement Syndical Autonome (GSA): Lomé.

Union Nationale des Syndicats Indépendants du Togo (UNSIT): Tokoin-Wuiti, BP 30082, Lomé; tel. 21-65-65; fax 25-95-66; f. 1991; 17 affiliated unions.

Confédération Nationale des Travailleurs du Togo (CNTT): 160 blvd du 13 janvier, BP 163, Lomé; tel. 21-57-39; f. 1973; affiliated to RPT until April 1991; Sec.-Gen. DOUEVI TCHIVIAKOU.

Transport

RAILWAYS

Société Nationale des Chemins de Fer du Togo (SNCT): BP 340, Lomé; tel. 21-43-01; telex 5178; fax 21-22-19; f. 1905; restructured under present name in 1995; total length 517 km, incl. lines running inland from Lomé to Atakpamé and Blitta (280 km), and a coastal line, running through Lomé and Aného, which links with the Benin railway system, but which was closed to passenger traffic in 1988 (a service from Lomé to Palimé—119 km—has also been suspended); passengers carried (1990): 630,000, freight handled (1990): 16,000 metric tons; Gen. Man. ROY GEMMELL.

ROADS

In 1995 there were some 7,519 km of roads, of which 2,376 km were paved. Principal roads run from Lomé to the borders of Ghana, Nigeria, Burkina Faso and Benin.

Africa Route International (ARI–La Gazelle): km 9, route d'Atakpamé, BP 4730, Lomé; tel. 25-27-32; fax 29-09-93; f. 1991 to succeed Société Nationale de Transports Routiers; Pres. and Man. Dir BAWA S. MANKOUBI.

SHIPPING

The major port, at Lomé, generally handles a substantial volume of transit trade for the land-locked countries of Mali, Niger and Burkina Faso, although political unrest in Togo has resulted in the diversion of much of this trade to neighbouring Benin. Lomé handled about 856,600 metric tons of goods (including transit trade) in 1994, compared with some 2m. tons in previous years. In 1995 the Banque ouest-africaine de développement approved a loan of 5,000m. francs CFA to help finance the rehabilitation of the infrastructure at Lomé port. The project aimed to re-establish Lomé as one of the principal transit ports on the west coast of Africa. There is another port at Kpémé for the export of phosphates.

Port Autonome de Lomé: BP 1225, Lomé; tel. 27-47-42; telex 5243; fax 27-02-48; f. 1968; Pres. IHOUI AGBOBOLI; Man. Dir KODJO AGBEJOMÉ.

Société Ouest-Africaine d'Entreprises Maritimes Togo (SOAEM-TOGO): Zone Industrielle Portuaire, BP 3285, Lomé; tel. 21-07-20; telex 5207; fax 21-34-17; f. 1959; forwarding agents, warehousing, sea and road freight transport; Pres. JEAN FABRY; Man. Dir JOHN M. AQUEREBURU.

Société Togolaise de Navigation Maritime (SOTONAM): place des Quatre Etoiles, rond-point du Port, BP 4086, Lomé; tel. 21-51-73; telex 5285; fax 27-69-38; Man. PAKOUM KPEMA.

SOCOPAO-Togo: 18 rue du Commerce, BP 821, Lomé; tel. 21-55-88; telex 5205; fax 21-73-17; f. 1959; freight transport, shipping agents; Pres. GUY MIRABAUD; Man. Dir HENRI CHAULIER.

SORINCO-Marine: 110 rue de l'OCAM, BP 2806, Lomé; tel. 21-56-94; freight transport, forwarding agents, warehousing, etc.; Man. AHMED EDGAR COLLINGWOOD WILLIAMS.

Togolaise d'Armements et d'Agence de Lignes SA (TAAL): 21 blvd du Mono, BP 9089, Lomé; tel. 22-02-43; telex 5329; fax 21-06-69; f. 1992; shipping agents, haulage management, crewing agency, forwarding agents; Pres. and Man. Dir LAURENT GBATI TAKASSI-KIKPA.

CIVIL AVIATION

There are international airports at Tokoin, near Lomé, and at Niamtougou. In addition, there are smaller airfields at Sokodé, Sansanné-Mango, Dapaong and Atakpamé.

Air Afrique: BP 111, Lomé; tel. 21-20-42; telex 5276; see under Côte d'Ivoire; Man. in Togo RAPHAËL BIAM.

Air Togo: rue du Commerce, Lomé; tel. 21-33-10; f. 1963; cap. 5m. francs CFA; scheduled internal services; Man. Dir AMADOU ISAAC ADE.

Peace Air Togo (PAT): Lomé; internal services and services to Burkina Faso and Côte d'Ivoire; Man. Dir M. DJIBOM.

Tourism

Some 44,000 tourists visited Togo in 1994, when receipts from tourism totalled US $18m. There were 4,163 hotel beds in 1993.

Direction des Professions Touristiques: BP 1289, Lomé; tel. 21-56-62; telex 5007; Dir GAMELI KETOMAGNAN.

Defence

In August 1996 Togo's armed forces officially numbered about 6,950 (army 6,500, air force 250, naval force 200). Paramilitary forces comprised a 750-strong gendarmerie. (However, at the time of the 1991 national conference, several sources put the strength of the armed forces at 12,000.) Military service is by selective conscription and lasts for two years. Togo normally receives assistance with training and equipment from France; however, French military assistance was suspended in late 1992, in view of the political crisis in Togo, and only resumed in September 1994.

Defence Expenditure: Budgeted at 14,000m. francs CFA in 1996.

Chief of the Armed Forces: Gen. GNASSINGBE EYADÉMA.

Education

In 1995, according to UNESCO estimates, the adult illiteracy rate averaged 48.3% (males 33.0%; females 63.0%). Primary education, which begins at six years of age and lasts for six years, is officially compulsory. Secondary education, beginning at the age of 12, lasts for a further seven years, comprisng a first cycle of four years and a second of three years. In 1993 enrolment at primary schools included 69% of children in the relevent age-group (80% of boys; 58% of girls). In the same year secondary enrolment was equivalent to only 23% of the appropriate age group (boys 34%; girls 12%). Proficiency in the two national languages, Ewe and Kabiye, is compulsory. Mission schools are important, educating almost one-half of all pupils. The Université du Bénin at Lomé had about 11,000 students in the mid-1990s, and scholarships to French universities are available. Current expenditure on education was an estimated 23,800m. francs CFA in 1995 (16.2% of total expenditure by the central government).

Bibliography

Cornevin, R. *Histoire du Togo.* Paris, 1962.

'Le Togo', in *Collection Que sais-je?* Paris, Presses Universitaires de France, 1967.

Le Togo: des origines à nos jours. Paris, Académie des sciences d'outre-mer, 1987.

Curkeet, A. A. *Togo: Portrait of a West African Francophone Republic.* Jefferson, McFarland, 1993.

Decalo, S. *Historical Dictionary of Togo.* Metuchen, NJ, Scarecrow Press, 1976.

Delval, R. *Les musulmans au Togo.* Paris, Académie des sciences d'outre-mer, 1984.

François, Y. *Le Togo.* Paris, Editions Karthala, 1993.

Harrison Church, R. J. *West Africa.* 8th Edn. London, Longman, 1979.

Piraux, M. *Le Togo aujourd'hui.* Paris, Editions Jeune Afrique, 1977.

Stoecker, H. (Ed.). *German Imperialism in Africa.* London, Hurst Humanities, 1987.

Thompson, V. *West Africa's Council of the Entente.* Ithaca, NY, and London, Cornell University Press, 1972.

Toulabor, C. *Le Togo sous Eyadéma.* Paris, Editions Karthala, 1986.

Verdier, R. *Le pays kabiyé Togo.* Paris, Editions Karthala, 1983.

UGANDA

Physical and Social Geography

B. W. LANGLANDS

PHYSICAL FEATURES AND CLIMATE

The Republic of Uganda is located on the eastern African plateau, at least 800 km inland from the Indian Ocean, and has a total area of 241,139 sq km (93,104 sq miles), including 44,081 sq km of inland water. There are several large freshwater lakes, of which Lakes Victoria, Edward and Albert are shared with neighbouring states. These lakes and most of the rivers form part of the basin of the upper (White) Nile, which has its origin in Uganda. At the point where the upper Nile leaves Lake Victoria, it is harnessed for hydroelectricity by the Owen Falls dam.

Of the land area (excluding open water), 84% forms a plateau at 900–1,500 m above sea-level, with a gentle downwarp to the centre to form Lake Kyoga. The western arm of the east African rift system accounts for the 9% of the land area at less than 900 m; this includes the lowlands flanking the rift lakes (Edward and Albert) and the course of the Albert Nile at little more than 620 m. Mountains of over 2,100 m occupy 2% of the land area and these lands are above the limit of cultivation. The highest point is Mt Stanley, 5,109 m, in the Ruwenzori group on the border with the Democratic Republic of the Congo, but larger areas of highland are included in the Uganda portion of the volcanic mass of Mt Elgon, near the Kenyan border. The remaining 5% of the land area lies at an altitude of 1,500–2,100 m, including both the eastern and western extremities which form the shoulders to their respective rift valley systems, and the foothills of the mountains already referred to. Some of the most heavily populated regions are located at this altitude, which is free of malaria.

Geologically the great proportion of the country is made up of Pre-Cambrian material, largely of gneisses and schists into which granites have been intruded. In the west, distinct series of metamorphosed rocks occur, largely of phyllites and shales, and in which mineralized zones contain small quantities of copper, tin, tungsten and beryllium. Deposits of gold, cobalt and nickel have also been identified, and in the east of the country there are extensive deposits of magnetite, apatite and crystalline limestone. The apatite provides the basis for a superphosphate industry and the limestone for a cement industry, both at Tororo.

NATURAL RESOURCES

The economy of Uganda depends upon agriculture and this, in turn, is affected by climate. The country's location, between 1° 30′S and 4°N, gives little variation in temperature throughout the year, affording an equatorial climate modified by altitude. Rainfall is greatest bordering Lake Victoria and on the mountains, where small areas have over 2,000 mm per year. The high ground of the west, the rest of the Lake Victoria zone, and the eastern and north-central interior all have more than 1,250 mm annually. Only the north-east (Karamoja) and parts of the south (east Ankole) have less than 750 mm. However, total amounts of rain are less significant agriculturally than the length of the dry season. For much of the centre and west there is no more than one month with less than 50 mm and this zone is characterized by permanent cropping of bananas for food, and coffee and tea for cash crops. To the south the dry season increases to three months (June to August); in the north it increases to four months (December to March) and in the north-east the dry season begins in October. Where the dry season is marked, as in the north and east, finger millet provides the staple food and cotton the main cash crop. In the driest parts pastoralism predominates, together with some sorghum cultivation.

Western Uganda, where there is a greater range of different physical conditions, and generally where population densities are below average, shows a diversity of land use, with tropical rain forest, two game parks, ranch lands, fishing, mining and the cultivation of coffee and tea. The north and east is more monotonous, savannah-covered plain with annually sown fields of grain and cotton. Most of the country's coffee comes from the Lake Victoria zone (*robusta*) and Mt Elgon (*arabica*). The economy relies heavily upon smallholding peasant production of basic cash crops.

POPULATION

The latest census, conducted in January 1991, enumerated a population of 16,671,705, giving a density of about 69 inhabitants per km. The total at the 1980 census had been 12.6m. The population is predominantly rural; at the 1980 census only about 7% of the populace resided in towns of more than 1,000 people. Kampala (population estimated at 458,423 in 1980), the capital and main commercial centre, and Jinja (45,060), an industrial town, are the only urban centres of any significance. The annual birth rate is just under 52 per 1,000 of the population. Average life expectancy in 1990–95 was 45 years, according to estimates by the UN. About 50% of the population are below the age of 16. Demographic patterns in the later 1990s and beyond are expected to be significantly affected by the high rate of incidence of the Acquired Immunodeficiency Syndrome (AIDS), which, by the early 1990s, had reportedly reached epidemic proportions in parts of Uganda.

In 1959 about two-thirds of the population, mainly in the centre and south, were Bantu-speaking, about one-sixth Nilotic-speaking and a further one-sixth Nilo-Hamitic (Paranilotic). In 1969 there were 74,000 people of Indian and Pakistani origin, engaged mainly in commerce, and 9,500 Europeans, mostly in professional services. Since the 1972 expulsions of non-citizen Asians (who comprised the majority of the resident Asian population), both of these totals have fallen substantially.

Recent History

ALAN RAKE

With revisions by the Editor

British penetration of Uganda began after 1860. In 1888 the United Kingdom's interests were assigned to the British East Africa Co, whose control over the area was consolidated in 1891 by a treaty with the kabaka (king) of Buganda, the principal kingdom. The company's responsibilities were taken over by the British government in 1894. Buganda was declared a protectorate and the same status was subsequently conferred on the kingdoms of Bunyoro, Toro, Ankole and Bugosa. For the next 50 years, debate over the position of Buganda within a future self-governing state inhibited the creation of a united nationalist movement. In 1956 the Democratic Party (DP) was formed, with a predominantly professional leadership and widespread support among the Roman Catholic peasantry. The DP favoured a unitary independent state of Uganda and opposed the ambitions of the Baganda people, who did not wish Buganda's influence to be diminished after independence. The Uganda National Congress (UNC), however, was a nationally-based party, derived from farmers' organizations and advocating greater African control of the economy in a federal independent state. In 1958 seven African members of the protectorate's legislative council, including two members of the UNC, joined another faction, led by Dr Milton Obote, to form the Uganda People's Congress (UPC). By 1960 the UPC, the DP (led by Benedicto Kiwanuka) and the Buganda council (lukiiko) were the principal political forces in Uganda.

In 1961, at the first nation-wide election to the legislative council, the DP won a majority of the seats. Kiwanuka was appointed chief minister, but he proved to be unacceptable to the ruling élite of Buganda. The Kabaka Yekka (KY, or 'King Alone'), a political party representing the interests of the lukiiko, was formed to ally with the UPC against the DP, and to obtain political advantage from the forthcoming constitutional negotiations. Uganda was granted self-government in 1962, with Kiwanuka as prime minister. At pre-independence elections to a national assembly, held in April, the UPC won a majority of seats. The UPC–KY coalition formed a government, led by Obote. The new constitution provided for a federation of four regions—Buganda, Ankole, Bunyoro and Toro—each with considerable autonomy. In October Uganda became independent, within the Commonwealth, and a year later, on 9 October 1963, the country became a republic, with Mutesa II, the kabaka (king) of Buganda, as non-executive president.

OBOTE AND THE UPC

During the first years of independence the UPC–KY alliance was placed under strain by controversy over levels of central government expenditure in Buganda, and over the 'lost counties', two districts of Bunyoro that had been transferred to Buganda in the late 19th century: in a referendum in November 1964 the inhabitants of the two districts voted to return to Bunyoro, but President Mutesa refused to endorse this result. By now, sufficient KY and DP members of the national assembly had defected to the UPC for the alliance to be no longer necessary. The UPC had also gained control of all district councils and kingdom legislatures, except in Buganda. The UPC itself, however, was affected by disagreements between conservative, centrist and radical elements of the party. In February 1966 the national assembly approved a motion demanding an investigation into gold-smuggling, in which Dr Obote, the minister of defence, and the second-in-command of the army, Col Idi Amin Dada, were alleged to be involved. Later in that month Obote led a pre-emptive coup against his opponents within the UPC. Five government ministers were arrested, the constitution was suspended, the president was deposed and all executive powers were transferred to Obote. In April an interim constitution was introduced, withdrawing regional autonomy and introducing an executive presidency. Obote became head of state. In May, when the lukiiko demanded the restoration of Buganda's autonomy, government troops, commanded by Amin, seized the palace of the kabaka (who escaped abroad), and a state of emergency was imposed in Buganda. A new constitution was adopted in September 1967, establishing a unitary republic and abolishing traditional rulers and legislatures. National elections were postponed until 1971.

During the late 1960s the Obote regime pursued an economic programme which aimed to achieve the redistribution of incomes through nationalization. At the same time the government came to rely increasingly on detention and armed repression by the paramilitary and intelligence services. Estrangement began to develop, however, between Obote and the army, which had remained under Amin's command since the suppression of the lukiiko. In 1969 Amin ignored Obote's order to cease channelling military aid to separatist guerrillas in Southern Sudan. In December Obote was wounded in an assassination attempt in Kampala: Amin immediately fled to an army base in his home area. In the following month Brig. Pierino Okoya, Amin's most forceful critic in the government, was murdered.

THE AMIN REGIME

In January 1971, while Obote was out of the country, Amin seized power. In February he declared himself head of state, promising a return to civilian rule within five years. Many Ugandans believed that Amin would bring about the national cohesion which the UPC had failed to provide, and at first he received substantial support, as well as obtaining ready recognition from Western governments. Amin consolidated his military position by massacring troops and police (particularly those of the Langi and Acholi tribes) who had supported the Obote regime. Soon after taking power Amin suspended political activity and most civil rights. The national assembly was dissolved, and Amin ruled by decree. The jurisdiction of military tribunals was extended to cover the entire population, and several agencies were established to enforce state security. In August 1972 Amin announced the expulsion of all non-citizen Asians (who comprised the majority of the resident Asian population). The order was subsequently extended to include all Asians, and although this was later rescinded, under internal and external pressure, all but 4,000 Ugandan Asians left the country. Most went to the United Kingdom, which severed diplomatic relations and imposed a trade embargo against Uganda. In December all British companies in Uganda were nationalized without compensation.

In September 1972 a group of pro-Obote guerrillas (former members of the army and police who had fled the country when Amin seized power) attempted unsuccessfully to oust Amin by an invasion, launched from Tanzania. The attempt was led by David Oyite-Ojok, the former chief of staff, and Yoweri Museveni, another senior officer. In retaliation, Amin's air force bombed Tanzanian towns. The Amin regime was supplied with military aid by Libya and the USSR, and by the end of 1972 virtually all Western aid had ceased. No coherent economic development policy existed, and the country's infrastructure was allowed to deteriorate. During 1972–75 there were sporadic occurrences of factional fighting within the army, including an unsuccessful coup attempt in March 1974. Attacks on the Langi and Acholi populations were perpetrated by the army between late 1976 and early 1977. In February 1977, after protesting at the massacres, the Anglican archbishop of Uganda, Janine Luwum, and two government ministers were murdered.

In October 1978 Amin sought to divert the attention of the armed forces from internal divisions (which had led to another abortive coup in August) by invading Tanzania, claiming the rightful possession of the Kagera salient. The attempt was unsuccessful and stimulated the Tanzanian government's efforts to remove Amin from power. Political exiles in Tanzania and elsewhere, including Obote, were encouraged by President

Nyerere of Tanzania to form a united political front to remove Amin. In January 1979 the Tanzanian armed forces invaded Uganda, assisted by the Uganda National Liberation Army (UNLA), which comprised exiled Ugandan volunteers under the command of Oyite-Ojok and Museveni. They met little resistance from Amin's forces (assisted by 1,500 Libyan troops) and captured Kampala in April. Amin fled the country, eventually taking refuge in Saudi Arabia.

TRANSITIONAL GOVERNMENTS

Attempts among Ugandan exiles to form a common political front in Tanzania had led to the Moshi Conference in March 1979. Nyerere, reluctant to support Obote's reinstatement, had persuaded Obote not to attend, although the UPC was represented at the conference by an associate of Obote, Paulo Muwanga. A compromise candidate, Dr Yusufu Lule (a distinguished academic who had formerly been associated with the KY) was chosen to lead a newly-created Uganda National Liberation Front (UNLF), on whose 30-member national consultative committee (NCC), all the 18 organizations participating at Moshi were represented. A national executive committee (NEC) was established under Lule's chairmanship, together with a military commission, headed by Muwanga. Lule was sworn in as president of Uganda in April.

In June 1979 attempts by Lule to reorganize the NEC led to his removal by the NCC. He was replaced as president by the former attorney-general, Godfrey Binaisa. A period of widespread anarchy followed: relations between the UNLA and the Tanzanian forces deteriorated, as did those between the military and civilian populations. The UNLA had been greatly enlarged by numbers of untrained recruits and ethnically-based militias, and was divided into supporters of Oyite-Ojok and of Museveni. In late 1979 Binaisa was persuaded by Obote and Muwanga to dismiss Museveni as minister of defence, thereby gravely weakening his own position in relation to the NCC. Binaisa announced that a general election would take place in December 1980: with the support of the NCC, he ruled that only UNLF candidates would be allowed to participate. In May 1980 Binaisa attempted to dismiss Oyite-Ojok from the command of the UNLA: UNLA soldiers began to arrest Binaisa's ministers, and in May power was assumed by the UNLF's military commission, under the chairmanship of Paulo Muwanga, supported by Oyite-Ojok and with Museveni as vice-chairman.

OBOTE AND OKELLO

The elections held in December 1980 were contested by four parties: the UPC, under Obote; the DP, led by Paul Ssemogerere; the Uganda Patriotic Movement (UPM), a regrouping of the radical faction of the UPC, led by Yoweri Museveni; and the Conservative Party (CP), a successor to the KY. The DP was prevented from registering a number of candidates for the 126 elective seats in the new legislature, with the result that the UPC gained a majority of 20 seats, and Obote was proclaimed president of Uganda on 15 December, with Paulo Muwanga as vice-president and minister of defence, Eric Otema Allimadi (a former minister of foreign affairs) as prime minister, and Tito Okello as army chief-of-staff.

The election of the UPC government did not bring military or political stability to Uganda. Although Amin himself had been easily dislodged, his legacy of corruption and rule by terror proved to be more difficult to eradicate. The new UPC government inherited neither political continuity nor an administrative framework; its leading members ranged from military war-lords to politically independent civilians who were committed to national development. Not surprisingly, the UPC was unable to formulate a consistent ideology. In its dealings with potential foreign donors, however, the government proclaimed its support of an IMF-sponsored economic reconstruction programme. This stance was successful in attracting goodwill and, initially, a certain amount of finance from Western countries and Arab sources. While the level of violence subsided considerably during 1981–82, domestic uncertainty was perpetuated by continued indiscipline in the army and by the proliferation of security agencies which were effectively beyond the law.

Following the removal of Binaisa in 1980, the UNLA openly participated in Ugandan politics. Its main preoccupation, however, was in internal counter-insurgency operations, as dissatisfaction with the conduct and outcome of the elections caused several factions to initiate guerrilla operations against the UPC government. The three main guerrilla movements were the Uganda National Rescue Front (UNRF), comprising supporters of Amin who were active in the West Nile area, the Uganda Freedom Movement (UFM), led by Balaki Kirya and Andrew Kayiira, and the National Resistance Army (NRA), led by Yoweri Museveni, with ex-president Lule, now in exile, as chairman of its political wing, the National Resistance Movement (NRM).

From 1981, NRA operations grew steadily in military expertise and political sophistication. Drawing on disaffected southern Ugandans, especially among the Banyarwanda and Baganda, and defectors from the increasingly disorganized UNLA, the NRA began to establish a reputation for military discipline. A UNLA campaign during 1983 attempted to deprive the NRA of civilian support by depopulating the area around Luwero—the 'Luwero Triangle'—where a large proportion of the population was forced to take refuge in government camps. Large numbers of 'displaced persons' made their way to Kampala and surrounding towns after the main camps were dismantled in early 1984, while others joined the NRA. The offensive against the NRA was renewed in late 1984, with civilians again suffering the main impact of attacks.

Meanwhile, tensions were developing within the UNLA between the two main ethnic groups from which the army was recruited, the Acholi and the Langi. Following the death of the Langi chief of staff, Oyite-Ojok, in December 1983, the appointment of a successor was delayed for eight months, creating further tensions. Some 200 Acholi officers were eventually promoted, in compensation for the appointment of another Langi as chief of staff, Lt-Col (later Brig.) Smith Opon-Acak, in late 1984.

By early 1985 the Obote government was under pressure on other fronts. When IMF funds had been exhausted, the resultant shortage of foreign exchange led to shortages of many commodities, and inflation rapidly increased. After allegations in 1984 at hearings of a US congressional committee that up to 100,000 people had been killed since the accession of the UPC government, a report by Amnesty International, in mid-1985, alleged widespread and systematic torture and murder of civilians by the security forces.

In the first week of July 1985 the Acholi-Langi rivalries led to an outbreak of fighting in the Kampala barracks, following rumours that Obote was planning a massacre of Acholi officers. A group of Acholi soldiers, led by Lt-Gen. (later Gen.) Tito Okello, escaped north to join the Acholi detachments of Brig. (later Lt-Gen.) Basilio Okello (not related to Tito Okello). After a confrontation near the Karuma Falls, these combined forces severed the route to the West Nile area and the major Acholi population centres. Despite the history of bitter rivalry between the Acholi and the West Nile tribes, the Acholi rebels had already agreed to join the UNRF in an attempt to oust Obote. When, in late July, troops under Basilio Okello began to march south on Kampala, Obote fled to Kenya (moving eventually to exile in Zambia).

At the close of July 1985 Tito Okello became Uganda's new president. He quickly formed an Acholi-dominated military council in which a small number of civilians (including Paul Ssemogerere of the DP) were included. There followed a brief period during which some control was exercised over army indiscipline, and political prisoners were released.

By the end of August 1985, however, the Okello government was facing serious difficulties. The NRA had occupied the main towns of the west (Fort Portal and Kasese), and by late September southern Uganda, up to the Katonga river, was under its control, while UNLA troops in the southern towns of Mbarara and Masaka remained under siege in their barracks. The discipline of the NRA forces contrasted starkly with the performance of the UNLA, while the NRA's control of southern Uganda, and the region's cash crops, placed an economic stranglehold on the Kampala government.

Against this volatile background, a series of peace talks opened in Nairobi, Kenya, between representatives of the NRA and the Okello government. It soon became apparent, however, that neither side was fully committed to a permanent peace settlement, and the accord that they eventually signed, in late December 1985, was intended mainly to pre-empt a *coup d'état* against Tito Okello by the minister of defence, Wilson Toko and his supporters in the West Nile. The subsequent attempt to disarm the West Nile troops prompted most of them to retreat north, leaving devastation in their path. Yoweri Museveni, who had become sole leader of the NRM and NRA following Lule's death earlier in the year, did not take up his alloted seat on the military council in Kampala, but returned to south-west Uganda to lead the NRA in a final offensive.

THE MUSEVENI PRESIDENCY

Claiming that law and order had broken down throughout Uganda, NRA troops surrounded Kampala, and took control in January 1986. Yoweri Museveni was sworn in as president and formed a National Resistance Council (NRC), with both civilian and military members. His cabinet, with Samson Kisekka as prime minister, included members as diverse as Paul Ssemogerere of the DP, Moses Ali, a former minister under Amin, and Andrew Kayiira of the UFM. Elections were postponed for at least three years. Political parties were not banned, although their activities were officially suspended in March. The defeat of Okello's remaining UNLA troops was officially completed by the end of March. They wreaked havoc in the areas through which they retreated into Sudan, where Lt-Gen. Basilio Okello died in exile in January 1990.

Museveni announced a policy of national reconciliation. He established a commission to investigate breaches of human rights during the regimes of Amin, Obote and Okello, under whom, he claimed, up to 800,000 Ugandans had been killed. Following an investigation of the activities of the police force, more than 2,500 of its members were dismissed in July 1986. During 1986 the Museveni government developed a system of resistance committees at local and district level; these were to be partly responsible for the maintenance of security and the elimination of corruption.

Lawlessness, banditry and indiscipline remained rife, especially in the north. In March 1986 an armed opposition movement seeking the overthrow of Museveni, the Uganda People's Democratic Movement (UPDM), was formed, with Obote's former prime minister, Eric Otema Allimadi, as chairman. This, together with raids by remnants of the UNLA, chronic problems with armed cattle-rustlers in the north-east and the lack of any basic infrastructure of law and order, prevented Museveni from consolidating his control over Uganda. Although he allowed the return from exile of Prince Ronald Mutebi, the claimant to the throne of Buganda, Museveni refused to restore Uganda's traditional monarchies until stability had returned to the country (see below). In August an alleged plot by Baganda monarchists was uncovered, and more than 20 were arrested.

In October 1986 it was announced that 26 people, including Paulo Muwanga, Obote's former vice-president, and Andrew Kayiira of the UFM, had been arrested for treason. Although charges against some of these were later withdrawn, the murder of Kayiira in March 1987 caused the UFM to withdraw its support from the government. The trial of seven of the 26 people who had been arrested in October 1986 began in August 1987, and in the following March three of the defendants were sentenced to death for treason, while the remaining four were acquitted. Muwanga, who was acquitted of abduction and murder, was released in October 1990 and died in April 1991.

The largest uprising in the period immediately following Museveni's accession to power was led by a charismatic cult leader, Alice Lakwena, whose religious sect attracted both peasant farmers from the Acholi tribe and former soldiers of the UNLA. The rebel 'Holy Spirit Movement', as it became known, engaged the NRA in attacks that were effectively suicidal. In late 1987, after several thousand of the rebels had been killed, the revolt was crushed, and Lakwena fled to Kenya. However, remaining members of the movement subsequently regrouped themselves as the Lord's Resistance Army (LRA). In August 1987 the UPDM joined with a faction of the Federal Democratic Movement and another opposition group, the United National Front, to form an alliance which aimed to overthrow Museveni, but by August 1988 this alliance had proved to be ineffective. Another rebel group, the Uganda Democratic Alliance (UDA), claimed responsibility for a bomb attack on diplomatic buildings in Kampala in January 1988, in which a Libyan diplomat was killed. An abortive mutiny by members of the NRA in April resulted in the detention of some 700 army officers and soldiers. In October 24 people were arrested and charged with plotting a coup.

In conjunction with the use of force to curb dissidence, Museveni also adopted a reconciliatory approach towards opponents of the NRC. In June 1987 an amnesty was declared for insurgents (except those accused of murder or rape), which was subsequently repeatedly extended; by April 1988 Ugandan officials reported that almost 30,000 rebels had surrendered. However, in December 1987, while on a mission to implement the amnesty in Soroti district, Stanislas Okurut, the minister of labour, and two deputy ministers were detained by rebels of the Ugandan People's Army (UPA), led by Peter Otai, a former minister in the Obote administration. The UPA's demands for the release of rebel prisoners in exchange for the ministers were not met; one of the deputy ministers escaped in March 1988, while a clash between NRA troops and the rebels in August led to the death of the other deputy minister and the injuring of Okurut. In early 1988 the NRA held peace talks with the armed wing of the UPDM, the Uganda People's Democratic Army (UPDA). The failure by the commander of the UPDA, Brig. Justin Odong Latek, to endorse the proposed peace agreement led to his removal, in May, from the leadership of the rebel army. In the following month his successor, Lt-Col John Angelo Okello, signed a peace agreement with the NRC; however, a faction of the UPDA regrouped, under the leadership of Odong Latek, and continued to oppose the government. In mid-1989 the NRC launched a major offensive against guerrilla forces.

Further efforts were made to consolidate the position of the Museveni administration. The president carried out a major cabinet reshuffle in February 1988, in which he increased the number of ministers originating from the north-east of Uganda, where opposition to the government was most prevalent. In May the NRC approved legislation validating the NRC as the country's official legislature. In the following month, draft legislation was introduced to prohibit the practice and promotion of sectarianism; other new legislation imposed heavy penalties for revealing military operations and strategies to the 'enemy'. A degree of press censorship was also introduced. It was stressed by Museveni that the prohibition of 'sectarianism' was not aimed at stifling political debate.

In February 1989 the first national election since 1980 was held. The NRC, which had previously comprised only members nominated by the president, was expanded from 98 to 278 members, to include 210 elected representatives. While a total of 20 ministerial posts were reserved for nominated members of the NRC, 50 were allocated to elected members. As a result of these changes, 10 cabinet ministers and four deputy ministers lost their posts. Following the election, Museveni appointed a constitutional commission to gauge public opinion on Uganda's political future and to draft a new constitution.

In October 1989 (despite opposition from the DP) the NRC approved draft legislation, submitted by the NRM, to extend the government's term of office by five years from January 1990, when its mandate had been due to expire: the NRM justified seeking to extend its rule by claiming that it required further time in which to prepare a new constitution, to organize elections, to eliminate continuing anti-government guerrilla activity, to improve the judiciary, police force and civil service, and to rehabilitate the country's infrastructure. It was announced in January 1990 that several army officers and civilians had been charged with plotting to overthrow the government. In March the NRM extended the ban on party political activity (imposed in March 1986) for a further five years. In February 1990 the minister of culture, youth and sports, Brig. Moses Ali, was dismissed and charged with plotting a *coup d'état*. (Ali was subsequently acquitted of this charge, but in January 1991 was found guilty of illegally possessing ammunition.) In July 1990 the leader of the UPDM, Eric Otema Allimadi, signed a peace accord with the government; nevertheless, some members of the group were reported to have rejected the government amnesty.

In January 1991 Samson Kisekka was replaced as prime minister by George Adyebo; Kisekka was appointed vice-president and minister of internal affairs. In April Daniel Omara Atubo, the minister of state for foreign affairs and regional co-operation, was arrested, together with two other members of the

NRC, and charged with plotting to overthrow the government by assisting anti-government rebels; 15 other people (including further members of the NRC) were subsequently detained on similar grounds. At the beginning of April the government initiated a campaign to eradicate continuing guerrilla activity in northern and eastern districts: by July it was reported that more than 1,500 rebels had been killed and more than 1,000 had been arrested. International observers accused the NRA of committing atrocities during the campaign.

In May 1991 Museveni formally invited all emigré Ugandan Asians, who had been expelled during the Amin regime, to return. This gesture was intended to attract both international approval and investment in the Ugandan economy by expelled Asians who had prospered since leaving Uganda. In July the cabinet was reshuffled, with the number of ministries substantially reduced as a measure to enhance efficiency. A report by Amnesty International, which was released in early December, accused the NRA of torturing and summarily executing prisoners during anti-insurgency operations.

In October 1992 the government launched a three-year programme to reduce the size of the NRA by about one-half, in response to pressure from the international donor community. In December negotiations on the restoration of the Bugandan monarchy commenced between Museveni and the claimant, Prince Ronald Mutebi. Later in the same month the constitutional commission which had been established in 1989 published a draft constitution, which was criticized by the opposition on the grounds that it would increase presidential powers still further. The commission recommended non-party presidential elections after two years followed by a further five-year ban on political parties.

In March 1993 the draft constitution was published; the document (which was strongly opposed by the UPC and the DP) provided for the proscription of party political activity for at least a further seven years and a continuation of 'non-party democracy', under the auspices of a national political movement to which all citizens would belong. In April the NRC passed legislation authorizing the establishment of a constituent assembly (see below).

In July 1993 legislation was approved which provided for the restoration of each of Uganda's traditional monarchies; these were, however, to be limited to ceremonial and cultural functions. At the end of that month Prince Ronald Mutebi was enthroned as the kabaka of Buganda, and in early August the lukiiko was re-established. A new omukama (king) of Toro, Patrick Olimi Kaboyo, was also installed in late July. The Ankole people similarly proceeded with the coronation of their omugabe (king), John Barigye, at a ceremony held in November. However, Museveni, although himself an Ankole, refused to recognize the new king, thereby increasing suspicions that his recognition of the kabaka of Buganda and the omukama (king) of Toro was based on short-term political expediency rather than a desire to revive Uganda's traditional kingdoms. In June 1994 Museveni agreed to the coronation of Solomon Gafabusa Iguru as omukama of the Bunyoro. Patrick Olimi Kaboyo died in August 1995, and was succeeded as omukama of Toro in September 1996 by his infant son Oyo Nyimba Iguru. The kingdom of Busoga was restored in February 1996, with Henry Wako Muloki installed as king

At the beginning of September 1993 nine army officers, who had been arrested on treason charges between 1988–90 and held without trial, were released. In the same month the government ordered a judicial review of the trials of those sentenced to death in the previous January by army tribunals which were now officially described as 'illegal and incompetent'. In October Lt-Col James Oponyo, the commander of the UPA in the Teso area in north-eastern Uganda, surrendered to government forces. In January 1994 the Ugandan Democratic Alliance (UDA) and the Uganda Federal Army (UFA) decided to suspend their guerrilla operations, under the provision of the government amnesty first granted in 1988. The commander-in-chief of the alliance, Sam Luwero, indicated that the organization was to be dissolved. Museveni stated that the government was determined to suppress the continuing insurgency in the Karamojong area, however, where bandits and cattle thieves were still active. In early 1994 Peter Otai, a minister under Obote and former leader of the UPA, formed a new rebel group, known as the Uganda People's Freedom Movement (UPFM).

In March 1994 renewed clashes occurred in northern Uganda between the forces of the LRA, now led by Joseph Kony, and the government. The rebels, who claimed to be fighting a 'holy war' against foreign occupation of Uganda, carried out ambushes and abductions which prompted the government to dispatch large numbers of security forces to the region.

The return of emigré Asians to reclaim the property which was expropriated by the Amin regime continued in 1994, although the process provoked jealousies and racial antagonism, with indigenous businessmen claiming that they had not been sufficiently compensated. Despite sporadic acts of violence, the government adhered to its compensation policy and extended from October 1993 to April 1994 the deadline for Asians to return and reclaim their expropriated assets.

Elections to the 288-member constituent assembly took place in March 1994, and were accepted by a majority of Ugandans to have been conducted fairly. In a turn-out of 7m. of the total 8m. registered voters, Museveni and the NRM won overwhelming support. Although candidates were officially required to stand on a non-party basis, tacit official tolerance of party campaigning was reflected in the leaders of three parties—the DP, the CP and the UPC—being given access to national radio and television during the weeks prior to the election. Of the 214 elective seats to the constituent assembly the government alliance won an estimated 150 seats, most of which were in Buganda, the Western region and parts of the East, while the opposition (supporters of the UPC and DP) secured most seats in the north and the north-east. Museveni and Samson Kisseka, the vice-president, who indicated that he was to retire from active politics, did not stand. Museveni's most senior government colleagues (including the prime minister, Cosmas Adyebo and his three deputies) won convincingly. Among five senior ministers who failed to obtain seats, however, was the minister of finance and economic planning, Jehoash Mayanja-Nkangi, and the katikiro (prime minister) of Buganda. The constituent assembly, which also comprised nominated representatives of the armed forces, political parties, trade unions and various special interest groups, was empowered to debate, amend and finally to enact the draft constitution. Amendments to the draft required a two-thirds majority of the assembly; changes that received majority support but less than two-thirds were to be submitted to referendum. The new constitution, under whose terms a national referendum on the future introduction of a multi-party political system was to be staged in 1999, was eventually promulgated in October 1995.

In November 1994 Museveni reshuffled the cabinet, replacing Adyebo as prime minister by Kintu Musoke, hitherto minister of state for security, and appointing Dr Speciosa Wandira Kazibwe, the minister of women's affairs and community development, as vice-president. Brig. Moses Ali rejoined the cabinet as minister of tourism, wildlife and antiquities. In June 1995 Paul Ssemogerere resigned from his posts of second deputy prime minister and minister of public service, announcing that he intended to prepare a campaign with which to contest the presidential election that was scheduled to take place, with legislative elections, in 1996. A minor cabinet reshuffle ensued in mid-July, at which Eric Adriko, hitherto minister of state for internal affairs, was appointed second deputy prime minister and minister of public service.

In June 1995 the constituent assembly rejected the immediate restoration of multi-party democracy, claiming that it would exacerbate existing ethnic and religious divisions. Consequently, candidates at the legislative and presidential elections would be required to seek election without official reference to their respective political affiliations. The constituent assembly's decision was strongly opposed by the UPC and other unofficial opposition parties.

It was announced in mid-1995 that defence expenditure would be increased by 40% (despite recent cutbacks) in order to combat continuing insurrection in northern Uganda by rebel groups (including the LRA, see below) which was hampering the economic development of the already impoverished region. Signs of serious tensions in the army were apparent at this time. A military report was published, which detailed deteriorating conditions and equipment, as well as corruption and low morale among soliders. For the first time since he had taken power, Museveni appeared to be losing the support of sections of the NRA; this had potentially serious implications, as disagreements within the armies of previous regimes had pre-empted a sudden collapse of the administration's power base. A number of opposition groups were established during the mid-1990s by Baganda with federalist aspirations.

Preparations for the forthcoming presidential and legislative elections proceeded at a leisurely pace during 1995 and early 1996. The election dates were postponed several times. Registration of the presidential candidates eventually took place in March 1996. The main challenger to Museveni was Paul Ssemogerere, the leader of the DP and former second deputy prime minister. While many of Ssemogerere's election rallies were banned, Museveni campaigned with the full backing of the army, police and security forces. The presidential election was held on 9 May; Museveni won convincingly, securing 74.2% of the votes (Ssemogerere took 23.7%). The incumbent president triumphed in most regions, including Buganda and other areas that had traditionally been loyal to the DP. As the unofficial representative of an electoral alliance between the DP and the UPC, Ssemogerere was widely perceived to be associated with the UPC's former leader, Dr. Milton Obote. This brought Ssemogerere some successes in the north but lost him support in Buganda and in the west. The election, which was declared free and fair by international observers, emphatically legitimized Museveni's presidency. He immediately declared that he would not restore multi-party government for at least five years. Legislative elections took place in June. The total membership of the NRC, redesignated the parliament under the new constitution, was reduced from 278 to 276, comprising 214 elected and 62 nominated representatives. Also in June elections were held for new local councils (to replace the resistance committees). In July Museveni appointed an enlarged 57-member cabinet (25 ministers and 32 junior ministers), disregarding pressure from international creditors to adhere to the constitutional limitation of 42 cabinet members. Museveni hoped to achieve national unity by appealing to as broad a base as possible, but he also owed a debt to his own party, the NRM, for supporting his election campaign. Dr. Speciosa Wandira Kazibwe retained the vice-presidency, despite a challenge by Jaberi Bidandi-Ssali, the minister of local government, who had hoped to be rewarded for organizing the successful campaign. Many other important ministers retained their portfolios. The president, notably, ceded responsibility for defence to two (non-cabinet) ministers of state.

The LRA became increasingly disruptive during the mid-1990s. In April 1995 the rebel group mounted a serious attack on Atiak in which 250 civilians were killed. Smaller incursions from Pataluka camp, across the Sudanese border, occurred during the course of 1995. Museveni took the threat seriously, announcing that the NRA would be re-equipped to fight mobile and modern warfare against the rebels (see above). In March 1996 the LRA raided the village of Pabo, some 230 miles from Kampala, killing at least 200 people. The Ugandan government has repeatedly accused Sudan of providing the LRA with refuge and support. Further skirmishes were reported in July, when the rebel group surrounded NRA troops at a barracks near Gulu and proceeded to attack targets in the town. Soon afterwards Museveni appointed his half-brother, Maj.-Gen. Salim Saleh, to oversee all military operations in the north. Saleh launched 'Operation Clean', a campaign to rout the rebels; although this had some early successes, the LRA resumed its attacks on Gulu in August. In early 1997 the continuing conflict in the north was considered to have contributed to food shortages there, with some 140,000 people being fed by the UN World Food Programme. During 1993–97 the LRA killed as many as 10,000 people, while a further 230,000 had sought refuge in protected camps.

From late 1996 the Uganda People's Defence Forces (UPDF, as the NRA had become) also fought intermittently with two rebel groups in the west of Uganda: the West Nile Bank Front (WNBF, led by a former minister of foreign affairs, Juma Oris) and the Allied Democratic Front (ADF), comprising Islamic fundamentalists and former soldiers of the defeated UNLA, reportedly assisted by Rwandan Hutu militiamen and by some 3,000 Zairean troops. The regional policy of the Ugandan government (see below), in particular in Sudan and in Zaire (renamed the Democratic Republic of the Congo in May 1997), reflected concerns that rebel groups were operating from within these countries. Ugandan rebel groups were reported to have suffered severe setbacks in the first half of 1997, with military advances by Zairean and Sudanese rebels on good terms with the Ugandan government. In June 1997 some 500 ADF soldiers, based in the Ruwenzori mountains, briefly occupied the town of Bundibugyo, before being dislodged by the UPDF. At the end of July, in an incident believed to be the work of a rebel organization, two bombs exploded in a suburb of Kampala, killing at least six people.

REGIONAL RELATIONS

During 1987 Uganda's relations with neighbouring Kenya deteriorated, with the Museveni government accusing Kenya of sheltering Ugandan rebels. In March the Kenyan authorities expelled hundreds of Ugandans. When, in October, Uganda stationed troops at the two countries' common border, Kenya threatened to retaliate with force against any attempts by Ugandan military personnel to cross the frontier in pursuit of rebels. In December clashes occurred between Kenyan and Ugandan security forces and the border was temporarily closed. Later in December, discussions between the heads of state of the two countries led to an improvement in relations, and in January 1988 Kenya and Uganda signed a joint communiqué, which provided for co-operation in resolving problems relating to the flow of traffic across the common border. However, several incursions into Kenya by Ugandan troops were reported in 1988 and 1989, and in July 1988 the Ugandan government accused Kenya of complicity in smuggling weapons to rebels in northern Uganda. In August 1980 President Moi of Kenya visited Museveni, indicating a renewed *détente* between Uganda and Kenya. Moi made a further visit to Uganda in November 1993, at which a communiqué was signed providing for the exploration of areas of co-operation in both security and trade. In November 1994 the presidents of Uganda, Kenya and Tanzania met in Arusha, Tanzania, and established a permanent commission for co-operation between the three countries, with a view to reviving the defunct EAC; progress was hindered, however, by a sudden deterioration in relations between Uganda and Kenya. During early 1995 the Kenyan government protested strongly to the UN, following the granting of refugee status in Uganda to an alleged Kenyan guerrilla leader; the Ugandan authorities subsequently claimed to have deported the Kenyan to a third country (reported to be Ghana). Relations between Uganda and Kenya deteriorated further in late 1995, when the Kenyan president accused Uganda of recruiting South African mercenaries with a view to invading Kenya; the Museveni administration strongly denied the allegations. Following the intervention of the newly-elected President Mkapa of Tanzania, the Ugandan and Kenyan presidents were publicly reconciled in January 1996, and undertook to co-operate over the planned relaunch of the EAC. In March 1996 Museveni, Moi and President Benjamin Mpaka of Tanzania, meeting in Nairobi, Kenya, formally inaugurated the secretariat of the permanent tripartite commission for East African co-operation. The principal aims of this revival of the EAC were to enhance regional co-operation in political and economic affairs, and to reduce its members' reliance on foreign aid. In September, none the less, the Kenyan authorities suggested that the Ugandan government was supporting attempts to subvert the Moi administration; such allegations were strongly denied by Uganda. In April 1997 a four-year development strategy was launched for the three countries, along with a regional passport and flag. In August the government complained to Kenya regarding the detention without trial of some 100 Ugandans in that country.

During 1988 tension also arose on the border between Uganda and Zaire (now the Democratic Republic of the Congo), owing to a number of attacks by Zairean troops on NRA units; further border clashes occurred in 1992. In November 1996 Ugandan rebels were reportedly operating from within Zaire with the support of Zairean troops. In late 1996 and early 1997 the Ugandan authorities repeatedly denied allegations that Ugandan forces were occupying territory in eastern Zaire; however, it was widely reported that Uganda was supplying armaments and tactical support, if not troops, to Laurent-Désiré Kabila's Alliance des forces démocratiques pour la libération du Congo-Zaïre (AFDL), which overthrew the government of President Mobutu in May 1997.

During the late 1980s and early 1990s Sudanese troops reportedly made repeated incursions into Ugandan territory in pursuit of Sudanese rebels, and Sudanese aircraft were alleged to have dropped bombs in northern Uganda on several occasions. In early 1992 nearly 80,000 Sudanese refugees fled to Uganda, followed by a further 50,000 in August 1993. Relations between the two countries deteriorated seriously in 1994, when each Government accused the other of harbouring and supporting their respective outlawed guerrilla groups; in April 1995 Uganda severed diplomatic relations with Sudan, accusing several Sudanese diplomats of endangering Ugandan national security. In October 1995 intense fighting between Sudanese rebels and government forces resulted in the displacement of several thousand Ugandans residing in the border region. In November the Ugandan government dispatched troops to protect the area. Subsequent allegations by the Sudanese authorities that Ugandan forces were massing on the two countries' common border in order to invade southern Sudan were strongly denied by the Museveni regime. In the following month, however, Museveni threatened to launch military assaults into Sudan in retaliation for the Sudanese government's alleged continuing support for the LRA. Sudanese troops shelled the border area for three consecutive days in April 1996, provoking strong protest from the Ugandan government. In September 1996 Sudan and Uganda resumed diplomatic relations, and in the following month a preliminary accord was signed in the Iranian capital, Teheran. Relations between the two countries did not improve, however: in September 1996 and in February 1997 it was alleged that Sudanese aircraft had once again attacked northern Uganda, and in April, despite continuing discussions under the auspices of Iran and Libya, the Sudanese authorities claimed that their forces had killed several hundred Ugandan soldiers who had been assisting Sudanese rebels from within Sudan.

During the late 1980s an estimated 250,000 Rwandan refugees were sheltering in Uganda. Relations with Rwanda deteriorated in October 1990, following the infiltration of northern Rwanda by an invasion force of some 4,000 Rwandan rebels who had been based in Uganda; their leader, Maj.-Gen. Fred Rwigyema (who was killed by the Rwandan armed forces), was a deputy commander of the NRA and a former Ugandan deputy minister of defence. In November President Museveni dismissed all non-Ugandan members of the NRA. In February 1991 a conference was held on the Rwandan security situation; an amnesty was agreed for all Rwandans who were exiled abroad, and the rebels were urged to observe a cease-fire. Nevertheless, the allegedly Uganda-based Rwandan rebels continued to operate in northern Rwanda during 1991–93. In January 1992 it was reported that 64,000 Ugandans residing near the two countries' common border had been displaced, owing to cross-border shelling by Rwandan troops. In August 1993 the UN Observer Mission Uganda-Rwanda (subsequently disbanded) stationed troops on the Ugandan side of this border to verify that no military assistance reached Rwandan rebels. In May 1994 the Ugandan authorities appealed for emergency assistance, claiming that the corpses of thousands of victims of massacres taking place in Rwanda were contaminating the water supply of districts abutting Lake Victoria. The victory in Rwanda of the Front patriotique rwandais (FPR) in mid-1994 brought about a significant change in bilateral relations; Maj.-Gen. Paul Kagame, Rwandan vice-president and minister of national defence, had previously served in the Ugandan NRA, as had other members of the FPR administration. In August 1995 Museveni made an official visit to Rwanda, and both countries made commitments to enhance economic and social co-operation. The Ugandan government strenuously denied allegations that a military alliance had been formed between the countries with the ultimate aim of extending Tutsi rule as far as Burundi and Zaire. In July 1996 Uganda joined other regional governments in imposing economic sanctions on the military regime in Burundi; in April 1997 it was agreed that most of these sanctions should be lifted.

Economy

LINDA VAN BUREN

AGRICULTURE

Agriculture is overwhelmingly the most important sector of Uganda's economy. It accounts for some 90% of the country's export earnings, contributes about 46% of gross domestic product (GDP, combining subsistence and monetary agricultural production) and provides a livelihood for more than 80% of Uganda's labour force. Nearly two-thirds of government revenue is provided by the agricultural sector, mainly through export duties on coffee, the country's principal export. The development of the whole economy is therefore heavily influenced by the sector's performance. Coffee is, by far, the most important export crop, followed by cotton and tea. Tobacco was also an important crop until the 1970s. Soils are generally fertile and, apart from some parts of the north-east and north-west, the country has a climate favourable to both crops and livestock production. Smallholder mixed farming predominates, with estate production confined mainly to tea and sugar cane. Agricultural output was severely affected by the unstable security situation which prevailed during the 1970s and early 1980s; since assumption of power by Yoweri Museveni in January 1986 efforts have been made to rehabilitate the sector, although continuing security problems have slowed the pace of recovery. Growth in agricultural GDP reached a peak of 7.8% in 1987/88, but had fallen to 2.7% by 1991/92. The collapse of international coffee prices in 1989 had a particularly adverse effect on overall economic performance. A poor harvest in 1991/92 was followed by a greatly improved season in 1992/93; in 1993/94, however, output was again depressed by the effects of widespread drought. Agricultural production increased by an annual average of 3.3% in 1990–95.

Coffee

Coffee (mostly *robusta*) continues to dominate the monetary sector. It is grown by more than 1m. small farmers. Production fell steadily throughout the 1970s, from a record 225,200 metric tons in 1973 to only 97,500 tons in 1981. Lack of transport and spare parts, and smuggling into Kenya and Zaire were the main factors that limited coffee exports during this period.

Following the assumption of power by the National Resistance Army in January 1986, coffee exports were temporarily halted, with the unfortunate result that Uganda failed to benefit from the prevailing high prices for coffee on the world market. Although exports were resumed later in the year, the total quantity for the 1985/86 coffee year was only 2.4m. bags (each of 60 kg), leaving substantial unsold stocks. As a result of favourable weather and the introduction by the Coffee Marketing Board (CMB), in August 1987, of advance payments to farmers, Uganda easily fulfilled its International Coffee Organization (ICO) quota for 1987/88 of 2.1m. bags, and additional exports to non-ICO countries raised total exports for the year to 2.7m. bags. In 1988/89 a record 3.1m. bags were exported. However, despite the greatest coffee output for 14 years, export earnings declined to US $160m. in 1989, from $270m. in 1988, owing to the collapse of world prices, following the suspension of ICO quotas (see below). Production fell to 2.8m. bags in 1990 and to 2.3m. bags in 1991, with exports earning $141m. in 1990 and only $126m. in 1991. Output was 1.83m. bags in 1992, 2.35m. bags in 1993, 3.4m. bags in 1994 and about 3.7m. bags in 1995; production was expected to rise still further in 1996, with the maturing of a new higher-yielding strain. However, the spread of tracheomycosis, a coffee wilt disease, in 1997 represented a serious potential threat to production levels. The collapse of ICO quota arrangements in 1989 brought about a sharp decline in the international coffee market that continued into the early 1990s. Effective action to revive the market began in August 1993, when the Inter-African Coffee Organization, of which Uganda is a member, joined Latin American producers in a scheme to withhold 20% of output whenever market prices fell below an agreed limit; by September 1994 market quotations for all grades and origins of coffee had achieved their highest levels since 1986, although they subsequently fell back. While the value of coffee exports boomed, farmgate prices paid to coffee growers declined from sh. 1,200 per kg to sh. 600 in the mid-1990s. In February 1995 Uganda was among the five African coffee producers which agreed to participate in coffee price guarantee arrangements under the auspices of the Common Market for Eastern and Southern Africa (COMESA).

The CMB, which was the sole purchaser and exporter of coffee during the 1980s, had persistent problems with crop finance, which adversely affected deliveries from farmers. In 1990 the CMB's monopoly of coffee marketing was abolished. Five coffee co-operatives joined forces to form Union Export Services (UNEX), and by mid-1992 UNEX was handling 20% of coffee sales with the CMB handling the remaining 80%. By mid-1993 there were 12 coffee-marketing co-operatives. However, liberalization was slow, and in 1996 25 of a total 100 licensed exporters controlled an estimated 80% of the trade; growers were thus forced to accept low prices for their crop. In 1991 the Uganda Coffee Development Authority (UCDA) was established, with responsibility for policy-making, research and development in the coffee sector. The CMB was to be reorganized as a public limited company; bidding opened in mid-1997. In 1994 the government introduced a coffee stabilization tax, which aimed to alleviate the potential 'boom and bust' effect of soaring international coffee prices; in the 1994/95 financial year the tax produced revenue of sh. 14,300m. However, some exporters avoided payment of the tax by underselling coffee, at a rate of more than US $6.5m. per month, as a result of which a lower threshold of sh. 1,500m. per kg and a new rate of 25% were introduced from June 1995. In June 1996 the unpopular tax was abolished. In 1994 and 1995 the Uganda Investment Authority was seeking investors in coffee nurseries and enterprises for roasting, packaging, processing, blending and the utilization of coffee by-products. In 1996 the UCDA sought to encourage the wet-processing of coffee.

The United Kingdom is Uganda's largest customer for coffee, taking about one-third of the total. The USA, Japan and Germany are also important customers. Most of Uganda's coffee was formerly transported to Mombasa (Kenya) by road and rail. The Museveni government, however, has attempted to effect a transfer to rail freight for all Ugandan trade, in order to reduce costs.

Tea

Prior to the Amin regime and the nationalization of tea plantations in 1972, Uganda was second only to Kenya among African producers. However, production declined each year thereafter until 1980, by which time Uganda's tea exports were negligible. In 1980 the British-based company Mitchell Cotts, former owner of three groups of tea estates until these were nationalized by Amin, was invited back to establish a joint venture with the government to own and operate the estates. The Toro and Mityana Tea Co (Tamteco) was formed in 1980, with 51% of the shares owned by the government, and work began on a US $8.8m. programme to rehabilitate the overgrown plantations and near-derelict factories. Tamteco, the main producer of tea, with 2,300 ha under cultivation, was fully privatized in 1995. The second-largest producer is the Uganda Tea Corpn, which is state-owned and has plantations covering 900 ha. A parastatal body, Agricultural Enterprises Ltd (AEL), has 2,100 ha of estates and seven tea factories, which have been rehabilitated by a Netherlands company. The remaining government holdings in tea enterprises are awaiting transfer to the private sector, and investors in processing and packaging plants were being sought in the mid-1990s. Smallholders, with 9,440 ha under tea, market their output through the Uganda Tea Growers' Asscn. Plans to create a regulatory body for the sector and to organize research into growing methods were being discussed in 1997.

Output and exports of tea improved from 1981. By 1984 production of made tea had risen to 5,223 metric tons, with exports of 2,604 tons. Uganda derived some benefit from the record international tea prices of late 1983 and 1984 (although tea accounted for less than 1% of total export earnings in 1984). A sustained recovery began in 1989, when tea production totalled 4,620 tons and exports were 3,134 tons. By 1993 production totalled 12,289 tons, and 10,251 tons were exported. In 1994, when tea output advanced to 13,461 tons, exports of 10,971 tons exceeded those achieved in 1977. Production fell back to 12,692 tons in 1995, when 10,682 tons were exported. In 1996, however, tea output increased to 17,418 tons, with exports advancing to 14,982 tons. The principal markets for Ugandan teas are Kenya, Sudan, Saudi Arabia and the United Kingdom. The full realization of Uganda's production potential remains inhibited by a shortage of labour, caused mainly by very low wages.

Cotton

In the early 1970s Uganda ranked third among African cotton producers. However, production decreased from a peak of 467,000 bales (each of 480 lb or 217.7 kg) in 1970 to a low of 18,800 bales in 1981. The causes of the decline were the very low official prices paid to producers and the physical deterioration of the ginneries during Amin's rule. Exports ceased altogether during the 1970s, resuming in 1982. Output rose slowly, reaching 56,646 bales in 1983/84, of which 60% was exported. The 1984/85 harvest was slightly lower. In 1985 cotton exports earned US $15.4m., equivalent to 4.1% of total export earnings. The 1985/86 harvest fell to about 45,000 bales. In 1986 the government initiated the Emergency Cotton Production Programme, but the 1987 target of 140,000 bales was not even 50% achieved. Low producer prices and the poor security situation in the main cotton-growing areas in the north and east were mainly to blame for the disappointing result. The $15m. programme was funded by the World Bank, the United Kingdom and other donors. The production target for 1988/89 was 150,000 bales, but actual output was only 44,000 bales. Exports of cotton earned $3.1m. in 1988, compared with $4.1m. in 1987. Production reached 105,650 bales in 1989, but fell back to 51,000 bales in 1990, to 36,750 bales in 1991, to 32,150 bales in 1992, to 30,864 bales in 1993 and to 29,600 bales in 1994. In 1995 cotton output was estimated to have increased to 70,000 bales. Exports of cotton earned $14.7m. in 1996, an increase of more than 50% on the previous year's level. The derelict state of the ginneries frequently resulted in stockpiles awaiting ginning, despite the low harvests. Ginneries were privatized during 1995–97, and the ensuing competition, together with the distribution of free high-quality seed by the government in 1996 and the liberalization of seed distribution in 1997, was expected to contribute to increased yields. Production of cottonseed declined from 18,000 metric tons in 1991 to 15,000 tons annually in 1992–94, and to 12,000 tons in 1995. In addition, Uganda produced an estimated 12,000 tons of cotton lint, 26,000 tons of cottonseed and 2,830 tons of cottonseed oil in 1996. Main customers are the United Kingdom, Germany, Hong Kong and Portugal.

Other Crops

Tobacco output has frequently been adversely affected by unfavourable weather conditions and recurrent fighting in the West Nile region, where it is grown. Production was estimated at only 100 metric tons in 1981, compared with a peak of 5,000 tons in 1972, but by 1983 exports resumed on a very small scale. Following a rise in producer prices and the implementation of a US $5.5m. rehabilitation programme, production increased to 1,900 tons in 1984. Output fell to 925 tons in 1986, but recovered to about 4,000 metric tons annually during 1987–89. There was a further recovery in 1992, to 7,285 tons, the largest crop for more than two decades. Production fell back to just under 5,000 tons in 1993, and was estimated at 7,000 tons in 1994, when there was an increase in the availability of interest-free crop finance from British-American Tobacco (BAT). Phillip Morris of the USA was given permission in April 1994 to enter the

Ugandan market, thereby breaking a monopoly previously held by BAT. In 1996 exports of tobacco earned $7.4m.

Production of raw sugar had fallen to only 2,400 metric tons by 1984, compared with a peak of 152,000 tons in 1968. Local demand is estimated at 160,000–200,000 tons per year. Lack of transport and problems with the maintenance of mechanical equipment contributed to this drastic fall in output, but the major cause was the expulsion of the Asian families who ran much of the sugar industry, on three large estates. The Madhvani and Mehta families returned in 1980 to begin the rehabilitation of the estates and factories, in joint-venture companies with the government. The Lugazi sugar complex, 40 km east of Kampala, and now operated by the Uganda Sugar Corpn, is 51% owned by the government and 49% by the Mehta group. A new refinery, with a capacity of 60,000 tons per year, was opened in 1988. The complex (including a 9,180-ha plantation) has been rehabilitated in a US $90m. project, funded by the International Development Association (IDA), the African Development Bank (ADB), the Commonwealth Development Corporation (CDC), the Arab Bank for Economic Development in Africa (BADEA), Kuwait and India. In 1993, however, the factory suspended production, owing to competition from sugar which had been smuggled from western Kenya. The state-owned Kinyala sugar works are being rehabilitated in a project costing $58m., which is partly financed by Kuwait, BADEA and the Saudi Fund for Development. Once rehabilitated, Kinyala should produce 37,000 tons of sugar per year. In 1985 a branch of the Madhvani family signed an agreement with the government to establish a new company, Kakira Sugar Works (1985). The rehabilitation of the Kakira complex began in 1988, and trial production commenced in the following year. Upon completion of the rehabilitation work, Kakira is expected to have an annual capacity of 120,000 tons of cane sugar; in 1997 it produced an estimated 70,000 tons. In 1996 Uganda's output of raw sugar amounted to some 78,000 tons, up from 49,300 tons in 1993. In the early 1990s, large quantities of sugar grown and processed in western Kenya were being smuggled into Uganda. Cocoa production declined significantly during the Amin regime, and has subsequently not fully recovered. Exports increased from 100 tons in 1982 to 170 tons in 1984 and to 1,396 tons in 1990. Production remained steady at about 1,000 tons per year in 1991–95. Revenue from cocoa exports amounted to $442,000 in 1995, and to $1.1m. in 1996.

Uganda's principal food crops are matoke (a form of plantain), cassava, sweet potatoes, finger millet, maize, beans, sorghum, potatoes, groundnuts and simsim. Output of matoke was 9,519,000 metric tons in 1995. There are three rice-growing projects in the country. The largest, in Olwiny swamp in the north, covers 800 ha and is being implemented with help from the People's Republic of China, the ADB and the Islamic Development Bank. A further 680 ha is to be developed for smallholder production. Maize cultivation is rapidly expanding, both as a subsistence and as a cash crop. In 1984 maize became Uganda's third largest source of foreign exchange. Since the late 1980s, however, transport problems and the poor state of rural roads have hampered the collection of crops. In 1988, when output of maize was estimated at 600,000 tons, Uganda fell far short of fulfilling its commitments for the export of maize and beans under barter agreements which had been concluded with several countries, whereby crops were to have been exchanged for machinery, equipment or other essential imports. The maize harvest, according to official figures, totalled 804,000 tons in 1993, rising to 850,000 tons in 1994, and again, to 913,000 tons, in 1995. Uganda produced 610,000 tons of millet per year in 1993 and 1994, and 632,000 tons in 1995. Output of sorghum in the same period rose steadily, from 383,000 tons in 1993 to 390,000 tons in 1994 and 395,000 tons in 1995. Cassava production amounted to 2,224,000 tons in 1995.

Groundnuts and soya beans enjoyed an upsurge in production in the early 1990s. Output of groundnuts in shells totalled 153,000 tons in 1993, but declined to 142,000 tons in 1994, before recovering slightly, to 144,000 tons in 1995.Uganda also produced 5,097 tons of groundnut oil in 1995. Similarly, production of soya beans increased from 53,000 tons in 1992 to 79,000 tons in 1995. Uganda also harvests about 3,000 metric tons of sunflower seed each year. According to the FAO, production of dry beans stood at 115,000 tons in 1993, rising to 120,000 tons in 1994 and to 123,000 tons in 1995. Output of castor-bean oil declined from 437 tons in 1993 to 347 tons in 1995. In May 1992 the government confirmed that strategic food stocks were low. World Bank figures indicate that Uganda's receipts of food aid amounted to 17,000 tons in 1989, 35,000 tons in 1990, 61,000 tons in 1991 and 28,000 tons in 1992. In mid-1997 food shortages, caused by drought and political instability, were estimated to require US $24m. in aid. In 1996 investors were being sought to finance the cultivation of horticultural produce, including vanilla, chillies, papayas, asparagus, medicinal plants and fresh flowers.

Beef and dairy cattle are kept by smallholders and on large commercial ranches. The country has good-quality pasture, but the prevalence of several endemic diseases and the armed theft of cattle are continuing problems. The total number of cattle was estimated at 5.2m. in 1995. Following a decline in cattle numbers during the 1980s, the government initiated an artificial insemination programme to regenerate the herd, with funding from the European Union (EU). The dairy sector is being revitalized in a scheme funded by several UN agencies, the ADB, the European Development Fund (EDF) and Denmark. The project is aimed at improving the processing, collection and transport of dairy produce to urban markets. Poultry, pigs, sheep, goats and bees are also important. In the mid-1990s the government invited foreign companies to invest in cattle, sheep and goat ranching, chicken, Peking duck and ostrich farming, beekeeping, hide and skin processing, leather processing, cattle horn processing, preserved meat processing and crocodile farming and processing.

Uganda has an abundance of lakes and rivers, and fishing is an important rural industry, with considerable scope for further development, particularly in inshore fish farming, eels and freshwater prawns. In 1995 the total catch amounted to 208,807 metric tons. In 1989 an Italian company began to develop an integrated fisheries centre at Masese to smoke and dry tilapia and Nile perch. Concerns were raised in 1996 that the country's fish stocks were being depleted, and the licensing of processing factories was suspended (20 were currently licensed, although not all were operational). In the same year a fast-growing aquatic plant, water hyacinth, had covered large areas of Lake Victoria and had rendered the main landing at Port Bell inaccessible; a US company was brought in to control the problem. It was warned, however, that the use of herbicides could affect fish export earnings, Uganda's third most important export in 1996. Some 7.5m. ha are covered by forest and woodland. In early 1990 the government banned exports of timber, pending the implementation of legislation to regulate the forestry sector. By 1994 production of industrial roundwood had reached 2.22m. cu m, while output of non-coniferous sawnwood had recovered significantly, from 20,000 cu m in 1991 to 77,000 cu m in 1993.

INDUSTRY

The main industries are processing of cotton, coffee, tea, sugar, tobacco, edible oils and dairy products, grain milling, brewing, vehicle assembly and the manufacture of textiles, steel, metal products, cement, soap, shoes, animal feeds, fertilizers, paints, cigarettes and matches. The output of all these industries fell drastically during the 1970s. Much plant and machinery was in a bad state of repair and there were shortages of fuel, spare parts and technical and managerial skills. In January 1993 the European Investment Bank provided Uganda with a loan of ECU 5.4m. in support of industrial development. Copper refining was formerly very important, but production ceased during Amin's regime. Negotiations concerning a project to revive the copper-refining sector took place in 1991.

The rehabilitation of Uganda's industrial sector has proceeded very slowly, and in 1992 industry was still estimated to be operating at below 30% of capacity. However, in 1987 the government claimed that several industries, including grain-milling and the manufacture of hoes, beer, blankets and poultry feed, were operating at more than 50% of capacity. The output of the industrial sector increased by an annual average of 9.3% during the period 1990–94, according to estimates by the World Bank. According to the UN, manufacturing production increased by 20.1% in 1994 and by 27.5% in 1995. This growth is attributable to the food-processing, timber and paper, tobacco and leather and footwear sectors. Nevertheless, in 1991/92 manufacturing provided only 6.2% of gross domestic product (GDP), rising only slightly, to 7.7%, in 1995/96.

The textile industry is suffering a severe lack of skilled personnel and of spare parts but considerable amounts of aid, from the ADB, the EU and from certain Arab funds, are helping to establish new ginneries, spinning and weaving mills and to repair existing plants. There are four fully integrated textile mills, with a total rated capacity of 66m. linear metres of cloth per year. Yarn is also produced. In 1996 Uganda's largest textile factory, Nyanza Textiles Industries, at Jinja, reopened, after several years of dormancy, under private management.

The country's first vehicle-assembly plant, operated by GM Co, is a joint venture between the local Spear Motors and Peter Bauer of Germany. Capacity is 490 commercial vehicles and 360 trailers per year, with about 40% available for export. In 1983 the British-based Lonrho group resumed production at its Chibuku brewery, which had fallen into disuse after its expropriation by the Amin government. The group also opened negotiations for the repossession of its other expropriated assets in Uganda, including Consolidated Printers, which prints the government-controlled daily *New Vision,* and Printpak (Uganda). In November 1986 Lonrho signed an agreement with the government, under which it was to construct an oil pipeline from the Kenyan border to Kampala, and participate in the marketing of Ugandan coffee and cotton. In 1989 the Madhvani group began to bring nine of its 10 industrial companies back into production (only its textile firm, Mulco, was still operating). By 1997 the group was producing tea, beer, cooking oil, sugar, confectionery, steel bars, fencing, cables, matches, bottle tops, glassware, cut flowers, twine and cardboard boxes. In 1984 Uganda Breweries was returned to its original owners, Nairobi-based East African Breweries and Ind Coope and City Breweries of the UK. It subsequently started to rehabilitate its Port Bell plant. In 1995 the Madhvani group announced a sh. 9,000m. project to expand its Nile Breweries plant at Jinja, with the aim of increasing the factory's capacity to 500,000 crates of beer per month; a similar project of expansion at Uganda Breweries was also under way in the mid-1990s. In 1995 the government awarded KW Uganda Ltd a licence to import beer from South Africa, thereby opening the Ugandan beer market to foreign competition. In 1997 Nile Breweries announced a joint venture with South African Breweries, to produce South African brands of beer in Uganda. A local firm, Century Bottling Co, obtained the franchise to produce Coca-Cola in the Ntinda industrial area, outside Kampala. The East African Development Bank and Uganda Development Bank were major investors in the project. Crown Bottlers produces Pepsi-Cola. A tannery has been opened at Jinja, and it is hoped that Uganda will become self-sufficient in leather goods. Chloride (Uganda) has been expanded and it is expected that Uganda will eventually be self-sufficient in batteries. The country's second pharmaceutical plant, INLEX, opened in 1989.

A salt plant at Lake Katwe, built with German finance in 1974–78 for the production of table salt and potassium chloride, closed in 1980, owing to technical problems. Uganda has since had to import all its salt requirements. A US $20m. contract for the rehabilitation of the plant was awarded to a Swiss firm in 1986, but the government had difficulty in attracting private investors to be joint shareholders with the Uganda Development Corpn. Output of unrefined salt averaged 5,000 metric tons in 1989–91. There are two cement plants, at Tororo (near the Kenyan border) and at Hima (about 500 km to the west), with rated annual capacities of 150,000 tons and 300,000 tons respectively, although in 1995 their combined output was only 84,000 tons. Total domestic requirements are 650,000 tons per year. Some renovation work has been carried out, by a Turkish company at Tororo and by a German company at Hima. In 1995 the Kenya-based Rawal group bought the Hima plant for US $20.5m., while the Tororo complex was purchased for $5.7m. by the Kenyan company Corrugated Sheets Ltd.

During 1992–95 the Uganda Investment Authority identified 1,600 new investment projects in agro-processing, tourism, mining, banking and communications. It is seeking investors in radio, television and video assembly and in the manufacture of office equipment, household durables and electrical goods.

MINERALS

The Kilembe copper mines, in western Uganda, which produced about 17,000 metric tons of blister copper in 1970, became inactive in 1979, and the associated smelter at Jinja fell into disrepair. Exports of copper resumed in 1994. Reserves of copper ore were estimated in 1982 to exceed 4m. tons. Prior to the Amin period, a stockpile of copper pyrites accumulated at the Kilembe mines. The Kasese Cobalt Co, a joint venture between the state-owned Kilembe Mines Ltd and La Source of France, was established to extract cobalt from these tailings in a scheme with a projected cost of US $86.5m., scheduled to come into operation in 1998; target annual production is 1,000 tons of cobalt. Banff Resources, of Canada, subsequently acquired a 55% interest in the company. Prior to the Amin period, Uganda exploited substantial deposits of apatite (used in superphosphate fertilizers) at Tororo. Until the 1970s, the country also mined tungsten, beryl, columbo-tantalite, gold, bismuth, phosphate, limestone and tin, mostly on a small scale. It is hoped to reopen these mines. Extraction of small quantities of tungsten, tin concentrates and gold has recommenced. In 1996, following the removal of a 5% royalty on the metal, gold was Uganda's second largest export; an uncertain proportion, however, had allegedly been smuggled into the country from Zaire (subsequently the Democratic Republic of the Congo). In 1996 Branch Energy, a consortium of British and South African mining interests, was prospecting for gold in Karamoja, while Pangea Goldfields of Canada was prospecting for gold near Busia under 12 licences. A study, financed by the World Bank, was made by US and French consultants on a phosphate fertilizer project using phosphate deposits in the Sukulu hills, estimated at 220m.–225m. tons. The study recommended construction of a plant to make single superphosphates, with initial capacity of 80,000 tons per year. The total cost of the project was to be about US $102m. There are high-grade iron ore deposits at Kigezi but they have not yet been exploited. Geological surveys have been carried out in the Lake Albert and Rift Valley areas.

Petroleum exploration has proceeded slowly. In the early 1980s the IDA loaned US $5.1m. for exploration promotion, to attract bids from international oil companies and for consultancy services to evaluate these offers. Initially, there was little interest, and successive changes of government prevented any progress, until, in 1987, the Museveni government initiated a Petroleum Exploration Promotion Project. Bidding for exploration rights was opened in 1988. In 1990 Uganda and Zaire signed an agreement for the joint exploration and exploitation of petroleum reserves beneath Lakes Albert and Edward. Geological surveys in Lake Albert were completed in 1994, and were proceeding in the Lake Edward basin in 1995. In February 1995 the government awarded a US-affiliated company, the Uganda General Works and Engineering Co, a licence to exploit reserves in the Lake Albert area. A further exploration licence was awarded, in January 1997, to a British company, Heritage Oil and Gas Ltd.

POWER

Electricity is generated at the Owen Falls hydroelectric station at Jinja, which has an installed capacity of 180 MW, of which 30 MW has been exported, under contract, to Kenya since 1955. Plans have been announced to modernize the Owen Falls plant, and to expand its capacity to 380 MW, under a US $282m. programme to rehabilitate the power grid, which received pledges of finance from the IDA and a number of Western European development agencies. In 1993 the Chinese company Sietco was awarded the contract for the principal construction work at the Owen Falls plant; by mid-1996, however, Sietco had departed. A successor was to be chosen; meanwhile, the power station was refurbished and restored to full capacity in 1997. Energy consumption per caput grew by an annual average of 3.7% in 1980–92, a marked increase over the annual average of –7.0% in 1971–80. However, by the mid-1990s domestic demand for electricity was considerably in excess of supply, despite price rises amounting to some 300% during 1994–97; after exports of power, barely one-half of Uganda's domestic requirement was being met. With the need for further revenue to install new generators, protracted negotiations were held with Kenya concerning the price of that country's contractual imports from Uganda. An agreement was eventually reached in

June 1997. Electricity production was estimated at 756m. kWh in 1994. In that year Uganda imported 58% of its energy requirements and consumed 479,000 tons of petroleum equivalent. The monopoly held by the Uganda Electricity Board (UEB) over electricity supply was removed from September 1996, opening the sector to competition. Companies in all fields were encouraged to establish 'build, own and operate' schemes to provide electricity to meet their own demands, while selling power to others as a means of recouping some of their investment. A new 250-MW dam at Bijagari Falls has been proposed by the Madhvani group and AES, of the USA; finance was being sought in 1997.

TOURISM

During the 1960s and until 1972, tourism was, after coffee and cotton, the third most important source of foreign exchange. In 1971 there were 85,000 visitors and receipts were US $27m. Tourism ceased during Amin's rule, with wildlife parks and hotels totally neglected. Under the Obote government, the sector began to be slowly rehabilitated. The number of visitors rose from 8,622 in 1982 to an estimated 193,000 in 1995 and 250,000 in 1996. Revenue from the sector totalled some $90m. in 1995.

The state-owned Uganda Hotels Corpn (which is to be transferred to private-sector ownership) owns four hotels. In early 1988 a consortium of Italian companies, led by Viginter, agreed to construct four four-star hotels, in Masaka, Fort Portal, Jinja and Mbale. The 264-room Sheraton Kampala was refurbished by the Yugoslav company, Energoprojekt, at a cost of US $27.5m., and it is now managed by Sheraton Corpn of the USA. In 1996 it was undergoing a $4m. renovation. In 1995 the 76-room Nile Hotel International announced plans to build a 16-storey, 150-room tower block. The 109-room luxury Grand Imperial Hotel opened in Kampala in October 1995. Uganda has eight national parks. In 1995 there were 29 tour operators in Uganda.

TRANSPORT AND COMMUNICATIONS

The Third Highway Project, costing US $32.6m. (with financing by the IDA) was inaugurated in August 1987. It involved repair of existing surfaced and unsurfaced roads. The road link with Rwanda was to be improved with EU finance, as part of the 'northern corridor' scheme to link eastern Zaire, Rwanda and Uganda with the Kenyan port of Mombasa. The EDF has pledged funding for the second phase of a project to repair Kampala's roads. Other major programmes of road repairs have received financial backing from Germany, under its bilateral aid programme. In February 1987 the government signed an agreement with Yugoslavia's Energoprojekt, for the construction of a 250-km road in western Uganda, from Mityana to Fort Portal, as part of the Trans-African Highway. Under a US $150m. road rehabilitation project, launched in 1994, some 15 roads were to be improved by mid-1998. The rehabilitation of the Kampala-Entebbe road encountered some difficulties, and, as well as an upwards revision of the cost, the completion date was postponed to September 1997. Several hundred new lorries were imported, many under barter agreements, in the early 1990s. India, France and Germany supplied locomotives and rolling stock, which were urgently needed by the Uganda Railways Corpn (URC), established following the dissolution of East African Railways. The United Kingdom, France, Italy, Germany and the EU have all assisted with a programme to rehabilitate the railway system, which also forms part of the 'northern corridor'. The URC operates a wagon-ferry service on Lake Victoria between Jinja and Mwanza, in Tanzania. This provides a much needed alternative route to the sea, via the Tanzanian ports of Tanga and Dar es Salaam. The URC carried an officially estimated 1m. tons of freight in 1995. In 1996 the company was following a strategy of 'privatisation from within,' selling off non-core activities such as locomotive maintenance.

In 1976 Uganda Airlines Corpn (UAC) was established by the government, and in 1978 the airline inaugurated its first international scheduled service, between Entebbe and Nairobi. In May 1980 a scheduled passenger and cargo service started operating from Uganda to Rome, Brussels and London, using a Boeing 707 airliner. The airline subsequently introduced new routes, to Cologne, Dubai and Bombay. In January 1988 the weekly service to London was halted because the 707s failed to satisfy new European noise regulations. This service was resumed in February 1989, using a leased aircraft. By 1991 UAC had only a single Fokker F-27 passenger aircraft. The airline's route coverage was considerably curtailed. The government appointed a new management team in 1991, and soon afterwards UAC leased an Air Zimbabwe Boeing 737-200. The number of passengers carried by the airline increased from 32,000 in 1992 to 100,000 in 1995. In the latter year UAC leased a Boeing 737-500 from Ansett of Australia. UAC holds 10% of the equity in Alliance, a joint venture with South African Airways, Air Tanzania Corpn, the Ugandan and Tanzanian governments and private investors. Attempts to transfer UAC to private ownership were taking place in the mid-1990s. A US $52m. project to modernize Entebbe airport began in 1994, and included the construction of a new passenger terminal.

Kampala's telephone network has been modernized and expanded in a US $13m. project, financed mainly by a concessionary loan from France. In 1993 there was one telephone line per 1,000 inhabitants. An IDA credit, worth about $52.3m., was approved in 1989 to finance part of the rehabilitation programme of the Uganda Posts and Telecommunications Corpn (UP & TC), which is expected to cost about $100m. UP & TC is to be privatized. Mobile telephone services were available in Kampala in 1995 from Celtel (which had approximately 3,000 customers in 1996), and in 1994 Kenya's Wilken Group received a licence to establish a V-Sat (a small-aperture satellite terminal), to provide voice, data and fax links in remote areas of the country.

EXTERNAL TRADE

Traditionally, Uganda's four leading export commodities were coffee, tea, cotton and copper. However, copper exports dwindled from US $20.6m. in 1970 to nil by 1979, with the halting of production at Kilembe. Coffee alone once accounted for about 95% of total export earnings. However, the value of coffee exports declined sharply in 1993, when coffee contributed about 53% of total export revenue. In 1996 the principal export commodities were coffee (accounting for 62.5% of the total), gold (6.9%), fish (4.0%) and maize (2.8%). The substantial increase in gold exports (from US $224,000 in 1994 to $43.9m. in 1996) could, in part, be attributable to metal smuggled into the country from Zaire. In the eastern provinces of that country (now renamed the Democratic Republic of the Congo), the Ugandan shilling was being used as currency in 1997. The United Kingdom is Uganda's main supplier after Kenya, which provides refined petroleum products and also re-exports goods to Uganda through Mombasa. Other principal suppliers in 1996 were Japan, the United Arab Emirates, India and Germany. The main customers for Uganda's exports in 1992 were the United Kingdom, Belgium-Luxembourg, Spain, the USA and France.

The deficit on merchandise trade was US $60.4m. in 1983, but there was an estimated surplus of $65.7m. in 1984. This surplus rose sharply to $115m. in 1985, with exports down to $379m. and imports declining at an even faster rate to $264m. These trends were mainly due to the fall in the value of the shilling and the slowdown in the economic recovery programme. In 1986, with improved export earnings, as a result of high world coffee prices, and a severe reduction in imports, the surplus totalled about $2.2m. Owing to the scarcity of foreign exchange and to the over-inflated value of the shilling, legitimate imports had slowed to a trickle by the time that the currency was devalued by 76% in May 1987. The continuing foreign exchange crisis led to the signing, in 1987, of a series of barter agreements with several countries (including Libya) and companies, whereby Uganda was supplied with goods and services in return for commodities: coffee, in particular, but also cotton, timber, maize, beans and sesame seed. The total value of such agreements had reached about $500m. by the end of 1989. By early 1988 it was clear that there was not enough surplus agricultural produce to fulfil commitments, which, for 1987, had totalled 140,000 metric tons of produce. Although it had been hoped that barter agreements would be a means of diversifying exports, coffee remained the main commodity involved. In 1988 the value of exports was estimated at $272.9m., of which coffee earned $264.3m., cotton $3.1m. and tea $1.2m. Imports cost $627.4m. The value of exports fell to an estimated $259.2m. in 1989, while the value of imports rose to $727.7m., leaving a trade deficit of $468.5m. In 1991 exports earned $196m., while imports cost $523m., leaving a trade deficit of $327m. In 1992 total merchandise exports, at $171m., covered only one-third of total merchandise imports, at $524m., leaving a visible trade deficit of $353m. According to the IMF, exports amounted to $200m. in 1993, covering 45% of imports, at $442m. (f.o.b.), leaving a visible trade deficit of $242m. In 1994 exports more than doubled, to $441m., while imports soared to $672m., causing the visible trade deficit to decline slightly, to $231m. In 1995 exports increased to $549m., but imports soared to $867m., leaving an increased trade deficit of $318m. In June 1996 Uganda implemented an 80% tariff reduction on trade with other COMESA members, four months ahead of the October 1996 deadline set by COMESA. From July 1996, however, Uganda imposed a 10% surtax on all commodities entering the country from COMESA sources.

East African Community

Uganda was a partner, with Kenya and Tanzania, in the East African Community (EAC), which came into existence in December 1967. The EAC disintegrated, however, as a result of continual disagreements between the partners over financial and political issues. By mid-1977 the various common services, such as railways, harbours and the airline, had ceased to function and the EAC had collapsed. In November 1983 agreement was finally reached, after nearly six years of negotiations, on the division of the EAC's assets and liabilities. The final accounts of the EAC, produced by the World Bank, were approved by the three heads of state in July 1986. The surviving EAC institution, the East African Development Bank (which has its headquarters in Kampala), was given a new charter in August 1980 and is gradually expanding its lending programme. In January 1996 the presidents of Uganda, Kenya and Tanzania undertook to co-operate over an initiative to relaunch the EAC. In March the permanent tripartite commission for East African co-operation was formally inaugurated, and in April 1997 a four-year East African development strategy was launched, to encourage trade between the three member states.

PUBLIC FINANCE

The 1985/86 budget introduced rises of 11%–31.5% in producer prices for export crops, but these increases were insufficient to offset inflation, which soared to an average annual rate of 200% in 1986. In May 1986 the Museveni government reintroduced a two-tier system of exchange rates, with a low priority rate, at sh. 1,400 = US $1, for basic consumer imports, and a higher market rate, at sh. 5,000 = US $1 (a 72% devaluation), for all other imports. This measure, designed to encourage exports and to curb the 'black market', was complemented by a nominal increase in producer prices for coffee, tea, tobacco and cocoa. The 1986/87 budget abandoned this dual exchange rate, fixing the shilling instead at the previous 'priority' rate of sh. 1,400 = US $1, representing a large revaluation. This decision encountered strong disapproval from multilateral and bilateral donors, who were also dismayed at the tripling of the envisaged budget deficit, to sh. 349,500m.

Measures under the three-year rehabilitation and development programme for 1987/88–1989/90 (see below), announced in May 1987, included the devaluation of the currency by 76%, and the introduction of a 'new' shilling, equivalent to 100 'old' shillings. The main aim of the rehabilitation programme, to reduce government spending, was echoed in the 1987/88 budget. The budget deficit, envisaged at 'new' sh. 8,600m. ($143.3m.), although three times that of the previous year, represented only 15% of total planned expenditure, projected at sh. 53,200m. ($886.7m.). The increase in budgetary spending was moderate in real terms, when set against the estimated rate of inflation of 300%. The revenue from taxes was expected to rise as a result of increased earnings from exports owing to the devaluation of the shilling, and because of additional taxes on private sector businesses. However, the removal of the sales tax from basic essentials, such as sugar, salt and kerosene, was expected to reduce government revenue considerably. The lifting of import duties on raw materials and industrial equipment, and the reduction of interest rates were aimed at encouraging investment in industry.

Interim budget proposals, announced in February 1988, included the reduction of expenditure in several government departments, partly because of Uganda's failure to achieve levels of agricultural output sufficient to fulfil barter agreements with other countries. The 1988/89 budget, announced in July 1988, represented continuing efforts by the government to encourage economic rehabilitation of the country, while curbing inflation. The shilling was devalued by 60%, so that the exchange rate stood at sh. 150 = US $1, in place of the previous rate of sh. 60 = US $1. The shilling was further devalued, by 10% in December 1988 and by 21% in March 1989, bringing it to sh. 200 = US $1. The rate on the parallel market fell to sh. 530 = US $1 from sh. 420 = US $1 following the March devaluation. In July a two-tier foreign exchange system was reintroduced. The Bank of Uganda was to sell foreign currency to importers at a rate of about sh. 400 = US $1, undercutting the parallel market rate, which was about sh. 600 = US $1 at that time. The selling rate was to be adjusted weekly.

Total expenditure under the 1989/90 budget, announced in July 1989, was projected at sh. 212,555m., while revenue was forecast at sh. 118,899m. The deficit of sh. 93,656m. was to be offset by external borrowing. Also included in the budget was a 40% salary increase for civil servants and an increase in producer prices.

Five further devaluations reduced the value of the shilling to sh. 620 = US $1 by end-March 1991. The budget for 1990/91 envisaged total expenditure of sh. 320,800m. and revenue of sh. 206,960m., leaving a deficit of sh. 113,840m. Budgetary measures included a wage increase of 22% for civil servants and improved public access to foreign exchange.

In February 1992 Uganda re-introduced the auctioning of foreign currency, with the Bank of Uganda auctioning the currency to commercial banks. Initially this produced an exchange rate of sh. 980 = US $1. By May 1992, however, inflation was running at 52% over the rate at the beginning of the year, projecting an annual rate of 139%. The government announced the licensing of foreign exchange bureaux, and by September 1992 there were 59 in operation. (By September 1993 there were 79, of which 26 were owned by commercial banks and 53 were privately-owned.) In June 1992 the official exchange rate was sh. 1,300 = US $1. By July 1992 the government claimed that inflation had been brought under control. In mid-1993 the IMF assessed the annual average rate of inflation at 3%. In June 1993 the shilling had stabilized and was trading at sh. 1,197 = US $1. At the beginning of November 1993, the government abandoned the auction of foreign exchange and introduced the Foreign Exchange Inter-Bank Market. By July 1994 the exchange rate had improved to sh. 937 = US $1. By July 1995 the exchange rate was sh. 950 = US $1, demonstrating a degree of stability unknown previously. By September 1996 the exchange rate had weakened to sh. 1,040 = US $1. In mid-1996 the IMF estimated that inflation stood at 7.4% on an annual average basis. Uganda, Kenya and Tanzania are considering plans for full currency convertibility. The 1995/96 budget involved total expenditure of sh. 1,010,782m., of which sh. 563,963m. was recurrent. Revenue under the 1995/96 budget was sh. 646,042m. The 1996/97 budget, introduced in June 1996, envisaged total revenue of sh. 824,300m., of which sh. 728,700m. was to be derived from taxes, and total expenditure of sh. 1,233,200m., of which sh. 660,500m. was recurrent. The projected budgetary deficit was forecast at 6.7% of GDP, lower than the actual deficit for 1995/96 (equivalent to 7% of GDP), but higher than the ceiling set by the IMF (5% of GDP). Under the 1996/97 budget the former sales tax (at 15%) was replaced by a value-added tax (VAT), at an initial rate of 17%. The government was also to pay VAT on its purchases, thereby providing a means for businesses to claim refunds where applicable. Although the new tax was proclaimed a success, and company registration was high, traders protested that they felt unable to pass on the increased cost to their customers. The level of taxation in Uganda—reportedly the highest in Africa—has given rise to concern that GDP growth may be stunted. The 1997/98 budget envisaged total revenue of sh. 840,000m., of which sh. 828,000m. was to be derived from taxes; expenditure was to be reduced by some 23%. Civil service salaries were 'frozen'; with the introduction of universal primary schooling, education expenditure, in particular on teachers' salaries, was to be a spending priority. However, a revenue shortfall was expected, owing to smuggling and tax evasion.

BALANCE OF PAYMENTS

The balance of payments in 1983 showed a current account deficit of US $72.2m., but this was transformed into a surplus of $103.5m. in 1984, when export earnings were slightly higher and the import bill much lower, producing a surplus on the merchandise trade balance. The current account surplus was only $4.6m. in 1985, and a deficit of $4.0m. was recorded in 1986. The current account deficit widened to $131.1m. in 1987, owing to low international prices for coffee and an increased volume of imports in that year. The deficit grew to $199.4m. in 1988, and to an estimated $247.9m. in 1989. In 1990 the current account deficit amounted to $434m. before, and $255m. after, official transfers. In 1991 the deficit was $393m. before, and $182m. after, official transfers. An improvement was achieved in 1992 when the current account deficit was $346m. before, and $113m. after, official transfers. In 1993 the current account deficit was $369m. before, and $107m. after, official transfers, and in 1994 the deficit before official transfers amounted to $264m. The 1995/96 budget speech reported that the current account deficit narrowed from the equivalent of 2.4% of GDP in 1993/94 to 0.2% in 1994/95, owing to a large increase in private transfers, from $311.9m. to $397.0m. The 1996/97 budget speech indicated that there was a surplus of $110m. on the overall balance of payments in 1995/96. The 1997/98 budget speech indicated an overall balance-of-payments surplus of $106.6m. in 1996/97. Foreign reserves at the end of 1989 totalled $28.3m. At the end of 1991 they stood at $59m., enough to cover four weeks' worth of imports. Foreign reserves edged upwards to $146m. by the end of 1993, equivalent to six weeks' worth of imports. The June 1995 budget speech reported that gross reserves increased by $172.8m. in 1994/95, bringing the total to $382m. at 30 June 1995, which was described as sufficient to cover 4.8 months' worth of imports. It was reported in the June 1996 budget speech that foreign reserves were enough to cover just over four months' worth of imports. Foreign reserves stood at $527m. in mid-December 1996, enough to cover four months' worth of imports. Total external debt was officially estimated at about $1,800m. at the end of 1989, $2,830m. at the end of 1991, $2,997m. at the end of 1992, $3,056m. at the end of 1993, $3,473m. at the end of 1994, $3,384m. at the end of 1995 and $3,200m. at the end of 1996, when it was reported that Uganda spent 10 times as much on debt-servicing as on health care. Debt-servicing throughout the 1970s had remained as low as 5% of export earnings, owing to a low level of foreign investment and lending. In 1981, however, the debt-service ratio was about 60%, but subsequently, as export revenue increased more quickly than borrowing, the ratio declined. According to the World Bank, debt-servicing costs amounted to 62.2% of exports in 1988 and to 59.9% of exports in 1990. The ratio was 57.3% in 1992, rising to 64.7% in 1993. In 1994, however, it fell to 43.8%, and in 1995 it fell to 21.3%. Under the 1996/97 budget, debt-servicing costs were estimated at about $110m. Of the $194.1m. of medium- and long-term debt due for repayment in 1989, $93.1m. was rescheduled by four members of the 'Paris Club' of official creditors (France, Italy, the United Kingdom and the USA) and Libya. In July 1993 Uganda repurchased $153m. of commercial debt at a substantial discount. In February 1995 international creditor governments agreed to cancel some two-thirds of Uganda's bilateral government-guaranteed debt. In April 1997 the IMF and the World Bank approved a $338m. debt-relief programme for Uganda, to be released in April 1998; however, it was argued that, because the payments were to be spread over a number of years, actual year-on-year cash savings would be minimal; moreover, the Ugandan government had budgeted for such relief to be disbursed in 1997, and it was feared that plans to introduce universal primary education would be set back.

AID

During the rule of Idi Amin there was a drastic decline in receipts of aid except, after 1974, from Arab countries, in particular Libya. After the overthrow of Amin, several countries and multilateral agencies signed agreements with Uganda to provide official assistance. In June 1981 the World Bank arranged a reconstruction credit for Uganda. Negotiations were concluded in April 1982 for a second arrangement covering reconstruction credit, totalling US $120m.–$130m., with $70m. from the World Bank and the remainder from co-financiers. In May 1982 the World Bank announced a $35m. line of credit for industrial rehabilitation, and in January 1983 it agreed to lend $70m. for agriculture and $32m. for education. A third IDA reconstruction credit, of about $50m., was agreed in May 1984. The UN Development Programme provided about $30m. in 1977–81 and agreed to double this for 1982–86. The EC (now restructured as the EU) pledged $78.9m. under Lomé I, $104m. under Lomé II and $125m. under Lomé III. It has also given emergency food aid. Agencies which have provided concessional loans include the ADB, BADEA and other Arab funds.

The IMF agreed a US $197m. stand-by facility in June 1981, and a second stand-by arrangement, for $122m. over one year, was agreed in August 1982; a third stand-by facility, for 12 months and totalling nearly $105m., was approved by the IMF in September 1983. Negotiations on a new facility, of about $60m., reached deadlock, however, reportedly because the IMF disapproved of some of the government's policy trends, particularly the large rise in public spending. Almost one-third of the 1983/84 facility was unused by the time that the arrangement had expired.

In May 1982, at a World Bank Consultative Group meeting in Paris, Uganda presented its 1982–84 recovery programme, requiring US $557.5m. in finance. A further meeting of the Consultative Group took place in January 1984. The government presented the revised recovery programme, covering 1983–85 (see below). For this, additional project finance, totalling $199m., was required, and consolidation of the programme beyond 1985 required a total of $729m. In March 1986 representatives of donor countries and organizations attended a meeting in Kampala, at which the government presented proposals for a $160m. programme of emergency relief and rehabilitation, aimed at repairing the damage resulting from five years of civil war. During 1986, however, international donors waited for the new government to formulate its economic policies before pledging any new funds, and the IDA suspended disbursement of part of its committed funds. Discussions with the IMF and the World Bank were resumed in early 1987. Following the introduction of the three-year rehabilitation programme in May 1987 (see below), the IMF agreed to provide $24m. as a structural adjustment facility (SAF) for the first year, then $32m. over the following 24 months, in addition to $20m. from its compensatory financing facility (CFF) fund. The World Bank agreed in principle to a $100m. arrangement to support the recovery plan, and a Consultative Group meeting of donors, held in June 1987, resulted in new commitments amounting to $310m. for the first year of the three-year rehabilitation programme. Later in the month the 'Paris Club' rescheduled $66m. of debts due to be repaid in 1987/88. Non-members of the 'Paris Club' also rescheduled debts of up to $45m. In July 1988 the World Bank formally approved the draw-down of the second tranche, worth $50m., of its economic recovery credit (ERC), which had been agreed in September 1987. In February 1988 the IMF approved a CFF equivalent to SDR 24.8m. (about $33.7m.), in connection with Uganda's shortfall in export earnings in the year ended September 1987, caused mainly by low world coffee prices in 1987. In October 1988 a Consultative Group meeting of international donors committed $550m. in loans and grants for 1989, in addition to existing commitments. The donors were presented with the government's economic recovery programme for 1988–92, which replaced the 1987–90 rehabilitation programme (see below). In September 1988 the IMF released the second tranche of its SAF, following repayment by Uganda of $18m. of arrears to the Fund. In April 1989 the IMF approved a three-year low-interest enhanced structural adjustment facility (ESAF) worth SDR 179.3m., replacing the SAF arranged in 1987. The World Bank agreed a $25m. supplement to the first ERC. At a meeting on Uganda in late 1989 of the Consultative Group, international donors pledged $640m. The World Bank committed $265m. for 1990, of which $125m. represented balance-of-payments support which had been withheld during 1989, pending the implementation of measures to reduce inflation. In April 1989 the IMF approved a SDR 199.2m. ESAF to support economic recovery. The facility was due to last until late

November 1992, and by April 1992 all but the last SDR 19.92m. tranche had been drawn. Disbursement of aid pledged by the international donor community was slow in the late 1980s, but improved in 1990. The Consultative Group held a donors' meeting in Paris during May 1992, at which Uganda received up to $830m. in financial support for its economic development and adjustment programme for 1992/93. A further Consultative Group meeting in May 1993 pledged $825m. in support for 1993/94, and in 1995 and 1996 the Consultative Group meeting pledged a similar level of support. The government's introduction of VAT under the 1996/97 budget, as part of its structural reform strategy, received the approval of the IMF.

ECONOMIC DEVELOPMENT

During 1965–71 Uganda's GDP expanded at an average rate of about 4.2% annually in real terms, as a result of the excellent performance of the agricultural sector and the food-processing industry, although the rate of increase was lower from the late 1960s. Uganda's third Five-Year Development Plan (1971–76) envisaged 5.6% annual growth; however, both government spending and economic performance fell considerably short of targets, with real GDP declining each year during the Plan period. There was a slight recovery in 1977, as a result of the strong advance in coffee prices. The Three-Year Plan (1976–79) had little chance of being fulfilled, since the economy was by that time operating at the most basic level. The dire state of the economy was due, in large measure, to ex-President Amin's policies of expulsion of non-citizen Asians and mass expropriations of foreign firms. The disruption that was caused by the war of liberation early in 1979 produced a further fall in output in every sector during that year.

Emergency aid began to arrive in Uganda several months after Amin's overthrow, and large sums of development aid appeared to be waiting for the moment when the country was again in a position to absorb it. However, the nascent economic recovery came to a virtual halt with the May 1980 coup, which ousted President Binaisa.

In March 1981 President Obote announced an economic recovery plan which aimed at, among other things, providing greater encouragement and protection for foreign investors. This was followed in March 1982 by a two-year recovery programme, which concentrated on the strengthening of the main export commodity sectors, on projects which would bring a quick return, either in export earnings or foreign exchange savings, and on schemes of an urgent humanitarian or social nature. The Obote government declared its intention to encourage a mixed economy and expected industrial revival to come mainly through the private sector. In July 1982 it ordered a study on the country's 97 parastatal enterprises, to decide which should be sold off to private investors, and to devise means of strengthening the remainder and making them more efficient. During 1983 the government decided to 'roll over' the recovery programme, and in November a revised programme was announced, covering 1983–1985. Uganda's annual inflation rate, which was 104% in 1980, was reduced to 30% in 1983, the government claimed. However, by the mid-1980s inflation had increased sharply. After President Museveni came to power in January 1986, he commissioned a report on the economy from a Canadian team. The Rehabilitation and Development Programme for 1987/88–1989/90, which was finally announced in May 1987, had the approval of the IMF and the World Bank, and was the first sign that the government was getting to grips with the country's economic problems. The programme included the introduction of a 'new' shilling, to equal 100 'old' shillings, and at the same time devalued the currency by 76%. The programme was replaced by an Economic Recovery Programme for 1988–92, presented to donors in October 1988. Total investment was scaled down to $1,674m., compared with $2,866m. for the previous plan. Projected average annual growth during the period of the programme was 5%; the plan aimed to revive exports and to boost non-traditional exports. Of total investment, transport and communications were allocated 27%, social infrastructure 25.7%, agriculture 23.8% and industry and tourism 17.2%. The World Bank estimated that Uganda's GDP grew by 5.6% per year, in real terms, during 1990–94.

In July 1995 the World Bank put pressure on the Ugandan government to privatize or close 15 commercial banks. All of the banks were to raise a minimum capital base of sh. 500m. (for domestic banks) or sh. 1,000m. (for foreign banks) by mid-1997; any bank that failed to do so would be wound up. All 15 banks reportedly had high levels of 'non-performing loans'; Uganda Commercial Bank (UCB) was in the worst bad-debt situation, with non-performing loans amounting to sh. 105,000m. in 1995. In preparation for privatization, UCB was reduced in size; of its 189 branches in 1993, 50 had been closed and 54 had been put on a part-time basis by 1996. Opponents of UCB's privatization feared that future private-sector owners may close the bank's unprofitable rural network, leaving the banking requirements of large areas of the country unserved. By the end of April 1996, 1,885 non-performing UCB loans totalling sh. 66,900m. had been transferred to a Non-Performing Assets Recovery Trust, and during 1996 the British merchant bank Morgan Grenfell was brought in to advise on the reform and privatization of the bank; it was decided that 60% of UCB's equity would be reserved for Ugandan nationals. In 1995 Nile Bank Ltd and Sembule Investment Bank were placed under the supervision of the Bank of Uganda (the central bank) while undergoing restructuring. Meanwhile, the Bank of Uganda itself had financial difficulties. Its sh. 40,000m. loss in 1993/94 was attributed primarily to currency conversion operations. However, the bank was also owed money by the government, and in need of recapitalization. In the June 1996 budget speech it was announced that the government had made an outstanding payment to the central bank, and that it planned to pay sh. 60,000m. towards the first phase of the bank's recapitalization. In mid-1997 all banks except the UCB satisfied the minimum capital requirement; however, the minister of finance announced that he would seek to have it doubled.

The Expropriated Properties Act, governing the return of (or compensation for) property confiscated during Idi Amin's rule (mainly from Asian owners), came into force in 1983. Unclaimed or unverified property was to be sold to Ugandan nationals or to foreign investors in joint ventures with Ugandans. In May 1991 the government announced further measures to benefit dispossessed Asian Ugandans. Any investment code to protect foreign investors was promulgated in 1991. By January 1993 some 524 properties had reportedly been returned to their original owners. In April 1993, responsibility for the Asian-owned entities was entrusted to the Departed Asians' Property Custodian Board (DAPCB). In the mid-1990s the Asian-controlled Madhvani group became one of the most active industrial investors in the country.

In early 1995 the government established a Privatization Unit, and transferred to the Ministry of Finance and Economic Planning responsibility for those parastatals which were to be divested. It was hoped that 85% of current public enterprises would be transferred to private ownership by June 1997. Some 13 former state-owned enterprises had already been privatized in 1994/95, realizing combined gross proceeds of sh. 57,720m. Net proceeds will, however, be at a much lower level, because the government is required to settle the large debts which some of the organizations had accumulated. In September 1996 73 of the 140 companies scheduled for privatization were still awaiting disposal; among them were UCB, CMB Ltd (formerly the Coffee Marketing Board) and Uganda Air.

On the basis of gross national product (GNP) per head (only US $240 in 1995), Uganda is among the poorest countries in the world. Uganda's GNP per caput, in real terms, expanded by an annual average of 2.6% in 1985-95, according to World Bank estimates. Over the same period GDP increased, in real terms, by an annual average of 5.8%. GDP grew by 3.4% in 1991/92, 8.3% in 1992/93, 6.3% in 1993/94, 11.5% in 1994/95 and 9.8% in 1995/96, according to the Ugandan ministry of finance and economic planning. The annual rate of inflation, which stood at 200% in 1986 when the NRM took power, had been brought under control by mid-1993. According to government figures, inflation stood at an annual rate of 9.2% in 1993, although by the time of the June 1994 budget speech, finance minister Jehoash Mayanja-Nkangi admitted that it had crept back up to an annual 16%. By September 1994 it was officially reported that inflation had been reduced to an annual rate of 5.2%, and in mid-1995 it was officially assessed at just 3%. Official figures indicated that inflation stood at 6.1% in 1995 and 7.4% in 1996.

Inflation increased slightly in 1996/97, owing to a 30% rise in food prices (resulting from widespread drought).

The Museveni administration's implementation of effective economic recovery plans, supported by the IMF and World Bank, has been greeted with approval by Uganda's donors and business partners. By mid-1990 the short-term prospects for recovery seemed to be reasonably favourable; there had been a considerable influx of aid, and inflation was greatly reduced. In May 1996 a Capital Markets Authority began operating, in order to oversee the establishment of a stock exchange in Kampala; discussions were lengthy and ongoing, however. The government has made efforts to encourage investment from abroad, in order to reduce Uganda's significant dependence on aid. Although economic growth was consistent from the early 1990s, obstacles to economic recovery include the cost of continued fighting against rebel groups, and continuing reliance on coffee, and hence international commodity prices and weather conditions, for most of Uganda's export revenue. These and many other problems will have to be overcome before the country can begin to benefit from its unquestionable advantages: a generally favourable climate, fertile soils and an abundance of natural resources.

Statistical Survey

Source (unless otherwise stated): Statistics Department, Ministry of Planning and Economic Development, POB 13, Entebbe.

Area and Population

AREA, POPULATION AND DENSITY

Area (sq km)	
Land	197,058
Inland water	44,081
Total	241,139*
Population (census results)	
18 January 1980	12,636,179
12 January 1991	
Males	8,185,747
Females	8,485,958
Total	16,671,705
Density (per sq km) at January 1991	69.1

* 93,104 sq miles. Source: Lands and Surveys Department.

DISTRICTS (population at 1991 census)

Apac	454,504	Kumi	236,694
Arua	637,941	Lira	500,965
Bundibugyo	116,566	Luwero	449,691
Bushenyi	579,137	Masaka	838,736
Gulu	338,427	Masindi	260,796
Hoima	197,851	Mbale	710,980
Iganga	945,783	Mbarara	798,774
Jinja	289,476	Moroto	174,417
Kabale	417,218	Moyo	175,645
Kabarole	746,800	Mpigi	913,867
Kalangala	16,371	Mubende	500,976
Kampala	774,241	Mukono	824,604
Kamuli	485,214	Nebbi	316,866
Kapchorwa	116,702	Ntungamo	289,222
Kasese	343,601	Pallisa	357,656
Kibaale	220,261	Rakai	383,501
Kiboga	141,607	Rukungiri	390,780
Kisoro	186,681	Soroti	430,390
Kitgum	357,184	Tororo	585,574
Kotido	196,006		

PRINCIPAL TOWNS (population at census of 18 August 1969)

Kampala (capital)	330,700	Mbale	23,544
Jinja and Njeru	52,509	Entebbe	21,096
Bugembe planning area	46,884	Gulu	18,170

1980 (provisional census results): Kampala 458,423; Jinja 45,060; Masaka 29,123; Mbale 28,039; Mbarara 23,155; Gulu 14,958.

BIRTHS AND DEATHS (UN estimates, annual averages)

	1980–85	1985–90	1990–95
Birth rate (per 1,000)	49.5	51.5	51.8
Death rate (per 1,000)	17.8	18.4	19.2

Expectation of life (UN estimates, years at birth, 1990–95): 44.9 (males 43.6; females 46.2).

Source: UN, *World Population Prospects: The 1994 Revision*.

ECONOMICALLY ACTIVE POPULATION
(ILO estimates, '000 persons at mid-1980)

	Males	Females	Total
Agriculture, etc.	2,950	2,340	5,290
Industry	222	50	272
Services	353	247	600
Total	3,525	2,637	6,162

Source: ILO, *Economically Active Population Estimates and Projections, 1950–2025*.

Mid-1995 (estimates in '000): Agriculture, etc. 8,856; Total 10,626 (Source: FAO, *Production Yearbook*).

Agriculture

PRINCIPAL CROPS ('000 metric tons)

	1993	1994	1995
Wheat	9	9	9
Rice (paddy)	74	77	80
Maize	804	900	950
Millet	610	610	643
Sorghum	383	390	398
Potatoes	320	368	386
Sweet potatoes	1,958	2,129	2,235
Cassava (Manioc)	3,139	2,080	2,625
Beans (dry)	428	378	387
Other pulses	115	120	123
Soybeans	67	75	78
Groundnuts (in shell)	153	142	143
Sesame seed	75	70	71
Cottonseed*	24	25	26
Vegetables and melons†	413	418	424
Sugar cane†	950	950	1,450
Bananas†	570	580	580
Plantains	8,222	9,000	9,519
Other fruit†	46	47	48
Coffee (green)	145	198	220*
Tea (made)	12	13	15*
Tobacco (leaves)	5	7	7†
Cotton (lint)	11*	12	12

* Unofficial figure(s). † FAO estimates.

Source: FAO, *Production Yearbook*.

LIVESTOCK ('000 head)

	1993	1994	1995
Cattle	5,370	5,106	5,233
Sheep	871	897	924
Goats	5,227	5,383	5,545
Pigs	1,266	1,304	1,343
Poultry	21,214	21,404	21,832

Asses (FAO estimates, '000 head): 17 in 1993; 17 in 1994; 17 in 1995 (Source: FAO, *Production Yearbook*).

LIVESTOCK PRODUCTS (FAO estimates, '000 metric tons)

	1993	1994	1995
Beef and veal	90	89	90
Mutton and lamb	9	9	9
Goat meat	14	14	15
Pig meat	49	50	51
Poultry meat	35	35	36
Other meat	16	19	17
Cows' milk	455	446	455
Poultry eggs	17.2	17.6	18.0
Cattle hides	12.6	12.4	12.6

Source: FAO, *Production Yearbook*.

Forestry

ROUNDWOOD REMOVALS
(FAO estimates, '000 cubic metres, excl. bark)

	1992	1993	1994
Sawlogs, veneer logs and logs for sleepers	150	150	150
Other industrial wood	1,931	1,999	2,068
Fuel wood	13,514	13,994	14,464
Total	15,595	16,143	16,682

Source: FAO, *Yearbook of Forest Products*.

SAWNWOOD PRODUCTION
('000 cubic metres, incl. railway sleepers)

	1992	1993	1994*
Coniferous (softwood)	6	7	7
Broadleaved (hardwood)	76	77	77
Total	82	83	83

* FAO estimates, unchanged since 1993.

Source: FAO, *Yearbook of Forest Products*.

Total wood production ('000 cubic metres): 19,050 in 1993; 19,724 in 1994; 20,420 in 1995.

Fishing

('000 metric tons, live weight)

	1993	1994	1995
Tilapias	74.3	80.2	83.2
African lungfishes	3.9	7.9	7.7
Characins	10.0	10.0	10.4
Naked catfishes	10.1	4.7	4.9
Other freshwater fishes	26.4	9.2	9.9
Nile perch	95.0	101.2	92.7
Total catch	219.8	213.1	208.8

Source: FAO, *Yearbook of Fishery Statistics*.

Mining

(metric tons, unless otherwise indicated)*

	1992	1993	1994
Tin concentrates†	30	30	30
Tungsten concentrates†	66	60	60
Salt—unrefined ('000 metric tons)†	5	5	5

* Estimates from the US Bureau of Mines.

† Figures refer to the metal content of concentrates.

Source: UN, *Industrial Commodity Statistics Yearbook*.

Industry

SELECTED PRODUCTS
('000 metric tons, unless otherwise indicated)

	1993	1994	1995*
Beer (million litres)	23.9	30.8	51.2
Soft drinks (million litres)	280.0	459.0	505.1
Cigarettes (million)	1,412.5	1,458.9	1,575.8
Sugar	49.3	59.2	70.1
Soap	47.6	48.5	55.7
Cement	52.0	45.2	88.5
Paint	1,221.0	1,502.0	1,831.6
Edible oil and fat ('000 litres)	1,654.0	6,265.0	13,963.6
Animal feed	18.2	35.4	43.8
Footwear ('000 pairs)	326.0	660.0	1,207.2
Wheat flour	10.1	8.3	6.0
Electricity (million kWh)	977.9	1,017.9	1,057.4

* Provisional figures.

1996: Raw sugar ('000 metric tons): 78; Cigarettes (million): 1,702; Cement ('000 metric tons): 175.

Finance

CURRENCY AND EXCHANGE RATES

Monetary Units

100 cents = 1 new Uganda shilling.

Sterling and Dollar Equivalents (31 March 1997)

£1 sterling = 1,682.6 new Uganda shillings;
US $1 = 1,024.7 new Uganda shillings;
10,000 new Uganda shillings = £5.943 = $9.759.

Average Exchange Rate (new Uganda shillings per US $)

1994	979.4
1995	968.9
1996	1,046.1

Note: Between December 1985 and May 1987 the official exchange rate was fixed at US $1 = 1,400 shillings. In May 1987 a new shilling, equivalent to 100 of the former units, was introduced. At the same time, the currency was devalued by 76.7%, with the exchange rate set at $1 = 60 new shillings. Further adjustments were implemented in subsequent years. Foreign exchange controls were mostly abolished in 1993.

BUDGET (million new shillings, year ending 30 June)

Revenue*	1993/94	1994/95	1995/96
Tax revenue	392,387	522,229	635,266
Non-tax revenue	6,765	8,965	10,776
Total	399,152	531,194	646,042

Expenditure†	1993/94	1994/95	1995/96
Current expenditure	416,767	501,263	563,963
Wages and salaries	86,900	128,721	164,886
Interest payments	44,631	53,362	42,765
Other current expenditure	285,236	319,180	356,312
Capital expenditure	431,878	404,014	446,819
Total	848,645	905,277	1,010,782

* Excluding grants received (million shillings): 282,487 in 1993/94; 253,876 in 1994/95; 268,446 in 1995/96.

† Excluding lending minus repayments (million shillings): 2,800 in 1993/94; 11,347 in 1994/95; 2,798 in 1995/96.

INTERNATIONAL RESERVES (US $ million at 31 December)

	1994	1995	1996
IMF special drawing rights	3.1	0.5	1.1
Foreign exchange	318.3	458.4	527.3
Total	321.4	458.9	528.4

Source: IMF, *International Financial Statistics*.

MONEY SUPPLY (million new shillings at 31 December)

	1994	1995	1996
Currency outside banks	176,522	204,519	221,094
Demand deposits at commercial banks	177,498	204,182	229,742
Total money (incl. others)	363,352	419,151	460,797

Source: IMF, *International Financial Statistics.*

COST OF LIVING
(Consumer Price Index for all urban households; base: 1990 = 100)

	1993	1994	1995
Food	196.5	227.7	238.1
Clothing	175.3	164.5	163.8
Rent*	225.0	248.7	284.7
All items (incl. others)	207.4	228.3	243.3

* Including fuel and light.

Source: ILO, *Yearbook of Labour Statistics.*

1996: All items 260.5 (Source: UN, *Monthly Bulletin of Statistics*).

NATIONAL ACCOUNTS
(million new shillings at current prices, year ending 30 June)

Expenditure on the Gross Domestic Product

	1993/94	1994/95	1995/96
Government final consumption expenditure	453,929	504,008	594,881
Private final consumption expenditure	3,730,985	4,447,233	5,154,110
Increase in stocks	2,091	44,692	49,431
Gross fixed capital formation	641,311	819,893	1,062,422
Total domestic expenditure	4,828,316	5,815,826	6,761,982
Exports of goods and services	384,788	631,227	734,365
Imports of goods and services	−850,477	−1,105,522	−1,363,759
GDP in purchasers' values*	4,366,721	5,273,248	6,077,035
GDP at constant 1991 prices	2,572,413	2,868,209	3,150,019

* Including statistical discrepancy (million shillings): 4,094 in 1993/94; −68,282 in 1994/95; −55,554 in 1995/96.

Gross Domestic Product by Economic Activity

	1993/94	1994/95	1995/96
Agriculture, hunting, forestry and fishing	1,998,986	2,401,274	2,519,382
Mining and quarrying	13,320	14,801	15,891
Manufacturing	265,353	311,510	397,874
Electricity, gas and water	45,725	60,239	65,167
Construction	238,898	290,318	402,317
Trade, restaurants and hotels	493,427	616,472	742,024
Transport, storage and communications	160,408	185,663	213,857
General government services	180,882	212,046	248,231
Education	174,906	188,340	223,149
Health	58,989	62,948	70,245
Other services	404,966	484,577	622,986
GDP at factor cost	4,035,860	4,828,189	5,521,123
Indirect taxes	330,861	445,059	555,912
GDP in purchasers' values	4,366,721	5,273,248	6,077,035

Source: Bank of Uganda.

BALANCE OF PAYMENTS (US $ million)

	1993	1994	1995
Exports of goods f.o.b.	200.0	440.9	548.9
Imports of goods f.o.b.	−441.7	−672.2	−866.7
Trade balance	−241.7	−231.3	−317.8
Exports of services	93.6	64.1	99.4
Imports of services	−269.8	−409.5	−528.0
Balance on goods and services	−417.9	−576.7	−746.4
Other income received	6.4	13.8	17.7
Other income paid	−65.3	−71.0	−113.3
Balance on goods, services and income	−476.8	−633.9	−842.0
Current transfers received	306.0	476.2	566.3
Current balance	−170.8	−157.7	−275.7
Capital account (net)	42.4	36.1	48.3
Direct investment from abroad	54.6	88.2	121.2
Investment assets	−5.0	−40.3	−9.9
Other investment liabilities	−61.8	−52.0	3.8
Net errors and omissions	−11.1	52.5	47.5
Overall balance	−151.7	−73.2	−64.8

Source: IMF, *International Financial Statistics.*

External Trade

PRINCIPAL COMMODITIES (US $'000)

Imports c.i.f. (by SITC)	1994	1995	1996*
Food and live animals	70,837	90,226	53,951
Cereals and cereal preparations	38,336	39,741	31,696
Sugar, sugar preparations and honey	16,355	26,694	7,540
Crude materials (inedible) except fuels	28,532	37,098	38,469
Textile fibres and waste	19,648	23,421	22,445
Mineral fuels, lubricants, etc.	30,105	16,664	10,890
Petroleum, petroleum products, etc.	29,949	16,254	10,519
Animal and vegetable oils, fats and waxes	35,712	47,047	31,737
Fixed vegetable fats and oils	21,042	27,376	21,899
Chemicals and related products	67,711	105,407	116,839
Medicinal and pharmaceutical products	29,239	40,365	46,372
Basic manufactures	164,022	205,684	161,985
Rubber manufactures	15,937	16,885	17,015
Paper, paperboard, etc.	14,470	20,719	17,508
Textile yarn, fabrics, etc.	28,740	37,599	25,242
Non-metallic mineral manufactures	32,241	41,847	33,267
Iron and steel	44,653	49,439	35,033
Other metal manufactures	20,681	29,086	21,353
Machinery and transport equipment	220,047	327,321	248,519
Machinery specialized for particular industries	25,322	53,062	30,449
General industrial machinery, equipment and parts	20,466	29,614	26,835
Office machines and automatic data-processing machines	19,496	11,856	10,436
Telecommunications and sound equipment	13,739	26,210	16,427
Other electrical machinery, apparatus, etc.	28,838	39,556	32,637
Road vehicles (incl. air-cushion vehicles) and parts (excl. tyres, engines and electrical parts)	94,955	149,055	115,525
Miscellaneous manufactured articles	67,916	78,887	72,002
Clothing and accessories (excl. footwear)	15,614	14,754	12,819
Total (incl. others)	686,465	909,428	735,080

Domestic exports f.o.b.	1994	1995	1996
Traditional export crops	366,847	409,913	435,208
Coffee	343,289	384,122	396,100
Cotton	3,485	9,696	14,659
Tea	11,804	8,698	17,058
Tobacco	8,269	7,397	7,391
Non-traditional exports	93,092	150,592	198,462
Maize	28,666	19,302	17,818
Beans and other legumes	12,900	10,847	15,231
Fish and fish products	10,403	17,541	25,194
Cattle hides	10,549	8,886	7,835
Gold and gold compounds	224	23,197	43,914
Total†	459,939	560,505	633,670

* Provisional figures.
† Includes some re-exports, and therefore overstates the true level.

PRINCIPAL TRADING PARTNERS (US $ '000)

Imports c.i.f.	1994	1995	1996*
Austria	n.a.	10,699	n.a.
Bangladesh	7,275	n.a.	n.a.
Belgium-Luxembourg	15,354	27,474	15,164
Canada	14,360	12,066	11,248
China, People's Repub.	9,216	20,146	9,953
Denmark	13,705	19,306	16,796
France (incl. Monaco)	10,895	25,376	18,997
Germany	30,965	37,261	30,712
Hong Kong	15,893	30,060	21,800
India	46,762	61,448	47,229
Italy	21,891	46,845	22,745
Japan	57,679	99,432	66,332
Kenya	196,883	213,445	157,132
Korea, Republic	3,389	12,519	6,360
Malaysia	1,786	17,014	18,499
Netherlands	9,583	19,841	10,514
Singapore	6,570	17,336	10,824
South Africa	5,873	27,674	19,445
Switzerland (incl. Liechtenstein)	6,628	7,642	9,309
Tanzania	8,709	11,583	5,082
United Arab Emirates	35,482	61,717	44,437
United Kingdom	91,116	126,922	103,500
USA	30,379	31,478	22,291
Total (incl. others)	686,475	1,047,649	729,410

* Provisional figures.

Exports f.o.b.	1990	1991	1992
Belgium-Luxembourg	16,906	11,392	21,139
France (incl. Monaco)	23,229	24,643	10,912
Germany	8,030	8,813	7,408
Italy	25,207	21,586	7,290
Korea, Repub.	189	329	2,225
Netherlands	8,030	8,813	7,408
Spain	27,183	17,436	15,859
United Kingdom	14,545	30,767	35,557
USA	19,348	19,708	13,961
Total (incl. others)	190,102	196,009	171,353

Source (for exports): UN, *International Trade Statistics Yearbook*.

Transport

RAILWAYS (traffic)

	1994	1995	1996
Passenger-km (million)	35	30	28
Freight ton-km (million)	208	236	187

ROAD TRAFFIC (estimates, '000 motor vehicles in use)

	1994	1995	1996
Passenger cars	24	30	35
Commercial vehicles	35	42	50

CIVIL AVIATION (traffic on scheduled services)

	1992	1993	1994
Kilometers flown (million)	1	1	2
Passengers carried ('000)	32	40	63
Passenger-km (million)	17	24	52
Total ton-km (million)	2	2	5

Source: UN, *Statistical Yearbook*.

Tourism

	1992	1993	1994
Tourist arrivals ('000)	76	103	119
Tourist receipts (US $ million)	38	50	61

Source: UN, *Statistical Yearbook*.

Communications Media

	1992	1993	1994
Radio receivers ('000 in use)	2,040	2,130	2,210
Television receivers ('000 in use)	193	220	230
Telephones ('000 main lines in use)	30	21	35
Book production*			
Titles	162	314	n.a.
Copies ('000)	n.a.	2,229	n.a.
Daily newspapers:			
Number	6	n.a.	2
Average circulation ('000 copies)	80†	n.a.	35†

* Not including pamphlets or government publications.
† Estimate.

Sources: UN, *Statistical Yearbook*; UNESCO, *Statistical Yearbook*.

Education

(1995)

	Teachers	Students
Primary	76,134	2,636,409
Secondary:		
General	14,447	255,158
Vocational*	766	13,360
Primary teacher training colleges	1,022	22,703
Higher:		
University	955	11,469
Other†	1,051	17,874

* Technical schools and institutes.
† Includes secondary teacher training colleges.

Directory

The Constitution

Following the military coup in July 1985, the 1967 Constitution was suspended, and all legislative and executive powers were vested in a Military Council, whose Chairman was Head of State. In January 1986 a further military coup established an executive Presidency, assisted by a Cabinet of Ministers and a legislative National Resistance Council (NRC). In September 1995 a Constituent Assembly (comprising 214 elected and 74 nominated members) enacted a draft Constitution. The new Constitution was promulgated on 8 October 1995. Under its terms, a national referendum on the introduction of a multi-party political system was to take place in 1999. A direct presidential election took place in May 1996, followed in June of that year by legislative elections to the Parliament. This body, comprising 214 elected members and 62 nominated members, replaced the NRC.

The Government

HEAD OF STATE

President: Lt-Gen. Yoweri Kaguta Museveni (took office 29 January 1986; elected 9 May 1996).

THE CABINET

(August 1997)

President and Minister of Defence: Lt-Gen. Yoweri Kaguta Museveni.

Vice-President and Minister of Agriculture, Animal Industry and Fisheries: Dr Speciosa Wandira Kazibwe.

Prime Minister: Kintu Musoke.

First Deputy Prime Minister and Minister of Foreign Affairs: Eriya Kategaya.

Second Deputy Prime Minister and Minister of Tourism and Wildlife: Brig. Moses Ali.

Third Deputy Prime Minister and Minister of Labour and Social Services: Paul Orono Etiang.

Minister of Education and Sports: Maj. Amanya Mushega.

Minister of Finance: Jehoash Mayanja-Nkangi.

Minister of Gender and Community Development: Janet B. Mukwaya.

Minister of Health: Dr Crispus W. C. B. Kiyonga.

Minister of Information: Dr Ruhakana Rugunda.

Minister of Internal Affairs: Maj. Tom Butime.

Minister of Justice and Attorney-General: Balthazar Magundi Katureebe.

Minister of Lands, Housing and Urban Development: Francis Ayume.

Minister of Local Government: Jaberi Bidandi-Ssali.

Minister of Natural Resources: Gerald Sendawula.

Minister of Planning and Economic Development: Richard Kajuka.

Minister of Public Service: Prof. Apolo Sebambi.

Minister of Trade and Industry: Henry Muganwa Kajura.

Minister of Works, Transport and Communications: John Nasasira.

Minister without Portfolio: Ali Kirunda Kivejinja.

MINISTRIES

Office of the President: Parliament Bldgs, POB 7108, Kampala; tel. 234881; telex 61389; fax 235459.

Office of the Prime Minister: POB 341, Kampala; tel. (41) 259518; telex 62001; fax (41) 242341.

Ministry of Agriculture, Animal Industry and Fisheries: POB 102, Entebbe; tel. (42) 20752; telex 61287; fax (42) 21042.

Ministry of Defence: Republic House, POB 3798, Kampala; tel. (41) 270331; telex 61023; fax (41) 245911.

Ministry of Education and Sports: Crested Towers, POB 7063, Kampala; tel. (41) 234440; telex 61298; fax (41) 244594.

Ministry of Finance: POB 8147, Kampala; tel. (41) 234700; telex 61170; fax (41) 230163.

Ministry of Foreign Affairs: POB 7048, Kampala; tel. (41) 258251; telex 61007; fax (41) 258722.

Ministry of Gender and Community Development: POB 7136, Kampala; tel. (41) 254253.

Ministry of Health: POB 8, Entebbe; tel. (42) 20201; telex 61373; fax (42) 20274.

Ministry of Information: POB 7142, Kampala; tel. (41) 254461; telex 61373; fax (41) 256888.

Ministry of Internal Affairs: POB 7191, Kampala; tel. (41) 233811; telex 61331; fax (41) 231188.

Ministry of Justice: POB 7183, Kampala; tel. (41) 233219; fax (41) 254828.

Ministry of Labour and Social Services: POB 7009, Kampala; tel. (41) 242837; telex 62167.

Ministry of Lands, Housing and Urban Development: POB 7122, Kampala; tel. (41) 242931; telex 61274.

Ministry of Local Government: POB 7037, Kampala; tel. (41) 241763; telex 61265; fax (41) 258127.

Ministry of Natural Resources: POB 7270, Kampala; tel. (41) 234995; telex 61098; fax (41) 243508.

Ministry of Planning and Economic Development: POB 13, Entebbe; tel. (42) 20165; fax (42) 20147.

Ministry of Public Service: POB 7168, Kampala; tel. (41) 254881.

Ministry of Tourism and Wildlife: Parliament Ave, POB 4241, Kampala: tel. (41) 232971; telex 62218; fax (41) 242188.

Ministry of Trade and Industry: POB 7103, Kampala; tel. (41) 258202; telex 61183; fax (41) 245077.

Ministry of Works, Transport and Communications: POB 10, Entebbe; tel. (42) 20101; telex 61313; fax (42) 20135.

President and Legislature

PRESIDENT

Election, 9 May 1996

Candidate	Votes	%
Lt-Gen. Yoweri Kaguta Museveni	4,428,119	74.2
Paul Kawanga Ssemogerere	1,416,139	23.7
Kibirige Mohamed Mayanja	123,290	2.1
Total	5,967,548	100.0

PARLIAMENT

Speaker: James Wapakhabulo.

The National Resistance Movement, which took office in January 1986, established a National Resistance Council (NRC), initially comprising 80 nominated members, to act as a legislative body. National elections were held on 11–28 February 1989, at which 210 members of an expanded NRC were elected by members of district-level Resistance Committees (themselves elected by local-level Resistance Committees, who were directly elected by universal adult suffrage). The remaining 68 seats in the NRC were reserved for candidates nominated by the President (to include 34 women and representatives of youth organizations and trades unions). Political parties were not allowed to participate in the election campaign. In October 1989 the NRC approved legislation extending the Government's term of office by five years from January 1990, when its mandate was to expire. The Constituent Assembly (see Constitution) extended further the NRM's term of office in November 1994. Under the terms of the Constitution that was promulgated in October 1995, the NRC was to be restyled as the Ugandan Parliament, and a national referendum on the future introduction of a multi-party political system was to be staged in 1999. Legislative elections to the Parliament took place in June 1996 (again officially on a non-party basis). The total membership of the Parliament was reduced from 278 to 276, comprising 214 elected and 62 nominated representatives.

Political Organizations

Political parties were ordered to suspend active operations, although not formally banned, in March 1986. A referendum on the future restoration of a plural political system was scheduled to take place in 1999. The following parties were in existence in mid-1997:

Bazzukulu ba Buganda (Grandchildren of Buganda): Bagandan separatist movement.

Buganda Youth Movement: f. 1994; seeks autonomy for Buganda; Leader STANLEY KATO.

Conservative Party (CP): f. 1979; Leader JEHOASH MAYANJA-NKANGI.

Democratic Party (DP): POB 7098, Kampala; tel. (41) 230244; f. 1954; main support in southern Uganda; seeks a multi-party system; Pres. PAUL KAWANGA SSEMOGERERE; Sec.-Gen. MARY MUTAGAMBA.

Federal Democratic Movement (FEDEMO): Kampala.

Forum for Multi-Party Democracy: Kampala; Gen. Sec. JESSE MASHATTE.

Movement for New Democracy in Uganda: based in Zambia; f. 1994 to campaign for multi-party political system; Leader DAN OKELLO-OGWANG.

National Resistance Movement (NRM): f. to oppose the UPC Govt 1980–85; also opposed the mil. Govt in power from July 1985 to Jan. 1986; its mil. wing, the National Resistance Army (NRA), led by Lt-Gen. YOWERI KAGUTA MUSEVENI, took power in Jan. 1986; Chair. Dr SAMSON KISEKKA.

Nationalist Liberal Party: Kampala; f. 1984 by a breakaway faction of the DP; Leader TIBERIO OKENY.

Uganda Democratic Alliance: opposes the NRM Govt; Leader APOLO KIRONDE.

Uganda Democratic Freedom Front: Leader Maj. HERBERT ITONGA.

Uganda Freedom Movement (UFM): Kampala; mainly Baganda support; withdrew from NRM coalition Govt in April 1987; Sec.-Gen. (vacant).

Uganda Independence Revolutionary Movement: f. 1989; opposes the NRM Govt; Chair. Maj. OKELLO KOLO.

Uganda Islamic Revolutionary Party (UIRP): Kampala; f. 1993; Chair. IDRIS MUWONGE.

Uganda National Unity Movement: opposes the NRM Govt; Chair. Alhaji SULEIMAN SSALONGO.

Uganda Patriotic Movement: Kampala; f. 1980; Sec.-Gen. JABERI SSALI.

Uganda People's Congress (UPC): POB 1951, Kampala; f. 1960; socialist-based philosophy; ruling party 1962–71 and 1980–85, sole legal political party 1969–71; Leader CECILIA OGWAL.

Ugandan People's Democratic Movement (UPDM): seeks democratic reforms; support mainly from north and east of the country; includes mems of fmr govt armed forces; signed a peace accord with the Govt in 1990; Chair. ERIC OTEMA ALLIMADI; Sec.-Gen. EMMANUEL OTENG.

Uganda Progressive Union (UPU): Kampala; Chair. ALFRED BANYA.

The following organizations are in armed conflict with the Government:

Lord's Resistance Army (LRA): f. 1987; claims to be conducting a 'holy war' against the Govt; forces est. to number up to 6,000, operating mainly from bases in Sudan; Leader JOSEPH KONY.

Uganda People's Freedom Movement (UPFM): based in Tororo and Kenya; f. 1994 by mems of the fmr Uganda People's Army; Leader PETER OTAI.

Diplomatic Representation

EMBASSIES AND HIGH COMMISSIONS IN UGANDA

Algeria: POB 4025, Kampala; tel. (41) 232918; telex 61184; fax (41) 341015; Ambassador: MOHAMED EL AMINE DERRAGUI.

Burundi: POB 4379, Kampala; tel. (41) 221697; telex 61076; Ambassador: GEORGES NTZEZIMANA.

China, People's Republic: POB 4106, Kampala; tel. (41) 236895; fax (41) 235087; Ambassador: TAN XINGJIN.

Congo, Democratic Republic: POB 4972, Kampala; tel. (41) 233777; telex 61284; Chargé d'affaires a.i.: BWANAMAZURI KAMONGU.

Cuba: POB 9226, Kampala; tel. (41) 233742; Chargé d'affaires a.i.: ANGEL NICHOLAS.

Denmark: Plot 5, Lumumba Ave, POB 11234, Kampala; tel. (41) 250926; telex 61560; fax (41) 254979; Ambassador: THOMAS SCHJERBECK.

Egypt: POB 4280, Kampala; tel. (41) 254525; telex 61122; fax (41) 232103; Ambassador: SAMIR ABDALLAH.

Ethiopia: Kampala; tel. (41) 231010; Ambassador: DAWIT KEBEDE.

France: POB 7112, Kampala; tel. (41) 242120; telex 61079; fax (41) 241252; Ambassador: (vacant).

Germany: 15 Philip Rd, POB 7016, Kampala; tel. (41) 256767; telex 61005; fax (41) 243136; Ambassador: HANS-JOACHIM HELDT.

Holy See: POB 7177, Kampala (Apostolic Nunciature); tel. (41) 221167; fax (41) 221774; Apostolic Pro-Nuncio: Most Rev. LUIS ROBLES DÍAZ, Titular Archbishop of Stephaniacum.

India: Bank of Baroda Bldg, 1st Floor, POB 7040, Kampala; tel. (41) 344631; fax (41) 254943; High Commissioner: S.S. GILL.

Italy: POB 4646, Kampala; tel. (41) 241786; telex 61261; fax (41) 250448; Ambassador: MARCELLO RICOVERI.

Kenya: POB 5220, Kampala; tel. (41) 258235; telex 61191; fax (41) 258239; High Commissioner: PETER OLE NKURAIYIA.

Korea, Democratic People's Republic: POB 3717, Kampala; tel. (41) 233667; telex 61017; Ambassador: RI KWANG ROK.

Korea, Republic: Baumann House, POB 3717, Kampala; tel. (41) 233667; telex 61017; Ambassador: KIM JAE-KYU.

Libya: POB 6079, Kampala; tel. (41) 244924; telex 61090; fax (41) 244969; Sec. of People's Bureau: ABU ALLAH ABDUL MULLAH.

Netherlands: Plot 8A, Kisozi Complex, 4th floor, Nakasero Lane, POB 7728, Kampala; tel. (41) 231859; fax (41) 231861; Chargé d'affaires a.i.: S. E. DE LANG.

Nigeria: 33 Nakasero Rd, POB 4338, Kampala; tel. (41) 233691; telex 61011; fax (41) 232543; High Commissioner: MAMMAN DAURA.

Pakistan: Kampala.

Russia: POB 7022, Kampala; tel. (41) 233676; telex 61518; Ambassador: STANISLAV N. SEMENENKO.

Rwanda: POB 2468, Kampala; tel. (41) 244045; telex 61277; fax (41) 258547; Ambassador: SAGAHUTU MURASHI ISAIE.

Tanzania: POB 5750, Kampala; tel. (41) 256756; telex 61062; High Commissioner: JOSHUA OPANGA.

United Kingdom: 10–12 Parliament Ave, POB 7070, Kampala; tel. (41) 257054; fax (41) 257304; High Commissioner: MICHAEL COOK.

USA: POB 7007, Kampala; tel. (41) 259795; Ambassador: NANCY J. POWELL (designate).

Judicial System

Courts of Judicature: POB 7085, Kampala.

The Supreme Court: Mengo; hears appeals from the High Court.

Chief Justice: SAMUEL WILLIAM WAKO WAMBUZI.

Deputy Chief Justice: S. T. MANYINDO.

The High Court: POB 7085, Kampala; tel. (41) 233422; has full criminal and civil jurisdiction over all persons and matters in the country. The High Court consists of the Principal Judge and 20 Puisne Judges.

Principal Judge: J. H. NTABGOBA.

Magistrates' Courts: These are established under the Magistrates' Courts Act of 1970 and exercise limited jurisdiction in criminal and civil matters. The country is divided into magisterial areas, presided over by a Chief Magistrate. Under the Chief Magistrate there are three categories of Magistrates. The Magistrates preside alone over their courts. Appeals from the first category of Magistrates' Court lie directly to the High Court, while appeals from the second and third categories of Magistrates' Court lie to the Chief Magistrate's Court, and from there to the High Court.

Religion

It is estimated that more than 60% of the population profess Christianity (with approximately equal numbers of Roman Catholics and Protestants). About 5% of the population are Muslims.

CHRISTIANITY

The Anglican Communion

Anglicans are adherents of the Church of the Province of Uganda, comprising 27 dioceses. There are about 4m. adherents.

Archbishop of Uganda and Bishop of Kampala: Most Rev. LIVINGSTONE MPALANYI-NKOYOYO, POB 14123, Kampala; tel. (41) 270218; fax (41) 250922.

Greek Orthodox Church

Archbishop of East Africa: NICADEMUS of IRINOUPOULIS (resident in Nairobi, Kenya); jurisidiction covers Kenya, Tanzania and Uganda.

The Roman Catholic Church

Uganda comprises one archdiocese and 15 dioceses. At 31 December 1995 there were an estimated 7,892,782 adherents (an estimated 43.1% of the total population).

Uganda Episcopal Conference: Uganda Catholic Secretariat, POB 2886, Kampala; tel. (41) 268458; fax (41) 268713; f. 1974; Pres. Rt Rev. PAUL L. KALANDA, Bishop of Fort Portal.

Archbishop of Kampala: Cardinal EMMANUEL WAMALA, Archbishop's House, POB 14125, Mengo, Kampala; tel. (41) 270184; fax (41) 245441.

ISLAM

The Uganda Muslim Supreme Council: POB 3247, Kampala; Mufti of Uganda IBRAHIM SAID LUWEMBA; Chief Kadi and Pres. of Council HUSAYN RAJAB KAKOOZA.

BAHÁ'Í FAITH

National Spiritual Assembly: POB 2662, Kampala; tel. (41) 540511; mems resident in 3,522 localities.

The Press

DAILY AND OTHER NEWSPAPERS

The Citizen: Kampala; official publ. of the Democratic Party; English; Editor JOHN KYEYUNE.

The Economy: POB 6787, Kampala; weekly; English; Editor ROLAND KAKOOZA.

Financial Times: Plot 17/19, Station Rd, POB 31399, Kampala; tel. (41) 245798; bi-weekly; English; Editor G. A. ONEGI OBEL.

Focus: POB 268, Kampala; tel. (41) 235086; telex 61284; fax (41) 242796; f. 1983; publ. by Islamic Information Service and Material Centre; 4 a week; English; Editor HAJJI KATENDE; circ. 12,000.

Guide: POB 5350, Kampala; tel. (41) 233486; fax (41) 268045; f. 1989; weekly; English; Editor-in-Chief A. A. KALIISA; circ. 30,000.

The Monitor: POB 12141; Kampala; tel. (41) 231541; fax (41) 251352; f. 1992; daily; English; Editor-in-Chief WAFULA OGUTTU; Editor CHARLES ONYANGO-OBBO; circ. 30,000.

Mulengera: POB 6787, Kampala; weekly; Luganda; Editor ROLAND KAKOOZA.

Munnansi News Bulletin: POB 7098, Kampala; f. 1980; weekly; English; owned by the Democratic Party; Editor ANTHONY SGEKWEYAMA.

Munno: POB 4027, Kampala; f. 1911; daily; Luganda; publ. by the Roman Catholic Church; Editor ANTHONY SSEKWEYAMA; circ. 7,000.

New Vision: POB 9815, Kampala; tel. (41) 235846; fax (41) 235221; f. 1986; official govt newspaper; daily; English; Editor WILLIAM PIKE; circ. 40,000.

Ngabo: POB 9362, Kampala; tel. (41) 42637; telex 61236; f. 1979; daily; Luganda; Editor MAURICE SEKAWUNGU; circ. 7,000.

The People: Kampala; weekly; English; independent; Editor AMOS KAJOBA.

The Star: POB 9362, Kampala; tel. (41) 42637; telex 61236; f. 1980; revived 1984; daily; English; Editor SAMUEL KATWERE; circ. 5,000.

Taifa Uganda Empya: POB 1986, Kampala; tel. (41) 254652; telex 61064; f. 1953; daily; Luganda; Editor A. SEMBOGA; circ. 24,000.

Weekly Topic: POB 1725, Kampala; tel. (41) 233834; weekly; English; Editor JOHN WASSWA; circ. 13,000.

PERIODICALS

Eastern Africa Journal of Rural Development: Dept of Agriculture, Makerere University, POB 7062, Kampala; 2 a year; circ. 800.

The Exposure: POB 3179, Kampala; tel. (41) 267203; fax (41) 259549; monthly; politics.

Leadership: POB 2522, Kampala; tel. (41) 221358; fax (41) 221576; f. 1956; 6 a year; English; Roman Catholic; circ. 7,400.

Mkombozi: c/o Ministry of Defence, Republic House, POB 3798, Kampala; tel. (41) 270331; telex 61023; f. 1982; military affairs; Editor A. OPOLOTT.

Musizi: POB 4027, Mengo, Kampala; f. 1955; monthly; Luganda; Roman Catholic; Editor F. GITTA; circ. 30,000.

Pearl of Africa: POB 7142, Kampala; monthly; govt publ.

Uganda Confidential: Kampala; monthly; Editor TEDDY SSEZI-CHEEYE.

NEWS AGENCIES

Uganda News Agency (UNA): POB 7142, Kampala; tel. (41) 32734; telex 61188; Dir (vacant); Editor-in-Chief F. A. OTAI.

Foreign Bureaux

Inter Press Service (IPS) (Italy): Plot 4, 3rd St, Industrial Area, POB 16514, Wandegeya, Kampala; tel. (41) 235846; fax (41) 235211; Correspondent DAVID MUSOKE.

Rossiiskoye Informatsionnoye Agentstvo—Novosti (RIA—Novosti) (Russia): POB 4412, Kampala; tel. (41) 232383; telex 62292; Correspondent Dr OLEG TETERIN.

Xinhua (New China) News Agency (People's Republic of China): Plot 25, Hill Drive, Kololo, POB 466, Kampala; tel. (41) 254951; telex 61189; Correspondent ZHANG YINGSHENG.

Publishers

Centenary Publishing House Ltd: POB 2776, Kampala; tel. (41) 41599; f. 1977; religious (Anglican); Man. Dir Rev. SAM KAKIZA.

Fountain Publishers Ltd: POB 488, Kampala; tel. (41) 259163; fax (41) 251160; general, school textbooks, children's books, academic; Man. Dir JAMES TUMUSIIME.

Longman Uganda Ltd: POB 3409, Kampala; tel. (41) 42940; f. 1965; Man. Dir M. K. L. MUTYABA.

Uganda Printing and Publishing Corporation: POB 33, Entebbe; tel. (42) 20639; fax (42) 20530; f. 1993; Man. Dir P.A. BAKER

Radio and Television

According to estimates by UNESCO, there were 2,210,000 radio receivers and 230,000 television receivers in use in 1994.

RADIO

91.3 Capital FM: POB 7638, Kampala; tel. (41) 344556; fax (41) 235092; independent station broadcasting nationally.

Central Broadcasting Service (CBS): Kampala; f. 1996; independent station broadcasting to Buganda.

Radio Uganda: Ministry of Information, POB 2038, Kampala; tel. (41) 257256; telex 61084; fax (41) 257252; f. 1954; state-controlled; broadcasts in 24 languages, including English, Swahili and Ugandan vernacular languages; Commr for Broadcasting: JACK TURYAMWIJUKA.

Sanyu Radio: Katto Plaza, Nkrumah Rd, Kampala; f. 1993; independent station broadcasting to Kampala and its environs.

TELEVISION

Sanyu Television: Naguru; f. 1994; independent station broadcasting to Kampala and its environs.

Uganda Television Service: POB 4260, Kampala; tel. (41) 254461; telex 61084; f. 1962; state-controlled commercial service; programmes mainly in English, also in Swahili and Luganda; transmits over a radius of 320 km from Kampala; five relay stations are in operation, others are under construction; Controller of Programmes FAUSTIN MISANVU.

Finance

(cap. = capital; auth. = authorized; res = reserves; dep. = deposits; m. = million; brs = branches; amounts in new Uganda shillings unless otherwise indicated).

BANKING

Central Bank

Bank of Uganda: 37–43 Kampala Rd, POB 7120, Kampala; tel. (41) 258441; telex 61059; fax (41) 230878; f. 1966; bank of issue; auth. cap. 15,050m. (1994); Gov. CHARLES NYONYINTONO KIKONYOGO; Dep. Gov. EMMANUEL LULE; Exec. Dir ERIAB RUKYALEKERE.

State Banks

The Co-operative Bank Ltd: 9 William St, POB 6863, Kampala; tel. (41) 258323; telex 61263; fax (41) 234578; f. 1970; cap. 7,741m. (Dec. 1994); Chair. S. M. RUGATSIMBANA.

Uganda Commercial Bank: Plot 12, Kampala Rd, POB 973, Kampala; tel. (41) 234710; telex 61073; fax (41) 259012; e-mail ucb@starcom.co.ug; f. 1965; 49% state-owned; cap. and res 37m., dep. 190,364m. (Sept. 1995); Chair. ELLY RWAKAKOOKO; 82 brs.

Uganda Development Bank: UDB Towers, 22 Hannington Rd, POB 7210, Kampala; tel. (41) 230740; telex 61143; fax (41) 258571; f. 1972; state-owned; cap. 11m. (Dec. 1993); Man. Dir JOHN K. TWINO-MUSINGUZI.

Commercial Banks

Crane Bank Ltd: Kampala Rd, POB 22572, Kampala; tel. (41) 241414; telex 61627; fax (41) 231578; cap. and res 3,014m. (Dec. 1996); Chair. SAMSON MUWANGUZI; Man. Dir A. N. NAIR.

Gold Trust Bank Ltd: 13 Kimathi Ave, POB 70, Kampala; tel. (41) 231784; telex 61300; fax (41) 231687; f. 1984; cap. and res 221m., dep. 6,841m. (Dec. 1994); Chair. MANZUR ALAM: Gen. Man. SIVARAMAN VISVANATHAN.

Greenland Bank Ltd: Greenland Towers, Plot 30, Kampala Rd, POB 6021, Kampala; tel. (41) 242872; telex 61424; fax (41) 242872; f. 1991; cap. and res 3,674m., dep. 37,775m. (July 1996); Chair. MAJID BAGALAALIWO; Gen. Man. NASSER LUBEGA.

International Credit Bank Ltd: Katto Plaza, Plot 11/13, Nkrumah Rd, POB 22212, Kampala; tel. (41) 230050; fax (41)

230408; f. 1977 as Credit Finance Bank; cap. and res 2,060m., dep. 9,794m. (June 1996); Chair. THOMAS I. KATTO; Gen. Man. S. BALARAMAN.

Nile Bank Ltd: Spear House, Plot 22, Jinja Rd, POB 2834, Kampala; tel. (41) 231904; telex 61240; fax (41) 257779; f. 1988; cap. 1,606m. (Dec. 1992), dep. 26,170m. (Dec. 1994); CEO JAN ASMAN.

Orient Bank Ltd: Uganda House, Plot 10, Kampala Rd, POB 3072, Kampala; tel. (41) 236012; telex 61342; fax (41) 236066; e-mail orient@starcom.co.ug; br in Jinja.

Sembule Commercial Bank Ltd: 24 Jinja Rd, POB 2750, Kampala; tel. (41) 236535; telex 61365; fax (41) 230439; reorg. in 1996; 35% owned by Banque Belgolaise SA; cap. and res 1,308m. (Dec. 1996); Chair. Prof. J. EPELU-OPIO; Man. Dir J. J. LAING.

Development Banks

East African Development Bank (EADB): East African Development Bank Bldg, 4 Nile Ave, POB 7128, Kampala; tel. (41) 230021; telex 61074; fax (41) 259763; f. 1967; provides financial and tech. assistance to promote industrial development within Uganda, Kenya and Tanzania, whose govts each hold 25.8% of the equity, the remaining 22.6% being shared by the African Development Bank, Barclays Bank, the Commercial Bank of Africa, Grindlays Bank, Standard Chartered Bank, Nordbanken of Sweden and a consortium of institutions in fmr Yugoslavia; regional offices in Nairobi and Dar es Salaam; cap. SDR 26.7m., dep. SDR 33m. (Dec. 1995); Chair. R. KUINDWA; Dir-Gen. F. R. TIBEITA.

Development Finance Co of Uganda Ltd: Rwenzori House, Lumumba Rd, POB 2767, Kampala; tel. (41) 244059; telex 61196; fax (41) 259435; owned by Commonwealth Devt Corpn, Uganda Devt Corpn, Int. Finance Corpn and DEG (25% each); cap. and res 6,953m. (Dec. 1995); Chair. RICHARD KEMOLI; Gen. Man. DEREK ELSE.

Foreign Banks

Bank of Baroda (Uganda) Ltd (India): 18 Kampala Rd, POB 2971, Kampala; tel. (41) 233680; telex 61315; fax (41) 258263; f. 1969; 49% govt-owned; cap. and res 2,063m., dep. 46,540m. (Dec. 1995); Chair. and Man. Dir K. U. YAJNIK; 6 brs.

Barclays Bank of Uganda Ltd (United Kingdom): 16 Kampala Rd, POB 2971, Kampala; tel. (41) 232594; telex 61014; fax (41) 259467; f. 1969; 49% govt-owned; cap. and res 6,248m., dep. 70,970m. (Dec. 1995); Man. Dir J. N. B. LISTER; 2 brs.

Stanbic Bank Uganda Ltd: 45 Kampala Rd, POB 7131, Kampala; tel. (41) 230811; telex 61018; fax (41) 231116; f. 1906 as National Bank of India, adopted present name in 1993; wholly owned by Standard Bank Investment Corpn; cap. and res 5,520m. (Sept. 1995); Chair. A. D. B. WRIGHT; Man. Dir J. M. MILLER.

Standard Chartered Bank Uganda Ltd (United Kingdom): 5 Speke Rd, POB 7111, Kampala; tel. (41) 258211; telex 61010; fax (41) 231473; f. 1969; cap. 2,000m., res 5,525m., dep. 48,124m. (Dec. 1995); Chair. T. GROAG; Man. Dir E. N. ESSOKA.

Tropical Africa Bank Ltd (Libya): Plot 27, Kampala Rd, POB 7292, Kampala; tel. (41) 241408; telex 61286; fax (41) 232296; f. 1972; 50% govt-owned, 50% owned by Libyan Arab Foreign Bank; cap. 1,000m. (Jan. 1994); Chair. SULAIMAN SEMBAJJA; Gen. Man. ABD AL-GADER RAGHEI.

STOCK EXCHANGE REGULATOR

Capital Markets Authority: Kampala; f. 1996 to license, regulate and oversee proposed stock exchange; Chair. LEO KIBIRANGO.

INSURANCE

East Africa General Insurance Co Ltd: 14 Kampala Rd, POB 1392, Kampala; telex 61378; life, fire, motor, marine and accident.

National Insurance Corporation: Plot 3, Pilkington Rd, POB 7134, Kampala; tel. (41) 258001; telex 61222; fax (41) 259925; f. 1964; general and life; Man. Dir F. F. MAGEZI.

Pan World Insurance Co Ltd: Plot 28, Jinja Rd, POB 2750, Kampala; tel. (41) 341618; fax (41) 341593; e-mail pwico@imul.com; Gen. Man. GORDON SENTIBA.

Uganda American Insurance Co Ltd: Kampala; telex 61101; f. 1970.

Uganda Co-operative Insurance Ltd: Plot 10, Bombo Rd, POB 6176, Kampala; tel. (41) 241836; fax (41) 258231; f. 1982; general.

Trade and Industry

Export and Import Licencing Division: POB 7000, Kampala; tel. (41) 258795; telex 61085; f. 1987; advises importers and exporters and issues import and export licences; Prin. Commercial Officer JOHN MUHWEZI.

Uganda Advisory Board of Trade: POB 6877, Kampala; tel. (41) 33311; telex 61085; f. 1974; issues trade licences and service for exporters.

Uganda Export Promotion Board: POB 5045, Kampala; tel. (41) 230233; telex 61391; fax (41) 259779; e-mail Uepc@starcom.co.ug; f. 1983; provides market intelligence, organizes training, trade exhbns, etc.; Exec. Dir ROBERT K. RUTAAGI.

Uganda Investment Authority: Investment Centre, Plot 28, Kampala Rd, POB 7418, Kampala; tel. (41) 251562; telex 61135; fax (41) 242903; f. 1991; promotes foreign and local investment, issues investment licences and provides investment incentives to priority industries; Exec. Dir G. W. RUBAGUMYA.

CHAMBER OF COMMERCE

Uganda National Chamber of Commerce and Industry: Plot 17/19 Jinja Rd, POB 3809, Kampala; tel. (41) 258791; telex 61272; fax (41) 258793; Chair. BADRU BUNKEDDEKO; Sec. GEORGE RUJOJO.

DEVELOPMENT CORPORATIONS

Agriculture and Livestock Development Fund: f. 1976; provides loans to farmers.

National Housing and Construction Corporation: Crested Towers, POB 659, Kampala; tel. (41) 230311; telex 61156; fax (41) 258708; f. 1964; govt agent for building works; also develops residential housing; Chair. D. LUBEGA; Gen. Man. M. S. KASEKENDE.

Ugandan Coffee Development Authority: Coffee House, Plot 35, Jinja Rd, POB 7267, Kampala; tel. (41) 256940; telex 61412; fax (41) 256994; f. 1991; enforces quality control and promotes coffee exports, maintains statistical data, advises govt on local and world prices and trains processors and quality controllers.

Uganda Industrial Development Corporation Ltd (ULDC): 9–11 Parliament Ave, POB 7042, Kampala; telex 61069; f. 1952; Chair. SAM RUTEGA.

EMPLOYERS' ORGANIZATION

Federation of Uganda Employers, Commerce and Industry: POB 3820, Kampala; Chair. BRUNO ABALIWANO; Exec. Dir J. KASWARRA.

MARKETING ORGANIZATIONS

CMB Ltd (Coffee Marketing Board): POB 7154, Kampala; tel. (41) 254051; telex 61157; fax (41) 230790; state-owned; purchases and exports coffee; Chair. Dr DDUMBA SSENTAMU; Man. Dir SAM KIGGUNDU.

Cotton Development Organization: POB 7018, Kampala; tel. (41) 232968; fax (41) 232975; Man. Dir JOLLY SABUNE.

Produce Marketing Board: POB 3705, Kampala; tel. (41) 236238; Gen. Man. ESTHER KAMPAMPARA.

Uganda Manufacturers' Association (UMA): POB 6966, Kampala; tel. (41) 221034; fax (41) 220285; promotes mfr's interests; Chair. JAMES MULWANA.

Uganda Tea Authority: POB 4161, Kampala; tel. (41) 231003; state-owned; controls and co-ordinates activities of the tea industry; Gen. Man. MIRIA MARGARITA MUGABI.

CO-OPERATIVE UNIONS

In 1993 there were 5,775 co-operative societies, grouped in 44 unions. There is at least one co-operative union in each administrative district.

Uganda Co-operative Alliance: Kampala; co-ordinating body for co-operative unions, of which the following are among the most important:

Bugisu Co-operative Union Ltd: Plot 2, Court Rd, Private Bag, Mbale; tel. (45) 2235; telex 66042; fax (45) 3565; f. 1954; processors and exporters of Bugisu arabica coffee; 226 mem. socs; Gen. Man. P. J. MUYIYI.

East Mengo Growers' Co-operative Union Ltd: POB 7092, Kampala; tel. (41) 270383; fax (41) 243502; f. 1968; processors and exporters of coffee and cotton; 280 mem. socs; Chair. FRANCIS MUKAMA; Man. JOSEPH SSEMOGERERE.

Kakumiro Growers' Co-operative Union: POB 511, Kakumiro; processing of coffee and cotton; Sec. and Man. TIBIHWA-RUKEERA.

Masaka Co-operative Union Ltd: POB 284, Masaka; tel. (481) 20260; f. 1951; coffee, dairy farming, food processing, carpentry; 245 primary co-operative socs; Chair. J. M. KASOZI; Gen. Man. EDWARD C. SSERUUMA.

Mubende District Co-operative Union: coffee growers.

Wamala Growers' Co-operative Union Ltd: POB 99, Mityana; tel. (46) 2036; f. 1968; coffee and cotton growers; 250 mem. socs; Gen. Man. HERBERT KIZITO.

West Mengo Growers' Co-operative Union Ltd: POB 7039, Kampala; tel. (41) 567511; f. 1948; cotton growing and buying, coffee buying and processing, maize milling; 250 mem. socs; Chair. H. E. KATABALWA MIIRO.

MAJOR INDUSTRIAL COMPANIES

The following are some of the largest companies in terms either of capital investment or employment.

The African Textile Mill Ltd: POB 242, Mbale; tel. (45) 34373; telex 66274; fax (45) 33380; f. 1970; cap. sh. 11.25m.; textile mfrs; operates one mill.

Blenders Uganda Ltd: POB 7054, Kampala; tea- and coffee-blending, packaging and distribution; Gen. Man. T. D. MUZITO.

British-American Tobacco (BAT) Uganda 1984 Ltd: POB 7100, Kampala; f. 1928; tel. (41) 243231; telex 61075; jtly owned by the Uganda govt and BAT London; tobacco mfrs and exporters; Man. Dir PHILIP PAYNE.

Bugirinya United Steel Co: POB 1321, Kampala; tel. (41) 245279; iron and steel producers.

Fina Exploration Uganda Ltd: wholly-owned by Petrofina Ltd (Belgium); petroleum exploration.

International Distillers Uganda Ltd: POB 3221, Kampala; tel. (41) 221111; f. 1965; cap. US $15m.; production of potable spirits; Gen. Man. I. H. KINSTON.

Kakira Sugar Works (KSW): POB 54, Jinja; jtly owned by Madhvani Group (70%) and Uganda govt; mfrs of some 70,000 metric tons of sugar annually.

Lonrho Motors Uganda Ltd: Plot 45, Jinja Rd, POB 353, Kampala; tel. (41) 231395; fax (41) 236769; mfrs of motor vehicles and parts.

Mitchell Cotts Uganda Ltd: 8 Burton St, POB 7032, Kampala; telex 61003; UK trading group active in tea sector, in which it part-owns the Toro and Mityana Tea Co, a jt venture with the Govt to rehabilitate the tea industry began in 1980; also operates freight services.

Nile Breweries Ltd: POB 762, Jinja; tel. (43) 20179; telex 64223; fax (43) 20759; f. 1951; mem. of Madhvani Group of Cos; Man. Dir RONI MADHVANI.

Nyanza Textile Industries Ltd: POB 408, Jinja; telex 64133; f. 1949; cap. sh. 80m.; textile mfrs; Man. Dir Mr ONEG-OBEL.

Pamba Textiles Ltd: POB 472, Jinja; f. 1963; cap. sh. 46m.; mfrs of cotton textiles.

Sembale Steel Mill: POB 4627, Kampala; tel. (41) 270147; iron and steel producers.

Steel Corpn of East Africa Ltd: POB 1023, Jinja; tel. (43) 21452; telex 64223; fax (43) 21453.

Tororo Industrial Chemicals and Fertilisers Ltd: POB 254, Tororo; f. 1962; mfrs of single super-phosphate fertilizer, sulphuric acid and insecticide.

Uganda Bata Shoe Co Ltd: POB 422, Kampala; tel. (41) 258911; fax 241380; f. 1966.

Uganda Breweries Ltd: POB 7130, Kampala; tel. (41) 220224; telex 61218; produces Bell, Pilsner and Guinness beers for the domestic market.

Uganda Grain Milling: POB 895, Jinja; tel. (43) 20054; millers.

Uganda Metal Products and Enamelling Co Ltd: POB 3151, Kampala; f. 1956; cap. £225,000; mfrs of enamelware, furniture, signs, etc.; 110 employees.

TRADE UNION

National Organization of Trade Unions (NOTU): POB 2150, Kampala; tel. (41) 256295; f. 1973; Chair. E. KATURAMU; Sec.-Gen. MATHIAS MUKASA.

Transport

RAILWAYS

In 1992 there were 1,241 km of 1000-mm-gauge track in operation. A programme to rehabilitate the railway network is under way.

Uganda Railways Corporation: Nasser Rd, POB 7150, Kampala; tel. (41) 254961; telex 61111; fax (41) 244405; formed after the dissolution of East African Railways in 1977; Man. Dir E. K. TUMUSIIME.

ROADS

In 1985 there was a total road network of 28,332 km, including 7,782 km of main roads and 18,508 km of secondary roads. About 22% of roads were paved. By early 1997 about 60% of main roads (by then totalling some 10,000 km) had been rehabilitated, and it was planned to invest some US $1,500m. in a further 10-year rehabilitation project.

INLAND WATERWAYS

A rail wagon ferry service connecting Jinja with the Tanzanian port of Tanga, via Mwanza, was inaugurated in 1983, thus reducing Uganda's dependence on the Kenyan port of Mombasa. In 1986 the Uganda and Kenya Railways Corporations began the joint operation of Lake Victoria Marine Services, to ferry goods between the two countries via Lake Victoria.

CIVIL AVIATION

The international airport is at Entebbe, on Lake Victoria, some 40 km from Kampala. In 1995 the airport was undergoing modernization. There are also several small airfields.

Civil Aviation Authority (CAA): Entebbe International Airport, POB 5536, Kampala; tel. (41) 243940; fax (41) 256807; Man. Dir AMBROSE AKANDONDA.

Principal Airlines

Alliance Airlines (African Joint Air Service); Impala House, 13 Kimathi Ave, POB 2128, Kampala; tel. (41) 244011; fax (41) 251681; f. 1994; jtly owned by South African Airways (40%), Air Tanzania Corpn (10%), Uganda Airlines Corpn (10%), the Ugandan and Tanzanian govts (30%) and private investors (10%); operates scheduled passenger and cargo services to Africa, Europe, the Middle East and Asia; Chair. ADRIAN SIBO; Man. Dir CHRISTO ROODT.

Eagle Aviation Uganda Ltd: Entebbe Internationl Airport; f. 1995; domestic services, charter flights to neighbouring countries; Man. Dir Capt. ANTHONY RUBOMBORA.

Uganda Airlines Corporation: Airways House, 6 Colville St, POB 5740, Kampala; tel. (41) 232990; telex 61239; fax (41) 257279; f. 1976; state-owned; scheduled cargo and passenger services to Africa, Europe and the Middle East; scheduled cargo and passenger domestic services; Chair. Dr EZRA SURUMA (acting); Gen. Man. BENEDICT MUTYABA.

Tourism

Uganda's principal attractions for tourists are the forests, lakes and wildlife and an equable climate. A programme to revive the tourist industry by building or improving hotels and creating new national parks began in the late 1980s. There were an estimated 175,000 tourist visitors in 1995 (compared with 12,786 in 1983). Revenue from tourism in 1995 was estimated at US $100m.

Ministry of Tourism and Wildlife: Parliament Ave, POB 4241, Kampala; tel. (41) 232971; telex 62218; provides some tourist information.

Uganda Tourist Board: Parliament Ave, POB 7211, Kampala; tel. (41) 242196; telex 61150; fax (41) 242188; Chair. PETER KAMYA; Gen. Man. FRANK S. KARAKE.

Defence

In August 1996 the Uganda People's Defence Forces (UPDF, formerly the National Resistance Army) was estimated to number 50,000 men, including paramilitary forces (a border defence unit of about 600 men, a police air wing numbering approximately 800, and about 400 marines). In October 1991 the police force numbered 16,890 men; the force was to be expanded to 30,000 members by the mid-1990s. It was announced in mid-1995 that defence expenditure would be increased by 40%, in order to combat insurrection in northern Uganda. In July 1997 some 50 US military staff arrived in Kampala to train a batalion of the UPDF to act as an African peace-keeping force under the African Crisis Response Initiative programme.

Defence Expenditure: Budgeted at 140,000m. shillings in 1996.

Commander of the UPDF: Maj.-Gen. MUGISHA MUNTU.

Education

Education is not compulsory. Most schools are sponsored by the government, although a small proportion are sponsored by missions. All schools charge fees; however, the government aims to begin the phased introduction of free primary school education in 1997. Primary education begins at six years of age and lasts for seven years. Secondary education, beginning at the age of 13, lasts for a further six years, comprising a first cycle of four years and a second of two years. In 1993 the number of pupils attending government-aided primary and secondary schools was equivalent to 44% of children in the relevant age-group. In 1995 there were 2,636,409 pupils enrolled at primary schools, and 255,158 pupils attending general secondary schools. In addition to Makerere University in Kampala, there is a university of science and technology at Mbarara, and a small Islamic university is located at Mbale. In 1993 enrolment in tertiary education was equivalent to 1.3% of students in the relevant age-group (males 1.9%; females 0.8%). In 1995, according to UNESCO estimates, the average rate of adult illiteracy was 38.2% (males 26.3%; females 49.8%). Education received 15.0% of budgetary expenditure by the central government in 1991. Education expenditure in the financial year ending 30 June 1995 accounted for approximately 11.0% of government current expenditure.

Bibliography

Ahluwalia, D. P. S. *Plantations and the Politics of Sugar in Uganda.* Kampala, Fountain Publishers, 1995.

Armstrong, J. *Uganda's AIDS Crisis: Its Implications for Development.* Washington, DC, World Bank, 1995.

Bernt, H., and Twaddle, M. (Eds). *Uganda Now.* London, James Currey, 1988.

Hansen, H. B. *Mission, Church and State in a Colonial Setting, Uganda 1890–c.1925.* London, Heinemann Educational, 1984.

Hansen, H. B., and Twaddle, M. (Eds). *Changing Uganda: The Dilemmas of Structural Management Adjustment and Revolutionary Change.* London, James Currey, 1991.

Jørgensen, J. J. *Uganda: A Modern History.* Croom Helm, 1981.

Kabwegyere, T. B. *The Politics of State Formation and Destruction in Uganda.* Kampala, Fountain Publishers, 1995.

Karugire, S. R. *A Political History of Uganda.* London, Heinemann, 1980.

Kasozi, A. B. K. *Social Origins of Violence in Uganda, 1964–1985.* London, University College London Press, 1995.

Langlands, B. W. *Notes on the Geography of Ethnicity in Uganda.* Kampala, 1975.

Langseth, P., and Katotobo, J. (Eds). *Uganda: Landmarks in Rebuilding a Nation.* Kampala, Fountain Publishers, 1993.

Low, D. A., and Pratt, R. C. *Buganda and British Overrule.* London, Oxford University Press, 1960.

Mamdani, M. *Politics and Class Formation in Uganda.* London, Heinemann Educational, 1977.

Imperialism and Fascism in Uganda. London, Heinemann Educational, 1983.

Martin, D. *General Amin.* London, Faber and Faber, 1974.

Mudoola, D. *Religion, Ethnicity and Politics in Uganda.* Kampala, Fountain Publishers, 1995.

Mukholi, D. *A Complete Guide to Uganda's Fourth Constitution: History, Politics and the Law.* Kampala, Fountain Publishers, 1995.

Mutibwa, P. *Uganda since Independence: A Story of Unfulfilled Hopes.* London, Hurst, 1992.

Nabudere, D. Wadada. *Imperialism and Revolution in Uganda.* Tanzania Publishing House/Onyx, 1980.

Nzita, R., and Mbaga-Niwampa. *Peoples and Cultures of Uganda.* 2nd edn. Kampala, Fountain Publishers, 1995.

Ofcansky, T. *Uganda: The Tarnished Pearl of Africa.* Boulder, CO, Westview Press, 1996.

Okoth, G. P., and Muranga, M. (Eds). *Uganda: A Century of Existence.* Kampala, Fountain Publishers, 1995.

Pirouet, M. L. *Historical Dictionary of Uganda.* Metuchen, NJ, Scarecrow Press, 1995.

Robertson, A. F. (Ed.). *Uganda's First Republic: Chiefs, Administrators and Politicians 1967–1971.* Cambridge, African Studies Centre, 1982.

Roth, M., Cochrane, J., and Kisamba-Mugerwa, W. *Tenure Security, Credit Use and Farm Investment in the Rujumbura Pilot Land Registration Scheme, Rukungiri District, Uganda.* Madison, University of Wisconsin, 1993.

Sathymurthy, T.V. *The Political Development of Uganda 1980–86.* Aldershot, Gower Publishers, 1986.

Soghayroun, I. E.-Z. *The Sudanese Muslim Factor in Uganda.* Khartoum University Press, 1981.

World Bank. *Uganda: Growing out of Poverty.* Washington, DC, World Bank, 1993.

The Challenge of Growth and Poverty Reduction. Washington DC, World Bank, 1996.

ZAMBIA

Physical and Social Geography

GEOFFREY J. WILLIAMS

The Republic of Zambia is a land-locked state occupying elevated plateau country in south-central Africa. Zambia has an area of 752,614 sq km (290,586 sq miles). The country is irregularly shaped, and shares a boundary with no fewer than eight other countries. For many years the 'line of rail' extending south from the Copperbelt, through Lusaka, to the Victoria Falls has been the major focus of economic activity.

PHYSICAL FEATURES

The topography of Zambia is dominated by the even skylines of uplifted planation surfaces. Highest elevations are reached on the Nyika plateau on the Malawi border (2,164 m). Elevations decline westward, where the country extends into the fringe of the vast Kalahari basin. The plateau surfaces are interrupted by localized downwarps (occupied by lakes and swamp areas, such as in the Bangweulu and Lukanga basins), and by the rifted troughs of the mid-Zambezi and Luangwa. An ancient rift structure probably underlies the Kafue Flats, an important wetland area to the south-west of Lusaka.

Katangan rocks of upper-Pre-Cambrian age yield the copper ores exploited on the Copperbelt. Younger Karoo sedimentaries floor the rift troughs of the Luangwa and the mid-Zambezi rivers, while a basalt flow of this age has been incised by the Zambezi below the Victoria Falls to form spectacular gorges. Coal-bearing rocks in the Zambezi trough are of this same system. Over the western third of the country there are extensive and deep wind-deposited sands, a relic of periods when the climate was drier and desert conditions in southern Africa were more widespread than at present.

The continental divide separating Atlantic from Indian Ocean drainage forms the frontier with the Democratic Republic of the Congo, then traverses north-east Zambia to the Tanzanian border. Some 77% of the country is drained to the Indian Ocean by the Zambezi and its two main tributaries, the Kafue and Luangwa, with the remainder being drained principally by the Chambeshi and Luapula via the River Congo to the Atlantic. Rapids occur along most river courses so that the rivers are of little use for transportation. The country's larger lakes, including the man-made Lakes Kariba and Itezhitezhi, offer possibilities of water use as yet relatively little developed.

Zambia's climatic year can be divided into three seasons: a cool dry season (April-August), a hot dry season (August-November) and a warm wet season (November-April). Temperatures are generally moderate. Mean maximum temperatures exceed 35°C only in southern low-lying areas in October, most of the country being in the range 30°–35°C. July, the coldest month, has mean minima of 5°–10°C over most of the country, but shows considerable variability. Rainfall is highest on the high plateau of the Northern Province and on the intercontinental divide west of the Copperbelt (exceeding 1,200 mm per year). In the south-west and the mid-Zambezi valley, annual mean rainfall is less than 750 mm.

The ancient rocks of the eastern two-thirds of the country have generally poor soils. Soils on the Kalahari Sands of the west are exceptionally infertile, while seasonal waterlogging of soils in basin and riverine flats makes them difficult to use. Savannah vegetation dominates, with miombo woodland extensive over the plateau, and mopane woodland in the low-lying areas. Small areas of dry evergreen forest occur in the north, while treeless grasslands characterize the flats of the river basins.

RESOURCES AND POPULATION

Zambia's main resource is its land, which, in general, is underutilized. Although soils are generally poor, altitudinal modifications of the climate make possible the cultivation of a wide range of crops. Cattle numbers are greatest in the southern and central areas, their range being limited by large tsetse-infested areas in the Kafue basin and the Luangwa valley. In the Western Province their numbers are less, but their importance to the local economy is even greater. Subsistence farming characterizes most of the country, with commercial farming focusing along the line of rail. Commercial forestry is important on the Copperbelt, where there are extensive softwood plantations, and in the south-west, where hardwoods are exploited. The main fisheries are located on the lakes and rivers of the Northern Province, with the Kafue Flats, Lukanga and Lake Kariba also contributing significantly. Game parks cover 7.9% of the country.

For many years, the mining of copper has dominated the Zambian economy, although its contribution has declined significantly since the mid-1980s, reflecting price fluctuations on international commodity markets. The country is the world's fifth-largest producer, although it has been estimated that, at current production rates, Zambia's economically recoverable reserves will be virtually exhausted by the year 2010. Cobalt, a by-product of copper mining, has recently gained in significance, and Zambia has been steadily expanding its cobalt production in an attempt to offset falls in copper output. Lead and zinc are produced at Kabwe, although the reserves of the Broken Hill Mine are nearing exhaustion. Coal, of which Zambia has the continent's largest deposits outside South Africa, is mined in the Zambezi valley, although this industry is in need of re-equipment and modernization. Manganese, silver and gold are produced in small quantity. Deposits of uranium have been located, and prospects exist for the exploitation of iron ore. No petroleum deposits have yet been identified. Zambia is rich in hydropower, developed and potential.

At mid-1995, according to an official estimate, Zambia's population was 9,373,000, equivalent to 12.5 inhabitants per sq km. This level of population density is low, by African standards, for a state which contains no truly arid area. However, this average figure is misleading, for Zambia is the third most urbanized country in mainland sub-Saharan Africa, with 41% of its population of 5,661,801 at the September 1980 census residing in towns of more than 5,000 inhabitants (42% in 1993, according to World Bank figures). Some 78% of the urban population was, in fact, located in the 10 largest urban areas, all situated on the 'line of rail'. Lusaka is the largest single urban centre, but the Copperbelt towns together constitute the largest concentration of urban population (47.1% of the total). While the increasing rate of population growth for the country as a whole (2.6% per annum in 1985–95) is a problem, the sustained influx to urban areas is even more acute as this growth has not been matched by employment and formal housing provision.

There are no fewer than 73 different ethnic groups among Zambia's indigenous population. Major groups are: the Bemba of the north-east, who are also dominant on the Copperbelt; the Nyanja of the Eastern Province, also numerous in Lusaka; the Tonga of the Southern Province and the Lozi of the west. Over 80 languages have been identified, of which seven are recognized as 'official' vernaculars. English is the language of government.

Recent History

ANDREW D. ROBERTS

Revised for this edition by the Editor

In the late 19th century the British government, concerned with maintaining British supremacy at the Cape, was anxious to prevent the Boers, Portuguese or Germans from forming hostile alliances further north. In 1889 it granted a charter to the British South Africa Co (BSA), which had recently been formed by Cecil Rhodes, a South African mining entrepreneur, empowering the company to make treaties and conduct administration north of the Limpopo river. In 1890 the BSA occupied the eastern part of what became Southern Rhodesia (now Zimbabwe), south of the Zambezi river, and meanwhile it had concluded treaties with, and obtained mining concessions from, various African chiefs to the north of the Zambezi. These agreements served to place most of what became Northern Rhodesia firmly within the British sphere of influence.

In 1924 the BSA, which had obtained little profit from exploiting the copper deposits in the territory, transferred its administrative responsibilities in Northern Rhodesia to the British government. However, by the mid-1930s, following discoveries of a vast deposits of copper ores, the large-scale exploitation of the region known as the Copperbelt was firmly established, using Northern Rhodesia as a vast labour reserve. African trade unions were not permitted, and in the absence of any other means of negotiation Africans formed 'welfare societies' throughout the country. The Federation of Welfare Societies was formed, and two years later reconstituted itself as a political body, the Northern Rhodesia Congress (renamed the Northern Rhodesia African National Congress in 1951). Under the leadership of Harry Nkumbula, it campaigned vigorously but unsuccessfully against British government proposals, supported by the white settlers, for a federation with Southern Rhodesia. In 1953 Northern Rhodesia became part of the Central African Federation (CAF) with Southern Rhodesia and Nyasaland (now Malawi).

Initially the CAF attracted new investment, and the copper-mining industry expanded. The Africans in Northern Rhodesia, however, could claim neither economic nor political advantages from the federation. During the first few years of the CAF the Congress organization sustained a loss of popular support. In 1958 Nkumbula's leadership was challenged by the secession from the Congress of a group of young radicals, led by Kenneth Kaunda, a former schoolteacher. They demanded the dissolution of the CAF and the independence of Northern Rhodesia, under the name of Zambia. The Congress was proscribed in 1959, and Kaunda was imprisoned. On his release, a few months later, he assumed the leadership of the newly-formed United National Independence Party (UNIP). In 1962, following a massive campaign of civil disobedience, organized by UNIP, the British government introduced a constitution for Northern Rhodesia, which would create an African majority in the legislature. UNIP agreed to participate in the ensuing elections, and formed a coalition government with the remaining supporters of Congress. The CAF was formally dissolved in December 1963.

INDEPENDENCE AND THE IMPACT OF UDI

Following pre-independence elections in January 1964 Kaunda formed a government comprising members of UNIP. The territory became independent as the Republic of Zambia on 24 October, with Kaunda as president. The new republic inherited an economy in which great mineral wealth had contributed very little to overall national development, and which was dependent on the massive industrial complex of white-ruled southern Africa. Before independence the government obtained the mineral rights whereby the BSA had exacted massive royalties from the mineral companies. Southern Rhodesia's unilateral declaration of independence in November 1965, and the subsequent imposition of international sanctions, stimulated Zambian efforts to reduce dependence on imports from the south: coal deposits were exploited to replace imports from Rhodesia, new hydroelectric schemes were developed, and new communications links were established between the Copperbelt region and the port of Dar es Salaam in Tanzania, notably the Tazara railway, opened in 1975.

The numerous whites who remained after independence were content to accept a minority role, but the relative ethnic harmony in Zambia was largely a result of the substantial wage increases granted to the African miners and other urban workers in the mid-1960s. The far more numerous subsistence farmers, and the many unemployed, however, were neglected. Plans for rural development achieved little success, and failed to halt migration to the towns. Although UNIP was returned to power in 1968, popular support for the party had declined.

Zambia gave support to guerrilla opposition groups in Rhodesia and Mozambique, thereby becoming a target for counter-subversion. Violent incidents occurred along the borders with both countries, and there were also outbreaks of internal political violence, particularly in the Copperbelt area. In 1971 Simon Kapwepwe, a former vice-president of Zambia, left UNIP and formed the United People's Party (UPP). The UPP was suppressed, and in December 1972 Zambia was declared a one-party state. Legislative elections took place in December 1973, and President Kaunda was re-elected for a third term of office. A new constitution gave UNIP responsibility for formulating strategies for national political development.

In January 1973 the Rhodesian administration closed the border along the Zambezi for everything except Zambia's copper exports; the government's subsequent decision to divert copper exports resulted in a severe deterioration in the economy, which was compounded, following the outbreak of civil war in Angola in late 1975, by the closure of the Benguela railway. Between 1974–76, moreover, world copper prices fell, and Zambia's revenues accordingly declined. By the end of the year, there was widespread discontent resulting from high food prices, import restrictions and increasing unemployment. Fears that this unrest was being exploited by external forces prompted Kaunda to declare a state of emergency in January 1976.

Constitutional changes, introduced in October 1978, effectively eliminated all organized political opposition, and in December Kaunda was returned for a fourth term as president. During that year Simon Kapwepwe, the former UPP leader, rejoined UNIP; as a recognized leader of the Bemba ethnic group (who were traditionally hostile to Kaunda), his support was considered vital for Kaunda at a time of acute political and economic instability. There remained, however, disagreement within UNIP over national policy, and, in particular, over Zambia's economic relations with Rhodesia, in view of the worsening economic crisis. In October 1978 rail links with Rhodesia were restored, and an agreement was reached on the shipping of exports via South Africa. Since 1977, however, Zambia had openly harboured members of the Zimbabwe African People's Union (ZAPU) wing of the Patriotic Front, and in 1978 and 1979 Rhodesian forces attacked ZAPU bases in Zambia and carried out air raids on Lusaka. Zambia continued to suffer severe disruption from Rhodesian bombing until the implementation, in December 1979, of an agreement, providing for the independence of Southern Rhodesia, as Zimbabwe, which came into effect in April 1980.

ECONOMIC PROBLEMS AND POLITICAL UNREST

Political dissent increased towards the end of 1980, following a further deterioration in economic conditions. In October several prominent businessmen, government officials and UNIP members allegedly staged a coup attempt. Kaunda claimed that South Africa had supported the plot, but many of those arrested after the incident were ethnic Bemba.

In January 1981 the suspension from UNIP of 17 officials of the Mineworkers' Union of Zambia (MUZ) and the Zambia

Congress of Trade Unions (ZCTU) prompted a widely-observed strike, and riots. Further strikes occurred in July, in protest at the continuing poor economic situation. The chairman of the ZCTU was arrested in July, along with several other trade union leaders, and was not released until October, when the high court ruled that the detention had been illegal. In 1980–83 several reorganizations of the cabinet and the central committee of UNIP were carried out.

Despite the introduction of unpopular austerity measures, necessitated by worsening economic problems, Kaunda retained a strong following; in October 1983 he was again re-elected president, receiving, as sole candidate, 93% of the votes cast, compared with 81% in 1978. Shortly afterwards, a campaign (which was to continue throughout that decade) was launched against corruption and inefficiency within the government and in industry; in a reorganization of the cabinet in December 1983, Kaunda personally assumed the industry portfolio.

In March 1985, following a series of strikes by public-sector employees demanding higher wages, Kaunda took emergency powers to ban strikes in essential services. In an extensive government reorganization in April, Kebby Musokotwane was appointed prime minister, while Alexander Grey Zulu became secretary-general of UNIP. Efforts to eradicate corruption continued later in that year, with the arrest of about 30 prominent businessmen, diplomats and former politicians on charges of smuggling illicit drugs to South Africa. In October a judicial tribunal was established to investigate the charges, but 24 of the detainees were released in April 1986.

In response to the continuing economic crisis, further austerity measures were imposed in 1985, leading to an increase in retail prices, which provoked angry demonstrations in Lusaka in October. Student demonstrations, which began in December, led to the closure of the university in the following May. In December 1986 the removal of the government subsidy on refined maize meal, the staple food, resulted in an increase of 120% in the price of this essential commodity. After violent rioting in the Copperbelt towns of Kitwe and Ndola, the subsidy was restored. Although peace in the region was restored by the end of December, strikes in support for wage increases occurred in early 1987, and in April of that year the government was forced to rescind a 70% increase in the price of fuel, following protests in Lusaka. In May Kaunda announced that an economic austerity programme advocated by the IMF was to be replaced by a government-devised strategy involving greater state controls, and a new minister of finance was appointed.

Meanwhile, the government became increasingly preoccupied with internal security. In April 1987 Kaunda alleged that the South African government, with the assistance of Zambian businessmen and members of the Zambian armed forces, had conspired to destabilize the Zambian government. In the following month a long-standing opponent of Kaunda, Alfred Masonda Chambeshi, was arrested, following allegations in court that he planned to overthrow the government, in collusion with Angolan rebels of the União Nacional para a Independência Total de Angola (UNITA). In July three members of the Zambian air force and a businessman were charged with having engaged in espionage for the South African government. In March 1988 a former South African soldier was sentenced to 50 years' imprisonment on espionage charges, and in June a New Zealand national, also convicted of spying for South Africa, was deported. In October three civilians and six military officers, including Lt-Gen. Christon Tembo, a former commander of the Zambian army, were arrested on suspicion of plotting a coup. (Tembo and a further three military officers were subsequently charged with treason, but were pardoned in July 1990.)

In August 1988, the UNIP central committee was enlarged to include a number of military commanders and industrialists, together with the chairman and secretary-general of the MUZ. In late October presidential and legislative elections took place. Kaunda, the only candidate, received 95.5% of all votes cast in the presidential election; however, four cabinet ministers lost their seats in the elections to the national assembly. In November Kaunda reorganized the cabinet, merging or abolishing five portfolios, apparently in an attempt to reduce government costs. In March 1989 Kebby Musokotwane, widely considered to be a potential rival to the president, was removed from the post of prime minister and briefly relegated to the ministry of general education, youth and sport, before being transferred to an overseas diplomatic posting; he was succeeded as prime minister by Gen. Malimba Masheke, minister of home affairs and a former minister of defence.

In early 1989 continued unrest among workers and students was reported, and the government threatened to ban trade unions involved in strike action. Increases in the prices of essential goods were implemented in mid-1989, prompting renewed rioting in the Copperbelt region in July. In June 1990 an announcement that the price of maize meal was to increase by more than 100% resulted in severe rioting in Lusaka, in which at least 30 people were reported to have been killed. In the same month the minister of defence, Frederick Hapunda (who was widely believed to favour a multi-party system), was dismissed, while several other prominent state officials were similarly removed from office. On 30 June a junior army officer, Lt Mwamba Luchembe, announced on the state radio that Kaunda had been overthrown by the armed forces. Luchembe was immediately arrested, although he was subsequently pardoned and released. In early July Lt-Gen. Hannaniah Lungu was appointed minister of defence.

In April 1990 the UNIP general conference rejected proposals for the introduction of a multi-party political system in Zambia. In the following month, however, Kaunda announced that a popular referendum on the subject of multi-party politics would be conducted in October of that year, and that proponents of such a system would be permitted to campaign and hold public meetings. Accordingly, in early July the Movement for Multi-party Democracy (MMD), an unofficial alliance of political opponents of the government, was formed, under the leadership of a former minister of finance, Arthur Wina, and the chairman of the ZCTU, Frederick Chiluba. In addition, the ZCTU demanded an end to the existing state of emergency, the creation of an independent body to monitor the referendum, and equal access to the media for both those supporting and those opposing the introduction of a multi-party system. In July 1990, however, Kaunda announced that the referendum was to be postponed until August 1991 to facilitate full electoral registration. Although he welcomed the registration procedure, Wina severely criticized the referendum's postponement and requested that it take place before December 1990. In August 1990 the national assembly proposed the introduction of a multi-party system, to which Kaunda again expressed his opposition. In the following month, however, Kaunda abandoned his opposition to the restoration of a plural political system, and proposed that multi-party presidential and legislative elections be organized, that the national referendum be abandoned, and that a commission be appointed to revise the constitution. Later in September UNIP endorsed the proposals for multi-party elections, which were scheduled for October 1991, and accepted recommendations for the restructuring of the party.

CONSTITUTIONAL TRANSITION

In December 1990 Kaunda formally adopted constitutional amendments, approved by the national assembly earlier that month, which permitted the formation of political parties other than UNIP to contest the forthcoming elections. Shortly afterwards, the MMD was granted official recognition as a political organization; the establishment of a further 11 opposition movements followed in subsequent months. In early 1991 several prominent members of UNIP resigned from the party and declared their support for the MMD, while the ZCTU officially transferred its allegiance to the MMD. In February Kaunda announced that he would permit other members of UNIP to contest the presidential election, despite previous statements to the contrary.

In early June 1991 the constitutional commission presented a series of recommendations, which included the establishment of a bicameral system of parliament, the creation of the post of vice-president, and the expansion of the national assembly from 135 to 150 members. Kaunda accepted the majority of the proposed constitutional amendments, which were subsequently submitted for approval by the national assembly. However, the MMD rejected the draft constitution, and threatened to boycott the elections in October if the national assembly accepted the proposals. Opposition supporters objected in particular to amendments permitting the appointment of non-elected ministers from outside the national assembly, and the vesting of supreme authority in the president rather than in the national assembly. The government also rejected opposition demands that foreign observers be invited to monitor the elections. In July, following discussions between Kaunda, Frederick Chiluba and delegates from seven other opposition parties, under the chairmanship of the deputy chief justice, Mathew Ngulube, Kaunda agreed to suspend the review of the draft constitution in the national assembly, pending further discussions; it was also decided that state subsidies would be granted to all registered political parties. Subsequent negotiations between the MMD and UNIP, resulted in the formation of a joint commission of experts to revise the draft constitution. Later in July, following a meeting of the two parties under the auspices of the constitutional commission, Kaunda conceded to opposition demands that ministers be appointed only from members of the national assembly and that the proposed establishment of a constitutional court be abandoned; presidential powers to impose martial law were also to be rescinded. On 2 August the national assembly formally adopted the new draft constitution, which included these amendments.

In late July 1991 Kaunda's leadership of UNIP was challenged by Enoch Kavindele, a businessman, and member of the central committee of UNIP. In addition, allegations of the misuse of state funds by government officials threatened to increase opposition to Kaunda. Two days prior to UNIP's party congress, however, Kavindele withdrew his canditure, allegedly in the interests of party unity. In early August the party congress re-elected Kaunda as president. However, several prominent party officials, including Alexander Grey Zulu, hitherto secretary-general of the party, refused to contest the elections. Later in August Kaunda agreed to permit foreign observers to monitor the forthcoming elections, in an attempt to counter opposition allegations that UNIP would perpetrate electoral fraud. In addition, Kaunda announced that the armed forces were henceforth disassociated from UNIP, in accordance with the tenets of political pluralism; leaders of the armed forces were obliged to retire from membership of the party's central committee.

In September 1991 the national assembly was dissolved, in preparation for the presidential and legislative elections, which were scheduled for 31 October. On the same day Kaunda officially disassociated UNIP from the State; workers in the public sector were henceforth prohibited from engaging in political activity. However, international observers, who arrived in Zambia in September, expressed concern that the elections would not be conducted fairly, on the grounds that the government-owned media and parastatal organizations continued to support UNIP in its electoral campaign, and that the state of emergency remained in force. During October numerous outbreaks of violence were reported; in one incident four supporters of the MMD were killed by members of UNIP. Kaunda warned that UNIP's failure to win the election would provoke a civil conflict, while Chiluba accused Kaunda of amassing troops on the border with Malawi to fight the MMD in the event of its accession to power. Chiluba also claimed that an attempt to assassinate him had been staged, and appealed to the Organization of African Unity (OAU) to deploy peace-keeping forces in Zambia during the election period. In late October Kaunda accused the international observers of involvement in a conspiracy to remove UNIP from power.

THE CHILUBA PRESIDENCY

Contrary to previous indications, international observers reported that the elections, which took place on 31 October 1991, had been conducted fairly. In the presidential election Chiluba, who received 75.79% of votes cast, defeated Kaunda, who obtained 24.21% of the vote. In the legislative elections, which were contested by 330 candidates representing six political parties, the MMD secured 125 seats in the national assembly, while UNIP won the remaining 25 seats; only four members of the previous government were returned to the national assembly. Kaunda's failure to be re-elected to the presidency was attributed to widespread discontent at the deterioration of economic conditions, as a result of the government's continued mismanagement. On 2 November Chiluba was inaugurated as president. Chiluba appointed Levy Mwanawasa, a constitutional lawyer, as vice-president and leader of the national assembly, and formed a new 22-member cabinet. In addition, a minister was appointed to each of the country's nine provinces, which were previously administered by governors. Two days later the government allowed the state of emergency to lapse. During his first month in office Chiluba began to carry out a major restructuring of the civil service and parastatal organizations, as the first step in his programme of economic revival.

Internal 'Conspiracies' and Official Investigations

In December 1991, following a road accident in which Mwanawasa was severely injured, the minister without portfolio, Brig.-Gen. Godfrey Miyanda, was accused of plotting his death. A commission of inquiry was later informed that Miyanda had previously conspired with members of the former government to assassinate Chiluba and to abduct Mwanawasa. It was alleged that after the failure of this plan he had arranged the road accident, in an attempt to kill Mwanawasa, and subsequently to assume the vice-presidency. In March 1992, however, following an investigation by detectives from the United Kingdom of the circumstances of the accident, Miyanda was exonerated. Later in December 1991 Kaunda announced that he was to relinquish the leadership of UNIP; a new president was to be elected at a party congress in August 1992. In January 1992 Kaunda denied allegations that he had misappropriated public funds during his tenure of office, and moved to institute legal proceedings against the state, members of the media and leading government officials, following accusations of his complicity in a number of offences. Later in January the minister of defence, Ben Mwila, claimed that UNIP was promoting a coup attempt by former army officers.

In May 1992, amid widespread opposition to government, a dissident faction of academics within the MMD, known as Caucus for National Unity (CNU), emerged. The CNU, which claimed support from several members of the government, requested that Chiluba review his appointment of cabinet ministers and heads of parastatal organizations, to ensure that all ethnic groups were represented. The CNU, together with the Zambia Research Foundation and the Women's Lobby, also advocated the establishment of a constitutional commission to curtail the executive powers of the president and the cabinet. However, Chiluba refused to initiate a review of the constitution, on the grounds of expense. The government was also criticized for its rigid enforcement of the structural adjustment programme supported by the IMF and World Bank, which had resulted in an increase in economic hardship.

In June 1992 a breakaway faction of UNIP formed a new opposition group, the United Democratic Party (UDP). In July, following the rejection by the national assembly of a report that implicated several members of the government in alleged financial malpractice, two cabinet ministers (who were believed to have links with the CNU) resigned in protest at the government's failure to eradicate corruption and to implement democratic reform; Chiluba subsequently reshuffled the cabinet. Later that month the CNU registered as an independent political party, after the resignation of its leader, Dr Muyoba Macwani, from the MMD. In August Kaunda and the secretary-general of UNIP, Kebby Musokotwane, were temporarily detained, on the grounds that they had convened an illegal gathering. At a party congress in late September, Kaunda formally resigned as leader of UNIP, and was replaced by Musokotwane. In local government elections which took place in late November, the MMD won the majority of seats. There was, however, a high rate of abstention (the turnout was less than 10% of registered voters); this was widely attributed to disillusionment with the Chiluba administration.

In early March 1993 Chiluba declared a state of emergency, following the discovery of UNIP documents detailing an alleged conspiracy (referred to as the 'Zero Option') to destabilize the government by inciting unrest and civil disobedience. A number of prominent members of UNIP, including Kaunda's three sons, were subsequently arrested. Musokotwane conceded the existence of the documents, but denied that UNIP officials were involved in the conspiracy, which he attributed to extreme factions within the party. Kaunda, however, claimed that the conspiracy had been fabricated by Zambian security forces, with the assistance of US intelligence services, in an attempt to discredit the opposition. Later that month, following allegations by the Zambian government that Iran and Iraq had financed subversive elements within UNIP, diplomatic relations with the two countries were suspended. Shortly afterwards, the national assembly approved the state of emergency, which was to remain in force for a further three months. Owing to pressure from Western governments, however, Chiluba reduced the maximum period of detention without trial from 28 to seven days.

In April 1993, with the stated intention of eradicating government corruption, Chiluba extensively reshuffled the cabinet. Although four senior ministers were dismissed, a number of ministers who were implicated in alleged malpractice remained in the government. In the same month 15 members of UNIP, who had been arrested in connection with the alleged conspiracy in March, appealed to the high court against their continued detention without trial; seven of the detainees were subsequently released. In May the detention orders on the remaining eight members were revoked; however, they were immediately rearrested and charged with related offences. Later that month the state of emergency was lifted.

Political Realignments

In July 1993 UNIP, the UDP and the Labour Party (LP) established an informal alliance, and advocated a campaign of civil disobedience in protest at the economic austerity measures. In the same month Kaunda announced that he was to retire from political activity. Divisions within the MMD became apparent in August, when 15 members (11 of whom held seats in the national assembly and including several former cabinet ministers) left the party. The rebels accused the government of protecting corrupt cabinet ministers and of failing to respond to numerous reports linking senior party officials with the illegal drugs trade. Their opposition to Chiluba's government was consolidated later in the month by the formation of a new political group, the National Party (NP). An existing organization, the National Party for Democracy, merged with the new party.

In January 1994 two prominent cabinet ministers announced their resignations, following persistent allegations of their involvement in high-level corruption and drugs-trafficking, and increasing domestic and international pressure for the government to take action over the allegations. One of the ministers, Vernon Mwaanga, a founder member of the MMD, who had held the foreign affairs portfolio, had been accused of drugs-trafficking by a tribunal in 1985, although he had not been convicted of the alleged offences. Both ministers denied any misconduct and declared they had resigned pending an official investigation. The resignations were followed by an extensive reorganization of cabinet portfolios, in which a further two ministers were removed. At by-elections for 10 of the 11 vacated seats in the national assembly, which were held in November 1993 and April 1994, the MMD regained five seats, while the NP secured four and UNIP one.

In June 1994 seven opposition parties, including UNIP, formed the Zambia Opposition Front (ZOFRO) to co-ordinate the various groups' activities. In early July Levy Mwanawasa resigned as vice-president, citing long-standing differences with Chiluba, and was replaced by Godfrey Miyanda. In the same month ex-president Kaunda announced that he was considering renouncing political retirement to contest the presidential election in 1996. However, UNIP officials indicated that he would be allowed to resume the leadership of the party only if he were officially elected by members. (Kaunda's decision to return to active politics subsequently led to factional division within UNIP.) In August 1994 Kaunda was allegedly warned against inciting revolt, after he conducted a number of rallies in the Northern Province (where the MMD traditionally attracted considerable support). Later that month the government announced that Kaunda had been placed under surveillance in the interests of national security, following reports that he had received support from foreign diplomatic missions in Zambia.

In October 1994 two deputy government ministers were dismissed, after criticizing the modalities of government plans to privatize the country's principal industrial enterprise, Zambia Consolidated Copper Mines. At a by-election in December UNIP secured the remaining vacant seat in the national assembly. In January 1995 Chiluba dismissed the minister of lands, Dr Chuulu Kalima, on grounds of misconduct; Kalima had apparently accused the president of involvement in a transaction in which a deputy minister had acquired land formerly owned by the University of Zambia. In early February Chiluba ordered members of the government to declare their financial assets and liabilities within a period of two days. In the same month Kaunda was charged with convening an illegal political gathering, after he had addressed a public rally. Later in February the governor of the Bank of Zambia was replaced, following a sharp depreciation in the value of the national currency. In March increasing divisions became evident within the MMD between the Bemba ethnic group (to which Chiluba belonged) and the traditionalist Nsenga; it was reported that MMD factions had circulated pamphlets criticizing Chiluba and Mwanawasa (who remained as vice-president of the MMD). In April a former cabinet minister, Dean Mung'omba, announced that he intended to contest Chiluba's leadership of the MMD. In the same month a pro-Kaunda faction of UNIP indicated that it would challenge the leadership of the incumbent party president, Musokotwane. Later in April the MMD retained two parliamentary seats contested in further partial elections. In late June, at an extraordinary congress of UNIP, Kaunda was elected UNIP president by a large majority. Kaunda's avowed aim on election was to contest the country's presidential election scheduled for 1996; he subsequently demanded that both the presidential and general elections be brought forward to October 1995. It was widely expected, however, that proposed constitutional reforms would include a clause banning any president from a third term of office, and bar candidates from seeking election as president if their parents were not both of Zambian origin (Kaunda's parents were reported to have come from Malawi, of which country Kaunda was subsequently himself alleged to have been a national at the time of his election as president in 1964). In mid-June the leader of the Movement for Democratic Process (MDP), Chama Chakomboka, had also declared his intention of standing in the forthcoming elections.

In mid-July 1995 Chiluba reshuffled the cabinet, appointing a new minister of foreign affairs. Later in that month the minister of home affairs, Chitalu Sampa, warned Kaunda to desist from 'inciting violence' or risk being arrested, following Kaunda's urging of a public campaign of civil disobedience against the government. It appeared, however, that there were growing signs of divisions within UNIP itself when, by the end of August, three opposition MPs had resigned, including the opposition parliamentary leader, Dingiswayo Banda, who defected to the MMD. Banda's defection followed reports of a plot within UNIP, after the election of Kaunda, to have Banda removed as opposition parliamentary leader. Two other UNIP officials also joined the MMD in that month.

In early September 1995 the Munyama Commission on Human Rights, established by Chiluba in 1993 to review allegations of abuses during the Kaunda presidency, alleged that torture and other abuses of human rights had been carried out in cells beneath the presidential residence which were subsequently opened to public inspection. The report further asserted that torture and other violations of human rights were still taking place in Zambia. At by-elections held in 13 constituencies in September and early October 1995, the MMD secured seven seats, and UNIP six. In October the minister of legal affairs announced that Kaunda had not officially relinquished Malawian citizenship until 1970 (and had therefore governed illegally for six years), and that he had not obtained Zambian citizenship through the correct procedures. Later that month, however, following widespread reports that the authorities intended to deport Kaunda, the government ordered the security forces to suspend investigations into his citizenship (apparently owing to fears of civil unrest). In the same month opposition parties criticized the government's failure to establish a constituent assembly to approve the draft constitution. At the end of October much of the Asian population of the southern town of Livingstone fled to Lusaka or neighbouring Zimbabwe, following an outbreak of racial violence prompted by the alleged involvement of two Asian traders in the ritual murder of two minors. (The two Asians were, however, later acquitted of murder.)

Electoral Controversies

In January 1996 seven opposition parties, including UNIP and the NP, established an informal alliance to campaign in favour of democratic elections and the establishment of a constituent assembly to approve the draft constitution by a process of national consensus. In March a parliamentary edict sentenced three journalists to indefinite imprisonment on charges of contempt of parliament. The charges concerned the publication of newspaper articles commenting on criticism by Miyanda in the national assembly of a supreme court ruling that restrictions on public gatherings were unconstitutional. The three journalists subsequently went into hiding (although two of them later surrendered to security forces), while the International Press Institute condemned the convictions, which it declared to be invalid; the edict was later overturned by the high court, and the journalists were released. In early May division emerged within the MMD regarding the draft constitution when the minister of works and supply resigned from office in protest at the amendment barring foreign nationals and those with foreign parentage from contesting the presidency. (The same issue had already prompted the resignation, in February, of the minister of commerce, trade and industry.) The cabinet was reorganized at the end of May. Opposition parties, moreover, demanded that the government abandon the draft constitution and negotiate with them regarding electoral reform. Later that month UNIP deputies withdrew from a parliamentary debate on the draft, which was subsequently approved by a large majority in the national assembly. On 28 May, despite continuing criticism of the new constitution, it was officially adopted by Chiluba. In early June the USA and Norway announced a reduction in aid to Zambia, in protest at the constitutional amendment that effectively procluded Kaunda from contesting the presidential election. Other Western donor governments subsequently announced their decision to review aid disbursements to Zambia in the light of the new constitution. Despite this set-back, Chiluba announced that the forthcoming presidential and legislative elections would be conducted according to the terms of the new constitution, while Kaunda announced that he intended to contest the presidency despite the ban. In the same month eight senior UNIP officials, including the vice-president of the party, were arrested and charged in connection with a series of bomb attacks against official buildings, which were attributed to a clandestine anti-government organization, known as 'Black Mamba'.

In August 1996 Chiluba and Kaunda met for discussions in Lusaka as part of a programme of dialogue between the government and opposition parties. Following Kaunda's decision to boycott a scheduled second round of discussions in September, the government made minor concessions regarding the conduct of forthcoming elections, including assurances that votes would be counted at polling stations and that the electoral commission (appointed by Chiluba) would be independent; UNIP's request that the elections be conducted according to the 1991 constitution was rejected. In mid-October 1996 Chiluba dissolved the national assembly and announced that presidential and legislative elections would take place on 18 November. UNIP, still dissatisfied with the electoral system, announced its intention to boycott the elections and organize a campaign of civil disobedience; by early November a further six political parties had also decided to boycott the elections. There was widespread criticism of the voter registration process (conducted by an overseas computer company), in which fewer than one-half of the estimated 4.6m. eligible voters had been listed. The government ordered the temporary closure of the University of Zambia, after two days of rioting by students who were attempting to force Chiluba to reopen negotiations with the opposition and reach agreement on the electoral process.

Despite appeals for a postponement, the elections took place, as planned, on 18 November 1996, and Chiluba and the MMD were returned to power by a large majority. In the presidential election Chiluba defeated the four other candidates with 72.5% of the valid votes cast. His nearest rival (with only 12.5%) was Dean Mung'omba of the Zambia Democratic Congress (ZADECO), an erstwhile opponent of Chiluba within the MMD. The MMD secured 131 of the 150 seats in the national assembly. Of the eight other parties that finally contested the legislative elections, only the NP (five seats), ZADECO (two seats) and Agenda for Zambia (two seats) won parliamentary representation, with independent candidates taking the remaining 10 seats. The rate of participation was low. Despite the electoral commission's verdict that the elections had been conducted fairly, allegations of fraud were made by opposition parties and local monitoring groups, which criticized voter registration procedures and accused the MMD of buying votes. The chairmen of two electoral monitoring groups were taken into custody for questioning, but were later released without charge. A former senior official of one of the groups claimed that the monitoring groups had been influenced by donor governments attempting to discredit the elections, and six journalists working in the state media were suspended for allegedly conspiring to undermine the elections.

Chiluba was inaugurated for a second presidential term on 21 November 1966. Amid demands for his resignation and for fresh elections to be held, Chiluba dissolved the cabinet and put the military on alert at the end of the month. In early December a new government was appointed: there were no changes to the main portfolios, except for the appointment of Lawrence Shimba (a professor of law at the University of Zambia) as minister of foreign affairs. Opposition parties continued their campaign of civil disobedience throughout December, although nation-wide marches of solidarity with the government were reported to have been widely supported. Four opposition parties filed petitions with the supreme court challenging Chiluba's citizenship (and therefore his eligibility as president), and accusing the electoral commission of conspiring with the MMD to commit electoral fraud; the petitions were dismissed in early 1997. In response to reports in late December that a senior army commander had been placed under house arrest as a result of rumours of a military takeover, Chiluba warned the media against attempting to incite the security forces to challenge his leadership.

In early February 1997 a human rights report prepared for the US department of state condemned police brutality and prison conditions in Zambia, but claimed there had been no evidence of significant electoral fraud in the 1996 elections. In the same month an African human rights group released a report, in which it asserted that further investigation was required into the deaths of five opposition politicians during 1995–96. In March 1997 the government established a permanent commission to investigate human rights violations, although opposition parties refused to participate. (In October 1996 the human rights commission established by Chiluba in 1993 had presented its final report, disclosing evidence of the violation of the human rights of political detainees under both Kaunda's and Chiluba's governments.)

Student protests in support of demands for an increase in allowances from the government for the purchase of books caused the temporary closure of the University of Zambia in early March and of the Copperbelt University in early April. UNIP expelled three central committee officials from the party on disciplinary charges in early April 1997, provoking clashes involving the security forces later that month as the expelled officials and their supporters attempted to gain entry to party headquarters. Also in April the government, in response to public pressure, suspended a proposed bill that was to have increased official control over the media. In early May the MMD retained three parliamentary seats unopposed at by-elections, owing to an opposition boycott. In June the decision of Emmanuel Kassonde, a former minister of finance, to resign from the NP and rejoin the MMD prompted the resignation of the NP leadership in the Northern Province.

Political tension intensified in June 1997. In response to reports claiming that Kaunda and Roger Chongwe, the leader of the Liberal Progressive Front, were appealing for international assistance to overcome a political crisis in Zambia, the MMD refuted the existence of any such crisis. Later that month the MMD's chairman in Lusaka called for the declaration of a state of emergency, on the grounds that the opposition were advocating a civil war by refusing to enter into talks with the MMD. The opposition denounced his claims and Chongwe insisted that they would welcome dialogue, but only if the 1996 elections were annulled and the constitution repealed. Meanwhile, the opposition's campaign of civil disobedience continued. Joint ralles were held, at which voter cards from the

November elections were burnt, and in late July security forces intervened to disperse demonstators at a protest march against the MMD after government vehicles were stoned. In mid-August the government accused the opposition of inciting unrest, as market-traders rioted after their stalls were destroyed by fire; 56 people were arrested in the disturbances. Later that month Kaunda and Chongwe were shot and wounded when the security forces opened fire on an opposition gathering, following the cancellation of a rally in Kabwe, north of Lusaka. Kaunda's subsequent allegation that the shooting was an assassination attempt organized by the government was strongly denied by Chiluba. Two senior police-officers were suspended pending the completion of an investigation.

REGIONAL RELATIONS

Relations between Zambia and a newly independent Zimbabwe were initially tense, owing to Kaunda's long-standing support for Robert Mugabe's political rival, Joshua Nkomo. Contacts between the two states were considerably improved, however, following reciprocal state visits in 1981. In 1987 the first state visit to Zambia by the Tanzanian president, Ali Hassan Mwinyi, reinforced economic and technical co-operation between the two countries.

Kaunda assumed a leading role in peace initiatives in southern Africa, and supported both the South West Africa People's Organisation of Namibia (SWAPO), allowing it to operate from Zambian territory, and the African National Congress of South Africa (ANC), which, until its return to South Africa in mid-1990, maintained its headquarters in Lusaka. In 1984 Kaunda was joint chairman of a conference on the issue of Namibian independence, which was held in Lusaka and involved the South African administrator-general in Namibia, together with representatives from SWAPO and some of Namibia's internal political parties. In September 1985 Kaunda was appointed chairman of the 'front-line' states, and in July 1987 he was elected to the chairmanship of the OAU. Owing to Kaunda's support for SWAPO and the ANC, Zambia was frequently subjected to military reprisals by South Africa. In May 1986 an air attack on an alleged ANC base near Lusaka, resulting in two deaths, was carried out by South African defence forces. Intermittent bomb attacks in Lusaka in 1987, 1988 and 1989 were generally viewed as attempts at destabilization by South Africa. Following the initiation of a programme of political reforms in South Africa in 1990, however, the Zambian government envisaged the restoration of diplomatic relations between the two countries. In mid-1993 the South African president, F. W. de Klerk, made an official visit to Zambia (the first by a South African head of state).

Zambia's support for the governments of Angola and Mozambique also resulted in retaliatory attacks by UNITA rebels and by Mozambican guerrillas of the Resistência Nacional Moçambicana (Renamo). In May 1986 landmine explosions in the Zambezi district, which killed three people, were reportedly the responsibilty of UNITA; attacks by UNITA rebels continued in the late 1980s and early 1990s. Over the same period, a number of Zambian civilians were reported to have been killed in repeated raids by members of Renamo, while Zambian troops entered Mozambican territory in pursuit of the rebels. In September 1992 the governments of Zambia and Angola signed a security agreement providing for joint border controls. Following a peace accord, signed by the Mozambican government and Renamo in October of that year, Zambia contributed some 950 troops to a UN peace-keeping force, which was deployed in Mozambique. In May 1993 the Zambian government dispatched troops to the border with Angola, in an attempt to prevent further attacks by UNITA rebels. In July 1994 it was alleged that Zambia was violating UN sanctions against UNITA rebels by supplying arms and oil to the movement. The allegation was rejected by President Chiluba. In early 1996 Zambia contributed some 1,000 troops to the UN Angola Verification Mission.

In early March 1997 the Zambian government appealed for international assistance in coping with the influx of refugees fleeing the civil conflict in Zaire (now the Democratic Republic of the Congo); by March some 6,000 Zairean refugees had arrived in Zambia.

Economy

LINDA VAN BUREN

The Zambian economy expanded rapidly during the 1960s and early 1970s, owing to high levels of the international price of copper. Despite considerable investment in physical and social infrastructure, however, the government failed to develop other sectors of the economy, and a reduction in the international price of copper in the mid-1970s resulted in a severe economic decline. Development was subsequently constrained by a shortage of foreign exchange with which to buy essential inputs and by a lack of skilled manpower, a poor transport network and high debt-service obligations. The economic mismanagement of the Kaunda administration contributed to a further deterioration in domestic conditions, with severe food shortages, and a dramatic increase in inflation and unemployment. In the early 1990s an economic recovery was expected, following the establishment of a new government and the resumption of an IMF-approved austerity programme; however, signs of improvement were slow to appear.

AGRICULTURE

Zambia's topography, with its variations in elevation, enables a variety of crops to be grown, although only about 7% of the surface area is under cultivation, while some 40% serves as permanent pasture and 43% is under forest. The principal crops are maize, sugar cane, cassava, millet, sorghum, beans, groundnuts, cotton, tobacco, sunflowers, rice, wheat, arabica coffee and horticultural products. A number of lakes and rivers, particularly those in the Northern Province and at Lake Kariba on the southern border, offer considerable potential for fishing. Zambia has 323,000 sq km of forest land, of which 265,000 sq km are open to exploitation. Commercial forestry is important on the Copperbelt, where there are numerous softwood tree plantations, and in the hardwood areas of the south-west, which are rich in African teak.

Zambia has a few hundred large commercial farms, situated mostly near the railway lines, which account for about 45% of the country's agricultural output. The number of smallholders who cultivate cash crops is increasing, while most subsistence farmers in all parts of the country use traditional methods, without adequate inputs or infrastructural support. Agriculture accounted for 11% of gross domestic product (GDP) in 1970, and for 19.8% in 1996; the sector employed some 73.6% of the labour force at mid-1995, according to FAO estimates. Food production per caput remained static throughout the 1980s, even registering a decline of 0.7%. The agricultural sector is frequently affected by drought but grew by an annual average of 2.1% in 1970–80, by an annual average of 3.3% in 1980–91, and by an annual average of 2.1% in 1990–94. Drought returned in 1994/95 and, following growth of 6.8% in 1994, the agricultural sector registered a decline of 11.3% in 1995. After a recovery in early 1996, drought in some parts of the country, flooding in other parts, and a lack of fertilizers at a crucial time in the growing period, all combined to damage the maize crop, leaving Zambia with a 3m.-bag maize deficit for 1996/97. Arrangements were made to import 120,000 metric tons of maize from Zimbabwe, but in July 1997 Zimbabwe announced that it could only supply 50,000 tons and the Zambian government confirmed that this time, unlike in 1994, no maize would be available from South Africa. Moreover, it was discovered that some of the country's stored grain in Luapula Province had been infested by an insect larva.

Production of maize (the staple food of most Zambians) exhibited a remarkable recovery after a particularly severe drought in 1991/92. Output in 1992/93 (year ending 30 April) amounted to a record level of 17.8m. 90-kg bags, to 9.3m. bags in 1994/95, and to 9.1m. bags in 1996/97. National consumption is about 15.5m. bags per year. In April 1993 the Zambia National Union of Farmers complained that the basic guaranteed price of K5,000 per 90-kg bag was uneconomical and warned that commercial farmers might abandon the cultivation of maize unless the government were to increase the price to at least K8,000 per bag; the government subsequently agreed to review the price. In the event, in preference to increasing the guaranteed price, the government chose to introduce two types of promissory note. The first, a rediscountable promissory note, allowed farmers to collect, after 15 February 1994, money owed to them on maize they had produced up to 31 October 1993, together with interest equivalent to the prevailing rate on 182-day treasury bills (at the time, 125% per annum). Farmers could, alternatively, sell the notes to a commercial bank at a discount, or they could use them as collateral on loans or to purchase agricultural inputs such as fertilizers. The farmers' other option was to accept a forward-contract promissory note, guaranteeing a price of K7,500 per 90-kg bag on 15 February 1994, which was intended to reflect the market price plus interest and a storage allowance. The farmers had then to decide whether they would lose or gain by waiting to accept the undertaking to buy on 15 February. The scheme was immediately criticized for being both complicated and costly. According to the FAO, the area planted with maize declined by 23.4% between 1994–95, from 679,000 ha to 520,000 ha. Financial losses, principally resulting from over-production, continued to pose a problem, and experts have advocated a comprehensive strategic maize policy that would assure adequate stocks to meet domestic requirements in times of drought, and sufficient storage for that purpose, while avoiding costly maintenance of excessive stocks. However, the new government, which took office in 1991, reacted effectively to the drought in 1991/92, distributing emergency supplies far more efficiently than the governments of neighbouring countries, and subsequently arranging the timely supply of seed to effect a quick recovery.

Wheat is grown almost exclusively on large commercial farms, usually under irrigation. Production increased from 37,000 metric tons in 1988 to 47,000 tons in 1989, and 54,500 tons in 1990, before reaching a record 71,000 tons in 1993. Production then declined to 43,000 tons in 1994, before recovering slightly to 50,000 tons in 1995. The country's flour mills require some 120,000 tons per annum to keep the nation supplied with bread. In September 1997 the government imposed a ban on the import of wheat flour, with the stated aim of curtailing the smuggling of 'expired products' into Zambia from unnamed 'neighbouring countries'. The wheat sector was assisted by Canadian agricultural advisers, who maintained that Zambia had the potential to meet much more of its wheat requirement from local production. The Zambian government lifted controls over the producer price of wheat in June 1988, precipitating a dramatic increase in the price, to K370 per 90-kg bag in October (compared with K190 in June). However, liberalization also meant that the National Milling Co (the country's only miller of wheat, although no longer with a statutory monopoly) was free to obtain its wheat at lower prices from elsewhere, notably from South Africa. Zambian farmers also grew 55,000 metric tons of millet and 27,000 metric tons of sorghum in 1995. Smallholders grow most of the nation's cotton crop. Textile factories in the country require about 12,000 metric tons of cotton lint per annum, and in most years, the domestic cotton crop is large enough to meet all of the demand and allow for cotton exports. However, output declined from 21,000 tons in 1988 to 17,000 tons in 1989, and to 10,000 tons in 1990, even before the 1991/92 drought. Textile companies complained that the best cotton was exported, leaving lower-quality raw material for the local industry; another problem was that, following the liberalization of trade, cheap imports reduced demand for local textiles, and therefore the textile companies' demand for local cotton. Unofficial figures indicated that Zambian farmers harvested 16,000 tons of cotton lint, and 44,000 tons of cottonseed, in 1995. Production of cottonseed oil fell from 5,460 metric tons in 1993 to 1,969 metric tons in 1994, before recovering to 4,030 tons in 1995. In July 1997 the Zambia Agricultural High Value Crops Association was formed, with the aim of encouraging Zambian smallholders to grow high-value cash crops such as cotton, castor-bean seed, simsim (sesame seed) and paprika. The tobacco sector has experienced problems in the last decade, with reduced yields (owing to drought) in 1983, 1985 and 1992. Yields averaged 1,034 kg per ha annually in 1979-81 and rose to 1,776 kg per ha in 1991. Drought reduced the yields to 438 kg per ha in 1992, and the effects were still being felt in 1993, when yields were 514 kg per ha, and in 1994 and 1995, when yields were 538 kg per ha. Tobacco price controls were lifted in 1989. Production of Virginia tobacco in 1992 was only 2m. kg; in 1993, however, output recovered to 5.6m. kg of Virginia tobacco and to 1.4m. kg of burley tobacco. FAO estimates indicate production of 7m. kg of tobacco per annum in 1994 and 1995. Zambia's sugar sector recovered much more quickly from the 1991/92 drought than in neighbouring countries. The 1992/93 crop totalled 143,204 metric tons, sufficient to cover the national demand of about 93,000 tons and to allow 50,000 tons to be exported, of which 40,000 tons went to Zimbabwe. In 1995/96 the sugar crop totalled 150,503 tons, of which 69,887 tons were exported. A US $63m. rehabilitation and expansion programme, which received new impetus following the privatization of the state sugar company in mid-1995, was expected to increase annual production to 200,000 tons per annum by 2000. Tate and Lyle of the United Kingdom acquired a 40% share in Zambia Sugar PLC, which was one of the 10 companies whose shares were being traded on the Lusaka stock exchange in July 1997. The coffee sector has suffered, as a result of both lower output and reduced international prices. Exports declined from 1,772 metric tons in 1991/92 (year ending 31 March), to 1,675 tons in 1992/93; in 1990/91 exports totalled 1,310 tons. Earnings from coffee exports amounted to US $2.65m. in 1991/92 (compared with $2.43m. in 1990/91). The horticultural sector has experienced strong growth, with the export of fruits and vegetables to Europe. In October 1992, however, the Zambia Export Growers' Asscn (ZEGA) suspended the export of certain types of vegetables, owing to excessively high airfreight charges. Production of other crops in 1993 amounted to: 13,993 tons of rice (more than the annual national demand for rice, which is 9,450 tons); 42,301 tons of groundnuts in shells; and 21,176 tons of sunflower seeds. In 1994 Zambia produced 6,358 tons of paddy rice, 35,000 tons of groundnuts in shells, 2,000 tons of groundnut oil, 10,336 tons of sunflower seeds, 2,500 tons of sunflower oil, 24,630 tons of soya beans and 3,510 tons of soya-bean oil. In 1995 Zambia produced 36,000 tons of groundnuts in shells, 2,000 tons of groundnut oil, an estimated 16,000 tons of sunflower seeds, 875 tons of sunflower-seed oil and 1,260 tons of soya-bean oil.

The livestock sector suffered as a result of the drought in 1991/92, when a higher number of animals were slaughtered than in most years; in 1992/93, however, herds began to reach normal levels. A small amount of beef is generally exported. Foot-and-mouth disease constitutes a problem in some areas of the country. An outbreak of African swine fever in 1992 threatened the destruction of 10,000 pigs and prompted the government to establish a K3,200m. fund to compensate pig farmers for their losses from the disease. Trans-Zambezi Industries, whose shares were also quoted on the Lusaka stock exchange in 1997, owns 90% of Zambezi Ranching and Cropping, whose 100,000-ha holding is the largest ranch in Zambia, grazing some 25,000 head of cattle.

Although rural development was accorded a high priority by the Kaunda administration, most of the schemes and programmes yielded disappointing results. Nearly 18% of total development expenditure in 1980 was for agriculture. However, poor organization, lack of skills, inadequate marketing and transport infrastructure, and migration to urban areas have all impeded growth. The sector was additionally constrained by low producer prices, late and unreliable payments to farmers for their crops, inefficient marketing and inadequate supply of inputs from the state-owned National Agricultural Marketing Board (NAMBOARD), which maintained a statutory monopoly over all aspects of agricultural marketing until January 1986, when private companies and co-operatives were allowed to compete for the first time. Ten years after liberalization was introduced, however, farmers continued to face most of these impediments. In 1994 larger-scale traders in agricultural commodities established the Zambian Grain Growers and Marketing Association. In that year the government ceased setting floor prices for commodities, allowing prices to be determined entirely by supply and demand. In 1995, in order to address the problem of the lack of effective agricultural credit, the government launched a Pilot Credit Management Scheme and appointed 117 'credit co-ordinators' to distribute seed, fertilizers and other agricultural inputs to farmers.

MINING

Copper accounted for about 93% of all Zambia's foreign exchange earnings in 1991, but the proportion declined to 68% in 1994, before recovering slightly to 72% in 1995. Other minerals exploited include cobalt (found in association with copper), zinc, lead, gold, silver, selenium, marble, emeralds and amethyst. In 1996 mining and quarrying contributed 5.8% of GDP and engaged some 10% of the total labour force. The mining industry in Zambia was established during the colonial period, with the opening in 1906 of the Broken Hill lead and zinc mine at Kabwe. Copper mining was begun in the 1920s by Zambian Anglo American (later Nchanga Consolidated Copper Mines) and Roan Selection Trust (later Roan Consolidated Mines), which, in 1982, united to form Zambia Consolidated Copper Mines (ZCCM), in which the government took a 60.3% share. Growth continued after independence in 1964, and by 1969 Zambia had become a leading producer of unrefined copper, with a record level of output of 747,500 metric tons (accounting for 12% of international production). (ZCCM, together with its holding company, Zambia Industrial and Mining Corpn (ZIMCO), is still among the world's largest copper companies.) Since the mid-1970s, however, copper output and revenues have declined significantly; production declined from 700,000 metric tons in 1976 to 338,000 tons in 1993 and to 265,000 tons in 1994. Output in 1995 was about 308,000 tons. Earnings from copper exports declined from US $840m. in 1995 to $567.7m. in 1996. ZCCM recorded a gross profit of K31,551m. in the financial year to 31 March 1992, compared with K18,539m. in the previous financial year. However, the company ultimately incurred financial losses during both these years, despite operating at well below capacity at the mining, smelting and refining stages. Ageing capital equipment, shortages of skilled labour, poor maintenance and inadequacy of reinvestment all adversely affected productivity. In 1983 the government introduced an export levy in order to compensate for lack of tax revenue during the company's loss-making years. The levy initially contributed 4% of gross sales revenue, but increased to 8% in 1983, and to 10% in 1985. ZCCM resorted to borrowing to cover this export levy and other high costs, resulting in accruing debts. The largest purchaser of ZCCM copper is Japan (which accounted for 18% of total exports in 1993), followed by Thailand (12%) and France (10%). Following Zambia's change of government in 1991, a number of remedial measures, including the proposed transfer of ZCCM to private-sector ownership, have been announced. A range of reforms within ZCCM have been carried out, and higher production targets for copper have been set. Plans are also proceeding for the expansion of productive capacity and a wide-ranging programme of exploration and modernization. Nevertheless, in 1994 ZCCM experienced 'operational problems', which caused mineral revenue to the government for that year to fall 35% below target. In 1995 'geo-technical problems' were experienced at the Mufilira, Luanshya and Konkola mines. In that year Nchanga was operating at a loss, due to the low grade of ore extracted. Owing to these problems, Zambia was unable to take advantage of the high world copper prices that year. In 1996 the government finally determined to initiate the partial privatization of ZCCM. The conglomerate was to be divested as four separate entities, and the process was expected to be completed by late 1998. In mid-1996 an international consortium, led by Anglo American, was negotiating with ZCCM to develop the Konkola Deep copper belt, with envisaged investment of $650m. and production forecast at 180,000 tons of finished copper per annum. Also involved were Falconbridge of Canada, Gencor of South Africa and Western Mining Corpn (WMC) of Australia; however, Gencor and WMC both subsequently withdrew. The adjacent Konkola North reserve was to be developed by Anglovaal Minerals of South Africa. A fire in 1996 destroyed one of the two smelters at Mufulira and forced the closure of the plant. In December 1996 First Quantum of Canada acquired the Bwana Mkubwa open-pit copper mine, which had been inoperative since 1984. The move was described as the first private-sector copper project in Zambia for 25 years.

The production of cobalt increased from 4,447 metric tons in 1990 to 4,674 tons in 1991, and to 5,078 tons in 1992, stimulating revenue of K14.15m. in 1992. Cobalt output declined to 4,100 tons in 1993 and to 2,546 tons in 1994, but recovered slightly to 2,934 tons in 1995. In 1994 Apollo Enterprises Ltd of Zambia formed a joint venture with Claim Minerals NL of Australia, to study and potentially exploit nickel-sulphide deposits at Munali, 65 km south-west of Lusaka. The site is now estimated to contain some 11.69m. tons of ore and is situated close to power, water, road and rail infrastructures. Output of zinc declined from 13,637 tons in 1990 to 13,387 tons in 1991 (owing, in part, to power generation cuts), and to just 6,459 tons in 1992, while international prices of zinc were low in 1992 and 1993. Production of lead amounted to 2,332 tons in 1992, stimulating revenue of K93m. Output of precious metals totalled 38,902 kg in 1992, stimulating revenue of K286m. Production of zinc and lead at Kabwe was undertaken by the Kabwe division of ZCCM until its closure in 1994. Konkola is potentially the richest of Zambia's copper mines, possessing reserves of 44.3m. tons, with a copper content of 3.92%, while Nchanga has a copper content of 3.75%, and Mufulira of 3.16%; Nkana is the largest mine, with 95.5m. tons of reserves, which, however, have a copper content of only 2.3%. Nchanga also produces cobalt. Zambia mines emeralds, aquamarines, amethysts and some diamonds. A new deposit of diamonds was discovered in Western Province in 1992, and it was hoped that investigations would reveal further reserves. In the mid-1990s Zambia's emeralds accounted for a significant and growing share of the coloured-gem market, and by 1997 held a dominant position near the top end of the market. Exploration for oil took place in the 1980s, but no significant discoveries were announced. In April 1995 the government announced that it was to sell 27.4% of the shares in Chilanga Cement on the Zambia Stock Exchange. Total production levels in the mining sector were declining in the mid-1990s, with output falling by 16.3% in 1994 and by 7.8% in 1995.

INDUSTRY

Zambia's manufacturing sector has suffered from a variety of problems, not least a chronic shortage of foreign exchange with which to import raw materials and inputs. The sector was also constrained by state intervention in many manufacturing activities, investment in inappropriate schemes and corresponding lack of funds to invest in more suitable undertakings. The state-owned Industrial Development Corpn of Zambia (INDECO) acquired 26 companies in 1968, and continued to take majority shareholdings in a number of other enterprises thereafter. By 1991 INDECO accounted for 75% of Zambia's manufacturing activity. The industrial sector contributed 31.3% of Zambia's GDP in 1996, while the manufacturing sector accounted for 25.5% of total GDP in that year. In 1989 the industrial sector engaged 37.4% of the total labour force; in 1996 it employed just 21%. At the time of the Kaunda administration, the government, usually through INDECO, formed a number of joint ventures with foreign enterprises, in order to establish a chemical-fertilizer plant, a petroleum refinery, an explosives plant, a glass-bottle factory, a battery factory, a brickworks, a textile factory, a copper-wire factory, two vehicle-assembly operations, and an iron-and-steel project; however, a number of these subsequently ended in failure. Nitrogen Chemicals of Zambia opened a sulphuric-acid plant, at a cost of K32m. in 1983, while its fertilizer operation, with an estimated cost of K300m., was the country's largest non-mining enterprise. Operations at Kapiri Glass Works, which produced glass bottles, declined to less than 50% of its installed capacity by 1984. Mansa Dry Batteries began production in 1979, but was operating at only 33% of its capacity by 1984. Kafue Textiles of Zambia faced intense competition from cheap imported cloth and clothing from the Far East and from elsewhere in Africa in the early 1990s. The Tika iron-and-steel project, conceived in 1972, was abandoned in 1979, after the accumulation of large debts in foreign currency to overseas companies that had participated in the expensive planning of the project. Rover Zambia's plant at Ndola assembles Toyota, Mitsubishi and Volkswagen trucks, while Leyland Zambia's assembly plant in Lusaka produces

2,000 commercial vehicles per annum. Privatization of the tyre manufacturer Dunlop Zambia was under way in mid-1997. A tractor-assembly factory, with the capacity to produce 2,500 tractors per annum, was established, with the assistance of the Czechoslovak government, in 1983. Livingstone Motor Assemblers produces Fiat, Peugeot and Mazda saloon cars. In April 1993 Refined Oil Products of Ndola opened a glycerine plant, at a cost of K68m., with the capacity to produce 240 metric tons of glycerine per annum (equivalent to about 20% of national annual demand). Swarp Spinning Mills in Ndola received a loan of $10m. from the European Investment Bank in December 1992 for the expansion of its cotton-spinning and associated yarn-dyeing facilities.

The liberalization of prices, imposition of an import tariff and allocation of foreign exchange helped to alleviate some of the major problems in the manufacturing sector after 1983, but other aspects of liberalization, such as allowing the kwacha to depreciate according to the dictates of market forces, negated some of these gains. The government, deprived of some of its tax revenue from ZCCM during its loss-making period, attempted to compensate for the shortfall by charging import duties on the c.i.f. (cost, insurance and freight) value of imports, rather than on their f.o.b. (free on board) value, thereby further reducing companies' narrowing profit margins.

In 1983, the government introduced an arrangement whereby companies that exported non-traditional items were allowed to retain 50% of foreign exchange from those exports for use in paying for imported inputs, thereby compensating for lack of foreign currency. After only one year, exports of non-metal products exhibited a fivefold increase. In 1987, however, companies lost this concession, after the Kaunda government adopted the former system of strict import licensing, an artificially revalued exchange rate and similar measures. The Investment Act of 1991, promulgated at the end of the Kaunda regime, partially restored the facility, allowing companies holding investment licences to retain 70% of gross foreign-exchange earnings for three years, 60% for the following two years and 50% for the remaining period of the investment licence's validity. The Chiluba government subsequently revised the Investment Act to allow the full retention of foreign-exchange earnings by investors.

Nominally, manufacturing in Zambia provided revenue of US $1,392m. in 1992, compared with $181m. in 1970 and $847.6m. in 1993. The largest manufacturing sector was food, beverages and tobacco, which contributed 45% of total revenue in 1992, compared with 49% in 1970. Textiles and clothing accounted for 12% in 1992, while chemicals contributed 11% and machinery and transport equipment contributed 7%. In 1990, according to the World Bank, gross output per manufacturing employee (1980 = 100), was 90 in Zambia, compared with 135 in Zimbabwe and 235 in Kenya.

Manufacturing production declined by 9.0% in 1994 and by 4.5% in 1995. Only fabricated metal products, non-metallic mineral products and basic metal products registered any growth in those years. The downturn in manufacturing output was largely due to competition from imported goods, as reforms dismantled trade barriers, and the high cost of borrowing, which deterred investment in new technology. In mid-1996 the government announced that it had designated US $45m. of World Bank funding to facilitate loans to the textile industry in a bid to rehabilitate and increase the competitiveness of the industry. In June the People's Republic of China granted a loan of $21.6m., principally for the rehabilitation of the Mulungushi textile mill complex in Kabwe. Meanwhile, spearheading the privatization drive was the Zambia Privatization Agency. Of 257 companies on the privatization list, 157 had been transferred to the private sector by December 1996.

ENERGY

Zambia became self-sufficient in hydroelectric power in 1974 and began exporting power to Zimbabwe (then Rhodesia) and the Democratic Republic of the Congo (then Zaire). In that year a major expansion of output from Kafue Gorge resulted in an increase of 82% in domestic energy production. Long delays occurred in the construction of the Kariba North power station, but 150 MW of capacity were operational by 1977, with a further 150 MW for later completion. New 150 MW generators came into service at Kafue Gorge in 1976 and 1977, bringing the facility's total installed capacity to 900 MW. The construction of an additional dam at Itezhi-Tezhi provided a more reliable flow of water to the Kafue Gorge power plant. However, a fire in March 1989 inflicted major damage on this installation, destroying the main power cables; rehabilitation of the facility cost more than US $20m., and exports of power to Zimbabwe (valued at $1m. per month) were suspended for more than a year. Zimbabwe, meanwhile, proceeded with the construction of its own Kariba South facility to end its dependence on Zambia for imported power. Low water levels throughout the region during the 1991/92 drought significantly reduced power output in Zambia, resulting in the suspension of exports, and Zambia was one of several countries which arranged to import power from South Africa and Zaire. (Imports from Zaire ceased in February 1993.) In 1995 drought again reduced water levels at hydroelectric facilities, necessitating the introduction of electricity rationing and the renewed import of power from Zaire, at a cost of more than $1m. per month. A Norwegian company was engaged in November 1991 to conduct feasibility studies for the construction of electricity interconnection lines from Zambia to Malawi and Tanzania. Rural electrification is a stated priority, and some extension of the national grid has been achieved, but many areas of rural Zambia still do not have access to mains power supply. Charcoal and fuelwood remain the main sources of energy supply for cooking and heating purposes for most people in both urban and rural areas. Both energy production and energy consumption declined in 1980–93, by 3.0% and 2.5% respectively per annum. Zambia used 146 kg per caput in 1993, compared with 471 kg per caput in Zimbabwe, 99 kg per caput in Kenya and 2,399 kg per caput in South Africa. The Zambia Electricity Supply Corpn (Zesco) completed several township and rural electrification projects during 1994. The country generated 5,791.8m. kWh, and consumed 5,221.0m. kWh, in 1994. Norway granted Zesco 15m. kroner (some K2,500m.) in September 1997 to help boost its output.

Coal production commenced in 1965, but was subsequently affected by shortages of equipment and spare parts. The remaining colliery, at Maamba, operated substantially below capacity in 1987. Following a rehabilitation programme, however, the mine met its production target of 560,000 metric tons in 1987/88, and began exporting coal to Zaire, Malawi and Tanzania. By 1994, however, annual output of hard coal had declined to an estimated 380,000 tons. Thereafter output declined further, and in 1997 a 70% share in Maamba Collieries Ltd was to be transferred to the private sector.

TRANSPORT

At independence in 1964, Zambia had only one tarred road, and one railway line, which extended from the Copperbelt, in the north, through Lusaka and Livingstone to Zimbabwe (then Southern Rhodesia), and connected with the Rhodesian Railway, providing access to South African ports. In 1965 the unilateral declaration of independence by Rhodesia prompted sanctions against that country, which severely disrupted the flow of Zambia's traffic on its only transport link to the outside world.

The Zambian government invested substantial sums in improving infrastructure, with the construction of the TanZam oil pipeline from the Tanzanian port of Dar es Salaam, which was completed in 1968. The Great North Road to Tanzania (which was previously only a dirt track) was tarred, and a Great East Road to Malawi, which connected with the Mozambican ports of Nacala and Beira, was constructed (although civil war in Mozambique subsequently prevented Zambia from making full use of this route). A railway to Dar es Salaam, known as the Tanzania-Zambia Railway Authority (Tazara), which was built and financed by the People's Republic of China with an interest-free loan, was used in early 1974 to transport goods, following the closure of the Rhodesian border. The complete route was opened to regular service in October 1975, ahead of the original schedule, and proved to be essential, after the closure of the Lobito railway to Angola in August 1975. However, limited port facilities at Dar es Salaam and unavailability of rolling stock resulted in severe delays, and Tazara incurred losses for the Zambian government in its first eight years of operation. In October 1978 Zambia resumed its use of the Rhodesian rail route to South Africa. Tazara finally moved into profit in the June quarter of 1983, although it did not consistently achieve profits until 1988. In 1991 Zambia Railways rehabilitated about 80% of its rolling stock, with the assistance of loans totalling US $13.5m. from Japan and the USA, but additional funds were required for signalling and communications equipment. Zambia's only port, Mpulungu, is on Lake Tanganyika; in 1997 the Mpulungu Harbour Authority was due to be privatized.

The BotZam Highway, linking Kazungula with Nata, in Botswana, was opened in 1984, and in 1989 Botswana completed the tarring of the road that extended south from Nata to connect with its own road system. In 1992 Japan provided US $13.9m. for the reconstruction of the ageing Kafue Road Bridge. In 1968 the Zambian government nationalized the country's two main road-haulage companies and merged them into a single enterprise, Contract Haulage. In July 1992 it was estimated that Contract Haulage owned 85% of the 1,200 commercial trucks in Zambia. The public passenger and cargo road-transport sectors were opened to private enterprise in 1992, and in 1995 the state-owned United Bus Company of Zambia ceased operations, owing to private-sector competition. In 1994 a road agreement was signed with Namibia, which included a plan to build a bridge across the Zambezi river to facilitate cross-border passage and to enable Zambia to use Namibia's Walvis Bay port for cargo transportation. In 1995 the government released K2,100m. for the tarring of the Luanshya–Mpongwe and Choma–Namwala roads, to be completed within two years. In 1996 Japan granted K16,000m. towards an ongoing road rehabilitation project in Lusaka.

The national airline, Zambia Airways, which was established in 1967, operated domestic, regional and long-haul passenger and airfreight services. In 1992 the government indicated that the airline would henceforth have to service its external and domestic debt from its own revenue. Supplies of aviation fuel to Zambia were subsequently suspended until payment was received, forcing all carriers flying to Zambia to divert to Zimbabwe, where they could buy aviation fuel for hard currency. In February 1993 the government announced the implementation of extensive measures at Zambia Airways, including the retrenchment of staff, to compensate for continuing financial losses. In March 1993, however, the National Airports Corpn announced that it was to spend US $30m. towards the rehabilitation of four airports, situated at Lusaka, Ndola, Livingstone and Mfuwe. In addition, equipment, valued at $7m., was to be installed at airports at Kaoma, Solwezi, Kasama, Livingstone and Mfuwe. In 1994 Zambia Airways reduced its regional routes and introduced other cost-cutting measures, although the government still had to provide K2,500m. in subsidies to the airline. In 1995 the loss-making carrier entered liquidation. Some 3,000 creditors in 50 countries presented claims to the company's assets. By January 1996 most of the assets had been sold, including overseas operations in 13 countries. In 1997 British Airways, KLM Royal Dutch Airlines, Kenya Airways and South African Airways were operating long-haul flights to Lusaka.

FOREIGN TRADE AND PAYMENTS

Zambia generally maintained a visible trade surplus from independence until 1991. Exports f.o.b. totalled US $974.9m. in 1996, down from $1,190m. in 1995 and $1,066.4m. in 1994, while imports c.i.f. cost $1,198.6m. in 1996, compared with $1,278m. in 1995, $1,002.5m. in 1994 and $1,018.5m. in 1993. The resultant visible trade balance registered a $223.7m. deficit in 1996, after a $88m. shortfall in 1995. The principal export commodity was copper, which accounted for $840m., or 71% of total export revenue, in 1995, followed by $567.7m., or 58%, in 1996. In total, more than 80% of export revenue is derived from mineral products. The principal non-mineral export is tobacco, though other commodities, such as sugar, coffee and horticultural produce, are exported on a modest scale.

In 1995 the principal imports were machinery, transport equipment and other manufactures, followed by maize (8.6%) and petroleum (7.9%). South Africa is the largest supplier of imports (22% in 1993), followed by the United Kingdom (12%), Japan (6%) and Zimbabwe (6%). Japan, as a result of its purchases of Zambian copper, is the principal market for exports (18% in 1993). Owing to some improvement in the international price of copper, Zambia's terms of trade improved by an annual average of 9% between 1987–92. The global copper price rose from US $0.82 per pound in January 1994 to $1.36 per pound in December 1994, and stood at an annual average price of $1.19 per pound in 1995.

In 1991 the current account of the balance of payments registered a significant deficit of US $487m. before official transfers (compared with a surplus of $107m. in 1970), but an overall surplus of $1m. was recorded (compared with a surplus of $108m. in 1970). The overall figure in 1991 represented a major improvement, compared with that in 1990, when, even after official transfers, a deficit of $343m. on the overall balance of payments was recorded. In 1995 the current account registered a deficit of $344.5m. before official transfers and a deficit of $207.2m. after official transfers. The overall balance of payments recorded a deficit of $84.1m. in 1995, following a deficit of $242.5m. in 1994. Gross international reserves amounted to $210m. at the end of 1995, equivalent to the cost of 10 weeks of imports; at the end of 1990, according to the World Bank, larger reserves of $201m. covered only the equivalent of 0.9 month of the total cost of imports.

GOVERNMENT FINANCE

The 1997 budget proposals forecast total spending of K1,427,606m., up 23% on the level of the previous year, when the budget envisaged expenditure and revenue balanced at K1,161,600m. Of total projected expenditure in 1996, K421,600m. (36.3%) was to be funded by donors. According to an IMF report issued in 1996, total expenditure, including net lending, by the central government in 1995 was provisionally assessed at K908,204m., of which K783,264m. was current expenditure. Expenditure on the domestic budget in 1995 was K603,469m., while external budget spending was K304,735m. In that year, according to provisional figures, government revenue reached K583,402m., with a further K155,689m. received in the form of grants. The resultant deficit (on a commitment basis) was K169,113m., equivalent to 4.8% of GDP. In 1994 the budget deficit had been K144,619m. (5.7% of GDP): expenditure and net lending were K713,907m. (including current expenditure of K624,735m.), while revenue and grants totalled K569,289m. In 1993 the deficit was 5.1% of GDP, whereas in 1992 it had been only 2.5% (despite unforeseen expenditure on emergency drought relief). These ratios compare with budget deficits of 7.2% in 1991 (the final year of the Kaunda administration) and 8.3% in 1990. In real terms, Zambia's GDP contracted by 3.4% in 1992, as a result of the drought, but achieved positive growth of 8.2% in 1993. However, GDP contracted again by 3.1% in 1994, and by 3.9% in 1995, but increased by an estimated 6.4% in 1996. GDP increased by an annual average of 0.6% in 1985–95. In the first year of the Chiluba administration, the government indicated that it had made considerable progress in the reduction of the country's high external debt, which was estimated at US $7,300m. in October 1991, when Chiluba succeeded Kaunda. Only three months later, the government was able to pay back arrears totalling $51m., which had been overdue for more than six months, on loans from the World Bank and the International Development Association (IDA). The payment resulted in the resumption of disbursements on previously approved loans and credits. By August 1992, owing to rescheduling by the 'Paris Club' of official creditors, together with cancellations of debt by bilateral creditors, Zambia's total debt had fallen to $6,500m. At 30 September 1993 Zambia's total debt stood at $6,750m., of which $2,640m. was owed to bilateral lenders, $1,740m. to multilateral lenders (of which $1,300m. was owed to the IMF), $822m. comprised short-term loans, $149m. was owed to foreign suppliers and $97m. to the 'London Club' of Western commercial creditors. In mid-1994 Zambia's debt-servicing requirements were absorbing, on an annualized basis, about 40% of the country's export earnings. The government subsequently embarked upon a 'debt buy-back' operation, which removed $652m.-worth of commercial debt. Zambia's external public debt totalled US $6,853m. at the end of 1995, of which $5,078m. was long-term public debt. In that year the cost of debt-servicing was equivalent to 201.9% of the value of exports of goods and services. The government estimated the country's total debt stock at $6,300m. in January 1996. In March 1996 the 'Paris Club' of official creditors was reported to have cancelled 67% of the debt owed to it by Zambia. Nevertheless, in July 1996 the World Bank and the IMF named Zambia among 11 countries whose debt burdens were 'unsustainable'. Zambia's total foreign debt was estimated at that time to be $6,400m.

In 1987 the IMF declared Zambia to be ineligible for credit facilities, owing to its failure to meet loan repayments. In 1992 the Chiluba administration adopted a three-year structural adjustment programme, in agreement with the IMF and the World Bank, which emphasized the decentralization of social services, the reorganization of the civil service and the transfer of parastatal organizations to the private sector. In addition, the new government negotiated a Rights Accumulation Programme (RAP) with the IMF, giving Zambia the potential to convert nearly US $1,220m. in arrears owed to the IMF into a concessional facility carrying only 0.5% annual interest. In June the World Bank agreed to new loans, totalling $200m., and the IMF extended funds of $100m. in July. In the same month donors pledged $300m. in drought relief. In September the IDA extended $200m. in support of the government's privatization programme. At a conference of donors, convened by the World Bank Consultative Group for Zambia in April 1993, $800m. was pledged in support of the country's reform programme; additional bilateral pledges were expected to compensate for a shortfall of $115m. Several of the donors had visited Lusaka in March to urge the government to accelerate the pace of its privatization programme and to implement measures to restrict inflation. Also in March, Germany cancelled loans totalling DM 135.2m., and rescheduled an equivalent amount over a period of 23 years.

The World Bank Consultative Group for Zambia reconvened in Paris on 9 December 1993 and pledged a further US $800m. to the country for 1994. The donors issued a statement praising the Zambian government for 'maintaining its commitment to the country's economic recovery programme under difficult conditions' but cautioning that formidable challenges lay ahead, not least Zambia's heavy debt burden. The group also expressed concern at the slow pace of privatization. The $800m. pledge fell short of the $1,100m. which Zambia had requested, however. In March 1994 the IDA extended a SDR 108.9m. ($150m.) three-year contract, which included badly-needed balance-of-payments support. In December 1995 following the successful completion of the RAP, the IMF announced that Zambia was again eligible for credit, and subsequently approved a three-year enhanced structural adjustment facility of $1,043m. and a one-year structural adjustment facility of $270m. In mid-1996 a number of Western donor governments temporarily suspended aid to Zambia, in protest at the political situation (see Recent History), but in July 1997, at a World Bank Consultative Group meeting, donors pledged $435m. in support of the government's Economic Recovery and Investment Programme.

The rate of inflation was unofficially estimated at an average of 400% in October 1991. (According to the IMF, however, consumer prices increased by an average of 92.6% in 1991.) The Chiluba government's pledge to halve the official rate by the end of 1992 was not achieved, and, although estimates varied considerably, the rate of inflation increased to an average of 197.4% in that year, according to the IMF. Despite government plans to reduce inflation to 35% in 1993, IMF figures indicate inflation of 189.0% in that year. According to the IMF, the rate was reduced to an annual average of 53.6% in 1994, to 34.2% in 1995, and to 43.9% in 1996, although the government recorded inflation of 35% in that year. Many economists contend that the true inflation rate in 1996 and 1997 was 70% or more.

As part of the reform programme, Zambia has liberalized its exchange-rate policy. The first bureaux de change, which opened in October 1992, were permitted to set their own rates for the buying and selling of foreign currency; Zambian residents were initially limited to purchases of US $2,000 per transaction. The exercise proved extremely successful, and the kwacha fared far better during its initial period as a free-market currency than any other African currency had in similar circumstances. In February 1993 91-day treasury bills were introduced as a means of stimulating finance for the 1993 budget, replacing the former method of borrowing direct from the Bank of Zambia. Zambian business interests had complained that heavy government borrowing on the domestic market had caused a shortage of loanable funds for the private sector. New banknotes were introduced in February 1993, followed by a new coinage in March. The new notes replaced those bearing the likeness of Kenneth Kaunda but did not demonetize 'old' banknotes, which remained in circulation. In the last quarter of 1993 and the first quarter of 1994, the kwacha weakened on the exchange markets. It fell from K347 = US $1 in mid-October 1993 to K435 = US $1 in early December and to K657 = US $1 in early January 1994. The descent was much less rapid thereafter, however, reaching K695 = US $1 in late May 1994 and stabilizing at about that level. The currency depreciated by 26.5% between January and December 1994, compared with its decline of 28.1% in 1993. However, in the first half of 1995 the currency depreciated by 26%, reaching K920 = US $1. The exchange rate stabilized in the second half of 1995, ending the year at K950.5 = US $1. Pressure on the currency in 1995 was exacerbated by the collapse of Meridien BIAO Bank Zambia Ltd, which, in turn, precipitated the closure of a further two banks. Further depreciation, of 24%, followed in the first nine months of 1996, and in September the exchange rate stood at K1,252 = US $1. Thereafter it levelled off, and a year later, in September 1997, the rate was K1,294 = US $1.

Statistical Survey

Source (unless otherwise indicated): Central Statistical Office, POB 31908, Lusaka; tel. (1) 211231; telex 40430.

Area and Population

AREA, POPULATION AND DENSITY

Area (sq km)	752,614*
Population (census results)	
1 September 1980	5,661,801
20 August 1990	
Males	3,617,577
Females	3,765,520
Total	7,383,097
Population (official estimate at mid-year)	
1995	9,373,000
Density (per sq km) at mid-1995	12.5

* 290,586 sq miles.

PRINCIPAL TOWNS (estimated population 1990 census)

Lusaka (capital)	982,362	Chingola	162,954
Ndola	376,311	Mufulira	152,944
Kitwe	338,207	Luanshya	146,275
Kabwe	166,519		

Source: UN, *Demographic Yearbook*.

BIRTHS AND DEATHS (UN estimates, annual averages)

	1980–85	1985–90	1990–95
Birth rate (per 1,000)	49.0	47.4	44.6
Death rate (per 1,000)	14.8	14.1	15.1

Expectation of life (UN estimates, years at birth, 1990–95): 48.9 (males 48.0; females 49.7).

Source: UN, *World Population Prospects: The 1994 Revision*.

ECONOMICALLY ACTIVE POPULATION
(ILO estimates, '000 persons at mid-1980)

	Males	Females	Total
Agriculture, etc.	959	438	1,398
Industry	174	14	188
Services	257	69	326
Total labour force	1,390	522	1,912

Source: ILO, *Labour Force Estimates and Projections, 1950–2025*.

1980 census (persons aged 12 years and over): Total employed 1,302,944 (males 908,606, females 394,338); Unemployed 492,999 (males 247,013, females 245,986); Total labour force 1,795,943 (males 1,155,619, females 640,324).

Mid-1984 (official estimates): Total labour force 2,032,300 (males 1,464,800; females 567,500).

Mid-1995 (estimates in '000): Agriculture, etc. 2,944; Total 3,999 (Source: FAO, *Production Yearbook*).

Agriculture

PRINCIPAL CROPS ('000 metric tons)

	1993	1994	1995
Wheat	71	43	50
Rice (paddy)	14	6	12
Maize	1,598	1,021	738
Millet	37	63	55
Sorghum	35	35	27
Sugar cane	1,220	1,311	1,380*
Potatoes*	10	11	11
Sweet potatoes*	56	57	57
Cassava (Manioc)*	570	600	600
Pulses	24	23	24
Onions (dry)*	26	27	20
Tomatoes*	26	27	20
Soybeans (Soya beans)	28	25	21
Sunflower seed	21	10	16*
Groundnuts (in shell)	42	35	36
Cottonseed	58	26†	44†
Cotton (lint)	21	9†	16†
Tobacco (leaves)	7	7*	7*

* FAO estimate(s). † Unofficial figure.

Source: FAO, *Production Yearbook*.

LIVESTOCK ('000 head, year ending September)

	1993	1994†	1995†
Cattle	3,204*	3,300	3,300
Sheep	67*	69	69
Goats	600*	620	620
Pigs†	293	295	295

* Unofficial figure. † FAO estimates.

Poultry (FAO estimates, million): 21 in 1993; 22 in 1994; 22 in 1995.

Source: FAO, *Production Yearbook*.

LIVESTOCK PRODUCTS (FAO estimates, '000 metric tons)

	1993	1994	1995
Beef and veal	41	42	42
Pig meat	9	9	9
Poultry meat	25	26	26
Other meat	33	34	34
Cows' milk	87	89	89
Hen eggs	33.4	35.2	35.2
Cattle hides	5.4	5.5	5.5

Source: FAO, *Production Yearbook*.

Forestry

ROUNDWOOD REMOVALS ('000 cubic metres)

	1992	1993	1994
Sawlogs, veneer logs and logs for sleepers	356	450	606
Pulpwood	59	67	67*
Other industrial wood*	497	512	527
Fuel wood*	12,707	13,093	13,465
Total	13,619	14,122	14,665

* FAO estimate(s).

Source: FAO, *Yearbook of Forest Products*.

SAWNWOOD PRODUCTION
('000 cubic metres, incl. railway sleepers)

	1992	1993	1994
Coniferous (softwood)	78	300	340
Broadleaved (hardwood)	34	18	27
Total	112	318	367

* FAO estimates.

Source: FAO, *Yearbook of Forest Products*.

Fishing

('000 metric tons, live weight)

	1993	1994	1995
Freshwater fishes	52.2	60.0	59.1
Dagaas	13.1	10.0	10.0
Total catch (inland waters)	65.3	70.1	69.1

Source: FAO, *Yearbook of Fishery Statistics*.

Mining

(metric tons)

	1992	1993	1994
Hard coal	395,000	400,000§	380,000§
Cobalt ore*†	6,910	4,750	3,500
Copper ore*‡	432,600	431,500	384,400
Lead ore*‡	6,100	7,600	600
Zinc ore*‡	19,200	19,700	1,000
Gold (kg)*†	271	235	210

* Figures relate to the metal content of ores and concentrates (or, for cobalt, the metal recovered).
† Data from the US Bureau of Mines.
‡ Data from *World Metal Statistics*, London.
§ Estimate.

Source: UN, *Industrial Commodity Statistics Yearbook*.

Industry

SELECTED PRODUCTS (metric tons, unless otherwise indicated)

	1992	1993	1994
Raw sugar	155,000*	147,000*	150,000†
Cigarettes (million)‡	1,500	n.a.	n.a.
Nitrogenous fertilizers§	4,000	6,000	n.a.
Cement§‖	347,000	350,000	350,000
Copper (unwrought)			
Smelter¶**	380,200	337,800	265,200
Refined	441,600	424,800	369,500**
Lead (primary)‖	3,400	2,900	500
Zinc (primary)	7,300	4,700**	100**
Electric energy (million kWh)§	7,780	7,785	7,785

* Data from the Food and Agriculture Organization, Rome.
† Data from the International Sugar Organization, London.
‡ Data from US Department of Agriculture.
§ Estimates.
‖ Data from the US Bureau of Mines.
¶ Including copper obtained from ores by leaching in electrowinning plants.
** Data from *World Metal Statistics*, London.

Source: UN, *Industrial Commodity Statistics Yearbook*.

Finance

CURRENCY AND EXCHANGE RATES

Monetary Units
100 ngwee = 1 Zambian kwacha (K).

Sterling and Dollar Equivalents (31 March 1997)
£1 sterling = 2,105.1 kwacha;
US $1 = 1,282.1 kwacha;
10,000 Zambian kwacha = £4.750 = $7.800.

Average Exchange Rate (Zambian kwacha per US $)
1994 669.37
1995 857.23
1996 1,203.71

BUDGET (K million)*

Revenue†	1993	1994	1995‡
Tax revenue	227,248	418,879	545,911
Company income tax	39,487	43,011	38,355
Personal income tax	41,859	86,202	134,154
Excise taxes	33,067	70,204	84,616
Sales taxes	34,394	76,104	107,678
Taxes on trade	78,441	138,536	163,155
Extraction royalty	n.a.	4,821	17,954
Other revenue	8,008	30,739	37,490
User fees and charges	n.a.	12,292	17,255
Total	235,256	449,618	583,402

Expenditure§	1993	1994	1995‡
Domestic budget	296,645	500,479	603,469
General public services	83,368	145,482	156,552
Defence	23,149	42,083	47,756
Public order and safety	15,711	5,998	8,349
Education	36,418	46,539	85,310
Health	24,818	44,409	86,008
Social security and welfare	11,788	19,659	23,597
Housing and community amenities	79	5,992	13,048
Recreation, cultural and religious affairs and services	4,254	9,587	11,889
Economic affairs and services	23,097	78,192	93,931
Fuel and energy	652	16,875	31,814
Agriculture, forestry and fishing	7,926	53,171	51,453
Mining, manufacturing and construction	2,351	4,842	7,349
Transport and communications	12,168	3,304	3,315
Other purposes	73,963	102,538	77,029
Interest payments	71,463	102,538	77,029
External budget‖	139,812	213,428	304,735
Total	436,457	713,907	908,204
Current	389,568	624,735	783,264
Capital	46,889	89,173	124,940

* Figures refer to the consolidated accounts of the central Government's Recurrent and Capital Budgets.
† Excluding grants received (K million): 118,250 in 1993; 119,671 in 1994; 155,689 (provisional) in 1995.
‡ Figures are provisional.
§ Including lending minus repayments.
‖ Including interest payments abroad and foreign-financed capital expenditure.

Source: IMF, *Zambia—Statistical Annex* (August 1996).

INTERNATIONAL RESERVES (US $ million at 31 December)

	1986	1987	1988
Gold*	1.0	1.8	4.1
Foreign exchange†	70.3	108.8	134.0
Total	71.3	110.6	138.1

* Valued at market-related prices.
† Foreign exchange (US $ million at 31 December): 116.2 in 1989; 193.1 in 1990; 184.6 in 1991; n.a. in 1992; 192.3 in 1993.

IMF special drawing rights (US $ million at 31 December): 12.1 in 1995; 2.0 in 1996.

Source: IMF, *International Financial Statistics*.

MONEY SUPPLY (K million at 31 December)*

	1993	1994	1995
Currency outside banks	40,400	56,300	77,800
Demand deposits at commercial banks	56,800	83,800	140,200
Total money (incl. others)	97,300	141,000	227,900

1996 (K million at 31 December)*: Demand deposits at commercial banks 163,100.

* Figures are rounded to the nearest K100 million.

Source: IMF, *International Financial Statistics*.

COST OF LIVING (Consumer Price Index; base: 1990 = 100)

	1994	1995	1996
All items	2,300.4	3,086.8	4,440.7

Source: IMF, *International Financial Statistics*.

NATIONAL ACCOUNTS (K million at current prices)

Expenditure on the Gross Domestic Product

	1994	1995	1996
Government final consumption expenditure	440,500	572,300	720,700
Private final consumption expenditure	1,475,300	1,683,900	3,499,000
Increase in stocks	77,100	112,500	163,900
Gross fixed capital formation	207,200	281,200	450,800
Total domestic expenditure*	2,200,200	2,650,000	4,834,600
Exports of goods and services	410,200	908,800	633,000
Less imports of goods and services	490,200	732,500	1,389,900
GDP in purchasers' values	2,120,200	2,826,300	4,077,700

* Including adjustment.

Source: IMF, *International Financial Statistics*.

Gross Domestic Product by Economic Activity

	1993	1994	1995*
Agriculture, forestry and fishing	451,732	644,206	581,164
Mining and quarrying	129,785	191,974	318,438
Manufacturing	477,313	737,720	1,286,745
Electricity, gas and water	18,095	23,988	45,663
Construction	61,310	65,758	65,335
Wholesale and retail trade, restaurants and hotels	191,773	302,064	439,634
Transport and communications	65,241	103,283	172,969
Finance, insurance, real estate and business services	96,020	158,044	251,767
Community, social and personal services	102,369	197,050	270,680
Sub-total	1,593,639	2,424,086	3,432,395
Import duties	30,165	78,000	116,833
Less imputed bank service charge	10,066	15,812	27,505
GDP in purchasers' values	1,613,738	2,486,274	3,521,723

* Figures are provisional.

Source: IMF, *Zambia—Statistical Annex* (August 1996).

BALANCE OF PAYMENTS (US $ million)

	1989	1990	1991
Exports of goods f.o.b.	1,340	1,254	1,172
Imports of goods f.o.b.	–774	–1,511	–752
Trade balance	566	–257	420
Exports of services	85	107	83
Imports of services	–444	–386	–363
Balance on goods and services	208	–537	140
Other income received	1	2	10
Other income paid	–509	–439	–696
Balance on goods, services and income	–300	–974	–546
Current traders received	114	398	262
Current transfers paid	–32	–18	–22
Current balance	–219	–594	–306
Direct investment from abroad	164	203	34
Other investment assets	26	–275	–125
Other investment liabilities	1,637	569	108
Net errors and omissions	–1,712	322	110
Overall balance	–106	222	–179

Source: IMF, *International Financial Statistics*.

External Trade

PRINCIPAL COMMODITIES (US $ million)

Imports f.o.b.	1984	1985	1986
Food and live animals	27.7	25.3	n.a.
Cereals and cereal preparations	21.0	14.3	10.1
Crude materials (inedible) except fuels	13.1	10.9	n.a.
Mineral fuels, lubricants, etc.	180.6	156.1	n.a.
Petroleum and petroleum products	175.0	153.7	80.1
Crude petroleum	n.a.	n.a.	71.7
Chemicals and related products	82.8	106.0	n.a.
Fertilizers (manufactured)	24.2	29.2	3.0
Plastic materials, etc.	9.5	15.6	9.8
Basic manufactures	99.0	116.0	n.a.
Rubber manufactures	9.6	17.6	16.0
Textile yarn, fabrics, etc.	25.5	19.6	14.5
Iron and steel	27.4	25.4	20.6
Machinery and transport equipment	174.1	232.1	n.a.
Power-generating machinery and equipment	11.9	17.6	18.2
Machinery specialized for particular industries	35.8	60.0	46.8
General industrial machinery, equipment and parts	46.6	57.8	56.5
Telecommunications and sound equipment	9.9	6.5	20.8
Other electrical machinery, apparatus, etc.	16.4	21.5	24.1
Road vehicles and parts	42.3	52.3	74.2
Miscellaneous manufactured articles	13.0	23.8	n.a.
Total (incl. others)	595.6	713.8	602.8

Total imports (K million, f.o.b.): 6,627.5 in 1987; 6,898.1 in 1988; 10,901.8 in 1989; 37,627.6 in 1990; 59,988.0 in 1991; 172,871.7 in 1992.

Source: UN, *International Trade Statistics Yearbook*.

Exports f.o.b.	1993	1994	1995
Copper	717	741	840
Cobalt	149	169	134
Total (incl. others)	970	1,066	1,190

Source: IMF, *Zambia—Statistical Annex* (August 1996).

PRINCIPAL TRADING PARTNERS (US $'000)*

Imports f.o.b.	1988	1989	1990
Algeria	—	—	20,451
Belgium-Luxembourg	17,891	17,496	13,694
Finland	7,195	29,627	23,184
France	31,574	15,937	12,471
Germany	53,058	184,038	144,015
India	34,931	29,302	22,930
Iran	122	—	35,134
Italy	39,368	38,706	30,289
Japan	84,440	105,590	82,627
Kuwait	—	—	33,697
Madagascar	93	82	66,700
Netherlands	7,482	19,771	15,472
Southern African Customs Union†	169,801	286,500	224,177
Sweden	12,443	24,553	19,213
United Kingdom	19,596	256,049	200,365
USA	213,075	67,071	125,522
Zimbabwe	35,392	73,948	57,866
Total (incl. others)	886,054	1,258,321	1,237,717

Exports f.o.b.	1988	1989	1990
Belgium-Luxembourg	31,776	48,619	34,405
France	50,310	98,121	81,008
Greece	36,144	19,648	16,221
India	55,785	44,141	36,443
Indonesia	18,143	24,070	19,872
Italy	46,822	32,243	26,620
Japan	193,150	223,194	184,268
Kenya	4,007	9,360	7,728
Malayasia	22,178	27,689	22,860
Saudi Arabia	47,595	38,732	31,977
Singapore	95	161	11,004
Thailand	27,814	—	40,673
United Kingdom	29,652	14,712	12,147
USA	206,158	13,781	9,752
Zaire	5,061	10,105	8,342
Zimbabwe	19,985	21,833	18,025
Total (incl. others)	866,711	667,811	594,765

* Imports by country of production; exports by country of last consignment.
† Comprising Botswana, Lesotho, Namibia, South Africa and Swaziland.

Source: UN, *International Trade Statistics Yearbook*.

Transport

ROAD TRAFFIC (estimates, '000 motor vehicles in use at 31 December)

	1993	1994	1995
Passenger cars	111.0	123.0	142.0
Lorries and vans	60.3	68.0	73.5

Source: International Road Federation, *World Road Statistics*.

CIVIL AVIATION

(scheduled services: Passengers carried—thousands; others—millions)

	1992	1993	1994
Kilometres flown	5	4	4
Passengers carried	246	219	235
Passenger-km	509	393	428
Total ton-km	63	47	54

Source: UN, *Statistical Yearbook*.

Tourism

	1992	1993	1994
Tourist arrivals ('000)	159	157	134
Tourist receipts (US $ million)	51	44	43

Source: UN, *Statistical Yearbook*.

Communications Media

	1992	1993	1994
Radio receivers ('000 in use)*	705	730	760
Television receivers ('000 in use)*	225	237	245
Telephones ('000 main lines in use)	76	78	80
Daily newspapers:			
Number	2	n.a.	2
Circulation ('000 copies)	70	n.a.	70

* Estimates.

Sources: UNESCO, *Statistical Yearbook*; UN, *Statistical Yearbook*.

Education

(1989)

	Institutions	Pupils	Teachers
Primary	3,715*	1,507,660*	36,697*
Secondary	480	199,081*†	5,786†‡
Trades and technical	12	3,313§	438
Teacher training	14	4,669§	408
University	2	7,361§	320‖

* 1994 figures.
† Figures refer to government-maintained and aided schools only.
‡ 1988 figures.
§ 1990 figures.
‖ Excluding part-time lecturers and teaching assistants.

Sources: the former Ministry of Higher Education and the former Ministry of General Education, Lusaka; University of Zambia; UNESCO, *Statistical Yearbook*.

Directory

The Constitution

The Constitution for the Republic of Zambia, which was formally adopted on 28 May 1996 (amending the Constitution of 1991), provides for a multi-party form of government. The Head of State is the President of the Republic, who is elected by popular vote at the same time as elections to the National Assembly. The President's tenure of office is limited to two five-year terms. Foreign nationals and those with foreign parentage are prohibited from contesting the presidency. The legislature comprises a National Assembly of 150 members, who are elected by universal adult suffrage. The President appoints a Vice-President and a Cabinet from members of the National Assembly.

The Constitution also provides for a House of Chiefs numbering 27: four from each of the Northern, Western, Southern and Eastern Provinces, three each from the North-Western, Luapula and Central Provinces and two from the Copperbelt Province. It may submit resolutions to be debated by the Assembly and consider those matters referred to it by the President.

The Supreme Court of Zambia is the final Court of Appeal. The Chief Justice and other judges are appointed by the President. Subsidiary to the Supreme Court is the High Court, which has unlimited jurisdiction to hear and determine any civil or criminal proceedings under any Zambian law.

The Government

HEAD OF STATE

President: FREDERICK J. T. CHILUBA (took office 2 November 1991; re-elected 18 November 1996).

THE CABINET
(September 1997)

Vice-President: Brig.-Gen. GODFREY MIYANDA.

Minister of State: ERIC S. SILWAMBA.

Minister of Defence: BENJAMIN YORAM MWILA.

Minister of Foreign Affairs: Prof. LAWRENCE SHIMBA.

Minister of Finance and Economic Development: RONALD D. S. PENZA.

Minister of Home Affairs: CHITALU M. SAMPA.

Minister of Mines and Mineral Development: Gen. CHRISTON SIPAFI TEMBO.

Minister of Agriculture, Food and Fisheries: EDITH NAWAKWI.

Minister of Health: Dr KATELE KALUMBA.

Minister of Education: SYAMUKAYUMBU SYAMUJAYA.

Minister of Local Government and Housing: BENNIE MWIINGA.

Minister of Labour and Social Security: Dr PETER D. MACHUNGWA.

Minister of Legal Affairs: VINCENT MALAMBO.

Minister of Community Development and Social Services: NEWSTEAD ZIMBA.

Minister of Tourism: AMUSA MWANAMWABWA.

Minister of Commerce, Trade and Industry: ALFEYO HAMBAYI.

Minister of Communications and Transport: DAWSON LUPUNGA.

Minister of Energy and Water Development: SURESH DESAI.

Minister of Lands: (vacant).

Minister of Information and Broadcasting Services: DAVID MPAMBA.

Minister of Works and Supply: KELI WALUBITA.

Minister of Science, Technology and Vocational Training: ENOCH KAVINDELE.

Minister of Sport, Youth and Child Development: SAMUEL MIYANDA.

Minister of the Environment and Natural Resources: WILLIAM HARRINGTON.

Minister without Portfolio: MICHAEL CHILUFYA SATA.

MINISTRIES

Office of the President: POB 30208, Lusaka; tel. (1) 218282; telex 42240.

Ministry of Agriculture, Food and Fisheries: Mulungushi House, Independence Ave, Nationalist Rd, POB RW50291, Lusaka; tel. (1) 213551; telex 43950.

Ministry of Commerce, Trade and Industry: Kwacha Annex, Cairo Rd, POB 31968, Lusaka; tel. (1) 213767; telex 45630.

Ministry of Communications and Transport: Fairley Rd, POB 50065, Lusaka; tel. (1) 251444; telex 41680; fax (1) 253260.

Ministry of Community Development and Social Services: Lusaka.

Ministry of Defence: POB 31931, Lusaka; tel. (1) 252366.

Ministry of Education: 15102 Ridgeway, POB RW50093, Lusaka; tel. (1) 227636; telex 42621; fax (1) 222396.

Ministry of Energy and Water Development: Mulungushi House, Independence Ave, Nationalist Rd, POB 36079, Lusaka; tel. (1) 252589; telex 40373; fax (1) 252589.

Ministry of the Environment and Natural Resources: Lusaka.

Ministry of Finance and Economic Development: Finance Bldg, POB RW50062, Lusaka; tel. (1) 213822; telex 42221.

Ministry of Foreign Affairs: POB RW50069, Lusaka; tel. (1) 252640; telex 41290; e-mail mfalus@zamnet.zm.

Ministry of Health: Woodgate House, 1st–2nd Floors, Cairo Rd, POB 30205, Lusaka; tel. (1) 227745; fax (1) 228385.

Ministry of Home Affairs: POB 32862, Lusaka; tel. (1) 213505.

Ministry of Information and Broadcasting Services: Independence Ave, POB 51025, Lusaka; tel. (1) 228202; telex 40113; fax (1) 253457.

Ministry of Labour and Social Security: Lechwe House, Freedom Way, POB 32186, Lusaka; tel. (1) 212020.

Ministry of Lands: POB 50694, Lusaka; tel. (1) 252288; telex 40681; fax (1) 250120.

Ministry of Legal Affairs: Fairley Rd, POB 50106, 15101 Ridgeway, Lusaka; tel. (1) 228522; telex 40564.

Ministry of Local Government and Housing: Lusaka.

Ministry of Mines and Mineral Development: Chilufya Mulenga Rd, POB 31969, 10101 Lusaka; tel. (1) 251402; telex 40539; fax (1) 252095.

Ministry of Science, Technology and Vocational Training: POB 50464, Lusaka; tel. (1) 229673; telex 40406; fax (1) 252951.

Ministry of Sport, Youth and Child Development: Lusaka.

Ministry of Tourism: Electra House, Cairo Rd, POB 30575, Lusaka; tel. (1) 227645; telex 45510; fax (1) 222189.

Ministry of Works and Supply: POB 50003, Lusaka; tel. (1) 253088; fax (1) 253404.

President and Legislature

PRESIDENT

Presidential Election, 18 November 1996

Candidate	Votes	% of votes
FREDERICK CHILUBA (MMD)	917,382	72.51
DEAN MUNG'OMBA (ZADECO)	158,756	12.55
HUMPHREY MULEMBA (NP)	88,766	7.02
AKASHAMBATWA LEWANIKA (AZ)	59,379	4.69
CHAMA CHAKOMBOKA (MDP)	40,843	3.23
Total	1,265,126	100.00

In addition, a total of 55,184 invalid votes were cast.

NATIONAL ASSEMBLY

Speaker: ROBINSON NABULYATO.

General Election, 18 November 1996

	Seats
Movement for Multi-party Democracy (MMD)	131
National Party (NP)	5
Agenda for Zambia (AZ)	2
Zambia Democratic Congress (ZADECO)	2
Independents	10
Total	150

House of Chiefs

The House of Chiefs is an advisory body which may submit resolutions for debate by the National Assembly. There are 27 Chiefs, four each from the Northern, Western, Southern and Eastern Provinces, three each from the North Western, Luapula and Central Provinces, and two from the Copperbelt Province.

Political Organizations

During 1972–90 the United National Independence Party was the sole authorized political party. In 1990 constitutional amendments permitted the formation of other political associations. Among the most prominent political organizations in 1997 were:

Agenda for Zambia (AZ): Lusaka; f. 1996 by fmr mems of National Party; Pres. AKASHAMBATWA LEWANIKA.

Democratic Party (DP): Lusaka; f. 1991; Pres. EMMANUEL MWAMBA.

Independent Democratic Front: Lusaka; Pres. MIKE KAIRA.

Labour Party (LP): Lusaka; Leader CHIBEZA MUFUNE.

Liberal Progressive Front (LPF): Leader ROGER CHONGWE.

Movement for Democratic Process (MDP): Lusaka; f. 1991; Pres. CHAMA CHAKOMBOKA.

Movement for Multi-party Democracy (MMD): POB 365, 10101 Lusaka; f. 1990; governing party since Nov. 1991; Pres. FREDERICK CHILUBA; Sec. MICHAEL SATA.

Multi-Racial Party (MRP): Lusaka; Leader AARON MULENGA.

National Democratic Alliance (NADA): Lusaka; f. 1991; Pres. YONAM PHIRI.

National Lima Party (NLP): f. 1996; Leader GUY SCOTT.

National Party (NP): Lusaka; f. 1993 by fmr mems of MMD; Pres. HUMPHREY MULEMBA; Chair. (vacant).

National Party for Democracy (NPD): Lusaka.

National People's Salvation Party (NPSP): Lusaka; Pres. LUMBWE LAMBANYA.

New Democratic Party (NDP): Lusaka; f. 1995; Pres. DAVID LIMAKA.

United Democratic Congress Party: Lusaka; f. 1992; Leader DANIEL LISULO.

United National Independence Party (UNIP): POB 30302, Lusaka; tel. (1) 221197; telex 43640; fax (1) 221327; f. 1958; sole legal party 1972–90; Pres. Dr KENNETH D. KAUNDA; Chair. Gen. MALIMBA MASHEKE; Sec.-Gen. SEBASTIAN ZULU.

Zambia Democratic Congress (ZADECO): Lusaka; f. 1995; Leader DEAN MUNG'OMBA; Gen. Sec. DERRICK CHITALA.

Diplomatic Representation

EMBASSIES AND HIGH COMMISSIONS IN ZAMBIA

Angola: Plot 5548, Lukanga Rd, Kalundu, POB 31595, Lusaka; tel. (1) 254346; telex 41940; Ambassador: MANUEL DOMINGOS AUGUSTO.

Austria: 30A Mutende Rd, Woodlands, POB 31094, Lusaka; tel. (1) 260407; telex 43790; Ambassador: Dr H. SCHURZ.

Botswana: 2647 Haile Selassie Ave, POB 31910, Lusaka; tel. (1) 250804; telex 41710; High Commissioner: SOBLEM MAYANE (acting).

Brazil: 74 Anglo-American Bldg, Independence Ave, POB 33300; tel. (1) 250400; telex 40102; fax (1) 251652; Chargé d'affaires a.i.: PAULO M. G. DE SOUSA.

Bulgaria: 4045 Lukulu Rd, POB 31996, Lusaka; tel. and fax (1) 263295; telex 40215; Chargé d'affaires a.i.: YULI MINCHEV.

Canada: Plot 5199, United Nations Ave, POB 31313, Lusaka; tel. (1) 250833; telex 42480; fax (1) 254176; High Commissioner: AUBREY L. MORANTZ.

China, People's Republic: Plot 7430, Haile Selassie Ave, POB 31975, Lusaka; tel. (1) 253770; telex 41360; Ambassador: YANG ZENGYE.

Congo, Democratic Republic: Plot 1124, Parirenyatwa Rd, POB 31287, Lusaka; tel. (1) 213343; Ambassador: Dr ATENDE OMWARGO.

Cuba: Plot 5509, Lusiwasi Rd, Kalundu, POB 33132, Lusaka; tel. (1) 251380; telex 40309; Ambassador: JUAN CARRETERO.

Denmark: 18 Dunduza Chisidza Crescent, Prospect Hill, POB 50299, Lusaka; tel. (1) 254277; telex 43580; fax 254618; Ambassador: JØRN KROGBECK.

Egypt: Plot 5206, United Nations Ave, POB 32428, Lusaka; tel. R.i.(1) 253762; telex 40021; Ambassador: KHALED M. ALY OSMAN.

Finland: Anglo-American Bldg, 6th Floor, POB 50819, 15101 Ridgeway, Lusaka; tel. (1) 228492; telex 43460; fax (1) 261472; Chargé d'affaires a.i.: HANNU IKONEN.

France: Anglo-American Bldg, 4th Floor, 74 Independence Ave, POB 30062, Lusaka; tel. (1) 251322; telex 41430; fax (1) 254475; Ambassador: PHILIPPE PERRIER DE LA BATHIE.

Germany: Plot 5209, United Nations Ave, POB 50120, 1501 Ridgeway, Lusaka; tel. (1) 250644; telex 41410; fax (1) 254014; Ambassador: Dr PETER SCHMIDT.

Holy See: Hussein Saddam Blvd, POB 31445, Lusaka; tel. (1) 251033; telex 40403; fax (1) 250601; Apostolic Pro-Nuncio: Most Rev. GIUSEPPE LEANZA, Titular Archbishop of Lilibeo.

India: 5220 Haile Selassie Ave, POB 32111, Lusaka; tel. (1) 253152; telex 41420; fax (1) 254118; High Commissioner: RINZINGWANGDI.

Ireland: Katima Mulilo Rd, Olympia Park, POB 34923, Lusaka; tel. (1) 290650; telex 43110; Chargé d'affaires a.i.: BRENDAN ROGERS.

Italy: Embassy Park, Diplomatic Triangle, POB 31046, Lusaka; tel. (1) 260382; telex 43380; fax (1) 260329; Ambassador: Dr G. MINGAZZINI.

Japan: Plot 5218, Haile Selassie Ave, POB 34190, Lusaka; tel. (1) 251555; telex 41470; fax (1) 253488; Ambassador: YOSHIHIRO NAKAMURA.

Kenya: Harambee House, Plot 5207, United Nations Ave, POB 50298, Lusaka; tel. (1) 227938; telex 42470; High Commissioner: JACKSON TUMWA.

Korea, Democratic People's Republic: Lusaka; Ambassador: PAK BYONG JONG.

Malawi: Woodgate House, Cairo Rd, POB 50425, Lusaka; tel. (1) 228296; telex 41840; High Commissioner: B. H. KAWONGA.

Mozambique: Mulungushi Village, Villa 46, POB 34877, Lusaka; tel. (1) 250436; telex 45900; High Commissioner: M. JAMO.

Namibia: Lusaka; High Commissioner: ANDREAS GUIBEB.

Netherlands: 5028 United Nations Ave, POB 31905, Lusaka; tel. (1) 253819; telex 42690; fax (1) 253733; Ambassador: J. P. DIJKSTRA.

Nigeria: 52034 Haile Selassie Ave, Longacres, POB 32598, Lusaka; tel. (1) 253177; telex 41280; fax (1) 253560; High Commissioner: Chief L. O. C. AGUBUZU.

Portugal: Plot 25, Yotom Muteya Rd, POB 33871, Lusaka; tel. (1) 252996; telex 40010; Ambassador: A. LOPES DA FONSECA.

Romania: 2 Leopard's Hill Rd, POB 31944, Lusaka; tel. (1) 262182; Ambassador: L. FLORESCU.

Russia: Plot 6407, Diplomatic Triangle, POB 32355, Lusaka; tel. (1) 252183; Ambassador: MIKHAIL N. BATCHARNIKOV.

Saudi Arabia: Premium House, 5th Floor, POB 34411, Lusaka; tel. (1) 227829; telex 45550; Ambassador: (vacant).

Somalia: G3/377A Kabulonga Rd, POB 34051, Lusaka; tel. (1) 262119; telex 40270; Ambassador: Dr OMAN UMAL.

South Africa: 4th Floor, Bata House, Cairo Rd, Private Bag W369, Lusaka; tel. (1) 228443; fax (1) 223268; High Commissioner: WALTER THEMBA THABETHE.

Spain: Lusaka; Ambassador: JESÚS CARLOS RIOSALIDO.

Sweden: POB 30788, Lusaka; tel. (1) 251249; telex 41820; fax (1) 254049; Ambassador: KRISTINA SVENSSON.

Tanzania: Ujamaa House, Plot 5200, United Nations Ave, POB 31219, Lusaka; tel. (1) 227698; telex 40118; fax (1) 254861; High Commissioner: NIMROD LUGOE.

Uganda: Kulima Tower, 11th Floor, Katunjila Rd, Lusaka; tel. (1) 214413; telex 40990; High Commissioner: VALERIANO KARAKUZA-BAGUMA.

United Kingdom: Plot 5201, Independence Ave, POB 50050, 15101 Ridgeway, Lusaka; tel. (1) 251133; telex 41150; fax (1) 253798; High Commissioner: PATRICK NIXON.

USA: cnr Independence and United Nations Aves, POB 31617, Lusaka; tel. (1) 250955; telex 41970; fax (1) 252225; Ambassador: ROLAND KUCHEL.

Yugoslavia: Plot 5216, Diplomatic Triangle, POB 31180, Lusaka; tel. (1) 250247; Chargé d'affaires a.i.: STANIMIR JOVANOVIĆ.

Zimbabwe: Memaco House, 4th Floor, Cairo Rd, POB 33491, Lusaka; tel. (1) 229382; telex 45800; fax (1) 227474; High Commissioner: T. J. KANGAI.

Judicial System

Supreme Court of Zambia: Independence Ave, POB 50067, Ridgeway, Lusaka; tel. (1) 251330; telex 40396; fax (1) 251743; the final Court of Appeal. Judges of the Supreme Court include the Chief Justice and the Deputy Chief Justice. The High Court consists of the Chief Justice and 30 Judges. Principal Resident, Senior Resident and Resident Magistrates' Courts also sit at various centres. The Local Courts deal mainly with customary law, although they have a certain limited criminal jurisdiction.

Chief Justice: MATHEW M. S. W. NGULUBE.

Deputy Chief Justice: B. K. BWEUPE.

Supreme Court Judges: E. L. SAKALA, M. S. CHAILA, E. K. CHIRWA, W. M. MUZYAMBA, D. M. LEWANIKA.

Religion

CHRISTIANITY

Christian Council of Zambia: Church House, Cairo Rd, POB 30315, Lusaka; tel. (1) 224308; telex 45160; f. 1945; 17 mem. churches and 18 other Christian orgs; Chair. Rt Rev. CLEMENT SHABA (Anglican Bishop of Central Zambia); Gen. Sec. VIOLET SAMPA-BREDT.

The Anglican Communion

Anglicans are adherents of the Church of the Province of Central Africa, covering Botswana, Malawi, Zambia and Zimbabwe. The Church comprises 12 dioceses, including four in Zambia. The Archbishop of the Province is the Bishop of Botswana. There are an estimated 40,000 adherents in Zambia.

Bishop of Central Zambia: Rt Rev. CLEMENT SHABA, POB 70172, Ndola; fax (2) 615954.

Bishop of Eastern Zambia: Rt Rev. JOHN OSMERS, POB 510514, Chipata; fax (1) 262379.

Bishop of Lusaka: Rt Rev. STEPHEN MUMBA, Bishop's Lodge, POB 30183, Lusaka.

Bishop of Northern Zambia: Rt Rev. BERNARD AMOS MALANGO, POB 20173, Kitwe; tel. (2) 223264; fax (2) 224778.

Protestant Churches

African Methodist Episcopal Church: POB 31478, Lusaka; tel. (1) 264013; 400 congregations, 80,000 mems; Presiding Elder Rev. D. K. SIMFUKWE.

Baptist Church: Lubu Rd, POB 30636, Lusaka; tel. (1) 253620.

Baptist Mission of Zambia: 3061/62 cnr Makishi and Great East Rds, POB 50599, 15101 Ridgeway, Lusaka; tel. (1) 222492; fax (1) 227520.

Brethren in Christ Church: POB 115, Choma; tel. (3) 20278; f. 1906; Bishop Rev. SHAMAPANI; 116 congregations, 8,000 mems.

Reformed Church of Zambia: POB 32301, Lusaka; tel. (1) 231206; f. 1899; African successor to the Dutch Reformed Church mission; 147 congregations, 400,000 mems.

Seventh-day Adventists: POB 31309, Lusaka; tel. (1) 219775; telex 43760; 66,408 active mems.

United Church of Zambia: Synod Headquarters, Nationalist Rd at Burma Rd, POB 50122, Lusaka; tel. (1) 250641; f. 1967; c. 1m. mems; Synod Bishop Rev. A. SIATURINDA; Gen. Sec. Rev. SILISHEBO SILISHEBO.

Other denominations active in Zambia include the Assemblies of God, the Church of Christ, the Church of the Nazarene, the Evangelical Fellowship of Zambia, the Kimbanguist Church, the Presbyterian Church of Southern Africa, the Religious Society of Friends (Quakers) and the United Pentecostal Church.

The Roman Catholic Church

Zambia comprises two archdioceses and seven dioceses. At 31 December 1995 there were an estimated 2,677,471 adherents in the country, equivalent to 26.7% of the total population.

Bishops' Conference: Zambia Episcopal Conference, Catholic Secretariat, Unity House, cnr Freedom Way and Katunjila Rd, POB 31965, Lusaka; tel. (1) 212070; telex 43560; fax (1) 220996; f. 1984; Pres. Rt Rev. TELESPHORE GEORGE MPUNDU, Bishop of Mbala-Mpika; Sec.-Gen. Rev. IGNATIUS MWEBE.

Archbishop of Kasama: Most Rev. JAMES SPAITA, Archbishop's House, POB 410143, Kasama; tel. (4) 221248; fax (4) 222202.

Archbishop of Lusaka: Most Rev. MEDARDO JOSEPH MAZOMBWE, 41 Wamulwa Rd, POB 32754, Lusaka; tel. (1) 239257; fax (1) 290631.

ISLAM

There are about 10,000 members of the Muslim Association in Zambia.

BAHÁ'Í FAITH

National Spiritual Assembly: POB 227, Ridgeway, Lusaka; tel. and fax (1) 254505; mems resident in 1,456 localities.

The Press

DAILIES

The Times of Zambia: POB 30394, Lusaka; tel. (1) 229076; telex 41860; fax (1) 222880; f. 1943; govt-owned; English; Man. Editor CYRUS SIKAZWE; circ. 65,000.

Zambia Daily Mail: POB 31421, Lusaka; tel. (1) 211722; telex 44621; f. 1968; govt-owned; English; Man. Editor EMMANUEL NYIRENDA; circ. 40,000.

PERIODICALS

African Social Research: Institute of Economic and Social Research, University of Zambia, POB 32379, Lusaka; tel. (1) 294131; fax (1) 253952; f. 1944; 2 a year; Editor MUBANGA E. KASHOKI; circ. 1,000.

Chipembele Magazine: POB 30255, Lusaka; tel. (1) 254226; 6 a year; publ. by Wildlife Conservation Soc. of Zambia; circ. 20,000.

Chronicle: Lusaka; bi-weekly; independent.

Farming in Zambia: POB 50197, Lusaka; tel. (1) 213551; telex 43950; f. 1965; quarterly; publ. by Ministry of Agriculture, Food and Fisheries; Editor L. P. CHIRWA; circ. 3,000.

Icengelo: Chifubu Rd, POB 71581, Ndola; tel. (2) 680456; telex 30054; fax (2) 680484; e-mail mpress@zamnet.zm; f. 1970; monthly; Bemba; social, educational and religious; Roman Catholic; edited by Franciscan friars; circ. 40,000.

Imbila: POB RW20, Lusaka; tel. (1) 217254; f. 1953; monthly; publ. by Zambia Information Services; Bemba; Editor D. MUKAKA; circ. 20,000.

Intanda: POB RW20, Lusaka; tel. (1) 219675; f. 1958; monthly; general; publ. by Zambia Information Services; Tonga; Editor J. SIKAULU; circ. 6,000.

Journal of Adult Education: University of Zambia, POB 50516, Lusaka; tel. (1) 216767; telex 44370; f. 1982; Exec. Editor FRANCIS KASOMA.

Leisure Magazine: Farmers House, Cairo Rd, Woodlands, Lusaka; general interest.

Liseli: POB RW20, Lusaka; tel. (1) 219675; monthly; publ. by Zambia Information Services; Lozi; Editor F. AMNSAA; circ. 8,000.

Lukanga News: POB 919, Kabwe; tel. (5) 217254; publ. by Zambia Information Services; Lenje; Editor J. H. N. NKOMANGA; circ. 5,500.

Mining Mirror: POB 71505, Ndola; tel. (2) 640133; f. 1973; monthly; English; Editor (vacant); circ. 15,000.

National Mirror: Bishops Rd, Kabulonga, POB 320199, Lusaka; tel. (1) 261193; telex 40630; fax (1) 263050; f. 1972; weekly; publ. by Multimedia Zambia; Editor FANWELL CHEMBO; circ. 40,000.

Ngoma: POB RW20, Lusaka; tel. (1) 219675; monthly; Lunda, Kaonde and Luvale; publ. by Zambia Information Services; Editor B. A. LUHILA; circ. 3,000.

Orbit: POB RW18X, Lusaka; tel. (1) 254915; f. 1971; publ. by Ministry of Education; children's educational magazine; Editor ELIDAH CHISHA; circ. 65,000.

The Post: POB 352, Lusaka; tel. (1) 225455; fax (1) 224250; f. 1991; independent; Editor-in-Chief FRED M'MEMBE; Man. Editor BRIGHT MWAPE; circ. 22,000.

Speak Out: POB 70244, Ndola; tel. (2) 612241; fax (2)610556; f. 1984; bi-monthly; Christian; circ. 40,000.

The Sportsman: POB 31762, Lusaka; tel. (1) 224250; telex 40151; f. 1980; monthly; Man. Editor SAM SIKAZWE; circ. 18,000.

The Sun: Lusaka.

Sunday Express: Lusaka; f. 1991; weekly; Man. Editor JOHN MUKELA.

Sunday Times of Zambia: POB 30394, Lusaka; tel. (1) 229076; telex 41860; fax (1) 222880; f. 1965; owned by UNIP; English; Man. Editor ARTHUR SIMUCHOBA; circ. 78,000.

Tsopano: POB RW20, Lusaka; tel. (1) 217254; f. 1958; monthly; publ. by Zambia Information Services; Nyanja; Editor S. S. BANDA; circ. 9,000.

Workers' Challenge: POB 270035, Kitwe; tel. and fax (2) 220904; f. 1981; 2 a month; publ. by the Workers' Pastoral Centre; English and Bemba; Co-Editors Fr MISHECK KAUNDA, JUSTIN CHILUFYA; circ. 16,000.

Workers' Voice: POB 652, Kitwe; tel. (2) 211999; f. 1972; fortnightly; publ. by Zambia Congress of Trade Unions.

Youth: POB 30302, Lusaka; tel. (1) 211411; f. 1974; quarterly; publ. by UNIP Youth League; Editor-in-Chief N. ANAMELA; circ. 20,000.

Zambia Government Gazette: POB 30136, Lusaka; tel. (1) 228724; telex 40347; fax (1) 224486; f. 1911; weekly; English; official notices.

NEWS AGENCY

Zambia News Agency (ZANA): Mass Media Complex, POB 30007, Lusaka; tel. (1) 219673; telex 42120; Editor-in-Chief DAVID KASHWEKA.

Foreign Bureaux

Agence France-Presse: POB 33805, Lusaka; tel. (1) 212959; telex 45960; Bureau Chief ABBE MAINE.

Informatsionnoye Telegrafnoye Agentstvo Rossii–Telegrafnoye Agentstvo Suverennykh Stran (ITAR–TASS)

(Russia): POB 33394, Lusaka; tel. (1) 254201; telex 45270; Correspondent ANDREY K. POLYAKOV.

Reuters (UK): POB 31685, Lusaka; tel. (1) 253430; telex 41160.

Rossiiskoye Informatsionnoye Agentstvo—Novosti (RIA—Novosti) (Russia): Lusaka; tel. (1) 252849; telex 45190; Rep. VIKTOR LAPTUKHIN.

Xinhua (New China) News Agency (People's Republic of China): United Nations Ave, POB 31859, Lusaka; tel. (1) 252227; telex 40455; fax (1) 251708; Chief Correspondent DU ZHENFENG.

PRESS ASSOCIATION

Press Association of Zambia (PAZA): c/o The Times of Zambia, POB 30394, Lusaka; tel. (1) 229076; f. 1983; Chair. ROBINSON MAKAYI.

Publishers

Africa: Literature Centre, POB 21319, Kitwe; tel. (2) 210765; fax (2) 210716; e-mail alc@zamnet.zm; general, educational, religious; Dir JACKSON MBEWE.

African Social Research: Institute of Economic and Social Research, University of Zambia, POB 32379, Lusaka; tel. (1) 294131; fax (1) 253952; social research in Africa; Editor MUBANGA E. KASHOKI.

Daystar Publications Ltd: POB 32211, Lusaka; f. 1966; religious; Man. Dir S. E. M. PHEKO.

Directory Publishers of Zambia Ltd: POB 30963, Lusaka; tel. (1) 233404; fax (1) 289738; f. 1958; trade directories; Gen. Man. W. D. WRATTEN.

Multimedia Zambia: Woodlands, POB 320199, Lusaka; tel. (1) 261193; telex 40630; fax (1) 263050; f. 1971; religious and educational books, audio-visual materials; Exec. Dir JUMBE NGOMA.

Temco Publishing Co: 10 Kabelenga Rd, Lusaka; tel. (1) 211883; telex 45250; f. 1977; educational and general.

University of Zambia Press: POB 32379, 10101 Lusaka; tel. (1) 292884; telex 44370; fax (1) 253952; f. 1938; academic books, papers and journals.

Zambia Educational Publishing House: Chishango Rd, POB 32664, Lusaka; tel. (1) 229211; telex 40056; f. 1967; educational and general; Dir H. LOMBE.

Zambia Printing Co Ltd: POB 34798, 10101 Lusaka; tel. (1) 227673; telex 40068; fax (1) 225026; Gen. Man. BERNARD LUBUMBASHI.

Government Publishing Houses

Government Printer: POB 30136, Lusaka; tel. (1) 228724; telex 40347; fax (1) 224486; official documents and statistical bulletins.

Zambia Information Services: POB 50020, Lusaka; tel. (1) 219673; telex 41350; state-controlled; Dir BENSON SIANGA.

PUBLISHERS' ASSOCIATION

Booksellers' and Publishers' Association of Zambia: POB 31838, Lusaka; tel. (1) 222647; fax (1) 225195; Chair. RAY MUNAMWIMBU; Sec. BASIL MBEWE.

Radio and Television

In 1994, according to UNESCO, there were an estimated 760,000 radio receivers and 245,000 television receivers in use. In mid-1997 plans were announced for the transmission of two Egyptian satellite television channels in Zambia.

Zambia National Broadcasting Corporation: Broadcasting House, POB 50015, Lusaka; tel. (1) 254989; telex 41221; fax (1) 254317; f. 1961; state-controlled; radio services in English and seven Zambian languages; television services in English; Dir-Gen. DUNCAN H. MBAZIMA.

Educational Broadcasting Services: Headquarters: POB 50231, Lusaka; tel. (1) 251724; radio broadcasts from Lusaka; television for schools from POB 21106, Kitwe; audio-visual aids service from POB 50295, Lusaka; Controller MICHAEL MULOMBE.

Finance

(cap. = capital; auth. = authorized; res = reserves; dep. = deposits; m. = million; br. = branch; amounts in kwacha)

BANKING

Capitalization of banks must total at least K500,000 in the case of any commercial bank wholly or partially owned by the Government, and not less than K2m. in the case of any other commercial bank. At least one-half of the directors of these latter banks must be established residents in Zambia. All foreign-owned banks are required to incorporate in Zambia. All banks operating in Zambia were required to have capital of K2,000m. or more by 30 June 1996 in order to obtain a banking licence or to continue to function.

Central Bank

Bank of Zambia: POB 30080, Lusaka; tel. (1) 228888; telex 41560; fax (1) 226822; f. 1964; bank of issue; cap. and res 35.3m., dep. 7,832m. (Oct. 1985); Gov. JACOB MWANZA; Gen. Man. GODFREY MBULO; br. in Ndola.

Commercial Banks

Finance Bank Zambia Ltd: 2101 Chanik House, Cairo Rd, POB 37102, 10101 Lusaka; tel. (1) 229736; telex 40338; fax (1) 224450; cap. and res 3,055.7m., dep. 25,570.8m. (Dec. 1994); Chair. Dr R.L. MAHTANI; Man. Dir M. WADOOD; 21 brs.

Manifold Investment Bank Ltd: Cusa House, Cairo Rd, POB 36595, Lusaka; tel. (1) 224109; telex 40368; fax (1) 224071; f. 1988; cap. and res 144.4m., dep. 540.9m. (June 1994); Chair. HELLINS V. CHABI; Man. Dir RICHARD N. MUTUKWA; 1 br.

National Savings and Credit Bank of Zambia: Plot 248, Cairo Rd, POB 30067; Lusaka; tel. (1) 227534; telex 40089; fax (1) 223296; f. 1973; dep. 2,973m. (Dec. 1996); Man. Dir G. J. M. CHEMBE.

New Capital Bank: Lotti House, Cairo Rd, Lusaka; tel. (1) 229508; telex 43830; fax (1) 224055; cap. 250m. (March 1994); Chair. W. D. MUNG'OMBA; Man. Dir ANTHONY STORROW.

Union Bank Zambia Ltd: Zimco House, Cairo Rd, POB 34940, Lusaka; tel. (1) 229392; telex 40112; fax (1) 221866; cap. 320m. (Dec. 1993); Chair. J. R. NAYEE; Man. Dir S. A. J. RIZVI.

Zambia National Commercial Bank Ltd: Plot 2118, Cairo Rd, POB 33611, Lusaka; tel. (1) 228979; telex 42360; fax (1) 223082; f. 1969; govt-controlled; cap. and res 26,467.4m., dep. 116,333.4m. (March 1995); Chair. K. P. CHUNGU; Man. Dir J. M. MTONGA; 41 brs.

Foreign Banks

Barclays Bank of Zambia Ltd (UK): Kafue House, Cairo Rd, POB 31936, Lusaka; tel. (1) 228858; telex 41570; fax (1) 222519; f. 1971; cap. and res 16,621.3m., dep. 108,733.0m. (Dec. 1995); Chair. A. B. MUNYAMA; Man. Dir M. M. MCNIE; 32 brs.

Citibank Zambia Ltd (USA): Citibank House, Cha Cha Cha Rd, POB 30037, Southend, Lusaka; tel. (1) 229025; telex 45610; fax (1) 226264; f. 1979; cap. 521.2m., dep. 38,862m. (Dec. 1996); Man. Dir SANJEEV ANAND; 1br.

Indo-Zambia Bank (IZB): Plot 6907, Cairo Rd, POB 35411, Lusaka; tel. (1) 224653; fax (1) 225090; e-mail izb@zamnet.zm; f. 1984; cap. and res 2,276.4m., dep. 14,794.9m. (March 1996); Chair. Prof. B. MWEENE; Man. Dir K. C. MEHTA; 7 brs.

Stanbic Bank Zambia Ltd: Woodgate House, Nairobi Place, Cairo Rd, POB 31955, Lusaka; tel. (1) 229071; telex 42461; fax (1) 221152; f. 1971; wholly-owned by Standard Bank Investment Corpn; cap. 300m. (Sept. 1995), dep. 14,499m. (Sept. 1994); Chair. D. A. R. PHIRI; Man. Dir A. B. MEARS; 6 brs.

Standard Chartered Bank Zambia Ltd (UK): Standard House, Cairo Rd, POB 32238, Lusaka; tel. (1) 229242; telex 41660; fax (1) 222092; f. 1971; cap. and res 17,276m., dep. 90,441m. (Dec. 1996); Chair. A. K. MAZOKA; Man. Dir J. A. H. JONES; 15 brs.

Development Banks

Development Bank of Zambia: Development House, Katondo St, POB 33955, Lusaka; tel. (1) 228576; telex 45040; fax (1) 222426; f. 1973; 99% state-owned; provides medium- and long-term loans and offers business consultancy and research services; cap. 6,984.0m. (March 1996); Chair. J. M. MTONGA; Man. Dir G. M. B. MUMBA; 2 brs.

Lima Bank: Kulima House, Chachacha Rd, POB 31977, Lusaka; tel. (1) 213111; telex 43280; fax (1) 228077; cap. 57m. (March 1986); Chair. N. MUKUTU; Man. Dir K. V. KASAPATU.

Zambia Agricultural Development Bank: Society House, Cairo Rd, POB 30847, Lusaka; tel. (1) 219251; telex 40126; f. 1982; loan finance for development of agriculture and fishing; auth. cap. 75m.; Chair. K. MAKASA; Man. Dir AMON CHIBIYA.

Zambia Export and Import Bank Ltd: Society House, Cairo Rd, POB 33046, Lusaka; tel. (1) 229486; telex 40098; fax (1) 222313; f. 1987; state-owned; privatization pending in 1997; cap. 50m. (March 1992), dep. 50.9m. (March 1990); Man. Dir. LIKANDO NAWA.

STOCK EXCHANGE

Lusaka Stock Exchange: Plot 2A, Cairo Rd, POB 34523, Lusaka; tel. (1) 228594; fax (1) 228608; e-mail luse@zamnet.zm; f. 1994; Gen. Man. CHARLES MATE.

INSURANCE

Zambia State Insurance Corporation Ltd: Premium House, Independence Ave, POB 30894, Lusaka; tel. (1) 229343; telex 42521; fax (1) 222263; f. 1968; took over all insurance business in Zambia in 1971; transfer to private sector pending in 1997; Chair. E. WILLIMA; Man. Dir MWENE MWINGA.

Trade and Industry

STATE PROPERTY AGENCY

Zambia Privatization Agency: Privatization House, Nasser Rd, POB 30819, Lusaka; tel. (1) 223859; fax (1) 225270; e-mail zpa@zamnet.zm; f. 1992; responsible for the divestment of various state-owned enterprises; CEO VALENTINE CHITALU.

CHAMBER OF COMMERCE

Lusaka Chamber of Commerce and Industry: POB 30844, Lusaka; tel. (1) 252369; telex 40124; f. 1933; Chair. R. D. PENZA; Sec. Dr E. BBENKELE; 400 mems.

INDUSTRIAL AND COMMERCIAL ASSOCIATIONS

Copper Industry Service Bureau Ltd: POB 22100, Kitwe; tel. (2) 214122; telex 52620; f. 1941 as Chamber of Mines.

Zambia Association of Manufacturers: POB 30844, Lusaka; tel. (1) 252369; telex 40124; f. 1985; Chair. MARK O'DONNELL; Sec. N. NAMUSHI; 250 mems.

Zambia Confederation of Industries and Chambers of Commerce: POB 30844, Lusaka; tel. (1) 252369; telex 40124; fax (1) 252483; f. 1938; Chair. R. D. FROST; CEO THEO BULL; 2,000 mems.

Zambia Farm Employers' Association: V.T.A. House, Chachacha Rd, POB 30395, Lusaka; tel. (1) 213222; telex 40164; Chair. D. FLYNN; Vice-Chair. M. J. H. BECKETT; 300 mems.

Zambia Seed Producers' Association: POB 30013, Lusaka; tel. (1) 223249; telex 40164; fax (1) 223249; f. 1964; Chair. BARRY COXE; 300 mems.

STATUTORY ORGANIZATIONS

Industry

Industrial Development Corporation of Zambia Ltd (INDECO): Indeco House, Buteko Place, POB 31935, Lusaka; tel. (1) 228463; telex 41821; fax (1) 228868; f. 1960; auth. cap. K300m.; c. 47 subsidiaries and assoc. cos in brewing, chemicals, property, manufacturing, agriculture and vehicle assembly; Chair. R. L. BWALYA; Man. Dir S. K. TAMELÉ.

Metal Marketing Corporation (Zambia) Ltd (MEMACO): Memaco House, Sapele Rd, POB 35570, Lusaka; tel. (1) 228131; telex 40070; fax (1) 223671; f. 1973; sole sales agents for all metal and mineral production; Chair. R. L. BWALYA; Man. Dir U. M. MUTATI.

National Import and Export Corporation (NIEC): National Housing Authority Bldg, Lusaka; tel. (1) 2288018; telex 44490; fax (1) 252771; f. 1974.

Small Industries Development Organization (SIDO): Sido House, Cairo Rd, POB 35373, Lusaka; tel. (1) 229707; telex 40169; fax (1) 224284; e-mail sido@zamnet.zm; f. 1981 to promote development of small and village industries.

Zambia Electricity Supply Corporation (Zesco): Lusaka; Man. Dir ROBINSON MWANSA.

Zambia Investment Centre: Ndeke House, POB 34580, Lusaka; tel. (1) 252130; fax (1) 252150; e-mail invest@zamnet.zm; Dir Gen. BWALYKA NG'ANDU.

Zambia Telecommunications Co Ltd: POB 71630, Ndola; tel. (2) 612399; telex 30360; fax (2) 615855; transfer to private sector pending in 1997.

Agriculture

The Dairy Produce Board of Zambia: Kwacha House, Cairo Rd, POB 30124, Lusaka; tel. (1) 214770; telex 41520; f. 1964; purchase and supply of dairy products to retailers, manufacture and marketing of milk products.

Department of Marketing and Co-operatives: POB 50595, Lusaka; tel. (1) 214933; a dept of Ministry of Agriculture, Food and Fisheries; Dir S. B. CHIWALA.

Tobacco Board of Zambia: POB 31963, Lusaka; tel. (1) 288995; telex 40370; Sec. L. C. SIMUMBA.

Zambia Co-operative Federation Ltd: Co-operative House, Chachacha Rd, POB 33579, Lusaka; tel. (1) 220157; telex 43210; fax (1) 222516; agricultural marketing; supply of agricultural chemicals and implements; cargo haulage; insurance; agricultural credit; auditing and accounting; property and co-operative development; Chair. B. TETAMASHIMBA; Man. Dir G. Z. SIBALE.

MAJOR INDUSTRIAL COMPANIES

The following are among the largest companies in terms either of capital investment or employment. The government has a controlling interest in major strategic industries, although it has been undertaking an ambitious privatization programme since 1992.

Chilanga Cement PLC: Head Office: POB 32639, 10101 Lusaka; tel. (1) 278501; fax (1) 252655; f. 1949; works at Chilanga and Ndola; manufacture and marketing of cement. CEO PATRICK R. GORMAN; Finance Man./Co. Sec. TERENCE A. MORDUE; 750 employees.

Dunlop Zambia Ltd: POB 71650, Ndola; tel. (2) 650789; telex 34110; fax (2) 650138; f. 1964; cap. K563m.; transfer to private sector pending in 1997; mfrs and distributors of car, truck, tractor, earthmover and mining as well as cycle tyres and tubes; also of contact adhesives, floor tiles and other allied rubber products; Man. Dir ROBERT MAY; 460 employees.

Kafue Textiles of Zambia Ltd: POB 360131, Kafue; tel. (1) 311501; telex 70020; fax (1) 311514; f. 1969; 99.9% of shares owned by state; transfer to private sector pending in 1997; mfrs of drills, denims, twills and poplins; dress prints and African prints; industrial and household textiles; Gen. Man. JEAN PAUL BONDAZ; 600 employees.

Minestone (Zambia) Ltd: POB 31870 Lusaka; tel. (1) 228748; telex 40210; fax (1) 222301; f. 1954; cap. K1.9m.; building, civil and mechanical contractors; Gen. Man. D. J. C. O'LEARY; 2,000–3,000 employees.

National Breweries Ltd: POB 22699, Kitwe; tel. (2) 211333; telex 51740; inc 1968; subsidiary of INDECO; operates 14 breweries; Chair. D. H. LUZONGO; Gen. Man. H. G. MUZABAZI; 680 employees.

National Milling Co Ltd: Box 20646, Kitwe; tel. (2) 3304.

Nitrogen Chemicals of Zambia Ltd: POB 360226, Kafue; tel. (1) 311531; telex 70004; fax (1) 311313; f. 1967; cap. K509m.; 70% shareholding to be transferred to private sector in 1997; production of ammonium nitrate for fertilizer and explosives, nitric acid, ammonium sulphate, sulphuric acid, methanol, compound fertilizers and liquid carbon dioxide; Chair. Dr K. MULEYA; Man. Dir F. M. KAMBOBE; 1,200 employees.

Non-Ferrous Metal Works (Zambia) Ltd: Box 72283, Ndola; tel. (65) 5603; telex 34321; fax (2) 5777.

ROP Ltd: POB 71570, Nakambala Rd, Ndola; tel. (2) 650549; telex 33120; fax (2) 650162; f. 1975 by merger of Refined Oil Products Ltd and Lever Brothers, Zambia; mfrs of soaps, detergents, toilet preparations and edible oils; Gen. Man. (vacant).

Zambezi Sawmills (1968) Ltd: POB 60041, Livingstone; tel. (3) 322853; telex 24003; fax (3) 322853; subsidiary of ZIMCO; sawmillers and mfrs of railway sleepers, mining timbers, sawn timber, wooden parquet tiles, etc.

Zambia Breweries Ltd: POB 70091, Ndola, 74 Independence Ave, Lusaka; tel. (1) 3601; telex 42330; f. 1951, opened in Lusaka 1966; cap. K5.6m.; state-owned; transfer to private sector pending in 1997; brewing, bottling and distribution of lager beers; Gen. Man. ZACKS MUSONDA; 1,300 employees.

Zambia Consolidated Copper Mines Ltd (ZCCM): 5309 Dedan Kimathi Rd, POB 30048, Lusaka; tel. (1) 229115; fax 221057; f. 1982 by merger of Nchanga Consolidated Copper Mines and Roan Consolidated Mines; auth. cap. K900m.; Govt holds 60.3% of shares; transfer to private sector scheduled for completion in 1998; Chair. L. MWANANSHIKU; CEO EDWARD SHAMUTETE.

TRADE UNIONS

Zambia Congress of Trade Unions: POB 20652, Kitwe; tel. (2) 211999; telex 52630; f. 1965; 18 affiliated unions; c. 400,000 mems; Pres. JACKSON SHAMENDA; Sec.-Gen. ALEC CHIORMA.

Affiliated Unions

Airways and Allied Workers' Union of Zambia: POB 30272, Lusaka; Pres. F. MULENGA; Gen. Sec. B. CHINYANTA.

Guards Union of Zambia: POB 21882, Kitwe; tel. (2) 216189; f. 1972; 13,500 mems; Chair. D. N. S. SILUNGWE; Gen. Sec. MICHAEL S. SIMFUKWE.

Hotel Catering Workers' Union of Zambia: POB 35693, Lusaka; 9,000 mems; Chair. IAN MKANDAWIRE; Gen. Sec. STOIC KAPUTU.

Mineworkers' Union of Zambia: POB 20448, Kitwe; tel. (2) 214022; telex 52650; 50,000 mems; Chair. (vacant); Gen. Sec. K. G. SHENG'AMO.

National Union of Building, Engineering and General Workers: POB 21515, Kitwe; tel. (2) 213931; 18,000 mems; Chair. LUCIANO MUTALE (acting); Gen. Sec. P. N. NZIMA.

National Union of Commercial and Industrial Workers: 87 Gambia Ave, POB 21735, Kitwe; tel. (2) 217456; f. 1982; 16,000 mems; Chair. P. L. NKHOMA; Gen. Sec. I. M. KASUMBU.

National Union of Plantation and Agricultural Workers: POB 80529, Kabwe; tel. (5) 224548; 15,155 mems; Chair. L. B. IKOWA; Gen. Sec. S. C. SILWIMBA.

National Union of Postal and Telecommunications Workers: POB 70751, Ndola; tel. (2) 611345; 6,000 mems; Chair. G. C. MWAPE; Gen. Sec. F. U. SHAMENDA.

National Union of Public Services' Workers: POB 32523, Lusaka; tel. (1) 215167; Chair. W. CHIPASHA; Gen. Sec. WILLIE MBEWE.

National Union of Transport and Allied Workers: POB 32431, Lusaka; tel. (1) 214756; Chair. B. MULWE; Gen. Sec. L. K. MABULUKI.

Railway Workers' Union of Zambia: POB 80302, Kabwe; tel. (5) 224006; 10,228 mems; Chair. H. K. NDAMANA; Gen. Sec. CALVIN J. MUKABAILA.

University of Zambia and Allied Workers' Union: POB 32379, Lusaka; tel. (1) 213221; telex 44370; f. 1968; Chair. BERIATE SUNKUTU; Gen. Sec. SAINI PHIRI.

Zambia Electricity Workers' Union: POB 70859, Ndola; f. 1972; 3,000 mems; Chair. COSMAS MPAMPI; Gen. Sec. ADAM KALUBA.

Zambia National Farmers' Union: TAZ House, Chiparamba Rd, POB 30395, Lusaka; tel. (1) 222797; telex 40164; fax (1) 222736; Gen. Sec. G. R. GRAY.

Zambia National Union of Teachers: POB 31914, Lusaka; tel. (1) 216670; 2,120 mems; Chair. JACKSON MULENGA; Gen. Sec. A. W. CHIBALE.

Zambia Typographical Workers' Union: POB 71439, Ndola; Chair. R. SHIKWATA; Gen. Sec. D. NAWA.

Zambia Union of Financial Institutions and Allied Workers: POB 31174, Lusaka; tel. (1) 219401; Chair. B. CHIKOTI; Gen. Sec. GEOFFREY ALIKIPO.

Zambia Union of Local Government Officers: f. 1997; Pres. ISAAC MWANZA.

Zambia United Local Authorities Workers' Union: POB 70575, Ndola; tel. (2) 615022; Chair. A. M. MUTAKILA; Gen. Sec. A. H. MUDENDA.

Principal Non-Affiliated Unions

Civil Servants' Union of Zambia: POB 50160, Lusaka; tel. (1) 221332; f. 1975; 26,000 mems; Chair. W. D. PHIRI; Gen. Sec. J. C. MOONDE.

Zambian African Mining Union: Kitwe; f. 1967; 40,000 mems.

Transport

RAILWAYS

Total length of railways in Zambia was 2,164 km (including 891 km of the Tanzania–Zambia railway) in 1988. There are two major railway lines: the Zambia Railways network, which traverses the country from the Copperbelt in northern Zambia and links with the National Railways of Zimbabwe to provide access to South African ports, and the Tanzania–Zambia Railway (Tazara) system, linking New Kapiri-Mposhi in Zambia with Dar es Salaam in Tanzania. The Tazara railway line increased its capacity from 1986, in order to reduce the dependence of southern African countries on trade routes through South Africa. In April 1987 the Governments of Zambia, Angola and Zaire declared their intention to reopen the Benguela railway, linking Zambian copper-mines with the Angolan port of Lobito, following its closure to international traffic in 1975 as a result of the guerrilla insurgency in Angola.

Tanzania–Zambia Railway Authority (Tazara): POB 98, Mpika; Head Office: POB 2834, Dar es Salaam, Tanzania; tel. 62191; telex 41059; f. 1975; operates passenger and freight services linking New Kapiri-Mposhi, north of Lusaka, with Dar es Salaam in Tanzania, a distance of 1,860 km of which 891 km is in Zambia; jtly owned and administered by the Tanzanian and Zambian Govts; a 10-year rehabilitation programme, assisted by the USA and EC countries, began in 1985; it was announced in 1990 that a line linking the railway with the Zambian port of Mpulungu was to be constructed; Chair. RICHARD MARIKI; Gen. Man. A. S. MWEEMBA.

Zambia Railways: cnr Buntungwa St and Ghana Ave, POB 80935, Kabwe; tel. (5) 222201; telex 81000; fax (5) 224411; f. 1967; controlled by ZIMCO; a 10-year rehabilitation programme, estimated to cost US $200m., was initiated in 1990; Chair. PATRICK S. CHAMUNDA; Man. Dir CLEMENT C. F. MANBWE.

ROADS

At December 1995 there was an estimated total road network of 38,898 km, including 58 km of motorways, 6,790 km of main roads and 8,750 km of secondary roads; an estimated 18.3% of the road network was paved. The main arterial roads run from Beit Bridge (Zimbabwe) to Tunduma (the Great North Road), through the copper-mining area to Chingola and Chililabombwe (hitherto the Zaire Border Road), from Livingstone to the junction of the Kafue river and the Great North Road, and from Lusaka to the Malawi border (the Great East Road). In 1984 the 300-km BotZam highway linking Kazungula with Nata, in Botswana, was formally opened. A 1,930-km main road (the TanZam highway) links Zambia and Tanzania. The Government was to invest US $500m. in road rehabilitation and development in the late 1990s.

Department of Roads: POB 50003, Lusaka; tel. (1) 253088; fax (1) 253404; Dir of Roads T. NGOMA.

SHIPPING

Zambia National Shipping Line: Lusaka; f. 1989; state-owned; cargo and passenger services from Dar es Salaam in Tanzania to northern Europe; Gen. Man. MARTIN PHIRI.

CIVIL AVIATION

In 1984 there were 127 airports, aerodromes and air strips. An international airport, 22.5 km from Lusaka, was opened in 1967.

Aero Zambia: ZNIB House, Dedan Kimathi Rd, Private Bag E717, Lusaka; f. 1995 to acquire business of Zambia Airways; majority ownership by private Belgian interests; 10% held by Govt of Zambia; operates domestic routes and international services to United Kingdom and Johannesburg; Chair and Man. Dir D. TOKOPH.

National Air Charters (Z) Ltd (NAC): POB 33650, Lusaka; tel. (1) 229774; telex 43840; fax (1) 229778; f. 1973; air cargo services; Gen. Man. STAFFORD MUDIYO.

Tourism

Zambia's main tourist attractions are its wildlife and unspoilt scenery; there were 19 national parks in 1990. In 1994 an estimated 134,000 tourists visited Zambia and tourist receipts totalled an estimated US $43m.

Zambia National Tourist Board: Century House, Cairo Rd, POB 30017, Lusaka; tel. (1) 229089; telex 41780; fax (1) 225174; e-mail zntb@zamnet.zm; CEO AGNES SEENKA (acting).

Zambia Tourism Council: Lusaka; Dep. Pres. MARK HARVEY.

Defence

In August 1996 Zambia's armed forces officially numbered about 21,600 (army 20,000, airforce 1,600). Paramilitary forces numbered 1,400. Military service is voluntary. There is also a national defence force, responsible to the government.

Defence Expenditure: K47,756m. allocated for 1995.

Commander of the Army: Brig.-Gen. NOBLE SIMBEYE.

Commander of the Air Force: Lt-Gen. RONNIE SIKAPAWASHA.

Education

Between 1964–79 enrolment in schools increased by more than 260%. Primary education, which is compulsory, begins at seven years of age and lasts for seven years. Secondary education, beginning at the age of 14, lasts for a further five years, comprising a first cycle of two years and a second of three years. In 1994 an estimated 69% of children (70% of boys; 68% of girls) in the relevant age-group attended primary schools, while enrolment at secondary schools was equivalent to 25% of children (31% of boys; 19% of girls) in the relevant age-group. Some 1,507,660 pupils were enrolled at primary schools in 1994, while about 199,081 pupils were enrolled at secondary schools. There are two universities: the University of Zambia at Lusaka, and the Copperbelt University at Kitwe (which is to be transferred to Ndola). There are 14 teacher training colleges. In 1995, according to estimates by UNESCO, the average rate of adult illiteracy was 21.8% (males 14.4%; females 28.7%). Of total estimated budgetary expenditure by the central government in 1995, education was allocated K85,310m. (9.4%).

Bibliography

Akashambatwa, M.-L. *Milk in a Basket: The Political-Economic Malaise in Zambia.* Lusaka, Zambia Research Foundation, 1990.

Clark, J., and Allison, C. *Zambia: Debt and Poverty.* Oxford, Oxfam, 1989.

Daloz, J.-P., and Chileshe, J. D. (Eds). *La Zambie contemporaine.* Paris, Editions Karthala, 1996.

Gulhati, R. *Impasse in Zambia: The Economics and Politics of Reform.* Washington, DC, World Bank, 1989.

Hamalengwa, M. *Class Struggle in Zambia, 1884–1989 and the Fall of Kenneth Kaunda, 1990–1991.* Lanham, MD, University Press of America, 1992.

Ihonvbere, J. O. *Economic Crisis, Civil Society and Democratization: The Case of Zambia.* Trenton, NJ, Africa World Press, 1996.

Moore, H., and Vaughan, M. *Cutting Down Trees: Gender, Nutrition and Agricultural Change in Northern Province, Zambia, 1890–1990.* Zambia, University of Zambia Press, 1994.

Moore, R. C. *The Political Reality of Freedom of the Press in Zambia.* Lanham, MD, University Press of America, 1992.

Mwanakatwe, J. M. *End of Kaunda Era.* Lusaka, Multimedia, 1994.

Mwanza, A. M. (Ed.). *The Structural Adjustment Programme in Zambia: Lessons from Experience.* Harare, SAPES Books, 1992.

Nag, P. *Population, Settlement and Development in Zambia.* New Delhi, Concept Publishing Co, 1989.

Rakner, L. *Trade Unions in Processes of Democratisation: A Study of Party Labour Relations in Zambia.* Bergen, Norway, Michelsen Institute, 1992.

Saasa, O., and Carlsson, J. *The Aid Relationship in Zambia: A Conflict Scenario.* Uppsala, Nordiska Afrikainstitutet, 1996.

Saasa, O., Wilson, F., and Chingambo, L. *The Zambian Economy in Post-Apartheid Southern Africa: A Critical Analysis of Policy Options.* Lusaka, IAS Consultancy Services, 1992.

Turok, B. *Mixed Economy in Focus: Zambia.* London, IFAA, 1989.

Van Binsbergen, W. *Tears of Rain: Ethnicity and History in Central Western Zambia.* London, Kegan Paul International, 1992.

Virmani, K. K. *Zambia: The Dawn of Freedom.* Delhi, Kalinga, 1989.

Wood, A. P. (Ed.). *Dynamics of Agricultural Policy and Reform in Zambia.* Ames, Iowa State University Press, 1990.

World Bank. *Zambia: Country Assistance Review.* Washington, DC, World Bank, 1996.

Zambia: Prospects for Sustainable Growth, 1995–2005. Washington, DC, World Bank, 1996.

ZIMBABWE

Physical and Social Geography

GEORGE KAY

The Republic of Zimbabwe, covering an area of 390,757 sq km (150,872 sq miles), is land-locked and is bounded on the north and north-west by Zambia, on the south-west by Botswana, by Mozambique on the east and on the south by South Africa. It depends largely for its overseas trade on rail routes to Mozambique and South African ports. The census of August 1992 enumerated 10,412,548 persons. In August 1997 the population was officially estimated at 12,293,953, giving a population density of 31.5 inhabitants per sq km.

Zimbabwe lies astride the high plateaux between the Zambezi and Limpopo rivers. It consists of four relief regions. The highveld, comprising land more than 1,200 m above sea-level, extends across the country from south-west to north-east; it is most extensive in the north-east. The middleveld, land of 900 m–1,200 m above sea-level, flanks the highveld; it is most extensive in the north-west. The lowveld, land below 900 m, occupies the Zambezi basin in the north and the more extensive Limpopo and Sabi-Lundi basins in the south and south-east. These three regions consist predominantly of gently undulating plateaux, except for the narrow belt of rugged, escarpment hills associated with faults along the Zambezi trough. Also, the surfaces are broken locally where particularly resistant rocks provide upstanding features. For example, the Great Dyke, a remarkable intrusive feature over 480 km in length and up to 10 km wide, gives rise to prominent ranges of hills. The fourth physical region, the eastern highlands, is distinctive because of its mountainous character. Inyangani rises to 2,594 m and many hills exceed 1,800 m.

Temperatures vary by altitude. Mean monthly temperatures range from 22°C in October and 13°C in July on the highveld to 30°C and 20°C in the low-lying Zambezi valley. Winters are noted for a wide diurnal range; night frosts can occur on the high plateaux and can occasionally be very destructive.

Rainfall is largely restricted to the period November–March and, except on the eastern highlands, is extremely variable; in many regions it is low for commercial crop production. Mean annual rainfall ranges from 1,400 mm on the eastern highlands, to 800 mm on the north-eastern highveld and to less than 400 mm in the Limpopo valley. The development of water resources for economic uses is a continually pressing need which, to date, has been met by a major dam-building programme. Underground water resources are limited. Large-scale irrigation works in the south-eastern lowveld have overcome climatic limitations, and the area around Chiredzi, once suitable only for ranching, is now a major developing region.

Soils vary considerably. Granite occurs over more than half of the country and mostly gives rise to infertile sandy soils; these are, however, amenable to improvement. Kalahari sands are also extensive and provide poor soils. Soil-forming processes are limited in the lowveld and, except on basalt, soils there are generally immature. Rich, red clays and loams occur on the limited outcrops of Basement Schists, which are also among the most highly mineralized areas of Zimbabwe.

Climatic factors are the chief determinants of agricultural potential and six broad categories of land have been defined largely on bio-climatic conditions: Region I (1.6% of the country) with good, reliable rainfall; suitable for specialized and diversified farming, including tree crops; Region II (18.7%) with moderately high rainfall; suitable for intensive commercial crop production with subsidiary livestock farming; Region III (17.4%) with mediocre rainfall conditions; suitable for semi-extensive commercial livestock farming with supplementary production of drought-resistant crops; Region IV (33%) with low and unreliable rainfall; suitable for semi-extensive livestock production; Region V (26.2%) semi-arid country; suitable only for extensive ranching; and Region VI (3.1%—probably underestimated) which, because of steep slopes, skeletal soils, swamps, etc., is unsuitable for any agricultural use.

Zimbabwe possesses a wide variety of workable mineral deposits, which include gold, platinum, asbestos, copper, chrome, nickel, palladium, cobalt, tin, iron ore, limestone, iron pyrites and phosphates. Most mineralization occurs on the highveld and adjacent parts of the middleveld. There are plentiful supplies of coal. No deposits of hydrocarbons have yet been discovered.

The population of Zimbabwe is diverse. At mid-1980 it was estimated to include some 223,000 persons of European descent and some 37,000 Asians and Coloureds, all of them a legacy of the colonial era. The indigenous inhabitants, who accounted for over 98% of the population at mid-1987, broadly comprise two ethnic or linguistic groups, the Ndebele and the Shona. The Shona, with whom political power now rests, outnumber the Ndebele by 4:1. There are, in addition, several minor ethnic groups, such as the Tonga, Sena, Hlengwe, Venda and Sotho. The official languages are English, Chishona and Sindebele.

In recent years, urban growth has proceeded rapidly. The urban poor, operating within the highly competitive 'informal economy', are now a large and increasing part of the urban social structure. During 1982–92 the population of Harare, the capital, grew from 656,000 to 1,189,103, while that of Bulawayo increased from 413,800 to 621,742.

In the rural districts of Zimbabwe, a relatively small number of white farmers and companies continue to hold extensive interests in commercial farming. However, in recent years the communal lands that are occupied by indigenous households have increased their contribution to national sales of crops and livestock. Official resettlement schemes on to the land of erstwhile commercial holdings (many of which had been unused or under-used), and colonization in the form of squatter movements on to such lands, have been formally encouraged, although resettlement has not proceeded as rapidly as planned. Legislation came into force in 1992 which empowered the government compulsorily to acquire land; it was hoped that this would facilitate the redistribution of land ownership from white commercial farmers (who then owned more than 40% of farming land producing about 80% of the country's cash crops) to African smallholders.

Most rural African households still reside on communal lands, where they have traditionally depended upon subsistence production, augmented by small irregular sales of surplus produce, by casual employment and by remittances from migrant labourers. However, the cohesion of this rural society is being eroded by the selective effects of migration.

The socio-economic difficulties of rural African society are compounded by ecological problems. While some extensive areas (notably in remote northern parts of the country) remain sparsely populated, the greater part of the communal lands suffers from overpopulation and overstocking. Deforestation, soil erosion and a deterioration of wildlife and water resources are widespread; and in some areas they have reached critical dimensions. 'Desertification' is a real danger in the semi-arid regions of the country.

Recent History

RICHARD BROWN

Revised for this edition by the Editor

The former colony of Southern Rhodesia, which now forms the Republic of Zimbabwe, was established on the strength of its rumoured mineral potential by the British South Africa Co (BSA) in 1890. Disappointed by the limited scale of gold discoveries, the BSA encouraged white farming and a reckless alienation of land to individual settlers and to speculative companies. When BSA administration ended in 1923, the British government was reluctant to accept direct responsibility for the colony, and permitted the white settlers to choose between joining South Africa or themselves taking over the administration from the BSA. The settlers, mainly British and South African in origin, elected to remain separate, and were subsequently permitted by the United Kingdom to develop a racially stratified and segregated society similar to that in South Africa. The foundation of the segregation policy was the Land Apportionment Act of 1930, which severely restricted the access of Africans to land by dividing the country very unequally in relation to population into two racially exclusive parts, with consequences which are evident in land tenure to the present day. Measures were taken to prevent Africans from competing in the markets for agricultural produce and skilled labour. Taxation, pass laws and pressures on land collectively ensured that the main role of Africans in the economy was as temporary unskilled labour migrants to the towns, farms and mines located in the 'European' areas.

INDUSTRIALIZATION AND DISCONTENT

The Second World War helped to promote industrialization and make manufacturing the leading growth sector. Rapid urbanization took place and some modifications to the policy of segregation were accepted by the overwhelmingly white electorate in the post-war period. In particular education for Africans became more widespread in recognition of the need for a more skilled black labour force. Settler immigration was also encouraged, and by the late 1950s the white population was well over 200,000, and becoming increasingly prosperous. The African population then numbered about 4m. and was growing rapidly. As strong economic growth continued after 1945, Africans increasingly resented their social, economic and political subordination. Strikes and rural discontent multiplied: by the late 1950s and early 1960s unrest was being channelled into a mass nationalist movement demanding equal rights. The government reacted with a series of bannings, and refused to allow Africans more than a limited voice in a new constitution agreed with the United Kingdom in 1961.

Meanwhile, attracted by the copper revenues of Northern Rhodesia and by the labour resources of Nyasaland, Southern Rhodesia became the dominant member of the Central African Federation (CAF), established by the United Kingdom in 1953. The territorial governments of the two northern protectorates remained under direct British control, a situation provoking much conflict with the settler-dominated federal and Southern Rhodesian governments. The federation's declared policy of racial partnership was viewed as meaningless by Africans in all three territories. The British government eventually recognized the strength of African hostility in Northern Rhodesia and Nyasaland, and conceded independence, breaking-up the federation in the process (1963). Whites in Southern Rhodesia interpreted these developments as the outcome of British appeasement and redoubled their own opposition to African political advancement. In 1962 they abandoned the party which had governed almost without interruption since 1923 and voted into office the newly-formed Rhodesian Front (RF), dedicated to upholding white supremacy and demanding full independence from the United Kingdom and the retention of the existing minority-rule constitution. When the United Kingdom refused independence on this basis, the RF appointed the intransigent Ian Smith as prime minister.

In November 1965 Smith carried out the long-threatened unilateral declaration of independence (UDI). Retaining the unswerving support of the majority of the whites, Smith maintained UDI for 14 years, until finally being brought down in 1980 by a combination of guerrilla war and international pressure. For the first half of this period Smith could claim a degree of success: international economic sanctions proved ineffective and economic prosperity for most whites continued. Smith obtained the practical support of Portugal (which still controlled neighbouring Mozambique) and South Africa (which provided his regime with material and, later, military assistance). An attempted constitutional settlement with the United Kingdom in 1971 was decisively rejected when African opinion was consulted by the Pearce Commission. Thereafter, the guerrilla war dominated events.

ARMED STRUGGLE

Repressive measures preceding UDI had virtually neutralized the African nationalist opposition, which had been further weakened by a split in 1963 into the Zimbabwe African People's Union (ZAPU), led by Joshua Nkomo, and the breakaway Zimbabwe African National Union (ZANU), led by Rev. Ndabaningi Sithole and later by Robert Mugabe. Nevertheless, shortly after UDI, elements of the banned nationalist parties in exile sent guerrilla units into the country from Zambia in the hope of provoking external intervention to remove the Smith regime. When these actions proved ineffectual, the nationalists sought to develop a 'people's war' in an attempt to overthrow the Smith regime. ZAPU, based mainly in Zambia, received training and armaments from the USSR, although its operations within Zimbabwe were confined mainly to majority Ndebele areas. ZANU developed strong links with the Frente de Libertação de Moçambique (Frelimo) movement fighting the Portuguese in Mozambique, and with the People's Republic of China. It concentrated on infiltration and rural mobilization in the Shona-speaking areas in the north-east, and later in the eastern and central areas of the country. Active operations began in December 1972, and ZANU's initial successes were enhanced when a Frelimo-dominated government took control in Mozambique in September 1974.

Alarmed at the apparent radicalization of the nationalist movement in the context of the cold war, the United Kingdom, the USA, South Africa and Zambia each sought to bring about a settlement; however, after a confused period of *détente* politics in the mid-1970s, the war resumed with new intensity. From 1976 it was waged in the name of the Patriotic Front (PF), an uneasy alliance formed by ZAPU and ZANU, and backed by the 'front-line' states, i.e. those African countries most involved in the Zimbabwean conflict. Within the country, the regime relied on terror and propaganda in a vain attempt to counter the growing civilian support for the armed struggle. Nevertheless, mounting unemployment and the guerrillas' own excesses helped to provide numerous black recruits into the government's security forces. By 1979 economic difficulties, declining white morale and guerrilla inroads in the rural areas led Smith to fashion what was termed an 'internal settlement', which took the form of a black surrogate regime under the leadership of Bishop Abel Muzorewa. 'Zimbabwe Rhodesia', as the country was briefly known under Muzorewa, was unable to improve conditions for ordinary Africans, obtain international recognition or end the war. Within less than a year all the parties to the conflict agreed to participate in the Lancaster House constitutional conference, under the chairmanship of the British secretary of state for foreign and commonwealth affairs, which was to lead to the birth of the independent state of Zimbabwe on 18 April 1980.

THE INDEPENDENCE SETTLEMENT

The conference, which also had to negotiate a cease-fire and mutually acceptable transitional arrangements, began on 10 September 1979 and lasted for 14 weeks, an agreement being signed on 21 December, nine days after UDI had been renounced. The British and their allies, including South Africa, were convinced of the need to end the war through negotiations which would involve the PF in the political process, but still believed that an outright PF government could be avoided. The PF was itself under intense pressure to negotiate from the 'front-line' states, which themselves had come under attack from Zimbabwe Rhodesia's increasingly well-equipped military forces. These attacks, together with the war inside the country and the other pressures, continued throughout the conference and helped the British to obtain their own settlement proposals more or less without alteration. Continuity was stressed in the adoption of the prime ministerial system in preference to an executive presidency, in the disproportionate political influence reserved to the white minority (20 of the 100 seats in the house of assembly), and in such matters as citizenship and state pensions. In particular, the compensation clause attached to land reform was strongly opposed by the PF, and was accepted only after vague assurances had been given about a future multinational fund to assist in the urgent problems of land redistribution.

Arrangements for the transitional period and the cease-fire also caused considerable friction. The cease-fire, involving the assembly of more than 20,000 guerrillas at 16 designated sites, could only be supervised, not enforced, by the small Commonwealth monitoring force. Nor could the appointment as governor of Lord Soames (a senior British politician and diplomatist), to replace the Muzorewa-Smith administration and to direct the transition, hide the fact that he remained dependent on the former regime and its notorious security forces, sections of which conducted a campaign of bombing and vilification directed against Mugabe and his party. Cease-fire violations, intimidation, rumours of a possible white coup and threatening statements from South Africa also contributed to an atmosphere of crisis. None the less, following elections in February 1980, a substantially peaceful transition was accomplished.

The ZANU wing of the PF, confident of the allegiance of the population in the large part of the country in which its guerrillas had operated, decided to contest the election as a separate party under the leadership of Robert Mugabe. His main rival, Joshua Nkomo, hoped that his reputation as the 'father' of Zimbabwean nationalism would help ZAPU–PF win support throughout the country and a majority in parliament. The two PF parties were challenged by Muzorewa's United African National Council (UANC), whose campaign received financial support from business interests and from South Africa. A number of minor parties which had supported the 'internal settlement' also put up candidates. The hopes which various anti-Mugabe interests inside and outside the country had in keeping him from power disappeared when ZANU–PF won 57 of the 80 'common roll' (African) seats in the house, receiving 63% of the votes. Nkomo's PF, which won 20 seats, mainly in Matabeleland, became the junior partner in the coalition government formed under Mugabe's premiership. This left only three seats for the UANC. Between them the two parties which had conducted the armed struggle received 87% of the votes in a turn-out estimated at 94% (in an earlier and separate election, the RF won all 20 seats reserved for whites). Rev. Canaan Banana, a prominent figure in the nationalist struggle, became Zimbabwe's first president, with ceremonial duties only.

RECONCILIATION

In the immediate period following his massive victory, Mugabe adopted a markedly conciliatory stance. To restore stability, he quickly stressed the need for reconciliation; disavowed rapid change towards his stated socialist goals; emphasized non-alignment in foreign affairs; and included two whites in his cabinet. Nevertheless, the new government was faced with formidable problems arising from the ravages of war and the expectations aroused in the struggle against settler rule.

As in other newly independent African countries, the rapid growth of educational opportunities for blacks offered one of the clearest signs of change. Scope for extensive Africanization was provided by the emigration of whites and by the expansion of government services (four years after independence, the white population had dropped by one-half, to about 100,000, not without causing grave shortages of skilled labour). Black labour unrest surfaced even before the independence celebrations, but may have been lessened by legislation on minimum wages and by a temporary reduction in the burden of direct taxation. Improvements in social welfare, however, did not prevent later strikes by transport workers, teachers and nurses. These challenges were forcefully met by the government. In 1985 criticism of the Labour Relations Act for unduly strengthening government control led to the arrest of union activists.

Land redistribution and the rehabilitation of the trust lands seemed likely to provide the greatest challenges to the government's aspirations and authority. For most Zimbabweans the struggles of recent decades have been about recovering the land, and the later stages of the war had much of the character of a peasant uprising. The strategic power and importance of the established commercial farming sector make the problem of meeting peasant needs daunting. The pace of official resettlement, slowed by drought, manpower shortages, restrictive provisions in the Lancaster House agreement and perhaps by lack of will, was not sufficient to head off extensive uncontrolled resettlement or to prevent the land issue from fuelling the dissidence in Matabeleland.

In the international field, the new Zimbabwe quickly made its mark. Extensive diplomatic relations were established with other countries in Africa, with the West, with the People's Republic of China and its allies and, more hesitantly, with the USSR and its allies. The Zimbabwe Conference on Reconstruction and Development (Zimcord), held in March 1981, was a notable success in substantially meeting its targets for aid. Zimbabwe also began to play a prominent part in the Southern African Development Co-ordination Conference (SADCC, now the Southern African Development Community–SADC). Mugabe made it clear that political and diplomatic support would be given to the opposition movements in neighbouring South Africa which were backed by the OAU.

POLITICS AND SECURITY

At independence it was necessary to consolidate the peace by integrating the three large, hostile and undefeated armies. British instructors were called in, but progress was slow at first and serious clashes, on party lines, between guerrilla groups in the vicinity of Bulawayo led to several hundred deaths. Nevertheless, by late 1981 the integration appeared to have been successfully completed. From outside ZANU–PF there was criticism of the creation of a specialist army brigade (the Fifth), of largely Shona composition trained by advisers from the Democratic People's Republic of Korea. However, Mugabe cited, in justification, the internal and external threats posed by disaffected supporters of the former regime, by unresolved tensions within the governing coalition, and by South Africa. In December 1981 the ZANU–PF headquarters were destroyed in a bomb attack. Subsequently, vital transport routes and petroleum facilities in Mozambique were sabotaged, the homes of government ministers attacked, and a substantial part of the air force destroyed.

Meanwhile, there was increasing discussion of the need for a one-party state. The prime minister stated that such a development should come about through persuasion, but other members of his party urged the need for speed and attacked the restrictive clauses of the Lancaster House constitution. Nkomo, who later made it known that he did not consider the election results to be valid and who had rejected Mugabe's offer of the presidency following the independence elections, refused to accept that a ZAPU merger with ZANU–PF was the best solution to the sharp regional polarization between the two coalition parties. In January 1981 Nkomo was demoted from his home affairs portfolio to a lesser cabinet office, and one year later he and some of his colleagues were dismissed altogether, following the discovery of substantial illegal arms caches on properties belonging to ZAPU in Matabeleland. Although there were some immediate outbreaks of pro-Nkomo dissident violence in the province, it was also significant that the remaining members of the coalition from the minority party failed to heed Nkomo's wish that they should resign. Mugabe threatened to bring

Nkomo to trial on charges of plotting a coup, but he also went out of his way to stress again his policy of reconciliation. The ZAPU ministers who had remained were promoted, and Mugabe also added two ex-RF members of parliament to his government. The RF, restyled the Republican Front in 1981, was still led by Ian Smith, having undergone a sizeable secession from its parliamentary ranks in protest at RF negativism since independence. In 1983 an RF faction sympathetic to the Mugabe government broke away to form the Independent Zimbabwe Group. By the June 1985 elections, the RF had reconstituted itself as the Conservative Alliance of Zimbabwe (CAZ).

Mugabe emerged from the crisis over the arms discoveries in a strong position, but the government's authority was increasingly challenged by events in Matabeleland. The acute land problems of the province, allied to the effects of a devastating drought, heightened the tense political situation. During 1982 dissidents from ZIPRA, ZAPU's former guerrilla army, and former colleagues who had deserted from the new national army, perpetrated numerous indiscriminate acts of violence. Their exact links with Nkomo and his party could not be fully established, but the government held ZAPU largely to blame for the worsening situation. It was also alleged that members of the former regime's forces who had moved to South Africa were providing a ready supply of personnel for covert operations, which the South African government was also suspected of supporting.

Early in 1983, and again in 1984, serious allegations of indiscipline and atrocities against civilians were made against the Fifth Brigade as it sought to suppress the dissidents and to protect the mainly white, commercial farming sector on which so much of the government's overall economic strategy rested. The allegations were supported by local churchmen, including the Roman Catholic authorities who had previously played a major part in exposing atrocities committed by the security forces of the Smith regime. Controversy over human rights issues continued when adverse reports, from Amnesty International, in 1985, and from the US-based Lawyers' Committee for Human Rights, were rejected by the prime minister.

In addition to the desire to oust ZAPU from its regional stronghold, the fear that a South African-backed dissident movement might reach the same devastating proportions as those already operating in Angola and Mozambique probably lay behind the government's decision to mount a forceful military campaign in Matabeleland in spite of the risk of alienating the province's mainly Ndebele-speaking population, Zimbabwe's principal minority language group. The prolonged nature of the operations in Matabeleland suggested more civilian support for the dissidents than was officially admitted, but, as the first general election since independence approached, there was increasing emphasis on the ruling party's need to achieve genuine political support in the province. The approaching election also intensified political violence elsewhere in the country.

A new party constitution, adopted by a ZANU–PF congress held in August 1984, greatly enlarged the central committee and introduced a new 15-member politburo. The congress dedicated itself to the 'victory of socialism over capitalism' and endorsed the aim of achieving a one-party Marxist-Leninist state under the leadership of ZANU–PF.

The first general elections since independence were held at the end of June 1985 (for the 20 'guaranteed' white seats) and in early July (for the 80 'common roll' seats). Ian Smith's CAZ won 15 of the 20 reserved seats. (However, following the elections, several CAZ representatives in the house of assembly either joined the ruling party or became independents.) In the election for the 80 black 'common roll' seats, almost 3m. votes were cast, 76% for ZANU–PF candidates, an increase of more than 12% on the proportion won in the 1980 elections. ZANU–PF increased its representation in the house of assembly by six seats to 64, although it failed to gain any of the Matabeleland seats held by Joshua Nkomo's ZAPU. Outside Matabeleland, however, ZAPU lost all five of the seats that it held in the previous parliament. ZANU–Sithole secured one seat, but Muzorewa's UANC failed to gain any representation.

ZANU–PF CONSOLIDATES

Following the elections, the drive towards a *de facto* one-party state was resumed, with reprisals against supporters of minority parties. The government's vigorous campaign against ZAPU led to the adverse report by Amnesty International referred to above, but it did not prevent the resumption of unity talks between ZAPU and ZANU–PF. Success seemed to be imminent on several occasions, especially following the release in 1986 of prominent ZAPU detainees. In April 1987, however, Mugabe abruptly abandoned the unity negotiations on the grounds that they had been deadlocked for too long. A resurgence of violence in Matabeleland and further measures against ZAPU's political activities followed the cancellation of the unity talks. Nkomo, however, continued to deny any involvement with the dissidents, and in July ZAPU indicated its continuing wish for negotiations with the ruling party by voting in favour of renewing the state of emergency.

A particularly brutal massacre in Matabeleland in November 1987 and the worsening security situation on the eastern border (see below) at last precipitated a unity agreement between ZAPU and ZANU–PF, healing the split of almost 25 years in the nationalist ranks. The agreement to merge the two parties, under the name of ZANU–PF, was signed by Mugabe and Nkomo in December, and was ratified by both parties in April 1988. According to the agreement, the new party was to be committed to the establishment of a one-party state with a Marxist-Leninist doctrine. The party was to be led by Mugabe, with Nkomo as one of two vice-presidents. Nkomo was offered a senior position in a new cabinet, while two other ZAPU officials were given government posts. An amnesty, proclaimed in April 1988, led to a rapid improvement in political and security conditions in Matabeleland.

Meanwhile, significant constitutional changes were moving Zimbabwe nearer to becoming a one-party state. The reservation for whites of 20 seats in the house of assembly and 10 seats in the senate was finally abolished in September 1987. In the following month the 80 remaining members of the assembly elected 20 candidates who were all nominated by ZANU–PF, including 11 whites, to fill the vacant seats. Candidates nominated by ZANU–PF, including four whites, were then elected to the vacancies in the senate by the new house of assembly. In October parliament adopted another major constitutional reform, whereby the ceremonial presidency was replaced by an executive presidency incorporating the post of prime minister. Robert Mugabe was nominated as sole candidate for the office, and on 31 December he was inaugurated as Zimbabwe's first executive president. His new enlarged cabinet included Joshua Nkomo as one of three senior ministers in the president's office who were to oversee policy and review ministerial performance, in association with the president. In November 1989 the house of assembly voted by the necessary majority to abolish the upper chamber of parliament, the senate. The single chamber was then enlarged from 100 to 150 seats, with effect from the next general election. In addition to 120 elected members, the change provided for eight provincial governors, 10 chiefs and 12 presidential nominees to be members of the assembly.

DISCONTENT AND 'CORRUPTION'

As unemployment and prices rose in 1988, open public and parliamentary criticism of corrupt government officials mounted. An anti-government demonstration by students in September resulted in many arrests. In October a former secretary-general of ZANU–PF, Edgar Tekere, was expelled from the party for his persistent denunciation of its leadership and policies, including the plans to introduce a one-party state; this action resulted in further student protest. In the same month allegations that government ministers had obtained new cars from the state-owned vehicle assembly plant in order to re-sell them at a profit, an illegal activity, first appeared in the Bulawayo *Chronicle*. The newspaper's editor was subsequently removed from his post. Amid intense public concern, Mugabe appointed a judicial commission of inquiry to investigate the newspaper's allegations: as a result of the commission's findings, five cabinet ministers and one provincial governor resigned from their posts in March and April 1989. Mugabe's establishment of the judicial commission of inquiry attracted initial public approval. At the behest of the ZANU–PF central committee, however, the charges against the former ministers were withdrawn, precipitating widespread protests and contributing to a tense political atmosphere, especially in urban areas.

Following publication of the judicial commission's report, Edgar Tekere, who had previously disavowed any intention of forming a new party, challenged the government's plans for a one-party state by founding the Zimbabwe Unity Movement (ZUM). Tekere denounced the government as corrupt, and proposed economic liberalization and the withdrawal of Zimbabwean troops from Mozambique. Although the new party was unable seriously to challenge ZANU–PF in five by-elections (held in July and October 1989)—partially, at least, owing to alleged official harassment and obstruction—the low level of electoral participation suggested a significant decline in the popularity of the governing party.

The government was embarrassed during 1989 by a series of conflicts with the judiciary and by strikes in the public service sector, but it was criticism by students which provoked the most serious political disturbances. In July a clash occurred between students and security police during a rally of ZUM supporters at the University of Zimbabwe, and, following further serious clashes, the university was closed from October 1990–April 1991. Unconvincingly, the government related the trouble to subversion from South Africa. When the Zimbabwe Congress of Trade Unions (ZCTU) issued a statement supporting the students, its secretary-general, Morgan Tsvangirai, was arrested and detained for six weeks (the cause of one particular conflict with the judiciary). During July 1990, however, the state of emergency was discontinued, owing to the reduction of tension in South Africa, although it was noted that the government retained wide powers of arrest and detention.

Political debate intensified during the ZANU–PF congress in December 1989. The congress was convened to complete the merger process with ZAPU, begun two years earlier (see above), but it required strong directive action from Mugabe to resolve the contentious issue of the distribution of party posts. There was also controversy concerning a proposed constitutional amendment to create a second vice-presidency, specifically for Joshua Nkomo, the former ZAPU leader. (Nkomo was officially appointed vice-president, in addition to the existing vice-president, Simon Muzenda, in August 1990.) Although Mugabe recommitted the new ZANU–PF to Marxism-Leninism and the one-party state, opposition to a one-party state was expressed within and outside the congress. Indeed, in August 1990 the ZANU–PF politburo voted to reject plans for the creation of a one-party state in Zimbabwe.

For the general election of March 1990, ZANU–PF chose to campaign against ZUM, its only serious opponent among the four opposition parties, on the general issue of national unity rather than on that of the one-party state. The election was marred by political violence, in which a ZUM candidate was seriously wounded, but the result of the poll appeared to be a fair reflection of the government's popularity. ZANU–PF secured 117 of the 120 elective seats (including one seat in which polling was initially postponed). However, electoral participation—estimated to be in the range of 54%–65%—had declined sharply in comparison with turn-outs of 95% and above in the two previous general elections. Moreover, ZUM, despite a controversial alliance with the CAZ and the disruption of some of its campaign activities, received almost 20% of the total votes. Significantly, ZUM performed even better in urban areas, especially in Harare, where it secured 30% of the votes. However, ZANU–PF's control of the seats was disrupted only in eastern Manicaland (owing, at least in part, to the difficulties occasioned by Mozambican guerrillas—see below), where ZUM obtained two seats and ZANU–Ndonga (formerly ZANU–Sithole) retained one. Overall, the distribution of votes in the election indicated that ZUM had achieved something approaching national status as an opposition party. However, its leader, Edgar Tekere, was overwhelmingly defeated in the contest for the remaining seat, even though the constituency was located in his home province of Manicaland. At the concurrent election for the presidency itself, Tekere received 413,840 votes, and Mugabe 2.03m. votes.

Mugabe's new cabinet included three whites as ministers, but its overall composition, to the annoyance of former ZAPU members, was little altered. Nevertheless, few doubted that, under the surface, the final year of the decade since independence had witnessed a substantial political shift. With more than 50% of the population below the age of 25 years, and with severe unemployment and other domestic problems, appeals by ZANU–PF to the heroism of the pre-independence struggle could no longer be regarded as relevant or powerful.

IDEOLOGICAL REASSESSMENTS

Meanwhile, following the adoption in 1991 of an Economic Structural Adjustment Programme (ESAP), 'Marxism-Leninism' was increasingly replaced in official discourse by references to 'pragmatic socialism' and 'indigenous capitalism'. Vigorous debate was also aroused by the expiry of the remaining restrictions of the Lancaster House agreement on 18 April 1990. Constitutional amendments which restored corporal and capital punishment and which denied recourse to the courts in cases of compulsory purchase of land by the government were enacted in April 1991, despite fierce criticism from the judiciary and from human rights campaigners.

Student unrest erupted once more following the publication in October 1990 of proposals for a substantial increase in government control of universities. A student boycott of classes on the issue in May 1991 won support in many quarters, but an attempt to march on the Commonwealth Prime Ministers' Conference held in Harare in October led to violence following heavy-handed police actions to prevent the students from leaving the campus. In May 1992, students, angry at eroded grants and the imposition of fees, found themselves once again in confrontation with the police. Subsequently, the 10,000 students of the University of Zimbabwe were expelled. Student protest was the most visible part of much wider discontent. In June, police prevented trade unionists from holding anti-government demonstrations. For workers, the extent and severity of the 1991/92 drought added to the economic difficulties already being blamed on the ESAP. Shortages, inflation, unemployment, corruption, government inertia and the stalled programme of land resettlement were the main grievances expressed. The discovery of extensive human remains, thought to date from the activities of the Fifth Brigade in its operations in Matabeleland in the 1980s (see above), added to the political *malaise*.

However, despite the government's evident unpopularity, the disorganized and divided state of the opposition continued to protect the government from serious challenge. A split in ZUM led to the formation in September 1991 of the ineffective Democratic Party. The unenthusiastic response outside his home area to the return to the country in January 1992 from self-imposed exile of Ndabaningi Sithole, ZANU's original leader and now leader of ZANU–Ndonga, underlined the discredit in which the older generation of nationalist politicians were now held.

In July 1992 ZANU–Ndonga, the UANC, ZUM and the CAZ formed an informal alliance, the United Front (UF), with the aim of defeating the government at the general elections due in 1995. Divisions soon emerged within the new grouping, whose manifesto, which attacked the executive presidency, eventually appeared in February 1993. Bishop Abel Muzorewa (see above) returned to active politics in January 1994 and merged the UANC with ZUM; later in that year Muzorewa founded a new opposition grouping, the United Parties (UP). In spite of efforts by another former prime minister, Ian Smith, the UF remained ineffective. Meanwhile, a non-party Forum for Democratic Reform, led by a former chief justice, Enoch Dumbutshena, and supported by a number of prominent Zimbabweans, was formed in May 1992. Following some controversy within the group, a separate Forum Party of Zimbabwe (FPZ), led by Dumbutshena, emerged in March 1993. Lacking a distinctive policy and a popular base, the FPZ made little headway subsequently, but continued to press for electoral reform. The expulsion of 22 of its members in March 1994 underlined the party's disarray.

The ZCTU found itself unable to capitalize on the widespread industrial unrest which took place in 1994. The organization was weakened by the resignation of its secretary-general, Morgan Tsvangirai, and by the loss of members due to the recession. When the ZCTU rejected the suggestion that it form its own party, a group of non-union figures opposed to the ESAP announced the formation of a Movement for Democracy in June 1994.

Meanwhile, amid the rising urban discontent fuelled by corruption scandals, falling real wages and the social consequences of the ESAP, the government was increasingly preoccupied by the land issue, which it continued to regard as the key to retaining its grip on power. The Land Acquisition Act (LAA), drafted following the expiry of the Lancaster House provisions, passed its final legislative phase on 19 March 1992 (see Economy). The new legislation, which paved the way for the compulsory acquisition of land by the state, brought the government into conflict with the powerful white-dominated Commercial Farmers' Union (CFU) and with Western aid donors. Both groups were angered by the decision in April 1993 to designate 70 commercially owned farms for purchase. Many of them were productive holdings which, it had been understood, were to be exempt from compulsory purchase. The government eventually allowed appeals in a sufficient number of cases—22—to suggest that an uneasy compromise had been reached. For its part, the CFU announced in September that it would assist in the government's resettlement programme, and its members were represented on the commission set up in November to make proposals for land tenure reforms. However, in March 1994, the government found itself once again under intense pressure when it was revealed that the first of the farms acquired under the LAA had been allocated to the government minister, Witness Mangwende, who had been minister of agriculture when the act was passed. The scandal escalated when the press revealed that most of the first 98 farms acquired by compulsory purchase had been leased to prominent party figures and civil servants and were not being used for peasant resettlement. The president responded by ordering the cancellation of all relevant leases. In November the high court ruled against three white farmers who had attempted to prove that the confiscation of their land was unconstitutional; the farmers subsequently lost an appeal to the supreme court against the verdict. Although the government has announced that land redistribution is to be accelerated, lack of resources make its target of resettling 100,000 smallholders over five years highly improbable. Indeed, the funds made available for resettlement were more than halved in the 1995/96 budget. In mid-1996 Mugabe requested financial assistance from the United Kingdom for the implementation of the land redistribution programme.

In spite of the popular discontent which had characterized its last term of office, the government won a fourth decisive general election victory on 8–9 April 1995. Eight opposition groups, including ZUM and the UP, boycotted the election, but, at 57%, the turnout of voters was much higher than expected. Of the six opposition parties which did contest the election, only the regionally-based ZANU–Ndonga won any seats in the house of assembly (two). ZANU–PF received more than 82% of the votes cast and secured 118 of the 120 elective seats (55 of them uncontested), as well as control of the 30 nominated and reserved seats. Most independent observers agreed that the elections had been largely 'free and fair', but they criticized aspects of the registration procedures, the ruling party's domination of the media and the Political Parties (Finance) Act of 1991, under which only organizations with at least 15 assembly members are entitled to state support. In August 1995 the high court nullified the election result in the bitterly contested Harare South constituency, when it was established that more votes had been cast than there were registered electors. This lent credence to opposition claims of widespread electoral malpractices by the Mugabe administration (despite the favourable pronouncement of the majority of independent observers—see above), and calls were made for both the annulment of all the results and the convening of an all-party constitutional conference to debate means of improving the implementation of democratic principles in the *de facto* one-party state.

The effects of a recurrence of drought and the impending implementation of the second stage of the unpopular SAP were the immediate problems which faced the new government. Against the known wishes of the IMF and World Bank, the president enlarged his government substantially in a post-election reshuffle, creating 13 new cabinet posts. Two women were included in the cabinet, and the number of former ZAPU members was doubled to four. The long-serving minister of finance, Dr Bernard Chidzero, was replaced by Ariston Chambati, reportedly to the satisfaction of the country's major business interests. Chambati, however, died suddenly in October 1995; he was replaced by Dr Herbert Murerwa, hitherto minister of industry and commerce. Meanwhile, during June–August 1995 a series of protests were made by students at the University of Zimbabwe in Harare who were dissatisfied with the level and administration of their grants; such student action frequently escalated into violent confrontations with the security forces.

At local elections which took place in October 1995 some 15 independent and dissident ZANU–PF candidates won representation on local councils. During that month Rev. Sithole, the leader of ZANU–Ndonga, was arrested and charged with conspiracy to assassinate Mugabe, in association with the Chimwenjes, a group of mainly Zimbabwean dissidents based in Mozambique; Sithole strongly denied the accusation. In early November there was rioting in Harare, reportedly instigated by ZANU–PF supporters who infiltrated a peaceful protest against alleged brutality by the security forces.

Mugabe ws returned to office at a presidential election on 16–17 March 1996, winning 92.7% of the votes cast. There was, however, a turnout of only 31.7% of the eligible electorate. The election was also unwillingly contested by Muzorewa (who took 4.7% of the votes) and Sithole, who had been released on bail (2.4%); they had been denied permission to withdraw their candidacies prior to the ballot. In late March Mugabe was sworn in for a third term as president. In early May the cabinet was extensively reorganized. In June Nkomo announced his intention to resign his position as one of Zimbabwe's two vice-presidents in the near future, on the grounds of ill health.

In late August and early September 1996 thousands of civil servants demanding salary increases organized a national strike; in October and November there were further strikes by nurses and junior doctors (who claimed that agreed pay increments had not been implemented), as a result of which many of Zimbabwe's hospitals were unable to function. In October it was announced that ZANU–PF was officially abandoning Marxism-Leninism as its guiding principle. In December the minister of education, Edmund Garwe, resigned; he was replaced by Gabriel Machinga, previously a deputy minister. In February 1997 a former aide-de-camp to Banana in the early 1980s, Jefta Dube, made allegations that the then president had sexually assaulted him, and in April 1997 Dube lodged a civil suit for damages against Banana. In July it was announced that criminal charges were to be brought against the former president. The allegations received considerable international attention, since Mugabe had of late made a number of much-publicized condemnations of homosexual practices. Meanwhile, in April the white minister of agriculture, Dennis Norman, resigned, reportedly because he had lost support among the white farming community; he was also said to be dissatisfied that his advice was not being heeded by the government. In May a report compiled by the Legal Resources Foundation and the Catholic Commission for Justice and Peace emerged (prior to official publication), detailing atrocities allegedly committed by security forces in Matabeleland in the early 1980s (see above). A reorganization of the cabinet in July, in which a number of ministries were merged, was attributed to pressure from international creditors. In the midst of a number of protests in July and August by veterans of the armed struggle for independence, a commission of inquiry was set up to investigate the alleged misappropriation by members of government and their families of funds intended to assist such veterans; in late August it was announced that the veterans were to be awarded a number of unpriced benefits, as well as tax-free pensions and gratuity payments. Corruption once again became a prominent issue in 1997, with allegations that official contracts were being unfairly tendered and that ministerial funds were being used to finance the construction of homes for civil servants and government ministers.

THE SOUTHERN AFRICAN CRISIS

Regional instability and the issue of South Africa dominated Zimbabwe's foreign relations in the first decade of independence. High priority was given to co-operation with Zimbabwe's other neighbours through the SADCC (now the SADC—see above) and the Preferential Trade Area for Eastern and Southern African States (later superseded by the Common Market for Eastern and Southern Africa). Robert Mugabe's strong support for mandatory sanctions against South Africa brought him into conflict with the United Kingdom and the USA, but enhanced Zimbabwe's standing in the Non-Aligned Movement.

The activities of the South African-backed insurgent guerrilla group, the Resistência Nacional Moçambicana (Renamo) in Mozambique posed a threat to Zimbabwe's alternative access to the sea via the Beira corridor during the 1980s and early 1990s, and as a result, Zimbabwe provided military assistance to the Mozambique government. Following the death of President Machel of Mozambique in an air crash in October 1986, Mugabe reiterated his support for the Mozambique government. Renamo consequently declared war on the Zimbabwe government, and cross-border incursions and civilian deaths became a regular occurence. In late 1992–early 1993, under the terms of a cease-fire between Renamo and the Mozambique government, Zimbabwean troops, who had been stationed in Mozambique since 1982, were withdrawn. By 1992 it was estimated that 250,000 Mozambican refugees were sheltering in Zimbabwe. Plans for the repatriation of some 145,000 Mozambican refugees were announced in March 1993; this scheme, under the auspices of UNHCR, was completed during the mid-1990s. By January 1997 Zimbabwe's refugee population had dwindled to an estimated 1,400. The SADC has enlisted the support of private business interests, including Zimbabwean companies, and of Western governments, for the Beira corridor rehabilitation project in Mozambique, which is of great importance to Zimbabwe's economy. President Mugabe played a leading role in mediating the cease-fire between the Mozambique government and Renamo. Following the end of the Mozambican conflict, the Zimbabwe government announced in May 1993 that the size of the country's armed forces was to be reduced from almost 49,000 troops to 35,000 over a five-year period. It was confirmed in April 1995 that a group of armed Zimbabwean dissidents (known as 'Chimwenjes') had occupied abandoned Renamo bases in Mozambique; in July it was reported that hundreds of former Renamo rebels had joined them. In June 1996 the Zimbabwean and Mozambican governments agreed to co-operate in combating the Chimwenjes, who were mounting attacks in both countries. A dispute with Zambia in 1997 over the possession of two islands in the Zambezi river was to be submitted to international arbitration.

The support given by Zimbabwe to the Mozambique government, and the leading role taken by Mugabe in advocating the imposition of economic sanctions against South Africa, resulted in direct retaliatory action against Zimbabwe by the South African government during the 1980s. In May 1987 South African defence forces launched two raids, within a week, on alleged bases of the African National Congress of South Africa (ANC) in Harare. Bomb explosions in Harare in October 1987 and in Bulawayo in January 1988 were widely regarded as further attempts by South Africa to destabilize the Zimbabwe government. In June 1988 an attempt by a South African commando unit to release five alleged South African agents who were awaiting trial in Zimbabwe was thwarted by Zimbabwean security forces; three of the detainees were found guilty in June 1989 of taking part in bomb attacks on ANC targets. The detainees were eventually released in July 1990. Diplomatic relations with South Africa were resumed following the holding of democratic elections in that country in April 1994. With democratic government finally established in South Africa, Zimbabwe lost some of the regional pre-eminence it had enjoyed since its independence in 1980. Political and economic relations with its mighty, if now friendly neighbour, will continue to be a dominant concern for Zimbabwe in the future.

In a wider international context, Zimbabwe's supportive role as a member of the UN security council during the Gulf war and its IMF-approved economic liberalization policies helped to overcome the tension with the USA which had surfaced in the mid-1980s (see above). Mugabe's meeting in Washington, DC, with President Bush in July 1991 confirmed the new relationship. In February 1993 a small number of troops from both countries engaged in joint training manoeuvres. During the 1990s Zimbabwe has contributed troops to UN operations in Mozambique, Rwanda, Somalia and Angola. In May 1995 Mugabe visited President Clinton and drew attention (as he had also done on a state visit to the United Kingdom in the previous year) to Zimbabwe's pressing need for foreign capital.

Economy

LINDA VAN BUREN

In the decade following independence, economic growth in Zimbabwe was uneven, fluctuating in conformity with the effect of rainfall on agricultural production, with world prices for the country's main exports, and with changes in government economic policy. None the less, with an abundance of natural resources, a well-developed infrastructure and a diversified industrial sector, Zimbabwe is better placed than most African economies to withstand the effects of commodity price fluctuations, and to recoup short-term set-backs.

High levels of economic growth were recorded in the first two fiscal years following independence on 18 April 1980. Gross domestic product (GDP) grew in real terms by 11% in 1980 and by 13% in 1981. A major factor in these growth levels was the withdrawal, in 1980, of economic sanctions (which had crippled the economy during the 15 years of unilaterally declared independence–UDI); increased trade with the outside world rapidly stimulated economic activity.

The degree to which the phenomenal growth levels of 1980 and 1981 were artificially caused by the temporary overinflation of the economy was illustrated graphically in the following three fiscal years. GDP stagnated in real terms in 1982 and retreated by 3.5% in 1983. There was positive growth in 1984, but only at a very low level of 1% in real terms. This downturn also reflected the onset of a serious drought that lasted three years and was to postpone until 1984/85 the entry of Zimbabwe's 800,000 peasant farmers into the formal agricultural economy. Real GDP growth advanced to 7.3% in 1985. The country's first Five-Year Development Plan, introduced in April 1986 and covering the period 1986–90, was based on an average annual real GDP growth of 5.1% for the term of the Plan. This target proved to be optimistic. GDP growth in 1986, which had been projected at 3%, reached only 0.18%. In 1987 GDP growth remained virtually stagnant, at 0.3%. In 1988 GDP grew by 5.3%, exceeding the Plan target of 5%. The recovery was attributable to an increase of 20% in the value of agricultural production, owing to improved rainfall, and to high commodity prices. GDP growth slowed slightly in the following three years, to 4% in 1989, 3.8% in 1990 and 2.9% in 1991. As a result of the region's drought, GDP fell by 8.9% in 1992. Positive growth returned in 1993, at 3.0%, increasing to 6.1% in 1994. The government's growth target for 1995 was reduced from 5% to 1%, owing to a recurrence of drought in the 1994/95 growing season; in the event negative real GDP growth was recorded (–2.3%). Rainfall was abundant in 1995/96; real GDP growth of 8.1% was estimated for 1996 and 5% growth forecast for 1997, although this projection was later revalued downwards, owing to excessive rainfall in 1996/97. The annual average growth rate of GDP during the first 13 years of Zimbabwean independence was 2.7%.

NATIONAL INCOME

Zimbabwe's GDP at current prices grew steadily from Z.$3,224m. in 1980 to Z.$7,303m. in 1985 and, according to the IMF, to Z.$16,655m. in 1990, increasing further to Z.$56,864m. in 1995 and to Z.$74,700m. in 1996.

The population, which was officially estimated to be 12.29m. at August 1997, increased by some 3.3% per annum, according to official figures, during 1982–97, so population growth has slightly exceeded economic growth. Real GDP per caput grew by an estimated 1.5% annually during 1980–85; it declined sharply, by 11%, in 1986, and it fell again, although less steeply, in 1987. A return to positive growth in 1988, at 1.1%, was followed by a negligible growth rate of 0.4% in 1989 and 0.2% for 1990. Subsequently, real GDP per caput declined, by 2.3% in 1991, by 11.3% in 1992 (influenced by drought) and by 0.5%

in 1993; in 1994 it increased by 2.6%, before decreasing by 5.5% in 1995. In 1996 real GDP per caput grew by some 4.7%.

Although Zimbabwe has one of sub-Saharan Africa's most successful agricultural sectors, agriculture ranks only third, behind services and manufacturing, in terms of contribution to GDP. Services accounted for 48% of GDP in 1993, followed by manufacturing at 30%, agriculture at 15% and mining at 6%.

The most notable trend in domestic expenditure in the 1980s was the decline in the private sector's share, from 63% in 1980 to 53% in 1986, and to 44% in 1989. The downward trend was reversed in 1990, however, when the private sector accounted for 53% of total spending; the sector's share grew to 61% in 1991 and to 71% in 1992, reflecting almost immediately the Economic Structural Adjustment Programme (ESAP) introduced in 1991, which envisaged continued growth of private consumption. The private sector's share in domestic expenditure had increased to 78% in 1996.

The World Bank Consultative Group for Zimbabwe held a donors' conference in Paris in February 1992, at which donors pledged about US $1,000m., of which US $500m. was in the form of balance of payments support. A further Consultative Group meeting, held in Paris in December 1992, pledged US $1,400m. for 1993, of which US $800m. was in support of the balance of payments. The Consultative Group convened again in December 1993 in Paris and pledged US $789m. in loans and grants to Zimbabwe in 1994. By 1995, however, relations between the Zimbabwe government and the Bretton Woods institutions had deteriorated significantly, and the IMF suspended assistance worth US $100m. in mid-1995, pending a reduction in Zimbabwe's budgetary deficit. Multilateral credit and bilateral balance-of-payments support remained suspended in 1996/97 and in 1997/98, following a failure to attain targets for economic reform.

LAND POLICIES

Access to productive land in Zimbabwe remains, 16 years after independence, of crucial importance in determining the degree to which the vast majority of the Zimbabwean people can contribute to the country's national production.

Before independence, the country's land was divided into five grades; the most productive cropland was classified as Grade I, the least productive as Grade V. Whites were allocated 78% of all Grade I and II land, and, in the early 1990s, 4,000 commercial farmers, the overwhelming majority of them white, still occupied over one-half of the most productive land. Grade IV and V land, deemed fit only for the grazing of livestock, accounted for 75% of the land allocated to smallholders, in what are known as the 'communal areas'. In March 1992 some 7.5m. black Zimbabweans were still crowded on 16m. ha (40m. acres).

After independence, the government undertook to 'resettle' landless Zimbabweans on commercial farmland acquired from willing sellers among the white commercial farmers. By 1990, about 52,000 families had been resettled on 2.7m. ha—only about 32% of the target set in the 1982–85 Transitional National Development Plan, which envisaged the resettlement of 162,000 families by 1985. Under the 1980 constitution, the government was permitted, until 1990, to acquire land compulsorily for purposes of resettlement if it was 'under-utilized'. After 1990 expectations were directed towards an acceleration in land reform measures. In March 1992 the house of assembly unanimously passed the Land Acquisition Act, which permitted the compulsory acquisition of land by the state, smoothing the way for the compulsory purchase of 5.5m. ha of the 11m. ha of land then still held by white farmers. The purchased land was to be used to resettle small-scale farmers from the communal areas. After much debate, the Act stopped short of detailing the white farmers' guarantee of fair compensation. In April 1993 the government announced that it was to acquire 70 farms, covering some 190,000 ha; protests ensued from the white-dominated Commercial Farmers' Union. The high court subsequently ruled against three white farmers who had attempted to prove that the confiscation of their land was unconstitutional. (A later appeal to the supreme court was also lost.) In March 1994 it emerged that a former cabinet minister and other senior politicians and government officials had obtained favourable leases to some of the forcibly purchased farms. President Mugabe abrogated the leases and announced a detailed study of the land-tenure and land-use system. In mid-1996 Mugabe requested financial assistance from the United Kingdom for the acceleration of the resettlement process. In 1996 the acquisition of land by foreign investors was only permissible in areas of low rainfall, and only in cases (subject to government approval) where a project would upgrade an economically marginal area, bring significant industrialization to a primary agricultural region, create major employment opportunities or introduce a new form of export processing; plans were announced in mid-1997 to bar foreigners and companies from owning land, following the announcement in June that the National Land Acquisition Committee had concluded its programme of identifying land for reallocation. Further plans to tax large agricultural holdings were also proposed. By August 1997 only 3.4m. ha of land had been acquired since independence; it was reported that some 450,000 ha had been overrun by squatters. In the same month, plans were announced to acquire 1,072 farms, covering 3.2m. ha, to resettle landless peasants, and a further 700 farms, covering 1.3m. ha, for indigenous commercial farming.

AGRICULTURE

Zimbabwe has a diversified and well-developed agricultural sector, in terms of food production, cash crops and livestock. About 67% of the total labour force and 27% of the formal-sector labour force were engaged in agricultural activity in 1995. Agriculture (including forestry) contributed 14% of GDP in 1996 (compared with 17% in both 1980 and 1985 and 12.4% in 1990), rising to 20% in 1991 and 22% in 1992; in 1993 the sector's contribution to GDP fell back to 15%. Agricultural output declined by some 12% in 1995, but an expansion of 18% was forecast for 1996. Sales of crops and livestock rose from Z.$1,164.7m. in 1988 to Z.$2,374.3m. in 1990 and, further, to Z.$3,412m. in 1991 and to Z.$6,041m. in 1992, falling back slightly to Z.$5,663m. in 1993.

The staple food crop is maize, and other cereal crops grown include wheat, millet, sorghum and barley. Despite the fact that the country's best farmland was still concentrated overwhelmingly in the commercial sector, the share of agricultural output contributed by small-scale farmers in the communal areas rose from 9% in 1983 to 25% in 1988. Communal and small-scale farmers contributed 50% of total agricultural production in 1989/90.

In 1996 Zimbabwe enjoyed a bumper harvest of 2.6m. metric tons of maize, more than three times as much as had been harvested in 1995 (some 840,000 tons), when crops had been affected by drought. In 1994/95 deliveries of maize to the marketing organizations reached 1.42m. metric tons, compared with deliveries of 1.1m. tons in 1993/94, 13,000 tons in 1992/93 (owing to severe drought), 1.19m. tons in 1991/92 and 675,000 tons in 1990/91. Total output of maize was 2.6m. tons in 1995/96, compared with 1.75m. tons in 1994/95, 1.8m. tons in 1993/94, 362,000 tons in 1992/93, 1.6m. tons in 1990/91, 1.99m. tons in 1989/90, 2.05m. tons in 1985/86 and 2.5m. tons in 1984/85. Zimbabwe also produces some 11,250 tons of maize oil annually. In 1985 the Grain Marketing Board (GMB) initiated a silo-development programme, costing Z.$65m., which aimed to increase its storage capacity from 435,000 tons to 1m. tons. Silos were built in the communal areas, with a view to eliminating the necessity of importing storage bags, and thereby potentially saving some Z.$27m. in foreign exchange per year. The first stage of the programme, covering 1985–90, involved the construction of seven silos with a combined capacity of 300,000 tons. The programme continued into the 1990s.

Added storage is also needed to help Zimbabwe meet its food storage requirements in times of plenty, so as to provide adequate food security for periods of drought. With domestic maize demand running at about 2m. tons a year, Zimbabwe had accumulated a surplus of 1.3m. tons by mid-1985 and stocks of 1.9m. tons by April 1987. Exports began in earnest in 1985 (see below), and continued until October 1987, when they were suspended as a precaution against the effects on the maize crop of the drought in the 1986/87 growing season. After good rains in December 1987 (excessive in some areas), exports resumed in April 1988. In 1990/91 poor rains restricted farmers' deliveries to the GMB to only 675,000 tons, causing the Board to use some of the country's strategic maize stocks of 714,000 tons, carried over from the 1989/90 season. The GMB in mid-1991 expected to have closing maize stocks of 300,000 tons at March 1992, 40% less than the minimum carry-over requirement of 500,000 tons. This shortfall was extremely untimely, as the 1992/93 drought reduced deliveries in that crop year to a mere 13,000 tons, finding the government unprepared despite its expenditure of substantial sums to ensure a higher level of preparedness than in previous seasons. The November 1993–March 1994 rains were shorter than usual, causing maize output to fall slightly below the country's annual requirement; however, strategic stocks were adequate to meet the shortfall. In mid-1996 the strategic grain reserve was set at a statutory 936,000 tons and a strategic grain reserve fund (initially totalling more than Z.$1,000m.) was established.

In May 1985 Zimbabwe became the first African country to donate its own food aid to Ethiopia, sending 25,000 metric tons to famine victims in that country. The World Food Programme (WFP) bought 100,000 tons of Zimbabwean grain in 1988 for distribution to Malawi, Botswana and Mozambique. In 1990 the WFP undertook to transport at least 60,000 tons of Zimbabwe maize to drought victims in Angola, Malawi, Mozambique and Zaire. The almost complete failure of the long rains in the November 1991–March 1992 rainy season, however, plunged Zimbabwe, as well as its neighbours in the region, into the worst drought of the century. Having imported maize only three times in the previous 75 years, Zimbabwe faced the necessity of importing 2m. tons of maize—and this time it had to come from overseas, as South Africa's crop was also affected by the drought. The food crisis affected Zimbabwe until the second quarter of 1993, when, owing to the generous November 1992–March 1993 rains, the next crop rose above expectations. Although drought was the most serious factor leading to lower maize output, the shortages were also influenced by the reduced volume of maize intake by the GMB in 1991, down by 23% from the 1990 figure, primarily because low official prices payable to producers had led many farmers to abandon planting maize (in favour of groundnuts, sunflower seeds and, especially, soya beans). The government's policy had been a deliberate bid to keep what then seemed to be more and more excess maize from pouring into the country's overstretched storage facilities. Producer prices were raised in March 1992 from Z.$325 per metric ton of maize to Z.$550. In June 1993 controls on maize prices were abolished.

Zimbabwe consistently fails to meet its high domestic requirement of wheat (350,000 metric tons per annum), and imports are necessary. Output rose to a record 326,823 metric tons in 1990/91 before falling back to 259,000 tons in 1991/92. During the 1991/92 season, the government raised the producer price for wheat by 20.6% and the price to the flour mills by 119%. Owing to the severe drought, wheat output for 1992/93 fell to only 58,000 tons, or enough to supply the milling industry for two months. Some 340,000 tons of wheat were to be imported in 1992. Wheat output in 1993/94 was 300,000 tons. Output in 1995 was only 83,000 tons, but in 1996 production was estimated at 275,000 tons; the export quota was doubled to 100,000 tons.

In the financial year to 31 March 1996 the GMB recorded a preliminary profit of Z.$50m., compared with a Z.$1,000m. loss in 1994/95. The government's decision to take responsibility for debts amounting to Z.$4,000m. owed collectively by the GMB, the Cotton Marketing Board (CMB) and the Cold Storage Commission (CSC) contributed to the GMB's improved performance.

National Breweries Ltd produces 8,000–10,000 metric tons of malt per year for export (although output was considerably lower following the devastating effect of the 1991/92 drought on the barley crop). Zimbabwe's barley output was 28,000 tons in 1985, up from 8,500 tons in 1984 and 11,500 tons in 1983. According to FAO estimates, production reached 29,000 tons in 1987 and 1988 and 30,000 tons in 1989. However, the drought-affected 1992 barley crop was only about 15% of normal levels, or 4,500 tons. Output improved to an estimated 24,000m. tons in 1993, but was estimated at only 8,000 tons in 1994. In the latter year production of all cereals declined by 5.4%, and in 1995 total cereal output slumped by 54.3%, owing to a recurrence of drought. In 1995 Zimbabwe produced: 30,400 metric tons of millet, 29,500 tons of sorghum, 52,000 tons of groundnuts in shells, 77,000 tons of soya beans, 22,000 tons of sunflower seeds and 46,000 tons of dry beans, as well as 3,780 tons of groundnut oil, 5,250 tons of soya bean oil and 2,664 tons of sunflower seed oil. The horticultural sector performed well in 1994, producing 850 tons of peaches and nectarines, 350 tons of pears, 120 tons of plums, 40 tons of apricots and 40 tons of papayas. Horticultural produce is regularly freighted to Europe; in 1997 exports of flowers were expected to amount to some 15,000 tons, while horticultural exports as a whole earned Z.$514m. in 1994/95.

Zimbabwe's principal cash crops are tobacco, cotton and sugar. Tobacco contributes about 66% of the agricultural export revenue and employs 12% of the work-force. Zimbabwe's golden-yellow 'lemon leaf' variety is highly prized by blenders. Tobacco auctions each year normally begin in April, and last for 25 weeks. Output marketed in 1989/90 was 129,900 metric tons, an increase of 8% in volume terms from marketed output of 119,913 tons in 1988/89. The crop marketed in 1988/89 was of exceptionally high quality, attaining an average price per kg of Z.$4.30 and a total value of Z.$640m., compared with an average price per kg of Z.$2.15 and a total value in export earnings of Z.$278.9m. in 1987/88. The crop marketed in 1989/90, which earned Z.$971m. in export revenue, attained an even higher average price, of Z.$6.48 per kg, producing almost Z.$860m. for the total crop. The 1990/91 crop amounted to 155m. kg of flue-cured tobacco, raising anticipated tobacco revenue to more than Z.$1,000m. Despite the drought, growers produced 201m. kg in 1991/92, in a year when 19% more farmers planted tobacco on 17% more hectarage than in 1990/91. Exports of tobacco reached their highest quarterly level ever in October–December 1991, at more than 51m. kg. The crop in 1992/93 totalled a record 210m. kg, and was of superior quality. However, prices obtained at the opening of the 1993 auctions were only 97 US cents per kg, about one-half the levels of a year previously. This adverse development was the result of substantially reduced world demand for tobacco. Prices fetched did not even cover most growers' costs, and, consequently, they incurred an aggregate debt of Z.$400m. In the 1993/94 season, output fell to 182m. kg, but prices subsequently recovered. Tobacco production totalled 200m. kg in 1994/95, rising to 210m. kg in 1995/96. Exports of tobacco in 1996 earned Z.$6,800m., with the European Union and the Far East the most important destinations. The area under tobacco cultivation was 85,000 ha in 1995, down from the record level of 93,000 ha in 1993. Smallholders have become increasingly involved in the cultivation of burley tobacco. The flue-cured sector is far larger, with commercial farmers accounting for most of the output. In 1996 the government imposed a 10% tax on tobacco sales, which was bitterly opposed by farmers and merchants, who claimed that it would damage the sector.

The proportion of cotton produced by communal farmers rose from 46% in 1987/88 to 60% in 1989/90, before falling back to 55% in 1990/91, as low real producer prices led farmers to plant other crops instead. Commercial area under cotton fell from 55,700 ha in 1988/89 to 40,666 ha in 1989/90, and communal area declined from 12,000 ha in 1988/89 to 11,000 ha in 1989/90. Deliveries of seed cotton amounted to a record 323,239 metric tons in 1987/88, but slumped to 262,000 tons in 1988/89 and to 219,000 tons in 1989/90, before recovering to 280,000 tons in 1990/91. (The crop year runs from 1 March to 28 February.) Heavy rains during the cotton-picking season contributed to the 1988–90 disappointment, but also blamed by many farmers was the seed that they had purchased from the CMB. Growers reported that the plants from these seeds wilted soon after germination, and the crops of both large- and small-scale growers were affected. The drought of 1992 further reduced cotton output, to 21,000 tons in that year. Output recovered, however, to 67,000 tons in 1993, stabilizing at 65,000 tons in 1994. Zimbabwe was unable to profit from high global cotton prices in 1995, as drought reduced the size of the domestic crop in that year. In 1996 output recovered considerably, to 283,000 tons, and production in 1997 was expected to be slightly less. Output of cottonseed declined to 39,000 tons in the drought-affected year of 1992, but recovered to 119,000 tons in 1993. Cottonseed production totalled 109,000 tons in the 1994 growing season, falling back to 64,000 tons in 1995. Output of cotton lint declined to 36,000 tons in 1995, from 60,000 tons in 1994. Production of cottonseed oil was only 7,230 tons in 1995 (compared with 17,280 tons in 1994).

Sugar earned an estimated Z.$308m. in 1990, compared with earnings of Z.$186.9m. in 1989 and of Z.$157.1m. in 1988. Drought affected the 1988 crop, but production nevertheless exceeded the national demand of 170,000 metric tons per annum. The 1992 drought cut the country's output of milled sugar to 35,000 tons, just 10% of normal levels. Cane production in 1992 fell to only 300,000 tons (compared with 3.2m. tons in 1991), necessitating the import of 132,000 tons from Cuba. Even after the return of rains in November 1992, the sugar industry did not make an immediate full recovery, and the 1993 cane harvest, at 538,000 tons, was still only a small proportion of normal levels of output. By 1994, however, the recovery was complete, with growers producing 3.4m. tons of cane (yielding 507,000 tons of milled sugar—900% of the 1993 level). Output of milled sugar in 1995 was 465,000 tons, with sugar imports forecast at 115,000 tons (expected to cost Z.$23m.). Cane production in that year totalled 3.48m. tons. An irrigation scheme has been proposed to make this very thirsty crop less vulnerable to drought in future. In 1993 the Commonwealth Development Corpn (CDC) loaned a total of £11m. for the re-establishment of canefields at Hippo Valley Estates Ltd and at Triangle Ltd, and a further £2m. to the Agricultural Finance Corpn of Zimbabwe for on-lending to the Chipiwa Growers' Co-operative Society Ltd. The 1992 drought is estimated to have killed up to 90% of the sugarcane plants in Zimbabwe's Lowveld region; despite good climatic conditions in 1996, the sector was unable to recover in time to benefit from them.

Coffee export revenue for Zimbabwe's mild arabicas rose from Z.$34m. in the 1984/85 season to Z.$50m. for the 1985/86 season, in which 11,000 metric tons were produced. Earnings from exports of arabica coffee reached Z.$75m. in the 1986/87 marketing year, but were estimated to have fallen to some Z.$45m. in 1987/88, reflecting the impact of drought on coffee production. The arabica crop doubled in 1988/89 to 12,500 tons, following favourable weather conditions; however, the value of exports was only Z.$54m., because of depressed world prices. The 1991/92 coffee crop was severely depressed, owing both to the severe drought and to low global prices. The 1992/93 coffee crop returned to near-normal levels, and world prices finally improved in May 1994, reaching a five-year high. However, production plummeted to an estimated 4,000 tons in 1995; in 1996, following good rains, output was forecast at more than 11,000 tons.

Zimbabwe is one of only a few sub-Saharan African countries allowed to export beef to the European Union (EU, formerly the European Community–EC) member states. Exports began in 1985; however, Zimbabwe was unable to meet its quota of 8,100 metric tons in the first two years (1985 and 1986), owing to a severe shortage of beef in the country. Beef allocations to butchers were reduced by 30% in 1986, when total beef sales realized some Z.$48m. (US $29.2m.). In an attempt to help the parastatal CSC survive in the face of competition from private-sector abattoirs, the government granted it a virtual monopoly of the urban market for beef from January 1987. However, producers argued that they needed a higher gazetted producer price in order to make their efforts economic. In April an increase of 38% in producer prices for beef was duly announced. Meanwhile, the government initiated major efforts to improve the financial position of the CSC, after a trading deficit of Z.$27.6m. was recorded in 1986 (increasing to Z.$28.9m. in 1987). With financing from the European Investment Bank (ECU 14m., or US $15.82m.) and from the Arab Bank for Economic Development in Africa (US $9.21m.), the CSC embarked upon a US $102m. project, under which a processing and distribution complex was to be built in Harare, a new abattoir was to be constructed in Bulawayo (with a daily capacity of 600 head of cattle), and the Masvingo abattoir was to be rehabilitated, with a planned capacity of 400 head of cattle per day. Zimbabwe fulfilled its EC quota of 8,100 metric tons of beef exports in 1987 (earning Z.$80m. from this source) and in 1988 (earning Z.$66.6m.). In 1989, however, the EC suspended its beef imports from Zimbabwe, owing to an outbreak of foot-and-mouth disease in April and May of that year. Exports were resumed in January 1992. In late 1987 domestic consumption of beef was restricted by the introduction of rationing. The 1992 drought led to a doubling of the intake of cattle at all abattoirs as herders rushed to sell their stock before they died of starvation. The CSC slaughtered 257,360 head of cattle during January–June 1992, more than double the number killed in July–December 1991. The drought reduced the national herd to 1.7m. head of cattle, but Zimbabwe was still able to meet its EU quota of high-quality beef, which had by then been increased to 14,600 tons. Zimbabwe produced 7,000 tons of dry milk, 2,000 tons of cheese and 3,000 tons of butter in 1995. Output of vegetable oils and margarines was 8,976 tons in that year.

In 1994 Zimbabwe's forestry sector produced 29,000 cu m of non-coniferous sawnwood, 3,000 cu m of non-coniferous sawlogs and veneer logs and 1.8m. cu m of industrial roundwood. Heavy rains in 1997 were expected substantially to reduce timber export earnings, which had amounted to more than US $10.9m. in 1996.

MINING AND MANUFACTURING

Mining contributed 7% of Zimbabwe's GDP in 1996 and generated Z.$6,500m. of export revenue in 1995 (45% of the total value of exports), up from Z.$4,500m. in the previous year. The value of mineral production was Z.$3,450m. in 1993 (of which gold accounted for Z.$1,370m.), Z.$1,836m. in 1991, Z.$1,324m. in 1990, Z.$1,197m. in 1989 and Z.$985.7m. in 1988. Steady performance is expected over the medium term, with the entry into full production of the Hartley platinum mine in June 1997 giving cause for optimism.

Zimbabwe currently produces more than 40 different minerals. Gold, nickel, asbestos, coal, copper, chromite, iron ore, tin, silver, emeralds, graphite, lithium, granite, cobalt, tungsten, quartz, silica sands, kyanite, vermiculite, corundum, magnesite, kaolin and mica are the main mineral products. Gold is the primary source of revenue in the mining sector, accounting for 40% of mineral sales by value in 1992. Production of gold amounted to 23.8 metric tons in 1996, well below the annual target figure and less than the 24.3 tons mined in 1995, but up from 20.5 metric tons in 1994, 18.7 tons in 1993, 18.5 tons in 1992, 17.34 tons in 1991, 16.9 tons in 1990 and 16.0 tons in 1989. In value terms, gold earned Z.$414.4m. in 1989, Z.$502.2m. in 1990, Z.$731.6m. in 1991, Z.$968m. in 1992, Z$1,400m. in 1993 and Z.$2,400m. in 1995. In November 1993 Cluff Resources of the UK (later acquired by Ashanti Goldfields of Ghana) reached an agreement with the Eastern and Southern African Trade and Development Bank for a 52,000–ounce gold loan to finance underground development of the Freda Rebecca gold mine, which had become Zimbabwe's largest gold mine by the end of 1994. The loan is repayable over five years and gives the borrower the choice of repaying in gold or US dollars. Nickel ranks second in export revenue, accounting for about 15.1% of total mineral export earnings in 1992. Output of nickel, spurred by a global upturn in demand, rose from 11,489 tons (valued at Z.$198m.) in 1988 and to 11,600 tons (valued at Z.$284m.) in 1989, before levelling off to 11,441 tons (valued at Z.$236.1m.) in 1990 and to 11,371 tons (valued at Z.$338.9m.) in 1991. Nickel production increased by 11% in 1993, but export value increased by only 7%. World prices for nickel remained depressed during 1992–94. Asbestos earned Z.$195.9m. in 1991 and Z.$145.8m. in 1990; output was 157,000 tons in 1993, compared with 187,066 tons in 1989. The association of asbestos with lung cancer has led to a decline in the value of exports. Coal output was 5.3m. tons in 1993 (compared with 2.9m. tons in 1981). Revenue from coal exports rose from Z.$119.2m. in 1989 to Z.$162.2m. in 1990 and to Z.$174.8m. in 1991. Rio Tinto Zimbabwe began operations in 1990 to develop the Sengwa coalfield in western Zimbabwe, which has a projected annual output of 100,000 tons of low-sulphur coal. Production of methane, or coal-bed gas, was expected to commence in the mid-1980s. Copper production fell in volume terms, from 15,659 tons in 1989, to 14,689 tons in 1990 and to 13,451 tons in 1991 although the value of output rose from Z.$74.9m. in 1989 to Z.$85.3m. in 1990 and to Z.$99.3m. in 1991. A declining trend in world copper prices culminated in a five-year price 'low' in May 1993. In 1997 it was reported that the Mhangura copper mine was no longer economical to run; loans and grants secured in that year were necessary to ensure its continued operation. Volume output of chromite fell slightly in 1991, to 570,749 tons from 573,103 tons in 1990, although in value terms earnings rose to Z.$101.5m. in 1991, a 68% rise over the Z.$60.3m. yielded in 1990. Chromite accounted for 5.2% of the total value of mineral production in 1992. Earnings from nickel, copper and chromite all suffered from the release of low-price supplies by Russia in 1992 and 1993. Output of iron ore (metal content 64%) was 1.16m. tons valued at Z.$49.83m. in 1991, compared with 1.26m. tons valued at Z.$44m. in 1990, 1.02m. tons valued at Z.$25.6m. in 1988 and 1.33m. tons valued at Z.$28.8m. in 1987. Output volume for silver declined from 21,154 tons in 1990 to 12,000 tons in 1993. Earnings from silver totalled Z.$10.94m. in 1991. Tin output declined from 808 tons in 1990 to 658 tons in 1993. Earnings from tin amounted to Z.$15.26m. in 1991. Platinum holds significant revenue potential. Substantial reserves of platinum are located in the Great Dyke mineral belt in central Zimbabwe. In 1990 Delta Gold announced plans to exploit them at the Hartley mine; development, which cost US $264m., began in that year, and trial mining was carried out in 1992. In December 1993, BHP of Australia made an investment of A$311m. (US $211m.)—said to be the largest single private sector investment in Zimbabwe since independence—to enable the Hartley project to go ahead. An underground mine came into operation in April 1996 and reached full production of 180,000 tons of platinum-bearing ore per month in June 1997. The mine, which has a projected lifespan of 70 years, has been forecast to produce annually by 1997 150,000 ounces of platinum metal, plus 110,000 ounces of palladium, 23,000 ounces of gold, 11,500 ounces of rhodium, 3,200 tons of nickel, 23,000 tons of copper, and 2,000 tons of cobalt. Hartley is projected to earn more than Z.$700m. annually. Areas adjacent to Hartley are also being assessed for possible exploitation. In May 1995 Delta Gold announced plans to develop a further platinum and gold project at Ngezi, 57 km south of the Hartley complex. While reserves of platinum at Hartley are assessed at 14m. ounces, those at Ngezi are evaluated at 24m. ounces. The Ngezi Mine is scheduled to come on stream, in late 1998. In 1996 the Zimbabwe Mining and Smelting Co was reported to be developing a smaller platinum mine in Midlands province.

The parastatal Zimbabwe Mining Development Corpn is developing the copper deposits at the Copper Queen and King mines, and it is planned to manufacture copper cable locally as an import-substitution measure, aimed at saving Z.$6.6m. in foreign exchange annually. There is also import-substitution potential in the manufacture of ferrochrome derivatives, chemicals and pesticides. Another parastatal organization, the Minerals Marketing Corpn of Zimbabwe, markets all the country's minerals, except gold, abroad. Established in 1982, its operations have been consistently profitable since 1983. Major private-sector mining companies, such as the Anglo American Corpn, Rio Tinto-Zinc and Lonrho, are also active in Zimbabwe. The medium-term outlook for Zimbabwe's mining sector is encouraging, helped by the government's decision, in 1990, to allow mining companies to retain 5% of the value of their export earnings to finance imported inputs. In 1989 a gold refinery, with a capacity of 50 tons per year, was opened in Harare. Built at a cost of Z.$4m., the refinery is owned by the Reserve Bank of Zimbabwe and operated by Fidelity Printers and Refiners. It is expected to lessen Zimbabwe's dependence on South Africa, which had previously possessed the only gold refineries in Africa. Gemstones hold considerable growth potential. In May 1991 the British company Reunion Mining began prospecting for diamonds on a 43,597 sq km area near Beitbridge. In the following month Auridiam Consolidated of Australia obtained a permit to develop the River Ranch diamond concession at a cost of US $10m.–$12m. The company completed its exploration activities in 1992, confirming that diamonds had been found at the concession and announcing plans to build a small-scale production plant. A 500,000 ton-per-annum processing plant at River Ranch was commissioned in January 1994. The River Ranch mine was expected to reach full production of 1.5m. tons of ore annually in 1996. It is forecast that River Ranch will produce 500,000 carats a year during its projected 10-year life span. Auridiam is also exploring for diamonds at Chinhu on the Highveld.

Zimbabwe produces a wide variety of manufactured products, both for the local market and for export. Growth of manufactured exports on a regional basis has been hindered by lack of foreign exchange in neighbouring countries, and by reductions as large as 55% in the amount of foreign exchange allocated to manufacturers for the import of essential raw materials. The ESAP, introduced in 1991, significantly alleviated the foreign-exchange constraint, although subsequent tensions between the Zimbabwe government and multilateral donors put further pressure on the country's foreign exchange position (see below). The manufacturing sector accounted for 23% of GDP in 1996, a decline from 30% annually in 1992–93. The sector also provided employment for 5.1% of the labour force in 1994.

The volume index of manufacturing production (1980 = 100) reached 153.3 in the October quarter of 1990, the highest level since independence. The annual index figure was 138.1 for 1990, 144 for 1991, 123 for 1992, 123.4 for 1993 and 128.3 for 1994. In the 1993 calendar year, as compared with the calendar year 1992, the only sectors to register positive growth were textiles and ginning (up by 9%), paper and printing (up by 14.6%), and clothing and footwear (up by 2.6%). All other sectors experienced a decline, the most pronounced being transport equipment (down by 41.8%), followed by metals and metal products (down by 18.2%, largely reflecting production problems at the parastatal Ziscosteel), foodstuffs (down by 17.9%) and non-metallic minerals (down by 17.7%). In 1991 the country began a three-phase measure to place more products under Open General Import Licence (OGIL). The first phase began on 1 April 1991, and the government had placed 50% of imported raw materials under OGIL by January 1992. Other products followed, and in January 1994 the government removed a 10% temporary duty on OGIL imports. The government also reduced the surtax on imports from 20% to 15%. While many manufacturers have welcomed aspects of the ESAP reforms, they are less fond of measures such as the removal of the Export Incentive Scheme, which the government now recognizes as a subsidy and a distortion of a free-market economy. Ziscosteel's problems have remained, and bailing out the company has placed some strain on public-sector expenditure. In the five-year period 1990/91–1995/96 government spending on parastatals amounted to Z.$6,500m. In 1997 the Confederation of Zimbabwe Industries was encouraging larger companies to contract out subordinate activities to smaller firms.

INTERNATIONAL TRADE AND BANKING

In 1988 the economy registered surpluses in the trade, current-account and overall payments balances. There was a visible trade deficit of US $157m. in 1994, compared with a surplus of US $122.1m. in 1993, a deficit of US $254.5m. in 1992 and a small surplus of US $48m. in 1991. The current account of the balance of payments registered a defict of US $603.7m. in 1992, up from a shortfall of US $457m. in 1991. The current account deficit was reduced to US $115.7m. in 1993 and to US $226m. in 1994. In 1995 the current account deficit was equivalent to 5.2% of GDP. The government had warned that the 1992 current account deficit could be as high as US $1,000m., even before the full extent of the effects of the drought were taken into account. In 1984 Zimbabwe's terms of trade rose by 15.7%, to 120.6 (1980 =100)—the highest figure for 20 years. Zimbabwe's exports equalled only 90% of its imports in 1982, but import cover subsequently improved to 108% in 1983, to 120% in 1986 and to 136% in 1987; import cover was estimated to have remained at 136% in 1988. Although the trade balance was in surplus, the overall balance of payments was in deficit for eight years up to 1984, when an overall balance-of-payments surplus of Z.$164m. was achieved. This followed deficits of Z.$159m. in 1983 and Z.$124m. in 1982. The overall balance of payments was again positive in 1985, and registered a Z.$205m. surplus in that year, a Z.$73m. surplus in 1986, a Z.$236m. surplus in 1987, a Z.$19m. surplus in 1988, a Z.$107m. deficit in 1989, a Z.$231m. deficit in 1990, a Z.$670m. deficit in 1991, a Z.$853m. deficit in 1992, a Z.$1,160m. surplus in 1993, a Z.$2,200m. surplus in 1994 and a Z.$1,520m. surplus in 1995. However, a Z.$349.3 deficit on the overall balance of payments was forecast for 1996. The value of exports increased from Z.$1,380m. in 1984 to Z.$1,615m. in 1985, to Z.$1,760m. in 1986, to Z.$1,840m. in 1987, to Z.$2.860m. in 1988, to Z.$3,334m. in 1989 and to Z.$4,231m. in 1990 before falling back to Z.$2,210m. in 1991, all at current prices. On a percentage basis, growth was 17.5% in 1984, 17% in 1985, 9% in 1986 and 5% in 1987, again at current prices. Exports were estimated to have risen by 25% in 1989, owing to increased sales of non-traditional exports and an effective 11% depreciation in the official value of the Zimbabwe dollar. Further currency depreciation led to a 33.6% rise in export value in 1990. Exports declined in US dollar terms by 6% in 1991, but currency depreciation turned export performance into positive growth in Zimbabwe dollar terms. Visible export value was US $1,967m. in 1994 and US $1,895m. in 1995. Tobacco and gold are the largest two items, but together they contribute less than 50%; other export earners are cotton lint, textile products, footwear, ferro-alloys, food and live animals, crude inedible non-food materials, chrome, nickel, asbestos, copper, raw sugar, iron and steel bars, ingots and billets, electric cables and radios. This list illustrates an unusually high level of export diversity for an African country. Exports of ivory (to Japan only) were to recommence on a limited scale in mid-1997, following a vote at a conference of the Convention on International Trade in Endangered Species.

Imports have also grown steadily but more slowly in most years. The value of imports rose from Z.$1,087m. in 1983 to Z.$2,043.2m. in 1988 and to Z.$4,528.2m. in 1990. The main imports in 1993 were machinery and transport equipment (35%), manufactured goods (14.8%) and food and live animals (14.7%). Imports in US dollar terms cost US$1,852m. in 1990, rising to US $2,030m. in 1991, US $2,213m. in 1992, but falling back to US $1,817m. in 1993. Imports amounted to US $2,241m. in 1994 and to US $2,726m. in 1995, leaving a visible trade deficit of some US $831m. in that year.

Zimbabwe's principal trading partners vary significantly from year to year. In 1995 the most important was the Southern African Customs Union (41% of imports and 18% of exports), followed by the United Kingdom (8% of imports and 13% of exports), Japan (7% of imports and 8% of exports), Germany (5% of imports and 8% of exports) and the USA (5% of both imports and exports); France was an important supplier in that year, whilst Zambia and Italy were major markets.

Zimbabwe's membership of the Common Market for Eastern and Southern Africa (COMESA), formerly the Preferential Trade Area for Eastern and Southern Africa, has, in theory, provided access to new directions in regional trade, but, in practice, Zimbabwean exporters have been somewhat disappointed. Zimbabwe produces many items which the other member states need to import, but the potential trade partners lack the foreign exchange to pay for them. The member state in the best position to pay for imports from Zimbabwe is Kenya, with which a bilateral trade treaty was signed in 1984. Kenya itself has a fairly wide manufacturing base, and is therefore in competition with Zimbabwe in supplying some items to the other COMESA states. The historic change of government in South Africa has created many opportunities for companies to work in a country which is widely regarded as a formidable competitor for investment and as a ready source of imported goods. South Africa is able to take an even larger share of Zimbabwe's domestic market, following the recent increase in trade liberalization.

Zimbabwe's external debt rose sharply during the 1980s, totalling US $4,485m. at the end of 1995, compared to US $4,007m. in 1992 and US $2,959m. in 1990, and with US $276m. at independence in April 1980. In 1987 debt-servicing costs exceeded 33% of export earnings; in 1988, however, the proportion had fallen to 27.5%, and it declined to 21.3% in 1989 before rising to 22.6% in 1990, 27.2% in 1991, 30% in 1992 and to 31% in 1993. There was a decline, to 26.9%, in 1994, and economists forecast a further narrowing of the ratio onwards to the year 2001. Zimbabwe owed US $190m. in repayments on its foreign debt during 1989 and US $220m. in 1990. Shortages of foreign exchange have persisted throughout the post-independence period.

The domestic banking sector is diversified, with major foreign banks participating, as well as the Zimbabwe government. Of the commercial banks, two are long-established foreign banks—Barclays Bank of Zimbabwe and Standard Chartered Bank Zimbabwe. Zimbabwe Banking Corpn (Zimbank) is state-controlled and in 1990 expanded internationally, opening offices in Ghana and Botswana. Merchant banks include the Merchant Bank of Central Africa, Syfrets Merchant Bank (a wholly-owned affiliate of Zimbank), First Merchant Bank of Zimbabwe, Standard Chartered Merchant Bank Zimbabwe and National Merchant Bank. The Zimbabwe Development Bank began operations in 1985; the government has a controlling interest, in partnership with the African Development Bank and other multilateral development institutions. In November 1991 the Zimbabwe Building Society was launched; by June 1995 deposits had grown to Z.$1,880m., with capitalization at Z.$2,120m. In July 1993 exchange controls were relaxed, allowing foreign investors to repatriate investment proceeds, providing a major boost to the Zimbabwe Stock Exchange. The share purchase limit was also raised to 35%. The exchange was capitalized at US $1,900m. in May 1994. In August 1995 some 66 local industrial and mining companies were listed, and at the end of 1996 the exchange had a market capitalization of US $4,719m. with an annual turnover of some US $250m. Bureaux de change require a minimum paid-up capital of US $10,000, and must submit weekly statements of all transactions to the Reserve Bank of Zimbabwe.

ENERGY

Petroleum and petroleum products accounted for 8.8% of all imports in 1995. Petroleum products enter the land-locked country through a 300-km pipeline running between Mutare and the Mozambique port of Beira. Work began in 1989 to extend the pipeline to Harare. Operations by Renamo insurgents during the conflict in Mozambique occasionally disrupted the flow of fuel for short periods, despite the presence of some 10,000 Zimbabwean troops to defend the pipeline. The most serious stoppage occurred in late 1982, when the Mozambican guerrillas bombed the storage tanks and pumping station at Beira; on that occasion, repairs took two months to complete, and fuel shortages ensued. Zimbabwe consumes some 800,000 metric tons of petroleum products (including diesel fuel) annually.

Zimbabwe's sole coal producer is the Wankie Colliery Co, which mines coal at Hwange (formerly Wankie). The company was producing at only about 50% of capacity in the first half of the 1980s, and by 1985 only 15 of its 32 ovens were in operation. The coke-oven battery was closed from 1986 until late 1987 for rehabilitation, but the company had stockpiled sufficient coke to maintain supplies during the closure. The colliery's output was 160,000 metric tons of coke in the year to February 1989, while domestic demand was 68,000 tons per annum. The company's operations are being expanded to exploit a deposit estimated at 400m. tons. In October 1996 a new coke oven gas plant at Wankie Colliery was formally commissioned, after it had already been fully operational for six months. The new facility enabled the company to sell 25.38m. cu m of coke oven gas to the national electricity grid in the last eight months of 1996. Reserves at Lubimbi coalfield are estimated to exceed 20,000m. tons, and an oil-from-coal project is in operation there. Zimbabwe's total coal reserves are estimated at 28,000m. tons.

Zimbabwe shares with Zambia the huge Kariba dam, on the Zambezi river. For many years, Kariba's only hydroelectric power plant was on the Zambian side, and Zimbabwe imported some Z.$20m. worth of energy annually from its northern neighbour. In 1987, however, Zimbabwe added 920 MW of new thermal capacity to its own national grid, eliminating the need for these imports; in July 1987 the Zimbabwean government notified Zambia of its intention to terminate the supply contract. This termination was brought about abruptly in early 1989, however, when a fire seriously damaged Zambia's Kafue station, eliminating its export capacity. The Hwange thermal power station, constructed at a cost of Z.$230m., accounted for 920 MW of total national generating capacity of 1,900 MW in 1989. However, the Hwange facility's performance has been disappointing owing to design faults and a shortage of spare parts. Work to refurbish units 1–4 of the facility during the first half of the 1990s was funded by the World Bank. The shared Central African Power Corpn was replaced in 1986 by the Zimbabwe Electricity Supply Authority (ZESA), which has aimed to maximize the operational efficiency of existing installed capacity, while furthering a longer-term development programme directed towards a forecast demand of 2,800 MW by 2004. (Maximum demand in 1988/89 was about 1,400 MW.) In April 1991, after many delays, the government agreed to the construction of a Z.$500m. hydroelectric extension facility at Kariba South, due for completion in 1998, and of a joint Zambia-Zimbabwe Batoka Gorge hydroelectric facility costing Z.$1,000m. which was to add 1,600 MW by 2003; however, the Zambian government withdrew from the project, and in 1997 the Zimbabwean authorities were seeking private finance for the scheme. A Z.$154m. plan to rehabilitate three thermal power plants was also approved. The 1992 drought lowered the water level for all hydroelectric facilities in the region, necessitating the unusual step of rationing electricity in Zimbabwe. Urgent negotiations were initiated to obtain power imports from Zaire and Zambia, and in May 1992 ZESA arranged for the import of 500 MW from Mozambique. Work on an interconnector linking Mozambique's Cahora Bassa facility to Matimba and Bindura in Zimbabwe began in 1994 and was to add 500 MW to Zimbabwe's national grid by the end of 1996. Further work on Hwange, stages 7 and 8, is to be completed in 1998, and a coal-fired project at Sengwa is to add 600 MW by 2004. In September 1997 ZESA raised electricity tariffs by 30%; multilateral institutions had long been advocating higher tariffs as a means to funding the capital investment needed to increase the efficiency of electricity supply, for which there was a growing demand.

LABOUR, WAGES AND INFLATION

Inflation has, with the exception of 1988, affected lower-income urban families more than it has higher-income urban families in every year since independence in 1980. Inflation was stimulated in 1991 by the government's relaxation of price controls as part of its 1991–95 economic reform programme. According to the consumer price index, in the year ended 30 June 1991, prices for all items rose by 22% for the higher-income group, compared with the same period a year earlier, while they rose by 23% for the lower-income group. The cost of living for lower income families rose by 16.4%, compared with 11.5% for higher-income families. In the year ended 31 December 1990, prices for all items rose by 16.1% for the higher-income group, but they rose by 18.5% for the lower income group. Analysis reveals that transport prices rose fastest for the lower-income group, at 50.9%, followed by food at 19.4% and beverages and tobacco at 20.3%. In the higher-income group, clothing and footwear prices rose fastest, at 19.0%, followed by food at 18.6%. In December 1990 the consumer price index (1980 = 100) for all items was 359 for the higher-income group and 394.5 for the lower-income group. In December 1991 the consumer price index was 457 for lower-income urban dwellers and 408 for higher-income urban dwellers. In early 1993 the government introduced a new consumer goods weighting structure (1990 = 100) to reflect a 'more representative' combination of goods and services than previously. However, even the new index reflected a high level of consumer price inflation: the annual figure for 1993 reached 206.9. The 1994 and 1995 annual figures were even higher, at 273.4 and 335.1. Food prices rose by 71.8% between January 1992 and January 1993. Overall inflation rates were 22% in 1995, 22% in 1994, 24.2% in 1993, 45% in 1992, 28.1% in 1991, 15.5% in 1990, 11.6% in 1989, 7.7% in 1988, 9% in 1987, 15% in 1986 and 10% in 1985. The post-independence peak was 25% in 1983 until this was exceeded in 1991. By January 1996 the average annual inflation rate had risen to 28%; however, it fell back to 23.7% in March and to 22.5% in June. In June 1997 inflation was officially assessed at an average annual rate of 21.4%. The Zimbabwe dollar was devalued by 17% at 1 January 1994. Since independence, the government has endeavoured to narrow the wide gap in incomes between rich and poor Zimbabweans. The Minimum Wage Act of 1980 established a wages minimum of Z.$85 per month for workers who came under the Industrial Conciliation Act, Z.$70 per month for others in industry, Z.$58 per month for mineworkers and Z.$30 per month for agricultural and domestic workers. In January 1982 minimum wages were again raised, and in 1986 the upper limit for the wages 'freeze' was raised to include only those earning more than Z.$36,000 per year. Wage rises were announced on a graduated scale, ranging from 3% for those earning between Z.$30,000 and Z.$36,000 per year upwards, to 10% for those earning between Z.$100 and Z.$500 per month. Those earning less than Z.$100 per month were granted a uniform monthly increase of Z.$10. Before the wage increases, an employee receiving Z.$36,000 per year was paid Z.$34,800 more annually than a worker earning Z.$100 per month; after the wage rises, the gap between the two earners was wider, at Z.$35,760 per year. The differential between the industrial minimum wage and the agricultural minimum wage reflects, among other factors, the higher cost of urban life. In 1995 the statutory monthly minimum wage was Z.$242 in agriculture, Z.$472 in commerce, Z.$498 in mining and Z.$514 in manufacturing.

In June 1987 the government announced a six-month 'freeze' on wages and prices, which was extended on 31 December 1987. The wages 'freeze' was lifted in February 1988, and that on prices was relaxed in May 1988. A study by the University of Zimbabwe, released in March 1988, forecast that as much as 24% of the country's labour force would be unemployed by 1990. It warned that, between 1986 and 1990, 857,000 school leavers would enter the job market, while only 144,000 new jobs were to be created. In the event, an estimated 1m. Zimbabweans were unemployed in 1990, and an additional 300,000 school-leavers entered the job market in that year. Unemployment was estimated at 22% in 1992 and at 35% in July 1996. Pressure to cut payrolls under the 1991–95 ESAP exacerbated unemployment, and banking sources estimate that in March 1994 current incomes were, on average, only 68% of their 1990 levels in real terms. The ESAP called for a 25% reduction in the civil service, necessitating the elimination of 32,000 jobs by 1994. In May 1992, 1,170 government posts were abolished, and a further 6,154 public-sector jobs were described as 'superfluous': their abolition was forecast to reduce government expenditure by Z.$32.5m. annually. In July 1992 the government reduced the number of ministries as part of its streamlining of the administration; in April 1995, however, despite reported pressure from the IMF and the World Bank to halve the number of cabinet posts, 13 new positions were created. In 1992 approximately 10,000 textile workers and 7,000 agricultural workers lost their jobs, and in June 1993 only 11% of the working population was employed in the formal sector, the lowest percentage in over 23 years. Government provisions of Z.$20m. to offset the social effects of the austerity accompanying structural adjustment were widely regarded as unrealistic and inadequate. In June 1994 the government granted substantial allowances and salary increases of between 10%–20% to members of the civil service and armed forces. In August–September 1996 civil servants staged a national strike in support of demands for higher salary increases and further industrial action in many sectors took place during 1996–97. Multilateral creditors expressed disappointment at unscheduled salary increases awarded to civil servants in late 1996, which undermined efforts to limit the budgetary deficit. The government's record in harnessing expenditure has been disappointing. The 1994/95 budget envisaged total spending of Z.$17,900m.; the actual figure was, however, Z.$22,257m., exceeding the target by 24%. With actual revenue totalling Z.$15,257m. in 1994/95, the budget deficit reached Z.$7,000m., equivalent to 13.4% of GDP—far in excess of the IMF and World Bank target of 5%. Under the 1995/96 budget, total expenditure was envisaged at Z.$22,574m., compared with projected revenue of Z.$18,300m. In September 1995 the IMF announced the suspension of Zimbabwe's balance-of-payments loans pending a reduction in the budget deficit. The IMF was critical of the government's expenditure on the creation of new ministries earlier in the year (see above), and of the fiscal contribution to political parties for which only the ruling party was, effectively, eligible. A mid-year revision of the 1995/96 budget, announced in December 1995, raised the spending projection to Z.$25,474m.; actual expenditure was Z.$26,024m., leaving a deficit of Z.$6,560m., equivalent to 10.1% of GDP (well above the target of 6.7%). The 1996/97 budget, announced in July 1996 by the new minister of finance, Dr Herbert Murerwa, envisaged recurrent expenditure of Z.$25,903m. and capital expenditure of Z.$4,557m., totalling Z.$30,173m. (less recoveries). Revenue was forecast at Z.$23,350m., producing a projected deficit (exclusive of grants) of Z.$6,823m., which was envisaged to be equivalent to 8.5% of GDP. The 1997/98 budget, announced by Dr Murerwa on 24 July 1997, covered the 18-month period to 31 December 1998. It called for total expenditure of Z.$63,900m., against total anticipated revenues of Z.$48,800m., leaving a budgetary deficit of Z.$15,100m. On an annualized basis, this deficit represented about 20% of GDP, as against the IMF target of 5% of GDP. The out-turn for 1996/97 represented the fiscal deficit for that 12-month period at 7.1% of GDP, apparently based on the government's reported revision of its GDP estimates to Z.$100,000m. In any case, the need to finance the deficit was expected to enlarge the public-sector borrowing requirement on the domestic market to Z.$11,000m. in the 18-month period, as against Z.$5,000m. during the previous 12-month period. Several new taxes were introduced in the budget, which also implemented the value-added tax that had been announced in the previous year. The new tax measures included a motor-vehicle benefit tax and a 15% tax on pension funds.

Statistical Survey

Source (unless otherwise stated): Central Statistical Office, Kaguvi Bldg, Fourth St, POB CY 342, Causeway, Harare; tel. (4) 706681; fax (4) 728529.

Area and Population

AREA, POPULATION AND DENSITY

Area (sq km)	390,757*
Population (census results)	
18 August 1982	7,608,432
18 August 1992	
Males	5,083,537
Females	5,329,011
Total	10,412,548
Population (official estimate at 18 August)	
1997	12,293,953
Density (per sq km) at August 1997	31.5

* 150,872 sq miles.

PRINCIPAL TOWNS (population at census of August 1992)

Harare (capital)	1,189,103	Masvingo	51,743
Bulawayo	621,742	Hwange (Wankie)	42,581
Chitungwiza	274,912	Chinhoyi (Sinoia)	43,054
Mutare (Umtali)	131,367	Marondera (Marandellas)	39,384
Gweru (Gwelo)	128,037	Zvishavane (Shabani)	32,984
Kwekwe (Que Que)	75,425	Redcliff	29,959
Kadoma (Gatooma)	67,750		

BIRTHS AND DEATHS (UN estimates, annual averages)

	1980–85	1985–90	1990–95
Birth rate (per 1,000)	43.1	41.2	39.1
Death rate (per 1,000)	11.7	10.9	12.0

Expectation of life (UN estimates, years at birth, 1990–95): 53.7 (males 52.4; females 55.1).

Source: UN, *World Population Prospects: The 1994 Revision*.

ECONOMICALLY ACTIVE POPULATION
(sample survey, '000 persons aged 15 years and over, 1994)

	Males	Females	Total
Agriculture, hunting, forestry and fishing	1,216.9	1,587.9	2,804.8
Mining and quarrying	63.8	5.0	68.8
Manufacturing	190.0	31.0	221.0
Electricity, gas and water	12.9	0.9	13.8
Construction	80.3	5.7	86.0
Trade, restaurants and hotels	80.2	50.0	130.2
Transport, storage and communications	73.4	5.2	78.6
Financing, insurance, real estate and business services	20.2	11.9	32.1
Community, social and personal services	354.0	290.5	644.5
Activities not adequately defined	7.4	4.1	11.5
Total employed	2,099.1	1,992.2	4,091.3
Unemployed	153.3	62.2	215.5
Total labour force	2,252.4	2,054.4	4,306.8

Mid-1995 (estimates in '000): Agriculture, etc. 3,480; Total labour force 5,233 (Source: FAO, *Production Yearbook*).

EMPLOYMENT ('000 persons)*

	1993	1994	1995
Agriculture, forestry and fishing	324.1	329.5	326.9†
Mining and quarrying	47.7	52.5	59.1
Manufacturing	187.7	199.7	185.9
Construction	90.5	85.2	71.8
Electricity and water	7.9	8.6	9.5
Transport and communications	49.8	52.5	50.9
Trade	95.9	105.1	100.6
Finance, insurance and real estate	20.2	21.9	21.1
Community, social and personal services	416.5	408.7	406.8
Total employees	1,240.3	1,263.7	1,227.7
Males	997.6	1,014.7	n.a.
Females	242.7	249.0	n.a.

* Excluding small establishments in rural areas.
† IMF estimate.

Source: Mainly IMF, *Zimbabwe—Recent Economic Developments* (July 1997).

Agriculture

PRINCIPAL CROPS ('000 metric tons)

	1993	1994	1995
Wheat	276	239	83
Barley	24	8*	8*
Maize	2,012	2,326	840
Millet	95	78	21
Sorghum	90	122	29
Potatoes*	30	31	30
Cassava (Manioc)*	130	130	130
Dry beans*	45	46	40
Soybeans (Soya beans)	101	109	77
Groundnuts (in shell)	67	66	52
Sunflower seed	49	49	22
Cottonseed	119	109†	63†
Vegetables (incl. melons)*	143	146	143
Sugar cane	538†	3,420	3,943†
Oranges	72*	75*	70
Other citrus fruits	19*	22*	19
Bananas	82*	85*	80
Coffee (green)	4	9†	4†
Tea (made)	14†	13†	15
Tobacco (leaves)	205	182	198
Cotton (lint)	67	60†	37

* FAO estimate(s). † Unofficial figure.

Source: FAO, *Production Yearbook*.

LIVESTOCK ('000 head, year ending September)

	1993	1994	1995
Horses*	23	24	24
Asses*	103	104	104
Cattle	4,180†	4,300*	4,500
Sheep	420*	450*	487
Pigs	210†	246†	277
Goats	2,500*	2,580*	2,615

* FAO estimate(s). † Unofficial figure.

Poultry (FAO estimates, million): 13 in 1993; 14 in 1994; 14 in 1995.

LIVESTOCK PRODUCTS (FAO estimates, '000 metric tons)

	1993	1994	1995
Beef and veal	75	64	53
Goat meat	9	9	9
Pig meat	8	10	11
Poultry meat	17	18	18
Other meat	20	21	20
Cows' milk	388	420	420
Butter	2.4	2.6	2.6
Cheese	2.0	2.2	2.2
Poultry eggs	16.8	17.4	17.4
Cattle hides	8.2	6.9	6.0

Source: FAO, *Production Yearbook*.

Forestry

ROUNDWOOD REMOVALS
(FAO estimates, '000 cubic metres, excl. bark)

	1992	1993	1994
Sawlogs, veneer logs and logs for sleepers*	525	525	525
Pulpwood*	157	157	157
Other industrial wood	1,070	1,098	1,125
Fuel wood†	6,269	6,269	6,269
Total	8,021	8,049	8,076

* Assumed to be unchanged since 1991.
† Assumed to be unchaged since 1988.

Source: FAO, *Yearbook of Forest Products*.

SAWNWOOD PRODUCTION
(FAO estimates, assumed to be unchanged since 1991, '000 cubic metres, incl. railway sleepers)

	1992	1993	1994
Coniferous (softwood)	221	221	221
Broadleaved (hardwood)	29	29	29
Total	250	250	250

Source: FAO, *Yearbook of Forest Products*.

Fishing

('000 metric tons, live weight)

	1993	1994	1995*
Dagaas	20.0	19.2	19.3
Other fishes	1.4	1.1	1.2
Total catch	21.4	20.3	20.5

* FAO estimates.

Source: FAO, *Yearbook of Fishery Statistics*

Mining

('000 metric tons, unless otherwise indicated)

	1992	1993	1994
Antimony ore (metric tons)*	254	95†	35†
Asbestos	150	157	152
Chromium ore*	160	120	155‡
Clay	65	123	170
Coal	5,548	5,285	5,469
Cobalt ore (metric tons)*	101	110	130
Copper ore*	9.6	8.2	9.4†
Gold (kilograms)*	18,278	18,565	20,528
Iron ore*	710	225‡§	2‡
Limestone	1,365	1,036	n.a.
Magnesite	9.0	6.0	n.a.
Nickel ore (metric tons)*	10,115	11,889	13,518
Niobium ore (metric tons)*‡	14	14	14
Phosphate rock	142	153	160§
Silver (metric tons)*	17	12	14
Tantalum (metric tons)*‡	33	33	2
Tin ore (metric tons)*	716	658	82

* Figures refer to the metal content of ores and concentrates.
† Data from *World Metal Statistics* (London).
‡ Data from the US Bureau of Mines.
§ Estimated figure.

Source: mainly UN, *Industrial Commodity Statistics Yearbook*.

1995 ('000 metric tons, unless otherwise indicated): Asbestos 170; Coal 5,539; Cobalt (metric tons) 111; Copper 8.1; Gold (kilograms) 23,950.

Industry

SELECTED PRODUCTS
('000 metric tons, unless otherwise indicated)

	1992	1993	1994
Raw sugar*	9*†	56*	523‡
Cigarettes (million)	3,025	n.a.	n.a.
Coke	578	521	540
Cement	829	816	n.a.
Pig-iron§	507	500	—
Ferro-chromium§	211	140	200
Crude steel§	547	221	180
Refined copper—unwrought§	17.9	16.4	16.0
Nickel—unwrought (metric tons)	10,115	11,889	11,500§
Tin—unwrought (metric tons)‖	716	658	82§
Electric energy (million kWh)	8,617	7,643	7,334

* Data from the FAO.
† Estimate(s).
‡ Data from the International Sugar Organization (London).
§ Data from the US Bureau of Mines.
‖ Primary metal only.

Source: UN, *Industrial Commodity Statistics Yearbook*.

1995: Electric energy (million kWh) 7,871 (Source: UN, *Monthly Bulletin of Statistics*).

Finance

CURRENCY AND EXCHANGE RATES

Monetary Units

100 cents = 1 Zimbabwe dollar (Z.$).

Sterling and US Dollar Equivalents (31 March 1997)

£1 sterling = Z.$ 18.398;
US $1 = Z.$ 11.204;
Z.$ 1,000 = £54.36 = US $89.25.

Average Exchange Rate (US $ per Zimbabwe dollar)

1994 0.1227
1995 0.1155
1996 0.1008

BUDGET (Z.$ million, year ending 30 June)

Revenue*	1993/94	1994/95	1995/96
Taxation	11,153	13,066	16,121
Taxes on income and profits	6,157	6,966	8,147
Personal income	3,399	3,912	4,486
Business profits	2,303	2,378	2,847
Customs duties	2,425	2,438	3,050
Excise duties	497	693	896
Sales tax	1,891	2,741	3,730
Other revenue	1,601	1,692	2,782
Entrepreneurial and property income	799	801	1,547
Parastatal interest and dividends	691	691	723
Total	12,754	14,758	18,903

Expenditure†	1993/94	1994/95	1995/96
Recurrent expenditure:			
Goods and services:			
Salaries, wages and allowances	4,682	6,144	7,737
Subsistence and transport	470	553	407
Incidental expenses	594	589	440
Other recurrent expenditure	2,120	2,393	3,677
Total	7,866	9,679	12,261
Transfers:			
Interest	2,992	4,582	6,955
Subsidies	360	146	93
Pensions	402	867	1,308
Grants and transfers	1,375	2,391	2,427
Total	5,129	7,986	10,783
Capital expenditure:			
Buildings	621	741	765
Civil engineering	645	567	432
Plant, machinery and equipment	21	113	212
Other capital expenditure	390	387	356
Total	1,677	1,808	1,764
Grand Total*	14,672	19,473	24,808

* Excluding grants received (Z.$ million): 923 in 1993/94; 1,247 in 1994/95; 973 in 1995/96.

† Excluding lending minus repayments (Z.$ million): 1,260 in 1993/94; 1,810 in 1994/95; 1,507 in 1995/96.

Source: IMF, *Zimbabwe—Recent Economic Developments* (July 1997).

INTERNATIONAL RESERVES (US $ million at 31 December)

	1994	1995	1996
Gold*	89.7	139.7	117.2
IMF special drawing rights	0.1	0.8	9.8
Reserve position in IMF	0.1	0.1	0.2
Foreign exchange	405.1	594.6	588.9
Total	495.0	735.2	716.1

* Valued at a market-related price which is determined each month.

Source: IMF, *International Financial Statistics.*

MONEY SUPPLY (Z.$ million at 31 December)

	1994	1995	1996
Currency outside banks	1,467.1	1,823.5	2,440.3
Demand deposits at deposit money banks	5,791.1	9,351.8	11,290.0
Total money (incl. others)	7,396.0	11,269.8	13,874.5

Source: IMF, *International Financial Statistics.*

COST OF LIVING (Consumer Price Index; base: 1990 = 100)

	1993	1994	1995
Food and beverages	267.4	336.8	429.3
Clothing and footwear	185.6	207.8	239.9
Rent, fuel and light	204.4	236.7	n.a.
All items (incl. others)	223.6	273.4	335.1

Source: ILO, *Yearbook of Labour Statistics.*

1996: Food 544.8; All items 406.9 (Source: UN, *Monthly Bulletin of Statistics*).

NATIONAL ACCOUNTS (Z.$ million at current prices)

Expenditure on the Gross National Product (IMF estimates)

	1994	1995	1996
Government final consumption expenditure	8,773	10,970	14,424
Private final consumption expenditure	30,074	37,738	47,209
Increase in stocks	252	—	790
Gross fixed capital formation	9,233	10,009	12,724
Total domestic expenditure	48,332	58,717	75,147
Exports of goods and services	19,826	25,317	33,372
Less Imports of goods and services	20,732	26,838	33,021
GDP in purchasers' values	47,426	57,196	75,498

Source: IMF, *Zimbabwe—Recent Economic Developments* (July 1997).

Composition of the Gross National Product

	1987	1988	1989
Compensation of employees	4,847	5,611	6,572
Operating surplus / Consumption of fixed capital	3,172	4,573	5,542
GDP at factor cost	8,019	10,184	12,114
Indirect taxes	1,346	1,645	2,093
Less Subsidies	426	388	413
GDP in purchasers' values	8,939	11,441	13,794
Net factor income from abroad	–355	–478	–538
GNP at market prices	8,584	10,963	13,256

Source: UN, *National Accounts Statistics.*

Gross Domestic Product by Economic Activity (at factor cost)

	1990	1991	1992
Agriculture, hunting, forestry and fishing	2,391	3,709	5,692
Mining and quarrying	676	939	1,226
Manufacturing	4,130	5,585	7,760
Electricity and water	394	520	687
Construction	362	499	499
Trade, restaurants and hotels	1,569	1,898	2,145
Transport, storage and communications	1,067	1,243	1,865
Finance, insurance and real estate	977	1,133	1,271
Government services	1,057	1,230	1,311
Other services	2,423	3,197	3,616
Sub-total	15,046	19,953	26,072
Less Imputed bank service charges	344	366	366
Total	14,702	19,587	25,706

Source: UN, *National Accounts Statistics.*

BALANCE OF PAYMENTS (US $ million)

	1992	1993	1994
Exports of goods f.o.b.	1,527.6	1,609.1	1,961.1
Imports of goods f.o.b.	−1,782.1	−1,487.0	−1,803.5
Trade balance	−254.5	122.1	157.6
Exports of services	305.1	372.1	383.2
Imports of services	−660.9	−563.8	−711.7
Balance on goods and services	−610.3	−69.6	−170.9
Other income received	26.0	35.0	27.5
Other income paid	−302.3	−287.1	−321.2
Balance on goods, services and income	−886.6	−321.6	−464.5
Current transfers received	347.3	270.6	69.4
Current transfers paid	−64.4	−64.7	−29.8
Current balance	−603.7	−115.7	−424.9
Capital account (net)	−1.4	−0.4	284.4
Direct investment abroad	—	—	−4.7
Direct investment from abroad	15.0	28.0	34.7
Portfolio investment assets	27.6	—	—
Portfolio investment liabilities	−37.1	−5.1	50.2
Other investment assets	15.9	99.9	−260.3
Other investment liabilities	352.0	204.4	154.7
Net errors and omissions	37.2	14.9	80.2
Overall balance	−194.6	225.9	−85.8

Source: IMF, *International Financial Statistics*.

External Trade

PRINCIPAL COMMODITIES

(distribution by SITC, US $'000, excl. stores and bunkers for aircraft)

Imports f.o.b.	1993	1994	1995
Food and live animals	152,140	53,915	100,260
Cereals and cereal preparations	113,204	23,036	46,202
Maize (unmilled)	69,981	884	717
Crude materials (inedible) except fuels	91,674	73,127	94,654
Mineral fuels, lubricants, etc. (incl. electricity)	267,398	222,369	245,937
Petroleum, petroleum products, etc.	265,190	215,659	239,722
Refined petroleum products	256,771	210,164	234,423
Motor spirit (gasoline) and other light oils	77,138	50,103	70,095
Motor and aviation spirit	76,271	48,739	69,129
Kerosene and other medium oils	41,807	32,577	29,274
Gas oils	110,133	109,069	117,349
Animal and vegetable oils and fats	36,607	42,161	45,422
Chemicals and related products	248,919	360,505	367,234
Inorganic chemicals	44,413	54,126	57,794
Artificial resins, plastic materials, etc.	49,740	72,299	91,692
Products of polymerization, etc.	39,422	57,935	75,342
Basic manufactures	268,567	369,411	469,450
Textile yarn, fabrics, etc.	73,360	96,361	118,460
Iron and steel	54,900	84,033	104,935
Machinery and transport equipment	636,781	934,633	1,134,747
Power-generating machinery and equipment	32,525	60,414	65,476
Machinery specialized for particular industries	103,418	183,478	253,233
General industrial machinery, equipment, etc.	107,876	162,999	175,184

Imports f.o.b. — *continued*	1993	1994	1995
Telecommunications and sound equipment	61,703	66,472	81,310
Other electrical machinery, apparatus, etc.	70,212	131,660	148,301
Switchgear, etc., and parts	22,521	44,915	38,238
Road vehicles and parts*	163,481	256,971	324,627
Passenger motor cars (excl. buses)	48,127	76,664	77,351
Motor vehicles for goods transport, etc.	55,993	108,248	157,450
Goods vehicles	48,301	101,366	144,000
Other transport equipment*	55,937	18,767	24,852
Aircraft, associated equipment and parts*	52,289	15,980	22,696
Miscellaneous manufactured articles	75,265	120,895	149,698
Total (incl. others)	1,817,329	2,241,267	2,726,180

*Excluding tyres, engines and electrical parts.

Exports f.o.b.	1993	1994	1995
Food and live animals	148,836	389,159	314,374
Cereals and cereal preparations	43,263	171,742	67,237
Maize (unmilled)	31,190	146,222	34,372
Vegetables and fruit	15,146	24,673	42,056
Sugar, sugar preparations and honey	4,564	101,832	85,577
Sugar and honey	327	96,704	78,275
Raw beet and cane sugar	230	88,540	63,739
Coffee, tea, cocoa, spices, and manufactures thereof	18,277	28,922	42,826
Beverages and tobacco	393,075	668,957	498,100
Tobacco and tobacco manufactures	379,452	665,584	494,649
Unmanufactured tobacco, incl. refuse	370,237	649,005	483,534
Unstripped tobacco	102,021	133,596	48,895
Wholly or partly stripped tobacco	261,518	509,173	431,950
Crude materials (inedible) except fuels	185,049	217,933	239,118
Cotton	24,162	60,445	51,810
Crude fertilizers and crude minerals	73,583	72,904	98,879
Asbestos	55,300	56,418	71,847
Cut flowers	26,740	19,298	33,410
Chemicals and related products	37,643	36,120	47,864
Basic manufactures	370,934	411,994	545,774
Textile yarn, fabrics, etc.	61,678	76,149	64,416
Iron and steel	155,503	137,437	240,427
Pig-iron, etc.	101,802	115,164	219,837
Ferro-alloys	97,122	115,164	219,790
Non-ferrous metals	73,929	109,313	113,196
Nickel and nickel alloys	49,615	80,533	90,100
Other metal manufactures	34,413	31,636	45,435
Machinery and transport equipment	39,830	49,278	50,527
Miscellaneous manufactured articles	124,811	159,786	166,254
Clothing and accessories (excl. footwear)	49,681	63,864	62,814
Total (incl. others)	1,318,922	1,967,464	1,895,475

Source: UN, *International Trade Statistics Yearbook*.

PRINCIPAL TRADING PARTNERS (US $'000)*

Imports f.o.b.	1993	1994	1995
Argentina	22,509	10,688	40,775
Belgium-Luxembourg	24,593	27,080	34,009
China, People's Repub.	32,147	20,597	28,508
France (incl. Monaco)	44,756	45,875	102,375
Germany	88,629	131,643	138,437
Hong Kong	12,354	24,319	33,554
Italy	27,497	43,483	50,421
Japan	120,406	140,060	187,887
Korea, Repub.	6,612	24,304	27,855
Netherlands	46,827	43,461	47,158
SACU†	553,125	782,417	1,118,890
Sweden	37,597	31,208	33,824
Switzerland (incl. Liechtenstein)	34,970	67,072	40,226
United Kingdom	183,690	230,409	219,652
USA	161,926	118,929	121,884
Total (incl. others)	1,812,744	2,236,030	2,712,703

Exports f.o.b.	1993	1994	1995
Belgium-Luxembourg	32,736	48,054	55,285
Canada	3,306	19,738	3,863
China, People's Repub.	22,832	47,106	57,908
Egypt	20,832	334	9,372
France (incl. Monaco)	19,815	31,978	32,496
Germany	78,941	140,258	155,961
Indonesia	12,509	26,601	23,247
Italy	48,790	58,432	89,996
Japan	95,506	124,975	149,462
Malawi	42,709	78,275	51,211
Mozambique	54,018	60,830	52,983
Netherlands	46,281	88,900	66,950
Philippines	10,904	30,390	11,033
Poland	7,489	25,479	18,727
Portugal	10,890	28,619	37,379
SACU†	267,462	356,236	349,967
Spain	17,227	26,277	31,868
Switzerland (incl. Liechtenstein)	44,382	38,120	21,333
United Kingdom	144,307	251,869	243,424
USA	94,210	124,438	89,989
Zambia	66,855	65,667	95,414
Total (incl. others)	1,316,881	1,958,902	1,895,030

* Imports by country of production; exports by country of last consignment. Figures exclude trade in gold.

† South African Customs Union, comprising Botswana, Lesotho, Namibia, South Africa and Swaziland.

Source: UN, *International Trade Statistics Yearbook*.

Transport

RAIL TRAFFIC
(National Railways of Zimbabwe, including operations in Botswana)

	1992	1993	1994
Total number of passengers ('000)	2,355	2,200	2,034
Revenue-earning metric tons hauled ('000)	13,038	10,464	11,250
Gross metric ton-km (million)	11,913	9,649	9,397
Net metric ton-km (million)	5,887	4,581	4,489

ROAD TRAFFIC ('000 motor vehicles in use, estimates)

	1993	1994	1995
Passenger cars	388	461	492
Commercial vehicles	101	102	108

Source: IRF, *World Road Statistics*.

CIVIL AVIATION (traffic on scheduled services)

	1992	1993	1994
Kilometres flown ('000)	14,000	13,000	10,000
Passengers carried ('000)	678	558	605
Passenger-km (million)	880	735	666
Total ton-km (million)	171	154	209

Source: UN, *Statistical Yearbook*.

Tourism

	1992	1993	1994
Number of tourist arrivals	737,885	942,723	1,099,332
Tourist receipts (US $ million)	108	138	153

Source: UN, *Statistical Yearbook*.

Communications Media

	1992	1993	1994
Radio receivers ('000 in use)	890	920	945
Television receivers ('000 in use)	280	290	297
Telephones ('000 main lines in use)	127	128	135
Book production:			
Titles	232	n.a.	n.a.
Daily newspapers:			
Number	2	n.a.	2
Circulation ('000 copies)	195	n.a.	195

Sources: UNESCO, *Statistical Yearbook*; UN, *Statistical Yearbook*.

Education

(1995)

	Schools	Teachers	Students
Primary	4,633	63,475	2,655,564
Secondary	1,535	27,320	711,094
Higher	n.a.	3,581	46,492

Source: Ministry of Education, Causeway, Harare.

Directory

The Constitution

The Constitution of the Republic of Zimbabwe took effect at independence on 18 April 1980. Amendments to the Constitution must have the approval of two-thirds of the members of the House of Assembly (see below). The provisions of the 1980 Constitution (with subsequent amendments) are summarized below:

THE REPUBLIC

Zimbabwe is a sovereign republic and the Constitution is the supreme law.

DECLARATION OF RIGHTS

The declaration of rights guarantees the fundamental rights and freedoms of the individual, regardless of race, tribe, place of origin, political opinions, colour, creed or sex.

THE PRESIDENT

Executive power is vested in the President, who acts on the advice of the Cabinet. The President is Head of State and Commander-in-Chief of the Defence Forces. The President appoints two Vice-Presidents and other Ministers and Deputy Ministers, to be members of the Cabinet. The President holds office for six years and is eligible for re-election. Each candidate for the Presidency shall be nominated by not fewer than 10 members of the House of Assembly; if only one candidate is nominated, that candidate shall be declared to be elected without the necessity of a ballot. Otherwise, a ballot shall be held within an electoral college consisting of the members of the House of Assembly.

PARLIAMENT

Legislative power is vested in a unicameral Parliament, consisting of a House of Assembly. The House of Assembly comprises 150 members, of whom 120 are directly elected by universal adult suffrage, 12 are nominated by the President, 10 are traditional Chiefs and eight are Provincial Governors. The life of the House of Assembly is ordinarily to be six years.

OTHER PROVISIONS

An Ombudsman shall be appointed by the President, acting on the advice of the Judicial Service Commission, to investigate complaints against actions taken by employees of the government or of a local authority.

Chiefs shall be appointed by the President, and shall form a Council of Chiefs from their number in accordance with customary principles of succession.

Other provisions relate to the Judicature, Defence and Police Forces, public service and finance.

The Government

HEAD OF STATE

President: Robert Gabriel Mugabe (took office 31 December 1987; re-elected March 1990 and 16–17 March 1996).

THE CABINET
(September 1997)

Vice-Presidents: Simon Vengayi Muzenda, Joshua Mqabuko Nkomo.

Minister of Defence: Moven Enock Mahachi.

Minister of Home Affairs: Dumiso Dabengwa.

Minister of Justice, Legal and Parliamentary Affairs: Emmerson Dambudzo Mnangagwa.

Minister of Finance: Dr Herbert Muchemwa Murerwa.

Minister of National Affairs, Employment Creation and Co-operatives: Virginia Thenjiwe Lesabe.

Minister of Public Service, Labour and Social Welfare: Florence Lubalendlu Chitauro.

Minister of Local Government and National Housing: John Landa Nkomo.

Minister of Lands and Agriculture: Kumbirai Manyika Kangai.

Minister of Industry and Commerce: Nathan Marwirakuwa Shamuyarira.

Minister of Mines, Environment and Tourism: Simon Khaya Moyo.

Minister of Information, Posts and Telecommunications: Chenhamo Chakezha Chimutengwende.

Minister of Foreign Affairs: Dr I. Stanislaus Gorerazvo Mudenge.

Minister of Higher Education and Technology: Dr Ignatius Morgan Chiminya Chombo.

Minister of Education, Sports and Culture: Gabriel Machinga.

Minister of Health and Child Welfare: Dr Timothy Stamps.

Minister of Transport and Energy: Enos Chamunorwa Chikowore.

Minister of Rural Resources and Water Development: Joyce Mujuru.

Ministers without Portfolio: Joseph Msika; Eddison Jonas Mudadirwa Zvogbo.

Minister of State in the President's Office: Cephas Msipa.

Minister of State for National Security: Dr Sidney Tigere Sekeremayi.

Planning Commissioner: Richard Chemist Hove.

MINISTRIES

Office of the President: Munhumutapa Bldg, Samora Machel Ave, Private Bag 7700, Causeway, Harare; tel. (4) 707091; telex 22141.

Office of the Vice-Presidents: Munhumutapa Bldg, Samora Machel Ave, Private Bag 7700, Causeway, Harare; tel. (4) 707091; telex 24235.

Ministry of Defence: Munhumutapa Bldg, Samora Machel Ave, Private Bag 7713, Causeway, Harare; tel. (4) 700155; telex 22141; fax (4) 796762.

Ministry of Education, Sports and Culture: Ambassador House, Union Ave, POB CY 121, Causeway, Harare; tel. (4) 734051; telex 26430; fax (4) 734075.

Ministry of Finance: Munhumutapa Bldg, Samora Machel Ave, Private Bag 7705, Causeway, Harare; tel. (4) 794571; telex 22141; fax (4) 792750.

Ministry of Foreign Affairs: Munhumutapa Bldg, Samora Machel Ave, POB 4240, Causeway, Harare; tel. (4) 727005; telex 22141; fax (4) 705161.

Ministry of Health and Child Welfare: Kaguvi Bldg, Fourth St, POB CY 198, Causeway, Harare; tel. (4) 730011; telex 22141; fax (4) 729154.

Ministry of Higher Education: Old Mutual Centre, Union Ave, POB UA 275, Harare; tel. (4) 796441; fax (4) 728730.

Ministry of Home Affairs: Mukwati Bldg, Samora Machel Ave, Private Bag 7703, Causeway, Harare; tel. (4) 703641; fax (4) 726716.

Ministry of Industry and Commerce: Mukwati Bldg, Fourth St, Private Bag 7708, Causeway, Harare; tel. (4) 702731; telex 24472; fax (4) 729311.

Ministry of Information, Posts and Telecommunications: Linquenda House, Baker Ave, POB CY825, Causeway, Harare; tel. (4) 703894; telex 24142; fax (4) 707213.

Ministry of Justice, Legal and Parliamentary Affairs: Mapondera Bldg, Samora Machel Ave, Private Bag 7751, Causeway, Harare; tel. (4) 790905; telex 22141; fax (4) 790901.

Ministry of Lands and Agriculture: Ngungunyana Bldg, Private Bag 7701, Causeway, Harare; tel. (4) 792223; telex 22455; fax (4) 734646.

Ministry of Local Government and National Housing: Mukwati Bldg, Private Bag 7706, Causeway, Harare; tel. (4) 790601; telex 22179; fax (4) 708848.

Ministry of Mines, Environment and Tourism: Karigamombe Centre, Private Bag 7753, Causeway, Harare; tel. (4) 751720; telex 26430; fax (4) 734075.

Ministry of National Affairs, Employment Creation and Co-operatives: ZANU–PF Bldg, Private Bag 7762, Causeway, Harare; tel. (4) 734691; fax (4) 732709.

Ministry of Public Service, Labour and Social Welfare: Compensation House, cnr Central Ave and Fourth St, Private Bag 7707, Causeway, Harare; tel. (4) 790871; telex 22079.

Ministry of Rural Resources and Water Development: Makombe Complex, Private Bag 7701, Causeway, Harare; tel. (4) 706081.

Ministry of State Security: Chaminuka Bldg, POB 2278, Harare; tel. (4) 700501; fax (4) 732660.

Ministry of Transport and Energy: Kaguvi Bldg, POB CY595, Causeway, Harare; tel. (4) 700991; fax (4) 708225.

PROVINCIAL GOVERNORS

Manicaland: Kenneth Vhundukayi Manyonda.

Mashonaland Central: Border Gezi.

Mashonaland East: David Ishemunyoro Karimanzira.

Mashonaland West: Peter Chanetsa.

Masvingo: Josiah Dunira Hungwe.

Matabeleland North: Welshman Mabhena.

Matabeleland South: Stephen Jeqe Nyongolo Nkomo.

Midlands: Lt-Col Herbert Mahlaba.

President and Legislature

PRESIDENT

Election, 16–17 March 1996

Candidate	% of total votes cast
Robert Gabriel Mugabe	92.7
Bishop Abel Muzorewa	4.7
Rev. Ndabaningi Sithole	2.4

HOUSE OF ASSEMBLY

Speaker: Cyril Ndebele.

Election, 8–9 April 1995

	Seats*
Zimbabwe African National Union–Patriotic Front . .	118†
Zimbabwe African National Union–Ndonga . . .	2
Total	120

* In addition to the 120 directly elective seats, 12 are held by nominees of the President, 10 by traditional Chiefs and eight by Provincial Governors.

† ZANU–PF ceded one seat to an independent politician at a by-election in November 1995.

Political Organizations

Committee for a Democratic Society (CODESO): f. 1993; Kalanga-supported grouping, based in Matebeleland; Leader SOUL NDLOVU.

Conservative Alliance of Zimbabwe (CAZ): POB 242, Harare; f. 1962, known as Rhodesian Front until 1981, and subsequently as Republican Front; supported by sections of the white community; Pres. GERALD SMITH; Chair. MIKE MORONEY.

Democratic Party: f. 1991 by a breakaway faction from ZUM; Nat. Chair. GILES MUTSEKWA; Pres. DAVIDSON GOMO.

Forum Party of Zimbabwe (FPZ): Harare; f. 1993; conservative; Pres. WALTER SANSOLE (acting).

Front for Popular Democracy: f. 1994; Chair. Prof. AUSTIN CHAKAWODZA.

Independent Zimbabwe Group: f. 1983 by a breakaway faction from the fmr Republican Front; Leader BILL IRVINE.

National Democratic Union: f. 1979; conservative grouping with minority Zezeru support; Leader HENRY CHIHOTA.

National Progressive Alliance: f. 1991; Chair. CANCIWELL NZIRAMASANGA.

United National Federal Party (UNFP): Harare; f. 1978; conservative; seeks a fed. of Mashonaland and Matabeleland; Leader Chief KAYISA NDIWENI.

United Parties (UP): f. 1994; Leader Bishop ABEL MUZOREWA.

Zimbabwe Active People's Unity Party: Bulawayo; f. 1989; Leader NEWMAN MATUTU NDELA.

Zimbabwe African National Union - Patriotic Front (ZANU–PF): 88 Manica Rd, Harare; f. 1989 by merger of PF–ZAPU and ZANU–PF; Pres. ROBERT GABRIEL MUGABE; Vice-Pres SIMON VENGAYI MUZENDA, JOSHUA MQABUKO NKOMO.

Zimbabwe African National Union–Ndonga (ZANU–Ndonga): POB UA525, Union Ave, Harare; tel. and fax (4) 614177; f. 1977; breakaway faction from ZANU, also includes fmr mems of United African National Council; supports free market economy; Pres. Rev. NDABANINGI SITHOLE; Sec.-Gen. GODFRY MUMBAMARWO.

Zimbabwe Congress Party: Harare; f. 1994; Pres. KENNETH MANO.

Zimbabwe Democratic Party: Harare; f. 1979; traditionalist; Leader JAMES CHIKEREMA.

Zimbabwe Federal Party (ZFPO): Nketa 6, Po Nkulumane, Bulawayo; f. 1994; aims to create nat. fed. of five provinces; Leader TWOBOY JUBANE.

Zimbabwe National Front: f. 1979; Leader PETER MANDAZA.

Zimbabwe Peoples' Democratic Party: f. 1989; Chair. ISABEL PASALK.

Zimbabwe Unity Movement (ZUM): f. 1989 by a breakaway faction from ZANU–PF; merged with United African National Council in 1994; Leader EDGAR TEKERE.

Diplomatic Representation

EMBASSIES AND HIGH COMMISSIONS IN ZIMBABWE

Angola: 26 Speke Ave, POB 3590, Harare; tel. (4) 790070; fax (4) 790077; e-mail 101663.2177@compuserve.com; Ambassador: ALBERTO RIBEIRO.

Argentina: Club Chambers Bldg, cnr Baker Ave and Third St, POB 2770, Harare; tel. (4) 730075; telex 22284; fax (4) 730076; Ambassador: VALENTIN LUCO ORIGONE.

Australia: Karigamombe Centre, 4th Floor, 53 Samora Machel Ave, POB 4541, Harare; tel. (4) 757774; fax (4) 757770; High Commissioner: K. W. SIBRAA.

Austria: 216 New Shell House, 30 Samora Machel Ave, POB 4120, Harare; tel. (4) 702921; telex 22546; Ambassador: Dr FELIX MIKL.

Bangladesh: 9 Birchenough Rd, POB 3040, Harare; tel. (4) 727004; telex 24806; High Commissioner: HARUN AHMED CHOWDHURY.

Belgium: Tanganyika House, 5th Floor, 23 Third St, POB 2522, Harare; tel. (4) 793306; telex 24788; fax (4) 703960; Ambassador: LEOPOLD CARREWYN.

Botswana: 22 Phillips Ave, Belgravia, POB 563, Harare; tel. (4) 729551; telex 22663; High Commissioner: PHENEAS M. MAKEPE.

Brazil: Old Mutual Centre, 9th Floor, Jason Moyo Ave, POB 2530, Harare; tel. (4) 730775; fax (4) 737782; Ambassador: ANTÔNIO CARLOS DINIZ DE ANDRADA.

Bulgaria: 15 Maasdorp Ave, Alexandra Park, POB 1809, Harare; tel. (4) 730509; telex 24567; Ambassador: CHRISTO TEPAVITCHAROV.

Canada: 45 Baines Ave, POB 1430, Harare; tel. (4) 733881; telex 24465; High Commissioner: CHARLES BASSET.

China, People's Republic: 30 Baines Ave, POB 4749, Harare; tel. (4) 724572; telex 22569; fax (4) 794959; Ambassador: LIU GUIJIN.

Congo, Democratic Republic: 24 Van Praagh Ave, Milton Park, POB 2446, Harare; tel. (4) 724494; telex 22265; Ambassador: BEMBOY BABA.

Cuba: 5 Phillips Ave, Belgravia, POB 4139, Harare; tel. (4) 720256; telex 24783; Ambassador: EUMELIO CABALLERO RODRÍGUEZ.

Czech Republic: 11 Walmer Drive, Highlands, POB 4474, Harare; tel. (4) 700636; telex 22413; fax (4) 737270.

Denmark: UDC Centre, 1st Floor, cnr 59 Union Ave and First St, POB 4711, Harare; tel. (4) 758185; telex 24677; fax (4) 758189; Ambassador: ERIK FIIL.

Egypt: 7 Aberdeen Rd, Avondale, POB A433, Harare; tel. (4) 303445; telex 24653; Ambassador: Dr IBRAHIM ALY BADAWI EL-SHEIK.

Ethiopia: 14 Lanark Rd, Belgravia, POB 2745, Harare; tel. (4) 725822; telex 22743; fax (4) 720259; Ambassador: MAHIMUD DIRIR.

France: Ranelagh Rd, Highlands, POB 1378, Harare; tel. (4) 48096; telex 24779; fax (4) 45657; Ambassador: HADELIN DE LA TOUR DU PIN CHAMBLY DE LA CHARGE.

Germany: 14 Samora Machel Ave, POB 2168, Harare; tel. (4) 731956; telex 24609; fax (4) 790680; Ambassador: Dr NORWIN Graf LEUTRUM VON ERTINGEN.

Ghana: 11 Downie Ave, Belgravia, POB 4445, Harare; tel. (4) 738652; telex 24631; fax 738654; High Commissioner: Prof. P. A. TWUMASI.

Greece: 8 Deary Ave, Belgravia, POB 4809, Harare; tel. (4) 793208; telex 24790; Ambassador: ALEXANDROS SANDS.

Holy See: 5 St Kilda Rd, Mount Pleasant, POB MP191, Harare (Apostolic Nunciature); tel. (4) 744547; fax (4) 744412; Apostolic Nuncio: Most Rev. PETER PAUL PRABHU, Titular Archbishop of Tituli in Numidia.

Hungary: 20 Lanark Rd, Belgravia, POB 3594, Harare; tel. (4) 733528; telex 24237; fax (4) 730512; Ambassador: TAMÁS GÁS PÁR GÁL.

India: 12 Nathal Rd, Belgravia, POB 4620, Harare; tel. (4) 795955; telex 24630; fax (4) 722324; High Commissioner: SIDDHARTH SINGH.

Indonesia: 3 Duthie Ave, Belgravia, POB 3594, Harare; tel. (4) 732561; telex 24237; Ambassador: SAMSI ABDULLAH.

Iran: 8 Allan Wilson Ave, Avondale, POB A293, Harare; tel. (4) 726942; telex 24793; Chargé d'affaires a.i.: ALIREZA GAKARANI.

Israel: 54 Jason Moyo Ave, POB CY3191, Harare; tel. (4) 756808; fax (4) 756801; e-mail israel@harare.iafrica.com; Ambassador: GERSHON GAN.

Italy: 7 Bartholomew Close, Greendale North, POB 1062, Harare; tel. (4) 498190; telex 24380; fax (4) 498199; Ambassador: Dr LUCA BROFFERIO.

Japan: Karigamombe Centre, 18th Floor, 53 Samora Machel Ave, POB 2710, Harare; tel. (4) 790108; telex 24566; fax (4) 727769; Ambassador: MITSUO IIJIMA.

Kenya: 95 Park Lane, POB 4069, Harare; tel. (4) 790847; telex 24266; fax (4) 723042; High Commissioner: C. A. MWAKWERE.

Korea, Democratic People's Republic: 102 Josiah Chinamano Ave, Greenwood, POB 4754, Harare; tel. (4) 724052; telex 24231; Ambassador: RI MYONG CHOL.

Kuwait: 1 Bath Rd, Avondale, POB A485, Harare; Ambassador: NABILA AL-MULLA.

Libya: 124 Harare St, POB 4310, Harare; tel. (4) 728381; telex 24585; Ambassador: M. M. IBN KOURAH.

Malawi: Malawi House, Harare St, POB 321, Harare; tel. (4) 705611; telex 24467; High Commissioner: ANSLEY D. KHAUYEZA.

Malaysia: 12 Lawson Ave, Milton Park, POB 5570, Harare; tel. (4) 796209; fax (4) 796200 High Commissioner: A. K. S. YEO KEAT SEON.

Mozambique: 152 Herbert Chitepo Ave, cnr Leopold Takawira St, POB 4608, Harare; tel. (4) 790837; telex 24466; High Commissioner: CORREIA FERNANDES SUMBANA.

Netherlands: 2 Arden Rd, Highlands, POB HG601, Harare; tel. (4) 776701; telex 24357; fax (4) 776700; Ambassador: WIM WESSELS.

New Zealand: Eastgate Centre, 8th Floor, Second St, cnr Robert Mugabe Rd, POB 5448, Harare; tel. (4) 759221; telex 22747; fax (4) 759228; High Commissioner: MAUREEN O'MEEGHAN.

Nigeria: 36 Samora Machel Ave, POB 4742, Harare; tel. (4) 790765; telex 24473; High Commissioner: MUHAMMED LAMEEN METTEDEN.

Norway: 5 Lanark Rd, Belgravia, POB A510, Avondale, Harare; tel. (4) 730916; telex 24550; fax (4) 729844; Ambassador: JOHAN H. DAHL.

Pakistan: 11 Van Praagh Ave, Milton Park, POB 3050, Harare; tel. (4) 720293; fax (4) 722446; High Commissioner: TARIQ FATEMI.

Poland: 16 Cork Road, Belgravia, POB 3932, Harare; tel. (4) 732159; telex 22745; fax (4) 732159; e-mail ambrphre@somaro.co.zw; Chargé d'affaires a.i.: JACEK CHODOROWICZ.

Portugal: 10 Samora Machel Ave, POB 406, Harare; tel. (4) 725107; telex 24714; Ambassador: Dr EDUARDO NUNEZ DE CARVALHO.

Romania: 105 Fourth St, POB 4797, Harare; tel. (4) 700853; telex 24797; Ambassador: Dr GHEORGHE POPESCU.

Russia: 70 Fife Ave, POB 4250, Harare; tel. (4) 720358; telex 22616; fax (4) 700534; Ambassador: LEONID A. SAFONOV.

Slovakia: 32 Aberdeen Rd, Avondale, POB HG72, Harare; tel. (4) 302636; telex 22460; fax (4) 302236; Ambassador: Dr JÁN VODERADSKÝ.

South Africa: Temple Bar House, cnr Baker Ave and Angwa St, POB 121, Harare; tel. (4) 757908; fax (4) 757908; High Commissioner: J. N. MAMABOLO.

Spain: 16 Phillips Ave, Belgravia, POB 3300, Harare; tel. (4) 738681; telex 24173; fax (4) 795440; Ambassador: TOMÁS SOLÍS GRAGERA.

Sudan: 4 Pascoe Ave, Harare; tel. (4) 725240; telex 26308; Ambassador: ANGELO V. MORGAN.

Sweden: Pegasus House, 52 Samora Machel Ave, POB 4110, Harare; tel. (4) 790651; telex 24695; fax (4) 754265; Ambassador: LENNARTH HJELMÅKER.

Switzerland: 9 Lanark Rd, POB 3440, Harare; tel. (4) 703997; fax (4) 794925; Ambassador: CATHERINE KRIEG POLEJACK.

Tunisia: 5 Ashton Rd, Alexandra Park, POB 4308, Harare; tel. (4) 791570; telex 24801; fax (4) 727224; Ambassador: HAMID ZAOUCHE.

United Kingdom: Corner House, cnr Leopold Takawira St and Samora Machel Ave, POB 4490, Harare; tel. (4) 772990; fax (4) 774617; High Commissioner: MARTIN WILLIAMS.

USA: 172 Herbert Chitepo Ave, POB 3340, Harare; tel. (4) 794521; fax (4) 796488; Ambassador: (vacant).

Yugoslavia: 1 Lanark Rd, Belgravia, POB 3420, Harare; tel. (4) 738668; fax (4) 738660; Ambassador: LJUBISA KORAC.

Zambia: Zambia House, cnr Union and Julius Nyerere Aves, POB 4698, Harare; tel. (4) 790851; telex 24698; fax (4) 790856; High Commissioner: NCHIMUNYA SIKAULU.

Judicial System

The legal system is Roman-Dutch, based on the system which was in force in the Cape of Good Hope on 10 June 1891, as modified by subsequent legislation.

The Supreme Court has original jurisdiction in matters in which an infringement of Chapter III of the Constitution defining fundamental rights is alleged. In all other matters it has appellate jurisdiction only. It consists of the Chief Justice and four Judges of Appeal. A normal bench consists of any three of these.

The High Court consists of the Chief Justice, the Judge President, and 11 other judges. Below the High Court are Regional Courts and Magistrates' Courts with both civil and criminal jurisdiction presided over by full-time professional magistrates.

The Customary Law and Local Courts Act, adopted in 1990, abolished the village and community courts and replaced them with customary law and local courts, presided over by chiefs and headmen; in the case of chiefs, jurisdiction to try customary law cases is limited to those where the monetary values concerned do not exceed Z.$1,000 and in the case of a headman's court Z.$500. Appeals from the Chiefs' Courts are heard in Magistrates' Courts and, ultimately, the Supreme Court. All magistrates now have jurisdiction to try cases determinable by customary law.

Chief Justice: ANTHONY R. GUBBAY.

Judges of Appeal: A. M. EBRAHIM, N. J. MCNALLY, K. R. A. KORSAH, S. C. G. MUCHECHETERE.

Judge President: WILSON R. SANDURA.

Attorney-General: PATRICK ANTHONY CHINAMASA.

Religion

AFRICAN RELIGIONS

Many Africans follow traditional beliefs.

CHRISTIANITY

About 55% of the population are Christians.

Zimbabwe Council of Churches: 128 Mbuya Nehanda St, POB 3566, Harare; tel. (4) 791208; telex 26243; f. 1964; 20 mem. churches, nine assoc. mems; Pres. Rt Rev. JONATHAN SIYACHITEMA (Anglican Bishop of Harare); Gen. Sec. MUROMBEDZI KUCHERA.

The Anglican Communion

Anglicans are adherents of the Church of the Province of Central Africa, covering Botswana, Malawi, Zambia and Zimbabwe. The Church comprises 12 dioceses, including four in Zimbabwe. The Archbishop of the Province is the Bishop of Botswana.

Bishop of Central Zimbabwe: Rt Rev. TITUS ZHENJE, POB 25, Gweru; tel. (54) 51030; fax (54) 3658.

Bishop of Harare: Rt Rev. JONATHAN SIYACHITEMA, Bishop's Mount, Bishopsmount Close, POB UA7, Harare; tel. (4) 487413; fax (4) 700419.

Bishop of Manicaland: Rt Rev. ELIJAH MUSEKIWA PETER MASUKO, 115 Herbert Chitepo St, Mutare; tel. (20) 64194; fax (20) 63076.

Bishop of Matabeleland: Rt Rev. THEOPHILUS T. NALEDI, POB 2422, Bulawayo; tel. (9) 61370; fax (9) 68353.

The Roman Catholic Church

For ecclesiastical purposes, Zimbabwe comprises two archdioceses and five dioceses. At 31 December 1995 there were an estimated 1,022,226 adherents.

Zimbabwe Catholic Bishops' Conference: General Secretariat, Africa Synod House, 29 Selous Ave, POB 738, Causeway, Harare; tel. (4) 705368; fax (4) 739619; f. 1969; Pres. Mgr FRANCIS MUGADZI, Bishop of Gweru.

Archbishop of Bulawayo: Most Rev. HENRY ERNEST KARLEN, cnr Lobenguela St and Ninth Ave, POB 837, Bulawayo; tel. (9) 63590; fax (9) 60359.

Archbishop of Harare: Most Rev. PATRICK FANI CHAKAIPA, POB CY330, Causeway, Harare; tel. (4) 727386; fax (4) 721598.

Other Christian Churches

City Presbyterian Church: 60 Samora Machel Ave, POB 50, Harare; tel. (4) 790366; fax (4) 620431; f. 1904; Minister Rev. I. D. FAUCHELLE; Session Clerk H. SHEPHERD; 240 mems.

Dutch Reformed Church (Nederduitse Gereformeerde Kerk): 35 Samora Machel Ave, POB 967, Harare; tel. (4) 774748; fax (4) 774739; f. 1895; 16 parishes; Moderator Rev. A. S. VAN DYK; Gen. Sec. Rev. F. MARITZ; 2,500 mems.

Evangelical Lutheran Church: POB 2175, Bulawayo; tel. (9) 62686; f. 1903; Sec. Rt Rev. D. D. E. SIPHUMA; 57,000 mems.

Greek Orthodox Church: POB 808, Harare; tel. (4) 791616; Archbishop (vacant).

Methodist Church in Zimbabwe: POB 71, Causeway, Harare; tel. (4) 724069; fax (4) 723709; f. 1891; Pres. Bishop FARAI J. CHIRISA; Sec. of Conference Rev. MARGARET M. JAMES; 109,232 mems.

United Congregational Church of Southern Africa: POB 2451, Bulawayo; Synod Sec. for Zimbabwe Rev. J. R. DANISA LATE.

United Methodist Church: POB 3408, Harare; tel. (4) 704127; f. 1890; Bishop of Zimbabwe ABEL TENDEKAYI MUZOREWA; 45,000 mems.

Among other denominations active in Zimbabwe are the African Methodist Church, the African Methodist Episcopal Church, the African Reformed Church, the Christian Marching Church, the Church of Christ in Zimbabwe, the Independent African Church, the Presbyterian Church, the United Church of Christ, the Zimbabwe Assemblies of God and the Ziwezano Church.

JUDAISM

There were 968 members of the Jewish community in 1994.

Zimbabwe Jewish Board of Deputies: POB 1954, Harare; tel. (4) 702506; Pres. M. C. ROSS; Gen. Sec. Mrs E. ALHADEFF.

BAHÁ'Í FAITH

National Spiritual Assembly: POB GD380, Greendale, Harare; tel. (4) 495945; fax (4) 744244; mems resident in more than 3,000 localities.

The Press

DAILIES

The Chronicle: POB 585, Bulawayo; tel. (9) 540071; telex 33481; fax (9) 75522; f. 1894; circulates throughout south-west Zimbabwe; English; Editor STEPHEN A. MPOFU; circ. 74,000.

The Herald: POB 396, Harare; tel. (4) 795771; telex 26196; fax (4) 791311; f. 1891; English; Editor TOMMY SITHOLE; circ. 122,166.

PERIODICALS

Africa Calls Worldwide: POB BW1500, Harare; tel. (4) 728256; telex 26334; fax (4) 792932; f. 1960; travel; 6 a year; Man. Editor DONETTE KRUGER.

Business Herald: Harare; weekly; Editor ANDREW RUSINGA.

Central African Journal of Medicine: POB A195, Avondale, Harare; tel. (4) 791631; f. 1955; monthly; Editor-in-Chief Dr J. A. MATENGA.

Chaminuka News: POB 251, Marondera; f. 1988; fortnightly; English and Chishona; Editor M. MUGABE; circ. 10,000.

City Observer: POB 990, Harare; tel. (4) 706536; telex 26189; fax (4) 708544; monthly.

Commerce: POB 1683, Harare; tel. (4) 736835; journal of Zimbabwe Nat. Chambers of Commerce; monthly; Editor J. MAKAMURE; circ. 1,500.

Computer and Telecom News: Thomson House, cnr Speke Ave and Harare St, POB 1683, Harare; tel. (4) 736835; fax (4) 749803; monthly.

CZI Industrial Review: POB 1683, Harare; tel. (4) 736835; fax (4) 749803.

Economic Review: c/o Zimbabwe Financial Holdings, POB 3198, Harare; tel. (4) 751168; telex 24163; fax (4) 757497; 4 a year; circ. 3,000.

Executive: POB 2677, Harare; tel. (4) 755084; fax (4) 752162; bimonthly; Editor: MICHAEL J. HAMILTON.

The Farmer: POB 1622, Harare; tel. (4) 753278; telex 22084; fax (4) 750754; f. 1928; commercial farming; weekly; English; Editor FELICITY WOOD; circ. 6,100.

Farming World with Kurima Ukulima: POB MP 1283, Mount Pleasant, Harare; tel. (4) 745955; f. 1975; monthly; English; Editors S. DICKIN, D. H. B. DICKIN; circ. 7,500.

Financial Gazette: 27–29 Charter Rd, POB 66070, Kopje, Harare; tel. (4) 738722; weekly; independent; Editor (vacant); circ. 28,000.

Horizon Magazine: POB UA196, Union Ave, Harare; tel. (4) 704645; monthly; circ. 35,000.

Hotel and Catering Gazette: POB 2677, Kopje, Harare; tel. (4) 738722; telex 26334; fax (4) 707130; monthly; Editor PAULA CHARLES; circ. 2,000.

Indonsakusa: POB 150, Hwange; f. 1988; monthly; English and Sindebele; Editor D. NTABENI; circ. 10,000.

Insurance Review: POB 1683, Harare; tel. (4) 736835; fax (4) 749803; monthly; Editor M. ZHUWAKINYU.

Jassa: POB MP 203, Mount Pleasant, Harare; tel. (4) 303211; telex 26580; fax (4) 333407; applied science journal of the Univ. of Zimbabwe; 2 a year; Editor Prof. C. F. B. NHACHI.

Journal on Social Change and Development: POB 4405, Harare; tel. (4) 720417; telex 22055; f. 1981; quarterly; Chair. JOYCE KAZEMBE; circ. 4,500.

Just for Me: POB 66070, Kopje, Harare; tel (4) 704715; f. 1990; family and women's interest; Editor BEVERLEY TILLEY.

Karoi News: POB 441, Karoi; tel. 6216; fortnightly.

Kwayedza: POB 396, Harare; tel. (4) 795771; weekly; Editor G. M. CHITEWE; circ. 34,000.

Look and Listen: POB UA589, Harare; tel. (4) 756160; fax (4) 723792; f. 1965; radio and TV programmes, entertainment and reviews; fortnightly; Editor GAVIN PETER; circ. 23,000.

Mahogany: POB UA589, Harare; tel. (4) 752144; telex 24748; fax (4) 752062; f. 1980; English; women's interest; 6 a year; Editor AULORA STALLY; circ. 33,000.

Makonde Star: POB 533, Kwekwe; tel. (55) 2248; f. 1989; weekly; English; Editor FELIX MOYO; circ. 21,000.

Makoni Clarion: POB 17, Rusape; monthly.

Manica Post: POB 960, Mutare; tel. (20) 61212; telex 81237; fax (20) 61149; 2274; f. 1893; weekly; Editor J. GAMBANGA; circ. 20,000.

Masiye Pambili (Let Us Go Forward): POB 591, Bulawayo; tel. (9) 75011; telex 50563; fax (9) 69701; f. 1964; English; 2 a year; Editor M. M. NDUBIWA; circ. 21,000.

Masvingo Mirror: POB 171, Masvingo; tel. (39) 64372; fax (39) 64484; weekly; independent.

Midlands Observer: POB 533, Kwekwe; tel. (55) 2248; f. 1953; weekly; English; Editor FELIX MOYO; circ. 5,000.

Monthly Bulletin: POB 1283, Harare; tel. (4) 70300; publ. by the Reserve Bank of Zimbabwe.

Moto: POB 890, Gweru; tel. (54) 4886; fax (54) 51991; Roman Catholic; Editor JOHN HAASBROEK (acting); circ. 30,000.

Nehanda Guardian: POB 150, Hwange; f. 1988; monthly; English and Chishona; Editor K. MWANAKA; circ. 10,000.

Nhau Dzekumakomo: POB 910, Mutare; f. 1984; publ. by Mutare City Council; monthly.

North Midlands Gazette: POB 222, Kadoma; tel. (68) 2021; fax (68) 2841; f. 1912; weekly; Editor C. B. KIDIA.

On Guard: National Social Security Authority, POB 1387, Causeway, Harare; tel. (4) 728931; fax (4) 796320; Editor C. C. MUSHAMBI.

The Outpost: POB HG106, Highlands; tel. (4) 724571; f. 1911; English; monthly; Editor WAYNE BVUDZIJENA; circ. 21,000.

Parade Magazine: POB 3798, Harare; tel. (4) 736835; fax (4) 749803; f. 1953; monthly; English; Editor C. NGWIRA; circ. 91,000.

Prize Africa: POB UA460, Harare; tel. (4) 705411; telex 24748; f. 1973; monthly; English; Editor STEPHAN DZIVANE; circ. 15,000.

Quarterly Guide to the Economy: First Merchant Bank of Zimbabwe, FMB House, 67 Samora Machel Ave, POB 2786, Harare; tel. (4) 703071; telex 26025; fax (4) 738810; quarterly.

RailRoader: POB 596, Bulawayo; f. 1952; tel. (9) 363526; telex 33173; fax (9) 363502; monthly; Editor M. GUMEDE; circ. 10,000.

The Record: POB 179, Harare; tel. (4) 708911; journal of the Public Service Asscn; 6 a year; Editor GAMALIEL RUNGANI; circ. 30,000.

Southern African Economist: POB MP1005, Harare; tel. (4) 704952; monthly; circ. 16,000.

Southern African Political and Economic Monthly: POB MP111, Harare; tel. (4) 704952; fax (4) 732735; monthly; Editor-in-Chief IBBO MANDAZA; circ. 16,000.

Sunday Gazette: POB 66070, Kopje, Harare; tel. (4) 738722; weekly; Editor FRANCIS MDLONGWA.

Sunday Mail: POB 396, Harare; tel. (4) 795771; telex 26196; fax (4) 791311; f. 1935; weekly; English; Editor CHARLES CHIKEREMA; circ. 154,489.

Sunday News: POB 585, Bulawayo; tel. (9) 65471; telex 33481; fax (9) 75522; f. 1930; weekly; English; Editor LAWRENCE CHIKUWIRA; circ. 66,000.

Teacher in Zimbabwe: POB 350, Harare; tel. (4) 497548; fax (4) 497554; f. 1981; monthly; circ. 47,000.

The Times: 71 Seventh St, POB 66, Gweru; tel. (54) 3285; telex 77753; fax (54) 51614; f. 1897; weekly; English; Editor SHEPARD SAMASUWO; circ. 5,000.

Tobacco News: POB 1683, Harare; tel. (4) 736836; fax (4) 749803; circ. 3,000.

Vanguard: POB 66102, Kopje; tel. 751193; every 2 months.

The Worker: POB 8323, Causeway, Harare; tel. 700466.

World Vision News: POB 2420, Harare; tel. 703794; quarterly.

Zambezia: POB MP203, Harare; tel. (4) 303211; telex 26580; fax (4) 333407; humanities journal of the Univ. of Zimbabwe; 2 a year; Editor Prof. M. C. M. BOURDILLON.

Zimbabwe Agricultural Journal: POB CY594, Causeway, Harare; tel. (4) 704531; telex 22455; fax (4) 728317; f. 1903; 6 a year; Editor R. J. FENNER; circ. 2,000.

Zimbabwe Defence Forces Magazine: POB 7720, Harare; tel. (4) 722481; f. 1982; 6 a year; circ. 5,000.

The Zimbabwe Engineer: POB 1683, Harare; tel. (4) 736835; fax (4) 749803; Editor M. ZHUWAKINYU.

Zimbabwe Independent: Harare; f. 1996; weekly; Editor TREVOR NCUBE; Publisher CLIVE WILSON.

Zimbabwe News: POB CY3206, Causeway, Harare; tel. (4) 790148; fax (4) 790483; monthly.

Zimbabwean Government Gazette: POB 8062, Causeway, Harare; official govt journal; weekly; Editor L. TAKAWIRA.

NEWS AGENCIES

Zimbabwe Inter-Africa News Agency (ZIANA): POB CY511, Causeway, Harare; tel. (4) 730151; telex 26127; fax (4) 794336; f. 1981; owned and controlled by Zimbabwe Mass Media Trust; Editor-in-Chief HENRY E. MURADZIKWA.

Foreign Bureaux

Agence France-Presse (AFP): Robinson House, Union Ave, POB 1166, Harare; tel. (4) 758017; telex 26161; fax (4) 753291; Rep. FRANÇOIS-BERNARD CASTÉRAN.

ANGOP (Angola): Mass Media House, 3rd Floor, 19 Selous Ave, POB 6354, Harare; tel. (4) 736849; telex 22204.

Agenzia Nazionale Stampa Associata (ANSA) (Italy): Harare; tel. (4) 723881; telex 74177; Rep. IAN MILLS.

Associated Press (AP) (USA): POB 785, Harare; tel. (4) 706622; telex 24676; fax (4) 703994; Rep. JOHN EDLIN.

Deutsche Presse-Agentur (dpa) (Germany): Harare; tel. (4) 700875; telex 24339; Correspondent JAN RAATH.

Informatsionnoye Telegrafnoye Agentstvo Rossii—Telegrafnoye Agentstvo Suverennykh Stran (ITAR—TASS) (Russia): Mass Media House, 19 Selous Ave, POB 4012, Harare; tel. (4) 790521; telex 26022; Correspondent YURII PITCHUGIN.

Inter Press Service (IPS) (Italy): 127 Union Ave, POB 6050, Harare; tel. (4) 790104; telex 26129; fax (4) 728415; e-mail ipshre@harare.iafrica.com; Rep. KENNETH BLACKMAN.

News Agency of Nigeria (NAN): Harare; tel. (4) 703041; telex 24674.

Pan-African News Agency (PANA) (Senegal): 19 Selous Ave, POB 8364, Harare; tel. (4) 730971; telex 26403; Bureau Chief PETER MWAURA.

Prensa Latina (Cuba): Mass Media House, 3rd Floor, 19 Selous Ave, Harare; tel. (4) 731993; telex 22461; Correspondent HUGO RIUS.

Press Trust of India (PTI): Mass Media House, 3rd Floor, 19 Selous Ave, Harare; tel. (4) 795006; telex 22038; Rep. N. V. R. SWAMI.

Reuters (United Kingdom): 901 Tanganyika House, Union Ave, Harare, POB 2987; tel. (4) 724299; telex 24291; Bureau Chief DAVID BLOOM.

Rossiiskoye Informatsionnoye Agentstvo—Novosti (RIA—Novosti) (Russia): 503 Robinson House, cnr Union Ave and Angwa St, POB 3908, Harare; tel. (4) 707232; telex 22293; fax (4) 707233; Correspondent A. TIMONOVICH.

Tanjug (Yugoslavia): Mass Media House, 19 Selous Ave, Harare; tel. (4) 479018; Correspondent DEJAN DRAKULIĆ.

United Press International (UPI) (USA): Harare; tel. (4) 25265; telex 24177; Rep. IAN MILLS.

Xinhua (New China) News Agency (People's Republic of China): 4 Earls Rd, Alexander Park, POB 4746, Harare; tel. (4) 731467; telex 22310; fax (4) 731467; Chief Correspondent LU JIANXIN.

Publishers

Academic Books (Pvt) Ltd: POB 567, Harare; tel. (4) 706729; fax (4) 702071; educational.

Amalgamated Publications (Pvt) Ltd: POB 1683, Harare; tel. (4) 736835; fax (4) 749803; f. 1949; trade journals; Man. Dir A. THOMSON.

Anvil Press: POB 4209, Harare; tel. (4) 751202; f. 1988; general; Dirs PAUL BRICKHILL, PAT BRICKHILL, STEVE KHOZA.

The Argosy Press: POB 2677, Harare; tel. (4) 755084; magazine publrs; Gen. Man. A. W. HARVEY.

Baobab Books (Pvt) Ltd: POB 1559, Harare; tel. (4) 706729; fax (4) 702071; general, literature, children's.

Books of Zimbabwe Publishing Co (Pvt) Ltd: POB 1994, Bulawayo; tel. (9) 61135; f. 1968; Man. Dir LOUIS W. BOLZE.

College Press Publishers (Pvt) Ltd: POB 3041, Harare; tel. (4) 754145; telex 22558; fax (4) 754256; f. 1968; educational and general; Man. Dir B. B. MUGABE.

Directory Publishers Ltd: POB 1595, Bulawayo; tel. (9) 78831; telex 33333; fax (9) 78835; directories; Man. BRUCE BEALE.

Graham Publishing Co (Pvt) Ltd: POB 2931, Harare; tel. (4) 752437; f. 1967; general; Dir GORDON M. GRAHAM.

Harare Publishing House: Chiremba Rd, Hatfield, POB 4735, Harare; tel. (4) 570613; f. 1984; Dir Dr T. M. SAMKANGE.

HarperCollins Publishers (Zimbabwe) Pvt) Ltd: Union Ave, POB UA 201, Harare; tel. (4) 721413; fax (4) 732436; Man. S. D. McMILLAN.

Longman Zimbabwe (Pvt) Ltd: Tourle Rd, Harare Drive, Ardbennie, Harare; tel. (4) 621661; telex 22566; fax (4) 621670; f. 1964; general and educational; Man. Dir N. L. DLODLO.

Mambo Press: Senga Rd, POB 779, Gweru; tel. (54) 4016; fax (54) 51991; f. 1958; religious, educational and fiction in English and African languages; Gen. Man. PATRICK RUKODZI.

Modus Publications (Pvt) Ltd: Modus House, 27-29 Charter Rd, POB 66070, Kopje, Harare; tel. (4) 738722; Man. Dir ELIAS RUSIKE.

Munn Publishing (Pvt) Ltd: POB UA460, Harare; tel. (4) 752144; telex 24748; fax (4) 752062; Man. Dir A. F. MUNN.

Standard Publications (Pvt) Ltd: POB 3745, Harare; Dir G. F. BOOT.

Southern African Printing and Publishing House (SAPPHO): Mass Media House, 1st Floor, 19 Selous Ave, POB MP1005, Mt Pleasant, Harare; tel. (4) 704951; fax (4) 704953; Editor-in-Chief Dr IBBO MANDAZA.

University of Zimbabwe Publications: POB MP203, Mount Pleasant, Harare; tel. (4) 303211; telex 26580; fax (4) 333407; f. 1969; Dir MAURICE K. MUTOWO.

Zimbabwe Newspapers (1980) Ltd: POB 396, Harare; tel. (4) 704088; telex 26196; fax (4) 702400; f. 1981; state-owned; controls largest newspaper group; Chair. HONOUR MKUSHI.

Zimbabwe Publishing House: POB 350, Harare; tel. (4) 497548; telex 26035; fax (4) 497554; f. 1982; Chair. DAVID MARTIN.

Government Publishing House

The Literature Bureau: POB 749, Causeway, Harare; tel. (4) 333812; f. 1954; controlled by Ministry of Education; Dir B. C. CHITSIKE.

Radio and Television

In 1994, according to UNESCO estimates, there were 945,000 radio receivers and 297,000 television receivers in use.

RADIO

Broadcasts in English, Chishona, Sindebele, Kalanga, Venda, Tonga and Chewa; four programme services comprise a general service (predominantly in English), vernacular languages service, light entertainment, educational programmes.

TELEVISION

The main broadcasting centre is in Harare, with a second studio in Bulawayo; broadcasts on two channels (one of which serves the Harare area only) for about 190 hours per week. A commercial television channel was scheduled to commence operations in the late 1990s.

Zimbabwe Broadcasting Corporation: POB HG444, Highlands, Harare; tel. (4) 498630; fax (4) 498613; f. 1957; Chair. HOSEA MAPONDERA; Dir-Gen. EDWARD M. MOYO (acting).

Finance

(cap. = capital; res = reserves; dep. = deposits; m. = million; br. = branch; amounts in Zimbabwe dollars)

BANKING

Central Bank

Reserve Bank of Zimbabwe: 80 Samora Machel Ave, POB 1283, Harare; tel. (4) 703000; telex 26075; fax (4) 707800; f. 1964; bank of issue; cap. and res 8m., dep. 7,496m. (April 1997); Gov. Dr LEONARD TSUMBA.

Commercial Banks

Barclays Bank of Zimbabwe Ltd: Barclay House, First St and Jason Moyo Ave, POB 1279, Harare; tel. (4) 729811; telex 24185; fax (4) 707293; cap. and res 377m., dep. 4,132m. (Dec. 1995); Chair. D. M. ZAMCHIYA; Man. Dir I. G. TAKAWIRA.

Commercial Bank of Zimbabwe: POB 3313, Harare; tel. (4) 758081; telex 24245; fax (4) 758085; state-owned; cap. and res 37m. (Dec. 1992); Man. Dir GIDEON GONO; 9 brs.

Stanbic Bank Zimbabwe Ltd: Ottoman House, 1st Floor, 59 Samora Machel Ave, POB 300, Harare; tel. (4) 759480; telex 26103; fax (4) 751324; f. 1990; cap. and res 74m., dep. 2,506m. (Dec. 1996); Chair. C. M. D. SANYONGA; Man. Dir A. A. JAYES; 14 brs.

Standard Chartered Bank Zimbabwe Ltd: John Boyne House, 38 Speke Ave, POB 373, Harare; tel. (4) 753212; telex 22115; fax (4) 758076; f. 1983; cap. and res 487m., dep. 4,729m. (Dec. 1995); Chair. H. P. MKUSHI; CEO J. M. MCKENNA; 42 brs and sub-brs; 10 agencies.

Trade and Investment Bank Ltd: Cabs Centre, 10th Floor, Jason Moyo Ave, POB CY 1064, Causeway, Harare; tel. (4) 793455; telex 26757; fax (4) 793454; f. 1995; cap. and res 20m. (Sept. 1996); Chair. Dr B. CHIDZERO; CEO Dr K. J. MOYANA.

Zimbabwe Banking Corporation Ltd: Zimbank House, 46 Speke Ave, POB 3198, Harare; tel. (4) 757471; telex 24163; fax (4) 757497; f. 1951; wholly-owned subsidiary of Zimbabwe Financial Holdings Ltd, which is 59% govt-owned; cap. and res 120m., dep. 4,468.3m. (Sept. 1995); Group CEO E. N. MUSHAYAKARARA; 48 brs, sub-brs and agencies.

Development Bank

Zimbabwe Development Bank (ZDB): ZDB House, 99 Rotten Row, POB 1720, Harare; tel. (4) 750171; telex 26279; fax (4) 774225; f. 1985; 33.3% state-owned; cap. and res 171m. (June 1996); Chair. Dr T. MASAYA; Man. Dir R. JARAVAZA; 3 brs.

Merchant Banks

First Merchant Bank of Zimbabwe Ltd: FMB House, 67 Samora Machel Ave, POB 2786, Harare; tel. (4) 703071; telex 26025; fax (4)

738810; f. 1956; cap. and res 305m., dep. 778m. (Dec. 1996); Chair. R. P. Lander; Man. Dir R. Feltoe; br. in Bulawayo.

Heritage Investment Bank: Karigamombe Centre, 6th Floor, 53 Samora Machel Ave, POB CY813, Causeway, Harare; tel. (4) 749750; fax (4) 749413.

Merchant Bank of Central Africa Ltd: Old Mutual Centre, 14th Floor, cnr Third St and Jason Moyo Ave, POB 3200, Harare; tel. (4) 738081; telex 26568; fax (4) 708005; f. 1956; cap. and res 87m., dep. 812m. (March 1996); Chair. E. D. Chiura; Man. Dir David Hatendi.

National Merchant Bank of Zimbabwe Ltd: Unity Court, 1st Floor, cnr Union Ave and First St, POB 2564, Harare; tel. (4) 759651; telex 26392; fax (4) 759648; f. 1993; cap. 25m. (Dec. 1995); Chair. P. T. Zhanda; Man. Dir J. T. Makoni.

Standard Chartered Merchant Bank Zimbabwe Ltd: Standard Chartered Bank Bldg, Second St, POB 60, Harare; tel. (4) 708585; telex 22208; fax (4) 725667; f. 1971; cap. and res 78m., dep. 193m. (Dec. 1995); Chair. J. M. McKenna; Man. Dir W. Matsaira.

Syfrets Merchant Bank Ltd: Zimbank House, 46 Speke Ave, POB 2540, Harare; tel. (4) 757535; telex 26292; fax (4) 751741; f. 1967; subsidiary of Zimbabwe Financial Holdings Ltd, which is 59% govt-owned; cap. and res 90m., dep. 768m. (Sept. 1995); Chair. A. F. Nhawu; Man. Dir A. D. Henchie.

Discount Houses

Bard Discount House Ltd: Club House, 47 Samora Machel Ave, POB 3321, Harare; tel. (4) 752756; telex 24326; fax (4) 750192; cap. and res 90m. (April 1997); Chair M. A. Masunda; Man. Dir R. G. Paterson.

The Discount Co of Zimbabwe (DCZ): 70 Park Lane, POB 3424, Harare; tel. (4) 705414; fax (4) 731670; cap. 5.1m. (Feb. 1995); Chair. S. J. Chihambakwe.

Intermarket Discount House: Unity Court, 5th Floor, Union Ave, Harare.

National Discount House Ltd: Chancellor House, 10th Floor, 69 Samora Machel Ave, POB CY 2245, Causeway, Harare; tel. (4) 700771; fax (4) 792927; cap. and res 7m. (Sept. 1995); Man. Dir E. Matienga.

udc Ltd: udc Centre, cnr First St and Union Ave, POB 1685, Harare; tel. (4) 750597; telex 24405; fax (4) 758179; cap. and res 73m. (Dec. 1995); Man. Dir J. W. Dick.

Banking Organization

Institute of Bankers of Zimbabwe: POB UA521, Harare; tel. (4) 752474; fax (4) 737499; f. 1973; Pres. P. Sigsworth; Dir S. A. H. Brown.

STOCK EXCHANGE

Zimbabwe Stock Exchange: Southampton House, 8th Floor, Union Ave, POB UA234, Harare; tel. (4) 736861; fax (4) 791045; f. 1946; Chair. M. J. S. Tunmer.

INSURANCE

Commercial Union Insurance Co of Zimbabwe Ltd: Harare; tel. (4) 730041; telex 24194; fax (4) 790214; e-mail cuzimb@harare.iafrica.com; mem. of Commercial Union group; Chair. H. P. Mkushi.

Fidelity Life Assurance of Zimbabwe (Pvt) Ltd: 66 Julius Nyerere Way, POB 435, Harare; tel. (4) 750927; telex 24189; fax (4) 704705; Chair. M. Sifelani; Gen. Man. J. P. Weeks.

National Insurance Co of Zimbabwe (Pvt) Ltd: cnr Baker Ave and First St, POB 1256, Harare; tel. (4) 704911; telex 24605; fax (4) 704914.

Old Mutual: POB 70, Harare; tel. (4) 308400; telex 22118; fax (4) 308468; f. 1845; life assurance; Chair. J. S. Brown; CEO G. D. Hollick; Gen. Man. L. E. M. Ngwerume.

RM Insurance Co (Pvt) Ltd: Royal Mutual House, 45 Baker Ave, POB 3599, Harare; tel. (4) 731011; telex 24683; fax (4) 731028; f. 1982; cap. p.u. 2m.; Chair. C. Wright; Gen. Man. D. K. Beach.

Southampton Assurance Co of Zimbabwe Ltd: Southampton Life Centre, 77 Jason Moyo Ave, POB 969, Harare; tel. (4) 708801; fax (4) 703186; life assurance.

Zimnat Life Assurance Co Ltd: Zimnat House, cnr Baker Ave and Third St, POB 2417, Harare; tel. (4) 737611; fax (4) 790726; Gen. Man. R. G. Muirimi.

Trade and Industry

CHAMBER OF COMMERCE

Zimbabwe National Chambers of Commerce (ZNCC): Equity House, Rezende St, POB 1934, Harare; tel. (4) 753444; telex 22531; fax (4) 753450; f. 1983; Pres. Danny Meyer.

INDUSTRIAL AND EMPLOYERS' ASSOCIATIONS

Bulawayo Agricultural Society: PO Famona, Bulawayo; tel. (9) 77668; fax (9) 77668; f. 1907; Pres. C. P. D. Goodwin.

Bulawayo Landowners' and Farmers' Association: Bulawayo.

Cattle Producers' Association: Harare; Pres. G. Franceys.

Chamber of Mines of Zimbabwe: 4 Central Ave, POB 712, Harare; tel. (4) 702843; telex 26271; fax (4) 707983; f. 1939; CEO Derek Bain.

Coffee Growers' Association: Leopold Takawira St, POB 4382, Harare; tel. and fax (4) 750238; Dir Jules Lang.

Commercial Cotton Growers' Association: 113 Leopold Takawira St, POB 592, Harare; tel. (4) 772726; fax (4) 772735; Pres. J. M. H. Kemple.

Commercial Farmers' Union: POB 1241, Harare; tel. (4) 772726; telex 22084; f. 1942; Pres. Peter MacSporran; Dir D. W. Hasluck; 4,200 mems.

Confederation of Zimbabwe Industries: Fidelity Life Tower, cnr Luck and Raleigh Sts, Harare; tel. (4) 739833; telex 22073; fax (4) 750953; f. 1957; Pres. J. Blanchfield; CEO Joe Foroma; 1,000 mems.

Construction Industry Federation of Zimbabwe: POB 1502, Harare; tel. (4) 746661; fax (4) 746937; e-mail cifoz@id.co.zw; Pres. P. M. Power; CEO M. B. Narotam.

Employers' Confederation of Zimbabwe: POB 158, Harare; tel. (4) 224070; fax (4) 223942; Pres. Lazarus Dhlakama; Exec. Dir Peter F. Kunjeku.

Employment Council for the Motor Industry: POB 1084, Bulawayo; tel. (9) 78161.

Industrial Development Corporation of Zimbabwe Ltd: POB CY1431, Causeway, Harare; tel. (4) 706971; telex 24409; fax (4) 796028; f. 1963; Chair. J. B. Wakatama; Gen. Man. M. N. Ndudzo.

Kadoma Farmers' and Stockowners' Association: Kadoma; tel. (68) 3658; Chair. A. Reed; Sec. P. M. Reed; 66 mems.

Kwekwe Farmers' Association: POB 72, Kwekwe; tel. (55) 247721; f. 1928; Chair. D. Edwards; Sec. J. Tapson; 87 mems.

Manicaland Chamber of Industries: POB 92, Mutare; tel. (20) 62300; f. 1945; Pres. L. Baxter; 60 mems.

Mashonaland Chamber of Industries: POB 3794, Harare; tel. (4) 739833; telex 22073; fax (4) 750953; f. 1922; Pres. A. I. S. Ferguson; Sec. M. Mubataripi; 729 mems.

Matabeleland Chamber of Industries: POB 2317, Bulawayo; tel. (9) 60642; fax (9) 60814; f. 1931; Pres. E. V. Matikiti; Sec. N. McKay; about 300 mems.

Matabeleland Region of The Construction Industry Federation of Zimbabwe: POB 1970, Bulawayo; tel. (9) 65787; f. 1919; Sec. M. Barron; 124 mems.

Midlands Chamber of Industries: POB 213, Gweru; tel. (54) 2812; Pres. J. W. Pringle; 50 mems.

Minerals Marketing Corporation of Zimbabwe: 90 Mutare Rd, Msasa, POB 2628, Harare; tel. (4) 486945; fax (4) 487261; f. 1982; sole authority for marketing of mineral production (except gold); Chair. E. Mutowo; Gen. Man. Liz Chitiga.

Mutare District Farmers' Association: POB 29, Mutare; tel. (20) 64233; Chair. R. C. Truscott; Sec. Mrs J. Froggatt; 45 mems.

National Association of Dairy Farmers: Agriculture House, 113 Leopold Takawira St, POB 1241, Harare; tel. (4) 772724; fax (4) 752614; Chair. I. M. Webster; CEO D. R. Pascoe.

National Employment Council for the Construction Industry of Zimbabwe: St Barbara House, Moffat St, POB 2995, Harare; tel. (4) 726740; Gen. Sec. F. Chitsva.

National Employment Council for the Engineering and Iron and Steel Industry: Chancellor House, 5th Floor, Samora Machel Ave, POB 1922, Harare; tel. (4) 705607; fax (4) 791221; f. 1943; Gen. Sec. E. E. Sharpe.

Tobacco Industry and Marketing Board: POB UA214, Union Ave, Harare; tel. (4) 666311; telex 24656; fax (4) 666384.

Zimbabwe Farmers' Union: POB 3755, Harare; tel. (4) 704763; telex 26217; fax (4) 700829; Chair. Gary Magadzire.

Zimbabwe Tobacco Association: POB 1781, Harare; tel. (4) 727441; fax (4) 724523; e-mail zta@id.co.zw; Pres. Robert Webb; CEO Chris R. L. Molam; 4,620 mems.

Zimtrade: POB 2738, Harare; tel. (4) 732974; telex 26677; fax (4) 706930; f. 1991; nat. export promotion org.; Chair. P. T. Zhamda; CEO S. K. Hwindingwi.

MAJOR INDUSTRIAL COMPANIES

Almin Metal Industries: POB 394, Southernton, Harare; tel. (4) 620110; fax (4) 620123; semi-fabricators in non-ferrous metals.

Bindura Nickel Corporation Ltd: POB 1108, Harare; tel. (4) 704461; telex 26048; fax (4) 703734; mining, smelting and refining of nickel; Chair. R. P. LANDER.

Circle Cement Ltd: POB GD160, Greendale, Harare; tel. (4) 498156; telex 26570; fax (4) 498553; Exec. Chair. G. I. GEORGE; Man. Dir I. COULTER.

Delta Corporation Ltd: POB BW294, Borrowdale, Harare; tel. (4) 883865; telex 22126; fax (4) 883864; f. 1946; brewers, soft drink mfrs, supermarket and furniture retailing and the hotel industry; Chair. Dr R. M. MUWAPOSE; CEO J. P ROONEY.

Hippo Valley Estates Ltd: POB 1, Chiredzi; tel. (31) 2381; telex 92301; fax (31) 2554; production of sugar from cane; Chair. P. M. BAUM; Gen. Man. B. R. BURBIDGE.

Mhangura Copper Mines: 90 Mutare Rd, POB 2370, Harare; tel. (4) 487014; telex 26372; fax (4) 487022; f. 1947; copper mining.

Rio Tinto Zimbabwe Ltd: POB CY1243, Causeway, Harare; tel. (4) 746141; telex 26081; fax (4) 746228; custom refining nickel and copper; gold mining; also diamonds and coal prospecting; Chair. S. C. TAWENGWA.

Wankie Colliery Co Ltd: POB 123, Hwange; coal mining at Hwange (fmrly Wankie); Chair. N. KUDENGA; Man. Dir O. K. BWERINOFA.

ZIMASCO (Pvt) Ltd: Pegasus House, 6th Floor, Samora Machel Ave, POB 3110, Harare; tel. (4) 739622; fax (4) 707758; f. 1923; chromite mining at Shurugwi and Mutorashanga, smelting at Kwekwe; 3,500 employees.

Zimbabwe Iron and Steel Co Ltd (Ziscosteel): Private Bag 2, Redcliff; tel. (55) 62401; telex 70038; fax (55) 68666; largest integrated steelworks in sub-Saharan Africa, with annual capacity of 1m. tons of liquid steel.

TRADE UNIONS

All trade unions in Zimbabwe became affiliated to the ZCTU in 1981. The ZCTU is encouraging a policy of union amalgamations.

Zimbabwe Congress of Trade Unions (ZCTU): Chester House, 10th Floor, Speke Ave at Third St, POB 3549, Harare; tel. (4) 794742; fax (4) 728484; f. 1981; co-ordinating org. for trade unions; Pres. GIBSON SIBANDA.

Zimbabwe Federation of Trade Unions: Harare; f. 1996 as alternative to ZCTU; Co-ordinator CUTHBERT CHISWA.

Principal Unions

Air Transport Union: POB AP40, Harare Airport, Harare; tel. (4) 52601; f. 1956; Pres. J. B. DEAS; Gen. Sec. C. J. GOTORA; 580 mems.

Associated Mineworkers' Union of Zimbabwe: POB 384, Harare; tel. (4) 700287; Pres. J. S. MUTANDARE; 25,000 mems.

Building Workers' Trade Union: St Barbara House, POB 1291, Harare; tel. (4) 720942; Gen. Sec. E. NJEKESA.

Commercial Workers' Union of Zimbabwe: Travlos House, 3rd Floor, Harare; tel. (4) 751451; Gen. Sec. S. D. R. CHIFAMBA; 6,000 mems.

Federation of Municipal Workers' Union: Bulawayo; tel. (9) 60506; Gen. Sec. F. V. NCUBE.

Furniture and Cabinet Workers' Union: POB 1291, Harare; Gen. Sec. C. KASEKE.

General Agricultural and Plantation Workers' Union: Harare; tel. (4) 792860; Gen. Sec. M. MAWERE.

Graphical Association: POB 27, Bulawayo; tel. (4) 62477; POB 494, Harare; Gen. Sec. A. NGWENYA; 3,015 mems.

Harare Municipal Workers' Union: Office No 12, Harare Community, Harare; tel. (4) 62343; Gen. Sec. T. G. T. MAPFUMO.

National Airways Workers' Union: POB AP1, Harare; tel. (4) 737011; telex 40008; fax (4) 231444; Gen. Sec. B. SPENCER.

National Engineering Workers' Union: POB 4968, Harare; tel. (4) 702963; Pres. I. MATONGO; Gen. Sec. O. KABASA.

National Union of Clothing Industry Workers' Union: POB RY28, Raylton; tel. 64432; Gen. Sec. C. M. PASIPANODYA.

Railways Associated Workers' Union: Bulawayo; tel. (9) 70041; f. 1982; Pres. SAMSON MABEKA; Gen. Sec. A. J. MHUNGU.

Technical & Salaried Staff Association: POB 33, Redcliff; tel. (55) 68798; Gen. Sec. J. DANCAN.

Transport and General Workers' Union: Dublin House, POB 4769, Harare; tel. (4) 793508; Gen. Sec. F. MAKANDA.

United Food and Allied Workers' Union of Zimbabwe: Harare; tel. (4) 74150; f. 1962; Gen. Sec. I. M. NEDZIWE.

Zimbabwe Amalgamated Railwaymen's Union: Unity House, 13th Ave, Herbert Chitepo St, Bulawayo; tel. (9) 60948; Gen. Sec. T. L. SHANA.

Zimbabwe Banks and Allied Workers' Union: POB 966, Harare; tel. (4) 703744; Pres. SHINGEREI MUNGATE; Gen. Sec. C. C. GWIJO.

Zimbabwe Catering and Hotel Workers' Union: Nialis Bldg, POB 3913, Harare; tel. (4) 794627; Gen. Sec. N. E. MUDZENGERERE.

Zimbabwe Chemical & Allied Workers' Union: POB 4810, Harare; Gen. Sec. R. MAKUVAZA.

Zimbabwe Domestic & Allied Workers' Union: Harare; tel. (4) 795405; Gen. Sec. G. SHOKO.

Zimbabwe Educational, Welfare & Mission Workers' Union: St Andrews House, Samora Machel Ave, Harare; Pres. I. O. SAMAKOMVA.

Zimbabwe Leather Shoe & Allied Workers' Union: Harare; tel. (4) 793173; Gen. Sec. I. ZINDOGA.

Zimbabwe Motor Industry Workers' Union: POB RY00, Bulawayo; tel. (9) 74150; Gen. Sec. M. M. DERAH.

Zimbabwe Posts and Telecommunications Workers' Union: POB 739, Harare; tel. (4) 721141; Gen. Sec. GIFT CHIMANIKIRE.

Zimbabwe Textile Workers' Union: POB UA245, Harare; tel. (4) 705329; Sec. F. C. BHAIKWA.

Zimbabwe Tobacco Industry Workers' Union: St Andrews House, Samora Machel Ave, Harare; Gen. Sec. S. MHEMBERE.

Zimbabwe Union of Musicians: POB 232, Harare; tel. (4) 708678; Gen. Sec. C. MATEMA.

Transport

In 1986 a Zimbabwe-registered company, the Beira Corridor Group (BCG), was formed to develop the transport system in the Beira corridor as an alternative transport link to those running through South Africa. The transport sector received 4.1% of total expenditure in the government budget for 1991/92. In 1991 National Railways of Zimbabwe (NRZ) announced a Z.$700m. development programme which included plans to electrify and extend some railway lines to previously uncovered areas.

RAILWAYS

In 1992 the rail network totalled 2,759 km. Trunk lines run from Bulawayo south to the border with Botswana, connecting with the Botswana railways system, which, in turn, connects with the South African railways system; north-west to the Victoria Falls, where there is a connection with Zambia Railways; and north-east to Harare and Mutare connecting with the Mozambique Railways' line from Beira. From a point near Gweru, a line runs to the south-east, making a connection with the Mozambique Railways' Limpopo line and with the Mozambican port of Maputo. A connection runs from Rutenga to the South African Railways system at Beitbridge.

National Railways of Zimbabwe (NRZ): cnr Fife St and 10th Ave, POB 596, Bulawayo; tel. (9) 363111; telex 33173; f. 1899, reorg. 1967; rationalization pending in 1997; Chair. JOHN LAURIE; Gen. Man. ALVORD MABENA.

ROADS

In 1995 the road system in Zimbabwe totalled an estimated 91,810 km, of which 5,710 km were primary roads and 11,600 km were secondary roads; some 19% of the total network was paved.

CIVIL AVIATION

International and domestic air services connect most of the larger towns. Construction of a new airport for Harare was scheduled to begin in 1997.

Air Zimbabwe Corporation (AirZim): POB AP1, Harare Airport, Harare; tel. (4) 575111; telex 40008; fax (4) 575053; f. 1967; scheduled domestic and international passenger and cargo services to Africa, Australia and Europe; Chair. D. M. ZAMCHIYA; CEO BRENDAN DONOHOE.

Affretair: POB AP13, Harare; tel. (4) 575000; fax (4) 575011; f. 1965 as Air Trans Africa; state-owned; freight carrier; scheduled services to Europe, and charter services world-wide; Chair. D. M. ZAMCHIYA; Man. Dir G. T. MANHAMBARA.

Manicaland Air Charter: f. 1996; operates charter service between Harare and Mutare.

Zimbabwe Express Airlines: Kurima House, Ground Floor, 89 Baker Ave, POB 5130, Harare; tel. (4) 705265; fax (4) 737117; e-mail zimexair@harare.iafrica.com; f. 1995; domestic routes and service to Johannesburg (South Africa); Man. Dir EVANS NDEBELE.

Tourism

In 1995 an estimated 1.6m. tourists visited Zimbabwe. Revenue from tourism in 1994 totalled about US $153m. The principal tourist attractions are the Victoria Falls, the Kariba Dam and the Hwange Game Reserve and National Park. Zimbabwe Ruins, near Fort Victoria, and World's View, in the Matapos Hills, are also of interest. There is trout-fishing and climbing in the Eastern Districts, around Umtali.

Zimbabwe Tourism Authority (ZTA): POB CY286, Causeway, Harare; tel. (4) 793666; telex 26082; fax (4) 793669; f. 1984 as Zimbabwe Tourist Development Corpn; promotes tourism domestically and abroad; Chair. ISIDORE GWASHURE.

Defence

Total armed forces numbered about 43,000 in August 1996: 39,000 in the army and 4,000 in the air force. Zimbabwe receives military aid and training from the United Kingdom and the Democratic People's Republic of Korea. There is a police force of 19,500, a police support unit of 2,300 and a national militia of 1,000. In February 1993 Zimbabwe and the USA commenced joint military manoeuvres. In April 1997 Zimbabwe hosted and participated in the first multinational peace training operation of the Southern African Development Community. The size of the armed forces is scheduled to be reduced to about 35,000 troops during the late 1990s.

Defence Expenditure: Allocated 8.8% of total budgetary expenditure in 1995/96.

Commander-in-Chief of the Armed Forces: ROBERT GABRIEL MUGABE.

Head of the Armed Forces: Gen. VITALIS ZVINAVASHE.

Commander of the Zimbabwe National Army: Lt-Gen. CONSTANTINE CHIWENGA.

Education

Primary education, which begins at seven years of age and lasts for seven years, is free, and has been compulsory since 1987. Secondary education begins at the age of 14 and lasts for six years. Between 1980 and 1995 the numbers of primary school pupils increased from 1,235,036 to 2,655,654. There were 711,094 pupils at secondary schools in 1995, compared with 74,746 in 1980. In 1993 the number of pupils attending primary and secondary schools was equivalent to 86% of children in the relevant age group (males 90%; females 81%). The number of primary schools rose from 2,411 at independence to 4,633 in 1995, and the number of secondary schools increased from 177 at independence to 1,535 in 1995. In 1995 some 46,495 students were attending institutions of higher education. There are two universities, the University of Zimbabwe, which is located in Harare, and the University of Science and Technology, at Bulawayo. The estimated rate of adult literacy in 1995 was 80.3% (males 86.1%; females 75.1%). Education received about 19.3% of total budgetary expenditure in 1995/96.

Bibliography

Auret, D. *A Decade of Development: Zimbabwe 1890–1990.* Gweru, Zimbabwe, Mambo Press in association with the Catholic Commission for Justice and Peace in Zimbabwe, 1990.

Baynham, S. *Zimbabwe in Transition.* Stockholm, Almqvist and Wiksell International; Pretoria, Africa Institute of South Africa, 1992.

Bhebe, N., and Ranger, T. (Eds). *Society in Zimbabwe's Liberation War.* Portsmouth, NH, Heinemann, 1993.

Soldiers in Zimbabwe's Liberation War. Heinemann, 1993.

Bourdillon, M. F. C. *Where are the Ancestors? Changing Culture in Zimbabwe.* Harare, University of Zimbabwe Publications, 1993.

Carver, R. *Zimbabwe: A Break with the Past? Human Rights and Political Unity.* New York, Africa Watch, 1989.

Chung, F., and Ngara, E. *Socialism, Education and Development.* Harare, Zimbabwe Publishing House, 1995.

De Waal, V. *The Politics of Reconciliation: Zimbabwe's First Decade.* London, Hurst, 1990; Harare, Longman Zimbabwe, 1992.

Engel, U. *Foreign Policy of Zimbabwe.* Hamburg, Institute of African Affairs, 1994.

Gibbon, P. (Ed.). *Structural Adjustment and the Working Poor in Zimbabwe: Studies on Labour, Women, Informal Sector Workers and Health.* Uppsala, Nordiska Afrikainstitutet, 1995.

Gore, C. *The Case for Sustainable Development in Zimbabwe: Conceptual Problems, Conflicts and Contradictions.* Harare, Zero, 1992.

Herbst, J. *State Politics in Zimbabwe.* Berkeley, University of California Press; Harare, University of Zimbabwe Publications, 1990.

Kriker, N. *Zimbabwe's Guerrilla War: Peasant Voices.* Cambridge, Cambridge University Press, 1991.

Lindenthal, R. *Co-operative Development and Economic Structural Adjustment in Zimbabwe.* Geneva, International Labour Organization, 1994.

Lopes, C. (Ed.). *Balancing Rocks: Environment and Development in Zimbabwe.* Uppsala, Nordiska Afrikainstitutet, 1996.

Mararike, C. G. *Grassroots Leadership: The Process of Rural Development in Zimbabwe.* Harare, University of Zimbabwe Publications, 1995.

Masters, W. A. *Government and Agriculture in Zimbabwe.* London, Greenwood; Westport, CT, Praeger, 1994.

Mbiba, B. *Urban Agriculture in Zimbabwe: Implications for Urban Management and Poverty.* Aldershot, Avebury; Brookfield, VT, Ashgate Publishing, 1995.

Mlambo, A. S., and Pangeti, E. S. *The Political Economy of the Sugar Industry in Zimbabwe, 1920–1990.* Harare, Zimbabwe Publishing House, 1996.

Morris-Jones, E. H. (Ed.). *From Rhodesia to Zimbabwe.* London, Cass, 1980.

Moyana, H. V. *The Political Economy of Land in Zimbabwe.* Gweru, Mambo Press, 1984.

Moyo, J. N. *Voting for Democracy: A Study of Electoral Politics in Zimbabwe.* Harare, University of Zimbabwe Publications, 1992.

Moyo, S. *Economic Nationalism and Land Reform in Zimbabwe.* Harare, Southern African Printing and Publishing House, 1994.

The Land Question in Zimbabwe. Harare, Southern African Printing and Publishing House, 1995.

Mudenge, S. I. G. *A Political History of Munhumutapa, c.1400–1902.* Portsmouth, NH, Heinemann, 1989.

Mungazi, D. A. *Colonial Policy and Conflict in Zimbabwe: A Study of Cultures in Collision, 1890–1979.* New York, Crane Russak, 1992.

Munkonoweshuro, E. G. *Zimbabwe: Ten Years of Destabilisation: A Balance Sheet.* Stockholm, Bethany Books, 1992.

Mutizwa-Mangiza, N. D., and Helmsing, A. H. J. *Rural Development and Planning in Zimbabwe.* Aldershot, Avebury, 1991.

Ncube, M. *Development Dynamics: Theories and Lessons from Zimbabwe.* Aldershot, Avebury, 1991.

Ndhlovu, T. *Zimbabwe: A Decade of Development.* London, Zed Books, 1992.

Palmer, R., and Birch, I. *Zimbabwe: A Land Divided.* Oxford, Oxfam, 1992.

Patel, H. *The Transfer of Power.* Harare, College Press, 1990.

Patsanza, A. J. D. *Our Zimbabwe: An Element of Political Economy.* Harare, GMP Publishing House, 1988.

Phimister, I. *Wangi Kolia: Coal, Capital and Labour in Colonial Zimbabwe, 1894–1994.* Harare, Baobab Books, 1994.

Rasmussen, R. K., and Rubert, S. C. *Historical Dictionary of Zimbabwe.* 2nd Edn., Metuchen, NJ, Scarecrow Press, 1991.

Roussos, P. *Zimbabwe: An Introduction to the Economics of Transformation.* Harare, Baobab Books, 1988.

Schatzburg, M. G. (Ed.). *The Political Economy of Zimbabwe: An SAIS Study on Africa.* New York, Praeger, 1984.

Schmidt, E. *Peasants, Traders and Wives: Shona Women in the History of Zimbabwe, 1870–1939.* London, James Currey; Portsmouth, NH, Heinemann, 1992.

Seidman, G., and Johnson, M. *A New History of Zimbabwe.* Harare, Zimbabwe Publishing House, 1982.

Shadur, M. A. *Labour Relations in a Developing Country: A Case Study on Zimbabwe.* Aldershot, Avebury, 1994.

Sithole, M. *Democracy and the One-Party State in Africa: The Case of Zimbabwe.* Harare, SAPES Books, 1992.

Staunton, I. (Ed.). *Mothers of the Revolution: War Experiences of Thirty Zimbabwean Women.* Harare, Baobab Books, 1991.

Stoneman, C., and Cliffe L. *Zimbabwe: Politics, Economics and Society.* London, Pinter, 1989.

Sylvester, C. *Zimbabwe: The Terrain of Contradictory Development.* Boulder, CO, Westview Press, 1991.

Tamarkin, M. *The Making of Zimbabwe.* London, Frank Cass, 1990.

Verrier, A. *The Road to Zimbabwe, 1890–1980.* London, Jonathan Cape, 1986.

Weiss, R. *Zimbabwe and the New Elite.* London, British Academic Press, 1994.

Whyte, B. *Yesterday, Today and Tomorrow: A 100 Year History of Zimbabwe, 1890–1990.* Harare, David Burke, 1990.

World Bank. *Zimbabwe: Achieving Shared Growth: Country Economic Memorandum.* Washington, DC, World Bank, 1995.

Zvobgo, R. J. *Colonialism and Education in Zimbabwe.* Harare, SAPES Books, 1994.